N Webster

NOAH WEBSTER

OCTOBER 16, 1758 — MAY 28, 1843

THE significance of Noah Webster's *Dictionary* and his *Spelling Book* can be appreciated only when they are viewed against the background spanned by his life. He was born on an eighty-acre Connecticut farm the year before Wolfe's victory on the Plains of Abraham, and lived to see American pioneers penetrate overland into California and Oregon. He was a small boy when the Stamp Act aroused the colonists, and a student at Yale when college classes were dispersed into the interior towns by the menace of British landing parties. He marched with his father against Burgoyne. In 1785, moved by the incompetence of the Confederation of thirteen sovereign states, he wrote a widely circulated argument for national union. In 1787 he issued an influential pamphlet advocating the adoption of the Federal Constitution. From 1793 to 1798 he owned, managed, and edited a daily and a weekly newspaper in New York City, supporting the Federalist policies of Washington and Adams. Living under the first ten presidents, he witnessed the acquisition of Louisiana Territory and Florida, the admission of thirteen additional states, and the approaching annexation of Texas.

Out of the patriotism and nationalism inspired by this sweep of events came the conviction that lusty young America needed its own school books, its own uniform language, and its own intellectual life. Into the attainment of these ends Webster flung himself with insatiable curiosity and indomitable energy. His *Blue-Backed Speller* (which taught not only spelling but pronunciation, common sense, morals, and good citizenship) was partly provoked by his efforts to use Dilworth's English spelling book while he was teaching school in Connecticut, New York, and Philadelphia. His dictionaries (*Compendious*, 1806; *American*, 1828) were suggested partly by his resentment against the ignorance concerning American institutions shown in contemporary British dictionaries. All his life he was a defender and interpreter of the American political "experiment", with all its cultural implications.

His dictionaries and his *Spelling Book* grew out of an intimate and vital familiarity with American life. He knew the farm, the law, the city, the school, and politics. He knew the country as a whole—he had traveled (1785–1786) by horse, by carriage, and by sailing vessel from Massachusetts to South Carolina, persuading state legislatures to pass laws for the protection of copyright. He was a spelling reformer, an orchardist, a gardener, and an experimental scientist. He was admitted to practice before the United States Supreme Court. He became and remained a devoted Calvinistic churchman. He wrote scores of articles, books, and pamphlets on literary, economic, political, philological, practical, and scientific subjects —on banks, epidemics, insurance, the French Revolution, the decomposition of white-lead paint, the Jay Treaty, and the rights of neutral nations in time of war. He edited Governor Winthrop's Journal. He wrote and published a revised and emended version of the Bible.

He assumed all the local duties and responsibilities of a citizen. He was clerk and committeeman of his Hartford school district. He was a member for a time of the General Assembly of Connecticut and for a time of the General Court of Massachusetts. He was councilman and alderman in New Haven and judge of the County Court. In Amherst he was town moderator. He was a director of the Hampshire Bible Society, a vice-president of the Hampshire and Hampden Agricultural Society, and a founder of the Connecticut Academy of Arts and Sciences. He was active in the establishment of both Amherst Academy and Amherst College, and was president of the Board of Trustees of the Academy. In New Haven he campaigned for the introduction of an adequate water supply, and took active part in a movement to plant elms along the streets.

In 1807 he wrote: "I hope to be able to finish my Complete Dictionary. . . . It will require the incessant labor of from three to five years." In 1812 he moved to Amherst, Massachusetts, where for ten years he labored from point to point about the large circular table that held the dictionaries and grammars of twenty languages. In 1824 he sailed to spend a year in the libraries of Paris, London, and Cambridge in order to consult books not available in America. In 1828, at the age of seventy, he at length published *An American Dictionary of the English Language* in a two-volume edition of 2500 copies.

The *American Dictionary* stands practically beyond praise or comparison. The excellence of the definitions has received ample acknowledgment. But some other features of Webster's work have never been adequately recognized: First, the inclusion of thousands of modern technical and scientific terms, making it more than a purely literary dictionary. Second, the discovery of the correct principle for arranging the definitions, with the etymologically primary meaning first. And third, the etymologies, which are mines of pertinent and valuable information, as appears when they are compared, not only with the results of an added century of research, but especially with the scanty or fragmentary treatment of Johnson, Junius, and Skinner, and the speculations of Horne Tooke.

Webster brought out a revised edition of the *Dictionary* in 1841, just before his death. The *Spelling Book* had meanwhile undergone many revisions and improvements. These two books, written to illuminate and explain to the American people both their language and their culture, were his contribution to American civilization.

The publishers and the editors of this latest edition of *Webster's Dictionary* have worked under the constant responsibility of maintaining Noah Webster's standards of integrity and clarity in meeting the needs of the whole modern English-speaking world.

a living language must keep pace with improvements in knowledge and with the multiplication of ideas
—Noah Webster, *A Letter to John Pickering*, 1817

DICTIONARY . . . A book containing the words of a language arranged in alphabetical order, with explanations of their meanings; a lexicon
—Noah Webster, *An American Dictionary of the English Language*, 1828

dictionary . . . **1 :** a reference book containing words usu. alphabetically arranged along with information about their forms, pronunciations, functions, etymologies, meanings, and syntactical and idiomatic uses ⟨a general ~ of the English language⟩ ⟨a monolingual ~⟩ — compare VOCABULARY ENTRY **2 a :** a reference book listing terms or names important to a particular subject or activity along with discussion of their meanings and applications ⟨a law ~⟩ ⟨a ~ of sports⟩; *broadly* **:** an encyclopedic listing ⟨a ~ of dates⟩ **b :** a reference book giving for words of one language equivalents in another ⟨an English-French ~⟩ ⟨a bilingual ~⟩ **c :** a reference book listing terms as commonly spelled together with their equivalents in some specialized system (as of orthography or symbols) ⟨a ~ of shorthand⟩ ⟨a pronouncing ~⟩ **3 a :** a general comprehensive list, collection, or repository ⟨a ~ of biography⟩ ⟨a usage ~⟩ **b :** vocabulary in use (as in a special field) **:** TERMINOLOGY ⟨the ~ of literary criticism⟩ **c :** a vocabulary of accepted terms ⟨in the ~ of the French Academy⟩ **d :** a vocabulary of the written words used by one author ⟨systematic *dictionaries* of individual authors —Hillis Miller⟩ **e :** LEXICON 4
—*Webster's Third New International Dictionary*

Webster's Third New International Dictionary

OF THE ENGLISH LANGUAGE

UNABRIDGED

A Merriam-Webster

REG. U.S. PAT. OFF.

Utilizing all the experience and resources of more than one hundred years of Merriam-Webster dictionaries

EDITOR IN CHIEF

PHILIP BABCOCK GOVE, Ph.D.

AND

THE MERRIAM-WEBSTER

EDITORIAL STAFF

G. & C. MERRIAM COMPANY, *Publishers*

SPRINGFIELD, MASSACHUSETTS, U.S.A.

Standard Book Numbers:
0-87779-001-9 (buff buckram)
0-87779-002-7 (dark tan Fabrikoid)
0-87779-003-5 (2 volumes, buff buckram)
0-87779-005-1 (tan buckram, India paper)
0-87779-006-X (dark brown Fabrikoid, India paper)

MADE IN THE U. S. A.

CONTENTS

PLATES AND FULL-PAGE ILLUSTRATIONS

INDEX TO TABLES

(at or near italicized word)

PREFACE

WEBSTER'S THIRD NEW INTERNATIONAL DICTIONARY is a completely new work, redesigned, restyled, and reset. Every line of it is new. This latest unabridged Merriam-Webster is the eighth in a series which has its beginning in Noah Webster's *American Dictionary of the English Language*, 1828. On Webster's death in 1843 the unsold copies and publishing rights of his dictionary were acquired by George and Charles Merriam, who in 1847 brought out a revision edited by Noah Webster's son-in-law, Professor Chauncey A. Goodrich of Yale College. The 1847 edition became the first Merriam-Webster unabridged dictionary*. G. & C. Merriam Company now offers WEBSTER'S THIRD NEW INTERNATIONAL DICTIONARY to the English-speaking world as a prime linguistic aid to interpreting the culture and civilization of today, as the first edition served the America of 1828.

As the number of students in school and college jumps to ever-increasing heights, the quantity of printed matter necessary to their education increases too. Not only are more words used more often with these increases; words must be used more economically and more efficiently both in school and out. More and more do people undertaking a new job, practicing a new hobby, or developing a new interest turn to how-to pamphlets, manuals, and books for both elementary instruction and advanced guidance. Where formerly they had time to learn by doing, they now need to begin by reading and understanding what has been recorded. A quick grasp of the meanings of words becomes necessary if one is to be successful. A dictionary opens the way to both formal learning and to the daily self-instruction that modern living requires. It is the key also to the daily newspaper and to a vast number of other periodicals that demand our attention. This edition has been prepared with a constant regard for the needs of the high school and college student, the technician, and the periodical reader, as well as of the scholar and professional. It undertakes to provide for the changes in public interest in all classes of words as manifested by what people want to read, discuss, and study. The dictionary more than ever is the indispensable instrument of understanding and progress.

G. & C. Merriam Company have produced this THIRD NEW INTERNATIONAL at a cost of over $3,500,000. The budgetary and technical planning underlying its production has been directed and coordinated since 1953 by the Company's president, Mr. Gordon J. Gallan. His activity, understanding, and cooperation have contributed indispensably to its editorial completion and have made possible the maintenance of a Merriam-Webster permanent office staff constituted according to need. This staff is in effect a faculty which specializes in different branches of knowledge much as a small college faculty does. Listed among the resident editors are a mathematician, a physicist, a chemist, a botanist, a biologist, a philosopher, a political scientist, a comparative religionist, a classicist, a historian, and a librarian as well as philologists, linguists, etymologists, and phoneticians whose specialty is the English language itself. Their academic affiliations and their degrees can be seen one by one in the "Merriam-Webster Editorial Staff" that follows this preface. Besides the office staff over two hundred other scholars and specialists have served as outside consultants in supplementary reviewing, revising, and submitting new definitions in subjects in which they are authorities. The range and experience of this special knowledge appear in the listing of their names alphabetically after the editorial staff.

In conformity with the principle that a definition, to be adequate, must be written only after an analysis of usage, the definitions in this edition are based chiefly on examples of usage collected since publication of the preceding edition. Members of the editorial staff began in 1936 a systematic reading of books, magazines, newspapers, pamphlets, catalogs, and learned journals. By the time of going to press the collection contained just under 4,500,000 such new examples of recorded usage, to be added to more than 1,665,000 citations already in the files for previous editions. Further, the citations in the indispensable many-volume *Oxford English Dictionary*, the new citations in Sir William Craigie's four-volume *Dictionary of American English* and Mitford M. Mathews' two-volume *Dictionary of Americanisms*, neither of which was available to the editors of the preceding edition, and the uncounted citations in dozens of concordances to the Bible and to works of English and American writers and in numerous books of quotations push the citation background for the definitions in this dictionary to over ten million. This figure does not include freely consulted text matter in the office library of reference books. Nor does it include thousands of textbooks in the private and academic libraries of the editors and consultants, nor books consulted in the Springfield City Library whose librarians have generously given the editorial staff ready and frequent access to its large and valuable word-hoard.

While dictionaries of special subjects, glossaries, indexes, and checklists are collected and examined to verify the existence of special words, no word has been entered in this dictionary merely on the authority of another dictionary, special or general, and no definition in this dictionary has been derived from any other dictionary (except, of course, Merriam-Webster predecessors). Learned and industrial organizations have created numerous committees of nomenclature to collect, define, and standardize the terminology in their fields. Some of the staff editors serve as advisory members of such committees. Nevertheless prescriptive and canonical definitions have not been taken over nor have recommendations been followed unless confirmed by independent investigation of usage borne out by genuine citations.

The primary objective of precise, sharp defining has been met through development of a new dictionary style based upon completely analytical one-phrase definitions throughout the book. Since the headword in a definition is intended to be modified only by structural elements restrictive in some degree and essential to each other, the use of commas either to separate or to group has been severely limited, chiefly to units in apposition or in series. The new defining pattern does not provide for a predication which conveys further expository comment. Instead of encyclopedic treatment at one place of a group of related terms, each term is defined at its own place in the alphabet. Every phrase in lowercase roman type following a heavy black colon and running to the next heavy colon or to a divisional number or letter is a complete definition of one sense of the word to which it is attached. Defining by synonym is carefully avoided by putting all unqualified or undifferentiated terms in small capital letters. Such a term in small capitals should not be considered a definition but a cross-reference to a definition of equivalent meaning that can be substituted for the small capitals.

A large number of verbal illustrations mostly from the mid-twentieth century has been woven into the defining pattern with a view to contributing considerably to the user's interest and understanding by showing a word used in context. The illustration is often a brief combination of words that has actually been used in writing and when this is so the illustration is attributed to its author or source. More than 14,000 different authors are quoted for their use of words or for the structural pattern of their words but not for their opinions or sentiments.

A number of other features are (1) the recognition and separate entry (with part-of-speech label) of verb-plus-adverb compounds (as *run down*) that function like one-word verbs in every way except for having a separable suffix, (2) the recognition (by using the label *n* for noun) that substantive open compounds (as *clothes moth*) belong in the same class as nouns written solid or hyphened, (3) the recognition (by using the label *often attrib*) of nouns that often function as adjectives but otherwise do not behave like the class of adjectives, (4) the indication (by inserting suffix-symbols, as -S or -ES, -ED/-ING/-S or -ES, -ER/-EST) of the inflectional forms of nouns, verbs, adjectives, and adverbs at which the forms are not written out in full, (5) the recognition (by beginning entries with a lowercase letter and by inserting either the label *cap*, *usu cap*, *often cap*, or *sometimes cap*) that words vary considerably in capitalization according to circumstances and environment, (6) the recognition (by not using at all the status label *colloquial*) that it is impossible to know whether a word out of context is colloquial or not, and (7) the incorporation of abbreviations alphabetically in the main vocabulary.

In continuation of Merriam-Webster policy the editors of this new edition have held steadfastly to the three cardinal virtues of dictionary making: accuracy, clearness, and comprehensiveness. Whenever these qualities are at odds with each other, accuracy is put first and foremost, for without accuracy there could be no appeal to WEBSTER'S THIRD NEW INTERNATIONAL as an authority. Accuracy in addition to requiring freedom from error and conformity to truth requires a dictionary to state meanings in which words are in fact used, not to give editorial opinion on what their meanings should be.

In the editorial striving for clearness the editors have tried to make the definitions as readable as possible. Even so, the terminology of many subjects contains words that can be adequately and clearly explained only to those who have passed through preliminary stages of initiation, just as a knowledge of algebra is prerequisite for trigonometry. A dictionary demands of its user much understanding and no one person can understand all of it. Therefore there is no limit to the possibilities for clarification. Somewhat paradoxically a user of the dictionary benefits in proportion to his effort and knowledge, and his contribution is an essential part of the process of understanding even though it may involve only a willingness to look up a few additional words.

Comprehensiveness requires maximum coverage with a minimum of compromise. The basic aim is nothing less than coverage of the current vocabulary of standard written and spoken English. At the same time the scientific and technical vocabulary has been considerably expanded to keep pace with progress especially in physical science (as in electronics, nuclear physics, statistics, and soil science), in technology (as in rocketry, communications, automation, and synthetics), in medicine, and in the experimental phases of natural science. Therefore space has been found not only for new terms but also for new uses of old terms, for English like other living languages is in a metabolic process of constant change. The changes affect not only word stock but meaning, syntax, morphology, and pronunciation.

The demands for space have made necessary a fresh judgment on the claims of many parts of the old vocabulary. This dictionary is the result of a highly selective process in which discarding material of insubstantial or evanescent quality has gone hand in hand with adding terms that have obtained a place in the language. It confines itself strictly to generic words and their functions, forms, sounds, and meanings as distinguished from proper names that are not generic. Selection is guided by usefulness, and usefulness is determined by the degree to which terms most likely to be looked for are included. Many obsolete and comparatively useless or obscure words have been omitted. These include in general words that had become obsolete before 1755 unless found in well-known major works of a few major writers.

In definitions of words of many meanings the earliest ascertainable meaning is given first. Meanings of later derivation are arranged in the order shown to be most probable by dated evidence and semantic development. This arrangement applies alike to all meanings whether standard, technical, scientific, historical, or obsolete. No definitions are grouped alphabetically by subject labels. In fact this edition uses very few subject labels. It depends upon the definition for incorporating necessary subject orientation.

The pronunciation editor is Mr. Edward Artin. This edition shows as far as possible the pronunciations prevailing in general cultivated conversational usage, both informal and formal, throughout the English-speaking world. It does not attempt to dictate what that usage should be. It shows a

---

*The successors in the Merriam-Webster series are *American Dictionary of the English Language*, popularly known as the *Unabridged*, 1864, edited by Dr. Noah Porter, president of Yale College; *Webster's International Dictionary*, 1890, Noah Porter, editor in chief; *Webster's New International Dictionary*, 1909, Dr. William Torrey Harris, U. S. Commissioner of Education, editor in chief, and F. Sturges Allen, general editor; *Webster's New International Dictionary, Second Edition*, 1934, Dr. William Allan Neilson, president of Smith College, editor in chief, and Dr. Thomas A. Knott, general editor.

wide variety of acceptable pronunciations based on a large file of transcriptions made by attentive listening to actual educated speech in all fields and in all parts of the country—the speech of those expecting to be completely understood by their hearers. The facility with which such speech can be checked today by television, radio, and recordings has made it possible to show more representative and more realistic pronunciations than in the past.

To this end the Merriam-Webster pronunciation key has been revised. Many of the symbols of preceding editions have been retained, some with slight alteration, a few substitutions have been made, and some symbols that have outlived their usefulness have been dropped altogether. It is still fundamentally a diacritical key that makes use of many of the conventions of English spelling and is based on the principles that every distinct significant sound should have a distinct symbol to represent it and that no sound should be represented in more than one way. The elimination of symbols for all nonsignificant differences in sound makes it possible for transcriptions to convey to speakers in different parts of the English-speaking world sounds proper to their own speech. The new pronunciation alphabet is designed to represent clearly the standard speech of educated Americans.

It should be clearly understood that in striving to show realistic pronunciations definite limitations are fixed by the very nature of a dictionary. Each word must be isolated and considered apart from its place in connected spoken discourse. It is impracticable to show in a dictionary many kinds of variations—rising or falling pitch, syllabic emphasis or lack of emphasis, contraction or prolongation of sounds—to which the pronunciation of a word is susceptible under the influence of other words temporarily associated with it. Some of these variations are discussed under several headings in "Guide to Pronunciation", which contains also several paragraphs on the subject of correctness in pronunciation.

The etymologist for this edition is Dr. Charles R. Sleeth. In the etymologies the aim has been to retrace step by step the line of transmission by which the words have come down to modern English from the language in which they are first recorded. The present work adheres in this respect to the sound general principles governing the presentation of word histories in previous editions and indeed applies them with a consistency that has not previously been attained. With particular care it traces back to Middle English every word which is recorded in Middle English; also it carefully distinguishes the age of borrowings from French by giving the source language as Old French if the word came into English before 1300, as Middle French if it came into English between 1300 and 1600, and as French only if it came into English in the seventeenth century or later.

The etymologies fall into four general groups based on the origins of English words. Native words (as *hound*) that have been in the language as long as it has existed are traced back first through Middle English to Old English and then to Germanic languages other than English and to Indo-European languages other than Germanic. Old and well-established borrowings (as *chief*, *add*, and *dialect*) that have been in English since medieval or Renaissance times and come from languages, usually French, Latin, or often indirectly Greek, which belong, like English, to the Indo-European language family are traced back through their immediate source to their ultimate source in as much detail as native words. Many more recent borrowings (as *éclair*, *anile*, *hubris*, *sforzando*, *lariat*, *dachshund*, *smorgasbord*, *galore*, *muzhik*, and *karma*) are incorporated into the network of Indo-European etymology more thoroughly than in earlier dictionaries by going beyond the immediate source to either a list of cognates or a cross-reference to another entry. Borrowings (as *bushido*, *tepee*, *sheikh*, *sampan*, and *taboo*) from non-Indo-European languages are traced to the immediate source and analyzed into their parts if in the source language they are compounds or derivatives.

In the modern technical vocabulary of the sciences it is difficult if not impossible to adhere strictly to the principle of tracing step by step the line of transmission of a word, because such vocabulary has expanded rapidly in numerous fields and has been transmitted freely across language boundaries. Very few works of reference give full or systematic information about the language of origin of technical terms in any one field, and consequently it is impossible for the etymological staff of a general dictionary to garner and present such information about the technical terms of all fields. The present work attempts a new solution of this problem by introducing the label ISV (for International Scientific Vocabulary), for use in the etymology of such words when their language of origin is not positively ascertainable but they are known to be current in at least one language other than English. Examples of the use of ISV and further details about it are given in "Explanatory Notes", 7.6. Some ISV words (like *haploid*) have been created by taking a word with a rather general and simple meaning from one of the languages of antiquity, usually Latin or Greek, and conferring upon it a very specific and complicated meaning for the purposes of modern scientific discourse. More typically, however, ISV words are compounds or derivatives, made up of constituents that can be found entered in their own alphabetical position with their own ulterior etymology, again generally involving Latin or Greek. In either case an ISV etymology as given in the present work incorporates the word into the system of Indo-European etymology as well as if the immediate source language were known and stated. At the same time, use of ISV avoids the often untenable implication that the word in question was coined in English, and recognizes that the word as such is a product of the modern world and gets only its raw materials, so to speak, from antiquity.

The scheme of biological classification used has been concerted in consultation between Dr. Mairé Weir Kay, staff biologist, and specialists in the several divisions of taxonomy. It is planned to coordinate in the broadest way with current professional usage and specifically avoids undue reliance on any single school or system. The total taxonomic coverage is far more extensive than this characterization might imply and is designed to include and link with the preferred scheme both historically important though now disused terminology and the more important terms pertinent to divergent schools of professional thought (as in the question of whether the leguminous plants constitute one or several families).

Words that are believed to be trademarks have been investigated in the files of the United States Patent Office. No investigation has been made of common law trademark rights in any word since such investigation is impracticable. Those that have current registrations are shown with an initial capital and are also identified as trademarks. The inclusion of any word in this dictionary is not, however, an expression of the publishers' opinion on whether or not it is subject to proprietary rights. Indeed, no definition in this dictionary is to be regarded as affecting the validity of any trademark.

This dictionary has a vocabulary of over 450,000 words. It would have been easy to make the vocabulary larger although the book, in the format of the preceding edition, could hardly hold any more pages or be any thicker. By itself, the number of entries is, however, not of first importance. The number of words available is always far in excess of and for a one-volume dictionary many times the number that can possibly be included. To make all the changes mentioned only to come out with the same number of pages and the same number of vocabulary entries as in the preceding edition would allow little or no opportunity for new words and new senses. The compactness and legibility of Times Roman, a typeface new to Merriam-Webster dictionaries, have made possible more words to a line and more lines to a column than in the preceding edition, and a larger size page makes a better proportioned book.

The preparation of this edition has absorbed 757 editor-years. This figure does not include the time of typists, photocopiers, and clerical assistants or the time of over 200 consultants. The book appears, like its predecessor, after more than ten years of active full-time preparation. It is hardly necessary to observe that no one editor could harmonize all the diverse and disparate matter by reading and criticizing every line or even determine and keep firm control over editorial policy, nor could an editorial board of fixed membership. Instead the editor in chief has used his editors one by one and has delegated multiple responsibilities to them individually as occasion required. In this way members of the Merriam-Webster staff have been grouped and regrouped to form hundreds of task forces performing simultaneously thousands of missions. The editor can say with gratitude and relief that the accomplishment is not a one-man dictionary. "What individual", asks Noah Webster in his preface, "is competent to trace to their source, and define in all their various applications, popular, scientific, and technical, sixty or seventy thousand words!"

WEBSTER'S THIRD NEW INTERNATIONAL DICTIONARY is a collaborative effort. Without the cooperation of the scholarly, scientific, and technical world, the specialized guidance of our outside consultants, and the ingenuity of the compositors and printers, G. & C. Merriam Company and its permanent editorial staff could not have brought the work to its successful culmination. Those most deeply involved with overall responsibility deserve special mention here. Three associate editors, Mr. Artin, Dr. Kay, and Dr. Sleeth, have already been named in this preface. Among others who have shared large responsibilities are these associate editors: Miss Anne M. Driscoll, Dr. Philip H. Goepp, Mr. Hubert P. Kelsey, Dr. Howard G. Rhoads, and Dr. H. Bosley Woolf; two assistant editors, Miss Ervina E. Foss and Mrs. Laverne W. King; and the departmental secretary, Mrs. Christine M. Mullen.

It is now fairly clear that before the twentieth century is over every community of the world will have learned how to communicate with all the rest of humanity. In this process of intercommunication the English language has already become the most important language on earth. This new Merriam-Webster unabridged is the record of this language as it is written and spoken. It is offered with confidence that it will supply in full measure that information on the general language which is required for accurate, clear, and comprehensive understanding of the vocabulary of today's society.

Springfield, Mass.
June 1, 1961

PHILIP B. GOVE

MERRIAM-WEBSTER EDITORIAL STAFF

EDITOR IN CHIEF

PHILIP B. GOVE (1946–1972)
A.B., Dartmouth College; A.M., Harvard University; Ph.D., Columbia University; Litt.D., Dartmouth College
Formerly teacher at Rice Institute and at New York University
(managing editor 1950–1952; general editor 1952–1960)

ASSOCIATE EDITORS

EDWARD ARTIN (*from 1934)
Harvard University

JOHN P. BETHEL (*1934–1958)
B.A., McGill University; A.M., Ph.D., Harvard University
Formerly teacher at Buffalo (N.Y.) State Teachers College
(general editor 1935–1952; senior associate editor 1952–1958)

DANIEL COOK (1952–1957)
B.S.(Ed.), M.A., University of Wisconsin; Ph.D., University of California
Formerly teacher at Duke University and at University of California

ANNE M. DRISCOLL (1937–1961)
A.B., Smith College

PHILIP H. GOEPP (1952–1967)
Ph.D., Johns Hopkins University
Formerly teacher at City College (N.Y.) and at University of Rochester

LUCIUS H. HOLT (*1934–1946) **
B.A., M.A., Ph.D., Yale University
Formerly teacher at United States Military Academy
(managing editor 1934–1946)

MAIRÉ WEIR KAY (from 1946)
B.A., University of Kansas; M.A., Ph.D., University of Washington
Formerly teacher at Wells College

HUBERT P. KELSEY (1935–1972)
B.A., M.A., University of Michigan

DONALD W. LEE (1946–1948; 1953–1957)
B.A., Pennsylvania State College; M.A., Duke University; Ph.D., Columbia University
Formerly teacher at United States Naval Academy and at University of Pittsburgh

EDWARD F. OAKES (*1934–1957)
B.A., M.A., Williams College; A.M., Harvard University
Formerly teacher at Union College and at University of Michigan

HOWARD G. RHOADS (1952–1965)
A.B., University of Pennsylvania; A.M., Harvard University; Ph.D., University of Pennsylvania
Formerly teacher at Beaver College, at College of Wooster, at Harvard University, at Lehigh University, at Lingnan University (China), and at Temple University

CHARLES R. SLEETH (1951–1962)
A.B., A.M., West Virginia University; B.A., Oxford University; M.A., Ph.D., Princeton University
Formerly teacher at Greensboro College, at University of Oklahoma, and at Princeton University

H. BOSLEY WOOLF (from 1955)
A.B., Emory & Henry College; Ph.D., Johns Hopkins University; Litt. D., Emory & Henry College
Formerly teacher at Louisiana State University
(managing editor from 1960)

ASSISTANT EDITORS

FREEMAN B. ANDERSON (1952–1953)
A.B., Bucknell University; Ph.D., Stanford University

WARREN B. AUSTIN (1958–1963)
B.A., City College (N.Y.); Ph.D., Columbia University
Formerly teacher at City College (N.Y.)

MILDRED F. BAXTER (1954–1960)
A.B., Vassar College; M.A., Ph.D., University of Michigan

WARREN B. BEZANSON (1954–1956)
B.A., Guilford College; B.Ed., Central Connecticut State College; M.A., University of North Carolina; Ph.D., University of Maryland
Formerly teacher at Washington College and at University of Maryland

LUCILLE C. BROUILLET (1940–1956)
B.S., University of Massachusetts

ROBERT B. COSTELLO (1960–1962)
B.A., Wesleyan University

F. STUART CRAWFORD (from 1959)
B.A., Amherst College; M.A., Oxford University; Ph.D., Harvard University
Formerly teacher at Amherst College, Miami University (Ohio) and at Boston University

PHILIP W. CUMMINGS (1958–1962)
B.A., Bowdoin College; M.A., Ph.D., University of Pittsburgh

VIRGINIA L. DONIGIAN (1950–1961)
B.S., Boston University

AUDREY R. DUCKERT (1953–1956)
B.S.(Ed.), M.A., University of Wisconsin; Ph.D., Radcliffe College

ROSE F. EGAN (*1934–1945)
B.A., Syracuse University; M.A., Columbia University
Formerly teacher at Smith College

This table contains only those who have been in full-time residence for at least one year.

FRANK FLETCHER (1953–1959)
A.B., M.A., Brown University; Ph.D., University of Michigan
Formerly teacher at University of Michigan and Cornell University

ERVINA E. FOSS (*1934–1968)
A.B., Mount Holyoke College

MARIAN M. FOX (1958–1962)
B.A., University of Massachusetts
Formerly teacher at Dalton (Mass.) High School

EDWARD A. H. FUCHS (1943–1952)
Ph.B., Ph.D., University of Chicago
Formerly teacher at Indiana University and Centre College of Kentucky

JEROME J. FUSSELL (1951–1955)
B.J., University of Missouri; M.A., Ph.D., University of Chicago

J. EDWARD GATES (1956–1962)
B.A., Maryville College; B.D., Yale University; S.T.M., Harvard University; Ph.D., Hartford Seminary Foundation
Formerly teacher at Gerard Institute (Sidon, Lebanon)

E. WARD GILMAN (from 1958)
B.A., Bowdoin College; A.M., Boston University

MYRON J. GLADSTONE (1952–1956)
S.B., M.A., Harvard University

SAMUEL J. GOLUB (1947–1949)
B.S., M.S., University of Massachusetts; Ph.D., Harvard University
Formerly teacher at University of Massachusetts

LUCILE GREBENC (1952–1960)
University of California

---

* also on the editorial staff of WEBSTER'S NEW INTERNATIONAL, Second Edition, 1934
** also on the editorial staff of WEBSTER'S NEW INTERNATIONAL, 1909

WILLIAM H. HAWLEY (1959–1961)
A.B., Dartmouth College; M.A., Middlebury College; LL.B., Western New England College
Formerly teacher at Mt. Hermon School, at St. Paul's School, at Williston Academy, and at the Peddie School

CHRISTOPHER T. HOOLIHAN (1955–1959)
B.A., St. Meinrad Seminary; M.A., Catholic University of America
Formerly teacher at St. Meinrad Seminary

BETTIE (SHULL) HUGHES (1956–1957)
B.S. in Ed., A.M., University of Missouri
Formerly teacher at Westboro (Mo.) Consolidated High School, at Lathrop (Mo.) High School, and at University of Missouri

BENJAMIN KEEN (1956–1959)
B.A., Muhlenberg College; M.A., Lehigh University; Ph.D., Yale University
Formerly teacher at Yale University, at Amherst College, and at University of West Virginia

GRACE A. KELLOGG (from 1941)
B.A., American International College

FRANCIS M. KELLY, JR. (1959–1961)
B.A., University of Rochester; M.A., Ph.D., Columbia University
Formerly teacher at Hunter College and at University of Michigan

LAVERNE W. KING (from 1949)

HENRY KRATZ (1955–1960)
A.B., State University College of Education at Albany, New York; A.M., Ph.D., Ohio State University
Formerly teacher at Ohio State University, at University of Michigan, and at University of Massachusetts

MALCOLM R. LEETE (1935–1937)
B.A., Harvard University

ELSIE MAG (*1934–1968)
A.B., Smith College
Formerly teacher at Ludlow (Mass.) High School

MILDRED A. MERCIER (1956–1962)
B.S. in Ed., Ohio University; M.A., Western Reserve University; B.S. in L.S., Columbia University
Formerly teacher at South High School (Lima, Ohio) and at Celina (Ohio) High School

RALF F. MUNSTER (1951–1955)
A.B., M.A., Ph.D., Duke University
Formerly teacher at Duke University and at University of Georgia

HAROLD E. NIERGARTH (1959–1965)
B.A., University of Michigan

JOSEPH A. PALERMO (1940–1943)
A.B., Temple University; A.M., Ph.D., Princeton University
Formerly teacher at Temple University

FRANK G. PICKEL (1957–1959)
A.B., Oberlin College; Ph.D., University of Chicago
Formerly teacher at Washington University (St. Louis), at University of Washington, and at University of Vermont

ROBERT J. QUINLAN (1958–1962)
A.B., M.A., Ph.D., Yale University

RAYMOND RHINE (1953–1958)
A.B., A.M., Syracuse University
Formerly teacher at Felt Mills (N.Y.) High School, at Black River (N.Y.) High School, at Babylon (N.Y.) High School, at Syracuse University, and at Springfield College

M. ELUNED ROBERTS (1952–1962)
A.B., M.A., University of Vermont
Formerly teacher at Westbrook Junior College

THOMAS H. B. ROBERTSON (1958–1962)
A.B., Bluffton College
Formerly teacher at Wilbraham (Mass.) Academy

HUBERT H. ROE (*1934–1967)

MIRIAM H. ROOT (1946–1962)
A.B., Keuka College; B.S., Columbia University

DONALD B. SANDS (1953–1957)
B.A., Lehigh University; A.M., Ph.D., Harvard University
Formerly teacher at University of Arkansas, at University of Maine, at Bowdoin College, and at Harvard University

JANET D. SCOTT (1955–1960)
A.B., Vassar College; S.M., University of Chicago

DONALD J. SHARF (1957–1961)
B.A., M.A., Wayne State University; Ph.D., University of Michigan

LESTER C. SHERMAN (1950–1959)
B.A., Wayne State University; M.A., University of Michigan
Formerly teacher at Drake University

SIDNEY A. SIMMONS (1950–1956)
B.S.A., Ontario College of Agriculture; M.A., University of Toronto
Formerly teacher at Ontario College of Agriculture

HARRIET SMITH (1957–1961)
A.B., Mt. Holyoke College; M.S., Columbia University; M.A., University of Massachusetts

ADELE K. SULLIVAN (1951–1968)
B.A., Connecticut College

SOL STEINMETZ (1958–1961)
B.A., Yeshiva University
Formerly teacher at Yavne Academy (Brooklyn, N.Y.)

GEORGE M. SWANSON (1955–1958)
A.B., Drake University

SIDNEY THOMAS (1958–1961)
B.A., City College (N.Y.); M.A., Ph.D., Columbia University
Formerly teacher at City College (N.Y.), at Brooklyn College, and at Queens College

EVERETT E. THOMPSON (*1934–1949)
B.A., M.A., Amherst College; Litt. D., Syracuse University **

JARVIS TODD (1947–1951)
A.B., Wabash College; M.A., University of Kentucky
Formerly teacher at University of Dayton

LEROY D. WELD (1951–1955)
B.S., M.S., Ph.D., State University of Iowa
Formerly teacher at Coe College

BAXTER D. WILSON (1952–1955)
A.B., The Citadel; M.A., Ph.D., University of Virginia

RAYMOND R. WILSON (from 1950)
B.A., Northwestern State College (Oklahoma); M.A., West Texas State College

RENATE (WOLFF) WOLF (1952–1956)
B.A., Goucher College; M.Ed., Smith College; M.A., Ph.D., Bryn Mawr College
Formerly teacher at Wilkes College and at Wellesley College

EDITORIAL ASSISTANTS

DOROTHY L. ARTIN (*1934–1942; 1957)
B.S., University of Massachusetts

JOHN D. BARLOW (1954–1956)
B.A., Bates College

HOWARD K. BATTLES (1951–1955)
B.A., M.A., University of Minnesota

RUTH Y. BERRY (1958–1962)
S.B., Simmons College; M.A., American International College

GRACE E. BROPHY (1960–1963)
A.B., Grove City College

DOLORES D. CIERI (1951–1954)
Beaver College

MIRIAM E. COHEN (1957–1959)
New England Conservatory of Music

ROBERT W. CONBOY (1952–1970)
A.B., University of Miami; A.M., Vanderbilt University
Formerly teacher at Pfeiffer Junior College and at Riverside Military Academy

HILDA H. CONKLING (1959–1960)

THERESE (HAFEY) CORRIDAN (1946–1952)
B.A., College of Our Lady of the Elms

DOROTHY K. CRONE (1954–1955)
A.B., Smith College

MARIANNE E. DUFRESNE (1957–1959)
A.B., University of Vermont
Formerly teacher at Delevan (N.Y.) High School

ERWIN L. EISOLD (1940–1943)
B.A., Centre College of Kentucky

JOHN T. FLAHIVE (1951–1954)
B.S., Arnold College of Hygiene and Physical Education; M.A., Columbia University

HAROLD J. FLAVIN (1956–1957)
B.A., Tusculum College; M.F.S., University of Maryland; M.S. in L.S., Drexel Institute

LUCILLE B. GILCREAST (1958–1959)
B.S., Boston University

RITA L. GOYETTE (1946–1952)

HARVEY R. GRAVELINE (1959–1960)
A.B., Boston University

RUTH F. GREEN (1951–1954)
B.S.E., Massachusetts State Teachers College (Westfield); M.Ed., Springfield College

ALICE A. GUIMOND (1953–1954; 1955–1957)
B.A., American International College; M.A., University of Illinois; Ph.D., University of Wisconsin

MABEL B. HANCHETT (1942–1952)

SHIRLEY H. HENDERSON (1954–1955)
B.S., State Teachers College at Edinboro (Penn.)

JAMES M. HENRY, JR. (1958–1960)

BARBARA A. HOLLAND (1953–1955)
A.B., M.A., University of Pennsylvania

VERNON L. INGRAHAM (1951–1953)
B.A., University of New Hampshire; M.A., Amherst College

RUTH S. JOHNSON (1959–1961)
A.B., Oberlin College
Formerly teacher at Connellsville (Penn.) High School and at Northampton (Mass.) High School

CHARNA (LYTELL) KATZMAN (1952–1954)
B.A., American International College

IRENE (BARONIAN) KING (1950–1956)
B.A., American International College

DORIS R. KNIGHT (1958–1959; 1960–1961)
B.A., M.A., University of Massachusetts

MARY ELLEN KNIGHT (1957–1964)
B.A., University of New Hampshire; A.M., Boston University

ARTHUR G. LAMIRANDE (1959–1961)
B.A., American International College

EMILE O. LARUE (1956–1957)
B.A., Université Laval
Formerly teacher at Loyola College (Montreal), at Assumption College, and at Clark University

EDITH M. LOWE (1959–1966)
B.A., Milwaukee-Downer College
Formerly teacher at Wausau (Wis.) High School and at Bay Path Junior College

EULELAH G. LYON (1957–1963)
A.B. in Th., Gordon College

CHARLES P. MCCORMICK, JR. (1958–1961)
B.S., M.Ed., Springfield College

JUDITH (LEITCH) MARQUESS (1958–1959)
B.A., Queens College

PATRICIA F. MARTIN (1957–1971)
Wayne State University

JEAN (YOUNGDALE) MAYER (1953–1954)
B.S., University of Minnesota; M.Ed., University of Massachusetts

JOHN O. MAYHUGH (1941–1942)
B.A., M.A., University of Texas

BETTY MELTZER (1959–1967)
B.A., Goddard College

M. PORTIA MICKEY (1951–1954)
A.B., Oberlin College
Formerly teacher at North China Union Women's College and at Doshisha University (Japan)

LORNA (HOLBROOK) MUI (1953–1955)
B.S., M.A., Columbia University

EMILY (NOSS) MUTTER (1951–1952)
A.B., Mt. Holyoke College

GERTRUDE F. NEW (1957–1964)
Massachusetts State Teachers College (Westfield)

ANNE (BAKER) O'BRIEN (1951–1956)

RAYMOND L. PANIGHETTI (1959–1960)
B.A., American International College

JOHN E. PETRONE (1957–1961)
B.A.(J.), University of Wisconsin

MARIE T. PLOUFFE (1959–1960)
B.A., American International College

CHARLEEN A. PRENTICE (1952–1953)
B.A., American International College; M.Ed., Springfield College

WALTER A. REPPUCCI (1958–1959)
B.S.F.S., Georgetown University; M. Ed., Massachusetts State College at Westfield; J.D., Western New England College

BARBARA A. RICHMOND (1952–1956)
A.B., Smith College

ALICE (DUNN) ROBERTS (1952–1953)
A.B., Smith College

HAZEL B. ROSSI (1957–1959)
University of Massachusetts

WALTER E. SEARS (1951–1955)
A.B., Harvard University

DORIS N. SHERWOOD (1954–1966)

WALTER J. SKOCZOLEK (1951–1955)
B.S. in Ed., Massachusetts State Teachers College (Hyannis); A.M., Boston University
Formerly teacher at Springfield (Mass.) Technical High School and at Boston (Mass.) High School of Commerce

JANE F. SMITH (1958–1962)
B.A., Cornell University

GEORGIANA (WARD) STRICKLAND (1955–1957)
B.A., Middlebury College

THOMAS J. SULLIVAN (1954–1956)
A.B., Holy Cross College
Formerly teacher at Holy Cross College

KATHLEEN W. THOMPSON (1957–1958)
A.A., A.B., George Washington University

LUCY (RICH) THOMPSON (1940–1942)
A.B., Vassar College

ELSIE A. TOURVILLE (1951–1952)

CHARLES WESTCOTT (*1934–1946)

IDA N. WOLFSON (1954–1956)

DOROTHY M. ZIEMANN (1951–1955)
B.A., American International College; A.M., Ed.M., Boston University

ETHEL S. ZIMMERMAN (1958–1959)
B.S., University of Massachusetts

SECRETARIAL AND CLERICAL ASSISTANTS

MAUDE L. BARNES (from 1960)
Massachusetts State Teachers College (Framingham)

LILLIAN (BOUDREAU) CARPENTER (1953–1957)

ANNA M. CURTO (1953–1961)

BEATRICE (BREAULT) DAUNAIS (1951–1956)

MARY C. DILLON (1959–1968)
Massachusetts State Teachers College (Westfield)

ESTHER (HARRINGTON) GAUTHIER (1958–1962; 1969–)

MARY A. GRIFFIN (1953–1961)

ELEANOR (BRAULT) HARVEY (1952–1957)

EDITH (MOORE) HEATHCOTE (1938–1941)

ALICE HOYT (*1934–1940)

HELEN (MCGUIRE) JUTT (1943–1957)

SHEILA M. KELLY (1955–1961)

FLORIDA L. KING (1956–1961)

SADIE LAGODITZ (1946–1952)

CHRISTINE (MAYHER) MULLEN (*1934–1964)

MAE C. NIELSEN (1956–1965)

ARABELLE POLLOCK (1952–1957)

ROSAMOND (LYLE) PORTER (1948–1951)
B.A., Wells College

NELL (SABALASKA) SHERWOOD (1947–1952)

ROSE D. STICKEL (1959–1962)

EVELYN G. SUMMERS (from 1959)

FRANCES V. SUNDQUIST (1952–1956)

ROBERTA M. TEEHAN (1935–1944)

ROSE (DEWEY) THERRIEN (1954–1959)

BERTHA P. TIMBIE (1946–1962)
Sargent School of Physical Education

SARA N. TRACY (1954–1963)

MARIE P. TRUE (1953–1957)

MARGARET (COLE) VANCINI (1947–1951)

HELEN F. VYE (1952–1956)

NELLIE T. WILLCUTT (1958–1964)

PEARL (GREEN) WYMAN (*1934–1946)

OUTSIDE CONSULTANTS

THIS LIST of outside consultants contains 201 names. It is a partial list of specialists not on our own Merriam-Webster staff, for it includes only those who were asked to handle a considerable body of related terms as distinguished from other hundreds of outsiders whose opinions were sought by letter, telephone, or visit. To all these others we are grateful, but it would be impracticable to name every one. Those who are named have worked on terms in the subject mentioned opposite their name. This does not necessarily mean that they actually phrased the definitions in that subject. Because of the requirements of styling and of integrating definitions with each other and with overall policies not always easily explained to outsiders, responsibility for any definition cannot in fairness be placed on an outside consultant. The staff editors are solely responsible for the printed form of all definitions in this dictionary.

ABBOTT, KENNETH M. **Etymology: Greek and Latin**
A.B., Harvard University; Ph.D., University of Illinois
Professor of Classical Languages, Ohio State University
Coauthor: *Index Apuleianus; Index Verborum Ciceronis Epistularum*

ALLEN, MARTHA F. **Camp Fire Girls**
A.B., Mississippi State College for Women; A.M., Columbia University
National Director, Camp Fire Girls Inc.

ANDERSON, FRANK W., JR. **Air Force**
B.A., Birmingham-Southern College; M.A., Ph.D., University of North Carolina
Managing Editor: *Air University Quarterly Review*
Editor: *Great Flying Stories*

ANDERSON, RUTH TRIPP **Salvation Army**
Member of Salvation Army Editorial Staff

ARAND, LOUIS A. **Roman Catholicism**
A.B., A.M., S.T.B., St. Mary's Seminary and University; S.T.L., Catholic University of America; S.T.D., Anglico University (Rome)
President, Divinity College, Catholic University of America
Author: *St. Augustine: Faith, Hope and Charity*
Coauthor: *Doctrine and Devotion*
Editor: *The Spiritual Life*

ARENSBERG, CONRAD M. **Peoples and Tribes of Europe**
A.B., Ph.D., Harvard University
Professor of Anthropology, Columbia University
Author: *Irish Countryman; Family and Community in Ireland*
Coauthor: *Measuring Human Relations; Trade and Markets in the Early Empires*
Editor: *Human Organization*

BANNER, PAUL H. **Economics**
B.A., University of Michigan; M.P.A., Ph.D., Harvard University
Chairman, Research Committee, Western and Southwestern Trunkline Railroads
Lecturer in Economics, Washington University

BARROWS, ROBERT S. **Physics of Photography**
B.A., Kalamazoo College
Research Physicist, Eastman Kodak Company
Author: chapters or sections in *Theory of the Photographic Process* (Mees, rev.ed.) and *Fundamentals of Photographic Theory* (James and Higgins); several papers on photographic sensitometry

BASOLO, FRED **Chemical Elements Table, Periodic Table**
B.Ed., Southern Illinois Normal University; M.S., Ph.D., University of Illinois
Professor of Chemistry, Northwestern University
Author: numerous scientific publications
Coauthor: *Mechanisms of Inorganic Reactions*

BAUER, EDWARD E. **Concrete and Masonry**
B.S., C.E., M.S., University of Illinois
Professor of Civil Engineering, University of Illinois
Author: *Plain Concrete; Highway Materials*
Contributor: *Engineering News Record*

BECKMAN, THEODORE N. **Marketing**
B.S., A.M., Ph.D., Ohio State University
Professor of Marketing, Ohio State University
Author: *Credits and Collections in Theory and Practice*
Coauthor: *Principles of Marketing; Wholesaling; Cases in Credits and Collections*

BENDER, ERNEST **India and Pakistan**
A.B., Temple University; Ph.D., University of Pennsylvania
Research Associate Professor of Modern Indo-Aryan Languages and Literatures, University of Pennsylvania
Editor and translator: *The Nalarāyadavadantīcarita*

BITTINGER, CHARLES *Color:* **Spectrum**
Student, Massachusetts Institute of Technology; student, École des Beaux Arts; Academician, National Academy of Design; Captain, U.S.N.R. (Ret.)
Contributor: *U.S. Naval Institute Proceedings; National Geographic Magazine*

BLACK, KNOX C. **Communications**
A.B., A.M., Ph.D., Harvard University
Scientific Advisor to SACEUR, Supreme Headquarters Allied Powers Europe and to SHAPE in Paris, France

BLACK, MAX **Logic**
B.A., University of Cambridge; Ph.D., D. Lit., University of London
Professor of Philosophy, Cornell University
Author: *Language and Philosophy; The Nature of Mathematics; Critical Thinking; Problems of Analysis*
Editor: *Philosophical Analysis; The Social Theories of Talcott Parsons*
Coeditor: *Journal of Symbolic Logic; Philosophical Review*

BLAKELEY, HAROLD W. **Military Science**
Graduate: Field Artillery School; Command and General Staff School; Army War College
Major General, U.S. Army (Ret.)
Author: *The Employment of Land Mines; The 32d Infantry Division in World War II*
Contributor: *N. Y. Times, N. Y. Herald Tribune, Reporter*, and misc. military journals

BOGEN, JULES I. **Finance and Banking**
B.S., A.M., Ph.D., Columbia University
Professor of Finance, Graduate School of Business Administration, New York University
Author: *Corporation Finance*
Coauthor: *Investment Banking; Money and Banking*
Editor: *Financial Handbook*

BOUDREAU, RICHARD P. **Etymology: Romance**
B.A., Seton Hall University;
M.A., Ph.D., Princeton University
Assistant Professor of French, La Salle College

BOWIE, HAROLD E. **Mathematics**
B.A., M.A., University of Maine
Professor of Mathematics, American International College
Contributor: misc. mathematics publications

BOYD, WILLIAM C. **Immunology and Serology**
A.B., A.M., Harvard University;
Ph.D., Boston University
Professor of Immunochemistry, Boston University School of Medicine
Author: *Genetics and the Race of Man; Races and People;* textbooks and articles in technical journals

BREWER, ALLEN F. *Color Plate:* **Horses**
B.F.A., Yale University
Free-lance artist; president of EQUI-LITH
Contributor: *Encyclopaedia Britannica;* veterinary manuals; national turf and harness horse publications

BROWN, JAMES M., III **Glass**
B.A., (hon.) M.A., Amherst College; M.A., Harvard University
Director, Corning Glass Center

BROWN, KARL **Library Science**
A.B., University of Kansas; B.S., New York State Library School
Free-lance editor and bibliographer; Library Consultant, St. Martin's Press (N.Y.C.)
Author: *Guide to Reference Collections of the New York Public Library*
Editor: *New York Public Library; Library Journal*

BROWN, ROY H. **Art**
A.B., Queens College; A.M., Columbia University
Instructor, Garland Junior College; Art Director, Houghton Mifflin Company

BRUMMITT, WYATT B. **Amateur Photography**
B.Litt., Columbia University
Manager, Historical Projects, Eastman Kodak Company
Coauthor: *This Is Photography*
Editor: *Pictures*

BUSSOW, CARL **Pavement Construction**
B.S., Cooper Union; B.S., Polytechnic Institute of Brooklyn
Consulting Chemist and Paving Engineer
Contributor: misc. articles

CALAMIA, ERIC **Pipes and Tobacco**
Managing Director, Retail Tobacco Dealers of America Inc.

CARPENTER, FRANK M. **Entomology**
A.B., M.S., D.Sc., Harvard University
Professor of Entomology, Alexander Agassiz Professor of Zoology, and Curator of Fossil Insects, Museum of Comparative Zoology, Harvard University
Author: misc. articles on insect evolution and taxonomy

CASKEY, JAMES E., JR. **Meteorology**
B.S., Furman University; M.A., Duke University; Certificate of Professional Competence in Meteorology, University of Chicago
Meteorologist Editor: U.S. Weather Bureau
Editor: *Monthly Weather Review*

CHAMBERLAIN, NEIL W. **Labor**
A.B., M.A., Western Reserve University; Ph.D., Ohio State University
Professor of Economics, Yale University
Author: *The Union Challenge to Management Control; Collective Bargaining; Social Responsibility and Strikes; The Impact of Strikes; A General Theory of Economic Process; Labor*

CHILD, EDWIN B. *Portrait of Noah Webster*
A.B., (hon.) M.A., Amherst College
Artist

CHRISTENSEN, CLYDE M. **Mycology**
B.S., M.S., Ph.D., University of Minnesota
Professor of Plant Pathology, University of Minnesota
Author: *Common Edible Mushrooms; Molds and Man; Keys to the Common Fleshy Fungi;* numerous research papers in plant pathology, mycology

CLENCH, WILLIAM J. **Mollusks**
B.S., (hon.) D.Sc., Michigan State University; M.S., Harvard University; M.S., Ph.D., University of Michigan
Curator of Mollusks, Harvard Museum of Comparative Zoology
Special Editor in Zoology, *Webster's New International Dictionary, Second Edition*
Editor and contributor: *Johnsonia;* occasional papers on mollusks

COBURN, C. GILBERT **Coffee**
B.J., University of Missouri
Director of Public Relations, Pan-American Coffee Bureau

COLE, FAY-COOPER **Archaeology**
B.S., Sc.D., Northwestern University; Ph.D., Columbia University; LL.D., University of Chicago; LL.D., Beloit College
Professor Emeritus of Anthropology, University of Chicago
Author: *Peoples of Malaysia; The Bukidnon*
Coauthor: *Kincaid, A Prehistoric Illinois Metropolis*
Contributor: articles for encyclopedias

CONKLIN, HAROLD C. **Etymology and Definitions: Austronesian**
A.B., University of California (Berkeley); Ph.D., Yale University
Associate Professor of Anthropology, Columbia University
Author: *Hanunóo-English Vocabulary; Hanunóo Agriculture*

CORNEY, GEORGE M. **Radiography**
B.A., Cornell University
Research Associate, Eastman Kodak Company
Contributor: *Handbook of Nondestructive Testing; Radiation Hygiene Handbook*

CREED, ROBERT P. **Etymology: Derivative and Germanic**
B.A., Swarthmore College;
M.A., Ph.D., Harvard University
Assistant Professor of English, Brown Univ.
Author: articles and reviews on Old English

DALL, WILLIAM B. **Textile Machinery and Processes**
B.A., Amherst College
Managing Editor, *Textile World*

DARKIS, FREDERICK R. **Tobacco**
B.S., M.S., Ph.D., University of Maryland
Vice-president and Director of Research, Liggett and Myers Tobacco Company
Author: misc. articles on tobacco

DAY, CYRUS L. **Knots**
B.S., Harvard University; A.M., Columbia University; Ph.D., Harvard University
Professor of English, University of Delaware
Author: *The Art of Knotting and Splicing*
Editor: *Songs of Dryden; Songs of D'Urfey*
Cocompiler: *English Song-Books*

DECAMP, DAVID **Etymology: Scientific**
B.A., Hillsdale College; M.A., University of New Mexico; Ph.D., University of California
Assistant Professor of English, University of Texas
Author: *Jamaican Creole*
Contributor: *Orbis*

DEIGNAN, HERBERT G. **Ornithology**
A.B., Princeton
Curator, Birds, U.S. National Museum, Smithsonian Institution
Author: *The Birds of Northern Thailand; Type Specimens of Birds in the United States National Museum; Check-list of the Birds of Thailand*

DILGER, WILLIAM C. *Color Plates:* **State Birds, Water Birds**
B.S., M.S., Ph.D.,
Cornell University
Director of Research and Assistant Professor of Ornithology, Cornell University
Contributor: *Wilson Bulletin; Auk; Evolution; Zeitschrift für Tierpsychologie*

DIXON, ALBERT, JR. **Accounting**
C.P.A., Massachusetts, Connecticut; B.C.S., Northeastern University; LL.D., Western New England College
Partner, Ernst & Ernst
Trustee, Western New England College

DODGE, AUSTIN A. **Pharmacy**
Ph.C., Valparaiso University; B.S., Ph.D., University of Wisconsin
Professor of Pharmacognosy, School of Pharmacy, University of Mississippi
Assistant Editor: *Remington's Practice of Pharmacy*

DRAVES, CARL Z. **Dye Table**
B.S., M.S., Ph.D., University of Washington
Instructor in Chemistry, Brooklyn College
Author: "Textile Chemical Specialties," *1933 Technical Manual and Year Book of American Association of Textile Chemists and Colorists*
Contributor: *Journal of Optical Society of America; American Dyestuff Reporter; Melliand Textilberichte; Encyclopedia of Chemical Technology*

DUNNIGAN, MARY CATHERINE **Brewing**
B.A., Mary Washington College; M.L.S., Columbia University
Librarian, U.S. Brewers Foundation, Inc.
Author: *Beer and Ale in Old New York*

EATON, GEORGE T. **Chemistry of Photography**
B.A., Brandon College; B.S.,
Acadia University; M.A., McMaster University
Head of Processing Research Department; Assistant Head of Applied Photography Division, Research Laboratories, Eastman Kodak Company
Author: *Photochemistry; in Black-and-White and Color Photography*
Contributor: *Americana Annual*

ELBERT, SAMUEL H. **Etymology and Definitions: Polynesian**
A.B., Grinnell College;
Ph.D., Indiana University
Professor of Pacific Languages and Linguistics, University of Hawaii
Coauthor: *Hawaiian-English Dictionary*

EMENEAU, MURRAY B. **Etymology: Indic and Dravidian**
B.A., Dalhousie University; B.A., M.A., Oxford University; Ph.D., Yale University
Professor of Sanskrit and General Linguistics, University of California (Berkeley)
Author: *Kota Texts; Kolami, a Dravidian Language; Sanskrit Sandhi and Exercises; Studies in Vietnamese (Annamese) Grammar*
Coauthor: *A Dravidian Etymological Dictionary*
Contributor: educational publications

FAIRBAIRN, HAROLD W. **Petrology and Geochronology**
B.Sc., Queen's University; A.M., Ph.D., Harvard University
Professor of Geology, Massachusetts Institute of Technology
Author: *Structural Petrology of Deformed Rocks*

FEDERER, CHARLES A., JR. **Astronomy**
B.S., City College of New York
Editor and Publisher: *Sky and Telescope*

FERGUSON, CHARLES A. **Language Tables: Afro-Asiatic (Arabic)**
A.B., A.M.,
Ph.D., University of Pennsylvania
Director, Center for Applied Linguistics (Washington, D.C.)
Coauthor: *Lessons in Contemporary Arabic*
Editor: *Contributions to Arabic Linguistics*
Coeditor: *Linguistic Diversity in South Asia*

FERGUSON, WALTER W. *Color Plates:* **Gems, Insects, Monkeys**
Artist; formerly a
staff artist for the American Museum of Natural History

FLOROVSKY, GEORGES **Eastern Orthodoxy**
Diploma, Graduate Studies, University of Odessa; D.D., St. Andrews University; S.T.D., Boston University; Th.D., University of Salonika
Professor of Eastern Church History, Harvard Divinity School
Author: *Eastern Fathers of the Fourth Century; Byzantine Fathers of the Fifth through the Eighth Centuries; Ways of Russian Theology*
Contributor: *Cahiers théologiques de l'actualité protestante; A History of the Ecumenical Movement*

FORD, ROBERT S. **Taxation**
A.B., Texas Christian University; A.M., University of California; Ph.D., Columbia University
Associate Dean, Rackham Graduate School and Professor of Economics, University of Michigan
Author: *Michigan Highway Finance*
Contributor: technical and professional journals

FOSTER, FRED W. **Cartography**
A.B., M.S., Ph.D., University of Michigan
Professor of Geography, University of Illinois
Editor: *Atlas of Illinois Resources; Commercial Atlas*
Contributor: numerous articles on interpretation of aerial photographs

FRIED, HENRY B. **Horology**
Graduate of the University of the State of New York Industrial Teachers' Training College
Technical Director: American Watchmakers' Institute; Watch Material Distributors' Association of America
Horological Consultant: *Jewelers' Circular-Keystone*
Author: *Watch Repairers' Manual; Bench Practices for Watch Repairers; The Watch Escapement; The Universal Watch Parts Catalogue*

FULFORD, MARGARET **Mosses and Liverworts**
B.A., B.E., A.M., University of
Cincinnati; Ph.D., Yale University
Professor of Botany, Fellow of the Graduate School, University of Cincinnati
Author: *Bazzania in Central and South America; Young Stages in the Leafy Hepaticae; Distribution Patterns of the Genera of Leafy Hepaticae of South America*

GARRATT, GEORGE A. **Forestry**
B.S., Michigan State College; M.F., Ph.D., Yale University; (hon.) Sc.D., University of the South
Dean, School of Forestry, and Pinchot Professor of Forestry, Yale University
Author: *The Mechanical Properties of Wood*
Coauthor: *Wood Preservation*

GILLETTE, GEORGE A. **Photographic Trade Names**
E.E., Rensselaer Polytechnic Institute; LL.B., Fordham University Law School
Assistant Director of Patent Department, Eastman Kodak Company

GLEASON, HENRY A. **Plant Taxonomy (Flowering Plants)**
B.S., A.M., University of Illinois; Ph.D., Columbia University
Head Curator Emeritus, New York Botanical Garden
Author: *A Revision of the North American Vernonieae; The Vegetation of the Inland Sand Deposits of Illinois; Some Applications of the Quadrat Method; The Vegetational History of the Middle West; The Individualistic Concept of the Plant Association; Botan-*

ical Results of the Tyler-Duida Expedition; Plants of the Vicinity of New York
Coauthor: *The New Britton and Brown Illustrated Flora of the Northeastern United States and Adjacent Canada; Plant Ecology of Porto Rico*
Contributor: numerous articles on botanical research

GLEASON, HENRY A., JR. **Language Names**
B.S., Cornell; Ph.D., Hartford Seminary Foundation
Professor of Linguistics, Hartford Seminary Foundation
Author: *An Introduction to Descriptive Linguistics*

GODLOVE, ISAAC H. **Color**
B.S., A.M., Washington University; Ph.D., University of Illinois
Chemist and Physicist, DuPont Company and General Aniline and Film Corporation
Special Editor in Color, *Webster's New International Dictionary, Second Edition*
Author: articles on color physics and psychology
Coauthor: *The Science of Colors; The Smithsonian Tables of Physical Constants*

GOLLON, FRANK R. **Photographic Trade Names**
B.S., C.E., City College of New York; LL.B. George Washington University
Patent Attorney, Eastman Kodak Company

GORDON, LEWIS H. **Etymology: Italian and French**
A.B., A.M., Princeton University; Ph.D., Cornell University
Professor of Italian and French, Brown Univ.
Author: *Supplementary Concordance to Minor Italian Works of Dante*

GRIMWOOD, W. K. **Sound Motion Pictures**
B.S., Massachusetts Institute of Technology
Research Associate, Eastman Kodak Company
Contributor: articles on sound recording and television

GRISWOLD, ERWIN N. **Law**
A.B., A.M., Oberlin College; LL.B., S.J.D., Harvard University; L.H.D., Tufts College and Case Institute of Technology; LL.D., thirteen universities and colleges
Dean and Langdell Professor of Law, Harvard Law School
Author: *Spendthrift Trusts; Cases on Federal Taxation; The Fifth Amendment Today*
Coauthor: *Cases on Conflict of Laws*
General Editor: American Casebook Series
Contributor: legal periodicals; *Geographical Review*

GROSSENHEIDER, RICHARD P. *Color Plates:* **Butterflies and Moths, Cats, Shells**
Free-lance artist

GUMPERTZ, WERNER H. **Building and Building Materials**
S.B., S.M., Bldg. E., Massachusetts Institute of Technology
Consulting Engineer and President, Simpson Gumpertz and Heger Inc.
Contributor: *Technology Review, Journal of Engineering Education, Civil Engineering*

GUNN, HAROLD D. **Africa: Peoples and Tribes**
B.A., Southern Methodist University; M.A., University of London
Assistant Professor of Anthropology and African History, Lincoln University (Pa.)
Author: *Peoples of the Plateau Area of Northern Nigeria; Pagan Peoples of the Central Area of Northern Nigeria; Handbook of the African Collections of the Commercial Museum of Philadelphia*
Coauthor: *Peoples of the Middle Niger Region, Northern Nigeria*

HAMILTON, RICHARD W. *Star Charts*
B.S., Polytechnic Institute of Brooklyn
Chart Curator of the American Association of Variable Star Observers

HARRIS, ZELLIG S. **Language Tables: Afro-Asiatic**
A.B., A.M., Ph.D., University of Pennsylvania
Professor of Linguistic Analysis, University of Pennsylvania
Author: *Development of Canaanite Dialects; Methods in Structural Linguistics;* several monographs
Contributor: articles to technical journals

HARRISON, G. DONALD **Pipe Organs**
President of Aeolian-Skinner Company

HECKMAN, RICHARD C. **Physics**
B.S., Antioch College; M.A., Ph.D., Duke University
Research Physicist, C. F. Kettering Foundation
Associate Professor of Physics, Antioch College

HEDGES, J. EDWARD **Insurance**
A.B., Baker University; M.B.A., University of Kansas; Ph.D., Johns Hopkins University; LL.D., Baker University
Professor of Insurance, Indiana University
Author: *Practical Fire and Casualty Insurance; Commercial Banking and the Stock Market before 1863*
Coauthor: *Compensation of Life Insurance Agents; Public Law 15 and the Insurance Agent*
Contributor: *Economic Problems of War;* educational and business publications

HENRY, ROBERT S. **Railroads**
A.B., LL.B., Vanderbilt University; Litt.D., University of Chattanooga
Vice-president, Association of American Railroads
Author: *Trains; This Fascinating Railroad Business; The Story of the Confederacy; "First with the Most" Forrest; The Story of the Mexican War; The Story of Reconstruction*
Editor: *As They Saw Forrest*

HIBBS, FENELLA W. **Girl Guiding**
Public Relations Secretary, Girl Guides Association, London

HIMMELSBACH, G. R. **Brewing**
B.A., M.A., Indiana University
Head, Department of Information, U.S. Brewers' Foundation Inc.

HINE, WADSWORTH C. *Line drawings for cuts*
Student, Cleveland Institute of Art
Commercial artist

HOENIGSWALD, HENRY M. **Etymology: Greek and Latin**
D.Litt., University of Florence (Italy)
Professor of Linguistics, Univ. of Pennsylvania
Author: *Spoken Hindustani; Language Change and Linguistic Reconstruction*

HOOTMAN, JAMES A. **Aeronautics**
B.S., Randolph-Macon College; M.S., Mississippi State College; Ph.D., University of Virginia
Executive Secretary, Inventions and Contributions Board, National Aeronautics and Space Administration
Contributor: *American Journal of Science, Physics Review*, National Advisory Committee for Aeronautics reports

HUGHES, CHARLES H. **Nautical**
Student, Massachusetts Institute of Technology
Naval Architect and Engineer
Author: *Motor Boats; Handbook of Ship Calculations and Construction*
Contributor: *New International Year Book*

HURD, CHARLES D. **Chemistry**
B.S., Syracuse University; Ph.D., Princeton University; (hon.) Sc.D., Syracuse Univ.
Clare Hamilton Hall Research Professor of Chemistry, Northwestern University
Author: *The Pyrolysis of Carbon Compounds; Open-Chain Nitrogen Compounds*
Contributor: articles in various fields of chemistry

HURD, FRED W. **Traffic Regulations**
B.S., University of Missouri; Certificate in Highway Traffic, Yale University
Director, Bureau of Highway Traffic, Yale University
Coauthor: *Traffic Engineering*

HYMES, DELL H. **Etymology: American Indian**
B.A., Reed College; M.A., Ph.D., Indiana University
Associate Professor of Anthropology and Linguistics, Univ. of California (Berkeley)
Contributor: *Anthropological Linguistics, Current Anthropology*

IVES, CHARLES E. **Motion Picture Technology**
Research Associate, Eastman Kodak Company
Coauthor: papers on motion picture film, instrument design, and photographic development

JACKSON, Robert J. **Rugs**
B.Ch.E., Northeastern University; M.S., Massachusetts Institute of Technology
Director of Engineering and Research, Bigelow-Sanford Carpet Company Inc.

JAMES, THOMAS H. **Photo Theory and Development Theory**
A.B., M.A., Ph.D., University of Colorado
Senior Research Associate, Eastman Kodak Company
Author: *Fundamentals of Photographic Theory*
Editor: *Photographic Science and Engineering*
Contributor: *Encyclopedia of Chemical Technology;* numerous research papers

JONES, WILLIAM R. **Etymology: Greek and Latin**
A.B., A.M., Ph.D., Univ. of Illinois
Associate Professor of Classical Languages, Ohio State University

JOOS, MARTIN **Cryptography**
A.M., Ph.D., University of Wisconsin
Professor of German and Linguistics, University of Wisconsin
Author: *Acoustic Phonetics; Middle High German Courtly Reader; Readings in Linguistics*
Contributor: articles in linguistic journals

JUDD, DEANE B. **Color**
A.B., M.A., Ohio State University; Ph.D., Cornell University
Physicist, Colorimetry, National Bureau of Standards; President, Munsell Color Foundation
Author: *Colór in Business, Science, and Industry*
Editor: *Journal of the Optical Society of America*
Contributor: chapters in science books and articles

KELLENBERGER, HUNTER **Etymology: Romance**
A.B., Kenyon College; A.M., Ph.D., Princeton University
Professor of French, Brown University
Author: *The Influence of Accentuation on French Word Order*
Contributor: *The Case for Basic Education*

KIMPTON, KENNETH **Hardware**
B.S., University of Rochester
Associate Professor, Electrical Department, Rochester Institute of Technology

KINGSLAKE, RUDOLF **Optics of Photography**
B.Sc., M.Sc., D.Sc., Imperial College of Science and Technology (London)
Director of Optical Design, Eastman Kodak Company
Author: *Lenses in Photography*
Contributor: scientific papers, articles, and chapters in books

KNOWLTON, ARCHER E. **Engineering**
B.S., M.S., Trinity College (Conn.); E.E., Yale University
Associate Professor of Electrical Engineering, Yale University
Electrical Engineer, Connecticut Public Utilities Commission
Author: *Electrical Power Metering*
Senior Associate Editor: *Electrical World*

KORAB, HARRY E. **Soft Drinks**
B.S., University of Maryland
Technical Service Director, American Bottlers of Carbonated Beverages
Author: *Technical Problems of Bottled Carbonated Beverage Manufacture; Outline of Water Treating Methods*
Contributor: *American Society of Refrigeration Engineers Data Book*

KOSSOFF, A. DAVID **Etymology: Romance**
A.B., Amherst College; A.M., Ph.D., Brown University
Associate Professor of Spanish, Brown University
Author: *The Poetic Vocabulary of Fernando de Herrera*
Contributor: articles on Herrera

KRONEN, LEIF C. **Leather**
A.B., Nebraska Wesleyan University; LL.B., University of Nebraska
Secretary of Tanners' Council of America Inc.

KURATH, GERTRUDE PROKOSCH **Dance Ethnology**
B.A., M.A., Bryn Mawr College
Dance Editor: *Ethno-musicology*
Director: Dance Research Center
Author: books on Indian musicology and dance, folkways records
Dance Editor: *Topical Encyclopedia*
Contributor: articles on music and dance ethnology in journals, encyclopedias and the *Dictionary of Folklore*

LADRIÈRE, JAMES C. **Prosody**
Ph.B., University of Detroit; A.M., Ph.D., University of Michigan
Professor of English, Catholic University of America; Visiting Professor of Comparative Literature, University of Louvain and Harvard University
Author: *Directions in Contemporary Criticism and Literary Scholarship*
Coauthor: *English Institute Essays; Sound and Poetry*
Contributor: various articles on prosody

LAFAR, ARTHUR B. **Cocktails**
Formerly, President, Angostura-Wuppermann Corporation

LAMBDIN, THOMAS O. **Etymology: Semitic and Hamitic**
A.B., Franklin and Marshall College; Ph.D., Johns Hopkins University
Assistant Professor of Hebrew, Harvard Univ.
Contributor: articles on the Semitic and Egyptian languages

LAWSON, RICHARD H. **Etymology: Scientific**
B.A., M.A., University of Oregon; Ph.D., University of California
Assistant Professor of German, San Diego State College
Contributor: articles on Old High German and Modern German literature

LEBEL, C. J. **Audio Devices**
S.B., S.M., Massachusetts Institute of Technology
Vice-president, Audio Devices Inc.; President and Chief Engineer, Audio Instrument Company Inc.
Contributor: articles in engineering and scientific journals

LEROUX, ANDRE **Liquors and Cordials**
B.A., Lehigh University
President, Leroux and Company Inc.

LESLAU, WOLF **Language Tables: Afro-Asiatic (Ethiopic, Cushitic)**
Lic. ès Lettres, Dr. ès Lettres, Sorbonne
Professor of Hebrew and Semitic Linguistics, University of California (Los Angeles)
Author: *Short Grammar of Tigre; A Dictionary of Moca*

LEWIS, HENRY **Etymology: Celtic**
M.A., D. Litt., University College (Cardiff); (hon.) D.Litt.Celt., National University of Ireland
Professor Emeritus of University of Wales; formerly, Professor of Welsh Languages and Literature, University College of Swansea
Author: *Llawlyfr Cernyweg Canol; Llawlyfr*

Llydaweg Canol; Datblygial yr Iaith Gymraeg; Brut Dingestow
Coauthor: *A Concise Comparative Celtic Grammar*
Editor: *Peniarth 53; Welsh New Testament; Welsh Old Testament; Welsh Apocrypha;* etc.
Coeditor: *Welsh Congregational Hymnbook;* etc.
Contributor: *Encyclopaedia Britannica;* Welsh journals

LOVELAND, ROGER P. **Photomicrography**
B.A., Grinnell College; M.Sc., Ohio State University
Head, Photomicrography Department, Eastman Kodak Company
Author: *Photomicrography*
Contributor: misc. papers

LOWE, RONALD L. **Matches**
A.B., DePauw University
Sales Promotion Manager, Diamond Match Division, Diamond National Corporation

LUNN, HERBERT W. **Boy Scouts**
Assistant to the Director, Editorial Service, National Council of Boy Scouts of America

LUTZ, HAROLD J. **Forestry**
B.S., Michigan State College; M.F., Ph.D., Yale University
Morris K. Jesup Professor of Silviculture, Yale University
Coauthor: *Forest Soils*

LYMAN, HENRY **Marine Sport Fisheries**
A.B., Harvard University
Publisher: *Salt Water Sportsman*
Author: *Bluefishing*
Coauthor: *Striped Bass Fishing; Weakfishing*

LYMAN, TAYLOR **Metals**
A.B., Stanford University; S.M., Harvard University; Ph.D., Notre Dame University
Editor: *Metals Handbook*

MCGHEE, ADDISON F., JR. **Distilling**
B.S., Alabama Polytechnic Institute
Director of Public Relations, Kentucky Rural Electric Corporation; formerly, Community Relations Manager, Brown-Forman Distilling Corporation
Author: *He's in the Armored Force; History of Fort Knox*
Contributor: misc. articles in magazines, newspapers

MCLANATHAN, RICHARD B. K. **Minor Arts**
A.B., Ph.D., Harvard University
Director, Munson-Williams-Proctor Institute; formerly, Curator, Museum of Fine Arts, Department of Decorative Arts of Europe and America (Boston)

MCMILLAN, DONALD M. **Salvation Army**
Graduate, Salvation Army Officers' Training College
National Commander, Salvation Army in U.S.

MARTIN, GEORGE WILLARD **Mycology**
Litt.B., M.S., Rutgers University; Ph.D., University of Chicago
Emeritus Professor of Botany, State University of Iowa
Author: *Outline of the Fungi*
Coauthor: *The Myxomycetes*
Contributor: articles in botanical journals; *Dictionary of the Fungi*

MARTIN, JOHN H. **Agriculture**
B.S., Oregon State College; M.S., University of Maryland; Ph.D., University of Minnesota
Agriculturist, Research Service, U.S. Department of Agriculture
Author: *Principles of Field Crop Production*
Contributor: *Encyclopaedia Britannica, Cyclopedia American*

MATHER, KIRTLEY F. **Geology**
B.S., Sc.D., Denison University; Ph.D., University of Chicago; Sc.D., Colby College; Litt.D., Union College; L.H.D., Bates College; LL.D., Beloit College
Professor Emeritus of Geology, Harvard University
Author: *Old Mother Earth;* numerous other books
Coauthor: *Source Book of Geology*
Contributor: U.S. Geological Survey papers and bulletins; papers in technical periodicals; popular articles

MATTHEWS, GLENN E. **Photography and Motion Pictures**
B.Sc., M.Sc., University of Minnesota
Technical Editor, Research Laboratories, Eastman Kodak Company
Special Editor in Photography, *Webster's New International Dictionary, Second Edition*
Coauthor: *Photographic Chemicals and Solutions*
Contributor: *New International Encyclopedia, National Encyclopedia Yearbook, Americana Encyclopedia Yearbook, American Annual of Photography, Yearbook of Science, Photography Yearbook, Photographic Progress*

MEES, CHARLES E. K. **Photography**
B.Sc., D.Sc., University of London; (hon.) D.Sc., University of Rochester, Alfred University
Vice-president in charge of Research, Eastman Kodak Company
Special Editor in Photography, *Webster's New International Dictionary, Second Edition*
Author or coauthor of several books

MEGARGEE, EDWIN *Color Plate:* **Dogs**
Student, Georgetown University, Drexel Institute, Art Students League
Painter, Author, and Illustrator: *Dogs; Horses; The Dogs' Dictionary; Gun Dogs at Work*

MERRILL, LINDSEY **Music**
Mus.M., Yale University
Professor of Music, Bucknell University
Editor: *Trio Sonatas by J. S. Bach*

MERTON, ROBERT K. **Sociology**
A.B., LL.D., Temple University; M.A., Ph.D., Harvard University
Professor of Sociology, Columbia University
Author: *Social Theory and Social Structure; Science, Technology, and Society in 17th Century England; Mass Persuasion*
Coauthor: *The Focussed Interview*
Coeditor: *Continuities in Social Research; Reader in Bureaucracy; The Student-Physician; Sociology Today*

MEYER, WALTER H. **Forestry**
B.A., M.F., Ph.D., Yale University
Harriman Professor of Forest Management, Yale University
Coauthor: *Forest Mensuration; Forest Valuation*

MILLER, PAUL R. **Plant Pathology**
B.S., Indiana University; M.S., Purdue University; Ph.D., George Washington University
Plant Pathologist, Crops Research Division, U.S. Department of Agriculture
Author: numerous scientific papers

MINSHALL, ROBERT **Etymology: Romance and Celtic**
A.B., M.A., Ph.D., Princeton University
Assistant Professor of German, University of Scranton
Author: *Indo-European */y in Armenian; Indo-European */y in Albanian*

MITCHELL, GEORGE F. **Tea**
B.S., Clemson Agricultural College
Tea consultant; formerly, Plant Manager, Maxwell House Tea Division, General Foods Corporation
Author: monographs and articles on tea

MONACHINO, JOSEPH **Taxonomy**
B.S., St. John's University (N.Y.)
Associate Custodian of the Herbarium, New York Botanical Gardens
Author: taxonomic studies on *Manilkara, Ryania,* and various genera of Apocynaceae

MOREHEAD, ALBERT H. **Card Games, Gambling Games**
Bridge Editor, New York Times
Author: *The New Complete Hoyle; Official Rules of Card Games;* numerous other books

MORGAN, ANN H. **Zoology**
A.B., Ph.D., Cornell University
Professor of Zoology, Mount Holyoke College
Author: *Field Book of Ponds and Streams; Animals in Winter; Kinships of Animal and Man*

MORGRET, CHARLES O. **Railroads**
B.A., George Washington University; M.A., American University
Manager, Public and Special Services, Association of American Railroads
Author: *Careers in the American Railroad Industry*

MORRIS, ROBERT A. **Color and Colorimetry**
B.S., University of Michigan
Technical Associate, Eastman Kodak Company
Contributor: *Progress in Photography; Television Engineering Handbook*

MORTON, CONRAD V. **Ferns**
A.B., University of California
Curator, Division of Ferns, United States National Museum

MOYES, VICTOR J. **Applied Photography and Equipment**
S.B., S.M., Massachusetts Institute of Technology
Curator, Patent Department Museum, Eastman Kodak Company

MUEHLER, LOWELL E. **Chemistry of Photography**
B.S., Rose Polytechnic Institute
Research Associate: Photographic Chemistry, Research Laboratories, Eastman Kodak Company
Coauthor: papers on the chemistry and technology of photographic processing and after-treatments

MUNROE, W. O. **Industrial Management**
A.B., St. Mary's College (Kansas)
Formerly, Works Manager, The Baldwin Locomotive Works (1929–38)
Author: shop manuals and procedure instructions for various industries

MYERS, GEORGE S. **Ichthyology**
A.B., A.M., Ph.D., Stanford University
Professor of Biology and Curator of Zoology Collections, Stanford University
Editor: *Stanford Ichthyological Bulletin*
Associate Editor: *The Aquarium*
Managing Editor: *Aquarium Journal*

NELSON, CLARENCE N. **Physics of Photography**
B.A., St. Olaf College; M.S., Ohio State University
Research Physicist, Eastman Kodak Company
Contributor: articles on sensitivity of photographic materials, aerial photography, color photography

NEWHALL, BEAUMONT **History of Photography**
A.B., A.M., Harvard University
Director, George Eastman House
Author: *The History of Photography; The Daguerreotype in America*
Coauthor: *Masters of Photography*

NICKERSON, DOROTHY **Colorimetry**
Color Technologist, Chief of Standardization Section, Cotton Division, United States Department of Agriculture
Contributor: articles on color measurements and specifications, color, and illumination problems in color grading and standardization

NOEL, JOHN V., JR. **Navigation and Seamanship**
B.S., United States Naval Academy; M.A., Stanford University
Captain, United States Navy
Author: *Naval Terms Dictionary; Division Officer's Guide; Watch Officer's Guide*
Coauthor: *Shiphandling*
Editor: *Knight's Modern Seamanship*

ODELL, LOREN B. **Paints and Varnish**
B.S., North Dakota Agricultural College
President, James Bute Company

ODUM, EUGENE P. **Ecology**
A.B., A.M., University of North Carolina; Ph.D., University of Illinois
Alumni Foundation Distinguished Professor of Zoology, University of Georgia
Author: *Fundamentals of Ecology*
Contributor: articles in scientific journals

OWEN, GWILYM E. **Physics**
Ph.B., Lafayette College; Ph.D., University of Pennsylvania
Professor of Physics, Antioch College
Special Editor in Physics, *Webster's New International Dictionary, Second Edition*
Contributor: articles on the growing of quartz crystals, the conductivity of electrolytes at temperatures near the critical temperature of water, the responsibility of scientists, history of science, and the teaching of physics

PARKER, HAYWOOD, JR. **Applied Photography and Equipment**
A.B., M.S., University of North Carolina
Supervisor of Technical Publications, Eastman Kodak Company

PATTERSON, AUSTIN M. **Chemistry**
A.B., Princeton University; Ph.D., Johns Hopkins University; (hon.) D.Sc., Antioch College
Vice-president and Professor of Chemistry, Antioch College
Special Editor in Chemistry, *Webster's New International Dictionary* and *Webster's New International Dictionary, Second Edition*
Author: *French-English Dictionary for Chemists; German-English Dictionary for Chemists*
Coauthor: *Ring Index: A List of Ring Systems Used in Organic Chemistry; Guide to the Literature of Chemistry*
Editor: *Chemical Abstracts*
Contributor: numerous articles on chemistry

PEEL, ROBERT **Christian Science**
A.B., A.M., Harvard University
Formerly, editorial writer for *Christian Science Monitor*
Author: *Christian Science: Its Encounter with American Culture*

PENZL, HERBERT **Etymology: Iranian**
Ph.D., Vienna University
Professor of German, University of Michigan
Author: *A Grammar of Pashto*
Contributor: articles in general, Germanic, and Oriental linguistics

PERROT, PAUL N. **Glass**
Director, The Corning Museum of Glass, Corning Glass Center
Author: *Three Great Centuries of Venetian Glass*
Contributor: *Antiques*

PERRY, JAMES W. **Non-numerical Computer Applications**
B.S., M.S., North Carolina State College; S.M., Massachusetts Institute of Technology
Professor, College of Engineering, University of Arizona
Author: *Chemical Russian, Self-Taught; Scientific Russian*
Coauthor: *Surface Active Agents; Machine Literature Searching; Centralized Information Services*
Coeditor: *Punched Cards; Information Systems in Documentation; Tools for Machine Literature Searching*

PHILLIPS, CRAIG *Color Plates:* **Fishes, Tropical Fishes**
A.B., University of Miami
Assistant Director, National Aquarium, United States Fish and Wildlife Service
Coauthor: *Sea Pests*

PIOTRASCHKE, CHARLES F. **Hardware**
A.A.S., Rochester Institute of Technology; B.S., University of Rochester
Assistant Professor of Electrical Engineering, Rochester Institute of Technology

PLUMMER, GAYTHER L. **Plant Ecology**
B.S., Butler University; M.S., Kansas State College; Ph.D., Purdue University
Assistant Professor, Department of Botany, University of Georgia
Contributor: articles on plant species

POSTER, FRANCES W. **Girl Scouts**
A.B., University of Maryland; M.A., Columbia University
Director of Publications, Girl Scouts of the United States of America

PRESCOTT, G. W. **Phycology**
B.A., University of Oregon; M.A., Ph.D., University of Iowa
Professor of Botany and Plant Pathology, Michigan State University
Author: *Algae of the Western Great Lakes Area; How to Know the Fresh-water Algae*
Coauthor: *Fundamentals of Plant Science*

QUIMBY, HAROLD R. **Shoes**
Formerly, Executive Secretary, National Shoe Manufacturers' Association

RASCHIG, F. ELMER **Freemasonry**
A.B., Indiana University
Grand Secretary General Supreme Council 33 Scottish Rite of Northern Masonic Jurisdiction U.S.A.

RASHKIS, HAROLD A. **Psychiatry, Neurology**
A.B., University of Miami; A.M., Ph.D., Columbia University; M.D., University of Pennsylvania
Senior Research Psychiatrist, Eastern Pennsylvania Psychiatric Institute
Author: articles on psychology and psychiatry

RASKIN, EUGENE **Architecture**
A.B., B.Arch., Columbia University
Associate Professor of Architecture, School of Architecture, Columbia University
Author: *Architecturally Speaking*

REMINGTON, CHARLES L. **Entomology**
B.S., Principia College; A.M., Ph.D., Harvard University
Associate Professor of Zoology, Yale University
Associate Curator of Entomology, Peabody Museum
Author: several articles on entomology

RUDGE, WILLIAM E. **Printing**
President, Rudge Associates Inc.
Editor and Publisher: *Print*

SCHNERR, WALTER J. **Etymology: Romance**
A.B., A.M., Ph.D., University of Pennsylvania
Associate Professor of Romance Languages, Brown University

SCHOLES, SAMUEL R. **Ceramics**
A.B., Ripon College; Ph.D., Yale University; (hon.) Sc.D., Alfred University
Formerly, Dean of New York State College of Ceramics
Emeritus Professor, Alfred University
Author: *Modern Glass Practice; Opportunities in Ceramics*
Editor: *Glass Industry Handbook*

SCHOPF, JAMES M. **Paleobotany**
B.A., University of Wyoming; M.S., Ph.D., University of Illinois
Supervising Geologist, Fuels Branch, Coal Laboratory, United States Geological Survey, Ohio State University
Author: technical articles on conifer embryology, paleobotany, and coal geology

SEEMANN, HERMAN E. **Radiography**
A.B., Oberlin College; Ph.D., Cornell University
Physicist, Eastman Kodak Company
Author: papers on physical problems of medical and industrial radiography

SEYMOUR, MERRILL W. **Color and Colorimetry**
B.S., University of Minnesota; M.A., Ph.D., Princeton University
Research Associate, Eastman Kodak Company

SHAND, ERROL B. **Glass**
B.S., McGill University
Technical Consultant, formerly Staff Research Engineer, Corning Glass Works
Author: *Glass Engineering Handbook*

SHIPMAN, FRANK M. **Distilling**
B.S., Georgetown College; M.S., University of Louisville; Ph.D., Iowa State College
Technical Director and Vice-president, Brown-Forman Distillers Corporation

SMITH, DAVID M. **Forestry**
B.S., University of Rhode Island; M.F., Ph.D., Yale University
Associate Professor, School of Forestry, Yale University
Coauthor: *Practice of Silviculture*

SMITH, GILBERT M. **Phycology**
B.S., (hon.) Sc.D., Beloit College; Ph.D., University of Wisconsin
Formerly, Professor of Botany, Stanford University
Author: *A Textbook of General Botany; Fresh Water Algae of the United States; Marine Algae of the Monterey Peninsula; Cryptogamic Botany*

SNELL, HAMPTON K. **Transportation**
A.B., A.M., University of Wisconsin; Ph.D., Yale University
Professor of Marketing and Transportation, College of Business Administration, University of Texas
Author: *Coordination of Rail, River, and Road Transportation in Egypt; Air Transportation;* numerous monographs, papers, reports of studies

SOUTHWICK, CHARLES A., JR. **Packaging**
B.S., Massachusetts Institute of Technology
Technical Editor: *Modern Packaging; Modern Packaging Encyclopedia*
Contributor: *Colloid Chemistry; Storage of Cereal Grains and Their Products;* numerous articles in packaging field

SPRAGUE, ATHERTON H. **Mathematics**
B.A., Amherst College; M.A., Ph.D., Princeton University
Professor of Mathematics, Amherst College
Author: *Plane and Spherical Trigonometry; Trigonometry and Analytical Geometry; Calculus*

STALLINGS, JAMES H. **Soils**
B.S., Agricultural and Mechanical College of Texas; M.S., Ph.D., Iowa State College
Principal Soil Conservationist, Agricultural Research Service, U.S. Department of Agriculture
Author: *Soil Conservation; Soil: Use and Improvement*
Contributor: numerous technical articles and reviews

SUTERMEISTER, EDWIN **Paper and Paper Manufacturing**
B.S., Massachusetts Institute of Technology
Chief Chemist, S. D. Warren Company
Author: *Chemistry of Pulp and Paper Making; The Story of Papermaking*
Contributor: numerous articles to technical journals

TARKINGTON, RAIFE G. **Photogrammetry, Military Photography**
B.S., Virginia Polytechnic Institute
Associate Head, Applied Photography Division, Kodak Research Laboratories
Contributor: *Photogrammetric Engineering; Signal*

TAYLOR, NORMAN **General Botany**
Student, Cornell University; (hon.) D.Sc., Washington College
Curator, Brooklyn Botanic Garden
Special Editor in Botany, *Webster's New International Dictionary, Second Edition*
Author: *Taylor's Encyclopedia of Gardening; Taylor's Garden Guide; Flight from Reality; Cinchona in Java; Guide to Garden Flowers; Guide to the Wild Flowers*

TAYLOR, ROBERT E. **Etymology: French**
A.B., Reed College; A.M., Ph.D., Columbia University
Associate Professor of French, New York University
Seminar Associate, Columbia University
Associate Editor, Renaissance Society of America
Author: studies on Sade, French 17th & 18th centuries; bibliographies of French literature and general Renaissance literature

TAYLOR, ROY W. **Wine**
B.S., University of Illinois
Public Relations Director, Wine Institute

THAYER, CLARK L. **Horticulture**
B.S., University of Massachusetts
Head of Department of Floriculture, University of Massachusetts
Author: *Spring Flowering Bulbs*

THOMPSON, J. ERIC S. **Maya Calendar**
Student, Cambridge University; LL.D., University of Yucatan
Member of Department of Archaeology, Carnegie Institution of Washington
Author: *The Rise and Fall of Maya Civilization*
Contributor: numerous articles on Maya and Mexican archaeology and ethnology

THOMSON, C. L. **Horticulture**
B.S.A., University of Toronto; M.S., University of Minnesota
Professor of Vegetable Crops, University of Massachusetts

THORSEN, MARGARET A. **Sports**
B.A., Carleton College; M.S., Wellesley College; Ph.D., New York University
Associate Professor of Physical Education, Springfield College

TRIBOLET, HAROLD W. **Bookbinding**
Manager, Department of Extra Binding, R. R. Donnelley and Sons Company
Contributor: magazine articles, reviews of technical books

TUIT, FRANK E., II **Law**
A.B., Amherst College; student, Harvard Law School
Lawyer, Register of Probate Court for County of Hampshire, Massachusetts

TURNER, LORENZO D. **Etymology: African**
A.B., A.M., Harvard University; Ph.D., University of Chicago
Professor of English, Roosevelt University
Author: *Anti-Slavery Sentiment in American Literature Prior to 1865; Africanisms in the Gullah Dialect*
Coauthor: *Readings from Negro Authors*

TWADDELL, W. FREEMAN **Grammar, Linguistics**
A.B., Duke University; A.M., Ph.D., Harvard University
Professor of Linguistics and German, Brown University
Author: numerous monographs, textbooks (German language, *Faust*), teacher training materials in Egypt and Japan
Contributor: articles and reviews on linguistics and philology

TYSON, VICTOR E., JR. **Navigation**
B.S., University of New Hampshire; B.S., U.S. Merchant Marine Academy
Captain, United States Marine Service
Assistant Superintendent, United States Merchant Marine Academy

VAN DEUSEN, W. P. **Graphic Reproduction Photography**
A.B., Princeton
Technical Staff Assistant to Research Director's Office, Eastman Kodak Company

VOEGELIN, CHARLES F. **Etymology: American Indian**
A.B., Stanford University; Ph.D., University of California
Professor of Anthropology, Indiana University
Author: monographs and papers on aboriginal languages of native Americans and anthropological theory
Editor: *International Journal of American Linguistics;* Indiana University publications in anthropology and linguistics

WANGAARD, FREDERICK F. **Forestry**
B.S., University of Minnesota; M.S., Ph.D., New York State College of Forestry; (hon.) M.A., Yale University
Professor of Forest Products, Yale University
Author: *Mechanical Properties of Wood*

WATERS, EVERETT O. **Tools**
A.B., Ph.B., M.E., Yale University
Emeritus Strathcona Professor of Mechanical Engineering, Yale University
Special Editor in Tools, *Webster's New International Dictionary, Second Edition*
Coauthor: *Principles of Machine Design*

WERNER, H. O. **Naval Science**
A.B., M.A., Brown University; M.A., Ph.D., Harvard University
Professor, United States Naval Institute
Coauthor: *The United States and World Sea Power; Men in Arms; Sea Power*

WEXLER, HARRY **Meteorology**
S.B., Harvard University; Sc.D., Massachusetts Institute of Technology
Director of Meteorological Research, United States Weather Bureau
Author: scientific articles

WIENS, HEROLD J. **Peoples of Asia**
A.B., University of California; A.M., Ph.D., University of Michigan
Associate Professor of Geography, Yale University
Author: *China's March toward the Tropics*
Coauthor: *Pattern of Asia*

WILLEY, NORMAN L. **Etymology: Scientific and Technical**
A.B., Syracuse University; A.M., Harvard University; LL.B., People's College; Ph.D., University of Michigan
Professor Emeritus of Germanic languages, University of Michigan
Contributor: articles in technical journals

WINCHELL, HORACE **Mineralogy, Crystallography, Gemmology**
B.A., M.A., University of Wisconsin; M.A., Ph.D., Harvard University
Associate Professor of Mineralogy, Yale University
Contributor: articles on physical and systematic mineralogy and optical crystallography

WINER, HERBERT I. **Forestry**
B.A., M.F., Ph.D., Yale University
Assistant Professor of Lumbering, Yale University

WOOLSTON, HELENE **Etymology: Maori**
M.A., University of Hawaii
Lecturer, Auckland University

EXPLANATORY CHART

THE CENTER COLUMN on this page contains entries taken from the dictionary. One or more parts of each entry has an oval line linked to a box in the margin. The term in the box is our name for the circled convention. The number in the box refers to a section in the "Explanatory Notes" following.

abbr 3.3, 19.1
angle bracket 13.1
author quoted 13.2.1, 13.2.2
binomial 14.1, 14.2
boldface type 1.1, 22.1
capitalization label 5.2
centered period 1.6
cognate cross-reference 1.7.3, 16.3.1
comb form 3.3, 21.1
definition
directional cross-reference 16.1, 16.1.2
ditto marks 2.8.1
double hyphens 2.7.2
equal variant 1.7.1
etymology 7.
functional label 3.1
homographs 1.4
hyphened compound 1.1, 2.7.2
inflectional cross-reference 4.6, 4.12, 16.4
inflectional form 4.1
lightface type 1.1
lowercase 5.1
main entry 1.1, 22.1
often attrib 6.
open compound 1.1, 2.7.2
pl but sing in constr 4.3
prefix 3.3, 21.1

pa *abbr* **1** paper **2** piaster

⁴pa·ce \ˈpāsē\ *prep* [L, abl. of *pac-, pax* peace — more at PEACE] **:** with all due respect or courtesy to ⟨~ the feminists, I believe my own sex is largely responsible for this . . . impertinent curiosity —Katharine F. Gerould⟩

pacific herring *n, usu cap P* **:** a herring (*Clupea pallasii*) of the northern Pacific ocean

¹pac·tion \ˈpakshən\ *n* -s [MF, fr. L *paction-, pactio,* fr. *pactus* (past part. of *pacisci* to agree, contract) + *-ion-, -io* -ion] **1** *chiefly Scot* **:** AGREEMENT, COMPACT, BARGAIN ⟨made ~ tween them twa⟩ — **pac·tion·al** \-shənᵊl, -shnəl\ *adj*

pants \ˈpants, ˈpaan-, ˈpain-\ *n pl but sometimes sing in constr, often attrib* [short for *pantaloons,* pl. of *pantaloon*] **1** *also* **pant a** (1) **:** PANTALOON 2 (2) **:** TROUSERS, SLACKS **b** *chiefly Brit* **:** men's short underpants **c :** PANTIE **2 pant** *n sing* **:** half or one leg of a pair of pants — **with one's pants down :** in an embarrassing position (as of being unprepared for an emergency) ⟨caught *with its pants down* by the surprise attack⟩

panty *var of* PANTIE

pa·per·ful \ˈpāpə(r),ˌfu̇l\ *n, pl* **paperfuls** *also* **papersful** \-(r),fu̇lz, -(r)z,fu̇l\ **:** as much as will fill a paper ⟨a ~ of pins⟩

papyro- *comb form* [Gk, fr. *papyros* papyrus] **1 :** papyrus

pas·to·ral·ize \ˈpast(ə)rə,līz\ *vt* -ED/-ING/-S *see -ize in Explan Notes* **1 :** to render pastoral or rural; *specif* **:** to convert to a pastoral economy or social organization

pas·tor·ate \ˈpast(ə)rət, ˈpaas-, ˈpais-, ˈpȧs-, *usu* -əd.+V\ *n* -s [ML *pastoratus,* fr. LL *pastor* pastor (fr. L, shepherd) + L *-atus* -ate] **1** (**a**) **:** the office, state, jurisdiction, or tenure of office of a pastor **b :** a body of pastors (**2**) **:** PARSONAGE

¹pat·a·go·ni·an \ˌpad·əˈgōnyən, -atə̇-, -nēən\ *adj, usu cap* [*Patagonia,* region in southern So. America belonging partly to Argentina and partly to Chile + E *-an*] **1 :** of, relating to, or characteristic of Patagonia **2 a :** of, relating to, or characteristic of the people of Patagonia **b** *obs* **:** GIGANTIC

²patagonian \ˈ"\ *n* -s **1** *cap* **:** a native or inhabitant of Patagonia; *esp* **:** one of the aboriginal Indian stock — compare TEHUELCHE

pat·e·fac·tion \ˌpad·əˈfakshən\ *n* -s [L *patefaction-, patefactio,* fr. *patefactus* (past part. of *patefacere*) + *-ion-, -io* -ion] *archaic* **:** DISCLOSURE, MANIFESTATION, REVELATION

patent-coated \ˈ==,==\ *adj, of paperboard* **:** vat-lined on one or both sides with an uncoated white liner

patent hammer *or* **patent ax** *n* **:** BUSHHAMMER

pat·er·is·sa \ˌpad·əˈrisə\ *n* -s [NGk *pateritsa,* fr. MGk *pateriza,* perh. dim. of Gk *pater-, patēr* father — more at FATHER] *Eastern Church* **:** a crosier surmounted by a small cross from whose base issue two serpents

¹pa·tine \pəˈtēn\ *n* -s [F, fr. ML & NL *patina* — more at PATINA] **1 :** PATEN **2 :** PATINA ⟨time has bestowed a ~ of oxidation on these vessels —Dorothy Adlow⟩

²patine \"\ *vt* -ED/-ING/-S **:** PATINATE

¹pa·to·la \pəˈtōlə\ *n* -s [Gujarati *paṭolū,* fr. Skt *paṭola*] **1 :** a silk cloth of India **2 :** a wedding sari woven in Gujarat, India, in chiné technique

²patola \"\ *n* -s [Tag] *Philippines* **:** a dishcloth gourd (*Luffa acutangula*) that is eaten green or cooked

patty-cake \ˈ==,=\ *n* [by alter.] **:** PAT-A-CAKE

paul·in·ize \-lə,nīz\ *vb* -ED/-ING/-S *often cap* [*pauline* + *-ize*] *vi* **:** to follow the teachings of the apostle Paul ~ *vt* **:** to indoctrinate with Paulinism

pawky \ˈpȯkē\ *adj* [obs. E (northern dial.) *pawk* trick + E *-y*] **1** *chiefly Brit* **:** artfully shrewd **:** CANNY ⟨that favorite of fiction, the ~ rich old lady who incessantly scores off her parasitical descendants —*Punch*⟩ **2** *chiefly Scot* **a :** LIVELY, UNINHIBITED **b :** BOLD, FORWARD ⟨a rude and ~ child⟩

paws *pl of* PAW, *pres 3d sing of* PAW

paymaster general *n, pl* **paymasters general** **1 :** a military officer in command of the pay department of an army or navy

Pb *symbol* [L *plumbum*] lead

peanut tube *n* **:** a small vacuum tube

peanut worm *n* **:** SIPUNCULID

pen·ni·less \ˈpenᵊlə̇s, -nəl-\ *adj* [ME *peniles,* fr. *peni* penny + *-les* -less] **:** destitute of money **:** extremely poor ⟨in one day the rich man . . . saw himself ~, landless, a bankrupt among creditors —J.G.Lockhart⟩ **syn** see POOR

phy·sique \fə̇ˈzēk\ *n* -s [F, fr. *physique,* adj., physical, bodily, fr. L *physicus* natural, fr. Gk *physikos* — more at PHYSIC] **1 :** bodily makeup or type **:** the structure, constitution, appearance, or strength of the human body ⟨a muscular ~⟩

syn BUILD, CONSTITUTION, HABIT: PHYSIQUE designates the total bodily or physical construction or qualities of an individual ⟨tall of stature, slender in *physique* —H.W.H.Knott⟩ ⟨his five-foot-nine-inch *physique* —*Current Biog.*⟩ BUILD, usu. interchangeable with PHYSIQUE, often stresses the geometrically determinable qualities of the physique ⟨a man of rather square *build*⟩ ⟨leisure and heredity gave me a husky *build*⟩ CONSTITUTION is the overall makeup of an individual comprising both mental and physical qualities ⟨extremely high-spirited, my greatest advantage was that my *constitution* did not allow me to be depressed —Osbert Sitwell⟩ ⟨a frail *constitution* necessitated his living in the South —H.E.Starr⟩ ⟨wealthy by inheritance but saving by *constitution* —Ellen Glasgow⟩ HABIT, usu. occurring with a qualifier, is generally confined to characteristic mental or moral quality, makeup, or disposition ⟨the country is where he has gone to indulge a contemplative *habit* —L.J.Halle⟩

²poster \"\ *n* -s *often attrib* [²*post* + *-er*] **1 :** a bill or placard intended to be posted in a public place; *specif* **:** one that is decorative or pictorial **2 :** POSTER STAMP

post flag *n* [⁷*post*] **:** the national flag measuring 19 feet fly by 10 feet hoist ordinarily used at a military post (as of the U.S. Army)

¹posthaste \(ˈ)=ˈ=\ *n* [⁴*post* (courier) + *haste*] **:** speed in traveling (as of a post or courier) **:** great haste — used chiefly in the phrase *in posthaste*

practical politics *n pl but sing or pl in constr* **1 :** matter for concrete action as distinguished from theoretical discussion

prac·tic·ing *or* **prac·tis·ing** \ˈpraktə̇siŋ, -sēn\ *adj* **:** actively engaged in an indicated career or way of life ⟨a ~ physician⟩ ⟨~ Catholics⟩

¹pro- *prefix* [ME, fr. OF, fr. L, fr. Gk, fr. *pro* — more at FOR] **1 a :** earlier than **:** prior to **:** before ⟨*pro*anthropus⟩ ⟨*pro*baptismal⟩ ⟨*Pro*mammalia⟩ **b :** rudimentary **:** PROT- ⟨*pro*embryo⟩ **2 :** situated before **:** located in front of **:** anterior to

pro-and-con \ˌ==ˈ=\ *vb* **pro-and-conned; pro-and-conned; pro-and-conning; pro-and-cons** **:** DEBATE

primary stress 2.2
pronunciation 2.
regional label 8.3.4
run-on entry (derivatives) 17.1.1
run-on entry (phrasal) 17.2
secondary stress 2.2
secondary variant 1.7.2
see -ize in Explan Notes 23.1
sense letter 12.2
sense number 12.1
small capitals 16.0, 16.2
status label 8., 8.1.2
subject guide phrase 10.1
subject label 9.1
suffixal cross-reference 4.4, 4.10, 16.5
superscript 1.4, 1.5
swung dash (boldface) 3.2
swung dash (lightface) 13.1
symbol 3.3, 20.1
symbolic colon 11.1
synonymous cross-reference 16.2
synonymy cross-reference 18.2
synonymy paragraph 18.1
uppercase
usage note 15.1
verbal illustration 13.1
verb principal parts 4.7

EXPLANATORY NOTES

A careful reading of these explanatory notes will make it easier for the user of this dictionary to comprehend the information contained at each entry. Here are brief explanations of the different typefaces, different labels, significant punctuation, symbols, and other conventions by which a dictionary can achieve compactness. The chief divisions are:

1. THE MAIN ENTRY
2. THE PRONUNCIATION
3. FUNCTIONAL LABELS
4. INFLECTIONAL FORMS
5. CAPITALIZATION
6. ATTRIBUTIVE NOUNS
7. THE ETYMOLOGY
8. STATUS LABELS
9. SUBJECT LABELS
10. SUBJECT GUIDE PHRASES
11. THE SYMBOLIC COLON
12. SENSE DIVISION
13. VERBAL ILLUSTRATIONS
14. THE TAXONOMIC ENTRY
15. USAGE NOTES
16. CROSS-REFERENCES
17. RUN-ON ENTRIES
18. SYNONYMIES
19. ABBREVIATIONS
20. SYMBOLS
21. COMBINING FORMS
22. THE VOCABULARY ENTRY
23. -ER, -OR, -IZE
24. FACTOTUMS

1. THE MAIN ENTRY

1.1 A heavy black letter or a combination of heavy black letters (**boldface type**) set flush with the left-hand margin of each column of type is a main entry or entry word. The combination consists usually of letters set solid (*about*) or of letters separated by one or more spaces (*art song*) or of letters joined by a hyphen (*air-dry*). What follows each such boldface entry in lightface type on the same line and on indented lines below explains and justifies its inclusion in the dictionary. The boldface entry together with this added matter is also called an entry.

1.2 The main entries follow one another in this dictionary from *a* to *zyzzogeton* in alphabetical order letter by letter. For example, *above the line* follows *abovestairs* (not *above all*) as if it were printed *abovetheline* with no spaces in the middle. Entry words containing an arabic numeral (*3-D, 1080* "ten-eighty") are alphabetized as if the numeral were spelled out. Entry words derived from proper names beginning with abbreviated forms of *Mac-* (*McCoy*) are alphabetized as if spelled *mac-*. Entries often beginning with *St.* or *Ste.* in common usage have the abbreviation spelled out *saint* (*Saint Martin's summer*).

1.3 A thumb index with tabs lettered from *A* through *Z* is cut into the fore edge of this dictionary to aid in locating the pages beginning with each letter. As a further aid to finding a wanted entry, a pair of guide words is printed at the top of nearly every page. These are the first and last words of a sequence of boldface words on one page of the dictionary. Entries alphabetically between the word in the upper left corner (as *addressee* on page 25) and the word in the upper right corner (as *adhere*) are defined on the same page.

1.4 When one entry has exactly the same written form as another that follows it, the two are distinguished by superior numbers preceding each word:

[1]arc
[2]arc

Sometimes such homographs are related, like the two *arcs*, which are different parts of speech derived from the same root. At other times, there is no relationship beyond the accident of spelling:

[1]are ⟨the boys *are* here⟩
[2]are ⟨one *are* equals 100 square meters⟩

Whether homographs are related or not, their order is usually historical: the one first used in English, insofar as the dates can be established, is entered first.

1.5 Such superscripts are used only when all the letters, spaces, and hyphens of two or more entries are identical (except for foreign accent marks). A variation in form calls for a new series of superscripts. In general, words precede word elements made up of the same letters, and lowercase type precedes uppercase type.

1.6 The centered periods within entry words indicate division points at which a hyphen may be put at the end of a written line, thus for *ar·chae·ol·o·gy:*

ar-
chaeology
archae-
ology
archaeol-
ogy
archaeolo-
gy

Such periods are not shown after a single initial letter (*aplomb*, not *a·plomb*) or before a single terminal letter (*ar·ea*, not *ar·e·a*) because printers seldom cut off one letter only. Many printers try to avoid cutting off two letters only, especially at the end. They might divide *ar·cha·ic* into *ar-/chaic* but not into *archa-/ic*. Other words (*April, apron*) that are not often divided in printing do not show a centered period. For a full discussion of word division, see the following article headed "Divisions in Boldface Entry Words".

1.6.1 A double hyphen ⸗ at the end of a line (as between *pro* and *British* at [1]*hyphen* 1b) stands for a hyphen that belongs normally at that point in a hyphened word (as *pro-British*) and should be retained when the word is written out as a unit on one line.

1.7.1 When a main entry is followed by the word *or* and another spelling or form, the two spellings or forms are equal variants. Their order is usually alphabetical, and the first is no more to be preferred than the second, or third, or fourth, if three or four are joined by *or*. Both or all are standard and any one may be used according to personal inclination or personal style preferences:

an·gel·ic . . . *or* **an·gel·i·cal**
ar·dor *or* **ar·dour**
arc of recess *or* **arc of recession**
angel cake *or* **angel food** *or* **angel food cake**

If the alphabetical order of variants joined by *or* is reversed, they remain equal variants. The one printed first may be slightly more common but not enough to justify calling them unequal:

cad·dis *or* **cad·dice**

1.7.2 When another spelling or form is joined to the first entry by the word *also* instead of *or*, the spelling or form after *also* is a secondary variant and occurs less frequently than the first form:

car·bo·ther·mic . . . *also* **car·bo·ther·mal**

The secondary variant belongs to standard usage and may be for personal or regional reasons be preferred by some. If there are two secondary variants, the second is joined to the first by *or*. Once the italic *also* is used to signal a secondary variant, all following variants are joined by *or:*

aso·ka . . . *also* **as·ak** *or* **as·ok**

No evaluation below secondary is implied. Absence of a variant does not mean that there is no variant; for example, some variants have been arbitrarily omitted.

1.7.3 Standard variants are reentered at their own places alphabetically whenever their spelling places them alphabetically more than five inches away from the main entry. The form of entry is

loth *var of* LOATH
rime *var of* RHYME

in which *var of* stands for "variant of". These two entries result from the main entries *loath or loth* and *rhyme or rime*.

2. THE PRONUNCIATION

2.1 The matter between reversed virgules \\ is the pronunciation in symbols shown in the chart headed "Pronunciation Symbols" and discussed in greater detail in the "Guide to Pronunciation". A centered period · shows syllable divisions only when a given sequence of sounds can be syllabified in more than one way without employing deliberate pause, as discussed in detail in the section on "Divisions in Boldface Entry Words". All other sequences have only one reasonably possible syllabication (as in the sounds of *admit*) or have no determinable syllabication (as in the sounds of *easter*). In either case they are pronounceable in a normal manner when the sound sequence is pronounced. These centered periods in the respelling for pronunciation often do not correspond with centered periods in the boldface entry. Thus in our analysis the first syllable of the pronunciation of *metric* ends with \e\ and the second syllable begins with \t\, but printers usually divide the word between the *t* and the *r*.

2.2 A high-set mark ˈ indicates primary accent or stress; a low-set mark ˌ indicates a secondary accent. The two are often set one over the other ¦ to indicate stress variation. Two occurrences of ¦ within a pronunciation indicate that in some contexts the first syllable so marked has secondary stress and the second so marked has primary stress, in other contexts vice versa:

ben·e·fi·cial \¦benə¦fishəl\

The occurrence of (ˈ) on the first syllable and of ¦ on the second syllable indicates that in some contexts the first syllable has a degree of stress we would leave unmarked and that the second syllable has primary stress but that in other contexts the first syllable has primary stress and the second has secondary stress:

fic·ti·tious \(ˈ)fik¦tishəs\

The order primary-secondary is especially common when another word, especially one with stress on the first syllable, follows without pause, as when the first word is attributive. Stress marks show the stress of the first vowel that follows; they are not necessarily indicators of syllable division and often do not correspond with the centered periods in the boldface entry.

2.3 The presence of variant pronunciations simply indicates that not all educated speakers pronounce the word the same way. Some variant pronunciations (as \ˈbərd\ and \ˈbə̄d\ for *bird*) are the kind that one speaker uses but another does not for the reason that their dialects are different and that the speech habits of one are different from those of the other. One of these pronunciations is predictable from a knowledge of a speaker's pronunciation of other words. Other variants (as for *disparate*) are not predictable from a speaker's pronunciation of other words. Some speakers stress *disparate* on the second syllable; others stress it on the first. Words with predictable variant pronunciations usually show them when the word is of frequent occurrence in highly literate language but only one pronunciation when it is not. Words with unpredictable variant pronunciations show any that has currency, whatever the frequency of the word.

2.4 When a word shows more than one unpredictable variant, variants not preceded by *also* or *sometimes* or by a label (as *substand*) do not differ greatly in frequency in educated speech. The order in which they appear has no significance. Variants preceded by *also* are appreciably less frequent. Variants preceded by *sometimes* are infrequent. Before predictable variants no *also* or *sometimes* occurs, whatever the frequency of a variant, except that *also* precedes a variant that is less common in one class of words than in another. Thus \er\, which is variant to \ar\ with fewer speakers in *harry* than in *hairy*, is preceded by *also* at the first but not at the second.

2.5.1 Parentheses mean that whatever is indicated by the symbol or symbols between them is present in the pronunciation of some speakers and absent from the pronunciation of other speakers, or that it is present in some utterances and absent from other utterances of the same speaker, or that its presence or absence is uncertain:

nu·mer·ous \ˈn(y)üm(ə)rəs\
floc·cu·lence \ˈfläkyələn(t)s\

Such pronunciations could alternatively have been shown, at greater cost of space, as \ˈnümərəs, ˈnyü-, -mrəs\

2.5.2 The symbols (r, with no closing parenthesis, at the end of the transcription of a word, as *seminar*, means that speakers who do not usually pronounce the \r\ when a consonant or a pause follows may pronounce it when a vowel follows without pause.

2.6.1 When a defined word that is at its own alphabetical place has less than a full pronunciation, the missing part is to be supplied from a pronunciation in a preceding entry, from a preceding pronunciation for a variant spelling in the same entry, or from a preceding pronunciation within the same pair of reversed virgules:

floc·cu·lence \ˈfläkyələn(t)s\ *also* **floc·cu·len·cy** \-nsē\
[1]floc·cu·lent \-nt\

The hyphen at *flocculency* and at *flocculent* indicates that the first part of the pronunciation is missing. The missing part is to be supplied from the pronunciation at *flocculence*.

2.6.2 The lightface vertical bar is used to facilitate the placement of a variant pronunciation. It occurs chiefly at a point immediately preceding or immediately following a variation.

flight·i·ly \ˈflīd·|ᵊlē, -īt|, |ᵊli, |ə̇l-\
flight·i·ness \|ēnə̇s, |in-\

At *flightily* in the four-character unit -īt| (hyphen + bar i + t + vertical bar) the īt is a variation of īd· and the hyphen stands for the ˈfl that precedes īd· and the vertical bar stands for the ᵊlē that follows īd·; in the unit |ᵊli the ᵊli is a variation of ᵊlē and the vertical bar stands for both ˈflīd· and ˈflīt; in the unit |ə̇l- the vertical bar stands for both ˈflīd· and ˈflīt and the hyphen stands for the variants ē and i of the final syllable. This system makes it possible to show economically several variant pronunciations for *flightily:*

\ˈflīd·ᵊlē, ˈflītᵊlē, ˈflīd·ᵊli, ˈflītᵊli, ˈflīd·ə̇lē, ˈflītə̇lē, ˈflīd·əli, ˈflītəli\

At *flightiness* the vertical bar in the unit |ēnə̇s stands for both ˈflīd· and ˈflīt from the pronunciation at *flightily;* the vertical bar in the unit |in- stands for ˈflīd· and ˈflīt and the hyphen stands for ə̇s from the preceding ēnə̇s.

2.7.1 A slanted double hyphen in transcriptions represents all the sounds of a syllable:

per·pet·u·ate \pə(r)ˈpechəˌwāt . . . \
per·pet·u·a·tion \⸗ˌ⸗⸗ˈwāshən\
per·pet·u·a·tor \⸗ˈ⸗⸗ˌwād·ə(r) . . . \

The first three syllables of each of these consecutive entries have the same sounds. The double hyphens at *perpetuation* and *perpetuator* show this sameness. The stress, however, differs. The stress on the second syllable is primary in *perpetuate* and *perpetuator* but secondary in the middle word.

2.7.2 Open compounds of two or more English words usually have no pronunciation (as at *barn dance*). Such members of solid or hyphened compounds as are whole English words often show only the stress indicated by double hyphens and stress marks:

heartache \\'=ˌ=\\
waterworthy \\'==ˌ==\\
fort·let \\'=lət\\
cata·baptist \\¦kad·ə¦==\\

The sounds of the syllables represented by such double hyphens can be found at the main entry of the elements (as at *heart* and *ache*, at *fort*, and at *baptist*). Thus in the consecutive entries

den·e·ga·tion \\ˌdenə'gāshən\\
denehole \\'=ˌ=\\

the value of the syllables of the second should be sought at *dene* and at *hole*, not in the representation of the first two syllables in the pronunciation at *denegation*.

2.8.1 A ditto mark " in a pronunciation stands for the sounds of the nearest preceding pronounced entry. The orthographic division for this preceding entry also applies unless another is shown. For an entry having the same sequence of letters as a preceding entry but not followed by reversed virgules, no commitment about pronunciation is made:

1**carp** \\'kärp, 'kȧp\\
2**carp** \\"\\
carp *abbr*

1**in·dict** \\ən'dīt, *usu* -īd·+V\\ *vt*
2**indict** *vt* . . . *obs*

keelboat \\'=ˌ=\\
keel·boat·man \\"mən\\

1**keel·er** \\'kēlə(r)\\
2**keeler** \\"\\
3**keeler** \\"\\
kee·ler polygraph \\"-\\

2*carp* has the same pronunciation as 1*carp*, but no pronunciation is to be understood for *carp* the abbreviation. No pronunciation is to be understood for the obsolete 2*indict*. (In general, words obsolete in their entire range of meaning have an indicated pronunciation only if they occur in Shakespeare.) The stress on the first two syllables of *keelboatman* is the same as for *keelboat;* the sounds for *keel* and *boat* should be sought at the entry for each. 2*keeler* and 3*keeler* have the same pronunciation and division as 1*keeler; keeler* in *keeler polygraph* has the same pronunciation as 1*keeler* but its division differs.

2.8.2 If the entry at which the value of a ditto mark is to be sought contains variants not identical in pronunciation, the value of the ditto mark is the pronunciation of the variant of the same spelling in a preceding entry:

1**ap·o·dal** \\'apədᵊl\\ *also* **ap·o·dan** \\-dən, -dᵊn\\ *or* **ap·o·dous** \\-dəs\\
2**apodal** \\"\\ *also* **apodan** \\"\\

2.9 When a word is composed of a combining form or prefix and a whole English word, often the transcription consists of a pronunciation for the first element followed by a plus sign. The plus sign means that the sounds and the orthographic division for the second element should be sought at the entry for that word. If other compounds with the same first element follow, their pronunciation may be shown by the formula \\"+\\:

geo·positive \\¦jē(ˌ)ō+\\
geo·potential \\"+\\

In many contexts a primary stress shown for the second element at its entry may alter to secondary in the compound.

2.10 The symbol *R* preceding variants indicates the pronunciation of speakers who consistently pronounce most postvocalic *r*'s; –*R* indicates the pronunciation of speakers who consistently have no \\r\\ sound for any *r* for which educated usage sanctions pronunciation without the sound. At

gov·er·nor *R* 'gəv(ə)nər *also* -vərnər, –*R* -v(ə)nə(r\\

the purpose of the labeling is to indicate that speakers who ordinarily have \\r\\ for postvocalic *r* (as for the last *r* in *governor*) often do not have \\r\\ for the first *r* in the word (see DISSIMILATION in "Guide to Pronunciation"). Some speakers sometimes drop, sometimes retain \\r\\ in the same environment (as in *card, art*), many consistently drop \\r\\ in some environments (as in *card, art*) but consistently pronounce it in others (as in *bird, hurt*). Our –*R* transcriptions, however, do not record this usage.

2.11 The low-set minus sign ₋ cancels a stress at the same point in a pronunciation shown elsewhere, as in a preceding variant or in a pronunciation for a preceding word in another entry:

cam·era·man \\'=(=)=ˌman, -₋mən . . . \\
1**mer·cu·ri·al** \\¦mər¦kyůrēəl, ₋mə(r)'k- . . . \\
ac·tiv·ism \\'aktəˌvizəm . . . \\
1**ac·tiv·ist** \\-₋vəst\\

2.12 The symbol ÷ precedes variants which occur in educated speech but to the acceptability of which many take strong exception, as to the second variant at *cu·po·la* \\'kyüpələ, ÷ -pəˌlō\\ because of the rarity or unprecedentedness of \\ō\\ for *a*, or to the second variant at *gon·do·la* \\'gändələ, ÷ gän'dōlə\\ because the stress in the language of origin is on the first syllable. Sometimes the variant to which exception is taken is the commonest of all and is given first, as at *sacrilegious*. If not repeated, ÷ applies only to the variant that it immediately precedes.

3. FUNCTIONAL LABELS

3.1 An italic label that indicates part of speech or some other functional classification follows the pronunciation or, if no pronunciation is given, the main entry. The eight traditional parts of speech are thus indicated:

ac·tive . . . *adj*	(adjective)
across . . . *adv*	(adverb)
al·though . . . *conj*	(conjunction)
alas . . . *interj*	(interjection)
act . . . *n*	(noun)
across . . . *prep*	(preposition)
he . . . *pron*	(pronoun)
act . . . *vb*	(verb)

3.2 If a verb is both transitive and intransitive, the labels *vt* and *vi* introduce the subdivisions:

act . . . *vb* . . . *vt* . . . **~** *vi*

The character **~** is a boldface swung dash used to stand for the main entry (as *act*) and mark the subdivisions of the verb.
If there is no subdivision, *vt* or *vi* takes the place of *vb:*

ac·ti·fy . . . *vt*

Definition of a verb as transitive does not preclude intransitive usage, although it may be uncommon. On occasion most transitive verbs get used intransitively.

3.3 Other italicized labels sometimes occurring in the same position as the part-of-speech label are:

atty *abbr*	(abbreviation, see 19)
anth- . . . *comb form*	(combining form, see 21)
ante- . . . *prefix*	
Ac *symbol*	(symbol, see 20)
may . . . *verbal auxiliary*	
whoa . . . *v imper*	(imperative verb)
me·thinks . . . *vb impersonal*	(impersonal verb)

Occasionally, two or more functional labels are combined, as *n or adj;* see also 19.3.

4. INFLECTIONAL FORMS

4.1 A plural for nearly all standard nouns is explicitly or implicitly shown in this dictionary. If a plural is irregular in any way, the form is given in full in boldface following the label *n, pl:*

man . . . *n, pl* **men**
mouse . . . *n, pl* **mice**
da·tum . . . *n, pl* **da·ta**
mother-in-law . . . *n, pl* **mothers-in-law**

4.2 If there are two or more plurals, all are written out in full and joined by *or* or *also* to indicate whether the forms are equal or secondary variants (see also 1.7.1 and 1.7.2):

fish . . . *n, pl* **fish** *or* **fishes**
court-martial . . . *n, pl* **courts-martial** *also* **court-martials**
fun·gus . . . *n, pl* **fun·gi** . . . *also* **funguses**
beef . . . *n, pl* **beefs** . . . *or* **beeves** . . . *also* **beef**
crux . . . *n, pl* **cruxes** . . . *also* **cru·ces**

4.3 Nouns that are plural in form and regularly used in plural construction are labeled *n pl* (without a comma):

en·vi·rons . . . *n pl*
feazings *n pl*
da·na·i·dae . . . *n pl*

If the plural form is not always construed as a plural, the label continues with an applicable qualification:

ge·net·ics . . . *n pl but sing in constr*
pol·i·tics . . . *n pl but sing or pl in constr*
math·e·mat·ics . . . *n pl but usu sing in constr*

in which *sing in constr* stands for "singular in construction" and means that the entry word takes a singular verb.

4.4 A noun that has only a regular English plural formed by adding the suffix *-s* or the suffix *-es* or by changing a final *-y* to *-i-* and adding the suffix *-es* is indicated by an -S or -ES following the label *n:*

bird . . . *n* -S
love . . . *n* -S
wish . . . *n* -ES
sky . . . *n* -ES
ba·by . . . *n* -ES

All standard English nouns can have regular English plurals. Such endings are given analogically in this dictionary to nouns that may be little used in the plural. All that their presence means in cases of doubtful frequency is that these plurals are available for use if needed; it does not bar the use of a non-English plural if known.

4.5 Plurals are usually omitted at compounds containing a terminal element that corresponds to a whole English word whose plural is regular and is shown at its own place. At

blackbird . . . *n*
arrow grass *n*
cake-eater . . . *n*
bio·ecology . . . *n*

the plurals are omitted because they can be found at *bird, grass, eater,* and *ecology*. At words (as *bioecology*) that may be unfamiliar, an etymology consisting of the elements of a compound word shows the element at which an omitted plural can be looked up. Plurals are often not indicated at nonstandard terms. At compounds with doubtful irregular plurals, the plural forms are written out in full. For a full discussion on the way English plurals are formed see the following article headed "Plurals".

4.6 A plural form that falls alphabetically more than five inches from the main entry is entered at its own alphabetical place:

bows *pl of* BOW
boxes *pl of* BOX
mice . . . *pl of* MOUSE
geni·i *pl of* GENIUS

Such an entry does not specify whether it is the only plural; it simply tells where to look for relevant information. At *genius* the variant plurals *geniuses* and *genii* are shown. The plural *geniuses* is not a main entry because it falls within five inches alphabetically of the main entry of *genius.*

4.7 The principal parts of all standard verbs are explicitly or implicitly given in this dictionary. These principal parts, besides the main entry, are four: the past, the past participle, the present participle, and the present 3d singular. They are printed in that order in boldface whenever any one of them has an irregular or unexpected combination of letters:

see . . . *vb* **saw** . . . **seen** . . . **seeing** . . . **sees**
make . . . *vb* **made** . . . **made** . . . **making** . . . **makes**
hit . . . *vb* **hit** . . . **hit** . . . **hitting** . . . **hits**
trap . . . *vb* **trapped** . . . **trapped** . . . **trapping** . . . **traps**
cha·grin . . . *vt* **chagrined** . . . **chagrined** . . . **chagrining** . . . **chagrins**
dye . . . *vb* **dyed** . . . **dyed** . . . **dyeing** . . . **dyes**
tie . . . *vb* **tied** . . . **tied** . . . **tying** . . . **ties**
volley . . . *vb* **volleyed** . . . **volleyed** . . . **volleying** . . . **volleys**
emcee . . . *vb* **emceed** . . . **emceed** . . . **emceeing** . . . **emcees**

4.8 Whenever any of the four parts has a variant all parts are written out in full:

sky . . . *vb* **skied** *or* **skyed** . . . **skied** *or* **skyed** . . . **skying** . . . **skies**
burn . . . *vb* **burned** . . . *or* **burnt** . . . **burned** *or* **burnt** . . . **burning** . . . **burns**
ring . . . *vb* **rang** . . . *also* **rung** . . . **rung** . . . **ringing** . . . **rings**
show . . . *vb* **showed** . . . **shown** . . . *or* **showed** . . . **showing** . . . **shows**
dwell . . . *vb* **dwelt** . . . *also* **dwelled** . . . **dwelt** *also* **dwelled** . . . **dwelling** . . . **dwells**
drink . . . *vb* **drank** . . . *or dial* **drunk** . . . **drunk** . . . *or archaic* **drunk·en** . . . **drinking** . . . **drinks**

4.9 If the four spaces usually occupied by inflectional forms cannot (for lack of evidence) all be filled, the surviving forms that can be given are identified by an italic label:

aby or **abye** . . . *vb, past or past part* **abought**

4.10 Verbs are considered regular when they have in their past a terminal *-ed* which is added with no other change except dropping a final *-e* or changing a final *-y* to *-i-*. The principal parts for these verbs are indicated by adding -ED/-ING/-S or -ED/-ING/-ES to represent the past and past participle endings (*-ed*), the present participle ending (*-ing*), and the present 3d singular ending (*-s* or *-es*):

bark . . . *vb* -ED/-ING/-S
wish . . . *vb* -ED/-ING/-ES
stone . . . *vb* -ED/-ING/-S
ba·by . . . *vt* -ED/-ING/-ES

4.11 Principal parts are usually omitted at compounds containing a terminal element or related homograph whose principal parts are regular and are shown at its own place. At

freewheel . . . *vi*
overdrive . . . *vt*
un·wrap . . . *vt*

the principal parts are not given because they can be found at *wheel, drive,* and *wrap*. An etymology consisting of the elements of a compound verb shows the element at which omitted principal parts can be looked up. Principal parts are often not given at nonstandard terms or at verbs of relatively low frequency.

4.12 A principal verb part that falls alphabetically more than five inches away from the main entry is entered at its own alphabetical place if there is no entry that is a homograph:

burned *past of* BURN
shoving *pres part of* SHOVE
denies *pres 3d sing of* DENY

4.13 All adjectives and adverbs that have comparatives and superlatives with the suffixes *-er* and *-est* have these forms explicitly or implicitly shown in this dictionary. They are written out in full in boldface when they are irregular or when they double a final consonant:

red . . . *adj* **redder** . . . **reddest**
cheer·ful . . . *adj, sometimes* **cheerfuller** . . . *sometimes* **cheerfullest**
well . . . *adv* **bet·ter** . . . **best**

4.14 When they are formed by simple addition of *-er* and *-est* with no change except dropping of final *-e* or changing of final *-y* to *-i-*, these forms are indicated by -ER/-EST following the part-of-speech label:

green . . . *adj* -ER/-EST
lucky . . . *adj* -ER/-EST
re·mote . . . *adj, often* -ER/-EST
soon . . . *adv* -ER/-EST
ear·ly . . . *adv* -ER/-EST

4.15 Comparatives and superlatives are usually omitted at compounds containing a constituent element whose inflection is shown at its own place. At

kindhearted . . . *adj*
un·lucky . . . *adj*

kinderhearted and *unluckiest* are omitted because -ER and -EST are shown at *kind* and at *lucky*. Similarly the comparatives and superlatives of adverbs are often omitted when an adjective homograph shows them, as at *flat* and *hot*.

4.16 Comparatives and superlatives that fall alphabetically more than five inches away from the main entry are entered at their own alphabetical places:

hotter *comparative of* HOT
hottest *superlative of* HOT

4.17 Showing *-er* and *-est* forms does not imply anything more about the use of *more* and *most* with a simple adjective or adverb than that the comparative and superlative degrees can often be expressed in either way (*luckier* or *more lucky*, *smoothest* or *most smooth*).

4.18 A few pronouns have identified case forms:

her . . . *pron, objective case of* SHE

5. CAPITALIZATION

5.1 Except for trademarks and some abbreviations and symbols the main entries in this dictionary are set lowercase. The extent to which usage calls for an initial uppercase letter is indicated in one of five ways. Four of these consist of an italic label:

cap = almost always capitalized initially
usu cap = more often capitalized than not; capitalized approximately two to one
often cap = as likely to be capitalized as not; acceptable one way or the other
sometimes cap = more often not capitalized than capitalized; not usually capitalized

The fifth is absence of one of these labels, which indicates that the word is almost never capitalized except under irrelevant circumstances (as beginning a sentence):

french . . . *n, cap*
christian . . . *adj, usu cap*
french . . . *adj, usu cap*
french·ify . . . *vb* . . . *often cap*
die·sel . . . *adj, sometimes cap*

5.2 When an entry has more than one letter in question, the label specifies the capitalization required by usage:

french anemone . . . *usu cap F*
black-eyed su·san . . . *usu cap S*
brown betty . . . *usu cap 2d B*
french canadian . . . *usu cap F&C*
neo-thomist . . . *often cap N & usu cap T*

6. ATTRIBUTIVE NOUNS

6.1 The label *often attrib* in italics added to the label *n* at a main entry indicates that the noun is often used as an adjective equivalent in attributive position before a substantive (as in *air passage*, *cabbage soup*):

air . . . *n* -S *often attrib*
cab·bage . . . *n* -S *often attrib*
din·ner . . . *n* -S *often attrib*
fox . . . *n, pl* **foxes** *or* **fox** *often attrib*
pep·per . . . *n* -S *often attrib*
shoul·der . . . *n* -S *often attrib*
va·ca·tion . . . *n* -S *often attrib*

6.2 While any noun is likely to get used attributively sometimes, the label *often attrib* is confined to those having such widespread general frequent attributive use that they could be entered and defined as adjectives or adjectival elements. The label is not used when there is an entered adjective homograph (as *milk, adj* and *dog, adj*). Also, it is not used at open compounds that may be often used attributively when hyphened (as *X ray* in *X-ray microscope*).

7. THE ETYMOLOGY

7.1 The matter in boldface square brackets preceding the definition is the etymology. Meanings given in roman type within these brackets are not definitions of the main entry, but meanings of the Middle English, Old English, or non-English words within the brackets. Such etymological meanings may or may not be the same as one or more of the meanings of the main entry. For the meanings of abbreviations in an etymology, see the pages headed "Abbreviations Used in This Dictionary".

7.2 It is the purpose of the etymology to trace a main vocabulary entry as far back as possible in English, as to Old English; to tell from what language and what form it came into English; and to trace the pre-English source as far back as possible. These etyma (or a part of them) are printed in italic type.

7.3 The etymology usually gives the Middle English and Old English forms of native words in the manner illustrated by the following examples:

earth . . . *n* . . . [ME *erthe*, fr. OE *eorthe* . . .]
day . . . *n* . . . [ME, fr. OE *dæg* . . .]

7.3.1 When a word is traced back to Middle English but not to Old English, it is found in Middle English but not in the texts that have survived from the Old English period, even though it cannot be shown to have been borrowed from any other language, and even though it may have cognates in the other Germanic languages:

girl . . . *n* . . . [ME *girle, gerle, gurle* young person of either sex]
poke . . . *vb* . . . [ME *poken;* akin to MD *poken* to poke, stick . . .]

7.3.2 When a word is traced back directly to Old English with no intervening mention of Middle English, it has not survived continuously from Old English times to the present, but died out after the Old English period and has been revived in modern times for its historical or antiquarian interest:

ge·mot *or* **ge·mote** . . . *n* . . . [OE *gemōt* . . .]

7.4 For words borrowed into English from other languages, the etymology gives the language from which the word is borrowed and the form or a transliteration of the word in that language if the form differs from that in English:

etch . . . *vb* . . . [D *etsen* . . .]
flam·boy·ant . . . *adj* [F . . .]
judge . . . *vb* . . . [ME *juggen*, fr. OF *jugier* . . .]
ab·bot . . . *n* . . . [ME *abbod, abbed*, fr. OE *abbod, abbad*, fr. LL *abbat-, abbas* . . .]

7.5.1 Sometimes no etymology is given for words (including open compounds) created in Modern English by the combination of existing constituents. This generally indicates that the identity of the constituents is expected to be evident to the user without guidance. Examples:

blackfish . . . *n* **1 :** any of several dark-colored fishes
black·ly *adv* **:** in a black manner

7.5.2 At other times the etymology states one or both of the constituents of such words, especially when it is felt that their identity is not necessarily self-evident:

ac·ti·va·ble . . . *adj* [*activate* + *-able*]
man·ga·nite . . . *n* . . . [*mangan-* + *-ite*]
black·guard . . . *n* [^{1}*black* + *guard*]
indian bison *n* . . . [^{2}*indian* 1]

No hard-and-fast line, however, can be drawn between these two methods of treatment.

7.6 A considerable part of the technical vocabulary of the sciences and other specialized studies consists of words or word elements that are current in two or more languages with only such slight modifications as are necessary to adapt them to the structure of the individual language in each case. Many words and word elements of this kind have become sufficiently a part of the general vocabulary of English to require entry in a general dictionary of our language. On account of the vast extent of the relevant published material in many languages and in many scientific and other specialized fields, it is impracticable to ascertain the language of origin of every such term, yet it would not be accurate to formulate a statement about the origin of any such term in a way that could be interpreted as implying that it was coined in English. Accordingly, whenever a term that is entered in this dictionary belongs recognizably to this class of internationally current terms, and no positive evidence is at hand to show that it was coined in English, the etymology recognizes its international status and the possibility that it originated elsewhere than in English by use of the label ISV (for International Scientific Vocabulary). In some instances a statement as to probable language of origin is added after a semicolon. Examples:

end·oral . . . *adj* [ISV *end-* + *oral*]
en·do·scope . . . *n* [ISV *end-* + *-scope;* prob. orig. formed in F]
hap·loid . . . *adj* [ISV, fr. Gk *haploeidēs* single . . .] **1 :** having the gametic number of chromosomes or half the number characteristic of the somatic cells
-ene . . . *n suffix* . . . [ISV, fr. Gk *-ēnē* (fem. patronymic suffix)] **:** unsaturated carbon compound

7.6.1 Occasionally the label ISV is used, not to indicate that the entire entry form belongs to the International Scientific Vocabulary, but to identify as internationally current (though non-Latin) one of the constituents of a compound word formed in New Latin:

cho·les·ter·ol·emia *also* **cho·les·ter·ol·ae·mia** . . . *n* . . . [NL, fr. ISV *cholesterol* + NL *-emia, -aemia*]

7.7.1 An etymology beginning with the name of a language (including ME or OE) and not giving the foreign (or Middle English or Old English) form indicates that the foreign (or Middle English or Old English) form is the same as that in present-day English:

for . . . *prep* [ME, fr. OE . . .]
fos·sa . . . *n* . . . [L, cavity, ditch, trench . . .]

7.7.2 An etymology beginning with the name of a language (including ME or OE) and not giving the foreign (or Middle English or Old English) meaning indicates that the foreign (or Middle English or Old English) meaning is the same as that expressed in the first or only definition in the entry:

bea·con . . . *n* . . . [ME *beken*, fr. OE *bēacen* sign . . .] **1 :** a signal fire
de·note . . . *vt* . . . [MF *denoter*, fr. L *denotare* . . .] **1 :** to serve as indication of

7.8.1 Small superscript figures preceding forms mentioned in an etymology identify them in each case as a particular member of a set of numbered homographic entries in this dictionary. Such figures are normally used with unlabeled (Modern English) forms; but sometimes, for convenience, they are used with forms labeled OE, ME, NL, or ISV, provided these are completely identical in spelling with the corresponding Modern English form. Examples:

chucker . . . *n* . . . [^{6}*chuck* + *-er*]
in·definable . . . *adj* [^{1}*in-* + *definable*]
in·dec·or·ous . . . *adj* [L *indecorus*, fr. *in-* ^{1}in- + *decorus* decorous]
bi·fluoride . . . *n* . . . [ISV ^{1}*bi-* + *fluoride*]
sad·ness *n* . . . [ME *sadnesse* seriousness, firmness, fr. ^{1}*sad* + *-nesse* -ness]

7.8.2 Small superscript figures following words or syllables in an etymology refer in each case to the tone of the word or syllable which they follow, and accordingly are used only with forms cited from tone languages:

sam·pan *also* **san·pan** . . . *n* . . . [Chin(Pek) *san*^{1} *pan*^{3}, fr. *san*^{1} three + *pan*^{3} board, plank]
voo·doo *also* **vou·dou** . . . *n* . . . [. . . Ewe *vo*^{1}*du*^{3} tutelary deity, demon]

7.9 When the source of a word appearing as a main entry is unknown, the formula "origin unknown" is usually used. Only rarely and in exceptional circumstances does absence of an etymology mean that it has not been possible to furnish any informative etymology; this is the case, however, with some ethnic names. More usually it means that no etymology is felt to be necessary; this is the case, for instance, with a very large proportion of the entries identified as variants or taxonomic synonyms and with Modern English coinages of the kind mentioned in paragraph 7.5.1. In one situation, absence of an etymology has a distinct and positive significance, namely in the second and later items in a set of homographic entries; here it indicates derivation by functional shift, in Modern English, from the last preceding homograph that has an etymology.

7.10.1 For native words the etymology gives cognates where possible from other Germanic or Indo-European languages, especially Old High German, Old Norse, Gothic, Latin, Greek, and Sanskrit. Similarly, for a very large proportion of the words borrowed into English from other Indo-European languages, not only Latin and Greek but also Sanskrit, the Germanic languages, the Romance languages, the Slavic languages, and the rest, the etymology gives a like indication of the Indo-European cognates. Examples:

bench . . . *n* . . . [ME, fr. OE *benc;* akin to OHG *bank* bench, ON *bekkr*]
bear . . . *vb* . . . [ME *beren*, fr. OE *beran;* akin to OHG *beran* to carry, ON *bera*, Goth *bairan*, L *ferre*, Gk *pherein*, Skt *bharati* he carries]
dic·tion . . . *n* . . . [LL & L; LL *diction-, dictio* word, fr. L, delivery in public speaking, fr. *dictus* (past part. of *dicere* to say) + *-ion-, -io* -ion; akin to OE *tēon* to accuse, OHG *zīhan* to accuse, ON *tjā* to show, Goth *gateihan* to tell, L *dicare* to dedicate, Gk *deiknynai* to show, *dikē* right, judgment, Skt *diśati* he shows]
meld . . . *vb* . . . [G *melden* to announce, report, fr. OHG *meldōn;* akin to OE *meldian* to announce, reveal, inform on, *meld* proclamation . . . OHG *melda* betrayal, OSlav *moliti* to ask for, request, pray . . .]

7.10.2 Considerations of space of course make it inadvisable to give a full display of cognates at every possible entry; what is more usually done is to direct the user by a "more at" cross-reference to another entry where such a full display of cognates is given:

edict . . . *n* . . . [L *edictum*, fr. neut. of *edictus*, past part. of *edicere* to declare, decree, fr. *e-* + *dicere* to say — more at DICTION]

7.11 Besides the use of "akin to" to denote ordinary cognate relationship, as in several examples in the preceding paragraph, there is in some etymologies a somewhat special use of "akin to" as part of a longer formula "of — origin; akin to —". This longer formula indicates that a word was borrowed from some language belonging to a group of languages, the name of the group being inserted in the blank just before *origin;* that for some reason it is not possible to say with confidence that the word in question is a borrowing of a particular attested word in a particular language of the source group; and that the word or words cited in the blank after "akin to" are a cognate or cognates of the word in question as attested within the source group. Examples:

guard . . . *vb* . . . [MF *garder*, fr. OF *garder, guarder* to ward, guard, of Gmc origin; akin to OHG *wartēn* to watch, take care — more at WARD]
cant . . . *n* . . . [ME, prob. fr. MD or ONF; MD, edge, fr. ONF, fr. L *cantus, canthus* iron ring round a carriage wheel, perh. of Celt origin; akin to W *cant* rim, Bret *cant* circle; akin to Gk *kanthos* corner of the eye, Russ *kut* corner]

This last example shows the two uses of "akin to" in explicit contrast with each other. The words cited immediately after "of Celt origin; akin to" are Celtic cognates of the presumed Celtic source word from which the Latin word was borrowed; the words cited after the second "akin to" are further cognates from other Indo-European languages.

8. STATUS LABELS

8.0 A status label in italics sometimes appears before a definition. It provides a degree of usage orientation by identifying the character of the context in which a word ordinarily occurs. Status labels are of three kinds: temporal, stylistic, and regional.

8.1.1 The temporal label *obs* for "obsolete" means that no evidence of standard use since 1755 has been found or is likely to be found:

abastardize *vt* . . . *obs*
abhorrency *n* . . . *obs*
absume *vt* . . . *obs*

obs is a comment on the word being defined, not on the thing defined by the word. When obsoleteness of the thing is in question, it is implied in the definition (as by *onetime*, *formerly*, or historical reference):

longbow . . . *n* . . . **:** the great bow of medieval England
man·tel·et . . . *n* . . . **:** a movable shelter formerly used by besiegers as a protection when attacking

8.1.2 The temporal label *archaic* means standard after 1755 but surviving in the present only sporadically or in special contexts:

be·like . . . *adv* . . . *archaic*
oak·en . . . *adj* . . . *archaic*
spir·i·tu·ous . . . *adj* . . . *archaic*

archaic is a comment on the word being defined, not on the thing the word represents.

8.2.1 The stylistic label *slang* is affixed to terms especially appropriate in contexts of extreme informality, having usually a currency not limited to a particular region or area of interest, and composed typically of clipped or shortened forms or extravagant, forced, or facetious figures of speech:

clary . . . *n* . . . *slang*
cornball . . . *n* . . . *slang*
happy dust *n* . . . *slang*
lu·lu . . . *n* . . . *slang*

There is no completely satisfactory objective test for slang, especially in application to a word out of context. No word is invariably slang, and many standard words can be given slang connotations or used so inappropriately as to become slang.

8.2.2 The stylistic label *substand* for "substandard" indicates status conforming to a pattern of linguistic usage that exists throughout the American language community but differs in choice of word or form from that of the prestige group in that community:

drown . . . *vb* . . . *substand* **drownd·ed**
his·self . . . *also* **his·sel** . . . *pron* . . . *substand*

This label is not regional.

8.2.3 The stylistic label *nonstand* for "nonstandard" is used for a very small number of words that can hardly stand without some status label but are too widely current in reputable context to be labeled *substand:*

ir·regardless . . . *adj* . . . *nonstand*

8.3.1 The regional label *dial* for "dialect" when unqualified indicates a regional pattern too complex for summary labeling usually because it includes several regional varieties of American English or of American and British English:

husky . . . *n* . . . *dial*

8.3.2 The combined label *dial Brit* and the combined label *dial Eng* indicate substandard currency in a provincial dialect of the British Commonwealth or England:

clart . . . *dial Brit*
slape . . . *adj* . . . *dial Eng*

8.3.3 A standard word requiring a specified regional restriction in the U.S. will have one of the seven labels *North, NewEng, Midland, South, West, Southwest,* and *Northwest.* These correspond loosely to the areas in Hans Kurath's *Word Geography of the Eastern United States* (1949). Examples:

dreadful . . . *adv, chiefly North*
jolt–wagon . . . *n, Midland*
can·ni·kin . . . *n* . . . *NewEng*
mountain pheasant *n, South*
cay·use . . . *n* . . . *West*
jor·na·da . . . *n* . . . *Southwest*
muck·a·muck . . . *vb* . . . *Northwest*

No collective label (as *U.S.*) is used to indicate currency in all regions of the U.S.

8.3.4 A regional label that names a country indicates standard currency in the named part of the whole English language area. Examples:

derry . . . *n* . . . *Austral*
cau·been . . . *n* . . . *Irish*
abeigh . . . *adv* . . . *Scot*
cabbage tree *n* . . . *NewZeal*
ca·nuck . . . *n* . . . *chiefly Canad*
pet·rol . . . *n* . . . *Brit*

9. SUBJECT LABELS

9.1 A prefixed subject label in italics names an activity or branch of knowledge in relation to which a word usually has a special meaning not identical with any other meaning it may have apart from the labeled subject. An abbreviated subject label can be found in the list of "Abbreviations Used in This Dictionary". Examples:

con·junct . . . *adj* . . . **5** *music*
break . . . *vt* . . . **4** . . . **c** *cricket*
con·choi·dal . . . *adj* . . . **2** *mineralogy*
con·sec·u·tive . . . *adj* . . . **3** . . . **b** *Semitic grammar*

10. SUBJECT GUIDE PHRASES

10.1 More common than the subject label in this dictionary is the subject guide phrase. This is a brief italicized phrase that points to something with which the word is associated:

con·chyl·i·at·ed . . . *adj* . . . *of a dye*
con·cor·dant . . . *adj* . . . **3** *of twins*
fire . . . *vi* . . . **1** . . . **d** (1) *of flax*
break *vi* . . . **6** . . . **d** (1) *of a fish or whale*

11. THE SYMBOLIC COLON

11.1 This dictionary uses a boldface character recognizably distinct from the usual roman colon as a linking symbol between the main entry and a definition. It stands for an unexpressed simple predicate that may be read "is being here defined as (or by)". It indicates that the supporting orientation immediately after the main entry is over and thus facilitates a visual jumping from word to definition:

black·ly *adv* **:** in a black manner
blackfish \\ˈ⸗,⸗\\ *n* **1 :** any of several dark-colored fishes
bis·cay·ner \\ˈbi(,)skānər\\ *also* **bis·cay·neer** \\,⸗⸗ˈni(ə)r\\ *n* -s *usu cap* [obs. *Biskaine, Biscayne* Biscayan (fr. *Biscay*, province of Spain) + *-er* or *-eer*] **:** a seaman or ship from Biscay

11.2 Words that have two or more definitions have two or more symbolic colons. The signal for another definition is another symbolic colon:

daunt·less . . . **:** marked by courageous resolution **:** incapable of being daunted, intimidated, or subdued
avail·a·ble . . . **3 :** such as may be availed of **:** capable of use for the accomplishment of a purpose **:** immediately utilizable

11.3 If there is no symbolic colon, there is no definition. For what sometimes takes the place of a definition see 15.2, 16.3, 19.1, 20.1.

12. SENSE DIVISION

12.1 Boldface arabic numerals separate the senses of a word that has more than a single sense:

x . . . **1 :** . . . **2 :** . . . **3 :**
sev·en·teenth . . . *adj* . . **1 :** being number 17 in a countable series . . . **2 :** being one of 17 equal parts into which something is divisible

12.2 Boldface lowercase letters separate coordinate subsenses of a numbered sense or sometimes of an unnumbered sense:

x . . . **1 :** . . . **2 a :** . . . **b :** . . . **c :** . . . **3 :**
howl . . . *n* . . . **1 :** a loud protracted mournful rising and falling cry . . . **2 a :** a prolonged cry of distress . . . **b :** a yell or outcry of disappointment, rage, or protest

x . . . **1 :** . . . **2 :** . . . : as **a :** . . . **b :** . . . **c :**
bridge·man . . . *n* . . . **1 :** one who works on a bridge: as **a :** one who tends the landing bridge where a ferryboat docks . . . **b :** one who operates the machinery for opening and closing drawbridges . . . **c :** a member of a construction crew that builds bridges . . . **2 :** one who works on the loading platform of an icehouse

x . . . **:** . . . : as **a :** . . . **b :** . . . **c :**
huge . . . *adj* . . . **:** very large or extensive: as **a :** of great size or area . . . **b :** of sizable scale or degree . . . **c :** of limitless scope or character

x . . . **1 :** . . . **2 :** . . . : **a :** . . . **b :** . . . **c :**
gag . . . *vb* . . . *vt* **1 :** to apply a gag to: **a :** to stop the mouth of . . . **b :** to pry or hold open . . . **c :** to silence by the force of authority . . . **2 :** to cause to heave

12.2.1 The lightface colon (as in the preceding formulas) indicates that the definition immediately preceding it binds together or subsumes the coordinate subsenses that follow it:

main stem *n* **:** a main trunk or channel: as **a :** the main course of a river or stream . . . **b :** the main line of a railroad **c :** the main street of a city or town

12.2.2 The word *as* may or may not follow this lightface colon. Its presence indicates that the subsenses following are typical or significant examples which are not exhaustive. Its absence indicates that the subsenses following are exhaustive with respect to evidence for dictionary inclusion.

12.3 Lightface numbers in parentheses indicate a further division of subsenses:

x . . . **1 a :** . . . **b** (1) **:** . . . (2) **:** . . . **c :** . . . **2 :**
lead . . . *vi* . . . **2 a :** to be first or foremost in some respects . . . **b** (1) **:** to begin or open a passage or course of action . . . (2) **:** to play the first card of a trick, round, or game (3) **:** to direct the first of a series of blows at an opponent in boxing

12.4 The system of separating by numbers and letters reflects something of the semantic relationship between various senses of a word. It is only a lexical convenience. It does not evaluate senses or establish an enduring hierarchy of importance among them. The best sense is the one that most aptly fits the context of an actual genuine utterance.

12.5 The order of senses is historical: the one known to have been first used in English is entered first. This ordering does not imply that each sense has developed from the immediately preceding sense. Sense 1 may give rise to sense 2 and sense 2 to sense 3. As often as not, however, each of several senses derived in independent lines from sense 1 has served as the source of a number of other meanings. Sometimes an arbitrary arrangement or rearrangement is the only reasonable and expedient solution to the problems of ordering senses.

12.6.1 An italic functional label or other information given between a main entry and the etymology of a multisense word applies to all senses and subsenses unless a limiting label (as *pl*) or symbol (as -s) is inserted immediately after a divisional number or letter and before the symbolic colon or unless in any way clearly inapplicable. Examples of limiting labels:

can·tha·ris . . . *n* . . . **1** *pl* **can·thar·i·des** . . . **2 canthar-ides** *pl but sing or pl in constr* . . . **3** *cap*
frit·il·lar·ia . . . *n* . . . **1** *cap* **:** a genus of bulbous herbs . . . **2** -s **:** any plant, bulb, or flower of the genus *Fritillaria*
alexandrian . . . *adj* . . . **1 a** *usu cap* **:** of or relating to Alexander the Great **b** *often cap* **:** characterized by the ideas prevalent after Alexander the Great
front . . . *adj* . . . **2** *comparative sometimes* **fronter :** articulated at or toward the front of the oral passage

12.6.2 The etymology also applies to all senses and subsenses unless another etymology in boldface brackets is given after a sense number or letter:

can·on . . . *n* . . . [ME *canoun* . . .] . . . **6** [LGk *kanōn*, fr. Gk] **:** a contrapuntal musical composition

12.6.3 An italic status label, subject label, or guide phrase does not apply to all the senses of a multisense word. When divisional numbers are present, such a label is inserted after the number:

daisy cutter *n* **1** *slang* **:** . . . **2** *slang* **:** . . . **3** *slang* **:**
de·ject . . . *vt* . . . **2 a** (1) *obs* **:** to lower esp. in rank or condition **:** ABASE, HUMBLE (2) *archaic* **:** to reduce esp. in force, degree, or quality **:** WEAKEN, LESSEN **b :** to make gloomy
de·fine . . . *vb* . . . **6 a** *math* **:** . . . **b :**
fish . . . *vb* . . . *vi* . . . **4** *of a Salvationist* **:** to speak with individuals

It then applies to lettered and parenthetically numbered subsenses that follow. It does not apply to succeeding boldface-numbered senses:

glance . . . *vt* . . . **2** *obs* **a :** to allude to **b :** to barely touch **:** GRAZE **3 :**

Senses 2a and 2b are both obsolete but not sense 3. If it falls between a boldface letter and the symbolic colon or between a lightface number in parentheses and the symbolic colon, it applies only to the immediately following sense.

13. VERBAL ILLUSTRATIONS

13.1 The matter enclosed in a pair of angle brackets illustrates an appropriate use of the word in context. The word being illustrated is replaced by a swung dash which stands for the same form of the word as the main entry or by a swung dash plus an italicized suffix which can be added without any change of letters to the form of the main entry. Otherwise the word is written in full and italicized:

av·id . . . *adj* . . . **2** . . . ⟨an ~ reader⟩ ⟨an ~ gardener⟩
firm . . . *adj* . . . **1** . . . **b** (1) . . . ⟨walked with a ~ tread⟩ ⟨a ~ handshake⟩
fix . . . *vb* . . . *vt* . . . **4** . . . **c** . . . (2) . . . ⟨the jury had been ~*ed*⟩
fritter . . . *vb* . . . **1** . . . ⟨foolishly ~*ing* away time and energy⟩
shake . . . *vb* . . . **3 a :** . . . ⟨were *shaking* in their shoes⟩

13.2.1 A person's name or an italicized title included in the angle brackets acknowledges the authorship or source of a quoted verbal illustration:

just . . . *adv* . . . **4 a** . . . ⟨I'm ~ your interpreter —Ernest Hemingway⟩
lim·it . . . *n* . . . **1a** . . . ⟨at the exact northern ~ of this valley —*Amer. Guide Series: Minn.*⟩
shake . . . *vb* . . . **3 a** . . . ⟨his voice *shook* and became shrill —Kenneth Roberts⟩

13.2.2 Suspension periods indicate an omission in quoted matter. Sometimes spelling, punctuation, or capitalization has been normalized without notation usually because the brief quotation is so far removed from its original context that such matters are no longer significant and may be actually misleading.

14. THE TAXONOMIC ENTRY

14.1 A main entry that defines the name of a kind of plant or animal (as rose) or a technical category of plants or animals (as Rosaceae) is a taxonomic entry. Such entries employ in part a formal codified New Latin terminology developed and used by biologists in accord with international codes of botanical and of zoological nomenclature to identify and to indicate the relations of plants and animals. In this terminology each kind of organism has one and only one correct name that for a species (binomial or species name) consists of a singular capitalized genus name combined with an uncapitalized specific epithet or trivial name which is an appositive or genitive noun or an adjective agreeing in case, number, and gender with the genus name (as in *Rosa setigera*). For a variety or subspecies (trinomial or variety name or subspecies name) the name adds a similar varietal or subspecific epithet (as in *Rosa setigera tomentosa*). Such binomials and trinomials are in this dictionary routinely italicized and enclosed in parentheses and ordinarily immediately follow the primary orienting noun:

ca·ran·dá . . . *n* . . . **1 :** a tropical palm (*Copernicia australis*)
bar·row's goldeneye . . . *n* . . . **:** a No. American goldeneye (*Bucephala islandica*)
red–shafted flicker *n* **:** a flicker (*Colaptes caper collaris*)

By their use an absolute technical identification is made.

14.2 A binomial or trinomial so used is a technical device and does not have separate entry. The name of a genus used in such a combination normally does have an entry unless directly or indirectly oriented (as by specific mention of a higher category or through another vernacular or a technical adjective) to a higher taxonomic category (as a family, order, or class):

northern anthracnose *n* . . . caused by a fungus (*Kabatulla caulivora*) of the family Tuberculariaceae
man·go . . . *n* . . . **4 :** a hummingbird of the genus *Anthracothorax*
rainbow runner *n* **:** a . . . carangid food and sport fish (*Elegatis bipinnulatus*)
but
indian laurel . . . *n* . . . **1 :** an Asiatic tree (*Persea indica*)

14.3 Occasionally two binomials appear in one parenthesis in a taxonomic entry:

redstart . . . *n* . . . **2** . . . birds of the genus *Phoenicurus* (as the black redstart, *P. ochruros* syn. *P. titys* of Europe)
blacknose dace . . . *n* **:** a common No. American dace (*Rhinichthys atronasus* or *Atratulus atronasus*)

The first form indicates that the binomial following *syn* (for "synonym") is technically invalid but so widely known or generally used as to justify mention. The second is used when there is professional lack of agreement about the correct name.

14.4 A genus name used more than once in an unnumbered entry or in a numbered sense of an entry is routinely abbreviated in uses after the first:

go·ran . . . *n* . . . **:** either of two Indian mangroves (*Ceriops roxburghiana* and *C. candolleana*)
nas·tur·tium . . . *n* . . . **2** -s **:** any plant of the genus *Tropaeolum* (as *T. majus* and *T. minus*)
ich·thy·oph·thir·i·us . . . *n* . . . *cap* **:** a genus of oval holotrichous ciliates comprising a single species (*I. multifiliis*)

14.5 Names of taxonomic categories higher than the genus are capitalized plural nouns often used with singular verbs, are not italicized or abbreviated in normal use, and in this dictionary are routinely oriented in rank when used in defining:

turtle . . . *n* . . . **1 :** a reptile of the order Testudinata
scar·a·bae·oid . . . **1 :** a beetle of Scarabaeidae or a closely related family
achari·ace·ae . . . a family of herbs and subshrubs (order Parietales)

Such names when used in other entries will be found entered at their own alphabetical place.

14.6 A taxonomic entry of the form X *syn of* Y means that *x* is in all respects (as grammatical number, capitalization, meaning, and taxonomic rank) equivalent to *y* but that it is for some reason (as a flaw of spelling or form, a faulty application, or a lack of priority) technically inferior to and less valid than *y*.

14.7 An italic guide phrase (as *in some classifications*) used to introduce the text of a taxonomic entry is a warning device and implies that the taxon defined though not strictly a synonym in the taxonomic sense is not as generally acceptable as one lacking such a qualifier.

15. USAGE NOTES

15.1 A usage note is introduced by a lightface dash. Two or more successive usage notes are separated by a semicolon. A usage note provides information about the use of the word being defined and so always modifies the word that is the main entry. It may be in the form of a comment on idiom, syntax, semantic relationship, status, or various other matters:

fresh·en . . . *vt* . . . **4 :** . . . — usu. used with *up*
collar . . . *vb* . . . *vi* **:** . . . — used of a steel bar in a rolling mill
al·le·gro . . . *adv (or adj)* . . . **:** . . . — used as a direction in music
free·ma·son . . . *n* . . . **2 :** . . . — called also *Mason*
co·he·sion . . . *n* . . . **3 :** . . . — distinguished from *adhesion*

15.2 A usage note may stand in place of a definition and without the symbolic colon. Some function words have little or no semantic content, and most interjections express feelings but otherwise are untranslatable into substitutable meaning. Many other words (as some oaths and imprecations, calls to animals, specialized signals, song refrains, and honorific titles), though genuinely a part of the English language, have a usage note instead of a definition:

gee . . . *interj* . . . — often used as an introductory expletive for emphasis and sometimes to express surprise or enthusiasm
at . . . *prep* . . . **1** — used as a function word to indicate presence in, on, or near
ahoy . . . *interj* . . . — used in hailing ⟨ship ~⟩
hey . . . *interj* . . . — used to call attention or to incite, to express interrogation, surprise, or exultation, or with indefinite meaning in the burden of a song

16. CROSS-REFERENCES

16.0 Various word relationships requiring that matter at one place in a dictionary show special awareness of matter at another place are taken care of by a system of cross-references. A sequence of lightface small capitals used anywhere in a definition is identical letter-by-letter with a boldface main entry (or with one of its inflectional forms) at its own alphabetical place. This sequence is a cross-reference; its boldface equivalent elsewhere is what is cross-referenced to and is not itself a cross-reference.

16.1 A cross-reference following a lightface dash and beginning with either *see* or *compare* is a directional cross-reference. It explicitly directs one to look somewhere else for further information. It never stands for a definition but (with a few exceptions) is always appended to one. Such a cross-reference is separated from another cross-reference or from a usage note by a semicolon.

16.1.1 A cross-reference using the verb *see* means that the boldface entry word to which it is appended is mentioned in the same meaning and function at the entry cross-referenced to. The information at this entry which is cross-referenced to adds to the meaning of the boldface word to which the cross-reference is attached or supplements it in some significant way (as by adding to one definition of *house* the cross-reference "see BUNGALOW, COTTAGE, MANSION; APARTMENT BUILDING, BOARDINGHOUSE, DWELLING HOUSE, LODGING HOUSE, ROOMING HOUSE, TENEMENT HOUSE"):

horn . . . *n* . . . **1 a** (1) **:** one of the paired bony processes that arise from the upper part of the head of many ungulate mammals . . . — see ANTLER
ant·ler . . . *n* . . . **:** a horn of an animal of the deer family

16.1.2 A cross-reference using the verb *compare* means that the boldface entry word to which it is appended is not mentioned (except perhaps incidentally) at the entry cross-referenced to. The additional information at this entry which is cross-referenced to is related in some pertinent way (as by similarity, contrast, or complement):

apoc·o·pe . . . *n* . . . **:** the loss of one or more sounds or letters at the end of a word . . . — compare APHAERESIS, SYNCOPE
syn·co·pe . . . *n* . . . **2 a :** the loss of one or more sounds or letters in the interior of a word

16.2 A cross-reference following a symbolic colon is a synonymous cross-reference. It may stand alone as the only definitional matter for a boldface entry or for a sense or subsense of an entry. It may be one of a group of definitions joined in series by symbolic colons. In either case the cross-reference means that the definitions at the entry cross-referenced to are substitutable as definitions for the boldface entry or the sense or subsense at which the cross-reference appears:

con·cep·ti·ble . . . *adj* . . . **:** CONCEIVABLE
con·cen·tra·tion . . . *n* . . . **4 :** DENSITY 1
concentric cable *n* **:** COAXIAL CABLE
con·cen·tric . . . *adj* . . . **1** . . . **b :** having a common axis (as of two or more cones or moraines) **:** formed about the same axis **:** COAXIAL
in·vent . . . *vt* . . . **2 :** to think up or imagine **:** concoct mentally **:** FABRICATE

16.2.1 Two or more synonymous cross-references are sometimes introduced by a symbolic colon and joined to each other by a comma. This indicates that there are two or more sets of definitions at other entries which are substitutable in various contexts:

con·cept . . . *n* . . . **:** THOUGHT, IDEA, NOTION
con·cede . . . *vb* . . . **2 :** ADMIT, ACKNOWLEDGE

16.2.2 A synonymous cross-reference sometimes accounts for a usage note introduced by *called also* at the entry cross-referenced to:

ra·ad . . . *n* . . . **:** ELECTRIC CATFISH
electric catfish *n* . . . — called also *raad*
fairy bell *n* **1** . . . **:** FOXGLOVE 1
foxglove . . . *n* . . . **1** . . . — called also *fairy bell, fingerflower, fingerroot*

16.3.1 A cross-reference following an italic *var of* is a cognate cross-reference. It is explained and illustrated in 1.7.3 as applied to standard variants.

16.3.2 A limiting label before the *var of* in a cognate cross-reference indicates in what way an entry word is nonstandard:

air *Scot var of* EYRE
alarum clock *chiefly Brit var of* ALARM CLOCK
ast . . . *dial var of* ASK
colour . . . *chiefly Brit var of* COLOR
defuse *obs var of* DIFFUSE

16.3.3 A cross-reference following an italic *syn of* is also a cognate cross-reference. See 14.6.

16.4 A cross-reference following an italic label identifying an entry as an inflectional form of a singular noun, of an adjective or adverb, or of an infinitive verb is an inflectional cross-reference. These are illustrated in 4.6, 4.12, and 4.16.

16.5 A cross-reference following a functional label is a suffixal cross-reference. These are illustrated at 4.4, 4.10, and 4.14. Each of these suffixes is an entry at its own alphabetical place where the way in which it is suffixed is explained.

16.6 A cross-reference may or may not be identified by a superscript number before it or by a lightface sense number or letter after it. A synonymous cross-reference to a homograph is not identified by part of speech: nouns refer to nouns, adjectives to adjectives. Cross-references to verbs sometimes distinguish between *vt* and *vi*.

17. RUN-ON ENTRIES

17.1.1 A main entry may be continued after a lightface dash by a boldface derivative of itself. This is a run-on entry. Its boldface is always in alphabetical order with respect to the word it is run on to. It has a functional label but no definition:

en·vi·able . . . *adj* . . . — **en·vi·able·ness** . . . *n* -ES
epi·phenomenal . . . *adj* . . . — **epi·phenomenally** . . . *adv*
equi·distant . . . *adj* . . . — **equidistantly** *adv*

17.1.2 An additional run-on entry sometimes follows:

er·ro·neous . . . *adj* . . . — **er·ro·neous·ly** *adv* — **er·ro·neous·ness** *n* -ES

17.2 A main entry may be continued after a lightface dash by a boldface phrase containing the main entry word or an inflected form of it. This also is a run-on entry. It often is not in alphabetical order. It may or may not have a functional label but it has a definition:

ac·count . . . *n* . . . — **in account with** *prep* . . . — **on account of** *prep*
bad . . . *adj* . . . — **in a bad way** . . . — **too bad**
deep . . . *adj* . . . — **in deep water**
run . . . *vb* . . . — **run across** . . . — **run a temperature** . . . — **run foul of** . . . — **run riot** . . . — **run to seed** . . . — **run wild**
set . . . *vb* . . . — **set about** . . . — **set aside** . . . — **set forth** . . . — **set one's cap for** . . . — **set one's hand to**

17.3 A run-on entry is an independent entry with respect to function and status. Labels at the main entry do not apply unless they are repeated.

18. SYNONYMIES

18.1 This dictionary contains over a thousand paragraphs in which synonymous words are briefly discriminated and given verbal illustrations. Each paragraph follows the entry of one of the words of a group under consideration and is signaled by the boldface abbreviation **syn** indented. The paragraph is a synonymy. The first one appears at the word *abjure* and considers *abjure, renounce, forswear, recant*, and *retract*.

18.2 Words considered in a synonymy refer at their own alphabetical places to its location by running on the boldface letters **syn** and the word:

re·nounce . . . **syn** see ABJURE
for·swear . . . **syn** see ABJURE

19. ABBREVIATIONS

19.1 An entry having the label *abbr* is an abbreviation and what follows it is an expansion rather than a definition. No symbolic colon is used:

bbl *abbr* barrel
abp *abbr, often cap* archbishop

19.2 An abbreviation formed from the initial letters of two or more words appears in unspaced capital letters.

BCD *abbr* bad conduct discharge
GA *abbr* **1** general agent **2** general assembly

19.3 Some abbreviations function also as substantives and have a combined label:

TD *abbr or n* -s . . . touchdown

20. SYMBOLS

20.1 An entry having the label *symbol* has an expansion or interpretation rather than a definition. No symbolic colon is used:

Ga *symbol* gallium
y *symbol* **1** unknown quantity **2** an ordinate **3** *cap* admittance **4** *cap* yttrium

21. COMBINING FORMS

21.1 A main entry that begins or ends with a hyphen is a word element that forms part of an English compound. The identifying label, besides the hyphen, is *comb form* for "combining form", or if the element is used only as an affix, the label is *prefix* or *suffix*. A suffix or terminal combining form that always determines syntactic function is further identified by addition of a part-of-speech label (as *adj suffix* or *n comb form*):

nas- *or* **naso-** *also* **nasi-** *comb form*
pre- *prefix*
-able *also* **-ible** . . . *adj suffix*
-age . . . *n suffix* -s
cephal- *or* **cephalo-** *comb form* . . . **1 :** head ⟨*cephal*itis⟩ ⟨*cephalo*meter⟩ **2 :** cephalic and ⟨*cephalo*facial⟩

21.2 This dictionary enters combining forms for two reasons: chiefly to make easier the writing of etymologies of words in which they occur over and over again; and to recognize meaningful elements that are constantly being used to form new words not yet authenticated for dictionary inclusion. A compound consisting of a known word and a known combining form is not censurable merely by being absent from the dictionary.

22. THE VOCABULARY ENTRY

22.1 The following definition appears at its own alphabetical place in the dictionary:

vocabulary entry *n* **:** a word (as the noun *book*), hyphened or open compound (as the verb *book-match* or the noun *book review*), word element (as the affix *pro-*), abbreviation (as *agt*), verbalized symbol (as *Na*), or term (as *man in the street*) entered alphabetically in a dictionary for the purpose of definition or identification or expressly included as an inflectional form (as the noun *books* or the verbs *booked* and *saw*) or as a derived form (as the noun *godlessness* or the adverb *globally*) or related phrase (as *one for the book*) run on at its base word and usu. set in a type (as boldface or small capitals) readily distinguishable from that of the running text which defines, explains, or identifies the entry

As defined, this term applies to all the entries as they are printed alphabetically from *a* to *zyzzogeton*, with or without hyphens, all their boldface variants, all the run-on entries, and all inflectional forms whether written out in boldface or indicated by small-capital suffixes.

23. -ER, -OR, -IZE

23.1 -ER, -OR, or -IZE. A "*see -er in Explan Notes*" as at *center*, a "*see -or in Explan Notes*" as at *honor*, or a "*see -ize in Explan Notes*" as at *synchronize* refers to variant spellings discussed in sections 2.7, 2.12, and 2.10 in the article headed "Spelling".

24. FACTOTUMS

24.1 The letter-forms illustrated at the beginning of each letter of the alphabet are a capital surrounded by lowercase roman (upper left), lowercase italic (upper right), and small and large script or black letter (across the bottom).

DIVISIONS IN BOLDFACE ENTRY WORDS

1. The centered periods in boldface main entries indicate places at which a hyphen may be put as the last character in a line of print or writing when the rest of the word must be put at the beginning of the following line. We have made an effort to insert the periods only at places where hyphens would actually be used by publishing houses whose publications show a conscientious regard for end-of-the-line divisions. Such publishers probably never divide *oleo* between the *e* and the *o* (if there is room for a hyphen, there is room for the *o*). They avoid dividing between the *o* and the *l* except in extremely narrow measure (as when an illustration narrows a column). They avoid divisions like *pre·adamic* and *cardi·ovascular*, in which a letter from one element of a compound containing an English word is placed with the other element. We show no division marks at all in the word *oleo*, none between the *a* and *d* of *adamic* or *preadamic*, and none between the *i* and *o* of *cardiovascular*. Divisions avoided by publishers are sometimes printed in dictionaries probably as a concession to those who believe that syllabic division is a guide to pronunciation. However, it is the pronunciation of a word that governs its orthographic division rather than the other way around. This summary of the division practices followed in this dictionary includes a few alternatives that may recommend themselves for use and discusses objections to some of the division practices that have long been followed by dictionaries and in turn by publishers.

2.1 A compound formed of two elements each of which is an independent English word may be divided between the two elements: *nose·bleed, up·end*. No divisions have been shown for these compounds in this dictionary under a belief that no writer or printer need consult a dictionary for such information.

2.2 Compounds formed of an English word and an element (prefix, suffix, or combining form) that is not an independent English word are difficult to reduce to rule. In general, the more freely attachable those elements are to English words, the more apt compounds containing them are to be divided between the two constituents if the consonant or consonant group at the point of junction is one that could be either word-final or word-initial in English with the phonetic value it has in the compound. Thus, compounds with syllable-increasing inflectional suffixes are divided before the suffix: *stat·ed, stat·ing, fil·ing, fill·ing, whit·er, whit·est*. Such divisions are too well known to be shown in this dictionary. Divisions are made before such suffixes as the noun-forming suffix *-er* and the adjective-forming suffix *-ish: stat·er, whit·ish*. Most words in *-or* with a consonant preceding are usually divided before the preceding consonant when the break must be made between the vowels of the last and next-to-the-last syllables (as in *mortga·gor*) although a variant spelling in *-er* is usually divided after the consonant (as in *mortgag·er*). A more realistic procedure would be to show alternative divisions for words which, like *tribal, affective, defendant*, and *zincoid*, exhibit variation, just as we show variant spellings and variant pronunciations. But even the minimal number of divisions that it has long been traditional to show constitutes a disfigurement of the entry word, which in reading matter has syllable indications only at the end of a line.

3. The unsatisfactoriness of the practice of allowing pronunciation to determine place of division when no morpheme boundary is involved is best illustrated by words of the type of *apparatus* and *cyclic*, which have pronunciation variants that call for inconsistent divisions. Thus, \ˈsīklik\ calls for *cy·clic*, but \ˈsiklik\ calls for *cyc·lic*. To print the word as *cy·c·lic* is something so precedentless that it would arouse strong resistance among dictionary users. An alternative that is less disturbing, that has good precedent in other parts of the English-speaking world, and that promises to require a minimum of dictionary thumbing for the typesetters and proofreaders who are the ones most concerned with orthographic divisions, is the divorcing of such division from pronunciation as much as possible. All dictionaries and all careful dividers use such divisions as *offi·cial, posi·tion*, and *divi·sion*, in which a short vowel stands at the end of a line or syllable.

4. If divisions such as these are accepted with equanimity, it seems unlikely that a short vowel would be strongly resisted at the end of a syllable when the consonant between it and the following vowel is one other than *c, t*, or *s* with the phonetic values they have in the words cited. Books published recently in Great Britain contain such line-final short vowels which not only do not disturb the reader but are not even noticed by him in the course of reading at normal tempo. (British publishers seem not to attach much importance to consistency of division, and most British dictionaries do not show divisions in entry words.) Any publisher who would like to reduce the expense of division checking by typesetter and proofreader and of resetting could start with the following practice: When no morpheme boundary is involved, put a single consonant (except *x*, which is really two consonants: compare *toxin, tocsin*) with the vowel that follows it. Examples:

ap·pa·ra·tus	*Co·lo·ra·do*
cy·clic	*pa·na·te·la*
ci·ty	*di·gi·ta·lis*
mi·li·ta·ry	*Abi·ti·bi*

In *Abi·ti·bi*, there is no division between the *A* and the following *b* because leaving a single letter at the end of a line is usually avoided, now probably from custom but originally probably from the obvious fact that the reader can seldom, if ever, know how to read a single letter without knowing what letters follow it.

5. We have eliminated many of the division marks called for by traditional dictionary practice—such division marks as *o·le·o, sepi·a, min·icamera*, and *mon·osyllable*. With less success at consistency, we have avoided showing a division at points where variant pronunciations would indicate two divisions, as at *process* (noun) whose *o* is both \ä\ and \ō\. If a dictionary user pronounces \ō\ in *process*, then he may find the division *proc·ess* disturbing and may wish for a system under which he can choose the division *pro·cess*. Because of the need for a maximum of division points, we have usually not omitted division marks out of regard for variant pronunciations if it would deprive the divider of a division point at the end of two consecutive syllables. A variant preceded by the qualifier *sometimes*, the sign ÷, or some such label as *dial* has also usually not been regarded as justifying omission of a divider. Although unavoidable inconsistencies may be noticed in our divisions, no reader is apt to notice any at the righthand margin of a printed page set in strictest accord with our divisions. The showing of alternative divisions (as for *process*) or a discussion of division in an entry is impracticable. Division, from whatever necessity, presents a problem that has no positive solution.

6. Other classes of words in which we are unable to avoid the appearance of inconsistency are hyphened compounds (as *self-centered*) and compounds composed of an English word and an initial combining form (as *rhinencephalon*). Because the hyphen used at the end of a line is identical with the hyphen that occurs between the *f* and *c* of a word like *self-centered*, many find objectionable the breaking of such a word at the end of a line at any point other than the hyphen. The reason no doubt is that *self-centered* looks as much like (*self-cen*)(*tered*) as it does like (*self*)-(*centered*), and may give the reader a slight pause. An end-of-the-line division that coincides with the orthographic hyphen is to be preferred, even at the expense of some contrivance, if the measure is wide enough to permit it. In *Mason-Dixon line*, for example, where the word preceding and the word following the orthographic hyphen are both quite short, every effort should be made to avoid dividing between *a* and *s* and between *x* and *o;* and in *master-at-arms*, which has two orthographic hyphens to start with, to avoid dividing between the *s* and *t* of *master*. But if a line will contain all except the last syllable of a word like *self-determination*, few will object to setting off *-tion*. If there are on either side of the orthographic hyphen two word components both of which occur freely in English, the boundary between these components is the next-best place for the typographic hyphen. In *self-centeredness*, for example, breaking the word between the *d* and *n* is much better than breaking it between the *n* and *t*. In fact, the word is really (*self-centered*)(*ness*) rather than (*self*)(*centeredness*). Divisions such as that between the *n* and *t*, however, occur in publications whose typography and proofreading are overall of a very high order. Probably no such publication would divide immediately before a single letter preceding or immediately after a single letter following an orthographic hyphen—for example, before the first *i* or after the second *i* of *semi-ionic*. Such divisions would also be avoided if the word were solid instead of hyphened.

7. Dictionaries have usually put a division mark before the final consonant of the combining form in such compounds as *rhinencephalon, otacoustic*, in which the vowel before that final consonant is long and in which the second element is an independent English word that begins with a vowel and that retains its pronunciation unchanged in the compound. Dividing *rhinencephalon* between the *i* and the immediately following *n* conceals the make-up of the word, difficult at best for any except the specialist, and fails to provide the resourceful reader with a clue for intelligent guessing that would be provided by a division between the first *n* and the *e*. Since a clue to meaning is more valuable to the average reader than a clue to pronunciation, we have departed from precedent in the division of words of this class. A division such as *hydr·argillite*, however, would confuse by suggesting a mispronunciation for the combining form. So we have not divided such words as these at the morpheme boundary.

8. The following brief summarization replaces the considerably longer list of rules contained in preceding editions of this work, a list so detailed as to be difficult to remember and follow.

8.1 A single lowercase letter at the end of a word is never separated from the rest of the word. (In *India* the *i* and *a* are never separated. In *grade-A milk* the *A* is possibly sometimes set at the beginning of a line in narrow measure.)

8.2 Dividing after a single letter at the beginning of a word in which an orthographic hyphen is not the second character is usually avoided except in narrow measure. (In *again* and *Abel* the first letter is found separated from the rest of the word in the publications of typographically careful publishers chiefly in such narrow columns as those of pocket New Testaments. Such publications would probably show greater toleration toward setting the "*H-*" of *H-shaped* and the "*2-*" of *2-celled* at the end of a line.)

8.3 Solid compounds that consist of whole English words and that require dividing between the last syllable of one component and the first syllable of the next are divided at the boundary between the components. (*Newspaper* is divided between the *s* and the first *p*, *breakup* between the *k* and the *u*. In a compound like *newspaper*, the between-component division between *s* and *p* is somewhat to be preferred to the within-component division between *a* and the following *p* if the measure is wide enough so that the first alternative is possible.)

8.4 When a word composed of a whole English word, with pronunciation unaltered from its lexical pronunciation, and a prefix freely attachable to English words (as *anti-, non-, post-, pre-, pro-, semi-*) or a syllable-increasing suffix freely attachable to English words (as the present participle suffix *-ing* of *holding*, the comparative and superlative suffixes *-er* and *-est* of *moister* and *moistest*, the adjective suffix *-ish* of *girlish*, the adjective and adverb suffixes *-ly* of *lowly* and *coyly*, the agent-noun suffix *-er* of *toiler*) requires division between vowels belonging to different components, the division is made at the boundary between the components.

8.5 A non-syllable-increasing suffix, as the *-ed* of *turned*, is not separated from the rest of the word by most U. S. publishers but divisions such as *turn-ed* are numerous in some books printed in Great Britain. A word is accounted unaltered when the sounds remain the same even though the stress in the compound may, at least in certain contexts, differ, as in *Hollywoodian*.

8.6 A word is accounted whole even though a final silent *e* is dropped. Thus, *whaling* belongs with the words mentioned in paragraph 8.4 and is divided between the *l* and *i*. The British appear to adhere as strictly to the division of these words between components as do careful American publishers. However, in American publications that take less care with division, one also sees such divisions as *toi·ler, fligh·ty*, in which something of the base is taken over with the suffix. Although the between-components division here seems logical, it is not easy to answer effectively an objection that *toi·ler* is not different from *rela·tion*. (The latter has a phonetic reason that the former does not. But the phonetics of *toiler* would not be a bar to the division *toi·ler:* compare *toi·let*.) Several dictionaries now or formerly put the *g* or *q* of words ending in *-gue* or *-que* with the suffix when a word-initial syllable-increasing suffix follows, showing such divisions as *pla·guing, pi·quing, pla·guy, cli·quish*.

8.7 *-y* as in *frisky* and *flighty* is a freely attachable suffix but would not be separated from the rest of the word any more than the single letter *a* of *India* would. Divisions such as *fris·ky, fligh·ty*, however, may be found in publications not much concerned about the matter. Publishers who follow the dictionaries for the division of words like *mangey* find such words treated sometimes as *mang(e)+-ey* and sometimes as *mange+-y*, and divide or refrain from dividing accordingly. There is probably a feeling that *mang·ey* suggests a first syllable rhyming with *fang*, but divisions like *rang·ing* appear not to elicit this feeling to the same extent.

8.8 The comparative adjectives *longer*, *stronger*, and *younger* are usually divided after the *g* although division before the *g* would be in better agreement with the standard pronunciation, which has a sound \g\ not found in the positive forms and not ascribable to the suffix. *England* and by extension *English* are often divided after the *g* to keep the *land* intact but we have adopted the division before the *g*.

8.9 *-en* is not as freely attachable as other suffixes mentioned. (As a past-participle and noun-plural ending it seldom or never occurs outside the small handful of words in which it has long been established) but it is of Old English origin and deserves comment. When *-en* is coupled with an English word to form a verb or an adjective (as in *broaden*, *oaken*), each component retains its own consonants, except in words like *hasten*, *moisten*, in which the \t\ of the base disappears and for which division between the *s* and *t* is usual. In past participles the *en* usually stands by itself when the pronunciation of what precedes is the same as that of the infinitive or past-tense form (as *tak·en*, *shak·en*, *fall·en*, *shrunk·en*) or takes a preceding consonant when the pronunciation of what precedes is different from that of the infinitive (as *cho·sen*, *fro·zen*).

8.10 In compounds of affix and whole English word, division immediately before a single vowel at the end of a prefix or immediately after a single vowel at the beginning of a suffix is better avoided (as between the *m* and *i* of *semicircle* or between the *d* and *i* of *Hollywoodian*). The alternative requires little or no more effort.

8.11 Except when morpheme-final, as in *missing*, divide between two consecutive identical intervocalic consonants: *ab·bot*, *al·lot*, *mis·sion*, *expres·sion*, *swim·ming*, *ad·der* ("snake"), *add·er* ("one that adds"). (Spanish-derived *ll*, when not anglicized \l\, is often divided before the first *l*, as in *Trujillo*.)

8.12 Some suffixes of frequent occurrence in words borrowed from other languages have been naturalized to the extent that they are freely added to whole English words to form words in which the boundary between the components is an optimum dividing place: *Russian·ize*, *social·ize*, *Shakespear·ean*, *Roosevelt·ian* (but *Jeffersonian*, in which the first component differs from its uncompounded phonetic form in more than mere stress, is much less often treated as so divisible).

8.13 In general, it is best not to regard English proper names as English word plus suffix in dividing. The safest course is to employ such divisions as *Ba·ker*, *Mil·ler*, *Wel·ler*, even though many such words are in origin suffix-containing compounds. Such names are ordinarily not taken literally today. The pitfalls of looking for suffixes in proper names is shown by a word like *Wheeling*, which is often divided *Wheel·ing*. But the name of the West Virginia city is probably of Indian origin and the identity of the first part with English *wheel* and of the second part with the English present-participle suffix pure accident.

9. Perhaps the most inconsistently divided class of words in English consists of words whose first part is a whole English word (except that the spelling may exhibit loss of a final silent *e* and the pronunciation may exhibit shift of stress) and whose second part is a suffix of frequent occurrence in words borrowed directly from a foreign language and of more or less definite meaning, or is a short sequence of letters of infrequent occurrence and of vague or no meaning except to a language specialist. Examples of this class of words are *pompous*, *labyrinthine*, *legendary*, *missionary*, *lemonade*, *servant*, *service*, *licensee*, *patentee*, *lobar*, *lubricator*, *mastoiditis*, *millionaire*, *meditative*. (Words of the type *momentous*, *laborious* do not belong because, although the spelling of the first part is that of an English word, the sounds are not.) Some words at least of this class so often show two divisions between the vowels of the abutting syllables of the components (the division being made either at the boundary between components or before the last letter of the first component) that the dictionary practice of showing no more than one division between two consecutive syllable cores is misleading. The members of this group that are most often subject to variation are those in which the first component ends in two consonants or in a long vowel (as *pompous*, *lobar*, *legendary*). The members that are least subject to variation are those in which the first component ends in a single consonant with a completely unstressed vowel preceding (as *legionary*, *lemonade*). In the second group, the single consonant is usually kept with the first component. *-ator* is usually divided between *a* and *t* (but *-ater*, with the same meaning, is usually divided between *t* and *e*).

10. Between two consecutive syllables not composed of two meaningful elements, the following basic rules are usually followed by American publishers. The latter often prescribe that a specific dictionary should be taken as a guide in such matters as division and spelling.

10.1 A single consonant or a digraph goes with the preceding vowel if the vowel is stressed and short, with the following vowel if the preceding vowel is long or has weaker stress than the vowel next following: *civ·ic*, *vap·id*, *Loch·invar*, *Ach·eson*, *feath·er; sa·vor*, *Si·nai*, *Gra·ham*, *Ra·chel*, *ei·ther*, *se·cede*, *ma·chine*.

NOTE: \ā\, \ȧ\, \au̇\, \ē\, \ī\, \ō\, \ȯ\, \ȯi\, \ü\ are long vowels, \a\, \aa\, \e\, \i\, \u̇\, \ˌə\ are short. An *a* pronounced \ä\ is in most cases treated as a long vowel (as in *fa·ther*, *sona·ta*) whereas an *o* pronounced \ä\ is treated as a short vowel (as in *both·er*). \ȯ\ is long when it does not immediately precede \r\ (as in *Ta·ney*, *Chautau·qua*). Before \r\, it is long when the spelling is other than *o* (as in *lau·rel*, *Law·rence*) or when an alternative pronunciation is \ō\ (as in *Dorian*); it is short when an alternative pronunciation is \ä\ (as in *Dor·ic*, *mor·al*). \i\ and \u̇\ are long before \r\ when their spelling is *e* and *u*, respectively (as in *se·rial*, *fu·rious; ser·ial*, *fur·ious* would suggest \ˈserēəl\, \ˈfər·ēəs\).

10.2 *x* (which ordinarily is pronounced as two consonants \ks\ or \gz\) goes with the preceding vowel (as in *ex·act*). Those who believe that a division that fits any of two or more variant pronunciations is acceptable may wish to divide *Artaxerxes* between *a* and the *x* immediately following, \z\ being one variant for the first *x* there.

10.3 A *c* not pronounced \k\ or \s\, an *s* not pronounced \s\ or \z\, a *t* not pronounced \t\ or \d·\, and a *g* not pronounced \g\ go with a following *i* or *e* even when the preceding vowel is short (*pre·cious*, *offi·cial*, *vi·sion*, *posi·tion*, *pi·geon*, *reli·gion*, *prodi·gious*). The same dividers have not usually, however, employed a parallel placement of the letter *s* when it is preceded by a short vowel and pronounced \zh\ but followed by the letter *u* (*cas·ual*, *vis·ual*, *meas·ure*, *pleas·ure*, *treas·ure;* in these last three, there is a variant with the long vowel \ā\ preceding), nor for *t* when its pronunciation is \ch\ and its environment is the same (*fat·uous*, *rit·ual*); nor for *d* when its pronunciation is \j\ (voiced cognate of \ch\) and its environment is the same (as in *grad·ual*, *decid·uous*). The explanation probably is that the divisions for these words were based on pronunciations that are not now and probably have never been usual or even common in this country. Thus, Jones's *English Pronouncing Dictionary*, based on southern British speech, shows, in its first pronunciation for *visual*, *ritual*, and *gradual*, characters whose equivalents in our alphabet are \zy\, \ty\, and \dy\ respectively, instead of the \zh\, \ch\, and \j\ respectively that are almost universal in U. S. speech. In the dictionary we have changed over to the divisions *ca·sual*, *vi·sual*, *mea·sure*, *plea·sure*, *trea·sure* but have retained such divisions as *rit·ual* and *grad·ual* for the reason that even in the pronunciations that have resulted from assimilation, \t\ and \d\ respectively are the sounds that immediately follow the short vowel (\ch\=\t+sh\, \j\=\d+zh\).

10.4 A single *r* immediately preceded by the letter *e* pronounced \-ə\ and immediately followed by another vowel is usually put with the preceding *e* (as in *feder·ation*, *ciner·ary*, *toler·able*), although when any other vowel letter precedes under the same circumstances the *r* is usually put with the vowel letter that follows (as in *ado·ration*, *admi·rable*, *decla·ration*, *satu·rable*). Probably responsible is an apprehension that a division like *cine·rary* would suggest a pronunciation like \ˈsīnˌrerē\, although such divisions as *dele·terious* and *ade·quate*, employed by the same dividers, are open to the same objection.

10.5 Practice has varied in the division of words in which a single consonant (usually *l* or *n*) is preceded by a long vowel and followed by an *i* pronounced \y\ (as in *Australian*, *communion*). In the past, the divisions *Austral·ian* and *commun·ion* have probably been the usual ones in dictionaries but *Austra·lian* and *commu·nion* appear to us to be better, especially since in some words of this class the *i* is alternatively pronounced \ē\ rather than \y\.

11. The practices followed for the division of two or more medial consonants (*consonants* is to be understood to include consonantal digraphs, as the *ch* of *puncheon* and the *ch* and *th* of *ichthyology*) are given in the following summary. These rules are for consonant clusters within which or at either end of which there is no boundary between the elements of a compound one or both of which is an English word.

11.1 When two identical consonants occur medially, a division is made between the consonants (as in *col·lie*, *mil·lion*, *camel·lia*). When two identical consonants are followed by another consonant but the entire consonant sequence is pronounced as a single sound, the division is also between the identical consonants (as in *Bud·dha*, *Mat·thew*, *bac·chanalian*, *sap·phire*). (These sequences are trigraphs.) When two identical consonants are followed by another consonant that is separately pronounced, the division is after the second identical consonant (as in *Press·ley*, *Meiss·ner*, *Hauss·mann*, *Hoff·mann*, *Ripp·mann*, *Will·kie*), except that before *le* pronounced \əl\ or \ᵊl\ the division is between the identical consonants (as in *bab·ble*, *mid·dle*, *baf·fle*, *tus·sle*, *muz·zle*). When the identical consonants are preceded by another consonant, the division is between the identical consonants *Nils·son*, *Jans·sen*.

11.2 When two consonants that are not identical are preceded by a short stressed vowel, the division is usually between the consonants (as in *bar·ley*, *ad·junct*, *whis·per*, *pub·lic*, *met·ric*, *arith·metic*, *expul·sion*, *conten·tion*). *ck* and *dg* are usually divided after the second member (as in *knick·er·bock·er*, *gadg·et*) but such treatment of *dg* (except in two-morpheme words like *edg·ing*) appears to us to be inconsistent with d-j in *adjunct*, and we have divided *gad·get*. When the first consonant is followed by *-le* pronounced \əl\ or \ᵊl\, the division is before the first consonant (as in *tre·ble*, *tri·ple*, *dou·ble*).

11.3 When two consonants that are not identical are preceded by a long stressed vowel or by a vowel that has less stress than the one immediately following, the division is before the first consonant if it is a stop (*p*, *t*, *c* or *k*, *b*, *d*, *g*) followed by *l* or *r* (except that *tl* and *dl*, which do not occur word-initially in English except in a few borrowed words, have the division before the first consonant only when this consonant is followed by *-le* or by an inflected form of *-le*, as in *ti·tle*, *enti·tling*, *noo·dle*, *At·lantic*, *ad·lumine*): *du·plicate*, *ca·pricious*, *ni·tric*, *trea·cle*, *mi·crometer*, *Bi·ble*, *cele·brate*, *hy·drant*, *hiero·glyphic*, *photo·graph*. The sequences *tl* and *dl* in *ti·tle* and *noo·dle* and *zl* in *muz·zle* are unusual in that they stand at the beginning of a syllable although they do not stand at the beginning of any except borrowed English words. The sequence *le* itself is unusual in that the phonetic items consisting of syllabic consonant and of vowel plus consonant are usually spelled with vowel letter first and consonant letter second. The sequence *ck* is usually treated as a digraph and kept together, with division after the *ck* (as in *knick·erbock·er*). *ck* is not, however, a digraph in the sense that the *ch* of *Wichita* is; it is much in the nature of a variant of *kk* (compare *chucker*, variant of *chukker*), and divisions like *grac·kle*, sometimes seen, can hardly be open to any serious objection. Dividing *lac·key* would parallel *lac·quer*. When two unidentical consonants other than those listed above occur, the division is usually between the consonants: *clois·ter*, *aus·picious*, *an·gel*, *Daim·ler*.

11.4 When three or more consonants occur between vowels, regardless of the nature of the preceding vowel, at least one consonant goes with it; if the placing of only one consonant with the preceding vowel would leave with the vowel that follows a consonant sequence that does not begin a genuine English word with the phonetic value it has intervocalically, two consonants are placed with the preceding vowel: *claus·trophobia*, *Neus·trian*, *mis·creant*, *im·bricated*, *ex·tricate*, *sump·ter*, *ad·script*. In a word like *sumpter* the \mpt\ is a difficult phonetic cluster and the \p\ is often lost by way of simplification, so that *pt* in *sumpter* often has the same pronunciation as the *pt* of *ptomaine*, but such accidental loss of a medial consonant does not constitute a reason for such divisions as *sum·pter*.

11.5 In words borrowed from foreign languages consonant sequences retaining a pronunciation close to that of the foreign language are sometimes divided as in that language (as they commonly are in our dictionary), and sometimes divided as they would be in English words: *vignette*, *tortilla*, *zabaglione*.

SPELLING

0. The following sections describe the spelling of English derivatives and variants. They do not aim to account for it. Examples are typical, not exhaustive.

The words *vowel* and *consonant* here refer to letters, not to sounds. The letters *a, e, i, o* are vowels; *u, w, y* are sometimes vowels, sometimes consonants; the other letters are consonants.

u is a consonant when it immediately follows *q* (*quit, liquid, quoin, pique*); when it is pronounced \w\ or is silent immediately following *g* (*anguish, guide*); when it is pronounced \w\ immediately following *s* (*suave*). Otherwise it is a vowel (*accuse, blue, snafu, suet, gulf, ague*).

w is a vowel when it immediately follows a vowel letter in the same syllable (*awe, law, ewe, dew, grow, cow*), and has no \w\ corresponding to it in the pronunciation as represented in this dictionary. It is a consonant in other positions (*way, swan, award*), where it has a \w\ corresponding to it in the pronunciation (but *answer* has no \w\ in the pronunciation).

y is a consonant when it is followed in the same syllable by any vowel except silent *e* (*yap, yet, youth, ye*). Otherwise it is a vowel (*dye, eye, boy, alley, gray, by, deny, gyp, synonym, many*).

1. DERIVATIVES

1.0.1 English derivatives are chiefly derivatives in which one element is an English word and the other is another English word or an affix that is readily attachable to a variety of English words. A number of suffixes from foreign languages (esp. from Greek and Latin) occur with great frequency in English words, often preceded by letters that spell an English word to whose meaning the suffix merely makes an addition. But such suffix-bearing formations have in the main been produced not by adding a suffix to an English word but by adding a suffix to the foreign source of the English word — unions either made in the foreign language and borrowed into English or made in English on the analogy of other unions in the foreign language. Accordingly, often the spelling of such suffixal formations is not the sum of the spelling of the English derivative of the foreign root plus the spelling of the anglicized form of the suffix, and such formations cannot be explained without a consideration of non-English spellings, which is beyond the province of these rules (except that a certain amount of such detail has been presented in the treatment of *-able/-ible*). Examples of spellings that these rules do not attempt to explain are: *crystallize* (has the meaning of *crystal* plus the meaning that *-ize* frequently gives, but the two *l*'s are on the analogy of Greek *krystallos*); *excellent* (from Latin *excellens, -entis;* compare English *excel* with one *l*); *libidinous* (traces orthographically to Latin *libidinosus* rather than English *libido*); *tranquillize* (the two *l*'s trace to Latin *tranquillus;* the more frequent one-*l* variant is based directly on English *tranquil*); *metallic* (from Greek *metallikos* and *metallon* rather than English *metal*); *pontifical* (from the Latin word *pontific-* rather than English *pontiff*).

1.0.2 In derivatives of the preceding type alteration of stress and vowel values is of frequent occurrence, whereas in most of the derivatives next discussed the addition merely adds sounds to the base without disturbing the latter's stress and sounds. Rules for adding a suffix to an English word are of such involvement and extent that the consultant who desires help on some one specific detail only is advised to locate that detail by the boldface subdivision.

1.1 Words ending in -x are unchanged before any suffix:

coax → *coaxed, coaxing*
fix → *fixable, fixed, fixer, fixing*
jinx → *jinxed, jinxing*
Manx → *Manxman*
Marx → *Marxist*
six → *sixty*

1.2 Words ending in -c remain unchanged

1.2.1 before *a, o, u* or a consonant:

frolic → *frolicsome*
sac → *saclike*
talc → *talcose, talcous*
zinc → *zincate, zincoid, zincous*

1.2.2 before suffixal *e, i,* and *y* add *k* if the pronunciation of the *c* remains hard but add nothing if the pronunciation of the *c* becomes soft:

bivouac → *bivouacked, bivouacking*
critic → *criticism, criticize*
frolic → *frolicked, frolicking*
mimic → *mimicked, mimicking*
music → *musician*
physic → *physicist*
picnic → *picnicked, picnicking*
toxic → *toxicity*

1.3 Words ending in consonant plus -c usually remain unchanged before any suffix, but forms with an inserted *k* occur occasionally:

arc → *arced*/sometimes *arcked,*
arcing/sometimes *arcking*
disc → *disced, discing*
zinc → *zinced/zincked, zinciferous,*
zincing/zincking, zincite, zincky/
zincy/but also *zinky*
talc → *talcky*

1.4 Some base words in this class have variants in which *-k* replaces *-c*. Such variants remain unchanged before any suffix.

1.4.1 Words ending in a single consonant except x or c immediately preceded by two or more vowels in the same syllable remain unchanged before any suffix:

air → *aired, airing, airy*
appeal → *appealed, appealing*
boil → *boiled, boiling*
brief → *briefed, briefer, briefly*
cloud → *clouded, cloudless*
cool → *cooled, cooler, coolest, cooling,*
coolly
curtail → *curtailed, curtailing,*
curtailment
head → *headed, headless, heady*
prowl → *prowled, prowler, prowling*
recoil → *recoiled, recoiling*
suit → *suitable, suitor*
tail → *tailed, tailless*
zeal → *zealot, zealous*
zoom → *zooming*

EXCEPTION:
wooly/but *woolly* is more frequent

1.4.2 Words ending in a single consonant immediately preceded by a single vowel bearing primary stress double the consonant before a suffixal vowel but not before a suffixal consonant:

abet → *abetted, abetting, abettor*
bag → *baggage*
begin → *beginner*
clan → *clannish*
drop → *droplet, dropped*
fit → *fitness, fitting*
glad → *gladden, gladly*
gyp → *gypped, gypping*
hot → *hotly, hotter*
lug → *luggage*
spot → *spotless, spotted*
trek → *trekker, trekking*

EXCEPTIONS:
chagrin → *chagrined, chagrining*
combat → *combated, combating*
(pronunciations having widespread currency in British speech, but little or none in U.S. are \shə'grēn\ or 'shagrin\ and \'kämbət\; see 1.4.3; the forms *combatted, combatting* are often found in U.S. writing; but *chagrinned, chagrinning,* though justifiable on the basis of logic and pronunciation, are less common variants).
control → *controled, controling*
(less frequent than the two *l* forms, but preferred by some to preserve the long vowel sound; for the same reason, derivatives of *extol* and *patrol* sometimes have single *l* spellings)
defer → *deference*
prefer → *preferable, preference*
refer → *reference*
transfer → *transference*
(when the stress is altered, the derivative has a single *r*, but some derivatives of *-er* verbs have an alternative single *r* spelling even when the stress remains the same: *transfer* → *transferable/transferrable*)
gas → *gaseous, gasify* but *gassed, gassing*

1.4.3 Words ending in a single consonant immediately preceded by a single vowel bearing secondary stress vary greatly in their derivatives:

some always double the consonant:

handicap → *handicapped, handicapping*
humbug → *humbugged, humbugging*
zigzag → *zigzagged, zigzagging*

some have single consonant only:

catalog → *cataloged, cataloging*
(but *catalogue* → *catalogued, cataloguing,* which present no problem)
chaperon → *chaperoned, chaperoning*
(the single *n* is probably due to the long vowel sound, as well as to the occasional appearance of the alternative form *chaperone*)
parallel → *paralleled, paralleling*
(the single *l* serves to avoid the awkward appearance of two pairs of *l*'s)
pyramid → *pyramided, pyramiding*

some have both forms:

bayonet → *bayoneted/bayonetted,*
bayoneting/bayonetting
benefit → *benefited/benefitted,*
benefiting/benefitting
carburet → *carbureted/carburetted,*
carbureting/carburetting,
carburetor/carburettor
combat → *combated/combatted,*
combating/combatting
kidnap → *kidnapped/kidnaped,*
kidnapping/kidnaping
nonplus → *nonplussed/nonplused,*
nonplussing/nonplusing
program → *programmed/programed,*
programming/programing
(the variant spellings may not have the same pronunciation; rather, the two-consonant spelling represents a pronunciation (or in *kidnap* a former pronunciation) with definite secondary stress on the last syllable of the base word, whereas the one-consonant spelling represents a pronunciation with no stress on the last syllable of the base word; in *carburetor* it may reflect the pronunciation \ˌrāt\ instead of \ˌret\

1.4.4 Words ending in a single consonant immediately preceded by one or more vowels without stress remain unchanged before any suffix:

bargain → *bargained, bargaining*
callous → *calloused, callously*
carom → *caromed, caroming*
credit → *credited, crediting, creditor*
gallop → *galloped, galloping*
gladden → *gladdened, gladdening*
solid → *solider, solidest, solidify, solidly*
waver → *wavered, wavering*

EXCEPTIONS:
(1) a large group of words doubles a final consonant immediately preceded by a single unstressed vowel before a suffixal vowel; in British use this is the regular practice; in U.S. use it is usually an accepted alternative to the one-consonant spelling. To this class belong words with unstressed final syllable ending in *-l* (except *parallel,* sometimes pronounced \-ləl\, esp. in Britain; compare 1.4.3) as well as some words ending in *-s* or *-t*. Derivatives of compounds of these words follow the same rules as derivatives of the simplex words. The following list includes the most important of these words:

apparel	*drivel*	*marshal*	*shovel*
barrel	*duel*	*marvel*	*shrivel*
bevel	*enamel*	*medal*	*signal*
bias	*equal*	*metal*	*snivel*
bowel	*focus*	*model*	*spiral*
cancel	*fuel*	*panel*	*stencil*
carol	*funnel*	*parcel*	*symbol*
cavil	*gambol*	*pedal*	*tassel*
channel	*gravel*	*pencil*	*tinsel*
chisel	*grovel*	*peril*	*total*
counsel	*gruel*	*pistol*	*towel*
cudgel	*jewel*	*pummel*	*trammel*
devil	*kennel*	*quarrel*	*travel*
dial	*label*	*ravel*	*trowel*
dishevel	*laurel*	*revel*	*tunnel*
dowel	*libel*	*rival*	*victual*

(2) two *l*'s are more common in adjectives like *gravelly, tinselly* than in derivatives with other suffixes; the double consonant prevents these words from being read as two-syllabled adverbs (*gravelly, adj; gravely, adv*)
(3) for derivatives of *worship* the one-*p* and two-*p* forms are about equally common:
worship → *worshiped/worshipped,*
worshiping/worshipping,
worshiper/worshipper

1.5 Words ending in a single consonant that is silent remain unchanged before any suffix:

chamois → *chamoised, chamoising*
crochet → *crocheted, crocheting*
hurrah → *hurrahed, hurrahing*
picot → *picoted, picoting*
pooh-pooh → *pooh-poohed, pooh-poohing*

EXCEPTION:
ricochet → *ricocheted/ricochetted,*
richocheting/ricochetting
(this is not a true exception, for whereas the single-consonant spelling reflects a pronunciation in which the *t* is silent (\ˈrikəˈshā\), the double-consonant form reflects the pronunciation \ˈrikəˈshet\— compare 1.4.3.

1.6 Words ending in two or more consonants the last of which is not c remain unchanged before any suffix:

art→ *artistic, artless*
attach→ *attached, attachment*
buzz→ *buzzed, buzzer, buzzing*
condemn→ *condemnatory, condemned, condemning*
length→ *lengthen, lengthy*
odd→ *oddity, oddly*
sighed→ *sighing*
stiff→ *stiffen, stiffer, stiffly, stiffness*
thrall→ *thralldom*
trick→ *tricked, tricking, trickster*
thirst→ *thirsty*
wrong→ *wronged, wrongly*

EXCEPTIONS:
(1) words ending in *-ll* often drop one *l* before a suffixal consonant and in forming compounds (in Britain the one *l* spelling is by far the more common for such words; in the U.S. it is a widespread variant):

dull→ *dulness* *skill*→ *skilful*
fill→ *fulfil, fulfilment* *will*→ *wilful*
roll→ *enrol* *thrall*→ *enthral, thraldom*

(2) the second *l* of final *-ll* frequently disappears before suffixal *l;* it always disappears before *-ly* (*droll*→ *drolly; dull*→ *dully; full*→ *fully*); before *-less* it may disappear, but hyphened forms, retaining all three *l*'s are more frequent (*hull-less, will-less*); with *-like*, the hyphened form, retaining all three *l*'s is usual (*bell-like, bull-like, scroll-like*)

1.7 Words ending in silent -e drop the vowel before a suffixal vowel but remain unchanged before a suffixal consonant:

bone→ *boned, boning*, but *boneless*
complete→ *completed, completing*, but *completeness*
curve→ *curvature, curved, curving*, but *curvesome*
imagine→ *imaginable, imagining*, but *imagines*
clique→ *cliquish*, but *cliques*
bugle→ *bugling, bugler*
gentle→ *gentler, gentlest*, but *gentleness*

Although both are often called silent, the *e* at the end of words of the type *bone* and *giraffe* differs from the *e* at the end of words of the type *bugle* and *tickle* in this respect: the vowel letter that immediately precedes the final consonant or consonant group of *bone* and *giraffe* stands for a vowel sound that is the nucleus of the final or only syllable of the word whereas the vowel letter in the same position in *bugle* and *tickle* does not. The *-e* in *bugle* may be regarded as a vowel letter that is pronounced but that is out of position in the orthography of the word. Although such an *e* is usually dropped from the spelling before a suffixal vowel, the extra syllable that it represents in the form of the word before suffixation may remain present in the pronunciation, *bugling* for example being either \'byügliŋ\ or \'byügəliŋ\ and *ticklish* being either \'tiklish\ or \'tikəlish\. Words ending in a single pronounced *-e* (other than those bearing an accent, covered in 1.9) are rare; the few existing examples drop the *-e* before a suffix beginning with an *e*, but remain unchanged before all other suffixes:

Dante→ *Dantesque*
dele (*vb*) → *deles, deled, deleing*

EXCEPTIONS:
(1) proper names ending in single *-e* preceded by one or more consonants usually keep the *e* before the suffix *-an;* in the derivatives so formed the *e* is sounded, whether or not it is silent in the base:

Coleridge→ *Coleridgean* usually preferred to */Coleridgian*
Europe→ *European* *Chile*→ *Chilean*
Nietzsche→ *Nietzschean*
Shakespeare→ *Shakespearean* usually preferred to */Shakespearian*

(2) *mile*→ *mileage* much more frequent than */milage*
nurse→ *nursling* the common form rather than */nurseling*

(3) before the suffix *-ly* words ending in consonantal *-le* usually drop the *-le:*
gentle→ *gently* *simple*→ *simply*
subtle→ *subtly*/but also *subtlely*
supple→ *supply*/but more frequently *supplely* probably to avoid confusion with the verb *supply*

(4) some words ending in *-re* retain the *-e* before a suffixal vowel:

acre→ *acreage* *nacre*→ *nacreous*

(5) words ending in *-ce* or *-ge* usually retain the *-e* before any suffixal letter except *e, i,* or *y,* thus preserving the softness of the *c* or *g:*

age→ *ageless* (but *aging/ageing*)
change→ *changeable, changeless* (but *changing*)
courage→ *courageous, encouragement* (but *encouraged, encouraging*)
grace→ *graceful* (but *disgraced, disgracing*)
peace→ *peaceable*
replace→ *replaceable* (but *replacing*)
range→ *rangy*/but also *rangey*

A *d* preceding *g* may in a few cases act as a preserver of the soft sound and permit the dropping of the *-e:*

abridge→ *abridgment*/but *abridgement* especially in Britain
acknowledge→ *acknowledgment*/but *acknowledgement* especially in Britain
judge→ *judgment*/but *judgement* especially in Britain
lodge→ *lodgment*/but *lodgement* especially in Britain

(6) although final *-e* regularly drops before the suffix *-able*, some adjectives in *-able* have alternatives retaining the *-e:*

like→ *likable/likeable*
live→ *livable/liveable*
love→ *lovable/loveable*
move→ *movable/moveable*
size→ *sizable/sizeable*

British usage is more inclined than U.S. usage to retain the form with *e;* recent or nonce formations, especially from polysyllabic base words, usually appear without the *e;* but formations based on verbs ending in *-le* or *-re* usually retain the *e:*

automobile→ *automobilable*
isolate→ *isolatable*

but:

handle→ *handleable* *whistle*→ *whistleable*
settle→ *settleable* *wrinkle*→ *wrinkleable*

(7) usage fluctuates considerably with regard to dropping or retaining final *-e* before derivatives formed with the suffix *-y;* many have both the *-ey* and the *-y* alternative:

cage→ *cagey/cagy* *phone*→ *phony/phoney*
home→ *homey/homy* *poke*→ *pokey/poky*
horse→ *horsey/horsy* *stage*→ *stagy/stagey*
mouse→ *mousy/mousey*
stone→ *stony/stoney*

and some words have only one form in common usage:

rose→ *rosy* *slave*→ *slavey*
shade→ *shady*

(8) the silent *-e* remains in some present participles to distinguish them from the corresponding forms of other verbs:

dye→ *dyeing* (in contrast to *dying*)
singe→ *singeing* (in contrast to *singing*)
springe→ *springeing* (in contrast to *springing*)
swinge→ *swingeing* (in contrast to *swinging*)

1.8 Words ending in -e preceded by a vowel drop the final *-e* before suffixal *-a-* and *-e-*:

argue→ *arguable, argued*
awe→ *awed* *toe*→ *toed*
blue→ *blued, bluer, bluest*
free→ *freed, freer, freest*
issue→ *issuance, issued*
lie→ *liar* *vie*→ *vied*

EXCEPTIONS:
(1) words ending in *-ee* usually retain both *e*'s before *a* and always before suffixal *-i-*:

agree→ *agreeable, agreeing*
flee→ *fleeing*
foresee→ *foreseeable*
free→ *freeing*

-ie in an accented syllable becomes *-y* before suffixal *-i-*:

die→ *dying* *lie*→ *lying*
tie→ *tying* *vie*→ *vying*

-ie in an unaccented syllable remains unchanged before suffixal *-i-*:

stymie→ *stymieing* *sortie*→ *sortieing*

-oe remains unchanged before suffixal *-i-*:

canoe→ *canoeing* *shoe*→ *shoeing*
hoe→ *hoeing* *toe*→ *toeing*

-ue usually drops *-e* before suffixal *-i-*:

accrue→ *accruing* *pursue*→ *pursuing*
argue→ *arguing* *true*→ *truing, truism*
ensue→ *ensuing*

-ye alternatively keeps or drops *-e* before suffixal *-i-*:

eye→ *eyeing/eying* (compare *dyeing*)

retain *-e* when forming adjectives with the suffix *-y:*

glue→ *gluey* *tissue*→ *tissuey*

usually remain unchanged before a suffixal consonant:

agree→ *agreement* *accrue*→ *accruement*
free→ *freedom* *blue*→ *blueness*
woe→ *woeful*/but also *woful*

but:

argue→ *argument* *true*→ *truly*
awe→ *awful* (but *awesome*) *due*→ *duly*

1.9 Verbs derived from the French and ending in -é usually form their past and past participle in *-éd*, less often in *-éed;* they form their present participle in *-éing:*

appliqué→ *appliquéd, appliquéing*
visé→ *viséd*/also *viséed*

1.10 Words ending in -y preceded by a consonant usually change the *-y* to *i* before any suffixal letter except *i* and the possessive sign *'s:*

beauty→ *beautiful, beautify*
body→ *bodily, embodiment*
cliquy→ *cliquier, cliquiest*
contrary→ *contrariwise*
copy→ *copyist* *icy*→ *iciest, icily*
defy→ *defiant, defying*
deny→ *denial, denying*
fancy→ *fanciful, fancying*
happy→ *happiness*
likely→ *likelihood* *mercy*→ *merciless*
merry→ *merrier, merriest, merriment*
thirty→ *thirtyish* *weary*→ *wearisome*

but:

everybody→ *everybody's*
Mary→ *Mary's*

Verbs of this classification form the third person singular by changing the *-y* to *i* and adding *-es*, in analogy with the past and past participle in which *-y* regularly changes to *i* before *-ed*.

EXCEPTIONS:
(1) one-syllable words usually retain *-y* before *-ly* and *-ness:*

dry→ *dryly, dryness* *sly*→ *slyly, slyness*
shy→ *shyly, shyness*
wry→ *wryly, wryness*

(2) comparatives and superlatives of one-syllable adjectives alternatively retain *-y* or replace it with *i:*

shy→ *shier/shyer, shiest/shyest*
dry→ *drier, driest*/more common than *dryer, dryest*

(3) *fly*→ *flier/flyer*

(4) *-y* remains unchanged
before *-like* and *-ship:*
lady→ *ladylike*
secretary→ *secretaryship*
in derivatives of *baby* and *lady:*
baby→ *babyhood* *lady*→ *ladykin*
in *busyness* (busy state) to distinguish it from *business* (enterprise)
in some rarely used forms:
hobby→ *hobbyless* *Tory*→ *Torydom*

(5) *-y* may be lost completely before suffixal *-i-*, especially when separated by one or more syllables from the primary stress of the base word:

accompany→ *accompanist/accompanyist*
military→ *militarism, militarist, militarize*
soliloquy→ *soliloquize*
voluntary→ *voluntarism*

1.11 Words ending in -y preceded by a vowel usually remain unchanged before any suffix:

alloy→ *alloys* *attorney*→ *attorneys*
convey→ *conveyance, conveyor*
enjoy→ *enjoying, enjoyment*
gray→ *graying, grayish, grayness*
play→ *played, playing, player, playful, playlet*

EXCEPTIONS:
(1) *day*→ *daily* *say*→ *saith*
lay→ *laid* *slay*→ *slain*
pay→ *paid*

(2) *gay*→ *gaiety/gayety, gaily/gayly*
stay→ *stayed*

(3) comparatives and superlatives of adjectives ending in *-ey* replace these two letters with *i:*

gluey→ *gluier, gluiest, gluily*
phoney→ *phonier, phoniest, phonily*

A number of adjectives ending in *-ey* preceded by a consonant have alternative forms without *e* (*phoney/phony*). For these alternatives the spellings *-ier, -iest* are covered in 1.10.

(4) adjectives ending in *-wy* change the *-y* to *i* before any suffix:

dewy→ *dewier, dewiest, dewily, dewiness*
showy→ *showier, showiest, showily, showiness*

1.12 Words ending in a vowel except e or y, when adding a suffix beginning with a consonant, remain unchanged:

China→ *Chinaman* *photo*→ *photostat*
coo→ *coos* *radio*→ *radiogram*
law→ *lawful* *taxi*→ *taximan*

1.13.1 Verbs ending in a vowel except e or y, when adding a suffix beginning with a vowel, remain unchanged before their inflectional suffixes:

alibi→ *alibied, alibiing*
boo→ *booed* *coo*→ *cooed, cooing*
radio→ *radioed, radioing*
shanghai→ *shanghaied, shanghaiing*
show→ *showed, showing*
ski→ *skied, skiing, skier*
snafu→ *snafus, snafued*
taboo→ *tabooed, tabooing*
tattoo→ *tattooed, tattooing*
taxi→ *taxis, taxiing*/but also *taxying*

EXCEPTIONS:
verbs ending in single *-o* usually insert *e* before adding *-s* for the third person singular:

echo→ *echoes* *lasso*→ *lassoes*

For the plural of nouns ending in a single *-o* (*potato*), see "Plurals".

1.13.2 Nouns ending in a vowel when adding one of the suffixes -esque, -ism, -ist usually remain unchanged especially if the base word is short and the final vowel is essential to its recognition:

Dada→ *Dadaism* *Tao*→ *Taoism*
Dali→ *Daliesque* *Tito*→ *Titoism*
solo→ *soloist* *Zola*→ *Zolaesque*

EXCEPTIONS:

cello→ *cellist*
chiaroscuro→ *chiaroscurist*
Leonardo→ *Leonardesque*
Michelangelo→ *Michelangelesque*
Nazi→ *Nazism*/but also *Naziism*
propaganda→ *propagandist*
quattrocento→ *quattrocentist*

1.13.3 Geographical and personal names ending in -a regularly drop the *-a* before the suffix *-an/-ian:*

Africa→ *African* *America*→ *American*
Alberta→ *Albertan* *Canada*→ *Canadian*
North Carolina→ *North Carolinian*
Seneca→ *Senecan* *Victoria*→ *Victorian*
Venezuela→ *Venezuelan*

1.13.4 Some geographical names ending in -o drop the *-o* before *-an/-ian:*

Borneo→ *Bornean*
Mexico→ *Mexican*
Morocco→ *Moroccan*
Ontario→ *Ontarian*
San Diego→ *San Diegan*
San Francisco→ *San Franciscan*

1.13.5 Scientific terms of Greek or Latin origin ending in -a regularly drop the *-a* before a suffix beginning with a vowel:

pleura→ *pleural*
urea→ *urease, ureic*
urethra→ *urethral*

1.13.6 Words ending in -o insert *e* before suffixal *-y:*

goo→ *gooey* *mosquito*→ *mosquitoey*

1.13.7 Geographical and personal names ending in -o or a combination of vowels pronounced \ō often insert *n* or *v* before *-an/-ian:*

Buffalo→ *Buffalonian*
Cicero→ *Ciceronian*
Draco→ *Draconian*
Harrow→ *Harrovian*
Marlow→ *Marlovian*
(compare *Peru*→ *Peruvian*)
Thoreau→ *Thoreauvian*
Toronto→ *Torontonian*

but some geographical names ending in *-o* remain unchanged before *-an:*

Chicago→ *Chicagoan*
Colorado→ *Coloradoan*

1.14 When adding a prefix that forms a new word, a base word usually remains unchanged:

act→ *enact*
call→ *recall*
change→ *exchange*
danger→ *endanger*
deck→ *bedeck*
fill→ *fulfill*
prove→ *disprove*
roll→ *enroll*
veil→ *unveil*

EXCEPTIONS:

words ending in *-ll* often drop one *l* when adding a prefix; this practice, common in Britain, is widespread also in the U.S., but the unchanged (*-ll*) forms prevail in this country:

fill→ *fulfil, fulfilment*
roll→ *enrol*
thrall→ *enthral*

By analogy even some infinitives which are not derivatives of English base words sometimes drop one *l.* For these words, too, the one *-l* spelling prevails in Britain, whereas in the U.S. it exists side by side with the *-ll* form:

distil/distill
instal/install
instil/instill

1.15 Two or more words joining to form a compound usually retain the full spelling of both component words:

billfold *self-conscious*
father-in-law *sidestep*
freedom-loving *well-bred*
love-lies-bleeding *wholehearted*
makeup *widespread*
man-of-war *workhouse*
narrow-minded

For the spelling of such compounds (separate, closed, or hyphened) see the section on "The Writing of Compounds".

EXCEPTIONS:

many compounds which are long-established in the language and in which the full literal force of one or both elements has been weakened or lost have dropped a letter from one, sometimes both, of the original elements:

almighty, almost, alone, already, also, although, altogether, always
withal, therewithal, wherewithal
welcome, welfare
Candlemas, Christmas, Lammas, Michaelmas
artful, hateful, rueful, woeful/woful
chilblain
fulfill
namesake
neckerchief
numskull/but also *numbskull*
pastime
until
wherever

Many words which are not readily recognizable as compounds resulted from the joining of two words in the Old or Middle English periods (*lord,* from OE *hlāfweard,* bread keeper; *threshold,* from ME *threshwold,* (a piece of) wood to tread (on); *woman* from OE *wīfmann,* a wife man).

2. VARIANTS

2.0 Many English words may be spelled in more than one way. The variant used may be a matter of individual choice, or it may be regional. One form may be usual in one region (as the U.S.), and a variant may be usual in another region (as Britain). Some of the more conspicuous U.S./British variations are:

U.S.	BRITISH	EXAMPLE	SEE
-ction	*-xion*	*connection/connexion*	**2.5**
-dg-	*-dge*	*judgment/judgement*	**1.7**
e	*ae, oe*	*eolian/aeolian* *ecology/oecology*	**2.2**
-er	*-re*	*theater/theatre*	**2.7**
-ize	*-ise*	*organize/organise*	**2.10**
-l-	*-ll-*	*leveling/levelling*	**1.4.4**
-ll-	*-l-*	*enrollment/enrolment*	**1.6**
-or	*-our*	*humor/humour*	**2.12**
-s-	*-c-*	*defense/defence*	**2.14**

The variations treated in the following sections are not regional unless the contrary is stated.

2.1 -able/-ible. English has a large group of adjectives in *-able,* another in *-ible;* the force of the suffix in both groups is the same. Many of these adjectives are from Latin adjectives in *-abilis* and *-ibilis; -abilis* occurs after first-conjugation stems, *-ibilis* after stems of the other conjugations. With *-abilis* the stem used is the present, with *-ibilis* it is sometimes the present, sometimes the participial. Examples: (first conjugation) *laudabilis;* (second, third, fourth conjugations respectively, present stem) *horribilis, credibilis, audibilis;* (second, third, fourth conjugations respectively, participial stem) *risibilis, defensibilis, sensibilis.* These and many other such Latin adjectives have been borrowed by English, with change of *-ilis* to *-le.* In addition, many others have been analogically formed in English, or in French and borrowed by English. Since Latin provides precedent for either the present or the participial stem with *-ibilis,* two quite or substantially synonymous *-ible* words with different stems have in some cases been introduced into English (*corrodible/corrosible, submergible/submersible*). Further, *-able* has become a productive suffix in English and has been attached to a multitude of English verbs. Many of these that are Latin-derived are (*a*) from second-, third-, and fourth-conjugation stems, or (*b*) from first-conjugation participial stems, with none of which *-abilis* occurs. Hence, English has a few variants of the type *preventible/preventable* (class *a*) and a probably larger number of the type *educable/educatable* (class *b*).

2.2 e/ae, o/oe. The digraphs *ae/æ* and *oe/œ* of Latin and of Greek transliterated into Latin are sometimes retained in English derivatives and borrowings, sometimes reduced to *e.* Sometimes one form strongly prevails throughout English, and variants are infrequent: *economy, enigma, estuary, ether, Caesar, Aegean, aer-* words (as *aerial, aeronautics*). When variants are frequent, the one-letter variant is nearly always in greater favor in U.S. use than in British:

anemia/anaemia
anesthetic/anaesthetic
diarrhea/diarrhoea
edema/oedema
esophagus/oesophagus
estrogen/oestrogen
etiology/aetiology
fetus/foetus
hemoglobin/haemoglobin
maneuver/manoeuvre (fr. French)

2.3.1 chemistry suffixes for compounds, classes of compounds, and radicals: -an/-ane, -id/-ide, -in/-ine, -ol/-ole, -on/-one, -oyl/-yl, -yne/-ine. Words in *-ane* usually designate saturated carbon compounds (as paraffin hydrocarbons and many cyclic hydrocarbons) and in the U.S. also completely hydrogenated parent heterocyclic compounds (as *dioxane*); words in *-an* designate other chemical compounds (as *furan, pyran*) including in Britain completely hydrogenated parent heterocyclic compounds (as *dioxan*). *-ide* has superseded *-id* except in a few terms (notably *lipid* as preferred by most biochemists). In organic chemical names *-ine* designates bases; *-in* designates compounds that are neutral or not distinctly basic or acidic (as glycerides, proteins, porphyrins, and some six-membered heterocyclic compounds). In systematic names *-ol* designates alcohols and phenols, whereas *-ole* designates other compounds (as most five-membered heterocyclic compounds and some others). Words in *-one* designate ketones, quinones, lactones, or other compounds containing a carbonyl group and also sulfones and sultones; in *-on,* other compounds (as *nervon*). *-oyl* is now preferred to *-yl* by the International Union of Pure and Applied Chemistry for most organic acid radicals (as *carbamoyl, phthaloyl*). With one or two exceptions *-yne* has superseded *-ine* in systematic names for carbon compounds containing triple bonds (as hydrocarbons of the acetylene series).

2.3.2 -ene/-en. The spelling *thiophene* is used in the U.S., whereas *thiophen* is used in Britain. (In both countries *-ene* is used especially for carbon compounds containing double bonds, as olefin hydrocarbons and aromatic hydrocarbons.)

2.3.3 -e. In systematic chemical names a final *e* (as in the name of a hydrocarbon) is dropped before a suffix beginning with a vowel (as *butane, butanol,* but *butanediol*).

2.4 -ant/-ent. English contains a large group of words ending in *-ant* and another in *-ent,* both pronounced \ənt\. Most of the *-ant* words stem from Latin present participles of the first conjugation (*radiant,* from Latin *radians, -antis*), the *-ent* words from Latin present participles of the other conjugations (*regent,* from Latin *regens, -entis*); but not always (*tenant,* ultimately from a Latin verb of the second conjugation, owes its *a* to Old French). The two endings do not differ in force, and, though usually all English words that derive from the present participle of the same Latin verb have *a* only or *e* only, in each of the following families of such derivatives there is variation:

a almost always	*e* almost always	*a* usually	*e* usually	*a* and *e* with about equal frequency
	repell...ncy		*repell...nt* *impell...nt*	
		propell...nt *expell...nt*		
pend...nt noun	*pend...ncy* *depend...nt* adj. *independ...nt* *-...nce, -...ncy*			*pend...nt* adj. *depend...nt* noun
ascend...nt, -...nce *descend...nt*				*ascend...ncy*
	transcend...nt, *-...nce, -...ncy*			
tend...nce "care" *intend...nt,* *-...nce, -...ncy* *attend...nt, -...nce*	*tend...ncy*			
	superintend...nt, *-...nce, -...ncy*			

2.5 -ction/-xion. Most nouns ending in \kshən\ are spelled *-ction* only; a few are alternatively *-ction/-xion;* a few are *-xion* only. Those that are *-ction* only are ultimately from a Latin verb whose participial stem ends in *-ct: direction,* from *directio* from *direct*(*us*). Those that are alternatively *-ction/-xion* are ultimately from a Latin verb whose participial stem ends in *-x* and whose present stem ends in *-ct;* the participial stem is the source of the *-xion* variant, the present stem is the source, usually via an English verb, of the *-ction* variant: thus *inflexion* is from *inflexio* from *inflex*(*us*); *inflection* is *inflexion* with *x* assimilated to the *ct* of English *inflect,* from *inflect*(*ere*), an assimilation catalyzed by the analogy of nouns like *direction.* Nouns that are *-xion* only are ultimately from Latin verbs of which the present stem does not end in *-ct* and which accordingly have not procreated English verbs in *-ct: crucifixion, transfixion,* and *fluxion.*

-CTION/-XION		
	U.S.	BRITISH
defle...ion	*ct* prevails *x* rare	*x* probably prevails
genufle...ion	*ct* prevails	*x* prevails
infle...ion	*ct* prevails *x* rare	*x* prevails
refle...ion	*ct* prevails *x* rare	*ct* prevails
conne...ion	*ct* prevails *x* rare	*x* prevails
comple...ion	*x* prevails *ct* rare*	*x* prevails *ct* rare

*in spite of the fact that there is a fairly common U.S. form *complected*

2.6.1 em-/im-, en-/in-. The Latin preposition or adverb *in,* in such English derivatives as *inoculate, intrude, invent,* occurs as a prefix in many Latin verbs and verb derivatives. Sometimes the *in-* is unchanged *(inoculare, intrudere, invenire).* At other times the phonetic influence of an initial consonant of the base that follows the *in-* changes the *n* to a consonant having the same articulation as the base-initial consonant. The change is to *m* before *m, b,* and *p (immigrare, imbibere, implorare),* to *l* before *l (illuminare),* to *r* before *r (irradiare).*

2.6.2 French — Old and Modern — has borrowed many of these compounds and retained the Latin spelling of the prefix *(inoculer, inventer, immigrer, imbiber, implorer, illuminer, irradier).* However, Latin *in* became *en* in French, and when similar compounds were constructed in French on French words as a base the vowel used in the prefix was *e.* The assimilation of the *n* to *m* before *m, b,* and *p* continued *(emmener, embaumer, employer);* the assimilation of the *n* to *l* and *r* before *l* and *r* respectively did not *(enlargier, enrager).*

2.6.3 English, like French, has borrowed many of the Latin compound verbs and retained the Latin spelling of the prefix *(inoculate, invent, immigrate, imbibe, implore, illuminate, irradiate).* English has borrowed also from French many forms in *em-* and *en- (embalm, employ, enlarge).* English has taken over also the prefixes *im-, in-, em-, en-* and attached them to English nouns and adjectives to make verbs, or to verbs to make other verbs *(imbed, encage, enkindle).* As in French formations, *-m* is usually used before *m, b, p (immarble/emmarble, imbed/embed, impanel/empanel)* but in the compound having *mesh* as base both *m* and *n* are found prefixally.

2.6.4 Of the borrowings from French *em-* and *en-* forms, and of the formations within English, some have now *e* now *i* as the prefixal vowel *(enclose/inclose, embed/imbed, embitter/imbitter);* others, some of which formerly showed the same variation, are found with *e* only or with *i* only *(embalm, encamp, impeach). i* is more frequent before *m* than before *n.*

2.6.5 In most of the intra-English formations the prefix adds little or nothing semantically to the base. Before an adjective or noun it serves chiefly as a sign that the adjective or noun has been made a verb. This verb-forming prefix is closest to being completely functionless when it is added to a verb: thus *kindle* and *enkindle* are not easily discriminable. If the prefix makes a substantial semantic contribution, usually the prefixal vowel is *i* and the prefixal consonant is *n* whatever letter follows *(inborn, inbound, inbuilt, inbred/*but *imbred* occasionally).

2.7 -er/-re. Some English words, mostly derived from French words in *-re,* which in turn are mostly derived from Greek or Latin, alternatively end in *-er/-re.* But the *-er,* of different origin, that is a productive suffix freely attachable to English bases *(writer, header, four-poster, New Yorker)* does not have the variant *-re.* Most of the variants are usually *-er* in U.S., *-re* in Britain:

caliber/calibre · *center/centre* · *fiber/fibre* · *luster/lustre* · *sepulcher/sepulchre* · *somber/sombre* · *specter/spectre*

EXCEPTIONS:

(1) in both U.S. and British use *-re* is usually the form after *c,* the immediately following *r* ensuring the hardness of the *c (acre, chancre, involucre, lucre, massacre, mediocre, nacre, wiseacre).* But after *g* (which, like *c,* may be hard or soft) the same is not true (U.S. *meager*/Britain *meagre;* but both countries prefer *eager, ogre).*

(2) U.S. and British usage both prefer *cadre* \ˈkadrē\, *macabre, timbre* "tone quality". The latter (often \ˈtambə(r)\) is not to be confused with *timber* "wood" (\ˈtimbə(r)\), a different word, which has only *-er* in both countries.

(3) although *meter/metre,* the metric-system unit of measurement (which is ultimately from Greek *metron),* and its compounds *(centimet-, decimet-, millimet-)* are *-re* in Britain, *meter* (which is *mete+ -er)* is universal in both countries for any device for measuring (electric *meter),* as is also *-meter* as the second element of many names for specific measuring devices *(altimeter, barometer, galvanometer, gasometer, ohmmeter, speedometer, thermometer, voltmeter, volumeter).* Some of these compounds are simply a joining or telescoping of an English first element and *meter* "measuring device", but most are not. In a few the quality of the *e* that follows the *m* is the same as in the simplex word; in most this *e* is of a different quality and without stress. In metric-system names the sound values in *-meter/-metre* are the same as in the simplex.

(4) although *meter/metre* "rhythm" is *metre* in Britain, for names of individual measures *(trimeter, tetrameter, pentameter, hexameter) -meter* is the spelling there as well as in the U.S. In these, too, the *e* following the *m* is without stress.

(5) both *theater/theatre* have wide currency in the U.S., only the second in Britain. In New York City, the theatrical center of the U.S., the spelling is usually *theatre.*

(6) *neuter* and *sober* are in both countries *-er* only.

2.8.1 -er/-or. These are the most common endings in English for agent nouns. This *-or* does not have a variant *-our* except in *saviour.* A few agent nouns have *a* rather than *e* or *o* before the *r (beggar, liar, pedlar* sometimes). Such nouns of this class as are based on a Latin perfect stem, whether the nouns are formed in English from an English verb so based or are taken from the Latin or, with somewhat altered spelling, from French *(author)* usually have *-or:*

actor · *arbitrator* · *collector* · *conductor* · *confessor* · *detector* · *fabricator* · *incisor* · *inspector* · *lubricator* · *mediator* · *motor* · *negotiator* · *objector* · *operator* · *supervisor* · *translator* · *victor*

2.8.2 Other agent nouns usually have *-er,* such as nouns based on Latin present stems and nouns based on verbs of Germanic origin:

convoker · *designer* · *digger* · *distiller* · *drawer* · *invader* · *commuter* (compare *commutator)* · *modifier* · *organizer* · *producer* · *rider* · *robber* · *redeemer* (compare *Redemptorist)* · *slicer* · *stitcher* · *subscriber* · *usurper* · *voyager*

2.8.3 Occasionally, however, an English agent noun, although its base is from a Latin perfect stem, has *-er* for suffix, as a less frequent variant of *-or.* In such pairs the *-or* form is on the analogy of Latin, the *-er* form is the English suffix added to an English verb that is from the same Latin perfect stem as the *-or* noun *(executor/* archaic *executer).* Conversely, sometimes an agent noun, though its base is from a Latin present stem, has *-or* alone or as a variant of *-er.* Sometimes false analogy may be responsible: some Latin present stems have the same final consonant or consonant cluster as some Latin perfect stems (compare the present participle *reflect[ere]* and the past participle *elect[us]);* the coiner of *reflector* may have used as his model a quite regular formation of the type *elector.* So also *adaptor* and *advisor* are unexpected (compare *adapt[are], advis[are]), captor* and *supervisor* are regular (compare *capt[us], supervis[us]).*

2.8.4 Old French is the source of numerous *-or* agent nouns. Many are law terms or have a legal sense, and of these many have correlatives in *-ee (bailor, bailee).* Most of the terms below have variants in *-er,* and *-er* is the usual spelling in nonlegal use of such terms as have both legal and nonlegal senses:

abettor · *alienor* · *bailor* · *bargainor* · *barrator* · *confirmor* · *consignor* · *donor* · *mortgagor* · *obligor* · *pawnor* · *pledgor/pledgeor* · *promisor* · *releasor* · *surrenderor* · *transferor* · *vendor* · *visitor*

bettor (avoidance of homography with *better* "more good" may have been a factor)

2.9. -ph-/-f-. \ˈsəlfə(r)\ as a chemical term and chemical terms based on it are usually spelled *sulf-* by U.S. scientists, *sulph-* by British scientists. Nonscientists in both countries usually spell *sulph-.*

2.10. -ize/-ise. Ancient Greek has a verb suffix *-izein,* which descended into postclassical Latin as *-izare* and into French as *-iser.* English has borrowed verbs (all of more than one syllable) containing this suffix from all three languages *(ostracize, pulverize, moralize).* In addition, English has isolated the suffix and used it quite freely, attaching it to bases both Greek *(criticize, mechanize)* and non-Greek (to Latin bases, *anglicize;* to English nouns, *victimize, memorize, dockize;* to English adjectives, *normalize, victorianize;* to proper names, *londonize, fletcherize).* In U.S. use the suffix is nearly always spelled *-ize,* even in words from French, in which the spelling is *-iser.* In Britain, however, many not only retain *s* in borrowings from French but use *s* instead of *z* in borrowings from Greek and Latin and in English formations. Many others in Britain, however, including several influential publications, use *-ize* in all words in which \īz\ is descended from Greek *-izein.*

EXCEPTIONS:

(1) although \īz\ in *exorci-e* and *chasti-e* derives (in the second somewhat circuitously) from Greek *-izein,* there is a strong preference for *s* over *z* in these words.

(2) the ending \īz\ in some English verbs (and a few nouns) not only is from etyma spelled with *s* rather than *z* but has no etymological relationship to the ending discussed in the preceding paragraph. For *appri-e* "inform" *s* strongly prevails in both the U.S. and Britain; for *appri-e* "evaluate", a rarer word, *z* seems to prevail in the U.S. and to be as common as *s* in Britain. For *adverti-e s* strongly prevails in both countries. In Britain *z* seems to prevail in *amorti-e, assi-e, recogni-e,* strongly prevails in *aggrandi-e, capsi-e, cogni-e, gormandi-e;* in the U.S. *z* alone occurs or strongly prevails in all seven words. The verb *merchandi-e* occasionally has *z,* the noun seldom. The following are usually found with *s:*

advise · *comprise* · *compromise* · *demise* · *despise* · *devise* · *disguise* · *enterprise* · *excise* · *franchise* · *improvise* · *revise* · *supervise* · *surmise* · *surprise*

(3) in the small group of words *analy-e, dialy-e, electroly-e, paraly-e,* in which *-ly-e* derives from the Greek noun *lysis, s* seems to be somewhat more common than *z* in Britain but *z* is much more common than *s* in the U.S.

2.11 -ol/-oul. In the words *mold/mould, molder/moulder, molt/moult,* and *smolder/smoulder,* the *u* is likely to be more often dropped than kept in the U.S., is almost always kept in Britain. *Molten* (from *melt)* has no variant with *u.*

2.12 -or/-our. English contains a group of *r*-final nouns that are descended from Latin nouns having nominative *-or,* that are not agent nouns (compare 2.8.1), and that are usually spelled *-or* in the U.S. but *-our* in Britain:

ardor/ardour · *color/colour* · *fervor/fervour* · *honor/honour* · *labor/labour* · *rigor/rigour* · *tumor/tumour*

The first such borrowings into English were from early Old French, and the termination in both lending and borrowing language was *-or* or *-ur.* In French as spoken in Britain after the Norman Conquest the ending became *-our.* English borrowings from this Anglo-French retained the *-our,* and earlier borrowings from continental French became *-our* by assimilation. After the Renaissance made Latin more widely known, words of this category were usually borrowed, in their Latin spelling, with *-or* as the ending. Many words once spelled *-our* in English are in Britain now written *-or,* but others are not. In the U.S. the *-our* spelling is seldom used in these words.

EXCEPTIONS:

(1) although the *-our* ending formerly occurred also in agent nouns, *saviour* is the only important survival.

(2) *glamour* and *saviour* are the only two *-our* forms that have wide currency in the U.S.

(3) not all *-or/-our* words derive ultimately from Latin *-or* words *(arbor* "latticework", *armor, behavior, harbor, neighbor).*

In Britain, *u* is usually retained before suffixes that had their origin within English *(favourer, flavourful, humourless, neighbourhood, neighbourly, vapourish);* before Latin suffixes that are not freely addable to English words *u* usually disappears *(coloration, honorary, honorific, odoriferous, odorous);* before Greek and Latin suffixes that have been naturalized *(-able, -ism, -ist, -ite, -ize)* the spelling varies.

2.13 -ped/-pede (from Latin *pes, pedis,* foot). *-pede* is more common than *-ped* after *milli-* and possibly the only form after *veloci-* and *centi-.* After other elements *-ped* is usual and is probably the only form that is now used after *bi-* and *quadru-.*

2.14 -c-/-s-.

defence/defense · *offence/offense* · *pretence/pretense* · *vice/vise* "tool"

In all four words *c* is the preference in Britain, *s* in the U.S.; *defensive, offensive,* and *pretension,* however, are the usual word forms in both countries.

licence/license
practice/practise

U.S. usually spells *license* both noun and verb with *s;* Britain almost invariably spells the noun with *c,* usually spells the verb with *s.* U.S. uses *c* more often than *s* in the noun *practice,* uses one letter about as often as the other in the verb *practise;* Britain strongly prefers *c* in the noun (*s* seems nonexistent), *s* in the verb. Although noun and verb were once undifferentiated, on both sides of the Atlantic *prophecy* is more common for the noun, *prophesy* for the verb.

PLURALS

1. The plurals of English nouns are regularly formed in writing by the suffixation of the letter *-s* (*hat*→*hats*) or the letters *-es* (*cross*→*crosses*) and in speaking by the addition of the sound \s\ (\hat→hats\), the sound \z\ (\bȯi→bȯiz\), or the sound \əz\ (\krȯs→krȯsəz\). Although there are many exceptions to be noted, this regularity is so dominant that in theory all English nouns may be said to be capable of an analogical plural in the letters *-s* or *-es*, and in practice little hesitation in so forming a new or unknown plural should be felt. Native speakers of English have no difficulty in using the sounds of pluralization in accordance with regular patterns. This treatment of plurals will be limited to written words, typically selected, not exhaustive.

2. -s. Most nouns simply add *-s:*

bag→*bags* — *button*→*buttons*
book→*books* — *violet*→*violets*

3. silent -e. Nouns ending in *-e* that is silent regularly add *-s:*

collapse→*collapses* — *race*→*races*
college→*colleges* — *ride*→*rides*
hedge→*hedges* — *size*→*sizes*

4. -es. Nouns ending in *-s, -z, -x, -ch,* or *-sh* regularly add *-es:*

buzz→*buzzes* — *gas*→*gases*
dash→*dashes* — *torch*→*torches*
fox→*foxes*

5. consonant + -y. Nouns ending in *-y* preceded by a consonant regularly change *-y* to *-i-* and add *-es:*

army→*armies* — *pity*→*pities*
baby→*babies* — *sally*→*sallies*
courtesy→*courtesies* — *sky*→*skies*
lady→*ladies*

except proper names:

Germany→*Germanys* — *Kinny*→*Kinnys*
Kathy→*Kathys* — *Mary*→*Marys*
Kentucky→*Kentuckys*

6. -quy. Nouns ending in *-quy* regularly change *-y* to *-i-* and add *-es:*

colloquy→*colloquies* — *soliloquy*→*soliloquies*

7. vowel + -y. Nouns ending in *-y* preceded by a vowel (except those ending in *-quy*) regularly add *-s:*

attorney→*attorneys* — *chimney*→*chimneys*
bay→*bays* — *guy*→*guys*
boy→*boys* — *key*→*keys*

8. vowel + -o. Nouns ending in *-o* preceded by a vowel regularly add *-s:*

cameo→*cameos* — *studio*→*studios*
duo→*duos* — *trio*→*trios*
embryo→*embryos* — *zoo*→*zoos*
Romeo→*Romeos*

9. consonant + -o. Most nouns ending in *-o* preceded by a consonant add *-s:*

alto→*altos* — *jocko*→*jockos*
bozo→*bozos* — *piano*→*pianos*
burro→*burros* — *poncho*→*ponchos*
chromo→*chromos* — *silo*→*silos*
ego→*egos* — *two*→*twos*
hippo→*hippos*

but other nouns ending in *-o* preceded by a consonant add *-es:*

bubo→*buboes* — *hero*→*heroes*
bucko→*buckoes* — *jo*→*joes*
echo→*echoes* — *potato*→*potatoes*
embargo→*embargoes*

The consonant or cluster preceding the *-o* does not determine whether the plural will add *-s* or *-es*. A few nouns add either:

banjo→{*banjos*, *banjoes*} — *innuendo*→{*innuendos*, *innuendoes*}
bravo→{*bravos*, *bravoes*} — *motto*→{*mottos*, *mottoes*}
buffalo→{*buffalos*, *buffaloes*} — *mulatto*→{*mulattos*, *mulattoes*}
calico→{*calicos*, *calicoes*} — *proviso*→{*provisos*, *provisoes*}
cargo→{*cargos*, *cargoes*} — *tobacco*→{*tobaccos*, *tobaccoes*}
domino→{*dominos*, *dominoes*} — *tornado*→{*tornados*, *tornadoes*}
halo→{*halos*, *haloes*} — *zero*→{*zeros*, *zeroes*}

10. -oo. Nouns ending in *-oo* regularly add *-s:*

coo→*coos* — *kangaroo*→*kangaroos*
cuckoo→*cuckoos* — *tattoo*→*tattoos*

11. -i. Most nouns ending in *-i* add *-s:*

macaroni→*macaronis* — *ski*→*skis*
rabbi→*rabbis*

but a few add either *-s* or *-es:*

alkali→{*alkalis*, *alkalies*} — *taxi*→{*taxis*, *taxies*}

12. -f. A few nouns ending in *-f* change the *-f* to *-v-* and add *-es:*

leaf→*leaves* — *thief*→*thieves*
self→*selves* — *wolf*→*wolves*

but some of these also add *-s* without consonant change:

beef→{*beeves*, *beefs*} — *loaf*→{*loaves*, *loafs*}
calf→{*calves*, *calfs*} — *wharf*→{*wharves*, *wharfs*}

13. -fe. A few nouns ending in *-fe* change *-f-* to *-v-* and add *-s:*

knife→*knives* — *life*→*lives*

14. uniliteral words. Single letters, numbers, figures, and signs add either apostrophe and *-s* or just *-s:*

A→{*A's*, *As*} — *1920*→{*1920's*, *1920s*}
A→{A'*s*, A*s*} — △→{△'*s*, △*s*}
a→{*a's*, *as*} — #→{#'*s*, #*s*}
4→{*4's*, *4s*}

15.1 nouns formed from abbreviations. Abbreviations formed by literation and used as nouns add either apostrophe and *-s* or more often just *-s:*

GI→{*GI's*, *GIs*} — *IQ*→{*IQ's*, *IQs*}
G. I.→{*G. I.'s*, *G. I.s*} — *Ph.D.*→{*Ph.D.'s*, *Ph.D.s*}

15.2 Abbreviations formed by truncation or contraction usually add *-s* without apostrophe:

apt→*apts* — *cap*→*caps*
bbl→*bbls* — *ms*→*mss*
bx→*bxs* — *mt*→*mts*

but some become plural without any change:

1 *hr*→4 *hr* — 1 *oz*→4 *oz*
1 *in*→4 *in* — 1 *qt*→4 *qt*
1 *mo*→4 *mo* — 1 *yd*→4 *yd*

15.3 Some single-letter abbreviations double an initial consonant:

c.→*cc.* (chapters) — *v.*→*vv.* (verses, violins)
p.→*pp.* (pages) — *M.*→*MM.* (Messieurs)

16. -en. One noun usually adds *-en:*

ox→*oxen*

and another changes the stem and adds *-en:*

child→*children*

and one sometimes changes the stem and adds *-en:*

brother→*brethren*

17. umlaut. Six nouns change the medial vowel:

foot→*feet* — *man*→*men*
goose→*geese* — *mouse*→*mice*
louse→*lice* — *tooth*→*teeth*

Compounds in which one of these is the final element likewise change:

dormouse→*dormice* — *eyetooth*→*eyeteeth*
Dutchman→*Dutchmen* — *forefoot*→*forefeet*
Englishman→*Englishmen* — *woman*→*women*

18. foreign endings. Many nouns of foreign origin retain the foreign plural; most of them have also a regular English *-s* or *-es* plural, which is often preferred, although sometimes a foreign plural signals a difference in meaning (compare *stadia* and *stadiums*).

18.1 Latin. Most of these common anglicized foreign words come from Latin:

alga→*algae* — *formula*→*formulae*
alumna→*alumnae* — *larva*→*larvae*
antenna→*antennae* — *minutia*→*minutiae*

alumnus→*alumni* — *focus*→*foci*
bacillus→*bacilli* — *fungus*→*fungi*
cactus→*cacti* — *radius*→*radii*

apex→*apices* — *executrix*→*executrices*
appendix→*appendices* — *index*→*indices*
codex→*codices* — *matrix*→*matrices*

addendum→*addenda* — *erratum*→*errata*
aquarium→*aquaria* — *medium*→*media*
datum→*data* — *ovum*→*ova*
emporium→*emporia* — *residuum*→*residua*

corpus→*corpora* — *genus*→*genera*
femur→*femora* — *opus*→*opera*

crux→*cruces* — *lex*→*leges*
dux→*duces* — *pons*→*pontes*
gens→*gentes* — *rex* "king"→*reges*
gravamen→*gravamina* — *nomen*→*nomina*

apparatus→*apparatus* — *nexus*→*nexus*
meatus→*meatus* — *series*→*series*
custos→*custodes* — *imago*→*imagines*

18.2 Greek. The second largest group of anglicized foreign words comes from Greek:

analysis→*analyses* — *nemesis*→*nemeses*
basis→*bases* — *parenthesis*→*parentheses*
crisis→*crises* — *thesis*→*theses*
ellipsis→*ellipses*
genesis→*geneses*

automaton→*automata* — *ganglion*→*ganglia*
criterion→*criteria* — *phenomenon*→*phenomena*
ephemeron→*ephemera*

carcinoma→*carcinomata* — *lemma*→*lemmata*
dogma→*dogmata* — *miasma*→*miasmata*
— *schema*→*schemata*

aphis→*aphides* — *iris*→*irides*
ephemeris→*ephemerides* — *proboscis*→*proboscides*

necropolis→*necropoleis*

cyclops→*cyclopes* — *phalanx*→*phalanges*
larynx→*larynges* — *sphinx*→*sphinges*

logos→*logoi*

18.3 Italian. A comparatively small number of Italian plurals have become anglicized:

bambino→ *bambini* — *palazzo*→ *palazzi*
bandit→ *banditti* — *seraglio*→ *seragli*
cicerone→ *ciceroni* — *solo*→ *soli*
dilettante→ *dilettanti* — *tempo*→ *tempi*
libretto→ *libretti*
monsignor→ *monsignori*

18.4 French. A small number of French plurals have been anglicized:

adieu→ *adieux* — *bureau*→ *bureaux*
beau→ *beaux* — *plateau*→ *plateaux*
madame→ *mesdames* — *monsieur*→*messieurs*

18.5 miscellaneous.

cherub→ *cherubim* (Hebrew)
fellah→ *fellahin* (Arabic)
halakah→ *halakoth* (Hebrew)
Kohen→ *Kohanim* (Hebrew)
señor→ *señores* (Spanish)
seraph→ *seraphim* (Hebrew)

19.1 compounds. Two-word compounds consisting of initial noun plus adjective hyphened or open customarily pluralize the noun:

cousin-german→ *cousins-german*
heir apparent→ *heirs apparent*
knight-errant→ *knights-errant*
vicar-general→ *vicars-general*

but not invariably; sometimes the adjective is construed as a noun and a regular suffix is alternatively added to it:

attorney general→{*attorneys general*, *attorney generals*}
battle royal→{*battles royal*, *battle royals*}
beau ideal→{*beaus ideal*, *beau ideals*}
court-martial→{*courts-martial*, *court-martials*}
notary public→{*notaries public*, *notary publics*}
poet laureate→{*poets laureate*, *poet laureates*}
sergeant major→{*sergeants major*, *sergeant majors*}

In similar-appearing compounds in which the second word is a noun a regular suffix is added at the end:

brigadier general→ *brigadier generals*
judge advocate→ *judge advocates*
lieutenant colonel→ *lieutenant colonels*

A few similar compounds have double plurals:

gentleman-usher→ *gentlemen-ushers*
lord justice→ *lords justices*
thing-in-itself→ *things-in-themselves*

19.2 Three-word compounds consisting of initial noun plus prepositional phrase hyphened or open customarily pluralize the initial noun:

aide-de-camp→ *aides-de-camp*
attorney-at-law→ *attorneys-at-law*
brother-in-law→ *brothers-in-law*
chargé d'affaires→ *chargés d'affaires*
coat of mail→ *coats of mail*
man-of-war→ *men-of-war*

20. animals. Many names of fishes, birds, and mammals have both a plural with a suffix and a zero plural that is identical with the singular. Some have one or the other. Some present a choice according to meaning or according to a special interest of the user

20.1 The following such names form a plural with a suffix (except occasionally when modified by an adjective like *wild, native, sea, mountain*):

bird → birds
cow → cows
crow → crows
cuckoo → cuckoos
dog → dogs
eagle → eagles
goat → goats
hawk → hawks
hen → hens
lark → larks
loon → loons
mole → moles
monkey → monkeys
owl → owls
parrot → parrots
penguin → penguins
pig → pigs
rat → rats
robin → robins
shark → sharks
sparrow → sparrows
starling → starlings
swallow → swallows
vulture → vultures

20.2 The following have both plurals of which the zero plural is likely to be preferred by those who hunt or fish:

albatross → albatross, albatrosses
antelope → antelope, antelopes
bear → bear, bears
beaver → beaver, beavers
buck → buck, bucks
buffalo → buffalo, buffalos
doe → doe, does
duck → duck, ducks
eel → eel, eels
flounder → flounder, flounders
fox → fox, foxes
hare → hare, hares
herring → herring, herrings
lobster → lobster, lobsters
mink → mink, minks
minnow → minnow, minnows
partridge → partridge, partridges
quail → quail, quails
rabbit → rabbit, rabbits
raccoon → raccoon, raccoons
sardine → sardine, sardines
seal → seal, seals
shrimp → shrimp, shrimps
skunk → skunk, skunks
smelt → smelt, smelts
squid → squid, squids
squirrel → squirrel, squirrels
stag → stag, stags
stork → stork, storks
swan → swan, swans
tiger → tiger, tigers
tortoise → tortoise, tortoises
tuna → tuna, tunas
turtle → turtle, turtles

20.3 The following have both plurals of which the zero plural is the commoner but the plural with a suffix is used to signify diversity in kind or species (*trouts* of the Rocky mountains; *fishes* of the Atlantic):

bass → bass, basses
bream → bream, breams
carp → carp, carps
cod → cod, cods
elk → elk, elks
fish → fish, fishes
haddock → haddock, haddocks
halibut → halibut, halibuts
mackerel → mackerel, mackerels
perch → perch, perches
pike → pike, pikes
pollack → pollack, pollacks
pout → pout, pouts
roe → roe, roes
springbok → springbok, springboks
trout → trout, trouts
waterbuck → waterbuck, waterbucks

20.4 The following customarily prefer the zero plural:

bison → bison
cattle → cattle
chamois → chamois
dace → dace
deer → deer
grouse → grouse
moose → moose
muskellunge → muskellunge
pickerel → pickerel
shad → shad
sheep → sheep
swine → swine

21. numbers. A small number of general terms for numbers or quantities have both a plural form with suffix and a zero plural used in some constructions:

brace → brace, braces
dozen → dozen, dozens
hundred → hundred, hundreds
million → million, millions
score → score, scores
thousand → thousand, thousands

22. peoples. Many names of tribal origin have a zero plural and also an anglicized plural with suffix:

Abnaki → Abnaki, Abnakis
Bantu → Bantu, Bantus
Carib → Carib, Caribs
Congo → Congo, Congos
Eskimo → Eskimo, Eskimos
Mohawk → Mohawk, Mohawks

23. -ese. Most names derived from a place name and ending in *-ese* have only a zero plural:

Burmese → Burmese
Cantonese → Cantonese
Ceylonese → Ceylonese
Chinese → Chinese
Genovese → Genovese
Japanese → Japanese
Maltese → Maltese
Portuguese → Portuguese
Sudanese → Sudanese
Tyrolese → Tyrolese
Viennese → Viennese

CAPITALIZATION

1. The essential distinction in the use of capitals and lowercase letters beginning words lies in the particularizing or individualizing significance of capitals as against the generic or generalizing significance of lowercase. A capital is used with proper nouns, that is, nouns that distinguish some individual person, place, or thing from others of the same class, and with proper adjectives, that is, adjectives that take their descriptive meaning from what is characteristic of the person, place, or thing named by the noun. Most proper nouns and proper adjectives used not in the primary signification but in a derived, secondary, or special sense (as *cashmere*, the fabric; *quixotism, herculean*) are written usually without capitalization.

2. A capital letter in normal practice in continuous textual matter:

2.1 begins the first word of a sentence or an expression standing for a sentence ⟨You urge in vain.⟩ ⟨Recant my views?⟩ ⟨Never!⟩

2.2 usually begins a direct formal quotation ⟨God said, Let there be light —Gen 1:3⟩

2.3 usually begins a direct question within a sentence even though not quoted ⟨The eighteenth century asked of any action, Is it decorous?⟩

2.4 often and traditionally begins a line of verse:

Our fears in Banquo
Stick deep; and in his royalty of nature
Reigns that which would be fear'd —Shak.

2.5 usually begins proper nouns, words used as proper nouns, and their derivatives used in the primary sense ⟨George→Georgian⟩ ⟨Spain→Spanish⟩ ⟨Americanism⟩ ⟨New-Yorky⟩ ⟨Roman customs⟩ but verbs are less often capitalized than adjectives or nouns ⟨anglicize⟩

2.6 represents the first person pronoun ⟨he and I disagree⟩

2.7 usually begins the names of peoples, races, tribes, and languages ⟨Phoenician⟩ ⟨Japanese⟩ ⟨Iroquois⟩ ⟨Indo-European⟩ ⟨Latin⟩

2.8 begins titles of honor, academic and religious titles, and professional and business titles used before proper nouns and epithets used in place of proper nouns ⟨Queen Elizabeth I⟩ ⟨His Eminence the Cardinal Archbishop of New York⟩ ⟨Iron Chancellor⟩ ⟨Citizen King⟩ ⟨Old Hickory⟩ ⟨the Hoosier Poet⟩ ⟨All-America team⟩ ⟨Associate Professor John Doe⟩ ⟨Chief Engineer John Doe⟩ ⟨Treasurer John Doe⟩ but not usually when used after ⟨Henry VIII, king of England⟩ ⟨King George V, emperor of India⟩

2.9 begins official and government titles and titles of nobility (as *president, governor, senator, speaker of the House, secretary for defense, postmaster general, prime minister*) when preceding a proper name or used in direct address; as ⟨U.S. Minister John Doe⟩ ⟨Secretary John Doe⟩ ⟨His Honor the Mayor⟩ ⟨Mr. President⟩

⟨Your Honor⟩ but ⟨John Adams, president of the U.S.⟩

2.10 begins official names of national or international governmental bodies or documents and sometimes short forms of these used specifically or with a capitalized name but not usually any short forms or modified forms of them in general reference ⟨The Constitution of the United States⟩ ⟨the Eightieth Congress⟩ ⟨the Federal Reserve system⟩ ⟨Federal Reserve banks⟩ ⟨the Federal Communications Commission⟩ ⟨Charter of the United Nations (*or* the Charter)⟩ ⟨the Security Council (*or* the Council)⟩ ⟨the International Bank⟩ but ⟨according to the constitution⟩ ⟨administration policies⟩ ⟨federal agency⟩

2.11 usually begins nouns and often also adjectives that refer to the Deity and pronouns and pronominal adjectives referring to the Deity when not closely preceding or following their antecedent naming Deity ⟨God⟩ ⟨the Supreme Being⟩ ⟨the Almighty⟩ ⟨Allah⟩ ⟨Great Manito⟩ ⟨Providence⟩ ⟨Lord⟩ ⟨the Trinity⟩ ⟨Holy Ghost⟩ ⟨trust Him who doeth all things well; take time to think about God and his beneficence⟩ ⟨The Almighty has his own purposes —Abraham Lincoln⟩ ⟨so lonely 'twas, that God himself scarce seemed there to be —S.T.Coleridge⟩ ⟨Lamb of God, who takest away the sins of the world, only in thy grace shall my soul be healed —Katherine Anne Porter⟩

2.11.1 Some writers and a few hymnals capitalize a pronoun or pronominal adjective referring to Deity, even when close to the antecedent naming Deity and thus not requiring a capital for clarity of reference ⟨a personal God, creator and governor of all, Who will bring His children into fellowship with Himself⟩ ⟨Jesus and His disciples⟩ ⟨"My Jesu, as Thou wilt"⟩ ⟨teach me, my God and King, in all things Thee to see —George Herbert⟩ ⟨God's in His heaven — all's right with the world —Robert Browning⟩ ⟨all Thy works, O Lord, shall bless Thee —*Oxford Amer. Hymnal*⟩

2.12 usually begins names for the Bible or parts, versions, or editions of it and names of other sacred books and often derivative adjectives when the adjective refers explicitly to the Bible or Scriptures (otherwise not capitalized) ⟨Bible⟩ ⟨Vedas⟩ ⟨the Scriptures⟩ ⟨Old Testament⟩ ⟨Pentateuch⟩ ⟨Apocrypha⟩ ⟨Gospel of Mark⟩ ⟨Apocalypse⟩

2.13 begins names of creeds and confessions, religious denominations, monastic orders, and *Church* when used to designate a specific body or edifice ⟨Apostles' Creed⟩ ⟨the Thirty-nine Articles of the Church of England⟩ ⟨Hunt Memorial Church⟩

2.14 usually begins holidays and holy days generally, the months of the year, and the days of the week ⟨Fourth of July⟩ ⟨Good Friday⟩ ⟨Holy Week⟩ ⟨Labor Day⟩ ⟨January⟩ ⟨next Tuesday⟩

2.15 begins names of congresses, councils, and expositions, of organizations and institutions, of governmental departments, and of political parties (but not the word *party*) ⟨the Yalta Conference⟩ ⟨the Security Council of the United Nations⟩ ⟨Louisiana Purchase Exposition⟩ ⟨the Progressive party⟩ ⟨the Smithsonian Institution⟩ ⟨Bureau of Engraving and Printing⟩ ⟨Congress of Industrial Organizations⟩

2.16 begins names of specific courts of law ⟨Circuit Court of the United States for the 2d Circuit (*but* the circuit court)⟩ ⟨the Michigan Court of Appeals (*but* the state court of appeals)⟩

2.17 begins names of treaties, laws, acts, important events, historical epochs, literary periods, wars ⟨Versailles Treaty⟩ ⟨the Crusades⟩ ⟨Middle Ages⟩ ⟨the Enlightenment⟩ ⟨the Civil War⟩ ⟨War of 1812⟩

2.18 usually begins names of geological eras, periods, epochs, strata, and names of prehistoric divisions ⟨Carboniferous⟩ ⟨Upper Jurassic⟩ ⟨Age of Reptiles⟩ ⟨Neolithic age⟩

2.19 begins names of genera but not of species in binomial scientific names in zoology and botany ⟨a marine worm (*Nereis diversicolor*)⟩ ⟨*Spiraea latifolia*⟩

2.20 begins New Latin names of classes, families, and all other groups above genera in zoology and botany but not derivative adjectives or nouns ⟨Gastropoda *but* gastropod⟩ ⟨Ranunculaceae *but* ranunculaceous⟩

2.21 usually begins a breed name ⟨Belgian hare⟩ ⟨Airedale terrier⟩ ⟨Guernsey bull⟩

2.22 begins names of planets, constellations, asteroids, stars, and groups of stars but not sun, earth, and moon unless listed with other astronomical names ⟨Mercury⟩ ⟨the planet Venus⟩ ⟨Pleiades⟩ ⟨Big Dipper⟩

2.23 usually begins generic geographical terms that form an integral part of a specific proper name (as *bay, borough, colony, continent, county, district, hemisphere, island, lake, mountain, pass,* and likewise *avenue, boulevard, bridge, park, road, square, street*) ⟨Hudson Bay⟩ ⟨Grand Canyon⟩ ⟨Niagara Falls⟩ ⟨Long Island⟩ ⟨Crater Lake⟩ ⟨Blue Ridge⟩ ⟨Park Drive⟩ but ⟨the Atlantic coast of Labrador⟩ ⟨Pacific islands⟩ ⟨Swiss mountains⟩ ⟨the Ohio river valley⟩ ⟨Indian ocean⟩ ⟨Florida keys⟩ ⟨Sahara desert⟩ ⟨born in Chekiang province⟩ ⟨on the Ohio river⟩ ⟨Oak avenue⟩ ⟨the Leeward and Windward islands⟩ ⟨at the confluence of the Missouri and Platte rivers⟩

2.24 usually begins generic political terms that form an integral part of a specific proper name, denoting a political division (as *colony, department, dominion, empire, kingdom, republic, state, territory*) ⟨the Holy Roman Empire⟩ ⟨the Province of Quebec⟩ ⟨the State of Ohio⟩ ⟨the Third Republic⟩

2.25 usually begins names of definite geographical divisions ⟨the Orient⟩ ⟨the Old World⟩ ⟨the Middle East⟩ ⟨the Middle West⟩

2.26 usually begins points of the compass used to designate geographical portions of a country or divisions of the world and also nouns or adjectives derived therefrom ⟨the South⟩ ⟨the Northwest⟩ ⟨a Northerner⟩ but not when used to denote direction only ⟨due east⟩ ⟨go west⟩

2.27 usually begins abstract ideas or inanimate objects personified and names of seasons only when personified or sometimes when referred to specifically or with special connotations ⟨do the bidding of Nature⟩ ⟨the Winter at Valley Forge⟩ ⟨the Plague Year of 1665⟩ ⟨where Spring her verdant mantle cast⟩

2.28 usually begins all words in titles of books, periodicals, essays, poems except unemphatic prepositions, conjunctions and articles ⟨Shakespeare's *Taming of the Shrew*⟩ ⟨the *Journal of the American Medical Association*⟩ ⟨"Phosphorus: Bearer of Light and Life," *Scientific American* 178:101 *ff.*⟩ and except in cataloging and often in bibliographies when only the first word and proper names are capitalized.

2.29 usually begins the article *the* when part of a proper name or title or when incorporated as part of the legal name but usually not in referring to newspapers and magazines in running text ⟨The Honorable John Doe⟩ but ⟨the *Chicago Daily News*⟩ ⟨the *Saturday Evening Post*⟩

2.30 usually begins particles in American names but in foreign names only when not preceded by a forename, a professional title, or title of nobility or of courtesy ⟨Reginald De Koven⟩ ⟨Della Crusca⟩ ⟨Von Moltke (Count von Moltke)⟩

2.31 usually begins German common nouns that have not been anglicized, when used in English text ⟨Frau⟩ ⟨Junker⟩ ⟨Luftwaffe⟩ but anglicized German nouns may be written with a small initial letter ⟨blitzkrieg⟩ ⟨gestalt⟩ ⟨leitmotiv⟩ ⟨pumpernickel⟩ ⟨rathskeller⟩ ⟨sauerkraut⟩ ⟨turnverein⟩

2.32 usually represents academic degrees ⟨A. B.⟩ ⟨LL.D.⟩ ⟨Ph.D.⟩

2.33 begins names of registered trademarks.

ITALICIZATION

1. Foreign words and phrases that are not fully naturalized are usually italicized in English context. This is done in manuscript or typescript by single underlining. The choice of roman or italic text properly belongs to the user on the basis of subject matter and expected readers. A dictionary cannot prescribe or even record in a matter so subjective. These examples simply show words and phrases that are often italicized in English context ⟨*ancien régime*⟩ ⟨*anschluss*⟩ ⟨*cognoscente*⟩ ⟨*de trop*⟩ ⟨*dolce far niente*⟩ ⟨*jeu d'esprit*⟩ ⟨*mañana*⟩ ⟨*noblesse oblige*⟩ ⟨*rapprochement*⟩ ⟨*zeitgeist*⟩

2. Titles of books (not parts of books), plays, works of art, magazines, newspapers are usually italicized but not the Bible or its books ⟨Stevenson's *Treasure Island*⟩ ⟨Verdi's *Il Trovatore*⟩ ⟨Michelangelo's *David*⟩ ⟨the *Christian Science Monitor*⟩ ⟨*Saturday Evening Post*⟩

3. Names of ships and aircraft are usually italicized ⟨Lindbergh's *Spirit of St. Louis*⟩ ⟨the carrier *Lexington*⟩

4. Names of long-range missiles and man-made satellites are often italicized.

5. A word spoken of as a word, a phrase as a phrase, a letter as a letter (except that a letter indicating shape is printed in type most nearly depicting the shape; thus, V-shaped; I beam) are usually italicized.

6. New Latin scientific names of genera, species, subspecies, and varieties (but not groups of higher rank, as phyla, classes, orders) in botanical and zoological names are italicized ⟨a thick-shelled quahog (*Mercenaria mercenaria*)⟩

THE WRITING OF COMPOUNDS

1. DEFINITION

1.1 A *compound*, as the term is used here, is a word or word group of two or more elements at least one of which is an independent word of the same language. The elements in an English compound are variously written solid, open, or hyphened when they are all English words that can be written independently. When one of the elements in an English compound is not an independent English word, the elements are usually solid (*watery, anticlerical, predate*) or hyphened (*de-emphasize*).

1.2 To show in a dictionary all of the stylings that are found for English compounds would necessitate excluding other information much more likely to be sought by the dictionary user. This dictionary therefore limits itself almost without exception to a single styling for a compound. When a compound occurs frequently and one styling predominates, this styling is used. When a compound is rare or when the examples indicate that two or three stylings are approximately equal in frequency, the choice is based on the analogy of parallel compounds or is made arbitrarily.

2. COMPOUNDS CONTAINING AN ELEMENT THAT IS NOT AN INDEPENDENT WORD

2.1 The dependent element in most compounds formed within English is a prefix or a suffix. It is added to several or many English words and exerts the same modification of sense on all of them.

2.1.1 Prefixes in borrowed compounds. In prefix-containing foreign-language compounds borrowed into English, if the prefix ends and the base word begins with the same vowel letter, a hyphen is often used between the two vowels, or a diaeresis is sometimes placed over the second vowel (*co-operate/coöperate*) but usually the form is solid (*cooperate*). If two vowels that are not identical come together at the point of juncture, usually neither hyphen nor diaeresis is used (*coalesce, coerce*). If the junctural letters are two consonants, or a vowel and a consonant, or a consonant and vowel, neither hyphen nor diaeresis is used (*collect, diagram, anarchy*).

2.1.2 Prefixes in compounds formed within English. In prefix-containing compounds formed in English a prefix and a base word are seldom open-styled. Some combinations are usually close-styled (*in-* and *un-*, as in *inexpressible, untenable*), some are usually hyphened (*ex-* in *ex-president*), some are frequently styled either way (*anti-, co-, extra-, non-, pre-, semi-*). With prefixes of this last class the hyphened styling is usual when the prefix ends with a vowel letter and the base word begins with the same letter (*anti-* + *intellectualism, infra-* + *angelic, semi-* + *independent*); the hyphened styling is less frequent when the junctural letters are two vowels that are not identical (*de-* + *adjectival, fore-* + *oath*); but solid styling is usual when the junctural letters are two consonants, or a vowel and a consonant (*non-* + *metallic, non-* + *alcoholic, extra-* + *legal*).

2.1.3 When the base word begins with a capital, a hyphen is usual (*un-* + *American*).

2.1.4 Some elements commonly regarded as prefixes function as adjectives when they stand open before a noun (*a pseudo liberal; quasi independence*). But a styling like *a semi annual sale* is seldom seen outside newspaper advertisements.

2.1.5 When a prefix governs two or more words, it is almost invariably followed by a hyphen, and the styling of the group of words to which the hyphen applies varies: sometimes the members of the group are left spaced, sometimes they are hyphened (*an ex-vice president/an ex-vice-president, pre-World War prices/pre-World-War prices, the ex-Republican majority leader/the ex-Republican-majority-leader*). Although spaced styling in such cases is often ambiguous, mere substitution of hyphens for spaces is not always a solution.

2.1.6 Sometimes the same succession of letters forms two words that contain the same prefix but that are different in sense, pronunciation, and styling, one word being solid and the other hyphened. In such cases the solid compound was formed in and borrowed from another language, the hyphened compound was formed in English; the second element may or may not be ultimately the same word etymologically in both cases (*recover* "to get back", *re-cover* "to cover again"; *recreation* "play", *re-creation* "a creating again").

2.2 Suffix-containing compounds. Suffixes are close-styled (*shoeless, meanness, freer*), except that a succession of three identical consonants is hyphened (*hull-less*) if one is not dropped (*hulless*).

2.2.1 Some independent English words (*like, worthy*) which are sometimes regarded as suffixes when they are joined to the word they govern may be joined by a hyphen: *Christlike/Christ-like, praiseworthy/praise-worthy*.

2.2.2 When a suffix is added to two or more words that are written separate before suffixation, the styling of these words varies (*baby farming/baby-farming, bitter-ender/bitter ender, otherworldly/other-worldly*). The composition of some of these compounds, especially those that end in *-er*, may be ambiguous. Thus *lime-juicer* "a British ship" is *lime juice* + *-er;* whereas *lime juicer* "a device for squeezing or juicing limes" is *lime* + *juicer*. Both words might appear in any of three stylings — hyphened, open, or solid.

2.3.1 Other real or apparent compounds of this category. In other compounds in which one element is also an independent English word and the other is not or seems not to be, some are usually solid (*raspberry, bonfire, bookmobile, cheeseburger*), others are usually spaced (*bez antler, tonka bean, shea tree*).

2.3.2 In some words that appear to be similar compounds the apparent independent English word is an assimilation to an English word (*crayfish, gillyflower, safflower, gridiron, andiron*). The solid styling is usual for such apparent compounds.

3. NOUN COMPOUNDS WHOSE COMPONENTS ARE WHOLE ENGLISH WORDS

3.1 Noun + noun, as in *fruit* + *cake, cherry* + *pie, ox* + *bow, shoulder* + *blade, car* + *load, calamity* + *howler, emancipation* + *proclamation.*

3.1.1 In most noun-plus-noun compounds the first noun is uninflected and singular. Some of these compounds are freely styled in all three ways (*prize fighter/prizefighter/prize-fighter*). Some are rarely seen, at least in American English, other than solid (*newspaper, typewriter, pineapple*). Some are usually open (*gunnery officer, secretary bird*). Since there is a long precedent for the purely uniting function of the hyphen, it is not out of place in almost any noun-plus-noun compound where both elements are lowercase (*ox-bow, power-transmission, security-regulations*), but it seems to be used less often today than it formerly was. The compounds in which it is most likely to be used are those that would be written solid except that they contain at the point of juncture letters in a sequence unusual within an English word so that apprehension of this point may be retarded. Thus the hyphen is often not so much a uniter of words as it is a separator of letters.

3.1.2 Typically, two-noun noun compounds that are often or usually solid are fairly short, are of frequent occurrence, are concrete rather than abstract, and have primary stress on the first element and secondary stress on the second element (*notebook, paperweight, grasshopper, battlewagon, newspaperman, holidaymaker*). Five-syllable solid compounds, such as the last, are comparatively rare. Compounds that sometimes have even stress usually solidify only if short and very common (*corn* + *meal, air* + *mail, life* + *blood, arm* + *chair, eye* + *tooth, pot* + *luck, bed* + *rock, jaw* + *bone, barb* + *wire, car* + *load, bow* + *knot, death* + *bed, bell* + *wether*).

3.1.3 Falling accentuation (primary stress on first element and secondary stress on second element) is almost a prerequisite to solidification. Observation of how compounds in the spoken language are stressed provides information of possibly more value than an examination of how compounds in the written language are styled. A large proportion of the compounds that are written solid may with equal acceptability be open or hyphened (*matchbox/match box/match-box*); but in the spoken language falling stress may be acceptable whereas even stress may not be, except when one is making a contrast between one compound and another with the same first element (*matchbox, matchstick*); in such contrasts supersession of the "normal" stress is regular. But the accentuation of compounds, like the accentuation of noncompound phrases, is a matter of usage, which does not fall into neat patterns. In some cases the meaning of a compound is a reliable guide to its accentuation, in other cases not. The native speaker knows that if *wood* + *box* means "a box made of wood" the stress is \ˈ=ˈ=\ and that if it means "a box in which wood is placed" the stress is \ˈ=ˌ=\. On the other hand he may be unable to be sure of the stress of another compound even after reading a definition of it. Some speakers stress a compound one way, and other speakers another way. To make rules that would cover the stress of all compounds seems impossible. Certain conditions seem to make for one kind of stress or the other; these conditions leave the stress on many compounds unexplained.

3.1.4 In what follows

A= *1st half of a two-part compound*
B= *2d half of a two-part compound*
C= *3d part of a three-part compound*

The relative specificity of B seems to account for many variations in stress between compounds whose elements stand in the same logical relationship to each other: the more specific, the less general and inclusive B is, the more likely the compound is to have even stress; thus *ˈtown* + *ˈhall* but (in the same sense) *ˈtown* + *ˌhouse: hall* is a more specific term than *house*, whose wide applicability is shown by the combinations or phrases *doll* + *house, chicken* + *house, discount* + *house, mail* + *order* + *house*, the *houses* of Congress or Parliament, the *house* of Rothschild. Other examples: *ˈfinger* + *ˈnail* (sometimes) but *ˈfinger* + *ˌtip, ˈalligator* + *ˈpear* but *ˈalligator* + *ˌweed, ˈtimothy* + *ˌgrass* but *ˈtimothy* + *ˈhay, ˈchurch* + *ˌservice* but *ˈchurch* + *ˈliturgy, ˈcorner* + *ˈstore* but *ˈcorner* + *ˌstone, ˈkey* + *ˈsignature* but *ˈkey* + *ˌnote, ˈdesk ˈdrawer* but *ˈdesk ˌleg*.

3.1.5 Compounds that name something which requires the synchronous association or combination of what is named by A and what is named by B are usually even-stressed: *ˈleather* + *ˈshoe* but *ˈshoe* + *ˌleather* (*shoe* + *leather* can exist even though it may never be made into a shoe, or has ceased to exist in the form of a shoe), *ˈbottle* + *ˈbeer* but *ˈbeer* + *ˌbottle, ˈpaper* + *ˈbook* but *ˈbook* + *ˌpaper, ˈbeef* + *ˈsoup* and *ˈbeef* + *ˈstew* but *ˈbeef* + *ˌbroth* (the last is merely a product of beef flesh, which is not present in the broth as it is in the soup and stew). Among the most numerous members of this category are compounds in which A names a thing of a sort that is the sole or an essential ingredient of B: *ˈcherry* + *ˈpie* (cherries or something of the sort — berries, apples, apricots, peaches — are a necessary part of a pie), *ˈgold* + *ˈcup, ˈglass* + *ˈpendant, ˈkid* + *ˈgloves, ˈrye* + *ˈbread*. When A is a thing of a sort that is secondary or incidental to B, falling stress is more likely: *ˈfruit* + *ˌcake, ˈraisin* + *ˌbread* (cake and bread can be quite plain, without anything of the order of raisins or other fruit). Compounds of the first category mentioned in this paragraph may have falling stress if B is lacking in specificity: *ˈglass* + *ˌware, ˈpaper* + *ˌgoods.*

3.1.6 When A and B stand in an appositive relationship to each other, the stress is usually even: *ˈbaby* + *ˈboy, ˈwoman* + *ˈdriver. Boy* + *friend*, however, has falling stress. It differs from the first two compounds in not being literal when it does not mean any friend who is a boy.

3.1.7 Metonymic compounds (compounds that name an entire thing by naming some feature of the thing, the first element sometimes being metaphorical) invariably have falling stress. They rarely have open styling. If they are not long and if there is no troublesome series of letters at the juncture, they are commonly solid: *sheath* + *bill, frog* + *mouth, paper* + *back, egg* + *head, leather* + *neck, butter* + *fingers;* otherwise they are usually hyphened: *violet* + *ear.*

3.1.8 There is a numerous class of words in which the second element is a verb plus *-er* or *-ing* and in the definition of which the first element is the object of the verb or the object of a preposition following the verb: *orange* + *sucker, potato* + *digger, baby* + *sitter*. These nearly always have falling accent, and appear quite freely in all three possible stylings. The hyphen is more often used in this class than it is in most other classes.

3.1.9 The relationship of the three elements in the preceding class of compounds can be represented thus: (A) (B, suffix). There is another class of compounds in which two elements are followed by a suffix (one of which may be *-er*, as in the preceding class) but in which the relationship of the three elements is different. Such compounds are *broad jumper* and *Bay Stater* in which the relationship is (A,B) (suffix), not (A) (B, suffix). Another such compound is *gold* + *medal* + *-ist*. Such compounds follow the accentuation of the two-part compound to which the suffix is added: *ˈbroad* + *ˌjump (er), ˈBay* + *ˌState (r), ˈgold* + *ˈmedal (ist)*. Such compounds exhibit all three stylings. In noun compounds of the class (A,B) (suffix), both of the first two elements need not be nouns: *bitter* + *end* + *-er, America* + *first* + *-er.*

3.2 Noun+(')s+noun, as in *fool(')s+cap, cock(')s* + *comb, woman(')s* + *club, women(')s* + *club*, or **noun+s(')+noun**, as in *boys(')+club, ladies(')+room.*

3.2.1 When these have a literal meaning, they are often written open, and with an apostrophe before the *s* if the first element is in the singular (*red as a cock's comb, a man's house is his castle*) or in the plural but not ending in *-s* (*children's clothes*). A few literal compounds of this class, however, are solid and without apostrophe, especially by assimilation to a form that is usual or frequent for an extended sense; thus *cockscomb* occurs for both the comb of a cock and a garden plant; *menswear* and *womenswear* occur usually. If the elements are written solid the apostrophe is not used, whether the first element is singular or plural (*foolscap*/never *fool'scap, menswear*/probably never *men'swear*). If the first element is singular and the elements are spaced, the apostrophe is not omitted: *a fool's cap, a man's thoughts, a woman's thoughts.*

3.2.2 When the compound is literal in meaning and open, and the first element is a plural ending in *-s* or is the possessive of a collective singular, the apostrophe is often omitted in titles in which the first element means "for the use of" or "operated by": *farmers(') cooperative, a students(') dictionary, People(')s Industrial Bank, Ladies(') Aid Society.* When the first element is the possessive of a plural that does not end in *-s*, omission of the apostrophe seems to be less frequent: *women's club/womens club.*

3.2.3 The first element may in some cases be either singular or plural: *woman's club/women's club/womens club.*

3.2.4 Compounds in which the first element has a possessive *s* are very common in an extended or figurative sense, especially in plant names. Use of the apostrophe seems to be usual for such compounds and the hyphen is sometimes used. There is often variation between a singular and a plural first element: *baby's breath/babies' breath, lady's slipper/ladies' slipper, lady's-eardrop/ladies'-eardrop.* The solid form without apostrophe also occurs: *cockscomb, foolscap, swansdown.*

3.3 Adjective + noun, as in *blue + bird, black + tern, red + head, blue + blood.*

3.3.1 When an adjective and an immediately following noun are used with full literalness of meaning and nonattributively, the two are written with a space between and are spoken with level stress: *I saw a 'blue 'bird* (a bird that was blue; variety unknown), *a doll with a 'red 'head.* But when there is some abridgment of full literalness, the adjective and the noun may be written solid or hyphened and be spoken with falling stress: *I saw one jay and two 'blue,birds* (two *'blue 'birds* of the variety known to scientists as *Sialis sialis;* the jay is also a *'blue 'bird*); *redheads are proverbially hot-tempered.* Here again, however, as in the case of noun + noun compounds, specificity is important: the more specific the second element of the compound, the more likely the compound is to be written spaced and pronounced with even stress. Thus a typical dictionary definition of *blue + bird* begins "any of several birds more or less blue above", and a typical definition of *black + tern* begins "any of several small terns with black plumage"; but the first is usually *'blue,bird,* the second is usually *'black 'tern.*

3.3.2 Metonyms with an adjective as the first element, like those with a noun as the first element, have falling stress and are usually solid or hyphened: *'red + ,head, 'hot + ,spur, 'free + ,stone, 'blue + ,stocking, 'yellow + ,jacket.*

3.3.3 Adjective + noun pairs in which the application of the adjective to the noun is not a literal one commonly have falling stress and may be hyphened or solid; but the solid styling is less frequent than for specifying compounds like *black + bird: sick + call, cold + chisel, easy + chair.* Some of these can also be analyzed as noun + noun compounds (a call for the sick).

3.3.4 A few literal even-stressed adjective + noun compounds are styled in any of the three possible ways: *good + will, long + suffering, loving + kindness.*

3.4 Verb + noun, as in (a) *kill + joy, pick + pocket, cure + all, turn + coat, skin + flint, sling + shot, tattle + tale,* and (b) as in *bake + shop, turn + table, drip + coffee, try + square.*

3.4.1 In the (a) class the second element is the direct object of the verb. Words of this class have falling stress and are not open-styled. They are usually solid if short and if there are no troublesome letter combinations, like *e + a* in *cure + all,* which makes a hyphen usual.

3.4.2 In the compounds in class (b) the second element is not the direct object of the first element. It is impossible to be sure whether the first element of many compounds of this class is to be regarded as a verb or a noun. No practical difficulty arises from this because the styling and stress of these compounds parallels that of noun + noun compounds: all three stylings occur, and the stress is falling in some cases, level in others.

3.5 Particle + noun, as in *down + pour, down + draft, down + card, out + come, out + house, on + rush, on + going, on + position.*

3.5.1 A particle, as used here, is one of a small class of words that have sometimes adverbial, sometimes adjectival, sometimes prepositional force. When a verbal idea is present in the noun that is the second element, as it commonly is when the second element is identical in spelling with a corresponding verb, or when the second element ends in *-ing,* such compounds are rarely open, and the solid styling is more frequent than the hyphened: *down + pour, on + going.* When the second element is a concrete noun without any verbal idea and the first element has adjective force, all three stylings may occur: *down + card, down + pipe, off + horse, out + garrison, through + street, up + train.*

3.6 Noun + adjective, as in *battle + royal, court + martial, cousin + german, letters + patent, postmaster + general, sum + total.* These occur both hyphened and spaced.

3.7 Verb or verb derivative + adverb, as in *write + up, lean + to, pin + up, cut + up, shoo + in, follow + through, grown + up, get + together, shut + in, damping + off, goings + on, passer + by, hanger + on.*

3.7.1 Both the solid and the hyphened stylings are common for such of these nouns as do not have a first element ending in the suffix *-ing* or *-er.* The hyphen prevails when both junctural letters are vowels, as in *write + up, shoo + in.* For compounds whose first element ends in the suffix *-ing,* both the hyphened and the open styling are common. For compounds whose first element ends in the suffix *-er,* the hyphened or solid styling is usual, the open styling occasional.

4. VERB COMPOUNDS WHOSE COMPONENTS ARE WHOLE ENGLISH WORDS

4.1 A verb and an adverb that accompanies and follows it usually have a space between them: *to throw out a ball, to throw a ball out, to talk loudly.* An adverb preceding a verb usually has a space following: *he loudly demanded reform, I well remember the day, he soon returned;* but the words considered as particles (in 3.5.) are usually not followed by a space but are close-styled, less often hyphened: *to uproot*/less often *up-root an evil.*

4.2 When a solid or hyphened noun compound is used as a verb by functional change, the styling of the noun compound is generally retained. Thus one who uses the solid or hyphened styling for the nouns *snow + shoe, sand + bag, court + martial* will probably use the same styling in *to snow + shoe across a field, to sand + bag a dike, to court + martial a soldier.*

4.3 For compound verbs that do not belong to any of the categories enumerated in the preceding paragraphs all three stylings are found. The hyphened styling is the most frequent; the open styling seems to be less common in formal than in informal English. Examples: *to double + space a manuscript, to heat + treat a metal, to cold + roll steel, to rotten + egg a speaker.*

4.4 A verb compound that has a verb as its second element and that has the suffix *-ing* at the end of the verb may be hyphened when an object follows but either hyphened or spaced when no object follows. Thus the same writer may write *heat-treating these metals is not recommended* but *for these metals, heat treating is not recommended.* In the latter, *heat + treatment,* whose usual styling is probably open, could be substituted.

5. ADVERB COMPOUNDS

5.1 Compound adverbs of the type illustrated by *to run hot + foot to the window, to go bare + foot, recommended sight + unseen, to win hands + down, to dive in head + first* are infrequently found, and at least two stylings can be found for all of these and for some, three. Combinations of adjective + noun are likely to be solid (*hotfoot*), but if the first element is a plural noun or the second a past participle, the form is likely to be open (*arms akimbo, feet first, sight unseen*).

5.2 Compound adverbs like *light + hearted + -ly* usually follow the styling of the corresponding compound adjective. See 6.5.

5.3 Some compounds with adverbial force consist of a preposition followed by a noun, with loss of the commonly preceding article: *down + town, up + stream, below + stairs, between + decks, over + board.* Although each of the three stylings occurs, the solid is probably usual for most.

6. ADJECTIVE COMPOUNDS

6.1 Noun or adjective + adjective or participle, as in *snow + white, home + grown, red + hot, rusty + red, bitter + sweet, acrid + smelling, smoke + filled.* These are usually hyphened, occasionally solid (when the compound is short and common), or less frequently open (more often in predicative than in attributive position).

6.2 Adverb + adjective or participle, as in *well + known, better + known, widely + acclaimed, very + ignorant, twice + told.* The solid styling sometimes occurs for these compounds when the first element is a word freely usable as an adverb (*straight + forward, plain + spoken*). Most adverb + adjective compounds are either hyphened or open. In attributive position an adverb + adjective compound is most likely to be open if the first element is an adverb ending in *-ly* (*an extremely + important matter*); is most likely to be hyphened if the first element is an adverb that is identical in spelling with an adjective: *a slow + moving van.* Here a hyphen between *slow* and *moving* tells the reader that the writer has in mind a van of no particular variety that is moving slowly; a space between *slow* and *moving* would leave the expression open to the interpretation that the van is a variety known as a moving van and that it is slow; if the latter were the writer's intent, he might very well make it clear by inserting a hyphen between *moving* and *van,* even though he might use the open styling in *the moving + van has arrived.* In predicative position, open styling is more frequent than in attributive position; it is the most frequent styling by far when the first element has only adverbial use (*his hair is now + gray, he was once + wealthy*); it is less frequent when the first element is a form that is used as both adverb and adjective (*the van was large and slow + moving, he is plain + spoken*).

6.3 Particle + participle, as in *out + spoken, up + swept, in + curving, out + bound.* These are solid or, less often, hyphened, whether attributive or predicative.

6.4 Noun or adjective + noun, as in *home + town boy, seed + case integument, stove + pipe hat, grandfather + clock collector, short + term loan, small + store owner.* Pairs that are consistently solid or hyphened in nonattributive position are usually so in attributive position: *the seedcase/seed-case is tough, the seedcase/seed-case integument, twenty blackbirds, a blackbird hater.* Sometimes a writer who uses the spaced styling nonattributively uses the solid styling attributively: *cut with a jig saw; a jigsaw puzzle.* Ordinarily, however, noun pairs that are open-styled nonattributively are either hyphened or open attributively; the open styling is more common in informal than formal English. Noun + noun + noun groups are probably less often ambiguous than adjective + noun + noun groups and accordingly are probably less often written with a space between A and B. Thus *feed + store owner* presents little or no ambiguity, whereas *small + store owner* written with a space between *small* and *store* is apprehensible, if the context affords no help, either as "owner of a small store" or "store owner who is small". If the first is the meaning intended, many would insert a hyphen between *small* and *store;* if the second many would insert a hyphen between *store* and *owner.*

6.5 Adjective or noun + noun + -ed, as in *red + head + -ed, club + foot + -ed, hot + temper + -ed, cloud + cap + -ped.* In these the middle element and the suffix are always solid. The first and middle elements are seldom spaced, whether in predicative or attributive position; are usually hyphened; are solid in a few short compounds of frequent occurrence.

6.6 Adjective or participle + particle, as in *to be hard + up, to be done + in, to be fed + up, warmed + over cabbage, a turned + down collar.* These are usually spaced in predicative position, hyphened in attributive position. When a prefix is added, the prefix and the middle element are usually written solid; the middle element and the particle are either spaced or hyphened in predicative position, hyphened in attributive position: *an un + heard + of accomplishment, such appliances were un + dreamed + of in those days.*

6.7 Preposition-initial adjective compounds, as in *down + stream, up + hill, over + seas, out + of + date, on + the + house, down + in + the + mouth.* Two-part compounds with no article between are usually solid, less often hyphened or open, in attributive position; in predicative position both solid and open stylings are common: *an up + hill pull, over + seas possessions, the race will be down + stream.* Compounds having three or more parts are open or hyphened in predicative position, usually hyphened in attributive position: *book is out + of + date, an out + of + date book, looked down + in + the + mouth.*

6.8 When something in the typography makes the interrelationship of a multiple-word adjective obvious, the hyphen is usually omitted:

A Jim Crow law	(capital letters)
an *a priori* argument	(italics)
his "big shot" talk	(quotation marks)

In an expression like *April + fool joke, Indian + club enthusiast,* where the typography of one member of the attributive (*April*) does not parallel that of the other (*fool*), the hyphen is frequently or usually present (*April-fool joke*).

6.9 Compound adjectives not covered by any of the categories enumerated above are usually hyphened: *a pop + up toaster, a middle + of + the + road course, his never + the + twain + shall + meet policy.* The solid styling is found occasionally for some shorter compounds, as *pop + up.* The open styling is more common in informal than formal English: *a middle of the road course.*

MERRIAM-WEBSTER PRONUNCIATION SYMBOLS

For greater detail and for some symbols not shown below see "Guide to Pronunciation"

ə .....banana, collect

ˈə, ˌə humdrum

ə̄ .....as in one pronunciation used by *r*-droppers for bird (alternative \əi\)

ə̇ .....two-value symbol equivalent to the unstressed variants \ə\, \i\, as in habit, duchess (\ˈhabə̇t\ = \ˈhabət, -bit\)

^{ə} .....immediately preceding \l\, \n\, \m\, \ŋ\, as in battle, mitten, and in one pronunciation of cap and bells \-^{ə}m-\, lock and key \-^{ə}ŋ-\; immediately following \l\, \m\, \r\, as in one pronunciation of French table, prisme, titre

əi ....as in one pronunciation used by *r*-droppers for bird (alternative \ə̄\)

ər ....operation; stressed, as in bird as pronounced by speakers who do not drop *r;* stressed and with centered period after the \r\, as in one pronunciation of burry (alternative \ə̄r\) and in one pronunciation of hurry (alternative \ə·r\); stressed and with centered period between \ə\ and \r\, as in one pronunciation of hurry (alternative \ər·\)

a .....mat, map

ā .....day, fade, date, aorta

ä .....bother, cot; most American speakers have the same vowel in father, cart

ȧ .....father as pronounced by speakers who do not rhyme it with bother; farther and cart as pronounced by *r*-droppers

aa ...bad, bag, fan as often pronounced in an area having New York City and Washington, D. C., on its perimeter; in an emphatic syllable, as before a pause, often \aaə\

ai ....as in some pronunciations of bag, bang, pass

au̇ ...now, loud, some pronunciations of talcum

b .....baby, rib

ch ....chin, nature \ˈnāchə(r)\ (actually, this sound is \t\ + \sh\)

d .....elder, undone

d· ....as in the usual American pronunciation of latter, ladder

e .....bet, bed

ˈē, ˌē beat, nosebleed, evenly, sleepy

ē .....as in one pronunciation of evenly, sleepy, envious, igneous (alternative \i\)

ee ....(in transcriptions of foreign words only) indicates a vowel with the quality of *e* in *bet* but long, not the sound of *ee* in *sleep: en arrière* \ä^{n}nàryeer\

eu̇ ...as in one pronunciation of elk, helm

f .....fifty, cuff

g .....go, big

h .....hat, ahead

hw ...whale as pronounced by those who do not have the same pronunciation for both *whale* and *wail*

i ......tip, one pronunciation of banish (alternative unstressed \ē\), one pronunciation of habit (alternative \ə\; see ə̇)

ī .....site, side, buy (actually, this sound is \ä\ + \i\, or \ȧ\ + \i\)

iu̇ ....as in one pronunciation of milk, film

j .....job, gem, edge, procedure \prəˈsējə(r)\ (actually, this sound is \d\ + \zh\)

k .....kin, cook, ache

k̲ .....as in one pronunciation of loch (alternative \k\), as in German ich-laut

l ......lily, pool

m ....murmur, dim, nymph

n .....no, own

^{n} .....indicates that a preceding vowel is pronounced with the nasal passages open, as in French *un bon vin blanc* \œ^{n}bō^{n}va^{n}blä^{n}\

ŋ .....sing \ˈsiŋ\, singer \ˈsiŋə(r)\, finger \ˈfiŋgə(r)\, ink \ˈiŋk\

ō .....bone, snow, beau; one pronunciation of glory

ȯ .....saw, all, saurian; one pronunciation of horrid

œ ....French bœuf, German Hölle

œ̄ ....French feu, German Höhle

ȯi ....coin, destroy, strawy, sawing

ōō ...(in transcriptions of foreign words only) indicates a vowel with the quality of *o* in *bone* but longer, not the sound of *oo* in *food: comte* \kōō^{n}t\

p .....pepper, lip

r .....rarity, one pronunciation of tar

s .....source, less

sh ....with nothing between, as in shy, mission, machine, special (actually, this is a single sound, not two); with a stress mark between, two sounds as in death's-head \ˈdeths,hed\

t .....tie, attack; one pronunciation of latter (alternative \d·\)

th ....with nothing between, as in thin, ether (actually, this is a single sound, not two); with a stress mark between, two sounds as in knighthood \ˈnīt,hu̇d\

th̲ ....then, either (actually, this is a single sound, not two)

ü .....rule, fool, youth, union \ˈyünyən\, few \ˈfyü\

u̇ .....pull, wood, curable \ˈkyu̇rəbəl\

ue ....German füllen, hübsch

ue̅ ....French rue, German fühlen

v .....vivid, give

w ....we, away

y .....yard, cue \ˈkyü\, union \ˈyünyən\

^{y} .....(in transcriptions of foreign words only) indicates that during the articulation of the sound represented by the preceding character the tip of the tongue has substantially the position it has for the articulation of the first sound of *yard*, as in French *digne* \dēn^{y}\

yü....youth, union, cue, few

yu̇....curable

z .....zone, raise

zh... with nothing between, as in vision, azure \ˈazhə(r)\ (actually, this is a single sound, not two); with a stress mark between, two sounds as in rosehill \ˈrōz,hil\

For greater detail on most of the following see the beginning of "Guide to Pronunciation" and that part of "Explanatory Notes" dealing with pronunciation (section numbers for the latter are included below)

\ .....slant line used in pairs to mark the beginning and end of a transcription: \ˈpen\

ˈ .....mark preceding a syllable with primary (strongest) stress: \ˈpenmən,ship\

ˌ .....mark preceding a syllable with secondary (next-strongest) stress: \ˈpenmən,ship\

ˈˌ .....combined marks preceding a syllable whose stress varies between primary and secondary: *backbone* \ˈ≈ˈˌ≈\ (§2.2)

ˍ .....inferior minus sign canceling a stress in the same position in a preceding pronunciation or emphasizing that a following syllable is without stress: *optimism* \ˈäptə,mizəm\, *optimist* \-ˍməst\ (§2.11)

· .....mark of syllable division inserted in a sequence of sounds that can have more than one syllable division: *nitrate* \ˈnī·,trāt\ (§2.1)

≈ .....symbol for the sounds of a syllable: *backbone* \ˈ≈ˈˌ≈\ (§§2.7.1, 2.7.2)

(), (.indicate that what is symbolized between or after is present in some utterances but not in others: *factory* \ˈfakt(ə)rē\, *bar* \ˈbär, ˈbȧ(r\ (§§2.5.1, 2.5.2)

" .....ditto mark, indicating that a preceding pronunciation is to be repeated: [1]*poise* \ˈpȯiz\ *v*, [2]*poise* \"\ *n* (§§2.8.1, 2.8.2)

+ ....in an incomplete pronunciation signifies that the missing part is to be sought elsewhere in the vocabulary: *geopositive* \ˈˌjē(ˌ)ō+\ (pronunciation of *-positive* is to be sought at POSITIVE) (§2.9)

+V..means "when a vowel sound follows without pause, as in a suffix or another word"

| .....facilitates the placement of a variant pronunciation: *flightily* \ˈflīd·|^{ə}lē, -īt|, |^{ə}li, |əl-\ (§2.6)

R ....labels certain pronunciations used by speakers who do not drop *r* (§2.10)

−*R*...labels certain pronunciations used by speakers who drop *r* (§2.10)

÷ ...indicates that many regard as unacceptable the one pronunciation immediately following: *cupola* \ˈkyüpələ, ÷-pə,lō\, *sacrilegious* \÷ˈˌsakrəˈˌlijəs, -lēj-\ (§2.12)

....indicates an omission to be supplied from a preceding entry or an entry elsewhere: *dilettantish* \ˈˌ≈≈ˈˌt. . .ntish\ (four variants for the *a* are to be supplied from [1]DILETTANTE)

GUIDE TO PRONUNCIATION

By Edward Artin, Pronunciation Editor

This is a presentation of facts adequate, it is hoped, to explain the way we use our symbols in pronunciation indications in the vocabulary and to enable the consultant to infer certain pronunciations not actually shown from pronunciations that we do show. This is not a treatise on phonetics; many elementary facts of phonetics are not discussed at all (for example, the nature of most articulations). Those who desire such information should consult any of a number of good textbooks on phonetics.

The matter in this "Guide" is arranged under headings that so far as possible are in alphabetical order. Criteria for the alphabetization of some of the items have not been established by usage.

Headings that are not, that do not contain, or that are not formed by addition to, the 26 letters of the English alphabet appear ahead of everything else. Between the beginning of the first of such items and the end of the last no scheme of ordering is attempted.

The character \ə\ and modifications of it appear next.

The character \ŋ\ appears between the *n*, \n\ items and the *o*, \ō\, \ȯ\ items.

Ligatured characters are alphabetized as if they were separate letters (e.g., \œ\ is alphabetized as if it were \oe\).

A character entered as an orthographic letter appears ahead of the same character entered as a symbol of our pronunciation alphabet.

The same symbol may appear in two or more of the following forms: plain or unmodified; with diacritic above or below; reduced in size and set high as a superior character. For a symbol having two or more of these forms the alphabetization is as follows:

(1) single plain symbol, as \a\, \th\
(2) single symbol with horizontal bar above or below, as \ā\, \t͟h\
(3) single symbol with two dots, as \ä\
(4) single symbol with one dot, as \ȧ\
(5) single symbol set as a small superior, thus: \ᵊ\, \ᵊ̄\, \ᵊ̇\, \ᵊ\
(6) multiple-character symbols come at the end of the last single symbol based on the first character of the multiple symbol. Thus \aa\ comes at the end of the series \a\, \ā\, \ä\, \ȧ\, not between \a\ and \ā\. Such multiple symbols are alphabetized without regard to diacritics or to the size of any component character, except that when such disregard results in duplication the order is as stated in (1)–(5) above. Thus \ai\ precedes \äi\ and \ōō\ precedes \ȯȯ\

\ \ see the section on phonemicity.

( ) two parentheses mean that whatever is indicated by the symbol or symbols between them is present in the pronunciation of some speakers and absent from the pronunciation of other speakers, or that it is present in some utterances and absent from other utterances of the same speaker, or that its presence or absence is something difficult to be sure of.

nu·mer·ous \ˈn(y)üm(ə)rəs\
floc·cu·lence \ˈfläkyələn(t)s\
chick·a·dee \ˈchikə(ˌ)dē, . . .\

Such pronunciations could alternatively have been shown, at greater cost of space, as \ˈnümərəs, ˈnyü-, -mrəs\, etc.

Parentheses are often placed around one of the members of a digraph symbol when there are two pronunciation variants one of which is symbolized by the digraph and the other of which is symbolized by one member of the digraph.

var·i·ous \. . ., ˈva(a)r-, . . .\ [\ˈva(a)r-\ = \ˈvar-, ˈvaar-, *or vice versa*\]
su·mac \ˈs(h)ü,mak, . . .\ [\ˈs(h)ü-\ = \ˈshü-, ˈsü-, *or vice versa*\]
fair \ˈfa(a)(ə)r, . . .\ [\ˈfa(a)(ə)r\ = \ˈfaər, ˈfar, ˈfaaər, ˈfaar, *or any other order*\]

There will possibly be those who will object to such symbolization on the ground that, for example, \sh\ is a single sound, not two, that \sh\ really has no \h\ in it, and that it is bad to suggest that \sh\ can be converted to \s\ by omitting a final \h\ sound. Our view is that \s(h)\ is no more objectionable than \sh\, and that dictionary users who demand \sh\ should be prepared to accept \s(h)\.

In an abbreviated variant pronunciation following a punctuation mark one of two parentheses in a preceding pronunciation may be repeated simply to provide a locator for the substitution of the second variant in a preceding pronunciation.

cre·do \ˈkrē(ˌ)dō, ˈkrā(-\ [the \ā\ replaces \ē\ between \ˈkr\ and the first parenthesis]

An r that stands at the end of a transcription will often be found parenthesized, and the parenthesizing takes either of two forms: a left-handed parenthesis stands before the r and no right-handed parenthesis follows, as in \ˈmär, ˈmȧ(r\ at ¹*mar;* a parenthesis stands on either side as in \ˈbät͟hə(r)\ at ¹*bother.* The single parenthesis will be found only in a pronunciation in which there are at least two variants separated by a comma, and never in the first variant. A preceding variant ending in r without parenthesis shows the pronunciation of those who have as many \r\ sounds in their speech as there are letters *r* and letter sequences *rr* in the spelling (but see the section on dissimilation). A variant with a single parenthesis preceding the r shows the pronunciation of those who often do not have or who never have immediately before a consonant or a pause the sound, made usually by a lifting and curling backward of the tip of the tongue, that is transcribed \r\. For details of the environments in which \(r\ is pronounced and those in which it is not, see the section on \r\.

A transcription with a parenthesis on each side of a final r, as \ˈbät͟hə(r)\ at *bother,* is an abbreviated way of writing the transcription \ˈbät͟hər, ˈbät͟hə(r\, with explanation as for \ˈmär, ˈmȧ(r\ in the preceding paragraph. The abbreviated transcription can be used for *bother* but not for *mar* for the reason that the vowel symbol immediately preceding the r is the same for both kinds of speech in *bother* but not in *mar.* Since by definition above the single parenthesis means that r occurs in some environments but usually not in others, we could not use \ˈbät͟hə(r\ alone as our transcription, which would not hold for those who have r in all environments. Our explanation of double parenthesis, however, in the first sentence of this section makes the two-parenthesis transcription applicable to both *r*-keepers and *r*-droppers.

= see 2.7.1, 2.7.2 in "Explanatory Notes".

+ see 2.9 of "Explanatory Notes", and stress marks and ". . ." in this "Guide".

When a stress marking (ˈ) or ¦ appears on a syllable in the item that precedes the plus sign, the marking ¦ is to be understood as superseding a primary stress in the pronunciation that is to be supplied for the last part of the compound.

The plus sign is not necessarily an indicator of the etymological make-up of the word in whose pronunciation it is used. The etymology in square brackets, immediately following the pronunciation, is the proper source of such information. Thus the etymology of *su·per·naturalism* is plainly shown as [¹*supernatural* + *-ism*] but as a time-saving and space-saving device the pronunciation is shown as \ˌsüpə(r)+\ (that is, "+ the pronunciation at *naturalism*").

When the spelling that the plus sign directs the consultant to refer to in order to complete the pronunciation has two or more entries belonging to different parts of speech not identical in pronunciation, the pronunciation to be supplied is that of the spelling whose part of speech is the same as that of the compound. Thus for ¹*concorporate,* an adjective, add the pronunciation given for the adjective *corporate,* and for ²*concorporate,* a verb, add the pronunciation given for the verb *corporate.* If the compound has inflected forms for which the pronunciation is desired, this information should be sought at the entry for the word that is the last part of the compound.

When the second syllable of a word has primary stress, anything less than primary stress is not marked on the first syllable (except when the vowel of the first syllable is \ə\), although first syllables often have a degree of stress that we mark as secondary stress on any syllable except the first. Thus no stress mark appears before the \mī-\ at *microscopist* and *microscopy,* although ˌ would appear before the \-mī\ of *biomicroscopy* if we were transcribing that compound in full. We usually forgo such nicety of stress indication when we use the plus formula, however, and the pronunciation of *biomicroscopy* is shown as \"+\ (read ¦bīō for the ditto).

The reason for the use of \"+\ instead of \"\ alone as the pronunciation of a word for which the value of the ditto is to be picked up from a preceding entry is illustrated by the following sequence of entries:

neo-arsphenamine \¦nē(ˌ)ō+\
neo-assyrian \"+\
¹*neo-babylonian* \"+\
²*neo-babylonian* \"\

Use of \"\ alone at *neo-assyrian* and ¹*neo-babylonian* could mean that these two words have the same pronunciation as *neoarsphenamine.* Use of \"\ alone at ²*neo-babylonian* means that that word does have the same pronunciation as the entry preceding, ¹*neo-babylonian.*

When an initial combining form has variants and appears in a number of compounds, we often list the variants in the entry for the combining form alone, devise a formula that we equate to the variants, and pronounce compounds in which the combining form so pronounced appears by means of the formula and a plus sign.

elec·tro- *in pronunciations below,* =¦== = ə¦lek(ˌ)trō *or* ē¦- *or* -ˌtrə\
. . .
¹*electrodeposit* \=¦== *at* ELECTRO- +\

The principal stress in the combining-form entry is altered if the stress in the compound differs.

In entries pronounced with the plus formula, usually no division marks are shown in the second part. This part may be divided at the places indicated at the entry where the pronunciation is to be sought. Divisions between the beginning of the compound and the beginning of the second element are usually shown, except that in compounds like ¹*electrodeposit* both the pronunciation and the divisions for the first part are to be sought at the entry for the initial combining form. In such compounds a division may also be made between the two components; in fact, this division is preferable to any other.

Many printers avoid dividing after a single initial letter, and no division is shown between the components of a compound when the first is a single letter, as in *asexual.*

| the vertical bar, ascender-high and descender= deep so that it will be as distinct as possible from \l\, is frequently used in transcriptions in which one or more variants are shown as an orientation mark to make it easier for the consultant to locate the part of the pronunciation in which the variation occurs. Our usual method of fixing the point of variation is to repeat, to both the left and the right of the variation or to one side only, one or more characters that are common to the variants and that fulfill other functions in the transcription (sound symbol, stress mark, parenthesis). But when contiguous variations occur, or when a character that would ordinarily be used occurs more than once in a transcription, a character whose sole function is that of a locator is desirable. The vertical locator is inserted in the first variant and is repeated in the same position in one or more variants that follow:

flight·i·ly \ˈflīd·|ᵊlē, -īt|, |ᵊli, |əl-\. See 2.6 in "Explanatory Notes".

Two vertical bars have been used with some frequency to facilitate the presentation of three contiguous variations, as in

gen·er·a·tive \ˈjenəˌrā|d·|iv, ˈjen(ə)rə|, |t|, |ēv *also* |əv\

In the variants presented after the first mark of punctuation variants of the first of the three contiguous parts end with a vertical bar, variants of the second have a vertical bar on each side, and variants of the third begin with a vertical bar.

ʻʻ see 2.8.1, 2.8.2 in "Explanatory Notes".

. see "Divisions in Respelled Pronunciations".

We hear a difference between the usual American pronunciation of the two items *fly twitch* and *flight witch* and the two items *sent reagents* and *sentry agents,* for the members of each of which pairs most transcribers would show identical sequences of sound symbols. On the other hand, we do not hear a difference between the two items *wool fox* and *wolf ox,* nor between the two items *wool freight* and *wolf rate,* for the members of each of which pairs most transcribers would also show identical sequences of sound symbols. (The qualification is to be understood that our observations are based upon the pronunciation of all items without pause, punctuative or hesitative. That some are nonsense items is of no moment.) We conclude therefore that an alteration of the boundary between meaningful elements in a sequence, or that the introduction of such a boundary into a sequence that lacks it, can cause a phonetic difference in some sequences but not in others. It makes sense to treat this phonetic difference as a difference of syllable division rather than as a difference between certain sounds in the pairs of sequences, which actually it is: such an interpretation will be more readily understood by those who do not know phonetics, and a single symbol for syllable division will do work that alternatively requires several additional sound symbols. Our symbol for a syllable division is a centered period, • ; we would use it in one position in a full transcription of items like *fly twitch* and *sentry agents* (\-ī•tw-\, \-n•tr-\) and in another position in items like *flight witch* and *sent reagents* (\-īt•w-\, \-nt•r-\); we would not use it at all in a full transcription of any of the items *wool fox, wolf ox, wool freight, wolf rate.* (Actually, we usually omit it in items of the first group when they are compounds of two English words and the pronunciation is limited to stress indication.) Our stress marks are not simultaneously indicators of syllable division, as they are in some systems of transcription, and their placement when no • accompanies them is arbitrary (see "Divisions in Respelled Pronunciations"). Thus our transcription at *astronomer* is \ə'stränəmə(r)\ but it is impossible to know from a comparison of normally pronounced English items containing the sequence \st\ whether the syllable division is before the \s\, between the \s\ and \t\, or after the \t\. In short, our policy in this book is to indicate a syllable division (use the mark •) only in sequences.

Examples of our use of •:

be•tween \bə̇•'twēn . . .\ [\tw\ different from that of *rabbit warren.*]

sight \. . . *usu* -īd•+V\ [The voiced sound that most Americans have between the first two vowels of *sight over* is different from the voiced sound that some speakers (e.g., some British speakers) have between the first two vowels of *side over* or *Cy Dover*.]

bur•ry \'bər•|ē . . .\ . . . : abounding in or containing burs . . . [Many have \'bər•ē\ for this but \'hə•rē\ for *hurry*.]

alma-ata \¦almə•ə¦tä\ [The centered period is necessary here because in our system a doubled symbol with nothing between indicates a long monosyllabic vowel.]

For \r(•)\ at the end of a transcription, as at *knur*, see the section on \r(•)\.

₋ the low-set minus sign usually cancels a stress at the same point in a pronunciation shown elsewhere, as in a preceding variant within the same reversed virgules or in a pronunciation for a preceding word in the same or another entry.

cam•era•man \'=(=)=,man, -₋mən\

[1]*mer•cu•ri•al* \¦mər¦kyu̇rēəl, ₋mə(r)'k-, . . .\

ac•tiv•ism \'aktə̇,vizəm\

[1]*ac•tiv•ist* \-₋və̇st\

Occasionally ₋ merely emphasizes that the syllable that follows is without stress, as when it stands at the beginning of the first pronunciation shown for a monosyllable.

from \₋f(r)əm, . . . \

[1]*-y also -ey* \₋ē, i\

If the compound word *binaural* had been transcribed in full in the vocabulary, the stress indication would have been ¦ and would have been placed immediately ahead of the symbol \n\, as explained in "Divisions in Respelled Pronunciations". In some areas of the vocabulary we used a formula of the type \(')bī¦n+₋-\ for such compounds (see the plus sign), in which the purpose of the mark ₋ is to cancel the stress appearing before the first vowel at the entry *aural* in favor of the placement of stress indication for the same syllable before the \n\ in the compound, and so to guard against the interpretation that our intention as to stress is \(')bī¦n'ȯrəl\. However, since we do not employ stress marks to double as syllable dividers, formulas of the type \(')bī¦n+₋-\ may carry nicety of stress-mark placement to excess. The shift of stress indication for *au* from ' at *aural* to ¦ at *binaural* is implied by (') or ¦ in the first member of the compound, as it of necessity must be when the plus formula is used for a compound whose second member has no stress on the first syllable. Hence in most of the vocabulary we use a formula of the type found at *exostracize*, \eks+\ (instead of \ek's+₋-\).

÷ see 2.12 in "Explanatory Notes".

. . . the three-dot ellipsis is often used between sound symbols preceding and following for a pronounced part that will be found in a corresponding position in a preceding pronunciation either within the same or in a preceding entry.

humpty-dumpty \¦həm(p)tē¦dəm(p)tē, -ti . . . ti\

It may be so used for one or more of the following reasons: what it stands for may be of such length that to repeat it would consume space and distract the reader's attention from the part of the word to which we wish to draw it; it may emphasize that the pronounced parts preceding and following are concomitant variants; a duplication of sound symbols in the part of the pronunciation the ellipsis stands for may make the provision of orienting symbols from this part difficult. For additional examples see *dilettantist* and *catalogue raisonné* in the vocabulary.

Occasionally . . . is used at the end of a pronunciation consisting of stress indication only for a multiplicity of variants that it would be clumsy to indicate otherwise.

high-temperature \'=¦= . . .\ [see *temperature*]

In a formula such as that found in the pronunciation of the three-part entry

sul•fo•benzoic acid \¦səl(,)fō+. . . -\

the three dots stand for the second of the three parts. The dots together with the hyphen that follows tell the consultant that to find the pronunciation of the entire entry he must look at two other entries, *benzoic* or *benzoic acid*, and *acid*.

\ə when a stress mark (' or ,) stands at the beginning of the syllable in which it occurs, this symbol, called *schwa*, is pronounced as in *bud* or *nut* or the last syllable of *aqueduct;* when the syllable in which it stands is without stress mark, it is pronounced as in the first syllable of *alone* or *occur* or as in the second syllable of *colony* or as in the last syllable of *abbot* or *famous* or *sabbath* or *circus*.

Formerly nearly all phonetic alphabets used for the vowel of *bud* a symbol different from that for the vowel of the second syllable of *abbot*, and some alphabets still do. Some who are familiar only with these alphabets find the use of \ə\ in stressed syllables objectionable when they encounter it for the first time. But use of \ə\ as a symbol for both unstressed and stressed vowel is rapidly increasing, and abandonment of a separate symbol for the vowel of *bud* parallels abandonment of former symbols for half-long a, e, and o in whose stead ā, ē, and ō without stress mark are entirely adequate.

\ə̄ used by *r*-droppers for the *-ir* of *stir* and the *-irre-* of *stirred*, and used by many *r*-droppers for the *-ur-* of *sturdy* and the *-ir-* of *bird*. It is a single sound and not a diphthong.

An *r*-dropper, symbolized by *–R* in transcriptions in this dictionary, in no case makes immediately before a pause or a consonant the *r*-sound that is characterized by the raising and bending backward of the tongue tip. Complete *r*-droppers are comparatively rare, and in the U.S. possibly nonexistent. A not uncommon phenomenon is a speaker who pronounces *bird* and the first syllable of *further* the way an *r*-keeper does but who drops the *r* of the second syllable of *further* and of words like *farm* and *form*.

In words like *bird* and *sturdy* (words not having *r* as the last letter in the orthography and not derived from such words) but not in words like *stir, stirred, stirs,* many *r*-droppers in the New York City area and in the southeastern U.S. have instead of the vowel \ə̄\ the diphthong \əi\ (see the section on \əi\). A variant vowel used by some speakers for words like *bird* and *stir* but not shown in this dictionary is \əə\ — that is, \'ə\, the vowel of *bud*, lengthened. With such speakers *bud* and *bird* have the same vowel, but it is appreciably longer in *bird*. With *r*-droppers in the U.S. the pronunciation of words like *furry* and *stirring* (two-element words whose second element is a vowel suffix or a vowel-initial suffix) is either \'fə̄rē\, \'stə̄riŋ\ or more often \'fər-ē\, \'stər•iŋ\, the latter being also the pronunciation of *r*-keepers. See the section on \ər(•)\.

\ə̄\ is often used by *r*-droppers as an anglicization of any of the vowels \œ\, \œ̄\, \œœ\, \œ̄œ in words borrowed from a foreign language. Example: \-sə̄z\ for the second syllable of *berceuse* which in French is \-sœ̄œz\. This \ə̄\ anglicization is even used to some extent by *r*-keepers although it is not a sound that they use in fully English words. See \œ\.

\ə̇ used in unstressed syllables only; the dot is not a diacritic indicating that \ə̇\ stands for something different from \ə\. Rather \ə̇\ is a compound or two-part symbol, the two components being \ə\ and the dot of the symbol \i\. \ə̇\ is used when \ə\ occurs in some dialects and \i\ in others, or when the same speaker may have \ə\ in ordinary speech but \i\ in formal speech, or in an initial position where either \ə\ or \i\ may occur depending on what precedes. Less space is required to transcribe, for instance, *rapid* as \'rapə̇d\ than to transcribe it as \'rapəd, -pid\. In positions in which we show \ə̇\, most dictionaries have long shown only \i\ — or even \e\ alternatively or alone when the orthography has *e*, as in the second syllable of *ticket*. \i\ is the pronunciation of some Americans and of most speakers of Received Standard, but most Americans make exact rhymes of *quotaed* and *quoted*, of *ballad* and *valid*, of *abbot* and *rabbit* and *rabbet*. The first member of each of these groups is shown with only \ə\ or its equivalent as the unstressed vowel.

Our system includes the three symbols \ə\, \i\, and \ə̇\ and uses \ə̇\ to mean either \ə\ or \i\. A system (or a modification of it) used by many linguists includes the three symbols \ə\, \i\, and "barred *i*", produced by overprinting the \i\ with a hyphen), and uses barred *i* in most of the places where we use \ə̇\. As used by most, it appears to be intended as a symbol for a sound distinct from \ə\ and \i\ — articulated with the tongue higher than for \ə\ and farther back than for \i\. Although it is quite true that the unstressed sound we symbolize \ə\ varies in its articulation more than any other vowel, the variation seems purely a matter of phonetic environment. If speakers do not consistently articulate within the same environment three distinct vowels symbolized by \ə\ and \i\ and barred *i*, then we need no equivalent for an unstressed barred *i*.

Barred *i* has also been used to symbolize a stressed vowel heard from some Southern speakers in the first syllable of *sister*, produced by drawing the tongue back in the direction of \u̇\. We have not used a symbol for this vowel in the vocabulary because the geographical and lexical incidence of the vowel does not seem to be well enough known. Some students of American speech insist that a symbol for such a stressed vowel is necessary for adequate transcription of the full range of variants heard for the adverb *just* from speakers in all parts of the U.S., on the ground that this adverb frequently has a vowel that is not the vowel of the adjective *just*, not the vowel of the noun *gist*, and not the vowel of the noun or verb *jest*. We agree but we are not convinced that (outside those areas of the South where the first vowel of *sister* is not \i\) pronunciations of the adverb *just* when the vowel is not stressed \ə\, \i\, or \e\ have any more stress to them than does the pronunciation of the *gest* of *largest*. The full range of variants for the adverb *just* is reasonably well covered for the English-speaking world as a whole when it is indicated that the vowel is \ə\, \i\, or (less frequent than the other two in standard speech) \e\, all either stressed or unstressed.

In transcriptions of uncommon words, as a space-saving device, \ə̇\ only is used where \ē\ is heard as a variant of \ə\ and \i\ as in the antepenultimate syllable of words in *-ical* or in the second syllable of *Libyco-Berber*. Such practice is not inconsistent with the widely followed practice of transcribing as \i\ the last vowel of words like *happy*, a vowel for which the symbol \ē\ better represents the usual U.S. pronunciation. The \ē\ variant is usually included in transcriptions of common words.

If we were attempting to cover British as well as American pronunciation, we would use \ə̇\ much more freely than we do in vocabulary pronunciations. In British usage an unstressed vowel whose orthographic counterpart is *i* or *e* is usually \i\, but American usage more often has \ə\ than \i\ in unstressed syllables. Even with American speakers who most often have \i\, its range is much more restricted.

\ᵊ (preceding \l\, \n\, \m\, \ŋ\; for ᵊ following \l\, \m\, \r\, see \lᵊ\, \mᵊ\, \rᵊ\) printed as a superior character means that a consonant following it is a syllabic consonant, that is, a consonant that immediately follows another consonant without any vowel between. Nearly all phoneticians are agreed that \n\ and \l\ are often syllabic in English although some use no symbol that indicates syllabicity. Some transcribers of pronunciations in dictionaries who use a special symbol for syllabicity with \n\ and \l\ find no occasion to attach the symbol to \m\ or \ŋ\, but this does not necessarily mean that they deny the existence of syllabic \m\ and \ŋ\. There is variation in the interpretation and transcription of the sound of the *er* in the three-syllabled pronunciation of *coppery* and in *r*-keepers' pronunciation of *copper*, some phoneticians regarding these sounds as a syllabic \r\.

Apparently there are many, especially among writers of textbooks on phonics and teachers in the elementary schools, who are of the opinion that there can be no syllable without a vowel. Every dictionary in line of succession from, and including, Noah Webster's original dictionary of 1828 shows vowelless syllables. For instance, the unabridged Webster dictionaries that preceded this pronounce the word *kitten* as follows:

1828	kit'n
1847	kit'tn
1864	kĭt'tn
1890	kĭt't'n
1909	kĭt"n
1934	kĭt"n

As a realistic representation of what takes place in articulation when a syllabic consonant is pronounced, the representation employed by Noah Webster in 1828 is difficult to improve: the consonant alone is used without the addition of any symbol for syllabicity. Something additional must be used when the syllabic consonant is not final in a sequence and is followed by a vowel; thus \kitnish\ does not adequately represent a three-syllabled pronunciation of *kittenish*, but its inadequacy can be rectified by inserting a hyphen after the syllabic consonant, thus: \kitn-ish\). Our latest school dictionaries transcribe *kitten* as \'kit-n\, and with the abolition of unnecessary marks of syllable division in this book our transcription could have been \'kitn\. However, this book departs from this method of transcribing syllabic consonants for two reasons:

(1) In some environments some monosyllabic particles (for example, *and*) often have no vowel sound but have a syllabic consonant as their first or only sound. Although in the transcription of words of more than one syllable a special symbol for syllabicity is not essential, without one the indication of a syllabic consonant in a monosyllable is a matter of some difficulty, and in this book the user has a right to expect a minute listing of all the variants commonly heard for such monosyllabic particles as *and*.

(2) In our school dictionaries, a syllabic consonant followed in the same word by a vowel is indicated as syllabic by the printing of a hyphen (in these books a mark of syllable division) after the consonant, as in \'fas-n-,āt\ for *fascinate* and \,fas-n-'āsh-n\ for *fascination*. We have found that these transcriptions have been often understood to show *fascinate* as having two syllables only or *fascination* three syllables only, so we attempt to forestall misinterpretations such

as these by using a small superior schwa before the syllabic consonant.

Some transcribers symbolize a syllabic consonant by a full-size \ə\ followed by the symbol for the consonant, for example, the sound that follows the second consonant of *wooden* being transcribed \ən\. Either or both of two lines of reasoning seem to motivate this procedure:

(1) There are speakers who have a vowel between the \d\ and \n\ of words like *wooden*. Even those who rarely or never have the vowel-plus-\n\ pronunciation would not apprehend that pronunciation as anything but the word *wooden*. There are few if any speakers who consistently have \d\ plus syllabic \n\ in one kind of context and have \d\ plus \ə\ plus \n\ in another context, and therefore the two pronunciations are seldom in contrast. Why then go to the trouble of having an additional method of symbolization for a syllabic consonant?

(2) The pronunciation without any vowel in the second syllable of *wooden* is the usual one, but a speaker's ingrained pronunciation habits can be depended upon to make him pronounce a syllabic consonant in the right places even though the transcription shows \ə\ before the consonant.

Against these arguments several counter arguments can be posed:

In the pronunciation heard, with few exceptions, for a word like *wooden* from speakers who are communicating with friends and are not trying to impress, there is no vowel in the syllable that contains the \n\. Some speakers do insert the vowel \ə\ before the consonant especially when they have a large audience containing hearers who may expect a more formal kind of pronunciation than the speaker ordinarily uses. That there are others in any such audience, however, who do not expect the speaker to alter his normal style of speech to this extent must be the experience of many or most who have done a great deal of radio or television listening in the company of others. When a television news broadcaster pronounces *threaten* with a vowel in the second syllable, a listener, although ignorant of phonetics, must be instantly aware that the pronunciation differs from what years of hearing English spoken have shown to be the usual pronunciation of *threaten*. Most speakers of English who pronounce a vowel in the second syllable of *wooden* or *threaten* probably do so because the spelling contains a vowel letter before the *n*. These speakers make a literal-minded interpretation of the presence of the written vowel, and do not see that they have introduced a vowel sound unnaturally. They can point to transcriptions that represent the same succession of symbols — \tən\ — the initial sounds of *tonight* and the final sounds of *threaten*. The utterances *lye denotes* and *Leyden oats* differ in that the first would ordinarily be pronounced with a vowel between the \d\ and the \n\ (with American speakers this vowel would often or usually be \ə\) whereas the second would ordinarily not have a vowel between the \d\ and the \n\. Some linguists would assert that there would be a difference of juncture between these two items whether there is or is not a vowel \ə\ in the second syllable of the second item — that in spite of identity of sounds and stresses and intonation there is something in the way these otherwise identical items are uttered that makes it clear to a hearer that the word boundaries are not the same. However, as readers know who are familiar with our vocabulary pronunciations or who have read the section on *juncture* in this "Guide", it is our view that often it is impossible to identify word boundaries phonetically. The difference between *lye denotes* consistently pronounced with \ən\ after the \d\ and *Leyden oats* consistently pronounced with a syllabic \n\ after the \d\ is the only one consistently made. Such a consistently made difference is phonemic.

Transcribers who use the symbol \ə\ in the second syllable of words like *wooden* will apparently be in difficulty if they decide to record certain widespread pronunciations that all of them seem to have thus far avoided — the pronunciation of *seven*, for instance, in which the second consonant is \b\ rather than \v\ and the last consonant is \m\ rather than \n\. The consultant who interprets a transcription like \'thretən\ literally and pronounces the word with a vowel in the last syllable will be saying something that may be heard from numerous other speakers but the consultant who interprets a transcription like \'sebəm\ in the same way would be using a pronunciation almost without precedent.

There can be no better way of indicating no vowel between two consonants than to print them with nothing between them — e.g., to transcribe \'sebm\ (one pronunciation of *seven*) and \'käntn-ənt\ (one pronunciation of *continent*), or to follow the long-established IPA practice of using a modifier underneath the symbol for the syllabic consonant, at least whenever the syllabic consonant is followed by an unstressed vowel in the same word. Some dictionary users, however, prefer some sort of symbol between the two consonants, and the raised symbol \ᵊ\ should provide an acceptable compromise between the extreme of no modifier at all and the extreme of a full-sized \ə\, which tends to encourage over-pronunciation.

Transcribers of dictionary pronunciations who employ a special way of indicating that a consonant is syllabic treat \n\ and \l\ as syllabic in a high percentage of cases. Some dictionaries show no syllabic \m\ or \ŋ\ in any of their pronunciations, although the very best speakers from time to time use a syllabic \m\ and less often a syllabic \ŋ\. (On these, see the entries \ᵊm\ and \ᵊŋ\.) The phonetic entity that corresponds to the *er* of the spelling *differ* or to the *or* of the spelling *honor* in the speech of *r*-keepers, and often in the speech of *r*-droppers when a word beginning with a vowel sound follows without pause, is variously interpreted. Some phoneticians regard this entity as the vowel \ə\ pronounced with a raising or turning back (retroflexion) of the tip of the tongue and use for it the symbol \ə\ with a symbol for retroflexion attached. Other phoneticians regard the sound as a syllabic \r\ and use a transcription that parallels that for syllabic \n\ or \l\. Still others transcribe \ər\. Of this number some regard the item as two sounds, others are willing to grant its singleness but find the two-symbol transcription more practicable since it more closely parallels the orthographic spelling, does not require the additional specially made symbol that use of a single symbol might, and makes it possible to show both the *r*-keepers' and the *r*-droppers' pronunciation by merely parenthesizing or italicizing the r. Whereas the latest school dictionaries in the Merriam-Webster series transcribe the *er* of *wither* as a syllabic r — \'with-r\ — this dictionary transcribes the same word \'withə(r)\. In the school dictionaries only the pronunciation of *r*-keepers is shown and it seemed advisable to attempt to indicate syllable boundaries in pronunciations (*attempt* because the exact location of many syllable boundaries in speech is highly uncertain). If these had been the only considerations affecting the transcription of words like *wither*, any of the three mentioned methods of transcribing the final part of the word would have served equally well. But there was the further consideration that derivatives formed by the addition of a vowel or vowel-initial suffix to many such words have pronunciation variants one of which has one syllable less than the other, *withering* and *withery*, for example, being either three-syllabled or two-syllabled. Such variation occurs often, especially in the present participle of verbs. By treating the sound of the *er* in the three-syllabled pronunciation of *withery* as a syllabic consonant \r\ we can show the variation thus: \'with-r(-)ē\, which means \'with-r-ē, 'with-rē\ or \'with-rē, 'with-r-ē\, the parentheses indicating the alternative presence or absence of the phonetic item symbolized between them. For the present participle *withering*, following after *wither* transcribed \'with-r\ at the beginning of the main entry, the indication of this variation can even be reduced to \-r(-)ing\. If the transcription of *wither* had been given as \'with-ər\, a parentheses formula for the two variants of *withering* would have entailed either \'with-(-ə)r(-)ing\ or \'with-(ə-)ring\, the first clumsy with its two pairs of parentheses one of which encloses two characters instead of one, the second having two characters parenthesized instead of one and having one division changed from what it is in the form without a suffix. The alternative to a parentheses formula would have been one of the two fairly long ones \'with-ər-ing, 'with-ring\ or \-ər-ing, 'with-ring\. Omission of the first syllable from the second variant in the last formula would have been ambiguous and even if done would have yielded a formula that is still longer than the \-r(-)ing\ formula. Primarily because the \-r(-)ing\ formula for the present-participle variation is the shortest one we were able to contrive for use in a transcription system in which syllable boundaries are indicated, \r\ is treated as being capable of being a syllabic consonant in the school dictionaries, in one of which the formula is extensively used.

The present book shows for well-known entries the pronunciation of both *r*-keepers and *r*-droppers and does not attempt to show boundaries for all syllables. Because of these two practices in this book we transcribe *wither* as \'with-ə(r)\ and *withering* as \'with(ə)riŋ\. This last is to be regarded as merely one of several possible ways of representing exactly the same two variant pronunciations that are represented by \'with-r(-)ing\ in our other dictionaries. We could achieve somewhat closer parallelism between the two systems by representing in this book the *r*-keepers' pronunciation of *wither* as \'withᵊr\ and the two variants of *withering* as \'with(ᵊ)riŋ\ (paralleling \'bət(ᵊ)niŋ\ for *buttoning*), but a transcription \'withᵊ(r)\ is impossible since \'withᵊ\ is impossible.

In this dictionary we use the same symbols for the *r*-keepers' pronunciation of the stressed *ur* in the first syllable of *murmur* and the unstressed *ur* in the second syllable of that word, \'mərmər\. In the school dictionaries we do not, transcribing \'mərm-r\, for two reasons:

(1) Primarily, there might be strong opposition to showing a syllabic consonant in a stressed syllable, since the average dictionary user has never encountered a system that so employs a syllabic consonant.

(2) Although the sound of the stressed *ur* in *murmur* is a single sound, the sound of the *ir* in *firm* and the *ur* of *fur* is often a double sound when these monosyllables are in prepausal position, particularly if they are emphasized, and transcribing the *ir* of *firm*, the *ur* of *fur*, and the first *ur* of *murmur* as two sounds has phonetic justification. The vowel of *ray* is apt to be diphthongal and the vowel of the first syllable of *raking* is apt to be monophthongal in most American speech, but sound phonetic practice calls for regarding these variations as nonsignificant and using the same symbol or symbols in both situations.

We transcribe the *ir* of *firm* and *firmer* as if it were pronounced as two successive sounds. We are not certain that this is the only phonetic item answering to a vowel letter and an *r* in the spelling that is sometimes pronounced as a single sound. We often pronounce the *ar* of *army* so, and if we use a single symbol for the *ir* in *firm(er)* we ought also to use a single symbol for the *ar* of *army*. But to add symbols to a pronunciation alphabet unnecessarily seems unwise and useless. It is simpler and adequate to use a vowel symbol followed by \r\, with the understanding that the \r\ may represent either a second, independent sound or merely a modification of the preceding sound. Of the four consonants — \l\, \n\, \m\, \ng\ — that we treat as capable of being syllabic, the first three are shown as syllabic in the school dictionaries in many environments in which they are treated as \ə\ plus consonant in this book. The chief reason for this is the same as for treating the *er* of *wither* as a syllabic \r\: if we show the pronunciation of *hyphen* as \'hīf-n\ and of *rival* as \'rīv-l\, we can show the two variant pronunciations of the present participles by simply parenthesizing a single character in the brief formulas \-n(-)ing\ and \-l(-)ing\. When syllable divisions in transcriptions are dispensed with, as in this book, it is possible to treat the *al* of *rival* as vowel plus \l\, the double pronunciation of the present participle being shown by the simple parenthesizing of a single character \'rīv(ə)liŋ\.

If the reader will pronounce each of the following items with the consonant between the two vertical bars as a syllabic consonant and then as \ə\ plus consonant, there should be no doubt that the two pronunciations of each word are markedly different:

(1) \'kit|n|\ (*kitten*)
(2) \'red|n|\ (*redden*)
(3) \'kēp|m|\ (*keep 'em*)
(4) \'grab|m|\ (*grab 'em*)
(5) \,kəp|m|'sȯsə(r)\ (*cup and saucer*)
(6) \'seb|m|\ (*seven*)
(7) \,läk|ŋ|'kē\ (*lock and key*)
(8) \,eg|ŋ|'kəp\ (*egg and cup*)

For items (1) and (2) a pronunciation \ən\ instead of \ᵊn\ is heard with some frequency especially in formal speech, but even in such speech it does not sound quite natural to many listeners. For items (3) and (4) both \ᵊm\ and \əm\ sound natural. For items (5) and (6) the \əm\ pronunciation sounds utterly unnatural, as does the \əŋ\ pronunciation for items (7) and (8). For the phonetic entity between vertical bars in items (5)–(8) \ən\ is a perfectly natural alternative (in item (6), when \v\ precedes) and if any experimenters believe that \əm\ and \əŋ\ sound normal in these items they are probably pronouncing or hearing \ən\ instead. In all eight items the first vertical bar is immediately preceded by a stop consonant that is homorganic with (i.e., that has the same basic articulation as) the consonant between the two. This book treats the nasal consonants \n\, \m\, and \ŋ\ as capable of being syllabic after such a homorganic consonant. If the preceding homorganic consonant is in turn preceded by a consonant, in many cases the first of the three consonants inhibits the syllabicity of the third. Thus *London* is nearly always \'ləndən\, although *fountain* is as often \'fau̇ntᵊn\ as \'fau̇ntən\.

The same criteria used for the possible syllabicity of the nasal consonants after homorganic stops point to the advisability of treating \l\ as capable of syllabicity after the homorganic stops \t\ and \d\ and also after the homorganic nasal \n\ (which is classifiable as a nasal stop), as in *metal, meddle,* and *final*. As with \n\, pronunciation of these words with \əl\ instead of \ᵊl\ is sometimes heard in formal speech. With most American speakers such pairs as *metal : medal* are quite identical in pronunciation, the consonant preceding the \l\ being a variety of \d\ (see the section on \d·\).

We have found it difficult to decide about the transcription of the group of words in which the consonant sound preceding \n\, \l\, or \m\ is a homorganic consonant other than a stop.*

---

*\ŋ\ is not involved here because it is the only velar consonant other than stops. Consonant successions like \ln\, \rn\, \rl\ in words like *sullen, barren, barrel* are not considered, for this reason: these successions can be pronounced monosyllabically, as in one pronunciation of *kiln*, in *barn*, and in one pronunciation of *Carl* (see section on *rl*), and the usual practice among phoneticians for these two-consonant successions capable of monosyllabic pronunciation (as successions like \tn\ and \bm\ are not) is to transcribe a vowel between them when they are pronounced as in *sullen, barren,* and *barrel*, just as \v\ and \d\ are \-vd\ in the monosyllable *lived* but \-vəd\ in the disyllable *livid*.

The following words illustrate this classification:

(1) \ˈbās|n|\ (*basin*)
(2) \ˈrēz|n|\ (*reason*)
(3) \ˈōsh|n|\ (*ocean*)
(4) \ˈvizh|n|\ (*vision*)
(5) \ˈskəch|n|\ (*scutcheon*)
(6) \ˈpij|n|\ (*pigeon*)
(7) \ˈnāth|n|\ (*Nathan*)
(8) \ˈhē<u>th</u>|n|\ (*heathen*)

---

(9) \ˈgris|l|\ (*gristle*)
(10) \ˈēz|l|\ (*easel*)
(11) \ˈsōsh|l|\ (*social*)
(12) \ˈyüzh|l|\ (*usual*)
(13) \ˈsach|l|\ (*satchel*)
(14) \ˈaj|l|\ (*agile*)
(15) \ˈeth|l|\ (*ethyl*)
(16) \bəˈkwē<u>th</u>|l|\ (*bequeathal*)

{ (17) \ˈstəf|m|\ (*stuff ’em*)
{ (18) \ˌdef|m|ˈāsh|n|\ (*defamation*)
{ (19) \ˈlēv|m|\ (*leave ’em*)
{ (20) \ˈsev|m|\ (*seven*)

The two chief kinds of data used in determining what our transcription of each of these types of word should be were (1) our records, accumulated over an extended period of listening, of our impression as to whether a consonant was syllabic or was preceded by a vowel \ə\ and (2) the impression arrived at after much pronouncing by ourselves such items (often containing made-up words or nonsensical names) as *May Sinnott: mace a knot: Maysa Nott: Mason Ott*, which could differ from one another only in the presence or absence of a vowel before the consonant being explored (items containing a pause were out of order). After repeated alternate attempts to pronounce \ən\ and then \ᵊn\ in the consonant successions in items (3)–(6), the successions all sound alike whether in our made-up test items there is a word boundary before the first member of the consonantal succession, after the second member, or between the two. Such an outcome determines an arbitrary choice of either \ən\ or \ᵊn\ for these words, and the equivalent of \ᵊn\ is used in the school dictionaries; in this book the syllable core of these words is represented, except for a few interjections, in all cases where the consonants \n\, \l\, \m\, and \ŋ\ are not involved, by a vowel symbol. Such representation also avoids transcribing the last part of *fission* as \-ᵊn\ and the first part of *another* as \əˈn-\, with their suggestion that *fission others* and *fish another's* do not sound alike.

Words of the type illustrated in (1) and (2) are transcribed with ᵊn because pairs like *Mason Ott* and *May Sinnott* seem distinct and because our records contain notations of pronunciations of words like *reason* with overpronunciations having \ən\ at the end. The difference between \zᵊn\ and \zən\, however, is by no means as easy to hear as the difference between \dᵊn\ and \dən\, and when an unstressed vowel precedes the \s\ or \z\ a clear distinction between \sən\ and \sᵊn\ seems impossible, *Jefferson Ott* and *Jeffersa Nott* and *Jeffer Sinnott* all sounding the same to us. Hence we transcribe \ˈgärsᵊn\ (*Garson*) but \ˈjefərsən\ (*Jefferson*).

Items (7) and (8) are more difficult, but a distinction can be heard between \thən\ and \thᵊn\ and between \<u>th</u>ən\ and \<u>th</u>ᵊn\; \ən\ is regular when a vowel follows the \n\ without pause, being heard in *unearth a nape, unearth an ape, Bertha Nape*, and *earthen ape;* and either \ən\ or \ᵊn\ is apt to occur when a consonant or a pause follows the \n\, \ən\ and \ᵊn\ in such position being in free variation. We have therefore shown \ən\ after \th\ and \<u>th</u>\, to the exclusion of \ᵊn\.

To make \əl\ and \ᵊl\ in items (9)–(16) sound distinct and like normal English is also difficult, and we accordingly transcribe \əl\ after the consonants listed there. A number of transcribers show a syllabic \l\ in words like *gristle* and *dazzle*, but this may be primarily because of the analogy of the orthography, in which there is no vowel letter immediately before the *l*.

After \v\ in items (19) and (20) \ᵊm\ and \əm\ are possible and are quite distinct: \ˈsevəm\ for *seven* would sound strange to probably all educated persons whose native language is English whereas \ˈsevᵊm\ sounds quite natural to nearly all and is a part-time pronunciation of many, most of whom are entirely unaware that they are hearing or pronouncing an \m\ at the end of the word, are unwilling to believe that any educated speaker so pronounces, and actually denounce the pronunciation as worthy only of the most illiterate.

The syllabic \m\ of \vᵊm\ has an articulation different from that of most \m\'s in English, being formed not with the lips but with the lower lip and the upper front teeth, by assimilation to the \v\. The same kind of \m\ is heard in *nymph* and *symphony*. Its lip-teeth articulation is an almost inevitable result of its environment and in most transcription requires no special symbol. \vᵊm\, however, has a very strong tendency to become \bᵊm\ which is somewhat easier to utter and has the usual two-lip variety of \m\.

Certain common speech items having *v* and *m* in the orthography may have any of the three variants \vəm\, \vᵊm\, \bᵊm\, as *government, leave ’em* (these three pronunciations for *government* are not limited to *r*-droppers). Possibly even an uncommon item like *Novum Organum* would be heard with all three. It seems likely that an item like *Neva Martin*, in which what precedes the letter *M* is a word that in isolation is pronounced with a final vowel, would usually have only the variant \vəm\, although it might be generalizing too much to rule out \vᵊm\ and \bᵊm\ altogether. For all *v . . . m* items a pronunciation \bəm\ does not sound natural.

A number of *v . . . n* items have any of the three variants \vən\, \vᵊm\, \bᵊm\, as *seven, eleven, davenport*. For these, either \vəm\ or \bəm\ does not sound natural. *b . . . m* items like *rob ’em* are either \bᵊm\ or \bəm\. For these, \vᵊm\ or \vəm\ would not sound natural.

Items of the type illustrated in (17) and (18) — *stuff ’em, defamation* — do not offer as many complications as do those just discussed. The \f\ does not tend to become \p\, as \v\ does to become \b\, and the \m\ does not tend, to an extent at least that would appear to require notice in transcriptions in this dictionary, to appear in words in which the corresponding orthograpic item is *n*, as *hyphen*. The variants \fəm\ and \fᵊm\ both occur freely for items like *stuff ’em* and *sophomore* (the last also has a two-syllable variant) but \fᵊm\ would probably be a pretty rare variant in an item like *Josepha Moore*.

In words exemplified in the following list, there is a syllable core between an \l\, \n\, or \m\ and the next preceding consonant, which is not homorganic (successions in which a nasal is preceded by a nasal are discussed later; no words in which unstressed \əŋ\ is a possibility are shown because such a succession probably does not occur in normal English, and \ᵊŋ\ occurs only as an occasional variant):

(1) *triple*	(9) *ribbon*	(17) *ligament*
(2) *babble*	(10) *weaken*	(18) *blossom*
(3) *fickle*	(11) *wagon*	(19) *chasm*
(4) *struggle*	(12) *stiffen*	(20) *Gotham*
(5) *baffle*	(13) *seven*	(21) *rhythm*
(6) *bevel*		(22) *Beecham*
(7) *camel*	(14) *bottom*	(23) *Bridgham*
	(15) *madam*	(24) *Gresham*
(8) *happen*	(16) *oakum*	

Although words of the type *triple* and *babble*, and of the type *chasm* and *rhythm*, have been shown as having syllabic \l\ or syllabic \m\ in many books containing transcriptions, an \əl\, \ən\, or \əm\ in these words distinct from an \ᵊl\, \ᵊn\, or \ᵊm\ is undetectable, and we accordingly transcribe all these words with \əl\, \ən\, \əm\. Some of these words having an *n* in the spelling have pronunciation variants in which, by assimilation to the preceding consonant, the \n\ becomes \m\ (homorganic with preceding \v\, \p\, or \b\) or \ŋ\ (homorganic with preceding \k\ or \g\). In such variants the \m\ or \ŋ\ is syllabic and is transcribed \ᵊm\ or \ᵊŋ\. Such variants are shown for common words (as *happen* and *seven*), but for other words they are to be understood as occasional pronunciations largely limited to extremely rapid speech or to predisposing environments. (Thus, \-gᵊŋ\ would be less frequent for *dragon* immediately before a pause than for *dragon* in *dragon claw*, an environment in which the nasal is not merely preceded but also followed by a consonant having the same place of articulation as \ŋ\).

It seems likely that some who transcribe words like *triple, fickle, chasm*, and *prism* with a syllabic consonant \l\ or \m\ do so in continuance of a tradition that originated in a day when transcribers stood more in awe of spelling than the more enlightened do today. Transcriptions of *rifle* and *supple* that do not parallel those of *rival, opal*, and *oval*, and transcriptions of *chasm* and *prism* that do not parallel those of *blossom* and *gruesome* are suspect. There are of course passages of poetry in which the pronunciation of an *-sm* word as \-zəm\ would roughen the meter — a phrase like "a chasm of granite rock" in a line requiring iambics. But what is required in such a passage is not the use of \ᵊm\ instead of \əm\ but the use of a pronunciation in which the \z\ and the \m\ stand to each other in the same relationship as in the word *jazzman*. Such a pronunciation is easy enough to make clear by the use of spaces in the transcription: \ə kaz məv granə̇t räk\. Any attempt at the entry *chasm* to transcribe such a pronunciation of the *sm* would probably elude even most of the phonetically sophisticated, unless an explanation were given. Some might say that such a pronunciation is merely an example of poetic license and as deserving of ready dismissal as the pronunciation \<u>th</u>\ required for the definite article in "and dashed th' ambitious hopes" or the pronunciation required for *loathed* in "the loathèd hut they left behind". Such elision of a vowel between certain consonants and a following word-final \m\ that precedes an unstressed vowel occurs in prose utterance as well (the more rapid the utterance, the more likely its occurrence) and it also occurs before word-final \l\, \n\, and even \ŋ\, despite the fact that its occurrence before \ŋ\ would require that \ŋ\ be regarded as preceding a vowel in the same syllable, something that \ŋ\ is supposed never to do in normal English. Thus such pronunciations as the following are heard frequently:

\ə mit nə(v) wu̇l\ (*a mitten of wool*)
\tə sēz nə rōst\ (*to season a roast*)
\ə kak lə(v) gēs\ (*a cackle of geese*)
\<u>th</u>ə pē plə(v) rōm\ (*the people of Rome*)
\<u>th</u>ə {sev nə(v) | sev mə(v) | seb mə(v)} kləbz\ (*the seven of clubs*)
\<u>th</u>ē ə̇nthüzēaz mə vȯl\ (*the enthusiasm of all*)
\<u>th</u>ə ri<u>th</u> mə velēəts līn\ (*the rhythm of Eliot's line*)
\ə̇t wōn(t) hap {nəgen | məgen}\ (*it won't happen again*)
\ə wag ŋə dā\ (*a wagon a day*)
\bak ŋəp <u>th</u>ə kär\ (*backing up the car*)

Except for an occasional entry word (as ²*couple*) that has prevocalic occurrence in a frequently pronounced phrase, such variants are not shown. Such information is more likely to be sought in a discussion of phonetics than at individual entries in a dictionary, and constant repetition of a formula adequate to make this difficult-to-transcribe variation clear is felt to be unjustified.

The preceding remarks have touched on the pronunciation of a word like *chasm* in prevocalic position. Also to be found in poetry are such passages as "the chasm 'twixt rock and rock" (Browning), with *chasm* preconsonantal and in a position where optimally smooth meter requires a monosyllable. Uttering *chasm* here in a way that would be normal in any prose passage produces a very jarring rhythm.

Transcriptions of *chasm* that have appeared in some of our earlier dictionaries are (kăzm) and (kăz'm). (kăz'm) parallels the transcription of words like *dazzle* and *button* in having an apostrophe (symbol indicating a following consonant as syllabic) before the final consonant but differs from them in having no stress mark before the apostrophe (in our earlier dictionaries a stress mark following any syllable except the last indicated not merely stress but also a syllable boundary). The transcribers of both (kăzm) and (kăz'm) may have been influenced by an awareness of the monosyllabicity desirable for *chasm* in some poetic passages and may have intended these transcriptions to represent either a disyllabic or a monosyllabic pronunciation. The orthography may have caused them not to realize that the variations occurring for *chasm* are paralleled in words like *couple* and *mitten* (which have a vowel letter either after or immediately before the last consonant whereas *chasm* has such a letter in neither position). The briefest possible transcription for such variation is \ˈkaz(ə)m\, \ˈkəp(ə)l\, \ˈmit(ᵊ)n\, although the intent of such a transcription would probably be lost on most dictionary users.

Many or most *r*-droppers have syllabic consonants not only in words of the type *cotton* and *curtain* (in which the orthography has a vowel letter or vowel letters between the two consonants involved) but also in words of the type *modern* \-dᵊn\, *pattern* \-tᵊn\, *lantern* \-ntᵊn\, *international* \ˌintᵊn-\, *utterly* \ˈəd-ᵊlē\, and *government* \ˈgəvᵊmənt, ˈgəbᵊmənt\ (in which there is a vowel letter and an *r* between the two consonant letters in the orthography). The two pronunciations just shown for *government* occur frequently in the speech of *r*-keepers as well. Although it has been claimed or implied in transcriptional practice that there are *r*-droppers who consistently keep the members of such a pair as *Patton: pattern* distinct in their pronunciation, making the first \ˈpatᵊn\ and the second \ˈpad·ən\ or \ˈpatən\, there can be no doubt that pronunciations such as \ˈpatᵊn\ for *pattern* are common in *r*-dropping speech in both the U.S. and Great Britain.

Between some successions of two sounds, the minimum transition in English is a non-syllable-forming one: for example, the transition from \ī\ to \n\ in *brine*, from \r\ to \n\ in *r*-keepers' *barn*, from \g\ to \d\ in *drugged*, from \l\ to \n\ in one pronunciation of *kiln*, all monosyllabic words. Between other successions of two sounds (the successions discussed in some detail in the preceding paragraphs), the minimum transition is a syllable-forming one: for example, the transition from \d\ to \n\ in *hidden*, from second \p\ to \l\ in *people*, from \z\ to \m\ in *chasm*, from \k\ to \r\ in *acre**. When both a minimum and a more-than-minimum transition can be heard, a vowel is present in the more-than-minimum transition and a vowel symbol should be shown in the transcription. Thus *Bryan* is \ˈbrīən\ not \ˈbrīᵊn\ (compare monosyllabic \ˈbrīn\ *brine*), *baron* is \ˈbarən\ not \ˈbarᵊn\ (compare monosyllabic \ˈbärn\ *barn*), *rugged* is \ˈrəgəd\ or \ˈrəgid\ not \ˈrəgᵊd\ (compare monosyllabic \ˈdrəgd\ *drugged*). Successions incapable of less than disyllabic transition offer the complications that some are clearly capable of both a minimum disyllabic transition and a more-than-minimum disyllabic transition (\d\ and \n\ for instance, as in *hidden*) whereas others are not. Some phoneticians, feeling it unnecessary to take cognizance of such

---

*In some other languages, as French, \l\, \m\, and \r\ are in such position pronounced in such a way as to make possible a monosyllabic transition between them and a preceding consonant of the type illustrated. The qualification should also be added that we are speaking of successions of sounds in which the second is in prepausal position: since the desideratum in these considerations is to see what happens to a succession when an attempt is made to attach it to a single vowel, to introduce a word like *jitney*, in which the members of the succession are susceptible to distribution between a preceding and a following vowel, is to introduce a different criterion.

transitional variation, transcribe alike all transitions that are disyllabic, either treating the second consonant of all such successions as having a vowel before it or as being syllabic. Transcribers who record both types of transition do not always agree to which classification a given succession belongs. Those who wish to distinguish them should use \ᵊ\ between consonant symbols for the minimum transition and \ə\ for the more-than-minimum — for example, \ˈhidᵊn\ for the minimum, \ˈhidən\ for the more-than-minimum, in *hidden*.

For words like *linen, allyl, minimum,* and *goaded,* in which the two sounds of the succession are identical consonants, the transcription is with a vowel (\ə\ or in many cases either \ə\ or \i\) rather than \ᵊ\, the transition being more-than-minimum. The minimum transition for such a consonant pair is that heard in a word like *meanness,* where the transition from \n\ to \n\ consists of a mere holding or prolongation of the articulation of the \n\ that is also regardable as a doubling of the consonant and is usually transcribed by writing the symbol twice. Citing *meanness* (a word with a vowel both preceding and following the consonant pair) violates the criteria announced earlier as a basis for this particular part of our discussion, but it is only in such words that this type of transition ordinarily occurs in English. In some languages, however, it occurs within the bounds of a single syllable as a regular phenomenon, and is occasionally used in English for effect. Thus Carl Sandburg pronounces *Lincoln* \ˈliŋŋkən\ in reading from his works.

Although there are those who use transcriptions of the type \ˈkämᵊn\ *common* and \ˈvenᵊm\ *venom* (just as there are those who use transcriptions of the type \ˈbrīᵊn\ *Bryan* and \ˈmelᵊn\ *melon*), such transcriptions are out of line with the criteria we have used in that they employ the symbol of syllabicity for a more-than-minimum transition. The minimum transition for two different nasals is one in which the mouth closure for the second is simultaneous with a part or all of the closure for the first. Presumably only the articulation that is nearest the breath stream is acoustically identifiable, the outer one being blocked off by the inner one from forming any part of the resonance chamber. Such transitions do not occur in normal English nor in any of the languages with whose phonetics we have any firsthand acquaintance but they are quite easy to make. Mischa Elman once pronounced his surname over the radio as \ˈelm\ plus a nasal \n\ whose articulation began during the closure for \m\ and was held until the pause that follows the surname, as was also apparently the closure for the \m\. Whether this pronunciation should be considered disyllabic or monosyllabic is something easily argued.

**\ ᵊ ** (following \l\, \m\, \r\; for ᵊ preceding \l\, \n\, \m\, \ŋ\, see the sections \ᵊl\, \ᵊn\, \ᵊm\, \ᵊŋ\) in some foreign languages, of which French is the best known, two consonants the second of which is \l\, \m\, or \r\ can occur at the end of a word without any vowel between them. However, whereas in English the second member of the pair is voiced and the pair is disyllabic, in French the second member of the pair is voiceless (even when the first member is voiced) and the pair is monosyllabic. We indicate such a pronunciation of a pair of consonants by placing the symbol ᵊ after rather than before the second member. Examples from French of words for which such a pronunciation is one variant:

couple \küplᵊ\ *titre* \tētrᵊ\
table \tȧblᵊ\ *mordre* \mȯrdrᵊ\
prisme \prēsmᵊ, -ēzmᵊ\

In French such words may have any of four pronunciation variants, representable in our system as follows:

table \tȧbl(ᵊ), -b(lə)\

The four variants shown are

1. \tȧblᵊ\
2. \tȧbl\
3. \tȧblə\
4. \tȧb\

In French prose, 1 occurs before a pause, as does 4 chiefly in rapid or informal speech; 2 occurs before a word that begins with a vowel sound and that follows without pause; 3 and 4 occur before a word that begins with a consonant sound and that follows without pause, 4 occurring esp. in rapid or informal speech and in set phrases such as *maître d'hôtel.* The meaning of a transcription like 2 will be misunderstood by many, who will interpret it as disyllabic. In the following examples, spaces are used to indicate where the syllable boundaries are usually regarded as being in French, in order to facilitate an understanding of our transcriptions. Examples:

1. *amour-propre* \ȧ mür prȯprᵊ— *three syllables*\
2. *la table est belle* \lȧ tȧ ble bel —*four syllables*\
3. *table de bois* \tȧ blə də bwä —*four syllables*\
4. { *amour-propre* \ȧ mür prȯp— *three syllables*\
   table de bois \tȧb də bwä — *three syllables*\ }

**\ əi ** as in a pronunciation of *bird* that is widely used in greater New York City and in a strip of the deep South extending from North Carolina to Louisiana. This pronunciation is commonly represented by the letters *oi,* as in the spelling *boid* for *bird,* but the \ȯi\ suggested by this spelling is rarely or never the pronunciation actually used. In the South this pronunciation appears to be less regarded by educated speakers as one to be avoided than in the New York City area.

\əi\ does not occur as a variant of \ər\ and \ə̄\ in words having no sound after the \ər\ or \ə̄\, nor in formations based on such words — that is, \əi\ does not occur, in educated speech at least, in words like *spur, spurred, spurring, furry.* Nor does \əi\ occur in educated speech as a variant of \ər\ in words in which \ər\ is followed by a vowel, as *hurry, flourish.*

**\ ᵊl ** the usual sound of the *le* of *battle* and *muddle,* of the *al* of *vital,* of the *el* of *model* and *funnel,* of the *ile* of *futile.* The \ᵊ\ is a diacritic and \ᵊl\ is a single sound, not two, an \l\ sound that serves as the nearest thing to a vowel in its syllable. Especially on formal occasions and with speakers not fully sure of themselves the two sounds \əl\ do sometimes occur instead of \ᵊl\. The \əl\ variant is usually not shown. When a word ending in \t\, \d\, or \n\ precedes without pause, words shown as beginning \əl-\ (as *allow, alone*) may have \ᵊl-\ instead, as in *not alone.*

**\ ᵊm ** often heard for the words *'em* and *and* when \p\, \b\, or \v\ precedes, as in *stop 'em, grab 'em, save 'em, up and down, rub and buff, stove and poker.* A preceding \v\ may be assimilated to \b\, as in the third and sixth examples above; if the \v\ remains \v\, the \ᵊm\ articulation is lip-teeth rather than lip-lip. \vᵊm\ and \bᵊm\ are also often heard for the *ven* of words like *seven* and *eleven* and for the *vernm* of *government.* The \ᵊ\ is a diacritic and \ᵊm\ is a single sound, not two, an \m\ sound that serves as the nearest thing to a vowel in its syllable. The two sounds \əm\ are not heard as a variant for \ᵊm\ when the orthographic correlate is *n* (*government* is not an exception because the orthographic correlate there is *m* not *n,* the first \n\ being lost possibly through the dissimilatory influence of the second \n\). When a word ending in \p\, \b\, or \m\ precedes without pause, words shown in the vocabulary as beginning \əm-\ sometimes have \ᵊm-\ instead, as in *save ammonia.*

**\ ᵊn ** as the usual *an* of *Satan* and *en* of *wooden.* The \ᵊ\ is a diacritic and \ᵊn\ is a single sound, not two, an \n\ sound that serves as the nearest thing to a vowel in its syllable. Especially on formal occasions and with speakers not fully sure of themselves the two sounds \ən\ do sometimes occur instead of \ᵊn\. The \ən\ variant is usually not shown. When a word ending in \d\ or \t\ precedes without pause, words shown as beginning \ən-\, \əṅ-\, or \in\ (as *announce, engage*) may have \ᵊn\ instead, as in *made announcements, can't engage.*

**\ ᵊŋ ** sometimes heard as a variant for vowel plus \n\ or \ŋ\ when \k\ or \g\ precedes and somewhat more often when \k\ or \g\ also follows, as in *chicken coop, breaking ground, dog and gun.* The \ᵊ\ is a diacritic and \ᵊŋ\ is a single sound, not two, an \ŋ\ sound that serves as the nearest thing to a vowel in its syllable. When a word ending in \k\ or \g\ precedes without pause, words shown as beginning \əṅk-\ or \əṅg-\ sometimes have \ᵊŋk\ or \ᵊŋg\ instead, as in *break engagements, big encouragement.*

**\ ər ** (see also the section on \ər·, ə·r\) when in a syllable bearing either of the stresses ˈ ˌ, and when word-final or followed by a consonant sound, \ər\ is the sound used by *r*-keepers for the *ir* of *stir,* the *ear* of *search,* or the *ir* of *circularity.* When the \ə\ of \ər\ is not preceded by a stress mark, \ər\ is the sound used by *r*-keepers for the *er* of *walker* and by both *r*-keepers and *r*-droppers for the *ar* of *arise,* the *er* of *veneration,* and the *er* of *bakery* when that word is pronounced in three syllables and not two.

Many transcribers regard what we transcribe as \ər\ as a single sound (stressed or unstressed) and use a single symbol instead of \r\ preceded by a vowel symbol. Such transcribers regard the articulation as a single one in which the body of the tongue is in the position for some such vowel as \ə\ or \ə̄\ at the same time that the tip is in substantially the position for the sound following the \n\ in *unroll.* Even if the pronunciation that we symbolize \ər\ is one sound, there appears to be no great objection to transcribing it as if the components of the articulation were successive rather than simultaneous, and such a transcription is now the usual practice of many linguists in this country. Such a practice makes it possible to show both the *r*-keepers' and the *r*-droppers' pronunciation of a word like *winner* by merely parenthesizing the \r\, thus: \ˈwinə(r)\.* Furthermore, it is by no means sure that, if \ər\ is a single sound, it is the only such sound in English: *arc* may be just as much a two-sound word as *irk.*

**\ ər·, ə·r ** used in words in which \ə\ is stressed and a vowel immediately follows the \r\. The first of the two transcriptions is also used at the end of words, since any word is capable of being followed by a vowel-initial word.

\ər·\ with a vowel sound following is the same sound as that written without the centered dot when a consonant sound follows — that is, it is the sound used by *r*-keepers for the *ir* of *bird* or the *irre* of *stirred.* It is also the sound used by *r*-keepers for the *irr* of *stirring* (most U.S. *r*-droppers have the same sound in this word, a smaller number have \ə̄r\) and by *r*-keepers for the *ir* of *Sir Albert* (some U.S. *r*-droppers have the same sound, some say \sə̄ˈalbət\, and fewer say \sə̄ˈralbət\, the usual pronunciation in southern British speech, as is \ə̄r\ for *stirring*). \ər·\ is also the pronunciation used by most *r*-keepers for the *urr* of *hurry* and the *our* of *courage,* words that differ from the linguistic items *stirring* and *Sir Albert* in not being composed of two meaningful English units.

Most U.S. *r*-droppers, speakers of southern British, and *r*-keepers in some areas of the U.S. pronounce the *urr* of *hurry* and the *our* of *courage* in a way that we transcribe \ə·r\. Whatever it is that we represent by the \ə\ and the \r\ is in the same syllable: the syllable division occurs after the \r\. But in the pronunciation that we represent \ə·r\ the \ə\ and the \r\ seem very definitely to be distributed between successive syllables. Therefore, we have made the distinction between the two by a difference in the placement of the centered period, a syllable-boundary indicator. One of the most expected places for the occurrence of the \ə·r\ pronunciation is in the circus barker's spiel "Hurry! Hurry! Hurry!" where, it seems likely, \ə·r\ is used even by speakers who ordinarily have \ər·\ in such words. This sound may be produced by saying the first two sounds of *hum* without sounding the \m\ and then adding the first two sounds of *react.*

In transcriptions of uncommon words rhyming with *stir,* like *claqueur* \klaˈkər(·)\, the parenthesized period means that the period is to be omitted when a consonant or a pause follows (as in \klaˈkərz\ *claqueurs*) but is to be retained, without the parentheses, when a vowel sound follows without pause (as in \əklaˈkər·əṅthə-ˈbalkənē\ *a claqueur in the balcony*). \-ˈkə·rəṅ-\ for this last phrase would be a pronunciation that does not ordinarily occur in educated standard speech.

In words as common as *hurry* both the \ər·\ and the \ə·r\ variant are shown, in the expectation that it will be chiefly in the more frequent words that phonetic detail will be sought in this book. But for a word having as little currency among nonspecialists as *gurry* the transcription is shown simply as \ˈgərē\, since either of two likely interpretations placed on the \ər\ will be acceptable.

In words like *stirring, burry,* formed by adding an active vowel or vowel-initial suffix to words of the type *stir,* the \ə·r\ variant is not usually heard, although it appears to be an occasional, and the usual British, variant of the noun *furrier* and a rare variant of *furry* (and therefore of the comparative adjective *furrier*) in British speech. In words of the type *occurrence,* which are from, or which parallel words existing in, a foreign language, notably Latin, and which if formed in English were formed by using a suffix now relatively inactive in English, an \ə·r\ variant is quite regular with speakers who have \ə·r\ in *hurry.*

**\ əu̇ ** as in one pronunciation of *bulb* — see section on \l\.

**\ əw ** this succession of symbols followed by a vowel symbol (as in \ˈstrenyəwəs\ for *strenuous,* \ˌsichəˈwāshən\ for *situation*) occurs instead of the \u̇\ or \ō\ followed by a vowel that is employed by a number of transcribers. The starting point in the reasoning that led to a decision to use \əw\ was a very strong conviction that the members, or that the shorter member and a part of the longer member, of such pairs as the following are exact rhymes (some of the words and names below are made up and some of the combinations are nonsensical):

silhouette
Scylla wet
Genoese
Jenna Weeze
Manuella
Manya Weller
Halloween
Valhalla wean
willowy Ona
Willa Weona
habituate
bitch a wait
Venezuela
Venn is a weal (or *wale*)

Granting the homophony of the members of those pairs, without any attempt to explore the phonetics of the matter, we transcribe \əw\ for the following two reasons: (1) Transcribers have been unanimous, or nearly so, in using \ə\ and \w\ in transcriptions of items of the sort we have shown in each pair as the second member, but the same transcriber ordinarily uses \u̇\ when the spelling has *u* and \ō\ when the spelling has *o.* If homophony is granted, then it must be that transcribers are using two symbols (\u̇\ and \ō\) for what is really the same sound or succession of sounds. Such variation violates one of the most fundamental tenets of transcription. (2) If we decide to transcribe *silhouette* and

*Parenthesizing of \r\ after a vowel in a stressed syllable will in most cases not yield the *r*-droppers' pronunciation.

Scylla wet both \silu̇et\ or \silōet\ rather than \siləwet\, then providing variant transcriptions at both words of the type *Scylla* and words of the type *wet* that will take care of their pronunciation in isolation and their pronunciation in succession, with the *w*-initial word second, is a task so formidable as to be prohibitive. If we transcribe both *silhouette* and *Scylla wet* with \əw\, however, then the transcription for *Scylla* and for *wet* in isolation is also the transcription for them in succession in that order. Thus only at words of the type *follow* and *value* must variants be provided for isolation and succession differences where a variant in \-əw\ is provided to take care of the usual or a common pronunciation in items like *following, follow up, valuer, value alteration.*

**\ a ** as in *hat, gap, has-been, have-not;* some speakers have \a\ also in one, two, or all of the three words *hash, hang, ask*. Other speakers have in *hash* and *ask* a vowel that we symbolize \aa\ or \aaə\; they have the latter vowel also in *halve* and in the emphatic pronunciation of the verb *can*, words which may be distinct from the emphatic form of *have* and from the noun *can* ("container"), the latter two having \a\. Other speakers have in *hash, hang, ask* a vowel that we symbolize \ai\; they also have the latter vowel in *halve* and, if the word is in their vocabulary, probably also in *salvy*, words which if so pronounced are distinct in the vocabulary of most from the emphatic form of *have* and from *savvy*, the latter two usually having \a\. Still other speakers have in *ask* a vowel that we symbolize \ȧ\; they also usually have the latter vowel in one or more of the words *halve, heart, salvy*, words which then are distinct from the emphatic form of *have*, from *hat*, and from *savvy*, the latter three having \a\. See the sections on \aa(ə)\, \ai\, and \ȧ\.

The sound in the vowel of *hat* may vary according to the dialect, but our symbol for all varieties is \a\. To speakers who have \aa(ə)\ in their vocabulary the vowel used in *hat* in other dialects may sound to them like or much like their \aa(ə)\. The \a\ of speakers whose vocabulary includes both \a\ and \aa(ə)\ may sound to speakers of other dialects like or much like \ȧ\. The vowel of *hat* in Scottish dialect is a sound that has a quality like that often heard for the *ear* of *heart* in eastern New England or southern British speech or for the *o* of *hot* in most U.S. speech (that is, that has an \ȧ\ or \ä\ quality) but that is always very short. For the Scottish vowel, a symbol different from that for the standard vowel of *hat* is often employed in dictionaries. However, since the standard-English vowel of *hat* does not occur in the type of Scottish transcribed in this dictionary and it and the Scottish vowel of *hat* are not in contrast, there is no necessity for using a different symbol to transcribe the Scottish sound. The speaker of Scottish will use the sound natural to him in *hat* when he sees \a\ in a transcription, just as the American and the southern Englishman each interprets \ō\ for the vowel of *toe* in his own way, although their vowels are usually markedly different.

**\ ā ** as the vowel of *day, fade, date, aorta*, when emphatic usually more diphthongal in British speech than in most American speech. When it is a diphthong, the second element is \i\ and the first element is either the vowel of *debt* or the vowel used in *day* when that vowel is a monophthong.

**\ ä ** as used in *cot* and *cod* by those who pronounce these words differently from *caught* and *cawed*. The quality of the vowel of *cot* and *cod* varies, in length and in quality. In southern British speech, it is consistently short but in the U.S. may be quite long, especially before a voiced consonant. The vowel of most southern Englishmen and of many eastern New Englanders is pronounced with the tongue higher and further back and with the lips more rounded than the vowel of the average American, to whom the others' vowel may sound more like that of his *caught* or *cawed*. Our symbol \ä\ is to be interpreted as covering all varieties of vowel used in the English-speaking world for the vowel of *cot* and *cod* by speakers who pronounce these words differently from *caught* and *cawed*. Although this vowel is more often spelled with *o* in English than with any other letter, we use \ä\ rather than \o\ or an *o*-based character in our transcription for this reason: We must be able to show that in the speech of most or many Americans the first two italicized items in each of the groups of three below are identical in sound and that the third item in each group consists of the same sounds in the same order but with the additional sound \r\ present immediately after the vowel under discussion:

*Fother*gill	*bock* beer
father	*Bach*
farther	*bark*
bomb	*mock*
balm	*mach*
barm	*mark*

The first two orthographies in each group show that either \a\ or \o\ with or without a diacritic would be a symbol with precedent in English orthography for the words without *r* in the spelling or \r\ in the pronunciation. For this last class of words, however, \a\ is a better symbol than \o\ because \o\ before an \r\ suggests the vowel of *cord* rather than of *card*.

When one transcribes, as sound transcriptional practice requires, on the principle of one symbol to a sound, it is impossible to have all transcriptions of a language as orthographically lawless as English look right. A vowel with an articulatory position as far forward as that of *fair* and *fare* is usually represented orthographically by *a* or a letter group containing *a* and has traditionally been represented in transcriptions by \a\ with a diacritic over it. On the other hand, a vowel with an articulatory position as far back as that of *all* and *saw* is often represented orthographically by *a* or a letter group containing *a* and is represented in some pronunciation systems by \a\ with a diacritic over it. The use of \a\ with a diacritic over it to represent a vowel with an in-between articulatory position should therefore occasion no surprise. In a phonetic alphabet widely used by American linguists today, the vowel of *cot* is \a\. In the alphabet of the International Phonetic Association, which is used by many transcribers of American speech, the symbol used for the vowel in this word is one that resembles a script or italic *a* or Greek alpha.

For any who may require in their transcribing a symbol for the unrounded vowel that occurs in *cot* and a symbol for the rounded vowel that occurs in the same word and is distinct from the vowel of *caught*, we suggest \ä\ for the unrounded vowel and \o\ for the rounded. It was common practice in dictionaries, and is still the practice in some dictionaries, to use symbols for four distinct vowels in the range from front \ȧ\ to back \ȯ\ — symbols equivalent to \ȧ\, \ä\, \o\, and \ȯ\ respectively. Although there may be dialects of English in which a distinction is consistently made between four classes of words on the basis of four vowels representable by \ȧ\, \ä\, \o\, and \ȯ\, we have no reason to believe that there are speakers enough who make such a distinction to justify its notice in our dictionary. Perhaps a knowledge that the usual or a frequent British vowel and the usual American vowel in *cot* are different accounts for some American transcribers' employing four symbols rather than three. The desideratum in the formulation of a phonetic alphabet, however, is not the provision of a one-character symbol for every minute shade of sound but the provision of the barest minimum necessary to represent the distinctions consistently made in the speech of any one speaker. For distinctions any finer than this, the phonetician may use modifiers. When the explanation is made that \ä\ is the vowel of *cot*, whatever the quality of that vowel may be; that any whose vowel (in *cart*, for example, in the speech of *r*-droppers) is consistently between that of *cot* and the further-forward and higher vowel of *cat* have a vowel that we symbolize \ȧ\; that any whose vowel (in *caught* or *quart*, for example) is consistently between that of *cot* and the further-back and higher vowel of *coat* have a vowel that we symbolize \ȯ\, we have provided symbols enough to transcribe all the vowel distinctions that most speakers make in this range.

Of the best-known dialects of English, none appears to have more than three vowels in this range, and some appear to have only two. Any who may have concluded from the presence in southern British of a rounded vowel in *cot* which is distinct from the unrounded vowel of *cart* and from the even more rounded vowel of *caught* that there are four vowels between \a\ and \ō\ should observe that Daniel Jones and Henry Wyld transcribe only three. The number of such words that are phonetically distinct in southern British probably does not differ materially from the number that are distinct in the speech of U.S. *r*-keepers who do not level pairs like *cot* and *caught*. Such U.S. speakers make no distinction between such words as *Spaak* and *Spock* but southern British speakers make no distinction between such words as *Spaak* and *spark*. It seems likely that the mistaking of one word for another in this group is greater than average. If so, an explanation is to be sought not merely in the fact that some speakers have two vowels instead of the three of other speakers but also in the fact that with speakers who have the same number of vowels the distribution of the vowels is subject to much variation, as was just illustrated in the words *Spaak, Spock*, and *spark*. Ordinary words known in all dialects cause little difficulty, for the same reason that such identically pronounced words as *meet* and *meat* seldom cause difficulty: the context in nearly every case leaves the hearer in no doubt as to what word the speaker is using. But unknown or little-known words — surnames and the names of small geographical entities, for example — can sometimes cause perplexity.

In our transcriptions we have attempted to use only the minimum number of symbols required to show the distinctions that occur in any one major dialect of English. Since the discussion that follows involves the comparative phonetics of a group of words showing a high degree of variation and overlapping in some of the major dialects of English, we will use symbolizations that do not occur in the dictionary. Those that do we will enclose in lightface square brackets rather than in our usual reverse slant lines. [ȧ] represents a vowel that has a tongue position somewhat lower and further back than \a\; it is the vowel usually heard in *part* and usually or often heard in *pass* in eastern New England speech. [ä] is the vowel that the majority of Americans use in *pot*. [o] is the vowel that is used in southern British speech in *pot*. It differs from the usual American vowel in the same word in being pronounced with the lips rounded and often or usually in having a tongue position slightly higher and further back. [ȯ] is the vowel used in the first syllable of *order* and in *sawed* by speakers with whom *sawed* and *sod* are distinct. Doubling a vowel symbol indicates a lengthening of the sound it represents; [oo] indicates a vowel of the same quality as [o] but longer; [oo] does not represent the vowel of *hoot* or *hook*.

Such pairs as *order : ardor, born : barn*, in which a consonant sound immediately follows whatever pronunciation is given the *or* or *ar*, are no more than sporadically leveled in any well-known dialect. There appears to be some leveling in the Southern Mountain dialect and perhaps in Utah. In a section of southern Illinois the first part of the word *Borneo* is pronounced exactly like *barn*. Speakers of the dialects of the Atlantic and Gulf coasts and of Texas, from New York City to El Paso, in which [o] occurs with some frequency in the first syllable of *ardor* and in *barn*, with or without an \r\ following the vowel, are apt to be misunderstood as pronouncing *order* and *born* instead by the speakers of dialects in which *ardor* and *barn* have [ä] or [ȧ]; but the percentage of misunderstandings appears to be no higher when both speaker and listener have the same distinction than in the case of other vowel pairs equally close in articulation.

With the majority of American speakers, such pairs as *Mahler : Moller, father : Fother*gill, *Brahms : Brom's, khaki : cocky* (when the *a* of *khaki* is not \a\), and *Bach's : box* (when the *ch* of *Bach's* is not \k̲\) are exact rhymes. When they are, the vowel of both is usually [ä], but in Southern Mountain speech may be [o]. These two vowels are represented by \ä\ in our dictionary transcriptions.

In some dialects of English (especially those in which *r*-dropping occurs, as eastern New England, southern Coastal, southern British, and New York City), the vowels of such pairs are usually or often not homophonous. The stressed vowel of *Mahler* may be [ȧ] (as in eastern New England and southern British), a vowel articulated further forward in the mouth than the stressed vowel of *Moller*, lacking the rounding that usually or often accompanies the vowel of *Moller*, and in southern British at least usually longer than that vowel. The vowel of *Mahler* may be [ää] or [äə] (as in southern Coastal and New York City), a vowel having the same quality at the beginning as the vowel of *Moller* but appreciably longer because of prolongation or because of the presence of a slight [ə] off-glide at the end. The vowel of *Mahler* may be [oo] (as also in southern Coastal and New York City), a vowel with the quality of [o], the rounded vowel heard in southern British *not*, but longer. All of these three vowels or vowel characteristics that make the stressed vowel of *Mahler* distinct from the stressed vowel of *Moller* are symbolized in the dictionary pronunciations by \ȧ\. If only southern Coastal and New York City speech were being transcribed, the vowel of *Mahler*, when it differs from that of *Moller*, could very well be transcribed as \ää\. This could be made to provide for the [oo] variant as well by an explanation that lengthened \ä\ is often accompanied by rounding. That *Mahler* and *Moller* are sometimes homophonous and sometimes not could be shown by the transcriptions \ˈmä(ä)lə(r)\ and \ˈmälə(r)\ respectively. Speakers of dialects in which the stressed vowel of *Mahler* is [oo] may easily be misunderstood by hearers not familiar with the dialect as saying *mauler* instead of *Mahler*. Whether within such dialects the stressed vowels of *Mahler, mauler*, and *Morley* are ever completely leveled is doubtful. With southern speakers who have [oo] in *Mahler*, the stressed vowel of *mauler* (but not, it appears, that of *Morley*) is often a diphthong [ȯu̇], acoustically quite distinct from [oo].

In *r*-keeping speech pairs like *Spaak : spark* are distinct because one member contains an \r\ and the other does not. In *r*-dropping speech such pairs usually are homophones, but sometimes in such speech *Spaak* goes with *Spock* rather than with *spark*, as it does in most *r*-keeping speech. Our symbol for the vowel of *Spaak* when it is homophonous with that of *Spock* is \ä\; for the vowel of *Spaak* when it is not homophonous with that of *Spock*, \ȧ\.

In *r*-keeping speech pairs like *spark : Spock, Farley : folly, harmony : hominy* are distinct because one member contains an \r\ and the other does not. In some such dialects (as Middle Atlantic and the *r*-keeping speech of Texas), the vowel of *spark* is apt to be rounded (['spork]) whereas the vowel of *Spock* is apt to be unrounded (['späk)]), but we can transcribe \ˈspärk\ and \ˈspäk\ and explain that \ä\ followed by \r\ may be rounded. Such an explanation holds both for words like *spark*, in which a consonant follows the \r\, and for words like *moral* and *horrid*, in which a vowel follows the \r\.

In some *r*-dropping dialects (as eastern New England and southern British) a pretty consistent qualitative distinction is made between the vowels of *spark* and *Spock*, and often in addition a quantitative or durational distinction as well. If the quantitative difference is lacking, the qualitative one sets the words apart. (Incidentally, the eastern New England vowel of *spark* is usually markedly different in quality from the southern British vowel in the same word, \ȧ\ standing in the former for a vowel much closer to that of *cat* and \ȧ\ being in the latter a vowel much the same in quality, and often in quantity also, as the vowel that most Americans have in *cot*.) Although some American phoneticians have observed that the southern British vowel in *cot* does not always have the rounding that the writings and transcriptions of British phoneticians seem to claim for it, the extent of the leveling of *spark* and *Spock* is beyond much question not as great as in the dialects next discussed.

With *r*-dropping speakers (as in the coastal Southern states and in New York City) who never have more than a quantitative difference between the vowels of *spark* and *Spock*, this difference of duration frequently breaks down, with the resultant homophony of such pairs. Some who have written on this type of leveling attribute it to a lengthening of the [ä] of the *r*-less member of the pair, chiefly before voiced consonants, the tendency to lengthening being greater before these than before voiceless consonants. But the leveling may be due also to a shortening of the vowel of *spark*. The tendency of a vowel to be short in duration increases with its distance from the last syllable of a word, and such words at least as *harmony* and *hominy*, in which the [ä] is in the third syllable from the end, both sometimes have a fairly short [ä] and are homophonous. Such leveling is not indicated in our transcription. A variant \ä\ is to be understood as occurring with varying frequency for all words transcribed with the variants \är\ and \ȧ\ (in uncommon words, with \är\ only) before a consonant. Our omission of the third variant does not mean that we regard the variant as substandard but rather reflects the uncertainty that exists as to the extent of the variation.

In some areas (as western Pennsylvania, eastern New England, and parts of the Far West) the members of such pairs as *cod : cawed, rot : wrought* may have the same vowel, or may undergo a range of variation from [ä] through [o] to [ȯ]. In *r*-dropping dialects, as that of eastern New England, such leveling may extend not merely to *cod* and *cawed* but to *cord* as well. *Card* and *cord* probably are not leveled to any great extent, although, as pointed out earlier, the vowel of *card* has some degree of rounding in some dialects. For a transcription of the speech of *r*-keepers who level *cod : cawed*, but not *card : cawed*, two symbols (as \ä\ and \ȯ\) are necessary in the range between \a\ and \ō\ to take care of the *card : cawed* distinction. For a transcription of the speech of *r*-droppers who level *cod : cawed : cord*, two symbols (as \ȧ\ and \ä\ or \ȧ\ and \o\ or \ȧ\ and \ȯ\) are necessary in the range between \a\ and \ō\ to take care of the distinction between *card* and *cod : cawed : cord*. For any speakers who may level *card : cord* as well as *cod : cawed*, only one symbol (\ȧ\ or \ä\ or \o\ or \ȯ\) is necessary in the range between \a\ and \ō\.

The leveling of words like *cod* and of words like *cawed* and *cord* is not transcribed after the entry words. We have refrained from transcribing it in order to simplify the transcriptions. Users of the pronunciations are to understand that the symbol \ȯ\ and the symbol \ä\, when the latter corresponds to the letter *o* in the spelling (as in *cod*), or corresponds to the letter *a* in the spelling and is preceded by the sound \w\ or \y\ and is not followed by the sound \r\ plus a consonant (as in *watch, yacht, warrant* but not in *yarn*), are merely, as far as certain dialects are concerned, two symbols for the same sound.

A further complication is the fact that the first vowel of *utter* in southern British speech is usually more like the usual American [ä] in *otter* than the usual American first vowel in *utter*, so that in an ambiguous context an Englishman's *utter* is apt to be heard by an American as *otter*.

**\ ȧ ** as any of several phonetically different vowel sounds that in the speech of *r*-droppers make *card* distinct from *cad* on the one hand and from *cod* on the other, or from *cod* on the one hand and from *cawed* on the other.

In the speech typical of eastern New England and southern England, the vowel transcribed \ȧ\ at *card* is articulatorily between the \a\ of *cad* and the \ä\ of *cod*. The New England vowel is closer to the vowel of *cad* than is the British vowel. In both eastern New England and southern British speech \ȧ\ is usual or frequent in a small group of words that have come to be known as the *ask* words. In all but a few words of this group, the vowel, orthographically *a* or *au*, is followed by one of the voiceless fricatives \f\, \s\, \th\, or by \m\ or \n\ plus a consonant. They are more often pronounced by American speakers with \a\ or (with a few exceptions, at least for \ai\) \aa(ə)\ or \ai\.

In one kind of *r*-dropping speech heard in the southeastern U.S. and in New York City, the vowel transcribed \ȧ\ at *card* is the same in quality as the vowel transcribed \ä\ at *cod* but usually of greater duration (see the statement about exceptions at the section on \ä\). Some transcribers treat the greater duration as a prolongation of the \ä\ sound, others as a diphthongization of the \ä\ sound to \äə\. In the South, with the exception of a small area of coastal Virginia, \ȧ\ occurs in the *ask* words only in conscious imitation of the speech of areas in which its use is natural. Its occurrence in New York City is also chiefly imitative, but *aunt* and *rather* have \ȧ\ (or \ä\) with some frequency. Because any word for which only an \a\ pronunciation is shown in this book may with many New York City speakers have a vowel of a quality like that of eastern New England \ȧ\, this latter vowel is perhaps to be regarded as merely a nonsignificant variant of \a\ in their speech.

In another kind of *r*-dropping speech heard in the southeastern U.S. and in New York City, the vowel transcribed \ȧ\ at *card* is articulatorily between that of *cod* and that of *cawed*. Speakers with whom the \ȧ\ is of such quality do not have \ȧ\ in the *ask* words. Any New York City speakers who may use in the *ask* words a vowel of the quality that is transcribed \ȧ\ for other dialects are to be regarded as using a nonsignificant variety of \a\. See the preceding paragraph.

Some transcribers use the symbol \ȧ\ for the vowel of most Scottish speakers in words which in most dialects are pronounced with \a\, \aa(ə)\, or \ai\, as *cat, man, bag*. This Scottish vowel is of much the same quality as eastern New England \ȧ\ but usually markedly shorter. We use for it the symbol \a\. See the section on \a\.

See also the section on \ä\.

**\ aa \, \ aaə ** chiefly in what is known as the Middle Atlantic region, an area that has New York City and Washington, D.C. on its perimeter. This vowel occurs in one or more of the following groups of words:

(1) words like *bare, fair*, and *Sayre*.

(2) words like *Cary, hairy, vary*, in which typically the sound \r\ represented by a single *r* in the spelling is followed by a vowel sound and is preceded by a vowel sound whose orthographic representation is *a* or a vowel sequence containing *a*. With speakers who have \aa(ə)\ in these words the members of the following groups are usually or often distinct: *Cary, carry, Kerry; hairy, Harry; vary, very*.

(3) words like *sail, sailor, Haley*, which in other dialects usually contain the sequence \āl\ or (when not immediately followed by a vowel sound) \āəl\. With speakers who have \aa(ə)l\ in these words, *barely* and *Bailey* may be exact rhymes. \aa(ə)\ in this group of words is reported to be less frequent among cultivated speakers.

(4) most words that have in other dialects the vowel \a\ or \ai\ in the last syllable immediately followed by one of the following consonants:

\b\, \d\, \g\, \j\
\f\, \v\, \th\, \t͟h\, \s\, \z\, \sh\
\m\, \n\

When a suffix is added to such words, the vowel usually remains the same, except that the \ə\ final element is usually lost. Before some of the above consonants or some consonant groups of which one of the above is the first member, \aa\ also occurs in syllables that are not final without the help of a suffix addition. The consonants just shown are classified into three groups as an aid to the memory. The first group consists of voiced stops (\j\ is actually a double sound, \d\ + \zh\, the first constituent of which is a voiced stop), the second group consists of voiced and unvoiced fricatives (\zh\ is not listed because there is no fully English word that ends in \aa(ə)zh\), and the third group consists of two of the three nasal consonants. With speakers who have \aa(ə)\ in these words, the vowel of *cab* is readily perceived as markedly different from the vowel of *cap* (although those who do not have \aa(ə)\ may have trouble hearing the distinction); *can* ("container" or "to put in a container") may be distinct from the emphatic form of *can* ("to be able"), and *halve* may be distinct from the emphatic form of *have*, in that the first member of each pair has \aa(ə)\ whereas the second has \a\; *fad* and *fared* when they are identical in stress may be exact rhymes.

In accord with our system of doubling a symbol to indicate duration, \aa\ is longer than \a\. In one variant it is of substantially the same quality as \a\, in a second and possibly commoner variant it is formed with a higher tongue position than \a\ (approaching the tongue position for \e\), and in a third and comparatively infrequent variant it is \ȧ\ (see section on \ȧ\). Sometimes \aa\ is followed by a distinct \ə\ off-glide, indicated by three transcriptions \aa\, \aa(ə)\, \aaə\. When the \ə\ is present, it is the overall length of the diphthong that distinguishes or helps to distinguish the vowel from \a\, but to indicate that what we transcribe \aa\ is longer when the \aa\ is a monophthong than when it is the first part of a diphthong would unnecessarily complicate the transcription.*

**\ ää ** as the sound \ä\ when it is appreciably long in duration and is distinct from the shorter \ä\ for the reason that both may occur in the same environment. Thus, the German words *Stadt* and *Staat*, in the dialect of German usually regarded as standard, consist of the sounds \sh\, \t\, a vowel of \ä\ quality, and \t\, but the \ä\ in *Stadt* is not as long as the \ä\ in *Staat*. In our system the German pronunciations are transcribed \ˈshtät\ and \ˈshtäät\ respectively. When such foreign words are pronounced in an English context by one whose native language is English, the durational difference is often lost.

Although the [ä] : [ää] difference in duration serves to distinguish otherwise identical words, as *cod* and *card*, in the *r*-dropping dialects of the southeastern U.S. and New York City, we do not employ [ää] in our symbolization of this difference. In *r*-dropping English speech as a whole there are several values of the vowel spelled *ar* in *card* that make that word distinct from *cod*, and all of these values, including [ää], are subsumed under the symbol \ȧ\.

**\ a(a)(ə) ** \e(ə)\ is to be understood as a variant when it does not appear in a vocabulary transcription, as at *cudbear*.

**\ aa^{n} ** as the sound of the *ein* in the French pronunciation of French *enceinte* — that is, a lengthened \a^{n}\. See section on \$^{n}$\.

**\ ää^{n} ** as the sound of the *ande* in the French pronunciation of French *bande* — that is, a lengthened \ä^{n}\. See section on \$^{n}$\.

**\ a(a)rV ** \erV\ and \ārV\ are to be understood as variants when they do not appear in a vocabulary transcription, as at *myaria*.

accentuation see the section on stress marks.

**\ ai ** articulated as a tense monophthong with the tongue higher than for \a\ or as a diphthong having approximately the beginning and ending limits indicated by the \ai\ transcription. Although using the two-symbol transcription is more convenient than devising another diacritic, the sound is in its less emphatic utterances at least a monophthong.

It occurs before some but not all of the consonants listed in classification (4) in the section on \aa\ and \aaə\; it does not occur in words that belong to the other three classifications there; and it occurs before one consonant not listed in any of the four classifications there — the nasal \ŋ\. The occurrence of \ai\ in the dialect of a native of southern Illinois compares as follows with the occurrence of \aa(ə)\ : \ai\ is almost invariable before \g\ even in syllables far removed from the last but does not occur before \b\ and \j\ and occurs before \d\ only in a few words (*bad, glad, mad*), chiefly when they are emphatic. \ai\ occurs before \f\, \v\, \th\, \t͟h\, and \s\ chiefly in final and near-final syllables (as in *half, bath, baths*, the variant \ˈshaivz\ of *shafts*, and *pass*) and before \sh\ even in syllables distant from the last (as in *passionate*); it does not occur before \z\ (in *jazz* for instance) nor in emphatic *have* or *has to*. \ai\ does not occur before \m\ or \n\ when one of these is the only consonant that follows (as in *ram, ran*, except that *man* may have \ai\ when it is emphatic, as in the interjectional phrase "Man oh man!") but it does occur before certain consonant sequences of which \m\ or \n\ is the first member (as in *sample, answer*). Before \ŋ\, \ai\ may occur in any syllable whereas \aa(ə)\ appears not to occur before \ŋ\ at all. In some parts of the southern U.S., particularly in uncultivated speech, the incidence of \ai\ seems to be wider than in the speech just described.

Precisely what the phonetic relationship is between \aa(ə)\ and \ai\ is uncertain. If both are diphthongs in their maximum-stress occurrences, then the difference in the ending positions of the diphthongs (\ə\ in one case, \i\ in the other) constitutes a distinction. If both vowels are in some of their occurrences monophthongs, then the difference is not so palpable. Both are fairly long vowels, and length therefore is an unlikely basis of difference. With some speakers \aa\ is of the same quality and tongue height as \a\ but longer, whereas with speakers who have \ai\, that vowel is always higher than the speaker's \a\ during all or a part of its articulation — *all* if \ai\ is a monophthong, *a part* if \ai\ is a diphthong. When one adds to this the fact that the \a\ (as in *cap*) of many Middle Atlantic speakers is an appreciably different vowel from the \a\ (as in *cap*) of speakers in most of the rest of the country, it is obvious that \aa\ must often be a quite different vowel from monophthongal \ai\. The \a\ in *cap* of many Middle Atlantic speakers is obviously a vowel with considerable \ȧ\ coloration in it. Speakers in other parts of the country use in *cap* a vowel that is much the same in quality (if not in length) as the monophthongal variety of \aa\ vowel in *cast*. Before certain consonants and with some speakers, the Middle Atlantic vowel that we transcribe \aa\ may be the same as the vowel that we transcribe \ai\. Since the words in which \aa(ə)\ is used instead of \a\ and \ai\ is used instead of \a\ are far from being always the same, it would cause difficulty to try to make only one of these two symbols do the work of both in a given transcription.

There are even fewer pairs of words that are distinguished solely by the difference between \a\ and \ai\ than there are pairs that are distinguished solely by the difference between \a\ and \aa(ə)\. In the speech of some *halve* is usually distinct from emphatic *have* and *salvy* from *savvy* in that the first member of each pair

*This account is based to a large extent on that of Allan F. Hubbell in his *Pronunciation of English in New York City* (1950) but he is in no way responsible for our interpretation of his data.

has \ai\ and the second \a\. The same is probably true of the pair *bad : bade* in the speech of many.

\ äi\, \ ȧi in the dictionary we have shown no pronunciation for the present participle of the few verbs which have as a final sound \ä\ or \ȧ\ (as *sol-fa*), with the implication that the transcription if shown would be \-äiŋ\, \-ȧiŋ\, \-äəŋ\, \-ȧəŋ\. Since, as stated in the section on \ī\, the first component of the diphthong represented \ī\ is usually \ä\ or \ȧ\ and the second component is or may be \i\, the question arises as to whether the vowel sequence immediately preceding the \ŋ\ of such present participles may not be identical with the sequence in *fine*. For the reasons stated in the section on \ȯi\, random-listening evidence on this matter is difficult to come by. When the last syllable of a verb ending in \ä\ or \ȧ\ is under primary stress (as in *hurrahing*), the \ä\ or \ȧ\ usually seems longer than the \ä\ or \ȧ\ of *fine;* when the \ä\ or \ȧ\ syllable has less than primary stress (as in some utterances of *sol-faing*) the two sequences are more apt to be leveled.

**\ āl ** words transcribed with this succession of symbols, as *sail, alien*, often have \aa(ə)l\ instead in Middle Atlantic speech. The \aa(ə)l\ variant is not shown in transcriptions in the vocabulary.

**\ aⁿ ** see section on \ⁿ\.

**\ äⁿ ** see section on \ⁿ\.

anglicization see section on foreign words.

**\ ār ** occurs in the deep South and in Scotland in words like *barbarian* and *various*, and in Scotland in words like *fair*. In the dictionary \ār\ is not shown for any except Scottish words of the latter type, and is shown only for common words of the former type.

**\ au̇ ** as the sound of *ow* in *now*, *ou* in *loud*, and *ou* in *out*, and used by many instead of \al\ in some words when certain labial or velar consonants follow, as in *scalp, Ralph, album, valve, talcum.* When \au̇\ is not an alternative to \al\, the first part of the diphthong may have a range from unrounded \ä\ to \e\, the \e\ occurring especially in dialect. The in-between varieties with \a\ or \ȧ\ are commoner, and it is difficult to be sure whether one is hearing \a\ or \ȧ\ unless there is prolongation of this part of the diphthong, as in the speech of some areas. \ȧ\ or an equivalent is the symbol usually employed for the first part of the sound, but fully as good a case can be made for \a\. There may be prejudice against the use of \a\ because of the exaggerated length of this sound in the diphthong often heard in styles of Southern speech regarded by many as substandard. Such length is not a necessary concomitant of the sound in this diphthong.

In a coastal area of the southern U.S. extending from Virginia to So. Carolina and in some areas of eastern Canada, still another variety of this diphthong occurs — one in which the first element is \ə\ or \ə̄\ or \ō\. Those who have this variety in their speech have the other also, the first occurring before voiceless consonants (as in *out*) and the second before voiced consonants and finally (as in *loud, now*). Although the two varieties strike even the most untrained ear as widely different, it is not necessary to have two different symbols since their occurrence is determined by the phonetic context.

When \au̇\ is alternative to \al\, the range of \a\ is no wider than that of \a\ when it is followed by a sound other than \u̇\. Although using \au̇\ in the transcription of one class of words in which there is and of another class in which there is not a wide range of variation is not an ideal procedure, neither are the other two possibilities: (1) using \au̇\ as the alternative to \al\ but \ȧu̇\ or some other variant for words of the type *out* and *loud;* this would not as readily convey the information that the diphthong in the two classes may be identical; (2) giving the full range of at least five variants for words like *out* and *loud* but only \au̇\ when the variant is \al\. This would have made transcribing too space- and time-consuming.

Although we do not show the possibility in vocabulary pronunciations, with some speakers who have \a\ as the first element of their diphthong in *loud*, the sequence of sounds that we transcribe \al\ in some words and \au̇l\ in others, depending on the spelling, is probably actually \au̇l\ in both classes. Such pairs as *Al : owl, Cal : cowl, Hal : howel, Halley : Howley, Alice Ide : owl aside* are sometimes identical (the second member of the \l\-final pairs is subject to the intrusion of a parasitic \ə\ sound after the \u̇\, the first is not). The variety of \l\ used by most Americans outside the South in words such as those cited is known as the dark variety, in which the back of the tongue is in a position for \u̇\ or a neighboring vowel. Since the back of the tongue must reach this position before the tip makes the contact for the articulation of an \l\, the intrusion of an \u̇\ or of a closely related vowel sound seems highly probable.

The use of \au̇\ instead of \al\ before \y\, as in *medallion, Italian*, belongs chiefly to substandard speech. See section on \l\.

**\ b ** as in *baby, knob.*

**\ b̲ ** as in the Spanish pronunciation of *hablar*. Whereas for \b\ the lips are in contact and form a closure along their entire extent, for \b̲\ the lips are close together without closure.

brackets, square [ ] lightface square brackets are used in this guide instead of slant enclosures to enclose transcriptions that are phonetic rather than phonemic.

British dialect see section on foreign words.

centered period see separate section on "Divisions in Respelled Pronunciations".

**\ ch ** based on English orthography, for the sound \t\ followed by the sound \sh\ in the same syllable, as in *chin, pitcher, fixture, Christian.* The sounds that come between the two vowels in the words *cha-cha* (dance) and *hotshot* can in both cases be regarded as \t\ followed by \sh\ but as being in the same syllable in the first (\ˈchä,chä\) and distributed between the two syllables in the second (\ˈhät,shät\). If our transcription for what precedes the first vowel in *cha-cha* had been \tsh\, the transcription for *cha-cha* and *hotshot* would have been \ˈtshä·,tshä\ and \ˈhät·,shät\ respectively.

For words of the type *mention, essential,* and *provincial*, transcriptions of the type \-nshən\ and \-nshəl\ have enjoyed a long tradition in dictionaries. At least in American speech and in common words of this type \t\ almost always intrudes between the \n\ and \sh\, and we transcribe \-nchən\ and \-nchəl\.

comparatives of adjectives see sections on INFLECTED FORMS, DIVISION OF and on INFLECTED FORMS, PRONUNCIATION OF.

correctness in pronunciation

The term *correct pronunciation* is often used. Yet it is probable that many who use the term would find it difficult to give a precise and clear definition of the sense in which they use it. As every kind of correctness implies a standard of measurement, so in pronunciation it is intimately bound up with the question of standard pronunciation. It has been stated that there are certain extensive regional types of cultivated English speech that have spread far beyond the area of their local origin, as the southern British or American speech is which *r* is not dropped. It might be reasonably maintained that it would be incorrect for an educated native of London or Oxford to say \ˈask\ or to pronounce the *r* in *farm*, just as it would be incorrect for the midwestern American to say \ˈȧsk\ or \ˈfȧm\; for in both cases it is contrary to the standard which prevails in each region. From the nature of the case, when the essential facts are considered, correctness of pronunciation must be a flexible term. It is perhaps as accurate a definition as can be made to say that a pronunciation is correct when it is in actual use by a sufficient number of cultivated speakers. This is obviously elastic, depending both on knowledge — never accurately ascertainable — of the number of users, and on judgment as to the cultivation of the speakers. Mere majorities, without consideration of historical linguistic background and regional distribution, are not decisive. For example, the fact that more speakers in the English-speaking world habitually use *R* American than any other single type cannot vitiate the standing of the southern British pronunciation for the educated Englishman.

It has been frequently maintained, and more often assumed, that some single type should be looked upon as solely standard. But this is not the prevailing view of those who are familiar with the essential facts (the detailed differences of pronunciation in the different types, their historical development and relations, the various conditions — chiefly uncontrollable — which in the past have brought certain types into prominence) and who, therefore, possess that breadth of view and freedom from local prejudice that result from acquaintance with those phonetic features, often strikingly different, that have attained to approved usage in the standard types of English and other languages. The following statements are worthy of consideration:

Daniel Jones, M.A., emeritus head of the department of Phonetics, University College, London:

"I have no intention of becoming either a reformer of pronunciation or a judge who decides what pronunciations are 'good' and what are 'bad'. My aim is to observe and record accurately, and I do not believe in the feasibility of imposing one particular form of pronunciation on the English-speaking world. I take the view that people should be allowed to speak as they like. And if the public wants a standardized pronunciation, I have no doubt that some appropriate standard will evolve itself. If there are any who think otherwise, it must be left to them to undertake the invidious task of deciding what is to be approved and what is to be condemned" — from *English Pronouncing Dictionary*, N.Y., 1956, p. xvi.

"I do not consider it possible at the present time to regard any special type as 'Standard' or as intrinsically 'better' than other types." . . . "The term 'Received Pronunciation' . . . is often used to designate this type of pronunciation. This term is adopted here for want of a better. I wish it, however, to be understood that other types of pronunciation exist which may be considered equally 'good' " — from *An Outline of English Phonetics*, 8th ed., N.Y., 1956, p. 12.

A. Lloyd James, M.A., late University reader in Phonetics, School of Oriental Studies, London; linguistic adviser to the British Broadcasting Corporation; and secretary of the B.B.C. Advisory Committee on Spoken English:

"The listener who writes to ask the 'correct way' of pronouncing a word quite evidently assumes that there *is* a 'correct way'. In all these queries and criticisms there is implied the idea of a standard pronunciation. We have a standard yard, a standard pound weight, a standard sovereign, and a standard pint. The yard does not vary from Aberdeen to Plymouth, and the pint pot contains as much in Mayfair as in Bethnal Green. Unfortunately speech is not capable of rigid measurement, and there is no standard of pronunciation. Pronunciation varies from district to district, from class to class, from character to character, in proportion to the local, social, or moral difference that separates them. . . . It is quite evident that we are not entitled to conclude that there is *one* standard pronunciation, *one* and *only one* right way of speaking English. There are varieties that are acceptable throughout the country, and others that are not" — from *Broadcast English*, I., 2d ed., London, 1931, pp. 11 f.

Samuel Moore, Ph.D., late professor of English in the University of Michigan, and editor of the *Middle English Dictionary:*

"When we consider all the varieties of English spoken by those who are admitted to speak 'good English' in the different British colonies and in different parts of the United States, we must recognize that there is still no Standard Spoken English in any strict sense of the term. In every part of the English-speaking world some type of spoken English, that which is used by the educated and superior class within the community, is considered 'good English', as contrasted with the 'Vulgar English' and local dialects spoken by other classes of the community. If we use the term Standard Spoken English at all we must recognize that it is merely a convenient way of speaking of the various kinds of 'good English' that are current in various parts of the English-speaking world" — from *Historical Outlines of English Phonology and Morphology*, 1929, p. 114.

George Philip Krapp, Ph.D., late professor of English in Columbia University:

"A sufficient definition of the term standard will perhaps be found in the statement that speech is standard when it passes current in actual use among persons who must be accounted as among the conservers and representatives of the approved social traditions of a community" — from *The English Language in America*, N.Y., 1925, II, 7.

Edward S. Sheldon, late professor of Romance Languages in Harvard University, and editor of etymologies for Webster's *International*, 1909, and *New International Dictionaries*, Second Edition, 1934:

"The so-called standard language is not a fixed and infallible standard, but is itself constantly changing with the course of time, and is different in the different places where it is spoken" — from "What is a Dialect?" *Dialect Notes*, I, 287.

Otto Jespersen, late professor of English in the University of Copenhagen:

"Our chief concern will be with the normal speech of the educated class, what may be called Standard English" — from *Essentials of English Grammar*, N.Y. [1933], p. 16.

The question, what degree of uniformity exists in the various cultivated types of English speech, depends on what differences one chooses to emphasize, and what to ignore. At present all cultivated types, when well spoken, are easily intelligible to any speaker of English, and there is a very large percentage of practical identity in the speech sounds used. For example, it has been found that, in a thousand words from *The Legend of Sleepy Hollow* as they would be pronounced by a native of Rochester, N.Y., and a native of London, respectively, there are 125 words that would differ in the use of \r\, 36 in the sound of *o* as in *not*, 11 in the sound of *a* as in *ask*, and 4 in the use of the secondary accent. These four differences may be looked upon as the differences of pronunciation in the two types most noticeable to the average person, and one of these, the short *o*, might often pass unnoticed. In most other respects the same phonetic symbols would be used to represent the two types.

Since the establishment of orthoepy as a feature of English dictionaries, the standard assumed has been considerably changed, and has of necessity been made broader. While usage is still and must always be the standard, it is no longer the usage of a particular locality, since the pronunciation of no one locality can now claim admitted precedence. Nor can the pronunciation of any one person, or group of persons, be taken as a standard for all, for such pronunciation is in some cases more advanced, in others more archaic, than the average. Orthoepists of former generations are authorities for the present generation only in so far as their work agrees with good present usage.

The standard of English pronunciation, then, so far as a standard may be said to exist, is the usage that now prevails among the educated and cultured people to whom the language is vernacular; but, as shown above, since somewhat different pronunciations are used by the cultivated in different regions too large to be ignored, we must admit the fact that uniformity of pronunciation is not to be found throughout the English⸗speaking world, though there is a very large percentage of practical uniformity.

The function of a pronouncing dictionary is to record as far as possible the pronunciations prevailing in the best present usage rather than to attempt to dictate what that usage should be. In so far as a dictionary may be known and acknowledged as a faithful recorder and interpreter of such usage, so far and no farther may it be appealed to as an authority.

In the case of diverse usages of extensive prevalence, the dictionary must recognize each of them.

There is a constantly increasing body of technical terms which, being more often written than spoken, are often called "book words". For many of these no accepted usage can properly be said to exist, and their pronunciations must be determined on the analogies of words more often spoken, or according to the accepted rules of pronunciation for the languages from which they are derived.

**\ d ** as in *dried, deduce.* See section on \d·\ immediately following.

**\ d· ** when one starts from pause and utters the word *die,* the consonant is produced by breaking a closure produced by the tongue against the front of the palate, to the accompaniment of vibration of the vocal cords. When one starts from pause and utters the word *tie,* the consonant is produced by breaking the same closure but without vibration of the vocal cords. The basic difference between the two sounds is that one is voiced and the other is voiceless, and when hearing conditions are not unfavorable, the two can usually be easily enough distinguished without the help of context. In the pronunciation of the *dd* of *ladder* and of the *tt* of *latter* used by some speakers (British, most consistently), the same readily heard distinction is made. Most U.S. speakers, however, do not use closure (stop) consonants in the words *ladder* and *latter* but a voiced flap consonant and the two words cannot be distinguished out of context. This flap consonant is either very similar to or identical with the sound often heard from British speakers for the *r* of *very,* the spelling *veddy* often being used by Americans to mimic this pronunciation.

The voiced flap consonant appears to be normal for *d(d)* in American speech when a vowel immediately precedes and a vowel or \ᵊl\ immediately follows, regardless of the stress of the two syllables (*ladder, tidal, parody, made-up, grade A, adorn*). It also appears to be normal for *t(t)* in American speech in the same environment when the second vowel is unstressed (*latter, title, parity*) and when the second word is stressed and *t(t)* ends a word or a word within a word (*at Omaha, pick it up, great A, butt end, separatism*). In words in which *t(t)* is not word-final, a vowel with primary stress precedes, and a vowel with secondary stress follows, both the flap and the voiceless stop (\t\) are quite common (*veto, Hittite, Mithridates*). Exceptionally, the flap is fairly frequent for the first *t* of *potato* (and is, of course, usual for the second *t*).

Some speakers seem to level *d(d)* and *t(t)* before \ᵊn\, in pairs like *ridden : written.* Such leveling is not as familiar to us and has not been shown in our transcriptions. The leveling sound before \ᵊn\ is probably a voiced stop rather than a flap.

Most transcribers use a special symbol for the flapped sound. We have employed another approach, however. As previously pointed out, when one starts from pause and pronounces *die* or *tie,* the beginning sound is a stop, voiced for *die,* voiceless for *tie.* The voiced flap sound does not occur finally before a pause but a typical occurrence of it is for word-final, and hence syllable⸗final, *t(t)* before a vowel. The flap that occurs for *d(d)* and *t(t)* in American English is always a single sound that follows a vowel and precedes a vowel or syllabic consonant (the \r\ that occurs in *r*-keeping speech in a word like *forty* is more vowel than consonant — see the section on \r\). Vowels and syllabic consonants are syllable nuclei, and there is accordingly a syllable boundary between what precedes and what follows the voiced flap sound. It has seemed altogether practicable to treat the alveolar voiced stop \d\ as a syllable-initial \d\ (transcription \·d\) and to treat the alveolar voiced flap as a syllable-final \d\ (transcription \d·\). Since both the flap and the voiced alveolar stops are heard for intervocalic *d(d),* the syllable divisor · is not used in the transcription of such words. Since a voiced stop is not used for *t(t)* before a vowel or \ᵊl\, the flap pronunciation of such words is always indicated by placing the · after the \d\. For all *t(t)* words that are commonly pronounced with the voiced flap in American English, a pronunciation with the voiceless alveolar stop is usual in some dialects (as British) and occurs with more or less frequency, especially for emphasis, as an alternative pronunciation. Examples of our transcription of *d(d)* and *t(t)* before a vowel or \ᵊl\:

ladder \ˈladə(r)\ (=\ˈlad·ə(r)\ *or* \ˈla·də(r)\)

latter \ˈlad·ə(r), -atə(r)\ (\ˈla·də(r)\ is not a normal pronunciation)

editor \ˈedəd·ə(r), -ətə(r)\

competitor \kəmˈped·əd·ə(r), -etətə(r)\ (this formula is to be understood as also covering a permutation like \-ed·ətə(r)\)

adapt \əˈdapt\ (=\ə·ˈdapt\ *or* \əd·ˈapt\)

attack \əˈtak\

For uncommon *t(t)* words, usually only the \d·\ variant is shown in the vocabulary. \t\ is always to be understood as an acceptable variant of \d·\.

Some observers who grant the leveling of the consonant in pairs like *ladder : latter* insist that the pairs are nevertheless distinct in that the vowel preceding the consonant is longer for the *d(d)* than for the *t(t)* word. We have not been sufficiently convinced of such a distinction to show it.

When *t* is initial in a word with an unstressed vowel or first vowel and follows without pause a word ending with a voiced consonant, or when in the same word *t* precedes an unstressed vowel and is preceded by a voiced consonant which in turn is preceded by an unstressed vowel, the *t* is probably often a stop \d\ (not \d·\), as in *a dog to watch, hang together, seventy.*

dissimilation see the vocabulary definition. \r\ dissimilation by *R* speakers (see section on *R*) is the most frequent kind in English. When the \r\ affected is preconsonantal, or word-final and therefore potentially prepausal, it is necessary to use the labels *R* and –*R* in order to make it clear that the omission occurs in *R* speech. A mere transcription \sə(r)ˈprīz\ at *surprise,* for example, would justifiably be interpreted as meaning that \sərˈprīz\ is the *R* and \səˈprīz\ the –*R* pronunciation, whereas actually \səˈprīz\ is frequent *R* as well.

Dissimilation of \l\ is probably next most frequent after \r\ in English, probably accounting, for example, for the frequent pronouncing of only the second *l* of *ophthalmologist* and *Guadalcanal* and of only the first *l* of *Wilhelmina.* (The last two words are not included in the vocabulary.)

ditto mark see 2.8.1, 2.8.2 in "Explanatory Notes".

division see "Divisions in Respelled Pronunciations" following \zü\. There is also an earlier section entitled "Divisions in Boldface Entry Words", not strictly in the field of pronunciation although to a great extent determined by pronunciation.

double hyphen (⸗) see 2.7.1, 2.7.2 in "Explanatory Notes".

doubling the doubling or repeating of a symbol indicates a sound of greater duration than is indicated by the symbol standing single. In the variants \ˈmanlē\ and \ˈmaanlē\ for *manly,* \aa\ is a vowel of greater duration than \a\; in \ˈshtäät\, German pronunciation of German *Staat,* and \ˈshtät\, German pronunciation of German *Stadt,* \ää\ is a vowel of greater duration than \ä\; in \ˈhīnəs\ *highness* and \ˈfīnnəs\ *fineness,* \nn\ is a consonant of greater duration than \n\. In the case of vowels, there may be a slight difference of quality in addition to the difference in duration but it is not necessary to transcribe this too: it can be regarded as a by-product of the lengthening.

Because of the practices of English orthography and of other pronunciation alphabets, a word of warning is necessary about certain of these doubled symbols that will be found in transcriptions of foreign words and phrases. \ee\ is a vowel having a quality like that of the *e* in *red* but of greater duration, not a vowel having the quality of the *ee* in *reed;* \ō ō\ and \ȯȯ\ are long vowels having a quality like that of the *o* in *coerce* and the *o* in *sort* respectively, not vowels having the quality of the *oo* in *boot* or *foot.*

**\ e ** as in *bet, bed,* and the first syllable of *merry;* in some American speech, the vowel of the first syllable of *marry* and the vowel or the core vowel of words like *bear* and *bare.*

Some speakers who have \a\ or \aa\ in most words of the type *bear, bare,* have \e\ in a small number of words of this type (among them *care, chair, scare, scarce,* emphatic *where*) in which the preceding sound is articulated with the tongue high in the mouth. Apparently by assimilative influence, the \a(a)\ is replaced by the higher \e\.

Some speakers have \a\ or \aa\ in emphatic *there* but \e\ in emphatic *their* and in *theirs.*

In words of the type *barbarian, various,* the same speakers have \e\ in some and \a(a)\ in others. Some appear to interchange \e\ and \a(a)\ in the same word. In the deep South and in Scottish, \ā\ occurs in these words. For uncommon words, we have usually transcribed \a(a)\. \e\ and \ā\ are always to be understood as variants of this \a(a)\.

**\ ē ** as in *beat, bead,* and the first syllable of *beady,* and the unstressed vowel used by most American speakers, and apparently also by most Canadian and Australian speakers, in the second syllable of *lady, cities,* and as a prevocalic in *piano, serious, meander.* In some parts of the southern U.S., \i\ appears to prevail in these unstressed syllables, and British phoneticians transcribe \i\ although reporting that the British vowel is sometimes \e\ (vowel of *bet*) or something approaching it. \i\ is favored by some who, while admitting that \ē\ better represents the quality of the usual American vowel, have misgivings that \ē\ in transcriptions may foster a tendency to overpronounce (i.e., to pronounce an \ē\ with full secondary stress).

To hold down the number of variants in transcriptions, only \ē\ has been shown for the *i* of *piano* and *serious* and the first *e* of *meander.* It may be, as some transcribers appear to believe, that \ē\ is used in such words by speakers who have \i\ in *lady,* but \i\ is surely frequent enough to justify the blanket recognition here of \i\ as an always-to-be-understood variant of unstressed \ē\.

**\ ee ** used only in the transcription of words from foreign languages; of long duration and with a quality like that of the *e* in English *red,* not like that of *ee* in English *reed.*

**\ ēr ** occurs in the deep South and in Scotland in words like *serial, serious, weary,* and in Scotland in words like *hear, mere, veer.*

It is not shown for any except Scottish words of the latter type, and is shown only for common words of the former type.

**\ eu̇ ** as a frequent variant of \el\ when certain consonant sounds follow, as in *elk, elm, help, twelve.* The use of \eu̇\ instead of \el\ before \y\, as in *hellion, rebellious,* belongs chiefly to substandard speech. See section on \l\.

**\ f ** as in *five, traffic, puff.*

foreign words for foreign words borrowed unchanged into English and italicized by some writers to signify that they are regarded as falling short of complete naturalization, we nevertheless often show in the vocabulary a pronunciation somewhat anglicized. Even an approximation to some foreign sounds is difficult or impossible for the average speaker of English who does not have a speaking knowledge of the foreign language, and even when a sound close to the foreign sound exists in English it may be passed over in favor of one that is usual in the same environment in English words. Thus the Italian name *Garibaldi* is usually pronounced by English speakers with the first vowel as in *garrison* and the third as in *bald,* although the vowel of *garb* is closer to the one vowel that occurs in both syllables in Italian. The speaker who is sufficiently conversant with the phonetics of a foreign language to be capable and desirous of using the full foreign pronunciation is unlikely to use an English dictionary as a source, and we have accordingly often not given the foreign pronunciation even as a variant. In general we give foreign pronunciations when known usage has shown them or similar pronunciations to be within the capabilities of educated English speakers inexpert in the foreign language, or when no anglicization is known to us to be established and the foreign pattern is such that there is insufficient analogy to make an anglicized pattern safely predictable.

For the same reasons we also show a standard⸗English pronunciation pattern for words or parts of words belonging to British dialect, including Scottish. Thus the vowel of *clat* is shown as \a\, the vowel of *fat* in standard English, and the vowel of *darg* is shown as \ä\, one of the vowels of *bargain* in standard English, although the two words have the same vowel in much British dialect. It seems pointless to give only \a\ for words like *fat* that belong to standard English as well as to British dialect and to give some other vowel for a word like *clat* that belongs exclusively to British dialect and that rhymes with *fat* in that dialect. A dictionary key that tells the speaker of standard English who is completely ignorant of British dialect that *clat* has the vowel of *fat* provides that consultant with a pronunciation that in his ignorance of dialect he would be well advised to use; a speaker of the British dialect Scottish who finds \a\ for *clat* in a dictionary and finds *fat* cited as a key word for \a\ is not misled; a speaker of standard English who knows something about Scottish knows that his vowel in *fat* is not Scottish dialect's vowel in *fat,* and also knows what vowel does occur there instead of his vowel.

French words fully French pronunciations are shown without any stress marks, in accord with the usual practice of transcribers of French.

**\ g ** as in *get, got, tiger, big.*

**\ g̅ ** as for *g* in Spanish *luego;* a non-English voiced fricative sound, made with the tongue in approximately the position for \g\ in English *go* but without closure.

glottal stop a phonetic effect (symbol \ʔ\) produced by a complete closure in the throat (more specifically, a closure of the vocal cords) that makes it impossible for breath to issue from the lungs. It is the same phenomenon that bottles up the breath before a cough or before the clearing of the throat. In speech it may occur between silence and a sound, between two sounds, or between a sound and silence. In some languages (as standard English, with the exception of a few interjections — see section on interjections), the glottal stop occurs only as an accidental, in some cases almost inevitable, sound, and adds no significance to the context in which it occurs: if it were omitted the meaning of the context would not be altered. Thus, this sound often occurs between \ə\ and a following vowel sound (as in *ultra-atomic, ultraism*) or before the vowel in a vowel-initial word that is under emphasis (as "Eggs!" or, with an intonation of annoyance or disbelief, "Eggs?"). In speech usually regarded as nonstandard and not recorded in this book, the glottal stop in certain contexts replaces \d·\ or \t\ of standard speech, as in \'wȯə(r)\ for *water*. Omission of the stop in such cases might cause misunderstanding if the context were ambiguous enough, since \'wȯə(r)\ is a pronunciation of *war*. In the type of German speech usually regarded as standard, a glottal stop occurs with great frequency before or at the beginning of words stressed on the first syllable and having no consonant letter preceding the first-syllable vowel; it is usually retained when the word follows another member in a compound. Such a glottal stop is symbolized by some transcribers but not by others. Whether it is phonemic or not, it is symbolized in this book in fully German transcriptions of words in which it occurs because its absence hinders ready comprehension by a German listener. We believe that a certain number of departures from strict phonemicity are advisable in the sporadic fully foreign pronunciations.

-gu-, -qu-; division of words containing for the end-of-the-line division of words like *leaguing* and *cataloguer* and *piquing*, in which *gu* is pronounced \g\, *qu* is pronounced \k\, and a following *e* is dropped before a syllable-increasing English suffix is added, see section on inflected forms, division of.

When the pronounced vowel that follows the *u* is not an English suffix or a part of one, the most satisfactory division between the two syllables is immediately preceding the *g* or *q*, as in *belea·guer, li·quor, che·quered.*

\gy in at least three coastal areas of the South — Virginia, South Carolina, eastern Texas — a \y\ sound often intrudes between \g\ and certain or all of the members of the vowel series from \ē\ to \ä\. Thus, *garden* is often \'gyȧdᵊn\ in Charleston. These variants are not shown in this book.

\h as in *hat, ahead;* in the anglicized pronunciation of Spanish-derived words, \h\ is the usual pronunciation before a stressed vowel of a sound that in some dialects at least of Spanish is \k̲\ — for example, for the *x* of *Don Quixote.*

\hw used for the *wh* of *whet* by speakers whose *whet* and *wet* are not pronounced the same. Some phoneticians regard \hw\ not as two sounds but as one, a voiceless \w\. With most American speakers *whet* and *wet* differ in pronunciation but with most southern British speakers they do not.

\i as in *bit, bid, here, hear.*

\ī as in *try, light, guide, aisle.* \ī\ is a diphthong, not a single sound, with heaviest stress on the first element. Its beginning position ranges from the position for the \ȧ\ heard in *ask* in eastern New England to the position for the unrounded \ä\ heard from most U.S. speakers for the vowel of *hot, heart;* its ending position ranges from that for monophthongal \ā\ to that for \i\. In eastern Virginia and in an area of Canada having Toronto as its metropolis, the position of the first element before voiceless consonants is approximately that of the \'ə\ of *nut*. In the southern U.S., the second part of the \ȧi\ or \äi\ variety of the diphthong may disappear, and finally and before voiced consonants, less often before voiceless consonants, the pronunciation may be simply \ȧ\ or unrounded \ä\, as in \'wȧvz\ or \'wävz\ for *wives.*

See section on \äi\.

incomplete pronunciations many of the pronunciations shown in this dictionary are for a part of the entry only and the user is to seek the missing part somewhere else in the dictionary. Two of the most frequently used indicators that a sound symbol or a sequence of sound symbols is not a complete pronunciation for the whole of a boldface entry are the ordinary single hyphen and the vertical bar (for the latter see the paragraph on | and 2.6 of "Explanatory Notes"). A hyphen at the left-hand side of a roman-type item within reversed virgules means that something is missing at the beginning (\-līn\); a hyphen at the right-hand side means that something is missing at the end (\'kōd-\); a hyphen to both left and right means that something is missing at both beginning and end (\-tȯr-\). If the missing part is the pronunciation of a word or of words pronounced at its or their own alphabetical place in the vocabulary, the missing part should be sought there.

law of ti·ti·us \-'tētsēəs\ [missing part at *law* and *of*]
gresh·am's law \'greshəmz-\ [missing part at *law*]

Otherwise the missing part is to be supplied from the corresponding part of a variant pronunciation that appears before a preceding punctuation mark within the same reversed virgules, or from a pronunciation for another spelling that precedes in the same or another entry.

[1]*sa·line* \'sā,lēn, -līn\ [substitute \'sā\ for the hyphen]
cod·i·fy \'kädə,fī, 'kōd-\ [substitute \ə,fī\ for the hyphen]
sen·a·to·ri·al \¦senə¦tōrēəl, -tȯr-\ [substitute \¦senə¦\ for the first hyphen and \ēəl\ for the second]
anal·y·sis \ə'naləsəs\ *n, pl* *analy·ses* \-ə,sēz\ [substitute \ə'nal\ for the hyphen]

[1]*or·gan·ic* \(')ȯ(r)¦ganik, -nēk\ . . .
[2]*organic* \" \ . . .
or·gan·i·cal \-nəkəl, -nēk-\ . . .
or·gan·i·cal·ly \-k(ə)lē, -li\ [for the first hyphen at *organical* substitute \(')ȯ(r)¦ga\ from [1]*organic;* for the first hyphen at *organically* substitute \(')ȯ(r)¦ganə, -nē\ from [1]*organic* and *organical*]

We usually repeat something from the preceding pronunciation to indicate where in this pronunciation that which is different in the following pronunciation is to serve as a replacement. Often both something to the left and something to the right of the variant part is repeated. Thus in \'sā,lēn, -līn\ the repeated \l\ and \n\ show that \ī\ may replace the \ē\ between those two characters. A locator repeated may be something other than a sound symbol, as a stress mark or a parenthesis.

per·sist \pə(r)'sist *also* -'zi-\
cre·do \'krē(,)dō, 'krā(-\

When we use a consonantal locator on one side of a vowel variant and no locator on the other side, it is to be understood that the vowel adjacent to the locator in a following pronunciation replaces the vowel adjacent to the locator in a preceding pronunciation and is not inserted after that vowel. Thus in \'kōdə,sēz, -äd-\ for *codices* at *codex*, \-äd-\ is to be read \'käd-\ not \'kōäd-\.

Variants of the vowel of a monosyllable or of a sound whose symbolization differs from that of the variant in that one has a diacritic and the other does not or has a different diacritic are sometimes shown without a locator on either side.

bask \'bask, -aa(ə)-,-ai-,-ȧ-\
broomy \'brümē, -u̇-\
hu·chen \'hükən, -k̲-\

Printing the last three variants for *bask* without spaces between is merely a space-saving device that we often employ when two or more variants of each other are printed in succession.

If no hyphen or vertical bar appears at the beginning of a pronunciation, the pronunciation for the first part of the word is complete and nothing is to be supplied ahead of what is shown; if no hyphen or vertical bar appears at the end of a pronunciation, the pronunciation for the last part of the word is complete and nothing is to be supplied at the end of what is shown.

[1]*good-bye or good-by* \gu̇d'bī, gəd'bī, gə'bī, 'bī\ [the last variant, \'bī\, is a pronunciation for the entire word and not for only the part *bye* or *by.*]
[2]*pretty* \. . ., *before 'near' often* 'pru̇t *or* 'prit\ [\ē\ or \i\ is not to be supplied at the end of the last two variants. The pronunciations intended are \pru̇tni(ə)r\, etc.]

A user who is familiar with the pronunciation practices of the preceding edition of this work should observe that the giving of variants differs in the two in that in this book no attempt is made to always have a variant begin at a syllable beginning and end at a syllable ending.

inflected forms, division of when no division is shown for an inflected form, a form with zero inflection or a form inflected by the addition of an ending that does not add a syllable may be divided at any point where a division is shown in the inflectional base:

[2]*mul·let*→ pl *mul·let* or *mul·lets*
in·ter·vene→ *in·ter·vened*→ *in·ter·venes*

If the ending adds a syllable and the spelling of the base does not change, a division may be made between the two components, as well as at any point at which a division is shown in the base:

church→ *church·es*
con·strain→ *con·strained*→ *con·strain·ing*→ *con·strains*
ap·proach→ *ap·proached*→ *ap·proach·ing*→ *ap·proach·es*
re·tort→ *re·tort·ed*→ *re·tort·ing*→ *re·torts*
[2]*stout*→ *stout·er*→ *stout·est*

In a syllable-increased form in which the final consonant of the inflectional base is doubled, a division is made between the doubled consonants:

re·but→ *re·but·ted*→ *re·but·ting*→ *re·buts*

When both of two identical consonants immediately preceding a syllable-increasing ending belong to the inflectional base, a division is made after the second consonant:

bluff·ing

For variants like *conn/con* a syllable-increased form can be divided in either of two ways:

conn also *con, conn·ing* or *con·ning*

In a syllable-increased form in which a final *e* of the base is dropped before the ending, a division is made between the letter that preceded the *e* and the ending:

rate→ *rat·ed*→ *rat·ing*
glue→ *glu·ing*
plague→ *plagu·ing*
pique→ *piqu·ing*
gro·tesque→ *gro·tesqu·er*→ *gro·tesqu·est*

In syllable-increased forms like those in the last three lines, in which *gu* or *qu*, with *u* silent, appears immediately before the ending, some prefer to divide immediately before the *g* or *q* if it is not immediately preceded by a short vowel or, in the case of *g*, by *n* (*haran·guing* would suggest the substandard pronunciation \hə'raŋgiŋ\):

pi·quing
pla·guing
grotes·quer

For plurals identical in form with the singular, or formed by adding *-s* or *-es*, usually neither pronunciation nor division is shown. For other plurals pronunciation and division are shown, except that (1) divisions common to both plural and singular are usually omitted and (2) the pronunciation and division of the last part of a compound whose last part is an independent English word must usually be sought at the entry for the independent word. The last or the only centered period in a plural is the last point at which a division should be made in it:

ep·i·the·li·um→ pl *epithe·lia*

The plural may be divided like the singular except that no division should be made after that between the *e* and *l.*

The centered period between two consecutive vowels in the plural supersedes a differently placed period between the same two vowels in the singular. In *ge·nus*, pl *gen·era* a division is not to be understood between the *e* and *n* of the plural as well as between the *n* and *e*. It is true, as explained in the section on "Divisions in Boldface Entry Words", that divisions such as *ge·nera* do occur, especially in British publications, but our policy is to show only one division between two consecutive vowels. A plural of the type not needing division and pronunciation does have pronunciation when it is the first variant plural (as at [2]*virtuoso* where *virtuosos* is first and *virtuo·si* second). When a plural of this type is the second variant plural, pronunciation and division are omitted (as at *tibia* where *tibi·ae* is first and *tibias* second).

inflected forms, pronunciation of

The pronunciation of any inflected forms not pronounced is the pronunciation shown at the entry for the inflectional base plus the pronunciation or one of the pronunciations shown for the inflectional ending. These ending entries are, for nouns, [1]-S, [1]-ES; for verbs, [1]-ED, [1]-ING, [3]-S, [2]-ES, [2]-EST, [1]-ETH; for adjectives, [1]-ER, [1]-EST. The definitions at some of these contain information that will facilitate the ascertainment of the pronunciation for the entire word.

-ing in vocabulary words formed by attaching this ending to a verb, usually no pronunciation is shown, whether the inflected form is a main entry or is a run-on entry, if the pronunciation of that part of the word preceding the *-ing* is the same as the pronunciation of the base verb. When such is not the case, usually the only pronunciation shown for the *-ing* is \-iŋ\ or, for common words entered with hanging indention, \-iŋ, -ēŋ\. It is to be understood, however, that in some dialects or under some circumstances the *-ing* may be otherwise pronounced. See the entry [1]-ING in the vocabulary for a detailed list of variants.

\iŋ when stressed, as in *sing, forefinger,* \āŋ\ and perhaps less often \eŋ\ are variants especially in the southern U.S. These variants are not shown. When unstressed, as in *running*, \ēŋ\ is a frequent variant and is shown for words that are common.

\ir\, \iər\, \iə in words of the type of *inferior, hear, pierce,* variants occur that are not shown in the vocabulary or that are not shown for uncommon words.

Words of the type of *inferior* are shown in the vocabulary as containing the sequence \ir\ followed by a vowel. In the deep South they may contain \er\ instead of \ir\, and the \ēr\ variant is to be understood for uncommon words for which it is not shown. In southern British speech all words of this type usually have \ə\ between the \i\ and \r\, and some may be pronounced with \yə̄\ instead of \iə\.

Words of the type of *hear* are shown in the vocabulary as having \ir\ or \iər\ in *R* speech and before a vowel in –*R* speech, and as having \iə\ in –*R* speech elsewhere. Words of the type of *pierce* are shown as having \iə\, with no \r\ following, in –*R* speech. In some words of both types \yə̄\ may occur instead of \iə\ in southern

British speech. The same variant occurs in a very few words in which the part of the orthography that answers to \iə\, \yə̄\ in the pronunciation contains no *r*, as in the *thea* fragment of *theater*.*

\ iu̇ \ as in one pronunciation of the *il* in *film, milk*. See section on \l\.

\ j \ as in *j*ug, ba*dg*e, a*g*ile. Some linguists treat the sound of the italicized letters in the words cited as the sound \d\ followed by the sound \zh\ in the same syllable, others transcribe it with a single symbol.

\ k \ as in *k*i*ck*, pa*ch*yderm, ba*cch*ic.

\ k̲ \ as for *ch* in German *siech* and *Buch;* a non-English voiceless fricative sound, made with the tongue in a range of positions from approximately that of the \k\ in English *keep* to that of the \k\ in English *cool* but without closure.

With particular reference to German, it was formerly the usual transcriptional practice to have two symbols for this range of sounds, one symbol for the front varieties and another for the back varieties. It is now common practice, however, to regard a single symbol as adequate to the phonemic transcription of the entire range of sounds, and the symbol \k̲\ is so used in the transcription of the comparatively small number of words for which a full German pronunciation, or something approaching it, is given. Whether or not a single symbol is adequate for transcribing German for Germans, a single symbol suffices in this book, in which any word or phrase borrowed unchanged in spelling from a foreign language is treated as an item occurring in English context. Whatever variety of \k̲\ may come naturally in a particular word to an educated speaker of English addressing another speaker of English is unlikely to seem out of place in English context. In German the use of one symbol instead of two presents the problem that certain pairs of words (very small in number, apparently) which when spoken in isolation are distinguishable are transcriptionally identical (*Pfauchen, pfauchen,* both \'pfau̇k̲ən\ but with a front \k̲\ in the first and a back \k̲\ in the second). If, as it appears may be the case for all except the intervocalic occurrences of \k̲\, a simple set of rules can be drawn up that will fix its front or back position on the basis of phonetic environment alone, an expediential device for transcribing its quality intervocalically is to treat the front variety as syllable-final, and the back variety as syllable-final, and to employ such transcriptions as \'pfau̇·k̲ən\ *Pfauchen*, \'pfau̇k̲·ən\ *pfauchen*, \äk̲·'ālis\ *Achelis*.

\ ky \ in at least three coastal areas of the South — Virginia, South Carolina, eastern Texas — a \y\ sound often intrudes between \k\ and certain or all of the members of the vowel series from \ē\ to \ä\. Thus, *card* is often \'kyȧd\ in Charleston. These variants are not shown.

\ l \ as in *leaf, loot, police, allude, feel, fool.* Articulations of \l\ vary widely, from the clear *l* in some pronunciations of *leaf* to the dark *l* of *fool*. In both sounds the tip of the tongue is in contact with the teethridge. For the clear *l* the top of the tongue is convex; for the dark *l* the top of the tongue is concave and at the back is in the articulatory position for \ü\ or a neighboring vowel. The clearest *l* in American speech is not as clear as in some foreign languages, and some phoneticians treat all occurrences of \l\ in the speech of most Americans as dark. The almost invariable practice of all transcribers, whatever their views, is to use only one symbol for all varieties in English. In the U.S. the clearest \l\'s occur in the speech of some Southern speakers, whose pronunciation of the intervocalic \l\ in words like *salad, Alice, willing* contrasts sharply with that of Northern speakers. The difference between the two can be shown by the transcriptions \'sa·lid\, \'a·lis\, \'wi·liŋ\ for the Southern speakers and \'sal·əd\, \'al·əs\, \'wil·ēŋ\ for the Northern. It is possible that \'sau̇l·əd\ and \'au̇l·əs\ (in which \a\ is the vowel of *apt*) would be proper transcriptions for the dark *l* articulations of the first two words and that *Alice* and *owl us* would be rhymes with some speakers. Such transcriptions have not been shown in this book.

When the vowel articulation preceding an \l\ is one that pulls the back of the tongue forward of the dark *l* articulatory position, a very clear \ə\ may result while the tongue is in transition between the two positions. Words like *ale, eel,* and *oil,* in which the last vowel represented by the spelling is front, often have as much of an \ə\ as *betrayal, perigeal,* or *loyal,* especially when a pause or a consonant follows. Before a pause or a consonant, pairs like *reel : ideal, trail : betrayal, vile : vial, oil : royal* may be exact rhymes. The pronunciation with epenthetic \ə\ is shown as a variant for such words. The back vowel \u̇\ in a word like *owl* is so far fronted when the first half of the diphthong has the quality of the \a\ in *pat* that a clear \ə\ frequently intrudes, and the variant with \ə\ is shown in this book. Between other back vowels and \l\ the \ə\ has not been shown although the \ə\ sometimes appears after \ü\ when that vowel is fronted by the articulation of a preceding tongue-front consonant, as in *schedule, mule.*

\u̇\ often occurs, in some dialects at least, instead of \l\ before the lip consonants \p\, \b\, \m\, \f\, \v\, and before the back-of-the-tongue consonant \k\, especially when these consonants are word-final — that is, only the back half of the articulation of a dark *l* occurs, the contact between tongue tip and teethridge being absent: *help, bulb, elm, self, twelve, elk.* With some Southern speakers, *help, self,* and *twelve* have nothing whatever corresponding to an *l*.

Less often than in the class of words just mentioned, \u̇\ occurs instead of \l\ when \y\ immediately follows, as in *million, hellion.* The \u̇\ variant is not shown before \y\ in this book.

\ l^{ə} \ as in one pronunciation of French *peuple.* Like \$^{ə}$l\, \l^{ə}\ is a single sound differing from \$^{ə}$l\ in being voiceless rather than voiced and in not adding an extra syllable, the \pœpl^{ə}\ pronunciation of *peuple* being a single syllable. The \$^{ə}$\ after the \l\ is always parenthesized to indicate the usual pronunciation when a vowel-initial word follows without pause. Thus *peuple anglais* is \pœ plä^{n} glā\, three syllables, with \pl\ as in French *plaisir.* Compare section on \$^{ə}$\.

\ lch \ as in *belch, gulch;* sometimes \lsh\ in U.S. speech and more often so in British speech.

-lds usually no pronunciation is shown for noun and verb inflected forms produced by adding *-s* to a base in *-ld*, as *fields, welds.* The pronunciation \l(d)z\ is to be understood.

\ lü \ as in *lute, lewd, clue, ablution, absolute, revolution;* that is, words in which the orthographic representation is not *loo* and which are mostly from Latin and Greek. In words like the first three, the variant \lyü\ (=\lyü\ or \liü\) appears to be frequent in southern British speech but is rare in U.S. speech and is not shown. In words like the last two, in which the \l\ is intervocalic and the sequence \lyü\ can easily be syllabicated \l·yü\ instead of \·lyü\, the variant with \y\ is less rare in the U.S. and is shown after an *also*.

\ l^{y} \ as *gli* in Italian *figlio* and *ll* in the Castilian Spanish pronunciation of *olla;* the sound can be approximated by trying to pronounce \l\ while the tip of the tongue is held behind the lower front teeth.

\ m \ as in *maim, hammer, nymph;* the usual articulation of \m\ is with the lips in contact to form a closure but when an \f\ or \v\ sound immediately precedes or follows the closure is made by the lower lip against the upper front teeth, as in *nymph, triumph, triumvir, Hoffman(n)* and the pronunciation \'sev^{ə}m\ for *seven.*

\ m^{ə} \ as in one pronunciation of French *prisme;* \m^{ə}\ is a single sound differing from \$^{ə}$m\ in being voiceless rather than voiced and in not adding an extra syllable, the \prēsm^{ə}\ or \-ēzm^{ə}\ pronunciation of *prisme* being a single syllable. The \$^{ə}$\ after the \m\ is always parenthesized to indicate the usual pronunciation when a vowel-initial word follows without pause. Thus *prisme oblique* is \prē smȯ blēk\ or \prēz mȯ blēk\, three syllables, with \m\ as in French *smille* or *mille.* Compare section on \$^{ə}$\.

\ n \ as in *known, manly, enrage, tenth.*

\ ^{n} \ indicates that the preceding vowel is pronounced through the nose, that is, with the velum lowered and the nostrils open at the back. Vowels are not infrequently so uttered in American English but the nasality is an accident and a nasal vowel does not function as something different from the same vowel without the nasality. In some languages, however, as French and Portuguese, the difference between a vowel without nasality and the same vowel with nasality may make two different words of two sequences of sounds otherwise identical. French has four nasal vowels and they are often exemplified by the four-word phase *un bon vin blanc* ("a good white wine"), which in our symbols would be transcribed \œ^{n}bō^{n}va^{n}blä^{n}\.

In a transcription like \kō͞o^{n}t\ at *comte,* in which \ō͞o\ indicates a sound the same in quality as \ō\ but of greater duration (not a vowel with the quality of *oo* in English *boot*), the diacritic \$^{n}$\ applies to both preceding characters.

-nds usually no pronunciation is shown for noun and verb inflected forms produced by adding *-s* to a base in *-nd*, as *friends, sends.* The pronunciation \n(d)z\ is to be understood.

ng see section on \ŋ\.

\ n^{y} \ as *gn* in French *agneau* and Italian *bagno* and *ñ* in Spanish *cañón.* The sound can be approximated by trying to pronounce \n\ while the tip of the tongue is held behind the lower front teeth.

\ ŋ \ as in *hang* \'haŋ\, *hanger* \'haŋə(r)\, *anger* \'aŋgə(r)\, *singer* \'siŋə(r)\, *finger* \'fiŋgə(r)\, *linger* \'liŋgə(r)\. The sound of the *ng* in *hang* and of the *n* in *anger* is a single sound not the sound \n\ followed by the sound \g\, although the transcription \ng\ for this single sound is used in some of the smaller members of this series to avoid the use of characters that are not letters of the ordinary English alphabet.

\ ō \ as in *bone, snow, coerce;* \ō\ has a strong tendency to become diphthongal, with \u̇\ as a second element, when it is in a position of emphasis, as when it is word-final, under primary stress, and before a pause. In southern British speech and in some American speech, especially in the Philadelphia area, the diphthongization is more frequent and the first element is often \ə\ or \ə̄\. The symbol \ō\ is to be understood to cover all these variants.

In a group of some fifty words, chiefly monosyllables, and their derivatives, transcribed with \ō\, some New England speakers, chiefly rural, have a vowel that has been described, and that apparently is articulated, in more than one way but that sounds to most ears unaccustomed to it like the vowel of *cut.* At least some New England speakers make homophones of *cut* and *coat.* The users of this vowel constitute only a small fraction of the English-speaking world and appear to be on the decrease, and so this variant is not shown.

In a small area that includes the cities of Charleston and Savannah, words transcribed with \ō\ followed by a consonant often have \ōə\ instead, as in \'kōət\ for *coat.* This variant is not shown.

\ ȯ \ as in *corn, saw, all, cause.* In the southern U.S., there is often a diphthongal variant (not used in this book) for at least all of the key words cited except *corn.* In this variant the first element is much the same as the monophthong that occurs with other speakers in these words and the second element is \u̇\ or even \ü\.

\ œ \ as in French *bœuf,* German *Hölle;* \œ\ can be approximated by pronouncing \e\ with moderately rounded lips.

\ œ̄ \ as in French *feu,* German *Höhle;* \œ̄\ can be approximated by pronouncing \ā\ with strongly rounded lips.

\ œ^{n} \ see section on \$^{n}$\.

\ ȯi \ as in *coin, boy.* In the southern U.S. and chiefly before a consonant in the same word, the second element is sometimes lost or replaced by \ə\. Random listening for misapprehension of two-morpheme items as one-morpheme and vice versa is not as productive of evidence for these pairs as it is for certain other pairs whose identity is disputed — e.g., for *latter : ladder* and *a name : an aim.* Even for these common items, highly ambiguous contexts are infrequent, and there are no or few words in *-oing* in English and but few in *-awy.* With most Americans speaking at normal tempo occurrences of \ȯ\ followed by \i\ without pause are phonetically identical, regardless of whether the two components belong to the same morpheme or to two. Whether, however, such sequences are to be regarded as one syllable or two is a more difficult matter. But *strawy* and the last part of *destroy* are identical, and *coin* and *boy* are more disyllabic than monosyllabic. In the speech of New York City the first half of the diphthong \ȯi\ is overlong.

In transcriptions of the full German pronunciation of German words, \ȯi\ is used for the vowel sequence of words like *neu,* whose second member in German is usually a lip-rounded vowel more properly transcribed \ȯue\ or \ȯœ\.

\ ō^{n} \ see section on \$^{n}$\.

\ ō͞o \ used only in the transcription of words from foreign languages; of long duration and with a quality like that of the *o* in English *coerce,* not like that of *oo* in English *boot.*

\ ȯȯ \ used only in the transcription of words from foreign languages; of long duration and with a quality like that of the *o* in English *sort,* not like that of *oo* in English *foot* or *boot.*

\ ō͞o^{n} \ as \ō͞o\ nasalized, as in French *comte.* See sections on \ō͞o\ and on \$^{n}$\.

\ ōr \ as in *board, boarder, glory;* many speakers have this sequence in their speech only when the \ō\ and the \r\ belong to separate phonemes, as in *pro rata* and the \ə\-less pronunciation of *grower.* With these speakers, in other items \ȯ\ occurs instead of \ō\. For words common in the literary language, both the \ō\ and \ȯ\ variants are shown. For other words, usually only the \ō\ variant is shown and the \ȯ\ variant is to be understood. Thus, only \-ōr-\ is shown at *auctorial* and \-ȯr-\ is to be understood, as can be ascertained

*Daniel Jones, *Outline of English Phonetics,* New York (1956), §442*a.*

by examining the transcription at the entry for a common word (like *editorial*) for which \-ōrēəl\ is the first variant shown; only \-fō(ə)r\ is shown at *gonophore* and \-fȯ(ə)r\ is to be understood, as well as \-fōə\ and \-fȯ(ə)\ for *r*-droppers, as can be seen by examining the transcription for a common word like *semaphore*.

In words like *glory* and *glorious*, in which a vowel follows the \ōr\, the pronunciation of many speakers in the deep South, whose vowel is \ō\, is appreciably different from the pronunciation of others in the South and from that of speakers in other parts of the country who have \ōr\ rather than \ȯr\, in that with the first group the \r\ is more consonantal than with the second group, whose \r\ is in the nature of the second half of a diphthong. The first variant may be transcribed \ˈglō·ri\, the second and probably more common variant \ˈglōr·ē, -ōr·i\.

**\ ȯr ** as in *moral, horrible*, in which a vowel follows the \r\. Both \ȯr\ and \är\ occur in these words in U. S. speech. \är\ strongly predominates in the South, and is frequent along the Atlantic coast in the North. \är\ strongly predominates in British speech, where the \ä\ is usually somewhat lip-rounded and different from the \ä\ of most U. S. speech. \ȯr\ probably prevails in the U. S. and is shown first for nearly all words for which both variants are shown. For words of this group not common in literary English, usually only the \ȯr\ variant is shown but the \är\ variant is to be understood. For a few such words in which the \r\ is or may be followed by \ō\, as *borrow* and *sorrow*, many have \är\ who have \ȯr\ in other words of the group. The pronunciation for words like *borrow* is shown as \är *also* ȯr\. Dissimilation has been suggested as an explanation of the difference. \är\ is not to be understood for \ȯr\ in words in which the vowel that follows the \r\ is that of a suffix freely addable to English words. \är\ is quite normal for *abhorrence* and *abhorrent*, but if it occurs for *abhorring* or *abhorrer* it probably does so from the analogy of a word like *abhorrence*. The analogy of *horror*, for example, for which \är\ is a normal variant, may sometimes produce \är\ in *abhorrer*.

**\ p ** as in *pay, lip, upper*.

phonemicity our endeavor has been to make the transcriptions of fully English items phonemic. Because of the inevitability, however, that they will not in every respect agree with every evaluator's ideas of phonemicity, and because we have deliberately not striven for phonemicity in our transcription of certain nonanglicized pronunciations, we enclose our transcriptions in virgules having a slant the opposite of the virgules conventionally employed for phonemic transcription. In the comparatively small number of nonanglicized pronunciations of words from foreign languages that occur in this dictionary of the English language, we have transcribed a variant that is purely allophonic in the foreign language (for example, the [ŋ] variant of \n\ in Spanish and Italian) if the variation is phonemic in English.

plurals see sections on INFLECTED FORMS, DIVISION OF and on INFLECTED FORMS, PRONUNCIATION OF.

present participles many present participles have two pronunciations, one that is the pronunciation of the base verb or of one form of it plus the pronunciation shown in the vocabulary for *-ing*, a second with one syllable less.

[1]*flick·er* \ˈflikə(r)\ . . . *flickering* \-k(ə)riŋ\ [i.e., the present participle is \ˈflikəriŋ\ or \ˈflikriŋ\]

fat·ten \ˈfatᵊn\ . . . *fattening* \-t(ᵊ)niŋ\ [i.e., the present participle is \ˈfatᵊniŋ\ or \ˈfatniŋ\]

When such a variation occurs, at all but wholly dialect or very rare verbs the present participle is subentered and pronounced. Usually only \-iŋ\ is shown at the end but it is to be understood that other variants of \-iŋ\ may occur; see [1]-ING in the vocabulary. When more than one identically spelled verb is entered the present-participle pronunciation may be shown only for the common one or ones or for the first.

principal parts of verbs see sections on INFLECTED FORMS, DIVISION OF and on INFLECTED FORMS, PRONUNCIATION OF.

punctuation marks variants are usually separated by a comma in the vocabulary but sometimes by a semicolon. See the paragraph on variants.

-qu-: division of words containing see sections on *-gu-* and on inflected forms, division of.

R used in vocabulary pronunciations and in this "Guide" as a label for the speech of those who always have the sound \r\ before a consonant or pause when *r* or *rr* in the spelling provides justification, except for occasional loss by dissimilation as in the first syllable of *surprise*. The term "*r*-keeper" has been used in a few places for a speaker of this type of speech, to supply the need for an antonym of "*r*-dropper".

–R used in vocabulary pronunciations and in this "Guide" as a label for the speech of those who have no \r\ sound before a consonant or pause. Our use of this label ignores speakers who in this position sometimes have \r\ and sometimes do not in the same class of words, or who usually have \r\ only in a limited number of classes from which educated usage sanctions its omission. Thus some speakers usually have \r\ before consonant or pause only in syllables of the type of *spurn* or *spur*. Speakers whose omission of \r\ is maximal and those whose omission is only partial are both known as "*r*-droppers" but in this "Guide" the term is restricted to the former.

**\ r ** as in *rid, arouse, merry* as pronounced by all speakers of standard English, and as in one pronunciation of *carbarn, lizard, murder*.

Words such as the last three are not uniformly pronounced. Most Americans have for these *r*'s a sound which, though it may usually differ appreciably from the prevocalic second sound in *crow*, is distinct from any other sound in the language and can be symbolized by \r\. The \r\ and the vowel sound that answers to a letter preceding the *r* in the orthography may be articulated simultaneously, as in *purr* and perhaps also in *par*, and some transcribers prefer a single symbol for the double articulation. Favoring the use of \r\ preceded by a vowel symbol, however, is the fact that the articulations, usually or often simultaneous, may alternatively be successive, particularly under emphasis, and that the two-symbol transcription parallels the transcription for items like *dear*, whose corresponding articulations are only or usually successive. Other speakers (as in the southeastern United States, eastern New England, New York City, and southern England) with varying degrees of regularity do not make in words like *carbarn, lizard, murder* the articulation that we transcribe \r\. The sum total of what they do instead is commonly called *r*-dropping, a term that is misleading to the extent that it may suggest that syllables in which some have \r\ and some do not are identical except that with the latter one member of a linear series has been removed, with consequent durational shortening. Trying to gauge the comparative duration of what *R* and *–R* speakers respectively say for what is between the \k\ and \d\ of *card* runs into complications. A vowel of the quality of that in *card*, if it occurs and is of substantially the same quality in the speech of both in items in which the spelling does not have *r*, may not be of the same duration in the two dialects. Further, it may be difficult or impossible to dissociate the vowel and the \r\ in *R* speech: the \r\ may be simultaneous with the whole or the last part of the vowel, or may be initiated after the vowel begins and continue after the vowel ends. In most classes of words with postvocalic *r* in the orthography things happen in the pronunciation that make these words as distinct from maximally similar words spelled without *r* as in *R* speech. The relationships in *–R* speech between the vowels used for items containing postvocalic *r* in the spelling and the vowels used for items not containing such an *r* are:

(1) The pronunciation of a spelling item containing the letter *r* may be identical with the pronunciation of an item not containing *r*:

tort and *taut* may be identical, with [ȯ] or [ȯȯ] (long [ȯ]) or [ȯə] for both *or* and *au*. *Card* and *cod* are often identical (as in the speech of New York City), with [ää] for both *ar* and *o*, [ää] occurring for the latter because of the tendency of certain final consonants, as voiced stops, to lengthen a preceding vowel. The consonants that when word-final tend to lengthen a preceding vowel and to produce such leveling are \b\, \d\, \g\, \j\, \m\, \n\, \sh\. Although published statements on *–R* speech take little note of the possible leveling of *ar* and *o* as in *cart* and *cot* for the opposite reason that the vowel for the *r*-containing item has the shortness normal for the *o* of an item like *cot*, in certain contexts at least that are most favorable to vowel shortness (distance in syllables from the end of a word as in *parsimony*, stress weaker than primary as in *arcade*) such leveling may occur. To hold down the amount of detail in our vocabulary transcriptions, we have not indicated there the levelings here discussed.

Pairs like *manners : mannas* \-nəz\, *scapulars : scapulas* \-ləz\, *rushers : Russia's* \-shəz\, *goer : Goa* \-ōə\, *Ballard : ballad* \-ləd\ are identical.

The following pairs may be identical, some chiefly in eastern New England and southern British speech, both members containing [ää] or [ȧ] ([ȧ] here, in square brackets, transcribes a vowel that is between \ä\ and \a\ in quality; within reversed virgules in vocabulary transcriptions, \ȧ\ stands for both [ää] and [ȧ]; see the section on \ȧ\): *farther : father, spars : spas, aren't : aunt, arms : alms, carve : calve, farced : fast, parsed : past.*

(2) The pronunciations of both items with and items without *r* in the spelling may contain the same sounds in the same sequence but be distinct because the vowel is longer in the items with *r*.

Pairs like *cart* and *cot* so differ with a high degree of consistency in the South and in New York City, pairs like *card* and *cod* with much less consistency. See (1) preceding.

Pairs like *bird* and *bud* may so differ, and the difference may be shown by the transcriptions [ˈbəəd] and [ˈbəd] respectively. The words more often differ in that *bird* has [ə̄] instead of [əə], [ə̄] indicating a vowel differing in quality from that of *bud*. Within reversed virgules in transcriptions, \ə̄\ stands for both [ə̄] and [əə].

(3) Items with and items without orthographic *r* may differ in that in the pronunciation of the former the vowel common to both has \ə\ following: *beard* \ˈbiəd\ : *bid* \ˈbid\, *erred* \ˈeəd\: *Ed* \ˈed\, *court* \ˈkōət\ : *coat* \ˈkōt\, *poorly* \ˈpu̇əlē\ : *pulley* \ˈpu̇lē\, *sired* \ˈsīəd\ : *side* \ˈsīd\, *scour* \ˈskau̇ə\ : *scow* \ˈskau̇\, *coir* \ˈkȯiə\: *coy* \ˈkȯi\. Some speakers may frequently have \ȯə\ in words like *tort* but usually only \ȯ\ in words like *taut*. Because of a tendency for English vowels to shorten in proportion to their distance in syllables from the end of a word, it was decided at the beginning of transcription to show \ȯə\ as well as \ȯ\ for *r* words of this class only in the ultima and penultima — e.g., in *norm* and *normal* but not in *normalize* or *normality*. The precedent, however, of words that show \ȯə\ only or alternatively in at least all stressed syllables and of other words that show only \ȯ\ in all syllables has made for some inconsistency in the transcriptions.

The \ȯə\ of some transcribers and the \ȯȯ\ of others (see 2) may sometimes be merely a difference of interpretation of the same phonetic entity. We do not show a transcription \ȯə\ for words of the type *taut, law*. For *–R* dialects in which *tort* and *taut* are both \ˈtȯət\ the variant \ȯ\ should be regarded as having the value \ȯə\. Some transcribers might regard the entity transcribed \ää\ in (1) as in pairs like *card : cod, cart : cot*, as \äə\ instead.

The Middle Atlantic vowel symbolized \aa\ is often followed by \ə\ in monosyllables or in the last syllable of words without *r* in the spelling, with leveling of pairs like *paired : pad*, as indicated by the variants \ˈpaaə\ at *pair* and \ˈpaa(ə)d\ at *pad*.

In drawled speech, especially common in the South but not here transcribed, the vowel \ə\ frequently occurs between certain vowels and a following consonant, as in \ˈbiəd\ for *bid*. Whether pairs like *beard : bid* are leveled in the South and if so to what extent is a question that needs further investigation.

(4) An item containing *r* may differ in *–R* pronunciation from all items not containing *r* in that a vowel is used for the *r* item that lacks \r\ quality and that is different from any other the speaker uses. Thus the vowel \ə̄\ is limited to words like *bird, German*, except as it may occur as a replacement for \œ\, \œ̄\, \œœ\, \œ̄œ\ in words originating in a foreign language, as *Goebbels, Goethe*. The diphthong \əi\ is used for the *ir* of *bird* by many speakers in the New York City area and in the deep South.

(5) The speech of some is partly *–R* and partly *R*. Speakers whose speech habits were formed near a boundary between *–R* and *R* areas sometimes have and sometimes lack \r\ in words of the same class (*card, cart, hearth*) or even in the same word. Many speakers have in words of the class *bird, dirt, mirth* the same pronunciation as *R* speakers — \ər\ — but a basically *–R* pronunciation in other classes of words.

What happens before a vowel in *–R* speech to a word in which \r\ is the last symbol shown in transcriptions for *R* speech needs some discussion.

When before an initial vowel in a following word there is a pause whose correlate in the written language is a punctuation mark, there usually is no \r\ at the end of a preceding word when there would be no \r\ if a consonant followed: *Why should I care? Others don't.*

When there is no pause between two such words, *–R* speech may have an \r\ or may not: *a door opened*. When there is no \r\ a glottal stop may occur between the two words. Such a glottal stop is not transcribed in this dictionary.

When the vowel that follows is a suffix or the first sound of a suffix, \r\ regularly occurs in all standard *–R* speech: *starry, starring*.

A word like *dear* is not pronounced with an \r\ at the end in *–R* speech when a consonant or pause follows ("*dear friend*", "*Dear? Eighty dollars!*"), but is often pronounced with an \r\ when a vowel word follows without pause (*dear experience*). A word like *idea* also is not pronounced with an \r\ when a consonant or pause follows, but like *dear* frequently does have an \r\ before a closely following vowel with many speakers who pronounce an \r\ in *dear* in the same situation, in spite of the fact that *idea* has no *r* in the orthography. Such an \r\, called "intrusive *r*", is frequent in the northeastern United States and southern England but is rare or nonexistent in the southern United States. It usually follows \ə\, \ȯ\, \ȧ\, or \ä\ and may occur before a vowel in a following word or, perhaps less often and with greater deprecation from some listeners, before a suffixed vowel: *idea of importance, law and order, Omaha and Lincoln, drawing, withdrawal, sol-faing*. Our transcriptions have taken notice of intrusive *r* probably only at *idea*, where the variant with \r\ was mentioned both because it seemed a distortion to omit it from a complement of variants so sizable and because *idea* has come to be regarded as something of a shibboleth for the occurrence of intrusive *r*. Two kinds of parenthesizing of an \r\ at the end of a transcription will be found: "(r)", with a parenthesis on each side, and "(r", with no closing parenthesis:

dod·der \ˈdädə(r)\
¹*bar* \ˈbär, ˈbȧ(r\

In transcriptions with two parentheses the form with r is the *R* pronunciation and in some environments the *–R* pronunciation also, the form without r is the *–R* pronunciation in other environments. In that fraction of a transcription that follows a comma or semicolon and that ends with r preceded but not followed by a parenthesis, the form with as well as the form without r is limited to *–R* speech (as \ˈbȧr\ as well as \ˈbȧ\); the form preceding the comma or semicolon (as \ˈbär\) is the *R* pronunciation and with *–R* speakers whose \ȧ\ is to be construed as [ää] is alternative to [ää] before a vowel.

In words that rhyme with *spur* and are common enough to call for maximum variant coverage, the *R* and *–R* pronunciations are labeled.

In a pronunciation like that at

fear \ˈfi(ə)r, -iə\

\ˈfi(ə)r\ is the *R* pronunciation in all environments and the *–R* pronunciation in some, \ˈfiə\ is the *–R* pronunciation in other environments.

To provide a degree of clarification of the pronunciations of such words impossible in most of our transcriptions, to enable the consultant to be sure of our intent as to the pronunciation of inflected forms not transcribed, and to enable the consultant to supply the *–R* pronunciation of uncommon words for which that pronunciation is not shown, we transcribe in detail below the infinitive, past, and present participle of one verb of each of the classes into which verbs are divisible on the basis of the pronunciation of the last syllable.

fear *R, –R+suffixal vowel, some –R+following-word vowel* ˈfir, ˈfiər; *–R+consonant or pause, some –R+following-word vowel* ˈfiə\ *feared* *R* ˈfi(ə)rd, *–R* ˈfiəd\ *fearing* *R & –R* ˈfi(ə)riŋ\ (the greater the stress or emphasis the greater the likelihood of \-iər(-)\ rather than \-ir(-)\)

bare *R, –R+suffixal vowel, some –R+following-word vowel* ˈbar, ˈber, ˈbaar, ˈbaər, ˈbeər, ˈbaaər; *–R+consonant or pause, some –R+following-word vowel* ˈbaə, ˈbeə, ˈbaaə\ *bared* *R* ˈba(ə)rd, ˈbe(ə)rd, ˈbaa(ə)rd, *–R* ˈbaəd, ˈbeəd, ˈbaaəd\ *bearing* *R & –R* ˈba(ə)riŋ, ˈbe(ə)riŋ, ˈbaa(ə)riŋ\

bar *R* ˈbär; *–R+consonant or pause, some –R+following-word vowel* ˈbȧ; *some –R+suffixal vowel, some –R+following-word vowel* ˈbȧr; *some –R+suffixal or following-word vowel* ˈbär (*with some speakers whose* ˈbȧ = ˈbää)\ *barred* *R* ˈbärd, *–R* ˈbȧd\ *barring* *R* ˈbȧriŋ, *–R* ˈbȧriŋ *or* ˈbäriŋ\

spur *R+consonant* ˈspər, *+vowel* ˈspər·; *–R+consonant or pause* ˈspə̄, *+suffixal vowel* ˈspər· *also* ˈspə̄r, *+following-word vowel* ˈspər· *or* ˈspə̄ *also* ˈspə̄r\ *spurred* *R* ˈspərd, *–R* ˈspə̄d\ *spurring* *R* ˈspər·iŋ, *–R* ˈspər·iŋ *also* ˈspə̄riŋ\ (the centered period means that only one of the two variants that occur for the *urr* of a word like *hurry* occurs in *spurring*; see the section on \ˌər\; the variants \ər·\, \ə̄r\ differ in that although both have substantially the same two articulations the articulations are simultaneous or overlapping for \ər·\ but consecutive for \ə̄r\, the latter being of greater duration than the former)

dodder *R, –R+suffixal vowel, some –R+following-word vowel* ˈdädər; *–R+consonant or pause, some –R+following-word vowel* ˈdädə\ *doddered* *R* ˈdädərd, *–R* ˈdädəd\ *doddering* *R & –R* ˈdäd(ə)riŋ\ (in most words of this class, with unstressed final syllable, a variation occurs for the present participle that it is more convenient to record at the subentry for that form)

war, warred, warring *as for variants with* ȯ *at* STORE *below*\

store *R, –R+suffixal vowel, some –R+following-word vowel* ˈstōr, ˈstōər, ˈstȯr, ˈstȯər; *–R+consonant or pause, some –R+following-word vowel* ˈstōə, ˈstȯ, ˈstȯə\ *stored* *R* ˈstō(ə)rd, ˈstȯ(ə)rd, *–R* ˈstȯ(ə)d\ *storing* *R & –R* ˈstō(ə)riŋ, ˈstȯ(ə)riŋ\

tour *R, –R+suffixal vowel, some –R+following-word vowel* ˈtu̇r, ˈtu̇ər; *–R+consonant or pause, some –R+following-word vowel* ˈtu̇ə\ *toured* *R* ˈtu̇(ə)rd, *–R* ˈtu̇əd\ *touring* *R & –R* ˈtu̇(ə)riŋ\

tire *R, –R+suffixal vowel, some –R+following-word vowel* ˈtīr, ˈtīər; *–R+consonant or pause, some –R+following-word vowel* ˈtīə\ *tired* *R* ˈtī(ə)rd, *–R* ˈtīəd\ *tiring* *R & –R* ˈtī(ə)riŋ\

tower *R, –R+suffixal vowel, some –R+following-word vowel* ˈtau̇r, ˈtau̇ər; *–R + consonant or pause, some –R+following-word vowel* ˈtau̇ə\ *towered* *R* ˈtau̇(ə)rd, *–R* ˈtau̇əd\ *towering* *R & –R* ˈtau̇(ə)riŋ\

**\ r(·) ** see \ə·r, ər·\ and \r\. Words that rhyme with *stir* and that are not common often have \r(·)\ as the final items in their transcriptions, as *knur* \ˈnər(·)\. The parenthesized centered period means that before a following vowel such words do not have one of the two pronunciations that are common in standard speech for the *urr* of *hurry*. For the full range of pronunciations that are heard for a word like *knur* see \r\ in this "Guide" or the pronunciation of rhyming words in the vocabulary.

**\ rᵊ ** as in one pronunciation of French *lustre*. \rᵊ\ is a single voiceless sound that does not add an extra syllable, the \ˈlūstrᵊ\ pronunciation of *lustre* being a single syllable. The \ᵊ\ after the \r\ is always parenthesized to indicate the usual pronunciation when a vowel-initial word follows without pause. Thus *lustre antique* is \lūe strä^{n} tēk\, three syllables, with \str\ as in French *strate*. See section on \ᵊ\.

***r*-dropper** see section headed *–R*.

***r*-keeper** see section headed *R*.

**\ rr ** in some languages, as Spanish, the difference between a trilled *r* (made with two or more taps of the tongue) and a single-tap *r* is phonemic, distinguishing words otherwise identical. In transcriptions of the Spanish pronunciation of words borrowed from the Spanish \rr\ has been used for the trilled *r*. For languages which have a trilled *r* only or in which the difference between two varieties is of no significance, \r\ alone is adequate.

**\ rü ** as in *rude, peruse, verruca;* that is, words in which the orthographic representation is not *roo* and that are mostly from Latin and Greek. The variant \ryü\ or \rïü\ occurs in such words to a very limited extent in U.S. speech and so is not shown for any of the words listed above. Occasionally when \ˈrü\ and \ˌr(y)ə\ are gradational variants (as in *garrulity, garrulous*), the \ryü\ variant may be less limited in its extent and then is shown.

**\ s ** as in *so, less, lesser.*

On the showing of \z\ and \s\ variants for the *s* of words like *abstain, teamster, instigate* (in which a voiced consonant precedes and a voiceless sound follows), see the section on \z\.

sandhi see the vocabulary definition. Only to a very limited extent is account taken in vocabulary pronunciations of the variations that occur at the beginning of words because of the nature of the last sound of a preceding word, or of the variations that occur at the end of words because of the nature of the first sound of a following word. In common words whose last sound is \t\ when the word is pronounced in isolation, we record that before vowels \d·\ usually occurs instead, as at *complete*. At *and* and *you* we record variations that these words undergo as a result of environment. At *'em* we record that a preceding word ordinarily \v\-final may before \ᵊm\ have \b\ instead of \v\. We do not, however, record at words whose final sound is shown as \s\ or \z\ that instead the sound is usually \sh\ or \zh\ respectively when a word following without pause begins with \sh\, \y\, or \zh\, as in *horseshoe, the pace you've set, the size you want, this gendarme*. We do not record at words whose first sound is shown as \b\, \d\, or \g\ that when a word ending in \s\ precedes without pause these three stops may not differ in pronunciation from the stops respectively transcribed \p\, \t\, and \k\ in *spy, stay, sky*, with frequent homophony of such pairs as *this buy : the spy, this day : the stay, this guy : the sky* (compare our transcriptions at *disband, disdain*, and *disguise*). We do not record at words shown as having a given consonant at the end of an unstressed final syllable and at words shown as having the same consonant as their first sound that when such a consonant-final word precedes such a consonant-initial word without pause often only one consonant is articulated, with homophony of such pairs as *Asian nights : Asia nights*. We do not record at words shown as beginning with unstressed \əl-\ or \il-\, \əm-\ or \im-\, \ən-\ or \in-\ that when certain consonants precede without pause some of the words of the first group may begin \ᵊl-\ instead (as in *not allowed*), some of the words of the second group may begin \ᵊm-\ instead (as in *the help employed*), and some of the words of the third group may begin \ᵊn-\, \ᵊm-\, or \ᵊŋ\ instead (as in *good encyclopedia, stop entirely*, and *dog encountered* respectively). These sandhi variants that we omit from vocabulary entries are more satisfactorily covered by being cataloged in a discussion of phonetics. Most of them happen automatically and usually without any awareness of the speaker that he is not using the pronunciations that dictionary vocabularies usually limit themselves to.

**\ sch ** as in *mischief, exhaustion*. Many transcribe only \sch\ in such words but a sequence whose first member is \sh\ rather than \s\, or at least whose first member seems to be closer to \sh\ than to \s\, is frequent when the vowel that precedes is front and is as high as \e\, as in *mischief, question*, the tongue position for a vowel of this height being closer to the tongue position for \sh\ than for \s\. After other vowels, whose tongue position is less conducive to \sh\, that consonant is less frequent and is not shown as a variant in the vocabulary, as at *bastion, combustion, exhaustion*.

Scottish see section on foreign words.

semicolon a semicolon rather than a comma sometimes separates variant pronunciations. A semicolon does not mean that what follows it is less acceptable or less frequent than what precedes it. It is in general used as a safeguard against regarding a variant or a label as applicable to an item or a part of an item following the semicolon. Examples:

adversary *R* ˈadvə(r)ˌserē, *–R* -vəˌs-; -ri\ (if a comma had been used instead of the semicolon, the meaning would be that the variant -ri is limited to *–R* speech)

cayuga \kēˈügə, ˈkyü-; kāˈ(y)üˌ, kīˈ(y)ü-, *attrib* (ˈ)=¦==\ [the *attrib* (ˈ)=¦== does not apply to anything before the semicolon]

aficionada \əˌfisēəˈnädə, əˌfēsēə-ˌəˌfishə-, aˌf-, -ädə; -ˌfēthēəˈnäthə, -nä-\ (such variants as \i\, \s\, and \sh\ are unlikely when the last consonant in the word is th)

luxembourg or *luxemburg* \ˈlu̇ksəmˌbu̇rg, -bu̇əg *also* ˈlük- *or* -ˌbərg *or* -ˌbə̄g *or* -ˌbəig; ˈləksəmˌbərg, -bə̄g, -ˌbəig *also* -bu̇rg *or* -bu̇əg\ (the label *also* does not apply to ˈləksəmˌbərg, which is probably as frequent as the ˈlu̇k- variant; and construing the *also* to apply to the last four final-syllable variants would produce a contradiction with the first part of the pronunciation. Use of the semicolon facilitates the presentation of the relationship between the vowel quality of the first and final syllables)

**\ sh ** as in *shy, dish, sure, mission*. \sh\ is a single sound, not two, and has in it no \s\ sound or \h\ sound.

**\ shch ** see section on \sch\.

-sia, -sian as in *magnesia, euthanasia, Andalusian*. For many words ending in *-sia* or *-sian* as many as ten variants occur: \-zhə(n), -zhēə(n), -shə(n), -shēə(n), *chiefly Brit* -ziə(n), -zyə(n), -zhyə(n), -siə(n), -syə(n), -shyə(n)\. We do not show this range of variants at any entry in the vocabulary. For common words for which we have records we limit the transcriptions to the variants that appear to be most frequent in American speech, and for uncommon words we often show \-zh(ē)ə\ as the two variants that an averaging of the records of commoner words suggests as most likely.

stress marks see 2.2 in "Explanatory Notes"; on the placement of stress marks, see "Divisions in Respelled Pronunciations"; the mark ˌ is treated in a separate part of the "Guide". The brief discussion of stress in "Explanatory Notes", while true as far as it goes, omits some details. Actually, words like *beneficial* (vocabulary stress marking \¦==¦==\), *fictitious* (vocabulary stress marking \(ˈ)=¦==\), and *campaign* (vocabulary stress marking \(ˈ)=¦=\) undergo an even wider variation of stress than "Explanatory Notes" shows. Thus *beneficial* may also be \ˈ==ˈ==\ (as in *Beneficial though it is . . .*) or \ˌ==ˌ==\ (as in *beneficial diet*), *fictitious* may also be \ˈ=ˈ==\ or \ˌ=ˌ==\ (as in *fictitious story*), and *campaign* may be \=ˈ=\ (as in *a hard campaign*), \ˈ=ˌ=\, \ˈ=ˈ=\, or \ˌ=ˌ=\ (as in *campaign promises*).

A high percentage of adjectives traditionally transcribed with a primary stress as the last of two or more stresses (as *beneficial, scrophulariaceous*), and many adjectives traditionally transcribed with a primary stress on the second syllable but no stress on the first (as *fictitious, magnanimous, dissociative*) are marked in the vocabulary with the indicators of variation of stress. (Two successive primary stresses were mentioned as a possible stress variant for *beneficial;* three successive primaries seem unlikely but three successive secondaries may easily occur, as in the fourth word of *one of the scrophulariaceous herbs.*) A high percentage of words belonging to other parts of speech and traditionally transcribed with two or more stresses the last of which is a primary on the last syllable (as *campaign, acquiesce, catamaran*) are transcribed with the markings for stress variation because of the frequency with which primary stress recedes in them or is reduced to secondary when another word follows without pause (*acquiesce readily, catamaran sailing*). It is possibly a safe generalization to say that there is no word having two or more stresses the last of which is primary when the word is pronounced in isolation that does not in some contexts undergo recession or reduction of the last stress, whatever the part of speech and whichever the syllable that bears the last stress. Thus in the item *Smith's explanation, Johnson's explanation, Wilson's explanation — they're all questionable*, probably neither of the two stressed syllables in any of the three words *explanation* would be uttered with primary stress. But such a stress pattern would occur in fewer contexts for a noun that in isolation lacks primary on the ultima than for a noun that possesses it, and our stress marking for *explanation* is \ˌ==ˈ==\.

For two-member compounds the second member of which is an independent English word the vocabulary usually shows only the pronunciation of the first member followed by a plus sign. If ¦ or (ˈ) occurs in the transcription of the first member, it is to be understood that the compound as a whole is subject to stress variation. When in compounds whose pronunciation is shown by the plus-sign formula the second member normally has secondary stress only, the plus sign is followed by ˌ-.

mac·ro·fauna \ˈmakrō+\
mac·ro·prism \ˈmakrō+ˌ-\

Many words for which variable stress is indicated are both adjective and noun. If for such a word that has no stress on the last syllable the adjective entry is first, we usually show the pronunciation of the noun following simply as \"\. If the noun entry is first, we usually show for it a pronunciation in which the only primary stress is the last and show variation of stress for the adjective following by means of stress marks and double hyphens. Thus our pronunciation for [1]*organic, adj* is \(ˈ)ȯ(r)ˈganik, -nēk\ and for [2]*organic, n* is \"\. If [1]*organic* had been the noun instead our pronunciation would have been \ȯ(r)ˈganik, -nēk\ and the pronunciation for [2]*organic, adj* would have been \(ˈ)=ˈ==\. Showing no stress variation for the noun in such cases is an oversimplification: even a noun without stress on the last syllable does sometimes undergo stress recession but much less often than does the adjective.

The nouns that usually have last-syllable primary stress when pronounced immediately before a pause are shown with the marks for recession of stress. If, in words with last-syllable stress, this stress is often secondary rather than primary before a pause their stress may be indicated by two variants separated by a comma.

[1]*av·oir·du·pois* \ˌavə(r)dəˈpȯiz, ˈ===ˌ=\

**\ sü ** as in *sue, suit, assume;* that is, words in which the orthographic representation is not *soo* and that are mostly from Latin and Greek. The variant \syü\ or \siü\ appears to be frequent in southern British speech but is rare in U.S. speech and so is not shown.

superlatives of adjectives see sections on INFLECTED FORMS, DIVISION OF and on INFLECTED FORMS, PRONUNCIATION OF.

syllables see separate section on "Divisions in Boldface Entry Words" and "Divisions in Respelled Pronunciations".

symbol names the terms *bar, one-dot,* and *two-dot* can be used with the name of a character in this way: \ā\ is "bar a", \t͟h\ is "bar t-h", \ȯ\ is "one-dot o", \ü\ is "two-dot u". Symbols with no modifier are *plain:* \a\ is "plain a", \i\ is "plain i" because the dot is not a modifier.

**\ t ** as in *tights, attend, Atlantic.* See section on \d·\.

With chiefly substandard speakers in the New York City area the precise phonetic form of the consonant answering to *t* or *tt* between a preceding stressed vowel and a following \ᵊl\ is the glottal stop, as in *title, battle* (symbol, not shown in the transcription of such words in the vocabulary, [ʔ]). In Scotland the glottal stop is used in the same environment, and before an unstressed vowel as in *water, bitter,* by a higher percentage of cultured speakers than in New York City.

In words like *winter, plenty, gentlemen,* in which what corresponds to the *nt* of the spelling is preceded by a stressed vowel and followed by an unstressed vowel or \ᵊl\, the \t\ is either feebly articulated or absent in much American speech, pairs like *winter : winner* being difficult or impossible to distinguish without the help of context. Certainly the usual American pronunciation is in strong contrast to the usual southern British pronunciation, in which there is a strongly articulated, aspirated, distinctly heard \t\ that probably is to be regarded as the first sound of the syllable to which the unstressed vowel or \ᵊl\ belongs, any \t\ that may occur in the American pronunciation probably being best regarded as belonging to the syllable that contains the \n\. One way of transcribing the difference between the two pronunciations would be \ˈwin(t)·ə(r), ˈwin·tə(r\. Orthoepic commentary usually decries the absence or weakness of the \t\ in such words but the pronunciation is too widespread in all levels of American speech to be ignored. The \t\-less pronunciation is noticed in the vocabulary only in an occasional word for which multiple variants are shown or from which the absence is regarded as apt to be especially conspicuous, as at *gentleman,* the emphasis on the plural of this word in the formula "Ladies and Gentlemen" at the beginning of an address making the absence quite noticeable. A two-variant pronunciation such as that shown above for *winter* is to be understood in the vocabulary for all words of this class, with the label "÷" preceding the \-n(t)·-\ variant to signify the deprecation of orthoepists.

With chiefly substandard speakers in the New York City area a pronunciation somewhat like the British often occurs, except that the tongue position is further forward, the tip frequently being against the lower front teeth.

**\ th ** as in *thin, ether.* \th\ is a single sound, not two, and has in it no \t\ sound or \h\ sound. The basic difference between \th\ and \t͟h\ is that the first is pronounced without and the second with vibration of the vocal cords.

**\ t͟h ** as in *then, either.* \t͟h\ is a single sound, not two, and has in it no \t\ sound or \h\ sound. The basic difference between \th\ and \t͟h\ is that the first is pronounced without and the second with vibration of the vocal cords.

-ths plurals of singulars ending in *-th* pronounced \th\ with vowel preceding and without pronunciation in the vocabulary are to be understood to be \ths\, as *myths.* Plurals with the variants \t͟hz\ and \ths\ (not always in this order) are pronounced in the vocabulary. The \t͟h\ of \t͟hz\ is often weakly articulated; in fact, it may be that in some pronunciations regarded as containing \t͟h\ what is so regarded is an extension of the length of the preceding vowel rather than a consonantal articulation.

**\ ū ** this symbol, used in most diacritical alphabets for the sounds following the \f\ of *few* and often for the sounds between the \f\ and \r\ of *fury,* is replaced in this dictionary by \yü\ and \yu̇\, which are not only phonetically more realistic but also transcriptionally more economical in permitting the showing of two variants by parenthesization, as in \ˈn(y)ü\ for *new.*

**\ u̇ ** as in *pull, wood, injurious.* See section on \u̇r\.

\u̇\ is usually shown as the second part or ending position of the diphthong of *loud* but in most articulations a point this high is not reached, the ending position being closer to \ō\. Other diphthongs with this ending position occur as variants in certain classes of words in which other speakers pronounce a vowel followed by \l\. See section on \l\.

**\ œ ** as in German *füllen, hübsch;* \œ\ can be approximated by pronouncing \i\ with moderately rounded lips.

**\ ᵫ ** as in French *rue,* German *fühlen;* \ᵫ\ can be approximated by pronouncing \ē\ with strongly rounded lips.

**\ ü ** as in *rule, moon, few* \ˈfyü\, *union* \ˈyünyən\. Compare the section on \yü\.

\ ü \ plus unstressed vowel in vocabulary pronunciations, \u̇\ if not shown is to be understood as a variant of \ü\ in such position, as in *fluid, gluey, skua.*

**\ u̇r \, \ u̇ər \, \ u̇ə ** in words of the type of *injurious, furious, tour, pure,* variants occur that are not shown in the vocabulary or that are not shown for uncommon words.

Words of the type of *injurious* are shown in the vocabulary as containing the sequence \u̇r\ followed by a vowel. In the deep South they may contain \ür\ instead of \u̇r\, and the \ür\ variant is to be understood for uncommon words for which it is not shown. In southern British speech all words of this type usually have \ə\ between the \u̇\ and \r\ and may have \ōər\ as a variant; the most common words may also have \ȯr\ or \ȯər\ as a variant, and for one such word at least (*injurious*) \ər\ is also shown.

Words of the type of *pure* are shown in the vocabulary as having \u̇r\ or \u̇ər\ in *R* speech and before a vowel in *–R* speech, and as having \u̇ə\ in *–R* speech elsewhere. In southern British speech the \ə\ appears to be usually present between \u̇\ and \r\; in all such words a variant \ōə(r\ is heard, and the most common words may also have \ȯə(r\ or \ȯ(r\.

V used in the formula "*usu* -ăd·+V" as at *wait;* chosen for the formula as being an abbreviation for "vowel" but "+V" is to be interpreted as meaning "*+ vowel or* ᵊl *following without pause*".

**\ v ** as in *vote, level, give.* Under the assimilative influence of a following \ᵊm\, the lip-teeth sound \v\ may have as a variant the two-lip sound \b\, as in *give 'em, government.* See section on \ᵊm\.

variants see 2.3, 2.4 in "Explanatory Notes". If the consultant knows or has reason to believe that an uncommon word has less than a full complement of the predictable variants that we usually give for common words, he can supply the omitted variants by examining the variants for better-known words that rhyme or the variants for a rhyming part of such words. He will need to observe certain precautions mentioned in this "Guide". The \əi\ variant shown at a word of the type of *bird,* for example, does not hold for a word of the type of *preferred.* See \əi\.

**\ w ** as in *we, sweep, away.* See sections on \əw\, \hw\.

**\ wʸ ** as *hu* in French *huile* or *u* in French *nuit;* \wʸ\ can be approximated by rounding the lips as for \w\ while the tongue makes the articulation for \y\.

x for words of the type of *exact, exult,* in which the sounds that correspond to the *x* of the spelling are preceded by an unstressed and followed by a stressed vowel, the vocabulary usually shows only the value \gz\ for the *x.* For such words some speakers have \ks\ instead.

**\ y ** as in *yard, yours, European* \ˌyu̇rəˈpēən\, *cue* \ˈkyü\, *union* \ˈyünyən\. See section on \yü\.

**\ ʸ ** not a symbol for a sound but a diacritic signifying a modification of the sound of the preceding symbol, the modification consisting of articulating the sound while the tongue is in approximately the position for the sound \y\, with the tip back of the lower front teeth. See the sections on \lʸ\, \nʸ\, \wʸ\.

Frequently at the end of the articulation of \nʸ\ or \lʸ\ an independent \y\ sound is heard, without anything else accompanying, [nʸy], [lʸy], but it is usually considered unnecessary to transcribe this off-glide.

The sound \wʸ\ could with equal logic have been symbolized by a full-size y followed by a superior w to denote lip rounding, but \wʸ\ is preferred because \w\ is the usual anglicization, as in \swăd\ for *suede,* from a French word pronounced \swʸed\.

**\ yə ** as in *ammunition.* Some transcribers prefer \yu̇\ to \yə\ as the transcription in an unstressed medial syllable of *u* or *eu.* In normal-tempo speech it is difficult to hear the difference between unstressed \yə\ and \yu̇\. A distinct \yu̇\ is probably more common in British speech than in American and is heard in the latter in emphatic or deliberate utterance. In initial syllables, as in *unite* and *uranium,* \yü\, \yu̇\, and \yə\ are all three heard although the vocabulary does not show all three. When such words are pronounced starting from pause, the \yə\ variant is more apt to occur before \r\ than before other consonants, and the vocabulary transcriptions for the initial vowel are not identical for all words.

**\ yü \, \ yu̇ ** these two transcriptions replace the ū of previous editions of this dictionary, \yu̇\ occurring before \r\ as in *European* and \yü\ elsewhere as in *unity.* These two transcriptions not only better display the nature of the sounds but also make it possible to show two pronunciations for a word like *new* simply by parenthesizing, \ˈn(y)ü\, the (y) signifying that *new* may either be pronounced like the *noo-* of *noose* or have between \n\ and \ü\ a sound that does not occur in *noose.* See sections on \lü\, \sü\.

When certain consonants precede in the same syllable the first component may be [i] instead of [y]. In the variety with [y] the second component has greater stress than the first but in the variety with [i] the first component has stress equal to or greater than that of the second. It is not necessary to show in the vocabulary the variant [iü] or [iu̇], which is merely the variety of \yü\ or \yu̇\ that occurs under certain conditions.

See section on \yə\.

**\ z ** as in *zone, freezer, raise.*

Most transcribers treat as \s\ the sound of the *s* in words like *abstain, teamster, instigate, redskin, brownstone,* in which a voiced consonant precedes and a voiceless sound follows. But it is doubtful that there is any difference between most utterances of the *-mst-* of *teamster* and the *-m's t-* of *the team's terrific,* of the *-dsk-* of *redskin* and the *-d's k-* of *Red's kin,* of the *-nst-* of *brownstone* and the *-n's t-* of *Brown's tone,* in the second member of which pairs transcribers just as regularly treat the sound of the *s* as \z\. What happens in both *brownstone* and *Brown's tone* when they are identical is probably the same thing that phoneticians agree happens to the last sound of *Brown's* or *brows* when those words have only pause following, as at the end of a sentence: the last sound starts out voiced, by carryover from the voiced sound preceding, but becomes voiceless.

This devoicing might be shown in minute transcription intended primarily for scholars by the symbol \z\ with a small circle underneath, such a circle being widely used by phoneticians for devoicing, or even by a transcription \brau̇nz-stōn\, but for an item like *Brown's* which has at the end the same sequence of voice and voicelessness a plain \z\ alone is usually employed. For items like *abstain, teamster, instigate* we show two variants for the *s,* \z\ and \s\, the latter probably being frequent or usual in emphatic utterance. We provide only stress indications at the vocabulary entries of compounds like *redskin* and *brownstone,* although only \s\ is shown at SKIN and STONE. If transcriptions with sound symbols were shown for such compounds our transcription at REDSKIN would be \ˈredzˌkin, -dˌsk-\. Compare the section on sandhi.

When the preceding voiced consonant is a nasal, when the next vowel is without stress, and when the *s* is definitely \s\ and not \z\, the voiceless stop homorganic with the nasal often occurs parasitically before the \s\: *teamster* \ˈtēmpstə(r)\, *monster* \ˈmäntstə(r)\, *gangster* \ˈgaŋkstə(r)\.

**\ zh ** as in *vision.* \zh\ is a single sound, not two, and has in it no \z\ sound or \h\ sound.

**\ zü ** as in *presume, resume;* that is, words in which the orthographic representation is not *zoo* and which are mostly from Latin and Greek. The variant \zyü\ or \ziü\ appears to be frequent in southern British speech but is rare in U.S. speech and so is not shown.

DIVISIONS IN RESPELLED PRONUNCIATIONS

1. American general dictionaries have for a long time attempted to mark the boundaries of all the syllables in a respelled pronunciation. Many linguists and phoneticians, however, have no certainty as to precisely where these divisions are and sometimes no certainty even as to how many syllables a word has. The three words *gore, goer, Goa* are pronounced alike by many U. S. speakers, and yet it is general practice to treat the first as a monosyllable only and the other two as disyllables only. It has also been general practice to treat a single consonant as being in the following syllable when preceded by a long stressed vowel or an unstressed vowel and as being in the same syllable with a preceding short stressed vowel, although consonantal quality has more to do with syllable boundaries than does vocalic quality.

2. Because of the extremes of opinion with regard to syllable boundaries, whatever course a dictionary adopts will meet with some opposition. Some students maintain that in some languages there is no such thing as a phonetically recognizable boundary between words when they follow one another without pause. Other students of language and probably most laymen believe that if practically any succession of two words is pronounced in isolation, the boundary is determinable from the pronunciation alone, even though a sequence like *a never-ready* may be misapprehended as *an ever-ready* (and vice versa) when the context is ambiguous. The word *adder* originally had an initial *n* whereas *nickname* originally lacked an initial *n*, the respective loss and gain resulting from mistaking the constituents when such words as *a* or *an*, *my* or *mine* preceded.

3. In most American speech the sound used for the letter *t* varies according to its position in a word. This variance is a basis of our treatment of syllables in the respellings. Thus most Americans would not speak *ten trips/tent rips* or *Kay Tolliver/Kate Oliver* identically. Our treatment does not attempt to cover in full southern British speech in which a *t* is often pronounced the same whether it appears to the left or to the right of a word boundary.

4. In American speech the following consonant sounds when preceded by a stressed vowel usually sound one way when a word boundary is immediately to the left of the corresponding orthographic *t* and another way when the boundary is to the immediate right of the *t:*

\t,d•\ *wry tangle/right angle*
\nt\ *men told/meant old*
\tr\ *stay trite/state right*
\ltr\ *bell trick/belt Rick*
\ntr\ *ten trips/tent rips*
\tw\ *no twill/note Will*
\ltw\ *Hall twin/halt Wynn*
\ntw\ *Doane twin/don't win*
\ty\ *why Tunis/white Eunice* (*when Tunis is* \'tyü-\ and not \'tü-\)
\lty\ *spell Tunis/spelt Eunice*
\nty\ *scan Tunis/scant Eunice*
\tsh(=t•sh)\ *Leete shin*
\ch(=•tsh)\ *Lee chin/Leech Inn*

5. When any consonant except \r\ occurs immediately before any of the preceding sequences except the last, the sequence resulting, if it is not one of those listed above, sounds the same regardless of word boundary. The following sequences sound the same: *black tie/blacked eye, cur stray/curse tray/curst ray, lop twigs/lopped wigs, miff Tunis/miffed Eunice.*

6. When the \l\ or \n\ in the preceding list is syllabic or is preceded by an unstressed vowel, the difference usually heard when a stressed vowel precedes is reduced or may disappear. A complication for the \nt\-plus-vowel sequence is the possibility that a difference heard may be due to complete loss of the \t\ when a word boundary follows rather than to a difference in the syllable placement of the \t\, as in the second item in *flew and told/fluent old.*

7. When any of the sequences in the preceding list susceptible of two syllabifications occurs within a word at a point where there is no boundary between meaningful elements that a speaker may be trying to maintain, the syllabification is usually that which occurs when a *t* is to the right of a word boundary: \t\ instead of \d•\ for the *tt* of *attack*, \n•t\ instead of \nt•\ for the *nt* of *entire*, \•tr\ instead of \t•r\ for the *tr* of *metric*, \•tyu̇\ instead of \t•yu̇\ for the *tu* of *mature* (when \y\ is not absent from the word). Exceptions are \d•\, sometimes heard instead of \t\ for the first *t* of *potato;* \t•w\ instead of \•tw\ for the *tw* of *Antwerp* (though \•tw\ possibly occurs sometimes in British speech); \nt•r\, sometimes heard instead of \n•tr\, chiefly in substandard speech for the *ntr* of words like *country* and *contribution.*

8. If in our transcriptions our symbol for the *ch* of *chin* and *each* were \tsh\, in order to make it clear that this \tsh\ differs from the \t•sh\ of *Leete shin* and to be consistent with our use of two differently placed dots in all the other divisionally different items, it would be necessary to use a dot in another position when the sequence is intervocalic (as in *Lee chin/Leech Inn*) and to make a commitment as to the syllable division of these two morpheme-different homophonous pairs, something that we do not do for other such pairs. In that case consistency could have been achieved by removing all pre-\t\ dots.

9. Presumably the sounds represented by the *d* preceding and the *g* following the space in *bad gendarme* (when the speaker's pronunciation of the *g* is \zh\) stand to the sound represented by the *dge* of *badge of honor* as the corresponding parts of *Leete shin/Leech Inn/Lee chin* do, the first being \d•zh\ and the second \j=•dzh\. But words beginning with \zh\ are so rare in English that random listening will yield little or nothing in the way of evidence.

10. In this dictionary the roles of the stress mark and the syllable divider are kept distinct; the stress mark does not simultaneously serve as a syllable divider as in some pronunciation systems. Our stress marks are ' and ˌ, our syllable divider is •. For a consonant or for a sequence of consonants preceding a stressed vowel that is not the first vowel in a word, our procedure is as follows: If the consonant or sequence is one that always sounds the same wherever the corresponding word division may be, no divider is used, and the stress mark is placed before the first consonant sound or sequence of consonant sounds that can begin English words that are not mere borrowings: *astrology* \ə'sträləjē\, *mellite* \'meˌlīt\, *guest rope* \'geˌstrōp\, *Rhode Island* \(')rō'dīlənd\, *McCoy* \mə'ku̇i\, *hypnosis* \hip'nōsə̇s\, *agnostic* \ag'nästik\. If, for a given sequence, a difference of word boundary in the orthography is paralleled by a difference in the pronunciation, we indicate for each occurrence of the sequence which of the two pronunciations it has by inserting the syllable divider and placing the stress mark immediately after the divider: *antagonize* \an•'tagəˌnīz\, *contrive* \kən•'trīv\, *between* \bə̇•'twēn\, *solitude* \'sälə•ˌtyüd\, *patrician* \pə•'trishən\. When the vowel that follows the consonants is without stress, only the divider is used: *metric* \'me•trik\, *matriarch* \'mā•trēˌärk\, *country* \'kən•trē\, *contribution* \ˌkän•trə'byüshən\. In derivatives formed by adding the suffix *-ry* to an English word ending in *t* immediately preceded by a vowel, *l*, or *n*, the division is sometimes before, sometimes after, the \t\, and no divider is used: *puppetry* \'pəpə̇trē\.

10.1 The sequence \ntr\ in a word like *country* is sometimes, chiefly in substandard speech, \'kənt•rē\ rather than \'kən•trē\. The \nt•r\ variant is not shown for these.

10.2 For \nt\ followed by an unstressed vowel, both \nt•\ and \n•t\ occur, and no divider has been used in the transcription: *winter* \'wintə(r)\, *bunting* \'bəntiŋ\. The \n•t\ division for these is much less frequent in American than in British speech. In American speech what many hear as \nt•\ is probably often simply \n\, pairs like *winter/winner* probably often being homophonous. \nt\ is often subject to variation in American speech when a vowel with secondary stress follows. There has been some inconsistency in the transcribing of these, and both of the following formulas, which are the same in intent, will be found: *pimento* \pə̇'ment•(ˌ)ō,-en•(ˌ)tō\, *adventism* \'adˌvenˌtizəm\.

10.3 \d\ is one of two single consonants with which the divider is used. When the orthographic correspondent of \d\ is *t*(*t*), the \d\ is always followed by the divider: *lattice* \'lad•ə̇s\, *at all* \əd•'ȯl\. When the orthographic correspondent of \d\ is *d*(*d*), no divider is used and the \d\ is to be interpreted as transcribing the variation \d•, •d\: *modest* \'mädə̇st\, *adopt* \ə'däpt\ (for words like the latter it is to be understood that for the \d•\ variant the stress is on the other side of the \d\). See the section on \d•\.

10.4 \r\ is the other single consonant with which the divider is used. The preceding vowel is always a stressed \ə\. For *hurry* the transcription \'hər•ē\ indicates a pronunciation in which the quality of the \ə\ is strongly affected by the \r\ and the two sounds may be regarded as in the same syllable, as they are in stressed *her* (in fact, the \ə\ and the \r\ may be simultaneously articulated and a single sound). The transcription \'hə•rē\ indicates a pronunciation in which the quality of the \'ə\ is much the same as the quality it has when it precedes any other consonant than \r\. \ə•r\ is probably familiar to some of the many Americans in whose speech it does not normally occur as the pronunciation usually used by circus-sideshow barkers (or by actors enacting the part) for the middle of *Hurry!* (See the section on \ər\.) In transcriptions of words not widely known in the literary language, no divider is used with the \r\, and this is to be interpreted as transcribing the same \ər•, ə•r\ variation: *dhurrie* \'dərē\.

10.5 When stressed \ər\ is followed by a consonant or a pause, the variety that occurs in American speech is the variety heard in stressed *her*. In the transcription of words like *piqueur* \-'kər(•)\, the parentheses mean that the divider is to be dispensed with when a consonant follows, as in transcribing the plural \-'kərz\, but retained when a vowel follows without pause, as in "the piqueur assisted" \-'kər•ə'sistə̇d\.

10.6 An \r\ within a word preceded by stressed \ō\ and followed by a stressed vowel is placed before, rather than after, the stress mark, as at *dorad* \'dōrˌad\, because in the prevailing pronunciation in the U. S. the division seems definitely to be \ōr•\. The centered period is not used, however, because the \ō•r\ variant is frequent in the deep South. See the section on \ōr\.

10.7 With some British speakers the sequence \tl\, as in *Atlantic*, very definitely sounds as it does at the beginning of a borrowed word like *Tlascala*, but because such a pronunciation of the \tl\ is not often heard in this country, we have transcribed \ət'lantic\. British practice could be shown by either of the two formulas mentioned above, \ət•'lantik, ə•'tl-\ or \ə'tlantik\.

10.8 Two successive identical vowels that are not in the same syllable are separated by a divider: *Alma-Ata* \ˌalmə•əˌtä\. Two successive identical vowel symbols not so separated indicate a same-syllable vowel that is or that may be regarded as of the same quality as the vowel indicated by only one of the symbols but longer: *champion* \'chaampēən\, *feuille* \fœœy\. See the section on \aa\.

10.9 In some cases the divider is put to a quite different use, serving merely to make up for deficiencies caused by the use of a digraph for a single sound. Thus, \sh\ is used to represent a single sound in *shoe* but two sounds in *gas house* and *less heroic*. \th\, likewise, is used to transcribe a single sound in *think* but two sounds in *knothole* and *not heroic*. In a transcription of sequences like *gas house* and *knothole*, in which the vowel following the \h\ is stressed, the presence of a stress mark between the two letters is sufficient. When the vowel following the \h\ is unstressed, the centered period needs to be used, as in one of the pronunciations for *imposthume* \ə̇m'päs•thəm\.

10.10 It is impracticable to attempt to show, in the transcription of single words, where a stress mark and where and when the divider would occur in connected discourse. Except for final stressed \ər\, this has not been attempted. When only part of an entry has been transcribed because the other part is pronounced at its own alphabetical place, it has usually not been practicable to position the stress mark as it would have been positioned if the entry had been transcribed in full. Thus, the transcription *Bartram oak* is \'bär•trəm-\. If a pronunciation had been shown for the second word, the full respelling would have been \'bär•trə'mōk\, with stress mark before rather than after the \m\. When an entire pronunciation or a part of a pronunciation consists of double hyphens only, full-transcription placement of stress marks is often impossible and the divider has also usually been omitted: *boathook* \'=ˌ=\, *sightworthy* \'=ˌ==\.

PUNCTUATION

The chief marks of punctuation and reference, with their names

The chief uses of the most important punctuation marks are explained in the numbered sections below.

, comma
; semicolon
: colon
. period *or* full stop
— dash *or* em dash
– dash *or* en dash
∼ swung dash
? question mark *or* interrogation point
¿? question marks, Spanish
! exclamation point
( ) parentheses *or* curves
[ ] brackets, square
⟨⟩ brackets, angle
’ *or* ' apostrophe
- hyphen
= *or* ⸗ double hyphen
´ (é) acute accent
` (è) grave accent
^ (ô) *or* ⁀ *or* ~ circumflex
~ (ñ) tilde
¯ (ō) macron
˘ (ŭ) breve
¨ (oö) diaeresis
¸ (ç) cedilla
∧ caret
“ ” *or* " " quotation marks
« » quotation marks, French
» « *or* „ “ quotation marks, German
‘ ’ *or* ' ' quotation marks, single
“ *or* ” *or* " ditto marks
/ virgule *or* slant
\ reversed virgule
{ *or* } *or* ⏟ brace
. . . *or* * * * *or* —— ellipsis
. . . suspension points
* asterisk
† dagger
‡ double dagger
§ section *or* numbered clause
‖ parallels
¶ *or* ⁋ paragraph
☞ index *or* fist
⁂ *or* ⁂ asterism

0.1 Speech consists not merely of sounds but of organized sound sequences that follow various structural patterns and are uttered with significant modifications of pitch and stress and significant pauses. Besides representing the basic sounds of speech, the English writing system accordingly utilizes signs called punctuation marks to separate groups of words and to convey some indication of the varying pitch and volume and especially the pauses in the flow of speech sounds.

0.2 A pause in speech is accompanied by a significant adjustment in the pitch of the voice, which may rise, fall, or remain the same. There may also be an increase or decrease in stress with or without actual cessation of sound. Three principal types of pauses are readily perceptible in English speech:

(1) The fading pause, a falling into silence with a full stop, is marked by a lowering of pitch and decrease of stress until the production of sound ceases. This pause signifies the termination of an utterance and in writing is usually indicated by the period or the semicolon. (2) The rising pause is characterized by an upturn in pitch often combined with a lengthening of word sounds just before the break. This pause is used to set off word groups within utterances, especially whenever there is anticipation of supplementary or explanatory matter to follow, and is usually indicated in writing by a comma or, at the end of a question, by a question mark. (3) The sustained pause occurs whenever there is a break without any change in the pitch of the voice or when the same pitch is continued across a break. This pause is often indicated in writing by a comma, particularly when a rising pause would also be appropriate. The sustained pause is indicated also by such marks as a dash or ellipsis where a person stops speaking without altering the pitch of his voice, as when he is interrupted.

0.3 Much written expression consists of discourse never actually spoken but formulated in the writer's mind and immediately expressed in writing. Somewhat more formal in its structural patterns than actual speech, such written expression is nevertheless a reflection of the spoken language, is itself capable of being spoken, and is therefore punctuated as the written expression of actual speech.

0.4 As will be indicated, punctuation marks are often used in an arbitrary or mechanical manner not directly related to language structure or to patterns of speech sounds. To a considerable extent, however, punctuation may be explained in terms of the structural divisions of speech — sentences, clauses, phrases, and other word groups — and some of the more obvious elements of pitch, stress, and pause that indicate their separation or their relationship.

1. THE PERIOD

1.1 Like a fading pause and full stop in speech, a period usually terminates a sentence that is neither interrogative nor exclamatory ⟨The mountain is 5,000 feet high. If the climbers have a good day, they will reach the top in a few hours. At the summit they will eat the lunch which has been prepared, and then they will start down early enough to reach the bottom before dark.⟩

1.1.1 Utterances terminated by a fading pause do not always have a complete subject-predicate structure. In the context of consecutive speech, however, the meaning of such utterances is entirely clear, and in writing they are usually terminated with a period ⟨"Tell me when you came in." "Just now."⟩ ⟨"Please close the door." "Certainly."⟩

1.1.2 Structurally incomplete or fragmentary elements terminating in a period occur frequently in modern narrative writing and are usually terminated with a period ⟨The sound of artillery through the night. The enemy again. Banging away to keep everyone nervous and awake.⟩

1.2 A period often follows an abbreviation ⟨Reedville, Mass., pop. 879⟩ ⟨cap. or l. c.⟩ ⟨7 a. m.⟩ ⟨30 mins.⟩ ⟨lg. pkg.⟩ ⟨no. 72⟩ ⟨5s. 6d.⟩ ⟨bks. marked o. p.⟩ ⟨dept. bulls.⟩ ⟨50 pp.⟩ ⟨U. S. S. *Wyoming*⟩ ⟨Dr. John H. Doe, 7 Pine St., New York, N. Y.⟩ ⟨Dec. 7, 1941⟩ ⟨Lt. Col. John Doe⟩

1.2.1 Periods do not usually follow abbreviations of compound names of international organizations and government agencies, official abbreviations designating equipment, and a large number of similar compound abbreviations usually written without spaces ⟨NATO⟩ ⟨UN⟩ ⟨UNESCO⟩ ⟨TVA⟩ ⟨VT fuze⟩ ⟨pfc⟩ ⟨EST⟩

1.2.2 Periods usually follow common contractions made by omitting medial letters ⟨secy.⟩ ⟨advt.⟩ ⟨mfg.⟩ ⟨recd.⟩

1.2.3 Some publishers, chiefly British, often do not put a period after *Mr, Mrs,* and *Dr* ⟨Dr and Mrs John H. Doe⟩

1.2.4 A period does not follow symbols of chemical elements ⟨*Al*⟩ ⟨*Cu*⟩ ⟨*U 235*⟩

1.2.5 Such terms as 1st, 2d, 3d, 4th, 8vo, and 12mo are not abbreviations and do not require a period.

1.2.6 Isolated letters of the alphabet used as designations do not require a period ⟨T square⟩ ⟨A 1⟩ ⟨I beam⟩

1.2.7 After titles of books and articles, after headings, and in display printing, printers usually omit a period at the ends of lines, as well as other punctuation except an essential question mark or an exclamation point.

1.3 A period is necessary before a decimal and between dollars and cents in figures ⟨16.63 ft.⟩ ⟨.32 cal.⟩ ⟨$12.17⟩

1.4 A period may or may not follow a Roman numeral. In particular contexts usage is often quite uniform; thus a period is used after a roman numeral designating a chapter of a book in the Bible ⟨2 Sam. xix. 12⟩ but no period is used after a roman numeral following a personal name ⟨Elizabeth II of England⟩

1.5 Dictionaries use centered periods to indicate division between syllables of words where division is not otherwise indicated by accent marks or hyphens.

2. THE QUESTION MARK

2.1 A question mark usually indicates in writing the incompleteness or anticipation conveyed in speech by any of various intonation patterns and frequently though not exclusively by a rising pause. The word order may be that of a question or a statement ⟨When did he leave?⟩ ⟨You say he never came back?⟩ ⟨An Oxford degree — or was it foreign travel? — lured him to England.⟩

2.1.1 A question mark does not follow an indirect question, which has the intonation pattern and fading pause of a positive statement ⟨They are asking him where he plans to go.⟩

2.1.2 A request expressed in interrogative form for the sake of courtesy usually ends in a period corresponding to the fading pause of a positive statement ⟨Will you kindly fill out this questionnaire and return it to the personnel office.⟩

2.1.3 When used as the terminal mark of a direct quotation, the question mark, as well as the exclamation point, usually takes the place of a comma or period which would otherwise be used at that point in the sentence ⟨After he had affixed the title "What is Progress?" he folded the manuscript of his speech.⟩

2.2 A question mark, usually enclosed in parentheses, often follows arbitrarily after a word, phrase, or date to indicate uncertainty of its accuracy or to mark a gap in available information ⟨Omar Khayyám, Persian poet (?–1123?)⟩

3. THE EXCLAMATION POINT

3.1 An exclamation point follows an expression or statement that is an exclamation and corresponds to a heavy, relatively high-pitched terminal stress in speech ⟨Oh no! Not that!⟩ ⟨I wish he would!⟩ ⟨Do you think we will stand for this any longer!⟩ ⟨Hurry! We need help!⟩

4. THE COMMA

4.0 Of all the marks of punctuation the comma offers the most difficulty in use and the widest range for individual choice. Though often marking rhetorical or elocutionary pauses, the comma is used primarily to separate or to set off in a group. It sometimes distinguishes nonrestrictive modifiers from restrictive modifiers. Since the genus-terms of definitions in this dictionary are intended to be modified only by differentiae that are restrictive in some degree, the use of commas either to separate or to group is severely limited chiefly to units in apposition or in series.

4.1 *Commas That Set Off.* A word, phrase, or clause is often inserted in a sentence to supply explanatory or supplementary information. In speech the rising pause or sometimes the sustained pause sets off such material when it is of relatively minor importance and is not essential to the main idea. In writing commas usually indicate the subordinate status of such matter. These commas always make a pair unless the element set off begins or ends a sentence.

4.1.1 Commas usually set off words, phrases, and other sentence elements that are parenthetical or independent. Items of this sort are contrasting expressions, prefatory exclamations, the name of a person directly addressed, and expressions like *he said* in direct quotations ⟨Work, not words, is what is needed.⟩ ⟨The outcome, though hardly to our liking, is better than expected.⟩ ⟨The animals, nervous and restless, pace interminably in their cages.⟩ ⟨He is often late, to be sure, but we can rely on him in a crisis.⟩ ⟨"Listen, John," he said, "drive carefully."⟩ ⟨Oh bosh, pay no attention to him (the comma that goes with the comma after *bosh* gives way to the capital *O*).⟩

4.1.2 Commas usually set off appositional or modifying words, phrases, or clauses that do not limit or restrict the main idea of a sentence. Such constructions are termed nonrestrictive ⟨George, his own brother, is turning against him.⟩ ⟨John, whom we saw yesterday, is away today.⟩ ⟨His father, dressed in a new gray suit, came early for the ceremony.⟩
The second of the pair of commas in the next three gives way to the period that closes the sentence ⟨There stood John, smiling quietly to himself.⟩ ⟨We leave at 3 o'clock, when the bell rings.⟩ ⟨The formation is of great interest to geologists, although most of us would hardly notice it.⟩

4.1.2.1 When inserted or appended words, phrases, or clauses are restrictive or essential to the main idea of a statement, they are spoken without the pauses or other significant intonation that would indicate matter of minor importance. In writing, commas are likewise unnecessary ⟨His friend George is turning against him.⟩ ⟨The man whom we saw yesterday is not here today.⟩ ⟨The man dressed in the new gray suit is his father.⟩ ⟨John is the boy standing in the rear and smiling to himself.⟩ ⟨We leave when the bell rings.⟩ ⟨He will come if his safe-conduct is guaranteed.⟩

4.1.2.2 Sometimes the presence or absence of commas corresponding to spoken pauses constitutes the sole means of determining whether a phrase or clause is essential or nonessential, restrictive or nonrestrictive ⟨Our friends, who live out of town, do not like the new parking laws/ Our friends who live out of town do not like the new parking laws.⟩ ⟨The men, draining the swamp, searched all day for the boy/The men draining the swamp searched all day for the boy.⟩ ⟨We do not visit him, because he always serves liquor/We do not visit him because he always serves liquor.⟩

4.1.3 Commas set off transitional words and expressions (as *on the contrary*, *on the other hand*, *consequently*, *furthermore*, *moreover*, *nevertheless*, *therefore*) whenever they are or would be spoken with the adjacent rising or sustained pauses that indicate subordinate matter ⟨The question, however, remains unsettled.⟩ ⟨Nevertheless, we shall go.⟩ ⟨On the contrary, under the rules a vote is in order.⟩

4.1.3.1 Such expressions may occur in context so as to be spoken without significant pauses and may likewise require no punctuation ⟨We shall therefore proceed with the operation.⟩ ⟨The weaklings will consequently be forced to drop out.⟩ ⟨A clear-cut decision is on the other hand too much to expect.⟩

4.2.1 *Commas That Separate*. Various expressions are often used in sentences to introduce or qualify something that follows. To separate these elements in speech a rising or sustained pause denotes the end of the introductory information and the beginning of the main part of the statement. In writing, a comma accordingly often separates an introductory word or phrase from the rest of the sentence, particularly when the introductory material is long or when ambiguity might otherwise occur ⟨Unfortunately, we shall have to decline the invitation.⟩ ⟨In the first place, you will get very little information from him.⟩ ⟨To gain popularity, he betrayed his convictions.⟩ ⟨Immediately upon reaching the surface, he swam to shore.⟩ ⟨Seeing the dog approaching, he ran off down the street.⟩

4.2.2 Whenever in spoken English there is an enumeration of items, a rising or sustained pause separates and distinguishes each member of the series. In writing, a comma likewise usually separates words, phrases, or clauses that occur in a series ⟨The estate is to be divided among Robert, John, and William.⟩ ⟨Trees, trees, trees were all we could see.⟩ ⟨He opened the can, removed the contents, and replaced the lid.⟩ ⟨The one who befriended us, watched over us, and gave us help is now no more.⟩ ⟨The prisoner will not talk, he refuses to eat, and he pounds the bars continually.⟩

4.2.2.1 Before *and* or *or* introducing the final term in a closed series, writers usually put a comma ⟨*a*, *b*, and *c*⟩ ⟨a coat, a hat, and a pair of gloves⟩ ⟨scientific, technical, and learned periodicals⟩ but sometimes omit it in a short series ⟨a coat, a hat and a pair of gloves⟩ ⟨*a*, *b* and *c*⟩

4.2.2.2 Modifying words in an open series preceding a noun are often separated and distinguished in speech by pauses and in writing by commas ⟨a rural, agricultural, idyllic life⟩ ⟨journalistic, literary, popular publications⟩. Sometimes, however, the pause and hence the comma may be unnecessary when the second modifier relates more closely to the noun than the first, or when the first modifier applies to the second modifier and the noun as a unit ⟨a quiet rural atmosphere⟩ ⟨a vivid red tie⟩ ⟨a brilliant military strategist⟩

4.2.3 Statements or clauses joined by a coordinating conjunction are separated in speech by a sustained or rising pause. In writing, a comma usually effects this separation ⟨He seemed inattentive, but not a word escaped him.⟩ ⟨His face showed his disappointment, for he knew he had failed.⟩ ⟨He did not like intruders of the sort that now confronted him, nor did he see any way of avoiding them.⟩ ⟨She knew very little about him, and he volunteered nothing.⟩

4.2.3.1 When the statements or clauses joined by a coordinating conjunction are brief and unambiguous, and usually when the subject is the same, the comma may be omitted ⟨He will suffer but he will recover.⟩

4.2.3.2 A comma alone without the conjunction sometimes separates brief and closely related statements or clauses. In such instances a sustained or slightly falling pause may occur in speech rather than the fading pause and full stop designated by the period ⟨The boy went to the store, then he went home.⟩ ⟨Don't bother, it doesn't make any difference.⟩ ⟨He would always remember, the experience was now a part of him.⟩ This comma may or may not be permissive in the treatment of the comma fault in various handbooks of composition.

4.2.3.3 When a conjunction joins two predicative constructions that have the same subject, the clarifying pause in speech may be slight or imperceptible. In writing, a comma is likewise not considered necessary except to avoid ambiguity ⟨The car teetered for a moment on the edge of the road and then plunged down the embankment.⟩ ⟨Sailing an iceboat is thrilling sport but requires great skill.⟩

4.2.4 Corresponding to the rising or sustained pause necessary in speech to distinguish items in addresses and dates, a comma usually separates such matter in writing ⟨Born January 1, 1900, in Delhi, India, the university's outstanding student received his college degree in June, 1922.⟩ ⟨Apply for the booklet at the Superintendent of Documents, Washington 25, D. C.⟩

4.2.4.1 Usage is about evenly divided, however, when the day is not given ⟨in June 1922⟩ or ⟨in June, 1922⟩

4.2.4.2 Sometimes writers omit the comma after the year ⟨born January 1, 1900 in India⟩

4.2.5 When such expressions as *namely*, *that is*, *i. e.*, *e. g.*, *viz.* introduce an illustration or example, a comma that corresponds in function to a rising or sustained pause in speech usually separates it from what follows ⟨There are two ways to do the job: namely, a right way and a wrong way.⟩ ⟨He forbade future forays; that is, there were to be no more raids on the neighbors' gardens.⟩

4.2.6 A comma usually indicates the place of an omitted word or word group to achieve a separation like that effected in speech by a sustained or rising pause ⟨The tractor is used for hauling; the bulldozer, for excavating.⟩

4.2.7 Like a sustained or rising pause in speech, a comma usually separates a direct quotation from the rest of a sentence or context ⟨"Make way for liberty," he cried.⟩ ⟨He asked abruptly, "Which way do you vote?"⟩ ⟨As some say, "Virtue is its own reward."⟩

4.3 *Commas Used Arbitrarily*. The comma often functions in an arbitrary manner as a mechanical device.

4.3.1 In numbers the comma usually separates thousands, millions, and other groups of three digits except in dates, page numbers, and street numbers, and in numbers of four digits ⟨an altitude of 7525 feet⟩ ⟨3600 rpm⟩

4.3.2 A comma usually sets off inverted names in bibliographies and reference lists ⟨Doe, John, Jr.⟩

4.3.3 A comma usually separates a proper name and an academic or honorary title, also two or more such titles in succession ⟨John Doe, M.A., Ph.D., President⟩

4.3.4 A comma is the customary mark after the salutation in personal letters and after the complimentary close in all letters ⟨Dear Jack,⟩ ⟨Sincerely yours,⟩ ⟨Yours very truly,⟩

4.4.1 One may avoid excessive or uncertain use of the comma by eliminating commas, excepting those used arbitrarily, where there are no significant pauses. In terms of structure, a comma does not usually separate closely related grammatical sequences ⟨The advice his father gave him/ remained long in his mind.⟩ ⟨The result of the long and detailed planning was/ that the forces were well prepared for the battle.⟩ ⟨The flea-bitten, shaggy/ dog padded desolately down the alley.⟩ ⟨The long, happy, and successful trip/ was one he will never forget.⟩ ⟨His new car is a fast/ and powerful machine.⟩

4.4.2 It is equally important to insert a comma to prevent misreading or ambiguity. The need for a rising or sustained pause in speech usually indicates that a comma is necessary in writing ⟨Inside, the fire was burning brightly.⟩ ⟨Ever since, the little man comes at dark to clean the kitchen.⟩ ⟨Whoever lost it, lost an invaluable treasure.⟩ ⟨To Ruth, John appeared as a mighty warrior on a white horse.⟩ ⟨In 1925, 25 percent of the graduates of the school went on to college.⟩ ⟨The railroad had no resources, but the trains were somehow kept running.⟩ ⟨As the car struck, the utility pole fell with a crash.⟩

5. THE SEMICOLON

5.1 In general the semicolon functions as a weak period or as a strong comma. As a weak period the semicolon corresponds to a fading pause and full stop in speech similar to but perhaps not quite as final as that represented by a period. As a strong comma the semicolon corresponds to a rising or sustained pause in speech possibly longer or slightly more definitive than that represented by a comma.

5.1.1 As a weak period a semicolon usually separates independent statements or clauses joined together in one sentence without a conjunction. Such statements or clauses are usually closely related ⟨Make no terms; resist until the last breath.⟩ ⟨A fool babbles continuously; a wise man holds his tongue.⟩

5.1.2 As a weak period a semicolon usually separates two statements or clauses when the second begins with a sentence connector or conjunctive adverb, as *accordingly*, *also*, *consequently*, *furthermore*, *hence*, *however*, *indeed*, *moreover*, *nevertheless*, *otherwise*, *so*, *still*, *then*, *therefore*, *thus*, *yet* ⟨You have recommended this man; therefore I will give him a trial.⟩ ⟨His conduct has always been exemplary; nevertheless he will not be permitted to go.⟩

5.1.3 As a strong comma a semicolon usually separates phrases or clauses that are themselves broken up by punctuation ⟨The country's resources consist of large ore deposits; lumber, waterpower, and fertile soils; a favorable climate; and a strong, rugged people.⟩ ⟨When the presently available natural resources are greatly depleted, man will have to develop new sources of food and power; and then will come the real test of his energies his imagination, and his ingenuity.⟩

5.1.4 A semicolon sometimes separates arbitrarily in lists of names with addresses, titles, or figures where a comma alone would not clearly separate items or references ⟨Genesis 3:1–19; 4:1–16⟩

6. THE COLON

6.1 The colon, corresponding to a fading or sustained pause in speech, is a rhetorical mark of supplementation. It links clauses, phrases, or less often single words; it indicates that what follows it coordinates with some element of what precedes or sometimes with all of what precedes back to the beginning of a sentence. Specific types of supplementation are mentioned in parentheses after the examples ⟨The same forced yes-or-no choice appears on referenda on public questions: the voter cannot express approval of some parts and disapproval of others unless amended. (elaboration)⟩ ⟨It vigorously opposes clandestine marriages: that is, marriages which were made outside the auspices of the Church. (definition)⟩ ⟨His ambition must be stirred: his greed must be played upon. (balance)⟩ ⟨The following items of equipment are necessary: sleeping bag, ground cloth, cooking utensils, and a small axe. (enumeration)⟩ ⟨Representatives of ten countries presented papers at the formal meetings, including: Brazil, England, France, Holland, India, Italy, Japan, the United States, the U. S. S. R., and West Germany —Allen Kent. (enumeration)⟩ ⟨The author never exploits any whimsical or romantic elements in this subject: he maintains throughout the decent, workmanlike attitude he has set himself. (restatement)⟩ ⟨Local currencies, like local laws, were not suppressed: they were encouraged to improve. (antithesis)⟩ ⟨His death raised the possibility that his political heirs might seek the final solution for insolvent, disorganized governments: war. (summation)⟩ ⟨The question is this: will the removal of restrictions lead to freedom or license? (apposition)⟩
Usually what precedes a colon is general and what follows is specific but sometimes the relation is reversed ⟨Physics and biology, evolution and anthropology, conservation and religion: he discusses them all.⟩
Sometimes paired colons correlate ⟨He has ambition: it must be stirred. He has a belief in fair play: it must be honored.⟩
Frequently the colon is reinforced by anticipatory phrasing (as *thus*, *namely*, *for example*, *as follows*).

6.2 A colon functions as a mechanical device in set formulas involving separation of parts, as when relating the antecedent of a ratio to its consequent ⟨12 : 19⟩ or one ratio to another ⟨12 : 19 : : x : 57⟩ or when relating subdivisional units in a descending series to specify or particularize one member, especially in time-telling by hour, minute, and second ⟨2:31:30⟩, in bibliographical reference by volume and page ⟨*National Geographic* 33:89⟩ or by chapter and verse ⟨Luke 2:12⟩ or by place and publisher ⟨Springfield : G. & C. Merriam Co.⟩, or in accounting by pounds, shillings, and pence ⟨46 : 6 : 11⟩

6.3 A colon symbolizes a conventional separation or emphatic pause after a formal salutation in a letter ⟨Dear Sir:⟩ or an address ⟨Mr. Chairman, Ladies and Gentlemen:⟩ or between a book title and a subtitle not otherwise differentiated ⟨*Victory : A History of the Recent Struggle*⟩

6.4 A colon introduces a quotation especially when quotation marks are omitted and when the quoted matter is indented ⟨We quote from the text: "Greater love hath no man".⟩:

He reads these words from Ruth:
  Whither thou goest, I will go.

Mother: Where did you go?
Child: I won't tell.

A colon joins terms that are being contrasted or compared and is sometimes centered or spaced ⟨Seventeenth century rhymes include *prayer: afar* and *brass : was : ass.*⟩ ⟨The stature of the two sexes shows very nearly the same female : male proportions.⟩

7. THE DASH

7.0 In its function in writing and in the speech intonation to which it corresponds, the dash is similar to the comma and the colon, and a pair of dashes is similar to parentheses.

7.1 A dash usually marks an abrupt change or suspension in the thought or structure of a sentence ⟨If you will listen I will explain — but perhaps another time will be better.⟩ ⟨The mountain we climbed is higher than — oh, never mind how high it is.⟩ ⟨He was — how shall I put it — a controversial figure to say the least.⟩ ⟨"Yes, but I — er — I'll have to —" and he stopped hopelessly.⟩

7.2 A dash often makes parenthetic, appositional, or explanatory matter stand out clearly or emphatically ⟨Three of the country's most important products — oil, steel, and wheat — are produced in greater quantities than ever before.⟩ ⟨Two of our group — Eddie and John — came walking down the street.⟩ ⟨He is willing to discuss all problems — those he has solved and those for which there is no immediate solution.⟩

7.3 A dash often occurs before a summarizing statement or clause ⟨Oil, steel, and wheat — these are the sinews of industrialization.⟩

7.4 A dash sometimes sets off appositional or parenthetic matter that is introduced by such expressions as *namely, for example, that is* ⟨Sports develop two valuable traits — namely, self-control and the ability to make quick decisions.⟩

7.5 A dash often mechanically precedes the name of an author or source at the end of a quoted passage ⟨There is a tide in the affairs of men which, taken at the flood, leads on to fortune —William Shakespeare⟩ ⟨"In the beginning God created the heavens and the earth" —Genesis 1:1⟩

7.6 A long dash often functions as a notational device to indicate the omission of a word or of letters in a word ⟨yelling —— loudly⟩ ⟨Mr. M—— of New York⟩ ⟨go to the d——l⟩

7.7 A short dash — slightly larger than a hyphen — often serves as an arbitrary equivalent of *to and including* between numbers or dates and in compounding capitalized two-word names with the hyphen ⟨pages 40–98⟩ ⟨the decade 1951–60⟩ ⟨the New York–Lisbon plane⟩

8. PARENTHESES

8.1 Parentheses often set off parenthetic matter when the interruption is more marked than that usually indicated by commas ⟨Three old destroyers (all now out of commission) will be scrapped.⟩ ⟨He is hoping (as we all are) that this time he will succeed.⟩

8.2 Parentheses often set off supplementary or explanatory matter that is not a part of the main statement or not a structural element of the sentence ⟨The more distant mountain (I think you have climbed it before) is our goal.⟩ ⟨The diagram (Fig. 3) illustrates the action of the pump.⟩ ⟨The Springfield (Illinois) stop is the first on the tour.⟩

8.3 Parentheses often mechanically enclose sequential numbers or letters in a series (but do not take the place of required punctuation) ⟨We must clearly set forth (1) our long-term goals, (2) our immediate objectives, and (3) the means at our disposal.⟩

8.4 Parentheses usually arbitrarily enclose an arabic number confirming a number expressed in words ⟨Delivery will be made in thirty (30) days.⟩ ⟨Payment due is twenty dollars ($20.00).⟩

9. BRACKETS

9.1 Brackets usually set off mechanically a word or phrase that is extraneous or incidental to the context, such as editorial interpolations ⟨He wrote, "I am just as cheerful as when you was [sic] here".⟩ ⟨A fly is said to be a two-winged dipterous [does that make four wings?] insect.⟩ ⟨The officer in charge [General Doe] had to countersign the order.⟩

9.2 Brackets often function as parentheses within parentheses ⟨Bowman Act (22 Stat., ch. 4, § [or sec.] 4, p. 50).⟩

10. ELLIPSIS *or* SUSPENSION POINTS

10.1 Consisting usually of three spaced periods or asterisks and corresponding in effect to a sustained pause in speech, an ellipsis often indicates an interrupted or unfinished sentence. Wherever an ellipsis is terminal, a period follows ⟨"I shall . . . that is . . . if we can only . . . ." He faltered and stopped speaking.⟩ ⟨"Cut the line and cast. . . ." His voice was lost in the crash of the next wave.⟩

10.2 An ellipsis often occurs as a notational device to indicate an omission in quoted matter, as a word or a group of consecutive words unessential or undesirable for quotation ⟨"Oh say can you see . . . what so proudly we hailed . . .?"⟩

10.3 An ellipsis on a line by itself in poetry indicates the omission of one or more lines of verse. Sometimes it consists of periods spaced and extended in number to the full measure of the line:

Thus driven
By the bright shadow of that lovely dream,
. . . .
He fled
—P. B. Shelley

11. THE CENTERED PERIOD

11.1 A centered period in a dictionary entry indicates syllabic or end-of-line division ⟨dy·nam·ic⟩. (For discussion and examples see "Divisions in Respelled Pronunciations" and "Divisions in Boldface Entry Words".)

12. THE HYPHEN (For discussion and examples of hyphens see "The Writing of Compounds".)

12.1.1 A hyphen is a mark of separation or division at the end of a line which terminates with a syllable of a word that is to be carried over to the next line ⟨mill- [end of line] stone⟩ ⟨pas-sion⟩

12.1.2 A hyphen divides letters or syllables to give the effect of stuttering, sobbing, or halting ⟨S-s-sammy⟩ ⟨ah-ah-ah⟩ ⟨y-y-es⟩

12.1.3 A hyphen suspends the second part of a hyphened compound used in combination with another hyphened compound ⟨a six- or eight⸗cylindered engine⟩ ⟨in ten- and twenty-dollar bills⟩

12.1.4 Hyphens indicate a word spelled out letter by letter ⟨p-r-o-b-a-t-i-o-n⟩

12.2 A hyphen before a word element indicates that it is a suffix or a terminal combining form ⟨-ous⟩ ⟨-ship⟩

12.3 A hyphen after a word element indicates that it is a prefix or initial combining form ⟨anti-⟩ ⟨fore-⟩

12.4 Hyphens before and after a word element indicate that it is a medial word element ⟨-o-⟩

13. QUOTATION MARKS

13.1 Quotation marks often enclose a direct quotation from a speaker or from a text or other written matter ⟨"When I am dead," said one of the keenest of modern minds, one of the greatest of modern poets, "lay a sword on my coffin, for I was a soldier in the war for the liberation of humanity."⟩
Quotation marks are not used to enclose oft⸗quoted familiar phrases (as *to err is human*).
Quotation marks are not used to enclose indirect quotations ⟨*direct* — The man said, "I am going home."⟩ ⟨*indirect* — The man said that he was going home.⟩

13.2 In long quotations, excepting extracts from plays, left-hand quotation marks are placed at the beginning of every paragraph included in the quotation in addition to those placed at the beginning and at the end of the selection.

13.3 Quotation marks are usually not used when the quoted matter is set in smaller type or in paragraphs indented on both sides.

13.4 Single quotation marks enclose a quotation within a quotation; or if single quotation marks are used primarily, double quotation marks enclose a quotation within a quotation ⟨The witness said, "I distinctly heard him say, 'Don't be late'; then I heard the door close".⟩

13.5 Quotation marks usually enclose titles of short poems, paintings, lectures, articles, and parts or chapters of books. (Titles of whole books, periodicals, and newspapers are usually italicized in context.)

13.5.1 In American usage printers usually place a period or comma inside closing quotation marks whether it belongs logically to the quoted matter or to the whole sentence or context ⟨The package is labeled "Handle with Care."⟩ ⟨The golden rule, "Do unto others as you would have them do unto you," is easier to remember than to practice.⟩
But when a logical or exact distinction is desired in specialized work in which clarity is more important than usual (as in this dictionary), a period or comma can be placed outside quotation marks when it belongs not to the quoted matter but to a large unit containing the quoted matter ⟨The package is labeled "Handle with Care".⟩ ⟨This act may be cited as the "Army-Navy Medical Services Corps Act of 1947".⟩ ⟨The Prime Minister, after reporting the negotiations, declared resolutely, "Our only course is to resist aggression".⟩ ⟨Replying with the one word "Bunk", he subsided.⟩

13.5.2 Only one other mark accompanies closing quotation marks, whether the quotation and the whole sentence or context call for the same mark or for different marks ⟨Did he keep asking you, "What is your number?"⟩ ⟨We shouted in unison, "Where do you think you're going?"⟩ ⟨Just as he screamed, "I will not!" he slammed the door.⟩ ⟨Is this the gratitude I receive, to have you bellow, "Get out of here and don't come back!"⟩

13.5.3 A colon or semicolon is usually placed outside of quotation marks ⟨"Fame is proof that people are gullible"; with this quotation he retired in silence.⟩

13.5.4 A colon or semicolon is sometimes placed inside the quotation marks when it belongs inseparably to the quotation ⟨"Sirs:" is a salutation used in letters to a newspaper.⟩; however, a terminal colon or semicolon of quoted matter incorporated in a sentence usually gives place to appropriate end punctuation.

13.5.5 A question mark or exclamation point is usually placed inside or outside the quotation marks according to whether it belongs to the quoted matter or to the whole sentence or clause that includes the quotation ⟨Can you forget his angry exit after he shouted "Include me out"?⟩ ⟨"And what do you think of this new novel?" his friend asked.⟩

13.6 Quotation marks, often single quotation marks, sometimes enclose technical terms unfamiliar to the reader; words used in an unusual sense; and coined words, trade or shop jargon, or slang for which the writer implies a slight apology ⟨An "em" is a unit of measure used in printing.⟩ ⟨The plates of copper are hung by "corrosion hooks" in the acid.⟩ ⟨This venture is a "wildcat" invented to prey upon the unwary.⟩ ⟨We've had enough of your "unshrinkable" shirts.⟩ ⟨He is "goofy" according to their lingo.⟩

14. THE APOSTROPHE

14.0 An apostrophe and *s* are usually added to a noun to indicate ownership or a relation analogous to ownership. This possessive form is a survival of the *es* ending in Old and Middle English, from which the vowel sound has disappeared in Modern English except in nouns ending with the sound \s\, \z\, \sh\, \zh\, \ch\, or \j\. In early Modern English the *s* of the possessive was often dropped from the possessive of nouns already ending in an *s* or *z* sound, both in speaking and in writing, leaving only the apostrophe in writing, as is evident in various idioms and in poetry. Since the middle of the 19th century, however, the form with the apostrophe and *s* has been generally adopted for the possessives in which the extra syllable is not awkward to pronounce in context.

14.1 An apostrophe and *s* form the possessive case of singular or plural nouns that do not end in an *s* or *z* sound ⟨boy's⟩ ⟨carpenter's⟩ ⟨dog's⟩ ⟨president's⟩ ⟨at his wit's end⟩ ⟨garage's responsibility⟩ ⟨Senator Doe's constituency⟩ ⟨the church's policy⟩ ⟨men's⟩ ⟨Descartes's philosophy⟩ ⟨Delacroix's painting⟩

14.2 An apostrophe either with or without *s* forms the possessive case of singular nouns ending in an *s* or *z* sound.

14.2.1 Singular nouns ending in an *s* or *z* sound that consist of one syllable or have a primary or secondary accent on the last syllable usually add an apostrophe and *s* to form the possessive case ⟨the class's recitation⟩ ⟨the press's description⟩ ⟨the fox's tail⟩ ⟨King James's reign⟩ ⟨Laplace's theories⟩ ⟨the marquise's jewels⟩

14.2.2 Singular nouns ending in an *s* or *z* sound that consist of more than one syllable and have no primary or secondary accent on the last syllable often add the apostrophe and *s* to form the possessive case unless the additional syllable with the *s* or *z* sound would be unpleasant or difficult to pronounce in context. Sometimes such a syllable is necessary to avoid ambiguity in pronunciation. Usage is divided in this matter (1) ⟨an audience's/

audience' reaction⟩ ⟨the waitress's/ waitress' duties⟩ ⟨the phoenix's/ phoenix' nest⟩ ⟨for appearance's/ appearance') sake⟩ (2) ⟨Dr. Adams'/ Adams's services⟩ ⟨the octopus'/ octopus's snaky appearance⟩ ⟨Dickens'/ Dickens's novels⟩

14.2.3 With some exceptions various classical and biblical names are treated as in 14.2.1 and 14.2.2 ⟨Zeus's son⟩ ⟨Mars's help⟩ ⟨Venus's/ Venus'⟩ ⟨Judas's/ Judas'⟩ but ⟨Brutus'/ Brutus's⟩ ⟨Odysseus'/ Odysseus's⟩, and ⟨Jesus'⟩ ⟨Moses'⟩ ⟨Pythagoras's/ Pythagoras'⟩ ⟨Herodotus's/ Herodotus'⟩⟨Oedipus's/Oedipus'⟩, but ⟨Aristophanes'/ Aristophanes's⟩ ⟨Socrates'/ Socrates's⟩ ⟨Thucydides'/ Thucydides's⟩

14.3 An apostrophe without *s* usually forms the possessive case of plural nouns ending in an *s* or *z* sound ⟨consumers' protest⟩ ⟨foxes' holes⟩ ⟨the Joneses' invitation⟩ ⟨the two chateaux' occupants⟩ but ⟨geese's⟩ ⟨lice's⟩ ⟨mice's⟩

14.4 An apostrophe and *s* usually form the possessive case of various indefinite pronouns ⟨anybody's⟩ ⟨anyone's⟩ ⟨everybody's⟩ ⟨everyone's⟩ ⟨somebody's⟩ ⟨someone's⟩ but no apostrophe is used in the possessive pronouns *his, hers, its, ours, yours, theirs.*

FORMS OF ADDRESS

An exhaustive list of all alternative forms of address permissible in polite correspondence would extend far beyond the scope of this dictionary; especially in informal correspondence there is a great variety of possible salutations. In the table below we have usually put the most formal address and salutation first. Differences of local usage, however, inevitably introduce many exceptions. In the United States "My dear Mrs. Smith" is more formal than "Dear Mrs. Smith"; in Great Britain the reverse is true. In business correspondence the addressee's address is placed before the salutation; in most official and some social correspondence, it is placed at the foot of the letter, below and to the left of the signature. Social invitations to a married man are customarily addressed to the man and his wife; as, Senator and Mrs. ——; The President and Mrs. ——; Lord and Lady ——; Their Excellencies, the German Ambassador and Madam ——; etc.

It will be noted that some of the addresses given below begin with the word "To," whereas most do not. There is no hard-and-fast rule. We have tried to suggest merely the more customary usage. Insertion or omission of the word "To" is optional. It will also be noted that the same word may be spelled differently according to the residence of the persons addressed. For example, in the United States the spellings *honor* and *honorable* are preferred; but in Great Britain, *honour* and *honourable.* In the address abbreviations are commonly used but they should never be used in the salutation or beginning of a letter.

*Such salutations as My Lord, Your Lordship, etc., are not ordinarily used in the United States of America, but should be used by an American writing to dignitaries of foreign countries entitled to such a title or mark of respect.

†When the person addressed holds several titles, as one from birth, another by marriage, and another by profession, the highest title should be preferred.

‡Clerical, naval, and military prefixes are written before other titles; initials indicative of distinction are written after the title and name; an officer should be addressed by his official title when the communication refers to official business.

A

abbot
address: The Right Reverend —— ——, O.S.B. (or other initials of the order), Abbot of ——; *or* The Right Rev. Abbot ——
begin: Right Reverend and dear Father

administrator same as governor

air force officers like army officers

alderman (in Canada and U.S.)
address: Honorable —— ——
begin: Dear Sir

ambassador†
address: His Excellency, The American Ambassador; *or* The Honorable —— ——, American Ambassador; *or* His Excellency, —— ——, Ambassador of Brazil at ——; *or* His Excellency, Her Majesty's Ambassador for the United Kingdom (the personal name or hereditary or professional title may be added after the words *His Excellency; His Excellency* is usually abbreviated to *H.E.*)
begin: Sir (*or* with the personal title, as Your Grace, etc.); *or* Excellency

ambassador and his wife
address: His Excellency, The —— Ambassador and Mrs. —— ——; *or* The Honorable —— ——, —— Ambassador and Madam —— ——
begin: Your Excellencies

apostolic delegate see papal nuncio

archbishop (Anglican)
address: The Most Reverend His Grace the Lord Archbishop of ——
begin: My Lord Archbishop; *or* Your Grace
In formal documents the archbishops of Canterbury and York are addressed as The Most Reverend Father in God ——, by Divine Providence Lord Archbishop of ——

archbishop (Roman Catholic)
address: The Most Reverend —— ——, D.D., Archbishop of ——
begin: Your Excellency

archdeacon
address: The Venerable The Archdeacon of ——; *or* The Venerable —— ——, Archdeacon of ——
begin: Venerable Sir

army officers
In the United States in letters from civilians:
address: The Commander in Chief, Army of the United States; *or* Lieutenant General ——, Commanding Officer, Army of the United States; Colonel (highest rank and full title) —— ——, U.S.A.; Lieutenant ——, U.S.A. (in case of retired officers U.S.A. is omitted)
begin: Sir; *or* (informal) My dear General —— (not My dear Lieutenant General ——); *or* Dear Commander —— (not Dear Paymaster Commander ——); and for all officers below the rank of captain, My dear (*Rank*) —— ——
In the British army and navy when an officer has a hereditary title or rank, his military or naval rank will ordinarily be prefixed to this; as, Admiral the Right Honourable the Earl of ——; General the Right Honourable Lord ——; but lieutenants in the army and sublieutenants in the navy are not addressed by their military or naval rank; thus, —— ——, Esq., 10th Hussars (not Lieutenant —— ——)
begin: Sir; *or* Dear General ——; *or* Dear Lord —— (but not Dear General Lord ——)

assemblyman
address: The Honorable —— ——, Member of Assembly; *or* Assemblyman ——
begin: Sir; *or* Dear Sir; *or* My dear Mr. ——

assistant secretary (assistant to a cabinet officer)
address: Honorable —— ——, Assistant Secretary of ——; *or* The Assistant Secretary of the —— Department
begin: Sir; *or* Dear Sir; *or* My dear Mr. ——; *or* Dear Mr. —— (never Mr. Secretary)

associate justice
address: The Honorable —— ——, United States Supreme Court; *or* Mr. Justice ——, The Supreme Court
begin: My dear Mr. Justice; *or* Dear Justice ——

attorney general see cabinet officers

auditor of the treasury
address: The Honorable —— ——, Auditor of the Treasury; *or* The Auditor of the Treasury
begin: Sir; *or* Dear Sir

B

baron
address: The Right Honourable Lord ——; *or* The Lord ——
begin: My Lord

baroness
address: The Right Honourable the Baroness ——; *or* The Right Honourable Lady ——; *or* The Lady ——
begin: Madam

baronet
address: Sir John ——, Bt. *or* Bart.
begin: Sir

baronet's wife see lady

baron's daughter
address: (if unmarried) The Honourable Helen ——; *or* (if married to a commoner or to the son of a baron or viscount or the younger son of an earl) The Honourable Mrs. ——; *or* (if her husband has a married brother) The Honourable Mrs. John ——; *or* (if married to a knight or baronet) The Honourable Lady ——. If she is married to a man of higher title, use feminine of husband's title
begin: Madam (or use higher title if one exists)

baron's son
address: The Honourable —— ——
begin: Sir
(in Scotland the eldest son is sometimes addressed as Master of ——)

baron's son's wife† like baron's married daughter

baron's wife = baroness

Benedictine see priest

bishop (Anglican)
address: The Right Reverend the Lord Bishop of ——; *or* The Lord Bishop of ——; *or* (very formal) The Right Reverend Father in God, ——, by Divine Permission Lord Bishop of ——
In formal documents the Bishop of Durham is addressed as The Most Reverend Father in God ——, by Divine Providence Lord Bishop of Durham
begin: My Lord Bishop; *or* My Lord

bishop (Methodist)
address: The Reverend —— ——, D.D.
begin: Reverend Sir; *or* Dear Sir; *or* Dear Bishop ——; *or* My dear Bishop ——

bishop (Protestant Episcopal)
address: To the Right Reverend —— ——, Bishop of ——
begin: Right Reverend and Dear Sir; *or* (informal) Dear Bishop ——; *or* My dear Bishop

bishop (Roman Catholic)
In England
address: The Lord Bishop of ——; *or* The Right Reverend —— ——, Bishop of ——
begin: My Lord Bishop; *or* My Lord
In the U.S.
address: The Most Reverend —— ——, Bishop of ——
begin: Your Excellency
In Italy
address: To His Excellency, the Most Illustrious and Most Reverend Monsignor —— ——, Bishop of ——
begin: Most Illustrious and Most Reverend Lord; *or* Excellency

brother of a religious order
address: Brother ——, (followed by the initials of the order)
begin: Dear Brother ——

C

cabinet officers (United States)
address: The Honorable the Secretary of State (or Defense, Agriculture, etc.); The Honorable the Secretary of the Treasury; The Honorable the Postmaster General; *or* The Honorable —— ——, Secretary of State, etc.; *or* The Secretary of State; The Attorney General, etc.
begin: Sir; *or* Dear Sir; *or* My dear Mr. Secretary; *or* My dear Mr. Attorney General

canon
address: The Very Reverend Canon —— ——; *or* The Very Reverend ——, Canon of ——
begin: Very Reverend Canon; *or* Dear Canon ——
canon regular see priest regular
cardinal
address: His Eminence John Cardinal H——
begin: Your Eminence*
cardinal (if also an archbishop)
address: His Eminence —— Cardinal ——, Archbishop of ——
Carthusian see priest
chargé d'affaires
address: The Chargé d'Affaires of ——; *or* ——, Esq., Chargé d'Affaires; *or* Mr. —— ——, Chargé d'Affaires
begin: Dear Sir; *or* Sir; *or* My dear Mr. —— (use military, naval, or hereditary title, if there is one)†
chief justice of the Supreme Court of Canada
address: The Honourable —— ——, Chief Justice of Canada
begin: Sir
chief justice of the United States
address: The Chief Justice of the United States; *or* The Chief Justice, The Supreme Court, Washington, D.C.; *or*, if to the chief justice and his wife, The Chief Justice and Mrs. ——
begin: Sir; *or* My dear Mr. Chief Justice
children see baron's daughter, baron's son, duke's eldest son; children of a peeress in her own right married to a commoner receive the same courtesy titles as though their father were a peer of the mother's rank
Cistercian see priest
clergyman
address: The Reverend —— —— (Rev. and Mrs. —— ——); *or* (if a doctor of divinity) The Rev. Dr. —— ——; *or* The Reverend —— ——, D.D.
begin: Dear Sir; *or* Reverend Sir; *or* My dear Mr. (or Dr.) ——; *or* Dear Mr. (or Dr.) ——; see also archbishop, bishop, priest (most authorities disapprove the use of *Rev.* with the last name alone)
clerk (Anglican Church)
address: The Reverend —— ——; *or* (if the son of a duke or marquess) The Reverend Lord —— ——; *or* (if the son of an earl, viscount, or baron) The Rev. The Hon. —— ——†
begin: Reverend Sir; *or* Sir
clerk (below the order of priesthood in Roman Catholic Church)
address: The Reverend —— ——
begin: Reverend Sir; *or* Dear Mr. ——
clerk of the Senate *or* House
address: The Honorable —— ——, Clerk of ——
begin: Sir; *or* Dear Sir
commissioner of a bureau (as U.S. Commissioner of Education)
address: The Honorable —— ——, Commissioner of the Bureau of Education
begin: Sir; *or* Dear Sir
common forms
man
address: Mr. —— ——
begin: Dear Sir; My dear Sir; My dear Mr. ——; *or* Dear Mr. ——
pl. address: Messrs. —— —— and —— ——
begin: Gentlemen
married woman
address: Mrs. John Doe
begin: Dear Madam; My dear Madam; My dear Mrs. Doe; *or* Dear Mrs. Doe
pl. address: Mmes. —— —— and —— ——
begin: Mesdames; *or* Ladies
unmarried woman
address: Miss Doe (eldest daughter); *or* Miss Jane Doe (younger daughter)
begin: Dear Madam; My dear Miss Doe; etc.
pl. address: The Misses Doe
begin: Ladies; *or* Mesdames
comptroller of Treasury
address: The Honorable —— ——, Comptroller of the Treasury
begin: Sir; *or* Dear Sir
congressman
address: Honorable —— ——, House of Representatives, Washington, D.C.; *or* Honorable John Doe, Representative in Congress, Springfield, Mass.
(some authorities disapprove the use of the prefix Hon. without first name or initials)
begin: Sir; *or* Dear Sir; *or* My dear Mr. ——
consul
address: To the American Consul at ——; *or* —— ——, Esq., American Consul at ——; *or* Mr. —— ——, United States Consul at ——; *or* To —— ——, Esq., Her Majesty's Consul for the United Kingdom
begin: Dear Sir
countess
address: To the Right Honourable The Countess of ——; *or* The Countess ——
begin: Madam

D

dame
address: Dame —— —— (followed with initials of the order, or if the lady has a higher title, with these initials after that title)†
begin: Madam
deacon (Anglican and Protestant Episcopal)
address: The Reverend Deacon —— ——
begin: Reverend Sir
(for deacons of other churches there is no special form of address)
dean (cathedral)
address: The Very Reverend the Dean of ——
begin: Very Reverend Sir; *or* Sir
dean (Roman Catholic)
address: The Very Reverend —— ——, V.F.
begin: Very Reverend Father
dean of a college *or* graduate school
address: Dean —— ——
begin: Dear Sir (*or* Madam); *or* Dear Dean ——
diplomat see ambassador, chargé d'affaires, minister (diplomatic); for diplomats of lower rank, having no other title, use common forms
divorced woman
(ordinarily *Mrs.* with her maiden name as a prename instead of her ex-husband's prename is preferred; some divorced women prefer to resume the *Miss;* the form of address preferred by the woman herself, if that is known, should be used unless there has been a court decision; divorced peeresses lose officially any title gained by marriage; courtesy use of former title is optional)
doctor of divinity
address: —— ——, D.D.; *or* Dr. —— ——; *or* Rev. Dr. ——
begin: Dear Sir; *or* My dear Dr. ——; *or* Dear Dr. ——; *or* Reverend and Dear Sir; *or* Reverend Doctor
doctor of philosophy, laws, medicine, etc.
address: A—— B——, Ph.D. [LL.D.] [M.D.]; *or* Dr. A—— B——; (Dr. and Mrs. A—— B——; etc.)
begin: Dear Sir; *or* My dear Dr. B——; *or* Dear Dr. B——
(if a higher title is applicable, it should be preferred; see professor, president of a college)†
domestic prelate of the pope
address: The Right Reverend Monsignor —— ——, Domestic Prelate (or D.P.)
begin: Right Reverend Monsignor; *or* Dear Monsignor ——
dowager see widow
duchess
address: Her Grace the Duchess of ——; *or* The Most Noble the Duchess of ——
begin: Madam; *or* Your Grace
duchess of the blood royal
address: Her Royal Highness The Duchess of ——
begin: Madam; *or* May it please your Royal Highness
duke
address: His Grace the Duke of ——; *or* The Most Noble the Duke of ——
begin: My Lord Duke; *or* Your Grace
duke of the blood royal
address: His Royal Highness The Duke of ——
begin: Sir; *or* May it please your Royal Highness
duke's daughter†
address: The Lady Mary ——; *or* The Right Honourable Lady ——
begin: Madam; *or* My Lady
(if her husband holds a title of nobility, either by right or courtesy, the wife is ordinarily addressed according to her husband's title)
duke's eldest son
address: The Most Honourable the Marquess ——; *or* The Marquess of ——
begin: My Lord Marquess; *or* My Lord
duke's eldest son's daughter same as baron's daughter
duke's eldest son's eldest son use grandfather's third title
duke's eldest son's wife
address: The Most Honourable the Marchioness of ——
begin: My Lady Marchioness
duke's wife = duchess
duke's younger son
address: The Right Honourable Lord —— ——
begin: My Lord
duke's younger son's wife
address: Lady —— ——
begin: Madam; *or* My Lady; *or* Your Ladyship

E

earl
address: The Right Honourable The Earl of ——; *or* The Earl of ——
begin: My Lord
earl's daughter like duke's daughter
earl's eldest son
address: The Right Honourable the Viscount ——; *or* The Right Honourable Lord ——
begin: My Lord Viscount ——
earl's wife = countess
earl's younger son same as baron's son
earl's younger son's wife†
address: Honourable Mrs. ——
begin: Madam
envoy same as minister (diplomatic)
esquire
address: —— ——, Esq.
begin: Sir; *or* Dear Sir; *or* Dear Mr. ——
(*Esq.* is never used if the person is addressed by any other title, even *Mr.*)

F

French common forms
(these forms are acceptable for nearly all diplomats other than English-speaking)
man
address: M. —— ——
begin: Monsieur
pl. address: Messrs. ——
begin: Messieurs
married woman
address: Mme. —— ——
begin: Madame
pl. address: Mmes. —— —— et —— ——
begin: Mesdames
unmarried woman
address: Mlle. —— ——
begin: Madame (formal); *or* Mademoiselle (informal)
pl. address: Mlles. —— —— et —— ——
begin: Mesdames

G

German common forms
man
address: Herrn —— ——
begin: Sehr geehrter Herr
pl. address: Herren —— ——
begin: Geehrte Herren
married woman
address: Frau —— ——
begin: Sehr geehrte Frau ——
unmarried young woman
address: Fräulein —— ——
begin: Mein liebes Fräulein (cordial)
governor
address (in Massachusetts and in New Hampshire and by courtesy in some other states) His Excellency, The Governor of ——; *or* His Excellency —— ——; *or* (in other states of the U.S.) The Honorable the Governor of ——; *or* The Honorable —— ——, Governor of ——
begin: Sir; *or* Dear Sir
governor-general of an independent commonwealth
address: His Excellency —— —— (personal title and name), Governor-General of ——
begin: Sir (or according to rank)
governor-general of Canada†
address: His Excellency The Right Honourable —— ——, (plus personal rank or title, if any)
begin: My Lord; *or* Sir (according to rank)
governor-general's wife (British dominions)†
address: Her Excellency —— ——
begin: Madam

H

honorary chamberlain to the pope same as papal chamberlain

I

internuncio see papal nuncio
Italian common forms
man
address: Gentilissimo Signore ——
begin: Gentilissimo Signore
pl. address: Spettabile Ditta ——
begin: Spettabile Ditta
married woman
address: Distinta Signora —— ——
begin: Distinta Signora
unmarried woman
address: Esimia Signorina —— ——
begin: Esimia Signorina

J

judge (in Canada)
address: The Honourable Mr. Justice —— (if of a superior court or of the circuit court of Montreal); *or* His Honour Judge —— (if of a lower court)
begin: Sir
judge (in England and the British dominions [except as noted elsewhere in this table])
address: Honourable Mr. Justice ——; *or* (when a knight) Honourable Sir —— ——
begin: Sir
judge (in U.S.)
address: The Honorable —— ——, United States District Judge (or Chief Judge of the Court of Appeals, etc.)
begin: Dear Sir; *or* My dear Judge ——
see also chief justice, associate justice
judge of City of London court *or* of a county court in England *or* of a court in British colonies
address: His Honour Judge ——
begin: Sir; *or* Dear Sir
junior added to a son's name to distinguish him from his father with the same name, —— ——, Jr.; *or* —— ——, Jr., Ph.D.; *or* jr.
justice see associate justice, chief justice, judge

K

king
address: The King's Most Excellent Majesty; *or* His Most Gracious Majesty, King ——
begin: Sir; *or* May it please your Majesty
king's counsel
address: To —— ——, Esq., K.C.
begin: Sir; *or* Dear Sir
knight
address: Sir —— —— (initials of his order, if any, as K.C.B.)
begin: Sir
knight's wife see lady

L

lady
address: Lady ——; *or* (if the daughter of a baron or viscount) Hon. Lady ——; *or* (if the daughter

of an earl, marquess, or duke) Lady Florence ——
begin: Madam; My Lady; Your Ladyship
lady mayoress see lord mayor's wife
lawyer
address: —— ——, Esq.; *or* Mr. —— ——, Attorney-at-Law
begin: Dear Sir; My dear Mr. ——; etc.
(Mr. —— ——, Esq. is incorrect)
lieutenant governor
address: The Honorable —— ——, Lieutenant Governor of ——; (British) His Honour The Lieutenant Governor of ——†
begin: Sir; *or* Dear Sir
lord advocate†
address: To the Right Honourable the Lord Advocate; *or* The Right Honourable —— ——
begin: Sir
lord chancellor†
address: The Right Honourable the Lord High Chancellor; *or* The Right Honourable —— (hereditary title), Lord High Chancellor
begin: My Lord (or according to rank)
lord chief justice of England†
address: To the Lord Chief Justice of England; *or* To the Rt. Hon. Baron ——, Lord Chief Justice of England
begin: Sir
lord mayor (of London, York, Belfast, Melbourne, Sydney, Brisbane, Hobart, Adelaide, and Perth)
address: The Right Honourable Lord Mayor of ——; *or* The Right Honourable —— ——, Lord Mayor of ——
(all other lord mayors are addressed as The Right Worshipful)
begin: My Lord
lord mayor's wife
address: Mrs. —— ——
begin: Madam
lord of appeal in ordinary same as baron
lord of appeal in ordinary's children same as baron's children
lord of appeal in ordinary's wife same as baroness
lord of council and session
address: Honourable Lord ——
begin: My Lord
lord of council and session's wife
address: Lady ——
begin: Madam
lord provost
address: The Honourable the Lord Provost; *or* The Honourable ——, Lord Provost of ——; *or* (in Edinburgh and Glasgow) The Right Honourable the Lord Provost, etc.
begin: Sir

M

maid of honor
address: The Honourable Miss ——
begin: Madam
marchioness
address: The Most Honourable the Marchioness of ——
begin: Madam
marquess
address: The Most Honourable the Marquess of ——; *or* The Marquess of ——
begin: My Lord Marquess
marquess's children like duke's children
married woman see common forms
master of the rolls
address: To the Right Honourable the Master of the Rolls
begin: Sir
mayor (in Canadian cities and towns, and English boroughs)
address: His Worship, The Mayor of ——
begin: Sir
mayor (in English cities)
address: The Right Worshipful the Mayor of ——
begin: Sir (see also lord mayor)
mayor (in the U.S.)
address: The Honorable —— ——, Mayor of ——; *or* The Mayor of the City of ——
begin: Sir; *or* Dear Sir; *or* Dear Mr. Mayor; *or* My dear Mr. Mayor
member of parliament (or of a provincial legislative council *or* of a provincial legislature, etc.) the ordinary form of address followed by M.P. (*or* M.L.C., *or* M.P.P., *or* M.L.A., etc.)
military officers see army officers
minister (diplomatic)
address: The Honorable —— ——, Minister of Costa Rica; *or* Her Majesty's Minister for the United Kingdom
begin: Sir (or with personal title, as My Lord, Your Grace, etc.); *or* My dear Mr. Minister
minister of a provincial cabinet of Canada
address: The Honourable —— ——, Minister of ——
begin: Sir
minister of religion see clergyman, priest, rabbi
moderator (of the General Assembly of the Church of Scotland)
address: The Right Reverend ——
begin: Right Reverend Sir
monk see priest regular, clerk
monsignor see domestic prelate, papal chamberlain, protonotary apostolic, vicar general
mother superior of a sisterhood
address: The Reverend Mother Superior, Convent of ——; *or* Reverend Mother ——, O.S.D. (*or* other initials of the order); *or* Mother ——, Superior, Convent of ——
begin: Reverend Mother; *or* Dear Madam; *or* Dear Reverend Mother (informal); *or* My dear Reverend Mother ——

N

naval officers
address: The Admiral of the Navy of the United States; *or* Admiral ——, Commanding United States Navy; Captain —— ——, U.S.N.
begin: Sir; *or* (informal) My dear Admiral ——; Dear Commander ——; but for officers below the rank of commander, Dear Mr. ——
nun see sister of a religious order
nuncio see papal nuncio

P

papal ablegate
address: The Right Reverend Monsignor ——, Ablegate of His Holiness the Pope
begin: Right Reverend Monsignor
papal chamberlain
address: The Very Reverend Monsignor ——
begin: Very Reverend and dear Monsignor
papal chaplain same as papal chamberlain
papal nuncio *or* internuncio *or* apostolic delegate
address: His Excellency, The Papal Nuncio (*or* Internuncio *or* Apostolic Delegate) to ——
begin: Your Excellency
parliament, member of see member of parliament
patriarch (Eastern Church)
address: His Beatitude the Patriarch of ——; *or* His Beatitude the Lord ——, Patriarch of ——
begin: Most Reverend Lord; *or* Your Beatitude
patriarch (Roman Catholic Church)
address: His Excellency, the Patriarch (Archbishop) of ——
begin: Your Excellency
peer see duke, marquess, earl, baron
pope
address: To His Holiness Pope ——
begin: Most Holy Father; Your Holiness
postmaster general see cabinet officers
preacher general
address: The Venerable and Very Reverend Father —— ——, O.P., P.G.
begin: Very Reverend Father
premier of a province of Canada
address: The Honourable ——, Premier of the Province of ——
begin: Sir
president of a Canadian legislative council
address: The Honourable ——, The President of the Legislative Council
begin: Sir
president of a college *or* university
address: —— ——, LL.D. (*or* if he is not an LL.D., the initials of his highest degree), President of —— University (*or* President, —— University); *or* President —— ——
If he is a clergyman, Reverend —— ——, LL.D., President of —— University
begin: Dear Sir; *or* Dear President ——
president of a theological seminary
address: The Rev. President —— ——
begin: Dear Sir; *or* Dear President ——
president of state senate
address: The Honorable —— ——, President of the Senate of ——
begin: Sir
president of the Senate of the United States
address: The Honorable, The President of the Senate of the United States; *or* The Honorable —— ——, President of the Senate
begin: Sir
president of the United States
address: The President, The White House (*His Excellency* should not be used)
begin: Mr. President; *or* The President; *or* My Dear Mr. President
priest (Roman Catholic Church)
regular (except as noted below)
address: Reverend —— ——, O.S.M. (*or* other initials of his order)
begin: Dear Father —— (religious name)
Benedictine, Cistercian, *or* canon regular
address: The Reverend Dom —— ——, C.R.L. (*or* other initials of his order)
begin: Reverend Father; *or* Dear Father ——
Carthusian
address: The Venerable Father Dom —— ——, O.Cart.
begin: Venerable Father; *or* Dear Father ——
secular
address: Reverend —— ——, (followed by the initials of his degree)
begin: Reverend and dear Father ——
prime minister of Canada
address: The Right Honourable —— ——, P.C., Prime Minister of Canada
begin: Sir
prime minister of the United Kingdom
address: The Right Honourable —— ——, P.C., M.P., Prime Minister
begin: Sir
prince of the blood royal
address: His Royal Highness Prince —— (given name)
begin: Sir
see also duke of the blood royal
prince of Wales
address: His Royal Highness The Prince of Wales
begin: Sir; *or* May it please your Royal Highness
princess of the blood royal
address: Her Royal Highness the Princess —— (given name)
begin: Madam
see also duchess of the blood royal
princess of Wales
address: Her Royal Highness The Princess of Wales
begin: Madam
prior, claustral
address: The Very Reverend Dom —— ——, O.C. (*or* other initials of his order); *or* The Very Reverend Father Prior, —— Abbey
begin: Very Reverend Father; *or* Dear Father Prior
prior, conventual
address: The Very Reverend the Prior of ——; *or* The Very Reverend Father (*or* Dom) —— ——, O.P. (*or* other initials of his order), Prior of ——; *or* The Very Reverend Father Guardian, O.F.M.; *or* The Very Rev. —— ——, Prior (*or* Guardian) of ——
begin: Very Reverend Father; *or* Dear Father Prior; *or* Very Reverend and Dear Father
prioress
address: The Very Reverend the Prioress of —— *or* The Very Reverend Mother (*or* Dame) —— ——, (followed by the initials of her order), Prioress of ——
begin: Very Reverend Mother; *or* Dear Mother Prioress
privy chamberlain to the pope same as papal chamberlain
privy councillor (British imperial)†
address: To the Right Honourable —— ——, P.C.
begin: Sir
If other titles are used, they should come after *The Right Honourable;* as, The Right Honourable Sir John ——
privy councillor (of Canada)
address: The Honourable —— ——
begin: Sir
professor in a college *or* university
address: Professor —— ——; *or* —— ——, Ph.D. (*or* LL.D., M.D., etc., using only the initials of his highest degree, if the degrees are in the same field), Professor of ——
begin: Dear Sir; *or* My dear Professor ——; *or* Dear Professor ——; *or* My dear Professor; etc.
professor in a theological seminary
address: The Reverend Professor —— ——; *or* The Rev. —— ——, D.D.; *or* Professor —— ——
begin: Dear Sir; *or* Dear Professor ——
protonotary apostolic
address: The Right Reverend Monsignor —— ——, Protonotary Apostolic (or P.A.)
begin: Right Reverend Monsignor; *or* Dear Monsignor ——
provincial of a religious order
address: The Very Reverend Father Provincial, O.F.M. (*or* other initials of his order); *or* The Very Reverend Father —— ——, Provincial, S.J.
begin: Very Reverend and dear Father
provost see lord provost
provost (Roman Catholic Church)
address: The Very Reverend Provost ——
begin: Very Reverend Provost; *or* Dear Provost ——
puisne judge of the Supreme Court of Canada
address: The Honourable Mr. Justice ——
begin: Sir

Q

queen
address: The Queen's Most Excellent Majesty; *or* Her Gracious Majesty, The Queen
begin: Madam; *or* May it please your Majesty
queen mother
address: Her Gracious Majesty Queen ——
begin: Madam; *or* May it please your Majesty

R

rabbi
address: Rabbi —— ——; *or* Rev. —— ——
begin: Reverend Sir; *or* Dear Sir; *or* My dear Rabbi ——; *or* Dear Rabbi ——
(if he holds a doctor's degree, Dr. may be substituted for Rabbi)
recorder
address: His Honour Recorder ——
begin: Sir
rector of a religious house *or* of a seminary
address: The Very Reverend —— ——, O.S.B. (*or* other initials of the order), Rector, Brothers of St. Francis (*or* Brother)
begin: Very Reverend and dear Father
representative see congressman

S

Scottish land court chairman same as lord of council and session
secretary of agriculture, state, defense, etc. see cabinet officer
secretary of state (England)
address: His Majesty's Principal Secretary of State for the —— Department (this may be preceded by hereditary title)
begin: according to rank (Your Grace, My Lord, etc.)
senator (Canadian)
address: The Honourable —— ——
begin: Dear Sir; Dear Senator ——; etc.
senator (U.S.)
address: The Honorable —— ——, The United

States Senate, Washington, D.C.
begin: Dear Sir; *or* My dear Senator
senior added to a father's name to distinguish him from a son of the same name; as, —— ——, Sr.; *or* —— ——, Sr., Ph.D.; *or* sr.
señor see Spanish common forms
serjeant-at-law
address: Serjeant ——; *or* Mr. Serjeant ——
begin: Sir; *or* Dear Sir
sister of a religious order
address: Sister ——, (followed by the initials of the order)
begin: Dear Sister; *or* My dear Sister; *or* Dear Sister ——; *or* My dear Sister ——
solicitor general (Canada)
address: The Honourable ——
begin: Sir
solicitor general (U.S.)
address: The Solicitor General
begin: Sir; *or* Dear Sir; *or* Dear Mr. ——
Spanish common forms
man
address: Señor —— ——
begin: Muy señor mío
pl. address: Señores —— ——
begin: Muy señores nuestros
married woman
address: Señora de ——; or Señora Doña —— de ——
begin: Muy estimada señora
unmarried woman
address: Señorita ——; *or* Señorita Doña ——
begin: Muy distinguida señorita
speaker of a provincial legislature of Canada
address: The Honourable ——, The Speaker of (name of legislature)
begin: Dear Mr. Speaker
speaker of the House of Commons (Canada)
address: The Honourable ——, The Speaker of the House of Commons
begin: Dear Mr. Speaker
speaker of the House of Representatives of the United States
address: The Honorable —— ——, Speaker of the House of Representatives
begin: Sir; *or* Mr. Speaker; *or* My dear Mr. Speaker
speaker of the Senate (Canada)
address: The Honourable —— ——, Speaker of the Senate
begin: Dear Mr. Speaker
state senator like senator (U.S.)
superior general of a religious community of priests
address: The Most Reverend Father —— (followed by the initials of the order), Superior General of the —— Fathers
begin: Most Reverend Father General
superior general of a religious order (female)
address: The Reverend Mother ——, (followed by the initials of her order), Superior General of ——
begin: Reverend Mother
Supreme Court see chief justice, associate justice

U

undersecretary of state (U.S.)
address: The Undersecretary of State; *or* The Honorable —— ——, Undersecretary of State
begin: Sir; *or* Dear Sir; *or* Dear Mr. ——
unmarried woman see common forms

V

vicar-general
address: The Right Reverend Monsignor —— ——, V.G.; *or* The Right Reverend the Vicar-General
begin: Right Reverend and dear Monsignor
vice-chancellor (law) same as judge (in England)
vice-consul similar to consul
vice-president
address: The Vice-President; *or* The Honorable, The Vice-President of the United States; *or* The Honorable —— ——, Vice-President of the United States
begin: Mr. Vice-President; *or* Sir; *or* My dear Mr. Vice-President
viceroy
address: His Excellency, The Lord Lieutenant of Ireland (The Viceroy of India)
begin: Excellency
viscount
address: The Right Honourable the Viscount ——; *or* The Viscount ——
begin: My Lord
viscountess
address: The Right Honourable the Viscountess ——; *or* The Viscountess ——
Begin: Madam
viscount's children same as baron's children

W

widow
(ordinarily addressed by her former title: as, Mrs. John Doe, not Mrs. Jane Doe, unless the latter form is preferred by the person herself; but if her married son, stepson, or grandson now holds a title of nobility formerly held by her late husband, the word dowager may be added before (or after) her title to distinguish her from the younger lady of the same title; as, Her Grace the Dowager Duchess of ——; The Dowager Lady ——; when such relationship does not exist, she may be distinguished by using her given name; as, The Right Honourable Jane, Countess of ——; the latter form is now generally preferred by ladies entitled to the distinction *Dowager;* officially a widow who remarries is not recognized as having any claim to bear the title of her deceased husband, but courtesy usually accords her this title)

ABBREVIATIONS USED IN THIS DICTIONARY

AA .... Associate in Arts
AAS ...... Associate in Applied Science
ab .... about
AB .... Bachelor of Arts
abbr ...... abbreviation
Abd ...... Abdias
AB in Th .. Bachelor of Arts in Theology
abl .... ablative
AC .... alternating current
acad ...... academy
acc or *accus* ..... accusative
act .... active
A.D. .... anno Domini
adj .... adjective
adv .... adverb
advt .... advertisement
Aeol ...... Aeolic
AF .... Anglo-French
Afr .... Africa, African
Afrik ...... Afrikaans
Agg .... Aggeus
agric ...... agriculture
A.H. ...... anno Hegirae
Ala .... Alabama
Alb .... Albanian
alter ...... alteration
a.m. ...... ante meridiem
AM .... amplitude modulation, Master of Arts
Am or *Amer* ..... America, American
AmerF .... American French
AmerInd ... American Indian
AmerSp or *AmSp* .... American Spanish
anat ...... anatomy
anthrop .... anthropological, anthropology
aor .... aorist
Apoc ...... Apocalypse
appar ..... apparently
Apr .... April
Ar .... Arabic
Aram ..... Aramaic
archeol .... archeology
archit ..... architecture
arith ...... arithmetic
Ariz ...... Arizona
Ark .... Arkansas
Arm ...... Armenian
art .... article
assoc or *assn* ...... association
ASSR ..... Autonomous Soviet Socialist Republic
Assyr ..... Assyrian
Assyr-Bab .. Assyro-Babylonian
astrol ..... astrology
astron ..... astronomy
ASV ...... American Standard Version
at.no. ..... atomic number
attrib ..... attributive, attributively
at.wt. ..... atomic weight
aug .... augmentative
Aug .... August
Austral .... Australia
Av .... Avestan
AV .... Authorized Version
b .... born
BA .... Bachelor of Arts
Bab .... Babylonian
bacteriol ... bacteriology
BA(J) ..... Bachelor of Arts in Journalism
Bar .... Baruch
BArch ..... Bachelor of Architecture
bart .... baronet
BBC ...... British Broadcasting Corporation
B.C. ...... before Christ, British Columbia
BChE ..... Bachelor of Chemical Engineering
BCS ...... Bachelor of Commercial Science
BD .... Bachelor of Divinity
Bé .... Baumé
BE .... Bachelor of Education, Bachelor of Engineering
BEd ...... Bachelor of Education
bef .... before
Bel .... Bel and the Dragon
Belg ...... Belgian, Belgium
Beng ...... Bengali
BFA ...... Bachelor of Fine Arts
biochem ... biochemistry
biog ...... biographical, biography
biol .... biologic, biological, biology
BJ .... Bachelor of Journalism
bk .... book
BldgE ..... Building Engineer
BLitt or *BLit* ..... Bachelor of Letters, Bachelor of Literature
bot .... botany
Braz ...... Brazilian
Bret ...... Breton
brig .... brigadier
Brit .... Britain, British
bros .... brothers
BS .... Bachelor of Science
BSA ...... Bachelor of Science in Agriculture
BSc ...... Bachelor of Science
BSEd or *BSE* ..... Bachelor of Science in Education
BSFS ..... Bachelor of Science in Foreign Service
BS in CE .. Bachelor of Science in Chemical Engineering, Bachelor of Science in Civil Engineering
BS in ChE . Bachelor of Science in Chemical Engineering
BS in Ed ... Bachelor of Science in Education
BS in LS .. Bachelor of Science in Library Science, Bachelor of Science in Library Service
bt .... baronet
Btu .... British thermal unit, British thermal units
Bulg ...... Bulgarian
bull .... bulletin
C .... centigrade
cal .... calendar, caliber
Calif ...... California
Canad ..... Canada, Canadian
CanF ..... Canadian French
Cant ...... Cantonese
cap .... capital, capitalized
capt ...... captain
Cast ...... Castilian
cat .... catalog
Catal ...... Catalan
caus ...... causative
cc .... cubic centimeter, cubic centimeters
CE .... Chemical Engineer, Civil Engineer
Celt .... Celtic

cen ....central
cent ....century
cgs ....centimeter-gram-second
Chald ....Chaldean
chem ....chemical, chemistry
Chin ....Chinese
Chron ....Chronicles
cm ....centimeter, centimeters
co ....company, county
col ....colonel
Col ....Colossians
coll ....college
colloq ....colloquial
Colo ....Colorado
com ....common
comb ....combination, combining
compar or *comp* ....comparative
conj ....conjunction
Conn ....Connecticut
cons ....consonant
constr ....construction
contr ....contraction
Copt ....Coptic
Cor ....Corinthians
Corn ....Cornish
corp ....corporation
cos ....cosine
CPA ....Certified Public Accountant
CRL ....Canons Regular of the Lateran
crystallog ....crystallography
cu ....cubic
cwt ....hundredweight
cycl ....cyclopedia
Czech ....Czechoslovak, Czechoslovakia, Czechoslovakian
d ....denarius, denarii, penny, pence
D ....Dutch
Dan ....Daniel, Danish
dat ....dative
D.C. ....District of Columbia
DC ....direct current
DD ....Doctor of Divinity
Dec ....December
def ....definite
Del ....Delaware
dept ....department
Deut ....Deuteronomy
dial ....dialect
dict ....dictionary
dim ....diminished, diminutive
DLitt or *DLit* ....Doctor of Letters, Doctor of Literature
dom ....dominant
Dor ....Doric
doz ....dozen
DP ....domestic prelate
dr ....debit, doctor
DSc ....Doctor of Science
Du ....Dutch
DV ....Douay Version
E ....east, eastern, English
eccl ....ecclesiastic, ecclesiastical
Eccles ....Ecclesiastes
Ecclus ....Ecclesiasticus
ecol ....ecological, ecology
econ ....economics
ed ....edition
EdM ....Master of Education
educ ....education, educational
EE ....Electrical Engineer
EFris ....East Frisian
e.g. ....exempli gratia
EGmc ....East Germanic
Egypt ....Egyptian
embryol ....embryology
emu ....electromagnetic unit, electromagnetic units
encyc ....encyclopedia
Eng ....England, English
engin ....engineering
Eph ....Ephesians
Esd ....Esdras
Esk ....Eskimo
esp ....especially
esq ....esquire
EST ....eastern standard time
Esth ....Esther
esu ....electrostatic unit, electrostatic units
etc ....et cetera
Eth ....Ethiopic
ethnol ....ethnology
eve ....evening
Exod ....Exodus
explan ....explanatory
Ezech ....Ezechiel
Ezek ....Ezekiel
f ....following
F ....Fahrenheit, French
FBI ....Federal Bureau of Investigation
Feb ....February
fem ....feminine
ff ....following
fig ....figurative, figuratively, figure
Finn ....Finnish
fl ....flourished
Fla ....Florida
Flem ....Flemish
FM ....frequency modulation
fo or *f* ....folio
f.o.b. ....free on board
fps ....foot-pound-second
fr ....from
Fr ....French
freq ....frequent, frequentative, frequently
Fri ....Friday
Fris ....Frisian
ft ....feet, foot
fund ....fundamental
fut ....future
g ....acceleration of gravity
G ....German
Ga ....Georgia
gal ....gallon, gallons
Gal ....Galatians
gaz ....gazette
gen ....general, genitive
Gen ....Genesis
geog ....geographic, geographical
geol ....geologic, geological, geology
geom ....geometry
Ger ....German
GI ....government issue
Gk ....Greek
gm ....gram, grams
Gmc ....Germanic
Goth ....Gothic
govt ....government
Gt Brit ....Great Britain
h ....hour, hours
Hab ....Habacuc, Habakkuk
Hag ....Haggai
handbk ....handbook
HE ....his excellency
Heb ....Hebrew, Hebrews
HG ....High German
hist ....historical, history
Hitt ....Hittite
HMS ....His Majesty's Ship, Her Majesty's Ship
hon ....honorable, honorary
hort ....horticulture
Hos ....Hosea
hp ....horsepower
ht ....height
Hung ....Hungarian
Icel ....Icelandic
i.e. ....that is
IE ....Indo-European
Ill ....Illinois
IMF ....International Monetary Fund
imit ....imitative
imp or *imper* ....imperative
imperf ....imperfect
in ....inch, inches
inc ....incorporated
incho ....inchoate
Ind ....Indiana
indic ....indicative
infin ....infinitive
infl ....influenced
inst ....institute, institution, institutional
instr ....instrumental
interj ....interjection
internat or *internatl* ....international
interrog ....interrogative
intrans ....intransitive
inv ....inversion
Ion ....Ionic
IPA ....International Phonetic Alphabet
Ir ....Irish
Ire ....Ireland
IrGael ....Irish Gaelic
irreg ....irregular
Isa ....Isaiah, Isaias
ISV ....International Scientific Vocabulary
It or *Ital* ....Italian
ital ....italic, italicized
Jan ....January
Jap ....Japanese
Jas ....James
Jav ....Javanese
Jer ....Jeremiah, Jeremias
jg ....junior grade
Jn ....John
JND ....just noticeable difference
Jos ....Josue
Josh ....Joshua
jour ....journal
JPS ....Jewish Publication Society
jr ....junior
Jth ....Judith
Judg ....Judges
K ....Kelvin (scale)
Kans ....Kansas
KC ....king's counsel
KCB ....Knight Commander of the Bath
kg ....kilogram, kilograms
kgps ....kilogram per second, kilograms per second
km ....kilometer, kilometers
KP ....kitchen police
kt ....knight
Ky ....Kentucky
L ....Latin
La ....Louisiana
LaF ....Louisiana French
Lam ....Lamentations
lang ....language, languages
lat ....latitude
lb ....pound, pounds
l.c. ....lowercase
Lev ....Leviticus
lg ....large
LG ....Low German
LGk ....Late Greek
LH ....lower half
LHD ....Doctor of Humanities
LHeb ....late Hebrew
lieut ....lieutenant
lit ....literal, literally, literary
Lith ....Lithuanian
LittB or *LitB* ....Bachelor of Letters, Bachelor of Literature
LittD or *LitD* ....Doctor of Letters, Doctor of Literature
Lk ....Luke
LL ....Late Latin
LLB ....Bachelor of Laws
LLD ....Doctor of Laws
loc ....locative
long ....longitude
LP ....long-playing
lt. ....lieutenant
ltd ....limited
LXX ....Septuagint
m ....meridies (L., noon), meter, meters, minute, minutes
M ....monsieur
MA ....Master of Arts
Macc ....Maccabees
Maced ....Macedonian
Mach ....Machabees
mag ....magazine
maj ....major
Mal ....Malachi, Malachias
manuf ....manufacture, manufacturing
Mar ....March
masc ....masculine
Mass ....Massachusetts
math ....mathematics
MBA ....Master of Business Administration
MBret ....Middle Breton
Md ....Maryland
MD ....Doctor of Medicine, Middle Dutch
Me ....Maine
ME ....Middle English
mech ....mechanical
med ....medical, medicine
MEd ....Master of Education
met ....metropolitan
meteorol ....meteorology
Mex ....Mexican, Mexico
MexSp ....Mexican Spanish
MF ....Master of Forestry, Middle French
mfg ....manufacturing
MFlem ....Middle Flemish
MFS ....Master of Foreign Study
mg ....milligram, milligrams
MGk ....Middle Greek
MHeb ....Middle Hebrew
MHG ....Middle High German
Mic ....Micah
Mich ....Micheas, Michigan
mil ....military
min ....minor, minute, minutes
Minn ....Minnesota
MIr ....Middle Irish
misc ....miscellaneous
Miss ....Mississippi
Mk ....Mark
mks ....meter-kilogram-second
ml ....milliliter, milliliters
ML ....Medieval Latin
MLA ....member of the legislative assembly
MLC ....member of the legislative council
MLG ....Middle Low German
Mlle ....mademoiselle
MLS ....Master of Library Science
mm ....millimeter, millimeters
Mme ....madame
Mo ....Missouri
mod ....modern
modif ....modification
Mon ....Monday
Mont ....Montana
MP ....member of parliament, military police
MPA ....Master of Public Administration
MPer ....Middle Persian
mph ....miles per hour
MPP ....member of provincial parliament
MS ....manuscript, Master of Science
MSc ....Master of Science
MS in LS ....Master of Science in Library Science
MSS ....manuscripts
MSw ....Middle Swedish
mt ....mount, mountain
Mt ....Matthew
MusM ....Master of Music
MW ....Middle Welsh
mythol ....mythology
n ....noun
N ....north, northern
Nah ....Nahum
nat or *natl* ....national
NATO ....North Atlantic Treaty Organization
naut ....nautical
N.C. ....North Carolina
NCAA ....National Collegiate Athletic Association
NCE ....New Catholic Edition
N. Dak. ....North Dakota
NE ....northeast
Nebr ....Nebraska
Neh ....Nehemiah
neut ....neuter
Nev ....Nevada
NewEng ....New England
NewZeal ....New Zealand
NGk ....New Greek
NGmc ....North Germanic
N.H. ....New Hampshire
NHeb ....New Hebrew
N.J. ....New Jersey
NL ....New Latin
N. Mex. ....New Mexico
no ....north, number
nom ....nominative
nonattrib ....nonattributively
nonstand ....nonstandard
Norw ....Norwegian
Nov ....November
n pl ....noun plural
N.S. ....Nova Scotia
NT ....New Testament
Num ....Numbers
numis ....numismatic, numismatical, numismatics
NW ....northwest
NWT ....Northwest Territories
N.Y. ....New York
NYC ....New York City
N.Z. ....New Zealand
O ....Ohio, old
Obad ....Obadiah
obs ....obsolete
OBulg ....Old Bulgarian
OC ....Cistercian Order
O Cart ....Carthusian Order
OCatal ....Old Catalan
occas ....occasionally
OCorn ....Old Cornish
Oct ....October
OD ....Old Dutch
ODan ....Old Danish
OE ....Old English
OF ....Old French
OFM ....Order of Friars Minor
OFris ....Old Frisian
OFrk ....Old Frankish
OHG ....Old High German
OIcel ....Old Icelandic
OIr ....Old Irish
OIt ....Old Italian
Okla ....Oklahoma
OL ....Old Latin
old-fash ....old-fashioned
OLF ....Old Low Franconian
ON ....Old Norse
ONF ....Old North French
ONorw ....Old Norwegian
Ont ....Ontario
o.p. ....out of print
OP ....Order of Preachers
OPer ....Old Persian
OPg ....Old Portuguese
OPol ....Old Polish
OProv ....Old Provençal
OPruss ....Old Prussian
Oreg ....Oregon
orig ....originally
ORuss ....Old Russian
OS ....Old Saxon
OSB ....Order of St. Benedict
Osc ....Oscan
OScan ....Old Scandinavian
OSD ....Order of St. Dominic
OSlav ....Old Slavic
OSM ....Order of the Servants of Mary
OSp ....Old Spanish
OSw ....Old Swedish
OT ....Old Testament
OTurk ....Old Turkish
OW ....Old Welsh
oz ....ounce, ounces
p ....page
Pa ....Pennsylvania
PA ....protonotary apostolic
PaG ....Pennsylvania German
paleontol ....paleontology
Par ....Paralipomenon

part .... participle
pass .... passive
pathol ..... pathology
PC .... privy councilor
Pek .... Pekingese
Per or *Pers* ..... Persian
perf .... perfect
perh .... perhaps
pers .... person
Pet .... Peter
pfc .... private first class
Pg or *Port* ..... Portuguese
PG .... preacher general
pharm ..... pharmacy
PhB .... Bachelor of Philosophy
PhC ...... Pharmaceutical Chemist
PhD ...... Doctor of Philosophy
Phil .... Philippians
Philem .... Philemon
philos ..... philosophy
PhilSp .... Philippine Spanish
photog .... photography
phr .... phrase
physiol ..... physiology
pkg .... package
pl .... plural
p.m. .... post meridiem
Pol .... Polish
polit .... political
pop .... population
poss .... possessive
pp .... pages
prep .... preposition
pres .... present, president
Pr Man .... Prayer of Manasseh
prob .... probably
pron .... pronoun
prond ...... pronounced
pronunc .... pronunciation
protect .... protection
prov .... province
Prov ...... Provencal, Proverbs
prox .... proximo
Ps .... Psalms
psychol .... psychology
PTA ...... Parent-Teacher Association
pub .... public
publ .... publication
rap .... rapid
RD .... rural dean
recd ...... received
redupl ..... reduplication
ref .... reference
refl .... reflexive
rel .... relative
relig .... religion
rep .... republic
repr .... representatives
resp .... respectively
ret .... retired
rev .... reverend, review
Rev .... Revelation
rev. ed. ..... revised edition
R.I. .... Rhode Island
Rom ...... Roman, Romance, Romanian, Romans
ROTC .... Reserve Officers' Training Corps
rpm ...... revolutions per minute
RR .... railroad
RSV ...... Revised Standard Version
rt hon ..... right honorable
Rum ...... Rumanian
Russ ...... Russian
s .... shilling, shillings
S .... south, southern
S.A. .... South Australia
Sam .... Samuel
Sat .... Saturday
SB .... Bachelor of Science
Sc .... Scots
S.C. .... South Carolina
Scand ..... Scandinavian
ScD .... Doctor of Science
ScGael .... Scottish Gaelic
sci .... science
Scot .... Scotland, Scottish
S. Dak. .... South Dakota
SE .... southeast
sec .... second, seconds, section
secy ...... secretary
Sem .... Semitic
Sept .... September
Serb .... Serbian
Shak ...... Shakespeare
sin .... sine
sing .... singular
SJ .... Society of Jesus
SJD ...... Doctor of Juridical Science
Skt .... Sanskrit
Slav .... Slavic
SM .... Master of Science
so .... south
soc .... social, society
sociol ...... sociology
Sol .... Solomon
Soph ...... Sophonias
Sp or *Span* ..... Spanish
specif ..... specific, specifically
sp. gr. ..... specific gravity
sq .... square
sr .... senior
SSR ...... Soviet Socialist Republic
st .... saint, street
stand ...... standard
stat .... statute
STB ...... Bachelor of Sacred Theology, Bachelor of Theology
STD ...... Doctor of Sacred Theology
ste .... saint
STL ...... Licentiate of Sacred Theology
STM ...... Master of Sacred Theology, Master of Theology
subj .... subjunctive
substand ... substandard
Sun .... Sunday
superl ...... superlative
supp .... supplement
Sus .... Susanna
Sw or *Swed* ..... Swedish
SW .... southwest
syll .... syllable
syn .... synonym, synonymy
Syr .... Syriac
Tag .... Tagalog
tech .... technical, technologically, technology
technol .... technology
tel .... telegraph, telephone
Tenn ...... Tennessee
Tex .... Texas
ThD ...... Doctor of Theology
theol ...... theological
Thess ..... Thessalonians
Thurs ..... Thursday
Tim .... Timothy
Tit .... Titus
Tob .... Tobias
Toch ...... Tocharian
Toch A .... Tocharian A
Toch B .... Tocharian B
trans or *transl* ..... translated, translation
Tues ...... Tuesday
Turk ...... Turkish
TV .... television
TVA ...... Tennessee Valley Authority
UH .... upper half
Ukr .... Ukrainian
Umbr ..... Umbrian
UN .... United Nations
UNESCO .. United Nations' Educational, Scientific, and Cultural Organization
univ .... university
US .... United States
USA ...... United States of America
USN ..... United States Navy
USNR ..... United States Naval Reserve
USS ...... United States Ship
USSR ..... Union of Soviet Socialist Republics
usu .... usually
v .... velocity, verb, versus, vowel
Va .... Virginia
var .... variant
vb .... verb
VF .... vicar forane
VG .... vicar-general
vi .... verb intransitive
v imper .... verb imperative
viz .... videlicet
VL .... Vulgar Latin
voc .... vocative
vocab ..... vocabulary
vol .... volume
vt .... verb transitive
Vt .... Vermont
VT .... variable time
W .... Welsh, west, western
Wall ...... Walloon
Wash ...... Washington
Wed .... Wednesday
WFris ...... West Frisian
WGmc ...... West Germanic
Wis or *Wisc* ..... Wisconsin
Wisd ...... Wisdom
Wisd Sol ..... Wisdom of Solomon
W. Va. .... West Virginia
Wyo ...... Wyoming
YMCA ..... Young Men's Christian Association
yr .... year
yrbk ...... yearbook
YWCA .... Young Women's Christian Association
Zach ...... Zacharias
Zech ...... Zechariah
Zeph ...... Zephaniah
zool .... zoological, zoology

SPECIAL SYMBOLS

[ ].... boldface square brackets contain etymology
:...... boldface symbolic colon signals a definition or sense
~..... boldface or lightface swung dash stands for the preceding boldface entry word
⟨ ⟩.... lightface angle brackets contain a verbal illustration
⸗...... lightface double hyphen at end-of-line is a hyphen that should be retained
☞.... fistnote (see definition)
+..... plus sign in etymology joins words or word elements
†...... dagger precedes a death date

ADDENDA SECTION

WEBSTER'S THIRD NEW INTERNATIONAL DICTIONARY

a* *abbr* atto- *herein*
abe·lian group \ə¦bēlyən-, -lēən-\ *n, usu cap A* [*Abelian* fr. Niels *Abel* †1829 Norw. mathematician + E *-ian*] **:** a group whose elements obey the commutative law
ab·la·tor \a'blād·ə(r\ *n* -s [LL, one that removes, fr. *ablatus* (suppletive past part. of *auferre* to remove) + *-or* — more at ABLATE] **:** a material that provides thermal protection (as to the outside of a spacecraft on reentry) by ablating
abort* *n* **:** the premature termination of an action, procedure, or mission relating to a rocket or spacecraft ⟨a launch ~⟩
ab·scis·ic acid \(,)ab,sizik-\ *n* [*abscisic* fr. *abscision* + *-ic*] **:** a plant hormone widespread in nature and made synthetically that promotes leaf abscission and dormancy and has an inhibitory effect on cell elongation — called also *abscisin II, dormin*
ab·scis·in *also* **ab·scis·sin** \ab'sisᵊn\ *n* -s [*abscision, abscission* + *-in*] **:** any of a group of plant regulatory substances that tend to promote leaf abscission and inhibit various growth processes — compare ABSCISIC ACID *herein*
absurd* *adj* **1 :** having no rational or orderly relationship to man's life **:** MEANINGLESS; *also* **:** lacking order or values ⟨adults have condemned them to live in what must seem like an ~ universe —Joseph Featherstone⟩ **2 :** dealing with the absurd or with absurdism
absurd *n* -s [*absurd*, adj. (herein)] **:** the state or condition in which man exists in an irrational and meaningless universe and in which man's life has no meaning outside his own existence
ab·surd·ism \əb'sərd,izəm, ab-, -'z-, -ə̄d-\ *n* -s [*absurd* (herein) + *-ism*] **:** a philosophy based on the belief that man exists in an irrational and meaningless universe and that his search for order brings him into conflict with his universe
¹ab·surd·ist \-dəst\ *n* -s [*absurd* (herein) + *-ist*] **:** a proponent or adherent of absurdism; *esp* **:** a writer who deals with absurdist themes
²absurdist *adj* **:** of, relating to, or dealing with absurdism
aca·de·mese \ə¦kadə¦mēz, ¦akəd-, -ēs\ *n* -s [*academic* + ²*-ese*] **:** a style of writing held to be characteristic of those in academic life ⟨the usual scholarly biography written in barbarous ~ —Dwight Macdonald⟩
acceptable* *adj* **:** capable of being endured **:** SUPPORTABLE, TOLERABLE ⟨maximum ~ damage from nuclear attack⟩
ace·tyl·cho·lin·es·ter·ase \ə¦sēd·ᵊl,kō¦lə'nestə,rās, ¦asəd-, -käl-, -āz\ *n* **:** ACETYLCHOLINE ESTERASE
ace·tyl–co A \ə'sēd·ᵊl'kō'ā; 'asəd·ᵊl-, -ə,tēl-\ *abbr or n* -s [*acetyl* coenzyme *A*] acetyl coenzyme A
acid* *n* **:** LSD *herein*
acidhead \'==,=\ *n* [*acid* (herein) + *head*] **:** a person who frequently uses LSD
acid rock *n* [*acid* (herein) + *rock*] **:** rock music with lyrics having cryptic references to a drug (as LSD)
acoustic* *or* **acoustical*** *adj* **:** of, relating to, or being a musical instrument whose sound is not electronically modified
acquire* *vt* **:** to locate and hold (a desired object) in a detector ⟨~ a target by radar⟩
ac·ti·no·spec·ta·cin \,aktənō'spektəsən\ *n* -s [*actinomycete* + NL *spectabilis* (specific epithet of *Streptomyces spectabilis*, species of actinomycete) + E *-mycin*] **:** an antibiotic from a soil actinomycete (*Streptomyces spectabilis*) that is notably effective against penicillin-resistant venereal infections
action* *n* **:** the most vigorous, productive, or exciting activity in a particular field, area, or group ⟨go where the ~ is⟩
action painting *n* **:** nonrepresentational painting marked esp. by thickly textured surfaces and by the use of improvised techniques (as dribbling, splattering, or smearing) to create apparently accidental pictorial effects — **action painter** *n*
activation analysis *n* **:** a method of analyzing for chemical elements in a material by bombarding it with nuclear particles to produce radioactive isotopes whose radiations indicate the identity and quantity of the parent elements
additive identity *n* **:** an identity element (as 0 in the group of whole numbers under the operation of addition) that in a given mathematical system leaves unchanged any element to which it is added
additive inverse *n* **:** a number of opposite sign with respect to a given number so that addition of the two numbers gives zero ⟨the *additive inverse* of 4 is −4⟩
ad·e·no·vi·rus \¦adᵊnō¦vīrəs\ *n* [*adenoid* + *-o-* + *virus*] **:** any of a group of viruses that contain deoxyribonucleic acid, may cause respiratory disorders, and include at least two capable of inducing malignant tumors in experimental animals — compare PICORNAVIRUS *herein* — **ad·e·no·vi·ral** \-rəl\ *adj*
¹admass \'=,=\ *n* -ES [*advertising* + *mass*] **:** a system of commercial marketing that attempts to influence great masses of consumers by mass-media advertising; *also* **:** a society thus influenced
²admass *adj* **:** of, characterized by, or influenced by admass
ADP* *abbr* automatic data processing
adre·no·cor·ti·co·steroid \ə¦drēnō,kȯrd·ə̇kō'sti(ə),rȯid, -ren-, -te(-\ *n* [*adrenocortical* + *-o-* + *steroid*] **:** a steroid obtained from or resembling those of the adrenal cortex
aer·on·o·my \a(ə)'ränəmē, e(ə)'-, ,āə'-\ *n* -ES [*aer-* + *-nomy*] **:** a science that deals with the physics and chemistry of the upper atmosphere — **aer·on·o·mer** \-mə(r\ *n* — **aer·o·nom·ic** \,a(ə)rə'nämik, ,e(ə)r-, ,āər-\ *adj*
aero·space \'a(ə)rə,spās, 'e(ə)r-, 'āər-\ *n* [*aer-* + *space*] **1 :** space comprising the earth's atmosphere and the space beyond **2 :** a branch of physical science that deals with aerospace **3 :** the industry involved in the manufacture of aerospace vehicles — **aerospace** *adj*
aero·train \-rə,trān\ *n* [*aer-* + *train*] **:** a propeller-driven vehicle that rides on a cushion of air astride a single rail
af·la·tox·in \¦aflə¦täksən\ *n* [NL *Aspergillus flavus*, species of mold + E *toxin*] **:** a complex of toxic substances that develop (as in corn or oilseed meals) through the action of a mold (*Aspergillus flavus*), are implicated in the death of livestock, and are suspected of being carcinogenic
a–frame* *n, cap A* [fr. the resemblance of the shape of the facade to a capital A] **:** a building (as a house) that typically has a triangular front and rear wall and a roof reaching to or nearly to the level of the ground floor
af·ro \'a(,)frō\ *adj, usu cap* [*Afro-*] **:** having the hair shaped into a round bushy mass ⟨an *Afro* hairstyle⟩ — **afro** *n* -s *usu cap*
af·ro–asian \¦==¦==\ *adj, usu cap both As* [*Afr-* + *Asian*] **:** of or relating to a group of African and Asian nations that cooperate in the solution of common political problems
af·ter·tax \¦aftər¦taks, ¦aa-, ¦ai-, ¦á-\ *adj* [²*after* + *tax*] **:** remaining after payment of taxes and esp. of income tax
ag·gior·na·men·to \ə,jȯrnə'men(,)tō\ *n* -s [It, fr. *aggiornare* to bring up to date, fr. *a* to (fr. L *ad-*) + *giorno* day, fr. LL *diurnum* — more at JOURNEY] **:** a bringing up to date ⟨called a Council with ~ as its theme —*Times Lit. Supp.*⟩
¹a–go–go \ä'gō(,)gō\ *n* -s [*Whisky à Gogo*, café and discotheque in Paris, France, fr. F *whisky* whisky + *à gogo* galore, fr. MF] **1 :** DISCOTHEQUE *herein* **2 :** a usu. small intimate nightclub for dancing to live music and esp. rock 'n' roll
²a–go–go *adj* **1 :** of, relating to, or being an a-go-go or the music or dances performed there ⟨a-go-go dancers⟩ **2 :** characterized by rapid frenetic movement or tempo ⟨the *a-go-go* rhythm of change in our century —Ted Palmer⟩ **3 :** being in the latest style ⟨psychiatry *a-go-go* —Charles Schulz⟩
ago·ra \,ägə'rä\ *n, pl* **ago·rot** \-'rōt\ [NHeb *ăgōrāh*, fr. Heb, a small coin] **1 :** a monetary unit of Israel representing 1/100 of a pound — see MONEY table *in the Dict* **2 :** a coin representing one agora
agrav·ic \(')ā¦gravik\ *adj* [²*a-* + *gravity* + *-ic*] **:** of or relating to a theoretical condition of no gravitation
ai·ki·do \¦īkē¦dō, -kə-\ *n* [Jap *aikidō*, fr. *ai-* together, mutual + *ki* spirit + *dō* district, province, art] **:** a Japanese art of self-defense employing locks and holds and utilizing the principle of nonresistance to cause an opponent's own momentum to work against him
air bag *n* **:** a bag designed to inflate automatically in front of riders in an automobile in case of accident to protect them from pitching forward into solid parts
air battery *n* [so called fr. the oxidation's being produced by exposure to pressurized air] **:** a rechargeable battery in which current is generated as a result of oxidation of a metal
airbus \'=,=\ *n* **:** a short-range or medium-range subsonic jet passenger airplane
air cavalry *or* **air cav** \-'kav\ *n* **1 :** an army unit that is transported in air vehicles and carries out the traditional cavalry missions of reconnaissance and security **2 :** an army unit that is esp. equipped and adapted for transportation in air vehicles but is organized for sustained ground combat
air–cushion vehicle *also* **air–cushioned vehicle** *n* **:** GROUND-EFFECT MACHINE *herein*
air door *n* **:** a temperature-controlled strong usu. upward current of air used instead of a door
air·mo·bile \'a(ə)rmō,bēl, 'e(-\ *adj* [*air* + *mobile*, adj.] **:** of, relating to, or being a military unit whose members are transported to combat areas usu. by helicopter
air·tel \'a(ə)r,tel, 'e(-\ *n* -s [*air* + *hotel*] **:** a hotel situated at or close to an airport
al·dos·ter·on·ism \al'dästə,rō,nizəm, ,aldōstə'r-\ *n* -s [*aldosterone* + *-ism*] **:** a condition characterized by excessive aldosterone and marked by excessive loss of body potassium, muscular weakness, and elevated blood pressure
ale·a·tor·ic \¦ālēə¦tȯrik, -tär-\ *adj* [L *aleator* dice player, gambler (fr. *alea* dice game) + E *-ic*] *of music* **:** characterized by chance or random elements
aleatory* *adj* **:** ALEATORIC *herein*
alf·vén wave \,al(f)vän-, -ven-\ *n, usu cap A* [after Hannes *Alfvén*, 20th cent. Swed. astrophysicist] **:** a transverse electromagnetic wave that propagates along lines of force in a magnetized plasma
al·gol \'al,gäl, -gȯl\ *n* -s *usu cap A or all cap* [*algo*rithmic *language*] **:** an algebraic and logical language for programming a computer
algorithm* *n* **:** a problem-solving procedure (as for finding the greatest common divisor) involving a finite number of often repetitive steps or operations — **algorithmic*** *adj* — **al·go·rith·mi·cal·ly** \-mək(ə)lē, -mēk-, -li\ *adv*
ali·es·ter·ase \¦alē¦estə,rās, -āz\ *n* [*aliphatic* + *esterase*] **:** an esterase that promotes the hydrolysis of ester links esp. in aliphatic esters of low molecular weight
al·lo·ge·ne·ic \¦aləjə¦nēik\ *also* **al·lo·gen·ic** \-¦jenik\ *adj* [*allogeneic* fr. *all-* + *-geneic* (as in *syngeneic* — herein); *allogenic* fr. *all-* + *-genic*] **:** sufficiently unlike genetically to interact antigenically — compare SYNGENEIC *herein*
al·lo·graft \'alō,=\ *n* [*all-* + *graft*; fr. its being a graft from another individual] **:** HOMOGRAFT
al·lo·ster·ic \¦alə¦sterik, -ti(ə)r-\ *adj* [*all-* + *steric*] **:** of, relating to, or being alteration of the activity of a protein (as an enzyme) by combination with another substance at a point other than the chemically active site
alpha–adrenergic \¦==,==¦==\ *adj* **:** of, relating to, or being an alpha-receptor ⟨*alpha-adrenergic* blocking action⟩
alpha decay *n* **:** the radioactive decay of an atomic nucleus by emission of an alpha particle
alpha helix *n* **:** the coiled structural arrangement of many proteins consisting of a single spiral amino-acid chain that is stabilized by hydrogen bonds
al·pha·met·ic \¦alfə¦med·ik\ *n* -s [*alpha*betic + arith*metic*] **:** a mathematical puzzle consisting of a numerical computation with letters substituted for numbers which are to be restored through mathematical reasoning
alpha–receptor \'===,==\ *n* **:** a receptor that responds to or is activated by epinephrine and levarterenol but not isoproterenol and that is associated with vasoconstriction, relaxation of intestinal muscle, and contraction of the myometrium, nictitating membrane, iris dilator muscle, and splenic smooth muscle — compare BETA-RECEPTOR *herein*
aman·ta·dine \ə'mantə,dēn\ *n* -s [*amantad-* (fr. anagram of *adamantane*) + *amine*] **:** an antiviral drug used esp. to prevent infection (as by an influenza virus) by interfering with virus penetration into host cells
am·bi·sex·trous \¦ambə¦sekstrəs\ *adj* [*ambi-* + *sex* + *-trous* (as in *ambidextrous*)] **1 :** not distinguishable as male or female **:** common to males and females ⟨~ clothing⟩ **2 :** including both sexes ⟨an ~ party⟩
am·bu·la·to·ri·ly \¦ambyələ¦tōrəlē, -tȯr-, -li\ *adv* [*ambulatory* + *-ly*] **:** as or in a manner suitable to an ambulatory patient
am·er·asian \¦amər+¦\ *n, cap* [*Amer-* + *Asian*] **:** a person of mixed American and Asian descent; *esp* **:** one whose mother is Asian and whose father is American
am·e·thop·ter·in \,amə'thäpt(ə)rən\ *n* -s [*amin-* + *meth-* + *pteroyl* + *-in*] **:** METHOTREXATE *herein*
am·i·trip·ty·line \,amə-'triptə,lēn\ *n* -s [origin unknown] **:** an antidepressant drug
am·i·trole \'amə-,trōl\ *n* -s [*amin-* + *triazole*] **:** an herbicide that is esp. effective in controlling poison ivy
am·nio·cen·te·sis \,amnēōsen-'tēsə̇s\ *n* [NL, fr. *amnio-* + *centesis*] **:** the surgical insertion of a hollow needle through the abdominal wall and uterus of a pregnant female and into the amnion esp. to obtain amniotic fluid for the determination of sex or chromosomal abnormality in the fetus
am·pho·ter·i·cin \,amfə'terəsən\ *n* -s [*amphoteric* + *-in*] **:** either of two antibiotic drugs obtained from a soil actinomycete (*Streptomyces nodosus*) of which one (**amphotericin B**) is useful against deep-seated and systemic fungal infections
am·pi·cil·lin \¦ampə¦silən\ *n* -s [*amin-* + *penicillin*] **:** an antibiotic of the penicillin group that is effective against gram-negative bacteria
anagenesis* *n* **:** essentially progressive and linear evolutionary change — **ana·ge·net·i·cal·ly** \¦anəjə¦ned·ək(ə)lē\ *adv*
an·chorman \'==,man\ *n*. **1 :** a newscaster who coordinates the related activities of other usu. remotely located broadcasters (as at a political convention) so as to produce a coherent program **2 :** MODERATOR 2d
angel* *n* **:** a radar echo caused by something not visually discernible
an·gio·ten·sin \,anjēō'ten(t)sən\ *n* -s [blend of *angiotonin* and *hypertensin*] **:** a kinin with a marked vasoconstrictive action that occurs in two forms of which one (**angiotensin II** \-'tü\) is used in the treatment of shock
an·gio·ten·sin·ase \-sə,nās, -āz\ *n* [*angiotensin* + *-ase*] **:** any of several enzymes of the blood that hydrolyze angiotensin
angry young man *n* [*Angry Young Man*, autobiography (1951) of Leslie A. Paul *b*1905 Eng. journalist] **:** one of a group of mid-20th century British authors whose works express the bitterness of the lower classes toward the established sociopolitical system and toward the mediocrity and hypocrisy of the middle and upper classes
angular perspective *n* **:** TWO-POINT PERSPECTIVE
annihilate* *vb* **~** *vi* **:** to undergo annihilation ⟨an elementary particle and its antiparticle ~ when they meet⟩
annual percentage rate *n* **:** a measure of the annual percentage cost of consumer credit (as in installment buying or a charge account) that is required by law to appear on statements of credit accounts and is variously computed but always takes into consideration the amount financed, the amount of the finance charges, and the schedule of repayment
an·ovulant \(')an +\ *n* -s [*an-* + *ovulation* + *-ant*] **:** an anovulatory drug — **anovulant** *adj*
anovulatory* *adj* **:** suppressing ovulation
answering service *n* **:** a commercial service that answers telephone calls for its clients
an·thro·po·sere \an'thräpə,si(ə)r, 'an(t)thrəp-\ *n* -s [*anthrop-* + ⁵*sere*] **:** NOOSPHERE *herein*
an·ti·allergic *also* **an·ti·allergenic** \¦an,tī, ¦antē, ¦antə +\ *adj* [¹*anti-* + *allergic*] **:** tending to relieve or control allergic symptoms — **antiallergic** *also* **antiallergenic** *n*
an·ti–art \"+,-\ *n* [¹*anti-* + *art*] **:** art based on premises antithetical to traditional or popular art forms; *specif* **:** DADA
an·ti·authoritarian \" +\ *adj* [¹*anti-* + *authoritarian*] **:** opposing or hostile to authoritarians or authoritarianism — **an·ti·authoritarianism** \" +\ *n*
an·ti·auxin \" +\ *n* [¹*anti-* + *auxin*] **:** a plant substance that opposes or suppresses the natural effect of an auxin
an·ti·ballistic missile \" +-\ *n* **:** a missile for intercepting and destroying a ballistic missile
an·ti·baryon \" +\ *n* -s [¹*anti-* + *baryon* (herein)] **:** an antiparticle of a baryon (as an antiproton or antineutron)
an·ti·cancer *also* **an·ti·cancerous** \" +\ *adj* [¹*anti-* + *cancer*] **:** used or effective against cancer ⟨~ drugs⟩
an·ti·coagulate \" +\ *vt* [¹*anti-* + *coagulate*] **:** to treat with an anticoagulant — **an·ti·coagulation** \" +\ *n* — **an·ti·coagulative** \" +\ *adj*
an·ti·codon \" +\ *n* [¹*anti-* + *codon* (herein)] **:** a sequence of three nucleotides in transfer RNA that is complementary with a codon of messenger RNA
an·ti·convulsant \" +\ *or* **an·ti·convulsive** \" +\ *adj* [¹*anti-* + *convulsant* or *convulsive*] **:** used or tending to control or ward off convulsions (as in epilepsy) — **anticonvulsant** *n*
an·ti·crop \" +\ *adj* [¹*anti-* + *crop*] **:** destructive to or directed against crops ⟨~ chemical weapons⟩
an·ti·depressant \¦an,tī, ¦antē, ¦antə +\ *or* **an·ti·depressive** \" +\ *adj* [¹*anti-* + *depressant* or *depressive*] **:** used or tending to relieve psychic depression — **antidepressant** *n*
an·ti·deuteron \" +\ *n* [¹*anti-* + *deuteron*] **:** an antiparticle that consists of one antielectron and one antiproton
an·ti·dumping \" +\ *adj* [¹*anti-* + *dumping*] **:** designed to prevent the importation and sale of foreign goods at prices substantially lower than domestic prices ⟨~ tariffs⟩
an·ti·electron \" +\ *n* [¹*anti-* + *electron*] **:** POSITRON
an·ti·emetic \" +\ *adj* [¹*anti-* + *emetic*] **:** used or tending to prevent or check vomiting — **antiemetic** *n*
an·ti·environment \" +\ *n* [¹*anti-* + *environment*] **:** something (as a work of art) that points up aspects of the current environment by contrast — **an·ti·environmental** \" +\ *adj*
an·ti·fertility \" +\ *adj* [¹*anti-* + *fertility*] **:** intended to control excess or unwanted fertility **:** CONTRACEPTIVE
an·ti·flu·o·ri·da·tion·ist \" +,flu̇rə¦dāsh(ə)nəst, -ōr-, -ȯr-\ *n* [¹*anti-* + *fluoridation* + *-ist*] **:** one vigorously opposed to the fluoridation of public water supplies
an·ti·foul·ant \" + 'fau̇lənt\ *n* -s [¹*anti-* + ⁴*foul* + ¹*-ant*] **:** a substance designed to prevent, reduce, or eliminate fouling
¹an·ti·gravity \" +\ *adj* [¹*anti-* + *gravity*] **:** reducing or canceling the effect of gravity or protecting against it
²antigravity \"\ *n* **:** a hypothetical effect resulting from cancellation or reduction of a gravitational field
an·ti–hero \¦an,tī, ¦antē, ¦antə + \ *n* -ES [¹*anti-* + *hero*] **:** a protagonist who is notably lacking in heroic qualities (as resoluteness or effectiveness) — **an·ti–heroic** \" +\ *adj*
an·ti·hypertensive \" +\ *adj* [¹*anti-* + *hypertension* + *-ive*] **:** used or effective against high blood pressure
an·ti·lepton \" +\ *n* [¹*anti-* + ³*lepton*] **:** an antiparticle (as a positron or an antineutrino) of a lepton
¹an·ti·missile \" +\ *adj* [¹*anti-* + ²*missile*] **:** designed as a defense against missiles ⟨an ~ system⟩
²antimissile \"\ *n* **:** ANTIMISSILE MISSILE *herein*
an·ti·missile missile \" +-\ *n* **:** a missile for intercepting another missile in flight
an·ti·mitotic \¦an,tī, ¦antē, ¦antə+\ *adj* [¹*anti-* + *mitotic*] **:** inhibiting division of the cell nucleus — **antimitotic** *n*
an·ti·mutagenic \" +\ *adj* [¹*anti-* + *mutagenic*] **:** decreasing the frequency of mutation either by inhibiting the action of mutagens or reducing spontaneous mutation
an·ti·novel \" + \ *n* [¹*anti-* + ¹*novel*] **:** a work of fiction that lacks most or all of the traditional features (as coherent structure or character development) of the novel —**an·ti·novelist** \" +\ *n*
an·ti·nuclear \" +\ *adj* [¹*anti* + *nucleus* + *-ar*] **:** tending to react with cell nuclei ⟨~ antibodies⟩
an·ti·particle \'an,tī, 'antē, 'antə + ,\ *n* [¹*anti-* + *particle*] **:** an elementary particle identical to another elementary particle in mass but opposite to it in electric and magnetic properties
an·ti·pollution \¦an,tī, ¦antē, 'antə+\ *adj* [¹*anti-* + *pollution*] **:** intended to prevent, reduce, or eliminate pollution
an·ti·poverty \" +\ *adj* [¹*anti-* + *poverty*] **:** of or relating to action designed to relieve poverty ⟨~ programs⟩
an·ti·psychotic \" +\ *adj* [¹*anti-* + *psychotic*] **:** tending to alleviate psychosis or psychotic states ⟨an ~ drug⟩ — **antipsychotic** *n*
an·ti·racism \" +\ *n* [¹*anti-* + *racism*] **:** adherence to the view that racism is a social evil
an·ti·science \" +\ *n* [¹*anti-* + *science*] **:** a system or attitude or cult that rejects scientific methods or the value of science to man; *also* **:** one that denies the value of basic scientific research — **an·ti·scientific** \" +\ *adj*
an·ti·scientism \" +\ *n* [*anti-* + *scientist* + *-ism*] **:** ANTISCIENCE *herein*
an·ti·sex *or* **an·ti·sexual** \" +\ *adj* [¹*anti-* + *sex* or *sexual*] **:** antagonistic toward sex; *esp* **:** tending to reduce or eliminate the sex drive or sexual activity
an·ti·smog \" +\ *adj* [¹*anti-* + *smog*] **:** designed to reduce pollutants contributing to smog ⟨~ devices on automobiles⟩
an·ti·static \" +\ *adj* [¹*anti-* + *static*, n.] **:** preventing the buildup of static electricity **:** reducing or removing static electricity — **antistatic** *n*
an·ti·tuberculous *also* **an·ti·tuberculosis** *or* **an·ti·tubercular** \" +\ *adj* [*antituberculous* fr. ¹*anti-* + *tuberculous* + *-ous*; *antituberculosis* fr. ¹*anti-* + *tuberculosis*; *antitubercular* fr. ¹*anti-* + *tuberculous* + *ar*] **:** used against tuberculosis
an·ti·tumor *also* **an·ti·tumoral** \"+\ *adj* [*antitumor* fr. ¹*anti-* + *tumor*; *antitumoral* fr. ¹*anti-* + *tumor* + *-al*] **:** ANTICANCER *herein*
ape *adj* [¹*ape*] **:** being beyond restraint **:** CRAZY, MAD — usu. used in the phrase *go ape* ⟨went ~ over another girl —*Boston Sunday Globe Mag.*⟩
aperture card *n* **:** a punched card for data processing in which one or more frames of a microfilmed document are mounted
aph·o·late \'afə,lāt\ *n* -s [prob. fr. *az-* + *phosphine* + *-late* (of unknown origin)] **:** a chemosterilant esp. effective in controlling houseflies
aph·ox·ide \(')a¦fäk,sīd *also* -ksə̇d\ *n* [prob. fr. *az-* + *phosphine* + *oxide*] **:** TEPA *herein*
apo·apsis \¦apō + \ *n* [NL, fr. *apo-* + *apsis*] **:** the apsis that is the greatest distance from the center of attraction
apo·cyn·thi·on \,apə¦sin(t)thēən\ *n* -s [NL, fr. *apo-* + *Cynthia*, goddess of the moon (fr. Gk *Kynthia*) + *-on* (as in *aphelion*)] **:** APOLUNE *herein*
apo·lune \'apə,lün\ *n* -s [*apo-* + L *luna* moon — more at LUNAR] **:** the point in the path of a body orbiting the moon that is farthest from the center of the moon
apo·se·le·ne \,apəsə'lēnē, -pəs-\ *n* -s [ISV *apo-* + *-selene* (fr. Gk *selēnē* moon) — more at SELEN-] **:** APOLUNE *herein*
apo·se·le·ni·um \-nēəm\ *n* -s [NL, fr. Gk *apo-* apo- + *selēnē* moon + NL *-ium* (alter. of *-ion* — as in *aphelion*) — more at SELEN-] **:** APOLUNE *herein*
¹après–ski \¦a,prä¦skē\ *n* [F *après* after + *ski* ski, skiing — more at APRÈS] **:** social activity (as at a ski lodge) after a day's skiing
²après–ski *adj* **:** of, relating to, or suitable for après-ski
aqua·naut \'akwə,nȯt, 'äk-, -nät\ *n* -s [*aqua-* + *-naut* (as in *astronaut*)] **:** one that lives beneath the surface of water for

*additional definition **additional definition but change in form an extended period and carries on activities both inside and outside his underwater shelter

aqua·plan·ing \-ˌplāniŋ\ *n* -s [²*aquaplane* + *-ing*; fr. the riding of the tires on water like that of an aquaplane] **:** HYDROPLANING *herein*

arabesque* *n* **:** a contrived intricate pattern of verbal expression ⟨~s of alliteration —C.E.Montague⟩

ar·bo·vi·rus \ˌärbəˈvīrəs\ *n* [*arthropod-borne virus*] **:** any of various arthropod-borne viruses that cause encephalitis

arc–jet engine *n* **:** a rocket engine in which the propellant gas is heated by an electric arc

area code *n* [fr. its designation of major subdivisions of the territory of the United States] **:** a 3-digit code used in dialing long-distance telephone calls

arm–twist·ing \ˈ=ˌ==\ *n* **:** the use of direct personal pressure in order to achieve a desired end ⟨for all the *arm-twisting*, the . . . vote on the measure was unexpectedly tight —*Newsweek*⟩

ar·res·tant \əˈrestənt\ *n* -s [¹*arrest* + *-ant*] **:** one that checks a course or activity; *esp* **:** a substance that causes an insect to stop and begin to feed

art·mo·bile \ˈärtmōˌbēl\ *n* [*art* + *-mobile*] **:** a trailer that houses an art collection designed for exhibition on road tours

asphalt jungle *n* **:** a big city or a specified part of a big city ⟨the *asphalt jungle* around Times Square —E.R.Bentley⟩

as·sem·blage* \əˈsemblij, -lēj; ˌaˌsäⁿmˈbläzh, ˌäˌs-, -säⁿˈb-, -läzh\ *n* **1 :** an artistic composition made from scraps, junk, and odds and ends (as of paper, cloth, wood, stone, or metal) **2 :** the art of making assemblages — **as·sem·blag·ist** \-jəst, -zhə-\ *n*

assembler* *n* **:** a computer program that automatically converts instructions written in a mnemonic code into the equivalent machine code — compare COMPILER *herein*

assembly language *n* **:** a mnemonic language for programming a computer that is a close approximation of machine language

assist* *n* **:** a mechanical device that provides assistance

as·tri·on·ics \ˌastrēˈäniks\ *n pl but sing or pl in constr* [*astronautics* + *-ionics* (as in *avionics*)] **:** electronics applied to astronautics

as·tro·biology \ˈas(ˌ)trō +\ *n* [*astr-* + *biology*] **:** EXOBIOLOGY *herein* — **as·tro·biologist** \" +\ *n*

as·tro·bleme \ˈastrəˌblēm\ *n* -s [*astr-* + Gk *blēma* throw, missile, wound from a missile, fr. *ballein* to throw — more at DEVIL] **:** an ancient scar on the earth's crust made by the impact of a meteorite

as·tro·chemistry \ˈastrō +\ *n* [*astr-* + *chemistry*] **:** the chemistry of the stars and interstellar space

as·tro·dy·nam·ics \ˈas(ˌ)trō +\ *n pl but sing or pl in constr* [*astr-* + *dynamics*] **:** dynamics that deals with objects in outer space — **as·tro·dynamic** \" +\ *adj* — **as·tro·dy·nam·i·cist** \ˈas(ˌ)trō + dīˈnaməsəst *sometimes* də-\ *n*

as·tro·geology \ˈas(ˌ)trō +\ *n* [*astr-* + *geology*] **:** a branch of geology that deals with celestial bodies — **as·tro·geologic** \ˈastrō +\ *adj* — **as·tro·geologist** \ˈas(ˌ)trō +\ *n*

at·a·rax·ic \ˌadəˈraksik\ *adj* [*ataraxy* + *-ic*] **:** ATARACTIC

ath·er·o·gen·ic \ˌathərōˈjenik\ *adj* [*athero-* + *-genic*] **:** tending to produce degenerative changes in blood-vessel walls

at·lan·ti·cism \ətˈlantəˌsizəm\ *n* -s *usu cap* [*Atlantic* + *-ism*] **:** a policy of military cooperation between European and North American powers — **at·lan·ti·cist** \-ntəsəst\ *n* -s *usu cap*

at·mo·sphe·ri·um \ˌatməˈsfirēəm\ *n* -s [*atmosphere* + *-ium* (as in *planetarium*)] **1 :** an optical device for projecting images of meteorological phenomena (as clouds) on the inside of a dome **2 :** a room housing an atmospherium

at·om·ar·i·um \ˌadəˈmerēəm, -mar-\ *n* -s [NL, fr. Sw *atom* atom (fr. L *atomus*) + NL *-arium* (as in *planetarium*)] **1 :** a small nuclear reactor on permanent display for the public **2 :** a room for viewing an atomarium

attitude* *n* **:** the position or orientation (as of a missile or spacecraft) determined by the relationship between its axes and a reference datum (as the horizon or a particular star)

at·to- \ˈad·(ˌ)ō, -d·ə\ *comb form* [ISV, fr. Dan or Norw *atten* eighteen (fr. ON *āttjān*) + *-o-* — more at EIGHTEEN] **:** one quintillionth (10^{-18}) part of

attrition* *n* **:** a usu. gradual loss of personnel from causes normal or peculiar to a given situation (as death, retirement, and resignation in a labor force or failure and dropout among students) often without filling the vacancies

audible *n* -s [*audible*, adj.] **:** AUTOMATIC *herein*

au·dio–lingual \ˈȯdē(ˌ)ō+\ *adj* [*audio-* + *lingual*] **:** involving a drill routine of listening and speaking in language learning

au·dio·tape \ˈȯdēōˌtāp\ *n* [*audio-* + *tape*] **:** a tape recording of sound

au·dio·visuals \ˌȯdēō+\ *n pl* [*audiovisual*] **:** instructional materials (as filmstrips accompanied by recordings) that make use of both sight and sound

au pair girl *also* **au pair** *n* **:** a foreign girl living in England who does domestic work for a family in return for room and board and the opportunity to learn the English language

aus·form \ˈȯsˌfȯ(ə)rm\ *vt* [*austenitic* + *deform*; fr. the deformation's taking place while the steel is still in the austenitic form] **:** to subject (steel) to deformation and then to quenching and tempering in order to make stronger, more ductile, and more resistant to fatigue failure

au·teur theory \ōˈtər-, -tœr-\ *n* [part trans. of F *politique des auteurs*, fr. *auteur* author, fr. OF *autor*; fr. the view that directors are the true authors of a film — more at AUTHOR] **:** a cinematic technique characterized by the movie director's complete control over all aspects of production from the selection of a subject to the final editing of the film

au·to·drome \ˈȯd·əˌdrōm, -d·ō-\ *n* -s [²*auto* + ¹*-drome*] **:** a driving or racing course for automobiles

au·to·immune \ˈȯd·ō +\ *adj* [back-formation fr. *autoimmunization*] **:** of, relating to, or caused by autoantibodies ⟨~ diseases⟩ — **au·to·immunity** \" +\ *n*

au·to·manipulation \ˈȯd·ō +\ *n* [*aut-* + *manipulation*] **:** physical stimulation of the genital organs by oneself

automatic* *n* **:** a substitute play called by a football quarterback at the line of scrimmage; *also* **:** a substitute defensive formation called by a linebacker at the line of scrimmage

au·to·net·ics \ˌȯd·ōˈned·iks\ *n pl but usu sing in constr* [*aut-* + *-netics* (as in *cybernetics*)] **:** a branch of knowledge dealing with automatic guidance or control systems

au·toph·a·gy \ȯˈtäfəjē\ *n* [*aut-* + *-phagy*] **:** digestion of cellular constituents by enzymes of the same cell

au·to·regulation \ˈȯd·ō +\ *n* [*aut-* + *regulation*] **:** the maintenance of relative constancy of a physiological process under varying conditions by factors inherent in an organ or tissue — **au·to·regulative** \" +\ *adj* — **au·to·regulatory** \" +\ *adj*

au·to·stra·da \ˌaud·ōˈsträdə, ˌȯd·-\ *n*, *pl* **autostradas** *or* **autostra·de** \-ˈäd(ˌ)ā\ [It, fr. *automobile* automobile (fr. F) + *strada* street, fr. LL *strata* paved road — more at STREET] **:** a high-speed multilane motor road first developed in Italy

avale·ment \ävál(ə)mäⁿ\ *n* -s [F, lit., swallowing, fr. *avaler* to lower, swallow, fr. MF — more at AVALE] **:** a folding of the legs by a skier as he leans back and shoots his feet forward so as to keep the skis in contact with the snow in skiing and turning at high speed on bumpy terrain

avoid·ant \əˈvȯidᵊnt\ *adj* [*avoid* + ²*-ant*] **:** tending to draw away **:** negatively orienting with respect to a stimulus

aza·ser·ine \ˌazəˈseˌrēn, -sī,-, -ˌrən\ *n* [*diaz-* + *acetyl* + *serine*] **:** an antibiotic that is used to inhibit the growth of some tumors and is an immunosuppressive agent

back·ground·er \ˈbakˌgraündə(r\ *n* [*background* + ²*-er*] **:** an informal off-the-record news conference in which a government official talks freely to reporters

backup* *n* **:** one that serves as a substitute or alternative ⟨a ~ for a rocket⟩ — **backup** *adj*

bad–mouth \ˈ=ˌmauth, -th\ *vt* **:** to criticize severely, persistently, and often unjustifiedly

bag* *n* **1 :** frame or state of mind ⟨when a person acts stupidly, he is "in his stupid ~" —Junius Griffin⟩ **2 :** something suited to one's taste **:** something one likes or does well **:** SPECIALTY ⟨hasn't been my ~ so far, but I'm a very dedicated actor —Dick Van Dyke⟩ **3 a :** an individual's typical way of life ⟨can't expect people who are in another ~ to accept my ~ —Jerry Rubin⟩ **b :** a characteristic manner of expression ⟨more than any other singer in the soul ~ —Albert Goldman⟩ **4 :** something that frustrates or impedes **:** HANG-UP

bag·gies \ˈbagēz, -aag-, -aig-, -giz\ *n pl* [*baggy*] **:** long loose-fitting swim trunks — compare JAMS *herein*

ba·ha·sa in·do·ne·sia \bəˈhäsəˌindəˈnēzhə, -ēshə, -ēzēə, -äsēə\ *n*, *cap B&I* [Indonesian *bahasa indonésia*, fr. *bahasa* language (fr. Skt *bhāṣā*, fr. *bhāṣate* he speaks) + *indonésia* Indonesian, fr. *Indonesia*, republic in Malay archipelago; akin to Gk *phanai* to say — more at BAN] **:** INDONESIAN 3b

ba·ker–nunn camera \ˌbākə(r)ˈnən-\ *n*, *usu cap B&N* [after James G. *Baker* b1914 & Joseph *Nunn*, Amer. optical designers] **:** a large camera for tracking earth satellites

bal·lute \bəˈlüt, ˈbaˌlüt\ *n* -s [*balloon* + *parachute*] **:** a small inflatable parachute for stabilization and deceleration of a jumper or object before the conventional parachute opens

baltimore chop *n*, *usu cap B* [so called fr. its perfection by the Baltimore baseball team of the 1890s] **:** a batted ball in baseball that usu. bounces too high for an infielder to make a putout at first base

banana seat *n* **:** an elongated bicycle saddle that often has an upward-curved back and a tapered front

banquet lamp *n* **:** a tall elaborate kerosine table lamp

ban·tu·stan \ˈban·(ˌ)tüˌstan, ˈbantəˌs-, ˈbän·(ˌ)tüˌstän, ˌ=(ˌ)=ˈ=\ *n* -s *usu cap* [*Bantu* + *-stan* land (as in *Hindustan*)] **:** an all-black enclave in the Republic of So. Africa with a limited degree of self-government

barf \ˈbärf\ *vi* -ED/-ING/-S [origin unknown] **:** VOMIT

bar girl *n* **:** a prostitute who frequents bars

bar·i·at·rics \ˌbarēˈatriks\ *n pl but sing in constr* [*bar-* + *-iatrics*] **:** a branch of medicine that deals with the treatment of obesity — **bar·i·a·tri·cian** \-ēəˈtrishən\ *n* -s

bar mitzvah *vt*, *often cap B&M* **:** to administer the ceremony of bar mitzvah to

baro·re·cep·tor \ˈbarōrēˈseptə(r), -ōrē-\ *also* **bar·o·cep·tor** \ˈbarōˌs-\ *n* -s [*bar-* + *receptor*] **:** a neural receptor sensitive to changes in environmental pressure ⟨~s of the arterial walls⟩

bary·on \ˈbarēˌän\ *n* -s [ISV *bary-* + ²*-on*] **:** any of a group of elementary particles (as a nucleon or a heavier particle) that obey Fermi-Dirac statistics and satisfy the principle of conservation of baryon number — **bary·on·ic** \ˈbarēˈänik\ *adj*

baryon number *n* **:** a number equal to the number of baryons minus that of antibaryons in a system of elementary particles

base* *n* **:** a price level at which a security previously actively declining in price resists further price decline

base exchange *n* **:** a post exchange on an air force base

battered child syndrome *n* **:** the complex of grave physical injuries (as fractures, hematomas, and contusions) that results from gross abuse (as by a parent) of a young child

bayes·ian \ˈbāzēən, -āzhən\ *adj*, *usu cap* [Thomas *Bayes* †1761 Eng. mathematician + E *-ian*] **:** being or relating to a theory (as of decision or of statistical inference) in which probabilities are associated with individual events or statements and not merely with sequences of events (as in frequency theories)

beach bunny *n* **:** a girl who joins a surfing group but does not engage in surfing

beachwear \ˈ=ˌ=\ *n* **:** clothing for wear at a beach

beautiful people *n*, *often cap B&P* **:** people that are identified with the smart set ⟨you can make it if you're one of the *beautiful people* . . . or if you just have money —*Newsweek*⟩

behavioral scientist *n* **:** a specialist in behavioral science

bellyboard \ˈ==ˌ=\ *n* [¹*belly* + *board*; fr. the prone position of the rider] **:** a small buoyant board usu. less than three feet in length that is used in surf riding

belted–bias tire *n* **:** a pneumatic tire with a hooplike belt of cord around the tire underneath the tread and on top of the ply cords laid at an acute angle to the center line of the tread

bem·e·gride \ˈbeməˌgrīd, -ēm-\ *n* -s [*b*eta + *e*thyl + *m*ethyl + glutaric acid + im*ide*] **:** an analeptic drug used esp. to counteract the effect of barbiturates

ben·ning·ton \ˈbeniŋ(k)tən\ *or* **bennington ware** *also* **bennington pottery** *n* -s *usu cap B* **:** ceramic ware including earthenware, stoneware, and Parian ware produced at Bennington, Vt.; *esp* **:** earthenware with brown or mottled glaze

Bering time *n* [*Bering* (*sea*)] **:** the time of the 11th time zone west of Greenwich that includes western Alaska and the Aleutian islands

best–efforts \ˈ=ˈ=\ *adj*, *of security underwriting* **:** not involving a firm commitment on the part of an underwriter to take up any unsold shares or bonds of an issue being underwritten

beta–adrenergic \ˈ==ˌ==ˈ==\ *adj* **:** of, relating to, or being a beta-receptor ⟨*beta-adrenergic* blocking action⟩

beta decay *n* **1 :** a radioactive transformation of an atomic nucleus in which the atomic number is increased or decreased by 1 by the simultaneous emission of a beta particle and a neutrino or antineutrino without change in the mass number **2 :** the decay of an unstable elementary particle in which an electron or positron is emitted

beta–oxidation \ˈ==ˌ==ˈ==\ *n* [²*beta* + *oxidation*] **:** stepwise catabolism of fatty acids in which two-carbon fragments are successively removed from the carboxyl end of the chain

beta particle* *n* **:** a high-speed electron or positron

beta–receptor \ˈ===ˌ==\ *n* **:** a receptor that responds strongly to or is activated by epinephrine and isoproterenol but is relatively unresponsive to levarterenol and that is associated with positive cardiac chronotropic and inotropic effects, vasodilation, and inhibition of smooth muscle in the bronchi, myometrium, and intestine — compare ALPHA-RECEPTOR *herein*

bi·a·fran \bēˈafrən, bī-, -äf-, -āf-\ *n* -s *cap* [*Biafra*, name assumed by seceding region of Nigeria (1967–1970) + E *-an*] **:** a native or inhabitant of the onetime secessionist Republic of Biafra — **biafran** *adj*, *usu cap*

bi·aly \bēˈälē\ *n* -s [Yiddish, short for *bialystoker*, fr. *bialystoker* of Bialystok, fr. *Bialystok*, city in northeast Poland] **:** a flat breakfast roll that has a depressed center and is usu. covered with onion flakes

bias–belted tire *n* **:** BELTED-BIAS TIRE *herein*

bi·ath·lon \bīˈathlən, -ˌlän\ *n* -s [ISV ¹*bi-* + *-athlon* (as in *pentathlon*)] **:** a composite athletic contest consisting of cross-country skiing and rifle sharpshooting

bi·dialectal \ˈbī +\ *adj* [*bi-* + *dialectal*] **:** using two dialects of the same language

bi·dialectalism \" +\ *n* **:** the constant oral use of two dialects of the same language

bi·don·ville \ˌbēˌdōⁿˈvē(ə)l\ *n* [F, fr. *bidon* tin can (fr. MF, canteen, fr. OF, prob. fr. —assumed— ON *bidha* milk jug — whence Icel *bidha*) + *ville* city, fr. OF, village — more at FISCAL, VILLAGE] **:** a settlement of jerry-built dwellings on the outskirts of a city (as in France)

big bang theory *n* **:** a theory in astronomy: the universe originated billions of years ago from the explosion of a single mass of material so that the pieces are still flying apart — compare STEADY STATE THEORY *herein*

big beat *n*, *often cap both Bs* **:** ROCK 'N' ROLL

big·it \ˈbijət\ *n* -s [*binary digit*] **:** BINARY DIGIT

bi–level \ˈbī +\ *n* **:** a two-story house with the first floor beginning below ground level and divided into two areas by a ground-level entry situated between the stories of the adjoining areas

binary* *adj* **1 :** involving a choice between or condition of two alternatives only (as on-off, yes-no) **2 :** involving binary notation

binary notation *n* **:** expression of a number with a base of 2 using only the digits 0 and 1 with each digital place representing a power of 2 instead of a power of 10 as in decimal notation

bio- \ˈbīō\ *comb form* [*biological*] **:** being such biologically ⟨the *bio*mother gave up her baby for adoption⟩

bio·activity \ˈbīō +\ *n* [²*bi-* + *activity*] **:** the effect (as of an insecticide) on a living organism

bio·astronautics \" +\ *n pl but sing or pl in constr* [²*bi-* + *astronautics*] **:** the medical and biological aspect of astronautics — **bio·astro·nautical** \" +\ *adj*

bio·au·to·gra·phy \ˌbīōōˈtägrəfē\ *n* [²*bi-* + *autograph* + *-y*] **:** the identification or comparison of organic compounds separated by chromatography by means of their effect on living organisms and esp. microorganisms — **bio·au·to·graph** \-ˈōd·əˌgraf\ *n* — **bio·au·to·graph·ic** \ˈbīōˌȯd·əˈgrafik\ *adj*

bi·o·ci·dal \ˈbīəˈsīdᵊl\ *adj* [²*bi-* + *-cidal*] **:** destructive to life

bio·clean \ˈbīō +ˌ-\ *adj* [²*bi-* + *clean*] **:** free or almost free of harmful or potentially harmful organisms (as bacteria)

bio·de·grad·able \ˌbīōdəˈgrādəbəl, -ōdē-\ *adj* [²*bi-* + *degradable* (herein)] **:** capable of being broken down esp. into innocuous products by the action of living beings (as microorganisms) — **bio·de·grad·abil·i·ty** \ˈ===ˌ==ˈbiləd·ē\ *n* -ES — **bio·degradation** \ˈbīō + \ *n* — **bio·degrade** \" +\ *vb*

bio·elec·tro·gen·e·sis \ˈbīōəˌlektrəˈjenəsəs, -ōēˌl-\ *n* [NL, fr. ²*bi-* + *electr-* + *genesis*] **:** the production of electricity by living organisms

bio·electronics \ˈbīō +\ *n pl but sing in constr* [²*bi-* + *electronics*] **1 :** a branch of the life sciences that deals with electronic control of physiological function esp. as applied in medicine to compensate for defects of the nervous system **2 :** a branch of science that deals with the role of electron transfer in biological processes

bioengineering* *n* **:** the application of engineering principles and technology to the solution of biological and medical problems — **bioengineer** *n*

bio·environmental \ˈbīō +\ *adj* [²*bi-* + *environmental*] **:** concerned with the environment and esp. with deleterious factors in the environment of living beings

bio·geo·ce·nose \ˌbīōˌjēōsəˈnōz, -nōs\ *n* [Russ *biogeotsenoz*, fr. NL *bi-* ²*bi-* + *ge-* + *-coenosis* (as in *biocoenosis*)] **:** BIOGEOCOENOSIS *herein*

bio·geo·coe·no·sis *or* **bio·geo·ce·no·sis** \-ˌjēsəˈnōsəs\ *n*, *pl* **biogeocoeno·ses** *or* **biogeoceno·ses** \-ōˌsēz\ [NL, fr. ²*bi-* + *ge-* + *-coenosis* (as in *biocoenosis*)] **:** ECOSYSTEM — **bio·geo·coe·not·ic** \-nädˈik\ *adj*

bio·hazard \ˈbīō +\ *n* [²*bi-* + *hazard*] **:** biological material that constitutes a hazard to man or his environment — used esp. of infective material

bio·instrumentation \" +\ *n* [²*bi-* + *instrumentation*] **:** the development and use of instruments for recording and transmitting physiological data (as from astronauts in flight)

biological clock *n* **:** an inherent timing mechanism responsible for various automatic rhythmic responses of living beings

bio·material \ˈbīō +\ *n* [²*bi-* + *material*] **:** material used for or suitable for use in prostheses that come in direct contact with living tissues

bio·medical \" +\ *adj* [²*bi-* + *medical*] **1 :** of or relating to biomedicine ⟨~ studies⟩ **2 :** of, relating to, or involving biological, medical, and physical science ⟨~ engineering⟩

bio·medicine \" +\ *n* [²*bi-* + *medicine*] **:** a branch of medical science concerned esp. with the survival and function of human beings in abnormal environments

bi·on·ics \bīˈäniks\ *n pl but sing or pl in constr* [²*bi-* + *-onics* (as in *electronics*)] **:** a branch of science concerned with the application of data about the functioning of biological systems to the solution of engineering problems — **bi·on·ic** \-nik\ *adj*

bio·organic \ˈbīō +\ *adj* [²*bi-* + *organic*] **:** of or relating to the organic chemistry of biologically significant substances

bio·polymer \" +\ *n* [²*bi-* + *polymer*] **:** a polymer (as a protein) formed in a biological system

bio·rhythm \" +\ *n* [²*bi-* + *rhythm*] **:** an inherent rhythm that appears to control or initiate various biological processes — **bio·rhythmic** \" +\ *adj*

bio·satellite \" +\ *n* [²*bi-* + *satellite*] **:** an artificial satellite for experimental study of the effects of space on living beings

bio·science \ˈbīō +\ *n* [²*bi-* + *science*] **:** BIOLOGY 1a — **bio·scientific** \" +\ *adj* — **bio·scientist** \" +\ *n*

bio·sensor \" +\ *n* [²*bi-* + *sensor*] **:** a device sensitive to a physical stimulus (as heat or a particular motion) and transmitting information about a life process (as of an astronaut)

bio·speleology \" +\ *n* [²*bi-* + *speleology*] **:** the biological study of cave-dwelling organisms — **bio·speleologist** *n*

bio·telemetry \" +\ *n* [²*bi-* + *telemetry*] **:** the remote detection and measurement of a condition, activity, or function relating to a man or animal — **bio·telemetric** \" +\ *adj*

bio·transformation \" +\ *n* [²*bi-* + *transformation*] **:** the transformation of a chemical compound into another compound in a living system

bio·tron \ˈbīəˌträn\ *n* -s [²*bi-* + *-tron* (as in *cyclotron*)] **:** a climate control chamber used to study the effect of specific environmental factors on living organisms

bi·quinary \(ˈ)bī +\ *adj* [¹*bi-* + *quinary*] **:** of, being, or relating to a mixed-base system of numbers in which one digit of each pair is to the base 5 and the other digit to the base 2

birch·er \ˈbərchər, ˈbōchə(r, ˈbəichə(r\ *n* -s *usu cap* [the John *Birch* Society, conservative political organization + E *-er*] **:** a member or adherent of the John Birch Society — **birch·ism** \-ˌchizəm\ *n* -s *usu cap* — **birch·ist** \-ˌchəst\ *or* **birch·ite** \-ˌchīt, *usu* -īd· + V\ *n* -s *usu cap*

bird* *n* **1 :** AIRPLANE **2 :** ROCKET **3 :** SATELLITE **4 :** SPACECRAFT

birdy·back *also* **bird·ie·back** \ˈbərdēˌbak, -ə̄-, -əi-, -di-\ *n* [¹*bird* + *-yback* (as in *piggyback*)] **:** the movement of loaded truck trailers by airplane

bi·stable \(ˈ)bī +\ *adj* [¹*bi-* + *stable*, adj.] **:** having two stable states ⟨a ~ electrical element⟩ — **bi·stability** \ˈbī +\ *n*

bit* *n* **1 a :** a characteristic pattern of behavior ⟨book burning, unless it's an embassy library, is strictly a Fascist ~ —Gene Williams⟩ **b :** a standardized procedure ⟨the familiar "testing: 1 . . . 2 . . . 3 . . . 4 . . ." ~ to check sound level and room acoustics —David Curl⟩ **2 a :** a particular appearance or style ⟨sick of the bouffant ~ —H.B.Jacobs⟩ **b :** the aggregate of items, situations, or activities appropriate to a given style, genre, or role

bit* *n* **:** the physical representation (as in a computer tape or memory) of a bit by an electrical pulse, a magnetized spot, or a hole whose presence or absence indicates data

bi·zen ware \bēˈzen-\ *n*, *usu cap B* [part trans. of Jap *bizen-yaki*, fr. *Bizen*, former province in Japan, where it was made + Jap *yaki* pottery] **:** a Japanese ceramic ware produced since the 14th century that is typically a dark bronzy stoneware often with smears of natural ash glaze

black belt \ˈ=ˈ=\ *n* [so called fr. the color of the belt of the uniform worn by the holder of the rating] **1 :** a rating of expert in various arts of self-defense (as judo and karate) **2 :** one who holds a black belt — **black belt** *adj*

black box *n* **1 :** a usu. complicated electronic device (as a radar set) that can be inserted in or removed as a unit from a particular place in an assembly (as a spacecraft) **2 :** a usu. electronic device (as a control for a computer) which operates on an input to produce an output but whose internal mechanism is hidden from or mysterious to the user

black comedy *n* **:** comedy that employs black humor

black humor *n* **:** humor marked by the use of usu. morbid, ironic, grotesquely comic episodes that ridicule human folly — **black humorist** *n*

blacklight trap \ˈ=ˈ=ˌ=\ *n* **:** a trap for insects that uses a form of black light perceptible to particular insects as an attractant

black lung *n* **:** a disease of the lungs caused by habitual inhalation (as by miners) of coal dust **:** ANTHRACOSILICOSIS

black muslim *n*, *usu cap B&M* [so called fr. the adoption by members of the group of Muslim religious practices] **:** a member of a black group that professes Islamic religious belief and advocates a strictly separate black community

black nationalist *n*, *often cap B&N* **:** one of a group of militant blacks who advocate separatism from the whites and the formation of self-governing black communities — **black nationalism** *n*, *often cap B&N*

blackness* *n* **1 :** the aggregate of qualities characteristic of the Negro race **2 :** NEGRITUDE

black panther *n*, *usu cap B&P* **:** a member of an organization of militant American Negroes

black power *n* **:** the mobilization of the political and economic power of American Negroes esp. to further racial equality

black studies *n pl* **:** studies (as history and literature) relating to American Negro culture

blast* *n* **1 :** an enjoyably exciting occasion or event; *esp* **:** PARTY **2 :** HOME RUN

blast *n* [*-blast*] **:** an immature or imperfectly developed cell — **blastic** *also* **blast** *adj*

bleep \ˈblēp\ *n* -s [imit.] **:** a short high-pitched sound (as from electronic equipment)

blip* *vt* **:** to remove (recorded sound) from a videotape so that in the received television program there is an interruption in the sound ⟨swearwords *blipped* by a censor⟩

blitz* *n* **:** a defensive rush on a passer in football

blitz* *vb* ~*ed*; ~*ing*; ~*es* *vt* **1 :** to rush (a passer) in football **2 :** to cause (a linebacker) to blitz ~ *vi* **:** to make a rush on a passer in football — **blitz·er** *n* -s

block·bust·ing \ˈbläkˌbəstiŋ\ *n* -s [¹*block* (space in a city) + *-busting*, gerund of ²*bust*] **:** profiteering by inducing white property owners to sell hastily and often at a loss by appeals to fears of depressed values because of threatened minority encroachment and then reselling at inflated prices — **block·bust·er** *n*
blow* *vt* **:** SMOKE ⟨a few had started ~*ing* grass in their early teens —Daniel Greene⟩ — **blow one's cool :** to lose one's composure — **blow one's mind 1 :** to affect one with intense emotional excitement **2 :** to take one by surprise **:** SHOCK **3 :** to undergo a psychedelic experience
bluegrass \ˈ≈,≈\ *n* [fr. *Bluegrass State*, nickname of Kentucky, an important source of hillbilly music] **:** country music played at a rapid tempo on unamplified stringed instruments (as banjos and fiddles)
blue stellar object *n* **:** any of various blue celestial bodies that do not emit appreciable radio waves
board* *n* **boards** *pl* **:** the low wooden wall enclosing a hockey rink
boa·tel \bōˈtel\ *n* -s [blend of *boat* and *hotel*] **:** a waterside hotel equipped with docks to accommodate persons traveling by boat
bocage* *n* **:** a supporting and ornamental background (as of shrubbery and flowers) for a ceramic figure
body shirt *n* **:** a close-fitting high-collared shirt or blouse with curved front and back seams and deep cuffs
body stocking *n* **:** a sheer close-fitting one-piece garment for the torso that may have sleeves and legs
bodysurf \ˈ≈≈,≈\ *vi* [¹*body* + ²*surf*] **:** to ride on a wave without a surfboard by planing on the chest and stomach — **body·surf·er** \ˈ≈≈,≈≈\ *n*
bof·fo \ˈbäf(ˌ)ō\ *adj* [*boffo*, *n.*, short for *boffola*] **:** extraordinarily successful **:** SENSATIONAL
boilerplate \ˈ≈≈,≈\ *n* [*boiler plate*] **:** a model of a spacecraft whose structure is heavier than the flight version
bok·mål \ˈbu̇kˌmōl, ˈbōk-\ *n* -s [Norw, fr. *bok* book (fr. ON *bōk*) + *mål* language, fr. ON *māl* — more at BOOK, MAIL] **:** RIKSMÅL
bomb* *n* **1 :** an inept or unfavorably received performance **:** FLOP **2 :** a long pass in football
bomb* *vb* ~ *vi* **:** to fall flat; *esp* **:** to put on an unsuccessful or unfavorably received performance — often used with *out*
bomb·let \ˈbämlət\ *n* -s [¹*bomb* + *-let*] **:** a small bomb
bonded* *adj* **:** composed of two or more layers of the same or different fabrics held together by an adhesive **:** ⟨~ jersey⟩
bon·kers \ˈbäŋkə(r)z\ *adj* [origin unknown] *chiefly Brit* **:** CRAZY, MAD ⟨if I don't work, I go ~ —Zoe Caldwell⟩
boo \ˈbü\ *n* [origin unknown] **:** MARIJUANA
bootstrap* *n* **:** a computer routine consisting of a few initial instructions by means of which the rest of the instructions are brought into the computer
borough* *n* **:** a civil division of the state of Alaska corresponding to a county in other states
bos·sa no·va \ˌbäsəˈnōvə, ˌbȯs-\ *n* [Pg, lit., new trend, fr. *bossa* hump, bump, trend (fr. F *bosse* hump, fr. OF *boce*) + *nova*, fem. of *novo* new, fr. L *novus* — more at BOSS, NEW] **1 :** a Brazilian dance characterized by the sprightly step pattern of the samba and a subtle bounce **2 :** music resembling the samba with jazz interpolations
boston arm *n*, *usu cap B* [so called fr. its development by four institutions in Boston, Mass.] **:** an artificial arm that is activated by an amputee's nerve impulses which are electrically amplified and transmitted to a motor operating the arm
bottle-feed \ˈ≈≈,≈\ *vt* **:** to feed (as an infant) with a bottle
bottom out *vi*, *of a security market* **:** to decline to a point where demand begins to exceed supply and a rise in prices is imminent
bou·zou·ki *also* **bou·sou·ki** \bu̇ˈzükē\ *n*, *pl* **bouzoukia** *also* **bouzoukis** [NGk *mpouzouki*] **:** a long-necked stringed musical instrument of Greek origin
brace* *n* **brac·es** *pl* **:** wire fastened to teeth to correct irregularities in their position
bra·dy·ki·nin \ˌbrādəˈkīnən\ *n* [*brady-* + *kinin* (herein)] **:** a kinin that is formed in injured tissue, acts in vasodilation of small arterioles, is held to play a part in inflammatory processes, and is composed of a chain of nine amino acids
brain* *n* **:** an automatic device (as a computer) that performs one or more of the functions of the human brain for control, guidance, or computation ⟨the ~ of a missile⟩
brain drain *n* **:** the migration of professional people (as scientists, professors, or physicians) from one country to another usu. for higher salaries or better living conditions
breadboard \ˈ≈,≈\ *vt* **:** to make an experimental arrangement of (an electronic circuit) on a flat surface
brecht·ian \ˈbrektēən, -k-\ *adj*, *usu cap* [Bertolt *Brecht* †1956 Ger. dramatist + E *-ian*] **:** of, relating to, or suggestive of Bertolt Brecht or his writings
bride's basket \ˈ≈,≈\ *n* **:** an ornate, handled, usu. colored, and often cased glass bowl fitted with a silver-plated base
broadband \ˈ≈,≈\ *adj* **:** of, having, or involving operation with uniform efficiency over a wide band of frequencies
bro·me·la·in \ˌbrōməˈlāən, brōˈmeləən\ *n* -s [alter. (influenced by *papain*) of *bromelin*] **:** BROMELIN
brown bag·ging \ˈbrau̇nˈbagiŋ, -aag-, -aig-, -geŋ\ *n* [*brown bag* + *-ing*; fr. the brown paper bag used] **1 :** the practice of carrying a bottle of liquor into a restaurant or club where setups are available but where the sale of liquor by the drink is illegal **2 :** the practice of carrying (as to work) one's lunch usu. in a brown paper bag — **brown bag·ger** \-gə(r\ *n*
brown recluse spider *n* [*recluse* prob. fr. NL *reclusa*, specific epithet, fr. LL, fem. of *reclusus* shut up; fr. its living chiefly in dark corners — more at RECLUSE] **:** a venomous spider (*Loxosceles reclusa*) introduced into the southern U. S. that has a violin-shaped mark on the cephalothorax and produces a dangerous neurotoxin
brownware \ˈ≈,≈\ *n* [¹*brown* + *ware*] **1 :** a brown-glazed earthenware formerly widely used for utility pottery **2 :** typically primitive pottery that fires to a brown or reddish color
bru·tal·ism \ˈbrüd-ᵊlˌizəm, -üt³l-\ *n* -s [*brutal* + *-ism*] **:** a style in art and esp. architecture using exaggeration and distortion to create its effect (as of massiveness or power) — **brutalist** *adj or n*
bubble* *n* **:** something (as a plastic structure) that is more or less semicylindrical or dome-shaped
bubble car *n* **:** an automobile having a transparent bubble top
bum·mer \ˈbəmə(r\ *n* -s [⁸*bum* + ²*-er*] **:** an unpleasant drug-induced hallucinatory experience; *broadly* **:** an unpleasant event or situation
bunny* *n* [so called fr. the rabbit's ears and tail originally forming part of their costume] **:** a young, attractive, scantily attired waitress ⟨nightclub *bunnies*⟩
bun·ra·ku \bünˈräˌ(ˌ)kü, ˈbün(ˌ)r-\ *n*, *usu cap* [Jap] **:** Japanese puppet theater featuring large costumed wooden puppets, onstage puppeteers, and a chanter who speaks all the lines
burnout* *n* **1 a :** the process or an instance of burning out **b :** the cessation of operation of a jet engine as the result of exhaustion of or shutting off of fuel **2 :** the point in the trajectory of a rocket engine at which burnout occurs
bush hat *n* [¹*bush* (backcountry)] **:** a broad-brimmed hat worn esp. as part of an Australian military uniform
bust* *vt* **1 :** ARREST **2 :** RAID
bust* *n* **:** a police raid
butch* *n* [*butch*, adj. (herein)] **:** a butch lesbian
butch *adj* [prob. fr. *Butch*, a nickname for boys, esp. tough boys] **1** *of a lesbian* **:** playing the male role in a homosexual relationship **2** *of a male homosexual* **:** very masculine in appearance
butter pat* *n* **:** BUTTER CHIP
buy-in \ˈbīˌin\ *n* [*buy in*, v.] **:** the act or process of buying in to cover a short on a stock or commodity exchange
BX \(ˈ)bēˈeks\ *abbr or n* -s base exchange *herein*
byte \ˈbīt\ *n* -s [perh. alter. of ²*bite* (morsel)] **:** a group of adjacent binary digits often shorter than a word that a computer processes as a unit ⟨an 8-bit ~⟩
byzantine* *adj*, *usu cap* **:** of, relating to, or characterized by a devious manner of operation ⟨the government, with its own *Byzantine* sources of intelligence —Wesley Pruden⟩
BZ \(ˈ)bēˈzē\ *n* [*BZ*, army code name] **:** a gas that when breathed produces incapacitating physical and mental effects
cabana set *n* **:** a two-piece beachwear ensemble for men consisting of loosely fitting shorts and a short-sleeved jacket
cable TV *n* **:** COMMUNITY ANTENNA TELEVISION *herein*
caer·phil·ly \kärˈfilē\ *n*, *usu cap* [fr. *Caerphilly*, urban district in Wales] **:** a mild white whole-milk Welsh cheese
cae·sar salad \ˈsēzə(r)-\ *n*, *usu cap C* [fr. *Caesar's*, restaurant in Tijuana, Mexico, where it originated] **:** a tossed salad made typically with romaine, garlic, anchovies, and croutons and served with a dressing of olive oil, coddled egg, lemon juice, and grated cheese
cage* *n* **:** a sheer one-piece dress that has no waistline, is often gathered at the neck, and is worn over a close-fitting underdress or slip
cal·cia \ˈkalsēə, -lshə\ *n* -s [NL, fr. *calcium* + *-a*] **:** CALCIUM OXIDE
cal·ci·phy·lax·is \ˌkalsəfəˈlaksəs\ *n*, *pl* **calciphylax·es** \-akˌsēz\ [NL, fr. *calc-* + *-phylaxis* (as in *prophylaxis*)] **:** an adaptive response that follows systemic sensitization by a calcifying factor (as a D-vitamin) and a challenge (as with a metallic salt) and involves local inflammation and sclerosis with calcium deposition — **cal·ci·phy·lac·tic** \ˌ≈≈≈ˈlaktik\ *adj* — **cal·ci·phy·lac·ti·cal·ly** \-tək(ə)lē\ *adv*
cal·ci·to·nin \ˌkalsəˈtōnən\ *n* -s [*calci-* + ¹*tonic* + *-in*] **:** THYROCALCITONIN *herein*
callback** *n* **:** a recall by a manufacturer of a recently sold product (as an automobile) for correction of a defect
cal·li·graph \ˈkaləˌgraf\ *vt* -ED/-ING/-S [back-formation fr. *calligraphy*] **:** to produce or reproduce in a calligraphic style
cameo* *n* **:** a small theatrical role performed by a well-known actor or actress and often limited to a single scene
¹**camp** \ˈkamp, -aa(ə)-, -ai-\ *n* [origin unknown] **1 :** exaggerated effeminate mannerisms (as of speech or gesture) exhibited esp. by homosexuals **2 :** one that is so outrageously artificial, affected, inappropriate, or out-of-date as to be considered amusing — **camp·i·ness** *n* -ES — **campy** *adj* -ER/-EST
²**camp** *adj* **:** HOMOSEXUAL
³**camp** *vi* **:** to engage in camp **:** exhibit the qualities of camp ⟨he . . . was ~*ing*, hands on hips, with a quick eye to notice every man who passed by —Robert McAlmon⟩
camper* *n* **:** a portable dwelling (as a structure to fit in a pickup truck, a collapsible structure folded into a small trailer, or a specially equipped automotive vehicle) for use during casual travel and camping
camphor glass *n* **:** glass with a cloudy white appearance resembling gum camphor in lump form
C and W *abbr* country and western
can·dy strip·er \-ˌstrīpə(r\ *n* [*candy stripe* + *-er*; fr. the red and white stripes of her uniform] **:** a teen-age volunteer nurse's aide
can of worms : PANDORA'S BOX
canton china *n*, *usu cap 1st C* **:** porcelain Canton ware esp. when blue-and-white
canton enamel *n*, *usu cap C* [fr. *Canton*, China] **:** Chinese enamelware of Limoges type
capital gains distribution *n* **:** the part of the payout of an investment companyto its shareholders that consists of realized profits from the sale of securities and technically is not income
capital structure *n* **:** the makeup of the capitalization of a business in terms of the amounts and kinds of equity and debt securities **:** the equity and debt securities of a business together with its surplus and reserves
capri pants *n pl*, *often cap C* [fr. *Capri*, island in the Bay of Naples, Italy] **:** close-fitting pants that have tapered legs with a slit on the outside of the leg bottom, extend almost to the ankle, and are used for informal wear esp. by women
cap·sid \ˈkapsəd\ *n* -s [L *capsa* case + E *-id* — more at CASE] **:** the outer protein shell of a virus particle
cap·so·mere \ˈkapsəˌmi(ə)r\ *n* -s [*capsid* (herein) + *-o-* + *-mere*] **:** one of the discrete elements making up a capsid
car·a·van·eer \ˌkarə(ˌ)vaˈni(ə)r, -ˌvə-, -niə(r\ *n* -s [*caravan* + *-eer*] **:** CARAVANNER *herein*
car·a·van·ner \ˈkarəˌvanə(r, -vaan- *also* ˈker- *esp Brit* ˌ≈≈ˈ≈≈\ *n* -s [*caravan* + *-er*] **1** *or* **car·a·van·er :** one that travels in a caravan — called also *caravaneer* **2** *Brit* **:** one that goes camping with a trailer
car·ba·ryl \ˈkärbəˌril, -ˌrəl\ *n* [*carbamate* + *aryl*] **:** a carbamate insecticide effective against numerous crop, forage, and forest pests
carbon dating *n* **:** determination of age (as of an archaeological find) by means of the content of carbon 14
carbon spot* *n* **:** a small black spot on a coin
car coat *n* **:** a three-quarter-length overcoat
card-car·ry·ing \ˈ≈,≈≈≈\ *adj* [so called fr. the assumption that such a member carries a membership card] **1 :** being a full-fledged member of a Communist party **2 :** being strongly identified with a group (as of people in a common profession)
car·di·nal·i·ty \ˌkärdᵊnˈaləd-ē\ *n* -ES [²*cardinal* + *-ity*] **:** the number of elements in a given mathematical set
cardinal number* *n* **:** the property that a mathematical set has in common with all sets that can be put into one-to-one correspondence with it
cardinal's hat *n* **:** GALERO *herein*
car·dio·accelerator *or* **car·dio·acceleratory** \ˌkärdē(ˌ)ō +\ *adj* [*cardi-* + *accelerator* *or* *acceleratory*] **:** speeding up the action of the heart — **car·dio·acceleration** \"+\ *n*
car·dio·meg·a·ly \ˌkärdēōˈmegəlē\ *n* -ES [*cardi-* + *-megaly*] **:** enlargement of the heart
car·dio·myopathy \ˌkärdēō+\ *n* [*cardi-* + *myopathy*] **:** a typically chronic disorder of heart muscle that may involve hypertrophy and obstructive damage to the heart
carhop *vi* **:** to work as a carhop
ca·ri·so·pro·dol \kəˌrīsəˈprōˌdȯl, -īzə-, -dōl\ *n* -s [*car-* (prob. fr. *carbamate*) + *isopropyl* + *diol*] **:** a drug related to meprobamate that is used to relax muscle and relieve pain
carnival glass *n*, *often cap C* [so called fr. its frequent use for prizes at carnival booths] **:** pressed glass with an iridescent finish mass-produced in a variety of colors (as frosty white or deep purple) in the U. S. in the early 20th century
carryon \ˈ≈≈,≈\ *n* -s [¹*carry* + ²*on*] **:** a piece of luggage suitable for being carried aboard an airplane by a passenger
casebook* *n* **:** a compilation of primary and secondary documents relating to a central topic together with scholarly comments, exercises, and study aids that is often designed to serve as a source book for short papers (as in a course in composition) or as a point of departure for a research paper
ca·sette \kəˈset, ka-\ *n* -s [by alter.] **:** CASSETTE 3
cash flow *n* **:** a measure of corporate worth that consists of net income after taxes plus bookkeeping deductions involving no cash outlay and that is usu. figured in dollars per share of common stock outstanding
cassette* *n* **:** a usu. plastic case containing two small reels for insertion into a tape recorder with the tape on one reel passing to the other without having to be threaded
cas·tro·ism \ˈkas(ˌ)trōˌizəm *sometimes* -äs-\ *n* -s *usu cap* [Fidel *Castro* *b*1927 Cuban political leader] **:** the political, economic, and social principles and policies of Fidel Castro — **cas·tro·ite** \-ōˌīt\ *n* -s *usu cap*
C A T \ˌsē(ˌ)āˈtē\ *abbr* clear-air turbulence *herein*
cat·e·chol·amine \ˌkad-əˈchōləˌmēn, -əˈsh-, -əˈk-, -ōl-, -ˌmən\ *n* [*catechol* + *amine*] **:** any of various substances that are related to catechols but have one or more amine side groups and include physiologically active compounds (as adrenaline)
CATV \ˌsēˌāˌtēˈvē\ *abbr* community antenna television *herein*
CBW *abbr* chemical and biological warfare
CCTV *abbr*, *often not cap* closed-circuit television
ce·di \ˈsādē\ *n* -s [Akan *sedie* cowrie] **1 :** the basic monetary unit of Ghana — see MONEY table *in the Dict* **2 :** a note representing one cedi
center-of-mass system* *n* **:** a frame of reference in which the center of mass is at rest
cen·ti·second \ˈsentə + ˌ\ *n* [ISV *centi-* + *second*] **:** one hundredth of a second
central tendon *n* **:** a 3-lobed aponeurosis located near the central portion of the diaphragm caudal to the pericardium and composed of intersecting planes of collagenous fibers
cereal leaf beetle *n* **:** a small reddish brown black-headed Old World chrysomelid beetle (*Oulema melanopa*) that feeds on cereal grasses and is a serious threat to U. S. grain crops
ce·ru·lo·plas·min \səˌrüləˈplazmən, ˌser(y)əl-\ *n* [ISV *cerulo-* (fr. L *caeruleus* dark blue) + *plasma* + *-in*; prob. orig. formed in Sw] **:** a plasma oxidase that is an alpha globulin active in copper storage and transport
cesium clock *n* **:** an atomic clock regulated by the natural vibration frequency of a beam of cesium atoms
cesium 137 \-ˌwənˌthərd-ēˈsevən, -vᵊm, -bᵊm\ *n* **:** a radioactive isotope of cesium that has the mass number 137 and a half-life of about 12 months and is present in fallout
chamberlain* *n* **:** an often honorary papal attendant; *specif* **:** a priest having a rank of honor below domestic prelate
chan·dler's wobble \ˌchandlə(r)z-, -aan-, -än-, *rap.* -nl-\ *n*, *usu cap C* [after Seth Carlo *Chandler* †1913 Am. astronomer] **:** an elliptical oscillation of the earth's axis of rotation with a period of 14 months whose cause has not been determined
channel* *n* **:** a path along which information passes or an area (as of magnetic tape) on which it is stored
character* *n* **:** a symbol (as a letter or number) that represents information; *also* **:** a representation (as by a series of ones and zeros) of such a character that may be accepted by a computer
checkout** *n* **1 :** the process of examining and testing something as to readiness for intended use ⟨the ~ of a spacecraft⟩ **2 :** the process of familiarizing oneself with the operation of a mechanical thing (as an airplane)
che·la·tor *also* **che·lat·er** \ˈkēˌlād-ə(r)\ *n* -s **:** a binding agent that suppresses chemical activity by forming chelates
chemo·nuclear \ˌkemō, -ēmō +\ *adj* [*chem-* + *nuclear*] **:** being or relating to a chemical reaction induced by nuclear radiation or fission fragments
chemo·sphere \ˈkeməˌsfi(ə)r, -ēm-\ *n* [*chem-* + *sphere*] **:** a stratum of the upper atmosphere in which photochemical reactions are prevalent and which begins about 20 miles up
chemo·sterilant \ˌkemō, -ēm- +\ *n* [*chem-* + *sterilant*] **:** a substance that produces irreversible sterility (as of an insect) without evidently altering mating habits or life expectancy — see APHOLATE *herein* — **chemo·sterilization** \"+\ *n* — **chemo·sterilize** \"+\ *vb*
chemo·surgery \"+\ [*chem-* + *surgery*] **:** chemical removal of unwanted tissue — **chemo·surgical** \"+\ *adj*
chemo·taxonomy \" +\ *n* [*chem-* + *taxonomy*] **:** the classification of plants and animals based on similarities and differences in biochemical composition — **chemo·taxonomic** \" +\ *adj* — **chemo·taxonomically** \" +\ *adv*
cheong·sam \ˈcheu̇ŋˈsäm\ *n* -s [Chin (Cant) *cheung sam*, lit., long gown] **:** a dress with a slit skirt and a mandarin collar worn esp. by Oriental women
chiao \ˈjau̇\ *n*, *pl* **chiao** [Chin (Pek) *chiao*³] **1 :** a monetary unit of China equal to ¹⁄₁₀ yuan — see MONEY table *in the Dict* **2 :** a coin or note representing one chiao
chi·ca·no \chiˈkän(ˌ)ō, shi-\ *n* -s *usu cap* [modif. of Sp *mejicano* Mexican, fr. *Méjico* Mexico] **:** an American of Mexican descent — **chicano** *adj*, *usu cap*
chien ware \ˈchēˈen,-\ *also* **chien yao** \-nˈyau̇\ *n*, *usu cap C* [Chin (Pek) *ch'ien yao*², fr. *Ch'ien-an*, locality in China where it was first made + Chin (Pek) *yao*² pottery] **:** a dark Chinese stoneware dating from the Sung period, usu. having a black brown-mottled glaze, and usu. used for tea wares
chill factor *n* **:** WINDCHILL *herein*
chil·tern hundreds \ˌchiltə(r)n-\ *n pl*, *cap C&H* [fr. *Chiltern Hundreds*, three hundreds in the Chiltern hills of England appointment to the stewardship of which is a disqualification for membership in Parliament] **:** a nominal appointment granted by the British crown that serves as a legal fiction to enable a member of Parliament to relinquish his seat
chip* *n* **:** INTEGRATED CIRCUIT *herein*
chlor·am·bu·cil \klōrˈambyəˌsil, klȯr-\ *n* -s [*chloro*ethyl + *amin-* + *butyric* + *-cil* (of unknown origin)] **:** a nitrogen mustard derivative used esp. to treat leukemias and Hodgkin's disease
chlor·mer·o·drin \-rˈmerədrən\ *n* -s [*chlor-* + *mercury* + *-o-* + *-hydrin*] **:** a mercurial diuretic compound
chlor·pro·pa·mide \-rˈprōpəˌmīd, -ˌməd\ *n* [*chlor-* + *propane* + *amide*] **:** a sulfonyl urea compound used to reduce blood sugar in the treatment of mild diabetes
cho·le·sta·sis \ˌkōləˈstāsəs, ˌkäl-\ *n*, *pl* **cholesta·ses** \-āˌsēz\ [NL, fr. *chol-* + *-stasis*] **:** a checking or failure of bile flow — **cho·le·stat·ic** \ˌkōləˌstad-ik, ˌkäl-\ *adj*
cho·li·no·lyt·ic \ˌkōlənōˈlid-ik, ˌkäl-\ *adj* [ISV acetyl*choline* + *-o-* + *-lytic*] **:** interfering with the action of acetylcholine or cholinergic agents — **cholinolytic** *n*
cho·li·no·mi·met·ic \-məˌmed-ik, -(ˌ)mī-\ *adj* [ISV acetyl*choline* + *-o-* + *mimetic*] **:** resembling acetylcholine or simulating its physiologic action — **cholinomimetic** *n*
chrome* *n* **:** something plated with an alloy of chromium
chug·a·lug \ˈchəgəˌləg\ *vb* **chugalugged; chugalugged; chugalugging; chugalugs** [imit.] *vt* **:** to drink a whole container of in one swallow ~ *vi* **:** to drink a whole container (as of beer) in one swallow
church key *n* **:** a can opener with a triangular pointed head for piercing the tops of cans (as of beer)
churn* *vt* **:** to subject (a client's security account) to excessive numbers of purchases and sales primarily to generate additional commissions
chutz·pah *also* **chutz·pa** *or* **hutz·pah** *or* **hutz·pa** \ˈku̇tspə, ˈhu̇-, -(ˌ)spä\ *n* -s [Yiddish, fr. L Heb *ḥuṣpāh*] **:** supreme self-confidence **:** NERVE, GALL
cinema ve·ri·té \-ˌverəˈtā\ *n* [F *cinéma-vérité* truth cinema] **:** the art or technique of filming a motion picture (as a documentary) so as to convey candid realism
cir·ca·di·an \(ˌ)sərˈkadēən, ˌsərkəˈdīən\ *adj* [L *circa* about + *dies* day + E *-an* — more at CIRCA, DEITY] **:** being, having, or occurring at approximately 24-hour intervals ⟨*circadian* rhythms in insects⟩
cir·cum·planetary \ˈsərkəm +\ *adj* [*circum-* + *planet* + *-ary*] **:** surrounding and relatively close to a planet ⟨~ space⟩
cir·cum·solar \" +\ *adj* [*circum-* + *solar*] **:** revolving about or surrounding the sun
cir·cum·stellar \" +\ *adj* [*circum-* + *stellar*] **:** surrounding or occurring in the vicinity of a star
cir·cum·terrestrial \" +\ *adj* [*circum-* + *terrestrial*] **:** revolving about or surrounding the earth
cis·lu·nar \(ˈ)sis +\ *adj* [*cis-* + *lunar*] **:** of or relating to the space between the earth and the moon or the moon's orbit
cis·tron \ˈsiˌsträn\ *n* -s [*cis-trans* + ²*-on*] **:** a segment of a DNA molecule that carries the code for a single polypeptide — compare OPERON *herein* — **cis·tron·ic** \siˈstränik\ *adj*
citizen's arrest *n* **:** an arrest made by a citizen who derives his authority from the fact that he is a citizen
citizens band *n* **:** one of the frequency bands that in the U. S. is allocated officially for private radio communications
clad* *adj*, *of a coin* **:** consisting of outer layers of one metal bonded to a core of a different metal
clado·genesis \ˌkladō +\ *n* [NL, fr. Gk *klados* branch + *genesis* — more at GLADIATOR] **:** evolutionary change that is essentially adaptive to different ecological niches — **clado·genetic** \"+\ *adj* — **clado·genetically** \"+\ *adv*
clang·er \ˈklaŋə(r, -aiŋ-\ *n* -s [²*clang* + *-er*] *Brit* **:** a conspicuous blunder; *also* **:** an inappropriate remark — often used in the phrase *drop a clanger*
class action *n* **:** a legal action undertaken by one or more plaintiffs on behalf of themselves and all other persons having an identical interest in the alleged wrong
clathrate *n* -s [*clathrate*, adj.] **:** a clathrate compound
clath·ra·tion \klaˈthrāshən\ *n* -s [*clathrate* + *-ion*] **:** the process of clathrate formation
clean room \ˈ≈,≈\ *n* **:** a room for the manufacture or assembly of objects (as precision parts) that is maintained at a high level of cleanliness by special means
clear-air turbulence *n* **:** sudden severe turbulence occurring in cloudless regions that causes violent jarring or buffeting of aircraft passing through — abbr. *C A T*
cleaver* *n* **:** a rock ridge protruding from a glacier or snowfield
clio* *n*, *usu cap* **:** any of several statuettes awarded annually by a professional organization for notable achievement in radio and television commercials
clone *vt* **:** to grow as a clone or culture into a clone
closed* *adj* **1 :** traced by a moving point that returns to an arbitrary starting point ⟨~ curve⟩; *also* **:** so formed that every plane section is a closed curve ⟨~ surface⟩ **2 :** characterized by mathematical elements that when subjected to an operation produce only elements of the same set ⟨the set of whole numbers is ~ under addition and multiplication⟩
closed loop *n* **:** an automatic control system for an operation or process consisting of a closed transmission path or a group of

such paths linked together that by feedback acts to maintain the output at the desired level

closet queen *n* **:** one who secretly engages in homosexual activities while leading an ostensibly heterosexual life

closing* *n* **:** a meeting between parties to a real-estate deal usu. together with their attorneys and interested parties (as a mortgagor) for the purpose of formally transferring title

closing costs *n pl* **:** expenses (as for appraisal, title search, and title insurance) connected with the purchase of real estate that usu. constitute a charge against the purchaser additional to the cost of the property purchased

closure* *n* **:** the property of being mathematically closed

cloud nine *n* [perh. so called fr. the ninth and highest heaven of Dante's Paradise, whose inhabitants are most blissful because nearest to God] **:** a feeling of extreme well-being or elation — usu. used with *on* ⟨was on *cloud nine* after his victory⟩

clout* *n* **:** PULL, INFLUENCE ⟨had a lot of ~ with the governor⟩

clox·a·cil·lin \ˌkläksəˈsilən\ *n* -S [*chlorophenol* + *isoxazole* + *penicillin*] **:** a synthetic oral penicillin esp. effective against staphylococci

cloze \ˈklōz\ *adj* [by shortening & alter. fr. *closure*] **:** of, relating to, or being a test of reading comprehension that involves having the person being tested supply words which have been systematically deleted from a text

cluster* *n* **:** a group of buildings and esp. houses built close together on a sizable tract in order to preserve open spaces larger than the individual yard for common recreation

cluster college *n* **:** a small residential college constituting a semiautonomous division of a university and usu. specializing in one branch of knowledge (as history and the social sciences)

CN* *abbr* chloroacetophenone

co·an·da effect \kōˈandə-, -än-\ *n, usu cap C* [after Henri *Coanda* b1886 Romanian engineer] **:** the tendency of a jet of fluid emerging from an orifice to follow an adjacent flat or curved surface and to entrain fluid from the surroundings so that a region of lower pressure develops

co·bol \ˈkōˌbȯl\ *n* -S *usu cap C or all cap* [*common business oriented language*] **:** a standardized business language for programming a computer

cock·a·ma·my *or* **cock·a·ma·mie** \ˈkäkəˌmāmē\ *adj* [perh. fr. (assumed) *cockamamy* decalcomania, alter. of *decalcomania*] **:** RIDICULOUS, INCREDIBLE ⟨of all the ~ excuses I ever heard —Leo Rosten⟩

code* *n* **:** GENETIC CODE *herein*

co·don \ˈkōˌdän\ *n* -S [²*code* + ²*-on*] **:** a triplet of nucleotide units that specify a particular amino acid in the genetic code

coenzyme Q *n* [*Q* prob. fr. *quinone*] **:** a quinone that functions as an electron transfer agent between cytochromes in the citric acid cycle — called also *ubiquinone*

coes·ite \ˈkōˌzīt\ *n* -S [Loring *Coes*, Jr., b1915 Am. chemist + E *-ite*] **:** a dense crystalline silica formed from quartz under great heat and pressure and found in meteorite craters

coincident* *or* **coincident indicator** *n* **:** an economic indicator (as level of personal income or of retail sales) that more often than not correlates directly with the state of the economy

co·institutional \ˌkō + \ *adj* [*co-* + *institutional*] **:** of, relating to, or being a high school having separate class or activity areas for boys and girls

cold duck *n* [trans. of G *kalte ente*, a drink made of a mixture of fine wines] **:** a beverage that consists of a blend of sparkling burgundy and champagne

cold weld** *vi* **:** to adhere on contact without application of pressure or heat — used of metals in the vacuum of outer space

collegiality* *n* **:** the participation of bishops in the government of the Roman Catholic Church in collaboration with the pope — **collegial*** *adj* — **col·le·gial·ly** *adv*

color-field *adj* **:** of, relating to, or being abstract painting in which color is emphasized and form and surface are correspondingly de-emphasized ⟨*color-field* abstractionists⟩

color painting *n* **:** color-field painting — **color painter** *n*

combinatorial mathematics *n pl but sing in constr* **:** a study that deals with the arrangement, operation, and selection of mathematical elements within finite sets and configurations

combinatorial topology *n* **:** a study that deals with geometric forms based on their decomposition into combinations of the simplest geometric figures

com·bi·na·to·rics \kəmˌbīnəˈtȯriks, -ōr-\ *n pl but sing in constr* [*combinatorial mathematics*] **:** COMBINATORIAL MATHEMATICS *herein*

comb–out* *n* **:** the combing of hair into a desired hairdo

come·back·er \ˈkəmˌbakə(r\ *n* -S [*come back* + *-er*] **:** a grounder in baseball hit directly to the pitcher

come on* *vi* **:** to behave or perform in a specified manner **:** ACT ⟨*come on* strong⟩

command* *n* **1 :** an electrical or electronic signal that actuates a device (as a control mechanism in a spacecraft or one step in a computer) **2 :** the activation of a device in or the control of a vehicle (as a spacecraft) by means of a command

command module *n* **:** a space vehicle module designed to carry the crew, the chief communication equipment, and the equipment for reentry

commentator* *n* **:** a layman who leads a congregation in prayer at Mass or explains the rituals performed by the priest

common market *n* **:** an economic unit formed to remove trade barriers among members

common trust fund *n* **:** a fund which is managed by a bank or trust company and in which the assets of many small trusts are handled as a single portfolio with individual beneficiaries receiving returns proportionate to their share of the principal

communication theory *or* **communications theory** *n* **:** a theory that deals with the technology of the transmission of information (as in the printed word or a computer) between men or men and machines or machines and machines

community antenna television *n* **:** a system of television reception in which signals from distant stations are picked up by a tall or elevated antenna and sent by cable to the individual receivers of paying subscribers

com·mu·ta·tiv·i·ty \kəˌmyüd·əˈtivəd·ē, ˌkämyətəˈti-\ *n* -ES [*commutative* + *-ity*] **:** the property of being commutative

commute* *vi* **:** to yield the same result regardless of order — used of two mathematical elements undergoing an operation or of two operations on elements

com·mute \kəˈmyüt\ *n* -S [*commute*, v.] **1 :** an act or instance of commuting ⟨his usual morning ~ to work—*Newsweek*⟩ **2 :** the distance covered in commuting ⟨about an hour's ~ from the university —*College Composition & Communication*⟩

com·pact·ible \kəmˈpaktəbəl\ *adj* [²*compact* + *-ible*] **:** capable of being compacted ⟨~ soils⟩

compiler* *n* **:** a computer program that automatically converts instructions written in a higher-level language (as Fortran) into machine language

complementation* *n* **:** the determination of the complement of a given mathematical set

complex conjugate *n* **:** a complex number formed from another complex number by changing the sign of its imaginary part

computational linguistics *n* **:** linguistic research carried out by means of a computer

com·put·er·ese \kəmˌpyüd·əˈrēz, -ütə-, -ēs\ *n* -S [*computer* + *-ese*] **1 :** MACHINE LANGUAGE *herein* **2 :** jargon used by computer technologists

com·put·er·ize \kəmˈpyüd·əˌrīz, -ütə-\ *vt* -ED/-ING/-S [*computer* + *-ize*] **1 :** to carry out or conduct by means of a computer **:** control by means of a computer ⟨*computerized* typesetting⟩ ⟨~ a process⟩ **2 :** to equip with computers ⟨a *computerized* society⟩ — **com·put·er·iz·able** \-īzəbəl\ *adj* — **com·put·er·iza·tion** \-ˌpyüd·ərəˈzāshən, -ˌrīˈz-\ *n* -S

com·sat \ˈkämˌsat\ *n* -S [fr. *Comsat*, a service mark] **:** an artificial satellite of the earth used for reflecting or relaying radio waves (as for intercontinental communication)

concrete* *adj* **:** of or relating to concrete poetry ⟨~ poet⟩

concrete* *n* **1 :** CONCRETE POETRY *herein* **2 :** a concrete poet

concrete poetry *n* **:** poetry in which the poet's intent is conveyed by the graphic patterns of letters, words, or symbols rather than by the conventional arrangement of words

concretism* *n* -S **:** the theory or practice of concrete poetry — **con·cret·ist** \-ēd·əst, -ētə-\ *n* -S

cong *n, pl* **cong** *usu cap* [by shortening] **:** VIETCONG *herein*

conglomerate* *n* **:** a widely diversified company; *esp* **:** a corporation that acquires other companies whose activities are unrelated to the corporation's primary activity

conk \ˈkäŋk, ˈkȯŋk\ *vt* -ED/-ING/-S [origin unknown] **:** to treat (as kinky hair) so as to straighten

conservation of angular momentum : a principle in physics: the total angular momentum of a system free of external torque remains constant irrespective of transformations and interactions within the system

conservation of baryon number : a principle in physics: the baryon number of an isolated system of elementary particles remains constant irrespective of transformations or decays

conservation of lepton number : a principle in physics: the lepton number of an isolated system of elementary particles remains constant regardless of transformations or decays

conserve* *vt* **:** to maintain (a quantity) constant during a process of chemical or physical change ⟨~ energy⟩

consolidation* *n* **:** a period of backing and filling in a security or commodity market usu. following a strong run-up of prices and typically preceding a further active advance

con·sum·er·ism \kənˈsüməˌrizəm\ *n* -S [*consumer* + *-ism*] **:** the promotion of consumer's interests (as against false advertising or shoddy goods) — **consumerist** *n*

con·tain·er·iza·tion \kənˌtānərəˈzāshən, -ˌrīˈz-\ *n* -S [*containerize* (herein) + *-ation*] **:** a method of shipping whereby a considerable amount of material (as merchandise) is packaged together in one large container

con·tain·er·ize \kənˈtānəˌrīz\ *vt* -ED/-ING/-S [*container* + *-ize*] **:** to ship by containerization ⟨*containerized* freight⟩

con·tain·er·ship \-nə(r)ˌship\ *n* [*container* + ¹*ship*] **:** a ship esp. designed or equipped for carrying containerized cargo

continuous creation theory *n* **:** STEADY STATE THEORY *herein*

con·toid \ˈkänˌtȯid\ *n* -S [*consonant* + *-oid*] **:** a speech sound of a phonetic rather than phonemic classification that includes most sounds traditionally treated as consonants and that excludes those (as English \y\, \w\, \r\, and \h\) which like vowels are characterized by the escape of air from the mouth over the center of the tongue without oral friction — compare VOCOID *in the Dict*

con·tra·test \ˈkäntrəˌ=\ *adj* [*contra-* + *test*] **:** of, relating to, or serving as an experiment control

convenience foods *n pl* **:** packaged foods designed for quick and easy preparation

cooking top *n* **:** a built-in cabinet-top cooking apparatus consisting of four heating units for gas or electricity

cooktop \ˈ=ˌ=\ *n* [²*cook* + *top*] **:** the flat top of a range

cool* *adj* **:** employing understatement and a minimum of detail to convey information and usu. requiring the listener, viewer, or reader to complete the message ⟨another indication of the very ~ . . . character of this medium —Marshall McLuhan⟩

cool* *vb* — **cool it :** to cool one's temper **:** go easy

coordinate* *n* **coordinates** *pl* **:** articles (as of clothing or furniture) designed to be used together and to attain their effect through pleasing contrast (as of color, material, or texture)

cop out* *vi* **:** to back out (as of an unwanted responsibility) — often used with *on* or *of* ⟨young Americans who *cop out* on society —*Christian Science Monitor*⟩ ⟨*copping out* of jury duty through a variety of machinations —H.F.Waters⟩

cop–out \ˈ=ˌ=\ *n* [*cop out* (herein)] **1 :** an excuse for copping out **:** PRETEXT **2 :** the means for copping out **3 :** one who cops out **4 :** the act or an instance of copping out

cor·al·ene \ˈkȯrəˌlēn, ˈkär-\ *n* -S [irreg. fr. ¹*coral*] **1 :** a raised decoration of glass beading on glassware **2 :** glassware with coralene decoration

cord·less \ˈkȯ(ə)rdləs, -ō(ə)d-\ *adj* [¹*cord* + *-less*] **:** having no cord; *esp* **:** powered by a battery ⟨~ tools⟩

core city *n* **:** INNER CITY *herein*

corn chip *n* **:** a piece of a crisp dry snack food prepared from a seasoned cornmeal batter

corner* *adj* **:** of, relating to, or being a defensive football player who covers one of the flanks ⟨~ linebacker⟩ ⟨~ positions⟩

cornerback \ˈ=ˌ=ˌ=\ *n* [*corner* (herein) + ¹*back*] **:** a defensive halfback in football whose duties include defending the flank and covering a wide receiver

cor·ner·man \ˈ==ˌman\ *n, pl* **corner·men** \-ˌmen\ [*corner* + *man*] **:** one that is in a corner: as **a :** CORNERBACK *herein* **b :** a basketball forward

cor·pus al·la·tum \ˌkȯrpəsəˈlād·əm, -äd-\ *n, pl* **cor·po·ra al·la·ta** \ˌkȯrpərə·əˈlād·ə, -äd-\ [NL, lit., applied body] **:** one of a pair of separate or fused bodies in many insects that are sometimes closely associated with the corpora cardiaca and secrete hormones (as juvenile hormone)

corpus car·di·a·cum \-pəskärˈdīəkəm\ *n, pl* **cor·po·ra car·di·a·ca** \-pərəkärˈdīəkə\ [NL, lit., cardiac body] **:** one of a pair of separate or fused bodies of nervous tissue in many insects that lie posterior to the brain and dorsal to the esophagus and function in the storage and secretion of a hormonal substance which stimulates prothoracic gland secretion

cos·mo·drome \ˈkäzməˌdrōm\ *n* -S [Russ *Kosmodrom*, fr. *Kosmonaut* cosmonaut + *-drom* ¹-drome] **:** a Soviet aerospace center; *esp* **:** a Soviet spacecraft launching installation

cos·mo·gen·ic \ˌkäzməˈjenik\ *adj* [*cosmic* ray + *-o-* + *-genic*] **:** produced by the action of cosmic rays ⟨~ carbon 14⟩

cos·mo·nau·tics \ˌkäzməˈnȯd·iks, -ȯti-\ *n pl but usu sing in constr* [*cosmonaut* + *-ics*] **:** ASTRONAUTICS

cost–effective \ˈ=ˌ==\ *adj* **:** economical in terms of tangible benefits produced by money spent — **cost–effectiveness** *n*

cost–push \ˈ=ˌ=\ *n* **:** an increase or upward trend in production costs (as wages) that tends to result in increased consumer prices irrespective of the level of demand — compare DEMAND-PULL *herein* — **cost–push** *adj*

co·terminal \(ˈ)kō + \ *adj* [*co-* + *terminal*] **:** having different angular measure but with the vertex and sides identical—used of angles generated by the rotation of lines about the same point in a given line whose values differ by an integral multiple of 2π radians or of 360° ⟨~ angles measuring 30° and 390°⟩

cou·chette \küˈshet\ *n* -S [F, berth, bunk, dim. of *couche* bed, fr. MF — more at COUCH] **1 :** a compartment on a European passenger train so arranged that berths can be provided at night **2 :** one of the berths in a couchette

cou·lom·bic \(ˈ)küˈläm(b)ik, -lōm-\ *adj* [ISV *coulomb* + *-ic*] **:** of or relating to electrostatic coulomb forces

coun·ter* *n* **:** a football play in which the ballcarrier goes in a direction opposite to the flow of play

coun·ter·example \ˈ== + \ *n* [*counter-* + *example*] **:** an example that is inconsistent with or contrary to what is typical or usual **:** a disproving example

coun·ter·insurgency \ˈ" + \ *n* [*counter-* + *insurgency*] **:** organized activity designed to deal with insurgency — **coun·ter·insurgent** \ˈ" + \ *n*

country* *adj* **:** having or using lyrics or style identified with country music ⟨~ singer⟩

country and western *adj, sometimes cap C & often cap W* **:** having or using lyrics, style, or string instrumentation identified with country music of western U.S. origin

crambe* *n* -S **:** an annual Mediterranean herb (*Crambe abyssinica*) cultivated as an oilseed crop

cranberry glass *n* **:** clear ruby glass usu. with a blue-violet tint

crash pad* *n* **:** an apartment where free lodging is available

crashworthy \ˈ=ˌ==\ *adj* [²*crash* + *-worthy* (as in *seaworthy*)] **:** resistant to the effects of a collision ⟨~ cars⟩ — **crashworthiness** *n*

crawl·er·way \ˈ=ˌ=\ *n* [*crawler* + *way*; fr. its slow-moving traffic] **:** a road built esp. for moving heavy rockets and spacecraft

crawlway \ˈ=ˌ=\ *n* [¹*crawl* + *way*] **:** a low passageway (as in a cave) that can be traversed only by crawling

credibility gap *n* **1 a :** lack of trust ⟨a special *credibility gap* is likely to open between the generations —Kenneth Keniston⟩ **b :** lack of believability ⟨a *credibility gap* created by contradictory official statements —Samuel Ellenport⟩ **2 :** DISCREPANCY ⟨the *credibility gap* between the professed ideals . . . and their actual practices —Jeanne Noble⟩

creditworthy \ˈ=ˌ==\ *adj* [¹*credit* + *worthy*] **:** being financially sound enough to justify the extension of credit **:** having an acceptable credit rating — **creditworthiness** *n*

creeping* *adj* **:** developing or advancing by slow imperceptible degrees ⟨~ socialism⟩

cre·mains \krəˈmānz, krēˈ-\ *n pl* [blend of *cremated* and *remains*] **:** the ashes of a cremated human body

crew sock *n* [so called fr. its use by rowing crews] **:** a short bulky usu. ribbed sock

crista* *n* **:** any of the inwardly projecting folds of the inner membrane of a mitochondrion

cruise* *vi* **:** to search (as in public places) for a sexual partner

crunch* *n* **:** a tight or critical situation: as **a :** a critical point in the buildup of pressure between opposing elements **:** SHOWDOWN **b :** a severe economic squeeze (as on credit)

cryo·biology \ˌkrīō + \ *n* [*cry-* + *biology*] **:** the study of the effects of extremely low temperature on biological systems — **cryo·biological** \ˈ" + \ *adj* — **cryo·biologically** \ˈ" + \ *adv* — **cryo·biologist** \ˈ" + \ *n*

cryo·chemistry \ˈ" + \ *n* [*cry-* + *chemistry*] **:** chemistry dealing with processes carried out at very low temperatures — **cryochemical** *adj* — **cryochemically** *adv*

cryo·electronics \ˈ" + \ *n pl but sing in constr* [*cry-* + *electronics*] **:** a branch of electronics that employs cryogenic methods to bring about a desired effect (as superconductivity)

cryogenic* *adj* **1 :** being or relating to a very low temperature ⟨a ~ temperature of −50°C⟩ **2 a :** requiring or involving the use of a cryogenic temperature **b :** requiring cryogenic storage **c :** suitable for the storage of a cryogenic substance ⟨a ~ container⟩ — **cry·o·gen·i·cal·ly** \-nək(ə)lē\ *adv*

cry·on·ics \krīˈäniks\ *n pl but usu sing in constr* [*cryo*biology (herein) + *-onics* (as in *electronics*)] **:** the practice of freezing a dead diseased human being for the purpose of bringing him back to life at some future time supposedly when a cure for his disease has been developed — **cry·on·ic** \(ˈ)krīˈänik\ *adj*

cryo·precipitate \ˌkrīō + \ *n* [*cry-* + *precipitate*] **:** a precipitate that is formed by cooling a solution — **cryo·precipi·tation** \ˈ" + \ *n*

cryo·pump \ˈkrīōˌ=\ *n* [*cry-* + *pump*] **:** a vacuum pump whose operation involves the freezing and absorption of gases on cold surfaces at very low temperatures — **cryopump** *vi*

cryo·surgery \ˌkrīō + \ *n* [*cry-* + *surgery*] **:** surgical procedures in which extreme controlled chilling (as by use of liquid nitrogen) produces desired dissection — **cryo·surgeon** \ˈ" + \ *n* — **cryo·surgical** \ˈ" + \ *adj*

cryp·to·biosis \ˌkrip(ˌ)tō + \ *n, pl* **cryptobioses** [NL, fr. *crypt-* + *-biosis*] **:** the reversible cessation of metabolism under extreme environmental conditions (as low temperature)

cui·se·naire colored rod \ˌkwēzᵊnˈa(ə)r-, -ˈe(-\ *n, usu cap 1st C* [fr. *Cuisenaire*, a trademark] **:** any of a set of colored rods that are usu. of 1 centimeter cross section and of ten lengths from 1 to 10 centimeters and that are used for teaching number concepts and the basic operations of arithmetic

cup·pa \ˈkəpə\ *n* -S [short for *cuppa tea*, pronunciation spelling of *cup of tea*] *chiefly Brit* **:** a cup of tea

cu·ri·age \ˈkyürēij, kyəˈr-\ *n* -S [*curie* + *-age*] **:** the strength of radioactivity expressed in curies

curl* *n* **:** a hollow arch of water formed when the crest of a breaking wave spills forward — called also *tube, tunnel*

curve* *vt* **:** to throw a curve to (a batter) in baseball

custard glass *n* **:** opaque glass of creamy buff color

cut* *n* **:** BAND 8

cutback* *n* **:** a surfing maneuver in which a surfboard is turned back toward the crest of the wave

cy·ber·culture \ˈsībə(r) + ˌ\ *n* [*cyber*netics + *culture*] **:** a society that is served by cybernated industry — **cy·ber·cul·tural** \ˌsībə(r) + \ *adj*

cy·ber·nat·ed \ˈsībə(r)ˌnād·əd\ *adj* [fr. *cybernation* (herein); after such pairs as E *automation*: *automated*] **:** involving cybernation; *also* **:** characterized by the use of cybernation

cy·ber·na·tion \ˌsībə(r)ˈnāshən\ *n* -S [*cyber*netics + *-ation*] **:** the automatic control of a process or operation (as in manufacturing) by means of computers

cy·borg \ˈsīˌbȯrg\ *n* -S [*cyb*ernetic + *org*anism] **:** a human linked with mechanical devices that perform some of the vital physiological functions

cy·clo·phos·pha·mide \ˌsīkləˈfäsfəˌmīd, ˌsik-, -ˌməd\ *n* [prob. fr. *cycl-* + *phosph-* + *amide*] **:** a drug used esp. to suppress immunity reactions (as in tissue transplantation) and to induce temporary remission of some leukemias

cyclotron resonance *n* **:** the absorption of electromagnetic energy by a charged particle orbiting in a magnetic field when the electromagnetic and orbital frequencies are equal

cy·to·chimera \ˌsīd·ō + \ *n* [NL, fr. *cyt-* + *chimera*] **:** an individual (as a plant, an organ, or a tissue) having cells of varied genetic constitution and esp. of various ploidy levels

cyto·differentiation \ˈ" + \ *n* [*cyt-* + *differentiation*] **:** the development of specialized cells (as muscle, blood, or nerve cells) from undifferentiated precursors

cyto·ecology \ˈ" + \ *n* [*cyt-* + *ecology*] **:** the study of organismic adaptation at the molecular and cellular level — **cyto·ecological** \ˈ" + \ *adj*

cyto·kinin \ˈ" + \ *n* [*cyt-* + *kinin* (herein)] **:** any of various adenines with an amino group attached at the number six position that are plant growth substances

cy·to·stat·ic \ˌsīd·əˈstad·ik\ *adj* [*cyt-* + Gk *statikos* causing to stand — more at STATIC] **:** tending to retard cellular activity and multiplication — **cytostatic** *n* -S — **cy·to·stat·i·cal·ly** \-ad·ək(ə)lē\ *adv*

cy·to·technologist \ˌsīd·ō + \ *or* **cy·to·technician** \ˈ" + \ *n* [*cyt-* + *technologist* or *technician*] **:** a person trained to do preliminary screening of and to assist a pathologist in the study of cytological preparations for the detection of cancer

da* *abbr* deka-

dal·a·pon \ˈdaləˌpän\ *n* -S [prob. fr. *di-* + *alpha* + *propionic acid*] **:** an herbicide used esp. on unwanted grasses

dal·ton \ˈdȯlt-ᵊn\ *n* -S [after John *Dalton* †1844 Eng. chemist and physicist] **:** ATOMIC MASS UNIT

damsel bug *n* **:** any of a family (Nabidae) of small brown or black bugs that feed on pest insects

dan \ˈdän\ *n* -S [Jap, step, grade] **:** a proficiency grade in some Japanese arts of self-defense (as judo) and games (as shogi)

das *abbr* dekastere *herein*

da·shi·ki \däˈshēkē, -dəˈ-\ *n* -S [of African origin] **:** a usu. brightly colored loose-fitting one-piece pullover garment worn esp. by men

data processing *n* **:** the converting (as by electronic computers or mechanical sorting devices) of crude information into usable or storable form — **data processor** *n*

day trader *n* **:** a speculator who seeks profit from the intraday fluctuation in the price of a security or commodity and therefore completes double trades of buying and selling or selling and covering in the course of single sessions of the market — **day–trade** \ˈ=ˌ=\ *n or vb*

DDVP *n* -S [*d*imethyl + *d*ichlor- + *v*inyl + *p*hosphate] **:** a volatile organophosphate insecticide

dead drop *n* [so called fr. the absence of personal contact between the agents] **:** a prearranged hiding place for the deposit and pickup of information obtained through espionage

dear john \di(ə)rˈjän, diəˈj-\ *n, usu cap D&J* **:** a letter (as to a soldier) in which a wife asks for a divorce or a girl friend breaks off an engagement or a friendship

de·boost \(ˈ)dē, dē + \ *n* [*de-* + *boost*] **:** the process of slowing down a spacecraft ⟨before ~ into low orbit —C.J.Sitomer⟩

debrief* *vt* **:** to instruct not to reveal classified information after release from a sensitive position

debug* *vt* **:** to remove a concealed microphone or wiretapping device from ⟨~ a room⟩

deca·met·ric \ˌdekəˈme·trik\ *adj* [*decameter* + *-ic*; fr. the wavelength range being between 1 and 10 dekameters] **:** of, relating to, or being a radio wave of high frequency

deciding *adj* [fr. pres. part. of *decide*] **:** having the effect of settling a contest or controversy ⟨the ~ run⟩ ⟨the ~ vote⟩

deck* *n* **:** TAPE DECK *herein*

declining–balance method *n* **:** a method of calculating periodic depreciation that involves determining at regular (as annual) intervals throughout the expected life of an asset of equal percentage amounts of a cost balance which is progressively decreased by subtraction of each prior increment of depreciation from the original cost of the asset — compare STRAIGHT-LINE METHOD *in the Dict*

de·colonization \(ˌ)dē, dē + \ *n* [*de-* + *colonization*] **:** the act or process of granting independence to a colony

de·colonize \(ˈ)dē, dē + \ *vb* [*de-* + *colonize*] *vi* **:** to grant independence to a colony ~ *vt* **:** to free from colonial status

deep* *adv* **:** near the outer limits of an athletic playing area

deep space* *n* **:** space well beyond the limits of the earth's atmosphere including space outside the solar system

deep structure *n* **:** a formal representation of the underlying

semantic content of a sentence; *also* **:** the structure which such a representation specifies
de-escalate \(ˈ)dē+\ *vb* [*de-* + *escalate*] *vi* **:** to decrease in extent, volume, number, amount, or scope **:** DIMINISH ~ *vt* **:** to decrease the extent, volume, number, amount, or scope of ⟨my sister . . . tried to *de-escalate* our feud —H.A.Smith⟩
de-escalation \(ˌ)dē+\ *n* [*de-* + *escalation*] **:** a decreasing in extent, volume, number, amount, or scope
de-es·ca·la·tor \(ˈ)dē¦es¦ka,lād·ə(r)\ *n* -s [*de-escalate* + *-or*] **:** an advocate of de-escalation
de-es·ca·la·to·ry \-lə,tōrē\ *adj* [*de-escalate* + *-ory*] **:** of or relating to de-escalation
defensive* *adj* **:** of, relating to, or being industries (as foods, utilities, and insurance) which provide essential needs to the ultimate consumer and in which business activity is relatively insensitive to changes in general business activity
deferred income* *n* **:** current income forgone to produce a later higher income (as at retirement)
de·fibrillate \(ˈ)dē, də+\ *vt* [*de-* + *fibrillate*] **:** to restore the rhythm of (a fibrillating heart) — **de·fibrillation** \(ˌ)dē, də +\ *n* — **de·fi·bril·la·tor** \dēˈfibrə,lād·ə(r)\ *n*
¹de·focus \(ˈ)dē, də+\ *vb* [*de-* + *focus*] *vt* **:** to cause (as a beam of radiation or a lens) to deviate from an accurate focus ~ *vi* **:** to lose accuracy of focus **:** become defocused
²defocus \"\ *n* **:** a result of defocusing; *esp* **:** an image (as on motion-picture film) deliberately blurred for dramatic effect
de·fog \(ˈ)dē, də+\ *vt* [*de-* + *fog*] **:** to remove fog or condensed moisture from **:** keep free of fog — **de·fog·ger** *n*
de·grad·able \dəˈgrādəbəl, dē-\ *adj* [*degrade* + *-able*] **:** capable of being chemically degraded ⟨~ detergents⟩
de·industrialization \ˌdē+\ *n* [*de-* + *industrialization*] **:** the act or process of reducing or destroying the industrial organization and potential esp. of a defeated nation
deka·gram *n* -s [by alter.] **:** DECAGRAM
deka·li·ter *n* -s [by alter.] **:** DECALITER
deka·me·ter *n* -s [by alter.] **:** ²DECAMETER
deka·stere *n* -s [by alter.] **:** DECASTERE
delay* *n* **:** a play in football in which an offensive back delays momentarily as if to block and then runs his prescribed pattern
deli \ˈdelē, -li\ *or* **del·ly** *n, pl* **del·is** *or* **del·lies** [by shortening] **:** DELICATESSEN
deliver* *vi* **:** to produce the promised, desired, or expected results **:** come through ⟨failed to ~ on their promises⟩
demand-pull \=ˈ=,=\ *n* [¹*demand* + ²*pull*] **:** an increase or upward trend in spendable money that tends to result in increased competition for available goods and services and a corresponding increase in consumer prices — compare COST-PUSH *herein* — **demand-pull** *adj*
dem·e·ton \ˈdemə,tän\ *n* -s [prob. fr. *d*iethyl + *me*rcapt- + *thion*ate] **:** an organophosphate systemic insecticide
de·moth·ball \(ˈ)dē+\ *vt* [*de-* + *mothball*] **:** to remove the preservative covering in order to reactivate (as ships)
den·som·e·ter \denˈsäməd·ə(r)\ *n* -s [ISV *dens-* (fr. L *densus* dense) + *-o-* + *-meter*] **1 :** an instrument for measuring the porosity of paper by forcing air through it **2 :** DENSIMETER
de·nu·cle·ar·ize \(ˈ)dēˈn(y)üklēə,rīz\ *vt* -ED/-ING/-S *see -ize in Explan Notes* [*de-* + *nuclear* + *-ize*] **:** to remove nuclear arms from **:** prohibit the use of nuclear arms in
¹de·orbit \(ˈ)dē+\ *vb* [*de-* + *orbit*] *vi* **:** to go out of orbit ~ *vt* **:** to cause to deorbit ⟨~ a spacecraft⟩
²deorbit \"\ *n* **:** the process of deorbiting
de·pic·ture \dəˈpikchə(r), dē-, -ksh-\ *vt* [blend of *depict* and ²*picture*] **1 :** DEPICT **2 :** IMAGINE
de·politicize \ˌdē+\ *vt* [*de-* + *politicize*] **:** to remove the political character from **:** take out of the realm of politics
de·pressurize \(ˈ)dē+\ *vt* [*de-* + *pressurize*] **:** to release (as a pressurized aircraft) from pressure
de·rail·leur \ˌdāˌ(ˌ)rīˈyər\ *n* -s [F *dérailleur*, fr. *dérailler* to throw off the track (fr. *dé-* de- + *rail* rail, fr. E) + *-eur* -or] **1 :** a multiple-speed gear mechanism on a bicycle that involves the moving of the chain from one sprocket to another ⟨10-speed ~⟩ **2 :** a bicycle having a derailleur
de·repress \ˌdē+\ *vt* [*de-* + *repress*] **:** to activate (a gene) by releasing from a blocked state — **de·repression** \"+\ *n*
derrick* *vt* **:** to remove (a pitcher) from a baseball game **:** YANK
de·sa·li·nate \(ˈ)dēˈsalə,nāt, -sā-\ *vt* -ED/-ING/-S [*de-* + *salin-* + *-ate*] **:** to remove salt from ⟨~ seawater⟩ — **de·sa·li·na·tor** \-nād·ə(r)\ *n* -s
de·sa·li·nize \-,nīz\ *vt* [*de-* + *salinize*] **:** DESALINATE *herein*
descriptor* *n* **:** a word or phrase (as an index term) used to identify an item (as a subject or document) esp. in an information retrieval system; *also* **:** an alphanumeric symbol so used
de·select \ˌdē+\ *vt* [*de-* + *select*] **:** to dismiss (a trainee) from a training program
de·sta·lin·iza·tion \(ˌ)dē,stälənəˈzāshən, -tal-, -,nīˈz-\ *n* -s [*destalinize* + *-ation*] **:** the deflation of Stalin and his policies
de·struct \ˈdē,strəkt, dəˈs-, dēˈs-\ *n* -s [short for *destruction*] **:** the deliberate destruction of a rocket after launching esp. during a test; *also* **:** such destruction of a device or material (as to prevent its falling into enemy hands)
detonate* *vt* **:** to set off in a burst of activity **:** ACTIVATE
deu·ter·ate \ˈd(y)üd·ə,rāt\ *vt* -ED/-ING/-S [*deuterium* + *-ate*, vb. suffix] **:** to introduce deuterium into (a compound)
de·vel·op·ing *adj* **:** UNDERDEVELOPED 3 ⟨~ nations⟩
dexa·meth·a·sone \ˌdeksəˈmethə,sōn, -,zōn\ *n* -s [perh. fr. *Dexa*myl, a trademark + *meth*yl + *-sone* (as in *cortisone*)] **:** a synthetic steroid that is a cortisone analogue with comparable anti-inflammatory and antiallergic effects
dic·ey \ˈdīsē\ *adj* [²*dice* + *-y*] **:** RISKY, UNPREDICTABLE ⟨a very ~ operation —*Newsweek*⟩
dich·otic \(ˈ)dīˌkōd·ik\ *adj* [*dich-* + *-otic*] **:** affecting or relating to the two ears differently in regard to a conscious aspect (as pitch or loudness) or a physical aspect (as frequency or energy) of sound — **dich·oti·cal·ly** \-d·ək(ə)lē\ *adv*
di·functional \(ˈ)dī+\ *adj* [*di-* + *functional*] **:** of, relating to, or being a compound with two sites in the molecule that are highly reactive — **di·functionality** \(ˌ)dī+\ *n*
dig·i·tal·ize \ˈdijəd·ᵊl,īz\ *vt* -ED/-ING/-S [¹*digital* + *-ize*] **:** DIGITIZE
di·meth·o·ate \dīˈmethə,wāt\ *n* -s [*dimethyl* + *-thioic* + *-ate*] **:** an insecticide used on livestock and various crops
di·meth·yl·sulf·ox·ide \ˌdī,methəl,səlˈfäk,sīd, -,səd\ *n* [*dimethyl* + *sulfoxide*] **:** a compound obtained as a by-product in wood-pulp manufacture and used as a solvent and in experimental medicine — called also *DMSO*
di·meth·yl·tryptamine \ˌdī,methəl+\ *n* [*dimethyl* + *tryptamine*] **:** an easily synthesized hallucinogenic drug that is chemically similar to but shorter acting than psilocybin — called also *DMT*
dinch \ˈdinch\ *vt* -ED/-ING/-ES [origin unknown] **:** to extinguish by crushing ⟨~ a cigarette⟩
diner-out \ˌdīnəˈraůt\ *n, pl* **diners-out** [*dine out* + *-er*] **:** one who dines away from home esp. in the course of an active social life ⟨a constant *diner-out* —Thomas Wolfe⟩
director's chair *n* [so called fr. its use by movie directors] **:** a lightweight folding armchair with a back and seat usu. of cotton duck
directrix* *n* **:** a line or curve with which a generatrix of a surface remains in contact
dirham* *also* **dirhem*** *n* **1 :** the basic monetary unit of Morocco established in 1959 — see MONEY table *in the Dict* **2 :** a coin representing one dirham
dis·bound \(ˈ)dis+\ *adj* [¹*dis-* + ⁴*bound*] **:** no longer having a binding ⟨a ~ pamphlet⟩
dis·co·theque \ˈdiskəˈtek, ˌdēs-, -kōˈt-\ *n* -s [F *discothèque* collection of phonograph records, discotheque, fr. *disque* disk (fr. L *discus*) + *-o-* + *-thèque* (as in *bibliothèque* library, fr. L *bibliotheca*) — more at DISH, BIBLIOTHECA] **:** a usu. small intimate nightclub for dancing to recorded music; *broadly* **:** a nightclub often featuring psychedelic and mixed-media attractions (as slides, movies, and special lighting effects)
dis·cret·iza·tion \(ˌ)dis,krēd·əˈzāshən\ *n* -s [*discrete* + *-ization*] **:** the action of making mathematically discrete **:** the state of being mathematically discrete
dishware \ˈ=,=\ *n* [¹*dish* + *ware*] **:** tableware (as of china) used in serving food
dis·in·sec·tion \ˌdisənˈsekshən\ *n* -s [¹*dis-* + *insect* + *-ion*] **:** DISINSECTIZATION
dis·in·ter·me·di·a·tion \(ˌ)dis,intə(r),mēdēˈāshən\ *n* [¹*dis-* + *intermediate* + *-ion*; fr. the investor's bypassing of the intermediate institution] **:** diversion of savings from institutions (as savings banks) with governmentally imposed interest ceilings to direct investment in higher-yielding securities
disjoint* *adj* **:** lacking common members ⟨~ mathematical sets⟩
disposable *n* -s [*disposable*, adj.] **:** something (as a paper blanket) that is disposable
di·uron \ˈdīyə,rän\ *n* -s [*di-* + *urea* + ¹*-on*] **:** a persistent herbicide used esp. to control annual weeds
DMSO *n* [*d*i*m*ethyl*s*ulf*o*xide] **:** DIMETHYLSULFOXIDE *herein*
DMT *n* [*d*i*m*ethyl*t*ryptamine] **:** DIMETHYLTRYPTAMINE *herein*
dock* *vt* **:** to maneuver and bring (a spacecraft) together with something (as another spacecraft) in space
doggie-bag \ˈ=,=,=\ *n* [²*doggy* + *bag*; fr. the original assumption that such leftovers were destined for the diner's dog] **:** a bag used for carrying home leftover food and esp. meat from a meal eaten at a restaurant
do-good·ing \ˈdüˌgůdiŋ\ *n* -s **:** the activities of a do-gooder
dogs·body \ˈdògz,bädē *sometimes* ˈdäg-\ *n, chiefly Brit* [Brit. naval slang, midshipman, fr. slang *dog's body* pease pudding] **:** one who performs menial tasks **:** DRUDGE
do-it-your·self \ˌdüəchə(r)ˈself, -ətyə-\ *adj* **:** of, relating to, or designed for use in construction, repair, or artistic work done by an amateur or hobbyist ⟨a *do-it-yourself* car model kit⟩
do-it-your·self·er \-fə(r)\ *n* -s [*do-it-yourself* + ²*-er*] **:** one who engages in do-it-yourself activities
do·jo \ˈdō(ˌ)jō\ *n* -s [Jap *dōjō*, fr. *dō* way, art + *-jō* ground] **:** a place (as a gymnasium) where judo or karate is practiced or taught; *also* **:** a school that teaches judo or karate
dol·ce vi·ta \ˌdōlchēˈvē(ˌ)tä, -(ˌ)chā-\ *n* [It, lit., sweet life] **:** a life of indolence and self-indulgence
DOM \ˌdē(ˌ)ōˈem\ *n* [prob. fr. *d*imethoxy- + *m*ethyl] **:** STP *herein*
domestic prelate *n* **:** a priest having permanent honorary membership in the papal household and ranking above a papal chamberlain
domino effect *n* [so called from the fact that if a number of dominoes are stood on end one behind the other with a slight intervening space, a slight push on the first one will result in the toppling of all the others] **:** a cumulative effect produced when one event initiates a succession of related events
domino theory *n* [so called fr. the domino effect] **:** a theory that if one nation in Southeast Asia becomes Communist-controlled the neighboring nations will also become Communist-controlled
done·ness \ˈdənnəs\ *n* -ES [²*done* + *-ness*] **:** the condition of being cooked to the desired degree
do·pa·mine \ˈdōpə,mēn, -,mən\ *n* [*dopa* + *amine*] **:** dopa or a decarboxylated form of this found esp. in the adrenal
dop·ant \ˈdōpənt\ *n* -s [²*dope* + *-ant*, n. suffix] **:** an impurity added usu. in minute amounts to a pure substance to alter its properties
doppler radar *n, usu cap D* **:** a radar system utilizing the Doppler effect for measuring velocity
dor·min \ˈdòrmən\ *n* [*dormancy* + *-in*] **:** ABSCISIC ACID *herein*
double-blind \ˈ=;=ˈ=\ *adj* **:** of, relating to, or being an experiment or system of experimentation in which neither the subjects nor the experimenters know the makeup of the test and control groups during the actual course of the experimentation
doublet* *n* **1 a :** a pair of atomic, molecular, or nuclear quantum states that are usu. close together in energy and arise from two possible orientations of spin **b :** a pair of spectral frequencies of light arising from transitions to or from such quantum states **2 :** a pair of otherwise similar elementary particles (as a proton and a neutron) with different charge
dove* *n* **:** one who takes a conciliatory attitude (as in a dispute) and advocates negotiations and compromise — compare HAWK *herein* — **dov·ish** \ˈdəvish\ *adj* — **dov·ish·ness** *n* -ES
downrange \ˈ=ˈ=\ *adv (or adj)* [³*down* + ¹*range*] **:** away from a launching site and along the course of a test range
downer* *n* **:** a depressant drug; *esp* **:** BARBITURATE
downplay \ˈ=,=\ *vt* **:** to play down **:** DE-EMPHASIZE
dozen* *n* **dozens** *pl* **:** a game that consists of exchanging often obscene insults usu. about the members of the opponent's family — often used in the phrase *play the dozens*
draft* *vi* **:** to drive close behind another car while racing at high speed in order to take advantage of the reduced air pressure created by the leading car
drawdown* *n* **:** a lowering of the water level (as in a reservoir)
dream·scape \ˈdrēmz,kāp, -m,sk-\ *n* [¹*dream* + *-scape*] **:** a dreamlike usu. surrealistic scene ⟨seemed greener than he had remembered any jungle to be: a ~ out of neverland —Frank Yerby⟩; *also* **:** a painting of a dreamscape
drive-up \ˈ=,=\ *adj* [*drive up*, v.] **:** designed to allow patrons or customers to be served while remaining in their automobiles
drop* *vt* **:** to take (a drug) through the mouth **:** SWALLOW
drop-in \ˈdrä,pin\ *n* [fr. the verb phrase *drop in*] **1 :** one who drops in **:** a casual visitor **2 :** an informal social gathering at which guests are invited to drop in
drop out* *vi* **:** to withdraw from conventional society because of disenchantment with its values and mores
dropout* *n* **:** one who drops out from conventional society
drown·proof·ing \ˈdraůnˈprüfiŋ\ *n* -s [*drown* + ²*proof* + *-ing*] **:** a technique for staying afloat in water for an extended period with minimum effort through the use of a person's natural buoyancy
drunk tank *n* **:** a large detention cell for arrested drunks
dual fund *n* **:** a closed-end investment company whose capitalization consists half of income shares entitled to the entire income of the company and half of capital shares entitled to all capital appreciation — called also *dual purpose fund*
duc·ti·bil·i·ty \ˌdəktəˈbiləd·ē\ *n* -ES [*ductible* + *-ity*] **:** DUCTILITY
dune buggy *n* **:** BEACH BUGGY
durable press *n* **1 :** the process of treating a fabric with a chemical (as a resin) and heat for setting the shape and for aiding wrinkle resistance **2 :** material treated by durable press **3 :** the condition of material treated by durable press — **durable-press** *adj*
dyke *also* **dike** *n* [origin unknown] **:** LESBIAN; *esp* **:** one assuming an aggressively masculine role
dy·nap·o·lis \dīˈnapələs\ *n* -ES [NGk, fr. *dynamikos* dynamic (fr. Gk, powerful) + *polis* city, fr. Gk — more at DYNAMIC, POLICE] **:** a city planned for orderly growth along a main traffic artery by means of self-contained communities
dys·ba·rism \ˈdisbə,rizəm\ *n* -s [*dys-* + *bar-* + *-ism*] **:** the complex of symptoms (as bends, headache, or mental disturbance) that accompanies exposure to excessively low or rapidly changing environmental air pressure
dys·to·pia \disˈtōpēə\ *n* -s [*dys-* + *-topia* (as in *eutopia*)] **:** an imaginary place which is depressingly wretched and whose people lead a fearful existence — **dystopian** *adj*
earthrise \ˈ=,=\ *n* [*earth* + *rise*] **:** the rising of the earth above the horizon of the moon as seen from the moon
eb·ul·lism \ˈebə,lizəm\ *n* -s [L *ebullire* to come bubbling out + E *-ism* — more at EBULLIENT] **:** the formation of bubbles in body fluids under sharply reduced environmental pressure
ec·dy·sone \ˈekdə,sōn\ *n* -s [*ecdysis* + *hormone*] **:** an insect hormone affecting larval growth and molting
echo·virus \ˌekō+\ *n* [*e*nteric *c*ytopathogenic *h*uman *o*rphan + *virus*] **:** any of a group of picornaviruses sometimes associated with respiratory ailments or meningitis
eco·geographic \ˌekō, ˌēkō+\ *or* **eco·geographical** *adj* [*ecological* + *geographic* or *geographical*] **:** of or relating to both ecological and geographical aspects of the environment — **eco·geographically** \"+\ *adv*
economy *adj* **:** designed to save the buyer money ⟨~ cars⟩
eco·sphere \ˈekō,sfi(ə)r, ˈēk-\ *n* [²*ec-* + *sphere*] **:** the parts of the universe habitable by living organisms; *esp* **:** BIOSPHERE 1 — **eco·spher·ic** \ˌekōˈsfirik, ˌēk-, -fer-\ *adj*
ec·to·crine \ˈektəkrən; -,krin, -rīn, -rēn\ *n* -s [*ect-* + *-crine* (as in *endocrine*)] **:** a metabolite produced by an organism of one kind and utilized by one of another kind
ec·to·hormone \ˌektə+\ *n* [*ect-* + *hormone*] **:** a substance (as a pheromone) given off by one organism that is capable of affecting the behavior of other organisms of the same species — **ec·to·hormonal** \"+\ *adj*
ecu·me·nop·o·lis \ˌekyəmeˈnäpələs, ˌekyüm-\ *n* -ES [NGk *oikoumenopolis*, fr. Gk *oikoumenē* world + *-polis* — more at ECUMENE] **:** a global network of urbanized communities held to be a possibility of the future
ed·it \ˈedət\ *n* -s [*edit*, vb.] **:** an instance of editing
EDP *abbr* electronic data processing
educational park *n* **:** a large centralized educational complex of elementary and secondary schools
educational television *n* **1 :** PUBLIC TELEVISION *herein* **2 :** television that provides instructional material esp. for students sometimes by closed circuit
EHV *abbr* extra high voltage
eightfold way *n* **:** a unified theoretical scheme for classifying the relationship among strongly interacting elementary particles on the basis of isospin and hypercharge
ekis·tics \əˈkistiks, ēˈk-\ *n pl but sing in constr* [NGk *oikistikē*, fr. fem. of *oikistikos* relating to settlement, fr. Gk, fr. *oikizein* to settle, colonize, fr. *oikos* house — more at VICINITY] **:** a science dealing with human settlements and drawing on the research and experience of the architect, the engineer, the city planner, and the social scientist — **ekis·tic** \-tik\ *adj* — **ekis·ti·cian** \ə,kiˈstishən, (ˌ)ē,k-\ *n* -s
elec·tro·cor·ti·co·graph·ic \əˈlektrə,kòrd·əkōˈgrafik, ēˈl-\ *adj* [*electr-* + *cortico-* + *-graphic*] **:** of, relating to, or involving the use of an electrocorticogram — **elec·tro·cor·ti·co·graph·i·cal·ly** \-fək(ə)lē, -fēk-\ *adv* — **elec·tro·cor·ti·cog·ra·phy** \-d·əˈkägrəfē\ *n* -ES
elec·tro·fishing \əˈlektrō, ēˈl-+\ *n* [*electr-* + *fishing*] **:** the taking of fish by a system based on their strong galvanotactic attraction to a source of direct electric current
elec·tro·gas·dynamics \ə,lektrōˈgas, ē,l-+\ *n pl but sing in constr* [*electr-* + *gas* + *dynamic* + *-s*] **:** a method of generating electrical energy that is based on the conversion of the kinetic energy of the flow of a high pressure combustion gas — **elec·tro·gas·dynamic** \"+\ *adj*
elec·tro·hydraulic \əˈlektrō, ēˈl-+\ *adj* [*electr-* + *hydraulic*] **1 :** of, relating to, or involving a combination of electric and hydraulic mechanisms ⟨an ~ elevator⟩ **2 :** involving or produced by the action of very brief but powerful pulse discharges of electricity under a liquid resulting in the generation of shock waves and highly reactive chemical species ⟨an ~ effect⟩ — **elec·tro·hydraulically** \"+\ *adv*
elec·tro·hydraulics \"+\ *n* [*electrohydraulic* + *-s*] **:** the production of shock waves by electrohydraulic means
electromagnetic interaction *n* **:** a fundamental interaction experienced by most elementary particles that is responsible for the emission and absorption of photons and for electric and magnetic forces
electronic music *n* **:** music that consists of sounds electronically captured or originated, taped, and played through a loudspeaker
electron spin resonance *n* **:** the magnetic resonance of electrons that are either free or bound in atoms
elec·tro·pho·rese \ə,lektrəfəˈrēs, ē,l-, -ˈträfə,-, -ēz\ *vt* -ED/-ING/-S [back-formation fr. *electrophoresis*] **:** to subject to electrophoresis
elec·tro·pho·ret·o·gram \əˈlektrəfəˈred·ə,gram, ē,l-\ *n* -s [*electrophoretic* + *-gram*] **:** a record that consists of the separated components of a mixture (as of proteins) produced by electrophoresis in a supporting medium (as filter paper)
elec·tro·sensitive \əˈlektrō, ēˈl-+\ *adj* [*electr-* + *sensitive*] **:** being or using sensitive paper on which an image is produced by the passage of electric current through it
elec·tro·sleep \əˈlektrō, ēˈl-+,\ *n* [*electr-* + *sleep*] **:** profound relaxation or a state of unconsciousness induced by the passage of a very low voltage electric current through the brain
electrostatic printing *n* **:** a process (as xerography) for printing or copying in which electrostatic forces are used to form the image (as with powder or ink) directly on a surface
elementary particle* *n* **:** OXYSOME *herein*
el·hi \ˈel,hī\ *adj* [*el*ementary school + *hi*gh school] **:** of, relating to, or designed for use in grades 1 through 12
en·cap·su·lant \ənˈkapsələnt, en- *also* -syə-\ *n* -s [*encapsulate* + *-ant*] **:** a material used for encapsulating
end·ar·te·rec·to·my \ˌen,därd·əˈrektəmē\ *n* -ES [*endarterium* + *-ectomy*] **:** surgical entry into an artery (as of the heart) for the removal of occluding material (as intimal plaques)
en·do·cy·to·sis \ˌendō,sīˈtōsəs\ *n, pl* **endocyto·ses** \-ō,sēz\ [NL, fr. *end-* + *cyt-* + *-osis*] **:** incorporation of substances into a cell by phagocytosis or pinocytosis — **en·do·cy·tic** \ˈ==ˈsid·ik\ *adj* — **en·do·cy·tot·ic** \ˈ==,sīˈtäd·ik\ *adj*
end-of-day glass \ˈ==ˈ=,=\ *n* [so called from its resemblance to objects made by glassblowers at the end of the day's work to use up various odds and ends of glass left over] **:** glass of various colors (as red, blue, green, and white) mixed together
endogenic* *adj* **:** ENDOGENOUS
en·do·phil·ic \ˌendəˈfilik\ *adj* [*end-* + *-philic*] **:** ecologically associated with man and his domestic environment — compare EXOPHILIC *herein* — **en·doph·i·ly** \enˈdäfəlē\ *n* -ES
endoplasmic reticulum *n* **:** a system of interconnected vesicles or minute canals that occupy much of the cytoplasm esp. of metabolically active cells — compare RIBOSOME *herein*
en·do·radiosonde \ˌendō+\ *n* [*end-* + *radiosonde*] **:** a subminiature electron device introduced into the body to gather physiological information
en·do·sul·fan \ˌendōˈsəlfən, -,fan\ *n* -s [perh. fr. *endrin* + *-o-* + *sulf-* + ³*-an*] **:** a brownish crystalline insecticide $C_9H_6Cl_6O_3S$ that is used in the control of numerous crop insects and some mites, is relatively nontoxic to bees and warm-blooded vertebrates, and is potentially destructive to cold-blooded vertebrates (as fish)
endpoint* \ˈ=,=\ *n* [¹*end* + ¹*point*] **:** either of a pair of points that mark the limits of something (as a line segment or a sequence of values) or a point that marks the end of a ray
energetics* *n pl but sing in constr* **:** the total energy relations and transformations of a system (as a chemical reaction or an ecological community)
energizer* *n* **:** ANTIDEPRESSANT *herein*
energy budget *n* **:** an accounting of the income, use, and loss of energy in an ecosystem
en·tero·virus \ˌentərō+\ *n* [NL, fr. *enter-* + *virus*] **:** any of a group of picornaviruses that typically occur in the intestinal tract but may be involved in respiratory ailments, meningitis, and neurological disorders — **en·tero·viral** \"+\ *adj*
en·ven·om·ation \ən,venəˈmāshən, en,v-\ *n* -s [*envenom* + *-ation*] **:** an act or instance of impregnating with a venom (as of a snake or spider)
en·ven·om·iza·tion \-,mīˈzāshən\ *n* -s [*envenom* + *-ization*] **:** poisoning caused by a venomous bite or sting
environment* *n* **:** an artistic or theatrical work that involves or encompasses the spectator **:** an instance of environmental art or theater
environmental* *adj* **:** involving or encompassing the spectator rather than simply facing him ⟨~ art⟩ ⟨~ theater⟩
environmentalist* *n* **:** one concerned about the quality of the human environment; *specif* **:** a specialist in human ecology
epi·fauna \ˌepə, ˌepē+\ *n* [NL, fr. *epi-* + *fauna*] **:** benthic fauna living on the substrate and esp. on a hard sea floor — compare INFAUNA *herein* — **epi·faunal** \"+\ *adj*
episcopal vicar *n* **:** a bishop assigned to the pastoral supervision of a part of a Roman Catholic diocese
epi·some \ˈepə,sōm\ *n* -s [*epi-* + ³*-some*] **:** a genetic determinant or group of determinants (as of a bacterium) capable of existing autonomously or attached to a chromosome — **epi·som·al** \ˌepəˈsōməl\ *adj* — **epi·so·mic** \-ōmik\ *adj*
EPN \ˌē(ˌ)pēˈen\ *n* -s [*e*thyl *p*ara-*n*itro-phenyl] **:** a miticide and insecticide used esp. on cotton and orchard crops that enhances the toxicity of malathion to vertebrates
equi·gravi·sphere \ˌēkwəˈgravə,sfi(ə)r *sometimes* ˌek-\ *n* [*equi-* + *gravity* + *sphere*] **:** the area between the earth and a celestial body or between celestial bodies in which the gravitational influence of the bodies is equal
er·o·tol·o·gy \ˌerəˈtäləjē\ *n* -ES [Gk *erōt-*, *erōs* sexual love + *-logy* — more at EROS] **:** a description of lovemaking — **er·o·to·log·i·cal** \ˌerəd·ᵊlˈäjəkəl\ *adj*
er·y·thor·bate \ˌerəˈthòr,bāt\ *n* -s [*erythorbic acid* (prob. fr. *erythrose* + *ascorbic acid*) + *-ate*] **:** a salt of an optical isomer (**er·y·thor·bic acid** \-,thòrbik-\) of ascorbic acid that is used in various foods as an antioxidant
eryth·ro·poi·e·tin \ə,rithrəˈpòiətᵊn\ *n* -s [*erythropoietic* + *-in*] **:** a hormonal substance that is prob. formed in the kidney and stimulates red blood cell formation
escalate* *vb* ~ *vi* **:** to increase in extent, volume, number,

amount, or scope : EXPAND ⟨any limited nuclear war would rapidly ~ into full-scale disaster —*Sat. Eve. Post*⟩ ~ *vt* : to increase the extent, volume, number, amount, or scope of
escalation* *n* : an increasing in extent, volume, number, amount, or scope — **es·ca·la·to·ry** \ˈeskələ,tōrē\ *adj*
escudo* *n* -s **1** : the basic monetary unit of Chile established in 1960 — see MONEY table *in the Dict* **2** : a note representing one escudo
establishment* *n, often cap* **1** : a group of social, economic, and political leaders who form a ruling class (as of a nation) ⟨by *them* he meant not the English, but the governing classes, the *Establishment* —A.J.P.Taylor⟩ **2** : a controlling group ⟨the Welsh literary *Establishment* . . . kept him out of everything —Keidrych Rhys⟩
es·tro·ge·nic·i·ty \,estrəjəˈnisəd·ē\ *n* -ES [*estrogenic* + *-ity*] : capacity for estrogenic action or effect
eta particle *n* [¹*eta*] : an uncharged and spinless elementary particle with mass 1074 times the mass of an electron that decays rapidly into pions or gamma rays
etha·mi·van \eˈthamə,van, ,ethəˈmīvən\ *n* -S [di*ethyl* + *amide* + *vanillic* acid] : an analeptic drug related to vanillic acid and used in treating barbiturate poisoning
eth·no·musicology \ˌeth(,)nō+\ *n* [ISV *ethno-* + *musicology*] : a study of the music of non-European cultures — **eth·no·musicological** \"+\ *adj* — **eth·no·musicologist** \"+\ *n*
eth·no·science \"+\ *n* [*ethno-* + *science*] : the nature lore of primitive people
eth·o·sux·i·mide \,ethōˈsəksə,mīd\ *n* -S [*eth-* + *-suximide* (by shortening and alter. fr. *succinimide*)] : an antidepressant drug derived from succinic acid and used to relieve epilepsy
ETV *abbr* educational television *herein*
eu·phen·ics \yüˈfeniks, -nēks\ *n pl but sing in constr* [*eu-* + *phen-* (fr. *phenotype*) + *-ics*; after E *genotype*: *eugenics*] : a science that deals with the biological improvement of human beings after birth — **eu·phen·ic** *adj*
eu·ro·bond \ˈyu̇rō+,\ *n* -S *usu cap* [*euro*dollar (herein) + *bond*] : a bond of a U.S. corporation that is sold outside the U.S. and that is denominated and paid for in dollars and yields interest in dollars
eu·ro·crat \yu̇rə,krat\ *n* -S *usu cap* [ISV, fr. *Europe* + *-crat*] : a staff member of the administrative commission of the European Common Market
eu·ro·dollar \ˈyu̇rō+,\ *n* -S *usu cap* [*Europe* + *dollar*] : a U.S. dollar held outside the U.S. and esp. in Europe
eu·ro·po·centric \yəˌrōpə, ˌyu̇rəpə+\ *adj, usu cap* [*Europe*, continent + E *-o-* + *-centric*] : centered on Europe and the Europeans — **eu·ro·po·centrism** \-ˌsen·trizəm\ *n, usu cap*
EVA \,ē(,)vēˈā\ *abbr* extravehicular activity
ex·ac·ta \igˈzaktə, eg-\ *n* -S [AmSp *quiniela exacta* exact quiniela] : PERFECTA *herein*
exchange force *n* : a force between two elementary particles (as a neutron and a proton) arising from the incessant interchange between them of other particles (as pions)
exo·biology \ˌek(,)sō+\ *n* [*exo-* + *biology*] : extraterrestrial biology — **exobiological** \"+\ *adj* — **exo·biologist** \"+\ *n*
ex·o·cri·nol·o·gy \,eksəkrəˈnäləjē, -,krī-, -,krē-\ *n* -ES [*exocrine* + *-o-* + *-logy*] : the study of external secretions (as pheromones) that serve an integrative function
exo·nu·mia \,eksəˈn(y)ümēə\ *n pl* [NL, fr. *exo-* + E *numismatic* + NL *-ia* ³-ia] : numismatic items (as tokens, medals, or scrip) other than coins and paper money
exo·nu·mist \-məst, ˈ≠≠,≠≠\ *n* -S [*exonumia* + *-ist*] : a specialist in exonumia
exo·phil·ic \ˌeksəˈfilik\ *adj* [*exo-* + *-philic*] : ecologically independent of man and his domestic environment — compare ENDOPHILIC *herein* — **ex·oph·i·ly** \ekˈsäfəlē\ *n* -ES
exotic* *adj* : of or relating to striptease ⟨~ dancing⟩
exotic* *n* -S : a dancer who performs a striptease
explosive* *adj* : done by the force of a controlled explosion ⟨~ welding⟩ ⟨~ forming of metal parts⟩
ex·po \ˈek(,)spō\ *n* -S [by shortening] : EXPOSITION 3c
ex·tra·chromosomal \ˌekstrə+\ *adj* [*extra-* + *chromosomal*] : situated or controlled by factors outside the chromosomes
ex·tra·corporeal \ˌekstrə+\ *adj* [*extra-* + *corporeal*] : occurring or based outside the living body — **ex·tra·corporeally** \"+\ *adv*
ex·tra·solar \"+\ *adj* [*extra-* + *solar*] : originating or existing outside the solar system ⟨~ life⟩
ex·tra·vehicular \"+\ *adj* [*extra-* + *vehicular*] **1** : taking place outside a vehicle (as a spacecraft) ⟨~ activity⟩ **2** : relating to extravehicular activity ⟨an ~ assignment⟩
¹ex·trem·al \ikˈstrēməl, ekˈs-\ *n* -S [²*extreme* + *-al*, adj. suffix] : any curve that in the calculus of variations has the property of having the first variation of the integral of the given function over it equal to zero
²extremal \"\ *adj* : of, relating to, or being an extreme or an extremal
eyeliner \ˈ≠,≠\ *n* [¹*eye* + ¹*liner*] : makeup used to emphasize the contour of the eyes
f* *abbr* femto- *herein*
fab·ri·ca·ble \ˈfabrəkəbəl\ *adj* [LL *fabricabilis*, fr. L *fabricari* to fabricate — more at FABRIC] : capable of being shaped ⟨~ alloys⟩ — **fab·ri·ca·bil·i·ty** \,fabrəkəˈbiləd·ē\ *n* -ES
face fly *n* : a European fly (*Musca autumnalis*) similar to the housefly that is widely established in No. America and causes great distress to livestock by clustering about the face
face-off* *n* : CONFRONTATION
fading* *n* : the gradual withdrawal of hints or cues to the student in programmed instruction — called also *vanishing*
fag·got·ry \ˈfagə·trē\ *n* -ES [*faggot* + *-ry*] : HOMOSEXUALITY
fail* *n* : a failure (as by a security dealer) to deliver or receive securities within a prescribed period after a purchase or sale
fail-safe \ˈ≠,≠\ *adj* [*fail* + *safe*, adj.] **1** : incorporating some feature for automatically counteracting the effect of an anticipated possible source of failure **2** : being or relating to a safeguard that prevents continuing on a bombing mission according to a preconceived plan
fake book *n* [³*fake* (to improvise) + *book*] : a book that contains the melody lines of popular copyrighted songs without accompanying harmonies and that is published without the permission of the copyright owners
fallout* *n* : an incidental result or product ⟨the war . . . produced its own literary ~— a profusion of books —*Newsweek*⟩
family* *n* : a group constituting a unit of a crime syndicate (as the Mafia) and engaging in underworld activities within a defined geographical area
family planning *n* : planning of the number and spacing of one's children by effective methods of birth control
family room *n* : a large room designed as a recreation center for members of a family
fan-jet \ˈ≠,≠\ *n* [¹*fan* + *jet*] **1** : a jet engine having a ducted fan in its forward end that draws in extra air whose compression and expulsion provide extra thrust **2** : an airplane powered by a fan-jet engine
fantasy* *vi* : to imagine a sexually stimulating situation esp. as an adjunct to autoeroticism
faraday rotation *n, usu cap F* **1** : optical rotation of a beam of polarized light due to the Faraday effect **2** : rotation of a beam of polarized microwaves traversing an isotropic medium along the lines of force of a magnetic field
far-out \ˈ≠,≠\ *adj* [*far out* (adverbial phrase), fr. ME *fer oute*, fr. *fer* far + *out, oute* out] : marked by a considerable departure from the conventional or traditional : EXTREME ⟨a small, *far-out*, but fervent religious sect —Joseph Alsop⟩ — **far-out** \ˈ≠,≠\ *n* — **far-out·ness** \ˈ≠ˈ≠nəs\ *n*
far-red \ˈ≠,≠\ *adj* [²*far* + *red*] **1** : lying in the part of the infrared spectrum farthest from the red — used of radiations with wavelengths between 30 and about 1000 microns **2** : lying in the part of the infrared spectrum nearest to the red — used of radiations with wavelengths starting at about .8 micron
fastback *n* [¹*fast* + ¹*back*] **1** \ˈ≠,≠\ : a back roof on a closed passenger automobile sloping in a long unbroken line toward the rear bumper **2** \ˈ≠,≠\ : an automobile having a fastback
fa·ve·la *also* **fa·vel·la** \fəˈvelə\ *n* -S [Pg *favela*] : a settlement of jerry-built shacks lying on the outskirts of a Brazilian city
fax \ˈfaks\ *n* -ES [by shortening and alter.] : FACSIMILE 2
FDC* *abbr* fleur de coin *herein*
federal funds *n pl* : uncommitted reserves of a Federal Reserve member bank available for interbank loans esp. to enable other banks to maintain their legally required reserves
fem·to- \ˈfem(p)(,)tō\ *comb form* [ISV, fr. Dan or Norw *femten* fifteen (fr. ON *fimmtān*) + *-o-* — more at FIFTEEN] : one quadrillionth (10^{-15}) part of ⟨*femto*ampere⟩
fer·mi \ˈfer(,)mē\ *n* -S [after Enrico *Fermi* †1954 Ital. physicist] : a unit of length equal to 10^{-13} centimeter
fer·re·dox·in \,ferəˈdäksən\ *n* -S [L *ferrum* iron + E *redox* + *-in* — more at FARRIER] : an iron-containing plant protein that functions in intercellular electron transport
fertility pill *n* : a pill that tends to bring about the most fertile period of the female at an exact time and thereby enhances the effectiveness of the rhythm method of birth control
fetal position *n* : a resting position with body curved, legs bent and drawn toward the chest, head bowed forward, and arms tucked in in the manner of the fetus in the womb
fiberfill \ˈ≠≠,≠\ *n* [*fiber* + *fill*] : man-made fibers (as of polyester) used as a filling material (as for cushions)
fiber optic *n* : a very thin transparent homogenous fiber (as of plastic) that is enclosed by material of lower refractive index and transmits light throughout its length by internal reflections; *also* : a bundle of such fibers used in an instrument for bending light or seeing around corners
fi·bo·nac·ci number \,fēbəˈnächē-\ *n, usu cap F* [after Leonardo *Fibonacci* (Leonardo Pisano) †*ab* 1250 Ital. mathematician] : a number in the unending series 0, 1, 1, 2, 3, 5, 8, 13, . . . of which the first two terms are 0 and 1 and each succeeding term is the sum of the two immediately preceding
fi·bro·calcific \ˌfī(,)brō+\ *adj* [*fibr-* + *calcific*] : relating to or involving both fibrotic and calcific changes ⟨~ lesions⟩
fiche \ˈfēsh\ *n* -S [by shortening] : MICROFICHE
fiddle* *n* [Brit. slang *fiddle* to cheat, fr. ²*fiddle*] *Brit* : SWINDLE
fi·do \ˈfīd(,)ō\ *n* -S [*f*reaks + *i*rregulars + *d*efects + *o*ddities] : a coin having a minting error
fiduciary* *adj* : being a mark or set of marks in the reticle of an optical instrument used as a point of reference or for a measure
field* *n* : a particular area (as a column on a punched card) in which the same type of information is regularly recorded
field* *vt* : to give an impromptu answer or solution to ⟨~*ed* the questions with ease⟩
field ion microscope *n* : a high-magnification microscope in which an image of the atoms of a metal surface is formed on a fluorescent screen by means of usu. helium ions formed in a high-voltage electric field
filmcard \ˈ≠,≠\ *n* [¹*film* + *card*] : MICROFICHE
film·og·ra·phy \filˈmägrəfē\ *n* -ES [¹*film* + *-o-* + *-graphy*] : a list of motion pictures featuring the work of a prominent film figure (as an actor) or relating to a particular topic
filmsetting \ˈ≠,≠≠\ *n* [¹*film* + *setting*] : PHOTOCOMPOSITION — **filmset** \ˈ≠,≠\ *adj* — **filmset** *vt* — **filmsetter** \ˈ≠,≠≠\ *n*
finance company* *n* : a company that specializes in making small loans usu. to individuals
financial service *n* : an organization that studies the business situation and security market and makes investment recommendations usu. in a regularly issued publication
fink* *n* : one who is disapproved of or is held in contempt
fink out *vi* **1** : to fail miserably **2** : to back out : COP OUT ⟨others . . . *finked out* in the fat of middle-age—Seymour Krim⟩
fireflood \ˈ≠,≠\ *or* **fireflooding** \ˈ≠,≠≠\ *n* [¹*fire* + ¹*flood* or *flooding*] : the process of injecting compressed air into a petroleum reservoir and burning some of the oil so as to drive the rest of the oil into producing wells
fish-eye \ˈ≠,≠\ *adj* [so called fr. the resemblance of the lens to the protruding eye of a fish] : being, having, or produced by a wide-angle photographic lens that has a highly curved protruding front, that covers an angle of about 180 degrees, and that gives a circular image ⟨a ~ view⟩ ⟨a ~ camera⟩
fish protein concentrate *n* : FISH FLOUR
fixed-point \ˈ≠ˈ≠\ *adj* : involving or being a mathematical notation (as in a decimal system) in which the point separating whole numbers and fractions is fixed
flakeboard \ˈ≠,≠\ *n* [*flake* + *board*] : a composition board made of flakes of wood bonded with synthetic resin
flanker back *n* : a football back who on offense lines up on the flank slightly behind the line of scrimmage
flashcube \ˈ≠,≠\ *n* [²*flash* + *cube*] : a cubical device that incorporates four flashbulbs, is usu. attached to a camera, and can be turned for taking four pictures in rapid succession
flashed glass *n* : glass in which a very thin layer of colored glass or of a metallic oxide is flashed to clear glass
flash-forward \ˈ≠ˈ≠≠\ *n* -S [*flash* (as in ¹*flashback*) + *forward*, adv.] : a literary or theatrical technique used esp. in motion pictures and television that involves interruption of the chronological sequence of events by interjection of events or scenes of future occurrence; *also* : an instance of a flash-forward
fleur de coin \ˌflərdəˌkwaⁿ\ *adj* [F *à fleur de coin*, lit., with the bloom of the die] : being in the preserved mint condition
flex·a·gon \ˈfleksə,gän\ *n* -S [¹*flex* + *-agon* (as in *hexagon*)] : a folded paper figure that can be flexed into numerous arrangements of its faces
flight bag *n* **1** : a traveling bag usu. with zippered outside compartments for use esp. in air travel; *esp* : one that fits under an airplane seat **2** : a small thin lightweight canvas satchel decorated with the name of an airline
flip* *vi* **1** : to lose self-control ⟨when he ~*s* it takes three men to hold him —Eddie Krell⟩ **2** : to become extremely enthusiastic
flip side *n* [¹*flip* (to turn over)] : the reverse and usu. less popular side of a phonograph record
floating-point \ˈ≠≠ˈ≠\ *adj* [²*floating* + *point*] : involving or being a mathematical notation in which a quantity is denoted by one number multiplied by a power of the number base ⟨the fixed-point value 99.9 could be expressed in a *floating-point* system as .999 × 10^2⟩
flo·ka·ti \flōˈkätē\ *n, pl* **flokati** *or* **floka·tes** \-ā,tes\ [NGk *phlokatē*, fr. *phloko* strand of wool, prob. fr. G *flocke* flock of wool (fr. MHG *vlocke*) — more at FLOCK] : a hand-woven Greek rug with a thick shaggy pile
floor partner *n* : a member of a brokerage firm who owns a seat on an exchange and acts as floor broker for his firm
flower bug *n* : any of various small mostly black-and-white predaceous bugs (family Anthocoridae) that frequent flowers and feed on pest insects (as aphids and thrips)
flower child *n* : a hippie who indicates his belief in love, beauty, and peace by wearing or displaying flowers
flower people *n pl* : FLOWER CHILDREN
flu·er·ic \(ˈ)flüˈerik\ *adj* [irreg. fr. L *fluere* to flow + E *-ic* — more at FLUID] : FLUIDIC *herein*
flu·er·ics \flüˈeriks\ *n pl but usu sing in constr* [*flueric* (herein) + *-s*] : FLUIDICS *herein*
fluidic* *adj* : of, relating to, or being a device (as an amplifier or control) that depends for operation on the pressures and flows of a fluid in precisely shaped channels — **fluidic** *n* -S
flu·id·ics \flüˈidiks\ *n pl but usu sing in constr* [²*fluid* + *-ics*] : the technology of fluidic devices
flu·id·on·ics \,flüəˈdäniks\ *n pl but usu sing in constr* [²*fluid* + *-onics* (as in *electronics*)] : FLUIDICS *herein*
flu·o·ri·diz·er \ˈflu̇rə,dīzə(r), -lōr-, -lȯr-\ *n* -S [*fluoridize* + *-er*] **1** : one that fluoridizes **2** : a fluorine-containing water and oil repellent finish for textiles
flu·o·ro·uracil \" + \ *n* [*fluor-* + *uracil*] : a fluorine-containing pyrimidine base used to treat some kinds of cancer
flying crane *n* : a helicopter equipped with a crane and used esp. for lifting and transporting heavy cargoes
FOBS *abbr* fractional orbital bombardment system *herein*
foggy bottom *n, usu cap F & B* [fr. *Foggy Bottom*, section of Washington, D.C., in which the offices of the Department of State are located] : the U.S. Department of State
foil* *n* : HYDROFOIL
folk mass *n* : a mass in which traditional liturgical music is replaced by folk music
folk-rock \ˈ≠,≠\ *n* : folk songs sung to a rock 'n' roll background — **folk-rock** *adj* — **folk-rock·er** \ˈ≠,≠ə(r\ *n*
fondue fork *n* : a long slender usu. 2-tined fork used in eating or cooking fondue
food stamp *n* : a government-issued stamp that is sold or given to families on welfare and is redeemable for a specific type or amount of food
footpad* *n* : a flattish foot on the leg of a spacecraft for distributing weight to minimize sinking into a surface
format *vt* **formatted; formatted; formatting; formats** [*format*, n.] : to produce (as a book, printed matter, or data) in a particular form (as print) or style
formula *adj* [*formula*, n.] *of a racing car* : conforming to prescribed specifications of size, weight, and engine displacement and usu. having a long narrow body with a single seat
formula investing *n* : investing according to a plan (**formula plan**) under which more funds are invested in equity securities when the market is low and more are put into fixed-income securities when the market advances
for·tran \ˈfȯr-,tran\ *n* -S *usu cap F or all cap* [*for*mula *tran*slation] : an algebraic and logical language for programming a computer
fortune cookie *n* : a thin folded cookie containing a slip of paper on which is printed a fortune, proverb, or humorous statement
found object *n* [trans. of F *objet trouvé*] : a natural or discarded object (as a piece of driftwood or junk) found by chance and held to have aesthetic value esp. through the working of natural forces on it
found poem *n* : a poem consisting of words found in a nonpoetic context (as a telephone directory) and usu. rearranged by the poet into poetic form
FPC* *abbr* fish protein concentrate *herein*
fractional orbital bombardment system *n* : a system for delivering a nuclear warhead from orbit by slowing it down by a retrorocket before completion of an orbit
frame* *n* : a minimal unit of instruction or stimulus in a programmed instruction routine : a unit of programmed instruction calling for a response by the student
fran·chi·see \ˌfranchəˈzē, -,chī-, -raan- *sometimes* -ˈsē\ *n* -S [¹*franchise* + *-ee*] : one who is granted a franchise to operate a unit in a chain of business establishments
fran·co-american \ˌfraŋ(,)kō+\ *n, cap F&A* [*Franco-* + *American*] : an American of French or esp. French-Canadian descent — **franco-american** *adj, usu cap F&A*
fran·co·phone \ˈfraŋkə,fōn\ *adj, often cap* [F, fr. *franco-* Franco- + Gk *phōnē* voice, speech — more at BAN] : consisting of or belonging to a French-speaking population
fran·glais \fräⁿˈglā, -äŋˈg-\ *n, usu cap* [F, blend of *français* French and *anglais* English] : French marked by a considerable number of borrowings from English
freak* *n* **1** : ENTHUSIAST **2** : one who uses drugs
freak out *vb* [*freak*, n. (herein) + *out*, adv.] *vi* **1** : to withdraw from reality and society esp. by taking drugs **2** : to experience nightmarish hallucinations as a result of taking drugs : have a bad trip **3** : to behave irrationally or unconventionally under or as if under the influence of drugs ~ *vt* **1** : to put under the influence of a psychedelic drug **2** : to put into a state of intense excitement ⟨what he saw *freaked* him *out* so much that he still gets shaken when he remembers it —*Berkeley Barb*⟩
freak-out \ˈ≠,≠\ *n* [*freak out* (herein)] **1** : a withdrawal from reality esp. by means of drugs **2 a** : a drug-induced state of mind characterized by terrifying hallucinations : a bad trip **b** : an irrational act by one that freaks out **3** : a gathering of hippies **4** : one who freaks out
free-associate \ˌ≠≠ˈ≠≠,≠\ *vi* [back-formation fr. *free association*] : to engage in free association
free·bie *or* **free·bee** \ˈfrēbē, -bi\ *n* -S [by alter. fr. obs. slang *freeby* gratis, fr. *free* + *-by*, of unknown origin] : something (as a theater ticket) given or received without charge
freedom ride *n, often cap F&R* : a ride made by civil rights workers through states of the southern U.S. to ascertain whether public facilities (as bus terminals) are desegregated — **freedom rider** *n, often cap F&R*
free safety *n* : a safety man in football who has no specific pass receiver to guard in a man-to-man defense and who usu. helps wherever needed on defense
free university *n* : an unaccredited autonomous free institution established within a university by students to present and discuss subjects not usu. dealt with in the academic curriculum
frog* *n* : a small holder with perforations or spikes that is placed in a bowl or vase to keep cut flowers in position
front-end load \ˈ≠,≠-\ *n* [³*front* + ¹*end* + ¹*load*] : the part of the total load taken out of early payments under a contract plan for the periodic purchase of investment-company shares
fron·te·nis \ˌfränˈtenəs, (ˈ)frän-\ *n* [AmerSp, blend of Sp *frontón* pelota court and *tenis* tennis, fr. E *tennis* — more at FRONTON] : a game of Mexican origin played with rackets and a rubber ball on a 3-walled court
frosting* *n* : the lightening (as by chemicals) of small strands of hair throughout the entire head to produce a two-tone effect — compare STREAKING *herein*
fruit machine *n* [fr. the use of pictures of various fruits as symbols to be matched] *Brit* : SLOT MACHINE 2
fuel cell *n* : a device that converts the chemical energy of a fuel (as hydrogen) directly into electrical energy continuously
funk* *n* : funky music
funky* *adj* -ER/-EST : having an earthy unsophisticated style and feeling; *specif* : having the style and feeling of early blues
fu·tu·rol·o·gy \ˌfyüchəˈräləjē\ *n* [*future* + *-o-* + *-logy*] : a study that deals with future possibilities based on current trends — **fu·tu·rol·o·gist** \-jəst\ *n* -S
g* *abbr, cap* giga-
ga·ga·ku \gäˈgä(,)kü\ *n, often cap* [Jap, fr. *ga* elegance + *gaku* music] : the ancient court music of Japan
ga·le·ro \gəˈle(ə)r(,)ō\ *n* -S [It, fr. L *galerus*, *galera* cap of skin worn by certain flamens — more at GALERA] : the flat-crowned wide-brimmed tasseled red hat formerly worn by Roman Catholic cardinals — called also *cardinal's hat*
gallium arsenide *n* : a synthetic compound GaAs used esp. as a semiconducting material
gallows humor *n* : humor that makes fun of a very serious or terrifying situation
game ball* *n* : a ball (as a football) presented by the members of a team to a player or coach in recognition of his contribution to the team's victory
gamma decay *n* **1** : a radioactive transformation of an atomic nucleus in which the nucleus loses energy by emitting a gamma ray without change of mass number or atomic number **2** : the decay of an unstable elementary particle in which one or more photons are emitted
gamma ray* *n* : a high-energy photon
gang bang *n* -S : copulation by several persons with the same passive partner — **gang-bang** *vb*
gan·gle \ˈgaŋgəl, -aiŋ-\ *vi* -ED/-ING/-S [back-formation fr. *gangling*] : to move in an awkward ungraceful manner — **gangle** *n*
gang·sa \ˈgäŋ(,)sä\ *n* -S [Indonesian *gampang gangsa*, fr. *gampang* musical instrument consisting of bars struck by hammers + *gangsa* brass] : a Balinese metallophone with bamboo resonators
gantry* *n* : a movable scaffold with platforms at different levels for use in erecting and servicing rockets before launching
gar·çon·nière \ˌgärsᵊnˈye(ə)r\ *n* -S [F, fr. *garçon* boy, bachelor — more at GARÇON] : a bachelor apartment
gar·vey·ism \ˈgärvē,izəm\ *n* -S *usu cap* [Marcus *Garvey* †1940 Jamaican Black Nationalist + E *-ism*] : a 20th century racial and political doctrine advocating black separation and the formation of self-governing black nations in Africa — **gar·vey·ite** \-ē,īt\ *n* -S *usu cap*
gas chromatography *n* : chromatographic analysis in which the sample is carried in vapor form through a column of absorbing material usu. along with a carrier gas (as nitrogen or helium) — **gas chromatographic** *adj*
gas·dy·namics \ˌ≠ˈ≠≠\ *n pl but sing in constr* [*gas* + *dynamics*] : a branch of dynamics that deals with gaseous fluids including products of combustion and plasmas — **gasdynamic** *adj* — **gasdynamicist** *n* -S
gaudy ironstone *n* : a polychrome-decorated mid-19th century English ironstone ware
gaussian integer *n, usu cap G* [Karl Friedrich *Gauss* †1855 Ger. mathematician + E *-ian*] : a complex number $a + bi$ where a and b are integers and $i = \sqrt{-1}$
gaussian plane *n, usu cap G* : COMPLEX PLANE
GB \(ˈ)jēˈbē\ *n* -S [code name] : SARIN
gene pool *n* : the whole body of different genes available for exchange and recombination within a population
general obligation bond *n* : a municipal of which payment of interest and principal is backed by the taxing power and credit of the issuing governmental unit
general term *n* : a mathematical term composed of constants

and variables that when specific values are substituted for the variables yields the successive terms of a series

generative grammar *n* **1 :** a description in the form of an ordered set of rules for producing the grammatical sentences of a language **2 :** TRANSFORMATIONAL GRAMMAR

generic* *n* **:** a generic drug

genetic code *n* **:** the self-reproducing record of the specific protein pattern of an organism which is apparently stored in triplets of sequential nucleotides in the nuclear deoxyribonucleic acid and which is transmitted through a series of ribonucleic acids to the cytoplasmic seats of protein syntheses

genetic engineering *n* **:** alteration of hereditary defects by intervention in gene-controlled bodily processes and when practicable by directed changes in the genetic material

geno·plasm \ˈjēnə,plazəm, -en-\ *n* [*²gen-* + *-plasm*] **:** GERM PLASM

geo·corona \ˌjēō+\ *n* [*ge-* + *corona*] **:** the outermost part of the earth's atmosphere consisting primarily of hydrogen

geology* *n* **:** a study of the solid matter of a celestial body

geo·probe \ˈjēə,prōb\ *n* [*ge-* + *probe*] **:** a rocket for exploration near the earth but at distances of more than 4000 miles

geo·stationary \ˌjē(,)ō+\ *adj* [*ge-* + *stationary*] **:** of, relating to, or being an artificial satellite that travels from west to east at an altitude of over 22,000 miles above the equator and at the same speed as that of the earth's rotation so that the satellite seems to remain in the same place

geo·synchronous \"+\ *adj* [*ge-* + *synchronous*] **:** GEOSTATIONARY *herein*

give-up* *n* [*give up*, vb.; fr. the giving up by the first broker of part of the commission to the second] **1 :** a security or commodity market order which one broker executes for a client of a second broker and the commission for which is shared by the two brokers **2 :** the part of a commission due a broker from a major client (as a mutual fund) that he is directed by the client to turn over to another broker who has provided special services (as research or sale of fund shares) to the client

glitch \ˈglich\ *n* -ES [prob. fr. G *glitschen* to slip, slide, fr. MHG intensive of *gliten* to glide, fr. OHG *glītan* — more at GLIDE] **1 :** an unwanted brief surge of electric power **:** a false or spurious electronic signal **2 :** MALFUNCTION ⟨a ~ in the fuel cell of a spacecraft⟩ **3 :** MISHAP; *also* **:** a minor technical problem

glu·co·neo·gen·ic \ˌglükō,nēəˈjenik\ *adj* [*gluconeogenesis* + *-ic*] **:** GLUCONEOGENETIC

glu·teth·i·mide \glüˈtethə,mīd, -,məd\ *n* [*glutaryl* + *eth-* + *imide*] **:** a sedative-hypnotic drug chemically and physiologically related to phenobarbital

glyph* *n* [short for *hieroglyph*] **:** a symbol (as a curved arrow on a road sign) that carries information nonverbally

gno·to·biology \ˌnōd·ə+\ *n* [Gk *gnōtos* known + E *biology*] **:** GNOTOBIOTICS *herein* — **gno·to·biologist** \"+\ *n*

gno·to·bi·ot·ic \ˌnōd·ōbīˈäd·ik *also* -bēˈä-\ *adj* [Gk *gnōtos* known (fr. *gignōskein* to know) + *biotē* life, way of life + E *-ic* — more at KNOW, BIOTA] **:** of, relating to, living in, or being an environment containing one or a known few kinds of organisms; *also* **:** AXENIC — **gno·to·bi·ote** \ˌnōd·əˈbī,ōt\ *n* -S — **gno·to·bi·ot·i·cal·ly** \ˌnōd·ōbīˈäd·ək(ə)lē *also* -bēˈä-\ *adv*

gno·to·bi·ot·ics \ˈnōd·ōbīˈäd·iks\ *n pl but sing in constr* [*gnotobiotic* (herein) + *-s*] **:** the raising and study of animals under gnotobiotic conditions

go* *vb* — **go public** *of a close corporation* **:** to offer stock for sale to the general public

go *adj* [¹*go*] **:** functioning properly **:** being in good and ready condition ⟨declared all systems ~⟩

go-go \ˈgō-(,)gō\ *adj* [by shortening] **1 :** A-GO-GO *herein* ⟨*go-go* dancers⟩ **2 :** not conservative **:** UNRESTRAINED ⟨play *go-go* baseball⟩ **3 :** using such tools of speculation as leverage and short selling **:** SPECULATIVE ⟨a *go-go* mutual fund⟩

gold·en·ag·er \ˌgōldənˈājə(r)\ *n* -S [*Golden Age clubs*, organizations for recreational activities of the elderly + E *-er*] **:** an elderly person; *esp* **:** one who has retired

gold point* *n* **:** a fixed point on the international temperature scale equal to the melting point of gold or 1063°C

golf cart *n* **1 :** a small cart for carrying a golf bag around a golf course **2 :** a motorized cart for carrying a golfer and his equipment over a golf course

gondola* *n* **:** an enclosed car suspended from a cable and used for transporting passengers; *esp* **:** one used as a ski lift

go-no-go \ˈgōˈnō,gō\ *adj* [¹*go* + ¹*no* + ¹*go*] **1 :** being or relating to a required decision to continue or stop a course of action **2 :** being or relating to a point at which a go-no-go decision must be made

goof-off \ˈ=,=\ *n* [fr. the verb phrase *goof off*] **:** one who evades work or responsibility

goofy-foot \ˈgüfē,fu̇t\ *or* **goofy-foot·er** \-u̇d·ə(r\ *n, pl* **goofy-foots** *or* **goofy-footers :** a surfer who rides a surfboard with the right foot forward

gox *abbr* gaseous oxygen

grab* *vt* **:** to forcefully engage the attention of ⟨the technique of *grabbing* an audience —Pauline Kael⟩

grade point *n* **:** a numerical value assigned to each academic letter grade (as F=0, D=1, C=2, B=3, A=4) that is multiplied by the number of credits for the course

grade-point average *n* **:** the average obtained by dividing the total number of grade points by the total number of credits earned

gram·mat·i·cal·i·ty \grə,mad·əˈkaləd·ē\ *n* -ES [*grammatical* + *-ity*] **:** the quality or state of being grammatical

gram·my \ˈgramē, -mi\ *n, pl* **grammys** *or* **grammies** *usu cap* [*gramophone* + *-my* (as in *Emmy*)] **:** any of several gold-plated statuettes awarded annually by a professional organization for notable achievement in phonograph recording

granny glasses *n pl* **:** spectacles with usu. small oval, round, or square lenses and metal frames

grants·man·ship \ˈgran(t)smən,ship, -aa-,ai-,-á-\ *n* -S [*grants* + *-manship* (herein)] **:** the art of obtaining grants

graphic* *n* **:** a graphic representation displayed by a computer (as on a cathode-ray tube); *also* **:** the process whereby a computer displays such graphics and an operator can manipulate them (as with a light pen) — often used in pl.

grass* *n* **:** MARIJUANA

gravi·sphere \ˈgravə,sfi(ə)r\ *n* [*gravity* + *sphere*] **:** the sphere of space in which the gravitational influence of a particular celestial body is predominant

gravitational collapse *n* **:** the tendency of particles to move rapidly toward a common center of gravity that results in the formation of stars, star clusters, and galaxies from the dilute gas of interstellar space

gravitational interaction *n* **:** the weakest interaction of the four fundamental interactions in nature that is hypothesized to act between elementary particles but that has been observed only on a larger scale — compare ELECTROMAGNETIC INTERACTION, STRONG INTERACTION, WEAK INTERACTION *herein*

gravitational wave *n* **:** a hypothetical wave which travels at the speed of light and by means of which gravitational attraction effect is propagated

grav·i·ton \ˈgravə,tän\ *n* -S [ISV *gravity* + ²*-on*] **:** a hypothetical particle with zero charge and rest mass that is held to be the quantum of the gravitational field

gravity wave* *n* **:** GRAVITATIONAL WAVE *herein*

green beret *n, usu cap G&B* [so called fr. the green beret worn as part of his uniform] **:** a member of the U.S. Army Special Forces

greenhouse effect *n* **:** the warming of the lower layers of the atmosphere near the surface of the earth caused by a complicated process that starts with solar radiation and involves selective transmission, absorption, and emission of infrared radiation by the water vapor and carbon dioxide in the air

grem·mie *also* **grem·my** \ˈgremē, -mi\ *n, pl* **gremmies** [*gremlin* + *-ie*] **:** a young or inexperienced surfer; *esp* **:** one whose behavior is objectionable — called also *gremlin*

groove* *vb* [fr. the phrase *in the groove*] *vt* **1 :** to enjoy appreciatively ⟨~*s* exciting experiences⟩ **2 :** to excite pleasurably ⟨*grooving* their minds with cannabis —Stephen Nemo⟩ ~ *vi* **1 :** to enjoy oneself intensely **:** experience keen pleasure ⟨self-perception that informs you how and when to ~ in your own way —Al Calloway⟩ **2 :** to interact harmoniously ⟨contemporary minds and rock ~ together —Benjamin De Mott⟩

ground-effect machine *n* [so called fr. the support provided by the cushion of air as if the vehicle rode on the ground] **:** a vehicle for traveling over land or water a short distance above the surface supported on a cushion of air produced by downwardly directed fans

group* *n* **:** a mathematical system consisting of a set of elements and an operation such that the operation on any pair of elements yields an element of the set, the operation is associative, and for each element there is an inverse element such that the operation on the element and its inverse yields the identity element

group·ie \ˈgrüpē, -pi\ *n* -S [¹*group* + *-ie*] **:** a girl admirer of a rock group; *esp* **:** one who follows the group on tour

group theory *n* **:** a branch of mathematics dealing with the properties of groups

growth* *n* **:** anticipated progressive growth in capital value and income ⟨younger investors may prefer ~ to immediate income⟩

growth company *n* **:** a company that grows at a greater rate than the economy as a whole

gua·neth·i·dine \gwäˈnethə,dēn, -ədən\ *n* -S [*guanidine* + *eth-*] **:** a drug used esp. in treating severe high blood pressure

gun* *n* **:** a heavy surfboard that is usu. longer than a Malibu board, has a round nose and a tapered tail, and is used in big surf over 15 feet in height — called also *big gun*

gunn effect \ˈgən-\ *n, usu cap G* [after J. B. *Gunn* b1928 Brit. physicist] **:** the production of rapid fluctuations of current when the voltage applied to a semiconductor device exceeds a critical value with the result that microwave power is generated

gunship \ˈ=,=\ *n* **:** an armed helicopter used esp. for protecting troop transport helicopters against ground fire

gus·sy up \ˌgəsēˈəp\ *vt* [origin unknown] **:** to dress up

gut *adj* [¹*gut*] **1 :** arising from one's inmost self **:** VISCERAL ⟨a ~ reaction to the misery he has seen —J.A.Lukas⟩ **2 :** having strong impact or immediate relevance ⟨~ issues⟩

gyp·lure \ˈjip,lu̇(ə)r\ *n* [*gypsy* + *lure*] **:** a synthetic sex attractant used in trapping male gypsy moths

gy·ro·cop·ter \ˈjīrə,käptə(r\ *n* -S [*autogyro* + *helicopter*] **:** a usu. one-passenger rotary-wing aircraft that is driven forward by a conventional propeller

gy·ro·dynamics \ˌjī(,)rō+\ *n pl but sing in constr* [*gyr-* + *dynamics*] **:** a branch of dynamics that deals with rotating bodies and esp. gyroscopes

hacking pocket *n* [so called fr. its use on hacking coats] **:** a slanted coat pocket usu. with a flap

ha·dal \ˈhādᵊl\ *adj* [F, fr. *Hadès* Hades + *-al*] **:** of, relating to, or being the parts of the ocean below 6000 meters

had·ron \ˈha,drän\ *n* -S [ISV *hadr-* + ²*-on*] **:** any one of a class of elementary particles consisting of the pion and all heavier particles that takes part in the strong interactions

haf·nia \ˈhafnēə\ *n* -S [NL, fr. *hafnium* + *-a*] **:** a white refractory crystalline oxide HfO_2 of hafnium

hailer* *n* [short for *loud-hailer*] **:** BULLHORN

hairweaving \ˈ=,==\ *n* **:** the process of covering a bald spot with human hair and nylon thread woven into the wearer's own hair — **hairweave** \ˈ=,=\ *n* — **hair weaver** *n*

ha·la·la *also* **ha·la·lah** \həˈlälə\ *n, pl* **halala** *or* **halalas** [Ar] **1 :** a monetary unit of Saudi Arabia equal to 1/100 riyal — see MONEY table *in the Dict* **2 :** a coin representing one halala

halfway house* *n* **:** a center for formerly institutionalized individuals (as mental patients or drug addicts) that is designed to facilitate their readjustment to private life

hallucinate* *vt* **:** to perceive or experience as an hallucination

halo·cline \ˈhalə,klīn\ *n* -S [*hal-* + *-cline*] **:** a usu. vertical gradient in salinity

hal·o·thane \ˈhalə,thān\ *n* -S [*halogen* + *ethane*] **:** a nonexplosive inhalational anesthetic

handprint \ˈ=,=\ *n* **:** an impression of a hand on a surface

hang* *vb* — **hang five :** to ride a surfboard with the weight of the body forward and the toes of one foot turned over the front edge of the board — **hang ten :** to ride a surfboard with the weight of the body forward and the toes of both feet turned over the front edge of the board

hanging curve *n* **:** an intended curve ball that fails to break

hang-up* *n* **:** a source of mental or emotional difficulty

ha·ni·wa \ˈhänə,wä\ *n, pl* **haniwa** [Jap] **:** a large baked clay figure usu. in the form of a hollow cylinder or a crude human figure placed in groups on early Japanese grave mounds

happening* *n* **:** an event or series of events designed to evoke a spontaneous audience reaction to sensory, emotional, or spiritual stimuli: as **a :** the activities concurrent with or involved in the creation or presentation of a nonrepresentational art object (as an action painting) **b :** a usu. unrehearsed staged performance utilizing art objects and sound effects for chance and impromptu results

hap·to·glo·bin \ˈhaptə,glōbən\ *n* -S [Gk *haptein* to fasten, bind + E *-o-* + *hemoglobin* — more at APSIS] **:** a carbohydrate-containing serum alpha globulin that can combine with and may have a protective action toward hemoglobin

hard* *adj, of a drug* **:** being both addictive and gravely detrimental to health ⟨such ~ drugs as heroin⟩

hard copy *n* **:** copy (as that produced in connection with a computer) that is readable without use of a special device

hard-edge \ˈ=ˌ=\ *adj* **:** of or relating to abstract painting characterized by geometric forms with clearly defined boundaries

hardened* *adj* **:** protected from possible danger from blast or heat by means of concrete or earth or by being situated underground ⟨a ~ missile launching site⟩ ⟨a ~ missile⟩

hard-line \ˈ=ˈ=\ *adj* **:** advocating a persistently firm course of action **:** UNYIELDING ⟨*hard-line* policy toward polluters⟩

hard-lin·er \ˈhärdˈlīnə(r)\ *n* [*hard-line* (herein) + *-er*] **:** an advocate of a hard-line policy

hard rock *n* **:** basic rock 'n' roll in its original style

hardware* *n* **:** the physical components (as mechanical and electrical devices) of a vehicle or an apparatus

hawk* *n* **:** one who takes a militant attitude (as in a dispute) and advocates immediate vigorous action — compare DOVE *herein* — **hawk·ish** *adj* — **hawk·ish·ly** *adv* — **hawk·ish·ness** *n* -ES

haw·thorne effect \ˈhȯ,thȯrn-\ *n, usu cap H* [fr. the *Hawthorne* Works of the Western Electric Co., Cicero, Ill., where its existence was established by experiment] **:** the stimulation to output or accomplishment (as in an industrial or educational methods study) that results from the mere fact of being under concerned observation

hay·lage \ˈhālij\ *n* -S [²*hay* + *silage*] **:** a stored forage that is essentially a grass silage wilted to 35 to 50 percent moisture

head* *n* [short for *pothead* (herein) or *acidhead* (herein)] **:** one who uses a drug (as LSD or marijuana)

head dip *n* **:** a surfing feat in which a surfer squats on the board, leans forward, and dips his head into the wave

headrest* *n* **:** a resilient pad at the top of the back of an automobile seat esp. for preventing whiplash injury

head restraint *n* **:** HEADREST *herein*

heat pipe *n* **:** a closed container in which a continuing cycle of evaporation and condensation of a fluid takes place with the heat being given off at the condenser end and which is more effective in transferring heat than a metallic conductor

heat pollution *n* **:** THERMAL POLLUTION *herein*

heavy* *n* **heav·ies** *pl* **:** heavy surf; *esp* **:** waves over 10 ft. high

hedge fund *n* **:** an investing group usu. in the form of a limited partnership that employs speculative techniques (as short selling and leverage) in the hope of obtaining large capital gains

heli·borne \ˈhelə,bō(ə)rn, ˈhēl-, -bȯ(-\ *adj* [²*heli-* + ¹*borne*] **:** transported by helicopter ⟨~ infantry⟩

he·lic·i·ty \heˈlisəd·ē, hə-\ *n* -ES [*helic-* + *-ity*] **1 :** the motion of a particle about an axis parallel to its direction of motion **2 :** the component of the spin of a particle in its direction of motion measured in quantum units of spin

heli·lift \ˈhelə,lift, -hēl-\ *vt* [²*heli-* + *lift*] **:** to transport (troops) by helicopter

heli·pad \ˈ==,=\ *n* [²*heli-* + ¹*pad*] **:** a landing and takeoff surface for helicopters

heli·spot \ˈ==,=\ *n* [²*heli-* + ¹*spot*] **:** a temporary landing surface for helicopters

heli·stop \ˈ==,=\ *n* [²*heli-* + ²*stop*] **:** HELIPORT

helium-4 *n* [*helium* + *4*, mass number of the isotope] **:** HELIUM

helium-3 *n* [*helium* + *3*, mass number of the isotope] **:** the isotope of helium having the mass number three

hep·a·top·a·thy \ˌhepəˈtäpəthē\ *n* -ES [*hepat-* + *-pathy*] **:** an abnormal or diseased state of the liver

hep·a·to·tox·ic·i·ty \ˌhepəd·ō,täkˈsisəd·ē\ *n* -ES [*hepatotoxic* + *-ity*] **1 :** a state of toxic damage to the liver **2 :** capacity to cause hepatotoxicity — **hep·a·to·tox·in** \-ˈtäksən\ *n* -S

hexa·decimal \ˌheksə+\ *adj* [alter. (influenced by *hexa*) of *sexadecimal*] **:** SEXIDECIMAL *herein* ⟨a ~ number system⟩

hidden tax *n* **:** INDIRECT TAX

high energy physics *n* **:** physics that deals with the constitution, properties, and interactions of elementary particles as revealed by experiments involving particle accelerators

high-rise \ˈ=ˈ=\ *adj* **1 :** being multistory and equipped with elevators ⟨*high-rise* apartment buildings⟩ **2 :** of, relating to, or characterized by high-rise buildings — **high rise** *n*

hip* *n* [⁸*hip*] **:** HIPNESS *herein*

hip-hugger \ˈ=,==\ *n* **:** a low-slung usu. close-fitting outer garment (as slacks) that rests on the hips

hip·ness \ˈhipnəs\ *n* -ES [⁸*hip* + *-ness*] **:** the quality or state of being hip

hip·pie *or* **hip·py** \ˈhipē, -pi\ *n, pl* **hippies** [⁸*hip* + *-ie*] **:** a young person who rejects (as by dressing unconventionally or favoring communal living) the mores of established society, adheres to a nonviolent ethic, and often uses marijuana or psychedelic drugs; *broadly* **:** a long-haired unconventionally dressed young person

hip·pie·dom \-pēdəm, -pid-\ *n* -S [*hippie* (herein) + *-dom*] **:** the world of hippies

hip·ster·ism \ˈhipstə,rizəm\ *n* -S [*hipster* + *-ism*] **1 :** HIPNESS *herein* **2 :** the way of life characteristic of hipsters

his·to·compatibility \ˌhi(,)stō+\ *n* [*hist-* + *compatibility*] **:** a state of mutual tolerance that allows some tissues to be grafted effectively to others — **his·to·compatible** \"+\ *adj*

ho·dad \ˈhō,dad\ *n* [perh. alter. of *hodag*] **:** a nonsurfer who frequents surfing beaches and pretends to be a surfer

hold* *n* **:** a delay in a countdown (as in launching a missile)

holding pattern *n* **:** the usu. oval course flown (as over an airport) by aircraft awaiting clearance to land

ho·lid·ic \häˈlidik, -hōˈ-\ *adj* [*hol-* + *-idic* (as in *meridic* — herein)] **:** having the active constituents chemically defined ⟨~ diets⟩ — compare MERIDIC, OLIGIDIC *herein*

hol·o·gram \ˈhälə,gram, ˈhōl-\ *n* -S [*hol-* + *-gram*] **:** a three-dimensional picture produced in the form of an interference pattern on a photographic film or plate without use of a lens by two beams of coherent light (as from a laser) so that for reconstruction of the image the pattern is viewed by coherent light passing through the film or plate — **hol·o·graph** \-af\ *vt* -ED/-ING/-S — **hol·o·graph·ic** \ˌhäləˈgrafik, ˌhōl-\ *adj* — **hol·o·graph·i·cal·ly** \-fək(ə)lē\ *adv* — **ho·log·ra·phy** \häˈlägrəfē, hōˈ-\ *n* -ES

hom·i·ni·za·tion \ˌhämənəˈzāshən, -,nī'-\ *n* -S [*homin-* + *-ization*] **1 :** the evolutionary development of human characteristics that differentiate man from his primate ancestors **2 :** the progressive taking over and adapting of the world to his needs by man — **hominized** *adj*

ho·mo ha·bi·lis \ˌhō(,)mōˈhabələs\ *n, usu cap 1st H* [NL, fr. L *homo* man + *habilis* skillful, handy — more at HOMAGE, ABLE] **:** an extinct primate that is known from eastern African fossil remains associated with crude tools, is believed to have flourished some two million years ago, and is variously interpreted as the earliest true man or an australopithecine

homomorphism* *n* **:** a mapping of one mathematical group on itself or another so that the results of the group operations correspond

ho·mo·phile \ˈhōmə,fīl\ *adj* [*hom-* + ²*-phil*] **:** GAY 8b

hon·cho \ˈhän(,)chō\ *n* -S [Jap *hanchō* squad leader, fr. *han* squad + *chō* head, chief] **:** BOSS

hon·kie *or* **hon·ky** *also* **hon·key** \ˈhäŋkē, -ki *also* ˈhȯŋ-\ *n, pl.* **honkies** *also* **honkeys** [origin unknown] **:** a white man — usu. used disparagingly

hot·dog \ˈhät,dȯg *sometimes* -däg\ *vb* **hot·dogged; hot-dogged; hot·dog·ging; hot·dogs** [prob. fr. ²*hot dog*] *vi* **:** to perform stunts and fancy maneuvers while riding a surfboard ~ *vt* **:** to hotdog on (a wave) — **hotdogger** *also* **hotdog** *n* — **hotdogging** *n* -S

hotel china *n* **:** a high-fired well-vitrified American ceramic ware approaching hard-paste porcelain in composition

hot line *n* **:** a direct telephone line in constant readiness to operate so as to facilitate immediate communication (as between heads of two governments)

hung up* \ˌhəŋˈəp\ *adj* **1 :** having a hang-up **:** ANXIOUS ⟨sometimes I'm so *hung up* I can't function —*New Yorker*⟩ **2 :** being much involved with: as **a :** INFATUATED ⟨they get *hung up* on some fellow here —Jeff Brown⟩ **b :** ENTHUSIASTIC ⟨people who are *hung up* on French Provincial —Walter Goodman⟩ **c :** OBSESSED ⟨*hung up* on winning⟩

hunting* *n* **1 :** a self-induced and undesirable oscillation of a variable above and below the desired value in an automatic control system **2 :** a continuous attempt by an automatically controlled system to find a desired equilibrium condition

hutzpah *or* **hutzpa** *var of* CHUTZPAH

hydro* *n* [by shortening] **:** HYDROPLANE 2a

hy·dro·chlo·ro·thi·az·ide \ˌhīdrə,klōrəˈthīə,zīd\ *n* [*hydr-* + *chlor-* + *thi-* + *azide*] **:** a diuretic and hypotensive drug

hy·dro·crack·er *n* **:** an apparatus for hydrocracking

hy·dro·dy·nam·i·cist \ˌhīdrōdīˈnaməsəst\ *n* -S [*hydrodynamics* + *-ist*] **:** one who specializes in hydrodynamics

hydrofoil* *n* **:** a motorboat that has metal plates or fins attached by struts fore and aft so that they act in water as airplane wings do in air and lift the hull a short distance above the water

hy·dro·gasification \ˌhīdrō+\ *n* [*hydr-* + *gasification*] **:** the process of reacting hydrogen or a mixture of steam and hydrogen with coal at high temperature and high pressure so that the carbon in the coal reacts directly or indirectly to produce methane used for fuel — **hy·dro·gasifier** \"+\ *n*

hy·dro·magnetic \ˌhīdrō+\ *adj* [*hydr-* + *magnetic*] **1 :** MAGNETOHYDRODYNAMIC **2 :** being a wave in an electrically conducting fluid in a magnetic field

hy·dro·magnetics \"+\ *n pl but sing in constr* [*hydr-* + *magnetics*] **:** MAGNETOHYDRODYNAMICS

hy·dro·naut \ˈhīdrə,nȯt, -nät\ *n* -S [*hydr-* + *-naut* (as in *astronaut*)] **:** a member of the crew of a deep-sea vehicle (as a bathyscaphe) other than a submarine

hy·dron·ic \hīˈdränik\ *adj* [*hydr-* + *-onic* (as in *electronic*)] **:** of, relating to, or being a system of heating or cooling that involves transfer of heat by a circulating fluid in a closed system of pipes — **hy·dron·i·cal·ly** \-nək(ə)lē\ *adv*

hy·dron·ics \-niks\ *n pl but usu sing in constr* [*hydronic* + *-s*] **:** a hydronic system

hy·dro·plan·ing \ˈhīdrə,plāniŋ\ *n* -S [*hydroplaning*, gerund of ²*hydroplane*] **:** the riding of an automobile or airplane tire on a film of water on a wet surface when a critical speed is reached and when the lift between the tire and the pavement exceeds the weight riding on the tire with a resultant loss of directional stability and braking effectiveness

hy·dro·skimmer \ˈhīdrō+,\ *n* [*hydr-* + *skimmer*] **:** a ground-effect machine for use over water

hy·dro·space \"+,\ *n* [*hydr-* + *space*] **:** the regions beneath the surface of the ocean

hy·dro·treat \"+,\ *vt* [*hydr-* + ¹*treat*] **:** to subject to hydrogenation ⟨~ lube oil⟩ — **hy·dro·treat·er** *n*

hy·dro·trope \ˈhīdrə,trōp\ *n* -S [back-formation fr. *hydrotropic*] **:** a hydrotropic substance

hy·droxo·cobalamin \ˌhīˈdräksə, -(,)sō+\ *n* [*hydroxo-* + *cobalamin*] **:** a member of the vitamin B_{12} group used in treating and preventing B_{12} deficiency

hype* *n* **1 :** DECEPTION, PUT-ON ⟨had come upon some way I could work a ~ on the penal authorities —Malcolm X⟩ **2 :** ADVERTISEMENT, BLURB

hype *vt* -ED/-ING/-S [*hype*, n.] **1 :** to put on **:** MISLEAD, DECEIVE **2 :** STIMULATE, JAZZ 2a — usu. used with *up* ⟨his assignment is to ~ up the crowd —J.S.Radasta⟩

hy·per·al·dos·te·ron·ism \ˌhīpəralˈdästə,rō,nizəm, -ldōstəˈrō-\ *n* -S [*hyper-* + *aldosterone* + *-ism*] **:** ALDOSTERONISM *herein*

hyperbaric* *adj* **:** of, relating to, or utilizing greater than normal pressure esp. of oxygen ⟨~ medicine⟩

hy·per·charge \ˈhīpə(r)+,\ *n* [*hyper-* + *charge*] **:** a quantum characteristic of a closely related group of strongly interacting particles represented by a number equal to twice the average value of the electric charge of the group

hy·per·velocity \ˌhīpə(r)+\ *n, often attrib* [*hyper-* + *velocity*] **:** a high or relatively high velocity; *esp* **:** one greater than 10,000 feet per second

IC* *abbr* integrated circuit *herein*
ice* *n* **:** an undercover premium paid to a theater employee for choice theater tickets
ice-cream chair *n* [fr. its use in ice-cream parlors] **:** a small armless chair with a circular seat for use at a table
ice-out \ˈ=,=\ *n* -s [*ice* + ¹*out*] **:** the disappearance of ice from the surface of a body of water (as a lake) as a result of thawing
idem·po·tent \ˈīˈdempəd·ənt; ¦īdəm¦pōtᵊnt, ¦ī,dem-\ *adj* [ISV *idem-* same (fr. L *idem*) + L *potent-, potens* having power — more at IDENTITY, POTENT] **:** being a mathematical quantity which is not zero and every positive power of which equals itself — **idem·po·ten·cy** \-ənsē, -ᵊnsē\ *n* -ES
ike·ba·na \,ikəˈbänə, ,ēk-, -kēˈ-\ *n* [Jap, fr. *iki* alive + *hana* flower] **:** the Japanese art of flower arranging that emphasizes form and balance
illuminate* *vt* **:** to subject to radiation — **illumination*** *n*
im·bal·anced \(ˈ)im¦balən(t)st\ *adj* [*imbalance* + *-ed*] **:** not balanced; *esp* **:** having an unequal number of members of one racial or ethnic group ⟨~ schools⟩
imi·pra·mine \,iməˈpra,mēn, -,mən; ī'miprə-, əˈm-\ *n* [*imid-* + *propyl* + *amine*] **:** an antidepressant drug
im·mit·tance \iˈmitᵊn(t)s\ *n* -s [*impedance* + *admittance*] **:** ADMITTANCE; *also* **:** IMPEDANCE — used of transmission lines, networks, and measuring instruments
immuno-* *comb form* **:** immunologic ⟨*immuno*hematology⟩
im·mu·no·assay \¦imyənō, ə¦myünō+\ *n* [*immuno-* + *assay*] **:** the determination of a substance (as a protein or peptide hormone) through use of its capacity to act as an antigen
im·mu·no·competence \"+\ *n* [*immuno-* + *competence*] **:** the capacity for normal immune response — **im·mu·no·competent** \"+\ *adj*
im·mu·no·cytochemistry \"+\ *n* [*immuno-* + *cytochemistry*] **:** the biochemistry of cellular immunology — **im·mu·no·cytochemical** \"+\ *adj* — **im·mu·no·cytochemically** \"+\ *adv*
im·mu·no·diffusion \"+\ *n* [*immuno-* + *diffusion*] **:** the separating of a complex antigen into discrete parts by differential diffusion
im·mu·no·electrophoresis \"+\ *n, pl* **immunoelectrophore·ses** \-ē(,)sēz\ [*immuno-* + *electrophoresis*] **:** electrophoretic separation of proteins followed by identification through specific immunologic reactions — **im·mu·no·electrophoretic** \"+\ *adj* — **im·mu·no·electrophoretically** \"+\ *adv*
im·mu·no·fluorescence \"+\ *n* [*immuno-* + *fluorescence*] **:** antibody demonstration by use of a fluorescent dye to label the antibody — **im·mu·no·fluorescent** \"+\ *adj*
im·mu·no·globulin \"+\ *n* [*immuno-* + *globulin*] **:** IMMUNE GLOBULIN
im·mu·no·hematology \"+\ *n* [*immuno-* + *hematology*] **:** a branch of immunology that deals with the immunologic properties of blood — **im·mu·no·hematologic** \"+\ *adj* — **im·mu·no·hematological** \"+\ *adj*
im·mu·no·histochemical \"+\ *adj* [*immuno-* + *histochemical*] **:** of or relating to the application of histochemical and immunologic methods to chemical analysis of living cells and tissues — **im·mu·no·histochemically** \"+\ *adv*
im·mu·no·histology \"+\ *n* [*immuno-* + *histology*] **:** a branch of immunology that deals with the application of immunologic methods to histology — **im·mu·no·histologic** \"+\ *adj* — **im·mu·no·histological** \"+\ *adj* — **im·mu·no·histologically** \"+\ *adv*
im·mu·no·pathology \"+\ *n* [*immuno-* + *pathology*] **:** a branch of medicine that deals with immunologic abnormalities and disease — **im·mu·no·pathologic** \"+\ *adj* — **im·mu·no·patho·logical** \"+\ *adj* — **im·mu·no·pathologist** \"+\ *n*
im·mu·no·reactive \"+\ *adj* [*immuno-* + *reactive*] **:** reacting to particular antigens or haptens ⟨serum ~ insulin⟩ — **im·mu·no·reactivity** \"+\ *n*
im·mu·no·suppression \"+\ *n* [*immuno-* + *suppression*] **:** the suppression of natural immune responses — **im·mu·no·suppressant** \"+\ *n* — **im·mu·no·suppressive** \"+\ *adj*
impacted area *n* **:** an area in which a large number of public school students are from families living or working on nontaxable federal property
imported fire ant *n* **:** a small brown So. American fire ant (*Solenopsis saevissima richteri*) that is a destructive pest in the southeastern U.S.
in* *adj* **1 :** keenly aware of and responsive to what is new and smart ⟨the ~ crowd⟩ **2 :** highly approved by those who are au courant ⟨the ~ place to go⟩ — **in–ness** \ˈinnəs\ *n* -ES
-in \,in\ *n comb form* -s [²*in* (as in *sit-in*)] **1 :** organized public protest by means of or in favor of **:** demonstration ⟨teach-*in*⟩ ⟨love-*in*⟩ **2 :** public group activity ⟨swim-*in*⟩
in-and-out* *adj* **:** involving purchase and sale of the same security within a short period ⟨*in-and-out* trading⟩
in·ca·pac·i·tant \,inkəˈpasətənt, -sədə-\ *n* -s [*incapacitate* + *-ant*] **:** an incapacitating agent ⟨a chemical ~⟩
indicator* *n* **:** any of a group of statistical values (as level of employment and change in the price of industrial raw materials) that taken together give an indication of the health of the economy — compare COINCIDENT, LAGGER, LEADER *herein*
inducer* *n* **:** a substance capable of activating a structural gene by combining with and inactivating a genetic repressor
industrial–revenue bond *n* **:** a revenue bond issued to provide industrial facilities for lease and dependent on the lease revenue for amortization and interest payments
inertial platform *n* **:** an assemblage of devices used in inertial guidance together with the mounting
inertial space *n* **:** a part of space away from the earth assumed to have fixed coordinates so that the trajectory of an object (as a spacecraft or missile) may be calculated in relation to it
inertia welding *n* **:** the welding of metals by means of the heat produced by friction when one metallic piece is pressed while spinning against another
in·fauna \ˈin+,\ *n* [NL, fr. *in-*, ¹*in-* + *fauna*] **:** benthic fauna living in the substrate and esp. in a soft sea bottom — compare EPIFAUNA *herein* — **in·fau·nal** \"+\ *adj*
in-flight \(,)=¦=\ *adj* [fr. the phrase *in flight*] **:** made or carried out while in flight **:** provided for use or enjoyment while in flight ⟨*in-flight* movies⟩ ⟨*in-flight* calculations⟩
information science *n* **:** a study that deals with the properties of information and its storage, retrieval, and dissemination
in·fra·sound \ˈinfrə+,\ *n* [*infra-* + ³*sound*] **:** a wave phenomenon of the same physical nature as sound but with frequencies below the range of human hearing
in-house \(,)=¦=\ *adj* [¹*in* + ¹*house*] **:** of, relating to, or carried on within a group or organization
ini·tial·ism \əˈnishə,lizəm\ *n* -s [²*initial* + *-ism*] **:** an acronym formed from initial letters
initial teaching alphabet *n* [so called because it is used only in the initial stages of teaching reading] **:** a 44-symbol alphabet designed esp. for children who are learning to read English
injection* *n* **1 :** the placing of an artificial satellite or a spacecraft into an orbit — called also *insertion* **2 :** the time or place at which injection occurs
in-line \(¦)=¦=\ *adj* (*or adv*) [*in line*] **:** having the parts or units arranged in a straight line; *also* **:** being so arranged
inner city *n* **:** the usu. older and most densely populated central section of a city — **inner–city** *adj*
insertion* *n* **:** INJECTION *herein*
instruction* *n* **:** a code that tells a computer to perform a particular operation
insurance run *n* **:** a run scored in baseball that gives a team a two-run lead
integrated circuit *n* **:** a tiny complex of electronic components (as transistors, resistors, and capacitors) and their interconnections produced in or on a single small slice of material (as silicon) — called also *chip*
in·te·gro–differential \¦intə(,)grō, in¦te-, in¦tē-+\ *adj* [¹*integral* + *-o-* + ¹*differential*] **:** involving both mathematical integration and differentiation
intensive care *adj* **:** having special medical facilities, services, and monitoring devices to meet the needs of gravely ill patients ⟨*intensive care* unit⟩ — **intensive care** *n*
interface* *n* **1 :** the place at which two independent systems meet and act upon or communicate with each other ⟨the ~ between engineering and science⟩ ⟨the man-machine ~⟩; *broadly* **:** an area in which diverse things interact on each other ⟨~ between the known and unknown⟩ ⟨the high school-college ~⟩ **2 :** the means by which interaction or communication is effected at an interface ⟨an ~ between a computer and a typesetting machine⟩
interface* *vt* **1 :** to connect by means of an interface ⟨~ a machine with a computer⟩ **2 :** to serve as an interface for ~ *vi* **1 :** to become interfaced ⟨a system that ~s with a computer⟩ **2 :** to serve as an interface ⟨*interfacing* hardware⟩
in·ter·fer·on \,intə(r)ˈfi(ə),rän\ *n* -s [*interference* + ¹*-on*] **:** a heat-stable soluble basic antiviral protein of low molecular weight produced usu. by cells exposed to the action of a virus or experimentally to that of certain chemicals
in·ter·laboratory \¦intə(r)+\ *adj* [*inter-* + *laboratory*] **:** of, relating to, or engaged in by more than one laboratory
in·ter·me·dia \¦intə(r)¦mēdēə\ *adj* [*inter-* + ¹*media*] **:** involving the simultaneous use of several media and esp. several electronic media
in·ter·mod·al \-¦mōdᵊl\ *adj* [*inter-* + ¹*mode* + *-al*] **1 :** being or involving transportation by more than one form of carrier during a single journey **2 :** used for intermodal transportation
in·ter·ro·bang *also* **in·tera·bang** \inˈterə,baŋ, -aiŋ\ *n* -s [*interrogation point* + *bang* (printers' slang for *exclamation point*)] **:** a punctuation mark ‽ designed for use esp. at the end of an exclamatory rhetorical question
interrogate* *vt* **:** to give or send out a signal to (as a computer) for triggering an appropriate response
in·ter·sensory \¦intə(r)+\ *adj* [*inter-* + *sensory*] **:** involving two or more sensory systems ⟨~ factors in memory loss⟩
in·tra·cardiac \¦in·trə, -n·(,)trä+\ *also* **in·tra·car·di·al** \"+¦kärdēəl\ *adj* [*intracardiac* fr. *intra-* + *cardiac; intracardial* fr. *intra-* + *cardi-* + *-al*] **:** situated or occurring within the heart — **in·tra·car·di·al·ly** \-ēəlē\ *adv*
in·tra·day \¦==,=\ *adj* [*intra-* + *day*] **:** occurring in the course of a single day ⟨the market showed wide ~ fluctuations⟩
in·tra·personal \"+\ *adj* [*intra-* + *personal*] **:** occurring within the individual mind or self ⟨~ concerns of the aged⟩
in·tra·population \"+\ *adj* [*intra-* + *population*] **:** occurring within or taking place between members of a population
intrauterine device \¦==¦==(,)=-\ *n* [*intra-* + *uterine*] **:** a device (as a spiral of plastic or a ring of stainless steel) inserted and left in the uterus to prevent effective conception
in·tra·vascular \¦in·trə, -n·(,)trä+\ *adj* [ISV *intra-* + *vascular*] **:** occurring or situated within a vessel and esp. a blood vessel ⟨~ thrombosis⟩ — **in·tra·vascularly** \"+\ *adv*
in·tro·gres·sant \,in·trəˈgresᵊnt, -trō-\ *adj* [by alter.] **:** INTROGRESSIVE — **introgressant** *n* -s
investment letter stock *n* **:** LETTER STOCK *herein*
ionic propulsion *n* **:** ION PROPULSION *herein*
ion·o·mer \īˈänəmər\ *n* -s [*ion* + *-o-* + polymer] **:** any of a class of tough synthetic ethylene-based thermoplastic resins consisting of a long-chain polymer
ion·o·sonde \īˈänə,sänd\ *n* [ISV *ionosphere* + *sonde*] **:** a device for determining and recording the heights of ionized layers in the ionosphere by shortwaves reflected from them
ion propulsion *n* **:** propulsion of a body by the forces resulting from the rearward discharge of a stream of ionized particles
ion rocket *n* **:** ION ENGINE
iso·enzyme \¦īsō *also* ¦īzō+\ *n* [*is-* + *enzyme*] **:** ISOZYME *herein* — **iso·enzymic** \"+\ *adj*
isolated camera *n* [so called fr. its focusing on isolated activities of the game] **:** a television camera used to videotape an ongoing activity (as a play in football) for immediate replay
iso·met·rics \,īsəˈme·triks *also* ,īzə-\ *n pl but sing or pl in constr* [¹*isometric* + *-s*] **:** exercise or a system of exercises involving isometric contraction of muscles
isomorphic* *adj* **:** having mathematical elements in one-to-one correspondence with the elements of another set
iso·spin \ˈīsə,spin *also* ˈīzə-\ *n* -s [*isotopic spin* (herein)] **:** a quantum characteristic of a group of closely related elementary particles (as a proton and a neutron) handled mathematically like ordinary spin with the possible orientations in a hypothetical space specifying the number of particles of differing electric charge comprising the group
isotopic spin *n* **:** ISOSPIN *herein*
iso·zyme \ˈīsə,zīm *also* ˈīzə-\ *n* -s [*is-* + *-zyme*] **:** one of two or more chemically distinct but functionally like enzymes
ITA \,ī,tēˈā\ *abbr* initial teaching alphabet *herein*
iterative* *adj* **:** involving the repeated application of a procedure until a specified condition is satisfied with testing for the condition done after the completion of each iteration ⟨an ~ procedure in computer programming⟩ — compare RECURSIVE 2b *herein*
IUD \,īyüˈdē\ *abbr or n* -s intrauterine device *herein*
jams \ˈjamz\ *n pl* [prob. by shortening fr. *pajamas*] **:** knee-length loose-fitting swim trunks usu. having a drawstring waist and large brightly colored patterns — compare BAGGIES *herein*
jaw·bon·ing \ˈjō¦bōniŋ\ *n* [*jawbone* + *-ing*] **:** a strong appeal by a chief of state to national business and labor leaders for price and wage restraints
jazz* *n* **:** similar but unspecified things **:** STUFF ⟨I *love* sailing . . . that wind, and the waves, and all that ~ —John Updike⟩
jet·ava·tor \ˈjed·ə,vād·ə(r)\ *n* -s [irreg. fr. ⁶*jet* + *elevator*] **:** a control surface for deflecting a rocket's exhaust stream so as to change the direction of thrust
jet set *n* **:** an international social group of wealthy individuals who frequent fashionable resorts — **jet–set·ter** \ˈjet,sed·ə(r\ *n*
job-hopping \ˈ=,==\ *n* -s **:** the practice of moving (as for immediate financial gain) from job to job — **job-hopper** \ˈ=,==\ *n*
jock* *n* [so called fr. the wearing of jockstraps by such athletes] **:** ATHLETE; *esp* **:** a school or college athlete
jogging *n* -s [*jogging*, gerund of *jog*] **:** running at a slow even pace, *also* **:** exercise consisting of walking and jogging
john birch·er \ˈjän ˈbərchər\ *n, usu cap J & B* **:** BIRCHER *herein*
jo·mon \ˈjō,män\ *adj, often cap* [Jap *jōmon* straw rope pattern; fr. the characteristic method of forming designs on pottery of the period] **:** of, relating to, or typical of a Japanese neolithic cultural period extending from about 3000 B.C. or earlier to about 200 B.C. and characterized esp. by elaborately ornamented hand-formed unglazed pottery (**Jomon ware**)
jo·seph·son effect \ˈjōzəfsən- *also* -ōsə-\ *n, usu cap J* [after B. D. *Josephson*, 20th cent. Eng. physicist] **:** the passage of electrons at superconductivity temperatures through a thin insulator separating two superconductors so that when the electrons are accelerated through the barrier by application of a voltage the energy they gain is emitted as radiation
ju·do·ist \ˈjü(,)dōəst, -üdəwə-\ *n* -s [*judo* + *-ist*] **:** one who is trained or skilled in judo
jug band *n* **:** a band that plays jazz on usu. crude improvised instruments (as a jug, washboard, and stovepipe)
juice* *n* **1 :** LIQUOR **2 :** exorbitant interest exacted of a borrower under the threat of violence
juke* *vt* **:** to fake out of position (as in football)
jump cut *n* **:** a discontinuity or acceleration in the action of a filmed scene brought about by removal of medial portions of the shot
jumper* *n* **:** JUMP SHOT 3
jumping–jack* *n* **:** an exercise performed in a standing position in which the subject spreads his legs and throws his arms over his head with a jump and returns to his original position with another jump — called also *side-straddle hop*
jump suit* *n* **:** a one-piece garment consisting of a blouse or shirt with attached trousers or shorts
junk art *n* **:** three-dimensional art made from discarded material (as of metal, mortar, glass, or wood) — **junk artist** *n*
ju·ri·me·tri·cian \,jürəməˈtrishən\ *n* -s [*jurimetrics* (herein) + ¹*-an*] **:** a specialist in jurimetrics
ju·ri·met·rics \,jürəˈme·triks\ *n pl but usu sing in constr* [L *juri-, jus* law + E *-metrics* (as in *econometrics*) — more at JUST] **:** the application of scientific methods to legal problems
juvenile hormone *n* **:** a compound prob. related to farnesol that is widespread in nature, that is secreted by the corpora allata of insects in which it inhibits maturation to the imago and plays a role in reproductive phenomena, and that has been used experimentally to control pest insects by disrupting their life cycles
ju·ve·nil·ize \ˈjüvənᵊl,īz\ *vt* -ED/-ING/-S [*juvenile* + *-ize*] **:** to restrain from normal development and maturation **:** prolong the immaturity of ⟨chemicals that ~ insect larvae⟩ — **ju·ve·nil·iza·tion** \,jüvənᵊləˈzāshən, -ᵊl,īˈz-\ *n* -s
kaf·ka·esque \¦käfkə¦esk, ¦kaf-\ *adj, usu cap* [Franz *Kafka* †1924 Austrian writer + E *-esque*] **:** of, relating to, or suggestive of Franz Kafka or his writings
ka·lim·ba \kəˈlimbə, käˈ-\ *n* -s [of African origin; akin to Bemba *akalimba* zanza, Kimbundu *marimba* xylophone] **:** an African musical instrument that is derived from the zanza
kal·li·din \ˈkalədən\ *n* -s [G, fr. *kallikrein* + *-d-* (prob. fr. *dekapeptid* peptide having 10 amino acids, fr. *deka-* + *peptid* peptide) + *-in*] **:** any of several kinins formed from blood plasma globulin by the action of kallikrein
kal·li·kre·in \,kaləˈkrēən, kəˈlik-\ *n* -s [G, fr. *kalli-* calli- + *pankreas* pancreas (fr. Gk) + *-in*; prob. so called fr. its therapeutic use in pancreatic disorders] **:** an enzyme that liberates kinins from blood plasma
ka·na·my·cin \,kanəˈmīsᵊn, ,kän-\ *n* -s [NL *kanamyceticus* (specific epithet of *Streptomyces kanamyceticus*) + E *-in*] **:** a broad-spectrum antibiotic from a Japanese soil actinomycete (*Streptomyces kanamyceticus*)
ka·on \ˈkā,än\ *n* -s [ISV ¹*ka* (fr. *K-meson* — herein) + ²*-on*] **:** an unstable meson of cosmic radiation or produced in high-energy particle collisions with its charged forms being 966.3 times more massive than the electron and its neutral form being 974.6 times more massive than the electron
ka·ra·tsu ware \kəˈrät(,)sü-\ *n, usu cap K* [fr. *Karatsu*, city in Japan] **:** a Japanese ceramic ware traditionally made from the 7th century at Karatsu on Kyushu island that is probably the earliest glazed Japanese ceramic ware, includes both earthenware and stoneware, and comprises chiefly vessels for chanoyu
kart \ˈkärt\ *n* -s [prob. fr. *GoKart*, a trademark] **:** a miniature motorcar used esp. for racing
kart·ing \ˈkärd·iŋ\ *n* -s [*kart* (herein) + *-ing*] **:** the sport of racing miniature motorcars
kbar *abbr* kilobar *herein*
keeper* *n* **:** an offensive football play in which the quarterback keeps the ball and runs usu. around end
ken·ya·pi·the·cus \,kenyəpəˈthēkəs, -ˈpithək-\ *n, usu cap* [NL, genus name, fr. *Kenya*, country in Africa + *-pithecus*] **:** an ancient prehuman African primate that is held to belong to the human ancestral line and that is placed in a distinct genus (*Kenyapithecus*) or included in *Ramapithecus*
key club *n* [so called because each member is provided with a key to the premises] **:** an informal private club serving liquor and providing entertainment
kick out* *vi* **:** to turn a surfboard around and drive it over the top of a wave by pushing down on the rear of the board with the foot
kilo·bar \ˈkilə,bär\ *n* -s [ISV *kilo-* + ⁷*bar*] **:** a unit of pressure equal to one thousand bars — abbr. *kbar*
kilo·megacycle \¦kilə+\ *n* [ISV *kilo-* + *megacycle*] **:** one thousand megacycles **:** one billion cycles
kinetic art *n* **:** art (as sculpture or assemblage) having mechanical parts which can be set in motion (as by a motor) — **kinetic artist** *n*
ki·net·i·cism \kəˈned·ə,sizəm, kīˈ-\ *n* -s [*kinetic* (*art*) + *-ism*] **:** KINETIC ART *herein*
ki·net·i·cist \-,səst\ *n* -s [*kinetic* + *-ist*] **1 :** a specialist in kinetics **2 :** KINETIC ARTIST *herein*
ki·ne·tin \ˈkīnətən\ *n* -s [*kinet-* + *-in*] **:** a plant growth substance that increases mitosis and callus formation
ki·nin \ˈkīnən\ *n* -s [Gk *kinein* to move, stimulate + E *-in* — more at HIGHT] **1 :** any of various polypeptide hormones formed locally in the tissues and acting on smooth muscle **2 :** any of various plant growth factors prob. related to adenine that function in growth processes
ki·nin·o·gen \kīˈninəjən\ *n* [*kinin* (herein) + *-o-* + *-gen*] **:** an inactive precursor of a kinin — **ki·nin·o·gen·ic** \(¦)==¦==¦jenik\ *adj*
kinky* *adj, chiefly Brit* **:** FAR-OUT, OFFBEAT
klutz \ˈkləts\ *n* -ES [Yiddish *klotz, klutz*, fr. G *klotz*, lit., wooden block, fr. MHG *kloz* lumpy mass — more at CLOT] **:** a clumsy and awkward person — **klutzy** *adj* -ER/-EST
k–meson \ˈkā+\ *n, usu cap K* [¹*K* + *meson*] **:** KAON *herein*
kook \ˈkük\ *n* -s [by shortening and alter. fr. *cuckoo*] **:** one whose ideas or actions are eccentric, fantastic, or insane
kooky *also* **kook·ie** \ˈkükē, -ki\ *adj* **kook·i·er; kook·i·est** [*kook* (herein) + *-ie*] **:** having the characteristics of a kook **:** CRAZY, OFFBEAT — **kook·i·ness** *n* -ES
k particle *n, usu cap K* [¹*K*] **:** KAON *herein*
krem·lin·ol·o·gy \,kremləˈnäləjē\ *n* -ES *usu cap* [*Kremlin* + *-o-* + *-logy*] **:** the study of the policies and practices of the Soviet Russian government — **krem·lin·ol·o·gist** \-jəst\ *n* -s *usu cap*
ku·ta·ni \küˈtänē\ *or* **kutani ware** *n* -s *usu cap K* [fr. *Kutani*, village in Japan] **:** a Japanese porcelain produced in and about the village of Kutani on Honshu island since the mid-17th century and esteemed for originality of design and coloring
kwa·cha \ˈkwächə\ *n, pl* **kwacha** [native name in Zambia, lit., dawn] **1 :** the basic monetary unit of Zambia — see MONEY table *in the Dict* **2 :** a note representing one kwacha
la·combe \ləˈkōm\ *n, usu cap* [fr. *Lacombe* Experiment Station, Lacombe, Alta., Canada, where the breed was developed] **:** a breed of white bacon-type swine developed in Canada from Landrace, Chester White, and Berkshire stock
laggard* *n* **:** a security whose price has lagged for no obvious reason behind the average of its group or of the market
lagger* *n* **:** an economic indicator (as spending on new plants and equipment) that more often than not maintains an existent trend for some time after the state of the economy has turned onto an opposite trend — called also *lagging index*
lambda* *or* **lambda particle** *n* **:** an uncharged elementary particle that has a mass 2183 times that of an electron, is an unstable baryon, and decays typically into a nucleon and a pion with an average lifetime of 2.6×10^{-10} second
landmark* *n* **:** a structure (as a building) of unusual historical and usu. aesthetic interest; *esp* **:** one that is officially designated and set aside for preservation
language* *n* **:** MACHINE LANGUAGE *herein*
lan·tian man \,lan,tyan-\ *also* **lan·tien man** \-,tyen-\ *n usu cap L* [fr. *Lant'ien*, district in Shensi province, China] **:** an extinct man known from parts of a skull excavated in China and held to be an extremely primitive example of modern man
la·place transform \ləˈpläs-, -las-\ *n usu cap L* [after Pierre Simon de *Laplace* †1827 Fr. astronomer and mathematician] **:** a transformation of a function $f(x)$ into the function $g(t) = \int_0^\infty e^{-xt}f(x)dx$ that is useful esp. in reducing the solution of an ordinary linear differential equation with constant coefficients to the solution of a polynomial equation
lase \ˈlāz\ *vi* -ED/-ING/-S [back-formation fr. *laser*] **:** to emit coherent light
l–as·pa·rag·i·nase \¦e,laspəˈrajə,nās, -āz\ *n, usu cap L* [*L-* (levorotatory) + *asparagine* + *-ase*] **:** an enzyme that breaks down the L-form of asparagine, is obtained esp. from bacteria, and is used esp. to treat leukemia
law·ren·cium \lòˈren(t)sēəm, ləˈ-, -nch(ē)əm\ *n* -s [NL, fr. Ernest O. *Lawrence* †1958 Am. physicist + NL *-ium*] **:** a short-lived radioactive element of atomic number 103 that is produced artificially from californium — symbol *Lr*
lay·about \ˈlāə,baůt\ *n* -s [fr. the phrase *lay about*, nonstandard alter. of *lie about*] *chiefly Brit* **:** IDLER
lay–by* *n* **:** the final operation (as a last cultivating) in the growing of a field crop
lazy eye *n* **:** AMBLYOPIA
l–do·pa \(ˈ)elˈdōpə\ *n, usu cap L* [*l-* + *dopa*] **:** the levorotatory form of dopa found esp. in broad beans or prepared synthetically and used in treating Parkinson's disease
leader* *n* **:** an economic indicator (as the level of corporate profits or of stock prices) that more often than not shows a change in direction before a corresponding change in the state of the economy — called also *leading indicator*
LE M \ˈlem\ *abbr or n* -s lunar excursion module *herein*
le·one \lēˈōn\ *n* -s [fr. Sierra *Leone*, Africa] **1 :** the basic monetary unit of Sierra Leone — see MONEY table *in the Dict* **2 :** a note representing one leone
lep·ton·ic \(ˈ)lep¦tänik\ *adj* [*lepton* + *-ic*] **:** of, relating to, or producing a lepton ⟨~ decay of a hyperon⟩
lepton number *n* **:** a number equal to the number of leptons minus that of antileptons in a system of elementary particles

lesion *vt* -ED/-ING/-S [*lesion*, n.] **:** to produce lesions in
let·ter·set \ˈ==,set\ *n* -s [*letter*press + off*set*] **:** DRY OFFSET
letter stock *n* [so called fr. the letter signed by the purchaser stating that the stock is acquired for investment and not for public sale] **:** restricted and unregistered stock that may not be sold to the general public without undergoing registration
leu·ke·mic \lüˈkēmik, -mēk\ *n* -s [*leukemia* + ²*-ic*] **:** a person suffering from leukemia
lev·al·lor·phan \,levəˈlȯr,fan, -,fən\ *n* -s [*lev-* + *allyl* + *morphine* + ³*-an*] **:** a drug related to morphine that is used to counteract morphine poisoning
leverage *vt* -ED/-ING/-S [*leverage*, n.] **:** to provide (as a corporation) with leverage
lex·is \ˈleksəs\ *n, pl* **lex·es** \-k,sēz\ [Gk, speech, word — more at LEXICON] **:** VOCABULARY, WORD-STOCK
li·dar \ˈlī,där\ *n* -s [*light* + *radar*] **:** a device or system for locating an object that is similar in operation to radar but emits pulsed laser light instead of microwaves
life science *n* **:** the branch of science that deals with living organisms and life processes and that includes the biological, the medical, and the social sciences
life–support system *n* **:** a system that provides all or some of the items (as oxygen, food, water, control of temperature and pressure, disposition of carbon dioxide and body wastes) necessary for maintaining (as in a spacecraft or on the surface of the moon) the life and health of a person
lifting body *n* **:** a maneuverable rocket-propelled wingless vehicle that is capable of travel in aerospace or in the earth's atmosphere where its lift is derived from its shape and that can be landed on the ground
light pen *n* **:** a hand-held photosensitive device that is connected to a computer and used with the cathode-ray tube display for direct communication with the computer by adding, deleting, manipulating, or altering information
light show *n* **:** a kaleidoscopic display of colored lights, slides, and films that imitates the effects of psychedelic drugs
li·ku·ta \lə̇ˈküd·ə, (ˈ)lē¦k-\ *n, pl* **ma·ku·ta** \(ˈ)mä¦k-\ [of Niger-Congo origin; prob. akin to obs. Nupe *kuta* stone] **1 :** a monetary unit of the Republic of the Congo (Kinshasa) equal to $1/100$ zaire — see MONEY table *in the Dict* **2 :** a coin representing one likuta
lim·bo \ˈlim(,)bō\ *n* -s [native name in West Indies] **:** a West Indian acrobatic dance orig. for men that involves bending over backward and passing under a horizontal pole which is lowered slightly for each successive pass
limo \ˈlim·(,)ō\ *n* -s [by shortening] **:** LIMOUSINE
limp·en \ˈlimpən\ *vi* -ED/-ING/-S [³*limp* + ²*-en*] **:** to become limp ⟨~*ed* instantly and fell —Carson McCullers⟩
li·nac \ˈlī,nak\ *n* -s [*linear accelerator*] **:** LINEAR ACCELERATOR
lin·co·my·cin \,liŋkəˈmīsᵊn\ *n* -s [*linco-* (fr. *Streptomyces lincolnensis*, a streptomyces) + *-mycin*] **:** an antibiotic obtained from an actinomycete (*Streptomyces umbrinus* var. *cyaneoniger*) and found effective esp. against cocci
linear* *adj* **:** composed of simply drawn lines with little attempt at pictorial representation ⟨~ script⟩
linear a \-ˈā\ *n, usu cap L&A* **:** a linear form of writing used in Crete from the 18th to the 15th centuries B.C.
linear alkylate sulfonate *n* **:** a biodegradable salt of sulfonic acid used in detergents as a surface-active agent
linear b \-ˈbē\ *n, usu cap L&B* **:** a linear form of writing employing syllabic characters and used at Knossos on Crete and on the Greek mainland from the 15th to the 12th centuries B.C. for documents in the Mycenaean language
line score *n* **:** a score of a baseball game giving the runs, hits, and errors made by each team
lin·gui·ne \liŋˈgwēnē, -(,)nā\ *n* -s [It, pl. of *linguina*, dim. of *lingua* tongue, fr. L — more at TONGUE] **:** thin flat pasta
lin·u·ron \ˈlinyə,rän\ *n* [*lin-* (of unknown origin) + *urea* + ¹*-on*] **:** a selective herbicide used esp. to control weeds in crops of soybeans or carrots
lip·o·tro·pin \,lipəˈtrōpən, ,lī-\ *n* -s [*lipotropic* + *-in*] **:** an anterior pituitary hormone believed to function in the mobilization of fatty reserves
lip·pes loop \,lipəs- *also* ˈlips-\ *n, usu cap 1st L* [after Jack *Lippes*, 20th cent. Amer. physician] **:** an S-shaped plastic intrauterine device
litterbag \ˈ==,=\ *n* [¹*litter* + *bag*] **:** a bag used (as in an automobile) for refuse disposal
LM* *abbr* lunar module *herein*
locked–in* *adj* **:** unable or unwilling to shift invested funds because of the tax effect of realizing capital gains
logic* *n* **:** the fundamental principles and applications of truth tables and the interconnection of circuit elements and gating necessary for arithmetical computation in a computer
log·nor·mal \(ˈ)=¦==\ *adj* [⁴*log* + *normal*] **:** of, relating to, or being a logarithmic function (as the logarithm of a statistical variable or distribution) that has a normal distribution
long–term* *adj* **:** generated by assets held for longer than six months ⟨*long-term* capital gains⟩
look–in* *n* **:** a quick pass in football to a receiver running diagonally toward the center of the field
lookup \ˈ=,=\ *n* -s [*look up*] **:** the process or an instance of looking something up; *esp* **:** the process of matching by computer the words of a text against material stored in memory
loop* *n* **:** INTRAUTERINE DEVICE *herein; esp* **:** LIPPES LOOP *herein*
lo·rentz force \,lȯr|,en(t)s-, ,lōr|-\ *n, usu cap L* [after Hendrik A. *Lorentz* †1928 Du. physicist] **:** the force exerted on a moving charged particle in an electric and magnetic field
lowball \ˈ=,=\ *vt* **:** to give (a customer) a deceptively low cost estimate that one has no intention of honoring
low–rise \ˈ=¦=\ *adj* **:** being one or two stories and not equipped with elevators ⟨a *low-rise* classroom building⟩
LPN *abbr* licensed practical nurse
Lr *symbol* lawrencium *herein*
LSD \,e,lesˈdē\ *n* **:** LYSERGIC ACID DIETHYLAMIDE
lunar excursion module *or* **lunar module** *n* **:** a space vehicle module designed to carry astronauts from the command module to the surface of the moon and back
lu·nar·naut \ˈlünər,nȯt, -nät\ *n* -s [*lunar* + *astronaut*] **:** an astronaut who explores the moon
ly·ase \ˈlī,ās, -āz\ *n* -s [Gk *lyein* to loosen, release + E *-ase* — more at LOSE] **:** an enzyme (as a decarboxylase) that forms double bonds by removing groups from a substrate other than by hydrolysis or that adds groups to double bonds
lym·phan·gi·og·ra·phy \,lim,fanjēˈägrəfē\ *n* -ES [*lymphangi-* + *-graphy*] **:** LYMPHOGRAPHY *herein* — **lym·phan·gio·gram** \limˈfanjēə,gram\ *n* -s — **lym·phan·gio·graph·ic** \=¦==ə-ˈgrafik, ===¦==\ *adj*
lym·phog·ra·phy \limˈfägrəfē\ *n* -ES [*lymph-* + *-graphy*] **:** X-ray depiction of lymph vessels and nodes after use of a radiopaque material — **lym·pho·gram** \ˈlim(p)fə,gram\ *n* -s — **lym·pho·graph·ic** \¦==ˈgrafik\ *adj*
ly·sog·e·ny \līˈsäjənē\ *n* -ES [*lys-* + *-geny*] **:** the carrying and transmitting of an inactive phage by a bacterium to its descendants — **ly·sog·e·ni·za·tion** \-,säjənəˈzāshən,-,nīˈz-\ *n* -s
ly·so·some \ˈlīsə,sōm\ *n* -s [ISV *lys-* + ³*-some*; orig. formed in F] **:** a cellular organelle held to be the seat of various hydrolytic enzymes — **ly·so·som·al** \,līsəˈsōməl\ *adj*
ly·so·staph·in \,līsəˈstafən\ *n* -s [*lys-* + *staph* + *-in*] **:** an enzyme obtained from a strain of staphylococcus that is an effective antibiotic against other staphylococci
mac·chi·net·ta \,mäkəˈnetə\ *n* -s [It *macchinetta (da caffè)* coffee machine, fr. dim. of *macchina* machine, fr. L *machina* — more at MACHINE] **:** a drip-coffee maker in which water is heated in the upper part which is then inverted to allow the water to run through the coffee into the lower part
mace \ˈmās\ *vt* -ED/-ING/-S [fr. *Mace*, a trademark] **:** to attack with a temporarily disabling liquid that is usu. sprayed in the face and that causes tears, dizziness, confusion, immobilization, and sometimes nausea
machine language *n* **1 :** information recorded in a form usable by a machine (as a computer) **2 :** numbers or instructions expressed in a form directly usable by a computer
machine translation *n* **:** automatic translation from one language to another
ma·chis·mo \mäˈchēz(,)mō\ *n* -s [MexSp, fr. Sp *macho* male (fr. L *masculus*) + *-ismo* -ism — more at MALE] **:** a strong sense of masculine pride **:** an exaggerated awareness and assertion of masculinity
mac·ro·aggregate \¦makrō+\ *n* [*macr-* + *aggregate*] **:** a relatively large particle (as of soil or serum albumin) — **mac·ro·aggregated** \"+\ *adj*
macrobiotic* *adj* **:** of, relating to, or being an extremely restricted diet (as one containing chiefly whole grains) that is held to promote health and well-being even though deficient in essential nutrients
mac·ro·globulin \¦makrō+\ *n* [ISV *macr-* + *globulin*] **:** a highly polymerized globulin of high molecular weight
mac·ro·glob·u·lin·emia \,makrō,gläbyələˈnēmēə\ *n* -s [NL, fr. ISV *macroglobulin* + NL *-emia*] **:** a disorder characterized by increased blood serum viscosity and by macroglobulins in the serum — **mac·ro·glob·u·lin·emic** \-nēmik\ *adj*
mac·ro·lide \ˈmakrə,līd\ *n* -s [*macrocyclic* + *lactone* + *-ide*] **:** any of several antibiotics that contain a lactone ring and are produced by actinomycetes of the genus *Streptomyces*
mac·ro·organism \¦makrō+\ *n* [*macr-* + *organism*] **:** an organism large enough to be seen by the normal unaided human eye — compare MICROORGANISM *in the Dict*
mafia* *n, often cap* **:** a group of people of similar interests or backgrounds prominent in a particular field or enterprise **:** CLIQUE ⟨representation of what the inflamed imaginations . . . see as the homosexual *Mafia* of hairdressers, dress designers and decorators —Elenore Lester⟩
ma·fi·o·so \,mäfēˈō(,)sō, -af-, -)zō\ *n, pl* **mafio·si** \-sē, -zē\ *usu cap* [It, fr. *Mafia* + *-oso* -ous, fr. L *-osus*] **:** a member of the Mafia
magnetic bottle *n* **:** a magnetic field for confining plasma for experiments in nuclear fusion
magnetic core *n* **1 :** CORE 1i **2 :** a magnetic material in the shape of a doughnut that is strung on wires through which electric current is pulsed, that is capable of assuming and retaining one or more conditions of magnetization, and that is used esp. in computer memories
mag·ne·to·cardiograph \magˈnēd·ō, -ed·- +\ *n* [*magnet-* + *cardiograph*] **:** an instrument for recording the changes in the magnetic field around the heart that is used to supplement information given by an electrocardiograph — **mag·ne·to·cardiogram** \"+\ *n* — **mag·ne·to·cardiographic** \"+\ *adj*
mag·ne·to·gas·dy·nam·ics \mag,nēd·ō,gasdīˈnamiks, -ed·- *sometimes* -sdə'n-\ *n pl but sing in constr* [*magnet-* + *gas* + *dynamics*] **:** MAGNETOHYDRODYNAMICS — **mag·ne·to·gas·dy·nam·ic** \-ik\ *adj*
mag·ne·to·pause \magˈnēd·ə,pȯz, -ed·-\ *n* [*magnetosphere* (herein) + *pause*] **:** the outer boundary of a magnetosphere
mag·ne·to·plas·ma·dy·nam·ic \mag¦nēd·ō,plazmədī¦namik, -ed·- *sometimes* -mədə¦\ *adj* [*magnet-* + *plasma* + *dynamic*] **:** MAGNETOHYDRODYNAMIC — **mag·ne·to·plas·ma·dy·nam·ics** \-ks\ *n*
mag·ne·to·sphere \magˈnēd·ə, -ed·ə +,\ *n* [*magnet-* + *sphere*] **1 :** a region of the upper atmosphere that surrounds the earth, extends out for thousands of miles, and is dominated by the earth's magnetic field so that charged particles are trapped in it **2 :** a region that surrounds a celestial body (as a planet) and is comparable to the earth's magnetosphere in trapping charged particles — **mag·ne·to·spheric** \=¦== +\ *adj*
mail cover *n* **:** a postal monitoring and recording of information (as return address and postmark) on all mail going to a designated addressee
majolica* *n* **:** a 19th century earthenware modeled in naturalistic shapes and glazed in bright colors
major–medical \¦==¦==\ *adj* **:** of, relating to, or being a form of insurance designed to pay all or part of the medical bills of major illnesses usu. after deduction of a fixed initial sum
make* *vb* — **make it 1 :** to be successful ⟨trying to *make it* as writer-in-residence at the university —Gershon Legman⟩ **2 :** to have sexual intercourse ⟨one young couple who would . . . *make it* in a rear seat —Thomas Pynchon⟩
makuta *pl of* LIKUTA *herein*
mal·i·bu board \ˈmalə,bü-\ *n, usu cap M* [after *Malibu* Beach, California] **:** a lightweight surfboard 9 to 10 feet long with a round nose, square tail, and slightly convex bottom
man* *n, usu cap* **1 :** POLICE ⟨when I heard the siren, I knew it was the *Man* —*Amer. Speech*⟩ **2 :** the white establishment **:** white society ⟨surprise that any black man . . . should take on so about The *Man* —Peter Goldman⟩
man·eb \ˈma,neb\ *n* -s [*manganese* + *ethylene* + *bis-*] **:** a carbamate agricultural fungicide
ma·ni·cot·ti \,manəˈkäd·ē, ,mänēˈkȯd·ē\ *n, pl* **manicotti** [It, lit., muff, fr. *manica* sleeve, fr. L — more at MANCHE] **:** tubular pasta shells stuffed with ricotta
manifold* *n* **1 :** a space topologically equivalent to a sphere in euclidean space **2 :** an abstract generalization of a surface **3 :** a set of mathematical elements having properties common to various elementary configurations
-man·ship \mən,ship\ *n suffix* -s [*sportsmanship*] **:** the art or practice of maneuvering to gain a tactical advantage ⟨*gamesmanship*⟩
mao \ˈmau̇\ *adj, usu cap* [after *Mao* Tse-tung *b*1893 Chin. communist leader] **:** having a long narrow cut and a mandarin collar — usu. used of a jacket
mao·ism \ˈmau̇,izəm\ *n* -s *usu cap* [*Mao* Tse-tung + E *-ism*] **:** the theory and practice of Marxism-Leninism developed in China chiefly by Mao Tse-tung — **mao·ist** \ˈmau̇əst\ *n or adj, usu cap*
mar·ag·ing steel \ˈmär,ājiŋ-\ *n* [*martensite* + *aging* + *steel*] **:** a strong tough low-carbon martensitic steel which contains up to 25 percent nickel and in which hardening precipitates are formed by aging
mar·ga·ri·ta \,märgəˈrēd·ə\ *n* -s [MexSp, prob. fr. the name *Margarita* Margaret] **:** a cocktail consisting of tequila, lime or lemon juice, and an orange-flavored liqueur
mari·culture \ˈmarə+,\ *n* [*mari-* + *culture*] **:** the cultivation of marine organisms by exploiting their natural environment
mar·i·na·ra \,marəˈnärə\ *adj* [It *(alla) marinara* in sailor style, fr. *marinara*, fem. of *marinaro*, of sailors, fr. *marino* marine — more at MARINATE] **:** made with tomatoes, onion, garlic, and spices ⟨~ sauce⟩
mar·ko·vi·an \märˈkōvēən\ *adj, usu cap* [*Markov* (*process*) + *E -ian*] **:** of, relating to, or resembling a Markov process esp. by having probabilities defined in terms of transition from the possible existing states to other states
mar·kov process *also* **mar·koff process** \ˈmär,kȯf-\ *n, usu cap M* [after Andrei Andreevich *Markov* †1922 Russ. mathematician] **:** a stochastic process (as Brownian movement or a random walk) in which the probabilities of occurrence of various future states depend only on the present state of the system or on the immediately preceding state and not on the path by which the present state was achieved
mary greg·o·ry \ˈgreg(ə)rē, -rāg-, -ri\ *n, usu cap M & G* [perh. after *Mary Gregory fl* 1887 Am. glass painter] **:** colored glassware of a popular 19th century style marked by white enamel decoration usu. including children
mas·con \ˈmas,kän\ *n* -s [²*mass* + *concentration*] **:** one of the concentrations of large mass under the surface of the moon's maria whose gravitational effect is held to cause perturbations of the paths of spacecraft orbiting the moon
mass·cult \ˈmas,kəlt\ *n* [*mass culture*] **:** the artistic and intellectual culture associated with and disseminated through the mass media **:** mass culture
mass·less \ˈmasləs, ˈmaas-, ˈmais- *sometimes* ˈmȧs-\ *adj* [²*mass* + *-less*] **:** having no mass — **mass·less·ness** *n* -ES
matching funds *n pl* **:** funds provided (as by a government) that match funds provided by the recipient
mathematical biology *n* **:** a branch of knowledge concerned with the application of mathematics to the solution of problems in theoretical biology esp. by the construction of mathematical models — **mathematical biologist** *n*
matrix algebra *n* **:** generalized algebra that deals with the operations and relations among matrices
matrix sentence *n* **:** that one of a pair of sentences joined by means of a transformation that keeps its essential external structure and syntactic status ⟨in "the book that I want is gone", "the book is gone" is the *matrix sentence*⟩
ma·ven *or* **ma·vin** *or* **may·vin** \ˈmāvən\ *n* -s [Yiddish, fr. L Heb *mēbhīn*, perh. fr. Heb *mēbhī* one who has brought in] **:** one who is experienced or knowledgeable **:** EXPERT
maxi \ˈmaksē\ *n* -s [*maxi-* (herein)] **:** a long skirt or coat that usu. extends to the ankle — called also respectively *maxiskirt, maxicoat*
maxi- \ˈmaksē\ *comb form* [fr. *maximum*, after E *minimum*: *mini-* (herein)] **1 :** extra long ⟨*maxi*-dress⟩ ⟨*maxi*-kilt⟩ **2 :** extra large ⟨*maxi*-sculpture⟩ ⟨*maxi*-problems⟩
mbi·ra \emˈbirə\ *n* -s [native word in southern Africa; of Bantu origin] **:** ZANZA
mechanical bank *also* **mechanical*** *n* **:** a toy bank in which insertion of a coin activates a mechanism that goes through some amusing or absurd routine
mech·a·no·receptor \¦mekə(,)nō +\ *n* [*mechan-* + *receptor*] **:** a neural end organ (as a tactile receptor) that responds to a mechanical stimulus (as a change in pressure) — **mech·a·no·reception** \" +\ *n* — **mech·a·no·receptive** \" +\ *adj*
mech·lor·eth·a·mine \,me,klōrˈethə,mēn, -lȯr-, -,mən\ *n* [*methyl* + *chloroethyl* + *amine*] **:** a nitrogen mustard used as an insect chemosterilant, as a war gas, and in palliative treatment of some neoplastic diseases
media mix *n* **:** a presentation (as in a theater) in which several media (as films, tapes, and slides) are employed simultaneously
med·ic·aid \ˈmedə,kād, -dē,-\ *n* [*medical* + *aid*] **:** a program of medical aid designed for those unable to afford regular medical service and financed by the state and federal governments
medi·care \ˈmedə, -dē +,\ *n* [blend of *medical* and *care*] **:** a government program of medical care esp. for the aged
me·dul·lin \məˈdələn, me-; ˈmedᵊl-, ˈmejəl-\ *n* -s [NL *medulla* + E *-in*; fr. its isolation from the medulla of the kidney] **:** a renal prostaglandin effective in reducing blood pressure
mef·e·nam·ic acid \,mefə,namik-\ *n* [*dimethyl* + *fen-* (by shortening and alter. fr. *phenyl*) + *aminobenzoic acid*] **:** a crystalline compound $C_{15}H_{15}NO_2$ used esp. to relieve pain or inflammation
mega·buck \ˈmegə +,\ *n* [*mega-* + ¹*buck*] **:** one million dollars
mega·death \"+,\ *n* [*mega-* + *death*] **:** one million deaths — used as a unit in reference to atomic warfare
mega·rad \"+,\ *n* [*mega-* + ³*rad*] **:** one million rads
mega·unit \"+,\ *n* [*mega-* + *unit*] **:** one million units
mela·to·nin \¦meləˈtōnən\ *n* -s [prob. fr. *melanocyte* + *serotonin*; fr. its power to lighten melanocytes] **:** a substance produced in the pineal body that plays a role in sexual development and maturation
memory trace *n* **:** an alteration within the central nervous system that is held to constitute the physical basis of learning
men·a·zon \ˈmenə,zän\ *n* -s [perh. fr. *dimethyl* + *diamino-* + *triazine* + *thionate*] **:** an organophosphate insecticide used esp. against aphids, plant bugs, and cattle insects
meno·taxis \¦menə+\ *n* [NL, fr. ²*meno-* + *taxis*] **:** a taxis involving a constant reaction (as movement at a constant angle to a light source) but not a simple movement toward or away from the directing stimulus
me·rid·ic \məˈridik\ *adj* [Gk *merid-*, *meris* part + E *-ic*; akin to Gk *meros* part — more at MERIT] **:** having some but not all active constituents chemically defined ⟨insects reared on a ~ diet⟩ — compare HOLIDIC, OLIGIDIC *herein*
mer·i·toc·ra·cy \,merəˈtäkrəsē\ *n* -ES [¹*merit* + *-cracy*] **1 :** an educational system whereby the talented are chosen and moved ahead on the basis of their achievement (as in competitive examinations) **2 :** leadership by the talented — **mer·it·o·crat·ic** \¦merəd·əˈkrad·ik\ *adj*
meson* *n* **:** any of a group of strongly interacting particles that can be created and annihilated in arbitrary numbers and that obey the Bose-Einstein statistics
meso·pelagic \¦me|zō, ¦mē|, |sō+\ *adj* [*mes-* + *pelagic*] **:** of or relating to oceanic depths from about 600 feet to 3000 feet
mesosome* *n* **:** a cell organelle that appears in electron micrographs as an invagination of the plasma membrane and is a site of localization of respiratory enzymes
messenger RNA \-,ä,reˈnā\ *n* -s **:** a ribonucleic acid that carries the code for a protein from the nuclear deoxyribonucleic acid to the ribosome and acts as a template for the formation of that protein — compare TRANSFER RNA *herein*
met·al·lid·ing \ˈmed·ᵊl,īdiŋ, -etᵊl-\ *n* -s [*metall-* + *-iding* (prob. fr. ¹*-ide* + ³*-ing*)] **:** the process of diffusing atoms of a metal or metalloid into the surface of a metal by electrolysis in order to impart a desired surface property (as hardness) to the bulk metal
me·tal·lo·enzyme \mə¦talō+\ *n* [*metall-* + *enzyme*] **:** an enzyme consisting of a protein linked with a specific metal
metameric* *adj* **:** of, relating to, or being color metamers ⟨a ~ pair⟩ — **metamerism*** *n*
me·te·or·oi·dal \¦mēd·ēə¦rȯidᵊl\ *adj* [*meteoroid* + *-al*] **:** of or relating to meteoroids
me·tepa \mə, (ˈ)me+\ *n* -s [*methyl* + *tepa* (herein)] **:** an insect chemosterilant that is a methyl derivative of tepa
meter maid *n* **:** a female member of a police force who is assigned to write tickets for parking violations
meth·i·cil·lin \¦methəˈsilən\ *n* -s [*meth-* + *penicillin*] **:** a synthetic penicillin esp. effective against penicillinase-producing staphylococci
method* *n, usu cap* **:** a dramatic technique by which an actor seeks to gain complete identification with the inner personality of the character being portrayed so that all thoughts, feelings, and actions expressed in the portrayal are those of the character and not of the actor
meth·o·trex·ate \,methəˈtrek,sāt, -sət\ *n* -s [*meth-* + *trex-* (of unknown origin) + *-ate*] **:** a drug that is a folic acid analogue and antimetabolite used as an anticancer drug
meths \ˈmeths\ *n pl but sing in constr* [contr. of *methylated spirits*] *Brit* **:** METHYLATED SPIRIT
met·ri·cate \ˈmetrə,kāt\ *vt* -ED/-ING/-S [²*metric* + ⁴*-ate*] *Brit* **:** METRICIZE *herein*
met·ri·ca·tion \,me·trəˈkāshən\ *n* -s [²*metric* + *-ation*] **:** the act or process of metricizing
metricize* *vt* [²*metric* + *-ize*] **:** to change into or express in the metric system
met·ro \ˈme·(,)trō\ *n* -s [short for *metropolitan government*] **:** a regional government having authority over a city and outlying suburbs or towns
me·tyr·a·pone \məˈtirə,pōn\ *n* -s [perh. fr. *methyl* + *-rapone* (alter. of *propanone*)] **:** a metabolic hormone that inhibits biosynthesis of cortisol and is used to test for normal functioning of the hypothalamus and pituitary
mi·chae·lis constant \mīˈkāləs-, mə-\ *n, usu cap M* [after Leonor *Michaelis* †1949 Am. biochemist] **:** a constant that is a measure of the kinetics of an enzyme reaction and that is equivalent to the concentration of substrate at which the reaction takes place at one half its maximum velocity
mickey–mouse \,mikēˈmau̇s, -ki-\ *vt* -ED/-ING/-S [fr. *Mickey Mouse*, a trademark] **:** to provide (a film) with accompanying music that closely describes or mimics the action
mickey mouse *adj, usu cap both Ms* [fr. *Mickey Mouse*, cartoon character — more at ²MICKEY] **:** lacking importance or serious meaning **:** INSIGNIFICANT ⟨switch to *Mickey Mouse* courses, where you don't work too hard —Willie Cager⟩
micro·body \¦mīkrō+,\ *n* [*micr-* + *body*] **:** a subcellular organelle demonstrable by electron microscopy that is a site of localization of enzymes in the cell
mi·cro·capsule \¦mīkrō+\ *n* [*micr-* + *capsule*] **:** a tiny capsule containing material (as a medicine) that is released when the capsule is broken, melted, or dissolved
mi·cro·card \ˈmīkrō+,\ *vb* -ED/-ING/-S [fr. *Microcard*, a trademark] *vt* **:** to reproduce (as a book) on a Microcard card or a series of such cards ~ *vi* **:** to use Microcard cards in reproducing printed matter
mi·cro·circuit \"+,\ *n* [*micr-* + *circuit*] **:** a compact electronic circuit consisting of elements of small size — **mi·cro·circuitry** \" +\ *n*
mi·cro·circulation \¦mīkrō+\ *n* [*micr-* + *circulation*] **:** the part of the circulatory system made up of very fine channels (as capillaries or venules) — **mi·cro·circulatory** \"+\ *adj*
mi·cro·culture \¦mīkrō+,\ *n* [*micr-* + *culture*] **1 :** the culture of a small group of human beings with limited perspective **2 :** a microscopic culture of cells or organisms — **mi·cro·cultural** \¦mīkrō+\ *adj*
mi·cro·distribution \¦mīkrō+\ *n* [*micr-* + *distribution*] **:** the precise distribution of one or more kinds of organisms in a microhabitat or in part of an ecosystem ⟨~ of soil mites⟩
mi·cro·dot \ˈmīkrō+,\ *n* [*micr-* + *dot*] **:** a photographic reproduction of printed matter reduced to the size of a dot for ease or security of transmittal
mi·cro·ecology \¦mīkrō +\ *n* [*micr-* + *ecology*] **:** ecology of all or part of a small community (as a microhabitat or a housing development) — **mi·cro·ecological** \"+\ *adj*

microelectrode* *n* **:** a small electrode inserted in a living biological cell or tissue in studying its electrical characteristics
mi·cro·electronics \¦mīkrō+\ *n pl but sing in constr* [*micr-* + *electronics*] **:** a branch of electronics that deals with the miniaturization of electronic circuits and components — **mi·cro·electronic** \"+\ *adj*
mi·cro·encapsulate \¦mīkrō+\ *vt* [*micr-* + *encapsulate*] **:** to enclose a small amount of (a substance) in a microcapsule
microform* *n* **1 :** MICROCOPY **2 :** matter reproduced in microform
mi·cro·image \'mīkrō+,\ *n* [*micr-* + *image*] **:** an image (as on a microfilm) that is of greatly reduced size ⟨~*s* of documents⟩
mi·cro·machining \¦mīkrō+\ *n* [*micr-* + *machining*, gerund of ²*machine*] **:** the removing (as in drilling, planing, or shaping) of small amounts of metal by action other than that of a sharp-edged tool ⟨~ with an electron beam⟩
micrometeorite* *n* **:** a meteoritic particle of very small size — **mi·cro·meteoritic** \¦mīkrō+\ *adj*
mi·cro·meteoroid \¦mīkrō+\ *n* [*micr-* + *meteoroid*] **:** MICROMETEORITE *herein*
mi·cro·miniature \"+\ *adj* [*micr-* + *miniature*] **1 :** MICROMINIATURIZED *herein* **2 :** suitable for use with microminiaturized parts
mi·cro·miniaturization \"+\ *n* [*micr-* + *miniaturization*] **:** the process of producing microminiaturized things
mi·cro·miniaturized \"+\ *adj* [*micr-* + *miniaturized*] **:** reduced to or produced in a very small size and esp. in a size smaller than one considered miniature ⟨~ electronic circuit⟩
mi·cro·module \"+\ *n* [*micr-* + *module*] **:** a miniaturized module
mi·cro·morphology \"+\ *n* [*micr-* + *morphology*] **1 :** MICROSTRUCTURE — used esp. with reference to soils **2 :** the study of minute morphological detail esp. by electron microscopy — **mi·cro·morphologic** \"+\ *adj* — **mi·cro·morphological** \"+\ *adj* — **mi·cro·morphologically** \"+\ *adv*
mi·cro·population \"+\ *n* [*micr-* + *population*] **1 :** a population of microorganisms **2 :** the population of organisms within a small area
mi·cro·probe \'mīkrə+,\ *n* [*micr-* + *probe*] **:** a device for microanalysis that operates by exciting radiation in a minute area or volume of material so that the composition may be determined by means of the emission spectrum
mi·cro·programming \¦mīkrō+\ *n* [*micro-* + *programming*, gerund of ²*program*] **:** the use of data stored in memory rather than specialized circuits for controlling a device (as a computer) — **mi·cro·program** \"+\ *n or vt*
mi·cro·state \'mīkrō+,\ *n* [*micr-* + *state*] **:** a newly independent nation that is extremely small in area and population and poor in resources
mi·cro·surgery \¦mīkrō+\ *n* [*micr-* + *surgery*] **:** minute dissection or manipulation (as by micromanipulator or laser beam) of living structures (as cells) for surgical or experimental purposes — **mi·cro·surgical** \"+\ *adj*
mi·cro·tubule \"+\ *n* [*micr-* + *tubule*] **:** any of the minute tubular or possibly rodlike structures that are widely distributed in protoplasm, are made up of longitudinal fibrils, and are sometimes held to be specifically related to protoplasmic motility — **mi·cro·tubular** \"+\ *adj*
mi·cro·vascular \"+\ *adj* [*micr-* + *vascular*] **:** of, relating to, or constituting the part of the circulatory system made up of minute vessels (as venules or capillaries) that average less than 0.3 millimeters in diameter — **mi·cro·vasculature** \"+\ *n*
mi·cro·villus \"+\ *n* [NL, fr. *micr-* + *villus*] **:** a microscopic projection of a tissue, a cell, or a cell organelle; *esp* **:** one of the fingerlike outward projections of some cell surfaces — **mi·cro·vil·lar** \¦==¦vilər\ *adj* — **mi·cro·vil·lous** \-ləs\ *adj*
midcourse \¦=,=\ *adj* [*midcourse, n.*, fr. ¹*mid* + *course*] **:** being or relating to the part of a course (as of spacecraft) that is between the initial and final phases — **midcourse** \'=¦=\ *n*
mid·cult \'mid,kəlt\ *n* -s [*mid*dlebrow *cult*ure] **:** the artistic and intellectual culture that is neither highbrow culture nor lowbrow culture **:** middlebrow culture
middle america *n, often cap M& usu cap A* **1 :** the midwestern section of the U.S. **2 :** the middle-class segment of the U.S. population — **middle american** *n, cap M&A*
midi \'midē\ *n* -s [¹*mid* + -*i* (as in *mini* — herein)] **:** a dress, skirt, or coat that usu. extends to the mid-calf — called also respectively *midi dress, midi skirt, midi coat*
mim·eo \'mimē,ō\ *n* -s [by shortening fr. *mimeographed*] **:** a mimeographed publication
mim–mem \'mim'mem\ *adj* [*mim*icry + *mem*orization] **:** of, relating to, or being a drill pattern in which students repeat usu. in chorus a foreign language phrase supplied by their instructor
mind–expanding \'==,==\ *adj* **:** PSYCHEDELIC 1a *herein*
mini \'minē\ *n* -s [by shortening] **1 :** MINICAR **2 :** a short skirt or dress that usu. extends to the mid-thigh — called also respectively *miniskirt* or *minidress*
mini- \¦minē\ *comb form* [*miniature*] **:** very small **:** miniature
minibike \'==,=\ *n* [*mini-* (herein) + *bike*] **:** a small one-passenger motorcycle having a low frame and elevated handlebars
minibus \'==,=\ *n* [*mini-* (herein) + *bus*] **:** a small bus for comparatively short trips
minicab \'==,=\ *n* [*mini-* (herein) + *cab*] **:** a very small car used as a taxicab
minicomputer \¦===¦==\ *n* [*mini-* (herein) + *computer*] **:** a small comparatively inexpensive computer
minimal* *adj, often cap* **:** of, relating to, or being minimal art ⟨~ aluminum pieces —Grace H. Glueck⟩
minimal art *n* **:** abstract art (as painting or sculpture) consisting primarily of simple geometric forms executed in an impersonal style — **minimal artist** *n*
minimalist* *n* **:** MINIMAL ARTIST *herein*
mini·max \'minə,maks, -nē,m-\ *n* -ES [*mini*mum + *max*imum] **:** the minimum of a set of maxima; *esp* **:** the smallest of a set of maximum possible losses each of which occurs in the most unfavorable outcome of a strategy followed by a participant in a situation governed by the theory of games
minimax principle *n* **:** a principle of choice for a decision problem: one should choose the action which minimizes the loss that he stands to suffer even under the worst circumstances
minimax theorem *n* **:** a theorem in the theory of games: the lowest maximum expected loss equals the highest minimum expected gain
mini·pig \-,pig\ *n* [*mini-* (herein) + *pig*] **:** a miniature pig bred for use in scientific research
mini·ski \'minē+,\ *n* [*mini-* (herein) + *ski*] **1 :** a ski of less than normal length held to make skiing easier (as for beginners) **2 :** a miniature ski worn by a skibobber
mini·state \"+,\ *n* -s [*mini-* (herein) + *state*] **:** a small newly independent nation
mini·sub \"+,\ *n* -s [*mini-* (herein) + ⁴*sub*] **:** a very small submarine used esp. in research (as on the ocean bottom)
minnesota multiphasic personality inventory *also* **minnesota multiphasic test** *n, usu cap both Ms & P & I* [fr. the University of *Minnesota*, where it was developed] **:** a test of personal and social adjustment based on a complex scaling of the answers to an elaborate true or false test
MIRV \'mərv\ *n* -s [*m*ultiple *i*ndependently targeted *r*eentry *v*ehicle] **:** a missile with two or more warheads designed to reenter the atmosphere on the way to separate enemy targets; *also* **:** any of the warheads of such a missile
mis·communication \"+\ *n* [¹*mis-* + *communication*] **:** failure to communicate clearly
mis·orient \"+\ *vt* [¹*mis-* + *orient*] **:** to orient improperly or incorrectly — **mis·orientation** \"+\ *n*
mist* *n* **:** a drink of alcoholic liquor (as Scotch) served over cracked ice and garnished with a twist of lemon peel
mi·to·gen \'mīd·əjən\ *n* -s [*mit-* + -*gen*] **:** a substance that induces mitosis — **mi·to·gen·ic** \¦mīd·ə¦jenik\ *adj* — **mi·to·gen·ic·i·ty** \,mīd·əjə'nisəd·ē\ *n* -ES
mi·to·my·cin \,mīd·ə'mīsᵊn\ *n* -s [prob. fr. ISV *mit-* + -*mycin*] **:** an antibiotic produced by a Japanese streptomyces that in one form (**mitomycin C**) acts directly on deoxyribonucleic acid and shows promise as an anticancer agent
mito·spore \'mīd·ə+,\ *n* [*mit-* + *spore*] **:** a haploid or diploid spore produced by mitosis
mix* *n* **:** MIXER 2b
mixed–media \'=¦===\ *adj* [*mixed* + *media*, pl. of *medium*] **:** MULTIMEDIA *herein*
mixed media *n* [*mixed-media, adj* (herein)] **1 :** a work of art executed in more than one medium **2 :** MULTIMEDIA *herein*
¹**mod** \'mäd\ *adj, often cap* [short for *modern*] **:** MODERN; *esp* **:** bold, free, and unconventional in style or dress
²**mod** *n* -s *often cap* **:** one who wears mod clothes
model* *n* **:** a system of postulates, data, and inferences presented as a mathematical description of an entity or state of affairs ⟨a mathematical ~ of the physical world⟩
mo·dem \'mō,dem\ *n* -s [*mo*dulator + *dem*odulator] **:** a device that converts signals from one form to a form compatible with another kind of equipment ⟨a ~ for transmitting computer data over telephone lines⟩
modular arithmetic *n* **:** arithmetic that deals with whole numbers where the numbers are replaced by their remainders after division by a fixed number ⟨in a *modular arithmetic* with modulus 5, 3 multiplied by 4 would be 2⟩
mod·u·lar·ized \'mäjələ,rīzd\ *adj* [*modular* + -*ize* + -*ed*] **:** constructed of modules ⟨~ electronic equipment⟩
module* *n* **1 :** any in a series of standardized units for use together **2 :** an assembly of components that are packaged or mounted together and constitute a functional unit for an electronic or mechanical system ⟨a ~ for a computer⟩ **3 :** an independent unit that constitutes a part of the total structure of a space vehicle ⟨a propulsion ~⟩
modulus* *n* **:** the length of the radius vector from the origin to the point representing the number in the complex plane
mo·gul \'mōgəl\ *n* -s [prob. of Scand origin; akin to Norw dial. *muge* heap, pile, fr. ON *mūgi* — more at MOW] **:** a bump in a ski run
mois·tur·ize \'mȯischə,rīz\ *vt* -ED/-ING/-S [*moisture* + -*ize*] **:** to add moisture to ⟨~ the air⟩ — **mois·tur·iz·er** *n* -s
moldy fig *n* **:** a devotee of traditional jazz
moment of truth 1 : the final sword thrust in a bullfight **2 :** a moment of crisis on whose outcome much or everything depends ⟨the lift-off of a . . . space vehicle with three men aboard is an awesome *moment of truth* —R.A.Petrone⟩
¹**mono** \'mä(,)nō, 'mō(,)-\ *adj* [by shortening] **:** MONOPHONIC 3 ⟨a ~ phonograph record⟩
²**mono** *n* -s **1 :** a mono phonograph record **2 :** mono reproduction
³**mono** *n* -s [by shortening] **:** MONONUCLEOSIS
monoamine* *n* **:** PRIMARY AMINE; *esp* **:** one (as serotonin) that is functionally important in neural transmission
mono·am·i·ner·gic \¦mäno,amə¦nərjik, ¦mōn-\ *adj* [*monoamine* (herein) + *erg-* + -*ic*] **:** of, relating to, or being nervous mechanisms in which monoamines play a role in nerve impulse transmissions
monoamine oxidase *n* **:** an enzyme that deaminates primary amines oxidatively
monochrome* *adj* **:** BLACK-AND-WHITE 4b
mono·contaminate \¦mä(,)nō, ¦mō(,)-+\ *vt* [*mon-* + *contaminate*] **:** to infect (a germ-free organism) with one kind of pathogen — **mono·contamination** \"+\ *n*
mono·functional \¦mä(,)nō, ¦mō(,)-, -,nə- +\ *adj* [*mon-* + *functional*] **:** of, relating to, or being a compound with one highly reactive site in the molecule (as in polymerization)
monolayer* *n* **:** a single continuous layer of cells
monolithic* *adj* **1 :** formed from a single crystal ⟨a ~ silicon chip⟩ **2 :** produced in or on a monolithic chip ⟨a ~ circuit⟩ **3 :** consisting of or utilizing a monolithic circuit or circuits
mono·pole \'mänə,pōl, 'mōn-\ *n* -s [*mon-* + ⁴*pole*] **1 :** a single positive or negative electrical charge; *also* **:** a hypothetical north or south magnetic pole existing alone **2 :** a radio antenna in the form of a single often straight radiating element
mono·sexual \¦mä(,)nō, ¦mō(,)-+\ *adj* [*mon-* + *sexual*] **:** of, relating to, or intended for one sex only ⟨~ schools⟩: **a :** male or female rather than bisexual **b :** composed of individuals of one sex — **mono·sexuality** \"+\ *n*
montagnard* *n, often cap* **:** a member of a people inhabiting a highland region in southern Vietnam bordering on Cambodia — **montagnard** *adj, often cap*
mon·te car·lo method \,mäntē'kär(,)lō-, -tə'k-\ *n, usu cap 1st M&C* [fr. *Monte Carlo*, Monaco, city noted for its gambling casino] **:** a procedure that involves the use of sampling techniques based on probabilities to approximate the solution of mathematical or physical problems
mon·uron \'mänyə,rän, 'mōn-\ *n* -s [*mon-* + *urea* + ¹-*on*] **:** a persistent herbicide used esp. to control mixed weeds
mooncraft \'=,=\ *n* [*moon* + *craft*] **:** MOONSHIP *herein*
moon·fall \'mün,fȯl\ *n* [*moon* + -*fall* (as in *landfall*)] **:** a landing on the moon
moonflight \'=,=\ *n* [*moon* + *flight*] **:** a flight to the moon
moonport \'=,=\ *n* [*moon* + ¹*port*] **:** a place on earth equipped for sending spacecraft to the moon
moon·ship \'=,=\ *n* [¹*moon* + ¹*ship*] **:** a spacecraft for travel to the moon
moonshot \'=,=\ *or* **moon shoot** \'=,=\ *n* [*moon* + ¹*shot* or ²*shoot*] **:** the act or an instance of launching of an unmanned instrumented vehicle on a course to the moon or its vicinity
moonwalk \'=,=\ *n* [¹*moon* + ²*walk*] **:** an instance of walking on the moon — **moonwalker** \'=,==\ *n*
mo·ped \'mō,ped\ *n* -s [G, fr. ISV *mo*tor + ¹-*ped*] **:** a lightweight low-powered motorbike developed by Europeans
morning–after pill \,==¦==-\ *n* [so called fr. its being taken after rather than before intercourse] **:** an oral drug that blocks implantation of a fertilized egg in the human uterus and thereby interferes with pregnancy
morph \'mȯ(ə)rf, 'mȯ(ə)f\ *n* -s [Gk *morphē* form — more at FORM] **1 :** a local population of a species that consists of interbreeding organisms and is distinguishable from other populations by morphology or behavior though capable of interbreeding with them **2 :** a phenotypic variant of a species
mor·pho·physiology \¦mȯr(,)fō+\ *n* [ISV *morph-* + *physiology*] **:** a branch of biology that deals with the interrelationships of structure and function — **mor·pho·physiological** \"+\ *adj*
möss·bau·er effect \'mə(r)s,bau̇(ə)r-, ¦mōs-,¦mœs-,¦mes-\ *n usu cap M* [after Rudolf L. *Mössbauer* b1929 Ger. physicist] **:** the emission and absorption of gamma rays without recoil by various radioactive nuclei embedded in solids
motor home *n* **:** an automotive vehicle built on a truck or bus chassis and equipped as a self-contained traveling home
motor inn *n* **:** a usu. multistory urban motel — called also *motor hotel*
mox·i·bus·tion \¦mäksə¦bəschən\ *n* -s [NL *moxa* + E -*bustion* (as in *combustion*)] **:** medical use of a moxa
mri·dan·ga \mrē'däŋgə, ,marē-\ *or* **mri·dan·gam** \-gəm\ *n* -s [Skt *mṛdaṅga*, prob. of imit. origin] **:** a drum of India that is shaped like an elongated barrel and has tuned heads of different diameters
mul·ti·centric \¦məltə, -tē, -,tī+\ *adj* [*multi-* + -*centric*] **:** having multiple centers of origin ⟨a ~ tumor⟩ — **mul·ti·centrically** \"+\ *adv* — **mul·ti·centricity** \"+\ *n* -ES
mul·ti·company \"+\ *n* [*multi-* + *company*] **:** a large corporate enterprise with interests in two or more distinct industries
multi·hull \"+\ *adj* [*multi-* + *hull*] **:** having more than one hull ⟨a ~ boat⟩; *also* **:** of or relating to multihull boats
mul·ti·industry \"+\ *adj* [*multi-* + *industry*] **:** active in or concerned with two or more separate industries
mul·ti·market \"+\ *adj* [*multi-* + *market*] **:** MULTI-INDUSTRY *herein*
¹**mul·ti·media** \"+\ *adj* [*multi-* + *media*, pl. of ¹*medium*] **:** using, involving, or encompassing several media
²**mul·ti·media** \"+\ *n* **:** communication or entertainment in which several media are employed esp. simultaneously
mul·ti·national \"+\ *adj* **1a :** of, relating to, or involving more than two nations ⟨a ~ nuclear force⟩ **b :** having divisions in more than two countries ⟨a ~ corporation⟩ **2 :** of or relating to more than two nationalities ⟨a ~ society⟩
multiple store *n, chiefly Brit* **:** CHAIN STORE
multiplet* *n* **1 :** any of two or more atomic, molecular, or nuclear quantum states that are usu. close together in energy and that arise from different relative orientations of angular momenta **2 :** a group of spectral frequencies arising from transitions to or from a multiplet quantum state
multiplicative identity *n* **:** an identity element (as 1 in the group of rational numbers without 0 under the operation of multiplication) that in a given mathematical system leaves unchanged any element by which it is multiplied
multiplicative inverse *n* **:** the reciprocal of a given number
multiplier effect *n* **:** the effect of a relatively minor factor in precipitating a great change; *esp* **:** the effect of a relatively small change in one economic factor (as rate of saving or level of consumer credit) in inducing a disproportionate increase or decrease in another (as gross national product)
mul·ti·processing \¦məltə, -tē, -,tī +\ *n* [*multi-* + *processing*, gerund of ²*process*] **:** the processing of several computer programs at the same time esp. by a computer system with several processors sharing a single memory — **multiprocessor** *n*
mul·ti·programming \"+\ *n* [*multi-* + *programming*] **:** the simultaneous utilization of interleaved programs in a computer — **mul·ti·programmed** \"+\ *adj*
mul·ti·resistant \"+\ *adj* [*multi-* + *resistant*] **:** biologically resistant to several toxic agents ⟨~ falciparum malaria⟩ — **mul·ti·resistance** \"+\ *n*
mul·ti·ver·si·ty \¦məltə¦vərsəd·ē, -tē¦v-, -stē\ *n* -ES [*multi-* + -*versity* (as in *university*)] **:** a very large university with many component schools, colleges, or divisions, with widely diverse functions (as the teaching of freshmen and the carrying on of advanced research), and with a large staff engaged in activities other than instruction and esp. in administration
mu–meson* *n* **:** MUON *herein*
muon* *n* **:** an unstable lepton that is common in the cosmic radiation near the earth's surface, has a mass 206.77 times the mass of the electron and an average lifetime of 2.20×10^{-6} second, and exists in negative and positive forms related as particle and antiparticle — **mu·on·ic** \myü'änik\ *adj*
muslim* *n, usu cap* **:** BLACK MUSLIM *herein*
mu·ta·ge·nic·i·ty \,myüd·əjə'nisəd·ē\ *n* -ES [*mutagenic* + -*ity*] **:** the capacity to induce mutations
mu·ta·ro·tase \,myüd·ə'rō,tās, -āz\ *n* [*muta*rotation + -*ase*] **:** an isomerase found esp. in mammalian tissues that catalyzes the interconversion of anomeric forms of certain sugars
mu·ta·tor gene \¦myü,tād·ə(r)-\ *also* **mutator** \'=,==, =¦==\ *n* -s [L *mutator* one that changes, fr. *mutatus*, past part. of *mutare* to change + -*or* — more at MISS] **:** a gene modifier that increases the mutability of one or more genes
MVP *abbr* most valuable player
my·co·toxin \¦mīkə +\ *n* [*myc-* + *toxin*] **:** a poisonous substance produced by a fungus and esp. a mold — compare AFLATOXIN *herein* — **my·co·toxic** \"+\ *adj* — **my·co·toxicity** \"+\ *n* — **my·co·toxicosis** \"+\ *n*
my·e·lo·fibrosis \¦mīəlō+\ *n* [NL, fr. *myel-* + *fibrosis*] **:** an anemic condition in which bone marrow becomes fibrotic and the liver and spleen usu. exhibit a development of blood cell precursors — **my·e·lo·fibrotic** \"+\ *adj*
my·e·lo·proliferative \"+\ *adj* [*myel-* + *proliferative*] **:** of, relating to, or being a disorder (as leukemia) marked by excessive proliferation of the blood cell precursors
myo·electric \¦mīō+\ *also* **myo·electrical** \"+\ *adj* [*my-* + *electric*] **:** of, relating to, or utilizing electricity generated by muscle — **myo·electrically** \" +\ *adv*
myo·fibrillar \"+\ *adj* [*myofibril* + -*ar*] **:** of or relating to myofibrils
myo·filament \"+\ *n* [*my-* + *filament*] **:** a single contractile micelle of a myofibril
mys·te·ri·um \mə'stirēəm, -tēr-\ *n* -s [NL, fr. E *mystery* + NL -*ium*] **:** a source of fluctuating radio emissions in the Milky Way galaxy held to be excited hydroxyl radicals
myxo·virus \¦miksə+\ *n* [NL, fr. *myx-* + *virus*; fr. its affinity for certain mucins] **:** any of a group of rather large RNA-containing viruses that includes influenza and mumps viruses — **myxo·viral** \"+\ *adj*
n* *abbr* ²nano-
NAD \,e(,)nā'dē\ *abbr or n* -s nicotinamide-adenine dinucleotide *herein*
NADP \,e,nā(,)dē'pē\ *abbr or n* -s nicotinamide-adenine dinucleotide phosphate *herein*
naïve* *adj* **:** ignorant of relevant research hypotheses or of the purpose of a particular experiment; *also* **:** not previously subjected to experimentation or to a particular experimental situation ⟨experimentally ~ rats⟩
na·led \'nā,led\ *n* -s [origin unknown] **:** a short-lived insecticide of relatively low toxicity to warm-blooded animals that is used esp. to control crop pests and mosquitoes
name of the game : the thing to do or have **:** the essential quality or matter ⟨patience is the *name of the game* in coastal duck hunting —Dick Beals⟩
nano·second \¦nanō+\ *n* [ISV *nano-* + *second*] **:** one billionth of a second — *abbr. nanosec, nsec*
narc *or* **nark** \'närk\ *n* -s [short for *narcotic agent*] **:** one (as a government agent) who investigates narcotics violations
narcotic* *n* **:** a drug (as marijuana or LSD) subject to restriction similar to that of addictive narcotics whether in fact physiologically narcotic and addictive or not
na·tri·ure·sis \¦nā·trē(y)ə¦rēsəs, ¦na-\ *also* **na·tru·re·sis** \-trə¦rē-\ *n* [NL, fr. *natrium* or *natr-* + *uresis*] **:** excessive loss of cations and esp. sodium in the urine — **na·tri·uret·ic** \-trē(y)ə¦red·ik\ *adj or n*
natural language* *n* **:** the language of ordinary speaking and writing — distinguished from *machine language, herein*
neb·bish \'nebish\ *n* -ES [Yiddish *nebach, nebech* poor thing (used interjectionally), of Slav origin; akin to Czech *nebohý* wretched, Pol *nieboże* poor creature] **:** a timid, meek, or ineffectual person
negative income tax *n* **:** a system of federal subsidy payments to families with incomes below a stipulated level proposed as a substitute for or supplement to welfare payments
negative transfer *n* **:** the impeding of learning or performance in a situation by the carry-over of learned responses from another situation — called also *negative transfer effect;* compare INTERFERENCE 9, TRANSFER 6b
ne·gri·tude \'negrə,tüd, 'nēg-, -rə-,tyüd\ *n* -s [F *négritude*, fr. *nègre* Negro + -*i-* + -*tude* (fr. MF) — more at NEGRESS, -TUDE] **1 :** a consciousness of and pride in the cultural and physical aspects of the African heritage **2 :** the state of being a Negro
ne·gro·ness \'=(,)=nəs\ *n, usu cap* [*Negro* + -*ness*] **:** the quality or state of being Negro
neh·ru \'nā(,)rü, 'nā(,)rü\ *adj, usu cap* [after Jawaharlal *Nehru* †1964 Indian nationalist] **:** MAO *herein*
neo·colonialism \¦nē(,)ō+\ *n* [*ne-* + *colonialism*] **:** the economic and political policies by which a Great Power indirectly maintains or extends its influence over other areas or peoples — **neo·colonialist** \"+\ *n or adj*
neo–dada \"+\ *n, usu cap D* [*ne-* + *Dada*] **:** an anti-art movement esp. of the late 1950s and the 1960s based on tenets similar to those of Dada but having more interest in the object than Dada claimed to have; *broadly* **:** JUNK ART *herein* — **neo–dadaism** \"+\ *n* — **neo–dadaist** \"+\ *adj or n*
neur·amin·i·dase \,n(y)urə'minə,dās, -āz\ *n* -s [*neuramin*ic acid + -*idase* (as in *glucosidase*)] **:** a hydrolytic enzyme that is found esp. in microorganisms of the respiratory or intestinal tract and that splits mucoproteins by breaking a glucoside link
neu·ro·biology \¦n(y)ürō, -ü-\ *n* [*neur-* + *biology*] **:** a branch of the life sciences that deals with the anatomy, physiology, and pathology of the nervous system from a holistic viewpoint — **neu·ro·biological** \"+\ *adj* — **neu·ro·biologist** \"+\ *n*
neu·ro·chemistry \"+\ *n* [*neur-* + *chemistry*] **:** the study of the chemical makeup and activities of nervous tissue — **neu·ro·chemical** \"+\ *adj* — **neu·ro·chemist** \"+\ *n*
neu·ro·endocrinology \"+\ *n* [*neur-* + *endocrinology*] **:** a branch of the life sciences dealing with neurosecretion and the physiological interaction between the central nervous system and the endocrine system — **neu·ro·endocrinological** *adj*
neu·ro·he·mal organ *also* **neu·ro·hae·mal organ** \,n(y)ürō,hēməl-, -ü-\ *n* [*neur-* + *hem-* + -*al* + *organ*] **:** an organ (as a corpus cardiacum of an insect) that releases stored neurosecretory substances into the blood
neu·ro·ki·nin \¦n(y)ürō¦kīnən\ *n* -s [*neur-* + *kinin* (herein)] **:** a vasodilator kinin that may play a role in the causation of migraine headaches
neu·ro·lept·analgesia \¦n(y)ürō,lept, -ü- +\ *also* **neu·ro·lep·to·analgesia** \,n(y)ürō¦leptō, -ü- +\ *n* [NL, fr. ISV *neurolept-* or *neurolepto-* (fr. *neuroleptic* — herein) + *analgesic* + NL -*ia* (as in *analgesia*)] **:** joint administration of a tranquilizing drug and an analgesic esp. for relief of surgical pain — **neu·ro·lept·analgesic** *adj*
neu·ro·lep·tic \,n(y)ürō'leptik, -ü-\ *n* -s [ISV *neur-* + *psycholeptic*; orig. formed as F *neuroleptique*] **:** TRANQUILIZER 2 — **neuroleptic** \¦==¦==\ *adj*

neu·ro·pharmacology \ˌn(y)u̇rō, -ü- +\ *n* [*neur-* + *pharmacology*] **:** a branch of medical science dealing with the action of drugs on and in the nervous system — **neu·ro·pharmacologic** \"+\ *adj* — **neu·ro·pharmacological** \"+\ *adj* — **neu·ro·pharmacologist** \"+\ *n*

neu·ro·psychic \"+\ *also* **neu·ro·psychical** \"+\ *adj* [*neur-* + *psychic* or *psychical*] **:** of or relating to both the mind and the nervous system as affecting mental processes

neu·ro·science \"+\ *n* [*neur-* + *science*] **:** a branch of science (as neurology or neurophysiology) that deals with the anatomy, physiology, biochemistry, or molecular biology of nerves and nervous tissue and esp. with their relation to behavior and learning — **neu·ro·scientist** \" +\ *n*

neu·ro·sensory \"+\ *adj* [*neur-* + *sensory*] **:** of or relating to afferent nerves

neu·ro·transmitter \"+\ *n* [*neur-* + *transmitter*] **:** a substance (as norepinephrine) that transmits nerve impulses across a synapse

neutron star *n* [*neutron* + *star;* fr. the hypothesis that the cores of such stars are composed entirely of neutrons] **:** any of various hypothetical very dense celestial objects that consist of closely packed nuclear particles resulting from the collapse of a much larger stellar body and that may be detectable through their emission of X rays

new economics *n pl but usu sing in constr* **:** an economic concept that is a logical extension of Keynesianism and that holds that appropriate fiscal and monetary maneuvering can maintain healthy economic growth and prosperity indefinitely

new issue *n* **:** a new security or an additional amount of a security made available for the first time to the general public

new left *n, usu cap N&L* **:** a political movement originating in the U.S. in the 1960s that is composed chiefly of students and various extremist groups and that actively advocates (as by demonstrations) radical changes in prevailing political, social, and educational practices — **new leftist** *n, often cap N & L*

new math *n* **:** mathematics that is based on set theory esp. as taught in elementary and secondary school

newspeak \ˈ=,=\ *n, often cap* [*Newspeak*, a language "designed to diminish the range of thought" in the novel *Nineteen Eighty-Four* (1949) by George Orwell †1950 Eng. author, fr. [1]*new* + [2]*speak*] **:** inflated propagandistic language characterized by ambiguity and contradictions **:** DOUBLE-TALK 2

new town* *n* **:** an urban development comprising a small to medium-size city with a broad range of housing and planned industrial, commercial, and recreational facilities

new wave *n, often cap N & W* [trans. of F *nouvelle vague*] **:** a cinematic movement that is characterized by improvisation, abstraction, and subjective symbolism and that often makes use of experimental photographic techniques

-nik \(ˌ)nik\ *n suffix* [Yiddish, fr. Pol & Russ] **:** one connected with or characterized by being ⟨peace*nik*⟩ ⟨neat*nik*⟩

ngwee \enˈgwē, eŋ'-\ *n, pl* **ngwee** [native name in Zambia, lit., bright] **1 :** a monetary unit of Zambia equal to 1/100 kwacha — see MONEY table *in the Dict* **2 :** a coin representing one ngwee

nicotinamide–adenine dinucleotide *n* **:** DIPHOSPHOPYRIDINE NUCLEOTIDE

nicotinamide–adenine dinucleotide phosphate *n* **:** TRIPHOSPHOPYRIDINE NUCLEOTIDE

nit \ˈnit\ *n* -S [ISV, fr. L *nitēre* to shine — more at NEAT] **:** a unit of brightness equal to one candle per square meter of cross section perpendicular to the rays

nit·pick \ˈnit,pik\ *vi* -ED/-ING/-S [back-formation fr. *nit-picking*] **:** to engage in nit-picking — **nit·pick·er** *n* -S

nit–picking \ˈ=,==\ *n* [[1]*nit* + *picking*, gerund of [1]*pick*] **:** minute and usu. unjustified criticism

ni·tro·fu·ran·to·in \ˌnī-(ˌ)trōfyəˈrantəwən\ *n* -S [*nitrofuran* + hydan*toin*] **:** a nitrofuran derivative that is a broad-spectrum antimicrobial agent esp. valuable in urinary tract infections

nit·ty–grit·ty \ˌnidēˈgridē\ *n* [origin unknown] **:** the actual state of things **:** what is ultimately essential and true ⟨getting down to the *nitty-gritty*⟩

nobble* *vt, Brit* **:** to get hold of **:** CATCH

noise* *n* **1 :** electromagnetic radiation (as light or radio waves) that is composed of several frequencies and that involves random changes in frequency or amplitude **2 :** irrelevant or meaningless bits or words occurring along with desired information (as in a documentary search or a computer output)

noise pollution *n* **:** environmental pollution consisting of annoying or deleterious noise — called also *sound pollution*

no–load \ˈ=ˈ=\ *adj* **:** sold at net asset value

nominal* *adj* **:** being according to plan **:** falling within a range of acceptable planned limits **:** SATISFACTORY ⟨everything was ~ during the spacecraft launch⟩ ⟨satellite had a ~ orbit⟩

nominal* *n* **1 :** a linguistic form (as English *boy* or *he*) that inflects for number or case or for both **2 :** a word or word group functioning as a noun normally functions

non·additive \ˈnän *sometimes* ˈnən+\ *adj* [[1]*non-* + *additive*] **1 :** not having a numerical value equal to the sum of values for the component parts **2 :** of, relating to, or being a genic effect that is not additive — **nonadditivity** *n*

non·aligned \ˈnän *sometimes* ˈnən+\ *adj* [[1]*non-* + *aligned*, past part. of *align*] **:** not allied with other nations and esp. with one of the Great Powers

non·alignment \"+\ *n* **:** the condition of a state or government that is nonaligned

nonbook \ˈnän *sometimes* ˈnən+ˌ\ *n* **:** a book which has little literary merit or factual information, which is often a compilation (as of pictures or press clippings), and whose salability is usu. of primary interest

non·chromosomal \ˈnän *sometimes* ˈnən+\ *adj* **:** not situated on a chromosome **:** not involving chromosomes

non·destructive \"+\ *adj* **:** not destructive; *specif* **:** not causing destruction of material being investigated or treated ⟨~ testing of metal⟩ — **non·destructively** \" +\ *adv*

non·discrimination \"+\ *n* **:** the absence or avoidance of discrimination — **non·discriminatory** \"+\ *adj*

non·enzymatic \"+\ *or* **non·enzymic** \"+\ *also* **non·enzyme** \" +\ *adj* **:** not involving the action of enzymes ⟨~ cleavage of protein⟩ — **nonenzymatically** *adv*

non·fluency \ˈnän *sometimes* ˈnən+\ *n* **1 :** lack of fluency **2 :** an instance of nonfluency — **non·fluent** \"+\ *adj*

non·graded \"+\ *adj* **:** having no grade levels ⟨~ schools⟩

non·green \"+\ *adj* **:** not green; *specif* **:** containing no chlorophyll ⟨fungi and other ~ saprophytes⟩

non·hero \ˈnän *sometimes* ˈnən +\ *n* **:** ANTI-HERO *herein*

nonhost \"+\ *n* **:** a plant that is not attacked or parasitized by a particular organism

non·insecticidal \ˈnän *sometimes* ˈnən+\ *adj* **:** lacking an insecticidal action **:** not involving use of an insecticide

non·negative \"+\ *adj* **:** not negative **:** being either positive or zero ⟨a ~ integer⟩

non·neoplastic \"+\ *adj* [[1]*non-* + *neoplastic*] **:** not being or caused by neoplasms

non·nuclear \"+\ *adj* **1 :** not producing or involving a nuclear explosion ⟨a ~ bomb⟩ ⟨a ~ mining blast⟩ **2 :** not operating by or involving atomic energy ⟨a ~ propulsion system⟩ **3 :** not having developed or not having the atom bomb ⟨a ~ country⟩ **4 :** not involving the use of atom bombs ⟨~ war⟩

non·person \ˈnän *sometimes* ˈnən +ˌ\ *n* **1 :** a person who is regarded as nonexistent or as never having existed **2 :** UNPERSON *herein*

non·proliferation \ˈnän *sometimes* ˈnən+\ *adj* **:** providing for the stoppage of the worldwide spread of nuclear arms production ⟨~ treaty⟩ — **nonproliferation** *n*

non–u \"+\ *adj, cap U* [[1]*non-* + *U* (herein)] **:** not characteristic of the upper classes

non·vocoid \"+\ *n* [[1]*non-* + *vocoid*] **:** CONTOID *herein*

noo·sphere \ˈnōə+ˌ\ *n* [ISV *noo-* + *sphere;* prob. orig. formed as Russian *noosphera*] **:** the biosphere as altered consciously or unconsciously by human activities

nor·eth·in·drone \nȯˈrethən,drōn\ *n* -S [*nor-* + *ethinyl* + *-dr-* (perh. fr. *androgen*) + testoster*one*] **:** a synthetic progestational hormone used in oral contraceptives

nor·ethyn·o·drel \ˌnȯrəˈthinə,drel\ *n* -S [*nor-* + *ethynyl* + *-odrel* (of unknown origin)] **:** a progesterone derivative used in oral contraceptives and clinically in the treatment of abnormal uterine bleeding and the control of menstruation

nor·mo·ther·mia \ˌnȯrməˈthərmēə\ *n* -S [NL, fr. *norm-* + *-thermia*] **:** normal body temperature — **nor·mo·ther·mic** \ˈ==ˈ=mik\ *adj*

nose–ride \ˈ=,=\ *vi* **:** to ride or perform stunts on the nose of a surfboard — **nose–rider** *n*

notchback \ˈ=,=\ *n* [[1]*notch* + [1]*back*] **1 :** a back on a closed passenger automobile having a distinct deck as distinguished from a fastback **2 :** an automobile having a notchback

nou·velle vague \(ˌ)nü,velˈväg, -ȧg\ *n* [F, lit., new wave, fr. *nouvelle* (fem. of *nouveau* new, fr. L *novellus*) + *vague* wave, fr. OF *wage*, fr. ON *vāgr;* akin to OE *wǣg* wave, *wegan* to move — more at NOVELLA, WAY] **:** NEW WAVE *herein*

nsec *abbr* nanosecond *herein*

nuclear force *n* **1 :** the powerful force between nucleons that holds atomic nuclei together **2 :** STRONG INTERACTION *herein*

nuclear magnetic resonance *n* **:** the magnetic resonance of an atomic nucleus

nuclear resonance *n* **:** the resonance absorption of a gamma ray by a nucleus identical to the nucleus that emitted the gamma ray — compare MÖSSBAUER EFFECT *herein*

nu·cleo·capsid \ˈn(y)üklēō+\ *n* [*nucle-* + *capsid* (herein)] **:** the nucleic acid and surrounding protein coat in a virus

nu·cle·o·lo·ne·ma \n(y)ü,klēələˈnēmə\ *also* **nu·cle·o·lo·neme** \-ˈklēələ,nēm\ *n* -S [NL *nucleolonema* fr. *nucleolus* + *-o-* + Gk *nēma* thread — more at NEEDLE] **:** a filamentous network consisting of small granules in some nucleoli

nucleon* *n* **:** a hypothetical single entity with one-half unit of isospin capable of manifesting itself as either a proton or a neutron and of making transitions between these two states

nu·cleo·synthesis \ˈn(y)üklēō+\ *n* [NL, fr. *nucle-* + *synthesis*] **:** the production of a chemical element in nature from hydrogen nuclei or protons — **nu·cleo·synthetic** \"+\ *adj*

[1]**nud·ie** \ˈn(y)üdē\ *n* -S [[1]*nude* + *-ie*] **:** SKIN FLICK *herein*

[2]**nudie** *adj* **:** featuring nudes ⟨~ films⟩ ⟨~ magazines⟩

nu·mer·ate \ˈn(y)ümərət\ *adj* [L *numerus* number + E *-ate* (as in *literate*) — more at NIMBLE] *Brit* **:** marked by an understanding of the scientific approach and by the ability to think quantitatively — **nu·mer·a·cy** \-rəsē\ *n*

numerical control *n* **:** automatic control (as of a machine tool) by a digital computer — **numerically controlled** *adj*

nur·tur·ance \ˈnərchərən(t)s\ *n* -S [[2]*nurture* + *-ance*] **:** affectionate care and attention — **nur·tur·ant** \-rənt\ *adj*

ny·norsk \ˈn(y)üˈnȯ(ə)rsk, ˈnē-\ *n* -S [Norw, lit., new Norwegian, fr. *ny* new (fr. ON *nýr*) + *norsk* Norwegian — more at NEW, NORSKI] **:** LANDSMÅL

obie \ˈōbē\ *n* -S *usu cap* [*O.B.*, abbr. for *off-Broadway*] **:** any of several prizes awarded annually by a newspaper for excellence in off-Broadway theater

ob·jet trou·vé \ˌȯb,zhä(ˌ)trüˈvā\ *n, pl* **objets trouvés** *same*\ [F, lit., found object] **:** FOUND OBJECT *herein*

ocea·naut \ˈōshə,nȯt, -nät\ *n* -S [blend of *ocean* and *-naut* (as in *aquanaut* — herein)] **:** AQUANAUT *herein*

oce·an·ics \ˌōshēˈaniks\ *n pl but usu sing in constr* [*ocean* + *-ics*] **:** a group of sciences that deal with the ocean

odd–lot·ter \ˈädˈläd·ə(r\ *n* -S [*odd lot* + *-er*] **:** a speculator or an investor who habitually buys and sells stock in less than round lots

off broadway *n, usu cap B* [so called fr. its usu. being produced in smaller theaters outside of the Broadway theatrical district] **:** a part of the New York professional theater stressing fundamental and artistic values and formerly engaging in experimentation — **off–broadway** *adj, usu cap B*

offering price* *n* **:** the price at which an open-end mutual fund is sold consisting of its asset value plus a specified load

of·fi·ci·a·lis \ə,fishēˈāləs, -ˈal-\ *n, pl* **of·fi·ci·a·les** \-ˈä(ˌ)lās, -ˈa(ˌ)lēz\ [NL, fr. ML, official — more at OFFICIAL] **:** the presiding judge of the matrimonial court of a Roman Catholic diocese

off–off–broadway \(ˈ)=ˈ=ˈ=,=\ *n, usu cap B* [so called fr. its relation to off-Broadway being analogous to the relation of off-Broadway to Broadway] **:** an avant-garde theatrical movement in New York that stresses untraditional techniques and radical experimentation — **off–off–broadway** *adj, usu cap B*

off–putting \ˈ=ˈ==\ *adj* **:** that puts one off **:** DISCOURAGING

ol·fac·tron·ics \ˌōl,fakˈträniks\ *n pl but sing in constr* [*olfaction* + *-tronics* (as in *electronics*)] **:** a branch of physical science dealing with the detection and identification of odors

ol·i·gid·ic \ˌäləˈgidik, -ˈji-\ *adj* [*olig-* + *-idic* (as in *meridic* — herein)] **:** having the active constituents with the exception of water undefined chemically ⟨~ growth medium⟩ — compare HOLIDIC, MERIDIC *herein*

olig·o·mer \ōˈligəmə(r), əˈl-\ *n* -S [*olig-* + *-mer*] **:** a polymer or polymer intermediate that contains relatively few structural units — **olig·o·mer·ic** \ˈ=ˈ==ˈmerik, ˌäləgōˈm-\ *adj*

ol·i·go·nucleotide \ˈäləgō, əˈligə+\ *n* [*olig-* + *nucleotide*] **:** a chain of several nucleotides

om·buds·man \ˈäm,bùdzmən, ˈȯm-, -ˌbəd-, -ˌman\ *n, pl* **ombuds·men** \-mən,-ˌmen\ [Sw, lit., representative, commissioner, fr. ON *umbothsmathr*, fr. *umboth* commission (fr. *um* around + *bjōtha* to command) + *mathr* man — more at EMBER DAY, BID, MAN] **1 :** a government official (as in Sweden or New Zealand) appointed to receive and investigate complaints made by individuals against abuses or capricious acts of public officials **2 :** one that investigates reported complaints (as from students or customers), reports findings, and helps to achieve equitable settlements — **om·buds·man·ship** \-mən,ship\ *n*

omega* *or* **omega particle** *n* **1 :** a negatively charged elementary particle that has a mass 3280 times the mass of an electron and that is an unstable baryon decaying into a xi and a pion with an average lifetime of about 10^{-10} second **2** *or* **omega meson :** a very short-lived unstable meson with mass 1532 times the mass of an electron

om·ni·focal \ˈämnə, -nē+\ *adj* [*omn-* + *focal*] **:** of, relating to, or being a bifocal eyeglass that is so ground as to permit smooth transition from one correction to the other

onboard \ˈ=ˈ=\ *adj* [*on board*] **:** carried within a vehicle (as a rocket, satellite, or spacecraft) ⟨an ~ computer⟩

one–time pad \ˌ=,=-\ *n* [[1]*one* + [1]*time* + [1]*pad;* prob. fr. its original form's being a pad of keys whose sheets were torn off and discarded after a single use] **:** a random-number additive or mixed keying sequence to be used for a single coded message and then destroyed

one–up \ˈwənˈəp\ *vt* **one–upped; one–upping; one–ups** [back-formation fr. *one-upmanship*] **:** to practice one-upmanship on

on–line \ˈ=ˈ=\ *adj* [[1]*on* + [3]*line*] **1 :** located at a point served directly by a particular railroad ⟨*on-line* industry⟩ **2 :** being under the direct control of or in direct communication with a computer ⟨*on-line* equipment⟩ — **on–line** *adv*

op \ˈäp\ *or* **op art** *n* -S [by shortening] **:** OPTICAL ART *herein* — **op artist** *n*

open–circuit \ˈ=ˈ==\ *adj* **:** of or relating to an open circuit; *specif* **:** being or relating to television in which programs are broadcast so that they are available to all receivers within range

open enrollment *n* **1 :** the voluntary enrollment of a student in a public school other than the one he is assigned to on the basis of his residence **2 :** enrollment on demand as a student in an institution of higher learning irrespective of formal qualifications

open–heart \ˈ==ˈ=\ *adj* **:** of, relating to, or performed on a heart temporarily relieved of circulatory function and laid open for inspection and treatment ⟨*open-heart* surgery⟩

open loop *n* **:** a control system for an operation or process in which there is no self-correcting action

open sentence *n* **:** a statement (as in mathematics) containing at least one blank or unknown so that when the blank is filled or a quantity substituted for the unknown the statement becomes a complete statement that is either true or false

operand* *n* -S **:** the part of a computer instruction that indicates the quantities to be operated on; *also* **:** one of these quantities

op·er·a·tion·ist \ˌäpəˈrāsh(ə)nəst\ *n* -S [*operation* + *-ist*] **:** OPERATIONALIST

operator* *n* **:** OPERATOR GENE *herein*

operator gene *n* **:** a chromosomal region that triggers formation of messenger RNA by one or more structural genes and is itself subject to inhibition by a genetic repressor

op·er·on \ˈäpə,rän\ *n* -S [ISV *operator* + [2]*-on;* prob. orig. formed in F] **:** a group of linked cistrons

optical* *adj* **:** of, relating to, or being optical art

optical art *n* **:** nonobjective art characterized by the use of straight or curved lines or geometric patterns often for an illusory effect (as of perspective or motion)

op·to·electronic \ˌäp(ˌ)tō+\ *adj* [*optical* + *-o-* + *electronic*] **:** being or relating to a device in which light energy and electrical energy are coupled — **op·to·electronics** \"+\ *n pl but sing in constr*

oral history *n* **:** tape-recorded historical information obtained in interviews with persons who have led significant lives — **oral historian** *n*

order* *n* **:** a class of mutually exclusive linguistic forms any and only one of which may occur in a fixed definable position in the prescribed sequence of items forming a word

or·ga·no \ˈȯrgə(ˌ)nō, ȯrˈga(-\ *adj* [by shortening] **:** ORGANOMETALLIC

or·ga·no·phosphate \ˌȯrgənō-, ȯrˈganə-+\ *adj* [*organ-* + *phosphate*] **:** of, relating to, or being a phosphorus-containing organic insecticide (as malathion) that acts by inhibiting the action of cholinesterase — **organophosphate** *n*

or·ga·no·phosphorous \"+\ *or* **or·ga·no·phosphorus** \"+\ *adj* [*organ-* + *phosphorous* or *phosphorus*] **:** ORGANOPHOSPHATE *herein*

ori·en·teer·ing \ˌōrēən·ˈtiriŋ, -ē,en-\ *n* [modif. (influenced by *-eer*) of Sw *orientering*, fr. *orientera* to orient, fr. F *orienter*] **:** cross-country racing in which map and compass are used

or·thog·o·nal·iza·tion \ȯ(r),thägənᵊləˈzāshən, -ᵊl,īˈz-\ *n* -S [*orthogonalize* + *-ation*] **:** the replacing of a set of vectors by a linearly equivalent set of orthogonal vectors

or·tho·normal \ˌȯ(r)thə+\ *adj* [*orth-* + *normal*] **:** being a system of vectors in which each vector is of unit length and any two distinct vectors are orthogonal

or·thot·ics \ȯrˈthädiks\ *n pl but sing in constr* [fr. Gk *orthōsis* straightening; after such pairs as E *prosthesis; prosthetics* — more at ORTHOSIS] **:** a branch of mechanical and medical science dealing with the support and bracing of weak or ineffective joints or muscles — compare PROSTHETICS *in the Dict* — **or·thot·ic** \-ik\ *adj* — **or·tho·tist** \ˈȯrthətəst\ *n* -S

orthotropic* *adj* **1 :** being, having, or relating to properties (as strength, stiffness, and elasticity) that are symmetric about two or three mutually perpendicular planes ⟨a piece of straight-grained wood is an ~ material⟩ **2 :** designed so that the roadway serves as an orthotropic structural member **:** constructed with a steel-plate deck as an integral part of the support structure — used of a bridge

or·well·ian \ȯrˈwelēən\ *adj, usu cap* [George *Orwell* (pseudonym of Eric Blair †1950 Eng. writer) + E *-ian*] **:** of, relating to, or suggestive of George Orwell or his writings

os·mol \ˈäz,mōl, ˈä,smōl\ *n* -S [blend of *osmosis* and *mol*] **:** a standard unit of osmotic pressure based on the concentration of an ion in a solution — **os·mo·lal** \(ˈ)äzˈmōləl, (ˈ)äˈsmō-\ *adj* — **os·mo·lal·i·ty** \ˌäzmeˈlaləd·ē, ˌäsm-\ *n* -ES

os·mo·lar \(ˈ)äzˈmōlə(r), (ˈ)äˈsm-\ *adj* [*osmol* (herein) + *-ar*] **:** OSMOTIC — used chiefly of biological fluids — **os·mo·lar·i·ty** \ˌäzməˈlarəd·ē, ˌäsm-\ *n* -ES

out* *adj* **:** not approved of or accepted by those who are keenly aware of and responsive to what is new and smart **:** not in

outside* *adj* **:** made or done from the outside or from a distance ⟨borrowed a basketball and practiced his ~ shot all day⟩

over·achiev·er \R ˌōvərəˈchēvər, -R -və(r)əˈchēvə(r\ *n* -S [[1]*over* + *achieve* + *-er*] **:** one who achieves success over and above a standard or expected level

overbook \ˌ=ˈ=\ *vb* [[1]*over* + [2]*book*] *vt* **:** to issue reservations for (as an airplane flight) in excess of the space available ~ *vi* **:** to issue reservations in excess of the space available

overdub \ˈ==,=\ *vt* [[1]*over* + *dub*] **:** to transfer (sound already recorded) to a record that bears recorded sound for producing a combined effect

overkill \ˈ==,=\ *n* -S [*overkill*, v. (herein) fr. [1]*over* + [1]*kill*] **1 :** the capability of destroying an enemy or target with a nuclear force larger than is required **2 :** an excess of something (as a quantity or an action) beyond what is required or suitable for a particular purpose ⟨a propaganda ~⟩ ⟨an ~ in weaponry⟩ **3 :** killing in excess of what is intended or required **:** excessive killing — **overkill** \ˈ==,=, ˌ==ˈ=\ *vb*

overnutrition \ˈ===+\ *n* [[3]*over* + *nutrition*] **:** excessive food intake esp. when viewed as a factor in pathology

overshoot \ˈ=,=\ *n* [*overshoot*, v.] **:** the action or an instance of overshooting; *esp* **:** a going beyond an intended point

ovon·ic \ōˈvänik\ *n* -S [short for *ovonic device*] **:** a device that operates in accordance with the Ovshinsky effect

ovon·ics \-ks\ *n pl but usu sing in constr* [*Ovshinsky* effect (herein) + electr*onics*] **:** a branch of electronics that deals with applications of the Ovshinsky effect — **ovonic** *adj*

ov·shin·sky effect \ävˈshin(t)skē-, ōv-\ *n, usu cap O* [after Stanford R. *Ovshinsky* b1923 Amer. inventor] **:** the change from an electrically nonconducting state to a semiconducting state shown by glasses of special composition upon application of a certain minimum voltage

ox·a·cil·lin \ˌäksəˈsilən\ *n* -S [*isoxazole* + *penicillin*] **:** a semisynthetic penicillin that is esp. effective in the control of infections caused by penicillin-resistant staphylococci

ox·bridge \ˈäksbrij\ *adj, usu cap* [*Oxford* University, England + Cam*bridge* University, England] **:** of, relating to, or characteristic of Oxford and Cambridge universities — compare REDBRICK *herein*

oxy·some \ˈäksə,sōm\ *n* -S [[2]*oxy-* + [3]*-some*] **:** one of the structural units of mitochondrial cristae that appear usu. as spheres or stalked spheres and that are prob. sites of energy-producing reactions

ozone·sonde \ˈ=,=,=\ *n* -S [*ozone* + *sonde*] **:** a balloon-borne instrument that measures the concentration of ozone at various altitudes and broadcasts the data by radio

p* *abbr* pico-

pa·'anga \päˈäŋ(g)ə\ *n, pl* **pa'anga** [Tongan, lit., seed] **1 :** the basic monetary unit of Tonga — see MONEY table *in the Dict* **2 :** a coin or note representing one pa'anga

pa·leo·magnetism \ˈpālēō, ˈpalēō+\ *n* [*pale-* + *magnetism*] **1 :** the intensity and direction of residual magnetization in ancient rocks **2 :** a study that deals with paleomagnetism — **pa·leo·magnetic** \"+\ *adj*

pa·leo·temperature \"+\ *n* [*pale-* + *temperature*] **:** the temperature (as of the ocean) during a past geological age

pan·chres·ton \panˈkrestən, -ˌtän\ *n* -S [Gk *panchrēston* panacea, fr. neut. of *panchrēstos* good for all work, fr. *pan-* + *chrēstos* good — more at CHRESTOMATHY] **:** a broadly inclusive thesis that is intended to cover all possible variations within an area of concern and that in practice usu. proves to be an unacceptable oversimplification

pan·gram \ˈpangrəm, -aŋg-, -ˌgram\ *n* -S [*pan-* + Gk *grammat-, gramma* letter — more at GRAM] **:** a short sentence containing all 26 letters of the English alphabet — **pan·gram·mat·ic** \ˌpangrəˈmad·ik, -aŋg-\ *adj*

pantdress \ˈ=,=\ *n* [[4]*pant* + *dress*] **:** CULOTTE 2

pantsuit *or* **pants suit** \ˈ=,=\ *n* -S [[4]*pant* or *pants* + *suit*] **:** a woman's ensemble consisting usu. of a long jacket with sleeves reaching to the wrist and tailored pants of the same material

panty hose *also* **panti·hose** \ˈpantē,hōz\ *n* **:** a one-piece woman's garment combining the functions of panties and hose for wear esp. with a miniskirt

pa·pa·raz·zo \ˌpäpəˈrät(ˌ)sō\ *n, pl* **paparaz·zi** \-sē\ [It] **:** a news reporter or photographer who doggedly searches for a story that can be sensationalized

paper factor *n* **:** a substance orig. isolated from pulpwood of the balsam fir that is a selectively effective insecticide with activity like that of juvenile hormone

paper gold *n* **:** SDRS *herein*

pap smear *also* **pap test** \ˈpap-\ *n, usu cap P* [*pap* short for *Papanicolaou test*] **:** PAPANICOLAOU TEST

para·foil \ˈparə,fȯil\ *n* [*parachute* + *-foil* (as in *airfoil*)] **:** a self-inflating fabric device that resembles a parachute, behaves in flight like an airplane wing, is maneuverable, is capable of landing a payload at slow speed, and can be launched from the ground in a high wind like a kite

para·glider \ˈparə+ˌ\ *n* [*parachute* + *glider*] **:** a triangular device that consists of two flexible sections, resembles a kite, and is used for guiding and landing a spacecraft after reentry or for recovering a launching rocket

para·kite \ˈparə+ˌ\ *n* [*parachute* + *kite*] **:** a parachute with slits that is towed against the wind by an automobile or motorboat so that a person harnessed to the parachute is lifted into the air and pulled along — **para·kiting** \-ˌkīd·iŋ\ *n*

para·language \"+ˌ\ *n* [[1]*para-* + *language*] **:** optional vocal effects (as tone of voice) that accompany or modify the phonemes of an utterance and may communicate meaning

para·linguistic \ˌparə+\ *adj* [¹*para-* + *linguistic*] **:** of or relating to paralanguage or to the study of paralanguage

para·linguistics \"+\ *n* [¹*para-* + *linguistics*] **:** the study of paralanguage

paramagnetic resonance *n* **:** ELECTRON SPIN RESONANCE *herein*

parameter* *n* **1 :** any of a set of physical properties whose values determine the characteristics or behavior of a system ⟨~*s* of the atmosphere such as temperature, pressure, and density⟩ **2 :** something represented by a parameter **:** a characteristic element; *broadly* **:** ELEMENT, FACTOR

parametric* *adj* **:** depending on the usu. periodic variation of a parameter; *specif* **:** being or relating to a high-frequency amplifier whose operation is based on time variations in a parameter (as reactance) and which converts the energy at the frequency of an alternating current into energy at the input signal frequency in such a way as to amplify the signal

parametric equation *n* **:** any of a set of equations that express the coordinates of the points of a curve as functions of one parameter or that express the coordinates of the points of a surface as functions of two parameters

para·political \ˌparə+\ *adj* [*para-* + *political*] **:** existing alongside a political structure or group in a professedly nonpolitical capacity

para·professional \"+\ *n* [*para-* + *professional*] **:** a trained aide who assists a professional person; *esp* **:** a teacher's aide

para·wing \ˈparə+\ *n* [*parachute* + *wing*] **:** PARAGLIDER *herein*

parietal* *n* **parietals** *pl* **:** the regulations governing visiting by members of the opposite sex in campus dormitories

parity* *n* **1 :** the property of an integer with respect to being odd or even ⟨3 and 7 have the same ~ while 3 and 4 have different ~⟩ **2 :** the evenness or oddness of a quantum-mechanical wave function with respect to inversion of spatial coordinates **3 a :** the property of a physical system or process that indicates whether or not its mirror image occurs in nature **b :** the property of an elementary particle that is emitted or created during a nuclear process and that indicates whether or not the emission is in a preferred direction

parking orbit *n* **:** the orbit of an artificial satellite or a space vehicle traveling around a body (as the earth) in such a way as to serve as a station from which another vehicle is launched or as to be itself propelled later into a new trajectory

par·kin·son's law \ˌpärkənsənz-, ˌpäk-\ *n, usu cap P&L* [after C. Northcote *Parkinson* b1909 Eng. historian] **1 :** an observation in office organization: the number of subordinates increases at a fixed rate regardless of the amount of work produced **2 :** an observation in office organization: work expands so as to fill the time available for its completion

particle board *n* **:** a composition board made of very small pieces of wood bonded together (as with a synthetic resin)

par·y·lene \ˈparəˌlēn\ *n* -s [contr. of *paraxylene*] **:** any of several thermoplastic crystalline materials that are polymers of paraxylene and are used esp. as electrical insulation coating

passive satellite *n* **:** an artificial satellite without instruments; *esp* **:** one that simply reflects radio signals back to earth

pasteurization* *n* **:** partial sterilization of perishable food products (as fruit or fish) with radiation (as gamma rays)

past·ies \ˈpāstēz\ *n pl* [²*paste* + *-ie*] **:** small round coverings for a woman's nipples

pata·physics \ˌpad·ə+\ *n pl but sing in constr* [F *pataphysique*] **:** intricate and whimsical nonsense intended as a parody of science — **pata·physical** \"+\ *adj* — **pata·physician** \"+\ *n*

patch* *vt* **:** to connect (as circuits) by a patch cord

patchboard \ˈ=,=\ *n* [¹*patch* + *board*] **:** a plugboard in which circuits are interconnected by patch cords

patch panel *n* **:** PATCHBOARD *herein*

patterning* *n* **:** a technique designed to improve damaged neural controls by means of feedback from forced muscular activity imposed in physical therapy

payload* *n* **:** the load (as of passengers or instruments) directly related to the purpose of a rocket or space flight; *also* **:** the weight of such a load

payout ratio *n* **:** a ratio relating dividend payout of a company to its earnings or cash flow

pazazz *var of* PIZZAZZ *herein*

peaceful coexistence *n* **:** a living together in peace rather than in constant hostility

peace sign *n* **:** a sign made by raising the index finger and middle finger to form a V and used to indicate the desire for peace or as a greeting or farewell

pearl* *vi, of a surfboard* **:** to plunge headfirst into the trough of a wave

peat·land \ˈpēt,land\ *n* [*peat* + *land*] **:** land rich in peat

peek–a–boo* *adj* **:** of, relating to, or being a document retrieval system in which desired documents are identified by light shining through matching holes in index cards

pe·king·ol·o·gy \ˌpē(ˌ)kiŋˈäləjē\ *n* -ES *usu cap* [*Peking*, capital of Communist China + *-o-* + *-logy*] **:** the study of the policies and practices of the Chinese Communist government — **pe·king·ol·o·gist** \-jəst\ *n* -s *usu cap*

peloton* *or* **peloton glass** *n* **:** a European ornamental glass often with variegated metallized and satinized surface and usu. overlaid with strands of contrasting color

pemoline *n* -s [of unknown origin] **:** a synthetic organic drug that is usu. mixed with magnesium hydroxide, is a mild stimulant of the central nervous system, and is used experimentally to improve memory

percentile* *n* **:** a value on a scale of one hundred that indicates the percent of a distribution that is equal to or below it

per·fec·ta \pə(r)ˈfektə\ *n* -s [AmerSp *quiniela perfecta* perfect quiniela] **:** a system of betting on races in which the bettor must pick the first and second horses in this sequence in a specified race in order to win — called also *exacta*

per·for·ma·tive \pərˈfȯrməd·iv\ *n* -s [*perform* + *-ative* (as in ²*imperative*)] **:** an expression that serves to effect a transaction or that constitutes the performance of the specified act by virtue of its utterance ⟨. . . many ~*s* are *contractual* ("I bet") or *declaratory* ("I declare war") utterances —J.L.Austin⟩

peri·apsis \ˌperē+\ *n, pl* **periapsides** [NL, fr. *peri-* + *apsis*] **:** the apsis that is the least distance from the center of attraction

peri·cyn·thi·on \ˌperəˈsin(t)thēən\ *n* -s [NL, fr. *peri-* + *Cynthia*, goddess of the moon (fr. Gk *Kynthia*) + *-on* (as in *aphelion*)] **:** PERILUNE *herein*

peri·lune \ˈperə,lün\ *n* -s [*peri-* + L *luna* moon — more at LUNAR] **:** the point in the path of a body orbiting the moon that is nearest to the center of the moon

peri·se·le·ne \ˌperəsəˈlēnē\ *n* -s [ISV *peri-* + *-selene* (fr. Gk *selēnē* moon) — more at SELEN-] **:** PERILUNE *herein*

peri·se·le·ni·um \-lēnēəm\ *n* -s [NL, fr. Gk *peri-* peri- + *selēnē* moon + NL *-ium* (alter. of *-ion* — as in *aphelion*) — more at SELEN-] **:** PERILUNE *herein*

pe·ri·tus \pəˈrēd·əs\ *n, pl* **peri·ti** \-ēd·ē, -ē,tē\ [NL, fr. L *peritus*, adj., skilled, experienced — more at PERITE] **:** an expert (as in theology or canon law) who advises and assists the hierarchy (as in the drafting of schemata) at a Vatican council

permanent press *n* **:** DURABLE PRESS *herein* — **permanent-press** *adj*

personal tax *n* **:** DIRECT TAX

PERT \ˈpərt\ *n* -s [*p*rogram *e*valuation and *r*eview *t*echnique] **:** a technique for planning, scheduling, and monitoring a complex project esp. by graphically displaying the separate tasks and showing how they are interconnected

pe·se·wa \pəˈsäwə\ *n* -s [native name in Ghana] **1 :** a monetary unit of Ghana equal to 1/100 cedi — see MONEY table *in the Dict* **2 :** a coin representing one pesewa

petit bourgeois *adj* [*petit bourgeois*, n.] **:** of, relating to, or characteristic of the petite bourgeoisie

pet·nap·ping \ˈpet,napiŋ\ *n* [¹*pet* + *-napping* (as in *kidnapping*)] **:** the act of stealing a pet (as a cat or dog) usu. for profit

phar·ma·co·genetics \ˌfärməkō+\ *n pl but sing in constr* [ISV *pharmaco-* + *genetics*] **:** the study of the interrelation of hereditary constitution and response to drugs — **phar·ma·co·genetic** \"+\ *adj*

phase·out \ˈ=,=\ *n* -s [*phase out*] **:** a gradual stopping of operations or production **:** a closing down by phases

phe·naz·o·cine \fəˈnazə,sēn, -sən\ *n* -s [*phen-* + *-azocine* (perh. irreg. fr. ²*azo* + *-ine*)] **:** a drug related to morphine that has greater pain-relieving and slighter narcotic effect

phe·neth·i·cil·lin \fəˌnethəˈsilən\ *n* -s [*phen-* + *eth-* + *penicillin*] **:** a synthetic penicillin administered orally and used esp. in the treatment of respiratory infections

phe·ren·ta·sin \fəˈrentəsən\ *n* -s [Gk *pherein* to carry + *entasis* tension, stretching + E *-in* — more at BEAR, ENTASIS] **:** a pressor amine present in the blood in severe hypertension

pher·o·mone \ˈferə,mōn\ *n* [ISV *phero-* (fr. Gk *pherein* to carry) + *-mone* (as in *hormone*); orig. formed as G *pheromon*; fr. its conveying information from one individual to another — more at BEAR] **:** a chemical substance that is produced by an animal and serves as a specific stimulus to other individuals of the same species for one or more behavioral responses

phil·lips curve \ˌfiləps-\ *n, usu cap P* [after A.W.H. *Phillips* b1914 Brit. economist] **:** a graphic representation of the relation between inflation and unemployment which indicates that as the rate of either increases that of the other declines

pho·no·tac·tics \ˌfōnəˈtaktiks\ *n pl but sing in constr* [*phon-* + *tactics*] **:** the area of phonology that analyzes and describes the permitted phoneme sequences of a language — **pho·no·tac·tic** \ˌ==ˈ=tik\ *adj*

phor·ate \ˈfō(ə)r,āt, ˈfȯ(-\ *n* -s [*phosphor-* + *thionate*] **:** a very toxic organophosphate systemic insecticide

¹pho·to·chro·mic \ˌfōd·əˈkrōmik\ *adj* [*phot-* + *chrom-* + *-ic*] **1 :** capable of changing color on exposure to radiant energy (as light) ⟨~ glass⟩ **2 :** of, relating to, or utilizing the change of color shown by a photochromic substance ⟨a ~ process⟩ — **pho·to·chro·mism** \-,mizəm\ *n* -s

²photochromic *n* -s **:** a photochromic substance

pho·to·coagulation \ˌfōd·ō+\ *n* [*phot-* + *coagulation*] **:** surgical coagulation of tissue by means of a precisely oriented high-energy light source (as a laser beam) — **pho·to·coagulative** \"+\ *adj* — **pho·to·coagulator** \"+\ *n*

pho·to·scan \ˈfōd·ō+,\ *n* [*photoscan*, v. (herein), fr. *phot-* + ¹*scan*] **:** a photograph (as of a kidney) produced by converging scintillations from gamma rays given off by an injected radioactive substance into a beam of light that is recorded photographically to show variations in tissue state — **photoscan** *vb* — **pho·to·scanner** \"+,\ *n* -s

phrase marker *n* **:** a representation of the immediate constituent structure of a linguistic construction

phrase structure *n* **:** the arrangement of the constituents of a sentence

phy·to·chrome \ˈfīd·ə,krōm\ *n* -s [*phyt-* + *-chrome*] **:** a plant pigment; *specif* **:** a chromoprotein present in traces in many plants that when activated by red to far-red radiation plays a role in initiating floral and developmental processes

phy·to·tron \ˈfīd·ə,trän\ *n* -s [*phyt-* + *-tron* (as in *cyclotron*)] **:** a laboratory with facilities for growing plants under various combinations of strictly controlled conditions

PI* *abbr* programmed instruction

pi·cor·na·virus \pəˈkȯrnə+\ *n* [*pico-* + *RNA* + *virus*] **:** any of a group of tiny RNA-containing viruses including the enteroviruses and rhinoviruses — compare ADENOVIRUS *herein*

pig* *n* **:** POLICEMAN

piggyback* *adj* **:** being or relating to something (as a capsule or package) carried into space as an extra load by a vehicle (as a spacecraft or rocket) — **piggyback*** *adv*

pi·li·pi·no \ˌpil·əˈpē(ˌ)nō, ˌpēl-\ *n, cap* [Pilipino, fr. Sp *Filipino* Philippine] **:** the Tagalog-based official language of the Republic of the Philippines

pill* *n* **:** an oral contraceptive — usu. used with *the*

pill–head \ˈ=,=\ *n* [⁴*pill* + *head*] **:** a person who takes pills or capsules (as of amphetamines) for nonmedicinal reasons

pill pool *n* [⁴*pill*; fr. the drawing of small numbered balls from a bottle to determine order of play] **:** KELLY POOL

pinholder \ˈ=,==\ *n* [*pin* + *holder*] **:** a flower holder that consists of a substantial base topped with projecting pins

pinta \ˈpīntə\ *n* -s [*pint* + *-a* (as in *cuppa* — herein)] *Brit* **:** a pint of milk

pi·sci·cide \ˈpīsə,sīd, ˈpisə-, ˈpiskə-\ *n* -s [*pisci-* + *-cide*] **:** a substance used to kill fish — **pi·sci·ci·dal** \ˌ==ˈsīdᵊl\ *adj*

piz·zazz *or* **pi·zazz** *also* **pa·zazz** \pəˈzaz\ *n* -ES [origin unknown] **:** the quality of being exciting or attractive: as **a :** GLAMOUR, APPEAL ⟨bemoans the lack of color and provocative ~ in today's stars —Vernon Scott⟩ **b :** SPIRIT, VITALITY ⟨we had four numbers with ~ and the rest of the show died around them —Gower Champion⟩

placebo effect *n* **:** improvement in the condition of a sick person that occurs in response to treatment but cannot be considered due to the specific treatment used

¹planeside \ˈ=,=\ *n* [⁴*plane* + ¹*side*] **:** the area adjacent to an airplane ⟨speaking briefly at ~ —*Christian Science Monitor*⟩

²planeside \ˌ=ˈ=\ *adj* **:** engaged in or made at planeside

plan·e·tol·o·gy \ˌplanəˈtäləjē\ *n* -ES [*planet* + *-o-* + *-logy*] **:** a study that deals with the condensed matter (as the planets, comets, and meteorites) of the solar system — **plan·e·to·log·i·cal** \-tᵊlˈäjəkəl\ *adj* — **plan·e·tol·o·gist** \-ˈtäləjəst\ *n* -s

plasma jet *n* **1 :** a stream of very hot gaseous plasma; *also* **:** a device for producing such a stream **2** *or* **plasma engine :** a rocket engine designed to derive thrust from the discharge of a magnetically accelerated plasma

plasma torch *n* **:** a device that heats a gas by electrical means to form a plasma for high-temperature operations

plate* *vt* [fr. the crossing of home plate by the scoring runner] **:** to cause (as a run) to score in baseball

plated amberina *n* **:** an ornamental glass consisting of an amberina casing over a fiery opalescent or white lining

platform tennis *n* **:** a variation of paddle tennis that is played on a wooden platform enclosed by a wire fence

platoon* *vt* **:** to alternate (one player) with another player in the same position ⟨if I can't play him every day, I'll ~ him in left field —Leo Durocher⟩ ~ *vi* **:** to alternate with another player in the same position

playbook* *n* **:** a notebook containing the diagramed plays of a football team

plench \ˈplench\ *n* -ES [*pl*iers + *w*rench] **:** a combination pliers and wrench operated by squeezing the handle and used to make pulling and turning motions under zero gravity

p–marker *n, usu cap P* [*P*, symbol for *phrase*] **:** PHRASE MARKER *herein*

pocket* *n* **:** an area formed by blockers from which a football player (as a quarterback) attempts to pass

pod* *n* **:** a detachable compartment on a spacecraft

point* *n* **points** *pl* **:** a percentage of the face value of a loan often added as a placement fee or service charge

point of no return 1 : the point in the flight of an aircraft beyond which the remaining fuel will be insufficient for a return to the starting point with the result that the craft must proceed **2 :** a critical point (as in development or a course of action) at which turning back or reversal is not possible

point set *n* **:** a collection of geometrical points

point set topology *n* **:** a study that deals with the structure and properties of point sets as based on neighborhood

polar* *adj* **1 :** passing over the earth's north and south poles ⟨a ~ orbit⟩ **2 :** traveling in a polar orbit ⟨a ~ satellite⟩

pole lamp *n* **:** a lamp that consists of a pole to which light fixtures are attached and that usu. extends from floor to ceiling

po·lio·virus \ˌpōlē(ˌ)ō+\ *n* [NL, fr. *poliomyelitis* + *virus*] **:** an enterovirus that occurs in several antigenically distinct forms and is the causative agent of human poliomyelitis

political* *adj* **:** involving or charged or concerned with acts against a government or a political system ⟨a ~ offense⟩

poly·carbonate \ˌpälē, -lə+\ *n* [*poly-* + *carbonate*] **:** any of various tough thermoplastics characterized by high impact strength and high softening temperature

poly·cen·trism \ˌpälēˈsen·,trizəm, -lə-\ *n* -s [ISV *poly-* + *-centric* + *-ism*; prob. orig. formed in It] **:** the doctrine of a plurality of centers of Communist thought and leadership

polychromatic* *adj* **:** being or relating to radiation that is composed of more than one wavelength

poly·ether \ˌpälē+\ *n* [*poly-* + *ether*] **1 :** a polymer in which the repeating unit contains a carbon-oxygen bond **2 :** a polyurethane foam made by use of a polyether

poly·imide \ˌpälē+\ *n* [*poly-* + *imide*] **:** any of a class of polymeric synthetic resins resistant to high temperatures, wear, and corrosion and used esp. for coatings and films

poly I.poly C \ˌpälēˈī-ˌpälēˈsē\ *also* **poly I:C** \-ˌīˈsē\ *n* [*poly-* + *inosinic acid* + *poly-* + cytidylic acid] **:** a synthetic RNA that is held to induce interferon formation and that has been used experimentally as an anticancer and antiviral agent

poly·ribosome \ˌpälē, -lə+\ *n* -s [*poly-* + *ribosome* (herein)] **:** a protein-building unit consisting of a cluster of ribosomes held together by messenger RNA — **poly·ribosomal** \"+\ *adj*

poly·some \ˈpälē,sōm, -lə-\ *n* -s [*poly-* + *ribosome* (herein)] **:** POLYRIBOSOME *herein*

poly·unsaturated \ˌpälē+\ *adj* [*poly-* + *unsaturated*] *of a fat or oil* **:** rich in unsaturated bonds — **poly·unsaturate** \"+\ *n*

poor–mouth \ˈ=,maůth, -t͟h\ *vb* [*poor mouth*] *vi* **:** to plead poverty as a defense or excuse ⟨usually *poor-mouths* when it's his turn to contribute⟩ ~ *vt* **:** to speak disparagingly of

pop* *adj* **:** of, relating to, or constituting a voguish mid-20th century mass culture that is international in scope, receives wide dissemination through the mass media, and encompasses a broad range of cultural phenomena (as vinyl clothing, pop art, and comic books)

pop* *or* **pop art** *n* **:** art in which commonplace objects (as road signs, hamburgers, comic strips, or soup cans) are used as subject matter and are often physically incorporated in the work — **pop artist** *n*

pop·ster \ˈpäpstə(r\ *n* -s [*pop* (herein) + *-ster*] **:** a practitioner of pop art

pop–top \ˌ=ˈ=\ *adj* [¹*pop* + ¹*top*] **:** having a tab that can be pulled off to make an opening ⟨a *pop-top* beer can⟩

population explosion *n* **:** excessive population growth esp. of man aided by increase in both survival and reproduction

pornography* *n* **:** material (as a book) that is pornographic

po·ro·mer·ic \ˌpȯrəˈmerik, ˌpȯr-\ *adj* [*poro-* + *polymeric*] **:** full of very fine pores — used of a tough synthetic material (as for shoe uppers) — **poromeric** *n* -s

posi·grade \ˈpäzə,grād\ *adj* [*positive* + *-grade* (as in *retrograde*)] **:** being an auxiliary rocket used for imparting additional thrust to a spacecraft in the direction of motion

position paper *n* **:** a detailed report that recommends a course of action on a particular issue

pothead \ˈ=,=\ *n* [¹*pot* + *head*] **:** one who smokes marijuana

power broker *n* **:** a person (as in politics) able to exert strong influence because of votes or individuals that he controls

power series *n* **:** an infinite series whose terms are successive integral powers of a variable multiplied by constants

power structure *n* **1 :** a group of persons having control of an organization **:** ESTABLISHMENT **2 :** the hierarchical interrelationships existing within a controlling group

pre·capillary \(ˈ)prē+\ *adj* [*pre-* + *capillary*] **:** being on the arterial side of and immediately adjacent to a capillary

pre·determiner \ˌprē+\ *n* [*pre-* + *determiner*] **:** a limiting noun modifier (as *both* or *all*) characterized by occurrence before the determiner in a noun phrase

pre·diabetes \ˌprē+\ *n* [*pre-* + *diabetes*] **:** an inapparent abnormal state that precedes the development of clinically evident diabetes — **pre·diabetic** \"+\ *adj or n*

preemptive* *adj* **:** marked by the seizing of the initiative **:** initiated by oneself ⟨~ attack⟩ ⟨~ war⟩

prehistoric* *adj* **:** of or relating to a language in a period of its development from which contemporary records of its actual sounds and forms have not been preserved

prelate nul·li·us \-nüˈlēəs\ *n, pl* **prelates nullius** [part translation of NL *praelatus nullius dioeceseos* prelate of no diocese] **:** a Roman Catholic prelate having ordinary jurisdiction over a district independent of any diocese

pre·plant \ˈ=,=\ *also* **pre·planting** \ˈ=,==, ˌ=ˈ==\ *adj* **:** occurring or used before planting a crop ⟨~ fertilization⟩

pre·preg \ˈprē,preg\ *n* -s [*pre-* + *impregnated*] **:** a reinforcing or molding material (as glass cloth or paper) already impregnated with a synthetic resin

¹pre·soak \(ˈ)prē+\ *vt* [*pre-* + *soak*] **:** to soak beforehand

²presoak \ˈ=,=\ *n* **1 :** a preparation used in presoaking clothes **2 :** an instance of presoaking

pre·sort \(ˈ)prē+\ *vt* [*pre-* + *sort*] **:** to sort (outgoing mail) by zip code usu. before delivery to a post office

pre·teen \ˈprē+ˌ\ *n* -s [*pre-* + ³*teen*] **:** PREADOLESCENT — **preteen** *adj*

prevent defense *n* **:** a football defense in which linebackers and backs play deeper than usual in order to prevent the completion of a long pass

preventive detention* *n* **:** imprisonment without the right to bail of an arrested person awaiting trial for a felony who is considered dangerous to society

price–earnings ratio *n* **:** a measure of the value of a common stock determined as the ratio of its market price to its earnings per share and usu. expressed as a simple numeral (**price-earnings multiple**)

primary derivative *n* **:** a word (as *telegram*) whose immediate constituents are bound forms

primary structure *n* **:** sculpture in the idiom of minimal art — **primary structurist** *n*

prime rate *n* **:** an interest rate at which preferred customers can borrow from banks and which is the lowest commercial interest rate available at a particular time and place

print out *vt* [²*print* + ¹*out*] **:** to make a printout of

printout \ˈ=,=\ *n* -s [*print out*, v. (herein)] **:** a printed record produced automatically (as by a computer)

pri·va·tism \ˈprīvə,tizəm\ *n* -s [¹*private* + *-ism*] **:** the attitude of being uncommitted to or avoiding involvement in anything beyond one's immediate interests

pro·ac·tive \(ˌ)prō+\ *adj* [L *pro-* forward (fr. *pro* before, for) + E *active* — more at FOR] **:** preceding something in time and modifying that which is preceded ⟨amount of ~ facilitation — amount of ~ transfer to the second task — was related to the amount of practice on the initial task —Don Lewis⟩

pro·ben·e·cid \prōˈbenəsəd\ *n* -s [irreg. fr. *propyl* + *benzoic acid*] **:** a drug that acts on renal tubular function and is used to inhibit the excretion of some drugs (as penicillin) and to increase the excretion of urates in gout

pro·ges·to·gen \prōˈjestəjən, -,jen\ *n* -s [*progest*ational + *-ogen* (as in *estrogen*)] **:** a progestational steroid used esp. to control uterine bleeding and to inhibit ovulation

program* *n* **1 :** a sequence of coded instructions for insertion into a mechanism (as a data processor, language translator, machine tool, missile, or vehicle) for automatic control of its operation **2 :** a series of stimuli usu. in the form of written statements and questions relating to a specific subject presented to a student in a particular sequence so that responses are elicited from him and he is informed of the appropriateness of his response before going on to the next item

program* *vt* **1 :** to insert a program into ⟨~ a computer⟩ ⟨~ a machine tool⟩ ⟨~ a missile for guidance⟩ **2 :** to insert a program for (a particular action, operation, or process) into a mechanism ⟨~ a calculation⟩ ⟨~ a farming operation⟩

pro·gram·ma·ble *or* **pro·gram·able** \ˈprō,graməbəl\ *adj* [²*program* + *-able*] **:** capable of being programmed ⟨a ~ calculator⟩ — **pro·gram·ma·bil·i·ty** \ˌ=,==ˈbiləd·ē\ *n* -ES

pro·grammed *or* **pro·gramed** \ˈprō,gramd, -grəmd\ *adj* [fr. past part. of ²*program*] **1 :** being instruction or learning by means of an instructional program **2 :** produced in the form of an instructional program ⟨a ~ textbook of physics⟩

programmer* *or* **pro·gram·er** *n* **1 :** one that prepares a program for a mechanism **2 :** a device that programs a mechanism **3 :** one that prepares an educational program

programming* *or* **programing*** *n* **1 :** the process of instructing or learning by means of an instructional program **2 :** the process of preparing an instructional program

pro·jec·tu·al \prəˈjekchəwəl, prō-\ *n* -s [²*project* + *-ual* (as in *visual*)] **:** a usu. instructional material (as a transparency) to be projected (as onto a screen) by a projector

pros·ta·glan·din \ˌprästəˈglandən\ *n* [ISV *prostate gland* + *-in*; fr. its occurrence in the sexual glands of mammals] **:** any of various oxygenated unsaturated cyclic fatty acids of animals that may perform a variety of hormonelike actions (as in controlling blood pressure or smooth muscle contraction)

pro·tein·oid \ˈprō,tē,nȯid, ˈprōtᵊn,ȯid, ˈprōd·ēə,nȯid\ *n* -s [*protein* + ¹*-oid*] **:** a proteinaceous substance obtained by suitable polymerization of mixtures of amino acids

prothoracic gland *n* **:** one of a pair of thoracic endocrine organs in some immature insects that control molting

pro·to·continent \ˌprōd·ō+\ *n* [*prot-* + *continent*] **:** SUPERCONTINENT *herein*

pro·to·porcelain \ˌprōd·(ˌ)ō+\ *n* [*prot-* + *porcelain*; prob. trans. of G *urporzellan*] **:** a porcelaneous ware lacking some of the qualities of a true porcelain; *specif* **:** a hard-fired gray kaolinic Chinese stoneware known since Han times

prox·e·mics \präkˈsēmiks\ *n pl but sing in constr* [*prox*imity +

-emics (as in *phonemics*)] **:** a branch of study dealing with the personal and cultural spatial needs of man and his interaction with his environing space

psi·lo·cin \ˈsīləsən\ *n* -s [NL *Psilocybe mexicana*, fungus from which it is obtained + E *-in*] **:** a hallucinogenic tertiary amine obtained from a fungus (*Psilocybe mexicana*)

psi·lo·cy·bin \ˌsīləˈsībən\ *n* -s [NL *Psilocybe mexicana*, fungus from which it is obtained + E *-in*] **:** a hallucinogenic indole obtained from a fungus (*Psilocybe mexicana*)

psych* *also* **psyche** \ˈsīk\ *vt* -ED/-ING/-s **1 :** to make (oneself) psychologically ready for performance — usu. used with *up* ⟨~*ed* himself up for the race⟩ **2 :** to make psychologically uneasy **:** INTIMIDATE, SCARE ⟨pressure doesn't ~ me —Jerry Quarry⟩ — often used with *out*

psy·che·de·lia \ˌsīkəˈdēlyə\ *n* [NL, fr. E *psychedelic* (herein) + L *-ia* -y] **:** the world of people, phenomena, or items associated with psychedelic drugs

¹psy·che·del·ic \ˌsīkəˈdelik, -dēl-\ *adj* [Gk *psychē* soul + *dēloun* to show, reveal (fr. *dēlos* evident) + E *-ic* — more at PSYCHE, ADEL-] **1 a :** of, relating to, or causing an exposure of normally repressed psychic elements ⟨~ drugs⟩ **b :** of, relating to, involving, or resulting from the use of psychedelic drugs ⟨~ indulgences⟩ ⟨a ~ experience⟩ ⟨experimental ~ therapy⟩ **c :** of, relating to, or concerned with psychedelics ⟨hippies escaping to their ~ lairs —T.E.Mullaney⟩ ⟨~ medicine designed to help LSD users⟩ **2 a :** imitating or reproducing the effects (as distorted or heightened sense perception) of psychedelic drugs ⟨~ light show⟩ ⟨~ art⟩ **b** (1) **:** brightly colored ⟨ferryboats soon will take on a ~ look, with an overall coat of international orange and touches of red and yellow —*N.Y.Times*⟩ (2) *of colors* **:** FLUORESCENT **c :** making use of electronically distorted sounds ⟨~ rock⟩ **3 :** of, relating to, dealing in, or being the culture associated with psychedelic drugs ⟨~ shops⟩ — **psy·che·del·i·cal·ly** \-lək(ə)lē\ *adv*

²psychedelic *n* **1 :** a psychedelic drug (as LSD) **2 a :** a user or an advocate of psychedelic drugs **b :** a person with psychedelic social and cultural interests and orientation

psychic energizer *n* **:** an antidepressant drug

psy·cho·active \ˌsīkō+\ *adj* [*psych-* + *active*] **:** affecting the mind or behavior ⟨~ drugs⟩

psy·cho·chemical \"+\ *n* [*psych-* + ²*chemical*] **:** a chemical that alters mental functioning; *esp* **:** a chemical warfare agent (as a war gas) that acts on nervous centers and makes affected individuals temporarily helpless — **psychochemical** *adj*

psy·cho·pharmaceutical \"+\ *n* [*psych-* + ²*pharmaceutical*] **:** a drug having an effect on the mental state of a person

psy·cho·quack \ˈsīkō+,\ *n* [*psych-* + ³*quack*] **:** an unqualified psychologist or psychiatrist — **psy·cho·quackery** \ˌsīkō+\ *n*

psy·chot·o·gen \sīˈkädəjən\ *n* -s [*psychotic* + *-o-* + *-gen*] **:** a chemical agent (as a drug) that induces a psychotic state — **psy·chot·o·gen·ic** \(ˌ)sī,kädəˈjenik\ *adj*

psy·choto·mimetic \sīˌkädō +\ *adj* [*psychotic* + *-o-* + *mimetic*] **:** of, relating to, or involving psychotic alteration of behavior and personality — **psychotomimetic** *n* -s — **psy·choto·mimetically** \"+\ *adv*

psy·cho·toxic \ˌsīkō+\ *adj* [*psych-* + *toxic*] **:** damaging to the mind; *specif* **:** of, relating to, or being a habituating drug (as amphetamine) which is not a true narcotic but the use of which may be correlated with delinquency and crime

PTV *abbr* public television *herein*

public television *n* **:** television that provides cultural, informational, and instructional programs for the public and that does not promote the sale of a product or service except for identifying the donors of program funds **:** noncommercial television

pul·sar \ˈpəl,sär\ *n* -s [*pulse* + *-ar* (as in *quasar* — herein)] **:** any of various stellar objects characterized by the emission of very intense radio energy at short regular intervals

pump* *n* **1 :** electromagnetic radiation for pumping atoms or molecules **2 :** the process of pumping atoms or molecules **3 :** a device for pumping atoms or molecules

pump* *vt* **:** to change equilibrium populations of energy levels of (atoms or molecules) by strong electromagnetic radiation at one of the resonant frequencies so that stimulation of emission may occur at another frequency resulting in amplification or sustained oscillation — compare LASER, MASER *in the Dict*

put down* *vt* **1 a :** BELITTLE, DISPARAGE ⟨many writers want to *put down* not only their interviewers but their critics —Melvin Maddocks⟩ **b :** DISAPPROVE, CRITICIZE ⟨*put down* for the way he dressed⟩ **2 :** DEFLATE, SQUELCH ⟨nothing beastlier than a woman who *puts* a man *down* on the air —Pamela Mason⟩

put-down \ˈ≈,≈\ *n* -s [*put down* (herein)] **:** an act or instance of putting down; *esp* **:** a deflating remark

put-on* *n* -s **:** an instance of putting someone on ⟨couldn't decide whether the question was serious or just a *put-on*⟩; *also* **:** PARODY, SPOOF ⟨a kind of *put-on* of every pretentious film ever made —C.A.Ridley⟩

py·re·throid \pīˈrē,thrȯid, -reˈ-\ *n* -s [*pyrethrin* + ¹*-oid*] **:** any of various synthetic compounds related to and resembling in insecticidal properties the pyrethrins — **pyrethroid** *adj*

qi·vi·ut \ˈkēvē,üt\ *n* [Esk] **:** the wool of the undercoat of the musk-ox that is held to be comparable to cashmere

quan·ta·some \ˈkwäntə,sōm\ *n* -s [prob. fr. *quanta*, pl. of *quantum* + ³*-some*] **:** one of the chlorophyll-containing spheroids found in the grana of chloroplasts

quantized *adj* [fr. past part. of *quantize*] **:** characterized by the property of taking on only discrete values

quantum electronics *n pl but sing in constr* **:** a branch of physics that deals with the interaction of radiation with discrete energy levels in substances (as in a maser or laser)

quark \ˈkwärk\ *n* -s [coined by Murray Gell-Mann *b*1929 Amer. physicist] **:** a hypothetical particle that carries an electric charge and that is held to be a constituent of known elementary particles

qua·sar \ˈkwā,zär, ˈkwä-, -,sär\ *n* -s [*quasi-stellar* radio source (herein)] **:** QUASI-STELLAR RADIO SOURCE *herein*

qua·si·mo·do \ˌk(w)äzēˈmō(ˌ)dō, -äsō-\ *n* -s *usu cap* [after *Quasimodo*, hunchback in Victor Hugo's novel *Notre-Dame de Paris* (1831)] **:** a surfing feat in which a surfer squats on the board, leans forward, and extends one arm straight forward and the other straight back

qua·si·par·ti·cle \ˈ≈(ˌ)≈ˈ≈≈≈\ *n* [²*quasi* + *particle*] **:** a composite entity (as a vibration in a solid) that is analogous in its behavior to a single particle

quasi-stellar object \ˈ≈(ˌ)≈ˈ≈≈-\ *n* **:** QUASI-STELLAR RADIO SOURCE *herein*

quasi-stellar radio source \ˈ≈(ˌ)≈ˈ≈≈-\ *n* [*quasi-stellar* fr. ¹*quasi-* + *stellar*] **:** any of various very distant celestial objects which resemble a star but emit unusually bright blue and ultraviolet light and powerful radio waves

quas·qui·centennial \ˌkwäskwē, -kwȯ+\ *n* -s [fr. L *quadrans* quarter, after L *semis* half **:** E *sesquicentennial* — more at QUADRANT, SESQUI-] **:** a 125th anniversary — **quasquicentennial** *adj*

queen size *adj* **1 :** having dimensions of approximately 60 inches by 80 inches — used of a bed **2 :** of a size that fits a queen size bed ⟨a *queen size* bedspread⟩

quick kick *n* **:** a punt in football made on first, second, or third down from a running or passing formation and designed to take the opposing team by surprise

rack car* *n* **:** a railroad flatcar equipped with a 2-level or 3-level framework for transporting motor vehicles

radar astronomy *n* **:** astronomy dealing with investigations of celestial bodies in the solar system by comparing the characteristics of a reflected radar wave with the characteristics of one transmitted from the earth

radar telescope *n* **:** a radar transmitter-receiver with an antenna for use in radar astronomy

radial-ply tire *or* **radial tire** *n* **:** a pneumatic tire in which the ply cords that extend to the beads are laid at approximately 90 degrees to the center line of the tread

ra·di·esthesia \ˌrādē+\ *n* -s [NL, fr. L *radius* ray + NL *esthesia* — more at RAY] **1 :** sensitiveness held to enable a person with the aid of a divining rod or pendulum to detect things (as the presence of underground water, the nature of an illness, or the guilt of a suspected person); *also* **:** DOWSING, DIVINING **2 :** a study that deals with radiesthesia

ra·dio·ecology \ˌrādē(ˌ)ō+\ *n* [*radio-* + *ecology*] **:** the study of the interaction of ecological communities and radiations or radioactive substances — **ra·dio·ecological** \"+\ *adj* — **ra·dio·ecologist** \"+\ *n*

radio galaxy *n* **:** a visible or photographable galaxy that includes a source from which radio energy is detected

ra·dio·isotopic \ˌrādē(ˌ)ō+\ *adj* [*radioisotope* + *-ic*] **:** of, relating to, or being a radioisotope — **ra·dio·isotopically** \"+\ *adv*

ra·dio·pharmaceutical \"+\ *n* [*radio-* + ²*pharmaceutical*] **:** a radioactive drug used for diagnostic or therapeutic purposes

ra·dio·protective \"+\ *adj* [*radio-* + *protective*] **:** serving to protect or aiding in protecting against the injurious effect of radiations ⟨~ drugs⟩ — **ra·dio·protection** \"+\ *n*

ra·dio·sterilized \"+\ *adj* [*radio-* + *sterilized*] **:** sterilized by irradiation (as with X rays or gamma rays) ⟨~ mosquitoes⟩ ⟨~ syringes⟩ — **ra·dio·sterilization** \"+\ *n*

ra·dio-ulna \"+\ *n* [NL, fr. *radius* (fr. L) + *-o-* + *ulna*] **:** a bone in the forelimb of an amphibian (as a frog) representing the fused radius and ulna of higher forms

rand \ˈrand, -ä-\ *n, pl* **rand** *or* **rands** [fr. the *Rand* (*Witwatersrand*), gold-producing district in So. Africa] **1 a :** the basic monetary unit of the Republic of So. Africa established in 1961 — see MONEY table *in the Dict* **b :** the basic monetary unit of Botswana, Lesotho, and Swaziland **2 :** a coin or note representing one rand

R and B *abbr* rhythm and blues

R and D *abbr or n* **:** research and development — usu. written *R & D*

random-access *adj* **:** permitting access to stored data in any order the user desires ⟨*random-access* computer memory⟩

¹rap \ˈrap\ *n* [perh. by shortening & alter. fr. *repartee*] **:** TALK, CONVERSATION

²rap *vi* **:** to talk freely and frankly ⟨down at the corner bar *rapping* —*Newsweek*⟩ — **rap·per** *n* -s

rapid eye movement *n* **:** rapid conjugate movement of the eyes associated with a state of sleep characterized by changes in brain waves and heart rhythm, relaxed muscles, and dreaming

rapture of the deep **:** a confused mental state caused by nitrogen forced into a diver's bloodstream from atmospheric air under pressure

rate of change **:** a value that results from dividing the change of a function of a variable by the change in the variable

rat fink *n* **:** FINK *herein*

ratio *vt* -ED/-ING/-s [*ratio*, n.] **1 :** to express as a ratio **2 :** to make proportionate **3 :** to enlarge or reduce the size of (a photograph) in accordance with a ratio

RBE *abbr* relative biological effectiveness *herein*

read* *vt* **1 :** to sense the meaning of (information) in recorded and coded form (as in storage) **:** acquire (information) from storage — used of a computer or data processor **2 :** to read the coded information on (as tape or a punched card)

readout* *n* **1 :** the process of reading **2 a :** the process of removing information from an automatic device (as an electronic computer) and displaying it in an understandable form **b :** the information removed from such a device and displayed or recorded (as by magnetic tape or printing device) **c :** a device used for readout **3 :** the radio transmission of data or pictures from a space vehicle either immediately upon acquisition or later by means of playback of a tape recording

readymade** *n* -s **:** an artifact (as a comb or a pair of ice tongs) selected and displayed as a work of art

real time *n* **1 :** the actual time in which a physical process takes place — used in reference to a process controlled by a computer **2 :** the actual time in which an event takes place with the reporting on or recording of the event practically simultaneous with its occurrence — **real-time** *adj*

receptor* *n* **:** a cellular entity (as a beta-receptor or alpha-receptor) that is postulated as the intermediary between a chemical agent (as a neurohumor) acting on nervous tissue and the physiological or pharmacological response

re·charter \"+\ *vt* [*re-* + ²*charter*] **:** to grant a new charter to ⟨~*ed* the national bank⟩ — **recharter** *n*

recursion* *n* **:** the determination of a succession of elements (as numbers or functions) by operation on one or more preceding elements according to a rule or formula involving a finite number of steps

re·cur·sive \rəˈkərsiv, rēˈ-\ *adj* [²*recursion* + *-ive*] **1 :** of, relating to, or involving mathematical recursion **2 a :** capable of repeated application **b :** involving the repeated application of a procedure until a specified condition is satisfied with the testing for the condition included in the procedure itself ⟨~ techniques in computer programming⟩ — compare ITERATIVE *herein* — **re·cur·sive·ly** *adv* — **re·cur·sive·ness** *n*

re·cycle* \(ˈ)rē+\ *vb* ~ *vt* **1 :** to pass (as liquid body wastes) continuously through a purification process in order to produce a product fit for human use **2 :** to cause (as an electric generator) to accelerate gradually in bringing up to full power production ~ *vi* **1 :** to stop the counting and return to an earlier point in a countdown **2 :** to return to an original condition so that operation can begin again — used of an electronic device

redbrick \ˈ≈,≈, *attrib also* ˌ≈ˈ≈\ *adj, sometimes cap* [*red* + *brick*; fr. common use of red brick in constructing the buildings of recently founded universities] **:** of, relating to, or being the British universities founded in modern times — compare OXBRIDGE *herein*

red guard *n, usu cap R&G* [¹*red* (communist) + *guard*] **:** a member of a teen-age activist organization in China serving the Maoist party

redshirt* *n* [¹*red* + *shirt*; fr. the red jersey commonly worn by such a player in practice scrimmages against the regulars] **:** a college athlete who is kept out of varsity competition for a year in order to extend the period of his eligibility to a more mature age — **redshirting** \ˈ≈,≈≈\ *n* -s

redundant* *adj* **:** designed to serve as a substitute in case of failure (as of a subsystem) for preventing failure of an entire device or system ⟨~ electronic equipment on a spacecraft⟩

region* *n* **:** a set of points such that if a point belongs to the set then a neighborhood of the point also belongs to the set

reinforce* *vb* ~ *vt* **1 :** to stimulate (as an experimental animal or a student) with a reinforcer following a correct or desired performance **2 :** to encourage (a response) with a reinforcer

reinforcer* *n* **:** a stimulus (as a reward or the removal of discomfort) that is effective in operant conditioning because it regularly follows a desired response

rejective art *n* **:** MINIMAL ART *herein*

relative biological effectiveness *n* **:** the relative capacity of a particular ionizing radiation to produce a response in a biological system — abbr. *RBE*

relativistic* *adj* **1 :** moving at a high velocity exceeding one tenth that of light so that there is a significant change in mass and other properties in accordance with the theory of relativity ⟨a ~ electron⟩ **2 :** of or relating to a relativistic particle

REM \ˌär(ˌ)ēˈem, ˈrem\ *abbr or n* -s rapid eye movement *herein*

re·no·gram \ˈrēnə,gram\ *n* -s [*reno-* + *gram*] **:** a photographic depiction of the course of excretion of a radioactively labeled substance — **re·nog·ra·phy** \rēˈnägrəfē, rəˈ-\ *n* -ES

reo·virus \ˈrēō+\ *n* [respiratory enteric orphan *virus*] **:** any of a group of rather large, widely distributed, and possibly tumorigenic viruses with double-stranded RNA

repertory* *n* — **in repertory** *adv* **:** in the manner of a repertory theater ⟨presents four plays *in repertory*⟩

repressor* *n* **:** a product of the action of a regulator gene that interacts with an operator gene and inhibits its function

re·prog·ra·phy \rəˈprägrəfē, rēˈp-\ *n* -ES [ISV *reproduction* + *-graphy*] **:** the facsimile reproduction (as by photocopying) of graphic matter (as books or documents) — **re·prog·ra·pher** \-fə(r)\ *n* -s — **re·pro·graph·ic** \ˈrēprəˌgrafik, ˌrep-\ *adj*

re·segregation \(ˈ)rē+\ *n* [*re-* + *segregation*] **:** a return (as of a school) to a state of segregation after an initial period of desegregation

residual* *n* **:** a payment (as to an actor or writer) for each rerun (as of a TV tape) esp. of a commercial

residual security *n* **:** common stock or a security convertible into common stock

resilience* *n* **:** an ability to recover from or adjust easily to misfortune or change

resistance* *n* **:** RESISTANCE LEVEL *herein*

resistance level *or* **resistance area** *n* **:** a price level on a rising market at which a security resists further advance due to increased attractiveness of the price to potential sellers

re·sis·to·jet \rəˈzistō,jet, rēˈz-\ *n* [*resistance* + *-o-* + *jet*] **:** a small reaction engine that uses electrically heated hydrogen or ammonia as a propellant and that produces small thrust (as for satellite control)

resonance* *n* **1 a :** the enhancement of an atomic, nuclear, or particle reaction or a scattering event by excitation of internal motion in the system **b :** MAGNETIC RESONANCE **2 :** an extremely short-lived elementary particle

respondent* *n* **:** a reflex that occurs in response to a specific external stimulus ⟨the knee jerk is a typical ~⟩

res·sen·ti·ment \rəˈsäⁿ-tēˈmäⁿ\ *n* -s [G, fr. F, resentment — more at RESENTMENT] **:** resentment expressed indirectly esp. by belittling the values esteemed by the hated individual

ret·ro-engine \ˈreˈtrō *sometimes* -ē-+,\ *n* **:** a rocket engine on a space vehicle that thrusts in a direction opposite to that of the motion of the vehicle in order to decelerate it

ret·ro·fire \"+\ *vi* [*retro-* + ²*fire*] **:** to ignite a retro-engine — **retrofire** *n*

retrograde* *adj* **:** being or relating to the rotation of a satellite in a direction opposite to that of the body being orbited

ret·ro·reflector \ˌreˈtrō *sometimes* -ē-+\ *n* [*retro-* + *reflector*] **:** a device that reflects radiation (as light) so that the paths of the rays are parallel to those of the incident rays

reu·ben sandwich \ˌrübən-\ *n, usu cap R* [fr. the name *Reuben*] **:** a grilled sandwich consisting of corned beef, Swiss cheese, and sauerkraut usu. on rye bread

re·vanch·ism \rəˈväⁿ,shizəm\ *n* -s [*revanche* + *-ism*] **:** REVANCHE ⟨a policy of nationalistic ~ —Bernard Fall⟩

re·vascularization \(ˈ)rē+\ *n* -s [*re-* + *vascular* + *-ization*] **:** a surgical procedure for the provision of a new, additional, or augmented blood supply to a body part or organ

reverse osmosis *n* **:** the flow of fresh water through a semipermeable membrane when pressure is applied to a solution (as seawater) on one side of it

rheumatoid factor *n* **:** a gamma globulin of high molecular weight that is usu. present in rheumatoid arthritis and that behaves like an autoantibody

rhi·no·virus \ˈrīnō+\ *n* [NL, fr. *rhin-* + *virus*] **:** any of a group of picornaviruses that are related to the enteroviruses and associated with upper respiratory tract disorders

rho* *or* **rho particle** *n* **:** a very short-lived unstable meson with mass 1490 times the mass of an electron

rhythm and blues *n* **:** popular music with elements of blues and Negro folk music

ribosomal RNA \-ˌärˌeˈnā\ *n* -s **:** the part of the RNA that is a fundamental structural element to the ribosome

ri·bo·some \ˈrībə,sōm\ *n* -s [*ribo*nucleic acid + ³*-some*] **:** any of the RNA-rich cytoplasmic granules that function in protein and enzyme synthesis — **ri·bo·som·al** \ˈ≈ˈsōməl\ *adj*

rich·ter scale \ˈriktə(r)-\ *n, usu cap R* [after Charles F. *Richter b*1900 Am. seismologist] **:** a logarithmic scale for expressing the magnitude of a seismic disturbance (as an earthquake) in terms of the energy dissipated in it with 1.5 indicating the smallest earthquake that can be felt, 4.5 an earthquake causing slight damage, and 8.5 a very devastating earthquake

ricky-tick \ˈrikēˌtik\ *n* [imit.] **:** sweet jazz of a style reminiscent of the 1920s — **ricky-ticky** \-tikē\ *adj*

right-to-work law *n* **:** any of various state laws banning the closed shop and the union shop

RNAase \ˌärˌeˈnā,ās, -,āz\ *abbr or n* -s [*RNA* + *-ase*] **:** RIBONUCLEASE

ro·bot·ics \rōˈbädiks\ *n pl but sing in constr* [*robot* + *-ics*] **:** a field of interest concerned with the construction, maintenance, and behavior of robots ⟨~ is a major science fiction theme⟩

rock·a·bil·ly \ˈräkə,bilē\ *n* [*rock* and roll + *hillbilly*] **:** pop music marked by features of rock, country, and western styles

ro·la·mite \ˈrōlə,mīt\ *n* -s [*roll* + *-amite*, of unknown origin] **:** a nearly frictionless elementary mechanism consisting of two or more rollers inserted in the loops of a flexible metal or plastic band with the band acting to turn the rollers whose movement can be directed to perform various functions

roll bar *n* **:** an overhead metal bar on an automobile designed to protect an occupant in case of a turnover

roll cage *n* **:** a protective framework of metal bars encasing the driver of a racing car

roller hockey *n* **:** a variation of ice hockey that is played on roller skates

roll out* *vi* **:** to circle to the right or left before passing or running ⟨the quarterback would either hand off to the fullback or fake to him and *roll out* —Arthur Sampson⟩

rollout** *n* **:** an offensive play in football in which the quarterback rolls out

rose medallion *n* **:** a chiefly 19th century enamel-decorated Chinese porcelain with medallions of oriental figures surrounded and separated by panels of flowers and butterflies

ruly english *n, cap E* **:** an artificial English for use in computers in which each word has a single conceptual meaning and each concept a single word to describe it

rya \ˈrēə\ *n* -s [fr. *Rya*, village in southwest Sweden] **:** a Scandinavian handwoven rug with a deep resilient comparatively flat pile; *also* **:** the weave typical of this rug

sailboard \ˈ≈,≈\ *n* [*sail* + *board*] **:** a small flat sailboat that is designed for one or two passengers

sal·uret·ic \ˌsalyəˈredik\ *n* -s [L *sal* salt + E *diuretic* — more at SALT] **:** a drug that facilitates the urinary excretion of salt and esp. of sodium ion — **saluretic** \ˈ≈≈ˈ≈\ *adj* — **sal·u·ret·i·cal·ly** \-ˈredək(ə)lē\ *adv*

SAM \ˈsam, ˌe(ˌ)sāˈem\ *abbr or n* -s surface-to-air missile

san·da ware \ˈsandə-, ˈsän-\ *n, usu cap S* [fr. *Sanda*, town in western Honshu, Japan, where it originated] **:** a Japanese pottery and esp. porcelain ware produced since the late 17th century and noted for its celadons

sandwich shop *n* **:** LUNCHEONETTE

sanitize* *vt* **:** to make more acceptable by removing unpleasant or undesired features ⟨~ a document⟩

sa·ran·gi \ˈsärən,gē\ *n* -s [Skt *sāraṅgī*] **:** a bowed stringed musical instrument of India with a tone similar to that of the viola

satellite* *n* **:** a usu. independent urban community situated near but not immediately adjacent to a large city

saturated diving *n* **:** SATURATION DIVING *herein* — **saturated diver** *n*

saturation diving *n* **:** diving in which a person remains underwater at a certain depth breathing a mixture of gases under pressure until his body becomes saturated with the gases so that decompression time remains the same regardless of how long he remains at that depth — **saturation dive** *n*

scam·pi \ˈskampē, -ām-\ *n, pl* **scampi** [It, pl. of *scampo* Norway lobster] **:** SHRIMP; *esp* **:** large shrimp prepared with a garlic-flavored sauce

scan* *vt* **:** to make a detailed examination of (as a human body) for the presence or localization of radioactive material

scan* *n* **1 :** a depiction (as a photograph) of the distribution of radioactive material in something (as a body organ) **2 :** COLOR SEPARATION

scattering matrix *n* **:** S MATRIX

scene* *n* **:** a sphere of activity **:** a way of life ⟨the hippie ~⟩

schlepp \ˈshlep\ *or* **schlep·per** \-epə(r)\ *also* **shlepp** *or* **shlep·per** *n* -s [Yiddish *shlep*, *shlepper*, fr. *shlepen* to drag, pull, jerk — more at SCHLEPP, vb.] **:** an awkward or incompetent person

schlock *also* **shlock** \ˈshläk\ *adj* [Yiddish *shlak*, lit., blow, apoplectic stroke, curse, fr. MHG *slag*, *slac*, fr. OHG *slag*, fr. *slahan* to strike — more at SLAY] **:** of low quality or little worth ⟨~ books⟩ ⟨~ merchandise⟩ — **schlock** *n* -s

schussboomer \ˈ≈,≈≈\ *n* [¹*schuss* + ¹*boomer*] **:** one who skis usu. straight downhill at high speed

sci·en·tol·o·gy \ˌsīən·ˈtäləjē\ *n, usu cap* [L *scientia* science + E *-o-* + *-logy* — more at SCIENCE] **:** a religious movement begun in 1952 by L. Ron Hubbard which teaches that man has an immortal spirit that is subject to reincarnation and that increased spiritual awareness and cures for mental and physical illnesses can be achieved through a form of psychotherapy

sci-fi \ˈsīˈfī\ *adj* [*science fiction*] **:** of, relating to, or being science fiction ⟨*sci-fi* writers⟩ ⟨*sci-fi* stories⟩

scouse \ˈskau̇s\ *n* -s *cap* [back-formation fr. *Scouser* (herein)] **1 :** a dialect of English spoken in Liverpool **2 :** SCOUSER *herein*

scous·er \ˈskau̇sə(r)\ *n, cap* [*scouse* (in the Dict.) + *-er*; fr. the popularity of lobscouse in Liverpool] **:** a native or inhabitant of Liverpool

scramble* *vi, of a football quarterback* **:** to leave the protection of the blockers on a pass play and run with the ball
scramble* *n* **:** a motorcycle race over a rough hilly course
scram·jet \ˈskram,jet\ *n* [supersonic combustion *ramjet*] **:** a ramjet airplane engine in which thrust is produced by burning fuel in a supersonic airstream after the airplane has attained supersonic speed by other means of propulsion
screening test *n* **:** a preliminary or abridged test intended to eliminate the less probable members of an experimental series
screwbean mesquite \ˈ=,=-\ *n* [*screw bean* + *mesquite*] **:** SCREW BEAN 1
SDRs \,es(,)dēˈärz\ *n pl* [special drawing rights] **:** a proposed international means of exchange for use by governments in settling their international indebtedness
seat* *n* **:** a precise or accurate contact between parts or surfaces
secondary* *n* **:** SECONDARY DISTRIBUTION
secondary derivative *n* **:** a word (as *teacher*) whose immediate constituents are a free form and a bound form
secondary offering *n* **:** SECONDARY *herein*
seed money *n* **:** money used for setting up a new enterprise
sel·e·nod·e·sy \,seləˈnädəsē\ *n* [*selen-* + *-odesy* (as in *geodesy*)] **:** a branch of physical science that deals with determination of the shape and size of the moon and of the exact positions of points on it and with the variations of lunar gravity — **sel·e·no·det·ic** \ˌselənōˌdedik\ *adj*
self-dealing \ˈ=ˈ==\ *n* **:** financial dealing that is not at arm's length; *esp* **:** borrowing from or lending to a company by a controlling individual primarily to his own advantage
self-destruct \ˈ==ˈ=\ *vi* **:** to destroy itself
selling climax *n* **:** a sharp decline in stock prices for a short time on very heavy trading volume followed by a rally
semi·automated \ˌsemē, -,mī, -,mi+\ *adj* [*semi-* + *automated,* past part. of *automate*] **:** partly automated
semi·comatose \ˌsemē, -,mī, -mə+\ *adj* [*semi-* + *comatose*] **:** lethargic and disoriented but not completely comatose
send-up \ˈ=,=\ *n* [Brit slang *send up* to take off, parody] *chiefly Brit* **:** PARODY, TAKEOFF
sen·gi \ˈseŋgē\ *n, pl* **sengi** [native name in the Congo] **:** a monetary unit of the Republic of the Congo (Kinshasa) equal to 1/100 likuta or 1/10,000 zaire — see MONEY table *in the Dict*
sen·i·ti \ˈsenətē\ *n, pl* **seniti** [Tongan, modif. of E *cent*] **1 :** a monetary unit of Tonga equal to 1/100 pa'anga — see MONEY table *in the Dict* **2 :** a coin representing one seniti
sensitivity training *n* **:** training designed to enhance interpersonal relations based typically on exploration by a small interacting group of the behavior, needs, and responses of the individuals making up the group
sequential *n* -s [*sequential,* adj.] **:** an oral contraceptive in which the pills taken during approximately the first three weeks contain only estrogen and those taken during the rest of the cycle contain both estrogen and progestogen
se·ri·al·ism \ˈsirēə,lizəm, ˈsēr-\ *n* -s [¹*serial* + *-ism*] **:** serial music; *also* **:** the theory or practice of composing serial music
service module *n* **:** a space vehicle module containing propellant tanks, fuel cells, and the main rocket engine
se·to ware \ˈsā,tō-, ˈse-\ *also* **seto** *n, usu cap S* [fr. *Seto,* city in central Honshu, Japan, where it originated] **:** a Japanese ceramic ware traditionally produced since the 10th century comprising in its earlier period earthenwares often based on contemporaneous Chinese and Korean porcelains, later high-fired stonewares sometimes with notable brown, black, yellow, or celadon glazes, and from the end of the 18th century chiefly porcelain often decorated with underglaze blue
sex* *n* **:** GENITALIA
sexi·decimal \ˌseksə, -ksē+\ *adj* [*sex-* + *-decimal* (as in *duodecimal*)] **:** of, relating to, or being a system of numbers having 16 as a base ⟨use of a ~ notation in binary computers⟩
sey·fert galaxy \ˌsīfərt-\ *n, usu cap S* [after Carl K. *Seyfert* †1960 Amer. astronomer] **:** any of a class of spiral galaxies that have very compact and intensely bright nuclei whose emission spectra show that the atoms are in a high state of excitation and are travelling at high speeds
shade* *n* **shades** *pl* **:** SUNGLASSES
sha·ku·ha·chi \ˌshäkəˈhächē\ *n, pl* **shakuhachi** [Jap] **:** a Japanese bamboo flute
shatter cone *n* **:** a conical fragment of rock that has striations radiating from the apex and is formed by high pressure (as from volcanism or meteorite impact)
shell* *n* **:** a plain usu. sleeveless overblouse
shih tzu \ˈshēd-ˈzü\ *n, usu cap S&T* [Chin (Pek) *shih¹ tzŭ³ kou³* Pekingese dog, fr. *shih¹* lion + *tzŭ³* son + *kou³* dog] **:** a small alert active dog of an old Chinese breed that has a square short unwrinkled muzzle, short muscular legs, and massive amounts of long dense hair
ship* *n* **:** SPACECRAFT
shoot* *vt* **:** to inject (an addictive drug) directly into the bloodstream — **shoot the curl** *or* **shoot the tube :** to surf into or through the curl of a wave — **shoot the pier :** to surf between the pilings of an ocean pier
short position* *n* **:** the market position of a trader who has made but not yet covered a short sale
short-term* *adj* **:** generated by assets held six months or less
showboat* *n* **:** one who tries to attract attention by conspicuous behavior
showboat *vi* [*showboat* n. (herein)] **:** to show off
shrink-wrap \ˈ=ˈ=\ *vt* [¹*shrink* + ¹*wrap*] **:** to wrap (as a book or meat) in tough clear plastic film that is then shrunk (as by heating) to form a tightly fitting package
shtick *also* **schtick** \ˈshtik\ *n* -s [Yiddish *shtik,* lit., piece, fr. MHG *stücke,* fr. OHG *stucki* — more at STOCK] **:** a theatrical routine **:** BIT
shun·pik·er \ˈshən,pīkə(r)\ *n* -s [*shunpike* + ²*-er*] **:** one who engages in shunpiking
shun·pik·ing \-kiŋ\ *n* -s [*shunpike* + ³*-ing*] **:** the practice of avoiding superhighways esp. for the pleasure of driving on back roads
side-straddle hop *n* **:** JUMPING-JACK *herein*
sigma* *or* **sigma particle** *n* **:** an unstable elementary particle of the baryon family existing in positive, negative, and neutral charge states with masses respectively 2328, 2343, and 2333 times the mass of an electron
sign on* \(ˈ)=ˈ=\ *vi* **:** to announce the start of broadcasting for the day — **sign-on** \ˈ=,=\ *n* -s
silky terrier *n* **:** a low-set toy terrier that weighs 8 to 10 pounds, has a flat silky glossy coat colored blue with tan on the head, chest, and legs, and is derived from crosses of the Australian terrier with the Yorkshire terrier
sil·vex \ˈsil,veks\ *n* -ES [irreg. fr. L *silva* wood] **:** a selective herbicide that is esp. effective in controlling woody plants
sil·vi·chemical \ˌsilvə+\ *n* [L *silva* wood + E *-i-* + *chemical*] **:** any of numerous chemicals derived from a part of a tree
si·ma·zine \ˈsīmə,zēn\ *n* -s [*sim-* (prob. alter. of ²*sym-*) + *triazine*] **:** a selective herbicide used to control weeds
simulate* *vt* **:** to make a simulation of (as a physical system)
simulation* *n* **1 :** the imitative representation of the functioning of one system or process by means of the functioning of another ⟨a computer ~ of an industrial process⟩ **2 :** examination of a problem often not subject to direct experimentation by means of a simulator (as a programmed computer)
singlet* *n* **:** an elementary particle not part of a multiplet
situation comedy *n* **:** a radio or television comedy series that involves a continuing cast of characters in a succession of unconnected episodes
situation ethics *n* [trans. of G *situationsethik*] **:** a system of ethics which is based on love and by which acts are judged within their contexts instead of by categorical principles
skateboard \ˈ=,=\ *n* [²*skate* + ¹*board*] **:** a narrow board about two feet long mounted on roller-skate wheels — **skate·board·ing** \-iŋ\ *n* -s — **skate·board·er** \-ər\ *n* -s
skibob \ˈ=,=\ *n* [¹*ski* + ⁸*bob*] **:** a vehicle that has two short skis one behind the other, a steering handle attached to the forward ski, and a low upholstered seat over the rear ski and that is used for gliding downhill over snow by a rider wearing miniature skis for balance — **ski·bob·ber** \-ə(r)\ *n* — **ski·bob·bing** \-iŋ\ *n*
skif·fle \ˈskifəl\ *n* -s [perh. imit.] **:** jazz or folk music played by a group consisting of or including nonstandard instruments or noisemakers (as jugs, washboards, or jew's harps)
skimmer* *n* **:** a fitted sleeveless usu. flaring sheathlike dress
skimming* *n* **:** the practice of fraudulently reporting gambling income (as of a casino) so as to avoid full tax payments
skin flick *n* **:** a motion picture characterized by nudity and explicit sexual situations
skin·ny-dip·ping \ˈskinē,dipiŋ\ *n* [¹*skin* + ¹*-y* + *dipping,* gerund of ¹*dip*] **:** swimming in the nude — **skin·ny-dip·per** \-pər\ *n*
skiwear \ˈ=,=\ *n* [²*ski* + ²*wear*] **:** clothing suitable for wear while skiing
sky·div·ing \ˈskī,dīviŋ\ *n* -s [¹*sky* + *diving,* gerund of *dive*] **:** the sport of jumping from an airplane at a moderate altitude (as 6000 feet) and executing various tumbles and dives before pulling the rip cord of a parachute — **sky diver** *n*
sky·jack·er \ˈskī,jakə(r)\ *n* -s [*sky* + *-jacker* (as in *hijacker*)] **:** one who commandeers a flying airplane (as by coercing the pilot at gunpoint) — **sky·jack·ing** \-akiŋ\ *n* -s
skylounge \ˈ=,=\ *n* [*sky* + *lounge*] **:** a vehicle that picks up passengers and is then carried by a helicopter between a downtown terminal and an airport
slap shot *n* **:** a shot in ice hockey that is made with a swinging stroke so that the puck often leaves the ice
slot car *n* **:** an electric toy racing automobile that has an arm underneath fitting into a groove for guidance and metal strips alongside the groove for supplying electricity and that is remotely controlled by the operator's hand-held rheostat
slot racing *n* **:** the racing of slot cars — **slot racer** *n*
slow-pitch \ˈ=,=\ *also* **slo-pitch** *n* **:** softball played with 10 men on each side in which each pitch must describe an arc from 3 to 10 feet high in order to be legal and in which base stealing is not permitted
slugging average *n* **:** the average of a baseball batter determined by dividing the number of official times at bat into the total number of bases reached on hits
slumlord \ˈ=,=\ *n* -s [¹*slum* + land*lord*] **:** a landlord who receives inflated rents from substandard neglected properties
slurbs \ˈslərbz\ *n pl* [*sl-* (as in *sloppy, sleazy, slovenly, slipshod*) + sub*urbs*] **:** suburbs characterized by wearisomely uniform and usu. poorly constructed houses
s matrix *n, usu cap S* **:** a unitary matrix in quantum mechanics the absolute values of the squares of whose elements are equal to probabilities of transition between different states — called also *scattering matrix*
smog·less \ˈsmäg·ləs\ *adj* [*smog* + *-less*] **1 :** marked by the absence of smog ⟨a ~ city⟩ **2 :** emitting no fumes that would contribute to the production of smog ⟨~ cars of the future⟩
snow·mo·bil·ing \==,bēliŋ\ *n* [*snowmobile* + *-ing*] **:** the sport of driving or racing a snowmobile — **snow·mo·bil·er** \-lə(r)\ *also* **snow·mo·bil·ist** \-ləst\ *n* -s
socialist realism *n* [trans. of Russ *sotsialisticheskiĭ realizm*] **:** a theory of Soviet art, music, and literature that calls for the didactic use of artistic work to develop social consciousness in an evolving socialist state — **socialist realist** *n*
so·cio·linguistic \ˌsōs(h)ē(,)ō+\ *adj* [*socio-* + *linguistic*] **1 :** of or relating to the social aspects of language **2 :** of or relating to sociolinguistics
so·cio·linguistics \"+\ *n* [*socio-* + *linguistics*] **:** the study of linguistic behavior as determined by sociocultural factors (as social class or educational level)
so·cio·religious \ˌsōs(h)ēō+\ *adj* [*socio-* + *religious*] **:** involving a combination of social and religious factors
sodium stearate *n* **:** a white powdery salt $C_{17}H_{35}COONa$ that is soluble in water, is the chief constituent of some laundry soaps, and is used esp. in cosmetics and toothpaste
soft* *adj* **1 :** occurring at such a speed and under such circumstances as to avoid destructive impact ⟨~ landing of a spacecraft on the moon⟩ **2 :** not protected against enemy attack ⟨a ~ aboveground launching site⟩ **3** *of a detergent* **:** BIODEGRADABLE *herein* **4** *of a drug* **:** considered less detrimental than a hard narcotic ⟨marijuana is usu. regarded as a *soft* drug⟩
softbound \ˈ=ˈ=\ *adj* [¹*soft* + ⁴*bound*] **:** not bound in hard covers ⟨~ books⟩
soft-land \ˈ=ˈ=\ *vb* [back-formation fr. *soft landing*] *vi* **:** to make a landing on a celestial body (as the moon) at such a slow speed that there is neither destruction nor serious damage ~ *vt* **:** to cause to soft-land — **soft-land·er** *n* -s
soft paste* *n* **1 :** a fine-grained opaque Chinese ceramic ware related to true porcelain but having part of the kaolin replaced by pegmatite and usu. being fired twice **2 :** a lightweight soft opaque clay body (as of early Staffordshire)
software \ˈ=,=\ *n* [¹*soft* + ⁴*ware*] **:** the features of an apparatus or system that are not hardware ⟨the designing and installation of a computer and programs for a computer are ~⟩
soilborne \ˈ=,=\ *adj* [³*soil* + ¹*borne*] **:** transmitted by or in soil ⟨~ fungi⟩
so·ka gak·kai \ˌsōkəˈgäˌkī\ *n, usu cap S & G* [Jap *Sōka Gakkai,* fr. *sōka* creation + *gakkai* learned society] **:** a Japanese sect of Buddhism that emphasizes active proselytism and the use of prayer for the solution of all human problems
solar cell *n* **:** a photovoltaic cell (as one including a junction between two types of silicon semiconductors) that is able to convert sunlight into electrical energy and is used (as in artificial satellites) as a power source
solar panel *n* **:** a battery of solar cells (as in a spacecraft)
solar sail *n* **:** a propulsive device that consists of a flat material (as aluminized plastic) designed to receive thrust from solar radiation pressure and that can be attached to a spacecraft
solar wind *n* **:** the continuous ejection of plasma from the sun's surface into and through interplanetary space
solid-state \ˈ==,=\ *adj* **1 :** relating to the properties, structure, or reactivity of solid material; *specif* **:** relating to the arrangement or behavior of ions, molecules, nucleons, electrons, and holes in the crystals of a substance (as a semiconductor) or to the effect of crystal imperfections on the properties of a solid substance **2 :** utilizing the electric, magnetic, or photic properties of solid materials **:** not utilizing electron tubes
so·ma·to·sensory \ˌsōmədˌə+\ *adj* [*somat-* + *sensory*] **:** of, relating to, or being sensory activity having its origin elsewhere than in the special sense organs (as eyes or ears) and conveying information about the state of the body proper and its immediate environment
son·i·cate \ˈsänə,kāt\ *vt* -ED/-ING/-S [*sonic* + ⁴*-ate*] **:** to disrupt (as biological material) by treatment with high-frequency sound waves — **son·i·ca·tion** \ˌsänəˈkāshən\ *n* -s
sono·chemistry \ˌsänō, ˌsōnō+\ *n* [*son-* + *chemistry*] **:** a branch of chemistry that deals with the chemical effects of ultrasound — **sono·chemical** \"+\ *adj*
soul* *n* **1 :** a strong positive feeling (as of intense sensitivity and emotional fervor) conveyed esp. by American Negro performers **2 :** NEGRITUDE *herein* **3 :** SOUL MUSIC *herein*
soul *adj* [*soul,* n. (herein)] **1 :** of, relating to, or characteristic of American Negroes or their culture ⟨vocals are delivered in a raspy, ~ style —Ellen Sander⟩ **2 :** designed for or controlled by Negroes ⟨~ radio stations⟩
soul brother *n* **:** a male Negro — used by other Negroes
soul food *n* **:** food traditionally eaten esp. by southern American Negroes that usu. includes chitterlings, hogs' jowls, ham hocks, collard greens, catfish, and cornbread
soul music *n* **:** music that originated with American Negro gospel singing, is closely related to rhythm and blues, and is characterized by intensity of feeling and earthiness
sound pollution *n* **:** NOISE POLLUTION *herein*
soup* *n* **:** the fast-moving white water that moves shoreward after a wave breaks
spaceborne \ˈ=,=\ *adj* [¹*space* + ¹*borne*] **1 :** carried in space external to the atmosphere as a result of velocity ⟨~ satellites⟩ **2 :** involving the use of spaceborne equipment
space sickness *n* **:** unpleasant physiological effects occurring under the conditions of sustained spaceflight
space walk *n* **:** a moving about in open space outside a spacecraft by an astronaut protected by a space suit — **space walk** *vi* — **spacewalker** \ˈ=,==\ *n* — **spacewalking** \ˈ=,==\ *n*
spacewoman \ˈ=,==\ *n* [*space* + *woman*] **:** a female astronaut
spatter glass *n* **:** END-OF-DAY GLASS *herein*
speakerphone \ˈ==,=\ *n* [*speaker* + *phone*] **:** a combination microphone and loudspeaker device for two-way communication by telephone lines
spear·ing \ˈspiriŋ\ *n* -s [fr. gerund of ³*spear*] **:** a check in hockey in which one player jabs another in the body with the end of a hockey stick
special drawing rights *n pl* **:** SDRS *herein*
special situation *n* **:** an exceptional corporate condition or prospect that offers unusual chances for capital gains
speed* *n* **:** a form or derivative of amphetamine used esp. as a stimulant for the central nervous system
speed-reading \ˈ=,==\ *n* **:** a method of reading rapidly by skimming — **speed-read** \ˈ=,=\ *vt*
speed shop *n* **:** a shop that sells automotive equipment esp. to hot rodders and sometimes installs such equipment
spider hole *n* **:** a camouflaged foxhole
spinner* *n* **:** a surfing feat in which a standing surfer makes a complete turnaround while the board continues to move straight ahead
spin-off* *n* **1 :** the distribution by a business to its stockholders of particular assets and esp. of stock of another company **2 :** a usu. useful by-product ⟨new household products that are *spin-offs* from missile research⟩; *also* **:** a number of such by-products ⟨the *spin-off* from defense research⟩
spinout \ˈ=,=\ *n* -s [²*spin* + *out*] **:** a rotational skid by an automobile that usu. causes it to leave the roadway
spin resonance *n* **:** ELECTRON SPIN RESONANCE *herein*
spi·rono·lactone \spī,rānə+\ *n* [*spirono-* (of unknown origin) + *lactone*] **:** an aldosterone antagonist that promotes diuresis and sodium excretion and is sometimes used to relieve ascites
splashdown \ˈ=,=\ *n* -s [fr. the phrase *splash down*] **:** the landing of a manned spacecraft in water — **splash down** *vi*
split end *n* **:** a football end who on offense lines up on the weak side usu. several yards from the tackle
spoiler* *n* **:** an air deflector on the front or on the rear deck of an automobile and esp. a racer to reduce the tendency to lift off the road at high speeds
spongeware \ˈ=,=\ *n* [¹*sponge* + ⁴*ware*] **:** a typically 19th century earthenware with background color spattered or dabbed (as with a sponge) and usu. a freehand central design
spoon·er \ˈspünə(r)\ *n* -s [¹*spoon* + ²*-er*] **:** a container that is designed to hold extra teaspoons and forms part of a 19th century table service
spread end *n* **:** SPLIT END *herein*
sprint car *n* **:** a rugged racing automobile that is midway in size between midget racers and ordinary racers, has about the same horsepower as the larger racers, and is usu. raced on a dirt track
square out *n* **:** a pass pattern in football in which a receiver runs downfield a short distance and then breaks at a 90 degree angle for the sidelines
SST \,e(,)seˈstē\ *abbr or n* -s supersonic transport *herein*
stacked heel *n* [*stacked* (past part. of ²*stack*) + ¹*heel*] **:** a heel made of layers of leather and used on women's shoes
staging* *n* **:** the disengaging and discarding of a burned-out rocket unit from a space vehicle during flight
standing crop* *n* **:** the total amount or number of living beings or of one kind of living being in a particular situation at any given time ⟨the *standing crop* of fish in a farm pond⟩
standoff* *n* **:** a standoff insulator
stannous fluoride *n* **:** a white compound SnF_2 of tin and fluorine used in toothpaste to combat tooth decay
sta·pe·dec·to·my \ˌstāpəˈdektəmē, -pēˈd-\ *n* -ES [ISV *staped-* (fr. NL *staped-, stapes* stapes) + *-ectomy*] **:** surgical removal and prosthetic replacement of the stapes to relieve deafness
stark·ers \ˈstärkərz\ *adj* [¹*stark* + *-ers* (Oxford University slang suffix)] *chiefly Brit* **:** completely unclothed **:** NUDE
station* *n* **:** a pocket with its automatic signature-feeding equipment in a gathering machine
steady state theory *n* **:** a theory in astronomy: the universe has always existed and has always been expanding with hydrogen being created continuously and spontaneously — compare BIG BANG THEORY *herein*
stel·lar·ator \ˈstelə,rād·ə(r)\ *n* -s [*stellar* + *-ator* (as in *generator*); fr. its use of temperatures approaching those occurring in some stars] **:** a device for producing controlled nuclear fusion that involves the confinement of gaseous plasma in a usu. figure-eight-shaped tube by means of an externally applied magnetic field and the heating of the plasma
stellar wind *n* **:** hot gases ejected at varying rates from a star's surface into interstellar space
stere·ol·o·gy \ˌsterēˈäləjē, ˌstir-\ *n* -ES [ISV *stere-* + *-logy*] **:** a branch of science concerned with the development and testing of inferences about the three-dimensional properties and reactions of objects or matter ordinarily observed or observable from a two-dimensional point of view
stereotape \ˈ===ˌ=\ *n* [²*stereo* + *tape*] **:** a stereophonic magnetic tape
stereo·tax·ic \ˌsterēəˈtaksik, ˌstir-\ *adj* [NL *stereotaxis* stereotaxic technique (fr. *stere-* + Gk *taxis* arrangement) + E *-ic* — more at TAXIS] **:** of, relating to, involving, or being a technique or apparatus used in neurological research or surgery for directing the tip of a delicate instrument (as a needle or an electrode) in three planes in attempting to reach a predetermined locus in the nervous system
ste·ven·graph \ˈstēvən,graf\ *or* **ste·vens·graph** \-nz,g-\ *n* -s *usu cap* [Thomas *Stevens,* 19th cent. Am. weaver + E *-graph*] **:** a woven silk picture
stick shift *n* **:** a manually operated sticklike gearshift mounted on the steering column or floor of an automobile
stiletto heel *n* **:** a high thin heel that is narrower than a spike heel and is used on women's shoes
still bank \ˈ=,=\ *n* [¹*still* + ⁴*bank*] **:** a bank (as in the shape of an animal or a ship) with a slot for inserting coins
stish·ov·ite \ˈstishə,vīt\ *n* -s [S.M. *Stishov,* 20th cent. Russ. mineralogist + E *-ite*] **:** a dense silicon dioxide formed under great pressure
STOL *abbr* short takeoff and landing
stop* *vb* — **stop a stock** *of a stock-market specialist* **:** to agree to a later sale or purchase of a specified number of shares at the price current when the agreement is made
stop out* *vt* **:** to sell securities of (a shareowner) on a stop order
STP \,e(,)stēˈpē\ *n* -s [fr. *STP,* trademark for a motor fuel additive to which it is likened in its effects] **:** a psychedelic drug chemically related to mescaline and amphetamine — called also *DOM*
straight* *adj* **:** HETEROSEXUAL
strangeness* *n* **:** a quantum characteristic of a strongly interacting elementary particle indicated by a number that is equal to its hypercharge minus its baryon number
strange particle *n* **:** a short-lived unstable elementary particle (as a kaon) that is created in high-energy particle collisions and has a strangeness quantum number different from zero
strat·i·fi·ca·tion·al grammar \ˌstrad·əfəˌkāshnəl-, -shənᵊl-\ *n* [*stratification* + *-al* + *grammar*] **:** a grammar based on the theory that language consists of a series of hierarchically related strata linked together by representational rules
strawberry jar *n* **:** a usu. large upright ceramic jar with pocketed openings in the sides into which small plants can be inserted for growing in soil contained in the jar
streak·ing \ˈstrēkiŋ\ *n* -s [fr. gerund of ²*streak*] **:** the lightening (as by chemicals) of a few long strands of hair to produce a streaked effect — compare FROSTING *herein*
stream* *n, Brit* **:** ¹TRACK 3c
streaming* *n, Brit* **:** TRACKING *herein*
strep·to·ni·grin \ˌstreptəˈnīgrən\ *n* -s [NL *strepto-* (fr. *Streptomyces flocculus,* actinomycete from which it is produced) + L *nigr-, niger* black + E *-in;* prob. fr. its dark color] **:** a toxic antibiotic from an actinomycete (*Streptomyces flocculus*) that interferes with DNA metabolism
strike* *n* **:** a perfectly thrown ball ⟨fired a ~ to first base⟩
striking price *n* **:** a price agreed upon as that at which an option contract (as a put or call) can be exercised
strip city *n* **:** an urban area forming a long narrow strip
strong interaction *n* **:** a fundamental interaction experienced by elementary particles (as hadrons) that is more powerful than any other known force and is responsible for the binding together of neutrons and protons in the atomic nucleus and for processes of particle creation in high-energy collisions
structural gene *n* **:** a gene determining the amino acid sequence of a protein through a specific messenger RNA
strung out *adj* **1 :** addicted to a drug **2 :** physically debilitated from or as if from long-term drug addiction
student union *n* **:** a building on a college campus that is devoted to student activities and that usu. contains lounges, auditoriums, offices, and game rooms
sub·cellular \ˌsəb+\ *adj* [*sub-* + *cellular*] **:** of less than

cellular scope or level of organization ⟨~ particles⟩
sub·compact \ˈsəb+\ *n* [*sub-* + ³*compact*] **:** an automobile smaller than one commonly designated as a compact
sub·or·di·na·tor \səˈbȯrdᵊn,ād·ə(r)\ *n* -s [³*subordinate* + ¹*-or*] **:** one that subordinates; *esp* **:** a subordinating conjunction
sub·program \ˈsəb+\ *n* [*sub-* + *program* (herein)] **:** a semi-independent portion of a program (as for a computer)
sub·satellite \"+\ *n* [*sub-* + *satellite*] **1 :** a political entity within the sphere of influence of another entity that is itself a satellite of a stronger power **2 :** an object carried into orbit in and subsequently released from an artificial satellite
sub·shell \ˈsəb+,\ *n* [*sub-* + *shell*] **:** any of the one or more orbitals making up an electron shell of an atom
sub·to·pia \,səbˈtōpēə\ *n* -s [*sub*urbs + *-topia* (fr. Gk *topos* place) — more at TOPIC] *chiefly Brit* **:** the suburbs of a city — **sub·to·pi·an** \-ēən\ *adj, chiefly Brit*
succorance* *n* **:** a dependence on or an active seeking for nurturant care — **suc·cor·ant** \ˈsəkərənt\ *adj*
suicide pact *n* **:** an agreement between two individuals wherein they commit suicide together or one kills the other and then commits suicide
su·i·cid·ol·o·gy \,süə,sīˈdäləjē\ *n* -ES [*suicide* + *-o-* + *-logy*] **:** the study of suicide and suicide prevention
sul·fo·nyl·urea \,səlfə,nil+\ *n* -s [NL, fr. ISV *sulfonyl* + NL *urea*] **:** any of several hypoglycemic compounds related to the sulfonamides and used in the oral treatment of diabetes
sulphide* *n* **:** a ceramic form and esp. a portrait bas-relief enclosed in clear glass where it glitters like silver
sunroof \ˈ=,=\ *n* [so called fr. its letting in the sunlight] **:** an automobile roof having a panel that is openable
sunseeker \ˈ=,==\ *n* [¹*sun* + *seeker*] **1 :** a person who travels to an area of warmth and sun esp. in winter **2 :** a photoelectric device on a spacecraft or artificial satellite that maintains a constant fix on the sun and forms a part of the navigational system of the vehicle
su·per·alloy \ˈsüpər+\ *n* [*super-* + *alloy*] **:** any of various high-strength often complex alloys having resistance to high temperature
su·per·continent \"+\ *n* [*super-* + *continent*] **:** a hypothetical former large continent from which other continents broke off and drifted away — called also *protocontinent*
su·per·jet \ˈsüpə(r)+\ *n* [*super*sonic + *jet*] **:** a supersonic jet airplane
su·per·molecule \ˈsüpə(r)+\ *n* [*super-* + *molecule*] **:** MACROMOLECULE — **su·per·molecular** \"+\ *adj*
su·per·plasticity \"+\ *n* [*super-* + *plasticity*] **:** the quality or state of having enhanced ductility as a result of microstructural change brought about by heat and mechanical treatment — used of an alloy — **su·per·plastic** \"+\ *adj or n*
supersonic transport *n* **:** a supersonic transport airplane
support hose *n* **:** STOCKING 2a
support level *or* **support area** *n* **:** a price level on a declining market at which a security resists further decline due to increased attractiveness to traders and investors
suppressant *n* -s [*suppressant*, adj.] **:** an agent (as a drug) that tends to suppress rather than eliminate something undesirable
su·pra·cellular \ˈsüprə+\ *adj* [*supra-* + *cellular*] **:** of greater than cellular scope or level of organization
su·pre·mo \səˈprē(,)mō, süˈp-\ *n* -s *often cap* [Sp & It, fr. *supremo*, adj., supreme, fr. L *supremus*] *Brit* **:** one who is highest in rank or authority
surf·able \ˈsərfəbəl\ *adj* [²*surf* + *-able*] **:** suitable for surfing
surface-effect ship *n* **:** a ground-effect machine that operates over water
surface structure *n* **:** a formal representation of the phonetic form of a sentence; *also* **:** the structure which such a representation describes
surface-to-air missile *n* **:** a usu. guided missile launched from the ground against a target in the air
surfer's knot *n* **:** a knobby lump just below a surfer's knee or on the upper surface of his foot caused by friction and pressure between surfboard and skin
swing* *vi* **:** to be lively and up-to-date
swing* *n* **:** a play in football in which a backfield receiver runs to the outside to take a short pass — called also *swing pass*
swing-by \ˈ=,bī\ *n* -s **:** an interplanetary mission in which a space vehicle utilizes the gravitational field of a planet near which it passes for changing course
swing-wing \ˈ=,=\ *adj* **:** being or having a variable airplane wing whose outer portion for high speeds folds back along the fuselage and thereby gives the plane an arrowlike planform — **swing wing** *n*
switched-on \(ˈ)swichˈtȯn, -tän\ *adj* [fr. past part. of the verb phrase *switch on*] **:** attuned to what is new and exciting
synchrotron radiation *n* [so called from its having been first observed in a synchrotron] **:** radiation emitted by high-energy charged relativistic particles (as electrons) when they are accelerated by a magnetic field (as in the Crab nebula)
syn·ec·tics \səˈnektiks\ *n pl but usu sing in constr* [perh. fr. Gk *synektik*tein to bring forth together (fr. *syn-* + *ektiktein* to bring forth, fr. *ex-* out + *tiktein* to beget) + E *-s* (as in *dialectics*) — more at EX-, THANE] **:** a theory or system of problem-stating and problem-solving based on creative thinking that involves free use of metaphor and analogy in informal interchange within a carefully selected small group of individuals of diverse personality and areas of specialization — **syn·ec·tic** \-tik\ *adj* — **syn·ec·ti·cal·ly** \-tək(ə)lē\ *adv*
synergism* *n* **:** interaction of discrete agencies (as of industrial firms or physical equipment) in combination such that the total effect is greater than the sum of the individual effects
syn·ge·ne·ic \ˈsinjəˈnēik\ *adj* [Gk *syngeneia* kinship (fr. *syn-* + *genos* kind, kin) + E *-ic* — more at KIN] **1 :** genically identical **:** ISOGENIC **2 :** sufficiently alike genetically to be antigenically similar — compare ALLOGENIC *herein*
syntactic foam *n* [*syntactic* fr. Gk *syntaktikos* putting together — more at SYNTACTIC] **:** a plastic in which preformed cells (as tiny hollow glass spheres) have been incorporated, which can withstand great pressures (as at ocean depths), and which floats
synthetic division *n* **:** a simplified form of the division of a polynomial in *x* by *x* — *a* using only the coefficients of the polynomial and the number *a*
systems analysis *n* **:** the act, process, or profession of studying an activity (as a procedure, a business, or a physiological function) typically by mathematical means in order to determine its desired or essential end and how this may most efficiently be attained — **systems analyst** *n*
t* *abbr, cap* tera- *herein*
ta·bla \ˈtäblə, ˈtəb-\ *n* -s [Hindi *tabla*, fr. Ar *ṭabla*] **:** a pair of small different-sized hand drums used esp. in Hindu music
ta·can \ˈtā,kan\ *n* -s [*tactical air navigation*] **:** a system of navigation employing ultra-high frequency signals to determine the distance and bearing of an aircraft from a transmitting station
tach·ism \ˈta,shizəm\ *n* -s *often cap* [F *tachisme*, fr. *tache* stain, spot, blob + *-isme* -ism — more at TACHE] **:** ACTION PAINTING *herein* — **tach·ist** \ˈtashəst\ *adj or n, often cap*
tachy·on \ˈtakē,än\ *n* -s [*tachy-* + ²*-on*] **:** a hypothetical subatomic particle that travels faster than light and behaves in a manner opposite to that of ordinary particles so that with an increase in velocity its energy decreases
tag·me·mic grammar \(,)tag,mēmik-\ *n* [*tagmeme* + *-ic*] **:** a grammar that describes language in terms of the relationship between grammatical function and the class of items which can perform that function
take* *vb* — **take a position** *of a security dealer* **:** to hold in his own account stock bought in the course of trading
take-out \ˈ=,=\ *adj* [*take out*, v.] **:** designed for the sale of food that is not to be consumed on the premises ⟨*take-out* counter⟩
ta·la \ˈtälə\ *n* -s [Skt *tāla* hand-clapping, musical beat, alter. of *tāḍa* beating, fr. *tāḍayati* he beats] **:** one of the ancient traditional metrical patterns of Hindu music
tape deck *n* **1 a :** a mechanism that moves a tape past a magnetic head (as of a tape recorder) — called also *tape transport* **b :** a device that contains such a mechanism and that for the playback of recorded magnetic tapes usu. has to be connected to a separate audio system **2 :** TAPE PLAYER *herein*
tape player *n* **:** a self-contained device for the playback of recorded magnetic tapes
target language *n* **1 :** a foreign language that is the subject of study **2 :** a language into which a translation (as by machine) is made
tar pit *n* **:** an area in which natural bitumens collect and are exposed at the earth's surface and which forms a trap into which animals sink and in which their bones are preserved
taxi squad *n* [so called fr. the practice of a former owner of a professional team who employed such surplus players as drivers for a taxi fleet which he also owned] **:** a group of football players under contract who practice with a team but are ineligible to participate in official games
tax selling *n* **:** concerted selling of securities late in the year to establish gains and losses for income-tax purposes
tax shelter *n* **:** a factor (as special depreciation allowances) that reduces the taxes on current earnings either to a corporation or its stockholders — **tax-sheltered** \ˈ=,=\ *adj*
tea ceremony *n* **:** CHANOYU
teach-in \ˈ=,=\ *n* -s [*teach* + *-in* (herein)] **:** an extended meeting usu. held on a college campus for lectures, debates, and discussions on critical topics (as U. S. foreign policy)
teaching machine *n* **:** any of various mechanical devices for presenting a program of instructional material
tech·ne·tron·ic \ˈteknəˈtränik\ *adj* [*techno*logical + elec*tronic*] **:** of or being a society that is shaped by the impact of technology and electronics and esp. by the impact of computers and communications on its structure, culture, psychology, and economics
tech·no·structure \ˈteknō+\ *n* [*techno-* + *structure*] **:** a large-scale corporation or system of corporate enterprise; *also* **:** a group of professionals who control a technostructure
teeny \ˈtēnē\ *n, pl* **teen·ies** [*teen* + *-y*] **:** TEEN-AGER
teenybopper \ˈ==,==\ *n* -s [*teeny* (herein) + *bopper*] **1 :** a teen-aged girl **2 :** a teen-ager who rejects middle-class mores, dresses in the latest styles, is addicted to rock 'n' roll music, and is keenly aware of and interested in the use of drugs
TEFL \ˈtefəl\ *abbr* teaching English as a foreign language
tele·facsimile \ˈtelə+\ *n* [*tele-* + *facsimile*] **:** a system for the transmission and reproduction of fixed graphic matter (as printing) involving the use of signals transmitted (as between libraries) over telephone wires
tele·lecture \ˈtelə+,\ *n* [*tele-* + *lecture*] **1 :** a loudspeaker connected to a telephone line for amplifying voice communication **2 :** a lecture delivered to an audience by telelecture
tel·ex \ˈte,leks\ *n* -ES [*tel*eprinter + *ex*change] **:** a communication service involving teletypewriters connected by wire through automatic exchanges — **telex** *vt* -ED/-ING/-ES
ten·der·om·e·ter \,tendəˈräməd·ə(r)\ *n* -s [¹*tender* + *-o-* + *-meter*] **:** a device for determining the maturity and tenderness of samples of fruits and vegetables
ten·sio·met·ric \ˈten(t)sēəˈme·trik\ *adj* [*tension* + *-metric*] **:** of, relating to, or involving the measurement of tension or tensile strength — **ten·si·om·e·try** \,ten(t)sēˈämə·trē\ *n* -ES
tent-trailer \ˈ=,==\ *n* **:** a 2-wheeled automobile-drawn trailer having a canvas shelter that can be opened up above the body to provide camping facilities
te·pa \ˈtēpə\ *n* -s [*tri-* + *e*thylene + *p*hosphor- + *a*mide] **:** a compound related to ethylenimine that is a chemosterilant of insects and an alleviant in some kinds of cancer
tera- \ˈterə\ *comb form* [ISV, fr. Gk *teras* monster — more at TERAT-] **:** TRILLION ⟨*teraton*⟩
ter·a·to·gen \ˈterətəjən, -,jen; təˈrad·əjən\ *n* -s [*terat-* + *-gen*] **:** a teratogenic agent (as a drug or virus) — **ter·a·to·ge·nic·i·ty** \,terətəjəˈnisəd·ē, tə,rad·əj-\ *n* -ES
terminal* *n* **:** a device (as a teletypewriter) through which a user can communicate with a computer
ter·ran \ˈterən\ *n* -s *usu cap* [*Terra*, the planet Earth (fr. L *terra* earth) + E ¹*-an* — more at TERRACE] **:** EARTHMAN
TESL \ˈtesəl\ *abbr* teaching English as a second language
tes·la \ˈteslə\ *n* -s [ISV, after Nikola *Tesla* †1943 Am. electrician and inventor] **:** a unit of magnetic flux density in the mks system equivalent to one weber per square meter
test-drive \ˈ=,=\ *vt* **:** to drive (a motor vehicle) before buying in order to evaluate performance
tet·ra·functional \ˈte·trə+\ *adj* [*tetra-* + *functional*] **:** of, relating to, or being a compound with four sites in the molecule that are highly reactive (as in polymerization)
tet·ra·hy·dro·cannabinol \,te·trəˈhīdrə+\ *n* -s [*tetrahydr-* + *cannabinol*] **:** a physiologically active liquid from hemp plant resin that is prob. the chief intoxicant in marijuana
tet·ra·pyr·role *also* **tet·ra·pyr·rol** \ˈte·trəˈpi,rōl, -rōl, -pəˈr-\ *n* [*tetra-* + *pyrrole*] **:** a chemical group consisting of four pyrrole rings joined either in a straight chain (as in phycobilins) or in a ring (as in chlorophyll)
tha·lid·o·mide \thəˈlidə,mīd, -məd\ *n* -s [*phthalimide* + *-o-* + *imide*] **:** a sedative and hypnotic drug found to cause malformation of infants born to mothers using it during pregnancy
THC *n* [*t*etra*h*ydro*c*annabinol (herein)] **:** TETRAHYDROCANNABINOL *herein*
theater of the absurd **:** theater that seeks to represent the absurdity of man's existence in a meaningless universe by bizarre or fantastic means
therapeutic index *n* **:** a measure of the relative desirability of a drug for the attaining of a particular medical end that is usu. expressed as the ratio of the largest dose producing no toxic symptoms to the smallest dose routinely producing cures
thermal pollution *n* **:** the discharge of liquid (as waste water from a factory) into a natural body of water at such a high temperature that harm to the plant and animal life may result
ther·mo·form \ˈthərmə,fȯrm\ *vt* [*therm-* + ²*form*] **:** to give a final shape to (as a plastic) with the aid of heat and usu. pressure — **thermoform** *n*
ther·mo·gravimetry \ˈthər(,)mō+\ *n* [ISV *therm-* + *gravimetry*; prob. orig. formed in F] **:** the determination (as with a thermobalance) of weight changes in a substance at a high temperature or during a gradual increase in temperature — **ther·mo·gravimetric** \"+\ *adj*
ther·mo·physical \ˈthərmō, -mə+\ *adj* [*therm-* + *physical*] **:** of, relating to, or concerned with the physical properties of materials as affected by elevated temperatures
ther·mo·sphere \ˈthərmə+,\ *n* [ISV *therm-* + *sphere*] **:** the part of the earth's atmosphere that begins at about 50 miles above the earth's surface, extends to outer space, and is characterized by steadily increasing temperature with height — **ther·mo·spheric** \ˈ==+\ *adj*
thia·ben·da·zole \,thīəˈbendə,zōl\ *n* -s [*thia*zole + *benzimidazole*] **:** a drug used in the control of parasitic roundworms and in the treatment of fungus infections
thi·a·zide \ˈthīə,zīd, -,zəd\ *n* -s [*thia-* + dia*zi*ne + dioxi*de*] **:** any of several drugs used as oral diuretics esp. in the control of high blood pressure
thing* *n* **:** a personal choice of activity **:** SPECIALTY — often used with *do* ⟨letting students do their own ~ —*Newsweek*⟩
think tank *n* **:** an institute, corporation, or group organized for interdisciplinary research (as in military strategy or technological and social problems) — called also *think factory*
thin-layer chromatography *n* **:** chromatography in which the absorbent medium is in a thin layer (as of siliceous fibers)
thi·o·rid·a·zine \,thīəˈridə,zēn, -,zən\ *n* -s [*thio-* + piper*id*ine + phenothi*azine*] **:** a tranquilizer used in relief of anxiety states and in the treatment of schizophrenia
third market *n* [so called in distinction from the organized exchanges and the market in unlisted securities] **:** the over-the-counter market in listed securities
third-stream *adj* **:** of, relating to, or being music that incorporates elements of classical music and jazz
third world *n, often cap T&W* **1 :** a group of nations esp. in Africa and Asia that are not aligned with either the Communist or the non-Communist blocs **2 :** an aggregate of minority groups within a larger predominant culture
thread* *n* **threads** *pl* **:** CLOTHES
thrift shop *n* **:** a shop that sells secondhand articles and esp. clothes and is often run for charitable purposes
throughput* *n* **:** OUTPUT, PRODUCTION ⟨the ~ of a computer⟩
throwaway \ˈ==,=\ *adj* [*throw away*] **1 :** that may be thrown away **:** DISPOSABLE ⟨~ containers⟩ **2 :** written or spoken (as in a play) in a low-key or unemphasized manner ⟨~ lines⟩
thrust chamber *n* **:** ROCKET 4
thrus·tor *or* **thrust·er*** \ˈthrəstə(r)\ *n* -s [¹*thrust* + ¹*-or* or ²*-er*] **:** REACTION ENGINE
thrust stage *n* [*thread*, past part. of ¹*thrust*] **:** a stage surrounded on three sides by the audience; *also* **:** a forestage that is extended into the auditorium to increase the stage area
thy·mi·co·lymphatic \ˈthīməkō+\ *adj* [²*thymic* + *-o-* + *lymphatic*] **:** of, relating to, or affecting both the thymus and the lymphatic system
thy·ro·calcitonin \ˈthīrō+\ *n* -s [*thyr-* + *calcitonin* (herein)] **:** a polypeptide hormone from the thyroid gland that tends to lower the level of calcium in the blood plasma
tight end *n* **:** a football end who on offense lines up on the strong side usu. within two yards of the tackle
time dilation *also* **time dilatation** *n* **:** a slowing of time on a system moving at a velocity approaching that of light relative to an observer as predicted by the theory of relativity
time reversal *n* **:** a formal operation in mathematical physics that reverses the order in which a sequence of events occurs
time reversal invariance *n* **:** a principle in physics: if a given sequence of events is physically possible the same sequence in the opposite order is also possible
time-sharing \ˈ=,==\ *n* **:** simultaneous access to a computer by many users with programs being interspersed and processed so rapidly that answers to individual problems are obtained in seconds — **time-shared** \ˈ=,=\ *adj*
ting ware \ˈtiŋ,=\ *also* **ting yao** \-ˈyaü\ *n, often cap T* [*Ting* fr. *Ting Chou*, town southwest of Peking, China, where it was originally made; *Ting yao* fr. *Ting* + Chin (Pek) *yao*² pottery] **:** a Chinese porcelain ware known since Sung times that is typically expertly potted, often decorated with engraved underglaze designs, and characteristically glazed with a milk-white to creamy white or less often an iron-red glaze
tissue* *vt* **:** to remove (as cleansing cream) with a tissue
to·ken·ism \ˈtōkə,nizəm\ *n* -s [*token* + *-ism*] **:** the policy or practice of making only a token effort (as to desegregate)
tom \ˈtäm\ *n, usu cap* **:** UNCLE TOM
tool *n* -s [²*tool*] **:** a design (as on the binding of a book) made by tooling
toothpick* *n* **:** a small often elaborate container for a supply of toothpicks at table
topo·cen·tric \ˈtäpəˈsen·trik, ˈtōp-\ *adj* [*top-* + *-centric*] **:** relating to, measured from, or as if observed from a particular point on the earth's surface **:** having or relating to such a point as origin ⟨~ coordinates⟩ — compare GEOCENTRIC *in the Dict*
to·pos \ˈtō,päs, ˈtä,p-\ *n, pl* **to·poi** \-,pȯi\ [Gk, place, commonplace, topic — more at TOPIC] **:** a stock rhetorical theme or topic
torque *vt* -ED/-ING/-S [²*torque*] **:** to impart torque to **:** cause to twist (as about an axis) — **torqu·er** \ˈtȯrkə(r)\ *n* -s
total* *vt* **:** to make a total wreck of (a car) **:** DEMOLISH
total environment *n* **:** ENVIRONMENT *herein*
tow-away zone \ˈtōə,wā,=\ *n* [fr. the phrase *tow away*] **:** a no-parking zone from which parked vehicles are towed away
town house* *n* **:** a single-family house of two or sometimes three stories connected to another house by a common sidewall
track·ing \ˈtrakiŋ\ *n* -s [fr. gerund of ²*track*] **:** the grouping of children in classes or schools on the basis of their abilities and intelligence
track record *n* **:** a record of accomplishments ⟨a company with an excellent *track record* in public service⟩
trade-off \ˈ=,=\ *n* [*trade off*] **1 :** a balancing of factors all of which are not attainable at the same time ⟨the education versus experience *trade-off* which governs personnel practices —H.S.White⟩ **2 :** a giving up of one thing in return for another **:** EXCHANGE
train·ee·ship \trāˈnē,ship\ *n* -s [*trainee* + *-ship*] **:** the position or status of a trainee; *specif* **:** one involving a program of advanced training and study esp. in a medical science and usu. bearing a stipend and allowances (as for travel)
trans·am·i·nate \tran(t)ˈsamə,nāt, traan-, -nˈza-\ *vb* -ED/-ING/-S [back-formation fr. *transamination*] *vi* **:** to induce or catalyze a transamination ~ *vt* **:** to induce or catalyze the transamination of
transcription* *n* **:** construction of a messenger RNA molecule from the information contained in DNA
trans·duce \tran(t)sˈd(y)üs, traan-, -nzˈ-\ *vt* -ED/-ING/-S [L *transducere* to lead across, transfer, fr. *trans-* + *ducere* to lead — more at TOW] **1 :** to convert (as energy or a message) into another form **2 :** to bring about the transduction of **:** produce by transduction
transearth \ˈ=,=\ *adj* [*trans-* + *earth*] **:** of or relating to the entry of a spacecraft into a trajectory between a celestial body (as the moon) and the earth and to travel in the direction of the earth ⟨~ injection⟩ ⟨~ burn⟩ ⟨~ coast⟩
transfer RNA \-,ä,reˈnā\ *n* -s **:** a relatively small ribonucleic acid molecule that functions in the transfer of a particular amino acid to the site of protein synthesis
transform* *n* **:** a linguistic structure (as a sentence) produced by means of a transformation ("the duckling is killed by the farmer" is a ~ of "the farmer kills the duckling")
transformation* *n* **1 :** passage of small amounts of free genetically active DNA from one bacterial cell to another resulting in changes in the genetic potential of the recipient cells — compare TRANSDUCTION *in the Dict* **2 :** one of an ordered set of rules that specify how to convert the deep structures of a language into surface structures
trans·for·ma·tion·al \ˈtranzfə(r)ˈmāshənᵊl, ˈtraan-, -n(t)sf-\ *adj* [*transformation* + *-al*] **:** of, relating to, or based on linguistic transformation
transformational grammar *n* **:** a grammar that generates the deep structures of a language and relates these to the surface structures by means of transformations
trans·for·ma·tion·al·ist \,tranzfə(r)māshənᵊləst, ,traan-, -n(t)sf-, -shnəl-\ *n* -s **:** an exponent of transformational grammar
transistor* *or* **transistor radio** *n* **:** a transistorized radio
translation* *n* **:** construction of a protein molecule from the information contained in messenger RNA
translunar \(ˈ)=ˈ==\ *adj* [*trans-* + *lunar*] **:** of or relating to the entry of a spacecraft into a trajectory between a celestial body (as the earth) and the moon and to travel in the direction of the moon ⟨~ injection⟩ ⟨~ burn⟩ ⟨~ coast⟩
transmutation* *n* **:** the effect of controlled reduction firing on certain chiefly Oriental copper-containing and/or iron-containing ceramic glazes (**transmutation glazes**) that is typically a variegation of colors (as purple, blue, and red) and a thick often bubbly consistency
transpose* *n* **:** a matrix that differs from another mathematical matrix by having rows and columns interchanged
transsexual \(ˈ)=ˈ=(=)=\ *n* [*trans-* + *sexual*] **:** a person physically of one sex who desires to belong to the opposite sex — **transsexual** *adj* — **trans·sex·u·al·ism** *n*
trans·thoracic \ˈ=ˈ==\ *adj* [*trans-* + *thoracic*] **:** done or made by way of the thoracic cavity — **trans·tho·rac·i·cal·ly** \-ˈrasək(ə)lē\ *adv*
travel trailer *n* **:** a trailer drawn esp. by a passenger automobile and equipped for use (as while traveling) as a dwelling
trendy \ˈtrendē\ *adj* [²*trend* + *-y*] *chiefly Brit* **:** very fashionable **:** UP-TO-DATE ⟨he's a ~ dresser —*Sunday Mirror*⟩
tri·am·cin·o·lone \,trīamˈsinᵊl,ōn\ *n* -s [*tri-* + *-amcin-* (of unknown origin) + predniso*lone*] **:** a corticoid drug used esp. in treating psoriasis and allergic skin and respiratory disorders
tri·functional \(ˈ)trī+\ *adj* [*tri-* + *functional*] **:** of, relating to, or being a compound with three sites in the molecule that are highly reactive (as in polymerization)
tri·jet \ˈtrī+,\ *adj* [*tri-* + *jet*] **:** powered with three jet engines ⟨a ~ airplane⟩ — **trijet** \ˈ=,=\ *n*
tri·ma·ran \ˈtrīmə,ran\ *n* -s [*tri-* + *-maran* (as in *catamaran*)] **:** a fast pleasure sailboat with three hulls side by side
trip* *n* **:** an intense visionary experience undergone by a person who has taken a psychedelic drug (as LSD)
trip *vi* [*trip*, n. (herein)] **:** to get high on a psychedelic drug **:** turn on — often used with *out* — **trip·per** *n*
triplet* *n* **1 :** a group of three elementary particles (as positive, negative, and neutral pions) with different charge states but otherwise similar properties **2** *or* **triplet state :** any state of an elementary particle having one quantum unit of spin
trog·lo·bite \ˈträglə,bīt\ *n* -s [by alter. (influenced by *troglodyte*)] **:** TROGLOBIONT — **trog·lo·bit·ic** \ˈ==ˈbid·ik\ *adj*
troika* *n* **1 :** an administrative or ruling body of three ⟨replaced by a ~ of three coequal secretaries-general —*Newsweek*⟩ **2 :** a group of three ⟨astrology, yoga, and poetry are the ~ of humanities that most interest him —A.J.Liebling⟩
tropo·collagen \ˈträpə, -rōpə+\ *n* [¹*trop-* + *collagen*] **:** a

soluble precursor of collagen whose elongated molecules form the elementary building unit of collagen fibers
trust fund* *n* **:** a governmental fund consisting of moneys accepted for a specified purpose (as civil service retirement) that is administered as a trust separately from other funds and is expended only in furthering the specified purpose
truth set *n* **:** a mathematical or logical set containing all the elements that may be substituted in a given statement of relationships without altering the truth of the statement
t-time \'tē,=\ *n, usu cap 1st T* [prob. fr. ²*t* (abbr. for *time*)] **:** the time of initial firing of a rocket vehicle or missile
tube* *n* **1 :** TELEVISION TUBE; *broadly* **:** TELEVISION **2 :** CURL *herein*
tu·mor·i·gen·ic \,t(y)ümərə'jenik\ *adj* [*tumor* + *-i-* + *-genic*] **:** producing or tending to produce tumors; *also* **:** CARCINOGENIC — **tu·mor·i·genesis** \,t(y)ümərə+\ *n* — **tu·mor·i·ge·nic·i·ty** \,=== jə'nisəd-ē\ *n*
tunnel* *n* **:** CURL *herein*
tunnel diode *n* **:** a semiconductor device that has two stable states when operated in conjunction with suitable circuit elements and a source of voltage, is capable of extremely rapid transformations between the two by means of the tunnel effect of electrons, and is used for amplifying, switching, and computer information storage and as an oscillator
tur·bo·cop·ter \'tərbō,käptər, -bə,k-\ *n* -s [*turbo-* + *helicopter*] **:** a helicopter in which motive power for the rotor is provided by one or more gas turbine engines
tur·bo·electric \'tərbō+\ *adj* [*turbo-* + *electric*] **:** involving or depending as a power source on electricity produced by turbine generators ⟨ships with ~ drive⟩
tur·bo·fan \'tərbō+,\ *n* [*turbo-* + *fan*] **1 :** a fan that is directly connected to and driven by a turbine **2 :** a jet engine having a turbofan
tur·bo·pump \"+,\ *n* [*turbo-* + *pump*] **:** a pump that is driven by a turbine
tur·bo·shaft \"+,\ *n* -s [*turbo-* + ¹*shaft*] **:** a gas turbine engine that is similar in operation to a turboprop engine but that instead of being used to power a propeller is used through a transmission system for powering other devices
tu·ring machine \'t(y)u̇riŋ-\ *n, usu cap T* [after A. M. *Turing* †1954 Eng. mathematician] **:** a hypothetical computing machine that is not limited in use by a fixed maximum amount of information storage and is not subject to malfunctioning
turnaround* *n* **:** the readying of a pad and the installation of the booster for the next spacecraft launching
turn off* *vi* **:** to lose interest **:** WITHDRAW ⟨the kids *turn off* or drift into another world —Edwin Sorensen⟩ ~ *vt* **:** to cause to turn off ⟨dropouts who are *turned off* by . . . political phoniness —Hendrik Hertzberg⟩
turn on* *vt* **1 :** to cause to undergo an intense visionary experience esp. by taking a drug (as LSD or marijuana) **2 :** to excite pleasurably **:** STIMULATE ⟨the ballet . . . was *turning* the audience *on* like magic —Clive Barnes⟩ ~ *vi* **1 :** to undergo an intense visionary experience esp. as a result of taking a drug; *broadly* **:** to get high ⟨students have always *turned on* — it used to be on alcohol —Harvey Wasserman⟩ **2 :** to become pleasurably excited ⟨*turns on* instead with classical music or jazz —Julie M. Heldman⟩ — **turn-on** \'=,=\ *n* -s
twin double *n* **:** a system of betting (as on horse races) in which the bettor must select the winners of four consecutive races in order to win
ty·lo·sin \'tīləsən\ *n* -s [origin unknown] **:** an antibacterial antibiotic from an actinomycete (*Streptomyces fradiae*)
u \'yü\ *adj, cap* [upper class] **:** characteristic of the upper classes
ubi·qui·none \yü'bikwə,nōn; ¦yübəkwə'n-, -'kwi,n-\ *n* [blend of L *ubique* everywhere and E *quinone;* fr. its occurrence in nature — more at UBIQUITY] **:** COENZYME Q *herein*
ufol·o·gy \yü'fäləjē\ *n* -ES [*UFO* + *-logy*] **:** the study of unidentified flying objects — **ufol·o·gist** \-jəst\ *n* -s
ul·tra·high \¦əltrə+\ *adj* [*ultra-* + *high*] **:** very high **:** exceedingly high ⟨~ vacuum⟩ ⟨at ~ temperatures⟩
ul·tra·mi·cro·fiche \¦əltrə¦mīkrō,fēsh\ *n* [*ultramicro-* + *-fiche* (as in *microfiche*)] **:** a photographic reproduction of printed matter in greatly reduced (as 100 to one) form
ul·tra·mi·cro·tome \-rə,tōm\ *n* [*ultramicro-* + *-tome*] **:** a microtome for cutting extremely thin sections for electron microscopy — **ul·tra·microtomy** \"+\ *n*
ul·tra·miniature \¦əltrə+\ *adj* [*ultra-* + *miniature*] **:** SUBMINIATURE — **ul·tra·miniaturization** \"+\ *n*
ul·tra·pure \"+\ *adj* [*ultra-* + *pure*] **:** of the utmost purity **:** wholly free from foreign or contaminating matter
umbilical *n* -s **:** UMBILICAL CORD 2
uncle tom *vi* **uncle tommed; uncle tom·ming** *usu cap U&T* **:** to behave like an Uncle Tom
uncle tomism \,==¦tä,mizəm\ *n, usu cap U&T* [*Uncle Tom* + *-ism*] **:** behavior characteristic of an Uncle Tom — **uncle tom·ish** \-ämish\ *adj, usu cap U&T*
underachieve \¦===¦=\ *vi* [¹*under-* + *achieve*] **:** to perform below an expected level of proficiency — **underachievement** \¦===¦==\ *n* — **un·der·achiev·er** \-ə¦chēvər\ *n*
underclass \'==,=\ *n* [prob. trans. of Sw *underklass*] **:** the lowest stratum of society usu. composed of disadvantaged minority groups
undercoating* *n* **:** a waterproof coating applied to the undersurface of a vehicle
underground* *adj* **:** existing, produced, or published outside the establishment esp. by the avant-garde ⟨~ movies⟩; *also* **:** of or relating to the avant-garde underground
underground* *n* **:** a usu. avant-garde group or movement that functions outside the establishment
un·der·whelm \,əndə(r)'hwelm *also* -'w-\ *vt* [¹*under* + *-whelm* (as in *overwhelm*)] **:** to fail to impress or stimulate
undock* *vt* [²*un-* + *dock*] **:** UNCOUPLE ⟨~ the lunar module from the command module⟩
un·flap·pa·ble \,ən'flapəbəl\ *adj* [¹*un-* + ¹*flap* + *-able*] **:** marked by assurance and self-control ⟨the most ~ of politicians — Anthony Lewis⟩ — **un·flap·pa·bil·i·ty** \-,flapə'biləd-ē\ *n* — **un·flap·pa·bly** \-'flapəblē\ *adv*
union* *n* **1 :** a mathematical set that is formed by combining two other sets and that contains all their separate and shared elements **2 :** the mathematical or logical operation of converting separate sets to a union
¹**uni·sex** \'yünə,seks\ *n* [*uni-* + *sex*] **:** the state or condition of not being distinguishable (as by hair or clothing) as to sex
²**unisex** *adj* **:** AMBISEXTROUS *herein*
uni·tar·i·ty \,yünə'tarəd-ē, -ter-\ *n* -ES [*unitary* + *-ty*] **:** the requirement in quantum mechanics that the S matrix be a unitary transformation between initial and final states of motion
unitary matrix *n* **:** a matrix whose inverse is equal to the complex conjugate of its transpose
unitary transformation *n* **:** a linear transformation of a vector space that leaves scalar products unchanged
uni·term \'yünə,tərm\ *n* [*uni-* + *term*] **:** a single term used as a descriptor in document indexing
unit train *n* **:** a railway train that transports a single commodity
un·person \,ən+\ *n* [¹*un-* + *person*] **:** an individual who usu. for political or ideological reasons is removed completely from recognition, consideration, or memory ⟨became an ~ when he was removed from the Lenin Mausoleum —Henry Tanner⟩
up·date \'əp,dāt\ *n* -s [*update,* v.] **1 :** the act of updating **:** an instance of updating **2 :** current information for updating ⟨navigational ~ for a spacecraft computer⟩
upmanship *n* [by shortening] **:** ONE-UPMANSHIP
upper* *n* **:** a stimulant drug; *esp* **:** AMPHETAMINE
uptight \'=¦=\ *adj* [²*up* + ³*tight*] **1 :** being in financial difficulties **:** BROKE ⟨surtax was another blow to an industry already ~ —*Chem. & Engineering News*⟩ **2 a :** showing signs of tension or uneasiness **:** APPREHENSIVE ⟨I was a little ~ about it at first —Phyllis Craig⟩ **b :** ANGRY, INDIGNANT ⟨I've been doing that voice in Negro theaters for years. Nobody ever got ~ —Flip Wilson⟩ **3 :** rigidly conventional ⟨~ and antiseptic white community —J.M.Culkin⟩ — **up·tight·ness** *n*
ura·nia \yə'rānēə, yu̇r-, -nyə\ *n* -s [NL, fr. *uranium* + *-a*] **:** URANIUM OXIDE a
uranium dioxide *n* **:** URANIUM OXIDE a
ur·ban·ol·o·gist \,ərbə'näləjəst\ *n* [*urban* + *-o-* + *-logist*] **:** one who specializes in the problems of cities — **ur·ban·ol·o·gy** \-jē\ *n*
urban renewal *n* **:** a construction program to replace or restore substandard buildings in an urban area
urban sprawl *n* **:** the spreading of urban developments (as houses and shopping centers) on undeveloped land near a city
ureo·tel·ic \yə¦rēə¦telik, ¦yu̇r-\ *adj* [*ure-* + ²*tel-* + *-ic;* fr. the fact that urea is the end product] **:** excreting nitrogen mostly in the form of urea ⟨mammals are ~ animals⟩
uri·co·tel·ic \¦yu̇rəkō¦telik\ *adj* [*uric-* + ²*tel-* + *ic;* fr. the fact that uric acid is the end product] **:** excreting nitrogen mostly in the form of uric acid ⟨birds are ~ animals⟩
uro·kinase \¦yu̇rə+\ *n* [¹*ur-* + *kinase*] **:** an enzyme similar to streptokinase found in human urine and used to dissolve blood clots (as in the heart)
ur·ti·car·io·gen·ic \,ərd-ə¦ka(a)rēə¦jenik\ *adj* [*urticaria* + *-o-* + *-genic*] **:** being an agent or substance that induces or predisposes to urticarial lesions (as wheals on the skin)
vac·ci·nee \,vaksə'nē\ *n* -s [¹*vaccinate* + *-ee*] **:** VACCINATE
van·co·my·cin \,vaŋkə'mīsən\ *n* -s [*vanco-* (of unknown origin) + *-mycin*] **:** an antibiotic from an actinomycete (*Streptomyces orientalis*) that is effective against spirochetes
vanishing *n* -s **:** FADING *herein*
vanity plate *n* **:** an automobile registration plate bearing letters, numbers, or a combination of these chosen by the owner
va·rac·tor \və'raktər, (ˈ)va(a)|(ə)¦r-, (ˈ)ve|\ *n* -s [*varying* + *reactor*] **:** a semiconductor device whose capacitance varies with the applied voltage
variable annuity *n* **:** an annuity contract which is backed primarily by a fund of common stocks and the payments on which fluctuate with the state of the economy
vaso·active \¦vā(,)zō, ¦vā(,)sō, ¦va(,)zō, ¦va(,)zō+\ *adj* [*vas-* + *active*] **:** affecting the blood vessels esp. in respect to the degree of their relaxation or contraction
VC* *abbr* Vietcong
vector* *n* **:** a mathematical quantity with two or more numerical components obeying rules of transformation within a space of two or more dimensions
veg·an·ism \'vejə,nizəm\ *n* -s [by contraction fr. *vegetarianism*] **:** extreme vegetarianism
ver·nal·in \'vərnᵊlən\ *n* -s [*vernalization* + *-in*] **:** a plant hormone found after vernalization and held to function in flower initiation
vernier* *also* **vernier engine** *n* **:** any of two or more small supplementary rocket engines or gas nozzles mounted on a missile or rocket vehicle and designed to make fine adjustments in the speed or course or to control the attitude
vex·il·lol·o·gy \,veksə'läləjē\ *n* -ES [L *vexillum* flag + E *-o-* + *-logy* — more at VEXILLUM] **:** the study of flags — **vex·il·lo·log·i·cal** \,veksəlō¦läjəkəl, (ˈ)vek¦silə¦lä-\ *adj* — **vex·il·lol·o·gist** \,veksə'läləjəst\ *n* -s
vi·bron·ic \(ˈ)vī¦bränik\ *adj* [*vibration* + *electronic*] **:** electronic-vibrational — used of the state of a molecule and of spectra of molecules
vid·eo·phone \'vidēə,fōn\ *n* [*video* + ¹*phone*] **:** a telephone equipped for transmission of video as well as audio signals so that users can see each other
¹**vid·eo·tape** \-ēə,tāp, -ēō,t-\ *n* **1 :** VIDEO TAPE RECORDING **2 :** the magnetic tape used in a videotape
²**videotape** *vt* -ED/-ING/-S **:** to make a video tape recording of
vi·et·nam·iza·tion \vē,etnəmə'zāshən, ,vyet-, -,mī'z- *also* ,vēət- *or* ,vēt-\ *n, usu cap* [*Vietnam* country in Indochina + *-ization*] **:** the act or process of transferring to the responsibility of the Vietnamese ⟨*Vietnamization* of the war⟩ — **vi·et·nam·ize** \vē'etnə,mīz, 'vyet-, 'vēət-, 'vēt-\ *vb* -ED/-ING/-S *usu cap*
-ville \,vil *esp South* vəl\ *n suffix* -s [*-ville,* suffix occurring in names of towns, fr. F, fr. OF, fr. *ville* farm, village — more at VILLAGE] **:** place or category of a specified nature ⟨squares*ville*⟩
vin·blas·tine \vin'bla,stēn, -stən\ *n* -s [contr. of *vincaleukoblastine* (herein)] **:** an alkaloid from Madagascar periwinkle used to relieve human neoplastic diseases
vin·ca·leu·ko·blas·tine \,viŋkə¦lükō¦bla,stēn, -stən; -,lükə-(,)bla'stēn\ *n* -s [NL *Vinca* + E *leukoblast* + *-ine*] **:** VINBLASTINE *herein*
vin·cris·tine \vin'kri,stēn, viŋ'k-, -stən\ *n* -s [NL *Vinca* + L *crista* crest + E *-ine*] **:** an alkaloid from Madagascar periwinkle used to relieve human neoplastic diseases
vi·ri·on \'vīrē,än, 'vir-\ *n* -s [ISV *viri-* (fr. NL *virus*) + ²*-on*] **:** a complete virus particle with membrane intact **:** the extracellular infective form of a virus
vital signs *n pl* **:** the pulse rate, respiratory rate, body temperature, and sometimes blood pressure of a person
voice-over \'=,==\ *n* -s **:** the voice of an unseen narrator heard in a motion picture or television program; *also* **:** the voice of a visible character indicating his thoughts but without motion of his lips
voiceprint \'=,=\ *n* [¹*voice* + ¹*print*] **:** a spectrographically produced individually distinctive pattern of certain voice characteristics that is an effective agent of identification
V/STOL \'vē,stōl, -ōl\ *abbr* vertical short takeoff and landing
VTOL \'vē,tōl\ *abbr* vertical takeoff and landing
wafer* *vt* **:** to prepare (as hay or alfalfa) in the form of small compressed cakes suggestive of crackers
wahine* *n* **:** a girl surfer
wake surfing *n* **:** the sport of riding (as on a surfboard) the wake of a powerboat
walking catfish *n* **:** an Asiatic catfish (*Clarias batrachus*) able to scramble overland for some distance that has been inadvertently introduced into waters of the southern U.S.
walk-up* *adj* **:** designed to allow pedestrians to be served without entering a building ⟨the *walk-up* window of a bank⟩
wan·kel engine \'väŋkəl-, ,wä-\ *n, usu cap W* [after Felix *Wankel,* 20th cent. Ger. engineer] **:** an internal-combustion engine developed in Germany that has a rounded triangular rotor functioning as a piston and rotating in a space in the engine and that has only two major moving parts
warning track *or* **warning path** *n* **:** a usu. dirt or cinder strip around the outside edge of a baseball outfield to warn a fielder when he is approaching a wall, a fence, or bleachers
wasp \'wäsp, 'wȯsp\ *n* -s *usu all cap or cap W* [white Anglo-Saxon Protestant] **:** an American of English or other northern European stock and of Protestant religious background
waterford glass *n, usu cap W* [fr. *Waterford,* city in southern Ireland where it was originally made] **:** an 18th and 19th century hand-blown flint glass often with a bluish cast
wat·son-crick model \¦wätsən¦krik- *also* ¦wȯt-\ *n, usu cap W&C* [after J. D. *Watson* b1928 Amer. biologist and F.H.C. *Crick* b1916 Eng. biologist] **:** a model deoxyribonucleic acid structure in which the molecule is visualized as a double-stranded helix cross-linked by hydrogen bonds
wave function* *n* **:** a quantum-mechanical function whose absolute value squared is a relative probability
way-out \'=¦=\ *adj* [*way out* (adverbial phrase), fr. ⁴*way* + ¹*out*] **:** FAR-OUT *herein* — **way-out·ness** \(ˈ)=¦=nəs\ *n*
weak interaction *n* **:** a fundamental interaction experienced by elementary particles that is responsible for some particle decay processes, for nuclear beta decay, and for emission and absorption of neutrinos — compare STRONG INTERACTION *herein*
we·del \'vādᵊl, 'wā-\ *vi* -ED/-ING/-S [back-formation fr. *wedeln*] **:** to perform wedelns in skiing
we·deln \'vādᵊl(ə)n, 'wā-\ *n, pl* **wedelns** *or* **wedeln** [G, fr. *wedeln* to fan, wag the tail, fr. *wedel* fan, tail, fr. OHG *wadal;* akin to ON *vēl* bird's tail] **:** an oscillating movement of the body in skiing that involves short quick turns straight down the fall line ⟨if a skier is to learn *wedeln* —John Blatt⟩
wheel·er-dealer \¦hwēlə(r)¦dēlə(r) *also* ¦wē-\ *n* -s [irreg. fr. *wheel and deal* + *-er*] **:** a shrewd operator esp. in business or politics
wheel·ie \'hwēlē *also* 'wē-\ *n* -s [*wheel* + *-ie*] **:** a maneuver in which a wheeled vehicle (as a skateboard, bicycle, or dragster) is balanced momentarily on its rear wheel or wheels
whipsawed *adj* [fr. past part. of ²*whipsaw*] **:** subjected to a double market loss through trying inopportunely to recoup a loss by a subsequent short sale of the same security
whisker* *n* **:** a thin hairlike crystal of great strength
white backlash *n* **:** the hostile reaction of white Americans to the advances of the civil rights movement
white room \'=,=\ *n* **:** CLEAN ROOM *herein*
whit·ey \'hwīd-ē *also* 'wī-\ *n, often cap* [*white* + *-ie*] **:** the white man **:** white society ⟨Negro leaders who are seen as stooges for *Whitey* —*Times Lit. Supp.*⟩ — usu. used disparagingly
wig·let \'wiglət\ *n* -s [²*wig* + *-let*] **:** a small wig used esp. to enhance a hairstyle
wil·son's disease \'wilsənz=,=\ *n, usu cap W* [after Samuel A. K. *Wilson* †1937 Eng. neurologist] **:** a congenital disease marked esp. by cirrhotic changes in the liver and severe mental disorder due to inability to metabolize copper
windblast \'=,=\ *n* [¹*wind* + ¹*blast*] **:** a gust of wind; *esp* **:** a destructive effect on a pilot ejected from a high-speed airplane
windchill** \'=,=\ *or* **windchill index** *n* -s [¹*wind* + ³*chill*] **:** a still-air temperature that would have the same cooling effect on exposed human flesh as a given combination of temperature and wind speed — called also *chill factor*
window* *n* **1 :** a range of wavelengths in the electromagnetic spectrum to which the earth's atmosphere is transparent **2 :** an interval of time within which a rocket or spacecraft must be launched to accomplish a particular mission **3 :** an area at the limits of the earth's sensible atmosphere through which a spacecraft must pass for successful reentry
wipeout \'=,=\ *n* -s [fr. the phrase *wipe out*] **:** a fall from a surfboard caused usu. by losing control, colliding with another surfer, or being knocked off by a wave
wok \'wäk\ *n* -s [Chin (Cant) *wōk*] **:** a bowl-shaped cooking utensil used esp. in the preparation of Chinese food
wolf-ra·yet star \¦wu̇lfrī'ā-\ *n, usu cap W & R* [after Charles *Wolf* †1918 & Georges *Rayet* †1906 Fr. astronomers] **:** any of a class of white stars which are found mainly in the Milky Way and Magellanic Clouds and whose spectra are characterized by very broad bright lines esp. of hydrogen, helium, carbon, and nitrogen that indicate very hot unstable stars
won \'wȯn, 'wän\ *n, pl* **won** [Korean *wŏn*] **1 :** the basic monetary unit of Korea — see MONEY table *in the Dict* **2 :** a coin or note representing one won
wooden rose *n* **:** a tuberous half-hardy trailing vine (*Ipomoea tuberosa*) grown in warm regions esp. for its hard showy yellow rose-shaped calyx and seed capsule
word* *n* **:** a group of information-conveying characters that have a specific storage point and are handled as a unit by a data-processing machine
workload** \'=,=\ *n* **:** the amount of work performed or capable of being performed (as by a mechanical device) usu. within a specific period
world line *n* **:** the aggregate of all positions in space-time of any individual particle that retains its identity
worry beads *n pl* [so called fr. the belief that the fingering releases nervous tension] **:** a string of beads to be fingered so as to keep one's hands occupied
wraparound \¦==,=\ *adj* [fr. *wrap around,* v.] **:** of or relating to a flexible printing surface wrapped around a plate cylinder
write* *vt* **1 :** to introduce (information) into the storage device or medium of a computer **2 :** to transfer (information) from the memory store of a computer to its output storage device or medium
wu-ts'ai \'wüt'sī\ *n* -s [Chin (Pek) *wu*³ *ts'ai*³ five colors] **:** a 5-colored overglaze enamel decoration used on Chinese porcelain since the Ming period
xe·nate \'zē,nāt, 'ze-\ *n* -s [ISV *xenon* + ¹*-ate*] **:** a salt of xenic acid
xe·nic acid \,zēnik-, ,ze-\ *n* [*xenic,* ISV *xenon* + *-ic*] **:** a weak acid known only in the form of its hydrate ($XeO_3 \cdot xH_2O$) and obtained by hydrolysis from xenon fluorides
xeno·biology \¦zenō+\ *n* [*xen-* + *biology*] **:** EXOBIOLOGY *herein*
xenon hexafluoride *n* **:** a highly reactive colorless crystalline compound XeF_6
xenon tetrafluoride *n* **:** a colorless crystalline compound XeF_4 that sublimes readily in air and is formed by heating xenon with fluorine under pressure
xi* *or* **xi particle** *n* **:** an unstable elementary particle existing in negative and neutral charge states with masses respectively 2585 and 2572 times the mass of an electron
x-ray astronomy *n, usu cap X* **:** astronomy dealing with investigations of celestial bodies by means of the X rays they emit
x-ray diffraction *n, usu cap X* **:** a scattering of X rays by the atoms of a crystal that produces an interference effect so that the diffraction pattern gives information on the structure of the crystal or the identity of a crystalline substance
x-ray star *n, usu cap X* **:** a luminous starlike celestial object emitting a major portion of its radiation in the form of X rays
xu \'sü\ *n, pl* **xu** [Vietnamese, fr. F *sou* sou] **1 :** a monetary unit of North Vietnam equal to 1/100 dong **2 :** a coin representing one xu
ya·ma·to-e \yä'mäd-ə,wā\ *also* **ya·ma·to** \-'mä(,)tō\ *n* -s *usu cap* [Jap *yamato-e,* fr. *Yamato* Japan + *e* picture, painting] **:** a movement in Japanese art arising in medieval times and marked by the treatment of Japanese themes with Japanese taste and sentiment
ya·yoi \(ˈ)yä,yȯi\ *adj, often cap* [fr. *Yayoi,* site in Tokyo, Japan, where remains of the period were discovered] **:** of, relating to, or typical of a Japanese cultural period extending from about 200 B.C. to A.D. 200, being generally neolithic but including the beginning of work in metal, and characterized esp. by unglazed wheel-thrown pottery (**Yayoi ware**) usu. without ornamentation but often of florid shape
yellow pages *n pl, usu cap Y & P* **:** the section of a telephone directory that lists business and professional firms and people alphabetically by category and includes classified advertising
yé-yé \(ˈ)yā(,)yā\ *adj* [F, fr. E *yeah-yeah,* exclamation often interpolated in rock 'n' roll performances] **:** of, relating to, or featuring rock 'n' roll as it developed in France
yield to maturity *n* **:** the total rate of return to an owner holding a bond to maturity expressed as a percentage of cost
YIG \'yig\ *abbr or n* -s yttrium iron garnet *herein*
yi-hsing ware \'yē'shiŋ,-\ *also* **yi-hsing** \'=¦=\ *or* **yi-hsing yao** \,yē,shiŋ'yau̇\ *n, usu cap 1st Y* [*Yi-hsing* fr. *Yi-hsing* (*Ihing*), town in southern Kiangsu province, China; *Yi-hsing yao* fr. *Yi-hsing* + Chin (Pek) *yao*² pottery] **:** BOCCARO
yttrium iron garnet *n* **:** a synthetic magnetic crystal $Y_3Fe_5O_{12}$ that is used esp. as a filter for selecting or tuning microwaves
zaire \'zï(ə)r, zä'i(ə)r\ *n* -s [F *zaïre,* former name of Congo river] **1 :** the basic monetary unit of the Republic of the Congo (Kinshasa) — see MONEY table *in the Dict* **2 :** a note representing one zaire
¹**zap** \'zap\ *interj* [imit.] — used to express the sound made by or as if by a gun
²**zap** *vt* **zapped; zapped; zapping; zaps :** to make helpless or sterile esp. by shooting
zea·tin \'zēətən\ *n* -s [NL *Zea* + E *-tin* (as in *kinetin* — herein)] **:** a cytokinin first isolated from maize endosperm
zebra crossing *Brit sometimes* 'zebrə-\ *n, Brit* **:** a crosswalk marked by a series of broad white stripes
zelkova* *n* -s **:** a plant of the genus *Zelkova; esp* **:** a tall widely spreading Japanese tree (*Z. serrata*) resembling the American elm and replacing the latter as an ornamental and shade tree because of its resistance to Dutch elm disease
ze·ner diode \'zānə(r)-\ *n, often cap Z* [origin unknown] **:** a silicon semiconductor device used esp. as a voltage regulator
zinj·an·thro·pine \zin'jan(t)thrə,pīn\ *n* -s [*zinjanthropine* adj., fr. *zinjanthropus* + ¹*-ine*] **:** any of several closely related primitive extinct African hominids including zinjanthropus — **zinjanthropine** *adj*
zip code \'zip,-\ *n, often cap Z&I&P* [*ZIP* fr. zone improvement plan] **:** a 5-digit code that identifies each postal delivery area in the U.S.
zip-code *vt* **:** to furnish with a zip code
zir·ca·loy \'zərkə,lȯi\ *n* -s [*zirconium* + *alloy*] **:** any of several zirconium alloys notable for corrosion resistance and stability over a wide range of radiation and temperature exposures
zone melting *n* **:** a technique for the purification of a crystalline material and esp. a metal in which a molten region travels through the material to be refined, picks up impurities at its advancing edge, and then allows the purified part to recrystallize at its opposite edge
zone refine *vt* **:** to produce or refine by zone melting
zonked \'zäŋ(k)t, -ȯ-\ *adj* [origin unknown] **:** being under the influence of alcohol or a drug (as LSD) **:** HIGH
zo·ri \'zōrē, -ȯr-\ *n, pl* **zori** [Jap *zōri*] **:** a flat thonged sandal usu. made of straw, cloth, leather, or rubber

A DICTIONARY OF THE ENGLISH LANGUAGE

[1]a \'ā\ *n, pl* **a's** *or* **as** *also* **aes** \'āz\ *often cap, often attrib* **1 a :** the first letter of the English alphabet **b :** an instance of this letter printed, written, or otherwise represented **c :** a speech counterpart of orthographic *a* (as the different *a* sounds in *ape, pat, part*) ⟨mouthing out his hollow oes and *aes* —Alfred Tennyson⟩ **2 a :** the keynote of A major or A minor **b :** the tone A **3 :** a printer's type, a stamp, or some other instrument for reproducing the letter *a* **4 :** someone or something arbitrarily or conveniently designated *a,* esp. as the first in order or class ⟨*A* deeded land to B⟩ **5 a :** a grade assigned by a teacher or examiner rating a student's work as excellent, best, first, or superior in quality ⟨receiving an *A* in a science course⟩ **b :** one graded or rated with an A ⟨an *A* student⟩ ⟨those student papers are *A's*⟩ ⟨the movie was an *A*⟩ **6 :** something having the shape of the capital letter A — **from A to Z** *also* **from A to izzard :** from beginning to end **:** with coverage through the whole range or scope involved **:** THOROUGHLY, COMPLETELY

[2]a \ə, *esp emphatic or hesitating or after a pause* (ˈ)ā\ *indefinite article* [ME, fr. OE *ān* one — more at ONE] **1** — used as a function word before most singular nouns other than proper and mass nouns when the individual in question is undetermined, unidentified, or unspecified, esp. when the individual is being first mentioned or called to notice ⟨there was *a* tree in the field⟩ ⟨*a* man walked past him⟩ ⟨he bought *a* house, but this is not the house he bought⟩; used before words beginning with a consonant sound ⟨*a* man⟩ ⟨*a* union⟩ ⟨*a* one⟩ ⟨*a* heroic effort⟩ and in some dialects also before words beginning with a vowel sound ⟨*a* oak⟩ ⟨*a* apron⟩; used with a plural noun only if *few, very few, good many,* or *great many* is interposed ⟨*a* few hours⟩; used before adjectives modifying a noun to which it refers except that it follows *many, such, what* and any adjective or adjectives preceded by *as* or *how,* and usu. follows any adjective or adjectives preceded by *so* or *too* ⟨*a* long time⟩ ⟨such *a* day⟩ ⟨how good and brave *a* deed⟩ ⟨too long *a* time⟩; compare [1]AN **2 a** — used as a function word before noun and adjective uses of such number collectives as *dozen* and *score* and before such words as *hundred, thousand,* and *million* ⟨*a* gross of candles⟩ ⟨*a* hundred and twenty men⟩ ⟨*a* hundred and fifty thousand⟩ **b** — used as a function word before attributive adjectives expressing number to imply indefiniteness or approximation ⟨*a* twenty men⟩ ⟨*a* twelve hours⟩; now dial. except in constructions given in note following sense 1 ⟨*a* great many men⟩ **3 a :** ONE ⟨swords all of *a* length⟩ ⟨men all of *a* sort⟩ **b** — used as a function word to suggest limitation in number ⟨with only *a* brigade to defend the fort⟩ **c :** the same ⟨birds of *a* feather⟩ **4 a :** a particular illustration of **:** an example of (a named class) ⟨he is *a* man⟩ **b** — used as a function word before a singular noun followed by a restrictive clause or other identifying modifier ⟨*a* man who was here yesterday⟩ **c :** ANY, EACH — used with a following restrictive modifier ⟨*a* man guilty of kidnaping wins scant sympathy⟩ ⟨*a* man who is sick can't work well⟩ **d** — used as a function word before proper nouns to indicate lack of full knowledge concerning what is indicated by them ⟨*a* Mr. Smith called you yesterday⟩ ⟨among the towns of the area there is *a* Smithville, I believe⟩ **e** — used as a function word before proper nouns as a step in commonization, often to designate another having qualities like those of the person or thing named ⟨*a* Shakespeare in his dramatic skill⟩ ⟨*a* new Rome controlling the world⟩ **f** — used as a function word before a mass noun to suggest that a kind or type is under consideration ⟨*a* tobacco that grows well in cold areas⟩ ⟨*a* bronze made in ancient times⟩ **g :** an instance or case of ⟨the patient later developed *a* tonsillitis⟩ **:** a kind of ⟨copper is *a* metal⟩ **h** — used as a function word with form plurals to suggest a unifying notion ⟨*a* falls in the river⟩ ⟨*a* glassworks⟩ **5** [by folk etymology fr. [3]*a*] **:** in, to, or for each **:** for every ⟨twice *a* week⟩ ⟨a dollar *a* dozen⟩

[3]a \ə\ *prep* [ME *a, o,* fr. OE *a-, an, on* — more at ON] *now dial* **:** [1]ON, [1]IN, [1]AT, [1]TO ⟨*a* God's name⟩ ⟨*a* this fashion⟩ ⟨*a* to-side⟩ ⟨he that died *a* Wednesday —Shak.⟩ ⟨going to town *a* Monday⟩

[4]a *or* **'a** *in senses 1-3* ə, *in sense 4* ə *or* (ˌ)å\ *pron* [in sense 1, fr. ME *a, ha* he, unstressed var. of *he,* fr. OE *hē;* in sense 2, fr. ME *a, ha,* unstressed var. of *heo, hie, hi,* fr. OE *hēo, hīo, hī,* fem. of *hē;* in sense 3, fr. ME *a, ha,* unstressed var. of *hie, hi,* fr. OE *hīe, hī,* pl. of *hē;* in sense 4, fr. ME *a, ha,* unstressed vars. of *he, heo,* used to refer to inanimate objects of masc. or fem. gender; in sense 5, var. of *I* — more at HE, I] **1** *chiefly dial* **:** HE; *sometimes* **:** HIM — usu. used in spoken English in unemphatic positions **2** *dial chiefly Brit* **:** SHE; *sometimes* **:** HER **3** *chiefly dial* **:** THEY; *sometimes* **:** THEM **4** *chiefly dial* **:** IT **5** *chiefly dial* **:** I

[5]a *also* **'a** *or* **'a'** \ə, (ˈ)a\ *or* **ha** *or* **ha'** \hə, (ˈ)ha\ *vb* [ME *a, ha,* contr. of *have* (imper. & pres. subj.), *haven* (infin.)] **:** HAVE ⟨God '*a*' mercy on his soul —Shak.⟩ ⟨I'd *a* done it if I could⟩ — now usu. used as an unstressed auxiliary; often attached without hyphen to the preceding word ⟨could*a*⟩ ⟨might*a*⟩ ⟨would*a*⟩; not often in formal use

[6]a \ə\ *prep* [ME, contr. of *of*] **:** OF ⟨passing the time *a* day⟩ ⟨get it out *a* my locker —James Jones⟩ — often attached without hyphen to the preceding word ⟨kind*a*⟩ ⟨sort*a*⟩ ⟨coupl*a*⟩ ⟨lott*a*⟩; not often now in formal use

[7]a *or* **a'** \ˈó\ *adv (or adj)* [ME (northern dial.) *aw,* alter. of *all*] *chiefly Scot* **:** ALL

[8]a *abbr, often cap* **1** about **2** absent **3** absolute **4** academician; academy **5** acceleration **6** accepted **7** accommodation **8** ace **9** acre **10** act; acting; active; activity **11** adjective **12** adjutant **13** administration **14** adult **15** after **16** afternoon **17** age; aged **18** air **19** aircraft **20** airman **21** airplane **22** alto **23** amateur **24** American **25** ampere **26** amphibian; amphibious **27** amplitude **28** ana **29** angstrom unit **30** anna **31 a** [L *anno,* abl. of *annus*] in the year **b** [L *annus* — more at ANNUAL] year **32** anode **33** anonymous **34** answer **35** ante **36** anterior **37** approved **38** aqua **39** arctic **40** are **41** area **42** army **43** article **44** artillery **45** asked **46** assist **47** associate; association **48** asymmetric **49** at **50** atom; atomic **51** atomic weight **52** Australian **53** author **54** automobile **55** [F *avancé,* past part. of *avancer* to advance, be fast (used of a clock), fr. OF *avancier* — more at ADVANCE] fast

[9]a *symbol* **1** *cap* argon **2** [L *ad* — more at AT] at, to — often enclosed in an encircling loop **3** *cap* mass number

[1]a- \ə\ *prefix* [ME, fr. OE *a-, an, on*] **1 :** on **:** in **:** at ⟨*a*bed⟩ ⟨*a*foot⟩ ⟨*a*sunder⟩ — sometimes used in dialect speech in locutions not found in standard ⟨he did it *a*-purpose⟩ **2** *obs* **:** at (such) a time ⟨*a*-nights⟩ **3 :** in (such) a state or condition ⟨*a*fire⟩ ⟨*a*sleep⟩ — often used with *with* ⟨*a*crawl with ants⟩ **4 :** in (such) a manner ⟨*a*loud⟩ **5 :** in the act of **:** in the process of ⟨daddy's gone *a*-hunting⟩ ⟨the ship was still *a*-building⟩

[2]a- \(ˈ)ā, (ˈ)a *also* (ˈ)ä *or* (ˈ)å; *at individual entries variants other than the first are not shown unless believed to be frequent*\ *or* **an-** \(ˈ)an, ˌən\ *prefix* [L & Gk; L *a-, an-,* fr Gk — more at UN-] **:** not **:** without ⟨*a*chromatic⟩ ⟨*a*sexual⟩ — used chiefly with words of Gk or L origin; *a-* before consonants other than *h* and sometimes even before *h, an-* before vowels and usu. before *h* ⟨*a*historical⟩ ⟨*an*esthesia⟩ ⟨*an*hydrous⟩

-a- *comb form* [ISV] **:** replacing carbon esp. in a ring — in initial combining forms as second constituent after a first constituent designating a chemical element ⟨ars*a*-⟩ ⟨az*a*-⟩ ⟨sil*a*-⟩

-a *n suffix* -s [NL, prob. fr. originally nonsignificant *-a* in *magnesia,* fr. ML *-a* (in *magnesia,* alchemical substance), fr. Gk *-a, -ē* (in *magnēsia, magnēsiē,* alchemical substance, magnet), fr. nom. sing. fem. adjectival ending corresponding to nom. sing. masc. *-os* and nom. sing. neut. *-on*] **:** oxide ⟨ceri*a*⟩ ⟨lanthan*a*⟩ ⟨thori*a*⟩

aa \ˈä,ä\ *n* -s [Hawaiian *'a'ā*] **:** rough scoriaceous lava — contrasted with *pahoehoe*

AA *abbr* **1** achievement age **2** acting appointment **3** *often not cap* always afloat **4** *often not cap* ana **5** antiaircraft **6** approximate absolute **7** athletic association **8** author's alteration **9** automobile association

AAA *in sense 1 at least,* ˈā,āˈā *or* ˌtripəˈlā\ *abbr* **1** amateur athletic association **2** antiaircraft artillery

AAC *abbr* [L *anno ante Christum*] in the year before Christ

aa·chen \ˈäkən, ˈåk-\ *adj, usu cap* [fr. *Aachen,* Germany] **:** of or from Aachen, Germany **:** of the kind or style prevalent in Aachen

aa·lii \äˈlē,ē\ *n* -s [Hawaiian] *Hawaii* **:** a small tree (*Dodonaea viscosa*) sometimes valued for its hard dark wood

A and M *abbr* agricultural and mechanical

AAR *abbr, often not cap* against all risks

aard·vark \ˈärd,värk\ *also* **erd·vark** \ˈe(ə)rd,värk\ *n* -s [obs. Afrik *aardvark* (now *erdvark*), fr. *aard* earth + *vark* pig; akin to OE *eorthe* earth and to OE *fearh* little pig — more at EARTH, FARROW] **:** a burrowing nocturnal African mammal about five feet long that feeds on ants, has a long snout, a snakelike tongue, large ears, and a heavy tapering tail, and is usu. considered to form a single variable species (*Orycteropus afer*) that is the sole recent representative of the obscure mammalian order Tubulidentata — called also *ant bear, ant eater, earth pig*

aardvark (*Orycteropus afer*)

aard·wolf \-,wu̇lf\ *n, pl* **aard·wolves** \-lvz\ [Afrik, fr. *aard* earth + *wolf;* akin to OE *wulf* wolf — more at WOLF] **:** a hyenalike mammal (*Proteles cristata*) of southern and eastern Africa that has a striped coat, 5-toed forefeet, and a distinct mane, feeds chiefly on carrion and insects (as termites), and is usu. placed in the Hyaenidae though formerly separated in another family (Protelidae)

aar·hus \ˈó(ə)r,hüs\ *adj, usu cap* [fr. *Aarhus,* Denmark] **:** of or from Aarhus, Denmark **:** of the kind or style prevalent in Aarhus

aa·ron·ic \(ˈ)aˈränik, -eˈ-, -aaˈ-, -āˈ-\ *adj, usu cap* [*Aaron fl ab* 1200 B.C. Jewish patriarch & high priest, brother of Moses + E *-ic*] **1 :** of or stemming from Aaron the Levite, the first high priest of the Hebrews **2 :** of or belonging to the lesser order of priesthood in the Mormon church comprising the grades of deacon, teacher, and priest — compare MELCHIZEDEK

aa·ron·ite \ˈarə,nīt, ˈer-, ˈaar-, ˈār-\ *n* -s *usu cap* **:** a priestly descendant of Aaron

aaron's-beard \ˈ==ˈ=\ *n, pl* **aaron's-beards** *usu cap A* [so called fr. the reference to the patriarch Aaron's beard in Ps 133: 2] **:** any of several plants having numerous stamens or threadlike runners: as **a :** GREAT ST.-JOHN'S-WORT **b :** JERUSALEM STAR **c :** STRAWBERRY GERANIUM **d :** KENILWORTH IVY **e** *or* **aaron's-beard cactus :** a cactus (*Opuntia leucotricha*) that has white hairs on its joints

aaron's rod \ˈ==ˈ=\ *n, usu cap A* [so called fr. the reference (Num 17:8) to the patriarch Aaron's rod, which blossomed and yielded almonds] **1 :** any of several plants with tall flowering stems; *esp* **:** GREAT MULLEIN **2 :** an architectural ornament consisting of a rounded molding decorated by a single entwined serpent and sometimes vines and leaves

aas·vo·gel \ˈäs,fōgəl\ *also* **aas·vo·el** \-,fōəl\ *n* -s [obs. Afrik *aasvogel* (now *aasvoël*), fr. *aas* carrion + *vogel* (now *voël*) bird; akin to OE *etan* to eat and to OE *fugol* bird — more at EAT, FOWL] *Africa* **:** VULTURE

AAU *abbr* amateur athletic union

[1]ab *or* **av** \ˈäb, ˈäv\ *n* -s *usu cap* [Heb *ābh*] **:** the 11th month of the civil year or the 5th month of the ecclesiastical year in the Jewish calendar — see MONTH table

[2]ab \ˈab\ *n* -s *often cap* [alternate transliteration of Egypt *'ıb*] *Egyptian relig* **:** the spirit of the physical heart and the seat of the will and intentions conceived as proceeding at death to the future world where it gives evidence for or against its possessor

[1]ab- *prefix* [ME, fr. OF & L; OF, fr. L, fr. *ab* from — more at OF] **1 :** from **:** departing from ⟨*ab*normal⟩ **2 :** away **:** outside of ⟨*ab*enteric⟩

[2]ab- *prefix* [[1]*absolute*] — used for a cgs electromagnetic unit (as in the following table)

UNIT	NATURE	EQUIVALENT
abampere	current	10 amperes
abcoulomb	charge	10 coulombs
abfarad	capacitance	10^9 farads
abhenry	inductance	10^{-9} henrys
abohm	resistance	10^{-9} ohms
abvolt	potential	10^{-8} volts

ab *abbr* **1** *often cap* abbot **2** about

[1]AB \(ˈ)āˈbē\ *abbr or n* -s [abbr. of NL *artium baccalaureus*] Bachelor of Arts

[2]AB \"\ *abbr or n* -s able-bodied seaman

AB *abbr* **1** aid to blind **2** airbase **3** airborne **4** *often not cap* at bat

[1]aba \ˈabə\ *n* -s [after A. T. d'*Abbadie* †1897 Fr. explorer, its inventor] **:** an altazimuth for either astronomical or terrestrial use

[2]aba *or* **ab·ba** \əˈbä, aˈbä\ *or* **aba·ya** \-äyə\ *n* -s [Ar *'abā', 'abā'ah*] **1 :** a coarse often striped fabric woven in the Near East from wool or from the hair of camels or goats **2 :** a loose sleeveless outer garment of aba or of fine silk worn chiefly by Arabs

abab·da \əˈbabdə\ *or* **abab·deh** \-de\ *n, pl* **ababda** *or* **ababdas** *or* **ababdeh** *or* **ababdehs** *usu cap* [Ar *'Abābidah*] **1 :** an Arabic-speaking mostly nomadic Beja people of Upper Egypt **2 :** a member of the Ababda people

ab ab·sur·do \,abəbˈsər,dō, ,a,bab-, -ˈz-\ *adv (or adj)* [L] **:** from absurdity — used of an argument that an assertion is false because of its absurdity

ab·a·ca \ˌabəˈkä\ *n* -s [Sp *abacá,* fr. Tag *abaká*] **1 :** a fiber obtained from the leafstalk of a banana (*Musa textilis*) native to the Philippines — called also *Manila hemp* **2 :** the plant that yields abaca

aba·ca·te \,abəˈkäd·ē\ *n* -s [Pg] **:** AVOCADO

aba·ca·xi \ˌabəkəˈshē\ *n* -s [Pg *abacaxi*] **:** a large sweet pineapple grown esp. in Brazil

ab·a·cis·cus \,abəˈsiskəs, -ˈki-\ *n, pl* **abacis·ci** \-ˈsi,sī, -ˈki,skē, -ˈki,skī\ [NL, fr. LGk *abakiskos,* dim. of Gk *abak-, abax* slab, board] **:** ABACULUS

ab·a·cist \ˈabəsə̇st, -bə̇kə̇-, əˈbakə̇- *also* əˈbäk- *or* əˈbåk-\ *n* -s [ME, fr. ML *abacista,* fr. L *abacus* + *-ista* -ist] **:** one that uses an abacus

aback \əˈbak\ *adv* [ME *abak,* fr. OE *on bæc,* fr. *on* on, at, towards + *bæc* back — more at ON, BACK] **1** *archaic* **a :** toward or to the back or rear **:** BACKWARD, BACK ⟨all suddenly dismayed . . . he fled ~ —Edmund Spenser⟩ **b :** in the rear **:** BEHIND ⟨front and ~ there was nothing but sand⟩ **2 :** in a position to catch the wind upon the forward surface of a sail — usu. used of a square sail or yard ⟨the ship came up into the wind with all yards ~ —H.A.Chippendale⟩ **3 :** by surprise **:** UNAWARES — used with preceding *take* ⟨completely taken ~ at the question⟩

abacot *var of* BYCOKET

ab·ac·ti·nal \(ˈ)aˈbaktənᵊl, ˌa,bakˈtīnᵊl\ *adj* [[1]*ab-* + *actinal*] **:** of or relating to the surface or end opposite to the mouth in a radiate animal — **ab·ac·ti·nal·ly** \-nᵊlē\ *adv*

ab·ac·tor \ˈa,baktə(r), =ˈ==\ *n* -s [LL, lit., one that drives away, fr. L *abactus* (past part. of *abigere* to drive away, fr. *ab-* [1]ab- + *-igere,* fr. *agere* to drive) + *-or* — more at AGENT] **:** one that steals cattle

a ba·cu·lo \(ˈ)āˈbakyə,lō, (ˈ)äˈbäkə,-\ *adv (or adj)* [NL] **:** by means of the rod — used of an argument appealing to force rather than reason

abac·u·lus \əˈbakyələs\ *n, pl* **abacu·li** \-,lī, -ē\ [L, dim. of *abacus*] **:** a tile used in mosaic **:** TESSERA

ab·a·cus \ˈabə̇kəs, əˈbak- *also* əˈbäk- *or* əˈbåk-\ *n, pl* **aba·ci** \ˈabə,sī, -,kī, -,kē, əˈba,kī *also* əˈbä,kī *or* -bå- *or* -,kē\ *or* **aba·cus·es** [L, fr. Gk *abak-, abax,* lit., slab] **1 :** a slab that forms the uppermost member or division of the capital of a column and that supports the architrave **2 :** a calculating instrument for performing arithmetical processes by sliding counters by hand on rods or in grooves

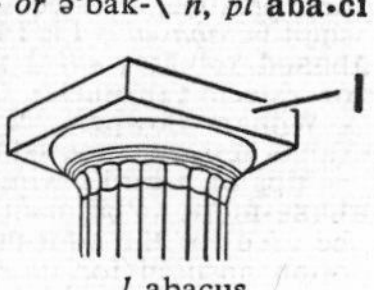

1 abacus

aba·dan \ˌabəˈdan, -dän; ˌäbəˈdän\ *adj, usu cap* [fr. *Abadan,* Iran] **:** of or from Abadan, Iran **:** of the kind or style prevalent in Abadan

abad·don \əˈbadᵊn\ *n* -s *usu cap* [fr. *Abaddon* "the angel of the bottomless pit" (Rev 9: 11), fr. ME, fr. LL, fr. Gk *Abaddōn,* fr. Heb *'ăbhaddōn,* lit., destruction] **:** a place of destruction **:** an underworld abode of lost souls **:** HELL

abadite *usu cap, var of* IBADITE

ab ae·ter·no \,abēˈtər(,)nō, ,ä,bīˈter-\ *adv* [NL, lit., from forever] **:** from a point in time that has no beginning

[1]abaft \əˈbaft, -ˈaa(ə)-, -ˈai-, -ˈå-\ *adv* [[1]*a-* + *baft*] **:** toward or at the stern **:** AFT, ASTERN ⟨ships with square sails sail fairly efficiently with the wind ~ —Elijah Baker⟩

[2]abaft \"\ *prep* **:** to the rear of **:** BEHIND ⟨selection by a better-than-average jazz band, taped in a small room ~ the 52d Street night spot —J.M.Conly⟩; *specif* **:** toward the stern from ⟨our deserter stood just ~ the foremast —Vincent McHugh⟩ ⟨a large explosion occurred just ~ B turret . . . which blew the back of the turret up over the bridge —Russell Grenfell⟩

abai·ser \?əˈbāsə(r)\ *n* -s [origin unknown] **:** IVORY BLACK

[1]abais·sé \əˈbā(,)sā\ *adj* [F, past part. of *abaisser* to lower — more at ABASE] *heraldry* **:** ABASED

[2]abaisse \əˈbās\ *n* -s [F, fr. *abaisser*] **:** a thin undercrust of pastry

ab·alien·ate \(ˈ)aˈbālyə,nāt, lēə-\ *vt* [L *abalienatus,* past part. of L *abalienare,* fr. *ab-* ab- + *alienare* to alienate — more at ALIENATE] **:** to transfer the title of **:** ALIENATE

ab·alien·ation \(ˈ)a,bālyəˈnāshən, -lēə-\ *n* [L *abalienation-, abalienatio,* fr. *abalienatus* + *-ion-, -io* -ion] **:** the act of transferring a legal title

ab·a·lo·ne \ˌabəˈlōnē, -i\ *n* -s [AmerSp *abulón*] **1 :** a gastropod mollusk of the genus *Haliotis* that clings to rocks tenaciously with a broad muscular foot and that has a nacre-lined shell of a flattened, oval, slightly spiral form perforated with a row of apertures for the escape of the water from the gills and covering the animal like a roof **2 :** the edible flesh of certain large abalones

shell of abalone

ab·am·pere \(ˈ)aˈbam,pi(ə)r, -aam-, -iə *also* ˌ=ˈ=\ *n* -s [ISV ²*ab-* + *ampere*] **:** the cgs electromagnetic unit of electric current equaling 10 amperes that flows in a circular path of one centimeter radius and produces a magnetic field of 2 π oersteds at the center of the circle — compare AB- table

¹aban·don \əˈbandən, -aand-\ *vt* **abandoned; abandoned; abandoning** \-andəniŋ, *rapid sometimes* -anniŋ\ **abandons** [ME *abandounen*, fr. MF *abandoner*, fr. *abandon*, n., surrender, abandonment, fr. *a bandon* in one's power, at one's discretion (in the phrase *metre a bandon* to put under someone's jurisdiction or at one's mercy), fr. *a* at, to (fr. L *ad* to) + *banon, bandon* power, authority, discretion, of Gmc origin; akin to OHG *ban* command, prohibition, authority — more at AT, BAN] **1 :** to cease to assert or exercise an interest, right, or title to esp. with the intent of never again resuming or reasserting it **:** YIELD, RELINQUISH ⟨∼*ed* the estates when he inherited them —Charles Dickens⟩ **2 :** to give up (as a position, a ship) by leaving, withdrawing, ceasing to inhabit, to keep, or to operate often because unable to withstand threatening dangers or encroachments ⟨the site was ∼*ed* after one year because of the number of rattlesnakes —*Amer. Guide Series: Calif.*⟩; *specif* **:** to bail out of (an aircraft about to crash) **3 :** to forsake or desert esp. in spite of an allegiance, duty, or responsibility ⟨endure the ignominy of his ∼*ing* her —D.H.Lawrence⟩ **:** withdraw one's protection, support, or help from ⟨a faithful member of the Democratic party, ∼*ing* it only once —W.W.Pierson⟩ **4** *obs* **:** to drive or cast out **:** BANISH, EXPEL, REJECT ⟨being all this time ∼*ed* from your bed —Shak.⟩ **5 :** to give (oneself) over to or yield (oneself) to without check, restraint, or control ⟨the girl ∼*ed* herself without restraint to a delicious wave of voluptuous contentment —J.C.Powys⟩ **6 :** to turn away from, give over, or permit to cease or lapse: as **a :** to desist from maintaining, adhering to, or following ⟨aristocratic families ∼*ed* paganism for Christianity —Will Durant⟩ **b :** to desist from practicing, doing, using ⟨they ∼*ed* their native speech and adopted the French tongue —T.B.Macaulay⟩ **c :** to turn from or relinquish (some course or action) ⟨he ∼*ed* the project with a sigh —Rudyard Kipling⟩ **7 :** to surrender to the insurer the insured's interest in (insured property) and to claim payment for a total loss sometimes permitted only when damage constitutes constructive total loss **syn** see RELINQUISH

²aban·don \ˈ", *F* abäⁿdōⁿ\ *n, pl* **abandons** \-ənz,-ōⁿ(z)\ [F, fr. OF] **:** a yielding to natural impulses **:** freedom from constraint ⟨with childish ∼ she gave herself over to grief —Sherwood Anderson⟩ **:** carefree ease or freedom often with disregard for consequences **:** ENTHUSIASM, EXUBERANCE ⟨smashed public property and burned private houses with an ever more ardent ∼ —Rose Macaulay⟩

aban·doned \əˈbandənd, -aand-\ *adj* [ME *abandouned*, fr. past part. of *abandounen* to abandon] **1 :** given up **:** DESERTED, FORSAKEN ⟨an ∼ child⟩ ⟨an ∼ house⟩ **2 :** SELF-ABANDONED **:** given over to vice **:** free from moral restraint ⟨an ∼ villain⟩ **3 :** showing abandon **:** free from constraint ⟨an ∼ sadness born of grief —Liam O'Flaherty⟩ **4** *of a geological formation* **:** no longer affected by the geologic agent that produced it ⟨an ∼ valley⟩ — **aban·doned·ly** \-ndən(d)lē, -i\ *adv*

aban·don·ee \ə¦=dəˈnē\ *n* -s **:** one that holds or claims abandoned property; *specif* **:** the person (as the insurer in marine insurance) to whom property or rights are relinquished

aban·don·ment \əˈ=dənmənt\ *n* -s [F *abandonnement*, fr. *abandonner* to abandon (fr. OF *abandoner*) + *-ment* — more at ABANDON] **1 a :** the act of abandoning **:** RELINQUISHMENT, RENUNCIATION ⟨such freedom meant the ∼ of many long-cherished phrases —I.M.Price⟩ **b** (1) **:** desertion of a spouse with the intention of creating a permanent separation (2) **:** desertion of a child by its parents **c** (1) **:** such relinquishment by an inventor of his right to secure a patent as will constitute a dedication of the invention to public use (2) **:** an author's relinquishment to the public domain of his copyright **d :** relinquishment by a nonuser for a specified period (as of an easement) **e :** the act of the insured in surrendering all rights to damaged or lost property to the insurer as a total loss **f :** refusal to accept from a delivering carrier a shipment so damaged in transit as to be worthless **g :** permission sought by or granted to a carrier by a state or federal agency to cease operation of all or part of a route or service **2 :** the quality or state of being abandoned **:** freedom from restraint **:** SELF-SURRENDER ⟨in a spirit of utter ∼ he carols his simple strain —John Burroughs⟩

aba·ñe·eme \əˌbänyəˈāmē\ *n* -s *usu cap* [Guarani] **:** the southern dialect of the Tupi-Guarani Indians

aban·ic \əˈbanik\ *adj, usu cap* [prob. fr. Ojibwa *Ab-boin-ug* Dakota (Sioux), lit., roasters; fr. their habit of torturing enemies] **:** SIOUAN

ab·ar·thro·sis \ˌaˌbärˈthrōsəs\ *n, pl* **abarthro·ses** \-ˌsēz\ [NL, fr. ¹*ab-* + *arthrosis*] **:** DIARTHROSIS

¹abas *or* **abassi** *var of* ABBASI

²abas *pl of* ABA

à bas \(ˈ)ä¦bä, (ˈ)a¦bä, *F* äbä\ [F] **:** down with ⟨*à bas* the profiteers⟩

abase \əˈbās\ *vt* -ED/-ING/-S [ME *abessen, abassen*, fr. MF *abaisser*, fr. (assumed) VL *abbassiare*, fr. L *ad-* + (assumed) VL *bassiare* to lower, fr. (assumed) VL *bassus* low (whence ML *bassus* fat, short, low)] **1** *archaic* **:** LOWER, DEPRESS **:** cast down ⟨∼ the eye⟩ **2 :** to lower or reduce in rank, office, prestige, or esteem **:** HUMBLE ⟨whosoever exalteth himself shall be *abased* —Lk 14:11 (AV)⟩ **:** DEGRADE

abased \əˈbāst\ *adj* **1 :** lowered esp. in rank, office, prestige, or esteem **:** HUMBLED ⟨I shrink ∼ and yet aspire to Thee —William Cowper⟩ **2** *heraldry* **a :** borne lower than usual ⟨an ∼ fess⟩ — opposed to *enhanced* **b :** turned downward ⟨the ∼ tips of a bird's wings⟩ — **abas·ed·ly** \-sədlē, -i\ *adv*

abase·ment \əˈbāsmənt\ *n* -s **1 :** the act of abasing ⟨these may be used for the adornment of life but he believes them more often misused for its ∼ —John Baillie⟩ **2 :** the quality or state of being abased ⟨each confession would bring her into an attitude of ∼ —H.L.Mencken⟩

abash \əˈbash, -ˈaa(ə)-,-ˈai-\ *vb* -ED/-ING/-ES [ME *abaisen, abaishen, abashen*, fr. (assumed) MF *abaisser* to be astonished, alter. (influenced by *abaisser* to abase) of *esbaiss-*, stem of *esbair* to be astonished, fr. *es-* (fr. L *ex-*) + *bair* to yawn, gape, bark — more at BAY] *vt* **:** to destroy the self-possession of **:** confuse or put to shame (as by arousing suddenly a feeling of guilt or inferiority) **:** DISCONCERT, DISCOMFIT ⟨a man whom no check could ∼ —T.B.Macaulay⟩ ∼ *vi, obs* **:** to lose self-possession **syn** see EMBARRASS

aba·shev \əˈbäshəf\ *adj, cap* [Russ] **:** belonging to a Bronze Age culture of the Chuvash Republic in the east central Soviet Union

abash·less \əˈ=ləs\ *adj* **:** UNABASHED — **abash·less·ly** *adv*

abash·ment \əˈ=mənt\ *n* -s [ME *abaishment, abashment*, fr. MF *abaissement* astonishment, alter. (influenced by *abaissement* abasing) of *esbaissement*, fr. *esbaiss-* + *-ment*] **:** the quality or state of being abashed

aba·sia \əˈbāzh(ē)ə\ *n* -s [NL, fr. ²*a-* + Gk *basis* step + NL *-ia* — more at BASE (bottom)] **:** inability to walk caused by a defect in muscular coordination — compare ASTASIA — **aba·sic** \əˈbāsik, -āzik\ *adj*

abastardize *vt* -ED/-ING/-S [MF *abastardir* (fr. OF, fr. *a-* — fr. L *ad-* — + *bastart* bastard) + E *-ize* — more at BASTARD] *obs* **:** BASTARDIZE, DEBASE

abat·able \əˈbād·əbəl, -ātə-\ *adj* [¹*abate* + *-able*] **:** capable of being abated

¹abate \əˈbāt, *usu* -ād· + V\ *vb* -ED/-ING/-S [ME *abaten*, fr. OF *abatre, abattre* to knock down, fell, slaughter, fr. *a-* (fr. L *ad-*) + *batre, battre* to beat, fr. L *battuere* — more at BAT] *vt* **1** *law* **a :** to bring entirely down **:** DEMOLISH **:** put an end to **:** do away with ⟨∼ a nuisance⟩ ⟨∼ an action⟩ **b :** NULLIFY **:** make void ⟨∼ a writ⟩ **2** *obs* **:** to lower in status **:** HUMBLE **3 a :** to reduce or lessen in degree or intensity **:** DIMINISH, MODERATE ⟨may . . . ∼ their zeal and give up their hopes of world conquest —Elmer Davis⟩ **b :** to reduce in value ⟨∼ a tax⟩ ⟨the legacies were *abated* pro rata to pay debts⟩ **4 :** DEDUCT, OMIT ⟨∼ part of a price⟩ **5 :** to beat down, cut away, or otherwise lower, so as to leave a figure in relief (as in metalwork or stonecutting) **6 :** DEPRIVE ⟨she hath *abated* me of half my train —Shak.⟩ **7** *obs* **:** to turn or dull the edge or point of **:** BLUNT ⟨∼*s* my sword's keen edge —Thomas Heywood⟩ ∼ *vi* **1 :** to decrease in force, intensity, or violence **:** LESSEN, SUBSIDE ⟨wait for a storm to ∼⟩ ⟨the fear of immediate war has measurably *abated*⟩ **2 a :** to become defeated or become null or void (as of a writ or appeal) **b :** to decrease in amount or value ⟨the legacies *abated* proportionately⟩ **syn** see ABOLISH, DECREASE

²abate \ˈ"\ *vi* -ED/-ING/-S [AF *abatre*, alter. of *enbatre*, fr. OF *en-* + *batre* to beat] *law* **:** to enter without right upon a tenement after the death of the last possessor and before the heir or devisee takes possession

¹abate·ment \əˈ=mənt\ *n* -s [ME, fr. AF, fr. *abatre* to abate + MF *-ment* — more at ABATE] *law* **:** the action of one that abates — compare ²ABATE

²abatement \ˈ"\ *n* -s [MF, fr. *abatre* to throw down + *-ment* — more at ABATE] **1 :** the act or process of abating or the state of being abated ⟨laws intended to speed up smoke ∼⟩ ⟨the ∼, if not the complete disappearance, of some long-standing mutual irritations —*New Yorker*⟩ **2** *heraldry* **:** any of various bearings emblematic of dishonor, degradation, or disgrace which were described by former writers on heraldry but never actually used **3 :** an amount abated **:** DECREASE, DEDUCTION; *esp* **:** a deduction from the full amount of a tax — **in abatement** *law* **:** seeking termination of the proceedings of an action by reason of some formal defect (as misnomer) ⟨a plea *in abatement*⟩

ab·a·tis *or* **ab·at·tis** \ˈabəˌtē, -ədˌəs; əˈbad·ē, -ad·əs\ *n, pl* **abatis** \-ēz\ *or* **abatises** \-əsəz\ *or* **abattis** *or* **abattises** [F, fr. *abattre* to fell, reduce — more at ABATE] **:** a defensive obstacle usu. formed by felled trees whose butts are secured towards the place defended with the often sharpened branches directed outwards against the enemy but sometimes made of live small trees bent down and often reinforced with barbed wire

ab·a·tised *or* **ab·at·tised** \-ēd,-əst\ *adj* **:** having an abatis

abat-jour \ˌäˌbäˈzhü(ə)r, *F* àbàzhüür\ *n, pl* **abat-jours** \-ü(ə)rz, -üür\ [F, fr. *abattre* to throw down + *jour* day, daylight, fr. (assumed) VL *diurnus*, fr. L, daily — more at ABATE, DIURNAL] **1 :** a device for deflecting daylight downward as it enters a window (as a sloping soffit of a lintel or a movable screen) **2 :** SKYLIGHT

¹aba·tor \əˈbād·ə(r), -ātə-\ *n* -s [²*abate* + *-or*] *law* **:** one that abates in a tenement

²abator \ˈ"\ *n* -s [¹*abate* + *-or*] *law* **:** one that abates a nuisance

abat-sons \ˌäˌbäˈsōⁿ, *F* àbàsōⁿ\ *n, pl* **abat-sons** \-ōⁿz, *F* -ōⁿ\ [F, fr. *abattre* + *sons*, pl. of *son* sound — more at SOUND] **:** a device for throwing sound downward (as louver boards in a belfry)

a battery \ˈā,-\ *n, usu cap A* **:** a battery used to heat the filaments or cathode heaters of electron tubes — called also *filament battery*; compare B BATTERY

ab·at·toir \ˈabəˌtwär, -twȧ(r,-t(w)ȯ(ə)r,-t(w)ȯ(ə), ˌ==ˈ=\ *n* -s [F, fr. *abattre* to slaughter + *-oir* -ory (fr. L *-orium*) — more at ABATE] **:** SLAUGHTERHOUSE

abat-vent \ˌäˌbäˈväⁿ, *F* àbàväⁿ\ *n, pl* **abat-vents** \-äⁿz, *F* -äⁿ\ [F, fr. *abattre* to throw down + *vent* wind, fr. L *ventus* — more at ABATE, WIND] **1 :** a series of sloping boards used (as in a belfry light) to break the wind without obstructing the passage of air or sound **2 :** a sloping roof (as of a penthouse) **3 :** a metal chimney cap

abat-voix \ˌäˌbäˈvwä, *F* àbàvwà *or* -wä\ *n, pl* **abat-voix** \-wäz, *F* -wà *or* -wä\ [F, fr. *abattre* + *voix* voice, fr. OF *vois* — more at VOICE] **:** a device for reflecting sound (as the sounding board over a pulpit or rostrum)

ab·ax·i·al \(ˈ)a¦baksēəl\ *also* **ab·ax·ile** \-səl,-ˌsīl\ *adj* [¹*ab-* + *axial* or *axile*] **:** situated outside of or facing away from the axis (as of an organ or organism) **:** DORSAL — opposed to *adaxial*

abaya *var of* ABA

abb \ˈab, ˈaa(ə)b\ *n* -s [(assumed) ME, fr. OE *āb, āweb, ōweb* — more at WOOF] **1 a :** coarse wool from the inferior parts (as the skirtings and edges) of a fleece **b :** a warp yarn made of abb wool **2** *Brit* **:** a filling pick in weaving

abb *abbr* abbess; abbey; abbot

¹abba *var of* ABA

²ab·ba \ˈabə, aˈbä\ *n* -s *often cap* [ME, fr. LL, fr. Gk, fr. Aram *abbā*] **:** FATHER — a title of honor given variously to the Deity in the New Testament, to bishops and patriarchs in many Eastern churches, and to Jewish scholars in the Talmudic period

ab·ba·cy \ˈabəsē, -i\ *n* -ES [alter. of ME *abbatie*, fr. LL *abbatia* — more at ABBEY] **:** the office, estate, jurisdiction, or term of tenure of an abbot

ab·bad·id \ˈabədəd, -(ˌ)did\ *n* -s *cap* [ʻ*Abbād* ibn-Muḥammad abu-ʻAmr †1042 founder of the dynasty + E *-id*] **:** a member of a Muslim dynasty that ruled at Seville from 1023 to 1091

ab·ba·si \əˈbäsē\ *or* **abas** \əˈbäs\ *also* **abas·si** əˈbäsē\ *n, pl* **abbasis** *or* **abas** *also* **abassis** [Per ʻ*abbāsī*, lit., of Abbās, fr. *Abbās* I †1628 shah of Persia] **1 :** a Persian silver coin first issued in the late 16th century **2 :** an old Persian unit of weight equivalent to about 0.8 pound **3 :** an Afghan yellow bronze coin equivalent to four shahi issued between 1921 and 1923 **4 :** an Afghan unit of value for postage stamps ⟨one-*abbasi* stamps⟩ ⟨two-*abbasi* stamps⟩

ab·bas·id \əˈbasəd, -ˈä-\ *n* -s *cap* [abu-al-*Abbas* †754 Islamic caliph, founder of the dynasty + E *-id*] **:** a member of a dynasty of caliphs that ruled the Islamic empire (750–1258) from Baghdad and claimed descent from Abbas, the uncle of Muhammad

ab·ba·tial \əˈbāshəl, (ˈ)a¦b-\ *adj* [F, fr. LL *abbatialis*, fr. *abbatia* abbey + L *-ialis* -ial — more at ABBEY] **:** of or belonging to an abbot, abbess, or abbey

abbaye *archaic var of* ABBEY

ab·bé \aˈbā, *F* àbā\ *n, pl* **abbés** \-āz, *F* -ā\ [F, fr. LL *abbat-, abbas* — more at ABBOT] **:** a member of the secular clergy of France **:** anyone wearing or entitled to wear the dress of a secular ecclesiastic — used chiefly as a title

ab·be condenser \ˈäbə-, ˈabē-\ *n, usu cap A* [after Ernst *Abbe* †1905 Ger. physicist] **:** an adjustable substage lens used as a condenser for a compound microscope

ab·be refractometer \ˈäbə-, ˈabē-\ *n, usu cap A* [after Ernst *Abbe*] **:** a refractometer in which the critical angle for total reflection at the interface of a film of a liquid between two similar glass prisms is utilized in determining the index of refraction

ab·bess \ˈabəs\ *n* -ES [ME *abbesse*, fr. OF *abbesse, abaesse*, fr. LL *abbatissa*, fem. of *abbat-, abbas* abbot — more at ABBOT] **:** a woman who is the superior of a convent of nuns

ab·bet·din *or* **ab·beth·din** \ˌävˌbātˈdēn\ *n* -s *often cap* [Heb *abh-bēth-dīn*, fr. *abh* chief (of) + *bēth* court of law, fr. *bēth* house (of) + *dīn* judgment] *in the rabbinical tradition* **:** the vice-president of the Sanhedrin

ab·be·vill·i·an *also* **ab·be·vill·e·an** \(ˈ)ab¦vilēən, ¦abə¦v-, -ēl-, -lyən\ *adj, usu cap* [*Abbeville*, town in Somme Dept., France + E *-ian* or *-an*] **:** of or belonging to the earliest epoch of the lower Paleolithic period characterized by the biface stone hand ax

ab·bey \ˈabē, -i\ *n* -s [ME, fr. OF *abeïe, abaïe*, fr. LL *abbatia*, abbacy, abbey, fr. *abbat-, abbas* abbot + L *-ia* — more at ABBOT] **1 :** a monastery ruled by an abbot or a convent ruled by an abbess **2 :** an abbey church ⟨buried in the ∼⟩

abbeystead *or* **abbeystede** *n* -s [*abbey* + *stead* or earlier *stede*] *archaic* **:** the seat of an abbey

ab·bot \ˈabət, *usu* -əd· + V\ *n* -s [ME *abbod, abbed*, fr. OE *abbod, abbad*, fr. LL *abbat-, abbas*, fr. LGk *abbas* (also, a title of respect given to monks), fr. Aram. *abbā* father] **:** the superior of an abbey for men

abbot general *n, pl* **abbots general :** the head of a monastic order ⟨the *abbot general* of the Cistercians⟩

abbot nul·li·us \-nuˈlēəs\ *n, pl* **abbots nullius** [part trans. of NL *abbas nullius*, short for *abbas nullius dioecesis*, abbot of no diocese] **:** an abbot who is exempt from diocesan control and under direct papal jurisdiction and who exercises the authority of an ordinary within the district in which his abbey is situated

abbot of misrule *usu cap A&M* [ME *abbot of mysreule*] **:** LORD OF MISRULE 1

abbot of unreason *usu cap A&U* [ME *abbot of unresoun*] **:** an elected leader in old Scottish popular revels — compare LORD OF MISRULE

abbot primate *n, pl* **abbot primates** *or* **abbots primate :** the representative head of all Benedictine congregations

ab·bot·ship \ˈ==ˌship\ *n* -s [ME, fr. *abbot* + *-ship*] **:** ABBACY

abbott-miller tube *n, usu cap A&M* **:** MILLER-ABBOTT TUBE

abbozzo *var of* ABOZZO

¹ab·bre·vi·ate \əˈbrēvēˌāt, aˈb-, *usu* -ād·+V\ *vt* -ED/-ING/-S [ME *abbreviaten*, fr. LL *abbreviatus*, past part. of *abbreviare* — more at ABRIDGE] **:** to make briefer **:** SHORTEN: **a :** to reduce the length of (as a book) by omitting some parts **:** ABRIDGE ⟨∼ a novel for very young readers⟩ **b :** to shorten by bringing to an end earlier than that planned or expected **:** cut short ⟨the ceremony, held during the annual Alumni Day, was *abbreviated* by rain —*N. Y. Times*⟩ **c :** to reduce (as an object or a form) in size or complexity by contraction or simplification ⟨in all these systems there was more or less tendency to ∼ the pictures, to contract them to a few strokes —A.L.Kroeber⟩ **d :** to reduce (as a word or phrase) to a shorter form intended to stand for the whole ⟨∼ *building* as *bldg*⟩ ⟨*United States of America* is commonly *abbreviated* to *U.S.A.*⟩ — compare ABBREVIATION **syn** see SHORTEN

²ab·bre·vi·ate \-ēˌət,-ˌāt\ *adj* [LL *abbreviatus*] **:** SHORTENED **:** relatively short **:** ABBREVIATED

³ab·bre·vi·ate \-ˌāt\ *n* -s [LL *abbreviatus*, past part.] *Scots law* **:** ABRIDGMENT, ABSTRACT

abbreviated *adj* **1 :** made briefer **:** SHORTENED **2 :** relatively short **:** shorter than others of its kind regarded as normal or conventional ⟨no adornment except an ∼ French tower —*Amer. Guide Series: Conn.*⟩ ⟨an ∼ dinner dress —*Mademoiselle*⟩

abbreviated number *n* **:** a number from which significant figures are omitted beyond a certain point determined by the degree of approximation desired or of accuracy attainable (as *5.667* for 5⅔ or *93,000,000* for the mean distance in miles to the sun)

ab·bre·vi·a·tion \=ˌ==ˈāshən\ *n* -s [ME *abreviacioun*, fr. MF *abbreviation*, fr. LL *abbreviation-, abbreviatio*, fr. *abbreviatus* + L *-ion-, -io* -ion] **1 :** the act or result of abbreviating **:** reduction in length or content **:** ABRIDGMENT ⟨our law, which shrinks from any ∼ of the span of life —B.N.Cardozo⟩ ⟨∼, leading to the omission of essential explanation —*Economist*⟩ **2 a :** a shortened form of a written word or phrase used for brevity in place of the whole made commonly by omission of letters from one or more parts of the whole (as *abbr* for *abbreviation*, *amt* for *amount*, *bldg* for *building*, *doz* or *dz* for *dozen*, *recd* for *received*, *H.E.* for *His Eminence* and *His Excellency*, *N.Y.* for *New York*, *r.p.m.* or *RPM* for *revolutions per minute*) sometimes showing substitution or other alteration in the part or parts retained (as *bbl* for *barrel*, *cwt* for *hundredweight*, *oz* for *ounce*, *Xmas* for *Christmas*) and sometimes doubling of initial letters to show plural form (as *ff* for *folios*, *pp* for *pages*, *SS* for *Saints*) — often extended to include signs and symbols (as ÷ for *divided by*, & for *and*, $ for *dollar*); compare CONTRACTION, SIGN, SYMBOL **b :** a shortened form of a spoken word or phrase (as *Smiffle* for *Smithfield*, *auto* for *automobile*) **3 a :** a device used in a music score as a direction (as *pp.*, *con 8 va*) **b :** a symbol used to shorten music notation by representing repeated notes or groups of notes **4 :** any convenient spoken or written short form or simple substitute for an understood or stipulated whole ⟨the phrase "civil rights" is an ∼ for a whole complex of relationships —*Pres. Truman's Committee on Civil Rights*⟩ **5 :** loss in the course of evolution of the final stages of the ancestral ontogenetic pattern — compare ACCELERATION, FETALIZATION

ab·bre·vi·a·tor \=ˈ==ˌād·ə(r), -ātə-\ *n* -s **:** one that abbreviates

ab·bre·vi·a·ture \-vēəˌchu̇(ə)r\ *n* -s [ML *abbreviatura*, fr. LL *abbreviatus* (past part. of *abbreviare* to abbreviate) + L *-ura* -ure — more at ABBREVIATE] **1** *obs* **:** ABBREVIATION **2 :** ABRIDGMENT, COMPENDIUM, ABSTRACT

abbs *pl of* ABB

abc \ˌāˌbēˈsē, ˌābēˈsē\ *n, pl* **abc's** *or* **abcs** \-ˈsēz\ *usu cap A & B & C* **1 a :** ALPHABET ⟨before I knew my *ABC* —A.L. Guérard⟩ — usu. used in pl. ⟨said his *ABC's* over and over —Mark Derby⟩ **b :** the rudiments of reading, writing, and spelling — usu. used in pl. ⟨a worker learned in little more than his *ABC's* —H.A.Overstreet⟩ **2 :** ABECEDARIUS **3** *obs* **:** a primer containing the alphabet and teaching the elements of reading **4 a :** the rudiments of any field of knowledge or practice ⟨the *ABC* of piano playing —H.W.Van Loon⟩ **b :** the first or basic principle ⟨distrust of everybody became the *ABC* of ordinary prudence in daily life —Willi Frischauer⟩ **5** *Brit* **:** an alphabetical guidebook of railway stations and their train service

ABC *abbr* atomic, biological, and chemical

ab·cha·la·zal \ˈabkə¦lāzəl\ *adj* [¹*ab-* + *chalazal*] **:** located or facing away from the chalaza of a seed — compare CHALAZAL

ab·cou·lomb \(ˈ)ab¦küˌläm, -lōm\ *n* -s [ISV ²*ab-* + *coulomb*] **:** the cgs electromagnetic unit quantity of electricity equal to 10 coulombs and being the charge that passes in one second through any cross section of a conductor carrying a steady current of one abampere — compare AB- table

abc soil \ˌāˌbēˈsē-\ *n, usu cap A & B & C* **:** a soil that has a well-differentiated profile, the A-, B-, and C-horizons being well developed

abd *abbr* abdicated

ab·der·hal·den reaction \ˈäpdə(r),häldən-\ *n, usu cap A* [trans. of G *Abderhaldensche reaktion*, after Emil *Abderhalden* †1950 Swiss chemist & physiologist] **:** the occurrence in body fluids of proteolytic enzymes specific for foreign proteins introduced into the body parenterally

ab·de·ri·an \(ˈ)ab¦dirēən\ *adj, usu cap* [*Abdera*, city of ancient Thrace (fr. Gk *Abdēra*) + E *-ian*] **1 :** of or belonging to Abdera or to its inhabitants **2 :** FOOLISH ⟨∼ laughter⟩

ab·de·rite \ˈabdəˌrīt\ *n* -s *usu cap* [L *Abderita, Abderites*, fr. Gk *Abdēritēs*, fr. *Abdēra*, whose inhabitants were reputedly stupid + Gk *-itēs* -ite] **1 :** a native or inhabitant of Abdera **2 :** SIMPLETON, SCOFFER

ab·di·ca·ble \ˈabdəkəbəl\ *adj* [*abdicate* + *-able*] **:** that may be abdicated ⟨∼ responsibilities⟩

ab·di·cate \ˈabdəˌkāt, *usu* -ād·+V\ *vb* -ED/-ING/-S [L *abdicatus*, past part. of *abdicare*, fr. *ab-* ¹ab- + *dicare* to proclaim — more at DICTION] *vt* **1 :** DISOWN, DISINHERIT ⟨a father who ∼*s* his son⟩ **2** *obs* **:** to separate (oneself) formally from or divest (oneself) of ⟨the ruler *abdicated* himself from the government⟩ **3 :** to cast off **:** DISCARD ⟨∼ an opinion⟩ **4 :** to relinquish formally (as sovereign power) **:** RENOUNCE **:** lay down **:** SURRENDER ∼ *vi* **:** to renounce a throne, high office, dignity, or function ⟨leadership that ∼*s*⟩

ab·di·ca·tion \ˌabdəˈkāshən\ *n* -s [L *abdication-, abdicatio*, fr. *abdicatus* + *-ion-, -io* -ion] **:** act of abdicating **:** RENUNCIATION, SURRENDER

ab·di·ca·tor \ˈabdəˌkād·ə(r), -ātə-\ *n* -s **:** one that abdicates

ab·do·men \ˈabdəmən; abˈdōmən, əb-\ *n, pl* **abdo·mens** \-nz\ *also* **abdom·i·na** \abˈdämənə, əb-\ [MF & L; MF, fr. L; perh. akin to L *abdere* to conceal, fr. *ab-* ¹ab- + *-dere* to put — more at DO] **1 a :** the part of the body, excepting the back, between the thorax and the pelvis or in certain lower vertebrates between the cardiac and caudal regions **:** BELLY **b :** the cavity of this part of the trunk lined by the peritoneum, enclosed by the body walls, the diaphragm, and the pelvic floor, and containing the stomach, intestines, liver, and other visceral organs **c :** the portion of this cavity between the diaphragm and the brim of the pelvis — distinguished from *pelvic cavity* **2 a :** the posterior often elongated region of the body behind the thorax in arthropods consisting of up to 10 segments in insects or of 7 or less in crustaceans and being usu. unsegmented in arachnids — see INSECT illustration **b :** the section of the zooid of a compound ascidian next behind the branchial sac

abdomin- *or* **abdomino-** *comb form* [L *abdomin-, abdomen*] **:** abdomen **:** abdominal ⟨*abdomin*algia⟩ ⟨*abdomino*perineal⟩ ⟨*abdomino*cardiac⟩

¹ab·dom·i·nal \ab'dämən°l, əb-\ *adj* [F, fr. *abdomin-* + *-al*] **1 :** of or belonging to the abdomen **:** VENTRAL ⟨~ muscle⟩ **2** *of a fish* **:** having the pelvic or ventral fins under the abdomen and behind the pectoral fins

²abdominal \"\ *n* -s **:** an abdominal element (as a vein or muscle)

abdominal fin *n* **:** one of the posterior paired fins of fishes **:** PELVIC FIN

ab·dom·i·nal·ly *adv* **:** in the area of the abdomen

abdominal pore *n* **:** an excretory usu. paired aperture opening within or behind the cloacal region in many fishes and affording communication between the abdominal cavity and the exterior

abdominal pouch *n* **:** MARSUPIUM 1

abdominal region *n* **:** one of the nine areas into which the abdomen is divided by imaginary planes, two vertical through the middle of Poupart's ligament and two horizontal through the junction of the ninth rib and costal cartilage and through the top of the iliac crest — compare EPIGASTRIC, HYPOCHONDRIAC, HYPOGASTRIC, INGUINAL, LUMBAR, UMBILICAL

abdominal respiration *n* **:** DIAPHRAGMATIC RESPIRATION

abdominal rib *n* **:** any of the riblike structures extending across the abdomen beneath the skin in certain reptiles

abdominal ring *n* **:** either of two external and internal openings in the fasciae of the abdominal muscles on either side, being the outlet and inlet of the inguinal canal, giving passage to the spermatic cord in the male and the round ligament in the female, and constituting a frequent site of hernia formation

abdominal regions: *1* epigastric; *2* right hypochondriac; *3* left hypochondriac; *4* right lumbar; *5* umbilical; *6* left lumbar; *7* right iliac; *8* hypogastric; *9* left iliac

ab·dom·i·no·per·i·ne·al resection \ab¦dämə(,)nō,perə¦nēəl-, əb-\ *n* [*abdomin-* + *perineal*] **:** resection of a part of the lower bowel together with adjacent lymph nodes through abdominal and perineal incisions

ab·dom·i·nous \ab'dämənəs, əb-\ *adj* [L *abdomin-, abdomen* + E *-ous*] **:** big-bellied

ab·duce \ab'd(y)üs, əb-\ *vt* -ED/ -ING/ -S [L *abducere* — more at ABDUCT] **:** ABDUCT ⟨*abducing* the forelimb⟩

ab·du·cens nerve \-,senz-\ *also* **abducent nerve** *or* **abducens** *n, pl* **abducen·tes** \,==(,)='sen(,)tēz\ [L *abducent-, abducens,* pres. part. of *abducere*] **:** either of the 6th pair of cranial nerves, being a motor nerve arising beneath the floor of the 4th ventricle and supplying the external rectus muscle of the eye

ab·du·cent \(')ab¦d(y)üs°nt, əb'd-\ *adj* [L *abducent-, abducens,* pres. part. of *abducere*] *of a muscle* **:** ABDUCTING — opposed to *adducent*

ab·duct \ab'dəkt, əb-\ *vt* -ED/ -ING/ -S [L *abductus,* past part. of *abducere* lit., to lead away, fr. *ab-* ¹ab- + *ducere* to lead — more at TOW (pull)] **1 :** to carry off (a person) by force **:** lead away (a child) wrongfully — compare ABDUCTION, KIDNAP **2** [back-formation fr. *abduction*] **:** to draw away (as a limb) from a position near or parallel to the median axis of the body ⟨the peroneus longus extends, ~*s,* and everts the foot —C.R.Bardeen⟩ ⟨the deltoid muscle plays a major part in ~*ing* the arm⟩; *also* **:** to separate (similar parts) ⟨~ adjoining fingers⟩

ab·duc·tion \ab'dəkshən, əb-\ *n* -s [in sense 1, fr. F, fr. L *abductus* + F *-ion;* in sense 2, fr. LL *abduction-, abductio,* fr. L *abductus* + *-ion-, -io* -ion; in sense 3, fr. NL *abduction-, abductio* (trans. of Gk *apagōgē*), fr. L *abductus* + *-ion-, -io* -ion] **1 :** the action of abducting or condition of being abducted ⟨~ of a limb⟩ **2 :** the unlawful carrying away of a man's wife or child or ward for the purpose of marriage or immoral intercourse — variously defined in statutory law but generally stated to include taking away or detention of a woman under a certain age, usu. 16 or 18, with or without her consent or knowledge of her age; compare KIDNAP **3 :** a syllogism in which the major premise is evident but the minor premise and therefore the conclusion only probable — called also *apagoge*

ab·duc·tive \(')ab¦dəktiv, əb'd-\ *adj* [*abduction* + *-ive*] *logic* **:** involving abduction

ab·duc·tive·ly *adv* **:** in an abductive manner

¹ab·duc·tor \ab'dəktə(r) *also* -,tȯ(ə)r *or* -,tō(ə)\ *n, pl* **ab·duc·to·res** \,ab,dək'tōr(,)ēz, -'tȯ-\ *or* **abductors** [NL, fr. L *abductus* + *-or*] **:** a muscle that draws a part away from the median line of the body or from the axis of an extremity

²abductor \"\ *n* -s [*abduct* + *-or*] **:** one that abducts ⟨protecting women from ~*s*⟩

abe \ə'bē\ *vi* [prob. fr. *a-* (in *alone*) + *be*] *dial Brit* **:** BE — used only as infinitive ⟨let ~⟩

abeam \ə'-\ *adv* (*or adj*) [¹*a-* + *beam*] **:** on a line forming a right angle with a ship's keel **:** opposite the middle of a ship's side ⟨at noon we came ~ of the island⟩ ⟨the tug lay directly ~ of us⟩

abear \ə'ba(a)(ə)r, -be(ə)r\ *vt* [ME *aberen,* fr. OE *āberan,* fr. *ā-, ar-* (perfective prefix) + *beran* to bear; akin to OE *or-* out of, OHG *ir-, ur-, ur,* ON *ūr-, ör-, ūr,* Goth *us-, us,* and prob. to OE *ūt* out — more at OUT, BEAR] *chiefly dial* **:** ENDURE, ABIDE — usu. used with *can* and negative ⟨I can't ~ a sulk —H.G.Wells⟩

¹abe·ce·dar·i·an \,ābē(,)sē'da(a)rēən\ *n* -s [*abecedary* + *-an,* n. suffix] **1 :** one that is learning the alphabet **:** TYRO **2** *archaic* **:** one that teaches the alphabet and the rudiments of learning **3** *cap* **:** one of a 16th century Anabaptist sect that despised human learning on the ground that the illiterate needed no more than the guidance of the Holy Spirit to interpret Scripture

²abecedarian \¦==(,)=¦===\ *adj* [*abecedary* + *-an,* adj. suffix] **1 :** having reference to the alphabet **:** alphabetically arranged **:** RUDIMENTARY **2 :** of or relating to an abecedarius **:** resembling an abecedarius

abe·ce·dar·i·um \,==(,)='ērēəm\ *n, pl* **abecedar·ia** \-rēə\ [ML] **:** ALPHABET BOOK, PRIMER

abe·ce·dar·i·us \-rēəs\ *n* -ES [NL, fr. LL, adj.] **:** a poem in which the lines or stanzas begin with the letters of the alphabet in regular order (as the 119th Psalm in Hebrew or Chaucer's *A B C*)

¹abe·ce·da·ry \,ā(,)bē'sēdərē\ *n* -ES [ME, fr. ML *abecedarium* alphabet, primer, fr. neut. of LL *abecedarius* of the alphabet, fr. the names of the letters *a* + *b* + *c* + *d* + L *-arius* -ary] **1 :** ABECEDARIUM **2 :** ABECEDARIAN

²abecedary \¦=(,)=¦===\ *adj* **:** ABECEDARIAN

abed \ə'=\ *adv* (*or adj*) [ME *abedde,* fr. earlier *on bedde,* fr. OE, fr. *on* + *bedde,* dat. of *bedd* bed — more at BED] **:** in bed ⟨sick ~⟩ ⟨~ and asleep⟩

abegg's rule \'ä,begz-, -eks-\ *n, cap A* [after Richard *Abegg* †1910 Ger. chemist] **:** a rule in chemistry: the sum of the hydrogen valence and the maximum oxygen valence of a chemical element is often equal to 8 [as of silicon in SiH_4 (−4) and SiO_2 (+4) or of sulfur in H_2S (−2) and H_2SO_4 (+6)]

abeigh \ə'bēk\ *adv* [prob. fr. ¹*a-* + ON *beigr, beygr* fear; akin to ON *beygja* to bend — more at BOW] *Scot* **:** cautiously aloof

abel·am \ə'beləm\ *n, pl* **abelam** *or* **abelams** *usu cap* [native name in New Guinea] **1 :** a Papuan people in the Sepik district, Territory of New Guinea **2 :** a member of the Abelam people

abele \ə'bēl, ə'bāl, 'ābəl\ *n* -s [D *abeel,* fr. MD, fr. ONF *abiel,* irreg. fr. L *albus* white — more at ALB] **:** WHITE POPLAR 1 a

abe·lia \ə'bēlyə, ā'-, -lēə\ *n* [NL, fr. Clarke *Abel* †1826 Eng. botanist + NL *-ia*] **1** *cap* **:** a genus of chiefly eastern Asian shrubs (family Caprifoliaceae) having opposite leaves and white, pink, or reddish flowers in cymes **2** -s **:** a plant of the genus *Abelia*

abel·ite \'ābə,līt\ *n* -s [Sir Frederick *Abel* †1902 Eng. chemist + *-ite*] **:** an explosive consisting essentially of ammonium nitrate and a nitro derivative of some aromatic hydrocarbon

abel·mos·chus \,ābəl'mäskəs, '==,==\ *n, cap* [NL, fr. Ar *abū-l-misk* father (source) of the musk] **:** a genus of tropical coarse herbs (family Malvaceae) having large lobed leaves, a spathelike calyx, and often yellow flowers

abel·mosk \'ābəl,mäsk\ *also* **abel·musk** \-,məsk\ *n* -s [NL *abelmoschus*] **:** a bushy herb (*Hibiscus moschatus*) native to tropical Asia and the East Indies whose musky seeds are used in perfumery and to flavor coffee

abel test \'ābəl-\ *n, usu cap A* [after Sir Frederick *Abel*] **1 :** a test for determining the flash point of a volatile oil by use of a closed cup in which the oil is heated over a fixed flame and by use of a small movable flame that passes at regular intervals of temperature over the surface of the oil **2 :** a test for the stability of smokeless powder and similar explosives in which a ground sample is heated in a test tube with potassium iodide–starch paper, the time required for discoloring the paper being the measure of the stability

abel·tree \'ābəl·,trē\ *n* [part trans., part modif. of D *abeelboom,* fr. *abeel* white poplar + *boom* tree — more at ABELE] **:** WHITE POPLAR 1 a

ab·em·bry·on·ic \¦a,bembrē¦änik\ *adj* [¹*ab-* + *embryonic*] *of an embryonic structure* **:** remote from the embryo proper; *sometimes* **:** VEGETATIVE

abenaki *usu cap, var of* ABNAKI

abend·mu·sik \'äbənt(,)mü,zēk\ *n, pl* **abendmusi·ken** \-kən\ [G, lit., evening music, fr. *abend* evening + *musik* music] **:** an evening performance of music usu. of a religious or semisacred character **:** the music for such a performance

a be·ne pla·ci·to \,ä,benē'pläch ə,tō\ *adv* [It] **:** at pleasure **:** ad libitum — used as a direction in music

aben·len \ə'ben,len\ *n, pl* **abenlen** *or* **abenlens** *usu cap* [native name in the Philippines] **1 :** a predominantly pagan Negrito people in the Zambales mountains of western Luzon, Philippines **2 :** a member of the Abenlen people

¹ab·er·deen \¦abə(r)¦dēn\ *adj, usu cap* [fr. *Aberdeen,* city & county in Scotland] **1 :** of or from the city of Aberdeen, Scotland **:** of the kind or style prevalent in the city of Aberdeen **2 :** ABERDEENSHIRE

²aberdeen \"\ *n* -s *usu cap* **1 :** a fishhook of a wide evenly curved pattern — see FISHHOOK illustration **2** *or* **aberdeen terrier :** SCOTTISH TERRIER

aberdeen an·gus \-dē'naŋgəs, -aiŋ-\ *n* [fr. *Aberdeen & Angus,* counties in Scotland where the breed originated] **1** *usu cap both As* **:** a breed of black hornless beef cattle originating in Scotland **2** *often cap both As* **:** an animal of the Aberdeen Angus breed

ab·er·deen·shire \,==¦=,shi(ə)r, -,shər\ *adj, usu cap* **:** of or from the county of Aberdeen, Scotland **:** of the kind or style prevalent in the county of Aberdeen

ab·er·de·vine *also* **ab·er·da·vine** *or* **ab·er·du·vine** \'abə(r)-də,vīn, ,==='=\ *n* -s [origin unknown] **:** SISKIN 1

¹ab·er·do·ni·an \,abə(r)'dōnyən, -nēən\ *n* -s *cap* [ML *Aberdonia* Aberdeen + E *-an*] **:** a native or resident of Aberdeen, esp. Aberdeen, Scotland

²aberdonian \¦==¦=(=)=\ *adj, usu cap* **:** of or belonging to Aberdeen, Scotland

ab·er·ne·thy biscuit \'abə(r),nēthē-, -ne-\ *n, usu cap A* [prob. after John *Abernethy* †1831 Eng. surgeon who treated maladies by diet] **:** a hard biscuit containing caraway seeds

ab·er·rance \(')a'berən(t)s\ *or* **ab·er·ran·cy** \-sē, -i\ *n, pl* **aberrances** *or* **aberrancies** [obs. E *aberr* to stray (fr. L *aberrare*) + *-ance* or *-ancy*] **:** DEVIATION

¹ab·er·rant \(')a¦berənt\ *adj* [L *aberrant-, aberrans,* pres. part. of *aberrare* to wander from the way, go astray, fr. *ab-* ¹ab- + *errare* to wander, go astray, err — more at ERR] **1 :** straying from the right or normal way **:** deviating from truth, rectitude, propriety **2 :** deviating from the usual or natural type **:** EXCEPTIONAL, ABNORMAL

²aberrant \"\ *n* -s **1 :** an aberrant natural group, individual, or structure; *esp* **:** an individual with a chromosome number atypical for its species **2 :** a person whose behavior departs substantially from the standards for behavior in his group **:** DEVIANT, DEVIATE

ab·er·rant·ly *adv* **:** in an aberrant manner

ab·er·ra·tion \,abə'rāshən\ *n* -s [L *aberratus* (past part. of *aberrare*) + E *-ion*] **1 :** act of wandering away or of going astray **:** deviation from truth or a moral standard, from the natural state, or from a normal type ⟨~*s* of character⟩ ⟨~*s* of structure⟩ **2 :** failure of a mirror, refracting surface, or lens to produce exact point-to-point correspondence between an object and its image **3 :** unsoundness of the mind; *esp* **:** unsoundness insufficient to constitute insanity **4 :** a small periodic change of apparent position in the stars and other heavenly bodies due to the combined effect of the motion of light and the motion of the observer **5 :** an aberrant organ or individual **:** SPORT 6

ab·er·ra·tion·al \¦==¦=shən°l, -shnəl\ *adj* **:** characterized by aberration

ab·er·ra·tive \'==,rād·iv\ *adj* [*aberration* + *-ive*] **:** having or showing a tendency to aberration

abert's towhee \'ābə(r)ts-\ *also* **abert's finch** *or* **abert's pipilo** *n, usu cap A* [after J. W. *Abert* †1897 Am. soldier and scientist] **:** a rather large distinctly brown towhee (*Pipilo aberti*) of southwestern No. America

ab·es·sive \(')a¦besiv\ *adj* [L *abesse* to be absent + E *-ive* — more at ABSENT] *of a grammatical case* **:** denoting absence or lack

abet \ə'bet *also* a'-; *usu* -ed· + V\ *vt* **abetted; abetted; abetting; abets** [ME *abetten,* fr. MF *abeter,* fr. *a-* (fr. L *ad-*) + *beter* to bait, of Gmc origin; akin to OHG *beizen* to bait — more at BAIT] **1 :** to incite, encourage, instigate, or countenance — now usu. used disparagingly ⟨~ the commission of a crime⟩ **2 :** to assist or support in the achievement of a purpose ⟨the singer was ably *abetted* by her skillful accompanist⟩ **syn** see INCITE

abet·ment \-tmənt\ *n* -s [ME *abetement,* fr. AF, fr. OF *abeter* + *-ment*] **:** act of abetting ⟨~ of crime⟩

abet·tor *or* **abet·ter** \-ed·ə(r), -etə-\ *n* -s [*abettor* fr. AF *abettour,* fr. OF *abeter* + *-our* -or; *abetter* fr. *abet* + *-er*] **:** one that abets

ab ex·tra \(')a'bekstrə\ *adv* [LL] **:** from without

abey·ance \ə'bāən(t)s\ *n* -s [MF *abeance* desire, expectation, fr. *abaer, abair* to desire (fr. *a-* — fr. L *ad-* — + *baer, bair* to yawn, gape, stare, desire, fr. ML *batare* to yawn, perh. of imit. origin) + *-ance*] **1 :** a lapse in succession during which there is no person in existence in whom a freehold estate, dignity, or title is vested ⟨a peerage revived after an ~ of many years⟩ — usu. used with *in* ⟨the estate was in ~⟩ **2 :** temporary inactivity or suppression **:** cessation or suspension (as of a customary practice) ⟨statutes fallen into ~⟩ ⟨a rule in ~ since 1935⟩ — used chiefly in the phrases *in abeyance* or *into abeyance*

abey·an·cy \-sē, -i\ *n* -ES **:** ABEYANCE

abey·ant \-ənt\ *adj* [back-formation fr. *abeyance*] **:** in abeyance **syn** see LATENT

ab·far·ad \(')ab'fa,rad, -rəd\ *n* [ISV ²*ab-* + *farad*] **:** a cgs electromagnetic unit of capacitance equal to one billion farads that measures the capacitance of a condenser that when charged to a potential difference of one abvolt has a charge of one abcoulomb — compare AB- table

ab·ge·sang \'äpgə,zäŋ\ *n* -s *usu cap* [G, fr. *ab-* down, from + *gesang* song] **:** EPISTROPHE; *specif* **:** the concluding section of the medieval bar

ab·hen·ry \(')ab'henrē\ *n* [ISV ²*ab-* + *henry*] **:** a cgs electromagnetic unit of inductance equal to one billionth of a henry that measures the self-inductance of a circuit or the mutual inductance of two circuits in which the variation of current at the rate of one abampere per second results in an induced electromotive force of one abvolt — compare AB- table

abhi·na·ya \ə'binəyə\ *n* -s [Skt, acting, dramatic action] **:** the expressive use of face or hands characteristic of the kathakali dance style of India

abhi·se·ka \,əbē'shäkə\ *n* -s [Skt *abhiṣeka,* fr. *abhiṣecate* he sprinkles, fr. *abhi* to, toward + *secate* he pours — more at BY, SACK (wine)] *India* **:** LUSTRATION; *also* **:** coronation of a king

abhominable *adj* [alter. (influenced by L *ab homine* from the man, its supposed etymology) of *abominable*] *obs* **:** ABOMINABLE

ab·hor \əb'hȯ(ə)r, ab-, -ȯ(ə)\ *vt* **abhorred; abhorred; abhorring; abhors** [ME *abhorren,* fr. L *abhorrēre,* fr. *ab-* ¹ab- + *horrēre* to bristle, shiver, shudder — more at HORROR] **1 :** to regard with repugnance **:** detest extremely **:** LOATHE ⟨they ~ the thought of going to war⟩ **2** *obs* **:** to fill with horror or disgust ⟨mine own clothes shall ~ me — Job 9:31 (AV)⟩ **3 :** to turn aside or keep away from esp. in scorn **:** AVOID, REJECT ⟨the university should ~ mediocrity —Walter Moberly⟩ **syn** see HATE

ab·hor·rence \-hȯrən(t)s, -här-\ *n* -s **1 :** the act or state of abhorring **:** the feeling of one who abhors **:** LOATHING ⟨the good man has an ~ of evil —M.H.Weseen⟩ **2 :** one that is abhorred **:** object of loathing ⟨disguise of every sort is my ~ —Jane Austen⟩

abhorrency *n* -ES *obs* **:** ABHORRENCE

ab·hor·rent \-hȯrənt, -här-\ *adj* [L *abhorrent-, abhorrens,* pres. part. of *abhorrēre*] **1 a** *archaic* **:** strongly opposed **:** at variance — used with *from* ⟨a man most ~ from violence⟩ **b :** feeling or showing abhorrence **:** LOATHING, ABHORRING — used with *of* ⟨~ of compromises⟩ **2 :** not in accord **:** not agreeable **:** CONFLICTING, DISCORDANT — used with *to* ⟨a strange notion ~ to their scheme of things⟩ **3 :** DETESTABLE, REPUGNANT ⟨a repugnant, ~, and outrageous procedure for hiring government servants —Wayne Morse⟩ **syn** see HATEFUL

ab·hor·rent·ly *adv* **:** in an abhorrent manner

ab·hor·rer \-hȯrə(r)\ *n* -s *sometimes cap* **:** one of the signers of an address to Charles II of England in 1679 in which those who had petitioned for the reconvening of Parliament were abhorred and condemned

abib \ä'vēv\ *n* -s *usu cap* [Heb *ābhībh,* lit., ear of grain] **:** the 1st month of the ancient Hebrew calendar coming in the spring and corresponding to Nisan — see MONTH table

abid·ance \ə'bīd°n(t)s\ *n* -s **1 :** a state of abiding or staying **:** CONTINUANCE **2 :** COMPLIANCE ⟨~ by rules⟩

abide \ə'bīd\ *vb* **abode** \-bōd\ *or* **abid·ed** \-bīdəd\ **abode** *or* **abided** *also* **abid·den** \-bid°n\ **abiding; abides** [ME *abiden,* fr. OE *ābīdan,* fr. *ā-* (perfective prefix) + *bīdan* to bide, wait — more at ABEAR, BIDE] *vt* **1** *archaic* **a :** to wait for **:** await expectantly **:** watch for **:** EXPECT ⟨I will ~ the coming of my lord —Alfred Tennyson⟩ **b :** to stand ready for **:** AWAIT — used of things awaiting persons ⟨the fate which ~*s* him⟩ **2 a** *obs* **:** to stand up under **:** endure or undergo (a hard trial or task) ⟨material able to ~ hard use⟩ **b :** to endure without yielding **:** await defiantly **:** WITHSTAND, FACE ⟨~ the onrush of the enemy⟩ ⟨~ one's doom⟩ **c :** to endure or bear patiently **:** TOLERATE, STAND — used in negative construction ⟨cannot ~ such people⟩ ⟨can't ~ the taste of caraway⟩ sometimes with *to* and the infinitive ⟨cannot ~ to stay in one position for long —T.B.Costain⟩ **3 :** to await submissively **:** accept without question or objection ⟨unwilling to ~ the decision of the court⟩ **:** submit to ⟨works securely established among the classics have had to ~ the question of a new criticism⟩ **4** [by folk etymology fr. *aby*] **:** to atone for **:** pay for **:** suffer for ⟨dearly I ~ that boast so vain —John Milton⟩ **~ *vi*** **1 :** to wait in expectation or before proceeding **:** TARRY, DELAY, STOP ⟨the sawyer did not participate . . . but *abided* at a little distance —Charles Dickens⟩ ⟨we shall ~ till the battle is won —Rudyard Kipling⟩ **2 a :** to be or remain stable or fixed in some state or constant in some relationship **:** CONTINUE ⟨let every man ~ in the same calling wherein he was called — 1 Cor 7:20 (AV)⟩ ⟨a love that ~*s* with him all his days⟩ **b :** to continue to be **:** LAST, ENDURE ⟨though many features were *abiding,* the changes were much felt⟩ **3 :** to be left **:** REMAIN ⟨tho' much is taken, much ~*s* —Alfred Tennyson⟩ **4 :** to continue in a place **:** have one's abode **:** DWELL, SOJOURN, STAY ⟨I repented my rashness in venturing to ~ in town —Daniel Defoe⟩ **syn** see BEAR, CONTINUE, STAY — **abide by :** to act or behave in accordance with or obedience to (as a rule or promise) ⟨accept a limitation and *abide by* it⟩ **:** conform to **:** acquiesce in ⟨*abide by* a decision⟩

abid·ing \ə'bīdiŋ, -ēŋ\ *adj* [ME, fr. pres. part. of *abiden* to abide] **:** continuing or persisting in the same state without changing or diminishing **:** CONTINUING, ENDURING ⟨the theater has ~ value and importance⟩ **:** great or lasting ⟨music is his ~ passion⟩ — **abid·ing·ly** *adv*

ab·i·djan \¦abə¦jän\ *adj, usu cap* [fr. *Abidjan,* Ivory Coast] **:** of or relating to Abidjan, capital of the Ivory Coast **:** of the kind or style prevalent in Abidjan

ab·i·ence \'abēən(t)s\ *n* -s *psychol* **:** tendency to withdraw from a stimulus object or situation — opposed to *adience*

ab·i·ent \'abēənt\ *adj* [L *abient-, abiens,* pres. part. of *abire* to go away, fr. *ab-* ¹ab- + *-ire* to go — more at ISSUE] *psychol* **:** characterized by avoidance or withdrawal ⟨an ~ response⟩ — opposed to *adient*

abi·es \'ābē,ēz, 'ab-\ *n* [NL, fr. L, silver fir] **1** *cap* **:** a genus of north temperate evergreen trees which are the true firs (family Pinaceae) distinguished from spruces by flattish leaves, smooth circular leaf scars, and erect cones — see BALSAM FIR, FIR **2** *pl* **abies :** a tree of the genus *Abies*

ab·i·e·tate \'abēə,tāt\ *n* -s [ISV *abiet-* (fr. *abietic acid*) + *-ate*] **1 :** a salt or ester of abietic acid **2 :** RESINATE — used chiefly commercially

ab·i·e·tene \-,tēn\ *n* -s [*abietic* + *-ene*] **:** the hydrocarbon mixture, chiefly $C_{19}H_{30}$ with two double bonds in the molecule, that results from heating resin acids

ab·i·et·ic acid \¦abē¦ed·ik-\ *n* [ISV *abiet-,* (fr. L *abiet-, abies* silver fir) + *-ic*] **:** a colorless crystalline tricyclic acid $C_{19}H_{29}COOH$ with two double bonds that constitutes the major component of rosin, that is formed from certain other resin acids by heat and acid treatment, and that is used chiefly in making esters for plasticizers

ab·i·e·tin·e·ae \,abēə'tinē,ē\ *n pl, cap* [NL, fr. *Abiet-, Abies,* type genus + *-ineae*] **:** a tribe of the family Pinaceae including the pines, spruces, hemlocks, and firs — **ab·i·e·tin·e·ous** \¦==¦=¦nēəs\ *adj*

ab·i·gail \'abə,gāl\ *n* -s *sometimes cap* [after *Abigail,* serving woman in the play *The Scornful Lady,* by Francis Beaumont †1616 and John Fletcher †1625 English dramatists] **:** a lady's waiting maid

ab·i·lene \'abə,lēn\ *adj, usu cap* [fr. *Abilene,* Tex., near where the artifacts were discovered] **:** of or belonging to a prehistoric culture of central Texas characterized by long slender roughly flaked weapon points and by scrapers and oval grinding stones

abiliment *obs var of* HABILIMENT

abil·i·ty \ə'biləd·ē, -ətē, -i\ *n* -ES [ME *abilite* suitability, aptitude, ability, fr. MF *habilité,* fr. L *habilitat-, habilitas* aptness, ability, fr. *habilis* fit, apt, skillful + *-itat-, -itas* -ity — more at ABLE] **1 :** the quality or state of being able **:** physical, mental, or legal power to perform **:** competence in doing **:** SKILL ⟨a writer's ~ to interest readers⟩ **2 :** natural talent or acquired proficiency esp. in a particular work or activity **:** APTITUDE — usu. used in pl. ⟨children whose *abilities* warrant higher education⟩

-ability *also* **-ibility** \"\ *n suffix* -ES [ME *-ablete, -abilite, -iblete, -ibilite,* fr. MF *-ableté, -abilité, -ibleté, -ibilité,* fr. L *-abilitas, -ibilitas,* fr. *-abilis, -ibilis* + *-tas* -TY] **:** -ABLENESS ⟨avail*ability*⟩ ⟨*risibility*⟩

abi·lla \ə'bē(y)ə\ *n* -s [AmerSp] **:** the oily seed of a So. American plant (*Fevillea trilobata*) that is used in making candles

abi·lo \'abə,lō\ *or* **abi·lao** \-,laů\ *n* -s [Tag] **:** BOGO

ab in·con·ve·ni·en·ti \¦a,binkən,vēnē'entē, -n,tī\ *adv* [NL] **:** from inconvenience or hardship — referring to a rule in law that an argument from inconvenience has great weight

ab in·i·tio \,abə'nishē,ō, -nid·ē,ō\ *adv* [L] **:** from the beginning **:** from the instant of the act ⟨an act outside one's legal competence is void *ab initio*⟩ **:** at the outset (of an inquiry or investigation) ⟨assumes *ab initio* that the idea is worthless⟩

ab in·tra \a'bin·trə\ *adv* [NL] **:** from within

abio- *comb form* [²*a-* + *bio-*] **:** whatever is lifeless ⟨*abiogenesis*⟩

abio·gen·e·sis \¦ā,bīō'jenəsəs\ *n, pl* **abiogene·ses** \-ə,sēz\ [NL, fr. *abio-* + *genesis*] **:** the origination of living organisms from lifeless matter — called also *spontaneous generation*

abio·ge·net·ic \¦ā,bīōjə¦ned·ik\ *adj* [fr. NL *abiogenesis,* after E *genesis: genetic*] **:** of or relating to abiogenesis **:** originating by abiogenesis — **abio·ge·net·i·cal·ly** \'ək(ə)lē\ *adv*

abi·og·e·nist \¦ā,bī'äjənəst\ *n* -s [*abiogenesis* + *-ist*] **:** one who believes that life can be produced independently of antecedent life

abi·ot·ic \¦ā,bī'äd·ik\ *adj* [²*a-* + *biotic*] **1 :** characterized by the absence of life **2 :** ANTIBIOTIC 1

abio·troph·ic \¦ā,bīō¦träfik, -ōf-\ *adj* **:** relating to or involving abiotrophy ⟨the ~ nature of certain diseases⟩

abi·ot·ro·phy \¦ā,bī'ä·trəfē\ *n* -ES [ISV *abio-* + *-trophy*] **:** degeneration or loss of function or vitality in an organism or in cells or tissues not due to any apparent injury

abi·pón \ˈabə,pän, ,==ˈ=\ n, pl **abi·po·nes** \,abəˈpōnēz\ or **abipón** \like sing\ usu cap [Sp abipón, of AmerInd origin] **1 a :** an extinct people of Paraguay and Argentina **b :** a member of such people **2 :** the Guaicuruan language of the Abipones

abir \əˈbi(ə)r\ n -s [Hindi abīr] India **:** a perfumed red powder used at the Holi festival

ab·i·tibi \,abəˈtibē\ n, pl **abitibi** or **abitibis** usu cap [of Algonquian origin; akin to Fox or Ojibwa abiʹta-bi-g, lit., halfway across water, fr. abiʹta halfway + bi water + -g (locative suffix)] **1 :** an Algonkian people of the region about Lake Abitibi, Ontario **2 :** a member of the Abitibi people — compare ALGONKIAN

abi·u·ret \(ˈ)āˌbīyə,ret\ adj [²a- + biuret] **:** not giving the biuret reaction

¹**ab·ject** \ˈab,jekt also, esp nonattrib, =ˈ=\ adj [ME, fr. L abjectus, fr. past part. of abicere to cast off, fr. ab- ¹ab- + -icere (fr. jacere to throw) — more at JET (to spout)] **1 :** sunk to or existing in a low state or condition **2 a :** cast down in spirit **:** without spirit or pride **:** SERVILE ⟨~ knuckling down to the demands of . . . pressure groups —Elmer Rice⟩ **b :** unrelieved by any sign of independence, courage, or originality ⟨~ imitation of foreign ideas⟩ **:** showing utter resignation **:** HOPELESS, HELPLESS ⟨~ surrender⟩ ⟨~ frustration⟩ — **ab·ject·ness** n -ES

²**abject** vt -ED/-ING/-S [ME abjecten, fr. abject, adj.] **1** obs **:** to cast off or out **:** REJECT **2** obs **:** to cast down **:** ABASE

³**ab·ject** \ˈab,jekt\ n -s [¹abject] **:** one cast off **:** OUTCAST

ab·jec·tion \abˈjekshən\ n -s [ME abjeccioun, fr. MF or LL; MF abjection, fr. LL abjection-, abjectio, fr. L abjectus cast down + -ion-, -io -ion — more at ABJECT] **1 :** a low or downcast state **:** DEGRADATION, HUMILIATION **2 :** the act of making abject: as **a :** HUMBLING ⟨I protest against this vile ~ of youth to age —G.B.Shaw⟩ **b :** a casting out or off **:** REJECTION ⟨the ~ of Satan from heaven⟩ **3 :** the discharge or casting (as of the spores of certain fungi) — compare ABSTRICTION

ab·ject·ive \(ˈ)abˌjektiv\ adj [²abject + -ive] **:** tending to make abject

ab·ject·ly \(ˈ)abˌjek(t)lē, -li\ adv [ME, fr. ¹abject + -ly] **:** in an abject manner

ab·joint \(ˈ)abˌjȯint\ vb [¹ab- + joint] vt **:** to form by cutting off (as a protuberance from a mother cell) ~ vi **:** to separate by means of a cross wall (as of certain cells and of fungus spores cut off from hyphal tips)

ab·judge \(ˈ)abˌjəj\ vt -ED/-ING/-S [¹ab- + judge; part trans. of L abjudicare] **:** to take away by judicial decision — opposed to adjudge (sense 3)

ab·junc·tion \(ˈ)abˌjəŋ(k)shən\ n -s [¹ab- + junction] bot **:** ABSTRICTION

ab·ju·ra·tion \,abjəˈrāshən\ n -s [ME abjuracioun, fr. ML abjuration-, abjuratio, fr. L abjuratus (past part. of abjurare) + -ion-, -io -ion] **1 :** the act of abjuring **2 :** an oath taken on the occasion of abjuring

ab·jure \abˈju̇(ə)r, əb-, -u̇ə\ vt -ED/-ING/-S [ME abjuren, fr. MF or L; MF abjurer, fr. L abjurare, fr. ab- ¹ab- + jurare to swear — more at JURY] **1 :** to disclaim formally or renounce upon oath ⟨solemnly ~s his allegiance to his former country⟩ **:** give up **:** REJECT ⟨~ his old beliefs⟩ **2 :** to take oath to leave (as a realm or country) ⟨the criminal was allowed to claim immunity by abjuring the realm⟩ **3 :** to abstain from **:** AVOID ⟨~ extravagant claims for a product⟩

syn RENOUNCE, FORSWEAR, RECANT, RETRACT: ABJURE indicates a firm, final rejecting or abandoning made with measured conviction and, often, signalized by oath or other formality ⟨the friar concluded with beseeching the Peruvian monarch to receive him kindly, to abjure the errors of his own faith, and embrace that of the Christians now proffered to him —W.H. Prescott⟩ ⟨Galileo was summoned before the Inquisition at Rome, and there he was made to abjure the Copernican theory —S.F.Mason⟩ RENOUNCE indicates a giving up or casting off of something previously believed, practiced, or adhered to, with some spoken or tacit indication of the change of position ⟨abandoning wife and children, home and business, and renouncing normal morality and humanity —G.B.Shaw⟩ ⟨he was later to renounce impressionism, and to quarrel with most of the most impressionists —Herbert Read⟩ ⟨they made a monk of me; I did renounce the world, its pride and greed —Robert Browning⟩ FORSWEAR may indicate resolute rejection; it may apply to dishonorable or ill-advised rejection of that to which one should adhere ⟨Mr. Dulles grants by implication that the Peking regime is the government of China. He insists that it forswear the use of force in advancing its ambitions —New Republic⟩ ⟨support him in an apostasy, in a forswearing of honor and principle, for personal power —J.C.Fitzpatrick⟩ RECANT is likely to indicate rejection of a previously adhered-to belief or position accompanied by admission of error and acceptance of a sanctioned belief ⟨Shostakovich, as our newspapers have told us, has suffered from official criticism and been forced to recant and rewrite —W.C.Huntington⟩ ⟨if Christians recanted they were to be spared, but if they persisted in their faith they were to be executed —K.S.Latourette⟩ RETRACT indicates a withdrawing or calling back, often of a statement or implication to someone's discredit ⟨give the present writer an opportunity of retracting criticism from his own pen which he now feels to have been unjust —Richard Garnett⟩ ⟨they . . . retract what they have said, and say publicly that they were mistaken —Rose Macaulay⟩

ab·kar \ˈäb,kär\ n -s [Per ābkār, fr. āb water, liquid (fr. OPer āpi-) + -kār doer (fr. MPer); akin to Av āfsh (acc. sing. āpəm) water, Skt ap-, Lith ùpė, OPruss ape river, Gk Apia Peloponnesus and to Skt kāra doing — more at KARMA] India **:** a wine seller **:** DISTILLER; also **:** one whose trade is subject to abkari tax

ab·ka·ri also **ab·ka·ry** \äbˈkärē\ n -s [Per ābkārī, fr. ābkār] **1** India **:** manufacture or sale of intoxicating liquors or drugs **2** India **:** an excise or internal revenue tax on the manufacture or sale of intoxicating liquors or drugs

ab·khas \abˈkäs\ or **ab·kha·sian** \-ˈkāzhən,-ˈkāzēən\ n, pl **abkhas** or **abkhasians** usu cap [Abkhas fr. Russ; Abkhasian fr. Russ Abkhas + E -ian] **1 a :** a Georgian people living on the eastern shore of the Black sea **b :** a member of this people **2 :** the North Caucasic language of the Abkhas people

abl abbr ablative

ablach \ˈablək, ˈä-\ n -s [ScGael, mangled carcass, brat; akin to IrGael, carcass, corpse, carrion] Scot **:** an insignificant person

ab·lac·ta·tion \,a,blakˈtāshən\ n [ME ablactacioun, fr. LL ablactation-, ablactatio (past part. of ablactare to wean, fr. L ab- ¹ab- + lact-, lac milk) + -ion-, -io -ion — more at GALAXY] **:** the act of weaning

ablare \əˈ-\ adj [¹a- + blare, v.] **:** BLARING ⟨with trumpets ~⟩

ablas·te·mic \ˌā,blaˈstēmik, -em-\ adj [²a- + blastemic] **:** not germinal **:** incapable of blastema formation

ablas·tin \əˈblastən, (ˈ)āˈ- \n -s [Gk ablastos not germinating + E- in] **:** a substance in the blood of infected animals that inhibits the reproduction of the infecting organism

ablas·tous \(ˈ)āˌblastəs\ adj [Gk ablastos] **:** having no germ or bud

ab·late \(ˈ)aˌblāt\ vb -ED/-ING/-S [L ablatus (suppletive past part. of auferre to remove), fr. ab- ¹ab- + latus, suppletive past part. of ferre to bear — more at BEAR, TOLERATE] vt **:** to carry away **:** remove by cutting or by erosion, melting, or evaporation ~ vi **:** to undergo ablation **:** become melted or vaporized and removed at a very high temperature

ab·la·tion \aˈblāshən\ n -s [MF & LL; MF, fr. LL ablation-, ablatio, fr. L ablatus + -ion-, -io -ion] **1 :** REMOVAL **2 :** removal of an organ or part by surgery ⟨~ of the appendix⟩ or of an activity by other means ⟨~ of ovarian function by radiation⟩ **3 a :** decrease in volume of ice, névé, or snow in or on a glacier primarily as a result of melting and evaporation — compare ALIMENTATION **b :** lowering of a land surface by wind erosion or weathering agents ⟨the warming of the polar seas leads to ~ of the ice caps⟩ **4 :** the process of ablating

ab·la·ti·val \ˌabləˌtīvəl\ adj [ablative + -al] **:** connected with the ablative case or any of the relations frequently expressed by it **:** of or belonging to the ablative case

¹**ab·la·tive** \ˈablәd·iv, -ətiv\ adj [ME, fr. MF or L; MF ablatif, fr. L ablativus, fr. ablatus + -ivus -ive] **1** of a grammatical case **:** expressing typically the relations of separation and source (as L metu in liberari metu "to be freed from fear"; L ea familia in ea familia ortus "descended from that family") and also frequently esp. in Latin such relations as cause (as L gaudio in exsilire gaudio "to jump for joy"), instrument (as L pugnis in certare pugnis "to fight with fists"), time (as L constituta die "on the appointed day"), place (as L media urbe "in the middle of the city"), accordance (as L meo modo "in my fashion"), specification (as L altero pede in claudus altero pede "lame in one foot"), difference by comparison (as L Ennio in veracior Ennio "more truthful than Ennius"), difference in measure (as L annis in aliquot ante annis "several years before"), or price (as L pecunia in regna addicere pecunia "to sell kingdoms for money") — used esp. in the grammar of Latin, Sanskrit, Hungarian, and Finnish **2 :** of or belonging to the ablative case ⟨an ~ suffix⟩

²**ablative** \"\ n -s **:** the ablative case or a form in it

³**ab·la·tive** \", (ˈ)aˌblā-\ adj [ablate + -ive] **:** tending to ablate ⟨~ material on a rocket nose cone⟩

ablative absolute n **:** a construction in Latin in which a noun or pronoun and its adjunct both in the ablative case form together an adverbial phrase expressing generally the time, cause, or an attendant circumstance of an action (as acceptis litteris in Caesar, acceptis litteris, nuntium mittit "the letter having been received, Caesar sends a messenger")

ab·laut \ˈä,plau̇t, ˈa,bl-\ n -s [G, fr. ab off, away from, down from (fr. OHG aba) + laut sound, fr. MHG lūt; akin to OE hlūd loud — more at OF, LOUD] **:** a systematic variation of vowels in the same root or affix or in related roots or affixes in the Indo-European languages usu. paralleled by differences in use or meaning (as sing, sang, sung, song; Gk petomai "I fly", potē "flight", ptesthai "to fly", pōtaomai "I fly around"; -es- in assumed IE genesa, L genera "kinds", -os in assumed IE genos, L genus "kind") **:** a similar variation in any language or language family — called also apophony, gradation

ablaze \əˈ-\ adj [¹a- + blaze, v.] **1 :** on fire ⟨forests are sometimes set ~ by lightning —John Tyndall⟩ **2 :** radiant with light or bright color ⟨~ with lighted Christmas trees⟩ **3 :** glowing or inflamed esp. with emotion ⟨his face all ~ with excitement —Bram Stoker⟩

¹**able** \ˈābəl\ adj **abler** \-b(ə)lə(r)\ **ablest** \-b(ə)ləst\ [ME, fr. MF, fr. L habilis easily managed, apt, skillful, fr. habēre to have, hold — more at HABIT] **1 a :** possessed of needed powers (as intelligence or strength) or of needed resources (as means or influence) to accomplish an objective ⟨~ to solve a problem⟩ ⟨~ to buy a house⟩ **b :** designed, constructed, or naturally endowed with the power to perform a task or achieve an end ⟨machines ~ to lift 10 tons⟩ ⟨owls ~ to see in the dark⟩ **c :** having freedom from restriction or obligation or from conditions preventing an action ⟨American women are ~ to vote⟩ ⟨we were ~ to meet her at noon⟩ **d :** constituted or situated so as to be susceptible or readily subjected to some action or treatment ⟨a shoe ~ to be repaired⟩ ⟨a hill ~ to be climbed⟩ **2 a** obs **:** having physical strength **:** ROBUST **b** now dial **:** WELL-TO-DO, RICH **3** dial **:** fit to cope with — usu. used with for ⟨~ for four helpings of dessert⟩ **4 :** marked by intelligence, knowledge, skill, or competence ⟨an ~ and rapacious tyrant —H.O.Taylor⟩ ⟨an ~, moving, and fascinating portrait —B.D.Wolfe⟩ **5 :** legally qualified **:** possessed of legal competence ⟨~ to inherit property⟩

syn CAPABLE, COMPETENT, QUALIFIED: placed after the noun modified, ABLE is likely to indicate only the power, strength, skill, or resources needed for an indicated action ⟨some day I would be like one of themselves, able to kill animals and catch fish —W.H.Hudson⟩ Placed before the noun modified, it may suggest a combination of superior qualities, esp. as demonstrated in practice ⟨Cleveland was an able leader, honest, courageous . . . a fine exponent of Manchester liberalism —Allan Nevins & H.S.Commager⟩ ⟨a priest . . . an able one, by all means, not only devoted, but resourceful and intelligent —Willa Cather⟩ CAPABLE is commonly interchangeable with ABLE in this sense. It is more likely than ABLE to be used in situations involving possibilities and potentialities ⟨democracy alone has constructed an unlimited civilization capable of infinite progress —F.D.Roosevelt⟩ ⟨a being . . . more capable of feeling than even the most gifted of common men —Aldous Huxley⟩ Often it suggests powers of adjustment, adaptability, or resourcefulness adequate for treating satisfactorily whatever matter is under consideration ⟨it was impossible even to recall the house of mourning without a grateful memory of Louisa's capable dealing with funerals —Ellen Glasgow⟩ ⟨only people who valued machines more than men were capable under these conditions of governing men to their profit and advantage —Lewis Mumford⟩ COMPETENT suggests complete fitness for adequate performance ⟨Tolstoy and Turgenev were quite competent in Russian, though they learned English, French, and German in infancy —Bertrand Russell⟩ Sometimes the word connotes special professional or technical training ⟨the associated workers must be competent scholars in language and palaeography —F.N.Robinson⟩ Sometimes COMPETENT is used to suggest adequacy but to deny outstanding superiority and hence may be derogatory ⟨the difference between a great dancer and a merely competent dancer is in the vital flame, that impersonal and . . . inhuman force which transpires between each of the great dancer's movements —T.S.Eliot⟩ ⟨they were all competent practical mechanics, but Gay was an inspired mechanic —John Steinbeck⟩ QUALIFIED suggests either adequate experience and knowledge, satisfactory special training, or formal certification as being especially trained ⟨Poky . . . was . . . my guide . . . no mortal could be better qualified; his native country was not large, and he knew every inch of it —Herman Melville⟩ ⟨being a qualified doctor, she knew all the facts of life —Upton Sinclair⟩

²**able** vt -ED/-ING/-S [ME ablen, fr. able, adj.] **1** obs **:** to make capable **:** ENABLE, STRENGTHEN **2** obs **:** to vouch for

³**able** \ˈābəl\ usu cap — a communications code word for the letter a

-able also **-ible** \əbəl\ adj suffix, see Explan Notes [ME, fr. OF, fr. L -abilis, -ibilis, fr. -a-, -i- (thematic vowels of various conjugations of verbs) + -bilis capable or worthy of (being acted upon)] **1 :** capable of, fit for, or worthy of (being so acted upon or toward) — chiefly in adjectives derived from verbs ⟨breakable⟩ ⟨connectible⟩ ⟨eatable⟩ ⟨lovable⟩ **2 :** tending to, given to, favoring, causing, able to, or liable to ⟨agreeable⟩ ⟨changeable⟩ ⟨knowledgeable⟩ ⟨peaceable⟩ ⟨perishable⟩ — **-a·ble·ness** \əbəlnəs\ n suffix -ES — **-a·bly** also **-i·bly** \əblē, -li\ adv suffix

able-bod·ied \ˈ==ˌ==\ adj **:** having a sound body **:** not incapacitated for work or service **:** HEALTHY, ROBUST

able-bodied seaman or **able seaman** n **:** an experienced deck-department seaman qualified to perform routine duties at sea and rated in the British navy and on British and American commercial ships between ordinary seaman and leading seaman or boatswain's mate — abbr. A.B.

ableeze \əˈblēz\ adj [¹a- + bleeze (v.)] Scot **:** ABLAZE

ab·le·gate \ˈabləgət, -lē-, -,gāt\ n -s [F ablégat, fr. L ablegatus, past part. of ablegare to send away, fr. ab- ¹ab + legare to send on a commission, dispatch — more at LEGATE] **:** a papal envoy on a special mission (as the conveying of the insignia of office to a newly named cardinal)

aleph·a·rus \āˈblefərəs\ n, cap [NL, irreg. fr. ²a- + Gk blepharon eyelid] **:** a genus of Old World scincoid lizards with the lower eyelid reduced to a transparent cover fused to the upper lid

abler comparative of ABLE

ablest superlative of ABLE

ablins \ˈāblənz\ var of AIBLINS

abloom \əˈ-\ adj [¹a- + bloom, v.] **:** BLOOMING

¹**ablow** \əˈ-\ adj [¹a- + blow, v.] **:** BLOWING

²**ablow** \əˈblō\ prep [a- (as in above) + blow, alter. of below] Scot **:** BELOW

ablush \əˈ-\ adj [¹a- + blush, v.] **:** BLUSHING

ab·lu·tion \əˈblüshən, aˈb-\ n -s [ME, fr. MF or L; MF ablution, fr. L ablution-, ablutio, fr. ablutus (past part. of abluere to wash away, fr. ab- ¹ab- + -luere, fr. lavere to wash) + -ion-, -io -ion — more at LYE] **1 a** obs **:** the cleansing of bodies by distillation **b :** the washing of one's body or part of it as a religious rite ⟨historically, the practice of ~s is common to many people —W.B.Duckat⟩ **c :** the ceremonial washing of the sacred vessels (as the chalice) and of the priest's thumb and forefinger after communion **d :** the washing of one's body or part of it ⟨he was finished with his ~s now —Douglas Woolf⟩ **2 :** the portion of wine or of water used in the ceremonial washing of the sacred vessels after communion **3 ablutions** pl, Brit **:** the building housing bathing and toilet facilities on a military base — **ab·lu·tion·ary** \-ə,nerē\ adj

ably \ˈāb(ə)lē, -li\ adv [ME, fr. able + -ly] **:** in an able manner **:** with ability

ab·mi·gra·tion \ˌab,mīˈgrāshən\ n -s [¹ab- + migration] **:** northward summer migration of birds that have not made a corresponding southward journey in the previous autumn

abn abbr airborne

ab·na·ki \abˈnäkē\ also **ab·e·na·ki** \,abəˈnäkē\ or **wa·ba·na·ki** \,wäbəˈn-\ n, pl **abnaki** or **abnakis** usu cap [of Algonquian origin; akin to Fox and Kickapoo Wâpanaʹkia, lit., eastern land, fr. wâpan light, dawn, east + aʹkia land] **1 a :** an Indian people of Maine and southern Quebec **b :** a member of such people **2 :** an Algonquian language of the Abnaki and Penobscot peoples

ab·ne·gate \ˈabnē,gāt, -ə,g-\ vt -ED/-ING/-S [back-formation fr. abnegation] **:** to surrender or relinquish (as a right, belief, or idea) ⟨he asked the assembly to ~ its financial powers⟩ ⟨~ high hope for the sake of barren convenience —A.T. Quiller-Couch⟩ **:** deny or renounce (as desire or self-interest) ⟨communities dedicated to the living of a humble and self-abnegating life —Lewis Mumford⟩ **syn** see FORGO

ab·ne·ga·tion \ˌab=ˈgāshən\ n -s [LL abnegation-, abnegatio, fr. L abnegatus (past part. of abnegare to refute, deny, fr. ab- ¹ab- + negare to say no, deny) + -ion-, -io -ion — more at NEGATION] **:** renunciation or denial ⟨prepared to move in the direction of early ~ of federal responsibility —D'Arcy McNickle⟩ **:** restraint or denial of desire or self-interest ⟨cold lines, but penned by what heartbroken ~ —George Meredith⟩ **:** SELF-DENIAL, HUMILITY

ab·ne·ga·tor \ˈ==,gād·ə(r)\ n -s [LL, fr. L abnegatus + -or] **:** one that abnegates

ab·ney level \ˈabnē-\ n, usu cap A [after Wm. de Wiveleslie Abney †1920 Eng. scientist] **:** a surveying clinometer consisting of a short telescope, bubble tube, and graduated vertical arc used esp. for measuring tree heights

¹**ab·nor·mal** \(ˈ)abˈnȯrməl, -ó(ə)m- also əbˈ-\ adj [alter. (influenced by L abnormis) of anormal] **1 :** deviating from the normal **:** differing from the typical ⟨the large family is ~ today⟩ **:** IRREGULAR, UNUSUAL **2 :** greater than or superior to the normal **:** EXCESSIVE ⟨~ profits⟩ ⟨~ ambition⟩ **:** EXCEPTIONAL ⟨~ powers of recollection⟩ **3 :** less than or inferior to the normal **:** deficient in intellectual powers **:** characterized by mental defect or disorder ⟨a school for ~ children⟩ **:** SUBNORMAL **4 :** departing from the accepted standards of social behavior — **ab·nor·mal·ly** \-əlē, -i\ adv

²**abnormal** \"\ n -s **:** an abnormal person

ab·nor·mal·cy \abˈnȯrməlsē, -ó(ə)m-, -si also əb-\ n -ES [fr. abnormal, after normal: normalcy] **:** ABNORMALITY

ab·nor·mal·ism \=ˈ==,lizəm\ n -s **:** ABNORMALITY

ab·nor·mal·i·ty \,abnó(r)ˈmaləd·ē, -bnə(r)ˈ-, -ətē, -i\ n -ES **1 :** the quality or state of being abnormal **:** IRREGULARITY, DEVIATION **2 :** something abnormal (as a malformation or aberration)

ab·nor·mal·ize \=ˈ==,līz\ vt -ED/-ING/-S **:** to make abnormal

abnormal psychology n **:** a branch of psychology that deals with disorders of experience and of behavior (as in neuroses, psychoses, and mental deficiency) or with certain incompletely understood normal phenomena (as dreams and hypnosis)

ab·nor·mi·ty \=ˈ=məd·ē, -ətē, -i\ n -ES [LL abnormitas, fr. L abnormis irregular, abnormal (fr. ab- ¹ab- + norma rule, pattern) + -itas -ity — more at NORMAL] archaic **:** ABNORMALITY

ab·nor·mous \(ˈ)abˌnȯrməs, -ó(ə)m- also əbˈ-\ adj [irreg. (influence of enormous) fr. L abnormis, fr. ab- ¹ab- + norma rule — more at NORMAL] archaic **:** ABNORMAL, IRREGULAR

abo \ˈa(,)bō\ n -s [by shortening] Austral **:** ABORIGINE, ABORIGINAL

¹**aboard** \əˈ-\ adv [ME abord, fr. ¹a- + bord board, side of a ship — more at BOARD] **1 a :** on board **:** on, onto, or within a ship, a railway car, or a passenger vehicle ⟨all ~⟩ ⟨climb ~⟩ **b :** ASTRIDE ⟨swing ~⟩ ⟨sling a saddle ~⟩ **2 :** ALONGSIDE ⟨another ship close ~⟩

²**aboard** \"\ prep [ME abord, fr. abord, adv.] **:** on board ⟨go ~ ship⟩ ⟨~ a horse⟩

abococket var of BYCOKET

¹**abode** past of ABIDE

²**abode** \əˈbōd\ n -s [ME abod waiting, stay, fr. abod, past of abiden to abide — more at ABIDE] **1** obs **:** act of waiting **:** DELAY **:** temporary stay **2 :** continued stay in a place **:** RESIDENCE, SOJOURN ⟨during one's ~ in the country⟩ **3 :** place where one abides or dwells **:** HOME ⟨a cottage became their ~⟩

³**abode** vb -ED/-ING/-S [alter. (influenced by bode) of ME abeden to announce, fr. OE ābēodan to command, proclaim, fr. ā- (perfective prefix) + bēodan to command, proclaim — more at ABEAR, BID] vt, obs **:** FOREBODE, PRESAGE ~ vi, obs **:** to be ominous

abo·ga·do \,abəˈgäd·(,)ō\ n -s [Sp, fr. L advocatus — more at ADVOCATE] Southwest **:** COUNSEL 6

abo group n, usu cap A&B&O **:** ABO SYSTEM

ab·ohm \(ˈ)aˈbōm\ n -s [ISV ²ab- + ohm] **:** the cgs electromagnetic unit of resistance equal to one billionth of an ohm that measures the resistance of a conductor that with a constant current of one abampere flowing through it maintains between its terminals a potential difference of one abvolt — compare AB- table

aboi·deau \ˌabwäˈdō\ or **aboi·teau** \-tō\ n, pl **aboi·deaux** \-dō\ or **aboi·teaux** \-tō\ [CanF aboiteau] Canad **:** a tide gate or dam to prevent the overflow of water into marshland

aboil \əˈ-\ adj [¹a- + boil, v.] **:** BOILING

abol·ish \əˈbälish, -ēsh, esp in pres part -əsh\ vt -ED/-ING/-ES [MF aboliss-, stem of abolir to abolish, fr. L abolēre to abolish, destroy, prob. back-formation fr. abolescere to disappear, fr. ab- ¹ab- + -olescere (as in adolescere to grow up) — more at ADULT] **1 :** to do away with wholly **:** ANNUL — used chiefly of laws, customs, institutions, traditions ⟨~ slavery⟩ ⟨~ed bedtime during the holidays⟩ **2 :** to destroy completely ⟨a fog . . . ~ed the landscape —Aldous Huxley⟩

syn ANNIHILATE, EXTINGUISH, ABATE: ABOLISH indicates the definitive ending or causing a cessation of being or operating; it is used typically but not always with customs, traditions, conditions, conceptions rather than with more tangible items like things or persons ⟨abolish racial discrimination⟩ ⟨trying to abolish child labor⟩ ⟨abolishing a primitive custom⟩ ⟨no plan will be acceptable unless it abolishes poverty —G.B.Shaw⟩ ⟨the political liberalism which threatened to abolish some of the most flagrant abuses in the Church of England —W.R.Inge⟩ ⟨unfair that the anonymous churl, with an iron tube and some gunpowder and a great slug of lead, could abolish a knight —Tom Wintringham⟩ ANNIHILATE indicates utter destruction precluding any chance of re-creation, reforming, revivifying ⟨the events of this week annihilated the immature plans of last week —Charles Dickens⟩ ⟨the pollution of the Delaware river and bay by sewage and chemicals has practically annihilated the sturgeon —Amer. Guide Series: Del.⟩ ⟨the realization that for the first time the homes and cities of the U.S. itself can be annihilated by enemy attack —Aidan Crawley⟩ EXTINGUISH may suggest a putting out, choking off, stifling, smothering, as water extinguishes fire ⟨Italy, where the instincts of ancient Rome never were extinguished —H.O.Taylor⟩ ⟨a religion of their own which was thoroughly and painfully extinguished by the Inquisition —T.S.Eliot⟩ ⟨though the literal extirpation of a nation is an impossibility, there is every reason to believe that the Celtic inhabitants of those parts of Britain which had become English at the end of the sixth century had been as nearly extinguished as a nation could be —A.T.Quiller-Couch⟩ ABATE, now almost always a synonym for lessen or decrease, in legal usage may indicate abolishing or bringing to an end ⟨abate a nuisance⟩

abol·ish·ment \-shmənt\ n -s [MF abolissement, fr. aboliss- + -ment] **:** ABOLITION

ab·o·li·tion \,abəˈlishən\ n -s often attrib [MF, fr. L abolition-, abolitio, fr. abolitus (past part. of abolēre) + -ion-, -io -ion] **:** act of abolishing or state of being abolished **:** ABROGATION ⟨~ of imprisonment for debt⟩; specif **:** the abolishing of slavery

ab·o·li·tion·ary \-ə,nerē\ *adj* **:** relating to or favoring abolition

ab·o·li·tion·dom \-əndəm\ *n* -S **:** ABOLITIONISTS; *specif* **:** the northern states in the American Civil War

ab·o·li·tion·ism \-ə,nizəm\ *n* -S **:** the principles or measures favoring abolition (as of slavery or capital punishment) **:** the tenets or practices of abolitionists

ab·o·li·tion·ist \-ənəst\ *n* -S *often attrib* **:** an advocate of abolition

ab·o·li·tion·ize \-ə,nīz\ *vt* -ED/-ING/-S **:** to make abolitionists of (the members of a corporate body) ⟨~ Kansas⟩

abo·ma \əˈbōmə\ *n* -S [Pg, F, & AmerSp, prob. modif. of Kongo *mboma* python] **:** any of several large So. American snakes of the genus *Constrictor* or of related genera

ab·o·ma·sal \ˌabōˈmāsəl, -bə-\ *adj* [NL *abomasum* + E *-al*] **:** of, belonging to, or involving the abomasum

ab·o·ma·sum \ˌ=ˈ=səm\ *also* **ab·o·ma·sus** \-səs\ *n, pl* **aboma·sa** \-sə\ *also* **aboma·si** \-ˌsī,-ˌsē\ [NL, fr. ¹*ab-* + L *omasum* tripe of a bullock] **:** the fourth or true digestive stomach of a ruminant

¹**a–bomb** \ˈā,-\ *n, usu cap A* [by abbr.] **:** ATOM BOMB

²**a–bomb** \"\ *vb, usu cap A* **:** ATOM BOMB

a–bomber \ˈ=,==\ *n, usu cap A* **1 :** an aircraft capable of delivering an atom bomb on a target **2 :** an aircraft capable of delivering nuclear weapons on a target

abom·i·na·ble \əˈbäm(ə)nəbəl\ *adj* [ME, fr. MF, fr. L *abominabilis*, fr. *abominari* + *-abilis* -able] **1 :** worthy of or causing loathing or hatred **:** revoltingly unnatural **:** DETESTABLE, LOATHSOME **2 :** quite disagreeable or unpleasant ⟨~ weather⟩ — **abom·i·na·bly** \-əblē, -i\ *adv*

abominable snowman *n, often cap A&S* [prob. intended as trans. of Tibetan *mi-te*, lit., man-bear] **:** an animal reported as existing in the high Himalayas and usu. thought to be a bear

¹**abom·i·nate** \əˈbämə,nāt, *usu* -ād.+V\ *vt* -ED/-ING/-S [L *abominatus*, past part. of *abominari* to deprecate as an ill omen, to detest, fr. *ab-* ¹ab- + *ominari* to forebode, presage, fr. *omin-, omen* omen] **:** to hate or loathe intensely **:** ABHOR ⟨~ a crime⟩ **syn** see HATE

²**abom·i·nate** \-mənət, -ˌnāt\ *adj* [L *abominatus*] **:** ABOMINATED

abom·i·na·tion \ə,bäməˈnāshən\ *n* -S [ME *abominacioun*, fr. MF *abomination*, fr. LL *abomination-, abominatio*, fr. L *abominatus* + *-ion-, -io* -ion] **1 :** something that is abominable ⟨guilty of ~s⟩ ⟨a wonderful wooden statue . . . now replaced by the usual metal ~ —Norman Douglas⟩ **2 :** a feeling of extreme disgust and hatred **:** ABHORRENCE, DETESTATION, LOATHING ⟨tobacco . . . was held in ~ —T.B.Macaulay⟩

abom·i·na·tor \əˈbämə,nād·ə(r), -ātə-\ *n* -S **:** one that abominates

abon·go \əˈbäŋ(,)gō\ *n, pl* **abongo** *or* **abongos** *usu cap* **1 :** a Negrillo people on the Ogowe river, Gabon, French Equatorial Africa — called also *Obongo* **2 :** a member of the Abongo people — compare PYGMY

aboon \əˈbün, -ˈœn\ *adj or adv or prep* [ME *abone*, fr. earlier *aboven, abuven* — more at ABOVE] *chiefly dial* **:** ABOVE

ab·oospore \(ˈ)aˈbōə,spō(ə)r\ *n* [¹*ab-* + *oospore*] **:** an oomycete spore functioning as an oospore but produced without sexual union

abor \ˈä,bȯ(ə)r\ *n, pl* **abor** *or* **abors** *usu cap* **1 :** a primitive people inhabiting the Brahmaputra river region about 100 miles north of the town of Dibrugarh in northern Assam **2 :** a member of the Abor people

ab·orad \(ˈ)aˈbōr,ad, -ȯ,r-\ *adv* [¹*ab-* + *orad*] **:** away from the mouth

ab·oral \(ˈ)aˈbōrəl, -ȯr-,-är-\ *adj* [¹*ab-* + *oral*] **:** opposite to or away from the mouth — **ab·oral·ly** \-əlē, -i\ *adv*

¹**abord** *vt* -ED/-ING/-S [ME *aborden*, fr. *abord*, adv., aboard — more at ABOARD] *archaic* **:** APPROACH, ACCOST

²**abord** *n* -S *archaic* **:** APPROACH **:** manner of approach

abordage *n* -S [¹*abord* + *-age*] *archaic* **:** boarding a ship in an attack

¹**ab·orig·i·nal** \ˌabəˈrijənᵊl, -jnəl\ *adj* [*aborigine* + *-al*] **1 :** first according to historical record or scientific analysis **:** INDIGENOUS ⟨~ flora⟩ **:** PRIMITIVE ⟨~ tribes⟩ ⟨a great safety valve for the ~ human impulses—Lewis Mumford⟩ **2 :** of or belonging to aborigines ⟨~ languages⟩ ⟨~ weapons⟩ **syn** see NATIVE

²**aboriginal** \"\ *n* -S **:** ABORIGINE

ab·orig·i·nal·i·ty \ˌabə,rijəˈnaləd·ē\ *n* -ES **:** the quality or state of being aboriginal

ab·orig·i·nal·ly \ˌ=ˈ=ᵊnᵊlē, -jnəlē, -i\ *adv* **:** from the beginning **:** from earliest known times

ab·orig·i·ne \ˌabəˈrijə(,)nē, -əni\ *also* **ab·or·i·gen** \aˈbȯrəjən, -är-\ *n* -S [back-formation fr. *aborigines*, pl., fr. L, perh. irreg. fr. *ab origine* from the beginning] **1 :** an indigenous inhabitant of a country **:** one of the native people esp. as contrasted with an invading or colonizing people **2 aborigines** *pl* **:** the original fauna and flora of a geographical area

ab orig·i·ne \"\ *adv* [L] **:** from the beginning

abor–miri \ˌä,bȯrˈmirē\ *n, usu cap A&M* **:** a language spoken in northern Assam

¹**aborn·ing** \əˈbȯrniŋ, -ȯ(ə)n-, -nēŋ, -nən\ *adv* [¹*a-* + *borning*] **:** while being born or produced **:** at the moment of birth **:** before coming to completion **:** used esp. in the phrase *die aborning* ⟨a resolution that died ~⟩

²**aborning** \"\ *adj* **:** being born or produced ⟨the ~ social evolution of the girls —Fannie Hurst⟩ ⟨a new world was ~ overseas —B.D.Wolfe⟩

¹**abort** \əˈbȯ(ə)rt, -ȯ(ə)t, *usu* -d.+V\ *vb* -ED/-ING/-S [L *abortare*, fr. *abortus* abortion] *vi* **1 :** to bring forth premature or stillborn offspring ⟨cows with brucellosis often ~⟩ **2 :** to become checked in development so as to remain rudimentary or to shrink away ⟨pollen grains that ~⟩ **3 :** to stop or fail in the early stages ⟨many colds ~ without treatment⟩ ⟨the plans have ~*ed*⟩ ⟨the bomber ~*ed* from its mission⟩ ~ *vt* **1 :** to bring forth (offspring) prematurely ⟨~*ed* a 3-month-old fetus⟩ **:** cause to be delivered of a stillborn or nonviable fetus ⟨~ a malformed patient⟩; *esp* **:** to terminate pregnancy of before term **2 a :** to terminate prematurely ⟨~ a project⟩ **:** stop in the early stages ⟨~ a disease⟩ **b :** to turn back without completion **3 :** to check so as to produce rudimentary development or a shrinking away ⟨~ branches of trees⟩

²**abort** \"\ *n* -S [ME, fr. L *abortus*, fr. *abortus*, past part. of *aboriri* to disappear, miscarry, fr. *ab-* ¹ab- + *oriri* to rise, be born — more at ORIENT] **1** *obs* **:** ABORTION **2 :** an abortive flight by an aircraft on a combat or bombing mission; *also* **:** an aircraft making such a flight

abor·ti·cide \əˈbȯrd·ə,sīd\ *n* -S [²*abort* + *-i-* + *-cide*] **1 :** act of destroying a fetus within the uterus **2 :** an agent that destroys the fetus and causes abortion

¹**abor·ti·fa·cient** \əˈbȯrd·əˈfāshənt, =,==ˈ==\ *adj* [²*abort* + *-i-* + *-facient*] **:** inducing abortion

²**abortifacient** \"\ *n* -S **:** a drug or other agent that induces abortion

abort·in \əˈbȯrtᵊn\ *n* -S [NL *abortus* (specific epithet of *Brucella abortus*, fr. L, past part.) + E *-in*] **:** an extract made from cultures of a bacterium (*Brucella abortus*) and used in the diagnosis of contagious abortion of cattle

abor·tion \əˈbȯrshən, -ȯ(ə)sh-\ *n* -S [L *abortion-, abortio*, fr. *abortus* (past part.) + *-ion-, -io* -ion] **1 :** the expulsion of a nonviable fetus: **a :** expulsion of a human fetus during the first 12 weeks of gestation — compare MISCARRIAGE **b :** criminal expulsion of a human fetus **c :** expulsion often due to infection of a fetus by a domestic animal at any time before completion of pregnancy — see CONTAGIOUS ABORTION, VIBRIONIC ABORTION; TRICHOMONIASIS **2 :** a misshapen thing or person **:** MONSTROSITY **3 :** something that fails to attain full development or that ceases to progress before it is matured or perfect ⟨his attempt proved an ~⟩ **4 a :** arrest of development of an organ so that it remains imperfect or is absorbed **b :** the result of such arrest of development (as a fruit that fails to reach maturity or a potential leaf reduced to a scale) **5 :** the arrest of a disease in its earliest stage ⟨~ of a cold⟩

abor·tion·ist \-nəst\ *n* -S **:** one that induces criminal abortions

¹**abort·ive** \əˈbȯr|d·iv, -ȯ(ə)|, |tiv, -ēv\ *adj* [ME, fr. L *abortivus*, fr. *abortus* (past part.) + *-ivus* -ive] **1** *obs* **:** prematurely born ⟨an ~ child⟩ **2 :** failing of purpose or effect **:** MISCARRYING, FRUITLESS, UNSUCCESSFUL ⟨an ~ enterprise⟩ **3 :** imperfectly formed or developed **:** RUDIMENTARY **4 a :** ABORTIFACIENT **b :** cutting short ⟨~ treatment of pneumonia⟩ **c :** failing to develop completely or typically ⟨an ~ case of poliomyelitis⟩ — **abort·ive·ly** \-əvlē, -li\ *adv* — **abortiveness** \-ivnəs, -ēv-\ *n*

²**abortive** \"\ *n* -S [ME, fr. L *abortivus*, adj.] **:** one that is abortive (as a bombing mission)

abor·to·gen·ic \əˌbȯrd·əˈjenik\ *adj* [²*abort* + *-o-* + *-genic*] **:** causing abortion **:** ABORTIFACIENT ⟨~ necrosis⟩

abor·tus \əˈbȯrd·əs\ *n* -ES [NL, fr. L, abortion] **:** an aborted fetus; *specif* **:** a human fetus less than 12 weeks old or weighing at birth less than 17 ounces

abos *pl of* ABO

abo system \ˌāˌbēˈō-, ˌabēˈō-\ *n, usu cap A&B&O* **:** the basic system of antigens of human blood behaving in heredity as an allelic unit to produce any of the four blood groups A, B, AB, or O according to the particular antigens passed from parents to child — called also *ABO group*; compare ISOANTIBODY, RH FACTOR

à bouche \äbüsh\ *adj* [F, with a bouche] *heraldry, of a shield* **:** having a bouche on the dexter side

abought *past of* ABY

aboulia *var of* ABULIA

abound \əˈbau̇nd\ *vi* -ED/-ING/-S [ME *abounden*, fr. MF *abonder*, fr. L *abundare* to abound, overflow, fr. *ab-* ¹ab- + *undare* to rise in waves, fr. *unda* wave — more at WATER] **1 :** to be present or available in large numbers or in great quantity ⟨wild animals ~⟩ ⟨iron ore ~*s*⟩ ⟨~*ing* confidence⟩ **2 a** *obs* **:** to be wealthy ⟨feed the poor while he ~*s*⟩ **b :** to be full to overflowing ⟨~*ing* streams⟩ **c :** to be highly productive ⟨~*ing* soil⟩ **3 :** to become copiously supplied — used with *in* or *with* ⟨the city ~*s* in historic remains⟩ ⟨the fields ~ with stones⟩

¹**about** \əˈbau̇t, *usu* -d.+V\ *adv* [ME *about, abouten*, fr. OE *abūtan*, fr. ¹*a-* + *būtan* outside, without — more at BUT] **1 :** on all sides **:** in every direction **:** AROUND ⟨'tis time to look ~ —Shak.⟩ **2 a :** in rotation **:** ROUND ⟨they go ~ in circles⟩ **b :** around the outside **:** in circumference ⟨the lake is a mile ~ and a half mile across⟩ **c :** in a circuitous way **:** ROUNDABOUT ⟨the sure way (though most ~) to make gold —Francis Bacon⟩ **3 a :** with some approach to exactness in quantity, number, or time **:** APPROXIMATELY ⟨~ four feet of snow⟩ ⟨~ eight o'clock⟩ **b :** ALMOST **:** NEARLY ⟨~ as serious⟩ **:** little less than ⟨~ starved⟩ **4 :** here and there at random ⟨tools lying ~⟩ **:** from one place to another ⟨carry money ~ with him⟩ **5 :** in the vicinity **:** NEAR ⟨he spoke to the people standing ~⟩ **6 :** in rotation or succession **:** one after the other **:** ALTERNATELY ⟨turn ~ is fair play⟩ **7 a :** in the opposite direction ⟨face ~⟩ ⟨bring a ship ~⟩ **:** in reverse order ⟨arranged the other way ~⟩ **:** from the contrary point of view ⟨put the matter the other way ~⟩ **b :** on the opposite tack — see COME ABOUT

²**about** \"\ *prep* [ME, fr. OE *abūtan*, fr. *abūtan*, adv.] **1 :** in a circle around **:** AROUND ⟨our thoughts revolve ~ ourselves⟩ **:** on every side of ⟨he found ~ him innumerable flowers⟩ **2 a :** in the immediate neighborhood of **:** NEAR ⟨fish are abundant ~ the reefs⟩ **b :** near or not far from in time ⟨a night ~ midsummer⟩ **c :** by or on (one's person) ⟨secreting money ~ him⟩ **d :** in or as a part of the makeup of ⟨a mature wisdom ~ him⟩ **e :** at the command of **:** in readiness for the use of ⟨he has his wits ~ him⟩ **3 a :** in the act or process of doing **:** engaged in ⟨I put it in the form of a poem while I was ~ it —Eudora Welty⟩ **:** concerned with ⟨no idea of what American music is ~⟩ **b :** on the point or verge of — usu. used with following infinitive ⟨~ to enter the army⟩ ⟨~ to be graduated⟩ **4 a** — used as a function word to indicate that which is dealt with as the object of thought, feeling, or action ⟨resentment ~ this state of affairs⟩ or that to which reference is made ⟨the most exciting thing ~ the adventure⟩ **b :** with regard to **:** CONCERNING **c :** on the subject of ⟨a novel ~ Spain⟩ **5 :** over or in different parts of ⟨he traveled ~ the country⟩ **:** THROUGHOUT ⟨a well-known figure ~ the town⟩ **:** here and there upon ⟨the knife wounded him ~ the face and throat⟩

³**about** \"\ *adj* [ME, fr. *about*, adv.] **1 :** stirring or moving from place to place **:** ASTIR ⟨few people were ~ on the streets⟩ **2 :** being in evidence, in existence, or in circulation **:** ABROAD ⟨plenty of money ~⟩ ⟨more reason and less emotion ~ —Herbert Hoover⟩ **3 :** normally active or capable (as after a confining illness) ⟨eager to be up and ~ again⟩

¹**about–face** \ˈ=ˈ=ˌ=\ *n* -S [fr. the imper. phrase *about face*, fr. ¹*about* + *face*, *v.*] **1 :** the act of facing in the opposite direction as a military maneuver ⟨soldiers did an *about-face* and marched away —Dorothy C. Fisher⟩ **2 a :** a reversal of direction ⟨the river does an *about-face*⟩ **b :** a reversal of attitude or point of view ⟨an *about-face* on national policies⟩

²**about–face** \"\ *vi* -ED/-ING/-S **:** to execute an about-face

about ship *vi* [fr. the imper. phrase *about ship*, fr. ¹*about* + *ship*, n.] **:** TACK — usu. used as an order

about–turn \ˈ=ˈ=ˌ=\ *vi* [fr. the imper. phrase *about turn*, fr. ¹*about* + *turn*, v.] **:** ABOUT-FACE

¹**above** \əˈbəv\ *adv* [ME *above, aboven*, fr. OE *abufan*, fr. ¹*a-* + *bufan* above (akin to OS *bi-oƀan*, MD *bōven*, OFris *bova*, MHG *bobene*), fr. *be-* + *ufan* above — more at OVER] **1 a :** in a higher place **:** OVERHEAD ⟨he lay under the tree and looked at the branches ~⟩ **:** in the sky ⟨the stars ~⟩ **:** in or to heaven ⟨gone ~⟩ **:** UPSTAIRS ⟨a stairway leading ~⟩ **b :** farther up (as on a mountain or river) ⟨the bridge is two miles ~⟩ **c :** on the upper or dorsal surface ⟨these young birds are light brown ~⟩ **2 :** higher on the same page or on a preceding page ⟨except as stated ~⟩ **3 :** higher or superior in rank, position, or power ⟨a vacancy in the rank ~⟩ **:** higher in number ⟨50 and ~⟩ **4** *archaic* **:** in addition **:** BESIDES

²**above** \"\ *prep* [ME *above, aboven*, fr. *above, aboven*, adv.] **1 a :** in or to a higher place than ⟨the house perched ~ the road⟩ **:** directly over ⟨a room ~ the store⟩ **:** higher than **b :** farther up than (as on a mountain or river) ⟨anchored 10 miles ~ the city⟩ **:** on the other side of **:** BEYOND ⟨hunted ~ the farm⟩ **c :** farther north than ⟨the ship sank just ~ the Azores⟩ **d :** on top of — used of clothing ⟨aprons ~ a motley of borrowed . . . raiment —Ellen Glasgow⟩ **2 a :** superior to or surpassing in any respect **:** higher than (as in rank, position, quality, or degree) ⟨filial piety is ~ self-interest⟩ **:** out of reach of **:** not likely to be affected by **:** not exposed to ⟨be ~ suspicion⟩ **:** in preference to **:** over against ⟨preoccupation with design ~ all other elements⟩ **b :** too proud or honorable to stoop or condescend to ⟨~ taking profits for himself⟩ **:** averse to **:** disinclined to ⟨she is not ~ reading her poems⟩ **3 :** exceeding in number, quantity, or size **:** more than ⟨men ~ 50 years old⟩ **4 :** in addition to **:** BESIDES ⟨~ and beyond his good nature⟩ — **above oneself :** showing or feeling self-importance ⟨when he gets a bit *above himself* . . . he inclines to be a nuisance —*Atlantic*⟩

³**above** \"\ *n* -S [ME *above, aboven*, fr. *above, aboven*, adv.] **1 a :** something that is located, written, or discussed higher on the same page or on a preceding page ⟨a diagram like the ~⟩ **b :** a person whose name is written higher on the same page or on a preceding page ⟨the ~ is the owner of this car⟩ **2 a :** higher esp. arbitrary authority ⟨the policy was imposed from ~⟩ **b :** HEAVEN ⟨every perfect gift is from ~ —Jas 1:17 (AV)⟩

⁴**above** \"\ *adj* [¹*above*] **1 :** being located, written, or discussed higher on the same page or on a preceding page ⟨the ~ chart⟩ **2 :** of heaven **:** HEAVENLY ⟨think on things ~⟩

above all *adv* **:** before every other consideration **:** ESPECIALLY ⟨this *above all*⟩

¹**above·board** \ˈ=ˌ=ˈ=\ *adv* [²*above* + *board*; fr. the difficulty of cheating at cards when the hands are above the table] **:** in a straightforward manner **:** OPENLY

²**aboveboard** \"\ *adj* **:** without concealment or deception **:** in open sight **:** STRAIGHTFORWARD ⟨open and ~ in his opposition⟩

above·ground \ˈ=ˌ=ˈ=\ *adj* **1 :** located on or above the surface of the ground **2 :** not dead and buried **:** ALIVE

above–proof \ˈ=ˌ=ˈ=\ *adj* **:** OVERPROOF

¹**above·stairs** \ˈ=ˌ=ˈ=\ *adv* **:** in or on an upper story ⟨they sat ~⟩

²**abovestairs** \"\ *adj* [¹*abovestairs*] **:** located on an upper story ⟨a room ~⟩

³**abovestairs** \"\ *n pl but sing in constr* [¹*abovestairs*] **:** the part of a building above the ground floor ⟨a shout from ~⟩

above the line *or* **above–line** \əˈbəv,līn\ *adv (or adj)* **1 :** in that part of the score sheet in bridge that is reserved for the scoring of honors, penalties, and premiums — used of any score that does not count toward game; compare CONTRACT BRIDGE **2 :** classified as an ordinary or routine expense or revenue item or as a current expense or asset ⟨an *above-line* surplus⟩

above–wa·ter \ˈ=ˌ=ˈ==\ *adj* **1 :** above the surface of the water **2 :** above the waterline of a ship

ab ovo \(ˈ)abˈō(ˌ)vō\ *adv* [L, lit., from the egg] **:** from the beginning ⟨develops every thought *ab ovo*, leading the reader up to the finest ramifications —Arnold Brecht⟩

abox \əˈbäks\ *adj* [¹*a-* + *box* (to boxhaul)] **:** braced aback — used of head yards when the headsails only are aback

aboz·zo *also* **ab·boz·zo** \əˈbȯt(ˌ)sō\ *n, pl* **aboz·zi** \-(ˌ)sē\ [It *abbozzo*, fr. *abbozzare* to make a rough sketch or draft, fr. *a-* (fr. L *ad-*) + *bozzare* to make a rough sketch or draft, fr. *bozza* boss, swelling, roughhewn stone, rough sketch or draft — more at BOSS] **:** a rough sketch or draft (as of a picture or a poem)

abp *abbr, often cap* archbishop

abr *abbr* abridged; abridgment

ab·ra·ca·dab·ra \ˌabrəkəˈdabrə\ *n* -S [LL] **1 :** a charm or incantation **:** magical formulas ⟨relied on effigies and ~ to produce results —E.A. Hoebel⟩ — used as a word to ward off calamity esp. when written on an amulet in a mystical design **2 :** confused or unintelligible language **:** JARGON, NONSENSE ⟨pseudoscientific ~⟩

A B R A C A D A B R A
A B R A C A D A B R
A B R A C A D A B
A B R A C A D A
A B R A C A D
A B R A C A
A B R A C
A B R A
A B R
A B
A

abracadabra

¹**abrad·ant** \əˈbrādᵊnt, aˈ-\ *n* -S [*abrade* + *-ant*] **:** ABRASIVE

²**abradant** \"\ *adj* **:** ABRASIVE

abrade \əˈbrād, aˈ-\ *vb* -ED/-ING/-S [L *abradere* to scrape off, fr. *ab-* ¹ab- + *radere* to scrape — more at RAT] *vt* **1 a :** to rub or wear away esp. by friction **:** ERODE ⟨the waves ~ the rocks⟩ **b :** to irritate by rubbing **:** CHAFE ⟨broad crape . . . *abraded* her soft skin —Arnold Bennett⟩ **c :** to roughen the surface of ⟨*abraded* yarns⟩ **2 :** to wear down or exhaust (as a person or a person's spirit) **:** IRRITATE ⟨the affront to his pride *abraded* him more and more —Robert Shaplen⟩ ~ *vi* **:** to undergo abrasion

abrad·er \-də(r)\ *n* -S **1 :** a tool or machine for abrading **2** *or* **abrading stone** *archaeol* **:** a primitive stone artifact usu. of sandstone for smoothing, sharpening, or shaping

abra·ham–man \ˈābrə,ham,man, -haa(ə)m,maa(ə)n; ˈābrəm,-, ˈābrəhəm,-\ *also* **abram–man** \ˈābrəm,-\ *n, pl* **abra·ham–men** *also* **abram–men** *usu cap A* [after *Abraham* or *Abram*, Biblical patriarch of the Jews; prob. fr. the New Testament reference (Lk 16: 19–31) to the beggar Lazarus, who is said to have rested in Abraham's bosom after death] **:** one of a class of vagrant beggars who roamed through England esp. in the 16th and 17th centuries usu. feigning lunacy to obtain alms

abraham's bosom *n, usu cap A* [trans. of LL *sinus Abrahae*, trans. of Gk *kolpos Abraam*] **:** the abode of bliss in the other world **:** PARADISE — so called in Jewish writings and in the New Testament, in Lk 16:22 (RSV)

abram *obs var of* ¹AUBURN

ab·ra·mis \ˈabrəməs\ *n, cap* [NL, fr. Gk, a kind of mullet] **:** a genus of fishes (family Cyprinidae) including the European freshwater bream

abran·chia \(ˈ)āˈbraŋkēə\ *n pl, cap* [NL, fr. ²*a-* + *-branchia*] **:** a former division of annelids comprising forms without specialized respiratory structures (as most of the oligochaetes and leeches)

abran·chi·al \(ˈ)āˈbraŋkēəl\ *adj* [²*a-* + *branchial*] **:** ABRANCHIATE

abran·chi·al·ism \(ˈ)=ˈ===,lizəm\ *n* -S [*abranchial* + *-ism*] **:** the condition of being without gills (as certain mollusks of the genus *Firoloida*)

¹**abran·chi·a·ta** \ˌ=ˌ=kēˈäd·ə, -ād·ə\ [NL, fr. ²*a-* + *branchi-* + *-ata*] *syn of* ABRANCHIA

²**abranchiata** \"\ *n pl, cap* **:** any of several groups of gill-less animals other than Abranchia

abran·chi·ate \(ˈ)=ˈ=kēət, -ē,āt\ *also* **abran·chi·ous** \-kēəs\ *adj* [²*a-* + *branchi-* + *-ate* or *-ous*] **:** lacking gills ⟨various ~ salamanders⟩

abrase \əˈbrāz, aˈ-\ *vt* -ED/-ING/-S [L *abrasus*, past part. of *abradere* — more at ABRADE] **:** to wear down or rub off **:** smooth off **:** ABRADE

abras·er \-zə(r)\ *n* -S **:** ABRADER

abrash \ˈä,brash, -rash\ *n* -ES [Ar, mottled] **:** a variation or deviation of a color in Oriental rugs

ab·ra·sin oil \ˈabrəzə̇,n-\ *n* [part trans. of F *huile d'abrasin*] **:** TUNG OIL

abra·si·om·e·ter \ə,brāzēˈämәd·ə(r), a,-\ *n* -S [*abrasion* + *-meter*] **:** a device for measuring the resistance of surfaces to abrasion

abra·sion \əˈbrāzhən, aˈ-\ *n* -S [ML *abrasion-, abrasio*, fr. L *abrasus* (past part. of *abradere* to scrape off) + *-ion-, -io* -ion — more at ABRADE] **1 :** wearing, grinding, or rubbing away by friction **2 a :** the rubbing or scraping of the surface layer of cells or tissue from an area of the skin or mucous membrane; *also* **:** a place so abraded **b :** the mechanical wearing away of the tooth surfaces by chewing

abrasion platform *n* **:** the portion of the submerged margin of a continent or island that has been planed off by marine abrasion as distinct from the portion that has been built up to its present level by the deposit of marine sediments

¹**abra·sive** \-āsiv, -ziv, -ēv\ *adj* [*abrase* + *-ive*] **:** tending to abrade **:** producing abrasion

²**abrasive** \"\ *n* -S **1 a :** any of a wide variety of natural or manufactured substances used to grind, wear down, rub away, smooth, scour, clean, or polish often combined with a binder to make grinding wheels or affixed with glue to the surface of paper or cloth **b :** something made of an abrasive (as sandpaper) **2 :** rock fragments, mineral particles, or sand grains used by running water, wind, waves and currents, and glaciers in abrading a land surface

ab·raum \ˈä,prau̇m\ *n* -S [G, lit., rubbish, fr. *ab* off (fr. OHG *aba* away) + *raum* space, fr. OHG *rūm* — more at OF, ROOM] **:** a red ocher used to darken mahogany

abrax·as \əˈbraksəs\ *n* [LL *Abraxas*, a god, fr. Gk *Abrasax*, *Abraxas*; perh. regarded as a charm fr. the numerical value of the Greek letters, which is 365] **1 —** used as a charm on an amulet or talisman in Europe, Asia Minor, and No. Africa from the 2d century B.C. until the 13th century **2** *also* **abraxas stone** -ES **:** a gem engraved with the word *abraxas*

abra·zo \əˈbrä(ˌ)sō, äˈb-\ *n* -S [Sp, fr. *abrazar* to embrace, fr. *a-* (fr. L *ad-*) + *brazo* arm, fr. L *brachium* — more at BRACE] **:** an embrace (as of salutation) employed in Latin America

ab·re·act \ˌabrēˈakt\ *vt* -ED/-ING/-S [part trans. of G *abreagieren*, fr. *ab* off, away from, down from (fr. OHG *aba*) + *reagieren* to react — more at OF] **:** to release or express ⟨an emotion previously repressed or forgotten⟩ ⟨~ his resentment over a childhood slight⟩

ab·re·ac·tion \ˌabrēˈakshən\ *n* -S [part trans. of G *abreagierung*, fr. *ab* + *reagierung* reaction] **:** the discharge of the emotional energy supposed to be attached to a repressed idea esp. by the conscious verbalization of that idea in the presence of a therapist — compare CATHARSIS 3a

ab·re·ac·tive \-ktiv\ *adj* [*abreaction* + *-ive*] **:** relating to or capable of producing abreaction ⟨~ technique⟩

¹**abreast** \əˈ-\ *adv (or adj)* [ME *abrest*, fr. ¹*a-* + *brest* breast] **1 a :** beside one another with bodies in line ⟨four cars standing ~ so as to block the street⟩ ⟨with seats two ~ on each side of the aisle⟩ **b** *naut* **:** in or to a position with the bearing of another object 90 degrees from the bow **:** directly abeam ⟨~ of the tip of the island⟩ **2 :** up to or equal to a particular standard or level (as of performance or development) ⟨kept wages ~ of the rising living costs⟩ **:** in a condition of acquaintance with events or developments in a particular field **:** UP-TO-DATE ⟨the researcher keeps ~ with related work in his field⟩ ⟨~ of current thinking⟩

²**abreast** \"\ *prep, naut* **:** abreast of ⟨lying ~ the island⟩

abreed *or* **abreid** \əˈbrēd\ *chiefly Scot var of* ABROAD

abrenunciation *n* -s [ML *abrenuntiation-, abrenuntiatio,* fr. LL *abrenuntiatus* (past part. of *abrenuntiare* to renounce), fr. L *ab-* ¹ab- + *renuntiare* to renounce — more at RENOUNCE] *archaic* : RENUNCIATION, REPUDIATION

abri \ˈabrē\ *n, pl* **abris** \-ē(z)\ [F, fr. OF, fr. *abrier* to shelter, fr. LL *apricari* to sun oneself, fr. *apricus* exposed to the sun] : SHELTER; *esp* : a dugout or cavity in a hillside

abri au·dit \ˌa(ˌ)brē,ōˈdē\ *adj, usu cap both As* [fr. F *Abri Audit* (lit., Audit Shelter), a rock shelter in Dordogne dept., France] : of or belonging to a prehistoric culture transitional between late Mousterian and Aurignacian

abridge \əˈbrij\ *vt* -ED/-ING/-S [ME *abregen, abriggen,* fr. MF *abregier,* fr. LL *abbreviare,* fr. L *ad-* + *breviare* to shorten, fr. *brevis* short — more at BRIEF] **1 a** *archaic* : DEPRIVE — usu. used with *of* ⟨~ a man of his rights⟩ **b** : to diminish (as a right) by reducing ⟨the danger of *abridging* the liberties of the people —Abraham Lincoln⟩ **2** : to shorten in duration ⟨I have other reasons for *abridging* my stay at Bath —Tobias Smollett⟩ : shorten or cut down in extent ⟨the airplane ~s distance⟩ ⟨~ library service during the summer⟩ **3** : to shorten by omission of words without sacrifice of principal meaning : CONDENSE ⟨an *abridged* version of the novel⟩ **syn** see SHORTEN

abridg·er \-jə(r)\ *n* -s : one that abridges

abridg·ment *or* **abridge·ment** \-jmənt\ *n* -s **1** : action of abridging : state of being abridged **2 a** : a shortened form of a work produced by condensation and omission but retaining the general meaning and manner of presentation of the original : COMPENDIUM **3** : a brief statement of a subject : an epitome of general outlines or principles : SYNOPSIS; *specif* : any of various brief statements of case law made before modern reporting of cases

syn ABRIDGMENT, ABSTRACT, BRIEF, SYNOPSIS, CONSPECTUS, EPITOME: these terms all denote a condensation of a larger work or more extended, although often only prospective, treatment. ABRIDGMENT implies reduction in compass yet retention of relative completeness, usu. with the retention too of something of the manner of the original ⟨all *abridgments* of encyclopedic treatments, even when they are the work of their own authors, must inevitably suffer —Paul Radin⟩ ⟨he delivers an *abridgment* of the famous opening soliloquy with little regard for metrical or musical values —Henry Hewes⟩ ⟨a 50-page *abridgment* of a full-length novel⟩ An ABSTRACT is a summary of a document, treatise, or proposed treatment giving the salient points, usu. in the order of presentation, with usu. no claim to independent worth ⟨accounts of ancient and modern political unions . . . He made *abstracts* of them —H.E.Scudder⟩ ⟨this pamphlet contains an *abstract* of the hunting and trapping law as contained in the Biennial Revision —*Maine Hunting & Trapping Laws*⟩ A BRIEF is an abstract of a case or argument, esp. in law ⟨prepared an extended *brief* to support his position —*Amer. Guide Series: Oregon*⟩ ⟨two *briefs* submitted by lawyers —M.R.Cohen⟩ ⟨it became in time the principal *brief* and basic blueprint for the expansion of the Air Force —Gordon Harrison⟩ SYNOPSIS usu. implies a skeletal presentation, esp. of a narrative or proposed narrative, that can be apprehended in a moment or rapidly ⟨a *synopsis* of an argument⟩ ⟨the *synopsis* is an outline of three or four typewritten pages containing the barest summary of character and action . . . made for the convenience of the producer —V.I.Pudovkin⟩ CONSPECTUS implies a quick overall but relatively complete view of something complex or extremely detailed on more leisurely careful examination ⟨a detached and objective *conspectus* of the ideological background and basis of Soviet communism —*Times Lit. Supp.*⟩ ⟨the book . . . will contain a full *conspectus* of the published treatises —*Mediaeval Academy News*⟩ ⟨a detailed *conspectus* of this society's values —J.J.Spengler⟩ EPITOME suggests the briefest possible condensation yet extreme accuracy in presentation, a complex whole in miniature, usu. with an independent value as a whole ⟨having an *epitome* of all these findings upon a single sheet —L.F.Barker⟩ ⟨*epitomes* of British novels circulated widely —H.R.Warfel⟩ ⟨the title is a neat *epitome* of the contents —*Current Biog.*⟩

abrim \əˈ-\ *adj* [¹*a-* + *brim,* v.] : BRIMMING

abrin \ˈābrən, ˈa-, -(ˌ)brin; äˈbrin, aˈb-\ *n* -s [ISV *abr-* (fr. NL *Abrus,* genus name of *Abrus precatorius* Indian licorice) + *-in*] : a toxic protein obtained from jequirity

abrine \ˈāˌbrēn, ˈaˌb-; ⸗ˈ⸗\ *n* -s [alter. of *abrin*] : a toxic crystalline amino acid $C_{12}H_{14}N_2O_2$ obtained from jequirity; *N*-methyltryptophan — distinguished from *abrin*

abris *pl of* ABRI

abris·tle \əˈ-\ *adj* [¹*a-* + *bristle,* v.] : BRISTLING

abroach \əˈbrōch\ *adv (or adj)* [ME *abroche,* fr. ¹*a-* + *broche* pointed rod, perforation — more at BROACH] **1** *of a cask* : in a condition for letting out liquor : TAPPED ⟨set the cask ~⟩ **2** : in a state to be diffused or propagated ⟨mischiefs that I set ~ —Shak.⟩

¹**abroad** \əˈbrȯd\ *adv (or adj)* [ME *abrood,* fr. ¹*a-* + *brood* broad] **1** : over a wide area : at large ⟨a tree spreading its branches ~⟩ : widely apart ⟨flinging his arms wildly ~ —Nathaniel Hawthorne⟩ **2** : out of the house : away from one's home ⟨walk ~ after lunch⟩ : in circulation or movement from place to place : on the street or public ways : here and there ⟨at this hour the few people ~ go quickly on their ways⟩ ⟨the enemy is ~ in the land⟩ : out in the open ⟨insects awakened from torpor and ~ in the spring sun —Walter Pater⟩ **3** : beyond the boundaries of a country ⟨travel ~ in many lands⟩ : in or to foreign countries ⟨a university well known ~⟩ **4** : in circulation throughout society or the world ⟨the idea has got ~⟩ : in evidence : ABOUT ⟨plenty of enthusiasm ~⟩ **5** : wide of the mark : ASTRAY : in confusion ⟨I'm much ~ in my ciphering —Francis Hoover⟩ **6** : contested elsewhere than on the home grounds ⟨the team wears a different uniform for games ~⟩

²**abroad** \"\ *prep* : THROUGHOUT, OVER ⟨and then ~ the world he goes —Emily Dickinson⟩

ab·ro·come \ˈabrəˌkōm\ *n* -s [NL *Abrocoma,* irreg. fr. Gk *habrokomēs* with delicate hair, fr. *habro-* + *komē* hair] : either of two ratlike hystricomorph rodents having fine soft fur and large rounded ears and constituting a genus (*Abrocoma*) restricted to the Andes mountains — called also *rat chinchilla*

¹**abrogate** *adj* [ME *abrogat,* fr. L *abrogatus*] *obs* : ABROGATED

²**ab·ro·gate** \ˈabrəˌgāt, *usu* -ād.+V\ *vt* -ED/-ING/-S [L *abrogatus,* past part. of *abrogare,* fr. *ab-* ¹ab- + *rogare* to ask, propose a law — more at RIGHT] **1** : to abolish by authoritative, official, or formal action : ANNUL, REPEAL ⟨neither a court decision nor a statute can, however, ~ a treaty as an international contract —F.A.Ogg & P.O.Ray⟩ ⟨special legal privileges for foreigners should be *abrogated* —*New Republic*⟩ **2** : to put an end to : do away with : set aside ⟨we are not thereby called upon to ~ the standards of values that are fixed —J.L.Lowes⟩ ⟨he declined to ~ his conscience —Walter H. Page⟩ **syn** see NULLIFY

ab·ro·ga·tion \ˌabrəˈgāshən\ *n* -s [MF or L; MF *abrogation,* fr. L *abrogation-, abrogatio,* fr. *abrogatus* + *-ion-, -io* -ion] : the act of abrogating : definitive repeal

abro·ma \əˈbrōmə\ *n, cap* [NL, fr. ²*a-* + Gk *brōma* food; akin to Gk *bibrōskein* to devour — more at VORACIOUS] : a genus of Asiatic and Australian woody plants (family Sterculiaceae) the bark of which yields a strong white fiber — see DEVIL'S-COTTON

abro·nia \əˈbrōnēə\ *n* [NL, irreg. fr. Gk *habros* graceful, delicate + NL *-ia* — more at HABRO-] **1** *cap* : a genus of herbs (family Nyctaginaceae) native to western No. America having showy fragrant flowers in bracted heads and with the salver-shaped calyx having a 3-winged base — see SAND VERBENA **2** -s : any plant of the genus *Abronia*

abrood \əˈbrüd\ *adv* [ME *abrod,* fr. ¹*a-* + *brod* brood — more at BROOD] *now dial Eng* : on a hatch

abrot·a·num \əˈbrätənəm\ *n* -s [ML, alter. of L *abrotonum,* fr Gk *abrotonon* southern wormwood, southernwood] : SOUTHERNWOOD

ab·ro·tine \ˈabrəˌtēn\ *n* -s [ISV *abrot-* (fr. ML *abrotanum*) + *-ine;* prob. orig. formed as G *abrotin*] : a colorless crystalline alkaloid $C_{21}H_{22}N_2O$ obtained from southernwood

¹**abrupt** \əˈbrəpt, *also* (ˈ)aˌb-\ *adj, sometimes* -ER/-EST [L *abruptus,* fr. past part. of *abrumpere* to break off, fr. *ab-* ¹ab- + *rumpere* to break — more at REAVE] **1** : broken off : suddenly terminating as if cut or broken off ⟨short and ~ plant filaments⟩ **2 a** : characterized by or producing the effect of a sharp break or sudden ending ⟨act with ~ decision⟩ : UNEXPECTED ⟨at ~ intervals in the performance⟩ **b** : unceremoniously curt ⟨~ in manner⟩ **c** : lacking transition from one subject to another : DISCONNECTED ⟨an ~ literary style⟩ **3** : rising or dropping sharply as if broken off : PRECIPITOUS, STEEP ⟨an ~ peak rising from the ocean⟩ **syn** see PRECIPITATE, STEEP — **abrupt·ness** *n* -ES

²**abrupt** \"\ *vt* -ED/-ING/-S *archaic* : to break off ⟨let brazen bands ~ their din —W.H.Auden⟩ : SEPARATE

abrup·tion \əˈbrəpshən, aˈb-\ *n* -s [L *abruption-, abruptio,* fr. *abruptus* (past part.) + *-ion-, -io* -ion] **1** *archaic* : sudden termination or interruption ⟨~ in a narrative⟩ ⟨total ~ of all relations between them⟩ **2** : a sudden breaking off : detachment of portions from a mass ⟨placental ~⟩

ab·rup·tio pla·cen·tae \əˈbrəpshēˌōpləˈsenˌtē, äˈbrüptēˌōpläˈkenˌtī\ *n, pl* **abruptio pla·cen·ta·rum** \-ˌplasənˈta(a)rəm, ˌpläˌkenˈtäˌrüm\ *or* **abrupti·o·nes placentarum** \-shēˈō(ˌ)nēz-,-tēˈōˌnās-\ [NL, a breaking off of the placenta] : premature detachment of the placenta from the wall of the uterus

abrupt·ly \əˈbrəp(t)lē, -li *also* (ˈ)aˌb-\ *adv* [¹*abrupt* + *-ly*] : in an abrupt manner

abrus \ˈābrəs, ˈä-\ *n, cap* [NL, irreg. fr. Gk *habros* graceful, delicate — more at HABRO-] : a genus of tropical vines (family Fabaceae) having pinnate leaves, purplish flowers with a 4-lobed calyx, and flat pods — see INDIAN LICORICE

abruz·zi ware \äˈbrütsē, əˈb-\ *n, usu cap A* [fr. *Abruzzi e Molise,* compartimento of central Italy where it was first made] : an ornate Italian pottery chiefly of the 15th century

abs *pl of* AB

abs *abbr* **1** absent **2** absolute **3** abstract

ab·sa·ro·ka \abˈsärəkə\ *or* **ab·sa·ro·ke** *or* **ab·sa·ro·kee** \-särəkē,-sȯrkē\ *n, pl* **absaroka** *or* **absarokas** *or* **absaroke** *or* **absarokes** *or* **absarokee** *or* **absarokees** *usu cap* [Dakota, lit., crow people, bird people] : ¹CROW 8

ab·scess \ˈabˌses *also* -ˌsəs\ *n* -ES [L *abscessus,* lit., act of going away, fr. *abscessus,* past part. of *abscedere* to go away, fr. *abs-* (var. of *ab-* ¹ab-) + *cedere* to go — more at CEDE] : a localized collection of pus surrounded by an area of inflamed tissue in which hyperemia and infiltration of leukocytes is marked

ab·scessed \-est, -əst\ *adj* : afflicted with an abscess or abscesses

ab·scess·root \ˈ⸗(ˌ)⸗ˌ⸗\ *n* : a perennial herb (*Polemonium reptans*) of the eastern U. S. with compound leaves and blue flowers

ab·scind \abˈsind\ *vt* -ED/-ING/-S [L *abscindere* to cut or tear off, fr. *ab.* ¹ab- + *scindere* to cut, tear — more at SHED (to throw off)] : to cut off

ab·scise \abˈsīz\ *vb* -ED/-ING/-S [L *abscisus,* past part. of *abscidere,* fr. *abs-* (var. of *ab-* ¹ab-) + *-cidere* (fr. *caedere* to cut) — more at CONCISE] *vt* : to cut off by abscission (sense 2) ~ *vi* : to separate (as of a leaf from a twig) by abscission

ab·sciss \abˈsis\ *vb* -ED/-ING/-S [back-formation fr. *abscission*] : ABSCISE

ab·scis·sa \abˈsisə, əb-\ *n* -s [NL, fr. L, fem. of *abscissus,* past part. of *abscindere* — more at ABSCIND] : the horizontal coordinate of a point in a plane Cartesian coordinate system obtained by measuring parallel to the x-axis — compare ORDINATE

AP abscissa of point *P*

ab·scis·sio in·fi·ni·ti \abˈsisēˌōˌinfəˈnīˌtī\ *n, pl* **abscissi·o·nes infiniti** \-ˌsisēˈōˌnēˌzin-\ [NL, abscission of that which is infinite] : a logical process using successive exclusions of the inapplicable for the purpose of determining a true conclusion or the classification of a subject — compare METHOD OF EXCLUSION

ab·scis·sion *also* **ab·sci·sion** \abˈsizhən, əb-, -ish-\ *n* -s [L *abscission-, abscissio,* fr. *abscissus* + *-ion-, -io* -ion] **1** : a cutting off or removal : ABLATION **2** : the natural separation of flowers, fruit, and leaves from plants by the development and subsequent disorganization of the separation layer

abscission layer \"-\ *also* **ab·sciss layer** \ˈabˌsis-\ *n* : SEPARATION LAYER

abscission zone *n* : the zone in a leaf petiole, fruit stalk, or branch often marked by a constriction within which is developed the separation layer, the vascular bundles in the zone usu. being reduced in diameter, the sclerenchyma being weak or absent, the collenchyma lacking, and the cytoplasm of some of the parenchyma cells being denser than in adjacent cells

ab·scond \abzˈkänd, abˈsk-, əb-\ *vb* -ED/-ING/-S [L *abscondere* to hide, fr. *abs-* (var. of *ab-* ¹ab-) + *condere* to found, construct, store up, conceal — more at CONDITE] *vi* **1** : WITHDRAW, FLEE ⟨valleys from which the evil spirits had long ago ~*ed* —Herbert Read⟩ **2** : to depart secretly : withdraw and hide oneself ⟨homesickness which . . . drives so many recruits to ~ —T.B. Macaulay⟩; *specif* : to evade the legal process of a court by hiding within or secretly leaving its jurisdiction ⟨~ from New York⟩ ⟨~ to Canada⟩ ~ *vt, archaic* : CONCEAL **syn** see ESCAPE

ab·scond·ence \-dən(t)s\ *n* -s : fugitive concealment : secret retirement : HIDING

ab·seil \ˈäpˌzīl, -ˌīəl\ *n* -s [G *abseil-,* fr. *abseilen* to descend by a rope, fr. *ab-* down + *seil* rope] : descent in mountaineering by means of a rope looped over a projection above — compare RAPPEL

ab·sence \ˈabsən(t)s\ *n* -s [ME, fr. MF, fr. L *absentia,* fr. *absent-, absens* + *-ia*] **1** : state of being absent or missing from a place or from companionship : failure to be present — opposed to *presence* **2** : failure to be present (as in an accustomed place) or where one is needed, wanted, or normally expected ⟨frequent ~s from a job⟩ ⟨drawings executed with ~ of detail⟩ ⟨a noticeable ~ of enthusiasm for his task⟩ : NONATTENDANCE ⟨~ from school⟩ : NONAPPEARANCE ⟨called on to speak in his brother's ~⟩ : DEFICIENCY ⟨the ~ of trained leaders⟩ **3** : inattention to things present ⟨~ of mind⟩ **4** : transient loss or impairment of consciousness beginning and ending abruptly, unremembered afterward, and seen chiefly in mild types of epilepsy **5** : lack of contact between blades in fencing

syn LACK, DEFECT, WANT, PRIVATION: ABSENCE usu. is used to indicate the fact that a thing is not present ⟨absolute liberty is *absence* of restraint —Henry Adams⟩ ⟨in the *absence* of a force strong enough to challenge the Federals, the towns submitted quietly —*Amer. Guide Series: La.*⟩ ⟨the serenity or *absence* of distorting passion in classic art —M.R.Cohen⟩ ⟨a complete *absence* of any thinking on fundamental problems of methodology —René Wellek⟩ LACK, although often interchangeable with ABSENCE, suggests an absence that constitutes a deficiency or falling short ⟨the *lack* of applause seemed a criticism of her work —*Current Biog.*⟩ ⟨he had become impressed by the *lack* of adequate textbooks in the schools —H.E.Starr⟩ ⟨production in other industries was similarly slowed by the power shortage and by a *lack* of raw materials —*Collier's Yr.Bk.*⟩ ⟨the mud and the *lack* of bridges made travel almost impossible —*Amer. Guide Series: Minn.*⟩ DEFECT implies the absence or the lack of something necessary to completeness or perfection ⟨each little fault of temper and each social *defect* —W.S.Gilbert⟩ ⟨*defects* of understanding based on ignorance and unfamiliarity —J.R. Oppenheimer⟩ ⟨those countries which are invaded suffer from the *defects* of the invader's civilization —Stephen Spender⟩ WANT implies the absence of something essential, usu. indispensable, often, however, indicating something only considered essential and, therefore, coming close to signifying something merely desired ⟨a certain *want* of confidence in his superiors⟩ ⟨the country was going to the dogs because of the *want* of education —F.M.Ford⟩ ⟨war production occas. suffered from *want* of hands to tend the machines or harvest the crops —Oscar Handlin⟩ PRIVATION in the sense pertinent here (as opposed to the sense of deprivation or destitution) has a use mainly confined to the fine philosophical definition of a negative state or quality in terms of its opposite ⟨cold is the *privation* of heat⟩ ⟨vice may be called the *privation* of virtue⟩

absence without leave : the military offense of being absent without leave — compare AWOL

¹**ab·sent** \ˈabsənt\ *adj* [ME, fr. MF, fr. L *absent-, absens,* pres. part. of *abesse* to be away, be absent, fr. *ab-* ¹ab- + *esse* to be — more at IS] **1** : not present or not attending ⟨~ committee members⟩ : being elsewhere : MISSING ⟨~ at roll call⟩ : being away ⟨~ from home⟩ ⟨~ friends⟩ **2** : not existing in a place ⟨a species totally ~ in the Great Lakes⟩ : LACKING ⟨danger in a situation where power is ~ —M.H.Trytten⟩ **3** *sometimes* -ER/-EST : INATTENTIVE ⟨his look had grown ~, as if he were calling up memories —William Black⟩ : PREOCCUPIED ⟨drew near to the fireplace, and looked into the flames in an ~ mood —Thomas Hardy⟩ — **ab·sent·ly** *adv*

²**absent** \abˈsent, əb-\ *vt* -ED/-ING/-S [ME *absenten,* fr. MF *absenter,* fr. LL *absentare,* fr. L *absent-, absens*] : to keep away ⟨~s himself entirely from all fellowship —R.L.Stevenson⟩

³**ab·sent** \ˈabsənt\ *prep* [¹*absent*] : in the absence of ⟨under this definition, ~ any other facts, there arises an implied contract —*Jour. Amer. Med. Assoc.*⟩

ab·sen·ta·tion \ˌabsənˈtāshən, -ˌsen-\ *n* -s [ML *absentation-, absentatio,* fr. LL *absentatus* (past part. of *absentare* to be absent) + L *-ion-, -io* -ion] : an absenting of oneself

ab·sen·tee \ˌabsənˈtē\ *n* -s *often attrib* **1** : one that is absent or that absents himself (as a pupil from school or a worker from a job) ⟨sick ~s⟩; *specif* : a proprietor that lives elsewhere — often used disparagingly ⟨~ landlords⟩ **2** : one that is nonexistent or lacking ⟨trees are notable ~s in the perpetually drought-stricken landscape —George Farwell⟩ ⟨in this anthology, these two authors being among the ~s⟩

absentee ballot *n* : a ballot cast (as by mail) by a voter unable to be present in person at the polls

ab·sen·tee·ism \ˌ⸗⸗ˈ⸗ˌizəm\ *n* -s **1** : protracted or permanent absence of an owner from his property ⟨~ of landlords⟩ **2** : continual interruption of attendance ⟨effect of ~ on factory production⟩ ⟨~ of school children⟩ ⟨his record of ~⟩

absentee ownership *n* : ownership esp. of corporation stock by one residing elsewhere than in the locality where income is derived

absentee voter *n* : ABSENT VOTER

ab·sen·te reo \abˌsentēˈrē(ˌ)ō\ [NL] : the defendant being absent

ab·sent·mind·ed \ˈabsəntˌmīndəd\ *adj, sometimes* -ER/-EST : preoccupied to the point of failure to respond to ordinary demands on the attention — **ab·sent·mind·ed·ly** *adv* — **ab·sent·mind·ed·ness** *n* -ES

absent over leave *adj* : having failed to return from liberty or leave on time — abbr. *AOL*

absent treatment *n* : treatment that ignores one's presence : SNUB, COLD SHOULDER

absent voter *n* : a qualified voter who is legally permitted to vote by mail because of illness or unavoidable and necessary absence from the voting district

absent without leave *adj* : absent from one's place of duty in the armed forces without authority — abbr. *AWOL*

absidiole *var of* APSIDIOLE

ab·sinthe *or* **ab·sinth** \ˈabˌsin(t)th *also* -ˌsən-\ *n* -s [F *absinthe,* fr. L *absinthium* — more at ABSINTHIUM] **1** : WORMWOOD **2** : a green bitter liqueur formerly flavored with wormwood, anise, and other aromatics but now usu. with a substitute for wormwood **3** *or* **absinthe green** : a moderate yellow green that is greener and lighter than average moss green, yellower and less strong than average pea green, and yellower and duller than apple green (sense 1)

absinthe oil *n* : WORMWOOD OIL

absinthe yellow *n* : a grayish greenish yellow that is slightly stronger and very slightly darker than hay, deeper than yellow stone, and greener and duller than dusty yellow

ab·sin·thin \(ˈ)abˈsin(t)thən\ *also* **ab·sin·thi·in** \⸗ˈ⸗thēən\ *n* -s [ISV *absinth-* or *absinthi-* (fr. L *absinthium*) + *-in;* orig. formed as G *absinthin*] : a bitter white crystalline compound $C_{15}H_{20}O_4$ constituting the bitter principle of wormwood

ab·sin·thine \(ˈ)abˈsin(t)thən, ˈabsənˌthīn\ *adj* [*absinthe* + *-ine*] : like absinthe

ab·sin·thism \ˈabsənˌthizəm, -ˌsin-\ *n* -s [F *absinthisme,* fr. *absinthe* + *-isme* -ism] : a diseased condition resulting from habitual excessive use of absinthe that contains oils of wormwood — **ab·sin·this·mic** \⸗(ˌ)⸗ˈ⸗zmik\ *adj*

ab·sin·thi·um \abˈsin(t)thēəm\ *n, pl* **absinthium** [ME, fr. L, fr. Gk *apsinthion*] **1** : WORMWOOD **2 a** : the dried leaves and flowering tops of a common wormwood (*Artemisia absinthium*) once used as a bitter tonic and stomachic **b** : oil of wormwood used as an ingredient of absinthe

ab·sin·thol \ˈabsənˌthōl, -ˌsin-, -ōl\ *n* -s [ISV *absinthe* + *-ole*] : THUJONE

ab·sit omen \ˌabsədˈōmən\ *interj* [L, may (evil) omen be absent, i.e., may what is said not come true] — used as a mild invocation (if he should fail, *absit omen,* all will be lost); compare *God forbid* at ²GOD

¹**ab·so·lute** \ˈabsəˌlüt *also* -əlˌyüt *or* ˌ⸗⸗ˈ⸗; *usu* -üd.+V\ *adj, sometimes* -ER/-EST [ME *absolut,* fr. L *absolutus,* fr. past part. of *absolvere* to set free, absolve — more at ABSOLVE] **1** *obs* : ABSOLVED, FREE ⟨~ from necessity⟩ **2 a** : free from imperfection or fault : PERFECT ⟨equally ~ is his meticulous taste in choosing the books —Christopher Morley⟩ **b** : free or relatively free from admixture : PURE ⟨~ alcohol contains one percent or less of water⟩ : OUTRIGHT, THOROUGHGOING, UNMITIGATED ⟨~ villainy⟩ ⟨an ~ lie⟩ **3** : marked by freedom from restraint or control by any governing or commanding agent or instrumentality: as **a** : having supreme power effectively or formally without constitutional or other restrictions ⟨an ~ ruler⟩ **b** : marked by extreme concentration of complete power and jurisdiction ⟨an ~ government⟩ ⟨an ~ dictatorship⟩ **c** : proceeding from or characteristic of an absolute ruler or state ⟨~ edicts⟩ ⟨~ power⟩ **d** : possessing or marked by absolute power : in sole control ⟨a ship captain ~ on the high seas⟩ **e** : ABSOLUTIST **4** : characterized by the lack of a particular (as the normal or usual) syntactical connection: **a**(1) *of a case form* : syntactically connected with the rest of its sentence in an atypical manner ⟨a nominative that is not the subject of a finite verb or a genitive that is not dependent on another substantive is an ~ nominative or an ~ genitive⟩ — see ABLATIVE ABSOLUTE, ACCUSATIVE ABSOLUTE, GENITIVE ABSOLUTE, NOMINATIVE ABSOLUTE (2) : standing by itself in loose syntactical connection with the rest of its sentence and qualifying the sentence as a whole rather than any single word in it ⟨*anyhow* in "anyhow, there is still time to catch the train" and *to say the least* in "to say the least, this procedure is unusual" are ~ constructions⟩ **b** *of an adjective or possessive pronoun* : standing alone without a modified substantive ⟨*blind* in "help the blind"; *ours* in "your work and ours" are ~⟩ ⟨*ours* is the ~ form of *our*⟩ **c** *of a comparative or superlative* : expressing a relatively high or an unsurpassed degree without definite comparison to any other under view ⟨*older* in "an older person should be treated with respect"; *greatest* in "I have the greatest confidence in him" are ~⟩ **d** *of a verb* : having no object in the particular construction under consideration though normally transitive ⟨*kill* in "if looks could kill" is an ~ verb⟩ ☞ In this dictionary absolute verbs are treated as intransitive **e** *in Irish and Welsh verb inflection* : belonging to or characteristic of a verb that is not preceded by any of a particular set of particles nor compounded with a preverb ⟨the ~ form⟩ ⟨an ~ ending⟩ — opposed to *conjunct* **5** : free from conditional limitation : operating or existing in full under all circumstances without variation or exception : COMPLETE ⟨an ~ requirement⟩ ⟨an ~ prohibition⟩ ⟨~ agreement⟩ ⟨~ freedom⟩ ⟨experience proved that man's power of choice in action was very far from ~ —Henry Adams⟩ **6** : free from doubt: as **a** *obs* : convinced and certain **b** : POSITIVE, UNQUESTIONABLE ⟨~ proof⟩ ⟨~ facts⟩ ⟨~ standards of righteousness —Rose Macaulay⟩ **c** : PEREMPTORY ⟨an ~ command⟩ **7 a** : independent of arbitrary standards of measurement ⟨an ~ coefficient in an equation⟩ **b** : having reference to or derived in the simplest manner from the fundamental units of length, mass, and time ⟨~ electric units⟩ **c** : relating to the absolute-temperature scale ⟨10° ~⟩ **8** : free from qualification: as **a** : final and not liable to modification or termination : FULL ⟨an ~ denial⟩ ⟨an ~ resignation⟩ ⟨~ divorce⟩ ⟨~ ownership⟩ ⟨rights that even seem ~ have these qualifications —O.W.Holmes †1935⟩ **b** : TOTAL ⟨~ loss⟩ ⟨~ perfection is denied to us humans —M.R.Cohen⟩ ⟨calm and ~ assurance —Arnold Bennett⟩ ⟨~ master of the raciest elements of the vernacular —J.L. Lowes⟩ **c** *of democracy* : ²DIRECT 4b **9 a** : free of relation-

ship or relativity : not compared : not dependent on or modified or affected by circumstances or by anything outside itself ⟨an ~ term in logic⟩ ⟨truth . . . is no ~ thing, but always relative —John Galsworthy⟩ **b** : FUNDAMENTAL, ULTIMATE, INTRINSIC : self-contained and self-sufficient : free from the variability and error natural to human perception and human ways of thinking ⟨God's ~ knowledge⟩ **10** : perfectly realizing or typifying the nature of the thing in question ⟨~ justice⟩ ⟨~ hate⟩ ⟨the abstract of beauty ~ —P.E.More⟩ **11 a** : concerned entirely with the expression of beauty or of pure feeling and devoid of meaningful reference ⟨~ poetry⟩ — see ABSOLUTE MUSIC **b** *of the dance* : relying on the medium of the human body for the expression of an idea independent of music, costumes, stage sets

syn AUTOCRATIC, ARBITRARY, DESPOTIC, TYRANNICAL, TYRANNOUS: ABSOLUTE indicates the fact of having or constituting complete power or authority without external restraint or control ⟨he ruled as an *absolute* monarch⟩ ⟨it was possible for Signor Mussolini to be made *absolute* managing director (Dictator or Duce) of the Italian nation —G.B.Shaw⟩ ⟨they held their subjects with an *absolute* hand as all communistic leaders do —F.M.Brown⟩ AUTOCRATIC and AUTOCRATICAL, likewise designating complete, unchecked power, may be derogatory in implying overwhelming domination or imperious attitudes ⟨*autocratic* prerogatives could be exercised, under the president, by military officers authorized to arrest without warrants, imprison, and mete out penalties at the drumhead —Charles & Mary Beard⟩ ⟨let the emperor turn his nominal sovereignty into a real central and *autocratic* power, subjecting every rebel city and noble —Hilaire Belloc⟩ ARBITRARY is often derogatory in suggesting caprice, unreason, and lack of consideration in exercising power ⟨as absolute a master of all their professional actions as ever was the most *arbitrary* general of the professional actions of his soldiery —W.H.Mallock⟩ ⟨irresponsible in its unrestraint, the majority vote may easily outdo an Oriental despot in *arbitrary* rule —V.L.Parrington⟩ ⟨that *arbitrary* idealism which knows no law —Josiah Royce⟩ DESPOTIC is likely to imply imperious and oppressive misuse of absolute power ⟨a *despotic* government based on fear or blind obedience is a state of slavery —M.R. Cohen⟩ ⟨his manner was imperious, and his administration had been arrogant and *despotic* —Willa Cather⟩ TYRANNICAL and TYRANNOUS, always quite condemnatory, imply cruel, harsh oppression by an absolute ruler or power ⟨the *tyrannical* rule of Porfirio Díaz, who reduced his own people to peonage while he sold out his country to foreign mining and business interests —Allan Nevins & H.S. Commager⟩ ⟨I remember recent instances where *tyrannical* judges sitting in local courts rode roughshod over the civil liberties of defendants charged with crime —W.O.Douglas⟩ **syn** see in addition PURE

²absolute \"\ *n* -S **1** : something that is absolute: **a** : something that is independent of human perception, valuation, and cognition **b** : something that is not dependent on anything else (as the Spinozistic substance, the first cause, or the primordial) — usu. used with *the* **2** *usu cap* **a** : one of various concepts: as (1) : ABSOLUTE EGO (2) : the underlying unity of spirit and nature **b** : the whole of reality considered as the final or total fact : that totality to which everything may be reduced or which in the estimation of its proponent constitutes the ultimate or final referent — usu. used with *the* **3** : a concentrated natural flower oil used in perfumery ⟨~ of rose⟩: as **a** : a concentrate prepared by removal of plant waxes from a concrete (sense 5) **b** *also* **absolute of enfleurage** : a concentrate obtained in the enfleurage process by removal of the alcohol from alcoholic extracts of the pomade

absolute altimeter *n* : an aircraft altimeter emitting a radio wave, distance to the earth being calculated by the time needed for the wave to reach the earth and reflect back to the aircraft

absolute altitude *n* : the vertical distance between an aircraft and the surface over which it is flying

absolute blocking *n* : BLOCK SYSTEM

absolute ceiling *n* : the maximum height above sea level at which a particular airplane can maintain horizontal flight under standard air conditions — called also *ceiling*

absolute constant *n* : a constant (as π) that has the same value wherever it occurs in mathematics

absolute ego *n* : the Fichtean ego that posits its own existence and through the opposition of subject and object thus created dialectically evolves the universe

absolute endorsement *n* : an endorsement that binds the endorser to pay only on failure of the prior parties to do so and on due notice thereof to him

absolute fee simple *n* : FEE SIMPLE ABSOLUTE

absolute form *n* **1** : the Platonic form of the supreme idea or unity in which all other ideas participate **2** : the subject-object relation

absolute humidity *n* : the amount of vapor actually present in the air usu. expressed in grams per cubic meter or grains per cubic foot

absolute idealism *n* : the Hegelian philosophy of the absolute mind or any one of a group of metaphysical idealisms deriving primarily from Hegel which affirm that fundamental reality is an all-embracing spiritual unity — see IDEALISM; compare HEGELIANISM

absolute impediment *n*, *canon & civil law* : a diriment impediment that makes it impossible for a person to enter into a marriage but does not require punishment or a decree of annulment

ab·so·lute·ly \ˈ=ˌ=ˈ=\ *adv* [ME, fr. *absolute* + *-ly*] : in an absolute manner or condition : INDEPENDENTLY, UNCONDITIONALLY, ENTIRELY, POSITIVELY ⟨~ unmolested inquiry —J.B. Conant⟩ ⟨iron is ~ necessary —Morris Fishbein⟩

absolutely convergent *adj*, *of an infinite series* : remaining convergent even if the signs of negative terms are changed

absolutely privileged communication *n* : PRIVILEGED COMMUNICATION 2

absolute magnitude *n* : the intrinsic luminosity of a celestial body expressed on a scale for which the distance is arbitrarily established (as of a star observed from a standard distance of 10 parsecs) ⟨the *absolute magnitude* of the sun is about +5 visual⟩

absolute majority *n* **1** : more than half of the votes: as **a** : more than half of the votes actually cast **b** : more than half of the number of qualified voters **2** : MAJORITY 3a

absolute music *n* : instrumental music independent of the objective suggestion of title, text, or program and dependent on structure alone for its subjective comprehension

ab·so·lute·ness \ˈ=ˌ=ˈ=\ *n* -ES : the quality or state of being absolute ⟨the ~ of the dictator's decrees⟩

absolute of enfleurage : ²ABSOLUTE 3b

absolute personal equation *n* : the deviation between a value obtained by an observer and a standard value assumed as true — compare RELATIVE PERSONAL EQUATION

absolute pitch *n* **1** : the position of a tone in reference to the whole range of pitch or to a standard scale and independently determined by its rate of vibration — distinguished from *relative pitch* **2** : the sense or memory of absolute pitch : the ability to sing or name a note asked for or heard ⟨that singer has *absolute pitch*⟩

absolute pressure *n* : total pressure at a point in a fluid equaling the sum of the gage and the atmospheric pressures

absolute privilege *n* : a privilege that arises in the law of libel and slander and that protects members of a lawmaking body (as Congress) in their statements made on the floor without regard to whether spoken in good faith — compare QUALIFIED PRIVILEGE

absoluter *comparative of* ABSOLUTE

absolute reality *n* **1** : ultimate reality as it is in itself unaffected by the perception or knowledge of any finite being **2** *Scholasticism* : reality in relation to the divine mind

absolute right *n* : an unqualified right : a legally enforceable right to take some action or to refrain from acting at the sole discretion of the person having the right

absolutes *pl of* ABSOLUTE

absolute scale *n* : a temperature scale based on absolute zero, the units of measurement being equivalent to centigrade degrees on the Kelvin scale or to Fahrenheit degrees on the Rankine scale

absolute space *n* : space independent of what occupies it : the space in which positions are finally determined

absolutest *superlative of* ABSOLUTE

absolute state *n*, *in the grammar of the Semitic languages* : the form that is characteristic of a noun when it is not linked in a grammatical construction with another noun (as Hebrew *bēn* "son") — compare CONSTRUCT STATE, EMPHATIC STATE

absolute system *n* : a system of physical units (as cgs units) based on a unit of force independent of the value of acceleration of gravity

absolute temperature *n* : temperature measured on the absolute scale — symbol *T*

absolute term *n*, *math* : the constant term of a polynomial

absolute threshold *n* : the smallest magnitude at which a sensory stimulus can reliably evoke a sensation

absolute time *n* : empty time apart from the events that occupy it

absolute value *n* **1** *of a real number* : the value irrespective of sign **2** *of a complex number* : the positive square root of the sum of the squares of the real and imaginary parts of the number

absolute weight *n* : the weight of a definite number of seeds used in calculating the average weight of a single seed

absolute zero *n* : a hypothetical temperature characterized by complete absence of heat: **a** *on the Kelvin scale* : approximately −273.16°C or −459.69°F at which no heat for performance of work could be derived **b** *on the scale of the constant-volume hydrogen thermometer* : approximately −273.03°C at which hydrogen pressure would become zero if a linear temperature-pressure relation were maintained **c** *in classical kinetic theory* : a point at which mutual linear motions of all the molecules of a substance would cease

ab·so·lu·tion \ˌabsəˈlüshən *also* -lyü-\ *n* -S [ME *absolucioun*, fr. OF *absolution*, fr. L *absolution-*, *absolutio*, fr. *absolutus* (past part. of *absolvere* to absolve) + *-ion-*, *-io* -ion — more at ABSOLVE] **1** : an absolving or setting free from guilt, sin, or penalty : forgiveness of an offense **2** *civil law* : ACQUITTAL **3 a** : a remission of sins imparted or pronounced by a priest in the sacrament of penance to a person who has confessed his sins **b** : a releasing from religious censure (as from excommunication) **4** : a rite, ceremony, or form of words in which a remission of sins is pronounced, proclaimed, or prayerfully implored by a priest or minister **syn** see PARDON

ab·so·lut·ism \ˈabsəˌlüˌtizəm, -əl,yü-, -üd·ˌiz-\ *n* -S **1** : the doctrine of what is absolute, unconditional, or independent: **a** : the doctrine of God's absolute sovereignty esp. as exhibited in predestination **b** : the political doctrine or practice of unlimited power and absolute sovereignty vested esp. in a monarch, dictator, or oligarchy **c** : a philosophy of an axiological or metaphysical absolute **2** : ABSOLUTENESS, POSITIVENESS ⟨an ~ of pure aestheticism is artistic and spiritual death —R.W.Stallman⟩

¹ab·so·lut·ist \-üd·əst, -ütə-\ *n* -S : one that propounds or advocates a doctrine of absolutism

²absolutist \"\ *or* **ab·so·lu·tis·tic** \ˈ=ˌ=ˈtistik\ *adj* : of, relating to, or in the nature of absolutism : ARBITRARY, DESPOTIC ⟨~ principles⟩ — **ab·so·lu·tis·ti·cal·ly** \-ək(ə)lē\ *adv*

ab·so·lut·i·za·tion \ˌabsəˌlüd·əˈzāshən, -əlˌyü-\ *n* -S : the process of rendering something absolute or converting it into an absolute

ab·so·lu·tize \ˈabsəˌlüd·ˌīz, -əlˌyü-, -ü,tīz\ *vt* -ED/-ING/-S [¹*absolute* + *-ize*] : to make absolute : convert into an absolute

ab·solve \əbˈzälv, ab-, -ˈs-, -ólv *also* -ä(ü)v *or* -óv\ *vt* -ED/-ING/-S [ME *absolven*, fr. L *absolvere*, fr. *ab-* ¹ab- + *solvere* to loosen, release — more at SOLVE] **1** : to set free or release from some obligation, debt, or responsibility or from the consequences of guilt or from such ties as it would be guilt to violate : pronounce free ⟨~ a subject from his allegiance⟩ **2** : to adjudge or pronounce not guilty : ACQUIT ⟨Halifax was *absolved* by a majority of fourteen —T.B.Macaulay⟩ **3** : to free from a religious penalty : PARDON : remit (a sin) by absolution **4** *obs* : FINISH, ACCOMPLISH **5** *obs* : to resolve or explain (as a difficulty) **6** : to qualify in (an academic requirement) : pass or obtain credit for passing (a course or an examination) **syn** see EXCULPATE

ab·solv·er \-və(r)\ *n* -S : one that absolves

ab·sol·vi·tor \-ˈälvəd·ər, -ól-\ *n* -S [L, let him be absolved, 3d pers. sing. pass. imper. of *absolvere* to absolve — more at ABSOLVE] *in Scots law* : a dismissal of an action : ACQUITTAL — **ab·sol·vi·to·ry** \-vəˌtōri\ *adj*

ab·so·nant \ˈabsənənt\ *adj* [¹*ab-* + *-sonant* (as in *consonant*)] *archaic* : DISCORDANT, CONTRARY, UNREASONABLE ⟨~ to nature — Francis Quarles⟩ — compare CONSONANT

ab·sorb \əbˈsó(ə)rb, -ˈz-, -ó(ə)b *also* ab-\ *vt* -ED/-ING/-S [MF *absorber*, fr. L *absorbēre*, fr. *ab-* ¹ab- + *sorbēre* to suck up, swallow; akin to Gk *rhophein* to sup up, MIr *srub* snout, Lith *srėbti* to sip, and perh. to MHG *sürpfeln* to sip, Norw *slurpe*] **1** *archaic* : to swallow up : ENGULF ⟨~*ed* by oblivion⟩ **2** : ASSIMILATE, INCORPORATE ⟨the power of Chinese civilization to ~ new arrivals —G.W.Johnson⟩ **3 a** : to suck up : take up by various means (as by capillary, osmotic, solvent, or chemical action) ⟨water ~*ed* by plant roots⟩ ⟨~ ammonia gas in water⟩ — distinguished from *adsorb* **b** : to take in : IMBIBE ⟨convictions ~*ed* in youth —M.R.Cohen⟩ ⟨the prudential morality he had ~*ed* from Puritanism —R.H.Gabriel⟩ **4** : to engage wholly ⟨~*ed* in thoughts of poetry —E.W.H.Lumsden⟩ : occupy fully ⟨work ~*s* most of his time⟩ **5 a** : to receive the impact of or undergo the shock of without recoil ⟨~ the vibration of machinery⟩ ⟨capable of ~*ing* punishment⟩ **b** : to receive without repercussion or echo ⟨walls lined with material that ~*s* sound⟩ **c** : to transform (radiant energy) into a different form usu. with a resulting rise of temperature (as when the earth receives energy from the sun) ⟨neutrons ~*ed* by cadmium rods⟩ **6 a** : to take up by purchase ⟨the business being ~*ed* by a competitor⟩ ⟨the market ~*ed* the entire production⟩ **b** : to take over (a cost) ⟨traveling expenses ~*ed* by the employer⟩ **syn** see MONOPOLIZE

ab·sorb·a·bil·i·ty *n* -ES : the quality or state of being absorbable

ab·sorb·able *adj* : capable of being absorbed

ab·sorb·ate \-bət, -ˌbāt\ *n* -S [*absorb* + *-ate*] : an absorbed substance (as a gas absorbed in a liquid)

ab·sorbed \-bd\ *adj* : obliviously engaged or occupied ⟨the mere sight of that engrossed look, that ~ and rapt delight —J.C.Powys⟩ ⟨so ~ in the business of his journey —Thomas Hardy⟩ — **ab·sorb·ed·ly** \-bədlē, -li\ *adv*

¹ab·sor·be·fa·cient \ˈ=ˌbəˈfāshənt\ *adj* [*absorb* + *-efacient* (as in *rubefacient*)] : causing or promoting absorption

²absorbefacient \"\ *n* -S : an agent causing or promoting absorption

ab·sorb·en·cy \ˈ=ˈbənsē, -si\ *n* -ES **1** : the quality or state of being absorbent **2** *or* **ab·sorb·ance** \-ən(t)s\ *or* **ab·sorb·an·cy** \-ənsē, -si\ : the ability of a layer of a substance to absorb radiation expressed mathematically as the negative common logarithm of transmittance — compare ABSORPTANCE

¹ab·sorb·ent \-bənt\ *adj* [L *absorbent-*, *absorbens*, pres. part. of *absorbēre* to absorb — more at ABSORB] : having power, capacity, or tendency to absorb ⟨as ~ as a sponge⟩

²absorbent \"\ *n* -S **1** : a substance that absorbs (as starch in pharmaceutical compounds) : a means of absorption ⟨surgical dressings used as ~*s*⟩ **2** : a liquid (as a petroleum oil) used in separating gases or volatile substances (as gasoline) in gas manufacture and petroleum refining

absorbent cotton *n* : cotton made absorbent by chemically freeing it from its fatty matter

absorbent paper *n* : a soft unsized paper used for absorbing water or other fluids

ab·sorb·er \-bə(r)\ *n* -S : a device for absorbing gases or vapors in a liquid (as in an absorption system or a petroleum-refining unit)

ab·sorb·er·man \-ˌman\ *n*, *pl* **absorbermen** : one that tends an absorber

absorbing *adj* : fully taking attention : ENGROSSING ⟨an ~ book⟩ ⟨an ~ task⟩ **syn** see INTERESTING

absorbingly *adv* : in an absorbing manner

ab·sorp·tance \əbˈsórptən(t)s, ab-, -ˈz-\ *n* -S [*absorption* + *-ance*; trans. of G *absorptionsvermögen*] : the proportion of radiant energy absorbed before it reaches the further boundary of a layer of absorbing matter, being equal to 1 minus the transmittance — compare ABSORBENCY 2

ab·sorp·ti·om·e·ter \əbˌsórpshēˈäməd·ər, (ˌ)ab-, -ˌzó-, -ptē-\ *n* [*absorption* + *-meter*] **1** : an instrument for measuring the reduction of pressure in a gas as it is absorbed by a liquid to determine the absorption rate **2** : a colorimeter for transparent fluids usu. employing photoelectric means of comparison — **ab·sorp·ti·o·met·ric** \ˈ=ˌ=ōˈme·trik\ *adj*

ab·sorp·tion \əbˈsórpshən, ab-, -ˈz-, -ó(ə)p-\ *n* -S [F & L; F, fr. L *absorption-*, *absorptio*, fr. *absorptus* (past part. of *absorbēre* to absorb) + *-ion-*, *-io* -ion — more at ABSORB] **1** : the process of absorbing or of being absorbed: as **a** *obs* : a swallowing up or engulfing (as of land due to subterranean movements) **b** : ASSIMILATION, INCORPORATION ⟨~ of immigrants⟩ ⟨~ of one railroad by another⟩ **c** : taking up by capillary, osmotic, chemical, or solvent action ⟨~ of moisture from the air⟩ ⟨~ of gas by water⟩ ⟨~ of nourishment in the small intestine⟩ ⟨~ by plant roots of nutrients from the soil solution⟩ — distinguished from *adsorption*; compare SORPTION **d** : interception (as of light or sound waves) ⟨the light of an average star in the Milky Way band . . . was dimmed through interstellar ~ —B.J.Bok⟩ ⟨high ~ of certain types of wallboard⟩ **2** : entire occupation of the mind ⟨~ in his employment⟩ **3** : the retention of electric polarization by some dielectrics for a measurable time after an exciting field has been removed — called also *dielectric absorption* **4** : the assumption by a freight carrier of special charges (as for switching) assessed by another carrier usu. without increasing the rate charged the shipper **5** : reduction of power of radio waves through dissipation (as in the atmosphere) — compare ATTENUATION 4

absorption band *n* : a dark band in an absorption spectrum

absorption cell *n* : a transparent container in which liquids are placed for the study of their optical absorption

absorption coefficient *n* **1** : the fractional rate at which flux density of radiation decreases by absorption with respect to the thickness of the absorbing medium traversed **2** : ABSORPTIVITY

absorption dynamometer *n* : any of several dynamometers in which the energy measured is absorbed by frictional or electrical resistances — see PRONY BRAKE

absorption edge *n* : a clear-cut long-wavelength boundary of an absorption band in an X-ray spectrum

absorption factor *n* : ABSORPTIVITY

absorption hygrometer *n* : a hygrometer that utilizes the elongation and shrinkage of organic tissue or fiber to indicate increasing or decreasing atmospheric humidity — see HAIR HYGROMETER

absorption line *n* : a dark line in the absorption spectrum of a gas or a vapor

absorption pipette *n* : a pipette for the absorption of gases

absorption spectrum *n* : an electromagnetic spectrum whose intensity distribution has been modified by passage through selectively absorbing substances — compare EMISSION SPECTRUM

absorption system *n* : a refrigerating system in which refrigeration is effected by the expansion of liquid ammonia into gas in evaporating coils, the expanded gas then being absorbed by water and used again after the water is evaporated

ab·sorp·tive \ˈ=ˈ=tiv, -ēv\ *adj* [*absorption* + *-ive*] : relating to absorption : ASSIMILATIVE ⟨problem for several generations was that of maintaining Canada's independence against the ~ powers of the U.S. —B.K.Sandwell⟩ : ABSORBENT

ab·sorp·tiv·i·ty \ˌabˌsó(r)pˈtivəd·ē, -ətē, -i *also* əb-\ *n* -ES : the fraction of a medium and of its surface that determines what fraction of normally incident radiation or sound flux will penetrate the surface of the medium and be absorbed therein — called also *absorption coefficient*, *absorption factor*

ab·squat·u·late \abzˈkwächəˌlāt, abˈsk-\ *vi* -ED/-ING/-S [¹*ab-* + *squat* + *-ulate* (as in *speculate*)] **1** *slang* : DECAMP ⟨a frontiersman preparing to ~ and head for the wilderness⟩ **2** *slang* : ABSCOND ⟨the cashier *absquatulated* with the funds⟩ — **ab·squat·u·la·tion** \(ˌ)=ˌ=ˈlāshən\ *n* -S

abs·que im·pe·ti·ti·o·ne va·sti \ˈabzkwē,impə,tishēˈōnēˈva-ˌstī\ [NL] *law* : without impeachment of waste

ab·stain \əbzˈtān, ab-, -bˈst-\ *vb* -ED/-ING/-S [ME *absteinen*, *abstenen*, fr. MF *abstenir*, fr. L *abstinēre*, fr. *abs-* (var. of *ab-* ¹ab) + *tenēre* to hold — more at THIN] *vi* : to withhold oneself from participation : refrain voluntarily : withhold oneself deliberately from an action ⟨a vote of nine million in favor, eight million against, and nine million ~*ing* —E.J.Knapton⟩ : FORBEAR — often used with *from* ⟨they ~*ed* from comment⟩ ⟨a lifelong pledge to ~ from drinking —M.V.Reidy⟩ ~ *vt*, *obs* : WITHHOLD **syn** see REFRAIN

ab·stain·er \-nə(r)\ *n* -S [ME *absteiner*, fr. *absteinen* to abstain + *-er*] : one that abstains esp. from the use of intoxicating liquors — used esp. in the phrase *total abstainer*

ab·ste·mi·ous \abzˈtēmēəs, əb-, -bˈst-\ *adj* [L *abstemius*, fr. *abs-* (var. of *ab-* ¹ab-) + *-temius* (fr. *temetum* mead, wine, intoxicating beverage); akin to G *dämlich* stupid, silly, ON *thām* mugginess, OIr *tām* death, Skt *tāmyati* he becomes stunned, exhausted, and perh. to L *tenebrae* darkness — more at TEMERITY] **1** : sparing in eating and drinking ⟨the pleasures of the table, never of much consequence to one naturally ~ —John Galsworthy⟩ ⟨he was not a teetotaler, but ~ —A.W. Long⟩ : generally refraining from indulgence of pleasures and cravings ⟨the most ~ of men . . . he held old-fashioned and rather puritanical views —Virginia Woolf⟩ : ABSTINENT **2** : used with or in conformity with temperance or moderation : marked by abstinence ⟨the Roman Empire appropriated far more energy than Greece, with its sparse ~ dietary —Lewis Mumford⟩ — **ab·ste·mi·ous·ly** *adv*

ab·sten·tion \əbzˈtenchən, ab-, -bˈst-\ *n* -S [LL *abstention-*, *abstentio*, fr. L *abstentus*, past part. of *abstinēre* to abstain + *-ion-*, *-io* -ion — more at ABSTAIN] **1** : act or practice of abstaining; *specif* : withholding of a vote ⟨seven votes in favor, three against, and one ~ —A.W.Rudzinski⟩ **2** : nonparticipation in political life or (as by a government) in international affairs ⟨cooperation versus isolation in the 'twenties, intervention versus ~ in the late thirties —H.J.Morgenthau⟩ — **ab·sten·tion·ism** \-ˌnizəm\ *n* -S — **ab·sten·tion·ist** \-ˌnəst\ *n* -S

ab·sten·tious \-enchəs\ *adj* [*abstention* + *-ous*] : ABSTINENT : self-restraining

ab·sterge \abˈstərj, əb-, -bˈst-\ *vt* -ED/-ING/-S [MF or L; MF *absterger*, fr. L *abstergēre*, fr. *abs-* (var. of *ab-* ¹ab-) + *tergēre* to wipe off — more at TERSE] *archaic* : to cleanse esp. by wiping : PURGE

¹ab·ster·gent \-jənt\ *adj* [F or L; F, fr. L *abstergent-*, *abstergens*, pres. part. of *abstergēre*] : CLEANSING, DETERGENT

²abstergent \"\ *n* -S : a substance used in cleansing : DETERGENT ⟨scoured with an ~⟩

ab·ster·sion \-rzhən, -rsh-\ *n* -S [MF, fr. L *abstersus* (past part. of *abstergēre*) + MF *-ion*] *archaic* : the action or process of absterging

¹ab·ster·sive \-rsiv, -rz-\ *adj* [MF *abstersif*, fr. L *abstersus* + MF *-if* -ive] : ABSTERGENT

²abstersive *n* -S *obs* : ABSTERGENT

ab·sti·nence \ˈabztənən(t)s, -bst-\ *n* -S [ME, fr. OF, fr. L *abstinentia*, fr. *abstinent-*, *abstinens* + *-ia*] **1** : the act or practice of abstaining: **a** : self-restraint or self-denial with regard to hunger, pleasure, or craving ⟨after long ~ from the movies —Edmund Wilson⟩ ⟨~ from narcotics⟩ **b** : the abstaining from certain foods (as meat) in obedience to ecclesiastical law or as a matter of religious discipline — distinguished from *fast*, *fasting* **c** : habitual abstaining from intoxicating liquors — called also *total abstinence* **2** : postponement of expenditure so as to accumulate capital

abstinence syndrome *n* : the physical effects that result from depriving an addict of the drug to which he is habituated

abstinence theory *n* : a theory in economics: interest is a reward for economic abstinence

ab·sti·nen·cy \-nənsē\ *n* -ES [L *abstinentia*] *archaic* : ABSTINENCE

¹ab·sti·nent \-nənt\ *adj* [ME, fr. MF, fr. L *abstinent-*, *abstinens*, pres. part. of *abstinēre* to abstain — more at ABSTAIN] : practicing abstinence : ABSTEMIOUS, CONTINENT, TEMPERATE — **ab·sti·nent·ly** *adv*

²abstinent \"\ *n* -S [ME, fr. *abstinent*, adj.] **1** : one that abstains **2** *usu cap* : one of a 4th century Christian ascetic sect in southwestern Europe that rejected meat eating and held that the relation between the sexes should be purely spiritual — compare PRISCILLIANIST

[1]**ab·stract** \(ˈ)abz¦trakt, əbzˈ-, -ab¦st-, əbˈst-\ *adj, sometimes* -ER/-EST [ME, fr. L *abstractus*, past part. of *abstrahere* to draw away, withdraw, fr. *abs-* (var. of *ab-* [1]ab-) + *trahere* to pull, draw — more at TRACE] **1** *archaic* **:** absent in mind **:** ABSTRACTED 3 ⟨~, as in a trance —John Milton⟩ **2** [ML *abstractus*, fr. L, past part.] **a :** considered apart from any application to a particular object or specific instance **:** separated from embodiment ⟨an ~ entity⟩ ⟨arguments from ~ probability —P.E.More⟩ **b :** difficult to understand **:** ABSTRUSE ⟨more ~ problems involving judgment and ability to reason —*Saturday Rev.*⟩ **c :** IDEAL ⟨to shed tears over ~ justice and generosity . . . and never to know these qualities when you meet them in the street —William James⟩ **d :** insufficiently factual **:** FORMAL ⟨she possessed all civil rights — but these were ~ and empty —H.M.Parshley⟩ ⟨~ and doctrinaire instruction⟩ **e** *of a unit or number* **:** having no reference to a thing or things — opposed to *concrete* **3** *archaic* **:** drawn away **:** REMOVED, SEPARATE **4 :** expressing a property, quality, attribute, or relation viewed apart from the other characteristics inhering in or constituting an object ⟨*honesty, whiteness, triangularity* are ~ words⟩ **5 :** dealing or tending to deal with a subject in the abstract: as **a** *of a science* **:** PURE, THEORETICAL — contrasted with *applied* **b :** IMPERSONAL, DETACHED ⟨I should have remained mainly academic and ~ but for the war —Bertrand Russell⟩ ⟨the ~ compassion of a surgeon —*Time*⟩ **6 a** *of a fine art* **:** presenting or possessing schematic or generalized form frequently suggested by and having obscure resemblance to natural appearances through a contrived ordering of pictorial or sculptural elements — contrasted with *academic;* compare NONOBJECTIVE **b** *music* **:** ABSOLUTE 11a **c** *of dance composition* **:** lacking concrete program or story **7 :** signifying a logical predicate or a class esp. of higher order (as number when conceived of as a class property)

[2]**ab·stract** \" *in sense 2; in other senses usu* ˈ=,=\ *n* -S [ME, fr. L *abstractus*, past part.] **1 :** a summary or an epitome (as of a book, a scientific article, or a legal document) **2 :** an abstract term or idea **:** the result of abstraction **3 :** something that comprises or concentrates in itself the essential qualities of a larger thing or of several things ⟨a man who is the ~ of all faults that all men follow —Shak.⟩ ⟨trial by jury . . . the very ~ and essence of . . . democratic government —W.H. Mallock⟩ **4 :** ABSTRACT OF TITLE **5** *pharmacy* **:** a preparation made by mixing a powdered solid extract of a vegetable substance with sugar of milk in such proportion that one part of the final product represents two parts of the original drug from which the extract was made **6** *fine art* **:** ABSTRACTION 6 **syn** see ABRIDGMENT — **in the abstract :** with reference to theoretical considerations only **:** apart from practical or actual conditions

[3]**ab·stract** *in vt senses 3 & 6 usu* ˈ=,=; *in other senses usu like adj*\ *vb* -ED/-ING/-S [[1]abstract] *vt* **1 :** to draw away **:** take away **:** REMOVE, SEPARATE ⟨add or ~ baser metal in minting⟩ ⟨a vast cigar-shaped body of gas was raised and eventually ~*ed* from the surface of the sun —W.E.Swinton⟩ **2 :** to separate (as an idea) by the operation of the mind **:** consider (as a quality or attribute) apart from any application to a particular object or instance ⟨~ the notion of dimension from that of space⟩ **3 :** to make an abstract of **:** EPITOMIZE, SUMMARIZE **4 :** to draw away the interest or attention of **:** DIVERT ⟨his imagination had so ~*ed* him that his name was called twice before he answered —James Joyce⟩ **5 :** to take secretly or dishonestly **:** STEAL, PURLOIN ⟨Shaftesbury's son seems to have ~*ed* important documents for Cavour —*Times Lit. Supp.*⟩ **6** *in life insurance* **:** to summarize (an insurance contract) esp. in the effort to induce a policyholder to cancel a policy and substitute another **7** *fine art* **:** to create abstractions suggested by (a concrete or natural object) ~ *vi* **1 :** to perform the process of abstraction or of abstracting something ⟨we naturally ~ when two similar objects are presented to us —Frank Thilly⟩ **2** *fine art* **:** to create abstractions **syn** see DETACH — **abstract from :** to leave out of consideration

abstracta *pl of* **abstractum**

ab·stract·ed \(ˈ)=¦==\ *adj* **1** *archaic* **:** ABSTRACT 2 **2 :** drawn away **:** REMOVED, SEPARATE, APART ⟨the evil one ~ stood from his own evil —John Milton⟩ ⟨possibility is that in which stands achievability, ~ from achievement —A.N.Whitehead⟩ **3 :** withdrawn in mind **:** inattentive to surrounding objects **:** PREOCCUPIED, ABSENTMINDED ⟨sitting silent and ~⟩ ⟨their pallid ~ air of human beings devoted to a difficult ideal —Herman Wouk⟩ — **ab·stract·ed·ly** *adv* — **ab·stract·ed·ness** *n* -ES

abstracter *var of* ABSTRACTOR

abstract expressionism *n* **:** the theory or practice of freely creating (as in painting) abstractions characterized by sinuous linearity, organic shape, and highly decorative surface

ab·strac·tion \abzˈtrakshən, əb-, -bˈst-\ *n* -S [MF or ML; MF, fr. ML *abstraction-, abstractio*, fr. LL, abduction, fr. L *abstractus* (past part. of *abstrahere* to draw away, withdraw) + *-ion-, -io* -ion — more at ABSTRACT] **1 :** the act of drawing or taking away **:** the state of being drawn or taken away **:** REMOVAL, SEPARATION ⟨labels bearing a clearly printed notice of addition or ~⟩ ⟨in search of seclusion, of loneliness, of . . . ~ from the trivial round —*Times Lit. Supp.*⟩ ⟨suspected of the ~ of money from the mail⟩ **2 a :** the act or process of leaving out of consideration one or more qualities of a complex object so as to attend to others (as when the mind considers the form of a tree by itself or the color of the leaves independently of their size or figure) **b :** the act or process of imaginatively isolating or considering apart the common properties or characteristics of distinct objects ⟨~ is necessary for the classification of things into genera and species⟩ **c :** the formation of a concept or an idea by such an act **:** the construction of a class name **3** [prob. fr. [1]*abstract* + *-ion*] **:** the result of a mental process of abstracting **:** an abstract idea or a term expressing such an idea ⟨his style was dense with ~*s*⟩; *sometimes* **:** a visionary or unrealistic idea **4 :** inattention to present objects or surroundings **:** absence of mind ⟨lost in ~⟩ ⟨an air of complete ~⟩ **5 :** abstract quality or character ⟨pantomime with a symbolic ~ that approached ballet⟩ **6** *fine art* **:** an abstract composition or creation **7 :** the merging of two or more streams into a single stream course by the deepening and widening of one valley so that it engulfs a shallower and smaller neighboring valley

ab·strac·tion·ism \-shə,nizəm\ *n* -S **1 :** the creation of abstractions esp. in art **2 :** the principles or ideals of abstract art

[1]**ab·strac·tion·ist** \-sh(ə)nəst\ *n* -S **1 :** one that deals with abstractions rather than with concrete things **:** one that takes abstractions for realities **2 a :** an abstract artist **b :** a supporter of abstractionism in art

[2]**abstractionist** \"\ *adj* [[1]*abstractionist*] *fine art* **:** showing tendencies toward abstractionism

ab·strac·tive \(ˈ)abzˈtraktiv, əbzˈ-, -ab¦st-, əbˈst-, -ēv\ *adj* [ML *abstractivus*, fr. L *abstractus* + *-ivus* -ive] **1 a :** having the power of abstracting **:** of an abstracting nature ⟨~ analysis⟩ **2 a :** derived by a process of abstraction ⟨an ~ element⟩ **b :** belonging to or formed by abstraction — **ab·strac·tive·ly** *adv*

ab·stract·ly \(ˈ)=¦==\ *adv* [ME, fr. *abstract*, adj. + *-ly*] **:** in an abstract state or manner **:** SEPARATELY, ABSOLUTELY **:** by itself

abstract music *n* **:** ABSOLUTE MUSIC

ab·stract·ness *n* -ES **:** the quality or state of being abstract

abstract of title : a summary statement of the successive conveyances and other facts upon which a person's title to a piece of land rests

ab·strac·tor or **ab·stract·er** \(ˈ)=¦=tə(r)\ *n* -S [[3]*abstract* + *-or* or *-er*] **:** one that abstracts or makes abstracts (as of records, documents, or scientific articles): as **a :** an accounting clerk who records payroll allotments, deductions, and disbursements **b :** a person who searches out and summarizes information to be used as reference or proof in legal or insurance cases

abstract plant *n* **:** a comprehensive record maintained by a title-insurance company indicating liens, encumbrances, and defects affecting the title to properties located in the community where the company operates as insurer — not often in formal use

abstracts *pl of* ABSTRACT, *pres 3d sing of* ABSTRACT

ab·strac·tum \=ˈ=təm\ *n, pl* **abstrac·ta** \-tə\ [NL, fr. ML, neut. of *abstractus* abstract — more at ABSTRACT] **:** an abstract entity (as a universal, a relation, a class name) ⟨whiteness and virtue are *abstracta*⟩ — contrasted with *concretum*

abstract universal *n* **:** [2]UNIVERSAL 2a(1)

ab·strict \abzˈtrikt, abˈst-, əb-\ *vt* -ED/ -ING/ -S [[1]*ab-* + L *strictus*, past part. of *stringere* to draw tight — more at STRAIN] **:** ABJOINT

ab·strict·ed \(ˈ)=¦==\ *adj* **:** cut off by abstriction

ab·stric·tion \=ˈ=shən\ *n* [[1]*ab-* + LL *striction-, strictio* act of pressing together, fr. L *strictus* + *-ion-, -io* -ion] **:** the formation of spores by the cutting off of usu. successive terminal portions of the sporophore through the growth of septa — see CONIDIUM

ab·struse \əbzˈtrüs, (ˈ)abz¦t-, əbˈst-, -ab¦st-\ *adj, sometimes* -ER/ -EST [L *abstrusus* concealed, fr. past part. of *abstrudere* to push away, conceal, fr. *abs-* (var. of *ab-* [1]ab-) + *trudere* to push, thrust — more at THREAT] **1** *obs* **:** CONCEALED, HIDDEN ⟨the eternal eye whose sight discerns *abstrusest* thoughts —John Milton⟩ **2 :** difficult to comprehend or understand **:** RECONDITE ⟨the ~ calculations of mathematicians⟩ ⟨involved and ~ language⟩

ab·struse·ly *adv* **:** in an abstruse manner

ab·struse·ness *n* -ES **:** ABSTRUSITY

ab·stru·si·ty \=ˈ=sədē, -ətē, -i\ *n* -ES **1 :** the quality or state of being abstruse ⟨the intrinsic ~ of the material with which the poem grapples —J.H.Wheelock⟩ **2 :** something abstruse

absume *vt* -ED/ -ING/ -S [L *absumere*, fr. *ab-* [1]ab- + *sumere* to take — more at CONSUME] *obs* **:** to consume gradually

ab·surd \əbˈsərd, ab-, -ˈz-, -ˈsəd\ *adj, sometimes* -ER/-EST [MF *absurde*, fr. L *absurdus* harsh-sounding, incongruous, absurd, fr. *ab-* [1]ab- + *surdus* dull-sounding, silent, deaf — more at SURD] **1 :** marked by an obvious lack of reason, common sense, proportion, or accord with accepted ideas **:** ridiculously unreasonable, unsound, or incongruous ⟨the ~ predicament of seeming to argue that virtue is highly desirable but intensely unpleasant —Walter Lippmann⟩ ⟨don't be so ~ as to forget you're a man, and to act like a child —Anthony Trollope⟩ **2 :** SELF-CONTRADICTORY **:** fallacious by reason of contradiction **syn** see FOOLISH

ab·surd·i·ty \-dədē, -ətē, -i\ *n* -ES [ME *absurdite*, fr. MF or LL; MF *absurdité*, fr. LL *absurditat-, absurditas*, fr. L *absurdus* + *-itat-, -itas* -ity] **1 :** the quality or state of being absurd ⟨to retain unmarred the sense of the ~ of all life —Rose Macaulay⟩ **2 :** something that is absurd ⟨the *absurdities* of social pretense —T.S.Eliot⟩ **:** a logical contradiction ⟨a new set of inconsistencies, not to say *absurdities* —P.E.More⟩

ab·surd·ly \-lē, -i\ *adv* **1 :** in an absurd manner **2 :** to an absurd degree ⟨an ~ rich young lady⟩

ab·surd·ness *n* -ES **:** the quality or state of being absurd

abt *abbr* about

abt system \ˈäp(t),s-, ˈa-\ *n, usu cap A* [after Roman *Abt* †1933 Swiss railroad engineer who devised it] **:** a system of tracking for mountain railroads in which two or more cograils are used and so arranged that the teeth are not opposite on any two of the rails

ab·u·def·duf \,abüˈdef(,)dəf\ *n, cap* [NL] **:** a genus of small ovate short-headed marine teleost fishes commonly found about rocks and other submerged objects and usu. included in the percoid family Pomacentridae but sometimes made the type of a separate family (Abudefdufidae)

abuild·ing \əˈbildiŋ, -ēŋ\ *adj* [[1]*a-* + *building*, pres. part. of *build*] **:** in the process of building or of being built ⟨formidable discontents, some already strong and some ~ —*N. Y. Times*⟩ ⟨low-cost housing now ~ at the edge of town⟩

ab·u·ku·ma·lite \,abəˈkümə,līt, əˈbükəmə-\ *n* -S [*Abukuma*, river on Honshu Island, Japan + E *-lite*] **:** a mineral $(Ca,Y)_5(P,Si)_3O_{12}(OH,F)$ consisting of a phosphate-silicate of calcium and yttrium sometimes containing uranium or thorium

abu·lia or **abou·lia** \(ˈ)āˈb(y)ülēə\ *n* -S [NL, fr. [2]*a-* + *-bulia, -boulia*] **:** loss of will power **:** abnormal lack of ability to act or to make decisions characteristic of certain psychotic and neurotic conditions — **abu·lic** *also* **abou·lic** \(ˈ)ā¦b(y)ülik\ *adj*

abu·lo·ma·nia *also* **abou·lo·ma·nia** \ā,b(y)üləˈmānēə\ *n* -S [NL, fr. *abulo-, aboulo-* (fr. *abulia, aboulia*) + *-mania*] **:** a form of mental disorder characterized by abulia

abun·dance \əˈbəndən(t)s\ *n* -S [ME *abundaunce, habundaunce*, fr. MF *abundance*, fr. L *abundantia*, fr. *abundant-, abundans* + *-ia*] **1 a :** a great quantity or amount **:** large number **:** plentiful supply ⟨an ~ of water power⟩ ⟨illustrated with an ~ of figures and diagrams⟩ — not commonly used of persons **2 :** overflowing fullness **:** great plenty **:** PROFUSION ⟨the ~ that pours from our factories and our farms —*New Republic*⟩ ⟨the whole bucolic ~ of the well-kept country seat —Vicki Baum⟩ **3 :** plentiful supply of means or resources **:** AFFLUENCE, WEALTH ⟨a life of ~⟩ ⟨the economics of the new ~⟩ **4 :** relative quantity or amount (as with respect to an observed or supposed norm) **:** degree of plentifulness ⟨information about the ~ of various species⟩ ⟨measurements on meteorites also indicate very low ~*s* of uranium and thorium —H.C.Urey⟩ **5** *ecol* **:** the relative number of individuals of one kind (as of a species) in an area under consideration

abun·dant \-ənt\ *adj* [ME *abundaunt, habundaunt*, fr. MF *abundant*, fr. L *abundant-, abundans*, pres. part. of *abundare* to abound —more at ABOUND] **1 a :** possessing (as resources) in great quantity **:** having great plenty **:** RICH ⟨a fair and ~ land⟩ ⟨the promise of a more ~ life⟩ **b :** amply supplied **:** ABOUNDING ⟨~ with fly life and other natural trout food —Alexander MacDonald⟩ — used with *in* and *with* **2 :** more than sufficient ⟨~ and well-distributed rainfall⟩ **:** occurring or existing in great quantity **:** AMPLE, PLENTIFUL, COPIOUS ⟨life, in all its forms, is most ~ near water —John Burroughs⟩ ⟨her forthright manner and her ~ common sense —C.G.Bowers⟩ **syn** see PLENTIFUL

abun·dant·ly \-lē, -i\ *adv* [ME *abundauntly, habundauntly*, fr. *abundaunt, habundaunt* + *-ly*] **:** in sufficient or more than sufficient measure **:** FULLY, AMPLY, PLENTIFULLY

abundant number *n* **:** an imperfect number that is less than the sum of all its divisors (as 12)

abundant year *n* **:** PERFECT YEAR

abune \əˈbᵫn\ *chiefly Scot var of* ABOON

abu·ra \əˈb(y)ürə\ *n* -S [Yoruba *aˈbuˈraˈ*] **:** a medium-sized tropical African tree (*Mitragyne macrophylla*) of the family Loganiaceae having large elliptical leaves, greenish flowers, and soft wood

abu·ra·chan seed \,äbərəˈchän-\ *n* [Jap *abura*.*han*, fr. *abura* oil + *chan* pitch] **:** the seed of a Japanese shrub (*Benzoin praecox*) yielding an aromatic medicinal oil

abu·ra·giri \,äbərəˈgirē\ *n* -S [Jap *abura-kiri*, fr. *abura* oil + *kiri* paulownia] **:** CANDLENUT 2

aburst \əˈ-\ *adj* [[1]*a-* + *burst*, v.] **:** BURSTING

abur·ton \əˈbərtᵊn\ *adv* (*or adj*) [prob. fr. [1]*a-* + *burton*] **:** with the length athwartship ⟨stowed the barrels and casks ~⟩

abus·a·ble \əˈbyüzəbəl\ *adj* [[1]*abuse* + *-able*] **:** capable of being abused

abus·age \əˈbyüsij, -zij\ *n* -S [[2]*abuse* + *-age*] **:** improper or incorrect use of language **:** bad usage

[1]**abuse** \əˈbyüz\ *vt* -ED/-ING/-S [ME *abusen*, fr. MF *abuser*, fr. *abus*, n., abuse, fr. L *abusus*, past part. of *abuti* to consume, abuse, misuse, fr. *ab-* [1]ab- + *uti* to use — more at USE] **1 a :** to attack or injure with words **:** reproach coarsely **:** DISPARAGE ⟨~ a person in the most violent terms⟩ **b** *obs* **:** to speak falsely of **:** MISREPRESENT ⟨*abused* her to her friends⟩ **2** *obs* **:** to cause to believe the false **:** lead into error **:** DECEIVE ⟨the Moor's *abused* by some most villainous knave —Shak.⟩ **3 a :** to put to a use other than the one intended **:** MISAPPLY ⟨*abusing* the privilege by invoking it for ends not sanctioned by law —Bernard Meltzer⟩ **:** use or apply improperly or to excess ⟨farmers have learned not to ~ the soil⟩ **b :** to put to a bad use **:** PERVERT ⟨*abused* his power by profiting at the expense of others⟩ **:** take unfair or undue advantage of ⟨he has *abused* my confidence in letting this secret become known⟩ **4 :** to use or treat so as to injure, hurt, or damage **:** MALTREAT ⟨~ a horse by overworking it⟩ ⟨~ one's eyes by reading in dim light⟩ **:** treat without consideration or fairness ⟨those left behind felt themselves *abused*⟩ **5 a :** MASTURBATE **b** *archaic* **:** to violate sexually **:** RAPE **c :** to commit indecent assault on — compare [2]ABUSE 5

[2]**abuse** \-üs\ *n* -S [ME, fr. MF *abus*] **1 :** a corrupt practice or custom **:** OFFENSE, FAULT ⟨the buying of votes and other election ~*s*⟩ **2 :** improper or incorrect use **:** MISUSE ⟨to call that state a democracy is an ~ of terms⟩ **:** application to a wrong or bad purpose ⟨the arbitrary punishments were an ~ of his power⟩ **3** *obs* **:** a deceitful act **:** DECEPTION, DELUSION ⟨or is it some ~, and no such thing —Shak.⟩ **4 :** language that condemns or vilifies usu. unjustly, intemperately, and angrily ⟨*bolshevist* had become . . . a vague term of ~ —Rose Macaulay⟩ ⟨the political harridans would . . . attack every possible leader with scandal and ~ —H.G.Wells⟩ **5 a :** the act of violating sexually **:** RAPE **b** *under some statutes* **:** rape or indecent assault not amounting to rape — compare CARNAL ABUSE, SELF-ABUSE **6 :** physically harmful treatment **:** MALTREATMENT, ILL-USAGE ⟨to be arrested for ~ of an animal⟩ ⟨~ of one's health⟩

syn INVECTIVE, OBLOQUY, VITUPERATION, SCURRILITY, BILLINGSGATE: ABUSE, the most general word in this list of terms, may frequently indicate a speaker's angry intent to wound; it usually suggests lack of anything that is fair or temperate ⟨now there is one word in the extended vocabulary of barrack-room *abuse* that cannot pass without comment . . . you must not call a man a bastard unless you are prepared to prove it on his front teeth —Rudyard Kipling⟩ INVECTIVE may apply to any denunciatory diatribe, but it often connotes a certain command of cogent language ⟨John Bull stopped at nothing in the way of insult; but its blazing audacity of *invective* never degenerated into dull abuse —Agnes Repplier⟩ ⟨Cicero replied in that masterpiece of *invective* known as the Fifth Philippic —John Buchan⟩ This suggestion is not necessarily present ⟨not the rapier of sarcasm but the bludgeon of *invective* —W.S.Maugham⟩ OBLOQUY may suggest language designed to shame another, language casting shame upon another ⟨those who . . . stood by me in the teeth of *obloquy*, taunt and open sneer, or insult even —Oscar Wilde⟩ ⟨to a symbol of *obloquy*, to an unanswerable epithet of derogation —Bliss Perry⟩ VITUPERATION suggests fluent, ready, and sustained abuse and castigation nastily delivered ⟨hag, nuisance, shrew, termagant let loose, she assailed everybody who violated in the least her prejudices. Presidents were nagged beyond endurance, and senators, and congressmen: no one could escape the vials of her *vituperation* —F.L.Pattee⟩ ⟨avoid reflections on the chastity of your opponent's female relations . . . Once you have gone so far it is impossible to retrace your steps and resort to minor forms of *vituperation* —Robert Graves⟩ SCURRILITY, the most uncomplimentary of these words, implies meanness or viciousness in attack and coarseness or foulness in language ⟨interrupted in his defense by ribaldry and *scurrility* from the judgment seat —T.B.Macaulay⟩ BILLINGSGATE may indicate very ready, easy profanity and obscenity delivered with practiced ease ⟨the *billingsgate* slang they certainly have acquired in perfection, and no white would think of competing with them in abuse or hard swearing —Sidney Baker⟩ ⟨an assortment of *billingsgate* that would have paralyzed a fishwife and brought blushes to a character in a Jim Tully novel or a Eugene O'Neill play —Herbert Asbury⟩

abuse of process *law* **:** the malicious use of a regular judicial proceeding without probable cause

abus·er \-zə(r)\ *n* -S [ME, fr. *abusen* to abuse + *-er*] **:** one that abuses

abusion *n* -S [ME *abusioun*, fr. MF *abusion*, fr. L *abusion-, abusio*, fr. *abusus* (past part. of *abuti* to misuse, abuse) + *-ion-, -io* -ion — more at ABUSE] *obs* **:** ABUSE, MISUSE; *specif* **:** abuse of the truth **:** DECEPTION

abu·sive \əˈbyüsiv, -ēv *also* -üz-\ *adj* [MF *abusif*, fr. LL *abusivus*, fr. L *abusus* + *-ivus* -ive] **1 a :** characterized by wrong or improper use or action **:** constituting an abuse **:** PERVERTED ⟨~ financial practices⟩ **b** *archaic* **:** CATACHRESTIC **c** *obs* **:** tending to deceive **:** FRAUDULENT, CHEATING ⟨an ~ treaty —Francis Bacon⟩ **2 a :** employing harsh insulting language ⟨an ~ spectator⟩ **:** characterized by or serving for abuse **:** SCURRILOUS ⟨~ jibes⟩ **b :** physically injurious **:** tending to damage or weaken **:** ROUGH ⟨tools made for ~ use⟩ — **abu·sive·ly** *adv* — **abu·sive·ness** *n* -ES

abus·tle \əˈ-\ *adj* [[1]*a-* + *bustle*, v.] **:** showing great activity **:** stirring busily ⟨a store ~ with crowds⟩

ab·u·sua \,abəˈsüə\ *n* -S [Ashanti] **:** a matrilineal exogamous clan among the Ashanti people

abut \əˈbət, *usu* -d·+V\ *vb* **abutted; abutted; abutting; abuts** [ME *abutten*, partly fr. OF *aboter, abouter* to touch at one end, border on (fr. *a-* — fr. L *ad-* — + *bout* end, blow, fr. *boter, bouter* to strike), partly fr. OF *abuter* to come to an end, aim, reach, fr. *a-* + *but* end, aim, purpose, of Gmc origin; akin to ON *butr* piece of wood — more at BUTT (to strike), BUTT (end)] *vi* **:** to touch (as of contiguous estates) along a border or with a projecting part ⟨his land ~*s* on the road⟩ **:** terminate at a point of contact (as with an adjacent structure) **:** lean or rest for support (as upon another structure) — used with *on*, *upon*, or *against* ~ *vt* **1 :** to border on **:** reach or touch with an end ⟨two lots that ~ each other⟩ **2 :** to cause to abut **:** support by abutment ⟨~ a timber against a post⟩

abu·ta \əˈb(y)üd·ə\ *n, cap* [NL, prob. fr. Sp, a plant of this genus] **:** a genus of tropical American woody vines (family Menispermaceae) — see WHITE PAREIRA, YELLOW PAREIRA

ab uti·li \aˈbyüd·ᵊl,ī\ [NL] *adv, of an argument* **:** from utility

abu·ti·lon \əˈbyüdᵊl,än, ,abyəˈtīlən\ *n* [NL, fr. Ar *awbūtīlūn*, a plant of this genus] **1** *cap* **:** a large genus of mostly tropical plants (family Malvaceae) having usu. lobed leaves and solitary showy bell-shaped flowers — see FLOWERING MAPLE, INDIAN MALLOW **2** -S **:** any plant of the genus *Abutilon*

abut·ment \əˈbətmənt\ *n* -S **1 :** the place at which abutting occurs ⟨at the ~ of two properties⟩ **2 a :** the part of a structure that directly receives thrust or pressure (as of an arch, vault, beam, or strut) **b :** an anchorage for the cables of a suspension bridge or aerial railway **c :** a tooth to which a denture or other prosthetic appliance is attached for support **3 :** the action of abutting ⟨~ of two braces upon the post⟩ **4 :** a fixed point, surface, or body from which resistance or reaction is obtained (as the cylinder head of a steam engine or the fulcrum of a lever)

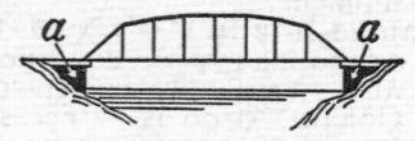

a, a, abutments of a bridge

abut·tals \əˈbəd·ᵊlz, -bətᵊlz\ *n pl* **:** the boundaries of lands with respect to other contiguous lands or highways by which they are bounded

abut·ter \-d·ə(r), -tə-\ *n* -S **:** one that abuts; *specif* **:** the owner of a contiguous property ⟨the ~*s* on a street⟩

abutting *adj* **:** that abuts or serves as abutment **syn** see ADJACENT

abuzz \əˈ-\ *adj* [[1]*a-* + *buzz*, v.] **:** buzzing or filled with buzzing **:** filled or resounding with talk and excitement ⟨London was ~ over the new appointment⟩

abv *abbr* above

ab·volt \ˈab,vōlt\ *n* -S [[2]*ab-* + *volt*] **:** the cgs electromagnetic unit of electrical potential and electromotive force equal to one one-hundred-millionth of a volt and being the potential difference through which transference of one abcoulomb of electricity involves a change of one erg in energy — compare AB- table

ab·wab \əbˈwäb\ *n* -S [Hindi *abwāb*, fr. Ar, doors, sources of public revenue, pl. of *bāb* door] *India* **:** any of various fines, cesses, or imposts levied by a native chief upon a landowner or subject

aby or **abye** \əˈbī\ *vb, past or past part* **abought** \əˈbȯt\ [ME *abien, abiggen*, fr. OE *ābycgan*, fr. *ā-* (perfective prefix) + *bycgan* to buy — more at ABEAR, BUY] *vt* **1** *archaic* **:** to suffer for or pay for (an offense) ⟨lest to thy peril thou ~ it dear —Shak.⟩ **2** *archaic* **:** to pay, suffer, or endure (as a penalty) ~ *vi* **1** *obs* **:** to pay the penalty **:** SUFFER **2** *obs* **:** ENDURE, LAST, CONTINUE ⟨but naught that wanteth rest can long ~ —Edmund Spenser⟩

abysm \əˈbizəm *also* aˈ-\ *n* -S [alter. (influenced by *abyss*) of ME *abime*, fr. OF *abisme*, modif. (influenced by words ending in *-isme* -ism) of LL *abyssus*] **:** ABYSS ⟨the dark backward and ~ of time —Shak.⟩

abys·mal \-zməl\ *adj* **1 :** having the characteristics of an abyss **:** BOTTOMLESS ⟨mountain roads . . . within a few inches of ~ precipices —W.R.Arnold⟩ **:** immeasurably great **:** UNENDING, PROFOUND ⟨~ ignorance⟩ **:** immeasurably low or wretched ⟨~ living conditions of the poor⟩ **2 :** ABYSSAL **syn** see DEEP

abys·mal·ly \-zməlē, -li\ *adv* **:** far down in the scale of acceptability **:** to an extreme degree **:** WRETCHEDLY, DREADFULLY

— used as a pejorative intensive ⟨~ poor⟩ ⟨~ cynical⟩ ⟨~ wretched⟩

abyss \ə'bis *also* a'-\ *n* -ES [alter. of ME *abissus*, fr. LL *abyssus*, fr. Gk *abyssos*, fr. *abyssos*, adj., bottomless, fr. *a-* ²a- + *byssos* depth, fr. *bythos* deep; akin to Gk *bathys* deep — more at BATHY-] **1 :** the bottomless gulf, pit, or chaos of the old cosmogonies: as **a :** a confined subterranean body of water that according to the Old Testament was once an ocean surrounding the earth **b :** the infernal regions including the abode of the dead and the place of punishment of the wicked **:** the abode of the evil powers **:** HELL **c :** the formless chaos out of which the earth and the heavens were created **2 a :** any vastly or immeasurably deep gulf or great space ⟨a road running close to the ~⟩ ⟨the ~*es* of sky and sea —Joseph Conrad⟩ ⟨the ~ . . . between the artist and the public —Harry Levin⟩ ⟨across the ~ of years⟩ **b :** intellectual or spiritual profundity ⟨in the ~ of his mind he apprehends the world's minuteness —W.L.Sullivan⟩ **:** moral depths **:** a condition of vast moral depravity ⟨an ~ of dark impulses⟩ **3 :** the bottom water of the deep sea — compare ABYSSAL ZONE

abyss·al \-səl\ *adj* [ML *abyssalis*, fr. LL *abyssus* + L *-alis* -al] **1** *archaic* **:** having the characteristics of an abyss **:** UNFATHOMABLE **2 a :** of, relating to, occurring in, or being in the abyssal zone ⟨~ sediments⟩ **b :** resulting from crystallization at a considerable depth within the earth ⟨~ igneous rocks⟩

abys·sal·benthic \ə¦bisəl + ¦-\ *also* **abys·so·benthic** \ə¦bi(,)sō + ¦-\ *adj* [*abyssal* or *abyss* + *-o-* + *benthic*] **:** of, relating to, or occurring on the sea bottom of the abyssal zone

abys·sal·pelagic \ə¦bisəl + ≈¦≈≈\ *also* **abys·so·pelagic** \ə¦bi(,)sō + ≈¦≈≈\ *adj* [*abyssal* or *abyss* + *-o-* + *pelagic*] **:** of, relating to, or occurring in the open water of the abyssal zone

abyssal rock *n* **:** PLUTONIC ROCK

abyssal zone *n* **:** the biogeographic realm consisting of the deep sea, lacking higher plant life because of the absence of light, and occupied chiefly by carnivorous animals that are often blind or have special luminous organs and are structurally adapted to withstand the great pressures of this level

ab·ys·sin·ia \¦abə¦sinēə, -nyə\ *adj, usu cap* **:** ETHIOPIAN, ABYSSINIAN

¹ab·ys·sin·i·an \¦abə¦sinēən, -nyən\ *adj, usu cap* [*Abyssinia*, kingdom in eastern Africa + E *-an*] **:** of or relating to Abyssinia **:** ETHIOPIAN **:** ETHIOPIC

²abyssinian \"\ *n* -s *cap* **:** ETHIOPIAN **:** ETHIOPIC

abyssinian banana *n, usu cap A* **:** a banana (*Musa ensete*) having leaves about 20 feet long, inedible fruit, and edible young flower stalks

abyssinian cat *n, usu cap A* **:** a domestic cat of a breed of African origin comprising small slender cats with short silvery gray or brown hair ticked with darker color and with a black stripe down the spine

abyssinian primrose *n, usu cap A* **:** a Chinese primrose (*Primula sinensis*) common in cultivation

abyssinian tea *n, usu cap A* **:** an infusion from the leaves of the kat

abys·so·lith \ə'bisə,lith\ *n* -s [*abyss* + *-o-* + *-lith*] **:** a deep-seated igneous body lacking a floor of crystalline rock — **abys·so·lith·ic** \≈¦≈≈¦≈ik\ *adj*

ac- — see AD-

ac *abbr* **1** account **2** acre **3** alicyclic **4** money of account

AC *abbr* **1** absolute ceiling **2** account current **3** after Christ **4** air corps **5** aircraftsman **6** alternating current **7** [L *anno Christi*] in the year of Christ **8** [L *ante Christum*] before Christ **9** *often not cap* [L *ante cibum*] before meals **10** army corps **11** athletic club **12** author's correction **13** automobile club **14** aviation cadet

Ac *symbol* actinium

aca·cat·e·chin \¦akə'kad·əchən, -əsh-,-ək-\ *n* -s [*ac-* (fr. NL *Acacia*, genus name of *Acacia catechu*) + *catechin*] **:** a crystalline substance that is obtained from acacia catechu, that is held to be a mixture containing catechin, and that is an antioxidant for fatty oils

ac·ac·e·tin \ə'kasət³n, a'k-\ *n* -s [ISV *acacia* (locust) + *acetin*] **:** a pale yellow crystalline compound $C_{16}H_{12}O_5$ occurring in the form of glycosides esp. in the leaves of the common locust; apigenin 4′-methyl ether

aca·cia \ə'kāshə\ *n* [NL, fr. L, acacia tree, Egyptian thorn, fr. Gk *akakia* shittah] **1** *cap* **:** a genus of woody plants (family Leguminosae) of warm regions having pinnate leaves and white or yellow flower clusters, the leaves in many Australian members being reduced to phyllodes — see CATECHU, COOBA, WATTLE **2** -s **:** any plant of the genus *Acacia* **3** -s **:** LOCUST 3a(2) **4** -s **:** GUM ARABIC **5** -s **:** a light to moderate greenish yellow that is redder and less strong than liqueur green — called also *weld*

acacia gum *n* **:** GUM ARABIC

¹aca·cian \ə'kāsh(ē)ən\ *n* -s *usu cap* [*Acacius* †ab A.D. 366 bishop of Caesarea in Palestine + E *-an*] **:** a follower of Acacius who taught likeness of will alone in the Father and Son in the Christian godhead

²acacian \"\ *adj, usu cap* **:** of or relating to the Acacians

³acacian \"\ *adj, usu cap* [*Acacius* †A.D. 489 patriarch of Constantinople + E *-an*] **:** of or relating to a schism occurring 484-519 between Eastern and Western Christian churches

acacia veld *n* **:** TREE VELD

aca·ci·in \ə'kās(h)ēən, -shən\ *n* -s [ISV *acacia* (locust) + *-in*] **:** a crystalline glycoside $C_{28}H_{32}O_{14}$ that is found in the leaves of a common No. American locust tree (*Robinia pseudoacacia*) and that yields acacetin on hydrolysis

ac·a·deme \'akə,dēm\ *n* -s [irreg. fr. NL *academia* — more at ACADEMY] **1** *sometimes cap* **a :** a place of study and instruction **:** SCHOOL **b :** academic environment ⟨the pleasant walks of ~ —R.M.Lovett⟩ **2 :** one with a marked leaning toward intellectualism and the academic environment; *esp* **:** PEDANT

ac·a·de·mia \,akə'dēmyə, -em-\ *n* -s [NL, university — more at ACADEMY] **:** academic life and interests **:** academic environment ⟨the complacent paddocks of ~, clubdom, or social status —Lucien Price⟩

¹ac·a·dem·ic \¦akə¦demik, -ēk\ *also* **ac·a·dem·i·cal** \-əkəl\ *adj* [MF & L; MF *académique* (influenced in meaning by *académie*), fr. L *academicus* of the school of Plato, fr. Gk *akadēmeikos*, fr. *Akadēmeia*, a place where Plato taught + *-ikos* -ic, -ical — more at ACADEMY] **1** *usu cap* **:** belonging or relating to the philosophy of Plato **2 a :** of, belonging to, or associated with an academy or school esp. of higher learning ⟨the ~ curriculum⟩ ⟨~ interests⟩ **b :** formed by school training or associations **:** SCHOLARLY ⟨an ~ mind⟩ **c :** very learned but inexperienced in or unable to cope with the world of practical reality **:** VISIONARY ⟨~ thinkers and schoolmen, men whom the free spaces of thought frightened and who felt safe only behind secure fences —V.L.Parrington⟩ **d :** based on formal study at an institution of learning, esp. of higher learning ⟨though I have no ~ qualifications, I am in fact much more highly educated than most university scholars —G.B. Shaw⟩ **3 :** of or belonging to literary or art studies ⟨the state might free the ~ high schools of those who do not belong there, either through an expanded apprentice training program or through vocational guidance —*Amer. Child*⟩ **4 a :** conforming usu. overrigidly to the traditions or rules of a school esp. of literature or art **:** CONVENTIONAL, FORMALISTIC ⟨I call them ~ because I think the composer's interest in the musical devices he was employing was greater than his effort toward a direct . . . expression of anything in particular —Virgil Thomson⟩ **b :** meeting the standards or deriving from the teachings of an official academy **c :** of a conservative nature **:** REALISTIC, REPRESENTATIONAL — compare ABSTRACT, MODERN **5 a :** theoretical and not expected to produce an immediate or practical act or result **:** SPECULATIVE, ABSTRACT ⟨the problem of truth is more than an ~ problem of rational, objective, neutral knowledge —J.L.Hromádka⟩ **b :** of no practical or useful significance **6 :** conforming to the architectural theories of Vitruvius (1st century B.C.) and later classical theorists as embodied in the doctrines of the Italian and French academies **:** marked by conventional use of the classical orders — **ac·a·dem·i·cal·ly** \-mək(ə)lē, -ēk-, -li\ *adv*

²academic \"\ *n* -s **1** *usu cap* **a :** a philosopher of the Academy **b :** one adhering to the philosophy of Plato **2 a :** one (as a professor or student) that is associated with or a member of an institution of learning (as a university) **b :** one that is academic in background, outlook, actions, or procedure

ac·a·dem·i·cals \,≈≈'≈əkəlz\ *n pl* **:** ACADEMIC COSTUME

academic costume *n* **:** a costume consisting typically of cap,

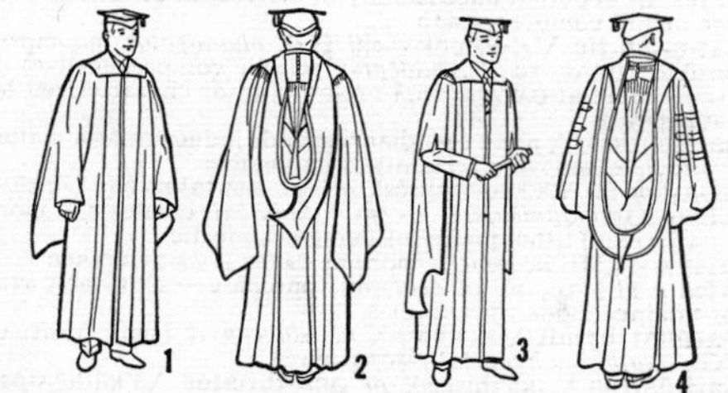

academic costume: *1* undergraduate, *2* bachelor, *3* master, *4* doctor

gown, and sometimes hood worn on occasion by students, holders of academic degrees, and faculty of a school, college, or university

academic freedom *n* [trans. of G *akademische freiheit*] **1 :** freedom (as of a professor) to teach according to personal convictions without what is or appears to be the truth without fear of hindrance, loss of position, or other reprisal **2 :** freedom (as of a student) to learn and inquire fully in any field of investigation without fear of hindrance, dismissal, or other reprisal

ac·a·de·mi·cian \,akədə'mishən, -(,)de'-; ə,kadə'-\ *n* -s [F *académicien*, fr. *académie* academy + *-icien* -ician — more at ACADEMY] **1 a :** a member of an academy **b :** a follower of an artistic or philosophical tradition or a promoter of its ideas **2 :** ACADEMIC

ac·a·dem·i·cism \,akə'demə,sizəm\ *also* **acad·e·mism** \ə'kadə,mizəm\ *n* -s **1** *sometimes cap* **:** a tenet of Academic philosophy **2 :** academic manner, style, or content **:** FORMALISM, CONVENTIONALITY ⟨writing lacks freshness if it is weighted down with ~⟩ ⟨a modernistic composer who broke away from the fixed norms of musical ~⟩ **3 :** purely speculative thoughts and attitudes divorced from immediate or practical effect ⟨he lived in a dreamy, unrealistic world of ~⟩

academic year *n* **:** the annual period of sessions of an educational institution usu. beginning in September and ending in June — called also *school year*

acad·e·mist \ə'kadəməst\ *n* -s [F *académiste*, fr. *académie* academy + *-iste* -ist] **:** ACADEMIC

acad·e·my \ə'kadəmē, -mi\ *n* -ES *often attrib* [in sense 1, fr. L *academia*, fr. Gk *Akadēmeia*, *Akadēmia*, fr. the name of the gymnasium near Athens where Plato taught, fr. *Akadēmos* Attic mythological hero + Gk *-eia* or *-ia* -y; in sense 2, partly fr. NL *academia* university, partly fr. F *académie* university, academy, fr. It & NL; It *accademia* university, academy, fr. NL; in senses 3 & 4, fr. F *académie*, fr. NL *academia*, lit., university] **1** *usu cap* **:** the school of philosophy founded by Plato **2 a :** a school above the elementary level; *esp* **:** HIGH SCHOOL **b :** a high school or college in which a special art, technical skills, or business courses are taught often to the exclusion of a liberal curriculum in languages and sciences ⟨an ~ of business⟩ ⟨a military ~⟩ **3 :** a society of learned individuals united for the advancement of the arts and sciences and literature or of some particular art or science **4 :** a body of established opinion in any particular field widely accepted as authoritative and often tending to stifle initiative ⟨the modern movement has been stiffening prematurely into an ~ —Lewis Mumford⟩

academy blue *n* **:** a moderate greenish blue that is greener, lighter, and stronger than average peacock and greener and deeper than Brittany

academy board *n* [fr. the Royal *Academy* of Painting, Sculpture, and Architecture, England, where it was much used] *n* **:** a heavy cardboard having a surface prepared for painting in oil

aca·dia·lite \ə'kādēə,līt\ *n* -s [*Acadia* + E *-lite*] **:** a mineral consisting of a flesh-red chabazite found in Nova Scotia

¹aca·di·an \ə'kādēən; *apparently formerly also* ə'kājən — *compare* CAJUN\ *n* -s *cap* [*Acadia*, Fr. colony of 17th and 18th cent. consisting principally of what is now Nova Scotia (fr. F *Acadie*) + E *-an*] **1 :** a native or inhabitant of Acadia **2 a :** a Louisianian descended from French-speaking immigrants from Acadia **b :** a dialect of French spoken by Acadians

²acadian \"\ *adj, usu cap* **1 a :** of or relating to the one-time French colony of Acadia **b :** of or relating to the Acadians **2 :** of or relating to the mountain-making movements in No. America in or near the Devonian period

acadian chickadee *n, usu cap A* **:** a brown-capped chickadee (*Parus hudsonicus littoralis*) of northern New England and Canada

acadian flycatcher *n, usu cap A* **:** a small No. American flycatcher (*Empidonax virescens*) that is olive-green above and whitish below and tinged with yellow on the belly and sides

acadian owl *n, usu cap A* **:** SAW-WHET OWL

acae·na \ə'sēnə\ *n, cap* [NL, fr. Gk *akaina* spike, goad, fr. *akē* point — more at EDGE] **:** a genus of herbs or low shrubs (family Rosaceae) mostly native to south temperate regions and having compound leaves and spiny calyces — see NEW ZEALAND BUR

ac·a·jou \'akə,zhü, -,jü\ *n* -s [F, fr. Pg *acajú* — more at CASHEW] **1 a :** CASHEW **b :** CASHEW NUT **1** **2 :** any of several mahoganies; *esp* **:** MAHOGANY **1** **3 :** LAUREL OAK **2**

acal·cu·lia \,ā,kal'kyülēə\ *n* -s [NL, fr. ²a- + LL *calculare* to calculate + NL *-ia* — more at CALCULATE] **:** lack or loss of the ability to perform simple arithmetical tasks

ac·a·leph \'akə,lef\ *n* -s [NL *Acalepha*] **:** a coelenterate of the group Acalepha

ac·a·le·pha \,akə'lēfə\ *n pl, cap* [NL, alter. of *Acalephae*] *in old classifications* **:** a class or other group of coelenterates including the jellyfishes, hydroids, and related forms and sometimes the ctenophores

ac·a·le·phae \,akə'lē(,)fē\ [NL, fr. Gk *akalēphai*, pl. of *akalēphē* stinging nettle, sea anemone] *syn of* ACALEPHA

aca·ly·cine \(')ā¦kāləˌsīn, -al-\ *or* **aca·lyc·i·nous** \¦ākə¦lisənəs\ *adj* [*acalycine* fr. ²a- + L *calyc-*, *calyx* + E *-ine*; *acalycinous* fr. *acalycine* + *-ous*] **:** without a calyx

ac·a·ly·pha \,akə'līfə, ə'kaləfə\ *n, cap* [NL, fr. Gk *akalyphē*, alter. of *akalēphē* nettle] **:** a genus of herbs and shrubs (family Euphorbiaceae) found in warm regions and having alternate leaves and monoecious apetalous flowers which are showy in cultivated species — see CHENILLE 2

aca·lyp·te·rae \,ākə'liptə,rē\ *or* **acal·yp·tra·ta** \¦ā,kaləp'trād·ə, -ād·ə\ [NL, alter. of *Acalyptratae*] *syn of* ACALYPTRATAE

acal·yp·tra·tae \¦ā,kaləp'trād·(,)ē, -ād·-\ *n pl, cap* [NL, irreg. fr. ²a- + *calypter* + L *-atae* (fem. pl. of *-atus* -ate)] **:** a group of two-winged flies having the alula small or wanting and including a number of pests (as fruit flies, many leaf miners, frit flies, and the cheese skipper) — **aca·lyp·trate** \¦ākə¦lip,trāt, (')ā¦kaləp,trāt\ *adj*

aca·na \'akənə, -,nä\ *n* -s [Sp *ácana*, prob. fr. Ciboney or Taino] **:** either of two West Indian trees (*Manilkara albescens* and *M. bidentata*) of the family Sapotaceae that yield valuable timber

acanth- *or* **acantho-** *comb form* [NL, fr. Gk *akanth-*, *akantho-*, fr. *akantha;* akin to ON *ǫgn* awn — more at AWN] **:** thorn **:** spine ⟨*acanthocephalous*⟩ ⟨*Acanthophis*⟩

acan·tha \ə'kan(t)thə\ *n* -s [NL, fr. Gk *akantha* thorn, spine of a fish] **:** a spine or spinous fin

ac·an·tha·ce·ae \,a,kan'thāsē,ē, ,akən-\ *n pl, cap* [NL, fr. *Acanthus*, type genus + *-aceae*] **:** a family of widely distributed herbs, shrubs, and trees (order Polemoniales) having opposite leaves and tubular bracted irregular flowers with two or four stamens — **ac·an·tha·ceous** \¦a,kan¦thāshəs, ¦akən-\ *adj* — **acan·thad** \ə'kan(t)thad, -n,thad\ *n* -s

ac·an·thar·ia \,a,kan'tha(a)rēə, ,akən-\ *n pl* [NL, fr. *acanth-* + *-aria*] *syn of* ACTIPYLEA

ac·an·thar·i·an \-rēən\ *n* -s [NL *Acantharia* + E *-an*] **:** a protozoan of the suborder Actipylea

ac·an·thel·la \-'thelə\ *n, pl* **acanthellas** \-ləz\ *also* **acan·thel·lae** \-(,)lē\ [NL, fr. *acanth-* (fr. *Acanthocephala*) + *-ella*] **1 :** a transitional larva of the acanthocephalan intermediate between the acanthor and the juvenile infective form — called also *preacanthella* **2 :** the juvenile infective form of an acanthocephalan

acanthi *pl of* ACANTHUS

acan·thi·al \ə'kan(t)thēəl\ *adj* [NL *acanthion* + E *-al*] **:** of or belonging to the acanthion

acan·thine \ə'kan(t)thən, -n,thīn\ *adj* [L *acanthinus*, fr. *acanthus* + *-inus* -ine] **1 :** of or relating to the acanthus plant **2 :** resembling the leaves of the acanthus plant

acan·thi·on \ə'kan(t)thēən, -ē,än\ *n* -s [NL, fr. Gk *akanthion* thorn, spinous process of the vertebrae, dim. of *akantha* thorn — more at ACANTHA] **:** a point at the base of the anterior nasal spine — see CRANIOMETRY illustration

acan·thi·sit·ti·dae \ə,kan(t)thə'sid·ə,dē\ *n pl, cap* [NL, fr. *Acanthisitta*, type genus (fr. Gk *akanthis* goldfinch, linnet + *sitta* nuthatch) + *-idae*] **:** a family (type genus *Acanthisitta*) of passerine New Zealand birds including the rock wren, rifleman bird, and certain related birds

acan·thite \ə'kan,thīt, 'akən,-\ *n* -s [ISV *acanth-* + *-ite;* fr. the thornlike shape of its crystals; orig. formed as G *akanthit*] **:** a mineral Ag_2S consisting of a silver sulfide like argentite but crystallizing in slender prisms (sp. gr. 7.2–7.3)

acantho- — see ACANTH-

acan·tho·ceph·a·la \ə,kan(t)thə'sefələ\ *n pl, cap* [NL, fr. *acanth-* + *-cephala* (neut. pl. of *-cephalus*)] **:** a group of elongated unsegmented bilaterally symmetrical parasitic worms that lack a digestive tract, have a hooked proboscis by which as adults they attach themselves to the intestinal wall of various vertebrates, and live out their larval stages as interstitial or digestive parasites, the group being of uncertain systematic position formerly considered a class of Nemathelminthes but now usu. made a separate phylum near Platyhelminthes or associated with or included in Aschelminthes — **acan·tho·ceph·a·lan** \-ələn\ *adj or n* — **acan·tho·ceph·a·lid** \-ləd\ *adj or n*

acan·tho·ceph·a·li \-ə,lī, -,lē\ [NL, alter. of *Acanthocephala*] *syn of* ACANTHOCEPHALA

acan·tho·ce·re·us \-'sirēəs\ *n, cap* [NL, fr. *acanth-* + L *cereus* candle — more at CEREUS] **:** a genus of tropical American weak often trailing cacti (family Cactaceae) having nocturnal funnel-shaped white flowers and 3-angled spiny stems — see PITAHAYA

acan·tho·chei·lo·ne·ma \ə¦kan(t)thə,kīlə'nēmə\ *n, cap* [NL, fr. *acanth-* + *cheil-* + *-nema*] **:** a common genus of tropical filarial worms parasitic in man and monkeys

acan·tho·cyb·i·um \ə,kan(t)thə'sibēəm\ *n, cap* [NL, fr. *acanth-* + L *cybium* tunny, fr. Gk *kybion* flesh of the young tunny, fr. *kybos* piece of salted fish, cube] **:** a genus (sometimes made the type of a separate family Acanthocybiidae though usu. placed in Scombridae) of large predaceous marine fishes that includes the wahoo and other food and game fishes

ac·an·tho·dea \,a,kan'thōdēə, ,akən-\ *or* **ac·an·tho·dei** \-dē,ī\ *or* **ac·an·thod·i·ni** \-'thäd³n,ī\ *syn of* ACANTHODII

ac·an·tho·des \-'thō(,)dēz\ *n, cap* [NL, fr. Gk *akanthōdēs* thorny, spiny, fr. *akanth-* acanth- + *-ōdēs* -ode] **:** a genus of small slender possibly degenerate fishes having generalized toothless jaws and a single small dorsal fin and found in the Carboniferous and Permian formations

¹ac·an·tho·di·an *also* **ac·an·tho·de·an** \¦a,kan¦thōdēən, ¦akən-\ *adj* [NL *Acanthodii*, *Acanthodei* + E *-an*] **:** of or belonging to the subclass Acanthodii

²acanthodian *also* **acanthodean** \"\ *n* -s **:** an animal or fossil belonging to the subclass Acanthodii

ac·an·tho·dii \,a,kan'thōdē,ī, ,akən-\ *n pl, cap* [NL, fr. *Acanthodes*] **:** a subclass of Placodermi comprising primitive Paleozoic fishes having the anterior margin of each fin supported by a stout spine and often having one or more pairs of spines similar to the fin spines along the lower lateral part of the body between the paired fins of each side

acan·thoid \ə'kan,thȯid\ *adj* [*acanth-* + *-oid*] **:** shaped like a spine **:** SPINY, SPINOUS

acan·tho·li·mon \ə,kan(t)thə'lī,män, -,mən\ *n, cap* [NL, fr. *acanth-* + *Limonium*] **:** a genus of stiff oriental herbs (family Plumbaginaceae) having basal leaves and small stalked heads of white or rosy flowers

ac·an·thol·o·gy \,a,kan'thäləjē, ,akən-\ *n* -ES [*acanth-* + *-logy*] **:** the study of spines (as of sea urchins) esp. as an adjunct of taxonomy

ac·an·thol·y·sis \,a,kan'thäləsəs, ,akən-\ *n, pl* **acantholy·ses** \-ə,sēz\ [NL, fr. *acanth-* + *-lysis*] **:** atrophy of the prickle-cell layer of the epidermis

ac·an·tho·ma \-'thōmə\ *n, pl* **acanthomas** \-məz\ *or* **acanthoma·ta** \-məd·ə\ [NL, fr. *acanth-* + *-oma*] **:** a neoplasm originating in the skin and developing through excessive growth of skin cells esp. of the prickle-cell layer

ac·an·thop·a·nax \-'thäpə,naks\ *n, cap* [NL, fr. *acanth-* + *Panax*] **:** a genus of prickly shrubs and trees (family Araliaceae) native to temperate Asia that have handsome palmate leaves and produce green flowers in much-branched clusters

acan·tho·phis \ə'kan(t)thəfəs\ *n, cap* [NL, fr. *acanth-* + Gk *ophis* snake — more at OPHIDIA] **:** a genus of venomous Australian snakes (family Elapidae) having a long horny upturned spine at the end of the tail and consisting of the death adder (*A. antarcticus*)

acan·tho·pod \ə'kan(t)thə,päd\ *adj* [*acanth-* + *-pod*] **:** spiny-footed

ac·an·thop·o·dous \¦a,kan¦thäpədəs, ¦akən-\ *adj* [*acanth-* + *-podous*] **1 :** spiny-footed **2 :** having spiny petioles or peduncles

acan·tho·pore \ə'kan(t)thə,pō(ə)r\ *n* -s [*acanth-* + *-pore*] **:** a tubular spine in some fossil bryozoans

ac·an·thopt \'a,kan,thäpt, 'akən-\ *n* -s [irreg. fr. NL *Acanthopteri*] **:** an acanthopterygian fish

ac·an·thop·te·ri \,a,kan'thäptə,rī, ,akən-\ [NL, alter. of *Acanthopterygii*] *syn of* ACANTHOPTERYGII

¹ac·an·thop·te·ryg·i·an \-,thäptə'rijēən\ *or* **ac·an·thop·te·ran** \¦a,kan¦thäptərən, ¦akən-\ *adj* [NL *Acanthopterygii* or *Acanthopteri* + E *-an*] **:** of or belonging to the Acanthopterygii

²acanthopterygian \"\ *or* **acanthopteran** \"\ *n* -s **:** ACANTHOPT

ac·an·thop·te·ryg·ii \,a,kan,thäptə'rijē,ī, ,akən-\ *n pl, cap* [NL, fr. *acanth-* + *-pterygii* (fr. Gk *pterygion* fin, small wing)] *in many classifications* **:** a superorder or other category of teleost fishes containing orig. all those having the anterior rays of the dorsal and anal fins stiff and spiny (as the basses, perches, and mackerels) or now those usu. lacking a duct to the air bladder, having no mesocoracoid bone, and having the pectoral arch suspended from the skull, the ventral fins attached to the clavicular arch, and the gill opening in front of the pectoral fin (as most of the spiny-finned and some soft-finned fishes)

acan·thor \ə'kan,thȯ(ə)r\ *n* -s [NL, fr. *acanth-* (fr. *Acanthocephala*) + *-or*] **:** the mature embryo of an acanthocephalan just previous to hatching — compare ACANTHELLA

acan·tho·scel·i·des \ə,kan(t)thə'selə,dēz\ *n, cap* [NL, fr. *acanth-* + Gk *skelos* leg + *-ides* (pl. of *-id-*, *-is*, patronymic suffix)] **:** a genus of weevils (family Bruchidae) native to America but of cosmopolitan distribution and including the destructive bean weevil

ac·an·tho·sis \,a,kan'thōsəs, ,akən-\ *n, pl* **acanthoses** \-ō,sēz\ [NL, fr. *acanth-* + *-osis*] **:** a benign overgrowth of the prickle-cell layer of the skin — **ac·an·thot·ic** \¦a,kan¦thäd·ik, ¦akən-\ *adj*

acanthosis nig·ri·cans \-'nigrə,kanz, -'nīg-\ *n* [NL, lit., blackish acanthosis] **:** a skin disease characterized by gray-black wartlike patches usu. situated in the axilla or groin or on elbows or knees and sometimes associated with cancer of abdominal viscera

acan·tho·so·ma \ə'kan(t)thə'sōmə\ *n, pl* **acanthosomas** \-ōməz\ *or* **acanthosoma·ta** \-ōməd·ə\ [NL, fr. *acanth-* + *-soma;* fr. its spiny carapace] **:** a peneid zoea

acan·tho·style \ə'kan(t)thə,stīl\ *n* -s [*acanth-* + *-style*] **:** a monaxon sponge spicule rounded at one end and bearing tiny spines

acan·thous \ə'kan(t)thəs\ *adj* [*acanth-* + *-ous*] **:** SPINOUS

ac·an·thu·ri·dae \,a,kan'th(y)ürə,dē, ,akən-\ *n pl, cap* [NL, fr. *Acanthurus*, type genus + *-idae*] *syn of* TEUTHIDIDAE

ac·an·thu·rus \-rəs\ [NL, fr. *acanth-* + *-urus*] *syn of* TEUTHIS

acan·thus \ə'kan(t)thəs\ *n* [NL, fr. Gk *akanthos* (*Acanthus mollis, Acanthus spinosus*), fr. *akantha* thorn — more at ACANTHA] **1 a** *cap* **:** a genus of prickly herbs (family Acanthaceae) of the Mediterranean region that have spiny-bracted flowers **b** *pl* **acanthuses** \-n(t)thəsəz\ *also* **acan·thi** \-n,thī, -,thē\ **:** any plant of the genus *Acanthus* **2** *pl* **acanthuses** *also* **acanthi :** a usu. sculptured ornamentation representing or suggesting the leaves of the acanthus (as in a Corinthian capital)

acanthus 2

-a·can·thus \"\ *n comb form* [NL, fr. Gk *akantha* thorn] **:** animal having (such) a spine or (such or so many) spines ⟨Cephal*acanthus*⟩ ⟨Cten*acanthus*⟩ — in generic names esp. of fishes

acanthus family *n, usu cap A* **:** ACANTHACEAE

acap·nia \ə'kapnēə, (')ā'-\ *n* -S [NL, fr. L *acapnos* without smoke, used to mean "without carbon dioxide", which is contained in smoke (fr. Gk *akapnos*, fr. *a-* ²a- + *kapnos* smoke) + NL *-ia* — more at COVET] **:** a condition of carbon dioxide deficiency in blood and tissues — **acap·ni·al** \-ēəl\ *adj*

¹**a cap·pel·la** *also* **a ca·pel·la** \,äkə'pelə, ,ā-\ *adv* [It *a cappella* in chapel or choir style] **1 :** in a style marked by the absence of instrumental accompaniment ⟨sing *a cappella*⟩ **2** *obs* **:** in alla breve time

²**a cappella** *also* **a capella** \¦==¦==\ *adj* **1 :** unaccompanied by instruments **:** marked by or specializing in unaccompanied singing ⟨an *a cappella* choir⟩ **2** *obs* **:** ALLA BREVE

a ca·pric·cio \,äkə'prē(,)chō, -ri-, -,che,ō\ *adv* [It, at one's caprice] **:** in any interpretation that appeals to the performer — used as a direction in music

acap·su·lar \(')ā¦kapsələ(r)\ *adj* [²a- + *capsular*] *bot* **:** having no capsule

aca·pu \,äkə¦pü\ *n* -S [Pg *acapú*, fr. Tupi] **1 a :** any of several tropical American timber trees of the genus *Andira* (esp. *A. americana*) **b :** the dark chocolate-brown wood of the acapu tree widely used esp. in Brazil for flooring and heavy construction **2 a :** an Amazonian leguminous tree (*Clathrotropis nitida*) **b :** the wood of this tree used for heavy construction

aca·pul·co \,äkə'pül(,)kō\ *n* -S [PhilSp, fr. *Acapulco*, Mexico, its point of export] **:** a Mexican plant (*Cassia alata*) introduced into Guam and the Philippines the leaves of which are used as a folk remedy for ringworm and other skin diseases

acar- *or* **acari-** *or* **acaro-** *comb form* [NL, fr. *Acarus*] **:** mite ⟨*acar*oid⟩ ⟨*acari*cide⟩

aca·ra \,äkə¦rä\ *n* -S [Pg *acará*, fr. Tupi] **:** any of several So. American and Central American fishes (family Cichlidae) that build nests and guard their young — see BLUE ACARA

acar·a·pis \ə'karəpəs\ *n, cap* [NL, fr. *acar-* + L *apis* bee] **:** a genus of minute mites that are chiefly parasitic on insects and include a species (*A. woodi*) that invades the tracheae of honeybees causing Isle of Wight disease

acar·dite \ə'kär,dīt\ *n* -S [origin unknown] **:** a crystalline compound $(C_6H_5)_2NCONH_2$ used as a stabilizer in smokeless powder; 1,1-diphenyl-urea

¹**ac·a·ri** \'akərē, -,rī\ [NL, fr. Gk *akari*, a mite] *syn of* ACARINA

²**acari** *pl of* ACARUS

¹**acar·i·an** \ə'ka(a)rēən\ *adj* [NL *Acari* + E *-an*] **1 :** of or relating to the order Acarina **2 :** of, relating to, caused by, or having the characteristics of a mite or tick

²**acarian** \"\ *n* -S **:** an arachnid of the order Acarina **:** MITE, TICK

ac·a·ri·a·sis \,akə'rīəsəs\ *n, pl* **acaria·ses** \-ə,sēz\ [NL, fr. *acar-* + *-iasis*] **:** infestation with or disease caused by mites

acar·i·cid·al \ə¦karə¦sīdᵊl\ *adj* [*acaricide* + *-al*] **:** that kills mites ⟨an ~ compound⟩

acar·i·cide *also* **acar·a·cide** \ə'karə,sīd\ *n* -S [*acaricide* fr. *acar-* + *-cide*; *acaracide*, alter. of *acaricide*] **:** a substance or preparation that kills mites

¹**ac·a·rid** \'akərəd, -,(,)rid\ *adj* [NL *Acarida*] **1 :** ACARIAN **2 :** of or relating to the family Acaridae

²**acarid** \"\ *n* -S **1 :** ACARIAN **2 :** a mite of the family Acaridae

acar·i·da \ə'karədə\ *or* **ac·a·rid·ea** \,akə'ridēə\ [NL, fr. *Acarus* + *-ida* or *-idea*] *syn of* ACARINA

acar·i·dae \ə'karə,dē\ *n pl, cap* [NL, fr. *Acarus*, type genus + *-idae*] **:** a large and widely distributed family of mites that feed on organic substances (as preserved meats, hides, seeds, and grains) and are sometimes responsible for dermatitis in persons exposed to repeated contacts with infested products — see GROCER'S ITCH

¹**acar·i·dan** \ə'karədᵊn, -dən\ *also* **ac·a·rid·e·an** *or* **ac·a·rid·i·an** \¦akə¦ridēən\ *adj* [NL *Acaridae* + E *-an, -ean, -ian*] **:** ACARIAN; *esp* **:** ACARID 2

²**acaridan** \"\ *also* **acaridean** *or* **acaridian** \"\ *n* -S **:** ACARIAN; *esp* **:** ACARID 2

acar·i·dol·o·gist \ə,karə'däləjəst\ *n* -S [*acarid* + *-o-* + *-logist*] **:** ACAROLOGIST

acar·i·form \ə'karə,fȯrm\ *adj* [*acar-* + *form*] **:** shaped like a mite

ac·a·ri·na \,akə'rīnə, -ēnə\ *n pl, cap* [NL, fr. *Acarus* + *-ina*] **:** a cosmopolitan and very large order of Arachnida comprising the mites and ticks most of which lack distinct demarcation into cephalothorax and abdomen and have no book lungs, many of which are parasites of plants, animals, or man, and some of which are vectors of important diseases — compare TEXAS FEVER, TYPHUS

ac·a·ri·nar·i·um \-rə'na(a)rēəm\ *n, pl* **acarinar·ia** \-ēə\ *or* **acarinariums** \-ēəmz\ [NL, fr. *Acarina* + *-arium*] **:** a chamber of the body wall of insects (as wasps) frequently infested by tiny nonparasitic mites

ac·a·rine \'akə,rīn, -,rēn, -rən\ *adj or n* [NL *Acarina*] **:** ACARIAN

acarine disease *n* **:** Isle of Wight disease of honeybees; *also* **:** any disease caused by ticks or mites

ac·a·ri·nol·o·gy \,akərə'näləjē\ *n* -ES [NL *Acarina* + E *-o-* *-logy*] **:** ACAROLOGY

ac·a·ri·no·sis \-'nōsəs\ *n, pl* **acarino·ses** \-ō,sēz\ [NL, fr. *Acarina* + *-osis*] **:** ACARIASIS

acar·i·o·sis \ə,karē'ōsəs\ *n, pl* **acario·ses** \-ō,sēz\ [NL, by alter.] **:** ACARIASIS

ac·a·ro·ce·cid·i·um \¦akə(,)rōsə'sidēəm\ *n, pl* **acarocecid·ia** \-ēə\ *or* **acarocecidiums** \-ēəmz\ [NL, fr. *acar-* + *cecidium*] **:** a plant gall caused by an acarid

ac·a·roid \'akə,rȯid\ *adj* [*acar-* + *-oid*] **:** resembling a mite

acaroid resin *n* [NL *acaroides*] **:** a red or yellow balsamic alcohol-soluble resin from Australian grass trees used chiefly in varnishes, printing inks, and paper sizes — called also *accroides, gum accroides*

ac·a·rol·o·gist \,akə'räləjəst\ *n* -S [*acarology* + *-ist*] **:** a student of or specialist in acarology

ac·a·rol·o·gy \-jē\ *n* -ES [*acar-* + *-logy*] **1 :** a branch of zoology that treats of mites and ticks **2 :** a treatise on mites and ticks

ac·a·ro·pho·bia \,akərə'fōbēə\ *n* -S [NL, fr. *acar-* + *-phobia*] **1 :** an abnormal dread of skin infestation with small crawling organisms **2 :** a delusion that the skin is infested with small crawling organisms

acar·pel·ous *or* **acar·pel·lous** \(')ā¦kärpələs\ *adj* [²a- + *carpel* + *-ous*] **:** having no carpels

acar·pous \(')ā¦kärpəs\ *adj* [Gk *akarpos*, fr. *a-* ²a- + *-karpos* -carpous] *bot* **:** not producing fruit **:** STERILE

ac·a·rus \'akərəs\ *n* [NL, fr. Gk *akari*, a mite; prob. akin to Gk *keirein* to cut off, shear — more at SHEAR] **1** *cap* **:** a genus of arachnids including a number of small mites and formerly including all mites and ticks **2** *pl* **aca·ri** \-,rī, -,rē\ **:** MITE; *usu* **:** a mite of the genus *Acarus*

¹**acat·a·lec·tic** \¦ā,kad·ᵊl¦ektik\ *adj* [LL *acatalecticus*, fr. *acatalectus* (fr. Gk *akatalēktos*, fr. *a-* ²a- + *-katalēktos*, fr. *katalēgein* to leave off) + L *-icus* -ic — more at CATALECTIC] *prosody* **:** not defective in the last foot **:** complete in the number of syllables ⟨an ~ line of verse⟩

²**acatalectic** \"\ *n* -S **:** a line of verse complete in the number of its syllables

acat·a·lep·sy \(')ā'kad·ᵊl,epsē\ *n* -ES [Gk *akatalēpsia*, fr. *a-* ²a- + *katalēpsis* comprehension, seizing + *-ia* — more at CATALEPSY] **1 :** an ancient Skeptic doctrine that human knowledge amounts only to probability and never to certainty **2 :** real or apparent impossibility of arriving at certain knowledge or full comprehension

¹**acat·a·lep·tic** \¦=,==¦eptik\ *adj* [Gk *akatalēptos* incomprehensible (fr. *a-* ²a- + *katalēptos* seized, comprehensible) + E *-ic* — more at CATALEPTIC] **:** relating to or characterized by acatalepsy

²**acataleptic** \"\ *n* -S **:** one that suspends judgment as a matter of principle believing certainty is impossible

acat·a·lex·is \¦ā,kad·ᵊl'eksəs\ *n, pl* **acatalex·es** \-k,sēz\ [LL, fr. Gk *akatalēxis*, fr. *a-* ²a- + *katalēxis* catalexis — more at CATALEXIS] **:** the quality of being acatalectic

acater *n* -S [ME *acatour* — more at CATER] *obs* **:** CATERER

acates *n pl* [ME, pl. of *acat*, lit., purchase — more at CATE] *obs* **:** dainty foods **:** DELICACIES

ac·a·thist hymn \'akə,thəst-\ *n, usu cap A* [part trans. of MGk *akathistos hymnos*] **:** ACATHISTUS

ac·a·this·tus \,akə'thistəs\ *or* **aca·thi·stos** \ä'käthē,stōs\ *also* **ak·a·thist** \'akə,thist\ *or* **aka·thi·stos** \ä'käthē,stōs\ *n, pl* **ac·a·this·ti** \,akə'thi,stī, -(,)stē\ *or* **aca·thi·stoi** \ä'käthē,stē\ *also* **ak·a·thists** \'akə,this(t)s\ *or* **aka·thi·stoi** \ä'käthē,stē\ *usu cap* [MGk *akathistos* (*hymnos*), lit., standing hymn, fr. *akathistos* standing, fr. *a-* ²a- + *-kathistos* (fr. Gk *kathizein* to seat, set, sit, fr. *kata* down + *-izein* -ize) — more at CATA-] **:** any of several Lenten hymns of the Eastern Orthodox Church sung with the people standing in honor of Christ, the Virgin Mary, or one of the saints

acau·dal \(')ā¦kȯdᵊl\ *or* **acau·date** \(')ā'kȯ,dāt\ *adj* [²a- + *caudal, caudate*] **:** without a tail

acau·les·cence \¦ā(,)kȯ'lesᵊn(t)s\ *n* -S **:** state of being acaulescent

acau·les·cent \¦ā(,)kȯ¦lesᵊnt\ *or* **acau·line** \(')ā'kȯ,līn\ *adj* [²a- + *caulescent* or *-cauline* (fr. L *caulis* stem + E *-ine*) — more at COLE] **:** stemless or apparently stemless — opposed to *caulescent*

aca·wai *or* **aka·wai** \'äkə,wī\ *n, pl* **acawai** *or* **acawais** *or* **akawai** *or* **akawais** *usu cap* **1 a :** a Cariban people of northwestern British Guiana **b :** a member of such people **2 :** the language of the Acawai people

aca·xee \'ä'käkē\ *n, pl* **acaxee** *or* **acaxees** *usu cap* [Sp *acaxe, acajé*, fr. Nahuatl] **1 a :** a Taracahitian people of western Mexico **b :** a member of such people **2 :** the language of the Acaxee people

acc *abbr* **1** acceleration **2** acceptance; accepted **3** accompanied; accompaniment **4** according **5** account **6** accusative

ac·ca \'akə\ *n* -S [ML, prob. fr. *Acca, Accho*, ancient city of Syria (now *Acre*, Israel), its place of export] **:** a gold and silk brocade of medieval origin

accadian *usu cap, var of* AKKADIAN

acce *abbr* acceptance

ac·ce·das ad cu·ri·am \ä'kādə,säd'k(y)ůrē,äm\ *n* [ML, lit., that you go to the court] *in English legal practice* **:** a common-law writ to remove a cause from an inferior court not of record to a higher court

ac·cede \ak'sēd, ək-, *chiefly substand* ə's-\ *vi* -ED/-ING/-S [ME *acceden*, fr. L *accedere*, fr. *ad-* + *cedere* to go, yield — more at CEDE] **1** *archaic* **:** to come forward **:** APPROACH **2 a** (1) **:** to become a party (as to an agreement) by associating oneself with others ⟨they were invited to ~ to the covenant⟩ (2) *of a people or territory* **:** to join in political union (as with another country) ⟨Kashmir was said to have *acceded* to India⟩ **b :** to express approval or give consent **:** ASSENT ⟨ready to ~ to his proposal — Jane Austen⟩ **3 :** to assume an office or position **:** attain an honor ⟨he *acceded* to the governorship⟩ **:** come or succeed to the throne ⟨the queen *acceded* in 1918⟩ **4** *law* **:** to become added by way of accession **syn** see ASSENT

¹**ac·ce·le·ran·do** \(,)ä,chelə'ran(,)dō, -än-\ *adv* (*or adj*) [It, lit., accelerating, fr. L *accelerandum*, gerund of *accelerare*] **:** gradually faster — used as a direction in music

²**accelerando** \"\ *n* -S **:** a gradual increase in tempo ⟨examples of the ~s . . . our metrical ear seems willing to accept —P.F. Baum⟩

ac·cel·er·ant \ik'selərənt, ak- *sometimes* ek-\ *n* -S [*accelerate* + *-ant*] **:** one that accelerates

¹**ac·cel·er·ate** \-lə,rāt, *chiefly substand* ə's-; *usu* -ād· + V\ *vb* -ED/-ING/-S [L *acceleratus*, past part. of *accelerare*, fr. *ad-* + *celerare* to hasten, fr. *celer* swift — more at CELERITY] *vt* **1 :** to bring about at an earlier point of time ⟨anxious to ~ our departure —James Cook⟩ **2 :** to add to the speed of or quicken the motion of ⟨the voice caused me to ~ my steps —W.H.Hudson⟩ **3 :** to hasten the ordinary progress or the development of ⟨war *accelerated* the old trends⟩ ⟨hot weather *accelerated* their efforts to adjourn⟩ **:** increase the rate or amount of ⟨he decided to ~ his advertising⟩ **4 a :** to enable (a student) to complete a course of study more rapidly than usual **b :** to modify (as a course of study) by decreasing the time usu. taken to complete the normal amount of work **5 :** to cause to undergo acceleration; *esp* **:** to increase the velocity of (a body) ~ *vi* **1 a :** to become faster **:** move faster **:** gain speed ⟨a pace that neither ~s nor lags⟩ **b :** to increase in number or amount ⟨the number of newspapers *accelerated*⟩ **c :** to open the throttle or accelerator ⟨the driver *accelerated* gradually on the highway⟩ **2 :** to follow a speeded-up educational program **:** progress from grade to grade more rapidly than usual **:** complete requirements (as for a diploma) more rapidly than usual **syn** see SPEED

²**ac·cel·er·ate** \-lərət, -,rāt, *usu* -d·+V\ *n* -S **:** an accelerated pupil or student

accelerated *adj* **:** beyond one's years in development ⟨~ in intelligence⟩

accelerated amortization *n* **:** a deduction from taxable income in lieu of normal depreciation on qualified facilities based on writing off capital investment over a stated period representing the duration of war or emergency, the higher write-off resulting in a tax advantage

accelerated depreciation *n* **:** depreciation of assets at a higher rate than that normally assigned to cover use and exhaustion

ac·cel·er·a·tion \=,=='rāshən\ *n* -S [L *acceleration-, acceleratio*, fr. *acceleratus* + *-ion-, -io* -ion] **1 :** the act or process of accelerating ⟨the unusual ~ of economic activity⟩ **:** state of being accelerated **2 :** the time rate of change of velocity (as in speed or direction) **:** the vector derivative of the velocity with respect to time — see ANGULAR ACCELERATION **3 :** gradual appearance in the course of evolution of an ancestral adult character in the immature descendant — compare ABBREVIATION **4 :** advancement in mental growth or achievement beyond the average of one's age

acceleration clause *n* **:** a clause (as in a loan contract) providing for advancement of the date of payment under specified circumstances

acceleration coefficient *n* **:** ACCELERATOR 2

acceleration lane *n* **:** a speed change area or lane consisting of added pavement at the edge of through-traffic lanes to permit vehicles to accelerate before merging with the through-traffic flow — compare DECELERATION LANE

acceleration of gravity : acceleration of a body falling in a vacuum under the influence of the earth's gravity expressed as the rate of increase of velocity per unit of time, its value at sea level in latitude 45 degrees being 980.616 centimeters per second per second which is designated as *g*45 as distinguished from g_0 = 980.665 centimeters per second per second, an arbitrary value adopted in 1901 by the International Committee of Weights and Measures — abbr. *g*

acceleration of the tide : priming of the tide

acceleration principle *n* **:** a principle in economics: an increase or decrease in income induces a corresponding change in investment

ac·cel·er·a·tive \=¦==,rād·iv, -,rə-\ *adj* **:** relating to or tending to cause acceleration **:** ACCELERATING

ac·cel·er·a·tor \-,rād·ə(r), -ātə-\ *n* -S **1 :** one that accelerates: as **a :** any muscle or nerve that speeds the performance of an action ⟨cardiac ~⟩ **b :** a chemical (as an alkali) used in photography for speeding the action of a developer — called also *activator* **c :** any of several devices for increasing the speed of a motor vehicle engine; *esp* **:** a foot-operated throttle that varies the supply of fuel-air mixture to the combustion chamber **d :** an attachment to a dry-pipe valve for accelerating its operation when sprinkler heads are opened **e :** a substance that speeds a chemical reaction; *esp* **:** one that speeds the vulcanization of rubber or the curing of a plastic **f :** a substance added to stucco, plaster, mortar, concrete, or similar materials to hasten the set **g :** an apparatus for imparting high velocities by electromagnetic or electrostatic means to charged particles (as electrons) which are generated in the apparatus, accelerated in controlled paths to a state of high energy, and focused continuously until they emerge as a stream of high-speed projectiles — see CYCLOTRON **2 :** the ratio of increase or decrease in investment to an increase or decrease in income — called also *acceleration coefficient;* compare ACCELERATION PRINCIPLE

accelerator globulin *n* **:** a globulin occurring in inactive form in blood plasma that in its active form is one of the factors accelerating the formation of thrombin from prothrombin in the clotting of blood

ac·cel·er·a·to·ry \-,rə,tōrē\ *adj* **:** ACCELERATIVE

ac·cel·ero·graph \-,rə,graf\ *n* -S [ISV *acceleration* + *-o-* + *-graph;* orig. formed as F *accélérographe*] **1 :** an apparatus for measuring and recording the pressure developed by combustion of an explosive in a closed space **2 :** an instrument for recording the acceleration in velocity of earthquake vibrations

ac·cel·er·om·e·ter \=,=='rämədə(r)\ *n* -S [ISV *acceleration* + *-o-* + *-meter;* orig. formed as F *accéléromètre*] **1 :** an instrument for measuring acceleration (as of a moving vehicle) or for detecting and measuring mechanical vibrations (as of machinery) **2 :** an apparatus for measuring the gas pressure at any particular point in a gun

ac·cen·sion \ak'senchən\ *n* -S [LL *accension-, accensio*, fr. L *accensus* (past part. of *accendere* to set on fire, fr. *ad-* + *-cendere*, fr. *candēre* to glow) + *-ion-, -io* -ion — more at CANDID] *archaic* **:** KINDLING, IGNITION, COMBUSTION

¹**ac·cent** \'ak,sent, *Brit usu* -sənt\ *n* -S [MF, fr. L *accentus* (trans. of Gk *prosōidia*), fr. *ad-* + *-centus* (fr. *cantus* song, fr. *cantus*, past part. of *canere* to sing) — more at CHANT, PROSODY] **1 :** a distinctive manner of usu. oral expression: as **a :** the inflection, tone, or choice of words associated with a particular situation, event, emotion, or attitude or taken to be unique in or highly characteristic of an individual — usu. used in pl. ⟨the authoritative ~s of a ruling class —*Time*⟩ ⟨I knew Heathcliff's ~s —Emily Brontë⟩ **b :** speech habits typical of the natives or residents of a region or of any other group (as social, professional, or business) ⟨a heavy foreign ~⟩ ⟨a southern ~⟩ ⟨the staccato ~ of a circus barker⟩ **2 a :** an articulative effort (as an increase of stress or a change of pitch) giving prominence to one syllable of a word or group of words over adjacent syllables **b :** the prominence given a syllable through the use of accent **3 :** rhythmically significant stress on the syllables of a verse usu. at approximately regular intervals **:** ICTUS **4** *archaic* **:** a word or group of words **:** UTTERANCE **5 a :** a mark (as ´, `, ˆ) used in writing or printing to indicate a specific sound value, stress, or pitch, to distinguish words otherwise identically spelled, or to indicate that an ordinarily mute vowel should be pronounced; *broadly* **:** any mark, point, or sign used with a letter whether functional or not — see ACUTE, CIRCUMFLEX, GRAVE; compare DIACRITIC **b :** a letter with a diacritical mark (as é, ç, ä, ñ) — a printers' term; compare PIECE ACCENT **c :** a letter not used in the ordinary alphabet — a printers' term **6 a :** greater stress or emphasis given to one musical tone than to its neighbors **b :** the principle of regularly recurring stresses which serve to distribute a succession of pulses into equal groups or measures — called also *grammatical accent* **c :** special emphasis placed exceptionally upon tones not subject to grammatical accent — called also *rhetorical accent* **d :** the rhythmical principle of grammatical accent operating over such longer spans of time as to mark alternate strong and weak measures or phrase relationships — called also *rhythmical accent* **e :** ACCENT MARK 2 **7 a :** emphasis laid on a part of an artistic design or composition **b :** a detail or area emphasized **:** a striking detail; *esp* **:** a small detail in sharp contrast with its surroundings (as in color or texture) **c :** a substance or object used for emphasis ⟨a plant used for ~ in a landscape design⟩ **8 :** a mark placed to the right of a letter or number and usu. slightly above it: **a :** a mark used singly with letters to distinguish either different mathematical variables (as x and x') or singly, doubly, and triply to distinguish different values of the same variable (as y' and y'') — compare DOUBLE PRIME, PRIME **b :** a mark used singly with numbers to denote minutes and doubly to denote seconds of time (as a 4′3″ interval) or to denote minutes and seconds of an angle or arc **c :** a mark used singly with numbers to denote feet and doubly to denote inches (as 6′3″ tall) **9 :** any distinguishing characteristic or individualizing stamp ⟨his peculiar ~ of wistful naïveté —Edmund Wilson⟩ **10 :** attribution of special importance **:** special concern or attention **:** EMPHASIS — usu. used with *on* ⟨the ~ on air power in the defense program⟩

²**ac·cent** \'ak,sent, =ˈ=\ *vt* -ED/-ING/-S [MF *accenter*, fr. *accent*, n.] **1 a :** to utter (as a syllable) with accent **:** STRESS ⟨~*ing* the first syllable of each word he spoke⟩ **b :** to mark with a written or printed accent ⟨each word of the list was neatly ~*ed* with a typed stress mark⟩ **2** *archaic* **:** to give voice to **:** ARTICULATE, UTTER, SPEAK ⟨sounds ~*ed* by a thousand voices —Sir Walter Scott⟩ **3 a :** to give prominence to or increase the prominence of **:** make more emphatic, noticeable, or distinct ⟨columns ~ the vertical lines of the building⟩ **:** heighten in effect (as by contrast) **:** bring out **:** set off ⟨a background of mountains ~s the quiet beauty of the landscape⟩ **:** increase in degree **:** INTENSIFY, SHARPEN ⟨hostility that was ~*ed* by inbred antagonism⟩ **b :** to make of special interest or concern **:** give special attention to **:** EMPHASIZE ⟨a defense program ~s air power⟩ ⟨~s the practical utility of science —Frank Thilly⟩

accent mark *n* **1 :** ACCENT 5a, 8 **2 a :** one of several symbols used in music to indicate that stress is to be given to a tone or chord (as > may be used for indicating sforzando) **b :** a mark placed after a letter designating a note of music to indicate in which octave the note occurs (as *a′* indicates A above middle C)

ac·cen·tor \ak'sentə(r), '=,==\ *n* -S [NL, fr. ML, cosinger, fr. L *ad-* + ML *-centor* (fr. L *cantor* singer) — more at CANTOR] **:** a bird of the genus *Prunella; esp* **:** the European hedge sparrow

accents *pl of* ACCENT, *pres 3d sing of* ACCENT

ac·cen·tu·al \(')ak¦senchəwəl\ *adj* [¹*accent* + *-ual* (as in *manual, visual*)] **:** of, relating to, characterized by, or formed with accent; *specif* **:** based upon accent rather than upon quantity or syllabic recurrence ⟨~ hexameters⟩ — compare QUANTITATIVE — **ac·cen·tu·al·ly** \-wəlē, -li\ *adv*

ac·cen·tu·ate \ak'senchə,wāt, ək-, + V\ *vt* -ED/-ING/-S [ML *accentuatus*, past part. of *accentuare*, fr. L *accentus* accent — more at ACCENT] **:** ACCENT

ac·cen·tu·a·tion \=,=='wāshən\ *n* -S [F, fr. ML *accentuatus* + F *-ion*] **1 :** the act or the result of accentuating **2 a :** the correspondence between the accents of a melody and those of the text to which it is written **b :** the placing of an accent in a musical phrase either coinciding with or independent of the basic meter

ac·cen·tu·a·tor \=ˈ==,wād·ə(r), -ātə-\ *n* -S **:** one that accentuates

ac·cen·tus \ak'sentəs\ *n, pl* **accentus** [ML, fr. L, accent] **:** the part of the church service sung or recited by the priest and his assistants at the altar usu. in monotone — contrasted with *concentus*

ac·cept \ik'sept, ak- *also* ək- *or* ek-\ *vb* -ED/-ING/-S [ME *accepten*, fr. MF *accepter*, fr. L *acceptare*, freq. of *accipere* to take, receive, accept, perceive, explain, undertake, fr. *ad-* + *-cipere* (fr. *capere* to take) — more at HEAVE] *vt* **1** *obs* **:** to treat with partiality or favoritism ⟨God ~*eth* no man's person —Gal 2:6 (AV)⟩ **2 a :** to receive with consent (something given or offered) ⟨~*ed* the medal⟩ **:** assent to the receipt of ⟨~*ed* lower wages than the native workers⟩ **b :** to be able to take or hold or be designed to take or hold (something applied, affixed, or impressed) ⟨a glazed surface that will not ~ ink⟩ **3 :** to give admittance to (as into one's company or into a particular group) ⟨the town's best families ~*ed* her⟩ **:** give approval to ⟨those people will never ~ abstract sculpture⟩ **4 a :** to take without protest **:** endure or tolerate with patience ⟨queueing is one aspect of English life he will never wholly ~ —*London Calling*⟩ **b :** to regard as proper, suitable, or normal ⟨it came to be ~*ed* that there should be universal education⟩ **:** acknowledge or recognize as appropriate, permissible, or inevitable **:** agree to ⟨refused to ~ the dangerous working conditions —P.E.James⟩ **c :** to regard and hold as true **:** believe in ⟨by *~ing* the proposition that all men are created equal⟩ **d :** to receive into the mind **:** UNDERSTAND ⟨words mean . . . what we ~ them as meaning —J.L.Lowes⟩ **5 a :** to make an affirmative or favorable response to (as an invitation or offer) ⟨*~ing* an invitation to speak⟩ **:** undertake the responsibility of (as a task or employment) ⟨if he *~s* a junior partnership in the firm⟩ **b :** to allow (a train) onto the particular section of a line under local control — used of a block operator in the manual block-signal system **6 :** to assume orally, in writing, or by conduct an obligation to pay ⟨*~ing* a bill of exchange⟩ **7** *of a deliberative body* **:** to receive (a report) officially (as from a committee) **8 :** to be sexually responsive to; *esp* **:** to allow to mount and copulate — usu. used of a female domestic mammal **~** *vi* **:** to receive favorably something offered — usu. used with *of* ⟨no person . . . shall . . . ~ of any present —*U. S. Constitution*⟩ **syn** see RECEIVE —**accept service :** to agree that a writ or process shall be considered as regularly served when it has not been

ac·cept·abil·i·ty \\ˌ⁼ˌ⁼⁼'bilǝd·ē, -ǝtē, -i\\ *n* -ES **:** the quality or state of being acceptable

ac·cept·able \\⁼'⁼tǝbǝl\\ *adj* [ME, fr. MF, fr. LL *acceptabilis*, fr. L *acceptare* + *-abilis* -able] **1 :** capable or worthy of being accepted ⟨no compromise could ever be ~⟩ **:** SATISFACTORY ⟨~ living conditions⟩ **:** conforming to or equal to approved standards ⟨~ English usage⟩ **2 a :** WELCOME, PLEASING ⟨compliments . . . are always ~ to ladies —Jane Austen⟩ **b :** barely satisfactory or adequate ⟨performances varied from excellent to ~⟩ —**ac·cept·ably** \\-blē, -i\\ *adv*

ac·cept·ance \\⁼'⁼tǝn(t)s\\ *n* -S [MF, fr. *accepter* to accept + *-ance*] **1 :** the act of accepting ⟨~ of an offer⟩ **:** favorable reception ⟨~ by society⟩ **:** APPROVAL ⟨the theory found wide ~⟩ **:** ACQUIESCENCE ⟨passive ~⟩ **2 :** the quality or state of being accepted or acceptable or esp. of being received favorably or with approval **:** ACCEPTABILITY ⟨some men cannot be fools with so good ~ as others —Robert South⟩ **3 :** an agreeing either expressly or by conduct to the act or offer of another so that a contract is concluded and the parties become legally bound — compare CONTRACT, MEETING OF THE MINDS, OFFER **4 a :** the act of accepting a time draft or bill of exchange for payment when due according to the specified terms, the drawee usu. indicating acceptance by writing *accepted* and his signature across the face of the draft or bill **b :** a draft or bill of exchange drawn by the seller either on the purchaser or on a bank in accordance with previous arrangement made with it by the buyer for the purchase price of the goods — see BANK ACCEPTANCE, TRADE ACCEPTANCE **5 :** ACCEPTATION 2 **6 acceptances** *pl, Brit* **:** entries in a horse race the handicap weights for which have been accepted by the owners or their agents **7 :** the period during which the female esp. of a domestic mammal will permit copulation **:** HEAT, ESTRUS

acceptance credit *n* **:** an authorization given by a bank to a specified beneficiary to draw drafts upon the bank up to a specified amount

acceptance for honor *or* **acceptance supra protest :** the action of an acceptor for honor

acceptance house *or* **accepting house** *n* **:** a banking institution in England specializing in financing foreign trade by allowing the use of its name as drawee on bills of exchange and by frequently acting also as fiscal agent and financial adviser (as for foreign nations or municipalities) — compare MERCHANT BANKER

ac·cept·ant \\⁼'⁼tǝnt\\ *adj* [F, fr. pres. part. of *accepter* to accept] **:** willing to accept **:** RECEPTIVE **:** tending to accept passively ⟨an ~ type of mind⟩

ac·cep·ta·tion \\ˌakˌsep'tāshǝn\\ *n* -S [ME *acceptacioun*, fr. MF *acceptation*, fr. *accepter* + *-ation*] **1 :** ACCEPTANCE; *esp* **:** favorable reception or approval **:** BELIEF ⟨a faithful saying and worthy of all ~ —1 Tim 1:15 (AV)⟩ **2 :** the generally accepted meaning of a word or understanding of a concept ⟨the term . . . will be used in its common ~ —H.O.Taylor⟩

accepted *adj* [ME, fr. past part. of *accepten* to accept] **:** generally approved **:** widely used or found ⟨there are three ~ types of pump⟩ **:** generally agreed upon **:** UNCHALLENGED, CONVENTIONAL ⟨~ interpretation of the poem⟩ —**ac·cept·ed·ly** *adv*

ac·cept·er \\ik'septǝ(r), a-,ǝ-,e-, 'akˌs-\\ *n* -S [ME, fr. *accepten* + *-er*] **1 :** one that accepts **2 :** ACCEPTOR 2

ac·cep·ti·late \\ak'septǝˌlāt\\ *vt* -ED/-ING/-S [back-formation fr. *acceptilation*] **:** to discharge (a claim) by acceptilation

ac·cep·ti·la·tion \\(ˌ)akˌseptǝ'lāshǝn\\ *n* -S [L *acceptilation-*, *acceptilatio*, fr. *accepti lation-*, *latio*, lit., bringing the receipt, fr. *accepti* (gen. of *acceptum* receipt, fr. neut. of *acceptus*, past part. of *accipere* to accept) + *lation-*, *latio* act of bringing, fr. *latus* (suppletive past part. of *ferre* to bear) + *-ion-*, *-io* -ion — more at ACCEPT, BEAR, TOLERATE] **1** *Roman or civil law* **:** a formal verbal acknowledgment by a creditor or other obligee that his claim has been satisfied with or without payment **2** [ML *acceptilation-*, *acceptilatio*, fr. L] *in the theology of Duns Scotus* **:** the act of God by which the merit of Jesus Christ was accepted as sufficient for man's salvation

accepting *pres part of* ACCEPT

ac·cep·tion \\ak'sepshǝn\\ *n* -S [ME *accepcioun*, fr. MF or L; MF *acception*, fr. L *acception-*, *acceptio*, fr. *acceptus* + *-ion-*, *-io* -ion] **:** ACCEPTATION

ac·cept·ive \\(')ak¦septiv\\ *adj* **1 :** RECEPTIVE ⟨~ of every new idea⟩ **2 :** acceptable or appropriate ⟨a psychologically ~ way of living⟩

ac·cep·tor \\ik'septǝ(r), a-,ǝ-,e-, 'akˌs-\\ *n* -S [L, fr. *acceptus* + *-or*] **1 :** ACCEPTER 1 **2 :** one (as the drawee) that accepts an order or a bill of exchange **3 :** a substance or particle capable of combining with another specified substance or particle ⟨oxygen is a hydrogen ~⟩ ⟨ammonia and bases are proton *~s*⟩ ⟨a proton is an electron pair ~⟩ ⟨wool is a dye ~⟩ — compare DONOR 2 **4 a :** a circuit that combines inductance and capacitance in series so as to resonate to a given impressed frequency — compare REJECTOR **b :** HOLE 2e(1) **c :** an impurity occurring in a semiconducting material and containing holes that contribute to the conductivity of the material

acceptor for honor *or* **acceptor supra protest :** one who accepts a protested bill of exchange on which he is not already liable for the honor of some party to the bill, the acceptor being liable to the holder and all parties subsequent to the one for whose honor he accepts

accepts *pres 3d sing of* ACCEPT

ac·cess \\'akˌses *also* ik's- *or* ak's-\\ *n* -ES *often attrib* [ME, fr. MF & L; MF *acces* arrival, fr. L *accessus* approach, access, admittance, fr. *accessus* past part. of *accedere* to approach — more at ACCEDE] **1** [influenced in meaning by MF *accession* & L *accessio* — more at ACCESSION] **a :** an attack or onset of illness or disease ⟨an ~ of paralysis the afternoon previous —George Ticknor⟩ **b :** a fit or spell of intense feeling ⟨he had such an ~ now —Oliver La Farge⟩ **:** OUTBURST ⟨*~es* of pessimism —S.H.Adams⟩ **2 a** (1) **:** permission, liberty, or ability to enter, approach, communicate with, or pass to and from ⟨~ to every room⟩ ⟨~ to the president⟩ ⟨a country with ~ to the sea⟩ (2) **:** admission to sexual intercourse (3) **:** a landowner's legal right to pass from his land to a highway and to return without being obstructed **b :** freedom or ability to obtain or make use of ⟨give them ~ to jobs of confidence or trust —*N.Y. Times*⟩ **:** ability or means to participate in, work in, or gain insight into ⟨~ to the liberal arts⟩ **c :** a way by which a thing or place may be approached or reached **:** PASSAGEWAY ⟨a lock built to give ~ to the sea⟩ **d** (1) **:** the action of going to or reaching **:** APPROACH, ENTRANCE **:** passage to and from ⟨provide a means of ~ to the lake⟩ ⟨completed plans for ~ tracks to the factory⟩ (2) **:** approach to God through Jesus Christ — used esp. in titles of prayers ⟨the Anglican prayer of humble ~⟩ **3 :** an increase by addition ⟨a sudden ~ of wealth⟩ **4** *obs* **a :** an assembling or meeting esp. of the British Parliament **b :** a coming to office or sovereignty

accessary *var of* ACCESSORY

access clerk *n* **:** a safe-deposit attendant who is responsible for admitting to the vault only properly accredited persons whose signatures he has verified

access control *n* **:** a condition in which the common-law rights of property owners and others to access, light, air, or view in connection with a public road are controlled by public authority by means of physical construction, legal restrictions, toll requirements, or other limitations

ac·ces·si·bil·i·ty \\ikˌsesǝ'bilǝd·ē, (ˌ)ak-,ǝk-, *chiefly substand* ǝˌs-\\ *n* -ES **:** the quality or state of being accessible

ac·ces·si·ble \\⁼'⁼ǝbǝl\\ *adj* [F, fr. LL *accessibilis*, fr. L *accessus* (past part. of *accedere* to approach) + *-ibilis* -ible — more at ACCEDE] **1 :** capable of being used as an entrance **:** providing access ⟨one ascent ~ from earth —John Milton⟩ **2 a :** capable of being reached or easily approached ⟨a town ~ by rail⟩ **:** easy to meet **b :** easy to get along with, talk to, or deal with **:** APPROACHABLE, COMMUNICATIVE ⟨an ~ and genial man⟩ **3 :** capable of being influenced or affected **:** OPEN ⟨~ to the flattery of this honest praise —Elinor Wylie⟩ **4 :** capable of being used, seen, known, or experienced **:** AVAILABLE ⟨a book ~ to all students⟩ **:** COMPREHENSIBLE ⟨readily ~ to the nonprofessional reader —J.K.Galbraith⟩ —**ac·ces·si·bly** \\-blē, -i\\ *adv* —**ac·ces·si·ble·ness** \\-bǝlnǝs\\ *n* -ES

[1]ac·ces·sion \\ik'seshǝn, ak-,ǝk-\\ *n* -S [MF, fr. L *accession-*, *accessio*, fr. *accessus* + *-ion-*, *-io* -ion] **1 a :** something added as to a collection or formal group **:** ACQUISITION ⟨new *~s* in the paintings department of the museum⟩ **b :** a specimen under consideration or study **:** examination sample ⟨all *~s* of volunteer tomatoes were susceptible⟩ **2 a :** the act of becoming joined (as in a confederacy or union) **:** ADHERENCE ⟨French ~ to the European Defense Community⟩ **b :** the act by which one nation becomes party to engagements already in force between other powers **c :** the mode of acquiring property by which the owner of a corporeal substance (as land or cattle) becomes the owner of an addition by growth, increase, or labor **3 :** increase by something added **:** augmentation from without ⟨the greatest ~ of positive knowledge has come in our own time —W.R.Inge⟩ **4 :** the act of assenting or agreeing ⟨~ to the determination made by Congress —Samuel Williams⟩ **5 a :** a coming near or to **:** APPROACH, ARRIVAL **:** ADMISSION ⟨marriage represents full ~ to adult life —H.M.Parshley⟩ **b :** the act of attaining or coming to high office or a position of honor or power ⟨the ~ of a new queen⟩ **6 :** a sudden fit or spell (as of feeling) **:** OUTBURST ⟨sharp *~s* of impatience —Mary Austin⟩ **7 :** a hiring or rehiring of an employee

[2]accession \\"\\ *vt* **accessioned; accessioned; accessioning** \\-sh(ǝ)niŋ\\ **accessions :** to record in the order of acquisition listing essential data (as author, title, and publication date of a book) **:** enter (an accession) in a special record book, list, or file ⟨each book in the library had been carefully *~ed*⟩ ⟨the art gallery has an efficient way of *~ing* newly received paintings⟩

ac·ces·sion·al \\-shǝnᵊl, -shnǝl\\ *adj* **:** of or constituting an accession **:** ADDITIONAL

accession book *n* **:** a record book used for accessioning

accession number *n* **:** a number assigned to an acquisition (as a library book) indicating the order of its receipt

accession service *n* **:** a form of service used in the Church of England on the anniversary of the accession of the sovereign to the throne

accessions register *n, Brit* **:** ACCESSION BOOK

ac·ces·sit \\ak'sesǝt\\ *n* -S [L, he came near, 3d pers. sing. perf. ind. of *accedere* to come near, approach, accede — more at ACCEDE] **:** a distinction awarded in British and other European schools to one who has come nearest to a prize **:** an honorable mention

ac·ces·so·ri·al \\¦aksǝ¦sōrēǝl\\ *adj* [[2]*accessory* + *-al*] **1 :** of or relating to an accessory ⟨~ guilt⟩ **2 :** relating to an accession or increase **:** SUPPLEMENTARY, ADDITIONAL ⟨~ services included sorting and packing⟩

ac·ces·so·ri·us \\ˌ⁼⁼'⁼ēǝs\\ *n, pl* **accesso·rii** \\-ēˌī, -ēˌē\\ [NL, fr. ML, accessory] **1 :** a muscle reinforcing the action of another **2 :** ACCESSORY NERVE

ac·ces·so·rize \\ik'sesǝˌrīz, ak-, ǝk-\\ *vt* -ED/-ING/-S [*accessor*ies + *-ize*] **:** to furnish or provide with accessories ⟨dress . . . was *accessorized* for after-dark wear with rhinestone and pearl earrings —*Fashion Accessories*⟩

[1]ac·ces·so·ry *also* **ac·ces·sa·ry** \\ik'ses(ǝ)rē, ak-,ǝk-, *chiefly substand* ǝ's-\\ *n* -ES [ME *accessorie*, *accessarie*, fr. ML *accessorius*, fr. L *accessus* (past part. of *accedere* to accede) + *-orius* -ory — more at ACCEDE] **1 a :** a thing of secondary or subordinate importance (as in achieving a purpose or an effect) ⟨the pelican's pouch is an ~ to catching fish⟩ **:** an adjunct or accompaniment ⟨some counsel regard the jury as . . . impersonal and inanimate *accessories* of the court —E.M. Lustgarten⟩ **b** (1) **:** an object or device that is not essential in itself but that adds to the beauty, convenience, or effectiveness of something else ⟨spotlights, reflectors, and other auto *accessories* ⟩ ⟨household *accessories* such as small tables and lamps⟩ ⟨the *accessories* of the estate include a putting green and a tennis court⟩ (2) **:** any of several mechanical devices (as pistons or tablets) that assist in operating or controlling the tone resources of an organ (3) **:** any of various articles of apparel (as a scarf, belt, or piece of jewelry) that accent or otherwise complete one's costume **2 :** one that is accessory: as **a :** a person who is not actually or constructively present but contributes as an assistant or instigator to the commission of an offense — called also *accessory before the fact;* compare PRINCIPAL 1d **b :** one who knowing that a crime has been committed aids, assists, or shelters the offender with the intent to defeat justice — called also *accessory after the fact;* compare PRINCIPAL 13c **3 :** a mineral that is accessory

[2]accessory *also* **accessary** \\"\\ *adj* **1** *of a thing* **a :** aiding or contributing in a secondary or subordinate way ⟨~ substances in nutrition⟩ **:** supplementary or secondary to something of greater or primary importance ⟨an ~ function of the tongue⟩ **:** ADDITIONAL ⟨sidewalks lead to ~ buildings⟩ **b :** incidental to a main contract or some other obligation (as by being given as security) ⟨a mortgage is ~ to the main obligation⟩; *specif* **:** constituting a subordinate contract (as a mortgage or pledge) designed to assure the fulfillment of a prior principal contract ⟨an ~ contract⟩ ⟨an ~ obligation⟩ **2** *of a person* **:** assisting or aiding as a subordinate; *esp* **:** uniting in or contributing to a crime, but not as the chief agent ⟨charged . . . with being ~ to the felony —Sir Walter Scott⟩ **3 :** present in a minor amount and not essential as a constituent ⟨an ~ mineral in a rock⟩

accessory body *n* **:** a differentiated structure originating in the Golgi material and included in the neck of the spermatozoon

accessory bud *n* **:** a bud growing near and in addition to a normal axillary bud

accessory cell *n* **:** one of the epidermal cells surrounding and adjacent to the guard cells, differing in configuration from other epidermal cells, and apparently functioning as part of the stomatal apparatus

accessory chromosome *n* **:** a sex chromosome; *specif* **:** an X chromosome that is solitary and unpaired in one sex (as in certain insects)

accessory fruit *n* **:** a fruit (as the apple, strawberry, or fig) of which a conspicuous portion consists of tissue other than that of the ripened ovary — called also *pseudocarp*

accessory gland *n* **:** any of certain glands (as the colleterium) associated with the reproductive organs of insects

accessory nerve *also* **accessory** *n* **:** either of the 11th pair of cranial nerves, being a motor nerve, arising partly from the lateral wall of the medulla and partly from the cervical spinal cord, supplying the pharynx, trapezius, and sternocleidomastoid muscles as well as sending fibers to the vagus nerve in higher vertebrates, and being absent from lower forms

accessory nucleus *n* **:** any of certain small masses or layers of gray matter adjacent to the inferior olivary body, there being typically two on each side — called also *accessory olivary body*

accessory pancreatic duct *n* **:** DUCT OF SANTORINI

accessory scale *n* **:** a modified scale or elongate scalelike projection at the base of the pectoral or pelvic fins of certain bony fishes

accessory shoot *n* **:** a shoot developed from an accessory bud

accessory stop *n* **:** a stop knob used on an organ to control a coupler or other mechanical device rather than a register of pipes

access road *n* **:** a public road affording access to a particular area (as a military establishment or source of raw materials) or to a through highway ⟨the route will have several *access roads* and exits — *N.Y. Times*⟩

ac·ciac·ca·tu·ra \\(ˌ)äˌchäkǝ'türǝ\\ *n, pl* **acciaccaturas** \\-ürǝz\\ *or* **acciaccatu·re** \\-üˌrā, -ürē\\ [It, lit., crushing, fr. *acciaccare* to crush (prob. fr. Sp *achacar* to impute falsely, accuse, fr. Ar dial. *'atshakka*, 5th form of Ar *shaka* to complain) + *-ura* -ure] **1** *in early keyboard music* **:** a short grace note sounded with a principal note or chord before which it appears and immediately released while the tone of the principal note or chord is sustained **2 :** SHORT APPOGGIATURA

ac·ci·dence \\'aksǝdǝn(t)s *also* -dᵊn(t)s, *or* -ˌden(t)s\\ *n* -S [L *accidentia* inflections of words, nonessential qualities or circumstances, pl. of *accident-*, *accidens* nonessential quality or circumstance] **:** the part of grammar that deals with inflections

ac·ci·dens \\'aksǝˌdenz; 'ä(t)chēˌdenz, -nts\\ *n, pl* **acciden·tia** \\ˌaksǝ'denchēǝ; ˌä(t)chē'dentsēǝ\\ [L] *logic* **:** ACCIDENT

ac·ci·dent \\'aksǝdǝnt *also* -dᵊnt *or* -ˌdent\\ *n* -S [ME, fr. MF, fr. L *accident-*, *accidens* nonessential quality or circumstance, accident, chance, fr. pres. part. of *accidere* to happen, fr. *ad-* + *-cidere* (fr. *cadere* to fall) — more at CHANCE] **1 a :** an event or condition occurring by chance or arising from unknown or remote causes ⟨by the ~ that it was observed and noted down —Havelock Ellis⟩ ⟨happenings outside the range of probability which we would term historical *~s* —M.J. Herskovits⟩ **b :** lack of intention or necessity **:** CHANCE — often opposed to *design* ⟨by ~ rather than with an intention to utilize —Arnold Bennett⟩ **c :** an unforeseen unplanned event or condition ⟨by a charming ~ he had disposed of them to a chance buyer —Arnold Bennett⟩ **2 a :** a usu. sudden event or change occurring without intent or volition through carelessness, unawareness, ignorance, or a combination of causes and producing an unfortunate result ⟨a traffic ~ in which several persons were injured⟩ **b :** an unexpected medical development esp. of an unfavorable or injurious nature occurring in apparently good health or during the course of a disease or a treatment ⟨the paralytic ~ occurred between the 8th and 21st day after the initial injection —*Jour. Amer. Med. Assoc.*⟩ ⟨a cerebral ~⟩ **c :** an unexpected happening causing loss or injury which is not due to any fault or misconduct on the part of the person injured but from the consequences of which he may be entitled to some legal relief **3 :** an adventitious characteristic that is either inseparable from the individual and the species or separable from the individual but not the species; *broadly* **:** any fortuitous or nonessential property, fact, or circumstance ⟨~ of appearance⟩ ⟨~ of reputation⟩ ⟨~ of situation⟩ **4 :** an irregularity of a surface (as of the moon) **syn** see CHANCE, QUALITY

[1]ac·ci·den·tal \\¦aksǝ¦dentᵊl\\ *adj* [ME, fr. MF, fr. *accident* + *-al*] **1 :** arising from or produced by extrinsic, secondary, or additional causes or forces **:** not innate, intrinsic, or of the real nature of **:** NONESSENTIAL ⟨some of the colors were mineral, in the rock itself: but others were ~ due to water from the melting snow —T.E.Lawrence⟩ ⟨whether this paralogistic procedure is essential or ~ to his doctrine —T.H.Green⟩ **2 :** occurring sometimes with unfortunate results by chance alone: **a :** UNPREDICTABLE **:** proceeding from an unrecognized principle, from an uncommon operation of a known principle, or from a deviation from normal **b :** happening or ensuing without design, intent, or obvious motivation or through inattention or carelessness ⟨~ collision⟩ ⟨~ shooting⟩ ⟨~ loss⟩ **3 :** having reference to a logical accident **:** not essential **:** CONTINGENT, EXTRINSIC ⟨being dark-haired is an ~ property of a man —Arthur Pap⟩ **4 :** relating to an accidental in music or to its prefixed sign **5** *of a bird* **:** found outside the normal geographic range or season ⟨a common migrant, ~ in winter⟩

syn FORTUITOUS, ADVENTITIOUS, CONTINGENT, CASUAL, INCIDENTAL: when it is used in reference to events, ACCIDENTAL may stress lack of intent or indicate an unusual operation of natural causes ⟨so plain that Thady's presence . . . was *accidental*, and that the attack could not have been premeditated —Anthony Trollope⟩ In reference to qualities, ACCIDENTAL indicates absence of an essential or innate characteristic ⟨their search for the typical and their avoidance of anything that might be considered *accidental* —John Dewey⟩ FORTUITOUS stresses chance and minimizes the idea of definite analyzable cause ⟨I do not look upon public events either as *fortuitous* or absolutely derivable either from the wisdom or folly of man —William Cowper⟩ ADVENTITIOUS stresses the extrinsic, additional, irrelevant, or nonessential ⟨regular repetition of forms, uniformly spaced, the architect depending only upon *adventitious* ornamentation for variety —John Dewey⟩ ⟨in works of imagination and sentiment . . . meter is but *adventitious* to composition —William Wordsworth⟩ CONTINGENT stresses unpredictability and uncertainty, esp. in future events ⟨countless *contingent* difficulties . . . many of which must necessarily arise, though the exact nature of them could not be anticipated —J.A.Froude⟩ It also indicates dependence on something else for existence or occurrence ⟨the resistance that we may meet with is *contingent* on the enemy's continued strength⟩ INCIDENTAL stresses a secondary or minor nature, regardless of manner of origin ⟨war . . . the comprehensive business of the German . . . to the British . . . was an *incidental* adventure —H.G.Wells⟩ CASUAL stresses dependence on chance and lack of prearrangement or predictability ⟨it was no *casual* reencounter. He had been enticed into the place —J.A.Froude⟩ ⟨the *casual* allusion, the chance reference —Henry Adams⟩ CASUAL and INCIDENTAL may indicate occurrences actually planned and intended but presented as if by chance ⟨the pupil must be aroused . . . his curiosity must be awakened by an *incidental* explanation, a *casual* remark —C.H.Grandgent⟩

[2]accidental \\"\\ *n* -S [ME, fr. *accidental*, adj.] **1** *logic* **:** a nonessential property **2 :** NONESSENTIAL **3 a :** a chromatically altered note (as a sharp or flat) in a musical composition that is usu. foreign to the key indicated by the signature **b :** the prefixed sign (as ♯ or ♭) indicating a chromatically altered note **4 :** warp ends not usu. included in the treadling pattern in hand weaving **5 :** a fingerprint showing two or more pattern types or other peculiarities making classification difficult

accidental death *n* **:** death by accidental means usu. sudden and violent; *sometimes* **:** death occurring as the unforeseen and chance result of an intended act — compare DOUBLE INDEMNITY

accidental error *n* **:** an error of observation that cannot be controlled

accidental injury *n* **:** injury occurring as the unforeseen and chance result of a voluntary act

ac·ci·den·tal·ism \\ˌ⁼⁼'⁼⁼ˌizǝm\\ *n* -S **:** a theory in philosophy: events can or do occur without cause — compare INDETERMINISM, TYCHISM

ac·ci·den·tal·ist \\-ˌǝst\\ *n* -S **:** a believer in accidentalism

ac·ci·den·tal·i·ty \\ˌaksǝdǝn'talǝd·ē, -(ˌ)den-\\ *n* -ES **:** the quality or state of being accidental ⟨the ~ of history⟩

ac·ci·den·tal·ly \\¦aksǝ¦dentlē, -tᵊlē, -li\\ *adv* [ME, fr. *accidental* + *-ly*] **1** *archaic* **:** INCIDENTALLY **2 :** by accident **:** in an accidental manner

accidental means *n* **:** an act or event preceding harm or damage to an insured that is sudden, unexpected, and not intended or designed by any person

accidentary *adj, obs* **:** ACCIDENTAL

ac·ci·dent·ed \\'aksǝˌdentǝd\\ *adj* **:** of uneven surface ⟨~ topography⟩

accidentia *pl of* ACCIDENS

accident insurance *n* **:** insurance against loss through accidental bodily injury to the insured — compare DISABILITY INSURANCE

ac·ci·dent·ly \\¦aksǝ¦dentlē, -li\\ *adv* [prob. alter. of *accidentally*] **:** ACCIDENTALLY

accident-prone \\'⁼⁼(ˌ)⁼¦⁼\\ *adj* **1 :** having a greater number of accidents than would be expected of the average individual under the same conditions ⟨older people are less *accident-prone* than we customarily think —Graenum Berger⟩ **2 :** having personality traits that predispose to accidents ⟨importance of identifying *accident-prone* persons —*Jour. Amer. Med. Assoc.*⟩

accidents *pl of* ACCIDENT

ac·cid·ia \\ak'sidēǝ\\ *n, pl* **accidias** \\-ēǝz\\ *also* **accidi·ae** \\-ēˌē\\ [ML, alter. of LL *acedia* — more at ACEDIA] **:** [2]ACEDIA

ac·ci·die \\'aksǝdē\\ *n* -S [ME *accidie*, *accide*, fr. OF, fr. ML *accidia*, alter. of LL *acedia* — more at ACEDIA] **:** [2]ACEDIA

ac·cinge \\ak'sinj\\ *vt* -ED/-ING/-S [L *accingere*, fr. *ad-* + *cingere* to gird — more at CINCTURE] *archaic* **:** to brace (oneself) up ⟨may ~ ourselves for a supreme effort —A.T.Quiller-Couch⟩

ac·cip·i·ter \\ak'sipǝd·ǝ(r), ⁼a's-,⁼ǝ's-\\ *n* [NL, fr. L, hawk, falcon, prob. by folk etymology (influence of *accipere* to take, accept) fr. (assumed) OL *acupeter*, lit., fast flier, fr. *acu-* fast (akin to L *ocior* faster) + *-peter* flier (akin to Gk *pteron* wing) — more at ACCEPT, FEATHER, OCYPODE] **1** *cap* **:** the type genus of Accipitridae comprising small or medium-sized hawks that have rather short wings and comparatively long legs and tail and that usu. fly low darting in and out among trees **2** -s **:** any hawk of the genus *Accipiter* (as the Cooper's hawk, sharp-shinned hawk, goshawk); *also* **:** any hawk resembling a member of this genus in appearance or habits of flight

ac·cip·i·tral \-pə·trəl\ *adj* [L *accipitr-, accipiter* + E *-al*] **:** resembling that of a hawk

ac·cip·i·tres \-pə,trēz\ [NL, fr. L, pl. of *accipitr-, accipiter* hawk, falcon] **1** *syn of* FALCONIFORMES **2** *syn of* FALCONES

ac·cip·i·trid \-pə·trəd\ *n* -s *often attrib* [NL, *Accipitridae*] **:** a bird of the family Accipitridae

ac·ci·pit·ri·dae \,aksə'pi·trə,dē, ÷,asə-\ *n pl, cap* [NL, fr. *Accipitr-, Accipiter*, type genus + *-idae*] **:** a large family (order Falconiformes) of carnivorous birds having comparatively rounded wings, long legs, and an unnotched bill and including the typical hawks and goshawks, the kites, and usu. the eagles — compare FALCONIDAE

¹ac·cip·i·trine \ak'sipə,trīn, -,trən, ÷a's-,÷ə's-\ *adj* [F, fr. L *accipitr-, accipiter* + F *-ine*] **:** of or relating to the genus *Accipiter* or to the typical hawks ⟨the distinctive features of the ∼ head⟩ — compare BUTEONINE, CATHARTINE

²accipitrine \"\ *n* -s **:** ACCIPITER 2

accite *vt* -ED/-ING/-S [ME *acciten*, fr. L *accitus*, past part. of *accire* to call, summon, fr. *ad-* + *cire, ciere* to move, rouse, call upon — more at CITE] *obs* **:** CITE, SUMMON

¹ac·claim \ə'klām *also* a'-\ *vb* -ED/-ING/-S [in sense 1, fr. ME *acleimen*, fr. ML *acclamare*, fr. L, to shout at, approve, applaud, fr. *ad-* + *clamare* to shout, call; in senses 2 & 4, fr. L *acclamare;* in sense 3, fr. ML, fr. L — more at CLAIM] *vt* **1** *obs* **:** CLAIM **2 :** PRAISE ⟨a book widely ∼ *ed* by critics⟩ **:** welcome with praise or applause ⟨∼*ed* the guest of honor⟩ **3 :** to declare or proclaim approvingly — usu. used with a complement now usu. preceded by *as* ⟨on the formation of the National Sculpture Society, he was ∼*ed* its president —Adeline Adams⟩ ⟨his eyes too openly ∼*ed* her a fair woman —Mary Webb⟩ ⟨the hearings have been ∼*ed* as something of a model of dignified and fair procedure —*New Republic*⟩ **4** *archaic* **:** to call out loudly **:** SHOUT ⟨∼*ing* my joy⟩ ∼ *vi* **:** to shout praise **:** APPLAUD

²acclaim \"\ *n* -s **1 :** the act of acclaiming **2 :** PRAISE ⟨deserves the ∼ he has received —Lewis Mumford⟩

ac·cla·ma·tion \,aklə'māshən\ *n* -s [L *acclamation-, acclamatio*, fr. *acclamatus* (past part. of *acclamare*) + *-ion-, -io* -ion] **1 :** a loud eager expression of approval, praise, or assent ⟨she was received with ∼*s* —Walter Bagehot⟩ **2 :** an overwhelming approving vote by cheering, shouts, or hand clapping rather than by ballot ⟨made a motion to elect the popular candidate to the chairmanship by ∼⟩

ac·cli·ma·ta·tion \ə,klīmə'tāshən, (,)a,k-\ *n* -s [F, fr. *acclimater* + *-ation*] **:** ACCLIMATIZATION

ac·cli·mate \ə'klīmət *also* a'-; 'aklə,māt; *usu* -d·+V\ *vt* -ED/-ING/-S [F *acclimater*, fr. *a-* to (fr. L *ad-*) + *climat* climate — more at CLIMATE] **:** ACCLIMATIZE **syn** see HARDEN

ac·cli·ma·tion \,a,klī'māshən, ,aklə'-\ *n* -s [*acclimate* + *-ion*] **1 :** ACCLIMATIZATION **2 :** the usu. physiological adjustment that an individual organism exhibits to a change in its immediate environment — compare ACCLIMATIZATION 2

ac·cli·ma·ti·za·tion \ə,klīmәd·ə'zāshən, -əd·,ī'z-, -ətə'z-, -ə,tī'z- *also* a,k-\ *n* -s [*acclimate* + *-ization*] **1 :** the process of acclimatizing **:** the result of acclimatizing **2** *ecol* **:** adaptation or increased tolerance of a species to a changed environment in the course of several generations — compare ACCLIMATION 2

ac·cli·ma·tize \ə'klīmə,tīz *also* a'-\ *vb* -ED/-ING/-S *see -ize in Explan Notes* [F *acclimater* + E *-ize*] *vt* **1 :** to adapt to a new temperature, altitude, climate, environment, or situation ⟨gradually *acclimatized* to temperatures that prove unsuited . . . under ordinary conditions —*Popular Science Monthly*⟩ ⟨sufficiently *acclimatized* to altitudes of 24,000 feet —*Geog. Jour.*⟩ ⟨American varieties have been *acclimatized* in experimental farms operated by Japanese agriculturists —*Nat'l Geographic*⟩ ⟨the ultimate outcome of this movement to ∼ psychical research in the universities —*Jour. of Parapsychology*⟩ ⟨∼ the mind to a world of natural beauty —*Times Lit. Supp.*⟩ **2 :** to increase the stability of (a sol) toward a precipitant by adding the latter slowly ⟨yeast *acclimatized* during preparation⟩ ∼ *vi* **:** to become acclimatized **syn** see HARDEN

ac·cliv·i·tous \ə'klivəd·əs, (')a¦k-\ *adj* [*acclivity* + *-ous*] **:** sloping upward

ac·cliv·i·ty \ə'klivəd·ē, a'-\ *n* -ES [L *acclivitas*, fr. *acclivus, acclivis* ascending (fr. *ad-* + *clivus* slope) + *-itas* -ity — more at DECLIVITY] **:** an ascending slope (as of a hill) — opposed to *declivity*

ac·cli·vous \ə'klīvəs, (')a¦k-\ *adj* [L *acclivus*] **:** sloping upward — opposed to *declivous*

accloy *vt* -ED/-ING/-S [ME *acloien*, fr. MF *encloer* to drive in a nail, fr. ML *inclavare*, fr. L *in* + *clavare* to nail, fr. *clavus* nail — more at CLAVUS] *obs* **:** CLOY

accoast [MF *accoster* — more at ACCOST] *obs var of* ACCOST

ac·co·lade \'akə,lād, ,==¦= *also* -ăd *or* -äd\ *n* -s [F, fr. *accoler* to embrace (fr. — assumed — VL *accollare*, fr. L *ad-* + *collum* neck) + *-ade* — more at COLLAR] **1 :** a gesture of greeting; *esp*: a ceremonial embrace and kiss on both cheeks ⟨seized me by the hand and, drawing me toward him, gave me the ∼ —Frederick O'Brien⟩ **2 a :** a ceremony to mark the conferring of knighthood consisting of an embrace, a kiss, or a tap on each shoulder with the flat of a sword **b :** a ceremony marking the recognition of special merit, distinction, or achievement **3 a :** a mark of acknowledgment ⟨effectively cut short his chances of promotion and the ultimate ∼ which might have been his —James Leasor⟩ **b :** AWARD ⟨the Iffland Ring, the highest ∼ of the German theater —*Americana Annual*⟩ **c :** a bestowal of praise ⟨receive the ∼ of the newspapers⟩ **4 :** a molding in the shape of an ogee arch above a door or window **5 :** a brace or a line used in music to join two or more staffs carrying simultaneous instrumental or voice parts

ac·co·lat·ed \'akə,lād·əd\ *adj* [F *accoler* + E *-ated*] **:** ACCOLÉ

ac·col·é *or* **ac·col·lée** \¦akə¦lā\ *adj* [F *accolé*, past part. of *accoler* to embrace] **1** *heraldry* **:** entwined about the neck; *also* **:** COLLARED, GORGED **2** *heraldry* **:** joined or touching at the neck **:** side by side (as sets of arms on a shield or profiles on a coin or medal)

ac·com·mo·da·ble \ə'kämədəbəl *also* a'-\ *adj* [F, fr. *accommoder* to accommodate (fr. L *accommodare*) + *-able*] **:** capable of being accommodated or fitted ⟨anthropologists regard the Upper Paleolithic period as ∼ between 25,000 B.C. and 8000 B.C.⟩

¹ac·com·mo·date \-dət, -,dāt\ *adj* [L *accommodatus*] *archaic* **:** ADAPTED, SUITABLE, FIT

²ac·com·mo·date \-,dāt, *usu* -ād·+V\ *vb* -ED/-ING/-S [L *accommodatus*, past part. of *accommodare*, fr. *ad-* + *commodare* to make fit, give, lend — more at COMMODATUM] *vt* **1 :** ADAPT ⟨words ∼ their meanings to the other words that accompany them —I.A.Richards⟩ **:** make fit, suitable, or congruous ⟨observations had to be *accommodated* to these preconceptions —S.F.Mason⟩ **2 :** to show the correspondence of **:** account for ⟨to ∼ the new findings physicists have had to elaborate the theory —*Scientific American Reader*⟩ **:** MATCH ⟨*accommodating* a statement to facts⟩ **3 :** to bring into agreement or concord **:** RECONCILE, ADJUST ⟨he had to ∼ his step to hers —Michael Arlen⟩ ⟨∼ his religious and cultural life to the culture of the majority while avoiding complete assimilation —F.J.Brown⟩ **4 :** to furnish with something desired, needed, or suited **:** OBLIGE ⟨Rosamond *accommodated* him, taking his picture over and over again to please him —Thomas Barbour⟩ **a :** to grant a loan to esp. without security **b :** to provide with lodgings **:** HOUSE ⟨how are travelers *accommodated* in villages and towns —*Notes & Queries on Anthropology*⟩ **:** make room for ⟨the door was reluctantly opened wide enough to ∼ a small brown wet hand —L.C. Douglas⟩ **:** HOLD ⟨the mailbox is huge — obviously designed to ∼ packages from mail-order houses —G.R.Stewart⟩ ∼ *vi* **:** to adapt oneself ⟨normal and neurotic both ∼ to the same situations by different techniques —Abram Kardiner⟩ ⟨try in some way to ∼ — morally, intellectually — to the world —Edmund Wilson⟩; *specif, of the eye* **:** to undergo accommodation **syn** see ADAPT, CONTAIN, OBLIGE

accommodating *adj* **:** disposed to be helpful or obliging **:** PLIANT — **ac·com·mo·dat·ing·ly** *adv*

ac·com·mo·da·tion \=,==¦dāshən\ *n* -s [F or L; F, fr. L *accommodation-, accommodatio*, fr. *accommodatus* + *-ion-, -io* -ion] **1 a :** something that is supplied for convenience or to satisfy a need ⟨huts with no sanitary ∼ or running water —S.G.O'Kelly⟩: as (1) **:** ROOM, SPACE ⟨the library ∼ is leased —*Library Science Abstracts*⟩ (2) **:** lodging, food, and services (as at a hotel) or seat, berth, or other space occupied together with services available (as on a train) — usu. used in pl. ⟨tourist ∼*s* on the boat⟩ ⟨overnight ∼*s* for visitors⟩ **b :** a public conveyance (as a railroad train) that stops at all or nearly all points ⟨I drove around the town in a horse-drawn ∼ —Mary H. Vorse⟩ ⟨on the ∼ local —Bennett Cerf⟩ **2 :** the provision of what is needed or desired for convenience ⟨tables and benches are installed for the ∼ of picnickers —*Amer. Guide Series: N. H.*⟩ **3 :** ADAPTATION, ADJUSTMENT ⟨an ∼ to transient conditions —W.R.Inge⟩: **a :** application of a writer's language on the ground of analogy to a meaning not orig. referred to or intended ⟨by the very greatest ∼ of language —C.M.Crawford⟩ **b :** functional adjustment of an organism to its environment through modification of its habits ⟨a long period of migration, ∼, and contest for supremacy among species —C.L.White & G.T.Renner⟩ **c :** a process of functional adjustment of conflict between individuals and groups through change of habits and customs **4 :** an adjustment of differences **:** state of agreement **:** SETTLEMENT ⟨the question of reaching an ∼ with Japan —*N.Y.Times*⟩ **5 :** LOAN **6 :** the automatic adjustment of the eye for seeing at different distances effected in the eye of higher animals chiefly by changes in the convexity of the crystalline lens; *also* **:** the range over which such adjustment is possible for a particular eye

ac·com·mo·da·tion·al \=¦=¦=¦dāshən°l, -shnəl\ *adj* **:** relating to or caused by accommodation of the eye ⟨∼ strain⟩

accommodation bill *or* **accommodation paper** *n* **:** a bill, draft, or note made, drawn, accepted, or endorsed by one person for another without consideration to enable that other to raise money or obtain credit thereby

accommodation coefficient *n* **:** the efficiency of a gas in removing heat from a surface expressed as the ratio of the actual heat loss from the surface to the ideal loss

accommodation house *n* **:** a house for boarding and lodging travelers

accommodation ladder *n* **:** a light ladder or similar structure hung over the side of a ship at the gangway for use in ascending from or descending to small boats

accommodation ladder

accommodation line *n* **:** an insurance policy issued on an unsatisfactory risk by a company that wishes to accommodate a particular agent or broker

accommodation train *n* **:** a train that stops at all or nearly all stations **:** a local train

ac·com·mo·da·tive \ə'kämə,dād·iv, a'-, -ātiv, -ēv\ *adj* **:** tending to accommodate **:** relating to accommodation

ac·com·mo·da·tor \-,dād·ə(r), -ātə-\ *n* -s **:** one who substitutes for a regularly employed domestic worker

ac·com·pa·ni·er \ə'kəmp(ə)nēə(r) *also* a'- *or* -käm-\ *n* -s **:** ACCOMPANIST

ac·com·pa·ni·ment \-nēmənt, -nim- *also* -nəm-\ *n* -s [modif. (influenced by *accompany*) of F *accompagnement*, fr. OF *acompaignement* sharing, fr. *acompaignier* to accompany + *-ment*] **1 :** an instrumental or vocal part subordinate to and designed to support, amplify, or complement a principal voice or instrument **2 :** something added to the principal thing to give it completeness or symmetry (as an ornament) **:** COMPLEMENT **3 :** an accompanying situation or occurrence **:** CONCOMITANT ⟨we can no longer live without an ∼ of noise —Wynford Vaughan-Thomas⟩ ⟨to the ∼ of booming guns —*Amer. Guide Series: Maine*⟩

ac·com·pa·nist \ə'=p(ə)nəst\ *also* **ac·com·pa·ny·ist** \-p(ə)nēəst\ *n* -s [*accompany* + *-ist*] **:** one (as a pianist) that plays the accompaniment for a vocalist or instrumentalist; *sometimes* **:** one that sings an accompaniment

ac·com·pa·ny \-p(ə)nē, -ni\ *vb* -ED/-ING/-ES [ME *accompanien*, fr. MF *accompaignier*, fr. *a-* (fr. L *ad-*) + *compaing, compain* companion, fr. LL *companio* — more at COMPANION] *vt* **1 :** to go with or attend as an associate or companion **:** go along with ⟨will you do me the honor to ∼ me home for supper? —Laura Krey⟩ ⟨servants came to ∼ us to the nobleman's house —Heinrich Harrer⟩ **2 :** to play or sing an accompaniment to or for **3 :** to add or join to often incidentally or casually ⟨he *accompanied* the advice with a warning⟩ **4 :** to exist or occur in conjunction or association with ⟨the text which *accompanies* these pictures —John Haverstick⟩ ∼ *vi* **:** to perform an accompaniment

ac·com·plice \ə'kämpləs *also* a'- *or* -əm-\ *n* -s [alter. (resulting from incorrect division of *a complice*, and influenced by *accomplish*) of *complice*] **1 :** one associated with another in wrongdoing **:** one that participates with another in a crime either as principal or accessory ⟨the ∼ of the burglar⟩ ⟨an ∼ in a robbery⟩ **2 :** an associate in any undertaking

ac·com·plish \ə'kämplish, -ēsh *also* a'- *or* -əm-\ *vt* -ED/-ING/-ES [ME *accomplissen, accomplisshen*, fr. MF *accompliss-*, stem of *acomplir*, fr. (assumed) VL *accomplēre*, fr. L *ad-* + *complēre* to fill up, complete — more at COMPLETE] **1 :** to execute fully **:** PERFORM, ACHIEVE, FULFILL ⟨I have ∼*ed* all that God has given me the strength to do —Henry Baerlein⟩ **2 a :** to attain to ⟨I have ∼*ed* 92 years of my life —P.B.Kyne⟩ **b :** TRAVERSE ⟨he would starve before ∼*ing* half the distance —W.H.Hudson †1922⟩ **3** *archaic* **a :** to equip thoroughly **b :** PERFECT ⟨qualities ∼*ing* a proper gentlewoman⟩ **syn** see PERFORM

accomplished *adj* **1 a** *archaic* **:** fully attained **:** COMPLETED ⟨∼ term of servitude⟩ **b :** ESTABLISHED ⟨by the 10th century the modern alphabet was an ∼ fact —Joseph Blumenthal⟩ **2 :** having or displaying social graces to a marked degree ⟨an ∼ hostess⟩ **:** made highly proficient by practice or training ⟨one of Hollywood's most ∼ producers —Arthur Knight⟩ **:** marked by proficiency or finish ⟨an ∼ dancer⟩

ac·com·plish·ment \-shmənt\ *n* -s [ME, fr. MF *acomplissement*, fr. *accompliss-* + *-ment*] **1 a :** the act of accomplishing **:** COMPLETION, FULFILLMENT ⟨I beheld the ∼ of my toils —Mary W. Shelley⟩ **b** *obs* **:** the act of bringing to perfection ⟨the ∼ of the soul⟩ **2 :** DEED, ACHIEVEMENT ⟨his force all spent, he counts his small ∼ —Amy Lowell⟩ **3 a :** a quality or ability that equips one for society ⟨an ∼ of which he was a perfect exponent, the interchange of humorous and agreeable civilities —Agnes Repplier⟩ **b :** a special skill or ability acquired by training or practice ⟨a young lady of the early Victorian period, with china painting as one of her ∼*s*⟩

accomplishment quotient *n* **:** the ratio usu. multiplied by 100 of achievement age to mental age

accompt *archaic var of* ACCOUNT

accomptant *archaic var of* ACCOUNTANT

accompting *archaic var of* ACCOUNTING

¹ac·cord \ə'kȯ(ə)rd, -ȯ(ə)d *also* a'-\ *vb* -ED/-ING/-S [ME *accorden, acorden*, fr. OF *acorder*, fr. (assumed) VL *accordare*, fr. L *ad-* + *cord-, cor* heart — more at HEART] *vt* **1 :** to bring into agreement **:** RECONCILE, HARMONIZE ⟨the scientists' conclusions seem contradictory but can be ∼*ed* by calm reasoning⟩ **2 a :** to grant as suitable or proper **:** render as due ⟨parents have rights which are not ∼*ed* to strangers or neighbors —A.I. Melden⟩ ⟨formerly, historians ∼*ed* to "justice" less than its due place —J.G.Edwards⟩ **b :** ALLOW, CONCEDE ⟨the law ∼*s* them favored status⟩ ⟨he decided to ∼ himself the delight of breaking the news —P.B.Kyne⟩ **c :** AWARD ⟨the President ∼*ed* him an honorary title⟩ **d :** ALLOT ⟨in spite of the injustices ∼*ed* him⟩ ∼ *vi* **1** *archaic* **:** to arrive at an agreement **:** come to terms ⟨proceed as we ∼*ed* before dinner —Sir Walter Scott⟩ — often used with *with* ⟨the Queen ∼*ed* with this view of the matter —Thomas Carlyle⟩ **2** *obs* **:** to give consent — used with *to* ⟨you to his love must ∼ —Shak.⟩ **3 :** to be in harmony **:** be consistent — usu. used with *with* ⟨find whether or not the treatment which they have received ∼*s* with freedom of speech —Zechariah Chafee b.1885⟩ **syn** see AGREE, GRANT

²accord \"\ *n* -s [ME *accord, acord*, fr. OF *acort, acorde*, fr. *acorder*] **1 a :** agreement (as in opinion, will, or action) ⟨engineers have reached a certain ∼ in regard to ethical principles —H.A.Wagner⟩ **:** CONFORMITY ⟨scholars studying human languages in ∼ with accepted scientific principles —H.R.Warfel⟩ **b :** a formal act of agreement **:** RECONCILIATION, UNDERSTANDING, TREATY ⟨the Munich ∼⟩ **c :** an agreement between parties in controversy by which satisfaction for an injury is stipulated and which when executed bars a lawsuit **2 :** balanced interrelationship (as of ideas, dimensions, colors, or musical tones) **:** PROPORTION, HARMONY ⟨a persuasive ∼ in his arguments⟩ ⟨the gentle ∼ of rolling plains⟩ ⟨the ∼ of voices⟩ **3** *obs* **:** ASSENT ⟨this gentle and unforc'd ∼ of Hamlet sits smiling to my heart —Shak.⟩ **4 :** voluntary or spontaneous impulse to act **:** completely free or unprompted will to act ⟨they gave generously of their own ∼⟩ — **with one accord** *adv* **:** with unanimity ⟨*with one accord* the crowd shouted its approval⟩

ac·cord·ance \-d°n(t)s\ *n* -s [ME *accordaunce, acordaunce*, fr. MF *acordance*, fr. *acordant*] **1 :** AGREEMENT, ACCORD — now used chiefly in the phrase *in accordance with* ⟨in ∼ with their instructions, they took an early plane for New York⟩ **2 :** the act of granting ⟨the ∼ of a privilege⟩ **3 :** ACCORDATURA

ac·cord·an·cy \-d°nsē, -si\ *n* -ES **:** ACCORD, ACCORDANCE

ac·cord·ant \-d°nt\ *adj* [ME *accordaunt, acordaunt*, fr. MF *acordant*, fr. pres. part. of *acorder*] **1 a :** AGREEING, CONSONANT, CONFORMABLE — now usu. used with *with* ⟨a place perfectly ∼ with man's nature —Thomas Hardy⟩ ⟨more ∼ with natural growth than with human planning —W.B.Adams⟩ **b** *obs* **:** of the same mind **:** UNOPPOSED **2 :** correspondent or harmonious ⟨∼ tones⟩ **3** *geol* **:** of the same or nearly the same elevation ⟨∼ mountain summits⟩ —**ac·cord·ant·ly** *adv*

ac·cor·da·tu·ra \ə,kȯrdə'tùrə, (,)a,k-\ *n* -s [It, lit., act of tuning, fr. *accordato* (past part. of *accordare* to tune, accord, fr. (assumed) VL) + *-ura* -ure — more at ACCORD] **:** the tuning scheme of a stringed musical instrument ⟨g d′ a′ e″ is the usual ∼ of a violin⟩

accorded *past of* ACCORD

¹according *adj* [ME, fr. pres. part. of *accorden* to accord] *archaic* **:** AGREEING, HARMONIOUS ⟨this ∼ voice of national wisdom —Edmund Burke⟩

²according *adv, obs* **:** ACCORDINGLY

according as *conj* [²*according*] **1 :** just as **:** proportionately as ⟨you'll receive *according as* you give⟩ **:** depending on how ⟨*according as* this question is answered, there are two suggestions to be made —*Publ's Mod. Lang. Assoc. of America*⟩ **2 :** depending on whether **:** IF ⟨*according as* he gives a favorable answer, you can plan to see him⟩

ac·cord·ing·ly *adv* [ME, fr. ¹*according* + *-ly*] **1 :** in conformity with a given set of circumstances **:** CORRESPONDINGLY ⟨it helps us to understand him and it helps us to act ∼ —W.J. Reilly⟩ **2 :** as a consequence **:** CONSEQUENTLY **:** as a logical outcome **:** SO ⟨later the club also accepted amateurs and ∼ changed its name⟩

according to *prep* [ME, fr. ¹*according* + *to*] **1 :** in conformity with **:** consistently with ⟨seated *according to* their rank⟩ **2 :** as attested, maintained, or declared by ⟨*according to* the best authorities⟩ ⟨the Gospel *according to* St. Mark⟩ **3** *obs* **:** with regard to ⟨his Son, who was descended from David *according to* the flesh —Rom 1:3 (RSV)⟩ **4 :** contingently upon **:** depending on ⟨we'll go or we won't, *according to* circumstances⟩ —**according to cock·er** \-'käkə(r)\ *usu cap C* [after Edward *Cocker* †1675 Eng. engraver & teacher, author of *Tutor to Arithmetic* (1664), a much-used textbook] **:** ACCURATE, CORRECT —**according to hoyle** \-'hȯil, -ȯi(ə)l\ *usu cap H* [after Edmond *Hoyle* †1769 Eng. writer and authority on games, whose treatises, esp. on whist (1742), became famous] **:** in agreement with standard practice or rules **:** in conformity with accepted usage or with an accepted procedure or system **:** CONVENTIONALLY ⟨playing the game *according to Hoyle*⟩ ⟨the girl did not behave *according to Hoyle* —Maude Hutchins⟩

¹ac·cor·di·on *also* **ac·cor·de·on** *or* **ac·cor·di·an** \ə'kȯ(r)dēən *also* a'-\ *n* -s [G *akkordion*, fr. *akkord* chord (fr. F *accord*) + *-ion* (as in *melodion*)] **:** a portable keyboard wind instrument in which the wind is forced past free metallic reeds by means of a hand-operated bellows

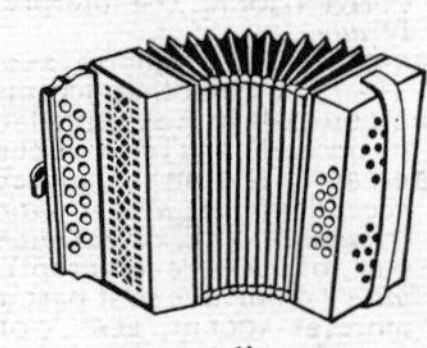

accordion

²accordion \"\ *adj* **:** folding like an accordion **:** creased or hinged so as to fold like an accordion ⟨an ∼ pleat⟩ ⟨an ∼ map⟩ ⟨an ∼ door⟩

accor·di·on·ist \-əst\ *n* -s **:** an accordion player

accords *pres 3d sing of* ACCORD, *pl of* ACCORD

¹ac·cost \ə'kȯst, -äst *also* a'-\ *vb* -ED/-ING/-S [MF *accoster*, prob. fr. OProv *acostar*, fr. LL *accostare*, fr. L *ad-* + *costa* rib, side — more at COAST] *vi, obs* **:** to lie alongside ⟨all the shores which to the sea ∼ —Edmund Spenser⟩ ∼ *vt* **1 :** to approach and speak to ⟨they were ∼*ed* by the immigration officials⟩ **:** speak to without having first been spoken to ⟨the host walked up and ∼*ed* the two silent guests⟩ **2 :** to confront, usu. in a somewhat challenging or defensive way ⟨Mrs. Berry, wishing first to see herself as she was, mutely ∼*ed* the looking glass —George Meredith⟩ **3 :** to address abruptly (as in a chance meeting) and usu. with a certain degree of impetuosity or boldness ⟨a beggar ∼*ed* me in the street⟩ **4 :** to solicit (as a man) for sexual immorality

²accost \"\ *n* -s *archaic* **:** GREETING ⟨she shrunk with fastidious pride from their hail-fellow ∼ —Elizabeth C. Gaskell⟩

ac·cost·a·ble \-təbəl\ *adj* [F, fr. *accoster* + *-able*] **:** capable of being approached **:** easily accessible

ac·cost·ed \-təd\ *adj* **1** *heraldry* **:** supported on both sides by other charges **2** *heraldry* **:** side by side

ac·couche \a'küsh, ə'-\ *vt* -ED/-ING/-S [F *accoucher*] **:** to assist during an accouchement

ac·couche·ment \,a,küsh'mäⁿ; a'küsh,mäⁿ, ə'-, -,mənt\ *n* -s [F, fr. *accoucher* to deliver a child, to be delivered of a child (fr. OF *acouchier* to lay down) + *-ment* — more at COUCH] **:** LYING-IN; *esp* **:** PARTURITION

accouchement for·cé \-(,)fȯr'sā\ *n, pl* **accouchements forcés** \-äⁿ(z)(,)f-,-ən(t)s(,)f-\ [F, lit., forced delivery] *med* **:** artificially forced and hastened delivery

ac·cou·cheur \,a,kü'shər(·), a'kü,sh-, -shə(r, ə'=,=\ *n, pl* **accoucheurs** \-ərz,-əz\ [F, fr. *accoucher* + *-eur* -or] **:** one that assists during an accouchement **:** OBSTETRICIAN

¹ac·count \ə'kaùnt *also* a'-\ *n* -s [ME *acount, accompt*, fr. OF *aconte*, fr. *aconter*, v.] **1** *archaic* **:** COUNTING, ENUMERATION, COMPUTATION ⟨a pupil good at ∼⟩ **2 a :** a record of debit and credit entries chronologically posted to a ledger page from books of original entry to cover transactions involving a particular item (as cash or notes receivable) or a particular person or concern **b :** a statement of transactions during a fiscal period showing the resulting balance **3 :** a collection of items to be balanced — usu. used in pl. **4 :** a statement or explanation of one's activities, conduct, and discharge of responsibilities esp. in financial administration ⟨he could give no satisfactory ∼ of what he had done with the money⟩ **5 a :** a periodically rendered reckoning (as one listing charged purchases and credits) ⟨a grocery ∼⟩ **b :** the patronage involved in establishing or maintaining an account **:** BUSINESS **:** business relationship ⟨glad to secure that customer's ∼⟩; *also* **:** PATRON, CUSTOMER, CLIENT ⟨a salesman with many good ∼*s*⟩ **6 a :** value or importance esp. as attributed by others ⟨an official of considerable ∼⟩ **b :** ESTEEM, JUDGMENT ⟨he stands high in their ∼⟩ **7 :** PROFIT, ADVANTAGE ⟨he turned his wit to good ∼⟩ **8 a :** a statement or exposition of underlying or explanatory reasons, causes, grounds, or motives ⟨no satisfactory ∼ has been given of these phenomena⟩ **b :** a reason giving rise to an action, decision, opinion, or any other result **:** BASIS ⟨on that ∼ he refused the offer⟩ ⟨on all ∼*s* you must do it⟩ **c :** ATTENTION, CONSIDERATION **:** careful thought ⟨don't leave that point out of ∼⟩ ⟨take ∼ of what you are doing⟩ **d :** a usu. mental record based on close observation

⟨keep careful ~ of all you do⟩ **9 a :** a statement of facts or events ⟨a newspaper remarkable for its sober ~*s* of the theater world⟩ **b :** an informative report or descriptive narration ⟨an ~ of the varieties of tropical vegetation⟩ ⟨the ~ of a battle⟩ **c :** a study or narrative usu. nonfictional and wholly objective ⟨an illuminating ~ of colonial days⟩ **10 :** HEARSAY — usu. used in pl. ⟨by all ~*s* he is very rich⟩ ⟨he has been quite successful, from all ~*s*⟩ **11 :** a sum of money or its equivalent deposited in the common cash of a bank and subject to withdrawal at the option of the depositor **12 :** a common-law action for a statement of receipts and disbursements and the recovery of any balance due; *also* **:** the writ by which it was brought **13 :** the fortnightly or monthly settlement between buyers and sellers on the London Stock Exchange; *also* **:** the period from one such settlement to another — usu. used with *the;* compare ACCOUNT DAYS, TERM SETTLEMENT **14 :** performance or rendition (as of a musical composition) ⟨the pianist gave a sensitive ~ of it⟩ **syn** see ²USE — **for account of** *prep* **:** on behalf of — **for the account :** not for settlement until the end of the term-settlement period — **for the account and risk of :** on behalf of and at the hazard of — used by a stock-exchange broker to indicate that he is solely an agent in buying or selling for a customer — **in account with** *prep* **:** in reckoning with **:** in the relationship of creditor or debtor to — **on account of** *prep* **:** for the sake of **:** by reason of **:** because of ⟨*on account of* her love for her children, she did all that was possible⟩ — **on one's own account 1 :** for one's own interest or on one's own behalf ⟨I'm doing it *on my own account,* not for anyone else⟩ **2 :** at one's own risk ⟨it's a dangerous plan, one you'll have to follow up *on your own account*⟩ **3 :** on one's own intelligence or strength **:** on one's own motivation **:** by oneself ⟨she left her parents and lived in the city entirely *on her own account*⟩

²**account** \"\ *vb* -ED/-ING/-S [ME *accounten, acounten, accompten,* fr. MF *aconter, acompter,* fr. *a-* (fr. L *ad-*) + *conter, compter* to count — more at COUNT] *vt* **1 a** *obs* **:** to calculate the numerical quantity of **:** COUNT ⟨my father and my mother ~ the days —William Caxton⟩ **b** *obs* **:** to determine or establish by comparison with a fixed point or standard **c** *obs* **:** to include in an enumeration or calculation ⟨~*ing* the Lent season —Thomas Cogan⟩ **d** *archaic* **:** CREDIT, ALLOT **e :** to probe into **:** give an analytical report on **:** take or render account of ⟨the report will be ~*ed* by the finance committee⟩ **2 :** to think of as **:** look upon as **:** rate, regard, or classify as — usu. used passively or reflexively ⟨he was ~*ed* a lawyer of ability —G.S.Bryan⟩ ⟨they ~*ed* themselves fortunate⟩ ~ *vi* **1** *obs* **:** COUNT **2** *archaic* **:** to give or receive a financial account **:** settle an account **3 :** to furnish a justifying analysis or a detailed explanation of one's financial credits and debits or of the discharge of any of one's responsibilities — used with *for* ⟨the broker ~*ed* satisfactorily for his expenditures⟩ ⟨he could not ~ for the time spent away from his post⟩ **4 :** to furnish substantial reasons or a convincing explanation **:** make clear or reveal basic causes — used with *for* ⟨a consistent theory which would ~ for the facts —G.C.Sellery⟩ **5 a :** to be the sole or primary factor in the existence, acquisition, supply, use, or disposal of an indicated thing — used with *for* ⟨the region ~*s* for a large part of usable timber⟩ **b :** to bring about the capture, death, or destruction of an indicated thing — used with *for* ⟨his dog ~*ed* for two of the rabbits⟩ **syn** see CONSIDER, EXPLAIN

ac·count·a·bil·i·ty \ə,kau̇nt-ə'biləd-ē, -ətē, -i\ *n* -ES **:** the quality or state of being accountable, liable, or responsible

ac·count·a·ble \ə'kau̇ntəbəl\ *adj* [ME, fr. AF, fr. MF *aconter* to account + *-able*] **1 :** subject to giving an account **:** ANSWERABLE ⟨every sane man is ~ to his conscience for his behavior⟩ **2 :** capable of being accounted for **:** EXPLAINABLE ⟨their apparently strange customs are now ~⟩ **syn** see RESPONSIBLE

ac·count·a·bly \-blē, -i\ *adv* **:** in an accountable manner

ac·count·an·cy \ə'kau̇nt³nsē, -tən-, -si\ *n* -ES **1 :** the profession of accounting **2 :** the practice of accounting

¹**ac·count·ant** \-t³nt,-tənt\ *n* -S [ME *accountaunt, accomptaunt,* fr. MF *acontant, acomptant,* fr. pres. part. of *aconter, acompter* to account, compute — more at ACCOUNT] **1 a :** one that gives an account **:** one that is accountable **b** *archaic* **:** the defendant in an action of account **2** *archaic* **:** one that counts or calculates **3 :** one that is skilled in the practice of accounting **:** one that has charge of public or private accounts — distinguished from *bookkeeper;* see CERTIFIED PUBLIC ACCOUNTANT, CHARTERED ACCOUNTANT, PUBLIC ACCOUNTANT

²**accountant** *adj* [ME *accountaunt, accomptaunt,* fr. MF *acontant, acomptant,* pres. part.] *obs* **:** liable to account **:** ACCOUNTABLE ⟨~ to the law —Shak.⟩

account book *n* **:** a book in which accounts are kept **:** LEDGER

account current *n, pl* **accounts current :** CURRENT ACCOUNT

account day *n* **:** the final day of the account days **:** SETTLEMENT DAY

account days *n pl* **:** the several days at the end of each term-settlement period on the London Stock Exchange when arrangements are made for carrying over the transactions to the next period or for making final settlement

accounted *past of* ACCOUNT

account executive *n* **:** a business executive responsible for the management of a client's account

accounting *n* -S [ME, fr. gerund of *accounten* to account] **1 a :** the system of classifying, recording, and summarizing business and financial transactions in books of account and analyzing, verifying, and reporting the results **b :** the body of principles, conventions, and procedures underlying accounting — distinguished from *bookkeeping* **2 a :** practical application of accounting — see COST ACCOUNTING, PUBLIC ACCOUNTING **b :** an instance of applying the principles, conventions, and procedures of accounting to the financial condition of an individual or individual organization **3 :** the presenting or stating of accounts ⟨the treasurer rendered his annual ~⟩ **4 :** the process of devising and installing systems of accounts

accounting equation *n* **1 :** the equality of debits and credits as used in the double-entry system **2 :** a statement of net worth as equal to assets minus liabilities

accounting machine *n* **1 :** a key-operated machine which dates, codes, tabulates, adds, subtracts, or totals chiefly in the process of keeping business records (as accounts payable or receivable) **2 :** a business machine that selects information from punched cards fed into it, tabulates, adds, subtracts, or totals in various predeterminable ways, and prints the results

account payable *n, pl* **accounts payable :** the balance due to a creditor on a current account

account receivable *n, pl* **accounts receivable :** a balance due from a debtor on a current account

account render *n* **:** ACCOUNT 12

account rendered *n, pl* **accounts rendered :** an account presented by a creditor to his debtor for examination and settlement

accounts *pl of* ACCOUNT, *pres 3d sing of* ACCOUNT

account sale *or* **account sales** *n* **1 :** a statement showing the net result of a purchase or sale transaction made by one person on another's account or behalf with commission and all other charges included **2 :** a sale on credit

account stated *n, pl* **accounts stated :** an account rendered which by implied or express acceptance has been agreed upon by both parties as correct

accouple *vt* -ED/-ING/-S [ME *acouplen,* fr. MF *accoupler, acopler,* fr. *a-* (fr. L *ad-*) + *cople* couple — more at COUPLE] *obs* **:** JOIN, COUPLE

ac·cou·ple·ment \ə'kəpəlmənt, a'-\ *n* -S [MF, fr. *accoupler* + *-ment*] **1 :** action of joining together **:** COUPLING ⟨proposing an ~ of the two great labor organizations —Edwin Lahey⟩ **2** *archit* **:** placement of two columns very close together or in contact **3 :** something that couples (as a tie or brace)

ac·cou·ter *or* **ac·cou·tre** \ə'küd-ə(r), -ütə- *also* a'k-\ *vt* **accoutered** *or* **accoutred; accoutered** *or* **accoutred; accou·ter·ing** *or* **accou·tring** \-üd-əriŋ, -ütər-,-ü·tr-\ **accouters** *or* **accoutres** [F *accoutrer,* fr. MF *acoustrer,* fr. *a-* (fr. L *ad-*) + *costure* seam, fr. (assumed) VL *consutura,* fr. L *consutus* (past part. of *consuere* to sew together, fr. *com-* + *suere* to sew) + *-ura* -ure — more at SEW] **:** to fit out **:** DRESS **:** provide with equipment or furnishings **:** equip esp. for military service — usu. used passively ⟨they were properly ~*ed* for the trip⟩ ⟨~*ed* for battle⟩ **syn** see FURNISH

ac·cou·ter·ment \-üd-ə(r)mənt, -ütə(-\ *or* **ac·cou·tre·ment** \", -ü·trəm-\ *n* -S [MF *accoutrement,* fr. *accoutrer* + *-ment*] **1 :** the act of accoutering or state of being accoutered **2 a :** any article of equipment or dress esp. when used merely as an accessory ⟨she carried a pink parasol, a rather startling ~⟩ **b :** OUTFIT, FURNISHINGS, EQUIPMENT, TRAPPINGS, REGALIA; *specif* **:** a soldier's outfit (as a rifle belt, pack, and other accessories) usu. not including clothes and weapons ⟨the ~*s* of war⟩ — usu. used in pl. **3 a :** an identifying but usu. extraneous characteristic **:** a nonessential but usual accompaniment ⟨political demagoguery accompanied by its unsurprising ~ of prejudice and stupidity⟩ **b :** a typical device or procedure ⟨the lurid ~*s* employed by the average comic artist —Coulton Waugh⟩

accpt *abbr* acceptance

¹**ac·cra** \ə'krä, a'-,ä'-\ *adj, usu cap* [fr. *Accra, Akkra,* Ghana] **:** of or from Accra, the capital of Ghana **:** of the kind or style prevalent in Accra

²**accra** *usu cap, var of* AKRA

accra copal *n, usu cap A* **:** a hard resin obtained from certain trees in the coastal forests of western Africa and used in varnishes

accrd *abbr* accrued

ac·cred·it \ə'kredət *also* a'-; *usu* -dəd+V\ *vt* -ED/-ING/-S [F *accréditer,* fr. *ad-* + *crédit* credit — more at CREDIT] **1 :** to put (as by common consent) into a reputable or outstanding category **:** consider, recognize, or acclaim as rightfully possessing an uncontested status ⟨sages so fully ~*ed* as Mr. Bertrand Russell —C.E.Montague⟩ **2 :** to give official authorization to or approval of: **a :** to order or permit to proceed on an official mission or on one otherwise officially recognized ⟨in the course of service as an air attaché at several capitals . . . governments to which he was ~*ed* gave him medals —J.G. Cozzens⟩ **b :** to vouch for officially **:** recognize or clear officially as bona fide, approved, or in conformity with a standard ⟨only a few counties in the state had been ~*ed* with reference to tuberculosis in cattle —*Jour. Amer. Med. Assoc.*⟩ **c :** to recognize (an educational institution) as maintaining standards that render it eligible for membership in an association of similar institutions and that qualify its graduates for admission to higher or more specialized institutions or for professional practice **3 :** CREDIT **:** to give credit for **:** ascribe or attribute esp. favorably ⟨rare and treasured possessions ~*ed* with magical properties —C.D.Forde⟩ ⟨nobility not generally ~*ed* to him by the coarse world —Bernard DeVoto⟩ **syn** see APPROVE, ASCRIBE, AUTHORIZE

ac·cred·i·ta·tion \ə,kredə'tāshən\ *n* -S *often attrib* **:** the act or process of accrediting ⟨recently developed standards for the ~ of junior colleges⟩ ⟨a joint commission on ~ of hospitals⟩ **:** the state or fact of being accredited ⟨ambassador in Rome with concurrent ~ to Italy and Yugoslavia —*Current Biog.*⟩ ⟨the ~ status of an educational institution⟩

accredited *adj* **1 a :** publicly sanctioned or recognized ⟨take it as a personal insult if any of their neighbors break away from ~ custom —W.R.Inge⟩ **b :** officially authorized or recognized **:** provided with credentials ⟨an ~ war correspondent⟩ ⟨~ observers at the United Nations⟩ **c :** accepted as valid or authoritative ⟨theories in keeping with the ~ science of the day⟩ **2 :** officially vouched for or guaranteed as conforming to a prescribed or desirable standard ⟨an ~ hospital⟩: as **a** *of an educational institution* **:** approved by an accrediting agency ⟨an ~ college⟩ **b** *of livestock* **:** guaranteed as free from a usu. specified disease ⟨an ~ herd⟩

ac·cred·i·tee \ə,kredə'tē\ *n* -S **:** one that has received accreditation ⟨UN ~*s* —*Newsweek*⟩

accrediting agency *n* **:** a state-controlled or privately supported agency authorized to grant accreditation to educational institutions

ac·cred·it·ment \ə'kredətmənt\ *n* -S **:** ACCREDITATION

ac·cresce \ə'kres, a'-\ *vi* -ED/-ING/-S [L *accrescere,* fr. *ad-* + *crescere* to grow — more at CRESCENT] **:** ACCRUE *vi* 1

ac·cres·cence \-s³n(t)s\ *n* -S [ML *accrescentia,* fr. L *accrescent-, accrescens* (pres. part. of *accrescere*) + *-ia*] **1 :** continuous growth **2 :** ACCRETION

ac·cres·cent \-s³nt, 'a,k-\ *adj* [L *accrescent-, accrescens*] **:** growing continuously; *specif* **:** growing larger after flowering — used esp. of a calyx

¹**ac·crete** \ə'krēt, a'-\ *vb* -ED/-ING/-S [back-formation fr. *accretion*] *vi* **1 :** to grow together **:** UNITE, COMBINE **2 :** to become attached by accretion **:** ADHERE ~ *vt* **1 :** to cause to adhere or become attached ⟨a desire to ~ to himself symbols of status —Edward Sapir⟩ **2 :** to gather and attach to oneself or itself ⟨as the story traveled, it *accreted* emotion —E. M.Forster⟩

²**ac·crete** \", 'a,k-\ *adj* [L *accretus*] **1 :** formed by accretion **2** *bot* **:** grown together

ac·cre·tion \ə'krēshən, a'-\ *n* -S [L *accretion-, accretio* increase, increment, fr. *accretus* (past part. of *accrescere* to increase) + *-ion-, -io* -ion — more at ACCRESCE] **1 :** the process of growth or enlargement: **a :** organic growth **:** continued development from within **b :** increase by external addition or accumulation (as by adhesion of external parts or particles) **c** (1) **:** the increase or extension of the boundaries of land or the consequent acquisition of land accruing to the owner by the gradual or imperceptible action of natural forces (as by the washing up of sand or soil from the sea or a river or by a gradual recession of the water from the usual watermark) **:** accession in which the boundaries of land are enlarged by this process; *sometimes* **:** increase in the amount or extent of any kind of property or in the value of any property — compare AVULSION (2) **:** gain to an heir or legatee by failure of a coheir or a colegatee to take his share **2 a :** the result of the process of accretion ⟨every culture is an ~ —A.L. Kroeber⟩ ⟨a complex ~ of rules —Edmund Wilson⟩ **b :** the matter added; *esp* **:** an extraneous addition ⟨~*s* of grime⟩ ⟨the immense ~ of flesh which had descended on her in middle life —Edith Wharton⟩ **c** *forestry* **:** INCREMENT; *sometimes* **:** increase in diameter as contrasted with increase in volume **3 :** CONCRETION **:** coherence of separate particles

ac·cre·tion·ary \-,nerē\ *adj* **1 :** marked by or involving accretion **2 :** produced by accretion

accretionary hypothesis *n* **:** any explanation of the origin of the earth that involves the hypothesis of gradual growth by the gravitational infall of solid bodies (as asteroids, planetesimals, or meteorites) — compare PLANETESIMAL HYPOTHESIS

accretion borer *n* **:** a hollow auger used for cutting out from a tree a core from which accretion is estimated by counting annual rings

accretion cutting *or* **accretion thinning** *n* **:** thinning of trees in order to secure greater growth in girth of those left standing

ac·cre·tive \ə'krēd-iv, (')a¦k-\ *adj* [*accretion* + *-ive*] **1 :** relating to accretion ⟨made up by a sort of ~ process —*N.Y. Times*⟩ **2 :** growing by accretion

ac·croach \ə'krōch, a'-\ *vt* -ED/-ING/-ES [ME *acrochen* to draw, acquire, fr. MF *acrochier,* fr. *a-* (fr. L *ad-*) + *crochier* to hook, get hold of, fr. *croc* hook, of Gmc origin; akin to ON *krōkr* hook — more at CROOK] **:** ASSUME, APPROPRIATE, USURP ⟨~ to themselves royal power —William Stubbs⟩

ac·croi·des \ə'krȯi(,)dēz, a'-\ *or* **accroides resin** *or* **accroides gum** *n* [modif. of NL *acaroides*] **:** ACAROID RESIN

ac·cru·al \ə'krüəl *also* a'-\ *n* -S *often attrib* [¹*accrue* + *-al*] **1 :** the action or process of accruing **2 a :** something that accrues; *esp* **:** an amount of money that periodically accumulates for a specific item (as taxes, interest, or anticipated expenses) **b :** something that has accrued during a specified period

accrual basis *n* **:** the method of keeping accounts that recognizes income when earned and expenses when incurred regardless of when cash is received or disbursed — compare CASH BASIS

¹**ac·crue** \ə'krü *also* a'-\ *vb* -ED/-ING/-S [ME *acreuen, acruwen,* prob. fr. MF *acreue, accreue* increase, fr. fem. of *acreu,* past part. of *acreistre* to increase, grow, fr. L *accrescere,* fr. *ad-* + *crescere* to grow — more at CRESCENT] *vi* **1 :** to come into existence as an enforceable claim **:** vest as a right ⟨a cause of action has *accrued* when the right to sue has become vested⟩ **2 :** to come by way of increase or addition **:** arise as a growth or result — usu. used with *to* or *from* ⟨advantages *accruing* to society from the freedom of the press⟩ **3 :** to be periodically accumulated in the process of time whether as an increase or a decrease ⟨the *accruing* of taxes⟩ ⟨allowing the receivable interest to ~⟩ ~ *vt* **1 :** GATHER, COLLECT, ACCUMULATE ⟨authorized by law to ~ leave . . . in the maximum amount of 120 days —*U.S.Code*⟩ **2 :** to enter in the books as an accrual

²**accrue** \"\ *n* -S [MF *accreue, acreue*] *obs* **:** ACCRUAL, ADDITION

accrued dividend *n* **:** a dividend earned or assumed earned at a specified rate on cumulative preferred stock but not declared or paid

accrued interest *n* **:** interest earned since last settlement date but not yet due or payable

accrued liability *n* **:** the portion of an accruing liability that has become definitely ascertainable and chargeable though actual payment thereof is not yet due

ac·crue·ment \-ümənt\ *n* -S [¹*accrue* + *-ment*] **:** ACCRUAL, INCREMENT

acct *abbr* account; accountant

ac·cul·tur·ate \ə'kəlchə,rāt\ *vb* -ED/-ING/-S [back-formation fr. *acculturation*] *vt* **:** to cause to change through acculturation ~ *vi* **:** to become changed through acculturation

ac·cul·tur·a·tion \ə,kəlchə'rāshən, (,)a,k-\ *n* -S [*ad-* + *culture* + *-ation*] **1 :** a process of intercultural borrowing marked by the continuous transmission of traits and elements between diverse peoples and resulting in new and blended patterns; *esp* **:** the resultant modifications occurring in a primitive culture through direct and prolonged contact with an advanced society — distinguished from *assimilation;* compare TRANSCULTURATION **2 :** the process of socialization — compare ENCULTURATION

ac·cul·tur·a·tion·al \-shən³l,-shnəl\ *adj* **:** of or relating to the process of acculturation or to the modifications in culture resulting from acculturation

ac·cul·tur·a·tion·ist \-sh(ə)nəst\ *n* -S **:** a student of acculturation

ac·cul·tur·a·tive \ə'kəlchə,rād-iv, a'-\ *adj* **:** of, relating to, or contributing to acculturation

ac·cul·tur·ize \-chə,rīz\ *vt* -ED/-ING/-S [*acculturation* + *-ize*] **:** to cause (a people) to adopt the culture of another

ac·cum·ben·cy \ə'kəmbənsē, a'-\ *n* -ES [L *accumbent-, accumbens* + E *-cy*] **:** the state of being accumbent

ac·cum·bent \ə'kəmbənt, (')a¦k-\ *adj* [L *accumbent-, accumbens,* pres. part. of *accumbere* to lie down, recline at table, fr. *ad-* + *-cumbere* to lie down (akin to *cubare* to lie down) — more at HIP] **1 :** leaning or reclining esp. at meals ⟨the Roman ~ posture in eating⟩ **2** *bot* **:** lying against something — used chiefly of cotyledons having their edges folded against the hypocotyl (as in many crucifers) — compare CONDUPLICATE, INCUMBENT **3** *zool* **:** closely applied to a surface (as of the wing scales of certain insects)

ac·cu·mu·la·ble \ə'kyümyələbəl, ÷-mə- *also* a'-\ *adj* [*accumulate* + *-able*] **:** capable of being accumulated

¹**ac·cu·mu·late** \-,lāt, *usu* -ād·+V\ *vb* -ED/-ING/-S [L *accumulatus,* past part. of *accumulare,* fr. *ad-* + *cumulare* to heap up — more at CUMULATE] *vt* **:** to heap up in a mass **:** pile up ⟨the sands then had their own way, and *accumulated* the barrier which now exists between the two rivers —Douglas Carruthers⟩ ⟨they . . . ~ blame upon the conditions imposed on them by fate —A.C.Benson⟩ **:** AMASS ⟨*accumulated* a fortune as a tea planter⟩ **:** COLLECT, GATHER ⟨true poetry ~*s* meaning every time it is read —C.D.Lewis⟩ ⟨dismantled the spinning wheel and carried it to the attic to ~ antiquity —John Gould⟩ ~ *vi* **:** to grow or increase in quantity or number ⟨where wealth ~*s* and men decay —Oliver Goldsmith⟩ ⟨snow *accumulated* to a depth of 10 feet⟩

syn AMASS, HOARD: ACCUMULATE suggests a gradual piling up or increasing so as to make a store or great quantity ⟨to *accumulate* dust⟩ ⟨he who *accumulates* objects of value —Herbert Spencer⟩ ⟨*accumulated* major collections of important Arabic manuscripts —*Amer. Council of Learned Soc. Newsletter*⟩ ⟨to *accumulate* wisdom⟩ AMASS stresses the size, esp. the great size, of the accumulation, usu. of things of value; it may imply rather rapid acquisition ⟨great wealth was *amassed* through steel, railroad, coal, and other industries —*Amer. Guide Series: Pa.*⟩ ⟨scientific knowledge, painstakingly *amassed* by many devotees over an extended period of human history —F.A.Geldard⟩ HOARD always implies a holding or storing up after acquisition, and usu. concealment, sometimes suggesting miserly retention ⟨*hoarding* money is not a safe way of saving —G.B.Shaw⟩ ⟨some delicacy that has been *hoarded* for weeks is brought forth for a guest —Maeanna Cheserton-Mangle⟩ ⟨newspapermen, *hoarding* their eloquent comments for their own typewriters —Leonard Lyons⟩

²**ac·cu·mu·late** \-,lət, -,lāt\ *adj* [L *accumulatus*] **:** heaped or piled up **:** ACCUMULATED

accumulated surplus *n* **:** the surplus of a corporation that has been earned or has accrued after incorporation

accumulated temperature *n* **:** CUMULATIVE TEMPERATURE

ac·cu·mu·la·tion \ə,-'lāshən\ *n* -S [F or L; F, fr. L *accumulation-, accumulatio,* fr. *accumulatus* + *-ion-, -io* -ion] **1 :** the action or process of accumulating **:** state of being or having accumulated **:** a collecting together **:** AMASSING ⟨the steady ~ of snow throughout the night⟩ ⟨fabrics subject to the ~ of static electricity⟩ ⟨current theories about the ~ of the sun and stars from dust clouds —H.C.Urey⟩ **2 :** increase or growth by addition esp. when continuous or repeated (as of interest to principal): as **a :** the increase of a fund or property by the continuous addition to it of the interest or income of it, subject in England to a rule analogous to the rule against perpetuities and in the U. S. allowed in many states only during the minority of the person for whom the property is held **b** (1) *in life insurance* **:** retention of dividends for distribution at some later date (2) *in accident insurance* **:** an increase in the principal sum that sometimes takes effect without change of premium upon each renewal of a policy (3) *in marine insurance* **:** an increase in the limit of liability under open-cargo policies to double the normal amount if two or more cargoes at a port are loaded on the same vessel **c :** the gradual purchase of large quantities of securities in anticipation of a rise in price or for investment or control purposes **d :** appreciation between the date of purchase and maturity in the value of a bond bought at a discount **3 :** something that has accumulated or has been accumulated **:** an accumulated mass, quantity, or number ⟨huge ~*s* of mouse-gray clouds —Ira Wolfert⟩ ⟨clearing away the ~ of centuries from the base of the pyramid —*London Calling*⟩ ⟨the giant ~*s* of stars known as galaxies —George Gamow⟩ **4 :** the movement of a substance into a cell against a concentration gradient or from a lower to a higher potential for the specific substance — used esp. of movement of ions into plant cells

accumulation factor *n* **:** the factor $(1 + r)^n$ by which any principal must be multiplied to give its amount at compound interest after *n* periods, *r* being the interest for one period ⟨the *accumulation factor* for 10 years at 6 percent compounded quarterly is $(1.015)^{40}$⟩

accumulation of energy *or* **accumulation of power :** the storing of energy by various means (as by weights lifted, masses put in motion, or chemical changes effected)

ac·cu·mu·la·tive \ə'==,lād·iv, -,lə|, |tiv, -ēv\ *adj* **1 :** marked by accumulation **:** produced by accumulation **:** CUMULATIVE ⟨~ toxic effects⟩ ⟨~ rainfall⟩ **2 :** tending to or given to accumulation **:** ACCUMULATING ⟨nations are imperialistic in their ~ stage —D.L.Kemmerer⟩ **3 :** CUMULATIVE 4 — **ac·cu·mu·la·tive·ly** *adv*

ac·cu·mu·la·tor \-,lād·ə(r), -ātə-\ *n* -S *often attrib* **:** one that accumulates: as **a :** an apparatus for storing energy (as a cylinder containing water under the pressure of a weighted piston for hydraulic presses) **b :** a contrivance to take up the force of a sudden strain (as a system of springs or an elastic section in a chain) **c** *Brit* **:** STORAGE CELL **d :** a vessel for collecting a gas or liquid usu. for temporary storage **e :** a mechanism or electrical circuit on a cash register, adding machine, computer, or similar machine that automatically stores or collects certain classes of figures **:** COUNTER

ac·cu·ra·cy \'akyərəsē, -si, ÷-k(ə)rəs-\ *n* -ES [*accurate* + *-cy*] **1 :** the quality, state, or degree of being accurate: **a :** freedom from mistake or error **:** CORRECTNESS ⟨answers will be marked for neatness as well as for ~⟩ ⟨to achieve ~, errors or their repetition must be avoided —*English Language Teaching*⟩ **b :** conformity to truth or to some standard or model ⟨an account, the general ~ of which could hardly be doubted⟩ ⟨the ~ of a firearm is its ability to deliver a close group of hits on a target⟩ **:** EXACTNESS ⟨impossible to state with ~ the number of casualties⟩ ⟨a play much admired for the ~ of its idiom⟩ ⟨the highly approximate reconnaissance ~ of the map—*Geog. Rev.*⟩ **c** *of measurement* **:** the degree of conformity to some recognized standard value **:** deviation of a result obtained by a particular method from the value accepted as true ⟨elevations have been extended as far as 50 miles across rugged mountainous terrain with an ~ of about 2 feet —*Science*⟩ — contrasted with *precision*

ac·cu·rate \-rət, *rapid* ˈakyərt, *usu* -d·+V\ *adj* [L *accuratus* prepared with care, careful, exact, fr. past part. of *accurare* to take care of, do carefully, fr. *ad-* + *curare* to take care of, heal — more at CURE] **1 :** free from error or mistake esp. as the result of care ⟨an ~ estimate of expenses⟩ ⟨new inventions . . . had made it possible to chart and to hold a more ~ course at sea —Lewis Mumford⟩ ⟨sound and ~ observers⟩ ⟨~ methods⟩ **:** in exact conformity to truth or to some standard **:** CORRECT, EXACT, PRECISE ⟨the report was dry, factual, painstakingly ~, crabbedly truthful —Carl Sandburg⟩ ⟨a mathematically ~ distribution⟩ ⟨the instruments were sensitive and marvelously ~ —E.K.Gann⟩ **2** *obs* **:** precisely fixed **:** executed with care **:** CAREFUL **syn** see CORRECT

ac·cu·rate·ly \-tlē, -i\ *adv* **:** in an accurate manner **:** PRECISELY, EXACTLY

ac·cu·rate·ness \-tnəs\ *n* -ES **:** the quality or state of being accurate

ac·curse \əˈkərs, -kōs *also* aˈ-\ *vt* **accursed; accursed** *see* ACCURSED\ *or* **accurst; accursing; accurses** [alter. (influenced by such words as *accord, account*) of ME *acursen*, fr. *a-* (fr. OE *ā-*, perfective prefix) + *cursen* to curse — more at ABIDE, CURSE] **:** to consign to destruction, misery, or evil by a curse **:** ANATHEMATIZE — now used chiefly as past part. ⟨looked upon her as a thing *accursed* —Charles Kingsley⟩

ac·cursed \-st,-səd; -səd *usu when a stressed syllable follows without pause*, "-səd *breed*" *for instance being more frequent than* "-st *breed*"\ *or* **ac·curst** \-st\ *adj* [ME *acursed*, fr. past part. of *acursen*] **1 :** CURSED ⟨this ~ devil —Shak.⟩ **2 :** bad enough to be under a curse **:** DETESTABLE, DAMNABLE ⟨dry, unhealthy, and ~ was the road —Eve Langley⟩ — **ac·curs·ed·ly** \-sədlē, -i\ *adv* — **ac·curs·ed·ness** \-sədnəs\ *n* -ES

ac·cus·a·ble \əˈkyüzəbəl *also* aˈ-\ *adj* [F, fr. L *accusabilis* blameworthy, fr. *accusare* + *-abilis* -able] **:** liable to be accused — **ac·cus·a·bly** \-blē\ *adv*

ac·cus·al \-zəl\ *n* -s **:** ACCUSATION ⟨lurid and rather unlikely scenes of ~, confession, and remorse —*New Yorker*⟩

ac·cus·ant \-zᵊnt\ *n* -s [F, fr. L *accusant-, accusans*, pres. part. of *accusare*] **:** one that accuses

ac·cu·sa·tion \ˌakyəˈzāshən, -yüˈ-\ *n* -s [ME *accusacioun*, fr. MF *accusation*, fr. L *accusation-, accusatio*, fr. *accusatus* (past part. of *accusare* to call to account) + *-ion-, -io* -ion — more at ACCUSE] **1 :** the act of accusing **:** the state or fact of being accused ⟨his basic premise that ~ equals proof of guilt —*New Republic*⟩ **2 a :** a charge of wrongdoing, delinquency, or fault **:** the declaration containing such a charge **:** ALLEGATION, INDICTMENT ⟨with the calumnies were mingled ~*s* much better founded —T.B.Macaulay⟩ ⟨~*s* in the press⟩ **b :** the offense or fault of which one is accused ⟨the ~ was murder⟩

ac·cu·sa·ti·val \əˌkyüzəˈtīvəl *also* aˌ-\ *adj* [²*accusative* + *-al*] **:** ¹ACCUSATIVE

¹**ac·cu·sa·tive** \ə=ˈzəd·iv, -ətiv, -ēv\ *adj* [ME, fr. MF or L; MF *accusatif*, fr. L *accusativus* (trans. of Gk *aitiatikos*, lit., accusing, causal), fr. *accusatus* (past part. of *accusare*) + *-ivus* -ive] **1 a** *of a grammatical case* **:** marking typically the direct object of a verb (as Latin *filium* in *mater amat filium* "the mother loves her son"; German *mich* in *er sieht mich* "he sees me") or the object of any of several prepositions (as Latin *eos* in *ad eos* "toward them"; German *den stuhl* in *ohne den stuhl* "without the chair") — used esp. in the grammar of those Indo-European languages that have relatively full inflections **b** *of a word or word group* **:** being the direct object of a verb or the object of a preposition even when this relation is not marked by any inflectional element (as *Robert* in "John met Robert") — not now used technically **c :** of or belonging to the accusative case ⟨an ~ ending⟩ **2 :** ACCUSING, ACCUSATORY ⟨indicating their opponent with ~ forefingers —Stephen Crane⟩ — **ac·cu·sa·tive·ly** *adv*

²**accusative** \"\ *n* -s [ME, fr. MF or L; MF, fr. L *accusativus*, fr. *accusativus*, adj.] **:** the accusative case of a language or a form in the accusative case

accusative absolute *n* **1 :** a construction in German consisting of a noun in the accusative case joined with a predicate that does not include a finite verb and usu. capable of being construed as the modifier of the principal verb in its sentence (as *den hut in der hand* in *den hut in der hand ging er ins haus* "hat in hand he went into the house") **2 :** a construction in English, esp. colloquial English, consisting of a pronoun in the accusative case joined with a predicate that does not include a finite verb and otherwise identical with the nominative absolute (as *him being my friend* in "him being my friend, I granted his request")

accusative-dative *adj, of a case of English pronouns* **:** marking typically the object of a verb (as *me* in "he saw me", *him* in "I gave him the book") or of a preposition (as *us* in "with us")

ac·cu·sa·to·ri·al \əˌkyüzəˈtōrēəl, aˈ-, ˌaˌk-\ *adj* [*accusatory* + *-al*] **:** of or relating to an accuser; *specif* **:** indicating the form of criminal prosecution in which the alleged criminal is publicly accused of his crime and is tried in public by a judge who is not also the prosecutor — contrasted with *inquisitorial* — **ac·cus·a·to·ri·al·ly** \-əlē\ *adv*

ac·cus·a·to·ry \əˈkyüzəˌtōrē, aˈ-, -tō-, -ri\ *adj* [L *accusatorius* of an accuser, fr. *accusator* accuser, fr. *accusatus* (past part. of *accusare* to call to account, accuse) + *-or*] **1 :** containing or expressing accusation **:** tending to accusation **:** ACCUSING ⟨black ~ looks —Corra Harris⟩ ⟨the ~ generalities uttered during the war —R.H.Jackson⟩ **2** *law* **:** ACCUSATORIAL

ac·cu·sa·trix \ˌakyəˈzātriks, -yüˈ-\ *n* -ES [L, fem. of *accusator*] **:** a female accuser

¹**ac·cuse** \əˈkyüz *also* aˈ-\ *vb* -ED/-ING/-S [ME *accusen, acusen*, fr. OF *acuser*, fr. L *accusare* to call to account, fr. *ad-* + *-cusare* (fr. *causa* cause, lawsuit) — more at CAUSE] *vt* **1 a :** to charge unequivocally with a specified or implied wrong or fault often in a condemnatory or indignant manner ⟨the courtiers *accused* their queen⟩ ⟨the planes were *accused* of spreading cholera, typhus, and bubonic plague—*Current History*⟩ **b :** to charge with an offense judicially or by a public process **c :** to speak censoriously against as culpable or reprehensible ⟨*accused* the brazen corruptions of the capital —Carl Van Doren⟩ ⟨~*s* a system rather than any specific persons —Bruce Catton⟩ **2 :** REVEAL, BETRAY ⟨sometimes, as she passed a high window, the *accusing* light fell for a moment on her oval face —Edith Sitwell⟩ **~** *vi* **:** to bring an accusation **:** prefer charges ⟨he *accused* no more, but dumbly shrank before *accusing* throngs of thought —George Eliot⟩ ⟨where thought ~*s* and feeling mocks—W.H.Auden⟩ ⟨the "war party" fretted and *accused*—*New Republic*⟩

syn CHARGE, INDICT, IMPEACH, ARRAIGN, INCRIMINATE, CRIMINATE: ACCUSE and CHARGE are frequently interchangeable in meaning to declare a person guilty of a fault or offense. CHARGE may suggest a certain formality in the declaration ⟨*charging* him with impiety —J.A.Froude⟩ ⟨suppose the petitioner falsely and unjustly *charged* the judge with having excluded him from knowledge of the facts —O.W.Holmes †1935⟩ ACCUSE may suggest stronger personal feeling or interest ⟨Louvet . . . took his station in the Tribune, saying, "I, Robespierre, *accuse* thee!" —William Wordsworth⟩ INDICT indicates formal accusation in or as if in holding for trial ⟨you are here *indicted* . . . Lord Dudley [and] Lady Jane Grey, of capital and high treason —Thomas Wyatt⟩ IMPEACH implies a charge, esp. one involving corruptness, poor judgment, or malfeasance through duplicity, calling for a defense or answer ⟨any intelligent and noble-minded American can with reason take that side . . . without having either his reason or his integrity *impeached* —Kenneth Roberts⟩ ⟨why should he be *impeaching* the Reverend George Barnard for exceptional futility? —Compton Mackenzie⟩ ARRAIGN suggests formal presentation of charges with a demand for a plea, defense, or explanation ⟨I was carried down to the sessions house, where I was *arraigned* —Daniel Defoe⟩ ⟨Davies's career . . . affords the perfect grounds for *arraigning* both capitalism and socialism —Osbert Sitwell⟩ INCRIMINATE and CRIMINATE once commonly meant to charge with a crime; in today's use they are more likely to mean involving or inculpating in crime, laying open to charges ⟨the answer need not reveal a crime in order to be *incriminating*. It is enough if it might furnish a clue . . . that leads to proof of an illegal act —*New Republic*⟩

²**accuse** *n* -s *obs* **:** ACCUSATION

accused *n, pl* **accused :** one charged with an offense; *esp* **:** the defendant in a criminal case ⟨the ~ shall enjoy the right to a speedy and public trial —*U.S.Constitution*⟩ ⟨one of the ~ in a notorious conspiracy case⟩

accusement *n* -s [ME, fr. MF *acusement*, fr. *acuser* + *-ment*] *obs* **:** ACCUSATION

ac·cus·er \-zə(r)\ *n* -s [ME *accusour, accuser*, fr. MF *acuseor*, fr. *acuser* + *-eor* -or] **:** one that accuses; *specif* **:** one that formally accuses another of a crime

accusingly *adv* **:** in an accusing manner

ac·cus·ive \-ziv, -siv\ *adj* **:** tending to accuse **:** ACCUSING ⟨his ~ shoes and telltale trousers —O.Henry⟩

ac·cus·tom \əˈkəstəm *also* aˈ-\ *vb* -ED/-ING/-S [ME *accustomen*, fr. MF *acustumer, acostumer*, fr. *a-* (fr. L *ad-*) + *costume* custom — more at CUSTOM] *vt* **:** to make familiar through use or experience **:** HABITUATE, FAMILIARIZE, INURE ⟨~*ing* one's ears to the din⟩ ⟨opportunity to ~ the girl to sea life —Joseph Conrad⟩ ⟨she would go back to the districts . . . she knew so well, and ~ herself again to the old ways —Israel Zangwill⟩ — usu. used with *to* and an object but sometimes with an infinitive ⟨taught how to ~ themselves to use books and enjoy them —*Library Science Abstracts*⟩ **~** *vi, obs* **:** to be wont

accustomable *adj* [ME, fr. *accustomen* + *-able*] *obs* **:** CUSTOMARY — **accustomably** *adv, obs*

accustomary *adj* [obs. *accustom* custom (fr. ME, fr. *accustomen*, v.) + *-ary*] *archaic* **:** CUSTOMARY

accustomed *adj* [ME, fr. past part. of *accustomen*] **1 :** familiar through use or long and repeated experience **: a :** often used or practiced **:** CUSTOMARY, HABITUAL, USUAL ⟨her ~ cheerfulness⟩ ⟨cut off from its ~ sources of manufactured articles —P.E.James⟩ **b :** HABITUATED, INURED ⟨great wicker baskets balanced easily on ~ heads —Claudia Cassidy⟩ — often used with *to* and an object ⟨eyes not fully ~ to the darkness⟩ ⟨nations become ~ to the use of collective action —Vera M. Dean⟩ **2 :** in the habit or custom **:** established in the practice **:** USED, WONT — used with *to* and an infinitive or gerund ⟨~ to paint their faces before battle⟩ ⟨~ to making decisions⟩ **3** *archaic* **:** frequented by customers **syn** see USUAL

¹**ace** \ˈās\ *n* -s [ME *as*, fr. OF, fr. L *ass-, as* unity, unit, copper coin; akin to L *asser* beam, pole, stake, *assis* board, plank] **1 a :** a die face marked with one spot **b :** a playing card marked in its center with one large pip and usu. having the index *A* in its corners **c :** such a card ranking highest in its suit **d :** a domino end marked with one spot — usu. used in compounds ⟨double-*ace*⟩ ⟨*ace*-blank⟩ **e aces** *pl* (1) **:** a throw of 2 in craps (2) **:** a pair of aces in poker; *also* **:** three aces — used in the phrase *aces full* (3) **:** honors in no= trump ⟨easy ~*s*⟩ ⟨150 ~*s*⟩ (4) **:** one ace of each suit in pinochle **2 :** a very small amount or degree **:** PARTICLE, BIT ⟨I'll not wag an ~ further —John Dryden⟩ **3 :** a score won by a single stroke; *specif* **:** a point (as in tennis or handball) scored on a shot (as a service) that an opponent fails to touch **4 :** a score in golf of one stroke on a hole or a hole made in one stroke **5 :** an airplane combat pilot who has brought down at least five enemy airplanes **6 a :** a person who excels at something ⟨a football ~⟩ **b :** an important or outstanding thing or event ⟨speed is the ~ of air transport —*Forum*⟩ — **within an ace of :** on the point of **:** very near to ⟨*within an ace of* hitting a telephone pole⟩

aces 1b

²**ace** \"\ *vt* -ED/-ING/-S **1** *in tennis or handball* **:** to score an ace against (an opponent) **2** *in golf* **:** to make (a hole) in one stroke

³**ace** \"\ *adj* **:** of first or high rank or quality **:** OUTSTANDING ⟨an ~ reporter⟩

ace- *comb form* [ISV, fr. *acetic*] **:** acetic ⟨*ace*naphthene⟩; *specif* **:** related to acenaphthene ⟨*ace*anthrene⟩

-a·ce \ə,sē\ *n comb form* -s [LGk *akē* point — more at EDGE] **:** apex having (so many) faces ⟨hept*ace*⟩⟨tessar*ace*⟩

-a·cea \ˈāshēə\ *n pl suffix* [NL, fr. L, neut. pl. of *-aceus* -aceous] **:** animals characterized by **:** animals of the nature of ⟨Cet*acea*⟩ ⟨Crust*acea*⟩ — in names of zoological divisions larger than a genus, esp. orders and classes

-a·ce·ae \ˈāsē,ē\ *n pl suffix* [NL, fr. L, fem. pl. of *-aceus* -aceous] **:** plants of the nature of ⟨Acanth*aceae*⟩ ⟨Ros*aceae*⟩ — in names of families of plants; formerly in names of orders of plants

¹**-acean** *adj suffix* [NL *-acea, -aceae* + E *-an*] **:** -ACEOUS ⟨ros*acean*⟩

²**-acean** *n suffix* -s **:** organism characterized by **:** organism of the nature of ⟨crust*acean*⟩ ⟨ros*acean*⟩ — in singular corresponding to plurals in *-acea, -aceae*

¹**ace·dia** \ˌasəˈdēə\ *n* -s [Sp *acedia*] **:** a flatfish (*Symphurus plagiusa*) of the West Indies and the So. American Atlantic coast

²**ace·dia** \əˈsēdēə\ *n* -s [LL, fr. Gk *akēdia, akēdeia*, fr. *a-* ²*a-* + *kēdos* care, anxiety, grief + *-ia, -eia* — more at HATE] **1 :** the deadly sin of sloth **2 :** spiritual torpor and apathy

ace·di·ast \əˈsēdē,ast, -ˌəst\ *n* -s **:** one afflicted with acedia

ace-high \ˈ=ˈ=\ *adj* **1 :** having an ace as its highest card — used esp. of a hand of cards **2 :** high in esteem or favor ⟨he is *ace-high* with me⟩

ace in the hole 1 : an ace when it is a player's hole card in stud poker **2 :** an effective or decisive argument or resource held in reserve

acei·tu·na \ˌasəˈtünə\ *n* -s [Sp, olive, fr. Ar *az-zaytūnah* the olive, fr. *zayt* oil] **1 :** a West Indian tree (*Symplocos martinicensis*) having a soft light wood **2 :** PARADISE TREE 1

acel·da·ma \əˈseldəmə *also* əˈke-\ *also* **akel·da·ma** \əˈke-\ *n* -s *sometimes cap* [fr. *Aceldama*, field bought with the money received by Judas for betraying Christ (Acts 1: 18-19), fr. Gk *Akeldama*, fr. Aram *ḥăqēl dĕmā*, lit., field of blood] **:** a field of bloodshed **:** a place of highly disagreeable associations

acel·lu·lar \(ˈ)āˈselyələ(r)\ *adj* [²*a-* + *cellular*] **:** not cellular **:** not made up of cells

acenaphth- *or* **acenaphtho-** *comb form* [ISV, fr. *acenaphthene*] **:** acenaphthene **:** acenaphthylene ⟨*acenaphtho*phen-anthrene⟩

ace·naph·thene \ˌasəˈnap,thēn, -af,th-\ *n* -s [ISV *ace-* + *naphthene*] **:** a crystalline tricyclic hydrocarbon $C_{12}H_{10}$ obtained esp. from coal tar and used chiefly as a dye intermediate and in biology for inducing polyploidy

ace·naph·the·nyl \-,thə,nil\ *n* -s [*acenaphthene* + *-yl*] **:** a univalent radical $C_{12}H_9$ formed by removal of one hydrogen atom from acenaphthene

ace·naph·thy·lene \-,thə,lēn\ *n* -s [ISV *acenaphth-* + *-ylene*] **:** a yellowish crystalline hydrocarbon $C_{12}H_8$ made by dehydrogenation of acenaphthene

-a·cene \ə,sēn\ *n suffix* -s [ISV, fr. *anthracene*] **:** aromatic polycyclic hydrocarbon containing three or more fused benzene rings in straight linear sequence ⟨naphth*acene*⟩ ⟨pent*acene*⟩

acenesthesia *var of* ACOENESTHESIA

acen·tric \(ˈ)āˈsen·trik\ *adj* [²*a-* + *-centric*] **1 :** lacking a centromere ⟨an ~ chromosome fragment⟩ **2 :** ACENTROUS

acen·trous \(ˈ)āˈsen·trəs\ *adj* [²*a-* + *centr-* + *-ous*] *of some primitive fishes* **:** having the notochord persistent through life and lacking vertebral centra

-a·ceous \ˈāshəs\ *adj suffix* [L *-aceus*] **:** characterized by ⟨aren*aceous*⟩ ⟨argill*aceous*⟩ **:** of the nature of ⟨herb*aceous*⟩ **:** belonging to or connected with a division of animals characterized by or of the nature of ⟨cet*aceous*⟩ ⟨crust*aceous*⟩ **:** belonging to or connected with a family of plants of the nature of ⟨solan*aceous*⟩ — often in adjectives corresponding to biological classification names in *-acea, -aceae*

aceph·al \(ˈ)āˈsefəl\ *n* -s [NL *Acephala*] **:** LAMELLIBRANCH

aceph·a·la \(ˈ)āˈsefələ\ [NL, fr. Gk *akephala*, neut. pl. of *akephalos* headless] *syn of* LAMELLIBRANCHIA

aceph·a·lan \(ˈ)āˈsefələn\ *adj or n* [NL *Acephala* + E *-an*] **:** LAMELLIBRANCH

¹**acephali** *pl of* ACEPHALUS

²**aceph·a·li** \(ˈ)āˈsefə,lī, əˈ-, -,lē\ *n pl, usu cap* [ML, fr. LGk *Akephaloi*, pl. of *Akephalos*, fr. Gk *akephalos* headless — more at ACEPHALOUS] **:** various groups of 5th century and 6th century Christians that recognized no patriarch; *esp* **:** Egyptian Monophysites after about A.D. 482

ace·pha·lia \ˌāsəˈfālēə\ *n* -s [NL, fr. Gk *akephalos* + NL *-ia*] **:** HEADLESSNESS ⟨~ of a fetus⟩

ace·phal·ic \ˌāsəˈfalik\ *adj* [²*a-* + *-cephalic*] **:** ACEPHALOUS

aceph·a·li·na \(,)ā,sefəˈlīnə, ə,s-, -lē-\ *n pl, cap* [NL, fr. Gk *akephalos* + NL *-ina*] **:** a tribe or other division of gregarines comprising forms with nonseptate trophozoites that do not undergo schizogony (as earthworm parasites of the genus *Monocystis*) — see MONOCYSTIS — **aceph·a·line** \(ˈ)āˈsefə,līn, -əl-, -,lən\ *adj*

aceph·a·lo·cyst \(ˈ)āˈsefəlō,sist, əˈ-\ *n* -s [NL *Acephalocystis*, genus of worms, fr. L *acephalus* + NL *-cystis*] **:** a hydatid or echinococcus cyst that has not developed a head — **aceph·a·lo·cyst·ic** \ˌā,sefə(,)lōˈsistik, ə,s-\ *adj*

aceph·a·lous \(ˈ)āˈsefələs, əˈs-\ *adj* [Gk *akephalos*, fr. *a-* ²*a-* + *kephalē* head — more at CEPHALIC] **1 a :** without a head or headlike structure **b :** lacking a distinct head (as in lamellibranch mollusks or amphioxus) or having the head reduced and retracted into the thorax (as in certain larval diptera) **2 :** without a governing head or chief ⟨an ~ village⟩ **3 :** lacking an expected initial element; *specif* **:** having the first foot in a line of verse abbreviated or missing — compare TRUNCATION **4** *bot* **:** having (as of the mints) the style issuing from the base instead of from the apex of the ovary

aceph·a·lus \(ˈ)āˈsefələs, əˈ-\ *n, pl* **acepha·li** \-,lī, -,lē\ [NL, fr. Gk *akephalos* headless] **:** a headless fetal monster

ace point *n* **:** the first point in backgammon

acepots \ˈ=,=\ *n pl but sing in constr* [*ace* + *-pots* (as in *jackpots*)] **:** draw poker similar to jackpots except that a player is not permitted to open without a pair of aces or better

ace·quia \äˈsākyä\ *n* -s [Sp, fr. Ar *as-sāqiyah* the irrigation stream, fr. *saqa* to irrigate] *Southwest* **:** an irrigation ditch or canal

acer \ˈāsər, ˈä,ke(ə)r\ *n, cap* [NL, fr. L, maple tree; akin to OHG, OS, & MLG *ahorn* maple tree, ODan *ær*, Gk *akastos*, a maple tree, *akarna* laurel, and prob. to L *acer* sharp — more at EDGE] **:** a widely distributed genus of trees and shrubs (family Aceraceae) having simple or compound leaves, polygamous or dioecious flowers, and winged fruits — see BOX ELDER, MAPLE

ac·er·a·ce·ae \ˌasəˈrāsē,ē\ *n pl, cap* [NL, fr. *Acer*, type genus + *-aceae*] **:** a family of trees and shrubs (order Sapindales) having opposite leaves and small clustered flowers succeeded by fruits consisting of two united samaras — compare MAPLE — **ac·er·a·ceous** \ˌasəˈrāshəs\ *adj*

ac·er·ae \ˈasə,rē\ [NL, fr. ²*a-* + Gk *kera* horn] *syn of* ACERATA

ac·er·a·ta \ˌasəˈrād·ə, ,as-, -rā-\ *n pl, cap* [NL, fr. Gk *akeratos* without horns, fr. *a-* ²*a-* + *kerat-, keras* horn — more at HORN] *in old classifications* **:** a class of arthropods comprising the Merostomata and Arachnida

ac·er·ate \ˈasə,rāt, -,rət\ *or* **ac·er·ose** \-,rōs\ *also* **ac·er·ous** \-,rəs\ *adj* [L *acer* sharp + E *-ate* or *-ose, -ous* — more at EDGE] **1 :** having needlelike leaves **2** *usu acerose* **:** NEEDLELIKE

acera·there \(ˈ)əˈserə,thi(ə)r\ *n* -s [NL *Aceratherium*] **:** a rhinoceros or fossil of the genus *Aceratherium*

acera·the·ri·um \əˌserəˈthirēəm\ *n, cap* [NL, irreg. fr. Gk *akeratos* + NL *-therium*] **:** a genus of extinct hornless rhinoceroses of the Oligocene, Miocene, and Pliocene

acerb \əˈsərb, aˈ-, -əb\ *adj, sometimes* -ER/-EST [F or L; F *acerbe*, fr. L *acerbus*, fr. *acer* sharp — more at EDGE] **1 :** acid or sour to the taste ⟨~ apples⟩ **2 :** acid in temper, mood, or tone **:** sharply or bitingly ironic, sarcastic, or critical ⟨an ~ time of it sticking pins in the balloons of his pretensions —*Time*⟩

¹**ac·er·bate** \ˈasə(r),bāt\ *vt* -ED/-ING/-S [L *acerbatus*, past part. of *acerbare*, fr. *acerbus*] **:** IRRITATE, EXASPERATE

²**acer·bate** \əˈsərbət, -səb-\ *adj* [L *acerbatus*] **:** IRRITATED, EXASPERATED **:** HARSH ⟨~ and profane writing⟩

acer·bic \-bik\ *adj* [*acerb* + *-ic*] **:** ACERB

acer·bi·ty \əˈsərbəd·ē, aˈ-, -səb-, -ətē, -i\ *n* -ES [MF *acerbité*, fr. L *acerbitat-, acerbitas*, fr. *acerbus* sour + *-itat-, -itas* -ity — more at ACERB] **:** the quality of being acerb **: a :** acidity of taste **b :** acidity of temper or tone **:** astringency or sharpness of manner

ace·ria \əˈsirēə\ *n, cap* [NL, fr. L *acer* sharp + NL *-ia*] **:** a large genus of eriophyid mites including a number of parasites of economic plants — see CITRUS BUD MITE

ac·er·o·la \ˌasəˈrōlə\ *n* -s [AmerSp, fr. Sp, azarole — more at AZAROLE] **:** BARBADOS CHERRY 1

¹**acerous** *var of* ACERATE

²**ace·rous** \(ˈ)āˈsirəs, -ēr-\ *adj* [Gk *akeros*, fr. *a-* ²*a-* + *keras* horn — more at HORN] **1 :** without horns **2 :** without antennae **3 :** without tentacles

ac·er·tan·nin \ˌasə(r)ˈtanən\ *n* [ISV *acer-* (fr. NL *Acer*, genus name of *Acer ginnala*) + *tannin*; orig. formed in G] **:** a crystalline tannin $C_{20}H_{20}O_{13}$ found in the leaves of the Amur maple

acer·vate \əˈsərvət, ˈasər,vāt\ *adj* [L *acervatus*, past part. of *acervare* to heap up, fr. *acervus* heap] **:** growing in heaps or closely compacted clusters ⟨~ fungous sporophores⟩ — **acer·vate·ly** *adv*

ac·er·va·tion \ˌasə(r)ˈvāshən\ *n* -s [L *acervation-, acervatio*, fr. *acervatus* + *-ion-, -io* -ion] **:** a heaping up **:** ACCUMULATION

acer·vu·line \əˈsərvyələn, -,līn\ *adj* [NL *acervulus* + E *-ine*] **:** resembling little heaps **:** HEAPED

acer·vu·lus \-,ləs\ *n, pl* **acervu·li** \-,lī, -,lē\ [NL, dim. of L *acervus* heap] **1 :** a fungous fruiting body consisting of a compacted and often saucer-shaped mass of threads lacking a well-developed stromatic base and with the conidiophores not tufted — compare SPORODOCHIUM **2** *also* **acervulus cer·e·bri** \-ˈserə,brē, -brī\ **:** BRAIN SAND

aces *pl of* ACE, *pres 3d sing of* ACE

-aces *pl of* -ACE

aces·cen·cy \əˈsesᵊnsē, aˈ-\ *n* -ES **:** the quality or state of being acescent

aces·cent \-ᵊnt\ *adj* [F, fr. L *acescent-, acescens*, pres. part. of *acescere* to turn sour, incho. of *acēre* to be sour, fr. *acer* sharp — more at EDGE] **1 :** turning sour or tending to turn sour ⟨~ milk⟩ **2 :** slightly sour ⟨an ~ flavor⟩

ace-showing \ˈ=,==\ *n* **:** the bidding of a suit in contract bridge to show possession of the ace but not necessarily length or other high-card strength in the suit

aces·o·dyne \əˈsesə,dīn\ *adj* [Gk *akesōdynos*, fr. *akesis* healing, cure + *odynē* pain] **:** mitigating or relieving pain **:** ANODYNE

acet- *or* **aceto-** *comb form* [F & L; F *acét-*, fr. L *acet-*, fr. *acetum* vinegar — more at ACETIC] **:** acetic acid **:** acetic **:** acetyl ⟨*acet*aldehyde⟩ ⟨*acet*amide⟩ ⟨*aceto*benzoic⟩

aceta *pl of* ACETUM

ac·e·tab·u·lar \ˌasəˈtabyələ(r)\ *adj* [NL *acetabulum* + E *-ar*] **:** of or relating to an acetabulum

ac·e·tab·u·lar·ia \ˌasə,tabyəˈla(a)rēə\ *n, cap* [NL, fr. L *acetabulum* + NL *-aria*] **:** a genus of delicate more or less calcified green algae (family Dasycladaceae) native to the warmer seas and resembling small mushrooms

acetabular notch *n* **:** a notch in the rim of the acetabulum through which blood vessels and nerves pass

ac·e·tab·u·late \ˌasəˈtabyələt\ *adj* [NL *acetabulum* + E *-ate*] *anat* **:** possessing an acetabulum

ac·e·tab·u·lif·era \ˌasə,tabyəˈlif(ə)rə\ [NL, fr. *acetabulum* + *-i-* + *-fera* (neut. pl. of *-fer*)] *syn of* DIBRANCHIA

ac·e·tab·u·lif·er·ous \ˌasə,tabyəˈlif(ə)rəs\ *adj* [NL *acetabulum* + E *-i-* + *-ferous*] **:** ACETABULATE

ac·e·tab·u·lum \ˌasəˈtabyələm\ *n, pl* **acetabulums** \-ləmz\ *or* **acetabu·la** \-lə\ [L, fr. *acetum* vinegar — more at ACETIC] **1 :** a little cup used in ancient Rome to hold vinegar or sauce at the table **2 a :** the cup-shaped socket in the hip bone that receives the head of the thigh bone **b :** the cavity into which the leg of an insect is inserted at its articulation with the body **3** [NL, fr. L] **:** one of the cotyledons or lobes of the placenta in ruminating animals **4** [NL, fr. L] **:** a sucker of certain invertebrates: as **a :** a ventral sucker of many trematodes **b :** one of the suckers on the scolex of a tapeworm **5** [NL, fr. L] **:** the posterior sucker of a leech

acetacetic acid *var of* ACETOACETIC ACID

ac·e·tal \ˈasə,tal\ *n* -s [G *azetal*, fr. *azet-* acet- + *al*kohol alcohol] **1 :** any of a class of organic compounds characterized by the grouping $>C(OR)_2$ and usu. made from aldehydes or ketones by reaction with alcohols; *specif* **:** any acetal derived from acetaldehyde (as by the catalytic addition of an alcohol to acetylene or a vinyl ether) ⟨dimethyl ~ $CH_3CH(OCH_3)_2$⟩ **2 :** a colorless liquid $CH_3CH(OC_2H_5)_2$ made by the reaction of ethyl alcohol with acetaldehyde and used as a solvent

ac·et·al·de·hyd·ase \\,asəd·,aldə'hī,dās, -ə,tal-\\ *n* -s [*acetaldehyde* + *-ase*] **:** an enzyme that accelerates the oxidation of acetaldehyde to acetic acid

ac·et·al·de·hyde \\,==ˈ==,hīd\\ *n* -s [ISV *acet-* + *aldehyde*] **:** a colorless volatile water-soluble liquid aldehyde CH_3CHO of pungent odor made usu. by oxidation of ethyl alcohol or by catalytic hydration of acetylene and used chiefly in organic synthesis

acetaldehyde ammonia *n* **:** ALDEHYDE AMMONIA

ac·et·al·dol \\-l,dōl, -ōl\\ *n* -s [*acetaldehyde* + *-ol*] **:** ALDOL 1

ac·e·tal·ize \\'asə,ta,līz\\ *vt* -ED/-ING/-S [*acetal* + *-ize*] **:** to convert (as an aldehyde) into an acetal

acet·a·mide \\ə'sed·ə,mīd, ,asəd·'a,m-, -,məd\\ *n* -s [G *azetamid*, fr. *azet-* acet- + *amid* amide] **:** the white deliquescent crystalline amide CH_3CONH_2 of acetic acid used chiefly as a solvent and in organic synthesis

ac·et·am·i·dine \\,asəd·'amə,dēn, -ə'tam-, -,dən\\ *n* -s [ISV *acet-* + *amidine*] **:** the unstable amidine $CH_3C(=NH)NH_2$ of acetic acid that forms crystalline salts with acids

ac·et·ami·do- \\¦asəd·ə'mē(,)dō, -d·'amə,dō\\ *comb form* [*acetamide* + *-o-*] **:** containing the univalent radical CH_3CONH- derived from acetamide ⟨*α-acetamido*cinnamic acid⟩

ac·et·ami·no- \\¦asəd·ə'mē(,)nō, -d·'amə,nō\\ [*acet-* + *amine* + *-o-*] **:** ACETAMIDO-

Ac·et·am·i·nol \\,asəd·'amə,nōl, -ōl\\ *trademark* — used for an antiseptic powder

ac·et·an·i·lide *or* **ac·et·an·i·lid** \\,asəd·'anᵊl,īd, -ə'tan-, -,əd\\ *n* -s [ISV *acet-* + *anilide*; prob. orig. formed as G *azetanilid*] **:** a white crystalline compound $CH_3CONHC_6H_5$ derived from aniline and acetic acid and used chiefly in organic synthesis and in medicine as an analgesic and antipyretic — called also *phenylacetamide*

ac·et·anis·i·dide \\,asəd·ə'nisə,dīd, -dəd\\ *n* -s [ISV *acet-* + *anisidine* + *-ide*] **:** any of three isomeric crystalline compounds $CH_3CONHC_6H_4OCH_3$ derived from anisidine and acetic acid

ac·e·tan·nin \\,asə'tanən\\ *n* -s [*acet-* + *tannin*] **:** ACETYLTANNIC ACID

ac·e·tar·i·ous \\¦asə¦ta(a)rēəs\\ *adj* [L *acetaria*, pl., salad (fr. *acetum* vinegar + *-aria*, pl. of *-arium* -ary) + E *-ous*] **:** used in salads ⟨~ plants⟩

ac·et·ar·sone \\,asəd·'är,sōn\\ *also* **ac·et·ar·sol** \\-sōl, -ōl\\ *n* -s [ISV *acet-* + *ars-* + *-one* or *-ol*] **:** a white powder $C_8H_{10}AsNO_5$ sometimes used in the treatment of amebiasis; 3-acetamido-4-hydroxy-benzene-arsonic acid

ac·e·tate \\'asə,tāt, 'aas-, *usu* -ād·+V\\ *n* -s [prob. fr. F *acétate*, fr. *acét-* acet- + *-ate*] **1 :** a salt, ester, or acylal of acetic acid **2 :** cellulose acetate or its products: as **a** (1) **:** a textile fiber made from partly hydrolyzed cellulose acetate in filament and staple form and characterized by faster drying properties and better electrical insulating properties than rayon made from viscose and usu. by poorer resistance to softening by heat — called also *acetate fiber*; formerly called *acetate rayon* (2) **:** yarn or fabric made of acetate fiber — formerly called *acetate rayon* **b :** a plastic used esp. in the manufacture of film and phonograph records **3** *or* **acetate disk a :** a phonograph recording disk made of various acetate compounds; *esp* **:** one coated with cellulose acetate **b :** a disk recording consisting of a stiff core (as of aluminum) usu. coated on both sides with cellulose nitrate and used esp. for immediate playback

acetate butyrate *n* **:** a mixed acetate and butyrate; *specif* **:** CELLULOSE ACETATE BUTYRATE

ac·e·ta·tion \\,asə'tāshən\\ *n* -s [by contr.] **:** ACETIFICATION

ac·e·ta·to- \\¦asə¦tād·(,)ō\\ *comb form* [ISV, fr. *acetate* + *-o-*] **:** acetate — in names of minerals and coordination complexes ⟨*acetato*-sodalite⟩ ⟨*acetato*pentamminecobalt(III) nitrate $[Co(NH_3)_5C_2H_3O_2](NO_3)_2$⟩

ac·et·azol·amide \\,asəd·ə'zōlə,mīd, -,məd\\ *n* -s [*acet-* + *azole* + *amide*] **:** a white crystalline sulfonamide $CH_3CONHC_2N_2SSO_2NH_2$ derived from thiadiazole and used as a diuretic and antiepileptic drug

acet·e·nyl \\ə'sed·ə,nil, -etᵊnəl\\ *n* -s [ISV, contr. of *acetylenyl*] **:** ETHYNYL

ac eti·am \\(')ak·'ed·ē,am, (')ä...äm; (')ak·'ēshē,am\\ [L] *English law* **:** and also — formerly used in certain actions to introduce a clause stating the real cause of the action after a fictitious cause had been alleged in order to establish jurisdiction

ace·tic \\ə'sēd·ik, -ētik, -ēk *also* a'- *or* -se-\\ *adj* [prob. fr. F *acétique*, fr. L *acetum* sour wine, vinegar, fr. *acēre* to be sour, fr. *acer* sharp — more at EDGE] **:** relating to or producing acetic acid or vinegar

acetic acid *n* **:** a colorless liquid acid CH_3COOH with a pungent odor constituting the chief acid of vinegar, made usu. by oxidation of acetaldehyde, by fermentation of alcohol, or by distillation of wood, and used chiefly in manufacturing cellulose acetate plastics and fibers, in making salts, esters, and other derivatives, in the textile and paint and pigment industries, and occas. in medicine as an astringent and styptic — see GLACIAL ACETIC ACID, PYROLIGNEOUS ACID, VINEGAR; compare KREBS CYCLE

acetic aldehyde *n* **:** ACETALDEHYDE

acetic anhydride *n* **:** a colorless mobile liquid $(CH_3CO)_2O$ with a pungent odor and lacrimatory and vesicant action used in organic synthesis, esp. in making acetyl derivatives (as cellulose acetate and aspirin) and in condensations

acetic ester *n* **:** any ester of acetic acid; *esp* **:** ETHYL ACETATE

acetic ether *n* **:** ACETIC ESTER — not now used scientifically

acetic ferment *n* **:** any microorganism or enzyme capable of producing acetic fermentation

acetic fermentation *n* **:** a process of oxidation in which alcohol is converted into acetic acid by the agency of bacteria of the genus *Acetobacter*, esp. *A. aceti* (as in the production of vinegar from cider or wine)

acetic nitrile *n* **:** ACETONITRILE

ac·e·ti·fi·ca·tion \\ə,sēd·əfə'kāshən, a,s-, -,se-\\ *n* -s [*acet-* + *-i-* + *-fication*] **1 :** a turning sour or into vinegar esp. through the action of bacteria **2 :** the production of acetic acid by acetic fermentation **:** the growth in an alcoholic medium of bacteria that produce acetic and lactic acids

ace·ti·fi·er \\ˈ==,fī(ə)r\\ *n* -s **:** an apparatus in which vinegar is produced (as from wine or cider)

ace·ti·fy \\-,fī\\ *vb* -ED/-ING/-ES [*acet-* + *-ify*] **:** to turn into acetic acid or vinegar

acetimeter *var of* ACETOMETER

ac·e·tin \\'asətᵊn, -əd·ən, -ətən\\ *n* -s [ISV *acet-* + *-in*] **:** any of three liquid acetates formed when glycerol and acetic acid are heated together: **a :** the monoacetate $C_3H_5(OH)_2C_2H_3O_2$ used chiefly in the manufacture of explosives — called also *monoacetin* **b :** the diacetate $C_3H_5(OH)(C_2H_3O_2)_2$ used chiefly as a plasticizer and solvent — called also *diacetin* **c :** the triacetate $C_3H_5(C_2H_3O_2)_3$ used chiefly as a plasticizer and solvent and as a fixative in perfumes — called also *triacetin*

ac·e·tize \\'asə,tīz\\ *vb* -ED/-ING/-S [*acet-* + *-ize*] **:** ACETIFY

aceto- — see ACET-

ac·e·to·ac·et·an·i·lide \\¦asə(,)tō,asəd·'anᵊl,īd, ə¦sēd·ō-, -ə'tan-, -,əd\\ *n* -s [ISV *acet-* + *acetanilide*] **:** a crystalline compound $CH_3COCH_2CONHC_6H_5$ made by reaction of aniline with acetoacetic ester or with diketene and used as a dye intermediate

ac·e·to·ac·e·tate \\-'asə,tāt\\ *n* -s [ISV *acetoacet-* (fr. *acetoacetic acid*) + *-ate*] **:** a salt or ester of acetoacetic acid

ac·e·to·ace·tic acid \\¦asə(,)tōə¦sēd·ik-, ə¦sēd·ō- *also* -ed·ik-\\ *also* **ac·et·ace·tic acid** \\¦asəd·ə¦-\\ *n* [part. trans. of G *azetessigsäure*, fr. *azet-* acet- + *essigsäure* acetic acid] **:** an unstable acid CH_3COCH_2COOH sometimes found in urine in disease — see KETONE BODY

acetoacetic ester *n* **:** ETHYL ACETOACETATE

ac·e·to·ace·tyl \\¦asə(,)tōə'sēd·ᵊl, ə,sēd·ō-, -ō'asəd·ᵊl\\ *n* -s [*acet-* + *acetyl*] **:** the radical CH_3COCH_2CO- of acetoacetic acid

ac·e·to·ar·se·nite \\-'ärsᵊn,īt\\ *n* -s [*acet-* + *arsenite*] **:** a combined acetate and arsenite — see PARIS GREEN

ace·to·bac·ter \\ə'sēd·ō,baktə(r)\\ *n* [NL, fr. *acet-* + *-bacter*] **1** *cap* **:** a genus of aerobic ellipsoidal to rod-shaped bacteria (family Pseudomonadaceae) growing in the presence of alcohol and securing energy by oxidizing organic compounds to organic acids (as alcohol to acetic acid) **2** -s **:** a bacterium of the genus *Acetobacter*

ac·e·to·bu·ty·rate \\¦asə(,)tō'byüd·ə,rāt, ə,sēd·ō-\\ *n* -s [*acet-* + *butyrate*] **:** ACETATE BUTYRATE

ac·e·to·car·mine \\-'kärmən, -,mīn *also* -,mēn\\ *n* -s [*acet-* + *carmine*] **:** a saturated solution of carmine in 45 percent acetic acid used esp. for the rapid staining of fresh unfixed chromosomes

ac·e·to·glyc·er·ide \\'glisə,rīd, -,rəd\\ *n* [*acet-* + *glyceride*] **:** an acetylated glyceride

acet·o·in \\ə'sed·əwən\\ *n* -s [ISV *acet-* + *-oin*] **:** a colorless liquid hydroxy ketone $CH_3COCHOHCH_3$ formed from various carbohydrates by fermentation — called also *acetylmethylcarbinol*

ac·e·to·ki·nase \\¦asə(,)tō'kī,nās, ə,sēd·ō-, -ki,n-\\ *n* -s [*acet-* + *kinase*] **:** TRANSACETYLASE

ac·e·tol \\'asə,tōl, -ōl\\ *n* -s [ISV *acet-* + *-ol*] **:** a colorless liquid hydroxy ketone CH_3COCH_2OH obtained indirectly from acetone — called also *acetylcarbinol*

ac·e·tol·y·sis \\,asə'täləsəs\\ *n*, *pl* **acetoly·ses** \\-ə,sēz\\ [NL, fr. *acet-* + *-lysis*] **1 :** any chemical reaction analogous to hydrolysis in which acetic acid plays a role similar to that of water **2 :** simultaneous acetylation and hydrolysis

acet·o·lyze \\ə'sed·ᵊl,īz\\ *vt* -ED/-ING/-S [blend of *acetolysis* and *-ize*] **:** to subject to acetolysis

ac·e·to·me·roc·tol \\¦asə(,)tōmə'räk,tōl, ə,sēd·ō-, -ōl\\ *n* -s [*acetoxymercuri* + *octyl* + *phenol*] **:** a white crystalline mercury derivative $C_{16}H_{24}HgO_3$ of phenol used in solution as a topical antiseptic

ac·e·tom·e·ter \\,asə'tämədə(r)\\ *also* **ac·e·tim·e·ter** \\-tim-\\ *n* -s [F *acétimètre*, fr. *acét-* acet- + *-i-* + *mètre* meter] **:** an instrument for estimating the amount of acetic acid in any solution of it (as in vinegar)

ac·e·tom·e·try *also* **ac·e·tim·e·try** \\-mə·trē\\ *n* -ES [F *acétimétrie*, fr. *acét-* acet- + *-i-* + *-métrie* -metry] **:** the act or method of ascertaining the amount of acetic acid present esp. in vinegar

ac·e·to·mor·phine \\¦asə(,)tō-,ə,sēd·ō-\\ *n* -s [*acet-* + *morphine*] **:** HEROIN

ac·e·to·naph·thone \\-'nap,thōn, -af,th-\\ *n* -s [ISV *acet-* + *naphth-* + *-one*] **:** either of two isomeric colorless crystalline ketones $C_{10}H_7COCH_3$ — called also *methyl naphthyl ketone*

ac·e·ton·ate \\'asə(,)tō,nāt, -ətə,n-\\ *also* **ac·e·ton·ize** \\-,nīz\\ *vt* -ED/-ING/-S [*acetone* + *-ate* or *-ize*] **:** to combine with acetone

ac·e·tone \\'asə,tōn, 'aas-\\ *n* -s [G *azeton*, fr. *azet-* acet- + *-on* -one] **:** a volatile fragrant flammable liquid ketone CH_3COCH_3 occurring in pyroligneous acid, made by dehydrogenation of isopropyl alcohol or by bacterial fermentation (as of molasses or corn mash), and used chiefly as a solvent (as for cellulose acetate or cellulose nitrate) and in organic synthesis — called also *dimethyl ketone*, *propanone*; see KETONE BODY

acetone body *n* **:** KETONE BODY

acetone chloroform *n* **:** CHLOROBUTANOL 2

acetone cyanohydrin *n* **:** a colorless liquid $(CH_3)_2C(OH)CN$ made from acetone and hydrogen cyanide and used in organic synthesis esp. of esters of methacrylic acid; α-hydroxy-isobutyro-nitrile

ac·e·ton·emia *also* **ac·e·ton·aemia** \\¦asə(,)tō'nēmēə\\ *n* -s [NL, fr. ISV *acetone* + NL *-emia*, *-aemia*] **:** KETONEMIA — **ac·e·ton·emic** *also* **ac·e·ton·aemic** \\-¦nēmik\\ *adj*

acetone number *n* **:** the number of grams of acetone that must be added to 100 grams of a thermally treated drying oil in order to cause separation of the acetone-insoluble polymerized phase

acetone oil *n* **:** an oil of complex composition obtained in the distillation of acetone and used as a solvent

ac·e·ton·ic \\¦asə¦tänik, -ōn-\\ *adj* [ISV *acetone* + *-ic*] **:** of or related to acetone

ac·e·to·ni·trile \\¦asə(,)tō'nī·trəl, ə,sēd·ō-, -ī-,trēl, -īl\\ *n* -s [ISV *acet-* + *nitrile*] **:** the colorless liquid nitrile CH_3CN of acetic acid usu. made by dehydration of acetamide and used chiefly in organic synthesis and as a solvent — called also *methyl cyanide*

ac·e·ton·uria \\¦asə(,)tō'n(y)ürēə\\ *n* -s [NL, fr. ISV *acetone* + NL *-uria*] **:** KETONURIA

ac·e·ton·yl \\'asə(,)tō,nil, ə'sed·ə,-\\ *n* -s [ISV *acetone* + *-yl*] **:** the univalent radical CH_3COCH_2 formed by removal of a hydrogen atom from acetone

ac·e·ton·yl·ac·e·tone \\-'asə,tōn\\ *n* -s [ISV *acetonyl* + *acetone*] **:** a mobile fragrant liquid diketone $(CH_3COCH_2)_2$ obtained by hydrolysis of 2,5-dimethyl-furan and in other ways; 2,5-hexane-dione

ac·e·ton·yl·i·dene \\,asətō'nilə,dēn, ə,sed·ə'-\\ *n* -s [*acetonyl* + *-idene*] **:** the bivalent radical $CH_3COCH<$ formed by removal of two hydrogen atoms from the same carbon atom of acetone

ac·e·to·phe·net·i·dide \\¦asə(,)tōfə'ned·ə,dīd, ə,sēd·ō-\\ *also* **ac·e·to·phen·e·tide** \\-'fenə,tīd\\ *n* -s [ISV *acet-* + *phenetidine* or *phenetidine* + *-ide*] **:** any of three isomeric compounds $CH_3CONHC_6H_4OC_2H_5$ made by acetylating the three phenetidines — see ACETOPHENETIDIN

ac·e·to·phe·net·i·din \\-fə'ned·ədən\\ *also* **ac·et·phe·net·i·din** \\¦asətfə-\\ *n* -s [ISV *acet-* + *phenetidin*] **:** a white crystalline compound $C_{10}H_{13}NO_2$ used as an analgesic and antipyretic; *p*-acetophenetidide — called also *phenacetin*

ac·e·to·phe·none \\¦asə(,)tōfə'nōn, ə,sēd·ō-\\ *n* -s [ISV *acet-* +*-phenone*; prob. orig. formed as F *acétophénone*] **:** a colorless liquid ketone $CH_3COC_6H_5$ found in certain essential oils but prepared synthetically (as from acetic anhydride and benzene in the presence of aluminum chloride) and used chiefly in perfumery — called also *hypnone*, *phenyl methyl ketone*

ac·e·to·pro·pi·o·nate \\-'prōpēə,nāt, -,prə'pīənət\\ *n* -s [*acet-* + *propionate*] **:** a mixed acetate and propionate; *specif* **:** CELLULOSE ACETATE PROPIONATE

ac·e·to·pur·pu·rine 8B \\-'pərpyə,rēn, -,rən\\ *n*, *usu cap A* [ISV *acet-* + *purpurine*] **:** a direct dye — see DYE table I (under *Direct Red 46*)

ac·e·to·py·rine \\-'pī,rēn, -,rən\\ *n* -s [ISV *acet-* + *antipyrine*; orig. formed as G *azetopyrin*] **:** a crystalline combination of aspirin and antipyrine used as an analgesic and antipyretic

ac·e·tose \\'asə,tōs, ə'sē,-\\ *adj* [LL *acetosus* vinegary — more at ACETOUS] **:** ACID, SOUR, ACETOUS

ac·e·to·sol·u·ble \\¦asə(,)tō¦-, ə¦sēd·ō-\\ *adj* [*acet-* + *soluble*] **:** soluble in acetic acid

ac·e·to·thi·enone \\¦asə(,)tō'thīə,nōn, ə,sēd·ō-\\ *n* -s [ISV *acet-* + *thienone*] **:** an oily liquid ketone $CH_3COC_4H_3S$ formed by the acetylation of thiophene; methyl 2-thienyl ketone

ac·e·to·to·lu·i·dide \\-,tə'lüə,dīd\\ *also* **ac·e·to·tol·u·ide** \\-'tälyə,wīd\\ *n* -s [ISV *acet-* + *-toluidide* (fr. *toluid-* + *-ide*) or *toluide*] **:** any of three crystalline isomeric compounds $CH_3CONHC_6H_4CH_3$ made by acetylating the toluidines

ace·tous \\ə'sēd·əs, 'asəd·-\\ *adj* [F *acéteux* vinegary, fr. LL *acetosus*, fr. L *acetum* vinegar — more at ACETIC] **:** having the characteristics of vinegar **:** producing vinegar ⟨~ fermentation⟩ **:** VINEGARY ⟨~ comments⟩

acetous acid *n*, *obs* **:** VINEGAR

ac·e·to·va·nil·lone \\¦asə(,)tōvə'ni,lōn, ə,sēd·ō-, -'vanᵊl,ōn\\ *n* -s [ISV *acet-* + *vanillin* + *-one*] **:** a crystalline ketone $C_9H_{10}O_3$ formed as a by-product in the commercial synthesis of vanillin from lignin; 3-methoxy-4-hydroxy-acetophenone — called also *apocynin*

ac·e·to·ver·a·trone \\-'verə-,trōn\\ *n* -s [ISV *acet-* + *veratrole* + *-one*] **:** a white crystalline ketone $CH_3COC_6H_3(OCH_3)_2$ made by acetylating veratrole; 3,4-dimethoxy-acetophenone

ac·et·ox·ime \\,asəd·'äk,sēm, -,səm\\ *n* -s [ISV *acet-* + *oxime*; prob. orig. formed as G *azetoxim*] **:** a colorless crystalline volatile compound $(CH_3)_2C{=}NOH$ formed from acetone by the action of hydroxylamine

ac·e·toxy- \\¦asə¦täksē\\ *comb form* [ISV, fr. *acet-* + *oxy-*] **:** containing the univalent acetate radical CH_3COO- — in names of organic compounds ⟨*acetoxy*naphthoic acid⟩; compare ACETO-

ac·e·tox·yl \\,asə'täksəl\\ *n* -s [*acet-* + *oxyl*] **:** a group or radical derived from acetic acid: as **a** *obs* **:** ACETYL **b :** the acetate group CH_3COO-

ac·e·tract \\'asə·,trakt\\ *n* -s [*acet-* + *extract*] **:** a powdered extract prepared by exhausting a vegetable drug with an alcoholic menstruum containing 5 to 10 percent of acetic acid ⟨~ of nux vomica⟩

ace·tum \\ə'sēd·əm\\ *n*, *pl* **ace·ta** \\-d·ə\\ [L, sour wine, vinegar — more at ACETIC] **1 :** VINEGAR **2 :** a solution of aromatic substances in a mixture of acetic acid, alcohol, and water **3 :** a liquid preparation made by extracting a vegetable drug with dilute acetic acid

ac·e·tu·ric acid \\¦asə·¦tyürik-, ¦asə¦tür-\\ *n* [ISV *acet-* + *-uric*] **:** a crystalline acid $CH_3CONHCH_2COOH$ — called also *acetylglycine*

ace·tyl \\ə'sēd·ᵊl, 'asəd·ᵊl, 'asə,tēl\\ *n* -s [ISV *acet-* + *-yl*] **:** the radical CH_3CO- of acetic acid

ace·tyl·ac·e·ton·ate \\-'asə(,)tō,nāt, -ətə,n-\\ *n* -s [*acetylacetone* + *-ate*] **:** a metallic derivative of the enol form of acetylacetone

ace·tyl·ac·e·tone \\-'asə,tōn\\ *n* -s [ISV *acetyl* + *acetone*] **:** a colorless liquid diketone of pleasant odor known in two forms [keto form $CH_3COCH_2COCH_3$ and enol form $CH_3COCHC(OH)CH_3$] made in various ways (as by the reaction of sodium with acetone and ethyl acetate); 2,4-pentanedione

ace·tyl·ami·no- \\-ə'mē(,)nō,-'amə,nō\\ *comb form* [*acetyl* + *amine* + *-o-*] **:** ACETAMIDO-

acet·y·lase \\ə'sed·ᵊl,ās\\ *n* -s [*acetyl* + *-ase*] **:** any of a class of enzymes that accelerate the synthesis of acetic esters (as acetylcholine) ⟨choline ~⟩

acet·y·late \\-,āt\\ *or* **acet·y·lize** \\-,īz\\ *vb* -ED/-ING/-S [*acetyl* + *-ate* or *-ize*] *vt* **:** to introduce the acetyl radical into (a compound) by any of various processes (as by the use of a mixture of acetic acid and acetic anhydride) ~ *vi* **:** to become acetylated

acet·y·la·tion \\ə,sed·ᵊl'āshən\\ *n* -s **:** the act or process of acetylating ⟨~ of cellulose⟩

acet·y·la·tor \\ə'sed·ᵊl,ād·ə(r)\\ *n* -s **:** an acetylating apparatus used esp. in making cellulose acetate

acetyl benzoyl peroxide *n* **:** a white crystalline compound $CH_3CO_2CO_2C_6H_5$ that is explosive when pure and is used in germicidal preparations and for initiating polymerization processes

acetyl bromide *n* **:** a liquid CH_3COBr similar to acetyl chloride in properties and use

ace·tyl·car·bi·nol \\ə,sēd·ᵊl'kärbə,nōl, -nōl; ¦asəd·ᵊl-, -ə,tēl-\\ *n* -s [*acetyl* + *carbinol*] **:** ACETOL

acetyl cellulose *n* **:** CELLULOSE ACETATE

acetyl chloride *n* **:** a colorless pungent fuming liquid CH_3COCl made by chlorination of acetic acid or its derivatives (as by distilling a mixture of acetic acid and phosphorus trichloride) and used chiefly in preparing acetyl derivatives

ace·tyl·cho·line \\-'kō,lēn, -'kä-\\ *n* -s [ISV *acetyl* + *choline*] **:** a compound $(CH_3)_3N(CH_2CH_2OOCCH_3)OH$ that is released at many autonomic nerve endings, is believed to have a specific function in the transmission of the nerve impulse, and is formed enzymatically in the tissues from choline with the aid of an acetylase or in vitro by reaction of choline chloride with acetic anhydride

acetylcholine esterase *n* **:** an enzyme that accelerates hydrolysis of acetylcholine

acetyl coenzyme A *n* **:** the coenzyme $C_{21}H_{35}N_7O_{16}P_3SOCCH_3$ of transacetylase that is formed as an intermediate in metabolism and that takes part in various biological acetylations and is oxidized in the Krebs cycle

acet·y·le·na·tion \\ə,sed·ᵊlə'nāshən\\ *n* -s [*acetylene* + *-ation*] **:** the process of combining with acetylene

acet·y·lene \\ə'sed·ᵊlən, -etᵊl-, -l,ēn\\ *n* -s [*acetyl* + *-ene*] **1 a :** a colorless gaseous hydrocarbon $HC{\equiv}CH$ containing a triple bond that is explosive when compressed but safe if diluted with nitrogen or acetone, that is made by the action of water on calcium carbide or by pyrolysis or oxidation of other hydrocarbons, and that is used in welding and soldering, for removing paint and for illuminating, and for many organic syntheses — called also *ethyne* **b :** ALKYNE **2 a :** the tetravalent radical $>CHCH<$ **b :** the bivalent radical $-CH{=}CH-$

acetylene black *n* **:** a carbon black characterized by relatively high electrical conductivity, made by decomposing acetylene (as by pyrolysis in a retort or by explosion), and used chiefly as a filler in dry cells, rubber, and plastics

acetylene linkage *n* **:** a carbon-to-carbon triple bond

acetylene series *n* **:** the homologous series of unsaturated aliphatic hydrocarbons C_nH_{2n-2} of which acetylene is the lowest member — compare ALKYNE

acetylene tetrachloride *n* **:** TETRACHLOROETHANE

acet·y·le·nic \\¦==¦ēnik, -en-\\ *adj* [ISV *acetylene* + *-ic*] **:** relating to or derived from acetylene **:** like acetylene esp. in having a triple bond ⟨~ acids⟩

acet·y·le·nyl \\¦sed·ᵊlə¦nil\\ *n* -s [ISV *acetylene* + *-yl*] **:** ETHYNYL

ace·tyl·gly·cine \\ə¦sēd·ᵊl'glī,sēn, ¦asəd·-\\ *n* -s [ISV *acetyl* + *glycine*] **:** ACETURIC ACID

acet·y·lide \\ə'sed·ᵊl,īd\\ *n* -s [ISV *acetyl* + *-ide*] **:** a carbide derived from acetylene by the replacement of hydrogen by a metal ⟨cuprous ~ C_2Cu_2⟩

acet·y·li·za·tion \\ə,sed·ᵊlə'zāshən, -l,ī'z-\\ *n* -s **:** ACETYLATION

acetylize *var of* ACETYLATE

acet·y·liz·er \\ə'sed·ᵊl,īzə(r)\\ *n* -s **:** ACETYLATOR

ace·tyl·meth·yl·car·bi·nol \\ə'sēd·ᵊl'methəl'kärbə,nōl, 'asəd·ᵊl-, -nōl\\ *n* -s [*acetyl* + *methyl* + *carbinol*] **:** ACETOIN

acetyl peroxide *n* **:** a low-melting crystalline compound $(CH_3CO)_2O_2$ used esp. for initiating vinyl-type polymerizations

ace·tyl·phen·yl·hy·dra·zine \\ə'sēd·ᵊl'fenᵊl'hīdrə,zēn, 'asəd·ᵊl-, -'fēn-\\ *n* -s [ISV *acetyl* + *phenylhydrazine*] **:** a white crystalline compound $C_6H_5NHNHCOCH_3$ less toxic than phenylhydrazine and used in the symptomatic treatment of polycythemia

ace·tyl·sa·lic·y·late \\-sə'lisə,lāt, -,lət, -,salə'si-\\ *n* -s [*acetylsalicylic* + *-ate*] **:** a salt or ester of acetylsalicylic acid

ace·tyl·sal·i·cyl·ic acid \\-¦salə¦silik-\\ *n* [ISV *acetyl* + *salicylic*] **:** ASPIRIN 1

ace·tyl·tan·nic acid \\-¦tanik-\\ *n* [*acetyl* + *tannic*] **:** a yellowish white or grayish white powder obtained by the acetylation of tannin and used as an intestinal astringent

ace·tyl·tan·nin \\-'tanən\\ *n* -s [ISV *acetyl* + *tannin*] **:** ACETYLTANNIC ACID

acetyl value *or* **acetyl number** *n* **:** a measure of the free hydroxyl groups in a substance (as a fat or oil) as determined by acetylation, being the number of milligrams of potassium hydroxide required for neutralization of the acetic acid formed by hydrolysis of one gram of the acetylated substance

ac·ey-deuc·ey \\¦āsē'd(y)üsē\\ *n* -s [*acey* (fr. *ace* + *-y*) + *deucey*, fr. *deuce* + *-y*] **:** backgammon in which a roll of 3 entitles the player to name and play any set of doublets he chooses and roll the dice again

acft *abbr* aircraft

ac-glob·u·lin \\'ā'sē,-, 'ak,-\\ *n*, *often cap A* [by shortening] **:** ACCELERATOR GLOBULIN

[1]**achae·an** \\ə'kēən\\ *also* **achai·an** \\ə'kīən, ə'kā(y)ən\\ *adj*, *usu cap* [*Achaea*, *Achaia*, ancient region of the Peloponnesus, Greece (fr. L & Gk; L *Achaea*, fr. Gk *Achaia*) + E *-an*] **:** of or relating to Achaea; *broadly* **:** of or relating to Greece

[2]**achaean** \\"\\ *also* **achaian** \\"\\ *n* -s *cap* **:** a native or inhabitant of Achaea; *broadly* **:** GREEK

ach·ae·me·ni·an \\¦akə¦mēnēən, -nyən\\ *adj*, *usu cap* [*Achaemenid* + *-an*] **:** of or relating to the Achaemenids or the Persian language of their inscriptions

achae·me·nid \\ə'kēmənəd, a'-, -kem-, -,nid\\ *n*, *pl* **achaemenids** \\-dz\\ *also* **ach·ae·men·i·dae** \\,akə'menə,dē\\ *or* **ach·ae·men·i·des** \\,akə'menə,dēz\\ *usu cap* [Gk *Achaimenidēs*, fr. *Achaimenēs* (Achaemenes), 7th cent. B.C. Persian king, founder of the dynasty + Gk *-idēs* (patronymic suffix)] **:** a member of the ruling house of ancient Persia from 553 B.C. during the reign of Cyrus the Great to the overthrow of Darius III in 330 B.C. — **ach·ae·me·nid·i·an** \\¦akəmə¦nidēən\\ *adj*, *usu cap*

achae·no·don \\ə'kēnə,dän\\ *n*, *cap* [NL, fr. [2]*a-* + Gk *chainein* to yawn + NL *-odon* — more at YAWN] **:** a genus of extinct Eocene piglike mammals related to *Entelodon*

1achae·ta \(ˈ)āˈkēd·ə\ [NL, fr. 2a- + -chaeta] *syn of* SIPUNCULOIDEA 2

2achaeta \"\ *n, cap* [NL, fr. 2a- + -chaeta] **:** a genus of oligochaete worms completely lacking setae

achaetous *also* **achetous** \(ˈ)āˈkēd·əs, əˈk-\ *adj* [2a- + Gk *chaitē* hair + E *-ous* — more at CHAET-] **:** having no setae

acha·gua \əˈchägwə\ *n, pl* **achagua** *or* **achaguas** *usu cap* [Sp, of AmerInd origin] **1 a :** an Arawakan people of the upper valley of the Orinoco **b :** a member of such people **2 :** the Arawakan language of the Achagua people

achak·zai \əˈchäk,zī\ *n, pl* **achakzai** *or* **achakzais** *usu cap* [prob. Pashto] **1 :** a division of the Afghans **2 :** a member of the Achakzai

ach·a·la·sia \,akəˈlāzh(ē)ə\ *n* -s [NL, fr. 2a- + Gk *chalasis* loosening, relaxation (fr. *chalan* to loosen + *-sis*) + NL *-ia*] **:** failure of a ring of muscle (as a sphincter) to relax ⟨~ of the esophagus⟩ ⟨~ of the anal sphincter⟩

achang \ˈä,chäŋ\ *n, pl* **achang** *or* **achangs** *usu cap* **:** a sinicized Shan ethnic group occupying two valleys in the western frontiers of Yunnan province in southwest China

achar \(ˈ)äˈchär\ *n* -s [Per *āchār*] **:** a pickled article of food as prepared in India **:** a pickle or relish

acha·ra \äˈchärə\ *also* **atsa·ra** \", ätˈsä-\ *n* -s [Tag *atsara*] **:** a pickled article of food as prepared in the Philippines **:** a pickle or relish

achari·ace·ae \ə,karēˈāsē,ē\ *n pl, cap* [NL, fr. Erik *Acharius* †1819 Swedish botanist + NL *-aceae*] **:** a family of erect herbs or subshrubs (order Parietales) with palmately lobed leaves and monoecious flowers — **achari·aceous** \ə¦karēˈāshəs\ *adj*

achar·ne·ment \àshärnəmäⁿ\ *n* -s [F, ardor, relentlessness, ferocity, fr. *acharner* to bait, excite (fr. OF, fr. *a-* — fr. L *ad-* — + *charn-*, stem of *char* meat, fr. L *carn-, caro*) + *-ment* — more at CARNAL] **:** FEROCITY

achar·ya \äˈchäryə\ *n* -s [Skt *ācārya*, lit., one who knows the rules, fr. *ācāra* custom, rule of conduct, fr. *ācarati* he approaches, proceeds, acts, fr. *ā* towards + *carati* he moves, goes; akin to Gk *o-* (in *okellein* to run aground), Av & OPer *ā* toward, OE *ō-* back, behind, OHG *ā-*, OSlav *ja-* (in *jaskudĭ* ugly) — more at WHEEL] **1 :** a Hindu religious teacher **:** one versed in the sacred writings of the Hindus **2 :** any illustrious or learned person in India

ach·ate \ˈakət\ *or* **acha·tes** \əˈkād·ēz\ *n, pl* **achates** \ˈakəts, əˈkād·ēz\ [ME *achate*, fr. OF, fr. L *achates* — more at AGATE] **:** AGATE 1

achates *var of* ACATES

ach·a·ti·na \,akəˈtīnə, -ēnə\ *n* [NL, fr. L *achates* agate + NL *-ina* — more at AGATE] **1** *cap* **:** a genus (the type of the family Achatinidae) comprising very large air-breathing land snails native to Africa but introduced for food in parts of southeast Asia and the Pacific islands where they have become serious pests of agricultural crops **2** -s **:** a snail of the genus *Achatina* — compare AGATE SNAIL

ach·a·ti·nel·la \,akətəˈnelə\ *n* [NL, fr. *Achatina* + *-ella*] **1** *cap* **:** a genus comprising many species and varieties of air-breathing land snails peculiar to the Hawaiian islands **2** -s **:** a snail of the genus *Achatinella*

a·chat·ter \əˈ-\ *adj* [1a- + *chatter* (v.)] **:** CHATTERING ⟨his teeth ~⟩

1ache \ˈāk\ *vb* -ED/-ING/-S [alter. (influenced by 2ache) of ME *aken* to ache, fr. OE *acan*; akin to LG *äken* to hurt, fester, MD *ākel* pain, damage, and perh. to Gk *agos* sin, guilt, Skt *āgas*] *vi* **1 a :** to suffer a usu. dull persistent and sometimes throbbing pain ⟨his muscles *ached* from chopping wood⟩ ⟨*aching* with fatigue⟩ **b :** to become distressed as if with dull persistent pain ⟨~ with the deep sadness of it all —H.A. Overstreet⟩ **:** become disturbed (as with anxiety, remorse, or regret) ⟨~ at the very thought of what may happen⟩ **c :** to feel compassion **:** become moved with pity, sympathy, or grief ⟨her heart *ached* for the homeless children⟩ **2 :** to become filled with persistent desire that is dully painful in intensity ⟨his heart *ached* for her love⟩ **:** desire very strongly **:** YEARN ⟨*aching* to see you again⟩ **3 :** to move with dully painful effort **:** STRAIN ⟨eyes *ached* along the shining rails so surely not to miss the . . . flash of speed —Harriet B. Barbour⟩ ~ *vt, archaic* **:** to cause to ache ⟨snowflakes *aching* my eyes —P.D.Boles⟩

2ache \ˈāk; *in early Modern Eng the -che was prond* -ch\ *n* -s [ME, fr. OE *ece, ece*, fr. *acan* to ache] **:** a usu. dull persistent and sometimes throbbing pain ⟨his loathing of the room became a dull ~ in his brain —Morley Callaghan⟩ **:** a condition marked by aching ⟨an ~ in his heart like the farewell to a dear woman —John Steinbeck⟩ **syn** see PAIN

3ache *n* -s [ME, fr. OF, fr. L *apium* celery — more at APIUM] *obs* **:** any of several umbelliferous plants (as wild celery or parsley)

ach·e·mon sphinx \ˈakə,män-, əˈkēmən-\ *n* [NL *achemon* (specific epithet of *Pholus achemon*), prob. fr. Gk, neut. of *achemōn, acheumōn*, pres. part. of *achein, acheuein* to grieve, annoy, fr. *achos* pain, distress — more at AIL] **:** a large hawk moth (*Pholus achemon*) having a caterpillar that feeds on the grapevine and Virginia creeper

achene *also* **akene** \əˈkēn\ *n* -s [NL *achaenium, achenium*, fr. 2a- + Gk *chainein* to yawn + NL *-ium* — more at YAWN] **:** a small dry indehiscent one-seeded fruit developed from a simple ovary and usu. having a thin pericarp attached to the seed at only one point (as in the buttercup) — **ache·ni·al** \əˈkēnēəl\ *adj*

1 a head of buttercup achenes, *2* single achene, *3* cross section of achene

ach·er·o·ni·an \¦akə¦rōnēən, -nyən\ *adj, usu cap* [*Acheron*, river in Hades (fr. L, fr. Gk *Acherōn*) + E *-ian*] **:** dark and gloomy **:** DISMAL ⟨in the depths of an *Acheronian* forest⟩

ach·er·on·tic \¦akə¦räntik\ *adj, usu cap* [LL *Acheronticus*, fr. L *Acheront-, Acheron* + *-icus* -ic] **:** ACHERONIAN

ach·e·ta \ˈakəd·ə\ *n, cap* [NL, fr. L, male cicada, fr. Gk (Dor dial.) *acheta, achetas* (Gk *ēcheta, ēchetēs*), lit., chirping one, fr. *acheta, achetas*, adj., shrill, chirping, fr. (Dor dial.) *achein* to sound, ring (Gk *ēchein*) — more at ECHO] **:** a genus of crickets including the common American house crickets and field crickets

achet·i·dae \əˈked·ə,dē\ [NL, fr. *Acheta*, type genus + *-idae*] *syn of* GRYLLIDAE

achetous *var of* ACHAETOUS

acheu·le·an *also* **acheu·li·an** \əˈshülēən, -ə(r)l-,-ōl-\ *adj, usu cap* [F *acheuléen*, fr. St. Acheul, near Amiens, France, location of the type station + F *-éen* -ean] **:** of or belonging to the epoch of the Lower Paleolithic period following Abbevillian and characterized by biface tools with cutting edges all around

à che·val \¦äshəˈväl, *F* àshvàl\ *adv* [F, lit., on horseback] **1 :** with a part on each side **:** ASTRIDE ⟨climbing a narrow ridge *à cheval*⟩ **2 :** in such a way as to straddle a line on the layout of a game of chance (as roulette) or be split between two numbers, cards, or events

achier *comparative of* ACHY

achiest *superlative of* ACHY

achie·va·ble \əˈchēvəbəl\ *adj* **:** capable of being achieved **:** ATTAINABLE

achieve \əˈchēv\ *vb* -ED/-ING/-S [ME *acheven*, fr. MF *achever* to finish, fr. *a-* (fr. L *ad-*) + *-chever* (fr. *chef, chief* end, head) — more at CHIEF] *vt* **1 a :** to bring to a successful conclusion **:** carry out successfully **:** ACCOMPLISH ⟨*achieving* his purpose⟩ **b** *obs* **:** to cause to end **:** make to cease **:** bring about the end of **:** FINISH **2 :** to get as the result of exertion **:** succeed in obtaining or gaining **:** WIN, REACH, ATTAIN ⟨he *achieved* greatness⟩ ~ *vi* **:** to attain a desired end or aim **:** reach a certain level of performance ⟨pupils who fail to ~ after promotion⟩ **syn** see PERFORM, REACH

achieve·ment \-mənt\ *n* -s [MF *achevement*, fr. *achever* + *-ment*] **1 :** the act of achieving **:** successful completion **:** ACCOMPLISHMENT, FULFILLMENT ⟨~ of an ambition⟩ **2 a :** a result brought about by resolve, persistence, or endeavor ⟨a major scientific ~⟩ **b :** a great or heroic deed **:** FEAT ⟨the ~ of Christopher Columbus⟩ **3 :** performance by a student in a course **:** quality and quantity of a student's work during a given period ⟨standardized tests to measure ~⟩ **4 :** an escutcheon of arms with the adjuncts (as helm, crest, mantling, motto, and supporters) with which it is displayed

achievement age *n* **:** the level of an individual's educational achievement as measured by an achievement test and related to the norm for his chronological age

achievement quotient *n* **1 :** the ratio usu. multiplied by 100 of achievement age to chronological age **2 :** ACCOMPLISHMENT QUOTIENT

achievement test *n* **:** a standardized test for measuring the skill or knowledge attained by an individual in one or more fields of work or study — compare INTELLIGENCE TEST

achi·la·ry \(ˈ)ā¦kīlərē, əˈk-\ *adj* [2a- + *chil-* + *-ary*] **:** having the labellum or lip of the flower undeveloped or lacking as in some orchids

ach·il·lea \,akəˈlēə, əˈkilēə\ *n, cap* [NL, fr. L *achillea, achilleos*, a plant, fr. Gk *achilleios*, a plant supposed to have been used medicinally by Achilles, fr. *achilleios* of Achilles, fr. *Achilleus* Achilles] **:** a large genus of north temperate herbs (family Compositae) having divided leaves, small heads of tubular and ray flowers, and flattened achenes — see SNEEZEWORT, YARROW

ach·il·le·an \¦akə¦lēən, əˈkilēə\ *adj, usu cap* [*Achilles*, hero of Homer's *Iliad* (fr. L, fr. Gk *Achilleus*) + E *-an*] **:** like Achilles (as in strength, invincibility, or moody and resentful wrath)

ach·il·le·ine \,akəˈlēən, -lē,ēn, əˈkilē-\ *n* -s [ISV *achille-* (fr. NL *Achillea*, genus name of *Achillea millefolium*) + *-ine*] **:** a brownish red bitter alkaloid $C_{20}H_{38}N_2O_{15}$, found in plants of the genus *Achillea*

achil·les' heel \əˈkilēzˈh-\ *n, usu cap A* [so called fr. the story that Achilles was invulnerable except in the heel] **:** a vulnerable point

achilles tendon *n, usu cap A* **:** the strong tendon formed by the united tendons of the large muscles in the calf of the leg of mammals and inserted into the bone of the heel — compare HAMSTRING

achim·e·nes \əˈkimə(,)nēz\ *n* [NL, alter. of L *achaemenis*, a plant (prob. *Euphorbia antiquorum*) used in magic rites, fr. Gk *achaimenis*] **1** *cap* **:** a genus of tropical American herbs (family Gesneriaceae) commonly cultivated for their gloxinialike flowers **2** *pl* **achimenes :** a plant of the genus *Achimenes*

achi·nese \,achəˈnēz, ¦ä-, -ēs\ *n, pl* **achinese** *usu cap* [by alter.] **:** ATJEHNESE

aching *adj* [ME *aking*, fr. pres. part. of *aken* to ache] **:** that aches **:** causing pain or distress ⟨what peaceful hours I once enjoyed . . . but they have left an ~ void —William Cowper⟩ ⟨for shade there is only this ~ and hollow waste of rock —Edith Sitwell⟩ **:** VEXATIOUS ⟨a useful work of reference in a field where students have long been conscious of an ~ gap —*Economist*⟩ — **ach·ing·ly** *adv*

achi·o·te \,ächēˈōd·ē\ *also* **achu·e·te** \,ächəˈwād·ē\ *n* -s [Sp, fr. Nahuatl *achiotl*] **1 :** the seed of the annatto tree **2 :** ANNATTO 1a **3 :** ANNATTO TREE **4 :** a tropical American tree (*Oncoba laurina*) valued for its hard yellow-brown wood

achi·ra \əˈchirə, -ērə\ *n* -s [AmerSp, fr. Quechua] **:** a canna (*Canna edulis*) with rootstocks bearing edible tubers from which an arrowroot is made

ach·kan \ˈächkən\ *n* -s [Hindi *ackan*] **:** a three-quarter-length coat or tunic worn by men in India

achlam·y·date \(ˈ)ā¦klamə,dāt, -,dət\ *adj* [2a- + *chlamydate*] **:** without a mantle — used of gastropods

achla·myd·e·ae \¦āklə¦midē,ē, ,akl-\ *n pl, cap* [NL, fr. 2a- + *chlamyd-* + *-eae*] *in some classifications* **:** a group of Apetalae comprising plants with flowers that lack a perianth

achla·myd·e·ous \-¦midēəs\ *adj* [2a- + *chlamyd-* + *-eous*] **:** of, relating to, or characteristic of the Achlamydeae; *often, of flowers* **:** lacking both calyx and corolla

ach–laut \ˈäk,laůt\ *n* -s *sometimes cap A* [G, fr. *ach* ah,alas + *laut* sound, fr. MHG *lūt*; akin to OE *hlūd* loud — more at LOUD] **:** the voiceless velar fricative sound represented by the *ch* of German *ach* or the *ch* of Scottish *loch*, phonemically often allophonic with the ich-laut

achlor·hy·dria \¦ā,klōrˈhīdrēə\ *n* -s [NL, fr. 2a- + *chlorhydria*] **:** absence of hydrochloric acid from the gastric juice — **achlor·hy·dric** \-¦hīdrik\ *adj*

achlo·ro·phyl·lous \(ˈ)ā¦klōrə,filəs, ¦==¦==\ *adj* [2a- + *chlorophyllous*] **:** having no chlorophyll ⟨a parasitic ~ plant⟩

achmimic *usu cap, var of* AKHMIMIC

acho·li \əˈchōlē\ *n, pl* **acholi** *or* **acholis** *usu cap* **1 a :** a nomadic pastoral people of northern Uganda **b :** a member of such people **2 :** a Nilotic language of the Acholi people

achol·ic \(ˈ)ā¦kälik\ *or* **acho·lous** \(ˈ)ā¦kōləs, -äl-, ˈakəl-\ *adj* [2a- + *chol-* + *-ic* or *-ous*] **:** exhibiting deficiency of bile

achol·uria \¦ākōˈlůrēə, ¦ā,kōlˈyů-, -kä-\ *n* -s [NL, fr. Gk *acholos* lacking gall, deficient in bile (fr. *a-* 2a- + *cholē* gall, bile) + NL *-uria* — more at GALL] **:** absence of bile pigment from the urine in one type of jaundice — **achol·uric** \¦=(,)=¦=rik\ *adj*

acho·ma·wi \əˈchōmə,wē\ *or* **achu·ma·wi** \-üm-\ *n, pl* **achomawi** *or* **achomawis** *or* **achumawi** *or* **achumawis** *usu cap* [Achomawi, fr. *achóma* river] **1 a :** an Indian people of the Pit river valley in northern California **b :** a member of such people **2 :** a Shastan language of the Achomawi people

achon·drite \(ˈ)āˈkän,drīt\ *n* -s [2a- + *chondrite*] **:** a stony meteorite devoid of chondrules — **achon·drit·ic** \¦ā,kän¦drid·ik\ *adj*

achon·dro·pla·sia \¦ā,kändrəˈplāzh(ē)ə\ *n* -s [NL, fr. 2a- + *chondr-* + *-plasia*] **:** failure of normal development of cartilage resulting in dwarfism and occurring in many animals including man, cattle, and fowls — called also, in man, *fetal rickets*; compare ATELIOSIS, CREEPER 9, 3DEXTER — **achon·dro·plas·tic** \-¦plastik\ *adj*

achor *n* -ES [LL, fr. Gk *achōr* dandruff, scurf] *archaic* **:** PUSTULE

achor·dal \(ˈ)ā¦kȯrdᵊl\ *adj* [2a- + *chordal*] **:** ACHORDATE

achor·da·ta \¦ā,kȯrˈdād·ə, -ȧd·ə\ *n pl, cap* [NL, fr. 2a- + *Chordata*] **:** an arbitrary subdivision of the animal kingdom including all animals lacking a notochord — opposed to *Chordata* — **achor·date** \(ˈ)ā¦kȯrdət, (ˈ)āˈkȯr,dāt\ *adj or n*

acho·ri·on \əˈkōrē,än\ *n, cap* [NL, fr. Gk *achor-, achōr* scurf, dandruff + *-ion* -ium] **:** a genus of imperfect fungi (order Moniliales) that is often regarded as a subgenus of either *Oidium* or *Oospora* and is parasitic on the skin of man, other mammals, and birds

ach·o·ru·tes \,akəˈrüd·ēz\ *n, cap* [NL] **:** a genus of springtails (order Collembola) including several destructive to mushrooms, various roots and bulbs, and seedlings, and also including the cosmopolitan snow flea (*A. nivicolus*)

ach·ras \ˈakrəs, -,ras\ *n* [NL, fr. L, a wild pear tree (prob. *Pyrus amygdaliformis*), fr. Gk; akin to Alb *dardhe* pear tree] **1** *cap* **:** a monotypic genus of tropical American trees (family Sapotaceae) having papery leaves and small white flowers followed by a large one-seeded fruit **2 :** SAPODILLA

achres·tic anemia \əˈkrestik-\ *n* [2a- + Gk *chrēstikos* knowing how to use, understanding the use of; fr. the hypothesis that the body of a sufferer from this disease is unable to use the antianemic principle contained in the body] **:** chronic progressive macrocytic anemia characterized by a refractoriness to liver therapy

achro- *or* **achroö-** *comb form* [Gk *achroos*, fr. *a-* 2a- + *-chroos* colored — more at -CHROOUS] **:** colorless ⟨*achro*dextrin⟩ ⟨*achroö*cyst⟩

achroa·cyte \(ˈ)āˈkrōə,sīt\ *n* -s [2a- + Gk *chroa* color + E *-cyte*] *anat* **:** a colorless cell; *specif* **:** LYMPHOCYTE

achrochordidae *syn of* ACROCHORDIDAE

achrodextrin *var of* ACHROÖDEXTRIN

ach·ro·ite \ˈakrə,wīt\ *n* -s [G *achroit*, fr. *achro-* + *-it* -ite] **1 :** a colorless variety of tourmaline **2 :** a gem cut from achroite

achroma *var of* ACHROMIA

achro·ma·cyte \(ˈ)āˈkrōmə,sīt\ *n* -s [2a- + Gk *chrōma* color + E *-cyte*] **:** a decolorized red blood cell

achro·ma·sia \¦ākrōˈmāzh(ē)ə, ,ak-\ *n* -s [NL, fr. 2a- + *-chromasia*] **1 :** ACHROMIA **2** *of cells or tissues* **:** loss of the usual reaction to stains

ach·ro·mat \ˈakrə,mat\ *n* -s [prob. fr. G, short for *achromatische linse* achromatic lens] **:** ACHROMATIC LENS

achromat- *or* **achromato-** *comb form* [Gk *achrōmatos* colorless, fr. *a-* 2a- + *-chrōmatos* colored, fr. *chrōmat-, chrōma* color — more at CHROMATIC] **:** achromatic ⟨*achromat*uria⟩ **:** something achromatic ⟨*achromato*lysis⟩

ach·ro·mati·ace·ae \,akrō,mad·ēˈāsē,ē, -māshē-\ *n pl, cap* [NL, fr. *Achromatium*, type genus (fr. *achromat-* + *-ium*) + *-aceae*] **:** a family usu. placed in the order Beggiatoales that includes large motile aquatic bacteria containing sulfur or calcium carbonate inclusions but no photosynthetic pigments

ach·ro·mat·ic \¦akrə¦mad·ik, -rō, -atik, -ēk\ *adj* [Gk *achrōmatos* + E *-ic*] **1 :** free from color **:** refracting light without dispersing it into its constituent colors **:** giving images practically free from extraneous colors ⟨an ~ telescope⟩ ⟨an ~ microscope objective⟩ **2** *biol* **:** UNCOLORED **:** not readily colored by the usual staining agents ⟨~ part of a cell⟩ — see ACHROMATIC FIGURE **3 a :** possessing no hue **:** totally lacking in saturation **:** NEUTRAL **b :** black, gray, or white **4** *music* **:** without accidentals or modulation **:** DIATONIC — **ach·ro·mat·i·cal·ly** \-ək(ə)lē, -ēk-, -li\ *adv*

achromatic figure *n* **:** the mitotic spindle and associated cell structures that do not stain with the usual microtechnical dyes

ach·ro·ma·tic·i·ty \,==məˈtisəd·ē\ *n* -ES **1 :** the quality or state of being achromatic (as grayness of a color) **2 :** degree of being achromatic

achromatic lens *n* **:** a compound lens made by combining lenses of different material (as flint glass and crown glass) having different focal powers, the light that emerges from the lens forming images practically free from prismatic colors

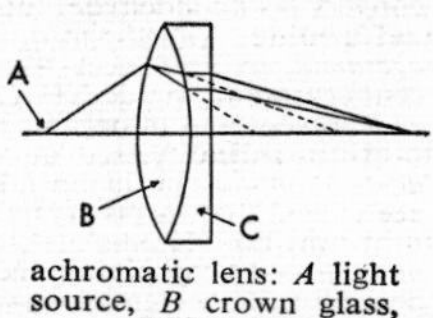

achromatic lens: *A* light source, *B* crown glass, *C* flint glass

achromatic prism *n* **:** a prism made by combining two or more prisms of different refractive index so designed and placed that a ray of white or other nonhomogeneous light passing through the prism is deviated but not dispersed into a spectrum — compare AMICI PRISM

achro·ma·tin \(ˈ)āˈkrōmətən\ *n* -s [*achromat-* + *-in*] **:** the part of the cell nucleus that is not readily colored by basic stains — opposed to *chromatin* — **achro·ma·tin·ic** \¦ā,krōmə¦tinik\ *adj*

achro·ma·tism \(ˈ)āˈkrōmə,tizəm, aˈ-\ *n* -s [*achromat-* + *-ism*] **:** the quality or state of being achromatic

ach·ro·ma·ti·um \,akrəˈmāshēəm\ *n, cap* [NL, fr. *achromat-* + *-ium*] **:** the type genus of the family Achromatiaceae

achro·ma·ti·za·tion \,ā,krōməd·əˈzāshən, (,)a,k-, -mə,tīˈz-\ *n* -s **:** the act or process of achromatizing

achro·ma·tize \(ˈ)āˈkrōmə,tīz, aˈ-\ *vt* -ED/-ING/-S [*achromat-* + *-ize*] **:** to deprive of color **:** make achromatic

achromato- — see ACHROMAT-

achro·mat·o·cyte \¦ākrōˈmad·ə,sīt, ¦ak-; (ˈ)āˈkrōməd·-, aˈ-\ *n* -s [*achromat-* + *-cyte*] **:** ACHROMACYTE

achro·ma·tol·y·sis \¦ā,krōməˈtäləsəs, a,-\ *n, pl* **achromatoly·ses** \-ə,sēz\ [NL, fr. *achromat-* + *-lysis*] **:** disorganization of the achromatic part of a cell

1achro·mat·o·phil \¦ākrōˈmad·ə,fil, ¦ak-; (ˈ)āˈkrōməd·-, aˈ-\ *adj* [*achromat-* + *-phil*] *of cells or tissues* **:** having no affinity for stains

2achromatophil \"\ *n* -s **:** an achromatophil individual

achro·ma·to·phil·ia \¦ā,krōməd·əˈfilēə, a,k-; ¦ākrō,mad·ə-, ,ak-\ *n* -s [NL, fr. *achromat-* + *-philia*] *biol* **:** the property of having no affinity for stains

achro·ma·top·sia \¦ā,krōməˈtäpsēə\ *n* -s [NL, fr. *achromat-* + *-opsia*] **:** a visual defect marked by total color blindness the colors of the spectrum being seen in tones of white-gray-black

achro·mia \(ˈ)āˈkrōmēə\ *also* **achro·ma** \-mə\ *n* -s [*achromia*, NL, fr. 2a- + *chrom-* + *-ia*; *achroma*, NL, fr. 2a- + Gk *chrōma* color] **:** absence of normal pigmentation esp. in red blood cells and skin — **achro·mic** \(ˈ)ā¦krōmik\ *adj*

achro·mo·bac·ter \(ˈ)āˈkrōmə,baktə(r)\ *n* [NL, fr. Gk *achromos* colorless + NL *-bacter*] **1** *cap* **:** a genus (the type of the family Achromobacteriaceae) of saprophytic usu. gram-negative rod-shaped bacteria that are common in water and soil, form no pigment, cause putrefaction of various organic substrates, and are often active denitrifying bacteria **2** -s **:** any bacterium of the genus *Achromobacter*

achro·mo·trich·ia \¦ā,krōməˈtrikēə\ *n* -s [NL, fr. Gk *achromos* + NL *-trichia*] **:** absence of pigment in the hair

achroö- — see ACHRO-

ach·ro·ö·dex·trin \,akrə(,)wōˈdekstrən\ *also* **ach·ro·dex·trin** \,akrōˈd-\ *n* -s [ISV *achro-* + *dextrin*] **:** a dextrin that does not give a color with iodine

ach·ter \ˈäktə(r)\ *adj* [obs. Afrik *achter-* (as in *achterveld* interior, backcountry — now *agter, agterveld*), fr. *achter*, adv., behind, after; akin to OE *æfter* — more at AFTER] *Africa* **:** REAR, HINDMOST — often used in combination ⟨*achter*-oxen⟩

achua \äˈchüə\ *n, pl* **achua** *or* **achuas** *usu cap* **1 :** a pygmy people of the Belgian Congo **2 :** a member of the Achua

achuete *var of* ACHIOTE

achumawi *usu cap, var of* ACHOMAWI

achy \ˈākē\ *adj, sometimes* -ER/-EST [2ache + *-y*] **:** afflicted with aches

achy·lia \(ˈ)āˈkīlēə\ *n* -s [NL, fr. 2a- + *-chylia*] **:** ACHYLIA GASTRICA — **achy·lous** \(ˈ)ā¦kīləs\ *adj*

achylia gas·tri·ca \-ˈgastrikə\ *n* -s [NL, gastric achylia] **1 :** partial or complete absence of gastric juice **2 :** ACHLORHYDRIA

ach·y·ran·thes \,akəˈran(,)thēz\ *n* [NL, fr. Gk *achyron* chaff, husk + NL *-anthes*] **1** *cap* **:** a genus of tropical herbs (family Amaranthaceae) having white or silvery spicate flowers **2** *pl* **achyranthes :** any of several plants of the genera *Iresine* and *Telanthera*

aci- *comb form* [G *azi-*, fr. NL *acidum* acid] acid — in names of acid forms of tautomeric compounds or groups ⟨*aci*-nitro group =NO(OH)⟩

acic·u·la \əˈsikyələ\ *n, pl* **acicu·lae** \-,lē, -,lī\ *or* **aciculas** [NL, fr. LL, small pin for a headdress, dim. of L *acus* needle — more at ACUTE] **:** a needlelike spine, bristle, or crystal

acic·u·lar \-lə(r)\ *adj* [LL *acicula* + E *-ar*] **1 a :** like a needle in shape **:** slender and pointed ⟨~ leaves⟩ ⟨~ crystals⟩ **b :** having a sharp needlelike point **2 :** ACICULATE 1

acic·u·late \-lət, -,lāt\ *adj* [NL *acicula* + E *-ate*] **1 a :** furnished with or composed of aciculae **b :** marked with fine irregular streaks like needle scratches **2 :** ACICULAR 1

acic·u·lum \-,ləm\ *n, pl* **acicu·la** \-lə\ *or* **aciculums** [NL, alter. of LL *acicula* small pin for a headdress] **:** a needlelike spine or bristle of an animal or plant **:** ACICULA; *specif* **:** one of the stiff setae in the base of a parapodium of an annelid

1ac·id \ˈasəd, ˈaa-\ *adj* [F or L; F *acide*, fr. L *acidus*, fr. *acēre* to be sour — more at ACUTE] **1 a :** sharp or biting to the taste ⟨~ lemons⟩ **:** SOUR, TART ⟨the ~ juice of unripe grapes⟩ ⟨an ~ apple⟩ **b :** sharp, biting, or sour in manner, disposition, or nature ⟨his ~ way of dealing with people⟩ ⟨an ~ misanthrope⟩ **:** prone to antagonize, wound, or humiliate **:** repellently disagreeable **:** UNPLEASANT, OFFENSIVE ⟨an ~ individual, unable to get along with anyone⟩ **:** CUTTING, CAUSTIC ⟨~ remarks⟩ ⟨~ gibes⟩ **:** CORROSIVE ⟨~ hatred⟩ **c :** sharply clear, discerning, pointed, and usu. more or less mocking or sarcastic ⟨~ criticism⟩ ⟨an ~ analysis of the situation⟩ ⟨~ wit⟩ **:** PENETRATING, TRENCHANT, INCISIVE **:** quick in perception ⟨his cold and ~ intelligence⟩ **:** SHREWD, ACUTE **d :** severe and uncompromising **:** HARSH, RIGID, INFLEXIBLE, UNYIELDING ⟨a censorious and ~ attitude toward freedom of thought⟩ **e :** piercingly intense ⟨the ~ radiance of the bright sunlight⟩ and often jarring ⟨~ splashes of brilliant yellows⟩ or shrill ⟨a singing voice that unfortunately becomes sometimes ~ in the upper register⟩ **2 :** of, relating to, or having the characteristics of an acid: as **a :** having an acid reaction **:** having a pH of less than 7 ⟨~ soil⟩ ⟨a slightly ~ solution⟩ **b** (1) **:** derived from an acid ⟨~ iodide⟩ (2) *of salts and esters* **:** derived by partial exchange of replaceable hydrogen ⟨~ potassium sulfate $KHSO_4$⟩ **c :** containing or involving the use of an acid ⟨~ bath⟩ ⟨~ sludge⟩ ⟨~ hydrolysis⟩ **d :** characterized by or resulting from an abnormally high concentration of acid ⟨~ condition of the stomach⟩ ⟨~ indigestion⟩ — not used technically **e :** relating to or made by an acid process ⟨~ steel⟩ **3 :** rich in silica **:** PERSILICIC ⟨~ rocks⟩ — opposed to *basic* **syn** see SOUR

2acid \"\ *n* -s [NL *acidum*, fr. L, neut. of *acidus*, adj.] **1 :** a sour substance **2 a :** a compound (as hydrochloric acid, sulfuric acid, or benzoic acid) capable of reacting with a base to form a salt, its aqueous solutions if it is water-soluble tasting sour, reddening litmus, and evolving hydrogen on reaction with certain metals (as iron, zinc, tin) **:** a compound (HX) containing hydrogen that in aqueous solution yields hydrogen ion (H^+) hydrated to hydronium ion (as H_3O^+), together with the anion (X^-), the degree of ionization in dilute solutions of strong acids (as nitric, hydrochloric, or trichloroacetic acid) being virtually complete, that of weak acids (as acetic or benzoic acid) being possibly one percent, and that of very weak acids (as hydrocyanic or boric acid) being much less than one percent — compare HYDROGEN-ION CONCENTRATION, PH **b** *according to the Brønsted-Lowry system* **:** a hydrogen-containing molecule (as nitric acid) or ion (as hydronium, ammonium, or bicarbonate) that can give up a proton to a base **:** a proton donor ⟨hydrogen chloride is the conjugate ~ of the chloride ion⟩ **c** *according to the G. N. Lewis system* **:** a substance capable of accepting from a base an unshared pair of electrons which then form a covalent chemical bond, many compounds (as boron fluoride, sulfur trioxide, or carbon dioxide) as well as protons and other positive ions being thus included in this class — called also *Lewis acid* **3 :** dilute sulfuric acid used in storage batteries **4 :** something sharp, biting, sour, or corrosive ⟨a social satire dripping with ~⟩ ⟨destroying freedom with the ~ of narrow-mindedness⟩

acid alizarin red B *n, often cap both As & R* **:** an acid chrome monoazo dye that dyes wool Bordeaux red — see DYE table (under *Pigment Red 60*)

ac·i·dan·the·ra \ˌasə'danthərə\ *n* [NL, fr. Gk *akid-, akis* pointed object, needle + NL *-anthera;* akin to Gk *akē* point — more at EDGE] **1** *cap* **:** a genus of African herbs (family Iridaceae) having slender-tubed flowers in loose spikes — see EXOTICA **2** -s **:** any plant of the genus *Acidanthera*

ac·i·das·pis \ˌasə'daspəs\ *n, cap* [NL, fr. Gk *akid-, akis* + NL *-aspis*] **:** a genus of trilobites mostly with long spines found in the Ordovician, Silurian, and Devonian

acid–binding *adj* **:** having the capacity of combining with acids

acid blast *n* **:** a method of etching a photoengraving in which sprays of acid are forced against the face of the plate

acid cell *n* **1** *anat* **:** a gastric parietal cell **2 a :** an electric storage cell with an acid electrolyte (as dilute sulfuric acid) **b :** LEAD-LEAD ACID CELL

acid chloride *n* **:** a chloride (as acetyl chloride, sulfuryl chloride) derived from an acid by replacement of hydroxyl by chlorine and yielding the acid on hydrolysis

acid drop *n, Brit* **:** any tart piece of candy (as one made of sugar flavored with tartaric acid) — compare SOUR BALL

acid dye *or* **acid color** *n* **:** any of a large class of dyes that contain acidic groups (as sulfonic or carboxyl groups) usu. in the form of sodium or potassium salts, that are soluble in water, and that are used in an acid bath for dyeing esp. textile fibers of animal origin and leather or in aqueous or alcoholic solution for staining cytoplasm and various acidophilic structures of cells and tissues — see DYE table I

acid egg *n* **:** a globular or cylindrical receptacle from which acid is forced by compressed air (as in manufacturing sulfuric acid) but which has been largely superseded by centrifugal pumps — called also *blowcase*

ac·i·de·mia \ˌasə'dēmēə\ *n* -s [NL, fr. *acidum* + *-emia*] **:** a condition in which the hydrogen-ion concentration in the blood is increased

acid–fast \'==,=\ *adj* **:** not easily decolorized by acids (as when stained or dyed) — used esp. of bacteria and tissues

acid fuchsine *or* **acid magenta** *n, often cap A&F&M* **:** an acid triphenylmethane dye that is now usu. obtained by sulfonation of fuchsine and is used in the form of a salt chiefly in histology as a general cytoplasmic stain and for demonstration of special elements (as mitochondria) and in photographic films as an antihalation dye — see DYE table I (under *Acid Violet 19*)

acid gloss *n* **:** a polish produced (as in stonecutting) with the aid of acids

acid green B *n, usu cap A & G* **:** GUINEA GREEN B

acid halide *n* **:** a halide (as an acid chloride) derived from an acid

acid heat test *n* **:** a test used in petroleum refining for indicating the amount of unsaturated hydrocarbons in gasoline and performed by noting the increase in temperature caused by adding one volume of 93 percent sulfuric acid to five volumes of gasoline in a Dewar flask

acid humus *n* **:** humus with a pH below 7.0

acid·ic \ə'sidik, (')a¦s-, -ēk\ *adj* [[2]*acid* + *-ic*] **1 :** acid-forming ⟨silicon is the chief ~ element of rocks⟩ ⟨~ oxides⟩ **2 :** ACID

ac·i·dif·er·ous \¦asə¦dif(ə)rəs\ *adj* [[2]*acid* + *-i-* + *-ferous*] **:** containing or yielding an acid

acid·i·fi·a·ble \ə¦sidə¦fīəbəl, a¦-\ *adj* **:** capable of being acidified

acid·i·fi·ant \='==,=ənt\ *adj* [F, fr. pres. part. of *acidifier* to acidify] **:** ACIDIFYING

acid·i·fi·ca·tion \əˌsidəfə'kāshən, aˌ-\ *n* -s [F, fr. *acidifier* to acidify] **:** the act or process of acidifying

acid·i·fi·er \='==,fī(ə)r, -īə\ *n* -s [*acidify* + *-er*] **:** one that acidifies: as **a :** a chemical element or group whose presence produces acidity — orig. used of oxygen **b :** a substance (as sulfur or aluminum sulfate) used to increase soil acidity

acid·i·fy \-ˌfī\ *vb* -ED/-ING/-ES [prob. fr. F *acidifier*, fr. *acide* acid + *-ifier* -ify — more at ACID] *vt* **:** to make acid (as by the addition of sufficient quantity of an acid) **:** convert into an acid ~ *vi* **:** to become acid

ac·i·dim·e·ter \ˌasə'dimədə(r)\ *n* -s [[2]*acid* + *-i-* + *-meter*] **:** an apparatus for measuring the strength or the amount of acid present in a solution

acid·i·met·ric \ə¦sidə¦me·trik, a-\ *adj* **:** relating to or involving acidimetry

ac·i·dim·e·try \ˌasə'dimə·trē\ *n* -ES [[2]*acid* + *-i-* + *-metry*] **1 :** measurement of the strength of an acid or of the amount of free acid in a solution — compare ALKALIMETRY 2 **2 :** measurement by titration of the amount of alkali in a solution by use of a standard solution of an acid — compare ALKALIMETRY 1

acid·i·ty \ə'sidəd·ē, a'-, -ətē, -i\ *n* -ES [F or L; F *acidité*, fr. L *aciditat-, aciditas*, fr. *acidus* acid, sour + *-itat-, -itas* -ity — more at ACID] **1 a :** the quality, state, or degree of being sour or chemically acid **:** SOURNESS, TARTNESS ⟨the ~ of lemon juice⟩ **b :** the quality or state of being abnormally or excessively acid **:** HYPERACIDITY ⟨~ of the stomach⟩ — not used technically **c :** a tartness or sharpness in the taste of wine due to the presence of fruit acids **2 :** the quality, state, or degree of being acid (as in manner) ⟨talking with her usual slightly envious ~ —Mary Deasy⟩

acidity coefficient *n, of rocks* **:** the ratio of the oxygen of the bases to the oxygen in the silica — called also *oxygen ratio*

ac·id·i·za·tion \ˌasədə'zāshən, -ˌdī'z-\ *n* -s **:** the act or process of acidizing

ac·id·ize \'asəˌdīz\ *vb* -ED/-ING/-S [[2]*acid* + *-ize*] *vt* **:** to treat with acid **:** ACIDIFY; *specif* **:** to charge (an oil or gas well) with hydrochloric acid, sometimes with hydrofluoric acid added, for dissolving the lime out of the sand in order to facilitate and increase production ~ *vi* **:** to become acidized

ac·id·iz·er \-zə(r)\ *n* -s **:** one that acidizes oil or gas wells

ac·id·ly \'asədlē, 'aa-, -li\ *adv* **:** SHARPLY, SARCASTICALLY

acid man *n* **:** a worker who mixes or controls acid solutions used in industrial processes

acid·ness *n* -ES **:** the quality or state of being acid

acid number *n* **:** a measure of the amount of free acids (as fatty acids) in a substance (as an oil or resin) usu. expressed as the number of milligrams of potassium hydroxide required to neutralize one gram of the substance — called also *acid value*

ac·i·do·gen·ic \¦asədō¦jenik, ə¦sid-\ *adj* [[2]*acid* + *-o-* + *-genic*] **:** acid-forming ⟨~ bacteria⟩

[1]**ac·id·oid** \'asəˌdȯid\ *adj* [[2]*acid* + *-oid*] *of certain soil substances* **:** like acid **:** potentially acid

[2]**acidoid** \"\ *n* -s **:** an acidoid substance

ac·i·dol·y·sis \ˌasə'däləsəs\ *n, pl* **acidoly·ses** \-əˌsēz\ [NL, fr. *acidum* acid + *-o-* + *-lysis*] **:** any chemical reaction analogous to hydrolysis in which an acid plays a role similar to that of water

ac·i·dom·e·ter \ˌasə'dämad·ə(r)\ *n* -s [by alter.] **:** ACIDIMETER

[1]**acid·o·phile** \ə'sidəˌfīl, a'-\ *or* **acid·o·phil** \-ˌfil\ *adj* [*acid* + *-o-* + *-phile, -phil*] **:** ACIDOPHILIC

[2]**acidophile** \"\ *or* **acidophil** \"\ *n* -s **:** an acidophilic substance, tissue, or organism

ac·i·do·phil·ia \¦asə(ˌ)dō'filēə, əˌsidə'-\ *n* -s [NL, fr. *acidum* + *-o-* + *-philia*] **:** EOSINOPHILIA

ac·i·do·phil·ic \¦asə(ˌ)dō¦filik, ə¦sidə¦filik\ *or* **ac·i·doph·i·lous** \¦asə¦däf(ə)ləs\ *adj* [[2]*acid* + *-o-* + *-philic, -philous*] **1** *biol* **:** staining readily with acid stains **2 :** preferring or thriving (as of certain bacteria) in a relatively acid environment — see ACIDURIC

ac·i·doph·i·lus milk \¦asə¦däf(ə)ləs-\ *n* [NL *acidophilus* (specific epithet of *Lactobacillus acidophilus*, one of the species of bacteria causing this fermentation), fr. *acidum* + *-o-* + *-philus*] **:** milk fermented by any of several bacteria and used therapeutically to change the intestinal flora

ac·i·do·pro·te·o·lyte \¦asə(ˌ)dō'prōd·ēəˌlīt\ *n* -s [back-formation fr. *acidoproteolytic*] **:** any bacterium attacking protein in an acid medium including certain bacteria used for the ripening of cheeses and other dairy products

ac·i·do·pro·te·o·lyt·ic \'==(ˌ)=¦===¦lid·ik\ *adj* [[2]*acid* + *-o-* + *proteolytic*] **:** of, relating to, or being an action in which there is both acid production and proteolytic digestion (as in the action of certain bacteria on milk)

ac·i·do·sis \ˌasə'dōsəs\ *n, pl* **acido·ses** \-ōˌsēz\ [NL, fr. *acidum* acid + *-osis*] **:** a condition of decreased alkalinity of the blood and tissues marked by sickly sweet breath, headache, nausea and vomiting, and visual disturbances and usu. a result of excessive acid production — opposed to *alkalosis;* compare KETOSIS 1

ac·i·dot·ic \¦asə¦däd·ik\ *adj* [fr. NL *acidosis*, after such pairs as NL *hypnosis:* E *hypnotic*] **:** having or characterized by acidosis

acid phosphate *n* **:** SUPERPHOSPHATE

acid process *n* **:** a process carried on in a furnace lined with acidic or highly siliceous material and under a slag that is predominantly siliceous — used esp. of steelmaking processes; opposed to *basic process*

acid radical *n* **1 :** the negative ion (as the sulfate ion SO_4^{--}) of an acid **:** ANION — now used esp. by analysts **2 :** a radical formed by removal of all hydroxyl or analogous groups (as mercapto) from an acid ⟨benzoyl C_6H_5CO– is the *acid radical* corresponding to benzoic acid C_6H_5COOH⟩ ⟨sulfuryl $>SO_2$ is the *acid radical* of sulfuric acid H_2SO_4⟩ — compare ACYL

acid resist *n* **:** RESIST 2c

acids *pl of* ACID

acid sludge *n* **:** gummy material that separates from a petroleum oil on treatment with sulfuric acid

acid sodium carbonate *n* **:** SODIUM BICARBONATE

acid test *n* [so called fr. the use of nitric acid to determine the gold content of jewelry] **:** a severe or crucial test (as of value, authenticity, or effectiveness) ⟨the *acid test* of our . . . good faith —A.H.Vandenberg⟩ ⟨rationally testing our hypothesis by the *acid test* of seeing how it works —Gardner Murphy⟩ ⟨reading papers is the *acid test* of the teacher —*English Jour.*⟩

acid·u·lant *or* **acid·u·lent** \ə'sijələnt\ *n* -s [F *acidulant*, fr. *acidulant*, adj.] **:** an acidulating or acidifying agent ⟨vinegar is an ~⟩

acid·u·late \-ˌlāt, *usu* -ād· + V\ *vt* -ED/-ING/-S [L *acidulus* + E *-ate*] **:** to make acid, esp. slightly acid **:** treat with acid ⟨~ water by adding hydrochloric acid⟩ — **acid·u·la·tion** \əˌsijə'lāshən\ *n* -s

acidulated *adj* **:** ACID 1b ⟨a morose ~ individual⟩

acidulated drop *n, Brit* **:** ACID DROP

[1]**acid·u·lent** \ə'sijələnt\ *adj* [F *acidulant*, fr. pres. part. of *aciduler* to acidulate, fr. L *acidulus*] **:** ACIDULOUS

[2]**acidulent** *var of* ACIDULANT

acid·u·lous \-ləs\ *adj* [L *acidulus* sourish, fr. *acidus* sour — more at ACID] **:** acid in taste or manner **:** BITING, CAUSTIC, HARSH ⟨tasting the pungent ~ wood sorrel —John Burroughs⟩ ⟨~ spinsterish pen⟩ ⟨thin ~ voice⟩ **syn** see SOUR

ac·i·du·ric \¦asə¦d(y)u̇rik\ *adj* [[2]*acid* + L *durare* to endure + E *-ic*] **:** tolerating an environment more acid than the optimum; *also* **:** ACIDOPHILIC

acid value *n* **:** ACID NUMBER

acid wood *n* **:** CHEMICAL WOOD

ac·idy \'asədē, 'aa-, -di\ *adj* [[2]*acid* + *-y*] **:** of a somewhat acid quality ⟨an ~ flavor⟩

ac·id·yl \'asəˌdil, -ēl\ *n* -s [by alter.] **:** ACYL

acier \'asēˌā\ *n* -s [F, steel, fr. (assumed) VL *aciarium*, fr. L *acies* point, sharp edge, fr. *acer* sharp — more at EDGE] **:** QUAKER GRAY

ac·i·er·age \'asēərij\ *n* -s [F *aciérage*, fr. *acier* + *-age*] **:** the process of coating the surface of a metal plate (as a stereotype plate) with a thin layer of iron by electrolysis, the iron becoming hard like steel **:** STEELING

ac·i·form \'asəˌfȯrm\ *adj* [L *acus* needle + E *-iform* — more at ACUTE] **:** ACICULAR

acil·i·ate \(')ā¦silēət, -ēˌāt\ *or* **acil·i·at·ed** \-ēˌād·əd\ *adj* [[2]*a-* + *ciliate, ciliated*] **:** without cilia

ac·i·na·ceous \¦asə¦nāshəs\ *adj* [*acinus* + *-aceous*] *bot* **:** containing seeds or kernels

ac·i·nac·i·form \ˌasə'nasəˌfȯrm\ *adj* [L *acinaces* short sword (fr. Gk *akinakēs*) + E *-iform*] *bot* **:** shaped like a scimitar — used of a leaf

ac·i·nar \'asənər, -ˌnär\ *also* **ac·i·nal** \'asənəl\ *or* **acin·ic** \ə'sinik, a'-\ *adj* [NL *acinus* + E *-ar* or *-al* or *-ic*] *anat* **:** of or relating to an acinus

ac·i·nar·i·ous \¦asə¦na(a)rēəs\ *adj* [prob. fr. F *acinaire*, fr. L *acinus* berry, grape, grape or berry seed + F *-aire* -arious] **:** covered (as of certain algae) with globose vesicles like grape seeds

[1]**ac·i·ne·ta** \ˌasə'nēd·ə, ˌakə'nā-\ *or* **ac·i·ne·tae** \-nēˌtē, -nāˌtī\ [NL, fr. Gk *akinētos* motionless, fr. *a-* [2]a- + *kinētos* moving — more at KINETIC] *syn of* SUCTORIA

[2]**acineta** \"\ *n, cap* [NL, fr. Gk *akinētos*] **:** a widely distributed genus of loricate usu. stalked suctorian protozoa with tentacles in two or three bundles at the anterior end

acing *pres part of* ACE

acin·i·form \ə'sinəˌfȯrm\ *adj* [L *acinus* + E *-iform*] **1 :** shaped like a cluster of grapes **:** clustered like grapes **2 :** full of small kernels like a grape

acin·o·nyx \ə'sinəˌniks\ *n, cap* [NL, fr. Gk *akinētos* motionless + NL *-onyx* — more at ACINETA] **:** the genus of cats comprising the cheetahs which are distinguished by the absence of cutaneous sheaths for guarding the claws

ac·i·nose \'asəˌnōs\ *adj* [L *acinosus*] **:** ACINOUS ⟨an ~ gland⟩

ac·i·no·tu·bu·lar \¦asə(ˌ)nō¦-\ *adj* [NL *acinus* + E *-o-* + *tubular*] **:** of or relating to a gland or other structure made up of tubular acini

ac·i·nous \'asənəs\ *adj* [F or L; F *acineux*, fr. L *acinosus*, fr. *acinus* + *-osus* -ous] **:** consisting of or containing acini

ac·i·nus \'asənəs, ə'sīnəs\ *n, pl* **aci·ni** \-ˌnī\ [NL, fr. L, berry, grape, berry or grape seed] **1 a :** a small seed or kernel (as of the grape) **b :** an individual drupelet in a multiple fruit (as in the raspberry) **2** *anat* **:** one of the small sacs or alveoli in which the ultimate ramifications of the duct of a racemose gland terminate and which are lined or filled with the secreting cells

ac·i·pen·ser \¦asə¦pen(t)sə(r)\ *n, cap* [NL, fr. L, a fish (prob. sturgeon)] **:** a genus (the type of the family Acipenseridae) of ganoid fishes that includes most sturgeons — **ac·i·pen·ser·id** \-rəd\ *n or adj* — **ac·i·pen·ser·ine** \ˌ=='==ˌrīn\ *adj*

ac·i·pen·ser·es \ˌasə'pen(t)səˌrēz\ *or* **ac·i·pen·ser·oi·dei** \ˌ==ˌ=='rȯidēˌī\ [*Acipenseres*, NL, fr. pl. of *Acipenser; Acipenseroidei*, NL, fr. *Acipenser* + *-oidei*] *syn of* CHONDROSTEI

ac·i·pen·ser·oid \ˌ=='==ˌrȯid\ *adj or n* [NL *Acipenseroidei*] **:** CHONDROSTEAN

ack *abbr* acknowledge; acknowledgment

ack–ack \'ak·¦ak\ *n* -s *often attrib* [Brit. signalmen's telephone pron. of *AA*, abbr. of *antiaircraft*] **:** an antiaircraft gun or its fire **:** antiaircraft guns or their fire ⟨batteries of *ack-ack*⟩

ackee *var of* AKEE

ack em·ma \(')ak·'emə\ *adv* [fr. Brit. signalmen's telephone pron. of *A.M.*] *Brit* **:** before noon

ack·er \'ākər, 'a-\ *n* -s [ME *aker* tidal wave, sea current] *now dial Eng* **:** a ripple or a patch of ruffled water

ack·ey \'akē\ *n* -s [alter. of *akee*, the seeds of which were used as weights roughly equivalent to 20 grains of gold dust] **1 :** a silver coin struck in England in 1796 and 1818 for use on the Gold Coast in western Africa **2 :** a unit of value equivalent to one ackey ⟨½-*ackey* and ¼-*ackey* coins were struck⟩

ackgt *abbr* acknowledgment

acknow *vt* **acknew; acknown; acknowing; acknows** [alter. (influenced by such words as *accord, account*) of ME *aknowen*, fr. OE *oncnāwan* to recognize, confess, fr. *on* + *cnāwan* to know — more at ON, KNOW] *obs* **:** to confess knowledge of

ac·knowl·edge \ik'nälij, ak-,ək-, -ēj,-əj, *Brit sometimes* -ōl-\ *vb* -ED/-ING/-S [*ac-* (as in *acknow*) + *knowledge*] *vt* **1 :** to show by word or act that one has knowledge of and agrees to (a fact or truth) ⟨ends generally *acknowledged* to be good —T.B.Macaulay⟩ **:** concede to be real or true ⟨~ that the bombing . . . was a mistake —Norman Cousins⟩ **:** ADMIT **2 a :** to show by word or act that one has knowledge of and respect for the rights, claims, authority, or status of ⟨~ an important contribution to the work⟩ **:** recognize, honor, or respect esp. publicly ⟨*acknowledged* him first citizen of the town⟩ **b :** to take notice of **:** indicate recognition and acceptance of ⟨she *acknowledged* his greeting by a slight inclination of the head⟩ **3 a :** to show by word or act that one has knowledge of and regard for (a duty, obligation, or indebtedness) ⟨~ their moral obligation to the people⟩ **:** express or admit gratitude or obligation for (as a gift, favor, or obligation) ⟨~ his services⟩ **b :** to make known to a sender or giver the receipt of (what has been sent or given) or the fact of (one's having received what has been sent or given) ⟨~ a gift⟩ ⟨~ receipt of a letter⟩ **4 :** to recognize as genuine **:** assent to (as a legal instrument) so as to give validity **:** avow or admit in legal form ⟨~ a deed⟩ ~ *vi* **:** to indicate the receipt and understanding of a message ⟨the pilot *acknowledged* by dipping the plane's wings⟩

syn ADMIT, OWN, AVOW, CONFESS: ACKNOWLEDGE indicates making known to others or recognizing to one's self what might be kept back, suppressed, or left uncertain, esp. under the influence of stress, pressure, or persuasion ⟨I was still smarting at his too candid criticism, all the more because in my heart I *acknowledged* its truth —W.H.Hudson⟩ ⟨with a perversity which he *acknowledged* frankly, he imagined that he had been devoted to her —Jean Stafford⟩ ⟨he started life as the illegitimate son of a Florentine lawyer and a woman of humble origin. His father *acknowledged* him —Stringfellow Barr⟩ ADMIT may be used in situations involving greater reluctance to make known, disclose, grant, or concede and greater stress or pressure ⟨those in whom reason is weak are often unwilling to *admit* this as regards themselves, though all *admit* it in regard to others —Bertrand Russell⟩ ⟨principally because of false pride few people will *admit* being apprehensive or airsick in flight and except in extreme circumstances these cases usually pass unnoticed —H.G.Armstrong⟩ ⟨at last the government at Washington *admitted* its mistake — which governments seldom do —Willa Cather⟩ OWN lacks any special suggestion about the manner or circumstances of an admission or acknowledgment but may apply to admissions having a certain closeness to the personality or individuality of whoever is making them ⟨then let me *own* I'm an aesthetic sham —W.S.Gilbert⟩ ⟨here we *own* to a little private preference —Olin Downes⟩ ⟨I *own* that I had sustained myself through this journey on thoughts of the cheery welcome ahead —Elizabeth Bowen⟩ AVOW suggests not unwilling disclosure but bold, firm declaration, with willingness to repeat or assert in the face of hostility ⟨in a pamphlet defending his political activity, he *avowed* beliefs and displayed a fearlessness that were to make him a national figure thirty years later —F.W.Scott⟩ ⟨let me *avow* at once that I enter this discussion as a layman speaking to laymen —J.S.Dickey⟩ CONFESS may apply to an acknowledgment, often reluctant, of a weakness, failure, omission, guilt, or sin ⟨in his potterings over occultisms he was *confessing* the sterility of intellectual interests —V.L. Parrington⟩ ⟨must I go on weakly *confessing* to you things a woman ought to conceal —Thomas Hardy⟩ ⟨I *confess* myself guilty of this error —J.S.Kenyon⟩ ⟨to *confess* a crime⟩

ac·knowl·edge·a·ble \-əbəl\ *adj* **:** capable of being acknowledged

acknowledged *adj* **:** generally known and openly stated to be real or true **:** RECOGNIZED, ACCEPTED, ADMITTED ⟨~ leader of the community⟩ ⟨~ existence of errors⟩ — **ac·knowl·edged·ly** \-j(ə)dlē, -li\ *adv*

ac·knowl·edg·ment *also* **ac·knowl·edge·ment** \-jmənt\ *n* -s **1 a :** the act of acknowledging **b :** recognition or favorable notice of an act or achievement ⟨received the ~ he deserved as a poet⟩ **2 :** a thing done or given in recognition of something received ⟨an ~ came in the mail⟩ ⟨an author's ~*s* of assistance⟩ **3 a :** a declaration or avowal of one's act or a fact to give it legal validity; *specif* **:** a declaration before a duly qualified public officer by one who has executed an instrument that the execution was his free act and deed **b :** the formal certificate made by an officer before whom one has acknowledged a deed including as an essential part the signature and seal of the officer

acknown *past part of* ACKNOW

acknows *pres 3d sing of* ACKNOW

ac·le \'aklē, ə'klā\ *n* -s [Tag *aklé*] **1 :** a tall Asiatic tree (*Xylia xylocarpa*) **2 :** the very heavy hard durable wood of the acle — called also *pyinkado* **3 :** a Philippine timber tree (*Albizzia acle*) used for cabinetwork and furniture

aclei·di·an \(')ā¦klīdēən, ə'k-\ *or* **aclid·i·an** \-id-,-īd-\ *adj* [F *acléidien, aclidien*, fr. *a-* [2]a- + Gk *kleid-, kleis* key, bar, clavicle + F *-ien* -ian] **:** having no clavicles

acli·nal \(')ā¦klīnᵊl\ *adj* [[2]*a-* + *-clinal*] **:** having no inclination **:** HORIZONTAL

aclin·ic line \(')ā¦klinik-\ *n* [[2]*a-* + *-clinic*] **:** an imaginary line on the earth's surface roughly parallel to the geographical equator and passing through those points where a magnetic needle if suspended freely has no dip or inclination and assumes a horizontal position — called also *magnetic equator;* compare AGONIC LINE, ISOCLINIC LINE

ac·maea \ak'mēə, 'akmēə\ *n* [NL, fr. Gk *akmaios* at the height, in full bloom, in the prime, fr. *akmē*] **1** *cap* **:** a cosmopolitan genus (the type of the family Acmaeidae) comprising small conical usu. dark-colored limpets **2** -s **:** a limpet of the genus *Acmaea*

ac·mae·idae \ak'mēəˌdē\ *n pl, cap* [NL, fr. *Acmaea*, type genus + *-idae*] **:** a family of gastropod mollusks (suborder Docoglossa) comprising the typical limpets with conical shell, fringed mantle, and a single plumelike ctenidium — see ACMAEA

ac·me \'akmē\ *n* -s [Gk *akmē* point, highest point, culmination; akin to Gk *akē* point — more at EDGE] **1 :** the highest point or stage (as of growth or development) ⟨reached the ~ of its power⟩ **:** the utmost degree **:** HEIGHT, PEAK, SUMMIT ⟨the ~ of perfection⟩ **2** *archaic* **:** the period of maturity or full growth **3 :** a hypothetical period of maximum evolutionary activity intermediate in the phylogenetic history of a stock between an initial emergent phase and a terminal aging phase

acme harrow *n* **:** a harrow having curved stiff blades attached to a transverse horizontal frame and projecting rearward that crush the clods in front and stir the surface soil in the rear — called also *blade harrow, curved knife-tooth harrow, pulverizer*

ac·mes·the·sia *also* **ac·maes·the·sia** \ˌakˌmes'thēzh(ē)ə\ *n* -s [NL, fr. Gk *akmē* point + NL *esthesia, aesthesia*] *psychol* **:** cutaneous sensation of a sharp point but without pain

acme thread *n* **:** an American screw thread having a section that is a mean between the V threads and square threads

ac·mic \'akmik\ *also* **ac·mat·ic** \(')ak¦mad·ik\ *adj* [*acme* + *-ic* or *-atic* (as in *automatic*)] **:** of or relating to the acme or an acme

ac·mite \'akˌmīt\ *n* -s [G *achmit*, fr. Gk *akmē* + G *-it* -ite] **:** a mineral consisting of a brown or green silicate of sodium and iron $NaFe(SiO_3)_2$ belonging to the pyroxene group and often found in long prismatic crystals characteristically pointed (hardness 6–6.5, sp. gr. 3.50–3.55) — called also *aegirite*

ac·mon·i·tal \ak'mänəˌtal\ *n* -s [It, fr. *acciaio monetario italiano* Italian monetary steel] **:** a stainless steel alloy used esp. for low-denomination coins esp. in Italy and Albania

ac·ne \'aknē\ *n* -s [Gk *aknē* eruption on the face, MS var. of *akmē*, lit., point — more at ACME] **:** any of several inflammatory diseases involving the oil glands and hair follicles of the skin; *specif* **:** ACNE VULGARIS — compare COMEDO, PIMPLE

ac·ne·form \'aknēˌfȯrm\ *or* **ac·ne·iform** \'aknēəˌfȯrm, ak'n-\ *adj* [NL *acne* + E *-form, -iform*] **:** resembling acne

ac·ne ro·sa·cea \ˌaknērōˈzās(h)ēə\ *n, pl* **ac·nae rosace·ae** \-(ˌ)nērōˈzās(h)ēˌē\ [NL, rose-colored acne] **:** acne involving the skin of the nose, forehead, and cheeks common in middle age and characterized by congestion, flushing, telangiectasis, and marked nodular swelling of tissues esp. of the nose

ac·ne vul·gar·is \ˌaknē,vəlˈga(a)rəs\ *n, pl* **ac·nae vulgar·es** \-(ˌ)nē,vəlˈga(a)(ˌ)rēz\ [NL, lit., common acne] **:** a chronic acne involving mainly the face, chest, and shoulders common in adolescent humans and various domestic animals and characterized by the intermittent formation of discrete papular or pustular lesions often resulting in considerable scarring — compare ACNE ROSACEA

ac·ni·da \akˈnīdə\ *n, cap* [NL, fr. ²a- + Gk *knidē* nettle — more at CNIDA] **:** a genus of American herbs (family Amaranthaceae) having entire leaves, greenish spicate flowers, and small utricles — see WATER HEMP 1

ac·ni·dar·ia \ˌaknəˈda(a)rēə\ [NL, fr. ²a- + Gk *knidē* nettle + NL *-aria*] *syn of* CTENOPHORA

ac·ni·do·spo·rid·ia \akˌnīdəspōˈridēə\ *n pl, cap* [NL, fr. ²a- + *cnid-* (fr. Gk *knidē* nettle) + *-sporidia*] **:** a subclass of Sporozoa comprising a number of forms of questionable relationship including the orders Sarcosporidia and Haplosporidia all having simple spores formed in a manner unlike that of the Telosporidia — **ac·ni·do·spo·rid·i·an** \ˌ≈≈≈≈ˌ≈ēən\ *adj or n*

ac·o·as·ma \ˌa(ˌ)kōˈazmə\ *n, pl* **acoasmas** \-məz\ *or* **acoasma·ta** \-mədˑə\ [NL, by alter.] **:** ACOUSMA

ac·o·can·thera \ˌakōˈkanthərə\ *n, cap* [NL, fr. Gk *akōkē* point, cutting edge (fr. *akē* point) + NL *-anthera* — more at EDGE] **:** a genus of African shrubs or trees (family Apocynaceae) most of them very poisonous having thick leathery leaves and odorous white flowers

acock \əˈ-\ *adj* [¹a- + *cock* (to turn up)] **:** turned up or tilted **:** COCKED ⟨with ears ~⟩

acock·bill \əˈkäk,bil\ *adv (or adj)* [*acock* + *bill* (end of an anchor)] **1** *of an anchor* **:** in place at the cathead or bow and ready to be dropped **2** *of a ship's yards* **:** in a tipped-up position **:** at an angle to the deck

acoel \āˈsēl\ *n* -s [NL *Acoela*] **:** a marine flatworm of the Acoela

acoe·la \(ˈ)āˈsēlə\ *n pl, cap* [NL, fr. ²a- + *coeloma* coelom] **:** an order or other division of Turbellaria that is sometimes regarded as a suborder of Rhabdocoela and comprises marine flatworms that lack a digestive cavity with definite walls and that receive food into a porous mass of endodermal tissue

acoe·lo·ma·ta \ˌāsēˈlōmədˑə\ *n pl, cap* [NL, fr. ²a- + *coeloma* + *-ata*] *in some classifications* **:** the Metazoa lacking a true body cavity regarded as a natural group (1) including the sponges and coelenterates and often the lower worms or (2) including only certain worms

acoe·lom·ate \(ˈ)āˈsēlə,māt; ˌāsēˈlōmət, -sə-\ *also* **acoe·lom·a·tous** \ˌāsēˈlämədˑəs, -sə-, -ōm-\ *adj* [²a- + *coelomate, coelomatous*] **:** without a coelom — compare EUCOELOMATE

acoe·lom·ous \(ˈ)āˈsēləməs\ *adj* [²a- + NL *coelom* + E *-ous*] **:** ACOELOMATE

acoe·lous \-ləs\ *adj* [²a- + *coelom* + *-ous*] **1 :** lacking a true stomach or digestive tract **2 :** lacking a true body cavity

acoem·e·ti \əˈsemə,tī\ *also* **acoem·e·tae** \-,tē\ *n pl, usu cap* [ML, fr. LGk *akoimētoi*, fr. pl. of Gk *akoimētos* sleepless, fr. *a-* ²a- + (assumed) *koimētos*, verbal of *koiman* to lull, put to sleep, go to sleep; akin to Gk *keisthai* to lie — more at HOME] **:** monks of large 5th century and 6th century Eastern monasteries who were noted esp. for their choral singing or recitation of the divine office in constant and never interrupted relays

acoe·nes·the·sia *or* **ace·nes·the·sia** \ˌā,sēnəsˈthēzhə, -en-\ *n* -s [NL, fr. ²a- + *coenesthesia, cenesthesia*] **:** loss of awareness of one's own bodily parts or organs **:** absence of coenesthesia

ac·o·ine \ˈakə,wēn, -,wən\ *n* -s [prob. fr. G *akoin*, prob. anagram of *kokain* cocaine — more at COCAINE] **:** a white crystalline derivative $C_{23}H_{26}ClN_3O_3$ of guanidine used as a local anesthetic

ac·o·la·pis·sa \ˌakələˈpisə\ *n, pl* **acolapissa** *or* **acolapissas** *usu cap* [Choctaw *Okla pisa*, lit., watchmen, guardians, spies, fr. *okla* people, tribe + *pisa* one who sees, observer] **1 :** an extinct Muskogean people of Louisiana and Mississippi **2 :** a member of the Acolapissa people

acold \əˈ-\ *adj* [ME, prob. alter. (influenced by *cold*, adj.) of *acoled*, past part. of *acolen* to become cold, fr. OE *ācōlian*, fr. *ā-* (perfective prefix) + *cōlian* to become cold — more at ABEAR, COOL] *archaic* **:** COLD, CHILLED

acol·hua \əˈkōl,wä\ *n, pl* **acolhua** *or* **acolhuas** *usu cap* [Sp, fr. Nahuatl, lit., strong men, fr. *acollo* shoulder + *hua* having] **1 :** a Nahuatl people of Mexico allied with the Aztec and Tlacopan **2 :** a member of the Acolhua people — **acol·huan** \-,wän\ *adj, usu cap*

ac·o·lu·thic \ˌakəˈlüthik\ *adj* [Gk *akolouthos* following + E *-ic* — more at ACOLYTE] **:** following immediately (as a visual afterimage) upon the primary activity aroused by a stimulus

ac·o·lyte \ˈakə,līt, *usu* -īd·+V\ *n* -s [ME *acolite, acolyt*, fr. OF & ML; OF *acolite*, fr. ML *acoluthus, acolythus, acolytus, acolitus*, fr. MGk *akolouthos*, fr. Gk, adj., following, fr. *a-* (var. of *ha-* together) + *-kolouthos* (akin to *keleuthos* path); akin to Gk *homos* same and to Gk *kellein* to drive — more at SAME, HOLD] **1 a** *Roman Catholicism* **:** a cleric ordained to the highest of the four minor orders in the Latin Church, his duties being to light and carry candles, prepare the wine and water used at mass, and assist the ministers at mass; *also* **:** one not ordained who performs the duties formerly reserved to an ordained acolyte **:** ALTAR BOY, SERVER **b :** one who assists the celebrant or other officiating ministers in a religious service of any Christian church by the performance of minor duties **2 :** one who attends or assists **:** FOLLOWER ⟨admiring teen-age ~*s* helping him about the depot —Ben Riker⟩

acol·y·thate \əˈkälə,thāt, -,thət\ *n* -s [NL *acolythatus*, fr. ML *acolythatus, acolytatus*, adj., of an acolyte, fr. *acolythus, acolytus* acolyte + L *-atus* -ate] **:** the office or state of an acolyte

acol·y·thist \-,thəst\ *n* -s [ML *acolythus* + E *-ist*] *archaic* **:** ACOLYTE

¹**aco·ma** \ˈäkə,mō, ˈak-\ *n, pl* **acoma** *or* **acomas** *usu cap* [Sp, fr. Acoma *Akóme*, lit., people of the white rock] **1 :** a Keresan pueblo people of New Mexico **2 :** a member of the Acoma people

²**aco·ma** \əˈkōmə\ *n* -s [AmerSp] **:** MASTIC BULLY

aco·man \ˈäkəmən, ˈak-\ *or* **aco·ma·ni·an** \ˌ≈≈ˈmānēən, -nyən\ *n* -s *usu cap* [¹*Acoma* + *-an, -ian*] **:** ¹ACOMA

acone \ˈā,kōn\ *adj* [²a- + *cone*] *of insect eyes* **:** having ommatidia that lack the crystalline cone of the lens system and that form the image by apposition — compare EUCONE

acon·ic acid \əˈkänik-, aˈ-\ *n* [contr. of *aconitic*] **:** a crystalline lactonic acid $C_4H_3O_2COOH$ formed indirectly from aconitic acid

ac·o·nine \ˈakə,nēn, -,nən\ *n* -s [ISV, contr. of *aconitine*] **:** a colorless alkaloid $C_{25}H_{41}NO_9$ obtained by hydrolysis of aconitine

ac·o·nit·al \ˌakəˈnīdˑəl\ *adj* [*aconite* + *-al*] **:** having the characteristics of aconite

acon·i·tase \əˈkänə,tās\ *n* -s [*aconitic* + *-ase*] **:** an enzyme occurring in many animal and plant tissues that accelerates the conversion of citric acid first into aconitic acid and then into isocitric acid

acon·i·tate \-,tāt\ *n* -s [*aconitic* + *-ate*] **:** a salt or ester of aconitic acid

ac·o·nite \ˈakə,nīt, *usu* -īd·+V\ *n* -s [MF or L; MF, fr. L *aconitum*, fr. Gk *akoniton*, perh. fr. neut. of *akonitos* without dust, without struggle, fr. *a-* ²a- + *-konitos* (fr. *konis* dust) — more at INCINERATE] **1 :** a plant of the genus *Aconitum; esp* **:** the common monkshood (*A. napellus*) — see WINTER ACONITE **2 :** the dried tuberous root of a monkshood (*Aconitum napellus*) formerly much used as a cardiac and respiratory sedative

aconite violet *n* **:** a moderate purple that is redder and duller than heliotrope (sense 4a), bluer, less strong, and slightly darker than average amethyst, and bluer and duller than average lilac (sense 3a)

ac·o·ni·tia \ˌakəˈnish(ē)ə\ *n* -s [NL, fr. *Aconitum* + *-ia*] **:** ACONITINE

ac·o·nit·ic acid \ˌakəˌnid·ik-\ *n* [ISV *aconite* + *-ic*] **:** a white crystalline acid $C_3H_3(COOH)_3$ known in cis and trans forms that occurs in aconite, sugar cane, and beet root and is obtained as a byproduct in sugar manufacture or by dehydration of citric acid; 1,2,3-propene-tricarboxylic acid

acon·i·tine \əˈkänə,tēn, -,tən\ *n* -s [G *akonitin*, fr. *akonit* aconite + *-in* -ine] **:** a white crystalline intensely poisonous alkaloid $C_{34}H_{47}NO_{11}$ from the root and leaves of aconite

ac·o·ni·tum \ˌakəˈnīd·əm\ *n* [NL, fr. L] **1** *cap* **:** a genus of poisonous herbs (family Ranunculaceae) found in temperate regions and having palmately divided leaves and very irregular blue, purple, or yellow flowers **2** -s **:** a plant of the genus *Aconitum* — see MONKSHOOD, WOLFSBANE **3** -s **:** ACONITE 2

acon·ti·as \əˈkänchēəs\ *n, cap* [NL, fr. Gk *akontias*, a snake, fr. *akont-, akōn* javelin, dart, fr. *akē* point — more at EDGE] **:** a genus of scincoid lizards with the limbs rudimentary or lacking

acon·ti·um \əˈkänchēəm\ *n, pl* **acon·tia** \-ēə\ *or* **acontiums** [NL, fr. Gk *akontion* javelin, dim. of *akont-, akōn*] *zool* **:** one of the free threads continued from the lower ends of the septa of certain actinians, histologically similar to cnidoglandular bands, protruding through the mouth when the animal contracts, and prob. defensive

a con·trar·io \ˌäkənˈtra(a)rē,ō\ *adv* [L] **:** by or from contraries — used of an argument based on contrast

aco·pa \əˈkōpə\ [NL, fr. ²a- + Gk *kōpē* oar; fr. the belief that they are without directive organs] *syn of* ASCIDIACEA

acorn \ˈā,kȯrn, -ō(ə)n *also* ˈākə(r)n\ *n* -s [ME, alter. (influenced by *corn*) of *akern*, fr. OE *æcern*; akin to MHG *ackeran* acorns collectively, ON *akarn* fruit of forest trees, Goth *akran* fruit, produce, IrGael *āirne* sloe, Russ *yagoda* berry] **1 :** the nut of the oak usu. seated in or surrounded by a hard woody cupule of indurated bracts **2 :** a small conical or globular object (as of wood or metal): as **a :** a turned ornamentation commonly used as a finial or pendant in Jacobean furniture **b :** an ornamental piece of wood fixed above the vane of a masthead or a piece of metal used at the top of an upright in a ship's railing **3 :** a grayish yellowish brown that is darker than deer and slightly yellower and lighter than olive wood — called also *meadowlark*

acorns

acorn barnacle *also* **acorn shell** *n* **:** any of numerous conical sessile barnacles (family Balanidae) common on littoral rocks

acorn calf *n* [so called fr. the belief the condition is caused by an excess of acorns in prenatal diet] **:** a calf exhibiting a congenital anomaly involving shortening of the limbs, malformation of the skull, incoordination, and intestinal tympany

acorn cup *n* **:** the cupule of an acorn

acorn disease *n* **:** a virus disease of citrus (as oranges) considered identical with or an expression of stubborn disease and characterized by malformed and more or less acorn-shaped fruit

acorn duck *n* [so called fr. its eating acorns] **:** WOOD DUCK 1

acorn squash *n* **:** a winter squash about four to six inches in width, oval to somewhat acorn-shaped, having a longitudinally grooved and ridged surface, with skin usu. dark green in color but varying to orange yellow esp. at maturity or in storage, and with sweet yellow to orange flesh

acorn tube *n* **:** a very small vacuum tube resembling an acorn in shape and used at extremely high frequencies

acorn weevil *n* **:** any of several long-snouted weevils (genus *Balaninus*) whose larvae feed on acorns

acorn worm *n* [so called fr. the shape of the front part of the body] **:** a worm of the group Enteropneusta

à corps per·du \äkȯȯrperdüe\ *adv* [F, lit., with lost body] **:** IMPETUOUSLY, DESPERATELY

ac·o·rus \ˈakərəs\ *n, cap* [NL, fr. L, an aromatic plant (perh. sweet flag), fr. Gk *akoros* (*Iris pseudacorus*)] **:** a genus of rushlike herbs (family Araceae) with the flowers in a close spadix — see SWEET FLAG

acos·mic \(ˈ)āˈkäzmik\ *adj* [²a- + *cosmic*] **:** denying the objective reality of the temporal world **:** transcendental in a world-negating sense ⟨the Hindu's two aspects of God: cosmic and ~, relative and transcendental⟩

acos·mism *or* **akos·mism** \(ˈ)āˈkäz,mizəm\ *n* -s [G *akosmismus*, fr. *a-* ²a- + *kosmos* cosmos + *-ismus* -ism — more at COSMOS] **:** a theory that denies that the universe possesses any absolute reality or that it has any existence apart from God — compare PANTHEISM

acos·mist \-zməst\ *n* -s [*acosmism* + *-ist*] **:** one who believes in or teaches acosmism — **acos·mis·tic** \ˌā,käzˈmistik\ *adj*

acot·y·le·don \ˌā,käd·ᵊlˈēd·ᵊn, ˈā≈≈,≈≈, ˈ≈,≈≈,≈≈\ *n* -s [F *acotylédone*, fr. *a-* ²a- + *cotylédone* cotyledon] **:** a plant without cotyledons (as the dodder) — **acot·y·le·don·ous** \ˌ≈,≈≈ˈ≈≈əs, -ˈed-\ *adj*

acou- *or* **acouo-** *comb form* [F *acou-*, fr. Gk *akouein* to hear — more at HEAR] **:** hearing **:** listening ⟨*acou*meter⟩ ⟨*acouo*phonia⟩

acou·chi *also* **acu·chi** \əˈküshē\ *or* **acouchi resin** *n* -s [native name in Guiana] **:** a resin similar in nature and uses to elemi and obtained from various So. American trees of the genus *Protium*

acou·me·ter \əˈkümēd·ə(r), aˈ-, ˈa,kü,mēd·-\ *n* -s [F *acoumètre*, fr. *acou-* + *-mètre* -meter] **:** AUDIOMETER

acou·me·try \əˈkümə·trē, aˈ-\ *n* -ES [F *acoumétrie*, fr. *acou-* + *-métrie* -metry] **:** AUDIOMETRY

-acusia *or* **-acusia** *n comb form, pl* **-acousiae** *or* **-acusiae** [NL, fr. Gk *akousis* (fr. *akouein* to hear + *-sis*) + NL *-ia*] **:** hearing ⟨presby*acousia*⟩ ⟨hyper*acusia*⟩

acous·ma \əˈküzmə, aˈ-\ *n, pl* **acousmas** \-məz\ *or* **acousma·ta** \-mədˑə\ [NL, fr. Gk, something heard, fr. *akouein* to hear] **1 :** an auditory hallucination of a simple nonverbal character (as a buzzing or ringing) **2** *acousmata pl* **:** exoteric teachings

ac·ous·mat·ic \ˌa,küzˈmad·ik\ *n* -s [Gk *kousmatikos*, fr. *akousmat-, akousma* + *-ikos* -ic] **:** one who received the exoteric teachings of the Pythagoreans

¹**acous·tic** \əˈküstik, -tēk *also* -kyüs- *or* -kaùs-\ *or* **acous·ti·cal** \-əkəl, -ēk-\ *adj* [*acoustic* fr. Gk *akoustikos* of hearing, fr. *akoustos* heard, audible (fr. *akouein* to hear) + *-ikos* -ic; *acoustical* fr. *acoustic* + *-al* — more at HEAR] **1 a :** of, relating to, adapted to, or affecting the sense of hearing or the organs of hearing ⟨the ~ apparatus of the human ear⟩ — compare AUDITORY, AURAL **b :** of or relating to sound or sound waves ⟨the ~ intensity of a shrill voice⟩ **:** deriving from sound ⟨~ energy⟩ **c :** controlled or actuated by sound or sound waves ⟨the ship was blown up by an ~ mine⟩ **d :** influencing sound or sound waves (as in direction or speed) ⟨their voices rang back from the ~ barrier of the high cliff before them⟩ **e :** of, relating to, or concerned with acoustics ⟨~ engineering⟩ **:** specializing in acoustics ⟨an ~ contractor⟩ **2 a :** made for, designed for, or having the quality of facilitating or improving the perception of sound ⟨a tiny ~ device very efficient in promoting hearing⟩ **:** designed or serving to produce, carry, or diffuse sound ⟨a highly efficient ~ system⟩ **b :** made for, designed for, or having the quality of controlling sound; *esp* **:** designed to eliminate or lessen noise and other unwanted sound (as reverberations or echoes) **:** noise-absorbent or sound-absorbent ⟨an ~ ceiling⟩ ⟨~ wallboard⟩ ⟨~ tile⟩ **3 a** (1) **:** of, relating to, adapted to, or produced by a method of recording sound by the use of a thin diaphragm vibrated directly by sound waves, the vibrations being in turn transmitted directly by the diaphragm to a recording stylus that cuts corresponding grooves (as in a revolving disc) (2) **:** of, relating to, adapted to, or produced by a method of reproducing sound by the use of a reproducing stylus whose vibrations are transmitted directly to a thin diaphragm, the corresponding vibrations of the diaphragm being directly amplified to produce audible sound ⟨an ~ recording⟩ — compare ELECTRIC 1b **b :** of, relating to, or adapted to measurement of depth (as of the ocean) by means of sonic or ultrasonic vibrations ⟨~ soundings⟩ — **acous·ti·cal·ly** \-k(ə)lē, -li\ *adv*

²**acoustic** *var of* ACOUSTICS

acoustical feedback *n* **:** a rumbling, whining, or whistling sound resulting esp. from excessive leakage of sound from the output of an electroacoustical system to the input

acoustic area *or* **acoustic center** *n* **:** a sensory area of the temporal lobe of the cerebral cortex receiving afferent projection fibers concerned with the sense of hearing

acoustic bass *n* **:** a 32-foot or 64-foot organ register obtained by the production of resultant tones by smaller pipes — compare COMBINATION TONE

acoustic duct *or* **acoustic meatus** *n* **:** the external auditory meatus

ac·ous·ti·cian \ˌa,küˈstishən, ə,k- *also* -kyü- *or* -kaù-\ *n* -s [*acoustics* + *-ian*] **1 :** one versed in the science of acoustics **2 :** one versed in the practice of acoustics **:** one who designs, makes, or repairs acoustic materials, instruments, and apparatus or who sets up or looks after acoustic installations

acoustic impedance *n* **:** the ratio of sound-pressure amplitude to volume-velocity amplitude across a given surface in a medium transmitting sound, the relationship being measured in acoustic ohms and commonly treated as a complex quantity whose components are acoustic reactance and acoustic resistance **:** the acoustic analogue of reactance in alternating-current circuits

acoustic inertance *or* **acoustic mass** *n* **:** the impeding effect of inertia upon the transmission of sound in a conduit, equal in a tubular conduit (as an organ pipe) to the mass of the vibrating medium divided by the square of the cross section **:** the acoustic analogue of alternating-current-circuit inductance — called also *inertance*

acoustic interferometer *n* **:** an instrument similar in principle to the interferometer and adapted to the accurate measurement of sound wavelengths and velocities

acoustic nerve *n* **:** AUDITORY NERVE

acoustic ohm *n* **:** OHM

acous·ti·co·lat·er·al \əˌküstə(ˌ)kōˈ-, -stē- *also* -kyüs- *or* -kaùs-\ *adj* [¹*acoustic* + *-o-* + *lateral*] **:** of or relating to the lateral-line organs and their central connection with the ear

acoustic organ *n* **:** ORGAN OF CORTI

acoustic radiation pressure *n* **:** a feeble net increase in atmospheric pressure experienced by a surface upon which sound waves are incident — compare SOUND PRESSURE

acoustic reactance *n* **:** the imaginary component of acoustic impedance measured in acoustic ohms and concerned with the effects of inertia and elasticity of a medium transmitting sound and differing one-quarter cycle in phase from acoustic resistance **:** the acoustic analogue of reactance in alternating-current circuits

acoustic resistance *n* **:** the real component of acoustic impedance measured in acoustic ohms and involving dissipation of energy through internal friction of a medium transmitting sound and differing one-quarter cycle in phase from acoustic reactance **:** the analogue of resistance in alternating-current circuits

acous·tics \≈ˈ≈tiks, -ēks\ *n pl but sing or pl in constr* **1 :** a science that deals with the production, control, transmission, reception, and effects of sound and of the phenomena of hearing **2 a** *also* **acoustic :** the aggregate of qualities (as absence of echo or reverberation) of an enclosure (as an auditorium) or other area that affects production, control, transmission, reception, and perception of sound **:** acoustic properties or peculiarities **:** acoustic environment ⟨the ~ of this room are excellent⟩ ⟨in the clear, dead *acoustic* of such halls every musical fault is audible —Virgil Thomson⟩ **b :** the science of planning, building, equipping, or using an enclosure or other area with the object of achieving good acoustics

acoustic tubercle *n* **:** a pear-shaped prominence on the restiform body including the dorsal nucleus of the cochlear nerve

acpt *abbr* acceptance

¹**ac·quaint** \əˈkwānt *also* aˈ-\ *adj* [ME *aquointe, aquainte*, fr. OF *acointe*, fr. LL *accognitus*, past part. of *accognoscere* to know perfectly, fr. L *ad-* + *cognoscere* to know — more at COGNITION] *archaic* **:** ACQUAINTED

²**acquaint** \"\ *vb* -ED/-ING/-S [ME *acoynten, aquainten*, fr. OF *acointier*, fr. ML *accognitare*, fr. LL *acccognitus*] *vt* **1 :** to make known socially **:** INTRODUCE ⟨someone should make them ~*ed*⟩ ⟨I am not ~*ed* with him⟩ ⟨the manager wishes to get ~*ed* with every employee⟩ **2 :** INFORM, APPRISE ⟨~ a new employee with his duties⟩ ⟨we ~*ed* him with our plans⟩ ⟨~ oneself with the facts of a case⟩ **3** *obs* **:** ACCUSTOM, HABITUATE ~ *vi, archaic* **:** to become acquainted — usu. used with *with*
syn see INFORM

ac·quaint·ance \-ᵊn(t)s, -tən-\ *n* -s [ME *acointaunce, aquaintaunce*, fr. MF *acointance*, fr. *acointier* + *-ance*] **1 a :** personal knowledge ⟨an ~ with all types of men⟩ **:** FAMILIARITY, EXPERIENCE ⟨long ~ with Amazon river Indians⟩ **b :** the quality or state of being acquainted **:** mutual knowledge or familiarity ⟨their ~ was of long standing⟩ **2 a :** persons with whom one is acquainted ⟨let your men-*acquaintance* be of your husband's choice —Jonathan Swift⟩ — sometimes pl. in constr. ⟨the ~ . . . were unworthy of her —Jane Austen⟩ **b :** a not particularly close or intimate friend **:** a person with whom one has had some social contact but for whom one has no strong personal attachment **syn** see FRIEND

ac·quaint·ance·ship \-ānt³n(s),ship, -tən-\ *n* -s **:** ACQUAINTANCE 1b

acquaintant *n* -s [obs. F *acointant*, fr. pres. part. of *acointier*] *obs* **:** ACQUAINTANCE 2

acquainted *adj* [ME *acointed, aquainted*, fr. past part. of *acointen, aquainten*] **1 a :** being known to and having knowledge of ⟨he was here so little, we never really got ~ —Mary Austin⟩ ⟨thoroughly ~ with him⟩ **b** *archaic* **:** personally known **:** FAMILIAR **2 :** having personal knowledge of **:** being somewhat familiar with ⟨reveals herself as not too well ~ with the conditions of women in America —M.F.A.Montagu⟩

ac·quent \əˈkwent\ *adj* [ME *aquente*, var. of *aquainte*] *Scot* **:** ACQUAINTED

ac·quest \əˈkwest, aˈ-\ *n* -s [obs. F (now *acquêt*), fr. (assumed) VL *acquaesitum*, fr. neut. of *acquaesitus*, past part. of *acquaerere* to acquire, alter. of L *acquirere* — more at ACQUIRE] **1** *archaic* **:** the act or action of acquiring **2** *archaic* **:** ACQUISITION **3 :** property acquired through means other than inheritance

ac·qui·esce \ˌakwēˈes\ *vi* -ED/-ING/-S [F *acquiescer*, fr. L *acquiescere* to rest, rejoice in, acquiesce, fr. *ad-* + *quiescere* to be quiet — more at QUIET] **1** *obs* **:** to rest satisfied physically or mentally **2** *obs* **:** to remain submissive — used with *under* **3 :** to accept or comply tacitly or passively **:** accept as inevitable or indisputable — often used with *in*, sometimes with *to*, and formerly with *with* ⟨led by the influence of his upbringing to ~ too much —*Times Lit. Supp.*⟩ ⟨if we ~ in this poorly disguised swindle —Sam Hunter⟩ ⟨political sociologists today are often reluctant to ~ to Michels' law —L.S.Feuer⟩ **syn** see ASSENT

ac·qui·es·cence \ˌakwēˈesᵊn(t)s\ *n* -s [obs. F, fr. (assumed) VL *acquiescentia*, fr. L *acquiescent-, acquiescens* + *-ia*] **1 :** the act or action of acquiescing ⟨his immediate ~ to every demand⟩ — often used with *in*, sometimes with *to*, and formerly with *with* **2 :** the quality or state of being acquiescent **:** passive assent or submission ⟨too great an ~ in American foreign policy —Woodrow Wyatt⟩

acquiescency *n* -ES [obs. F *acquiescence* + E *-y*] *obs* **:** ACQUIESCENCE

ac·qui·es·cent \ˌakwēˈesᵊnt\ *adj* [L *acquiescent-, acquiescens*, pres. part. of *acquiescere*] **:** acquiescing or disposed to acquiesce ⟨they are, if anything, too law-abiding and too ~ —H. S. Commager⟩ — **ac·qui·es·cent·ly** *adv*

ac·quire \əˈkwī(ə)r, -īə *also* aˈ-\ *vt* -ED/-ING/-S [alter. (influenced by L *acquirere*) of earlier *acquere*, fr. ME *aqueren*, fr. MF *aquerre*, fr. L *acquirere*, fr. *ad-* + *-quirere* (fr. *quaerere* to seek, gain, obtain, ask)] **1 :** to come into possession, control, or power of disposal of often by some uncertain or unspecified means ⟨had accumulated for her about as much money as she had herself *acquired* —Arnold Bennett⟩ **2 :** to come to have as a characteristic, attribute, trait, or ability often by sustained effort ⟨he had taken kindly to these languages and had rapidly and easily mastered what many boys take years in *acquiring* —Samuel Butler †1902⟩ **syn** see GET

acquired *adj* **1 :** gained by or as a result of effort or experience ⟨~ wealth⟩ ⟨~ knowledge⟩ ⟨~ response⟩ — compare INNATE, NATIVE **2 :** attained by the individual by or as if by his own efforts: as **a** *of bodily qualities or characters* **:** relating to or being a part of the individual soma **:** caused by environmental forces (as use and disuse) and not subject to transmission from parent to offspring — distinguished from *hereditary* and *genic* **b** *of disease or abnormal states* **:** developed after birth ⟨~ heart disease⟩ — opposed to *congenital*

acquired immunity *n* **:** immunity taken on by a member of a naturally susceptible group (as following an attack of some diseases or as induced by injection of suitable antigens or antibodies) — compare ACTIVE IMMUNITY, NATURAL IMMUNITY

ac·quire·ment \-ī(ə)rmənt, -īəm-\ *n* -s **1 :** the act or action of acquiring **2 :** an attainment of mind or body usu. resulting from continued endeavor and self-cultivation **:** ACHIEVEMENT ⟨our men of the greatest genius have not been most distinguished for their ~*s* at school or at the university —William Hazlitt⟩

acquisite *adj* [L *acquisitus*] *obs* **:** ACQUIRED

ac·qui·si·tion \ˌakwə'zishən\ *n* -s [ME *acquisicioun*, fr. MF or L; MF *acquisition*, fr. L *acquisition-*, *acquisitio*, fr. *acquisitus* (past part. of *acquirere* to acquire) + *-ion-*, *-io* -ion — more at ACQUIRE] **1 :** the act or action of acquiring ⟨power resulting from the ~ of wealth⟩ ⟨the early ~ of self-control in the matter of fear —Bertrand Russell⟩ **2 :** a thing acquired or gained **:** ACQUIREMENT, GAIN — **ac·qui·si·tion ist** \-əst\ *n* -s

acquisition cost *n* **:** commissions and other selling expenses in insurance production

acquisititious *adj* [L *acquisit*us + E *-itious*] *obs* **:** ACQUIRED

ac·quis·i·tive \ə'kwizəd·iv, -ətiv *also* a'-\ *adj* [*acquisit*ion + *-ive*] **1 :** capable of acquiring **2 :** strongly desirous of acquiring and possessing **:** GRASPING ⟨in an ~ society the form that selfishness predominantly takes is monetary greed —Edgar Johnson⟩ **syn** see COVETOUS

ac·quis·i·tive·ness *n* -ES **:** the quality or state of being acquisitive

ac·quist \ə'kwist, a'-\ *n* -s [ML *acquistum*, alter. of L *acquisitum*, neut. of *acquisitus*, past part. of *acquirere* to acquire — more at ACQUIRE] **:** ACQUISITION 1

[1]ac·quit \ə'kwit *also* a'-; *usu* -id·+V\ *vt* **acquitted; acquitted; acquitting; acquits** [ME *aquiten*, fr. OF *aquiter*, fr. *a-* (fr. L *ad-*) + *quite* acquitted, free of, tranquil — more at QUIT] **1 a** *archaic* **:** to pay off (as a claim or debt) **b** *obs* **:** to pay back (something done for or to one) **:** REPAY, REQUITE **2 a** *obs* **:** to set free (as by ransoming) **b** *obs* **:** to free or rid (oneself) of anything **c :** to discharge completely (as from an obligation or accusation) ⟨the court *acquitted* the prisoner⟩ ⟨~ a man of liability⟩ **3 :** to perform (one's part) or conduct (oneself) usu. satisfactorily ⟨in their first battle the recruits *acquitted* themselves like veterans⟩ **syn** see BEHAVE, EXCULPATE

[2]acquit \"\ *adj* [ME, short for *aquited*, past part. of *aquiten*] *archaic* **:** ACQUITTED **:** set free **:** RID ⟨to be ~ fro my continual smart —Edmund Spenser⟩

acquitment *n* -s [F *acquittement*, fr. *acquitter* to acquit (fr. OF *aquiter*) + *-ment*] *obs* **:** ACQUITTAL

ac·quit·tal \ə'kwid·ᵊl, -itᵊl *also* a'-\ *n* -s [ME *aquitaille*, *aquital*, fr. AF *aquitaille*, fr. OF *aquiter* to acquit] **1** *obs* **:** PAYMENT, REQUITAL **2 :** release or discharge from debt or other liability **3 :** a setting free or deliverance from the charge of an offense by verdict of a jury, sentence of a court, or other legal process

[1]ac·quit·tance \-itᵊn(t)s\ *n* -s [ME *aquitaunce*, fr. MF *aquitance*, fr. *aquitant* (pres. part. of *aquiter*) + *-ance*] **1** *obs* **:** the settlement of a debt or other obligation **:** REPAYMENT **2** *archaic* **:** ACQUITTAL 2 **3 :** a writing evidencing a discharge **:** a receipt in full — compare RELEASE 2b **4 :** ACQUITTAL 3

[2]acquittance *vt* -ED/-ING/-S [ME *aquitauncen*, fr. *aquitaunce*, n.] *obs* **:** ACQUIT, DISCHARGE

acquittance roll *n*, *Brit* **:** a military payroll

acr- *or* **acro-** *also* **akr-** *or* **akro-** *comb form* [MF or Gk; MF *acro-*, fr. Gk *akr-*, *akro-*, fr. *akros* topmost, extreme; akin to Gk *akmē* point — more at EDGE] **1 :** beginning **:** end **:** tip ⟨*acro*logy⟩ **2 a :** top **:** peak **:** summit ⟨*acro*petal⟩ ⟨*acro*cephaly⟩ **b :** height ⟨*acro*phobia⟩ **c :** extremity of the body, esp. the human body ⟨*acro*cyanosis⟩

acrae·in \ə'krēən\ *n* -s [NL *Acraeinae* + E *-in*] **:** a self-defensive substance secreted by butterflies of the subfamily Acraeinae that is distasteful to birds and other predators

ac·rae·i·nae \ˌakrē'ī(ˌ)nē\ *n pl*, *cap* [NL, fr. *Acraea*, type genus (fr. L, fem. of *acraeus* living on the heights, fr. Gk *akraios*, fr. *akron* height) + *-inae*] **:** a subfamily of Nymphalidae consisting of chiefly African butterflies possessing distastefulness to predators and mimicked by many more edible butterflies

ac·ral \'akrəl\ *adj* [Gk *akra* end, extremity, highest point + E *-al*] **:** of or belonging to the extremities of peripheral body parts ⟨~ cyanosis⟩

acral·de·hyde \ə'kraldəˌhīd, a'-\ *n* -s [L *acr-*, *acer* sharp + E *aldehyde*] **:** ACROLEIN

[1]acra·nia \(')ā'krānēə\ *n* -s [NL, fr. [2]*a-* + *-crania*] **:** congenital partial or total absence of the skull

[2]acrania \"\ *n pl*, *cap* [NL, fr. [2]*a-* + *-crania* (fr. Gk *kranion* skull) — more at CRANIUM] *in some classifications* **:** a division of Chordata comprising Hemichordata, Urochordata, and Cephalochorda and including all the chordates without true heads and anterior brains — compare VERTEBRATA

[3]acrania \"\ [NL, fr. [2]*a-* + *-crania* (fr. Gk *kranion* skull)] *syn of* CEPHALOCHORDA

acra·ni·al \(')=¦==əl\ *adj* [NL [2]*Acrania* + E *-al*] **:** ACRANIATE

acra·ni·a·ta \¦āˌkrānē'äd·ə, -ād·ə\ [NL, fr. [2]*a-* + *Craniata*] *syn of* [2]ACRANIA

[1]acra·ni·ate \(')=¦==ˌət, -ˌāt\ *adj* [NL *Acraniata*] **:** of or relating to the major division Acrania

[2]acraniate \"\ *n* -s **:** a chordate of the major division Acrania

acra·sia \ə'krāzh(ē)ə\ *n*, *cap* [NL, prob. fr. Gk *akrasia* bad mixture, fr. *akratos* unmixed + *-ia*] **:** a genus (the type of the family Acrasiaceae) of saprophytic fungi of the order Acrasiales having amoeboid cells produced from spores and aggregated without fusion into a pseudoplasmodium and having a fruiting body, often with a sterile stalklike portion, formed by rounding up and contraction of the pseudoplasmodium

acra·si·a·les \əˌkrāz(h)ē'ā(ˌ)lēz\ *n pl*, *cap* [NL, fr. *Acrasia* + *-ales*] **:** an order of lower fungi related to the slime molds but having swarm spores without flagella that do not fuse into a true plasmodium — see ACRASIA; compare PSEUDOPLASMODIUM

acras·i·da \ə'krasədə\ *n pl*, *cap* [NL, fr. *Acrasia* + *-ida*] *in some classifications* **:** a suborder or order of Mycetozoa equivalent to Acrasiales

acra·si·e·ae \əˌkrāz(h)ē'ēˌē\ *n pl*, *cap* [NL, fr. *Acrasia* + *-eae*] *in some classifications* **:** Acrasiales regarded as a class distinct from Myxomycetes

acras·pe·da \(')ā'kraspədə\ *n pl*, *cap* [NL, fr. Gk *akraspeda*, neut. pl. of *akraspedos* without fringes, fr. *a-* [2]a- + *kraspedon* edge, border] *in former classifications* **:** a division of coelenterates comprising medusae lacking a swimming velum — compare SCYPHOZOA

acras·pe·dae \-ˌdē\ *syn of* ACRASPEDA

[1]acras·pe·dote \(')=¦==ˌdōt\ *adj* [NL *Acraspeda* + E *-ote*] **:** of or relating to the division Acraspeda

[2]acraspedote \"\ *adj* [[2]*a-* + *craspedote*] *of the segments of a tapeworm* **:** not overlapping

ac·ra·sy \'akrəsē, -əzē\ *n* -ES [Gk *akrasia* incontinence, debility, fr. *akratēs* powerless, incontinent, intemperate (fr. *a-* [2]a- + *kratos* strength) + *-ia* -y] *archaic* **:** EXCESS, INTEMPERANCE

acrawl \ə'-\ *adj* [[1]*a-* + *crawl*, v.] **:** CRAWLING ⟨like young black india-rubber kittens — all ~ —H.G.Wells⟩ ⟨highways ~ with cars⟩

acre \'ākə(r)\ *n* -s [ME, fr. OE *æcer;* akin to OHG *ackar* field, ON *akr* arable land, Goth *akrs* field, L *ager*, Gk *agros*, Skt *ajra*, L *agere* to drive — more at AGENT] **1 a :** a field esp. of arable or pasture land — archaic except in proper names or in compounds or phrases ⟨Long *Acre*⟩ ⟨black*acre*⟩ **b acres** *pl* **:** LANDS, ESTATE ⟨he commuted between his country ~*s* and his Madison Avenue office —*Time*⟩ ⟨these skills, like fat flocks or ancestral ~*s*, were passed from father to son —Harriot B. Barbour⟩ **2 :** any of various units of area based on an old approximate unit equal to the amount of land plowed by a yoke of oxen in a day; *esp* **:** a unit in the U.S. and England equal to 160 square rods ⟨a field of six ~*s*⟩ ⟨a 10-*acre* field⟩ — see MEASURE table; compare ARPENT **3 :** a broad expanse ⟨smiling valleys were turned into ~*s* of slums —Gilbert Highet⟩ **:** a large quantity — usu. used in pl. ⟨I have read ~*s* of source material on European history —H.E.Barnes⟩

acre·age \'āk(ə)rij, -ēj\ *n* -s **:** area in acres **:** ACRES

acre–foot \'==¦=\ *n*, *pl* **acre–feet :** the volume (as of irrigation water) that would cover one acre to a depth of one foot

acre–inch \'==¦=\ *n* **:** the volume (as of water or soil) equivalent to a depth of one inch over an acre of land

acre·man \'ākə(r)mən\ *n*, *pl* **acremen** [ME, fr. OE *æcerman*, fr. *æcer* field + *man* — more at ACRE, MAN] **:** the leader of the plow team on a medieval English manor

ac·rid \'akrəd\ *adj*, *usu* -ER/-EST [modif. (influenced by *acid*) of L *acr-*, *acer* sharp — more at EDGE] **1 :** unpleasantly or irritatingly sharp or strong to the taste ⟨strong brine is ~⟩ ⟨~ alum⟩ or to the smell ⟨~ sulfur fumes⟩ **:** stingingly bitter **:** CAUSTIC **2 :** deeply or violently bitter **:** excessively caustic, rancorous, or acrimonious ⟨an ~ temper⟩ ⟨an ~ denunciation⟩ **syn** see BITTER

ac·ri·dan \'akrəˌdan\ *also* **ac·ri·dane** \-ˌdān\ *n* -s [ISV, blend of *acridine* + *-an*, *-ane*] **:** a colorless crystalline base $C_{13}H_{11}N$ made by reducing acridine

acrid·i·an \ə'kridēən\ *adj* [NL *Acrida* + E *-ian*] **:** of or relating to the family Acrididae

ac·ri·did \'akrəˌdid\ *n* -s [NL *Acrididae*] **:** a grasshopper of the family Acrididae

acrid·i·dae \ə'kridəˌdē\ *n pl*, *cap* [NL, fr. *Acrida*, type genus (fr. Gk *akrid-*, *akris* grasshopper) + *-idae*] **:** a family of orthopterous insects that includes the true locusts and the grasshoppers with short antennae

ac·ri·di·idae \ˌakrə'dīəˌdē\ *syn of* ACRIDIDAE

ac·ri·dine \'akrəˌdēn, -ˌdən\ *n* -s [*acrid* + *-ine*] **:** a colorless crystalline feebly basic tricyclic compound $C_{13}H_9N$ occurring in crude anthracene fractions from coal tar and important as the parent compound of dyes and pharmaceuticals (as acriflavine and quinacrine) — compare STRUCTURAL FORMULA

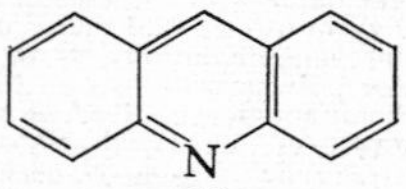

acridine

acridine dye *n* **:** any of a small class of basic dyes containing the acridine nucleus, most of them being yellow, orange, red, or brown, that are fluorescent in solution and are used chiefly for dyeing leather and mordanted cotton

acridine orange *n* **:** an orange acridine dye — see DYE table I (under *Basic Orange 14*)

ac·ri·din·i·um \ˌakrə'dinēəm\ *also* **ac·ri·do·ni·um** \-dōn-\ *n* -s [*acridinium*, NL, fr. ISV *acridine* + NL *-ium; acridonium*, NL, fr. ISV *acridone* + NL *-ium*] **:** a univalent radical $C_{13}H_{10}N$ analogous to ammonium derived from acridine

acrid·i·nyl \ə'kridᵊn(ˌ)il, -ˌəl\ *or* **ac·ri·dyl** \'akrəˌdil, -ˌdəl\ *n* -s [*acridinyl*, alter. of *acridyl; acridyl*, ISV *acrid*ine + *-yl*] **:** the univalent radical $C_{13}H_8N$ of acridine

acrid·i·ty \a'kridəd·ē, ə'-\ *n* -ES **:** the quality or state of being acrid **:** irritating sharpness **:** extreme bitterness ⟨the ~ of alkali⟩ ⟨the ~ of a critic's words⟩

ac·rid·ly \'akrədlē, -li\ *adv* **:** in an acrid manner

ac·rid·ness *n* -ES **:** ACRIDITY

ac·ri·dol·o·gy \ˌakrə'däləjē\ *n* -ES [Gk *akrid-*, *akris* grasshopper + E *-o-* + *-logy*] **:** the study of migratory locusts and other grasshoppers

ac·ri·done \'akrəˌdōn\ *n* -s [ISV, blend of *acridine* + *-one;* prob. orig. formed as G *akridon*] **:** a yellow crystalline ketone $C_6H_4(CO)(NH)C_6H_4$ yielding acridine on reduction

ac·ri·do·the·res \ˌakrədō'thi(ˌ)rēz\ *n*, *cap* [NL, modif. of Gk *akridothēra* locust trap, fr. *akrid-*, *akris* grasshopper, locust + *-o-* + *thēra* hunt, fr. *thēr* wild beast — more at FIERCE] **:** a genus of chiefly Asiatic passerine birds (family Sturnidae) that include the common myna of southeastern Asia and that are not permitted in the U.S. by private or commercial import because of their destructive feeding habits — compare STARLING

ac·ri·fla·vine \ˌakrə'flāˌvēn, -ˌvən\ *n* [*acri*dine + *flavine*] **:** a yellow acridine dye $C_{14}H_{14}N_3Cl$ obtained by methylation of proflavine as red crystals or usu. in admixture with proflavine as a deep orange powder and used often in the form of its reddish brown hydrochloride as an antiseptic esp. for wounds — called also *neutral acriflavine*, *trypaflavine*

ac·ri·mo·ni·ous \¦akrə¦mōnēəs, -nyəs\ *adj* [F *acrimonieux*, fr. ML *acrimoniosus*, fr. L *acrimonia* + *-osus* -ous] **1** *archaic* **:** bitter, irritating, or caustic esp. to the taste **2 :** caustic, biting, or rancorous esp. in feeling, language, or manner **:** BITTER ⟨an ~ dispute⟩ **syn** see ANGRY

ac·ri·mo·ny \'akrəˌmōnē, -ni, *US also & Brit usu* -ˌmən-\ *n* -ES [MF or L; MF *acrimonie*, fr. L *acrimonia*, fr. *acr-*, *acer* sharp — more at EDGE] **1** *archaic* **:** bitterness or sharpness esp. to the taste **2 :** sharpness or rancor esp. in words or manner ⟨timeworn controversies . . . are apt to revive . . . with an ~ undimmed by age — *Times Lit. Supp.*⟩

ac·ri·nyl \'akrəˌnil, -ˌnəl\ *n* -s [origin unknown] **:** a univalent radical C_7H_7O; *p*-hydroxy-benzyl

acro- — see ACR-

ac·ro·ama \ˌakrō'amə, -ämə\ *n*, *pl* **acroam·a·ta** \-məd·ə\ [Gk *akroama*, lit., something heard, fr. *akroasthai* to listen; prob. akin to Gk *akros* topmost and to Gk *ous* ear — more at ACR-, EAR] **:** an acroamatic teaching or doctrine

ac·ro·a·mat·ic \¦akrōə¦mad·ik\ *also* **ac·ro·a·mat·i·cal** \-əkəl\ *adj* [Gk *akroamatikos*, fr. *akroamat-*, *akroama* + *-ikos* -ic] **:** told orally to chosen disciples only **:** ESOTERIC

ac·ro·a·mat·ics \ˌakrōə'mad·iks\ *n pl* **:** acroamatic doctrines formerly ascribed to Aristotle

ac·ro·ba·cy \'akrəbəsē\ *n* -ES [*acrobat* + *-cy*] **:** ACROBATICS

ac·ro·bat \'akrəˌbat, *usu* -ad·+V\ *n* -s [F & Gk; F *acrobate*, fr. Gk *akrobatēs* tightrope walker, acrobat, fr. *akrobatos* walking on tiptoe, walking up high, fr. *akros* highest + *-batēs* (fr. *bainein* to go); akin to Gk *akē* point — more at EDGE, COME] **1 :** one that performs (as on a trapeze or bars) gymnastic feats or exercises **2 :** one adept at swiftly changing his position or viewpoint ⟨an intellectual ~⟩

acrob·a·tes \ə'kräbəˌtēz\ *n*, *cap* [NL, fr. Gk *akrobatēs* acrobat] **:** a genus of very small Australian marsupials having flattened tails and the lateral skin of the body extended into a supporting membrane like that of the flying squirrel and used similarly in gliding — see FLYING PHALANGER

ac·ro·bath·o·lith·ic \¦akrōˌbathə¦lithik\ *adj* [*acr-* + *batholith* + *-ic*] *of ore deposits* **:** located or formed in or near the upward-projecting domes or cupolas of batholiths

[1]ac·ro·bat·ic \¦akrə¦bad·ik, -atik, -ēk\ *adj* [F *acrobatique*, fr. *acrobate* + *-ique* -ic] **1 :** relating to or suggestive of an acrobat or acrobatics **2 :** performed with body contortions, back bends, high kicks, somersaults, or tossing of one dancer by a partner — **ac·ro·bat·i·cal·ly** \-ək(ə)lē, -li\ *adv*

[2]acrobatic \"\ *n* -s **:** an acrobatic trick, performance, or exercise ⟨indulges in every kind of ~ —*Ford Times*⟩

ac·ro·bat·ics \ˌ=='=iks, -ēks\ *n pl but sometimes sing in constr* **1 a :** the art, performance, or activity of an acrobat ⟨to perform ~ in a circus⟩ **b :** spectacular, showy, or startling ability esp. in performing something difficult or complex ⟨a politician's mental ~⟩; *also* **:** an instance of such ability ⟨an audience spellbound by a contralto's vocal ~⟩ **2 :** an aircraft maneuver other than that required for normal flight and usu. resulting in an abnormal position, speed, or altitude

ac·ro·bat·ism \'akrəˌbad·ˌizəm\ *n* -s **:** ACROBATICS 1

ac·ro·blast \'akrəˌblast\ *n* -s [ISV *acr-* + *-blast*] **:** a Golgi remnant that gives rise in spermatogenesis to the acrosome

ac·ro·car·pi \ˌakrə'kärˌpī\ *n pl*, *cap* [NL, fr. Gk *akrokarpoi*, pl. of *akrokarpos*] **:** an artificial group of mosses comprising acrocarpous forms (as most members of the orders Dicranales, Pottiales, and Eubryales) — compare PLEUROCARPI

ac·ro·car·pous \¦==¦=ˌpəs\ *adj* [NL *acrocarpus*, fr. Gk *akrokarpos* bearing fruit at the top, fr. *akr-* acr- + *-karpos* -carpous] *of a moss* **:** having the archegonia and hence the capsules terminal on the stem — compare PLEUROCARPOUS

ac·ro·cen·tric \¦akrə¦sen·trik\ *adj* [*acr-* + *centric*] **:** having or relating to a subterminal centromere

ac·ro·ce·phal·ic \¦akrōsə¦falik\ *adj* [ISV *acrocephaly* + *-ic;* orig. formed as F *acrocéphalique*] **:** OXYCEPHALIC

ac·ro·ceph·a·ly \ˌakrə'sefəlē\ *also* **ac·ro·ce·pha·lia** \ˌakrōsə'fālyə\ *n*, *pl* **acrocephalies** *also* **acrocephalias** [*acrocephaly* fr. F *acrocéphalie*, fr. *acr-* + *-céphalie* -cephaly; *acrocephalia*, NL, fr. F *acrocéphalie*] **:** OXYCEPHALY

acroc·e·ra \ə'kräsərə\ *n*, *cap* [NL, fr. *acr-* + *-cera*] **:** a genus of two-winged flies with very small heads and larvae that feed on spiders or their eggs

acroc·e·rat·i·dae \əˌkräsə'rad·əˌdē\ [NL, fr. Acrocerat-, *Acrocera*, type genus + *-idae*] *syn of* CYRTIDAE

ac·ro·chor·di·dae \ˌakrə'kördəˌdē\ *n pl*, *cap* [NL, fr. *Acrochordus*, type genus (fr. Gk *akrochordōn* wart with a thin neck, fr. *akr-* acr- + *chordē* intestine, catgut) + *-idae* — more at YARN] **:** a small family often considered a colubrid subfamily of aglyphous aquatic snakes of the eastern Asiatic coast comprising the wart snakes

[1]ac·ro·clin·i·um \ˌakrə'klinēəm\ [NL, fr. *acr-* + *-clinium*] *syn of* HELIPTERUM

[2]acroclinium \"\ *n* -s **:** a plant of the genus *Helipterum*

ac·ro·co·mia \ˌakrə'kōmēə\ *n*, *cap* [NL, fr. *acr-* + Gk *komē* hair, foliage + NL *-ia*] **:** a small genus of tall pinnate-leaved Central American and So. American palms with spiny trunk, long pendant clusters of flowers, and nutlike fruits

ac·ro·cra·ni·al \¦akrō¦krānēəl\ *or* **ac·ro·cra·nic** \-nik\ *adj* [*acr-* + *cranial*, *cranic*] *of a skull* **:** being pyramidal or pointed at the top with a breadth-height index of 98 or above — **ac·ro·cra·ny** \'akrōˌkrānē\ *n* -ES

ac·ro·cy·a·no·sis \¦akrōˌsīə'nōsəs\ *n*, *pl* **acrocyano·ses** \-ōˌsēz\ [NL, fr. *acr-* + *cyanosis*] **:** blueness or pallor of the extremities usu. associated with pain and numbness and caused by vasomotor disturbances (as in Raynaud's disease); *specif* **:** a disorder of the arterioles of the exposed parts of the hands and feet involving abnormal contraction of the arteriolar walls intensified by exposure to cold and resulting in bluish mottled skin, chilling, and sweating of the affected parts — **ac·ro·cy·a·not·ic** \-¦näd·ik\ *adj*

ac·ro·cyst \'akrōˌsist\ *n* -s [*acr-* + *-cyst*] **:** a chitinous cystlike expansion of the gonophore at the top of the gonotheca in certain hydroids

ac·ro·der·ma·ti·tis \¦akrōˌdərmə¦tīd·əs\ *n* -ES [NL, fr. *acr-* + *dermatitis*] **:** inflammation of the skin of the extremities

[1]ac·ro·dont \'akrəˌdänt\ *adj* [*acr-* + *-odont*] *of teeth* **:** consolidated with the summit of the alveolar ridge without sockets; *also* **:** having such teeth — compare PLEURODONT — **ac·ro·dont·ism** \-nˌtizəm\ *n* -s

[2]acrodont \"\ *n* -s **:** an acrodont animal

ac·ro·drome \'akrəˌdrōm\ *or* **acrod·ro·mous** \ə'krädrəməs, a'-\ *adj* [*acr-* + *-drome*, *-dromous*] **:** running to a point — used of a form of venation in which the principal veins terminate at the leaf tip (as in plants of the genus *Ziziphus*)

ac·ro·dus \'akrədəs\ *n*, *cap* [NL, fr. *acr-* + *-odus*] **:** a widely distributed genus of Mesozoic sharks (family Hybodontidae) with numerous rounded teeth

ac·ro·dyn·ia \ˌakrō'dinēə\ *n* -s [NL, fr. F *acrodynie*, fr. *acr-* + *-odynie* -odynia] **:** a disease of unknown cause seen in young children characterized by dusky pink discoloration of hands and feet with local swelling and intense itching and accompanied by insomnia, irritability, and sensitiveness to light — **ac·ro·dyn·ic** \¦==¦=ik\ *adj*

ac·ro·gen \'akrəjən\ *n* -s [*acr-* + *-gen;* fr. the growing point's being at the tip of the stem] **:** a plant of the higher cryptogams predominant in the Carboniferous era including ferns, fern allies, mosses, and liverworts and distinguished by growth from a special cell or growing point — compare THALLOGEN, THALLOPHYTE

acrog·e·nous \ə'kräjənəs, a'-\ *also* **ac·ro·gen·ic** \¦akrə¦jenik\ *adj* [*acr-* + *-genous*, *-genic*] **1 :** increasing by growth from the summit or apex **2** [*acrogen* + *-ous* or *-ic*] **:** relating to an acrogen — **acrog·e·nous·ly** *adv*

acrog·y·nae \ə'kräjə(ˌ)nē\ *n pl*, *cap* [NL, fr. *acr-* + *-gynae* (fr. Gk *gynē* woman) — more at QUEEN] *in some classifications* **:** a group of liverworts including all the leafy members of the Jungermanniaceae — compare ANACROGYNAE

acrog·y·nous \-ˌnəs\ *adj* [*acr-* + *-gynous*] **:** having the archegonia at the apex of the stem and involving the apical cell in their formation resulting in determinate growth of the gametophyte — used of certain liverworts

acro·le·in \ə'krōlēən\ *n* -s [L *acr-*, *ocer* sharp + *olēre* to smell + ISV *-in* — more at EDGE, ODOR] **:** a toxic colorless mobile liquid aldehyde $CH_2{=}CHCHO$ with acrid odor and irritating vapors that is obtained by dehydration of glycerol, by destructive distillation of fats, or by oxidation of allyl alcohol, that polymerizes readily into resins, and that is used chiefly in organic synthesis (as of methionine) — called also *acrylaldehyde*

ac·ro·lith \'akrəˌlith\ *n* -s [L *acrolithus*, fr. Gk *akrolithos* with ends of stone, fr. *akr-* acr- + *lithos* stone] **:** an acrolithic statue

ac·ro·lith·ic \¦==¦=ik\ *adj*, *of a statue* **:** having a trunk of wood usu. covered with metal or drapery and extremities of stone

ac·ro·log·ic \¦akrə¦läjik\ *adj* [F *acrologique*, fr. *acrologie* + *-ique* -ic] **:** ACROPHONIC — **ac·ro·log·i·cal·ly** \-jək(ə)lē\ *adv*

acrol·o·gy \ə'kräləjē\ *n* -ES [F *acrologie*, fr. *acr-* + *-logie* -logy] **:** ACROPHONY

ac·ro·ma·nia \ˌakrə'mānēə\ *n* [NL, fr. Gk. *akros* extreme + *mania* — more at ACR-] **:** violent incurable insanity

[1]ac·ro·me·gal·ic \¦akrōmə¦galik\ *adj* [ISV *acromegaly* + *-ic;* orig. formed as F *acromégalique*] **:** exhibiting acromegaly ⟨the oldest human skeleton yet discovered has an ~ skull —C.A.Doan⟩

[2]acromegalic \"\ *n* -s **:** one affected with acromegaly

ac·ro·meg·a·loid \¦akrō¦megəˌlȯid\ *adj* [*acromegaly* + *-oid*] **:** resembling acromegaly

ac·ro·meg·a·ly \ˌakrō'megəlē, -li\ *also* **ac·ro·me·ga·lia** \-ˌmə'gālyə\ *n*, *pl* **acromegalies** *also* **acromegalias** [*acromegaly* fr. F *acromégalie*, fr. *acr-* + *-mégalie* -megaly; *acromegalia*, NL, fr. F *acromégalie*] **:** a chronic disease of adult life that is characterized by a gradual and permanent enlargement of the flat bones (as the lower jaw) and of the hands and feet, abdominal organs, nose, lips, and tongue, that develops after ossification is complete, and that results from a disorder of the pituitary gland — compare GIGANTISM

acro·mi·al \ə'krōmēəl\ *adj* [NL *acromi*on + E *-al*] **:** of or relating to the acromion

acromial process *n* **:** ACROMION

acromial thoracic artery *n* **:** THORACICOACROMIAL ARTERY

ac·ro·mic·ria \ˌakrō'mikrēə, -mī-\ *n* -s [NL, fr. *acr-* + *micr-* + *-ia*] **:** abnormal smallness of the extremities

acromio- *comb form* [NL, fr. *acromion*] **:** acromial and ⟨*acromio*deltoid⟩ ⟨*acromio*sternal⟩

acro·mi·on \ə'krōmēˌän, -ˌən\ *or* **acromion process** *n* -s [NL, fr. Gk *akrōmion*, fr. *akr-* acr- + *ōmion* small shoulder, dim. of *ōmos* shoulder — more at HUMERUS] **:** the outer end of the spine of the scapula and in man protecting the glenoid cavity, forming the outer angle of the shoulder, and articulating with the clavicle

ac·ro·mon·o·gram·mat·ic \¦akrōˌmänəgrə¦mad·ik\ *adj* [*acr-* + Gk *monogrammatos* consisting of one letter (fr. *mon-* + *grammat-*, *gramma* letter) + E *-ic* — more at GRAMMAR] **:** having each verse beginning with the same letter that ends the preceding verse

ac·ro·my·o·di \¦akrōˌmī'ōˌdī\ *n pl*, *cap* [NL, fr. *acr-* + *-myodi* (fr. Gk *myōdēs* muscular, fr. *mys* mouse, muscle) — more at MOUSE] *in some classifications* **:** a group of birds nearly equivalent to Passeres having the syringeal muscles attached to the ends of the bronchial half rings

[1]ac·ro·my·o·di·an \-¦ōdēən\ *or* **ac·ro·my·o·dic** \-¦ōdik, -äd-\ *or* **ac·ro·my·o·dous** \-¦ōdəs\ *adj* [NL *Acromyodi* + E *-an* or *-ic* or *-ous*] **:** of or relating to the Acromyodi

[2]acromyodian \"\ *n* -s **:** a bird of the group Acromyodi

ac·ron \'aˌkrän, 'akrən\ *n* -s [NL, fr. Gk *akron* mountain top, end, fr. neut. of *akros* sharp; akin to Gk *akē* point — more at EDGE] **:** the unsegmented preoral part of the body of a segmented animal (as an arthropod) — **ac·ro·nal** \'akrənəl\ *adj*

[1]ac·ro·nar·cot·ic \¦akrəˌ=¦==\ *adj* [*acr*id + *-o-* + *narcotic*] **:** possessing both acrid and narcotic properties

[2]acronarcotic \"\ *n* -s **:** an acronarcotic substance

ac·ro·nym \'akrəˌnim\ *n* -s [*acr-* + *-onym*] **:** a word formed from the initial letter or letters of each of the successive parts or major parts of a compound term (as *anzac*, *radar*, *snafu*)

ac·ro·nym·ic \¦akrə¦nimik\ *adj* **:** marked by the use of acronyms

ac·ro·pachy \'akrōˌpakē, ə'kräpəkē\ *n* -ES [Gk *akropachēs* thick at the end (fr. *akr-* acr- + *-pachēs*, fr. *pachys* thick) + E *-y*] **:** OSTEOARTHROPATHY

ac·ro·par·es·the·sia \¦akrōˌparəs¦thēzh(ē)ə\ *n* -s [NL, fr. *acr-* + *paresthesia*] **:** a condition of burning, tingling, or pricking sensations or numbness in the extremities present on awaking and of unknown cause or produced by compression of nerves during sleep

acrop·e·tal \ə'kräpəd·ᵊl, a'-\ *adj* [*acr-* + *-petal*] *bot* **:** from the base toward the apex or from below upward ⟨~ differentiation of an inflorescence⟩ ⟨~ spread of a pathogen in a plant body⟩ — compare BASIPETAL — **acrop·e·tal·ly** \-ᵊlē\ *adv*

ac·ro·pho·bia \ˌakrəˈfōbēə\ *n* -s [NL, fr. *acr-* + *phobia*] : abnormal dread of being at a great height

ac·ro·pho·net·ic \ˈakrə+\ *adj* [*acr-* + *phonetic*] : ACROPHONIC

ac·ro·phon·ic \ˌakrəˈfänik\ *adj* **1** : having to do with acrophony **2** : instituted or used on the basis of acrophony — **ac·ro·phon·i·cal·ly** \-nək(ə)lē\ *adv*

acroph·o·ny \əˈkräfənē, aˈ-\ *n* -ES [*acr-* + *-phony*] **1** : the application in the evolution of an alphabet of a pictorial symbol or hieroglyph for the name of an object to the initial sound alone of that name **2** : the naming of a letter by a word whose initial sound is the same as that which the letter represents

acrop·o·lis \əˈkräpələs\ *n* -ES [Gk *akropolis*, fr. *akr-* acr- + *polis* city — more at POLICE] **1** : the upper fortified part of an ancient Greek city (as Athens) **2** : a height of a city or district fortified or strengthened as a place of refuge ⟨one magnificent photograph of Edinburgh — its ~ in the foreground —Kimon Friar⟩

ac·ro·po·ra \ˌakrəˈpōrə, əˈkräpərə\ *n, cap* [NL, fr. *acr-* + *-pora*] : a genus of corals consisting of the typical madrepores

¹ac·ro·pore \ˈakrəˌpō(ə)r\ *adj* [NL *Acropora*] : of or relating to the genus *Acropora*

²acropore \"\ *n* -s : a coral of the genus *Acropora*

ac·ro·rha·gus \ˌakrə+\ *n, pl* **acrorha·gi** \-ˌjī, -ˌgī\ [NL, fr. *acr-* + *-rhagus* (irreg. fr. Gk *rhag-, rhax* berry)] : one of a series of marginal tubercles found on certain sea anemones each consisting of a local accumulation of nematocysts

ac·ro·scop·ic \ˈakrə¦skäpik\ *adj* [*acr-* + *-scopic*] *bot* : facing or on the side toward the apex ⟨a plant with ~ branches⟩ — compare BASISCOPIC

ac·rose \ˈaˌkrōs\ *n* -s [ISV *acrolein* + *-ose*; orig. formed as G *akrose*] : either of two sugars $C_6H_{12}O_6$: **a** : a racemic fructose — called also *alpha-acrose* **b** : inactive sorbose — called also *beta-acrose*

ac·ro·some \ˈakrəˌsōm\ *n* -s [ISV *acr-* + *-some*; orig. formed as G *akrosom*] : an anterior cap or hooklike prolongation of a spermatozoon usu. regarded as a derivative of the Golgi apparatus

ac·ro·spire \-ˌspī(ə)r\ *n* -s [alter. (influenced by *acr-*) of earlier *akerspire, acherspire*, fr. E dial. *aker, acher* ear of grain (fr. OE *æhher, æcher, ēar*) + *spire* (sprout, blade of grass) — more at EAR (spike of grain)] : the spiral plumule in a germinating grain

ac·ro·spore \ˈakrəˌspō(ə)r\ *n* -s [F, fr. *acr-* + *-spore*] : a spore (as a basidiospore) borne at the extremity of the sporophore — **ac·ro·spor·ous** \ˌakrə¦spōrəs, əˈkräspərəs\ *adj*

¹across \əˈkrȯs *also* -ˈäs\ *adv* [ME *acrois, acros*, fr. AF *an crois*, fr. *an* in, on (fr. L *in*) + *crois* cross, fr. L *crux* — more at IN, CROSS] **1** : so as to cross transversely : CROSSWISE ⟨boards sawed directly ~⟩ **2** : to or on the opposite side ⟨a stretch of islandless ocean fully 500 miles ~ —F.C.Lincoln⟩ **3** : so as to be understandable, acceptable, or successful : OVER ⟨a highly individual style which comes ~ even in translation —K.I. Lansner⟩ ⟨failed to get his thoughts ~⟩ ⟨the carefully studied and rehearsed technique for putting himself ~ —T.C.Worsley⟩ **4** *dial Eng* : at odds ⟨to get ~ with his friends⟩

²across \"\ *prep* **1 a** : from one side to the opposite side of : OVER ⟨to swim ~ the channel⟩ ⟨to peer ~ the barricade⟩ ⟨to sweep her fingers ~ the strings of a harp⟩ **b** : from one point in time to another ⟨I can remember, ~ the years —W.A.White⟩ **2 a** : so as to intersect or pass at an angle (as a right angle) : crosswise of : at an angle with the length, direction, or course of ⟨to lay one stick ~ another⟩ ⟨~ the grain of the wood⟩ ⟨a lake lying ~ the state line⟩ **b** : so as to intrude upon ⟨to flash ~ his mind⟩ **3** : on the other side of ⟨~ the street⟩

³across \"\ *adj* : CROSSED ⟨with arms ~⟩

across-the-board \ˌ=¦==¦=\ *adj* **1** *of a racing bet* : placed in combination to win, place, or show **2** : embracing all classes or categories without exception : BLANKET ⟨an *across-the-board* tax cut⟩ **3** *of a radio or television program* : scheduled at the same time on consecutive days (usu. Monday through Friday) each week

acrost \əˈkrȯst *also* -ˈäst\ *dial var of* ACROSS

ac·ro·ster·nite \ˌakrōˈstərˌnīt\ *n* -s [*acr-* + *sternite*] : the precostal lip of the sternum of a typical segment of an arthropod

¹acros·tic \əˈkrȯstik, -ēk, -ˈäs-\ *n* -s [MF & Gk; MF *acrostiche*, fr. Gk *akrostichis*, fr. *akr-* acr- + *-stichis* (fr. *stichos* line); akin to *steichein* to go — more at STAIR] **1** : a composition usu. in verse in which one or more sets of letters (as the initial, middle, or final letters of the lines) when taken in order form a word, a connected group of words (as a sentence), or the regular sequence of the letters of the alphabet — compare ABECEDARIUS **2 a** : ACRONYM **b** : a word made from any of the letters in the words of a phrase **3** : a series of words of equal length, the number of words being the same as the number of letters in each word, so arranged that it is the same when read horizontally or vertically

H E A R T
E M B E R
A B U S E
R E S I N
T R E N D

acrostic 3

²acrostic \"\ *also* **acros·ti·cal** \-əkəl\ *adj* : characterized by, containing, or made up by means of an acrostic ⟨a ~ name⟩ ⟨an ~ poem⟩ ⟨an ~ anagram⟩ — **acros·ti·cal·ly** \-tək(ə)lē, -li\ *adv*

acros·ti·chal \əˈkrȯstəkəl, -ˈäs-\ *adj* [*acr-* + *-stich* + *-al*] : situated in the highest rank or row — used of certain bristles on the mesonotum of muscoid flies

acros·ti·chum \-kəm\ *n, cap* [NL, irreg. fr. Gk *akrostichis*; fr. the arrangement of the spores on the leaflets] : a genus of tropical ferns (family Polypodiaceae) with varied habit but with the sporangia covering all the underside of the frond

ac·ro·tar·si·al \¦akrō¦tärsēəl\ *adj* [NL *acrotarsium* + E *-al*] : of or relating to the acrotarsium

ac·ro·tar·si·um \ˌakrōˈtärsēəm\ *n, pl* **acrotar·sia** \-ēə\ [NL, fr. *acr-* + *tarsus* + *-ium*] : the instep of the foot

ac·ro·ter·gite \-ˈtərˌjīt\ *n* -s [*acr-* + *tergite*] : the precostal sector of the typical dorsal plate of a segment of an arthropod

ac·ro·te·ri·al \¦akrə¦tirēəl\ *adj* [*acroterion* + *-al*] : of or like an acroterion

ac·ro·te·ri·on \ˌakrəˈtirēˌän, -ēən\ *or* **ac·ro·te·ri·um** \-ēəm\ *or* **ak·ro·te·ri·on** \-ēˌän, -ēən\ *or* **ac·ro·ter** *also* **ak·ro·ter** \ˈakrətə(r)\ *n, pl* **acrote·ria** *or* **akrote·ria** \ˌakrəˈtirēə\ *or* **ac·roters** *also* **akro·ters** \ˈakrətə(r)z\ [*acroterion*, *akroterion*, fr. Gk *akrotērion*, fr. *akros* topmost, extreme; akin to Gk *akē* point; *acroterium* fr. L, fr. Gk *akrotērion*; *acroter, akroter* fr. F *acrotère*, fr. L *acroterium* — more at EDGE] : a pedestal placed on a pediment to support a statue or other ornamentation; *also* : an ornament similarly placed (as on the prow of a galley)

pediment showing three acroteria

ac·ro·tho·rac·i·ca \¦akrōthəˈrasikə\ *n pl, cap* [NL, fr. *acr-* + *Thoracica*] : a small order or suborder of barnacles that have the body surrounded by a chitinous mantle and that bore and inhabit cavities (as in mollusk shells or corals)

ac·ro·tre·ta \ˌakrōˈtrēdə\ *n, cap* [NL, fr. *acr-* + *-treta* (fr. Gk *trētos* perforated)] : a genus of brachiopods known from small fossil shells common in Cambrian rocks

ac·ro·troph·ic \¦akrō¦träfik, -ōf-\ *adj* [*acr-* + *-trophic*] : having nutritive cells grouped at the apex of the follicular tube — used of the ovariole of certain insects; compare POLYTROPHIC

ac·ryl·al·de·hyde \ˌakrəˈlaldəˌhīd\ *n* [ISV *acrylic* + *aldehyde*] : ACROLEIN

ac·ryl·am·ide \ˌakrəˈlaˌmīd, əˈkriləˌm-, -ˌməd\ *n* -s [*acrylic* + *amide*] : the crystalline amide $CH_2{=}CHCONH_2$ of acrylic acid used industrially (as in the manufacture of synthetic textiles) because of its ready polymerization

ac·ry·late \ˈakrəˌlāt, -ˌlət\ *n* -s [ISV *acrylic* + *-ate*] **1** : a salt or ester of acrylic acid **2** *or* **acrylate resin** : ACRYLIC RESIN

¹acryl·ic \əˈkrilik, aˈ-\ *adj* [ISV *acrolein* + *-yl* + *-ic*] : relating to acrylic acid or its derivatives ⟨~ polymers⟩

²acrylic \"\ *n* -s **1** : ACRYLIC RESIN **2** : ACRYLIC FIBER

acrylic acid *n* : an unsaturated liquid acid $CH_2{:}CHCOOH$ obtainable by oxidation of acrolein, by hydrolysis of acrylonitrile, and otherwise and polymerizing readily to useful products (as water-soluble thickening agents and constituents for varnishes and lacquers) — compare METHACRYLIC ACID

acrylic fiber *n* : any of various synthetic textile fibers made by polymerization of acrylonitrile usu. with other monomers that are quick-drying and resistant to the action of weather and moths and that are used esp. in fabrics for clothing and for outdoor exposure

acrylic resin *or* **acrylic plastic** *n* : a glasslike thermoplastic made by polymerizing acrylic or methacrylic acid or a derivative of either, esp. an ester (as methyl methacrylate), and used chiefly for cast and molded transparent parts and in solutions or emulsions as coatings (as for textiles and leather) and adhesives

ac·ry·lo·ni·trile \¦akrə(ˌ)lōˈnī·trəl; -ˌtrēl, -ˌtrīl\ *n* -s [*acrylic* + *-o-* + *nitrile*] : a colorless volatile flammable liquid nitrile $CH_2{=}CHCN$ soluble in most organic solvents that is usu. made by reaction of hydrogen cyanide with acetylene or with ethylene oxide with subsequent dehydration of the ethylene cyanohydrin formed and that is used chiefly in organic synthesis (as in cyanoethylation), as an insecticide, and as a raw material for polymerizations esp. to synthetic rubbers (as nitrile rubbers) and acrylic fibers — called also *vinyl cyanide*

acrylo·yl \əˈkriləˌwil, -ēl\ *or* **ac·ry·lyl** \ˈakrəˌlil\ *n* -s [*acryloyl* fr. *acrylic* + *-o-* + *-yl*; *acrylyl* fr. *acrylic* + *-yl*] : the univalent radical $CH_2{=}CHCO{-}$ of acrylic acid

ACS *abbr* **1** antireticular cytotoxic serum **2** autograph card signed

¹act \ˈakt\ *n* -s [ME *acte*, partly fr. L *actus* doing, driving, performance, recital, part of a play (fr. *actus*, past part. of *agere* to drive, do), partly fr. L *actum* thing done, public transaction, record, fr. neut. of *actus*, part. — more at AGENT] **1 a** : a thing done or being done : DEED, PERFORMANCE ⟨one of the first ~s of the new commission⟩ ⟨if some understanding of the ~ is not present, comment on the result may well be irrelevant —Ronald Bottrall⟩ ⟨an ~ of folly⟩ **b** *law* : an external manifestation of the will : something done by a person pursuant to his volition ⟨the effect may be negative, in which case the ~ is properly described as a "forbearance" —T.E.Holland⟩ **c** *psychol* (1) : a motor performance leading to a definite result (2) : a dealing with objects (as by moving, perceiving, or desiring them) **d** *sociol* : a sequence of human behavior considered as a unit that is directed toward a goal and is regulated by standards of conduct **2** *in Scholasticism* : an activity in process of completion; *also* : a state of reality or real existence attained — contrasted with *possibility*; compare ACTUS, ENERGY, ENTELECHY **3** *often cap* : the formal product of a legislative body : the formally declared will of a legislature the final requirement of which is usu. the signature of the proper executive officer : STATUTE ⟨an ~ of Congress⟩; *sometimes* : a decision or determination of a sovereign, a legislative council, or a court of justice : DECREE, EDICT, JUDGMENT, RESOLVE, AWARD — compare ⁴BILL, EX POST FACTO LAW, PRIVATE LAW, PUBLIC LAW **4** : process of doing : ACTION — now used chiefly in the phrase *in the act* ⟨caught in the ~⟩ ⟨they were always on the verge, or in the ~, of civil war —G.L.Dickinson⟩ **5** *often cap* [ME *acte*, fr. MF or L; MF *acte*, fr. L *actum*] : a formal record of something done or transacted ⟨given as my free ~ and deed⟩ ⟨*Acts* of the Apostles⟩ ⟨the following section is added to the *Act* of December 22, 1928, supra —*U.S. Code*⟩ **6** [L *actus*] **a** : one of the principal divisions of a play or opera — see SCENE **b** (1) : one of the successive parts or performances each complete in itself making up an entertainment program (as of a variety show or circus) (2) : the performer or performers in such an act ⟨common sense dictates that flying-trapeze ~s work over nets⟩ **c** (1) : something done for the sake of its intended impression upon others esp. when imitative or suggestive of a theatrical performance ⟨to do the neglected-wife ~⟩ (2) : a display of affected esp. insincere behavior : PRETENSE ⟨his iconoclasm became a trademark and an ~ —*Time*⟩ ⟨put on an ~ that deceived nobody⟩ **7** : an exercise formerly required of candidates for a degree at Oxford and Cambridge universities consisting of a thesis to be publicly maintained **8** : a voluntary inward prayer serving to express such things as faith in God or contrition for one's sins; *also* : the expressed form of such prayer — **in act** *archaic* : on the point : READY, ABOUT — used with *to* and the infinitive ⟨a tiger cat *in act* to spring —Alfred Tennyson⟩ — **into the act** *adv* : into an undertaking or situation as an active participant esp. with a view to securing a share in some supposed profit or advantage ⟨many were eager to get *into the act*⟩

²act \"\ *vb* -ED/-ING/-S *vt* **1** *obs* : to move to action : ACTUATE, ANIMATE ⟨self-love, the spring of motion, ~s the soul —Alexander Pope⟩ **2** *archaic* : to carry out into action : PERFORM, EXECUTE, DO ⟨had Satan been able to have ~*ed* anything by force —Daniel Defoe⟩ **3 a** : to represent (as an incident or an emotion) by action esp. on the stage ⟨I could have ~*ed* what swept through me then —Mary Austin⟩ ⟨he is handsome and he can ~ neurotic intensity —E.R. Bentley⟩ **b** : to perform (a dramatic work or role) as an actor ⟨beautifully staged and admirably ~*ed*⟩ ⟨~*ing* the part of Ophelia⟩ ⟨every company that ~s that operetta has the time of its life —Virgil Thomson⟩ **c** : to make a pretense of : FEIGN, COUNTERFEIT, SIMULATE ⟨~ dismay⟩ ⟨~*ed* a reluctance he did not feel⟩ **4 a** : to play the part of (a character in a dramatic work) : PERSONATE ⟨~*ed* Desdemona⟩ ⟨~*ing*, as usual, a crotchety octogenarian⟩ **b** : to play the part of as if in a play : assume the character of ⟨~ the man of the world⟩ ⟨contentedly ~ a self-sacrificing mother⟩ **c** : to behave in a manner suitable to ⟨~ your age⟩ ~ *vi* **1 a** : to perform on the stage : represent a character in the production of a dramatic work ⟨frequently ~s in his own plays⟩ ⟨she began ~*ing* as a child of eight⟩ **b** : to behave as if performing on the stage : PRETEND, FEIGN, DISSEMBLE ⟨wanted people who would be behaving rather than ~*ing* —*New Yorker*⟩ ⟨watching closely, one had a feeling that she was ~*ing*⟩ **2** : to carry into effect a determination of the will : take action : MOVE ⟨to think carefully before ~*ing*⟩ ⟨called on the government to ~ quickly⟩ ⟨in a position to ~ in the light of experience —*London Calling*⟩ ⟨found the truth too unbearable to face, much less to ~ upon —Hamilton Basso⟩ **3** : to conduct or comport oneself (as in morals or manners or in private life or public office) : BEHAVE ⟨to be judged by the way one ~s⟩ ⟨~*ed* with becoming modesty⟩ ⟨~ like a fool⟩ ⟨~*ed* as if he felt ill⟩ — often used with an adjective complement ⟨~*ed* tired⟩ ⟨~ superior⟩ **4** : to discharge the duties of a specified office or post : perform a specified function : SERVE — used with a prepositional phrase ⟨declaring what officer shall then ~ as President —*U.S.Constitution*⟩ ⟨appointed by the chairman to ~ for him⟩ ⟨~*ed* in this capacity throughout the winter⟩ ⟨trees left standing to ~ as a windbreak⟩ **5 a** : to exert power or influence : produce an effect ⟨the gas appears to ~ principally by causing pain —H.G.Armstrong⟩ ⟨forms of magic . . . which are supposed to ~ at a distance —J.G.Frazer⟩ — often used with *on* ⟨caused by acid ~*ing* on metal⟩ ⟨abnormal stimuli, ~*ing* on a neurotic temperament —V.L.Parrington⟩ **b** : to produce a desired effect : perform the function for which designed or employed : WORK ⟨the brake sometimes ~s too quickly⟩ ⟨wait for a medicine to ~⟩ **6** *of a play* : to be capable of being performed ⟨this play ~s as well as it reads⟩ **7** : to give a decision or award (as by vote of a deliberative body or by judicial decree) — often used with *on* ⟨adjourned with several important matters still not ~*ed on*⟩

syn BEHAVE, WORK, OPERATE, FUNCTION, REACT: these all have in common the indication of the way in which a person or thing performs, independently or in response to a stimulus. ACT, the most general of this group, stresses the specific nature of the movements or activity or what they indicate in terms of attitude or condition ⟨the child *acted* strangely when his teacher called⟩ ⟨how does the chemical *act* when mixed with water?⟩ ⟨the automobile *acted* all right on the trip⟩ BEHAVE commonly applies to persons and, in that application, commonly implies a standard of what is right, proper, or decorous ⟨*behaved* in a decent and polite way⟩ but has come also to apply more generally as more or less interchangeable with ACT ⟨how does the car *behave* on long trips?⟩ ⟨how the thyroid gland *behaves* under emotional excitement⟩ ⟨a study of how groups *behave* under war conditions⟩ FUNCTION, OPERATE, and WORK agree in meaning to act in a way natural or intended ⟨when the fuse blew, the electric stove ceased to *function*⟩ ⟨under the strain of fatigue his brain refused to *operate*⟩ ⟨the clock no longer *works*⟩ FUNCTION emphasizes the activity itself for which a thing exists or is designed, sometimes also applying to activity that is official or as if official ⟨in order to *function*, man's organism requires a specific temperature, a specific quality of climate, air, light, humidity, and food —Siegfried Giedion⟩ ⟨they have *functioned* as observers rather than participants —J.M.Brown⟩ OPERATE sometimes emphasizes more the degree of efficiency of the activity ⟨the device for lifting heavy objects did not *operate* to anyone's satisfaction⟩ ⟨if the machine is kept oiled, it will *operate* smoothly⟩ WORK emphasizes the degree of success or effectiveness of the activity ⟨the plan for promoting money did not *work* and so was not tried again⟩ ⟨the faucet, partly plugged with rust, did not *work* well⟩ REACT, as the etymology would imply, generally suggests action in response or with reciprocal or counteractive effect ⟨he had found that laboratory animals *reacted* to tests with the chemical by showing various forms of mental disturbances —*Current Biog.*⟩ ⟨we lived there blissfully happy, *reacting* upon one another, stimulating one another —W.A.White⟩ although it has come to be often almost interchangeable with ACT or BEHAVE ⟨at this threat the civil service *reacted* in the way which is always open to any civil service, under any regime —C.P.Fitzgerald⟩ esp. in a desired way ⟨children *react* under kind treatment⟩

— **act a part** **1** : to perform one of the roles in a play **2** : PRETEND, FEIGN, DISSEMBLE ⟨one would never guess that this paragon of virtue was *acting a part*⟩ — **act the part** **1** : to assume the role : perform the function or duties — used with *of* ⟨temporarily *acting the part of* janitor⟩ ⟨has the property of *acting the part* of an acid⟩ **2** : to exhibit the qualities that characteristically accompany a particular role ⟨now that he's rich he certainly *acts the part*⟩

¹-act \ˌakt\ *adj comb form* [Gk *aktis* ray — more at ACTIN-] : having (such or so many) rays ⟨polyact⟩ ⟨tetract⟩ — in terms applied to sponge spicules

²-act \"\ *n comb form* -s : one having (such or so many) rays ⟨hexact⟩ ⟨triact⟩ — in names of sponge spicules

act *abbr* **1** acting **2** active **3** actual **4** actuary

ac·ta \ˈaktə\ *n pl* [L, pl. of *actum* — more at ACT] **1** : recorded proceedings : official acts : TRANSACTIONS ⟨the ~ of the conference⟩ **2** : narratives of deeds ⟨the Christian ~⟩

act·a·bil·i·ty \ˌaktəˈbiləd·ē\ *n* -ES : the quality or state of being actable

act·a·ble \ˈaktəbəl\ *adj* : capable of being acted; *esp* : suitable for performance on the stage ⟨an ~ scene⟩ ⟨an ~ role⟩

ac·taea \akˈtēə\ *n, cap* [NL, fr. L, a plant (prob. *Actaea spicata*), fr. Gk *aktaia* baneberry (*Actaea spicata*), elder tree (*Sambucus nigra*)] : a small genus of herbs comprising the baneberries (family Ranunculaceae) and having twice-compound leaves, small white racemose flowers, and acrid poisonous berries

ac·tae·on \akˈtēən\ *n, cap* [NL, fr. L *Actaeon*, a hunter in Greco-Roman mythology turned into a stag by Diana and torn to pieces by his own dogs, fr. L, fr. Gk *Aktaiōn*] : a genus (the type of the family Actaeonidae) of tectibranchiate mollusks having the viscera twisted to a figure 8 and the shell large and spiral with the spire usu. prominent — compare TECTIBRANCHIA

act curtain *n* : a curtain in a theater drawn or lowered between acts

act drop *n* : a drop in a theater lowered between acts

acted *past of* ACT

actg *abbr* **1** acting **2** actuating

ACTH *abbr* adrenocorticotrophic hormone

ac·ti·as \ˈaktēəs, ˈakshē-\ *n, cap* [NL] : a genus of moths (family Saturniidae) comprising the luna moth and certain Asiatic relatives

Ac·ti–di·one \ˌaktəˈdīˌōn\ *trademark* — used for cycloheximide

ac·ti·fi·ca·tion \ˌaktəfəˈkāshən\ *n* -s [fr. *actify*, after such pairs as E *edify: edification*] : ACTIVATION

ac·ti·fi·er \ˈaktəˌfī(ə)r\ *n* -s : the part of the equipment for liquid purification of gases in which alkaline scrubbing solutions are reactivated (as by use of steam) by driving out hydrogen sulfide — called also *reactivator*

ac·ti·fy \-ˌfī\ *vt* -ED/-ING/-S [irreg. fr. *active* + *-fy*] : ACTIVATE

ac·tin \ˈaktən\ *n* -s [ISV *act-* (fr. L *actus* motion) + *-in*; orig. formed as G *aktin* — more at ACT] : a protein in muscle that is active in muscular contraction, is separable from the muscle structure along with myosin by use of strong salt solutions in the presence of adenosine triphosphate, and is known in both globular and fibrous forms

actin- *or* **actini-** *or* **actino-** *comb form* [NL *actin-* ray, fr. Gk *aktin-, aktino-*, fr. *aktin-, aktis*; akin to OE *ūhte* morning twilight, OHG *ūhta*, ON *ōtta*, Goth *ūhtwo*, Skt *aktu* light, night, L *noct-, nox* night — more at NIGHT] **1 a** : having a radiated structure ⟨*Actino*poda⟩ ⟨*Actino*myces⟩ **b** : actinian ⟨*actini*form⟩ ⟨*Actino*zoa⟩ **2 a** : actinic ⟨*actino*autography⟩ **b** : of, relating to, or caused by actinic radiation (as X rays) ⟨*actino*therapy⟩

ac·ti·nal \ˈaktənəl, (ˈ)ak¦tīnᵊl\ *adj* [*actin-* + *-al*] : belonging to the part of a radiate animal from which the tentacles or arms radiate and where the mouth is situated — often used as an equivalent of oral — **ac·ti·nal·ly** \-əlē, -ᵊlē\ *adv*

-ac·ti·nal \¦=ˌ==, ˌ=¦==\ *adj comb form* [Gk *aktin-, aktis* ray + E *-al*] : -ACTINE

ac·ti·nar·ia \ˌaktəˈna(a)rēə\ [NL, fr. *Actinia* + *-aria*] *syn of* ACTINIARIA

ac·tin·au·to·graph·ic \ˌaktəˌnȯd·əˈgrafik\ *adj* [*actin-* + *autographic*] : capable of producing a developable impression on light-sensitive material without contact — used of substances (as zinc) — **ac·tin·au·tog·ra·phy** \ˌaktəˌnȯˈtägrəfē\ *n* -ES

ac·tine \ˈakˌtīn, -ˌtən\ *n* -s [Gk *aktin-, aktis* ray — more at ACTIN-] : a star-shaped spicule (as of a sponge)

-actine \¦=(ˌ)=\ *adj comb form* [Gk *aktin-, aktis*] : having (such or so many) rays ⟨disco*actine*⟩ ⟨penta*ctine*⟩ — esp. in terms applied to sponge spicules

¹acting *adj* **1** : holding a temporary rank or position : performing services temporarily ⟨~ president⟩ ⟨served in an ~ capacity⟩ **2 a** : suitable for stage performance ⟨the best ~ play he ever wrote⟩ **b** : prepared with directions for acting or performing ⟨an ~ text of a play⟩

²acting *n* -s **1 a** : the art or practice of representing a character on the stage or in a motion picture or radio or television play ⟨to choose ~ as a career⟩ **b** : a particular mode or style of such representation ⟨the conventions of 19th century ~⟩ **2** : SIMULATION ⟨his affability is a piece of ~⟩

acting area *n* : the area of a stage left visible to the audience by the stage setting and usable by actors in the performance of a scene

actini- — see ACTIN-

ac·tin·ia \akˈtinēə\ *n* [NL, fr. *actin-* + *-ia*] **1** *cap, in some classifications* : a genus of sea anemones nearly coextensive with the order Actiniaria **2** *pl* **actini·ae** \-ēˌē\ *or* **actinias** : any sea anemone or related animal

¹ac·tin·i·an \(ˈ)ak¦tinēən\ *or* **ac·ti·ni·ar·i·an** \¦akˌtinē¦a(a)rēən, akˌt-\ *or* **ac·ti·nar·i·an** \¦aktəˈna(a)r-\ *adj* [NL *Actinia* or *Actiniaria, Actinaria* + E *-an*] : of or relating to the Actiniaria

²actinian \"\ *or* **actiniarian** \"\ *or* **actinarian** \"\ *n* -s : one of the Actiniaria : SEA ANEMONE

ac·tin·i·ar·ia \(ˌ)akˌtinēˈa(a)rēə\ *n pl, cap* [NL, fr. *Actinia* + *-aria*] : an order or suborder of Anthozoa (subclass Zoantharia) comprising the sea anemones which differ from the corals in forming no hard skeleton and in existing as separate individuals

ac·tin·ic \(ˈ)ak¦tinik\ *adj* [*actin-* + *-ic*] : having photochemical properties or effects : possessing or exhibiting actinism — **ac·tin·i·cal·ly** \-nək(ə)lē\ *adv*

actinic focus *n* : the focus at which the chemically most effective rays as distinguished from the visually most effective are brought together (as by a lens) — called also *chemical focus*

actinic glass *n* : glass that transmits light of high visibility (as green) but reduces the intensity of both infrared and ultraviolet and is often used for protecting the eyes of industrial workers

actinic ray *n* **:** a radiation (as the green, blue, violet, and ultraviolet rays of the spectrum) having marked photochemical action

ac·ti·nide \ˈaktəˌnīd\ *n* -S [ISV *actin-* + *-ide*] **:** a chemical element of the actinide series

actinide series *n* **:** a series of heavy radioactive metallic elements of increasing atomic number considered to be analogous to the lanthanide series and to begin with actinium (89) or thorium (90) and end with element of atomic number 103 — compare ACTINIUM SERIES, PERIODIC TABLE

ac·ti·nid·ia \ˌaktəˈnidēə\ *n, cap* [NL, fr. *actin-* + *-idia* (pl. of *-idium*)] **:** a small genus (the type of the family Actinidiaceae) of Asiatic woody vines having alternate simple leaves, dioecious or polygamous axillary flowers, and many-seeded berries — see SILVERVINE

ac·ti·nid·i·a·ce·ae \ˌaktəˌnidēˈāsēˌē\ *n pl, cap* [NL, fr. *Actinidia*, type genus + *-aceae*] **:** a family of trees, shrubs, or woody vines (order Parietales) with stamens distinct or in fascicles adnate to the petals and a single multiloculate pistil

ac·ti·nif·er·ous \ˌaktəˈnif(ə)rəs\ *adj* [NL *actinium* + E *-ferous*] **:** containing actinium

ac·tin·i·form \akˈtinəˌfȯrm\ *adj* [*actin-* + *-form*] **:** having a radiated form **:** like a sea anemone

ac·ti·nine \ˈaktəˌnēn, -ˌnən\ *n* -S [NL *Actinia* (genus name of *Actinia equina*) + E *-ine*] **:** a base $C_7H_{15}NO_2$ found in a sea anemone (*Actinia equina*)

actinio- *comb form* [*Actinia*] **:** actinian ⟨*actinio*chrome⟩ ⟨*actinio*hematin⟩

ac·tin·i·o·chrome \akˈtinēəˌkrōm\ *n* [ISV *actinio-* + *-chrome*] **:** a reddish pigment found in certain Anthozoa or Actinozoa

ac·tin·i·o·hem·a·tin \akˈtinē(ˌ)ō-\ *n* -S [*actinio-* + *hematin*] **:** a respiratory pigment obtained from a sea anemone (*Actinia equina*) and now considered to be a mixture of cytochromes

ac·tin·i·o·mor·pha \akˌtinēōˈmȯrfə\ [NL, fr. *actinio-* + *-morpha*] *syn of* ZOANTHARIA

ac·ti·nism \ˈaktəˌnizəm\ *n* -S [*actin-* + *-ism*] **:** the property of radiant energy esp. in the visible and ultraviolet spectral regions by which chemical changes are produced (as in light-sensitive photographic emulsions) — compare ACTINIC RAY

ac·ti·nis·tia \ˌaktəˈnistēə\ *n pl, cap* [NL, fr. *actin-* + *-istia* (fr. Gk *histion* web, cloth, sail); akin to Gk *histos* mast, weaver's beam, web — more at STAMEN] **:** an order (superorder Crossopterygii) of chiefly Mesozoic fishes including the family Coelacanthidae having the interspinous bones supporting each dorsal and anal fin fused into one piece — compare LATIMERIA

ac·tin·i·um \akˈtinēəm\ *n* -S [NL, fr. *actin-* + *-ium*; fr. the darkening effect of light on some zinc sulfide] **1 :** a supposed chemical element once thought to occur in commercial zinc **2 :** a radioactive trivalent metallic element resembling lanthanum in chemical properties formed by alpha radiation from protactinium and found esp. in pitchblende — symbol *Ac;* see ACTINIDE SERIES, ACTINIUM SERIES; ELEMENT table

actinium emanation *n* **:** ACTINON

actinium series *n* **:** a radioactive series beginning with actinouranium, constituting the isotope of uranium of mass number 235, and ending with actinium D, constituting the nonradioactive isotope of lead of mass number 207: actinouranium, at. no. 92 (syn. uranium 235)→ uranium Y, at. no. 90 (syn. thorium 231)→ protactinium 231, at. no. 91 → actinium 227, at. no. 89→ radioactinium, at. no. 90 (syn. thorium 227) [or actinium K, at. no. 87 (syn. francium 223)]→ actinium X, at. no. 88 (syn. radium 223)→ actinon, at. no. 86 (syn. radon 219)→ actinium A, at. no. 84 (syn. polonium 215)→ actinium B, at. no. 82 (syn. lead 211) [or astatine 215, at. no. 85] → actinium C, at. no. 83 (syn. bismuth 211)→ actinium C, at. no. 84 (syn. polonium 211) [or actinium C, at. no. 81 (syn. thallium 207)] → actinium D, at. no. 82 (syn. lead 207) — compare ACTINIDE SERIES

ac·tin·i·zoa \(ˌ)akˌtinəˈzōə\ [NL, fr. *actin-* + *-zoa*] *syn of* ANTHOZOA

ac·ti·ni·zo·an \ˌakˌtinəˈzōən, akˈt-\ *adj* [NL *Actinizoa* + E *-an*] **:** ANTHOZOAN

actino- — see ACTIN-

ac·ti·no·bac·il·lary \ˌaktə(ˌ)nōˈbasəˌlerē *also* -ˌbəˈsilərē\ *adj* [*actin-* + *bacillary*] **:** caused by actinobacilli

ac·ti·no·bac·il·lo·sis \-ˌbasəˈlōsəs\ *n, pl* **actinobacilloses** \-ōˌsēz\ [NL, fr. *actinobacillus* + *-osis*] **:** a disease of cattle, swine, and occas. of other domestic animals or man resembling actinomycosis and caused by a true bacterium (*Actinobacillus lignieresi*)

ac·ti·no·bac·il·lot·ic \-ˈlädik\ *adj* [fr. NL *actinobacillosis*, after such pairs as NL *psychosis:* E *psychotic*] **:** of or relating to actinobacillosis

ac·ti·no·ba·cil·lus \-ˌbəˈsiləs\ *n* [NL, fr. *actin-* + *bacillus*] **1** *cap* **:** a genus of aerobic gram-negative parasitic bacteria (family Brucellaceae) forming filaments resembling streptobacilli — see ACTINOBACILLOSIS **2** *pl* **actinobacil·li** \-iˌlī\ **:** a bacterium of the genus *Actinobacillus*

ac·tin·o·branch \akˈtinəˌbraŋk\ *or* **ac·ti·no·bran·chia** \ˌaktə(ˌ)nōˈbraŋkēə\ *n* -S [NL *actinobranchia*, fr. *actin-* + *branchia*] **:** a gill-like organ of certain Anthozoa

ac·ti·no·chem·is·try \ˌaktə(ˌ)nōˈ-\ *n* -ES [*actin-* + *chemistry*] **:** chemistry in its relations to actinism **:** PHOTOCHEMISTRY

ac·ti·no·cri·nite \ˌaktə(ˌ)nōˈkrīˌnīt\ *n* -S [prob. fr. F, fr. NL *Actinocrinus* + F *-ite*] **:** a fossil crinoid of *Actinocrinus* or a related genus

ac·ti·no·cri·nus \-ˈkrīnəs\ *n, cap* [NL, fr. *actin-* + *-crinus*] **:** a genus (the type of the family Actinocrinidae) of crinoids abundant in the Mississippian rocks of America and Europe

ac·tin·o·drome \akˈtinəˌdrōm\ *or* **ac·ti·nod·ro·mous** \ˌaktəˈnädrəməs\ *adj* [*actin-* + *-drome, -dromous*] *of a leaf* **:** palmately veined

ac·ti·no·elec·tric \ˌaktə(ˌ)nō+\ *adj* [*actin-* + *electric*] **:** exhibiting photoconductivity

ac·tin·o·graph \akˈtinəˌgraf\ *n* -S [*actin-* + *-graph*] **:** an instrument operating on the principle of the slide rule and used for calculating suitable exposure time in photography — **ac·ti·nog·ra·phy** \ˌaktəˈnägrəfē\ *n* -ES

ac·ti·noid \ˈaktəˌnȯid\ *adj* [*actin-* + *-oid*] **1 :** resembling a ray esp. of a radially symmetrical animal **2 :** exhibiting radial symmetry

ac·ti·noi·da \ˌaktəˈnȯidə\ *or* **ac·ti·noi·dea** \-dēə\ [NL, fr. *actin-* + *-oida, -oidea*] *syn of* ANTHOZOA

ac·tin·o·lite \akˈtinəˌlīt\ *n* -S [*actin-* + *-lite;* trans. of G *strahlstein*] **:** a mineral consisting of a bright green or grayish green variety of amphibole containing calcium, magnesium, and iron $Ca(Mg,Fe)_5Si_8O_{22}(OH)_2$ and occurring often in fibrous, radiated, or columnar forms (sp. gr. 3–3.2) — **ac·tin·o·lit·ic** \ˌakˌtinəˈlidik, akˈt-\ *adj*

ac·tin·o·logue \akˈtinəˌlȯg *also* -äg\ *n* -S [back-formation fr. *actinology*] **:** an organ or part of an actinomere that corresponds to another in a different actinomere — **ac·ti·nol·o·gous** \ˌaktəˈnäləgəs\ *adj*

ac·ti·nol·o·gy \ˌaktəˈnäləjē\ *n* -ES [ISV *actin-* + *-logy*] **1 :** a science that deals with actinism and photochemical effects **2 :** correspondence of similar parts of a radiate animal (as of the different actinomeres) **:** radial homology

ac·tin·o·mere \akˈtinəˌmi(ə)r\ *n* -S [prob. fr. F *actinomère*, fr. *actin-* + *-mère* -mere] **:** one of the radial segments composing the body of a radiate animal — **ac·tin·o·mer·ic** \-ˌtinəˈmerik\ *adj*

ac·ti·nom·e·ter \ˌaktəˈnäməd·ə(r)\ *n* -S [*actin-* + *-meter*] **1 :** an instrument for measuring the direct heating power of the sun's rays **2 :** an instrument for measuring the actinic power of radiant energy usu. by means of light-sensitive paper that darkens on exposure to light; *specif* **:** a photographic instrument for measuring the exposure to be given — compare PHOTOMETER — **ac·ti·no·met·ric** \ˌaktənōˈmetrik\ *adj* — **ac·ti·nom·e·try** \ˌaktəˈnämətrē\ *n* -ES

ac·ti·no·mor·phic \ˌaktə(ˌ)nōˈmȯrfik\ *also* **ac·ti·no·mor·phous** \-fəs\ *adj* [ISV *actin-* + *-morphic* or *-morphous*] **:** radially symmetrical — used of organisms, organs, or parts capable of division into essentially symmetrical halves by any longitudinal plane passing through the axis; compare ZYGOMORPHIC

ac·ti·no·mor·phy \-fē\ *n* -ES [*actin-* + *-morphy*] **:** the quality or state of being actinomorphic

ac·ti·no·my·ces \ˌ==(ˌ)=ˈmīˌsēz\ *n* [NL, fr. *actin-* + *-myces*] **1** *cap* **:** a genus of filamentous bacteria (family Actinomycetaceae) including numerous soil-inhabiting saprophytes and various disease-producing plant and animal parasites that form a much-branched mycelium which may break up into segments functioning as conidia and which in lesions of the animal body may conspicuous rosettes of radiating clavate threads — see ACTINOMYCOSIS **2** *pl* **actinomyces :** a bacterium of the genus *Actinomyces*

ac·ti·no·my·ce·ta·ce·ae \ˌ==(ˌ)=ˌmīsəˈtāsēˌē\ *n pl, cap* [NL, fr. *Actinomycet-, Actinomyces*, type genus + *-aceae*] **:** a family of filamentous bacteria of the order Actinomycetales, often branched, sometimes forming a mycelium that readily breaks up into bacillary elements, and sometimes producing conidia

ac·ti·no·my·ce·tal \-ˌmīˈsēdᵊl\ *adj* [NL *Actinomycetales*] **:** of or belonging to the Actinomycetales

ac·ti·no·my·ce·ta·les \-ˌmīsəˈtā(ˌ)lēz\ *n pl, cap* [NL, fr. *Actinomycet-, Actinomyces* + *-ales*] **:** an order of filamentous or rod-shaped bacteria tending strongly to the development of branches and true mycelium and lacking photosynthetic pigment — see MYCOBACTERIACEAE, STREPTOMYCETACEAE

ac·ti·no·my·cete \-ˈmīˌsēt, -ˌmīˈsēt\ *n* -S [ISV *actin-* + *-mycete*] **:** any organism belonging to the order Actinomycetales — **ac·ti·no·my·ce·tous** \-ˌmīˈsēd·əs\ *adj*

ac·ti·no·my·ce·tin \-ˌmīˈsētᵊn\ *n* -S [*actin-* + *mycetin*] **:** an enzymelike antibiotic obtained from a soil actinomycete (*Streptomyces albus*) that lyses various bacteria (as living streptococci or heat-killed colon bacilli)

ac·ti·no·my·cin \ˌ==(ˌ)=ˈmīsᵊn\ *n* -S [NL *Actinomyces* + E *-in*] **:** any of various red or yellow-red mostly toxic crystalline polypeptide antibiotics isolated from various soil bacteria (esp. *Streptomyces antibioticus*) — usu. followed by a distinguishing letter ⟨~ C is one of the less toxic members of the group⟩

ac·ti·no·my·co·ma \ˌ==(ˌ)=ˌmīˈkōmə\ *n, pl* **actinomycomas** \-məz\ *or* **actinomycoma·ta** \-məd·ə\ [NL, fr. *actin-* + *myc-* + *-oma*] **:** the characteristic granulomatous lesion of actinomycosis

ac·ti·no·my·co·sis \-ˌmīˈkōsəs\ *n, pl* **actinomyco·ses** \-ōˌsēz\ [NL, fr. *Actinomyces* + *-osis*] **:** infection with actinomycetes esp. of the genus *Actinomyces:* **a :** a chronic infectious disease of cattle, swine, and man characterized by the formation in mouth and jaw and sometimes also in chest, intestines, skin, mammary tissue, or brain of hard granulomatous masses that may break down and discharge pus containing the causative actinomycetes (usu. *Actinomyces bovis* in domestic animals and presumably *A. israeli* in man) — see ACTINOMYCOMA **b :** POTATO SCAB

ac·ti·no·my·cot·ic \-ˈkädik\ *adj* [fr. NL *actinomycosis*, after such pairs as NL *psychosis:* E *psychotic*] **:** of or relating to actinomycosis

ac·ti·no·myx·i·da \-ˈmiksədə\ *syn of* ACTINOMYXIDIA

ac·ti·no·myx·id·ia \-(ˌ)mikˈsidēə\ *n pl, cap* [NL, alter. of *Actinomyxida*, fr. *actin-* + *myx-* + *-ida*] **:** a small order of cnidosporidian protozoan parasites of worms distinguished by spores with trivalve shells and three polar capsules — **ac·ti·no·myx·id·i·an** \-ˈsidēən\ *adj or n*

ac·ti·no·myx·i·di·i·da \ˌ==(ˌ)=ˌmiksəˈdīədə\ *syn of* ACTINOMYXIDIA

ac·ti·non \ˈaktəˌnän\ *n* -S [NL, fr. *actinium* + *-on*] **:** a heavy radioactive gaseous isotope of the group of inert gases that is isotopic with radon and thoron, is formed from actinium X, emits alpha rays, and lives only a few seconds (mass number 219) — called also *actinium emanation;* see ACTINIUM SERIES

ac·ti·no·ne·ma \ˌaktə(ˌ)nōˈnēmə\ *n, cap* [NL, fr. *actin-* + *-nema*] **:** a form genus of imperfect fungi (order Melanconiales) having hyaline 2-celled spores

ac·tin·o·phage \akˈtinəˌfāj\ *n* -S [*actinomycete* + *-phage*] **:** a phage that develops in and lyses an actinomycete — compare BACTERIOPHAGE

ac·tin·o·phore \-ˌfō(ə)r\ *n* -S [*actin-* + *-phore*] **:** a bony or cartilaginous element supporting the fin rays of fishes

ac·ti·noph·o·rous \ˌaktəˈnäf(ə)rəs\ *adj* [Gk *aktinophoros* ray-bearing, fr. *aktin-* actin- + *-phoros* -phorous] **:** having raylike spines

ac·ti·noph·ry·an \ˌaktəˈnäfrēən\ *adj* [NL *Actinophrys* + E *-an*] **:** of or belonging to *Actinophrys*

ac·ti·noph·rys \ˌaktəˈnäfrəs, akˈtinəf-\ *n* [NL, fr. *actin-* + Gk *ophrys* brow, rim — more at BROW] **1** *cap* **:** a genus of protozoans (order Heliozoa) widely distributed in stagnant water **2** *pl* **actinophrys :** a protozoan of the genus *Actinophrys*

actinophrys

ac·ti·no·phy·to·sis \ˌaktə(ˌ)nō-(ˌ)fīˈtōsəs\ *n, pl* **actinophyto·ses** \-ōˌsēz\ [NL, fr. *actin-* + *phytosis*] **:** STREPTOTRICHOSIS

ac·tin·o·pod \akˈtinəˌpäd\ *n* -S [NL *Actinopoda*] **:** a protozoan of the subclass Actinopoda

ac·ti·nop·o·da \ˌaktəˈnäpədə\ *n pl, cap* [NL, fr. *actin-* + *-poda*] **1** *in former classifications* **:** an order of holothurians with tentacles arising from radial ambulacral vessels **2 :** a subclass of Sarcodina comprising usu. freely floating protozoans with highly specialized pseudopodia and including the orders Heliozoa and Radiolaria — compare AXOPODIUM — **ac·ti·no·po·di·an** \ˌ==(ˌ)nōˈpōdēən\ *n* -S

ac·ti·nop·te·ran \ˌaktəˈnäptərən\ *n* -S [NL *Actinopteri* + E *-an*] **:** ACTINOPTERYGIAN

ac·ti·nop·te·ri \-təˌrī\ [NL, fr. *actin-* + *-pteri* (pl. of *-pterus*)] *syn of* ACTINOPTERYGII

¹ac·ti·nop·te·ryg·i·an \ˌ==ˌ==ˈrijēən\ *adj* [NL *Actinopterygii* + E *-an*] **:** of or relating to the Actinopterygii

²actinopterygian \ˈ"\ *n* -S **:** one of the Actinopterygii

ac·ti·nop·te·ryg·ii \ˌ==ˌ=ˈ=ēˌī\ *n pl, cap* [NL, fr. *actin-* + *-pterygii* (fr. Gk *pteryg-, pteryx* wing); akin to Gk *pteron* feather, wing — more at FEATHER] *in many classifications* **:** a subclass or other division of Teleostomi comprising fishes having the projecting part of the paired fins supported only by dermal rays and being coextensive with the Teleostomi excluding the Choanichthyes — **ac·ti·nop·te·ryg·i·ous** \ˌ==ˌ== ˈ=ēəs\ *adj*

ac·tin·o·some \akˈtinəˌsōm\ *also* **ac·ti·no·so·ma** \ˌaktə(ˌ)nōˈsōmə\ *n* -S [*actinosome* fr. *actin-* + *-some; actinosoma* fr. NL, fr. *actin-* + *-soma*] **:** the entire body of a simple or compound coelenterate

ac·ti·no·sphae·ri·um \ˌaktə(ˌ)nōˈsfirēəm\ *n, cap* [NL, fr. *actin-* + Gk *sphairion* little ball, dim. of *sphaira* ball, sphere — more at SPHERE] **:** a genus of large freshwater protozoans (order Heliozoa)

ac·ti·nost \ˈaktəˌnäst\ *n* -S [*actin-* + *-ost*] **:** one of certain small bones directly supporting the rays of paired fins of teleost and some ganoid fishes — called also *carpal, pterygiophore;* compare HYPERCORACOID

ac·tin·o·stele \akˈtinəˌstēl *also* ˌaktə(ˌ)nōˈstēlē\ *n* -S [*actin-* + *stele*] **:** a vascular core (as in most roots and some stems) having the xylem and phloem in alternating or radial groups within a pericycle — compare STELE

ac·ti·nos·to·mal \ˌaktəˈnästəməl\ *adj* [*actinostome* + *-al*] **:** relating or belonging to an actinostome

ac·tin·o·stome \akˈtinəˌstōm\ *n* -S [*actin-* + *-stome*] **1 :** the mouth of a radially symmetrical animal **2 :** the peristome of an echinoderm

ac·ti·no·ther·a·py \ˌaktə(ˌ)nōˈtherəpē-\ *n* -ES [ISV *actin-* + *therapy*] **:** application for therapeutic purposes of the chemically active rays of the spectrum (as ultraviolet light or X rays)

ac·ti·no·trich·i·um \ˌaktə(ˌ)nōˈtrikēəm\ *also* **ac·tin·o·trich** \akˈtinəˌtrik\ *n, pl* **ac·ti·no·trich·ia** \-ˈtrikēə\ *also* **ac·tin·o·trichs** \-ˌtriks\ [NL *actinotrichium*, fr. *actin-* + Gk *trich-, thrix* hair + NL *-ium* — more at TRICH-] **:** any of the hairy threadlike fibers in the fin fold of an embryo fish which fuse and form the base of the rays

ac·ti·not·ro·cha \ˌaktəˈnä·trəkə\ *n, pl* **actinotro·chae** \-ˌkē\ [NL, fr. *actin-* + *-trocha*] **:** the free-swimming larva of the genus *Phoronis*

ac·ti·no·ura·ni·um \ˌaktə(ˌ)nō-\ *n* [ISV *actino-* (fr. NL *actinium*) + *uranium*] **:** the uranium isotope of mass 235

ac·ti·no·zoa \ˌaktə(ˌ)nōˈzōə\ [NL, fr. *actin-* + *-zoa*] *syn of* ANTHOZOA

ac·ti·no·zo·an \ˌ==(ˌ)=ˈzōən\ *or* **ac·ti·no·zo·al** \-əl\ *adj* [NL *Actinozoa* + E *-an* or *-al*] **:** ANTHOZOAN

ac·ti·no·zo·on \ˌ==(ˌ)=ˈzōˌän\ *n* -S [NL, fr. *Actinaria* + *-zoon*] **:** ANTHOZOON

actins *pl of* ACTIN

ac·tin·u·la \akˈtinyələ\ *n, pl* **actinulas** \-ləz\ *or* **actinu·lae** \-ˌlē\ [NL, fr. *actin-* + *-ula*] **:** a creeping larva of the hydroid generation of certain coelenterates (as Tubularia) that finally attaches and develops into a polyp

ac·tio \ˈakshēˌō, ˈäktēˌō\ *n, pl* **ac·ti·o·nes** \ˌakshēˈōˌnēz, ˌäktēˈōˌnās\ [L] *Roman law* **:** an action or right of action — see FORMULA 5

ac·tio ad di·stans \-ˌadˈdiˌstanz, -ˌädˈdiˌstän(t)s\ *or* **actio in distans** \-ˌinˈd-\ *n* [NL] **:** action at a distance or without contact ⟨Leibnitz held that the apparent physical impossibility of *actio ad distans* was an objection to gravitation⟩

actio bo·nae fi·dei \-ˈbōnēˈfīdēˌī, -ˈbōˌnīˈfideˌē\ *n, pl* **actiones bonae fidei** [LL, lit., action of good faith] **:** an action in Roman law giving great power to the trial judge to take all matters of good faith, conscience, and equity into consideration of the whole case — contrasted with *actio stricti juris*

¹ac·tion \ˈakshən\ *n* -S [ME *accioun*, fr. MF *action*, fr. L *action-, actio*, fr. *actus* (past part. of *agere* to do) + *-ion-, -io* -ion — more at AGENT] **1 :** a deliberative or authorized proceeding: **a** (1) **:** a legal proceeding by which one demands or enforces one's right in a court of justice (2) **:** a judicial proceeding for the enforcement or protection of a right, the redress or prevention of a wrong, or the punishment of a public offense — usu. distinguished from *special proceeding* (3) **:** the right to bring or maintain such a legal or judicial proceeding — see SUIT **b** (1) **:** an award by a judicial body (2) **:** an act or decision by an executive or legislative body (as of a government or a political party) or by a supranational agency ⟨the ~ taken by Congress followed a lengthy debate⟩ ⟨strikes organized by ~ committees⟩ **2 a :** the bringing about of an alteration by force or through some natural agency ⟨the ~ of water on rocks⟩ **b :** the process of change or alteration considered as a natural condition **:** ACTIVITY ⟨intervals of ~ and repose⟩ **c :** the progressive alteration of mental states or of mental and physical states coordinately esp. when resulting in an observable effect on the external world — compare BEHAVIOR 1b **d :** a quantity expressed in cgs units of erg seconds relating to the change of a dynamic system from one configuration to another and regarded in classical dynamics as twice the product of the average kinetic energy during the change and the time interval in which the change takes place **e** *ecol* **:** the effect of the environment on the individuals exposed to it as a factor in community formation — see COACTION **3 :** the process of doing **:** exertion of energy **:** PERFORMANCE **:** manner of doing: **a :** the deportment of an actor or speaker or his expression by means of attitude, voice, gesture, and countenance ⟨an actor's words and ~*s* should agree⟩ **b :** the movement of the feet and legs (of a horse or dog) **c :** a function of the body or of one of its parts or organs; *specif* **:** DEFECATION **4 :** a voluntary act of will that manifests itself externally ⟨an emergency requiring ~⟩ or that may be completed internally (as in contemplation) — contrasted with *passion* **5 a :** a thing done **:** DEED **b actions** *pl* **:** BEHAVIOR, CONDUCT 3c ⟨somber ~*s*⟩ **c :** INITIATIVE, ENTERPRISE ⟨a man of ~⟩ **6 a** (1) **:** an engagement between troops ⟨two small ~*s* for control of the hill⟩ or ships ⟨decks cleared for ~⟩ (2) **:** combat in war ⟨he saw ~ on a destroyer⟩ **b** (1) **:** a real or imaginary event or series of events forming the subject of a play, poem, or other composition (2) **:** the unfolding of the events of a drama or work of fiction **:** PLOT (3) **:** the movement of incidents in a plot ⟨*action*-packed drama⟩ ⟨an ~ story⟩ **c :** the combination of circumstances that constitute the subject matter of a painting or sculpture **d** (1) **:** a religious ceremony **:** a sacramental or devotional performance (2) **:** the canon of the mass, the communion service, or the Lord's Supper **7 :** a share of stock **8 a :** an operating mechanism: (1) **:** a mechanism connecting the keys with the sounding or effective part (as strings, pipes, or type faces) of a keyboard instrument or machine (2) **:** a mechanism by means of which a firearm is loaded and fired — compare LOCK; AUTOMATIC, DOUBLE-ACTION, SEMIAUTOMATIC, SINGLE-ACTION **b :** the manner in which a mechanism operates: (1) **:** the response or resistance of keys in a keyboard-operated mechanism to the player's or operator's fingers ⟨a stiff ~⟩ ⟨a sluggish ~⟩ (2) **:** the amount of resiliency and flexibility in a fishing rod in relation to its length and diameter ⟨dry-fly ~⟩ ⟨wet-fly ~⟩ (3) **:** the relationship between the number of turns made by the reel spool in a fishing reel for every turn of the reel handle ⟨a single-*action* reel⟩ **9 a :** the price movement and trading volume of a commodity, security, or market **b :** the entire process of betting including essentially the offering and acceptance of a bet and determination of a winner

²action \ˈ"\ *vt* -ED/-ING/-S *archaic* **:** to bring a legal action against

ac·tion·abil·i·ty \ˌaksh(ə)nəˈbilәd·ē\ *n* -ES **:** the quality or state of being actionable

ac·tion·able \ˈaksh(ə)nəbəl\ *adj* **:** subject to or affording ground for an action or suit at law ⟨slander is ~⟩

ac·tion·al \ˈakshənᵊl, -shnəl\ *adj* **1 :** relating to action or an action **2** *of a passive verb form* **:** expressing an action (as *was closed* in "the door was closed at eight o'clock") — contrasted with *statal*

action current *n* **:** an electric current arising from a variation of potential occurring during activity in living tissue (as a muscle or nerve)

actiones *pl of* ACTIO

ac·tion·ing \ˈaksh(ə)niŋ, -ēŋ\ *n* -S **:** the providing of an action to a gun; *also* **:** ACTION 8a(2)

ac·tion·ist \-sh(ə)nəst\ *n* -S **:** an advocate of direct action esp. in politics

action noun *n* **:** a noun denoting action (as *belief, inspection, arrival*) — sometimes used to include verbal nouns (as the infinitive *to believe* or the gerund *believing*)

action on the case 1 : TRESPASS ON THE CASE **2 :** a remedy for recovery of damages for tort in instances where injury was neither immediate nor direct — usu. referring to an action ex delicto but sometimes to assumpsit; compare FORM OF ACTION

action-research *n* **:** the use of techniques of social and psychological research to identify social problems in a group or community coupled with active participation of the investigators in group efforts to solve these problems

action sermon *n* **:** the sermon preached immediately before communion in Scottish Presbyterian churches

action spectrum *n* **:** a graphic representation of a physiological reaction; *specif* **:** physiological activity plotted against light wavelength

action time *n* **:** the time during which a stimulus must act to produce maximum effect — compare PRESENTATION TIME

ac·tio stric·ti ju·ris \-ˈstrikˌtīˈjürəs, -kˌtēˈyürəs\ *n, pl* **actiones stricti juris** [LL, lit., action of strict law] **:** an action in Roman law that the judge was to decide according to the strict legal rules without reference to equitable considerations — contrasted with *actio bonae fidei*

ac·ti·py·laea \ˌaktəˌpīˈlēə\ *or* **ac·ti·py·lar·ia** \-ˈla(a)rēə\ [*Actipylaea* fr. NL, alter. of *Actipylea; Actipylaria* fr. NL, fr. *Actipylea* + *-aria*] *syn of* ACTIPYLEA

ac·ti·py·lea \ˌaktəˈpīlēə\ *n pl, cap* [NL, irreg. fr. Gk *aktis* ray + *pylē* gate — more at ACTIN-, PYLON] **:** a suborder of Radiolaria comprising protozoa with skeletons of spicules of strontium sulfate

ac·ti·va·ble \ˈaktəvəbəl\ *adj* [*activate* + *-able*] **:** capable of being activated

ac·ti·vate \ˈaktəˌvāt, *usu* -ād·+V\ *vb* -ED/-ING/-S [*active* + *-ate*] *vt* **:** to make active or more active: as **a** (1) **:** to render (molecules) capable of reaction or to increase the reactivity of (parts of molecules) by the presence of neighboring groups (2) **:** to convert (a compound, as a provitamin or enzyme) into an active form or different compound, esp. into one that has a particular biological action ⟨~ ergosterol by irradiation to vitamin D_2 for use in treating rickets⟩ **b :** to render (a substance) radioactive, luminescent, photosensitive, or photoconductive by treatment (as by radiation or electric oscillation) or by admixture of an impurity **c** (1) **:** to alter the nature of the surface of (specific mineral particles in the flotation of an ore pulp) so that certain reagents will adhere (2) **:** to treat (materials, as carbon, clay, alumina, silica gel) so as to improve esp. adsorptive properties (as for use in removing colors from sugar solutions and other solutions, chemicals from vapor lines, and odors from water) **d :** to treat by prolonged aeration so as to favor the growth of organisms that will decompose (sewage) **e** (1) **:** to start development of (an egg) by fertilization or experimentally by chemicals (2) **:** to stimulate to sexual activity **:** induce heat or rut in **f :** to set up or formally institute (a military unit) with the necessary personnel and equipment ~ *vi* **:** to become active **syn** see VITALIZE

activated alumina *n* **:** a porous highly adsorptive alumina made usu. by heating alumina hydrates and used chiefly in drying gases and liquids

activated carbon *or* **activated charcoal** *n* **:** a highly adsorbent powdered or granular carbon or charcoal made usu. by carbonization of carbonaceous materials (as wood or coconut shells) and chemical activation (as by oxidizing gases) and used chiefly for adsorbing gases, for purifying syrups, for removing undesirable colors and odors, and for solvent recovery — called also *active carbon;* compare BONE BLACK

activated sludge process *n* **:** a sewage treatment procedure in which the decomposition of the raw sewage is hastened by the addition to it of biologically active sewage sludge

ac·ti·va·tion \ˌaktəˈvāshən\ *n* -s **:** the act or process of activating

activation energy *n* **:** the minimum amount of energy required to convert a normal stable molecule into a reactive molecule

ac·ti·va·tor \ˈaktəˌvād·ə(r)\ *n* -s **:** one that activates: as **a :** a substance that renders another substance active in a specific manner: as (1) **:** a chemical (as an ethanolamine) that acts with an accelerator to increase the rate of vulcanization of rubber (2) **:** an impurity (as a metal) present in small amounts in a luminescent solid (as a phosphor) to which the luminescence is attributed (3) **:** a substance (as a chloride ion) that increases the activity of an enzyme — usu. distinguished from *coenzyme* and *kinase* **b** *embryol* **:** a substance given off by developing tissue that stimulates differentiation of adjacent tissue; *also* **:** a structure giving off such a stimulant **c :** ACCELERATOR 1b

¹**ac·tive** \ˈaktiv, -ēv *also* -əv\ *adj* [ME, fr. MF or L; MF *actif,* fr. L *activus,* fr. *actus* (past part. of *agere* to drive, do) + *-ivus* -ive — more at AGENT] **1 :** characterized by action rather than by contemplation or speculation ⟨an ~ man⟩ **2 :** productive of action or movement ⟨a dog very much awake and filled with ~ antagonism —Jack McLaren⟩ **3 a** *of a verb form or voice* **:** asserting that the person or thing represented by the grammatical subject performs the action represented by the verb ⟨*hits* in "he hits the ball" and *shone* in "the sun shone" are ~⟩ — contrasted with *middle* and *passive* **b** *of a verb or verb form* **:** expressing action as distinct from mere existence or state ⟨"he walks" and "he walked" have ~ verbs⟩ — now used esp. in the grammar of certain American Indian and African languages; compare NEUTER 1b, STATIC, STATIVE **c** *of a grammatical construction* **:** containing an active verb form **4 :** quick in physical movement **:** of agile and vigorous habit **:** NIMBLE, LIVELY ⟨an animal ~ in burrowing⟩ **5 :** requiring vigorous action or exertion ⟨an interest in ~ sports⟩ **6 a :** having practical operation or results **:** EFFECTIVE ⟨an ~ law⟩ **b** *of a volcano* **:** erupting at the present time or at intervals of a few years or having a crater that contains fluid lava — compare DORMANT, EXTINCT **7 a :** disposed to action **:** ENERGETIC, DILIGENT ⟨to take an ~ interest⟩ **b :** engaged in an action or activity **:** PARTICIPATING ⟨an ~ club member⟩ **8 :** engaged in full-time service esp. in the armed forces ⟨ordered to ~ duty⟩ **9 :** marked by present operation, transaction, movement, or use ⟨an ~ coal mine⟩ ⟨an ~ bank account⟩ ⟨~ titles in a publisher's catalog⟩ ⟨a student's ~ vocabulary⟩ **10 a :** capable of acting or reacting esp. in some specific manner or with more than ordinary vigor **:** REACTIVE, ACTIVATED ⟨~ nitrogen⟩ ⟨~ charcoal⟩ **b :** OPTICALLY ACTIVE **c :** RADIOACTIVE ⟨an ~ deposit⟩ **11 :** still eligible to win the pot in poker — used of a player who has not dropped **12 :** moving down the line or visiting in the set — used of couples in contredanses or square dances **13** *of a disease* **:** progressing or retrogressing ⟨~ tuberculosis⟩ — **ac·tive·ly** \-təvlē, -li\ *adv* — **ac·tive·ness** \-ivnəs, -ēv- *also* -əv-\ *n* -ES

²**active** \"\ *n* -s **1 :** one that is active ⟨fraternity alumni and ~*s*⟩ **2 a :** an active verb **b :** the active voice of a language or a form in it

active amyl alcohol *n* **:** a liquid levorotatory primary alcohol $C_2H_5CH(CH_3)CH_2OH$ occurring in fusel oil; *levo*-2-methyl-1-butanol

active bond *n, Brit* **:** a bond bearing a fixed rate of interest from date of issue

active carbon *n* **:** ACTIVATED CARBON

active component *n* **:** the average power of an alternating electric current divided by the effective voltage in a circuit

active door *n* **:** the one of a pair of doors that is ordinarily used alone

active duty *or* **active service** *n* **:** full-time service in the armed forces with regular duties and pay and subject to the Uniform Code of Military Justice and appropriate regulations

active immunity *n* **:** immunity commonly long-lasting acquired through production of antibodies within the organism in response to the presence of antigens (as by infection or injection) — see PASSIVE IMMUNITY

active list *n* **:** a list comprising the officers and enlisted personnel of the armed forces who are performing or normally available for military duties and are receiving full pay

active mass *n* **1 :** the concentration of a reacting substance expressed usu. in moles per liter **2 :** the concentration of the portion of a dissolved electrolyte that is dissociated into ions and hence is capable of carrying the electric current

active serum *n* **:** a serum that contains complement

active trust *n* **:** a trust in which the trustee is charged with the performance of some substantial duties in respect to the control, management, and disposition of the trust property

ac·tiv·ism \ˈaktəˌvizəm, -ēˌv-\ *n* -s [G *aktivismus,* fr. *aktiv* active (fr. L *activus*) + *-ismus* -ism — more at ACTIVE] **1 :** either of two philosophical doctrines: (1) the mind is active, not passive, in perception or (2) activity is creative or fundamental **:** ACTUALISM — compare PRAGMATISM, VOLUNTARISM **2 :** a doctrine or practice that emphasizes vigorous action (as the use of force for political ends)

¹**ac·tiv·ist** \-vəst\ *n* -s [G *aktivist,* fr. *aktiv* + *-ist*] **:** one that advocates or practices activism

²**activist** \"\ *also* **ac·tiv·is·tic** \ˌ⸗⸗ˈvistik, -ēk\ *adj* **:** of or belonging to or having the characteristics of activism or activists **:** advocating or practicing activism

ac·tiv·i·ty \akˈtivəd·ē, -ətē, -i\ *n* -ES [MF *activité,* fr. ML *activitat-, activitas,* fr. L *activus* active + *-itat-, -itas* -ity — more at ACTIVE] **1 :** the quality or state of being active ⟨the sphere of his ~⟩ **2 :** physical motion or exercise of force: as **a :** vigorous or energetic action **:** LIVELINESS ⟨to restrict his ~⟩ **b :** adroit or skillful physical action **:** AGILITY ⟨an athlete's ~⟩ **3 :** natural or normal function or operation ⟨~ on the stock exchange⟩: as **a :** a process (as moving or digesting) that an organism carries on or participates in by virtue of being alive **b :** any similar process (as searching, desiring, learning, or writing) that actually or potentially involves mental function; *specif* **:** an educational procedure designed to stimulate learning by firsthand experience or observation, experiment, inquiry, and discussion ⟨~ program⟩ — compare PROJECT, UNIT **4 a :** an actuating force ⟨solar ~⟩ **b** *sometimes cap* **:** a creative agency or process; *esp* **:** an ultimate or underived cosmic agency **5 a :** an occupation, pursuit, or recreation in which a person is active — often used in pl. ⟨business *activities*⟩ ⟨social *activities*⟩ **b :** a form of organized, supervised, and often extracurricular recreation (as athletic games, dramatics, or dancing) **6** *chem* **a :** the characteristic of acting rapidly or of promoting a rapid reaction ⟨the ~ of adsorbent carbon⟩ ⟨the ~ of a catalyst⟩ **b :** the apparent or effective concentration of a substance esp. in solution as judged by the behavior of the substance under given conditions, such concentration being equal to the actual concentration in very dilute ideal solutions — called also *relative fugacity* **7 :** an organizational unit for performing a specific function; *also* **:** its duties or function ⟨navy supplies procured from the nearest shore ~⟩ ⟨the food-inspection ~ of the health department⟩

activity cage *n* **:** a cage for a small animal with a treadwheel or other device by which it can exercise

activity coefficient *n* **:** the ratio of chemical activity to actual concentration **:** an arbitrary quantity that in the case of solutions is a measure of the deviation of a more or less concentrated solution from an ideal solution

activity group psychotherapy *or* **activity group therapy** *n* **:** group psychotherapy in which the subjects (as children) are permitted to act out their repressed impulses in the presence of a nonparticipating therapist

ac·tiv·ize \ˈaktəˌvīz, -ēˌv-\ *vt* -ED/-ING/-S **:** ACTIVATE

act of adjournal *Scots law, usu pl* **:** one of various ordinances issued by the Court of Justiciary for regulating the procedure in that court and the inferior criminal courts

act of bankruptcy *or* **act of insolvency :** an act specified by law as subjecting a person to be proceeded against as an involuntary bankrupt or insolvent

act of faith [trans. of Pg *auto-da-fé*] **:** an act requiring or displaying faith; *specif* **:** AUTO-DA-FÉ

act of god *cap G* **:** an extraordinary interruption by a natural cause (as a severe flood or earthquake) of the usual course of events that experience, prescience, or care cannot reasonably foresee or prevent — compare INEVITABLE ACCIDENT

act of grace : an act extending clemency to offenders before the law (as one at the beginning of a new reign granting pardon or amnesty to numerous offenders)

act of honor : an acceptance or payment for honor of a protested bill of exchange; *also* **:** the instrument reciting such protest and acceptance or payment

act of indemnity 1 : an act passed to relieve persons (as officials) from some penalty to which they have become liable by acting illegally or beyond the limits of their powers **2 :** an act passed to provide compensation for damage incurred in the service of the government or resulting from some public measure

act of law : a change of a person's legal rights, obligations, or liabilities (as in the acquisition of a right or exemption from a liability) arising from the legal effect of some event such as bankruptcy

act of sederunt *Scots law, usu pl* **:** one of various rules of the Court of Session for regulating procedure in that court

ac·to·my·o·sin \ˌaktəˈmīəsən\ *n* [ISV *actin* + *-o-* + *myosin;* orig. formed as G *aktomyosin*] **:** a viscous substance that consists of a complex of actin and myosin, has the property of contractility, and is postulated to be concerned together with adenosine triphosphate in muscular contraction — formerly called *myosin*

ac·ton \ˈaktən\ *n* -s [ME *aketoun,* fr. OF *aketon,* cotton wool, padding, padded jacket, fr. OProv or OSp; OProv *alcoton* cotton, fr. OSp, fr. Ar *al-quṭun* the cotton] **:** a stuffed jacket worn under the mail of medieval body armor; *also* **:** a jacket plated with steel

ac·tor \ˈaktə(r) *also* -ˌtȯ(ə)r *or* -ȯ(ə)\ *n* -s [ME *actour* doer, pleader, fr. L *actor,* fr. *actus* (past part. of *agere* to drive, do) + *-or* — more at AGENT] **1** *Roman law* **:** one that conducts a legal action **:** PLEADER **: a :** PLAINTIFF — opposed to *reus* **b :** an advocate in civil causes **c :** the officer of a Roman corporation charged with prosecuting lawsuits in its behalf and defending those brought against it **2 a :** one that acts in a stage play, motion picture, radio or television play, or dramatic sketch **b :** a theatrical performer ⟨a professional ~⟩ **c :** one that behaves as if acting a part **3 a :** one that takes part in any affair **:** PARTICIPANT ⟨the , apers and memoirs of the leading ~*s* are shedding new light on the inside story of government —J.A.R.Pimlott⟩ **b :** WRONGDOER, TORT-FEASOR **4 :** one that is noticed for poor behavior or performance or for harmful influence or effect ⟨he's a bad ~ when he's drunk⟩

ac·tor·ish \ˈaktərish\ *adj* **:** having the characteristics of a professional actor; *esp* **:** noticeably histrionic or stagy in appearance or mannerism — **ac·tor·ish·ly** *adv*

actor-proof \ˈ⸗⸗ˌ⸗\ *adj* **:** effective no matter how badly acted — usu. used of a play or a part

ac·tory \ˈaktərē\ *adj* **:** ACTORISH

act out *vt* **1 a :** to represent in action ⟨my childhood was spent in reading and *acting out* what I read⟩ **b :** to translate into action ⟨unwilling to *act out* their beliefs⟩ **2** *psychoanalysis* **:** to express (repressed or unconscious impulses) directly in overt behavior without awareness or insight esp. during psychoanalytic investigation

act psychology *n* **:** psychology conceived as the study of the individual act esp. for meaning and intent — called also *intentionalism;* contrasted with *content psychology*

ac·tress \ˈaktrəs\ *n* -ES [*actor* + *-ess*] **1** *obs* **:** a woman that takes part in any affair **2 :** a female actor

ac·tressy \-sē\ *adj* **:** having the characteristics of a professional actress; *esp* **:** noticeably histrionic or stagy in appearance or mannerism

acts *pl of* ACT, *pres 3d sing of* ACT

-acts *pl of* -ACT

¹**ac·tu·al** \ˈakchə(wə)l, -ksh-\ *adj* [ME *actuel* active, existing, fr. MF, fr. LL *actualis* active, practical, fr. L *actus* act + *-alis* -al — more at ACT] **1** *obs* **:** involving or relating to acts or deeds **:** ACTIVE ⟨her walking and other ~ performances —Shak.⟩ **2 a :** existing in act ⟨our ~ intentions⟩ **:** EXISTENT — contrasted with *potential* and *possible* **b :** existing in fact or reality **:** really acted or acting or carried out — contrasted with *ideal* and *hypothetical* ⟨in ~ life⟩ ⟨the ~ conditions⟩; distinguished from *apparent* and *nominal* ⟨the ~ cost of goods⟩ **3 :** not spurious **:** REAL, GENUINE ⟨an ~ blizzard⟩ ⟨~ falsehood⟩ ⟨hard-pressed but not in ~ poverty⟩ **4 :** in existence or taking place at the time **:** PRESENT, CURRENT ⟨caught in the ~ commission of the crime⟩ **5** *physics* **:** KINETIC; *also* **:** MOTIVE, SENSIBLE — used of energy **syn** see REAL

²**actual** \"\ *n* -s **1 :** something that is actual or exists in fact **:** REALITY **2 :** something actually received or at hand (as a cash receipt or a market commodity) as distinct from estimated or expected ⟨trading in both ~*s* and futures in grain⟩

actual cautery *n* **:** an agent (as a hot iron, electrocautery, or moxa) used to destroy tissue by heat — compare POTENTIAL CAUTERY

actual cost *n* **:** cost based on the most factual allocation of historical cost factors — compare ESTIMATED COST, STANDARD COST

actual fraud *n* **:** FRAUD 1a(1)

actual horizon *n* **:** HORIZON 1b(2)

ac·tu·al·ism \ˈakchə(wə)ˌlizəm, -ksh-\ *n* -s [¹*actual* + *-ism*] **1 :** a philosophical doctrine that all existence is active or spiritual, not inert or dead, or that reality is founded on activity or consists of process **2 :** the theory that the self is a bundle of successive perceptions rather than a unified substance or entity

ac·tu·al·ist \-ˌləst\ *n* -s [¹*actual* + *-ist*] **1 :** one who deals with, aims at, or considers actuality **2 :** an adherent of philosophical actualism — **ac·tu·al·is·tic** \ˌ⸗⸗(⸗)ˈlistik\ *adj*

ac·tu·al·i·ty \ˌakchəˈwaləd·ē, -ksh-, -ətē, -i\ *n* -ES [ML *actualitas,* fr. LL *actualis* + L *-itas* -ity] **1 :** the quality or state of being actual **:** FACT, REALITY; *esp* **:** phenomenal reality ⟨by each of these artists emotions and feelings have been given ~ in shape and form —Michael Kitson⟩ ⟨often what seems the most novel is, in ~, merely the revival of something old —R.B.West⟩ **2 :** something that is actual ⟨possible risks which have been seized upon as *actualities* —T.S.Eliot⟩ **3 a** *in Aristotelianism* **:** the being of an existent object insofar as it is not merely potential but is endowed with form — compare ENTELECHY **b** *in Hegelianism* **:** the status of an entity enjoying relative independence and self-sufficiency ⟨the ~ of a commonwealth⟩ **c :** the nature of a thing as realized in existence **d :** something that embodies actuality **4 :** a film record or radio or television broadcast of an event as it actually occurs ⟨~ film⟩ ⟨~ program⟩ — compare DOCUMENTARY

ac·tu·al·iz·a·ble \ˌakchə(wə)ˈlīzəbəl, -ksh-\ *adj* **:** capable of being made actual

ac·tu·al·i·za·tion \ˌakchə(wə)ləˈzāshən, -ksh-, -ˌlīˈz-\ *n* -s **:** the act or process of actualizing **:** REALIZATION

ac·tu·al·ize \ˈakchə(wə)ˌlīz, -ksh-\ *vb* -ED/-ING/-S *see -ize in Explan Notes, vt* **:** to make actual ⟨he was placed in a position calculated to ~ his worst potentialities —F.R.Leavis⟩ ~ *vi* **:** to become actual

ac·tu·al·ly \ˈaksh(ə)lē, ˈakchəl-, -li; ˈakchəwəl-, -chül-, -ksh-; *rap. or chiefly substand* ˈaks(ə)l-\ *adv* [ME, fr. ¹*actual* + *-ly*] **1 :** in act or in fact **:** REALLY ⟨nominally but not ~ independent — Karl Loewenstein⟩ **2 :** at the present moment **:** for the time being ⟨the transmission screen showing the picture that was ~ on the air —Denis Johnston⟩ **3 :** in point of fact **:** in truth — used to imply that one would expect the fact to be the opposite of what is stated ⟨she ~ spoke Latin⟩

actual neurosis *n* **:** a neurosis characterized by hypochondriacal complaints or somatic manifestations believed by Freud to be caused by organic changes resulting from sexual inhibition — distinguished from *psychoneurosis*

actual neurotic *n* **:** one suffering from an actual neurosis

actual sin *n, Roman Catholicism* **:** sin traceable to the personal will of the sinner — distinguished from *original sin*

actual tare *n* **:** tare determined by the actual weight of the container

actual time *n* **:** time taken by an employee to perform a given operation: as **a :** the time recorded for time and motion study before being compared with a normal working pace **b :** the time recorded on a timing device to be compared with a standard time or an allowed time

actual truth *n* **:** EMPIRICAL TRUTH

ac·tu·ar·i·al \ˌakchəˈwerēəl, -ksh-\ *adj* **:** of or relating to actuaries **:** determined by actuaries **:** relating to statistical calculation esp. of life expectancy ⟨a plan based on ~ principles⟩ — **ac·tu·ar·i·al·ly** *adv*

actuaries' table *n* **:** COMBINED EXPERIENCE TABLE

ac·tu·ary \ˈakchəˌwerē, -ksh-, -ri\ *n* -ES [LL *actuarius,* fr. L, shorthand writer, writer of accounts, fr. *actum* public transaction, record + *-arius* -ary — more at ACT] **1** *obs* **:** a clerk or registrar orig. of a law court **2 :** one trained in mathematics and statistics whose business it is to calculate insurance and annuity premiums, reserves, and dividends

ac·tu·ate \ˈakchəˌwāt, -ksh-\ *vb* -ED/-ING/-S [ML *actuatus,* past part. of *actuare,* fr. L *actus* act, deed — more at ACT] *vt* **1 :** to put into mechanical action or motion ⟨most of the hydraulically operated items of equipment are *actuated* by pistons and cylinders —W.R.Sears⟩ **2 :** to move to action ⟨cultural developments which ~ and guide stylistic trends in art —Ralph Wickiser⟩ **:** stir or inspire to activity ⟨motives which ~ religious fanatics —M.R.Cohen⟩ ⟨individuals *actuated* by economic self-interest —Douglas Bush⟩ ~ *vi* **:** to become active **syn** see MOVE

ac·tu·a·tion \ˌ⸗⸗ˈwāshən\ *n* -s **:** a bringing into action **:** IMPULSION, OPERATION

ac·tu·a·tor \ˈ⸗⸗ˌwād·ə(r), -ātə-\ *n* -s **:** one that actuates; *specif* **:** any of various electric, hydraulic, or pneumatic mechanisms by means of which something is moved or controlled indirectly instead of by hand (as a motor that turns the rudder of a large ship or moves the elevators of an airplane or an air-brake cylinder operated by a motorman)

act up *vi* **1 :** to act in a way different from that which is natural, normal, usual, or expected: as **a :** to behave in an unruly, recalcitrant, or capricious manner ⟨skittish and inclined to *act up* with an unaccustomed rider⟩ ⟨occasionally the river *acts up*⟩ ⟨I'd advise you not to *act up* with me⟩ **b :** to show off ⟨children *acting up* for the benefit of anyone who cared to notice⟩ **c :** to function improperly ⟨this typewriter is *acting up* again⟩ **2 :** to become active or acute (as of a physical infirmity) after being quiescent ⟨an old injury to his right forefoot began to *act up* again —*New Yorker*⟩

ac·tus \ˈaktəs, *esp in sense 2* ˈäkˌtu̇s\ *n, pl* **actus** [L, lit., driving, doing, act, deed — more at ACT] **1** *Roman law* **:** the right to drive a beast or a vehicle over another's land — distinguished from *iter* and *via* **2** [ML (trans. of Gk *energeia*), fr. L *actus* — more at ENERGY] **:** an act or thing done; *specif* **:** a mental or spiritual act — used in Scholasticism to render Aristotle's terms *energeia* and *entelecheia;* compare ENERGY, ENTELECHY

acu- *comb form* [ML, fr. L *acu,* abl. of *acus* needle; akin to L *acies* edge — more at EDGE] **:** with a needle ⟨*acu*puncture⟩

ac·u·ar·ia \ˌakyəˈwa(a)rēə\ *n, cap* [NL, fr. *acu-* + *-aria*] **:** a genus of spiruroid nematodes that include destructive parasites of the gizzard walls of gallinaceous birds having intermediate stages in grasshoppers or other insects or crustaceans

¹**ac·u·ate** \ˈakyəˌwāt\ *adj* [ME *acuat,* fr. (assumed) ML *acuatus,* fr. L *acus* needle + *-atus* -ate — more at ACUTE] **:** having a sharp point **:** shaped like a needle **:** SHARPENED

²**acuate** *vt* -ED/-ING/-S *obs* **:** to make pungent or sharp

acuchi *var of* ACOUCHI

acuer·do \əˈkwer(ˌ)dō, *Sp* äˈkwerthō\ *n, pl* **acuerdos** \-dōz, -thōs\ [Sp, fr. *acordar* to resolve, agree, fr. (assumed) VL *accordare* — more at ACCORD] **1 :** a resolution or decision of a deliberative body or a tribunal in certain Latin American countries **2 :** a session of a tribunal; *also* **:** the members of it

acu·i·ty \əˈkyüəd·ē, aˈ-, -ətē, -i\ *n* -ES [MF *acuité,* alter. (influenced by L *acutus* sharp, pointed) of OF *aguëté,* fr. *agu* sharp (fr. L *acutus*) + *-eté* -ity — more at ACUTE] **:** SHARPNESS, ACUTENESS **:** keenness of sense perception ⟨~ of hearing⟩ or acuteness or perceptiveness of mind ⟨Wordsworth's ~ is exercised on common objects —Herbert Read⟩ — see VISUAL ACUITY

acu·lea \əˈkyülēə\ *n, pl* **acule·ae** \-lēˌē\ [NL, alter. of L *aculeus* point, sting] **:** a minute spinous outgrowth on the wing membrane of certain insects

acu·le·a·ta \əˌkyülēˈäd·ə, -ād·ə\ *n pl, cap* [NL, fr. L, neut. pl. of *aculeatus* having stings or prickles, stinging, fr. *aculeus* + *-atus* -ate] **:** a division of Hymenoptera including the bees, ants, and true wasps all characteristically having the ovipositor modified into a sting

¹**acu·le·ate** \əˈkyülēət, -ˌāt\ *adj* [L *aculeatus*] **1 :** marked by incisiveness ⟨~ language⟩ **:** POINTED, STINGING **2 :** having a sting **3** [NL *Aculeata*] **:** of or belonging to the Aculeata **4** [NL *aculea* + E *-ate*] **:** furnished with spines or aculeae (as of the wings of certain moths)

²**aculeate** \"\ *n* -s **:** one of the Aculeata

acu·le·i·form \əˈkyülēəˌfȯrm, ˌakyəˈlē-\ *adj* [ISV *acule-* (fr. L *aculeus* prickle, sting) + *-iform*] **:** like a prickle in shape; *specif* **:** resembling an aculeus

ac·u·le·o·late \ˌakyəˈlēələt, -ˌlāt\ *adj* [L *aculeolus* small needle (dim. of *aculeus* prickle, sting) + E *-ate*] **:** having very small prickles; *specif* **:** having an aculeolus

ac·u·le·o·lus \ˌakyəˈlēələs\ *n, pl* **aculeo·li** \-ˌlī\ [NL, dim. of *aculeus*] **:** a small aculeus

acu·le·us \əˈkyülēəs\ *n, pl* **acu·lei** \-lēˌī\ [NL, fr. L, point, sting, dim. of *acus* needle — more at ACUTE] *zool* **:** a sharp-pointed process; *specif* **:** an insect's ovipositor esp. when modified into a sting

acu·men \əˈkyümən *also* aˈ-; ˈakyəmən *also* -ˌmen\ *n* -s [L, lit., point, fr. *acuere* to sharpen — more at ACUTE] **1 :** acuteness of mind **:** keenness of perception, discernment, or discrimination **:** shrewdness esp. in practical matters ⟨a test of the senator's political ~⟩ ⟨loses confidence in the ~ of reviewers —E.S.McCartney⟩ ⟨business ~ and judicious handling of capital —William McFee⟩ **2** *bot* **:** a tapering point (as of a leaf) **3 :** a short spine on the rostrum of a crayfish or other crustacean

¹**acu·mi·nate** \əˈkyümənət, -ˌnāt\ *adj* [L *acuminatus,* past part. of *acuminare* to make pointed, sharpen, fr. *acumin-, acumen* point] **:** tapering to a slender point **:** POINTED

²**acu·mi·nate** \-ˌnāt\ *vb* -ED/-ING/-S [L *acuminatus*] *vt* **:** to make sharp or acute ~ *vi* **:** to taper or come to a point

acu·mi·na·tion \əˌkyüməˈnāshən, ˌaˌk-\ *n* -s **:** a sharpening or giving point to; *also* **:** a tapering point

acu·mi·nous \əˈkyümənəs, aˈ-\ *adj* [L *acumin-, acumen* sharp point + E *-ous* — more at ACUMEN] **1 :** characterized by acumen **2 :** ACUMINATE

ac·u·min·u·late \ˌakyəˈminyələt, -ˌlāt\ *adj* [blend of ¹*acuminate* and *-ule*] **:** minutely acuminate

ac·u·punc·ture \ˈakyəˌ-, -(ˌ)yü-\ *n* -s [L *acus* needle + E *puncture*] **1 :** the orig. Chinese practice of puncturing the body with special usu. gold or silver needles to cure disease **2 :** puncture of the skin or tissue by a needle (as for vaccination or the removal of fluid)

acush·la \əˈku̇shlə, əˈk-\ *n* -s [IrGael *a cuisle* oh darling, fr. *a* oh + *cuisle* darling, lit., pulse, vein, fr. OIr *cusle;* akin to ScGael *cuisle* pulse, vein] *Irish* **:** DARLING

-acusia — see -ACOUSIA

acu·ta \ə'k(y)üd·ə, ä'kü-\ *n* -s *usu cap* [prob. fr. It, fr. *acuta* (fem. of *acuto* sharp), fr. L, fem. of *acutus*] : ACUTE MIXTURE

acut·ance \ə'kyüt°n(t)s\ *n* -s [¹*acute* + *-ance*] : a measure of the steepness or abruptness of an edge in a photographic image

¹acute \ə'kyüt, *usu* -üd·+V\ *adj, sometimes* -ER/-EST [L *acutus*, past part. of *acuere* to sharpen, fr. *acus* needle; akin to L *acer* sharp — more at EDGE] **1** : ending in a sharp point : not blunt at the end: as **a** *of an angle* : measuring less than 90 degrees : not right or obtuse ⟨fences . . . so laid out that ~ corners are avoided —Henry Wynmalen⟩ — see ANGLE illustration **b** *of a figure* : marked by or composed of acute angles ⟨an ~ triangle⟩ **c** *of a leaf apex* : abruptly pointed : not tapering **2 a** : marked by keen shrewd discernment or intellectual perception esp. of subtle distinctions : PENETRATING ⟨people of ~ judgment and refined sensibilities —Elinor Wylie⟩ ⟨the fame of an ~ thinker —V.L.Parrington⟩ **b** : sensing or perceiving accurately, clearly, effectively, or sensitively ⟨~ observer⟩ ⟨~ vision, the ability to see sharp instead of blurred, is uncommon . . . in the animal kingdom —A.L. Kroeber⟩ **3** *of a sound* : high in pitch : SHARP, SHRILL ⟨an ~ note⟩ **4** : felt, perceived, or experienced intensely or powerfully ⟨the stench was ~ —Norman Mailer⟩ ⟨the incident . . . seemed to cause . . . ~ distress —Dorothy Sayers⟩ **5 a** *med* (1) : characterized by sharpness or severity ⟨~pain⟩ ⟨~ infection⟩ (2) *of a pathologic process* : having a sudden onset, sharp rise, and short course ⟨~ disease⟩ ⟨~ inflammation⟩ — opposed to *chronic* (3) : for the treatment of acute diseases ⟨an ~ hospital⟩ **b** : serious, urgent, and demanding attention : intensified or aggravated nearly to a crisis, culmination, or breaking point ⟨there was an ~ shortage of houses after the war⟩ : EXTREME, SEVERE, CRITICAL **6 a** *of an accent mark* : having the form ´ **b** : marked with an acute accent ⟨an ~ *e* in *canapé*⟩ **c** : of the variety indicated by an acute accent ⟨an ~ intonation⟩

syn CRITICAL, CRUCIAL: ACUTE most commonly indicates intensification, sometimes rapid, of a situation demanding notice and showing signs of some definite resolution ⟨intimately associated with Indian affairs was the pressing question of defense. . . . Pontiac's rebellion made the issue *acute* —S.E. Morison & H.S.Commager⟩ ⟨when the food shortage became *acute* in New Haven, the junior class of Yale College was moved to Glastonbury —*Amer. Guide Series: Conn.*⟩ CRITICAL may describe an approach to a crisis or turning point and may imply an imminent outcome or resolution ⟨the war has reached a new *critical* phase . . . we have moved into active and continuing battle —F.D.Roosevelt⟩ ⟨the *critical* lack of rubber in the last war was finally beaten by the development of synthetic rubber plants capable of turning out 1,000,000 tons a year —*Collier's Yr. Bk.*⟩ CRUCIAL applies to an actual crisis situation, often one viewed with fear, worry, or suspense, and implies a speedily ensuing decisive or definitive outcome ⟨a continuous evolution, punctuated by the sudden flaming or flowering of a *crucial* moment now and then —J.L.Lowes⟩ ⟨the next few months are *crucial*. What we do now will affect our American way of life for decades to come —H.S.Truman⟩ **syn** see in addition SHARP

²acute \"\ *n* -s : an acute accent used to show that a vowel is pronounced with a rise of pitch (as in ancient Greek), that a vowel has a certain quality (as over *e* in French), that a vowel is long (as in Hungarian), that a syllable has the highest degree of stress (as in Spanish or in phonetic transcription), or that a final *e* in a word in an English context is not silent (as in *maté*)

³acute \"\ *vt* -ED/-ING/-S [²*acute*] : to mark with an acute accent : pronounce with higher pitch ⟨~ your inflection⟩

acute abdomen *n* : an acute intra-abdominal condition requiring immediate operation

acute alcoholism *n* : an acute syndrome resulting from intoxication by excessive consumption of alcoholic drinks that is characterized by depression of higher nervous centers with uncontrolled excitement often leading to stupor, incoordination, and impaired motor control and often nausea, dehydration, and other physical symptoms — distinguished from *chronic alcoholism*

acute bisectrix *n* : the bisectrix of the acute angle formed by the axes of a biaxial crystal

acutely *adv* : in an acute manner : KEENLY, INTENSELY

acute mixture *n* : a compound organ stop sounding the higher harmonics and of bright quality — called also *sharp mixture*

acute·ness *n* -ES : the quality or state of being acute ⟨~ of vision —F.A.Geldard⟩ ⟨~ of intellect —Irving Kristol⟩ ⟨~ of sound —Irving Kolodin⟩

acute yellow atrophy *n* : a severe usu. fatal disorder in which the liver degenerates and is reduced in size as a result of toxic chemicals, infection, or other agents

acuti- *comb form* [ML, fr. L *acutus* — more at ACUTE] : sharp-pointed ⟨*acuti*foliate⟩ : sharply angled ⟨*acuti*plantar⟩

acu·ti·plan·tar \ə¦kyüd·ə¦-, -d·ē¦-\ *adj* [*acuti-* + *plantar*] *of certain birds* : having the hinder part of the tarsus sharp angled — opposed to *latiplantar*

acuto- *comb form* [¹*acute*] : acute and ⟨*acuto*-grave⟩ : acutely ⟨*acuto*-nodose⟩

acu·ya·ri palm \,ä,kü'yärē-\ *n* : GRUGRU

acuyari wood *n* [AmerSp *acuyari*, prob. fr. Carib *acaiara*] : a fragrant wood obtained from a tree (*Bursera altissima*) of Guiana

ACW *abbr* **1** aircraftswoman **2** alternating continuous wave

acy·clic \(')ā¦sīklik, -si-\ *adj* [²*a-* + *cyclic*] **1** : not cyclic : not disposed in cycles or whorls : not occurring in cycles **2** *chem* : having an open-chain structure; *esp* : ALIPHATIC **3** *ecol* : lacking regularly recurring population pulses — used esp. of planktonic organisms

acyclic machine *n* : a direct-current dynamo in which there is no reversal of current in the armature and no commutator and which in principle resembles the Faraday disk — called also *homopolar machine*

acyclic motion *n* : irrotational motion in which the velocity potential is single valued (as the rectilinear flow of a fluid)

ac·yl \'asəl, -,sēl\ *n* -s [ISV *acid* + *-yl*; prob. orig. formed as G *azyl*] : a radical derived usu. from an organic acid by removal of the hydroxyl from all acid groups; *esp* : a radical (as benzoyl, adipoyl) derived from a carboxylic acid and having the general formula RCO— in the case of a monobasic acid ⟨~ halides⟩ — compare ACYLOXY

ac·yl·al \'asə,lal\ *n* -s [*acyl* + *aldehyde*] : an acid derivative of an aldehyde or a ketone containing the grouping >C-$(OOCR)_2$ or >C(OR)OOCR

ac·yl·ami·no \,asələ'mē(,)nō, -'lamə,nō\ *adj* [*acyl* + *amino-*] : relating to or containing any radical (as acetamido) formed by removal of one hydrogen atom from nitrogen in an organic acid amide and usu. having the general formula RCONH—

ac·yl·ase \'asə,lās, -āz\ *n* -s [*acyl* + *-ase*] : any of several enzymes (as histozyme) that hydrolyze acylated amino acids — compare CARBOXYPEPTIDASE

¹ac·yl·ate \'asə,lāt\ *vt* -ED/-ING/-S [*acyl* + *-ate*] : to introduce acyl into

²ac·yl·ate \-,lāt, -,lət\ *n* -s [*acyl* + *-ate*] : a salt or ester of an organic acid ⟨titanium ~*s*⟩

ac·yl·a·tion \,asə'lāshən\ *n* -s : the act or process of acylating

acyl·oin \ə'siləwən, -,wēn; 'asə,lōin, ,asə'lōən\ *n* -s [ISV *acyl* + *benzoin*] : an alpha-hydroxy ketone (as benzoin) of the general formula RCOCH(OH)R

ac·yl·oxy \¦asə¦läksē\ *adj* [*acyl* + *oxy-*] : relating to or containing any radical (as acetoxy) formed by removal of hydrogen from oxygen in an organic acid and usu. having the general formula RCOO-

acys·tic \(')ā¦sistik\ *adj* [²*a-* + *cystic*] : not enclosed in a bladder ⟨~ tapeworm larvae⟩

¹ad \'ad, 'aa(ə)d\ *n* -s *often attrib* [by shortening] : ADVERTISEMENT 2b

²ad \"\ *n* -s [by shortening] : ADVANTAGE 5 ⟨~ in⟩ ⟨my ~⟩

ad- *or* **ac-** *or* **af-** *or* **ag-** *or* **al-** *or* **ap-** *or* **as-** *or* **at-** *prefix* [*ad-* fr. ME, fr. L, fr. *ad*; *ac-* fr. ME, fr. OF, fr. L, fr. *ad*; *af-* fr. ME, fr. OF, fr. L, fr. *ad*; *ag-* fr. ME, fr. MF, fr. L, fr. *ad*; *al-* ME, fr. MF, fr. L, fr. *ad*; *ap-* fr. ME, fr. MF, fr. L, fr. *ad*; *as-* fr. ME, fr. OF, fr. L, fr. *ad*; *at-* fr. ME, fr. OF, fr. L, fr. *ad* — more at AT] **1** : to : toward — usu. *ac-* before *c, k,* or *q* ⟨acculturation⟩ and *af-* before *f* ⟨*af*formative⟩ and *ag-* before *g* ⟨aggradation⟩ and *al-* before *l* ⟨*al*lineation⟩ and *ap-* before *p* ⟨appersonation⟩ and *as-* before *s* ⟨asself⟩ and *at-* before *t* ⟨*at*tune⟩ and *ad-* before other sounds ⟨adnominal⟩ ⟨adverbial⟩ but sometimes *ad-* even before one of the listed consonants ⟨adpronominal⟩ **2** : near : adjacent to — in this sense always in the form *ad-* ⟨*ad*oral⟩ ⟨*ad*renal⟩

¹-ad \,ad, ,aa(ə)d, ,əd\ *n suffix* -s [MF & L; MF *-ade*, fr. L *-ad-*, *-as*, fr. Gk *-ad-*, *-as*, fem. suffix denoting descent from or connection with] **1 a** : period of time ⟨quinquenni*ad*⟩ **b** : group, aggregate, or unit of (so many) parts ⟨quint*ad*⟩ **c** : element, atom, or radical having (such or so great) a chemical valence ⟨arti*ad*⟩ ⟨periss*ad*⟩ ⟨dy*ad*⟩ **2** : epic of : poem celebrating ⟨Columbi*ad*⟩ **3** [prob. fr. NL *-ad-*, *-as* (used as final element in botanical genus names), fr. Gk] : member of (such) a botanical group ⟨magnoli*ad*⟩ ⟨moring*ad*⟩ **4** : kind of plant or animal produced by or associated with ⟨ec*ad*⟩ ⟨vari*ad*⟩ — **-ad·ic** \¦adik, -ēk\ *adj suffix*

²-ad \"\ *adv suffix* [L *ad*] *biol* : in the direction of : toward : -WARD ⟨cephal*ad*⟩ ⟨ventr*ad*⟩

ad *abbr* **1** adapted **2** administration **3** adult

AD *abbr* **1** active duty **2** *often not cap* after date **3** air-dried **4** alternate days **5** [L *anno domini*] in the year of our Lord — often printed in small capitals **6** *often not cap* [L *ante diem*] before the day **7** archduke **8** assembly district **9** autograph document **10** average deviation

ad ab·sur·dum \¦adəb'sərdəm\ *adv* [L] : to the point of absurdity ⟨not slavishly imitate it *ad absurdum* —Frank Weitenkampf⟩

adac·tyl·ia \¦ā,dak'tilēə\ *n* -s [NL, fr. ²*a-* + *-dactylia*] : congenital lack of fingers or toes

adac·ty·lous \(')ā¦daktələs\ *adj* [²*a-* + *-dactylous*] **1** : without fingers or without toes **2** : without claws on the feet — used of crustaceans

¹adad *interj* [prob. by alter.] *archaic* : EGAD

²adad \'ā,dād\ *n* -s [prob. fr. Marshallese *ādād*, a species of *Triumfetta*] : a coarse fiber made from the stems of pilewort

adag *abbr* adagio

¹ad·age \'adij, -ēj\ *n* -s [MF, fr. L *adagio, adagium*, fr. *ad-* + *-agio, -agium* (akin to *aio* I say, fr. — assumed — OL *agio*); akin to Gk *ē* he spoke, Arm *asem* I say] : a saying typically embodying common experience or observation often in metaphorical form (as *it is always darkest before the dawn*)

²adage \ädäzh\ *n* -s [F, modif. of It *adagio*] : ADAGIO 2

¹ada·giet·to \ə,däjē'ed·(,)ō, ä,-, -äzhē-, ,adə'je-\ *n* -s [It, dim. of *adagio*] : a short adagio

²adagietto \"\ *adv (or adj)* [It, fr. *adagietto*, n.] : less slow than adagio — used as a direction in music

¹ada·gio \ə'dä|(,)jō, ä'dä|,ä'dä|,ə'dä|, |(,)zhō,|jē,ō,|zhē,ō\ *adv (or adj)* [It, fr. *ad*, *a* to, at (fr. L *ad*) + *agio* ease, convenience, fr. Prov. *aize* comfort, fr. L *adjacens*, pres. part. of *adjacēre* to be near — more at AT, EASE] : SLOWLY : in an easy graceful manner : in a tempo between largo and andante — used chiefly as a direction in music

²adagio \"\ *n* -s [It, fr. *adagio*, adv.] **1** : a musical composition or a movement or division of a composition in adagio tempo ⟨the ~ of a symphony⟩ **2 a** : a series of sustained and perfectly controlled dance movements (as ballet exercises) displaying balance and grace **b** : a ballet duet by a man and woman or a ballet by a mixed trio displaying difficult feats of balance, lifting, or spinning; *also* : an acrobatic or ballroom duet with similar feats

adagy *n* -ES [L *adagium*] *obs* : ¹ADAGE

adai \a'dā\ *n, pl* **adai** \"\ *or* **adaize** \-āz\ *usu cap* [F, prob. fr. Caddo] **1** : a Caddo people of Louisiana **2** : a member of the Adai people

ada·lat \ə'dälət, -äl-\ *or* **adaw·lut** \-ōl-\ *n* -s [Hindi *'adālat*, fr. Ar, *'adālat, 'adālah* justice, equity] : any of several courts of justice operative in India until the late 18th century

¹ad·am \'adəm\ *n* -s *cap* [after *Adam*, the first man of the Bible, who sinned in the Garden of Eden (Gen 2 & 3), fr. ME, fr. LL, fr. Heb *Ādhām*] : the unregenerate nature of man : human frailty — used esp. in the phrase *the old Adam* ⟨a good deal of the old *Adam* in the rascal⟩

²adam \"\ *adj, often cap* [after Robert *Adam* †1792 & James *Adam* †1794 Scottish architects and designers] **1** *of furniture* : designed in a late 18th century style resembling Sheraton but differing from it in greater preference for straight lines and decoration of surfaces (as by carving, inlaying, and painting) and in more consistent use of conventional designs (as festooned garlands and medallions) and in occasional employment of superimposed ornaments (as vases and urns) **2** *of architecture* : in a late 18th century style characterized by an ordered use of classic ornament derived from contemporary archaeological discoveries in Italy

ad·a·man·cy \'adəmənsē\ *n* -ES [²*adamant* + *-cy*] : unyielding quality : condition or fact of being adamantine : STUBBORNNESS, OBSTINACY

ad·am-and-eve \¦==ən'(d)ēv\ *n* -s [so called fr. the resemblance of the bulbs to human figures] : any of several plants of the genera *Aconitum, Arethusa, Corallorhiza, Orchis,* and *Pulmonaria*; *esp* : PUTTYROOT

¹ad·a·mant \'adəmənt *also* -,mant *or* -,maa(ə)nt\ *n* -s [ME, a fabulous mineral, diamond, lodestone, fr. OF, fr. L *adamant-, adamas* hardest iron or steel, diamond, fr. Gk] **1** : an imaginary stone of impenetrable hardness — formerly used of the diamond and other substances of extreme hardness **2** : an unbreakable or extremely hard substance ⟨she became as rigid as ~ —J.C.Powys⟩ ⟨the sharp ~ of fate —Thomas Carlyle⟩

²adamant \"\ *adj* : unshakable or immovable esp. in opposition : ADAMANTINE ⟨~ against any . . . game on Sunday —Archibald Marshall⟩ : inflexible or insistent esp. in maintaining a position or opinion ⟨was ~ that he was fit to go —Nevil Shute⟩ — **ad·a·mant·ly** *adv*

ad·a·man·tane \,adə'man,tān\ *n* -s [ISV ¹*adamant* + *-ane*; prob. orig. formed as G *adamantan*] : a crystalline high-melting hydrocarbon $C_{10}H_{16}$ having the carbon atoms of its skeleton in the same tricyclic pattern found in the space lattice of the diamond; symmetrical tricyclo-decane

ad·a·man·tine \,adə'man,tīn, -ēn, ¦adə¦mant°n\ *adj* [ME, fr. L *adamantinus*, fr. Gk *adamantinos* of steel, like a diamond, fr. *adamant-, adamas* steel, diamond] **1** : made of or having the quality of adamant ⟨these ~ gates —John Milton⟩ **2** : rigidly firm : UNYIELDING **3** : resembling the diamond in luster **4** : of or relating to the enamel of the teeth

adamantine drill *n* : a tubular well-drilling bit with hardened steel shot that revolve under the rim of the rotating tube

ad·a·man·ti·no·ma \,adə,mant°n'ōmə\ *n, pl* **ad·a·man·ti·no·mas** \-məz\ *also* **ad·a·man·ti·no·ma·ta** \-məd·ə\ [NL, fr. E *adamantine* (of tooth enamel) + NL *-oma*] : a tumor of the jaw derived from remnants of the embryonic rudiment of tooth enamel — **ad·a·man·ti·nom·a·tous** \¦==,==¦ämäd·əs, -ōm-\ *adj*

adamantive *adj* [¹*adamant* + *-ive*] *obs* : ADAMANTINE

ad·a·man·to·blast \,adə'mantə,blast\ *n* -s [ISV *adamant* + *-o-* + *-blast*] : AMELOBLAST

ad·a·man·to·blas·to·ma \,adə¦mantə,bla'stōmə\ *n* -s [NL, fr. ISV *adamantoblast* + NL *-oma*] : ADAMANTINOMA

adamantoid *n* -s [¹*adamant* + *-oid*] *obs* : HEXOCTAHEDRON

ad·a·ma·wa-east·ern \,adə'mäwə'-, -maùə'-\ *n, usu cap A&E* : a branch of the Niger-Congo language family including Ngbaka, Sango, and Zande spoken from Cameroons eastward across French Equatorial Africa and northern Belgian Congo

¹ad·am·bu·la·cral \¦a,dambyə¦läkrəl, -lak-\ *adj* [*ad-* + NL *ambulacrum* + E *-al*] : adjacent to the ambulacra

²adambulacral \"\ *n* -s : any of a series of ossicles lying along the ambulacral grooves of starfishes

ad·a·mel·lite \,adə'me,līt\ *n* -s [G *adamellit*, fr. Monte *Adamello*, mountain in Italy, its locality + G *-it* -ite] : any of several minerals: as **a** : an orthoclase-bearing quartz-hornblende-mica-diorite **b** : silica-rich quartz-monzonite **c** : any quartz-monzonite

ad·am·esque \¦adə¦mesk\ *adj, usu cap* [Robert and James *Adam* + E *-esque* — more at ADAM] *of architecture and furniture* : derived from the style of the brothers Adam ⟨attenuated delicacies of Mount Vernon's ~ ceilings —Hugh Morrison⟩

adam·ic \ə'damik, a'-\ *or* **adam·i·cal** \-əkəl\ *adj, usu cap* [*Adam*, the first man of the Bible + E *-ic*, *-ical* — more at ADAM] : of or belonging to the biblical Adam : proceeding from, resembling, or suggestive of Adam ⟨my *Adamic* and fresh daughters —Walt Whitman⟩

¹ad·am·ite \'adə,mīt\ *n* -s *usu cap* [*Adam*, the biblical first man + E *-ite*] **1** : a person who imitates Adam in going naked; *specif* : a member of any of various ascetic sects noted for practicing ritual nakedness in secret religious assemblies and dispensing with marriage on the basis of having entered a reborn state of heavenly innocence **2** : a descendant of Adam : a human being

²adamite \"\ *adj, usu cap* : of, relating to, or descended from Adam

³adamite \"\ *also* **ad·am·ine** \'adə,mēn\ *n* -s [*adamite*, modif. (influenced by *-ite*) of F *adamine*, fr. Gilbert-Joseph *Adam* †1881 Fr. mineralogist + F *-ine*; *adamine* fr. F] : a mineral $Zn_2(OH)AsO_4$ consisting of a basic zinc arsenate (hardness 3.5, sp. gr. 4.34–4.35)

ad·am·it·ic \¦adə¦mid·ik\ *adj, usu cap* [¹*adamite* + *-ic*] : having the characteristics of or resembling Adam or the Adamites ⟨in a state of ~ nudity —Norman Douglas⟩

ad·am·it·ism \'adə,mīd·,izəm\ *n* -s *usu cap* : the practice of going naked : a state of being unclothed

adams *pl of* ADAM

adam's ale *n, usu cap 1st A* [after the biblical *Adam*; fr. its being provided by nature and thus presumably being the only drink in the Garden of Eden] : WATER

¹adam's apple *n, usu cap 1st A* **1** : PLANTAIN **2** : CRAPE JASMINE **3** : SHADDOCK 1

²adam's apple *n, usu cap 1st A* [trans. of NL *pomum Adami*, trans. of LHeb *tappūaḥ hā ādhām* bodily protuberance on a man, misinterpreted (because of double meanings in Heb) as the apple of Adam] : the projection formed by the thyroid cartilage in the neck particularly prominent in males — compare LARYNX

adam's cup *n, usu cap A* [so called fr. the shape of its leaves] : PITCHER PLANT a

adam's fig *n, usu cap A* : PLANTAIN

adam's flannel *n, usu cap A* [so called fr. the texture of the leaves] : MULLEIN

ad·ams·ite \'adəm,zīt\ *n* -s [Roger *Adams* b1889 Am. chemist + E *-ite*] : a yellow crystalline arsenical $C_{12}H_9AsClN$ similar in action to diphenylchloroarsine — called also *diphenylaminechlorarsine, phenarsazine chloride*

adam's needle *also* **adam's needle-and-thread** *n, usu cap A* [so called fr. the shape of the fruits] **1** : any of several species of the genus *Yucca* **2 adam's needles** *pl* : LADY'S-COMB

adam's pitcher *n, usu cap A* : PITCHER PLANT a

ada·na \¦äd°n¦ä\ *adj, usu cap* [fr. *Adana*, Turkey] : of or from Adana, Turkey : of the kind or style prevalent in Adana

ad·anal \(')a¦dān°l\ *adj* [*ad-* + *anal*] : near the anus ⟨~ setae⟩

adance \ə'-\ *adj* [¹*a-* + *dance* (v.)] : DANCING

adan·gle \ə'-\ *adj* [¹*a-* + *dangle* (v.)] : DANGLING

ad·an·so·nia \,ad°n'sōnēə, ,a,dan'-, -nyə\ *n* -s *cap* [NL, fr. Michel *Adanson* †1806 Fr. botanist + NL *-ia*] : a genus of trees (family Bombacaceae) having palmately divided leaves, white pendent flowers, and capsular fruits — see BAOBAB, CREAM-OF-TARTAR TREE

adap·i·dae \ə'dapə,dē\ *n pl, cap* [NL *Adapid-, Adapis*, type genus + *-idae*] : a family of extinct lemuroid primates widely distributed in the northern hemisphere during the Eocene and generally considered to be ancestral to modern lemurs

ad·a·pis \'adəpəs\ *n, cap* [NL] : a genus of primitive crested fossil lemurs from the Eocene of Europe

¹adapt \ə'dapt *also* a'-\ *vb* -ED/-ING/-S [F or L; F *adapter*, fr. L *adaptare*, fr. *ad-* + *aptare* to fit, fr. *aptus* fit — more at APT] *vt* **1 a** : to make suitable or fit (as for a particular use, purpose, or situation) : FIT, SUIT ⟨the toughness of the material ~*s* it for many uses⟩ **b** : to make suitable (for a new or different use or situation) by means of changes or modifications ⟨he ~*ed* the novel for the stage⟩ ⟨~ his instruction to meet individual needs —P.H.Furfey⟩ **2** : to adjust (oneself) to particular conditions or ways : bring (oneself) into harmony with a particular environment : ACCLIMATIZE ⟨I could ~ myself to the isolated life —Ella E. Clark⟩ ⟨a given environment with organisms ~*ing* themselves to it —A.N. Whitehead⟩ ~ *vi* : to become adjusted; *specif* : to bring oneself or esp. one's acts, behavior, or mental state into harmony with changed conditions or environment ⟨man ~*s* socially to an increasingly complicated . . . culture —J.F.Brown⟩

syn ADJUST, ACCOMMODATE, CONFORM, RECONCILE: to ADAPT to something or to ADAPT one thing to another implies a suiting or fitting by alteration or modification ⟨to see men only in terms of the geographical conditions to which they *adapt* themselves —Alfred Kazin⟩ ⟨our plans must change in *adapting* to the new situations —Hugo Wall⟩ ⟨the inside walls are all movable so that the interior can easily be *adapted* to meet new requirements —*London Calling*⟩ To ADJUST to something or to ADJUST one thing to another usu. suggests no significant alteration or modification but rather a bringing into a correspondence or harmony, prearranged or clearly possible but not quite achieved previously ⟨the main problem confronting the child is not yet to *adjust* to a cultural milieu but primarily to *adjust* to the rapidly changing phases of his biological growth —Franz Alexander⟩ ACCOMMODATE often suggests the special or transient adaptation of one thing to another or of two things to each other, implying a significant difference overcome in a specially arranged, temporary, or expedient harmony ⟨local building ordinances . . . had been adjusted to *accommodate* the new materials and methods —*Current Biog.*⟩ ⟨a water trough long enough to *accommodate* the noses of a barnful of thirsting cows —*Monsanto Mag.*⟩ ⟨a school auditorium must *accommodate* a large variety of acoustic activities —*Bull. of Amer. Inst. of Architects*⟩ CONFORM implies the achievement of harmony or correspondence by compliance as with a preexisting pattern, form, or principle, sometimes carrying the implication of slavish compliance ⟨to ensure that all work done *conforms* to the highest standards —Ivor Bulmer-Thomas⟩ ⟨certain lies are indulged in to *conform* to etiquette —D.C.Buchanan⟩ ⟨unwilling to *conform* to American ways —Oscar Handlin⟩ To RECONCILE one thing with another or to RECONCILE two things, in the sense pertinent to this comparison, is to persuade oneself or others of the fundamental congruity of things that are, or seem to be, incompatible or to adjust the two things so that they are compatible ⟨*reconcile* opposing points of view⟩ ⟨we can *reconcile* naturalism or, if you please, materialism with the piety which has distinguished genuinely spiritualistic views of life —M.R.Cohen⟩ ⟨the critical judgment of those who are suspicious of "best sellers" and unwilling to *reconcile* excellence with public taste —*College English*⟩

²adapt *adj, obs* : FITTED, SUITED

adapt·a·bil·i·ty \ə,daptə'biləd·ē, (,)a,d-, -ətē, -i\ *n* : the quality or state of being adaptable ⟨the ~ of the subject to varied art forms⟩ ⟨youth's ~ to new surroundings⟩

adapt·able \ə'daptəbəl *also* a'-\ *adj* **1** : capable of being adapted or of adapting oneself ⟨a frame ~ to cloth bolts of various widths⟩ ⟨an ~ person⟩ **2** : suitable without change ⟨soil and climate ~ to growth of nut trees⟩ **syn** see PLASTIC

adap·tate \ə'dap,tāt, 'a,dap-\ *vt* -ED/-ING/-S [L *adaptatus*, past part. of *adaptare*] : ADAPT

ad·ap·ta·tion \,a,dap'tāshən *also* ,adəp- *or* ə,dap-\ *n* -s [F, fr. ML *adaptation-, adaptatio*, fr. L *adaptatus* + *-ion-, -io* -ion] **1 a** : the act or process of adapting, fitting, or modifying ⟨his ingenious ~ of the electric cautery knife to . . . surgery —George Blumer⟩ ⟨~ is a basic principle of applied design⟩ **b** : the state or condition of being adapted or adjusted or of adapting or adjusting oneself ⟨the complete ~ of the clergyman to his work⟩ ⟨the characteristic ~ of the emigrant trail to the terrain —G.R.Stewart⟩ **2** : adjustment to environmental conditions: as **a** : adjustment of a sense organ (as the eye) to the intensity or quality of stimulation (as light) prevailing at the moment effected by changes in sensitivity and occurring as a heightened sensitivity ⟨dark ~ of the retina⟩ or as a physical adjustment to meet changed conditions ⟨contraction of pupil or pigment migration in light ~ of the eye⟩ or as decline or loss of sensitivity to a constant stimulus **b** : modification of an organism or of its parts or organs fitting it more perfectly for existence under the conditions of its environment and resulting from the action of natural selection upon variation — compare NATURAL SELECTION, VARIATION 6 **c** : the continuing process through which the organization of groups is modified to meet the requirements of their social and physical environment

3 : something that is adapted **:** a modification for a new use **:** an alteration or change in form or structure ⟨the cactus is an ~ to dry conditions⟩; *specif* **:** a composition rewritten into a new form ⟨a screen ~ of a novel⟩ — **ad·ap·ta·tion·al** \ˌaˌdap-ˈtāshənᵊl, -shnəl *also* ˌadˈapˈt- *or* əˌdapˈt-\ *adj* — **ad·ap·ta·tion·al·ly** *adv*

adaptation syndrome *n* **:** the defensive response of the body through the endocrine system to systemic injury evoked by stresses and worked out by an initial stage of shock, a stage of growing resistance or adaptation, and a stage of healing or of becoming exhausted if adaptation fails — see ALARM REACTION

adapt·a·tive \əˈdaptəd·iv, aˈ-\ *adj* [*adapt* + *-ative* (as in *imitative*)] **:** ADAPTIVE

adapt·ed \əˈdaptəd *also* aˈd- *or* (*attrib*) ˈaˌd-\ *adj* **:** suited by nature, character, or design to a particular use, purpose, or situation — used with *to* or *for* ⟨soil well ~ to the growing of wheat⟩ ⟨subjects . . . not well ~ *for* examinations —W.R.Inge⟩

adapt·er *also* **adap·tor** \əˈdaptə(r) *also* aˈ-\ *n* -s **1 :** one that adapts: as **a :** a writer who adapts novels or magazine stories to motion-picture use **b :** a music arranger **2 a :** any of various devices used in adjusting or fitting to each other the separate parts of a machine or apparatus whose design is such that adjustment or fitting would otherwise not be possible (as two pipes of different diameters) **b :** any of several attachments for a camera or other apparatus to fit it for uses for which it was not orig. made (as for a plate camera to permit the use of films) **c :** a fitting usu. of glass or metal that serves to connect one tube to another or to deliver an effluent from a condenser into a receiver in a distillation apparatus **d :** a circuit or circuit element added to change the performance of an electronic apparatus in response to different actuating conditions ⟨a color ~ for black-and-white television sets⟩ **e :** a device (as a bushing) used to obtain proper fit of the fuse for assembly and functioning of a shell or bomb

adap·tion \əˈdapshən, aˈ-\ *n* -s [by contr. (influence of *adoption*)] **:** ADAPTATION

adap·ti·tude \əˈdaptəˌtüd, -ptə-, ˌtyüd, aˈ-\ *n* -s [blend of *adapt* and *aptitude*] **:** a special fitness **:** APTITUDE

adapt·ive \əˈdaptiv, -ēv *also* aˈ-\ *adj* **:** suited to or contributing to adaptation ⟨unfavorable variants would tend to be lost and the ~ favorable variants preserved —W.H.Camp⟩ **:** showing or having a capacity for or tendency toward adaptation ⟨wolves disappeared and the clever ~ coyotes grew in numbers⟩ — **adapt·ive·ly** *adv*

adaptive radiation *n* **:** diversification of a group of organisms into subgroups as it evolves in the various directions provided by interaction of its genetic potentialities and the environments it encounters **:** the evolution of ecologically similar though taxonomically distant organisms to occupy equivalent niches in comparable habitats

ad·ap·tom·e·ter \ˌaˌdapˈtäməd·ə(r)\ *n* -s [ISV *adaptation* + *-o-* + *-meter*] **:** a device for determining the efficiency of dark adaptation in the human eye — **ad·ap·tom·e·try** \-mə·trē\ *n* -ES

adapts *pres 3d sing of* ADAPT

adar \ä'där, ˈōdər\ *n* -s *usu cap* [ME, fr. Heb *ădhār*] **:** the 6th month of the civil year or the 12th month of the ecclesiastical year in the Jewish calendar — see MONTH table

adar sheni \äˌdärshäˈnē, ˌōdərˈshānē\ *n, pl* **adar shenis** *usu cap A&S* [Heb *ădhār shēnī* second Adar] **:** VEADAR

adas *pl of* ADA

adat \ˈäˌdät\ *n* -s [Turk *ādāt*, pl. of *ādet* custom, fr. Ar *ʿādah*] **:** the traditional law of an Islamic region **:** an often unwritten code of local customs, traditional practices, and conventions

ad·at·om \ˈaˌdad·əm\ *n* -s [*ad*sorbed *atom*] **:** an adsorbed atom

adaw *vt* -ED/-ING/-S [ME *adawen* to put an end to, fr. *adawe*, adv., out of existence, fr. OE *of dagum*, fr. *of*, out of + *dagum*, dat. pl. of *dæg* day — more at OF, DAY] *obs* **:** SUBDUE, DAUNT

adawlut *var of* ADALAT

ad·ax·i·al \(ˈ)aˈdaksēəl\ *adj* [*ad-* + *axial*] **:** situated on the same side as or facing the axis of an organ or organism ⟨upper side of a leaf stalk is known as the ~ surface —R.E.Torrey⟩ — opposed to *abaxial;* compare POSTERIOR

a-day \ˈāˌdā\ *n, usu cap A* [¹*a* + *day*] **1 :** the day set for launching a particular military operation **2 :** the time of a possible enemy attack with atomic bombs

adays \əˈdāz\ *adv* [ME *a dayes*, fr. *a* (on) + *dayes*, gen. of *day*] *archaic* **:** during the day **:** in the daytime

adaz·zle \əˈ-\ *adj* [¹*a-* + *dazzle* (n.)] **:** DAZZLING, GLEAMING, SHINING

ADC *abbr* **1** aide-de-camp **2** aid to dependent children

ad cap·tan·dum *or* **ad captandum vul·gus** \ˌad,kapˈtandəm(ˈvəlgəs)\ *adj* [*ad captandum*, fr. L, for pleasing; *ad captandum vulgus*, fr. L, for pleasing the crowd] **:** designed to attract or please the crowd — used often of an argument directed chiefly to the emotions

¹add \ˈad, ˈaa(ə)d\ *vb* -ED/-ING/-S [ME *adden*, fr. L *addere*, fr. *ad-* + *-dere* to put — more at DO] *vt* **1 a :** to join, annex, or unite (as one thing to another) so as to bring about an increase (as in number, size, or importance) or so as to form one aggregate ⟨~*ed* music to the list of his interests⟩ ⟨~*s* form to substance and achieves artistic unity⟩ ⟨~*ing* a wing to the house⟩ **b :** to put together mentally **:** unite or form a single whole in the mind ⟨~ together the ideas of two days —John Locke⟩ **2 :** to say or write further **:** go on to say or write ⟨that, he ~*ed*, was a mistake⟩ **3** *obs* **:** GIVE, BESTOW ⟨all these things shall be ~*ed* unto you —Mt 6:33 (AV)⟩ **4 :** to combine (two or more numbers or quantities or a group or column of numbers or quantities) into one sum **:** find the total sum of by combining **5 :** to join or unite (another thing) to itself ⟨a chemical compound that ~*s* chlorine⟩ **6 :** to include (a person) as a member of a group or party **:** COUNT ⟨don't forget to ~ me in⟩ ~ *vi* **1 a :** to perform the mathematical operation of addition ⟨learn to ~⟩ **b :** to come together or unite in or as if in the mathematical process of addition ⟨the facts . . . ~*ed* together to build up a theory which was indisputable —Harvey Graham⟩ **2 :** INCREASE, AUGMENT **:** be or serve as an addition ⟨the novel ~*ed* to his reputation⟩ **:** make an addition **:** ENLARGE ⟨they ~*ed* to the house the next year⟩ — used with *to*

²add \ˈ"\ *n* -s **:** copy to be added to a news story ⟨a new ~ on the hurricane story⟩

add *abbr* **1** addendum **2** addition **3** address

ad·da \ˈadə\ *n* -s [Ar dial. (Egypt) *ʿaẓa*] **:** the common Egyptian skink (*Scincus officinalis*)

add·a·ble *or* **add·i·ble** \ˈadəbəl, ˈaad-\ *adj* [¹*add* + *-able, -ible*] **:** capable of being added or of added to

ad·dax \ˈaˌdaks\ *n, pl* **addaxes** *also* **addax** [L] **:** a large light-colored antelope (*Addax nasomaculata*) of No. Africa, Arabia, and Syria

addebted *adj* [ME *adettid*, alter. of *endetted* — more at INDEBTED] *obs* **:** INDEBTED

added *adj* **:** ADDITIONAL, FURTHER, SUPPLEMENTARY ⟨takes on ~ significance⟩ ⟨an ~ attraction⟩ — **add·ed·ly** *adv*

added money *n* **:** money added to stakes by a track or racing association as an additional inducement for entries as distinct from entrance fees or forfeits

added sixth *n* **1** *in classical harmony* **:** the chord of the subdominant with a major sixth from the root added **2 :** a triad with a major sixth from the root added

addax

added value *n* **:** VALUE ADDED

ad·dend \ˈaˌdend, əˈd-,aˈd-\ *n* -s [short for *addendum*] **:** a number or quantity to be added to a preceding one or in continued addition to the sum already accumulated

ad·den·dum \əˈdendəm, aˈ-\ *n, pl* **adden·da** *see sense 3* \-də\ [L, neut. of *addendus*, gerundive of *addere* to add — more at ADD] **1 :** a thing that is added or is to be added **:** ADDITION, SUPPLEMENT ⟨as an ~ . . . let me point out one fact —A.C. Eurich⟩ **2 a :** an explanation, comment, or additional item appended to a book ⟨these *addenda* fill six pages⟩ **b :** a list or section consisting of added material; *esp* **:** a supplement to a book sometimes issued separately ⟨the new edition includes a 10-page ~⟩ — sometimes pl. but sing. in constr. ⟨the *addenda* contains many new words⟩ **3** *pl* **addendums :** the part of a tooth of a gear wheel between pitch line and extreme point of the tooth; *also* **:** the distance between pitch line and addendum circle — compare DEDENDUM **4** *addenda pl* **:** ACCESSORIES, APPURTENANCES ⟨a dozen exciting *addenda* to culinary art —*Holiday*⟩

addendum circle *n* **:** a circle touching the extreme points of the teeth of a circular gear wheel — see PITCH LINE

¹ad·der \ˈadə(r)\ *n* -s [ME *addre*, alter. (resulting from incorrect division of *a naddre*) of *naddre*, fr. OE *nǣdre* adder, snake; akin to OHG *nātara* adder, ON *nathr*, Goth *nadrs*, L *natrix* water snake, and prob. to L *nēre* to spin — more at NEEDLE] **1 a :** the common viper (*Vipera berus*) of Europe **b :** any other snake (as a puff adder) of the family Viperidae **2 :** KRAIT **3 :** any of several harmless No. American snakes: as **a :** HOGNOSE SNAKE **b :** MILK SNAKE

²add·er \ˈadə(r), ˈaad-\ *n* -s [¹*add* + *-er*] **:** one that adds; *specif* **:** ADDING MACHINE

adder's-fern \ˈ**,**\ *n, pl* **adder's-ferns 1 :** the common polypody (*Polypodium vulgare*) **2 :** ADDER'S-TONGUE 1

adder's-flower \ˈ**,**\ *n, pl* **adder's-flowers** [prob. so called fr. the spotted leaves] **:** RED CAMPION

adder's meat *n* [so called fr. their poisonous quality] **1 :** CUCKOOPINT **2 :** GREATER STITCHWORT

adder's mouth *n* [so called fr. the shape of the leaf] **1 :** an orchid of the genus *Malaxis* **2 :** SNAKEMOUTH

adderspit \ˈ**,**\ *n* -s [so called fr. the salivalike appearance of the sori] **:** the common brake (*Pteridium aquilinum*)

adder stone *n* [so called fr. the belief that it is formed by adders and is efficacious against snakebite] **:** a precious stone formerly believed to be efficacious in drawing out poison; *usu* **:** a highly absorbent aluminous gem

ad·der's-tongue \ˈ**,**\ *also* **adder tongue** *n, pl* **adder's-tongues** *also* **adder tongues** [so called fr. the shape of its fruiting spike] **1 :** a fern of the genus *Ophioglossum* **2 :** any of several plants esp. in the genera *Achillea, Arum, Erythronium, Geranium, Orchis,* and *Peramium* having leaves or flower or fruiting spikes suggesting the fruiting spikes of adder's-tongue fern

addible *var of* **addable**

¹ad·dict \əˈdikt, (ˈ)aˈd-\ *vb* -ED/-ING/-S [L *addictus*, past part. of *addicere* to favor, adjudge, fr. *ad-* + *dicere* to say — more at DICTION] *vt* **1** *obs* **a :** to award or deliver by judicial decree — used in works on Roman law **b :** to give over **:** give up **:** SURRENDER **c :** to attach (oneself) as a follower to a person or adherent to a cause ⟨we sincerely ~ ourselves to Almighty God —Thomas Fuller⟩ **2 :** to apply or devote (as oneself or one's mind) habitually **:** give (oneself) up or surrender (oneself) as a constant practice **:** HABITUATE, DEVOTE ⟨the researches to which your taste ~*s* you —Sir Walter Scott⟩ ⟨such persons . . . will ~ themselves to history or science —J.S.Mill⟩ ⟨to forswear thin potations and to ~ themselves to sack —Shak.⟩ **3 :** to cause or induce (a person) to make habitual use of a drug ⟨addicts . . . find it convenient to ~ several other persons —D.W.Maurer & V.H.Vogel⟩ ~ *vi, of a drug* **:** to bring about or cause habitual use ⟨drugs . . . threaten us because they are . . . ~*ing* —D.W.Maurer & V.H.Vogel⟩

²ad·dict \ˈa(ˌ)dikt, ˈadēkt *also* əˈdikt *or* aˈd-\ *n* -s **1 :** one who is addicted to a habit; *specif* **:** one who habitually uses and has an uncontrollable craving for an addicting drug ⟨a morphine ~⟩ ⟨a barbiturate ~⟩ **2 :** one showing zealous interest (as in a sport or pastime) **:** an enthusiastic devotee

addicted *adj* **:** devoted or given up ⟨~ to wine⟩ ⟨~ to stealing⟩ **:** strongly disposed or inclined ⟨~ to reading mystery novels⟩ ⟨easygoing as a husband, . . . straightforward as a politician, and as a man, ~ to pleasure —John Galsworthy⟩

ad·dic·tion \əˈdikshən, aˈ-\ *n* -s [¹*addict* + *-ion*] **1** *obs* **:** INCLINATION, BENT **2 a :** the quality or state of being addicted; *specif* **:** the compulsive uncontrolled use of habit-forming drugs beyond the period of medical need or under conditions harmful to society ⟨the extent of ~ ranged from 2 months to 10 years⟩ **b :** enthusiastic devotion, strong inclination, or frequent indulgence ⟨his ~ to the comics⟩ ⟨his ~ to vivid metaphors⟩ **3** [L *addiction-, addictio*, fr. *addictus* + *-ion-, -io* -ion] **:** a formal award or assignment of a person or thing to another; *esp* **:** an award made by a praetor or other magistrate (as of a debtor to his creditor)

ad·dict·ive \əˈdiktiv, (ˈ)aˈd-\ *adj* **:** causing or characterized by addiction

adding machine *n* **:** a usu. key-operated machine that performs arithmetical addition — see CALCULATING MACHINE

ad·dis aba·ba \ˌadəˈsabəbə\ *adj, usu cap both As* [fr. *Addis Ababa*, Ethiopia] **:** of or from Addis Ababa, the capital of Ethiopia **:** of the kind or style prevalent in Addis Ababa

¹ad·di·so·ni·an \ˌadəˈsōnēən, -nyən\ *adj, often cap* [Joseph *Addison* †1719 Eng. essayist + E *-ian*] **1 :** of or resembling Addison or his characteristic writings **2 :** clear and polished in literary style

²addisonian \ˈ"\ *adj, usu cap* [Thomas *Addison* + E *-ian*] **:** of, relating to, or affected with Addison's disease ⟨~ crisis⟩ ⟨~ patient⟩

addisonian anemia *or* **addisonian pernicious anemia** \ˈ"-\ *also* **ad·di·son's anemia** \ˈadəsənz-\ *n, often cap 1st A* [²*Addisonian*] **:** PERNICIOUS ANEMIA 1

ad·di·son's disease \ˈadəsənz-\ *n, usu cap A* [after Thomas *Addison* †1860 Eng. physician] **:** a destructive disease marked by deficient secretion of the adrenal cortical hormone and characterized by extreme weakness, loss of weight, low blood pressure, gastrointestinal disturbances, and brownish pigmentation of the skin and mucous membranes

ad·dit·a·ment \əˈdid·əmənt, aˈ-\ *n* -s [ME, fr. L *additamentum*, fr. *additus* (past part. of *addere* to add) + connective *-a-* + *-mentum* -ment — more at ADD] **:** a thing added **:** ADDITION

ad·di·tion \əˈdishən, aˈ-\ *n* -s [ME *addicioun*, fr. MF *addition*, fr. L *addition-, additio*, fr. *additus* + *-ion, -io* -ion] **1 a :** the result of adding **:** anything added **:** INCREASE, AUGMENTATION ⟨the clerk was a recent ~ to the staff⟩ **b :** something added that improves or increases value ⟨that table is certainly an ~ to the room⟩ **2 :** the act or process of adding **:** the joining or uniting of one thing to another ⟨the subject stood in need of correction and ~ —Benjamin Farrington⟩ **3** *obs* **:** a designation (as of rank or place of residence) added to a person's name ⟨the names of those justices . . . with all their ~*s* and titles —William Penn⟩ **4 a :** the process denoted by the sign + of combining two or more numbers so as to obtain their sum **b :** the part of mathematics that treats of addition **5 a :** a part added to or joined with a building to increase available space **b :** a suburban area marked out into streets and lots as a future residential section **c additions** *pl* **:** facilities, structures, equipment, or other property added to what is already in service **6 :** direct chemical combination of two or more substances to form a single product ⟨the union of ethylene and chlorine to form ethylene dichloride is an ~ reaction: $C_2H_4 + Cl_2 \rightarrow C_2H_4Cl_2$⟩ — often contrasted with *substitution* **7 a :** the amalgamation in logic of classes or of terms considered with reference to their denotation ⟨the logical ~ of "white" and "sweet" results in "either white or sweet (or both)"⟩ **b :** ALTERNATION 2 **8 :** a material used in the manufacture of portland cement other than water and untreated calcium sulfate that is interground with the clinker in an amount not exceeding two percent **9 :** a dice game played with five dice the object being to achieve the highest numerical total in five or fewer casts — **in addition** *adv* **:** ¹BESIDES 1a — **in addition to** *prep* **:** over and above

addition agent *n* **:** ADDITIVE

ad·di·tion·al \əˈdishənᵊl, (ˈ)aˈd-, -shnəl\ *adj* **:** existing or coming by way of addition **:** ADDED, FURTHER

additional accompaniment *n* **:** a musical accompaniment or arrangement of a composition not in the original score but added in a later period

additional insured *n, pl* **additional insureds :** a person other than the one in whose name a policy is issued but who is also protected by that policy

ad·di·tion·al·ly \-ᵊlē,-əlē, -li\ *adv* **:** in or by way of addition **:** FURTHERMORE ⟨the book is ~ the history of an era⟩

additional tax *n* **:** SURTAX b

addition axiom *n* **:** an axiom in mathematics: if equal numbers are added to equal numbers, the results are equal

addition compound *n* **:** a compound formed by chemical addition; *esp* **:** MOLECULAR COMPOUND

ad·di·tion la·tente \ådēsyōⁿlätäⁿt\ *n, pl* **additions latentes** \ˈ"\ [F, lit., latent addition] **:** FACILITATION 3

addition polymerization *n* **:** polymerization without formation of a by-product — distinguished from *condensation polymerization*

addition product *n* **:** a product formed by chemical addition — see ADDUCT

addition theorem *n* **:** a formula or rule that expresses algebraically a function of the sum of two arguments in terms of the same or related functions of the separate arguments [as sin $(x + y) = \sin x \cos y + \sin y \cos x$]

¹ad·di·tive \ˈadəd·iv, -ətiv\ *adj* [LL *additivus*, fr. L *additus* (past part. of *addere* to add) + *-ivus* -ive — more at ADD] **1 :** tending to add or be added **:** admitting, involving, or characterized by addition ⟨the process of cultural development is . . . ~ —A.L.Kroeber⟩ **2** *philos* **:** having the distinctive character of extensive magnitudes **:** of the nature of an addition or aggregation rather than an organic union of parts ⟨this pluralistic view of a world of ~ constitution —William James⟩ **3 :** having a numeral value equal to the sum of the values for the component parts — used of a property; compare COLLIGATIVE, CONSTITUTIVE 3 ⟨molecular weight may be thought of as an ~ property⟩ **4 :** relating to the sum of the pharmacological responses produced by the concurrent administration of two or more drugs capable of producing the same kind of effect **5 :** relating to the controlled mixing of colored light sources (as red, green, and blue) to form a colored image **:** formed by superposition or other nondestructive combination of colored lights **:** relating to a method of making halftone color prints in which the dots for each color are placed beside each other **6 :** having a genic effect that is the sum of the individual effects — **ad·di·tive·ly** *adv*

²additive \ˈ"\ *n* -s **1 :** a substance added to another in relatively small amounts to impart or improve desirable properties or suppress undesirable properties: as **a :** a chemical added to a lubricating oil to make it suitable for use at extreme pressures or to prevent corrosion ⟨an extreme-pressure ~⟩ **b :** a chemical (as an antiknock agent or an agent for counteracting deposits on spark plugs) added to gasoline ⟨tetraethyl lead is a gasoline ~⟩ **c :** an agent added to a foodstuff to improve color, flavor, texture, or keeping qualities ⟨gelatin is an ~ in the manufacture of ice cream⟩ **d :** material added to soil or feeds to improve plant or animal growth by indirect action **2 :** an arithmetical key for superencipherment esp. when numeral code groups are enciphered by adding to them a numeral keying sequence usu. by noncarrying addition

additive primary *n* **:** one of a set of the colored lights red, green, and blue by addition of which in varying proportions lights of a maximum number of colors may be produced

ad·di·tiv·i·ty \ˌadəˈtivəd·ē\ *n* -ES **:** the quality or state of being additive

ad·di·to·ry \ˈadəˌtōrē\ *adj* [*addition* + *-ory*] **:** tending to add **:** making an addition

¹ad·dle \ˈadᵊl\ *n* -s [ME *adel*, fr. OE *adela;* akin to MLG *adele* liquid manure, Sw dial. *adel* animal urine, and perh. to Gk *onthos* animal dung] *now dial Brit* **:** stagnant or filthy liquid

²addle \ˈ"\ *adj* [ME *adel-*, fr. *adel*, n.] **1** *of an egg* **:** foul smelling and putrid **:** ROTTEN **2 a :** EMPTY, UNSOUND ⟨I wish him an ounce more wit in his ~ head —William Robertson †1686⟩ **b :** CONFUSED, MUDDLED ⟨the brains of the people growing more and more ~ —Edmund Burke⟩

³addle \ˈadᵊl\ *vb* **addled; addled; addling** \-d(ᵊ)liŋ\ **addles** *vt* **:** to throw into confusion or disorder **:** MUDDLE, CONFOUND **:** make addle ⟨no housing problem . . . to ~ our heads —Irwin Edman⟩ ⟨any thinking . . . is bound to be *addled* by inaccurate language —R.G.Swing⟩ ~ *vi* **1 :** to become addle **:** SPOIL ⟨not one of these eggs ever *addled* —Robert Southey⟩ **2 :** to confuse or become confused ⟨the object is to ~ and not to elucidate —G.B.Shaw⟩

⁴addle \ˈ"\ *vb* -ED/-ING/-S [ME *addlen*, fr. ON *öthlask* (refl. v.) to acquire as property, fr. *ōthal* property — more at ODAL] *vt, now dial Eng* **:** to earn by labor **:** GAIN ~ *vi, now dial Eng* **:** GAIN, THRIVE

addlebrained \ˈ**,**\ *adj* [²*addle* + *brained*] **:** ADDLEPATED

ad·dle·pate \ˈ**,**\ *n* **:** one who is addlepated

addlepated \ˈ**,**\ *adj* [²*addle* + *pated*] **:** stupid and confused, mixed up, or eccentric ⟨blathering like the ~ nincompoop that you are —D.G.Gerahty⟩

ad·dlings *or* **ad·dlins** \ˈadlənz, -liŋz\ *n pl* [pl. of *addling*, gerund of ⁴*addle*] *dial Eng* **:** EARNINGS, SAVINGS

addn *abbr* addition

ad·dorsed \əˈdörst, (ˈ)aˈd-\ *also* **ad·dossed** \-däst, -ȯst\ *adj* [modif. of F *adossé*, past part. of *adosser* to turn the back, set on one's back, fr. *a-* (fr. L *ad-*) + *dos* back, fr. L *dorsum*] **:** set or turned back to back (as in heraldry)

ad·dra \ˈadrə\ *also* **addra gazelle** *n* -s [prob. native name in Africa] **:** a large African gazelle (*Gazella dama*); *esp* **:** a member of the typical race (*G.d.dama*) that is white with reddish hair on the neck and upper back — compare MOHR

¹ad·dress \əˈdres *also* aˈd- *or* ˈaˌd-\ *vb* -ED/-ING/-ES [ME *adressen*, fr. MF *adrescer*, *adresser*, fr. *a-* (fr. L *ad-*) + *drescer*, *dresser* to straighten, arrange — more at DRESS] *vt* **1** *obs* **a :** to make straight **:** set in order **:** ARRANGE ⟨whose stately numbers are so well ~*ed* —Richard Barnfield⟩ **b :** to make right **:** CORRECT, REDRESS ⟨a parliament being called to ~ many things —John Milton⟩ **2 a :** DIRECT, AIM **:** make straight (as a course) ⟨the enemy of mankind . . . towards Eve ~*ed* his way —John Milton⟩ **b :** to direct to go **:** SEND, DISPATCH ⟨he was ~*ed* first to the Earl —Gilbert Burnet⟩ **3** *archaic* **a :** to make ready **:** PREPARE ⟨he did ~ himself to quit . . . this mountain land —Lord Byron⟩ **b** (1) **:** to make ready or prepare (as with proper clothing) (2) **:** CLOTHE, DRESS **c :** to put on **:** DON ⟨I have ~*ed* a frock of heavy mail —Robert Browning⟩ **4 :** to direct the efforts or turn the attention of (oneself) ⟨he ~*ed* himself to the remains of his chicken and salad —C.D.Lewis⟩ ⟨the speakers ~*ed* themselves to a common question⟩ **:** try to apply (oneself or one's powers) ⟨~ yourself to the task of behaving better —Aldous Huxley⟩ **5 a :** to direct by way of communication **:** communicate directly ⟨~*ing* his thanks to his host⟩ ⟨they ~*ed* to the governor a plea for clemency⟩ **b :** to direct the words of (oneself) ⟨~*ing* himself to the principal, he defended the students' behavior⟩ **6 a :** to speak, write, or otherwise communicate directly to ⟨~*ing* the chairman, he began his speech⟩ ⟨she ~*ed* the older woman respectfully⟩ **b :** to deliver a prepared or formal speech to ⟨he ~*es* the convention tonight⟩ **7 a :** to write or otherwise mark directions for delivery on **:** DIRECT ⟨~ a letter for mailing⟩ ⟨~ a package for delivery by messenger⟩ **b :** to consign or entrust to the care of another (as agent or factor) ⟨the ship was ~*ed* to a factor⟩ **8 :** to greet directly using a prescribed form either in speech or in writing ⟨many people are uncertain about how to ~ members of the nobility⟩ **9 :** to direct one's attentions to (as in courtship) **:** COURT, WOO ⟨she is too fine and too conscious of herself to repulse any man who may ~ her —J.R.Lowell⟩ **10 a :** to take one's stance and adjust the club preparatory to hitting (a golf ball) **b :** to stand ready to shoot (an arrow) with the body turned at right angles to the target **c :** to bow slightly to (one's square-dancing partner) in preparation for a dance **11** *law* **:** to unseat or remove (a judge) as unworthy of office by executive order in accordance with a formal petition from the legislature **12 a :** to put information into (a memory or storage device) **b :** to call upon (such a device) for information ~ *vi* **1** *obs* **:** to prepare oneself **:** set about ⟨let us ~ to tend on Hector's heels —Shak.⟩ **2** *obs* **:** to direct one's speech or attentions ⟨my lord of Burgundy, we first ~ toward you —Shak.⟩ **syn** see DIRECT

²ad·dress \əˈdres, *in sense 7 usu & in other senses often* ˈaˌd-; *also* aˈdres, *sometimes (esp in sense 7)* ˈadrəs\ *n* -ES **1** *obs* **a** (1) **:** the act of preparing or making ready (2) **:** the state of being prepared **b :** something that is prepared; *specif* **:** DRESS, ATTIRE **2 :** the quality or state of being ready or skillful **:** DEXTERITY, ADROITNESS ⟨to bring the thing off as well as Mike has done requires ~ —Herman Wouk⟩ **3** *obs* **:** the act or action of addressing oneself or one's words to a person **4 a :** the manner in which one conducts or carries oneself **:** BEARING, DEPORTMENT ⟨the education and social ~ of the propertied class —G.B.Shaw⟩ **b :** the manner or style of speaking or singing **:** DELIVERY ⟨a tenor who sang . . . with a remarkable freedom of voice and ease of ~ —Douglas Watt⟩ **5 :** courteous or dutiful attention esp. in courtship — usu. used in pl. ⟨ladies . . . to whom all the polite part of the court . . . paid their ~*es* —Jonathan Swift⟩ **6 :** a formal communication either spoken or written: as **a :** a usu. formal speech or talk esp. as prepared for delivery to a special group ⟨his commencement ~ was subsequently published⟩ **b :** a formal petition esp. by a legislative body to an executive or sovereign **c :** a formal statement of policy or opinion by a sovereign or president to the people or to a legislative body ⟨an ~ by the president to Congress⟩ **7 a :** the designation of a place (as a residence or place of business) where a person or organization may be found or communicated with ⟨the ~ of the company is 47 Federal St., Springfield, Mass.⟩ **:** a part of such a designation ⟨a street ~⟩ **b :** the directions for delivery given on the outside of an object to be delivered (as a letter or package) **c :** the name of the addressee and designation of place of delivery between the heading and the salutation of a business letter — called also *inside address* **8 :** the act of directing or dispatching a ship ⟨the agent at the port being given a commission of ~⟩ **9 :** DIRECTION 11 **10 :** the stance of the player and the position of the club preparatory to hitting a golf ball **11 :** a unit (as an accumulator or circuit) or a designation of a unit where particular information is stored (as in a computer) **syn** see TACT

ad·dress·ee \,a,dre'sē, ə,dre'sē\ *n* -s **:** one to whom something (as a letter, package, or document) is addressed

ad·dress·er \ə'dresə(r) *also* a'-\ *n* -s **:** one that addresses: as **a :** a clerk who addresses mail or shipments **b :** a machine for printing addresses for mailing

addressing machine *n* **:** a business machine that automatically imprints names, addresses, or other information on successive envelopes or forms

ad·dres·sor \ə'dresə(r), a'-; ə,dre'sȯ(ə)r, a,-, -ō(ə)\ *n* -s **:** ADDRESSER; *esp* **:** one that addresses a letter of credit

adds *pres 3d sing of* ADD, *pl of* ADD

ad·duce \ə'd(y)üs, a'-\ *vt* -ED/-ING/-S [L *adducere*, lit., to lead to, fr. *ad-* + *ducere* to lead — more at TOW (pull)] **:** to bring forward (as an example, reason, or proof) for consideration in a discussion, analysis, or contention **:** OFFER, PRESENT, CITE ⟨in the light of the parallels which I have *adduced*, the hypothesis appears legitimate —J.G.Frazer⟩ ⟨let me ~ more pleasing evidence —A.T.Quiller-Couch⟩ **syn** see CITE

ad·du·cent \(')a¦d(y)üs³nt, ə'd-\ *adj* [L *adducent-, adducens*, pres. part. of *adducere*] *physiol* **:** ADDUCTING — opposed to *abducent*

ad·duc·er \ə'd(y)üsə(r), a'-\ *n* -s **:** one that adduces

ad·duc·i·ble *also* **ad·duce·a·ble** \-səbəl\ *adj* **:** capable of being adduced

¹ad·duct \ə'dəkt, a'-\ *vt* -ED/-ING/-S [L *adductus*, past part. of *adducere*] **:** to draw (as a limb) toward or past the median axis of the body; *also* **:** to bring together (similar parts) ⟨~ the fingers⟩ — compare ABDUCT 2

²ad·duct \'a,dəkt\ *n* -s [G *addukt*, fr. L *adductus*, past part.] **:** a chemical addition product: as **a :** the cyclic product of the addition reaction of a diene with another unsaturated compound (as maleic anhydride) — compare DIELS-ALDER REACTION **b :** a crystalline complex (as one of urea with a straight-chain aliphatic compound)

ad·duc·tion \ə'dəkshən, a'-\ *n* -s [F, fr. ML *adduction-, adductio* act of bringing forward, fr. L *adductus* + *-ion-, -io* -ion] **1 :** the action of adducting or the condition of being adducted ⟨prolonged ~ of the arm⟩ **2 :** the act or action of adducing or bringing forward

ad·duc·tive \ə'dəktiv, (')a¦d-\ *adj* [L *adductus* + E *-ive*] **:** bringing toward or to (something) **:** ADDUCTING

ad·duc·tor \ə'dəktə(r), (')a¦d-\ *n* -s [NL, fr. LL, conductor, fr. L *adductus* + *-or*] **1 :** a muscle that draws a part toward the median line of the body or toward the axis of an extremity; *esp* **:** any of three powerful triangular muscles that contribute to the adduction of the human thigh: (1) **:** one arising from the superior ramus of the pubis and inserted into the middle third of the linea aspera (2) **:** one arising from the inferior ramus of the pubis and inserted into the iliopectineal line and the upper part of the linea aspera (3) **:** one arising from the inferior ramus of the pubis and the ischium and inserted behind the first two into the linea aspera — called also respectively *adductor longus, adductor brevis, adductor magnus* **2 :** a muscle that closes the valves of a bivalve shell (as in the oyster and the scallop) or one of a pair of such muscles (as in other mollusks)

adductor impression *n* **:** one of the scars on the valve of a bivalve shell marking the attachment of the adductors

addulce *vt* -ED/-ING/-S [alter. (influenced by L *dulcis*) of earlier *addoulce, adoulce*, fr. MF *adoulcer, adoulcier*, lit., to sweeten, fr. *a-* (fr. L *ad-*) + *doulce, douz* sweet, fr. L *dulcis* — more at DULCET] *obs* **:** to bring into harmony or agreement **:** MOLLIFY

add up *vi* **1 a :** to make up or comprise **:** amount to — used with *to* ⟨two and two *add up* to four⟩ ⟨tunes . . . still don't *add up* to a piece —Leonard Bernstein⟩ **b :** SIGNIFY, MEAN — used with *to* ⟨an uneasiness about whether the universe *adds up* to anything —Irwin Edman⟩ **2 a :** to make or come to the expected or correct total ⟨the figures wouldn't *add up* —Charles Dickens⟩ **b :** to form an intelligible pattern **:** be plausible or probable **:** make sense ⟨he was unaccountable, he didn't *add up* —Graham Greene⟩ ~ *vt* **:** to form an opinion or judgment of **;** size up ⟨she could not claim to have *added up* Constance yet —Arnold Bennett⟩

ade \'ād\ *n* -s [*-ade*] **:** a sweetened drink made from water and fruit juice (as citrus)

-ade \¦ād, ¦ad, ¦äd\ *n suffix* -s [ME, fr. MF, fr. OProv *-ada*, fr. LL *-ata*, fr. L, fem. of *-atus* -ate] **1 :** act **:** action ⟨block*ade*⟩ **2 a :** product ⟨jamros*ade*⟩ **b :** sweet drink ⟨orange*ade*⟩

ade·cid·u·ate \¦ādə¦sijəwət, -dē,-\ *adj* [²*a-* + *deciduate*] **1 :** NONDECIDUATE **2** *bot* **:** not falling **:** EVERGREEN ⟨~ leaves⟩

adeem \ə'dēm, a'-\ *vt* -ED/-ING/-S [fr. *ademption*, after such pairs as E *redemption: redeem*] **:** to revoke or satisfy (as a legacy, grant, or donation) by ademption

adel- *or* **adelo-** *comb form* [NL, fr. Gk *adēl-, adēlo-* unseen, fr. *adēlos*, fr. *a-* ²a- + *dēlos* visible, evident; akin to OE *tǣtan* to gladden, OHG *zeiz* dear, ON *teitr* glad, Skt *dīdeti* he shines, L *dies* day — more at DEITY] **:** concealed **:** not apparent ⟨*Adel*aster⟩ ⟨*adelo*pod⟩

ad·e·laide \'ad³l,ād\ *adj, usu cap* [fr. *Adelaide*, So. Australia] **:** of or from Adelaide, the capital of So. Australia **:** of the kind or style prevalent in Adelaide

ade·lan·ta·do \,adəl,än'täd(,)ō\ *n* -s [Sp, fr. past part. of *adelantar* to put ahead, advance, fr. *adelante* ahead, fr. *a-* (fr. L *ad-*) + *delante* before, in front of, alter. of obs. *denante*, fr. *de* of, from (fr. L) + *enante* before, in front of, fr. LL *in ante*, fr. L *in* + *ante* before] **:** a civil and military governor of a province in Spain or her colonies

ade·lea \ə'dēlēə\ *n, cap* [NL, fr. Gk *adēlos* unseen — more at ADEL-] **:** a large genus of protozoans of the order Coccidia that are parasitic on arthropods and have two sporozoites in each sporocyst

adele balls \ə'del-\ *n pl but sing or pl in constr, usu cap A* [origin unknown] **:** CONGO RUBBER

adel·ges \ə'del(,)jēz\ *n, cap* [NL, fr. *adel-* + *-ges* (prob. fr. Gk *gē* earth)] **:** a genus of aphids feeding chiefly on spruce and balsam on which they often cause damaging and unsightly galls — **adel·gid** \-jəd\ *adj or n*

ade·lia \ə'dēlēə, -lyə\ *n, cap* [NL, fr. *adel-* + *-ia*] **:** a genus of tropical American shrubs (family Euphorbiaceae) with toothed leaves and small yellowish flowers

adé·lie penguin *or* **adélie** \ə'dālē\ *n* -s *usu cap A* [fr. *Adélie* Coast, Antarctica] **:** a small Antarctic penguin (*Pygoscelis adeliae*)

ad·e·lite \'ad³l,īt\ *n* -s [ISV *adel-* + *-ite*] **:** a mineral consisting of a gray or grayish yellow calcium and magnesium arsenate $CaMg(OH)AsO_4$ (hardness 5, sp. gr. 3.74)

ade·lo·chor·da \ə,dēlə'kȯrdə, ,ad³l-\ [NL, fr. *adel-* + *chorda*] *syn of* HEMICHORDATA

ade·lo·co·don·ic \ə¦dēləkō¦dänik, ¦ad³l(,)ōk-\ *adj* [*adel-* + Gk *kōdōn* bell + E *-ic*] *zool* **:** remaining attached and developing no umbrella — used of sexual zooids of certain hydroids; opposed to *phanerocodonic*

ade·lo·mor·phic \-¦mȯrfik\ *or* **ade·lo·mor·phous** \-fəs\ *adj* [*adel-* + *-morphic, -morphous*] **:** of obscure or indefinite form — used of the central cells of the peptic glands

ade·lo·spon·dy·li \ə,dēlə'spändə,lī, ,ad³l(,)ō'-\ [NL, fr. *adel-* + *-spondyli*] *syn of* MICROSAURIA

adel·phi·an \ə'delfēən\ *n* -s *usu cap* [*Adelphius*, an early leader of the sect + E *-an*] **:** EUCHITE 1

adel·phic \-fik\ *adj* [Gk *adelphikos* brotherly, sisterly, fr. *adelphos* brother + *-ikos* -ic] **:** of or relating to a polygynous marriage in which the wives are sisters or to a polyandrous marriage in which the husbands are brothers

adelpho- *comb form* [Gk, fr. *adelphos*] **:** brother ⟨*adelpho*gamy⟩

ad·el·phoc·o·ris \,ad³l'fäkərəs\ *n, cap* [NL, fr. *adelpho-* + Gk *koris* bug] **:** a widely distributed genus of rather small mirid bugs including a number of species destructive to economic plants (as the alfalfa plant bug)

ad·el·phog·a·my \-ägəmē\ *n* -ES [*adelpho-* + *-gamy*] **1 :** polyandry in which brothers have a wife or wives in common **2** *zool* **:** mating of brothers and sisters (as in certain ants) **3 :** union between mother and daughter cells (as in some yeasts)

-adel·phous \ə¦delfəs\ *adj comb form* [prob. fr. NL *-adelphus*, fr. Gk *adelphos* brother, fr. *a-* (fr. assumed *ha-*, akin to *heis, mia, hen* one, *homos* same) + *-delphos* (akin to *delphys* womb) — more at SAME, DOLPHIN] **:** having (such or so many) stamen fascicles ⟨is*adelphous*⟩ ⟨mon*adelphous*⟩

ademp·tion \ə'dem(p)shən, a'-\ *n* -s [L *ademption-, ademptio*, fr. *ademptus* (past part. of *adimere* to take away, fr. *ad-* + *-imere*, fr. *emere* to buy, obtain) + *-ion-, -io* -ion — more at REDEEM] **:** revocation or satisfaction of a property transfer either by disposal (as sale or destruction) of the subject of the property transfer or by some other act (as previous payment) showing such an intention

aden- *or* **adeno-** *comb form* [NL, fr. Gk *adeno-*, fr. *aden-, adēn*; akin to ON *ǫkkr* lump, L *inguen* groin, Gk *nephros* kidney — more at NEPHRITIS] **1 :** gland **:** glandular ⟨*aden*itis⟩ ⟨*adeno*carcinoma⟩ **2 :** glandular and ⟨*adeno*neural⟩

ade·na \ə'dēnə\ *adj, usu cap* [after *Adena*, town in Jefferson co., Ohio, its type station] **:** of or belonging to a prehistoric culture centered in the Mississippi valley characterized by large conical burial mounds and thought to precede the Hopewell culture though in some areas it persisted later than Hopewell

ad·e·nan·the·ra \,ad³n'anthərə\ *n, cap* [NL, fr. *aden-* + *-anthera*] **:** a small genus of Asiatic timber trees (family Leguminosae) with twice-pinnate leaves and racemose flower clusters — see BARBADOS PRIDE, RED SANDALWOOD

ad·e·nase \'ad³n,ās\ *n* -s [ISV *adenine* + *-ase*] **:** an enzyme found esp. in animal tissue (as liver) that hydrolyzes adenine to hypoxanthine and ammonia

aden·i·form \ə'denə,fȯrm, -ēn-\ *adj* [*aden-* + *-iform*] **:** like a gland

ad·e·nine \'ad³n,ēn\ *n* -s [ISV *aden-* + *-ine*; orig. formed as G *adenin*] **:** a purine base $C_5H_3N_4NH_2$ extracted esp. from many glandular organs and from tea and obtained by hydrolysis of nucleic acids; 6-amino-purine

ad·e·ni·tis \,ad³n'īdəs\ *n* -ES [NL, fr. *aden-* + *-itis*] **:** inflammation of one or more lymph nodes

ad·e·no·car·ci·no·ma \¦ad³n(,)ō,kärs³n'ōmə\ *n, pl* **adenocarcinomas** \-məz\ *also* **adenocarcinoma·ta** \-məd·ə\ [NL, fr. *aden-* + *carcinoma*] **:** a malignant tumor originating in glandular epithelium ⟨~ of the breast⟩ — **ad·e·no·car·ci·nom·a·tous** \-s³n¦ämədəs, -ōm-\ *adj*

aden·o·chrome \ə'denə,krōm -ēn-\ *n* -s [*aden-* + *-chrome*] **:** an acidic red pigment found in the branchial hearts of the octopus

ad·e·no·dac·tyl \ə'denə,dakt³l, -ēn-\ *n* -s [*aden-* + Gk *daktylos* finger] **:** one of the penislike supplementary structures in the male reproductive system of certain turbellarians

ad·e·no·fi·bro·ma \¦ad³n(,)ō,fī'brōmə\ *n, pl* **adenofibromas** *or* **adenofibroma·ta** \-məd·ə\ [NL, fr. *aden-* + *fibroma*] **:** a benign tumor of glandular and fibrous tissue

ad·e·no·hy·poph·y·sis \-,hī'päfəsəs\ *n, pl* **adenohypophyses** \-ə,sēz\ [NL, fr. *aden-* + *hypophysis*] **:** the portion of the pituitary body that arises from the embryonic pharynx and is predominantly glandular in nature — compare NEUROHYPOPHYSIS

¹ad·e·noid \'ad³n,ȯid, 'ad,nȯid\ *or* **ad·e·noi·dal** \¦ad³n¦ȯid³l\ *adj* [Gk *adenoeidēs* glandular, fr. *aden-* + *-eidēs* -oid, -oidal] **1 :** of, like, or relating to glands or glandular tissue; *esp* **:** like or belonging to lymphoid tissue **2 :** of or relating to the adenoids ⟨in the ~ region of the pharynx⟩ **3 a :** of, relating to, or affected with abnormally enlarged adenoids ⟨a severe ~ condition⟩ ⟨an ~ patient⟩ **b** *usu adenoidal* **:** typical or suggestive of one affected with abnormally enlarged adenoids: as (1) **:** characterized by mouth breathing **:** GAPING ⟨we can't park here in the driveway like a couple of *adenoidal* tourists —Ellery Queen⟩ (2) **:** nasal, monotonous, or constricted in tone quality **:** BREATHY — used esp. of a singing voice ⟨an *adenoidal* tenor⟩ (3) **:** lacking vivacity esp. in facial expression **:** DULL, APATHETIC ⟨the mumbling of some *adenoidal* moron —Ben Hecht⟩

²adenoid \"\ *n* -s **1 :** an abnormally enlarged mass of lymphoid tissue at the back of the pharynx characteristically obstructing the nasal and ear passages and inducing mouth breathing, nasality, postnasal discharge, and dullness of facial expression — usu. used in pl.; see PHARYNGEAL TONSIL **2 :** PHARYNGEAL TONSIL

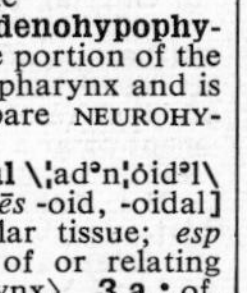

adenoids, *A*

ad·e·noid·ec·to·my \,ad³n,ȯi'dektəmē\ *n* -ES [²*adenoid* + *-ectomy*] **:** surgical removal of the adenoids

ad·e·noid·itis \,ad³n,ȯi'dīd·əs\ *n* -ES [NL, fr. ISV ²*adenoid* + NL *-itis*] **:** inflammation of the adenoids

ad·e·no·ma \,ad³n'ōmə\ *n, pl* **adenomas** *or* **ad·e·no·ma·ta** \-məd·ə\ [NL, fr. *aden-* + *-oma*] **:** a benign tumor of a glandlike structure or of glandular origin ⟨~ of the breast⟩ — **ad·e·nom·a·tous** \-ämədəs, -ōm-\ *adj*

ad·e·no·ma·to·sis \,ad³n,ōmə'tōsəs\ *n, pl* **adenomato·ses** \-ō,sēz\ [NL, fr. *adenomat-, adenoma* + *-osis*] **:** a condition marked by multiple growths consisting of glandular tissue

ad·e·no·my·o·ma \¦ad³n(,)ō,mī'ōmə\ *n, pl* **adenomyomas** *or* **adenomyoma·ta** \-məd·ə\ [NL, fr. *aden-* + *myoma*] **:** a benign tumor composed of muscular and glandular elements

ad·e·no·my·o·sis \¦ad³n(,)ō,mī'ōsəs\ *n, pl* **adenomyo·ses** \-ō,sēz\ [NL, fr. *aden-* + *myosis*] **:** ENDOMETRIOSIS

ad·e·no·neu·ral \¦ad³n(,)ō¦n(y)ùrəl\ *adj* [*aden-* + *neural*] **:** of or relating to a gland and nerve ⟨~ junction⟩

ad·e·nop·a·thy \,ad³n'äpəthē\ *n* -ES [*aden-* + *-pathy*] **:** any disease or enlargement involving glandular tissue; *esp* **:** a disease or enlargement involving lymph glands ⟨cervical ~⟩

ad·e·noph·o·ra \,ad³n'äfərə\ *n, cap* [NL, fr. *aden-* + *-phora*] **:** a genus of herbs (family Campanulaceae) of Europe and Asia that are distinguished by the cushionlike disk or gland around the base of the style

ad·e·nose \'ad³n,ōs\ *or* **ad·e·nous** \-¸əs\ *adj* [*aden-* + *-ose, -ous*] **1** *biol* **:** like a gland **2** *usu adenose, biol* **:** bearing or full of glands

aden·o·sine \ə'denə,sēn, -¸sən\ *n* -s [ISV, blend of *adenine* and *ribose*; orig. formed as G *adenosin*] **:** a crystalline nucleoside $C_{10}H_{13}N_5O_4$ isolated from various tissues, esp. muscle, and obtained by partial hydrolysis of ribonucleic acid, yielding on hydrolysis adenine and ribose and having a vasodilator effect in the vertebrate system; 6-amino-9-D-ribosyl-purine

adenosine diphosphate *also* **aden·o·sine·di·phos·phor·ic acid** \-¦dī,fä¦sfȯrik-\ *n* **:** an ester $C_{10}H_{12}N_5O_3H_2P_2O_7$ of adenosine and pyrophosphoric acid that is formed in living cells as an intermediate between adenosine triphosphate and adenylic acid, its formation from the triphosphate by loss of phosphate leading esp. to a transfer of energy to other compounds in glycolysis, and that reacts in muscle tissue with phosphocreatine or phosphoarginine to regenerate adenosine triphosphate — called also *ADP*

adenosine phosphate *also* **aden·o·sine·phos·phor·ic acid** \-¦fä¦sfȯrik-\ *n* **:** any of various esters of adenosine and a phosphoric acid; *esp* **:** ADENYLIC ACID

adenosine triphosphatase *n* **:** an enzyme that hydrolyzes adenosine triphosphate, esp. one that hydrolyzes the triphosphate to adenosine diphosphate and inorganic phosphate — compare APYRASE, MYOSIN

adenosine triphosphate *also* **adenosinetriphosphoric acid** *n* **:** an amorphous ester $C_{10}H_{12}N_5O_3H_4P_3O_9$ of adenosine and triphosphoric acid that occurs in living cells, esp. in muscle tissue, where its enzymatic hydrolysis to adenosine diphosphate and adenylic acid releases phosphate and available energy for the work of muscular contraction, and that plays a fundamental role in most other biochemical processes that either produce or require energy (as biological oxidations) — called also *adenylpyrophosphate, ATP*

ad·e·nos·to·ma \,ad³n'ästəmə\ *n, cap* [NL, fr. *aden-* + *-stoma*] **:** a small genus of California evergreen shrubs (family Rosaceae) having heathlike leaves and small white panicled flowers and comprising the chamiso and the ribbonwood

ad·e·no·troph·ic \¦ad³n(,)ō¦träfik, ə¦denə¦-, -ōf-\ *adj* [*aden-* + *-trophic*] **:** marked by retention of eggs within the mother until the larvae are hatched and nourished by special nutritive organs in the uterus — used of a form of ovoviviparous development in certain dipterous insects

aden ulcer \'äd³n-, 'ā-,'a-,'ā-\ *n, usu cap A* [fr. *Aden*, city and territory in Arabia, where it occurs] **:** TROPICAL ULCER 2

ad·e·nyl \'ad³n,il\ *n* -s [ISV *adenine* + *-yl*] **:** a univalent radical $C_5H_4N_5$ derived from adenine

ad·e·nyl·ic acid \¦ad³n¦ilik-\ *n* [ISV *adenyl* + *-ic*] **:** an amorphous nucleotide $C_{10}H_{12}N_5O_3H_2PO_4$ formed by partial hydrolysis of ribonucleic acid or of adenosine triphosphate, being an ester of adenosine and orthophosphoric acid known in three isomeric forms — called also *adenosine phosphate*; see ADENOSINE DIPHOSPHATE

ad·e·nyl·py·ro·phos·pha·tase \'ad³n,il¦pīrō'fäsfə,tās\ *n* -s [*adenylpyrophosphate* + *-ase*] **:** ADENOSINE TRIPHOSPHATASE

ad·e·nyl·py·ro·phos·phate \-,pīrō'fä,sfāt\ *n* -s [*adenyl* + *pyrophosphate*] **:** ADENOSINE TRIPHOSPHATE

ad·e·nyl·py·ro·phos·phor·ic acid \-¦pīrō,fä¦sfȯrik-\ *n* [ISV *adenyl* + *pyrophosphoric*] **:** ADENOSINE TRIPHOSPHATE

adeph·a·ga \ə'defəgə\ *n pl, cap* [NL, fr. Gk *adēphaga*, neut. pl. of *adēphagos* gluttonous, fr. *hadēn* enough + *-phagos* -phagous — more at SAD] **:** a suborder of Coleoptera containing certain predaceous beetles (as the tiger beetles, ground beetles, and water beetles) usu. with filiform antennae and the first ventral abdominal segment divided by the hind coxal cavities — **adeph·a·gan** \-gən\ *n* -s

adeph·a·gous \-gəs\ *adj* [NL *Adephaga* + E *-ous*] **:** of or relating to the Adephaga

adeps \'a,deps\ *n, pl* **adi·pes** \'adə,pēz\ [L — more at ADIP-] **1 :** animal fat **2 :** purified internal abdominal fat of the hog

adeps la·nae \¦a,dep'slā,(,)nē, ¦ä,dep'slä,nī\ *n, pl* **adi·pes lanae** \¦adə,pēz'lā-, ¦ädə,pā'slä-\ [NL, lit., wool fat] **:** LANOLIN

¹adept \'a,dept *also* ə'd- *or* a'd-\ *n* -s [NL *adeptus* alchemist that has attained the knowledge of how to change base metals into gold, fr. *adeptus*, adj., knowing how to change base metals to gold, fr. L, having attained, past part. of *adipisci* to arrive at, attain, fr. *ad-* + *apisci* to reach — more at APT] **1 a :** highly skilled or well-trained individual **:** EXPERT — usu. used with *at* or *in* ⟨an ~ in philosophy⟩ ⟨~*s* at traps and ambushes —Seth Agnew⟩ **2 :** an enthusiastic adherent, follower, or devotee (as of a specified philosophy) — usu. used with *of* **syn** see EXPERT

²adept \ə'dept *also* (')a¦d-\ *adj, sometimes* -ER/-EST [NL *adeptus* knowing how to change base metals into gold] **1 :** highly skilled **:** well trained **:** thoroughly proficient — usu. used with *at* or *in* ⟨~ at good newswriting⟩ ⟨~ in handicrafts⟩ **2 :** indicative of great skill or proficiency **:** marked by cleverness or aptitude ⟨an ~ save by the goalie⟩ ⟨an ~ transition from comedy to tragedy⟩ **syn** see PROFICIENT

adept·ly \ə'deptlē, -li *also* (')a¦d-, *rap.* -pl-\ *adv* **:** in an adept manner

adept·ness \-p(t)nəs\ *n* -ES **:** the quality or state of being adept ⟨showed great ~ at fencing⟩

ad·e·qua·cy \'adəkwəsē, -si\ *n* -ES [*adequate* + *-cy*] **:** the quality or state of being adequate **:** sufficiency for a purpose ⟨I do not believe in the ~ of the usual sentimental interpretation of the Golden Rule —M.R.Cohen⟩

¹adequate *vt* -ED/-ING/-S [L *adaequatus*] **1** *obs* **:** EQUAL **2** *obs* **:** to make equal or sufficient **:** EQUALIZE

²ad·e·quate \'adəkwət, -ēk-, *usu* -əd·+V\ *adj* [L *adaequatus*, past part. of *adaequare* to make equal, fr. *ad-* + *aequare* to equal — more at EQUATE] **1** *obs* **:** equal in size or scope **2 :** equal to, proportionate to, or fully sufficient for a specified or implied requirement; *often* **:** narrowly or barely sufficient **:** no more than satisfactory — often used with *to* and sometimes with *for* or *with* ⟨public issues are so large and so involved that . . . only a few . . . can hope to have any ~ comprehension of them —G.L.Dickinson⟩ ⟨with only six men covering two million acres, ~ fire prevention is impossible —*Amer. Guide Series: Minn.*⟩ ⟨a solution ~ to the problem⟩ **3 :** legally sufficient **:** such as is lawfully and reasonably sufficient ⟨~ grounds for a lawsuit⟩ **4** *logic* **:** fully representative ⟨an ~ definition⟩ **syn** see SUFFICIENT

adequate idea *n* **:** an idea that is commensurate to its object: as **a** *in Spinoza* **:** an idea having all the intrinsic marks of a true idea **b** *in Leibniz* **:** an idea clearly understood and analyzed into simple components

ad·e·quate·ly *adv* **:** in an adequate manner

ad·e·quate·ness *n* -ES **:** the quality or state of being adequate

adequate stimulus *n* **:** a stimulus that acts only on an esp. adapted end organ ⟨light is an *adequate stimulus* of the rods and cones of the retina⟩

ad·e·qua·tion \,=='kwāshən\ *n* -s [LL *adaequation-, adaequatio*, fr. L *adaequatus* + *-ion-, -io* -ion] **1 :** the result of making equal or adequate **:** EQUIVALENCE **2 :** the act of making adequate **:** the act of making equal or commensurate

ad·e·qua·tive \'==,kwād·iv\ *adj* **:** EQUIVALENT, ADEQUATE

ader·min \(')ā'dərmən\ *or* **ader·mine** \", -,mēn\ *n* -s [²*a-* + *derm-* + *-in*] **:** VITAMIN B_6

ader wax \'ädə(r)-\ *n* [prob. part trans. of G *aderwachs*, fr. *ader* vein (fr. MHG *āder*, fr. OHG *ādara*) + *wachs* wax; akin to OE *ǣdre* vein, ON *æthr*, Gk *ētor* heart] **:** OZOKERITE

ad·es·se·nar·i·an \(,)a,desə'na(a)rēən\ *n* -s *usu cap* [L *adesse* to be present (fr. *ad-* + *esse* to be) + connective *-n-* + E *-arian* — more at IS] **:** one who believes in the real presence of Christ's body in the eucharist but not by transubstantiation

ad·es·sive \(')a¦desiv\ *adj* [L *adesse* + E *-ive*] *of a grammatical case* **:** denoting presence at a place — used esp. in Finnish and Hungarian grammar

ad eun·dem *or* **ad eundem gra·dum** \,adē'əndəm('grādəm), -n,dem-, -räd-\ *adv (or adj)* [NL] **:** to, in, or of the same rank — used esp. of the honorary granting of an academic standing or degree by a university to one whose actual work for the standing or degree was done elsewhere

¹à deux \ä'də(r), -dǣ, *F* ädœ\ *adj* [F] **:** of, for, or between two individuals esp. privately or intimately ⟨a sly whisper of pretty nothings all *à deux* —Sinclair Lewis⟩

²à deux \"\ *adv* [F] **:** two together ⟨riding along *à deux*⟩; *esp* **:** privately or intimately with only two present ⟨dining *à deux*⟩

ADF *abbr* automatic direction finder

ad fi·lum aq·uae \äd'fēlə'mä,kwī\ [L] *law* **:** to the middle of the stream — often used in conveyancing in describing boundaries

ad fin *abbr* [L *ad finem*] at the end; to the end

ad·ha·mant \(')ad¦hamənt\ *adj* [L *adhamant-, adhamans*, pres. part. of *adhamare* to catch, secure, perh. fr. *ad-* + *hamus* hook] **:** clinging as if by hooks — used esp. of the feet of certain birds (as the swifts)

adhar·ma \ə'dərmə\ *n* -s *sometimes cap* [Skt, fr. *a-* ²a- + *dharma* virtue — more at DHARMA] **1** *Hinduism* **:** individual disharmony with the nature of things **:** nonconformity to one's worldly situation — opposed to *dharma* **2** *Jainism* **:** the uncreated and eternal substance that enables souls and matter to be inactive **:** the ontological principle of rest ⟨~ is compared to earth, on which creatures lie and stand —Heinrich Zimmer⟩ — compare DHARMA

ad·here \ad'hi(ə)r, əd-, -iə\ *vb* -ED/-ING/-S [MF or L; MF *adhérer*, fr. L *adhaerēre*, fr. *ad-* + *haerēre* to stick — more at HESITATE] *vi* **1 :** to hold, follow, or maintain loyalty steadily and consistently (as to a person, group, principle, or way) ⟨the agrarian party, to which he *adhered* to the end of his life —V.L.Parrington⟩ **2** *obs* **:** to be consistent or in accord ⟨nor time nor place did then ~ —Shak.⟩ **3 a :** to hold fast or stick by or as if by gluing, suction, grasping, or fusing ⟨paper *adhering* to the wall⟩ **b :** to become joined (as in pathological adhesion) ⟨the lung sometimes ~*s* to the pleura⟩ **4 :** to agree to join : bind oneself to observance (as of a treaty) ⟨other tribes *adhered* to the pact —P.M.Angle⟩ **5** *Scots law* : to cohabit as husband or wife **6** *bot* : to display adhesion ~ *vt* : to cause to stick fast ⟨paper that had been *adhered* to a surface with glue⟩

syn STICK, CLING, CLEAVE, COHERE: ADHERE is a general term somewhat more bookish in suggestion than STICK to indicate any holding to, esp. steadily and over a period of time ⟨the glue *adhering* to the frame⟩ ⟨dried blood still *adhering* to the cloth⟩ ⟨to revise our ideas and not to *adhere* to what passes for respectable opinion —J.H.Robinson⟩ STICK, more familiar and forceful, may more strongly indicate close tenacious holding to, as though fixed in, embedded, glued ⟨the barb *stuck* in the flesh⟩ ⟨the molasses *stuck* to his fingers⟩ ⟨both sides *sticking* obstinately to their old positions —*New Statesman & Nation*⟩ CLING suggests a hanging on or holding to tenaciously as though in danger or fear of losing one's grip ⟨tall spruce, their roots *clinging* tenaciously to the few inches of soil, crown the summit —*Amer. Guide Series: Maine*⟩ ⟨throwing men and women into the sea with a ship to *cling* to and a chance of reaching another country —G.B.Shaw⟩ ⟨hopes which Huxley cherished and to which many still *cling* —J.W.Krutch⟩ CLEAVE, a rather literary word, implies a close sticking or holding of or as if of flat layers glued or plastered together, a very close, lasting, and indissoluble attachment ⟨the soaked shirt *cleaving* to his shoulders⟩ ⟨to love one maiden only, *cleave* to her, and worship her by years of noble deeds —Alfred Tennyson⟩ COHERE may indicate either a physical sticking together in a mass or an abstract common principle or general consistency that facilitates joining or uniting; it applies to the holding together of like things, of parts of a whole ⟨the mortar will *cohere* to the bricks⟩ ⟨the parts of the exposition do not *cohere*⟩

ad·her·ence \-irən(t)s *also* -er- *or* -ēr-\ *n* -s [F or ML; F *adhérence*, fr. ML *adhaerentia*, fr. L *adhaerent-, adhaerens* (pres. part. of *adhaerēre*) + *-ia*] : the act, action, or quality of adhering: as **a** : ADHESION ⟨~ of paint to wood⟩ **b** : steady or faithful attachment (as to a party, principle, or cause) : continued observance : FIDELITY ⟨fierce ~ to what seemed true —*Times Lit. Supp.*⟩

ad·her·en·cy \-irənsē\ *n* -ES [ML *adhaerentia*] **1** *archaic* : the act of adhering or the quality of being adherent : ADHERENCE **2** *obs* : a person or thing that adheres

ad·her·end \-'hirend, -,hi'rend\ *n* -s [*adhere* + *-end* (as in *addend*)] : the surface to which an adhesive adheres; *also* : one of the bodies held to another by an adhesive

¹ad·her·ent \-'hirənt, -er- *also* -ēr-\ *adj* [ME, fr. MF or L; MF *adhérent*, fr. L *adhaerent-, adhaerens*, pres. part.] **1** : having the quality of adhering : tending to adhere ⟨an ~ coating of frost⟩ **2** : connected with or related to; *specif* : formally or contractually bound to or associated with ⟨nations ~ to the world organization⟩ **3** *bot* : having usu. separate parts united : ADNATE **4** : modifying a noun and standing before it ⟨*busy* in "a busy street", *tomato* in "tomato soup", *down* in "the down train", *pay-as-you-go* in "a pay-as-you-go plan" are ~⟩ — compare ¹APPOSITIVE 2, ¹ATTRIBUTIVE 1a, ¹PREDICATE 2 — **ad·her·ent·ly** *adv*

²adherent \"\ *n* -s [ME, fr. MF *adhérent*, adj., or L *adhaerent-, adhaerens*, pres. part.] **1** : one that adheres: as **a** : a follower of a leader, party, or profession ⟨the ~s of Charles the First —T.B.Macaulay⟩ ⟨~s to the Communist party —J.B.Conant⟩ **b** : a believer in or advocate of a particular thing, idea, or church ⟨~s of the respective faiths —B.K.Sandwell⟩ ⟨~s to a hostile foreign power —Vannevar Bush⟩ **2** : a person 14 years of age or older who has made the Salvation Army his place of worship and is listed on Army records but has not become a soldier because of reservations or inability to comply with requirements

ad·he·sion \ad'hēzhən, əd-\ *n* -s [F or L; F *adhésion*, fr. L *adhaesion-, adhaesio*, fr. *adhaesus* (past part. of *adhaerēre*) + *-ion-, -io* -ion] **1** : steady or firm attachment (as to a person, party, principle, or idea) : ADHERENCE ⟨unshakable ~ to one . . . individual —D.W.Brogan⟩ ⟨~ . . . to the federal party —H.E.Scudder⟩ **2** : the action or state of adhering; *specif* : a sticking together of substances (as of glue and wood or of parts united by growth) **3 a** : the abnormal union of surfaces normally separate by the formation of new fibrous tissue resulting from an inflammatory process; *also* : the newly formed uniting tissue ⟨pleural ~s⟩ **b** : the union of wound edges esp. by first intention **4** : something that adheres ⟨freeing the concept of executive functions from certain ~s sometimes confused with them —Harold Koontz & Cyril O'Donnell⟩ **5** : the act of joining, taking part in, or subscribing to ⟨~ of all countries to a copyright convention⟩ : agreement to join : CONCURRENCE ⟨the country announced its ~ to the pact⟩ **6** : the union of separate plant parts or organs — used chiefly of union between parts of different floral whorls (as between sepals and carpels); compare COHESION **7 a** : a grip or sticking effect produced by friction or the friction itself (as of a smooth locomotive wheel pulling on a smooth rail) **b** : the force that must be developed to overcome this grip before slip occurs **8** : the molecular attraction exerted between the surfaces of bodies in contact —distinguished from *cohesion* **9** : the association of apparently unrelated elements in a culture complex

ad·he·sion·al \-n°l\ *adj* : having or showing adhesion

¹ad·he·sive \ad'hēsiv, əd-, -ēz-, -ēv\ *adj* [*adhesion* + *-ive*] **1** : tending to keep close to or in association with ⟨the ~ character of calumny —J.A.Froude⟩ : tending to persist (as in the memory) ⟨an ~ witticism⟩ **2 a** : tending to adhere : STICKY, GLUEY ⟨~ mud⟩ : having the ability to stick things together ⟨powerfully ~ glue⟩ **b** : prepared for adhering (as by having a surface coated with a sticky substance) ⟨~ tape⟩ — **ad·he·sive·ly** *adv*

²adhesive \"\ *n* -s **1 a** : an adhesive substance; *esp* : a substance that bonds two materials together by adhering to the surface of each (as glue, starch paste, mucilage, rubber latex, or a synthetic resin composition) : CEMENT 2 **b** : ADHESIVE TAPE **2 a** : a postage stamp having a gummed back for sticking it onto postal matter as distinguished from one printed directly on a cover **b** : any stamp or seal having a gummed back

adhesive cell *n* : a glandular thread-bearing cell found only in ctenophores and used in capturing prey by adhesion — called also *colloblast, glue cell, lasso cell*

adhesively *adv* : in an adhesive manner : with adhesion

ad·he·sive·me·ter \-,mēd·ə(r)\ *n* -s : an instrument for testing the adhesive qualities of liquids

ad·he·sive·ness \-nəs\ *n* -ES **1** : the quality or state of being adhesive **2** *phrenology* : the propensity to form and maintain attachments to persons

adhesive organ *n* : a transient larval organ situated near the mouth in certain ganoids, African teleosts, and dipnoans and serving for attachment to the sea bottom — called also *cement organ*

adhesive plaster *n* : ADHESIVE TAPE; *sometimes* : a similar material made up in flat sheets

adhesive tape *n* : tape made usu. of woven cotton of various widths coated on one side with an adhesive mixture and used for many purposes in industry, manufacturing, and esp. in surgery to cover and hold dressings, hold wound edges together, or immobilize a limb or joint

ad·hib·it \ad'hibət\ *vt* -ED/-ING/-S [L *adhibitus*, past part. of *adhibēre* to bring to, summon, admit to consultation, apply, fr. *ad-* + *-hibēre* (fr. *habēre* to hold) — more at HABIT] **1** : to let in (as a person or thing) : bring in **2** : AFFIX ⟨~ a label⟩ **3** *archaic* : USE : ADMINISTER ⟨~ medicine⟩ — **ad·hi·bi·tion** \,adə'bishən, ,adhə'-\ *n* -s

¹ad hoc \(')ad'häk *also* -ōk\ *adv* [NL, lit., for this] : for the particular end or purpose at hand and without reference to wider application or employment ⟨a special number appointed *ad hoc* according to the problem under consideration⟩

²ad hoc \(')¦=¦=\ *adj* : made, established, acting, or concerned with a particular end or purpose ⟨a coordinated policy instead of *ad hoc* decisions⟩ ⟨an *ad hoc* commission of inquiry⟩

ad ho·mi·nem \(')ad'hämə,nem\ *adj* [NL, lit., to the man] **1** : directed at or appealing to one's hearer's or reader's personal feelings or prejudices rather than his intellect and reason ⟨an *ad hominem* argument⟩ **2** : marked by attack on an opponent's character rather than by answer to his contentions ⟨an *ad hominem* plea that his accuser had been in jail⟩

adhort *vt* -ED/-ING/-S [L *adhortari*, fr. *ad-* + *hortari* to incite — more at YEARN] *obs* : EXHORT

ad·i·a·bat \'adēə,bat\ *also* **ad·i·a·bat·ic** \,adēə'bad·ik, ,ā,dīə-\ *n* -s [*adiabat*, back-formation fr. *adiabatic*, adj.; *adiabatic*, fr. *adiabatic*, adj.] : a curve or line plotted using coordinates selected to represent the pressure and volume or the temperature and entropy of matter during an adiabatic process

ad·i·a·bat·ic \¦adēə¦bad·ik, ¦ā,dīə-\ *adj* [ISV *adiabat-* (fr. Gk *adiabatos* impassable, fr. *a-* ²a- + *diabatos* passable, fr. *diabainein* to go across, fr. *dia-* + *bainein* to go) + *-ic*; orig. formed as G *adiabatisch* — more at COME] *of a process* : occurring without loss or gain of heat by the substance concerned ⟨~ expansion⟩ ⟨~ compression⟩ — opposed to *diabatic*; compare ISENTROPIC — **ad·i·a·bat·i·cal·ly** \-ək(ə)lē\ *adv*

adiabatic chart *n* : a meteorological chart with coordinates usu. given as pressure and temperature on which adiabats have been superposed to assist in evaluating adiabatic energy transformations in the atmosphere

adiabatic gradient *n* : the rate at which the temperature of an ascending or descending body of air is changed by adiabatic expansion or compression, being about 1.6° F. for each 300 feet of change of height; *also* : a curve representing this

adi·ac·tin·ic \¦ā,dī,ak¦tinik, -īək-\ *adj* [²*a-* + *diactinic*] : not transmitting actinic rays

adi·ag·nos·tic \¦ā,dīəg¦nästik\ *adj* [ISV ²*a-* + *diagnostic*; orig. formed as G *adiagnostisch*] : having the constituents not distinctly separated but blending together in polarized light under the microscope — used of a rock texture

ad·i·an·tum \,adē'antəm\ *n, cap* [NL, fr. Gk *adianton* maidenhair, fr. neut. of *adiantos* unwetted, fr. *a-* ²a- + *diantos* capable of being wetted, fr. *diainein* to wet, moisten; prob. akin to Gk *deuein* to drench, steep] : a genus of plants comprising the maidenhair ferns (family Polypodiaceae) having dark and often polished stipes, much-divided fronds, and oblong sori borne on the upper margins of the pinnules, the margins of which are reflexed to form indusia

ad·i·a·phon \'adēə,fän\ *n* -s [G, fr. NL *adiaphonon*] : a keyboard instrument resembling the adiaphonon but having tuning forks instead of steel bars

ad·i·aph·o·non \,adē'afə,nän\ *n* -s [NL, fr. ²*a-* + Gk *diaphōnon*, neut. of *diaphōnos* discordant — more at DIAPHONY] : a keyboard instrument resembling the piano but having steel bars instead of strings

adiaphora *pl of* ADIAPHORON

ad·i·aph·o·rism \,adē'afə,rizəm\ *n* -s [*adiaphoron* + *-ism*] : indifference concerning religious or theological matters (as points of controversy)

ad·i·aph·o·rist \-,rəst\ *n* -s : one who adheres to adiaphorism — **ad·i·aph·o·ris·tic** \¦==¦==¦ristik\ *adj*

ad·i·aph·o·ron \,adē'afə,rän, -rən\ *n, pl* **adiapho·ra** \-rə\ [Gk, fr. neut. of *adiaphoros* indifferent, fr. *a-* ²a- + *diaphora* difference, fr. *diapherein* to carry across, bear to the end, make a difference, fr. *dia-* + *pherein* to bear — more at BEAR] **1** *Stoic philos* : a matter having no moral merit or demerit **2** : a religious ceremonial or ritual observance that is held to be an affair of the individual conscience because it is neither forbidden nor enjoined by the scriptures

ad·i·aph·o·rous \,adē¦af(ə)rəs\ *adj* [Gk *adiaphoros*] *obs* : INDIFFERENT, NEUTRAL; *esp* : neither right or beneficial nor wrong or harmful

ad·i·ate \'adē,āt\ *vt* -ED/-ING/-S [prob. back-formation fr. *adiation*] *Roman Dutch law* : to accept (an inheritance) as heir under a will, taking the liabilities and benefits of the estate

adi·a·ther·man·cy \¦a,dīə'thərmənsē\ *n* -ES [²*a-* + *diathermancy*] : imperviousness to infrared radiation

ad·i·a·tion \,adē'āshən\ *n* -s [modif. of L *adition-, aditio* act of entering upon an inheritance — more at ADITIO] : the act of adiating

adi·ba·si \,adə'bäsē\ *n* -s : a member of one of the aboriginal tribes of India

ad idem \a'dīdəm\ *adv (or adj)* [L, to the same] *law* : in agreement or at a meeting of minds on a point : at one — used in ref. to the making of a contract ⟨the parties were not *ad idem* —H.L.Robinson⟩

ad·i·ence \'adēən(t)s\ *n* -s *psychol* : a tendency to approach or accept a stimulus object or situation — opposed to *abience*

ad·i·ent \-ənt\ *adj* [L *adient-, adiens*, pres. part. of *adire* to go to, fr. *ad-* + *ire* to go — more at ISSUE] : characterized by adience : having or showing adience — opposed to *abient*

¹adieu \ə'd(y)ü\ *interj* [ME, fr. MF, fr. *a* to (fr. L *ad*) + *Dieu* God, fr. L *Deus* — more at AT, DEITY] — used to express farewell

²adieu \"\ *n, pl* **adieus** *or* **adieux** \-üz\ [ME, fr. *adieu*, interj.] : a civil or affable expression made upon parting : FAREWELL, LEAVE-TAKING ⟨to make one's ~s⟩

adi·ghe \¦ädə¦gā\ *n, pl* **adighe** *or* **adighes** *usu cap* [prob. fr. Circassian] : CIRCASSIAN

ad ig·no·ran·ti·am \¦a,dignə'ranshē,am\ *adv (or adj)* [L, to ignorance] : by use of unanswerable challenge to disprove rather than by serious attempt to prove ⟨an *ad ignorantiam* argument⟩

ad in·fi·ni·tum \¦a,dinfə'nīd·əm, ¦təm *also* -nē\ *adv (or adj)* [L] : to infinity : without end or limit ⟨talked on and on *ad infinitum*⟩

adin·i·da \ə'dinədə\ *n pl, cap* [NL, fr. ²*a-* + Gk *dinos* act of whirling, whirlpool + NL *-ida*] : a group of primitive flagellate protozoans of the order Dinoflagellata having two flagella but lacking a transverse groove — **adin·i·dan** \-dən\ *adj or n*

ad·i·nole \'ad°n,ōl\ *n* -s [F, fr. Gk *hadinos* close, thick + F *-ole*; akin to Gk *hadēn* enough — more at SAD] : a dense rock composed chiefly of quartz and albite being an alteration product produced by contact metamorphism

¹ad in·ter·im \(')a'dintərəm *also* -ntə,rim *or* -n·trəm\ *adv* [L] : for the intervening time : TEMPORARILY

²ad interim \(')¦=¦=(=)=\ *adj* : made or serving temporarily or for the time being : effective or functioning pending permanent disposition : TEMPORARY ⟨*ad interim* committees for research⟩

ad interim copyright *n* : a temporary copyright valid for five years from the date of first publication abroad of a book or periodical in the English language

ad·ion \a,dīən *also* -ī,än\ *n* -s [*adsorbed ion*] : an ion adsorbed on a surface

adi·os \,adē'ōs, ,ä-, ,a-\ *interj* [Sp *adiós* (prob. trans. of F *adieu*), fr. *a* to (fr. L *ad*) + *Dios* God, fr. L *Deus* — more at AT, DEITY] — used to express farewell

adip- *or* **adipo-** *comb form* [L *adip-, adeps*, fr. Gk *aleipha*; akin to Gk *lipos* fat, lard — more at LEAVE] **1** : fat : fatty tissue ⟨*adipic*⟩ ⟨*adipocele*⟩ **2** : connected with adipic acid ⟨*adipamide*⟩ ⟨*adiponitrile*⟩

adip·a·mide \ə'dipə,mīd, -məd\ *n* -s [*adip-* + *amide*] : the crystalline diamide $H_2NCO(CH_2)_4CONH_2$ of adipic acid that is best known in the form of its polymerized hexamethylene derivative — compare NYLON

ad·i·pate \'adə,pāt\ *n* -s [ISV *adip-* + *-ate*] : a salt or ester of adipic acid

adipes *pl of* ADEPS

adipes lanae *pl of* ADEPS LANAE

adip·ic acid \ə'dipik-\ *n* [ISV *adip-* + *-ic*] : a white crystalline dicarboxylic acid $HOOC(CH_2)_4COOH$ formed by oxidation of various fats and made usu. by oxidation of cyclohexanol or by hydrolysis of adiponitrile for use esp. in the manufacture of nylon

ad·i·po·cel·lu·lose \¦adə(,)pō'selyə,lōs\ *n* -s [*adip-* + *cellulose*] : cellulose associated with suberin in the cell walls of cork tissue

ad·i·po·cere \'adəpə,si(ə)r\ *n* -s [modif. of F *adipocire*, fr. *adip-* + *cire* wax, fr. L *cera* — more at CERATED] : a waxy or unctuous brownish substance consisting chiefly of fatty acids and calcium soaps produced by chemical changes affecting dead animal fat and muscle long buried or immersed in moisture — **ad·i·poc·er·ous** \¦adə¦päs(ə)rəs, ¦adəpə¦sirəs\ *adj*

ad·i·po·cyte \'adəpə,sīt\ *n* -s [*adip-* + *-cyte*] : TROPHOCYTE

ad·i·po·gen·e·sis \,adəpō'jenəsəs\ *n, pl* **adipogene·ses** \-ə,sēz\ [NL, fr. *adip-* + *genesis*] : the formation of fat or fatty tissue (as in the insect fat body)

ad·i·po·ge·net·ic \¦adə(,)pōjə'ned·ik\ *or* **ad·i·pog·e·nous** \-¦päjənəs\ *adj* [*adip-* + *-genetic* or *-genous*] : fat-producing

ad·i·po·leu·co·cyte \¦adə(,)pō'lükə,sīt\ *n* -s [*adip-* + *leucocyte*] : a blood cell typical of certain insects, having the cytoplasm packed with oil globules

ad·i·po·ni·trile \¦adə(,)pō'nī·trəl; -,trēl, -īl\ *n* -s [*adip-* + *nitrile*] : the high-boiling liquid dinitrile $NC(CH_2)_4CN$ of adipic acid made from 1,4-dichlorobutane and sodium cyanide and used to make the nylon intermediate hexamethylenediamine and adipic acid — called also *tetramethylene cyanide*

¹ad·i·pose \'adə,pōs\ *adj* [NL *adiposus*, fr. *adip-* + *-osus* -ose] : of or relating to animal fat : FATTY

²adipose \"\ *n* -s : the fat in the cells of adipose tissue

adipose body *n* : FAT BODY

adipose fin *n* : a soft fleshy rayless modification of the posterior dorsal fin found in certain fishes (as salmons, characins, and typical catfishes)

adipose tissue *n* : animal tissue in which fat is stored, consisting of connective tissue with the cells distended by droplets of fat and constituting the fat of meat

ad·i·po·sis \,adə'pōsəs\ *n, pl* **adipo·ses** \-ō,sēz\ [NL, fr. *adip-* + *-osis*] **1** : ADIPOSITY, OBESITY **2** : the condition of fatty infiltration or degeneration of single organs (as the heart or liver)

adiposis do·lo·ro·sa \-,dōlə'rōsə\ *n* [NL, lit., painful adiposis] : a condition of generalized obesity characterized by pain in the abnormal deposits of fat

ad·i·pos·i·ty \,adə'päsəd·ē\ *n* -ES : the quality or state of being fat : OBESITY

ad·i·po·so·gen·i·tal dystrophy \,adə¦pōsō¦jenəd·°l-\ *n* [*adipose* + *-o-* + *genital*] : a combination of obesity, retarded development of the sex glands, and changes in secondary sex characteristics that results from impaired function or disease of the pituitary body and hypothalamus — called also *Fröhlich's syndrome*

adipo·yl \ə'dipə,wil, a'-\ *or* **ad·i·pyl** \'adəpəl\ *n* -s [*adip-* + *-yl*] : the bivalent radical $-OC(CH_2)_4CO-$ of adipic acid

ad·i·ron·dack \,adə'rän,dak\ *n, pl* **adirondack** *or* **adirondacks** *usu cap* [Mohawk *Hatiróntaks*, lit., they eat trees] **1** : the Algonkian people formerly north of the St. Lawrence river **2** : a member of the Adirondack people

adirondack blackfly *n, usu cap A* : a common blackfly (*Prosimulium hirtipes*) widespread in eastern No. America

adirondack chair *n, often cap A* [prob. so called fr. its popular use in the Adirondack resort area] : a wooden slant-back lawn chair the seat of which usu. is higher at the front than at the back

Adirondack chair

ad·it \'adət\ *n* -s [L *aditus* approach, entrance, fr. *aditus*, past part. of *adire* to go to, approach, fr. *ad-* + *ire* to go — more at ISSUE] **1** : a nearly horizontal opening by which a mine is entered, drained, or ventilated — called also *tunnel*; compare DRIFT 6, GALLERY, INCLINE, LEVEL, SHAFT **2** : the act of coming to : APPROACH, ADMISSION, ACCESS ⟨gain ~ to the throne⟩

adi·tio \ə'dishē,ō\ *n* -s [LL, approach, fr. *aditus* (past part.) + *-io* -ion] *Roman law* : the informal acceptance by an outsider of heirship; *broadly* : the vesting of the inheritance in an heir to a testate or intestate estate or the entering into the inheritance

ad·i·tus \'adəd·əs\ *n, pl* **aditus** *or* **adituses** [L] : a passage or opening for entrance

adive \ə'dēv\ *n* -s [F] : CORSAC

adj *abbr* **1** adjacent **2** adjective **3** adjourned **4** adjudged **5** adjunct **6** adjustable; adjusted; adjustment **7** *often cap* adjutant

ad·jab \'a,jab\ *n* -s [prob. native name in Africa] : NJAVE

ad·ja·cence \ə'jās°n(t)s\ *n* -s [LL *adjacentia*] : ADJACENCY 2

ad·ja·cen·cy \-°nsē, -si\ *n* -ES [ML *adjacentia*, fr. LL, state of being adjacent, fr. L *adjacent-, adjacens* + *-ia* -y] **1 a** : whatever is adjacent in space **b** : nearby or neighboring places — usu. pl. **2** [LL] : the quality or state of being adjacent : CONTIGUITY **3** : a radio or television program or announcement immediately following or preceding ⟨his 9:30 program was helped by a popular ~ at 9:45⟩

adjacency effect *n* : a change in size, density, or other property of a photographic image sometimes observed when small adjacent images are close enough to influence each other and when such a change is not to be expected from the normal sensitometric properties of the material — compare BORDER EFFECT, EBERHARD EFFECT, MACKIE LINE

ad·ja·cent \-°nt\ *adj* [ME, fr. MF or L; MF, fr. L *adjacent-, adjacens*, pres. part. of *adjacēre* to lie near, border on, fr. *ad-* + *jacēre* to lie, fr. *jacere* to throw — more at JET (to spout)] **1 a** : not distant or far off ⟨the city square and the ~ streets⟩ : nearby but not touching ⟨the islands and the ~ mainland coast⟩ **b** : relatively near and having nothing of the same kind intervening : having a common border : ABUTTING, TOUCHING : living nearby or sitting or standing relatively near or close together ⟨hills . . . composed of oyster shells . . . the ~ inhabitants burn them —Mark van Doren⟩ **c** : immediately preceding or following with nothing of the same kind intervening **2** *of two angles* : having the same vertex and one side in common

syn ADJOINING, ABUTTING, CONTIGUOUS, CONTERMINOUS, COTERMINOUS, JUXTAPOSED: ADJACENT is sometimes merely a synonym for *near* or for *close to* ⟨the heavy lands *adjacent* to Paris —Charles Dickens⟩ ⟨Indian Pass, Mount Marcy, and the *adjacent* mountains —John Burroughs⟩ ⟨the safety of the western hemisphere and of the seas *adjacent* thereto —F.D. Roosevelt⟩ Applied to things of the same type, it indicates either side-by-side proximity or lack of anything of the same nature intervening ⟨the doors of the *adjacent* apartment were opened, and Egmont saw himself surrounded —J.L.Motley⟩ ADJOINING is quite similar to ADJACENT in meaning and suggestion but may more strongly indicate existence of common bounding lines or lines or points of junction ⟨in upstate New York and the *adjoining* counties of Pennsylvania —Hans Kurath⟩ ⟨the grayish white stone building and the *adjoining* graveyard —*Amer. Guide Series: Pa.*⟩ ABUTTING most strongly predicates actual contact at a bounding or dividing line ⟨*abutting* lots⟩ ⟨the state of Utah and the *abutting* state of Idaho —W.L.Sperry⟩ ⟨the north wall, to which *abutting* rooms were added —Christopher Hussey⟩ CONTIGUOUS shows variable usage but is likely to suggest touching along a dividing line; it may indicate an unbroken continuity ⟨Marsh and McDunn were each alone in *contiguous* labs, and McDunn attests that Marsh was still at the telephone when he entered his lab —Edith C. Rivett⟩ ⟨Tompkinsville and Stapleton are *contiguous* localities, virtually indistinguishable from each other —*Amer. Guide Series: N. Y. City*⟩ ⟨adjacent events need not be *contiguous*; just as there may be stretches of a string which are not occupied by beads, so the child may experience uneventful periods of time —James Jeans⟩ CONTERMINOUS may apply to a boundary strip in common; often it and COTERMINOUS indicate that all boundaries for two areas are the same and consequently that the two are practically identical ⟨*conterminous* with Philadelphia county, the Quaker City lies along the west bank of the Delaware river —*Amer. Guide Series: Pa.*⟩ ⟨the city and county of Philadelphia are *coterminous* —*American Yr. Bk.*⟩ ⟨the mythology of early man was not *conterminous* with the religion of early man —F.B.Gummere⟩ ⟨the history of Zionism, in fact, is *coterminous* with the history of Jewry —H.E.Wedeck⟩ JUXTAPOSED indicates placement face to face and may suggest likelihood of contrast or opposition ⟨opulence wildly *juxtaposed* to unbelievable poverty —Virginia A. Oakes⟩ ⟨disputes about water rights were almost inevitable between closely *juxtaposed* communities with expanding populations —V.G.Childe⟩

ad·ja·cent·ly *adv* : in an adjacent manner

ad·jag \'a,jag\ *n* -s [prob. native name in Java] : a wild dog (*Cuon javanicus*) found in Java

ad·ject \a'jekt, a'-\ *vt* -ED/-ING/-S [ME *adjecten*, fr. L *adjectus*, past part. of *adjicere* to throw to, add to, fr. *ad-* + *-jicere* (fr. *jacere* to throw) — more at JET (to spout)] *archaic* : to add or annex : JOIN — **ad·jec·tion** \-kshən\ *n* -s *archaic*

ad·jec·ti·val \,ajək¦tīvəl, -ēk-\ *adj* [²*adjective* + *-al*] **1** : of or belonging to an adjective : functioning as an adjective : ADJECTIVE ⟨~ phrase⟩ **2** : given to using adjectives ⟨an ~ poet⟩ : characterized by the use of numerous adjectives ⟨an ~ style⟩ ⟨~ language⟩ — **ad·jec·ti·val·ly** \-əlē, -li\ *adv*

¹ad·jec·tive \'ajəktiv, -ēk-, *rapid sometimes* 'ajəd·iv\ *adj* [ME, fr. MF or LL; MF *adjectif*, fr. LL *adjectivus*, fr. L *adjectus* + *-ivus* -ive] **1 :** being an adjective ⟨an ~ word⟩ : functioning as an adjective ⟨an ~ clause⟩ : fitting or suitable to an adjective ⟨~ uses of nouns⟩ ⟨~ inflections⟩ **2 a :** not standing by itself : DEPENDENT, DERIVATIVE **b :** QUALIFYING, LIMITING : ACCIDENTAL — contrasted with *essential* and *substantive* **3 :** relating to dyes that require a mordant or to the processes in which they are employed ⟨~ colors or dyes⟩ ⟨~ dyeing⟩ — opposed to *substantive* — **ad·jec·tive·ly** *adv*

²adjective \"\ *n* -s [ME, fr. MF or LL; MF *adjectif*, fr. LL *adjectivum*, fr. neut. of *adjectivus*] **1 :** a word belonging to one of the major form classes in any of a great many languages, typically used as a modifier of a noun to denote a quality of the thing named (as *brave* in "a brave man" or "the man is brave", *new* in "the new dress" or "the dress is new"), to indicate its quantity or extent (as *five* in "five cows", *every* in "every word"), or to specify or designate a thing as distinct from something else (as *these* in "these wheels") and in many languages declined for gender, number, and case and agreeing in all these respects with the noun it modifies but in English having no such inflections (except for *this*, plural *these*, and *that*, plural *those*) **2 :** something that has only dependent or qualifying status or existence ⟨a perceptual object is a true Aristotelian ~ of some event which is its situation —A.N. Whitehead⟩ : something that cannot stand alone : DEPENDENT

³adjective \"\ *vt* -ED/-ING/-S **1 :** to make an adjective of : furnish with an adjective or adjectives **2 :** to express or describe using many adjectives ⟨slick, glowingly *adjectived* phrases —Andy Logan⟩

adjective equivalent *n* **:** a word or word group that is not an adjective but has the noun-modifying function of an adjective (as *music* in "music teacher", *dancing* in "dancing teacher", *John's* in "John's dog", *on the wall* in "the picture on the wall", *the doctor* in "my friend the doctor", *who plays golf* in "a man who plays golf")

adjective law *n* **:** the portion of the law that deals with the rules of procedure governing evidence, pleading, and practice

ad·jec·tiv·ize \-tə,vīz\ *vt* -ED/-ING/-S [²*adjective* + *-ize*] **:** to make an adjective of : form an adjectival derivative from

ad·join \ə'jȯin *also* a'-\ *vb* -ED/-ING/-S [ME *ajoinen, adjoinen*, fr. MF *ajoindre*, fr. L *adjungere*, fr. *ad-* + *jungere* to join — more at YOKE] *vt* **1 a :** to add to or attach physically ⟨it is forbidden to ~ to a postcard any sample of merchandise —*Bahamas Official Gazette*⟩ **b :** to add, attach, or append esp. as a supplement ⟨he ~s the remark that God was . . . reconciling the world to himself —P.L.Holmer⟩ **2 :** to lie next to : be in contact with : abut upon ⟨his land ~s the sea —F.D.Smith & Barbara Wilcox⟩ **3 :** to add to a domain of numbers (a number not orig. belonging to it) thereby deriving a larger domain ⟨$x^2 - 2$ can be factored by *~ing* $\sqrt{2}$ to the domain of rational numbers⟩ ~ *vi* **:** to be close, next to, or in contact with one another ⟨the two lots ~⟩

adjoining *adj* [ME *ajoining, adjoining*, fr. pres. part. of *ajoinen, adjoinen*] **:** touching or bounding at some point or on some line : near in space ⟨islands . . . formed by owners living on the ~ shores —*Amer. Guide Series: N. H.*⟩ **syn** see ADJACENT

ad·journ \ə'jərn, -ən, -əin\ *vb* -ED/-ING/-S [alter. (influenced by such words as *adjoin, adjure*) of ME *ajornen, ajournen*, fr. MF *ajorner, ajourner*, fr. *a-* (fr. L *ad-*) + *jour* day, fr. LL *diurnum*, fr. L, neut. of *diurnus* daily — more at DIURNAL] *vt* **1 :** to suspend continuance of or action or decision on : put off : DEFER ⟨the simple plea that partisanship and selfishness be *~ed* —F.D.Roosevelt⟩ **2 :** to put off further proceedings of either indefinitely or until a later stated time : disband with or without an understanding about a future meeting : close formally ⟨*~ing* the session⟩ ~ *vi* **1 :** to suspend a session or meeting till another time or indefinitely : suspend formal business or procedure and disband ⟨the group *~ed* at 10 o'clock⟩ ⟨the congress will ~ next month⟩ **2 :** to move to another place ⟨we *~ed* to the library beside the fire —A.N. Whitehead⟩

ad·journ·al \-nᵊl\ *n* -s **:** ADJOURNMENT, POSTPONEMENT

adjourned summons *n, English law* **:** an originating summons that has been adjourned from chambers for a hearing in court

ad·journ·ment \-nmənt\ *n* -s [F *ajournement*, fr. *ajourner* + *-ment*] **1 :** the act of adjourning or state of being adjourned ⟨a motion for ~ of the meeting⟩ **2 :** the interval for which a body adjourns ⟨after the summer ~⟩

adjt *abbr, often cap* adjutant

ad·judge \ə'jəj *also* a'-\ *vt* -ED/-ING/-S [alter. (influenced by such words as *adjoin, adjure*) of ME *ajugen*, fr. MF *ajugier, ajuger*, fr. L *adjudicare*, fr. *ad-* + *judicare* to judge — more at JUDGE] **1 a :** to decide or rule upon as a judge or with judicial or quasi-judicial powers : ADJUDICATE ⟨~ a lawsuit⟩ ⟨~ a labor controversy⟩ **b :** to pronounce judicially : FIND, RULE ⟨he was *adjudged* insane⟩ ⟨*adjudging* that the defendant owns the land⟩ **2** *archaic* **:** to sentence or condemn (a person) to some punishment ⟨*adjudged* to death —John Milton⟩ ⟨*adjudged* to die⟩ **3 :** to regard, hold, or pronounce to be : JUDGE, DEEM ⟨studies . . . *adjudged* standard works in their field —A.D.H.Smith⟩ — opposed to *abjudge* **4 :** to award or grant judicially in a case of controversy ⟨the difficulty of *adjudging* the prize⟩ **5** *Scots law* **:** to award to a creditor by adjudication

ad·ju·di·ca·taire \ə,jüdəkə'ta(a)(ə)r\ *n* -s [F, fr. L *adjudicatus* + F *-aire* -ary] *Canadian law* **:** a purchaser at a judicial sale

ad·ju·di·cate \ə'jüdə,kāt, -ē,k-, *usu* -ād·+V\ *vb* -ED/-ING/-S [L *adjudicatus*, past part. of *adjudicare* — more at ADJUDGE] *vt* **1 a :** to settle finally (the rights and duties of the parties to a court case) on the merits of issues raised : enter on the records of a court (a final judgment, order, or decree of sentence) **b :** to decide (as an interlocutory matter) arising prior to a final decision **c :** to make (a decision) final or interlocutory in the course of quasi-judicial proceedings — compare ADJUDGE **2 :** to pass judgment on : settle judicially : JUDGE ⟨*adjudicating* a dispute⟩ ~ *vi* **:** to come to a judicial decision : act as judge ⟨the court *adjudicated* upon the case⟩

ad·ju·di·ca·tio \ə,jüdə'kād·ē,ō\ *n* -s [LL] **1 :** the part appearing at the end of the formula or written order of reference in an action in Roman law for partition of property held by common or joint owners that empowered the judge to adjudge the ownership of the property and to make the actual partition **2** *Roman & civil law* **:** a court decree awarding or establishing ownership; *also* **:** acquisition by operation of law

ad·ju·di·ca·tion \ə,jüdə'kāshən, -ē'k-\ *n* -s [F or LL; F *adjudication*, fr. LL *adjudication-, adjudicatio*, fr. L *adjudicatus* + *-ion-, -io* -ion] **1 :** the act or process of adjudicating ⟨the commission for the ~ of the interstate dispute —*Current Biog.*⟩ **2 :** a determination, decision, or sentence esp. without imputation of guilt (as a decree in bankruptcy or the disposition of a juvenile delinquent) **3** *Scots law* **:** an attachment of heritable estate (as for security or for a debt) **4** *Roman law* **:** the part of a formula that directed the judge to apportion shares in property — **ad·ju·di·ca·to·ry** \ə'==kə,tōrē, -ȯr-, -ri\ *adj*

ad·ju·di·ca·tive \ə'jüdəkəd·iv, -,kā-\ *adj* **:** tending to adjudicate or concerned with adjudication

ad·ju·di·ca·tor \,kād·ə(r), -ātə-\ *n* -s **:** one that adjudicates

ad·ju·di·ca·ture \-kə,chü(ə)r, -kəchər, -,kāchər\ *n* -s [*adjudicate* + *-ure*] **:** ADJUDICATION

¹ad·junct \'a,jəŋ(k)t\ *n* -s [L *adjunctum*, fr. neut. of *adjunctus*] **1 a :** something joined or added to another thing but not essentially a part of it ⟨meter and rhyme are not mere ~s of poetry —Samuel Alexander⟩ : an accompaniment or auxiliary to another thing ⟨road building . . . bridge building became necessary ~s of warfare —Lewis Mumford⟩ **b :** a valuable individual quality or attribute ⟨temperance is an ~ only of the wise⟩ **2** *logic* **:** an accidental or nonessential quality or characteristic (as the particular color of a body) **3 :** a word or word group that qualifies, amplifies, or completes the meaning of another word or other words and is not itself one of the principal structural elements in its sentence ⟨in the sentence "most children eat heartily", *most* is an ~ to the subject *children*, and *heartily* is an ~ to the predicate verb *eat*⟩ **4 :** a person associated with or assisting another in some duty or service : ASSOCIATE **5 :** ADJUVANT b

²adjunct \"\ *adj* [L *adjunctus*, past part. of *adjungere* to add, join — more at ADJOIN] **1 :** added or joined as an accompanying object or circumstance ⟨though that my death were ~ to my act, by heaven, I would do it —Shak.⟩ **2 :** added or accompanying in a subordinate capacity; *specif* **:** attached to a faculty or staff as a temporary member having for the time of his appointment the duties, privileges, and remuneration indicated by his rank ⟨~ psychiatrist⟩ ⟨~ associate professor⟩ — see ADJUNCT PROFESSOR — **ad·junct·ly** *adv*

adjunct accusative *n* **:** OBJECTIVE COMPLEMENT

ad·junc·tion \ə'jəŋ(k)shən *also* a'-\ *n* -s [L *adjunction-, adjunctio*, fr. *adjunctus* + *-ion-, -io* -ion] **1 :** a joining on or adding of a person or thing ⟨improve a sentence by ~ of a word⟩ **2 :** *Roman, civil, & Scots law* **:** a species of accession brought about by the activity or work of man as distinguished from that occurring in nature — compare INDUSTRIAL ACCESSION **3** *math* **:** the process of adjoining to a field a number not in it

ad·junc·tive \ə'jəŋ(k)tiv, (')a'j-\ *adj* [LL *adjunctivus*, fr. L *adjunctus* + *-ivus* -ive] **1 :** having the quality of joining : forming an adjunct **2 :** involving the medical use of an adjunct ⟨~ therapy⟩

adjunct professor *n, in some colleges and universities* **:** a teacher ranking next below a professor

ad·ju·ra·tion \,ajə'rāshən\ *n* -s [F or L; F *adjuration*, fr. L *adjuration-, adjuratio*, fr. *adjuratus* (past part. of *adjurare*) + *-ion-, -io* -ion] **1 :** a solemn charging on oath or under penalty of a curse ⟨an ~ by the living God⟩ **2 :** an earnest or solemn urging or charging (as in command, advice, or appeal) ⟨his father's ~ to him to work harder⟩

ad·jur·a·to·ry \ə'jürə,tōrē, 'ajər-\ *adj* [LL *adjuratorius*, fr. L *adjuratus* + *-orius* -ory] **:** having the characteristics of an adjuration : containing a solemn charge or appeal : suited to adjuration ⟨~ terms⟩

ad·jure \ə'jü(ə)r, -üə\ *vt* -ED/-ING/-S [ME *adjuren*, fr. MF & L; MF *ajurer*, fr. L *adjurare*, fr. *ad-* + *jurare* to swear — more at JURY] **1** *obs* **:** to put on oath : induce by the penalty of a curse **2 :** to charge or command solemnly as if under oath or penalty of a curse ⟨*adjuring* him by his belief in God to tell the truth⟩ **3 :** to entreat or advise earnestly : CHARGE ⟨these columns are *adjured* to have some bearing on literary matters —*Saturday Rev.*⟩ **syn** see BEG

ad·jur·er *also* **ad·ju·ror** \ə'jürə(r)\ *n* -s [ME *adjurer*, fr. *adjuren* to adjure + *-er*] **:** one that adjures

ad·just \ə'jəst\ *vb* -ED/-ING/-S [F *ajuster* (formerly also *adjuster*), fr. *a-* (fr. L *ad-*) + *juste* right, exact — more at JUST] *vt* **1 a** (1) **:** to bring to a more satisfactory state ⟨will not ~ their immigration policies for the empire —D.W.Brogan⟩ : SETTLE, RESOLVE ⟨orderly ways of *~ing* conflicts⟩ : RECTIFY ⟨*~ing* the error⟩ (2) **:** to determine the amount to be paid under an insurance policy in settlement of (a loss) ⟨agents who ~ losses⟩ **b** (1) **:** to make correspondent or conformable : ADAPT ⟨~ the books to include these unrecorded data —R.B.Kester⟩ ⟨he *~ed* his argument to meet the opposition⟩ (2) **:** to achieve an orientation of (oneself or itself) : ACCUSTOM ⟨writers *~ing* themselves to the demands of the "new order" —*Times Lit. Supp.*⟩ ⟨plants ~ themselves to many influences —*Encyc. Americana*⟩ : satisfy mental and behavioral needs of (oneself) ⟨characters who . . . ~ themselves better . . . in the army —Robert Lowry⟩ **2 :** to put in order : reduce to a system : REGULATE ⟨~ one's daily schedule to leave time for everything⟩ **3 a** (1) **:** to bring to a true or effective relative position (as the parts of a device) ⟨~ a carburetor⟩ (2) **:** to rearrange the relationship of components of (a watch movement) after complete assembly for improving performance with respect to temperature, positional, or balance-arc variations — distinguished from *regulate* **b :** to change the position of (as for better fit or appearance) ⟨*~ing* his hat on his head⟩ ⟨*~ing* the pillows on the couch⟩ **4 a :** to change the range and direction of (as an artillery piece) so as to move the center of impact of fire onto the target **b :** to send to (the firing unit) the information necessary to make changes in range and direction ~ *vi* **1 :** to come into conformity : adapt itself ⟨these groups . . . ~ freely to the opportunities of American life —Oscar Handlin⟩ : resolve itself : become settled ⟨differences have *~ed* easily —R.H.Jackson⟩ **2 :** to achieve a harmonious mental and behavioral balance between one's own personal needs and strivings and the demands of other individuals and of society **syn** see ADAPT

ad·just·a·ble \-əbəl\ *adj* **:** capable of being adjusted

adjustable-pitch \ə'==¦=\ *adj, of an airplane propeller* **:** having means of pitch adjustment of the blades while at rest but incapable of such adjustment while in motion

adjustable spanner *n, Brit* **:** MONKEY WRENCH

adjustable square *n* **:** a try square having a sliding connection between the two arms so that it may take the form of T as well as L — called also *double square*

adjustable wrench *n* **:** a wrench similar to an open end wrench but having one fixed jaw and one adjustable jaw

adjusted *adj* **1 a :** accommodated, altered, or revised to suit a particular set of circumstances or requirements **b :** having achieved a harmonious relationship with the environment or with other individuals (as by accommodation of physical characteristics or of personal desires) ⟨the ideally ~ plant form⟩ ⟨the well-*adjusted* school child⟩ **2** *of a river system or drainage pattern* **:** having the larger stream courses located for considerable distances in belts of relatively weak rocks

ad·just·er *also* **ad·jus·tor** \ə'jəstə(r)\ *n* -s **1 :** one that sets up or inspects and tunes machines, fits and assembles parts of furniture or electrical equipment, or inspects and adjusts completed products (as typewriters) **2 :** one that investigates claims for personal or property damage or complaints of unsatisfactory service, defective or damaged merchandise received, or improper billing and makes estimates for effecting settlement **3 :** any of various devices for adjusting the position of a part or object esp. with relationship to another part in a machine or apparatus (as one for attaching the rods of an oil-well pump to the walking beam and for adjusting the position of the rods) **4** *usu* **adjustor :** one of a set of muscles in some brachiopods that attach the peduncle to the shell and serve to raise the animal erect

ad·just·ive \ə'jəstiv\ *adj* **:** conducive or contributory to adjustment

ad·just·ment \ə'jəs(t)mənt\ *n* -s [F *ajustement* (formerly also *adjustement*), fr. *ajuster, adjuster* + *-ment*] **1 :** the act or process of adjusting: as **a :** the bringing into proper, exact, or conforming position or condition ⟨~ of a river to the underlying rock structure⟩ **b :** a harmonizing or settling ⟨the ~ of variant views —I.A.Richards⟩ ⟨the orderly ~ of disputes —F.A.Ogg & P.O.Ray⟩ **c** *ecol* **:** functional and often transitory alteration by which an organism is better adapted to its immediate environment — compare ADAPTATION 2b **2 :** a settlement of a claim or debt in a case in which the amount involved is uncertain or in which full payment is not made **3 :** the state of being adjusted: as **a :** a satisfactory or desirable solution or arrangement ⟨a series of emotional ~s —H.G. Armstrong⟩ ⟨the ~ of the boundary question —*Amer. Guide Series: Maine*⟩ **b :** a harmonized or balanced condition ⟨the nice ~ on either side of the scale —J.L.Lowes⟩ **4 :** a means (as a mechanism) by which things are adjusted one to another ⟨an ~ for focusing a microscope⟩ **5 a :** a correction or modification of an account to reflect the actual condition at the close of a given period by means of journal entries recording accruals, correction of errors, and depreciation **b :** an increase or decrease ⟨an ~ in his salary⟩; *sometimes* **:** a decrease in business activity : a mild depression **6** *psychol* **a :** the process by which one becomes adjusted **b :** the extent to which one is able to adjust — **ad·just·men·tal** \ə¦jəs(t)¦mentᵊl, ¦a,jə-\ *adj*

adjustment bond *n* **:** a bond issued in settlement of a prior obligation as part of a reorganization and on which interest payments are usu. contingent upon earnings

ad·ju·tage *or* **aj·u·tage** \'ajəd·ij, ə'jüd-\ *n* -s [alter. (influenced by *ad-*) of earlier *ajutage*, lit., adjustment, fr. MF *ajustage*, fr. *ajuster* to adjust + *-age* — more at ADJUST] **:** a tube or nozzle attached to facilitate or regulate the discharge of water (as in a fountain) or other fluids

ad·ju·tan·cy \'ajəd·ənsē, -ətən-, -si *also* -tᵊn-\ *n* -ES [¹*adjutant* + *-cy*] **:** the office or rank of an adjutant

¹ad·ju·tant \'ajəd·ənt, -ətənt *also* -tᵊnt\ *n* -s [L *adjutant-, adjutans*, pres. part. of *adjutare* to help — more at AID] **1 :** a staff officer acting as a general assistant to the commanding officer **2 :** a staff officer in charge of and responsible for all official correspondence except combat orders, all returns and records of personnel, strength reports, and the preparation and distribution of orders **3 :** one that helps : ASSISTANT ⟨sensibility, refinement, good taste, breeding: all are . . . ~s —Raymond Williams⟩ **4 :** ADJUTANT BIRD

²adjutant \"\ *adj* [L *adjutant-, adjutans*] **:** giving help : ASSISTING ⟨the regular army was aided by ~ irregular troops⟩

adjutant bird *or* **adjutant stork** *also* **adjutant crane** *n* [prob. so called fr. its fancied resemblance to a military figure pacing a parade ground] **:** any of several large upright storks (genus *Leptoptilos*) having the head and neck bare of feathers and feeding on carrion or on small aquatic animals or snakes: as **a :** an Indian stork (*L. dubius*) that attains a height of seven feet **b :** a smaller Indian stork (*L. javanicus*)

adjutant general *n, pl* **adjutants general 1 :** the chief administrative officer of the Army of the U. S. with the rank of major general who is head of the adjutant general's department and office and is responsible for the procedures affecting personnel procurement and for the administration and preservation of records of all army personnel **2 :** the chief administrative officer of a major military unit (as a division or corps)

adjutant's call *n* **:** a bugle call signaling a military unit to form for a ceremony

ad·ju·ta·tor \'ajə,tād·ə(r)\ *n* -s *usu cap* [by folk etymology (influence of *adjutant*)] **:** AGITATOR 1

ad·ju·van·cy \'ajəvənsē\ *n* -ES **:** the action of assisting : HELP

¹ad·ju·vant \-vənt\ *adj* [F or L; F, fr. L *adjuvant-, adjuvans*, pres. part. of *adjuvare* to aid — more at AID] **1 :** serving to aid or contribute : AUXILIARY ⟨an ~ discipline to . . . forms of mysticism —Havelock Ellis⟩ **2 :** involving the use of or functioning as a medical adjuvant ⟨the ~ action of certain bacteria⟩

²adjuvant \"\ *n* -s [F *adjuvant*, adj., or L *adjuvant-, adjuvans*, pres. part.] **:** one that helps or facilitates: as **a :** an ingredient (as in a prescription or solution) that facilitates or modifies the action of the principal ingredient ⟨an ~ that dries paint⟩ ⟨the beneficial activity of the spray is enhanced by ~s⟩ **b :** a method, drug, or other means that enhances the effectiveness of medical treatment ⟨X rays and antibiotics are ~s to surgery⟩

ad·lay *also* **ad·lai** \'ad,lī\ *n* -s [Bisayan] **:** any of several soft-shelled Job's tears (esp. *Coix lachryma-Jobi mayuen*) cultivated for food and for forage and fodder esp. in southeastern Asia, Japan, and the Philippines

adle *obs var of* ADDLE

ad·le·ri·an \(')ad¦lirēən\ *adj, usu cap* [Alfred *Adler* †1937 Austrian psychologist & psychiatrist + E *-ian*] **:** having to do with a theory of character, conduct, and neurosis and with a technique of psychotherapy that emphasize the importance of feelings of inferiority, a will to power, and overcompensation as a denial of personal weakness or inadequacy

ad·less \'adləs, 'aad-\ *adj* [¹*ad* + *-less*] **:** without an advertisement : lacking advertising material ⟨an ~ newspaper⟩

¹ad lib \(')ad'lib\ *adv* [modif. of NL *ad libitum*] **:** in accordance with one's wishes ⟨the skirt is . . . to be belted in *ad lib* —Lois Long⟩ : without restraint or imposed limit ⟨the animals were given water *ad lib* —*Science*⟩

²ad lib \(')=¦=\ *n, pl* **ad libs** [²*ad-lib*] **:** something ad-libbed ⟨the entire program was an *ad lib*⟩

¹ad-lib \(')=¦=\ *adj* **1 :** spoken or composed extempore ⟨free and easy *ad-lib* questioning —*N. Y. Times*⟩ **2 a :** available for free or spontaneous use or consumption ⟨dinner, with wine *ad-lib* —Bernard Smith⟩ **b :** made or done spontaneously : not controlled by a schedule ⟨*ad-lib* feeding of animals⟩

²ad-lib \(')=¦=\ *vb* **ad-libbed; ad-libbed; ad-libbing; ad-libs** *vt* **1 a :** to improvise as a part of something (as lines not in the script or music not in the score) **b :** to improvise all of (as a speech or a dance) **2 :** to devise (something) impromptu : employ offhand (as a makeshift) ⟨without spare parts the repairmen had to *ad-lib* material⟩ ~ *vi* **:** to improvise or deliver extempore esp. for filling in during a break in a program

ad-lib·ber \(')=¦=ə(r)\ *n* -s [²*ad-lib* + *-er*] **:** one that ad-libs

¹ad lib·i·tum \(')ad'libəd·əm\ *adv* [NL, in accordance with one's wishes] **:** ad lib

²ad libitum \(')=¦===\ *adj* **:** variable according to a performer's pleasure : OMISSIBLE — abbr. *ad lib;* used esp. of music; distinguished from *obbligato*

ad li·tem \(')ad'lī,tem\ [L] *adv (or adj)* **:** for the suit or action ⟨guardian *ad litem*⟩

ad·lit·to·ral \(')ad¦=\ *adj* [*ad-* + *littoral*] **:** of, relating to, occurring in, or being the shallow water adjacent to a shore ⟨~ mollusks⟩

ad lo·cum \(')ad'lōkəm\ *adv* [L] **:** to or at the place

ad·lu·mia \ad'lümēə\ *n, cap* [NL, fr. John *Adlum* †1836 Am. pioneer in viticulture + NL *-ia*] **:** a genus of climbing herbs (family Fumariaceae) with a spongy persistent corolla

ad·lu·mi·dine \-mə,dēn\ *n* -s [blend of *adlumine* and *-id*] **:** an alkaloid $C_{19}H_{15-17}NO_6$ found in the climbing fumitory

ad·lu·mine \-,mēn, -mən\ *n* -s [NL *adlumia* (genus name of *Adlumia fungosa*) + E *-ine*] **:** an alkaloid $C_{21}H_{21}NO_6$ found in the climbing fumitory

adm *abbr* **1** administration; administrative; administrator **2** *often cap* admiral; admiralty **3** admission

ad·man \'ad,man, -,mən, -,maa(ə)n\ *n, pl* **admen** [¹*ad* + *man*] **1 :** one that writes, solicits, or places advertisements **2 :** a compositor who sets advertisements

ad ma·num mor·tu·am \ȧd'mänəm'mȯrchə,wäm\ [ML, lit., to a dead hand] *adv* **:** in mortmain

ad·max·il·lary \(')ad¦maksə,lerē\ *adj* [*ad-* + *maxillary*] **:** near or connected with the maxilla

ad·mea·sure \ad'mezhə(r), -āzh-\ *vt* -ED/-ING/-S [alter. (influenced by such words as *administer, admit*) of ME *amesuren*, fr. MF *amesurer*, fr. *a-* (fr. L *ad-*) + *mesurer* to measure — more at MEASURE] **:** to determine the proper share of : APPORTION ⟨~ land among heirs⟩ : mete out ⟨the ally of the judge in the business of *admeasuring* the sentence —B.N. Cardozo⟩

ad·mea·sure·ment \=¦==mənt\ *n* -s **1 :** determination and apportionment of shares ⟨~ of common lands for pasturage⟩ **2 :** application of a measure to determine or compare dimensions ⟨land consisting of two acres by ~⟩ **3 :** DIMENSIONS, SIZE ⟨a ship of considerable ~⟩

ad·me·di·al \(')ad¦mēdēəl\ *or* **ad·me·di·an** \-ēən\ *adj* [*ad-* + *medial* or *median*] *biol* **:** near the median plane

ad·mi \'admē\ *n* -s [Berber (Touareg) *édemi*] **:** a gazelle (*Gazella cuvieri*) found in northeastern Africa

ad·min·i·cle \ad'minəkəl, əd-\ *n* -s [L *adminiculum* support, prop, perh. fr. *ad-* + *-miniculum* (fr. *minae* pinnacle of a wall + *-iculum*, dim. suffix)] **1 :** SUPPORT, AUXILIARY ⟨to serve as an ~ of the senate⟩ ⟨the ~s of modern culture⟩ **2** [ML *adminiculum*, fr. L] **a** *law* **:** corroborative or explanatory proof **b** *Scots law* **:** any writing tending to establish the existence or terms of a lost document

ad·mi·nic·u·lar \¦admə¦nikyələ(r)\ *also* **ad·mi·nic·u·lary** \-,lerē\ *adj* [L *adminiculum* + E *-ar* or *-ary*] **:** supplying help : AUXILIARY, CORROBORATIVE ⟨~ evidence⟩

ad·min·is·ter \əd'minəstə(r) *also* ad-\ *vb* **administered; administered; administering** \-st(ə)riŋ\ **administers** [ME *aministren, administren*, fr. MF *aministrer, administrer*, fr. L *administrare* to attend, manage, fr. *ad-* + *ministrare* to serve — more at MINISTER] *vt* **1 a** (1) **:** to manage the affairs of ⟨a government that is badly *~ed* can never be expected to last long —C.J.Friedrich⟩ (2) **:** to direct or superintend the execution, use, or conduct of ⟨*~ed* the regulations governing interstate travel —W.M.Emery⟩ ⟨in many Japanese homes the funds are *~ed* by the wife —D.C.Buchanan⟩ ⟨vocational interest tests are *~ed* to all students⟩ **b :** to act in lieu of an executor in settling (an intestate estate) **2 a :** to mete out : DISPENSE ⟨~ relief⟩ ⟨she was able to ~ a more piquant flattery —Ellen Glasgow⟩ ⟨~ justice⟩ ⟨disclaiming any intention to ~ any official rebuke —W.A.Slade⟩ ⟨*~ed* a public thrashing to the landlord who had mistreated his brother —C.V.Woodward⟩ **b :** to give ritually ⟨~ the last rites of the church⟩ **c :** to give remedially (as medicine) ⟨the amount of the antitoxin *~ed* is determined by the doctor —Morris Fishbein⟩ **3 :** TENDER ⟨the following questions were first *~ed* by the Archbishop of Canterbury —*Whitaker's Almanack*⟩ — often used with *to* ⟨the formal oath of office was *~ed* to him —*Current Biog.*⟩ ~ *vi* **1 :** to perform the office of administrator — sometimes used with *upon* ⟨A ~s upon the estate of B⟩ **2 :** to give or furnish a real or assumed benefit : MINISTER — used with *to* ⟨*~ing* to the last wants of his friend⟩ **3 :** to manage or conduct affairs ⟨the government ~s when it appoints an officer —F.J.Goodnow⟩

administered price *n* **:** a price determined by the conscious price policy of a seller rather than by impersonal competitive market forces

ad·min·is·te·ri·al \əd¦minə¦stirēəl, ad-, ¦ad,mi-\ *adj* **:** ADMINISTRATIVE

ad·min·is·tra·ble \əd'minəstrəbəl, ad-\ *adj* [*administrate* + *-able*] **:** capable of being administered

ad·min·is·trant \-strənt\ *n* -s [*administer* + *-ant*] **:** one that administers

ad·min·is·trate \-nə,strāt\ *vt* -ED/-ING/-S [L *administratus*, past part. of *administrare* — more at ADMINISTER] **:** ADMINISTER

ad·min·is·tra·tion \əd,minə'strāshən *also* (,)ad,m-\ *n* -s [ME *administracioun*, fr. MF or L; MF *administration*, fr. L *administration-*, *administratio*, fr. *administratus* + *-ion-*, *-io* -ion] **1 :** an act of administering: **a :** a furnishing or tendering according to a prescribed rite or formula ⟨~ of the sacraments⟩ ⟨~ of an oath⟩ **b :** a meting out ⟨~ of justice⟩ ⟨~ of discipline⟩ **c :** APPLICATION, DOSAGE ⟨~ of a medicine⟩ ⟨~ of sensory stimuli⟩ **2 a** *archaic* **:** performance of a service in any capacity **b :** performance of executive duties **:** MANAGEMENT, DIRECTION, SUPERINTENDENCE ⟨achieved a more businesslike ~⟩ ⟨engage in the ~ of public affairs⟩ ⟨~ of a relief fund⟩ — compare LOGISTICS **3 a :** the management and disposal under legal authority of the estate of an intestate or of a testator having no competent executor **b :** the management of an estate of a deceased person by an executor **c :** the management of an estate (as of an infant) by a trustee or guardian legally appointed to take charge of it **4 a :** the total activity of a state in the exercise of its political powers including the action of the legislative, judicial, and executive departments **:** GOVERNMENT 2 **b :** the management of public affairs as distinguished from the executive or political function of policy making **5 a :** the principles, practices, and rationalized techniques employed in achieving the objectives or aims of an organization **b :** administrative management **:** the phase of business management that plans, organizes, and controls the activities of an organization for the accomplishment of its objectives in the long run often as distinguished from operative management **6 a :** a body of persons who are responsible for managing a business or institution **b** *usu cap* **:** a group constituting the political executive in a presidential system ⟨even a supposedly friendly Congress may flout the *Administration's* program —F.A.Ogg & P.O.Ray⟩ — compare GOVERNMENT 8 c(1) **c :** a governmental agency or board **7 :** the term during which an administrative officer or body holds office; *specif* **:** the term or terms of office of a president of the U.S. — **ad·min·is·tra·tion·al** \əd¦minə¦strāshənᵊl, -shnəl *also* ¦ad,m-\ *adj*

ad·min·is·tra·tive \əd'minə,strād·iv, -,strə|, |tiv, -ēv *also* ad- *or* -əv\ *adj* [L *administrativus*, fr. *administratus* + *-ivus* -ive] **:** of, belonging to, proceeding from, or suited to administration or an administration **:** EXECUTIVE — **ad·min·is·tra·tive·ly** *adv*

administrative county *n* **:** a territorial division in Great Britain often not coincident with the older county and to which the administrative functions but not the judicial and political ones of the older counties have been transferred

administrative law *n* **:** law dealing with the establishment, duties, and powers of and available remedies against authorized agencies in the executive branch of government

administrative unit *n* **1 :** a military unit (as a company or regiment) whose headquarters is directly responsible for administration and supply of the unit **2 :** a geographic area having a single school administration over several schools

ad·min·is·tra·tor \-,strād·ə(r), -ātə-, -ā,tō(ə)r, -ā,tō(ə)r\ *n* -s [L, manager, fr. *administratus* + *-or*] **1 :** a person legally vested by a probate court with the right of administration of an estate — compare EXECUTOR **2 :** one that administers: as **a :** an officer appointed to govern (as a colony or dependency) **b :** an officer that directs or superintends affairs (as of a business, school, or government agency) **c :** a priest appointed to administer temporarily a diocese, parish, or ecclesiastical institution

administrator ad litem *n* [NL, administrator for the action] **:** a special administrator appointed to represent an estate in an action in which it must be represented when there is no executor or the executor for some reason cannot act

administrator with the will annexed : one appointed to administer an estate where the testator has appointed no executor or where his appointment of an executor has failed (as through death, incompetency, or refusal to act)

ad·min·is·tra·trix \əd¦minə¦strā·triks, ad-\ *n, pl* **adminis·tra·tri·ces** \⸗,⸗⸗'strā·trə,sēz, -,strə·'trī(,)sēz\ [ML, fem. of L *administrator*] **:** a female administrator esp. of an estate

¹ad·mi·ra·ble \'adm(ə)rəbəl\ *adj* [MF, fr. L *admirabilis*, fr. *admirari* to admire + *-abilis* -able — more at ADMIRE] **1** *obs* **:** worthy of being marveled at **:** WONDERFUL, SURPRISING ⟨it seemeth equally ~ to me, that holy king Henry the Sixth should do any wrong, or harsh Edward the Fourth do any right to the muses —Thomas Fuller⟩ **2 :** capable of exciting wonder united with approbation **:** deserving the highest esteem ⟨a record of a long, varied, and ~ career in the Foreign Service —R.H.Rovere⟩ **3 :** EXCELLENT **3** ⟨he is in many ways an ~ and even estimable figure —Irving Howe⟩ ⟨his taste was impeccable, his health ~ —Virginia Woolf⟩ — **admirableness** *n* -ES — **admirably** *adv*

²admirable *adv, obs* **:** ADMIRABLY

ad·mi·ral \'adm(ə)rəl\ *n* -s [ME *admiral*, *amiral*, fr. ML *admiralis* emir & OF *amiral* emir & MF *amiral* naval officer of high rank; ML *admiralis*, prob. by folk etymology (influence of L *admirabilis* admirable) fr. Ar *amīr* commander, *amīr-al-* commander of the (in such phrases as *amīr-al-baḥr* commander of the sea); OF & MF *amiral* fr. Ar *amīr*, *amīr-al-*] **1** *archaic* **:** the commander in chief of a navy **2 a :** a naval officer of high rank **:** FLAG OFFICER — see ADMIRAL OF THE FLEET, FLEET ADMIRAL, REAR ADMIRAL, VICE ADMIRAL **b :** a flag officer who is junior only to a fleet admiral, wears 4 stars and flies a 4-starred flag, and ranks with a four-star general in the army **3 :** a commander or officer having a certain general control of a fishing or merchant fleet; *specif* **:** a fisherman appointed to preserve order and decide differences in a fishing fleet **4** *archaic* **:** the chief ship of a fleet **:** FLAGSHIP **5 :** any of several brightly colored butterflies of the family Nymphalidae — see RED ADMIRAL **6 :** LOGWOOD 2

admiral of the fleet : the highest-ranking officer of the British navy corresponding to fleet admiral in the U. S. navy

¹ad·mi·ral·ty \'adm(ə)rəltē, -ti\ *n* -ES [alter. (influenced by *admiral*) of ME *amiralte*, fr. MF *amiralté*, fr. *amiral* admiral + *-té* -ty] **1** *archaic* **:** the office or jurisdiction of an admiral **2** *Brit, usu cap* **:** the executive department or officers having authority over naval affairs generally **3 :** the court having jurisdiction of maritime questions and civil and criminal maritime offenses, in the U. S. such jurisdiction being vested in the federal district court and in England in the probate, divorce, and admiralty division of the High Court of Justice; *also* **:** the system of law administered by admiralty courts

²admiralty \"\ *adj* **1 :** relating to maritime law ⟨~ jurisdiction⟩ ⟨~ practice⟩ **2** *usu cap* **:** of or belonging to British naval affairs or officials ⟨an *Admiralty* lord⟩ ⟨the *Admiralty* buildings⟩

admiralty bond *n* **:** a bond furnished by vessel or cargo owners in admiralty proceedings as security for the payment of legal claims to other vessel or cargo owners

admiralty brass *n* [*Admiralty Metal*] **:** a corrosion-resistant alloy containing about 71 percent copper, 28 percent zinc, and 1 percent tin

admiralty flag *n, usu cap A* [so called fr. its being flown on boats carrying members of the Board of *Admiralty*] **:** a British sea flag of red with an anchor and cable in yellow in the center

Admiralty Metal *trademark* — used for a corrosion-resistant alloy

admiralty mile *n, often cap A* **:** NAUTICAL MILE a

ad·mi·ra·tion \,admə'rāshən\ *n* -s [ME *admiracioun*, fr. MF or L; MF *admiration*, fr. L *admiration-*, *admiratio*, fr. *admiratus* (past part. of *admirari*) + *-ion-*, *-io* -ion] **1** *archaic* **:** WONDER, ASTONISHMENT **2 :** the object or source of wonder, astonishment, or esteem ⟨Poe was one of his greatest ~s —Amy Lowell⟩ **3 :** a feeling of mingled wonder, esteem, approbation, and delight ⟨my respect for him increased, and I looked on him almost with ~ —George Borrow⟩ ⟨there is perhaps a disproportionate ~ for the man who can produce original and good results —A.W.Haslett⟩ **4 :** act of viewing or contemplating with wonder, esteem, or approbation ⟨guided not by the giddy ~ of the shining accomplishments, but by the sober esteem of modesty —Adam Smith⟩ ⟨his persistence and courage won ~ even from those who thought him a madman —W.C.Ford⟩ ⟨he wagged his head and looked about for ~ —Pearl Buck⟩ **syn** see REGARD

admirative *adj* [F *admiratif*, fr. *admiration* + *-if* -ive] *archaic* **:** expressing admiration — **admiratively** *adv*

ad·mire \əd'mī(ə)r, -īə *also* ad-\ *vb* -ED/-ING/-S [MF *admirer*, fr. L *admirari*, fr. *ad-* + *mirari* to wonder — more at SMILE] *vt* **1** *archaic* **:** to regard with wonder or astonishment **:** view with surprise **:** marvel at ⟨how can we sufficiently ~ the stupidity and madness of these persons? —Joseph Addison⟩ **2 :** to regard with wondering esteem accompanied by pleasure and delight **:** regard with an elevated feeling of pleasure ⟨~ the beauty of the scene⟩ **3 :** to esteem or regard highly ⟨~ one's efficiency⟩ **4** *dial* **:** to take pleasure in **:** LIKE, ENJOY — usu. used with an infinitive ~ *vi* **:** WONDER, MARVEL — sometimes used with *at* ⟨his friends *admired* at his sudden success⟩

admired *adj* **:** regarded with admiration ⟨the most ~ single phrase that Shakespeare ever wrote —C.D.Lewis⟩ ⟨I was much about with a beautiful, ~ woman —W.B.Yeats⟩

ad·mir·er \-īrə(r)\ *n* -s **:** one that admires ⟨an ~ of the president⟩ ⟨among the ~s of his preaching⟩; *specif* **:** LOVER, BEAU ⟨one of the young lady's ~s⟩

admiring *adj* **:** feeling or showing admiration ⟨~ friends⟩ ⟨~ glances⟩ — **ad·mir·ing·ly** *adv*

admis *pl of* ADMI

ad mi·se·ri·cor·di·am \,admə,zerə'kȯrdē,am, -ēəm\ *adv (or adj)* [L] **:** to compassion or pity — used of an argument

ad·mis·si·bil·i·ty *also* **ad·mis·sa·bil·i·ty** \əd,misə'biləd·ē, (,)ad,-, -ətē, -i\ *n* -ES **:** the quality or state of being admissible

ad·mis·si·ble *also* **ad·mis·sa·ble** \əd'misəbəl *also* ad-\ *adj* [*admissible* fr. F, fr. ML *admissibilis*, fr. L *admissus* + *-ibilis* -ible; *admissable*, alter. of *admissible*] **1 a :** capable of being allowed or conceded **:** ALLOWABLE ⟨retelling the story, if done by a gifted writer, was felt to be ~ —N.A.McQuown⟩ ⟨a kind of speculation that was ~ in cosmology but inadmissible in medicine —Benjamin Farrington⟩ ⟨Buddhism, Taoism, and Confucianism are all ~ philosophies —C.P.Fitzgerald⟩ ⟨the difficulty would be lessened if entries in books of account were ~ as prima-facie evidence —B.N.Cardozo⟩ **b** *of a logical or mathematical value* **:** capable of producing a meaningful expression when substituted for a variable ⟨in the sentence "*X* is tall", *John* is an ~ substitute for *X* but *two* is not⟩ **2 :** entitled or worthy to be admitted ⟨handicapped persons ~ to industrial employment⟩ ⟨foreign products ~ to the domestic market⟩ ⟨hearsay evidence is not ordinarily ~ in court⟩

ad·mis·sion \əd'mishən *also* ad-\ *n* -s [in sense 1, fr. ME *admissioun*, fr. ML *admission-*, *admissio*, fr. L, admittance to an audience with a prince, fr. *admissus* (past part. of *admittere*) + *-ion-*, *-io* -ion; in other senses, fr. L *admissus* + E *-ion*] **1 a** *archaic* **:** acceptance into an office or position **b :** formal approval of a presentee to a benefice by a bishop of the Church of England; *sometimes* **:** the institution of such a presentee **2 a :** the granting of an argument or position not fully proved **:** the act of acknowledging something asserted **:** acquiescence or concurrence in the truth of an allegation **b** *in criminal law* **:** a concession that a fact or allegation is true without implying any acknowledgment of criminal intent — distinguished from *confession* **c :** a revealing statement (as of acknowledgment or fact) ⟨this ~ had the effect of an electric shock upon my older sister —Sidney Lovett⟩ **3 a :** an act of admitting **:** the fact of being admitted **:** permission or right to enter (as a place or a membership) **:** ACCESS **b** (1) **:** the act of admitting the working fluid (as steam) to the engine cylinder (2) **:** the point in the cycle of operations or on the corresponding indicator diagram at which this act occurs (3) **:** the period from this point to the completion of the cutoff **4 :** price of entrance **:** fee paid at or for entering

admission day *n, usu cap A&D* **:** the anniversary of the admission of a state to the U. S.

ad·mis·sive \-isiv\ *adj* [L *admissus* + E *-ive*] **:** characterized by or allowing admission ⟨an Elizabethan tragedy ~ of comic scenes —Rene Wellek & Austin Warren⟩

ad·mit \əd'mit *also* ad-; *usu* -id·+V\ *vb* **admitted; admitted; admitting; admits** [ME *admitten*, fr. L *admittere*, fr. *ad-* + *mittere* to send — more at SMITE] *vt* **1 a :** PERMIT ⟨the geological vocabulary ~s a less satisfactory treatment than does that of some of the other sciences —T.H.Savory⟩ **b :** to accept as true or valid **:** ACKNOWLEDGE ⟨Brunel was compelled to ~ failure —O.S.Nock⟩ ⟨*admitting* the possibility that the bomb might wipe out civilization —*Current Biog.*⟩ ⟨a reluctance to ~ any of the ample evidence —J.G.Cozzens⟩ ⟨another troublesome problem was settling a date after which no evidence would be *admitted* —W.O.Aydelotte⟩ — compare ADMISSION 2a **2 :** to allow entry (as to a place, membership, or privilege) ⟨this ticket ~s one person⟩ ⟨he was *admitted* a fellow of the Royal Society —Ella Lonn⟩ — often used with *to* or *into* ⟨he was *admitted* to the university⟩ ⟨*admitted* to candidacy⟩ ⟨states *admitted* to the Union⟩ ~ *vi* **1 :** to give entrance or access — used with *to* ⟨a gate that ~s to a yard⟩ **2 a :** ALLOW, PERMIT — often used with *of* ⟨indeterminate situations which ~ of answers —J.J.O'Connor⟩ ⟨many crucial dilemmas simply do not ~ of analysis on one page —Dorothy Fosdick⟩ **b :** to make acknowledgment — used with *to* ⟨they dare not publicly ~ to these doubts—Hessell Tiltman⟩ **syn** see ACKNOWLEDGE, RECEIVE

ad·mit·tance \-tᵊn(t)s\ *n* -s **1 a :** permission to enter (a place) **:** ENTRANCE **b :** ADMISSION 3a **2** *English law* **:** the act of giving possession of a copyhold **3 :** the reciprocal of the impedance of a circuit

ad·mit·ta·tur \,admə'tād·ə(r)\ *n* -s [L, let him be admitted (often the first word on such a certificate)] **:** a certificate of admission formerly given by a college or university

admitted *adj* **:** received as true or valid **:** CONCEDED, ACKNOWLEDGED — **ad·mit·ted·ly** *adv*

admitted asset *n* **:** any asset of an insurer allowed by state regulations to be reckoned in determining the financial condition of an insurance company

admitted company *n* **:** an insurance company that having complied with the laws is authorized to transact business within a certain state or country

¹ad·mix \(')ad¦miks, əd'm-\ *vt* -ED/-ING/-ES [back-formation fr. obs. *admixt* mingled with, fr. ME, fr. L *admixtus*] **:** MINGLE, MIX, BLEND — often used with *with* ⟨a saturated hydrocarbon that cannot be vulcanized unless ~*ed* with a little isoprene —J.W.McBain⟩

²ad·mix \'ad,miks\ *n* [by shortening] **:** ADMIXTURE 2b

admix *abbr* administratrix

ad·mix·ture \(')ad¦mikschə(r), əd'm-\ *n* [L *admixtus* (past part. of *admiscēre* to mix with, fr. *ad-* + *miscēre* to mix) + E *-ure* — more at MIX] **1 a :** the act of mixing ⟨a favorable result will be obtained only by careful ~ of ingredients⟩ **b :** the fact of being mixed ⟨repeated sifting is necessary to secure complete ~⟩ **2 a :** an element or substance added by mixing ⟨comic verses with an occasional ~ of mild bawdry —Alexander Cowie⟩ **b :** a substance other than cement, aggregate, or water that is mixed with concrete **3 :** a compound formed by mixing (as by using wool, silk, cotton, and linen fibers in various ~s —A.C.Morrison⟩

adml *abbr, often cap* admiral

ad·mon·ish \əd'mänish, -ēsh *also* ad-\ *vb* -ED/-ING/-ES [ME *admonissen*, *admonisshen*, alter. (*amonest-*, *admonest-* being taken as past & past part.) of *amonesten*, *admonesten*, fr. MF *amonester*, *admonester*, fr. (assumed) VL *admonestare*, alter. of L *admonēre* to remind, warn, fr. *ad-* + *monēre* to warn — more at MIND] *vt* **1 :** to indicate duties, obligations, or requisite action to (a person) **:** express warning or disapproval to about remissness or error esp. gently, earnestly, and solicitously in urging duty, caution, or amendment ⟨necessary to the decorum of her character that she should ~ her erring children —T.B.Macaulay⟩ **2 :** to express a direction or explanation or give advice or encouragement to esp. in friendly earnest counsel ⟨someone has ~*ed* you not to miss Brandon —E.W. Smith⟩ ~ *vi* **:** to give admonition **syn** see REPROVE

ad·mon·ish·ing·ly *adv* **:** in an admonishing manner

ad·mon·ish·ment \-mənt\ *n* -s [alter. of ME *admonestement*, *amonestement*, fr. OF, fr. *amonester* to admonish + *-ment*] **:** ADMONITION

ad·mo·ni·tion \,admə'nishən\ *n* -s [alter. (influenced by *admonish*) of ME *amonicioun*, fr. MF *amonition*, fr. L *admonition-*, *admonitio*, fr. *admonitus* (past part. of *admonēre*) + *-ion-*, *-io* -ion] **1 :** gentle or friendly reproof, warning, or reminder ⟨admirably took a middle key between ~ and philosophizing —Mary Austin⟩ ⟨a silent ~ to the guests to enjoy life while it lasted —T.L.Peacock⟩ **2 :** counsel against a fault, error, or oversight ⟨~s against the oversimplification, overdramatization, and lurking distortion of historiography —Ephraim Fischoff⟩ **3 :** expression of authoritative advice or warning esp. in ecclesiastical censure ⟨pressure is exerted largely through precept and ~ —Catherine H. Berndt⟩

ad·mon·i·to·ri·ly \əd¦mänə¦tōrəlē, ad-, -ȯr-, -ri\ ¦ad,m-\ *adv* **:** in an admonitory manner

ad·mon·i·to·ry \əd'mänə,tōrē, ad-, -ȯr-, -ri\ *adj* [ML *admonitorius*, fr. L *admonitus* + *-orius* -ory] **:** expressing admonition **:** WARNING, REPROVING ⟨the low, ~ growl of a fierce old dog —P.B.Kyne⟩ ⟨keep an ~ eye on the school children —Dorothy Sayers⟩ ⟨the king and queen received ~ letters from Pope Boniface V —F.M.Stenton⟩

admor *abbr* administrator

admr *abbr* administrator

admrx *abbr* administratrix

adms *or* **admstr** *abbr* administrator

admx *abbr* administratrix

ad·nate \'ad,nāt\ *adj* [L *adnatus*, past part. of *adnasci*, alter. of *agnasci* to be born in addition to — more at AGNATE] **1** *biol* **:** grown together — used esp. of unlike parts ⟨a coral zooid ~ to the stem⟩ ⟨a calyx ~ to the ovary⟩; compare CONNATE **2** *biol* **:** grown with one side adherent to a stem ⟨an ~ anther⟩

ad·na·tion \(')ad¦nāshən\ *n* -s **:** the state of being adnate — compare ADHESION 6

ad nau·se·am \ad'nȯzēəm *also* äd- *or* aad- *or* ȧd- *or* -s| *or* -zh| *or* -sh| *or* |ā *or* a(ə)d . . . ,a(əə)m *or* äd . . . ,ȧm *or* ȧd . . . ,ȧm; äd'nausä,äm, äd . . . ,ȧm *also* -zä- *or* a(ə)d'nauzēəm\ *adv* [L] **:** to a sickening degree **:** so as to disgust

ad·nexa \ad'neksə\ *also* **an·nexa** \ə'n-,a'n-\ *n pl* [NL, fr. L *adnexa*, *annexa*, neut. pl. of *adnexus*, *annexus*, past part. of *adnectere*, *annectere* to bind to — more at ANNEX] *anat* **:** conjoined, subordinate, or associated parts **:** APPENDAGES ⟨the fallopian tubes and ovaries are ~ of the uterus⟩; *specif* **:** the embryonic membranes and other temporary structures of the embryo — **ad·nex·al** \(')ad¦neksəl\ *also* **an·nex·al** \ə'neksəl, (')a¦n-\ *adj*

ad·nexed \(')ad¦nekst\ *adj* [L *adnexus* + E *-ed*] *bot* **:** reaching to the stem, but not attached to it — used of the gills of some agarics

ad·nex·i·tis \,ad,nek'sīd·əs\ *n* -ES [NL, fr. *adnexa* + *-itis*] **:** inflammation of adnexa, esp. those of the uterus

ad·nom·i·nal \(')ad¦nämənᵊl\ *adj* [*ad-* + *nominal*] **:** modifying a noun ⟨*hot* in "hot soup" or "this soup is hot", *John's* in "John's hat", *city* in "city limits", *for action* in "the time for action", *that Jack built* in "the house that Jack built" are ~⟩ **:** ¹ADJECTIVE 1 — **adnominally** *adv*

ad non ex·e·cu·ta \(,)ad¦nä,neksə'kyüd·ə\ *adv* [L] *law* **:** for the things not executed by an executor

ado \ə'dü\ *n* -s [ME, fr. *at do*, fr. *at* to, at + *do*, *don* to do — more at AT, DO] **1 a :** fussy excitement **:** TO-DO **b :** bustling about ⟨the annoying ~ of a political campaign⟩ **c :** confusing and wearying turmoil ⟨loath to plunge into the holiday ~⟩ **2 :** time-wasting bother over trifling details ⟨he answered the letter without much ~⟩ **3 :** difficulty esp. of a sort that makes special resourcefulness and stamina necessary ⟨in spite of the unexpected competition, he won the race without ~⟩ **syn** see STIR

ado·be \ə'dōbē\ *n* -s *often attrib* [Sp, fr. Ar *aṭ-ṭūb* the brick, fr. Copt *tōbe* brick] **1 :** a brick of sun-dried earth and straw **:** building material of sun-dried earth and straw **2 :** a heavy-textured clay soil (as that of the semiarid southwestern U.S.) used in making sun-dried bricks **:** alluvial or playa clay in desert or arid regions **3 :** a house or other structure made of adobe bricks **4 :** MUDCAP

adobe brown *n* **:** a moderate yellowish brown that is slightly paler than Bismarck brown, duller and very slightly yellower than maple sugar, and slightly yellower and paler than cinnamon brown

adobe bug *n* [so called fr. its distribution in areas where adobe is common] **:** a hemipterous insect pest (*Haematosiphon inodora*) of poultry in arid southwestern U.S. and adjacent Mexico — called also *coruco, Mexican chicken bug*

adobe lily *n* [so called fr. the typical soil of its locality] **:** a Californian bulbous herb (*Fritillaria pluriflora*) having pinkish purple flowers

adobe tick *n* [so called fr. its distribution in areas where adobe is common] **:** CHICKEN TICK

ad·o·les·car·ia \,adᵊl,es'ka(a)rēə\ *n, pl* **adolescariae** \-rē,ē\ *or* **adolescarias** [NL, fr. L *adolescere* + *-aria* (fem. of *-arius* -ary)] **:** a late larval trematode or a developing trematode not yet attained to sexual maturity — compare MARITA, PARTHENITA — **ad·o·les·car·i·al** \¦⸗⸗,⸗⸗ēəl\ *adj*

ad·o·lesce \¦adᵊl¦es\ *vi* -ED/-ING/-S [back-formation fr. *adolescent* & *adolescence*] **:** to grow toward maturity **:** pass through adolescence ⟨it is a young nation, still *adolescing*⟩

ad·o·les·cence \,adᵊl'esᵊn(t)s\ *n* -s [ME, fr. MF, fr. L *adolescentia*, fr. *adolescent-*, *adolescens* (pres. part. of *adolescere* to grow up) + *-ia* — more at ADULT] **1 :** the state or process of growing up **:** the period of life from puberty to maturity terminating legally at the age of majority **2 :** the transition from youth to maturity in the cycle of stream erosion, valley development, or regional sculpture by running water **syn** see YOUTH

ad·o·les·cen·cy \-ᵊnsē\ *n* -ES [ME *adolescencie*, fr. L *adolescentia*] *archaic* **:** ADOLESCENCE

¹ad·o·les·cent \,adᵊl'esᵊnt\ *n* -s [F, fr. L *adolescent-*, *adolescens*] **:** one that is in the state of adolescence

²adolescent \¦⸗⸗¦⸗⸗\ *adj* **1 :** in the state or process of adolescence **2 :** peculiar to, suggestive of, or relating to adolescence or an adolescent ⟨~ instability⟩ **:** developing during adolescence ⟨~ goiter⟩ — **adolescent·ly** *adv*

adolescent stream *n* **:** a stream in transition from the stage of youth to that of maturity in the erosion cycle characterized by a smoothly graded course without waterfalls or rapids and with only a very narrow valley flat

ado·nai *also* **ado·nay** \,ädə'nȯi, -'nä,ē, -'nī, ,ad- *also* ,adə'nā-,ī\ *n* -s *cap* [Heb *'ădhōnāy*] **:** GOD — a Hebrew word usu. translated in the Old Testament by *Lord*; see TETRAGRAMMATON

¹adon·ic \ə'dänik\ *also* **ado·ni·an** \ə'dōnēən\ *adj, often cap* [*Adonis*, mythological personage + E *-ic* or *-ian*] **1 :** of, relating to, or like Adonis; *esp* **:** exceptionally handsome ⟨the youth's ~ features⟩ **2 :** having a rhythm consisting of a dactyl followed by a spondee or by a trochee ⟨~ verse⟩

²adonic \"\ *n* -s *often cap* **:** a verse having adonic rhythm

adon·i·din \ə'dänədən\ *n* -s [ISV *adon-* (fr. NL *Adonis*, genus name of *Adonis vernalis*) + *-id* + *-in*; orig. formed in G] **:** a mixture of glucosides obtained from an adonis (*Adonis vernalis*) and used esp. formerly as a cardiac stimulant

adon·in \ə'dänən, -dō-\ *n* -s [ISV *adon-* (fr. NL *Adonis*, genus name of *Adonis autumnalis*) + *-in*; orig. formed in G] **:** a bitter gumlike glucoside $C_{24}H_{40}O_9$ found in the root of plants of the genus Adonis

¹adon·is \ə'dänəs, -dō-\ *n* [NL, after *Adonis*, in Greco-Roman mythology a beautiful youth beloved by Aphrodite and killed by a wild boar, fr. L, fr. Gk *Adōnis*; fr. the legend that a plant sprang forth from his blood] **1** *cap* **:** a small genus of herbs (family Ranunculaceae) having alternate finely dissected leaves and solitary red or yellow flowers **2** -ES *pharm* **:** the herbage of a plant (*Adonis vernalis*) formerly used like digitalis in dropsy

²adonis \"\ *n* -ES [after *Adonis*, mythological personage] **1** *usu cap* **:** an exceptionally handsome young man **2 :** an 18th century wig

adon·i·tol \ə'dänə,tōl, -ōl\ *n* -s [ISV *adon-* (fr. NL *Adonis*, genus name of *Adonis vernalis*) + *-itol*; orig. formed in G] **:** a crystalline pentahydroxy alcohol $HOCH_2(CHOH)_3CH_2OH$ occurring in a plant (*Adonis vernalis*) and obtainable by reduction of ribose — called also *ribitol*

ad·o·nize \'adᵊn,īz\ *vb* -ED/-ING/-S [F *adoniser*, fr. *Adonis*, mythological personage + F *-iser* -ize] **:** BEAUTIFY — usu. used of a man

adoors *adv* [earlier *a doors*, fr. ³*a* and/or *a* (fr. *at*) + *doors*]

obs **:** at the door **:** of the door ⟨run in ~ quickly —R.B. Sheridan⟩
adopt \ə'däpt\ *vt* -ED/-ING/-S [MF or L; MF *adopter*, fr. L *adoptare*, fr. *ad-* + *optare* to choose, desire — more at OPINE] **1 :** to take by free choice into a close relationship previously not existing esp. by a formal legal act; *specif* **:** to take voluntarily (a child of other parents) to be in the place of or as one's own child ⟨they ~*ed* him as their sole heir⟩ ⟨a country glad to have them as ~*ed* citizens⟩ **2 a :** to take up or accept esp. as a practice or tenet often evolved by another: as (1) **:** to come to believe in **:** MAINTAIN, SUPPORT ⟨one no longer ~*s* an idea unless it is driven in with hammers of statistics and columns of figures —Henry Adams⟩ (2) **:** to accept formally **:** acknowledge or enact as true, wise, fitting, germane ⟨no proposal for curtailment of the Supreme Court power over legislation has ever been ~*ed* —Felix Frankfurter⟩ (3) **:** to use as wonted or accustomed **:** EMPLOY, PRACTICE ⟨she had ~*ed* a blend of sisterly authority and business brusqueness —William McFee⟩ ⟨a precaution which . . . he had ~*ed* whenever he carried more than two or three shillings —Thomas Hardy⟩ **b :** to take over (a loanword) into general use esp. with little or no change in form **3** *of a deliberative body* **:** to endorse and assume official responsibility for (a resolution of a committee) **4 :** to choose (a textbook) for required study in a school subject
syn EMBRACE, ESPOUSE agree in indicating an accepting, taking, or receiving as a belief to be held or practice to be followed. ADOPT may stress the fact that the belief or practice is not of one's own invention but is voluntarily taken from another's example ⟨none seem to have yet *adopted* the utterly abominable European hat — Lafcadio Hearn⟩ ⟨Turkey . . . has *adopted* a Latin alphabet⟩ ⟨gave up old customs reluctantly, but once they had *adopted* a new one they found it impossible to understand why everyone else did not immediately do likewise —Edith Wharton⟩ It may refer to an attitude or gesture taken or to a bill or measure passed or accepted formally ⟨he noticed that now, far from looking glum, she had *adopted* a winning manner —Edith Sitwell⟩ ⟨Calhoun's address was *adopted*, the Whigs voting against it —R.P.Brooks⟩ EMBRACE may suggest ready, willing, or happy acceptance or reception of a belief or practice ⟨born on Manhattan's poverty-ridden East Side, they *embraced* the Communist movement in their teens —*N.Y.Times*⟩ ⟨"I hate inversions", declared Tennyson — a statement which, I fear, will lead some of the modernists forthwith to *embrace* them —J.L.Lowes⟩ ESPOUSE may indicate either genuine depth of attachment or lasting and participating acceptance and alliance ⟨when . . . Gobineau's *Essay* was resuscitated from comparative oblivion and its dogmas passionately and popularly *espoused* —Ruth Benedict⟩ ⟨the spirit of uncompromising individualism that would eventually *espouse* the principle of democracy in church and state —V.L. Parrington⟩
adopt·a·bil·i·ty \ə,däptə'biləd·ē\ *n* -ES **:** capability of being adopted
adopt·a·ble \ə'däptəbəl\ *adj* **:** capable of being adopted
adop·tee \ə,däp'tē, ə,däp¦tē\ *n* -S **:** one that is adopted
adop·tian \ə'däpshən\ *adj, sometimes cap* [ML *adoptianus*, fr. L *adoptare* + *-ianus* -ian] **:** of, relating to, or forming the doctrine of adoptionism
adop·tion \ə'däpshən\ *n* -S [ME *adopcioun*, fr. MF or L; MF *adoption*, fr. L *adoption-, adoptio*, fr. *ad-* + *option-, optio* choosing — more at OPTION] **1 :** act of adopting or state of being adopted **2 :** the taking of an outsider into a family, clan, or tribal group usu. by investing him with the rights and responsibilities of a member by birth but occas. by giving him only a subservient status
adop·tion·ism *also* **adop·tian·ism** \-shə,nizəm\ *n* -S *often cap* [*adoption* or *adoptian* + *-ism*] **:** the doctrine that Jesus of Nazareth became son of God by exaltation to a status that was not his by birth: as **a :** any of various theories in the first three centuries A.D. holding that Jesus was adopted to sonship at the time of his baptism or resurrection **b :** an 8th century doctrine of dual sonship holding that Christ as God is son by generation and nature but as man is son by adoption and grace
adop·tion·ist *also* **adop·tian·ist** \-,nəst\ *n* -S *often cap, often attrib* **:** one that adheres to adoptionism
adop·tive \-ptiv, -ēv *also* -əv\ *adj* [ME, fr. MF & L; MF *adoptif*, fr. L *adoptivus*, fr. *adoptare* to adopt + *-ivus* -ive — more at ADOPT] **1 :** of or relating to adoption **2 :** made or acquired by adoption ⟨an ~ father⟩ ⟨an ~ country⟩ **3 :** tending or inclined to adopt ⟨a gentle ~ matron⟩ — **adop·tive·ly** \-təvlē, -li\ *adv*
adoptive arms *n* **:** ARMS OF ADOPTION
adopts *pres 3d sing of* ADOPT
ador·a·bil·i·ty \ə,dōrə'biləd·ē, -ȯr-, -ətē, -i\ *n* -ES **:** the quality of being adorable
ador·a·ble \ə'dōrəbəl, -ȯr-\ *adj* [F, fr. L *adorabilis*, fr. *adorare* to adore + *-abilis* -able — more at ADORE] **1 :** worthy of being adored **2 :** inviting adoration **:** extremely charming or lovable **:** DELIGHTFUL ⟨an ~ child⟩ ⟨an ~ home⟩ — **ador·a·ble·ness** *n* -ES — **ador·a·bly** \-blē, -li\ *adv*
[1]**ad·oral** \(ˈ)a¦dōrəl\ *adj* [*ad-* + *oral*] **:** near the mouth ⟨~ cilia⟩ — **ad·oral·ly** \-əlē\ *adv*
[2]**adoral** \"\ *n* -S **:** an adoral plate, ossicle, or other part
[1]**ador·ant** \ə'dōrənt\ *adj* [L *adorant-, adorans*, pres. part. of *adorare* to adore — more at ADORE] **:** ADORING
[2]**adorant** \"\ *n* -S **:** one that adores
ad·o·ra·tion \,adə'rāshən\ *n* -S [MF or L; MF, fr. L *adoration-, adoratio*, fr. *adoratus* (past part. of *adorare*) + *-ion-, -io* -ion] **1 :** the act or state of adoring or of being adored **2 :** the object or recipient of the act of adoring ⟨she was his life, his ~⟩ **3 a :** worship given to God alone **:** LATRIA — distinguished from *veneration* **b :** HYPERDULIA **c :** DULIA **4 a :** a method of electing a pope by the obeisance to a candidate of two thirds of the cardinals in conclave
ador·a·to·ry \ə'dōrə,tōrē\ *n* -ES [ML *adoratorium*, fr. L *adoratus* + *-orium*] **:** a place of adoration ⟨a pagan ~⟩
adore \ə'dō(ə)r, -ō(ə)r, -ōə, -ō(ə)\ *vb* -ED/-ING/-S [MF *adorer*, fr. L *adorare*, fr. *ad-* + *orare* to speak, pray — more at ORATION] *vt* **1 :** to worship with profound reverence **:** pay divine honors to **:** honor as a deity or as divine **:** offer worship to **2 :** to regard with reverent admiration and devotion prompted by veneration, esteem, or love often with an accompanying outward expression of such regard ⟨he so *adored* his mother —Elizabeth Goudge⟩ **3 :** to be extremely fond of **:** be deeply attached to often to the point of excess ⟨to dance, to ride, she had *adored* all that —Virginia Woolf⟩ ~ *vi* **:** to become filled with a spirit of profound reverence (as toward a deity) often with an accompanying outward expression of such a spirit ⟨to bend, to tremble, and ~ —P.B.Shelley⟩ **syn** see REVERE
ador·er \ə'dōrə(r), ə'dȯr-\ *n* -S **:** one that adores
adoring *adj* **:** marked by, motivated by, or manifesting adoration — **ador·ing·ly** *adv*
adorn \ə'dȯ(ə)rn, -ȯ(ə)n\ *vt* -ED/-ING/-S [ME *adornen*, fr. MF *adorner*, fr. L *adornare*, fr. *ad-* + *ornare* to furnish, embellish — more at ORNATE] **1 a :** to make pleasing or attractive **b :** to add to the pleasantness, attractiveness, splendor, or beauty of ⟨a competence . . . ~*ed* by an unexcelled brilliance of vivid expression —A.H.Johnson⟩ **c :** to point up, highlight, or set off to advantage the pleasantness, attractiveness, splendor, or beauty of ⟨the simplicity with which great composers ~ their works —Warwick Braithwaite⟩ **2 :** to decorate with or as if with external ornamentation ⟨as a bride ~*s* herself with her jewels —Isa 61:10 (RSV)⟩ **3 :** to deck out or dress up esp. with a resultant sham splendor ⟨garish gin palaces that ~ all the suburbs —S.P.B.Mais⟩
syn DECORATE, ORNAMENT, EMBELLISH, BEAUTIFY, DECK, BEDECK, GARNISH: to ADORN signifies to give a certain attractiveness or beauty to (esp. to something already quite attractive) by being associated with, physically or otherwise, or by adding something beautiful to ⟨the painters who *adorned* the Minoan palaces with lovely frescoes —V.G.Childe⟩ ⟨her feet, stockingless, and *adorned* rather than clad in blue-satin slippers —Scott Fitzgerald⟩ To DECORATE, often interchangeable with ADORN, generally implies the adding of something of color or interest to relieve plainness or monotony ⟨the music was brief, gracefully *decorated* with trills and curlicues —*Time*⟩ ⟨pathways, *decorated* with ornamental trees and shrubs —Tom Marvel⟩ To ORNAMENT implies a decorating by means of some thing extraneous, as an adjunct or accessory ⟨columns *ornament* the front entrance —*Amer. Guide Series: Maine*⟩ To EMBELLISH, stressing more the act of an agent than an effect, suggests strongly the adding of superfluous or adventitious ornamental elements ⟨Gothic cathedrals . . . *embellished*, both inside and out, with grinning gargoyles —Lytton Strachey⟩ To BEAUTIFY is to make relatively beautiful, esp. by neutralizing, masking, or transforming a certain plainness or ugliness ⟨salt cedars and oleanders have been planted to *beautify* the highway —*Amer. Guide Series: Texas*⟩ To DECK or BEDECK implies the addition of something which contributes to gaiety, interest, splendor, or sometimes gaudiness ⟨*deck* the halls with boughs of holly⟩ ⟨he was as fine as any prince, ablaze with jewels, *bedecked* with yards of snowy lace and fine embroidery — Frank Yerby⟩ ⟨*bedecked* with cheap finery⟩ To GARNISH implies a decorating with something small but bright and attractive as a final touch in preparation for use or service ⟨a steak *garnished* with parsley⟩ ⟨the old-fashioned polemical sermon . . . *garnished* with quotations in Greek —Van Wyck Brooks⟩
adorned *adj* **1** *heraldry* **:** decorated with a specified accessory charge ⟨a double tressure ~ with roses⟩ **2** *heraldry* **:** ornamented in a specified tincture ⟨an antique shield azure ~ gold⟩
adorn·ment \ə'dȯrnmənt, -dȯ(ə)n-\ *n* -S [MF *adornement*, fr. *adorner* + *-ment*] **1 :** the action of adorning or state of being adorned **2 :** something with which one is adorned ⟨her hair was a lovely ~⟩
ador·no \ə'dȯr(,)nō\ *n* -S [Sp, ornament, ornamentation, back-formation fr. *adornar* to adorn, fr. L *adornare*] **:** an appliqué ornamentation; *esp* **:** a modeled or molded ornamentation appliquéd to pottery
ados *pl of* ADO
ad·os·cu·la·tion \(,)a,däskyə'lāshən\ *n* -S [LL *adosculatus* (past part. of *adosculari* to kiss, fr. L *ad-* + *osculari* to kiss) + E *-ion* — more at OSCULATE] **:** impregnation by external contact without intromission
[1]**adown** \ə'-\ *adv* [ME *adoun, adoune*, fr. OE *adūne, of dūne*, fr. *a-* (fr. *of*) or *of* off, from + *dūne*, dat. of *dūn* hill — more at OF, DOWN] *archaic* **:** DOWN
[2]**adown** \"\ *prep* [ME *adoun, adoune*, fr. *adoun, adoune*, adv.] **:** DOWN ⟨~ the long years —G.B.Shaw⟩
adoxa \ə'däksə\ *n, cap* [NL, fr. Gk *adoxos* without glory, fr. *a-* [2]*a-* + *doxa* glory; fr. the lack of showy flowers] **:** a genus (the type of the family Adoxaceae) of perennial rhizomatous herbs having berrylike fruit
ad·ox·a·ce·ae \,a,däk'sāsē,ē\ *n pl, cap* [NL, fr. *Adoxa*, type genus + *-aceae*] **:** a family of herbs (order Rubiales) by some included in the Caprifoliaceae but distinguished by having flowers without a calyx and with the stamens inserted in pairs on the tube of the corolla
ADP \¦ā,dē¦pē\ *abbr or n* -S adenosine diphosphate
adpressed *var of* APPRESSED
ad·pro·mis·sion \,adprō'mishən\ *n* -S [*adpromissor* + *-ion*] **:** a legal contract or relation of suretyship
ad·pro·mis·sor \,adprō'misər, -,sȯr\ *n, pl* **adpromissors** \-rz\ *also* **ad·prom·is·so·res** \,ad,prämə'sōr(,)ēz\ [LL *adpromissor, appromissor* one who gives bail, bail, fr. *ad-* + *promissor* promiser — more at PROMISSOR] **:** SURETY, BAIL
ad quod damnum \,ad,kwäd'damnəm, ,äd,kwōd'däm,nüm\ [L, to what damage] **:** a writ issued in proceedings (as of condemnation) to assess damages for land seized for public use
adrad *adj* [ME *adrad, adred*, fr. past part. of *adreden, adraden* to be afraid, fr. OE *adrǣdan, ondrǣdan* (fr. [1]*a-, on* + *drǣdan* to fear, dread) & *ofdrǣdan*, fr. *of-* (akin to OE *ofer* over) + *drǣdan* — more at DREAD] *archaic* **:** put in dread **:** AFRAID
ad·ra·di·al \(ˈ)ad·¦rādēəl\ *adj* **:** of or relating to the adradius in coelenterates — **ad·ra·di·al·ly** \-əlē\ *adv*
ad·ra·di·us \(ˈ)ad·'rādēəs\ *n, pl* **adra·dii** \-ē,ī\ *or* **adradiuses** [*ad-* + *radius*] **:** a radius of the third order in coelenterates
adream \ə'-\ *adj* [[1]*a-* + *dream*, v.] **:** DREAMING ⟨old people motionless and ~⟩
adreamed *past part* [prob. fr. *a-* (perfective prefix) + *dreamed*, past part. of *dream* — more at ABEAR] *obs* **:** visited by a dream ⟨I was ~ that I sat all alone —John Bunyan⟩
ad·rec·tal \(ˈ)ad·'rektᵊl\ *adj* [*ad-* + *rectal*] **:** adjacent to the rectum — used esp. of a gland in certain mollusks that secretes a fluid which turns purple on exposure to light; see TYRIAN PURPLE
[1]**ad rem** \(ˈ)ad·'rem, (ˈ)ä-\ *adv* [L, to the affair] **:** in a way that is marked by strict attention to essential points **:** without digression ⟨she seems incapable of speaking *ad rem*⟩
[2]**ad rem** \(ˈ)=¦=\ *adj* **:** pertinent to the matter at issue or under consideration **:** relevant or vital to the point or purpose ⟨a persuasive *ad rem* argument⟩
adren- *or* **adreno-** *comb form* [[1]*adrenal*] **1 :** adrenal glands ⟨*adrenocortical*⟩ ⟨*adrenomedullary*⟩ ⟨*adrenotropic*⟩ **:** adrenal and ⟨*adrenogenital*⟩ **2 :** adrenaline ⟨*adrenergic*⟩
[1]**ad·re·nal** \ə'drēnᵊl, (ˈ)a¦d-\ *adj* [*ad-* + *renal*] **1 :** adjacent to the kidneys; *specif* **:** relating to or derived from adrenal glands **2 :** having an effect like that of the secretion of adrenal glands **:** stimulating anger or energetic action
[2]**adrenal** \"\ *n* -S **:** ADRENAL GLAND
adrenal corticotrophic hormone *n* **:** ADRENOCORTICOTROPHIC HORMONE
ad·re·nal·ec·to·mize \ə,drēnᵊl'ektə,mīz, a-\ *vt* -ED/-ING/-S **:** to excise the adrenal glands of
ad·re·nal·ec·to·my \-təmē\ *n* -ES [[2]*adrenal* + *-ectomy*] **:** surgical removal of either adrenal gland or both
adrenal gland *n* **:** either of a pair of complex endocrine glands located near the anterior medial border of the kidney and comprising a yellowish lipoid-rich cortex of mesodermal origin and a darker highly vascular medulla of ectodermal origin, the hormone adrenaline being produced by specialized chromaffin cells of the medulla while the cortex forms several hormones significant in control of salt and water balance, sodium and potassium metabolism, and utilization of glucose and certain steroids related to or identical with sex hormones — called also esp. in man *suprarenal gland*
Adren·a·lin \ə'drenᵊlən\ *trademark* — used for a preparation of levorotatory epinephrine
adren·a·line \-ən *also* -,ēn\ *n* -S [[1]*adrenal* + *-ine*] **:** EPINEPHRINE — used esp. in physiology
adren·a·lone \-,ōn\ *n* -S [ISV *adrenaline* + *-one*] **:** a crystalline ketone $(HO)_2C_6H_3COCH_2NHCH_3$ that yields racemic epinephrine on hydrogenation; 3,4-dihydroxy-α-methylamino-acetophenone
adren·er·gen \ə'drenərjən\ *n* -S [*adren-* + *-ergen* (fr. Gk *ergon* work) — more at WORK] **:** a drug having a physiologic action resembling that of adrenaline
ad·re·ner·gic \,adrə¦nərjik\ *adj* [*adren-* + Gk *ergon* work + E *-ic*] **1** *of autonomic nerve fibers* **a :** liberating adrenaline or a substance like adrenaline **b :** activated by adrenaline — compare CHOLINERGIC **2** *of drugs and their action* **:** like or like that of adrenaline
adre·nin \ə'drēnən, -ren-\ *or* **adre·nine** \", ə'dre,nēn\ *n* -S [*adren-* + *-in, -ine*] **:** EPINEPHRINE
adreno·chrome \ə'drēnə,krōm, -ēn-\ *n* -S [*adren-* + *-chrome*] **:** a red-colored mixture of quinones derived from epinephrine by oxidation and yielding a melaninlike product on further oxidation
adre·no·cor·ti·cal \ə¦drēnō¦kȯrd·əkəl, -en-\ *also* **ad·re·nal·cor·ti·cal** \ə¦drēnᵊl¦-, (ˈ)a¦d-\ *adj* [*adren-* or [1]*adrenal* + *cortical*] **:** of, belonging to, or derived from the cortex of the adrenal glands ⟨~ hormones⟩
adre·no·cor·ti·co·troph·ic \ə'drē(,)nō¦kȯrd·əkō¦träfik, -e(,)n-, -ōf-\ *or* **adre·no·cor·ti·co·trop·ic** \-¦räpik\ *adj* [*adren-* + *cortico-* + *-trophic* or *-tropic*] **:** acting on or stimulating the adrenal cortex
adrenocorticotrophic hormone *n* **:** a protein produced by the anterior lobe of the pituitary gland that has a stimulatory effect on the adrenal cortex and a diabetogenic action — compare CORTICOTROPHIN
adre·no·gen·i·tal syndrome \ə¦drēnō¦jenəd·ᵊl-, -dren-\ *n* [*adren-* + *genital*] **:** CUSHING'S DISEASE
adre·no·lyt·ic \ə¦drēnᵊl¦id·ik, -en-\ *adj* [*adren-* + *-lytic*] **:** adrenaline-destroying — used of substances that check the release or action of adrenaline at nerve endings
adre·no·ste·rone \ə¦drēnō'stə,rōn, -dren-; ,adrə'nästə,rōn\ *n* -S [ISV *adren-* + *-sterone* (fr. *steroid* + *-one*); orig. formed as G *adrenosteron*] **:** a crystalline steroid $C_{19}N_{24}O_3$ obtained from the adrenal cortex and having androgenic activity
adre·no·sym·pa·thet·ic \ə¦drēnō,simpə¦thed·ik, -en-\ *adj* **1 :** of or relating to the adrenergic portion of the autonomic nervous system **2 :** of or involving interaction of the sympathetic nervous system and the adrenal gland
adre·no·troph·ic \ə¦drēnō¦träfik, -en-, -ōfik\ *or* **adre·no·trop·ic** \-äpik\ *adj* [*adren-* + *-trophic* or *-tropic*] **:** ADRENOCORTICOTROPHIC
ad·re·nox·ine \,adrə'näk,sēn\ *n* -S [*adren-* + *ox-* + *-ine*] **:** a cardiac inhibitor formed by enzymatic oxidation of either dextrorotatory or levorotatory epinephrine or of tyramine
adret \a'drā\ *n* -S [F, fr. F dial., lit., good side, obverse, fr. *a-* (fr. L *ad-*) + *dret* straight, direct, fr. L *directus* — more at DRESS] **:** a mountain slope so oriented as to receive considerable light and warmth from the sun during the day — used chiefly of the Alps
adri·a·no·ple red \¦ādrēə¦nōpəl- *also* ¦a-\ *n, often cap A* [fr. *Adrianople* (now *Edirne*), Turkey] **:** TURKEY RED
adri·at·ic \¦ādrē¦ad·ik, -atik, -ēk *also* ¦adr-\ *adj, usu cap* [L *Adriaticus, Hadriaticus*, fr. *Adria, Hadria*, ancient Etruscan settlement & seaport in northeast Italy] **:** of or relating to the sea that lies east of Italy
adriatic fig *n, usu cap A* **:** a cultivated fig that does not mature the first crop without caprification
adriatic oak *n, usu cap A* **:** TURKEY OAK
adrift \ə'-\ *adv (or adj)* [[1]*a-* + *drift*, v.] **1 :** without motive power and without anchor or mooring **:** DRIFTING ⟨~ for three days on the open ocean⟩ ⟨cut the boat ~⟩ **2 :** without guidance or means of orientation ⟨give to a people morally ~ a code and a belief —Elspeth Huxley⟩ **:** without ties, relations, or security or without a fixed place in society ⟨young men were ~ in a lawless society —Willa Cather⟩ **3 :** in or into a state of being free from restraint or freed from fastenings or supports **:** LOOSE ⟨poorly secured barrels came ~ in the storm⟩
adrip \ə'-\ *adj* [[1]*a-* + *drip*, v.] **:** DRIPPING ⟨he was ~ with perspiration⟩
ad·ro·gate \'adrō,gāt\ *vt* -ED/-ING/-S [L *adrogatus*, var. of *arrogatus*, past part. of *arrogare* to appropriate — more at ARROGATE] **:** ARROGATE 3
ad·ro·ga·tion \,adrō'gāshən\ *n* -S **:** ARROGATION 2
adroit \ə'drȯit\ *adj, sometimes* -ER/-EST [F, fr. *à droit* properly, fr. *à* to, at (fr. L *ad*) + *droit* right, fr. L *directus*, straight, direct — more at AT, DRESS] **1 :** dexterous in the use of the hands **2 :** marked by shrewdness, craft, resourcefulness, readiness at devising, or physical skill and address so that one is enabled to cope with difficulty or danger ⟨one of the most ~ technicians ever to have employed the English language —John Mason Brown⟩ ⟨~ leadership⟩ ⟨an ~ tennis player⟩ ⟨his ~ replies to hecklers soon won him a large following⟩ **syn** see CLEVER, DEXTEROUS
adroitly *adv* **:** in an adroit manner
adroitness *n* -ES **:** the quality or state of being adroit **:** skill and readiness **:** DEXTERITY
adroop \ə'-\ *adj* [[1]*a-* + *droop*, v.] **:** DROOPING
adrop *n* -S [ME] **1** *obs* **:** a substance (as lead) believed essential to evolving the philosophers' stone **2** *obs* **:** PHILOSOPHERS' STONE 1
ad·ros·tral \(ˈ)ad·'rästrəl\ *adj* [ISV *ad-* + *rostral*; orig. formed as F *adrostrale*] *zool* **:** near the rostrum
adry \ə'drī\ *adj* [[1]*a-* + *dry*, adj.] **1** *archaic* **:** THIRSTY **2** *archaic* **:** DRY
ads *pl of* AD
-ads *pl of* -AD
ads *abbr* [L *ad sectam*] at the suit of
ADS *abbr* autograph document signed
ad·sci·ti·tious \¦ad·sə¦tishəs\ *also* **as·ci·ti·tious** \¦asə-\ *adj* [L *adscitus, ascitus* derived, assumed, foreign (fr. past part. of *adsciscere, asciscere* to approve, receive, admit, appropriate, fr. *ad-* + *sciscere* to accept, approve, incho. of *scire* to know) + E *-itious* — more at SCIENCE] **1 :** originating, derived, or acquired from something extrinsic **:** ADVENTITIOUS ⟨an ~ habit rather than an inherent taste⟩ **2 :** SUPPLEMENTAL, ADDITIONAL ⟨~ remarks⟩ — **ad·sci·ti·tious·ly** *adv*
[1]**ad·script** \'adz,kript, -d,sk-\ *adj* [L *adscriptus, ascriptus*, past part. of *adscribere, ascribere* to ascribe, add to — more at ASCRIBE] **1** [influenced in meaning by ML *adscriptitius, adscripticius*] **:** irremovably attached — used of serfs bound to the soil, the right to their services passing with transfer of the land ⟨men ~ to their overlord's lands⟩ **2 :** written after ⟨iota ~⟩ **:** printed or written immediately to the right of another letter or character and aligning with it ⟨in the pronunciation transcription \lu:t\ *u* bears an ~ diacritic⟩ — distinguished from *subscript* and *superscript*
[2]**adscript** \"\ *n* -S **:** an adscript serf
ad·script·ed \(ˈ)=¦=əd\ *adj* **:** ADSCRIPT 1
ad·scrip·tion \(ˈ)=¦=pshən\ *n* -S [L *adscription-, adscriptio, ascription-, ascriptio* written addition (influenced in meaning by ML *adscriptitius*) — more at ASCRIPTION] **:** the quality or state of being added, annexed, or bound ⟨~ of serfs⟩ ⟨~ of an estate⟩
ad·scrip·ti·tious \¦=,=p¦tishəs\ *adj* [ML *adscriptitius, adscripticius* (in *adscriptitius glebae* attached to the soil), fr. LL *adscripticius* enrolled, fr. L *adscriptus, ascriptus*] **:** ADSCRIPT 1
ad·scrip·tive \(ˈ)=¦=ptiv\ *adj* [[2]*adscript* + *-ive*] **:** ADSCRIPT 1
ad·ses·sor \(ˈ)ad¦sesə(r)\ *n* -S [by alter.] **:** ASSESSOR
ad·smith \'=,=\ *n* -S [[1]*ad* + *smith*] **:** an advertising-copy writer
ad·sorb \ad'sȯrb, -'z-\ *vt* -ED/-ING/-S [*ad-* + *-sorb* (as in *absorb*)] **:** to take up and hold by adsorption — distinguished from *absorb*
ad·sorb·a·bil·i·ty \(,)=,=ə'biləd·ē\ *n* -ES **:** the ability to be adsorbed
ad·sorb·a·ble \=¦=bəbəl\ *adj* **:** capable of being adsorbed
ad·sorb·ate \-bət, -,bāt\ *n* -S [ISV *adsorb* + *-ate*] **:** an adsorbed substance
[1]**ad·sorb·ent** \=¦=bənt\ *adj* [*adsorb* + *-ent*] **:** having power, capacity, or tendency to adsorb
[2]**adsorbent** \"\ *n* -S **:** a solid or liquid substance that takes up and holds another substance by adsorption
ad·sorp·tion \ad'sȯrpshən, -'z-\ *n* -S [fr. *adsorb*, after E *absorb: absorption*] **:** a taking up by physical or chemical forces of the molecules of gases, of dissolved substances, or of liquids by the surfaces of solids or liquids with which they are in contact — distinguished from *absorption*; compare CHEMISORPTION, SORPTION
adsorption compound *n* **:** a more or less stable combination of varying chemical composition formed between an adsorbing surface and the adsorbed substance — compare [3]COMPOUND 2a
adsorption isotherm *n* **:** a curve obtained by plotting at constant temperature the quantity of adsorbate against the concentration of the substance in the original gas or solution
ad·sorp·tive \(ˈ)=¦=tiv\ *adj* **:** relating to adsorption **:** ADSORBENT — **ad·sorp·tive·ly** \-tәvlē\ *adv*
ad·stip·u·late \ad'stipyə,lāt\ *vi* -ED/-ING/-S [L *adstipulatus*, past part. of *adstipulari*, fr. *ad-* + *stipulari* to stipulate — more at STIPULATE] **:** to act as an adstipulator — **ad·stip·u·la·tion** \(,)=,==¦lāshən\ *n* -S
ad·stip·u·la·tor \=¦==,lād·ə(r)\ *n* -S [L, fr. *adstipulatus* + *-or*] **:** an additional party made accessory to a promise or contract in order to provide an agent or attorney or to enable a man to make an agreement that would take effect after his death
adsuki bean *var of* ADZUKI BEAN
ad·sum \'ad,səm, 'äd,sům\ *interj* [L, I am present, 1st pers. sing. pres. ind. of *adesse* to be present — more at ADESSENARIAN] — used to indicate one's presence esp. in answer to a roll call
a due \ä'dü,ä\ *adv* [It, lit., by two] **1 :** TOGETHER — used as a direction in music to two performers to play or sing the same part in unison **2 :** SEPARATELY — used as a direction in music to a group of performers to divide into two parts; compare DIVISI
ad·u·la·res·cence \,ajələ'resᵊn(t)s, -,lä'-\ *n* -S [*adularia* + *-escence* (as in *luminescence*)] **:** the changeable white to pale bluish luster of an adularia cut cabochon
ad·u·lar·ia \,ajə'la(a)rēə\ *also* **ad·u·lar** \'ajə,lär\ *n* -S [*adularia* fr. It, modif. of F *adulaire*, fr. *Adula*, mountain group in Switzerland + F *-aire* -ary; *adular*, modif. of It *adularia*] **:** a transparent or translucent variety of orthoclase of pseudo-orthorhombic crystal habit some specimens of which have pearly internal reflections — see MOONSTONE

ad·u·late \ˈajə,lāt *also* ˈadyə,l- *or* ˈad^{ə}l,-\ *vt* -ED/-ING/-S [back-formation fr. *adulation,* fr. ME *adulacioun,* fr. MF *adulation,* fr. L *adulation-, adulatio,* fr. *adulatus* (past part. of *adulari* to flatter, to wag a tail, perh. fr. *ad-* + a root akin to Skt *vāla, vāra* tail, Lith *valaĩ* horse's tail) + *-ion-, -io* -ion] **1 a :** to praise effusively and slavishly **:** flatter excessively **:** fawn upon ⟨sheepish fools that ~ every decision of their leaders⟩ **b :** to pay homage to without exercising a critical sense of values ⟨a man who respects science without *adulating* it⟩ **2 :** to admire or be devoted to abjectly and excessively ⟨teen-agers *adulating* the newest movie star⟩

ad·u·la·tion \,==ˈāshən\ *n* -s **:** the act of adulating ⟨feasted his self-esteem on their ~ —Aldous Huxley⟩

ad·u·la·tor \ˈ==,ād·ə(r), -atə-\ *n* -s [L, fr. *adulatus* + *-or*] **:** one that adulates

ad·u·la·to·ry \-,ə,tōrē, -ȯrē, -ri\ *adj* [L *adulatorius,* fr. *adulatus* + *-orius* -ory] **:** characterized by or given to adulation ⟨an ~ speech⟩

adul·lam·ite \əˈdələ,mīt\ *n* -s *usu cap* [(*Cave of*) *Adullam* + E *-ite* — more at CAVE OF ADULLAM] **:** one of a small group of seceders from a particular political or intellectual position; *esp* **:** one who withdraws to join with others in forming a new group

¹adult \əˈdəlt, ˈa,dəlt *also* aˈd- *or* ˈad^{ə}lt\ *adj* [L *adultus,* past part. of *adolescere* to grow up, fr. *ad-* + *-olescere* (fr. *alescere* to grow, incho. of *alere* to nourish) — more at OLD] **1 :** fully developed (as in size, strength, or intellectual capacity) **:** fully mature **:** GROWN-UP ⟨an ~ man⟩ ⟨an ~ lion⟩ ⟨an ~ plant⟩ **2 :** of or belonging to adults ⟨the standards of the ~ world —*Saturday Rev.*⟩ **3 :** evidencing the maturity (as the intellectual maturity) usu. associated with an adult ⟨his ~ approach to the problem⟩ **4 a :** on a par with the maturity usu. associated with an adult ⟨a thoroughly ~ comedy of manners⟩ **b :** designed for or restricted to adults ⟨~ murder mysteries that children wouldn't like⟩ — **adult·ness** *n* -ES

²adult \"\ *n* -s **1 :** one that has arrived at full development esp. in size, strength, or intellectual capacity **:** one that has reached full maturity **2 a** *civil law* **:** a human male after the age of 14 or a human female after the age of 12 **b** *common law* **:** a human male or female after a specific age (as 21)

adult education *n* **:** lecture or correspondence courses for adults usu. not otherwise engaged in formal study

¹adul·ter·ant \əˈdəltərənt, -l·trənt\ *n* -s [L *adulterant-, adulterans,* pres. part. of *adulterare*] **:** an adulterating substance or agent

²adulterant \"\ *adj* **:** ADULTERATING

¹adul·ter·ate \əˈdəltə,rāt, *usu* -ād·+V\ *vb* -ED/-ING/-S [L *adulteratus,* past part. of *adulterare* to pollute, defile, commit adultery, fr. *ad-* + *-ulterare* (fr. *alter* different, other) — more at ELSE] *vt* **1 a :** to corrupt, debase, or make impure by the addition of a foreign or a baser substance **:** prepare (as for sale) with one or more ingredients included that are not part of the alleged substance ⟨*adulterated* food⟩ **b :** to alter or treat (as an article) esp. deceptively in order to give a false value or to hide defects through some method or process not involving the addition of a spurious substance: (1) **:** to remove a valuable or necessary ingredient from ⟨*adulterating* milk by removing the cream⟩ (2) **:** to sell (a commodity) under the name of another commodity (3) **:** to offer as acceptable (what is in reality diseased, infected, or tainted) (4) **:** to conceal artificially the defects of (5) **:** to cause to simulate a better article **2 :** to lessen the full intensity of (as a state of happiness) through the addition of extraneous, incongruous, or discordant elements or through the removal of a vital element **:** lessen the purity of **:** make spurious ~ *vi, obs* **:** to commit adultery

²adul·ter·ate \-ltərət, -l·trət, -ltə,rāt\ *adj* [L *adulteratus*] **1 :** tainted with adultery **:** ADULTEROUS ⟨a perverse and ~ generation —H.M.Jones⟩ **2 :** ADULTERATED, SPURIOUS

adul·ter·a·tion \ə,dəltəˈrāshən\ *n* -s [L *adulteration-, adulteratio,* fr. *adulteratus* + *-ion-, -io* -ion] **1 :** the process of adulterating **:** the condition of being adulterated; *esp* **:** the partial substitution of one substance for another without acknowledgment **2 :** an adulterated product

adul·ter·a·tor \əˈdəltə,rād·ə(r), -ātə-\ *n* -s [*adulterate* + *-or*] **1 :** one that adulterates **2** [LL, fr. L *adulteratus* + *-or*] *law* **:** COUNTERFEITER

adul·ter·er \əˈdəltərə(r)\ *n* -s [alter. (influenced by *adultery* & L *adulter*) of ME *advouterer, avouterer,* alter. (influenced by L *adulter* & E words ending in *-er*) of MF *avoutre,* fr. L *adulter* — more at ADULTERY] **:** one that commits adultery; *esp* **:** a man who commits adultery

adul·ter·ess \-ltərəs, -l·trəs\ *n* -ES [alter. of earlier *advoutresse,* alter. of ME *avoutresse,* fr. MF, fr. *avoutre* + *-esse* -ess] **:** a woman who commits adultery

adul·ter·ine \-ltə,rīn, -,rēn, -,rən\ *adj* [L *adulterinus,* fr. *adulterare* + *-inus* -ine] **1 :** relating to or marked by adulteration **:** SPURIOUS ⟨~ drugs⟩ **2 :** without the support of law **:** ILLEGAL ⟨an ~ guild⟩ **3 :** born of adultery ⟨an ~ child⟩

adul·ter·ize \-ltə,rīz\ *vi* -ED/-ING/-S [obs. *adulter* adulterer (fr. L) + *-ize*] *archaic* **:** to commit adultery

adul·ter·ous \-ltərəs, -l·trəs\ *adj* [alter. of ME *advoutrous,* fr. *advoutrie* + *-ous*] **1 :** of, characterized by, or given to adultery ⟨she lived in what was legally an ~ relation —M.R.Cohen⟩ **2** *archaic* **:** ADULTERATED ⟨an ~ mixture, brewed up of nauseous ingredients —Tobias Smollett⟩ — **adul·ter·ous·ly** *adv*

adul·tery \əˈdəltərē, -l·trē, -ri\ *n* -ES [ME *adulterie,* alter. (influenced by L *adulterium*) of *advoutrie, avoutrie,* fr. MF *avoutrie,* alter. of OF *avoutire,* fr. L *adulterium,* fr. *adulter* adulterer, back-formation fr. *adulterare* to pollute, defile, commit adultery — more at ADULTERATE] **1 :** voluntary sexual intercourse between a married man and someone other than his wife or between a married woman and someone other than her husband ⟨if a man commits ~ with the wife of his neighbor, both the adulterer and the adulteress shall be put to death —Lev 20:10 (RSV)⟩ — compare FORNICATION **2 a :** unchastity of thought or act ⟨every one who looks at a woman lustfully has already committed ~ with her in his heart —Mt 5:28 (RSV)⟩ **b :** religious infidelity; *esp* **:** IDOLATRY ⟨she polluted the land, committing ~ with stone and tree —Jer 3:9 (RSV)⟩

adult·hood \əˈdəl,tu̇d, -lt,hu̇d\ *n* -s **:** the state or time of being an adult

adult·i·ci·dal \ə¦dəltəˈsīd^{ə}l\ *adj* **:** of, relating to, or being an adulticide

adult·i·cide \əˈdəltə,sīd\ *n* -s [*adult* + *-i-* + *-cide*] **:** an insecticide used to kill adult insects — compare LARVICIDE

adult·ly \əˈdəltlē, ˈa,d-, aˈd-, -li\ *adv* **:** in a manner typical of an adult ⟨you're too ~ serious —Aldous Huxley⟩ ⟨~ uncompromising⟩

adult·ness \-tnəs\ *n* -ES **:** the quality or state of being adult; *esp* **:** intellectual maturity usu. associated with an adult ⟨an ~ in the quality of his dialogue —R.A.Cordell⟩

adult·oid \əˈdəl,tȯid\ *n* -s *biol* **:** an immature individual that resembles an adult

ad·um·brate \ˈadəm,brāt, aˈd-, əˈd-\ *vt* -ED/-ING/-S [L *adumbratus,* past part. of *adumbrare,* fr. *ad-* + *umbra* shadow — more at UMBRAGE] **1 a :** to foreshadow, symbolize, or prefigure esp. in a not altogether conclusive or not immediately evident way ⟨social unrest *adumbrated* the French Revolution⟩ **b :** to suggest, indicate, or point out in advance ⟨an invention that *adumbrated* automation⟩ **c :** FORESEE, PREDICT **2 a :** to give a sketchy representation of **:** outline broadly, omitting details ⟨there was only time to ~ the plan⟩ **b :** to suggest, indicate, or disclose partially and with a purposeful avoidance of precision ⟨the meaning of the poem is *adumbrated* in its title⟩ **3 a :** SHADE **b :** to cast a shadow over **:** DARKEN **:** throw a gloomy pall upon ⟨bubbling optimism, not at all *adumbrated* by difficulties⟩ **2 :** to conceal partially **:** OBSCURE

ad·um·bra·tion \,a(,)dəmˈbrāshən\ *n* -s [L *adumbration-, adumbratio,* fr. *adumbratus* + *-ion-, -io* -ion] **1 :** the action of adumbrating or state of being adumbrated **2 a :** a faint sketch **:** an imperfect portrayal or representation **:** OUTLINE **b** *heraldry* **:** the shadow or outlines of a figure **3 :** a vague foreshadowing **4 :** OVERSHADOWING, SHADE

adum·bra·tive \aˈdəmbrəd·iv, əˈd-, ˈadəm,brād-\ *adj* **:** ADUMBRATING — **adum·bra·tive·ly** *adv*

Ad·u·rol \ˈadə,rōl, ˈajə-, -ōl\ *trademark* — used for either of two white crystalline photographic developing agents

¹adust \əˈdəst, (ˈ)a¦d-\ *adj* [ME, fr. L *adustus,* past part. of *adurere* to set fire to, inflame, fr. *ad-* + *urere* to burn — more at EMBER] **1 :** dried up with heat **:** BURNED, SCORCHED, PARCHED ⟨a vast desert all ~⟩ **2** *archaic* **:** of a burned or esp. sunburned appearance ⟨a tall, thin man, of an ~ complexion —Sir Walter Scott⟩ **3 :** of a gloomy appearance or disposition ⟨a wizened ~ old servant⟩

²adust \"\ *n* -s **:** LEATHER 4

adus·ti·o·sis \ə,dəstēˈōsəs, (,)a,d-, -dəschē-\ *n, pl* **adustioses** \-ō,sēz\ [NL, fr. L *adustus* + *-i-* + *-osis*] **:** a physiological breakdown of the rind of citrus fruit (as lemons) causing a reddish discoloration — called also *red blotch*

adv *abbr* **1** ad valorem **2** advance **3** *usu cap* advent **4** adverb; adverbial **5** advertisement; advertising **6** advice **7** advise; advisory **8** *often cap* advocate

advai·ta \ədˈvīd·ə\ *n, usu cap* [Skt, fr. *a-* ²a- + *dvaita* duality, fr. *dvi* two — more at TWO] **:** Vedantic nondualism that denies the separateness of any aspect of reality from the impersonal oneness of Brahma

ad va·lo·rem \¦advə¦lōrəm, -ȯr-, -,rem\ *adj* [L, according to the value] **1** *of a tax on goods* **:** imposed at a rate percent of the value as stated in an invoice rather than as a specific sum for a given quantity or number **2** *of a property tax* **:** levied according to assessed value — abbr. *ad val.*

¹ad·vance \ədˈvan(t)s, -aa(ə)n-, -ain-, -ān- *also* ad-\ *vb* -ED/-ING/-S [ME *advauncen,* alter. (influenced by L *ad-*) of *avauncen,* fr. OF *avancier,* fr. (assumed) VL *abantiare,* fr. L *abante* before, from before, fr. *ab-* + *ante* before — more at ANTE-] *vt* **1 :** to move forward along a course or toward a terminus or goal **:** make to proceed or to progress ⟨preparing to ~ his pawn⟩ **:** FORWARD ⟨finding ways to ~ the job more rapidly⟩**: a :** to accelerate the progress or hasten the development of ⟨~ the ripening of fruit⟩ **b :** to help on or aid the success or improvement of **:** FURTHER ⟨volunteers soliciting funds to ~ the work of the society⟩ ⟨used propaganda to ~ their cause⟩ ⟨*advancing* his own interests at the expense of his friend's⟩ **2 :** to raise in rank or position **:** PROMOTE ⟨the rank of lieutenant, to which he was *advanced* in 1940⟩ ⟨was *advanced* to the priesthood⟩ ⟨*advanced* him over the heads of his seniors⟩ **:** raise in importance ⟨in *advancing* the husband in the office, the corporation is quite likely to ~ him socially —W.H.Whyte⟩ **3** *obs* **:** EXTOL, MAGNIFY, LAUD ⟨greatly *advancing* his gay chivalry —Edmund Spenser⟩ **4 :** to supply or provide ahead of time: **a** *law* **:** to furnish by way of an advancement **b :** to supply (as money or other value) beforehand in expectation of repayment or other future adjustment ⟨~ an employee a week's pay as a loan⟩ ⟨to farmers willing to raise soybeans, seed is *advanced* by the company —*Amer. Guide Series: Mich.*⟩ **5** *archaic* **:** to lift up **:** RAISE, ELEVATE ⟨*advanced* their eyelids —Shak.⟩ **6 :** to bring forward in time: **a :** to make earlier (as an event or date) **:** HASTEN ⟨first scheduled for Nov. 1, then *advanced* to Oct. 15⟩ **b :** to bring or set forward to a later time **:** make or place later ⟨modern scholarship has *advanced* the date of composition from the first to the second century A.D.⟩ **c :** to readjust (the timing of an ignition spark) so that ignition occurs earlier with reference to top dead center in the piston stroke **7 a :** to set, push, or thrust forward, ahead, or to or toward the front **:** cause to go on ⟨cautiously *advancing* one foot⟩ ⟨*advanced* the tunnel 10 feet a day⟩ ⟨~ the hands of a clock⟩ **b** *phonetics* (1) **:** to move (the tongue) further forward (2) **:** FRONT **8 :** to bring forward for notice, consideration, or acceptance **:** bring to view **:** OFFER, PROPOSE ⟨~ an opinion⟩ ⟨explanations were *advanced* and rejected⟩ ⟨those *advancing* a claim to the vacant throne⟩ **9 :** to raise in rate **:** INCREASE ⟨measures to keep landlords from *advancing* rents unfairly⟩ ⟨*advancing* the price of gasoline twice in one week⟩ ~ *vi* **1 :** to move forward **:** go or come forward **:** PROCEED ⟨opened the door and *advanced* into the room⟩ ⟨saw in the distance another lantern *advancing* toward them —Anne D. Sedgwick⟩ ⟨the infantry *advanced* to the attack⟩ ⟨the physicist, accustomed to . . . *advancing* from certainty —*Amer. Scholar*⟩ **2 :** to increase or make progress ⟨a question on which knowledge is *advancing*⟩ ⟨as he *advanced* in age and stature he *advanced* in knowledge⟩ ⟨their children are *advancing* toward maturity⟩ ⟨sagebrush and juniper are *advancing* at the expense of grass —G.R.Stewart⟩ **3 :** to rise in rank, position, or importance ⟨at 30 he had already *advanced* to colonel⟩ ⟨the family has *advanced* to a position of influence in the community⟩ ⟨the self-made man . . . who *advanced* through his own unaided efforts —R.B.Morris⟩ ⟨have a fair chance to ~⟩ **4 :** to rise in rate or price ⟨as wages *advanced,* so did the cost of living⟩ ⟨government securities *advanced* steadily⟩ **5** *of a color* **:** to seem to come forward toward the viewer **:** stand out to the eye ⟨deep colors ~⟩ — contrasted with *recede*

syn FORWARD, FURTHER, PROMOTE: these four verbs signify in common to help to move ahead. ADVANCE, FORWARD, and FURTHER are virtually interchangeable. If a distinction exists it is perhaps that ADVANCE more than the others lays stress on the movement forward or the effectiveness of the assistance to that end ⟨these policies had been considerably *advanced* during the preceding year —*Americana Annual*⟩ ⟨ever alert to *advance* the cause of the freedom —W.H.Allison⟩ FORWARD is seldom applied to persons and perhaps stresses a little more than ADVANCE the activity or moral force intended to achieve the movement forward ⟨the high school as a means of *forwarding* the education of all youth —T.H.Briggs⟩ ⟨his military operations were successful, *forwarding* the Union cause —T.M. Spaulding⟩ FURTHER may be said, in comparison to ADVANCE and FORWARD, to put the least stress upon the movement forward and a great deal on the activity or force ⟨*furthering* no special school of art, the institute seeks to make the museum a compendium of the evolution and history of art as a whole —*Amer. Guide Series: Minn.*⟩ ⟨to *further* his selfish ends, he kept Monica from marrying the young man of her choice —Ann F. Wolfe⟩ PROMOTE, in the sense pertinent here, usu. implies nothing about a movement forward; it stresses solely the activity of assisting, encouraging, or fostering advancement, esp. openly ⟨she decided to *promote* a crusade to the Holy Land in a specially chartered liner —Carey McWilliams⟩ ⟨a sound forest economy *promotes* the prosperity of agriculture and rural life —A.F.Gustafson⟩ **syn** see in addition CITE

²advance \"\ *n* -s **1 :** a moving forward ⟨the ~ of the infantry⟩ ⟨the ~ of the polar caps⟩ ⟨the frontier ~ followed a well-defined pattern —R.A.Billington⟩ **2 a :** forward movement on a course of action or development **:** PROGRESS, IMPROVEMENT ⟨mistaking material ~ for spiritual enrichment —H.J. Laski⟩ ⟨the ~ of farm techniques⟩ ⟨recent ~s in social legislation⟩ **b :** a manifestation of progress or improvement **:** a step forward or beyond ⟨far from being an ~ on its predecessor, his new play is a regression⟩ ⟨a method which was a definite ~ over earlier practices⟩ **3 :** a rise or increase (as in price, value, or amount) **:** addition to the price ⟨during the year many workers won wage ~s⟩ ⟨a year-long ~ in stock prices⟩ **4 :** a first step toward the attainment of a result **:** an approach made (as to gain favor, form an acquaintance, adjust a difference) **:** OVERTURE, TENDER, OFFER ⟨an attitude that discouraged all ~s⟩ ⟨she would certainly misunderstand the most guarded words, the most careful ~s —Joseph Conrad⟩ **5 :** a furnishing of something (as money or goods) before a return is received **:** payment beforehand **:** the money or goods thus furnished **:** money or value supplied beforehand ⟨offered him an ~ to complete the book⟩ ⟨may also make cash ~ to the packers before shipment is made —E.A.Duddy⟩ **6 a :** the translational movement of a body in helical motion (as the forward motion of a screw) **b :** the interval by which an event in a cycle precedes a reference datum **7 :** a story written for a news medium before the actual event ⟨a Halloween ~ written early in October⟩ **8 :** the distance made parallel to the original course of a turning ship from the time of putting the rudder over until the ship is on the new course — **in advance** *adv* **:** BEFORE, AHEAD, BEFOREHAND ⟨the heavy luggage had been sent on *in advance*⟩ ⟨registered for the examination well *in advance*⟩ **:** before receiving an equivalent ⟨to pay *in advance*⟩ — **in advance of** *prep* **:** ahead of **:** BEFORE, BEYOND ⟨a thinker well *in advance of* his time⟩ ⟨designed to persuade customers *in advance of* their visit to the store —A.S.Igleheart⟩

³ad·vance \ədˈv-, (ˈ)ad¦v-\ *adj* [*²advance*] **1 :** given, made, sent, issued, furnished, or received ahead of time or of need ⟨~ payment⟩ ⟨an ~ copy of a book⟩ ⟨~ information⟩ **2 :** going before ⟨sent out an ~ party of soldiers **3 :** forward of major bases of supply ⟨an ~ depot⟩ ⟨~ base⟩

ad·vance·able \-səbəl\ *adj* **:** capable of being advanced

advance agent *also* **advance man** *n* **:** a business representative (as of a theatrical company or a lecturer) who travels ahead in order to make necessary arrangements for the public appearance of his employer

ad·vanced \ədˈv- *also* (ˈ)ad¦v-\ *adj* [ME *avaunced,* fr. past part. of *avauncen*] **1 :** far on in time or course ⟨a man ~ in years⟩ ⟨an ~ state of exhaustion⟩ ⟨the night was well ~⟩ **2 :** moved or set forward or in the front **:** ADVANCE ⟨~ air bases⟩ ⟨captured by an ~ unit of the infantry⟩ ⟨established a new ~ post⟩ **3 a :** beyond the elementary or introductory **:** carrying on from that which precedes ⟨an ~ course⟩ ⟨~ chemistry⟩ **b :** in front of or beyond others as regards progress or ideas ⟨the most ~ artists and critics⟩ ⟨believed himself to be very ~ in his views⟩ **c :** greatly developed beyond the initial stage ⟨a technologically ~ world⟩ ⟨turbines of an ~ construction⟩ **4 :** having altered from a presumed ancestral state ⟨he regards the jaw as more ~ than those of the Rhodesian group —R.W.Murray⟩ **syn** see LIBERAL

advanced charge *n* **:** a transportation service charge passed on by one carrier to another to be collected from the consignee

advanced credit *n* **:** academic credit allowed by an educational institution to students entering with higher than first-year standing for courses taken elsewhere usu. at a comparable institution

advanced degree *n* **:** a university degree higher than a bachelor's (as a master's or doctor's degree)

advanced fry *n* **:** young fishes having the yolk sac absorbed but not yet being developed into fingerlings

ad·vanc·ed·ly \=ˈ=sədlē\ *adv* **:** in an advanced manner or to an advanced degree

advanced score *n* **:** a partial score in the game of bridge

advanced standing *n* **1 :** the standing of a student who has been granted advanced credit **2 :** ADVANCED CREDIT

advance guard *n* **1 :** a detachment usu. divided into point, advance party, support, and reserve preceding a body of troops on the march to protect it and secure its uninterrupted advance **2 :** AVANT-GARDE — **advance guardist** *n*

ad·vance·ment \=ˈ=smənt\ *n* -s [alter. (influenced by L *ad-*) of ME *avauncement,* fr. OF *avancement,* fr. *avancier* to advance + *-ment* — more at ADVANCE] **1 :** the action of advancing or the state of being advanced: **a :** promotion or elevation to a higher rank or to a position of greater personal dignity or importance ⟨they came, not for personal ~ . . . but literally to establish a New France —B.K.Sandwell⟩ ⟨positions offering excellent opportunities for professional ~⟩ ⟨his ~ to captain came the following year⟩ **b :** furtherance or progression esp. toward perfection or to a higher stage of development **:** a helping or moving forward **:** IMPROVEMENT ⟨programs for the ~ and diffusion of knowledge⟩ ⟨leadership in the ~ of political and economic democracy —Vera M. Dean⟩ ⟨contributed greatly to the ~ of the new organization⟩ **2 :** property given usu. by a parent to a child in advance of a future distribution **:** an irrevocable gift by an intestate during his life of part or all of the donee's anticipated share in the donor's estate upon distribution, differing from an absolute gift in that it is charged against the donee's future share in the estate and from an advance in that the donee cannot be called upon to account for or repay it except by this charging of it **3 :** an advance of money or value

advance note *n* **:** a draft on owners or agents of a ship drawn by the master for the benefit of a seaman usu. for one month's advance wages

ad·vanc·er \=ˈ=sə(r)\ *n* -s **1 :** one that advances **2** [ME *avauncer,* fr. *avauncen* + *-er*] **:** a second branch of a buck's antler **3 :** PHASE ADVANCER

advances *pres 3d sing of* ADVANCE, *pl of* ADVANCE

advance track *n* **:** a track in a railroad yard for receiving a train as soon as made up

advancing *pres part of* ADVANCE

advancing color *n* **:** any of certain colors (as the yellows and colors closely related to yellow) that tend to appear nearer to the eye than other colors lying in the same plane

ad·van·cive \=ˈ=siv *also* ˈad,v-\ *adj* **:** tending to advance

¹ad·van·tage \ədˈvantij, -aan-, -ain-, -ān-, -ēj *also* ad-\ *n* -s [alter. (influenced by L *ad-*) of ME *avauntage,* fr. MF *avantage,* fr. *avant* before (fr. L *abante*) + *-age* — more at ADVANCE] **1 :** the quality or state of being superior **:** a more favorable or improved position or condition **:** SUPERIORITY ⟨control of the higher ground gave them an ~ over their opponents⟩ ⟨at the end of an hour's play the ~ lay definitely with the challenger⟩ ⟨our present ~ in the air⟩ ⟨gained the ~ by skillful maneuvering⟩ **2 a :** benefit, profit, or gain of any kind ⟨you will be given information to your ~⟩; *esp* **:** benefit resulting from some course of action ⟨a mistake which ironically turned out to his ~⟩ ⟨that can be done with ~ to all of us⟩ ⟨a manuscript that could be cut with ~⟩ **b** *obs* (1) **:** profit or gain in money **:** INTEREST ⟨you neither lend nor borrow upon ~ —Shak.⟩ (2) **:** excess quantity or number **:** SURPLUS ⟨it is but an ~ to the dozen —John Milton⟩ **3** *obs* **a** (1) **:** a place giving superiority **:** vantage ground (2) **:** high or higher ground **:** ELEVATION **b :** a favorable time or occasion **:** OPPORTUNITY **4 :** a factor or circumstance that gives superiority to its possessor or that puts him or it in a favorable or improved position ⟨among the ~s of a small college is its campus life⟩ ⟨a plan whose only ~ was its simplicity⟩ ⟨with none of the ~s of birth, wealth, or good health, he nevertheless rose quickly to the top⟩ ⟨a reputation that he later regarded as more of a handicap than an ~⟩ **5 :** the first point won in tennis after deuce; *also* **:** the score for it — called *advantage in* if won by the server, *advantage out* if won by the receiver **syn** see USE — **have the advantage of :** to have superiority over; *specif* **:** to have or profess a personal knowledge of (someone) that is not reciprocal — often used as a polite disclaimer of acquaintanceship ⟨I'm afraid you *have the advantage of* me⟩ — **to advantage** *adv* **:** so as to produce a favorable impression or effect **:** FAVORABLY, ADVANTAGEOUSLY ⟨shelves arranged to display the books *to advantage*⟩ ⟨a mountain seen *to advantage* in the morning light⟩

²advantage \"\ *vb* -ED/-ING/-S [alter. (influenced by L *ad-*) of ME *avauntagen,* fr. MF *avantager,* fr. *avantage,* n.] *vt* **:** to give an advantage to **:** be of benefit to **:** FURTHER, PROMOTE, PROFIT ⟨our present law of libel greatly ~s financial sharks —*Economist*⟩ ⟨considerably *advantaged* by his biological heritage —M.F.A.Montagu⟩ ~ *vi* **:** to derive advantage **:** BENEFIT ⟨the forces that would ~ —V.H.Burnstein⟩

ad·van·ta·geous \¦ad,van¦tājəs, -,vən- -,vaan-, -,vain-, -,vän-\ *adj* [*advantage* + *-ous*] **:** giving an advantage or the advantage **:** FAVORABLE, PROFITABLE, BENEFICIAL ⟨trade agreements ~ to both countries⟩ ⟨politically ~ to keep the other side guessing⟩ ⟨an unusually ~ financial settlement⟩ **syn** see BENEFICIAL

ad·van·ta·geous·ly *adv* **:** in an advantageous manner

advantage position *n* **:** a position in amateur wrestling in which a contestant has control of his opponent — compare NEUTRAL POSITION

ad·vec·tion \(ˈ)ad¦vekshən\ *n* -s [L *advection-, advectio* act of bringing, transportation, fr. *advectus* (past part. of *advehere* to carry to, fr. *ad-* + *vehere* to convey) + *-ion-, io* -ion — more at WAY] **:** the horizontal movement of a mass of air which causes changes in temperature or in other physical properties of air — compare CONVECTION — **ad·vec·tion·al** \-shən^{ə}l, -shnəl\ *adj*

ad·vec·tive \-ktiv\ *adj* **1 :** causing advection **2 :** relating to advection

ad·ve·hent \(ˈ)ad¦vēənt; ˈadvəhənt, -,hent\ *adj* [L *advehent-, advehens,* pres. part. of *advehere*] **:** AFFERENT

ad·vene \(ˈ)ad¦vēn\ *vb* -ED/-ING/-S [L *advenire* to come to, fr. *ad-* + *venire* to come — more at COME] *vi* **:** to become added to something or become a part of it ~ *vt* **:** to come to

ad·ve·nient \(ˈ)ad¦vēnyənt, -ēnēənt\ *adj* [L *advenient-, adveniens,* pres. part. of *advenire*] **:** coming from outward causes **:** SUPERADDED, ADVENTITIOUS

ad·vent \ˈad,vent, *esp Brit* -,vənt; *sometimes* ədˈvent\ *n* -s [ME, fr. ML *adventus,* fr. L, arrival, fr. *adventus,* past part. of *advenire* to come to] **1** *usu cap* **:** the period beginning four Sundays before Christmas and observed by many Christians as a season of prayer and fasting **2** *usu cap* **:** the coming of Christ: **a :** INCARNATION **b :** the coming of Christ as judge on the last day — called also *Second Advent, Second Coming* **3** [L *adventus*] **:** any coming or arrival ⟨the ~ of spring⟩ ⟨changes that followed the ~ of the railroad and the telegraph⟩ ⟨was watched in his ~ and departure —Mary Webb⟩ ⟨his ~ to the presidency was greeted by the guns of Fort Sumter —Edmund Wilson⟩ ⟨the ~ of the Cold War —*New Yorker*⟩

advent christian *n, usu cap A&C* **:** a member of the Advent Christian Church organized in 1861 under the original name of the Advent Christian Association

ad·ven·tial \(ˈ)ad¦venchəl\ *adj* [L *adventus* (past part.) + E *-ial*] **:** ADVENTITIOUS

ad·vent·ism \ˈad,ven,tizəm, -,vən-; əd'ven-, ad'-\ *n* -s *usu cap* **:** the doctrine that the second coming of Christ and the end of the world are near at hand; *specif* **:** the millenarian doctrine preached by William Miller and followers from 1831 on

[1]**ad·vent·ist** \ˈad,ventəst, -,vən-; əd'ven-, ad'-\ *n* -s *usu cap* [*advent* + *-ist*] **:** a believer in the doctrine of Adventism **:** a member of any of various religious bodies emphasizing this doctrine — called also *Second Adventist*

[2]**adventist** \"\ *adj, usu cap* **:** of or relating to the Adventists or Adventism

ad·ven·ti·tia \,advən'tish(ē)ə, -,ven-\ *n* -s [NL, alter. of L *adventicia*, neut. pl. of *adventicius* coming from outside, fr. *adventus* + *-icius* -icious] **:** an external covering or investment of an organ chiefly derived from the surrounding connective tissue; *esp* **:** the external coat or layer of a blood vessel consisting mostly of fibroelastic connective tissue

ad·ven·ti·tial \¦=(,)=¦tishəl\ *adj* [NL *adventitia* + E *-al*] **:** of or relating to an adventitia

adventitial cell *n* **:** MACROPHAGE

ad·ven·ti·tious \-shəs\ *adj* [L *adventicius*] **1 :** coming from another source **:** added or appended extrinsically and not sharing original, essential, and intrinsic nature **:** not inherent or innate ⟨we distinguish between borrowed, ~ energy in verse, and its natural energy —C.D.Lewis⟩ ⟨a disengagement of its own proper ideas from the ~ notions which have crept into it —A.N.Whitehead⟩ ⟨the ~ paraphernalia of 20th century living —*Time*⟩ **2** *biol* **a :** arising sporadically or in other than the usual location ⟨an ~ part in embryonic development⟩ **b :** occurring spontaneously or accidentally in a country or region to which it is not native ⟨~ weeds⟩ ⟨an ~ insect⟩ **3 :** ADVENTITIAL **4 :** not congenital **.** ACQUIRED ⟨~ deafness⟩ **syn** see ACCIDENTAL

adventitious bud *n, bot* **:** a bud arising in other than the normal position (as where elongation has ceased) and lacking a vascular trace — compare TRACE BUD

ad·ven·ti·tious·ly *adv* **:** in an adventitious manner

adventitious membrane *n* **:** a membrane connecting parts not usu. connected or of a different texture from the ordinary connection

ad·ven·ti·tious·ness *n* -ES **:** the quality or state of being adventitious

adventitious root *n* **:** a root that arises from any point other than the radicle or the root axis (as the prop roots of corn arising from the lower stem) — compare AERIAL ROOT; see ROOT illustration

adventitious vein *n* **:** a vein appearing irregularly between the accessory and intercalary veins of the wings of certain insects

[1]**ad·ven·tive** \(ˈ)ad¦ventiv, əd'v-\ *adj* [L *adventus* (past part.) + E *-ive*] **1 :** not native **:** imperfectly naturalized **:** IMMIGRANT ⟨an ~ weed⟩ **2 :** arising in an unusual position **:** ADVENTITIOUS — **ad·ven·tive·ly** *adv*

[2]**adventive** \"\ *n* -s **:** an exotic (as a plant) that is introduced often accidentally and imperfectly naturalized (as in being unable to bear fully mature fruit)

adventive crater *n* [¹*adventive*] **:** a small volcanic cone or crater on the flanks of a major volcanic cone

advents *pl of* ADVENT

advent sunday *n, usu cap A&S* **:** the first Sunday in Advent

[1]**ad·ven·ture** \əd'venchə(r) *also* ad-\ *n* -s [alter. (influenced by L *ad-*) of ME *aventure*, fr. OF, fr. (assumed) VL *adventura*, fr. L *adventus* (past part. of *advenire* to arrive, happen) + *-ura* -ure — more at ADVENE] **1** *obs* **a :** CHANCE, FORTUNE ⟨wished me fair ~ for the year —John Dryden⟩ **b :** a chance occurrence **:** an unplanned event **2 a** *chiefly marine insurance* **:** chance of loss **:** RISK, JEOPARDY, PERIL **b** *obs* **:** TRIAL, TEST **3 a :** a dangerous or risky undertaking **:** an enterprise or performance involving the uncertain or unknown ⟨an ~ in mountain climbing⟩ ⟨the time had come for drastic changes and bold ~s —Drew Middleton⟩ **b :** the encountering of risks **:** hazardous or exciting enterprise or experience ⟨the spirit of ~⟩ ⟨~ was gone from life in Mandalay —F.T. Jesse⟩ ⟨for the sake of the ~⟩ **4 :** a novel, exciting, or otherwise remarkable event or experience ⟨I found delightful ~s in the woods —W.B.Yeats⟩ ⟨long-forgotten childhood ~s⟩ ⟨hardly a day passed without its ~s⟩ **5 a :** an undertaking, enterprise, or venture involving financial risk or speculation esp. in mercantile or mining affairs; *also* **:** the risk incurred **b :** a shipment by a merchant on his own account

[2]**adventure** \"\ *vb* **adventured**; **adventured**; **adventuring** \-ch(ə)riŋ\ **adventures** [alter. (influenced by L *ad-*) of ME *aventuren, auntren*, fr. OF *aventurer*, fr. *aventure*] *vt* **1 :** to expose to possible danger or loss **:** RISK, VENTURE ⟨~ their capital in foreign trade⟩ ⟨so far had he *adventured* himself that I began to be afraid there might be no recovery —Hugh McCrae⟩ ⟨it is usual to ~ the very considerable cost of "wildcat" trial wells —W.G.Fearnsides⟩ ⟨~ himself gingerly into the water —Archibald Marshall⟩ **2 :** to venture upon **:** run the risks of **:** CHANCE, TRY ⟨durst not ~ such unknown ways —Edmund Spenser⟩ ⟨the last volume I have *adventured* is a very amusing book —H.J.Laski⟩ ⟨invites unbelievers . . . to retrace their steps and ~ Christianity —*Times Lit. Supp.*⟩ **3 :** to suggest venturesomely ⟨~ an opinion⟩ ~ *vi* **1 :** to proceed despite danger or risk **:** venture or hazard oneself (as in a dangerous or unknown region or risky undertaking) **:** DARE ⟨leaps at chances and . . . ~s to the shores washed with the farthest sea —J.L.Lowes⟩ ⟨only a madman would have *adventured* down the declivity —W.J.Locke⟩ ⟨David there *adventuring* in the blue, in the Middle Heaven —Mary Austin⟩ **2 :** to take the chance or risk **:** VENTURE ⟨I would ~ for such merchandise —Shak.⟩ ⟨wondering why the English theater is so slow to ~ with his last plays —*Irish Digest*⟩ — **ad·ven·ture·ment** \-mənt\ *n* -s

ad·ven·tur·er \-chərər, -ch(ə)rə\ *n* -s **1 :** one that adventures or seeks or engages in adventures: as **a :** a mercenary fighter **:** a free-lance volunteer **:** SOLDIER OF FORTUNE ⟨reported that the rebel command consisted largely of foreign ~s⟩ **b** (1) **:** one that engages or shares in commercial enterprises of considerable risk for profit esp. in foreign countries — compare MERCHANT ADVENTURER (2) *chiefly Brit* **:** a shareholder in a mining company **2 :** a person of uncertain qualifications seeking to attain unmerited wealth or position by sharp practice and dubious methods esp. by playing on the credulity or prejudices of others **:** one that lives by his wits ⟨if he had . . . no aim except to live at my expense, then I should regard him as an ~ —G.B.Shaw⟩ ⟨there were no courtesans . . . there were no ~s —F.L.Allen⟩ ⟨ring of political ~s —D.D.Martin⟩

ad·ven·ture·some \-chə(r)səm\ *adj* **:** given to incurring risks **:** ADVENTUROUS, VENTURESOME ⟨the risks — and gains — of an ~ economy —*Time*⟩ **syn** see ADVENTUROUS

ad·ven·ture·some·ly *adv* **:** in an adventuresome manner

ad·ven·tur·ess \-ch(ə)rəs\ *n* -ES [*adventurer* + *-ess*] **:** a female adventurer; *esp* **:** a woman who seeks position or livelihood by questionable means ⟨you just sit there . . . and let an ~ ruin your son's life —Josephine Pinckney⟩ ⟨a mercenary ~ who thought only of her 2000 guineas —Max Peacock⟩

ad·ven·tu·rine \əd'vench-\ *n* -s [by folk etymology] **:** AVENTURINE

ad·ven·tur·ism \-chə,rizəm\ *n* -s **1 :** the actions or attitudes of an adventurer **:** disregard of accepted standards of behavior **2 :** adventurous, dangerous, capricious, or haphazard improvisation or experimentation **:** ill-considered or rash adoption of expedients in the absence or in defiance of consistent plans or principles ⟨a personal ~ which is using the whole labor situation as a stamping ground for his own hatreds —*New Republic*⟩ ⟨a policy of sheer ~⟩

ad·ven·tur·ist \-chərəst\ *n* -s **:** one that adheres to adventurism — **ad·ven·tur·is·tic** \=¦=chə¦ristik\ *adj*

ad·ven·tur·ous \=¦=ch(ə)rəs\ *adj* [alter. (influenced by L *ad-*) of ME *aventurous*, fr. MF *aventureus*, fr. *aventure* adventure + *-eos* -ous — more at ADVENTURE] **1 :** having, enjoying, or seeking adventures **:** disposed to encounter dangers or risks or to cope with the new and unknown ⟨Caesar, the most skillful and prudent of generals, was yet as ~ as a knight-errant —J.A.Froude⟩ ⟨encouraged ~ Portuguese captains to push out into the Atlantic —G.C.Sellery⟩ **2 :** characterized by dangers and risks or by new or unknown situations ⟨an ~ period of river history⟩ ⟨my most ~ whaling voyage up to that time —H.A.Chippendale⟩ ⟨regions where life is still somewhat ~⟩

syn ADVENTURESOME, VENTURESOME, VENTUROUS, DARING, DAREDEVIL, TEMERARIOUS, FOOLHARDY, RECKLESS, RASH **:** ADVENTUROUS and the less common ADVENTURESOME may apply to a disposition to encounter danger or to explore the new and unknown ⟨the Dyaks . . . ferocious and *adventurous*, who had no equals in daring either in battles with rivers or in battles with enemies —Agnes N. Keith⟩ ⟨to be *adventurous* — to explore and discover in life as in art —Malcolm Cowley⟩ ⟨Admiral Byrd's *adventuresome* expeditions⟩ ⟨*adventuresome*, I sent my herald thought into a wilderness —John Keats⟩ VENTURESOME and VENTUROUS, the latter now somewhat uncommon, may imply greater willingness to chance danger or risk ⟨in 1919 Alcock and Brown undertook the first and highly *venturesome* crossing of the Atlantic by air —*Manchester Guardian*⟩ ⟨a faint pathway blazed through the wilderness by *venturesome* scouts and trappers from 1827 on —*Amer. Guide Series: Calif.*⟩ ⟨among these rocks that *venturous* feet could reach —William Wordsworth⟩ ⟨emancipation had some interest for *venturous* spirits —T.S.Eliot⟩ DARING may indicate fearlessness or boldness in greater dangers or most extreme ventures ⟨a *daring* and crafty captain, as careless of his own life as of other folk's —Charles Kingsley⟩ ⟨*daring* burglaries by armed men, and highway robberies, took place in the capital itself every night —Charles Dickens⟩ DAREDEVIL may imply the ostentatious, sensational, or bizarre in courting uncommon danger ⟨*daredevil* feats sometimes performed in the sperm-whale fishery —Herman Melville⟩ TEMERARIOUS, FOOLHARDY, RECKLESS, and RASH are mainly uncomplimentary. TEMERARIOUS, relatively uncommon in situations involving physical danger, may refer to actions or efforts ill-advised and overambitious ⟨summaries . . . more *temerarious* and experimental than the body of the book —George Saintsbury⟩ FOOLHARDY usu. describes the needless tempting or incurring of unnecessary dangers with virtually no chance of success ⟨the perfectly *foolhardy* feat of swimming the flood —Sinclair Lewis⟩ RECKLESS may apply to lack of concern about or consideration of the consequences of probable disaster and defeat ⟨he had frightfully dissipated his little capital. How wild and *reckless* he had been —W.M.Thackeray⟩ ⟨a *reckless*, devil-may-care individual who is ready for trouble, even looking for it, his advent into town is usually heralded by pistol shots and the splintering of glass —*Amer. Guide Series: Ariz.*⟩ RASH indicates imprudent haste and lack of thought ⟨like a *rash* exorcist, I was appalled by the spirit I had raised —L.P.Smith⟩ ⟨is it true that you were *rash* enough, mad enough, to speak to these men about murdering Keegan? —Anthony Trollope⟩

ad·ven·tur·ous·ly *adv* **:** in an adventurous manner

ad·ven·tur·ous·ness *n* -ES **:** the quality or state of being adventurous ⟨the insatiable ~ of man's imagination —H.G.Wells⟩

[1]**ad·verb** \ˈad,vərb, -ə̄b\ *n* -s [MF *adverbe*, fr. L *adverbium* (translation of Gk *epirrhēma*, lit., that which is said afterwards), fr. *ad-* + *-verbium* (fr. *verbum* word, verb) — more at EPIRRHEMA, WORD] **1 :** a word belonging to one of the major form classes in any of a great many languages typically used as a modifier of a verb, an adjective, another adverb, a preposition, a phrase, a clause, or a sentence and typically expressing some relation of manner or quality (as *well* in "she sings well", *surprisingly* in "surprisingly slow"), place (as *here* in "sit here"), time (as *now* in "now under consideration"), degree (as *too* in "too hastily", *rather* in "rather near us"), number (as *triply* in "triply bound"), cause (as *therefore* in "therefore the statement is true"), opposition (as *however* in "if however this proves impossible"), affirmation (as *certainly* in "he certainly did"), or denial (as *not* in "he did not"), sometimes having degrees of comparison expressed by affixation (as *soon, sooner, soonest*), suppletion (as *well, better, best*), or periphrasis (as *happily, more happily, most happily*) but otherwise uninflected, and frequently formed with a characteristic derivative affix (as *-ward, -wards* in "homeward", "homewards", *-wise* in "clockwise", and *-ly* in "aptly"), this last being esp. frequent since it is the principal means of forming adverbs from adjectives **2 adverbs** *pl but sing or pl in constr* **:** a game whose object is to guess an adverb by interpreting verbal or pantomimic answers given in the manner of the adverb chosen

[2]**adverb** \"\ *adj* **:** of or belonging to an adverb **:** functioning as an adverb usu. by modifying a verb or adjective ⟨an ~ phrase⟩ ⟨an ~ clause⟩

ad·verb·al \(ˈ)ad¦vərbəl, -ə̄b-\ *adj* [*ad-* + *verb* + *-al*] **:** modifying a verb

adverb equivalent *n* **:** a word not otherwise an adverb or a word group that has one of the typical functions of an adverb (as *months* in "we have waited months for this", *without leave* in "absent without leave", *in the corner* in "stand it there in the corner", *when I can* in "I'll write when I can")

ad·verb·i·al \(ˈ)ad¦vərbēəl, əd'v-, -ə̄b-\ *adj* [LL *adverbialis*, fr. L *adverbium* + *-alis* -al] **1 :** being an adverb ⟨in some sentences the word *likely* is ~ rather than adjectival⟩ **:** of or belonging to an adverb ⟨the ~ suffix *-ly*⟩ **2 :** having one of the typical functions of an adverb ⟨an ~ phrase⟩ ⟨an ~ clause⟩ ⟨the ~ noun *months* in "to wait months"⟩ — **ad·verb·i·al·ly** \-əlē, -li\ *adv*

ad ver·bum \(ˈ)ad'vərbəm, -er-\ [L] **:** to a word **:** VERBATIM

ad ve·re·cun·di·am \¦ad,verə'kendē,am -ēəm\ [L] **:** to modesty — used of an argument

ad·ver·sar·ia \,advə(r)'sa(a)rēə\ *n pl but sing or pl in constr* [L, journal, memorandum, fr. neut. pl. of *adversarius* turned toward] **1 :** commentaries or notes (as on a text or document) **2 :** a miscellaneous collection of notes, remarks, or selections **:** COMMONPLACE BOOK

[1]**ad·ver·sary** *R* ˈadvə(r),serē, *-R* -və,s-; -ri\ *n* -ES [ME, fr. MF & L; ME *aduersere*, fr. MF *adversier*, fr. L *adversarius*; ME *adversarie*, fr. L *adversarius*, fr. *adversarius*, adj., turned toward, antagonistic toward, fr. *adversus* (past part. of *advertere* to turn to) + *-arius* -ary — more at ADVERT] **1 :** one that contends with, opposes, or resists **:** ANTAGONIST, OPPONENT, ENEMY, FOE ⟨do as *adversaries* do in law, strive mightily but eat and drink as friends —Shak.⟩ ⟨powers of sarcasm that made him feared as an ~⟩ ⟨the sea powers have repeatedly succeeded in defeating their continental *adversaries* —G.H.Miller⟩ **2 a :** an opponent in a game **b :** an opponent of the declarer in the game of bridge or of the player who plays the dummy

[2]**adversary** \"\ *adj* [ME, fr. L *adversarius*] **1** *archaic* **:** OPPOSED, ADVERSE, ANTAGONISTIC **2 :** having or involving opposing antagonistic parties or interests **:** involving the Anglo-American system of procedure for conducting trials under strict rules of evidence with the right of cross-examination and argument, one party with his witnesses striving to prove the facts essential to his case and the other party striving to disprove those facts or to establish an affirmative defense **:** CONTESTED, LITIGATED

ad·ver·sa·tive \əd'vərsəd·iv, -ə̄s-, -əis-, ad-\ *adj* **:** expressive or indicative of antithesis, opposition, adverse circumstance, reservation, or contrary suggestion ⟨an ~ proposition⟩ ⟨the ~ conjunctions *but, only, still, yet*⟩ ⟨an ~ clause such as *although it was raining* in "although it was raining, the race started"⟩ — **ad·ver·sa·tive·ly** \-d·əvlē\ *adv*

[1]**ad·verse** \(ˈ)ad¦vərs, -ə̄s, -əis *also* əd'v-\ *adj* [ME, fr. MF *advers*, fr. L *adversus* (past part. of *advertere* to turn to) — more at ADVERT] **1 :** acting against or in a contrary direction **:** OPPOSING ⟨~ winds⟩ ⟨hindered by ~ forces⟩ **:** HOSTILE, OPPOSED, ANTAGONISTIC ⟨her feelings were still ~ to any man save one —Jane Austen⟩ ⟨a spirit ~ to class distinctions⟩ **2 a :** in opposition to one's interests **:** DETRIMENTAL, UNFAVORABLE ⟨an ~ balance of trade⟩ ⟨circumstances ~ to success⟩ ⟨~ fortune⟩ ⟨an ~ verdict⟩ **b :** tending to stress faults and withhold praise **:** CONDEMNATORY, CRITICAL ⟨irritated by ~ reviews of his play⟩ ⟨overheard several ~ comments⟩ **3 a :** opposite in position **:** CONFRONTING ⟨Calpe's ~ height —Lord Byron⟩ ⟨the two ~ carriages would therefore, to a certainty, be traveling on the same side —Thomas De Quincey⟩ **b** *bot* **:** turned toward the stem or axis ⟨~ leaves⟩ — opposed to *averse* **4** *law* **:** having opposing interests **:** having interests for the preservation of which opposition is essential

syn INIMICAL, ANTAGONISTIC, COUNTER, COUNTERACTIVE **:** ADVERSE describes what is unfavorable, harmful, difficult, detrimental; it may refer to opposition, often decisive or fateful opposition ⟨what very small things in *adverse* circumstances suffice to make people happy — a little food, warmth, and something to look forward to —Hervey Allen⟩ ⟨an *adverse* wind had so delayed him that his cargo brought but half its proper price —Amy Lowell⟩ INIMICAL may describe strongly adversative or prejudicial tendencies or effects or determinedly hostile persons, sometimes malevolent ⟨the fact of universal elementary education is *inimical* to poetry —C.D.Lewis⟩ ⟨nor was Miss Briggs, although forced to adopt a hostile attitude, secretly *inimical* to Rawdon —W.M.Thackeray⟩ ANTAGONISTIC, more frequently applied to persons than to things, may suggest incompatibility, antipathy, irreconcilability, or hostile opposition ⟨the West Indian planters, upon whom the successful working of the system largely depended, were not merely unsympathetic but violently *antagonistic* to it —*Times Lit. Supp.*⟩ ⟨the *antagonistic* principles of aristocracy and democracy —V.L.Parrington⟩ COUNTER may be applied to opposition, to action or tendency in an opposing direction, sometimes to parrying, retaliation, or reprisal ⟨as I reached the limit of my swing and prepared to rush back on the *counter* swing —Jack London⟩ ⟨currents and *counter* currents⟩ ⟨a *counter* threat that the interdict would be followed by the banishment of the clergy —J.R.Green⟩ COUNTERACTIVE refers to opposition tending to check, nullify, or destroy ⟨*counteractive* measures against the epidemic⟩

[2]**adverse** \"\ *vt* -ED/-ING/-S **:** OPPOSE ⟨~ a land patent⟩

ad·verse·ly \-lē, -li\ *adv* **1 :** in an adverse or hostile manner **:** with hostile effect **2 :** UNFAVORABLY, DISADVANTAGEOUSLY

adverse possession *n* **:** a possession that is hostile, under a claim or color of title, actual, open, notorious, exclusive, and continuous, continued for the required period of time (generally 20 years) thereby giving an indefeasible right of possession or ownership to the possessor by operation of the limitation of actions

adverse witness *n, law* **:** a hostile witness

ad·ver·si·ty \ad'vərsəd·ē, əd'v-, -ə̄s-, -əis-, -sətē, -i\ *n* -ES [ME *adversite* (also, opposition), fr. OF *adversité, aversité*, fr. LL *adversitat-, adversitas*, fr. L, opposition, fr. *adversus* + *-itat-, -itas* -ity] **1 :** a state of adverse fortune **:** a condition of suffering, destitution, or affliction often implying previous prosperity or well-being ⟨what fairy palaces we may build of beautiful thought — proof against all ~ —John Ruskin⟩ ⟨showed unexpected courage in ~⟩ **2 :** a stroke of ill fortune **:** a calamitous or disastrous experience — usu. used in pl. ⟨a period marked by *adversities* and *misfortunes*⟩

ad·ver·sive \(ˈ)ad¦vərsiv, əd'v-\ *adj* [¹*adverse* (opposite) + *-ive*] *anat* **:** OPPOSITE

[1]**ad·vert** \ad'vərt, əd'v-, -ə̄t, -əit, *usu* -d·+V\ *vb* -ED/-ING/-S [ME *averten, adverten*, fr. MF & L; MF *avertir, advertir*, fr. L *advertere*, fr. *ad-* + *vertere* to turn — more at WORTH] *vi* **1 :** to turn the mind or attention **:** pay heed or attention — used with *to* ⟨surely our present-day positivists can never indicate what is good for man without ~*ing* to his nature —J.A.McWilliams⟩ ⟨cosmologies that Freud, when he ~*ed* to them at all, regarded as too highbrow to be given the name of religion —David Riesman⟩ **2 :** to direct or call attention in the course of speaking or writing **:** REFER, ALLUDE — used with *to* ⟨will be ~*ed* to here, but will be dealt with more fully in other chapters —T.E.May⟩ ⟨~*ed* briefly to the circumstances of their first meeting⟩ ~ *vt* **1** *obs* **:** to turn the attention to **:** OBSERVE, CONSIDER **2 :** to give warning of **:** make aware **:** WARN

[2]**ad·vert** \ˈad,vərt, -ə̄t\ *n* -s [by shortening] *chiefly Brit* **:** ADVERTISEMENT

ad·vert·ence \ad'vərtᵊn(t)s, əd-, -ə̄t-, -əit-\ *n* -s [ME, fr. MF *avertence, advertence*, fr. *avertir, advertir* + *-ence*] **1 :** the action or process of adverting **:** ATTENTION, NOTICE, REFERENCE ⟨to this difference it is right that ~ should be had in regulating taxation —J.S.Mill⟩ ⟨selected samples with no ~ to the usefulness of controls in a scientific study —W.A.Harvey⟩ **2 :** ADVERTENCY 1

ad·vert·en·cy \-nsē, -i\ *n* -ES **1 :** the quality or state of being advertent **:** HEEDFULNESS **2 :** ADVERTENCE 1

ad·vert·ent \(ˈ)ad¦vərtᵊnt, əd'v-, -ə̄t-, -əit-\ *adj* [L *advertent-, advertens*, pres. part. of *advertere* to advert — more at ADVERT] **:** giving attention **:** HEEDFUL — **ad·vert·ent·ly** *adv*

ad·ver·tis·a·ble \¦advə(r)¦tīzəbəl\ *adj* **:** capable of being effectively advertised

ad·ver·tise \ˈadvə(r),tīz *also* ,==¦=\ *also* **ad·ver·tize** \"\ *vb* -ED/-ING/-S [ME *avertisen, advertisen*, fr. MF *avertiss-, advertiss-*, stem of *avertir, advertir* — more at ADVERT] *vt* **1 a :** to make known to (someone) **:** give notice to **:** INFORM, NOTIFY ⟨one does not need to ~ the squirrels where the nut trees are —J.R.Lowell⟩ ⟨the translators . . . were careful to ~ the reader that what they offered was Le Clerc's *Moreri* —*Times Lit. Supp.*⟩ — often used with *of* ⟨of which we have been *advertised* by the same authority —Jane Austen⟩ ⟨it seemed to Nathan as if the entire neighborhood were being *advertised* of the fact —Mary S. Watts⟩ **b** *obs* **:** WARN, ADMONISH — used with the infinitive ⟨St. Paul *advertised* all women to give a good ensample of . . . godly godliness —Hugh Latimer⟩ **2 :** to make generally known **:** call attention to **:** give notice of: **a :** to give publicity to ⟨extravagantly *advertised* by Swinburne —T.S.Eliot⟩ ⟨this renowned establishment, widely *advertised* in . . . works of fiction —N.F.Busch⟩ ⟨began deliberately *advertising* his willingness to make concessions —*Time*⟩ ⟨that higher *advertising* of England which has employed so many distinguished pens —F.R.Leavis⟩ **b :** to make conspicuous ⟨no tall man can be a successful pickpocket, because he must bend to his work, and so ~ it to every beholder —Arthur Morrison⟩ ⟨unrecognizable save by their fragrance and naked stamens, *advertised* neither by color nor form of blossom —William Beebe⟩ **c** (1) **:** to give public notice of **:** announce publicly esp. by a printed notice or through a radio or television broadcast ⟨the return of Sir Victor with Lady Pandolfo . . . had been officially *advertised* —W.J.Locke⟩ ⟨*advertised* him as their jail editor —Walter Lippmann⟩ ⟨a poster *advertising* forthcoming events⟩ ⟨enlist the aid of disc jockeys in *advertising* a rummage sale⟩ (2) **:** to call public attention to esp. by emphasizing desirable qualities so as to arouse a desire to buy or patronize ⟨~ a breakfast food⟩ ⟨spent a fortune *advertising* their filter-tip cigarettes⟩ ~ *vi* **:** to issue a public statement (as through printed notices, radio or television broadcasts) of something offered or wanted ⟨~ in the lost-and-found column⟩ ⟨~ for a stenographer⟩ ⟨business increased soon after they began to ~ on the radio⟩ **syn** see DECLARE, INFORM

ad·ver·tise·ment \,advə(r)'tīzmənt *also* '==,==; əd'vər|d·əz-, ad-, -və̄|, -vəi|, -|tə-, -əs-\ *also* **ad·ver·tize·ment** \"\ *n* -s [ME, fr. MF *avertissement, advertissement*, fr. *avertiss-, advertiss-* + *-ment*] **1 :** the action of advertising **:** a calling attention to or making known: as **a** *obs* **:** WARNING, ADMONITION **b** *obs* **:** an informing or notifying **:** NOTIFICATION **c :** a calling to public attention **:** PUBLICITY ⟨the limitations we have imposed will receive wide ~ in other parts of colonial Asia —*Atlantic*⟩ ⟨an unwarranted amount of ~ for an unattractive group —W.E.Swinton⟩ **2 a** *archaic* **:** a statement calling attention to something **:** NOTICE ⟨the publisher's ~ to the reader⟩ **b :** a public notice; *esp* **:** a paid notice or announcement published in some public print (as a newspaper, periodical, poster, or handbill) or broadcast over radio or television ⟨a full-page ~⟩ ⟨the classified ~s⟩ — compare COMMERCIAL

advertisement curtain *n* **:** a theater curtain covered with the advertisements of local businesses

ad·ver·tis·er \ˈadvə(r),tīzə(r) *also* ,==¦==\ *also* **ad·ver·tiz·er** \"\ *n* -s **:** one that advertises

advertising *also* **advertizing** *n* -s *often attrib* **1 :** the action of calling something (as a commodity for sale, a service offered or desired) to the attention of the public esp. by means of printed or broadcast paid announcements **2 :** ADVERTISEMENTS ⟨a magazine containing a great deal of ~⟩ ⟨the ~ pages of the Sunday paper⟩ **3 :** the business or profession

of designing and preparing advertisements for publication or broadcast ⟨an ~ firm⟩ ⟨a spectacular career in ~⟩
ad·ver·to·ri·al \ˌadvə(r)ˈtōrēəl\ *n* -s [blend of *advertisement* and *editorial*] **:** a factual report in the form of a paid advertisement intended to provide information of interest and importance to the public esp. about some aspect of business activity and usu. sponsored by a commercial or industrial organization or a group of allied organizations
adverts *pres 3d sing of* ADVERT, *pl of* ADVERT
ad·vice \ədˈvīs *also* ad-\ *n* -s [alter. of ME *avise, advise*, fr. OF *avis, advis* opinion, judgment, prob. fr. *a vis* apparent (as in *ce m'est a vis* that appears to me), fr. *a* to, at, in (fr. L *ad*) + *vis* view, opinion, fr. L *visus* appearance, probability, fr. *visus*, past part. of *vidēre*, to see — more at AT, WIT] **1** *obs* **:** the way in which one regards something **:** VIEW, OPINION ⟨with power to make known their ~ —Thomas Hobbes⟩ **2** *obs* **:** careful thought **:** CONSIDERATION, DELIBERATION ⟨consider of it, take ~, and speak your minds —Judg 19:30 (AV)⟩ **3 :** recommendation regarding a decision or course of conduct **:** COUNSEL ⟨among strangers, remote from the eye and ~ of my father —Benjamin Franklin⟩ ⟨the leader's commands, the priest's exhortations, and the philosopher's ~ —Alan Gregg⟩ ⟨my ~ to you is — don't do it⟩ ⟨to seek medical ~⟩ **4 :** information or notice given **:** INTELLIGENCE, NEWS ⟨and at last ~ had gone on a hunger strike —*Canadian Forum*⟩ — usu. used in pl. ⟨the latest ~s from our Paris correspondent⟩ ⟨had ~s that Casale was sufficiently provisioned to last for many months —Hilaire Belloc⟩ **5 :** a formal or official notice sent by one person or office to another concerning a business transaction ⟨a remittance ~⟩ ⟨shipping ~s⟩: as **a :** a letter by which the drawer of a bill of exchange notifies the drawee that the bill has been issued — called also *letter of advice* **b** (1) **:** a descriptive notice sent by a post office issuing an international money order to the post office which is to make payment (2) **:** a notice concerning a postal shipment (as one to the sender informing him of delivery to the addressee)
advice boat *n, archaic* **:** DISPATCH BOAT
adviceful *adj* **1** *obs* **:** THOUGHTFUL, ATTENTIVE **2** *obs* **:** skillful in giving advice
ad·vis·a·bil·i·ty \ədˌvīzəˈbilədē, -ətē, -i *also* ad,v-\ *n* -ES **:** the quality of being advisable **:** DESIRABILITY, EXPEDIENCY
ad·vis·a·ble \ə'ˈ=əbəl\ *adj* **1 :** proper to be advised or to be done **:** EXPEDIENT, PRUDENT ⟨neither necessary nor ~⟩ ⟨extreme caution is ~⟩ **2 :** ready to receive advice **:** open to advice **syn** see EXPEDIENT
ad·vis·able·ness *n* -ES **:** the quality of being expedient
ad·vis·a·bly \-əblē, -li\ *adv* **:** in an advisable manner **:** EXPEDIENTLY, PRUDENTLY
ad·vis·a·to·ry \-əˌtōrē\ *adj* **:** of or belonging to an adviser or to advice **:** ADVISORY
ad·vise \ədˈvīz *also* ad-\ *vb* -ED/-ING/-S [ME *avisen, advisen*, partly fr. OF *aviser, adviser* to give an opinion, inform, consider (fr. *avis* opinion), partly fr. OF *aviser, adviser* to observe, recognize, perceive, fr. *a-* (fr. L *ad-*) + *viser* to aim, fr. (assumed) VL *visare*, fr. L *visus*, past part. of *vidēre* to see] *vt* **1** *obs* **:** to look at **:** OBSERVE, CONSIDER ⟨abashed that her a stranger did ~ —Edmund Spenser⟩ **2** *obs* **:** BETHINK ⟨~ you what you say —Shak.⟩ **3 a :** to give advice to **:** COUNSEL ⟨among those *advising* the president⟩ ⟨was *advised* to try a warmer climate⟩ **:** CAUTION, WARN ⟨*advised* him of the danger⟩ ⟨against which a solemn trespass board *advised* us —Mary Austin⟩ **b :** RECOMMEND ⟨~ going slow⟩ ⟨*advised* prudence⟩ **4 :** to give information or notice to **:** INFORM, APPRISE ⟨had not *advised* his friends of his marriage —Willa Cather⟩ ⟨a note on the flyleaf *advised* that this was a limited edition —*Discovery*⟩ ⟨a stone guidepost *advised* him that Gaza was still eight miles distant —L.C.Douglas⟩ ~ *vi* **1** *obs* **:** to take thought **:** CONSIDER, DELIBERATE **2 :** to give advice **:** offer counsel ⟨an article written to inform, not to ~⟩ ⟨knowledge enabling them to ~ on actions designed to improve the well-being of people —Fritz Machlup⟩ **3 :** to take counsel **:** hold a consultation **:** CONSULT — used with *with* ⟨~ with friends⟩ ⟨by cooperating and *advising* with voluntary . . . nonprofit organizations —*U. S. Code*⟩ ⟨inspects their farms and ~s with them on the best farming methods —*Banking*⟩ **syn** see INFORM
ad·vised \-zd\ *adj* [ME *avised, advised*, fr. past part. of *avisen, advisen*] **:** characterized by or resulting from deliberation or reflection **:** thought out **:** CONSIDERED ⟨badly ~ conduct⟩ — used chiefly in the phrases *ill-advised, well-advised* **syn** see DELIBERATE
ad·vis·ed·ly \-zədlē, -li\ *adv* [alter. (influenced by *advised*) of ME *avisily, advisily*, fr. *avisy, advisy* well-advised, circumspect (fr. MF *avisé*, fr. past part. of *aviser*) + *-ly*] **:** with or after forethought or consideration **:** DELIBERATELY, INTENTIONALLY ⟨a strong term, but one used ~ and only after careful thought⟩
ad·vis·ee \ədˌvīˈzē, (ˌ)ad-\ *n* -s **:** one that is advised; *specif* **:** a student assigned to a faculty member for counseling
ad·vise·ment \ədˈvīzmənt *also* ad-\ *n* -s [ME *avisement, advisement*, fr. MF, partly fr. *aviser, adviser* to give an opinion, inform + *-ment*, partly fr. *aviser, adviser* to observe, recognize, perceive + *-ment*] **1 :** the process of observing or considering **:** CONSIDERATION, DELIBERATION ⟨take a matter under ~⟩ **2 a :** ADVICE, COUNSEL ⟨both ~ and aid are given to physically handicapped students⟩ **b :** the action or process of advising **:** the giving of advice or counsel ⟨a center for the vocational testing and ~ of veterans⟩
ad·vis·er *also* **ad·vi·sor** \-zə(r)\ *n* -s **1 :** one that gives advice ⟨served as special ~ to the American delegation⟩ ⟨the president's medical ~s⟩ ⟨a firm of investment ~s⟩; *specif* **:** one designated to advise students (as in the choice of studies, vocational preparation, or the conduct of research) or to supervise a student organization or activity ⟨the senior English teacher is ~ to the yearbook⟩ **2 :** an adult leader in a Horizon Club, the senior program of the Camp Fire Girls, Inc.
ad·vis·er·ship \-ˌship\ *n* -s **:** the office of an adviser
adviso *n* -ES [modif. (influenced by E *advice*) of Sp *aviso*, backformation fr. *avisar* to advise, inform, fr. F *aviser* — more at ADVISE] **1** *obs* **:** ADVICE 4 **2** *obs* **:** ADVICE 3 **3** *obs* **:** DISPATCH BOAT
ad·vis·o·ri·ly \ədˈvīz(ə)rəlē, -li *also* ad-\ *adv* **:** in an advisory manner or capacity
¹ad·vis·o·ry \-z(ə)rē, -ri\ *adj* [*advise* + *-ory*] **1 :** having or exercising power to advise ⟨an ~ council⟩ ⟨accompanied the president in an ~ capacity⟩ **2 :** containing or giving advice **:** intended to advise ⟨an ~ bulletin⟩ ⟨an ~ speed sign⟩
²advisory \"\ *n* -ES **:** a report giving information (as one issued by a weather bureau on the progress of a hurricane) ⟨the latest ~ from Miami⟩ ⟨after two days he emerges, receives an ~ on his battery-powered radio —R.E.Lapp⟩
advisory opinion *n* **:** a formal opinion by a judge, a court, or a law officer upon a question of law submitted by a legislative body or a governmental official but not presented in a concrete case at law and having no binding force
ad vi·tam aut cul·pam \ˌädˈwēˌtämˌau̇tˈku̇lˌpäm\ [L] **:** for life or until misbehavior — used to qualify orig. a feudal tenure and later an appointment to office
ad·vo·caat \ˈadvōˌkät\ *n* -s [D, short for *advocatenborrel*, fr. *advocaat* lawyer (fr. MD *advocaet*, fr. L *advocatus* one summoned to another) + *borrel* drink, bubble, fr. *borrelen* to bubble, alter. of MD *bordelen, bortelen*, of imit. origin; fr. its throat-soothing effect, esp. helpful for irritations caused by the traditional eloquence of lawyers — more at ADVOCATE] **:** an eggnog chiefly mixed and bottled in Holland made from eggs, sugar, and brandy with vanilla and coffee flavoring
ad·vo·ca·cy \ˈadvəkəsē, -si\ *n* -ES [ME *advocacie*, fr. MF *advocacie*, fr. ML *advocatia*, fr. L *advocatus* + *-ia*] **1 :** the profession or work of an advocate **2 :** the action of advocating, pleading for, or supporting ⟨devoted a lifetime to the ~ of economic reforms⟩ ⟨a consequence of his moving ~ —W.O. Douglas⟩
¹ad·vo·cate \-kət, -ˌkāt, *usu* -d·+V\ *n* -s [ME *avocat, advocat*, fr. MF, fr. L *advocatus*, fr. past part. of *advocare* to summon, call to one's aid, fr. *ad-* + *vocare* to call — more at VOICE] **1 :** one that pleads the cause of another **:** DEFENDER ⟨we have an ~ with the Father, Jesus Christ —1 Jn 2:1 (AV)⟩ ⟨accepted the responsibility of acting as a personal ~ for his chief⟩; *specif* **:** one that pleads the cause of another before a tribunal or judicial court **:** COUNSELOR ⟨never a close student of the law, his success was won as an ~⟩ — used as the technical name in Scotland, France, and various other countries whose legal system is based on the Roman law and in the English ecclesiastical courts and various other special courts; compare ATTORNEY, BARRISTER, COUNSEL **2 :** one that argues for, defends, maintains, or recommends a cause or proposal ⟨its warmest ~s agree in this with its severest critics —W.C. Brownell⟩ ⟨the ~s of classical education⟩ ⟨an ~ of air power⟩
²ad·vo·cate \-ˌkāt, *usu* -d·+V\ *vb* -ED/-ING/-S *vt* **:** to plead in favor of **:** defend by argument before a tribunal or the public **:** support or recommend publicly ⟨~ a permanent corps of civil servants⟩ ⟨~ changes be made⟩ ~ *vi* **:** to act as advocate
ad·vo·cate·ship \-ˌkətˌship, -ˌkāt-\ *n* -s **:** the office or duty of an advocate
ad·vo·ca·tion \ˌadvəˈkāshən\ *n* -s [L *advocation-, advocatio* act of calling, summoning, legal assistance, fr. *advocatus* + *-ion-, -io* -ion] **1 a :** SUMMONING **b** *Scots law* **:** the process whereby a superior court formerly reviewed cases brought in inferior courts **2 :** the act of advocating or pleading **:** PLEA
ad·vo·ca·tor \ˈadvəˌkād·ə(r)\ *n* -s **:** ¹ADVOCATE 2
ad·voc·a·to·ry \(ˈ)adˈväkəˌtōrē, ˈadvəˌkād·ərē\ *adj* **:** of or relating to an advocate
ad·vo·ca·tus dei \ˈadvəˌkäd·əsˈdēˌī; ˌadvəˌkäd·əsˈdāˌē, ˌädvōˌkäˌtu̇s-\ *n, usu cap D* [LL] **:** an official of the Roman Catholic Congregation of Rites whose duty is to refute the objections raised by the advocatus diaboli against the beatification or canonization of a person
advocatus di·a·bo·li \-kä...dīˈabəˌlī, -sdē'-; -kä...sdēˈäbə-(ˌ)lē\ *n* [ML] **:** DEVIL'S ADVOCATE
ad·vo·lu·tion \ˌadvəˈlüshən\ *n* -s [L *advolutus* (past part. of *advolvere* to roll to, fr. *ad-* + *volvere* to roll) + E *-ion* — more at WELL] **:** a rolling toward something **:** growth or development toward — contrasted with *evolution*
ad·vow·ee \ədˌvau̇ˈē, (ˌ)adˌ-\ *n* -s [*advowson* + *-ee*] **:** one that holds an advowson
ad·vow·son \ədˈvau̇zᵊn, ad-\ *n* -s [ME, *avoweson, advouson*, fr. OF *avoeson, avoueson*, fr. ML *advocation-, advocatio*, fr. L, act of summoning — more at ADVOCATION] *English law* **:** the right of presenting a nominee to a vacant ecclesiastical benefice
advt *abbr* advertisement
advtg *abbr* **1** advantage **2** advertising
ady·nam·ia \ˌādīˈnamēə, -ām-, ˌadə-\ *n* -s [NL, fr. Gk, fr. *a-* ²a- + *-dynamia*] **:** asthenia caused by disease
ady·nam·ic \ˌā,dīˈnamik, ˌadə-\ *adj* [NL *adynamia* + E *-ic*] **1 :** characterized by or relating to adynamia **2** *physics* **:** characterized by the absence of force
ad·y·tum \ˈadətəm\ *or* **ad·y·ton** \-ˌtän\ *also* **ad·yt** \-ət\ *n, pl* **ady·ta** \-ətə\ *also* **adyts** [L *adytum*, fr. Gk *adyton*, neut. of *adytos* not to be entered, fr. *a-* ²a- + *-dytos* (fr. *dyein* to enter, dive in, sink); akin to Gk *deielos* evening, Skt *upā-du-* to put on, and perh. to Skt *doṣā* evening, dark, Av *daoshatara-* toward the west] **:** the innermost sanctuary or shrine in ancient temples which was open only to priests and from which oracles were given **:** a private chamber **:** SANCTUM, HOLY OF HOLIES
¹adz *or* **adze** \ˈadz *also* ˈaa(ə)-\ *n, pl* **adz·es** [ME *adse, adese*, fr. OE *adesa*] **:** a cutting tool that has a thin arched blade sharpened on the concave side and set at right angles to the handle and is used principally for rough-shaping wood
²adz *or* **adze** \"\ *vt* **adzed; adzed; adzing; adzes :** to cut or shape with an adz
adz block *n* **:** the block in a wood-planing machine in which the cutters are fixed
adz-eye hammer *n* **:** a hammer having an extended eye for the handle

1 2 3

1 carpenter's adz with flat head, *2* ship carpenter's adz with spur head, *3* cooper's adz

adzhar \ˈajˌär\ *n, pl* **adzhar** *or* **adzhars** *usu cap* [Russ] **1 a :** a Georgian people of the southern Caucasus region — compare GURIAN, IMERITIAN **b :** a member of such people **2 :** the language of the Adzhar people
¹adzhar·i·an \əˈjärēən\ *adj, usu cap* [*Adzhar, Adzharia*, autonomous Soviet Socialist Republic (fr. Russ *Adzhar, Adzhariya*) + E *-ian*] **1 :** of, relating to, or characteristic of the Adzhar Republic **2 :** of, relating to, or characteristic of the people of the Adzhar Republic
²adzharian \"\ *n* -s *cap* **:** a native or inhabitant of the Adzhar Republic
ad·zu·ki bean \adˈzükē-\ *or* **ad·su·ki bean** \", -ˈs-\ *n* [Jap *azuki*] **:** an annual bushy bean (*Phaseolus angularis*) widely grown in Japan and China for the flour made from its seeds
ae \ˈā\ *adj* [ME (northern dial.) *a*, alter. (before consonants) of *an*, fr. OE *ān* — more at ONE] *chiefly Scot* **:** ONE
ae *abbr* [L *aetatis*, gen. of *aetas* age — more at AGE] of age; aged
AE \(ˈ)āˈē\ *abbr or n* -s **1** aeronautical engineer **2** agricultural engineer
ae·ae·an \ēˈēən\ *adj, usu cap* [*Aeaea*, island in the Tyrrhenian sea, legendary abode of Circe, fr. L, fr. Gk *Aiaia*] **:** of or belonging to the island of Aeaea
aeb·le·ski·ve \ˈebləˌskivə\ *n, pl* **aebleski·ver** \-və(r)\ [Dan *æbleskive*, lit., apple slice, fr. *æble* apple + *skive* slice; akin to ON *epli* apple and to ON *skīfa* slice — more at APPLE, SHEAVE] **:** a muffin-shaped pastry made of yeast-leavened batter baked in a special pan
ae·cial \ˈēsh(ē)əl, -sēəl\ *adj* [NL *aecium* + E *-al*] **:** of or belonging to an aecium
ae·cid·i·al \(ˈ)ēˈsidēəl\ *adj* [NL *aecidium* + E *-al*] **:** of or relating to an aecidium
ae·cid·i·o·spore \ēˈsidēəˌspō(ə)r\ *n* [ISV *aecidio-* (fr. NL *aecidium*) + *spore*] **:** AECIOSPORE
ae·cid·i·um \ēˈsidēəm\ *n* [NL, fr. Gk *aikia* + NL *-idium*] **1** *pl* **aecidia :** AECIUM; *esp* **:** a cup-shaped or spheroidal aecium with a peridial layer **2** *cap* **:** a form genus of rust fungi having only an aecial stage with toothed cup-shaped peridia
ae·ci·o·spore \ˈēs(h)ēəˌspō(ə)r\ *n* [NL *aecium* + E *-o-* + *spore*] **:** one of the spores in chainlike series within an aecium — **ae·ci·o·spor·ic** \ˌ==ˈspōrik\ *adj*
ae·ci·um \ˈēs(h)ēəm\ *n, pl* **ae·cia** \-ēə\ [NL, irreg. fr. Gk *aikia* torture, assault, fr. *aikēs, aeikēs* unseemly, shameful (fr. *a-* ²a- + *-eikēs* seemly, akin to *eoikōs, eikōs* fitting, apt) + *-ia*; akin to Gk *eikōn* picture, image — more at ICON] **:** the fruiting body of rust fungi sometimes flat and lacking peridial cells and in which the first binucleate spores are usu. produced — see CAEOMA; compare TELIUM, UREDINIUM
aecology *var of* ECOLOGY
ae·de·a·gal \ēˈdēəgəl, ˌēdēˈäg-\ *adj* [NL *aedeagus* + E *-al*] **:** of or relating to an aedeagus
ae·de·a·gus *also* **ae·doe·a·gus** \-gəs\ *n, pl* **aedea·gi** *also* **aedoea·gi** \-ˌgī, -ˌjī\ [NL, fr. Gk *aidoia* genitals + *agos* leader, fr. *agein* to lead — more at EDE-, AGENT] **:** the intromittent organ of a male insect **:** PHALLUS; *sometimes* **:** the distal part of this structure
ae·des \āˈē(ˌ)dēz\ *n, cap* [NL, fr. Gk *aēdēs* distasteful, nauseous] **:** a large cosmopolitan genus of mosquitoes distinguished from *Anopheles* by the trilobate scutellum and short palpi of the female and from *Culex* by the pointed abdomen of the female and including a number of species (as the yellow-fever mosquito) important as vectors of diseases of man and animals
ae·dic·u·la \ēˈdikyələ\ *also* **aed·i·cule** \ˈedəˌkyül, ˈēd-\ *n, pl* **aedicu·lae** \-əˌlē\ *also* **aedicules** *or* **edicules** \-ˌlēz\ [L *aedicula*, dim. of *aedes* temple, building — more at EDIFY] **:** a small structure used as a shrine **:** a niche for a statue — usu. used in pl.
ae·dic·u·lar \ēˈdikyələ(r)\ *adj* **:** of or relating to an aedicula **:** having niches ⟨an ~ façade⟩
ae·dile *also* **edile** \ˈēˌdīl, -īəl\ *n* -s [L *aedilis*, fr. *aedes* temple, pl. building + *-ilis* -ile — more at EDIFY] **:** an official in ancient Rome charged with policing the city, superintending public works and the grain supply, and providing for the public games — **ae·dil·i·tian** \ˌēdᵊlˈishən, ˌēˌdīˈli-\ *adj*
ae·dil·i·ty *also* **edil·i·ty** \ēˈdiləd·ē\ *n* -ES [L *aedilitas*, fr. *aedilis* + *-itas* -ity] **1 :** the office of an aedile **2 :** the superintendence of public buildings and works
ae·dine \āˈēˌdīn, -ēn\ *adj* [NL *Aedes* + E *-ine*] **:** of, related to, or involving the genus *Aedes* or mosquitoes of this genus
AeE *abbr or n* -s **:** an aeronautical engineer
ae·ga·grop·i·la \ˌēgəˈgräpələ\ *n* [NL, fr. Gk *aigagros* + L *pila* ball, fr. *pilus* hair — more at PILE] **1** *also* **ae·gag·ro·pile** *or* **egag·ro·pile** \ēˈgagrōˌpīl\ *pl* **aegagropilas** \ˌēgəˈgräpələz\ *or* **aegagropilae** \-ˌlē\ *also* **aegagropiles** *or* **egagropiles** \ēˈgagrōpīlz\ **:** a ball of hair or a concretion found in the stomach of the goat and other ruminants **2** *pl* **aegagropilas** *or* **aegagropilae :** a ball-shaped mass of hairlike filaments formed by some algae (as certain species of the genus *Cladophora*) **3** *cap, in some classifications* **:** a genus of algae comprising all forms forming aegagropilas — **ae·ga·grop·i·lous** \ˌēgəˈgräpələs\ *adj*
ae·gag·rus \ēˈgagrəs\ *n, pl* **aegag·ri** \-ˌgrī\ [NL, fr. Gk *aigagros*, fr. *aig-, aix* goat + *agrios* wild] **:** the wild goat (*Capra aegagrus*) of Asia Minor
ae·ge·an \ēˈjēən\ *adj, usu cap* [L *Aegaeus* (fr. Gk *Aigaios*) + E *-an*] **1 :** of or relating to the arm of the Mediterranean sea east of Greece **2 :** of or relating to the prehistoric civilization of the islands of the Aegean sea and the countries adjacent to it esp. in the Bronze Age (3000–1100 B.C.) — see MINOAN, MYCENAEAN; CYCLADIC, HELLADIC
¹ae·ge·ri·id \ēˈjirēəd\ *adj* [NL *Aegeriidae*] **:** of or relating to the Aegeriidae
²aegeriid \"\ *n* -s **:** CLEARWING MOTH
ae·ge·ri·i·dae \ˌējəˈrīəˌdē\ *n pl, cap* [NL, fr. *Aegeria*, type genus (fr. *Aegeria, Egeria*, a nymph, fr. L, fr. Gk *Ēgeria*) + *-idae*] **:** a family of small bright colored moths that resemble wasps and bees — see CLEARWING MOTH
ae·gi·lops \ˈējəˌläps, ˈej-\ *n, cap* [NL, fr. Gk *aigilōps* havergrass, Turkey oak (*Quercus cerris*) — more at OAK] *in some classifications* **:** a genus of grasses sometimes used to include the presumed wild ancestors of domestic wheat which are now usu. placed in the genus *Triticum*
¹ae·gi·ne·tan \ˌējəˈnētᵊn\ *adj, usu cap* [L *Aegineta* native of Aegina (fr. *Aegina*, island in the Saronic gulf off the SE coast of Greece, fr. Gk *Aigina*) + E *-an*] **:** of or relating to the island or ancient Greek state of Aegina or its inhabitants
²aeginetan \"\ *n* -s *cap* [L *Aegineta* inhabitant of Aegina (fr. Gk *Aiginētēs*, fr. *Aigina*) + E *-an*] **:** a native or inhabitant of the island or ancient Greek state of Aegina
aegir *var of* EAGRE
ae·gir·ite \ˈägəˌrīt, ˈējə-\ *also* **ae·gir·ine** \-ˌrēn\ *or* **aegirine-augite** *n, pl* **aegirites** *also* **aegirines** *or* **aegirine-augites** [*aegerite*, modif. (influenced by *-ite*) of G *aegerin*; *aegirine* fr. G *aegirin*, fr. *Aegir*, ancient Scand. sea god (fr. ON *Ægir*) + G *-in* -ine] **:** ACMITE
ae·gis *also* **e·gis** \ˈējəs\ *n, pl* **aegises** *also* **egises** [L, fr. Gk *aigis* goatskin, shield of Zeus, perh. fr. *aig-, aix* goat; akin to Arm *aic* goat, Av *izaēna* leathern] **1 :** a shield or breastplate emblematic of majesty that was orig. associated chiefly with the god Zeus but later, bordered with serpents and set with a Gorgon's head, associated mainly with the goddess Athena **2 a :** PROTECTION, DEFENSE ⟨the unfailing ~ of the law⟩ **b :** a set of favorable circumstances ⟨to live under the ~ of complete toleration and understanding⟩ **c :** controlling or conditioning influence ⟨literary activity under the ~ of symbolism —Carlos Lynes⟩ **3 a :** patronage, backing, or sponsorship esp. when afforded by a notable or authoritative organization, group, or individual **:** AUSPICES ⟨collective action under the ~ of the United Nations —J.S.Dickey⟩ **b :** LEADERSHIP ⟨the country rallying under the ~ of the prince⟩ **c :** control, guidance, or direction esp. as afforded by an organization, group, individual, system, or doctrine of notable or authoritative influence ⟨under the ~ of the government —R.A.Tybout⟩
ae·gi·tha·los \ˌējəˈthäˌläs, -ləs\ *n, cap* [NL, fr. Gk *aigithallos, aigithalos* titmouse] **:** a genus of titmice with very long tail feathers — see LONG-TAILED TIT
ae·gi·thin·i·dae \ˌējəˈthinəˌdē\ *n pl, cap* [NL, fr. *Aegithina*, type genus (fr. Gk *aigithos*, a kind of bird, perh. the linnet + NL *-ina*) + *-idae*] **:** a family of brightly colored passerine birds of the Oriental region that have stocky legs and curved bills and feed on fruits or insects — see IRENA
ae·gle \ˈē(ˌ)glē, ˈe-\ *n, cap* [NL, prob. fr. L, one of the Hesperides (nymphs who guarded the golden apples), fr. Gk *Aiglē*, lit., brightness; prob. fr. the apple-shaped fruit] **:** a genus of thorny trees (family Rutaceae) of tropical Asia and western Africa with compound leaves, greenish white flowers, and orangelike fruits — see BEL
ae·go·li·us \ēˈgōlēəs\ *n, cap* [NL, fr. L *aegolios*, an owl, fr. Gk *aigōlios*] **:** a genus of small northern owls including the saw-whet owl
ae·go·po·di·um \ˌēgəˈpōdēəm\ *n, cap* [NL, fr. Gk *aig-, aix* goat + NL *-o-* + *-podium*; prob. fr. the shape of the leaflets] **:** a small genus of herbs (family Umbelliferae) native to the north temperate zone with compound leaves, white flowers, and smooth 5-angled fruits — see GOUTWEED
ae·gro·tat \ēˈgrōˌtat, ˈēgrō-\ *n* -s [L, he is ill, 3d pers. sing. pres. indic. act. of *aegrotare* to be ill, fr. *aegr-, aeger* ill; akin to Toch A *ekro* ill, Toch B *aikre, aikare*, and perh. to OE *ācol* dismayed, Norw *eikla, eikla* to plague, pester, Alb *kë-ëk* evil, and perh. to OE *inca* suspicion, doubt, quarrel — more at INKLING] **1** *Brit* **:** a medical certificate testifying that a student is ill and unable to attend his lectures or examinations **2** *Brit* **:** the unclassified university degree granted to a candidate who is prevented by illness from attending examinations
ae·gy·pi·i·dae \ˌējəˈpīəˌdē\ *n pl, cap* [NL, fr. *Aegypius*, type genus (fr. Gk *aigypios* vulture) + *-idae*] *in some classifications* **:** a family (order Falconiformes) comprising the Old World vultures all with naked heads and longer wings and smaller tails than the typical eagles
ae·gyp·tia·nel·lo·sis \ēˌjipshə(ˌ)neˈlōsəs\ *n, pl* **aegyptianel·lo·ses** \-ōˌsēz\ [NL, fr. *Aegyptianella* (genus name of *Aegyptianella pullorum*, irreg. fr. L *Aegyptius* Egyptian + NL *-ella*) + *-osis* — more at EGYPTIAN] **:** a disease of domestic fowls marked by fever, anemia, jaundice, and typhoidlike symptoms and caused by a protozoan (*Aegyptianella pullorum*) related to the piroplasms and transmitted by the chicken tick esp. in the Mediterranean region
ae·gyp·til·la \ˌējəpˈtilə\ *n* -s [L, a gem formerly found in Egypt, fr. *Aegyptus* Egypt + L *-illa*, dim. suffix] **:** a gem produced from a 2-layered agate usu. cut so that one color is encircled by the other
aelodicon *var of* AEOLODICON
aelur- *or* **aeluro-** — see AILUR-
ae·lu·roid \ēˈlu̇ˌrȯid\ *n* -s *often cap* [NL *Aeluroidea*] **:** one of the Aeluroidea
ae·lu·roi·dea \ˌēl(y)əˈrȯidēə, ˌelyə-\ *n pl, cap* [NL, fr. *aelur-* + *-oidea*] **:** a superfamily of Carnivora comprising the cats, civets, hyenas, and related carnivorous mammals all distinguished from related forms by skull formations and by the absence or great reduction of the penis bone and Cowper's glands
aelurophile *var of* AILUROPHILE
aelurophobia *var of* AILUROPHOBIA
ae·lu·rop·o·dous \ˌēl(y)əˈräpədəs, ˌelyə-\ *adj* [*aelur-* + *-podous*] **:** having feet with retractile claws (like those of a cat)
ae·lu·ro·pus \ēˈlu̇rəpəs\ [NL, fr. *aelur-* + *-pus*] *syn of* AILUROPODA
ae·lu·rus \-rəs\ *syn of* AILURUS
-aemia — see -EMIA
ae·mu·la·tio vi·ci·ni \ˌīmüˈlädēˌōwəˈkē(ˌ)nē\ *n, pl* **aemulati·o·nes vicini** \-ˌläd·ēˈō(ˌ)nāsw-\ [L, malevolence or jealousy of a neighbor] *civil & Scots law* **:** the exercise of a legal right only to cause annoyance, harm, or injury to another
aen *abbr* [L *aeneus, aenus* — more at AENEOUS] of copper or bronze
aen·ach *or* **aon·ach** \ˈānək, -əḵ\ *n* -s [IrGael, fr. OIr *óenach*, lit., reunion, fr. *óen* one; akin to OE *ān* one — more at ONE] **:** an assembly in ancient Ireland for the promulgation of laws and for athletic contests
a end \ˈāˌend\ *n, usu cap A* **:** the end of a railway freight or passenger car opposite the end where the handbrake is located
ae·ne·o·lith·ic \āˌēnēōˈlithik\ *or* **ene·o·lith·ic** \ˈēn-\ *adj, usu cap* [L *aeneus* of copper or bronze + E *-o-* + *-lithic*] **:** of or belonging to a transitional period between the Neolithic and Bronze ages in which some copper was used
ae·ne·ous *also* **ae·ne·us** \āˈēnēəs\ *adj* [L *aeneus* of bronze, of copper, alter. of *aenus*, fr. *aes* bronze, copper — more at ORE] **:** like brass in color and luster **:** greenish gold ⟨~ beetles⟩
aenigma *var of* ENIGMA
aenigmatite *var of* ENIGMATITE
¹ae·o·li·an \ēˈōlēən, -lyən\ *adj, usu cap* [*Aeolis, Aeolia*, ancient country in Asia Minor (fr. L, fr. Gk *Aiolis*) + E *-an*] **1 :** of or relating to Aeolis or Aeolia, colonized by the Aeolians **2 :** of or relating to the inhabitants of Aeolis or Aeolia
²aeolian \"\ *n* -s *cap* **1 :** a member of a group of Greek

peoples that in early prehistoric times was settled in Thessaly and Boeotia, occupied some parts of the Peloponnesus before the Achaeans, and colonized Lesbos and the adjacent coast of Asia Minor **2 :** AEOLIC

³aeolian \"\ *adj* [*Aeolus*, god of the winds (fr. L, fr. Gk *Aiolos*) + E *-ian*] **1** *often cap* **:** of or relating to Aeolus **2 :** giving forth or marked by a soughing sound or musical tone produced by or as if by the wind ⟨trees with voices ~ —Richard Realf⟩

⁴aeolian *var of* EOLIAN

aeolian attachment *n* [³*Aeolian*] **:** a contrivance attached to a piano that prolongs vibrations and increases volume of sound by forcing a stream of air upon the strings

aeolian harp *n, sometimes cap A* [³*Aeolian*] **:** a box-shaped musical instrument having stretched strings usu. tuned in unison on which the wind produces varying harmonics over the same fundamental tone

ae·o·li·an·ly *adv* [³*Aeolian* + *-ly*] **:** with a soughing sound or musical tone produced by or as if by the wind ⟨distant voices humming ~ in the summer night⟩

aeolian minor scale *n, sometimes cap A* [¹*Aeolian*] **:** NATURAL MINOR SCALE

aeolian mode *n, sometimes cap A* [¹*Aeolian*] **:** an authentic ecclesiastical mode consisting of a pentachord and an upper conjunct tetrachord represented on the white keys of the piano by an ascending diatonic scale from A to A — see MODE illustration

¹ae·ol·ic \ē'älik\ *adj, usu cap* [L *Aeolicus*, fr. Gk *Aiolikos*, fr. *Aiolis* Aeolia + Gk *-ikos* -ic] **:** ¹AEOLIAN

²aeolic \"\ *n* -s *cap* **:** a group of dialects of ancient Greek used by the Aeolians

³aeolic \"\ *adj, usu cap* [L *Aeolicus*, lit., of Aeolia] **:** of or relating to lyric rhythms marked by isosyllabic balance and combination of dactyls and trochees with frequent variation or of tetrasyllabic units (as choriambs) — compare LOGAOEDIC, POLYSCHEMATIST DIMETER

ae·o·lid \'ēələd\ *n* -s [NL *Aeolid-, Aeolis*] **:** a nudibranch mollusk of the genus *Aeolis*

ae·o·lid·i·dae \,ēə'lidə,dē\ *n pl, cap* [NL, fr. *Aeolid-, Aeolis*, type genus + *-idae*] **:** a family that is made up of nudibranchs that have many nematocysts obtained from the hydroids on which they feed and that is sometimes placed with related families in a superfamily (Aeolidoidea)

aeo·light \'ēə,līt\ *n* [perh. fr. Gk *aiolos* quick-moving, glittering + E *light*] **:** a gas-discharge glow lamp which is used in optical sound recording and the luminous intensity of which can be varied by varying the terminal voltage

ae·o·line \'ēə,līn\ *also* **ae·o·li·na** \,ēə'līnə, -lē-\ *n* -s [*Aeolus*, god of winds + E *-ine, -ina* — more at AEOLIAN] **1 a :** a very soft organ stop of mild string quality — called also *aeolodicon* **b :** a soft free-reed stop in a European organ **2 :** a mouth harmonica

ae·ol·i·pile *also* **ae·ol·i·pyle** *or* **eol·i·pile** \ē'älə,pīl\ *n* -s [L & Gk; L *aeolipila*, by folk etymology (influence of L *pila* ball) fr. Gk *aiolipylē*, *Aiolon pylē*, fr. *aioli-* (fr. *Aiolos*, god of wind) or *Aiolon* (gen. of *Aiolos*) + *pylē* gate — more at PYLON] **:** an apparatus that was invented in the 2d century B.C. and is often called the first steam engine and that consisted essentially of a closed vessel (as a globe or cylinder) with one or more projecting bent tubes out of which steam is made to pass from the vessel, the action of the steam jets causing it to revolve

aeolipile

ae·o·lis \'ēələs\ *n, cap* [NL, irreg. fr. Gk *aiolos* quick-moving] **:** a genus (the type of the family Aeolididae) comprising nudibranch mollusks with an elongated sluglike body and a series of tufts of fingerlike gills, often brightly colored, along each side of the back

ae·o·lism \'ēə,lizəm\ *also* **ae·ol·i·cism** \ē'älə,sizəm\ *n* -s *usu cap* [²*Aeolian* or *Aeolic* + *ism*] **:** an idiom or peculiarity of the Aeolic dialect

ae·o·lod·i·con \,ēə'lädəkən\ *also* **ae·lod·i·con** \ē'lä-\ *or* **ae·o·lo·di·on** \,ēə'lōdēən\ *n* -s [*Aeolus* + *melodicon* or *melodion*] **1 :** a keyboard wind musical instrument similar to the harmonium **2 :** AEOLINE

ae·o·lo·me·lod·i·con \,ēə(,)lōmə'lädəkən\ *n* -s [*aeolo-* (fr. *Aeolus*) + *melodicon*] **:** an aeolodicon with tube resonators attached to the reeds

ae·o·lo·so·ma \,ēələ'sōmə\ *n, cap* [NL, fr. Gk *aiolos* quick-moving, glittering + NL *-soma*] **:** a nearly cosmopolitan genus (the type of the family Aeolosomatidae) comprising minute aquatic oligochaete worms with large prostomia and usu. with bright-colored oil globules in the integument — **ae·o·lo·so·ma·tid** \¦==='sōmətəd\ *adj or n* — **ae·o·lo·so·mid** \¦==='sōməd\ *adj or n*

ae·o·lo·trop·ic *also* **eo·lo·trop·ic** \¦ēəlō¦träpik\ *adj* **:** ANISOTROPIC 1

ae·o·lot·ro·py *also* **eo·lot·ro·py** \,ēə'lä·trəpē\ *n* -ES [Gk *aiolos* + E *-tropy*] **:** ANISOTROPY

ae·on *or* **eon** \'ēən, 'ē,än\ *n* -s [L *aeon*, fr. Gk *aiōn* age, lifetime — more at AYE] **1 :** an immeasurably or indefinitely long period of time **:** AGE ⟨the obscure ~s of prehistory⟩ **2** *in Gnosticism esp as taught by the Valentinians* **:** one of the group of eternal beings that together form the fullness of the supreme being from whom they emanate and between whom and the world they are intermediaries **3** *usu eon* **:** any large part of geological time usu. longer than an era **syn** see PERIOD

ae·o·ni·an *also* **eo·ni·an** \ē'ōnēən, -nyən\ *or* **ae·o·ni·al** \-ēəl, -yəl\ *or* **ae·on·ic** \(')ē¦änik\ *adj* **:** lasting for an immeasurably or indefinitely long period of time ⟨the ~ ages preceding our present universe⟩

ae·pi·or·nis \,ēpē'ȯrnəs\ *syn of* AEPYORNIS

ae·pyc·er·os \ē'pisərəs\ *n, cap* [NL, fr. MGk *aipykerōs* high-horned, fr. Gk *aipys* high + *-kerōs* (fr. *keras* horn)] **:** a genus of large African antelopes having the horns lyrate in the male — see IMPALA

ae·py·or·nis \,ēpē'ȯrnəs\ *n* [NL, fr. Gk *aipys* + NL *-ornis*] **1** *cap* **:** a genus (the type of the family Aepyornithidae coextensive with the order Aepyornithiformes of the superorder Palaeognathae) of gigantic ratite birds known only from remains found in Madagascar though believed to have survived into historic times and to have been the source of legends about the roc **2** -ES **:** a bird of the genus *Aepyornis* or the order Aepyornithiformes

aeq *abbr* [L *aequalis* — more at EQUAL] equal

aequator *archaic var of* EQUATOR

ae·qui \'ē,kwī, 'ī,kwē\ *or* **ae·quic·u·li** \ē'kwikyə,lī\ *n pl, cap* [L] **:** a people of ancient Latium east of Rome

aequi- — see EQUI-

¹ae·qui·an \'ēkwēən\ *adj, usu cap* [*Aequi* + *-an*] **1 :** of, relating to, or characteristic of the Aequi people **2 :** of, relating to, or characteristic of the Aequian language

²aequian \"\ *n* -s *usu cap* **1 :** a member of the Aequi people **2 :** the language of the Aequi people

ae·qui·dens \'ēkwə,denz, 'ek-\ *n, cap* [NL, fr. *aequi-* + L *dens* tooth — more at TOOTH] **:** a genus of small bright-colored So. American cichlid fishes including several species popular in the tropical aquarium — see BLUE ACARA

ae·quo·rea \ē'kwōrēə\ *n, cap* [NL, fr. L, fem. of *aequoreus* of the sea, fr. *aequor* sea, even surface, fr. *aequus* even, equal — more at EQUAL] **:** a cosmopolitan genus (the type of the family Aequoridae) of brilliantly luminescent hydrozoan jellyfish of moderate size

aer \'ā̇ə(r)\ *n* -s [MGk *aēr*, fr. Gk, air — more at AIR] **:** a large veil used in the Eastern Church to cover either the chalice or the paten

aer- *or* **aero-** *comb form* [ME *aero-*, fr. MF, fr. L, fr. Gk *aer-*, *aero-*, fr. *aer-*, *aēr* — more at AIR] **1 a :** air **:** atmosphere **:** aerial ⟨*aerate*⟩ ⟨*aerenchyma*⟩ ⟨*aerobic*⟩ **b :** aerial and ⟨*aerohydrous*⟩ **2 :** gas ⟨*aerometry*⟩ ⟨*aerosol*⟩ **3 :** aviation ⟨*aerodrome*⟩ ⟨*aerotechnical*⟩

aera *archaic var of* ERA

aer·ate \'a(ə),rāt, 'e(ə),-, 'aa(ə),-, 'āə,-; *chiefly substand* 'arē,āt *or* 'erē- *or* 'aarē- *or* 'ārē-; *usu* -ād·+V\ *vb* -ED/-ING/-S [*aer-* + *-ate*] *vt* **1 :** to supply (the blood) with oxygen by respiration **2 a :** to expose to air by passing air through (as an aquarium) **:** AERIFY **:** cause air to bubble through **b :** to introduce air into (a liquid) by stirring, spraying, or some similar method **c :** to supply or impregnate with air (as soil or sand) **d :** to expose to or as if to fresh air **:** VENTILATE, AIR ⟨a well-*aerated* room⟩ **3 a :** to combine or charge with gas, sometimes carbon dioxide **:** cause a gas to bubble through **b :** to make effervescent or sparkling ⟨*aerated* his writing with a persuasive colloquialism —H.T.Moore⟩ ⟨a kind of purposely clumsy charm, set off by *aerated* lyricism —*Atlantic*⟩ ~ *vi* **:** to be in a situation or condition that permits sufficient exposure to or adequate circulation of air ⟨the potatoes were set outside to ~⟩

aerated bread *n* **:** bread raised by introducing carbon dioxide into the water used for the dough

aerated water *n, chiefly Brit* **:** any water artificially impregnated with a large amount of gas (as carbon dioxide)

aer·a·tion \a(ə)'rāshən *etc (see* AERATE*)*; *chiefly substand* ,arē'ā- *etc*\ *n* -s **1 :** the act or process of aerating or the state of being aerated **:** exposure to air **2 :** the process of discharging hot milk or cream through one or more vacuum chambers of a vacuum pasteurizer for elimination of undesirable flavors followed by passage over a surface cooler

aer·a·tor \'a(ə),rād·ə(r) *etc (see* AERATE*)*, -ātə-; *chiefly substand* 'arē,ā- *etc*\ *n* -s **:** one that aerates: as **a :** any specialized apparatus for aerating a liquid, esp. water or milk **b :** a fumigator used to bleach grain, destroying fungi and insects **c :** a device with a roller equipped with hollow tines that remove cores of soil from turf

aerator c

aer·en·chy·ma \(,)a(ə)'reŋkəmə, |e(ə)-,|aa(ə)-,|āə-, -enk-\ *n* -s [NL, fr. *aer-* + *-enchyma*] **:** any of various tissues with large intercellular spaces; *specif* **:** the spongy modified cork tissue characteristic of many aquatic plants that develops large intercellular spaces as a result of elongation of certain cells and that facilitates gaseous exchange and maintains buoyancy

aeri- *comb form* [LL *aeri-*, fr. L *aer* — more at AIR] **:** air ⟨*aeriform*⟩ ⟨*aerify*⟩

¹aer·i·al \'a|rēəl, 'e|, 'aa|, 'ā| *also* ā'i| *or* ā'ē| *or* ā'e|\ *adj* [L *aerius* (fr. Gk *aerios*, fr. *aer-, aēr* air) + E *-al* — more at AIR] **1 a :** of or belonging to the air or atmosphere ⟨vast ~ gulfs —J.C.Powys⟩ **b :** consisting of air ⟨~ particles⟩ **c** (1) **:** existing in the air **:** moving through the air ⟨~ spirits⟩ (2) **:** existing, forming, or growing in the air rather than in the ground or in water ⟨~ plants⟩ **d :** found, placed, or suspended in the air ⟨an ~ supply of oxygen⟩ ⟨~ germicides⟩ **e :** produced by or performed in the air ⟨~ oxidation⟩ ⟨a hummingbird moving about in an ~ dance among the flowers —W.H.Hudson †1922⟩ **f :** rising high in the air **:** LOFTY ⟨~ spires⟩ **g :** operating or operated overhead on elevated cables or rails ⟨~ conveyors for transportation of raw materials⟩ ⟨an ~ railway⟩ **2 a :** resembling or suggestive of air: as (1) **:** THIN, ATTENUATED **:** lacking substance ⟨fine and ~ distinctions⟩ (2) **:** IMAGINARY, ETHEREAL, IDEAL ⟨visions of ~ joy —P.B.Shelley⟩ (3) **:** clear as air **:** LUCID ⟨compare the ~ texture of his essay with the . . . darkness of the original sources —John Russell⟩ **b :** representative of the effect of atmosphere **:** ATMOSPHERIC ⟨the principal charm of all Italian scenery, its graceful outlines and much of its delicate ~ tints —Norman Douglas⟩ **3 a :** of or relating to aircraft ⟨~ navigation⟩ **b :** designed for use in, taken from, or operating from or against aircraft ⟨~ camera⟩ ⟨~ photo⟩ ⟨~ gun⟩ **c :** by means of aircraft ⟨documents . . . for ~ transmission to the headquarters —*Punch*⟩ **4 :** using or resulting from a forward pass in football ⟨some fine ~ work⟩ ⟨an ~ attack that led . . . to their 27–20 victory —*N.Y. Times*⟩ — **aer·i·al·ly** \-ēəlē, -i\ *adv*

²aerial \"\ *n* -s **1 :** ANTENNA 3 **2 :** AERIAL LADDER **3 :** FORWARD PASS

aerial blue *n* **:** a delicate monochrome faïence ware having blue designs on a grayish ground

aerial bomb *n* **:** a bomb designed to be dropped from an aircraft

aerial cascade *n* **:** a swift wind passing down the side of a hill or mountain above surface eddies roughly following the major contours of the land

aerial drainage *n* **:** the downslope flow of surface air caused by its relatively high density produced by contact cooling, esp. prevalent on still clear nights in hilly or mountainous terrain

aerial farming *n* **:** the use of aircraft for seeding or for applying chemicals for weed or pest control

aerial funicular *n* **:** FUNICULAR RAILWAY; *esp* **:** one in which the cars are suspended from pulleys that run on an overhead cable

aerial gunner *n* **:** a gunner on an airplane **:** one qualified to fly as a gunner on a combat flight crew

aer·i·al·ist \-ləst\ *n* -s [¹*aerial* + *-ist*] **:** one that performs feats in the air or above the ground; *specif* **:** an entertainer on the flying trapeze

aer·i·al·i·ty \,=ē'aləd·ē, =ˈ=ē-\ *n* -ES **:** the quality or state of being aerial **:** UNSUBSTANTIALITY

aerial ladder *n* **:** a mechanically operated extensible fire ladder usu. mounted on a truck

aerial mine *n* **1 :** a mine designed to be dropped from the air esp. into water **2 :** a large light-case bomb dropped by parachute — called also *land mine*

aerial observation *n* **:** AIR OBSERVATION

aerial perspective *n* **1 :** the expression of space in painting by gradation of color or distinctness **2 :** the diminution of clarity of outline and intensity of color in a distant object as distance increases **:** the optical effect produced by diffusion of light whereby objects appear lighter in tone the farther away they are viewed

aerial photograph *n* **:** a photograph taken from an aircraft — **aerial photography** *n*

aerial potato *n* **:** a small tuber produced in the axil of a potato leaf

aerial root *n* **:** any root exposed to the air; *esp* **:** one of the roots found in epiphytes and climbers not in contact with the soil but usu. anchoring the plant to its support and often functioning in photosynthesis — compare PROP ROOT; see ROOT illustration

aerial survey *n* **:** a survey utilizing aerial photographs

aerial torpedo *n* **1 :** an explosive projectile fired from a trench mortar **2 :** a torpedo designed for launching from an airplane **3 :** a heavy aerial bomb **4 :** a guided missile capable of powered flight

aer·i·an \ā'irēən\ *n* -s *usu cap* [*Aerius* of Pontus, 4th cent. A.D. presbyter in Asia Minor + E *-an*] **:** one of a 4th century A.D. Arian sect that believed in the equality of bishops and priests and repudiated prayers for the dead and compulsory fasts

aer·i·des \'a(a)rə,dēz, ā'er-\ *n, cap* [NL, fr. *aer-* + L *-ides* (patronymic suffix) — more at -IDAE] **:** a genus of epiphytic orchids natives of tropical Asia having stiff 2-ranked leaves and white flowers in lateral clusters

ae·rie \'a(ə)rē, 'e(ə)-, 'i(ə)-,'a(ə)-, 'ērē, -ri\ *or* **ey·rie** \", 'īr-\ *or* **aery** *like* AERIE\ *n, pl* **aeries** *or* **eyries** [ML *aeria, aerea*, fr. OF *aire*, fr. L *area* open space, feeding place for animals — more at AREA] **1 :** the nest of a bird (as an eagle or hawk) on a cliff or a mountaintop **2** *obs* **:** a brood of birds, esp. birds of prey **3 :** a house or a dwelling or other quarters placed high up

aer·if·er·ous \(')a(ə)¦rif(ə)rəs, -e(ə)-,-aa(ə)-,-āə-\ *adj* [*aer-* + *-i-* + *-ferous*] **:** containing or conveying air

aer·i·fi·ca·tion \,arəfə'kāshən, ,er-, ,aar-, ,ār- *also* ā,er-\ *n* -s **1 :** the act of aerifying or of aerating **:** the state of being aerified or aerated **2 :** atomization of fuel oil

Aer·i·fi·er \'arə,fī(ə)r *etc (see* AERIFY*)*\ *trademark* — used for a machine used to dig or punch holes in sod to permit free movement of air

aer·i·form \-,fȯrm\ *adj* [*aer-* + *-iform*] **1 :** having the nature of air **:** GASEOUS **2 :** lacking substance or real existence **:** INTANGIBLE ⟨figures light and ~ come unlooked for and melt away —Thomas Carlyle⟩

aer·i·fy \'arə,fī, 'er-,'ā(ə)r-,ā'er-\ *vt* -ED/-ING/-ES [*aer-* + *-ify*] **1 :** to infuse or force air into **:** AERATE 2 **2 :** to change into an aeriform state **:** VAPORIZE

aer·i·ly \'a(ə)rəlē, 'er-,'ār-, -li\ *adv* [*aery* + *-ly*] **:** in an aery manner

aero \'a(ə)(,)rō, 'e(ə)-,'aa(ə)-,'āə-, *chiefly substand* 'arē(,)ō *or* 'erē- *or* 'aarē- *or* 'ārē-\ *adj* [*aer-*] **:** of or relating to aircraft or aeronautics ⟨~ club⟩ ⟨~ engine⟩ **:** designed for aerial use esp. in aerial photography ⟨~ lens⟩

aero- *in pronunciations below*, ¦=(=)= = ¦arə *or* ¦erə *or* ¦aarə *or* -rō *also* ¦aərə *or* ¦eə- *or* ¦aaə- *or* ¦āə- *or* -ə(,)rō, *chiefly substand* ¦arēə *or* ¦erēə *or* ¦aarēə *or* ¦ārēə *or* -rē(,)ō; =(=)ˈ= = (,)a(ə)¦rä *or* ,(,)e(ə)- *or* (,)aa(ə)- *or* ,āə-, *chiefly substand* ,arē¦ä *or* ,erē- *or* ,aarē- *or* ,ārē-\ — see AER-

aero·ba·cil·lus \¦=(=)=-\ *n, cap* [NL, fr. *aer-* + *bacillus*] *in some classifications* **:** a genus of bacteria (family Bacillaceae) including forms usu. placed in *Bacillus* but in some morphological and physiological characters resembling members of *Clostridium*

aero·bac·ter \'=(=)=,baktə(r)\ *n* [NL, fr. *aer-* + *-bacter*] **1** *cap* **:** a genus of aerobic gram-negative bacteria (family Enterobacteriaceae) producing acid and gas from many sugars (as dextrose and lactose), forming acetylmethylcarbinol, and being widely distributed in nature (as in feces, soil, water, and the contents of human and animal intestines) and often concerned in the natural souring of milk **2** -s **:** a bacterium of the genus *Aerobacter*

aero·bac·te·ri·ol·o·gy \¦=(=)=-\ *n* [*aer-* + *bacteriology*] **:** the branch of aerobiology that is concerned with the bacteria of the air

aero·bal·lis·tics \¦=(=)=-\ *n pl but sing in constr* [*aer-* + *ballistics*] **:** the study of the effects of aerodynamic forces upon the flight of missiles and projectiles

aero·bat·ic \¦=(=)=¦bad·ik\ *adj* [prob. back-formation fr. *aerobatics*] **:** of or relating to aerobatics **:** marked by, engaging in, or suitable for aerobatics

aero·bat·ics \,=(=)=ˈ=iks\ *n pl but sing in constr* [blend of *aer-* and *acrobatics*] **:** spectacular flying feats and evolutions (as rolls and dives); *also* **:** flying specializing in such performances

aer·obe \'a(ə),rōb, 'e(ə)-,'aa(ə)-,'āə-\ *n* -s [F *aérobie*, fr. *aér-* + *-bie* (fr. Gk *bios* life) — more at QUICK] **:** an organism that lives only in the presence of oxygen; *esp* **:** one of certain bacteria — compare ANAEROBE

aerobia *pl of* AEROBIUM

aer·o·bic \¦=(=)¦rōbik, -ēk\ *adj* [*aer-* + *bi-* + *-ic*] **1 :** living or active only in the presence of oxygen **2 :** taking place in the presence of oxygen **:** OXIDATIVE ⟨~ glycolysis⟩ **3** [*aerobe* + *-ic*] **:** of, relating to, or induced by aerobes ⟨~ fermentation⟩ — **aer·o·bi·cal·ly** \-ək(ə)lē, -ēk-, -li\ *adv*

aero·bi·o·log·i·cal \¦=(=)=,bīə¦l-\ *also* **aero·bi·o·log·ic** *adj* **:** belonging to, relating to, or for the purposes of aerobiology — **aero·bi·o·log·i·cal·ly** *adv*

aero·bi·ol·o·gy \¦=(=)=,-\ *n* [*aer-* + *biology*] **:** the branch of biology that deals with the occurrence, transportation, and effects of airborne microorganisms or biological objects (as viruses, pollen, or plant spores)

aero·bi·o·scope \¦=(=)=ˈbīə,skōp\ *n* [*aer-* + *bi-* + *-scope*] **:** an apparatus used to collect air for determination of its bacterial count

aero·bi·o·sis \¦=(=)=,bī'ōsəs\ *n, pl* **aerobioses** \-ō,sēz\ [NL, fr. *aer-* + *-biosis*] **:** life in the presence of air or oxygen

aero·bi·ot·ic \¦=(=)=,bī¦ä-\ *adj* [*aer-* + *-biotic*] **:** living only in the presence of free oxygen — **aero·bi·ot·i·cal·ly** *adv*

aero·bi·um \(,)a(ə)'rōbēəm, -e(ə)-,-aa(ə)-,-āə-\ *n, pl* **aero·bia** \-bēə\ [NL, modif. of F *aérobie* — more at AEROBE] **:** AEROBE

aero·cam·era \¦=(=)=-\ *n* [*aer-* + *camera*] **:** a camera specially designed for aerial photography

aero·car·to·graph \¦=(=)=-\ *n* [*aer-* + *cartograph*] **:** an apparatus for making contour maps from aerial photographs

aero·chem·i·cal \¦=(=)=¦-\ *adj* [*aer-* + *chemical*] **:** utilizing the projection of chemical warfare agents by aircraft ⟨an ~ attack⟩

aero·chlo·rin·a·tion \¦=(=)=-\ *n* [*aer-* + *chlorination*] **:** the treatment of sewage with compressed air and chlorine gas for removal of fatty matter

aero·craft \'=(=)=,-\ *n* [by alter.] **:** AIRCRAFT

Aero·crete \'=(=)=,krēt\ *trademark* — used for a lightweight concrete

aer·odon·tal·gia \a(ə),rō,dän'talj(ē)ə, ¦e(ə)-,aa(ə)-,¦āə-\ *n* -s [NL, fr. *aer-* + *odontalgia* toothache, fr. *odont-* + *-algia*] **:** the toothache resulting from atmospheric decompression (as in high-altitude flying or confinement in decompression chambers) — **aer·odon·tal·gic** \-¦taljik\ *adj*

aer·odon·tia \-rō'dänch(ē)ə\ *n* -s [NL, fr. *aer-* + *-odontia*] **:** the branch of dentistry associated with dental problems arising in connection with flying

aero·drome \'=(=)=,drōm\ *n* -s [*aer-* + *-drome*] *Brit* **:** AIRFIELD, AIRPORT

aero·drom·ics \,=(=)=ˈdrämiks\ *n pl but sing in constr* [obs. *aerodrome* airplane (fr. Gk *aerodromos* traversing the air, fr. *aer-* + *-dromos* -drome) + *-ics*] **:** the science or art of flying aircraft

aero·dy·nam·ic \¦=(=)(,)=¦==\ *adj* [back-formation fr. *aerodynamics*] **:** of or relating to aerodynamics — **aero·dy·nam·i·cal·ly** *adv*

aero·dy·nam·i·cist \-,dī'naməsəst, -,də'n-\ *n* -s **:** one who specializes in aerodynamics

aero·dy·nam·ics \¦=(=)=-\ *n pl but sing in constr* [*aer-* + *dynamics*] **:** the branch of dynamics that treats of the motion of air and other gaseous fluids and of the forces acting on bodies in motion relative to such fluids

aero·dyne \'=(=)=,dīn\ *n* -s [*aer-* + *-dyne* (fr. Gk *dynamis* power) — more at DYNAMIC] **:** a heavier-than-air aircraft that derives its lift in flight from aerodynamic forces — compare AEROSTAT

aero·elas·tic \¦=(=)==¦==\ *adj* [*aer-* + *elastic*] **:** subject to stretching or deformity under aerodynamic forces **:** relating to distortion through aerodynamic forces — **aero·elas·tic·i·ty** *n*

aero·em·bo·lism \¦=(=)=-\ *n* [*aer-* + *embolism*] **1 :** a gaseous embolism **2 :** a condition equivalent to caisson disease caused by rapid ascent to high altitudes and resulting exposure to rapidly lowered air pressure — called also *air bends*

aero·fil·ter \'=(=)=,-\ *n* [*aer-* + *filter*] **:** a sewage filter bed that employs coarse material and is operated at relatively high speed often with recirculation

aero·foil \'=(=)=,-\ *chiefly Brit var of* AIRFOIL

aero·gel \'=(=)=,-\ *n* [*aer-* + *gel*] **:** a highly porous solid formed by replacement of liquid in a gel with a gas so that there is little shrinkage — see SILICA AEROGEL; compare XEROGEL

aero·gen·er·a·tor \¦=(=)=¦-\ *n* [*aer-* + *generator*] **:** a wind-driven electric generator designed for utilization of wind power on a commercial scale

aero·gen·ic \¦=(=)=¦jenik\ *or* **aer·og·e·nous** \=(=)'jänəs\ *adj* [*aer-* + *-genic, -genous*] **:** forming gas — **aero·gen·i·cal·ly** \¦=(=)=¦jenək(ə)lē\ *adv*

aero·ge·og·ra·phy \¦=(=)=-\ *n* [*aer-* + *geography*] **1 :** the geography of air bases and air routes **2 :** the study of geographic features by aerial observation and aerophotography

aero·ge·ol·o·gist \¦=(=)=-\ *n* **:** a specialist in aerogeology

aero·ge·ol·o·gy \¦=(=)=-\ *n* [ISV *aer-* + *geology*] **:** the study of geological features by aerial observation and aerophotography

aero·gram \'=(=)=,gram\ *n* [*aer-* + *-gram*] **1 :** a message sent by wireless telegraphy, aircraft, or radio **2** *or* **aero·gramme** \"\ **:** AIR LETTER

aero·graph \'=(=)=,graf\ *n* [*aer-* + *-graph*] **:** METEOROGRAPH 1

¹aer·og·ra·pher \=(=)'grəfə(r)\ *n* -s [*aer-* + *-grapher*] **:** one that sprays with an airbrush

²aerographer \"\ *n* -s [*aerography* + *-er*] **:** a warrant officer in the U.S. Navy whose duties include the observation of weather and the preparation of weather and surf forecasts

aerographer's mate *n* **:** a petty officer in the U.S. Navy assisting or performing the duties of the aerographer

aer·og·ra·phy \=(=)'grəfē\ *n* -ES [*aer-* + *-graphy*] **:** METEOROLOGY

aero·hy·drous \¦=(=)=¦-\ *adj* [*aer-* + *hydrous*] *of minerals* **:** containing both air and water

aer·oi·des \(,)a(ə)'rȯi(,)dēz, -e(ə)-,-aa(ə)-,-āə-\ *n, pl* **aeroides** [Gk *aeroeidēs* like the air or sky, cloudy, fr. *aer-* + *-eidēs* -oid] **:** a pale blue beryl

aero·lite \'=(=)=,līt\ *also* **aero·lith** \'=(=)=,lith\ *n* -s [*aer-* + *-lite, -lith*] **:** a stony meteorite — **aero·lit·ic** \¦=(=)=¦lid·ik\ *adj*

aero·lith·ol·o·gy \¦=(=)=(ˌ)li'thäləjē\ *n* -ES [*aerolith* + *-o-* + *-logy*] **:** the science that deals with meteorites
aero·lit·ics \ˌ=(=)='lid·iks\ *n pl but sing in constr* [*aerolite* + *-ics*] **:** the science that deals with aerolites
aero·log·i·cal \¦=(=)=¦läjəkəl\ *adj* **:** of or relating to aerology
aer·ol·o·gist \=(=)'=ləjəst\ *n* -S **:** a specialist in aerology
aer·ol·o·gy \-əjē\ *n* -ES [*aer-* + *-logy*] **1 :** METEOROLOGY **2 :** the branch of meteorology that deals esp. with the description and discussion of the phenomena of the free air as revealed by kites, balloons, airplanes, and clouds
aero·mag·net·ic \¦=(=)=ˌmag¦n-\ *adj* [*aer-* + *magnetic*] **:** of, relating to, or derived from a study of the terrestrial magnetic field esp. from the air ⟨an ~ survey⟩ ⟨an ~ map⟩
aero·mancy \'=(=)=ˌman(t)sē\ *n* -ES [ME *aeromancie*, alter. (influenced by MF *aeromancie* or ML *aeromantia*) of *aeromaunce*, fr. (assumed) MF *aeromance*, fr. ML *aeromantia*, fr. L *aer-* + *-mantia* -mancy] **:** divination from the state of the air or from atmospheric substances; *also* **:** weather forecasting
aero·ma·rine \¦=(=)=mə¦rēn\ *adj* [*aer-* + *marine*] **:** of or relating to aerial navigation above sea or ocean ⟨under the conditions of ~ combat —Fletcher Pratt⟩
aero·me·chan·ic \¦=(=)=¦=¦==\ *n* -S [*aer-* + *mechanic*] **:** an aircraft mechanic
aero·me·chan·ics \¦=(=)==¦==\ *n pl but sing in constr* [*aer-* + *mechanics*] **:** the branch of mechanics that deals with the equilibrium and motion of gases and of solid bodies immersed in them — compare AERODYNAMICS, AEROSTATICS, PNEUMATICS
aero·med·i·cal \¦=(=)=¦-\ *adj* [*aer-* + *medical*] **:** of or relating to aeromedicine ⟨~ research⟩ ⟨~ laboratory⟩ ⟨~ historical museum⟩
aero·med·i·cine \¦=(=)=¦-\ *n* -S [ISV *aer-* + *medicine*] **:** the branch of medicine that deals with the diseases and disturbances arising from present-day flying and involves the study and solution of resulting physiologic, psychologic, pathologic, and epidemiologic problems
aero·me·te·or·o·graph \¦=(=)=-\ *n* -S [*aer-* + *meteorograph*] **:** METEOROGRAPH; *esp* **:** one adapted for use on an aircraft
aer·om·e·ter \=(=)'=məd·ə(r)\ *n* -S [prob. fr. F *aéromètre*, fr. *aér-* + *-mètre* -meter] **:** an instrument for ascertaining the weight or density of air or other gases
aero·met·ric \¦=(=)=¦me·trik\ *adj* [*aer-* + *-metric*] **:** relating to measurement of the properties or contaminants of air ⟨~ survey⟩
aero·mo·tor \'=(=)=ˌ-\ *n* [*aer-* + *motor*] **:** an aircraft motor
aero·naut \'=(=)=ˌnȯt, -ät, *usu* -d·+V\ *n* -S [F *aéronaute*, fr. *aéro-* aer- + Gk *nautēs* sailor — more at NAUTICAL] **:** one that operates or travels in an airship or balloon
aero·nau·ti·cal \-ədkəl, -ēk-\ *or* **aero·nau·tic** \¦=(=)=¦nȯ¦d·ik, -näl, ¦tik, -ēk\ *adj* [*aeronautical* fr. *aeronautic* + *-al*; *aeronautic* back-formation fr. *aeronautics*] **:** of or relating to aeronautics — **aero·nau·ti·cal·ly** \-ək(ə)lē, -ēk-, -li\ *adv*
aeronautical station *n* **:** a radio transmitting station usu. on the ground for communication with aircraft — compare AIRCRAFT STATION, LAND STATION
aero·nau·tics \¦=(=)='=iks, -ēks\ *n pl but sing in constr* [modif. (influenced by *-ics*) of NL *aeronautica*, fr. *aer-* + L *nautica*, neut. pl. of *nauticus* nautical — more at NAUTICAL] **1** *archaic* **:** the art or practice of sailing (as in lighter-than-air craft) through the air **2 :** the science that deals with the operation of aircraft **3 :** the art or science of flight
aero·na·val \¦=(=)=¦-\ *adj* [*aer-* + *naval*] **:** of or involving combined air and naval forces ⟨an ~ base⟩ ⟨~ war⟩
aero·neu·ro·sis \¦=(=)=-\ *n* [NL, fr. *aer-* + *neurosis*] **:** a functional nervous disorder of airmen caused by emotional stress and characterized by physical symptoms (as restlessness, pains in the abdomen, and diarrhea)
aero–oti·tis me·dia \¦=(=)=ō'tīd·ə'smēdēə\ *also* **aero–otitis** *or* **aer·oti·tis** \-rō'tīd·əs\ *n* [NL] **:** the traumatic inflammation of the middle ear resulting from differences between atmospheric pressure and pressure in the tympanic cavity and occurring in high-altitude flyers, caisson or tunnel workers, and deep-sea divers
aero·pause \'=(=)=ˌpȯz\ *n* -S [*aer-* + *pause*] **:** the level above the earth's surface where the atmosphere becomes ineffective for human and aircraft functions
aero·pha·gia \ˌ=(=)='fāj(ē)ə\ *also* **aer·oph·a·gy** \=(=)'=fəjē\ *n, pl* **aerophagias** *also* **aerophagies** [NL *aerophagia*, fr. *aer-* + *-phagia* -phagy] **:** the swallowing of air esp. in hysteria
aer·oph·a·gist \=(=)'=fəjəst\ *n* -S **:** one that swallows air
aero·phane \'=(=)=ˌfān\ *n* -S [prob. fr. F *aérophane*, fr. *aér-* aer- + *-phane*] **:** a fine silk gauze
aero·phil·a·tel·ic \¦=(=)=¦==¦==\ *adj* **:** of or relating to airmail stamps and flown covers
aero·phi·lat·e·list \¦=(=)=-\ *n* **:** a specialist in aerophilately
aero·phi·lat·e·ly \¦=(=)=-\ *n* -ES [*aer-* + *philately*] **:** the collection and study of airmail stamps and flown covers
aero·phile \'=(=)=ˌfīl\ *n* -S [*aer-* + *-phile*] **:** a lover of aviation
aero·pho·bia \ˌ=(=)='fōbēə\ *n* -S [NL, fr. *aer-* + *-phobia*] **:** abnormal or excessive fear of drafts or of fresh air — **aero·pho·bic** \¦=(=)=¦fōbik *also* -äb-\ *adj*
aero·phone \'=(=)=ˌfōn\ *n* -S [*aer-* + *-phone*] **:** a musical instrument (as a trumpet or flute) in which sound is generated by a vibrating column or eddy of air **:** WIND INSTRUMENT — **aero·phon·ic** \¦=(=)=¦fänik\ *adj*
aero·phor \'=(=)=ˌfō(ə)r\ *also* **aero·phore** \-ˌfō(ə)r, -ȯ(-\ *n* -S [G *aerophor*, fr. *aer-* + *-phor* -phore] **:** a device employing a foot bellows by means of which a tone may be sustained on a wind instrument for an indefinite period
aero·pho·to \'=(=)=ˌ-\ *n* -S [*aer-* + *photo*] **:** AERIAL PHOTOGRAPH
aero·pho·tog·ra·phy \¦=(=)=-\ *n* -ES [*aer-* + *photography*] **:** photography from aircraft
aero·phys·i·cal \¦=(=)=¦-\ *adj* **:** of or relating to aerophysics
aero·phys·ics \¦=(=)=¦-\ *n pl but sing in constr* [*aer-* + *physics*] **1 :** the physics of the air **2 :** physics dealing with the design, construction, and operation of devices that move rapidly through the air (as projectiles, guided missiles, rockets, and aircraft)
aero·plane \'=(=)=ˌplān, *or like* AIRPLANE\ *chiefly Brit var of* AIRPLANE
aero·pol·i·tics \¦=(=)=¦-\ *n pl but sing in constr* [*aer-* + *politics*] **:** politics as conditioned by considerations of air power ⟨the air future, a primer of ~ —Burnet Hershey⟩
aero·pulse \'=(=)=ˌ-\ *or* **aero·res·o·na·tor** \¦=(=)=¦=ˌ=\ *n* -S [*aer-* + *pulse* or *resonator*] **:** PULSE-JET ENGINE
aero·scep·sis \ˌ=(=)=ˌskepsəs\ *also* **aero·scep·sy** \'=(=)=ˌ=sē\ *n, pl* **aeroscep·ses** \-p(ˌ)sēz\ *also* **aerosceps·ies** \-psēz\ [*aeroscepsis*, NL, fr. *aer-* + Gk *skepsis* perception, consideration; *aeroscepsy*, modif. of NL *aeroscepsis*] **:** the power possessed by certain animals of observing the quality of the air by means of special organs
aero·sid·er·ite \¦=(=)=-\ *n* -S [*aer-* + *siderite*] **:** a meteorite composed chiefly of iron **:** SIDERITE
aero·sid·er·o·lite \¦=(=)=-\ *n* -S [*aer-* + *siderolite*] **:** a meteorite composed of both stone and iron **:** SIDEROLITE
aero·si·nus·i·tis \¦=(=)=-\ *n* [NL, fr. *aer-* + *sinusitis*] **:** the traumatic inflammation of the nasal sinuses resulting from the difference between atmospheric pressure and the pressure within the sinus cavities and occurring in high-altitude flyers, caisson or tunnel workers, or deep-sea divers
aero·sol \'=(=)=ˌsȯl, -ōl\ *n* -S [*aer-* + *sol*] **1 :** a suspension of ultramicroscopic solid or liquid particles in air or gas (as smoke, fog, or mist) **2 a :** a substance and a propellant (as compressed gas) in a container with a valve through which the substance is dispensed as an aerosol; *esp* **:** a liquid containing an active agent (as an insecticide, germicide, medicine, or cosmetic) **b :** a container for this
aerosol bomb *n* **:** a small container for dispensing an aerosol usu. by release of pressure
aero·sol·i·za·tion \ˌ=(=)=ˌsȯlə'zāshən, -sōl-,-säl-, -(ˌ)lī'z-\ *n* -S **:** dispersal (as of a medicine) in the form of an aerosol ⟨~ of penicillin⟩
aero·sol·ize \'=(=)=ˌsȯˌlīz, -sō-,-sä-\ *vt* -ED/-ING/-S **:** to disperse (as a medicine, bactericide, or insecticide) as an aerosol ⟨possible to ~ salt solutions, acids, bases, suspensions and emulsions —*Swiss Industry & Trade*⟩ — **aero·sol·iz·er** \-zə(r)\ *n* -S
aerosol therapy *n* **:** inhalation treatment using medicated aerosols
aero·sphere \'=(=)=ˌ-\ *n* -S [F *aérosphère*, fr. *aér-* aer- + *-sphère* -sphere] **:** the body of air around the earth **:** ATMOSPHERE
aero·stat \'=(=)=ˌstat\ *n* -S [F *aérostat*, fr. *aér-* aer- + *-stat*] **1 :** an aircraft (as a balloon or airship) that embodies one or more containers filled with a gas lighter than air and that is supported chiefly by buoyancy derived from the surrounding air — compare AERODYNE **2 :** either of a pair of pouches located at the base of the abdomen in dipterous flies
¹aero·stat·ic \¦=(=)=¦stad·ik\ *also* **aero·stat·i·cal** \-d·ə̇kəl\ *adj* [*aer-* + *static, statical*] **:** of or relating to aerostatics **:** PNEUMATIC
²aerostatic *also* **aerostatical** \"\ *adj* [F *aérostatique*, fr. *aérostat* + *-ique* -ic, -ical] **:** of or relating to aerial navigation
aero·stat·ics \¦=(=)=¦=iks\ *n pl but sing in constr* [modif. of NL *aerostatica*, fr. *aer-* + *-statica* -statics] **:** the branch of statics that deals with the equilibrium of gaseous fluids and of solid bodies immersed in them
aero·sta·tion \¦=(=)=¦stāshən\ *n* -S [F *aérostation*, irreg. fr. *aérostat* + *-ion*] **:** the art or science of operating lighter-than-air aircraft — compare AVIATION
aero·tac·tic \¦=(=)=¦taktik\ *adj* [fr. NL *aerotaxis*, after such pairs as NL *chemotaxis*: E *chemotactic*] **:** of or relating to aerotaxis
aero·tax·is \ˌ=(=)='taksəs\ *n* [NL, fr. *aer-* + *-taxis*] **:** a taxis in which air or oxygen is the directive factor
aero·tech·ni·cal \¦=(=)=¦-\ *adj* [*aer-* + *technical*] **:** of or relating to aeronautics
aero·ther·a·peu·tics \¦=(=)=-\ *n pl but sing in constr* [*aer-* + *therapeutics*] **:** the treatment of disease by varying pressure or composition of air breathed by the patient
aero·ther·a·py \¦=(=)=¦-\ *n* -ES [*aer-* + *therapy*] **:** AEROTHERAPEUTICS
aero·ther·mo·dy·nam·ics \¦=(=)=-\ *n pl but sing in constr* [*aer-* + *thermodynamics*] **:** the thermodynamics of gases and esp. air
aerotitis *var of* AERO-OTITIS
aer·ot·ro·pism \=(=)'=trəˌpizəm\ *n* -S [*aer-* + *tropism*] **:** response usu. by change in direction of growth of roots or other plant structures to changes in oxygen tension
aers *pl of* AER
ae·ru·gi·nous \ē'rüjənəs, i'-,ī'-\ *also* **e·ru·gi·nous** \ē'-, e'-, i'-\ *adj* [L *aeruginosus*, fr. *aerugin-*, *aerugo* + *-osus* -ous] **:** having the characteristics of or the color of verdigris
ae·ru·go \ē'rü(ˌ)gō, i'-,ī'-\ *n* -S [L, fr. *aer-*, *aes* copper, bronze, brass — more at ORE] **:** the rust of a metal and esp. brass or copper **:** VERDIGRIS
¹aery \'a(ə)rē, 'e¦,'aa¦,'ā¦, -ri\ *adj* [L *aerius*, fr. *aer* air — more at AIR] **:** having an aerial quality **:** ETHEREAL ⟨in ~ vision wrapped —James Thomson †1748⟩
²aery *var of* AERIE
aes *pl of* ¹A
AE's *pl of* AE
aesch·na \'esknə\ *n, cap* [NL, alter. of *Aeshna*] **:** a genus of large often bright-colored dragonflies including the blue darners
aes·chy·le·an \¦eskə¦lēən\ *adj, usu cap* [*Aeschylus* †456 B.C. Greek tragic poet (fr. L, fr. Gk *Aischylos*) + E *-ean*] **:** of, relating to, or suggestive of Aeschylus
aes·chy·nan·thus \ˌeskə'nan(t)thəs\ *n* [NL, fr. Gk *aischynē* shame + NL *-anthus*; fr. the red flowers, thought of as blushing] **1** *cap* **:** a genus of East Indian ornamental woody epiphytic plants (family Gesneriaceae) having red or orange flowers and seeds that bear one bristle or hair at the apex and one or more at the base **2** -ES **:** a plant of the genus *Aeschynanthus*
aeschynite *var of* ESCHYNITE
aes·chy·nom·e·ne \ˌeskə'nämə(ˌ)nē\ *n, cap* [NL, fr. Gk *aischynomenē* sensitive plant, fr. *aischynē* shame + *-menē* (fr. *menos* mind); fr. the fact that the leafstalks droop when touched] **:** a genus of shrubs and herbs (family Leguminosae) widely distributed in warm regions and having jointed pods and pinnate and often sensitive leaves — see SENSITIVE JOINT VETCH, SOLA
aes·cu·la·ce·ae \ˌeskyə'lāsēˌē\ *n pl, cap* [NL, fr. *Aesculus*, type genus + *-aceae*] *in some classifications* **:** a family of shrubs and trees of the order Sapindales that are usu. made a tribe of the family Hippocastanaceae or placed among the Sapindaceae — compare AESCULUS — **aes·cu·la·ceous** \¦==¦shəs\ *adj*
aes·cu·la·pi·an \¦eskyə¦lāpēən\ *adj, usu cap* [*Aesculapius*, the god + E *-an*] **:** of or belonging to Aesculapius or the healing art **:** MEDICAL, MEDICINAL
aesculapian staff *n, usu cap A* **:** STAFF OF AESCULAPIUS
aes·cu·la·pi·us \ˌeskyə'lāpēəs\ *n* -ES *usu cap* [after *Aesculapius*, Greco-Roman god of medicine, fr. L, fr. Gk *Asklēpios*] **:** PHYSICIAN
aesculapius' snake \-ēəs'sn-\ *or* **aesculapian snake** *n, usu cap A* [fr. *Aesculapius*, god of medicine] **:** a harmless European snake (*Coluber*, or *Elaphe*, *longissimus*) believed to have been held sacred to Aesculapius by the Romans
aesculetin *var of* ESCULETIN
aesculin *var of* ESCULIN
aes·cu·lus \'eskyələs\ *n, cap* [NL, fr. L, an oak — more at OAK] **:** a genus of trees and shrubs (family Hippocastanaceae) found in north temperate regions with palmately divided leaves, showy flowers in ample panicles, and large shiny seeds — see BUCKEYE, HORSE CHESTNUT
aes grave \'īs'grä,vā\ *n* [L, lit., heavy bronze] **:** a cumbersome bronze coinage used by the Romans and other Italic peoples and based on the as as unit of value
ae·sir \'āsir, 'aa-, 'ī-\ *n pl, usu cap* [ON *Æsir*, pl. of *āss* god; akin to OE *ōs* god (name of a rune), OS *ās-*, *ōs-* & OHG *ans-* (in proper names), (assumed) Goth *ans* (whence ML *ansis*, acc. pl., demigods), and prob. to Skt *asu* life, vital strength, *asura*, adj. & n., mighty, lord, demon, Av *ahurō* lord] **:** the chief gods of pagan Scandinavia
ae·so·pi·an \ē'sōpēən, -äp-\ *also* **ae·sop·ic** \ē'säpik\ *adj, usu cap* [*Aesop* (fr. L *Aesopus*, fr. Gk *Aisōpos*), legendary 6th cent. B.C. Greek author of fables + E *-ian* or *-ic*] **:** conveying an innocent meaning to an outsider but a concealed meaning to an informed member of a conspiracy or underground movement ⟨*Aesopian* language⟩
ae·sop prawn \'ēˌsäp-, -ˌsəp- *sometimes* 'ā-\ *n, usu cap A* [NL *aesopius*, lit., Aesopian (specific epithet of *Periclimenes aesopius*), fr. L *Aesopus*; fr. the belief that Aesop was humpbacked] **1 :** a small decapod crustacean of the genus *Hippolyte* **2** *Austral* **:** a small humpbacked prawn (*Periclimenes aesopius*)
aes ru·de \'īs'rüˌdā\ *n* [L, lit., crude bronze] **:** ancient money of Rome and Italy having as units rude uncoined masses of bronze
aes sig·na·tum \-ˌsig'näd·əm\ *n* [L, lit., marked bronze] **:** ancient money of Rome and Italy having as unit of exchange a bronze bar and usu. stamped with an animal figure
aesthacyte *var of* ESTHACYTE
aesthesia *var of* ESTHESIA
aesthesio- — see ESTHESIO-
aesthesis *var of* ESTHESIS
aes·thete *also* **es·thete** \'esˌthēt, *usu* -ēd·+V; *Brit usu* 'ēs-\ *n* -S [fr. *aesthetics*, after such pairs as E *athletics*: *athlete*] **:** one professing devotion to the beautiful **:** one having or affecting artistic perception or judgment or of sensitivity to the beautiful esp. in art
aes·thet·ic *or* **es·thet·ic** \es'thed·ik, is-,əs-, -etik, -ēk, *sometimes* 'es,th-, *Brit usu* ēs'-\ *or* **aes·thet·i·cal** *or* **es·thet·i·cal** \-ə̇kəl, -ēk-\ *adj* [G *ästhetisch*, fr. NL *aestheticus*, fr. Gk *aisthētikos* of sense perception — more at AESTHETICS] **1 :** relating to or dealing with aesthetics or its subject matter ⟨~ theories⟩ ⟨~ philosophers⟩ **2 a :** relating to the beautiful as distinguished from the merely pleasing, the moral, and esp. the useful and utilitarian ⟨a purely ~ reaction⟩ ⟨~ criteria⟩ **b :** ARTISTIC ⟨the illustrations made the book an ~ success⟩ **:** BEAUTIFUL **3 :** appreciative of, responsive to, or zealous about the beautiful ⟨an ~ person⟩ ⟨he lived in an ~ age⟩ **:** having a sense, real or affected, of beauty or fine culture **4 :** relating to sensuous cognition: **a :** involving pure feeling or sensation esp. in contrast to ratiocination ⟨the ~ component of knowledge⟩ **b :** based on or derived from immediate esp. sensuous experience ⟨gustatory and tactile ~ delights⟩ ⟨~ feeling⟩ **syn** see ARTISTIC
aes·thet·i·cal·ly *or* **es·thet·i·cal·ly** \-k(ə)lē, -li\ *adv* **:** in an aesthetic way ⟨a happy ending is morally and ~ satisfying —J.C.Bushman⟩
aesthetic distance *n* **:** the frame of reference that an artist creates by the use of technical devices in and around the work of art to differentiate it psychologically from reality
aes·the·ti·cian *also* **es·the·ti·cian** \ˌesthə'tishən, *Brit usu* ˌēs-\ *or* **aes·thet·i·cist** \es'thed·əsə̇st, is-,əs-, -etə-, *Brit usu* ēs-\ *n* -S **:** a specialist in aesthetics
aes·thet·i·cism *also* **es·thet·i·cism** \es'thed·əˌsizəm, is-,əs-, -etə-, *Brit usu* ēs-\ *n* -S **1 a :** the doctrine that the principles of beauty are basic and that other principles (as of the good or the right) are derived from them **b :** the advocacy of artistic and aesthetic autonomy, esp. of freedom of art from any interference on political, religious, social, or moral grounds **2 :** an extensive, singular, or excessive devotion to or emphasis on aesthetic experiences or the search for beauty esp. as evidenced by a cultivation of the arts to the neglect of other human interests
aes·thet·i·cize *also* **es·thet·i·cize** \-ˌsīz\ *vt* -ED/-ING/-S **:** to make aesthetic ⟨remodeled and *aestheticized* the old railroad station⟩
aes·thet·ics *also* **es·thet·ics** \-iks,-ēks\ *n pl but usu sing in constr, also* **aesthetic** *or* **esthetic** [G *ästhetik*, fr. NL *aesthetica*, fr. Gk *aisthētikē*, fem. of *aisthētikos* of sense perception, fr. *aisthanesthai* to perceive — more at AUDIBLE] **1 :** a branch of philosophy dealing with beauty and the beautiful esp. with judgments of taste concerning them: **a :** the science of sensuous knowledge whose goal is beauty — compare LOGIC **b :** TRANSCENDENTAL AESTHETIC **c :** a particular philosophical theory or conception of art ⟨a forward-looking ~⟩ ⟨an ~ of his own⟩ **2 :** the philosophy or science of art; *specif* **:** the science whose subject matter is the description and explanation of the arts, artistic phenomena, and aesthetic experience and includes the psychology, sociology, ethnology, and history of the arts and essentially related aspects
aesthetic truth *n* **:** NORMATIVE TRUTH
aes·thi·ol·o·gy \ˌesthē'äləjē, *Brit usu* ˌēs-\ *n* -ES [irreg. fr. Gk *aisthanesthai* to perceive + E *-logy* — more at AESTHETICS] **:** ESTHESIOPHYSIOLOGY
aes·tho–physiology \¦es(ˌ)thō-, *Brit usu* ¦ēs-\ *n* -ES **:** ESTHESIOPHYSIOLOGY
aes·ti·val *or* **es·ti·val** \'estəvəl, (')es¦tīvəl, *Brit usu* 'ēs-\ *adj* [ME *estival*, fr. MF or L; MF, fr. L *aestivalis*, fr. *aestivus* of summer (fr. *aestas* summer + *-ivus* -ive) + *-alis* -al; akin to L *aedes* temple — more at EDIFY] **:** of or belonging to the summer ⟨the sky was a burnished ~ blue —*Irish Statesman*⟩
aes·ti·vate *or* **es·ti·vate** \'estəˌvāt, *usu* -ād·+V; *Brit usu* 'ēs-\ *vi* -ED/-ING/-S [L *aestivatus*, past part. of *aestivare* to spend the summer, fr. *aestivus*] **1 :** to spend the summer usu. at one place and sometimes in relative inactivity ⟨*aestivating* at his mountain lodge⟩ **2 :** to pass the summer in a state of torpor — used esp. of animals ⟨crabs *aestivating* in the sand⟩; compare HIBERNATE
aes·ti·va·tion *or* **es·ti·va·tion** \ˌ=='vāshən\ *n* -S [L *aestivatus* + E *-ion*] **1 :** the state or condition of torpidity or dormancy induced by heat and dryness of summer (as in certain snails) — opposed to *hibernation* **2 :** the disposition or method of arrangement of floral parts in a bud — compare VERNATION
aes·ti·va·tor *or* **es·ti·va·tor** \'==ˌvād·ə(r)\ *n* -S **:** an animal that aestivates
aestivo–autumnal *var of* ESTIVO-AUTUMNAL
aet *or* **aetat** *abbr* [L *aetatis*, gen. of *aetas* age — more at AGE] of age; aged
ae·ta \'ēd·ə\ *n, pl* **aeta** *or* **aetas** *usu cap* [Tag] **1 :** a Negrito people inhabiting the central and southern Zambales mountains in Zambales, Papanga, and Bataan provinces of the Philippines **2 :** a member of the Aeta people
ae·tha·li·oid \ē'thālēˌȯid\ *adj* [NL ¹*aethalium* + E *-oid*] **:** resembling or belonging to an aethalium
¹ae·tha·li·um \-lēəm,lyəm\ *n, pl* **ae·tha·lia** \-ēə,-yə\ [NL, fr. Gk *aithalos* thick smoke, soot (fr. *aithein* to burn) + NL *-ium* — more at EDIFY] **:** a sessile flat encrusted fruiting body in several genera of the slime molds (class Myxomycetes) formed by the fusion of many plasmodia
²aethalium \"\ [NL] *syn of* FULIGO
aetheling *often cap, var of* ATHELING
aether *var of* ETHER
aethereal *or* **aetherial** *var of* ETHEREAL
aetheria *syn of* ETHERIA
aetheric *var of* ETHERIC
aetherin *var of* ETHERIN
aetherophone *var of* ETHEROPHONE
ae·thi·o·ne·ma \ˌēthēō'nēmə\ *n, cap* [NL, fr. *aethio-* (fr. Gk *aēthēs* strange) + *-nema*] **:** a genus of herbs (family Cruciferae) found in the Mediterranean region that have sessile glaucous leaves, some being cultivated for their white or rose-colored flowers
aethiopian *usu cap, var of* ETHIOPIAN
aethiops *var of* ETHIOPS
ae·thri·o·scope \'ēthrēəˌskōp, 'e-\ *n* [Gk *aithrios* clear + E *-scope*] **:** an instrument consisting in part of a differential thermometer for measuring changes of temperature produced by different conditions of the sky
aetio- — see ETIO-
aetiology *var of* ETIOLOGY
aetioporphyrin *var of* ETIOPORPHYRIN
ae·ti·tes \ˌāə'tīd·(ˌ)ēz\ *n, pl* **aetites** [L, fr. Gk *aetitēs*, fr. *aetitēs*, adj., of an eagle, fr. *aetos*, *aietos* eagle — more at AVIARY] **:** EAGLESTONE
aeto- *comb form* [NL, fr. Gk *aetos*; akin to L *avis* bird — more at AVIARY] **:** eagle ⟨*aetomorph*⟩ ⟨*Aetosaurus*⟩ — esp. in names of taxonomic groups in zoology
aeto·bat·i·dae \ˌāˌed·ə'bad·əˌdē, āˌē-\ [NL, fr. *Aetobatus*, type genus (fr. *aeto-* + Gk *batos*, a fish, prob. a skate) + *-idae*] *syn of* MYLIOBATIDAE
ae·to·li·an \ē'tōlēən, -lyən\ *adj, usu cap* [*Aetolia*, ancient district of Greece (fr. L, fr. Gk *Aitōlia*) + E *-an*] **1 :** of, relating to, or characteristic of Aetolia **2 :** of, relating to, or characteristic of the people of Aetolia
aeto·sau·rus \āˌed·ə'sȯrəs, āˌē-\ *n, cap* [NL, fr. *aeto-* + *-saurus*] **:** a genus of small extinct crocodiles of the Triassic period
-a·e·tus \'ēd·əs, 'āətəs\ *n comb form* [NL, fr. Gk *aetos* — more at AETO-] **:** eagle — in generic names of birds ⟨*Circaetus*⟩
aex \'eks\ *syn of* AIX
af- — see AD-
Af *abbr* Afghani
AF *abbr* **1** [L *actum fide*] done in faith **2** [L *ad finem*] at the end; to the end **3** admiral of the fleet **4** air force **5** [It *al fine*] to the end **6** audio frequency
afaint \ə'-\ *adj* [¹*a-* + *faint* (v.)] **:** FAINTING
afa·lou man \'afəˌlü-\ *n, usu cap A* [fr. *Afalou* bou Rummel, near Bougie, Algeria, where remains were found] **:** one of an Upper Paleolithic people of northern Africa closely related to Cro-Magnon man but having a broader nose, a sloping forehead, and heavy brow ridges
¹afar \ə'fär, -ä(r\ *adv* [ME *afer*, fr. *on fer* at a distance and *of fer* from a distance — more at FAR] **:** from or at a great distance **:** far away ⟨the world of books is something ~ —S.G. Shaw⟩ — often used with *off* ⟨I saw him ~ off⟩
²afar \"\ *n* -S **:** a great distance — usu. used with *from* ⟨saw him from ~⟩
³afar \'äˌfär\ *n, pl* **afar** \"\ *or* **afa·ra** \ə'färə\ *usu cap* **1 :** DANAKIL **2 :** the Cushitic language of the Danakil people — see AFRO-ASIATIC LANGUAGES table
afa·ra \ə'färə\ *n* -S [Yoruba *a²fa³ra³*] **:** ²LIMBA
AFB *abbr* air force base
AFC *abbr* **1** automatic flight control **2** automatic frequency control
¹afear \ə'fi(ə)r\ *vt* [ME *aferen*, fr. OE *āfǣran*, fr *ā-* (perfective prefix) + *fǣran* to frighten — more at ABEAR, FEAR] *now dial Eng* **:** FRIGHTEN
²afear \"\ *conj* [ME *afere*, adv., in fear, fr. ¹*a-* + *fere* fear] *now dial Brit* **:** for fear
afeard *or* **afeared** \-i(ə)rd\ *adj* [ME *afered*, fr. OE *āfǣred*, past part. of *āfǣran*] *now dial* **:** AFRAID
afebrile \(')ā+¦-\ *adj* [²*a-* + *febrile*] **:** free from fever **:** not marked by fever
af·er·nan \'afə(r)ˌnan\ *n* -S [Ar *al-farnān* the afernan] **:** a desert shrub (*Euphorbia balsamifera*) native to the Canary

islands that has leaves at the ends of the branches and inconspicuous yellow flowers

aff \'af\ *Scot var of* OFF

aff *abbr* **1** affectionate **2** affirmative

af·fa·bil·i·ty \,afə'biləd·ē, -ətē, -i\ *n* -ES [MF *affabilité*, fr. L *affabilitat-, affabilitas*, fr. *affabilis* + *-itat-, -itas* -ity] **:** the quality or state of being affable **:** SOCIABILITY

af·fa·ble \'afəbəl\ *adj* [MF, fr. L *affabilis*, fr. *affari* to speak to (fr. *ad-* + *fari* to speak) + *-abilis* -able — more at BAN] **1 a :** pleasant and at ease in talking to others ⟨an ~ person⟩ **b :** characterized by ease and friendliness ⟨on ~ terms with his neighbors⟩ **2 :** BENIGN ⟨an ~ smile⟩ **:** PLEASANT ⟨more of this composer's ~ music —Arthur Berger⟩ **syn** see GRACIOUS

af·fable·ness *n* -ES **:** the quality or state of being affable

af·fa·bly \-blē, -i\ *adv* **:** in an affable manner **:** COURTEOUSLY, PLEASANTLY

af·fair \ə'fa(a)(ə)r, -e(ə)r,-a(a)ə,-eə\ *n* -S [ME & MF; ME *afere, affaire*, fr. MF, fr. *a faire* to do, fr. *a* to (fr. L *ad*) + *faire* to do, fr. L *facere* — more at AT, DO] **1 a affairs** *pl* **:** commercial, professional, or public business ⟨the Federal Republic agrees to conduct its ~*s* in conformity with the principles stated in the charter —*Current History*⟩ ⟨a well-known man of ~*s*⟩ **b :** MATTER, CONCERN ⟨religion is also an ~ of the imaginative life —Roger Fry⟩ ⟨they don't want to get mixed up in it because it isn't their ~ —Brad Sebstad⟩ **2 a :** any procedure, action, or occasion not clearly distinguished or only vaguely specified ⟨an ~ of honor⟩ ⟨one of the most brilliant social ~*s* of the season⟩ ⟨public life had become so discreditable an ~ —F.M.Ford⟩ ⟨the whole ~ from start to finish did not occupy more than thirty seconds —S.H.Holbrook⟩ ⟨if he knew anything about rain, this was going to be an all-day ~ —Hamilton Basso⟩ — sometimes used in pl. ⟨an attempt to end this sad state of ~*s*⟩ **b** [F *affaire*] *also* **af·faire :** a romantic or passionate attachment typically of limited duration **:** an illicit sexual relationship **:** LIAISON, INTRIGUE ⟨a series of ~*s* before her marriage⟩ **c** [F *affaire*] *or* **affaire :** a matter or episode occasioning public anxiety or dispute or giving rise to scandalous report and speculation **:** CASE — used often with proper names ⟨the Doe ~⟩ ⟨the ~ Roeville⟩ **d :** any object or collection of objects not clearly distinguished or only vaguely specified ⟨a black-and-white checked wool ~ with a double collar —Lois Long⟩ ⟨the orchestra has arrived, no thin five-piece ~, but a whole pitful of oboes and trombones and saxophones —Scott Fitzgerald⟩

af·faire d'a·mour \"də'mu̇(ə)r, -u̇ə\ *n, pl* **affaires d'amour** \-(z)də-\ [F, love affair] **:** AFFAIR 2b

affaire de coeur \-də'kər, -kə̄\ *n, pl* **affaires de coeur** \-(z)də-\ [F *affaire de cœur*, lit., affair of the heart] **:** AFFAIR 2b

affaire d'hon·neur \-də'nər, -,dȯ'-, -nə̄\ *n, pl* **affaires d'honneur** \-(z)də-, -(z),dȯ-\ [F, lit., affair of honor] **:** a matter involving honor; *specif* **:** DUEL

affamish *vb* -ED/-ING/-ES [modif. (influenced by *famish*) of MF *affamer, afamer* — more at FAMISH] *vt, obs* **:** to cause to hunger **:** STARVE ~ *vi, obs* **:** to suffer or die from hunger **:** STARVE

[1]**af·fect** \'a,fekt, a'f-,ə'f-\ *n* -S [L *affectus* disposition, affection, desire, fr. *affectus*, past part. of *afficere*] **1** *obs* **:** FEELING, EMOTION **2** [G *affekt*, fr. L *affectus*] *psychol* **:** the conscious subjective aspect of an emotion considered apart from bodily changes

[2]**af·fect** \ə'fekt, (')a¦f-\ *vb* -ED/-ING/-S [MF & L; MF *affecter*, fr. L *affectare*, freq. of *afficere* to exert an influence, to bestow, apply oneself, fr. *ad-* + *-ficere* (fr. *facere* to do) — more at DO] *vt* **1** *archaic* **:** to aim at **:** aspire to **:** try to attain ⟨this proud man ~*s* imperial sway —John Dryden⟩ **2 a** *archaic* **:** to have affection for (a person or object) ⟨as for Queen Katharine, he rather respected than ~*ed*, rather honored than loved her —Thomas Fuller⟩ **b :** to be given to **:** FANCY ⟨~ a precise way of speaking⟩ ⟨~ brightly colored clothing⟩ **3 :** to make a display of liking or using **:** cultivate or profess ostentatiously ⟨it was the habit of the moment at Oxford to ~ irreverence —T.B.Costain⟩ **4 :** to assume the character or appearance of **:** put on a pretense of **:** PRETEND, FEIGN, COUNTERFEIT ⟨~ indifference⟩ ⟨youthfulness is something she has to ~ —E.R. Bentley⟩ ⟨Lewis at first ~*ed* to receive these propositions coolly —T.B.Macaulay⟩ **5 :** to tend toward ⟨drops of water ~ roundness⟩ **6 :** to be frequently or habitually found in **:** FREQUENT ⟨swallows that ~ chimneys⟩ ⟨she was employed far away from the table which I ~*ed* —Arnold Bennett⟩ ~ *vi, obs* **:** INCLINE 2 **syn** see ASSUME

[3]**affect** \"\ *vt* -ED/ING/-S [L *affectus*, past part.] **1 :** to act upon: **a :** to produce an effect (as of disease) upon ⟨a condition ~*ing* the heart⟩ **b** (1) **:** to produce a material influence upon or alteration in ⟨rainfall ~*s* plant growth⟩ ⟨areas to be ~*ed* by highway construction⟩ (2) **:** to have a detrimental influence on — used esp. in the phrase *affecting commerce* **c :** to make an impression on (as the mind or the feelings) ⟨the physical details that had once ~*ed* her so deeply —Ellen Glasgow⟩ **:** INFLUENCE ⟨the only law on the books ~*ing* the conduct of the individual —Zechariah Chafee⟩ **2 :** ASSIGN, ALLOT ⟨endowment funds ~*ed* to the provision of scholarships⟩

syn INFLUENCE, TOUCH, IMPRESS, STRIKE, SWAY: AFFECT applies to a stimulus strong enough to bring about a reaction, sometimes emotional, or bring about some modification, usu. without total change ⟨a sentence about the weather, and how it *affected* her joints —Floyd Dell⟩ ⟨I was more than a little unstrung. Those long weeks of solitude had *affected* my nerves —Jack McLaren⟩ ⟨the crop in China would have been larger had not flood damage adversely *affected* the yields —*Collier's Yr. Bk.*⟩ INFLUENCE applies to a force that brings about a change or determines a course or stand ⟨the general political views of John Quincy Adams strongly *influenced* him, though he was not attracted by the example and methods of the older man —W.C.Ford⟩ ⟨the British expressed views still strongly *influenced* by nineteenth-century concepts of diplomacy and imperialism —Vera M. Dean⟩ ⟨she *influenced* profoundly the history of her people by her political acumen as minister without portfolio —*Americana Annual*⟩ TOUCH, similar to AFFECT but more vivid, may suggest forceful or emotional arousing, stirring, or impinging on ⟨they do care! their hearts are *touched*. We can do anything with them now —Hugh Walpole⟩ ⟨a small object whose exquisite workmanship has *touched* me with its intimate charm —Jean S. Untermeyer⟩ IMPRESS may suggest a deep lasting effect ⟨the populace was *impressed* because the president in person had heeded the call of a poor farmer —H.F.Wilkins⟩ ⟨his appeal was to fear, and he so *impressed* his hearers that frequently they fell to the floor or shrieked in terror —H.E.Starr⟩ STRIKE is more likely to suggest sudden sharp perception or reaction ⟨with a note in her voice that *struck* them all awake and fearful —Grace Campbell⟩ ⟨she was *struck* silent by her love —Ethel Wilson⟩ ⟨we may be *struck* with a sense of otherness, of unfamiliarity, and we seek orientation in terms of what we already know —A.C.Danto⟩ SWAY often applies to influences that are either not resisted or have such force that resistance is overcome, with resulting change in the subject's nature or course ⟨capricious deities, *swayed* by human passions and desires —G.L.Dickinson⟩ ⟨it is generally conceded that phrasing can *sway* opinions most easily when those opinions are not strongly held —S.L.Payne⟩ ⟨the elemental forces which *sway* the spirit with immortal hopes and infinite terrors —Roger Fry⟩

af·fect·a·bil·i·ty *or* **af·fect·i·bil·i·ty** \ə,fektə'biləd·ē, (,)a,f-\ *n* -ES **:** ability or readiness to be affected

af·fect·a·ble *or* **af·fect·i·ble** \ə'fektəbəl, (')a¦f-\ *adj* **:** able to be affected **:** easily affected ⟨a material very ~ by sudden changes in temperature⟩

affectate *vt* -ED/-ING/-S [L *affectatus*] *obs* **:** [2]AFFECT 4

af·fec·ta·tion \,a,fek'tāshən *also* -,fik-,-,fēk-\ *n* -S [MF & L; MF *affectation*, fr. L *affectation-, affectatio* act of striving, conceit, fr. *affectatus* (past part. of *affectare* to aim) + *-ion-, -io* -ion — more at AFFECT] **1** *obs* **:** a striving after **:** aspiration toward **2** *obs* **:** FONDNESS, AFFECTION **3 :** the act of taking up or esp. displaying a feeling, attitude, opinion, or desire not natural to oneself or not genuinely felt ⟨his love of music was mere ~⟩ ⟨his ~ of righteous indignation fooled nobody⟩ **4 :** manner of speech or behavior not natural to one's actual personality or capabilities **:** artificiality of behavior esp. in display of feelings ⟨was there nothing in beautiful manners but foppery, prudery, starch, and ~, with false pride overtopping all? —Van Wyck Brooks⟩

affected *adj* [fr. past part. of [2]*affect*] **1 :** attached to **:** inclined or disposed toward ⟨the house of Gonzaga was already well ~ to the Spanish cause —J.A.Symonds⟩ ⟨events causing him to be differently ~ toward his brother⟩ **2 a** *obs* **:** deliberately chosen **b** *obs* **:** aimed at **:** sought after **:** wished for **c** *obs* **:** regarded with affection or liking **d :** FANCIED ⟨a republication of a diluted medical work much ~ by laymen —G.F. Whicher⟩ **3 a :** given to false show **:** assuming or pretending to possess what is not natural or real ⟨an ~ person⟩ ⟨too ~ in his manner to be convincing⟩ **b :** assumed artificially or falsely **:** not natural **:** PRETENDED ⟨with all the marks, real or ~, of intoxication —J.G.Frazer⟩ ⟨a sound and healthy revolt against an ~ and citified diction —J.L.Lowes⟩ ⟨titles for some of these paintings are ~ — closer to poetry than need be —H.D.Walker⟩ — **af·fect·ed·ly** *adv* — **affectedness** *n* -ES

af·fect·er \ə'fektə(r), a'-\ *n* -S [[2]*affect* + *-er*] **1** *obs* **:** one that affects or loves **2 :** one that strives after or pretends to something ⟨an ~ of unusual words⟩

affecting *adj* [fr. pres. part. of [2]*affect*] **1** *obs* **:** AFFECTED 3a **2** *obs* **:** IMPRESSING, ARRESTING **3 :** moving the emotions **:** TOUCHING, PATHETIC ⟨the scenes of disappointment are quite as ~ —Walt Whitman⟩ ⟨mounts . . . toward an extraordinarily ~ climax —Dan Wickenden⟩ **syn** see MOVING

affectingly *adv* **:** in an affecting manner **:** MOVINGLY

[1]**af·fec·tion** \ə'fekshən *also* a'-\ *n* -S [ME *affeccioun*, fr. OF & MF *affection*, fr. L *affection-, affectio*, fr. *affectus* (past part. of *afficere* to exert an influence, bestow, apply oneself) + *-ion-, -io* -ion — more at AFFECT] **1 :** any moderate feeling or emotion ⟨that serene and blessed mood in which the ~*s* gently lead us on —William Wordsworth⟩ **2 :** kind feeling **:** tender attachment **:** LOVE, GOOD WILL ⟨the young man warmly reciprocated her ~ —Elinor Wylie⟩ ⟨music played with ~ and understanding —Irving Kolodin⟩ ⟨you had some ~ for him —George Meredith⟩ — sometimes used in pl. ⟨he had been endowed with powerful family ~*s* that were progressively frustrated —Allen Tate⟩ ⟨the dearest object of their ~*s* —H.T. Buckle⟩ ⟨a powerful rival for the ~*s* of the working class —J.G.Colton⟩ **3** *obs* **a :** a strong emotion or passion (as anger, fear, or hatred) **b :** PARTIALITY, PREJUDICE ⟨'tis the curse of service, preferment goes by letter and ~, and not by old gradation, where each second stood heir to the first —Shak.⟩ **4** *psychol* **a :** the feeling aspect of consciousness (as in pleasure, displeasure) — distinguished from *conation;* compare COGNITION **b :** [1]AFFECT 2 **5 a :** bent of mind **:** feeling or natural impulse swaying the mind **:** PROPENSITY, DISPOSITION, INCLINATION ⟨my lawyer is bound by all his ~*s* to encourage me in litigation —G.B.Shaw⟩ **b** *archaic* **:** AFFECTATION 3, 4 ⟨they might discover themselves mock'd in these monstrous ~*s* —Ben Jonson⟩ **syn** see ATTACHMENT, FEELING

[2]**affection** \"\ *vt* -ED/-ING/-S [MF *affectionner*, fr. *affection*, n.] **:** to have affection for **:** LOVE

[3]**affection** \"\ *n* -S [MF, fr. L *affection-, affectio*] **1 :** action of affecting or state of being affected ⟨the reciprocal ~ of moving bodies⟩ **2 a** (1) **:** a bodily condition (2) **:** DISEASE, MALADY ⟨a pulmonary ~⟩ **b** (1) *archaic* **:** an alterable or nonessential state or mode of being ⟨veins that produce an accidental ~ of granite⟩ (2) **:** ATTRIBUTE, PROPERTY ⟨shape and weight are ~*s* of bodies⟩ **3 :** [1]UMLAUT 1 — used esp. in the grammar of the Celtic languages

af·fec·tion·al \-shənᵊl,-shnəl\ *adj* [[1]*affection* + *-al*] **:** belonging or relating to the affections — **af·fec·tion·al·ly** \-nᵊlē,-nəlē\ *adv*

[1]**af·fec·tion·ate** \-sh(ə)nət\ *adj* [[1]*affection* + *-ate*] **1** *obs* **:** mentally or emotionally affected: **a :** PREJUDICED, BIASED **b :** favorably disposed **:** FRIENDLY **c :** governed by passion **:** HEADSTRONG **d :** AMBITIOUS, EARNEST **2 :** having affection or warm regard **:** LOVING, FOND ⟨he watched the boy's quick descent with an ~ eye —T.B.Costain⟩ ⟨he flung an ~ arm around Hector's neck —Dorothy Sayers⟩ ⟨as ~ a pet as any you will find, the coati tends to be a devoted one-man animal —C.A.Nicholson⟩ **3 :** proceeding from affection **:** indicating love **:** TENDER ⟨Lafayette's ~ remembrance of the life there —H.E.Scudder⟩ ⟨his ~ care for his people was winning him love —John Buchan⟩ — **af·fec·tion·ate·ly** *adv*

[2]**af·fec·tion·ate** \-shə,nāt\ *vt* -ED/-ING/-S **1** *obs* **:** to feel or acquire affection for **2 :** to make affectionate ⟨he *affectionated* himself to the child⟩

affectionated *adj* **1** *obs* **:** favorably inclined **2** *obs* **:** AFFECTIONATE

affectioned *adj* [[1]*affection* + *-ed*] **1 a** *obs* **:** kindly disposed **:** well-affected **b** *archaic* **:** DISPOSED ⟨be kindly ~ one to another —Rom 12:10 (AV)⟩ **2** *obs* **a :** AMBITIOUS, ZEALOUS **b :** WILLFUL, OBSTINATE

af·fec·tive \(')a¦fektiv, ə'f-, -ēv\ *adj* [MF *affectif* (fr. L *affectus* disposition, affection + MF *-if* -ive) & G *affektiv*, fr. *affekt* emotion (fr. L *affectus*) + G *-iv* -ive — more at AFFECT] **1 :** relating to, arising from, or influencing feelings or emotions **:** EMOTIONAL ⟨sacrificing physical life and ~ life to mental life —Aldous Huxley⟩ **2 :** expressing emotion ⟨~ language⟩ ⟨the ~ force of a diminutive suffix⟩

af·fec·tiv·i·ty \,a,fek'tivəd·ē *also* ə,f-\ *n* -ES **:** ability to feel emotions **:** the division of mental life and activity relating to the emotions **:** EMOTION

affects *pres 3d sing of* AFFECT, *pl of* AFFECT

affectuous *adj* [ME, fr. MF or LL; MF *affectueux*, fr. LL *affectuosus*, fr. L *affectus* disposition, affection, desire + *-osus* -ous — more at AFFECT] *obs* **:** ARDENT, AFFECTIONATE

affectuously *adv* [ME, fr. *affectuous* + *-ly*] *obs* **:** ARDENTLY, AFFECTIONATELY

af·feer \ə'fi(ə)r\ *vt* -ED/-ING/-S [ME *afferen, affuren*, fr. MF *affeurer, afforer*, fr. *a-* (fr. L *ad-*) + *feur, fuer* market price, tax, fr. ML *forum* market price, fr. L, market place — more at FORUM] **1** *law* **:** to fix the amount of (an amercement) **:** ASSESS **2** *obs* **:** CONFIRM, ASSURE ⟨the title is ~*ed* —Shak.⟩

af·feer·er *or* **af·feer·or** \-irər\ *n* -S [ME *affurer*, fr. *affuren* + *-er* or *-or*] **:** one that affeers

af·feer·ment \-i(ə)rmənt\ *n* -S **:** the act of affeering

af·feir·ing \ə'firiŋ\ *adj* [fr. pres. part. of obs. E *affeir* to pertain, be proper, fr. ME *afferen, affieren*, fr. MF *afferir, aferir*, fr. (assumed) VL *afferire*, alter. of L *afferre*] *Scot* **:** PERTAINING, BEFITTING

af·fen·pin·scher \'afən,pinchə(r), 'äf-\ *n* -S [G, fr. *affe* monkey (fr. OHG *affo*) + *pinscher;* fr. its monkeylike face] **:** a small dog of a breed related to the Brussels griffon having a stiff red, gray, or black coat, pointed ears, and bushy eyebrows, chin tuft, and mustache

af·fer·ence \'af(ə)rən(t)s\ *n* -S **:** afferent activity

af·fer·ent \-nt\ *adj* [L *afferent-, afferens*, pres. part. of *afferre* to bring to, fr. *ad-* + *ferre* to bear — more at BEAR] *physiol* **:** bearing or conducting inward to a part or an organ; *specif* **:** conveying nervous impulses from a peripheral part toward a nerve center (as the brain or spinal cord) — opposed to *efferent* — **af·fer·ent·ly** *adv*

af·fet·tu·o·so \(,)a,fechə'wō(,)sō, -fed·ə'-, -zō\ *adj* (*or adv*) [It, fr. LL *affectuosus* — more at AFFECTUOUS] **:** tender or affecting — used as a direction in music

[1]**af·fi·ance** \ə'fīən(t)s, a'-\ *n* -S [ME *affiaunce*, fr. MF *affiance, afiance*, fr. *affier, afier* to trust (fr. ML *affidare*, fr. L *ad-* + *fidare* to trust) + *-ance;* akin to L *fides* faith, *fidere* to trust — more at BIDE] **1** *archaic* **:** TRUST, RELIANCE, FAITH, CONFIDENCE **2** *archaic* **:** plighted faith **:** marriage contract or promise **3** *obs* **:** close or intimate relationship

[2]**affiance** \"\ *vt* -ED/-ING/-S [MF *afiancer*, fr. *afiance*, n.] **:** to pledge one's faith to for marriage **:** solemnly promise (oneself or another) in marriage **:** BETROTH, ENGAGE ⟨the king *affianced* his daughter to the ruler of a neighboring principality⟩ ⟨the *affianced* couple will marry next month⟩

af·fi·ant \-nt\ *n* -S [MF *affiant, afiant*, fr. pres. part. of *affier, afier*] *law* **:** one that swears to an affidavit; *broadly* **:** DEPONENT

af·fiche \a'fēsh, ə'-\ *n* -S [F, fr. *afficher* to affix, fr. *a-* (f. L *ad-*) + *ficher* to drive in, fr. (assumed) VL *figicare*, fr. L *figere* to fasten, thrust in — more at DIKE] **:** POSTER, PLACARD

afficionado *var of* AFICIONADO

af·fi·da·vit \,afə'dāvət\ *n* -S [ML, he has made oath, 3d pers. sing. perf. indic. act. of *affidare* — more at AFFIANCE] **:** a sworn statement in writing made esp. under oath or on affirmation before an authorized magistrate or officer; *specif* **:** such a statement under oath made ex parte and without cross-examination — compare DEPOSITION

affidavit of merits : an affidavit made by a party to an action (as to prevent the automatic entry of judgment against that party) setting forth that the party has a substantial and genuine ground of action or defense and that the complaint or plea filed is not sham or dilatory

affidavit of verification : a short affidavit taking oath to the truth of the allegations in an instrument (as a petition or complaint) instead of including the allegations in extenso in a separate affidavit

af·fi·da·vy \-vē\ *n* -ES [by shortening & alter.] *dial* **:** AFFIDAVIT

af·fied *past of* AFFY

affies *pres 3d sing of* AFFY

[1]**af·fil·i·ate** \ə'filē,āt *also* a'-; -ād·+V\ *vb* -ED/-ING/-S [ML *affiliatus*, past part. of *affiliare* to adopt as a son, fr. L *ad-* + *filius* son — more at FEMININE] *vt* **1 a :** to attach as a member or branch **:** bring or receive into close connection ⟨the university would assist in organizing and *affiliating* high schools —*Amer. Guide Series: Texas*⟩ ⟨the number of *affiliated* schools or institutes varies from one university to another —R.J. Matthew⟩ ⟨a number of loose national federations with which the local bodies *affiliated* —Oscar Handlin⟩ ⟨everyone should be *affiliated* to the religious customs prevalent in his country —George Santayana⟩ **b :** to join as a member **:** ASSOCIATE ⟨detached in the sense of being neither politically *affiliated* nor yet antipathetic —Muriel Howlett⟩ ⟨*affiliated* himself with the social and literary circles —H.P.Willis⟩ ⟨lumbering and its *affiliated* activities form the city's chief industry —*Amer. Guide Series: Oregon*⟩ **2 :** to fix the paternity of (an illegitimate child) — used with *to* ⟨sufficient grounds for *affiliating* the child to its alleged father⟩; *broadly* **:** to connect in the way of descent **:** trace the origin of ⟨~ Shakespeare's *Hamlet* to earlier plays⟩ ~ *vi* **:** to connect or associate oneself **:** COMBINE — usu. used with *with* ⟨he refused to ~ with a political party⟩ ⟨these phenomena ~ with certain beliefs⟩

[2]**af·fil·i·ate** \-ēət *also* -ē,āt; *usu* -d·+V\ *n* -S **1 :** an affiliated person **:** ASSOCIATE ⟨~*s* and nonmembers attended the public ceremony⟩ **2 a :** a branch or unit of a larger organization ⟨the regional ~ of the national association⟩ **b** (1) **:** a company effectively controlled by another or associated with others under common ownership or control (2) **:** SUBSIDIARY

af·fil·i·a·tion \=,==ˈāshən\ *n* -S [F, fr. ML *affiliation-, affiliatio*, fr. L *affiliatus* + *-ion-, -io* -ion] **:** the act of affiliating **:** the state or relation of being affiliated

affinage *n* -S [F, fr. *affiner* to refine + *-age* — more at AFFINE] *obs* **:** act of refining (a metal)

af·fi·nal \(')a¦fīnᵊl, ə'f-\ *adj* [L *affin*is neighboring on, related by marriage + E *-al* — more at AFFINITY] **:** related by, based on, or involving marriage ⟨~ relatives⟩ ⟨~ relationships⟩ — distinguished from *consanguineous*

af·fi·na·tion \,afə'nāshən, ,a,fī'-\ *n* -S [[2]*affine* + *-ation*] **:** the treatment of raw sugar crystals with a heavy sugar syrup to remove the film of adhering molasses

[1]**af·fine** \a'fīn, ə'-\ *n* -S [MF *affin*, fr. *affin*, adj.] **:** a relative by marriage (as one's wife's brother)

[2]**af·fine** \"\ *vt* -ED/ -ING/ -S [F *affiner*, fr. *a-* (fr. L *ad-*) + *fin* fine, refined — more at FINE] **:** to subject (raw sugar) to affination

[3]**affine** \"\ *adj* [F *affin*, akin, connected, fr. L *affinis* related by marriage — more at AFFINITY] *math* **:** preserving finiteness [as in the transformation $y = ax + b$ (a not zero), where to every finite value of the variable x there corresponds a finite value of the variable y, and vice versa] — **af·fine·ly** *adv*

af·fined \-nd\ *adj* [MF *affin* + E *-ed*] **1 :** joined in a close relationship **:** CONNECTED ⟨syllable to blessed syllable ~ —Wallace Stevens⟩ **2 :** bound by obligation ⟨be judge yourself whether I in any just term am ~ to love the Moor —Shak.⟩

af·fin·i·tive \ə'finəd·iv, a'-\ *adj* [*affinity* + *-ive*] **:** closely related ⟨a situation ~ to his own⟩

af·fin·i·ty \ə'finəd·ē, -ətē, -i *also* a'-\ *n* -ES [ME *affinite, affinitie*, fr. MF or L; MF *afinité*, fr. L *affinitas*, fr. *affinis* bordering on, related by marriage (fr. *ad-* + *finis* border) + *-itas* *-ity* — more at FINAL] **1 :** relationship by marriage (as between a husband and his wife's blood relatives) — distinguished from *consanguinity* ⟨his kinsman, by blood, or by ~ —Lev 25:49 (DV)⟩ ⟨that grim friendliness which at last arises in all such cases of undesired ~ —Thomas Hardy⟩; *broadly* **:** any familial relationship ⟨every creature that bears any ~ to my mother is dear to me —William Cowper⟩ **2 a :** sympathy esp. as marked by community of interest **:** KINSHIP ⟨the strange *affinities* and hostilities of temperament —A.C.Benson⟩ — often used with *with* or *between* ⟨odd *affinities* she had with people she had never spoken to —Virginia Woolf⟩ ⟨her temperamental ~ with the stage —S.L.Gulick⟩ ⟨the mysterious ~ between them —Zane Grey⟩ **b :** attraction to or liking for ⟨metals without magnetic ~⟩ ⟨the special ~ of a virus for the nervous system⟩ ⟨he soon developed an ~ for politics⟩; *specif* **:** the attractive force exerted in different degrees between substances or particles that causes them to enter into and remain in chemical combination — usu. used with *for* ⟨basic dyes have an ~ for wool and silk⟩ ⟨hemoglobin has a greater ~ for carbon monoxide than for oxygen⟩ ⟨the tungsten surface has high electron ~ —V.K.Zworykin & E.G.Ramberg⟩ **c :** a person esp. of the opposite sex having a particular attraction for one ⟨she became his ~⟩ **3** *obs* **:** ASSOCIATION, ALLIANCE ⟨should we again break thy commandments, and join in ~ with the people of these abominations —Ezra 9:14 (AV)⟩ **4 :** causal connection or relationship **:** RESEMBLANCE ⟨reveals his Scandinavian *affinities* —Havelock Ellis⟩ ⟨a recognizable stylistic ~ between the extremes —Herbert Read⟩ ⟨essays arranged in groups by ~ of topic —H.W. Odum⟩ ⟨whatever bears ~ to cunning is despicable —Jane Austen⟩ ⟨this highly individual work of art bears ~ with diverse sources —Elizabeth Janeway⟩: **a** (1) **:** possession of common features as a result of descent from the same ancestral language ⟨the ~ of Dutch with English⟩ (2) **:** possession of common features not resulting from descent from the same ancestral language (as the uvular *r* which French shares with German but not with the other Romance languages) **b** *biol* **:** a relation between species or higher groups dependent on resemblance in the whole plan of structure and indicating community of origin

af·firm \ə'fərm, -ə̄m, -əim *also* a'-\ *vb* -ED/ -ING/ -S [alter. (influenced by L *affirmare*) of ME *affermen*, fr. MF *afermer*, fr. L *affirmare*, fr. *ad-* + *firmare* to make firm, fr. *firmus* firm — more at FIRM] *vt* **1 a :** VALIDATE, CONFIRM ⟨he was ~*ed* as a candidate⟩: **b :** to state positively or with confidence **:** declare as a fact **:** assert to be true ⟨science has become too complex to ~ the existence of universal truths —Henry Adams⟩ ⟨we cannot ~ that this is the later play —T.S.Eliot⟩ — opposed to *deny* **c :** to assert as valid or confirmed (as a judgment, decree, or order brought before an appellate court for review) — compare MODIFY, REVERSE **d :** to testify to or declare by affirmation — distinguished from *swear* ~ *vi* **1 a :** to declare or assert positively ⟨we must work and ~, but we have no guess of the value of what we say or do —R.W.Emerson⟩ **b :** to testify or declare by affirmation ⟨a court ruling that atheists may ~⟩ **2 :** to uphold a judgment or decree of a lower court ⟨the Court of Appeals ~*ed* —*N.Y. Certified Public Accountant*⟩ **syn** see ASSERT, SWEAR

af·firm·a·ble \-məbəl\ *adj* **:** capable of being affirmed — often used with *of* ⟨a quality ~ of every member of his family⟩

af·firm·ance \-mən(t)s\ *n* -S [MF *afermance*, fr. *afermer* + *-ance*] **:** a strong declaration **:** AFFIRMATION: **a :** an affirming of or assent to the existence, truth, or validity (as of a statement) **b :** a decision by a person to deal with an unauthorized act as though authorized **c :** a confirmation by a superior court of the validity and correctness of a judgment, decree, or order of a lower court

af·fir·ma·tion \,afə(r)'māshən\ *n* -S [MF, fr. L *affirmation-, affirmatio*, fr. *affirmatus* (past part. of *affirmare* to affirm) + *-ion-, -io* -ion — more at AFFIRM] **:** act of affirming, asserting as true, or confirming **:** a positive assertion ⟨~ of human dignity —*Time*⟩ ⟨~ by the vendor of the quality of goods⟩: **a** *logic* **:** an affirmative proposition, statement, or judgment **b :** a solemn declaration made under the penalties of perjury by a person who conscientiously declines taking an oath

affirmation of the consequent : the logical fallacy of inferring the truth of the antecedent of an implication from the truth of the consequent (as in, "if it rains, then the game is cancelled and the game has been cancelled, therefore it has rained") — called also *assertion of the consequent*

¹af·fir·ma·tive \ə'fərmәd·iv, -ə̄m-, -əim-, -ətiv *also* a'-\ *adj* [MF *affirmatif*, fr. L *affirmativus*, fr. *affirmatus* + *-ivus* -ive] **1** *obs* : CONFIRMATIVE, RATIFYING **2** *logic* : asserting a predicate of a subject or of a part of a subject; *also* : asserting the truth or validity of a statement ("All A is B", "Some A is B", and "It is true that A is B" are ~ propositions) — contrasted with *negative* **3 a** : asserting that the fact is so : declaratory of what exists ⟨~ proof that he was in fact a danger to public safety —David Fellman⟩ **b** : affirming the existence of certain facts or a particular state of things at the time a contract of insurance is made —used of representations and warranties; compare IMPLIED CONTRACT, PROMISSORY **4** : ASSERTIVE, POSITIVE ⟨an ~ approach to the problem⟩ — **af·firm·a·tive·ly** *adv*

²affirmative \"\ *n* -s [ME, fr. MF *affirmatif*, fr. *affirmatif*, adj.] **1** : an expression (as the word *yes* or the phrase *that's so*) of affirmation or assent — often used adverbially esp. in radiotelephone communication ("Is his wingman still with him?" "Affirmative." —J.A.Michener) **2** *logic* : AFFIRMATION a **3 a** : the side of a question that affirms or maintains the proposition stated — opposed to *negative* ⟨40 votes were in the ~⟩ **b** (1) : the speaker or speakers on the affirmative side in a debate (2) : the party in a legal proceeding upon whom falls the burden of proof

affirmative defense *n* : a defense setting up new matter that provides a defense against the plaintiff's case, assuming the complaint to be true

affirmative easement *or* **affirmative servitude** *n* : POSITIVE EASEMENT

affirmative pregnant *n, in pleading* : an affirmative allegation implying or not excluding some negative in favor of the adverse party

af·firm·a·to·ry \-mə,tōrē\ *adj* [*affirmation* + *-ory*] : giving affirmation ⟨an ~ gesture⟩

¹af·fix \ə'fiks, (')a¦f-\ *vt* -ED/-ING/-ES [ML *affixare*, fr. L *affixus*, past part. of *affigere* to fasten to, fr. *ad-* + *figere* to fasten — more at DIKE] **1** : to attach physically (as by nails or glue) : FASTEN — usu. used with *to* ⟨the king's seal dangled from the ribbon which ~*ed* it to the proclamation⟩ ⟨~ the label to the package⟩ **2** : to attach in any way : connect with : ADD, SUBJOIN — usu. used with *to* ⟨a penalty ~*ed* to hasty, superficial thinking —A.N.Whitehead⟩ ⟨a title of honor ~*ed* to a person's name⟩ ⟨~ your signature to the letter⟩ **3** : IMPRESS ⟨dropping a blob of wax upon the parchment, he ~*ed* his seal⟩ **4** *obs* : to fix upon : settle upon : FIX **syn** see FASTEN

²af·fix \'a,fiks\ *n* -ES [F *affixe*, fr. L *affixus*, past part.] **1 a** : a sound or sequence of sounds or, in writing, a letter or sequence of letters occurring as a bound form attached to the beginning or end of a word, base, or phrase or inserted within a word or base and serving to produce a derivative word (as *un-* in *untie*, *-ate* in *chlorate*, *-ish* in *morning-after-ish*) or an inflectional form (as *-s* in *cats*) or the basis of part or all of a paradigm (as L *-n-* in *vinco* "I conquer", *vincit* "he conquers" as contrasted with the perfect tense forms *vici* "I have conquered", *vicit* "he has conquered") — compare ²INFIX, PREFIX, SUFFIX 1 **b** *among animal breeders* : a registered generic or common name combined with the individual name of purebred animals to indicate the particular breeding or strain **2** : APPENDAGE, ADDITION **3** : a small decorative figure (as a flower) added to ceramic or bronze ware or to an architectural detail — **af·fix·al** \'a,fiksəl\ *or* **af·fix·i·al** \(')a'fiksēəl\ *adj*

af·fix·a·tion \,a,fik'sāshən\ *n* -s **1** : the action or process of affixing **2** : the use of an affix

affix-clipping *n* : METANALYSIS

af·fix·ion \ə'fikshən, a'-\ *n* -s [LL *affixion-*, *affixio*, fr. L *affixus* (past part. of *affigere* to fasten to) + *-ion-*, *-io* -ion — more at AFFIX] : the act of affixing : the state of being affixed

af·fix·ture \-kschə(r)\ *n* -s [¹*affix* + *-ture* (as in *fixture*)] : state of being affixed

af·flat·ed \ə'flād·əd, a'-\ *adj* [obs. *afflate* to blow on, fr. L *afflatus* + E *-ed*] : INSPIRED

af·fla·tion \-āshən\ *n* -s [L *afflatus* + E *-ion*] : a breathing into : INSPIRATION

af·fla·tus \-ād·əs,-ātəs\ *n* -ES [L *afflatus*, lit., act of blowing or breathing on, fr. *afflatus*, past. part. of *afflare* to blow on, fr. *ad-* + *flare* to blow — more at BLOW] : a divine imparting of knowledge or power : supernatural or overmastering impulse : INSPIRATION ⟨we imagine that a great speech is caused by some mysterious ~ that descends into a man from on high —Max Eastman⟩

af·flict \ə'flikt\ *vt* -ED/-ING/-S [ME *afflicten*, fr. L *afflictus*, past part. of *affligere* to cast down, deject, fr. *ad-* + *fligere* to strike — more at PROFLIGATE] **1** *obs* **a** : HUMBLE ⟨that we might ~ ourselves before our God —Ezra 8:21 (AV)⟩ **b** : to strike down : OVERTHROW ⟨in hope to find better abode, and my ~*ed* powers to settle here on earth —John Milton⟩ **2 a** : to distress severely so as to cause continued suffering ⟨cutting off the food supply and ~*ing* the people with dearth —J.G. Frazer⟩ ⟨strife between the Emperors and Popes which ~*ed* the Middle Ages —Herbert Agar⟩ **b** : TROUBLE ⟨the mummers themselves were not ~*ed* with any such feeling for their art —Thomas Hardy⟩ : INJURE, DAMAGE ⟨that debasement of the verbal currency which ~*s* terms used in advertising —*Times Lit. Supp.*⟩

syn TORTURE, TORMENT, RACK, GRILL, TRY: AFFLICT is a general term that is applicable to most situations involving distress or difficulty. It is often interchangeable with the following words although it lacks their more specific suggestions and stresses the fact of affliction rather than the manner. TORTURE is the strongest word in the group in suggesting most extreme infliction of pain, suffering, anguish, strain ⟨until his eye be *tortured* out with fire —P.B.Shelley⟩ ⟨and laid the strips and jagged ends of flesh even once more, and slacked the sinew's knot of every *tortured* limb —Robert Browning⟩ Although the two may be interchangeable, TORMENT may have a less extreme suggestion than TORTURE and may imply greater continuity or customary practice ⟨it was inevitable that the older boys should become mischievous louts; they bullied and *tormented* and corrupted the younger boys —H.G.Wells⟩ ⟨other epochs had been *tormented* by the misery of the existence and the terror of the unknown —*Humanist*⟩ RACK is likely to suggest a straining or wrenching with stress, duress, disease, pain, or emotion ⟨Thucydides' world was a place *racked* and ruined and disintegrated by war —Edith Hamilton⟩ ⟨a lean and nameless phantom *racked* by a consumptive cough —*Amer. Scholar*⟩ Although GRILL orig. suggested the torment of being broiled, it has weakened and is likely to suggest less pain than the preceding words; it is usu. used in situations involving stringent cross-examination or, in the present participle, in situations involving much vexation and agitation ⟨representatives of Intelligence . . . they gave his lordship a respectful but thorough *grilling* —Upton Sinclair⟩ ⟨a *grilling* afternoon trying to work despite confusions and interruptions⟩ TRY implies that which tests one's endurance, stamina, control ⟨other men were *tried* by puny ailments, were not searched and shaken by one tremendous shock —George Meredith⟩ ⟨it *tried* her that he gave her no encouragement —Willa Cather⟩

afflicted *adj* : grievously affected or troubled esp. by disease : mentally or physically impaired

afflictedness *n* -ES : AFFLICTION

af·flic·tion \-kshən\ *n* -s [ME *affliccioun*, fr. MF *affliction*, fr. L *affliction-*, *afflictio*, fr. *afflictus* + *-ion-*, *-io* -ion — more at AFFLICT] **1** *obs* : act of afflicting; *specif* : SELF-MORTIFICATION **2** : the state of being afflicted; a state of pain, distress, or grief ⟨some virtues are seen only in ~ —Joseph Addison⟩ **3** : the cause of continued pain or distress of body or mind (as illness or losses); *also* : the pain, distress, or grief resulting from such a cause ⟨the dark and senseless ~*s* of a nightmare —Kenneth Roberts⟩ **syn** see TRIAL

af·flict·ive \-ktiv\ *adj* [F *afflictif*, fr. L *afflictus* + F *-if* -ive] : giving pain : causing affliction : DISTRESSING — **af·flict·ive·ly** *adv*

aff loof \(')a'flüf\ *adv* [*aff* (alter. of *off*) + *loof*] *Scot* : without preparation : OFFHAND

af·flu·ence \'a,flüən(t)s, 'afləwən-\ *n* -s [ME, fr. MF, fr. L *affluentia*, fr. *affluent-*, *affluens* + *-ia*] **1 a** : an abundant flow or supply (as of words or feelings) : PROFUSION ⟨from the various falls and cataracts there is an ~ and variety of iris bows —John Muir⟩ **b** : abundance of property : WEALTH ⟨the heirs reduced from ~ to destitution —G.B.Shaw⟩ **2** : a flowing to or toward a point : INFLUX ⟨looking at the . . . constant ~ of newcomers —T.E.Lawrence⟩

¹af·flu·ent \-nt\ *adj* [ME, fr. MF, fr. L *affluent-*, *affluens*, pres. part. of *affluere* to flow abundantly, fr. *ad-* + *fluere* to flow — more at FLUID] **1 a** : flowing in abundance : ABUNDANT, COPIOUS ⟨his florid and ~ fancy was greatly admired —Van Wyck Brooks⟩ **b** : having an abundance of goods or riches : WEALTHY ⟨nor did the bankbook show that Mr. Oldacre was in such very ~ circumstances —A. Conan Doyle⟩ **2** : flowing toward ⟨~ breezes stirred the water⟩ **syn** see RICH

²affluent \"\ *n* -s [F, fr. L *affluent-*, *affluens*, pres. part] **1** : a stream or river flowing into a larger river or into a lake : a tributary stream — compare EFFLUENT **2** : the raw sewage entering a disposal plant

af·flu·ent·ly *adv* : with abundance : RICHLY

af·flux \'a,fləks\ *n* -ES [F or L; F, fr. L *affluxus*, past part. of *affluere* to flow to, flow abundantly] : AFFLUENCE 2 ⟨an ~ of blood to the head⟩ ⟨a regular ~ of laborers has been set up —James Bryce⟩

af·flux·ion \a'fləkshən, ə'-\ *n* -s [L *affluxus* + E *-ion*] : AFFLUX

affly *abbr* affectionately

af·force \ə'fō(ə)rs, ə'-\ *vt* -ED/-ING/-S [ML *afforciare*, fr. OF *aforcier* to strengthen, increase, fr. *a-* (fr. L *ad-*) + *forcier*, *forcer* to force — more at FORCE] : to strengthen (as a court or jury) by adding specially qualified members

af·force·ment \-mənt\ *n* -s : an afforcing (as of a court or jury)

af·ford \ə'fō(ə)rd, -ō(ə)rd,-ōəd,-ō(ə)d\ *vt* -ED/-ING/-S [ME *aforthen*, fr. OE *geforthian* to carry out, accomplish, further, fr. *ge-* (perfective prefix) + *forthian* to carry out, fr. *forth* forth, forward — more at CO-, FORTH] **1 a** : to manage to bear without serious detriment — used with infinitive ⟨a dictionary of an ancient language can ~ to embrace everything that can be called a word —R.W.Chapman⟩ ⟨you can't ~ to get out of balance —Lou Smyth⟩ ⟨most of us, however, can well ~ to look critically at our writing —Milton Hall⟩ ⟨she could ~ to be generous with Irene —Louis Auchincloss⟩ **b** : to manage to pay for or incur the cost of ⟨no country, however rich, can ~ the waste of its human resources —F.D. Roosevelt⟩ ⟨people who can ~ leisure sit in cafés by the hour —W.P.Webb⟩ ⟨our failure to recognize and foster promising students who cannot ~ college —Douglas Bush⟩ ⟨we can ~ only those threats that we are ready to carry out —*New Republic*⟩ **2 a** : GIVE, FURNISH ⟨history ~*s* us a wealth of examples —John Strachey⟩ ⟨an old building with grillwork elevators ~*ing* passengers a view of the cable —J.F.Powers⟩ — sometimes used with *to* ⟨their business is not to praise their age, but to ~ to the men who live in it the highest pleasure which they are capable of feeling —Matthew Arnold⟩ ⟨the bill was a measure necessary to ~ protection to labor as well as industry —*Current Biog.*⟩ **b** : to furnish or offer typically or as an essential concomitant ⟨apartments are small and ~ very little living space —D.P.O'Mahony⟩ ⟨by the great distribution ~*ed* by the printing press —R.A.Hall b.1911⟩ **3** *archaic* : to sell at a particular price

af·for·est \a'fȯrəst, ə'-, -ȧr-\ *vt* -ED/-ING/-S [ML *afforestare*, fr. L *ad-* + ML *forestis*, *foresta* forest — more at FOREST] **1** *English law* : to convert into a forest (sense 1) **2** : to establish forest cover on (as land not previously forested) — compare REFOREST

af·for·es·ta·tion \(,)a,fȯrəs'tāshən, ə,f-, -ȧr-\ *n* -s : the act or process of afforesting

¹af·form·a·tive \a'fȯ(r)məd·iv, ə'-\ *n* -s [*ad-* + *formative*] : SUFFIX 1 — used esp. in Semitic grammar; contrasted with *preformative*

²afformative \(')a¦f-, ə'f-\ *adj* : characterized by the use of suffixes ⟨the ~ conjugation⟩ : being an afformative ⟨an ~ element⟩

af·fran·chise \a'-,ə'-\ *vt* -ED/-ING/-S [modif. (influenced by *-ise*) of MF *afranchiss-*, stem of *afranchir*, fr. *a-* (fr. L *ad-*) + *franchir* to free — more at FRANCHISE] : ENFRANCHISE 1 **syn** see FREE

af·fray \ə'frā, a'f-, 'a,f-\ *n* -s [ME *afray*, *affray*, fr. MF *esfrei*, *effray*, *affray*, fr. *esfreer*, *effreer*, *affreer*, v.] **1** *obs* : ALARM, FRIGHT, TERROR **2** : a tumultuous assault : a violent engagement or action : FRAY, BRAWL, QUARREL ⟨the walls themselves were torn down in the fury of the ~ —M.J. O'Kelly⟩ ⟨European crises, diplomatic ~*s* —C.E.Montague⟩; *specif* : the fighting of two or more persons in a public place so as to frighten others, the offense under the law consisting in the disturbance of the public peace **syn** see CONTEST

²affray \"\ *vt* -ED/-ING/-S [ME *afraien*, *affraien*, fr. MF *esfreer*, *effreer*, *affreer*, fr. (assumed) VL *exfridare*, fr. L *ex-* + (assumed) VL *-fridare* (of Gmc origin; akin to OHG *fridu* peace) — more at FRITHBORH] **1** *archaic* : STARTLE, ALARM **2** *archaic* **a** : SCARE **b** : to frighten away **syn** see FRIGHTEN

af·freight \ə'frāt, ə'-\ *vt* -ED/-ING/-S [modif. (influenced by *freight*) of F *affréter*, fr. *a-* (fr. L *ad-*) + *fréter* to freight or charter a ship, fr. *fret* freight, fr. OF, fr. MD *vrecht*, *vracht* — more at FREIGHT] : to hire or charter (a ship) for the transportation of goods or freight — **af·freight·er** \-ād·ə(r)\ *n* -s

af·freight·ment \-mənt\ *n* -s [modif. of F *affrètement*, fr. *affréter* + *-ment*] : a mercantile lease of a vessel under which it remains in charge of the owners; *also* : the act of hiring a vessel under such a lease — compare CHARTER 5

af·fret·tan·do \,afrə'tän(,)dō, ,äf-\ *adj* [It, lit., hastening, verbal of *affrettare* to hasten, fr. *a-* (fr. L *ad-*) + *fretta* haste, fr. *frettare* to rub, fr. (assumed) VL *frictare*, fr. L *frictus*, past part. of *fricare* to rub — more at BRINE] : becoming faster, as if excited — used as a direction in music

af·fri·cate \'afrəkət, -ēk-, *usu* -əd·+V\ *n* -s [prob. fr. G *affrikata*, fr. L *affricata*, fem. of *affricatus*, past part. of *affricare* to rub against, fr. *ad-* + *fricare* to rub — more at BRINE] *phonetics* : a stop and its immediately following release through the articulatory position for a continuant nonsyllabic usu. homorganic consonant (as the \t\ and \sh\ that are the constituents of the \ch\ in *why choose* and that are different from the \t\ and \sh\ of *white shoes*)

af·fri·cat·ed \-,kād·əd\ *adj, phonetics* : changed in character from a simple stop into an affricate

af·fri·ca·tion \,==ˈkāshən\ *n* -s : conversion (of a simple stop sound) into an affricate

¹af·fric·a·tive \a'frikəd·iv, ə-; 'afrə,kād··\ *adj* [*affricate* + *-ive*] : having the articulation of an affricate or a fricative

²affricative \"\ *n* -s **1** : AFFRICATE **2** : FRICATIVE

¹affright *adj* [ME *afright*, alter. of *afyrht*, fr. OE *āfyrht*, past part. of *āfyrhtan* to frighten, fr. *ā-* (perfective prefix) + *fyrhtan* to fear — more at ABEAR, FRIGHT] *obs* : AFFRIGHTED

²af·fright \ə'frīt, ə'-, *usu* -īd·+V\ *vt* -ED/-ING/-S **1** : to impress with sudden fear : FRIGHTEN, ALARM ⟨a strange wild country that began a little to ~ us —Daniel Defoe⟩ ⟨the ~*ing* cycle of reincarnation —J.R.Ullman⟩ **2** : to make frightful ⟨casques that did ~ the air at Agincourt —Shak.⟩ ⟨these birds from their secret haunts ~ the quiet of the night —Sheridan Le Fanu⟩ **syn** see FRIGHTEN

³affright \"\ *n* -s [²*affright*] **1** : sudden and great fear approaching terror ⟨he looks behind him with ~ and forward with despair —Oliver Goldsmith⟩ **2** *archaic* : a cause of terror

affrighted *adj* : seized with affright : FRIGHTENED — **af·fright·ed·ly** *adv*

af·fright·en \-t°n\ *vt* -ED/-ING/-S [¹*affright* + *-en*] : AFFRIGHT

af·fright·ful \-tfəl\ *adj* [³*affright* + *-ful*] *archaic* : FRIGHTFUL — **af·fright·ful·ly** *adv*

af·fright·ment \-tmənt\ *n* -s [²*affright* + *-ment*] *archaic* : the act of affrighting : the state of being affrighted

¹af·front \ə'frənt, a'-\ *vt* -ED/-ING/-S [ME *afronten*, *afrounten*, fr. MF *afronter*, *affronter*, fr. (assumed) VL *affrontare*, fr. L *ad-* + *front-*, *frons* forehead — more at FRONT] **1 a** : to insult esp. to the face by behavior or language ⟨those who now smile upon and embrace would ~ and stab each other if manners did not interpose —Earl of Chesterfield⟩ **b** : to offend esp. by showing disrespect ⟨the prince ~*ed* his father by embarking on a love affair —Geoffrey Bruun⟩ **2 a** : to face in defiance : CONFRONT ⟨~ death⟩ **b** *archaic* : to meet in hostile encounter **c** *obs* : to meet or encounter face to face **3** : to appear directly before ⟨the still fresh scar on the hillside which ~*s* the traveler's eye —Norman Douglas⟩ **4** *archaic* : to front upon : border upon **syn** see OFFEND

²affront \"\ *n* -s [MF, back-formation fr. *affronter*] **1 a** : a deliberately offensive act or utterance ⟨in this heat every extra gesture was an ~ to the common store of life —Scott Fitzgerald⟩ **b** : an offense to one's self-respect ⟨for the Greeks, the Roman Empire was a necessity of life and at the same time an intolerable ~ —A.J.Toynbee⟩ **2** *obs* : a hostile encounter

syn INSULT, INDIGNITY: AFFRONT is a deliberate indication of disrespect calculated to offend ⟨an old *affront* will stir the heart through years of rankling pain —Jean Ingelow⟩ ⟨my determination to break this educational lockstep was an *affront* to their pride as schoolmasters —Sidney Lovett⟩ INSULT refers to a personal attack intended to rankle and humiliate ⟨the *insults* offered to the Federal troops by the women of New Orleans —W.C.Ford⟩ ⟨he suffered the greatest *insult* ever offered to a man in the House of Commons: when he entered with the Liberal party, the Conservatives rose to a man and left the House —O.S.J.Gogarty⟩ INDIGNITY indicates an outrageous or contemptuous offense to one's personal dignity ⟨that after all which had passed he should be compelled to accept his pardon at Caesar's hands was an *indignity* to which he could not submit —J.A.Froude⟩ ⟨to nearly all men serfdom was, without qualification, a degrading thing, and they found trenchant phrases to describe the *indignity* of the condition —R.W.Southern⟩

af·fron·té *or* **af·fron·tee** \¦a,frən¦tā; ə'frəntē, a'f-\ *adj* [F *affronté*, fr. past part. of *affronter* to confront, affront — more at AFFRONT] **1** *also* **af·fronty** \ə'frəntē, a'-\ *of two heraldic figures* : facing each other — compare COMBATANT, RESPECTANT **2** *of a heraldic figure* : facing to the front : full-faced : GARDANT

affrontedly *adv* [*affronted* (past part. of ¹*affront*) + *-ly*; intended as trans. of F *effrontément*] *obs* : IMPUDENTLY

af·front·ive \ə'frəntiv, a'-\ *adj, archaic* : OFFENSIVE

afft *abbr* affidavit

af·fuse \a'fyüz, ə'-\ *vt* -ED/-ING/-S [L *affusus*, past part.] *archaic* : POUR

af·fu·sion \-üzhən\ *n* -s [LL *affusion-*, *affusio* act of pouring on, fr. L *affusus* (past part. of *affundere* to pour on, fr. *ad-* + *fundere* to pour) + *-ion-*, *-io* -ion — more at FOUND (melt & pour)] : act of pouring a liquid upon (as in baptism)

affy *vb* -ED/-ING/-ES [ME *afien*, *affien*, fr. OF *afier* — more at AFFIANCE] *vt* **1** *obs* : CONFIDE, TRUST **2 a** *obs* : (1) : ESPOUSE (2) : AFFIANCE, BETROTH **b** *archaic* : to join closely (as in bonds of faith) ⟨souls *affied* by sovereign destinies —R.W. Emerson⟩ ~ *vi, obs* : CONFIDE, TRUST

¹af·ghan \'af,gan, -aa(ə)n *also* -,gən\ *n* -s [Pashto *afghānī*] **1** *cap* : a native or inhabitant of Afghanistan, in western Asia **2** *cap* : PASHTO **3** : a blanket or shawl of colored wool, knitted or crocheted in strips or squares which are joined by sewing or crocheting **4** : a Turkoman carpet of large size and long pile woven in geometric designs and predominantly wine red in color **5** *often cap* : CHIPPENDALE 2 **6** *usu cap* : AFGHAN HOUND

²afghan \"\ *adj, usu cap* : of, relating to, or like that of Afghanistan, its people, or its language

afghan fox *n, usu cap A* : CORSAC

afghan hound *n, usu cap A* : a swift greyhoundlike hunting dog of an ancient breed native to the Near East with a coat of silky thick hair of very fine texture, a head surmounted by a long silky topknot, and being about 26 inches tall

af·gha·ni \af'ganē, -änē\ *n* -s [Pashto *afghānī*, lit., Afghan] **1 a** : the basic monetary unit of Afghanistan — see MONEY table **b** : a silver coin no longer in active circulation representing the basic monetary unit of Afghanistan **2** *cap* : ¹AFGHAN 2

af·ghan·i·stan \af'ganə,stan, -taa(ə)n\ *adj, usu cap* [fr. *Afghanistan*, country in western Asia] : of or from Afghanistan : of the kind or style prevalent in Afghanistan

afi·brin·o·gen·emia \¦ā,=\ *n* -s [NL, fr. ²*a-* + E *fibrinogen* + NL *-emia*] : an abnormality of the blood-clotting mechanism caused by usu. congenital absence of fibrinogen in the blood and marked by a tendency to prolonged bleeding

afi·ci·o·na·da \ə,fisēə'nädə, ə,fēsēə'-,ə,fishə'-, a,f-, -ādə; -,fēthēə'nāthə, -nä-\ *n* -s [Sp, fr. fem. of *aficionado*, past part.] : a female aficionado

afi·ci·o·na·do *also* **af·fi·ci·o·na·do** \-ä(,)dō, -ā(-, -)thō\ *n* -s [Sp *aficionado*, fr. *aficionado*, past part. of *aficionar* to inspire devotion or affection (as in *aficionarse* to be fond of), fr. *afición* fondness, affection, fr. L *affection-*, *affectio* — more at AFFECTION] **1** : an enthusiastic follower of bullfighting ⟨the most important single thing for the beginning ~ to concentrate on is the matador's feet —Barnaby Conrad⟩ **2** : an ardent follower, supporter, or enthusiast : FAN ⟨an ~ of science fiction⟩ ⟨~*s* of progressive education argue that this has a frustrating effect on the children —Richard Joseph⟩

afield \ə'-\ *adv (or adj)* [ME *afelde*, fr. OE *on felda*, *on felde*, fr. *on* + *felda*, *felde*, dat. of *feld* field — more at FIELD] **1 a** : upon a field of battle ⟨the armies were ~, challenging the enemy's advance⟩ **b** : out to a field of battle ⟨fierce warriors rushing ~⟩ **2** : into or in a field : in or into the countryside ⟨unlawful to carry hunting rifles ~ until the open season⟩ ⟨~, too, he had a quick eye for scenery —*Times Lit. Supp.*⟩ **3 a** : away from home, usual surroundings, or native country : ABROAD ⟨looking for ~ for new lands to conquer —R.A.Hall b.1911⟩ **b** : to or at a distance : away from a given point — used esp. with *far* or *farther* ⟨they were at work far ~ —Russell Lord⟩ ⟨he did not want to go any farther ~⟩ **4 a** : outside the circle of one's immediate family, usual associates, or ordinary activities ⟨always looking ~ for new friends, new interests⟩ ⟨she did not go ~ for those who affected art and advanced ideas —Willa Cather⟩ **b** : beyond one's ordinary methods of procedure or patterns of behavior : out of the way : to extreme lengths ⟨an artist who has rarely gone ~ for his striking effects⟩ **5 a** : beyond the point at issue : off the subject : away from the line of reasoning or interest : ASTRAY — used esp. with *far* or *farther* ⟨inane remarks that were completely ~⟩ ⟨such a digression would lead us too far ~ —R.W. Murray⟩ **b** : beyond evident causes, reasons, or circumstances — usu. used with *farther* ⟨a social upheaval that can be understood only by going farther ~⟩ **c** : beyond the fundamental limitations or boundaries ⟨difficult problems that, so far as psychiatry is concerned, are quite ~⟩

afi·ko·men \,äfē'kōmən\ *n* -s [Heb *ăphīqōmān*] : a piece broken from the middle one of the three matzoth used by Jews at the Passover Seder service and set aside to be eaten at the end of the meal

afire \ə'-\ *adj* [ME *afire*, *afure*, fr. ¹*a-* + *fire*, *fure*, dat. of *fir*, *fur* fire] : on fire : BLAZING, FLAMING ⟨the building was ~⟩

afla·gel·lar \¦āflə¦jelə(r)\ *also* **aflag·el·late** \(')ā¦flajələt, -,lāt, ¦āflə¦jelət\ *adj* [²*a-* + *flagellar*, *flagellate*] *zool* : without a flagellum

aflame \ə'-\ *adj* [¹*a-* + *flame*, n.] : AFIRE

aflare \ə'-\ *adj* [¹*a-* + *flare*, v.] : FLARING, FLAMING ⟨~ with burning coals —Roderick Cameron⟩

a flat \'=¦=\ *n, usu cap A* **1** : the keynote of A-flat major or A-flat minor **2** : the tone a half step below A

a-flat major \'=,=¦==\ *n, usu cap A* : the major musical key having a signature of four flats

a-flat minor \'=,=¦==\ *n, usu cap A* : the minor musical key having a signature of seven flats

aflick·er \ə'-\ *adj* [¹*a-* + *flicker*, v.] : FLICKERING

afloat \ə'flōt, *usu* -ōd·+V\ *adv (or adj)* [ME *aflote*, *aflot*, fr. OE *on flote*, *on flot*, fr. *on* + *flote*, *flot*, dat. & acc. respectively of *flot* deep water, sea; akin to OE *flēotan* to float — more at FLOAT] **1 a** : borne on the water : not aground : FLOATING ⟨though badly battered, the boat remained ~⟩ **b** : at sea : away from port ⟨all the ships are still ~⟩ **c** : buoyed up, floating, or suspended on, in, or as if on or in water, air, or any similar medium ⟨water lilies placidly ~⟩ ⟨her hair ~ in the summer breeze⟩ ⟨~ on a tide of happiness —Marcia Davenport⟩ **d** : on shipboard — used of persons or goods ⟨preference for duty ~ —Louis Auchincloss⟩ ⟨a large quantity of wheat still ~⟩ **2** : free of difficulties, esp. financial ones or those requiring the intervention of outside assistance : self-sufficient ⟨the inheritance kept them ~ for years⟩ **3 a** : circulating about from one individual or place to another : RU-

MORED ⟨a story was ~ that they faced bankruptcy⟩ **b :** moving about haphazardly without guide or control **:** ADRIFT ⟨they were confused, ~, unable to plan for the future⟩ **4 :** flooded with or submerged under water **:** AWASH ⟨the ship's main deck was ~⟩ **5 :** actively functioning **:** fully operating ⟨a neat publishing venture, set ~ at the right time⟩

aflow \ə'-\ *adj* [¹*a-* + *flow*, v.] **:** FLOWING ⟨their founts ~ with tears —Robert Browning⟩

aflow·er \ə'-\ *adj* [¹*a-* + *flower*, v.] **:** FLOWERING ⟨meadows ~ in the warm sun⟩

aflut·ter \ə'-\ *adj* [¹*a-* + *flutter*, v.] **1 :** FLUTTERING ⟨with white wings ~⟩ **2 :** in a flutter **:** nervously excited ⟨all ~ at the thought of her return⟩ **3 :** filled with or marked by the presence of fluttering things ⟨the woods were ~ with unknown birds —Van Wyck Brooks⟩

afoam \ə'-\ *adj* [¹*a-* + *foam*, v.] **:** FOAMING ⟨brimming tankards all ~⟩

afo·cal \(')ā¦-\ *adj* [²*a-* + *focal*] *physics* **:** having focal points infinitely distant ⟨an ~ lens⟩

à fond \äfōⁿ\ *adv* [F, lit., to the bottom] **1 :** THOROUGHLY ⟨he knows his subject *à fond*⟩ **2 :** to the fullest extent **:** to the utmost ⟨supporting their party's principles *à fond*⟩

afoot \ə'-\ *adv (or adj)* [ME *afote*, fr. ¹*a-* + *fote*, dat. of *fot* foot — more at FOOT] **1 :** on foot ⟨traveling ~⟩ ⟨quail are hunted either ~ or on horseback —*Amer. Guide Series: Tenn.*⟩ **2 :** up and about **:** not bedridden ⟨she is ~ again, after her short illness⟩ **3 a :** on the move **:** in action **:** ASTIR ⟨there's trouble ~⟩ ⟨he knew that something out of the ordinary was ~ —Hamilton Basso⟩ **b :** under way **:** in progress ⟨there was much work ~ everywhere⟩ ⟨a plan to set ~ a new network of highways⟩

afore \ə'fō(ə)r, -ȯ(ə)r,-ōə,-ȯ(ə)\ *adv or conj or prep* [ME *aforen, aforn, afore*, fr. OE *onforan*, fr. *on* + *foran* before — more at BEFORE] *chiefly dial* **:** BEFORE

¹**afore·hand** \=ˈ=,=\ *adv* [ME, fr. *afore* + *hand*] *chiefly dial* **:** BEFOREHAND

²**aforehand** \"\ *adj, chiefly dial* **:** ready for the future ⟨sagacity that is ~ with events —Samuel Richardson⟩

afore·men·tioned \=ˈ=¦== *sometimes* ¦a,fōr¦- *or* ¦a,fōə¦- *or* ¦a,fȯ(r)¦- *or* ¦afə(r)¦-\ *adj* [*afore* + *mentioned*] **:** mentioned previously

afore·said \=ˈ=¦= *sometimes* ¦a,fōr¦- *or* ¦a,fōə¦- *or* ¦a,fȯ(r)¦- *or* ¦afə(r)¦-\ *adj* [ME *aforneseid*, fr. *aforn* afore + *seid* said] **:** AFOREMENTIONED

¹**afore·thought** \=ˈ=¦= *sometimes* ¦a,fōr¦- *or* ¦a,fōə¦- *or* ¦a,fȯ(r)¦- *or* ¦afə(r)¦-\ *adj* [*afore* + *thought*, past part. of *think*; prob. after *prepense*] **:** PREMEDITATED **:** previously in mind **:** DELIBERATE — usu. used postpositively ⟨with malice ~⟩ ⟨sheer falsehood, idle fables, allegory ~ —Thomas Carlyle⟩

²**afore·thought** \=ˈ=,=\ *n* -s [*afore* + *thought*, n.] **:** PREMEDITATION, DELIBERATION ⟨doing nothing without ~⟩

¹**afore·time** \=ˈ=,=\ *adv* [ME, fr. *afore* + *time*] *archaic* **:** FORMERLY

²**aforetime** \"\ *adj, archaic* **:** FORMER

a formation \'ā-\ *n, usu cap A* [¹*a*] **:** an offensive football formation in which the line is unbalanced to one side and the backfield strong to the other — compare FORMATION

¹**a for·ti·o·ri** \,ä,fȯ(r)|d·ē'ōr,ī, |ä...ōr(,)ē, ä...ōr(,)ē, -fōr|,-fōə|, |tē-,|shē-, -ē'ō-\ *adv* [L] **:** all the more certainly **:** with greater reason **:** with still more convincing force — used in drawing a reasoned conclusion which as compared with some other reasoned conclusion or recognized fact is inferred to be even more certain or inescapable ⟨the man of prejudice is, *a fortiori*, a man of limited mental vision⟩ ⟨if no major country has the resources for the enterprise, *a fortiori* neither has any lesser power⟩

²**a fortiori** \¦=,==¦=(,)=\ *adj* **1 :** marked by a certainty inferred from and taken to be even more conclusive than another reasoned conclusion or recognized fact ⟨*a fortiori* proof⟩ **2 :** making use of conclusions inferred from and taken to be even more conclusive than another reasoned conclusion or recognized fact ⟨*a fortiori* argumentation⟩

afoul \ə'-\ *adj* [¹*a-* + *foul* (entangled)] **:** FOULED, TANGLED ⟨a ship with its sails ~⟩

afoul of *prep* **:** in or into conflict with **:** in or into opposition to ⟨he fell *afoul of* the law⟩ **:** in or into collision or entanglement with ⟨one ship ran *afoul of* the other⟩

afr- *or* **afro-** *comb form, usu cap* [L *Afr-*, *Afer* African] **:** African ⟨*Afr*american⟩ **:** African and ⟨*Afro*-Asiatic⟩

afraid \ə'frād, *in S often* -re(ə)d\ *adj* [ME *affraied, afraied*, fr. past part. of *affraien* to frighten — more at AFFRAY] **1 :** FRIGHTENED **:** filled with fear, alarm, or apprehension ⟨running because they were ~⟩ ⟨~ of the dark⟩ ⟨~ he wouldn't live⟩ ⟨the author was ~ that he would lose his prestige⟩ ⟨to say bluntly what everyone else is ~ to say —T.S.Eliot⟩ — usu. used predicatively **2 :** filled with concern, regret, or sorrow over a situation that is or seems to be inescapable ⟨they said they were ~ they couldn't accept the invitation⟩ ⟨we have witnessed, I am ~, only the first phase of a basic conflict —J.B.Conant⟩ — often used to express a polite depreciation of one's own opinion or importance ⟨he told her he was ~ she was quite wrong⟩ **3 :** filled with annoyed expectation of an unwanted contingency ⟨he seemed ~, if he were kind, he might be ridiculed —E.A.Peeples⟩ **4 :** DISINCLINED, RELUCTANT, AVERSE ⟨he's ~ of even a little work⟩ ⟨~ to let his emotions seize upon his speech —V.L.Parrington⟩ ⟨not ~ of being declamatory in his fervor —Leslie Rees⟩

syn ANXIOUS, FEARFUL, AFRAID, FRIGHTENED, SCARED, TERRIFIED, and AGHAST all imply effects of apprehension, fear, or terror upon the one so described and form a roughly ascending order of intensity in the symptoms of such effects. ANXIOUS usu. suggests a mild fear amounting often to little more than a fretful though usu. persistent worry or mild apprehensiveness about possible misfortune ⟨your letter is a great relief to my mind for I still was *anxious* —O.W.Holmes †1935⟩ ⟨*anxious* for her own safety against dangers threatening from the Mediterranean —A.S.Esmer⟩ ⟨Cicero, *anxious* for his own safety, knowing now that he had made enemies of half the Senate, watching how the balance of factions would go —J.A.Froude⟩ FEARFUL, though often the same as ANXIOUS, usu. suggests a somewhat stronger and more generalized apprehensiveness stemming often rather from a natural timidity than particular objective causes and implying reactions of fear but fear usu. strongly mingled with shyness, uncertainty, and a more general tendency to foreboding and worry ⟨I was *fearful* lest we should strike the timbered edge of the plain —Francis Birtles⟩ ⟨they have been *fearful* of the unorthodox —S.E.Harris⟩ ⟨the average individual is somewhat *fearful* of high speeds —H.G.Armstrong⟩ ⟨it is timorous and *fearful* of challenge —H.L.Mencken⟩ ⟨now that he had these and a dozen other distinctions, he was *fearful* and insecure —Walter O'Meara⟩ AFRAID, FRIGHTENED, and SCARED are often interchangeable in meaning in common use; AFRAID, however, is the most general of the three and usu. implies a deep-seated though not necessarily outwardly apparent reaction of fear manifest in a strong sense of personal insecurity or danger or in a strong and usu. uncontrollable desire to avoid or evade the cause of the reaction ⟨*afraid*, in her extreme perturbation, of the loneliness of the deserted rooms, and of half-imagined faces peeping from behind every open door in them —Charles Dickens⟩ ⟨I was too *afraid* of her to shudder, too afraid of her to put my fingers to my ears —Joseph Conrad⟩ ⟨ten thousand regular soldiers of his wonderful army that everybody in the world was *afraid* of —Dorothy C. Fisher⟩ FRIGHTENED implies a fear that usu. gives rise to an inner disorder and temporary loss of self-command bordering on and often involving paralysis of muscle and will ⟨the men were *frightened* by the sudden and unexpected attack on the fort but they defended it valiantly⟩ ⟨*frightened* at the prospect of failure⟩ ⟨a child *frightened* by stories of the boogeyman⟩ ⟨*frightened* so that he broke out in a cold sweat and could hardly stand⟩ SCARED is the same as FRIGHTENED in intensity but suggests a more all-inclusive usu. childlike reaction as that of running away, trembling, or acting in ways that for adults would be foolish and irrational ⟨run like *scared* rabbits all the way down the hill to the Charles Street elevated station —Joseph Dever⟩ ⟨many of the houses here were still occupied by *scared* inhabitants, too frightened even for flight —H.G.Wells⟩ TERRIFIED and AGHAST, in this sense, suggest total paralysis of action and will. TERRIFIED implies the total reign of terror over the person resulting in stupefaction or in a total incapacity to act or think in any rational way ⟨a child *terrified* into screaming by the idea of going to the dentist⟩ ⟨*terrified* by the very sound of a plane after several months of steady bombings⟩ ⟨the mind, indeed, in its first blank outlook on life is *terrified* by the demoniac force of nature and the swarming misery of man —G.D.Brown⟩ AGHAST, a somewhat older use in this sense, puts strong emphasis on an immobility resulting from a terror or more usu. a horror or horrified disbelief esp. over the fate of someone or something other than oneself ⟨were *aghast* that in their own midst there were men capable of such barbarism —Ruth Gruber⟩ ⟨many who are *aghast* at the type of world which we are now entering, in which a war could cause obliteration —Vannevar Bush⟩ ⟨I stood *aghast*, unable to move, while the gravediggers uncovered a skeleton, cleaned the bones, laid them alongside the grave —J.A.Lomax⟩ ⟨an intelligent woman, remembering her own childhood, must stand *aghast* at the utter disregard of the children's ordinary human rights —G.B.Shaw⟩

a-frame \'=,=\ *n, cap A* [¹*A* + *frame*] **:** a 3-piece frame put together like the lines of a capital A and used to support or hold in position a heavy weight, a hoist, a shaft, or a pipe

aframerican *cap, var of* AFRO-AMERICAN

af·ra·sian \(')a¦frāzhən, -āsh-\ *adj, usu cap* [*Afr-* + *Asian*] **:** of or belonging to both Africa and Asia

afreet *or* **afrit** *also* **afrite** \'a,frēt, ə'f-\ *or* **efreet** \'e,f-, ə'f-\ *n* -s [Ar *'ifrīt*, prob. fr. Per *āfrīda* created being] **:** a powerful evil jinn, demon, or monstrous giant in Arabic mythology

afresh \ə'-\ *adv* [ME, fr. ¹*a-* + *fresh*] **1 :** ANEW **:** with fresh or unabated vigor, force, or impetus ⟨at every word her sobbing broke out ~⟩ **2 :** AGAIN **:** over again ⟨translation is a labor that must be done ~ for each succeeding age —J.C. Swaim⟩ **3 :** from a totally fresh beginning ⟨it is difficult to organize a school ~ in a primitive country⟩

¹**af·ric** \'afrik\ *adj, usu cap* [L *Africus*, fr. *Afr-*, *Afer* African (perh. back-formation fr. *Africa*) + *-icus* -ic] **:** AFRICAN

²**afric** \"\ *n* -s *cap* [L *Africus*] **:** AFRICAN

af·ri·ca \-rəkə, -rē-\ *adj, usu cap* [fr. *Africa*, the continent, fr. L] **:** of or from the continent of Africa **:** of the kind or style prevalent in Africa **:** AFRICAN

¹**af·ri·can** \-kən\ *adj, usu cap* [ME, fr. L *Africanus*, adj. & n., fr. *Africa* + L *-anus* -an] **1 :** of, relating to, or characteristic of Africa or its people **2 a :** being or constituting the biogeographic subregion that comprises Africa south of the Sahara; *broadly* **:** ²ETHIOPIAN 3 **b :** of, relating to, or native to the African subregion

²**african** \"\ *n* [ME, fr. OE, fr. L *Africanus*] **1** -s **a** *cap* **:** a native or inhabitant of Africa **b** *usu cap* **:** an individual of immediate or remote African ancestry; *esp* **:** NEGRO **2** -s *often cap* **:** a nearly neutral slightly brownish black that is darker than lava **3** *usu cap* **:** a breed of medium-sized ashy-brown geese with knobbed black bill, dewlap, and orange shanks possibly derived from the Chinese goose

african blackwood *n, usu cap A* **:** a tropical African tree (*Dalbergia melanoxylon*) with hard purple wood used esp. in the manufacture of musical instruments

african bladdernut *n* **:** a small evergreen tree (*Royena lucida*) of southern Africa with downy shoots, solitary pale yellow or white flowers, and small somewhat fleshy red or purple fruits

african bowstring hemp *n, usu cap A* **:** a bowstring hemp (*Sansevieria guineensis*) of tropical Africa

african boxthorn *n, usu cap A* **:** a tall shrub (*Lycium tetrandrum*) with spiny branchlets, rather thick leaves, and orange-red berries

african boxwood *n, usu cap A* **:** CAPE BOX

african breadfruit *n, usu cap A* **:** TRECULIA

african brown *n, often cap A* **1 :** a dark grayish brown that is very slightly redder, lighter, and stronger than average chocolate brown and paler and very slightly redder than Chippendale **2** *Brit* **:** a very dark chocolate brown

african buffalo *n, usu cap A* **:** CAPE BUFFALO

african cane *n, usu cap A* **:** PEARL MILLET 1

african cherry orange *n, usu cap A* **1 :** any of several small spiny central African citrus trees (genus *Citropsis*) with leathery unequally pinnate leaves and small sweet bright orange fruits growing in clusters **2 :** a fruit of the African cherry orange

african coast fever *n, usu cap A&C* **:** EAST COAST FEVER

african copaiba *n, usu cap A* **:** a copaibalike oleoresin supposedly derived from an African tree (*Hardwickia manii*)

african corn lily *n, usu cap A* **:** a plant of the genus *Ixia*

african cubeb *n, usu cap A* **:** the fruit of a tropical African shrub (*Piper clusii*) tasting like black pepper and used to adulterate it

african cypress *n, usu cap A* **:** any of several cypress pines of southern Africa that vary in size from moderate shrubs to tall trees and include some that produce a fragrant yellowish to brown wood suitable for cabinetwork and a resin that is used locally

african daisy *n, usu cap A* **1 :** a shrub (*Lonas inodora*) of the family Compositae having daisylike heads of flowers **2 :** a bushy perennial herb (*Arctotis stoechadifolia*) with white or violet rays **3 :** DIMORPHOTHECA 2

¹**af·ri·can·der** *or* **af·ri·kan·der** \,afrə'kandə(r), -rē-, -aan- *also* -ăn- *or* -ən-\ *n* -s *cap* [Afrik *Afrikaander*, alter. (prob. influenced by *Hollander*) of *Afrikaner*] **:** AFRIKANER

²**africander** *or* **afrikander** \"\ *n* -s *usu cap* [Afrik *Afrikaner*, *Afrikaander*, prob. short for *Afrikanerbees, Afrikaanderbees*, lit., African cattle, fr. *Afrikaner, Afrikaander* African + *bees* head of cattle — more at AFRIKANER] **1 :** a breed of tall red large-horned humped southern African cattle used chiefly for meat or draft **2 :** a breed of fat-rumped mutton-type southern African sheep

africanderism *var of* AFRIKANDERISM

african dominoes *n pl, usu cap A* [so called fr. the stereotypical popularity of dice games among American Negroes] **1** *slang* **:** DICE **2** *sing in constr, slang* **:** CRAPS

african elephant *n, usu cap A* **:** the very tall large-eared elephant (*Loxodonta africana*) that is widely distributed in tropical Africa

african fleabane *n, usu cap A* **:** any of several shrubby composite plants (genus *Tarchonanthus*) having stalked leathery leaves, small flower heads in axillary or terminal clusters, and usu. an odor like that of balsam

african ginger *n, usu cap A* **:** WHITE GINGER

african golf *n, usu cap A* [see AFRICAN DOMINOES] *slang* **:** CRAPS

african goose *n, usu cap A* **:** a goose of the African breed

african gray *n, usu cap A* **:** a parrot (*Psittacus erithacus*) that is native to equatorial Africa, has gray plumage, red tail, black primaries, and whitish face, and is very commonly domesticated esp. because of its aptness in learning to talk

african ground squirrel *n, usu cap A* **:** any of several large coarse-furred ground-dwelling squirrels of *Xerus* and related genera often conspicuously marked with white and widely distributed in drier parts of Africa

african hair *n, usu cap A* **:** a fiber obtained from the leaves of hemp palm and used for mattress stuffing and also made into a fabric resembling haircloth

african hemp *n, usu cap A* **1 :** AFRICAN BOWSTRING HEMP **2 :** a southern African shrub (*Sparmannia africana*) with white flowers

african holly *n, usu cap A, in California* **:** an arborescent woolly-stemmed biennial herb (*Solanum giganteum*) that is native to India but is grown in many warm regions as an ornamental for its large leaves with silky-white undersurface, clusters of showy blue or lilac flowers, and bright red fruits resembling holly berries

african horse sickness *n, usu cap A* **:** a serious and commonly fatal virus disease of horses endemic in parts of central and southern Africa, characterized by fever, edematous swellings, and internal hemorrhage, and spread by certain biting flies

african hunting dog *n, usu cap A* **:** a powerful doglike mammal (*Lycaon pictus*) brightly marked in black, white, and reddish yellow formerly abundant in southern and eastern Africa where it hunted in large packs but now becoming rare in settled areas

african incense *or* **african elemi** *n, usu cap A* **:** a fragrant oleoresin that is obtained from an Arabian tree (*Boswellia freeriana*)

af·ri·can·ism \'afrəkə,nizəm, -ēk-\ *n* -s *usu cap* **:** something that is characteristically African: as **a :** a characteristic feature of the Latin used by early Christian writers of northern Africa **b :** the theological doctrines of early Christian writers of northern Africa (as St. Augustine of Hippo †430) **c :** a characteristic feature of an African language occurring in a non-African language ⟨~s in the Gullah dialect —L.D. Turner⟩

af·ri·ca·nist \-nəst\ *n* -s *usu cap* **:** a specialist in African languages or cultures

af·ri·can·i·za·tion \,==kənə'zāshən, -,nī'z-\ *n* -s *often cap* **:** the action of africanizing esp. by bringing under the influence or domination of Negroes

af·ri·can·ize \'==kə,nīz\ *vt* -ED/-ING/-S *often cap* **1 :** to cause to acquire a trait regarded as distinctive of Negroes **2 :** to bring under the control or the cultural or civil supremacy of Africans, esp. Negroes

african juniper *n, usu cap A* **:** a tall evergreen tree (*Juniperus procera*) of the mountains of eastern Africa

african latin *n, cap A&L* **:** Latin of the style and idiom found in the earliest Latin version of the Bible

african lethargy *n, usu cap A* **:** SLEEPING SICKNESS 1

african lily *n, usu cap A* **1 :** AGAPANTHUS 2 **2 :** BLOOD LILY

african locust *n, usu cap A* **:** a plant of the genus *Parkia; esp* **:** a tree (*P. africana*)

african lynx *n, usu cap A* **:** CARACAL

african mahogany *n, usu cap A* **:** MAHOGANY 1b(1)

african marigold *n, usu cap A* **:** a stout branching annual herb (*Tagetes erecta*) with flower heads two to four inches across and yellow to orange in color

african milkbush *n, usu cap A* **:** a shrub (*Synadenium grantii*) of the family Euphorbiaceae that is cultivated for its red flowers

african millet *n, usu cap A* **1 :** a tall form of kafir **2 :** RAGGEE **3 :** PEARL MILLET 1

african mustard *n, usu cap A* **:** an Old World weedy annual plant (*Erysimum repandum*) that is related to the mustards, has bright yellow flowers, and is an adventive weed in much of No. America

african oak *n, usu cap A* **1 a :** an African timber tree (*Oldfieldia africana*) of the family Euphorbiaceae that yields a very heavy hard teaklike reddish brown or purplish brown timber **b :** the wood of this tree — called also *African teak* **2 :** EKKI

af·ri·can·oid \'afrəkə,nȯid, -rēk-\ *adj, usu cap A* **:** resembling or having characteristics of the peoples of Africa or their artifacts or cultures ⟨a long-headed member of the *Africanoid* races —W.Z.Ripley⟩

african oil palm *n, usu cap A* **:** a tall pinnate-leaved palm (*Elaeis guineensis*) with fruits yielding palm oil

african orthodox *adj, usu cap A&O* **:** of or relating to the African Orthodox Church, an independent church of Negro Episcopalians formed in 1921 under the leadership of the Rev. George A. McGuire

african padauk *n, usu cap A* [modif. of F *padouk*, fr. a native name in western Africa] **1 :** an African tree (*Pterocarpus soyauxii*) that yields a close-grained reddish brown wood important esp. as a source of red dyestuff — compare REDWOOD **2 :** the wood of African padauk — called also BARWOOD

african pepper *n, usu cap A* **1 :** AFRICAN CUBEB **2 :** CAYENNE PEPPER

african polecat *n, usu cap A* **:** MUISHOND

african rosewood *n, usu cap A* **1 :** an African tree (*Lingoum erinaceum*) **2 :** the close-grained fine-textured smooth and quite lustrous hard wood of the African rosewood **3 :** BUBINGA

african rue *n, usu cap A* **:** an African plant (*Peganum harmala*) yielding harmine and harmaline

africans *pl of* AFRICAN

african saffron *n, usu cap A* **1 :** a product formed by adulterating the true saffron with the flowers of other plants (as *Carthamus tinctorius* and *Calendula officinalis*) **2 a :** a shrub (*Lyperia crocea*) of southern Africa **b :** an orange dye obtained from the flowers of this shrub

african satinbush *n, usu cap A* **:** a southern African shrub (*Podalyria sericea*) grown for its silvery foliage and rosy purple pealike flowers

african scented mahogany *n, usu cap A* **:** MAHOGANY 1b(2)

african school *n, usu cap A* **:** an early ante-Nicene school of patristic philosophy developed in northern Africa of which Tertullian and Arnobius were chief representatives

african snail *n, usu cap A* **:** a large pulmonate land mollusk (*Achatina fulica*) introduced from the western coast of Africa into Ceylon, the East Indian region, and the Pacific islands — compare ACHATINA

african swallowwort *n, usu cap A* **:** a plant of the genus *Stapelia*

african tea *n, usu cap A* **:** KAT

african teak *n, usu cap A* **1 :** AFRICAN OAK **2 :** BUBINGA **3 :** IROKO

african tea tree *n, usu cap A* **:** an African shrub (*Lycium afrum*) having spiny branches, small linear leaves, and solitary purple flowers

af·ri·can·thro·pus \,afrə'kan(t)thrəpəs, -,kan'thrōpəs\ *n, cap* [NL, fr. *Africa* + *-anthropus* (as in *Pithecanthropus*)] *in some classifications* **:** a genus of primitive hominids from the Upper Pleistocene of Africa known from partial reconstruction of several shattered skulls found near Lake Eyasi in Tanganyika, considered in some respects intermediate between Neanderthal man and pithecanthropus and by some held congeneric with Florisbad man and Rhodesian man

african trypanosomiasis *n, usu cap A* **:** SLEEPING SICKNESS 1

african tulip *n, usu cap A* **1 :** BLOOD LILY **2 :** AGAPANTHUS 2

african valerian *n, usu cap A* **:** an herb (*Fedia cornucopiae*) of the family Valerianaceae cultivated for its red flowers or for use as a salad

african violet *n, usu cap A* **:** a tropical African plant (*Saintpaulia ionantha*) with long-petioled fleshy leaves in a basal cluster that is very popular as a house plant in color varieties of purple, pink, and white

african walnut *n, usu cap A* **1 :** a tropical African timber tree (*Lovoa klaineana*) of the family Meliaceae **2 :** the yellowish wood of the African walnut having the grain and figure of mahogany

africs *pl of* AFRIC

afri·di \ə'frēdē, a'-\ *n, pl* **afridis** *or* **afridi** *usu cap* [Pashto, prob. fr. Per *āfrīda* man, created being] **1 :** Pathan people occupying the hilly country about the Khyber Pass and found on both sides of the frontier between Pakistan and eastern Afghanistan **2 :** a member of the Afridi people

af·ri·kaans \'afrə,kän(t)s, -ǎn-, -ən-, -anz,-aa(ə)nz, ,==ˈ=\ *n, cap* [Afrik, fr. *afrikaans*, adj., African, fr. obs. Afrik *afrikaanisch*, fr. L *africanus* African + obs. Afrik *-isch* (now *-s*) -ish — more at AFRICAN] **:** a language that developed in southern Africa from 17th century Dutch and is one of the official languages of the Union of So. Africa — called also *Cape Dutch, Taal;* see INDO-EUROPEAN LANGUAGES table

afrikander *usu cap, var of* AFRICANDER

af·ri·kan·der·ism *or* **af·ri·can·der·ism** \,afrə'kandə,rizəm, -rē-, -aan- *also* -ăn- *or* -ən-\ *n* -s **1** *usu cap* **:** the principles, policies, or practices of Afrikaners **2** *often cap* **:** a characteristic feature of Afrikaans occurring in another language esp. in So. Africa

af·ri·ka·ner \,afrə'känə(r), -rē-, -an-,-ǎn- *also* ,äf- *or* ,ăf-\ *n* -s *cap, often attrib* [Afrik, lit., African, fr. L *Africanus* + Afrik *-er*] **:** a So. African native of European descent; *esp* **:** an Afrikaans-speaking descendant of the 17th century Dutch settlers who colonized Cape Province and neighboring regions of southern Africa

af·ri·ka·ner·dom *also* **af·ri·kan·der·dom** *or* **af·ri·can·der·dom** \-dəm\ *n* -s *cap* [Afrik *Afrikanerdom, Afrikaanderdom*, fr. *Afrikaner, Afrikaander* + *-dom*] **:** the Afrikaner section of the population of the Union of So. Africa

afrit *also* **afrite** *var of* AFREET

afro- *in pronunciations below*, ¦== = ¦a(,)frō\ — see AFR-

¹**af·ro–amer·i·can** \¦===¦=\ *or* **af·ra·mer·i·can** \¦afrə¦==\ *adj, usu cap initial As* [*Afr-* + *American*] **:** of or relating to Americans of African and esp. of Negroid descent

²**afro–american** \"\ *n, cap initial As* **:** an American of African and esp. of Negroid descent

AFRO-ASIATIC LANGUAGES

SUBFAMILY	BRANCH	DIVISION	SUBDIVISION	GROUP	SUBGROUP	LANGUAGES AND DIALECTS[1]	CHIEF LOCALITIES
SEMITIC	East Semitic					*Akkadian* (*Old Akkadian, Old Assyrian* or *Cappadocian, Assyrian, Old Babylonian, Middle Babylonian, Neo-Babylonian, Nuzi*)	Ancient Mesopotamia
	West Semitic	Northwest Semitic	Aramaic		Eastern Aramaic	*Babylonian Aramaic, Talmudic, Mandaean, Harranian,* Syriac	Ancient Mesopotamia and Syria, northwestern Iran, northeastern Turkey, northern Iraq, modern Syria and Lebanon
					Western Aramaic	*Old Aramaic, Biblical Aramaic, Jewish Palestinian Aramaic, Christian Palestinian Aramaic, Samaritan, Palmyrene, Nabataean, Sinaitic Aramaic,* Modern Western Aramaic	Ancient Syria, Palestine, and Sinai Peninsula, the Anti-Lebanon
			Canaanitic		Canaanite-Phoenician	*Canaanite, Phoenician, Punic, neo-Punic, Ugaritic*	Ancient Syria, Phoenicia, Carthage, ancient Palestine
					Hebraic	Hebrew (*Biblical, Mishnaic, Rabbinic, Medieval,* Modern), *Moabite, Ammonite, Edomite*	Ancient Palestine, Babylonia, modern Palestine
		Southwest Semitic	North Arabic			*Lihyanic, Thamudic, Safaitic, Nabataean Arabic,* classical Arabic, Modern Arabic (Maltese)	Arabia, Iraq, Syria, Lebanon, Palestine, North Africa, medieval Andalusia, Zanzibar, Madagascar, Malta
			Southeast Semitic	South Arabic	Old South Arabic	*Minaean, Sabaean, Qatabanian, Himyaritic, Hadhramautic*	Ancient Hejaz, Yemen, and Hadhramaut
					Modern South Arabic	Mahri, Sokotri, Qarawi, Shkhauri	Southern Arabia, Socotra
				Ethiopic	North Ethiopic	*Ethiopic* or *Geez,* Tigre, Tigrinya	Ethiopia, Eritrea
					South Ethiopic	Amharic, Argobba, Harari, *Gafat,* Gurage	Ethiopia
EGYPTIAN[2]						*Old Egyptian, Middle Egyptian, Late Egyptian, Demotic Egyptian, Coptic* (*Sahidic, Akhmimic, Subakhmimic, Fayumic, Memphitic, Bohairic*)	Egypt
BERBER[2]				Libyan		*Libyan*	Ancient North Africa and Canary islands
				Saharan		*Saharan*	Ancient Sahara
				Berber	Western Berber	Shluh (Shluh proper, Beraber, Draa), Tamashek, Zenaga, Kabyle	Morocco, central Sahara, southwestern Mauritania, Great Kabylia and Little Kabylia in Algeria
					Zenete	Zenete proper, Rif, Shawia, Siwi	In scattered areas of northern Africa from the Siwa oasis in Egypt west into Morocco
					Guanche	*Guanche*	Canary islands
CUSHITIC[2]	North Cushitic					Beja	Southeastern Egypt, northeastern Sudan, northwestern Eritrea
	Northeast Cushitic					Saho-Afar	Eritrea, French Somaliland, northeastern Ethiopia
	Central Cushitic					Agau (Bilin, Khamir, Quara, Awiya), Galla	Ethiopia, Kenya
	East Cushitic					Somali	French Somaliland, British Somaliland, Italian Somaliland, southeastern Ethiopia
	South Cushitic					Burji-Sidamo (Burji, Darasa, Kambatta; Alaba, Sidamo, Qabena), Konso-Geleba	Southern Ethiopia
	Southwest Cushitic					Ometo (Wolamo, Zala, Gofa, Basketo, Haruro, and other dialects), Janjero, Kafa, Gimira-Maji	Southwestern Ethiopia
CHAD						Hausa and numerous others	West and south of Lake Chad

[1]Parentheses denote dialects and periods; italics denote dead languages. [2]The Egyptian, Berber, and Cushitic subfamilies are often called collectively the Hamitic languages.

af·ro–asi·at·ic languages \\ˌ==ˌ==ˈ==-\\ *n pl, usu cap both As* **:** a family of languages widely distributed over southwestern Asia and northern Africa, comprising the Semitic, Egyptian, Berber, Cushitic, and Chad subfamilies — see HAMITIC LANGUAGES

af·ro–cu·ban \\ˈ==ˈ-\\ *adj, usu cap A & C* [*Afr-* + *Cuban*] **:** of or relating to Cubans of African, esp. Negroid, descent

af·ro–eu·ro·pe·an \\ˈ==ˌ==ˈ==\\ *adj, usu cap A & E* [*Afr-* + *European*] **:** of or relating to Africa and Europe

af·ro·gae·an \\ˈ==ˈjēən\\ *adj, usu cap* [NL *Afrogaea* the Ethiopian region of Africa (fr. *Afr-* + *-gaea*) + E *-an*] **:** ETHIOPIAN — used in biogeographic description

afront *adv* [ME, fr. [1]*a-* + *front*, n.] *obs* **:** ABREAST

af·ro·pa·vo \\ˌ=='pā(ˌ)vō, -pä-\\ *n* [NL, fr. *Afr-* + L *pavo* peacock] **1** *cap* **:** a genus of bronzy green and brown African birds that are about the size of the ring-necked pheasant but closely related to the peacocks though lacking the distinctive tail of the latter **2** -s **:** a bird of the genus *Afropavo* — called also *Congo peacock*

af·ro·pla·nor·bis \\ˈ==pləˈnȯrbəs\\ *n, cap* [NL, fr. *Afr-* + *Planorbis*] **:** a genus of African pulmonate freshwater snails (family Planorbidae) including important intermediate hosts of the blood fluke (*Schistosoma mansoni*)

af·shar \\ˈafˌshär\\ *n* -s **1** *cap* **:** AISSOR **2** *usu cap* **:** a Shiraz rug of coarse weave

[1]**aft** \\ˈaft, ˈaa(ə)-,ˈai-,ˈå-\\ *adv* [ME *afte* back, fr. OE *æftan* behind, from behind (akin to OHG *aftan*, ON *aptan*, Goth *aftana*), fr. the root of OE *æft* behind + *-an* (suffix denoting place from which) — more at AFTER, HENCE] **:** near, toward, or in the stern of a ship or the tail of an aircraft **:** ABAFT ⟨the captain would call all hands ~ —N.D.Ford⟩ ⟨midwing monoplane with a large vertical fin and rudder ~ —A.R.Weyl⟩; *broadly* **:** BEHIND ⟨a few trams were running, policemen posted fore and ~ —Christopher Isherwood⟩ ⟨a cloth Sherlock Holmes cap pulled down fore and ~ —Richard Joseph⟩ — sometimes used with *of* ⟨along the fairing ~ of the engines —Howard Nemerov⟩

[2]**aft** \\"\\ *adj* **:** REARWARD, REAR ⟨motion in the ~ direction⟩ **:** [4]AFTER 2 ⟨orders came for our unit to assemble on the ~ deck —H.D.Skidmore⟩

[3]**aft** \\ˈaft\\ *Scot var of* OFT

aft *abbr* afternoon

af·ten \\ˈafən\\ *Scot var of* OFTEN

[1]**af·ter** \\ˈaftə(r), ˈaa-,ˈai-,ˈå-, +V *sometimes* -ftr *as in* ˈaftrim *for "after him"*\\ *adv* [ME *after, efter*, fr. OE *æfter;* akin to OHG *aftar* after, ON *eptir* after, *aptr* back, Goth *aftaro* from behind, *aftra* backwards, and perh. to Skt *apataram* farther away, OPer, elsewhere, and perh. to OE *of* of, from, off — more at OF] **:** following in time or place **:** AFTERWARD, BEHIND ⟨we arrived shortly ~⟩ ⟨in Chaucer's day and for long ~ —G.M.Trevelyan⟩ ⟨along came a fox with the hounds following ~⟩

[2]**after** \\"\\ *prep* [ME *after, efter*, fr. OE *æfter*, fr. *æfter*, adv.] **1** — used as a function word to indicate the object or goal of a stated or implied action ⟨my soul thirsteth ~ thee —Ps 143:6 (AV)⟩ ⟨women go ~ causes harder than men do —Paul Engle⟩ ⟨he was too greedy ~ the treasures —Van Wyck Brooks⟩ ⟨it's serious work I'm ~ —Maurice Hewlett⟩ **2 a :** behind in place or time ⟨men in line one ~ another⟩ ⟨wave ~ wave beat on the shore⟩ ⟨the rains continued day ~ day⟩ **b :** below in rank **:** next in order to ⟨the richest and most splendid church in England ~ Westminster Abbey —Henry Riddell⟩ ⟨~ money, the biggest problem is personnel —*Time*⟩ **3 a** (1) **:** later than a particular time or period of time **:** following the expiration of ⟨20 minutes ~ 4⟩ ⟨at a quarter ~ 8⟩ ⟨it's half ~ 6⟩ ⟨events occurring ~ 1940⟩ ⟨~ three days⟩ ⟨condition of roads ~ the snow storm⟩ (2) **:** immediately following but not necessarily including the day, period, or date of event named ⟨thirty days ~ April 1⟩ ⟨two months ~ July⟩ ⟨ten days ~ sight of a draft⟩ **b** (1) **:** subsequent to and in consequence of ⟨~ what you have told me, I'll be careful⟩ ⟨net income ~ taxes⟩ (2) **:** subsequent to and notwithstanding ⟨even ~ the policeman's warning, the driver continued to speed⟩ **4 :** so as to resemble in some respect: **a :** in accordance with ⟨make me ~ thy will —Adelaide Pollard⟩ ⟨his ways are not ~ our expectations —Gilbert Kilpack⟩ ⟨Napoleon himself she admired as a man ~ her own heart —G.H.Genzmer⟩ **b** *obs* (1) **:** with reference to **:** in correspondence to **:** in proportion to (2) **:** at the rate of **c :** with the name of or by a name derived from that of ⟨John was named ~ his father⟩ ⟨called poinsettia ~ Joel R. Poinsett⟩ **d :** in imitation of **:** in the characteristic manner of **:** on the pattern of ⟨a great military power ~ the Western pattern —Ruth Benedict⟩ ⟨portrait of Charles I ~ Van Dyck —S.P.B. Mais⟩ ⟨he was built ~ his father —Conrad Richter⟩ **e :** derived from and shaped like ⟨malachite is a pseudomorph ~ cuprite⟩ **5** *chiefly Irish* **:** having just **:** in the act of **:** at the point of **:** given to — used with gerund ⟨it's a queer thing you wouldn't care to be hearing it and them girls ~ walking four miles to be listening to me now —J.M.Synge⟩ ⟨a pot of water they were ~ boiling potatoes in —Augusta Gregory⟩ ⟨you won't be ~ putting curses on people —Lucy M. Montgomery⟩ — **after a fashion** *adv* **:** in a careless, hasty, or perfunctory way **:** HAPHAZARDLY ⟨the house had been cleaned *after a fashion*⟩ ⟨cared for the children *after a fashion*⟩

[3]**after** \\"\\ *conj* [ME, short for *after that*, fr. *after*, prep. + *that*, conj.] **1 :** subsequently to the time when ⟨~ arrangements are made, we will follow⟩ **2** *obs* **:** in proportion as **:** just as

[4]**after** \\"\\ *adj* [ˈ*after*] **1 :** NEXT **:** later in time **:** SUBSEQUENT, SUCCEEDING ⟨in ~ years⟩ ⟨during his ~ life⟩ **2** [ME, prob. fr. *afte* aft + *-er*] **:** HINDER **:** nearer the rear **:** toward the stern of a ship or tail of an aircraft — used esp. of any object abaft midships ⟨~ cabin⟩ ⟨~ hatchway⟩

[5]**after** \\"\\ *n* -s [by shortening] **:** AFTERNOON

after all *adv* **:** in spite of considerations to the contrary **:** NEVERTHELESS ⟨they decided to go by the overland route *after all* —G.F.Hudson⟩ ⟨Asia, *after all*, is rich in raw materials —D.G.Bridson⟩

afterbath \\ˈ==ˌ=\\ *n* [[4]*after* + *bath*] **:** a solution for special treatment of photographic negatives or prints after fixation

afterbay \\ˈ==ˌ=\\ *n* -s [[4]*after* + *bay*] **:** TAILRACE; *also* **:** a reservoir into which it empties

afterbeat \\ˈ==ˌ=\\ *n, often attrib* [[4]*after* + *beat*] **:** a musical note or tone falling on a weak beat or on a weak portion of a beat

afterbirth \\ˈ==ˌ=\\ *n* [[4]*after* + *birth*] *in viviparous mammals* **:** the placenta and that part of the fetal membranes that are discharged from the uterus after the birth of offspring

afterblow \\ˈ==ˌ=\\ *n* [[4]*after* + *blow* (heat)] **:** the continuation of the blow after the complete oxidation of the carbon in the Bessemer process in order to oxidize and separate the phosphorus

afterbody \\ˈ==ˌ==\\ *n* [[4]*after* + *body*] **:** the after part of a body: as **a :** the part of a ship abaft midships **b :** the bottom portion of a seaplane hull or float aft of the main step

after–born \\ˈ==ˈ=\\ *adj* [[1]*after* + *born*] **1 a :** born after the father's death **:** POSTHUMOUS **b :** born after the making and publishing of the father's last will **2 :** born later **:** YOUNGER

afterbrain \\ˈ==ˌ=\\ *n* [[4]*after* + *brain*] **:** the posterior subdivision of the hindbrain **:** MYELENCEPHALON

afterburner \\ˈ==ˌ==\\ *n* [[4]*after* + *burner*] **:** an auxiliary burner attached to the tail pipe of a turbojet engine for injecting fuel into the hot exhaust gases and burning it to provide extra thrust — called also *tail-pipe burner*

afterburning \\ˈ==ˌ==\\ *n* [[4]*after* + *burning*] **1 :** the combustion that proceeds in an internal-combustion engine after the maximum pressure of explosion has occurred **2 :** the use of an afterburner — called also *reheat*

after–burthen *or* **after–burden** *n* [[4]*after* + *burthen, burden*] *obs* **:** AFTERBIRTH

aftercare \\ˈ==ˌ=\\ *n* [[4]*after* + *care*] **1 :** the care, nursing, or treatment of a convalescent patient (as the postoperative treatment of a surgical patient or the puerperal treatment of a mother after childbirth) **2 :** rehabilitative services for juvenile and adult offenders on parole or after release

aftercastle \\ˈ==ˌ==\\ *n* [[4]*after* + *castle*] **:** a ship's castle located at the stern — called also *sterncastle*

[1]**afterchrome** \\ˈ==ˌ=\\ *adj* [[4]*after* + *chrome*] **:** relating to a method of dyeing (as wool) by applying a chromium mordant after a dye **:** TOPCHROME

[2]**afterchrome** \\"\\ *vt* -ED/-ING/-S **:** to dye by the afterchrome method

afterclap \\ˈ==ˌ=\\ *n* [ME, fr. [1]*after* + *clap*] **:** an unexpected usu. untoward event resulting from or following a supposedly closed affair

aftercooler \\ˈ==ˌ==\\ *n* [[4]*after* + *cooler*] **1 :** an apparatus for cooling the discharge air from air compressors in order to remove its condensed moisture **2 :** a device for cooling the fuel mixture heated by compression in a supercharger

aftercrop \\ˈ==ˌ=\\ *n* [[4]*after* + *crop*] **:** a later crop of the same year from the same soil

afterdamp \\ˈ==ˌ=\\ *n* [[4]*after* + *damp*] **:** a toxic gas mixture remaining after an explosion of firedamp in mines and consisting principally of carbon dioxide, carbon monoxide, and nitrogen

afterday \\ˈ==ˌ=\\ *n* [[4]*after* + *day*] **:** a later day or period ⟨in this ~ these encounters and developments . . . appear to have made astonishingly little impression —A.B.Guthrie⟩ — often used in pl. ⟨he was known for his good works in his ~*s*⟩

afterdeath \\ˈ==ˈ=\\ *n* [[2]*after* + *death*] **:** an existence following death

afterdeck \\ˈ==ˌ=\\ *n* [[4]*after* + *deck*] **:** the part of a deck abaft midships

afterdinner *n* [ME *afterdiner*, fr. [2]*after* + *diner* dinner] *obs* **:** AFTERNOON

after–dinner cup *n* **:** DEMITASSE

afterdischarge \\ˈ==ˌ=ˌ=, ˈ===ˌ=\\ *n* [[4]*after* + *discharge*] **:** discharge of neural impulses (as by a ganglion cell) after termination of the initiating stimulus

aftereffect \\ˈ===ˌ=\\ *n* [[4]*after* + *effect*] **1 :** an effect that follows its cause after an interval **2 :** a secondary result esp. in the action of a drug coming on after the subsidence of the first effect **syn** see EFFECT

after–feather \\ˈ==ˌ==\\ *n* [[4]*after* + *feather*] **:** AFTERSHAFT

afterfeed \\ˈ==ˌ=\\ *n* [[4]*after* + *feed*] **:** aftergrass used for grazing

aftergame \\ˈ==ˌ=\\ *n* [ME, fr. [1]*after* + *game*] **:** a subsequent scheme or expedient undertaken to afford a chance of retrieval or improvement

afterglow \\ˈ==ˌ=\\ *n* [[4]*after* + *glow*] **1 a :** the light esp. in the western sky after sunset **b :** ALPENGLOW **2 :** a glow continuing after the disappearance of flame (as of a match) or electric discharge (as in a rarefied gas) and sometimes regarded as a type of phosphorescence **3 :** a reflection of past splendor, success, or emotion ⟨Budmouth still retained sufficient ~ from its Georgian gaiety and prestige —Thomas Hardy⟩ ⟨the mellow ~ of the septuagenarian —R.L.Strout⟩ ⟨the ~ of holidays spent in Europe —George Santayana⟩

aftergrass \\ˈ==ˌ=\\ *n* [[4]*after* + *grass*] **:** grass that grows after the first hay crop has been cut or among the stubble after harvest

aftergrowth \\ˈ==ˌ=\\ *n* [[4]*after* + *growth*] **:** a second growth or crop

afterguard \\ˈ==ˌ=\\ *n* [[4]*after* + *guard*] **1 :** the division composed usu. of ordinary seamen and apprentices stationed on the poop or after part of a ship to attend the after sails **2 :** the owner and other amateurs of a yacht's crew

after·hend \\ˈ==ˌhend\\ *adv* [ME *efterhend*, fr. *efter, after*, prep. + *hend*, pl. of *hand*] *chiefly dial* **:** AFTERWARD

after–hours \\ˈ==ˈ=\\ *adj* **1 :** engaged in after closing time ⟨they suddenly realized that there must be a great charm in *after-hours* drinking —Donagh MacDonagh⟩ **2 :** operating after a legal or conventional closing time ⟨a district notorious for *after-hours* clubs⟩

afterhouse \\ˈ==ˌ=\\ *n* [[4]*after* + deck*house*] **:** the deckhouse nearest the stern of a ship

afterimage \\ˈ==ˌ==\\ *n* [[4]*after* + *image;* trans. of G *nachbild*] **:** a usu. visual sensation occurring after the external stimulus causing it has ceased to operate — see COMPLEMENTARY AFTERIMAGE, HERING IMAGE, HESS IMAGE, NEGATIVE AFTERIMAGE, POSITIVE AFTERIMAGE, PURKINJE AFTERIMAGE

afterimpression \\ˈ===ˌ==\\ *n* [[4]*after* + *impression*] **:** AFTERIMAGE

af·ter·ings \\ˈaft(ə)riŋz, -rənz\\ *n pl* [[1]*after* + *-ings*] **1** *dial* **:** STRIPPING 2a **2 :** COLOSTRUM

afterlife \\ˈ==ˌ=\\ *n* [[4]*after* + *life*] **1 :** an existence after death ⟨it is doubtful whether the Egyptian conception of the ~ really enters into the background of Hebrew religion —S.H. Hooke⟩ **2 :** a later period in one's life ⟨he then laid a good foundation for his great work in that field in ~ —*World's Work*⟩

afterlifetime \\ˈ=='=ˌ=\\ *n* [[4]*after* + *lifetime*] **:** duration of life of an insured person subsequent to a specified age

afterlight \\ˈ==ˌ=\\ *n* [[4]*after* + *light*] **1 :** AFTERGLOW, TWILIGHT **2 :** RETROSPECT

aftermarket \\ˈ==ˌ==\\ *n* [[4]*after* + *market*] **:** the market for parts and accessories for a manufactured article (as an automobile) for repair and replacement as distinguished from the use of such parts as original components

aftermast \\ˈ==ˌ=\\ *n* [[4]*after* + *mast*] **:** the mast nearest the stern

af·ter·math \\ˈ==ˌmath, -aa(ə)th,-åth\\ *n, pl* **aftermaths** \\-ths,-t͟hz\\ [[4]*after* + *math* (mowing)] **1 :** a second-growth mowing **:** the crop of grass cut, grazed, or plowed under after the first crop of the season from the same soil **:** ROWEN ⟨the clover ~ being turned under —A.F.Gustafson⟩ **2 :** CONSEQUENCE, RESULT ⟨as a gratifying ~ of the recent aeronautical exposition —*N.Y.Times*⟩ **syn** see EFFECT

af·ter·most \\ˈ==ˌmōst, *esp Brit also* -ˌməst\\ *adj* [[4]*after* + *-most*] **:** nearest the stern of a ship **:** farthest aft

af·ter·nan \\ˈaftə(r)ˌnan\\ *n* -s [origin unknown] **:** a desert shrub (*Euphorbia balsamifera*) native to the Canary islands having leaves at the ends of the branches and inconspicuous yellow flowers

afternight \\ˈ==ˈ=\\ *n* [[2]*after* + *night* (nightfall)] *chiefly dial* **:** EVENING

[1]**afternoon** \\ˈ==ˈ=\\ *n* [ME *afternon*, fr. [2]*after* + *non* noon]

1 : the part of day between noon and sunset ⟨we were forced to make camp that ~ while it was still light —Kenneth Roberts⟩ ⟨during the late ~ and early evening —Frank Yerby⟩ **2 :** the part of the day between noon and midnight ⟨keeping open until after 10 in the ~⟩ — chiefly in legal use; abbr. *p.m.* **3 :** a relatively late period (as of time or life) ⟨a story that carries us through four wars, through the long Victorian ~ —Clifton Fadiman⟩ — compare EVENING 2

²afternoon \"\ *adj* **:** of, relating to, or intended primarily for use in the afternoon ⟨~ tea⟩ ⟨~ papers are issued from about 10:30 a.m. until about 5 p.m. —Bruce Westley⟩ ⟨~ dress⟩

af·ter·noon·er \ˌ⸗⸗ˈ⸗ə(r)\ *n* -s **:** an afternoon newspaper

afternoon lady *n* **:** FOUR-O'CLOCK

af·ter·noons \ˌ⸗⸗ˈnünz\ *adv* **:** in the afternoon repeatedly **:** on any afternoon ⟨~ he'd drop off to sleep —Helen Eustis⟩

afternoon watch *n* **:** the watch on a ship from noon to 4 p.m.

afterpain \ˈ⸗⸗ˌ⸗\ *n* -s [⁴*after* + *pain*] **1 :** pain that follows an exciting cause only after a distinct interval ⟨the ~ of a tooth extraction⟩ **2 afterpains** *pl* **:** pains that follow the termination of labor and are associated with contraction of the uterus towards its nonpregnant size

afterpart \ˈ⸗⸗ˌ⸗\ *n* [ME, fr. ⁴*after* + *part*] **:** the stern area of a ship

afterpeak \ˈ⸗⸗ˌ⸗\ *n* [⁴*after* + *peak*] **:** the extreme after compartment in a ship's hold where the ship narrows toward the sternpost

afterpiece \ˈ⸗⸗ˌ⸗\ *n* [⁴*after* + *piece*] **:** a short usu. comic entertainment performed after a play

afterpotential \ˈ⸗⸗⸗ˈ⸗⸗\ *n* [⁴*after* + *potential*] **:** the sequence of electrical events that follows the spike potential of nerve activity and that usu. takes the form of a negative followed by a positive potential with both being of much smaller amplitude than the spike potential

afterpressure \ˈ⸗⸗ˌ⸗⸗\ *n* [⁴*after* + *pressure*] **:** AFTERTOUCH

afterripen \ˌ⸗⸗ˈ⸗⸗\ *vb* [¹*after* + *ripen*] *vi* **:** to undergo afterripening ~ *vt* **:** to subject to afterripening

afterripening \ˌ⸗⸗ˈ⸗(ə)⸗\ *n* **:** a complex enzymatic process occurring in seeds, bulbs, tubers, and fruits after harvesting and often necessary for subsequent germination or palatable consumption

af·ters \-tə(r)z\ *n pl* [¹*after* + -*s*] *Brit* **:** DESSERT

aftersensation \ˈ⸗⸗(ˌ)⸗ˌ⸗⸗\ *n* [⁴*after* + *sensation*] **:** AFTERIMAGE

aftershaft \ˈ⸗⸗ˌ⸗\ *n* [⁴*after* + *shaft*] **:** an accessory plume arising from the posterior side of the stem of the feathers of many birds — **af·ter·shaft·ed** \ˈ⸗⸗ˌ⸗⸗\ *adj*

aftershock \ˈ⸗⸗ˌ⸗\ *n* [⁴*after* + *shock*] **:** a minor or accessory shock following the main shock of an earthquake

aftershow \ˈ⸗⸗ˌ⸗\ *n* [⁴*after* + *show*] **:** a short entertainment (as a band concert) presented in the main tent of a circus after the regular performance

aftersupper *n* [ME *aftersoper*, fr. ²*after* + *soper* supper] *obs* **:** the period of time after supper

afterswarm \ˈ⸗⸗ˌ⸗\ *n* [⁴*after* + *swarm*] **:** a swarm of honeybees that leaves a hive after the prime or first swarm

aftertack \ˈ⸗⸗ˌ⸗\ *n* [⁴*after* + *tack*] **:** residual tackiness or stickiness of a film (as of a varnish) after drying is complete

aftertaste \ˈ⸗⸗ˌ⸗\ *n* [⁴*after* + *taste*] **1 :** persistence of a sensation of flavor after the stimulating substance has passed out of contact with the sensory end organs for taste — used esp. of unpleasant flavors ⟨the powder leaves no bitter ~ —*Scientific Monthly*⟩ **2 :** a remnant or recurrence (as of an emotion) ⟨the ~ of hot anger⟩

afterthought \ˈ⸗⸗ˌ⸗\ *n* [⁴*after* + *thought*] **:** an idea or notion occurring later ⟨left space on every page for ~*s*⟩ **:** a part, feature, or device not present in a whole as first planned or made ⟨the porch was added as an ~⟩

aftertime \ˈ⸗⸗ˌ⸗\ *n* [⁴*after* + *time*] **:** time after the present **:** FUTURE

aftertouch \ˈ⸗⸗ˌ⸗\ *n* [⁴*after* + *touch*] **:** the sensation of pressure persisting for a time after actual pressure has ceased

aftertreat \ˈ⸗⸗ˌtrēt\ *vt* [back-formation fr. *aftertreatment*] **:** to subject to aftertreatment

aftertreatment \ˈ⸗⸗ˌ⸗⸗\ *n* [⁴*after* + *treatment*] **:** a secondary treatment to which a material (as film or dyed goods) is subjected after the primary treatment is finished

afterturn \ˈ⸗⸗ˌ⸗\ *n* [⁴*after* + *turn*] **:** the twist of the strands composing a rope — compare FORETURN

afterwale \ˈ⸗⸗ˌ⸗\ *n* [⁴*after* + *wale* (ridge of a horse collar)] **:** the body or pad of a horse collar that rests on the horse's shoulders

afterwar \ˌ⸗⸗ˈ⸗\ *adj* [²*after* + *war*] **:** POSTWAR

¹af·ter·ward *R* ˈ⸗tə(r)wərd, -*R* -təwəd\ *or* **af·ter·wards** \-dz\ *adv* [ME *afterward, afterwardes*, fr. OE *æfterweard*, fr. *æfter* behind + -*weard* -ward, -wards — more at AFTER] **:** at a later or succeeding time **:** SUBSEQUENTLY

²afterward \"\ *or* **afterwards** \"\ *n, pl* **afterwards :** FUTURE

afterwash \ˈ⸗⸗ˌ⸗\ *n* [⁴*after* + *wash*] **:** BACKWASH 2

afterwelt \ˈ⸗⸗ˌ⸗\ *n* [⁴*after* + *welt*] *in women's stockings* **:** the narrow strip between the welt and the leg knitted of medium-weight yarn

¹afterwhile \ˌ⸗⸗ˈ⸗\ *adv* [²*after* + *while* (n.)] **:** after a while **:** by and by **:** later on

²afterwhile \ˈ⸗⸗ˌ⸗\ *n* [⁴*after* + *while*] **:** AFTERTIME

afterwisdom \ˈ⸗⸗ˌ⸗⸗\ *n* [⁴*after* + *wisdom*] **:** wisdom after the event **:** wisdom arrived at when it is too late

afterwit *n* [⁴*after* + *wit*] **1** *obs* **:** later knowledge **2 :** wisdom or perception that comes after it can be of use

afterword \ˈ⸗⸗ˌ⸗\ *n* [⁴*after* + *word*; prob. translation of G *nachwort*] **:** EPILOGUE 1

afterwork \ˈ⸗⸗ˌ⸗\ *or* **afterworking** \ˈ⸗⸗ˌ⸗⸗\ *n* [⁴*after* + *work, working*] **:** ELASTIC AFTERWORK

afterworld \ˈ⸗⸗ˌ⸗\ *n* [⁴*after* + *world*] **:** a future world **:** a world after death

afteryears \ˈ⸗⸗ˌ⸗\ *n pl* [⁴*after* + *years*] **:** subsequent years **:** later times

aftn *abbr* afternoon

af·to·ni·an \(ˈ)afˈtōnēən\ *adj, usu cap A* [*Afton*, town in Iowa + E -*ian*] **:** belonging to the first interglacial interval during the glacial epoch in No. America

af·to·sa \afˈtōsə, -ōzə\ *n* -s [AmerSp, short for Sp. *fiebre aftosa* aphthous fever, fr. *fiebre* fever + *aftosa*, fem. of *aftoso* aphthous, fr. *afta* aphtha (fr. L *aphtha*) + -*oso* -ous — more at APHTHA] **:** FOOT-AND-MOUTH DISEASE

a·func·tion·al \(ˈ)āˈf-\ *adj* **:** lacking a normal function ⟨the ~ vestigial teeth of certain snakes⟩ ⟨having a stiff ~ knee⟩

af·wil·lite \ˈafwəˌlīt\ *n* -s [Alpheus Fuller *Williams b*1874 Am. mining engineer + E -*ite*] **:** a mineral $Ca_3Si_2O_4(OH)_6$ consisting of a hydrous calcium silicate and occurring in colorless monoclinic crystals (sp. gr. 2.6)

ag \ˈag, ˈaa(ə)g, ˈaig\ *adj* [short for *agriculture & agricultural*] **:** of or relating to agriculture ⟨~ school⟩

ag- — see AD-

ag *abbr* angolar

AG *abbr* **1** accountant general **2** adjutant general **3** agent-general **4** antigas **5** attorney general

Ag *symbol* [L *argentum*] silver

aga *also* **agha** \ˈägə, ˈa-\ *n* -s *often cap* [Turk *ağa* lord, master] **:** a man of authority who bears a title of respect: as **a :** a military or civil officer in the Ottoman Empire ⟨a vast body of dragoons . . . under . . . their great ~ —Jonathan Swift⟩ **b :** a Turkish chief ⟨the khans . . . and ~*s* . . . are probably the oldest landed aristocracy of the world —Harold Lamb⟩ **c :** a religious leader ⟨the *Aga* Khan . . . claims descent from Fatima —H.G.Rawlinson⟩

agaces *pl of* AGAZ

¹again \əˈgen *also* -ān *or* (*less often in stand than in substand speech*) -in\ *adv* [ME *again, agen, ayen*, fr. OE *ongēan, ongeagn, ongēn* towards, against, back (akin to OS *angegin*, OHG *ingagan, ingegin*), fr. *on* + (assumed) *gēan, geagn, gēn* against, toward (whence OE *gēan-, geagn-, gēn-*); akin to OHG *gegin, gagan* against, toward, ON *gegn* against, direct, OFris *jēn* against, toward] **1 a :** BACK; *specif* **:** in the opposite direction ⟨let us turn ~ and go home —John Bunyan⟩ **b** (1) **:** in return or in response **:** BACK ⟨soft eyes looked love to eyes which spake ~ —Lord Byron⟩ (2) **:** as a result or consequence ⟨the wind blowing . . . till every timber of the old house creaked ~ —Charles Dickens⟩ **2 :** another time **:** once more **:** ANEW ⟨I shall not look upon his like ~ —Shak.⟩ **3 :** as another point, fact, or instance: **a :** on the other hand ⟨he might go and ~ he might not⟩ **b :** in the next place **:** FURTHER ⟨~, these cases would not go to court —S.H.Hofstadter⟩ **4 a :** in addition **:** BESIDES ⟨that's something else ~⟩ **b :** by as much more ⟨his house is as big ~ as mine⟩ ⟨he has half ~ as much land as I do⟩

²again \"\ *prep* [ME *again, agen, ayen* toward, opposite, against, fr. OE *ongēan, ongeagn, ongēn*, fr. *ongēan, ongeagn, ongēn*, adv.] *now dial* **:** AGAINST ⟨sitting up with pillows behind her, leaning ~ them —Richard Llewellyn⟩

³again \"\ *conj* [ME *again, agen, ayen*, fr. *again, agen, ayen*, prep.] *now dial* **:** by the time that **:** AGAINST ⟨~ I got there, he was gone⟩

again and again *adv* **:** time after time **:** OFTEN, REPEATEDLY

¹against \əˈgen(t)st, -nzt *also* -ān- *or* (*less often in stand than in substand speech*) -in-\ *prep* [ME *against, agenst, avenst*, alter. of *againes, agenes, ayenes*, fr. *again, agen, ayen*, prep. + -es -'s] **1 a :** directly opposite **:** in front of **:** FACING ⟨America seems to stand ~ it with a fire extinguisher and . . . gets burned —E.A.Mowrer⟩ — often used with preceding *over* **b** *obs* **:** in the presence of **:** exposed to **:** WITH ⟨those boughs which shake ~ the cold —Shak.⟩ **2 a :** from an opposite direction and into contact with **:** UPON ⟨the fighter was knocked back ~ the ropes⟩ **b :** in contact with **:** TOUCHING ⟨~ the walls of . . . the houses . . . were pear trees —Ernest Hemingway⟩ **c :** close to **:** BESIDE, NEAR ⟨ships lay ~ the walls —Daniel Defoe⟩ **3 :** in a direction opposite to the course or motion of **:** counter to ⟨they sailed ~ the wind⟩ ⟨a ground swell running ~ the new education —Paul Woodring⟩ **4 a :** in opposition or hostility to ⟨stood steadfast ~ alumni pressure —J.B.Conant⟩ ⟨a successful campaign ~ the enemy⟩ **b :** not in conformity with **:** contrary to ⟨offenses ~ the law⟩ ⟨forced to act ~ his conscience⟩ **c :** in spite of **:** NOTWITHSTANDING ⟨succeeded ~ many handicaps⟩ **d :** in competition with ⟨a race run ~ the clock⟩ **5 a :** as a defense or protection from **:** in resistance to ⟨puffed his cigar ~ the mosquitoes —Claud Cockburn⟩ ⟨at wit's end what to do ~ the inexorable ticking of the clock —G.J.Nathan⟩ **b :** in the face of **:** FROM ⟨to protect their native subjects ~ the rapacity of some . . . business communities —W.T.Stace⟩ **6 :** compared with or contrasted to ⟨the importance of space as ~ time and of time as ~ space —A.N.Whitehead⟩ ⟨net profits of 80 cents a share ~ 70 cents last year⟩ **7 :** in preparation or provision for **:** in anticipation of ⟨silver coins hoarded ~ a day of need —W.P.Webb⟩ **8 :** with respect to **:** relating to **:** TOWARD ⟨customs which had the force of law ~ both lord and tenant —E.C.Smith⟩ **9 a :** in the opposite scale to **:** as a counterbalance to ⟨his pride in his own prestige is set ~ his kindness to younger writers —P.M. Fulcher⟩ **b :** in exchange for **:** in return for ⟨the free-market rate ~ dollars was 302 francs⟩ **c :** as a charge upon **:** to the debit of ⟨to make today's purchases ~ tomorrow's earnings⟩ **10 :** having as background: as **a :** before the surface or expanse of ⟨the rain is dark ~ the white sky —Amy Lowell⟩ ⟨~ this background the developments of the last two . . . years are . . . easy to grasp —Barbara Ward⟩ **b :** above the sound of ⟨talking ~ the music⟩ **11** *dial* **:** not later than **:** by the time of ⟨to leave ~ noon⟩ — **against the grain** *adv* **1 :** across the fiber of the wood **2 :** counter to one's inclination, disposition, or feelings ⟨the check he had imposed upon himself in the chapel, *against the grain* —Margery Bailey⟩ — **against the sun** *adv* **:** in a direction opposite to that of the sun's motion as it appears to one facing south in the northern hemisphere **:** COUNTERCLOCKWISE — opposed to *with the sun* — **against time** *adv* **1 :** in an attempt to approach, equal, or surpass a record or a previously recorded time ⟨they raced, not against each other, but *against time*⟩ **2 :** in an effort to complete an action before a certain time ⟨he wrote the essay hurriedly, as if *against time*⟩ ⟨were working *against time* to repair the levees⟩ **3 :** with the intention of effecting a delay by using up time ⟨the legislator was merely talking *against time*⟩

²against \"\ *conj* [ME *against, agenst, avenst*, fr. *against, agenst, ayenst*, prep.] **1** *now chiefly dial* **:** BEFORE **:** by the time that **2** *now chiefly dial* **:** in readiness for the time when

agal \əˈgäl\ *n* -s [Ar *ʻiqāl* bond, rope] **:** a cord usu. of goat's hair that Arabs (as the Bedouins) wind around their heads to hold down the kerchieflike headdress

aga·lac·tia \ˌāgəˈlaksh(ē)ə, -ktēə\ *n* -s [NL, fr. Gk *agalaktia* lack of milk, fr. *agalaktos* giving no milk (fr. *-a-* ²*a-* + *galakt-, gala* milk) + *-ia*] **:** the failure of the secretion of milk in mammals from any cause other than the normal ending of a lactation period — **aga·lac·tic** \ˌ⸗⸗ˈ⸗tik\ *adj* — **aga·lac·tous** \ˌ⸗⸗ˈ⸗təs\ *adj*

agal-agal \ˈägəlˈägəl\ *n* -s [of Indonesian origin; akin to Malay *agar-agar*] **:** AGAR 1a

aga·lax·ia \ˌāgəˈlaksēə\ *or* **ag·a·laxy** \ˈagəˌlaksē\ *n, pl* **agalaxias** *or* **agalaxies** [NL *agalaxia*, fr. Gk *agalax* giving no milk (fr. *a-* ²*a-* + *-galax*, fr. *gala* milk) + NL *-ia*] **:** AGALACTIA

ag·a·le·na \ˌagəˈlēnə\ *n, cap* [NL, fr. ²*a-* + Gk *galēnē* stillness, fr. fem. of *galēnos* calm, gentle] **:** a genus (the type of the family Agalenidae) of spiders that spin concave webs ending in a funnel-shaped tube where the spider hides — see GRASS SPIDER

ag·a·li·nis \ˌagəˈlīnəs\ *n, cap* [NL, irreg. fr. Gk *aga, agē* wonder + L *linum* flax] **:** a genus of flaxlike American herbs (family Scrophulariaceae) with opposite sessile leaves and irregular tubular mostly purple flowers

ag·a·lite \ˈagəˌlīt\ *n* -s [prob. fr. Gk *aga, agē* + E *-lite*] **:** a fine fibrous variety of talc

agal·lia \əˈgalēə\ *n, cap* [NL, fr. ²*a-* + LGk *gallia* guts] **:** a genus of leafhoppers that includes some species implicated as vectors of a virus disease of So. American sugar beets resembling curly top

agal·loch \əˈgalək, ˈagəˌläk\ *also* **agal·lo·chum** \əˈgaləkəm\ *n* -s [*agalloch* fr. LL or Gk; LL *agallochon*, fr. Gk, prob. by folk etymology (influence of *agallein* to adorn) fr. a word of Dravidian origin; akin to Tamil *akil* agalloch; *agallochum*, NL, fr. LL *agallochon*] **:** the soft resinous wood of an East Indian tree (*Aquilaria agallocha*) of the family Thymelaeaceae that is burnt as a perfume by the Orientals — called also *agalwood, agilawood, aloeswood, eaglewood*

agal·lop \əˈ-\ *adv* [¹*a-* + *gallop*, v.] **:** at a gallop

agal·ma \əˈgalmə\ *n, pl* **agalma·ta** \-mədə\ [Gk, fr. *agallein* to adorn; prob. akin to Gk *megas* large, great — more at MUCH] **:** MEMORIAL; *specif* **:** a primitive Greek statue of a god

ag·al·mat·o·lite \ˌagalˈmadᵊlˌīt, əˌgalˈ-, ˌagalˈ-\ *n* -s [NL *agalmatolithus*, fr. Gk *agalmat-, agalma* + NL *-lithus* -lite] **:** a soft compact stone of a grayish, greenish, or yellowish color, sometimes stained, carved into images or miniature pagodas by the Chinese — called also *figure stone, pagodite*

ag·al·wood \ˈagəlˌ-\ *or* **ag·a·la·wood** \ˈagələˌ-\ *n* [*agal-* or *agala-* (fr. *agalloch*) + *wood*] **:** AGALLOCH

agam- *or* **agamo-** *comb form* [NL, fr. LL *agamus* unmarried, fr. Gk *agamos*, fr. *a-* ²*a-* + *gamos* marriage — more at BIGAMY] **:** asexual ⟨*agamic*⟩ ⟨*agamogenesis*⟩

¹aga·ma \əˈgämə, ˈagəmə\ *n* [NL] **1** *cap* **:** a genus (the type of the family Agamidae) of Old World terrestrial lizards including many that are of bright and changeable colors **2** -s **:** a lizard of the genus *Agama*

²aga·ma \ˈägəmə\ *n* -s [Skt *āgama*, lit., arrival, acquisition of knowledge, fr. *āgacchati* he comes, arrives, fr. *ā* towards + *gacchati* he goes; akin to *gamati* he goes — more at ACHARYA, COME] **:** one of a class of tantric treatises accepted as scripture within Hinduism and Buddhism — compare TANTRA

ag·a·mae \ˈagəˌ(ˌ)mē\ [NL, fr. ²*a-* + *-gamae*] *syn of* CRYPTOGAMIA

aga·mete \ˌāgəˈmēt, (ˈ)āˈgaˌmēt, ˈagəˌmēt\ *n* -s [ISV, fr. Gk *agametos, agamētos* unmarried, fr. *a-* ²*a-* + *-gametos, -gamētos* married (fr. *gametēs* spouse, fr. *gamos* marriage) — more at BIGAMY] **:** an asexual reproductive cell (as a spore or a merozoite)

agam·ic \(ˈ)āˈgamik\ *adj* [*agam-* + *-ic*] **:** ASEXUAL, PARTHENOGENETIC — **agam·i·cal·ly** \-ək(ə)lē\ *adv*

¹ag·a·mid \ˈagəməd, -(ˌ)mid\ *adj* [NL *Agamidae*] **:** of or relating to the Agamidae

²agamid \"\ *n* -s **:** a lizard of the family Agamidae

agam·i·dae \əˈgaməˌdē\ *n pl, cap* [NL, fr. *Agama*, type genus + *-idae*] **:** a widely distributed family of Old World lizards related to the New World iguanas but distinguished by acrodont dentition and including arboreal, terrestrial, and semiaquatic forms most of which are insectivorous (as the frilled lizard, the flying dragon, and the Australian moloch)

agam·ma·glob·u·li·ne·mia \ˌāˌgaməˌgläbyələˈnēmēə\ *n* -s [NL, fr. ²*a-* + E *gamma globulin* + NL *-emia*] **:** a pathological condition in which the body forms no gamma globulins or antibodies or forms them only in minute amounts

agam·o·gen·e·sis \ˌāˌgaməˈjenəsəs, ˈagəmō-\ *n* [NL, fr. *agam-* + L *genesis*] **1 :** PARTHENOGENESIS **2 :** asexual reproduction — **agamo·ge·net·ic** \ˌāˌgaməjəˈnedˌik, ˈagəmō-\ *adj* — **agamo·ge·net·i·cal·ly** \-ək(ə)lē\ *adv*

ag·a·moid \ˈagəˌmȯid\ *adj* [NL *Agama* + *-oid*] **:** of or resembling *Agama* or lizards of this genus

aga·mog·o·ny \ˌāgəˈmägənē, ˌag-\ *n* -ES [*agam-* + *-gony*] **:** asexual reproduction; *specif* **:** SCHIZOGONY

ag·a·mo·mer·mid \ˌagəmōˈmərməd\ *n* -s [irreg. fr. NL *Agamomermith-, Agamomermis*] **:** a worm of the genus *Agamomermis*

ag·a·mo·mer·mis \-məs\ *n, cap* [NL, fr. *agam-* + Gk *mermis* cord, string — more at MERMIS] **:** a genus of nematode worms (family Mermithidae) that are normally free living as adults and larval parasites of insects and that may accidentally parasitize man

agam·ont \(ˈ)āˈgaˌmänt\ *n* -s [²*a-* + *gam-* + *-ont*] **:** SCHIZONT

ag·a·mo·spe·cies \ˈagəmō-\ *n* [*agam-* + *species*] **:** a group of obviously related asexually reproducing biotypes regarded as a group equivalent to a species

agamo·sperm·ic \(ˈ)āˈgaməˈspərmik, ˈagəmō-\ *also* **agamo·sperm·ous** \-məs\ *adj* [*agam-* + *-spermic, -spermous*] **:** exhibiting or reproducing by agamospermy

agamo·sper·my \āˈgaməˌspərmē, ˈagəmō-\ *n* -ES [*agam-* + *-spermy*] **:** APOGAMY 2; *specif* **:** apogamy in which sexual union is not completed because of abnormal development of both embryo sac and pollen, embryos being produced from the innermost layer of the integument — compare APOMIXIS 1

agam·o·spore \(ˈ)āˈgaməˌspō(ə)r, ˈagəmō-\ *n* -s [*agam-* + *spore*] **:** an asexual spore

ag·a·mous \ˈagəməs\ *adj* [Gk *agamos* unmarried, fr. *a-* ²*a-* + *-gamos* (fr. *gamos* marriage) — more at BIGAMY] **1 :** of or relating to agamy **2 :** AGAMIC

ag·a·my \ˈagəmē\ *n* -ES [Gk *agamia* celibacy, fr. *agamos* + *-ia*] **1 :** absence, nonregulation, or nonrecognition of marriage **2 :** AGAMOGENESIS

agan·gli·on·ic \(ˈ)āˈ⸗⸗ˈ⸗\ *adj* [²*a-* + *ganglionic*] **:** lacking ganglia

ag·a·on·i·dae \ˌagāˈänəˌdē\ [NL, fr. *Agaon*, type genus + *-idae*] *syn of* AGAONTIDAE

ag·a·on·ti·dae \ˌagāˈäntəˌdē\ *n pl, cap* [NL, alter. of *Agaonidae*] **:** a family of small chiefly tropical chalcid wasps having the fore and hind pairs of legs heavier than the middle pair and the male usu. wingless — see FIG WASP

ag·a·pan·thus \ˌagəˈpan(t)thəs\ *n* [NL, fr. Gk *agapē* love + NL *-anthus*] **1** *cap* **:** a small genus of southern African herbs (family Liliaceae) having radical leaves and scapose umbels of showy blue or purple flowers **2** -ES **:** a plant of the genus *Agapanthus* (esp. *A. africanus*) — called also *African lily, African tulip*

¹agape \əˈgāp *sometimes* -ap\ *adj* [¹*a-* + *gape*, v.] **1 :** wide open **:** GAPING ⟨his mouth was ~ in yokel fashion —Stephen Crane⟩ **2 :** in an attitude or state of wonder, expectation, or eager attention ⟨leaving him alone and ~ upon his feet —Dorothy Sayers⟩

²aga·pe \äˈgäˌpā, ˈägəˌ-, ˈagə-; ˈagəˌpē\ *n, pl* **aga·pae** \-ˌpī; -ˌpē\ *or* **aga·pai** \-ˌpī\ *also* **agapes** *sometimes cap* [LL, fr. Gk *agapē*, lit., love, back-formation fr. *agapan* to welcome, love; perh. akin to *agallein* to adorn — more at AGALMA] **1 :** a love feast or common meal of fellowship originating among the early Christians and including prayers, songs, the reading of Scripture, and offerings for the poor **2 :** spontaneous self-giving love expressed freely without calculation of cost or gain to the giver or merit on the part of the receiver: **a :** the love of God for man **b :** Christian brotherly love in its highest manifestation

ag·a·pem·o·ne \ˌagəˈpeməˌ(ˌ)nē\ *n* -s *often cap* [fr. *Agapemone*, a communistic establishment that was founded *ab*1849 at Spaxton, England, and had a reputation for immoral behavior, irreg. fr. Gk *agapē* love + *monē* stopping place, fr. *menein* to remain — more at MANSION] **:** a free-love institution ⟨allow Christopher to run an *Agapemone* in what was after all her own house —F.M.Ford⟩

aga·pe·tae \ˌägəˈpāˌtī, ˌagə-; ˌagəˈpēˌtē\ *n pl* [LL, fr. LGk *agapētai*, pl. of *agapētē*, fr. Gk, fem. of *agapētos* beloved, desirable, to be acquiesced in, fr. *agapan* to welcome, love] **:** women of the early church who lived under a pledge of spiritual love in the same house with men bound to strict celibacy

aga·pe·ti \-ˈpāˌtē, -ˈpēˌtī\ *n pl* [LGk *agapētoi*, pl. of *agapētos*, fr. *agapētos*, adj., beloved] **:** Christian monks of the early church who lived under vows of celibacy in the same house with nuns

ag·a·por·nis \ˌagəˈpȯrnəs\ *n, cap* [NL, fr. Gk *agapē* love + NL *-ornis*] **:** a genus of small short-tailed African parrots — see LOVEBIRD

agar \ˈäˌgär, ˈāˌgä(r), ˈa- *also* ˈā- *or* -ˌgə(r)\ *or* **agar-agar** \ˈ⸗(ˌ)⸗ˈ⸗(ˌ)⸗\ *n* -s [Malay *agar-agar*] **1 a :** any of various colloidal extractives of certain red algae (as of the genera *Gelidium, Gracilaria*, and *Eucheuma*) that are similar products both in appearance, being usu. in the form of translucent strips or flakes or a white powder, and in other physical properties (as ability to swell in cold water and to dissolve in hot water); that may differ in chemical structure, a common type being thought to be essentially a sulfuric acid ester of a linear galactan occurring as salts in the cell walls of the algae; and that are used chiefly in culture media, as bases for dental impression materials, as bulk producers in treating chronic constipation, and as gelling and stabilizing agents in foods (as jellies, dairy products, and canned meat and fish) — called also *Chinese gelatin, Chinese isinglass, Japanese gelatin, Japanese isinglass* **b :** any of the plants from which agar is obtained **2 :** any of various culture media having agar as a solidifying agent ⟨nutrient ~⟩ ⟨blood ~⟩

¹ag·a·ric \ˈagərik, ˈaig-; əˈgarik, -ēk *also* -ˈger-\ *n* -s [L *agaricum*, a fungus, fr. Gk *agarikon*] **1 :** a fungus of the family Agaricaceae and esp. of the genus *Agaricus* **2 :** any of several species of the genus *Fomes* (esp. *F. igniarius*) used in the preparation of punk **3 :** the dried fruit body of a mushroom (*Fomes officinalis* or *Polyporus officinalis*) formerly used in the treatment of excessive perspiration (as in the night sweats of tuberculosis)

²agaric \"\ *adj* **:** of or relating to agarics **:** like a fungus

agar·i·ca·ce·ae \əˌgarəˈkāsēˌē\ *n pl, cap* [NL, fr. *Agaricus*, type genus + *-aceae*] **:** a large family of fungi (order Agaricales) including many familiar mushrooms with the sporophore usu. consisting of a central stalk and an umbrellalike cap on the lower surface of which are numerous lamellae bearing the hymenium — **agar·i·ca·ceous** \ˌ⸗⸗⸗ˈshəs\ *adj*

agaric acid *or* **ag·a·ric·ic acid** \ˌagəˈrisik-\ *n* **1 :** a white powdery tribasic acid $C_{22}H_{40}O_7$ constituting the active principle of agaric — called also *agaricinic acid* **2 :** AGARINIC ACID

agar·i·ca·les \əˌgarəˈkā(ˌ)lēz\ *n pl, cap* [NL, fr. *Agaricus* + *-ales*] **:** an extensive order of basidiomycetous fungi that includes the typical gilled mushrooms and a number of related forms all having the basidia produced in a distinct hymenial fruiting layer usu. spread over the surface of a definite but transitory fruiting body which may be flat or be supinate, simply or compoundly club-shaped, or with the surface increased by pores, gills, or spines

ag·a·ric·i·form \ˌagəˈrisəˌfȯrm\ *adj* [ISV ¹*agaric* + *-iform*] **:** having the form of an agaric

agar·i·cin \əˈgarəsən\ *n* -s [¹*agaric* + *-in*] **:** an impure form of the active principle of agaric (sense 3)

agar·i·cine \-ˌsēn, -ˌsən\ *n* -s [ISV ¹*agaric* + *-ine*] **:** CHOLINE

agar·i·cin·ic acid \əˌgarəˈsinik-\ *n* [*agaricine* + *-ic*] **:** AGARIC ACID 1

agaric mineral *n* **:** a light chalky deposit of calcium carbonate formed in caverns or fissures of limestone — called also *rock milk*

agar·i·coid \əˈgarəˌkȯid\ *adj* [ISV ¹*agaric* + *-oid*] **:** resembling an agaric ⟨~ fungi⟩

agar·i·cus \-kəs\ *n, cap* [NL, alter. of L *agaricum*, a fungus — more at AGARIC] **:** a genus (the type of the family Agaricaceae) comprising gill fungi which have brown spores and including several members which are edible — see HORSE MUSHROOM, MEADOW MUSHROOM

ag·a·rin·ic acid \ˌagəˈrinik-\ *n* [*agar* + *-in* + *-ic*] **:** the free acid that is held to occur in agar — called also *agaric acid*

ag·a·ris·ti·dae \ˌagəˈristəˌdē\ *n pl, cap* [NL, fr. *Agarista*, type genus (perh. after *Agariste fl* 6th cent. B.C. daughter of Cleisthenes, tyrant of Sicyon, fr. Gk *Agaristē*) + *-idae*] **:** a family of mostly diurnal and brightly colored moths having the antennae thickened toward the tip and including the Australian whistling moths — see FORESTER

ag·a·ri·ta \ˌagəˈrēdə, ˌäg-\ *also* **agri·to** \əˈgrēd·(ˌ)ō\ *n* -s [MexSp *agrito*, prob. fr. Sp *agrio* sour, fr. OSp *agro*, fr. L *acr-, acer* — more at EAGER] **:** a shrub (*Mahonia trifoliata*) of Texas, New Mexico, and adjacent Mexico that yields a yellow dye, a tanning extract, and an ink and produces a bright red berry that is used to make jelly — compare OREGON GRAPE

ag·a·roid \ˈagəˌrȯid\ *n* -s **:** a substance similar to agar in properties that is obtained from certain red algae (as of the genus *Phyllophora*)

agar·o·phyte \əˈgarəˌfīt\ *n* -s [*agar* + *-o-* + *-phyte*] **:** an agar-yielding seaweed

ag·a·rum \ˈagərəm\ *n, cap* [NL, fr. E *agar*] **:** a genus of kelps (family Laminariaceae) inhabiting the colder oceans and having a branched holdfast, a brief stipe, and a lamina with smooth perforated margins

agar·wal \ˈägərˌwäl, ˈag-\ *n* -s [Hindi *aggarwāl*] **:** a mercantile caste of central India

ag·as·siz·o·cri·nus \ˌagəˌsē(z)əˈkrīnəs\ *n, cap* [NL, fr. Alexander *Agassiz* + NL *-o-* + *-crinus* (fr. L *crinis* hair) — more at CRINAL] **:** a genus of fossil crinoids known chiefly from Mississippian formations of No. America and characterized by a thick-walled ovoid cup

ag·as·siz trawl \ˈagə(ˌ)sē-\ *n, usu cap A* [after Alexander *Agassiz* †1910 Am. zoologist] **:** a dredge that consists of a heavy rectangular iron frame to which is fitted the mouth of a bag of stout netting and that is used in collecting plankton

agas·ta·che \əˈgastə(ˌ)kē\ *n, cap* [NL, irreg. fr. Gk *agan* very much + *stachys* ear of grain — more at STING] **:** a genus of No. American herbs (family Labiatae) having opposite toothed leaves and dense terminal spikes of 2-lipped flowers — see GIANT HYSSOP

agas·tric \(ˈ)āˈgastrik\ *adj* [²*a-* + Gk *gastr-, gastēr* stomach + E *-ic*] *zool* **:** having no stomach or distinct digestive canal ⟨the tapeworm is ~⟩

ag·a·ta \ˈagəd·ə\ *n* -s [It, agate, fr. L *achates*] **:** a late 19th century American glassware characterized by a mottled finish

¹ag·ate \ˈagət, ˈaig-\ *n* -s [MF, fr. L *achates*, fr. Gk *achatēs*] **1 :** a fine-grained chalcedony frequently mixed with opal and having various colors arranged in stripes or bands, blended in clouds, or showing mosslike forms — see FORTIFICATION AGATE, MOSS AGATE **2** *obs* **:** a very small person ⟨I was never manned with an ~ till now —*Shak.*⟩ **3 :** something made of or fitted with agate: as **a :** a drawplate having a drilled eye of agate used by gold-wire drawers **b :** a bookbinder's burnisher with an agate tip **c :** a playing marble of agate or of glass resembling agate **4 :** a size of type between pearl and nonpareil, approximately 5½ point — called also *ruby;* compare POINT SYSTEM **5 :** IRON-OXIDE RED

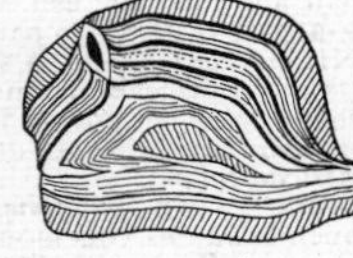
agate 1

²agate \"\ *adj* **:** of or resembling agate; *esp* **:** of the color of agate ⟨his brown ~ eyes —Oscar Wilde⟩

³agate \əˈgāt\ *adv (or adj)* [¹*a-* + *gate* (way)] **1** *dial Brit* **:** on the way; in motion **2** *dial Brit* **a :** going on **:** ASTIR **b :** AMISS, WRONG ⟨what's ~ now⟩

agate glass *n* **:** glass made by blending two or more colored glasses or by rolling transparent glass into powdered glass of various colors during the melting

agate gray *n* **:** a nearly neutral slightly yellowish medium gray that is lighter than flint gray, gull (sense 2 a), or old silver

agate jasper *n* **:** a chalcedonic quartz consisting of jasper and agate

agate line *n* **:** a space one column wide and 1⁄14 inch deep used as a unit of measurement in publication advertising — see ¹AGATE 4

agate opal *n* **:** opalized agate

agate shell *n* **1 :** the shell of the agate snail **2 :** AGATE SNAIL

agate snail *n* [so called from the variegated colors] **:** a member of the African family Achatinidae which includes the largest known land mollusks, some reaching 9 or 10 inches in length — compare ACHATINA

ag·ate·ware \ˈ==ˌ=\ *n* **1 :** pottery veined and mottled to resemble agate **2 :** an enameled iron or steel ware for household utensils

agath- *or* **agatho-** *comb form* [Gk, fr. *agathos;* perh. akin to OE *gōd* good — more at GOOD] **:** good ⟨*Agathosma*⟩ ⟨*agathology*⟩

ag·a·thau·mas \ˌagəˈthȯməs\ *n, cap* [NL, irreg. fr. Gk *agan* very much + *thaumasios* marvelous, fr. *thauma* marvel] **:** a genus of herbivorous dinosaurs related to and possibly not distinct from *Triceratops*

agath·ic acid \əˈgathik-\ *n* [NL *Agathis* + E *-ic*] **:** a crystalline diterpenoid dibasic acid $C_{18}H_{28}(COOH)_2$ obtained from Manila copal and from kauri

Ag·a·thin \ˈagəthən\ *trademark* — used for a yellow crystalline compound formerly used to relieve neuralgia and rheumatism

ag·a·this \ˈagəthəs\ *n, cap* [NL, fr. Gk *agathis* ball of thread; perh. akin to Skt *gadh-* to cling to, hang on to] **:** a small genus of evergreen timber trees (family Pinaceae) chiefly of Australasia and the Philippines that are distinguished from members of the genus *Araucaria* by having larger leaves with flat stalks and the seed free from the cone scale and are valued for their wood and fragrant resins

ag·a·thism \ˈagəˌthizəm\ *n* -s [*agath-* + *-ism*] **:** the doctrine that all things tend toward ultimate good — compare OPTIMISM

ag·a·thist \-ˌthəst\ *n* -s **:** an adherent of agathism

ag·a·tho·dae·mon *or* **ag·a·tho·de·mon** \ˌagə(ˌ)thōˈdēmən\ *n, often cap* [Gk *agathodaimōn*, fr. *agath-* + *daimōn* spirit, daemon — more at DEMON] **:** a good genius or beneficent divinity

ag·a·tho·kak·o·log·i·cal \ˌ==(ˌ)=ˌkakəˈläjəkəl\ *adj* [*agath-* + *kako-* (var. of *cac-*) + *-logical*] **:** composed of both good and evil

ag·a·thol·o·gy \ˌagəˈthäləjē\ *n* -ES [ISV *agath-* + *-logy*] **:** the science or doctrine of the good

ag·a·thos·ma \-ˈthäzmə\ *n* [NL, fr. *agath-* + *-osma*] **1** *cap* **:** a genus of southern African shrubs (family Rutaceae) having heathlike foliage from which a sulfur-containing oil used in folk medicine is obtained and numerous small flowers in dense heads **2** -s **:** any plant of the genus *Agathosma*, several of which are cultivated in the cool greenhouse

ag·a·tif·er·ous \ˌagəˈtif(ə)rəs\ *adj* [ISV ¹*agate* + *-i-* + *-ferous*] **:** bearing agate ⟨~ rocks⟩

ag·a·ti·form \ˈagəd·əˌfȯrm\ *adj* [¹*agate* + *-iform*] **:** like agate in form

ag·at·ine \ˈagəd·ˌīn, -əˌtīn, -ēn\ *adj* [ISV ¹*agate* + *-ine*] **:** of, relating to, or resembling agate

ag·at·ize \-d·ˌīz, -ˌtīz\ *vt* -ED/-ING/-S [ISV ¹*agate* + *-ize*] **:** to change into agate or give the appearance of agate to ⟨*agatized* wood⟩

ag·aty \-əd·ē, -ətē\ *adj* **:** resembling or containing agate ⟨a large piece of ~ flint⟩

agau *also* **agaw** \əˈgaù\ *n* -s *usu cap* **1 a :** a Cushitic-speaking Negroid peasant people of the northern highlands of Ethiopia **b :** a member of such people **2 :** the Cushitic language of the Agau people

ag·a·va·ce·ae \ˌagəˈvāsēˌē\ *n pl, cap* [NL, fr. *Agave*, type genus + *-aceae*] *in some classifications* **:** a family of the order Liliales that comprises chiefly tropical and xerophytic plants with fibrous linear leaves arranged in a basal rosette, rhizomatous rootstock, and usu. with flowers in large panicles, that includes species usu. divided between the families Liliaceae and Amaryllidaceae, and that has as its type the genus *Agave*

aga·ve \əˈgävē *also* -āvē\ *n* [NL, fr. Gk *agauē*, fem. of *agauos* noble, illustrious, brilliant] **1** *cap* **:** a genus of plants (family Amaryllidaceae) native to tropical America and to the southwestern U.S. having heavy stiff often spiny persistent leaves mostly in basal rosettes and tall panicles or spikes of flowers like candelabras and including some members that are cultivated for their fiber (as sisal), for other economic products (as mescal), or for ornament — see AGAVACEAE, CENTURY PLANT, MAGUEY, PULQUE **2** -s **:** a plant of the genus *Agave*

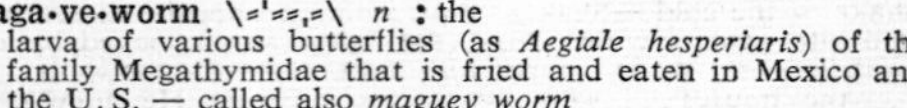
an agave (*A. americana*)

agave cactus *n* **:** a cactus (*Leuchtenbergia principis*) having columnar stems and persistent yellow terminal flowers

aga·ve·worm \=ˈ==ˌ=\ *n* **:** the larva of various butterflies (as *Aegiale hesperiaris*) of the family Megathymidae that is fried and eaten in Mexico and the U.S. — called also *maguey worm*

aga·vose \-ˌvōs\ *n* -s [ISV *agav-* (fr. NL *Agave*) + *-ose*] **:** a sugar $C_{12}H_{22}O_{11}$ obtained from the stalks of the century plant

agaz \əˈgäs\ *n, pl* **agaz** \"\ *or* **aga·ces** \əˈgäˌsās\ *usu cap* [Sp, of AmerInd origin] **1 :** an Indian people formerly living in southern Paraguay **2 :** a member of the Agaz people

agaze \əˈgāz\ *adj* [ME *a gase*, fr. ³*a* + *gasen* to gaze — more at GAZE] **:** GAZING

agazed *adj* [prob. alter. (influenced by *gaze*) of *aghast*] *obs* **:** struck with astonishment **:** AMAZED

ag·ba \ˈagbə\ *n* -s [native name in Africa] **:** a large African tree (*Gossweilerodendron balsamiferum*) having wood used for furniture and interior finish

AGC *abbr* automatic gain control

ag·chy·los·to·ma \ˌagkəˈlästəmə, ˌaŋk-\ *syn of* ANCYLOSTOMA

agcy *abbr* agency

agd *abbr* agreed

¹age \ˈāj\ *n* -s [ME, fr. OF *aage, eage*, fr. (assumed) VL *aetaticum*, fr. L *aetat-, aetas*, fr. OL *aevitas*, fr. *aevum* lifetime, age + *-itat-, -itas* -ity — more at AYE] **1 a** (1) **:** the length of time during which a being or thing has lived or existed **:** the length of life or existence from birth or beginning to the time spoken of or referred to ⟨the ~ of the student was 20⟩ ⟨the ~ of the wood was determined by measuring its radioactivity⟩ ⟨what is the ~ of your car⟩ (2) *of the moon* **:** the time that has elapsed since the last new moon **b :** the complete duration of the life or existence of a being or thing **:** LIFETIME ⟨the ~s of the Old Testament patriarchs were astonishingly long⟩ ⟨the normal ~ of a dog is reckoned as 12 years⟩ **c :** any one of the periods or stages of life ⟨Jaques' analysis of the seven ~s of man is one of the most familiar passages in Shakespeare⟩ **d** (1) **:** the time of life at which one becomes naturally or conventionally qualified or disqualified for something ⟨he was past the ~ for military service⟩ (2) **:** MATURITY; *specif* **:** the time of life at which one attains full legal rights and responsibilities ⟨last week he came of ~⟩ **e** (1) **:** an advanced stage of life **:** the latter part of life ⟨the child of his parents' ~ —Alan Paton⟩ ⟨the feebleness of ~⟩ (2) **:** the quality or state of being old ⟨~ cannot wither her, nor custom stale her infinite variety —*Shak.*⟩ **f :** a measure of the development, capacity, condition, or quality of an individual or of one of his traits or parts (as mentality or the skeleton) that tends to alter with age, expressed as the chronological age at which such state is mean or average ⟨a child of 7 with a mental ~ of 10⟩ ⟨X radiation revealed a bone ~ of 8 years and 5 months⟩ **g** *of a railroad employee* **:** seniority or time in service **2 a :** the period contemporary with a person's lifetime or with his active life ⟨the leading poet of his ~⟩ ⟨his ideas, considered radical in his own ~, seem almost reactionary in ours⟩ **b :** the period equal to the average span of human life **:** GENERATION ⟨actions of the last ~ are like almanacs of the last year —John Denham⟩ ⟨the mystery hidden for ~s and generations but now made manifest to his saints —Col 1: 26 (RSV)⟩ **c :** a period of 100 years **:** CENTURY ⟨be true to yourselves and this new 19th ~ —J.R. Lowell⟩ **d :** an indefinite but relatively long period of time in human affairs ⟨in that ~ before printing —G.F. Hudson⟩ ⟨the argument can continue on through the ~s —Deems Taylor⟩ **e :** a long time **:** many years ⟨it seemed an ~ though it was . . . only a few minutes —Sheila Kaye-Smith⟩ ⟨you haven't taken me to a nightclub in ~s —Louis Auchincloss⟩ ⟨the frames . . . stay smart for ~s —*Punch*⟩ — see COON'S AGE, DOG'S AGE **3 a :** a period of time in history or in the development of man esp. with reference to cultural evolution ⟨the golden ~⟩ ⟨the ~ of exploration⟩ ⟨the atomic ~⟩ **b :** a period of time in prehistory characterized by the use of artifacts made from a distinctive material — compare BRONZE AGE, IRON AGE, STONE AGE **4 a :** a period of time in the history of the earth often characterized by its dominant type of life **b :** the time during which a particular geologic event or series of events occurred — see ICE AGE **c :** one of the divisions of geologic time usu. included in an epoch ⟨the Lockport ~ of the Niagara epoch⟩ **5 a :** EDGE 7 **b :** the poker player having the edge **syn** see PERIOD — **act one's age** *or* **be one's age :** to behave in a reasonable manner

²age \"\ *vb* **aged** \ˈājd\ **aged** \"\ **aging** *or* **ageing** \ˈājiŋ\ **ages** [ME *agen*, fr. *age*, n.] *vi* **1 a :** to grow older **:** become old **:** show the effects of or undergo change with the passage of time ⟨no two people ~ alike⟩ ⟨his mind did not ~ —R.W. Firth⟩ **b :** to suffer with the passage of time a diminution of essential qualities or forces ⟨a car battery ~s during a severe winter⟩ **2 a :** to acquire a desirable quality by standing undisturbed for some time ⟨carbon paper . . . would easily pass the test if given time to ~ —C.E.Waters⟩ ⟨after flour is milled it ~s —S.C.Prescott⟩ **b :** to become mellow or mature **:** RIPEN ⟨this cheese has *aged* for nearly two years⟩ **c** *of metal* **:** to remain undisturbed at atmospheric temperature or at some higher temperature so that crystalline changes may occur ⟨an alloy ~s⟩ ~ *vt* **1 a :** to make old **:** cause or allow to grow old ⟨grief ~s a man⟩ **b :** to give the appearance of age to ⟨the painter sprayed the movie set with brown paint in order to ~ it⟩ **c :** to bring about with the passage of time a diminution of essential qualities or forces of ⟨excessive driving at night ~s a car battery⟩ **2 a :** to bring to a state fit for use ⟨the logwood chips had been properly *aged*⟩ **b :** to bring to a state of maturity or ripeness **:** MELLOW ⟨it's the tannic acid contained in . . . oak . . . that ~s the brandy—P.E.Deutschman⟩ **c :** to cause (an alloy) to remain at an appropriate temperature for a predetermined period of time in order to induce certain changes in structure and physical or mechanical properties ⟨~ duralumin alloys⟩ **d :** to develop (as a dye) by passage through or by hanging in warm moist air or by the use of steam ⟨*aged* aniline black⟩ **3 :** to determine the age of ⟨the forester is able to ~ trees —Wendell Lalime⟩ ⟨*aging* deer by dentition⟩ **4 :** to analyze (a customer's account) to rate entries as not yet due or as due for various given periods of time **syn** see MATURE

-age \ij,ēj *also* əj\ *n suffix* -s [ME, fr. OF, fr. L *-aticum*] **1 :** aggregate **:** collection ⟨cellar*age*⟩ ⟨surplus*age*⟩ ⟨track*age*⟩ ⟨word*age*⟩ **2 a :** action **:** process ⟨cover*age*⟩ ⟨haul*age*⟩ ⟨stopp*age*⟩ **b :** cumulative result of ⟨break*age*⟩ ⟨shrink*age*⟩ **c :** rate of ⟨dos*age*⟩ ⟨leak*age*⟩ ⟨out*age*⟩ ⟨slipp*age*⟩ **3 :** house or place of ⟨orphan*age*⟩ ⟨parson*age*⟩ **4 :** state **:** rank ⟨bond*age*⟩ ⟨peon*age*⟩ **5 :** charge for (an act or service) ⟨post*age*⟩ ⟨tow*age*⟩ ⟨wharf*age*⟩

age·a·ble \ˈājəbəl\ *adj* [¹*age* + *-able*] *chiefly Midland* **:** advanced in years **:** OLD

age and area concept *or* **age and area hypothesis** *n* **:** a principle of the diffusion of culture traits according to which those lying close to or at the center of distribution are considered relatively new and those lying farthest from it relatively old

age-area *adj* **:** of or relating to the age and area concept

age-class \ˈ=ˌ=\ *n* **1 :** a group of persons of the same sex and approximately the same age who have been initiated together or have passed through other social experiences together **2 :** an age-grade or a subdivision thereof

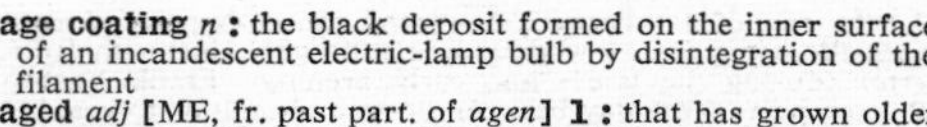

age coating *n* **:** the black deposit formed on the inner surface of an incandescent electric-lamp bulb by disintegration of the filament

aged *adj* [ME, fr. past part. of *agen*] **1 :** that has grown older or become old: **a** (1) \ˈājəd *also* ˈājd\ **:** having lived or existed long ⟨~ men⟩ ⟨an ~ oak⟩ (2) \ˈājəd\ **:** belonging to or characteristic of old age ⟨the ~ wrinkles in my cheeks —*Shak.*⟩ **b** \ˈājd\ **:** having lived **:** of or at the age of ⟨a man ~ 40 years⟩ **c** \ˈājd\ **:** having attained an age that is fixed for particular animals (as usu. 7 for horses, 3 or 4 for cattle, 2 for swine, 1 for sheep) **d** \ˈājəd\ **:** well advanced toward reduction to base level — used of topographic features **2** \ˈājd\ **:** having acquired a desirable quality or undergone an expected and desired change with the passage of time ⟨~ wine⟩ ⟨~ cheese⟩ — **ag·ed·ly** \ˈājədlē, -li\ *adv*

agee \əˈjē\ *adv* [¹*a-* + E dial. *gee, jee* to move to one side, turn, tilt] *dial Brit* **:** out of line **:** ASKEW, OBLIQUELY ⟨he wore his hat ~⟩

¹age-grade \ˈ=ˌ=\ *n* **1 :** a group of persons of the same sex and approximately the same age having certain definite duties and privileges in common and constituting a division of a tribe or society **2 :** a stage (as boyhood, adolescence, or manhood) through which an age-grade passes

²age-grade \"\ *vt* [¹*age-grade*] **:** to grade by age or organize by age-grades ⟨an *age-graded* tribe⟩

age-group \ˈ=ˌ=\ *n, chiefly Brit* **:** AGE-GRADE

age-harden \ˈ=ˌ==\ *vb* **:** to harden by aging

ageing *pres part of* AGE

ag·e·la·cri·ni·tes \ˌajələkrəˈnīd·ēz\ *n, cap* [NL, fr. Gk *agelē* herd + *krinon* lily + *-itēs* -ite] **:** a genus (the type of the family Agelacrinitidae) of saclike Devonian echinoderms with five covered food grooves on the oral side

ag·e·la·ius \ˌajəˈlā(y)əs\ *n, cap* [NL, fr. Gk *agelaios* gregarious, fr. *agelē* herd] **:** a genus of birds (family Icteridae) comprising the red-winged blackbirds

age·less \ˈājləs\ *adj* **1 :** not growing old or showing the effects of age ⟨a tall ~ . . . woman—Richard Wright⟩ **2 :** having no limits in time **:** ETERNAL ⟨the ~ theme of man and society —T.V.Smith⟩ — **age·less·ly** *adv* — **age·less·ness** *n* -ES

agel·i·cism \əˈjeləˌsizəm\ *n* -s [Gk *agelikos* of the herd, fr. *agelē* herd (fr. *agein* to lead) + E *-ism* — more at AGENT] **:** the doctrine that holds that society completely determines the thoughts, feelings, and acts of individuals

age-long \ˈ=ˌ=\ *adj* **:** lasting for an age **:** EVERLASTING, UNENDING ⟨man's ~ struggle for freedom⟩

age-mate \ˈ=ˌ=\ *also* **age-fellow** \ˈ=ˌ=(ˌ)=\ *n* **:** one who is a member of the same age-class as another

agen·cy \ˈājənsē, -si\ *n* -ES [²*agent* + *-cy*] **1 :** the capacity, condition, or state of acting or of exerting power **:** action or activity **:** OPERATION ⟨I have no intention to dispute her free ~ —Tobias Smollett⟩ **2 :** a person or thing through which power is exerted or an end is achieved **:** INSTRUMENTALITY, MEANS ⟨through the ~ of Benjamin Rush he renewed relations with Jefferson —W.C.Ford⟩ ⟨example is still . . . the greatest ~ by which men help each other —G.F.Kennan⟩ **3 a :** the office or function of an agent **b :** the relationship between a principal and his agent **4 a :** an establishment engaged in doing business for another ⟨an advertising ~⟩ ⟨an employment ~⟩ **b :** the place of business or the district of such an agency **5 a :** a department or other administrative unit of a government ⟨the War Department, the only ~ equipped to administer occupied areas —E.J.Hayward⟩ ⟨the independent *agencies* are generally regulatory in nature —H.M.Somers⟩ **b :** the office or headquarters of a government agent (as of an Indian agent) ⟨the house had once been used as an Indian ~⟩ **c :** the district administered by a government agent (as by a former British agent in India)

agency shop *n* **:** a shop in which the union serves as the agent for and receives dues and assessments from all employees in the bargaining unit regardless of union membership

agency tariff *n* **:** a tariff issued on behalf of two or more carriers by an authorized agent

agen·da \əˈjendə\ *n* -s [L, neut. pl. of *agendum*, gerundive of *agere* to drive, do — more at AGENT] **1 :** a memorandum book ⟨dragged a small ~ from his pocket and began flicking the pages —Monica Stirling⟩ **2 a :** a list or outline of things to be done, subjects to be discussed, or business to be transacted ⟨he sent out an ~ before each meeting⟩ **b :** a plan of procedure **:** PROGRAM ⟨military aggression was . . . on the ~ of international Communism —E.S.Furniss b.1890⟩ ⟨a brisk ~ of calisthenics —E.J.Kahn⟩

agen·dum \-dəm\ *n, pl* **agendums** *or* **agen·da** \-də\ [L] **1** *agenda pl* **a :** the forms and ceremonies of church liturgy **:** the ritual or order of worship ⟨the church constitutions and ~ of this period —G.C.Rietschel⟩ — used in Protestant Christianity **b :** matters of practical duty ⟨the ~ of a Christian —Ephraim Chambers⟩ — distinguished from *credenda* **2 :** AGENDA 2a ⟨the ~ for the conference was agreed upon⟩

ag·ene \ˈāˌjēn\ *n* -s [fr. *Agene*, a trademark] **:** commercially produced nitrogen trichloride for use in bleaching and aging flour

agen·e·sis \(ˌ)āˈjenəsəs\ *n, pl* **agene·ses** \-əˌsēz\ [NL, fr. ²*a-* + *genesis*] **1** *biol* **:** lack of development **:** faulty or incomplete development ⟨cerebral ~⟩ **2** *also* **age·ne·sia** \ˌājəˈnēzh(ē)ə\ -s *med* **:** the complete absence of an organ or part due to the absence of or a defect in its embryologic anlage — compare APLASIA

age·net·ic \ˌājəˈned·ik\ *adj* [²*a-* + *genetic*] **:** NONGENETIC

ag·en·ize \ˈājəˌnīz\ *vt* -ED/-ING/-S [*agene* + *-ize*] **:** to treat (flour) with nitrogen trichloride

age norm *n* **:** the norm (as for height, weight, or intellectual achievement) of individuals of a given chronological age

¹agent \ˈājənt\ *n* -s [in sense 1, fr. ME, fr. ML *agent-, agens*, fr. L, pres. part.; in senses 2, 3 & 4, fr. F or L; F, fr. L, pres. part.; in sense 5, fr. LL & ML, fr. L, pres. part.] **1 a :** something that produces or is capable of producing a certain effect **:** an active or efficient cause **:** a force effecting or facilitating a certain result ⟨the . . . emergence of the Christian church as the civilizing ~ of the western world —Helen Sullivan⟩ **b :** a substance capable of producing a chemical reaction or a physical or biological effect **:** an active principle ⟨chromic acid is an oxidizing ~⟩ ⟨detergents are surface-active ~s or wetting ~s⟩ **2 a :** one that acts or exerts power (as by driving, inciting, or setting in motion) **:** a moving force ⟨the distinction between ~ and patient, between something which acts and some other thing which is acted upon —Francis Bowen⟩ **b :** a person who originates a telepathic impulse or message — compare PERCIPIENT **3 :** one that acts or performs an act (as an act involving reason, conscience, and free will) **:** a person responsible for his acts or acts ⟨for that same deed now at Lorenzo's church both ~s, conscious and inconscious, lie —Robert Browning⟩ **4 :** a means or instrument by which a guiding intelligence achieves a result **:** a person governed, guided, or instigated by another in some action ⟨where the heads of departments are the political or confidential ~s of the executive, merely to execute the will of the president —John Marshall⟩ **5 :** one that acts for or in the place of another by authority from him: as **a :** a representative, emissary, or official of a government ⟨a crown ~⟩ ⟨an Indian ~⟩ ⟨a secret-service ~⟩ **b :** a special representative sent from one military organization to another to establish and maintain liaison **c :** a field worker from a welfare bureau **d :** a paid party worker who manages the financial and other affairs of a British political party during an election and is legally responsible for any corrupt practices **e :** a business representative: as (1) **:** a manager of an assigned territory or a branch office or plant of an industry (2) **:** one that sells and rents real estate on a commission basis (3) **:** an independent sales or service representative of an insurance company usu. paid on a commission basis **syn** see MEAN

²agent \"\ *adj* [L *agent-, agens*, pres. part. of *agere* to drive, lead, act, do; akin to ON *aka* to travel in a vehicle, Gk *agein* to lead, drive, OIr *ad-aig* to drive, Skt *ajati* (he) goes, drives] *archaic* **:** acting or exerting power — opposed to *patient*

agent cipher *n* **:** a cipher adapted for use in espionage

agent code *n* **:** a code adapted for use in espionage

agent de change \ȧzhäⁿtshäⁿzh\ *n, pl* **agents de change** \"\ [F, agent of the exchange] **:** a member of the board of licensed brokers who form the official bourse in France and some other European countries

agent-general \ˌājəntˈ=(=)=\ *n, pl* **agents-general :** a chief agent; *specif* **:** the representative in England of a British dominion acting in behalf of the political, economic, and commercial interests of the dominion

agen·tial \(ˈ)ā¦jenchəl\ *adj* [*agent* + *-ial*] **:** of, relating to, or expressive of an agent or agency — **a·gen·tial·ly** \-əlē\ *adv*

agent·ing \ˈājəntiŋ\ *n* -s **:** the work or activities of an agent ⟨the business of literary ∼⟩

agent intellect *n* [trans. of ML *intellectus agens*, trans. of Gk *nous poiētikos*] **:** INTELLECT 1d(2)

agen·ti·val \ˌājən¦tīvəl\ *or* **agent·ive** \ˈājəntiv\ *adj* [*agent* + *-ival*, *-ive*] **:** expressive of an agent or of agency **:** denoting the performer of an action ⟨*agentive* nouns⟩ ⟨an *agentive* suffix⟩

agent middleman *n* **:** a middleman who negotiates purchases or sales on an agency basis

agent noun *n* **:** a noun denoting the performer of an action (as *writer*, *inspector*, *patron*, *hanger-on*)

agent officer *n* **:** a military officer appointed to disburse funds

agent pro·vo·ca·teur \äzhäⁿprōvōkätœr; ˈājəntprō¦väkə¦tər, -tü(ə)r\ *n, pl* **agents provocateurs** \-äⁿp...œr; -ntsp...-ər(z), -ü(ə)r(z)\ [F, lit., provoking agent] **:** one employed to associate himself with members of a group or with suspected persons and by pretended sympathy with their aims or attitudes to incite them to some illegal or harmful action that will make them liable to apprehension and punishment **:** a secret agent or undercover man ⟨a city overrun with spies and *agents provocateurs*⟩

agent·ry \ˈājəntrē, -ri\ *n* -ES **:** the office, duties, or activities of an agent

agents *pl of* AGENT

age of consent : the age at which one is legally competent to give consent esp. to marriage or to unlawful sexual intercourse

age of copper *usu cap A&C* **:** the Aeneolithic period

age of discretion : the age at which the law imputes to a person the possession of sufficient knowledge for him to become responsible for certain acts or competent to exercise certain powers

age of fishes *usu cap A&F* **:** DEVONIAN

age of gold : GOLDEN AGE

age of mammals *usu cap A&M* **:** CENOZOIC

age of man *usu cap A&M* **:** QUATERNARY

age of reason : a period characterized by the dominance of reason and common sense; *esp* **:** the 18th century in England and France

age of reptiles *usu cap A&R* **:** MESOZOIC

age-old \ˈ=¦=\ *adj* **:** having existed for ages **:** ANCIENT ⟨an *age-old* problem⟩

ag·er \ˈājə(r)\ *n* -s **:** one that ages: as **a :** a chamber usu. containing rollers for aging material with steam **b :** one that inspects electric lamps in process **c :** a worker who puts radio tubes in an aging machine that passes current through them to stabilize their quality

ag·er·a·tum \ˌajəˈrād·əm, -ātəm\ *n* [NL, fr. L *ageraton*, a plant, fr. Gk *ageraton*, fr. neut. of *agēratos* ageless, fr. *a-* ²*a-* + *-gēratos* (fr. *gēras* old age) — more at GERIATRICS] **1** *cap* **:** a genus of tropical American herbs (family Compositae) having opposite leaves and small heads of blue or white flowers in terminal cymes **2** -s **:** a plant of the genus *Ageratum* (esp. *A. houstonianum*) **3** -s **:** any of several blue-flowered plants of the genus *Eupatorium*

ageratum blue *n* **:** FLOSSFLOWER BLUE

ages *pl of* AGE, *pres 3d sing of* AGE

-ages *pl of* -AGE

age score *n* **:** a test score translated into terms of a scale of age norms

age-set \ˈ=,=\ *n, chiefly Brit* **:** AGE-CLASS

age-society \ˈ=¦===\ *n* **:** AGE-GRADE 1

ageu·sia \əˈgyüzēə, (ˈ)āˈg-\ *n* -s [NL, fr. ²*a-* + Gk *geusis* taste (fr. *geuesthai* to taste) + *-ia* — more at CHOOSE] **:** the absence or impairment of the sense of taste — **ageu·sic** \(ˈ)=¦=zik\ *adj*

agg *abbr* aggregate

aggada *usu cap, var of* HAGGADA

ag·gag \ˈäˌgäg\ *n* -s [Chamorro] **1 :** a screw pine (*Pandanus tectorius*) with prop roots and sword-shaped spiny leaves covered with a whitish bloom **2 :** an article (as a mat or bag) made from the split leaves of the aggag

ag·ger \ˈajə(r)\ *n* -s **1** [L] **:** EARTHWORK: as **a :** MOUND, RAMPART **b :** a military or public road usu. raised and with sloping drainage embankments **2** [NL, fr. L] *anat* **:** PROMINENCE **3** [NL, fr. L] **:** a double tide: **a :** a high tide with two maxima separated by a slight lowering of water **b :** a low tide with two minima separated by a slight rise of water

¹**ag·gie** \ˈagē, ˈaig-, -gi\ *n* -s [alter. (influenced by *-ie*) of ¹*agate*] **:** a playing marble; *specif* **:** an agate marble

²**aggie** \"\ *n* -s *often cap* [*ag-* (as in *agricultural college*, *agricultural school*) + *-ie*] **1 :** a student at an agricultural school or college **2 :** an agricultural school or college

ag·glom·er·ant \əˈglämərant, a-\ *n* -s [L *agglomerant-*, *agglomerans*, pres. part. of *agglomerare*] **:** something that causes agglomeration

¹**ag·glom·er·ate** \-ˌrāt\ *vb* -ED/-ING/-S [L *agglomeratus*, past part. of *agglomerare* to heap up, join, fr. *ad-* + *glomerare* to wind into a ball, to assemble, fr. *glomus* ball — more at CLAM] *vt* **1** *obs* **:** to wind or collect into a ball **2 :** to gather into a mass or cluster ⟨∼ dust particles⟩ ∼ *vi* **:** to collect or come together in a mass ⟨caused the oxide film to ∼⟩

²**ag·glom·er·ate** \-rət\ *adj* [L *agglomeratus*] **:** collected into a ball, heap, or mass; *specif* **:** clustered or growing together but not coherent ⟨an ∼ head of flowers⟩

³**agglomerate** \"\ *n* -s **1 :** a confused or jumbled mass, heap, or collection ⟨this fine ∼ of duchies —Thomas Carlyle⟩ **2 :** a rock composed of volcanic fragments of various sizes and degrees of angularity; *esp* **:** a rock in which the constituent fragments were produced by explosions in the throat of a volcano — compare CONGLOMERATE

ag·glom·er·at·ic \=¦=ˈrad·ik\ *adj* [³*agglomerate* + *-ic*] **:** having the characteristics of an agglomerate ⟨∼ lavas⟩

ag·glom·er·a·tion \=,==ˈrāshən\ *n* -s **1 :** the action or process of collecting in a mass **:** an agglomerated condition ⟨protection against caking and ∼⟩ **2 :** an indiscriminately formed mass **:** a cluster of disparate elements ⟨the ∼ of buildings which somehow made up this town —Elizabeth Bowen⟩

ag·glom·er·a·tive \=ˈ==,rād·iv, ˌrəd·iv\ *adj* **:** tending to agglomerate **:** AGGLOMERATING

ag·glom·er·a·tor \-ˌrād·ə(r)\ *n* -s **:** one that agglomerates ⟨sonic ∼s⟩

ag·glu·ti·na·bil·i·ty \əˌglütᵊnəˈbiləd·ē, aˌ-\ *n* -ES [²*agglutinate* + *-ability*] **:** capacity (as of red blood cells, bacteria, or virus particles) to be agglutinated — **ag·glu·ti·na·ble** \=ˈ===bəl\ *adj*

ag·glu·ti·nant \=ˈ===nt\ *adj* [L *agglutinant-*, *agglutinans*, pres. part. of *agglutinare* to glue to, fr. *ad-* + *glutinare* to glue, fr. *glutin-*, *gluten* glue — more at CLAY] **:** uniting closely **:** causing or tending to cause adhesion

²**agglutinant** \"\ *n* -s **:** an agglutinating substance

¹**ag·glu·ti·nate** \-ət\ *adj* [L *agglutinatus*, past part. of *agglutinare*] **1 :** joined with or as if with glue ⟨∼ spores⟩ **2 :** AGGLUTINATIVE 2

²**ag·glu·ti·nate** \-ˌāt, *usu* -ād.+V\ *vb* -ED/-ING/-S *vt* **1 :** to cause to adhere **:** UNITE, FASTEN ⟨the town ∼s them all to its own atmosphere —Waldo Frank⟩ **2 :** to combine (words) into a compound **:** attach (a linguistic form) to a base as an affix **3 :** to cause (as blood cells) to undergo agglutination ∼ *vi* **1 :** to unite or combine into a group or mass ⟨groups . . . coalesced, fragmented, *agglutinated* again —John Hersey⟩ **2 :** to form words by agglutination **:** be agglutinative ⟨*agglutinating* languages⟩ ⟨the *agglutinating* state of language⟩ **3 :** to undergo agglutination

³**ag·glu·ti·nate** \-ət\ *n* -s **:** a clump of material (as blood cells or bacteria) that has undergone agglutination

ag·glu·ti·na·tion \=,==ˈāshən\ *n* -s **1 :** the action or process of uniting or adhering **:** an agglutinated condition ⟨the ∼ of foreign bodies⟩ **2 :** a mass or group formed by the union of separate elements ⟨a boundless ∼ of streets, dramshops, and low buildings —A.J.Liebling⟩ **3 :** the formation of derivative or compound words by putting together constituents of which each expresses a single definite meaning (as in Wishram, a Chinook dialect, in which *ačimlúda* "he will give it to you" has the constituents *a-* "future", *-č-* "he", *-i-* "him", *-m-* "thee", *-l-* "to", *-ud-* "give", and *-a* "future", as contrasted with Latin, in which the *-o* of *amo* "I love" expresses the meanings of first person, singular number, present tense, active voice, and indicative mood) **4 :** a reaction in which particles (as red blood cells, bacteria, virus particles, or rickettsiae) suspended in a liquid collect into clumps or floccules with loss of motility in the case of flagellated or ciliated organisms and which occurs when the suspension is treated with certain substances that combine with the surface of the particles — see AGGLUTINATION TEST, CROSS AGGLUTINATION

agglutination test *n* **:** any of several tests based on the ability of a specific serum to cause agglutination of a suitable system and used in the diagnosis of infections, the identification of microorganisms, and in blood grouping — compare WIDAL TEST

ag·glu·ti·na·tive \=ˈ==,ād·iv, -əd·iv\ *adj* **1 :** causing or produced by agglutination **:** ADHESIVE **2 :** characterized by agglutination ⟨an ∼ language⟩ — distinguished from *inflectional* and *isolating*

ag·glu·ti·nin \=ˈ=ᵊnən\ *n* -s [ISV *agglutination* + *-in*; prob. orig. formed in G] **:** a substance producing agglutination; *specif* **:** any antibody capable of effecting the agglutination of the agglutinogen that stimulated its production — see HEMAGGLUTININ

ag·glu·tin·o·gen \ˌa(ˌ)glüˈtinəjən\ *n* -s [ISV *agglutinin* + *-o-* + *-gen*] **:** any substance that acting as an antigen stimulates the production of an agglutinin — **ag·glu·tin·o·gen·ic** \¦=(ˌ)=,==¦jenik, ə¦glütᵊnə¦-\ *adj*

ag·glu·ti·noid \əˈglütᵊnˌȯid, a'-\ *n* -s [ISV *agglutinin* + *-oid*] **:** an agglutinin that has lost or never had the power to agglutinate but can still unite with its agglutinogen — compare ANTIBODY, BLOCKING ANTIBODY

ag·gra·da·tion \ˌagrəˈdāshən\ *n* -s [*aggrade* + *-ation*] **:** a modification of or the process of modifying the earth's surface in the direction of uniformity of grade or slope by deposition (as of detrital material in a river bed) — compare DEGRADATION

ag·gra·da·tion·al \¦==¦=shənᵊl, -shnəl\ *adj* **:** relating to, characterized by, or formed by aggradation

ag·grade \əˈgrād, a'-\ *vb* -ED/-ING/-S [*ad-* + *grade*] *vt* **:** to fill with detrital material ⟨silt has *aggraded* the river bed and waterlogged it for a hundred miles —Erna Fergusson⟩ ∼ *vi* **:** to build up by aggradation ⟨meltwater streams were *aggrading* beyond the moraines —R.J.Lougee⟩

ag·gran·dize \əˈgranˌdīz, -aan-; ˈagrən-, ˈaig-\ *vt* -ED/-ING/-S [modif. (influenced by *-ize*) of F *agrandiss-* stem of *agrandir*, fr. *a-* (fr. L *ad-*) + *grandir* to increase, fr. L *grandire*, fr. *grandis* great — more at GRAND] **1 :** to make great (as in degree, number, or size) **:** INCREASE, AUGMENT ⟨all he desired was to ∼ his estate —Hilaire Belloc⟩ **2 :** to make great or greater (as in power, honor, or wealth) ⟨to ∼ his family and his favorites Sixtus caused wars —R.A.Hall b. 1911⟩ **3 :** to make appear great or greater **:** EXALT ⟨in *aggrandizing* the one, he necessarily depreciated the other⟩ **syn** see EXALT

ag·gran·dize·ment \əˈgrandəzmənt, -aan- *also* əˈgra(a)nˌdīz-; *also* ˈagrənˌdīz- *or* ˈaig- *or* ,=='==\ *n* -s [modif. (influenced by *-ize*) of F *agrandissement*, fr. *agrandiss-* + *-ment*] **:** the act, action, or result of aggrandizing **:** ADVANCEMENT ⟨their ∼ from low estate to social prominence⟩ **:** ENLARGEMENT ⟨critics of his ∼ of federal power —B.N.Cardozo⟩

ag·gran·diz·er \əˈgra(a)nˌdīzə(r), ˈa(i)grən,-\ *n* -s **:** one that aggrandizes

aggrate *vt* -ED/-ING/-S [It *aggratare*, alter. of *aggradare*, fr. Prov *agradar*, fr. *a-* (fr. L *ad-*) + *grat* pleasing, agreeable (fr. L *gratus*) — more at GRACE] *obs* **:** to gratify or express gratitude to

ag·gra·vate \ˈagrəˌvāt, ˈaig-, *usu* -ād.+V\ *vt* -ED/-ING/-S [L *aggravatus*, past part. of *aggravare* to make heavier, fr. *ad-* + *gravare* to burden, fr. *gravis* heavy — more at GRIEVE] **1** *obs* **a :** to make heavy **:** weigh down **:** BURDEN ⟨a great grief *aggravateth* the heart that suffers it —Bartholomew Young⟩ **b :** to add weight to **:** INCREASE, MAGNIFY ⟨then, soul, live thou upon thy servant's loss and let that pine to ∼ thy store —Shak.⟩ **2** *archaic* **:** to give an exaggerated representation of **:** EXAGGERATE ⟨I have not . . . *aggravated* your sense or words —Andrew Marvell⟩ **3 :** to make worse, more serious, or more severe **:** INTENSIFY ⟨such a defense only *aggravated* the offense —R.W.Southern⟩ ⟨the war . . . had *aggravated* the confusions and social disasters of rapid industrial change —J.H.Plumb⟩ **4 a :** to arouse the displeasure, impatience, or anger of **:** PROVOKE, ANNOY ⟨nothing so ∼s an earnest person as a passive resistance —Herman Melville⟩ **b :** to produce inflammation in **:** IRRITATE ⟨the operation *aggravated* the ulnar nerve⟩ **syn** see INTENSIFY, IRRITATE

aggravated assault *n* **:** an assault regarded as more heinous than a common assault: as **a :** an assault combining an intent to commit a crime other than that involved in the mere assault itself **b :** any of various assaults so defined by statute

aggravated larceny *n* **:** larceny attended with aggravating circumstances (as when the theft is from the person)

aggravating *adj* **1 :** making worse **:** INTENSIFYING **2 :** arousing displeasure, impatience, or anger **:** EXASPERATING, IRRITATING — **ag·gra·vat·ing·ly** \¦==¦==\ *adv*

ag·gra·va·tion \ˌ=='vāshən\ *n* -s [ML *aggravation-*, *aggravatio*, fr. L *aggravatus* + *-ion-*, *-io* -ion] **1 :** the act, action, or result of aggravating; *esp* **:** an increasing in seriousness or severity ⟨in order to prevent an ∼ of the problem⟩ **2 :** an act or circumstance that intensifies or makes worse ⟨an ∼ to a person in slavery to reflect that he was sold by his parent —Thomas Paine⟩ **3** *obs* **:** an exaggerated statement or representation ⟨I from ∼s will forbear —George Wither⟩ **4 :** the act or action of irritating or annoying **:** PROVOCATION ⟨∼s between people South and North were getting worse —Carl Sandburg⟩

ag·gra·va·tor \ˈ==,vād·ə(r)\ *n* -s **:** one that aggravates

ag·gre·ga·ble \ˈagrəgəbəl, ˈaig-, -rē-\ *adj* [²*aggregate* + *-able*] **:** that may be aggregated ⟨property ∼ with other property⟩

¹**ag·gre·gate** \-gət *also* -ˌgāt; *usu* -d·+V\ *adj* [ME *aggregat*, fr. L *aggregatus*, past part. of *aggregare* to add to, fr. *ad-* + *greg-*, *grex* flock — more at GREGARIOUS] **1 :** formed by the collection of units or particles into a body, mass, or amount **:** COLLECTIVE ⟨the ∼ sentiments of mankind —J.F.Byrnes⟩: **a** (1) *of a flower* **:** clustered in a dense mass or head (2) *of a fruit* **:** formed from the several separate or fused ovaries of a single flower — distinguished from *multiple*; see FRUIT illustration **b** *of a rock* (1) **:** composed of mineral crystals of one or more kinds (2) **:** composed of mineral or rock fragments **c** (1) *of a colonial animal* **:** united in a somewhat continuous mass (2) *of a hibernating animal* **:** gathered into a compact mass **d :** formed into clusters or groups of lobules **2 :** AGGREGATIVE 2 — **aggregately** *adv* — **aggregateness** *n* -ES

²**ag·gre·gate** \-ˌgāt, *usu* -ād.+V\ *vb* -ED/-ING/-S *vt* **1 :** to collect or gather into a mass or whole **:** bring together ⟨wealth *aggregated* by their industrial and commercial skill —Will Durant⟩ **2 :** to make a part of the aggregate **:** unite as a constituent member ⟨these people are now *aggregated* with us —Thomas Jefferson⟩ **3 :** to amount in the aggregate to **:** form an aggregate of ⟨audiences *aggregating* a million people⟩ ∼ *vi* **:** to come together **:** ASSEMBLE ⟨people . . . abandon their normal occupations, ∼ in predesignated places —Anatol Rapoport⟩

³**ag·gre·gate** \-gət *also* -ˌgāt; *usu* -d·+V\ *n* -s **1 :** a mass or body of units or parts somewhat loosely associated with one another ⟨an ∼ of individuals actuated by economic self-interest —Douglas Bush⟩ **2 :** the whole sum or amount **:** SUM TOTAL ⟨the ∼ of knowledge . . . is greater than ever before —C.H.Grandgent⟩ **3 a :** an aggregate rock **b :** any of several hard inert materials used for mixing in various-sized fragments with a cementing material to form concrete, mortar, or plaster **c :** a clustered mass of individual soil grains or particles varied in shape, ranging in size from a microscopic granule to a small crumb, and usu. considered the basic structural unit of soil **4 a :** a total comprising all the elements or individuals in a particular category or a group of categories in an economy **b** *Brit* **:** the sum total of grades made by a student **5 :** a set of mathematical elements having some property in common ⟨the ∼ of rational numbers⟩ **syn** see SUM — **in the aggregate :** considered as a whole **:** COLLECTIVELY ⟨dividends for the year amounted *in the aggregate* to $60,000⟩

aggregated *adj* **1 :** gathered into a whole **:** AGGREGATE ⟨the ∼ masses in . . . the cells —C.R.Darwin⟩ **2 :** containing aggregates ⟨a highly ∼ soil⟩

aggregate mortality table *n* **:** an insurance mortality table based on both newly medically selected lives and lives from which the effect of selection has been eliminated

aggregate polarization *n* **:** polarization by a rock section in which the constituent minerals cannot be individually recognized

aggregate ray *n* **:** a group of rays in certain woods appearing at low magnification as a single vascular ray but consisting of smaller rays, fibers, and sometimes vessels — called also *compound ray*

ag·gre·ga·tion \ˌagrəˈgāshən, ˌaig-, -rē-\ *n* -s [MF or ML; MF *agregation*, fr. ML *aggregation-*, *aggregatio*, fr. L *aggregatus* + *-ion-*, *-io* -ion] **1 a :** the action or process of aggregating **:** the collection of units or parts into a mass or whole ⟨learning is . . the ∼ of many men's sentences —William Baldwin⟩ **b :** the state or condition of being aggregated or of having aggregates ⟨in most soils . . . there is only a partial ∼ of the various particles —L.D.Baver⟩ **2 :** a group, body, or mass composed of many distinct parts **:** ASSEMBLAGE ⟨one of the world's largest ∼s of industry⟩ ⟨a musical ∼ touring the small towns⟩: as **a :** a collection of individuals gathered together in response to the same external conditions **b :** an assemblage of animals of one or more species usu. come together in response to an external stimulus (as drought) **3** *patent law* **:** the bringing together of two or more separate parts without changing their function or producing any result other than the sum of the results of the separate operation of the parts **4 :** the condensation or movement of the contents of cells, esp. those of tentacles or tendrils of insectivorous or sensitive plants, in response to stimuli **5** *ecol* **a :** ASSOCIATION 8 **b :** SOCIETY

ag·gre·ga·tive \ˈ==,gād·iv, -ātiv, -ēv\ *adj* **1 :** of, relating to, or tending toward aggregation ⟨an ∼ process⟩ **2 :** of or relating to aggregates, specif. economic aggregates ⟨∼ terms⟩

aggrege *vt* -ED/-ING/-S [ME *aggreggen*, fr. MF *aggregier*, fr. (assumed) VL *aggraviare*, *aggreviare*, alter. of L *aggravare* to make heavier — more at AGGRAVATE] *obs* **:** to make graver **:** AGGRAVATE

ag·gress \əˈgres *also* a'-\ *vb* -ED/-ING/-S [LL *aggressus* attack, fr. L *aggressus*, past part. of *aggredi* to approach, attack, undertake, fr. *ad-* + *-gredi* (fr. *gradi* to step, go) — more at GRADE] *vi* **:** to make an attack **:** commit aggression ⟨westerners even ∼*ed* against one another —A.E.Stevenson b. 1900⟩ ∼ *vt* **:** to set upon **:** ATTACK ⟨lions . . . seeking whom they may ∼ —*Saturday Rev.*⟩

ag·gres·sin \-sᵊn\ *n* -s [ISV *aggress-* (fr. LL *aggressus*) + *-in*; orig. formed in G] **:** a hypothetical substance held to contribute to the virulence of pathogenic bacteria by paralyzing the defensive mechanisms of the host, esp. the leukocytes, and held to be produced by the bacteria in the body of the host

ag·gres·sion \əˈgreshən *also* a'-\ *n* -s [F & L; F *agression*, fr. L *aggression-*, *aggressio*, fr. *aggressus* + *-ion-*, *-io* -ion] **1 a :** an offensive action or procedure; *esp* **:** a culpable unprovoked overt hostile attack ⟨we have borne with their ∼s —Thomas Jefferson⟩ **b :** the practice of making attacks or encroachments **:** offensive tactics ⟨a war of ∼⟩ **2 :** the action of a nation in violating the rights, esp. the territorial rights, of another nation (as by unprovoked attack, invasion, or other unfriendly military action or sometimes by serious threat of or preparation for such action) ⟨that country was said to be guilty of ∼⟩ **3 :** a form of psychobiologic energy, either innate or arising in response to or intensified by frustration, which may be manifested by (1) overt destruction, fighting, infliction of pain, sexual attack, or forcible seizure, (2) covert hostile attitudes, covetousness, or greed, (3) introjection into one's self (as self-hate or masochism), (4) sublimation into play or sports, or (5) healthy self-assertiveness or a drive to accomplishment or to mastery esp. of skills

ag·gres·sive \-esiv, -ēv\ *adj* **1 a :** tending toward, characterized by, or practicing aggression ⟨her ∼ behavior⟩ ⟨an ∼ nation⟩ **b :** marked by combative readiness or bold determination **:** not conciliatory **:** MILITANT ⟨an ∼ fighter⟩ **2 a :** marked by driving forceful energy, ambition, or initiative **:** ENTERPRISING ⟨an ∼ salesman⟩ ⟨∼ leadership⟩ **b :** marked by obtrusive energy and self-assertiveness **:** demanding or attracting attention **:** SELF-CONFIDENT ⟨swaggering, blatant, and idiotically ∼ vulgarity —George du Maurier⟩ **3 a :** promoting or accessory to aggression in predaceous animals (as insects) esp. by concealment or disguise ⟨an ∼ trait⟩ **b** *bot* **:** spreading with vigor ⟨∼ weeds⟩ **c :** chemically active ⟨∼ waters⟩ **d :** tending or able to utilize a variety of habitats **:** able to encroach on occupied areas **:** variable and adaptable — used of organisms and taxa ⟨an extremely ∼ subspecies⟩

syn MILITANT, ASSERTIVE, SELF-ASSERTIVE, PUSHING, PUSHFUL: AGGRESSIVE may apply either to zealous loyalty to causes or to personal ambitions and aims; it suggests forceful and confident procedures and attitudes, sometimes truculent contentiousness or cavalier treatment of others ⟨positive in his convictions, *aggressive* and imperious, he became a zealot in any cause he embraced —F.L.Hise⟩ ⟨as intolerant and *aggressive* as any of the traditional satirists —C.D.Lewis⟩ MILITANT, complimentary except for suggestions of doctrinaire intractability, applies to fervent, resolute, devoted furthering of a cause ⟨the *militant* suffragist nuisance —Rose Macaulay⟩ ⟨*militant* in fighting to get for workers a larger share of the national income —*Time*⟩ ASSERTIVE suggests bold self-confidence and determination in expression of opinion ⟨an *assertive*, opinionated, likable fellow, ready to fight, drink, dance, shoot, or brag —V.L. Parrington⟩ ⟨to say, with some challenging *assertive* people, that trees are more beautiful than flowers —E.V.Lucas⟩ SELF-ASSERTIVE, usu. uncomplimentary, generally connotes obtrusive, crass forwardness or brash self-confidence ⟨the social and political revolt beginning in the new middle class against the Tory aristocracy found more vigorous expression in the *self-assertive* and ubiquitous energy of Henry Brougham —G.M.Trevelyan⟩ ⟨*self-assertive* and ill-bred bourgeois —Edmund Wilson⟩ PUSHING and PUSHFUL may praise by indicating ambition, energy, and enterprise ⟨an energetic, *pushing* youth, already intent on getting on in the world —Sherwood Anderson⟩ ⟨the *pushful* energetic man of business —Aldous Huxley⟩ or blame by indicating snobbish or crude intrusiveness ⟨a *pushing* sort, forever exposing themselves to the slights arising from their own undesirability —Mary Austin⟩ ⟨ignorant, *pushful*, impatient of restraint and precedent —H.L.Mencken⟩

aggressively *adv* **:** in an aggressive manner

ag·gres·sive·ness *or* **ag·gres·siv·i·ty** \əˌgreˈsivəd·ē, ˌa,g-\ *n* -ES **:** the quality or state of being aggressive **:** AGGRESSION

ag·gres·sor \əˈgresə(r), a'- *also* -ˌsō(ə)r *or* -ō(ə)\ *n* -s [LL, fr. L *aggressus* + *-or*] **1 :** one that commits or practices aggression; *esp* **:** a nation that commits an act of aggression ⟨economic insecurity and poverty . . . breed conflict and give ∼s their chance —E.R.Stettinius⟩ **2 a :** a military force organized, trained, and deployed to act as the enemy during a field problem or in maneuvers **b :** a member of such a force

ag·griev·ance \əˈgrēvən(t)s *also* a'-\ *n* -s [ME *agrevaunce*, fr. MF *agrevance*, fr. *agrever* + *-ance*] **:** GRIEVANCE

ag·grieve \əˈgrēv *also* a'-\ *vt* -ED/-ING/-S [ME *agreven*, fr. MF *agrever*, fr. L *aggravare* to make heavy — more at AGGRAVATE] **1 :** to give pain, sorrow, or trouble to **:** GRIEVE, DISTRESS ⟨I was *aggrieved* it did not include so notable a plant —Andrew Young⟩ **2 :** to inflict injury upon **:** OPPRESS, WRONG ⟨provisions should be made for recourse to the courts by parties who may be *aggrieved* by such orders —S.T.Powell⟩ **syn** see WRONG

aggrieved *adj* [ME *agreved*, fr. past part. of *agreven*] **1 :** troubled or distressed in spirit ⟨the spoke like one ∼⟩ **2 a :** showing grief, injury, or offense ⟨did not understand the ∼ attitude of the mate —Joseph Conrad⟩ **b :** having a grievance; *specif* **:** suffering from an infringement or denial of legal rights ⟨compensation paid to the ∼ party⟩ — **ag·griev·ed·ly** \-vədlē, -li\ *adv*

ag·group \əˈgrüp, a'-\ *vt* -ED/-ING/-S [F *agrouper*, fr. *a-* (fr. L *ad-*) + *groupe* group — more at GROUP] **:** to arrange in a group ⟨were ∼*ed* near the center of the group⟩ — **ag·group·ment** *n* -s

ag·gry bead *also* **ag·gri bead** \ˈagrē-\ *n* [of African origin; akin to Hausa *gori* snail shell used as an ornament, Twi *agyiratwefā*, a weight of gold, *gyirapaw*, a charm] **:** a variegated glass bead found buried in the earth in Ghana and in England

agha *often cap, var of* AGA

aghan \ə'gän\ *n* -s *usu cap* [Skt *Agrahāyaṇa*] **:** a month of the Hindu year — see MONTH table

aghast \ə'gast, -aa(ə)st, -aist, -ȧst\ *adj* [alter. (prob. influenced by Sc *ghast*, var. of E *ghost*) of ME *agast*, fr. past part. of *agasten* to frighten, be frightened, fr. *a-* (perfective prefix) + *gasten* to frighten — more at ABEAR, GAST] **1 :** seized with fear or terror **:** FRIGHTENED, TERRIFIED ⟨with shuddering horror pale and eyes ~ —John Milton⟩ **2 :** struck with amazement, bewilderment, disgust, or surprise **:** SHOCKED ⟨the trustees, ~ when he allowed pupils to study out-of-doors, demanded stricter discipline —E.W.Parks⟩ — usu. used predicatively ⟨he was ~⟩ but sometimes prepositively ⟨thousands of ~ Britons whose rage is concentrated on their government —Mollie Panter-Downes⟩ **syn** *see* AFRAID

agh·lab·ite \'aglə,bīt, ag'la,-\ *also* **agh·lab·id** \-,bəd\ *n* -s, *cap* [Ibrāhīm ibn- al- *Aghlab* (Ibrahim I) †A.D. 812 African sultan, founder of the dynasty + E *-ite* or *-id*] **:** a member of an Arab dynasty ruling at Kairouan, northern Africa, A.D. 800–909

ag·i·la·wood *also* **ag·ui·la·wood** \'agələ,wu̇d\ *n* [Pg *aguila* (fr. Tamil *akil*) + E *wood*] **:** AGALLOCH

ag·ile \'ajəl, *US also & Brit usu* 'a,jīl *or* -īəl\ *adj* [MF, fr. L *agilis*, fr. *agere* to move, act + *-ilis* -ile — more at AGENT] **1 :** characterized by ready ability to move quickly and easily with suppleness and grace ⟨as bright-eyed and ~ as the hares and slim gazelles —Elinor Wylie⟩ **2 :** characterized by quickness or liveliness of mind, resourcefulness, or adaptability in coping with new and varied situations ⟨the work of a . . . sympathetic intelligence, ~, humane, and . . . persuasive —A.D.Culler⟩

syn NIMBLE, BRISK, SPRY: AGILE suggests ease in quick motion along with smooth coordination and dexterous performance of sudden or difficult actions ⟨I saw her bounding down the rocky slope like some wild, *agile* creature possessed of padded hoofs and an infallible instinct —W.H.Hudson⟩ ⟨Silver, *agile* as a monkey, even without leg or crutch, was on the top of him next moment —R.L.Stevenson⟩ Applied to mental or intellectual matters it suggests ready adaptability and ability to change and adjust ⟨in a flow of racy comment, skimming from one topic to another with an *agile* irrelevance —Rose Macaulay⟩ NIMBLE stresses lightness and ease of sudden physical motion and suggests ability to dart, dash, or skip; applied to matters mental it suggests quick comprehension and ready responsiveness to change ⟨out ran the two maidens, their frocks flying, *nimble* feet scudding over the springy turf —Mary Webb⟩ ⟨the mind and the body have in this respect a striking resemblance of each other. In childhood they are both *nimble*, but not strong; they can skip and frisk about with wonderful agility —William Cowper⟩ BRISK suggests lively energetic activity or vivacity; it often applies to manner or attitude rather than physical capability or dexterity ⟨a *brisk* wind sending small white clouds scudding across the vast East Anglian sky —Osbert Lancaster⟩ ⟨that *brisk*, managing, lively, imperious woman —W.M.Thackeray⟩ SPRY indicates an ability for quick easy activity, esp. among the old or infirm in whom such ability may be unexpected ⟨I'm a little lame, I ain't as *spry* as I used to be —J.K.Jerome⟩ ⟨poor Canon Bonnyboat could only limp . . . whereas Reverend Mother was still as *spry* as a sparrow —Bruce Marshall⟩

agile gibbon *n* [*agile*, trans. of NL *agilis*, specific epithet of *Hylobates agilis*] **:** a gibbon (*Hylobates agilis*) of Malaysia and Sumatra that occurs in two color phases, one blackish brown, the other buffy brown, both with white brow and black face

ag·ile·ly \-əl(l)ē,-īllē, -i\ *adv* **:** in an agile manner

agil·i·ty \ə'jilad·ē, -ətē, -i *also* a'-\ *n* -ES [ME *agilite*, fr. MF *agilité*, fr. L *agilitat-*, *agilitas*, fr. *agilis* + *-itat-*, *-itas* -ity] **:** the quality or state of being agile: **a :** quickness and dexterity of movement ⟨a monkeylike ~⟩ **b :** quickness and resourcefulness of mind ⟨his ~ in debate⟩

agil·men·te \,ajəl'mentē, *It* äjēl'mān·tā\ *adv* [It, fr. *agile*, adj., fr. L *agilis*] **:** with agility — used as a direction in music

[1]agin \ə'gin\ *dial var of* AGAIN

[2]agin \"\ *dial var of* AGAINST

aging *pres part of* AGE

agio \'a(,)jō, 'ajē,ō, 'ä(,)jō\ *n* -s [It *aggio*, *agio*, alter. (by false word division, *l* being taken as the def. article) of It dial. *lajjë*, fr. MGk *allagion* exchange, fr. Gk *allagē* change, exchange, fr. *allos* other — more at ELSE] **1 a :** a premium or percentage paid for the exchange of one currency for another (as where gold is given for silver or metallic for paper currency) **b :** the premium or discount on foreign bills of exchange **2 :** MONEY CHANGING

agio·tage \'ajəd·ij, -ətij\ *n* -s [F, fr. *agioter* to practice stockjobbing (fr. *agio* stockjobbing, fr. It *aggio*, *agio*) + *-age*] **1 :** exchange business **2 :** speculative buying or selling of stocks **:** STOCKJOBBING

agist \ə'jist\ *vb* -ED/ -ING/ -s [MF *agister*, fr. *a-* (fr. L *ad-*) + *gister* to give lodging, fr. *giste* lodging, abode, fr. (assumed) VL *jacita*, fr. L *jacēre* to lie, fr. *jacere* to throw — more at JET] *vt* **1 :** to take in (livestock) for feeding or grazing and to collect the amount due therefor **2 :** to tax (land or owner) with a share of any public charge or burden ~ *vi* **:** to graze and feed for a specified period at a fixed rate

agist·er *or* **agis·tor** \-tə(r)\ *n* -s [ME *agister*, fr. AF *agistour*, fr. MF *agister* + *-our* -or] **:** one that agists livestock; *specif* **:** an officer of the royal forests in England who has the care of livestock agisted

agist·ment \-mənt\ *n* -s [MF *agistement*, fr. *agister* + *-ment*] **1 a :** the taking in of livestock for feeding at a specified rate **b :** the opening of a forest to livestock for a specified period **2 a :** the price paid for or the profit made from agisting livestock **b :** a charge or rate against lands

ag·i·ta·ble \'ajəd·əbəl\ *adj* [L *agitabilis*, fr. *agitare* + *-abilis* -able] **:** capable of being agitated

agi·ta·na·do \,ä,hētə'nä(,)thō\ *n* -s [Sp, gypsylike, fr. *a-* (fr. L *ad-*) + *gitano* gypsy (fr. — assumed — VL *Aegyptanus* Egyptian, fr. L *Aegyptius* + *-anus* -an) + *-ado* -ate — more at EGYPTIAN] **:** nonflamenco heelwork in dancing or a nonflamenco dance using heelwork

ag·i·tate \'ajə,tāt, *usu* -ād·+V\ *vb* -ED/ -ING/ -s [L *agitatus*, past part. of *agitare* to drive, agitate, turn over in the mind, freq. of *agere* to drive, do — more at AGENT] *vt* **1 a** *obs* **:** to give action or motion to **:** ACTUATE ⟨who fills, surrounds, informs, and ~*s* the whole —James Thomson⟩ **b :** to move to and fro **:** give regular motion to ⟨the ladies sigh and ~ their fans —J.E.Cooke⟩ **c :** to move with a brisk irregular action **:** shake or move rapidly or violently ⟨the convulsions and tremors which had *agitated* the body . . . were fewer —P.J.Phelan⟩ **2 :** to excite or trouble the mind or feelings of ⟨a discussion which has *agitated* thinkers —A.N.Whitehead⟩ **:** stir up **:** DISTURB ⟨questions which ~ modern states —G.L.Dickinson⟩ **3 :** to discuss or debate excitedly and earnestly ⟨the child and woman labor issues were *agitated* —H.M.Diamond⟩ **4** *obs* **:** to turn over in the mind **:** CONTRIVE, PLOT ⟨statesmen *agitating* new plans⟩ ~ *vi* **:** to attempt to arouse public feeling or influence public opinion (as by constant discussion) ⟨they were *agitating* for schools and the vote —V.G.Heiser⟩ **syn** see DISCOMPOSE, DISCUSS, SHAKE

agitated *adj* **1 :** moving to and fro **:** QUIVERING, SHAKING ⟨his ~ hand always gliding over the network of fine nerves about his mouth —Charles Dickens⟩ **2 :** troubled in mind **:** DISTURBED, EXCITED ⟨Wickham's alarm now appeared in a heightened complexion and ~ look —Jane Austen⟩ **3 :** kept before the public by extended discussion or debate ⟨the long ~ plan for a new high school⟩ — **ag·i·tat·ed·ly** \-ād·ədlē, -li\ *adv*

agitated depression *n* **:** a psychotic state characterized by restlessness, overactivity, anxiety, and despair but not accompanied by gross disorganization or deterioration — compare INVOLUTIONAL MELANCHOLIA

ag·i·tat·ing·ly \-ād·iŋlē, -ēŋ-, -li\ *adv* **:** in an agitating manner

ag·i·ta·tion \,ajə'tāshən\ *n* -s [MF or L; MF, fr. L *agitation-*, *agitatio*, fr. *agitatus* + *-ion-*, *-io* -ion] **1 a** *obs* **:** the action of moving **:** MOTION, ACTIVITY ⟨by exercise . . . I understand all . . . ~ of the body —Francis Fuller⟩ **b :** a moving back and forth **:** SHAKING, SWIRLING ⟨the ~ of milk can lead to a decrease in its keeping quality⟩ **c :** the state or condition of being moved to and fro violently, steadily, or with a fluttering effect ⟨a trifling ~ of the curtains —George Meredith⟩ **2 :** mental excitement or emotional perturbation **:** a tremulous and disturbed state ⟨in spite of his ~ his voice was low and quiet —Sherwood Anderson⟩ **3 :** earnest and thoughtful consideration **:** DISCUSSION, DEBATE ⟨this design was in ~ —Francis Parkman⟩ **4 :** the persistent and sustained attempt to arouse public feeling or influence public opinion (as by appeals, discussions, or demonstrations) ⟨no sudden revolt, but the culmination of a long ~ for national independence —W.R.Inge⟩ **syn** see COMMOTION

ag·i·ta·tion·al \¦ajə¦tāshən°l, -shnəl\ *adj* **:** of or concerned with agitation

ag·i·ta·tive \'ajə,tād·iv, -ātiv, -ēv\ *adj* **:** causing or tending to cause agitation

agi·ta·to \,ajə'täd·(,)ō, ,äjē'tä,tō\ *adj* (*or adv*) [It, lit., agitated, fr. L *agitatus*] **:** restless and agitated — used as a direction in music

ag·i·ta·tor \'ajə,tād·ə(r) *also* ¦ajə¦tā,tȯ(ə)r *or* -tȯ(ə)\ *n* -s [*agitate* (meaning also, in 17th cent., to administer, manage) + *-or*] **1** *usu cap* **:** an agent appointed by the Parliamentary army in Cromwell's time to look after the interests of the private soldiers — called also *Adjutator* **2 :** one that agitates: as **a :** one who stirs up political, economic, religious, or other social agitation ⟨an ~ for the rights of the common people⟩ **b :** an implement or apparatus (as one utilizing a propeller on a shaft) for mixing, stirring, or shaking — **ag·i·ta·to·ri·al** \¦ajətə¦tōrēəl\ *adj*

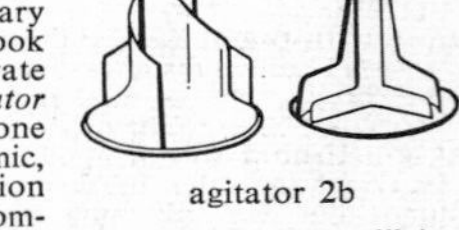
agitator 2b

agitator feed *n* **:** a device consisting of adjustable holes and rotating wheels used to prevent clogging in implements for broadcasting seed or fertilizer

[1]ag·it·prop \'ajət¦präp\ *n* -s [in sense 1, fr. Russ, fr. *agitatsiya-propaganda* agitation propaganda, fr. *agitatsiya* agitation (fr. F *agitation*) + *propaganda*, fr. G; in sense 2, Russ, a department of the Communist party, short for *Agitpropbyuro* Department of Agitprop — more at AGITATION, PROPAGANDA] **1 :** propaganda and agitation esp. in behalf of communism ⟨disillusioned ex-Communists who blame politics itself for their own earlier susceptibility to ~ —David Riesman⟩ **2 a :** a department or bureau in charge of agitprop ⟨he could no more be imagined cringing before a witch-hunting demagogue than taking orders from an ~ —*Nation*⟩ **b :** a person who engages in agitprop ⟨slogans chalked on walls by ~*s*⟩

[2]agitprop \"\ *adj* **:** of, relating to, or serving as a vehicle of agitprop ⟨~ officers⟩ ⟨the ~ drama⟩

ag·it·prop·ist \¦==¦=əst\ *n* -s **:** an agitprop agent

ag·it·punkt \'==,pu̇ŋ(k)t\ *n* -s [Russ, fr. *agitatsiya-punkt*, fr. *agitatsiya* + *punkt* point, place, fr. Pol or G; Pol, fr. G, fr. LL *puncta* — more at POINT] **:** an indoctrination and political propaganda center in the Soviet Union

ag·kis·tro·don \ag'kistrə,dän, aŋ'k-\ *n*, *cap* [NL, irreg. fr. Gk *ankistron* fishhook + NL *-odon*] **:** a genus of pit vipers including the American copperhead and water moccasin — used generally instead of the technically preferable *Ancistrodon*

ag·lao·ne·ma \,aglēō'nēmə\ *n*, *cap* [NL, fr. Gk *aglaos* shining, bright + NL *-nema*] **:** a genus of Indo-Malayan climbing herbs of the arum family having thick fleshy oblong leaves and naked unisexual flowers on a spadix shorter than the spathe — see CHINESE EVERGREEN

ag·lao·zo·nia \,aglēə'zōnyə, -nēə\ *n* [NL, fr. Gk *aglaos* + *zōnē* belt + NL *-ia*] **1** -s **:** the asexual stage of any brown alga of the genus *Cutleria* **2** *cap, in former classifications* **:** a genus of brown algae comprising those having aglaozonia stages

aglare \'ə-\ *adj* [[1]*a-* + *glare* (v.)] **:** GLARING ⟨with eyes ~⟩

aglas·pis \ə'glaspəs\ *n*, *cap* [NL, fr. Gk *aglaos* + NL *-aspis*] **:** a genus of extinct Cambrian Xiphosura related to the modern king crab

agleam \ə'-\ *adj* [[1]*a-* + *gleam* (v.)] **:** GLEAMING ⟨his face ~ in the sunlight⟩

ag·let \'aglət, 'aig- *or* **ai·glet** \'āg-\ *n* -s [ME *aglet*, fr. MF *aguillette*, dim. of *aguille* needle, fr. LL *acucula* ornamental pin, alter. of *acicula*, dim. of L *acus* needle, pin — more at ACUTE] **1 a** (1) **:** the plain or ornamental tag covering the ends of a point (sense 10a) (2) **:** an ornamental tag used for decoration on costumes **b :** any of various ornamental studs, cords, or pins worn on clothing **2 a :** HAWTHORN **b :** HAZEL 1a

agley \ə'glā, -lē,-lī, *Scot usu* -lē *or* -ləi\ *also* **aglee** \-lē\ *adv* [Sc, lit., squintingly, fr. E [1]*a-* + Sc & dial. E *gley*, *glee* to squint, fr. ME (northern dial.) *gleyen*] *chiefly Scot* **:** against hope, expectation, or plan **:** AWRY, WRONG ⟨the best-laid schemes o' mice an' men gang aft ~ —Robert Burns⟩

aglim·mer \ə'-\ *adj* [[1]*a-* + *glimmer*, v.] **:** GLIMMERING ⟨a city ~ with light⟩

aglint \ə'-\ *adj* [[1]*a-* + *glint*, v.] **:** GLINTING ⟨an island ~ in the sun⟩

[1]ag·li·pay·an \,aglə'pīən\ *n* -s *usu cap* [Gregorio *Aglipay* †1940 Philippine archbishop + E *-an*] **:** a member of the independent church of the Philippines organized on a national Catholic basis in 1902

[2]aglipayan \¦==¦==\ *adj*, *usu cap* **:** of or relating to Aglipayans

ag·li·pay·an·ism \,=='==,nizəm\ *n* -s *usu cap* **:** the doctrines, principles, and practices of Aglipayans

aglis·ten \ə'-\ *adj* [[1]*a-* + *glisten*, v.] **:** GLISTENING ⟨the garden ~ with dew⟩

aglit·ter \ə'-\ *adj* [[1]*a-* + *glitter*, v.] **:** GLITTERING ⟨a coronet ~ with diamonds⟩

aglo·mer·u·lar \¦ā=¦===\ *adj* [[2]*a-* + *glomerular*] **:** lacking glomeruli ⟨the ~ toadfish⟩

aglos·sa \(')ā'gläsə, -ȯsə\ *n pl*, *cap* [NL, fr. [2]*a-* + *-glossa*] **1** *in some classifications* **:** a suborder of amphibians including frogs or toads that have no tongue and have a common pharyngeal opening for the Eustachian tubes and comprising the families Pipidae and Xenopodidae **2** *in some classifications* **:** a division of mollusks having neither radula nor head coextensive with Lamellibranchia

[1]aglos·sate \(')ā¦gläsət, (')ā'glä,sāt, -lȯ-\ *or* **aglos·sal** \(')=¦=,səl\ *adj* [Gk *aglōssos* (fr. *a-* [2]a- + *glōssa* tongue) + E *-ate* or *-al*] **1** *zool* **:** having no tongue **2** [NL *Aglossa* + E *-ate* or *-al*] **:** of or relating to the Aglossa

[2]aglossate \(')='=(,)=\ *n* -s **:** one of the Aglossa

aglow \ə'-\ *adj* [[1]*a-* + *glow*, v.] **:** GLOWING ⟨a student ~ with liberalism⟩

aglu·con *or* **aglu·cone** \-lü-\ *n* -s [ISV *a-* (fr. Gk *a-*, *ha-* together) + *gluc-* + *-on*, *-one*] **:** AGLYCON; *esp* **:** one combined with glucose in a glucoside

agly·con \ə'glī,kän, ä'-,a'-\ *or* **agly·cone** \-ōn\ *n* -s [ISV *a-* (fr. Gk *a-*, *ha-* together) + *glyc-* + *-on*, *-one*] **:** an organic compound, usu. a phenol or an alcohol, combined with the sugar portion of a glycoside and obtainable by hydrolysis ⟨quercetin is the ~ of quercitrin⟩

ag·ly·pha \'agləfə\ *n pl*, *cap* [NL, fr. Gk *aglypha*, neut. pl. of *aglyphos* unhewn, fr. *a-* [2]a- + *-glyphos* (fr. *glyphein* to cut, hew) — more at CLEAVE (to cut)] **:** a primary division of the family Colubridae, in its widest sense nearly or exactly coextensive with the Aglyphodonta of other classifications

aglyph·o·don·ta \ə,glifə'däntə\ *n pl*, *cap* [NL, fr. *Aglypha* + *-odonta*] **:** a group of snakes without grooved fangs or venom glands and without limb vestiges, comprising the families Amblycephalidae, Acrochordidae, Colubridae (sensu stricto) and including the majority of common nonpoisonous snakes which are sometimes all placed in the family Colubridae

aglyph·o·don·tia \-nch(ē)ə\ *syn of* AGLYPHODONTA

ag·ly·phous \'agləfəs\ *adj* [NL *Aglypha* + E *-ous*] **1 :** of or relating to the Aglypha **2** *zool* **:** having solid teeth

ag·ma \'agmə\ *n* -s [LGk, fr. Gk, fragment] **1 :** the sound \ŋ\ in Greek or Latin **2 :** the Greek letter gamma (γ) when used to represent the sound \ŋ\ **3 :** ENG

ag·ma·tine \-,tēn\ *n* -s [ISV *agmat-* (fr. Gk *agmat-*, *agma* fragment) + *-ine*] **:** a base $C_5H_{14}N_4$ formed from arginine in putrefaction; (δ-amino-butyl)-guanidine

ag·mi·nate \'agmənət, -,nāt\ *or* **ag·mi·nat·ed** \-,nād·əd\ *adj* [L *agmin-*, *agmen* motion, march, troop + E *-ate*, *-ated*] **:** grouped together ⟨*agminated* glands are called Peyer's patches⟩

agn *abbr* again

ag·nail \'ag,nāl, 'aig-\ *n* -s [ME, fr. OE *angnaegl* corn, fr. *ang-* (akin to *enge* tight, painful) + *naegl* nail (of iron) — more at ANGER, NAIL] **1** *obs* **:** a corn on the foot or toe **2 :** a sore or inflammation about a fingernail or toenail **3 :** HANGNAIL

[1]ag·nate \'ag,nāt, 'aig-, *usu* -ād·+V\ *n* -s [L *agnatus*, fr. *agnatus*, past part. of *agnasci* to be born in addition to, fr. *ad-* + *nasci* to be born — more at NATION] **1 :** a relative whose kinship is traceable exclusively through males **2 :** any paternal kinsman — compare COGNATE, ENATE

[2]agnate \"\ *adj* [L *agnatus*] **1 :** related through male descent or on the father's side **2 :** having a kindred nature **:** ALLIED, AKIN

ag·na·tha \'agnəthə\ *n pl*, *cap* [NL, fr. [2]*a-* + *-gnatha*] **1 :** a superclass or other division of Vertebrata comprising those without jaws — compare GNATHOSTOMATA **2 :** a group of carnivorous air-breathing snails without jaws

ag·nath·ia \ag'nathēə, (')ā'n-, -āth-\ *n* -s [NL, fr. [2]*a-* + Gk *gnathos* + NL *-ia*] **:** the congenital complete or partial absence of one or both jaws

ag·na·tho·sto·ma·ta \,agnəthə'stōməd·ə, ¦ā,nath-\ [NL [2]*a-* + Gk *gnathos* jaw + NL *-stomata*] *syn of* AGNATHA

ag·na·tho·stom·a·tous \¦===¦stämad·əs, ¦=,==-, -ōm-\ *adj* [NL *Agnathostomata* + E *-ous*] **:** AGNATHOUS 2

ag·na·thous \'agnəthəs\ *also* **ag·nath·ic** \(')ag¦nathik, (')ā¦n-\ *adj* [[2]*a-* + Gk *gnathos* + E *-ous* or *-ic*] **1 :** having no jaws **2** [NL *Agnatha* + E *-ous* or *-ic*] **:** of or relating to the Agnatha

ag·nat·ic \(')ag¦nad·ik\ *adj* [[1]*agnate* + *-ic*] **:** of or relating to agnates **:** akin through male descent or on the father's side

ag·nat·i·cal·ly \-ək(ə)lē\ *adv* **:** in an agnatic manner

ag·na·tion \ag'nāshən\ *n* -s [F or L; F, fr. L *agnation-*, *agnatio*, fr. *agnatus* (past part. of *agnasci* to be born in addition to) + *-ion-*, *-io* -ion — more at AGNATE] **:** the relationship of agnates

ag·ne·an \'ägnēən\ *n* -s *cap* [*Agni*, ancient kingdom in Turkestan + E *-an*] **:** TOCHARIAN A

agnel \an'yel\ *n*, *pl* **agneaux** \-yō\ [F, fr. MF, lit., lamb, fr. L *agnellus* little lamb, dim. of *agnus* lamb — more at YEAN] **:** a gold coin of France, issued in the 13th to 16th centuries, bearing the figure of a lamb

ag·ni \'agnē\ *n*, *pl* **agni** *or* **agnis** *usu cap* **1 a :** a people of western Africa ethnologically allied to the Ashanti **b :** a member of such people **2 :** a Kwa language of the Agni people

ag·ni·fi·ca·tion \,agnəfə'kāshən\ *n* -s [L *agnus* lamb + E *-i-* + *-fication*] **:** the representation (as in painting) of persons as sheep or lambs

agnition *n* -s [L *agnition-*, *agnitio*, fr. *agnitus* (past part. of *agnoscere* to recognize, acknowledge, fr. *ad-* + *gnoscere* to know) + *-ion-*, *-io* -ion — more at KNOW] *obs* **:** RECOGNITION, ACKNOWLEDGMENT

ag·nize \(')ag¦nīz\ *vt* -ED/-ING/-s [fr. L *agnoscere*, after *recognoscere*: E *recognize*] *archaic* **:** RECOGNIZE, ACKNOWLEDGE ⟨I do ~ a natural and prompt alacrity —Shak.⟩

ag·no·e·tae \,ag(,)nō'ē,tē\ *n pl*, *usu cap* [LL *Agnoetae*, *Agnoitae*, fr. LGk *Agnoētai*, lit., ignorant ones, fr. Gk *agnoein* to be ignorant, fr. *a-* [2]a- + *-gnoein* (fr. *gignōskein* to know) — more at KNOW] **1 :** a 4th century A.D. sect of Arians that considered God's omniscience limited to the present **2 :** a 6th century sect of Severian Monophysites that denied the omniscience of Jesus Christ

ag·no·ete \'ag(,)nō,ēt\ *or* **ag·no·ite** \-,īt\ *n* -s *usu cap* [LL *Agnoetae*, *Agnoitae*, pl.] **:** one of the Agnoetae

ag·no·e·tism \,ag(,)nō'ē,tizəm, 'ag(,)nō,ēd·,iz-\ *n* -s *usu cap* **:** the doctrinal principles of the Agnoetae

ag·no·gen·ic \¦agnō¦jenik\ *adj* [[2]*a-* + Gk *gnōmē* means of knowing + E *-genic*] *med* **:** of unknown cause ⟨~ metaplasia⟩

ag·no·men \(')ag¦nōmən\ *n*, *pl* **ag·nom·i·na** \-nämənə, -nōm-\ *or* **agnomens** [L, irreg. (influence of *agnoscere* to acknowledge, fr. *ad-* + *noscere* to know) fr. *ad-* + *nomen* name — more at NAME] **:** an additional name or epithet; *specif* **:** an additional cognomen given to a person by the ancient Romans (as in honor of some achievement) — compare NOMEN, PRAENOMEN

ag·nom·i·na·tion \(,)ag,nämə'nāshən\ *n* -s [L *agnomination-*, *agnominatio*, fr. *ad-* + *nomination-*, *nominatio* naming; trans. of Gk *paronomasia* — more at NOMINATION] **1 :** the echoing of a sound of one word in another in close relationship with it (as in the same sentence) **2 :** the repetition of a word but in different senses often for purpose of wit (as in punning) or for emphatic contrast

ag·no·sia \ag'nōzh(ē)ə\ *n* -s [NL, fr. Gk *agnōsia* ignorance, fr. *a-* [2]a- + *-gnōsia* -gnosia] **:** the partial or complete loss of the ability to recognize familiar objects esp. by seeing, hearing, or touching and usu. as a result of brain damage

ag·no·sis \ag'nōsəs\ *n*, *pl* **agno·ses** \-ō,sēz\ [NL, fr. [2]*a-* + *-gnosis*] **:** AGNOSIA

ag·nos·te·rol \ag'nästə,rȯl, -ōl\ *n* -s [L *agnus* lamb + E *-o-* + *sterol*] **:** a crystalline tetracyclic triterpenoid alcohol $C_{30}H_{47}OH$ obtained from wool fat

[1]ag·nos·tic \ag'nästik, əg-,aig-, -ēk\ *n* -s [modif. (influenced by E *Gnostic*) of Gk *agnōstos* unknown, unknowable, not knowing, fr. *a-* [2]a- + *gnōstos* known, fr. *gignōskein* to know — more at KNOW] **:** one who professes agnosticism; *broadly* **:** one who maintains a continuing doubt about the existence or knowability of a god or any ultimates ⟨~ . . . came into my head as suggestively antithetic to the gnostic of church history who professed to know so much —T.H.Huxley⟩

syn AGNOSTIC, FREETHINKER, and ATHEIST can all apply to one who does not take an orthodox religious position. AGNOSTIC is the most neutral; it usu. implies only an unwillingness on available evidence to affirm or deny the existence of God or subscribe to tenets that presuppose such existence. FREETHINKER is broader; it can apply to one of no determinable religious position or to one who feels truth is made more available by not committing oneself to any orthodoxy, esp. a belief in God's existence. Often it can suggest a reprehensible and dangerous license of opinion. ATHEIST can apply strictly and neutrally to one who denies the existence of God or tenets presupposing it. More frequently than FREETHINKER, however, it has carried ideas of reprehensible license of opinion and menacing godlessness.

[2]ag·nos·tic \(')a(i)g¦n-, əg'n-\ *also* **ag·nos·ti·cal** \-təkəl, -ēk-\ *adj* **1 :** relating to or involving agnosticism; *esp* **:** professing ignorance or uncertainty about the ultimates usu. on the ground of unknowability ⟨so far as faith in God is concerned they are ~ rather than atheistic —W.L.Sperry⟩ **2 :** characterized by tolerance **:** UNDOGMATIC — **ag·nos·ti·cal·ly** \-ək(ə)lē, -ēk-, -li\ *adv*

[3]ag·nos·tic \(')ag¦nōstik\ *adj* [Gk *agnōstos* + E *-ic*] **:** of, relating to, or characterized by agnosia ⟨~ symptoms⟩

[4]agnostic \"\ *n* -s **:** one who is a subject of agnosia

ag·nos·ti·cism \ag'nästə,sizəm, əg-\ *n* -s **1 a :** the doctrine that the existence or nature of any ultimate reality is unknown and probably unknowable or that any knowledge about matters of ultimate concern is impossible or improbable; *specif* **:** the doctrine that God or any first cause is unknown and probably unknowable **b :** a doctrine affirming that the existence of a god is possible but denying that there are any sufficient reasons for holding either that he does or does not exist — compare ATHEISM, SKEPTICISM **2 :** SKEPTICISM 1b **3 :** an agnostic attitude or disposition

ag·nos·tid \ag'nästəd\ *adj* [NL *Agnostus* + E *-id*] **:** of or belonging to the genus *Agnostus*

ag·nos·tus \-təs\ *n*, *cap* [NL, fr. Gk *agnōstos* unknown] **:** a genus of small blind Cambrian and Ordovician trilobites that with a number of related forms in which the cephalon and pygidium are almost indistinguishable constitute an order (Agnostida) of highly specialized forms

ag·no·to·zo·ic \ag¦nōd·ə¦zōik, ¦ag,n-\ *n or adj*, *usu cap* [ISV *agnoto-* (fr. Gk *agnōtos* unknown) + *-zoic*] **:** ALGONKIAN, PROTEROZOIC

agnus *n* -ES [ME, short for *Agnus Dei*] **:** AGNUS DEI

ag·nus cas·tus \¦agnə'skastəs\ *n*, *pl* **agnus castuses** [ME, fr. L, by folk etymology (influence of L *agnus* lamb & *castus* chaste) fr. Gk *agnos* (confused with *hagnos* chaste, holy), perh. of Sem origin; akin to Heb *'āghan* to remain closed in or hidden — more at CASTE] **:** an ornamental shrub (*Vitex agnus-castus*) having blue or white flowers and fruit that has been used as a stimulant and carminative — called also *chaste tree*

ag·nus dei \ˌäg,nu̇s'dā,ē, -ˌnəs-, ¦än,yüs-, -yu̇s-; *sometimes, when not sung*, -'dā; ¦agnəs'dē,ī\ *n, usu cap A&D* [ME, fr. LL, lamb of God, trans. of Gk *Amnos tou Theou*] **1 :** an image of a lamb, often with a halo and bearing a banner or a cross, symbolizing Jesus Christ **2** *Roman Catholicism* **a :** a small cloth-covered disk of wax stamped with the figure of a lamb, blessed by the pope, and carried or worn through devotion **b :** a prayer in the ordinary of the mass beginning with the words "Agnus Dei" **3** *Anglicanism* **:** a liturgical prayer or anthem beginning "O Lamb of God"

Agnus Dei 1

ago \ə'gō\ *also* **agone** \ə'gȯn *also* -än\ *adj* (*or adv*) [ME *ago, agon*, fr. past part. of *agon* to go away, pass by, fr. OE *āgān* to pass away, fr. *ā-* (perfective prefix) + *gān* to go — more at ABEAR, GO] **:** gone by **:** PAST ⟨two days ~⟩ ⟨he lived here long ~⟩

agog \ə'gäg *also* -ȯg\ *adj* [MF *en gogues* merry, lively, lit., in mirth] **:** full of intense interest, ardent anticipation, or extreme excitement ⟨the abrupt announcement . . . left everybody . . . ~ —Bennett Cerf⟩ **:** EAGER ⟨always ~ for news —Virginia Woolf⟩ **syn** see EAGER

ago·ge \ə'gōjē, -ōgē, ¦ägō'gā\ *n* -s [Gk *agōgē*, lit., act of carrying away, fr. *agein* to lead — more at AGENT] *Greek music* **:** rate of speed **:** TEMPO

agog·ic \ə'gäjik, -gōjik\ *adj* [G *agogisch*, fr. Gk *agōgē* + G *-isch* -ish] **:** of or relating to agoge or agogics esp. to variations in tempo within a piece or movement ⟨tempos and ~ indications of an operatic score⟩

agogic accent *n* **:** stress secured through relative prolongation of the tones to be emphasized — compare AGOGICS

agog·ics \-iks\ *n pl but usu sing in constr* [G *agogik*, fr. Gk *agōgē* + G *-ik* -ics] **1 :** the musical theory that rhetorical emphasis involves not only dynamic stress but also the emphasis implied in the greater relative length of the tones to be emphasized — compare RUBATO **2 :** the quantitative aspect of musical nuances involving all variations from the rigid basic meter (as of retard, pause, accelerando)

-a·gogue \ə,gäg *also* -ȯg\ *also* **-a·gog** \"\ *n comb form* -s [F & NL; F *-agogue*, fr. LL *-agogus* promoting the expulsion of, fr. Gk *-agōgos*, fr. *agōgos* leading, drawing forth, fr. *agein* to lead; NL *-agogon*, neut. of *-agogus* promoting the expulsion of, fr. Gk *-agōgos* — more at AGENT] **:** substance that promotes the secretion or expulsion of ⟨chol*agogue*⟩ ⟨lymph*agogue*⟩

ago·ho *or* **ago·jo** \ə'gō,hō\ *n* -s [*agoho* fr. Tag *agohò*; *agojo* fr. PhilSp, fr. Tag *agohò*] **:** HORSETAIL TREE

agon \'ä,gän, ä'gōn, 'a,gän, 'ä,gän\ *n, pl* **agons** \-nz\ *also* **agones** \ä'gō,nes, ə'gō(,)nēz\ [Gk *agōn*, lit., gathering, assembly, contest — more at AGONY] **:** a struggle or contest: as **a :** a contest in athletics, chariot or horse racing, music, or literature at a public festival in ancient Greece **b :** the dramatic conflict between the chief characters in a Greek play **c :** the struggle between protagonist and antagonist in a literary work ⟨the central ~ of the novel⟩

ag·o·nal \'agən°l\ *adj* [*agony* + *-al*] **:** of, relating to, or associated with agony, esp. the death agony or period of dying ⟨the ~ state⟩ ⟨~ leukocytosis⟩

ago·ni·a·da \ə,gōnē'ädə, -adə\ *or* **agoniada bark** *n* -s [Pg *agoniada*] **:** the bark of a tropical So. American shrub (*Plumieria lancifolia*) yielding plumieride

ago·ni·a·ti·tes \(')ā,gōnēə'tīd·(,)ēz, ə,g-\ *n, cap* [NL, fr. ²*a-* + *Goniatites*] **:** a genus of Devonian ammonoid mollusks (family Goniatitidae)

agon·ic \(')ā¦gänik, ə'g-\ *adj* [Gk *agonos* without angle (fr. *a-* ²*a-* + *gonia* angle, corner) + E *-ic*] **:** not forming an angle

agonic line *n* **:** an imaginary line on the earth's surface connecting the north and south magnetic poles and passing through those points where there is no magnetic declination and where a freely suspended magnetic needle indicates true north — compare ACLINIC LINE, ISOGONIC LINE

agon·i·dae \ə'gänə,dē\ *n pl, cap* [NL, fr. *Agonus*, type genus + *-idae*] **:** a family of small slender fishes (order Scleroparei) having the body covered with overlapping striated often spiny plates

ag·o·nist \'agənəst\ *n* -s [LL *agonista*, fr. Gk *agōnistēs* combatant, fr. *agōnizesthai* to contend, fr. *agōn* gathering, assembly, contest — more at AGONY] **1 :** one that is engaged in a struggle: as **a :** a leading character (as the protagonist) in a literary work ⟨the chief interest of the novel . . . is an analysis of the nature and moods . . . of the four *~s* —Iris Barry⟩ **b :** one that is beset by intellectual or spiritual conflicts ⟨an ~, a self-tormentor who ran to meet suffering halfway —John Buchan⟩ **2** [back-formation fr. *antagonist* "a muscle"] **:** a muscle that on contracting is automatically checked and controlled by the opposing simultaneous contraction of another muscle — see ANTAGONIST 2a; compare SYNERGIST

ag·o·nis·tic \¦agə¦nistik\ *also* **ag·o·nis·ti·cal** \-təkəl\ *adj* [LL *agonisticus* of a contest, fr. Gk *agōnistikos* fit for combat, contentious, fr. *agōnistēs* + *-ikos* -ic, -ical] **1 :** of or relating to the athletic contests of ancient Greece ⟨~ inscriptions⟩ **2 :** seeking to overcome in discussion or debate **:** ARGUMENTATIVE ⟨a dialectical and ~ approach to knowledge⟩ **3 :** striving for effect **:** STRAINED ⟨~ poses⟩ — **ag·o·nis·ti·cal·ly** \-tək(ə)lē\ *adv*

ag·o·nize \'agə,nīz, 'aig-\ *vb* -ED/-ING/-S *see -ize in Explan Notes* [MF *agoniser* to be in agony, fr. LL *agonizare*, fr. Gk *agōnizesthai*, fr. *agōnia* agony — more at AGONY] *vt* **:** to cause to suffer agony **:** TORTURE ⟨he *agonized* himself with the thought —Aldous Huxley⟩ ~ *vi* **1 :** to suffer agony or torture **:** be in great pain or anguish ⟨who *agonized* and prayed and yet could not secure release from their guilt —Lillian Smith⟩ **2 :** to try desperately **:** STRUGGLE ⟨strive to do and ~ to do and fail in doing —Robert Browning⟩ **syn** see WRITHE

agonized *adj* **:** characterized by, suffering, or expressing agony ⟨an ~ search⟩ ⟨an ~ father⟩ ⟨an ~ cry⟩ — **ag·o·niz·ed·ly** \-zədlē, -li\ *adv*

agonizing *adj* **:** causing agony **:** PAINFUL ⟨an ~ reappraisal of the role and the future of the French Empire —D.W.Brogan⟩ — **ag·o·niz·ing·ly** *adv*

ag·o·nos·to·mus \,agə'nästəməs\ *n, cap* [NL, fr. Gk *agōnos* without angle + NL *-stomus*] **:** a genus of tropical freshwater mullets of the East and West Indies and Mexico much used as food

agon·o·thete \ə'gänə,thēt\ *n, pl* **agonothetes** \-ēts\ *or* **ag·o·noth·e·tae** \,agə'näthə,tē, -,tī\ [LL *agonotheta*, fr. Gk *agōnothetēs*, fr. *agōn* + *-thetēs* (fr. *tithenai* to appoint, make, do) — more at DO] **:** the judge or director of public games in ancient Greece

ag·o·ny \'agənē, 'aig-, -ni\ *n* -ES [ME *agonie*, fr. MF & LL; MF *agonie*, fr. LL *agonia*, fr. Gk *agōnia* contest, struggle, anguish, fr. *agōn* gathering, assembly at games, contest for a prize, fr. *agein* to lead, celebrate — more at AGENT] **1 a :** intense pain of mind or spirit **:** extreme distress **:** ANGUISH ⟨the ~ of being found wanting and exposed to the disapproval of others —Margaret Mead⟩ **b** *often cap* **:** the sufferings of Jesus in the garden of Gethsemane ⟨and being in an ~ he prayed more earnestly —Lk 22:44 (AV)⟩ **2 a :** intense pain of body **:** extreme torment **:** TORTURE ⟨left arm twisted upward behind him . . . in slow, deliberate ~ —Kay Boyle⟩ **b :** the throes of death **:** death struggle ⟨his final ~⟩ **3 :** a violent struggle, conflict, or contest ⟨the world is convulsed by the *agonies* of great nations —T.B.Macaulay⟩ **4 :** a strong sudden and often uncontrollable display (as of joy or delight) **:** OUTBURST ⟨my cousin . . . in an ~ of mirth —Edith Wharton⟩ **syn** see DISTRESS

agony column *n* **:** a newspaper column of personal advertisements relating esp. to lost objects, missing relatives or friends, and marriage separations

agood [¹*a-* + *good* (adj.)] *obs* **:** in earnest **:** HEARTILY

ag·o·ra \'agərə\ *n, pl* **agoras** \-rəz\ *or* **ag·o·rae** \-,rē, -,rī\ [Gk, fr. *ageirein* to assemble — more at GREGARIOUS] **:** a gathering place or assembly; *esp* **:** the market place in ancient Greece

ag·o·ra·pho·bia \,agərə'fōbēə\ *n* -s [NL, fr. Gk *agora* + NL *-phobia*] **:** abnormal fear of crossing or of being in the midst of open spaces — contrasted with *claustrophobia* — **ag·o·ra·pho·bic** \¦===¦fōbik *also* -äb-\ *adj*

agoua·ra *also* **agua·ra** \¦agwə¦rä\ *n* -s [Pg *aguara* & Sp *aguará*, fr. Guarani *aguará*] **1 :** any of several So. American wild dogs (genus *Chrysocyon*) **2 :** CRAB-EATING RACCOON

¹**agou·ti** *also* **agou·ty** \ə'güd·ē, -üte, -i\ *n, pl* **agoutis** *also* **agouties** [F *agouti*, fr. Sp *agutí*, fr. Guarani *acutí, agutí*] **1 :** a rodent of the genera *Dasyprocta* and *Myoprocta* being about the size of a rabbit and brownish or grizzled in color and peculiar to So. and Central America and the West Indies **2 a :** a grizzled color of the fur or hair of many rodents (as wild guinea pigs, rats, mice, and squirrels) consisting of the barring of each hair in several alternate dark and light bands blackish blue or brown at the base and yellowish at the tip **b :** an agouti-coated animal

²**agouti** \"\ *adj* **:** characterized by or bearing the color agouti

ag·pa·ite \'agpə,īt\ *n* -s [*Agpa*, locality in southern Greenland + E *-ite*] **:** any of a group of feldspathoid rocks (as naujaites, lujauvrites, or kakortokites) from Ilimausak, Greenland, which differ from normal nephelite-syenites in having alumina in excess of the alkalies — **ag·pa·it·ic** \¦==¦id·ik\ *adj*

agr *abbr* agriculture

¹**agra** \ə'grō\ *n* -s [IrGael *a grādh*, fr. *a* oh + *grādh* love, fr. MIr *grād*; akin to L *gratus* beloved, dear — more at GRACE] *Irish* **:** my dear **:** SWEETHEART

²**agra** \'ägrə\ *adj, usu cap* [fr. *Agra*, India] **:** of or from the city of Agra, India **:** of the kind or style prevalent in Agra

³**agra** \"\ *n* -s *usu cap* [fr. *Agra*, India, where it is made] **:** a carpet usu. distinguished by thick pile and heavy knotting

-ag·ra \'agrə, 'aig- *sometimes* 'äg-\ *n comb form, pl* **-ag·rae** \-,grē\ *also* **-agras** [ME, fr. L, fr. Gk, fr. *agra* hunting, catch; akin to W *aer* war, L *agere* to drive — more at AGENT] **:** seizure of pain ⟨cardi*agra*⟩ ⟨mel*agra*⟩

agrafe *or* **agraffe** \ə'graf\ *n* -s [F *agrafe*, fr. *agrafer* to hook, fasten, fr. MF, fr. *a-* (fr. L *ad-*) + *grafer* to hook, fr. *grafe* hook, fr. OHG *krāpfo*; akin to OHG *krampfo* hook — more at CRAMP] **1 :** a hook-and-loop fastening; *esp* **:** an ornamental clasp used on armor or costumes ⟨an ~ set with pearls⟩ **2 :** a hook, eyelet, or other device by which a piano wire is so held as to prevent the section between the pin and the bridge from vibrating **3 a :** a cramp used in building to hold stones together **b :** relief sculpture put upon the head of an arch **4 :** the iron clamp used to secure the cork in a champagne bottle or the closure in any jug, bottle, or carboy

agrafe 1

agra gauze \'ägrə-\ *n, usu cap A* [fr. *Agra*, India, where it was made] **:** a silk gauze with stiff finish used for trimming

agram·ma·tism \(')ā'gramə,tizəm\ *n* -s [ISV *agrammat-* (fr. Gk *agrammatos* illiterate, fr. *a-* ²*a-* + *grammat-, gramma* letter) + *-ism*; orig. formed as G *agrammatismus* — more at GRAMMAR] **:** the pathologic inability to use words in grammatical sequence

agran·u·lo·cyte \(')ā'granyələ,sīt\ *n* -s [ISV ²*a-* + *granulocyte*] **:** a leukocyte without cytoplasmic granules **:** a lymphocyte or monocyte — compare GRANULOCYTE

agran·u·lo·cyt·ic angina \¦=,===¦sid·ik\ *n* **:** GRANULOCYTOPENIA

agranulocytosis \¦=,===,sī'tōsəs\ *n, pl* **agranulocyto·ses** \-ō,sēz\ [NL, fr. ²*a-* + E *granulocyte* + NL *-osis*] **1 :** GRANULOCYTOPENIA **2** *Brit* **:** PANLEUCOPENIA

ag·ra·pha \'agrəfə\ *n pl* [Gk, neut. pl. of *agraphos* unwritten, fr. *a-* ²*a-* + *-graphos* (fr. *graphein* to write) — more at CARVE] **:** sayings of Jesus unrecorded in the canonical gospels but found in other parts of the New Testament or in early Christian writings

agraph·ia \(')ā'grafēə\ *n* -s [NL, fr. ²*a-* + *-graphia* -graphy] **:** the pathologic loss of the ability to write — **agraph·ic** \(')ā¦grafik\ *adj*

¹**agrar·i·an** \ə'grerēən, -ra(a)r-, -rär-\ *adj* [L *agrarius* (fr. *agr-, ager* field + *-arius* -ary) + E *-an* — more at ACRE] **1 :** of or relating to the land or landed property ⟨a policy of ~ redistribution was sketched out —G.A.Craig⟩ **2 a :** of, by, or characteristic of the farmer or his way of life ⟨the application of ~ virtues to . . . industrial economy —Lloyd Morris⟩ **b :** organized or designed to promote agricultural interests ⟨an ~ party drawing its original impulse from the grain growers and dairymen —H.R.Penniman⟩ **3 :** growing wild in fields **:** CAMPESTRAL — **agrarianly** *adv*

²**agrarian** \"\ *n* -s *often cap* **:** one who favors agrarianism; *esp* **:** a member of an agrarian party or movement

agrar·i·an·ism \-,nizəm\ *n* -s **1 a :** the doctrine of an equal division or equitable redistribution of landed property **b :** a social or political movement designed to bring about land reforms or to improve the economic status of the farmer **2 :** the way of life associated with a farm economy and country towns in contrast to that associated with an industrial economy

agré·a·tion \ägrāäsyōⁿ\ *n* -s [F, lit., approval, fr. *agréer* to agree + *-ation*] **:** a diplomatic procedure by which a state determines in advance whether a proposed envoy will be acceptable to the receiving state — compare AGRÉMENT

agree \ə'grē\ *vb* **agreed; agreed; agreeing; agrees** [ME *agreen*, fr. MF *agreer*, fr. *a-* (fr. L *ad-*) + *gré* will, pleasure, fr. L *gratum*, neut. of *gratus* beloved, dear, agreeable — more at GRACE] *vt* **1 a :** to concur in (as an opinion) **:** ADMIT ⟨all *agreed* that he was a man of stature⟩ **b :** to indicate willingness **:** CONSENT ⟨~ to abide by the interpretation of the court —M.R.Cohen⟩ **2** *chiefly Brit* **a :** to settle upon by arrangement **:** ARRANGE ⟨the following articles were *agreed* —Sir Winston Churchill⟩ **b :** to bring into settlement ⟨they have *agreed* their quarrel⟩ ~ *vi* **1 :** to give assent **:** express approval **:** ACCEDE — usu. used with *to* or *with* and sometimes with *in* ⟨~ to a plan⟩ ⟨~ with an opinion⟩ ⟨I ~ . . . in . . . what you say —Benjamin Jowett⟩ **2 a :** to achieve harmony (as of opinion, feeling, or purpose) **:** become of one mind ⟨no two of his admirers would . . . ~ in their selection of characteristic passages —Bliss Perry⟩ ⟨~ with classical antiquity in deeming a figure of speech to be worth frequent use —C.E. Montague⟩ **b :** to live or act together harmoniously **:** get along together ⟨the two managed to ~ fairly well and the next month passed very pleasantly —Elinor Wylie⟩ **c :** to reach a harmonious understanding **:** come to terms — usu. used with *on* or *upon* ⟨~ on a fair division of the profits⟩ ⟨the means of settling the dispute were finally *agreed* upon⟩ **3 a :** to be similar **:** CORRESPOND — used with *with* ⟨the photographs ~ exactly with the originals⟩ **b :** to resemble one another **:** correspond to each other ⟨the accounts of the wreck did not ~⟩ **c :** to be consistent or consonant **:** HARMONIZE — used with *with* ⟨popular poetry . . . *agreed* with the favorite fiction . . . in attitude —J.D.Hart⟩ **4 a** *obs* **:** to react suitably, pleasingly, or healthfully — used with *with* ⟨your appetites and your digestions do not ~ with it —Shak.⟩ **b :** to be fitting, pleasing, or healthful **:** SUIT — used with *with* ⟨a dry climate will ~ with the patient⟩ ⟨onions don't ~ with everyone⟩ **5 :** to have an inflectional form denoting either identity or some regular correspondence other than identity in such grammatical categories as gender, number, case, or person ⟨the German verb *~s* with its subject in person and number⟩ ⟨the Latin adjective *~s* with its noun in gender, number, and case⟩ ⟨in classical Greek a verb in the third person singular *~s* with a neuter plural subject⟩

syn CONCUR, COINCIDE: AGREE suggests an accord, harmony, or compatibility arrived at by a settling of differences, as in the making of a truce, or by acquiescence where there was or might have been opposition or contention ⟨*agree* upon a price⟩ ⟨I will presume that Mr. Murry and myself can *agree* that for our purposes these counters are adequate —T.S.Eliot⟩ CONCUR suggests a thinking, acting, or functioning cooperatively or harmoniously toward a given end or for a given purpose ⟨for the creation of a masterwork of literature two powers must *concur*, the power of the man and the power of the moment — Matthew Arnold⟩ ⟨all those who have been concerned in the administration of our finances have *concurred* in representing its importance or necessity —John Marshall⟩ COINCIDE emphasizes the identity or precise accord of nature, function, opinion, or attitude in much the same way that, applied to historical events, it signifies their occurrence at precisely the same time or place. It is infrequently used of persons ⟨private groups whose interests did not *coincide* with those of national defense —T.W.Arnold⟩ ⟨the hearty tones natural when the words demanded by politeness *coincide* with those of deep feeling — Thomas Hardy⟩

syn TALLY, SQUARE, CONFORM, CORRESPOND, HARMONIZE, ACCORD, JIBE: AGREE is a general term indicating a going, fitting, or matching together without significant difference, contradiction, or conflict ⟨in general, the two accounts *agree*⟩ ⟨their findings *agree* with his⟩ TALLY suggests an agreement like that between two correct sets of accounts or records matching in both itemized details and overall conclusions ⟨one thing must match another or representation must *tally* with thing represented, like items in a tradesman's account —R.M. Weaver⟩ SQUARE suggests an exact agreeing, as if one item could perfectly fit with the form or shape of another ⟨these two assertions *square* with orthodox tradition —T.S.Omond⟩ ⟨the facts of history exist; but they hardly trouble us. We select and interpret our documents till they *square* with our theories — Aldous Huxley⟩ CONFORM suggests an essential agreement in form or in action, nature, or import making differences or deviations unimportant ⟨a widely diffused popular story of a fairy wife or husband which *conforms* to the type known as the Swan Maiden, or Beauty and the Beast, or Cupid and Psyche —J.G.Frazer⟩ ⟨and since theology was philosophy's queen, medieval philosophy *conformed* to that system which Augustine employed in his theology —H.O.Taylor⟩ CORRESPOND may be used to indicate the matching of far-apart or dissimilar things in falling into the same category or in being analogous, as well as to apply to closely similar items ⟨remind ourselves that ideas and images and thoughts are merely the objects that *correspond* to certain impulses and conations of our own —Samuel Alexander⟩ ⟨conjurers, who *correspond* to the Siberian shamans, affect the usual mystery of the priestly craft —Edward Clodd⟩ HARMONIZE suggests a matching, juxtaposing, or combining agreeably or pleasurably without jarring or grating ⟨the advantage of the Ptolemaic scheme, complicated though it was, was that it *harmonized* fairly well with the observable phenomena of the heavens —G.C.Sellery⟩ ⟨such mortal impulses were so very difficult to *harmonize* with the eternal beatitude which consisted in the cognition and love of God — H.O.Taylor⟩ ACCORD suggests a general compatibility, a capacity for fitting, matching, or accompanying without friction, discord, difficulty ⟨the common doctrine of liberty *accorded* with the passions released by the Revolution —V.L. Parrington⟩ ⟨the splendid moving ritual, with a Queen who so perfectly *accorded* with its spirit, lifted the people of Britain out of their normal selves —*Britain Today*⟩ JIBE is more colloquial than the preceding; it suggests matching, fitting, or accord without serious difficulty or contradiction ⟨that the attempts at "reconciliation" were futile, that common sense and science simply wouldn't *jibe*, was not Mill's fault —Gail Kennedy⟩ **syn** see in addition ASSENT

agree·a·bil·i·ty \ə,grēə'bilәd·ē, -ətē, -i\ *n* -ES **:** the quality or state of being agreeable

¹**agree·a·ble** \ə'grēəbəl\ *adj* [ME *agreable*, fr. MF, fr. *agreer* + *-able*] **1 a :** pleasing to the mind or senses **:** to one's liking **:** PLEASANT ⟨an ~ manner⟩ ⟨an ~ garden⟩ ⟨~ people⟩ ⟨an occupation ~ to his tastes⟩ **b** *of an odor* **:** FRAGRANT **2 :** ready or willing to agree or consent **:** favorably disposed ⟨~ to the plan⟩ **3 :** in harmony or keeping **:** CONSISTENT, CONSONANT ⟨the theory . . . was ~ to the general evolutionary conceptions of the period —S.F.Mason⟩ **syn** see PLEASANT

²**agreeable** \"\ *n* -s **:** an agreeable person or thing — usu. used in pl. ⟨superficial advantages and outside *~s* —S.T.Coleridge⟩

agree·a·ble·ness *n* -ES **:** AGREEABILITY

agreeable to *prep* **:** in accordance with the requirements of **:** as provided by **:** according to ⟨chose officers *agreeable to* the laws of that province —*Amer. Guide Series: Vt.*⟩

agree·a·bly \-'blē, -li\ *adv* [ME *agreablely, agreably*, fr. *agreable* + *-ly*] **1 :** in an agreeable manner **:** PLEASANTLY **2** *obs* **:** in the same way **:** SIMILARLY

agreeably to *prep* **:** in conformity with **:** as provided by **:** according to ⟨disobedience of orders in not attacking the enemy . . . *agreeably to* repeated instructions —H.E.Scudder⟩

agreed *past of* AGREE

agreed case *n* **:** CASE STATED

agreed rate *n* **:** an esp. low rate granted by a carrier to a shipper in return for the allocation of a high proportion of the shipper's freight to that carrier

agreed valuation *n* **:** the value of articles or shipments agreed upon by shipper and carrier in order to obtain a specific rating or limited liability — compare RELEASED VALUATION

agreed weight *n* **:** the weight per package or unit agreed upon by shipper and carrier to avoid weighing each package or unit

agreeing *pres part of* AGREE

agreeingly *adv* **:** in an agreeing manner

agree·ment \ə'grēmənt\ *n* -s [ME *agrement*, fr. MF, fr. *agreer* to please, agree + *-ment* — more at AGREE] **1 a :** the act of agreeing or coming to a mutual arrangement ⟨never any solemn ~ amongst themselves —John Locke⟩ **b :** oneness of opinion, feeling, or purpose **:** harmonious understanding **:** CONCORD ⟨with which religious tradition . . . must come to some sort of ~ —W.R.Inge⟩ **c :** the state of agreeing or being in accord **:** HARMONY, CORRESPONDENCE ⟨~ between the measured ionospheric data and the indications of practical communication experience —*London Calling*⟩ **2 a :** an arrangement (as between two or more parties) as to a course of action ⟨entered into an ~ . . . to assist in planting a colony —R.J.Stanley⟩ **b :** a compact entered into by two or more nations or heads of nations **:** COVENANT, TREATY **3 a :** a contract duly executed and legally binding on the parties entering into it — see CONTRACT, MEETING OF THE MINDS **b :** the written or oral phraseology embodying reciprocal promises **c :** the written instrument that is the evidence of an agreement **4 :** the fact of agreeing grammatically ⟨the ~ of the English personal pronoun with its antecedent in gender and number⟩

agrees *pres 3d sing of* AGREE

agré·ga·tion \ägrāgäsyōⁿ\ *n, pl* **agrégations** \"\ *n* -s [F, lit., admittance, fr. ML *aggregation-, aggregatio* act of collecting, fr. L *aggregatus* (past part. of *aggregare*) + *-ion-, -io* -ion] **:** a competitive examination given at French universities which must be passed for admission to the rank of agrégé

agré·gé \ägrāzhā, -rezhā\ *n, pl* **agrégés** \"\ [F, fr. past part. of *agréger* to admit (influenced in meaning by *agrégation*), fr. L *aggregare* to add to — more at AGGREGATE] **:** an academic rank conferred by a French university on one who has passed a rigidly competitive examination and who is therefore entitled to appointment to the highest teaching post in a lycée or in one of the faculties of a university

agré·mens \ägrāmäⁿ\ *or* **agré·ments** *n pl* [F *agréments* (formerly also spelled *agrémens*), pl. of *agrément* pleasure, ornament, agreement, approval — more at AGREEMENT] **:** AMENITIES ⟨the ~ of social life⟩

agré·ment \ägrāmäⁿ\ *n, pl* **agréments** \"\ [F] **1:** GRACE NOTE, ORNAMENT **2 :** the approval of a diplomatic representative by the state to which he is to be accredited — compare AGRÉATION

agres·tal \ə'grest°l\ *or* **agres·tial** \-es(h)chəl\ *adj* [L *agrestis* (fr. *agr-, ager* field) + E *-al*] **:** dwelling or growing wild in the fields **:** WILD

agres·tic \-stik\ *adj* [L *agrestis* + E *-ic*] **:** of or relating to the fields or country **:** RUSTIC

ag·ri·business \'agrə, 'aigrə+,-\ *n* [blend of *agriculture* and *business*] **:** a combination of the producing operations of a farm, the manufacture and distribution of farm equipment and supplies, and the processing, storage, and distribution of farm commodities

ag·ri·cere \'agrə,si(ə)r\ *n* -s [L *agri* (gen. of *ager* field) + *-cere* (fr. *cera* wax) — more at ACRE, CERE] **:** a waxy or resinous coating of organic matter on soil particles

agric·o·lite \ə'grikə,līt\ *n* -s [G *agricolit*, fr. Georgius *Agricola* (Georg Bauer) †1555 Ger. mineralogist + G *-it* -ite] **:** monoclinic bismuth silicate **:** EULYTITE

ag·ri·cul·tur·al \¦agrə¦kəlch(ə)rəl, ¦aig-\ *adj* **1 a :** of, relating to, or used in agriculture ⟨~ production⟩ ⟨~ equipment⟩ **b :** characterized by or engaged in farming as the chief occupation ⟨an ~ community⟩ **c :** founded or designed to promote the interest or study of agriculture ⟨an ~ college⟩ ⟨an ~ magazine⟩ **2 :** of or having the characteristics of the farmer or his way of life ⟨the ~ life⟩ — **ag·ri·cul·tur·al·ly** \-rəlē, -li\ *adv*

agricultural agent *n* **1** : COUNTY AGENT **2** : an expert employed by a business organization (as a railroad) to promote agriculture in its trade territory

agricultural ant *n* [so called fr. its habit of clearing away all plants about its nest except those which provide its food] : HARVESTER ANT

agricultural dance *n* : a solo or group dance sometimes with mime of planting and harvesting that is related to the maturing of cultivated food plants and found in primitive cultures

agricultural economics *n* : the scientific study of methods, practices, conditions, and policies affecting agriculture

agricultural engineer *n* : an engineer specializing in agricultural engineering

agricultural engineering *n* : the branch of engineering that deals with the design of farm machinery, the location and planning of farm structures, farm drainage, soil management and erosion control, water supply and irrigation, rural electrification, and the processing of farm products

agricultural geology *n* : the branch of geology that deals with the character and origin of soils, the occurrence of mineral fertilizers, and the behavior of underground water

agricultural lien *n* : a lien securing a loan made esp. on the strength of growing crops

agricultural meteorology *n* : the branch of meteorology that deals with the relationship of weather and climate to crop and livestock production and soil management

agricultural paper *n* : negotiable paper created in granting loans for agricultural purposes

ag·ri·cul·ture \'agrə,kəlchə(r), 'aig- *also* ,=='==\ *n* -s [F, fr. L *agricultura*, fr. *agri* (gen. of *ager* field) + *cultura* cultivation — more at ACRE, CULTURE] **1 a** : the science or art of cultivating the soil, harvesting crops, and raising livestock : HUSBANDRY, FARMING **b** : the science or art of the production of plants and animals useful to man and in varying degrees the preparation of these products for man's use and their disposal (as by marketing) **2** : FARMERS

ag·ri·cul·tur·ist \¦==¦=ch(ə)rəst\ *or* **ag·ri·cul·tur·al·ist** \¦==¦=ch(ə)rələst\ *n* -s **1** : one trained in the theory or science of agriculture **2** : FARMER, HUSBANDMAN

ag·ri·lus \'agrələs\ *n, cap* [NL] : a genus of slender beetles (family Buprestidae) having larvae that bore in or girdle twigs and wood and the stems of semiwoody plants

ag·ri·mo·nia \,agrə'mōnēə, -nyə\ *n* [NL, fr. L, agrimony] **1** *cap* : a genus of herbs (family Rosaceae) found chiefly in north temperate regions that have pinnately compound leaves, yellow flowers, and bristly fruits **2** -s : a plant of the genus *Agrimonia*

ag·ri·mo·ny \'agrə,mōnē\ *n* -ES [ME *egrimoigne, agrimonie*, fr. MF & L; MF *aigremoine*, fr. L *agrimonia*, alter. of *argemonia*, fr. Gk *argemōnē, argemōnia*, a plant (prob. *Papaver argemone*), prob. fr. Heb *argāmān* red purple] : any of various plants: as **a** : a plant of the genus *Agrimonia* **b** : a plant of the genus *Bidens* **c** : HEMP AGRIMONY

ag·ri·mo·tor \'agrə,mōd·ə(r)\ *n* -s [*agricultural* + *motor*] : an agricultural tractor

agrin \ə'-\ *adj* [¹*a-* + *grin* (v.)] : GRINNING ⟨his face all ~⟩

agrio- *comb form* [Gk & NL; NL, fr. Gk, fr. *agrios*, fr. *agros* field — more at ACRE] : wild ⟨*agrio*logy⟩

ag·ri·o·choe·rus \,agrēō'kirəs\ *n, cap* [NL, fr. *agrio-* + *-choerus*] : a genus (the type of the large family Agriochoeridae) of extinct Oligocene ungulates resembling pigs but with teeth like those of camels

ag·ri·o·ecol·o·gy \¦agrē(,)ō-\ *or* **ag·ro·ecol·o·gy** \,agrō-\ *n* -ES [*agrio-* or *agro-* + *ecology*] : the ecology of cultivated plants esp. with respect to the relation of varietal characteristics to environmental adjustment and adaptation

ag·ri·o·li·max \,agrēō'lī,maks\ *n, cap* [NL, fr. *agrio-* + L *limax* snail] : a genus of slugs (family Limacidae) including a common garden pest (*A. agrestis*) and several forms that serve as intermediate hosts for worm parasites of vertebrates

ag·ri·ol·o·gy \,agrē'äləjē\ *n* -ES [*agrio-* + *-logy*] : the comparative study of the customs of nonliterate peoples

ag·ri·on·i·dae \,agrē'änə,dē\ *n pl, cap* [NL, fr. *Agrion*, type genus (fr. Gk, neut. of *agrios* wild) + *-idae*] : a family of slender-bodied usu. brilliantly colored damselflies

agri·o·tes \ə'grīə,tēz\ *n, cap* [NL, fr. Gk *agriotēs* wildness, fr. *agrios* wild] : a large cosmopolitan genus of beetles (family Elateridae) including several with larvae that are serious pests of the roots of crop plants — compare WIREWORM

ag·ri·o·type \'agrēə,tīp\ *n* -s [*agrio-* + *type*] : a wild form regarded as ancestral to a domesticated one ⟨an ~ of the domestic cat⟩

agrise *vt* -ED/-ING/-S [ME *agrisen*, fr. OE *āgrīsan* to shudder, fr. *ā-* (perfective prefix) + *-grīsan* — more at ABEAR, GRISLY] *obs* : TERRIFY, AFFRIGHT

agrite *var of* AGARITA

agrl *abbr* agricultural

agro- *comb form* [F, fr. Gk, fr. *agros* field — more at ACRE] **1** : of or belonging to fields or soil : agricultural ⟨*agro*nomy⟩ ⟨*agro*sterol⟩ **2** : agricultural and ⟨*agro*industrial⟩

ag·ro·anal·o·gous \¦a(,)grō=¦===\ *adj* [*agro-* + *analogous*] : having a similar climate and a suitability for similar crops

ag·ro·bac·te·ri·um \¦agrō,bak'tirēəm\ *n, cap* [NL, fr. *agro-* + *bacterium*] : a genus of small usu. gram-negative and motile bacterial rods (family Rhizobiaceae) including soil forms that vigorously reduce nitrates and several pathogens of cultivated plants that typically cause galls on stems — compare CROWN GALL

ag·ro·bi·o·log·ic \¦a(,)grō,=¦==\ — *or* **ag·ro·bi·o·log·i·cal** *adj* : of or relating to agrobiology — **ag·ro·bi·o·log·i·cal·ly** *adv*

ag·ro·bi·ol·o·gist \¦a(,)grō-\ *n* -s : a specialist in agrobiology

ag·ro·bi·ol·o·gy \¦a(,)grō-\ *n* -ES [*agro-* + *biology*] : the study of plant nutrition and growth and crop production in relation to soil management

ag·ro·city \'a(,)grō,-\ *n* [part trans. of Russ *agrogorod* — more at AGROGOROD] : AGRO-TOWN

ag·ro·cli·mat·ic \¦a(,)grō,=¦==\ *adj* [*agro-* + *climatic*] **1** : of or relating to the relationship between crop adaptation and climate ⟨~ studies⟩ **2** : characterized by similar agroclimatic status ⟨~ analogues in the New and Old Worlds⟩

ag·ro·cli·ma·to·log·i·cal \¦=(,)=,===¦===\ *adj* : of or relating to agroclimatology

ag·ro·cli·ma·tol·o·gy \¦=(,)=-\ *n* -ES [*agro-* + *climatology*] : the branch of climatology concerned esp. with agroclimatic factors and effects

ag·ro·eco·type \¦a(,)grō'ekə,tīp\ *n* [blend of *agrotype* and *ecology*] : a crop-plant type adapted to a particular environment

ag·ro·ge·o·log·i·cal \¦a(,)grō,=¦==\ *adj* : of or relating to agrogeology — **ag·ro·ge·o·log·i·cal·ly** *adv*

ag·ro·ge·ol·o·gist \¦a(,)grō-\ *n* -s : one trained in the structure, origin, and uses of soil

ag·ro·ge·ol·o·gy \¦a(,)grō-\ *n* -ES [*agro-* + *geology*] : AGRICULTURAL GEOLOGY

ag·ro·go·rod \,agrō'gȯrəd\ *n* -s [Russ, fr. *agro-* agro- + *gorod* city, town] : a group of amalgamated collective farms in the U.S.S.R.

ag·ro·log·ic \¦agrə¦läjik\ *or* **ag·ro·log·i·cal** \-jəkəl\ *adj* : of or relating to agrology — **ag·ro·log·i·cal·ly** \-jək(ə)lē\ *adv*

agrol·o·gist \ə'gräləjəst, a'-\ *n* -s : a specialist in agrology

agrol·o·gy \-əjē\ *n* -ES [ISV *agro-* + *-logy*; orig. formed as F *agrologie*] : the branch of agriculture that deals with the origin, structure, analysis, and classification of soils esp. in their relation to crop production

ag·ro·me·te·o·rol·o·gy \¦a(,)grō-\ *n* -ES [*agro-* + *meteorology*] : AGRICULTURAL METEOROLOGY

ag·ro·my·za \,agrō'mīzə\ *n, cap* [NL, fr. *agro-* + *-myza*] : the type genus of Agromyzidae including economically important leaf miners and certain flies that cause galls on wild and cultivated plants — see BEAN FLY

ag·ro·my·zid \¦agrō¦mīzəd\ *adj* [NL *Agromyzidae*] : of or relating to the Agromyzidae

ag·ro·my·zi·dae \,agrō'mīzə,dē, -miz-\ *n pl, cap* [NL, fr. *Agromyza*, type genus + *-idae*] : a family of small or minute acalyptrate two-winged flies having phytophagous larvae many of which are leaf miners on cultivated plants

ag·ro·nom·ic \¦agrə¦nämik\ *or* **ag·ro·nom·i·cal** \-məkəl\ *adj* [*agronomy* + *-ic, -ical*] : of, relating to, or designed to promote agronomy

agron·o·mist \ə'gränəməst, a'-\ *n* -s : a specialist in agronomy

agron·o·my \-əmē, -mi\ *n* -ES [prob. fr. F *agronomie*, fr. *agro-* + *-nomie* -nomy] : the branch of agriculture that deals with field-crop production and soil management

ag·ro·py·ron \,agrō'pī,rän\ *also* **ag·ro·py·rum** \-,rəm\ *n, cap* [NL, fr. *agro-* + *-pyron, -pyrum* (fr. Gk *pyros* wheat) — more at FURZE] : a widely distributed genus of chiefly perennial grasses with erect spikes of usu. solitary several-flowered sessile spikelets — see COUCH GRASS

ag·ro·stem·ma \,agrō'stemə\ *n, cap* [NL, fr. *agro-* + Gk *stemma* wreath, garland — more at STEMMA] : a genus of herbs (family Caryophyllaceae) with calyx lobes that are leaflike and extend far beyond the petals

agros·tis \ə'grästəs\ *n, cap* [NL, fr. L, couch grass, fr. Gk *agrōstis*, a grass] : a large and widely distributed genus of grasses having an open or contracted panicle with small one-flowered spikelets and including important pasture, hay, and lawn grasses — see BENT 2d, REDTOP

ag·ros·tog·ra·pher \,agrə'stägrəfə(r), ,a,grä'-, ə,grä'-\ *n* -s [*agrostography* + *-er*] : a specialist in agrostography

agros·to·graph·ic \ə¦grästə¦grafik\ *or* **agros·to·graph·i·cal** \-əkəl\ *adj* [*agrostography* + *-ic, -ical*] : of or relating to agrostography

ag·ros·tog·ra·phy \,agrə'stägrəfē, ,a,grä'-, ə,grä'-\ *n* -ES [Gk *agrōstis* + E *-o-* + *-graphy*] : a description of the grasses

agros·to·log·ic \ə¦grästə¦läjik\ *or* **agros·to·log·i·cal** \-əkəl\ *adj* : of or relating to agrostology

ag·ros·tol·o·gist \,agrə'stäləjəst, ,a,grä'-, ə,grä'-\ *n* -s : a specialist in agrostology

ag·ros·tol·o·gy \-ləjē\ *n* -ES [Gk *agrōstis* + E *-o-* + *-logy*] : the branch of systematic botany that deals with the grasses

ag·ro·tech·ny \'agrō,teknē\ *n* -ES [*agro-* + *-techny*] : the branch of agriculture that deals with the conversion of agricultural products into manufactured articles on or close to the farm

agrot·i·dae \ə'gräd·ə,dē\ [NL, fr. ²*Agrotid-, Agrotis*, type genus] *syn of* NOCTUIDAE

¹agro·tis \ə'grōd·əs\ [NL, fr. Gk *agrōtēs* wild, fr. *agros* field — more at ACRE] *syn of* EUXOA

²agrotis \"\ [NL] *syn of* NOCTUA

ag·ro-town \'a(,)grō,-\ *n* [part trans. of Russ *agrogorod* — more at AGROGOROD] : a group of collective farms in the U.S.S.R. that operate as a unit

ag·ro·type \'agrə,tīp\ *n* -s [*agro-* + *type*] **1** : any of various soils used in agriculture **2** : a cultivar esp. of an agricultural field crop

aground \ə'-\ *adv (or adj)* [ME, fr. ¹*a-* + *ground*] **1** : in or into a stranded condition esp. with the bottom lodged on the ground or on the shore ⟨ran his boat ~⟩ **2** : on the ground ⟨enemy air power aloft and ~ —G.R.Wilson⟩

agryp·nia \ə'gripnēə, a'-\ *n, pl* **agryp·ni·ai** \-ē,ī\ [LGk, fr. Gk, sleeplessness, time of watching, fr. *agrypnos* wakeful, sleepless + *-ia*] : a vigil before certain feasts (as Easter) in the Eastern Church

agst *abbr* against

agt *abbr* **1** against **2** agent **3** agreement

ag·ter \'äktə(r)\ *var of* ACHTER

agua \'ägwə\ *or* **agua toad** *n* -s [AmerSp *agua*, prob. fr. Tupi] : the largest known toad (*Bufo marinus*) reaching a length of eight inches and being native to Central America but introduced into Argentina, Hawaii, and the West Indies where its voracious habits make it a valuable destroyer of insect pests

agua·ca·te \,ägwə'käd·ē\ *n* -s [Sp — more at AVOCADO] : AVOCADO

agua·ca·tec \,ägwäkə,tek\ *n, pl* **aguacatec** *or* **aguacatecs** *usu cap* [Sp *aguacateca*, of AmerInd origin] **1 a** : an Indian people living in the region of Aguacatan, Guatemala **b** : a member of such people **2** : the Mayan language of the Aguacatec people

agua·ji \¦ägwə¦hē\ *n, pl* **aguaji** [Sp *aguají*, prob. fr. Taino] : any of several marine fishes (as the black grouper, the gag, or the rock hind) of the warmer parts of the western Atlantic

agua·miel \¦ägwəm¦yel\ *n* -s [MexSp, fr. Sp, honey water, fr. *agua* water (fr. L *aqua*) + *miel* honey, fr. L *mel* — more at ISLAND, MELLIFLUOUS] : the unfermented freshly gathered juice of any of several Mexican plants of the genus *Agave* that becomes pulque when fermented

¹agua·no \ə'gwä(,)nō\ *n, pl* **aguano** *or* **aguanos** *usu cap* [Sp, of AmerInd origin] **1 a** : an Indian people of Brazil **b** : a member of such people **2** : the language of the Aguano people

²aguano \"\ *n* -s [Pg] : a mahogany (*Swietenia macrophylla*)

aguara *var of* AGOUARA

aguar·di·en·te \,ä,gwärdē'entē, -d'yen(,)tā\ *also* **aguar·dien·te** \,ä,kw-\ *n* -s [Sp *aguardiente*, fr. *agua* water + *ardiente* burning, fr. L *ardent-, ardens*, pres. part. of *ardēre* to burn — more at ARDOR] : any of several distilled alcoholic beverages: as **a** : a coarse brandy made in Spain and Portugal **b** : a liquor that is usu. made from sugarcane and is common in So. America, Central America, and the southwestern U.S.

agua·ru·na \,ägwə'rünə\ *n, pl* **aguaruna** *or* **aguarunas** *usu cap* [Sp, of AmerInd origin] **1 a** : an Indian people of Peru **b** : a member of such people **2** : the Jivaroan language of the Aguaruna people

¹ague \'ā(,)gyü, *chiefly dial or old-fash* 'āgə(r); 'āg *by many to whom it is only a book word*\ *n* -s [ME, fr. MF *ague* (trans. of ML *acuta*, short for *febris acuta*, lit., sharp fever), fr. fem. of *agu* sharp, fr. L *acutus* — more at ACUTE] **1** : a fever of malarial character marked by paroxysms of chills, fever, and sweating that recur at regular intervals **2** : a fit or spell of shaking or shivering (as with cold) : CHILL ⟨people shaking with the ~ of the terrorized —W.L.Sullivan⟩

²ague \"\ *vt* -ED/ -ING/ -S : to affect with or as if with ague

ague bark *n* : HOP TREE

ague cake *n* : the enlarged hard spleen of chronic malaria

ague drop *n* : FOWLER'S SOLUTION

ague grass *or* **ague root** *n* : a colicroot (*Aletris farinosa*) with a scurfy or granuliferous perianth

ague tree *n* : SASSAFRAS

ague·weed \'ā(,)gyü,wēd\ *n* **1** : BONESET 1 **2** : FIVE-FLOWERED GENTIAN

agui·lar·ite \,ägə'lä,rīt\ *n* -s [P. Aguilar *fl* 1892 Mexican mine superintendent + E *-ite*] : a mineral consisting of silver selenide-sulfide Ag_4SeS (hardness 2, sp. gr. 7.59)

aguilawood *var of* AGILAWOOD

agui·nal·do \,ägə'näl(,)dō\ *n* -s [Sp (also, gift given on festive occasions, esp. Christmas and New Year's Day), alter. of earlier *aguilando, aguinando*, perh. fr. L *hoc in anno* in this year (a phrase common in the refrain of old popular songs sung on New Year's Day)] **1** : any of several ornamental plants of the morning-glory family native to Puerto Rico **2** : a Spanish-American Christmas carol

aguise *vt* -ED/-ING/-S [¹*a-* + *guise* (v.)] *obs* : DRESS, ARRAY

agu·ish \'āgyəwish, 'ā(,)gyüish\ *adj* [¹*ague* + *-ish*] **1** : productive of, subject to, or resulting from ague ⟨an ~ climate⟩ ⟨an ~ man⟩ ⟨~ pains⟩ **2** : somewhat chilly or quivering : SHAKY ⟨one candle with a small ~ beam shaking in the cold —Edith Sitwell⟩ — **agu·ish·ly** *adv*

agu·nah \,ägü'nä, ä'günə\ *n* -s [Heb *'ăghūnāh* prevented, restrained (from remarrying)] *Jewish law* : a woman whose husband has deserted her or has disappeared and who may not remarry until she gives proof of his death or obtains a bill of divorce

agust \'əgəst\ *n* -s [Hindi *agast*, fr. Skt *agasti*] : a bast fiber derived from a southern Indian plant (*Sesbania grandiflora*)

ah \'ä(ä), 'á(á); *when expressing displeasure, often* 'ò\ *interj* [ME *a, ah*] — used to express various emotions (as delight, relief, regret, or contempt)

AH *abbr* **1** *often not cap* ampere-hour **2** [ML *anno hegirae*] in the year of the hegira — often printed in small capitals

aha \ä'hä, á'há, ə'-\ *interj* [ME] — used to express surprise, triumph, or derision

aha·ai·na \,ä,hä'īnə\ *n* -s [Hawaiian, fr. *'aha* company + *'aina* meal] *Hawaii* : a banquet or feast

ahan·ka·ra \ə,həŋ'kärə\ *n* -s [Skt *ahaṁkāra*, fr. *aham* I + *kāra* act of making, fr. *karoti* he makes — more at I, KARMA] : the principle of individuation in Hinduism and Jainism; *specif* : the activity of attributing objective existence to the ego on the basis of subjective consciousness

ahantch·u·yuk \ə'hänchə,yük\ *n, pl* **ahantchuyuk** *or* **ahantchuyuks** *usu cap* [Kalapooia] **1 a** : a Kalapooian people of the Pudding river valley, Oregon **b** : a member of such people **2** : the language of the Ahantchuyuk people

ahau \ä'hau\ *n* -s *often cap* [Maya] : the last of the 20 day names of the Maya calendar that with its associated numbers 1 to 13 in a peculiar order (13, 11, 9, 7, 5, 3, 1, 12, 10, 8, 6, 4, 2) designated the 13 katuns of a series ⟨13 ~ the first⟩

¹ahead \ə'hed\ *adv* [¹*a-* + *head*] **1** : in or toward a position in advance ⟨set the clock ~⟩ : farther in the direction in which a person or thing is going ⟨send your dog ~ —Corey Ford⟩ ⟨the road stretches straight ~⟩ : FORWARD, ONWARD ⟨the propeller is turning ~⟩ **2** : at or toward a point of time before another ⟨he moves the spring starting of chicks ~ to late fall —*New England Homestead*⟩ : in advance ⟨plan ~⟩ **3** : in or toward a position of advantage ⟨facilities for pushing ~ talented students —*Saturday Rev.*⟩

²ahead \"\ *adj* **1** : farther in the direction in which a person or thing is going : farther forward in time — used postpositively ⟨advance to the next job ~ —W.J.Reilly⟩ **2** : leading toward a position of advantage — used postpositively ⟨a way ~ for aspiring youths⟩

ahead of *prep* **1** : in or into a position of advantage over ⟨helping to keep our country's weapons *ahead of* the rest of the world's⟩ **2** : in advance of : BEFORE ⟨*ahead of* the times⟩ ⟨a few days *ahead of* the German disclaimer —F.L.Paxson⟩ **3** : in excess of : ABOVE ⟨output had been *ahead of* estimates —*New Republic*⟩

aheight *adv* [¹*a-* + *height*] *obs* : AHIGH

ahem *a throat-clearing sound; often read as* ə'hem, *sometimes as* 'ā,hem\ *interj* [imit.] — used esp. to attract attention often as a humorously exaggerated warning to a minor social error or oversight

aher·ma·typ·ic \¦ā,hərmə¦tipik\ *adj* [²*a-* + Gk *herma* reef, prop + E *-typic*] *of corals* : not building reefs

ahey \ə'hā\ *interj* [*a* (as in *aha*) + *hey*] — used esp. to attract attention

ahi \'ä,hē\ *n* -s [Hawaiian *'ahi*] *Hawaii* : TUNA; *esp* : the Pacific yellowfin tuna

ahigh *adv* [ME, fr. ¹*a-* + *high*] *obs* : on high : ALOFT

ahim·sa \ə'him,sä, -iŋ,sä\ *n* -s *sometimes cap* [Skt *ahiṁsā* noninjury, fr. *a-* ²a- + *hiṁsā* injury, fr. *hiṁsati* he injures; akin to Skt *hinvati* he throws, urges on — more at GOAD] *Jainism, Hinduism, and Buddhism* : the doctrine of refraining from the harming of others or the taking of life

ahind \ə'hīnt, -in(d),-īn(d)\ *or* **ahint** \-int\ *prep* [¹*a-* + *hind*, adj.] *dial* : BEHIND

ahir \ə'hi(ə)r\ *n* -s *usu cap* [Hindi *Ahīr*, fr. Skt *Ābhīra*] : a member of a cattle-breeding and cattle-herding caste of India

ahis·tor·ic \¦ā=¦==\ *or* **ahis·tor·i·cal** \¦==¦===\ *adj* [²*a-* + *historic, historical*] **1** : free from or without regard for the temporal or finite world **2** : not concerned with or related to history, historical development, or tradition ⟨figures . . . born without a sense of the past . . . the *ahistorical* man —Clifton Fadiman⟩ : concerned only with the present and the immediately perceptible

ahl \'äl\ *n* -s [Ar] : the group of kinsmen of an Arabian consisting of three ascending and three descending generations

ah·med·abad *or* **ah·mad·abad** \'ämədə,bäd\ *adj, usu cap* [fr. *Ahmedabad, Ahmadabad*, India] : of or from the city of Ahmedabad, India : of the kind or style prevalent in Ahmedabad

ahn·felt·ia \än'feltēə, '=,===\ *n, cap* [NL, fr. Nils O. *Ahnfelt* †1837 Swed. botanist + NL *-ia*] : a small genus of dark-colored cartilaginous red algae (family Gigartinaceae) with tufted stemlike branchlets

¹ahold *adv* [¹*a-* + *hold*, v.] *obs* : near the wind

²ahold \ə'hōld, -lt\ *also* **aholt** \-lt\ *n* -s [prob. fr. ²*a* + *hold*, n.] *dial* : a hold ⟨take ~ of⟩ ⟨get ~ of⟩

aho·le·ho·le \ə,hōlē'hōlē\ *or* **aho·le** \ə'hōlē\ *n* -s [Hawaiian] : a small percoid food fish (*Kuhlia marginata*) widely distributed in brackish tropical waters

ahom \'ä,hōm\ *n, pl* **ahom** *or* **ahoms** *usu cap* **1 a** : a people of the Tai race who settled in Assam **b** : a member of such people **2** : the now extinct Thai language of the Ahom people

a-horizon \'ā=¦==\ *n, usu cap A* [¹*A* + *horizon*] : the outer dark-colored light-textured layer of a soil profile consisting typically of undeveloped soil rich in organic debris in varied stages of disintegration — see B-HORIZON, C-HORIZON

ahorse \ə'-\ *adv (or adj)* [¹*a-* + *horse*] : AHORSEBACK

ahorse·back \ə'-\ *adv (or adj)* [¹*a-* + *horseback*] *archaic* : on horseback

ahou·saht \ə'hau,sät\ *n, pl* **ahousaht** *or* **ahousahts** *usu cap* [Nootka] **1** : a Nootka people of Vancouver Island **2** : a member of the Ahousaht people

ahoy \ə'hȯi\ *interj* [*a-* (as in *aha*) + *hoy*, interj.] — used in hailing ⟨ship ~⟩

aht \'ät\ *n, pl* **aht** *or* **ahts** *usu cap* [Nootka] : NOOTKA

ah·te·na \'ät°nə\ *n, pl* **ahtena** *or* **ahtenas** *usu cap* [Ahtena, lit., ice people] **1 a** : an Athapaskan people of the Copper river valley in southeastern Alaska **b** : a member of such people **2** : the language of the Ahtena people

¹ahu \'ä,hü\ *n* -s [Per *āhū*, fr. MPer *āhūk*] : the common gazelle (*Gazella subgutturosa*) of central Asia

²ahu \"\ *n* -s [Hawaiian, Maori, Tahitian, & Marquesan] **1** *Polynesia* : a mound or stone heap serving as a boundary, waymark, or memorial **2** : a sacred Polynesian burial place

ahuat·le \ä,wätlē\ *n* [MexSp *ahuatle, ahuautle*, fr. Nahuatl *ahuautli*, fr. *atl* water + *huautli* wild amaranth] : water-insect eggs dried and used as food by Mexicans

ahue·hue·te \,äwē'wäd·ē\ *n* -s [Sp, fr. Nahuatl *ahuehueton*, lit., old man of the water, fr. *atl* water + *huehueton* old man, fr. *huehue* old] : a Mexican cypress (*Taxodium mucronatum*) of great girth

ahull \ə'-\ *adv* [¹*a-* + *hull*] : with sails furled and helm lashed alee — used in the phrase *lie ahull*

ahum \ə'-\ *adj* [¹*a-* + *hum*, v.] : HUMMING

ahung \'ä,hüŋ\ *n* -s [Chin a^4-*hong*^{4}, fr. Per *ākhūn* theologian, preacher] **1** : a Chinese mosque official **2** — used in China as a term of deference or esteem

ahun·gered \ə'həŋgə(r)d\ *adj* [ME *ahungred, anhungred*, fr. ¹*a-, an-* + *hungred* hungered] *archaic* : made hungry : very hungry

ahunt \ə'-\ *adj* [¹*a-* + *hunt*, v.] : HUNTING

ahu·ula \ä,hüˈülə, ,ä,hüˈü·lə\ *n* -s [Hawaiian, fr. *'ahu* garment + *'ula* red, regal] : a feather cloak or cape made of minute red or yellow bird feathers occas. trimmed with black or green and formerly worn in Hawaii by high chiefs and kings

¹ai \'ī\ *or* **aie** \'īē\ *or* **ai·ee** \'īē\ *interj* [ME] — used to express grief, despair, or anguish

²ai \'ī, 'ä,ē, ä'ē\ *n* -s [Pg *aí* or Sp *ai*, fr. Tupi *ai*] : a three-toed sloth of the genus *Bradypus* of So. America

³ai *var of* AYU

AI *abbr* **1** active ingredient **2** *often not cap* ad interim **3** air interception **4** artificial insemination

ai·blins \'āblənz\ *adv* [earlier *ablins*, fr. *able* + *-lins* (alter. of *-lings*)] *chiefly Scot* : PERHAPS

¹aid \'ād\ *vb* -ED/-ING/-S [ME *eyden*, fr. MF *aider*, fr. L *adjutare*, freq. of *adjuvare* to help, fr. *ad-* + *juvare* to help] *vt* : to give help or support to : FURTHER, FACILITATE, ASSIST ⟨he ~ed the cause⟩ ⟨the . . . Committee ~ed veterans in their applications for pensions —*Current Biog.*⟩ : contribute to ⟨finances are ~ed by rummage sales⟩ ~ *vi* : to give assistance : be of use : HELP ⟨he ~ed in the attempt⟩ **syn** see HELP

²aid \"\ *n* -s [ME *aide*, fr. MF, fr. *aider*, v.] **1** : a subsidy granted to the king by the English parliament until the 18th century for an extraordinary purpose **2** : the act of helping or the help given : ASSISTANCE, SUPPORT, RELIEF ⟨~ extended to Confederate privateers —Eleanor M. Sickels⟩ ⟨a rescue party sent to their ~⟩ **3 a** : a person who gives assistance : HELPER ⟨accepted the position of ~ in the U.S. Naval Observatory —W.J.Humphreys⟩ — compare AIDE **b** : something by which assistance is given (as in achieving an end) ⟨visual ~s in teaching⟩ **c** : an organization auxiliary to another organization; *esp* : a woman's local auxiliary church group (as a ladies' aid society) **4** : a tribute paid by a vassal to his lord for the lord's ransom from captivity, for knighting his eldest son, and for dowry of his eldest daughter **5** *English law* : assistance in defending an action that the defendant may or should legally claim from another having a joint interest in the defense **6 :** directive signals conveyed to a horse (as through the use of the hands, legs, shift of body weight, or voice)

aid·ance \ˈādᵊn(t)s\ *n* -s [MF, fr. *aider* + *-ance*] *archaic* **:** a means of help **:** AID

aid·ant \ˈādᵊnt\ *adj* [ME, fr. MF, pres. part. of *aider*] **:** furnishing or supplying aid

ai·da trumpet \ä,ēdə-\ *n*, *usu cap A* [after *Aida*, opera by Giuseppe Verdi †1901 Ital. composer, for which it was designed] **:** a long straight trumpet

aide \ˈād\ *n* -s [short for *aide-de-camp*] **:** a person who acts as an assistant (as to a diplomat or a nurse); *specif* **:** a military or naval officer acting as assistant to a superior

aide-de-camp *also* **aid-de-camp** \ˌāddəˈkamp, -aa(ə)mp, -aimp, -äⁿ\ *n*, *pl* **aides-de-camp** *also* **aids-de-camp** \ˌādz-də-\ [F *aide de camp*, lit., camp assistant] *mil* **:** AIDE

aided school *n* **:** a usu. denominational voluntary English school receiving one half of its maintenance costs from public funds but retaining control over appointments and religious instruction — compare CONTROLLED SCHOOL

aide-mé·moire \ˌād(ˌ)mām'wär, -(ˌ)mem-, -wȧ(r\ *n*, *pl* **aides-mémoire** \ˌād(z)-\ [F, fr. *aider* to aid + *mémoire* memory, fr. L *memoria* — more at MEMORY] **1 :** an aid to the memory (as a mnemonic device) **2 :** a written summary or outline of important items of a proposed agreement or diplomatic communication **:** MEMORANDUM

aid·er \ˈādə(r)\ *n* -s [prob. fr. MF *aider* to aid] **:** an act of aiding — used esp. in pleading in the phrase *aider by verdict*

aider by verdict : the presumption after a verdict that all facts necessary to the verdict were proved

aid·ful \ˈādfəl\ *adj*, *archaic* **:** abounding in aid **:** HELPFUL

ai·dle \ˈādᵊl\ *chiefly Scot var of* ADDLE

aid·less \ˈādləs\ *adj* **:** devoid of help **:** HELPLESS ⟨an ~ victim⟩

aid-major *n*, *obs* **:** the adjutant of a regiment

aid·man \ˈād,man, -mən\ *n*, *pl* **aidmen** [(*first*) *aid* + *man*] **:** a medical-corps enlisted man attached to a unit in the field to give first aid — compare HOSPITAL CORPSMAN

aid prayer *n*, *English law* **:** a defendant's appeal for aid

aids *pres 3d sing of* AID, *pl of* AID

aid station *n* [(*first*) *aid*] **:** an establishment for giving emergency medical treatment; *specif* **:** a forward medical installation where wounded receive emergency treatment

aie *or* **aiee** *var of* ¹AI

ai·el \ˈā(ə)l\ *n* -s [ME, grandfather, fr. MF *ael, aiuel*, fr. (assumed) VL *aviolus*, dim. of L *avus* grandfather — more at UNCLE] **:** a writ by which an heir entered into his grandfather's estate and dispossessed the third person who had attempted to gain possession

aiery *obs var of* AIRY

ai·ga \äˈēŋə, äˈēgə\ *n* -s [Samoan *ʼāiga*] *Samoa* **:** FAMILY

ai·gi·a·lo·saur \īˈjīə(ˌ)lōˌsȯ(ə)r\ *n* -s [NL *Aigialosaurus*] **:** an animal or fossil of the genus *Aigialosaurus* or family Aigialosauridae

ai·gi·a·lo·sau·rus \ˌī,jīə(ˌ)lōˈsȯrəs\ *n*, *cap* [NL, fr. Gk *aigialos* seashore + NL *-saurus*] **:** a genus (the type of the family Aigialosauridae) of fossil prob. semiaquatic lizards of the Lower Cretaceous

aiglet *var of* AGLET

ai·grette \(ˈ)āˌgret\ *n* -s [F — more at EGRET] **1 :** EGRET 1 **2 a :** a spray of feathers orig. those of the egret **b :** a spray of gems often worn on a hat or in a woman's hair **3 :** something resembling a plume or tuft (as a cluster of rays in the sun's corona seen during total eclipses) **4 :** a sharp point attached to an electrical conductor (as a lightning rod) to facilitate the formation of a corona discharge

aigue-marine *n* [F, trans. of (assumed) Prov *aiga marina*] *obs* **:** AQUAMARINE

aigues mortes *n pl* [F, lit., dead waters] *obs* **:** stagnant waters left by a river when it changes its channel — compare CUTOFF 4

ai·guière \(ˈ)āg,ye(ə)r\ *n* -s [F, fr. MF, fr. OProv *aiguiera*, fr. (assumed) VL *aquaria*, fr. L, fem. of *aquarius* of water — more at EWER] **:** a decorative pitcher-shaped usu. tall and slender vessel with a handle and spout

ai·guille \(ˈ)āˌgwēl, -ēəl, *F* äg(wʸ)ēēy\ *n* -s [F, lit., needle — more at AGLET] **1 :** a sharp-pointed pinnacle of rock commonly found in glaciated mountains **2 :** an instrument for boring holes in stone or other masonry materials or holes used in blasting

ai·guill·esque \ˌā(ˌ)gwēˈlesk\ *adj* **:** having the shape of an aiguille

ai·guil·lette \ˌāgwəˈlet\ *n* -s [F — more at AGLET] **1 :** AGLET; *specif* **:** a shoulder cord worn by a military aide to the president of the U.S. and to high-ranking officers — compare FOURRAGÈRE **2 :** long narrow strips of cooked food (as meat or fowl)

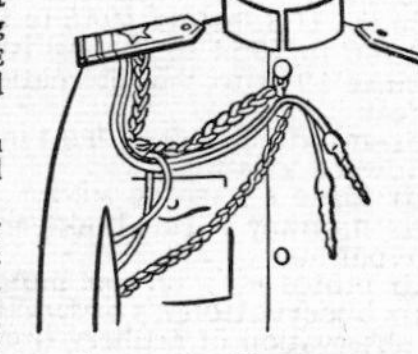

dress aiguillette of a presidential aide

ai·ka·ne \īˈkänē\ *n* -s [Hawaiian *aikāne*] *Hawaii* **:** a good friend **:** CHUM

ai·kin·ite \ˈākə,nīt\ *n* -s [Arthur *Aikin* †1854 Eng. chemist + E *-ite*] **:** a mineral $PbCuBiS_3$ consisting of lead, copper, bismuth, and sulfur occurring massive and in lead-gray needle-shaped orthorhombic crystals (hardness 2, sp. gr. 7.07)

¹**ail** \ˈāl, ˈāəl\ *vb* -ED/-ING/-S [ME *eilen*, fr. OE *eglan* to trouble, afflict; akin to OE *egle* hideous, loathsome, MLG *egelen* to annoy, Goth *usagljan* to oppress and perh. to MIr *ālad* wound, Skt *agha* evil and perh. to OE *ege* fear, OHG *egī*, ON *agi*, Goth *agis* fear, Gk *achos* pain, OIr *ad-āgor* I fear; basic meaning: fearing] *vt* **:** to affect with an unnamed disease or physical or emotional pain or discomfort **:** trouble or interfere with **:** be the matter with — used only of unspecified causes ⟨can the doctor tell what ~s the patient⟩ ⟨he will not concede that anything ~s his business⟩ ⟨what ~s that naughty boy⟩ **~** *vi* **:** to become affected with pain or discomfort **:** have something the matter ⟨he ~*ed* throughout his childhood⟩ ⟨the business is ~*ing*⟩ ⟨was ~*ing* from a cold⟩

²**ail** \"\ *n* -s [ME *eil*, fr. *eilen*, v.] **:** INDISPOSITION, AILMENT, TROUBLE

³**ail** \ˈī(ə)l\ *n* -s [ME *eile*, fr. OE *egl*; akin to OE *ecg* edge, sword — more at EDGE] *now dial Eng* **:** the beard of grain — usu. used in pl.

ai·lan·thus \āˈlan(t)thəs, īˈ-\ *n* [NL, fr. Amboinese *ai lanto*, lit., tree (of) heaven] **1** *cap* **:** a small genus of East Indian and Chinese trees (family Simaroubaceae) with odd-pinnate leaves and terminal panicles of greenish flowers succeeded by oblong twisted samaras **2** -ES **:** a tree of the genus *Ailanthus* (esp. *A. altissima*) — see TREE OF HEAVEN

ailanthus silkworm *n* **:** a large green silkworm (*Samia cynthia* or *S. walkeri*) native to eastern Asia but introduced into the U.S. that feeds on ailanthus leaves and has been used experimentally for the commercial production of silk — compare CYNTHIA MOTH

ai·lan·to \īˈlän,tō\ *n* -s [Amboinese *ai lanto*] **:** AILANTHUS 2

ai-lao \ˈī,laů\ *n*, *pl* **ai-lao** *or* **ai-laos** *usu cap A* **1 :** a West-Yunnan people of the Tai group who formed the Nan-chao kingdom in southwestern China from the 8th to 13th centuries **2 :** a member of the Ai-lao people

ai·la·va·tor *or* **ai·le·va·tor** \ˈālə,vād·ə(r)\ *n* -s [blend of *aileron* and *elevator*] **:** ELEVON

aild \ˈā(ə)ld\ *vi* -ED/-ING/-S [by alter.] *dial* **:** AIL ⟨what ~*ed* him⟩

aile *obs var of* AISLE

ai·le·ron \ˈālə,rän\ *n* -s [F, bird's pinion, aileron, dim. of *aile* wing, fr. L *ala* — more at AISLE] **1 :** a half gable or wing wall (as at the end of the aisle of a church) **2 :** a movable portion of an airplane wing or a movable airfoil external to the wing that is usu. located at the trailing edge near the wing tips and whose function is to impart a rolling motion to the airplane and thus provide lateral control

aileron roll *n* **:** a flight maneuver in which an airplane is rotated about its longitudinal axis through a full 360 degrees by means of the ailerons without altering its flight path

ailes de pi·geon \eldəpēzhōⁿ\ [F, lit., pigeon wings] **:** PIGEON-WING 3

ai·lette \āˈlet\ *n* -s [F, fr. OF *ailette, alette, elette* small wing, dim. of *ele* wing — more at AISLE] **:** a plate of forged iron or steel worn over a coat of mail to protect the shoulder

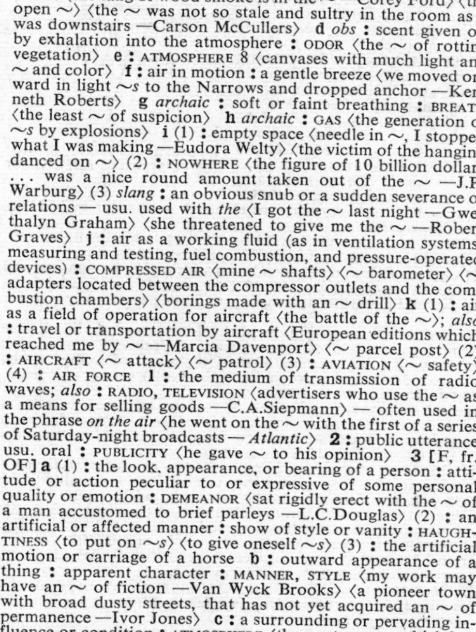

ailettes, *A*

ail·ing *adj* **:** having or suffering from an ailment

aillt \ˈīlt\ *n* -s [W] **:** one of a semiservile class among the early Cymry; *also* **:** TENANT FARMER

ail·ment \ˈālmənt\ *n* -s **1 :** a bodily sickness, disorder, or chronic disease ⟨always complaining of some ~ or other⟩ **2 :** UNREST, UNEASINESS ⟨symptomatic of the nation's ~⟩

ails *pres 3d sing of* AIL, *pl of* AIL

ail·syte \ˈāl,sīt\ *n* -s [*Ailsa* Craig, island off the coast of Scotland, its locality + E *-yte* (var. of *-ite*)] **:** a rock composed of an alkalic microgranite containing considerable riebeckite

ailur- *or* **ailuro-** *or* **aelur-** *or* **aeluro-** *comb form* [NL, fr. Gk *ailouro-*, fr. *ailouros*] **:** cat ⟨*ailur*odon⟩ ⟨*ailuro*phobia⟩

ai·lu·roi·dea \ˌīlyəˈrȯidēə, ˌāl-\ *syn of* AELUROIDEA

ai·lu·ro·phile \īˈlůrə,fīl, āˈ-\ *or* **ae·lu·ro·phile** \ēˈ-\ *n* -s [*ailur-, aelur-* + *-phile*] **:** a cat fancier **:** a lover of cats

ai·lu·ro·phobe *or* **ae·lu·ro·phobe** \-,fōb\ *n* -s [*ailur-, aelur-* + *-phobe*] **:** one that hates or fears cats **:** one suffering from ailurophobia

ai·lu·ro·pho·bia *or* **ae·lu·ro·pho·bia** \⸗,⸗⸗ˈfōbēə\ *n* -s [NL, fr. *ailur-, aelur-* + *-phobia*] **:** abnormal fear of cats

ai·lu·rop·o·da \ˌīlyəˈräpədə, ˌāl-\ *n*, *cap* [NL, fr. *ailur-* + *-poda*] **:** a genus of Procyonidae including only the giant panda

ai·lu·ro·pus \īˈlůrəpəs, āˈ\ [NL, fr. *ailur-* + *-pus*] *syn of* AILUROPODA

ai·lu·rus \-rəs\ *n*, *cap* [NL, fr. Gk *ailouros* cat] **:** a genus of mammals (family Procyonidae) comprising the panda and formerly regarded as the type of a separate family

¹**aim** \ˈām\ *vb* -ED/-ING/-S [ME *aimen, amen* to guess, estimate, aim, fr. MF *aesmer* & *esmer*; MF *aesmer* fr. OF, fr. *a-* (fr. L *ad-*) + *esmer*, fr. L *aestimare* to estimate — more at ESTEEM] *vi* **1 a :** to direct a course **:** point a weapon at an object **:** direct a missile so as to try to hit an object — usu. used with *at*, sometimes with *for* or *toward* ⟨scientific knowledge ~s at being wholly impersonal —Bertrand Russell⟩ ⟨that gun is ~*ing* straight at me —V.C.Aldrich⟩ ⟨this fact will give you something to ~ for —S.L.Payne⟩ ⟨officer-candidate schools toward which men . . . can ~ —J.J.O'Donnell⟩ **b :** ASPIRE — often used with *high* ⟨the monastic scholars did not ~ high —R.W.Southern⟩ **2** *obs* **:** to guess with intent to discover meaning or truth ⟨~ at another man's speech⟩ ⟨~ at suspected enmity⟩ **3 :** to have as a purpose **:** PLAN, INTEND — used only with infinitive ⟨he ~s to encourage mutual understanding —*Saturday Rev.*⟩ ⟨this book ~s to effect a partial remedy of this situation —E.A.Maziarz⟩ ⟨I ~ to finish up this job —I.S. Cobb⟩ **~** *vt* **1** *obs* **:** GUESS, CONJECTURE **2 a :** to direct or point (as a weapon or a missile) at or so as to hit an object ⟨on the lawn a small cannon was ~*ed* into space⟩ ⟨a camera was ~*ed* at the scene⟩ ⟨he ~*ed* the rock at the dog⟩ **b :** to direct (as an act or proceeding) at or toward a specified object or attainment ⟨the study was ~*ed* at developing a comparative picture —*N. Y. Times*⟩ ⟨the haphazard transcription inevitable in work ~*ed* solely at vocabulary collecting —Stanley Newman⟩ **c :** to intend for ⟨a new printing press ~*ed* at medium and small-sized newspapers —*Wall Street Jour.*⟩ ⟨radio and TV shows ~*ed* at juvenile audiences —*Current Biog.*⟩

²**aim** \"\ *n* -s [ME *aime, ame*, fr. *aimen, amen*, v.] **1** *obs* **:** the point intended to be hit (as by an arrow) **:** MARK, TARGET **2 :** the pointing of a weapon (as a gun) at an object intended to be hit ⟨to take ~ at the target⟩**: a :** the ability to hit a target ⟨his ~ was deadly⟩ **b :** effectiveness of a weapon ⟨the ~ is accurate up to 75 feet⟩ **3** *obs* **a :** CONJECTURE, GUESS ⟨man's ~ at the divine will⟩ **b :** the directing of effort toward an object in order to affect it ⟨ambitious ~s against the monarchy⟩ **c :** direction or guidance as to a course or procedure to be followed ⟨to give ~ to travelers on the road⟩ **4 :** the object intended to be attained **:** PURPOSE, DESIGN ⟨his ~ being the translation of certain religious and devotional writings —Edward Clodd⟩ ⟨the ~ of the Elizabethans was to attain complete realism —T.S.Eliot⟩ ⟨the only fault I find in the book is a certain lack of ~ —Geoffrey Boumphrey⟩ ⟨such exaggeration is purely impressionistic in ~ —R.M.Weaver⟩ **syn** see INTENTION

ai·mak \ˈī,mak, ˈā,-\ *n* -s [Mongolian, clan] **1 :** a clan or tribal band among Mongolian peoples **2 :** a province or administrative district of Outer Mongolia

aimara *usu cap*, *var of* AYMARA

aiming circle *n* **:** an instrument for measuring horizontal and vertical angles and magnetic azimuths in determining gunnery data and laying guns and in artillery surveying

aiming point *n* **:** the point at which the line of sight is directed when sighting (as for the dropping of bombs) or when a firing piece is being laid for direction

aiming stake *also* **aiming post** *n* **:** a stake used as an aiming point for laying mortars and artillery pieces for direction

aim·less \ˈāmləs\ *adj* [²*aim* + *-less*] **:** without aim or purpose ⟨an ~ existence⟩ — **aim·less·ly** *adv* — **aim·less·ness** *n* -ES

ai·mo·re \ˌīməˈrā\ *n*, *pl* **aimore** *or* **aimores** *usu cap* [Pg & Sp *aimoré*, of AmerInd origin] **:** BOTOCUDO

¹**ain** \ˈān\ *adj or n* [ME (northern dial.) *an*, fr. OE *ān* — more at ONE] *chiefly Scot* **:** ONE

²**ain** \"\ *adj or n* [prob. fr. ON *eiginn* — more at OWN] *dial Brit* **:** OWN

³**ain** *var of* AYIN

⁴**ain** *or* **aïn** *var of* ⁴AYN

aince \ˈān(t)s\ *adv* [ME (northern dial.) *anes* — more at ONCE] *chiefly Scot* **:** ONCE

ai·nhum \īˈnyüm, -üⁿ\ *n* -s [Pg, fr. Yoruba *eʹyunʹ*] **:** a tropical disease of unknown cause that results in increasing fibrous constriction and ultimately in spontaneous amputation of the toes, esp. the little toes

ai·ni \ˈīnē\ *n* -s [Quechua *áyni*, lit., recompense] **:** a Quechuan system of exchange of assistance usu. in the form of labor; *also* **:** a group that lends such assistance

ai·noi \ˈānē\ *n pl* [MGk, fr. Gk, pl. of *ainos* praise, tale — more at ENIGMA] **:** a part of the divine office concluding the orthros in the service of the Eastern Church

ai·noid \ˈī,nȯid\ *adj*, *usu cap* [*Ainu* + *-oid*] **:** resembling the Ainu

ain't \ˈānt\ *also* **an't** \" *also* ˈant *or like* AREN'T\ [prob. contr. of *are not, is not, am not, & have not*] **1 a :** are not ⟨you ~ going⟩ ⟨they ~ here⟩ ⟨things ~ what they used to be⟩ **b :** is not ⟨it ~ raining⟩ ⟨he's here, ~ he⟩ **c :** am not ⟨I ~ ready⟩ — though disapproved by many and more common in less educated speech, used orally in most parts of the U. S. by many cultivated speakers esp. in the phrase *ain't I* **2** *substand* **a :** have not ⟨I ~ seen him⟩ ⟨you ~ told us⟩ **b :** has not ⟨he ~ got the time⟩ ⟨~ the doctor come yet⟩

ai·nu \ˈī,nü *sometimes* -,nyü\ *also* **ai·no** \-,nō\ *n*, *pl* **ainu** *also* **ainus** *or* **ainos** *usu cap* [Ainu, lit., man] **1 a :** an indigenous Caucasoid people of Japan formerly occupying all or most of the archipelago but now confined to part of Hokkaido, Sakhalin, and parts of the Kurile islands **b :** a member of such people **2 :** the language of the Ainu people

¹**air** *var of* ¹ERE

²**air** \"\ *adj* -ER/-EST [ME (northern dial.) *ar, are*, fr. *ar*, adv. — more at ERE] *Scot* **:** EARLY

³**air** \a(a)(ə)r, ˈe(ə)r, ˈa(a)ə, ˈeə\ *n* -s *often attrib* [ME, fr. OF, fr. L *aer*, fr. Gk *aēr* air, mist; prob. akin to Gk *aētēs* wind, gale — more at WIND] **1 a :** the element described by early natural philosophers as having the qualities of moisture and heat **b :** a mixture of invisible odorless tasteless compressible elastic sound-transmitting and liquefiable gases composed chiefly of nitrogen and oxygen nearly in the ratio of four volumes to one together with 0.9 percent argon, about 0.03 percent carbon dioxide, varying amounts of water vapor, and minute quantities of helium, krypton, neon, and xenon, that surrounds the earth, half its mass being within four miles of the earth's surface, its pressure at sea level being about 14.7 pounds per square inch, and its weight being 1.293 grams per liter at 0°C and 760 mm. pressure **c :** the portion of the earth's atmosphere that immediately surrounds us and affects the senses ⟨the tang of wood smoke is in the ~ —Corey Ford⟩ ⟨the open ~⟩ ⟨the ~ was not so stale and sultry in the room as it was downstairs —Carson McCullers⟩ **d** *obs* **:** scent given off by exhalation into the atmosphere **:** ODOR ⟨the ~ of rotting vegetation⟩ **e :** ATMOSPHERE 8 ⟨canvases with much light and ~ and color⟩ **f :** air in motion **:** a gentle breeze ⟨we moved onward in light ~s to the Narrows and dropped anchor —Kenneth Roberts⟩ **g** *archaic* **:** soft or faint breathing **:** BREATH ⟨the least ~ of suspicion⟩ **h** *archaic* **:** GAS ⟨the generation of ~s by explosions⟩ **i** (1) **:** empty space ⟨needle in ~, I stopped what I was making —Eudora Welty⟩ ⟨the victim of the hanging danced on ~⟩ (2) **:** NOWHERE ⟨the figure of 10 billion dollars . . . was a nice round amount taken out of the ~ —J.P. Warburg⟩ (3) *slang* **:** an obvious snub or a sudden severance of relations — usu. used with *the* ⟨I got the ~ last night —Gwethalyn Graham⟩ ⟨she threatened to give me the ~ —Robert Graves⟩ **j :** air as a working fluid (as in ventilation systems, measuring and testing, fuel combustion, and pressure-operated devices) **:** COMPRESSED AIR ⟨mine ~ shafts⟩ ⟨~ barometer⟩ ⟨~ adapters located between the compressor outlets and the combustion chambers⟩ ⟨borings made with an ~ drill⟩ **k** (1) **:** air as a field of operation for aircraft ⟨the battle of the ~⟩; *also* **:** travel or transportation by aircraft ⟨European editions which reached me by ~ —Marcia Davenport⟩ ⟨~ parcel post⟩ (2) **:** AIRCRAFT ⟨~ attack⟩ ⟨~ patrol⟩ (3) **:** AVIATION ⟨~ safety⟩ (4) **:** AIR FORCE **l :** the medium of transmission of radio waves; *also* **:** RADIO, TELEVISION ⟨advertisers who use the ~ as a means for selling goods —C.A.Siepmann⟩ — often used in the phrase *on the air* ⟨he went on the ~ with the first of a series of Saturday-night broadcasts —*Atlantic*⟩ **2 :** public utterance usu. oral **:** PUBLICITY ⟨he gave ~ to his opinion⟩ **3** [F, fr. OF] **a** (1) **:** the look, appearance, or bearing of a person **:** attitude or action peculiar to or expressive of some personal quality or emotion **:** DEMEANOR ⟨sat rigidly erect with the ~ of a man accustomed to brief parleys —L.C.Douglas⟩ (2) **:** an artificial or affected manner **:** show of style or vanity **:** HAUGHTINESS ⟨to put on ~s⟩ ⟨to give oneself ~s⟩ (3) **:** the artificial motion or carriage of a horse **b :** outward appearance of a thing **:** apparent character **:** MANNER, STYLE ⟨my work may have an ~ of fiction —Van Wyck Brooks⟩ ⟨a pioneer town with broad dusty streets, that has not yet acquired an ~ of permanence —Ivor Jones⟩ **c :** a surrounding or pervading influence or condition **:** ATMOSPHERE ⟨the controversy which has been troubling the ~ about us —Victor Riesel⟩ ⟨the place had a little of the ~ of a college dormitory after the final exams —John Dos Passos⟩ ⟨steps it could take to clear the ~ considerably and give evidence before the world of its good intentions —*N.Y.Times*⟩ **4** [prob. trans. of It *aria*] **a** *Elizabethan and Jacobean music* **:** an accompanied song or melody in strophic form **b :** the chief voice part or melody in choral or other part music **c :** TUNE, MELODY **d :** a separate instrumental composition or one of the optional movements of the classical suite typically of a lyric character **5** [trans. of NGk *aēr*] **:** AER **6 :** airmail stamp ⟨an issue of new ~s⟩ — **in the air :** not protected by some substantial obstacle (as a river, mountain, or fortification) against flank attacks or turning movements — **on air** *adv* **:** in a state of elation **:** BUOYANTLY ⟨walking *on air*⟩ ⟨treading *on air*⟩ — **up in the air :** in a state of confusion, perturbation, or disorder **:** not yet settled or decided **:** in suspense ⟨the question was still *up in the air*⟩

⁴**air** \"\ *vb* -ED/-ING/-S *vt* **1 a** (1) **:** to expose to the air for the purpose of drying or purifying **:** VENTILATE ⟨~ damp clothing⟩ ⟨stench of whiskey and of things that were never ~*ed* —Ellen Glasgow⟩ ⟨~ the house⟩ (2) *archaic* **:** to expose to heat so as to expel dampness or to warm ⟨a brisk fire will soon ~ the room⟩ **b :** to expose to the air for the purpose of cooling or refreshing **:** exercise in the open air ⟨she left the overheated room to ~ herself⟩ ⟨take the dog out and ~ him⟩ **2 a :** to display ostentatiously **:** to expose to public view ⟨~ the latest fashions⟩ ⟨he constantly ~s his stupidity⟩ **b :** to expose for the sake of public notice **:** make open to the public ⟨he did not ~ his politics in the pulpit —K.B. Murdock⟩ ⟨the issue will be thoroughly ~*ed* —*Newsweek*⟩ **3 :** to transmit by radio or television **:** BROADCAST ⟨programs which will be ~*ed* in the future —*Musical Digest*⟩ **~** *vi* **1 :** to become exposed to the open air ⟨your suit is ~*ing* on the line⟩ **2 :** to become broadcast ⟨the program ~s daily⟩ **syn** see EXPRESS

⁵**air** \ˈär\ *n* -s [ME (northern dial.) *are, ar*, fr. OE & ON *ār* — more at OAR] *Scot* **:** OAR

⁶**air** *Scot var of* EYRE

⁷**air** \ˈär\ *n* -s [ON *eyrr* gravelly bank; akin to OE *ēar* earth, OHG *ōrah* gravelly, ON *aurr* sand, Goth *aurahjons* graves, and perh. to OIr *ūr* earth] *Scot* **:** SANDBANK, BEACH

⁸**air** *like* ³AIR\ *dial var of* ARE

⁹**air** \"\ *var of* ARY

ai·ra \ˈīrə\ *n*, *cap* [NL, fr. Gk, darnel] **:** a genus of delicate annual grasses with 2-flowered spikelets

air alert *n* **1 :** the period during which military and civilian agencies are required to be in readiness for an enemy air attack; *also* **:** the warning signal that begins such a period **2 :** combat or standby status of the aircraft, aircrew, and ground communications system that may have to repel the enemy air attack

ai·ram·po \īˈräm(ˌ)pō\ *n* -s [Sp, fr. Quechua *ayrampú*] **:** a prostrate cactus (*Opuntia soehrensii*) whose dried seeds yield a substance used in the Andes for coloring jellies red

ai·ran \īˈrän\ *n* -s [Turk *ayran*] **:** an Altaic and Turkish drink prepared from fermented milk

air-atomic \ˌ⸗⸗ˈ⸗⸗\ *adj* **:** capable of sending atomic weapons through space ⟨*air-atomic* power —Carl Spaatz⟩

air base *n* **:** a base of operations for military aircraft and for the housing and repairing of the craft, the storage of munitions, the housing of aviation personnel, and the administrative center of control over the operations of the aircraft

air bath *n* **1 :** a hygienic exposure of the body to the open air **2 :** a bath of air; *also* **:** a receptacle (as a small oven heated from below) containing such a bath

air bell *n* **1 :** an air bubble **2 :** an undeveloped spot on a negative or print caused by the adherence of an air bubble to the film surface during development

air bends *n pl* **:** AEROEMBOLISM

airbill *var of* AIRWAYBILL

air billow *n* **:** a wave at the interface of two horizontal layers of air caused by their difference in velocity

air bladder *n* **:** a bladder containing gas, esp. air: as **a :** a hydrostatic organ present in most fishes that consists of a gas-filled sac lying dorsal to the alimentary canal and sometimes being connected with the organ of hearing and that serves also as an accessory respiratory organ in dipnoans and some ganoids — called also *swim bladder*; compare LUNG **b :** FLOAT 4h

air bleed *n* **:** a slow escape or admission of air provided for in a mechanical system (as for equalizing pressure)

air blue *n* **:** AZURITE BLUE

airboat \ˈ⸗,⸗\ *n* **1 :** SEAPLANE **2 :** a shallow-draft boat driven by an airplane propeller and steered by an airplane rudder

airborne \ˈ⸗,⸗\ *adj* **1 :** supported wholly by aerodynamic and aerostatic forces ⟨an airplane is ~ after attaining flying speed in takeoff⟩ **2 :** transported or designed to be transported by air ⟨~ infantry⟩ ⟨~ bacteria⟩ **3 :** employing forces (as paratroops) that are transported by air ⟨an ~ attack⟩

air-bound \ˈ⸗,⸗\ *adj* **:** obstructed or inoperative because of air in a space normally filled with liquid ⟨an *air-bound* pipe⟩

air brake *n* **1 :** a brake operated by a piston driven by compressed air from reservoirs connected to brake cylinders by triple valves which upon reduction of air pressure in the brake pipe automatically admit air from the reservoirs into the brake cylinder **2 :** a surface (as an aileron) that may be projected into the airstream for increasing the resistance and lowering the speed of an airplane

air·bra·sive \ˈ⸗,brāsiv, -ziv\ *adj* [³*air* + *abrasive*] **:** relating to the grinding of tooth surfaces by means of a stream of abrasive particles under air or gas pressure ⟨the ~ method of preparing cavities for filling⟩

air-break switch *n* **:** an electrical switch that breaks the circuit in air — compare OIL-BREAK SWITCH

air brick *n* **:** a hollowed or perforated brick or a metal box of brick size with grated sides used for ventilation

¹airbrush \ˈ⸗ˌ⸗\ *n* **:** an often pencil-shaped atomizer for applying by compressed air a fine spray of paint, protective coating, or liquid color (as in shading drawings or retouching photographs)

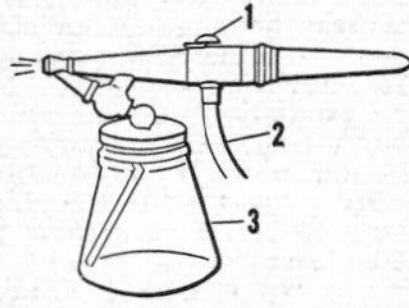

airbrush: *1* valve, *2* tube for compressed air, *3* color cup

²airbrush \ˈ"\ *vt* **:** to treat with an airbrush ⟨~ the print with gray paint to achieve a soft, high-key effect —*Popular Photography*⟩; *specif* **:** to take out (as a blemish in a photograph) — used with *out* ⟨freckles and awkward angles are ~*ed* out —*Time*⟩ **2 :** to paint (as a picture or a detail in a photograph) with an airbrush — often used with *on* or *in* ⟨orchids ~*ed* on towels⟩

airburst \ˈ⸗ˌ⸗\ *n* **:** the burst of a shell or bomb in the air

air cargo *n* **:** express, freight, or mail carried by aircraft

air carrier *n* **1 :** an organization transporting passengers and cargo by aircraft **:** AIRLINE **2 :** an aircraft certificated by a designated governmental agency to carry persons or cargo for hire

air casing *n* **1 :** a casing (as of sheet iron) surrounding a pipe or reservoir with an air space between to prevent transmission of heat **2 :** the coaming around the stack of a ship at the weather deck serving to ventilate the boiler room

air castle *n* **:** CASTLE IN THE AIR

air cell *n* **:** a cavity or receptacle for air: **a :** the air sac of a bird **b :** a dilation of a trachea of an insect **c :** a pulmonary alveolus **d :** the space between the membranes of an egg usu. at the large end that increases in size with age

air chamber *n* **:** a cavity filled with air: as **a :** a cavity containing air to act by its elasticity as a spring for equalizing the flow of a liquid in a pump or other hydraulic machine — see HYDRAULIC RAM illustration **b :** one of the chambers in the nautilus or other chambered cephalopods

air check *n* **:** a recording esp. of a radio broadcast

air chief marshal *n* **:** an officer of the British Royal Air Force equivalent in rank to a general in the army

air cleaner *n* **:** any of various devices for removing impurities (as suspended particles) from air (as by filtering, washing, or electrostatic precipitation)

air coach *n* **:** a passenger airliner offering service at less than first-class rates usu. with curtailed accommodations (as in space per passenger)

air command *n* **:** a unit of the highest echelon in the U. S. Air Force usu. composed of two or more air forces

air commodore *n* **:** an officer in the British Royal Air Force equivalent in rank to a brigadier in the army

air condenser *n* **:** a surface condenser in which steam or other vapor is cooled by contact with air-cooled surfaces

air–condition \ˈ⸗⸗ˌ⸗⸗\ *vt* [back-formation fr. *air conditioning*] **:** to equip with an apparatus for washing, humidifying, dehumidifying, and controlling the temperature of air ⟨*air-condition* a building⟩; *also* **:** to subject (air) to the process of washing, humidifying, and dehumidifying — **air–conditioned** *adj* — **air conditioning** *n* -s

air–conditioner *n* **:** one that air-conditions

air controller *n* **:** a military officer responsible for coordinating and directing close-support attacks of combat aircraft against enemy ground forces and installations

air controlman *n, pl* **air controlmen :** a petty officer in the U. S. Navy having as a specialty the control and coordination of air traffic on airfields, seadromes, and carriers

air–cool \ˈ⸗ˌ⸗\ *vt* [back-formation fr. *air-cooled* & *air cooling*] **:** to cool by means of air; *specif* **:** to cool the cylinder or cylinders of (an internal-combustion engine) by air without the use of any intermediate medium (as water or oil) — **air–cooled** *adj* — **air cooling** *n*

air–cooled storage *n* **:** COMMON STORAGE

air–core \ˈ⸗ˌ⸗\ *also* **air–cored** \ˈ⸗ˌ⸗\ *adj* **:** having no magnetic material (as iron) in its magnetic circuit — used esp. of certain coils, solenoids, or transformers

air cover *n* **:** a screen of fighter aircraft provided for a ground, sea, or air unit for protection esp. against enemy aircraft

aircraft \ˈ⸗ˌ⸗\ *n* [³*air* + *craft* (vessel)] **:** a weight-carrying machine or structure for flight in or navigation of the air and designed to be supported by the air either by the buoyancy of the structure or by the dynamic action of the air against its surfaces — used of airplanes, balloons, helicopters, kites, kite balloons, orthopters, and gliders but chiefly of airplanes or aerostats

aircraft carrier *n* **:** a warship equipped with a flight deck on which airplanes can be launched and landed and with a hangar deck for servicing airplanes

aircraft division *n* **:** a subdivision of a squadron of U.S. naval aircraft containing usu. from four to six planes

aircraft observer *n* **:** a person holding a rating in the U. S. Air Force for any aircrew position except that of pilot

aircraft section *n* **:** a subdivision of U.S. naval aircraft containing usu. two planes of the same type

air·crafts·man \-f(t)smən\ *also* **air·craft·man** \-f(t)mən\ *n, pl* **aircraftsmen** *also* **aircraftmen** *chiefly Brit* **:** an airplane mechanic who is a noncommissioned member of an air-force ground crew

aircraft station *n* **:** a radio transmitting station aboard an aircraft — compare AERONAUTICAL STATION

air·crafts·wom·an \-f(t)s+ˌ+\ *also* **air·craft·wom·an** \-f(t)+ˌ-\ *n, pl* **aircraftswomen** *also* **aircraftwomen** *chiefly Brit* **:** a woman who is a noncommissioned member of the air force

aircrew \ˈ⸗ˌ⸗\ *n* **:** the crew manning an aircraft

air·crew·man \-mən\ *n, pl* **aircrewmen :** a member of an aircrew often as distinguished from the pilot or other officers

air crossing *n* **:** a passage in a mine by which one airway crosses another — compare OVERCAST, UNDERCAST

air cushion *n* **1 :** an airtight inflatable cushion **2 :** a mechanical device using confined air for arresting motion without shock

air cylinder *n* **:** a cylinder in which air is compressed by a piston, in which compressed air is stored, or in which a piston is driven by air pressure

air defense *n* **:** the means, techniques, and organizations devoted to preventing or minimizing the effects of attack by enemy aircraft or guided missiles

Air·dent \ˈ⸗ˌdent\ *trademark* — used for an instrument designed to grind tooth surfaces by means of a jet of carbon dioxide carrying abrasive powder under pressure

air division *n* **:** a unit of that echelon of the U. S. Air Force that is higher than a wing and lower than an air force and is composed of a headquarters and usu. from two to five wings

airdock \ˈ⸗ˌ⸗\ *n* **:** HANGAR

air drainage *n* **:** AERIAL DRAINAGE

air·drau·lic \(ˈ)⸗ˈdrȯlik\ *adj* [³*air* + *hydraulic*] **:** combining pneumatic and hydraulic operation ⟨an ~ machine employing both air and oil in the same pressure enclosure⟩

air drill *n* **:** a drill driven by compressed air

air·drome \ˈ⸗ˌdrōm\ *n* [alter. (influenced by ³*air*) of *aerodrome*] **:** AIRPORT

air–drop \ˈ⸗ˌ⸗\ *vt* **:** to drop (troops or supplies) from an aircraft by parachute

airdrop \ˈ"\ *n* **:** delivery of cargo or personnel by parachute from an aircraft in flight

air–dry \ˈ⸗ˌ⸗\ *adj* **:** dry to such a degree that no further moisture is given up on exposure to air

air duct *n* **1 :** a tube or pipe for conveying air (as to the rooms of a house or ship for ventilation or to a furnace) **2 :** the duct connecting the air bladder and alimentary canal of certain fishes

ai·re \ˈärə\ *n, pl* **ai·rig** \-rik, -iḵ\ [IrGael, nobleman, chief, fr. OIr — more at ARYAN] **:** a person of any of various ranks in early Irish society above the common freeman and below the king

aired *past of* AIR

aire·dale \ˈ"\ *n* -s [*airedale* (*terrier*) (influenced in meaning by ³*air*)] **1** *slang* **:** a naval airplane pilot or aircrewman **2** *slang* **:** an airplane handler on a naval aircraft carrier

airedale terrier \ˈa(ə)(ə)rˌdāl-, ˈe(ə)r-,ˈa(ə)ə-,ˈeə-\ *or* **airedale** *n* -s *often cap A* [fr. *Airedale*, valley of the Aire river, Yorkshire, England] **:** a large terrier with hard and wiry coat of a breed supposedly produced by crossing the black-and-tan terrier, bullterrier, and otterhound being about 22 inches high, weighing from 35 to 45 pounds, and having a coat black or dark-grizzled on back and sides and tan elsewhere

air ejector *n* **1 :** a device that removes air and other gases from steam condensers through the suction action of a stream jet **2 :** a small jet pump (as a filter pump)

air embolism *n* **:** obstruction of the circulation by air that has gained entrance to veins usu. through wounds — compare AEROEMBOLISM

air engine *n* **1 :** an engine built like a steam engine but driven by compressed air **2 :** HOT-AIR ENGINE

air entrainment *n* **:** the incorporation in concrete or mortar of minute air bubbles (as by addition of soap or grease) to increase resilience and resistance to wear and weathering

air equivalent *n* **:** the absorbency of a layer of material in terms of the thickness of a layer of air that would have the same absorbency for the same radiation

airer *comparative of* AIR

airest *superlative of* AIR

air explorer *n* **:** a boy at least 14 years old who is enrolled in the air exploring program of the Boy Scouts of America

air express *n* [fr. *Air Express*, a service mark] **:** package transport service using airlines but distinct from airfreight because of special scheduling, handling, billing, pickup, and delivery; *also* **:** the packages so shipped

airfield \ˈ⸗ˌ⸗\ *n* **1 :** the landing field of an airport **2 :** AIRPORT

air fleet *n* **:** a group or assemblage of aircraft (as of military aircraft under a single command); *also* **:** the military aircraft of a nation

air float *n* **:** an air vesicle

airflow \ˈ⸗ˌ⸗\ *n* **:** the motion of air relative to the surface of a body immersed in it (as the wind passing an obstruction or the streamline flow of air around parts of an airplane in flight)

Airfoam \ˈ⸗ˌ⸗\ *trademark* — used for a fine-grained sponge rubber cushioning material

airfoil \ˈ⸗ˌ⸗\ *n* [³*air* + *foil*] **:** a body (as an airplane wing or propeller blade) designed to provide a desired reaction force when in motion relative to the surrounding air

air force *n* **1 :** one of the armed services of a state analogous to or part of the military and naval services and having the primary missions of gaining control of the air, interdicting the enemy lines of communication, supporting surface forces (as by bombing and strafing), and accomplishing strategic bombing objectives **2 :** a unit of that echelon of the U.S. Air Force that is higher than an air division and lower than an air command and is usu. composed of two or more air divisions

air force blue *often cap A&F* **:** an ultramarine blue

airframe \ˈ⸗ˌ⸗\ *n* [*aircraft* + *frame*] **:** the complete structure of an aircraft (as an airplane or rocket) without the power plant

¹airfreight \ˈ⸗ˌ⸗\ *n* **:** forwarding service by air for freight in volume **:** freight forwarded by a cargo-carrying airplane; *also* **:** the money charged or paid for this service

²airfreight \ˈ"\ *vt* [¹*airfreight*] **:** to ship by airfreight

airfreighter \ˈ⸗ˌ⸗\ *n* **1 :** an aircraft for transporting freight **2 :** a carrier operating airfreight service

air furnace *n* **:** a furnace that depends on a natural draft (as a reverberatory furnace) and not on blast

air gap *n* **1 :** an air-filled gap in a magnetic or electric circuit (as the space between the field-magnet poles and the armature in a dynamo or motor) **2 :** WIND GAP **3 :** the vertical distance between the point where water enters a plumbing fixture (as a tub or lavatory) and the level at which it would overflow

air gas *n* **1 :** a combustible gas made by charging air with the vapor of some volatile hydrocarbon mixture (as gasoline) and used for lighting and heating **2 :** a producer gas consisting chiefly of carbon monoxide and nitrogen and made by blowing air into a producer

air gauge *n* **1 :** a gauge for measuring air pressure **2 :** a comparator in which the rate of escape of air between the surface under test (as that of a gun bore) and one of known curvature approximately fitting it (as that of a spindle inserted in the bore) is used as a measure of the difference between the two

airglow \ˈ⸗ˌ⸗\ *n* **:** light from the nighttime sky originating in the high atmosphere

air·graph \ˈ⸗ˌgraf, -äf\ *n* -s [*air* + tele*graph*] *Brit* **:** V-MAIL

air group *n* **:** the two or more squadrons composing all of an aircraft carrier's airplanes

air gun *n* **1 :** AIR RIFLE, AIR PISTOL **2 :** AIR HAMMER; *esp* **:** one held in the hand like a pistol and controlled by a trigger **3 :** AIRBRUSH

air gunner *n* **:** AERIAL GUNNER

air hammer *n* **:** a portable tool in which a chisel, rivet set, or other tool is driven percussively by compressed air — called also *pneumatic hammer*

air harbor *n* **:** a landing place for seaplanes

air–hardening steel *n* **:** an alloy steel that can be hardened by cooling from a temperature higher than the transformation range either in air or or by quenching in a liquid — called also *self-hardening steel*

airhead \ˈ⸗ˌ⸗\ *n* [³*air* + *-head* (as in *beachhead*)] **1 :** an area in hostile territory secured usu. by airborne troops for further use in bringing in troops and materiel by air **2 :** an advance air base

air hoist *n* **:** a hoist operated by compressed air

air hole *n* **1 a :** a hole to admit or discharge air **b :** water not frozen over esp. because of a spring or current in a river or pond **2 :** a discontinuity produced in a foundry casting by a bubble of gas **:** BLOWHOLE **3 :** AIR POCKET 1

air horn *n* **1 :** a carburetor main air intake **2 :** a pneumatic horn (as on a motor vehicle or diesel locomotive)

air hostess *n* **:** a stewardess on an airplane

air hunger *n* **:** deep labored breathing at an increased or decreased rate (as in acidosis and other conditions)

airier *comparative of* AIRY

airiest *superlative of* AIRY

air·i·fied \ˈa(ə)rəˌfīd, ˈer-\ *adj* **1 :** fashioned in an airy style **2 :** affecting airs

airig *pl of* AIRE

air·i·ly \-rəlē, -li\ *adv* **:** in an airy manner **:** JAUNTILY, LIGHTLY, THINLY ⟨dismissed the idea ~⟩ ⟨~ graceful⟩

air·i·ness \-rēnəs, -rin-\ *n* -ES **:** the quality or state of being airy **:** SPRIGHTLINESS, DELICACY

airing *n* -s [fr. gerund of ⁴*air*] **1 :** exposure to air or heat for drying or freshening **:** VENTILATION ⟨give the clothes an ~⟩ ⟨this room needs an ~⟩ **2 :** exposure to or exercise in the open air esp. to promote health or fitness ⟨relief that this backyard had turned out to be as good a place for John's ~*s* as it had —Marcia Davenport⟩ ⟨she must take the dogs for an ~ —Arnold Bennett⟩ **3 :** exposure to public view or notice ⟨tolerant of his father's incessant ~ of his views —L.C. Douglas⟩ ⟨to get a congressional ~ soon —*Newsweek*⟩ **4 :** a radio or television broadcast ⟨series that have been booked for regular weekly ~*s* —Saul Carson⟩

air injection *n* **:** the injection of atomized fuel oil into the combustion chamber of a diesel engine by means of a jet of compressed air — compare SOLID INJECTION

air·ish \ˈa(ə)rish, ˈer-, -ēsh\ *adj* [ME, fr. *air* + *-ish*] **:** CHILLY, COOL, BREEZY

air knife *n* **:** a blade in a papermaking machine for removing excess coating from newly coated paper by means of an air blast

air–lance \ˈ⸗ˌ⸗\ *vt* **:** to remove (as clinkers from a boiler wall) by means of a stream of air under pressure

air lance *n* **:** a device (as a nozzle) used in air-lancing

airland \ˈ⸗ˌ⸗\ *vt* **:** to land (troops or materiel) in an area

air lane *n* **:** a path customarily followed by airplanes; *esp* **:** one made easy for navigation by steady winds

air–launch \ˈ⸗ˌ⸗\ *vt* **:** to launch (a rocket or missile) from a flying air vehicle

air law *n* **:** that part of the law dealing with air transport

air layer *n* **:** a plant propagated by air layering

air layering *n* **:** vegetative propagation of a plant (as one difficult or impossible to graft or bud) by enclosing a branch or shoot often after wounding or girdling in a moist medium (as sphagnum or soil) until roots have formed, the branch or shoot then being severed to form an independent plant — compare MARCOTTAGE

airle–pen·ny \ˈer(ə)l,-\ *n* [older Sc *arlis-penny*, fr. *arlis* (alter. of *arles*) + *penny* — more at ARLES] **:** ARLES

air·less \ˈa(ə)rləs, ˈe(ə)rl-,ˈa(ə)l-,ˈel-\ *adj* **1 :** lacking air **2 :** lacking fresh air or movement of air

air letter *n* **1 :** an airmail letter **2 :** a letter sheet esp. for airmail

air lift *n* **:** a pumping device consisting of two different-sized pipes, one within or adjacent to the other, compressed air or gas being forced down through the smaller pipe causing the fluid which is to be pumped to rise through the larger

¹airlift \ˈ⸗ˌ⸗\ *n* **1 :** a supply line operated by aircraft **2 :** air transportation esp. as improvised apart from regular schedules

²airlift \ˈ"\ *vt* [¹*airlift*] **:** to transport by means of an airlift

air line *n* **1 :** a straight line through the air between two points that disregards irregularities of the intervening ground or space **:** BEELINE; *also* **:** a great-circle arc between two points on the earth's surface **2 :** a pipe or hose used to supply air under pressure (as to a pneumatic tool or to a diver under water) **3** *usu* **airline** \ˈ⸗ˌ⸗\ **:** an established system of aerial transportation, its equipment, or the organization owning or operating it

airline hostess *n* **:** AIR HOSTESS

airliner \ˈ⸗ˌ⸗⸗\ *n* **:** an aircraft belonging to or operating over an airline

air load *n* **:** the aerodynamic load on a moving airfoil

air lock *n* **1 :** an air space with two airtight doors or openings for permitting entrance to or exit from a sealed-off space under pressure (as a ship's stokehole) or vacuum: as **a :** an intermediate chamber between the outer air and the working chamber of a pneumatic caisson **b :** the chamber in an electron microscope between outer air and inner vacuum **c :** the entrance chamber to a gas-proof shelter **2 :** a stoppage of flow (as in a pumping device) caused by air being in a part where liquid ought to circulate — compare VAPOR LOCK

air–lock \ˈ⸗ˌ⸗\ *vt* [*air lock*] **:** to stop (a flow) by an air lock

air locking *n* **:** materials (as weather stripping) and devices used in building construction for making enclosed spaces airtight

air log *n* **:** an instrument that records the distance traveled by an aircraft relative to the air through which it moves, the average true airspeed being computable from the distance traveled and the time elapsed

¹airmail \ˈ⸗ˌ⸗\ *n* [³*air* + *mail*] **1 :** the system of transporting mail by aircraft **2 :** mail transported or to be transported by air **3 :** an airmail stamp

²airmail \ˈ⸗ˌ⸗\ *adj* **:** relating to, for use with, or intended for airmail ⟨~ service⟩ ⟨~ stamp⟩ ⟨~ letter⟩

³airmail \ˈ⸗ˌ⸗\ *vt* **:** to send by airmail

airmail field *n* **:** an airport having a transfer office for sorting, distributing, dispatching, and transferring airmail; *also* **:** the office at such airport — abbr. *A.M.F.*

air·man \ˈ⸗mən, -ˌman, -ˌmaa(ə)n\ *n, pl* **airmen 1 :** BRATTICER **2 :** an icehouse worker who freshens the water in the cores of partially frozen blocks of ice to remove impurities and make the ice clear **3 :** one engaged in the operation, navigation, or maintenance of aircraft: as **a :** an enlisted man or woman in the U.S. Air Force; *specif* **:** one of any of four ranks below a staff sergeant **b :** an enlisted man in the U.S. Navy who performs general duties concerned with the operation of aircraft **c :** a civilian or military person who is a pilot or is associated with aviation

airman basic *n* **:** an enlisted man of the lowest rank in the air force

air·man·ship \-ˌmənˌship\ *n* **:** skill in piloting or navigating an aircraft

air map *n* **:** a map made up of a series of photographs taken from an aircraft

airmark \ˈ⸗ˌ⸗\ *vt* **:** to mark out (as a town) with ground location signs visible from the air as an aid to aerial navigation — **airmarker** \ˈ⸗ˌ⸗⸗\ *n*

air marshal *n* **:** an officer of the British Royal Air Force equivalent in rank to a lieutenant general in the army

air mass *n* **:** a body of air extending hundreds or thousands of miles horizontally and sometimes as high as the stratosphere and maintaining during transcontinental or transoceanic movements approximately uniform conditions of temperature and humidity at any given level ⟨a polar continental *air mass*⟩

air mass weather *n* **:** weather within an air mass in distinction from that occurring at its front

air mile *n* **:** the basic unit of distance in air navigation equal in the U.S. before 1946 to the statute mile of 5280 feet, from 1946 to 1954 to the British nautical mile of 6080 feet, and since 1959 to the international nautical mile of 6076.11549 feet

air–mind·ed \ˈ⸗ˌ⸗⸗\ *adj* **:** interested in or favorably disposed toward aviation

air mine *n* **:** AERIAL MINE

air monkey *n* [*air*-brake + (*grease*) *monkey*] **:** an air-brake repairman

air motor *n* **:** a turbine motor powered by compressed air

air observation *n* **:** observation from an aircraft; *specif* **:** such observation of artillery fire

air officer *n* **:** a naval officer who heads the air department of an aircraft carrier and is responsible for all aircraft operations

airpark \ˈ⸗ˌ⸗\ *n* **:** a small airport

air philately *n* **:** AEROPHILATELY

air photograph *n* **:** AERIAL PHOTOGRAPH — **air photography** *n*

air pistol *n* **:** a pistol that uses compressed air to propel shot or a slug

¹air·plane \ˈ⸗ˌplān\ *n* [alter. (influenced by ³*air*) of *aeroplane*, prob. fr. LGk *aeroplanos* wandering in air, fr. Gk *aer-* + *planos* wandering, fr. *planasthai* to wander — more at PLANET] **1 :** a fixed-wing aircraft heavier than air that is driven by a screw propeller or by a high-velocity jet and supported by the dynamic reaction of the air against its wings — commonly used of a landplane as distinguished from a seaplane; see MONOPLANE, BIPLANE **2 :** a piece of paper folded in three dimensions to be thrown (as by children) and made to swoop briefly through the air **3 :** pinochle in which partners may exchange certain cards

²airplane \ˈ"\ *vi* **:** to fly, glide, or soar in or as if in an airplane **:** travel by airplane ⟨*airplaning* across the continent⟩

airplane cloth *or* **airplane fabric** *n* **1 :** a cotton or linen fabric of firm plain weave doped for use on airplane parts **2 :** a shirting fabric resembling airplane cloth

airplane hostess *n* **:** AIR HOSTESS

airplane spin *n* **:** a professional-wrestling maneuver in which the opponent is picked up in a crotch-and-head hold, lifted onto the back, whirled about in the air, and thrown forward to the mat

air plant *n* **1 :** EPIPHYTE **2 :** any of several plants of the genus *Kalanchoe* (esp. *K. pinnata*) that propagate new plants from the leaves — called also *life plant*

air plot *n* **:** the room on an aircraft carrier from which all air operations are directed

air plug *n* **:** a removable plug screwed into a watertight manhole or scuttle cover

air pocket *n* **1 :** a condition of the atmosphere (as a local down current or an abrupt change of wind velocity in the direction of travel) that causes an airplane to drop suddenly **2 :** an air-filled section (as of a pipe) normally completely filled with liquid **3 :** a situation in the security market in which there is no nearby bid for an issue or for securities generally and which results in acute price weakness

air police *n* **:** an organized force in an air unit that exercises the function of police among air personnel and is responsible esp. for the security of the base, for prisoners, and for road traffic control — abbr. *A.P.*

air port *n* [³*air* + *port* (opening in a ship's side)] **:** an opening to release or admit air

airport \ˈ⸗ˌ⸗\ *n* [³*air* + *port* (harbor)] **:** a tract of land or water that is adapted and maintained for the landing and takeoff of aircraft and at which facilities for their shelter, supply, and repair are provided **:** a terminal point for air passengers and cargo — compare AIRFIELD

airport of entry : a port of entry for aircraft

airpost \ˈ⸗ˌ⸗\ *n* [prob. trans. of G *luftpost*] : AIRMAIL

air potato *n* : an Asiatic yam (*Dioscorea bulbifera*) sometimes cultivated for its large axillary potatolike tubers

air power *n* : the force that a nation is able to apply by military aviation to gain and secure its political and military ends : AIR FORCE

air pressure *n* : ATMOSPHERIC PRESSURE

¹airproof \ˈ⸗ˌ⸗\ *adj* [³*air* + *proof*] **1** : AIRTIGHT **2** : made impervious to air

²airproof \"\ *vt* **1** : to make airtight **2** : to protect from the injurious action of air

air propeller *n* : a rotary fan for circulating air

air pump *n* : a pump for exhausting air from a closed space or for compressing air or forcing it through other apparatus — compare VACUUM PUMP

air raid *n* : an attack by armed aircraft (as bombers) on a surface target

air receiver *n* : a storage tank for compressed air

air rifle *n* **1** : a rifle from which a projectile is propelled by air or carbon dioxide compressed usu. by a lever and pump system **2** : BB GUN

air right *n* : a property right to the space above a plane fixed a specified distance above the ground esp. when owned separately from the right to use the ground itself and the space immediately above it and usu. with a right to support from the ground below

air ring *n* : an inflatable rubber ring used as a cushion to relieve pressure on prominent bony points (as in helping to prevent bedsores)

air room *n* : a high-security room in an air headquarters displaying the latest air intelligence and estimates of the situation and used for the briefing of authorized personnel

air root *n* : AERIAL ROOT

airs *pl of* AIR, *pres 3d sing of* AIR

air sac *n* **1** : a cavity in the pollen grain of pines **2 a** : one of the spaces in different parts of the bodies of birds that are air-filled and connected with the air passages of the lungs and usu. with cavities in the bones and that serve to reduce the specific gravity of the body and assist respiration by the great increase of surface thus exposed to the air as well as by providing a space for the residual air so that the lungs may be completely filled with fresh air at each respiration **b** : paired bladderlike backward extensions of the branchial cavity of certain Indian fishes that are lined with vascular tissue and serve as accessory breathing organs **c** : the internal subumbrellar portion of the specialized inverted pneumatophore in siphonophores that contains air and keeps the colony afloat **3** : a thin-walled dilation of a trachea occurring in many insects **4** : a pulmonary alveolus

air-sac disease *n* : a serious inflammatory condition of the air sacs of poultry

air-sac mite *n* : a small pale oval nearly hairless mite (*Cytoleichus nudus*) having the legs ending in suckers and parasitizing the respiratory passages and air sacs of various wild and domesticated birds

air·scape \ˈ⸗ˌskāp\ *n* -S [³*air* + -*scape*] : a view or a picture taken from a position in an aircraft or on a height

air scoop *n* : an air-duct inlet or cowl that projects from an outer surface of an aircraft or automobile in such a way as to utilize the dynamic pressure of the airstream in maintaining a flow of air (as to a power plant or a ventilating system)

air scout *n* **1** : an airplane used for reconnaissance **2** : AIR EXPLORER

airscrew \ˈ⸗ˌ⸗\ *n* **1** : a screw or screw propeller designed to operate in air **2** *Brit* : an airplane propeller

air seal *n* : a seal to prevent passage of air or vapor

air service *n* **1** : the air arm of a nation **2** : mail, passenger, and freight service provided by the operation of aircraft

air-set \ˈ⸗ˌ⸗\ *vi* : to set in air at normal temperatures and pressures ⟨allowing mortar to *air-set*⟩

air shaft *n* : AIR WELL

airsheet \ˈ⸗ˌ⸗\ *n* : an air-letter sheet

airship \ˈ⸗ˌ⸗\ *n* : a lighter-than-air aircraft having a propelling system and a means for controlling the direction of motion

air shower *n* : cosmic rays formed into a shower by passage through the atmosphere

airsick \ˈ⸗ˌ⸗\ *adj* : affected with airsickness

airsickness \ˈ⸗ˌ⸗⸗\ *n* : motion sickness associated with flying and the modifying factors of high speed and altitude characterized by dizziness, nausea, headache, muscular weakness, faintness, anxiety, pallor, cold sweats, tremor, and vomiting — compare ALTITUDE SICKNESS

air-slake *also* **air-slack** \ˈ⸗ˌ⸗\ *vt* : to slake (lime) by exposure to the air

air sleeve *or* **air sock** *n* : WIND SOCK

air space *n* **1** : an enclosed space for or containing air: as **a** : space (as in a room) available for air for respiration **b** : a space between walls or in a wall to protect against dampness or to provide thermal insulation **c** : AIR SAC 2a **d** : the space between the powder charge and projectile in a firearm **e** : a cavity containing air in the cellular tissue of a plant **2** *usu* **airspace** : the space lying above the earth or above a certain area of land or water; *esp* : the space lying above a nation and considered as under its jurisdiction

airspace reservation *n* : a sector of airspace in which aerial navigation is restricted or prohibited by governmental authority

airspeed \ˈ⸗ˌ⸗\ *n* : the speed of an aircraft with relation to the air as distinguished from speed relative to the earth — compare GROUND SPEED

airspeed head *n* : a device mounted in the airstream and used to measure the airspeed of an aircraft — compare PRESSURE NOZZLE

airspeed indicator *or* **airspeed meter** *n* : a dial gauge showing the airspeed of an aircraft

air spot *n* : spotting and reporting from aircraft the fall of missiles in relation to a target; *also* : the aircraft and pilot assigned to this duty

air-spray \ˈ⸗ˌ⸗\ *adj* : applied or used to apply in the form of a spray by means of air under pressure ⟨*air-spray* lacquer⟩ ⟨*air-spray* equipment⟩

air stack *n* : planes circling at different assigned altitudes above an airport while waiting their turn to land

air stage *n*, *Canad* : the carrying of supplies to northern settlements by regularly scheduled airplane flights

air station *n* : a stopping place for aircraft equipped with facilities for receiving and servicing the craft — compare AIR BASE, AIRFIELD, AIRPORT

airstream \ˈ⸗ˌ⸗\ *n* **1** : AIRFLOW **2** : a current of air : WIND; *esp* : a high-velocity wind at high altitude

airstream engine *or* **airstream motor** *n* : a jet engine that unlike a rocket depends upon the oxygen in the surrounding atmosphere for combustion

air strike *n* : an air attack

airstrip \ˈ⸗ˌ⸗\ *n* [³*air* + *strip*] : a paved or unpaved runway that lacks normal airbase or airport facilities (as taxi strips, hangars)

air support *n* : air operations esp. in direct support of ground forces, naval forces, or other air forces

air surveillance *n* : the systematic scanning of a portion of the airspace esp. by electronic or visual means to detect and track flying aircraft or missiles

air survey *n* : AERIAL SURVEY

air system *n* : a system of mechanical refrigeration in which cold air is compressed, cooled, and permitted to expand and thus acts as the refrigerating agent

¹airt \ˈart, ˈe-\ *n* -S [ME *art*, fr. ScGael *āird* point of the compass, promontory; akin to OIr *aird* point, height — more at ARDISIA] *chiefly Scot* : point of the compass : DIRECTION

²airt \"\ *vb* -ED/-ING/-S *vt*, *chiefly Scot* : DIRECT, GUIDE ~ *vi*, *chiefly Scot* : to make one's way

airtight \ˈ⸗ˌ⸗\ *adj* **1** : so tight as to be impermeable or nearly so to air ⟨~ stove⟩ **2** : impenetrable esp. by an opponent; *also* : permitting no opportunity for an opponent to score ⟨an ~ argument⟩ ⟨an ~ defense⟩ — **air·tight·ness** *n* -ES

air-to-air \ˈ⸗⸗ˌ⸗\ *adv* (*or adj*) : from one aircraft to another while in flight ⟨*air-to-air* rockets⟩ ⟨refueling *air-to-air*⟩

air tourist *n* : air-coach service

air train *n* : SKY TRAIN

air transport *n* **1** : air transportation **2** : an aircraft designed for use in transporting esp. military personnel and cargo

air trap *n* **1** : a device for shutting off foul air or gas from drains or sewers **2** : AIR POCKET

air trumpet *n* : one of a pair of short breathing tubes that project from the thorax of mosquitoes and related insects

air twist *n* : a decorative spiral of air in the stem of a glass vessel formed during blowing and manufacture

air twist

air vehicle *n* : a man-made object that propels itself through the air (as an aircraft or a guided missile)

air vice-marshal *n* : an officer of the British Royal Air Force equivalent in rank to a major general in the army

airview \ˈ⸗ˌ⸗\ *n* : AERIAL PHOTOGRAPH

air volcano *n* : an eruptive sometimes volcanic opening in the earth from which large volumes of gas are discharged along with mud and stones — compare MUD VOLCANO

air war *n* : war waged by an air force or between opposing air forces

air warden *n* : a local civilian officer who supervises defensive measures against air raids during a war

air washer *n* : the part of an air-conditioning system in which the air is freed from dust and given the desired humidity by means of a spray of water

airwave \ˈ⸗ˌ⸗\ *n* **1** : the medium of radio and television transmission — usu. used in pl. **2** : AIRWAY 5 — not used technically

airway \ˈ⸗ˌ⸗\ *n* **1** : a passage for a current of air often underground (as in a mine) **2** : a designated route along which aircraft fly from airport to airport; *esp* : such a route equipped with navigational aids **3** : AIR LINE 3 **4** : a passageway for air into or out of the lungs; *specif* : a device passed into the trachea by way of the mouth or nose or through an incision to maintain a clear respiratory passageway (as during anesthesia, convulsions, or in obstructive laryngitis) **5** : a channel of a designated radio frequency for broadcasting or other radio communication

airway beacon *n* : a revolving beacon light of high intensity marking the course of an airway

airwaybill \ˈ⸗ˌ⸗ˌ⸗\ *also* **airbill** \ˈ⸗ˌ⸗\ *n* : a bill of lading issued by an air carrier

airway distance *n* : the distance by air between two points over a course chosen with due regard to airway aids and regulations, available equipment, and known hazards

air well *n* : a court enclosed within walls and open at the top for supplying air to windows — called also *air shaft*

air wing *n* : an organizational unit of military aircraft that may number up to 75 airplanes

air-wise \ˈ⸗ˌ⸗\ *adj* : skillful or experienced in aviation

airworthiness \ˈ⸗ˌ⸗⸗⸗\ *n* -ES : the quality or state of being airworthy

airworthy \ˈ⸗ˌ⸗⸗\ *adj*, *of an aircraft* : fit for operation in the air : able to bear the strains of flight and to withstand storms

airy \ˈa(a)rē, ˈer-, -ri\ *adj* -ER/-EST [ME, fr. ³*air* + -*y*] **1 a** : relating or belonging to air : ATMOSPHERIC ⟨the ~ clouds⟩ **b** : high in the air : LOFTY ⟨~ regions⟩ **c** : performed in air : AERIAL ⟨~ flight⟩ **2** : consisting of air ⟨~ phantoms⟩ **3 a** : resembling air in its immaterial character : without reality or solid foundation : EMPTY: (1) : TRIFLING, FLIPPANT (2) : VISIONARY **b** : resembling air in elasticity or lightness : AIRLIKE: (1) : light in movement or manner : SPRIGHTLY, VIVACIOUS (2) : delicate and graceful as air : ETHEREAL **4** : open to the free circulation of air : exposed to the air : BREEZY ⟨~ hillside⟩ **5** : having an affected manner : being in the habit of putting on airs : affectedly grand ⟨~ condescension⟩ **6** *of a sign of the zodiac* : having a hot and moist complexion

airy disk *n*, *usu cap A* : the bright central spot in the system of diffraction rings formed by an optical system with light from a point source (as a star)

airy-fairy \ˈ⸗⸗ˈ⸗⸗\ *adj* **1** : FAIRYLIKE, DELICATE ⟨*airy-fairy* beings⟩ **2** : VISIONARY ⟨*airy-fairy* notions⟩

¹ais \ˈās\ *n*, *pl* **ais** *usu cap* **1 a** : a people in the Indian river valley, Florida, thought to have been Muskogean **b** : a member of such people **2** : the language of the Ais people

²ais *pl of* AI

ais·chro·la·treia \ˌīskrōlə·ˈtrīə\ *n* -S [Gk *aischros* shameful, ugly (fr. *aischos* disgrace) + -*latreia* -latry; prob. akin to OE *ǣwisc*, *ǣwisce* disgrace, shame, *ǣwan* to despise, MHG *eisch* ugly, MLG *eichelen*, *ēchelen* to disgust, Goth *aiwiski* disgrace] : worship of filth : cult of the obscene

aise·weed \ˈāzˌwēd\ *n* [perh. fr. F *aise* ease (fr. OF, comfort) + E *weed* — more at EASE] : GOUTWEED

aisle \ˈīl, ˈīəl\ *n* -S [alter. (influenced by F *aile* wing, aisle) of earlier *isle*, alter. (influenced by *isle* "island") of ME *ile*, alter. (influenced by ME *ile* isle, island) of *ele*, *eile*, fr. MF *ele*, *aile* wing, wing of a building, fr. L *ala* wing, armpit; akin to OE *eaxl* shoulder, ON *öxl*, OHG *ahsala*, L *axilla* armpit — more at AXIS] **1** : the side of a church nave separated by piers from the nave proper — see BASILICA illustration **2** [influenced in meaning by *alley*] : a passage between sections of seats **3** : a long high narrow passage in a cave

aisle seat *n* : a seat on or next to an aisle

aisle·way \ˈ⸗ˌ⸗\ *n* : a cleared passageway (as in a store or warehouse) for inside traffic

ais·ling \ˈīshliŋ\ *n*, *pl* **aislings** \-ŋz\ *or* **ais·lingi** \-ŋē\ [IrGael, dream, vision, fr. OIr *aislinge*] : a poetical or dramatic description or representation of a vision

aissawa *usu cap*, *var of* ISAWA

ais·sor \ˈīsə(r)\ *n*, *pl* **aissor** *or* **aissors** *usu cap* **1** : a people in parts of Asiatic Turkey and in Persia calling themselves Syrians and believed to be descended from the Chaldeans **2** : a member of the Aissor people

¹ais·to·pod \āˈistəˌpäd\ *adj* [NL *Aistopoda*] : of or relating to the Aistopoda

²aistopod \"\ *n* -S : an amphibian or fossil of the Aistopoda

ais·top·o·da \ˌāsˈtäpədə\ *n pl*, *cap* [NL, fr. Gk *aistos* unseen + NL -*poda*] : an order or other group of extinct Carboniferous and Permian lepospondylous amphibians having a snakelike body and no limbs

¹ait \ˈāt\ *n* -S [ME *ait*, *eit*, fr. (assumed) OE *ǣget*, alter. of OE *īegoth*, *īgeth*, *īget*, fr. *īeg*, *īg*, *ēg* — more at ISLAND] *dial chiefly Brit* : a little island

²ait \"\ *n* [ME (northern dial.) *ate*, fr. OE *āte* — more at OAT] *Scot* : OAT

aitch \ˈāch\ *n* -ES [earlier *ache*, fr. F *hache*, fr. (assumed) VL *hacca*] : the letter *h*

aitch·bone \ˈāchˌbōn\ *also* **edge·bone** \ˈej,-\ *n* [ME *hachboon*, (assumed) *achebon*, alter. (resulting from incorrect division of *a nachebon*) of (assumed) *nachebon*, fr. *nache*, *nage* buttock (fr. MF, fr. LL *natica*, fr. L *natis*) + *bon* bone — more at NATES] **1** : the hipbone esp. of cattle **2** : the cut of beef containing the aitchbone

ait·en \ˈātᵊn\ *adj* [²*ait* + -*en*] *Scot* : OATEN

aith \ˈāth\ *n* [ME (northern dial.) *ath*, fr. OE *āth* — more at OATH] *chiefly Scot* : OATH

ai·thoch·roi \īˈthäkrəˌwī\ *n pl* [NL, fr. Gk *aithos* reddish brown + NL -*chroi* (fr. Gk *chrōa* color)] : people having dark red-brown skin

aitio- — see ETIO-

aitiology *var of* ETIOLOGY

ai·ti·on \ˈīd·ēˌän\ *n*, *pl* **ai·tia** \-ēə\ *or* **aiti·ons** [Gk *aition* cause, fr. neut. sing. of *aitios* responsible; akin to Gk *aitia* cause — more at EMULATE] : a tale devised to explain the origin of a religious observance

ait·ken·ite \ˈātkəˌnīt, ˈākə-\ *n* -S *usu cap* [Robert *Aitken* †1873 Scot. clergyman + E -*ite*] : a follower of Aitken in desiring to introduce into the Anglican Church certain Methodist practices and views esp. in regard to conversion

ait·meal \ˈāt,-\ *n* -S [²*ait* + *meal*] *Scot* : OATMEAL

ai·toff projection \ˈīˌtȯf-\ *or* **ai·toff's projection** \-fs-\ *n*, *usu cap A* [after David *Aitoff* †1933 Russ. geographer] : an equal-area projection similar in appearance to the Mollweide projection but with curved parallels

ai·tu \ˈīˌtü\ *n* -S [Samoan *āitu*] *Samoa* : SPIRIT, DEMON

¹ai·tu·ta·ki·an \ˌīd·əˌtäkēən\ *adj*, *usu cap* [*Aitutaki*, one of the Cook islands, So. Pacific ocean + E -*an*] : of or concerning Aitutaki Island

²aitutakian \"\ *n* -S *usu cap* : a native or inhabitant of Aitutaki Island

ai·ver *or* **aver** \ˈāvər\ *n* -S [ME *aver*, *aveyr* property, goods, fr. MF *aver*, *aveir*, fr. OF, fr. *aver*, *aveir* to have, fr. L *habēre* — more at HABIT] *now chiefly Scot* : a draft animal; *esp* : an old workhorse

aiwain *var of* AJOWAN

aix \ˈīks\ *n*, *cap* [NL, fr. Gk, a water fowl] : a genus of short-legged perching ducks having brilliant multicolored plumage in the male and including the mandarin duck and the wood duck (sense 1)

ai·zle \ˈāzəl, ˈaiz-\ *n* -S [ME *isel*, fr. OE *ysel*, *ysle* — more at EMBER] *chiefly Scot* : a glowing coal : SPARK, EMBER

ai·zo·a·ce·ae \āˌīzōˈwāsēˌē\ *n pl*, *cap* [NL, fr. *Aizoon*, type genus + -*aceae*] : a family of herbs or small shrubs (order Caryophyllales) with solitary or cymose flowers and capsular fruit (as the carpetweed and the fig marigolds) — **ai·zo·a·ceous** \āˌīzəˈwāshəs, ˌā,ī-\ *adj*

ai·zo·on \ˌā,īˈzōˌän\ *n*, *cap* [NL, fr. Gk *aei* always + NL -*zoon*] : a small genus (the type of the family Aizoaceae) of low-growing evergreen spreading plants found in Africa, Australia, and the Mediterranean region having fleshy entire leaves and containing some species that are cultivated for their yellow flowers or silvery foliage

AJ *abbr* associate justice

ajan·gle \əˈ-\ *adj* [¹*a-* + *jangle*, v.] : JANGLING ⟨you can hear the chains ~ —R.L.Stevenson⟩

¹ajar \əˈjä(r), -ā(r\ *adv* (*or adj*) [earlier *on char*, fr. *on* + *char* turn — more at CHARE] : slightly open ⟨the door stood ~⟩

²ajar \"\ *adj* [¹*a-* + *jar* (discord)] : in a state of discord ⟨~ with the world⟩

aja·ri \ˌäzhəˈrē\ *n* -S [prob. modif. of Pg *ajará*, fr. Tupi] : ¹TIMBO 1

ajax powder \ˈāˌjaks·ˌ-\ *n*, *usu cap A* [after *Ajax*, one of the Greek heroes in Homer's *Iliad*, possessed of great stature and strength, fr. L, fr. Gk *Aias*] : an explosive used in coal mining consisting chiefly of nitroglycerin, potassium perchlorate, ammonium oxalate, and wood flour

ajee \əˈjē\ *var of* **agee**

aji \äˈhē\ *n* -S [AmerSp *aji*, fr. Taino *axí*] *in Spanish America* : a plant of the genus *Capsicum*

aji·mez \ˌäkēˈmāth, -ās\ *n* -ES [Sp, fr. Ar *ash-shammīs* the ajimez] : a twin window derived from Arab architecture consisting usu. of two narrow windows separated by a slim mullion

ajin·gle \əˈ-\ *adj* [¹*a-* + *jingle*, v.] : JINGLING

ajit·ter \əˈ-\ *adj* [¹*a-* + *jitter*, v.] : JITTERY ⟨all ~ with fear —*Harper's*⟩

aji·va \əˈjēvə\ *n* -S *sometimes cap* [Skt *ajīva* lifeless, fr. *a-* ²*a-* + *jīva* living] *Jainism* : inanimate matter — opposed to *jiva*

ajivika \äˈjēvəkə\ *n* -S [Skt *ājīvika*, lit., following special rules with regard to livelihood, fr. *ājīva* livelihood, fr. *ājīvati* he lives on, fr. *ā* toward + *jīvati* he lives, fr. *jīva* living — more at ACHARYA, QUICK] : a member of a nontheistic religious sect greatly resembling Jainism that was founded by the Indian teacher Maskarin Gosala, a contemporary of the Buddha and Mahavira, and that flourished from the 6th to the 3d centuries B.C. as a rival of Buddhism and Jainism

aj·ma·line \ˈajməˌlēn\ *n* -S [origin unknown] : an amber crystalline alkaloid $C_{20}H_{26}N_2O_2$ obtained from trees or shrubs of the genus *Rauwolfia*, esp. from an Asiatic shrub (*R. serpentina*)

aj·mer \ˈəjˌme(ə)r, -mi(ə)r\ *adj*, *usu cap* [fr. *Ajmer*, India] : of or from the city of Ajmer, India : of the kind or style prevalent in Ajmer

ajo \ˈäˌhō\ *n* -S [Sp, fr. L *allium*, *alium* — more at ALLIUM] *chiefly Southwest* : GARLIC 1

ajoint \əˈ-\ *adj* [¹*a-* + *joint*] : twisting about as though on a pivot

ajon·jo·li \ˌäkȯnkōˈlē\ *n* -S [Sp *ajonjolí*, fr. colloq. Ar *jonjolīl* (classical Ar *juljulān*)] : SESAME 1

a jour \äˈzhü(ə)r\ *or* **ajou·ré** \ˌäˌzhu̇ˈrā\ *adj* [*a jour* fr. F *à jour*, lit., toward day; *ajouré* fr. F, fr. *ajour* perforation (fr. *à jour*) + -*é* (fr. L -*atus* -ate)] : pierced, cut away, or made translucent in such a way as to form a design : having figured openwork : decorated with translucent, pierced, or openwork designs — used of carving, metalwork, lace, drawnwork, or cutwork

ajou·ri·sé \(ˈ)äˌzhu̇rəˈzā\ *adj* [F, fr. *ajour* + -*isé* -ized] : OPEN-WORKED

aj·o·wan \ˈajəˌwän\ *also* **ai·wain** \ˈīˌwīn\ *n* -S [origin unknown] : the fruit of a plant (*Carum copticum*) used both as a medicine and as a condiment

ajowan oil *n* : an almost colorless essential oil containing thymol obtained from ajowan

aju·ga \ˈajəgə\ *n*, *cap* [NL, fr. ²*a-* + -*juga* (fr. L *jugum* yoke) — more at YOKE] : a large genus of herbs (family Labiatae) having verticillate flowers and a corolla with a short upper lip — see ¹BUGLE

ajutage *var of* ADJUTAGE

aka \ˈäkə\ *n* -S [Maori] *NewZeal* : any of several species of woody vines of the genus *Metrosideros*

aka·akai \ˌäˌkäˈäˈkī\ *n* -S [Hawaiian] : a stout European bulrush (*Scirpus lacustris*) adventive in Hawaii and used for making mats and baskets

akal \əˈkäl\ *n*, *usu cap* [Panjabi *Akāl*, fr. Skt *akāla* timeless, fr. *a-* ²*a-* + *kāla* time; perh. akin to Skt *carati* he moves, goes — more at WHEEL] *Sikhism* : the immortal or timeless one — an epithet of the Deity

aka·la \əˈkälə\ *also* **ake·la** \əˈkālə\ *n* -S [Hawaiian] : a shrub or climber (*Rubus macraei*) of Hawaii with very large red or purplish raspberrylike edible fruit

aka·li \əˈkälē\ *n* -S *usu cap* [Panjabi *Akālī*, fr. *Akāl*] : one of a militant sect of Sikhs

aka·mai \ˈäkäˈmī\ *adj* [Hawaiian] *Hawaii* : SMART, INTELLIGENT

aka·ma·tsu \ˌäkəˈmät(ˌ)sü\ *n* -S [Jap, fr. *aka* red + *matsu* pine] : JAPANESE RED PINE

aka·mu·shi mite \ˌäkəˈmüshē-\ *n* [Jap, fr. *aka* red + *mushi* bug] : TSUTSUGAMUSHI MITE

akan \ˈäˌkän\ *n*, *pl* **akan** *or* **akans** *cap* **1** : a Kwa language spoken over a wide area in Ghana and extending into the Ivory Coast — see FANTI, TWI **2** : the Akan-speaking peoples including the Akim, Akwapim, Ashanti, and Fanti

aka·roa \ˌäkəˈrōə\ *n* -S [Maori] : RIBBON TREE

akar·y·ote \(ˈ)āˈkarēˌōt\ *n* -S [modif. of NL *akaryoton*, fr. ²*a-* + *karyoton* nucleated cell, fr. Gk *karyōton*, neut. of *karyōtos* nut-shaped, fr. *karyon* nut — more at KARY-] : a cell lacking a nucleus

akathist *or* **akathistos** *usu cap*, *var of* ACATHISTUS

akawai *usu cap* [Carib] *var of* ACAWAI

¹ake (āk) *obs var of* ACHE

²ake \ˈäkä\ *adv* [Maori] *Austral* : FOREVER

ake·ake \ˌäkēˈäkē\ *or* **ake** \ˈäkē\ *n* -S [Maori] **1** : a small tropical tree (*Dodonaea viscosa*) with young twigs compressed or triangular and viscid **2** : either of two New Zealand trees (*Olearia avicenniaefolia* and *O. traversii*)

ake·bi \ˈäkəbē\ *n* -S [Jap] : an eastern Asiatic vine (*Akebia quinata*) valued for its oily seeds and as material for basketmaking

ake·bia \əˈkēbēə\ *n*, *cap* [NL, fr. Jap *akebi*] : a small genus of woody vines (family Lardizabalaceae) of eastern Asia having racemose purple-brown flowers and an oblong purple-violet bananalike berry — see AKEBI

akee *or* **ack·ee** \ˈaˌkē, aˈkē\ *n* -S [Kru *ā-kee*] : a tree (*Blighia sapida*) of the family Sapindaceae native to tropical West Africa and grown throughout the tropics for the white or yellowish spongy flesh of the aril which is attached to each of the many shiny black seeds and which is edible when cooked although other parts of the fruit esp. when fallen, unripe, or discolored and the seeds have been reported as deadly poisonous

ake·ki \ˈäkə(ˌ)kē\ *n* -S [Jap] : HIBA ARBORVITAE

¹a·ke·la *var of* AKALA

²ake·la \əˈkēlə\ *n* -S [after *Akela*, wolf-pack leader in Rudyard Kipling's *Jungle Book*] : a leader of a cub scout pack

akeldama *sometimes cap*, *var of* ACELDAMA

ake·ley \əˈkēlē\ *n* -S [modif. of NL *aquilegia*, *aquileia*] : any of several plants of the genus *Aquilegia*

akene *var of* ACHENE

ak·e·no·be·ite \,akə'nōbē,īt\ *n* -s [*Akenobe* district, Japan, its locality + E *-ite*] **:** a crisscross-granular leucocratic differentiation rock composed of oligoclase, orthoclase, a little biotite, and in the interstices considerable quartz

ake·pi·ro \,äkə'pi(,)rō\ *n* -s [Maori] **:** a showy New Zealand tree (*Olearia furfuracea*) with silvery leaves

aker·i·dae \ə'kerə,dē\ *n pl, cap* [NL, fr. *Akera*, type genus + *-idae*] **:** a family of gastropod mollusks comprising typical bubble shells — see HAMINOEA

aker·ite \'ōkə,rīt, 'ak-\ *n* -s [G *åkerit*, fr. *Åker*, former district near Oslo, Norway + G *-it* -ite] **:** a quartz-syenite rock containing oligoclase and augite besides soda-microcline

aker·man·ite \'ōkə(r)mə,nīt, 'ak-\ *n* -s [G *åkermanit*, fr. Richard *Åkerman*, 19th cent. Swedish mineralogist + G *-it* -ite] **:** a mineral $Ca_2MgSi_2O_7$ that consists of calcium magnesium silicate and is an end-member of the melilite series

akh \äk\ *n* -s *often cap* [alternate transliteration of Egypt *ꜣḫ(w)*] *Egyptian relig* **:** the spirit of a deceased person conceived as gloriously transfigured so as to reflect the deeds of the person in life

akha \'äkə\ *n, pl* **akha** *usu cap* **:** the most southerly group of Lolo-speaking Tibeto-Burman people forming a large part of the hill tribes of Shan State, Burma, and scattered in adjoining sections of southern Yunnan province of southern China, Laos, and northern Thailand

ak·his·sar \'äk(h)i¦sär\ *n* -s *usu cap* [after *Akhisar*, town in W Turkey near Izmir (Smyrna)] **:** a kind of heavy modern carpet made at Akhisar, near Izmir, Turkey

akh·mim·ic *also* **ach·mim·ic** \äk'mimik\ *n* -s *usu cap* [Ar *Aḫmīm* (of Hamitic origin; akin to Copt *Shmīm* Akhmimic, *Ahmīm* Egypt *ḫnty-mn*) + E *-ic*] **:** an Upper Egyptian dialect of Coptic

akhrot \ə'krōt\ *n* -s [Hindi *akhrot*; akin to Skt *akṣoṭa* walnut, Sindhi *akhiroṭu*] *India* **:** the English walnut tree

akhund·za·da \,ä,kün'zädə\ *n* -s [Hindi *ākhūndzāda*, fr. Per, fr. *ākhūnd* teacher + *zāda* son] *India* **:** the son of a head officer — used as a title

akia \ä'kēə\ *n* -s [Hawaiian] **:** any of several shrubs of the genus *Wikstroemia* with bark that is used as a fish poison

akim \'ä,kim, 'ä,chim\ *n, pl* **akim** *or* **akims** *usu cap* [Akan] **1 :** an African Negro Akan-speaking people of Ghana **2 :** a member of the Akim people

¹akim·bo \ə'kim(,)bō\ *adv* [ME *in kenebowe*] **:** in or into a position in which the hand is placed usu. on or near the hip so that the elbow projects outward at an angle ⟨to stand ~ surveying their little plots of land —John Galsworthy⟩ ⟨her arms went ~ on her hips —Donn Byrne⟩

²akimbo \"\ *adj* **1 :** placed akimbo ⟨with one elbow ~⟩ ⟨she stood with arms ~⟩ — usu. used postpositively **2 :** set in a bent position ⟨a tailor sitting with legs ~⟩ ⟨his hands folded under his head, his elbows ~⟩

akin \ə'kin\ *adj* [¹*a-* + *kin*] **1 a :** related by blood **:** of the same kind or family ⟨they discovered that they were ~ — cousins, in fact⟩ — used postpositively or predicatively **b :** descending from a common ancestor or prototype ⟨the dog and fox are closely ~⟩ **c :** ¹COGNATE 2 **2 :** showing the same nature **:** marked by similarity of essential characteristics suggesting a close relationship ⟨palsied by a feeling ~ to terror —Sheridan Le Fanu⟩ ⟨a state of feverish disorder ~ to that of a disturbed anthill —P.A.Sorokin⟩ **3 :** related and compatible, sympathetic, or close ⟨consanguinity there may have been . . . but the two were never spiritually ~ —Elinor Wylie⟩ **syn** see LIKE

aki·ne·sia \,ä,kī'nēzh(ē)ə, -,kə'-\ *n* -s [NL, fr. Gk *akinēsia* absence of motion, fr. *a-* ²*a-* + *-kinēsia* -kinesia] **:** loss or impairment of voluntary activity (as of a muscle or a death-feigning animal) — called also *akinesis*

aki·ne·sis \-nēsəs\ *n, pl* **akine·ses** *also* **aky·ne·sis** *or* **akyne·ses** \-ē,sēz\ [NL, fr. ²*a-* + *-kinesis*] **1 :** AKINESIA **2 :** AMITOSIS **3 :** a state of rest or nervous inhibition of muscular activity brought on by contact stimuli or experimental removal of the antennae of an insect

ak·i·nete \(')ā'kī,nēt, 'akə,-\ *n* -s [Gk *akinētos* motionless, fr. *a-* ²*a-* + *kinētos* moving, fr. *kinein* to move; akin to Gk *kiein* to go — more at HIGHT] *in certain algae* **:** a thick-walled single-celled nonmotile asexual resting spore formed by the thickening of the parent cell wall, corresponding to the chlamydospore of many fungi, and usu. germinating directly into a new filament — see APLANOSPORE

aki·net·ic \,ā,kī'ned·ik, -,kə'-\ *adj* [²*a-* + *kinetic*] **1 :** of, relating to, or affected by akinesia **2 :** AMITOTIC

¹aki·ta \ä'kēd·ə\ *n* -s [Jap] **:** a Japanese breed of spitzlike dogs

²aki·ta \"\ *adj, usu cap* [fr. *Akita*, Japan] **:** of or from the city of Akita, Japan **:** of the kind or style prevalent in Akita

ak·ka \'äkə, 'a-\ *n, pl* **akka** *or* **akkas** *usu cap* **1 :** a Pygmy people of the Vele basin in the Belgian Congo **2 :** a member of the Akka people

¹ak·ka·di·an \ə'kādēən, a'-, ä'-, -käd-\ *or* **accadian** *adj, usu cap* [*Akkad*, northern division of ancient Babylonia + E *-ian*] **1 :** of or relating to Akkad, the Accad of Gen 10:10, identified by some with Agade, near Sippar, north of Babylon **2** *archaic* **:** SUMERIAN **3 :** of or belonging to the Semitic inhabitants of central Mesopotamia before 2000 B.C. — compare ASSYRIAN, BABYLONIAN, SUMERIAN **4 :** of or relating to Akkadian

²akkadian \"\ *n* -s *cap* **1** *archaic* **:** SUMERIAN **2 :** one of the Semitic inhabitants of central Mesopotamia before 2000 B.C. **3 a :** an ancient Semitic language of Mesopotamia used from about the 28th to the 1st century B.C. as the vehicle of a widely varied literature in cuneiform writing — see ASSYRIAN, BABYLONIAN **b :** the earliest known stage of this language, used by the Akkadians **:** old Akkadian

ak·kum \'äkəm\ *n* -s [Heb *'akkum*, an acrostic (its details obscured by transliteration) of *'ōbhedh kōkhābhīm ūmazzālōth* worshiper of stars and constellations] **1 :** a Chaldean star worshiper **2** *in the Talmud* **:** HEATHEN, IDOLATER

aklan \'ä,klän\ *also* **akla·non** \'äklə,nän\ *n, pl* **aklan** *or* **aklans** *also* **aklanon** *or* **aklanons** *usu cap* [Aklan] **1 a :** a predominantly Christian Bisayan people on Panay Island, Philippines **b :** a member of such people **2 :** the Austronesian language of the Aklan people

akle *n* -s [var. of *acle*] **:** ACLE 3

ako·lu·thia *or* **ako·lou·thia** \,äkə(,)lü'thēə\ *n* -s [MGk *akolouthia*, fr. Gk, sequence, fr. *akolouthos* following, fr. *ha-, a-* together + *keleuthos* path; akin to Gk *homos* same and to Lith *keliáuti* to travel and perh. to Gk *kellein* to drive — more at SAME, HOLD] **1 :** a set order or traditional arrangement of a religious service in the Eastern Church **2 :** DIVINE OFFICE

akon·tae \ə'kän,tē\ *n pl, cap* [NL, fr. ²*a-* + *-kontae* (fr. Gk *kontos* punting pole)] *in former classifications* **:** a division of algae coextensive with the order Zygnematales

ako·ri \'äkərē\ *n* -s [prob. native name in western Africa] **1 :** a porous coral formerly used for ornaments by West African Negroes and Samoans **2 :** any one of several baser substitutes for akori

akosmism *var of* ACOSMISM

akr- *or* **akro-** — see ACR-

akra *also* **ac·cra** \ə'krä, a'-, ä'-\ *n, pl* **akra** *or* **akras** *also* **accra** *or* **accras** *usu cap* [Akra] **:** GA

ak·ro·chor·dite \,akrō'kȯr,dīt\ *n* -s [Gk *akrochordōn* wart + E *-ite*] **:** a mineral $MgMn_4(AsO_4)_2(OH)_4.4H_2O$(?) consisting of a hydrous basic manganese magnesium arsenate occurring in reddish brown rounded aggregates (hardness 3, sp. gr. 3.2)

ak·ron \'akrən\ *adj, usu cap* [fr. *Akron*, Ohio] **:** of or from the city of Akron, Ohio ⟨*Akron* factories⟩ **:** of the kind or style prevalent in Akron

ak·ro·po·di·on \,akrə'pōdēən, -ē,än\ *n* -s [NL, fr. Gk, dim. of *akropous* extremity of the leg, foot, fr. *akr-* acr- + *pous* foot — more at FOOT] **:** the most prominent point on the back of the heel

akroter *or* **akroterion** *var of* ACROTERION

aksumite *usu cap, var of* AXUMITE

ak·to·graph \'aktə,graf\ *n* -s [G, fr. L *actus* (past part. of *agere* to do, drive) + G *-graph* — more at AGENT] **:** a device for recording the movements of a caged but not restrained experimental animal

aku \'ä(')kü\ *n* -s [Hawaiian] *Hawaii* **:** OCEANIC BONITO

akua *var of* ATUA

aku·am·mine \,a,kü'a,mēn\ *n* -s [Tshi *akuamma* owala + E *-ine*] **:** a crystalline alkaloid $C_{22}H_{28}N_2O_4$ found in the seeds of a West African tree (*Picralima nitida*) of the dogbane family

aku·le \ä'külē\ *also* **atu·le** \ä't-\ *n* -s [Hawaiian] **:** BIG-EYED SCAD

akund \'ä,künd\ *n* -s [Hindi] **:** MUDAR

akvavit *var of* AQUAVIT

akwa·'ala \,äkwə'älə\ *n, pl* **akwa·'ala** *or* **akwa·'alas** *usu cap* **1 a :** an Indian people of Lower California, Mexico **b :** a member of such people **2 :** the Yuman language of the Akwa'ala people

akwa·pim \'äkwə,pim\ *n, pl* **akwapim** *or* **akwapims** *usu cap* [Akwapim *akuapem*] **1 :** an African Negro Akan-speaking people of Ghana **2 :** a member of the Akwapim people

akynesis *var of* AKINESIS

al \'äl\ *n* -s [Hindi *āl*] **:** INDIAN MULBERRY 1

al- — see AD-

¹-al \əl, ᵊl\ *adj suffix* [ME *-al, -el*, fr. OF & L; OF *-al, -el*, fr. L *-alis*] **:** of, relating to, or characterized by ⟨direction*al*⟩ ⟨fiction*al*⟩ ⟨hormon*al*⟩ ⟨organization*al*⟩ ⟨spectr*al*⟩ ⟨tid*al*⟩

²-al \"\ *n suffix* -s [ME *-aille*, fr. OF, fr. L *-alia*, neut. pl. of *-alis*] **:** action or process ⟨bestow*al*⟩ ⟨rehears*al*⟩ ⟨withdraw*al*⟩

³-al \,al, ,ȯl, ᵊl; *in sense 2* " *or* -,ōl *or* -,äl\ *n suffix* -s [F, fr. *alcool* alcohol, fr. ML *alcohol*] **1 a :** aldehyde ⟨butan*al*⟩ ⟨salicyl*al*⟩ — compare GENEVA SYSTEM **b :** acetal ⟨butyr*al*⟩ **2 :** pharmaceutical product ⟨barbit*al*⟩

al *abbr* **1** alias **2** alley

AL *abbr* **1** air letter **2** all lengths **3** [L *anno lucis*] in the year of light **4** autograph letter

Al *symbol* aluminum

a la *or* **à la** \¦ä(,)lä, ¦ä(,)lä, -lə *or, esp in some of the most frequently used phrases so beginning,* ,alə *or* ¦a(,)la\ [F *à la*] **:** after the fashion of **:** in the manner of — used freely with English nouns regardless of gender or number ⟨dangling from the rafters *a la* Douglas Fairbanks⟩ ⟨publicity shots *a la* Hollywood⟩ ⟨reciter of . . . "The Happy Prince", done *a la* Emlyn Williams and Dickens — Lewis Nichols⟩

¹ala \'ālə\ *n, pl* **alae** \'ā,lē\ [L — more at AISLE] **1 :** a wing ⟨an insect ~⟩ or a winglike process or part ⟨the *alae* of the nose⟩ ⟨the lateral *alae* of a nematode worm⟩ **2 :** one of the two side petals in a papilionaceous corolla **3 :** the membranous expansion found in some seeds **4 :** the basal lobes in the leaves of mosses

²ala \'ä(,)lä\ *or* **alal** \'ä,läl\ *n* -s [Sumerian *a-lal*] **:** a large ancient Sumerian drum

al·a·ba·do \,alə'bä(,)dō\ *n* -s [MexSp, fr. Sp, past part. of *alabar* to praise, fr. LL *alapari* to boast, perh. fr. L *alapa* slap on the cheek] **:** a Mexican hymn

¹al·a·bama \,alə'bamə *sometimes* -ämə *or* -āmə *esp in places distant from the state of Alabama; attrib* ¦==¦==\ *also* **al·i·ba·mu** \-(,)mü\ *n, pl* **alabama** *or* **alabamas** *also* **alibamu** *or* **alibamus** *usu cap* [prob. fr. Choctaw *alba ayamule* I make a clearing] **1 a :** a Muskogean people of central Alabama and of the Creek confederacy **b :** a member of such people **2 :** the language of the Alabama people

²alabama \"\ *adj, usu cap* [fr. *Alabama*, state in the southern U.S., prob. fr. the *Alabama* river, prob. fr. the *Alabama* people] **:** of or from the state of Alabama ⟨*Alabama* highways⟩ **:** of the kind or style prevalent in Alabama **:** ALABAMIAN

³alabama \"\ *n, cap* [NL, fr. *Alabama*, state] **:** a genus of moths (family Noctuidae) including a species of which the larva is the destructive cotton leafworm

alabama terrapin *or* **alabama turtle** *also* **alabama slider** *n, usu cap A* **:** a freshwater tortoise (*Pseudemys alabamensis*) having a range extending from the Gulf coast of Florida to Louisiana

¹al·a·bam·i·an \¦==¦=mēən\ *also* **alabaman** *adj, usu cap* [*Alabama* + E *-ian* or *-an*] **1 :** of, relating to, or characteristic of the state of Alabama **2 :** of, relating to, or characteristic of Alabamians

²alabamian \"\ *also* **alabaman** *n* -s *cap* **:** a native or resident of Alabama

al·a·bam·ine \,==¦=,mēn, -,mən\ *n* -s [*Alabama* (state) + *-ine*] **:** chemical element 85 — a name now superseded by *astatine*

al·a·ban·dite \,alə'ban,dīt\ *n* -s [G *alabandit*, fr. *Alabanda*, town in Turkey, its locality + G *-it* -ite] **:** manganese sulfide MnS usu. in iron-black massive form with cubic cleavage

al·a·barch \'alə,bärk\ *n* -s [L *alabarches*, fr. Gk *alabarchēs*, alter. of *arabarchēs*, fr. *Arabia* + Gk *-archēs* -arch] **:** the chief magistrate of the Jews at Alexandria under the Ptolemies and the Roman Empire

¹al·a·bas·ter \'alə,bastə(r), -aas-, -ais-, -ås- *also* ,==¦==\ *n* -s [ME *alabastre*, fr. MF, fr. L *alabaster*, *alabastrum*, fr. Gk *alabastros*, *alabastron* alabaster, vase made of alabaster] **1 a :** a compact variety of fine-textured gypsum usu. white and translucent but sometimes yellow, red, or gray that is carved into objects (as vases and mantel ornaments) **b :** a hard compact variety of calcite or aragonite that is translucent and sometimes banded — called also *Mexican onyx, onyx marble, oriental alabaster* **2 :** a pale yellowish pink to yellowish gray — called also *tilleul buff, white jade*

²alabaster \"\ *adj* **:** of or resembling alabaster; *specif* **:** having a nearly white color and a light-diffusing surface

alabaster tint *n* **:** a bluish white

al·a·bas·tine \¦==¦=strən\ *adj* [*alabaster* + *-ine*] *archaic* **:** of or like alabaster

al·a·bas·trum \,==¦=strəm\ *or* **al·a·bas·tron** \-,strän, -,strən\ *or* **al·a·bas·tos** \-,stäs, -stəs\ *n, pl* **alabas·tra** \-strə\ *or* **alabastrums** *or* **alabastrons** [L & Gk; L *alabastrum*, fr. Gk *alabastron*, *alabastos* — more at ALABASTER] **:** an ancient Greek or Roman jar for oils, ointments, or perfumes having a flattened lip with narrow orifice and an elongated body rounded at the bottom

alabastrum

alablaster *obs var of* ALABASTER

ala·ca·luf *or* **ala·ka·luf** *also* **ali·ku·luf** \¦aləkə¦lüf, ¦äl-\ *n, pl* **alacaluf** *or* **alacalufs** *or* **alakaluf** *or* **alakalufs** *usu cap* [Sp & Yahgan; Sp *alacaluf*, prob. fr. Yahgan (*Innalum*) *Aala Kaluf*, lit., western men with mussel-shell knives] **1 a :** a people of Tierra del Fuego **b :** a member of such people **2 :** a language of the Alacaluf people

a la carte \¦ä(,)lə¦kärt, -kät; *see* A LA\ *adj* [F *à la carte*] **:** by the card **:** by the bill of fare — used of a meal that is ordered dish by dish each of which has a separate price ⟨an *a la carte* dinner⟩

alack \ə'lak\ *interj* [ME *alacke*, prob. fr. *a* ah! + *lack* fault, loss — more at LACK] *archaic* — used to express sorrow or regret or formerly reproach ⟨of reading, ~, but little —H.J.Laski⟩

alack·a·day \ə'lakə,dā\ *also* **alack the day** *interj, archaic* — used to express sorrow or deprecation

al·a·cre·a·tine \,alə'krēə,tēn\ *n* -s [ISV *alanine* + *creatine*] **:** a white crystalline acid $C_4H_9N_3O_2$ formed from alanine and cyanamide; α-guanidino-propionic acid

alacrious *adj* [L *alacr-*, *alacer* swift, eager + E *-ious*] *obs* **:** BRISK, LIVELY — **alacriously** *adv, obs*

alac·ri·tous \ə'lakrəd·əs\ *adj* [*alacrity* + *-ous*] **:** characterized by alacrity

alac·ri·ty \ə'lakrəd·ē, -ətē, -i\ *n* -ES [L *alacritas*, fr. *alacr-*, *alacer* quick, lively, eager, happy + *-itas* -ity; akin to OE & OHG *ellen* zeal, courage, ON *eljan* power, Goth *aljan* zeal and perh. to L *adolēre* to burn up— more at ALTAR] **1 :** a promptness in responding **:** cheerful readiness **:** BRISKNESS, EAGERNESS ⟨to accept with ~⟩ ⟨the ~ with which he sprang from the vehicle —T.L.Peacock⟩

alac·ta·ga \ə'laktəgə\ *syn of* ALLACTAGA

alae *pl of* ALA

al·a·gui·lac \,aləgwē'läk\ *n, pl* **alaguilac** *or* **alaguilacs** *usu cap* [Sp, of AmerInd origin] **1 a :** a Nahuatlan people in eastern Guatemala **b :** a member of such people **2 :** the Uto-Aztecan language of the Alaguilac people

alai·mus \ə'līməs, a'-\ *n, cap* [NL, fr. ²*a-* + Gk *laimos* throat, gullet] **:** a nearly cosmopolitan genus of soil nematodes

al·a·ite \'alə,īt\ *n* -s [F *alaïte*, fr. *Alaï* mountains, Kirgiz S.S.R., U.S.S.R., Asia + F *-ite*] **:** a mineral $V_2O_5.H_2O$ consisting of a hydrous vanadium pentoxide occurring in blood-red mossy aggregates

alakaluf *usu cap, var of* ALACALUF

alake \ə'läk\ *chiefly Scot var of* ALACK

a la king \-'kiŋ; *see* A LA\ *adj* [*a la* + *king*] **:** in a cream sauce with mushrooms and pimiento or green peppers ⟨chicken *a la king*⟩ — used after the noun

alal *var of* ALA

ala·lau·wa \,älə'lau̇wə\ *n* -s [Hawaiian] **:** any of several food fishes (genus *Pocacanthus*) widely distributed in tropical seas

ala·lia \(')ā'lālēə, ə'-, -lal-\ *n* -s [NL, fr. ²*a-* + *-lalia*] **:** MUTISM, APHASIA

al·a·lite \'alə,līt\ *n* -s [F, fr. *Ala*, town & valley in northwestern Italy + F *-lite*] **:** a light-green variety of diopside from the Ala valley

al·a·lon·ga \,alə'lȯŋgə\ *also* **al·a·lun·ga** \-ləŋgə\ *or* **al·i·lon·ghi** \-lȯŋgē\ *n* -s [It; *alalonga*, *alalunga* fr. *ala* fin, wing (fr. L *ala* wing) + *longa*, *lunga*, fem. of *longo*, *lungo* long, fr. L *longus*; *alilonghi* fr. *ali* (pl. of *ala*) + *longhi*, pl. of *longo* — more at AISLE, LONG] **:** an albacore (*Thunnus germo*)

al·a·lus \'aləs; (')ā'lāləs, -'lal-\ *n, pl* **al·a·li** \-,lī\ *or* **al·a·loi** \-,lȯi\ [NL, fr. Gk *alalos* speechless, fr. *a-* ²*a-* + *lalos* loquacious] **:** a hypothetical lower order of man lacking the faculty of speech

al·a·man·dine \,alə'man,dēn, -,dən, -,dīn\ *n* -s [alter. of earlier *alabandine* — more at ALMANDINE] **:** GARNET — compare ALMANDINE

alamanni *usu cap, var of* ALEMANNI

alamannian *or* **alamannic** *usu cap, var of* ALEMANNIC

al·a·me·da \,alə'mēdə, -mādə\ *n* -s [Sp, fr. *álamo* poplar] **:** a public walk or promenade; *esp* **:** one with trees on each side

al·a·mi·qui \,aləmə'kē\ *n* -s [AmerSp *almiquí*] **:** a furry long-snouted Cuban insectivore (*Solenodon cubanus*) related to the tenrecs; *also* **:** a closely related Haitian form

al·a·mo \'alə,mō, 'äl-\ *n* -s [Sp *álamo*] *Southwest* **:** a tree of the genus *Populus*; *esp* **:** ASPEN

a la mode \-'mōd; *see* A LA\ *adj* [F *à la mode*] **1 :** according to the fashion **:** in fashion **:** FASHIONABLE ⟨costumes which are *a la mode* in the rest of Europe —Ernest Barker⟩ **2 :** topped or accompanied by a serving of ice cream — used of an individual portion of dessert (as pie)

ala·mode \"\ *n* -s **:** a thin glossy silk fabric (as for hoods and scarfs)

a la mort \-'mȯ(ə)rt; *see* A LA\ *adj* [MF *a la mort* to the death] **:** AMORT

al·a·mos·ite \'alə(,)mō,sīt, ,==¦=,=\ *n* -s [*Álamos*, Sonora, Mexico, its locality + E *-ite*] **:** a monoclinic lead silicate $PbSiO_3$ occurring in white or colorless radiating fibers (hardness 4.5, sp. gr. 6.5)

alamo vine *n* **:** a white-flowered morning-glory (*Ipomoea dissecta*) of the southeastern U.S.

alan *or* **alaunt** *also* **alant** *or* **alaun** *or* **alaund** *n* -s [ME *alaunt*, fr. MF *alant*, *alan*, fr. OSp *alán*, *alano*] **1** *archaic* **:** a large dog used to hunt wild animals **2** *heraldry* **:** a short-eared dog

aland *adv* [ME *aland*, *alande*, fr. ¹*a-* + *land*, acc. & dat. & *lande*, dat. of *land*] **1** *obs* **:** in the land or country **2** *obs* **:** on the land **3** *archaic* **:** to the land **:** ASHORE

alane \ə'lān\ *adj (or adv)* [ME (northern dial.) *alan*, var. of *alon*, *alone* — more at ALONE] *Scot* **:** ALONE

alang \ə'laŋ\ *Scot var of* ALONG

alang–alang \'ä,läŋ'ä,läŋ\ *n* -s [Java & Malay] **:** COGON

alán·gan \ə'laŋ,gän\ *n, pl* **alángan** *or* **alángans** *usu cap* [Tag] **1 :** a pagan people inhabiting the mountainous interior of northern Mindoro Island, Philippines **2 :** a member of the Alángan people

alang grass \'ä,läŋ-\ *n* [short for *alang-alang*] **:** COGON

alan·gi·um \ə'lanjēəm\ *n, cap* [NL, fr. Kanarese *alaṅgi*] **:** a genus (the type of the family Alangiaceae of the order Umbellales) of shrubs and trees found in warm regions of the Old World and having alternate leaves, axillary flowers, and one-seeded drupaceous fruit

al·a·nine \'alə,nēn\ *n* -s [G *alanin*, irreg. fr. *aldehyd* aldehyde + *-in* -ine] **1 :** a white crystalline amino acid $CH_3CH(NH_2)COOH$ that is known in three optically different forms, that is formed by the hydrolysis of proteins and made synthetically, and that takes part in transamination reactions in the living organism; α-amino-propionic acid **2 :** a white crystalline amino acid $NH_2CH_2CH_2COOH$ found in muscle in the form of carnosine and anserine, made synthetically, and used in making pantothenic acid; β-amino-propionic acid — used with an initial Greek beta ⟨β*-alanine*⟩

alans \'alənz, -,lanz\ *also* **ala·ni** \ə'lā,nī, ə'lä(,)nē\ *n pl, cap* [L *Alani*, fr. Gk *Alanoi*] **:** a Scythian people in pre-Slavic Russia and the Black sea regions

al·ant \'alənt, ə'lant\ *n* -s [G, fr. OHG, fr. (assumed) VL *iluna*, alter. of L *inula* — more at INULA] **:** SNEEZEWEED 1a

alan·tic acid \ə'lantik-\ *n* [ISV *alantic* (fr. *alant* + *-ic*) + *acid*; orig. formed as G *alantsäure*] **:** a crystalline acid $C_{15}H_{22}O_3$ obtained from alantolactone by hydration

alan·tin \ə'lantᵊn\ *n* -s [prob. fr. G, fr. *alant* + *-in*] **:** INULIN

alan·to·lac·tone \ə,lan(,)tō'lak,tōn\ *n* -s [ISV *alant* + *-o-* + *lactone*; prob. orig. formed as G *alantolakton*] **:** a white crystalline lactone $C_{15}H_{20}O_2$ obtained from elecampane root

al·an·tol·ic acid \¦alən¦tälik-\ *n* [*alantol*, liquid derived from alant (fr. *alant* + *-ol*) + *-ic*] **:** ALANTIC ACID

al·a·nyl \'alə,nil\ *n* -s [ISV *alanine* + *-yl*] **1 :** the acyl radical $CH_3CH(NH_2)CO$— of alanine **2 :** the acyl radical $NH_2CH_2CH_2CO$— of beta-alanine — used with an initial Greek beta ⟨β*-alanyl*⟩

al·a·ouite *also* **al·a·wite** \'alə¦wēt\ *n* -s *usu cap* [F] **:** one of a Muslim people living in Syria along the Turkish border

a la pou·pee \-,pü'pā; *see* A LA\ *adj* [F *à la poupée* in the ink-pad (lit., doll) manner] *of an engraving or etching* **:** having several areas of the plate inked in different colors by separate cloth pads for a single multicolor impression

alar \'ālə(r)\ *adj* [L *alaris*, fr. *ala* wing + *-aris* -ar — more at AISLE] **1 :** of or resembling a wing or wings **2** *bot* **:** belonging to the axil **:** AXILLARY

alar cartilage *n* **:** one of the pair of lower lateral cartilages of the nose

ala·re \ə'la(a)(,)rē, ə'lā(-\ *n* -s [NL, fr. L, neut. sing. of *alaris*] **:** the most lateral point on the ala of the nose

¹alar·ia \ə'la(a)rēə\ *n, cap* [NL, fr. L *ala* wing + NL *-aria*] **:** a genus (the type of the family Alariaceae) of olive-brown to black seaweeds found in northern seas, characterized by an elongate strap-shaped lamina, and having the sori restricted to tongue-shaped sporophylls borne at or near its apex — see BADDERLOCKS

²alaria \"\ *n, cap* [NL] **:** a genus of trematode worms (family Strigeidae) that is parasitic as adults in the intestines of carnivorous mammals but requires several intermediate hosts to complete the life cycle

alar ligament *n* **1 :** CHECK LIGAMENT **2 :** either of two fringe-like folds of the synovial membrane of the knee

¹alarm \ə'lärm, -ȧm\ *also* **alar·um** \-a(ə)rəm, -er-, -är-, -ar-\ *n* -s [*alarm* fr. ME *alarme*, fr. MF, fr. OIt *all' arme* to arms, lit., to the weapon, fr. *all'* to the (fr. *alla*, fr. L *ad illam* to that, fr. *ad* to + *illam*, accus. fem. of *ille* that, prob. alter. — influenced by *is* he, that — of OL *olle*, *ollus* that, akin to L *uls* beyond) + *arme* weapon, fr. L *arma* weapons; *alarum* fr. ME *alarom*, alter. of *alarme* — more at AT, ITERATE, ALL, ARM] **1** *usu alarum, obs* **:** a call to arms (as on the approach of an enemy) **2** *often alarum* **:** a disturbing noise **:** DISTRACTION, DIN — usu. used in pl. ⟨all is quiet, no *alarms* —A.E.Housman⟩ **3 a :** a signal giving notice of danger or calling attention to some event or condition ⟨the whole village heard the ~⟩ ⟨only one fire company will respond to the first ~⟩ **b :** a device that warns or signals by means of a noise (as a bell or siren) or visual effect (as a flashing light) ⟨set the ~ to wake me at seven⟩ ⟨a burglar set off the ~ at the bank⟩ **4** *obs* **:** a surprise attack **:** ASSAULT **5 a :** fear or terror resulting from a sudden sense of danger ⟨could not but observe with ~ the quickened motion of our horses —Thomas De Quincey⟩ **b :** apprehension of an unfavorable outcome, of failure, or of dangerous consequences ⟨viewed with ~ the growing power of the central government⟩ **c :** an occasion of excitement or apprehension ⟨the anxieties of common life began soon to succeed to the ~s of romance —Jane Austen⟩ **6 :** a notice, warning, or announcement calling attention to a circumstance or event ⟨police put out a two-state ~ for the missing car⟩ ⟨the dog's barking gave the ~ and the intruders were routed⟩ — see ALARUMS AND EXCURSIONS **syn** see FEAR

²alarm \"\ *also* **alarum** \"\ *vb* -ED/-ING/-S *vt* **1** *often alarum, obs* **:** to rouse to action **:** urge on ⟨I needed not the shout

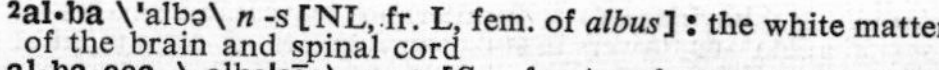

that should *alarm* all Asia militant —Thomas De Quincey⟩ **2** *often alarum, obs* **:** to call to arms **3** *sometimes alarum* **:** to arouse to a sense of danger **:** put on the alert ⟨before the battle of Trenton he crossed the river and *alarmed* the Hessians —E.M.Coulter⟩ **4 :** to strike with fear **:** fill with anxiety as to threatening danger or harm ⟨~*ed* by the sudden rumbling in the earth⟩ ⟨Southerners were ~*ed*, fearing slavery might be abolished —W.C.Ford⟩ **5 :** to keep in excitement or commotion **:** DISTURB ⟨heavy trucks ~*ed* one all night —Glenway Wescott⟩ ~ *vi* **1 :** to sound an alarm ⟨when one or both clocks ~ the trigger spring releases —W.F.Cloud⟩ **2 :** to serve as an alarm — used of a sound **syn** see FRIGHTEN

alarm·a·ble \ə'lärməbəl, -åm-\ *adj* **:** tending or disposed to become alarmed **:** EXCITABLE

alarm bird *n* **:** KOOKABURRA

alarm clock *n* **:** a clock that can be set to give an alarm (as by sounding a bell)

alarm·ed·ly \-mədlē, -li\ *adv* **:** with alarm **:** in an alarmed manner ⟨Britons . . . who ~ believe that too many leaders spoil a party —Mollie Panter-Downes⟩

alarm·ing·ly \-miŋlē, -ēŋ-, -li\ *adv* **:** in a manner or to a degree that excites alarm

alarm·ism \-ˌmizəm\ *n* -s **:** the practice of the alarmist **:** the needless raising or exciting of alarms

1alarm·ist \-ˌməst\ *n* -s [1*alarm* + *-ist*] **:** one inclined to raise or excite alarms esp. needlessly

2alarmist \"\ *adj* **:** characteristic of an alarmist **:** needlessly raising or exciting alarms ⟨to say this is not to be ~ or imaginative —A.P.Ryan⟩

alarm reaction *n* **1 :** the first stage of the adaptation syndrome during which the anterior pituitary gland is stimulated to increased secretory activity **2 :** a series of muscular movements frequently repeated according to a regular pattern that certain birds exhibit when disturbed

1al·a·ro·di·an \ˌalə'rōdēən\ *n* -s *usu cap* [Gk *Alarodios* + E *-an*] **1 :** a member of an Asian people mentioned by Herodotus who were predecessors and neighbors of the ancient Armenians and who are linguistically related to the contemporary Georgians of the Caucasus **2 :** the language of the Alarodians

2alarodian \¦==¦===\ *adj, usu cap* **1 :** of, relating to, or characteristic of Alarodians **2 :** of, relating to, or characteristic of the language of the Alarodians

alar septum *n* **:** one of the pair of lateral primary septa in the Paleozoic Tetracoralla from each of which the septa of one quarter of a corallite arise

alarum *var of* ALARM

alarum clock *chiefly Brit var of* ALARM CLOCK

alarums and excursions *n pl* **1 :** martial sounds and the movement of soldiers across the stage — used as a stage direction in Elizabethan drama **2 :** clamor, excitement, and feverish or disordered activity ⟨the *alarums and excursions* of the uneasy Manchu empire —*N.Y. Herald Tribune*⟩

ala·ry \'alərē, 'al-, -ri\ *adj* [L *alarius*, fr *ala* wing + *-arius* -ary — more at AISLE] **1 :** relating to a wing **2 :** wing-shaped or fan-shaped ⟨the ~ muscles of an insect⟩

1alas \ə'las, -aa(ə)s,-ais,-ås\ *interj* [ME, fr. OF, fr. *a* ah + *las* weary, wretched, fr. L *lassus* weary — more at LET] — used to express unhappiness, sorrow, pity, or concern; often used with *for* ⟨~ for their sad fate⟩; sometimes followed by *the day* ⟨~ the heavy day⟩

2alas \'äˌläs\ *n, pl* **alas** *usu cap* **1 :** an Indonesian people of northern Sumatra **2 :** a member of the Alas people

ala·sas \¦alə¦säs\ *n* -ES [Tag *alasás*] **:** any of several Philippine plants of the genus *Pandanus*

alas·can \ə'laskən, -aas-\ *n* -s *usu cap* [Johannes *a Lasco* (Jan Laski) †1560 Polish religious reformer in charge of foreign Protestants in London (*ab* 1550) + E *-an*] **:** a foreign Protestant in England during the reign of Edward VI

1alas·ka \ə'laskə, -laas-\ *adj, usu cap* [fr. *Alaska*, state of the U.S., fr. Russ *Alashka*, fr. Aleut *alakshak* peninsula] **:** of or from the territory or state of Alaska **:** of the kind or style prevailing in Alaska **:** ALASKAN

2alas·ka \"\ *n* -s *sometimes cap* **:** a storm rubber having a rubberized cloth vamp

alaska blackfish *n, usu cap A* **:** BLACKFISH 1f

alaska cedar *or* **alaska cypress** *n, usu cap A* **:** YELLOW CEDAR 1a

alaska cod *n, usu cap A* **:** a cod (*Gadus macrocephalus*)

alaska day *n, usu cap A&D* **:** October 18, the anniversary of the formal transfer of the territory of Alaska in 1867 by Russia to the U.S., celebrated as a legal holiday in Alaska

alaska goose *n, usu cap A* **:** LESSER SNOW GOOSE

alaska grayling *n, usu cap A* **:** a northern arctic grayling

alaska longspur *n, usu cap A* **:** a longspur (*Calcarius lapponicus alascensis*) of northwestern No. America

1alas·kan \ə'laskən, -aas-\ *adj, usu cap* [*Alaska* + E *-an*] **1 :** of, relating to, or characteristic of the territory or state of Alaska **2 :** of, relating to, or characteristic of the people of Alaska

2alaskan \"\ *n* -s *cap* **:** a native or resident of Alaska

alaskan malamute *n* **1** *usu cap A&M* **:** a breed of powerful heavy-coated deep-chested dogs that were developed from native Alaskan sled dogs and have erect ears, heavily cushioned feet, and plumy tail and are usu. colored wolf gray or black and white **2** *usu cap A & sometimes cap M* **:** a dog of the Alaskan Malamute breed

alaska pine *n, usu cap A* **:** a valuable timber hemlock (*Tsuga heterophylla*) of northwestern No. America

alaska pollack *n, usu cap A* **:** WALLEYE POLLACK

alas·kite \ə'laˌskīt, -aaˌs-\ *n* -s [*Alaska*, its locality + E *-ite*] **:** a leucocratic granite of medium or fine grain composed chiefly of quartz and alkali feldspars

ala spu·ria \¦ālə'spyůrēə\ *n* [NL, lit., false wing] **:** BASTARD WING

alas·tor \ə'lastər, -aas-, -ˌstȯ(ə)r\ *n* -s *usu cap* [Gk *alastōr*, fr. *a-* 2*a-* + *-lastōr* (prob. fr. *lan* to look); akin to Skt *lasati* he shines] **:** any of certain avenging deities or spirits esp. in Greek antiquity

alas·trim \¦alə¦strim\ *n* -s [Pg, fr. *alastrar* to spread, cover, fr. *lastro* covering, ballast, fr. F *laste*, a weight used in shipping, fr. D *last* load; akin to OHG *hlast* load — more at LAST] **:** a mild form of smallpox of low mortality

1alate \ə'lāt\ *adv* [ME, fr. 1*a-* + *late*] *archaic* **:** of late **:** LATELY

2alate \'āˌlāt, *usu* -ād·+V\ *also* **alat·ed** \'āˌlād·əd\ *adj* [L *alatus*, fr. *ala* wing + *-atus* -ate — more at AISLE] **1 :** having wings **:** WINGED ⟨an ~ horse in mythology⟩ **2 :** furnished with winglike expansions ⟨certain stems and fruits are ~⟩ **3 a :** having a broad expanded lip — used of shells **b :** having winged forms — used of certain insects (as ants and aphids) **c :** of or relating to alates

3alate \"\ *n* -s **:** a winged individual of a kind of insect (as ant or aphid) that has both winged and wingless forms

ala·tion \ā'lāshən\ *n* -s [2*alate* + *-ion*] *biol* **:** the state of having wings

alau·da \ə'lȯdə, -laůdə\ *n, cap* [NL, fr. L, lark, fr. Gaulish] **:** the type genus of Alaudidae comprising the skylark

alau·di·dae \-dəˌdē\ *n pl, cap* [NL, fr. *Alauda*, type genus + *-idae*] **:** a family of usu. brownish terrestrial gregarious passerine birds comprising the larks and having the hind claw elongated and more or less straight

alaun *or* **alaund** *or* **alaunt** *var of* ALAN

alawite *usu cap, var of* ALAOUITE

alb \'alb\ *n* -s [ME *albe*, fr. OE, fr. ML *alba*, fr. L, fem. of *albus* white — more at ELF] **1** *also* **albe :** a liturgical vestment worn by priests and certain other ecclesiastics consisting of a full-length close-sleeved tunic usu. of linen and usu. gathered at the waist with a cincture, now uniformly white in Western churches but of any of various colors in Eastern churches **2 :** a flat or gently inclined shelf high in a glaciated mountain valley

alb

alb- *or* **albo-** *comb form* [L, fr. *albus*] **:** white ⟨*alb*ite⟩ ⟨*albo*cinereous⟩

1al·ba \'älbə\ *n* -s [OProv, lit., dawn, fr. (assumed) VL *alba* dawn, fr. L, fem. of *albus*] **1 :** an often Provençal love lyric usu. dealing with a parting of lovers at dawn **2 :** the musical accompaniment of an alba

2al·ba \'albə\ *n* -s [NL, fr. L, fem. of *albus*] **:** the white matter of the brain and spinal cord

al·ba·cea \ˌalbə'sāə\ *n* -s [Sp, fr. Ar *al-waṣīyah* the thing designated in a will, fr. *waṣa* to entrust, make a will] *Spanish law* **:** the person designated by a testator to fulfill and execute the directions of the will **:** EXECUTOR

al·ba·co·ra \ˌalbə'kōrə\ *n, pl* **albacoras** *or* **albacora** [Sp, fr. Ar *al-bakūrah*] **1 :** ALBACORE **2 :** SWORDFISH

al·ba·core *or* **al·bi·core** \'albəˌkō(ə)r, -ȯ(ə)r,-ōə,-ȯ(ə)\ *n, pl* **albacores** *or* **albacore** *or* **albicores** *or* **albicore** [Pg *albacor*, fr. Ar *al-bakūrah* the albacore, perh. fr. *bākūr* precocious] **1 :** a large pelagic fish (*Thunnus germo*) of the family Thunnidae having long pectoral fins and noted for its fine flesh which is the source of most canned tuna **2 :** BLUEFIN TUNA **3 :** any of several smaller fishes related to the albacore (as a bonito) **4 :** any of several fishes of the family Carangidae

al·ba·da finder \al'bädə-\ *n, usu cap A* [after L.E.W. von *Albada fl* 1924, its inventor] **:** a camera viewfinder for use at eye level in which a white field-limiting frame is made to appear very distant by reflection at the rear surface of the front lens — called also *sport finder*

al·ba fir·ma \¦albə'fərmə\ *n* [ML, lit., white rent] **:** rent payable in silver in accordance with early English law

alba graeca *pl of* ALBUM GRAECUM

al·ba·ha·ca \ˌalbə'häkə, -akə\ *n* -s [Sp, fr. Ar *al-ḥabaqah* the basil] **:** any of several aromatic plants of the family Labiatae esp. of the genus *Ocimum*

al·bam \äl'bäm, 'alˌbam\ *n* -s [Heb] **:** a cipher used in Jewish mystical and allegorical writing in which each letter of the first half of the Hebrew alphabet is replaced by or replaces the letter occupying the corresponding position in the second half of the alphabet — compare ATHBASH

al·ba·nen·ses \ˌalbə'nenˌsēz\ *n pl, usu cap* [ML, pl. of *Albanensis*, lit., inhabitant of *Alba*, irreg. fr. *Alba*, Italy + L *-ensis* -ese] **:** members of a 12th century dualistic Catharistic sect closely related to the Albigenses — **al·ba·nen·sian** \¦==¦nenchən, -nen(t)sēən\ *adj, usu cap*

al·ba·nia \(')al¦bānēə, -nyə *sometimes* (')ȯl-\ *adj, usu cap* [fr. *Albania*, country in Balkan peninsula] **:** of or from Albania **:** of the kind or style prevalent in Albania **:** ALBANIAN

1al·ba·nian \-nēən,-nyən\ *adj, usu cap* [*Albania*, country in the Balkan peninsula + E *-an*] **1 a :** of, relating to, or characteristic of Albania **b :** of, relating to, or characteristic of the Albanians **2 :** of, relating to, or characteristic of the Albanian language

2albanian \"\ *n* -s *cap* **1 :** a native or inhabitant of Albania **2 a :** the language of the Albanian people **b :** a branch of the Indo-European language family containing only the Albanian language

3al·ba·ni·an \ȯl'bānēən, -nyən\ *n* -s *cap* [*Albany*, N.Y. + E *-an*] **:** a native or resident of Albany, N. Y.

albanian church *n, cap A & usu cap C* [1*Albanian*] **:** the autocephalous Church of Albania, a branch of the Orthodox Church

al·ban·ite \'ȯlbəˌnīt, 'al-\ *n* -s [*Alban* hills near Rome, Italy, its locality + E *-ite*] **:** a melanocratic leucitite

al·ba·ny \'ȯlbənē, -ni\ *adj, usu cap* [fr. *Albany*, N.Y.] **:** of or from Albany, the capital of New York ⟨*Albany* stores⟩ **:** of the kind or style prevalent in Albany

albany beef *n, usu cap A* [fr. *Albany*, N.Y.; fr. its former widespread use as a food in and near Albany] **:** the flesh of the sturgeon

albany slip *n, usu cap A* [fr. *Albany*, N.Y.] **:** a clay used by potters to produce a natural black or brown glaze on stoneware and large insulators

al·bar·co \al'bär(ˌ)kō\ *n* -s [modif. of AmerSp *abarco*] **:** COLOMBIAN MAHOGANY

al·ba red \'albə-\ *n, usu cap A&R* [fr. (assumed) VL *alba* dawn — more at ALBA] **:** an organic pigment — see DYE table I (under *Pigment Red 100*)

al·ba·rel·lo \ˌalbə're(ˌ)lō\ *n, pl* **albarel·li** \-(ˌ)lē\ *or* **albarellos** [It *alberello* bottle, phial, prob. dim. of *albero* poplar, fr. (assumed) VL *albarus* white poplar, fr. L *albus* white — more at ELF] **:** a majolica jar more or less cylindrical in form but with concave sides used orig. as a container esp. of drugs

al·bar·i·um \al'ba(a)rēəm\ *n* -s [L, fr. neut. of *albarius* of the whitening of walls, fr. *albus* + *-arius* -ary] **:** a thin white stucco

albas *pl of* ALBA

albas·pi·din \al'baspədən\ *n* -s [ISV *alb-* (fr. L *albus* white) + NL *Aspidium* + ISV *-in;* orig. formed in G] **:** a white crystalline compound $C_{25}H_{32}O_8$ extracted from aspidium

al·ba·tross \'albə·ˌtrȯs, -äs\ *n, pl* **albatrosses** *or* **albatross** [prob. alter. (prob. influenced by L *albus* white) of *alcatras*, fr. Pg or Sp *alcatraz* pelican, prob. fr. Ar *al-ghaṭṭās* the white-tailed sea eagle (*Haliaeetus albicilla*), fr. *al-* the + *ghaṭṭās* white-tailed sea eagle] **1 :** any of a number of large web-footed sea birds that are related to the petrels, that form a family (Diomedeidae) of the order Procellariiformes, and that include the largest of sea birds, being capable of long-continued flight and often appearing at great distances from land chiefly over southern seas — see BLACK-BROWED ALBATROSS, LAYSAN ALBATROSS, SOOTY ALBATROSS, WANDERING ALBATROSS **2 a :** a fine thin worsted fabric with a crepy surface made in various weaves **b :** a plain woven cotton cloth with a soft nap similar to cotton bunting

1albe *var of* ALB

2al·be \(')al¦bē, (')ȯl-\ *conj* [ME — more at ALBEIT] *archaic* **:** ALBEIT

al·be·do \al'bē(ˌ)dō\ *n* -s [LL, whiteness, fr. L *albus* white — more at ELF] **1 :** reflective power **2 a :** the fraction of incident light or electromagnetic radiation that is reflected by a surface or body (as the moon, a planet, a cloud, the ground, or a field of snow) **b :** the fraction of incident neutrons that are reflected by a surface **3 :** the whitish inner portion of the rind of citrus fruits that is a source of pectin used esp. in jelly and jam — compare FLAVEDO

al·be·dom·e·ter \ˌalbə'dämǝd·ə(r)\ *n* -s [*albedo* + *-meter*] **:** a device for measuring the reflection of light (as by snow)

al·be·it \(')al¦bēət, (')ȯl-\ *conj* [ME, lit., completely though it be, fr. *al* completely + *be* (3rd pers. sing. pres. subj. of *been* to be) + *it* — more at ALL, BE] **:** even though **:** ALTHOUGH ⟨destined to pass his fortieth year before fame saluted him — ~ his was a special genius —*Fashion Digest*⟩ ⟨passages of moving, ~ restrained, eloquence —*N. Y. Herald Tribune*⟩

Al·be·rene \'albəˌrēn\ *trademark* — used for a soapstone used to make acid-resistant or alkali-resistant surfaces

al·bers projection \'älbə(r)z-, -)s-\ *n, usu cap A* [after Heinrich C. *Albers* †1833 Ger. cartographer] **:** an equal-area projection with straight-line meridians and two standard parallels of true scale

al·bert \'albə(r)t\ *n* -s [after *Albert* †1861 prince consort of England] **:** a watch chain worn across the front of a vest

al·ber·ta \(')al¦bərd·ē\ *adj, usu cap* [fr. *Alberta*, province of Canada] **:** of or from the province of Alberta

1al·ber·tan \(')al¦bərtᵊn\ *adj, usu cap* [*Alberta*, province of Canada + E *-an*] **1 :** of or relating to Alberta **2 :** of or relating to a subage and substage of the Cambrian period

2albertan \"\ *n* -s *cap* **:** a native or resident of the province of Alberta

al·ber·ti bass \al'bərd·ē, äl'ber-\ *n, usu cap A* [after Domenico *Alberti* †*ab* 1740 It. musician] **:** a bass part in keyboard music consisting of broken chords in close position

al·ber·tist \al'bərd·əst, 'albər-\ *n* -s *usu cap* [*Albert*us Magnus (Albert, Count von Bollstädt) †1280 Ger. scholastic philosopher + E *-ist*] **:** a follower of Albertus Magnus, who adapted Aristotle's philosophy to Christian theology

al·bert·ite \'albərd·ˌīt\ *n* -s *sometimes cap* [*Albert* county, New Brunswick, Canada, its locality + E *-ite*] **:** a bituminous mineral resembling asphaltum (hardness 1-2, sp. gr. 1.097)

al·ber·tus·ta·ler \äl'berd·əsˌtälər\ *n, pl* **albertustaler** *or* **albertustalers** [G, fr. D *albertusdaalder*, fr. Albert VII (*Albertus*) †1622 archduke of Austria and regent of the Netherlands, its coiner + D *daalder* taler, fr. G *taler* — more at DOLLAR] **:** a silver coin worth three gulden

al·ber·type \'albər(t)ˌtīp\ *n* -s *sometimes cap* [part trans. of G *albertypie*, *alberttypie*, fr. Joseph *Albert* †1886 Ger. photographer, its inventor + G *-typie* -type] **:** COLLOTYPE

al·be·spine \'albəˌspīn\ *n* -s [ME, fr. MF, fr. (assumed) VL *albispina*, fr. L *alba* (fem. of *albus* white) + *spina* thorn — more at ELF, SPINE] **1 :** a European hawthorn (*Crataegus oxycantha*) **2 :** the wood of the albespine

al·be·tad \'albəˌtad\ *n* -s [prob fr. Ar *al-birzad*] **:** GALBANUM

1al·bi·an \'albēən\ *adj, usu cap* [*Alb-* (prob. fr. *Aube*, department of France, its type station) + E *-ian*] **:** of or relating to the lowest division of the Upper Cretaceous esp. in western Europe and the Mediterranean basin — see GEOLOGIC TIME table

2albian *n* -s *usu cap* **:** the Albian series or epoch

albicore *var of* ALBACORE

al·bi·gen·ses \ˌalbə'jenˌsēz\ *n pl, usu cap* [ML, pl. of *Albigensis*, lit., inhabitant of Albi, fr. *Albiga* (Albi), France + L *-ensis* -ese] **:** members of a Catharistic sect of southern France that arose in the 11th century and was exterminated in the 13th century through the influence of Pope Innocent III and the Inquisition — **al·bi·gen·sian** \¦albə¦jenchən. -en(t)sēən\ *adj or n, usu cap*

al·bi·gen·sian·ism \-ˌnizəm\ *n* -s *usu cap* **:** the principles and practices of the Albigenses

al·bin·ic \(')al¦binik\ *also* **al·bi·nis·tic** \¦albə¦nistik\ *or* **albinal** \'albənᵊl\ *adj* [*albino* + *-ic* or *-istic* or *-al*] **:** of, relating to, or affected with albinism

al·bi·nism \'albəˌnizəm\ *also* **al·bi·no·ism** \al'bī(ˌ)nōˌizəm, -bē-\ *n* -s [F or G; F *albinisme*, fr. G *albinismus*, fr. *albino* + *-ismus* -ism] **1 :** the state or quality of being an albino **2 :** complete inability to produce pigment, a recessive genetic condition of wide occurrence esp. in respect to coat, skin, and eye color of mammals — compare CHINCHILLA, HIMALAYAN, WILD TYPE

al·bi·no \al'bīˌnō, *Brit usu & US sometimes* -bē-\ *n* -s *often attrib* [Pg, fr. Sp, fr. *albo* white, fr. L *albus* — more at ELF] **1 :** any organism exhibiting deficient pigmentation: as **a :** a human being or other animal affected with albinism and typically having a milky or translucent skin, white or nearly colorless hair, and eyes with pink or blue iris and deep-red pupil; *sometimes* **:** an albinotic individual **b :** a member of a strain (as of mice or rabbits) developed by selectively breeding for pigment deficiency **c :** a plant lacking normal pigment or chromatophores: (1) **:** a plant that is pathologically deficient in chlorophyll and yellow leaf pigments (2) **:** an etiolated plant (3) **:** a plant whose flowers are white because of undeveloped chromoplasts **2 :** an impression of an embossed stamp (as on an envelope) made without ink

al·bi·not·ic \¦albə¦näd·ik\ *adj* [*albino* + *-tic* (as in *melanotic*)] **1 :** ALBINIC **2 :** tending toward albinism

al·bite \'alˌbīt\ *n* -s [Sw *albit*, fr. L *albus* white + Sw *-it* -ite — more at ELF] **:** a triclinic usu. white feldspar consisting of a sodium aluminum silicate $NaAlSi_3O_8$, occurring massive or in crystals, and forming a common constituent of granite and of various igneous rocks — **al·bit·ic** \(')al¦bid·ik\ *adj*

al·bi·tite \'albəˌtīt\ *n* -s [*albite* + *-ite*] **:** a granular dike rock consisting essentially of albite

al·bi·ti·za·tion \ˌalbəd·ə'zāshən\ *n* -s [*albite* + *-ization*] **:** a process in which albite replaces the plagioclase feldspar of an igneous rock

al·bit·o·phyre \al'bid·əˌfī(ə)r\ *n* -s [ISV *albite* + *-o-* + *-phyre;* orig. formed in F] **:** a porphyritic rock containing phenocrysts of albite in a groundmass usu. of albite and a little quartz and chlorite

al·biz·zia \al'bizēə\ *n* [NL, after Filippo degli *Albizzi fl*1749 It. naturalist who introduced it into Italy] **1** *cap* **:** a large genus of unarmed trees (family Leguminosae) found in warm regions of the Old World and having twice-pinnate leaves, solitary or panicled globelike clusters of flowers, and long flat pods — see SILK TREE **2** -s **:** a tree of the genus *Albizzia*

albo- — see ALB-

al·bo·ci·ne·re·ous \¦al(ˌ)bō=¦===\ *adj* [*alb-* + *cinereous*] *anat* **:** composed of white and gray matter

al·bo·lite \'albəˌlīt\ *or* **al·bo·lith** \-ˌlith\ *n* -s *often attrib* [ISV *alb-* + *-lite*, *-lith*] **:** a plastic cement consisting chiefly of magnesia and silica

al·bo·ra·da \ˌalbə'rädə\ *n* -s [Sp, fr. *alba* dawn, fr. fem. of *albo* white, fr. L *albus* — more at ELF] **:** an instrumental serenade usu. played on a bagpipe or oboe to the accompaniment of a small drum **:** AUBADE

al·bo·ran·ite \ˌalbə'raˌnīt\ *n* -s [G *alboranit*, fr. *Alborán* island, Spain, its locality + G *-it*, -ite] **:** a hypersthene-basalt having a porphyritic texture and containing phenocrysts of labradorite but no olivine

al·bright \'ȯlˌbrīt\ *n* -s *usu cap* [after Jacob *Albright* †1808 Am. preacher, founder of the association] **:** a member of a 19th century evangelical association now merged into the Evangelical United Brethren Church

al·bu·ca \al'byükə\ *n, cap* [NL, fr. L, asphodel] **:** a genus of bulbous plants (family Liliaceae) native to southern Africa and having pale yellow flowers in large clusters

al·bu·gi·na·ce·ae \(ˌ)alˌbyüjə'nāsēˌē\ *n pl, cap* [NL, fr. *Albugin-*, *Albugo*, type genus + *-aceae*] **:** a family of fungi (order Peronosporales) that produce whitish blisterlike conidial sori on certain flowering plants and that reproduce by forming conidia in chains within the sori or by producing oospores within the affected host tissue — compare WHITE RUST

al·bu·gi·na·les \-'nā(ˌ)lēz\ *n pl, cap* [NL, fr. *Albugin-*, *Albugo* + *-ales*] *in some classifications* **:** an order of fungi coextensive with the family Albuginaceae

al·bu·go \al'byü(ˌ)gō\ *n, cap* [NL, fr. L, white spot, fr. *albus* white — more at ELF] **:** a genus of fungi (the type of the family Albuginaceae) causing the white rusts

al·bu·la \'albyələ\ *n, cap* [NL, fr. L, fem. of *albulus* whitish, fr. *albus* white] **:** a genus (coextensive with the family Albulidae) of silvery marine fishes widely distributed in warm seas and prob. including only a single species (*A. vulpes*) — see BONEFISH

al·bum \'albəm, *rapid* 'albᵊm *or* 'aůbᵊm\ *n* -s [L, tablet on which edicts were written, list of names, fr. neut. of *albus* white — more at ELF] **1 a :** a bound or loose-leaf book usu. with mostly blank pages or some other volume or packet designed or used for making a collection (as of autographs, stamps, photographs, drawings, or specimens) usu. according to a selected theme, subject, or pattern — compare SCRAPBOOK **b :** a rigid or semirigid envelopelike, booklike, or boxlike container usu. made of strong paperboard and designed to hold and protect one or more phonograph records **c :** one or more phonograph records or tape recordings carrying either the whole of a long recording (as of a complete opera) or a grouped selection of shorter recordings (as of excerpts from a film score) **2 :** a usu. representative collection (as of literary selections, musical compositions, or pictures) **:** ANTHOLOGY; *esp* **:** a published collection of this kind usu. in book form

al·bum·blatt \'älbəmˌblät, 'albəmˌblat\ *n, pl* **albumblät·ter** \-led·ə(r)\ *or* **albumblatts** *usu cap* [G, lit., album leaf, fr. *album* (fr. L) + *blatt* leaf, fr. OHG *blat* — more at BLADE] **:** a short instrumental composition usu. for piano

album board *n* **:** a thick album paper often consisting of two layers of album paper pasted together

al·bu·men \al'byümən *sometimes* -ˌmen *or* 'albyə-\ *n* -s [L, fr. *albus* white — more at ELF] **1 a :** the white of an egg — see EGG illustration **b :** EGG ALBUMIN 2 **2** *archaic* **:** ENDOSPERM **3 :** ALBUMIN

albumen paper *n* **:** a light-sensitive paper prepared by coating with white of egg and a salt (as ammonium chloride) and sensitized by an after-treatment with a solution of silver nitrate

albumen plate *n* **:** a plate coated with bichromated albumen used in photolithography

al·bum grae·cum \¦albəm'grēkəm, -rīk-\ *n, pl* **al·ba grae·ca** \-bə...kə\ *usu cap G* [NL, lit., Greek white; fr. the fact that it becomes white when exposed to air] **:** dried dung of dogs or hyenas sometimes used in dressing leather

al·bu·min \al'byümən, -ˌmin *sometimes* 'albyə-\ *n* -s [ISV *album-* (fr. L *albumen*) + *-in;* orig. formed as F *albumine*] **:** any of a large class of simple proteins that are usu. characterized by their solubility in pure water, dilute salt solutions, and half-saturated ammonium sulfate or sodium sulfate solutions, that are coagulable by heat, thereby carrying coloring matters and impurities along with them, that form important constituents of human or animal blood plasma or serum and are found also in muscle, the whites of eggs, milk, and other animal substances and in many vegetable tissues and fluids, and that are used esp. for clarifying liquids, in photography, and in textile printing — see LACTALBUMIN, OVALBUMIN, SERUM ALBUMIN

al·bu·min- *or* **albumini-** *or* **albumino-** *comb form* [prob. fr. F, fr. L *albumin-, albumen*] **:** albumen **:** albumin ⟨*albumin*oid⟩ ⟨*albumini*ferous⟩ ⟨*albumino*lysis⟩
al·bu·mi·nate \alˈbyüməˌnāt, -nə̇t, *usu* -d·+V\ *n* -s [*albumin-* + *-ate*] **:** a compound derived from an albumin (as by the action of acids or alkalies or by combination with another substance)
al·bu·mi·nize *or* **al·bu·me·nize** \-ˌnīz\ *vt* -ED/-ING/-S [*albumin-* or *albumen* + *-ize*] **:** to cover or saturate with albumen **:** coat or treat with an albuminous solution
¹al·bu·mi·noid \-ˌnȯid\ *adj* [ISV *albumin-* + *-oid*] **:** resembling albumin in properties **:** PROTEIN
²albuminoid \"\ *n* -s **1 :** PROTEIN **2 :** SCLEROPROTEIN
al·bu·mi·nom·e·ter \alˌbyüməˈnäməd·ə(r)\ *also* **al·bu·mi·nim·e·ter** \-ˈnim-\ *n* -s [*albumin-* + *-meter*] **:** an instrument, usu. a graduated tube, for determining the presence and amount of protein (esp. albumin) in a liquid (as urine)
al·bu·mi·nous \alˈbyümənəs\ *adj* [*albumin-* + *-ous*] **1 :** relating to or containing albumin **:** having the properties of albumen or albumin **2 :** ENDOSPERMOUS
albuminous cell *n* **:** one of the parenchyma cells adjacent to the sieve cells in gymnosperm wood, distinguished by staining deeply with cytoplasmic stains, and apparently associated physiologically with the sieve cells and joined to them by sieve areas
albumin tannate *n* **:** a yellowish white powder used as an astringent in diarrhea
al·bu·min·uria \(ˌ)alˌbyüməˈn(y)u̇rēə\ *n* -s [NL, fr. *albumin-* + *-uria*] **:** the presence of albumin in the urine, usu. a symptom of disease of the kidneys but sometimes a response to other diseases or physiologic disturbances of benign nature — **al·bu·min·uric** \(ˈ)═ˌ══ˈn(y)u̇rik\ *adj*
al·bu·mose \ˈalbyəˌmōs\ *n* -s [F, fr. *albumine* albumin + *-ose*] **:** any of various protein derivatives formed by the action of hydrolytic enzymes, esp. pepsin, on proteins — compare PROTEOSE
album paper *n* **:** a plain usu. black or gray cover paper commonly used for the leaves of photograph albums
albums *pl of* ALBUM
al·bu·quer·que·an \ˌalbəˈkərkēən *also* -byə-\ *n* -s *cap* [*Albuquerque*, New Mexico + E *-an*] **:** a native or resident of Albuquerque, N. Mex.
al·bur·num \alˈbərnəm\ *n* -s [L, fr. *albus* white — more at ELF] **:** SAPWOOD
al·bus \ˈalbəs\ *n, pl* **albuses** [G, fr. ML, fr. L, white] **:** a minor billon coin of Germany and the Low Countries of the 13th and 14th centuries — compare BLANC
al·bu·tan·nin \ˌalbyəˈtanə̇n\ *n* -s [*albumin* + *tannin*] **:** ALBUMIN TANNATE
alc *abbr* alcohol
al·ca \ˈalkə\ *n, cap* [NL, fr. Sw *alka* auk, fr. Norw *alk, alka* — more at AUK] **:** the type genus of Alcidae usu. including solely the razor-billed auk
al·ca·de \älˈkädē\ *n* -s [obs. Sp (now *alcalde*) — more at ALCALDE] **:** ALCALDE
al·cae \ˈalˌsē\ *n pl, cap* [NL, fr. *Alca*] **:** a suborder of Charadriiformes coextensive with the family Alcidae and including the auks, murres, and puffins
alcahest *var of* ALKAHEST
¹al·ca·ic \(ˈ)alˈkāik\ *adj, often cap* [LL *Alcaicus* of Alcaeus, fr. Gk *Alkaikos*, fr. *Alkaios* (Alcaeus) *fl ab* 600 B.C. Greek lyric poet who used such verse forms + Gk *-ikos* -ic] **:** relating to or written in verse or strophe marked by complicated variation of a dominant iambic pattern by initial anacrusis and by spondees, trochees, and dactyls used mostly in medial or final positions
²alcaic \"\ *n* -s *often cap* **:** alcaic meter **:** an alcaic verse or strophe
al·cai·de *also* **al·cay·de** \älˈkīdē, al-\ *n* -s [Sp *alcaide*, fr. Ar *al-qāʼid* the captain, fr. *qād* to command] **:** a commander of a castle or fortress (as among Spaniards, Portuguese, or Moors)
al·cal·de \älˈkäldē, al-\ *n* -s *sometimes cap* [Sp, fr. Ar *al-qāḍī* the judge, fr. *qaḍā* to judge] **:** an administrative and judicial officer in villages, towns, or districts in Spain and regions under Spanish influence
al·ca·lig·e·nes \ˌalkəˈlijəˌnēz\ *n* [NL, fr. F *alcali* alkali + Gk *-genēs* -gen — more at ALKALI] **1** *cap* **:** a genus of usu. aerobic and gram-negative bacteria that are related to the achromobacters, do not ferment carbohydrates and are aerobes or facultative anaerobes, occur in the intestines of man and animals and in dairy products, and are probably all nonpathogenic though one species (*A. viscosum*) is economically important as a cause of a ropy condition of milk **2** *pl* **alcaligenes :** an organism of the genus *Alcaligenes*
al·ca·mine \ˈalkəˌmēn\ *n* -s [ISV alcohol + *amine*; orig. formed as G *alkamin*] **:** AMINO ALCOHOL
al·can·na \alˈkanə\ *n* -s [Sp *alcana* henna (shrub) — more at ALKANNA] **:** HENNA 3
al·cap·ton *var of* ALKAPTON
alcaptonuria *var of* ALKAPTONURIA
al·car·ra·za \ˌalkəˈräzə\ *n* -s [Sp, fr. Ar *al-karrāz* the jar] **:** a jug or similar container made of porous earthenware
al·ca·tras \ˈalkəˌtras, -az\ *n, pl* **alcatras** *or* **alcatrases** [Pg or Sp *alcatraz* pelican — more at ALBATROSS] **:** a large water bird (as the pelican or frigate bird)
al·ca·zar \alˈkazər, alˈkä-, älˈkä-, ˌalkəˈzär\ *n* -s [Sp *alcázar*, fr. Ar *al-qaṣr* the castle, fr. *al* the + *qaṣr* castle, fr. L *castrum* — more at CASTLE] **:** a Spanish fortress or palace
al·ce·din·i·dae \ˌalsəˈdinəˌdē\ *n pl, cap* [NL, fr. *Alcedin-, Alcedo*, type genus + *-idae*] **:** a large family of large-headed short-bodied birds comprising the kingfishers and constituting a suborder (Alcedines) of the order Coraciiformes
al·ce·do \alˈsē(ˌ)dō\ *n, cap* [NL, fr. L, kingfisher] **:** the type genus of Alcedinidae comprising Old World kingfishers including the small brightly colored European kingfisher
al·cel·a·phine \alˈseləˌfīn\ *adj* [NL *Alcelaphus* + E *-ine*] **:** of or belonging to the genus *Alcelaphus*
al·cel·a·phus \-fəs\ *n, cap* [NL, fr. L *alces* elk + Gk *elaphos* deer] **:** a genus of African antelopes including the hartebeest, bubalis, and related animals
al·ces \ˈalˌsēz\ *n, cap* [NL, fr. L, elk, of Gmc origin; akin to ON *elgr* elk — more at ELK] **:** the genus of mammals (order Artiodactyla) comprising the moose and the European elk
al·chem·ic \(ˈ)alˈkemik, -ēk\ *or* **al·chem·i·cal** \-ə̇kəl, -ēk-\ *adj* [*alchemy* + *-ic, -ical*] **:** of, relating to, marked by, or concerned with alchemy — **al·chem·i·cal·ly** \-ə̇k(ə)lē, -ēk-, -li\ *adv*
al·che·mil·la \ˌalkəˈmilə\ *n* [NL, perh. fr. ML *alchymia* alchemy; fr. the belief that the dew on the leaves of the plants is efficacious in alchemy] **1** *cap* **:** a genus of widely distributed perennial herbs (family Rosaceae) with compound serrate leaves and inconspicuous flowers — see LADY'S-MANTLE **2** -s **:** a plant of the genus *Alchemilla*
al·che·mist \ˈalkəmə̇st *sometimes* -ˌkem-\ *n* -s [ME *alkamist, alkamistre*, prob. fr. ML *alchymista*, fr. *alchymia* alchemy + L *-ista* -ist] **:** one that studies or practices alchemy
al·che·mis·tic \ˌalkəˈmistik, -ēk\ *also* **al·che·mis·ti·cal** \-ə̇kəl, -ēk-\ *adj* **:** ALCHEMIC
alchemistry *n* -ES [*alchemist* + *-ry*] *archaic* **:** ALCHEMY
al·che·mize *or* **al·che·mise** \ˈalkəˌmīz\ *vt* -ED/-ING/-S **:** to change by or as if by alchemy **:** TRANSMUTE ⟨trying to ∼ a base metal into gold⟩ ⟨pity *alchemized* her feeling —Richard Llewellyn⟩
al·che·my \ˈalkəmē, -mi\ *n* -ES [ME *alkamie, alquemie*, fr. MF or ML; MF *alquemie*, fr. ML *alchymia, alchimia*, fr. Ar *al-kīmiyā'* the philosopher's stone, the alchemy, fr. *al* the + *kīmiyā'*, fr. LGk *chēmeia*, prob. alter. of *chymeia*, prob. fr. Gk *chyma* fluid, fr. *chein* to pour — more at FOUND (to melt)] **1 :** the medieval chemical science and speculative philosophy whose aims were the transmutation of the base metals into gold, the discovery of a universal cure for diseases, and the discovery of a means of indefinitely prolonging life **2 a :** a great or magic power of transmutation ⟨no . . . dishonest candidate could, by an ∼ of election, be converted into an honest president —A.E.Stevenson †1965⟩ **3 a** *archaic* **:** a golden-colored alloy **b** *obs* **:** a golden-colored trumpet ⟨put to their mouths the sounding ∼ —John Milton⟩ **syn** see MAGIC
al·che·ra \ˈalchəˌrä\ *or* **al·che·rin·ga** \ˌalchəˈriŋgə\ *n* -s [native name in Australia] **:** DREAMTIME
al·chor·nea \alˈkȯrnēə\ *n* [NL, fr. Stanesby *Alchorne* †*ab* 1799 Eng. botanist] **1** *cap* **:** a genus of tropical trees and shrubs (family Euphorbiaceae) with alternate leaves and small unisexual apetalous flowers in spikes or racemes **2** -s **:** a plant of the genus *Alchornea*
alchymie *obs var of* ALCHEMY
al·cian blue 8GX \ˈalsh(ē)ən-\ *n, usu cap A&B* [*Alcian* of unknown origin] **:** an ingrain dye — see DYE table I (under *Ingrain Blue 1*)
al·ci·cor·ni·um \ˌalsəˈkȯrnēəm\ *n* [NL, fr. L *alces* elk + NL *-i-* + L *cornu* horn + NL *-ium*] *syn of* PLATYCERIUM
al·ci·dae \ˈalsəˌdē\ *n pl, cap* [NL, fr. *Alca*, type genus + *-idae*] **:** a family of diving birds (order Charadriiformes) having short wings and tail, webbed feet, a large head and heavy body, and thick compact plumage, being confined to the northern parts of the northern hemisphere, and including the auks, puffins, guillemots, murres, and related forms
al·clad \ˈalˌklad\ *n* -s [fr. *Alclad*, a trademark] **:** a duplex metal product made by cladding an aluminum alloy core with surface layers of pure aluminum or aluminum alloy usu. for giving increased resistance to corrosion
¹alc·ma·ni·an \(ˈ)alkˈmānēən\ *or* **alc·man·ic** \-manik\ *adj, usu cap* [*Alcmanian* fr. *Alcman* 7th cent. B.C. Greek lyric poet (fr. Gk *Alkman*) + E *-ian*; *Alcmanic* fr. Gk *Alkmanikos*, fr. *Alkman* + Gk *-ikos* -ic] **:** of or relating to Alcman or to verse composed wholly or partly of Alcmanians
²alcmanian \"\ *n* -s *usu cap* **:** a metrical line of four dactyls
al·co \ˈal(ˌ)kō\ *n* -s [Sp, fr. Quechua *állko, álkkho* dog] **:** a small long-haired dog with pendulous ears that is native to and sometimes domesticated in tropical America
alco- *or* **alcoo-** *comb form* [*alcohol*] **:** alcohol ⟨*alco*gel⟩ ⟨*alco*sol⟩ ⟨*alcoo*meter⟩
al·cock's canal \ˈalˌkäks-, ˈȯl-\ *n, usu cap A* [after Thomas *Alcock* †1833 Eng. anatomist] **:** a fascial compartment on the lateral wall of the ischiorectal fossa containing the pudendal arteries, veins, and nerves
alcock spruce *n, usu cap A* [after Sir Rutherford *Alcock* †1897 English diplomat] **:** a Japanese pyramidal evergreen tree (*Picea bicolor*) that has stiff branches and slightly flattened leaves and is cultivated for ornament
al·co·gel \ˈalkəˌjel\ *n* -s [*alco-* + *-gel* (fr. *gelatin*)] **:** a gel formed by the coagulation of an alcosol
al·co·hol \ˈalkəˌhȯl, ˈau̇k- *sometimes* -ˌhäl\ *n* -s [NL & ML; NL, liquid produced by distillation, fr. ML, finely pulverized antimony used by women to darken the eyelids, fr. OSp, fr. Ar *al-kuḥul, al-kuḥl* the powdered antimony] **1** *obs* **:** a fine powder of varying ingredients; *often* **:** KOHL **2** *obs* **:** the essence or spirit obtained by distillation **3 :** a colorless volatile flammable liquid C_2H_5OH formed by vinous fermentation and contained in wine, beer, whiskey, and the other fermented and distilled liquors of which it is the intoxicating principle, that is manufactured principally by fermentation of carbohydrate materials (as blackstrap molasses, various grains, esp. corn, and potatoes) and by hydration of ethylene, being obtained usu. by fractional distillation in a concentration of about 95 percent with about 5 percent water, and that in addition to its use in beverages and in medicines is used chiefly as a solvent (as for fats, oils, and resins), as an antifreeze, as a fuel (as for internal-combustion engines and rockets and for heating on a small scale), and as a raw material for many organic chemicals (as acetaldehyde, butadiene, ethers, and esters) — called also *ethanol, ethyl alcohol, grain alcohol*; see INDUSTRIAL ALCOHOL **4 :** any of a class of compounds analogous to ethyl alcohol in constitution and regarded as hydroxyl derivatives of hydrocarbons, being classed according to the number of hydroxyl groups (as monohydric, dihydric, trihydric, polyhydric) or according to structure — see GLYCOL 2, PRIMARY ALCOHOL, SECONDARY ALCOHOL, TERTIARY ALCOHOL; compare PHENOL
al·co·hol·ate \-ˌlāt, -lə̇t, ˌ══ˈ═(ˌ)═\ *n* -s [ISV *alcohol* + *-ate*] **1 a :** a crystallizable compound of a substance with alcohol in which the alcohol plays a part analogous to that of water of crystallization ⟨chloral ∼ $CCl_3CHO.C_2H_5OH$⟩ **b :** ALKOXIDE ⟨a sodium ∼⟩ **2** *pharmacy* **:** a preparation made by dissolving a volatile oil in alcohol or by distilling with alcohol the medicament containing a volatile principle — called also *spirit*
al·co·hol·a·ture \ˌ══ˈ═ləˌchu̇(ə)r\ *n* -s [F *alcoolature*, fr. *alcool* alcohol, fr. MF *alcohol* liquid produced by distillation, fr. NL — more at ALCOHOL] **:** an alcoholic tincture prepared from a fresh vegetable drug
¹al·co·hol·ic \ˌ══ˈhȯlik, -ˈäl-, -ēk\ *adj* [*alcohol* + *-ic*] **1 a :** of, relating to, or having the characteristics of alcohol ⟨an ∼ odor⟩ **:** having to do with alcohol ⟨∼ propensities⟩ **b :** composed of or containing alcohol ⟨an ∼ solution⟩ **:** INTOXICATING ⟨an ∼ drink⟩ **c :** derived from alcohol **:** caused by or showing the effects of alcohol ⟨suffering from ∼ depression⟩ **d :** preserved in or treated with alcohol ⟨an ∼ specimen⟩ **2 :** marked by the use of alcohol; *esp* **:** addicted to the use. excessive use of alcoholic drinks ⟨∼ expatriates in Paris —Carl Van Doren⟩ — **al·co·hol·i·cal·ly** \-ə̇k(ə)lē, -ēk-, -li\ *adv*
²alcoholic \"\ *n* -s **1 :** one who is addicted esp. compulsively to the excessive use of alcoholic drinks **:** one who suffers from alcoholism **2 :** a biological specimen preserved in alcohol
alcoholic fermentation *n* **:** a process in which certain kinds of sugar (as glucose) are converted into alcohol and carbon dioxide by the action of various yeasts, molds, or bacteria on carbohydrate materials (as dough or sugar solutions) some of which do not themselves undergo fermentation but can be hydrolyzed into fermentable substances (as in the production of alcohol and alcoholic beverages)
al·co·hol·ism \ˈalkəhȯˌlizəm *sometimes* -hä-\ *n* -s [NL *alcoholismus*, fr. NL *alcohol* + L *-ismus* -ism] **1 :** continuous and usu. excessive use of alcoholic drinks; *usu* **:** addiction esp. when compulsive to excessive use of alcoholic drinks **2 :** the state of being poisoned by alcohol; *specif* **:** the pathologic results of excessive use of alcoholic drinks — see ACUTE ALCOHOLISM, CHRONIC ALCOHOLISM
al·co·hol·ist \-lə̇st\ *n* -s **:** ALCOHOLIC
al·co·hol·i·za·tion \ˌ══ˌhȯlə̇ˈzāshən *sometimes* -ˌäl-\ *n* -s **:** the act or process of alcoholizing or the condition of being alcoholized
al·co·hol·ize \ˈ══ˌlīz\ *vt* -ED/-ING/-S **1 a :** to treat or saturate with alcohol **b :** to subject to the influence of alcohol **2 :** to convert into alcohol
alcohol of crystallization : alcohol, usu. ethyl alcohol, combined in a manner analogous to that of water of crystallization — see ALCOHOLATE 1a
al·co·hol·om·e·ter \ˌ══hȯˈläməd·ə(r) *sometimes* -äˈl-\ *also* **al·co·hol·me·ter** \ˌ══ˈhȯlˌmēd·ə(r) *sometimes* -äl-\ *or* **al·co·hol·im·e·ter** \ˌ══hȯˈlimədə(r) *sometimes* -äˈl-\ *n* -s [F *alcoolomètre*, fr. *alcool* alcohol + *-o-* + *-mètre* -meter] **:** a device for determining the alcoholic strength of liquids
al·co·hol·om·e·try \ˌ══hȯˈlämə·trē *sometimes* -äˈl-\ *n* -ES [*alcohol* + *-o-* + *-metry*] **:** the determining of the alcoholic strength of liquids
al·co·hol·y·sis \-ˈhäləsə̇s, -ȯl-\ *n, pl* **alcoholy·ses** \-əˌsēz\ [NL, blend of *alcohol* and *-lysis*] **:** any chemical reaction analogous to hydrolysis in which an alcohol plays a role similar to that of water ⟨∼ of an ester to a different ester⟩
al·co·hol·yt·ic \ˌ══hȯˈlid·ik, -hä'l-\ *adj* **:** of, relating to, or productive of alcoholysis
al·co·o- — see ALCO-
al·co·ran \ˌalkōˈran\ *n* -s *usu cap* [ME *alcoran, alkaron*, fr. MF or ML; MF *alcoran* & ML *alcoran, alcoranum*, fr. Ar *al-qur'ān*, lit., the recitation, the reading — more at KORAN] *archaic* **:** KORAN
al·cor·no·que \ˌal(ˌ)kȯrˈnōkē\ *n* -s [Pg (also, cork tree) & AmerSp *alcornoque*, both fr. Sp, cork tree, prob. fr. a 12th cent. Ar dial. (Spain) word formed fr. Ar *al* the + ML *quernus* oak tree (fr. L, oaken, fr. *quercus* oak tree) + ML *-occus* (dim. & pejorative suffix) — more at FIR] **:** any of several tropical American trees felt to resemble the cork oak
alcos *pl of* ALCO
al·co·sol \ˈalkəˌsȯl, -ˌōl\ *n* -s [*alco-* + *-sol* (fr. *solution*)] **:** a sol in which the liquid is alcohol
al·cove \ˈalˌkōv\ *n* -s [F *alcôve*, fr. Sp *alcoba*, fr. Ar *al-qubbah* the arch, vault] **1 a :** a recessed part (as a breakfast nook) of a room or a small room opening into a larger one (as in a library) **b :** a niche or similar arched opening (as in a wall) **:** a vaulted space (as a small clearing) **2 :** a small ornamental building usu. with seats (as in a park or garden) **:** SUMMERHOUSE
al·cres·ta ipecac \(ˈ)alˈkrestə-\ *n* [fr. *Alcresta*, a trademark] **:** a preparation of ipecac in which the alkaloids have been adsorbed on hydrous aluminum silicate
alcumy *obs var of* ALCHEMY
al·cy·on \ˈalsēən\ *n* -s [NL *Alcyonium*, genus of soft corals, fr. Gk *alkyoneion, alkyonion*, a zoophyte, fr. neut. of *alkyoneios* of a kingfisher, fr. *alkyōn* kingfisher; fr. its resemblance to a kingfisher's nest] **:** a soft coral of *Alcyonium* or a related genus
al·cy·o·na·cea \ˌalsēəˈnāsh(ē)ə\ *n pl, cap* [NL, fr. *Alcyonium* + *-acea*] **:** an order or other division of Alcyonaria comprising the soft corals — **al·cy·o·na·cean** \ˌ═══ˈ═shən\ *adj or n* — **al·cy·on·ic** \ˌ══ˈänik\ *adj* — **al·cy·on·i·form** \ˌ══ˈänəˌfȯrm\ *adj*
al·cy·o·nar·ia \-ˈna(a)rēə\ *n pl, cap* [NL, fr. *Alcyonium* + *-aria*] **:** a subclass or order of Anthozoa including chiefly compound coelenterates having polyps with 8-branched tentacles and eight septa and comprising the Stolonifera, Alcyonacea, Gorgonacea, and Pennatulacea — **al·cy·o·nar·i·an** \ˌ═══ˈ═rēən\ *adj or n*
al·cy·o·nes \alˈsīə(ˌ)nēz\ *n pl, cap* [NL, fr. Gk *alkyōn* kingfisher] *in some classifications* **:** a group of birds consisting of the kingfishers
al·cy·o·ni·a·ce·ae \ˌalsēˌōnēˈāsēˌē\ *syn of* ALCYONACEA
al·cy·o·ni·o·mor·pha \-nēōˈmȯrfə\ [NL, fr. *Alcyonium* + *-morpha*] *syn of* ALCYONARIA
al·cy·o·noid \ˈalsēəˌnȯid\ *n* -s [NL *Alcyonoidea*] **:** one of the Alcyonaria
al·cy·o·noi·dea \ˌalsēəˈnȯidēə\ [NL, fr. *Alcyonium* + *-oidea*] *syn of* ALCYONARIA
ald \ˈȯl(d), ˈō-\ *adj* [ME, var. of *old*] *now dial Brit* **:** OLD
ald- *or* **aldo-** *comb form* [prob. fr. F *ald-*, fr. *aldéhyde*, fr. G *aldehyd* — more at ALDEHYDE] **1 :** containing the aldehyde group — in names of classes of compounds ⟨*aldo*hexose⟩; compare ALDEHYDO- **2 :** related to an aldehyde ⟨*ald*imine⟩ ⟨*ald*oxime⟩
ald *abbr* alderman
al·da·zine \ˈaldəˌzēn\ *n* -s [ISV *ald-* + *azine*] **:** an azine RCH-NN-CHR formed from an aldehyde
al·de·hyde \ˈaldəˌhīd\ *n* -s [G *aldehyd*, fr. NL *al dehyd*, abbr. of *alcohol dehydrogenatum* dehydrogenated alcohol] **1 :** ACETALDEHYDE **2 :** any of a class of very reactive organic compounds typified by acetaldehyde and characterized by the group –CHO that are intermediate in state of oxidation, having two fewer hydrogen atoms in the molecule than primary alcohols and one less oxygen atom than carboxylic acids — **al·de·hyd·ic** \ˌaldəˈhīdik\ *adj*
aldehyde ammonia *n* **:** any compound formed by the union of an aldehyde with ammonia; *specif* **:** a crystalline compound $CH_3CH(OH)NH_2$ derived from acetaldehyde — called also *acetaldehyde ammonia*
aldehyde collidine *n* **:** METHYLETHYLPYRIDINE
aldehyde hydrate *n* **:** any compound (as chloral hydrate) formed by the union of an aldehyde with water and having the general formula $RCH(OH)_2$
aldehyde resin *n* **1 :** any resin produced from one or more aliphatic aldehydes by a condensation reaction brought about by concentrated alkali solutions **2 :** any resinous product made by interaction of an aldehyde (as formaldehyde or furfural) with another substance (as phenol or urea)
al·de·hyd·ine \ˈaldəˌhīˌdēn, ˌ══ˈ═ˌ═\ *n* -s [ISV *aldehyde* + *-ine*; orig. formed as G *aldehydin*] **1 :** METHYLETHYLPYRIDINE **2 :** any of a class of solid bases containing the imidazole ring formed by condensing aldehydes with aromatic *ortho*-diamines
al·de·hy·do \ˌaldəˈhī(ˌ)dō\ *adj* [*aldehydo-*] **:** of or relating to an aldehyde **:** containing the group —CHO **:** ALDEHYDIC
aldehydo- *comb form* [ISV, fr. *aldehyde* + *-o-*] **1** *usu ital* **:** containing the aldehyde group — in names of open-chain aldehydic forms of specific sugars ⟨*aldehydo*-D-galactose⟩; compare ALD- **2 :** formyl ⟨*aldehydo*benzoic acid⟩
al·der \ˈȯldə(r)\ *n* -s [ME *alder, aller*, fr. OE *alor, aler*; akin to OHG *elira, erila* alder, ON *ǫlr*, (assumed) Goth *alisa* (whence Sp *aliso*), L *alnus*, LGk (Maced dial.) *aliza* white poplar, Lith *alksnis* alder] **1 :** a tree or shrub of the genus *Alnus* **2 :** any of several shrubs resembling the alder
alder blight *n* **:** WOOLLY ALDER APHID
alder buckthorn *also* **alder dogwood** *n* [so called fr. its occurrence in the neighborhood of alders] **:** a common European tree (*Rhamnus frangula*) with flowers in sessile umbels
alder flea beetle *n* **:** a small metallic-colored beetle (*Altica ambiens*) feeding on alders and sometimes causing defoliation
alderfly \ˈ══ˌ═\ *n* **:** any of numerous insects (order Megaloptera) of the genus *Sialis* or related genera having aquatic larvae that are used for bait — compare DOBSONFLY
alder flycatcher *n* **:** a small greenish flycatcher (*Empidonax traillii*) with a dull white breast frequenting alder swamps and other moist secluded spots in much of eastern No. America
alder-leaved buckthorn *n* **:** either of two American shrubs (*Rhamnus alnifolia* or *R. caroliniana*)
alder-leaved dogwood *n* **:** a shrubby dogwood (*Cornus rugosa*) native to eastern No. America
alderliefest *adj* [ME *alderlevest*, fr. *alder-, aller-, alre-* (fr. OE *alra*, gen. pl. of OE *all, eall* all) + *levest*, superl. of *leef* dear — more at ALL, LIEF] *obs* **:** most beloved
al·der·man \ˈȯldə(r)mən\ *n, pl* **aldermen** \-mən\ [ME, fr. OE *aldorman, ealdorman*, fr. *aldor, ealdor* parent, head of a family (fr. *ald, eald* old) + *man* — more at OLD] **1 :** a person of rank, dignity, or authority; *specif* **:** one governing a former kingdom, a district, or a shire as the permanent representative of an Anglo-Saxon king **2** *obs* **:** a headman of a guild **3 a** *in England and Ireland* (1) **:** a magistrate ranking next to the mayor in cities and boroughs from medieval times until modern municipal reorganization (2) **:** a member of the smaller of the two classes composing the borough or county council — compare BAILIE 2b **b :** one of the 26 chief officers chosen for life who heads a ward of the City of London **c :** a member of a legislative body of a city ⟨a board of *aldermen*⟩
al·der·man·ic \ˌ══ˈmanik, -ēk\ *adj* **:** of, relating to, or like an alderman
alderman lizard *n* [so called fr. its large belly] **:** CHUCKWALLA
al·der·man·ly \ˈȯldə(r)mənlē\ *adj* **:** like or appropriate to an alderman ⟨∼ decorum⟩
al·der·man·ry \-rē\ *n* -ES [ME *aldermanrie*, fr. *alderman* + *-rie* -ry] **1 :** a kingdom, district, or shire in Anglo-Saxon England **2 a :** a district of an alderman **b :** the office or rank of an alderman
al·der·ney \ˈȯldə(r)nē, -ni\ *n* -s [fr. *Alderney*, one of the Channel islands in Guernsey bailiwick, England] **1** *usu cap* **:** an animal of any Channel island breed of cattle (as a Jersey or a Guernsey) **2** *often cap* **:** a moderate yellowish brown that is paler than Bismarck brown and less strong and very slightly yellower than maple sugar
al·der·wom·an \-ˌwu̇mən\ *n, pl* **alderwomen** [*alderman* + *woman*] **:** a woman with the office and rank of an alderman
al·di·mine \ˈaldəˌmēn\ *n* -s [*ald-* + *imine*] **:** any Schiff base of the general formula RCH—NH or RCH—NR' formed by condensation of an aldehyde with ammonia or a primary amine
¹al·dine \ˈȯlˌdīn, -ˌdēn *sometimes* ˈal-\ *adj, usu cap* [It *aldino*, fr. *Aldo* Manuzio or Manucci (Aldus Manutius) †1515 It. printer and scholar + It *-ino* -ine] **:** printed or published by Aldus Manutius of Venice or his family in the 16th century who produced fine editions of chiefly Greek, Latin, and Italian classics, each book usu. bearing an anchor and dolphin emblem ⟨an *Aldine* book⟩ ⟨an *Aldine* edition⟩
²aldine \"\ *n* -s *usu cap* **:** an Aldine book or edition
³al·dine \ˈalˌdēn\ *n* -s [ISV *ald-* + *-ine*] **:** PYRAZINE
Al·dis \ˈȯldə̇s\ *trademark* — used for a hand-carried signal lamp used to flash messages esp. from ships and aircraft

anchor and dolphin of Aldus

al·di·tol \ˈaldəˌtȯl, -ˌōl\ *n* -s [*aldose* + *-itol*] **:** a polyhydroxy alcohol (as mannitol) formed by reducing an aldose (as mannose)

aldm *abbr* alderman

al·do- — see ALD-

al·do·bi·on·ic acid \ˌal(ˌ)dō,bīˈänik-\ *n* [blend of *aldonic* and *bi-* (two)] **:** an aldonic acid (as lactobionic acid or maltoni acid) formed by simple oxidation of a reducing disaccharide (as lactose or maltose)

al·do·bi·u·ron·ic acid \-ˌbīyəˈränik-\ *n* [*ald-* + *bi-* + *-uronic*] **:** a disaccharide of acid nature in which one of the two sugar constituents is a uronic acid joined as a glycoside to a hexose or pentose unit

al·do·fu·ran·o·side \-fyüˈranə,sīd\ *n* -s [*ald-* + *furan* + *-oside*] **:** a glycoside containing a 5-member ring and hydrolyzable to an aldose

al·do·hex·ose \ˌaldōˈhek,sōs\ *n* -s [ISV *ald-* + *hexose*] **:** a hexose (as glucose or mannose) of an aldehyde nature

al·do·ke·tene \-ˈkē,tēn\ *n* -s [*ald-* + *ketene*] **:** any ketene having the general formula RHC:CO

al·dol \ˈal,dȯl, -ōl\ *n* -s [ISV *ald-* + *-ol;* orig. formed in F] **1 :** a colorless liquid $CH_3CH(OH)CH_2CHO$ obtained by condensation of two molecules of acetaldehyde and used in organic synthesis and in denaturing alcohol; *β*-hydroxy⸗butyraldehyde — called also *acetaldol* **2 :** any of a class of beta-hydroxy aldehydes typified by acetaldol

al·dol·ase \ˈaldə,lās\ *n* -s [*aldol* + *-ase*] **:** a crystalline enzyme that occurs widely in animal tissues (as muscle) and plant cells (as of bacteria and yeasts) and that accelerates both the cleavage of the 1,6-diphosphoric ester of fructose into two triose phosphates and the reverse reaction

al·dol·i·za·tion \ˌal,dȯləˈzāshən, -dōl-\ *n* -s **:** conversion into an aldol

al·dol·ize \ˈaldə,līz\ *vb* -ED/-ING/-S [*aldol* + *-ize*] *vt* **:** to convert into an aldol ~ *vi* **:** to undergo aldolization

aldon- *or* **aldono-** *comb form* [ISV, fr. *aldonic* (in *aldonic acid*)] **:** related to or derived from an aldonic acid ⟨*aldon*amide⟩ ⟨*aldono*lactone⟩

al·don·ic acid \(ˈ)alˈdänik-\ *n* [*ald-* + *-onic*] **:** any of a class of acids (as gluconic acid) formed from aldoses (as glucose) by oxidizing the aldehyde group to a carboxyl group

al·do·py·ran·o·side \ˌal(ˌ)dō,pīˈranə,sīd\ *n* -s [*ald-* + *pyran* + *-oside*] **:** a glycoside containing a 6-member ring and hydrolyzable to an aldose

al·dose \ˈal,dōs\ *n* -s [ISV *ald-* + *-ose*] **:** a sugar (as xylose, glucose, mannose) containing one aldehyde group per molecule — contrasted with *ketose;* see MONOSACCHARIDE

al·do·side \ˈaldə,sīd\ *n* -s [*ald-* + *-oside*] **:** any glycoside derived from an aldose

al·dos·ter·one \alˈdästə,rōn, ˌaldōstəˈrōn\ *n* -s [*ald-* + *sterol* + *-one*] **:** a steroid hormone $C_{21}H_{28}O_5$ extracted from the adrenal cortex that is very active in regulating the salt and water balance in the body

al·dox·ime \alˈdäk,sēm, -ˌsəm\ *n* -s [ISV *ald-* + *oxime*] **:** any oxime of an aldehyde

al·drin \ˈȯldrən\ *n* -s [Kurt *Alder* †1958 Ger. chemist + E *-in*] **:** a white crystalline insecticide consisting chiefly or entirely of a chlorinated tetracyclic derivative $C_{12}H_8Cl_6$ of naphthalene obtained by the Diels-Alder reaction

al·dro·van·da \ˌaldrōˈvandə\ *n, cap* [NL, fr. Ulisse *Aldrovandi* †1605 It. naturalist] **:** a genus of floating aquatic plants (family Droseraceae) found from southern Europe to Australia having small white flowers and whorls of leaves that act as traps for insects

ale \ˈāl, ˈāəl\ *n* -s [ME, fr. OE *alu, ealu;* akin to MHG *al*schaf vessel for beer, OS *alo*fat, ON *öl* beer, ale, and perh. to L *alumen* alum, Gk *alydimos* bitter] **1 :** a malted and hopped beverage that is usu. higher in alcoholic content than beer, heavier in body, and more bitter and is brewed by top fermentation **2 :** a country festival at which ale was the principal beverage ⟨at wakes and ~*s* —Ben Jonson⟩ — **in ale** *obs* **:** drunk with ale

aleak \əˈ-\ *adj* [¹*a-* + *leak* (v.)] **:** LEAKING ⟨hills ~ with thousands of cascades —Stephen Graham⟩

ale·a·to·ry \ˈālēə,tōrē, -ōr-, -ri\ *adj* [L *aleatorius* of a gambler, fr. *aleator* gambler, dice player, fr. *alea,* a dice game] **1 :** depending on an uncertain event or contingency as to both profit and loss ⟨an ~ contract⟩ **2 :** relating to good or bad luck, esp. the risks of bad luck ⟨the ~ element in life⟩

alebench \ˈ⸗,⸗\ *n* **:** a bench in or before an alehouse

alec·i·thal \(ˈ)āˈlesəthəl\ *also* **ale·cith·ic** \ˌāləˈsithik\ *adj* [²*a-* + Gk *lekithos* yolk + E *-al* or *-ic*] **:** without yolk — used of eggs with little or no food yolk embedded in their protoplasm (as those of placental mammals)

aleconner \ˈ⸗,⸗⸗\ *n* -s [*ale* + *conner*] **:** an English town official formerly charged with tasting and testing ale and beer and still a titular official in some communities

ale·cost \ˈā(ə)l,käst\ *n* -s [*ale* + obs. E *cost* costmary — more at COSTMARY] **:** COSTMARY 1

¹al·ec·to·ria \ˌaləkˈtōrēə\ *or* **al·ec·to·ry** \əˈlektərē\ *or* **al·ec·to·ri·an** \ˌaləkˈtōrēən\ *or* **al·ec·to·ri·us** \-ōrēəs\ *n, pl* **alectori·ae** \ˌaləkˈtōrē,ē\ *or* **allectories** *or* **alectorians** *or* **alecto·rii** \-ōrē,ī\ [*alectoria, allectory* fr. ML *alectoria,* short for L *alectoria gemma,* lit., cock's gem, fr. *alectoria* (fem. of *alectorius* of a cock, fr. Gk *alektōr* cock) + *gemma* gem; *alectorian* fr. L *alectorius* + E *-an; alectorius* fr. L, adj.] **:** a talismanic stone that is supposedly found in the crop of a cock and is believed to be magical

²al·ec·to·ria \ˌaləkˈtōrēə\ *n, cap* [NL, fr. Gk *alektōr* cock (prob. fr. *Alektōr,* a name) + NL *-ia*] **:** a genus of lichens (family Usneaceae) characterized by a dark brown erect or pendulous much-branched thallus of cylindrical form

alec·to·ris \əˈlektərəs\ *n, cap* [NL, fr. Gk *alektōr* cock] **:** a genus of Old World partridges including the chukars

alec·tri·on \əˈlektrē,än\ *n,* [NL, perh. fr. Gk *alektōr* cock] *syn of* NASSARIUS

alec·try·o·man·cy \əˈlektrēō,man(t)sē\ *or* **alec·to·ro·man·cy** \-tərō,-\ *n* -ES [Gk *alektryōn* or *alektōr* cock + E *-mancy*] **:** divination by means of a cock encircled by grains of corn placed on the letters of the alphabet which are then put together in the order in which the grains were eaten

alec·try·on \əˈlektrē,än\ *n, cap* [NL, fr. Gk *alektryōn* cock, fr. *Alektryōn,* a name] **:** a monotypic genus of New Zealand trees of the family Sapindaceae with alternate compound leaves and showy paniculate flowers — see TITOKI

aledraper *n* [*ale* + *draper* (as in *linen draper*)] *obs* **:** an alehouse keeper

alee \əˈlē\ *adv* (*or adj*) [ME, fr. ¹*a-* + *lee*] **1 :** on or toward the lee **:** to leeward ⟨put the helm ~⟩ ⟨with helm ~⟩ — opposed to *aweather* **2 :** ahead or in the direction of movement (as of a glacier or a current) ⟨sand is deposited ~ of the course base —*Jour. of Geol.*⟩

alef *var of* ALEPH

aleft \əˈ-\ *adv* [ME, fr. ¹*a-* + *left*] **:** to or on the left

ale gallon *n* **:** an old English unit of liquid capacity equal to 282 cubic inches or 4.62 liters — called also *beer gallon*

al·e·gar \ˈaligə(r), ˈāl-\ *n* -s [*ale* + *vinegar*] **:** sour ale **:** vinegar made of ale

al·e·gria \ˌaləˈgrēə\ *n* -s [MexSp *alegria,* fr. Sp, happiness, gaiety, fr. *alegre* happy, gay, fr. (assumed) VL *alecrus* — more at ALLEGRO] *Southwest* **:** any of certain herbs of the genus *Amaranthus* the red juice of which is sometimes used locally as a cosmetic

ale·gri·as \ˌaləˈgrēəs, ˌäl-\ *n pl but sing or pl in constr* [Sp *alegrias,* pl. of *alegria,* lit., gaiety, happiness] **:** a solo flamenco dance performed by a woman and marked by many intricate heelwork variations

alehouse \ˈ⸗,⸗\ *n* [ME *alehous,* fr. OE *ealahūs,* fr. *ealu* ale + *hūs* house — more at ALE, HOUSE] **:** a place where ale is sold to be drunk on the premises

aleknight *n* [*ale* + *knight*] *obs* **:** TIPPLER

al·e·man·ni *or* **al·a·man·ni** \ˌaləˈman,ī, -manē\ *n pl, usu cap* [LL, of Gmc origin; akin to Goth *alamans* totality of people] **:** a predominantly Suevian coalition of Germanic peoples first mentioned in the 3d century A.D. that settled in the area between the Main and Danube rivers and whose descendants are German-speaking inhabitants of Alsace, Switzerland, and southwestern Germany

¹al·e·man·nic *or* **al·a·man·nic** \ˌaləˈmanik\ *also* **al·e·man·ni·an** *or* **al·a·man·ni·an** \-nēən\ *n* -s *usu cap* [*Alemanni, Alamanni* + E *-ic* or *-an*] **:** the group of dialects of German spoken in Alsace, Switzerland, and southwestern Germany

²alemannic *or* **alamannic** *also* **alemannian** *or* **alamannian** *adj, usu cap* [*Alemanni, Alamanni* + E *-ic* or *-an*] **1 :** of, relating to, or characteristic of the Alemanni **2 :** of, relating to, or characteristic of the Alemannic dialects

alem·bert \ˌaləmˈbe(ə)r\ *n* -s *usu cap* [after Jean Le Rond d'*Alembert* †1783 Fr. mathematician] **:** a system of betting in gambling games whereby the player increases his stake by one unit each time he loses a bet and decreases it by one unit each time he wins one — called also *progressive system*

alem·bic \əˈlembik\ *n* -s [ME *alambic, alembic,* fr. MF & ML; MF *alambic* & ML *alembicum,* fr. Ar *al-anbiq* the still, fr. *al* the + *anbiq* still, fr. LGk *ambik-, ambix* alembic, fr. Gk, spouted cup, cap of a still] **1 :** an apparatus usu. made of glass or metal formerly much used in distillation **2 :** something that refines or transmutes as if by a process of distillation ⟨intellect as an ~ for the refinement of sensation —*Listener*⟩ ⟨philosophy of Asia and Greece as filtered through the ~ of Plato's mind —*Amer. Scholar*⟩

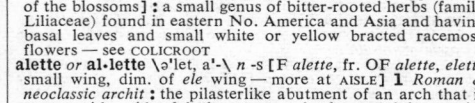

alembic: *a* head, *b* cucurbit, *c* receiver, *d* lamp

alem·bi·cate \-bə,kāt, *usu* -ād·+V\ *vt* -ED/-ING/-S **:** to distill as if in an alembic **:** refine to an essence

alembicated *adj* **:** overrefined as if by excessive distillation **:** excessively subtle **:** PRECIOUS ⟨highly sophisticated and ~ poetry —Richard Aldington⟩ ⟨the ~, the etiolate, the highly elaborated —Eric Partridge⟩

alem·bi·ca·tion \əˌlembəˈkāshən\ *n* -s **1 :** the action of alembicating or the state of being alembicated **:** DISTILLATION ⟨the ~ of a lifetime's thought and experience —Olin Downes⟩ **2 :** OVERREFINEMENT, PRECIOSITY

alem·broth \əˈlem,brȯth, ˈaləm,-\ *n* -s [ME *alembroth, alembroke, albrot*] **:** a double chloride of ammonium and mercury believed by the alchemists to be a universal solvent — called also *key of art, salt of wisdom*

alem·mal \(ˈ)āˈleməl\ *adj* [²*a-* + neuri*lemmal*] *of a nerve fiber* **:** without neurilemma

alen·çon \əˈlen,sän, -en(t)sən *also* ˈalənˈsän\ *n* -s *or* **alençon lace** *n* -s *usu cap A* [*Alençon* fr. F *alençon,* short for *point d'Alençon* Alençon lace, fr. *Alençon,* France, where it is made; *Alençon lace,* trans. of F *point d'Alençon*] **:** a delicate orig. handmade needlepoint lace characterized by the cordonnet outlining the floral designs on a fine mesh ground

alençon diamond *n, usu cap A* [fr. *Alençon,* France] **:** a smoky quartz sometimes valued as a jewel

aleph *also* **alef** \ˈä,lef, -ˌləf\ *n* -s [Heb *āleph,* prob. var. of *eleph* ox] **1 :** the first letter of the Hebrew alphabet — symbol א; see ALPHABET table **2 :** the letter of the Phoenician or of any of various other Semitic alphabets corresponding to Hebrew aleph **3 :** any transfinite cardinal number

aleph–null \ˈ⸗(ˌ)⸗ˈ⸗\ *also* **aleph–zero** \ˈ⸗(ˌ)⸗ˈ⸗(ˌ)⸗\ *n* **:** the smallest transfinite cardinal number **:** the power of the aggregate of all the finite integers

¹alep·i·dote \(ˈ)āˈlepə,dōt\ *adj* [Gk *a-* ²a- + *lepidōtos* covered with scales, fr. *lepid-, lepis* scale — more at LEPID-] *zool* **:** without scales

²alepidote \"\ *n* -s **:** a fish without scales

alep·i·sau·rus \ˌaləpəˈsȯrəs\ *n, cap* [NL, fr. Gk *alepis* without scales (fr. *a-* ²a- + *lepis* scale) + NL *-saurus*] **:** a genus (order Iniomi) of large slender scaleless active and predaceous deep-sea fishes comprising the handsaw fishes

¹alep·pine \əˈlepən, -ˌpen *also* -ˌpēn, -ˌpīn\ *adj, usu cap* [*Aleppo,* Syria + E *-ine*] **1 :** of, relating to, or characteristic of the city of Aleppo, Syria **2 :** of, relating to, or characteristic of the people of Aleppo

²aleppine \"\ *n* -s *cap* **:** a native or resident of Aleppo

alep·po \əˈle(ˌ)pō\ *adj, usu cap* [fr. *Aleppo,* Syria] **:** of or from the city of Aleppo, Syria **:** of the kind or style prevalent in Aleppo

aleppo boil *n, usu cap A* **:** ORIENTAL SORE

aleppo gall *n, usu cap A* **:** a hard brittle spherical body that is about the size of a hickory nut and is produced on the twigs of an oak (*Quercus infectoria*) by a gall wasp (*Cynips tinctoria*)

aleppo grass *n, usu cap A* **:** JOHNSON GRASS

aleppo pine *n, usu cap A* **:** a pine (*Pinus halepensis*) of southern Europe and the Levant that is of graceful habit, has usu. two leaves in each persistent sheath, and yields a wood that is much used for shipbuilding

aleppo stone *n, usu cap A* [so called fr. its use as a remedy for Aleppo boils] **:** an old oriental gem made by cutting an agate so that it suggests an eye — called also *eye agate*

aler·ce *or* **aler·se** \əˈlersə\ *n* -s [Sp *alerce* larch, fr. Ar *al-arz* the larch] **1 :** the wood of the sandarac tree of Morocco **2 :** an irregularly branched Patagonian timber tree (*Fitzroya patagonica*)

alerion *var of* ALLERION

¹alert \əˈlərt, -ət, -əit, *usu* -d·+V\ *adj, sometimes* -ER/-EST [It *all'erta* on the watch, lit., the ascent] **1 a :** marked by careful zealous watchfulness and promptness to counter threats and dangers and to cope with emergencies ⟨silent and ~, like a sentinel on duty —J.G.Frazer⟩ ⟨the ~ Washington who guided Braddock's army —Allan Nevins & H.S.Commager⟩ **b :** marked by ready perception and recognition and by promptness in perceiving, evaluating, responding ⟨~ to the script's theatrical possibilities —John Mason Brown⟩ ⟨~ to urge favorable legislation by Congress —Louis Pelzer⟩ **2 :** marked by ready activity, brisk liveliness, or quick reactions ⟨an ~ birdlike movement —Ellen Glasgow⟩ ⟨light, ~ step and a certain gamesome assurance of manner —G.B. Shaw⟩ **syn** see INTELLIGENT, WATCHFUL

²alert \"\ *n* -s **1 a :** an alarm or other signal to warn of danger (as from hostile aircraft or a violent storm) **b :** the period during which an alert is in effect **2 :** the state of readiness of those warned by an alert ⟨sirens brought the whole street to the ~⟩ — see BLUE ALERT, RED ALERT, WHITE ALERT, YELLOW ALERT — **on the alert :** on the lookout for or watch against attack or danger **:** ready to act

³alert \"\ *vb* -ED/-ING/-S *vt* **1 :** to call to a state of readiness: as **a :** to make watchful **:** put on guard **:** WARN ⟨hurricane warning systems for ~*ing* island residents⟩ ⟨vigilantes who could ~ each community to the threatened danger —*Atlantic*⟩; *esp* **:** to call to a state of readiness for an air raid ⟨sirens ~*ing* the cities long before the bombers arrived⟩ **b :** to give warning or notice to (as troops or their commanders) to prepare for movement or action ⟨~*ed* the division for shipment overseas⟩ **2 :** to make clearly perceptive to or aware of **:** AWAKEN, AROUSE ⟨~*ed* a community to the need for better schools⟩ ⟨a matter of ~*ing* teachers to their responsibility —*Educational Leadership*⟩ ~ *vi* **:** to give a warning signal esp. in the presence of an enemy — used chiefly of dogs employed in scouting ⟨after proceeding several hundred yards . . . the patrol's scout dog ~*ed*⟩ ⟨dogs ~ on all human beings, not the enemy alone —*Infantry Jour.*⟩

alert·ly *adv* **:** in an alert manner ⟨much enjoyment may be gained from listening to music ~ —Charles Johnson⟩

alert·ness *n* -ES **:** the quality or state of being alert

ales *pl of* ALE

-a·les \ˈā(ˌ)lēz\ *n pl suffix* [NL, fr. L, pl. of *-alis* -al] **:** plants belonging to or related to ⟨Chytridi*ales*⟩ ⟨Ros*ales*⟩ — in the names of orders of plants; in some classifications in the names of other superfamilial groups of plants (as alliances or cohorts)

al·e·san \ˈalə,san\ *n* -s [F *alezan,* fr. Sp *alazán*] **:** a light brown that is less strong and slightly yellower and lighter than blush, paler and slightly redder than French beige, and redder and paler than cork — called also *café au lait, French nude*

aleth·ic \əˈlethik, -ēth-\ *adj* [Gk *alēthikos,* fr. *alētheia* truth (fr. *alēthes* true, fr. *a-* ²a- + *-lēthēs,* fr. *lēthē* forgetfulness) + *-ikos* -ic — more at LETHE] **:** of or relating to truth ⟨~ modal⟩

al·e·thop·ter·is \ˌaləˈthäptərəs\ *n, cap* [NL, fr. Gk *alēthēs* (fr. *alēthēs* true) + NL *-pteris*] **:** a genus of large fossil seed ferns represented by abundant remains in Carboniferous coal measures and having large bipinnate to tripinnate fronds with the thick pinnules being inserted on the rachis by a broad decurrent base — **al·e·thop·ter·oid** \ˌaləˈthäptə,rȯid\ *adj*

al·e·tris \ˈalə·trəs\ *n, cap* [NL, fr. Gk, female slave who ground meal, noble Athenian maiden who prepared offering cakes, fr. *alein, aletreuein* to grind; fr. the floury appearance of the blossoms] **:** a small genus of bitter-rooted herbs (family Liliaceae) found in eastern No. America and Asia and having basal leaves and small white or yellow bracted racemose flowers — see COLICROOT

alette *or* **al·lette** \əˈlet, aˈ-\ *n* -s [F *alette,* fr. OF *alette, elette* small wing, dim. of *ele* wing — more at AISLE] **1** *Roman & neoclassic archit* **:** the pilasterlike abutment of an arch that is seen on either side of the large engaged column and that carries the entablature **2 :** a wing of a building

aleu·ke·mia *also* **aleu·kae·mia** \ˌā(ˌ)+\ *n* [NL, fr. ²*a-* + *leukemia, leukaemia*] **:** leukemia in which the circulating leukocytes are normal or decreased in number

aleu·ke·mic *also* **aleu·kae·mic** \ˌā(ˌ)⸗ˈ⸗⸗\ *or* **aleu·ce·mic** *or* **aleu·cae·mic** \-ˈsē-\ *adj* [ISV ²*a-* + *leukemic, leukaemic, leucemic, leucaemic*] **:** not marked by increase in circulating white blood cells

aleukemic leukemia *also* **aleukemic myelosis** *n* **:** leukemia resulting from changes in the leukocyte-forming tissues and characterized by a normal or decreased number of leukocytes in the circulating blood

aleu·ri·o·spore \əˈlürēə,spō(ə)r\ *also* **aleu·ro·spore** \əˈlürə,-\ *n* [*aleurio-* or *aleuro-* (fr. Gk *aleuron*) + *spore*] **:** an asexual spore in certain fungi produced terminally by septation but remaining attached until disintegration of the mycelium **:** a nondeciduous chlamydospore

al·eu·ri·tes \ˌalyəˈrīd·ēz\ *n, cap* [NL, fr. Gk *aleuritēs* of flour, fr. *aleuron* flour + *-itēs* -ite] **:** a genus of Asiatic trees (family Euphorbiaceae) having a milky juice, small white flowers, and rich oily seeds in drupes — see CANDLENUT

al·eu·rit·ic acid \ˌalyəˈrid·ik-\ *n* [NL *Aleurites* + E *-ic*] **:** a crystalline acid $C_{15}H_{28}(OH)_3COOH$ occurring in shellac; 9,10,16-trihydroxy-palmitic acid

aleuro- *comb form* [F, fr. Gk, fr. *aleuron* wheat flour, flour; akin to Arm *alam* I grind] **:** flour ⟨*aleuro*meter⟩

al·eu·ro·bi·us \ˌalyəˈrōbēəs\ *n, cap* [NL, fr. *aleuro-* + *-bius*] **:** a genus of mites (family Tyroglyphidae) including a species (*A. farinae*) common in flour and stored cereals and implicated as a cause of enteritis and dysentery in animals feeding on such contaminated grain products

aleu·ro·did \əˈlürədəd, -ˌdid\ *n* -s [NL *Aleurodidae*] **:** ALEYRODID

al·eu·rod·i·dae \ˌalyəˈrädə,dē\ [NL, alter. of *Aleyrodidae*] *syn of* ALEYRODIDAE

aleu·ro·man·cy \əˈlürə,man(t)sē\ *n* -ES [F *aleuromancie,* fr. Gk *aleuromanteion,* fr. *aleuro-* + *manteion* divination, oracle] **:** divination by means of flour

al·eu·rom·e·ter \ˌalyəˈrämədə(r)\ *n* -s [*aleuro-* + *-meter*] **:** an instrument for determining the expansive properties or the quality of gluten in flour

aleu·ro·nat \əˈlürə,nat\ *n* -s [G *aleuronat,* fr. *aleuron* aleurone + *-at* -ate] **:** a flour with a high gluten content

al·eu·rone \ˈalyə,rōn\ *also* **al·eu·ron** \-,rän\ *n* -s [G *aleuron,* fr. Gk *aleuron* flour — more at ALEURO-] **:** ergastic protein matter in the form of minute granules or grains produced by crystallization or solidification of the protein content of certain vacuoles, often associated with other substances (as calcium oxalate), and occurring chiefly in endosperm and in some seeds (as cereal grains) concentrated in a special peripheral layer of endodermal cells — **al·eu·ron·ic** \ˌalyəˈränik\ *adj*

¹aleut \əˈlüt, aˈ- *also* əlˈyüt *or* alˈy- *or* ˈalē,üt *or* ˈal,yüt\ *also* **aleu·tian** \əˈlüshən *also* əlˈyü-\ *n* -s *cap* [Russ, prob. fr. a native name in Asia] **1 a :** a people of the Aleutian and Shumagin islands and the western part of Alaska peninsula **b :** a member of such people **2 :** an Eskimo-Aleut language of the Aleut people

²aleut \"\ *adj, usu cap* **:** of or belonging to an early, middle, or late period of a prehistoric Aleutian culture of about 100 B.C. to A.D. 1750

aleu·tian \əˈlüshən *also* əlˈyü-\ *adj, usu cap* **:** of or belonging to the Aleutian islands

al·e·vin \ˈaləvən\ *n* -s [F, OF, fr. *alever* to lift up, rear (offspring), fr. L *allevare* to lift up, fr. *ad-* + *levare* to raise — more at LEVER] **:** a young fish; *esp* **:** the newly hatched salmon when still attached to the yolk mass

¹ale·wife \ˈāl,wīf\ *n, pl* **alewives** \-,wīvz\ [ME *alewif,* fr. *ale* + *wif* wife] **:** a woman who keeps an alehouse

²ale·wife \", sometimes ˈel-\ *n, pl* **alewives** \-,wīvz\ [prob. so called fr. its big belly] **1 a :** a food fish (*Pomolobus pseudoharengus*) of the herring family (Clupeidae) very abundant on the Atlantic coast **b :** any of several related fishes: as (1) **:** MENHADEN (2) **:** a pilchard (*Harengula pensacolae*) of the Florida coast (3) **:** ALLICE SHAD **2 :** ROUND POMPANO

¹al·ex·an·der \ˌaligˈzandə(r), ˌel-, -lēg- *sometimes* -ān-; *attrib* ⸗⸗ˈ⸗⸗\ *or* **al·i·san·der** \ˌaləˈsa- *also* -sā-\ *n* -s [ME *alexaundre, alisaundre,* fr. ML & OF; ME *alexaundre* fr. OF *alexandre,* fr. ML *alexandrum,* prob. by folk etymology (influence of L *Alexander* Alexander the Great †323 B.C. king of Macedonia) fr. L *holus atrum,* fr. *holus* vegetable (akin to L *helvus* light bay) + *atrum,* neut. of *ater* black; ME *alisaundre* fr. OF, fr. ML *alexandrum* — more at ATROCIOUS, YELLOW] **:** any of various plants of the family Umbelliferae: as **a :** a European plant (*Smyrnium olusatrum*) that somewhat resembles celery and was formerly cultivated as a potherb — usu. used in pl. **b :** COW PARSNIP — usu. used in pl.

²alexander \"\ *n* -s *usu cap* [by shortening & alter. fr. *Alexandrine silk*] **:** a striped silk of the 14th to 16th centuries

³alexander \"\ *also* **alexander cocktail** *n* -s *often cap A* [prob. fr. the name *Alexander*] **:** an iced cocktail made from crème de cacao, sweet cream, and gin or brandy

al·ex·an·dra palm \ˌaligˈzandrə-, ˌel-, -lēg- *sometimes* -ān-\ *n, usu cap A* [after *Alexandra* †1925 Danish princess, queen of England] **:** a lofty Australian pinnate-leaved palm (*Archontophoenix alexandrae*)

al·ex·an·dria \ˌ⸗⸗ˈ⸗drēə\ *adj, usu cap* [fr. *Alexandria,* Egypt] **:** of or from the city of Alexandria, Egypt **:** of the kind or style prevalent in Alexandria **:** ALEXANDRIAN

¹al·ex·an·dri·an \-ēən\ *adj, usu cap* [*Alexandria,* Egypt + E *-an*] **1 :** of, relating to, or characteristic of Alexandria, esp. Alexandria, Egypt **2 :** of, relating to, or characteristic of the people of Alexandria **3** [so called from the cultural prominence of Alexandria in the Hellenistic period] **:** HELLENISTIC **4 a :** of, belonging to, or like the Alexandrian school **b** *of a writer or literary work* (1) **:** overly recondite, derivative, or artificial (2) **:** concerned primarily with the technical perfection of language or literary form

²alexandrian \"\ *n* -s **1** *cap* **:** a native or resident of Alexandria **2** *usu cap* **:** a member of the Alexandrian school

³alexandrian \"\ *adj* [*Alexander* the Great †323 B.C. king of Macedonia + E *-ian*] **1 a** *usu cap* **:** of or relating to Alexander the Great **b** *often cap* [by alter.] **:** ALEXANDRINE **2** *usu cap* [*Alexander,* the name + E *-ian*] **:** of or relating to the name Alexander or any individual so named; *esp* **:** of or relating to Pope Alexander VI (about 1431–1503)

⁴alexandrian \"\ *n* -s *often cap* [by alter.] **:** ALEXANDRINE

alexandrian clover *n, usu cap A* [¹*Alexandrian* + *clover*] **:** BERSEEM

al·ex·an·dri·an·ism \ˌ⸗⸗ˈ⸗⸗⸗,nizəm\ *n* -s *often cap* [¹*Alexandrian* + *-ism*] **:** the teachings or tenets of the Alexandrian culture or theology — compare ALEXANDRIAN SCHOOL, PATRISTIC PHILOSOPHY

alexandrian laurel *n, usu cap A* [¹*Alexandrian* + *laurel*] **1 :** a leafless shrub (*Danaë racemosa*) of the Levant **2 :** POON TREE

alexandrian philosophy *n, usu cap A* [¹*Alexandrian*] **:** the philosophy that flourished at Alexandria in the early centuries of the Christian era and that was chiefly concerned with attempts to interpret oriental and esp. Hebrew religious beliefs in the light of Greek philosophy — compare NEOPLATONISM, NEO-PYTHAGOREANISM

alexandrian school *n, usu cap A* [¹*Alexandrian*] **1 :** the school of literature, science, and philosophy that flourished at Alexandria while that city was ruled by the Greeks and the Romans **2 :** an ante-Nicene school of patristic philosophy developed slightly later than the African school, taking its rise from Pantaenus, including Clement and Origen, and centered in Alexandria **3 :** a succession of Alexandrine Christian theologians who, in the 5th century and later, in the Christological debates against the theologians of Antioch, stressed the divinity and unity of Jesus Christ

al·ex·an·dria senna \¦==,-drēə-\ *n, usu cap A* [fr. *Alexandria*, Egypt, its chief place of export] **:** senna from a cassia (*Cassia acutifolia*)

[1]**al·ex·an·drine** \¦alig¦zandrən, ¦el-, -lēg-, -,drīn, -,drēn *sometimes* -zän-\ *adj, often cap* [MF *alexandrin*, fr. *Alexandre* Alexander the Great †323 B.C. king of Macedonia + MF *-in* -ine; fr. its use in an Old French poem on Alexander] **:** of, relating to, or having the structure of an alexandrine

[2]**alexandrine** \"\ *n* -s *often cap* **:** a verse of 12 syllables or of 13 syllables when with feminine rhyme consisting regularly of 6 iambics with a caesura after the 3d iambic — compare HEROIC VERSE

[3]**alexandrine** \"\ *adj, often cap* [L *Alexandrinus*, fr. *Alexandria*, Egypt + L *-inus* -ine] **:** ALEXANDRIAN

alexandrine rat *n, usu cap A* [[3]*Alexandrine;* fr. its original habitat; trans. of NL *rattus alexandrinus*] **:** ROOF RAT

al·ex·an·drite \,==¦=,drīt\ *n* -s [G *alexandrit*, fr. *Alexander I* †1825 Russ. emperor + G *-it* -ite] **:** a grass-green variety of chrysoberyl that shows a columbine-red color by transmitted or artificial light

alex·ia \ə'leksēə, (')ā'-\ *n* -s [NL, fr. [2]*a-* + Gk *lexis* speech (fr. *legein* to speak, but influenced in meaning by L *legere* to read) + NL *-ia* — more at LEGEND] **:** aphasia characterized by loss of ability to read

alex·ian \ə'lekshən, -ksēən\ *n* -s *usu cap* [St. *Alexius*, 5th cent. Roman Christian founder of the order + E *-an*] **:** a member of a Roman Catholic order devoted to care of the sick

alex·in \ə'leksən\ *also* **alex·ine** \", -,sēn\ *n* -s [G *alexin*, fr. Gk *alexein* to ward off, protect + G *-in* -in, -ine; akin to OE *ealh* temple, OS *alah*, Primitive Norse (Runic) *aluh* amulet, Goth *alhs* temple, Gk *alkar* protection, Skt *rakṣati* he protects, guards] **:** COMPLEMENT 10 — **al·ex·in·ic** \¦a,lek¦sinik\ *adj*

alexipharmac *n* -s *obs* **:** ALEXIPHARMIC

[1]**alex·i·phar·mic** \ə,leksə'färmik\ *n* -s [alter. of earlier *alexipharmac*, fr. Gk *alexipharmakos*, fr. *alexein* + *pharmakon* poison, drug, remedy — more at PHARMACY] **:** an antidote against poison or infection

[2]**alexipharmic** \=¦==¦==\ *or* **alex·i·phar·mi·cal** \-ə̇kəl\ *adj* **:** expelling or counteracting poison **:** ANTIDOTAL

ale yard *n* **:** a tall slender flaring drinking glass used also as a measure for liquids — compare YARD OF ALE

al·ey·ro·des \,alə'rō(,)dēz\ *n, cap* [NL, irreg. fr. Gk *aleurōdēs* like flour, fr. *aleuron* flour — more at ALEURO-] **:** the type genus of Aleyrodidae including several pests of cultivated plants

[1]**aley·ro·did** \ə'lārədəd, -,did\ *n* -s [NL *Aleyrodidae*] **:** an insect of the family Aleyrodidae **:** WHITEFLY

[2]**aleyrodid** \"\ *adj* **:** of or relating to the Aleyrodidae

al·ey·rod·i·dae \,alə'rädə,dē\ *n pl, cap* [NL *Aleyrodes*, type genus + *-idae*] **:** a family of minute homopterous insects winged as adults with the body and wings covered with a white powdery wax, the larvae being initially motile but after the first molt resembling unarmored scales and, like these, feeding on plant juices — compare CITRUS WHITEFLY, GREENHOUSE WHITEFLY

[1]**al·fa** \'alfə\ *or* **alfa grass** *n* -s [Ar *halfā'*] *Africa* **:** ESPARTO

[2]**alfa** \"\ *usu cap* — a communications code word for the letter *a*

al·fal·fa \al'falfə, *attrib* (')=¦==\ *n* -s [Sp., modif. of Ar dial. (Spain) *al-fasfaṣah* the alfalfa, alter. of *al-fiṣfiṣah*] **:** an important European leguminous forage plant (*Medicago sativa*) with trifoliate leaves and bluish purple flowers grown widely and principally for hay, capable of surviving dry periods because of its extraordinarily long root system, and adapted to widely varying conditions of climate and soil — called also *lucerne*

alfalfa butterfly *n* **:** an orange butterfly (*Colias eurytheme*) that is the adult form of the alfalfa caterpillar — compare CLOUDED SULPHUR

alfalfa caterpillar *n* **:** the green larva of the alfalfa butterfly that feeds on the foliage of alfalfa through most of No. America and is esp. abundant and destructive in the southwestern U. S.

alfalfa dwarf *n* **:** a virus disease of alfalfa that appears also as Pierce's disease of grapes and is characterized by dwarfing and usu. by darker color of leaves

alfalfa looper *n* **:** the caterpillar of a noctuid moth (*Autographa californica*) sometimes injurious to alfalfa

alfalfa meal *n* **:** ground alfalfa hay

alfalfa plant bug *n* **:** an Old World mirid bug (*Adelphocoris lineolatus*) accidentally introduced into Minnesota where it seriously damages flowering clover and alfalfa

alfalfa snout beetle *n* **:** a parthenogenetic wingless Old World weevil (*Brachyrhinus ligustici*) that attacks clovers, alfalfa, and other legumes and is esp. destructive to alfalfa since the larvae feed on the taproot while the adults consume the leaves

alfalfa webworm *n* **:** the small greenish or blackish larva of a pyralid moth (*Loxostege commixtalis*) that feeds on and webs together the leaves of various succulent plants and is esp. destructive on sugar beet and alfalfa

alfalfa weevil *n* **:** a small dark-brown European weevil (*Hypera postica*) now widely established in No. America having a yellowish or greenish white-striped larva that feeds on the foliage of alfalfa

al·fe·rez \al'ferəs, -ir-\ *n, pl* **alfere·ces** \,alfə'rāsēz, -sə̇z\ *also* **alferez** \al'ferəs, -ir-\ [Sp *alférez*, fr. Ar *al-fāris* the horseman, fr. *faras* horse] **:** ENSIGN, STANDARD-BEARER — used as a military title

al·fil·a·ria *or* **al·fil·e·ria** *also* **al·fil·e·ri·lla** \(')al,filə'rēə\ *n* -s [modif. of AmerSp *alfilerillo*, fr. Sp, dim. of *alfiler* pin, modif. of Ar *al-khilāl* the thorn, the pin] **:** a European weed (*Erodium cicutarium*) grown for forage in the dry regions of the southwestern U. S. — called also *pin grass*

al·fil·e·ri·llo \-'rē(,)(y)ō\ *n* -s [AmerSp, alfilerillo, alfilaria] **:** a Mexican cactus (*Peireskiopsis diguetii*) used for hedges

al·fin \'alfə̇n\ *adj* [alcohol + *olefin*] **:** of or relating to any of various catalysts made from sodium derivatives of alcohols (as isopropyl alcohol) and olefins (as propylene) and used in certain polymerizations (as of butadiene alone or with styrene and a high-viscosity oil) yielding synthetic rubbers

al·fi·o·na \,alfē'ōnə\ *or* **al·fi·o·ne** \-ōnē\ *n* -s [perh. fr. MexSp] **:** RUBBERLIP PERCH

al·for·ja \al'fórhə\ *n* -s [Sp, fr. Ar *al-khurj* the saddlebag, the wallet] *West* **:** SADDLEBAG

al·fre·di·an \al'frēdēən\ *adj, usu cap* [*Alfred* the Great †899 king of the West Saxons + E *-ian*] **:** belonging or relating to or originating with Alfred the Great ⟨the *Alfredian* Gospels⟩

[1]**al·fres·co** \(')al'fre(,)skō\ *adv* [It, lit., in the open] **1** *of painting* **:** in the fresco manner **2 :** in the open air ⟨what Paris . . . offered in its cloistered salons . . . Venice presented ~ amid its marble-walled canals —Janet Flanner⟩

[2]**alfresco** \(')al¦f-\ *adj* **1** *of a painting* **:** executed in fresco **2 :** OPEN-AIR ⟨an ~ dinner⟩

al·fur \'al,f(y)ů(ə)r\ *also* **al·fu·ro** \al'f(y)ů(,)rō\ *n* -s *usu cap* [Sp *alfur, alfor*, fr. Pg *alforro*, of Malayo-Indonesian origin; akin to Indonesian *alifuru*] **1 :** any one of a group of aboriginal peoples of mixed ancestry inhabiting interior regions of the Moluccas and parts of the Celebes **2 :** a member of an Alfur people

[1]**al·fu·rese** \¦alf(y)ə¦rēz, -ēs\ *n, usu cap* [*Alfur* + *-ese*] **:** the language of the Alfuros esp. those of the Celebes

[2]**alfurese** \"\ *adj, usu cap* **:** of or belonging to an Alfur people

alg- *or* **algo-** *comb form* [NL, fr. Gk *alg-, algos*] **:** pain ⟨*algesthesia*⟩ ⟨*alganesthesia*⟩ ⟨*algophobia*⟩

alg *abbr* algebra

al·ga \'algə\ *n, pl* **al·gae** \'al(,)jē\ *also* **algas** [L, seaweed] **:** a plant of the group Algae or of the divisions Chlorophyta, Euglenophyta, Pyrrophyta, Chrysophyta, Phaeophyta, Cyanophyta, and Rhodophyta

al·gae \'al(,)jē\ *n pl, cap* [NL, fr. L, pl. of *alga*] *in some classifications* **:** a major group of lower plants that is often included in Thallophyta, that comprises usu. photosynthetic plants of extremely varied morphology and physiology, and that is now commonly considered to be a heterogeneous assemblage — see ALGA, FUNGI

algaecide *var of* ALGICIDE

al·gal \'algəl\ *adj* **:** relating to, consisting of, or resembling an alga or algae

al·gal–al·gal \'algə'lalgəl\ *n* -s [alter. of *agar-agar*] **:** AGAR; *esp* **:** agar produced in the Malay archipelago from red algae of the genus *Eucheuma*

algal disease *n* **:** RED RUST 3a

algal fungus *n* **:** any fungus of the class Phycomycetes

algal layer *n* **:** GONIDIAL LAYER

algaroth *n* -s *usu cap* **:** POWDER OF ALGAROTH

al·gar·ro·ba *also* **al·ga·ro·ba** *or* **al·gar·ro·bo** *or* **al·ga·ro·bo** *or* **al·ge·ro·ba** \,algə'rōbə\ *n* -s [Sp, *algarroba*, fr. Ar *al-kharrūbah* the carob] **1 :** CAROB 1a **2** *or* **algarroba bean :** CAROB 1b **3** [MexSp *algarroba*, fr. Sp] **:** MESQUITE 1a **4** [MexSp *algarroba*, fr. Sp] **:** the sweet pulpy pods of the mesquite **5** [AmerSp, fr. Sp] **:** WEST INDIAN LOCUST **6** [AmerSp, fr. Sp] **:** RAIN TREE

al·gar·ro·bi·lla *or* **al·ga·ro·bi·lla** \,algə(,)rō'bē(y)ə\ *or* **al·ga·ro·bel·lo** \-'be(,)lō\ *also* **al·ga·ro·vi·lla** \-'vē(y)ə\ *n* -s [AmerSp *algarrobilla*, fr. Sp, carob tree, dim. of *algarroba*] **:** the seeds and pods of certain leguminous trees and shrubs (esp. of *Pithecolobium parvifolium*, *Caesalpinia brevifolia*, and *Prosopis juliflora*) having astringent properties and used for tanning and dyeing

al·gar·ro·bin \,algə'rōbə̇n\ *n* -s [*algarroba* + *-in*] **:** a brown dyestuff and mordant of Argentina said to be obtained from the wood of the carob tree

al·gates \'ól,gāts\ *adv* [ME *algate, algates* always, in all ways, entirely, fr. *al* all + *gate* (way), or *gates*, prob. pl. of *gate;* perh. influenced by ON *alla götu* always, throughout — more at GATE] **1** *now dial Brit* **:** WHOLLY, COMPLETELY **2** *obs* **:** NEVERTHELESS, NOTWITHSTANDING, YET

algazel *n* -s [Pg] *obs* **:** a gazelle or other antelope of Africa

al·ge·bra \'aljəbrə\ *n* -s [ML, algebra, bonesetting, fracture (whence ME, bonesetting, fracture), fr. Ar *al-jabr* the algebra, the bonesetting, lit., the reduction] **1 :** a branch of mathematics in which arithmetic relations are generalized and explored by using letter symbols to represent numbers, variable quantities, or other mathematical entities (as vectors and matrices), the letter symbols being combined, esp. in forming equations, in accordance with assigned rules **2** *logic* **:** a process of reasoning by the use of symbols — used esp. with reference to 19th century formulations in symbolic logic or the areas then dealt with; compare BOOLEAN ALGEBRA, SYMBOLIC LOGIC **3 :** a treatise on the science of algebra

al·ge·bra·ic \¦aljə¦brāik\ *also* **al·ge·bra·i·cal** \-ə̇kəl\ *adj* **1 :** of, relating to, involving, or according to the laws of algebra **2** *of a mathematical expression or equation* **:** involving only a finite number of algebraic operations — opposed to *transcendental* — **al·ge·bra·i·cal·ly** \-ə̇k(ə)lē, -li\ *adv*

algebraic arithmetic *n* **:** the part of the theory of numbers in which the methods of algebra are used to yield relations between integers

algebraic curve *n* **:** a curve the Cartesian coordinates of whose points are related by an algebraic equation

algebraic equation *n* **:** an equation obtained by equating to zero a sum of a finite number of terms each one of which is a product of positive integral powers (including the zero power) of the variables

algebraic expression *n* **:** an expression obtained by a finite number of the fundamental operations of algebra upon symbols representing numbers

algebraic form *n* **:** a homogeneous rational integral function of two or more variables

algebraic function *n* **:** a function whose dependence on the independent variable or variables is determined by an algebraic equation

algebraic geometry *n* **:** analytic geometry in which the graphs or curves considered can be represented by algebraic equations

algebraic logic *n* **:** ALGEBRA 2

algebraic number *n* **:** a root of an algebraic equation whose coefficients are rational

algebraic operation *n* **:** any combination of a finite number of the operations of addition, multiplication, subtraction, and division

algebraic sum *n* **:** the aggregate of two or more numbers or quantities taken with regard to their signs (as + or −) according to the rules of addition in algebra ⟨the *algebraic sum* of −2, 8, and −1 is 5⟩ — compare ARITHMETICAL SUM

algebraic surface *n* **:** a surface expressible analytically through an algebraic equation connecting its Cartesian coordinates

al·ge·bra·ist \'aljə,brāə̇st, ,==¦==\ *n* -s **:** a specialist in algebra

al·ge·bra·i·za·tion \,aljə,brāə'zāshən\ *or* **al·ge·bri·za·tion** \-,brə'z-, -,brī'z-\ *n* -s **:** the act or process of algebraizing

al·ge·bra·ize \'aljəbrə,īz, -rā,īz\ *vt* -ED/-ING/-S **:** to perform by algebra **:** reduce (a verbal or numerical statement) to algebraic form

algebra of classes : a branch of symbolic logic sometimes regarded as an independent discipline that deals with classes and has as its main operations the forming of logical products, sums, and complements — called also *calculus of classes;* compare INCLUSION, MEMBERSHIP

algebra of relations : a branch of symbolic logic dealing with relations analogously to the manner in which classes are dealt with in the algebra of classes — called also *calculus of relations*

al·ge·do·nic \¦aljə¦dänik\ *adj* [Gk *alg-* + *hēdonikos* pleasant — more at HEDONIC] **:** characterized by or relating to pain ⟨~ aesthetics⟩

al·ge·don·ics \,==¦niks\ *n pl but sing in constr* **:** HEDONICS 2

al·ge·ria \(')al¦jirēə, -ēr-\ *adj, usu cap* [fr. *Algeria*, country in NW Africa] **:** of or from the country of Algeria **:** of the kind or style prevalent in Algeria

[1]**al·ge·ri·an** \(')al¦jirēən, -ēr-\ *adj, usu cap* [F *algérien*, fr. *Algérie* Algeria, Africa] **1 :** of, relating to, or characteristic of Algeria or the former Barbary State of Algiers **2 :** of, relating to, or characteristic of the Algerians

[2]**algerian** \"\ *n* -s **1** *cap* **:** a native or inhabitant of Algeria or of the former Barbary State of Algiers **2** *usu cap* **:** a dialect of modern Arabic **3** *often cap* **:** TANBARK 2

algerian fir *n, usu cap A* **:** an evergreen tree (*Abies numidica*) having ornamental dark green white-banded leaves

algerian ivy *n, usu cap A* **:** a trailing or climbing vine or shrub (*Hedera canariensis*) resembling English ivy but having reddish twigs and petioles and thin, comparatively large, sometimes variegated leaves

algerian stripe *n, usu cap A* **:** a usu. cream-colored coating fabric with alternate stripes of coarse cotton and fine silk

[1]**al·ge·rine** \¦aljə¦rēn\ *adj, usu cap* [*Algeria* + *-ine*] **:** ALGERIAN

[2]**algerine** \"\ *n* -s **1** *cap* **:** a native or inhabitant of Algeria or of the former Barbary State of Algiers; *esp* **:** one of a native race **2 :** one with piratical characteristics ⟨~*s* of the black market⟩ **3** [fr. *Algerine*, British minesweeper, the first ship in this class] **:** a British or Canadian minesweeper of about 1000 tons displacement **4** *or* **al·ge·ri·enne** \(,)al¦jirē¦en\ [F *algérienne*, fr. fem. of *algérien* Algerian] **:** a soft woolen fabric with bright weftwise stripes used for shawls; *also* **:** this fabric in a heavier weight used in making Venetian blinds and awnings

al·ge·ri·ta \,aljə'rēd·ə\ *n* -s [MexSp, alter. of *agarita*, alter. of *agrita, agrito*] **:** AGARITA

algeroba *var of* ALGARROBA

al·ge·sia \al'jēzēə, -jēzhə\ *n* -s [NL, fr. Gk *algēsis* sense of pain (fr. *algein* to feel pain, fr. *algos* pain) + NL *-ia*] **:** sensitiveness to pain — **al·ge·sic** \-ēzik, -ēs-\ *adj*

al·ge·sim·e·ter \,aljə'simad·ə(r)\ *n* -s [NL *algesia* + E *-meter*] **:** an instrument used in determining acuteness of pain perception — **al·ge·sim·e·try** \-mə·trē\ *n* -ES

al·get·ic \al'jed·ik\ *adj* [ISV *alg-* + *-etic*] **:** relating to or causing pain

-al·gia \'alj(ē)ə\ *n comb form* -s [Gk *-algia*, fr. *algos*] **:** pain **:** painful condition ⟨cephal*algia*⟩ ⟨pod*algia*⟩ — **-al·gic** \,aljik, -ēk\ *adj comb form*

al·gic acid \'aljik-\ *n* [*alga* + *-ic*] **:** ALGINIC ACID

al·gi·cide \'aljə,sīd\ *or* **al·gae·cide** \", -jē,-\ *n* -s **:** a chemical (as copper sulfate) used to kill algae

al·gid \'aljə̇d\ *adj* [L *algidus*, fr. *algēre* to feel cold; akin to Icel *elgur* slush] **1 :** CHILL, COLD ⟨the river . . . grew colder . . . compressing their . . . lower limbs in an ~ vise —A.J. Cronin⟩ **2 :** marked by prostration, cold and clammy skin, and low blood pressure — used chiefly of a severe form of malaria — **al·gid·i·ty** \al'jidəd·ē\ *n* -ES

al·giers \(')al¦ji(ə)rz, -iəz\ *adj, usu cap* [fr. *Algiers*, Algeria] **1 :** of or from Algiers, the capital of Algeria **:** of the kind or style prevalent in Algiers **2 :** of or relating to the former Barbary State of Algiers

-algies *pl of* -ALGY

al·gin \'aljə̇n\ *n* -s [*alga* + *-in*] **:** any of various colloidal substances that occur in or are extracted from marine brown algae, esp. giant kelp: as **a :** a naturally occurring mixture held to contain alginic acid and certain of its salts **b :** ALGINIC ACID **c :** any soluble salt of alginic acid; *esp* **:** the sodium salt that forms a viscous solution with cold or hot water, that is obtained in the form of a white to brown powder by extraction from kelp with a soda solution, and that is used chiefly as a stabilizing, emulsifying, thickening, coating, or water-holding agent in foods (as ice cream), pharmaceuticals, cosmetics, and cold-water paints, in sizing textiles, in creaming rubber latex, and as a base for dental-impression materials

al·gi·nate \'aljə,nāt, -,nə̇t\ *n* -s [ISV *algin* + *-ate*] **:** a salt of alginic acid

alginate fiber *n* **:** any of various fibers made from alginates (as calcium alginate) that are characterized by nonflammability and in some cases by solubility in water or dilute alkaline solutions and are used in making yarns and textiles

al·gin·ic acid \(')al¦jinik-\ *n* [ISV *algin* + *-ic*] **:** an insoluble colloidal acid $(C_6H_8O_6)_n$ that in the form of salts is a constituent of the cell walls of marine brown algae and that is hard and horny when dry and is capable of absorbing large amounts of water when moist — called also *algic acid, algin*

al·giv·o·rous \(')al¦jiv(ə)rəs\ *adj* [*alga* + *-i-* + *-vorous*] **:** feeding on algae

algo- — see ALG-

al·go·cy·an \,algō'sī,an, -,ən\ *n* -s [*alga* + *-o-* + *-cyan*] **:** PHYCOCYANIN

al·go·don·ci·llo \,algə,dän'sē(,)(y)ō\ *n* -s [AmerSp, fr. Sp, milkweed, dim. of *algodón* cotton, fr. Ar dial. (Spain) *al-quṭun* the cotton] **:** MAJAGUA a

al·go·do·nite \,algə'dō,nīt\ *n* -s [*Algodones* mine, Coquimbo prov., Chile, its locality + E *-ite*] **:** a copper arsenide mineral Cu_6As allied to domeykite (sp. gr. 7.62)

[1]**al·go·gen·ic** \¦algō¦jenik\ *adj* [*alg-* + *-genic*] **:** producing pain

[2]**algogenic** \"\ *adj* [L *algor* cold + E *-genic*] **:** reducing body temperature

al·goid \'al,gȯid\ *adj* [ISV *alga* + *-oid*] **:** of the nature of or resembling an alga

al·go·lag·nia \,algō'lagnēə\ *n* -s [NL, fr. *alg-* + *-lagnia*] **:** the finding of sexual pleasure in inflicting or suffering pain — compare MASOCHISM, SADISM

al·go·lag·nic \¦==¦=nik\ *adj* **:** of or relating to algolagnia

al·go·lag·nist \'==,=nə̇st\ *n* -s **:** one who practices algolagnia

al·go·log·i·cal \¦algə¦läjə̇kəl\ *adj* **:** of or relating to algology

al·gol·o·gist \al'gäləjə̇st\ *n* -s **:** one that studies algology

al·gol·o·gy \-jē\ *n* -ES [*alga* + *-o-* + *-logy*] **:** the study or science of algae

al·gol variable \'al,gäl-, -ól-\ *n, usu cap A* [fr. *Algol*, an eclipsing binary star, fr. Ar. *al-ghūl*, lit., the ghoul, ogre] **:** a variable star with light variations resembling those of the binary star Algol

al·go·man *also* **al·go·mi·an** *or* **al·go·mic** *adj, usu cap* [*Algoma*, district in Ontario, Canada + E *-an* or *-ian* or *-ic*] **:** of or relating to the mountain-making movements and granitic intrusion commonly referred to the middle of the Proterozoic era

al·gom·e·ter \al'gäməd·ə(r)\ *n* [*alg-* + *-meter*] **:** an instrument for measuring the smallest pressure upon the skin that will arouse a sensation of pain

al·gom·e·try \-mə·trē\ *n* -ES [*alg-* + *-metry*] **:** the measurement of pain sensitivity (as by an algometer)

[1]**al·gon·ki·an** \al'gäŋkēən\ *or* **al·gon·kin** \-ŋkə̇n\ *or* **al·gon·qui·an** \-äŋkwēən, -äŋkwē-,-äŋkē-\ *or* **al·gon·quin** \-äŋkwə̇n,-äŋkwə̇n *sometimes* -ŋkə̇n\ *n, pl* **algonkian** *or* **algonkians** *or* **algonkin** *or* **algonkins** *or* **algonquian** *or* **algonquians** *or* **algonquin** *or* **algonquins** *usu cap* [*Algonkian, Algonquian*, blend of *Algonkin, Algonquin* + E *-ian; Algonkin, Algonquin* fr. CanF *Algonquin* (recorded by Champlain as *Algoumequin*), perh. fr. Micmac *algoomaking*, lit., at the place for spearing fish] **1 a :** an Indian people in the Ottawa river valley of Ontario and Quebec, Canada **b :** a member of such people **2** *usu algonquin* **:** a dialect of Ojibwa **3** *usu algonquian* **:** a stock of languages spoken from Labrador to Carolina and westward to the Great Plains, consisting of Cree, Ojibwa, Menomini, Fox, Potawatomi, Illinois, Shawnee; Pamlico, Powhatan, Nanticoke, Delaware; Mahican, Massachuset, Abnaki, Malecite, Micmac; Blackfoot; Cheyenne; Arapaho **4** *usu algonquian* **:** a member of any of the Indian peoples speaking Algonquian languages **5** *algonkian, geol* **:** the Algonkian era or system or group of systems

[2]**algonkian** \"\ *adj, usu cap* **:** of or relating to a geological era between the Archean and the Paleozoic, from both of which it is usu. separated by unconformities **:** PROTEROZOIC — used by the U.S. Geological Survey — see GEOLOGIC TIME table

al·goph·a·gous \al'gäfəgəs\ *adj* [*alga* + *-o-* + *-phagous*] **:** feeding on algae ⟨~ insects⟩

al·go·phil·ia \,algō'filēə\ *n* -s [NL, fr. *alg-* + *-philia*] **:** a morbid pleasure in the pain either of oneself or of others

al·goph·i·list \al'gäfələ̇st\ *n* -s **:** one who is subject to algophilia

al·go·pho·bia \,algə'fōbēə\ *n* -s [NL, fr. *alg-* + *-phobia*] **:** morbid fear of pain

al·go·rism \'algə,rizəm\ *n* -s [ME *augrim, algorisme*, fr. OF & ML; OF *augorisme*, fr. ML *algorismus*, fr. Ar *al-khuwārizmī*, after abu-Ja'far Mohammed ibn-Mūsa *al-Khuwārizmi fl* 825 A.D. Persian mathematician] **1 :** the system of Arabic numerals **:** the art of calculating by means of nine figures and zero **:** ARITHMETIC **2 :** the art of calculating with any species of notation ⟨the ~ of fractions⟩ — **al·go·ris·mic** \¦==¦rizmik\ *adj*

al·go·rist \'algərə̇st\ *n* -s [*algorism* + *-ist*] **:** one of a school of medieval mathematicians who made use of the algorismic notation — opposed to *abacist* — **al·go·ris·tic** \¦==¦ristik\ *adj*

al·go·rithm \'algə,rithəm, -th-\ *n* -s [alter. (influenced by *arithmetic*) of *algorism*] **:** ALGORISM — **al·go·rith·mic** \¦==¦rithmik, -th-\ *adj*

al·gous \'algəs\ *adj* [L *algosus*, fr. *alga* + *-osus* -ous] **:** relating to, of the nature of, or full of algae

al·gra·phy \'algrəfē\ *n* -ES [*aluminum* + *-graphy*] **:** a lithographic process in which an aluminum plate is used instead of a stone

al·gua·cil \¦algwə¦sēl, -il\ *or* **al·gua·zil** \-ə¦z-\ *n, pl* **alguacils** \-lz\ *or* **alguaci·les** \,==¦sē(,)lās\ *or* **alguazils** \-lz\ [Sp *alguacil* (formerly *alguazil*), fr. Ar *al-wazīr* the vizier] **1 :** an officer of justice in Spain, formerly of high rank, now of inferior rank **2 :** a sheriff or constable in Latin-American countries or in regions under Spanish influence

al·gum \'al,gəm *also* 'ól-\ *also* **al·mug** \-,məg\ *n* -s [fr. (assumed) Heb *algōm, almōg* (attested only in pl. as *algummīm, almuggīm*)] **1 :** a tree mentioned in the Old Testament, prob. cypress, perhaps sandalwood or walnut **2 :** RED SANDALWOOD

-al·gy \,aljē, -ji\ *n comb form* -ES [Gk *-algia*] **:** -ALGIA

al·ha·gi \al'häjē, -hä,jī\ *n, cap* [NL, fr. Ar *al-hāj* camel thorn] **:** a small genus of desert shrubs (family Leguminosae) found in northern Africa and Asia Minor having simple leaves, spiny branches, and tough pods — see CAMEL THORN

al·ham·bresque \¦al,ham¦bresk\ *or* **al·ham·bra·ic** \-¦brāik\ *adj, usu cap* [*Alhambra*, palace of the Moorish kings at Granada, Spain, erected in the 13th & 14th cents. (fr. Sp, fr. Ar *al-hamrā'* the red house) + E *-esque* or *-ic*] **:** made or decorated after the fanciful style of the ornamentation in the Alhambra

ali- *comb form* [L, fr. *ala* — more at AISLE] **1 :** wing ⟨*aliform*⟩ ⟨*alitrunk*⟩ **2 :** relating to the side parts of (a specified organ or structure) ⟨*aliethmoid*⟩ ⟨*alinasal*⟩

-a·lia \'ālēə, -lyə\ *n comb form* [NL, fr. Gk *halia* assembly & Gk *hal-, hals* sea; Gk *halia* akin to Gk *eilein* to compress, OSlav *veliků* great, and perh. to L *vulgus* common people; Gk *hals* sea akin to Gk *hals* salt — more at VULGAR, SALT] **:** realm of marine animal life — in names of biogeographic realms ⟨*Arctalia*⟩ ⟨*Bassalia*⟩ — **-a·li·an** \¦ālēən, -lyən\ *adj comb form*

[1]**ali·as** \'ālēəs, -lyəs\ *adv* [L, otherwise, at another time, fr.

alius other — more at ELSE] **1 :** otherwise called **:** otherwise known as — used esp. in legal proceedings to connect the different names of anyone who has gone by or been known by two or more names ⟨Smith, ~ Simpson⟩ **2 :** at another time

2alias \"\ *n* -ES **1 :** another name **:** an assumed name ⟨masquerading under an indeterminate number of ~*es* —A.E. Wier⟩ **2 :** ALIAS WRIT

alias writ *n* [L *alias* at another time, otherwise; fr. the occurrence in the writ (in its Latin form) of the phrase *sicut alias praecipimus* as we at another time commanded] *law* **:** a second writ issued after an earlier writ has been returned without action having been taken as commanded

alibamu *usu cap, var of* ALABAMA

1al·i·bi \'alə,bī\ *adv* [L] **:** in another place **:** ELSEWHERE ⟨the defendant was able to prove himself ~⟩

2alibi \"\ *n* -S **1** *law* **:** the plea of having been at the time of the commission of an act elsewhere than at the place of commission; *also* **:** the fact or state of having been elsewhere at the time **2 :** a plausible excuse esp. for failure or negligence **:** any excuse ⟨this sounds a little like the ~ which some editors make in defending . . . oversensational stories —F.L.Mott⟩ **syn** see APOLOGY

3alibi \"\ *vb* -ED/-ING/-ES [*2alibi*] *vi* **:** to offer an excuse ⟨they ~*ed* for not giving money to the teachers' organization —Victor Boesen⟩ ~ *vt* **:** to exonerate by an alibi **:** furnish an excuse for ⟨~*ed* themselves and accused other men —C.W.M.Hart⟩

al·i·ble \'aləbəl\ *adj* [L *alibilis*, fr. *alere* to nourish + *-ibilis* -ible — more at OLD] *archaic* **:** affording nourishment **:** NOURISHING

ali·can·te \,alə'käntē\ *adj, usu cap* [fr. *Alicante*, Spain] **:** of or from the city of Alicante, Spain **:** of the kind or style prevalent in Alicante

al·ice blue \'aləs-\ *n, often cap A* [after *Alice* Roosevelt Longworth *b*1884 daughter of Theodore Roosevelt] **:** a pale blue to grayish blue that is redder and stronger than forget-me-not (sense 2b)

alice clover \"-\ *usu cap A, var of* ALYCE CLOVER

alice's fern *n, usu cap A* [prob. fr. the name *Alice*] **:** CLIMBING FERN

al·i·cole \'alə,kōl\ *n* -S [*ali-* + *-cole* (fr. NL *-cola*)] *bot* **:** SPIKE, SPIKELET

al·i·cy·clic \,alə'sī-\ *adj* [ISV *aliphatic* + *cyclic;* orig. formed as G *alizyklisch*] **:** combining the properties of aliphatic and cyclic substances — used of organic compounds (as cycloparaffins and cycloolefins) containing a ring of carbon atoms but not belonging to the aromatic series — called also *cycloaliphatic;* see CARBOCYCLIC

al·id \'aləd, 'ā-\ *n* -S *usu cap* [prob. fr. (assumed) ML *Alides*, fr. *'Ali ibn-abi-Ṭālib* †661 Arab caliph + L *-ides* -id — more at -IDAE] **:** one that claims descent from the caliph Ali and Fatima, son-in-law and daughter respectively of Muhammad

al·i·dade \'alə,dād\ *also* **al·i·dad** \-,dad\ *n* -S [alter. (influenced by F *alidade*) of ME *allidatha*, fr. ML *alhidada*, fr. Ar *al-'iḍādah* the revolving radius of a circle] **:** a rule equipped with simple or telescopic sights and used for determination of direction: as **a :** a part of an astrolabe **b :** the ruler of a plane table **c :** a part of a surveying instrument (as a transit) consisting of the telescope, the telescope standards, the plate levels, the vernier and associated magnifiers, and the spindle **d :** a telescope mounted on a compass repeater and used as part of a ship's navigational equipment for taking bearings

1alien \'ālyən, -lēən\ *adj* [ME, fr. OF, fr. L *alienus*, fr. *alius* other — more at ELSE] **1 a :** belonging or relating to another person or place **:** STRANGE ⟨followed the crops north and back again year after year, ~ and set apart —Marjory S. Douglas⟩ **b :** relating, belonging, or owing allegiance to another country, land, or government **:** FOREIGN ⟨the government's attempt to expel all ~ agents⟩ **2 :** different in nature or character **:** far removed — used with *from* ⟨with an effect entirely ~ from the one intended⟩ **3 a :** of a foreign character or origin **:** belonging to something else ⟨a statement ~ to the topic under consideration⟩ **b :** repugnant in nature **:** HOSTILE, OPPOSED — used with *to* ⟨a political philosophy ~ to democracy⟩ **syn** see EXTRINSIC

2alien \"\ *n* -S [ME, fr. *alien*, adj.] **1 :** a person of another family, race, or place **:** STRANGER **2 :** one owing allegiance to another country **:** a foreign-born resident who has not been naturalized and is still a subject or citizen of a foreign country; *broadly* **:** a foreign-born citizen **3** *archaic* **:** one excluded from certain privileges **:** one alienated or estranged

3alien \"\ *vt* -ED/-ING/-S [ME *alienen*, fr. L *alienare*, fr. *alienus*] **1 :** ALIENATE, ESTRANGE ⟨~*ed* from all thoughts of . . . the marriage —Edward Hyde⟩ **2 :** to make over (as property or ownership)

alien·a·bil·i·ty \,==(=)nə'biləd·ē\ *n* -ES **:** the capability of being transferred to other ownership ⟨~ of property⟩

alien·a·ble \'=(=)nəbəl\ *adj* [prob. fr. F *aliénable*, fr. *aliéner* to transfer property, estrange (fr. L *alienare*) + *-able*] **:** that may be transferred to the ownership of another ⟨~ lands⟩

al·ien·age \-nij\ *n* -S [*1alien* + *-age*] **:** the status of an alien ⟨the government had sufficiently borne the burden of proving ~ to warrant deportation —*Amer. Labor Yr. Bk.*⟩

1alienate *adj* [ME *alienat*, fr. L *alienatus*, past part. of *alienare* to alienate, fr. *alienus* strange — more at ALIEN] *obs* **:** made unfriendly, hostile, or indifferent **:** ESTRANGED

2alien·ate \'ālyə,nāt, -lēə-, *usu* -ād.+V\ *vt* -ED/-ING/-S **1 :** to convey or transfer to another (as title, property, or right) **:** part voluntarily with ownership of **:** ALIEN — usu. used of the transfer of the title to property by act of the owner as distinguished from a transfer entirely by operation of law (as in case of descent) **2 :** to cause to be estranged **:** make unfriendly, hostile, or indifferent where attachment formerly existed ⟨her children are *alienated* from her —Ann F. Wolfe⟩ ⟨would ~ potential supporters among the faculty and student body —Sylvan Fox⟩ **3 :** to cause to be withdrawn or transferred ⟨~ capital from its natural channels⟩ **syn** see ESTRANGE

alien·a·tion \,=(=)'nāshən\ *n* -S [ME *alienacioun*, fr. L *alienation-, alienatio*, fr. *alienatus* + *-ion-, -io* -ion] **1 :** the act of alienating: as **a :** a transfer of ownership of title **:** a conveyance of property to another **b :** a withdrawing or separation of a person or his affections from an object or position of former attachment **:** ISOLATION, EXILE ⟨his ~ from the mainstream of American life —*Times Lit. Supp.*⟩ **2 :** the state of being alienated or diverted from normal function; *specif* **:** mental derangement

alienation of affection : the diversion of a person's affection from someone who has certain rights or claims to such affection to a third person who is held to be the instigator or cause of the diversion

alienation office *n* **:** an office in London where fees had to be paid upon the writs used in fine and recovery

alien corporation *n* **:** a corporation created and existing under the laws of some nation or state other than that wherein it is doing business

aliened *past of* ALIEN

al·ien·ee \,=(=)'nē\ *n* -S [*3alien* + *-ee*] **:** one to whom the title of property is transferred

alien enemy *n* **:** a person owing allegiance to an enemy state

alien·ic·o·la \,=(=)'nikələ\ *n, pl* **alienico·lae** \-,lē\ [NL, fr. L *alienus* foreign + *-i-* + *-cola* (fr. *colere* to cultivate, dwell)] **:** a foreign inhabitant; *specif* **:** an aphid of a seasonally migrating species (as *Aphis rumicis*) that is developed and lives on the secondary or summer host plants and reproduces young asexually

ali·e·ni ju·ris \,alē'ē,nī'jürəs, ,ālē'ā(,)nē'yü-\ *adj* [L, of another's law] *law* **:** subject to the authority of another — opposed to *sui juris*

aliening *pres part of* ALIEN

alien·ism \'ālyə,nizəm, -lēə,-\ *n* -S **:** the status of an alien

alien·ist \-,nəst\ *n* -S [F *aliéniste*, fr. *aliéné* insane, made insane (fr. L *alienatus*, lit., estranged, past part. of *alienare* to estrange) + *-iste* -ist — more at ALIEN] **:** one that treats diseases of the mind; *esp* **:** a physician specializing in legal problems of psychiatry

al·ien·or \,=(=)'nȯ(ə)r, '=(=)=nər\ *n* -S [fr. (assumed) AF *alienour*, fr. MF *aliener* to transfer property (fr. OF, fr. L *alienare* to transfer property, estrange) + AF *-our* -or — more at ALIEN] **:** one that transfers property to another

alien property custodian *n* **:** the person appointed in time of war to take charge of the property of alien enemies

aliens *pl of* ALIEN, *pres 3d sing of* ALIEN

1ali·eth·moid \,ālē'-, ,al-\ *or* **ali·eth·moi·dal** \,==;=;==\ *adj* [*ali-* + *ethmoid, ethmoidal*] **:** relating to or indicating the lateral expansions of the ethmoid bone or cartilage of certain birds

2aliethmoid \"\ *or* **aliethmoidal** \"\ *n* -S **:** an aliethmoid bone or cartilage

alif \'äləf\ *n* -S [Ar] **:** the first letter of the Arabic alphabet consisting of a simple vertical stroke — see ALPHABET table

alife *adv* [*1a-* + *life*] *obs* **:** DEARLY

alif·er·ous \ā'lif(ə)rəs, a'-,ə'-\ *adj* [*ali-* + *-ferous*] **:** having wings

ali·form \'ālə,fȯrm, 'al-\ *adj* [*ali-* + *-form*] **:** having winglike extensions **:** wing-shaped

ali·garh \'alə,gär\ *adj, usu cap* [fr. *Aligarh*, India] **:** of or from the city of Aligarh, India **:** of the kind or style prevalent in Aligarh

1alight \ə'līt, *usu* -d.+V\ *vi* **alighted** \-īd·əd, -ītəd\ *or sometimes* **alit** \ə'lit\ **alighted; alighting; alights** [ME *alighten* to alight, alighten, fr. OE *ālīhtan*, fr. *ā-* (perfective prefix) + *līhtan* to alight, lighten — more at ABEAR, LIGHT] **1 :** to spring down, get down, or descend (as from horseback or from a vehicle) **:** DISMOUNT **2 :** to descend and settle after falling or flying **:** LODGE, LAND ⟨a bird ~*s* on a twig⟩ ⟨snow ~*ing* on a roof⟩ **3** *archaic* **:** FALL **:** come down and strike **4** *archaic* **:** to come by chance — used with *upon* ⟨~ upon a solution⟩ **syn** see DESCEND

2alight \"\ *adj* [ME, alter. of *alighted*, past part. of *alighten* to light up, fr. OE *ālīhtan*, fr. *1a-* + *līhtan* to light — more at LIGHT] **:** lighted up **:** in a flame **:** LIGHTED ⟨the sky ~ with stars⟩ ⟨his face ~ with inspiration⟩

alighten *vt* -ED/-ING/-S [irreg. fr. ME *alighten* — more at ALIGHT] *obs* **:** to make lighter (as a boat) **:** relieve of care

align *also* **aline** \ə'līn\ *vb* -ED/-ING/-S [F *aligner*, fr. OF, fr. *a-* (fr. L *ad-*) + *ligne* line, fr. L *linea* — more at LINE] *vt* **1 :** to adjust or form to a line **:** range or form in line ⟨the tents were *aligned* in two rows —Norman Mailer⟩ **:** bring into line or alignment ⟨~ set type⟩ **2 :** to put (two or more parts of a machine or structure, esp. parts that should be parallel or in line with each other) into proper relative position or orientation ⟨~ the wheels⟩ **3 :** to make semipermanent adjustments in (a piece of electronic or radio equipment) in order to obtain optimum performance **4 :** to array on the side of or against a party or cause ⟨~ the nations of the world against warfare⟩ ~ *vi* **1 :** to get or fall into line ⟨~ with your friends against a common enemy⟩ **2 :** to be in or come into precise adjustment or correct relative position ⟨the wheels should ~ with the frame⟩ **3 :** to be in alignment (as of one printed character with another)

align·er *also* **alin·er** \-nə(r)\ *n* -S **:** one that aligns: as **a :** a device (as a telescope) for sighting an angle-measuring instrument used in surveying **b :** a sighter of small arms **c :** one that aligns type for use in typewriters

align·ment *also* **aline·ment** \-nmənt\ *n* -S [F *alignement*, fr. MF, fr. *aligner* + *-ment*] **1 :** the act of aligning or state of being aligned **2 a :** a forming in line (as of troops) **b :** the line thus formed; *specif* **:** an arrangement of soldiers in a line or lines **3 :** the ground plan (as of a railroad or fieldwork) in distinction from the profile **4 a :** the condition of being properly aligned **:** the condition of being in satisfactory adjustment or of having the parts in proper relative position **b :** the correct positioning of printed characters in horizontal lines and vertical columns **5** *dancing* **:** the reference of body movement to a vertical axis or directive horizontal line

alignment chart *n* **:** NOMOGRAM

al·i·greek \'alə,grēk\ *n* -S [modif. of It *alla greca* in the Greek manner] **:** a Greek ornamental fret

alii \ä'lē,ē\ *or* **ari·ki** \ä'rē(,)kē\ *or* **arii** \ä'rē,ē\ *n, pl* **alii** *or* **ariki** *or* **arii** [Hawaiian & Samoan *ali'i*, Maori & Rarotongan *ariki*, Tahitian *ari'i*] **:** a Polynesian chief, noble, or king

al·i·poe \ä,lē(,)ē'pō,ā\ *n* -S [Hawaiian] *Hawaii* **:** INDIAN SHOT

1alike \ə'līk\ *adj* [ME *ilik, alik*, alter. (influenced by ON *ālīkr*) of *ilich*, fr. OE *gelīc* (fr. *ge-* — collective prefix — + *līc* body) and *onlīc*, fr. *on* + *līc* — more at CO-, LIKE] **1 :** showing strong resemblance, likeness, or accord ⟨the two cars are much ~⟩ **2 :** showing no difference or no salient difference **:** ⟨the two dresses were quite ~⟩ ⟨the twins, ~ in face and manners —Charles Kingsley⟩ **syn** see LIKE

2alike \"\ *adv* [ME *ilike*, alter. (influenced by ON *ālīka*) of *iliche*, fr. OE *gelīce* and *onlīce*, fr. *gelīc*, adj., and *onlīc*, adj., respectively] **:** in the same manner, form, or degree **:** in common **:** EQUALLY ⟨we are all ~ concerned with religion⟩

alike·ness \-nəs\ *n* -ES [ME *aliknesse*, fr. *alik* + *-nesse* -ness] **:** the quality or state of being alike **:** mutual resemblance ⟨the ~ of mother and daughter was startling⟩

alikuluf *usu cap, var of* ALACALUF

alilonghi *var of* **alalonga**

alim \ä'lim\ *n* -S [Ar *'ālim*] **:** a Muslim learned in religious matters

al·i·ma \'aləmə\ *n* -S [NL, fr. *Alima*, in older classifications a genus of crustaceans, irreg. fr. Gk *halimos* of the sea, fr. *hals* sea] **:** the newly hatched larva of certain stomatopod crustaceans

1al·i·ment \'aləmənt\ *n* -S [ME, fr. L *alimentum*, fr. *alere* to nourish + *-mentum* -ment — more at OLD] **1 :** something that nourishes **:** FOOD, NUTRIMENT **2 :** a necessity for life **:** means of support ⟨luxuries are not an ~⟩ **3** *chiefly Scot* **:** an allowance for maintenance

2aliment \-,ment,-,mənt — *see* 2-MENT\ *vt* -ED/-ING/-S [MF *alimenter*, fr. *aliment*, n.] **:** to give aliment to ⟨raise money to ~ a cause⟩ ⟨force a man to ~ his wife⟩

al·i·men·tal \,alə'ment³l\ *adj, obs* **:** having the quality of nourishing **:** furnishing the materials for natural growth ⟨~ sap⟩

al·i·men·ta·ry \,alə'mentərē, -n·trē, -ri\ *adj* [L *alimentarius*, fr. *alimentum* + *-arius* -ary] **1 :** of, concerned with, or relating to nourishment or to the function of nutrition **:** NUTRITIOUS, ALIMENTAL ⟨~ processes of the body⟩ **2 :** having to do with sustenance or maintenance **:** furnishing maintenance ⟨that great ~ thoroughfare of the blossomed desert —A.B.Guthrie⟩

alimentary canal *n* **:** the tubular and in part sacculated passage that serves the functions of digestion, absorption of food, and elimination of residual waste products, being in man about 30 feet long and comprising the mouth, pharynx, esophagus, stomach, small intestine, and large intestine

alimentary castration *n* **:** inhibition of sexual development associated with nutritional deficiencies (as in worker bees)

alimentary paste *n* [trans. of It *pasta alimentaria*] **:** a shaped and dried dough (as macaroni, spaghetti, and vermicelli) prepared from semolina, farina, or wheat flour or a mixture of these with water or milk and with or without egg or egg yolk

alimentary system *n* **:** the organ system devoted to the ingestion, digestion, and assimilation of food and the discharge of residual wastes and consisting of the alimentary canal and those glands or parts of complex glands that secrete digestive ferments

al·i·men·ta·tion \,aləmən'tāshən, -(,)men-\ *n* -S [ML *alimentation-, alimentatio*, fr. LL *alimentatus* (past part. of *alimentare* to nourish, fr. L *alimentum* food) + L *-ion-, -io* -ion — more at ALIMENT] **1 :** the supplying with the necessities of life **:** MAINTENANCE **2 :** the process of giving nourishment ⟨intravenous ~ —M. S. Dunn⟩ **3 :** the act or process of receiving nourishment **4 :** an accumulation of snow (as from wind-blown drifts or avalanches) that tends to increase the volume of a glacier — compare ABLATION

al·i·men·ta·tive \,alə'mentəd·iv\ *adj* **:** having to do with the supply of aliment **:** NUTRITIVE — **al·i·men·ta·tive·ly** *adv*

al·i·men·ter \'alə,mentə(r)\ *n* -S **:** one that aliments; *specif* **:** a worker who feeds material into a machine

al·i·men·to·ther·a·py \,alə'mentō'therəpē\ *n* [*1aliment* + *-o-* + *therapy*] **:** the treatment of disease by dietetic methods

al·i·mo·ny \'alə,mōnē, -ni, *US also & Brit usu* -,mən-\ *n* -ES [L *alimonia* sustenance, fr. *alere* to nourish — more at OLD] **1 :** the means of living **:** MAINTENANCE **2 :** an allowance made to a woman for her support out of the estate or income of her husband (or to a husband from the property of the wife) or of him who was her husband upon her legal separation or divorce from him or during a suit for the same

alimony pendente lite *n* [L *pendente lite* pending suit] **:** alimony granted pending a suit for divorce or separation to include a reasonable allowance for the prosecution of the suit — called also *temporary alimony*

alims *pl of* ALIM

ali·na·sal \,ālə'-, ,al-\ *adj* [*ali-* + *nasal*] **:** relating to the lateral portions of the nose

aline *var of* ALIGN

alineation *var of* ALLINEATION

ali·no·tum \,ālə'nōdəm, ,al-\ *n, pl* **alino·ta** \-d·ə\ [NL, fr. *ali-* + *notum*] **:** the dorsal plate of the thoracic exoskeleton of a winged insect to which the wings are attached

alin·ta·tao \,alintä'taü\ *n* -S [PhilSp, fr. Tag *alintatáw*] **1 :** a tree (*Diospyros pilosanthera*) **2 :** the hard dark wood of the alintatao

ali·pa·ta \,alәpə'tä\ *n* -S [Sp, fr. Bisayan *alipatá*] **:** BLIND-YOUR-EYES

al·i·pat·ric \,alə'pa·trik\ *adj* [by alter.] **:** ALLOPATRIC

ali·ped \'ālə,ped, 'al-\ *adj* [*ali-* + *-ped*] **:** wing-footed ⟨the ~ bat⟩

al·i·phat·ic \,alə'fad·ik\ *adj* [ISV *aliphat-* (fr. Gk *aleiphat-, aleiphar* oil, fat, fr. *aleiphein* to smear) + *-ic*] **:** of, relating to, or derived from fat **:** FATTY, ACYCLIC — used of a large class of organic compounds characterized by an open-chain structure and consisting of the paraffin, olefin, and acetylene hydrocarbons and their derivatives (as the fatty acids); distinguished from *alicyclic, aromatic, heterocyclic* ⟨~ terpenes⟩

1al·i·quant \'alə,kwänt, -,kwənt\ *adj* [fr. (assumed) ML or NL *aliquantus* (as in — assumed — *pars aliquanta* aliquant part), fr. L, some, moderate, fr. *alius* some, other + *quantus* how great, how much — more at ELSE, QUANTITY] **:** being a part of a number or quantity but not dividing it without leaving a remainder ⟨5 is an ~ part of 16⟩ — opposed to *aliquot*

2aliquant \"\ *n* -S **:** an aliquant part

1al·i·quot \-,kwät, --kwət\ *adj* [ML *aliquotae* (as in *partes aliquotae* aliquot parts), fr. L *aliquot* some, several, fr. *alius* + *quot* how many — more at QUOTA] **1 :** contained an exact number of times in something else — used of a divisor or part ⟨5 is an ~ part of 15⟩; opposed to *aliquant* **2 :** FRACTIONAL ⟨an ~ portion of a chemical solution⟩ ⟨an ~ part of an estate⟩

2aliquot \"\ *n* -S **:** an aliquot part

3aliquot \"\ *vt* -ED/-ING/-S **:** to divide (a number or quantity) into equal parts

aliquot scaling *n* **:** a method of strengthening the tone of the upper notes of the piano by providing an extra sympathetic string for each note

aliquot tone *n, music* **:** a partial tone **:** HARMONIC

alisander *var of* ALEXANDER

ali·sep·tal \,ālə'-, ,al-\ *adj* [*ali* + *septal*] *anat* **:** relating to or designating lateral expansions of the nasal septum

ali·si·er \ə'lēzē,ā\ *n* -S [F, service tree, fr. *alise* sorb apple, of Gmc origin; akin to MD *else* alder, OHG *erila* — more at ALDER] **1 :** BLACK HAW 1 **2 :** SHEEPBERRY 1a

alis·ma \ə'lizmə\ *n* [NL, fr. L, water plantain, fr. Gk] **1** *cap* **:** a small genus (the type of the family Alismataceae) of aquatic or semiaquatic herbs with long-petioled often floating leaves and white flowers — see WATER PLANTAIN **2** -S **:** a plant of the genus *Alisma*

al·is·ma·ce·ae \,a(,)liz'māsē,ē\ *syn of* ALISMATACEAE

al·is·ma·les \,aləz'mā(,)lēz\ *or* **alis·ma·ta·les** \ə,lizmə'tā-(,)lēz\ [NL, fr. *Alisma* + *-ales*] *syn of* NAIADALES

alis·ma·ta·ce·ae \ə,lizmə'tāsē,ē\ *n pl, cap* [NL, fr. *Alismat-*, *Alisma*, type genus + *-aceae*] **:** a family of monocotyledonous aquatic or marsh herbs (order Naiadales) having regular perfect monoecious flowers

ali·so \ə'lē(,)zō, -sō\ *n* -S [Sp] **1 :** any of several shrubs or trees of the genus *Alnus* **2 :** the wood of an aliso

al·i·son \'aləsən\ *n* -S [by folk etymology (influence of name *Alison*)] **:** ALYSSUM

1ali·sphe·noid \,ālə'-, ,al-\ *or* **ali·sphe·noi·dal** \,===;==,==;=;==\ *adj* [*ali-* + *sphenoid, sphenoidal*] **:** belonging or relating to or forming the wings of the sphenoid or the pair of bones that becoming fused with other sphenoidal elements form in adult man the greater wings of the sphenoid

2alisphenoid \"\ *or* **alisphenoidal** \"\ *n* -S **:** an alisphenoid bone

alist \ə'-\ *adv (or adj)* [*1a-* + *list* (to incline)] *of a ship* **:** LISTED **:** in a list

alit *past of* ALIGHT

alite \'ā,līt\ *n* -S [*1a* + *-lite*] **:** a constituent of portland-cement clinker now identified as a calcium silicate approximately Ca_3SiO_5 containing small but essential amounts of aluminum and magnesium in substitution for silicon and empty holes in the crystal structure

al·i·ter \'alətər, -əd·ər, -ə,te(ə)r\ *adv* [L, fr. *alius* other — more at ELSE] **:** OTHERWISE

ali·trunk \'ālə,trəŋk, 'al-\ *n* -S [*ali-* + *trunk*] **:** the portion of the insect thorax that bears the wings, in the Hymenoptera including also the first abdominal segment

ali·tur·gic *also* **ali·tur·gi·cal** \,ā=;=-, ,a=;=-\ *adj* [*2a-* + *liturgic, liturgical*] *of a specified day* **:** marked by the omission of the celebration of the Christian liturgy or a portion of it ⟨an ~ day⟩

al·i·un·de \,alē'ən(,)dē\ *adv (or adj)* [L, fr. *alius* other + *unde* whence; akin to *ubi* where — more at ELSE, UBIQUITY] **:** from another source **:** from elsewhere

alive \ə'līv\ *adj* [ME *alive, on live*, fr. OE *on life*, fr. *on* + *life*, dat. of *līf* life — more at LIFE] **1 a :** having life **:** not dead or inanimate **:** LIVING; *esp* **:** marked by a state in which the organs perform their vital functions ⟨so good to be ~⟩ ⟨a large number were still ~ after the explosion⟩ — usu. used predicatively or postpositively **b :** LIVING — used for emphasis after the noun ⟨he was the proudest boy ~⟩ ⟨"Man ~!" he said. "You don't really mean that"⟩ ⟨sakes ~⟩ **2 a :** still in existence, force, or operation **:** effective at least to a degree **:** not dead, defunct, or extinct **:** EXISTENT, ACTIVE ⟨small farms kept ~ by judicious husbanding of the lake waters —*Amer. Guide Series: Calif.*⟩ ⟨keep ~ the conception of morals he preached —Havelock Ellis⟩ **b :** still in use **:** current to a degree **:** still exerting force or influence ⟨neither of these works is much ~ today —*Times Lit. Supp.*⟩ **c** *bowls* **:** in play **:** not dead **3 a :** marked by ready perception of **:** knowing or realizing the existence of **:** comprehending and vigilant about or appreciative of ⟨becoming ~ to the folly of what he had been doing —Samuel Butler⟩ ⟨consciousness of this danger . . . made her . . . ~ to the risks of an undesirable marriage —John Galsworthy⟩ **b :** quick to note or feel **:** readily impressed or influenced by **:** notably aware of, susceptible or sensitive to ⟨dreadfully ~ to nervous terrors —Charles Lamb⟩ ⟨veterans are as fully ~ to the romance . . . of newspaper work as any cub —Stanley Walker⟩ **4 a :** marked by alertness, activity, vitality, energy, animation, or briskness **:** not static, torpid, sluggish, or lifeless ⟨not sufficiently ~ to feel the tang of sense nor yet to be moved by thought —John Dewey⟩ ⟨the ~ promise of spring —H.D.Skidmore⟩ **b :** communicating a feeling of life, esp. of blended verisimilitude, activity, verve, and interestingness ⟨making the commonplaces of American culture . . . come ~ through his plain words —Babette Deutsch⟩ **5 :** FILLED, THRONGED, TEEMING **:** marked by much pulsating, stirring life, animation, or activity ⟨the sea was ~ with large whales —Herman Melville⟩ ⟨this decade was ~ with controversy and intellectual combat —*Amer. Guide Series: Ind.*⟩ **6 a :** electrically connected to a source of voltage or electrically charged **:** having a potential different from that of the earth or of the conducting ground of a radio or automobile **b :** not inactive, inactivated, shut off, or dead **:** operating and functioning **:** TRANSMITTING, BROADCASTING, RECORDING ⟨despite the hurricane the phone was still ~⟩ **7 :** LIVE 10 **syn** see AWARE

alive·ness \-nəs\ *n* -ES **:** the quality or state of being alive

ali·vin·cu·lar \,ālə'viŋkyələ(r), ,al-\ *adj* [*ali-* + *vinculum* + *-ar*] **:** having a short ligament with its longer axis transverse to the hinge line — used of certain bivalves

ali·yah \,ä'lē(,)yä, ə'lēyə, ,älē'yä\ *n, pl* **aliyahs** \-äz,-əz\ *or* **ali·yoth** *or* **ali·yot** \,älē'yōs, -ōt\ [Heb *'ălīyāh* ascent, act of going up] **:** the action of going up or of being called to the reading desk of the synagogue to read from the scriptures

al·i·zan·threne navy blue R \,alə'zan,thrēn-\ *n, usu cap A &N&B* [*alizanthrene* fr. *alizarin* + *-anthrene*] **:** a vat dye — see DYE table I (under *Vat Blue 18*)

al·i·za·ri \,alə'zärē\ *also* **li·za·ri** *or* **li·za·ry** \lə'zärē\ *n, pl* **alizaris** *also* **lizaris** *or* **lizaries** [F & Sp; F, *alizari*, fr. Sp] **:** the madder of the Levant

aliz·a·rin \ə'lizərən\ *also* **aliz·a·rine** \", -,rēn\ *n* -S [prob.

fr. F *alizarine*, fr. *alizari* (fr. Sp, prob. fr. Ar *al-'aṣārah* the juice, fr. *'aṣara* to squeeze) + *-ine*] **1 :** an orange or red crystalline compound $C_{14}H_6O_2(OH)_2$ formerly prepared from madder and now made synthetically from anthraquinone that with different mordants produces on cotton the Turkey reds and other shades (as pink and chocolate) but that is used now more in making red pigments than in dyeing; 1,2-dihydroxy-anthraquinone — see DYE table I (under *Mordant Red 11*) **2 :** any of a group of acid, mordant, and solvent dyes derived like alizarin proper from anthraquinone and used to produce various hues — see DYE table I **3 :** any of various dyes not derived from anthraquinone but somewhat similar to alizarin in dyeing properties

alizarine blue *n, often cap A&B* **:** any of various blue acid, mordant, and solvent dyes most of which are derived from anthraquinone — see DYE table I (under *Acid Blue* and *Solvent Blue*)

alizarine brown *n, often cap A&B* **:** ANTHRAGALLOL

alizarine carmine *n, often cap A&C* **:** ALIZARINE RED b

alizarine cyanine green *n, often cap A&C&G* **:** an acid anthraquinone dye derived from quinizarin that dyes wool and mordanted silk yellowish green to bluish green — see DYE table I (under *Acid Green 25* and *Solvent Green 3*)

alizarine lake *n, often cap A&L* **:** an organic pigment made from alizarin — see DYE table I (under *Pigment Red 83*)

alizarine red *n, often cap A&R* **:** any of various red mordant or acid dyes most of which are derived from anthraquinone: as **a :** TURKEY RED 1a **b :** an orange-yellow crystalline compound $C_{14}H_7NaO_7S$ used chiefly for dyeing and printing aluminum-mordanted wool scarlet red, as a biological stain, and as an analytical reagent (as for detecting aluminum); sodium 3-alizarin-sulfonate — called also *Alizarine Carmine, Alizarine Red S, Alizarine S;* see DYE table I (under *Mordant Red 3*)

alizarine S *n, often cap A* **:** ALIZARINE RED b

alizarine saphirol *n, often cap A&S* **:** either of two acid anthraquinone dyes — see DYE table I (under *Acid Blue 43 & 45*)

alizarine yellow *n, often cap A&Y* **:** any of various mordant dyes not related chemically to alizarin but applicable by similar methods: as **a :** a monoazo dye made by coupling diazotized *m*-nitroaniline with salicylic acid — called also *Alizarine Yellow 2G;* see DYE table I (under *Mordant Yellow 1*) **b :** a monoazo dye made by coupling *p*-nitroaniline with salicylic acid and used chiefly as an acid-base indicator — called also *Alizarine Yellow R;* see DYE table I (under *Mordant Orange 1*) **c :** GALLACETOPHENONE — called also *Alizarine Yellow C*

al·ja·ma \äl'hämə\ *n* -s [Sp, fr. Ar *al-jamā'ah* the assembly, congregation of people — more at AMALGAM] **:** a Jewish congregation or community in medieval Spain; *esp* **:** a Jewish (sometimes Moorish) quarter, school, or synagogue

al·ja·ma·do \,älhä'mä(,)thō\ *n, pl* **aljamados** [Sp, fr. *aljama* + *-ado*, n. & adj. suffix (fr. L *-atus* -ate)] **:** an inhabitant of an aljama

al·ja·mia *or* **al·ja·mi·ah** \,älhä'mēə\ *n* -s [Sp *aljamía*, fr. Ar *al-'ajamīyah* the non-Arab, barbarian] **1 :** Spanish written in Hebrew or esp. Arabic characters **2 :** the Arabic alphabet as adapted for writing Spanish

¹al·ja·mi·a·do \,äl,hämē'ä(,)thō\ *adj* [Sp, fr. *aljamía* + *-ado*] **:** written in Spanish with Arabic characters ⟨an ~ text⟩

²aljamiado \"\ *n* -s [Sp, fr. *aljamiado*, adj.] **:** a work written in Spanish with Arabic characters

alk \'alk\ *or* **alk gum** *n* -s [Ar *'ilk* resin] **:** resin of Chian turpentine

alk- *comb form* [*alkyl*] **:** alkyl ⟨*alk*acrylic⟩ ⟨*alk*iodide⟩

alk *abbr* alkaline

alka- *comb form* [*alkane*] **:** alkane ⟨*alka*diyne⟩ ⟨*alka*polyene⟩

al·ka·di·ene \,alkə'dī,ēn\ *n* -s [*alkali* + *di-* + *-ene*] **:** DIOLEFIN

al·ka·di·en·yl \,alkə'dī,ēnᵊl\ *n* -s [*alkadiene* + *-yl*] **:** a univalent aliphatic hydrocarbon radical containing two double bonds

al·ka·hest *also* **al·ca·hest** \'alkə,hest\ *n* -s [NL *alchahest*] **:** the universal solvent supposed by the alchemists to exist — **al·ka·hes·tic** \¦==¦=tik\ *adj*

alkakengi *var of* ALKEKENGI

al·ka·le·mia \,alkə'lēmēə\ *n* -s [NL, fr. ML *alkali* + NL *-emia*] **:** a condition in which the hydrogen ion concentration in the blood is decreased

al·ka·les·cence \,alkə'lesᵊn(t)s\ *also* **al·ka·les·cen·cy** \-ᵊnsē\ *n* -s **:** alkaline property **:** quality or degree of being alkaline

al·ka·les·cent \¦==¦=ᵊnt\ *adj* [*alkali* + *-escent*] **:** tending to the properties of an alkali **:** slightly alkaline

al·ka·li \'alkə,lī\ *n, pl* **alkalies** *or* **alkalis** \-īz\ *often attrib* [ME, fr. ML *alcali, alkali*, fr. Ar *al-qili* the ashes of the plant saltwort] **1 a :** a soluble salt obtained from the ashes of plants and consisting largely of potassium carbonate or (as from sea plants) of sodium carbonate **b :** a substance having marked basic properties like the above salts; *esp* **:** a hydroxide or carbonate of an alkali metal (as sodium or potassium) or less often of an alkaline-earth metal (as calcium) — see CAUSTIC ALKALI; compare BASE 8 **2 :** ALKALI METAL — used esp. in names of compounds ⟨~ cyanides⟩ **3 a :** a soluble salt or a mixture of soluble salts (as the sulfates and chlorides of sodium, potassium, and magnesium and the carbonates of sodium and potassium) present in some soils of arid or semiarid regions in quantity detrimental to ordinary agriculture ⟨~ soils⟩ **b :** a region in which the soil abounds in alkali

alkali bee *n* **:** a common solitary bee (*Nomia melanderi*) important as a pollinizer of alfalfa in the western U.S.

alkali blue *n* **1 :** any of various alkali-soluble triphenylmethane dyes that are essentially sodium salts of monosulfonic acids of phenylated pararosaniline and are used chiefly in making pigments — see DYE table I (under *Acid Blue 110*) **2 :** any of the fairly permanent pigments made from an alkali blue dye and used chiefly in printing inks

al·kal·ic \(')al¦kalik\ *adj* [*alkali* + *-ic*] *of igneous rocks* **:** containing a comparatively large proportion of the alkalies sodium and potassium

alkali cellulose *n* **:** a compound of cellulose with an alkali (as sodium hydroxide) formed during the mercerization of cotton and as the first step in the manufacture of viscose and cellulose ethers

alkali chlorosis *n* **:** a yellowing of the foliage of a plant caused by an excess of soluble salts in the soil

alkali disease *n* [so called fr. the belief that it was caused by alkaline water] **1 :** trembles of cattle — compare MILK SICKNESS **2 :** botulism of ducks — compare DUCK SICKNESS **3 :** chronic selenosis

al·ka·lied \-,līd\ *adj* **1 :** affected with alkali disease **2** *of grain or hay* **:** containing selenium

alkali fast green 10 G *n, usu cap A&F&G* **:** an acid dye — see DYE table I (under *Acid Green 22*)

alkali feldspar *n* **:** feldspar containing alkali metals (as sodium or potassium or both) but little calcium

alkali flat *n* **:** a level area in an arid or semiarid region that is encrusted with salt or alkali (as the dried bed of an evaporated pond or lake)

al·kal·i·fy \al'kalə,fī, 'alkə-\ *vb* -ED/-ING/-ES [*alkali* + *-fy*] *vt* **:** to convert or change into an alkali **:** make alkaline ~ *vi* **:** to become alkaline

alkali grass *n* [so called fr. its growth in alkaline soil] **1 :** a grasslike plant (*Zygadenus elegans*) with flowers in a loose cylindrical raceme **2 :** SALT GRASS a **3 :** any of several grasses of the genus *Puccinellia* that grow in saline situations

alkali heath *n* [so called fr. its growth in alkaline soil and fr. its heathlike leaves] **:** a California undershrub (*Frankenia grandifolia*) with revolute leaves, pinkish flowers in small terminal clusters, and linear many-seeded capsules

alkali lake *n* **:** a saline lake containing large amounts of sodium and potassium carbonates in solution as well as sodium chloride, commonly found in arid regions — called also *soda lake*

alkali mallow *n* **:** a low whitish scurfy perennial herb (*Sida hederacea*) having roundish or kidney-shaped leaves and cream-colored flowers

alkali metal *n* **:** any of the univalent mostly basic metals of group I of the periodic table comprising lithium, sodium, potassium, rubidium, cesium, and francium

al·ka·lim·e·ter \,alkə'limədə(r)\ *n* -s [F *alcalimètre*, fr. *alcali* alkali (fr. ML) + *-mètre* -meter] **1 :** an apparatus for measuring the strength or the amount of alkali in a mixture or solution **2 :** an apparatus for measuring the amount of carbon dioxide (as that liberated from a weighed sample of carbonate-containing material by reaction with acid)

al·ka·li·met·ric \¦alkələ¦me·trik\ *adj* **:** relating to or involving alkalimetry

al·ka·lim·e·try \-'limə·trē\ *n* -ES **1 :** the measurement of the strength of an alkali or of the amount of alkali in a mixture or solution — compare ACIDIMETRY 2 **2 :** the measurement by titration of the amount of acid in a solution by use of a standard solution of an alkali — compare ACIDIMETRY 1

alkali mustard *n* [so called fr. its growth in alkaline soil] **:** JACKASS CLOVER 2

al·ka·line \'alkələn, -,līn\ *adj* [*alkali* + *-ine*] **1 :** of, relating to, or having the properties of an alkali: as **a :** having an alkaline reaction **:** having a pH of more than 7 ⟨an ~ soil⟩ ⟨a strongly ~ solution⟩ **b :** containing or involving the use of alkali ⟨~ bath⟩ ⟨~ fusion⟩ — see BASIC 3, CAUSTIC 1 **2 :** of or relating to the alkali metals

alkaline detergent *n* **:** DETERGENT b

alkaline earth *n* **1 :** the oxide of any of a group of bivalent strongly basic metals comprising calcium, strontium, and barium and, according to some, magnesium, radium, and less often beryllium **2 :** ALKALINE-EARTH METAL

alkaline–earth metal *n* **:** any of the metals of group II of the periodic table whose oxides are the alkaline earths

alkaline metal *n* **:** ALKALI METAL

alkaline tide *n* **:** the period or condition of increased alkalinity of the body fluids and urine during digestion associated with the loss of acid by secretion of gastric juice

al·ka·lin·i·ty \,alkə'linəd·ē, -ətē, -i\ *n* -ES [*alkaline* + *-ity*] **:** the quality, state, or degree of being alkaline

al·ka·lin·i·za·tion \,alkə,linə'zāshən, -,lən-, -,līn-, -,lə,nī'z-\ *n* -s **:** the act or process of alkalinizing

al·ka·lin·ize \'alkələ,nīz\ *vt* -ED/-ING/-S [*alkaline* + *-ize*] **:** to make alkaline ⟨*alkalinized* the body by using sodium citrate as the agent⟩

alkali orange RT *n, usu cap A&O* **:** a direct dye — see DYE table I (under *Direct Orange 10*)

alkali sacaton *n* **:** a dropseed (*Sporobolus airoides*) that is abundant in dry alkali soils esp. in the southern U.S.

al·ka·li·troph·ic \¦alkələ¦träfik, -ōf-\ *adj* [*alkali* + *-trophic*] **:** exhibiting the alkaline state characteristic of lakes in arid regions — **al·ka·lit·ro·phy** \,alkə'li·trəfē\ *n* -ES

alkali weed *n* [so called fr. its growth in alkaline soil] **:** YERBA MANSA

al·ka·li·za·tion \,alkələ'zāshən, -,lī'z-\ *n* -s **:** ALKALINIZATION

al·ka·lize \'alkə,līz\ *vt* -ED/-ING/-S [F *alcaliser*, fr. *alcali* alkali (fr. ML) + *-iser* -ize] **:** ALKALINIZE

al·ka·loid \'alkə,lȯid\ *n* -s *often attrib* [G, fr. *alkali* + *-oid*] *chem* **:** any of a very large group of organic bases containing nitrogen and usu. oxygen that occur esp. in seed plants for the most part in the form of salts with acids (as citric, oxalic, or sulfuric acid), most of the bases being colorless and well crystallized, bitter tasting, complex in structure with at least one nitrogen atom in a ring (as a pyrrole, quinoline, or indole ring), and optically and biologically active, many of the bases or their salts being used as drugs (as morphine and codeine) ⟨ergot contains a number of closely related ~s⟩ — **al·ka·loi·dal** \¦==¦=dᵊl\ *adj*

al·ka·lom·e·try \,alkə'lämə·trē\ *n* -ES [ISV *alkaloid* + *-metry*] **1 :** the quantitative determination of alkaloids by chemical or other methods **2 :** the administration of alkaloids according to an exact system of dosage

al·ka·lo·sis \,alkə'lōsəs\ *n, pl* **alkalo·ses** \-ō,sēz\ [NL, fr. ML *alkali* + NL *-osis*] **:** a condition of increased alkalinity of the blood and tissues caused by excessive alkali intake or excessive loss of acid and resulting in muscular irritability and sometimes convulsions — opposed to *acidosis*

al·ka·lot·ic \¦alkə¦läd·ik\ *adj* **:** marked by the presence of or tendency toward alkalosis

al·ka·mine \'alkə,mēn, -,mən\ *n* -s [G *alkamin*, fr. *alk*ohol alcohol + *amin* amine] **:** AMINO ALCOHOL

al·ka·nal \'alkə,nal\ *n* -s [*alkane* + *al*dehyde] **:** any aliphatic aldehyde (as decanal) regarded as derived from an alkane and containing the same number of carbon atoms as the alkane

al·kane \'al,kān\ *n* -s [*alkyl* + *-ane*] **:** any of a series of saturated aliphatic hydrocarbons C_nH_{2n+2} (as methane) **:** PARAFFIN 2

al·ka·net \'alkə,net\ *n* -s [ME, fr. OSp *alcaneta*, dim. of *alcana*] **1 a :** a European plant (*Alkanna tinctoria*) **b :** the root of this plant **2 :** a red dyestuff prepared from alkanet root and used similarly to alkannin **3 :** BUGLOSS 1 **4 :** PUCCOON 1b

al·kan·na \al'kanə\ *n* [NL, fr. Sp *alcana* henna (shrub), fr. ML *alchanna*, fr. Ar *al-ḥinnā'* the henna] **1** *cap* **:** a genus of herbs (family Boraginaceae) native to southern Europe with funnel-shaped flowers and pitted or wrinkled nutlets **2** *also* **al·ken·na** \-ke-\ -s **:** HENNA 1

al·kan·nin \al'kanən\ *n* -s [ISV *alkann-* (fr. NL *Alkanna*) + *-in*] **:** a red crystalline coloring matter $C_{16}H_{16}O_5$ obtained from alkanet and used chiefly in coloring beverages and fatty and oily pharmaceutical and cosmetic preparations

al·ka·no·ic acid \¦alkə¦nōik-\ *n* [*alkane* + *-oic*] **:** an aliphatic acid (as hexanoic acid) regarded as derived from an alkane and containing the same number of carbon atoms as the alkane

al·ka·nol \'alkə,nȯl, -ōl\ *n* -s [ISV *alkane* + *-ol*] **:** an aliphatic alcohol (as methanol) regarded as derived from an alkane

al·ka·nol·a·mine \,==¦=ə¦mēn\ *n* -s [*alkanol* + *amine*] **:** a compound (as ethanolamine) that is both an alkanol and an amine

al·kap·ton *or* **al·cap·ton** \al'kap,tän, -,tən\ *n* -s [ISV *alkali* + Gk *kaptein* to gulp + ISV *-on*, orig. formed as G *alkapton*] **:** HOMOGENTISIC ACID

al·kap·ton·u·ria *or* **al·cap·ton·u·ria** \(,)al,kaptə'n(y)ürēə\ *n* -s [NL, fr. ISV *alkapton*, + *alcapton* + NL *-uria*] **:** a rare recessive metabolic anomaly in man marked by inability to complete the degradation of tyrosine and phenylalanine resulting in the presence of alkapton in the urine —**al·kap·ton·u·ric** \¦=,=¦==¦rik\ *adj*

al·ka·ryl \'alkə,ril, -ēl\ *n* [*alkyl* + *aryl*] **:** an alkyl-substituted aryl radical (as ethyl-phenyl)

al·ka·ver·vir \,alkə'vər,vi(ə)r, al'kavə(r),-\ *n* -s [*alka*loid + *vervir*, abbr. of NL *Veratrum viride*] **:** a preparation containing ester alkaloids obtained from a hellebore (*Veratrum viride*) and used in treating hypertension

al·ke·ken·gi *also* **al·ka·ken·gi** \,alkə'kenjē\ *n* -s [ME *alkenkengy*, fr. ML *alkekengi*, fr. Ar *al-kākanj* the ground-cherry, fr. Per *kākunaj*] **:** CHINESE LANTERN PLANT

al·kene \'al,kēn\ *n* -s [ISV *alkyl* + *-ene*] **:** any of a series of aliphatic hydrocarbons C_nH_{2n} (as ethylene) containing a double bond **:** OLEFIN

al·ke·nyl \'alkə,nil, -ēl\ *n* -s [*alkene* + *-yl*] **:** any univalent aliphatic hydrocarbon radical C_nH_{2n-1} (as 2-butenyl $CH_3CH{:}CHCH_2$–) derived from an alkene by removal of one hydrogen atom

al·ker·mes \al'kərmēz, -məs; ,alkər'mes\ *n* -ES [F *alkermès*, fr. Sp *alkermes* (now usu. *alquermes*), fr. Ar *al-qirmiz* the alkermes — more at CRIMSON] **1** *obs* **:** the kermes insect **2 :** an orig. Italian liqueur made of brandy flavored with bay leaves, mace, nutmeg, cloves, and cinnamon and colored a brilliant red with the kermes insect or with cochineal

alk gum *var of* ALK

al·kide \'al,kīd, -,kəd\ *n* -s [*alkyl* + *-ide*] **:** a binary compound of an alkyl esp. with a metal ⟨diethyl-zinc $(C_2H_5)_2Zn$ is an ~ of zinc⟩

alk·i·o·dide \al'kīə,dīd, -,dəd\ *n* -s [*alkyl* + *iodide*] **:** a compound (as a methiodide) with an alkyl iodide (as methyl iodide)

alk·ox·ide \al'käk,sīd, -,səd\ *n* -s [*alkoxy-* + *-ide*] **:** a binary compound (as a methoxide) of an alkoxyl; *esp* **:** a base formed from an alcohol by replacement of the hydroxyl hydrogen with a metal

alk·oxy \(')al¦käksē\ *adj* [fr. ISV *alkoxy-*, fr. *alkoxyl*] **:** of, relating to, or containing alkoxyl ⟨~ groups⟩

alk·ox·yl \al'käksəl\ *n* -s [blend of *alkyl* and *oxy-*] **:** an univalent radical RO (as methoxyl) composed of an alkyl group united with oxygen

alk·ox·yl·ate \al'käksə,lāt\ *vt* -ED/-ING/-S [*alkoxyl* + *-ate*] **:** to introduce alkoxyl into (a compound)

alk·ox·yl·a·tion \(,)=,==ˈlāshən\ *n* -s **:** the act or process of alkoxylating

al·ky \'alkē\ *n* -ES [by shortening & alter.] **1** *slang* **:** ALCOHOL **2** *slang* **:** ALCOHOLIC

al·kyd \'alkəd\ *or* **alkyd resin** *n* -s *often attrib* [blend of *alkyl* and *acid*] **:** any of a large group of thermoplastic or thermosetting synthetic resins that are essentially polyesters made by heating polyhydric alcohols (as glycerol, ethylene glycol, or pentaerythritol) with polybasic acids or their anhydrides (as phthalic anhydride, maleic anhydride, or sebacic acid) and used chiefly in making protective coatings characterized in general by their gloss, flexibility, and good weathering properties

al·kyl \'alkəl\ *n* -s [prob. fr. G, fr. *alkohol* alcohol (fr. ML *alcohol*) + *-yl*] **1 a :** a univalent aliphatic radical C_nH_{2n+1} (as methyl, ethyl) derived from an alkane by removal of one hydrogen atom **b :** any univalent aliphatic, aromatic-aliphatic, or alicyclic hydrocarbon radical **2 :** a compound of one or more alkyl radicals with a metal ⟨sodium ~s⟩

al·kyl·a·mine \¦alkələ¦mēn, ,==ˈlamən, -ˈla,mēn\ *n* -s [ISV *alkyl* + *amine*] **:** an amine (as methylamine) containing alkyl attached to amino nitrogen

al·kyl·a·mi·no \¦alkələ¦mē(,)nō, -kə¦lamə,nō\ *adj* [*alkylamino-*, fr. *alkylamine*] **:** of, relating to, or containing an alkylamine

alkyl aryl sulfonate *n* **:** a salt of an alkyl-substituted aromatic sulfonic acid — used chiefly commercially; see ANIONIC DETERGENT 2

¹al·kyl·ate \'alkə,lāt\ *vt* -ED/-ING/-S [*alkyl* + *-ate*] **:** to introduce one or more alkyl groups into (a compound)

²al·kyl·ate \", -,lət\ *n* -s **:** a product of alkylation; *esp, in petroleum refining* **:** a mixture of liquid paraffins (as isooctane) of high antiknock value used as a blending agent for gasoline (as aviation gasoline)

al·kyl·a·tion \,alkə'lāshən\ *n* -s **:** the act or process of alkylating; *esp, in petroleum refining* **:** a process in which gaseous paraffins (as isobutane) are converted into higher liquid branched-chain paraffins (as iso-octane) by reaction with gaseous olefins (as butylenes)

al·kyl·ene \'alkə,lēn\ *n* -s [ISV *alkyl* + *-ene*] **1 :** a bivalent saturated aliphatic radical (as ethylene) regarded as derived from an alkene by opening of the double bond or from an alkane by removal of two hydrogen atoms from different carbon atoms **2 :** ALKENE

alkyl halide *n* **:** a compound (as methyl iodide, ethyl bromide) of an alkyl group with a halogen

al·kyl·ic \(')al¦kilik\ *adj* [*alkyl* + *-ic*] **:** of or relating to an alkyl

al·kyl·i·dene \al'kilə,dēn\ *n* -s [ISV *alkyl* + *-idene*] **:** a bivalent aliphatic radical (as ethylidene) derived from an alkane by removal of two hydrogen atoms from the same carbon atom

al·kyl·ize \'alkə,līz, -,ki,-\ *vt* -ED/-ING/-S [*alkyl* + *-ize*] **:** ALKYLATE

al·kyl·o·gen \al'kilәjən, -,jen\ *n* -s [*alkyl* + *halogen*] **:** ALKYL HALIDE

al·kyl·ol \'alkə,lȯl, -ōl\ *n* -s [*alkyl* + *-ol*] **:** a hydroxy derivative of an alkyl radical **:** hydroxy-alkyl

al·kyl·ol·a·mine \,==¦=ə¦mēn\ *n* -s [*alkylol* + *amine*] **:** ALKANOLAMINE

al·kyne *also* **al·kine** \'al,kīn\ *n* -s [*alkyl* + *-yne, -ine*] **:** any of a series of aliphatic hydrocarbons C_nH_{2n-2} (as acetylene) containing a triple bond

al·ky·nyl \'alkə,nil, -ēl\ *n* -s [*alkyne* + *-yl*] **:** a univalent aliphatic hydrocarbon radical containing a triple bond

¹all \'ȯl\ *adj* [ME *all, ell*, fr. OE *all, eall;* akin to OHG *al* all, ON *allr*, Goth *alls*, and perh. to OIr *oll* large, beyond, L *uls* beyond, OSlav *lani* in the preceding year, Skt *araṇa* foreign; basic meaning: beyond] **1 a :** that is the whole amount or quantity of ⟨~ rubbish should be cleared out of cellars⟩ ⟨needed ~ the courage he had⟩ ⟨it ~ began one rainy afternoon⟩ **:** that is the whole extent or duration of ⟨~ the year round⟩ ⟨sat up ~ night⟩ ⟨one of the greatest victories in ~ history⟩ **b :** as much as possible **:** the greatest possible ⟨wished them ~ happiness⟩ ⟨traveled with ~ speed⟩ ⟨was told in ~ seriousness⟩ **2 a :** every member or individual component of **:** each one of — used distributively with a plural noun or pronoun to mean that a statement is true of every individual considered ⟨~ things to ~ men⟩ ⟨~ my friends were there⟩ ⟨a film suitable for ~ ages⟩ ⟨refugees ~, from one thing or another —*Punch*⟩ ⟨they ~ came late⟩ **b** *of members of a class* **:** each and every one of — used in logic as a verbalized equivalent of the universal quantifier **3 :** the whole number or sum of — used collectively with a plural noun or pronoun to mean that a statement is true of the sum of the individuals considered ⟨~ the angles of a triangle are equal to two right angles⟩ ⟨~ these together are not worth 10 dollars⟩ ⟨after ~ these years⟩ **4 :** EVERY — used chiefly in the phrases *all manner of, all kind of* ⟨endured ~ manner of hardship⟩ **5 :** any whatever ⟨beyond ~ doubt⟩ ⟨denied ~ responsibility⟩ **6 :** nothing but **:** ONLY, ALONE ⟨I was born to speak ~ mirth and no matter —Shak.⟩ **:** **a :** completely taken up with, given to, or absorbed by ⟨found him ~ gratitude⟩ ⟨suddenly became ~ attention⟩ **b :** having or seeming to have (some physical feature) in conspicuous excess or prominence ⟨a body ~ legs⟩ ⟨a face ~ pimples⟩ **c :** marked by acute or eager concentration on full perception by **:** paying full attention with ⟨at the mention of bicycles the boy was ~ ears⟩ **7** *dial* **:** used up **:** entirely consumed — used esp. of food and drink ⟨the keg of beer was ~⟩ **8 :** being more than one person or thing — used chiefly in speech esp. after interrogative and plural personal pronouns ⟨who ~ was there⟩ ⟨what ~ do you have to do⟩; often written with hyphen between pronoun and *all* ⟨we-*all* had better wait⟩; see YOU-ALL **syn** see WHOLE — **all the :** as much of . . . as **:** as much of a . . . as **:** the only ⟨*all the* home I ever had⟩ — **all two** *now dial* **:** all of two **:** BOTH ⟨walking hand in hand, *all two* of them⟩

²all \"\ *adv* [ME *al, all*, fr. OE *all, eall*, fr. *all, eall*, adj.] **1 :** WHOLLY, ALTOGETHER, QUITE ⟨sat ~ alone⟩ ⟨a statement that was not ~ true⟩ ⟨~ gone⟩ ⟨arrived ~ too late to be of service⟩ ⟨he was ~ for the racy phrase —W.S.Maugham⟩ — often used before other words and phrases or (chiefly in speech) after interrogative adverbs to intensify meaning ⟨dealers ~ across the country⟩ ⟨ran into the house ~ covered with mud⟩ ⟨could hear moaning ~ around him⟩ ⟨~ too few⟩ ⟨that's ~ very human and would harm nobody —Deems Taylor⟩ ⟨where ~ have you been⟩; often used in compounds to indicate representation of a whole area ⟨an *all*-British soccer team⟩ or selection of the best ⟨an *all*-girl team⟩ **2** *obs* **:** EXCLUSIVELY, ONLY ⟨I shall never marry like my sisters, to love my father ~ —Shak.⟩ **3** *archaic* **:** JUST **:** quite as indicated ⟨a damsel lay deploring, ~ on a rock reclined —John Gay⟩ — often merely intensive **4 :** by that amount **:** so much **:** very much — used with *the* and an adverb or adjective in the comparative degree ⟨~ the better for a night's sleep⟩ ⟨from private sources and therefore ~ the more revealing⟩ **5 :** for each side **:** APIECE, EACH ⟨the score is two ~⟩ — **all of 1 :** QUITE, FULLY ⟨a man *all of* 6 feet tall⟩ ⟨arrived *all of* 15 minutes ago⟩ ⟨this building cost *all of* five million dollars —Lewis Mumford⟩ **2 :** with marked signs of — used with *a* ⟨*all of* a flutter⟩ ⟨*all of* a tremble⟩ — **all the** *chiefly dial* **:** as . . . as — used with an adverb or adjective usu. comparative in form ⟨*all the* higher⟩ ⟨*all the* high⟩ but with the meaning of the positive (as high as) ⟨*all the* farther he could go was up to that fence⟩

³all \"\ *pron* [ME *al, all* (fr. *al, all*, adj.) & *alle*, pl. of *al, all*] **1 :** the whole number, quantity, or amount **:** TOTALITY — often used with a following relative clause ⟨~ that I have⟩ and with *of* and a pronoun and in recent usage with *of* and a noun ⟨~ of us⟩ ⟨~ of the books⟩ **2 :** EVERYBODY, EVERYTHING **:** everything in a particular scene or sequence of events ⟨through ~ he sat immovable⟩ ⟨sacrificed ~ for love⟩ ⟨to make it plain to one and ~⟩ ⟨that is ~⟩ ⟨when ~ is said and done⟩ — **and all :** and everything else esp. of a kind suggested by a previous context ⟨there he sat, pipe *and all*⟩ ⟨exhausted *and all* as he was —Gerrard MacDermott⟩ — often used merely to emphasize a previous context ⟨her friends was a queer lot, *and all* —Richard Llewellyn⟩

⁴all \"\ *n* -s [ME *all*, fr. *al, all*, adj.] **1 a :** the whole of one's possessions or of what one holds dear ⟨to lose one's

~⟩ **b alls** *pl, now chiefly dial* : BELONGINGS : personal possessions **2** *usu cap* **a** : WHOLE, TOTALITY **b** : the universe

all- *or* **allo-** *comb form* [Gk, fr. *allos* other, different — more at ELSE] **1** : other : different : dissimilar : extraneous ⟨*allergy*⟩ ⟨*allopathy*⟩ ⟨*allosematic*⟩ **2** *allo-* : isomeric form, close relative, or variety of (a specified chemical compound) ⟨*allo*-ocimene⟩ ⟨*allo*telluric acid⟩: as **a** : the more stable form (of two geometrical isomers) ⟨*allo*cinnamic acid⟩ **b** : TRANS- 3 — esp. in names of stereoisomeric compounds containing two fused saturated rings ⟨*allo*cholanic acid⟩ ⟨*allo*pregnane⟩ **3** *usu allo-* : having dissimilar genomes ⟨*allo*heteroploid⟩ ⟨*allo*ploid⟩ ⟨*allo*triploid⟩ — opposed to *aut-*

[1]**al·la breve** \ˌalə'brev(ə), ˌäl-, -re(ˌ)vā\ *adv (or adj)* [It, lit., according to the breve] : in duple or quadruple time, the beat being represented by the half note

[2]**alla breve** \"\ *n, pl* **alla breves** : the sign ₵ marking a piece or passage to be played alla breve; *also* : a passage so marked — called also *cut time*

al·lac·ta·ga \ə'laktəgə\ *n, cap* [NL] : a genus of small Asiatic jerboas having five toes on the hind feet

al·lac·tite \ə'lak,tīt\ *n* -s [ISV *allact-* (irreg. fr. Gk *allag-*, stem of *allassein* to change, fr. *allos* other) + *-ite*; orig. formed as Sw *allaktit* — more at ELSE] : a mineral consisting of a brownish red basic manganese arsenate $Mn_7(AsO_4)_2(OH)_8$

al·la·ha·bad \ˌaləhə'bad, -bäd\ *adj, usu cap* [fr. *Allahabad*, India] : of or from the city of Allahabad, India : of the kind or style prevalent in Allahabad

al·la·man·da \ˌalə'mandə\ *n* [NL, after Jean N.S. *Allamand* †1787 Swiss naturalist and physicist] **1** *cap* : a genus of tropical American woody vines (family Apocynaceae) having funnel-shaped flowers **2** -s : a plant of the genus *Allamanda*

al·la mar·cia \ˌälə'märˌchä; ˌälə'märchə, ˌäl-\ *adv (or adj)* [It] : in march style : like a march — used as a direction in music

[1]**all-amer·i·can** \ˌ==ˌ===\ *adj, cap 2d A* **1** : composed wholly of American elements ⟨played an *all-American* program⟩ **2** : thought of as representative of the U.S. as a whole ⟨the tales are not sectional or provincial in spirit; they are *all-American* —*Nation*⟩ ⟨a real *all-American* boy⟩; *esp* : selected (as by vote or nomination) as the best in the U.S. at a given time ⟨the *all-American* football team for the year⟩ ⟨suggested names for an all-time *all-American* relay team⟩ **3** : entirely within the U.S. ⟨access to the sea by an *all-American* system of waterways⟩ **4** : of or relating to the American nations collectively ⟨*all-American* research projects in Uruguay and Mexico⟩

[2]**all-american** \"\ *n, cap 2d A* [[1]*all-American*] **1** : a team or other unit composed of performers rated as best in the U.S. according to a vote or expert's choice **2** : a player or performer named to an all-American team

all-a-mort *adj* [by folk etymology (influence of [2]*all*) fr. MF *a la mort* to the death] *archaic* : AMORT

allanerly *var of* ALLENARLY

al·lan·ic acid \ə'lanik-\ *n* [ISV *allantoin* + *-ic*] : a crystalline acid $C_4H_5N_5O_5$ formed by the action of fuming nitric acid on allantoin

al·lan·ite \'alə,nīt\ *n* -s [Thomas *Allan* †1833 Eng. mineralogist, its discoverer + E *-ite*] : a mineral consisting of a brown or black monoclinic silicate allied to epidote and containing cerium, thorium, and other rare metals — **al·lan·it·ic** \ˌalə'nid·ik\ *adj*

allant- *or* **allanto-** *comb form* [NL, fr. Gk, sausage, fr. *allant-, allas*, prob. of Italic origin; akin to L *alium* garlic — more at ALLIUM] **1** : allantoic : allantoid ⟨*allanto*chorion⟩ ⟨*allant*oin⟩ **2** : sausage ⟨*allant*iasis⟩

al·lan·to·am·ni·ot·ic *or* **al·lan·to·am·ni·ot·ic** \ə¦lan(ˌ)tō-, ˌ==¦==\ *adj* [*allant-* + *amnionic* or *amniotic*] : relating to the allantois and amnion esp. when fused into a single membrane — compare CHORIOALLANTOIS

al·lan·to·ic \ˌalən·'tōik, ˌaˌlan-\ *adj* [ISV *allant-* + *-ic*] : relating to or contained in the allantois : characterized by an allantois

allantoic acid *n* : a crystalline acid $C_4H_8N_4O_4$ obtained by hydrolysis of allantoin; di-ureido-acetic acid

allantoic bladder *n* : a urinary bladder derived (as in certain vertebrates) from the allantois

allantoic vesicle *n* : the cavity of the allantois

[1]**al·lan·toid** \ə'lan,tȯid, -ntwȯd\ *adj* [F *allantoïde* allantois] : of or relating to the allantois

[2]**allantoid** \"\ *n* -s [F *allantoïde*, fr. Gk *allantoeidēs* sausage-shaped, fr. *allant-* + *-eidēs* -oid] : ALLANTOIS

[3]**allantoid** \"\ *adj* [Gk *allantoeidēs*] : shaped like a sausage

al·lan·toi·dal \¦alən·¦tȯidᵊl, ¦aˌlan-, -tōədᵊl\ *adj* [[2]*allantoid* + *-al*] : ALLANTOID

al·lan·toi·dea \ˌalən·'tȯidēə, ˌaˌlan-; əˌlantə'widēə\ *n pl, cap* [NL, fr. *allantoid-, allantois*] *in some classifications* : a division of Vertebrata comprising all forms in which the embryo develops a complete allantois

[1]**al·lan·toi·de·an** *or* **al·lan·toi·di·an** \¦alən·¦tȯidēən, ¦aˌlan-, ə¦lantə¦wid-\ *adj* [NL *allantoid-, allantois* + E *-ean, -ian*] : of, relating to, or derived from the allantois

[2]**allantoidean** \"\ *adj* [NL *Allantoidea* + E *-an*] : of or relating to the Allantoidea

al·lan·to·in \ə'lantəwən\ *n* -s [prob. fr. G, fr. NL *allantois* + G *-in*] : a crystalline oxidation product $C_4H_6N_4O_3$ of uric acid found in the allantoic liquid of cows, in the urine of most mammals, and in many plants (as sugar beets) and used in the treatment of wounds and ulcers

al·lan·to·in·ase \-ˌnās\ *n* -s [*allantoin* + *-ase*] : an enzyme occurring esp. in animals other than mammals that hydrolyzes allantoin

al·lan·to·is \ə'lantəwəs, -n,tōis\ *n, pl* **allanto·i·des** \ˌalən-'tōəˌdēz, ˌaˌlan-, -tōiˌdēz\ [NL, irreg. fr. MF *allantoide* — more at ALLANTOID] : a vascular fetal membrane of reptiles, birds, or mammals arising as a pouch or sac from the hindgut, in reptiles and birds expanding greatly between the amnion and chorion to serve as a respiratory organ while its cavity stores the fetal excretions and in placental mammals intimately associated with the chorion in formation of the placenta to which it contributes blood vessels and usu. a part of the cellular stroma

al·lant·ox·a·idin \ˌaˌlan,täk'säədᵊn\ *n* -s [ISV *allantoxa*nic + *-idin*] : a crystalline compound $C_3H_3N_3O_2$ derived from allantoxanic acid by decarboxylation; 5-imino-hydantoin

al·lant·ox·an·ic acid \ˌaˌlan,täk'sanik-\ *n* [ISV *allant-* + *oxanic*] : a crystalline acid $C_4H_3N_3O_4$ formed by the oxidation of allantoin or of uric acid — called also *oxonic acid*

al·lan·tu·ric acid \¦alən¦türik-, ¦aˌlan-, -tyü-\ *n* [ISV *allant-* + *-uric*] : an acid $C_3H_4N_2O_3$ obtained as a deliquescent mass by the oxidation of allantoin and in other ways; (carboxy-methylene)-urea

al·la po·lac·ca \ˌäləpə'läkə, ˌaləpə'la-\ *adv (or adj)* [It, lit., in the Polish manner] : in the manner of a polonaise — used as a direction in music

al·la pri·ma \ˌälə'prēmə, ˌal-\ *n* [It, at once] : a method of painting in which pigments are laid on in a single application instead of being built up by repeated paintings

al·lar·gan·do \ˌäˌlär'gän(ˌ)dō\ *adj (or adv)* [It, making slow, widening, verbal of *allargare* to make slow, widen, fr. *al-* (fr. L *ad-*) + *largare* to widen, fr. LL, to widen, loosen, fr. L *largus* abundant, generous — more at LARD] : becoming gradually broader with the same or greater volume — used as a direction in music

all-around \¦==¦=\ *also* **all-round** \(')=¦=\ *adj* [[2]*all*] **1** : not limited or specialized: as **a** : marked by competence in many fields ⟨an *all-around* athlete⟩ ⟨an *all-around* man of letters producing fiction, drama, poetry, and criticism⟩ **b** : marked by general utility : serviceable in various situations ⟨an *all-around* tool⟩ : meritorious for various reasons ⟨the best *all-around* breed⟩ **2 a** : INCLUSIVE, COMPREHENSIVE : not narrowly particularized ⟨taking an *all-around* view⟩ ⟨an *all-around* reduction in value⟩ **b** : comprising all charges including extras ⟨the *all-round* cost of the project⟩ **syn** see VERSATILE

all around *var of* ALL ROUND

al·lasch \'ä,läsh\ *n* -ES *usu cap* [G, fr. *Allasch* (*Allaži*), town near Riga, Latvia, where it originated] : a sweet kümmel prepared with flavoring agents not usu. found in kümmel (as bitter almonds, angelica root, anise, and orris root)

al·las·so·ton·ic \ə¦lasə¦tänik\ *adj* [ISV *allass-* (fr. Gk *allassein* to change) + *-o-* + *tonic* — more at ALLACTITE] *of the movements of mature plant organs* : temporarily induced by stimulus — opposed to *auxotonic*; compare IRRITOMOTILITY

al·la te·des·ca \ˌälətə'deskə, ˌal-, -tā'-\ *adv (or adj)* [It, in the German manner] **1** : in the style of the allemande **2** : in the style of the ländler or the waltz

[1]**al·la·tive** \'aləd·iv\ *adj* [L *allatus* carried to (suppletive past part. of *afferre* to carry to; *allatus* fr. *ad-* + *latus*, suppletive past part. of *ferre* to bear) + E *-ive* — more at BEAR, TOLERATE] *of a grammatical case* : denoting motion to or toward

[2]**allative** \"\ *n* -s : the allative case of a language or a form in the allative case

al·la tur·ca \ˌälə'türkə, ˌal-; ˌalə'tər-\ *adv (or adj)* [It, in the Turkish manner] : in the style of the Turkish military band

[1]**al·lay** \ə'lā, a'-\ *vb* -ED/-ING/-S [ME *alayen, aleggen*, fr. OE *ālecgan*, fr. *ā-* (perfective prefix) + *lecgan* to lay — more at ABEAR, LAY] *vt* **1** *obs* : OVERTHROW, SUBDUE ⟨~ this thy abortive pride —Shak.⟩ **2** : to subdue or reduce in intensity or severity : ALLEVIATE, RELIEVE, ABATE ⟨this ration is palatable, very rapidly ~s hunger —H.G.Armstrong⟩ ⟨widely used in our community to ~ aches —Ben Riker⟩ ⟨sought . . . to catch every river breeze to ~ the summer heat —Maxwell Mays⟩ **3** : to put at rest (as disquiet, fear, or suspicion) : make quiet : PACIFY, APPEASE, QUELL, CALM ⟨some answer to ~ all his anxieties —Norman Kelman⟩ ⟨the turmoil that had been partly ~ed returned —Elizabeth M. Roberts⟩ ⟨competition was embittered rather than ~ed —*Times Lit. Supp.*⟩ **4 a** : to limit the pleasurable or good effect of : moderate by something unpleasant ⟨the victors' joy was ~ed by the death of their prince⟩ **b** : WEAKEN, DIMINISH, QUALIFY ~ *vi, obs* : to diminish in strength : SUBSIDE ⟨when the rage ~s —Shak.⟩ **syn** see RELIEVE

[2]**allay** *n* -s **1** *archaic* : ALLEVIATION, ABATEMENT **2** *obs* : CHECK, STOPPAGE

[3]**allay** *vt* -ED/-ING/-S [ME *alayen*, fr. MF *alayer, aleier, aloier, alier* to combine, fr. L *alligare* to bind, bind to — more at ALLY] *archaic* : ALLOY

[4]**allay** *n* -s [ME *alay*, fr. MF *alay, aloi*, fr. *alayer, aloier*, v.] *archaic* : ALLOY

al·lay·ment \ə'lāmənt, a'-\ *n* -s [[1]*allay* + *-ment*] : the action of quieting or alleviating : the state of being quieted or alleviated : MITIGATION

al·la zin·ga·ra \¦äləˌt'siŋgərə, ¦al-; ¦alə¦zi-\ *adv (or adj)* [It] : in gypsy style — used as a direction in music

al·la zop·pa \¦älət'säpə, ¦al-, -ȯpə; ¦alə¦zäpə\ *adv (or adj)* [It, in a limping manner] : in syncopated style — used as a direction in music

all but *adv* : very nearly : ALMOST ⟨makes travel *all but* impossible⟩ ⟨*all but* fell in love with him⟩ ⟨marched forward *all but* unopposed⟩ ⟨the pain that is *all but* a pleasure —W.S. Gilbert⟩

all clear *n* : a signal that enemy aircraft have left

all-commodity rate *n* : a freight rate applied to all goods in a particular shipment regardless of particular classifications

all-court press *n* : FULL-COURT PRESS

all-day \'=¦=\ *adj* : lasting for, occupying, or appearing throughout an entire day ⟨an *all-day* picnic⟩ ⟨an *all-day* trip⟩ — used esp. of a newspaper that puts out editions throughout the day as contrasted with a morning or evening paper ⟨an *all-day* daily⟩

all-day sucker *n* : a piece of hard candy on a stick : a large lollipop

allectory *var of* ALECTORIA

alledge *obs var of* ALLEGE

al·lée \(')a¦lā\ *n* -s [F, fr. OF *alee* action of going, journey, fr. fem. of *alé*, past part. of *aler* to go — more at ALLEY] **1** : WALK; *specif* : a walk or path between two rows of formally planted trees or shrubs that are at least twice as high as the width of the walk or path **2** : a formal avenue or mall

al·lée cou·verte \(¦)aˌlā,kü'vert\ *n, pl* **allées couvertes** \-ā(z),k-\ [F, lit., covered passage] : a passage like a tunnel leading to a neolithic tomb

allegany *usu cap, var of* ALLEGHENY

al·le·ga·tion \ˌalə'gāshən, -ē'-\ *n* -s [ME *allegacioun*, fr. MF *allegation*, fr. L *allegation-, allegatio*, fr. *allegatus* (past part. of *allegare* to send on an errand, cite, adduce, fr. *ad-* + *legare* to send with a commission or charge, depute) + *-ion-, -io* -ion — more at LEGATE] **1** : the act of alleging or asserting positively often before a court **2** : something asserted or declared : a positive assertion : formal averment ⟨suffered dismissal . . . after unproved ~s of "pro-Germanism" —*Amer. Guide Series: Minn.*⟩; *specif* : a statement by a party to a legal action of what he undertakes to prove — usu. applied to each separate averment; see CHARGE, COUNT **3** : an assertion unsupported and by implication regarded as unsupportable ⟨the absurd and familiar ~ —*Encounter*⟩ ⟨there were several ~s . . . none of them creditable —Audrey Barker⟩ ⟨vague ~s of misconduct⟩

al·le·ga·tor \'==,gād·ə(r)\ *n* -s [*allegation* + *-or*] : one that alleges

al·le·ga·tum \ˌa=='gād·əm\ *n, pl* **allega·ta** \-d·ə\ [NL, fr. L, neut of *allegatus*, past part. of *allegare*] : ALLEGATION 2

[1]**al·lege** \ə'lej *also* a'-\ *vt* -ED/-ING/-S [ME *alleggen*, modif. (influenced by OF *alegier* to acquit, fr. LL *allegare* to free from servitude by adducing reasons, fr. L, to cite, adduce) of OF *alleguer*, fr. L *allegare* to cite, adduce] **1** *archaic* : to state under oath : plead in court ⟨a petition *alleging* that the conviction had been on perjured testimony⟩ **2 a** : to state or declare as if under oath positively and assuredly but without offering complete proof **b** : to assert, affirm, state without proof or before proving ⟨*alleged* that the suspect is a kidnaper⟩ ⟨the newspaper ~s the mayor's guilt⟩ **3** *archaic* : to adduce or bring forward (as a source or authority) esp. for or against ⟨*alleging* an old authority against the new science⟩ **4** : to bring forward as a cause or reason esp. for excusing oneself from blame, reproach, or dislike ⟨when she turned to him for help . . . he perhaps justly *alleged* that he had troubles of his own —Gamaliel Bradford⟩ **syn** see CITE

[2]**al·lège** \a'lezh\ *n* -s [F, fr. MF *alege* alleviation, fr. OF *alegier* to alleviate, lighten, fr. LL *alleviare* — more at ALLEVIATE] : a thinned part of a wall (as the spandrel under a window)

al·lege·able \ə'lejəbəl *also* a'-\ *adj* : capable of being alleged or affirmed

al·leged \-jd *also* -jəd\ *adj* **1** : asserted to be true or to exist ⟨an ~ miracle⟩ ⟨~ abuses of housing benefits —*Wall Street Jour.*⟩ ⟨ordering seizure of the steel mills under ~ "inherent" rights —*Current Biog.*⟩ **2** : questionably true or of the kind specified : SUPPOSED, SO-CALLED ⟨a program of ~ descriptive music⟩ ⟨another glass of that ~ brandy⟩ — **al·leg·ed·ly** \-jədlē, -li\ *adv*

al·lege·ment \-jmənt\ *n* -s [[1]*allege* + *-ment*] : ALLEGATION

al·le·gha·ny·ite \ˌalə'gānē,īt\ *n* -s *usu cap* [*Alleghany* county, N. C. + E *-ite*] : a mineral consisting of a pink basic silicate of manganese $Mn_5Si_2O_8(OH)_2$

al·le·ghe·ni·an *also* **al·le·gha·ni·an** \¦alə¦gānēən, -nyən\ *adj, usu cap* [*Allegheny, Alleghany* mts. + E *-an*] **1** : ALLEGHENY **1 2** : relating to or constituting the humid division of the biogeographic Transition zone that extends across the northern U. S. from New England to eastern No. and So. Dakota and includes also most of Pennsylvania and the mountainous region as far south as northern Georgia

al·le·ghe·ny *also* **al·le·gha·ny** *or* **al·le·ga·ny** \¦alə¦gānē, -ni\ *adj, usu cap* [fr. *Allegheny, Alleghany* mts., ranges of the Appalachian system in eastern U. S.] **1** : of or relating to the Allegheny mountains or the region where they are situated **2** : relating to or included in a subdivision of the Pennsylvanian coal measures

allegheny barberry *n, usu cap A* : AMERICAN BARBERRY

allegheny spurge *or* **allegheny mountain spurge** *n, usu cap A* : a low herb or subshrub (*Pachysandra procumbens*) with white or pinkish flowers in basal or axillary spikes native to southern U. S. but grown also elsewhere as a ground cover — compare JAPANESE SPURGE

allegheny vine *or* **allegheny fringe** *n, usu cap A* : CLIMBING FUMITORY

al·le·giance \ə'lējən(t)s *also* a'-\ *also* **al·le·gian·cy** \-nsē, -si\ *n* -s [ME *alligeaunce, allegeaunce*, modif. (influenced by ME *allegeaunce* allegation, fr. *alleggen* to allege + *-aunce* -ance) of MF *ligeance*, fr. OF, fr. *lige* liege + *-ance* — more at LIEGE] **1 a** : the relation or obligation of a feudal vassal to his liege lord — compare FEALTY **b** (1) : the duty of fidelity owed by a subject or citizen to his sovereign or government (2) : the obligation of an alien to the government under which he resides — see LOCAL ALLEGIANCE, NATURAL ALLEGIANCE; compare EXPATRIATE *vi* **2** : devotion or loyalty (esp. to a person, group, or cause entitled to obedience or service and respect ⟨wandered between . . . his ~s to political democracy and Marxist economics —*Time*⟩ ⟨the ~ of a poet to a specific philosophy —René Wellek⟩ ⟨rival powers compete for our ~; we are forever straining to serve two masters —Herbert Agar⟩ **syn** see FIDELITY

[1]**al·le·giant** \-jənt\ *adj* [*allegiance* + *-ant*] : giving allegiance : LOYAL ⟨it is impossible to be ~ to two opposing forces —*Christian Science Monitor*⟩

[2]**allegiant** \"\ *n* -s : one that owes allegiance

alleging *pres part of* ALLEGE

al·le·gor·i·cal \ˌalə¦gȯrəkəl, -lē¦-, -är-\ *also* **al·le·gor·ic** \-ik, -ēk\ *adj* [ME *allegorik*, fr. LL *allegoricus*, fr. Gk *allēgorikos*, fr. *allēgoria* allegory + *-ikos* -ic — more at ALLEGORY] **1** : of, relating to, or having the characteristics of allegory or an allegory : occurring in, constituting, or containing an allegory ⟨~ poetry⟩ ⟨~ figures⟩ ⟨an ~ interpretation⟩ **2** : stressing a hidden spiritual meaning transcending the literal sense of the text of sacred books — **al·le·gor·i·cal·ly** \-ək(ə)lē, -i\ *adv* — **al·le·gor·i·cal·ness** *n* -ES

al·le·go·rism \'==,gōr,izəm, -,gȯ,ri-, -gə,ri-\ *n* -s [fr. *allegorize*, after such pairs as E *baptize: baptism*] : the process or result of allegorizing : the allegorical method of literary interpretation

al·le·go·rist \-,rəst\ *n* -s [*allegory* + *-ist*] : one that allegorizes; *esp* : a writer of allegory

al·le·go·ri·za·tion \ˌ==,gōrə'zāshən, -ȯr-, -är-; -,gərə'z-, -,rī'z-\ *n* -s **1** : allegorical representation **2** : allegorical interpretation

al·le·go·rize \'==,gō,rīz, -,gȯ,rīz, -,gə,r-\ *vb* -ED/-ING/-S [ME *allegorisen*, fr. LL *allegorizare*, fr. L *allegoria* + *-izare* -ize] *vt* **1** : to make into allegory ⟨~ the history of a people⟩ **2** : to treat or explain as allegory ⟨their symbolic content can be *allegorized* for purposes of analysis —*Accent*⟩ ⟨*allegorizing* the ancient stories of their people⟩ ~ *vi* **1** : to give allegorical explanations **2** : to compose or use allegory ⟨the poets liked to ~ on the story⟩

al·le·go·riz·er \-zə(r)\ *n* -s : one that allegorizes

al·le·go·ry \'alə,gōrē, -ē,g-, -ȯr-, -ri\ *n* -ES [ME *allegorie*, fr. L *allegoria*, fr. Gk *allēgoria*, fr. *allēgorein* to speak figuratively, prob. fr. *alla* (neut. pl. of *allos* other) + *-agorein* to speak publicly, fr. *agora* assembly — more at ELSE, GREGARIOUS] **1 a** : the written, oral, or artistic expression by means of symbolic fictional figures and actions of truths or generalizations about human conduct or experience (as in Bunyan's *Pilgrim's Progress* and Spenser's *Faerie Queene*) **b** : an instance of such expression ⟨a poetic ~⟩ **2** : something resembling or suggestive of an allegory in its effect : symbolic representation : EMBLEM ⟨an organization that stands as an ~ of cooperation⟩

syn ALLEGORY, PARABLE, MYTH, FABLE, APOLOGUE: these five words apply in this comparison to literary forms typically telling a story for the sake of presenting a truth, a moral. ALLEGORY, the most general, applies to fiction in which action and character, usu. of a certain complexity, are symbolic or figurative, the characters usu. typical, the whole by its analogy to real-life situations or actual moral facts presenting a moral or spiritual truth or a normative generalization or a series of them. A PARABLE is a short, allegorical tale, usu. simple and homely, typically illustrating or reenforcing a single spiritual truth. MYTH in this application applies chiefly to Platonic myth, which was a brief explanation of a difficult philosophic truth by means of a short allegorical analogy. A FABLE or APOLOGUE is an allegorical tale, usu. a beast fable, that points up in its analogy the weaknesses or follies of man for the sake of a moral or normative generalization usu. formulated and appended at the end of the tale

[1]**al·le·gret·to** \ˌalə¦gred·(ˌ)ō, -e(ˌ)tō, ¦äl-\ *adv (or adj)* [It, fr. *allegro*] : faster than andante but not so fast as allegro — used as a direction in music

[2]**allegretto** \"\ *n* -s : a piece or movement in allegretto tempo

[1]**al·le·gro** \ə'le(ˌ)grō, -lā-, ä'-\ *adv (or adj)* [It, merry, gay, fr. (assumed) VL *alecrus* lively, alter. of L *alacr-, alacer* — more at ALACRITY] : in a brisk lively manner — used as a direction in music

[2]**allegro** \"\ *n* -s **1** : a piece or movement or division of a movement in allegro tempo **2 a** : ballet steps (as leaps, jumps, and turns) performed in a lively fast tempo **b** : rapid exercises and steps terminating a ballet class

allegro form *n* : a linguistic form shortened as a result of frequent occurrence in rapid speech (as *Miss* for *Mistress*)

al·lele \ə'lē(ə)l\ *also* **al·lel** \-lel\ *n* -s [G *allel*, short for *allelomorph*] **1** : either of a pair of alternative Mendelian characters (as smooth or wrinkled seed in the pea) — compare MENDEL'S LAW, MULTIPLE ALLELE **2** : GENE, FACTOR — used chiefly of a gene considered as the vehicle of an allele — **al·lel·ic** \-'lēlik, -lel-\ *adj* — **al·lel·ism** \-'lē,lizəm, -le,-\ *n* -s

allelo- *comb form* [Gk *allēlo-* each other, fr. *allēlōn* of each other, fr. *allos . . . allos* one . . . the other, fr. *allos* other — more at ELSE] **1** : alternative ⟨*allelo*morph⟩ **2** : of or for each other : reciprocal : reciprocally ⟨*allelo*catalytic⟩ ⟨*allelo*tropism⟩

al·lelo·ca·tal·y·sis \ə¦le(ˌ)lō, -ē(ˌ)-\ *n, pl* **allelocatalyses** [NL, fr. *allelo-* + *catalysis*] : the mutually stimulating effect on the rate of growth and reproduction of two or more microorganisms in a volume of medium as compared to the rate of a single microorganism in a like volume of the same medium — **al·lelo·cat·a·lyst** *n* -s — **al·lelo·cat·a·lyt·ic** \=¦=(ˌ)=,==¦==\ *adj*

al·lelo·morph \ə'lēlə,mȯrf, -lel-\ *n* -s [ISV *allelo-* + *-morph*] : ALLELE — **al·lelo·morph·ic** \=¦==¦fik\ *adj* — **al·lelo·morph·ism** \=¦==,=,fizəm\ *n*

al·le·lop·a·thy \ˌalə'läpəthē\ *n* -ES [F *allélopathie*, fr. *allélo-* allelo- + *-pathie* -pathy] : the reputed baneful influence of one living plant upon another due to secretion of toxic substances

[1]**al·le·lu·ia** *or* **al·le·lu·iah** *or* **al·le·lu·ja** \ˌalə¦lüyə\ *interj* [ME *alleluya*, fr. LL *alleluia*, fr. Gk *allēlouia*, fr. Heb *halalūyāh* praise ye Jehovah] : HALLELUJAH — used frequently in liturgies and hymns of praise and thanksgiving; used also as an expression of humble mourning in the Eastern Orthodox Church

[2]**alleluia** *or* **alleluiah** *or* **alleluja** \"\ *n* -s [ME *alleluia, alleluya*, fr. ML *alleluia*, fr. LL *alleluia*, interj.] *often cap* **1** : a responsory chant in various Christian liturgies **2** : the part of the Roman mass consisting of two or more alleluias and a verse usu. from a psalm and usu. sung or said after the gradual and before the gospel

[3]**alleluia** *also* **alleluja** \"\ *n* -s [[1]*alleluia*, repeatedly sung at Easter, when it blooms] **1** : a wood sorrel (*Opalis montana*) **2** : WOADWAXEN

al·le·lu·iat·ic \ˌalə,lü¦yad·ik\ *adj* [ML *alleluiaticus*, fr. *alleluia* (chant) + *-aticus* (as in LL *dramaticus*)] : of or relating to a religious alleluia

[1]**al·le·mande** \'alə,mand, -änd, -aa(ə)nd, ˌ==¦=; 'aləmən(d)\ *n* -s *often cap* [F, fr. fem. of *allemand* German, fr. LL *Alamannus* member of the Alamanni, sing. of *Alamanni*] **1 a** : a 17th century and 18th century court dance developed in France from a German folk dance and characterized by elaborate intertwinings of a couple's arms with joined hands **b** : a step with arms interlaced **c** : a quadrille figure in which each man turns his corner, then his partner, then usu. proceeds to a grand right and left **d** : a change of places by the first and second couples in Scottish country dancing **2 a** : music for the allemande **b** : a dance movement in moderate tempo and duple time (as in the classical suites of Bach and Handel)

[2]**allemande** \"\ *vi* -ED/-ING/-S : to perform an allemande

[3]**allemande** \"\ *also* **allemande sauce** *n* -s *often cap A* [F (*sauce*) *allemande*, lit., German sauce] : a rich yellow sauce made by adding egg yolks to velouté — compare BÉCHAMEL, BROWN SAUCE

all-embracing \¦==¦==\ *adj* : taking in or including everybody or everything : COMPLETE, UNQUALIFIED, SWEEPING ⟨explain in one grand *all-embracing* formula —*N. Y. Times Mag.*⟩ ⟨*all-embracing* disapproval⟩

al·le·mont·ite \ˌalə'män,tīt, '==,=,=\ *n* -s [F, fr. *Allemont, Allemond*, Isère dept., France, its locality + F *-ite*] : a mineral consisting of an arsenic antimony compound SbAs occurring in metallic-looking reniform masses

al·len·ar·ly \ə'lenərlī\ *also* **al·lan·er·ly** \-ān-\ *adv* [ME (northern dial.) *allanerly, allaneli,* var. of *allonely, allonly,* fr. *all* + *onely, only* — more at ONLY] *Scot* : SOLELY, ONLY

al·lene \'a,lēn\ *n* -s [ISV, contr. of *allylene*] **1** : a gaseous hydrocarbon $CH_2=C=CH_2$ — called also *propadiene, sym-allylene* **2** : a diolefin with its two double bonds in adjacent positions

al·len·ic \a'lēnik, ə'-, -en-\ *adj* : relating to or derived from allene : like allene esp. in having two double bonds in adjacent positions ⟨~ alkadienes⟩ — often distinguished from *conjugated*

al·len screw \'alən-\ *n* [fr. *Allen,* a proper name] : a screw with a hexagonal recess in the head

allen's hummingbird *n, usu cap A* [after Joel A. *Allen* †1921 Am. zoologist] : a hummingbird (*Selasphorus sasin*) of western No. America, the male being metallic green above with bright red throat and whitish breast, the female being variably marked with reddish brown, gray, and white

allen's rule *n, usu cap A* [after Joel A. *Allen*] : a statement in zoology: protruding body parts (as ears, tail, legs, bill) of warm-blooded animals are relatively shorter in cooler than in warmer parts of the range

al·len·tan·do \¦äl͟ən¦tän(,)dō, ¦al-, ¦alən¦ta-\ *adv (or adj)* [It, making slack, making slow, fr. (assumed) VL *allentandum,* gerund of (assumed) VL *allentare* to make slack, make slow, fr. L *ad-* + *lentare* to bend, prolong, fr. *lentus* flexible, slow, sluggish — more at LITHE] : in a manner becoming relaxed in tempo — used as a direction in music

[1]**al·len·ti·ac** \ə'lentē,ak\ *also* **al·len·ti·a·can** \¦alən¦tīəkən\ *adj, usu cap* [*Allentiac* fr. Sp, of AmerInd origin; *Allentiacan* fr. Sp *allentiac* + E *-an*] : of, relating to, or characteristic of a people of the San Juan province of western Argentina

[2]**allentiac** \"\ *n* -s *usu cap* **1 a** : a people of the San Juan province of western Argentina **b** : a member of such people **2** : the language of the Allentiac people

al·len·town \'alən,taun\ *adj, usu cap* [fr. *Allentown,* Pa.] : of or from the city of Allentown, Pa. : of the kind or style prevalent in Allentown

al·len wrench \'alən-\ *n* [fr. *Allen,* a proper name] : an L-shaped hexagonal bar of hardened steel either end of which fits the socket of a screw or bolt

al·ler·gen \'alə(r)jən\ *n* -s [G, fr. *allergie* allergy + *-gen*] : a substance that induces allergy — **al·ler·gen·ic** \¦==¦jenik\ *adj* — **al·ler·gen·ic·i·ty** \,==jə'nisəd·ē\ *n* -ES

al·ler·gic \ə'lərjik, -əj-,əij-, -ēk *also* a'-\ *adj* [ISV *allergy* + *-ic*] **1** : of, relating to, characterized by, or affected by allergy ⟨~ diseases⟩ ⟨an ~ reaction⟩ ⟨~ to actinic rays⟩ **2** : disagreeably sensitive (as to a person, thing, or idea) : responding with a feeling of irritation or annoyance : feeling antipathy, aversion, or repugnance ⟨deaf, if not ~, to ambitious music —John Mason Brown⟩ ⟨ ~ to work⟩ ⟨unmoved by oratory and ~ to double talk —*New Republic*⟩

al·ler·gin \'alə(r)jən\ *n* -s [alter. of *allergen*] **1** : ALLERGEN **2** : REAGIN

al·ler·gist \-jəst\ *n* -s : a specialist in allergy

al·ler·gol·o·gy \,alə(r)'gäləjē, -'gä-\ *n* -ES [ISV *allergy* + *-o-* + *-logy*] : the scientific study of allergy

al·ler·gy \'alə(r)jē, -ji, *sometimes* -,lərj-, -,lōj-, -,ləij-\ *n* -ES [G *allergie,* fr. *all-* + *-ergie* -ergy] **1** : altered bodily reactivity (as to antigens) **2** : exaggerated or pathological reaction marked by sneezing, respiratory embarrassment, itching and skin rashes, or other symptoms to substances (as germs, pollens, food, or drugs), situations (as mental or emotional excitement or exposure to sunlight), or physical states (as coldness) that are without comparable effect on the average individual ⟨sneezing follows inhalation of pollens by persons having an ~ to them⟩ ⟨*allergies* due to foods often cause hives⟩ — compare HYPERSENSITIVE **3** : medical practice concerned with the diagnosis and treatment of allergy ⟨he has practiced ~ for 15 years⟩ **4** : a feeling of antipathy or repugnance ⟨an ~ to controversy, and a strong distaste for crusading —Langdon Post⟩ ⟨a reputation of having an ~ to books —R.J.Crohn⟩

al·ler·i·on *also* **ale·ri·on** \ə'lirēən, -ē,än\ *n* -s [F *alérion*] : an eagle depicted in heraldry with expanded wings but without beak or feet

al·le·thrin \'aləthrən\ *n* -s [*allyl* + *pyrethrin*] : a light yellow viscous oily synthetic insecticide $C_{19}H_{26}O_3$ used esp. in household aerosols

allette *var of* ALETTE

al·le·vi·ant \ə'lēvēənt *also* a'-\ *n* -s [*alleviate* + *-ant*] : an alleviating agent : PALLIATIVE

al·le·vi·ate \ə'lēvē,āt *also* a'-; *usu* -ād·+V\ *vt* -ED/-ING/-s [LL *alleviatus,* past part. of *alleviare* to lighten, relieve, fr. L *ad-* + *levis* light — more at LIGHT] **1** : LIGHTEN, LESSEN : RELIEVE, MODERATE: as **a** : to make easier to be endured (as physical or mental suffering) ⟨does not cure but ~s the disease⟩ ⟨a lotion for *alleviating* the itching of poison ivy⟩ ⟨little can be done for the sufferer beyond *alleviating* his agony —V. G. Heiser⟩ ⟨helped slightly to ~ his sorrow⟩ **b** : to remove or correct in part (as a troublesome condition or state of mind) ⟨measures for *alleviating* the critical labor shortage⟩ ⟨could ~ the causes of conflicts among nations —Vera M. Dean⟩ ⟨efforts which do nothing to ~ that hate —*New Republic*⟩ — opposed to *aggravate* ⟨how these problems are aggravated or *alleviated* by advances in technical knowledge —Clyde Kennedy⟩ **2** *archaic* : EXTENUATE ⟨~s his fault by an excuse —Samuel Johnson⟩ **syn** see RELIEVE

al·le·vi·a·tion \-,==¦āshən\ *n* -s [ML *alleviation-, alleviatio,* fr. LL *alleviatus* + L *-ion-, -io* -ion] **1** : the action of alleviating or of being alleviated ⟨beyond correction or ~⟩ ⟨seeking ~ of his distress⟩ **2** : something that alleviates ⟨all the humane ~s of modern war ... was brutal violence ... were disregarded —W.R. Inge⟩

al·le·vi·a·tive \=¦==,ā|d·iv, -,ə|, |tiv, -ēv\ *or* **al·le·vi·a·to·ry** \-,ə,tōrē, -ōr-, -ri\ *adj* : tending to alleviate : PALLIATIVE

al·le·vi·a·tor \-,ād·ə(r), -ātə-\ *n* -s : one that alleviates ⟨the ~s, the doctors and nurses —Cyril Connolly⟩ ⟨snow can be a great ~ of the American restlessness —J.W.Krutch⟩; *specif* : a shock absorber in a hydraulic system

all–expense \'==¦=\ *adj* : involving the payment of all costs by the sponsor or the assessment of a fixed single charge for all costs (as of transportation, meals, hotels, and entertainment) ⟨winners of the contest will be awarded an *all-expense* trip⟩ ⟨railroads offering *all-expense* tours this summer⟩

[1]**al·ley** \'alē, -li\ *n* -s [ME *aley,* fr. ML *aleia* passage & MF *alee* action of going, journey, passage, fr. OF *alee* action of going, journey, passage, fr. fem. of *alé,* past part. of *aler* to go, prob. fr. (assumed) VL *amlare,* alter. of L *ambulare* to walk — more at AMBLE] **1** : a garden or park walk or passage bordered by trees or bushes **2 a** (1) : a grassed enclosure for bowling or skittles (2) : a hardwood lane at the end of which pins are set up for bowling and down which a ball is bowled (3) : the bowling unit consisting of surface lane, gutter, and backstop (4) : the building housing a group of such units **b** : the space on each side of a tennis doubles court between the sideline and the service sideline — see TENNIS illustration **c** : the strip of a field-hockey area between the 5-yard line and the sideline **3 a** : a passageway between buildings **b** : a lane wide enough only for persons on foot : a narrow street wide enough for only one vehicle **c** : a thoroughfare through the middle of a square or block giving access to the rear of lots or buildings **d** : a passage or covered way into or to a house or building **4** : a blank or open space between rows of any kind: as **a** *chiefly dial* : a passageway between rows of pews in a church : AISLE **b** : the floor space between the long sides of two parallel rows of compositors' stands **c** : the space between each two rows of a crop — **up one's alley** *also* **down one's alley** : adapted or suited esp. to one's abilities or tastes ⟨the ... fund-raising business is right *up his alley* —John Brooks⟩

[2]**alley** *also* **al·ly** \"\ *n* -s [by alter. and shortening fr. [1]*alabaster*] : a superior playing marble; *esp* : one made of alabaster, glass, or marble

alley cat *n* : a domestic short-haired cat esp. when of uncertain ancestry : any stray cat

al·leyed \'alēd, -id\ *adj* [ME *aleyed,* fr. *aley* + *-ed*] : furnished with alleys : forming an alley

alleyway \'==,=\ *n* -s : an alley or narrow passageway (as between houses or between rows of cabins on a ship)

all–father \'=,==\ *n* -s *usu cap A* : father of all — used of a deity — **all–fatherly** \(')=¦===\ *adj*

[1]**all–fired** \'=,=\ *adj, superlative often* **all–firedest** [euphemism for *hell-fired*] : INFERNAL, EXTREME, EXCESSIVE — used as a mild imprecation ⟨had the *all-fired* cheek to take my money away —Dorothy Sayers⟩ — **all–fired·ly** \-,fī(ə)rdlē, -īrəd-\ *adv*

[2]**all–fired** \"\ *adv* : EXTREMELY, EXCESSIVELY — used as a mild imprecation ⟨don't be so *all-fired* sure about it⟩ ⟨*all-fired* hot⟩

all fives *n pl but usu sing in constr* **1** : a form of all fours in which the five of trumps has a scoring value of five points **2** : MUGGINS 1b

all fools' day *n, usu cap A&F&D* : APRIL FOOLS' DAY

all fours *n pl* **1** : all four legs of a quadruped or the two legs and two arms of a person ⟨he explored it on *all fours* —John Buchan⟩ ⟨jumped and landed heavily on *all fours*⟩ **2** *sing in constr* : any of various card games whose essential feature is that points are scored for winning high, low, jack, and the game — see HIGH-LOW-JACK — **on all fours** *adv (or adj)* : in exact correspondence : on the same footing ⟨it is not easy to make a simile go *on all fours* —T.B.Macaulay⟩ — often used with *with* ⟨this principle is *on all fours* with that of the real-estate bloc —Stuart Chase⟩

all get–out \,ȯl(,)gid·'aut, -,ged-,(')=¦=,=\ *n, slang* : the extreme (as of extent, degree, quality, or condition) encountered or conceivable — used in comparisons to suggest something superlative ⟨a handbag big as *all get-out* —*New Yorker*⟩ ⟨stubborn as *all get-out*⟩

allgood \'=,=\ *n* -s : GOOD-KING-HENRY

all hail *interj* [ME *al hail,* fr. *al* all + *hail* (healthy)] — used to express greeting or welcome or sometimes acclamation

all–hail *vt* -ED/-ING/-s *archaic* : to greet with *all hail* ⟨who *all-hailed* me "Thane of Cawdor" —Shak.⟩

allhallond *usu cap, obs var of* ALLHALLOWS

allhallowmas *n* -ES *usu cap* [ME *Alhalwemesse, Alhalowmesse,* fr. OE *ealra halgena mæsse,* lit., all saints' mass] *archaic* : the feast of All Saints

allhallown *adj, usu cap* [*Allhallown-* (as in *Allhallowntide* & *Allhallownmas,* earlier variants of *Allhallowtide, Allhallowmas*)] *obs* : occurring at or near the time of Allhallows ⟨*Allhallown* summer —Shak.⟩

all·hal·lows \(')ȯl'ha(,)lōz, -,lə\ *also* **all·hal·low** *n, pl* **allhallows** *usu cap* [short for *All Hallows' Day, All Hallow Day,* fr. ME *Alhalwenday, Alhalowday, All Hallows Day*] : ALL SAINTS' DAY

allhallowtide *n -s usu cap* [ME *All Halewentid, All Halowtid,* lit., all saints' season] *archaic* : the time at or near All Saints' Day

all hands *n pl* **1** : an entire ship's company **2** : everybody engaged in the same pursuit

allheal \'=,=\ *n* -s **1** : VALERIAN **2** : SELF-HEAL **3** : MISTLETOE **4** : WOUNDWORT **5** : YARROW

all hours *n pl* **1** : an hour or time that one likes or that suits one's convenience ⟨he comes home to lunch at *all hours*⟩ **2** : the very late hours of the night ⟨stay up till *all hours*⟩

al·li·a·ble \ə'līəbəl *also* a'-\ *adj* [[1]*ally* + *-able*] : capable of being allied : able to enter into an alliance

al·li·a·ce·ae \,alē'āsē,ē\ *n pl, cap* [NL, fr. *Allium,* type genus + *-aceae*] *in some classifications* : a family of monocotyledonous plants comprising chiefly the genus *Allium* which is now usu. included in the family Liliaceae

al·li·a·ceous \¦alē¦āshəs\ *adj* [L *allium* garlic + E *-aceous* — more at ALLIUM] **1** : having the smell of garlic or onions **2** [NL *Alliaceae* + E *-ous*] : of or relating to the genus *Allium* or the family Alliaceae

al·li·ance \ə'līən(t)s *also* a'-\ *n* -s [ME *aliaunce,* fr. OF *aliance,* fr. *alier* to ally + *-ance* — more at ALLY] **1** : the state of being allied or the action of allying or uniting ⟨toleration at home and ~ with Protestantism abroad —Hilaire Belloc⟩ ⟨the two great men of letters stood in ~ —*Time*⟩ : union or connection esp. between families, states, parties, or individuals ⟨any ~ between church and state⟩ ⟨the dowry was small and the honor of the ~ great —Robert Graves⟩ ⟨a closer ~ between government and industry⟩ ⟨went through three marriages and several ~s of more doubtful character⟩ **2** : an association or union formed for the furtherance of the common interests and aims of the members ⟨an ~ among the independent unions⟩ ⟨a world ~ of interested groups⟩; *esp* : an association, confederation, or union of two or more independent states or nations that is created by a formal agreement (as a treaty or compact) in their common interest esp. for mutual assistance and protection ⟨~s and cooperative associations of states —C.K.Streit⟩ ⟨the ~ of western nations⟩ **3** : union by relationship in qualities : AFFINITY ⟨an indefinable sense of ~ draws one to books as to people —Allan McMahan⟩ ⟨between aesthetic and religious rapture there is a family ~ —Clive Bell⟩ **4** : a group of related botanical or zoological families; *esp* : a group of plants intermediate between a class and an order **5** : a treaty of alliance

alliance ring *n* : a wedding ring composed of two interlocking bands bearing the initials of the bride and groom and the date of the wedding

al·li·ar·ia \,alē'a(a)rēə\ *n, cap* [NL, fr. L *allium, alium* garlic + NL *-aria* — more at ALLIUM] : a genus of Old World herbs (family Cruciferae) having broad undivided leaves, white flowers, and long siliques — see GARLIC MUSTARD

al·lice shad \'aləs(h),sh-\ *also* **al·lice** *or* **al·lis** \'aləs\ *n* -s [alter. of earlier *allowes,* fr. F *alose,* fr. LL *alausa,* fr. Gaulish] : a European shad (*Alosa alosa*) of the Severn and other rivers

alliciency *n* -ES [ML *allicientia* fr. L *allicient-, alliciens* (pres. part. of *allicere* to allure, fr. *ad-* + *-licere,* fr. *lacere* to entice) + *-ia* -y — more at DELIGHT] *obs* : the quality or power of attracting : ATTRACTIVENESS

al·li·cin \'aləsən\ *n* -s [*alliin* + *-cin*] : a liquid compound $C_6H_{10}OS_2$ with a garlic odor and antibacterial properties formed from alliin by enzymatic action

al·lied \ə'līd, a'-; *freq in all senses & most freq in sense 2b* 'a,l-\ *adj* [ME, fr. past part. of *allien* to ally — more at ALLY] **1** : JOINED, CONNECTED ⟨closely ~ to his pride was his very strict sense of justice—R.A.Hall b.1911⟩ **2 a** : joined in alliance by compact or treaty ⟨all the ~ powers⟩ ⟨a party of ~ soldiers⟩ ⟨flags of the ~ nations⟩ **b** *usu cap* : of, by, or relating to the nations united against the Central European powers in World War I or those united against the Axis powers in World War II ⟨the largest *Allied* naval exercise ever held⟩ ⟨a unified *Allied* theater was created under British direction —R.M.Leighton⟩ **3 a** : related esp. by common properties or similar characteristics ⟨geography and ~ sciences⟩ ⟨agricultural and ~ workers⟩ **b** : genetically related; *specif* : presumed to share common ancestors ⟨~ groups of plants or animals⟩

allies *pl of* ALLY, *pres 3d sing of* ALLY

al·li·ga·tion \,alə'gāshən\ *n* -s [L *alligation-, alligatio* tying, band, fr. *alligatus* (past part. of *alligare* to tie to, fr. *ad-* + *ligare* to tie) + *-ion-, -io* -ion — more at LIGATURE] **1** : the action of attaching or the state of being attached **2** : a process or rule for the solution of problems concerning the compounding or mixing of ingredients differing in price or quality either (1) when a definite mixture is required or (2) when the price or quality of the mixture is to be determined — called also respectively (1) *alligation alternate,* (2) *alligation medial*

[1]**al·li·ga·tor** \'alə,gād·ə(r), -ē,g-, -ātə-\ *n* [alter. of earlier *aligarto, alagarto,* fr. Sp *el lagarto* the lizard, fr. *el* the (fr. L *ille* that) + *lagarto* lizard, fr. (assumed) VL *lacartus,* fr. L *lacertus, lacerta* — more at LIZARD] **1** -s **a** : either of two loricates comprising the genus *Alligator* having broad heads not tapering to the snout and a special pocket in the upper jaw for reception of the enlarged lower fourth tooth and being in general much more sluggish than the typical crocodiles (genus *Crocodylus*) **b** : CAIMAN **c** : LORICATE **2** [NL, fr. E] *cap* : the genus of Crocodylidae comprising the American and Chinese alligators **3** -s : any of various animals that resemble alligators (as an alligator lizard, a hellbender, or a hellgramite) **4** -s : leather made from alligator's hide ⟨a handbag of ~⟩ **5** -s : a machine with strong jaws (as a crocodile squeezer or rock breaker) one of which opens like the movable jaw of an alligator ⟨~ squeezer⟩ **6** -s **a** : a boat used in handling floating logs and provided with a windlass and cable for being drawn overland **b** : a small sled often made from the fork of a tree and used as an aid in skidding logs — called also *crotch, go-devil, lizard, travois* **7** -s : a devotee of current swing music

[2]**alligator** \"\ *adj* **1** : of, relating to, or like an alligator; *specif* : marked with a design resembling that of the skin of an alligator ⟨~ cloth⟩ **2** : opening like an alligator's jaws ⟨~ forceps⟩

[3]**alligator** \"\ *vi* -ED/-ING/-s : to develop intersecting cracks and ridges — used of films of paint, varnish, and similar coatings

alligator apple *n* [so called fr. the gnarled appearance of the fruits and its growth in the habitat of alligators] : POND APPLE

alligator bonnet *n* [so called fr. the appearance of the blossoms and its growth in the habitat of alligators] **1** : either of two water plants of the genus *Nymphaea*: **a** : a yellow pond lily (*N. sagittaefolia*) **b** : a fragrant water lily (*N. odorata*) **2** : the flower or fruit of alligator bonnets

alligator button *n* [so called fr. the appearance of the seeds and its growth in the habitat of alligators] **1** : WATER CHINQUAPIN **2** : the flower or fruit of the water chinquapin

alligator cacao *n* [so called fr. the resemblance of the pod to alligator hide] : a cacao (*Theobroma pentagona*) cultivated in Central America

alligator clip *n* : a wire or cable terminal having jaws resembling an alligator's and used for making temporary electrical connections — called also *crocodile clip*

alligator fish *n* [so called fr. its covering of bony plates] : a sea poacher (as *Podothecus acipenserinus*) of the Pacific coast of No. America

alligator gar *n* [so called fr. its size] : a large freshwater gar (*Lepisosteus spatula*) of the central U. S. that attains a length of over 7 feet and a weight in excess of 150 pounds; *also* : any of certain related Cuban and Central American fishes that are all valueless as food or game fishes and considered destructive of aquatic life and waterfowls

al·li·ga·tor·i·dae \,aləgə'tōrə,dē\ *n pl, cap* [NL, fr. *Alligator,* type genus + *-idae*] *in some classifications* : a family of crocodilians comprising the alligators and the caimans

alligator juniper *n* [so called fr. the ridged appearance of its bark] : an evergreen shrub or small tree (*Juniperus deppeana*) of the southwestern U. S. and adjacent Mexico having an edible sweet fruit

alligator lizard *n* : any of various small American lizards that resemble an alligator (as members of the genera *Anolis, Sceloporus,* or the western U. S. *Gerrhonotus*)

al·li·ga·tor·oid \'alə,gād·ə,rȯid\ *adj* [[1]*alligator* + *-oid*] **1** : resembling an alligator **2** : relating to alligators

alligator pear *n* [prob. so called fr. its growth near the habitat of alligators] : AVOCADO

alligator shears *n pl* [so called fr. its resemblance to an alligator's jaws] : LEVER SHEARS

alligator snapper *also* **alligator turtle** *or* **alligator terrapin** *n* **1** : a voracious snapping turtle (*Macrochelys temminckii*) of the rivers of the Gulf states differing from the common snapping turtle in its larger size which in old age reaches nearly 150 pounds in weight and 5 feet in length, its scaly head, and its numerous small scales beneath the tail **2** : a snapping turtle (*Chelydra serpentina*)

alligator tree *n* [so called fr. the ridged appearance of its bark] *South* : SWEET GUM

alligator weed *or* **alligator grass** *n* [so called fr. its long narrow leaves] : a prolific herbaceous weed (*Alternanthera phylloxeroides*) having opposite entire linear-lanceolate leaves and flowers in short headlike spikes and being esp. troublesome in irrigation canals and waterways which it clogs with a dense floating mass

alligatorwood \'==,==,=\ *n* -s [*alligator (tree)* + *wood*] **1** : SWEET GUM **2** : GUARAGUAO

alligator wrench *n* [so called fr. its resemblance to an alligator's jaws] : a wrench having a flaring jaw with teeth on one side

alligator wrench

al·lihn condenser \(')a¦lēn-\ *n, usu cap A* [fr. the name *Allihn*] : a condenser similar to a Liebig condenser with an inner tube consisting of a series of bulbs

allihn filter tube *n, usu cap A* [fr. the name *Allihn*] : a glass filtering funnel the top part of which is a cylindrical tube into which is sealed a fritted glass disk as a filter

al·li·in \'alēən\ *n* -s [ISV *alli-* (fr. NL *Allium,* genus name of the garlic *Allium sativum*) + *-in*] : a crystalline amino acid $C_6H_{11}NO_3S$ occurring in garlic oil

al·li·klik \'alə,klik\ *n, pl* **alliklik** *or* **allikliks** *usu cap* [Chumash] **1** : a Shoshonean people in the upper Santa Clara river valley, California **2** : a member of the Alliklik people

all–important \¦==¦==\ *adj* : of greatest or very great importance or significance ⟨the last and *all-important* bit of evidence⟩ ⟨discussing the *all-important* subject of disarmament⟩

all–in \'=¦=\ *adj* [short for *all-inclusive*] **1** *chiefly Brit* : ALL-INCLUSIVE ⟨*all-in* health insurance⟩ ⟨an *all-in* 10-day tour⟩ ⟨*all-in* cost⟩ ⟨*all-in* weight⟩ **2** : completely determined : sparing nothing ⟨an *all-in* effort⟩ **3** *of wrestling* : without restriction : having almost no holds barred

all in \(')=¦=\ *adj* [[2]*all* + *in* (adj.)] *slang* : completely tired : EXHAUSTED ⟨by the end of the day he was *all in*⟩ — used predicatively

[1]**all in all** : something that represents all things regarded as having value, significance, or importance : EVERYTHING ⟨the craft that was *all in all* to her —Rudyard Kipling⟩

[2]**all in all** *adv* **1** : as a whole : ALTOGETHER ⟨*all in all,* each article undergoes 20 inspections before leaving the plant⟩ ⟨take it *all in all,* this has been a hard week⟩ **2** : on the whole : all things considered : generally speaking ⟨*all in all,* the chautauqua was a tremendous force in American life —Russell Potter⟩ ⟨*all in all,* it might have been worse⟩

all–inclusive \¦==¦==\ *adj* : including everything : fully or broadly comprehensive ⟨a survey that was selective rather than *all-inclusive*⟩ ⟨the *all-inclusive* whole of our vast industrial machine —F.D.Roosevelt⟩ ⟨a broader and more nearly *all-inclusive* view⟩

al·lin·eate \ə'linē,āt, a'-\ *vt* -ED/-ING/-s [back-formation fr. *allineation*] : ALIGN

al·lin·eation *also* **alin·eation** \=,==¦āshən\ *n* -s [*ad-* + *-lineation* (as in *delineation*)] : ALIGNMENT

all–in–one \¦=¦=\ *n* -s : [2]CORSELET

al·li·o·nia \,alē'ōnēə, -nyə\ *n, cap* [NL, fr. Carlo *Allioni* †1804 Ital. physician and botanist + NL *-ia*] : a genus of chiefly American herbs (family Nyctaginaceae) having opposite entire leaves and small panicled flowers

al·li·o·ni·a·ce·ae \,alē,ōnē'āsē,ē\ [NL, fr. *Allionia,* type genus + *-aceae*] *syn of* NYCTAGINACEAE

allis *var of* ALLICE SHAD

al·li·sion \ə'lizhən, a'-\ *n* -s [LL *allision-, allisio,* fr. L *allisus* (past part. of *allidere* to strike against, fr. *ad-* + *-lidere,* fr. *laedere* to hurt) + *-ion-, -io* -ion — more at LESION] **1** *obs* : the action of dashing against or striking upon **2** : the running of one ship upon another ship that is stationary — distinguished from *collision*

al·li·son tuna \'aləsən-\ *or* **allison tunny** *n, usu cap A* [after James A. *Allison* *fl* 1920 Am. ichthyology enthusiast] : a yellowfin tuna

al·lit·er·al \a'lid·ərəl, ə'-, -itər-, -li·trəl\ *adj* [*alliterate* + *-al* (as in *literal*)] : ALLITERATIVE

[1]**al·lit·er·ate** \ə'lid·ə,rāt, -itər- *also* a'-; *usu* -ād·+V\ *vb* -ED/-ING/-s [back-formation fr. *alliteration*] *vi* **1** : to form an alliteration ⟨a sentence in which four of the six words *alliterated*⟩ **2** : to write or speak alliteratively ~ *vt* : to arrange or place so as to make alliteration ⟨with the stress falling on the *alliterated* syllables⟩

[2]**al·lit·er·ate** \a'lid·ərət, -itər-, -,rāt *also* ə'-\ *adj* [back-formation fr. *alliteration*] : characterized by alliteration : ALLITERATED

al·lit·er·a·tion \ə,lid·ə'rāshən, -itə- *also* a,-\ *n* -s [*ad-* + L *litera, littera* letter + E *-ation* — more at LETTER] : the repetition usu. initially of a sound that is usu. a consonant in two or more neighboring words or syllables (as wild and woolly, threatening throngs)

al·lit·er·a·tion·al \⸗¦⸗⸗¦⸗shən°l, -shnəl\ *adj* : ALLITERATIVE

al·lit·er·a·tive \⸗'⸗⸗,rā|d·iv, -‚rə|, |tiv, -ēv\ *adj* [*alliteration* + *-ive*] : of, related to, or marked by alliteration ⟨an ~ line⟩ — **al·lit·er·a·tive·ly** *adv*

alliterative verse *n* : verse usu. unrhymed having alliteration as a structural element ⟨Old English *alliterative verse*⟩

al·lit·er·a·tor \⸗'⸗⸗,rād·ə(r), -ātə-\ *n* -s [*alliteration* + *-or*] : one that alliterates esp. extensively or characteristically

al·lit·ic \ə'lid·ik, (')a¦l-\ *adj* [ISV *al*uminum + *-litic*] : lacking silica but having a high proportion of aluminum and iron compounds

al·li·um \'alēəm\ *n* [NL, fr. L *allium, alium* garlic; perh. akin to Skt *āluka* edible root of an aroid plant (*Amorphophallus campanulatus*)] **1** *cap* : a genus of bulbous herbs (family Liliaceae) distinguished by the characteristic odor, sheathing, mostly basal leaves, and umbellate white, yellow, or red flowers — see CHIVES, GARLIC, LEEK, ONION **2** -s : a plant of the genus *Allium*

al·li·va·lite \'alәvə,līt\ *n* -s [*Allival* Hill, Isle of Rum, Inner Hebrides, Scotland, its locality + E *-ite*] : a plutonic rock composed of anorthite and olivine in approximately equal amounts

all kinds of *adj* : many or much : plenty of ⟨*all kinds of* time to spend⟩ ⟨they say he has *all kinds of* money⟩ ⟨*all kinds of* opportunities to play golf⟩

allmouth \'⸗,⸗\ *n* -s [so called fr. its large mouth] : ANGLER 2

all·ness \'ȯlnəs\ *n* -ES *sometimes cap* : the quality or state of being complete or universal ⟨to learn it not in a specialized way but . . . in its relation to the ~ of things —D.C.Peattie⟩ ⟨he seemed at the center of the vast ~ —Irwin Edman⟩ : TOTALITY, COMPLETENESS, UNIVERSALITY

all-night *adj* **1** : lasting throughout an entire night ⟨an *all-night* sitting of the House of Commons⟩ ⟨an *all-night* card game⟩ **2** : open throughout the night ⟨an *all-night* lunch counter⟩

al·lo \'a(,)lō\ *adj* [*all-*] : isomeric or closely related — used esp. of one of two stereoisomers; sometimes contrasted with *normal;* compare ALL- 2

1allo- — see ALL-

2al·lo- *in pronunciations below,* ¦⸗⸗= ¦alō *or* ¦alə\ *comb form* [Gk *allos . . . allos* one . . . the other, fr. *allos* other — more at ELSE] : being one of a group whose members together constitute a structural unit esp. of a language ⟨*allo*phone⟩ ⟨*allo*morph⟩ — compare -EME

allo *abbr* allegro

al·lo·bar \'⸗⸗,bär\ *n* -s [*all-* + *-bar* (as in *isobar*)] **1** : barometric pressure change **2** : ISALLOBAR

al·lo·bar·bi·tal *also* **al·lo·bar·bi·tone** \¦⸗⸗-\ *n* -s [*all-* + *barbital, barbitone*] : DIALLYLBARBITURIC ACID

al·lob·ro·ges \ə'läbrə,jēz\ *n pl, cap* [L, pl. of *Allobrox*] : a people of Gaul inhabiting the region now known as Savoy and Dauphiné

al·lo·ca·bil·i·ty \,alәkə'biləd·ē, -lōk-\ *n* -ES : the quality or state of being allocable or assigned

al·lo·ca·ble \'⸗⸗kəbəl\ *or* **al·lo·cat·a·ble** \-,kād·əbəl\ *adj* [*allocable*, contr. of *allocatable; allocatable* fr. *allocate* + *-able*] **1** : capable of being allocated **2** *in accounting* : assignable to a particular account or to a particular period of time

al·lo·cate \'⸗⸗,kāt, *often* -ād·+V\ *vt* -ED/-ING/-S [ML *allocatus*, past part. of *allocare* to place, grant, fr. L *ad-* + *locare* to place fr. *locus* place — more at STALL] **1** : to apportion for a specific purpose or to particular persons or things ⟨if blame were to be *allocated* it must be apportioned elsewhere —F.W. Crofts⟩: as **a** : to give (a share of money, land, or responsibility) to a person **b** : to distribute or to divide and distribute according to relative contribution to an objective whether on an equal, proportional, or judiciously calculated basis ⟨~ a fortune to charitable foundations⟩ **c** : to apportion and distribute (as costs or revenues) among accounts according to some predetermined ratio or agreed measure of involvement (as degree of responsibility or benefit received) **d** : to deal out (something limited in supply) according to an allowance schedule established esp. by a public authority or major producer : RATION ⟨under a mobilization program metals may be *allocated* among manufacturers⟩ **2** : to set apart and earmark or designate : ASSIGN ⟨~ materials or facilities for a project⟩ ⟨government of the conscience is *allocated* to the clergy —*New Republic*⟩ **syn** see ALLOT

al·lo·ca·tee \¦⸗⸗kə¦tē\ *n* -s : one to whom material is allocated

al·lo·ca·tion \,⸗⸗'kāshən\ *n* -s [ML *allocation-, allocatio*, fr. *allocatus* + L *-ion-, -io* -ion] **1** *archaic* : the action of putting or adding one thing to another **2** : the action of apportioning : apportionment for specific purposes or to particular persons or organizations: as **a** *in accounting* : the apportionment of costs and expenses to accounts according to some arbitrary rule **b** : apportionment as a governmental or economic control measure ⟨the ~ of resources in a war economy⟩ **3** : a governmental or economic apportioning schedule or an assignment in it ⟨materials now on ~⟩ **4** : the amount allocated to one sharer

al·lo·ca·tive \'⸗⸗,kād·iv, -ātiv\ *adj* : serving to allocate ⟨an ~ analysis⟩ ⟨determination of ~ efficiency —Julius Margolis⟩

al·lo·ca·tor \-,kād·ə(r), -ātə-\ *n* -s : one that allocates

al·lo·ca·tur \,⸗⸗'kād·ər, -ā,tər\ *n* -s [ML, it is allowed, 3d pers. sing. pres. indic. pass. of *allocare*] : an order or writ of a court or of an assessor of damages or costs in a court granting something requested (as an order allowing an appeal, writ of certiorari, or a bill of costs or approving an assessment of damages)

al·lo·cen·tric \¦⸗⸗¦-\ *adj* [*all-* + *-centric*] : having one's interest and attention centered on other persons — compare EGOCENTRIC

al·lo·chet·ite \,alə'ked·,īt\ *n* -s [G *allochetit*, fr. *Allochet* valley, Tyrol, Austria + G *-it* -ite] : a porphyritic dike rock containing phenocrysts of labradorite, orthoclase, titanaugite, and nepheline in a dense groundmass of feldspar, augite, and hornblende

al·lo·chi·ria *also* **al·lo·chei·ria** \,⸗⸗'kīrēə\ *n* -s [NL, fr. *all-* + Gk *cheir* hand + NL *-ia* — more at CHIR-] : a confusion or transference of sides in the localization of sensation in which a person suffering from a central nervous lesion refers irritation of one point on the skin to some other point usu. corresponding to it on the other side of the body

al·lo·chlo·ro·phyll \¦⸗⸗-\ *n* -s [ISV *all-* + *chlorophyll*] : an isomer of chlorophyll easily formed from the latter

al·lo·chro·mat·ic \¦⸗⸗⸗¦⸗⸗\ *adj* [*all-* + *chromatic*] **1** : accidentally rather than inherently pigmented : variable in color — used of certain minerals that are without pigmentation when pure **2** : having or relating to photoelectric properties due to the presence of an impurity or as a result of irradiation

al·lo·chron·ic \¦⸗⸗¦kränik\ *adj* [*all-* + *chronic*] *of taxa* : occurring in different segments of geologic time : not contemporaneous — compare SYNCHRONIC

al·loch·ro·ous \ə'läkrəwəs, a'-\ *adj* [Gk *allochroos* changed in color, fr. *all-* + *chroa, chroia* color, skin; akin to Gk *chrōs* skin — more at GRIT] : changing color

al·loch·thon \ə'läkthən, a'-, -,thän\ *or* **al·loch·thone** \-,thōn\ *n* -s [back-formation fr. *allochthonous*] : an overthrust block of rocks that have been moved along a fault for a great distance from their place of origin

al·loch·tho·nous *also* **al·loc·tho·nous** \-‚thənəs\ *adj* [*all-* + *-chthonous* (as in *autochthonous*)] **1 a** : of or relating to the rocks of an allochthon **b** *of coal* : formed elsewhere than in situ and hence not autochthonous **c** *of limestone* : composed largely of organic debris moved far from the place where the base organisms lived **2** *biol* : of foreign origin : INTRODUCED — compare AUTOCHTHONOUS

al·lo·co·chick \'aləkə,chik\ *n* -s [Yurok *otl we-tsik*, fr. *otl* human beings + *we-tsik* their dentalium shells] : Indian shell money of northern California

al·lo·cor·tex \,⸗⸗-\ *n* [NL, fr. *all-* + L *cortex*] : ARCHIPALLIUM

al·lo·cryp·tic \¦⸗⸗¦⸗⸗\ *adj* [*all-* + *cryptic*] : imitating other objects for concealment by a covering of extraneous things ⟨an ~ hermit crab in a sponge⟩

al·lo·cute \'alə·,kyüt\ *vi* -ED/-ING/-S [back-formation fr. *allocution*] : to pronounce an allocution

al·lo·cu·tion \,alə·'kyüshən\ *n* -s [L *allocution-, allocutio*, fr. *allocutus* (past part. of *alloqui* to speak to, fr. *ad-* + *loqui* to speak) + *-ion-, -io* -ion] **1** : the act of addressing or exhorting ⟨a period eminently suited to exhortatory ~ —F.S.Crafford⟩ **2** : ADDRESS; *esp* : an authoritative or hortatory address ⟨a trio of centenary ~s —*Times Lit. Supp.*⟩ ⟨that other ~ delivered 15 years later, when he was pleading with the Americans for a loan —R.F.Harrod⟩ **3** : an address delivered by a pope in secret consistory and often later published

allod *var of* ALOD

al·lo·der·ma·nys·sus \¦⸗⸗,dərmə'nisəs\ *n, cap* [NL, fr. *all-* + *derma-* + *-nyssus* (fr. Gk *nyssein* to prick)] : a genus of bloodsucking mites parasitic on rodents including a species (*A. sanguineus*) that has been implicated as a vector of rickettsialpox in man

allodial *var of* ALODIAL

allodium *var of* ALODIUM

al·loe·o·coe·la \ə,lēə'sēlə\ *syn of* ALLOIOCOELA

al·loe·os·tro·pha \,alē'ästrəfə\ *n pl* [NL, fr. Gk, neut. pl. of *alloiostrophos* of irregular strophes, fr. *alloios* of another sort (fr. *allos* other) + *strophe* strophe — more at ELSE, STROPHE] : irregular strophes or stanzas

al·lo·erot·ic \¦alō⸗¦⸗⸗\ *adj* [*all-* + *erotic*] : of or relating to alloerotism ⟨~ impulses⟩

al·lo·er·o·tism *also* **al·lo·erot·i·cism** \,alō-\ *n* -s [*all-* + *erotism, eroticism*] : sexual feeling or activity finding its object in another person — contrasted with *autoerotism*

al·log·a·mous \ə'lägəməs, a'-\ *adj* [*all-* + *-gamous*] : reproducing by cross-fertilization

al·log·a·my \-mē\ *n* -ES [ISV *all-* + *-gamy*] : CROSS-FERTILIZATION

al·lo·ge·ne·i·ty \,⸗⸗jə'nēəd·ē\ *n* -ES : difference in nature or kind

al·lo·ge·ne·ous \¦alə¦jēnyəs, -nēəs\ *adj* [*all-* + *-geneous* (as in *heterogeneous, homogeneous*)] : different in nature or kind

al·lo·ge·net·ic \¦alōjə¦ned·ik\ *adj, of plankton* : produced elsewhere

al·lo·gen·ic \-¦jenik\ *adj* [*all-* + *-genic*] **1** : ALLOTHOGENIC **2** *of an ecologic succession* : resulting from factors (as a prolonged drought) that arise external to a natural community and alter its habitat ⟨~ changes in the vegetation⟩ — **al·lo·gen·i·cal·ly** *adv*

al·log·e·nous \ə'läjənəs, a'-\ *adj* [*all-* + *-genous*] : RELICT : persisting from an earlier floral and environmental situation — used of floras and their components

al·lo·gnath·o·su·chus \,alə,nathə'sükəs, ,a,läg,n-\ *n, cap* [NL, fr. *all-* + *gnath-* + *-suchus* (irreg. fr. Gk *sychnos* long, large)] : a genus of Eocene crocodilians sometimes regarded as ancestral to the true alligators

al·lo·graph \'⸗⸗,graf\ *n* -s [*all-* + *-graph*] **1** : a writing or signature made for a person by another — contrasted with *autograph* **2 a** : a letter of an alphabet in a particular shape (as A or a) **b** : any letter or combination of letters that is one of a number of ways of representing one phoneme (as *pp* in *hopping* representing the phoneme p) — compare GRAPH, GRAPHEME — **al·lo·graph·ic** \¦⸗⸗¦⸗ik, -ēk\ *adj*

al·loi·o·bi·o·gen·e·sis \ə¦lȯi(,)ō-\ *n* [NL, fr. Gk *alloios* different + NL *biogenesis*] : alternation of generations esp. of a sexual and an asexual generation — compare ALLOIOGENESIS

al·loi·o·coe·la \ə,lȯiə'sēlə\ *n pl, cap* [NL, fr. Gk *alloios* different, of another sort + NL *-coela* (irreg. fr. Gk *koilia* cavity of the body)] : an order of Turbellaria sometimes regarded as a suborder of Rhabdocoela comprising aquatic flatworms with a saclike intestine

al·loi·o·gen·e·sis \ə¦lȯiō'jenəsəs\ *n* [NL, fr. Gk *alloios* + NL *genesis*] : alternation of sexual and parthenogenetic generations esp. in certain flatworms

al·lo·isom·er·ism \,alō,ī's-\ *n* -s [*all-* + *isomerism*] **1** : isomerism not explainable by the ordinary structural formulas **2** : CIS-TRANS ISOMERISM a

al·lo·ki·ne·sis \,⸗⸗kə'nēsəs, -,kī-\ *n, pl* **allokine·ses** \-ē,sēz\ [NL, fr. *all-* + *kinesis*] : passive or reflex movement — **al·lo·ki·net·ic** \¦⸗⸗(,)⸗¦ned·ik\ *adj*

al·lo·lo·boph·o·ra \¦⸗⸗lō'bäfərə\ *n, cap* [NL, fr. *all-* + *lobo-* + *-phora*] : a common and widely distributed genus of earthworms (family Lumbricidae) not readily distinguished from *Lumbricus* and including one of the commonest earthworms (*A. caliginosa*) of temperate regions

al·lom·er·ism \ə'lämə,rizəm, a'-\ *n* -s [*all-* + *-merism*] : variability in chemical constitution without variation in crystalline form — **al·lom·er·ous** \-‚rəs\ *adj*

al·lo·met·ric \¦alə¦me·trik\ *also* **al·loi·o·met·ric** \ə¦lȯiō¦-\ *adj* : of or relating to allometry : exhibiting or marked by allometry

al·lom·e·tron \ə'lämə·,trän, a'-\ *n* -s [*all-* + Gk *metron* measure, rule] : quantitative alteration in the course of evolution of the proportional relation of body parts

al·lom·e·try \ə'lämə·trē, a'-\ *also* **al·loi·om·e·try** \,a,lȯi'äm-\ *n* -ES [*all-* or Gk *alloios* different + E *-metry*] : relative growth of a part in relation to an entire organism; *also* : the measure and study of such growth

1al·lo·morph \'alə,mȯrf, -ȯ(ə)f\ *n* -s [ISV *all-* + *-morph*] **1** : any of two or more distinct crystalline forms of the same substance ⟨calcium carbonate occurs in the ~s calcite and aragonite⟩ **2** : a pseudomorph that has undergone partial or complete change or substitution of material ⟨limonite is frequently an ~ after pyrite⟩ — **al·lo·mor·phic** \¦⸗⸗¦⸗fik, -ēk\ *adj* — **al·lo·morph·ism** \'⸗⸗,⸗,fizəm\ *n* -s

2allomorph \"\ *n* -s [*2allo-* + *morph*eme] : one of two or more forms that a morpheme has at different points in the language ⟨the *slep-* \slep\ of *slept* and the *sleep* \slēp\ of *sleep well, sleeping,* and *sleeper* are ~s of the same morpheme⟩ ⟨the *-es* \əz\ of *dishes*, the *-s* \z\ of *dreams*, the *-s* \s\ of *traps*, the *-en* \ən\ of *oxen*, the vowel modification distinguishing *teeth* from *tooth*, and the zero suffix of *sheep* in *those sheep* are ~s of the same morpheme⟩ — compare MORPH, MORPHEME 2 — **al·lo·mor·phic** \¦⸗⸗¦⸗fik, -ēk\ *adj* — **al·lo·morph·ism** \'⸗⸗,⸗,fizəm\ *n* -s

al·lo·mor·phite \,⸗⸗'mȯr,fīt\ *n* -s [G *allomorphit*, fr. Gk *allomorphos* of strange shape (fr. *all-* + *-morphos* -morphous) + G *-it* -ite] : a mineral consisting of barite that resembles anhydrite

al·lo·mor·pho·sis \-'mȯrfəsəs *sometimes* -,mȯr'fōsəs\ *n, pl* **allomorpho·ses** \-,sēz\ [NL, fr. *all-* + *morphosis*] : biological evolution marked by rapid increase of specialization : evolutionary allometry — compare AROMORPHOSIS

all one *adj* : of such a nature that no one possible outcome or course of events is more desirable than another ⟨it is *all one* to me what he does⟩

1al·longe \a'lōⁿzh\ *n, pl* **allonges** \-zhəz\ [F, lit., lengthening, fr. OF *alonge*, fr. *alongier* to make long, fr. (assumed) VL *allongare*, fr. L *ad-* + LL *longare* to make long, fr. L *longus* long — more at LONG] : a slip of paper attached to a bill of exchange or similar document to provide space for additional endorsements : RIDER

2al·lon·gé \¦a,lōⁿ¦zhā\ *adj* [F, fr. past part. of *allonger* to extend (an arm or leg), make long, fr. OF *alongier* to make long] *ballet* : with arms and one leg extended to form a long line ⟨an arabesque ~⟩

al·lo·nym \'alə,nim\ *n* -s [F *allonyme*, fr. *all-* + *-onyme* -onym] **1** : a name that is assumed by an author but that actually belongs to another person **2** : a work published under the name of a person other than the author

al·lo·pal·la·di·um \¦⸗⸗-\ *n* -s [*all-* + *palladium*] : palladium that is found in hexagonal tables with gold

al·lo·path \'alə,path, -aa(ə)th,-aith\ *n* -s [G, fr. *all-* + *-path*] : one who practices allopathy

al·lo·path·ic \¦⸗⸗¦pathik, -ēk\ *also* **al·lo·path·i·cal** \-əkəl, -ēk-\ *adj* [G *allopathisch*, fr. *all-* + *-pathisch* -pathic, -pathical] : of or relating to allopathy — **al·lo·path·i·cal·ly** \-ək(ə)lē, -ēk-, -li\ *adv*

al·lop·a·thy \ə'läpəthē, a'-, -thi\ *n* -ES [G *allopathie*, fr. *all-* + *-pathie* -pathy] **1** : a system of medical practice that aims to combat disease by use of remedies producing effects different from those produced by the special disease treated **2** : a system of medical practice making use of all measures that have proved of value in treatment of disease

al·lo·pat·ric \¦⸗⸗¦pa·trik, -pā·-\ *adj* [*all-* + Gk *patra* fatherland (fr. *patēr* father) + E *-ic* — more at FATHER] : biologically relating to or taking place in different areas — used esp. of speciation in which isolated populations evolve into good species; compare SYMPATRIC — **al·lo·pat·ri·cal·ly** \-ək(ə)lē\ *adv* — **al·lop·a·try** \ə'läpə·trē, 'alə,pa·t-\ *n* -ES

al·lo·pe·lag·ic \¦⸗⸗⸗¦⸗⸗\ *adj* [ISV *all-* + *pelagic;* orig. formed as G *allopelagisch*] : of or relating to marine organisms occurring irregularly at the surface or at varying depths in response to influences other than temperature

all-operator \'⸗,⸗⸗,⸗⸗\ *n* : a universal quantifier

al·lo·phan·a·mide \,alə'fanə,mīd, -‚məd\ *n* -s [*allophanic* + *amide*] : BIURET

al·loph·a·nate \ə'läfə,nāt\ *n* -s [*allophanic* + *-ate*] : a salt or ester of allophanic acid

al·lo·phane \'alə,fān\ *n* -s [Gk *allophanēs* appearing otherwise, fr. *all-* + *-phanēs* (fr. *phainesthai* to appear)] : an amorphous translucent mineral of various colors often in incrustations or stalactite forms consisting of a hydrous aluminum silicate (hardness 3, sp. gr. 1.85–1.89)

al·lo·phan·ic acid \¦alə¦fanik-\ *n* [ISV *allophan-* (after G *allophansäure* allophanic acid, fr. Gk *allophanēs* appearing otherwise + G *säure* acid) + *-ic*] : an acid $NH_2CONHCOOH$ known only in the form of derivatives (as esters)

al·lo·phone \'alə,fōn\ *n* -s [*2allo-* + *phone*] : one of two or more articulatorily and acoustically different forms of the same phoneme ⟨the aspirated *p* of *pin* and the nonaspirated *p* of *spin* are ~s of the phoneme *p*⟩ — compare PHONE, PHONEME — **al·lo·phon·ic** \¦alə¦fänik, -ēk\ *adj*

al·lo·phore \,⸗⸗,fō(ə)r\ *n* -s [*all-* + *-phore*] : a chromatophore containing an alcohol-soluble red pigment that occurs in the skins of fishes, amphibia, and reptiles

al·lo·phyl·i·an \¦⸗⸗¦filēən, -lyən\ *adj* [LL *allophylus* + E *-ian*] *archaic* : Asiatic or European but neither Indo-European nor Semitic ⟨an ~ language⟩ : Asiatic or European but speaking a language that is neither Indo-European nor Semitic ⟨an ~ people⟩

al·lo·phy·lus \,⸗⸗'fīləs\ *n, cap* [NL, fr. LL, of another tribe, foreign, fr. Gk *allophylos*, fr. *all-* + *phylē* tribe] : a genus of tropical trees (family Sapindaceae) with trifoliolate or rarely unifoliolate leaves and small white racemose tetramerous flowers

al·lo·plasm \,⸗⸗,plazəm\ *n* -s [ISV *all-* + *-plasm;* prob. back-formation fr. *alloplasmatic*, fr. *all-* + *plasmatic;* orig. formed as G *alloplasmatisch*] : differentiated active protoplasm (as myofibrils, tonofibrils, and cilia); *also* : certain protoplasmic derivatives (as cell walls or intercellular substances) — **al·lo·plas·mat·ic** \-,plaz¦mad·ik\ *adj* — **al·lo·plas·mic** \¦⸗⸗¦plazmik\ *adj*

al·lo·plas·tic \¦⸗⸗¦plastik\ *adj* [*all-* + *-plastic*] : molding or molded by external factors (as environment) ⟨man's evolution . . . is through ~ experiments with objects outside his own body —Weston La Barre⟩ — contrasted with *autoplastic* — **al·lo·plas·ti·cal·ly** \-ək(ə)lē\ *adv*

al·lo·plas·tic·i·ty \,⸗⸗,pla'stisəd·ē\ *or* **al·lo·plas·ty** \¦⸗⸗,plastē\ *n* -ES [*all-* + *plasticity* or *-plasty*] : the capacity for being molded or modified by the external world — contrasted with *autoplasticity*

1al·lo·pol·y·ploid \,⸗⸗'pälə,plȯid\ *n* -s [*all-* + *polyploid*] : an individual or strain exhibiting allopolyploidy

2al·lo·pol·y·ploid \¦⸗⸗¦⸗⸗,⸗\ *adj* : exhibiting allopolyploidy : being an allopolyploid

al·lo·pol·y·ploi·dy \,⸗⸗'⸗⸗,⸗dē\ *n* -ES : the state of having more than two genomes more or less dissimilar and derived from two or more different ancestral species — compare AUTOPOLYPLOIDY

al·lo·psy·chic \¦alō¦sīkik\ *adj* [*all-* + *psychic*] : related mentally to the outside world ⟨~ adjustment⟩ — contrasted with *autopsychic*

all-or-none \¦⸗⸗¦⸗\ *adj* : occurring either completely or not at all : marked either by entire, complete, inclusive, or unqualified operation or effect or by none at all ⟨in unequal degrees, rather than in *all-or-none* fashion —Walter Firey⟩ ⟨an *all-or-none* reaction⟩ ⟨a nerve cell has . . . an *all-or-none* response, like the trigger of a gun —E.C.Berkeley⟩

all-or-none law *n* : a principle in physiology: in any single nerve or muscle fiber the response to a stimulus above threshold level is maximal and independent of the intensity of the stimulus

all-or-nothing \¦⸗⸗¦⸗⸗\ *adj* **1** : ALL-OR-NONE **2 a** : accepting no less than everything ⟨an *all-or-nothing* attitude⟩ ⟨an *all-or-nothing* choice⟩ **b** : risking everything ⟨playing an *all-or-nothing* game⟩

al·lo·sau·rus \,alə'sȯrəs\ *n, cap* [NL, fr. *all-* + *-saurus*] : a genus of No. American Jurassic carnivorous dinosaurs having hind feet with three functional toes and sometimes being over 20 feet long

al·lose \'a,lōs\ *n* -s [ISV *all-* + *-ose;* orig. formed in G] : a sugar $C_6H_{12}O_6$ obtained synthetically as a syrup that is stereoisomeric with glucose and epimeric with altrose

al·lo·se·mat·ic \¦⸗⸗sə¦mad·ik\ *adj* [*all-* + *sematic*] : having protective coloration that imitates the coloration of some dangerous or inedible animal

al·lo·some \'⸗⸗,sōm\ *n* -s [*all-* + *-some*] : an atypical chromosome; *esp* : SEX CHROMOSOME — compare AUTOSOME

al·lo·sy·nap·sis \,⸗⸗sə'napsəs\ *n, pl* **allosynap·ses** \-p,sēz\ [NL, fr. *all-* + *synapsis*] : ALLOSYNDESIS

al·lo·syn·de·sis \,⸗⸗'sindəsəs\ *n, pl* **allosynde·ses** \-ə,sēz\ [NL, fr. *all-* + *syndesis*] : pairing at meiosis of nonhomologous chromosomes from the diverse sets of an allopolyploid individual — compare AUTOSYNDESIS — **al·lo·syn·det·ic** \¦⸗⸗(,)sin¦ded·ik\ *adj* — **al·lo·syn·det·i·cal·ly** \-ək(ə)lē\ *adv*

al·lot \ə'lät *also* a'-; *usu* -ăd·+V\ *vb* **allotted**; **allotted**; **allotting**; **allots** [ME *alotten*, fr. MF *aloter*, fr. *a-* (fr. L *ad-*) + *-loter* (fr. *lot*, of Gmc origin; akin to OE *hlot* lot) — more at AT, LOT] *vt* **1** : to assign as a portion or lot ⟨the right of society to ~ to each the work . . . that he should do —J.A. Hobson⟩: as **a** : to prescribe as one's lot (as in life) : ORDAIN, APPOINT ⟨man's *allotted* life span according to the psalmist⟩ ⟨nature . . . propels us like children through the role she has *allotted* us —D.C.Peattie⟩ ⟨each in his *allotted* place⟩ **b** : to assign as a share or portion to a particular person or thing or for a particular purpose : ALLOCATE ⟨business began to encroach upon the time *allotted* to rest —S.M.Crothers⟩ ⟨*allotted* to the civilian economy what was left over —*Current History*⟩ ⟨exceeded his *allotted* time by 15 minutes⟩; *specif* : to assign to a subscriber (his proportionate share of an issue of securities) **2** : to distribute by lot or as if by lot : parcel out in parts or portions or to each individual concerned : apportion esp. without regard to the choice or wishes of the recipients ⟨the council should not waste time on *allotting* blame between him and his junior officers⟩ ⟨some fairly good⸗sized parts to ~ among all those people who are coming to the tryout —Robertson Davies⟩ **3** : to assign as due or deriving : ATTRIBUTE ⟨~ diverse sets of instincts to the biological ego —P.A.Sorokin⟩ ~ *vi, North* : INTEND, RECKON, ANTICIPATE — usu. used with *on* or *upon* ⟨I ~ upon going⟩

syn ASSIGN, APPORTION, ALLOCATE: ALLOT may imply more or less arbitrary distribution ⟨*allotted* a task of vital importance —Sir Winston Churchill⟩ ⟨you will probably be *allotted* your seat for meals —Agnes M. Miall⟩ ⟨had been *allotted* a small sitting room —Compton Mackenzie⟩ ASSIGN may stress authoritative, usu. fixed, allotment suggesting no necessarily equitable distribution ⟨*assigns* to different departments their respective powers —John Marshall⟩ ⟨antiaircraft guns had been *assigned* the mission of protecting the bridge —P.W. Thompson⟩ ⟨an attic *assigned* to me as a playroom —R.M. Lovett⟩ APPORTION suggests a more or less equitable or proportionate distribution ⟨the duty of husbanding and *apportioning* the meager food stores of the party —W.J.Ghent⟩ ⟨works in which the violin and a keyboard instrument are *apportioned* equal musical interest —A.E.Wier⟩ ⟨to *apportion* the judicial power between the supreme and inferior courts —John Marshall⟩ ALLOCATE, chiefly applied to money, materiel, authority, or responsibility, implies appropriation to a particular person, group, or purpose ⟨various sums *allocated* to the different sciences —S.F.Mason⟩ ⟨*allocate* only part of the supply of the metals in order to affect civilian economy as little as possible —*Current Biog.*⟩ ⟨the Marine Corps would be *allocated* primary responsibility for amphibious development and doctrine pertaining to landing forces —*Collier's Yr. Bk.*⟩

al·lot·ee *var of* ALLOTTEE

al·lo·tet·ra·ploid \,⸗⸗'⸗⸗,⸗\ *n* -s [*all-* + *tetraploid*] : AMPHIDIPLOID — **al·lo·tet·ra·ploi·dy** \-dē\ *n* -ES

al·lo·the·ism \'⸗⸗(,)thē,izəm\ *n* -s [*all-* + *-theism*] : the worship of foreign or unsanctioned gods ⟨commandments against ~ and polytheism⟩

al·lo·the·ria \,==ˈthirēə\ *n pl, cap* [NL, fr. *all-* + *-theria*] **:** a subclass of Mammalia comprising small primitive forms extinct since the early Cenozoic, being usu. considered coextensive with the Multituberculata but sometimes extended to include the Protodonta and Triconodonta

al·lo·thig·e·nous \¦==¦thijənəs\ *adj* [G *allothigen* + E *-ous*] **:** ALLOTHOGENIC

al·loth·i·morph \əˈläthə,mȯrf\ *n* -s [ISV *allothi-* (fr. Gk *allothi* elsewhere, old loc. of *allos* other) + *-morph;* orig. formed in G — more at ELSE] **:** any constituent of a metamorphic rock that in the new rock still possesses its original crystal boundaries — **al·loth·i·mor·phic** \=¦==¦=fik\ *adj*

al·loth·o·gen·ic \ə¦läthə¦jenik\ *also* **al·lo·thog·e·nous** \¦alə¦thäjənəs\ *adj* [irreg. (influenced by E *-o-*) fr. G *allothigen* allothogenic (fr. Gk *allothi* elsewhere — fr. *allos* other — + *-genēs* born) + E *-ic* or *-ous* — more at ELSE, -GEN] **:** formed elsewhere **:** derived from preexisting rocks ⟨clastic rocks or their mineral particles formed elsewhere and transported to their present position are ~⟩ **:** ALLOGENIC — opposed to *authigenic*

al·lot·ment \əˈlätmənt *also* aˈ-\ *n* -s [MF *alotement*, fr. *aloter* to allot + *-ment*] **1 :** the act of allotting ⟨funds available and ready for ~⟩: as **a :** APPORTIONMENT **b :** assignment to a particular person or thing or for a particular use **2 :** something that is allotted **:** a part or portion distributed or assigned: as **a :** something that is assigned by or as if by lot or by destiny ⟨possessing a generous ~ of common sense —*Saturday Rev.*⟩ ⟨receiving . . . their varying ~*s* of discomfort and disappointment and discouragement —J.G.Cozzens⟩ **b :** something set apart by distribution or assignment for special use or for a distinct party: as (1) *chiefly Brit* **:** a small piece of land let or assigned to an individual (as by the town council) for cultivation as a family garden ⟨a disused railway siding that was turned into ~*s* —Anthony Powell⟩ ⟨an ~ garden⟩ (2) **:** a portion of range land, esp. of national forest, allotted to the use of a particular grazier or herd or flock of grazing animals (3) **:** a portion of a serviceman's salary paid, esp. with additional contributions, to a designated party at his request or to a bank for his account (4) **:** the portion of a newly issued security received by a subscriber **3 :** acceptance of an order to purchase or subscribe to securities of a new offering in part or whole

al·lo·top·o·type \,==ˈtäpə,tīp\ *n* -s [blend of *allotype* and *topotype*] *biol* **:** an allotype obtained from the type locality

al·lot·ri·og·na·thi \ə,lä·trēˈägnə,thī\ *n pl, cap* [NL, fr. Gk *allotrio-* (fr. *allotrios* strange) + *gnathoi*, pl. of *gnathos* jaw] **:** an order or suborder of oceanic teleost fishes comprising the opah, the dealfishes, ribbonfishes, and related forms

al·lot·ri·o·mor·phic \ə¦lä·trēə¦mȯrfik\ *adj* [Gk *allotrio-* + E *-morphic*] **:** marked by a form different from the normal or expected because of development in special circumstances — used esp. of mineral grains of igneous rocks whose mutual growths have prevented the assumption of outward crystal form; contrasted with *idiomorphic*

al·lot·ri·oph·a·gy \ə,lä·trēˈäfəjē\ *also* **al·lot·ri·o·pha·gia** \-ə¦fāj(ē)ə\ *n, pl* **allotriophagies** *also* **allotriophagias** [*allotriophagy* fr. G *allotriophagie*, fr. Gk *allotrio-* + G *-phagie* -phagy; *allotriophagia*, NL, fr. G *allotriophagie*] *med* **:** PICA

al·lo·trope \ˈalə,trōp\ *n* -s [ISV, back-formation fr. *allotropy*] **:** a form showing allotropy

al·lo·troph·ic \¦==¦träfik, -ōf-\ *adj* [ISV *all-* + *-trophic*] **1 :** having an altered, esp. lowered, nutritive value ⟨~ foods⟩ **2 :** HETEROTROPHIC

al·lo·trop·ic \¦==¦träpik\ *adj* [ISV *allotropy* + *-ic*] **1 :** of, relating to, or exhibiting allotropy ⟨~ chemical changes⟩ ⟨sulfur is known in a number of ~ forms⟩ **2 :** showing a variation of form **:** existent in a different form ⟨dialects with ~ developments⟩

al·lot·ro·pize \əˈlä·trə,pīz\ *vt* -ED/-ING/-S [*allotropy* + *-ize*] **:** to change from one allotropic form to another

al·lot·ro·py \əˈlä·trəpē\ *also* **al·lot·ro·pism** \-,pizəm\ *n, pl* **allotropies** *also* **allotropisms** [*all-* + *-tropy*, *-tropism*] **:** the phenomenon of the existence of a substance, esp. an element, in two or more different modifications usu. in the same phase (as different crystalline forms of carbon, iron, and phosphorus or as different kinds of molecules of oxygen and ozone) — compare POLYMORPHISM

allots *pres 3d sing of* ALLOT

al·lot·ta·ble \əˈläd·əbəl, -ätə- *also* aˈ-\ *adj* **:** capable of being allotted

all' ot·ta·va \¦älō¦tävə ¦al-\ *adv (or adj)* [It, at the octave] **:** OTTAVA

allotted *past of* ALLOT

al·lot·tee *or* **al·lot·ee** \ə¦läd·¦ē, -ä¦tē, ¦a,lä¦tē\ *n* -s **:** one that receives an allotment ⟨divided among the original ~*s* or their heirs —E.E.Dale⟩

allotting *pres part of* ALLOT

al·lo·type \ˈalə,tīp\ *n* -s [*all-* + *type*] **1 :** a type specimen of opposite sex to the holotype; *esp* **:** one designated by the original author **2 :** PARATYPE 1 — **al·lo·typ·ic** \¦alə¦tipik\ *adj*

all out *adv* **:** with full vigor, determination, or enthusiasm or with full use of one's powers, ingenuity, and influence, esp. in an effort or a cause — used chiefly in the phrase *go all out* ⟨went *all out* for excess-profits legislation —*New Republic*⟩ ⟨go *all out* to complete a job⟩ ⟨prevented them from going *all out*⟩

all-out \ˈ=¦=\ *adj* [*all out*] **:** exerting every energy and employing every resource (as military, economic, and political) ⟨an *all-out* offensive⟩ **:** thoroughgoing and unreserved ⟨the *all-out* support of the press⟩ ⟨*all-out* reformers⟩ **:** without reservation

all-out·er \ˈȯˈlaùdə(r), -aùtə-\ *n* -s **:** one that advocates an all-out policy or measure **:** EXTREMIST ⟨*all-outers* for "unconditional surrender" and "total victory" —J.R.Chamberlain⟩

all over *adv* [ME *alover*, fr. *al* all + *over*] **1 a :** over the whole extent ⟨decorated *all over* with a pattern of flowers⟩ ⟨felt tired *all over*⟩ **b :** EVERYWHERE ⟨looked *all over* for it⟩ **2 :** in every respect **:** THOROUGHLY, COMPLETELY ⟨she is her mother *all over*⟩ **3 :** everywhere on the outside ⟨he is *all over* dirt⟩ ⟨ragged and *all over* bruises⟩ — not often in formal use

[1]allover \ˈ=¦==\ *adj* **:** covering the whole extent of anything ⟨variations in solar radiation or some other ~ effect —*Time*⟩; *esp* **:** covering the entire surface (as of a fabric) — used esp. of designs or figuration ⟨~ quilting⟩ ⟨an ~ marbleized appearance⟩

[2]allover \"\ *n* -s **1 :** an embroidered, printed, or lace fabric with a design covering most of the surface **2 :** a pattern or design in which a single unit is repeated along two or more intersecting systems of lines so as to cover an entire surface

all-o·ver·ish \(ˈ)ȯ¦lōv(ə)rish\ *adj* [[1]*allover* + *-ish*] **1 :** vaguely uneasy **:** APPREHENSIVE **2 :** slightly indisposed

all-o·vers \ˈȯˈlōvə(r)z\ *n pl* [*all over* + *-s*] *chiefly South & Midland* **:** FIDGETS, CREEPS ⟨it gives me the *all-overs* just to think of it⟩

al·low \əˈlaù\ *vb* -ED/-ING/-S [ME *allowen*, fr. MF *aloer*, *alouer* to place, use, grant (fr. ML *allocare*) & *allouer* to approve, fr. L *adlaudare* to extol, fr. *ad-* + *laudare* to praise — more at ALLOCATE, LAUD] *vt* **1** *archaic* **a :** PRAISE **b :** APPROVE, SANCTION, ACCEPT ⟨truly ye bear witness that ye ~ the deeds of your fathers —Lk 11:48 (AV)⟩ **2 a** *obs* **:** to give or recognize as a right **b** (1) **:** to give or assign as a share or suitable amount (as of time or money) to a particular person or for a particular purpose ⟨~ an hour for lunch⟩ ⟨~*ed* each child one dollar a week as spending money⟩ (2) **:** to allot or assign as a deduction or an addition ⟨~ a gallon for leakage⟩ **3 :** to accept as true or as represented **:** ADMIT, CONCEDE, ACKNOWLEDGE ⟨a people of whom this is true must be ~*ed* to be musical —Wyn Griffith⟩ ⟨he will not ~ that we have eliminated these evils⟩ ⟨played a more important part in his life than his biographer ~*s*⟩ **4 :** PERMIT ⟨a pipe to ~ the heated air to escape⟩ ⟨occasional gaps ~ passage through the mountains⟩ ⟨pulled to the side to ~ us to pass⟩: **a :** to permit by way of concession ⟨no smoking ~*ed*⟩ ⟨he ~*s* himself many luxuries⟩ ⟨children too young to be ~*ed* out at night⟩ **b :** to permit by neglecting to restrain or prevent ⟨~ a garden to become overgrown with weeds⟩ ⟨conditions which should never have been ~*ed* to develop⟩ ⟨she had ~*ed* herself to become very fat⟩ **5** *dial* **a :** to be of the opinion **:** THINK, SUPPOSE ⟨we ~*ed* it was too late to start⟩ **b :** INTEND, PLAN — usu. used with an infinitive ⟨I ~ to go fishing tomorrow⟩ **~** *vi* **1 :** to make a possibility **:** provide opportunity or basis **:** ADMIT, PERMIT — used with *of* ⟨evidence that ~*s* of only one conclusion⟩ ⟨underbrush too dense to ~ of shooting⟩ **2 :** to give consideration **:** make allowance — used with *for* ⟨a distance, ~*ing* for detours, of about 10 miles⟩ **3** *dial* **:** SUPPOSE, CONSIDER **syn** see LET

al·low·a·bil·i·ty \ə,laùəˈbiləd·ē\ *n* -ES **:** the quality or state of being allowable

[1]al·low·a·ble \əˈlaùəbəl\ *adj* [ME, fr. MF *allouable*, fr. *allouer* to approve + *-able*] **1** *obs* **:** worthy of praise **:** LAUDABLE **2 :** PERMISSIBLE **:** not forbidden **:** not unlawful or improper ⟨the ~ rate of continuous descent of commercial airliners —H.G.Armstrong⟩ ⟨~ income tax deductions⟩ ⟨a degree of freedom ~ among friends⟩ — **al·low·a·ble·ness** *n* -ES

[2]allowable \"\ *n* -s **:** the amount of oil that an oil-well operator is permitted by law to take from a given well in any one day

al·low·a·bly \-əblē, -li\ *adv* **:** in an allowable manner

[1]al·low·ance \əˈlaùən(t)s\ *n* -s [ME *allowaunce*, fr. MF *allouaunce* approbation (fr. *allouer* to approve + *-aunce* -ance) & *alouaunce* action of leasing, fr. *aloer*, *alouer* to place, use, grant + *-aunce* -ance] **1 a** *archaic* **:** APPROVAL, APPROBATION **b** *obs* **:** ACKNOWLEDGMENT **2 :** something that is allowed **:** a share or portion allotted or granted ⟨an ~ of time for stopovers⟩ ⟨~*s* for depreciation⟩: **a** (1) **:** a sum granted as a reimbursement or a bounty or as appropriate for such purposes as personal or household expenses ⟨an officer's pay and ~*s*⟩ ⟨a schoolboy's weekly ~⟩ ⟨per diem ~*s* in lieu of subsistence —*U.S.Code*⟩ ⟨cost-of-living ~*s*⟩ ⟨spending the winter in California on the ~ he gets —Hamilton Basso⟩ (2) *law* **:** a sum in addition to the regular taxable costs awarded by court to a party in a difficult case — called also *extra allowance* **b :** a fixed amount allowed ⟨a sailor's daily ~ of grog⟩ ⟨the 66-pound free-luggage ~ granted by transatlantic air lines⟩ **c** (1) **:** a customary deduction from the gross weight of goods, different in different countries (2) **:** a reduction from a list price or stated price (as one granted on used products turned in or because of a previous credit) ⟨a trade-in ~⟩ **d :** a concession or privilege accorded a contestant to make his chances more nearly equal to his competitors': as (1) **:** an allowed deduction from the weight a racehorse is required to carry ⟨maidens were given special ~*s*⟩ (2) **:** a deduction from the actual elapsed time of a racing yacht computed against a scratch boat's elapsed time **e :** nonproductive time added in time study to the actual or base time of an operation to allow for fatigue, personal needs, and delays — compare BASE TIME, STANDARD TIME **f :** clearance in founding **g :** an allowed dimensional difference between mating parts of a machine (as between a shaft and a bearing in which it turns) — compare TOLERANCE 3 **3 :** the act of allowing **:** AUTHORIZATION, PERMISSION, SANCTION ⟨without the king's will or the state's ~ —Shak.⟩ ⟨no newspaper was suffered to appear without his ~ —T.B.Macaulay⟩ **4 :** the taking into account of circumstances (as mitigating circumstances) or of contingencies — often used with the verb *make* and the preposition *for* ⟨make ~*s* for the inexperience of youth⟩ ⟨~ must be made for what was then the fashionable pose —R.B.Merriman⟩ ⟨regional differences must be recognized and ~ made for them in any generalizations —C.R.Woodward⟩

[2]allowance \"\ *vt* -ED/-ING/-S **1 :** to put upon a fixed allowance (as of provisions and drink) ⟨the captain *allowanced* his crew⟩ **2 :** to supply in a fixed and limited quantity

allowance account *n* **:** RESERVE ACCOUNT 1

allowed *adj* **:** in accordance with selection principles in physics **:** PERMITTED — used of electron-energy states and transitions or spectrum lines

al·low·ed·ly \əˈlaùədlē, -li\ *adv* **:** by allowance **:** ADMITTEDLY

allowed time *n* **1** *industrial engin* **:** STANDARD TIME **2 :** the amount of time an employee is permitted to spend per work cycle for attending to personal needs — called also *time allowance*

allowing *pres part of* ALLOW

allows *pres 3d sing of* ALLOW

allox- *comb form* [ISV, fr. *alloxan*] **:** alloxan

al·lox·an \əˈläksən\ *n* -s [G, fr. *all*antoin + *ox*alsäure oxalic acid + *-an*] **:** a crystalline compound $C_4H_2N_2O_4$ or its monohydrate $C_4H_4N_2O_5$ formed by oxidation of uric acid and causing diabetes mellitus when injected into experimental animals

al·lox·an·ate \-sə,nāt, -,nət\ *n* -s [ISV *alloxan* + *-ate*] **:** a salt or ester of alloxanic acid

al·lox·an·ic acid \¦a,läk¦sanik-\ *n* [ISV *alloxanic* (fr. *alloxan* + *-ic*) + *acid;* orig. formed as G *alloxansäure*] **:** a crystalline acid $C_4H_4N_2O_5$ formed by hydrolysis of alloxan; 4-hydroxy-4-hydantoin-carboxylic acid

al·lox·an·tin \əˈläksən·tən\ *n* -s [ISV *alloxan* + connective *-t-* + *-in;* orig. formed in G] **:** a crystalline compound $C_8H_6N_4O_8 2H_2O$ formed by oxidation of uric acid and by reaction of alloxan and dialuric acid

al·lox·a·zine \əˈläksə,zēn\ *n* -s [*allox-* + *azine*] **:** either of two acidic compounds $C_{10}H_6N_4O_2$ containing a pyrimidine ring fused to quinoxaline: **a :** a grayish green powder obtained by reaction of alloxan with *ortho*-phenylenediamine **b :** ISOALLOXAZINE

al·lox·u·ric \¦a,läk¦sùrik, -ks¦yù-\ *adj* [ISV *allox-* + *uric*] **:** related to alloxan and urea

alloxuric base *n* **:** PURINE BASE

[1]al·loy \ˈa,lȯi, əˈl-, aˈl-; =ˈ= *is prob more freq for noun senses 4 & 5, and for the verb, than for noun senses 2 & 3*\ *n* -s [MF *aloi*, fr. *aloier*] **1** *obs* **:** essential quality or character **:** STANDARD **2 :** degree of mixture with base metals **:** comparative purity (as of gold or silver) **:** FINENESS **3 a :** a substance composed of two or more metals intimately mixed and united usu. by being fused together and dissolving in each other when molten ⟨brass is an ~ of copper and zinc⟩; *also* **:** the state of union of the components **b :** a similar substance with metallic properties, sometimes with limited malleability and conductivity, formed by union of a metal and a nonmetal ⟨steel is an ~ of iron and carbon⟩ **c** *archaic* **:** an inferior metal mixed with a more valuable one ⟨coins made of silver and ~⟩ **4 a :** admixture that lessens value or detracts from quality **b :** an impairing alien element or part ⟨no happiness is without ~⟩ ⟨had his ~, like other people, of ambition and selfishness —Rose Macaulay⟩ **5 :** any compound, mixture, or union of different things **:** AMALGAM ⟨an ethnic ~ of many peoples⟩

[2]alloy \"\ *vb* -ED/-ING/-S [obs. F *aloyer*, fr. OF *aleier*, *aloier*, *alier* to combine, fr. L *alligare* to bind, bind to — more at ALLY] *vt* **1 :** to reduce the purity of by mixing with a less valuable metal ⟨~ gold with copper⟩ **2 :** to mix with another metal or metals (as by melting together) **:** use as the constituent or constituents of an alloy **:** mix so as to form an alloy **3 :** to lower, impair, or debase by mixture ⟨~*ing* the splendor of the sight⟩ **:** ALLAY, MODERATE, TEMPER ⟨mercy should ~ our stern resentment —W.S.Gilbert⟩ **~** *vi* **:** to mix to form an alloy **:** lend itself readily to being alloyed ⟨iron ~*s* well⟩

al·loy·age \əˈlȯi·ij, aˈl-, ˈa,l-\ *n* -s [obs. F *aloyage*, fr. *aloyer* + *-age*] **:** the act or art of alloying

alloy steel *n* **:** a steel with modified properties made by incorporating with iron one or more elements in addition to carbon — contrasted with *carbon steel*

al·lo·zo·oid \,alə¦zō,ȯid\ *n* -s [*all-* + *zooid*] **:** a zooid differing from its parent — opposed to *isozooid*

all-points \ˈ=,=\ *adj* **:** directed to all points **:** sent in all directions **:** GENERAL — used esp. of police messages ⟨an *all-points* alarm⟩ ⟨broadcast an *all-points* bulletin⟩

all-possessed \¦==¦=\ *adj* **:** as if dominated by an evil spirit **:** DEMONIAC ⟨ran down the street like *all-possessed*⟩

all-powerful \(ˈ)ȯl¦-\ *adj* **:** having complete power or sole power ⟨perhaps dictators are not so *all-powerful* as they seem —Bertrand Russell⟩ ⟨an *all-powerful* arbiter —John Gunther⟩

all-purpose \ˈ=¦==\ *adj* **:** for all or many purposes **:** suited or adapted to various uses, including those uses ordinarily requiring special adaptations **:** not specialized ⟨an *all-purpose* wardrobe⟩ ⟨military *all-purpose* gasoline⟩ ⟨*all-purpose* emergency kits⟩

all-purpose flour *n* **:** flour made from a blend of hard or soft wheats suitable for all cookery except the finest cakes

all red *adj, usu cap A&R* [so called fr. the color of British territory on British official maps] **:** wholly within the British Commonwealth — used of connections between Britain and her overseas territories ⟨an *All Red* route⟩

[1]all right \ȯ(l)ˈrīt, *esp in senses 2 & 3* ˈ=,=; *usu* -īd·+V\ *adv* [ME *alright*, *alriht*, fr. *al* all + *right*, *riht* right — more at RIGHT] **1 :** SATISFACTORILY ⟨doing *all right*⟩ ⟨getting along *all right*⟩ **2 :** YES, AGREED **:** very well ⟨*all right*, let us suppose your plan is sound⟩ — often used as a generalized expression of assent ⟨*all right*, I'll meet you at 10 o'clock⟩; sometimes used in irritation by children ⟨*all right* for you. I'm going⟩ **3 :** beyond doubt **:** CERTAINLY ⟨the element has been conquered, *all right*, but it still hits back —*New Yorker*⟩ — often added as an expression of emphasis ⟨you've started *all right.* Right at the bottom —Louis Auchincloss⟩

[2]all right *nonattrib usu* =ˈ=, *attrib usu* ˈ=,=\ *adj* **1 :** SATISFACTORY: as **a :** AGREEABLE ⟨that is *all right* with me⟩ **b :** CORRECT ⟨checked his work and found it *all right*⟩ **c :** ADEQUATE ⟨not very good in his first role but *all right* in the second⟩ ⟨*all right* for the last century⟩ **d :** SUITABLE, PROPER ⟨a picture that is *all right* for children⟩ **2 :** SAFE, WELL ⟨he was ill but he is *all right* again⟩ **3** *slang* **:** GOOD, HONEST, DEPENDABLE — usu. used attributively as a generalized expression of approval ⟨an *all right* guy⟩ ⟨an *all right* party after it got started⟩

[3]all right \=ˈ=\ *n, chiefly Brit* **:** a signal (as a blue flag) raised over the number board to indicate that results of a horse race are official and that winning bets may be paid out

all risk *or* **all risks** *adj* **:** covering loss from all hazards insured against except those specif. excluded from coverage — compare BROAD FORM

all-round *var of* ALL-AROUND

all round *also* **all around** *adv* [*all-round*] **:** INCLUSIVELY **:** without concentration on one area or aspect **:** concerning or considering all members, units, parts, or phases ⟨some will fail *all round;* others will succeed in part⟩ ⟨our best athlete, if taken *all round*⟩

all-round·er \ˈȯlˈraùndə(r)\ *n* -s **:** one that is all-around **:** a person (as a workman or an athlete) or an animal (as a dog or horse) excelling or capable in many fields or in many departments of the same field ⟨he was an *all-rounder* at school (classics, science, history, languages) —Brian Dowling⟩ ⟨the working horse kept by the Irish farmer was a good *all-rounder* —Stanislaus Lynch⟩: as **a** *chiefly Brit* **:** an athlete, esp. a cricketer, who excels in several departments of play **b :** a show-dog judge considered capable of judging dogs of several different breeds

alls *pl of* ALL

all saints' cherry *n, usu cap A & S* [so called fr. its alleged blooming on All Saints' Day] **:** an ornamental horticultural variety (*Prunus cerasus semperflorens*) of the sour cherry blooming in spring and autumn

all saints' day *n, usu cap A & S & D* **:** a feast observed in various Christian churches on November 1 in honor of all the saints or all the blessed in heaven

all saints' summer *n, usu cap A & 1st S* **:** INDIAN SUMMER

allseed \ˈ=,=\ *n* -s **:** any of several many-seeded plants: as **a :** KNOTWEED **b :** a goosefoot (*Chenopodium polyspermum*)

all-sliming \ˈ=¦==\ *n* -s **:** grinding to the fineness of slime so that practically all material will pass through a 200-mesh screen — used of a common method of treating gold ores

all souls' day *n, usu cap A & S & D* **:** a day observed in the medieval Western church and in the modern Roman Catholic and some Anglican churches, usu. on November 2, by the solemn commemoration of and supplicatory prayers for the dead

all·spice \ˈȯl,spīs\ *n* -s [so called fr. the belief that it combines the flavor of cinnamon, nutmeg, and cloves] **1 :** the berry of the allspice tree yielding a pungent and aromatic spice; *also* **:** the spice prepared from this berry **2** *also* **allspice tree :** a West Indian tree (*Pimenta dioica*) of the family Myrtaceae that yields allspice **3 :** any of several aromatic shrubs: as **a :** CAROLINA ALLSPICE **b :** JAPAN ALLSPICE

allspice oil *n* **:** PIMENTO OIL

all standing *adv* **1 :** with all sail set — used of a ship brought suddenly to a stop while all sail is set ⟨to bring up *all standing*⟩ **2 :** in a fully clothed state ⟨to turn in *all standing*⟩

[1]all-star \ˈ=,=\ *adj* **:** composed wholly or chiefly of stars or of outstanding performers or participants ⟨an *all-star* team⟩ ⟨an *all-star* cast⟩ ⟨an *all-star* television program⟩ **:** participated in by stars ⟨an annual *all-star* game⟩

[2]all-star \"\ *n* -s [[1]*all-star*] **:** a member of an all-star team — usu. used in pl. ⟨major league *all-stars*⟩

all that *n* **:** everything of or related to the kind specified ⟨one last fling and he would put *all that* behind him⟩ ⟨believed in the stiff upper lip and *all that*⟩

all there *adj* **1 :** in full possession of one's mental faculties **:** SANE ⟨behaved in such a way as to make one wonder if he was quite *all there*⟩ — not often in formal use **2** *slang* **:** alert and well informed **:** QUICK-WITTED ⟨wide-awake, alert, *all there;* he knows just where he is and what he means and where he is going —*Times Lit. Supp.*⟩

all the same *adv* **:** NEVERTHELESS

all the world *n* **:** everybody or everything in existence; *esp* **:** everybody or everything regarded as of account ⟨convinced that *all the world* was against him⟩ — **for all the world 1 :** for the sake of gaining everything **:** for any consideration **2 :** in every respect **:** WHOLLY, EXACTLY ⟨whose posy was *for all the world* like cutler's poetry —Shak.⟩ ⟨with his father's pipe in his mouth and looking *for all the world* like him⟩

allthing *adv* [obs. *allthing* everything, fr. ME *althing*, fr. *alle thing* all things, fr. OE *ealle thing*] *obs* **:** ALTOGETHER

allthorn \ˈ=,=\ *n* -s **:** a spiny much-branched shrub (*Koeberlinia spinosa*) found in the southwestern U.S. and adjacent Mexico

all threes (thrēz) *n pl, but usu sing in constr* **:** a variety of muggins in which multiples of three are counted

all-time \ˈ=,=\ *adj* **1 :** FULL-TIME **2 a :** for or of all time up to and including the present ⟨an *all-time* average⟩; *esp* **:** exceeding all others of all time ⟨an *all-time* record⟩ ⟨receipts are expected to reach an *all-time* high⟩ **b :** the best, or hypothetically the best, in recorded sports history ⟨an *all-time* baseball team⟩

all to *adv* [ME *al to-* completely apart, completely to pieces, fr. OE *eall tō-*, fr. *eall* completely + *tō-*, *te-* apart, to pieces — more at ALL, DIS-] *obs* **:** all to pieces **:** THOROUGHLY, COMPLETELY ⟨a certain woman cast a piece of a millstone upon Abimelech's head, and *all to* brake his skull —Judg 9:53 (AV)⟩

all told *adv* **:** everything counted **:** in all **:** ALTOGETHER ⟨a town of perhaps 5000 people *all told*⟩ ⟨6 pounds of beef and 4 of lamb, 10 pounds *all told*⟩ ⟨*all told*, it had been one of the most frustrating experiences imaginable⟩

all-turned \ˈ=¦=\ *adj, of a piece of furniture* **:** having all the supporting members (as legs) shaped by turning in a lathe

al·lu·au·dite \,alyəˈwō,dīt\ *n* -s [G *alluaudit*, fr. François *Alluaud* †1865, Fr. mineralogist + G *-it* -ite] **:** a rare mineral $(Na,Fe,Mn)PO_4$ consisting of sodium-iron-manganese phosphate

al·lude \əˈlüd *sometimes* əlˈyüd *or* aˈ- *or* alˈ-\ *vi* -ED/ -ING/ -S [L *alludere* to play with, jest, refer to, fr. *ad-* + *ludere* to play — more at LUDICROUS] **:** to have or make indirect reference (as in passing or by suggestion) **:** refer indirectly — used with *to* ⟨proposals . . . always *alluded* to slightingly as innovations —Compton Mackenzie⟩ ⟨though any reference to his deformity annoyed him, there were times when she felt obliged to ~ to it —Ellen Glasgow⟩ ⟨a letter *alluding* to some unspecified family difficulties⟩

al·lu·lose \ˈalyə,lōs\ *n* -s [*all-* + *-ulose*] **:** a syrupy ketohexose sugar $C_6H_{12}O_6$ found in the unfermentable residue from cane molasses and related stereochemically to allose and altrose — called also *psicose*

all' uni·so·no \,ä(,)lüˈnēsə,nō\ *adv (or adj)* [It, lit., in unison] **:** in unison — used as a direction in music that several performers regularly grouped in parts are to play or sing a single part in unison

all up *adj* [[2]*all* + *up*, adj.] **1 :** at or very near an end **:** with death, defeat, or failure hopelessly or unalterably approaching — used predicatively and in impersonal constructions with *it* ⟨by night it was *all up* for the trapped miners⟩ **2 :** total inclusive of the weight of machine, necessary flight accessories, crew, passengers, and cargo ⟨a plane with an *all up* weight of 50,000 pounds⟩ **:** total inclusive of weight of oil, coolant, and necessary accessories ⟨the *all up* weight of the motor⟩ **3 :** paid for at first-class surface rates but carried by air ⟨*all up* mail to larger cities⟩ **:** of or relating to such carriage arrangements ⟨*all up* systems being planned⟩

[1]al·lure \əˈlù(ə)r, -ùə *also* əlˈyù- *or* aˈl- *or* alˈ-\ *vt* -ED/ -ING/ -S

[ME *aluren*, fr. MF *alurer, aleurrer*, fr. OF, fr. *a-* (fr. L *ad-*) + *loire, loirre* lure — more at LURE] **:** to influence, sway, or entice with some tempting appeal, some offered or suggested benefit or pleasure, genuine or specious ⟨ancient fables of men *allured* by beautiful forms and melodious voices to destruction —W.H.Hudson †1922⟩ **syn** see ATTRACT

[2]allure \"\ *n* -s **:** power of attraction or fascination **:** ALLUREMENT ⟨about the legends of the islands there is a glowing, haunting ~⟩ ⟨the neat ~ in mathematical formulae —Harlow Shapley⟩; *esp* **:** the power to entice or attract through personal charm ⟨is neatly made, has a cobra-cold ~ . . . and dances with the unerring grace of a cat —*Time*⟩ ⟨a female performer with no particular ~ —*New Yorker*⟩

al·lure·ment \-mənt\ *n* -s **1 :** a means of alluring **:** something that attracts or entices ⟨the social ~*s* of the city⟩ ⟨she had discarded forever the ~*s* of youth —Ellen Glasgow⟩ **2 :** the act of alluring **3 :** the power or quality of alluring **:** ALLURE, FASCINATION, CHARM ⟨the fatal gift of ~ —Idwal Jones⟩

al·lur·er \-u̇rə(r)\ *n* -s **:** one that allures

alluring *adj* **:** marked by allure **:** ATTRACTIVE, ENTICING, TEMPTING ⟨not an ~ prospect⟩ ⟨declines any path, however ~, that does not commend itself to his intellect —Brand Blanshard⟩ ⟨a land of mystery, remote and ~⟩ — **al·lur·ing·ly** *adv* — **al·lur·ing·ness** *n* -ES

al·lu·sion \ə'lüzhən, a'- *sometimes* əl'yü- *or* al'yü-\ *n* -s [ML *allusion-, allusio*, fr. LL, playing with, fr. L *allusus* (past part. of *alludere* to play with, jest, refer to) + *-ion-, -io* -ion — more at ALLUDE] **1** *obs* **:** a figurative or symbolical reference **2 :** an implied indication or indirect reference **:** ALLUDING ⟨the English habit of understatement, of ~ —D.W.Brogan⟩ **3 a :** a reference usu. by indirection or implication or in passing esp. as utilized in literature ⟨with historical ~*s* on every page⟩ ⟨Pope's ~*s* to Horace⟩ **b :** the use of such reference esp. in poetry

al·lu·sive \-siv,-sēv *also* -z- *or* -əv\ *adj* [L *allusus* (past part. of *alludere* to allude) + E *-ive* — more at ALLUDE] **1** *archaic* **:** FIGURATIVE, SYMBOLICAL **2 a :** of, having the character of, or marked by allusion **b :** containing allusions ⟨~ writing⟩ **3 :** PUNNING — **al·lu·sive·ly** *adv* — **al·lu·sive·ness** *n* -ES

alluvia *pl of* ALLUVIUM

[1]al·lu·vi·al \ə'lüvēəl, -vyəl *also* a'- *or* əl'yü- *or* al'yü-\ *also* **al·lu·vi·an** \-ən\ *adj* [*alluvium* + *-al* or *-an*] **1 :** relating to or composed of alluvium ⟨~ soil⟩ ⟨an ~ divide⟩ **2 :** found in alluvium ⟨~ diamonds⟩

[2]alluvial \"\ *n* -s **1 a :** alluvial soil **b** *Austral* **:** gold-bearing alluvial soil **2 :** a mineral occurring in placer deposits

alluvial cone *n* **:** an alluvial fan with steep slopes

alluvial deposit *n* **:** ALLUVIUM

alluvial fan *n* **:** the fanlike deposit of a stream where it issues from a gorge upon a plain or of a tributary stream near or at its junction with its main stream

alluvial plain *n* **1 :** a level or gently sloping flat or a slightly undulating land surface resulting from extensive deposition of alluvial materials by running water **2 :** a plain formed by lateral coalescence of alluvial fans ⟨a piedmont *alluvial plain*⟩ — compare BAJADA

alluvial terrace *n* **:** a river terrace composed of alluvium rather than carved in solid rock, resulting from a change in the regimen of the stream from alluviation to downcutting

al·lu·vi·ate \-vē,āt, *usu* -ād·+V\ *vb* -ED/-ING/-S [*alluvium* + *-ate*] *vt* **:** to cover with alluvium ⟨an *alluviated* valley⟩ ~ *vi* **:** to deposit alluvium

al·lu·vi·a·tion \=,==ʹāshən\ *n* -s **:** the process that results in deposits of clay, silt, sand, or gravel at places in rivers or estuaries, or along the shores of lakes or seas, where stream velocity is decreased

al·lu·vio \=ʹ==,ō\ *n, pl* **alluvi·o·nes** \=,==ʹō(,)nēz\ [L] *Roman law* **:** ALLUVION

al·lu·vi·on \=ʹ==ən, -,än\ *n* -s [L *alluvion-, alluvio*, fr. *alluere* to wash against (fr. *ad-* + *-luere*, fr. *lavere* to wash) + *-ion-, -io* -ion — more at LYE] **1 :** the wash or flow of water against the shore or bank **2 :** an overflowing **:** INUNDATION, FLOOD **3 :** ALLUVIUM **4 :** an accession to land by the gradual addition of matter by the action of water or sometimes by the gradual reliction of the water from its bank, the land so added belonging to the owner of the land to which it is added; *also* **:** the land so added — compare ACCESSION 2c, ACCRETION 1c

al·lu·vi·ous \-vēəs\ *adj* [LL *alluvius*] **:** ALLUVIAL

al·lu·vi·um \-vēəm\ *n, pl* **alluviums** \-ēəmz\ *or* **allu·via** \-ēə\ [LL, neut. of *alluvius* alluvial, fr. L *alluere*] **:** clay, silt, sand, gravel, or similar detrital material deposited by running water esp. during recent geologic time, the deposits ordinarily occurring on the floodplains of streams or as alluvial fans or cones at places where streams issuing from mountains lose velocity and deposit their contained sediment on a valley floor

all-weather \ʹ=¦==\ *adj* **:** of or for all kinds of weather **:** usable, operative, or practiced in all kinds of weather ⟨a good *all-weather* highway⟩ ⟨*all-weather* flying⟩

allwhere *adv* [ME *al wher*, fr. *al* all + *wher* where] *archaic* **:** EVERYWHERE

allwhither \ʹ=¦==\ *adv* [[2]*all* + *whither*] **:** in all directions

[1]al·ly \ə'lī, a'lī, 'a,lī; '=,= *is most freq for the form "allied" — see* ALLIED\ *vb* -ED/-ING/-S [ME *allien*, fr. OF *alier*, fr. L *alligare* to bind to, fr. *ad-* + *ligare* to bind — more at LIGATURE] *vt* **1 :** to unite or form a connection between (as one family and another by marriage or two or more states by treaty) **:** join in association or alliance — usu. used with *with* or *to* ⟨has *allied* herself to the West to attain certain economic aspirations —*New Republic*⟩ ⟨were so closely *allied* by prewar economic agreements —Alan Valentine⟩ ⟨the powerful family with which he had *allied* himself by marriage⟩ **2 :** to connect or form a relation between (as by likeness, resemblance, or compatibility) **:** ASSOCIATE, RELATE — usu. used with *with* or *to* ⟨the song of the kinglet is the only characteristic that *allies* it to the wrens —John Burroughs⟩ ⟨fear is an unbecoming affliction, *allied* to boasting —Herbert Agar⟩ ⟨functions which are complementary and closely *allied*⟩ ⟨sentiments are *allied* to the desire to achieve new goals —George Wythe⟩ ~ *vi* **:** to form or enter into an alliance ⟨a completely independent country free to choose with whom she would ~⟩ ⟨persuade the nation to ~ with the other democracies⟩ ⟨he again *allied* with his friends —S.L.A.Marshall⟩

[2]al·ly \'a,lī, ə'lī, a'lī; '=,= *is much more freq than* ='= *for the pl, & somewhat more freq than* ='= *for the sing*\ *n* -ES [ME *allie*, fr. *allien*, v.] **1 a** *obs* **:** KINSMAN, RELATIVE **b :** a plant or animal linked to another by natural genetic or evolutionary relationship ⟨the honey bees and *allies* as well as the more distantly related ants⟩ ⟨ferns and their *allies*⟩ **2 a :** one usu. a sovereign or state united, banded, or associated with another in a common cause or by treaty or league ⟨the duke and his *allies*⟩ ⟨an eastern empire with strong western *allies*⟩ **:** one of the subjects or citizens so united **b allies** *pl, usu cap* **:** the nations allied against the Central Powers in World War I or against the Axis in World War II **3 :** someone or something associated with another as a helper **:** AUXILIARY, SUPPORTER ⟨let the teacher appear always the ~ of the pupil, not his natural enemy —Bertrand Russell⟩ ⟨gained an ~ in organized labor —D.E.Clark⟩ ⟨time is at once the enemy and the ~ of life —F.B.Millett⟩

[3]ally *var of* ALLEY

-al·ly \(ə)lē, (ə)li\ *adv suffix* [[1]*-al* + *-ly*] **:** [2]-LY ⟨semantic*ally*⟩ — in adverbs formed from adjectives in *-ic* with no alternative form in *-ical*

all-year \ʹ=¦=\ *adj* **:** lasting, available, or suitable throughout the year **:** the whole year round ⟨a healthful *all-year* climate⟩ ⟨an *all-year* resort community⟩

al·lyl \'alə̇l\ *n* -s [ISV *all-* (fr. L *allium* garlic) + *-yl* — more at ALLIUM] **1 :** an unsaturated univalent radical $CH_2=CHCH_2-$ derived from allyl alcohol by removal of the hydroxyl group **2 :** ISOPROPENYL — used with an initial Greek beta ⟨*β-allyl*⟩ — **al·lyl·ic** \ə'lilik, a'-\ *adj*

allyl alcohol *n* **:** a colorless pungent liquid $CH_2=CHCH_2OH$ made chiefly by hydrolysis of allyl chloride and polymerized to a viscous substance by heating in the presence of oxygen

allyl aldehyde *n* **:** ACROLEIN

al·lyl·amine \¦alələ¦mēn, ,alə'la,mēn, ə'lilə,mēn\ *n* -s [ISV *allyl* + *amine*] **:** a pungent strongly basic liquid $CH_2=CHCH_2NH_2$ formed variously (as by hydrolysis of allyl isothiocyanate)

al·lyl·ate \'alə,lāt\ *vt* -ED/-ING/-S [*allyl* + *-ate*] **:** to introduce allyl into

al·lyl·a·tion \,alə'lāshən\ *n* -s **:** the act or process of allylating

allyl chloride *n* **:** a volatile pungent toxic flammable liquid $CH_2=CHCH_2Cl$ made by high-temperature chlorination of propylene and used chiefly in making glycerol and allyl derivatives (as allyl alcohol and allyl resins)

al·lyl·ene \'alə,lēn\ *n* -s [ISV *allyl* + *-ene*] **1 :** METHYLACETYLENE **2 :** ALLENE 1

allylic rearrangement *n* **:** the migration of an ion or radical from one end of a 3-carbon allyl sequence to the other with concurrent shifting of the position of the double bond (as $CH_2=CHCHRX \rightarrow XCH_2CH=CHR$)

allyl isothiocyanate *or* **allyl mustard oil** *n* **:** a colorless pungent irritating liquid ester $CH_2=CHCH_2NCS$ that is the chief constituent of mustard oil (sense 1b) and is used as a flavoring agent and as a medical counterirritant

al·lyl·nor·mor·phine \¦alə̇l,nȯr'mȯr,fēn\ *n* -s [*allyl* + *nor-* + *morphine*] **:** a white crystalline compound $C_{19}H_{21}NO_3$ derived from morphine and used as a respiratory stimulant in poisoning by morphine and similar narcotic drugs — called also *N-allylnormorphine, nalorphine*

allyl resin *or* **allyl plastic** *n* **:** any of a group of thermosetting transparent abrasion-resistant synthetic resins or plastics made usu. from esters derived from allyl alcohol or allyl chloride and used chiefly in making cast products (as sheets) and low-pressure laminated products

allyl starch *n* **:** any of various allyl ethers of starch made from starch and allyl chloride for use in coatings, printing inks, and plastics

al·lyl·thi·ou·rea \¦alə̇l,-\ *n* -s [NL, fr. ISV *allyl* + NL *thiourea*] **:** a white crystalline compound $C_3H_5NHCSNH_2$ made from allyl isothiocyanate and ammonia and used in photography esp. as a sensitizing agent — called also *allylthiocarbamide, thiosinamine*

al·ma-ata \¦almə·ə¦tä\ *adj, usu cap both As* [fr. *Alma-Ata*, U.S.S.R.] **:** of or from Alma-Ata, a city of Soviet Central Asia, U.S.S.R. **:** of the kind or style prevalent in Alma-Ata

almacantar *var of* ALMUCANTAR

al·ma·ci·ga \al'mäsēgə, -,gä\ *n* -s [Sp *almáciga* mastic, fr. Ar *al-maṣṭakah* the mastic, fr. Gk *mastichē* — more at MASTIC] **1 :** a tall Philippine timber tree (*Agathis alba*) yielding a dammar resin **2 :** the resin yielded by the almaciga tree

al·ma·ci·go \-,gō\ *n* -s [AmerSp *almácigo*, fr. Sp, mastic tree, fr. *almáciga*] *in the West Indies* **:** GUMBO-LIMBO 1

al·ma·gest \'almə,jest\ *n* -s *sometimes cap* [ME *almageste*, fr. MF & ML, fr. Ar *al-majusti* the almagest, fr. *al* the + Gk *megistē* (*syntaxis*) greatest (composition), fem. of *megistos*, superl. of *megas* great — more at MUCH] **:** any of several great early medieval treatises on a branch of knowledge (as the 9th century Arabic translation of Ptolemy's Greek work on astronomy)

almain *sometimes cap, obs var of* ALLEMANDE

al·main rivets \'al,mān-, 'ȯl-\ *n pl* [obs. *Almaine* Germany, fr. ME, fr. MF, fr. LL *Alamannia* land of the Alamanni, fr. *Alamannus* member of the Alamanni + L *-ia*] *archaic* **:** a flexible light armor of overlapping plates sliding on rivets

al·ma ma·ter \¦almə¦mä|d·ə(r), -mȧ|, |tə- *also* ¦äl- *or* -mā-\ *n, pl* **alma maters** \-ə(r)z\ *also* **al·mae ma·tres** \¦al,mī-¦mä·,trās, ¦äl-, -mȧ-; ¦al(,)mē¦mā·(,)trēz\ [L, fostering mother (applied as a title to such goddesses as Ceres and Cybele)] **1 :** a school (as a college or university) which one has attended and usu. from which one has graduated **2 :** the song or hymn of a school or college

alman *often cap, obs var of* ALLEMANDE

al·ma·nac *also* **al·ma·nack** \'ȯlmə,nak, 'al- *also* 'äl- *or* -,nik\ *n* -s [ME *almenak*, fr. ML *almanach*, prob. fr. Ar *al-manākh* the almanac, calendar] **1 a :** a publication containing astronomical and meteorological data arranged according to the days, weeks, and months of a given year and often including a miscellany of other information **b :** a publication containing statistical, tabular, and general information (as on world events, an individual society, or a religious body) related to a given calendar period, usu. a year ⟨*Nat'l Catholic Almanac*⟩ ⟨*Information Please Almanac*⟩ **c :** a publication containing a collection of useful or otherwise interesting facts or statistics usu. in the form of tables and often covering the period of a given year ⟨*The World Almanac*⟩ **2 :** a publication containing data on royal and titled families of Europe

al·man·dine \'almən,dēn, -,dīn\ *n* -s [alter. (influenced by ML *alamandina*, alter. of *alabandina*, or G *almandin*, fr. ML) of earlier *alabandine*, fr. ME, fr. ML *alabandina, alabandinus*, fr. *Alabanda*, ancient city in Asia Minor where gems were cut and sold + L *-ina, -inus* -ine] **1 :** ALMANDITE **2 :** a violet variety of the ruby spinel or sapphire **3 :** the purple Indian garnet

al·man·dite \'almən,dīt\ *n* -s [alter. (influenced by E *-ite*) of *almandine*] **:** a deep red variety of garnet consisting of an iron aluminum silicate $Fe_3Al_2(SiO_4)_3$

almc *abbr* almanac

al·me·mar \al'mē,mär\ *or* **al·me·mor** \-ȯ(ə)r\ *n* -s [Heb *almēmār*, fr. Ar *al-minbar* the pulpit] **:** a platform in a Jewish synagogue bearing the reading desk from which are read the Pentateuch and the Prophets — called also *bema, bimah*

al·men·dro \al'men(,)drō, äl-\ *n* -s [AmerSp, fr. Sp, almond tree, modif. of (assumed) VL *amyndulus*, alter. of LL *amygdalus*, fr. Gk *amygdalos*, fr. *amygdalē* almond] **:** MALABAR ALMOND

al·me·ri·an \¦almə¦rēən\ *adj, usu cap A* [*Almería*, province of Spain + E *-an*] *archaeol* **:** of or relating to Neolithic and Aeneolithic cultures of Almería province, Spain

al·me·ri·ite \,almə'rē,īt\ *n* -s [Sp *almeriita*, fr. *Almería*, city and province in Spain, its locality + Sp *-ita* -ite] **:** NATROALUNITE

alm·ery \'ämərē, 'alm-\ *n* -ES [ME *almerie, almarie* — more at AMBRY] **:** AMBRY 1a

al·mi·core \'almə,kō(ə)r\ *n* -s [origin unknown] **:** AMBERJACK 1

al·might·i·ly \(')ȯl¦mīd·ᵊlē, -ītᵊl-, -ᵊli\ *adv* **:** in an almighty manner

al·might·i·ness \-d·|ēnə̇s, -t|, |i-\ *n* -ES **:** the quality of being almighty

[1]al·mighty \(')ȯl¦mīd·ē, -ītē; *in "God Almighty" sometimes* ᵊl'm-\ *adj* [ME (akin to OHG *alamahtīg*, ON *almāttigr*), fr. OE *ælmihtig, ealmihtig*, fr. *æl-, eal-* all (akin to OE *eall* all) + *mihtig* mighty — more at ALL, MIGHTY] **1 a** *often cap* **:** having absolute power over all — used esp. of God **b :** relatively unlimited in power ⟨~ armies swept over the country⟩ **2** *slang* **:** very bad **:** EXTREME ⟨he's in one ~ fix⟩

[2]almighty \"\ *n* -ES *cap* **:** GOD — used with *the*

[3]almighty \"\ *adv, slang* **:** EXTREMELY ⟨~ cold⟩ ⟨took an ~ long time to make up his mind⟩

al·mi·que \¦almə¦kē\ *n* -s [modif. of AmerSp *almiqui*] **:** an acana (*Manilkara albescens*) with hard compact heavy deep red wood

al·mi·rah \al'mīrə\ *n* -s [Hindi *almārī*, fr. Pg *almario, armario*, fr. L *armarium* — more at AMBRY] *India* **:** CABINET, WARDROBE

al·mo·had \'almə,had\ *or* **al·mo·hade** \", -,hād, ,almə'hädē\ *n* -s *usu cap* [Ar *al-muwaḥḥid* the Almohad] **:** a member of a Muslim Berber sect and dynasty that established its rule in No. Africa and Spain in the 12th and 13th centuries, opposed anthropomorphic theology, and taught the absolute unity of God

al·moign *or* **al·moin** \(')al¦mȯin\ *n* -s [ME *almoyn*, fr. AF *almoigne*, fr. (assumed) VL *alemosina* alms — more at ALMONER] **:** FRANKALMOIGN

al·mon \'al,mōn\ *n* -s [Bisayan] **:** a tall Philippine timber tree (*Shorea eximia*) with soft yellowish white wood — called also *Philippine mahogany*

al·mond \'ämənd, 'a(l)m-,'ȧm- *also* 'älm- *or* 'ȧlm- *sometimes* 'ȯ(l)m-\ *n* -s *often attrib* [ME *almande*, fr. OF, fr. LL *amandula*, alter. of L *amygdala*, fr. Gk *amygdalē*] **1 :** the drupaceous fruit of a small tree (*Prunus amygdalus* syn. *Amygdalus communis*); *esp* **:** the ellipsoidal slightly compressed nutlike stone or kernel of this tree differing from the peach in having a dry instead of pulpy epicarp so that the nut or kernel is really the stone of the fruit — see ALMOND MEAL, AMYGDALIN **2 :** any tree that bears almonds **3 :** the fruit of any one of several trees in shape or flavor somewhat resembling the almond **4 :** any plant that bears almonds (sense 3) — usu. used with a descriptive attributive ⟨Malabar ~⟩ **5 :** an almond flavoring **6 a** *or* **almond brown :** a light grayish yellowish brown that is stronger and slightly redder and darker than gravel — called also *doe, pawnee, wood* **b :** a pale to moderate orange yellow

almond cake *n* **:** the residue of almonds from which the oil has been expressed

almond extract *n* **:** an alcoholic extract of macerated kernels (as of almonds, apricots, or peaches) used for flavoring

almond eye *n* **:** a somewhat triangular obliquely set eye ⟨a beautiful dark-skinned girl with the *almond eyes* of a Mongolian⟩; *specif, of dogs* **:** a slit-shaped eye (as in the bull terrier) with the outer corner pointing toward the ear

almond green *n* **:** a variable color averaging a moderate yellowish green that is greener and less strong than tarragon, duller than malachite green, and duller and slightly yellower than verdigris

almond-leaved willow \'==,=-\ *n* **:** PEACHLEAF WILLOW

almondlike \'==,=\ *adj* **:** resembling an almond

almond meal *n* **1 :** a powder obtained by grinding or pounding blanched almonds and used as an ingredient of various cosmetics and perfumes **2 :** ground almond cake

almond milk *n* **:** an emulsion (as from blanched almonds, acacia, sugar, and water) used as a demulcent

almond moth *n* **:** a small grayish brown-marked moth (*Cadra cautella*) having a larva that feeds on and mats together with webbing a variety of stored products of vegetable origin — called also *fig moth*

almond oil *n* **1 a :** a colorless or pale yellow bland and nearly odorless nondrying fatty oil expressed from sweet or bitter almonds and used as an emollient in pharmaceuticals and cosmetics and as a lubricant for delicate mechanisms (as in watches) — called also *expressed almond oil, sweet almond oil* **b :** a colorless to yellow essential oil owing its characteristic odor and flavor to benzaldehyde and its toxicity to hydrocyanic acid that is obtained from bitter almonds by steam distillation of almond cake or almond meal after decomposition of the amygdalin present and that is used in medicine (as for certain skin disorders) and after removal of the hydrocyanic acid as a flavoring agent — called also *bitter almond oil* **2 :** any of certain essential oils very similar in properties and uses to bitter almond oil and obtained from kernels other than almonds that contain amygdalin (as apricot and peach kernels) — called also *bitter almond oil* **3 :** BENZALDEHYDE

almond pink *or* **almond blossom** *n* **:** a pale pink

almonds *pl of* ALMOND

almond willow *n* **1 :** an Old World willow (*Salix amygdalina*) that has light green leaves and is cultivated for use in basketry — called also *black Hollander* **2 :** PEACHLEAF WILLOW

almondwood \'==,=\ *n* **:** a dark brown close-textured chittagong wood (*Chickrassia tabularia*) with lustrous surface

al·mondy \-dē\ *adj* **:** like an almond

al·mo·ner \'almənə(r), 'äm-\ *n* -s [ME *aumener*, fr. OF *aumosnier, almosnier*, fr. *aumosne, almosne* alms, fr. (assumed) VL *alemosina*, alter. of LL *eleemosyna* — more at ALMS] **1 :** one that distributes alms **2 :** a onetime official of a monastery or almshouse charged with distributing alms; *also* **:** one that dispenses alms for another ⟨the ~ of a king⟩ **3** *Brit* **:** a social-service worker in a hospital

al·mo·ning \-niŋ\ *n* -s [*almoner* + *-ing*] *Brit* **:** medical social work

al·mon·ry \-nrē\ *n* -ES [MF *almosnerie*, fr. OF, fr. *almosnier* + *-ie* -y] **:** a usu. ecclesiastical building set aside for the distribution of alms

almons *pl of* ALMON

al·mo·ra·vid \,almə'rävə̇d, al'mōrəv-\ *or* **al·mo·ra·vide** \,=='=və̇d, ='==,vīd\ *n* -s *usu cap* [Ar *al-murābiṭ* lit., the inhabitant of a fortified convent] **:** a member of a Muslim dynasty of No. African natives that flourished 1049–1145, led a religious reform along orthodox Islamic lines, and established political dominance over northwestern Africa and Spain

[1]al·most \(')ȯl¦mōst, -ȯ(u̇)¦m- *also* '=,məst\ *adv* [ME *almost, almest*, fr. OE *almǣst, ealmǣst*, fr. *al-, eal-* all (akin to OE *eall*) + *mǣst* most — more at ALL, MOST] **1 a :** close to the total of ⟨~ all the warriors were heathens⟩ **:** with few exceptions ⟨~ every man⟩ **b :** by far the greater part of ⟨~ the entire book⟩ **:** excepting only a small or minor section ⟨fire destroyed ~ the whole town⟩ **2 a :** not actually but very close to being **:** not really but deceptively near ⟨a cry ~ human⟩ **b :** what would amount to being ⟨he was after all ~ a failure⟩ **:** what would essentially approximate ⟨he paid ~ nothing for it⟩ **3 :** more than just approximately ⟨~ identical plans of attack⟩ **:** lacking by very little in being exactly ⟨~ half of the money⟩ **:** all but absolutely or utterly ⟨~ unique⟩

[2]almost \"\ *adj* **:** very close to being a ⟨an ~ bullseye⟩ **:** nearly a ⟨an ~ failure⟩ **:** NEAR

al·mous \'ȧməs, 'ȯ-\ *n, pl* **almous** [ME (northern dial.) *almouse, almus, awmus*, fr. ON *almusa, ölmusa*, fr. OS *almōsa* or OHG *alamuosan* — more at ALMS] *dial Brit* **:** ALMS

alms \'ä|mz, 'ȧ| *also* |lmz; *sporadic & old-fash* 'amz\ *n, pl* **alms** [ME *almesse, almes*, fr. OE *ælmesse, ælmes;* akin to OS *almōsa*, MD *aelmoese*, OHG *alamuosan;* all fr. a prehistoric WGmc word borrowed fr. LL *eleemosyna*, fr. Gk *eleēmosynē* pity, alms, fr. *eleos* pity] **1** *archaic* **a :** CHARITY ⟨such virtues as ~ and mercy⟩ **b :** charitable deeds ⟨when thou doest ~, let not thy left hand know what thy right hand doeth —Mt 6:3 (AV)⟩ **2 :** anything given freely to relieve the poor (as money, food, or clothing) **:** a charitable gift — usu. pl. in constr. **3 :** an offering of money received from the congregation during an Anglican religious service and usu. presented at the altar by the minister

alms basin *n* **:** a large plate on which the total offering received at a church service is presented at the altar

alms chest *n* **:** a box with a hole for alms and with three locks

alms·deed \'=,=\ *n* [ME *almesdede*, fr. *almes, almesse* + *dede* deed] **1** *archaic* **:** an act of giving alms ⟨this woman was full of good works and ~*s* —Acts 9:36 (AV)⟩ **2** *obs* **:** habitual practice of giving alms

alms dish *n* **1 :** a dish in which alms are collected **2 :** ALMS BASIN

alms fee *n* [trans. of OE *ælmesfēoh*, fr. *ælmes, ælmesse* alms + *fēoh* fee] **:** PETER'S PENCE

almsgiving \'=,==\ *n* **:** the giving of alms esp. as an habitual practice ⟨remarkably generous in his ~⟩

almshouse \'=,=\ *n* [ME *almeshous*, fr. *almes, almesse* + *hous* house] **1 :** a section of medieval religious houses set aside for distribution of alms **2 a** *Brit* **:** a privately financed home for the poor **b** *archaic* **:** POORHOUSE, WORKHOUSE

alms·man \-zmən\ *n, pl* **alms·men** [ME *almesman*, fr. OE *ælmesman*, fr. *ælmes, ælmesse* + *man*] **:** a recipient of alms

al·mu·can·tar \¦almyü¦kantə(r)\ *also* **al·ma·can·tar** \-mə-\ *n* -s [alter. (prob. influenced by ML *almucantarath*) of earlier *almicanter*, fr. ME *almicanteras* (pl.), fr. MF *almicantarath*, fr. ML *almicantarath, almucantarath*, fr. Ar *al-muqanṭarāt* the almucantars, fr. *al-* the + *muqanṭarāt*, pl. of *muqanṭarah* almucantar, sundial, fr. *qanṭarah* bridge, arch] **1 :** a small circle of the celestial sphere parallel to the horizon and connecting all points of equal altitude ⟨two stars on the same ~⟩ **2 :** a telescope mounted on a mercurial float and used for observing the heavenly bodies as they cross a given almucantar

almucantar staff *n* **:** an ancient instrument having an arc of 15 degrees and used at sea to take observations of the sun's amplitude and to find the variation of the compass

al·muce \'al,myüs\ *n* -s [MF *almuce, aumuce* — more at AMICE] **:** an ecclesiastical hood lined with fur worn commonly in the pre-Reformation era by canons and also by various other ecclesiastics

al·mud \(')al¦müd\ *or* **al·mu·de** \al'müdə\ *n* -s [Sp *almud* & Pg *almude*, fr. Ar *al-mudd*, a dry measure] **:** any of various old Portuguese and Spanish units of capacity varying as a dry measure from about 2 to 21 quarts and as a liquid measure from about 5 to 32 quarts

al·muer·zo \äl'mwer(,)sō\ *n* -s [Sp, fr. (assumed) VL *admordium*, fr. L *admordēre* to bite into, fr. *ad-* + *mordēre* to bite — more at SMART] *Southwest* **:** the first substantial meal of the day taken usu. just before noon

almug *var of* ALGUM

alnage *n* -s [ME *aulnage*, fr. MF, fr. *aulner* to measure by the ell (fr. *aulne* ell, of Gmc origin, akin to OHG *elina* ell) + *-age* — more at ELL] *old Eng law* **:** measurement of cloth by the ell esp. with official inspection and certification; *also* **:** a fee for such measurement

alnager *n* -s [*alnage* + *-er*] **:** a onetime officer in England whose duty it was to inspect and attest the measure and quality of woolen cloth

al·ni·co \'alnə,kō, -nē-; al'ni(,)kō\ *n* -s [*al*uminum + *ni*ckel + *co*balt] **:** a powerful permanent-magnet alloy containing iron, nickel, aluminum, and one or more of the elements cobalt, copper, and titanium

al·no·ite \'alnə,wīt\ *n* -s [G *alnöit*, fr. *Alnö*, island of Sweden, its locality + G *-it* -ite] **:** a rare basaltic dike rock of the composition of a melilite-basalt having phenocrysts of biotite, augite, and olivine in a groundmass of melilite and augite

al·nus \'alnəs\ *n* [NL, fr. L, alder — more at ALDER] **1** *cap* **:** a genus of alders (family Betulaceae) found in the north temperate zone and the Andes and having toothed leaves, a 4-parted calyx, and a woody conelike fruit **2** -s **:** any plant of the genus *Alnus*

al·o·ca·sia \,alə'kāzh(ē)ə\ *n* [NL, alter. of *Colocasia*] **1** *cap* **:** a genus of tropical Asiatic herbs (family Araceae) with basal long-petioled often showy leaves, a glaucous boat-shaped spathe, and reddish berries **2** -s **:** a plant of the genus *Alocasia*

al·o·cin·ma \,alə'sinmə\ *n, cap* [NL] **:** a genus of Asiatic pulmonate snails (family Helicidae) including a species (*A. longicornis*) which may serve as an intermediate host of the Chinese liver fluke

al·od *or* **al·lod** \'a,läd, 'aləd\ *n* -s [prob. fr. F *alode, allode*, fr. ML *alodium, allodium*] **:** ALODIUM

¹alo·di·al *or* **al·lo·di·al** \ə'lōdēəl, a'-\ *adj* [ML *allodialis*, fr. *allodium* + L *-alis* -al] **:** of or relating to alodium

²alodial *or* **allodial** \"\ *n* -s **:** land or property held in alodium

alo·di·al·ism *or* **al·lo·di·al·ism** \-,lizəm\ *n* -s **:** the alodial system

alo·di·al·ist *or* **al·lo·di·al·ist** \-ləst\ *n* -s **:** a proprietor holding an alodium

alo·di·al·i·ty *or* **al·lo·di·al·i·ty** \ə,lōdē'alədē, (,)a,l-\ *n* -ES **:** the quality or state of being alodial

alo·di·al·ly *or* **al·lo·di·al·ly** \ə'lōdēəlē, a'-\ *adv* **:** by alodial tenure

alo·di·ary *or* **al·lo·di·ary** \-dē,erē\ *n* -ES [ML *allodiarius*, fr. *allodium* + L *-arius* -ary] **:** one that holds an alodium

alod·i·fi·ca·tion *or* **al·lod·i·fi·ca·tion** \ə,lädəfə'kāshən, (,)a,l-\ *n* -s [*alodium, allodium* + *-fication*] **:** the change in the title to lands from feudal tenure to complete ownership

alo·di·um *or* **al·lo·di·um** \ə'lōdēəm, a'-\ *n* -s [ML, fr. OHG (Franconian) *alōd*, fr. *al* all + *-ōd* property (akin to OE *ēad* property, OS *ōd*, OHG *ōtac* rich, ON *authr* property, Goth *audags* blessed)] **1 :** a form of estate among 11th century Anglo-Saxons in which absolute possession and control were vested in the holder — opposed to *feodum* **2** *usu* **allodium :** land that is the absolute property of the owner **:** real estate held in absolute independence without being subject to any rent, service, or acknowledgment to a superior

al·oe *in sense 2* 'alə,wē, *in other senses* 'a(,)lō, *pl* 'a(,)lōz *or* 'aləz\ *n* [ME, agalloch, fr. LL, fr. L, dried juice of aloe leaves, fr. Gk *aloē* dried juice of aloe leaves, agalloch, prob. fr. a Sem word akin to Heb *ăhālīm, ăhālōth*, perh. fr. Skt *agaru*, prob. of Dravidian origin; akin to Tamil *akil* agalloch] **1 aloes** *pl* **:** AGALLOCH **2** [NL, fr. ML, aloe plant, fr. L, dried juice of aloe leaves] *cap* **:** a genus of succulent chiefly southern African plants (family Liliaceae) having basal leaves with a hemplike fiber and spicate often showy flowers **3** [ME, fr. ML, fr. L, dried juice of aloe leaves] -s **:** a plant of the genus *Aloe* **4** [ME, fr. L] -s **:** the dried bitter juice of the leaves of a plant of the genus *Aloe* used as a purgative, tonic, and emmenagogue — usu. pl. but sing. in constr. **5** -s **:** any of several plants of the genus *Furcraea* **6** *or* **aloes** *or* **aloes green :** a pale green that is stronger and slightly bluer than celadon gray, yellower and darker than spray green, and yellower, stronger, and slightly lighter than bayberry gray

an aloe (*Aloe succotrina*): *1* entire plant, *2* single flower

al·oe–em·o·din \,alə'wemədən, 'a,lō'e-, -dᵊn\ *n* -s **:** an orange-yellow crystalline compound $C_{15}H_{10}O_5$ derived from anthraquinone and obtained from many species of aloes, rhubarb, and senna leaves

aloe hemp *n* **1 :** any plant of the genus *Agave* that yields a hemplike fiber **2 :** BOWSTRING HEMP

al·oe·root \'=(,)=,=\ *n* **:** COLICROOT

al·oes·wood \'=(,)=,=\ *n* **:** AGALLOCH

alo·et·ic \,alə'wed·ik\ *adj* [*aloe* + *-etic* (as in *diuretic*)] **:** using, consisting of, containing, or belonging to aloes ⟨~ medicines⟩

al·oe·wood \'=(,)=,=\ *n* **:** GEIGER TREE

¹aloft \ə'lȯft *also* -äft\ *adv* [ME *aloft, alofte* fr. ON *ā lopt, ā lopti*, fr. *ā* on, in + *lopt, lopti*, acc. & dat. respectively of *lopt* air, sky — more at ON, LOFT] **1 a :** in the higher atmosphere above the earth ⟨weather conditions ~ are poor⟩ **b :** at a relatively great height **:** high up ⟨huge black buzzards hovered ~ —H.E.Rieseberg⟩ **2 a :** up into the air **:** away from or off the ground ⟨the air is filled with dust whirled ~ —P.E. James⟩ **b :** upward from an inferior position or from a depressing mood ⟨this happy news sent their spirits soaring ~⟩ **c :** in the air; *esp* **:** in flight (as of an airplane) ⟨an airline famous for the wonderful meals served ~⟩ **3** *naut* **:** at, on, or to the masthead or the higher rigging ⟨going ~ to unfurl the lighter sails —H.A.Chippendale⟩ **4** *archaic* **:** on or at the top ⟨a ladder with a man ~⟩

²aloft *prep* [ME *alofte*, fr. *alofte*, adv.] **1** *obs* **:** on the top of **2** *obs* **:** ABOVE, OVER ⟨they bear her still ~ men's heads —George Chapman⟩

alo·gi \(')ā'lō,gī, -lä-,-lō-\ *n pl, usu cap* [ML, fr. LGk *Alogoi*, pl. of *Alogos* (after Gk *alogos* absurd, speechless), fr. Gk *a-* ²a- + *logos* word of God, word, reason — more at LEGEND] **:** the early opponents of the Logos doctrine expressed in the Gospel of John and in the book of Revelation

alo·gia \(')ā'lōj(ē)ə\ *n* -s [NL, fr. LL, fr. Gk, fr. *alogos* speechless, absurd (fr. *a-* ²a- + *logos* word, reason) + *-ia*] **:** inability to speak esp. when caused by a brain lesion

alo·gi·an \(')ā'lāgēən, -lō-,-lō-\ *n* -s *usu cap* **:** one of the Alogi

alog·i·cal \(')ā'läjəkəl, -ēk-\ *adj* [²a- + *logical*] **:** outside the bounds of that to which logic can apply — **alog·i·cal·ly** \-k(ə)lē, -li\ *adv*

al·o·gism \'alə,jizəm\ *n* -s [LL *alogia* unreasonableness (fr. Gk, fr. *a-* ²a- + *-logia* -logy) + E *-ism*] **1 :** anything that is contrary or indifferent to logic; *specif* **:** an irrational statement or piece of reasoning **2 :** a view that denies to thought a place in the valid and final apprehension of reality

alo·ha \ə'lōə, ä'-,ə'-,ä'-; ä'lō,hä, ä'lō,há, ə'-, a'-\ *n* -s [Hawaiian] **:** LOVE, AFFECTION, KINDNESS — often used to express greeting or farewell

aloha party *n* **:** a farewell party (as in Hawaii); *also* **:** a party to welcome newcomers or visitors (as to Hawaii)

aloha shirt *n* **:** a loose brightly colored Hawaiian sport shirt

al·o·in \'aləwən\ *n* -s [*aloe* + *-in*] **:** a bitter yellow crystalline cathartic obtained from the aloe and containing one or more glycosides (as barbaloin and isobarbaloin) and used for the same purposes as aloes

alo·isi·ite \,alə'wi,shīt, -wis(h)ē,īt\ *n* -s [Prince Luigi (*Aloisius*) Amedeo †1933 duke of the Abruzzi + E *-ite*] **:** a mineral consisting of a hydrous subsilicate of calcium, ferrous iron, magnesium, and sodium occurring in amorphous brown-to-violet masses

alo·ma \ə'lōmə\ *n* -s [origin unknown] **:** a light brown to yellowish brown that is darker than bran and duller than pablo

alombrado *usu cap, var of* ALUMBRADO

¹alone \ə'lōn\ *adj* [ME *alon, alone*, fr. *al* all + *on, one* one] **1 a :** separated esp. physically from all other individuals or groups **:** ISOLATED ⟨the girl, intently listening, was ~ with her fear —G.D.Brown⟩ — usu. used predicatively or postpositively **b :** away from others of one's own kind ⟨~ except for his new gun and Ned, the setter —S.V.Benét⟩ **2 a :** exclusive of anyone or anything else **:** without anyone or anything else **:** ONLY ⟨Jack ~ arrived⟩ ⟨learning ~ produces not a university but a research institute —J.B.Conant⟩ **b :** considered apart and without reference to anyone or anything else ⟨in that country ~ 20 million bushels were produced⟩ **c :** lacking relative, friend, or helper ⟨a widow ~ in the world⟩ **d :** lacking the presence or support of those that are congenial to one's interests, temperament, viewpoint, or way of life ⟨~ in a crowded room⟩ **e :** lacking those that share one's situation ⟨he was not ~ in his ignorance⟩ **3 a :** lacking an equal or rival **:** INCOMPARABLE ⟨Hercules stood ~ in strength⟩ **b :** possessing radically distinctive qualities not found in others **:** UNIQUE ⟨of all the suggestions advanced, this theory is altogether ~ in its penetration of the problem⟩ **c :** acting without the influence or contribution of other factors ⟨that job ~ will take all your time⟩

syn SOLITARY, LONELY, LONESOME, LONE, LORN, FORLORN, DESOLATE may all refer to situations of being apart from others or emotions experienced while apart. In addition to indicating the physical fact of being apart, ALONE, less rich in suggestion than the other words, may connote feelings of isolation from others ⟨the captain of a ship at sea is a remote, inaccessible creature, something like a prince of a fairy tale, *alone* of his kind —Joseph Conrad⟩ SOLITARY may indicate a state of being apart that is desired and sought for ⟨Netta loved these *solitary* interludes . . . she could dream things there and tell herself stories there, untroubled —J.C.Powys⟩ It may lack connotation ⟨being *solitary* he could only address himself to the waiter —Virginia Woolf⟩ It may be used in indicating sadness at a lack of close intimate connections ⟨an only child, he was left *solitary* by the early death of his mother, Susan Sturgis, whose loss he felt severely —J.F.Fulton⟩ Sometimes LONELY simply indicates the fact of being alone ⟨he was *lonely*, but not in an unhappy sense . . . it was no hardship for him to be alone —H.S.Canby⟩ Sometimes it indicates a sense of isolation, often from intimate relatives or friends ⟨his grim look, his pride, his silence, his wild outbursts of passion, left William *lonely* even in his court —J.R.Green⟩ It may apply to feelings of deep sorrow and bereavement ⟨he felt more *lonely* and forsaken than at any time since his father's death —Archibald Marshall⟩ LONESOME, often more poignant, suggests sadness after a separation or bereavement ⟨you must keep up your spirits, mother, and not be *lonesome* when I'm not at home —Charles Dickens⟩ ⟨her flight . . . yet smote my *lonesome* heart more than all misery —P.B.Shelley⟩ LONE may indicate the mere fact of being alone ⟨in his *lone* course the shepherd oft will pause —William Wordsworth⟩ It may indicate a lack of close relatives ⟨the mother's dead and I reckon it's got no father; it's a *lone* thing —George Eliot⟩ LORN, now humorous or literary, suggests recent separation or bereavement ⟨when *lorn* lovers sit and droop —W.M.Praed⟩ FORLORN indicates dejection, woe, and listlessness at separation from someone dear ⟨as *forlorn* and stupefied as I was when my husband's spirit flew away —Thomas Hardy⟩ ⟨as *forlorn* as King Lear at the end of his days —G.W.Johnson⟩ DESOLATE is most extreme in suggesting inconsolable grief at loss or bereavement ⟨fatherless, a *desolate* orphan —S.T.Coleridge⟩ ⟨for her false mate has fled and left her *desolate* —P.B.Shelley⟩ SOLITARY, LONELY, LONESOME, and DESOLATE are applied to places and locations more than the other words are. SOLITARY may be applied either to that which is apart from things similar or to that which is uninhabited or unvisited by human beings ⟨a *solitary* chamber, or rather a cell, at the top of the house, and separated from all the other apartments by a gallery and staircase —Mary W. Shelley⟩ LONELY may be applied to what is either far apart from things similar and seldom visited or to that which is inhabited by only one person or group and conducive to loneliness ⟨heard not only in the towns but even in *lonely* farmhouses —Sherwood Anderson⟩ LONESOME has much the same suggestion. DESOLATE indicates either that a place is abandoned by people or that it is so barren and wild as never to have attracted them ⟨as if nothing had life by day, in that lifeless *desolate* spot —Anthony Trollope⟩

²alone \"\ *adv* [ME *alon, alone*, fr. *al* all + *on, one* one] **:** SOLELY, SIMPLY, EXCLUSIVELY; *often* **:** without the aid or support of another ⟨the proof does not rest ~ on that statement⟩ ⟨he said he could do it ~⟩

alonely *adv* [ME *alonly*, fr. *al* all + *only*] *obs* **:** ²ALONE

alone·ness *n* -ES **:** the state of being alone

¹along \ə'lȯŋ *also* -äŋ\ *prep* [ME, fr. OE *andlang, ondlang*, fr. *and-, ond-* against + *lang* long — more at ANTE-, LONG] **1 :** over the length of (a surface) ⟨he crawled ~ the fence until he reached the gate⟩ ⟨halfway ~ the street they stopped⟩ **2 :** in the course of (as time or distance) ⟨somewhere ~ the years —Ben Riker⟩ **3 :** in a line parallel with the length or direction of ⟨a ship sailing ~ the coast⟩ or on a line through the center or central axis of ⟨the boundary runs ~ the road⟩ — distinguished from *across* **4 :** in accordance with **:** IN ⟨research ~ certain specific lines —R.E.Barnaby⟩

²along \"\ *adv* [ME, fr. *along*, prep] **1 a :** onward with progressive movement **:** FORWARD, AHEAD, ON ⟨hurrying their education ~⟩ ⟨you'll see the hill as you ride ~⟩ ⟨rushing ~ through the speech⟩ — see COME ALONG, GET ALONG, GO ALONG **b :** on the way **:** OFF ⟨send a gift ~ to a friend⟩ **2 a :** in a line parallel with the length or direction — usu. used with *by* ⟨cottages ~ by the river⟩ **b :** down the line **:** from one to another ⟨word was passed ~ that the attack was coming⟩ **3 a** *obs* **:** at full length **:** LENGTHWISE ⟨Saul fell straightway all ~ on the earth —1 Sam 28:20 (AV)⟩ ⟨there lay he stretched ~ like a wounded knight —Shak.⟩ **b :** for the whole length — used with *all* ⟨the wall had crumbled all ~⟩; *specif* **:** with the thread stitches of a book passed direct from two opposed kettle stitches — used with *all* ⟨to handsew a book or section all ~⟩ **4 a :** in company or as company **:** as a companion ⟨he brought his wife ~⟩ — often used with *with* ⟨walking the fields ~ with his dog⟩ **b :** in association or accord — used with *with* ⟨working ~ with his colleagues⟩ **5 a :** at a loosely fixed point within a specified or implied extent of time, distance, or development — usu. used with *about* ⟨~ about the time the first leaves fall —*Saturday Rev.*⟩ ⟨~ about July 25⟩ **b :** at or to an advanced point; *esp* **:** at or to a point marked by a notable passage of time, increase of distance, or furtherance of development ⟨the morning was well ~⟩ ⟨farther ~ toward the goalpost⟩ ⟨plans are now far ~⟩ **c :** during the whole period **:** all the time — used with *all* ⟨the police knew all ~ who was guilty⟩ **6 :** in addition **:** ALSO ⟨food was sent to them and clothing went ~ in the package⟩ — often used with *with* ⟨a bill came ~ with the merchandise⟩ **7 :** in possession **:** at hand **:** as part of the equipment **:** as a necessary item, part, or feature ⟨the sheriff had his gun ~⟩ — often used with *with* ⟨a plane carrying heavy radar equipment ~ with full fuel tanks⟩ **8 :** in company **:** on hand **:** THERE ⟨sorry you weren't ~⟩ ⟨tell him I'll be ~ to see him⟩

along of *prep* [ME *along* (construed with *on*), alter. of *ilong* (construed with *on*), fr. OE *gelang* (construed with *on, æt*), fr. *ge-*, associative prefix + *lang* long — more at CO-, LONG] **1** *dial* **:** because of **:** on account of ⟨it's all *along of* mother leaving us like this —Joseph Conrad⟩ **2** *dial* **a :** WITH ⟨you come in here *along of* me —Richard Llewellyn⟩ **b :** TO ⟨they belong *along of* Snug here —G.A.Chamberlain⟩

¹alongshore \=¦=¦=\ *adv* (*or adj*) [¹*along* + *shore*] **:** along the shore or coast ⟨~ currents⟩ ⟨there are many trees ~⟩

²alongshore \=¦=,=\ *n* -s **:** WATERFRONT

¹alongside \=¦=¦=\ *adv* [¹*along* + *side*] **1 :** along the side **:** in parallel position ⟨a small cabin with logs piled ~⟩ **2 :** in company **:** at the side **:** close to ⟨a guard with his prisoner ~⟩

²alongside \"\ *prep* **1 a :** along the side of **:** at the side of or parallel to ⟨the tug drew up ~ the freighter⟩ **b :** in combination or company with **:** along with ⟨a pleasure to work ~ such men⟩ **2 :** in a position or manner comparable with ⟨a new writer who takes his place ~ the best⟩

alongside of *prep* **1 a :** side by side with **:** parallel to ⟨a car parked *alongside of* the curb⟩ **b :** in company with **:** at the side of ⟨the son fought *alongside of* his father⟩ **2 :** in comparison with ⟨a player who can stand up well *alongside of* the best⟩

alongst \ə'lȯŋ(k)st, -äŋ-, -ŋzt\ *adv or prep* [ME *alongest*, alter. of *alonges*, alter. (influenced by *-es* -s) of *along*] *dial* **:** ALONG

alon·soa \ə'länzəwə, -n(t)sə-\ *n, cap* [NL, fr. Zanoni *Alonso fl* 1798 Sp. official at Bogotá, Colombia] **:** a genus of often shrubby tropical American plants (family Scrophulariaceae) with showy red flowers in terminal racemes

¹aloof \ə'lüf\ *adv* [¹a + *loof*, var. of *luff* (side of a ship)] **1** *obs* **:** to windward ⟨keeping the ship ~⟩ **2** *archaic* **a :** from a distance ⟨barely visible, the mountains loomed up ~⟩ **b :** at a distance ⟨trying to keep failure ~⟩

²aloof \"\ *adj* **:** removed or distant either physically or spiritually and usu. by choice and with indifference to the feelings, opinions, or interests of others **:** APART, REMOTE ⟨he stood ~ from worldly success —John Buchan⟩ ⟨holding herself ~ in chosen loneliness —P.E.More⟩ ⟨a severe, ~ building —Green Peyton⟩ ⟨the ~ composer neither worried nor cared about public opinion —Mary Jane Matz⟩ **syn** see INDIFFERENT

³aloof *prep, obs* **:** away from **:** clear from

aloofly *adv* **:** in an aloof manner

aloof·ness *n* -ES **:** the quality or state of being aloof

al·o·pe·cia \,alə'pēsh(ē)ə\ *n* -s [alter. of ME *allopicia, allopucia* baldness, leprosy, fr. L *alopecia* baldness, fr. Gk *alōpekia* baldness, mange on foxes, fr. *alōpek-, alōpēx* fox + *-ia* — more at VULPINE] **:** loss of the hair, wool, or feathers **:** BALDNESS — **al·o·pe·cic** \¦=¦=¦sik\ *adj*

alopecia ar·e·a·ta \-,arē'ād·ə, -ē'ä-\ *n* [NL, circumscribed baldness] **:** sudden loss of hair in circumscribed patches accompanied by little or no inflammation

alop·e·coid \ə'läpə,kȯid\ *adj* [Gk *alōpekoeidēs*, fr. *alōpek-, alōpēx* fox + *-oeidēs* -oid] **:** like a fox **:** VULPINE

alop·e·cu·rus \ə,läpə'kyurəs, ,aləpə-\ *n, cap* [NL, fr. Gk *alōpekouros* beard grass (*Polypogon monspeliensis*), fr. *alōpek-, alōpēx* fox + *-ouros* -urous] **:** a genus of grasses found in temperate regions and having slender culms, flat leaves, and soft spikes — see MEADOW FOXTAIL

alo·pex \ə'lō,peks, 'alə,p-\ *n, cap* [NL, fr. Gk *alōpēx* fox — more at VULPINE] **:** a genus (family Canidae) comprising the arctic foxes

alo·pi·as \ə'lōpēəs\ *n, cap* [NL, modif. of Gk *alōpekias* thresher shark] **:** a monotypic genus of elasmobranch fishes that comprises the thresher sharks and is usu. included in the Lamnidae but sometimes made the type and sole representative of a separate family

al·o·rese \¦alə¦rēz, -ēs\ *n, pl* **alorese** *cap* [*Alor* island, Indonesia + E *-ese*] **:** an Indonesian native or resident of Alor Island in the Lesser Sundas, Indonesia

alo·sa \ə'lōsə\ *n, cap* [NL, fr. LL *alosa, alausa*] **:** a genus of fishes (family Clupeidae) comprising the shads

al·ou·at·ta \,alə'wad·ə\ *n, cap* [NL, fr. F *alouate*] **:** a genus of the howler monkeys

al·ou·atte \¦alə¦wat\ *n* -s [F *alouate*, of Cariban origin; akin to Galibi *aluáta*, Cumanagoto *araguata*] **:** HOWLER MONKEY

aloud \ə'lau̇d\ *adv* [ME, fr. ¹a- + *loud*] **1** *archaic* **:** LOUDLY ⟨singing ~ with joy⟩ **2 :** not in a whisper or undertone **:** with the distinctly audible normal speaking voice ⟨say it ~ — nobody will hear you⟩; *specif, of reading* **:** with visual scanning of words accompanied by their distinctly audible vocal utterance

aloun–aloun *var of* ALUN-ALUN

à l'outrance *var of* À OUTRANCE

¹alow *or* **alowe** \ə'lō\ *adj* [¹a + *low* (blaze)] *dial Brit* **:** AFIRE

²alow \"\ *adv* [ME, fr. ¹a + *low*] **:** in or to a lower part **:** BELOW ⟨work ~ and aloft was to my liking —Roland Barker⟩

alo·ys·ia \,alə'wish(ē)ə\ *n* -s [NL, after María Luisa (*Aloysia*) Teresa †1819 wife of Charles IV of Spain] **:** LEMON VERBENA

¹alp \'alp\ *n* -s [ME *alpe*] *dial Eng* **:** BULLFINCH

²alp \'alp, 'au̇p\ *n* -s [back-formation fr. *Alps*, mountain system of Europe, fr. ME *Alpes*, fr. L] **1 :** a high rugged mountain resembling topographically those in the Alps of Europe **2 :** something comparable to or suggesting comparison with an alp in height, size, or ruggedness ⟨intellectual ~s⟩ **3** [G, fr. MHG *albe*, pl. *alben*, fr. OHG *albūn*, *Alpūn* alps, fr. L *Alpes*] **:** a mountain pasture or mountain meadowland

al·paca \al'pakə, *attrib* (')al¦p-\ *n* -s [Sp, fr. Aymara *allpaca*] **1 :** an animal like a llama with fine long woolly hair domesticated in Peru and adjacent countries being possibly a variety of the guanaco **2 a :** the usu. brown or black or sometimes white woolly undercoat of the alpaca used in yarns and fabrics **b :** shearlings of alpaca **3 a :** a fine lightweight cloth of plain weave made of the hair of the alpaca often mixed with other fibers; *also* **:** any of various cotton or rayon imitations of this cloth **b :** a garment (as a coat) made of this cloth

alpaca 1

al·par·ga·ta \,alpə(r)'gäd·ə\ *n* -s [Sp, alter. of *alpargate*, fr. Ar dial. (Spain) *al-parghāt*, pl. of *al-parghah* the sandal, fr. Ar *al* the + *parghah* sandal, fr. Sp *abarca*] **:** ESPADRILLE

al·peen \al'pēn, əl-\ *n* -s [IrGael *ailpīn*] *Irish* **:** CUDGEL

al·pen·glow \'alpən,glō\ *n* -s [prob. part trans. of G *Alpenglühen*, fr. *Alpen* Alps + *glühen* glow] **:** a reddish glow or sometimes the entire series of light phenomena seen near sunset or sunrise on the summits of mountains; *specif* **:** a reillumination sometimes observed after the summits have passed into shadow and supposed to be due to a refraction of the light rays from the west resulting from the cooling of the air

al·pen·horn \'alpən,hȯrn, -ō(ə)n\ *or* **alp·horn** \'al,pȯ-,'alp-,hȯ-\ *or* **alpine horn** *n* -s [G, fr. OHG *Albūn*, fr. L *Alpen* Alps (fr. OHG *Albūn*, fr. L *Alpes*) + *horn* — more at HORN] **:** a straight wooden horn 7 to 15 feet in length with an upturned bell and a cupped mouthpiece used by Swiss herdsmen

alpenhorn

al·pen·stock \'alpən,stäk\ *n* -s [G, fr. *Alpen* Alps + *stock* staff, fr. OHG *stoc* — more at STOCK] **:** a long iron-pointed staff used in mountain climbing

al·pes·trine \(')al¦pestrən\ *adj* [ML *alpestris* mountainous (fr. L *Alpes* Alps) + E *-ine*] **:** growing at high elevations but not above the timber line **:** SUBALPINE

¹al·pha \'alfə, 'au̇fə\ *n* -s [ME, fr. L, fr. Gk, fr. a Phoenician word akin to Heb *āleph*, lit., ox] **1 :** the first letter of the Greek alphabet — symbol Α or α; see ALPHABET table **2 :** the first (as in sequence, order, classification) **:** BEGINNING ⟨the *Alpha* and the end —Rev 22:13 (RSV)⟩ — compare OMEGA **3 :** an alpha particle or alpha ray

²alpha *or* **α-** \"\ *adj* **1 :** of or relating to one of two or more closely related chemical substances ⟨α-yohimbine⟩ — used somewhat arbitrarily to specify ordinal relationship or to specify a particular physical form, esp. an allotropic modification (as in α-iron), or an isomeric or sometimes polymeric or stereoisomeric form (as in α-D-glucose); abbr. sometimes *a-* **2 :** first in position from or closest in the structure of an organic molecule to a particular group or atom or having a structure characterized by such a position ⟨the ~ positions of furan⟩ ⟨α-amino acids⟩ ⟨α-naphthol⟩ **3 :** producing green pigment when grown on blood media — used of certain hemolytic streptococci **4 :** first in order of brightness — used of a star in a constellation

alpha and omega *n* [so called with reference to Rev 1:8, fr. alpha and omega's being respectively the first and last letter of the Greek alphabet] **1 :** the beginning and ending **2 :** the principal element **:** the most important feature ⟨wheat is the *alpha and omega* of their diet —T.H.Fielding⟩

¹al·pha·bet \'alfə,bet, 'au̇f- *also* -,bət; *often* -d·+V\ *n* -s [ME *alphabete*, fr. LL *alphabetum*, irreg. fr. Gk *alphabētos*, fr. *alpha* + *bēta*, the first two letters of the Gk alphabet — more at BETA] **1 a :** any particular set of letters with which one or more languages are written; *esp* **:** such a set of letters arranged in a customary order — see LETTER **b :** any set of characters with which one or more languages are written whether these characters are letters (sense 1a), the signs of a syllabary, or other basic units of writing **c :** a set of the letters of an alphabet written, engraved, printed, or otherwise represented in some particular form or style, usu. one in which the characters are considered to have an artistic uniformity with one another

ALPHABET TABLE

Showing the letters of five non-Roman alphabets and the transliterations used in the etymologies

HEBREW[1,4]

Letter	Name	Transliteration
א	aleph	ʼ [2]
ב	beth	b, bh
ג	gimel	g, gh
ד	daleth	d, dh
ה	he	h
ו	waw	w
ז	zayin	z
ח	heth	ḥ
ט	teth	ṭ
י	yodh	y
כ ך	kaph	k, kh
ל	lamedh	l
מ ם	mem	m
נ ן	nun	n
ס	samekh	s
ע	ayin	ʻ
פ ף	pe	p, ph
צ ץ	sadhe	ṣ
ק	qoph	q
ר	resh	r
שׂ	sin	ś
שׁ	shin	sh
ת	taw	t, th

ARABIC[3,4]

Alone	Joined to preceding	Joined to both	Joined to following	Name	Transliteration
ا	ـا			alif	[5]
ب	ـب	ـبـ	بـ	bā	b
ت	ـت	ـتـ	تـ	tā	t
ث	ـث	ـثـ	ثـ	thā	th
ج	ـج	ـجـ	جـ	jīm	j
ح	ـح	ـحـ	حـ	ḥā	ḥ
خ	ـخ	ـخـ	خـ	khā	kh
د	ـد			dāl	d
ذ	ـذ			dhāl	dh
ر	ـر			rā	r
ز	ـز			zāy	z
س	ـس	ـسـ	سـ	sīn	s
ش	ـش	ـشـ	شـ	shīn	sh
ص	ـص	ـصـ	صـ	ṣād	ṣ
ض	ـض	ـضـ	ضـ	ḍād	ḍ
ط	ـط	ـطـ	طـ	ṭā	ṭ
ظ	ـظ	ـظـ	ظـ	ẓā	ẓ
ع	ـع	ـعـ	عـ	ʻayn	ʻ
غ	ـغ	ـغـ	غـ	ghayn	gh
ف	ـف	ـفـ	فـ	fā	f
ق	ـق	ـقـ	قـ	qāf	q
ك	ـك	ـكـ	كـ	kāf	k
ل	ـل	ـلـ	لـ	lām	l
م	ـم	ـمـ	مـ	mīm	m
ن	ـن	ـنـ	نـ	nūn	n
ه	ـه	ـهـ	هـ	hā	h[6]
و	ـو			wāw	w
ى	ـى	ـيـ	يـ	yā	y

GREEK[7]

Letter	Name	Transliteration
Α α	alpha	a
Β β	beta	b
Γ γ	gamma	g, n
Δ δ	delta	d
Ε ε	epsilon	e
Ζ ζ	zeta	z
Η η	eta	ē
Θ θ	theta	th
Ι ι	iota	i
Κ κ	kappa	k
Λ λ	lambda	l
Μ μ	mu	m
Ν ν	nu	n
Ξ ξ	xi	x
Ο ο	omicron	o
Π π	pi	p
Ρ ρ	rho	r, rh
Σ σ ς	sigma	s
Τ τ	tau	t
Υ υ	upsilon	y, u
Φ φ	phi	ph
Χ χ	chi	ch
Ψ ψ	psi	ps
Ω ω	omega	ō

RUSSIAN[8]

А а	a
Б б	b
В в	v
Г г	g
Д д	d
Е е	e
Ж ж	zh
З з	z
И и Й й	i, ĭ
К к	k
Л л	l
М м	m
Н н	n
О о	o
П п	p
Р р	r
С с	s
Т т	t
У у	u
Ф ф	f
Х х	kh
Ц ц	ts
Ч ч	ch
Ш ш	sh
Щ щ	shch
Ъ ъ[9]	"
Ы ы	y
Ь ь[10]	'
Э э	e
Ю ю	yu
Я я	ya

SANSKRIT[11]

Letter	Transliteration	Letter	Transliteration
अ	a	ञ	ñ
आ	ā	ट	ṭ
इ	i	ठ	ṭh
ई	ī	ड	ḍ
उ	u	ढ	ḍh
ऊ	ū	ण	ṇ
ऋ	ṛ	त	t
ॠ	ṝ	थ	th
ऌ	ḷ	द	d
ॡ	ḹ	ध	dh
ए	e	न	n
ऐ	ai	प	p
ओ	o	फ	ph
औ	au	ब	b
ं[12]	ṁ	भ	bh
ः[13]	ḥ	म	m
क	k	य	y
ख	kh	र	r
ग	g	ल	l
घ	gh	व	v
ङ	ṅ	श	ś
च	c	ष	ṣ
छ	ch	स	s
ज	j	ह	h
झ	jh		

1 See HEBREW ALPHABET and ALEPH, BETH, etc., in Vocab. Where two forms of a letter are given, the second one is the form used at the end of a word. 2 Not represented in transliteration when initial. 3 See ARABIC ALPHABET. In this table the first form given for each letter is used when it stands alone, the second when it is joined to the preceding letter, the third when it is joined to both the preceding and the following letter, and the fourth when it is joined to the following letter only. Many of the letters also have other forms which are used only in certain combinations; the number and nature of these differ from one style of handwriting or font of type to another. 4 The Hebrew and Arabic letters are all primarily consonants; a few of them are also used secondarily to represent certain vowels, but full indication of vowels, when provided at all, is by means of a system of dots or strokes adjacent to the consonantal characters. 5 Alif represents no sound in itself, but is used principally as a bearer of the hamza (transliterated ʼ medially and finally; not represented in transliteration when initial) and as the sign of a long *a*. 6 When ه has two dots above it (ة), it is called *tā marbūta* and, if it immediately precedes a vowel, is transliterated *t* instead of *h*. 7 See ALPHA, BETA, GAMMA, etc., in Vocab. The letter gamma is transliterated *n* only before velars; the letter upsilon is transliterated *u* only as the final element in diphthongs. 8 See CYRILLIC ALPHABET in Vocab. 9 This sign indicates that the immediately preceding consonant is not palatalized even though immediately followed by a palatal vowel. 10 This sign indicates that the immediately preceding consonant is palatalized even though not immediately followed by a palatal vowel. 11 The alphabet shown here is the Devanagari. When vowels are combined with preceding consonants they are indicated by various strokes or hooks instead of by the signs here given, or, in the case of short *a*, not written at all. Thus the character क represents *ka;* the character का, *kā;* the character कि, *ki;* the character की, *kī;* the character कु, *ku;* the character कू, *kū;* the character कृ, *kṛ;* the character कॄ, *kṝ;* the character के, *ke;* the character कै, *kai;* the character को, *ko;* the character कौ, *kau;* and the character क्, *k* without any following vowel. There are also many compound characters representing combinations of two or more consonants. 12 See ANUSVARA. 13 See VISARGA.

⟨a script ~⟩ ⟨a book printed in an old style ~⟩ **d :** the set of speech sounds that any particular language employs — not in technical use **e :** a series of words, paragraphs, phrases, stanzas of verse, or other units of composition the successive members of which have as their initial letters the letters of the alphabet in order or which deal with topics of which the initial letters of the names correspond to the letters of the alphabet in order; *specif* **:** an alphabetic acrostic poem **f :** the alphabetic system of writing as distinguished from syllabic, ideographic, and other systems — used with *the* ⟨the birthplace of the ~⟩ **g :** a series of words, phrases, names, or other units arranged in alphabetical order ⟨the suburban telephones are in a separate ~ in the directory⟩ ⟨the entries in this dictionary are all in one ~⟩ **h :** any system of signs or signals, visual, auditory, or tactile, that serve as equivalents for the usual written letters of an alphabet ⟨the ~ used in spelling words for the deaf⟩ ⟨the dots and dashes of the telegraphic ~⟩ **i :** a particular set of names used to designate the various letters of an alphabet ⟨the pronouncing ~ used in civil aviation⟩ **j** *cryptology* **:** a set of one-to-one equivalences between a sequence of plaintext letters and the sequence of their cipher substitutes; *sometimes* **:** one of these sequences ⟨a cipher ~⟩ — called also *substitution alphabet;* see VIGENÈRE CIPHER **2 :** the simplest rudiments **:** ELEMENTS, ABC ⟨the very ~ of our law —T.B.Macaulay⟩ **3** *obs* **a :** an index alphabetically arranged **b :** a complete or long series

²alphabet \"\ *vt* -ED/-ING/-S **:** ALPHABETIZE

al·pha·be·tar·i·an \ˌ⁼⁼ˌbə'ta(a)rēən\ *n* -S **:** a learner or student of the alphabet **:** ABECEDARIAN

alphabet block *n* **:** a cubical block of wood, plastic, or other material having letters of the alphabet on some of the sides, a set of which constitutes a toy for young children

alphabet book *n* **:** a book for teaching the alphabet

al·pha·bet·ic \ˌ⁼⁼¦bed·ik, -etik, -ēk\ *or* **al·pha·bet·i·cal** \-ə̇kəl, -ēk-\ *adj* **1 :** of or belonging to an alphabet or alphabets in general **2 :** written in an alphabet **:** employing an alphabet ⟨an ~ inscription⟩ ⟨an ~ language⟩ **3 :** employing letters that by and large represent single phonemes ⟨an ~ system of writing⟩ **4 :** arranged, subdivided, or proceeding according to the order of the letters of the alphabet ⟨an ~ acrostic poem⟩ ⟨arrangement in ~ sequence⟩ **5 a :** fulfilling the function of a letter of an alphabet ⟨an ~ character⟩ **b :** characteristic of a letter of an alphabet ⟨a sign having ~ value⟩ **6 :** frequently designated esp. in informal and unofficial use by a shortened name consisting of the initial letters of the several words that constitute the full official name ⟨the ~ agencies of the national government⟩

alphabetical code *n* **:** ONE-PART CODE

al·pha·bet·i·cal·ly \-ə̇k(ə)lē, -ēk-, -li\ *adv* **1 :** according to an arrangement or procedure based on alphabetical order **2 :** in an alphabetic method

al·pha·bet·i·co-classed catalog \¦⁼⁼¦⁼ə̇ˌkō,-\ *n* **:** a subject catalog in which main divisions are ordinarily arranged in some logically progressive order and subdivisions alphabetically

al·pha·bet·ics \ˌ⁼⁼'⁼iks, -ēks\ *n pl but sing in constr* **:** the science dealing with the representation of spoken sounds by means of letters

al·pha·bet·i·form \¦⁼⁼¦⁼əˌfȯrm\ *adj* [*alphabet* + *-iform*] **:** having the form of an alphabet **:** resembling letters — used specif. of certain figures on rocks of the cave period in Europe

al·pha·bet·ism \'⁼⁼ˌbəˌtizəm, -ˌbəd-ˌiz-, -ˌbed-ˌiz-\ *n* -S **:** the use of letters as symbols: **a :** the representation of speech sounds by vowel and consonantal rather than syllabic signs **b :** the use of groups of letters (as ABC or XYZ) as a signature or nom de plume

al·pha·bet·ist \-ˌbed·ə̇st *also* -ˌbəd-·\ *n* -S **:** one that studies or invents alphabets

al·pha·bet·i·za·tion \ˌ⁼⁼ˌbed·ə'zāshən, -etə'- *also* -ˌbəd-· *or* -bət- *or* -bəd-ˌī'z- *or* -bəˌtī'-\ *n* -S **1 :** the act or action of arranging alphabetically **2 :** an alphabetically arranged series, list, or file

al·pha·bet·ize \'⁼⁼ˌbəˌtīz, -bəd-ˌīz\ *vt* -ED/-ING/-S **1 :** to furnish with or express by an alphabet ⟨the revised system of *alphabetizing* Japanese —Cornelius Osgood⟩ **2 :** to arrange alphabetically ⟨~ a list of words⟩

alphabet length *n* **:** the total width of the 26 single lower-case unspaced letters of the alphabet in a particular font usu. given in points and used as an indicator of relative face width

al·pha·be·tol·o·gist \ˌ⁼⁼bə'täləjə̇st\ *n* -S **:** one that engages in alphabetology

al·pha·be·tol·o·gy \-ləjē\ *n* -ES [¹*alphabet* + *-o-* + *-logy*] **:** the study of alphabetic systems of writing

alphabets *pl of* ALPHABET, *pres 3d sing of* ALPHABET

alphabet soup *n* **:** a soup containing macaroni paste cut in the shapes of letters

alpha brass *n* **:** brass composed of a solid solution of zinc in copper and containing up to 39 or formerly 36 percent zinc

alpha cell *n* **:** an acidophile glandular cell (as of the pancreas or the adenohypophysis)

alpha cellulose *n* **:** CELLULOSE 2b

alpha globulin *n* **:** any of several globulins of human or animal plasma or serum that have at alkaline pH the greatest electrophoretic mobility next to albumin — compare BETA GLOBULIN, GAMMA GLOBULIN

al·pha·gram \'alfəˌgram\ *n* -S [¹*alpha* + *-gram* (as in *cryptogram*)] **:** a puzzle that consists in the defining of one phrase with another phrase made up of rhyming words that are spelled alike except for the first letters ⟨*boy toy* is an ~ for *male doll*⟩ ⟨*funny bunny* is an ~ for *amusing little rabbit*⟩

alpha hemolysis *n* **:** a greenish discoloration and partial hemolysis of the red blood cells immediately surrounding colonies of certain streptococci on blood agar plates

al·pha-hy·poph·a·mine \¦alfə,-\ *n* **:** OXYTOCIN

alpha iron *n* **:** the form of iron stable below 910°C and characterized by a body-centered cubic crystal structure — compare BETA IRON

al·pha·mer·ic \¦alfə¦merik\ *or* **al·pha·mer·i·cal** \-rə̇kəl\ *adj* [*alphabet* + *numeric, numerical*] **:** consisting of both letters and numbers; *specif* **:** capable of printing or otherwise using both letters and numbers in the same operation — used esp. of bookkeeping or computing machines

al·pha-naph·thol \ˌalfə-\ *n* [²*alpha* + *naphthol*] **:** NAPHTHOL 1a

al·pha-naph·thyl \ˌalfə-\ *n* [²*alpha* + *naphthyl*] **:** NAPHTHYL a

al·pha-naph·thyl·thio·urea \¦alfə¦n-\ *n* [NL, fr. ISV *alpha⁼ naphthyl* + NL *thiourea*] **:** ANTU

al·pha·nu·mer·ic \¦alfə(ˌ)⁼¦⁼⁼\ *adj* [*alpha*bet + *numeric*] **:** ALPHAMERIC

alpha particle *n* **:** a positively charged nuclear particle identical with the nucleus of a helium atom, consisting of 2 protons and 2 neutrons, having atomic mass 4 and atomic number 2, ejected at high speed in certain radioactive transformations

alpha privative *n* [trans. of MGk *alpha sterētikon*] **1 :** the Greek prefix *a-* or usu. before vowels *an-* expressing negation (as in Gk *abatos* "impassable" from *batos* "passable") **2 :** the English prefix *a-* expressing negation

alpha pulp *n* **:** chemical pulp that has been given a further chemical treatment to remove impurities and thus increase its alpha cellulose content

alpha quartz *n* **:** quartz with trigonal-trapezohedral symmetry **:** the stable form of quartz below about 573°C

alpha radiator *n* **:** a radioactive substance which radiates alpha rays

alpha ray *n* **1 :** an alpha particle moving at high speed (as in radioactive emission) **2** *or* **alpha radiation :** a stream of alpha particles

alpha rhythm *or* **alpha wave** *n* **:** a brain-wave current having a frequency of approximately 10 pulsations per second

alpha test *n* **:** a group intelligence test used esp. by the U.S. Army in World War I

al·pha-to·coph·er·ol \¦alfə-\ *n* **:** TOCOPHEROL a

al·phi·to·mor·phous \al¦fid·ə¦mȯrfəs, ¦alfə(ˌ)tō¦-\ *adj* [prob. fr. F *alphitomorphe*, fr. Gk *alphiton* barley meal + F *-morphe* -morphous] **:** resembling barley meal — used of certain parasitic fungi

al·phonse and gas·ton \'alˌfänz...'gastən, 'aủˌf, än(t)s-, -aast-\ *n, pl* **alphonses and gastons** *usu cap 1st A&G* [after *Alphonse* and *Gaston*, characters displaying excessive politeness and often uttering the phrases "after you, my dear Gaston" and "after you, my dear Alphonse" that appeared in the comic strip *Alphonse and Gaston* by Frederick B. Opper †1937 Amer. illustrator and cartoonist] **:** a pair of persons exhibiting an excessive usu. exaggerated politeness or deference to each other esp. about not taking precedence ⟨getting tired of being like *Alphonse and Gaston* at the door, the ambassador finally charged in ahead of the governor⟩ ⟨a beautiful imitation of *Alphonse and Gaston*—holding out their own bids . . . until they saw the other fellow's —*Time*⟩

al·phon·sine \(')al¦fän(t)sə̇n, -änzə̇n\ *adj, usu cap* [Sp *alfonsino*, fr. *Alfonso* X †1284 king of Castile and León + Sp *-ino* -ine] **:** relating to the set of astronomical tables prepared in 1252 by order of Alfonso X, king of León and Castile

alphorn *var of* ALPENHORN

¹al·pine \'alˌpīn *also* -ˌpə̇n\ *adj* [ME, fr. L *Alpinus*, fr. *Alpes* Alps + *-inus* -ine] **1** *often cap* **:** resembling or relating to the Alps or any lofty mountain or mountain system ⟨~ scenery⟩ ⟨~ winter⟩ **2** *usu cap* **:** of or relating to the mountain-making movements in Europe in the Tertiary period — see GEOLOGIC TIME table **3 a** *usu cap* **:** of, relating to, or being the biogeographic zone made up of elevated slopes above timber line and characterized by the presence of rosette-forming herbaceous plants and low shrubby slow-growing woody plants **b** *often cap* **:** growing in this zone ⟨~ plants⟩ **c** *often cap* **:** of, relating to, or made up of alpine plants ⟨an ~ forest⟩ **4** *usu cap* **:** of or relating to a broadheaded medium-statured brown-eyed or brown-haired white man of stocky build who is often regarded as representative of one of the three physical types of the white race ⟨a pure *Alpine* type⟩ — compare MEDITERRANEAN, NORDIC **5** *often cap* **:** devoted to mountaineering activities ⟨an ~ club⟩ — **al·pine·ly** *adv*

²alpine \"\ *n* -S **1 :** a plant native to mountain summits or boreal regions that is often grown in alpine or rock gardens **2** *sometimes cap* **:** a goat of a breed of large hardy milch goats originated in the Swiss Alps — see BRITISH ALPINE **3 :** any of several predominantly dark-brown or blackish butterflies (genus *Erebia*) of northern regions **4** *usu cap* **:** a person possessing Alpine physical characteristics

alpine anemone *n* **:** a silky-foliaged herb (*Anemone tetonensis*) of the Rocky mountains with bluish white flowers

alpine ash *n* **:** a tall Australian timber tree (*Eucalyptus gigantea*) having the lower part of the trunk covered with thick woolly gray bark

alpine aster *n* **:** a Rocky mountain herb (*Aster meritus*) with violet-purple flowers

alpine azalea *n* **:** a low-branching prostrate shrub (*Loiseleuria procumbens*) of the heath family found in high mountain regions in the northern hemisphere

alpine bartsia *n* [part trans. of NL *Bartsia alpina*] **:** a hemiparasitic herb (*Bartsia alpina*) of arctic America and northern Europe with opposite leaves and showy irregular purple flowers in a leafy spike

alpine bearberry *n* **:** a tufted or prostrate bearberry (*Arctostaphylos alpina*) of the mountainous regions of northeastern No. America

alpine beardtongue *n* **:** a common Rocky mountain perennial herb (*Pentstemon ellipticus*) with a partly woody stem and violet-purple flowers

alpine birch *n* **:** a low shrub (*Betula nana*) native in high northern regions

alpine bistort *n* **:** a slender perennial herb (*Bistorta vivipara*) with oblong leaves and reddish white flowers found in northern regions

alpine brook saxifrage *n* [¹*brook*, prob. part trans. of NL *Saxifraga rivularis*] **:** a white-flowered herb (*Saxifraga rivularis*) found on mountain summits and in arctic regions of the northern hemisphere

alpine campion *n* **:** a low tufted herb (*Lychnis alpina*) with pink flowers found throughout the north temperate zone esp. at high altitudes

alpine catchfly *n* **:** a European white-flowered herb (*Silene alpestris*) that is sometimes cultivated

alpine chough *n* **:** a small yellow-billed chough (*Pyrrhocorax graculus*) of mountainous parts of Europe

alpine clover *n* **:** a European mountain clover (*Trifolium alpinum*) with heads of pink flowers

alpine combined *n, usu cap A* **:** a competitive ski event consisting of both downhill racing and slalom — compare NORDIC COMBINED

alpine cress *n* **:** a low white-flowered perennial herb (*Cardamine bellidifolia*) found on mountain summits and in arctic regions of the north temperate zone

alpine currant *n* **:** a spreading dense European shrub (*Ribes alpinum*) often used as an ornamental or hedge plant esp. in shady locations — called also *mountain currant*

alpine dock *n* **:** a tall coarse rough-leaved dock (*Rumex alpinus*) of the Alps with drooping flowers and fruits in large branching clusters

alpine eyebright *n* **:** a showy New Zealand perennial herb (*Euphrasia monroi*) with yellow and white flowers

alpine fir *n* **:** a tall Rocky mountain evergreen timber tree (*Abies lasiocarpa*) having flat blue-green leaves and upright cones

alpine fireweed *n* **:** a perennial herb (*Epilobium latifolium*) with reddish white flowers found in arctic America and south through the Rocky mountains to Colorado

alpine forget-me-not *n* **:** a Rocky mountain perennial herb (*Eritrichium howardi*) with ashy yellowish foliage and dark blue flowers

alpine garden *n* **:** a garden on rock ledges or among rocks in the alpine zone or one (as in certain cool damp locations) intended to simulate such a garden; *broadly* **:** ROCK GARDEN

alpine glacier *n* **:** a glacier formed among summits and descending a mountain valley

alpine hemlock *n* **:** a valuable timber tree (*Tsuga mertensiana*) found in the northern Rocky mountains

alpine horn *var of* ALPENHORN

alpine lady fern *n* **:** a fern (*Athyrium americanum*) with deeply cut leaf segments found in the Rocky mountains

alpine larch *n* **:** a larch (*Larix lyallii*) growing in the higher mountains of the northwestern U.S. and British Columbia

alpine lift *n, often cap A* **:** T-BAR LIFT

alpine lousewort *n* **:** a white-flowered perennial herb (*Pedicularis contorta*) found on mountains of western No. America

alpine parnassia *n* **:** a white-flowered herb (*Parnassia kotzebuei*) found in Siberia, Greenland, and the Rocky mountains

alpine pine *n* **:** SWISS PINE

alpine poppy *n* **1 :** ICELAND POPPY **2 :** a tiny yellow-flowered Rocky mountain poppy (*Papaver pygmaeum*)

alpine rose *n* **1 :** any of various European and Asiatic alpine rhododendrons **2 :** EDELWEISS 1

alpine salamander *n, usu cap A* **:** an ovoviviparous tailed amphibian (*Salamandra atra*) occurring in the Alps that retains its one or two young in the uterus until metamorphosis is completed

alpine sedge *n* **:** a Rocky mountain sedge (*Carex scopulorum*) with sharply triangular culms

alpine spring beauty *n* **:** a fleshy perennial herb (*Claytonia megarrhiza*) found on summits of the Rocky mountains

alpine strawberry *n* **:** a variety (*Fragaria vesca monophylla*) of the wood strawberry with unifoliolate leaves

alpine structure *n, usu cap A* [so called fr. its prevalence in the Swiss Alps] **:** rock structure characterized by extensive overthrust faults and overturned folds

alpine totara *n* **:** a dense New Zealand shrub (*Podocarpus nivalis*) often low and widely spreading with leaves closely and irregularly arranged

alpine umbrella plant *n* **:** a Rocky mountain perennial herb (*Eriogonum androsaceum*) with white foliage and yellowish white flowers

alpine vole *n* **:** any of numerous European upland voles (genus *Microtus*)

alpine whitebark pine *n* **:** a timber tree (*Pinus albicaulis*) found in the Rocky mountains and in California

alpine woodsia *n* [part trans. of NL *Woodsia alpina*] **:** a slender fern (*Woodsia alpina*) of northern No. America with shining chestnut-colored stipes, bipinnate fronds, and usu. distinct marginal sori — called also *flower-cup fern*

al·pin·ia \al'pinēə\ *n* [NL, fr. Prospero *Alpini* †1617 Ital. botanist + NL *-ia*] **1** *cap* **:** a large genus of herbs (family Zingiberaceae) found in Asia, Australia, and Polynesia with showy very irregular flowers and large aromatic rootstocks — see GALINGALE **2** -S **:** a plant of the genus *Alpinia*

al·pin·ism \'alpəˌnizəm\ *n* -S *often cap* **:** mountain climbing in the Alps or other high mountain ranges

al·pin·ist \'alpənə̇st, -ˌpīn-\ *n* -S *often cap* **:** a mountain climber specializing in high difficult ascents

al·pi·no \al'pē(ˌ)nō\ *n, pl* **al·pi·ni** \-(ˌ)nē\ *usu cap* [It, fr. *alpino* of the Alps, fr. L *alpinus* — more at ALPINE] **:** a member of an Italian army unit trained to fight in mountainous terrain

al·pin·oid \'alpəˌnȯid\ *adj, usu cap* [¹*alpine* + *-oid*] **:** resembling or related to the Alpine race

al·pist \'alpə̇st, (')al¦pēst\ *also* **al·piste** \", al'pēstə\ *n* -S [Sp *alpiste*, fr. Mozarabic *al-bisht* the alpist, fr. *al-* the (fr. Ar) + *bisht* alpist, fr. ML *pistum*, fr. L, neut. of *pistus*, past part. of *pinsere* to pound, crush — more at PESTLE] **1 :** the seed of canary grass **2 :** the seed of any of various species of *Phleum*

alp·land \'alˌpland, -ˌplənd\ *n* **:** an area resembling the Alps in its topography

al·pu·jar·ra \ˌalpü'hārə\ *n* -S *usu cap* [*Las Alpujarras*, region of Spain where it is made] **:** an antique or modern Spanish rug embroidered in woolen or silken loops on canvas

al·raun \'alˌraủn, ⁼'⁼\ *n* -S [G, fr. MHG *alrūn*, alter. of OHG *alrūna* (perh. a fem. proper name), fr. *al-*, *all* all + *rūna* secret — more at ALL, RUNE] **:** MANDRAKE 1

al·ready \(')ȯl¦redē, -di\ *adv* [ME *al redy*, fr. *al redy*, adj., wholly ready, prepared, fr. *al* all + *redy* ready — more at ALL, READY] **:** prior to some specified or implied past, present, or future time **:** by this time **:** PREVIOUSLY — usu. used to refer to time that is past with respect to the verb modified ⟨if you stop to think, you'll find you ~ know the answer⟩ or to a condition that has been reached prior to the time of observation ⟨an ~ noticeable decrease⟩

alright *adv or adj* [ME *alright, alriht* — more at ALL RIGHT] **:** ALL RIGHT — in reputable use although *all right* is more common

al·root \'älˌr-\ *n* -S [Hindi *āl* + E *root*] **:** INDIAN MULBERRY 1

al rovescio *var of* A ROVESCIO

¹als *obs var of* ¹ALSO

²als *pl of* AL

-als *pl of* -AL

ALS *abbr* autograph letter signed

al·sace-lor·rain·er \¦alˌsaslə'rānə(r), -ˌsās-\ *n* -S *cap A&L* [*Alsace-Lorraine*, frontier region between Germany, France, Belgium, and Switzerland + E *-er*] **:** a native or inhabitant of Alsace-Lorraine

al·sa·tia \al'sāsh(ē)ə\ *n* -S *usu cap* [*Alsatia* (slang name for Whitefriars, a section of London that was a sanctuary for lawbreakers in the 17th cent.), fr. ML *Alsatia* Alsace, Rhenish province long in dispute between France and Germany] **:** any asylum or refuge for criminals **:** a region without law ⟨an *Alsatia* of dives, dance halls, and depravity —Herbert Asbury⟩

¹al·sa·tian \al'sāshən\ *n* -S *usu cap* [ML *Alsatia* Alsace + E *-an*] **1 :** a native or inhabitant of Alsatia or of Alsace **2** *also* **alsatian dog :** GERMAN SHEPHERD

²alsatian \(')⁼¦⁼⁼\ *adj, usu cap* **:** relating to, situated in, inhabiting, or coming from Alsatia or Alsace

alsatian clover *n, usu cap A* [by folk etymology] **:** ALSIKE CLOVER

als·bach·ite \'ȯlzˌbäˌkīt, 'älz-,'äls-\ *n* -S [G *alsbachit*, fr. *Alsbach*, village in Germany, its locality + G *-it* -ite] **:** a porphyritic aplite sometimes containing garnets

al·sea \al'sēə\ *n, pl* **alsea** *or* **alseas** *usu cap* [Alsea *Alsé*] **1 a :** an Indian people of the Pacific coast of Oregon **b :** a member of such people **2 :** the Yakonan language of the Alsea people

¹al sec·co \al'seˌkō\ *adj* [It, in a formal manner] *of a painting* **:** executed in the secco manner ⟨an *al secco* mural⟩ — compare ALFRESCO

²al secco \"\ *adv, of painting* **:** in the secco manner

al se·gno \äl'sān(ˌ)yō, al-\ *adv* [It, to the sign] **1 :** to the sign — used as a direction in music for the performer to continue as far as the sign :S: **2 :** DAL SEGNO

al·si·film \'alsəˌfilm\ *n* -S [*al*uminum *si*licate + *film*] **:** an oil-resistant and heat-resistant material produced in sheets from a gel of bentonite and used esp. for electrical insulation

al·sike clover *also* **alsike** \'alˌsak, -ˌīk *also* 'ȯlˌsīk\ *n* -S [fr. *Alsike*, Sweden, its locality] **:** a European perennial clover (*Trifolium hybridum*) much used as a forage plant and characterized by pinkish flowers that early become deflexed in the head

al·si·na·ce·ae \ˌalsə'nāsēˌē\ *n pl, cap* [NL, fr. *Alsine*, type genus + *-aceae*] *in some classifications* **:** a family of herbs having opposite entire leaves and small mostly perfect flowers with distinct sepals, clawless petals, and capsular fruits, often included in the Caryophyllaceae

al·si·na·ceous \¦alsə¦nāshəs, -ˌsī-\ *adj* [NL *Alsinaceae* + E *-ous*] **:** of or relating to the family Alsinaceae or genus *Alsine*

al·si·ne \al'sīnē\ *n, cap* [NL, fr. L, a plant (perh. chickweed), fr. Gk *alsinē* (*Parietaria lusitanica*)] *in some classifications* **:** a genus (the type of the family Alsinaceae) of herbs that includes the chickweeds and stitchworts and is equivalent to *Stellaria* or to a combination of *Stellaria* and *Arenaria* of other classifications

al si·rat \ˌalsə'rät\ *n, usu cap A&S* [Ar *al-sirāṭ* the road] **:** SIRAT

¹al·so \'ȯl(ˌ)sō, 'ȯlt(-\ *adv* [ME *also, alswa*, fr. OE *alswā, ealswā, ælswā* just as, likewise, fr. *al-, eal-, æl-* (akin to OE *eall* all) + *swā* so — more at ALL, SO] **1 :** in the same manner as something else **:** LIKEWISE ⟨another fallen prince, who is ~ not unknown to the students of literature —R.D.Altick⟩ ⟨they ~ serve who only stand and wait —John Milton⟩ **2 :** in addition **:** as well **:** BESIDES, TOO ⟨had immense dignity and reserve, but he ~ was self-sufficient —Harry Hansen⟩

²also \"\ *conj* [ME *also, alswa*, fr. *also, alswa*, adv.] **1** *obs* **:** as if **:** AS **2 :** AND ⟨his speech was tedious, ~ absurd⟩

als ob \äls'ˀōp\ *n, pl* **als obs** [G] **:** ASSUMPTION; *esp* **:** one made so that action, thought, or further assumption is possible

al·soph·i·la \al'säfələ\ *n* [NL, fr. Gk *alsos* grove + NL *-phila*; akin to Gk *aldēskein* to grow — more at OLD] **1** *cap* **:** a large genus of tree ferns (family Cyatheaceae) found in tropical mountainous regions having ample finely divided fronds bearing naked sori **2** -S **:** a fern of the genus *Alsophila* **3** *cap* **:** a genus of geometrid moths having wingless females and green-striped larvae that are loopers and include the common destructive fall cankerworm

also-ran \'⁼(ˌ)⁼ˌ⁼\ *n* -S **1 a :** a race horse or racing dog that finishes behind the first three contestants or out of the money **b :** a contestant in any actual or presumed competition that is not among the prize or point winners, is only moderately successful, or is a failure **c :** a failing or only moderately successful entry in any actual or presumed competition ⟨the book was an *also-ran* on the publisher's list⟩ **2 :** a person of little or no importance

al·sto·nia \ȯlz'tōnēə, ȯl'st-\ *n, cap* [NL, fr. Charles *Alston* †1760 Scottish botanist + NL *-ia*] **:** a genus of trees or shrubs (family Apocynaceae) found in tropical Asia, Australia, and Polynesia having white funnel-shaped flowers and seeds comose at both ends

al·sto·nine \'ȯlztəˌnēn, -lst-\ *n* -S [ISV *alston-* (fr. NL *Alstonia*, genus name of *Alstonia constricta*) + *-ine*; orig. formed as G *alstonin*] **:** an alkaloid $C_{21}H_{20}N_2O_4$ found in the bark of a tree (*Alstonia constricta*) — called also *chlorogenine*

al·ston·ite \'ȯlztəˌnīt, -lst-\ *n* -S [*Alston*, Cumberland, England + E *-ite*] **:** BROMLITE

al·stroe·me·ria \ˌalztrə'mirēə, -lst-\ *n* [NL, fr. Baron Klas von *Alstroemer* †1794 Swedish botanist + NL *-ia*] **1** *cap* **:** a genus of showy So. American herbs (family Amaryllidaceae) having leafy stems **2** -S **:** a plant of the genus *Alstroemeria*

alt *abbr* **1** alteration **2** alternate; alternating; alternative **3** altitude **4** alto

al·ta fescue \'altə-\ *n* [prob. fr. Mount *Alta*, peak in Kittitas co., central Wash.] **:** a variety (*Festuca elatior arundinacea*) of meadow fescue used esp. as a late hay and forage grass

al·tai \ˌal¦tī\ *n* [fr. *Altai* Mts., range in central Asia] **1** -S *usu cap* **:** a Turkic dialect of Kirghiz, U.S.S.R. **2** *usu cap* **:** an Asiatic breed of small shaggy sturdy horses **3** -S *often cap* **:** an animal of the Altai breed

[1]**al·ta·ic** \(ˈ)al¦tāik\ *or* **al·ta·ian** \(ˈ)al¦tā(y)ən, -tīən\ *adj, usu cap* **1 :** of or belonging to the Altai mountains of central Asia **2 :** of or relating to the Altaic peoples or languages

[2]**altaic** \"\ *or* **altaian** \"\ *n* -s *usu cap* **1 :** a language family comprising the Turkic, Tungusic, and Mongolic subfamilies **2 :** a member of the peoples belonging to the Altaic language group

al·ta·ist \al'tāəst\ *n* -s *usu cap* [[1]*altaic* + *-ist*] **:** a specialist in Altaic languages or cultures

al·ta·ite \al'tā‚īt, 'al‚tīt\ *n* -s [G *altait*, fr. *Altai* Mts., Asia, its locality + G *-it* -ite] **:** a mineral consisting of lead telluride PbTe tin-white when untarnished and usu. occurring massive with cubic cleavage

al·tar \'ȯltə(r)\ *n* -s [alter. (influenced by L *altare*) of ME *alter, auter;* ME *alter,* fr. OE *altar*, fr. L *altare* altar, materials for burning on an altar; ME *auter*, fr. OF, fr. L *altare;* akin to L *adolēre* to burn up, and perh. to Sw dial. *ala* to flame, burn, Skt *alāta* firebrand, coal] **1 :** a raised structure (as a block, pile of blocks, pillar, or stand) on which sacrifices are offered or incense burned (as in the worship of a deity or of the spirit of a deceased ancestor); *broadly* **:** any structure or place serving as a place of sacrifice or worship **2 a :** a tablelike construction used in the Christian church in celebrating the Eucharist **:** COMMUNION TABLE — called also *Lord's table, holy table* **b** *in the Eastern Church* **:** SANCTUARY 1a(2) **3 :** a piece of furniture resembling an altar and used in ritual and ceremonial practices in the Masonic and other fraternal societies **4 :** any of the steps, ledges, or offsets the flights of which form the inner sides of a graving dock or dry dock

al·tar·age \-rij\ *n* -s [alter. (influenced by *altar*) of ME *awterage*, fr. AF *auterage*, fr. OF *auter, alter* altar (fr. L *altare*) + *-age*] **1 :** the offerings made upon an altar or to a church **2 :** the honorarium received by a priest for services at the altar **3 :** endowments for masses for deceased persons

altar boy *n* **:** a boy who is or functions as an acolyte

altar brass *n* **:** a set of brass furnishings (as candlesticks, cross, and flower vases) for use on a Christian altar

altar bread *n* **:** bread or a piece of bread to be used in the Eucharist

altar call *n* **:** a general appeal issued by a preacher from the pulpit in evangelistic worship services inviting worshipers to come forward to the front of the church or meeting area to signify their decision to commit their lives to Jesus Christ

altar card *n* **:** one of three printed cards containing certain eucharistic prayers placed on the altar during Roman Catholic mass as an aid to the celebrant's memory

altar cloth *n* **:** a cloth used as a covering for an altar

altar desk *n* **:** MISSAL STAND

altar facing *or* **altar front** *n* **:** FRONTAL 2

altar girl *n* **:** a girl acting as a lay assistant in church services

al·tar·ist \'ȯltərəst\ *n* -s [ML *altarista*, fr. L *altare* altar + *-ista* -ist] **:** one that attends at an altar; *specif* **:** VICAR

altar ledge *n* **:** a raised ledge at the back of an altar for candles, flowers, cross, or ornaments

altar mound *n* **:** an Indian mound built over an altar on which sacrifices had been burned

altar of repose *often cap A&R* **:** REPOSITORY 1d

altarpiece \'==‚=\ *n* **:** a work of art to decorate the space above and behind an altar

altar plate *n* **:** plate used in the Eucharist

altar rail *n* **:** a railing in front of an altar separating the chancel from the body of the church

altars *pl of* ALTAR

altar screen *n* **:** a screen at the back of a church altar **:** REREDOS

altar slab *n* **:** MENSA 1

altar stone *n* **1 :** a stone slab serving as the top of an altar and often (as in the Roman Catholic Church) specially consecrated **2 :** a small rectangular consecrated stone used as an altar by the Roman Catholic Church

altar wine *n* **:** SACRAMENTAL WINE

altarwise \'==‚=\ *adv* **:** as an altar is usu. placed

alt·az·i·muth \al'tazəməth\ *n* -s [ISV *alt*itude + *azimuth*] **:** an instrument consisting of a telescope mounted so that it can swing horizontally and vertically and used for observing the altitude and azimuth of a celestial body; *also* **:** any of several other instruments (as a theodolite) mounted so that it swings in the same way

[1]**al·ter** \'ȯltə(r)\ *vb* **altered; altered; altering** \'ȯltəriŋ, 'ȯl-triŋ\ **alters** [ME *alteren*, fr. MF *alterer*, fr. ML *alterare*, fr. L *alter* other (of two); akin to L *alius* other — more at ELSE] *vt* **1 :** to cause to become different in some particular characteristic (as measure, dimension, course, arrangement, or inclination) without changing into something else ⟨the extent of a monosyllable the text has here been ~*ed* —J.B. Cabell & A.J.Hanna⟩ ⟨preserve it as it is or . . . ~ it out of all recognition —Aldous Huxley⟩ **2** *archaic* **:** to affect mentally **:** AGITATE ⟨the ~*ed* mood of terror⟩ **3 :** to castrate or spay (as a domestic mammal) ~ *vi* **:** to become different in some respect **:** undergo change usu. without resulting difference in essential nature ⟨the old witch had not ~*ed* by a wrinkle in twenty years —Compton Mackenzie⟩ ⟨people themselves ~ so much that there is something new to be observed in them for ever —Jane Austen⟩ ⟨customs that must ~ with every new invention —Herbert Agar⟩ **syn** see CHANGE

[2]**al·ter** \'ȯltə(r) *also* 'äl- *sometimes* 'al-\ *or* **al·te·rum** \-tərəm, -‚rüm\ *adj* [L] **:** OTHER — used of something that is distinguished from the ego or esp. of other persons as contrasted with the ego

al·ter·abil·i·ty \‚ȯltərə'biləd·ē, ‚ȯl-tr-\ *n* -ES **:** the quality or state of being alterable

al·ter·able \'ȯltərəbəl, 'ȯl-tr-\ *adj* **:** capable of being altered — **al·ter·ably** \-blē\ *adv*

al·ter·ant \'ȯltərənt\ *n* -s [LL *alterant-, alterans* pres. part. of *alterare*] **:** something that alters

al·ter·a·tion \‚ȯltə'rāshən\ *n* -s [ME *alteracioun*, fr. MF & ML; MF *alteration*, fr. ML *alteration-, alteratio*, fr. *alteratus* (past part. of *alterare*) + L *-ion-, -io* -ion] **1 a :** the act or action of altering **b :** the quality or state of being altered **2 :** the result of altering: as **a :** a change in a legal instrument that changes its legal effect either in the obligation it imports or its force as legal evidence — distinguished from *spoliation* **b :** a change made in fitting a new or old garment ⟨no charge for ~*s*⟩ **c :** a change marked on a proof that does not accord with the copy or with a previous proof — distinguished from *correction* **d :** a change or modification made on a building that does not increase its exterior dimensions

☞ In this dictionary the abbreviation "alter." for "alteration" is used in etymologies with reference only to changes occurring within a language

[1]**al·ter·a·tive** \'ȯltə‚rād·iv, -‚rəd-, ȯl'terəd-\ *n* -s [ME, fr. MF or ML; MF *alteratif*, fr. ML *alterativus*, fr. *alteratus*, adj.] **:** any drug used empirically to alter favorably the course of an ailment and to restore healthy body functions — now rarely used technically

[2]**alterative** \"\ *adj* [ME, fr. MF or ML; MF *alteratif*, fr. ML *alterativus*, fr. LL *alteratus* (past part. of *alterare*) + L *-ivus* -ive] **:** causing alteration

al·ter·cate \'ȯltə(r)‚kāt\ *vi* -ED/-ING/-S [L *altercatus*, past part. of *altercari*, fr. (assumed) *altercus* contending, fr. *alter* other — more at ALTER] **:** to contend wordily **:** dispute with zeal, heat, or anger **:** WRANGLE

al·ter·ca·tion \‚ȯltə(r)'kāshən\ *n* -s [ME *altercacioun*, fr. MF *altercation*, fr. L *altercation-, altercatio*, fr. *altercatus* + *-ion-, -io* -ion] **:** warm contention **:** dispute carried on with feeling (as anger) **:** noisy controversy **:** wordy strife **syn** see QUARREL

altered *past of* ALTER

altered chord *n* **:** a chord in music having one or more tones that are chromatic or foreign to the key of the passage

al·ter ego \'ȯltə'rē(‚)gō *also* ¦äl- *or* -'re- *or* -tə'ē *or* -tə'e- *sometimes* ¦al-\ *n, pl* **alter egos** [L, lit., second I] **:** a second self: **a :** a trusted friend ⟨John became his *alter ego*⟩ **b :** a confidential representative ⟨his political *alter ego*⟩ **c :** a guardian spirit often represented in So. and Central American Indian carvings by the figure of an animal on the head, back, or shoulders of a human being

al·ter·er \'ȯltərə(r)\ *n* -s **:** one that alters ready-made clothing to fit the customer

altering *pres part of* ALTER

al·ter·i·ty \ȯl'terəd·ē *also* al-\ *n* -ES [LL *alteritat-, alteritas* (trans. of Gk *heterotēs*), fr. L *alter* other + *-itat-, -itas* -ity — more at ALTER] **:** the quality or state of being other **:** OTHERNESS

al·tern \ȯl'tərn, al-, '=(‚)=\ *adj* [L *alternus* interchangeable, alternate, fr. *alter*] *archaic* **:** acting by turns **:** ALTERNATE

al·ter·na·cy \'ȯltərnəsē *also* 'al-; ='===\ *n* -ES [[1]*alternate* + *-acy*] *archaic* **:** ALTERNATENESS, ALTERNATION

al·ter·na·men·te \(‚)äl‚ternə'mentē\ *adv* [It, fr. *alterno* alternate, fr. L *alternus*] **:** ALTERNATELY — used as a direction in music

al·ter·nance \'ȯltərnən(t)s *also* 'al-; *chiefly Brit* ='==\ *n* -s **:** ALTERNATION ⟨the sun marks the ~ of day and night —S.L.Terrien⟩

[1]**al·ter·nant** \'ȯltə(r)nənt *also* 'al-; *chiefly Brit* ȯl'tən- *also* al't-\ *adj* [L *alternant-, alternans*, pres. part. of *alternare* to alternate — more at ALTERNATE] **:** ALTERNATING

[2]**alternant** \"\ *n* -s **1** *math* **:** a determinant the constituents of whose different rows are (in order) the same set of functions of different variables, the same variable appearing in each row and the same function in each column, the terms row and column here being interchangeable **2 :** one of the statements in logic composing an alternation **3 :** any of the nonsignificant variants (as an allomorph or allophone) that together constitute a significant linguistic category

al·ter·nan·the·ra \‚ȯltə(r)'nanthərə *also* ‚al-\ *n* [NL, fr. L *alternus* + NL *-anthera*] **1** *cap* **:** a genus of low herbs (family Amaranthaceae) chiefly of tropical America and Australia with inconspicuous flowers — see ALLIGATOR WEED **2** -s **:** a plant of the genus *Telanthera*

al·ter·nar·ia \-'na(ə)rēə\ *n, cap* [NL, fr. L *alternus* + NL *-aria*] **:** a genus of imperfect fungi (family Dematiaceae) producing chains of dark muriform conidia that taper at the upper end — compare EARLY BLIGHT, LEAF SPOT, MACROSPORIUM

al·ter·nat \älternä\ *n, pl* **alternats** \-nä(z)\ [F, fr. lit., alternation, prob. fr. NL *alternatus*, fr. L *alternatus*, past part. of *alternare*] **:** the practice among diplomats of regulating precedence among powers of equal rank by lot or in a certain regular order; *esp* **:** the practice in the signing of treaties and conventions of giving each power the copy on which it appears at the head of the list of signatories

[1]**al·ter·nate** \'ȯltə(r)nət *also* 'al-; *chiefly Brit* ȯl'tərn- *or* -'tən- *also* al't-; *usu* -əd-+V\ *adj* [L *alternatus*, past part. of *alternare*, fr. *alternus* interchangeable, alternate — more at ALTERN] **1 :** occurring or succeeding by turns **:** one following the other in time **:** by turns first one and then the other ⟨~ gain and loss⟩ ⟨~ periods of working and unemployment⟩ **:** changing back and forth by turns **:** RECIPROCATING ⟨~ favors between friends⟩ **2 a :** arranged first on one side and then on the other at different levels or points along an axial line **:** not side by side ⟨stems with ~ leaves⟩ ⟨~ pitting in cell walls⟩ — see PHYLLOTAXY; compare OPPOSITE **b :** disposed at intervals **:** arranged one above or alongside the other ⟨~ stamens and petals⟩ ⟨~ layers of brick and stone⟩ **3 :** composed of members that occur or succeed by turns ⟨recurring figures in an ~ pattern **4 :** belonging to a series in which the members regularly intervene between or follow by turns the members of another series (as the odd or even members of the numerals) **:** every other **:** every second ⟨the ~ members 1, 3, 5, and 7⟩ ⟨the ~ verses of a responsive reading⟩ ⟨a maid who works on ~ days⟩ **5 :** ALTERNATIVE, SUBSTITUTE ⟨this highway is an ~ route⟩ ⟨copper may be used as an ~ material⟩ ⟨make an ~ selection⟩ — **al·ter·nate·ly** *adv*

[2]**al·ter·nate** \'ȯltə(r)‚nāt *also* 'al-; *usu* -ād-+V\ *vb* -ED/-ING/-S *vt* **:** to perform by turns or in succession **:** cause to perform or succeed by turns **:** interchange regularly ⟨~ the melodies⟩ ⟨~ endurance tests⟩ ⟨~ pipe and cigar⟩ ~ *vi* **1 :** to vary by turns ⟨gravel and macadam ~ along the route⟩ **:** take turns ⟨singers who ~ in the leading role⟩ — often used with *between* ⟨the weather *alternated* between sunshine and storms⟩ ⟨~ between study and writing⟩ **2 :** to happen, succeed, or act by turns **:** follow reciprocally — used with *with* ⟨the flood and ebb tides ~ with each other⟩ **syn** see ROTATE

[3]**al·ter·nate** *like adj*\ *n* -s **1 :** a choice between two or among more than two objects or courses **:** ALTERNATIVE ⟨the port is the ~ to New York as a shipping terminus⟩ ⟨several basic ~*s* to expansion of the building⟩ **2 :** one that takes the place of another **:** one that alternates with another: as **a :** an extra person appointed to take the place of another who is unable to perform his duty **:** SUBSTITUTE ⟨delegates to the convention and their ~*s*⟩ **b :** a person that takes his turn often at regular intervals with another of equal rank in an occupation or in performing a duty ⟨appointed ~ to the chief of staff⟩

alternate angle *n* **:** either angle of a pair of nonadjacent angles that a transversal forms with two lines, the angles being on opposite sides of the transversal, two pairs lying within and two without the two lines

alternate interior angles a, a′ and b, b′; alternate exterior angles c, c′ and d, d′

alternate bearing *n* **:** biennial bearing (as in some varieties of apples)

alternate consciousness *n* **:** a conscious state dissociated from a person's usual state and not remembered when he has returned to the latter

alternate host *n* **:** a host belonging to a species different from the one usu. inhabited by a parasite

alternate proportion *n, math* **:** a proportion derived from another proportion by interchanging the means

alternate straight *n* **:** SKIP STRAIGHT

alternating *pres part of* ALTERNATE

alternating current *n* **:** an electric current that reverses its direction at regularly recurring intervals the frequency being determined by the frequency of the alternator supplying the current and the successive half waves being similar in shape and area — abbr. *A.C.*

alternating–current resistance *n* **:** the ratio of the average power dissipated to the square of the effective current in a conductor carrying an alternating current — called also *effective resistance*

alternating function *n, math* **:** a function in which the interchange of two variables changes only the sign of the function

al·ter·nat·ing·ly *adv* **:** ALTERNATELY

alternating personality *n* **1 :** MULTIPLE PERSONALITY **2 :** multiple personality in which the several conscious states are not present simultaneously but follow each other consecutively

alternating psychosis *n* **:** MANIC-DEPRESSIVE PSYCHOSIS

alternating series *n* **:** a series in mathematics whose terms are alternately positive and negative

al·ter·na·tion \‚ȯltə(r)'nāshən *also* ‚al-\ *n* -s [ME *alternacioun*, fr. LL *alternation-, alternatio*, fr. L *alternatus* + *-ion-, -io* -ion] **1 a :** the act or action of alternating or effecting alternate succession ⟨intelligent ~ of crops⟩ **b :** alternating occurrence **:** SUCCESSION ⟨the ~ of day and night⟩ **2 a :** a statement in logic of the form *p* v *q*, idiomatically rendered "*p* or *q*" and meaning "*p* or *q* or both" **b :** the sentential connective *v* or *or* used in logic in the inclusive sense **c :** the truth-function or operation symbolized or signified in logic by *or* or *v* **3 :** the occurrence of different allomorphs or allophones

alternation of generations : the occurrence of two or more forms differently produced in the life cycle of a plant or animal usu. involving the regular alternation of a sexual with an asexual generation but not infrequently consisting of alternation of a dioecious generation with one or more parthenogenetic generations, the alternative forms differing greatly in appearance (as in the gametophyte and sporophyte of higher plants or the hydroid and medusa of certain coelenterates) or being distinguished with difficulty (as the dioecious and parthenogenetic females of some aphids or the sexual and asexual generations of certain algae and fungi) — compare HETEROGENESIS, METAGENESIS

[1]**al·ter·na·tive** \ȯl'tərnəd·iv, -tən-,-tain-, -nətiv *also* al-\ *adj* [[1]*alternate* + *-ive*] **1 :** offering a choice of two or more things **:** offering for choice a second thing or proposition or other things or propositions ⟨a means of transportation ~ to the railroad⟩ ⟨several ~ plans⟩ **:** expressing a choice or choices ⟨~ proposition⟩ **2** *of a conjunction* **:** indicating that the terms connected are to be taken not together but one in place of the other (as *or* in "for dessert you may have cake or pie") **3 :** ALTERNATE — **al·ter·na·tive·ly** *adv*

[2]**alternative** \"\ *n* -s **1 a :** a proposition or situation offering a choice between two things wherein if one thing is chosen the other is rejected ⟨a government facing the ~ of high taxes or poor highways⟩ **b :** an opportunity or necessity for deciding between two courses or propositions either of which may be chosen but not both ⟨the ~ of going by train or by plane⟩ **2 a :** either of two paired or contrasted things, courses, or propositions offered for one's choice in a situation in which taking either necessarily entails rejecting the other ⟨that humanism is the ~ to religion —T.S.Eliot⟩ **b :** a counter case matched with one expressed or accepted and characterized by implicit or explicit unreality or implausibility ⟨if the states had any power, it was assumed that they had all power and that the necessary ~ was to deny it altogether —O.W.Holmes †1935⟩ **3 a :** one of a number of things or courses offered for choice ⟨a third ~⟩ ⟨certain customs in our culture are ~*s*⟩; *specif* **:** one of the subsidiary statements preceded or followed by *or* in an alternation **:** ALTERNANT **b :** a choice or an opportunity or necessity for choice among three or more things **syn** see CHOICE

alternative cost *n* **1 :** the determination of cost and value by comparison with the best alternative product rather than by totaling factor inputs **2 :** OPPORTUNITY COST

alternative denial *n* **:** the complex proposition that denies that both of two propositions are true ⟨the *alternative denial* "not both *p* and *q*" is true if either or both of *p* and *q* are false⟩ — compare JOINT DENIAL

alternative tariff *n* **:** a schedule of transportation rates each section of which provides that the rates in some other section may be used if they are lower

alternative title *n* **:** SUBTITLE 1a

alternative vote *n* **:** PREFERENTIAL VOTING

alternative writ *n* **:** a writ in the nature of an order to show cause commanding the person to whom it is addressed to perform some duty or show cause why a peremptory or final writ should not issue

al·ter·na·tiv·i·ty \(‚)ȯl‚tərnə'tivəd·ē *also* (‚)al-\ *n* -ES **:** the power to choose between two courses of action

al·ter·na·ti·vo \(‚)äl‚ternə'tē(‚)vō\ *n, pl* **alternati·vi** \-(‚)vē\ [It, alternative, fr. ML *alternativus* — more at ALTERNATIVE] **1** *music* **:** a contrasting middle section of a movement in the 18th century suite — compare TRIO **2 :** a second trio section played or to be played between repetitions of the first trio in 19th century music

al·ter·na·tor \'ȯltə(r)‚nād·ə(r), -nāt̬ə- *also* 'al-\ *n* -s **:** an electric generator for producing alternating current

alternats *pl of* ALTERNAT

al·terne \'ȯl‚tərn\ *n* -s [F, fr. *alterne*, adj., alternate, fr. L *alternus* — more at ALTERN] **:** one of a group of adjoining plant communities usu. sharply differentiated from one another ⟨a grass ~ on the southward-facing slope of a ridge contrasted with forest ~ on the northward-facing slope⟩

alterni- *comb form* [NL, fr. L *alternus* alternate — more at ALTERNATE] **:** alternate **:** alternately ⟨*alterni*foliate⟩ ⟨*alterni*petalous⟩ ⟨*alterni*pinnate⟩

al·ter·o·cen·tric \¦ȯltə(‚)rō¦sen·trik *also* ¦al-\ *adj* [L *alter* other + E *-o-* + *-centric*] **:** ALLOCENTRIC

alters *pres 3d sing of* ALTER

alterum *var of* ALTER

al·thaea \al'thēə\ *n* [NL, fr. L, marsh mallow, fr. Gk *althaia*] **1** *cap* **:** a genus of Old World herbs (family Malvaceae) with terminal spikelike clusters of showy flowers each with 6 to 9 bracteoles below the calyx — see HOLLYHOCK, MARSHMALLOW **2** *or* **althea** -s [L *althaea*] **a :** ROSE OF SHARON 3 **b :** a plant of the genus *Althaea* **c :** the dried root of the marsh mallow deprived of the brown corky layer and small roots and used as a demulcent and emollient

al·thae·in *or* **al·the·in** \al'thēən\ *n* -s [ISV *althae-, althe-* (fr. NL *Althaea*, genus name of *Althaea rosea*) + *-in*; orig. formed as G *althein*] **:** a crystalline pigment obtained from the hollyhock having a bronze luster but being blue in alkaline solution

alt hor *abbr* [L *alternis horis*] every two hours

alt·horn \'al‚tȯrn, 'alt‚hȯ-, -ȯ(ə)n\ *n* -s [G *althorn*, fr. *alt* alto (fr. It *alto*) + *horn*, fr. OHG — more at ALTO, HORN] **:** the alto member of the saxhorn family used most frequently in bands where it often replaces the French horn — called also *alto, alto saxhorn;* see BALLAD HORN

althorn

al·though *also* **al·tho** \(ˈ)ȯl¦t͟hō\ *conj* [ME *althogh, although*, fr. *al* all + *thogh, though* — more at ALL, THOUGH] **:** granting or supposing that **:** even if **:** even though **:** in spite of the fact that **:** notwithstanding that **:** THOUGH ⟨~ he is hungry, he will not eat⟩

alti *pl of* ALTUS

alti- *comb form* [ME, fr. L, fr. *altus* — more at OLD] **1 :** high ⟨*alti*sonant⟩ **2 :** altitude ⟨*alti*graph⟩ ⟨*alti*meter⟩

al·ti·ca \'altikə\ *n, cap* [NL, prob. irreg. fr. Gk *haltikos* good at leaping, fr. *hallesthai* to leap — more at SALLY] **:** a genus of flea beetles usu. of blue or green color

al·ti·ca·me·lus \‚altəkə'mēləs\ *n, cap* [NL, fr. *alti-* + *Camelus*] **:** a genus of large long-necked American Miocene camels

al·ti·graph \'altə‚graf\ *n* -s [*alti-* + *-graph*] **:** an altimeter equipped with a recording mechanism

al·ti·lik \'altə‚lik\ *n* -s [Turk *altılık*] **:** a coin, orig. of silver and equivalent to 6 piasters, formerly used in Turkey

al·tim·e·ter \al'timəd·ə(r), 'altə‚mēd·ə(r), ¦tə-\ *n* -s [*alti-* + *-meter*] **:** an instrument for measuring height (as above sea level or ground level) usu. in the form of an aneroid barometer designed to register changes in atmospheric pressure accompanying changes in altitude and calibrated in feet, yards, or meters

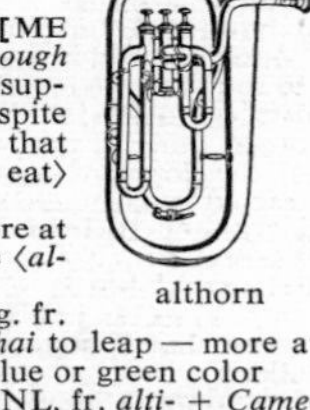
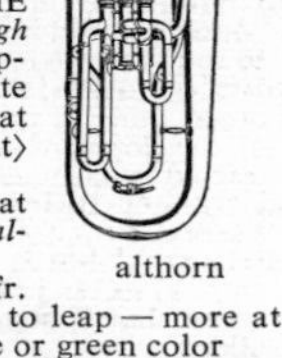

airplane altimeter, reading an indicated altitude of 500 feet: *1* barometer scale, reading 29.92 inches of mercury; *2* setting knob

al·tim·e·try \al'timə·trē\ *n* -ES [*alti-* + *-metry*] **:** the science of measuring altitudes

al·tin·gi·a·ce·ae \(‚)al‚tinjē'āsē‚ē\ [NL, fr. *Altingia*, type genus (fr. W. A. *Alting* †1800 governor-general of the Netherlands East Indies + NL *-ia*) + *-aceae*] *syn of* HAMAMELIDACEAE

al·tin·gi·a·ceous \¦=‚==¦āshəs, =¦==¦-\ *adj* [NL *Altingiaceae* + E *-ous*] **:** HAMAMELIDACEOUS

al·ti·pla·na·tion \‚altəplā'nāshən, -plə'-\ *n* -s [*alti-* + *planation*] **:** the erosion process that produces extensive flat surfaces at high altitudes

al·ti·pla·no \‚altə'plä(‚)nō\ *also* **al·ti·pla·ni·cie** \-plə'nēsē‚ā\ *n* -s [*altiplano* fr. AmerSp, fr. Sp *alti-* (fr. L) + *plano* plane, fr. *plano*, adj., flat, fr. L *planus* level, flat; *altiplanicie* fr. Sp, fr. *alti-* + *planicie* plain, fr. L *planities*, fr. *planus* — more at FLOOR] **:** a high plateau or plain **:** TABLELAND

al·tis·o·nant \(ˈ)al¦tisənənt\ *adj* [*alti-* + *sonant*] *archaic* **:** lofty or pompous **:** HIGH-SOUNDING

al·ti·ther·mal \‚altə¦thərməl\ *adj* [*alti-* + *thermal*] **:** of or belonging to a time during which the climate is relatively warm — often used of a part of postglacial time

al·ti·tude \'altə‚tüd, -ə‚tyüd\ *n* -s [ME, fr. L *altitudo*, fr. *alti-* + *-tudo* -tude] **1 a :** the angular elevation of a celestial object above the horizon measured by the arc of a vertical circle intercepted between the object and the horizon **b :** the vertical elevation of an object above a given level (as a foundation, the ground, or sea level) ⟨a city with an ~ of 2547 feet⟩ **c :** the perpendicular distance from the base of a geometric figure to the vertex ⟨the ~ of a triangle⟩ or to the side or face parallel to the base ⟨~ of a parallelogram⟩ **2 :** the height or an extremity of some quality or degree of excellence ⟨the ~ of human passion in Dante's poetry⟩ ⟨hopes raised to an ~ of tension⟩ ⟨standards in the College have been rising, and . . . despite their present ~, they continue to rise —N.M.Pusey⟩ **3 a :** vertical distance or extent **:** height or depth ⟨greater than the neighboring hills in ~⟩ ⟨~ of the fluid in the tube⟩ **b** (1) **:** position at a height ⟨the plane lost ~ rapidly⟩ (2) **:** exalted position (as in rank or power) ⟨a command issued from the ~ of the general staff⟩ **c :** an elevated region **:** EMINENCE — usu. used in pl. ⟨mountain ~s⟩ **4 altitudes** *pl, archaic* **:** haughty airs **:** POMPOSITY

altitude chamber *n* **:** a chamber having an interior that can be so controlled as to simulate the air pressure, humidity, and temperature encountered at various altitudes

altitude sickness *n* **:** the effects (as headache, lassitude, palpitation, nosebleed, nausea) of oxygen deficiency in the blood and tissues developed in rarefied air at high altitudes

al·ti·tu·di·nal \\ˌ==ˈ=d(ᵊ)nəl\\ *adj* [L *altitudin-, altitudo* + E *-al*] **:** of or relating to altitude — **al·ti·tu·di·nal·ly** \\-əlē\\ *adv*

al·ti·tu·di·nous \\ˌ==ˈ=d(ᵊ)nəs\\ *adj* [L *altitudin-, altitudo* + E *-ous*] **:** LOFTY, HIGH

al·ti·us non tol·len·di \\ˈältēəs·ˌnōn·təˈlen(ˌ)dē\\ *n* [L, of not raising higher] **:** the right to restrain another from building higher than a certain limit

alt·mann's granules \\ˈöltmənz-, ˈält,mänz-\\ *n pl, usu cap A* [trans. of G *Altmannsche granula*, after Richard *Altmann* †1901 Ger. histologist, their discoverer] **:** minute granules in protoplasm once regarded as its ultimate formative units but now physically equated with mitochondria

altn *abbr* **1** alteration **2** alternate

al·to \\ˈal(ˌ)tō\\ *n* -s *often attrib* [It, lit., high, fr. L *altus* — more at OLD] **1 a :** the part sung by the highest men's voices — compare COUNTERTENOR, FALSETTO **b :** the second highest of the four voice parts of the mixed chorus or choir or the lower part or parts in a women's chorus **2 :** a singer of alto parts; *esp, Brit* **:** a male alto singer (as in a cathedral choir) **3 :** the second highest member of a family of musical instruments ⟨the viola is the ~ of the violin family⟩ **4** *or* **alto horn :** ALTHORN

alto clarinet *n* **:** a large clarinet pitched a fifth below the standard B-flat clarinet

alto clef *n* **:** the C clef placed so as to designate the middle line of the staff in musical notation as middle C — called also *viola clef;* see CLEF illustration

al·to·cu·mu·lus \\ˌal(ˌ)tō+\\ *n, pl* **altocumuli** [NL, fr. L *altus* high) + NL *-o-* + *cumulus*] **:** a fleecy cloud or cloud formation consisting of large whitish or grayish globular cloudlets with shaded portions often grouped in flocks, rows, or layers and similar to cumulus clouds but at higher altitudes — see CLOUD illustration

altocumulus cas·tel·la·tus \\-ˌkastəˈlād·əs, -ȧd-\\ *n, pl* **altocumuli castella·ti** \\-ˈlād-ˌī, -ˈläd·(ˌ)ē\\ [NL, fr. *altocumulus* + ML *castellatus* past part. of *castellare* to fortify — more at CASTELLATED] **:** an altocumulus shaped like a tower

alto flute *n* **:** a large flute pitched a fourth lower than the ordinary flute — called also *bass flute*

¹al·to·geth·er \\ˌöltəˈgethə(r)\\ *adv* [ME *altogedere, al togedere,* fr. *al* all + *togedere* together] **1 :** WHOLLY, COMPLETELY, THOROUGHLY ⟨not ~ a fool⟩ ⟨~ stupid notions⟩ ⟨the evening was ~ pleasant⟩ **2 :** in all **:** all told ⟨losses amounting ~ to nearly a hundred dollars⟩ **3 :** on the whole **:** in the main **:** as a whole ⟨~ the institution compares favorably with others in the city⟩ — **al·to·geth·er·ness** *n* -ES

²altogether \\ˌ==ˈ==\\ *n* **:** NUDE — used with *the* ⟨swimming in the ~⟩

al·to·ist \\ˈal,tōəst, ˈaltəwəst\\ *n* -s **:** a player of the alto saxophone — called also *alto man*

al·to-re·lie·vo *or* **al·to-ri·lie·vo** \\ˌal(ˌ)tōrēˈlē(ˌ)vō; ˈäl(ˌ)tōrēlˈyā-, -ye-\\ *n, pl* **alto-relievos** \\-vōz\\ *or* **alto-rilie·vi** \\ˌäl(ˌ)tōrēlˈyā(ˌ)vē, -ye-\\ [It *alto rilievo*] **1 :** HIGH RELIEF ⟨adorned with columns and trophies in *alto-relievo* —Tobias Smollett⟩ **2 :** a sculpture executed in high relief; *esp* **:** a relief sculpture in which anatomical details (as arms or legs) are undercut so that, in part, they are detached from the background ⟨an *alto-relievo* by an unknown sculptor⟩ — opposed to *basso-relievo*

alto saxhorn *n* **:** ALTHORN

alto saxophone *or* **alto sax** *n* **:** the second highest member of the saxophone family pitched in F or E flat

al·to·stra·tus \\ˌal(ˌ)tō+\\ *n, pl* **altostrati** [NL, fr. L *altus* + NL *-o-* + *stratus*] **:** a cloud formation similar to cirrostratus but darker and at a lower level — see CLOUD illustration

alto tenor *n* **:** a boy's voice during the changing period which, while encompassing a limited tenor range, is neither alto nor tenor in tone quality and range

al·tri·ces \\alˈtrī(ˌ)sēz\\ *n pl, often cap* [L, pl. of *altric-, altrix* female nourisher, fr. *altor* male nourisher (fr. *altus,* past part. of *alere* to nourish + *-or* -or) + *-ic-, -ix* -trix — more at OLD] **:** altricial birds

al·tri·cial \\(ˈ)alˈtrishəl\\ *adj* [*altrices* + *-ial*] **:** having the young hatched in a very immature and helpless condition so as to require care for some time ⟨~ birds⟩ — compare PRECOCIAL

al·tri·gen·der·ism \\ˌal·trəˈjendə,rizəm\\ *n* -s [*altri-* (fr. L *alter* other, other of two) + *gender* + *-ism*] **:** the state or the period of development in which one becomes interested in or attracted to members of the opposite sex

al·tro-hep·tu·lose \\ˌal·(ˌ)trō-\\ *n* -s [*altrose* + *heptulose*] **:** SEDOHEPTULOSE

al·trose \\ˈal·ˌtrōs, -ōz\\ *n* -s [*altr-* (fr. L *alter* other) + *-ose* — more at ALTER] **:** a sugar $C_6H_{12}O_6$ obtained synthetically as a syrup that is stereoisomeric with glucose and epimeric with allose

al·tru·ism \\ˈal·trə,wizəm, -·,trü,iz-\\ *n* -s [F *altruisme,* fr. *altrui-* (alter. — influenced by L *alter* — of F *autrui* someone else, fr. OF, oblique case form of *autre* other, another, fr. L *alter* other) + *-isme* -ism] **:** uncalculated consideration of, regard for, or devotion to others' interests sometimes in accordance with an ethical principle ⟨Christianity, which is a religion of extreme ~ —R.M.Weaver⟩ ⟨the conflict is between selfishness and ~ —Estes Kefauver⟩ — compare EGOISM, EGOTISM

al·tru·ist \\-rəwəst, -rüə-\\ *n* -s **:** one that adheres to or practices altruism

al·tru·is·tic \\ˌal·trəˈwistik, ˌal·ˌtrüˈis-, -ēk\\ *adj* [*altruism* + *-istic*] **:** relating to or given to altruism **:** UNSELFISH — **al·tru·is·ti·cal·ly** \\-ək(ə)lē, -ēk-, -li\\ *adv*

alts *pl of* ALT

al·tus \\ˈaltəs\\ *n, pl* **al·ti** \\-,tī\\ *or* **altuses** [NL, fr. L, high — more at OLD] **:** ALTO

alu·chi resin \\əˈlüchē-\\ *n* [native name in Guiana] **:** ACOUCHI RESIN

al·u·del \\ˈalyə,del\\ *n* -s [MF *alutel, aludel,* fr. Sp & ML; Sp *aludel* & ML *alutel,* fr. Ar *al-uthāl* the vessel] **:** one of the pear-shaped or bottle-shaped pots open at both ends so that the neck can be fitted into the bottom of another similar pot in succession used to form a condenser in sublimation processes

al·u·la \\ˈalyələ\\ *n, pl* **alu·lae** \\-,lē,-,lī\\ [NL, fr. L, dim. of L *ala* wing — more at AISLE] **1 :** BASTARD WING **2 a :** a scalelike structure between the base of the wing and the halter of a two-winged fly — called also *calypter, squama* **b :** a small basal posterior lobe of the wing of such a fly; *also* **:** a similar lobe of the elytron of certain water beetles — **al·u·lar** \\-lə(r)\\ *adj*

al·u·let \\-,let,-ˌlət\\ *n* -s [irreg. fr. NL *alula* + E *-let*] **:** ALULA 2

¹al·um \\ˈaləm\\ *n* -s [ME, fr. MF *alum, alun,* fr. L *alumen* — more at ALE] **1 :** either of two colorless or white isomorphous crystalline double sulfates of aluminum having a sweetish-sourish astringent taste and used chiefly in medicine internally as emetics and locally as astringents and styptics: **a :** the potassium double sulfate $KAl(SO_4)_2.12H_2O$ occurring naturally and also made commercially (as by treating bauxite with sulfuric acid and then potassium sulfate) **:** potassium aluminum sulfate — called also *potash alum, potassium alum;* compare ALUNITE, KALINITE **b :** the ammonium double sulfate $NH_4Al(SO_4)_2.12H_2O$ made commercially (as from ammonium sulfate and aluminum sulfate) — called also *ammonia alum, ammonium alum* **2 :** any of a series of double salts isomorphous with potash alum that may contain analogous elements in place of the potassium, aluminum, and sulfur ⟨soda ~⟩ ⟨chrome ~⟩ ⟨selenium ~⟩ — compare PSEUDOALUM **3 :** ALUMINUM SULFATE — used chiefly commercially

²alum \\əˈləm\\ *n* -s [by shortening] **:** an alumnus or alumna

al·um·bloom \\ˈaləm,blüm\\ *n* -s **:** ALUMROOT 1

alum·bra·do *also* **alom·bra·do** \\ˌaləmˈbrä(ˌ)thō, -ä(ˌ)dō\\ *n* -s *usu cap* [Sp *Alumbrado,* lit., illuminated one, fr. *alumbrado* illuminated, fr. (assumed) VL *alluminatus,* past part. of *alluminare* to illuminate, fr. L *ad-* + *luminare* to illuminate, fr. *lumin-, lumen* light — more at LUMINARY] **:** a member of a 16th century mystical Spanish sect striving for spiritual illumination and union with God — called also *Perfectibilist*

alum cake *n* **:** a product of the action of sulfuric acid on clay consisting chiefly of silica and aluminum sulfate

alum carmine *n* **:** a red staining fluid composed of alum, carmine, ammonia, and water

alum cochineal *n* **:** a red staining fluid composed of alum, cochineal, and water

alu·men \\əˈlümən\\ *n, pl* **alumens** \\-mənz\\ *or* **alumi·na** \\-mənə\\ [L — more at *alum*] **:** ALUM

alumen us·tum \\-ˈəstəm, -ˈüs-\\ *n, pl* **alumi·na us·ta** \\-mənəˈəstə, -ˈüs-\\ [NL] **:** BURNT ALUM

alum flower *n* **:** powdered burnt alum

alum hematoxylin *n* **:** a staining fluid composed of hematoxylin, alum, alcohol, and water

al·u·mif·er·ous \\ˌalyəˈmif(ə)rəs\\ *adj* [*alum* or *aluminum* + *-i-* + *-ferous*] **:** ALUMINIFEROUS

alumin- *or* **alumino-** *comb form* [MF *alumin-,* fr. L, fr. *alumin-, alumen* — more at ALUM] **1 :** alum ⟨*alumini*form⟩ **2 :** aluminum ⟨*alumino*graphy⟩

alu·mi·na \\əˈlümənə\\ *n* -s [NL, fr. L *alumin-, alumen*] **:** the oxide of aluminum Al_2O_3 that occurs native as corundum and in hydrated forms, that is made, usu. from bauxite, in various forms (as a white powder obtained by calcination or a hard crystalline substance resembling natural corundum obtained by heating calcined aluminum oxide almost to the fusion point), and that is used chiefly as a source of metallic aluminum, as an abrasive and refractory, as a catalyst and catalyst carrier, and as an adsorbent (as in drying gases and liquids and in chromatography) — see ALUMINUM HYDROXIDE

alumina cement *n* **:** hydraulic cement having a higher alumina content, developing strength more rapidly, and being more resistant to heat and chemicals than portland cement

alumina porcelain *n* **:** a porcelain composed chiefly of alumina and used in spark plugs

¹alu·mi·nate \\əˈlümə,nāt\\ *vt* -ED/-ING/-S [*alumin-* (alum) + *-ate*] **:** to treat or combine with alum or alumina

²alu·mi·nate \\-ˌnət, -ˌnāt\\ *n* -s [*alumin-* + *-ate*] **:** a compound of alumina with a metallic oxide often regarded as a salt of an aluminum hydroxide⟨magnesium~$MgAl_2O_4$⟩—compare SPINEL

al·u·min·ic \\ˌalyəˈminik\\ *adj* [ISV *alumin-* + *-ic*] **:** of or relating to aluminum

alu·mi·nif·er·ous \\əˌlüməˈnif(ə)rəs\\ *adj* [*alumin-* + *-i-* + *-ferous*] **:** containing alum or aluminum

alu·mi·nite \\əˈlümə,nīt\\ *n* -s [G *aluminit,* fr. *alumin-* + *-it* -ite] **:** a hydrous aluminum sulfate $Al_2SO_4(OH)_4.7H_2O$ usu. occurring in white compact reniform masses

al·u·min·i·um \\ˌalyəˈminēəm, -nyəm\\ *n* -s [NL, by alter.] *chiefly Brit* **:** ALUMINUM

alu·mi·nize \\əˈlümə,nīz\\ *vt* -ED/-ING/-S [*alumin-* + *-ize*] **1 :** to treat (a metal) with aluminum or an aluminum compound to form a protective surface alloy ⟨~ steel⟩ **2 :** ALUMINATE **3 :** to coat (as glass) with a film of aluminum

alumino- — see ALUMIN-

alu·mi·nog·ra·phy \\əˌlüməˈnägrəfē\\ *n* -ES [*alumin-* + *-graphy*] **:** ALGRAPHY

alu·mi·non \\əˈlümə,nän\\ *n* -s [*aluminum ion*] **:** a precipitant for aluminum ion used in analytical work; ammonium aurintricarboxylate

alu·mi·no·sil·i·cate \\əˌlümə(ˌ)nō-\\ *n* -s [ISV *alumin-* + *silicate*] **:** a combined silicate and aluminate; *specif* **:** a silicate in which aluminum occurs in the crystalline structure in positions analogous to those of silicon, with four oxygen atoms as closest neighbors

alu·mi·no·sis \\əˌlüməˈnōsəs\\ *n, pl* **alu·mi·no·ses** \\-ō,sēz\\ [NL, fr. *alumin-* + *-osis*] **:** a lung disease caused by the inhalation of dusts of certain aluminum compounds

alu·mi·no·ther·mic \\əˌlümə(ˌ)nōˈthərmik\\ *adj* [*alumin-* + *thermic*] **:** of or belonging to aluminothermy

alu·mi·no·ther·mics \\=ˌ==(ˌ)=ˈ=miks\\ *n pl but sing in constr* **:** ALUMINOTHERMY

alu·mi·no·ther·my \\=ˈ==(ˌ)=ˌ=mē\\ *n* -ES [ISV *alumin-* + *-thermy;* orig. formed as G *aluminothermie*] **:** a process of producing great heat and strong chemical reduction by oxidizing finely divided aluminum with oxygen taken from another metal, this metal being thus reduced from its oxide (as molten iron is obtained from iron oxide in welding by the Thermit process)

alu·mi·no·type \\-,tīp\\ *n* -s [*alumin-* + *type*] **:** a relief-surface printing plate made by forcing molten aluminum alloy into a plaster-of-paris mold made from the surface to be duplicated

alu·mi·nous \\əˈlümənəs\\ *adj* [MF *alumineux* containing alum, fr. L *aluminosus,* fr. *alumin-, alumen* alum + *-osus* -ose] **:** relating to or containing alum or aluminum

aluminous cake *n* **:** ALUM CAKE

¹alu·mi·num \\əˈlümənəm *sometimes* alˈyü-\\ *n* -s [NL, alter. of *alumium,* fr. *alumina* + *-ium*] **1 :** a bluish silver-white trivalent metallic element, very malleable, ductile, and sonorous and noted for its lightness, good electrical and thermal conductivity, high reflectivity, and resistance to oxidation, that is the most abundant metal in the earth's crust, of which it forms over seven percent, always occurring in combination (as in bauxite, cryolite, corundum, alunite, diaspore, turquoise, spinel, kaolin, feldspar, mica), that is manufactured by electrolysis of a solution of alumina in molten fluorides, followed sometimes by electrolytic refining, that is used usu. in the form of alloys for structural purposes (as in the construction of aircraft, automobiles, and buildings), in the chemical and food-processing industries, in cooking utensils, and in electrical conductors, and that is used in the form of powder or flakes in pigments, pyrotechnic compositions, and explosives — symbol *Al;* see ELEMENT table **2 :** a nearly neutral medium-to-light gray

²aluminum \\"\\ *adj* **:** relating to, made of, or containing aluminum ⟨an ~ kettle⟩ ⟨~ earth⟩

aluminum brass *n* **:** an alloy containing about 76 percent copper, 22 percent zinc, and 2 percent aluminum

aluminum bronze *n* **:** a pale gold-colored alloy composed of copper and usu. five to ten percent aluminum with iron, nickel, and tin usu. being present in amounts less than one percent each and used esp. for corrosion-resistant parts, for wear-resistant bearings, bushings, gears, and dies, and for ornamental articles

aluminum chloride *n* **:** a deliquescent crystalline compound $AlCl_3$ or Al_2Cl_6, white when pure, that fumes in air and reacts explosively with water, that is obtained by chlorination (as of aluminum or a mixture of bauxite and carbon), and that is used in the anhydrous form chiefly as a catalyst — see CHLORALUM

aluminum hydrate *n* **:** the trihydrate of alumina — used chiefly commercially

aluminum hydroxide *n* **:** any of several white gelatinous or crystalline hydrates $Al_2O_3.nH_2O$ of alumina found in nature, esp. in bauxite, or obtained as precipitates by treating solutions of aluminum salts with hydroxides **:** hydrated alumina; *esp* **:** the trihydrate $Al_2O_3.3H_2O$ or $Al(OH)_3$ of alumina, regarded as acting both as a weak base and as a weak acid, that occurs as gibbsite and is used chiefly in ceramics, in pigments, and as a reinforcing agent for rubber

aluminum oxide *n* **:** ALUMINA

aluminum paint *n* **:** a paint composed of powdered aluminum and varnish

aluminum paper *n* **:** a paper of silvery appearance coated with powdered aluminum

aluminum soap *n* **:** any of various aluminum salts of higher carboxylic acids (as fatty acids) including aluminum stearate and aluminum resinate that are amorphous solids insoluble in water but soluble in hydrocarbon solvents and that are used chiefly in lubricating greases, in protective coatings, and in waterproofing compositions

aluminum sulfate *n* **:** a salt $Al_2(SO_4)_3$ colorless when pure that crystallizes with 18 molecules of water (as in alunogen) but is commonly desiccated to about 14 H_2O, that is usu. made by treating bauxite with sulfuric acid, and that is used chiefly in papermaking, in water purification, in sewage treatment, in tanning, in dyeing as a mordant, and in flameproofing — called also *alum, filter alum, papermakers' alum*

aluminum trihydrate *n* **:** the trihydrate of alumina — used chiefly commercially

alumite *var of* ALUNITE

alum leather *n* **:** leather tanned by the use of such substances as alum, egg yolk, and salt

alum·na \\əˈləmnə\\ *n, pl* **alum·nae** \\-(ˌ)nē *also* -,nī\\ [L, fem. of *alumnus*] **1 :** a girl or woman who has attended or has graduated from a particular school, college, or university **2 :** a woman who is a former member (as of an organization), employee (as in an office), or contributor (as to a magazine)

alum·nal \\-nəl\\ *adj* [*alumnus* or *alumna* + *-al*] **:** of or relating to alumni or alumnae

alum·nor \\-nər, -,nȯ(ə)r\\ *n* -s [*alumni* + *-or*] **:** a person employed to work with alumni and their organizations

alum·nus \\əˈləmnəs\\ *n, pl* **alum·ni** \\-,nī *sometimes* -(ˌ)nē\\ [L, pupil, nursling, foster son, fr. *alere* to nourish — more at OLD] **1 :** one that has attended or has graduated from a particular school, college, or university ⟨a Harvard ~⟩ ⟨an ~ of my college⟩ — usu. used of a man in the sing. but often of men and women in the pl. **2 :** one that is a former member (as of an organization), employee (as in an office), contributor (as to a magazine), or inmate (as of a penitentiary)

alu·mo·hy·dro·cal·cite \\əˌlümō,hīdrōˈkal,sīt, ˌalyə(ˌ)mō-\\ *n* [ISV *alumo-* (fr. *aluminum*) + *hydr-* + *calcite*] **:** a mineral consisting of a hydrous calcium aluminum carbonate $CaAl_2(CO_3)_2(OH)_4.2H_2O$ and occurring as white chalky radiating masses

alum rock *n* **:** ALUNITE

al·um·root \\ˈ==,=\\ *n* [¹*alum* + *root*] **1 :** any of several herbs of the genus *Heuchera; esp* **:** a No. American plant (*H. americana*) **2 :** a cranesbill (*Geranium maculatum*)

alums *pl of* ALUM

alum shale *or* **alum slate** *also* **alum schist** *n* **:** a shale or clay slate orig. containing pyrite and after weathering containing aluminum sulfate formed by the action of sulfuric acid from the decomposition of the pyrite on the aluminous materials of the rock

al·um·stone \\ˈ==,=\\ *n* **:** ALUNITE

alun-alun *also* **aloun-aloun** \\ˈä,lüˈnä,lün\\ *n* -s [Malay] **:** the public square in a Malaysian town usu. consisting of a grassplot surrounded by trees

Alun·dum \\əˈləndəm\\ *trademark* — used for a material made by fusing alumina in an electric furnace and used chiefly as an abrasive and refractory

al·u·nite \\ˈal(y)ə,nīt\\ *also* **al·um·ite** \\ˈalə,mīt\\ *n* -s [F *alunite,* fr. *alun* alum (fr. L *alumen*) + *-ite* — more at ALE] **:** a mineral consisting of a hydrous potassium aluminum sulfate $K(AlO)_3(SO_4)_2.3H_2O$ and occurring massive or in rhombohedral crystals

alu·no·gen \\əˈlünəjən\\ *n* -s [F *alunogène,* fr. *alun* + *-gène* -gen] **:** a mineral consisting of a white fibrous aluminum sulfate $Al_2(SO_4)_3.18H_2O$ frequently found on the walls of mines and quarries — called also *feather alum, hair salt*

alu·pag \\ˌä,lüˌpäg\\ *n* -s [Tag *alupág*] **:** a common Philippine timber tree (*Euphoria didyma*) with sweet edible fruit, the wood being used esp. for making combs

alur \\ˈä,lü(ə)r, äˈl-\\ *n, pl* **alur** *or* **alurs** *usu cap* **1 a :** a cattle-breeding Negro people north of Lake Albert **b :** a member of such people — called also *Luri* **2 :** the Nilotic language of the Alur people

al·ure *n* -s [ME *alour, alure,* fr. OF *aleor, aleoir* passage (fr. *aler* to go) & *aleure, alure* gait, course, gallery, fr. *aler* to go — more at ALLEY] *archaic* **:** PASSAGE, GALLERY, AMBULATORY

alur·gite \\əˈlər,jīt, ˈalər-\\ *n* -s [ISV *alurg-* (fr. Gk *halourgēs* genuine purple dye, lit., wrought in or by the sea, fr. *hals* salt, sea + *-ourgēs,* fr. *ergon* work) + *-ite;* orig. formed as G *alurgit* — more at SALT, WORK] **:** a manganese mica of purplish color

alush·tite \\əˈləsh,tīt, ˈaləsh-\\ *n* -s [Russ *alushtit,* fr. *Alushta,* town in the Crimea, its locality + Russ *-it* -ite] **:** a mineral consisting of a hydrous aluminum silicate and occurring in bluish or greenish claylike crusts and veins

alu·ta \\əˈlüd·ə\\ *n* -s [L] **:** a soft tawed leather

al·u·ta·ceous \\ˌalyəˈtāshəs\\ *adj* [irreg. (influence of *-aceous*) fr. LL *alutacius,* fr. L *aluta* soft leather, fr. *alumen* alum (used in tanning) — more at ALUM] **:** having the quality or color of tawed leather

¹al·var \\ˈal,vär, ˈäl-\\ *n* -s *usu cap* [Tamil *Āṛvār,* fr. *āṛ-* to sink, be immersed in meditation] **:** one of a group of southern Indian Vaishnava saints and devotional writers of the 7th to 9th centuries A.D.

²al·var \\ˈöl,vär\\ *n* -s [Sw *alvar*] **:** the plant community consisting typically of mosses and calciphilous herbaceous plants that grows on steppelike shallow alkaline soils overlying Scandinavian limestones

alvei *pl of* ALVEUS

al·ve·loz *also* **al·ve·los** \\ˌalvəˈlōz\\ *n* -ES [Pg *alveloz*] **:** the milky sap of a Brazilian plant (*Euphorbia heterodoxa*) used by the natives in the treatment of cancerous ulcers

alveol- *or* **alveolo-** *comb form* [L, fr. *alveolus*] **1 :** alveolus ⟨*alveol*ectomy⟩ **2 :** alveolar and ⟨*alveolo*labial⟩

al·ve·o·la \\alˈvēələ\\ *n, pl* **alveo·lae** \\-,lē,-,lī\\ [NL, alter. of L *alveolus* small cavity — more at ALVEOLUS] **1 :** a small depression or pit: as **a :** one of the pits in the naked receptacle of composite plants **b :** a pore of such fungi as *Polyporus* **c :** the pitted perithecium in certain fungi **2 :** ALVEOLUS

¹al·ve·o·lar \\alˈvēələ(r) *also* -,lär *or* -,lȧ(r *or* ˌalvēˈōl- *or* ˈalvēəl-\\ *adj* [prob. fr. F *alvéolaire,* fr. *alvéole* alveolus (fr. L *alveolus*) + *-aire* -ar] **1 :** of, relating to, resembling, made up of, or having an alveolus or alveoli **2 a :** of, relating to, or taking the form of a small pit or sac **b :** of or relating to the part of the jaw where the teeth arise, the air cells of the lungs, or glands in which the secretory cells are gathered about a central space **3 :** articulated with the tip of the tongue touching or near the teethridge (as the English consonant sounds \\t\\, \\d\\, \\n\\, \\s\\, and \\z\\) — **al·ve·o·lar·ly** *adv*

²alveolar \\"\\ *n* -s **1 alveolars** *pl* **a :** the alveolar processes in which the teeth are set **b** *or* **alveolar arch :** that part of the upper jaws in which the teeth are set; *esp* **:** the inner surface of such a part that is involved in the formation of certain speech sounds **2 a :** an alveolar consonant (as English \\t\\, \\d\\, \\n\\, \\s\\, or \\z\\) **b :** an alveolar sound

alveolar artery *n* **:** the branch of the internal maxillary artery that supplies the upper molar and bicuspid teeth

alveolar canals *n pl* **:** the canals in the jawbones for the passage of the dental nerves

alveolar ducts *also* **alveolar passages** *n pl* **:** the somewhat enlarged terminal sections of the bronchioles that branch into the terminal alveoli

al·ve·o·lar·i·form \\ˌalvēəˈlarə,fȯrm\\ *adj* [ISV *alveolar* + *-iform*] **:** ALVEOLIFORM

alveolar index *n* **:** GNATHIC INDEX

alveolar point *n* **:** a point on the alveolar process midway between the median upper incisor teeth — see CRANIOMETRY illustration

alveolar process *or* **alveolar ridge** *n* **:** the ridge or raised thickened border of the mandible and superior maxillary bones that contains the sockets of the teeth

alveolar surface *n* **:** a flat surface lying just within the cutting margin of the jaw of a turtle and functioning in mastication

alveolar theory *n* **:** a now discarded cytological theory that held protoplasm to be essentially an emulsion in which the apparent ground substance is the discontinuous phase

al·ve·o·lary \\alˈvēə,lerē, ˈalvē-\\ *adj* [*alveolar* + *-y*] **:** ALVEOLAR

al·ve·o·late \\-lət, -ə,lāt\\ *adj* [L *alveolus* + *-ate*] **:** pitted like a honeycomb

al·ve·o·la·tion \\al,vēəˈlāshən, ˌalvē-\\ *n* -s **:** the quality or state of being alveolate

al·ve·ole \\ˈalvē,ōl\\ *n* -s [F *alvéole,* fr. L *alveolus*] **:** ALVEOLUS

al·ve·o·lec·to·my \\al,vēəˈlektəmē, ˌalvē-\\ *n* -ES [*alveol-* + *-ectomy*] **:** the excision of a portion of the alveolar process usu. as an aid in fitting dentures

al·ve·o·li·form \\alˈvēələ,fȯrm, ˌalvēˈōl-\\ *adj* [*alveol-* + *-iform*] **:** shaped like an alveolus

al·ve·o·lite \\alˈvēə,līt, ˈalvē-\\ *n* -s [NL *Alveolites*] **:** a fossil coral of *Alveolites* or a related genus

al·ve·o·li·tes \\ˌalvēəˈlīd·ēz, (ˌ)al,vē-\\ *n, cap* [NL, fr. L *alveolus* small cavity + NL *-ites* -ite] **:** a genus of fossil corals of the Silurian and Devonian rocks having massive or branching bodies with compressed thin-walled corallites

alveolo- — see ALVEOL-

al·ve·o·lo·con·dyl·e·an \\alˌvēə,lō(ˌ)känˈdilēən, -ˌkändəˈlēən\\ *adj* [*alveol-* + *condyle* + *-an*] **:** of or relating to the plane which passes through the occipital condyles and the alveolar point — see CRANIOMETRY illustration

al·ve·o·lo·na·sal \-ˌnāzəl\ *adj* [*alveol-* + *nasion* + *-al*] **:** of or relating to the alveolar point and the nasion

al·ve·o·lus \al'vēələs\ *n, pl* **al·ve·o·li** \-ˌlī, -ˌlē\ [L, small hollow, tray, dim. of *alveus* tub, cavity, hollow, fr. *alvus* belly, hollow; akin to ON hvann*jōli* stalk of angelica, Gk *aulos* reed instrument like an oboe, OSlav *ulica* street, Arm *ul, uli* path; basic meaning: tube, long cavity] **1 :** a small cavity or pit: as **a :** a socket for a tooth **b :** an air cell of the lungs **c :** an acinus of a compound gland **d :** a cell or compartment of a honeycomb **e :** any of the pits in the wall of the stomach into which the glands open **2 :** the conical cavity in the anterior end of the guard of a belemnite **3 :** TEETHRIDGE **4 :** any of the converging tooth-bearing ossicles about the mouth of a sea urchin

al·ve·on \'alvēˌän\ *n* -s [*alveola* + *-on* (as in *prosthion, nasion*)] **:** ALVEOLAR POINT

al·ve·o·pal·a·tal \ˌalvē(ˌ)ō'-\ *or* **al·ve·o·lo·pal·a·tal** \al-ˌvēə(ˌ)lō-\ *adj* [*alveol-* + *palatal*] **:** in the more palatal of two positions between alveolar and palatal — compare PALATO-ALVEOLAR

al·ve·us \'alvēəs\ *n, pl* **al·vei** \-ēˌī, -ēˌē\ [NL, fr. L, tub, cavity, hollow] **:** a thin layer of medullary nerve fibers on the ventricular surface of the hippocampus major

al·way \'ȯl(ˌ)wā, ='=\ *adv* [ME *alwey, alway*] *archaic* **:** ALWAYS

al·ways \'ȯlwēz, 'ȯuw-, -wāz, -(ˌ)wāz, *before some consonants sometimes* -wəs\ *adv* [ME *alweyes, alwayes*, alter. (influenced by *-es* -s) of *alwey, alway*, fr. OE *ealne weg*, lit., all the way, fr. *ealne* (acc. of *eal, æl, al* all) + *weg* (acc.) way — more at ALL, WAY] **1 :** on every occasion **:** at all times **:** INVARIABLY, CONSTANTLY ⟨medieval spelling was ~ flexible —R.D.Altick⟩ **2 :** throughout all time **:** FOREVER, PERPETUALLY ⟨the cult of the superman will . . . ~ be with us —J.C.Wyllie⟩ **3 a :** in every circumstance or contingency **:** without exception ⟨an observed regularity will ~ hold —Edgar Zilsel⟩ **b :** at any rate **:** in any event **:** ANYHOW ⟨as a last resort one can ~ work⟩

al·yce clover *also* **al·ice clover** \'aləs-\ *n, usu cap A* [prob. by folk etymology fr. NL *Alysicarpus* (genus name of *Alysicarpus vaginalis*), fr. Gk *halysis* chain + NL *-carpus*] **:** a low spreading annual Old World legume (*Alysicarpus vaginalis*) of warm climates that is used in southern U.S. as a cover crop in citrus and tung orchards and for hay and pasturage

alyp·ia \ə'lipēə\ *n, cap* [NL, perh. fr. Gk, freedom from pain or grief, fr. *alypos* + *-ia*] **:** a genus of diurnal moths having black wings with brilliant white spots and including the eight-spotted forester

al·y·pin \'aləpən\ *also* **al·y·pine** \", -ˌpēn\ *n* -s [fr. *Alypin*, a trademark] *pharmacy* **:** amydricaine or its hydrochloride

alys·sum \ə'lisəm\ *n* [NL, fr. Gk *alysson* plant believed to cure rabies, fr. neut. of *alyssos* curing rabies, fr. *a-* [2]*a-* + *-lyssos* (fr. *lyssa* rage, rabies) — more at LYSSA] **1** *cap* **:** a genus of European and Asiatic herbs (family Cruciferae) having small yellow racemose flowers **2** -s **a :** a plant of the genus *Alyssum* **b :** SWEET ALYSSUM

al·y·tes \'alə,tēz\ *n, cap* [NL, prob. irreg. fr. Gk *alytos* not to be loosed or broken, fr. *a-* [2]*a-* + *lytos* capable of being loosed, fr. *lyein* to loose; prob. fr. the chainlike strings of eggs fastened to the male — more at LOSE] **:** a genus of toads (family Discoglossidae) comprising the obstetrical toads of southwestern Europe

alz·hei·mer's disease \'älts,hīmə(r)z-\ *n, usu cap A* [trans. of G *Alzheimersche krankheit*, after Alois *Alzheimer* †1915 Ger. physician] **:** senile dementia occurring at an early age

am [ME, fr OE *eam, am;* akin to ON *em* am, Goth *im*, L *sum*, Gk *eimi*, OIr *am*, Skt *asmi* am, *asti* is — more at IS] *pres 1st sing of* BE

-am \ˌam, ˌaa(ə)m\ *n comb form* -s [prob. fr. G, prob. fr. NL *ammonia*] **:** chemical compound related to ammonia ⟨lact*am*⟩ ⟨phosph*am*⟩

am *abbr* **1** ammeter; amperemeter **2** ammunition **3** amplitude

AM *abbr or n* -s [ML *artium magister*] Master of Arts

AM *abbr* **1** airmail **2** air marshal **3** amplitude modulation **4** [L *anno mundi*] in the year of the world — often printed in small capitals **5** *often not cap* [L] ante meridiem **6** associate member **7** Ave Maria

Am *symbol* americium

[1]**ama** \'ämə, 'a-, 'ā-\ *n* -s [LL *ama, hama*, fr. L, water bucket, fr. Gk *amē;* akin to L *sentina* bilge water, OIr to-eks-*sem* to pour out, Lith *semti* to draw up water] **:** AMULA

[2]**ama** \'ämə, 'ä,mä\ *n* -s [Hawaiian, Tahitian, Marquesan, Samoan, & Maori] **:** CANDLENUT 2

[3]**ama** \"\ *n, pl* **ama** *or* **amas** [Jap] **:** a Japanese woman diver who works usu. without diving gear

[4]**ama** \"\ *n* -s [Hawaiian] **:** the float of a Hawaiian outrigger canoe

amaas \'ä,mäs\ *n* -ES [Afrik] **:** ALASTRIM

ama·bi·le \ä'mäbə,lā, ə'-, -lē\ *adj* [It, lovable, fr. L *amabilis*, fr. *amare* to love + *-bilis* capable or worthy of (being so acted upon) — more at AMATEUR, -ABLE] **:** TENDER, GENTLE — used as a direction in music

ama·bi·lis fir \ə'mäbələs-\ *n* [part trans. of NL *Abies amabilis*] **:** a fir (*Abies amabilis*) of western No. America having deeply grooved leaves with a prominent midrib and a silvery-white lower surface — called also *white fir*

amability *n* -ES [L *amabilitat-, amabilitas*, fr. *amabilis* + *-tat-, -tas* -ty] *obs* **:** LOVABLENESS

am·a·cri·nal \ˌamə'krīnᵊl, ˌä,ma'k-\ *or* **am·a·crine** \'amə,krīn, \ä'ma,k-\ *adj* [*amacrinal* fr. [2]*a-* + *macr-* + Gk *in-, is* fiber, muscle, strength + E *-al; amacrine* fr. [2]*a-* + *macr-* + Gk *in-, is* — more at VIM] *anat* **:** of, relating to, or being an amacrine

amacrine \"\ *n* -s [[2]*a-* + *macr-* + Gk *in-, is*] **:** a unipolar nerve cell found in the retina, in the olfactory bulb, and in close connection with the Purkinje cells of the cerebellum

ama·dan \'ämə,thōn\ *var of* OMADHAUN

amadavat *var of* AVADAVAT

am·adel·phous \ˌamə'delfəs\ *adj* [irreg. fr. Gk *hama* together with + *adelphos* brotherly, fr. *adelphos* brother — more at SAME, -ADELPHOUS] **:** GREGARIOUS

am·a·dou \'amə,dü\ *n* -s [F, fr. Prov, amadou, lover, fr. L *amator* lover — more at AMATEUR] **:** [3]PUNK 2

ama·ga·sa·ki \ˌämə̇gə'säkē\ *adj, usu cap* [fr. *Amagasaki*, Japan] **:** of or from Amagasaki, Japan **:** of the kind or style prevalent in Amagasaki

ama·gat unit \ˌämə'gä-\ *n, usu cap A* [after Emile-Hilaire *Amagat* †1915, Fr. physicist] **1 :** a unit of the density of a substance (as gas or vapor) at 0°C and standard atmospheric pressure **2 :** a unit of the specific volume of a substance (as gas or vapor) at 0°C and standard atmospheric pressure

amag·mat·ic \ˌā,mag'mad·ik\ *adj* [[2]*a-* + *magmatic*] **:** not related to or involved in magmatic activity

amah \'ämə, 'ä(ˌ)mä, ä'mä\ *n* -s [Pg *ama* wet nurse, governess, fr. ML *amma* wet nurse, prob. of imit. origin] **:** a female servant typically Chinese; *esp* **:** NURSE ⟨Shanghai people . . . whole big families along with their cooks and ~s —Christopher Rand⟩

ama·hua·ca *or* **ama·wa·ca** \ˌämə'wäkə, ˌam-\ *n, pl* **amahuaca** *or* **amahuacas** *or* **amawaca** *or* **amawacas** *usu cap* [Sp, of AmerInd origin] **1 a :** a Panoan people of Brazil and Peru **b :** a member of such people **2 :** the Panoan language of the Amahuaca people

[1]**amain** \ə'mān\ *adv* [[1]*a-* + *main* (strength)] **1 :** with all one's might **:** with full force **:** VIOLENTLY ⟨he tugged and toiled ~ —Nathaniel Hawthorne⟩ **2 a :** at full speed ⟨they on the hill . . . came down ~ —John Milton⟩ **b :** in great haste **:** SUDDENLY ⟨left ~ their broken tasks —Joanna Baillie⟩ **3 :** to a high degree **:** GREATLY, EXCEEDINGLY ⟨pleased ~ —John Keats⟩

[2]**amain** *vi* -ED/-ING/-S [MF *amener* to lower, lead up (3d pers. sing. pres. indic. *ameine*) — more at AMENABLE] *obs* **:** to lower the topsail as a sign of surrender **:** YIELD

a ma·io·re \ˌä(ˌ)mä'yōrē, ˌā,mī'ō-\ *adj* [L *a majore* from the larger] **:** of or relating to an ionic foot beginning with two long syllables

amaist \ə'māst, a'-\ *adv* [ME (northern dial.) *almast*, alter. of *almost*] *Scot* **:** ALMOST

a major \'ā-\ *n, usu cap A* [[1]*a*] **:** the major musical key having a signature of three sharps

amakosa *pl of* XHOSA

ama·la \'ämələ\ *also* **am·lah** \'ämlə\ *n* -s [Hindi *'amala, 'amla*, fr. Ar *'amalah*, pl. of *'āmil* official] *India* **:** a minor official of a law court

ama·la·ka \ä'mələkə\ *n* -s [Skt *āmalaka* myrobalan] **:** a bulbous or melonlike ornament terminating the shikaras of medieval Indian temples

am·a·lek·ite \'amə,le,kīt, ə'malə,-\ *n* -s *usu cap* [Heb *'Ămālēqī*, after *'Ămālēq* (Amalek), grandson of Esau (Gen 36:12), from whom they were said to be descended] **:** a member of a powerful nomadic people living in the region around Kadesh south of Canaan by the time of the Exodus and wiped out by the Jews in the time of Hezekiah

[1]**amal·gam** \ə'malgəm\ *n* -s [ME *amalgame, malgame*, fr. MF *amalgame*, fr. ML *amalgama*, prob. modif. of Ar *al-jamā'ah* the assembly] **1 :** an alloy of mercury with another metal being made with most of the well-known metals except iron and platinum by merely bringing mercury and the other metal into contact, being solid or liquid at room temperature according to the proportion of mercury present, and being used esp. in making tooth cements; *specif* **:** a native alloy of mercury and silver occurring in isometric crystals or massive **2 :** a combination or mixture of different elements ⟨an ~ of wisdom and nonsense⟩ ⟨an ~ of peasants and businessmen —*N.Y. Times*⟩

[2]**amalgam** \"\ *vb* -ED/-ING/-S [ME *amalgamen*, fr. MF *amalgamer*, fr. *amalgame*] *vt* **1 :** AMALGAMATE **2 :** to cover with amalgam ~ *vi* **:** to unite, combine, or alloy — used with *with* ⟨mercury ~*ing* with an alloy⟩ — **amal·ga·ma·ble** \-gəməbəl\ *adj*

amalgama *n* -s [ML] *obs* **:** AMALGAM

[1]**amal·ga·mate** \-gəmət, -ˌmāt\ *adj* **:** AMALGAMATED ⟨two ~ natures⟩

[2]**amal·ga·mate** \-ˌmāt, *usu* -ād·+V\ *vb* -ED/-ING/-S *vt* **1 :** to compound or mix together **:** COMBINE, ALLOY ⟨silver *amalgamated* with mercury⟩ **2 a :** to unite or combine into a uniform and independent whole **:** INTEGRATE ⟨scattered fragments of humanity that had never shown any desire to be *amalgamated* with the social structure —Edith Wharton⟩ **b :** to unite or combine with an already existing whole **:** ABSORB, ANNEX ⟨policy of conciliating and *amalgamating* conquered nations —Agnes Repplier⟩ **3 :** to merge (as two societies) in a single body ⟨the two colleges were *amalgamated* to constitute a university⟩ ~ *vi* **1 :** to become amalgamated **:** become one **:** enter into close or intimate relations ⟨never united or *amalgamated* with man —*Commonweal*⟩ **2 :** to enter into a union (as by marriage) **:** INTERMARRY ⟨a tendency to ~ with the natives —C.W. Spencer⟩ **syn** see MIX

amalgamated union *n* **:** a union of smaller unions or of related crafts or occupations

amal·ga·ma·tion \əˌmalgə'māshən\ *n* -s [*amalgam* + *-ation*] **1 a :** the act or process of amalgamating **:** UNITING ⟨an opportunity for the ~ of Wales with England —G.M.Trevelyan⟩ **b :** the quality or state of being amalgamated ⟨in the 14th century the ~ of the races was all but complete —T.B. Macaulay⟩ **2 :** the result of amalgamating **:** AMALGAM ⟨an ~ of parishes to provide a workhouse for . . . the poor —G.E. Fussell⟩ **3 :** a consolidation or merger (as of two corporations) ⟨formed in 1844 by ~ of three smaller companies —O.S.Nock⟩ **4 :** a biological process of race mixture

amal·ga·ma·tion·ist \-shənəst\ *n* -s **:** an advocate of racial amalgamation

amalgamation process *n* **:** a process of extracting metals (as native gold and silver) from their ores by the addition of small quantities of mercury to the stamping or grinding unit so that the resulting amalgam is caught on mercury-coated copper plates from which it is then scraped, the precious metals in it being recovered by distilling off the mercury

amal·ga·ma·tive \ə'malgə,mād·iv\ *adj* **:** characterized by or tending to amalgamation

amal·ga·ma·tor \-ˌmād·ə(r)\ *n* -s **1 :** one that amalgamates ⟨henceforth Christianity was to be the prime ~ —H.O.Taylor⟩ **2 a :** a machine for use in the amalgamation process **b :** a person who tends such a machine

amal·ga·mize \-ˌmīz\ *vt* -ED/-ING/-S **:** AMALGAMATE

am·al·ri·cian \ˌaməl'rishən\ *n* -s *usu cap* [*Amalric* of Bena †*ab*1204 Fr. theologian and philosopher + E *-ian*] **:** a member of a sect of pantheists founded by the French philosopher Amalric of Bena

amal·tas \ə'məl,täs\ *n, pl* **amaltas** [Hindi *amaltās* drumstick tree] **1 :** CASSIA FISTULA **2 :** a tanning extract derived from the drumstick tree

ama·mau \ˌämə'maů\ *n* -s [Hawaiian *ama'uma'u*] **:** a small Hawaiian tree fern (*Sadleria cyatheoides*) of the family Cyatheaceae having petioles which yield soft hairs used for the same purposes as pulu

aman \'ämən\ *n* -s [Hindi *āman*] **:** long-stemmed rice grown in the rainy season in India

ama·na·yé \ˌämənä'yā\ *n, pl* **amanayé** *or* **amanayés** *usu cap* [Pg, of AmerInd origin] **1 a :** a Tupi-Guaranian people of the state of Maranhão in northeastern Brazil **b :** a member of such people **2 :** the language of the Amanayé people

amand *vt* -ED/-ING/-S [L *amandare*, fr. *a-* (fr. *ab-* [1]ab-) + *mandare* to send — more at MANDATE] *obs* **:** to send away **:** DISMISS

am·an·din \'amənd ən, 'äm-; ə'man-\ *n* -s [F *amandine*, fr. *amande* + *-ine* -ine, -in] **:** the typical protein of sweet almonds and peach kernels with the properties of a globulin

aman·dine \'ämən,dēn, ¦am-\ *adj* [F, fr. *amande* almond (fr. OF *almande*) + *-ine* — more at ALMOND] **:** prepared or served with almonds

amang \ə'maŋ\ *prep* [ME (northern dial.), alter. of *among*] *chiefly Scot* **:** AMONG

[1]**ama·ni** \ə'mänē\ *n* -s [Hindi & Per *amānī*, fr. Ar *amānah* security] **1 :** Indian government estates or other sources of revenue not leased or farmed out — compare ZAMINDARI **2 :** Indian government lands paying rent in kind instead of in money

[2]**ama·ni** \'ämənē\ *n* -s [Pashto, after *Amanullah* Khan *b*1892, amir of Afghanistan, 1919–29] **1 :** a gold coin of Afghanistan issued by Amanullah 1919–26 **2 :** a unit of value equivalent to one amani

aman·ist \ə'manəst\ *n* -s *usu cap* [*Amana* Society (prob. trans. of G *Amana-Gesellschaft*, fr. *Amana*, biblical name — Song of Sol 4:8 — for a range of the Lebanon mts.) + E *-ist*] **:** a member of the religious communal Amana Society organized in Germany in 1714, located at Amana, Iowa, in 1855, and known to the members as the Community of True Inspiration

am·a·ni·ta \ˌamə'nīd·ə, -ēd·ə\ *n, cap* [NL, prob. fr. Gk *amanitai* (pl.), a kind of fungus] **:** a genus of widely distributed white-spored agarics having an annulus and a volva that is separate from the pileus and with a few exceptions being poisonous

aman·i·top·sis \əˌmanə'täpsəs\ *n, cap* [NL, fr. *Amanita* + *-opsis*] **:** a genus of agarics distinguished by the absence of an annulus and being with a few exceptions poisonous

ama·no·ri \ˌämə'nōrē\ *n* -s [Jap] **:** an alga or a product prepared from algae of the genus *Porphyra* comprising purple gelatinous seaweeds that are dried and pressed and are important as food in Japan — called also *laver, nori*

am·a·nous \'amənəs, (')ā¦man-\ *adj* [[2]*a-* + L *manus* hand — more at MANUAL] **:** having no hands ⟨~ bipeds⟩

aman·u·en·sis \əˌmanyə'wen(t)səs\ *n, pl* **amanuen·ses** \-nˌsēz\ [L, fr. *a-* (fr. *ab-* [1]ab-) + *manus* hand, handwriting (as in *servus a manu* clerk) + *-ensis* -ese — more at MANUAL] **:** one who is employed to write from dictation or to copy what another has written **:** SECRETARY

ama·pa \ə'mäpə\ *n* -s [MexSp] **1 :** either of two Mexican timber trees (*Tabebuia chrysantha* and *T. palmeri*) used for veneering **2 a :** a large tree (*Parahancornia amapa*) of the family Apocynaceae of the Amazon valley **b :** a gum of this tree resembling chicle

am·a·ra \'amərə\ *n, cap* [NL, fr. Gk, trench; akin to Gk *amē* shovel, *diaman* to dig, OSlav *jama* pit] **:** a large genus of phytophagous ground beetles (family Carabidae) of oblong-ovate form, medium size, and usu. bronze color

am·a·ranth \'amə,ran(t)th, -aa(ə)n-\ *n* -s [in sense 1, alter. (prob. influenced by Gk *anthos* flower) of Gk *amaranton*, fr. neut. of *amarantos* immortal, fr. *a-* [2]*a-* + *-marantos* (fr. *marainein* to waste, wither, quench); in other senses, fr. NL *Amaranthus*, alter. (prob. influenced by Gk *anthos*) of L *amarantus*, a flower (prob. *Celosia cristata*), modif. of Gk *amaranton* — more at SMART] **1 :** an imaginary flower supposed never to fade ⟨beds of ~ and moly —Alfred Tennyson⟩ **2 a :** a plant of the genus *Amaranthus* **b :** PURPLEHEART **3 :** a dark reddish purple that is redder and less strong than patriarch and bluer and stronger than auricula purple or raisin purple **4 :** a red acid azo dye $C_{20}H_{11}N_2Na_3O_{10}S_3$ that is used chiefly in coloring foods, beverages, and pharmaceutical preparations and in dyeing wool and silk — see DYE table 1 (under *Acid Red 27*)

am·a·ran·tha·ce·ae \ˌaməˌran'thāsē,ē\ *n pl, cap* [NL, fr. *Amaranthus*, type genus + *-aceae*] **:** a cosmopolitan family of herbs and low shrubs (order Caryophyllales) having bracteate flowers in dense clusters for which many members are cultivated

amaranth family *n* **:** AMARANTHACEAE

am·a·ran·thine \ˌamə¦ran(t)thən, -n,thīn\ *adj* [*amaranth* + *-ine*] **1 a :** of or relating to amaranth ⟨~ bowers —Alexander Pope⟩ **b :** FADELESS, UNDYING ⟨the only ~ flower on earth is virtue —William Cowper⟩ **2 :** of the color amaranth

amaranth pink *n* **:** a deep purplish pink that is bluer and stronger than average orchid rose

amaranth purple *n* **:** a deep purplish red that is bluer and stronger than American beauty, redder and less strong than magenta (sense 2a), and redder, lighter, and slightly stronger than hollyhock

am·a·ran·thus \ˌamə'ran(t)thəs\ *n* [NL — more at AMARANTH] **1** *cap* **:** a large and widely distributed genus (the type of the family Amaranthaceae) of mostly coarse annual herbs having alternate leaves and small flowers with a 5-parted calyx and 2-celled anthers **2** -s **:** a plant of the genus *Amaranthus* — see PIGWEED

am·a·ran·tite \-ran,tīt\ *n* -s [ISV *amarant-* (fr. L *amarantus* amaranth) + *-ite;* orig. formed as G *amarantit* — more at AMARANTH] **:** a hydrous ferric sulfate $FeSO_4(OH).3H_2O$ of amaranth color

am·a·relle \ˌamə'rel\ *n* -s [G, fr. ML *amarellum*, fr. L *amarus* bitter, sour — more at AMAROID] **:** any of several cultivated cherries derived from the sour cherry (*Prunus cerasus*) and distinguished from the morellos by their colorless juice

ama·re·vo·le \ˌämə'revəlē\ *adv (or adj)* [It *amaro* bitter (fr. L *amarus*) + *-evole* -able (fr. L *-ibilis*)] **:** with bitterness **:** POIGNANTLY — used as a direction in music

amar·go·so \ˌämər'gō(ˌ)sō, -sə\ *also* **amar·go·sa** \-sə\ *n* -s [MexSp *amargoso* goatbush, fr. Sp, bitter, fr. (assumed) VL *amaricosus*, fr. L *amarus*] **1 :** the bark of the goatbush **2** [PhilSp, fr. Sp, bitter] **:** the balsam apple of the Philippines

am·a·ril·lite \ˌamə'ri,lit\ *n* -s [prob. fr. F, fr. Tierra *Amarilla*, Atacama province, Chile + F *-ite*] **:** a mineral $NaFe(SO_4)_2.6H_2O$ consisting of a hydrous sodium ferric sulfate

ama·ril·lo \ˌamə'ri(ˌ)lō; ˌamə'rē(ˌ)(y)ō, ˌäm-\ *n* -s [AmerSp, fr. Sp, yellow, fr. ML *amarellus* yellowish, pale, fr. L *amarus* bitter; perh. fr. association of the yellow skin color of jaundice with the bitterness of bile] **:** any of several tropical American timber trees: as **a :** a Venezuelan tree (*Aspidosperma vargasii*) **b :** either of two widely distributed Brazilian trees (*Terminalia obovata* and *Lafoensia punicifolia*) **c :** FUSTIC 1a

amar·na \ə'märnə\ *adj, usu cap* [fr. Tell el '*Almarna*, ancient station on the Nile river bet. Thebes and Memphis, Egypt] **:** of or belonging to the period of time about 1375–1360 B.C. that is described on the ancient Egyptian Tell el'Amarna tablets discovered 1887 and written in cuneiform characters containing the Asiatic correspondence of Amenhotep IV and his father Amenhotep III

am·a·roid \'amə,rȯid\ *n* -s [L *amarus* bitter + E *-oid;* akin to OE *ampre* sorrel, OHG *ampfaro*, ON *apr* sharp, Gk *ōmos* raw, cruel, Skt *amla, ambla* sour] **:** any bitter vegetable extractive of definite chemical composition other than an alkaloid or glucoside

am·a·roi·dal \ˌamə¦rȯidᵊl\ *adj* **:** relating to bitters or having a bitter taste

am·a·ryl·lid \ˌamə'riləd\ *n* -s [NL *Amaryllid-, Amaryllis*] **:** a plant of the family Amaryllidaceae — **am·a·ryl·lid·e·ous** \ˌamə¦ri¦lidēəs\ *adj*

am·a·ryl·li·da·ce·ae \ˌaməˌrilə'dāsē,ē\ *n pl, cap* [NL, fr. *Amaryllid-, Amaryllis*, type genus + *-aceae*] **:** a family of plants (order Liliales) found mostly in tropical regions and having perfect showy flowers with the tube of the perianth adnate to the ovary

am·a·ryl·li·da·ceous \ˌaməˌrilə¦dāshəs\ *adj* [NL *Amaryllidaceae* + E *-ous*] **:** of or relating to the family Amaryllidaceae

am·a·ryl·lis \ˌamə'riləs\ *n* [NL, prob. fr. L, the name of a shepherdess in Virgil] **1** *cap* **:** a genus (the type of the family Amaryllidaceae) of bulbous southern African plants having umbellate flowers with a corona of scales between the filaments — see BELLADONNA LILY **2** -ES **:** a plant of the genus *Amaryllis* or of any of several related genera formerly united with it (as *Hippeastrum, Sprekelia*, or *Vallota*)

amaryllis family *n* **:** AMARYLLIDACEAE

amas *pl of* AMA

amass \ə'mas, -aa(ə)s,-ais\ *vb* -ED/-ING/-ES [MF *amasser*, fr. OF, fr. *a-* (fr. L *ad-*) + *masser* to gather into a mass, fr. *masse* mass — more at MASS] *vt* **1 :** to collect for oneself **:** gather as one's own **:** ACCUMULATE ⟨~*ed* a large fortune⟩ **2 :** to collect into a mass **:** bring together **:** GATHER ⟨~*ing* daily trifles, writing down what came into her head —Virginia Woolf⟩ ~ *vi* **:** to come together **:** ASSEMBLE ⟨ivy . . . ~*ed* in bushes above . . . the porch —Elizabeth Bowen⟩ **syn** see ACCUMULATE

amas·sette \ˌamə'set\ *n* -s [F, fr. *amasser* + *-ette*] **:** a scraping instrument used in ancient and medieval painting for gathering on a slab colors intended to be ground

amass·ment \ə'masmənt, -aas-,-ais-\ *n* -s **:** the act or result of amassing **:** ACCUMULATION

amas·tia \(')ā'mastēə\ *n* -s [NL, fr. [2]*a-* + Gk *mastos* breast + NL *-ia* — more at MAMMA] **:** the absence or underdevelopment of the mammary glands

[1]**amate** *vt* -ED/-ING/-S [ME *amaten*, fr. MF *amatir*, fr. OF, fr. *a-* (fr. L *ad-*) + *matir* to overcome, fr. *mat* defeated, overcome — more at MAT] *archaic* **:** to cast down **:** DISHEARTEN, SUBDUE

[2]**amate** *vt* -ED/-ING/-S [*a-* (perfective prefix) + *mate* (to couple, match) — more at ABEAR] *obs* **:** to be a mate to **:** MATCH

[3]**ama·te** \ä'mäd·ē\ *n* -s [Sp, fr. Nahuatl *amatl*, short for *amacuahuitl*, lit., paper tree, fr. *amatl* paper + *cuahuitl* tree] **:** a Central American timber tree (*Ficus glabrata*) with lustrous foliage and edible fruits

[1]**am·a·teur** \'amə,tər (+V -ər-), -ˌtə(r) (*also* ˌ=='=), -d·ə(r), -ˌtə(r); -ˌtů(ə)r, -ˌtůə, -ˌtyů(ə)r, -ˌtyůə (*also* ˌ=='=); -ˌchů(ə)r, -ˌchůə, -ˌchə(r)\ *n* -s [F, fr. L *amator* lover, fr. *amatus* (past part. of *amare* to love) + *-or;* prob. akin to OHG *amma* mother, nurse, ON *amma* grandmother, L *amita* father's sister, Gk *amma* nurse, Phrygian adamnein to love] **1 :** one that has a marked fondness, liking, or taste **:** DEVOTEE, ADMIRER ⟨~s of this splendid wine will surely rejoice to learn that a limited quantity . . . will be available —*New Yorker*⟩ **2 a :** one that engages in a particular pursuit, study, or science as a pastime rather than as a profession ⟨the professional historians . . . have again let an ~ make off with a theme of real significance —T.H.Williams⟩ **b :** one that competes in sports or athletics for pleasure rather than for financial gain — compare PROFESSIONAL **3 a :** one that follows an art or science in a superficial way **:** DILETTANTE, DABBLER ⟨affected the pose of the gentleman ~ of the arts —F.H.Ellis⟩ **b :** one that engages in an activity in an inexperienced or incompetent manner ⟨the ~s, the green beginners . . . are naturally appalled by the shelfuls our curiosity persuades us to tackle —John Mason Brown⟩

[2]**amateur** \"\ *adj* **1 :** of, relating to, or having the status of an amateur ⟨football on an ~ basis⟩ ⟨an ~ writer⟩ **2 :** engaged in or performed by or as if by an amateur **:** NONPROFESSIONAL ⟨~ acting⟩

amateur band *n* **:** one of the bands of frequencies used by radio amateurs for communication

am·a·teur·ish \¦=='tər·ish, -¦tůr-, -¦tyůr-, '==ˌchůri-, -ēsh\ *adj* **:** having the characteristics of an amateur **:** lacking professional finish ⟨an ~ actor⟩ — **am·a·teur·ish·ly** *adv*

am·a·teur·ism \'==(ˌ)=ˌ==\ *n* -s **:** the practice, characteristics, or status of an amateur **:** NONPROFESSIONALISM ⟨~ in athletics⟩

am·a·tho·pho·bia \ˌaməthə'fōbēə\ *n* -s [NL, fr. Gk *amathos* sand + NL *-phobia*] **:** fear of dust

ama·ti \ä'mäd·ē, ə'-\ *n* -s *usu cap* [after *Amati*, 16th & 17th cent. Ital. family of violin makers] **:** a violin made by a member of the Amati family of Cremona

am·a·tive \'amədiv\ *adj* [ML *amativus*, fr. L *amatus*, past part. of *amare* to love + *-ivus* -ive — more at AMATEUR] **:** disposed or disposing to love **:** AMOROUS — **am·a·tive·ly** *adv*

am·a·tol \'amə,tȯl, -ăl\ *n* -s [ISV *ammonium* + connective *-a-* + trinitro*toluene*] **:** an explosive consisting of ammonium nitrate and trinitrotoluene

am·a·to·ry \'amə,tōrē, -ōr-, -ri\ *or* **am·a·to·ri·ous** \¦==¦=rēəs\ *also* **am·a·to·ri·al** \¦==¦==əl\ *adj* [*amatory, amatorious* fr. L *amatorius*, fr. *amatus* (past. part. of *amare* to love) + *-orius* -ory; *amatorial* fr. L *amatorius* + E *-al*] **:** of, relating to, or expressing sexual love ⟨the ~ affairs of youth⟩ ⟨an anthology of ~ poems⟩

ama·trice \ə'mä·trəs, (')a¦m-\ *n* -s [blend of *American* and *matrice*] **:** a gem cut from variscite and its surrounding matrix

am·a·tun·gu·la \,amə'təŋg(y)ələ\ *n* -s [Zulu *amatungulu*, pl.] **:** NATAL PLUM

am·au·ro·sis \,a,mȯ'rōsəs\ *n, pl* **amauro·ses** \-ō,sēz\ [Gk *amaurōsis*, lit., dimming, fr. *amauroun* to dim (fr. *amauros* dark, dim) + *-sis* -sis] **:** a partial or total loss of sight from disease of the optic nerve, retina, or brain without any perceptible external change in the eye — **am·au·rot·ic** \¦a,mȯ¦räd·ik\ *adj*

amaurotic idiocy *or* **amaurotic family idiocy** *n* **:** a recessive genetic defect manifested by mental deficiency associated with impaired vision or blindness

amau·ta \ə'mau̇də\ *n* -s *often cap* [Sp, fr. Quechua] **:** an Inca wise man and professional teacher

amawaca *usu cap, var of* AMAHUACA

amax·o·pho·bia \ə,maksə'fōbēə\ *n* -s [NL, fr. Gk *amaxo-*, *hamaxo-* (fr. *amaxa, hamaxa* wagon) + NL *-phobia*] **:** fear of being in or riding in a vehicle

amaxosa *pl of* XHOSA

¹amaze \ə'māz\ *vb* -ED/-ING/-S [ME *amasen*, fr. OE *āmasian*, fr. *ā-* (perfective prefix) + (assumed) *masian* to confuse — more at ABEAR, MAZE] *vt* **1** *obs* **a :** to fill with bewilderment **:** PERPLEX **b :** to fill with terror or alarm **:** CONFOUND **2 :** to fill with wonder **:** ASTONISH, ASTOUND ⟨proportions which continually ~ foreign observers —F.L.Mott⟩ ~ *vi* **:** to show or cause astonishment ⟨means by which they might astound or ~ —A.E.Wier⟩ **syn** see SURPRISE

²amaze \"\ *n* -s **1** *obs* **a :** mental confusion **b :** PANIC **2 :** AMAZEMENT ⟨with unfeigned wonder and ~ —J.L.Lowes⟩

amazed \-zd\ *adj* [ME *amased*, fr. past part. of *amasen*] **:** filled with wonder or astonishment **:** ASTOUNDED ⟨more and more ~ and not a little perplexed —T.L.Peacock⟩ — **amazed·ly** \ə'māz(ə)dlē, -li\ *adv*

amazeiner *n* -s [origin unknown] **:** a worker who feeds strips of shoe leather through a skiving machine to ensure thinner seams when strips are joined

amaze·ment \ə'māzmənt\ *n* -s **1** *obs* **a :** FRENZY, MADNESS **b :** BEWILDERMENT, PERPLEXITY **c :** CONSTERNATION, TERROR **2 :** the quality or state of being amazed ⟨left the squire staring after him in perfect ~ —Samuel Lover⟩ **:** great wonder or astonishment ⟨to her utter ~ she saw Mr. Darcy walk into the room —Jane Austen⟩ **3 :** something that amazes ⟨the wonders, the ~s of New York —H.H.Johnston⟩

¹amazing *adj* [fr. pres. part. of ¹*amaze*] **:** causing amazement, great wonder, or surprise **:** ASTONISHING — **amaz·ing·ly** *adv*

²amazing *adv, dial* **:** in a remarkable manner **:** EXCEPTIONALLY, WONDERFULLY ⟨the snow was ~ deep⟩

am·a·zon \'amə,zän *also* -,zən\ *n* -s [ME, fr. L, fr. Gk *Amazōn*] **1 a** *usu cap* **:** one of a race or nation of female warriors usu. associated with Scythia or Asia Minor with whom the ancient Greeks of mythology repeatedly warred **b :** a female warrior **c :** a tall strong masculine woman **:** VIRAGO **2 :** a member of a species or strain of animals known only as parthenogenetic females **3 :** a woolen dress goods in a satin or twill weave with the nap raised and shorn for softness **4** [NL *Amazona*] *sometimes cap* **a :** any of numerous parrots of *Amazona* and related genera of Central and So. America **b :** any of several brilliantly colored hummingbirds **c :** AMAZON ANT

am·a·zo·na \,amə'zōnə\ *n, cap* [NL, fr. *Amazon* river (Pg *Amazonas*)] **:** a large genus of tropical American parrots

amazon ant *n, usu cap 1st A* [so called fr. the legend that the Amazons captured children from other tribes and reared them as their own] **:** an ant of a genus (*Polyergus*) of slave-making ants of Europe and America which carry away and rear in their own nests the larvae and nymphs of other species

¹am·a·zo·ni·an \¦amə¦zōnēən, -nyən\ *adj* [*Amazon* + *-ian*] **1 a** *usu cap* **:** of, like, or befitting an Amazon **b** *of a woman* **:** having masculine characteristics **:** WARLIKE **2** *usu cap* **:** of or relating to the Amazon river or its valley

²amazonian \"\ *n* -s *usu cap* [*Amazonia*, regions about the *Amazon* river in So. America + E *-an*] **:** an Indian of the Amazon region in So. America

am·a·zon·ism \'amə,zä,nizəm, -,zə,-\ *n* -s *often cap* **:** the assumption by women of habits and occupations usu. regarded as masculine

am·a·zon·ite \-,nīt\ *or* **am·a·zon·stone** \'==(,)=¦=\ *n* -s [*Amazon* river, its locality + E *-ite* or *stone*] **:** a mineral consisting of a microcline of an apple-green or verdigris-green color

amazon lily *n, usu cap A* **:** a plant of the genus *Eucharis*

amazon sword *or* **amazon swordplant** *n, usu cap A* [fr. *Amazon* river] **:** an aquatic or marsh herb (*Echinodorus intermedius*) used as a table centerpiece and in aquariums

amazon terrapin *n, usu cap A* [fr. *Amazon* river] **:** a large tropical American river terrapin (*Podocnemis expansa*) whose eggs are a valuable source of oil

amazon water lily *n, usu cap A* [fr. *Amazon* river] **:** ROYAL WATER LILY

amb *abbr* **1** ambassador **2** ambulance

¹amba *var of* ANBA

²am·ba \'ambə, 'äm-\ *n, pl* **amba** *or* **ambas** *usu cap* **1 :** a Bantu-speaking people of southwestern Uganda of small stature and supposed to be of mixed Pygmy descent **2 :** a member of the Amba people

ambach *var of* AMBATCH

am·bage \'ambij\ *n, pl* **amba·ges** \am'bā,jēz, 'ambijəz\ [back-formation fr. ME *ambages*, fr. MF or L; MF, fr. L, roundabout way, circumlocution, ambiguity, fr. *amb-* (var. of *ambi-*) + *-ages* (fr. *agere* to drive, lead, act, do) — more at AGENT] **1** *archaic* **:** a roundabout way of speaking **:** AMBIGUITY, CIRCUMLOCUTION — usu. used in pl. **2** *ambages pl, archaic* **a :** winding or circuitous paths **b :** indirect ways or proceedings **c :** secret or mysterious ways of action

am·ba·gious \(')am¦bājəs\ *adj* [L *ambagiosus*, fr. *ambages* + *-osus* -ous] *archaic* **:** ROUNDABOUT, CIRCUITOUS — **am·ba·gious·ly** *adv*

am·ba·lam \'əmbələm\ *n* -s [Sinhalese *ambalama*] **:** a Ceylonese resthouse for travelers; *also* **:** a village meeting place in Ceylon

am·ba·ree *also* **am·ba·ri** \(,)əm'bärē\ *n* -s [Hindi *'ambārī*, *'amārī*, fr. Per *'amārī*, fr. Ar] *India* **:** a canopied howdah

am·ba·rel·la \,ambə'relə\ *n* -s [Sinhalese *æmbarælla*, fr. Skt *āmravāṭaka* (*Spondias mangifera*), fr. *āmra* mango (fr. *amla* sour) + *vāṭaka* enclosure, garden, fr. *vaṭa* surrounded; akin to Skt *valate* he turns — more at AMAROID, VOLUBLE] **:** OTAHEITE APPLE

am·ba·ri \am'bärē, ,əm-\ *or* **ambari hemp** \(')am¦b-, ¦əm¦b-\ *n* -s [Hindi *ambārā, ambārī*] **:** KENAF

am·bash·tha \(,)əm'bəshtə\ *n* -s *usu cap* [Skt *Ambaṣṭha*] **:** a member of a caste in India formed by persons descended from Brahman fathers and Vaisya mothers and having the practice of the art of healing as its prerogative

am·bas·sade \¦ambə¦sād, -äd\ *also* **em·bas·sade** \¦em-\ *n* -s [ME *ambassade*, fr. MF *ambassade, ambassiate*, fr. OIt *ambasciata* — more at EMBASSY] *archaic* **:** the mission of an ambassador or those sent on a mission

am·bas·sa·dor *also* **em·bas·sa·dor** \am'basədə(r), əm-, aam'baas- *also* em- *or* -sə,dȯ(ə)r *or* -sə,dō(ə) *or* -sdə(r) *or*, *rap.*, -stə(r)\ *n* -s [ME *ambassadour, embassadour, ambassatour, embassatour, ambassiatour, embassiatour*, fr. MF *ambassadeur, embassadeur, ambassateur, embassateur, ambassiateur*, fr. OIt *ambasciatore*, fr. OProv *ambaissador*, fr. (assumed) *ambaisa* mission — more at EMBASSY] **1** *sometimes cap* **:** an official representative of a sovereign or state: as **a :** a minister of the highest rank accredited to a foreign government or sovereign as the resident representative of his own government or sovereign **b :** a minister of the highest rank appointed for a special and often temporary diplomatic assignment **2 a :** an authorized or appointed representative or messenger ⟨the association . . . sends ~s to the state and national capitals to promote its interests —W.P.Webb⟩ **b :** an unofficial representative ⟨an effective ~ of American culture⟩

ambassador-at-large *n, pl* **ambassadors-at-large** *sometimes cap 1st A & L* **:** a minister of the highest rank not accredited to a particular foreign government or sovereign ⟨the *ambassador-at-large* . . . could assist . . . in important international negotiations —G.H.Stuart⟩

am·bas·sa·do·ri·al \(,)am,basə'dōrēəl, əm-, (,)aam-, -aas-, -ōr- *also* em-\ *adj* **:** of or relating to an ambassador or ambassadors — **am·bas·sa·do·ri·al·ly** \-əlē, -li\ *adv*

am·bas·sa·dor·ship \='===,ship\ *n* -s **:** the office, position, or function of an ambassador

am·bas·sa·dress *also* **em·bas·sa·dress** \am'basədrəs, əm-, aam'baas- *also* em-\ *n* -ES [*ambassador, embassador* + *-ess*] **1 :** a female ambassador **2 :** the wife of an ambassador

am·bas·sage *var of* EMBASSAGE

am·batch *also* **am·bach** \'am,bach\ *n* -ES [prob. of Ethiopic origin; akin to Tigrinya *ambasha, ambatcha*, Amharic *ambatcho*, names of various plants] **:** a rapidly growing thorny tree (*Aeschynomene elaphroxylon*) of the Nile valley valued for its white pithlike wood

am·ba·to·ar·i·nite \,ambə(,)tō'arə,nīt\ *n* -s [F, fr. *Ambatoarina*, town near Ambositra, Madagascar, its locality + F *-ite*] **:** a mineral $5SrCO_3.4(Ce,La,Di)_2(CO_3)_3.(Ce,La,Di)_2O_3$ consisting of an orthorhombic carbonate of the cerium metals and strontium

am·bay \'am,bī\ *n* -s [modif. of AmerSp *ambaiba*, fr. Tupi] **:** an Argentine timber tree (*Cecropia adenopus*) with light soft wood

am·beer \'am,bi(ə)r, -iə\ *n* -s [prob. alter. of *amber*; fr. its color] *chiefly South & Midland* **:** TOBACCO JUICE

¹am·ber \'ambə(r), 'aam-\ *n* -s [ME *ambra, ambre*, fr. MF & ML; MF *ambre*, fr. ML *ambra, ambar*, fr. Ar *'anbar* ambergris] **1** *obs* **:** AMBERGRIS **2 :** a very hard yellowish to brownish translucent fossil resin that is found in alluvial soils, in beds of lignite, or on some seashores, that takes a fine polish, and that is used chiefly in making ornamental objects (as beads and pipe mouthpieces) **3 a :** a variable color averaging a dark orange yellow that is yellower, lighter, and stronger than topaz **b :** the variable color of amber that averages the color lime **c :** AMBER YELLOW **4 a :** KLAMATH WEED **b :** SWEET GUM 1a

²amber \"\ *adj* **1 :** consisting of amber **2 :** resembling amber; *esp* **:** having the color amber ⟨on a special ~ afternoon of late November —Gladys B. Stern⟩

³amber \"\ *vt* **ambered**; **ambered**; **ambering** \-b(ə)riŋ\ **ambers** [²*amber*] **:** to make amber in color

⁴amber *n* -s [OE *amber, ambor, ember* vessel, pail, a dry measure; akin to OS *ēmbar* pail, OHG *ambar*; all fr. a prehistoric WGmc word borrowed fr. L *amphora* vessel with two handles — more at AMPHORA] **:** an Anglo-Saxon unit of capacity for dry or liquid measure

amber brown *n* **:** a brownish orange that is less strong and slightly yellower and lighter than spice, slightly yellower and lighter than prairie brown, Windsor tan, or Titian, and slightly redder and darker than gold pheasant

ambercane \'==,=\ *n* -s [so called fr. its color] **:** a sorghum (*Sorghum dochna*) used esp. in southern Africa as a fodder and grain crop

amberfish \'==,=\ *n* [so called fr. its color] **:** any of numerous tropical or subtropical fishes of *Seriola* or related genera (family Carangidae) — compare AMBERJACK, YELLOWTAIL

amber forest *n* **:** a forest whose trees yielded the resin that fossilized into amber

am·ber·gris \'ambə(r),gris, 'aam-, -,grēs, -,grəs *sometimes* -,grē *also* **am·ber·grease** \-,grēs\ *n, pl* **ambergrises** *also* **ambergreases** [*ambergris* fr. ME *ambregris*, fr. MF *ambre gris*, fr. *ambre* ambergris, amber + *gris* gray; *ambergrease* by folk etymology fr. *ambergris* — more at AMBER, GRIZZLE] **:** a white, ash-gray, yellow, or black and often variegated substance having a characteristic odor and the consistency of wax, found floating in or on the shores of the Indian ocean and other tropical waters, believed to originate as an accumulation in the intestines of the sperm whale, and used in perfumery as a fixative

am·ber·i·na \,=bə'rēnə\ *n* -s [fr. *Amberina*, a trademark] **:** a late 19th century American clear glassware of graduated color that shades from ruby to amber

am·ber·jack \'=bə(r),jak\ *n* -s [¹*amber* + *jack* (fish); fr. its color] **1 :** AMBERFISH: as **a :** a large vigorous sport fish (*Seriola zonata* or *dumerili*) of the western Atlantic from Massachusetts to Brazil **b :** a yellowtail (*S. dorsalis*) **2 :** SPHALERITE

am·ber·lite \-,līt\ *n* -s [prob. fr. *Amberlite*, a trademark for certain resins] **:** a light yellowish brown that is redder, lighter, and stronger than khaki, lighter, stronger, and slightly redder than walnut brown, and lighter and stronger than cinnamon

amber malt *n* **:** malt cured at a high temperature in the kiln, the diastase being greatly restricted

amber mica *n* **:** PHLOGOPITE

am·ber·oid \'=bə,rȯid\ *also* **am·broid** \'=,brȯid\ *n* -s [¹*amber* + *-oid*] **:** a material consisting of small pieces of amber or sometimes other resins united by heat and pressure

amber oil *n* **1 :** a pale yellow to brownish essential oil of empyreumatic odor and acrid taste made by destructive distillation of amber **2 :** a light essential oil obtained by destructive distillation of rosin

amber seed *n* **:** the seed of the abelmosk resembling millet and having a musky flavor — called also *ambrette, musk seed*

amber shell *or* **amber snail** *n* **:** a pulmonate land snail of the family Succineidae

amber tree *n* **1 :** a fossil tree (*Pinites succinifer*) **2 :** a southern African shrub of the genus *Anthospermum*

amber white *n* **:** a pale yellow green that is yellower, lighter, and stronger than smoke gray, slightly yellower, stronger, and slightly lighter than oyster gray, and yellower, lighter, and slightly stronger than average Nile

amber yellow *n* **:** a light to moderate yellow that is greener and stronger than buff (sense 4b) and greener than snapdragon — called also *Venetian yellow*

ambi- *prefix* [L *ambi-, amb-* both, on both sides, around; akin to L *ambo* both, Gk *amphō* both, *amphi* around — more at BY] **:** both ⟨*ambi*lateral⟩ ⟨*ambi*parous⟩

am·bi·col·or·ate \¦ambē¦kələrət, -,rāt\ *adj* [*ambi-* + *colorate*] **:** exhibiting ambicoloration

am·bi·col·or·a·tion \¦==,=='rāshən\ *n* -s [*ambi-* + *coloration*] **:** an abnormal development of color or pigmentation on the eyeless and ordinarily whitish side of any flatfish of the families Pleuronectidae and Soleidae

¹am·bi·dex·ter \¦ambə¦dekstə(r), ¦aam-\ *n* -s [in sense 1, fr. ME, fr. ML, fr. *ambidexter*, adj., fr. LL, skillful with both hands; in sense 2, fr. LL, fr. *ambidexter*, adj.] **1 a :** one that takes bribes or fees from both sides **b** *archaic* **:** one that practices duplicity **2** *obs* **:** one that uses both hands with equal facility

²ambidexter \"\ *adj* [ML & LL; ML, double-dealing, fr. LL, skillful with both hands (trans. of Gk *amphoterodexios*), fr. *ambi-* + *dexter* on the right, skillful — more at DEXTER] *archaic* **:** AMBIDEXTROUS

am·bi·dex·ter·i·ty \¦==,dek'sterəd·ē, -ətē, -i\ *n* -s **:** the quality or state of being ambidextrous

am·bi·dex·trous \¦==¦dekstrəs\ *adj* [LL & ML *ambidexter* + E *-ous*] **1 :** capable of using both hands with equal ease ⟨~ tennis players are rare⟩ **2 :** unusually skillful **:** VERSATILE, FACILE ⟨completely ~ . . . completely able to express himself in verse or prose —T.S.Eliot⟩ **3 :** characterized by duplicity **:** DOUBLE-DEALING ⟨unordained, uneducated, and theologically . . . ~ —G.H.Genzmer⟩ — **am·bi·dex·trous·ly** *adv*

am·bi·ence *or* **am·bi·ance** \ä^n^byä^n^s\ *n, pl* **ambi·ences** *or* **ambi·ances** \"\ [F *ambiance*, fr. *ambiant* surrounding (after such pairs as *confiant* confident: *confiance* confidence), fr. L *ambient-, ambiens* — more at AMBIENT] **:** a surrounding or pervading atmosphere **:** ENVIRONMENT, MILIEU ⟨moves out of provincial society and out of the ~ of exclusively female friendships —Lionel Trilling⟩

am·bi·ens \'ambē,enz\ *n, pl* **ambien·tes** \,=='en,tēz\ [NL, fr. L, pres. part. of *ambire*] **:** a thigh muscle of certain birds having the tendon passing over the knee and connecting with the tendon of a muscle that bends the toes so that the body weight on perching causes the knee to bend and the feet to clasp the perch on which the bird sits

¹am·bi·ent \'ambēənt, 'aam-\ *adj* [L *ambient-, ambiens*, pres. part. of *ambire* to go around, surround, encompass, fr. *ambi-* around + *ire* to go — more at AMBI-, ISSUE] **:** surrounding on all sides **:** ENCOMPASSING, ENVELOPING ⟨to exist in the ~ of space, to envelop him like a peculiar fragrance —Joseph Conrad⟩ ⟨voice communication in . . . high ~ noise —E.B. Newman⟩ ⟨~ temperature⟩

²ambient \"\ *n* -s **1 :** an encompassing sphere; *esp* **:** ATMOSPHERE **2 :** an encompassing atmosphere **:** ENVIRONMENT, AMBIENCE ⟨the re-creation of the various ~s in which Unamuno moved —Dudley Fitts⟩

am·bi·en·te \am'byentē, aam-; ,ambē'en-\ *n* -s [It & Sp, fr. L *ambient-, ambiens*, pres. part.] **:** surrounding atmosphere **:** MILIEU, ENVIRONMENT ⟨expert at portraying the spiritual ~ of Chile —Francis Herron⟩

am·bi·gu·i·ty \,ambə'gyüəd·ē, ,aam-, -ətē, -i\ *n* -ES [ME *ambiguite*, fr. MF *ambiguïté*, fr. L *ambiguitat-, ambiguitas*, fr. *ambiguus* + *-itat-, -itas* -ity] **1** *obs* **:** intellectual uncertainty **:** DOUBT ⟨resolve me of all *ambiguities* —Christopher Marlowe⟩ **2 a** (1) **:** the condition of admitting of two or more meanings, of being understood in more than one way, or of referring to two or more things at the same time ⟨their very ~ is one source of their use in defense of any measure —John Dewey⟩ (2) **:** looseness of signification or reference ⟨the technical writer must rigorously avoid all ~ —C.E.Kellogg⟩ **2 b** (1) **:** uncertainty of meaning or significance or of position in relation to something or somebody else ⟨a sufficiently detailed account . . . to remove all ~ —P.E.More⟩ ⟨the social ~ of his parents —Lionel Trilling⟩ (2) **:** mystery or mysteriousness arising esp. from a vague knowledge or understanding ⟨there was an ~ about this young lady —Nathaniel Hawthorne⟩ **3 :** the intellectual or emotional interplay or tension resulting from the opposition or contraposing of apparently incompatible or contradictory elements or levels of meaning in a poem or other literary work; *esp* **:** the opposition or contraposition of two or more meanings inherent in one word or symbol or in a consistent set of metaphoric or symbolic words **4 :** the maintaining of two or more logically incompatible beliefs or attitudes at the same time or alternately **:** inconsistency resulting from vacillation between two opposing views ⟨the inner ~ in each of us between reason and coercion —T.V.Smith⟩ **5 :** an ambiguous word or expression ⟨a poetical ~ depends on the reader's weighting the possible meanings according to their probability —William Empson⟩

am·big·u·ous \am'bigyəwəs, aam-\ *adj* [L *ambiguus*, fr. *ambigere* to wander about, waver, dispute, fr. *ambi-* around, about + *-igere* (fr. *agere* to drive, lead, act, do) — more at AMBI-, AGENT] **:** characterized by, suggestive of, or exhibiting ambiguity ⟨the ~ wording of a message⟩ ⟨an ~ smile⟩ ⟨an ~ position⟩; *specif* **:** capable of being classified in two or more categories ⟨an ~ insect⟩ **syn** see OBSCURE

ambiguous figure *n* **:** a picture of a subject which the viewer may see as either of two different subjects or as the same subject from either of two different viewpoints depending on his interpretation of the total configuration

am·big·u·ous·ly *adv* **:** in an ambiguous manner

ambiguous middle *n* **:** the fallacy of using the middle term of a syllogism in two different meanings **:** UNDISTRIBUTED MIDDLE

am·big·u·ous·ness *n* -ES **:** AMBIGUITY

am·bil·anak \¦ambə¦länə(k)\ *adj* [Malay *ambil-anak*, fr. *ambil* taking over + *anak* child] **:** of or relating to a form of Malayan marriage esp. in Sumatra where the husband in lieu of a bride-price enters the wife's family, has no property right in children or wife, and may be dismissed by her father

am·bi·lat·er·al \¦ambə¦-, -bē¦-\ *adj* [*ambi-* + *lateral*] **:** relating to or affecting both sides **:** BILATERAL — **am·bi·lat·er·al·i·ty** \-,ladə'raləd·ē\ *n* -ES — **am·bi·lat·er·al·ly** *adv*

am·bil·i·an \(')am¦bilyən, -lēən\ *adj* [Malay *ambil*-anak + E *-ian*] **:** AMBILANAK

am·bi·o·pia \,ambē'ōpēə\ *n* -s [NL, fr. *ambi-* + *-opia*] **:** DIPLOPIA

ambisexual *var of* AMBOSEXUAL

am·bi·sex·u·al·i·ty \¦==,=-\ *n* -ES [*ambi-* + *sexuality*] **:** partial hermaphroditism — used esp. of behavioral conditions

am·bi·syl·lab·ic \¦===¦==\ *adj* [*ambi-* + *-syllabic*] *of a sound or cluster of sounds* **:** partly in the first and partly in the second or not assignable to one only of two consecutive syllables ⟨the *n* in *cynic* is ~⟩

am·bit \'ambət\ *n* -s [ME, fr. L *ambitus* going around, circuit, circular edge, fr. *ambitus*, past part. of *ambire* to go round — more at AMBIENT] **1 :** CIRCUIT, COMPASS, CIRCUMFERENCE ⟨everywhere within an ~ of four feet —*Punch*⟩ **2 a :** the space surrounding a house, a castle, or a town **:** PRECINCTS **b :** the bounds or limits of a place or district **3 :** the sphere of action, expression, or influence **:** EXTENT, SCOPE ⟨going far outside his proper ~ as secretary —R.F.Harrod⟩ ⟨ranges freely throughout the entire ~ of universal history —Morris Watnick⟩

am·bi·tend·en·cy \'ambē,-, 'aam-\ *n* -ES [*ambi-* + *tendency*] **:** a tendency to act in opposite ways or directions **:** the presence of opposing behavioral drives

¹am·bi·tion \am'bishən, aam-\ *n* -s [ME *ambicioun*, fr. MF or L; MF *ambition*, fr. L *ambition-, ambitio* soliciting of votes, desire for honor or power, lit., going around, fr. *ambitus* (past part. of *ambire* to go around, solicit, strive for) + *-ion-, -io* -ion — more at AMBIENT] **1 a :** an ardent desire for rank, fame, or power ⟨his ruin was that ~ . . . had laid hold of him —Thomas Carlyle⟩ **b :** the will or desire to succeed or achieve a particular goal or end **:** ASPIRATION ⟨it was her ~ for me which proved the deciding factor — David Fairchild⟩ **2 :** the object of one's desire ⟨accomplished its curious ~ of breaking into and robbing the state prison —Dixon Wecter⟩ **3 :** a desire for activity or exertion **:** INITIATIVE, ENERGY ⟨I felt no ~ when I was under the weather for a few days —S.T. Byington⟩ **4** *chiefly Midland* **:** ILL WILL, SPITE, MALICE

²ambition \"\ *vt* **ambitioned**; **ambitioned**; **ambitioning** \-sh(ə)niŋ\ **ambitions :** to have as one's ambition **:** DESIRE ⟨I never ~*ed* it —Augusta Gregory⟩

am·bi·tion·less *adj* **:** having little or no ambition

am·bi·tious \am'bishəs, aam-\ *adj* [ME *ambicious*, fr. L *ambitiosus*, fr. *ambitio* + *-osus* -ous] **1 a :** having or controlled by ambition **:** eager for rank, fame, or power ⟨~ Rome —Edmund Spenser⟩ **b :** having a desire to succeed or to achieve a particular goal **:** ASPIRING ⟨~ youths . . . turned to the law as a congenial career —V.L.Parrington⟩ **2** *obs* **:** RISING, TOWERING ⟨the ~ ocean —Shak.⟩ **3 :** resulting from, characterized by, or showing ambition: as **a :** EXTENSIVE, ELABORATE ⟨the most ~ life of Washington . . . began appearing in 1948 —Walter Trohan⟩ **b :** PRETENTIOUS, SHOWY ⟨in a hard-cover book where I expect something more ~ —Marston Bates⟩ — **am·bi·tious·ly** *adv*

am·bi·ty \(')am¦bid·ē\ *adj* [prob. fr. F *ambité*] **:** DEVITRIFIED — used in glass manufacture of glass in the pot during manipulation

am·bi·tus \'ambətəs\ *n, pl* **ambitus** [L — more at AMBIT] **1 :** the exterior edge or periphery (as of a leaf, a bivalve shell, or the test of a sea urchin) **2 :** DENOTATION 4 **3 :** the compass of a melody in a Gregorian chant

am·biv·a·lence \am'bivələn(t)s, aam-\ *also* **am·biv·a·len·cy** \-nsē, -si\ *n, pl* **ambivalences** *also* **ambivalencies** [ISV *ambi-* + *valence, valency*; orig. formed as G *ambivalenz*] **1 :** contradictory emotional or psychological attitudes esp. toward a particular person or object and often with one attitude inhibiting the expression of another ⟨a heightened ~ which is expressed in behavior by alternating obedience and rebellion, followed by self-reproach —G.S.Blum⟩; *specif* **:** simultaneous attraction toward and repulsion from an object, person, or action ⟨Apache ~ in attitude and behavior toward death —C.K.Kluckhohn⟩ **2 a :** continual oscillation (as between one thing and its opposite) **:** FLUCTUATION ⟨Thackeray's major novels are vitiated by an ~ between satire and sentimentalism —J.L.Davis⟩ **b :** uncertainty as to which approach, attitude, or treatment to follow ⟨the English film . . . because of a nervous ~ toward its subject matter . . . fails to produce the chuckles —John McCarten⟩

am·biv·a·lent \-lənt\ *adj* [ISV *ambi-* + *valent;* orig. formed in G] **:** characterized by, suggestive of, motivated by, or exhibiting ambivalence ⟨an ~ nature⟩ ⟨~ feelings⟩ ⟨an ~ position toward religion⟩ ⟨the ~ aspects of the American spirit are reconciled —Louis le Fevre⟩ — **am·biv·a·lent·ly** *adv*

am·bi·ver·sion \ˌambēˈvərzhən, -bə- *also* -rsh-\ *n* -s [*ambi-* + *-version* (as in *introversion, extroversion*)] **:** the personality configuration of an ambivert **:** a state of balance between introversion and extroversion — **am·bi·ver·sive** \ˌ≈≈ˈ≈siv, -ziv\ *adj*

am·bi·vert \ˈ≈≈ˌvərt\ *n* -s [*ambi-* + *-vert* (as in *introvert, extrovert*)] **:** a type of person intermediate between the extrovert and the introvert

¹am·ble \ˈambəl, ˈaam-\ *vi* **ambled; ambled; ambling** \b(ə)liŋ\ **ambles** [ME *amblen,* fr. MF *ambler,* fr. L *ambulare* to walk, fr. *amb-* around + *-ulare* (verb base prob. akin to L *-ilium* in *exilium* exile); prob. akin to Gk *alasthai* to wander, Latvian *aluôt* to wander around — more at *ambi-*] **1 a :** to go at an amble ⟨the pony *ambled* down the lane⟩ **b :** to walk or move in an easygoing or leisurely manner **:** SAUNTER ⟨time to ~ back to the office⟩ **2 :** to go or proceed smoothly or easily ⟨the interpretation *~s* on —H.O.Taylor⟩

²amble \"\ *n* -s **1** *of a horse* **a :** an easy 4-beat gait with lateral motion **b :** ⁷RACK b **2 :** an easy gait **3 :** an easygoing or leisurely walking movement ⟨the aimless ~ of the . . . holiday crowd —L.C.Douglas⟩

am·bler \-b(ə)lə(r)\ *n* -s [ME, fr. *amblen* + *-er*] **:** one that ambles; *esp* **:** an ambling horse

am·bling \-b(ə)liŋ\ *adj* **:** moving at an easy pace ⟨~ carriages⟩ ⟨an ~ light novel⟩ — **am·bling·ly** *adv*

am·blop·li·tes \ˌamˌbläpˈlīdˌēz\ *n, cap* [NL, fr. Gk *amblys* blunt + *hoplitēs* hoplite] **:** a genus of sunfishes (family Centrarchidae) including the rock bass of the central U.S. and Great Lakes region

ambly- *or* **amblyo-** *comb form* [LL *ambly-,* fr. Gk, fr. *amblys;* akin to L *mollis* soft, *molere* to grind — more at MEAL] **1 :** blunt **:** obtuse ⟨*Amblycephalus*⟩ **2 :** dulled **:** dimmed ⟨*amblyacousia*⟩ **3 :** connected with amblyopia ⟨*amblyoscope*⟩

am·bly·ce·phal·i·dae \ˌamblēsəˈfalə,dē\ *n pl, cap* [NL, fr. *Amblycephalus,* type genus (fr. *ambly-* + *-cephalus*) + *-idae*] **:** a small family of tropical nonvenomous broad-headed snakes with extremely large eyes and very long delicate teeth occas. considered a colubrid subfamily Amblycephalinae — see BLUNTHEAD

am·bly·chro·mat·ic \ˌamblē≈ˈ≈≈, -lə-\ *adj* [ISV *ambly-* + *chromatic*] **:** lightly staining ⟨certain marrow cells are ~⟩

am·bly·dac·ty·la \ˌambləˈdaktələ\ [NL, fr. *ambly-* + *-dactyla* (fr. Gk *daktylos* finger, toe)] *syn of* AMBLYPODA

am·blyg·o·nite \amˈbligə,nīt\ *n* -s [G *amblygonit,* fr. Gk *amblygōnios* obtuse-angled (fr. *ambly-* + *-gōnios,* fr. *gōnia* angle) + G *-it* -ite] **:** a mineral $(Li,Na)AlPO_4(F,OH)$ consisting of basic lithium aluminum phosphate commonly containing sodium and fluorine and occurring in white cleavable masses

am·bly·om·ma \ˌamblēˈämə\ *n, cap* [NL, fr. *ambly-* + *-omma*] **:** a genus of ixodid ticks including the lone star tick of the southern U.S. and the African bont tick

am·bly·o·pia \-ˈōpēə\ *n* -s [NL, fr. Gk *amblyōpia* dimness of sight, fr. *ambly-* + *-ōpia* -opia] **:** dimness of sight without apparent change in the eye structures associated esp. with the toxic effects of certain drugs or chemicals or with dietary deficiencies — **am·bly·op·ic** \ˌ≈≈ˈäpik, -ōp-\ *adj*

am·bly·op·sis \ˌ≈≈ˈäpsəs\ *n, cap* [NL, fr. *ambly-* + *-opsis*] **:** a genus (the type of the family Amblyopsidae) of small blanched sightless fishes related to the killifishes and including the blindfish of Mammoth Cave

am·bly·o·scope \ˈamblēə,skōp\ *n* -s [ISV *amblyo-* (fr. NL *amblyopia*) + *-scope*] **:** an instrument for training amblyopic eyes to function properly

am·bly·pod \ˈambləˌpäd\ *n* -s [NL *Amblypoda*] **:** an ungulate of the order or suborder Amblypoda

am·blyp·o·da \amˈblipədə\ *n pl, cap* [NL, fr. *ambly-* + *-poda*] *in some classifications* **:** an order or suborder of extinct ungulates found in the Eocene rocks chiefly of No. America having very small smooth brains and some of them resembling the elephants in size and in the structure of their limbs but having horns as well as long tusks

am·blyp·o·dous \-dəs\ *adj* [NL *Amblypoda* + E *-ous*] **:** of or relating to the Amblypoda

am·bly·rhyn·chus \ˌambləˈriŋkəs\ *n, cap* [NL, fr. *ambly-* + *-rhynchus*] **:** a genus of iguanid lizards containing only one species (*A. cristatus*) of the Galápagos islands

am·bly·si·pho·nel·la \ˌ≈≈ˌsīfəˈnelə\ *n, cap* [NL, fr. *ambly-* + L *siphon-, sipho* + NL *-ella*] **:** a genus of thin-walled extinct calcareous sponges including important index fossils of Pennsylvanian age

am·blys·te·gite \amˈblistə,jīt\ *n* -s [ISV *ambly-* + Gk *stegos* roof + ISV *-ite;* orig. formed as G *amblystegit*] **:** a variety of hypersthene

am·blys·to·ma \-təmə\ [NL, alter. (influenced by *ambly-*) of *Ambystoma*] *syn of* AMBYSTOMA

¹am·bo \ˈam,bō\ *n, pl* **ambos** \-bōz\ *or* **ambo·nes** \amˈbō(,)nēz\ [ML *ambon-, ambo,* fr. LGk *ambōn,* fr. Gk, edge, rim] **:** a large pulpit or reading desk in early churches and in contemporary Greek and Balkan churches standing on the gospel side of the nave and often having its counterpart on the epistle side

²ambo \"\ *var of* AMBON

³am·bo \", ˈäm-\ *n, pl* **ambo** *or* **ambos** *usu cap* **1 :** a Bantu people of the northern part of southwestern Africa **2 :** the language of the Ambo people

am·bo·cep·tor \ˈambō,septə(r)\ *n* -s [ISV *ambo-* (alter. of *ambi-*) + *receptor;* orig. formed as G *ambozeptor*] **1 :** an intermediary body or antibody acting as a detached receptor **2 :** the lytic antibody used in complement-fixation tests

am·bo·coe·lia \ˌambōˈsēlēə\ *n, cap* [NL, prob. fr. Gk *ambōn* rim, edge + *koilia* cavity, fr. *koilos* hollow + *-ia*] **:** a genus of small smooth or spinose plano-convex fossil brachiopods characteristic of Devonian and Carboniferous rocks

am·boi·na button \(ˈ)amˈbȯinə-\ *n, usu cap A* [fr. *Amboina,* town, island, and division of the Moluccas] **:** YAWS

amboina pine *or* **am·boy·na pine** \"\ *n, usu cap A* **:** a tall tree (*Agathis alba*) native to the Moluccas and the Philippines and the chief source of dammar resin

¹am·boi·nese \ˌamˌbȯiˈnēz, -ēs, amˈbȯi,n-\ *also* **am·bo·nese** \ˌambəˈn-\ *adj, usu cap* [*Amboina, Ambon* + E *-ese*] **1 :** of, relating to, or characteristic of the island of Amboina **2 :** of, relating to, or characteristic of the people of Amboina

²amboinese \"\ *also* **ambonese** \"\ *n, pl* **amboinese** *also* **ambonese** *usu cap* **1 :** a native or inhabitant of Amboina **2 :** the language of the Amboinese people

am·bo·mal·le·al \ˌam(ˌ)bōˈmalēəl\ *adj* [*ambos* + *malleal*] **:** relating to the ambos and malleus ⟨the ~ articulation⟩

am·bon \ˈamˌbän\ *also* **am·bo** \-ˌbō\ *n, pl* **ambo·nes** \amˈbō(ˌ)nēz\ [NL, fr. Gk *ambōn* edge, rim] **:** the fibrocartilaginous ring around an articular cavity

am·bon·ite \ˈambə,nīt\ *n* -s [D *ambonīet,* fr. *Ambon,* its locality + D *-iet* -ite] **:** a mineral consisting of cordierite-bearing hornblende-biotite-andesite

am·bos \ˈam,bäs\ *n* -ES [G *amboss* anvil, fr. OHG *anabōz,* fr. *ana* on + *bōz* blow; akin to OHG *bōzzan* to beat] **:** INCUS

am·bo·sex·u·al \ˌam(ˌ)bōˈ-\ *also* **am·bi·sex·u·al** \ˌambēˈ-, -bəˈ-\ *adj* [L *ambo* both or E *ambi-* + *sexual* — more at AMBI-] **:** exhibiting or constituting sexual traits or characters common to male and female ⟨axillary hair is an ~ trait⟩

am·boy·na *or* **am·boi·na** \amˈbȯinə\ *n* -s [fr. *Amboina,* town, island, & division of the Moluccas, Indonesia] **1 :** a mottled curly-grained wood of a tree (*Pterocarpus indicus*) of India and the Malay archipelago — called also *Andaman redwood, rosewood* **2 :** the tree that yields amboyna

am·brein \ˈam,brān, -ˌbrēən\ *also* **am·brain** \ˈamˌbrān, -ˌbrə,in\ *n* -s [F *ambréine,* fr. *ambre* amber (fr. L *ambra*) + *-ine* -in] **:** a crystalline triterpenoid alcohol $C_{30}H_{51}OH$ obtained from ambergris

am·brette \(ˈ)amˈbret\ *n* -s [F, fr. OF, fr. *ambre* amber + *-ette*] **1 :** a French dessert pear having a musky odor **2 :** AMBER SEED **3 a :** an extract of amber seeds having a strong musky odor and used in perfumery as a fixative **b :** MUSK AMBRETTE

am·brite \ˈamˌbrīt\ *n* -s [ISV *amber* + *-ite;* orig. formed as G *ambrit*] **:** a fossil resin occurring in large masses in New Zealand

am·broid *var of* AMBEROID

am·bro·sia \amˈbrōzh(ē)ə, aam-, *attrib* (ˈ)≈ˈ≈(≈)≈\ *n* [L, fr. Gk, lit., immortality, fr. *ambrotos* immortal (fr. *a-* ²a- + *-mbrotos* — assumed — Gk *mbrotos* mortal — whence Gk *brotos*) + *-ia* — more at MURDER] **1** -s **a :** the food of the Greek and Roman gods ⟨a table where the heaped ~ lay —W.C.Bryant⟩ **b :** the ointment or perfume of the gods ⟨his dewy locks distilled ~ —John Milton⟩ **2** -s **:** something extremely pleasing to taste or smell ⟨with sweet ~ all besprinkled —Edmund Spenser⟩ **3** [NL, fr. L] *cap* **:** a genus of mostly American monoecious herbs (family Compositae) distinguished by the united involucre of the staminate heads of flowers and by the single row of spines on the involucre of the pistillate heads — see RAGWEED **4** -s **:** JERUSALEM OAK 1 **5** -s **:** a dessert of a fruit or of mixed fruits topped with shredded coconut **6** -s **:** a moderate reddish brown that is yellower and paler than roan and paler than mahogany

ambrosia beetle *n* [*ambrosia* (*fungus*)] **:** any of certain small semiosocial beetles (family Ipidae or Scolytidae) that bore deeply in dead or dying wood and tend and cultivate ambrosia fungus on which they feed and raise their larvae

am·bro·si·ac \≈ˈ≈zhē,ak\ *adj* [L *ambrosiacus,* fr. *ambrosia*] **:** AMBROSIAL ⟨an ~ odor⟩

am·bro·si·a·ce·ae \am,brōz(h)ēˈāsē,ē\ *n pl, cap* [NL, fr. *Ambrosia,* type genus + *-aceae*] *in some classifications* **:** a family of herbs comprising all the composites (as ragweeds) that have the flower head subtended by an involucre of separate or united bracts and the stamens separate or merely connivent — see COMPOSITAE

am·bro·si·a·ceous \≈ˌ≈ˌ≈ˈāshəs, ˌ≈ˌ≈≈ˈ-\ *adj* [NL *Ambrosiaceae* + E *-ous*] **:** of or relating to Ambrosiaceae

ambrosia fungus *also* **ambrosial fungus** *n* **:** a fungus upon which ambrosia beetles feed

am·bro·si·al \(ˈ)amˈbrōzh(ē)əl, (ˈ)aam-\ *or* **am·bro·si·an** \-(ē)ən\ *adj* [L *ambrosia* + E *-al* or *-an*] **1 a :** consisting of or like ambrosia ⟨fed by fair Iris with ~ food —Alexander Pope⟩ **b :** relating to or worthy of the gods or paradise **:** DIVINE ⟨these pure ~ weeds —John Milton⟩ **2 :** extremely pleasing to the senses esp. of taste or smell **:** DELICIOUS, FRAGRANT ⟨the ~ islands of the South Seas —Dixon Wecter⟩ ⟨an afternoon of warm ~ May weather —Elinor Wylie⟩ — **am·bro·si·al·ly** \-(ē)əlē, -li\ *adv*

¹am·bro·si·an \-(ē)ən\ *adj, usu cap* [LL *Ambrosianus,* fr. St. Ambrose (*Ambrosius*) †397 bishop of Milan and church father + L *-anus* -an] **1 :** of, relating to, established by, or ascribed to St. Ambrose ⟨the *Ambrosian* rite⟩ **2 :** characterized by the style of St. Ambrose ⟨the *Ambrosian* type of hymn is written in iambic tetrameter⟩

²ambrosian \"\ *n* -s *usu cap* [ML *Ambrosianus,* fr. LL, of St. Ambrose] **:** a member of a religious order (as of the Congregation of the Brethren of St. Ambrose founded by Crivelli in Milan in 1375, of the Oblates of St. Ambrose founded by Carlo Borromeo in 1578, or of the Sisterhood of St. Ambrose founded by Catherine Morigia in 1474)

ambrosian chant *n, usu cap A* **:** the plainsong associated with the liturgy of the church of Milan including antiphonal psalm chants ascribed to St. Ambrose

am·bro·sin \ˈambrə,zin, -ēn\ *n* -s [ML *Ambrosinus* (*nummus*), lit., Ambrosian coin, fr. St. Ambrose (*Ambrosius*) + L *-inus* -ine] **:** a Milanese gold or silver coin of the late 13th and early 14th centuries having as device a figure of St. Ambrose

am·bro·sine \-ˌzēn\ *n* -s [¹*amber* + *-rosine* (alter. of *rosin*)] **:** a resinous hydrocarbon mineral that is a variety of amber

am·bro·type \-ˌtīp\ *n* -s [Gk *ambrotos* immortal (fr. *a-* ²a- + *-mbrotos* — akin to *brotos, mortos* mortal —) + E *type* — more at MURDER] **:** a positive picture made by the collodion process on glass and viewed against a dark background

am·bry \ˈambrē, -ri, *dial Brit* " *or* ˈämr- *or* ˈōm(b)r-\ *n* -ES [earlier *aumbry, armorie,* fr. ME *almerie, almarie, awmerie, armarie,* fr. OF *almarie, aumaire, armarie,* fr. ML *almarium* & L *armarium;* ML *almarium* fr. L *armarium,* fr. *arma* weapons, tools + *-arium* -ary — more at ARM] **1 :** a place for keeping things: as **a :** a recess in a church wall for holding sacramental vessels, vestments, or books **b** *dial chiefly Brit* (1) **:** PANTRY (2) **:** a cupboard or chest in which food is kept **2** *obs* **:** ALMONRY

ambs·ace *also* **ames·ace** \ˈāmˌzās, ˈam-\ *n* -s [ME *ambes as,* fr. OF, fr. *ambes* both (fr. L *ambo*) + *as* aces, pl. of *as* ace — more at AMBI-, ACE] **:** the lowest throw at dice; *also* **:** something worthless or unlucky — **within ambsace of** *archaic* **:** within an ace of

ambulacra *pl of* AMBULACRUM

am·bu·lac·ral \ˌambyəˈlakrəl *also* -ˈāk-\ *adj* [NL *ambulacrum* + E *-al*] **:** of or relating to an ambulacrum

ambulacral brush *n* **:** a modified oral or anal ambulacral foot in heart urchins expanded into appendages resembling tentacles

ambulacral foot *n* **:** a tube foot of an echinoderm

ambulacral system *n* **:** the water-vascular system of echinoderms

am·bu·lac·ri·form \ˌambyəˈlakrə,fȯrm\ *adj* [NL *ambulacrum* + E *-iform*] **:** like an ambulacrum in shape

am·bu·lac·rum \ˌambyəˈlakrəm *also* -ˈāk-\ *n, pl* **ambulac·ra** \-rə\ [NL, fr. L, alley, covered way, fr. *ambulare* to walk — more at AMBLE] **1 :** one of the radially disposed areas of echinoderms along which run the principal nerves, blood vessels, and water tubes and which usu. bear rows of locomotive suckers or tentacles that protrude from regular pores **2 :** one of the suckers on the feet of mites

am·bu·lance \ˈambyələn(t)s, ˈaam-, *chiefly substand* -bəl-\ *n* -s *often attrib* [F, field hospital, fr. *ambulant* itinerant, traveling (esp. as used in the term *hôpital ambulant* field hospital, lit., traveling hospital), fr. L *ambulant-, ambulans,* pres. part. of *ambulare* to walk — more at AMBLE] **1 :** a vehicle equipped for transporting wounded, injured, or sick persons or animals **2 :** a passenger vehicle formerly used in the western U.S.

ambulance chaser *n* **:** a lawyer or lawyer's agent who incites accident victims to bring suit for damages

am·bu·lant \-byələnt\ *adj* [L *ambulant-, ambulans,* pres. part. of *ambulare* to walk — more at AMBLE] **1 :** walking or in a walking position; *specif* **:** AMBULATORY ⟨an ~ patient⟩ **2 :** moving or capable of being moved from place to place ⟨an ~ radio station⟩ **:** ITINERANT ⟨an ~ blacksmith⟩

am·bu·late \-ˌlāt, *usu* -ād·+V\ *vi* -ED/-ING/-S [L *ambulatus,* past part. of *ambulare*] **:** to move from place to place **:** WALK ⟨the patient was allowed to ~ in his room⟩

am·bu·la·tion \ˌ≈≈ˈlāshən\ *n* -s [L *ambulation-, ambulatio,* fr. *ambulatus* + *-ion-, -io* -ion] **:** the act or action of moving about or walking ⟨most surgeons encourage early ~⟩

am·bu·la·to·ri·al \ˌ≈≈ləˈtōrēəl\ *adj* [¹*ambulatory* + *-al*] **1 :** AMBULATORY **2** *of a forest animal* **:** adapted to progression by walking rather than by running, leaping, or crawling

¹am·bu·la·to·ry \ˈambyələ,tōrē, ˈaam-, -ōr-, -ri\ *adj* [L *ambulatorius,* fr. *ambulatus* (past part. of *ambulare* to walk) + *-orius* -ory — more at AMBLE] **1 a :** of or relating to walking ⟨~ exercise⟩ **b :** capable of, adapted to, or occurring while walking ⟨an ~ animal⟩ ⟨an ~ confession⟩ **2 a :** moving from place to place **:** ITINERANT, PERIPATETIC ⟨an ~ teacher⟩ **b :** having no fixed headquarters ⟨an ~ business⟩ **3 :** not yet fixed legally or settled past alteration **:** ALTERABLE ⟨a will is ~ until the testator's death⟩ **4 a :** able to walk about **:** not bedfast **:** AMBULANT ⟨the ~ clinic patient⟩ **b :** of, for, or involving an individual who is able to walk about ⟨~ treatment of tuberculosis⟩

²ambulatory \"\ *n* -ES [ML *ambulatorium,* fr. L, neut. of *ambulatorius*] **1 :** a sheltered place to walk in: as **a :** the gallery portion of a cloister **b :** the apse aisle of a church **c :** a passageway in some churches in back of the altar and behind the chancel used as an uninterrupted processional path **2 :** an appendage used for or adapted to walking (as a tube foot or one of the segmental abdominal appendages of a crustacean)

am·bu·lia \amˈbyülēə\ *n* -s [modif. of Malabar *amuli*] **:** any of several aquatic plants of the genus *Limnophora* (family Scrophulariaceae) having finely dissected submerged and peltate floating leaves and being often grown as an aquarium plant

¹am·bus·cade \ˈambə,skād, ˈaam-, ˌ≈≈ˈ≈\ *n* -s [MF *embuscade,* modif. (influenced by MF *embuschier* to place in ambush) of OIt *imboscata,* fr. fem. of *imboscato,* past part. of *imboscare* to place in ambush, fr. *in* (fr. L) + *-boscare,* fr. *bosco* forest, perh. of Gmc origin; akin to OHG *busc* forest — more at IN, BUSH, AMBUSH] *archaic* **:** AMBUSH 1

²ambuscade \"\ *vt* -ED/-ING/-S **:** to attack from an ambuscade

am·bus·ca·do \ˌ≈≈ˈskā(ˌ)dō\ *n* -s [alter. (influenced by *-ado,* as in *bastinado, bravado*) of *ambuscade*] *archaic* **:** AMBUSCADE

¹am·bush \ˈamˌbu̇sh, ˈaam-\ *vb* -ED/-ING/-ES [ME *embushen, abushen,* fr. OF *embuschier* to place in ambush, fr. *en* (fr. L *in*) + *-buschier,* fr. *busche* stick of firewood, prob. of Gmc origin; akin to MHG *büsch* cudgel — more at IN, BOAST] *vt* **1 :** to station in ambush ⟨he *~ed* his force in a canebrake —J.F.H.Claiborne⟩ **2 :** to lie in wait for and attack by surprise **:** WAYLAY ⟨units in superior strength had *~ed* . . . the 2d and 19th regiments —R.C.Cameron⟩ **~** *vi* **:** to lie in wait **:** LURK ⟨imaginary persons *~ed* in the fog—Marguerite Young⟩

²ambush \"\ *n* -ES [MF *embusche,* fr. OF, fr. *embuschier,* v.] **1 a :** a hidden or concealed station of troops lying in wait to attack an enemy by surprise ⟨attempt of a . . . boy to warn them of an ~ over the brow of the hill —Mary Gregoire⟩ **b :** the body of troops lying in wait for an enemy **2 a :** a hidden or concealed position ⟨trapped, baited, and shot from ~ like a criminal —D.C.Peattie⟩ **b :** a person occupying a concealed position **3 :** the act of lying in wait in or of attacking by surprise from a concealed position

ambush bug *n* **:** any of numerous carnivorous bugs that constitute the family Phymatidae, conceal themselves in flowers, and prey on other insects

am·bush·ment \-mənt\ *n* -s [ME *embushement,* fr. MF *embuschement,* fr. *embuschier* + *-ment*] **:** AMBUSH

am·bys·to·ma \amˈbistəmə\ *n* [NL, irreg. fr. *ambly-* + *-stoma*] **1** *cap* **:** a genus (the type of the family Ambystomidae) of common salamanders confined to America and characterized by amphicoelous vertebrae, short prevomers, and internal fertilization **2** -s **:** a salamander of the genus *Ambystoma* — see AXOLOTL — **am·bys·to·mid** \-məd, ˌ≈ˌmid\ *adj or n*

am·bys·to·moi·dea \(ˌ)amˌbistəˈmȯidēə\ *n pl, cap* [NL, fr. *Ambystoma* + *-oidea*] **:** the suborder of caudate amphibians that comprises the single family Ambystomidae — compare AMBYSTOMA

AMDG *abbr* [L *ad majorem Dei gloriam*] to the greater glory of God

amdt *abbr* amendment

ameba *var of* AMOEBA

am·e·bel·o·don \ˌaməˈbelə,dän\ *n, cap* [NL, fr. Gk *amē* shovel + *belos* missile, dart + NL *-odon*] **:** a genus of No. American Pliocene mastodonts having an elongated lower jaw and lower tusks flattened into broad scoops

am·e·bi·a·sis *or* **am·oe·bi·a·sis** \ˌaməˈbīəsəs\ *n, pl* **amebia·ses** *or* **amoebia·ses** \-əˌsēz\ [NL, fr. *ameba, amoeba* + *-iasis*] **:** infection with or disease caused by amoebas; *specif* **:** infection of the human colon with amoebas — see AMEBIC DYSENTERY

amebic *or* **ameban** *or* **amebous** *var of* AMOEBIC

amebic abscess *n* **:** a specific purulent invasive lesion commonly of the liver caused by parasitic amoebas esp. of the common species (*Endamoeba histolytica*)

amebic dysentery *n* **:** acute intestinal amebiasis of man caused by infection with the amoeba (*Endamoeba histolytica*) and marked by frequent passage of thin mucus-filled and blood-filled stools, griping pain, and more or less severe erosion of the intestinal wall and esp. the colon

ame·bi·ci·dal *also* **ame·ba·ci·dal** \əˌmēbəˈsīdᵊl\ *adj* **:** of, relating to, or being an amebicide

ame·bi·cide *also* **amoe·bi·cide** *also* **ame·ba·cide** \əˈmēbə,sīd\ *n* -s [NL *ameba, amoeba* + E *-i-* + *-cide*] **:** a substance used to kill or capable of killing amoebas (as parasitic amoebas)

amebid *var of* AMOEBID

amebiform *var of* AMOEBIFORM

amebocyte *var of* AMOEBOCYTE

ameboid *var of* AMOEBOID

amebula *var of* AMOEBULA

âme dam·née \ämdänā\ *n, pl* **âmes damnées** \-nā(z)\ [F, lit., damned soul] **:** a willing and devoted tool or slave of another ⟨a writer who is the *âme damnée* of certain interests⟩

ameen *or* **amin** \əˈmēn\ *n* -s [Hindi *amīn,* fr. Ar] *India* **:** a confidential agent; *esp* **:** a minor official of the judicial and revenue departments

ameer *var of* EMIR

ame haarez *pl of* AM HAAREZ

amei·o·sis \ˌāˌmīˈōsəs\ *n, pl* **ameio·ses** \-ōˌsēz\ [NL, fr. ²*a-* + *meiosis*] **:** suppression of one of the meiotic divisions resulting in nonreduction of chromosomes (as in parthenogenesis)

amei·ot·ic \ˌ≈ˌ≈ˈäd·ik\ *adj* [²*a-* + *meiotic*] **:** without meiosis

am·ei·u·rus \ˌa,mīˈyu̇rəs\ *n, cap* [NL, fr. ²*a-* + Gk *meiouros* tapering (used of a fish's snout), alter. (influenced by *meioun* to diminish) of *myouros,* lit., mouse-tailed, fr. *mys* mouse + *-ouros* (fr. *oura* tail)] **:** a genus of freshwater catfishes comprising the No. American bullheads

amei·va \əˈmāvə, -ˈīvə\ *n, cap* [NL, fr. Pg, lizard, fr. Tupi] **:** a genus of New World lizards (family Teiidae)

am·el \ˈaməl\ *n* -s [ME *amal, amel,* fr. MF *esmal, asmol, emal* — more at ENAMEL] *archaic* **:** ENAMEL

am·e·lan·chi·er \ˌaməˈlaŋkē(ə)r\ *n, cap* [NL, fr. F *amélanchier* shadbush, shadberry, of Celt origin; akin to Gaulish *avallo* apple, OIr *ubull* — more at APPLE] **:** a genus of shrubs and trees (family Rosaceae) with showy usu. racemose white flowers and sweet edible pomes resembling small berries — see JUNEBERRY

am·el·corn \ˈaməlˌkȯrn\ *n, pl* **amelcorn** [G *amelkorn,* fr. L *amylum* starch + *korn* grain, fr. OHG — more at AMYL-, CORN] **:** EMMER

ameli *pl of* AMELUS

ame·lio·rant \əˈmēlyərənt, -lēə-\ *n* -s [*ameliorate* + *-ant*] **:** a substance that aids plant growth primarily by improving the physical condition of the soil

ame·lio·rate \-ˌrāt, *usu* -ād·+V\ *vb* -ED/-ING/-S [alter. (influenced by F *améliorer,* alter. — influenced by L *melior* — of *ameilleurer,* fr. OF *ameillorer,* fr. *a-* — fr. L *ad-* — + *-meillorer,* fr. *meillor* better, fr. L *melior*) of *meliorate* — more at MELIORATE] *vt* **:** to make better **:** IMPROVE ⟨~ conditions⟩ **~** *vi* **:** to grow better **:** IMPROVE ⟨the situation *ameliorated*⟩ **syn** see IMPROVE

ame·lio·ra·tion \ˌ≈ˌ≈(≈)≈ˈrāshən\ *n* -s [F *amélioration,* fr. *améliorer* + *-ation*] **1 :** act of ameliorating or state of being ameliorated **:** IMPROVEMENT ⟨the ~ of human affairs —J.S. Mill⟩ **2** *Canadian law* **:** BETTERMENT 1a

ame·lio·ra·tive \əˈ≈(≈)≈ˌrād·iv, -ˌrəl, |tiv, -ēv\ *also* **ame·lio·ra·to·ry** \-rə,tōrē, -ōr-, -ri\ *adj* **:** tending to ameliorate

ame·lio·ra·tor \-ˌrād·ə(r), -ātə-\ *n* -s **:** one that ameliorates **:** AMELIORANT

am·e·lo·blast \ˈaməlō,blast\ *n* -s [*amel* + *-o-* + *-blast*] **:** one of the columnar cells of the inner layer of the enamel organ that produce and deposit enamel on the surface of a developing tooth — **am·e·lo·blas·tic** \ˌ≈≈≈ˈblastik\ *adj*

am·e·lo·blas·to·ma \ˌ≈≈(ˌ)≈ˌblaˈstōmə\ *n* -s [NL, fr. E *ameloblast* + NL *-oma*] **:** ADAMANTINOMA

am·e·lo·den·tin·al \ˌ≈≈(ˌ)≈ˈdenˌtēnᵊl, -ˌdenˈt-, *attrib often* ˈ≈≈(ˌ)≈ˌ≈ˌ≈≈\ *adj* [*amel* + *-o-* + *dentinal*] **:** of or relating to enamel and dentine ⟨the ~ junction of a tooth⟩

am·e·lo·gen·e·sis \ˌ≈≈(ˌ)≈ˈjenəsəs\ *n* [NL, fr. E *amel* + NL *-o-* + *genesis*] **:** the forming of tooth enamel

am·e·lung glass \ˈaməliŋ-, -ləŋ-\ *n, usu cap A* [after John F. Amelung *fl* 1784 Am. glass manufacturer] **:** a rare late 18th century American glassware often similar to fine engraved Stiegel glass

am·e·lus \ˈaməlǝs, (ˈ)āˈmel-\ *n, pl* **ame·li** \-ˌlī, -ē\ [NL, fr. ²*a-* + Gk *melos* limb] **:** a limbless fetus

¹amen *in religious use,* (ˈ)äˈmen *or* (ˈ)āˈ- *when sung,* (ˈ)äˈ- *or* (ˈ)äˈ- *or* (ˈ)āˈ- *when not sung; in nonreligious use usu* (ˈ)āˈ≈\ *interj* [ME, fr. OE, fr. LL, fr. Gk *amēn,* fr. Heb *āmēn*] — used to express solemn ratification (as of an expression of faith, a prayer, or an invocation) or hearty approval (as of an assertion)

²amen \" *also* ˈ=,=\ *n* -s [ME, fr. *amen*, interj.] **:** a response esp. of ratification, approval, conclusion, or termination ⟨as a sort of ~ to that, nine nations quickly recognized the new regime —*Time*⟩ ⟨he paused for a response of ~s —M.L. Bach⟩ ⟨responses including chants, doxologies, and ~s —Dwight Weldy⟩

ame·na·bil·i·ty \ə,mēnəˈbiləd·ē, -ətē, -i *also* -en-\ *n* -ES **:** the quality or state of being amenable **:** TRACTABLENESS

ame·na·ble \əˈ=nəbəl\ *adj* [prob. fr. (assumed) AF *amenable*, fr. MF *amener* to lead up, bring (fr. OF, fr. *a-* — fr. L *ad-* — + *mener* to lead, fr. L *minare* to drive, fr. *minari* to threaten) + *-able* — more at MOUNT] **1 a :** liable to be brought to account or judgment **:** liable to the legal authority of **:** ANSWERABLE, ACCOUNTABLE ⟨is it to be contended that the heads of departments are not ~ to the laws —John Marshall⟩ ⟨offenses ~ to the ecclesiastical judicature —Herman Melville⟩ **b :** liable to a claim or charge ⟨was ~ to the accusation⟩ **2 a :** capable of submission (as to a judgment or test) ⟨~ to the comparatively small-scale form of enquiry —K.E.Read⟩ ⟨~ data⟩ **b :** readily brought to yield or submit **:** RESPONSIVE, TRACTABLE ⟨a personality ~ to our desires —Mary Austin⟩ ⟨an ~ view on matters of mutual concern —Robert Trumbull⟩ **syn** see OBEDIENT, RESPONSIBLE

ame·na·bly \-blē, -li\ *adv* **:** in an amenable manner

amenance *n* -s [AF, action of bringing, fr. MF *amener* + *-ance*] *obs* **:** BEHAVIOR, BEARING

amen corner \ˈā,men- *sometimes* ˈä,- *or* ˈà,-\ *n* **:** a corner in a church near the pulpit formerly occupied by those leading in the responsive amens **:** a conspicuous corner occupied by fervent worshipers

amend \əˈmend\ *vb* -ED/-ING/-S [ME *amenden*, fr. OF *amender*, modif. (influenced by L *ad-*) of L *emendare*, fr. *e, ex* out + *-mendare* (fr. *menda* fault); akin to L *mendax* lying, false, *mendicus* beggar, Skt *mindā* physical defect] *vt* **1** *obs* **:** to reform, convert, or make better esp. in character ⟨may God ~ these sinful people⟩ **2** *archaic* **:** REPAIR, RESTORE, MEND **3 a :** to put right **:** CORRECT, RECTIFY ⟨~ such flaws⟩; *specif* **:** to make emendations in (as a text) **b** *archaic* **:** HEAL, CURE **c** (1) **:** to change or modify in any way for the better **:** IMPROVE, BETTER ⟨~ our situation⟩ (2) **:** to change or alter in any way esp. in phraseology ⟨~ a remark⟩; *specif* **:** to alter (as a motion, bill, or law) formally by modification, deletion, or addition ⟨~ the constitution⟩ **4** *obs* **:** to make amends or reparation for ~ *vi* **1 :** to reform oneself **:** become better by rectifying manners or morals ⟨when will you ~⟩ **2** *obs* **:** to recover from illness **3** *obs* **:** to become better **:** IMPROVE **syn** see CORRECT

amend·a·ble \-əbəl\ *adj* **:** capable of being amended

amend·a·to·ry \-ə,tōrē, -ōr-, -ri\ *adj* [*amend* + *-atory* (as in *emendatory*)] **:** designed or serving to amend **:** effecting amendment **:** CORRECTIVE

amende ho·no·ra·ble \àmäⁿdònòràbl³, -b(lə)\ *n, pl* **amendes honorables** \"\ [F, lit., honorable reparation] **:** reparation for a crime or injury formerly consisting in such a formal and humiliating acknowledgment of offense and apology as will restore the injured or offended honor of the one wronged; *broadly* **:** a full acknowledgment of error with apology

amend·ment \əˈmenmənt *also* -ndm-\ *n* -s [ME, fr. OF *amendement*, fr. *amender* to amend + *-ment* — more at AMEND] **1 :** act of amending esp. for the better **:** correction of a fault or faults **:** reformation (as of one's life) **2 :** a substance (as lime) that aids plant growth indirectly by improving the chemical condition of the soil (as by neutralizing soil acidity) **3 a :** the process of amending (as a motion, bill, act, or constitution) ⟨a well-drawn constitution will provide for its own ~ —C.J.Friedrich⟩ **b :** an alteration proposed or effected by such process ⟨the prohibition ~⟩

¹amends \əˈmen(d)z\ *pres 3d sing of* AMEND

²amends \"\ *n pl but usu sing in constr* [ME *amendes*, fr. OF, pl. of *amende* reparation, fr. *amender*] **1 :** compensation for a loss or injury **:** RECOMPENSE, REPARATION ⟨gesture which one hopes is the beginning of some fuller ~ —Virgil Thomson⟩ — rarely in sing. ⟨pay an *amend* of 50 pounds to the injured person⟩; often used with *make* ⟨he is ashamed and wants to make ~ —Glenway Wescott⟩ **2** *obs* **:** IMPROVEMENT **:** AMENDMENT

amene \əˈmēn\ *adj* [ME, fr. L *amoenus*, perh. akin to *amare* to love — more at AMATEUR] *archaic* **:** AGREEABLE, PLEASING

¹amen·i·ty \əˈmenəd·ē, -ēn-, -ətē, -i\ *n* -ES [ME *amenite*, fr. L *amoenitat-, amoenitas*, fr. *amoenus* pleasant + *-itat-, -itas* -ity; prob. akin to L *amare* to love — more at AMATEUR] **1 a :** the quality of being pleasant or agreeable (as in situation or climate or in manners or disposition) ⟨the ~ of the countryside⟩ ⟨large houses are divided up into smaller rooms with a lower standard of ~ —Stuart Piggott⟩ ⟨his ~ of temper⟩ **b** (1) **:** the attractiveness and aesthetic or nonmonetary value of real estate or of any structure for purely residential use ⟨woods . . . of which a good deal is capable of immediate realization without in the least detracting from the ~ —*Financial Times*⟩ (2) **:** a feature (as architectural distinction or desirability of location) conducive to such attractiveness and value ⟨the speculative builder who wants to put up a house regardless of its effect on the *amenities* —*Manchester Guardian Weekly*⟩ **2 a :** a feature, trait, or characteristic that makes for pleasantness ⟨the *amenities* of literature⟩ **b :** something that conduces to physical or material comfort or convenience or to a pleasant and agreeable life ⟨*amenities* like shops and community centers⟩ ⟨every ~ . . . including . . . showers, central heating, and first-class cuisine—Hugh G. Smith⟩ **c :** an area or location that provides comforts, conveniences, or attractive surroundings to residents or visitors ⟨a small . . . house in a choice ~ with clear bright sunny outlook —*Scotsman*⟩ ⟨preserving the region and . . . developing it as an ~ —*African Wild Life*⟩ **3** *usu pl* **a :** manner, civility, or relationship usu. expressive of or conducive to pleasantness or smoothness of social intercourse ⟨the *amenities* of diplomacy⟩ **b :** an act or form conventionally observed esp. in social intercourse ⟨the visitor got the *amenities* over quickly and got down to business⟩ ⟨one of the *amenities* which . . . lawyers have recognized . . . is the obligation to refrain from deliberately stealing each other's clients —H.S.Drinker⟩

²amenity \"\ *adj* **:** of, relating to, or providing an amenity ⟨~ values of the countryside —Hugh G. Smith⟩ ⟨an ~ tree for streets and parks⟩

amen·or·rhea *also* **amen·or·rhoea** \(ˌ)ā,menəˈrēə\ *n* -s [NL, fr. ²*a-* + Gk *mēn* month + NL *-o-* + *-rrhea, -rrhoea* — more at MOON] **:** absence or suppression of menstruation from any cause other than pregnancy or the menopause — **amen·or·rhe·al** *also* **amen·or·rhoe·al** \-ˈrēəl\ *adj* — **amen·or·rhe·ic** *also* **amen·or·rhoe·ic** \-ik\ *adj*

a men·sa et tho·ro \ˈäˈmen(t)sə,etˈt(h)ōr(,)ō, ä'm-\ *adj* [NL, lit., from table and bed] **:** relating to a separation in which the parties remain husband and wife but without cohabitation

amen seat \ˈā,men *sometimes* ˈä,- *or* ˈà,-\ *n* **:** a seat in the amen corner of a church

¹am·ent \ˈamənt, ˈām-, -,ment\ *n* -s [NL *amentum*, fr. L *amentum, ammentum* thong, strap, prob. fr. *apere* to fasten + *-mentum* -ment — more at APT] **:** an indeterminate spicate inflorescence bearing scaly bracts and apetalous unisexual flowers (as in the willow) — called also *catkin*

aments: *a* staminate, *b* pistillate

²ament \ˈā,ment, ˈāmə-\ *n* -s [L *ament-, amens* mad, fr. *a-* (fr. *ab-* ab-) + *ment-, mens* mind — more at MIND] **:** a person mentally deficient from birth (as an idiot, imbecile, or moron)

am·en·ta·ceous \ˌamənˈtāshəs,ˌām-, -,men-\ *adj* [¹*ament* + *-aceous*] **1 a :** resembling an ament **b :** consisting of aments ⟨an ~ inflorescence⟩ **2 :** AMENTIFEROUS

¹am·ent·al \ˈamənt³l, ˈāmə-, ˈa,men-\ *adj* [¹*ament* + *-al*] **:** AMENTACEOUS

²amen·tal \(ˈ)āˈment³l\ *adj* [²*a-* + *mental*] **:** devoid of mind ⟨a practically ~ hospital patient⟩

amen·tia \(ˈ)āˈmench(ē)ə, -nsh-\ *n* -s [NL, fr. L, madness, fr. *ament-, amens* + *-ia*] **:** mental deficiency; *specif* **:** a condition characterized by a primary lack of development of intellectual capacity — contrasted with *dementia*

am·en·tif·er·ae \ˌamənˈtifə,rē, ˌām-\ *n pl, cap* [NL, fr. *amentum* ament + *-i-* + *-ferae* (fem. pl. of *-fer*) — more at AMENT] *in some classifications* **:** a group, class, or other category including the dicotyledonous plants that bear aments

am·en·tif·er·ous \ˌ==ˈ=f(ə)rəs\ *adj* [ISV ¹*ament* + *-i-* + *-ferous*] **:** bearing aments

amen·ti·form \aˈmentə,fórm, ā-, ə-\ *adj* [¹*ament* + *-iform*] **:** having the shape of an ament

amen·tum \əˈmentəm\ *n, pl* **amen·ta** \-tə\ [L — more at AMENT] **:** a thong or cord attached to a javelin for aid in casting

amer- *or* **amero-** *comb form, cap* [*American*] **:** American ⟨*Amerophile*⟩ **:** American and ⟨*Amerasian*⟩

am·era \ˈamərə\ *n pl, cap* [NL, fr. ²*a-* + *-mera* (fr. Gk *meros* part)] *in certain classifications* **:** a major division of invertebrate animals comprising unsegmented more or less wormlike forms (as Platyhelminthes, Nemathelminthes, and certain Bryozoa) — compare OLIGOMERA, POLYMERA

amerce \əˈmərs, -3s,-əis\ *vt* -ED/-ING/-S [ME *amercien*, fr. AF *amercier*, fr. OF *a merci* at (one's) mercy, fr. *a-* (fr. L *ad-*) + *merci* mercy — more at MERCY] **:** to punish by a pecuniary penalty the amount of which is not fixed by law but is left to the discretion of the court ⟨the court *amerced* the criminal in the sum of $100⟩; *broadly* **:** PUNISH

amerce·ment \-mənt\ *n* -s [ME *amerciment, amerciament*, fr. AF, fr. *amercier* + OF *-ment*] **:** the infliction of a penalty at the discretion of the court; *also* **:** a mulct or penalty thus imposed — compare AFFEER

amer·ci·a·ble \əˈ=sēəbəl, -shəb-\ *adj* [alter. (influenced by *amerciament*) of earlier *amerceable*, fr. *amerce* + *-able*] **:** punishable by amercement

amer·ci·a·ment \-sēəmənt, -shəm-\ *n* -s [ME — more at AMERCEMENT] *archaic* **:** AMERCEMENT

amer·i·ca \əˈmerəkə *also* -rē-\ *adj, usu cap* [fr. *America*, the continental region, fr. NL, after *Americus* Vespucius, Latinized form of Amerigo Vespucci †1512 Ital. navigator once believed to be its discoverer] **1 :** of or from No. America or So. America **:** of the kind or style prevalent in No. America or So. America **:** AMERICAN 1 **2 :** of or from the U.S. **:** of the kind or style prevalent in the U.S. **:** AMERICAN 2

¹amer·i·can \-kən\ *n* -s *cap* [*America*, the continental region + E *-an*] **1 :** an Indian of No. America or So. America **2 :** a native or inhabitant of No. America or So. America — usu. used with a qualifying adjective ⟨Latin *Americans*⟩ ⟨North *Americans*⟩ of all except inhabitants of the U.S. **3 :** a citizen of the U.S. **4 :** AMERICAN ENGLISH

²american \"\ *adj, usu cap* **1 :** belonging to, inhabiting, coming from, or forming part of America ⟨*American* waters⟩ ⟨an *American* people⟩ ⟨*American* products⟩ ⟨the *American* land masses⟩ **2 :** belonging to, inhabiting, coming from, or forming part of the U.S., its possessions, or original territory ⟨*American* air bases⟩ ⟨the first *American* colonists⟩ ⟨*American* soldiers⟩ ⟨a typical *American* city⟩ **3 :** relating or belonging to the division of mankind that comprises the Indians of No. America and So. America now regarded as an offshoot of the Mongolian

amer·i·cana \ə,merəˈkanə, -ˈänə, -ˈānə *also* -ānə\ *n pl, usu cap* [*America* + E *-ana*] **:** materials (as literary or historical documents and relics) distinctively bearing on, concerning, or characteristic of America, its civilization, or its culture: *also* **:** a collection of such materials ⟨has collected Western *Americana*, especially old books and early firearms —*Current Biog.*⟩

american alder *n, usu cap 1st A* **:** SPECKLED ALDER

american alligator *n, usu cap 1st A* **:** the alligator (*Alligator mississipiensis*) of the southeastern U.S. occas. reaching 16 feet in length with a tough hide much sought for leather

american allspice *n, usu cap 1st A* **:** CAROLINA ALLSPICE

american aloe *n, usu cap 1st A* **:** CENTURY PLANT

american arborvitae *n, usu cap 1st A* **:** an evergreen tree (*Thuja occidentalis*) of eastern No. America having branchlets in horizontal planes — compare ORIENTAL ARBORVITAE

american ash *n, usu cap 1st A* **:** WHITE ASH 1a

american aspen *n, usu cap 1st A* **:** a slender tree (*Populus tremuloides*) with quaking leaves native to eastern No. America

american badger *n, usu cap A* **:** a badger (*Taxidea taxus*) of western No. America

american baptist *n, usu cap A&B* **:** a member of a body of Baptist churches in northern and western U.S. which was organized in 1907 as the Northern Baptist Convention and renamed American Baptist Convention in 1950

american barberry *n, usu cap A* **:** a shrub (*Berberis canadensis*) of the southeastern U.S. with brown branches and flowers in short umbelliform clusters — called also *Allegheny barberry*

american basement *n, usu cap A* **:** a basement story above the ground level containing the principal entrance to the building

american basswood *n, usu cap A* **:** an American tree of the genus *Tilia* (esp. *T. americana*)

american beauty *n, usu cap A* **:** a deep purplish red that is redder and paler than hollyhock, redder and less strong than magenta (sense 2a), and less strong and slightly redder and darker than Harvard crimson (sense 2)

american beech *n, usu cap A* **:** a forest tree (*Fagus grandifolia*) having smooth gray bark, light green leaves, and edible nuts

american bison *or* **american buffalo** *n, usu cap A* **:** the bison (*Bison bison*) of No. America that formerly ranged in great herds over much of temperate No. America but is now nearly extinct

american bittern *n, usu cap A* **:** a large No. American marsh bird (*Botaurus lentiginosus*) that is related to the herons and has a brown body, dark gray outer wings, and a black stripe down each side of the neck — called also *stake driver, thunder pumper*

american bladdernut *n, usu cap A* **:** a shrub or small tree (*Staphylea trifolia*) of eastern No. America with trifoliolate leaves, drooping clusters of white flowers, and a bladdery capsule

american blight *n, usu cap A, Brit* **:** WOOLLY APPLE APHID

american bond *n, usu cap A* **:** a masonry bond in which the headers recur every 5th or 6th course, the stretcher courses that come together being laid so as to break joints — called also *common bond*

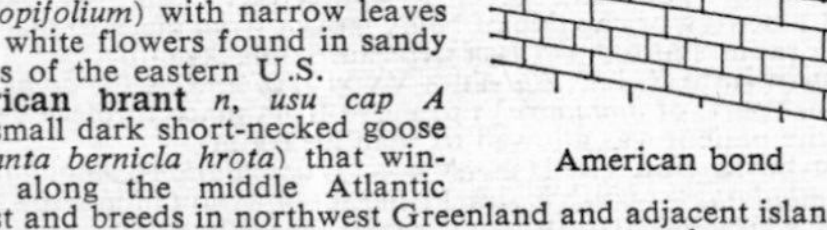
American bond

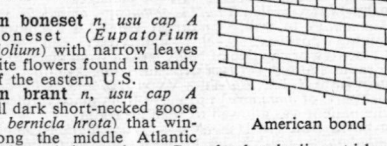

american boneset *n, usu cap A* **:** a boneset (*Eupatorium hyssopifolium*) with narrow leaves and white flowers found in sandy areas of the eastern U.S.

american brant *n, usu cap A* **:** a small dark short-necked goose (*Branta bernicla hrota*) that winters along the middle Atlantic coast and breeds in northwest Greenland and adjacent islands

american brown rot *n, usu cap A* **:** brown rot of stone and pome fruits caused by a fungus (*Sclerotinia fructicola*)

american catholic *adj, usu cap A&C* **:** of or relating to a church organized in 1885 for the purpose of bringing together American Catholics interested in the Old Catholic movement

american centaury *n, usu cap A* **:** either of two pink-flowered marsh plants (*Sabbatia angularis* and *S. stellaris*) of the eastern U.S. resembling the true centaury

american chameleon *n, usu cap A* **:** a lizard (*Anolis carolinensis*) of the southeastern U.S.

american cheese *n, usu cap A* **1 :** cheddar cheese made in America **2 :** a process cheese made from American cheddar

american cherry *n, usu cap A* **:** BLACK CHERRY 2

american chinaroot *n, usu cap A* **:** a greenbrier (*Smilax pseudo-china*) with large tuberous roots

american class *n, usu cap A* **:** a group of breeds of domestic fowls originated or developed chiefly in No. America — compare MEDITERRANEAN CLASS

american cloth *n, usu cap A, Brit* **:** a sturdy enameled oilcloth

american cockroach *n, usu cap A* **:** a free-flying cockroach (*Periplaneta americana*) that is a common pest infesting ships or buildings (as homes, warehouses, or bakeries) in the northern hemisphere

american columbo *n, usu cap A* **1 :** a perennial herb (*Frasera caroliniensis*) — called also *American gentian, columbo;* see DEER'S-EAR **2 :** the dried root of the American columbo formerly used as a bitter tonic

american coot *n, usu cap A* **:** a common American marsh bird (*Fulica americana*) having the bill, edge of wings, and upper tail coverts white, the rest of the plumage slaty and darker on the back than below — called also *blue peter, mudhen;* compare COOT 1

american copper *n, usu cap A* **:** a common copper butterfly (*Lycaena hypophlaeas*) widely distributed in central and eastern No. America north of the Gulf coast

american cotton *n, usu cap A* **:** UPLAND COTTON

american cowslip *n, usu cap A* **:** SHOOTING STAR

american crab apple *n, usu cap A* **:** a medium-sized tree (*Malus coronaria*) of the eastern U. S. with pink flowers and small hard yellow fruit — called also *garland crab*

american cranberry *n, usu cap A* **:** a trailing red-fruited cranberry (*Vaccinium macrocarpon*) with leaves oblong and obtuse, flowers in lateral clusters, and fruit ⅓ to ¾ inches in diameter — called also *large cranberry;* compare EUROPEAN CRANBERRY

american cranberry bush *n, usu cap A* **:** CRANBERRY BUSH 2

american crawl *n, usu cap A* **:** CRAWL 2; *specif* **:** a 6-beat crawl

american crocodile *n, usu cap A* **:** a tropical American crocodile (*Crocodylus acutus*) whose range extends to Florida

american dewberry *n, usu cap A* **:** a prostrate dewberry (*Rubus hispidus*) found in eastern No. America having persistent trifoliolate leaves, white flowers, and small reddish black fruit

american dog tick *n, usu cap A* **:** a common No. American tick (*Dermacentor variabilis*) attacking dogs, man, and other mammals and being an important vector of spotted fever and tularemia in man — called also *wood tick*

american dog violet *n, usu cap A* **:** a leafy-stemmed violet (*Viola conspersa*) with pale flowers found in moist woods

american dwarf birch *n, usu cap A* **:** a shrub (*Betula glandulosa*) of the colder parts of No. America with short aments and roundish glandular leaves

american eagle *n, usu cap A* **1 :** BALD EAGLE **2 :** a figure of a bald eagle with extended wings similar to that in the coat of arms of the U. S.

american ebony *n, usu cap A* **:** GRANADILLA TREE

american egret *n, usu cap A* **:** the common egret of No. America usu. being considered a variety (*egretta*) of the Old World egret (*Casmerodius alba* or *Egretta alba*)

american elder *n, usu cap A* **:** an elder (*Sambucus canadensis*) of eastern No. America with pale yellow branches, leaves with usu. seven leaflets, flat-topped flower clusters, and purplish black fruit about ¼ inch in diameter

american elm *n, usu cap A* **:** a large and well-known ornamental tree (*Ulmus americana*) common in eastern No. America with gradually spreading branches and pendulous branchlets

american empire *n, usu cap A* **:** a style of furniture of the second quarter of the 19th century influenced by contemporary French style, characterized by simple often heavy forms, and usu. finished in mahogany veneers

american english *n, cap A&E* **:** the native language of most inhabitants of the U. S. — used esp. with the implication that it is a variety of English clearly distinguishable from that used in Great Britain and not deriving its standards of usage from it, yet not so divergent as to be a separate language; compare AUSTRAL ENGLISH, AUSTRALIAN ENGLISH, BRITISH ENGLISH

amer·i·can·ese \əˌmerəkəˈnēz, -ēk-, -ēs\ *n* -s *cap A* **:** English speech or writing containing a high proportion of Americanisms — usu. used disparagingly

amer·i·can·ess \əˈ=== nəs\ *n* -s *cap A* **:** an American woman

american featherfoil *n, usu cap A* **:** an aquatic herb (*Hottonia inflata*) of the eastern U. S. with a spongy submerged stem, finely divided leaves, and white flowers

american feverfew *n, usu cap A* **:** a stout herb (*Parthenium integrifolium*) of the southeastern U. S. with whitish flowers resembling those of the feverfew

american fingering *n, usu cap A* **:** marking of piano music that uses the letter X to indicate the thumb and the figures 1, 2, 3, and 4 to indicate the other fingers — compare GERMAN FINGERING

american flag fish *n, usu cap A* **:** a small cyprinodont fish (*Jordanella floridae*) native to Florida swamps and mottled in blue and brown with white sides striped with red

american fluke *n, usu cap A* **:** the large liver fluke (*Fascioloides magna*) of cattle and related game mammals — compare LIVER FLUKE

american foulbrood *n, usu cap A* **:** foulbrood of the honeybee caused by a bacterium (*Bacillus larvae*) and characterized by a ropy or gummy condition of affected larvae

american foxhound *n, usu cap A* **:** a foxhound of a breed developed in America largely from English stock being slightly smaller than the English foxhound with longer ears, a dense hard glossy coat usu. of black, tan, and white, straight strong forelegs, and very powerful hindquarters

american fried potatoes *n pl, usu cap A* **:** HASHED BROWN POTATOES

american frog's-bit *n, usu cap A* **:** FROGBIT 2

american gentian *n, usu cap A* **:** AMERICAN COLUMBO 1

american germander *n, usu cap A* **:** an herb (*Teucrium canadense*) with serrate leaves, flowers in spikelike racemes, and calyx with a feltlike coat

american goldeneye *n, usu cap A* **:** a duck of the No. American subspecies (*americana*) of the goldeneye being stocky, medium sized, and large headed with the male chiefly black and white, the female brown and gray

american gooseberry *n, usu cap A* **:** any of several tropical American shrubs constituting a genus *Heterotrichum* of the family Melastomaceae and being often cultivated in warm regions for their showy panicles of white or pink flowers

american gooseberry mildew *n, usu cap A* **:** a powdery mildew (*Sphaerotheca mors-uvae*) of the gooseberry

american gray birch *n, usu cap A* **:** a medium-sized tree (*Betula populifolia*) of No. America having grayish or white bark, triangular leaves, and nearly valueless wood and occurring very commonly as a second-growth forest tree

american great valerian *n, usu cap A* **:** an herb (*Polemonium reptans*) of the eastern U. S. with pinnate leaves and blue flowers

american green *n, usu cap A* **:** a moderate yellowish green that is greener and duller than tarragon and yellower and duller than malachite green or verdigris — called also *jadesheen*

american gromwell *n, usu cap A* **:** a rough perennial herb (*Lithospermum latifolium*) of eastern No. America with hairy ovate leaves and axillary yellowish white flowers

american heather *n, usu cap A* **:** a beach heather (*Hudsonia tomentosa*)

american hellebore *n, usu cap A* **1 :** a white hellebore (*Veratrum viride*) of the eastern U. S. with dense spikelike flower clusters and rootstock that is the source of veratrum **2 :** the roots and rhizomes of the American hellebore

american hemp *n, usu cap A* **1 :** INDIAN MALLOW 1 **2 :** INDIAN HEMP 1

american holly *n, usu cap A* **:** a tree (*Ilex opaca*) of moist woodlands in the eastern U. S. having duller and less spiny leaves than the European holly

american hookworm *n, usu cap A* **:** a man-infesting hookworm (*Necator americanus*) discovered in No. America though probably native to Africa

american hornbeam *n, usu cap A* **:** a hornbeam (*Carpinus caroliniana*) of No. America with toothed leaves, winged fruit, and very hard durable wood

american horse chestnut *n, usu cap A* **:** OHIO BUCKEYE

amer·i·ca·ni *or* **amer·i·ka·ni** \ə,merəˈkänē\ *n* -s *often cap* [Swahili, fr. E ²*American*] **:** unbleached cotton sheeting orig. made in America and used in Africa and the Far East

american indian *n, cap A&I* **:** a member of any (except usu. the Eskimos) of the aboriginal peoples of the western hemisphere constituting one of the divisions of the Mongoloid stock **:** RED INDIAN, AMERIND

american ipecac *n, usu cap A* **:** INDIAN PHYSIC 1

amer·i·can·ism \əˈmerəkə,nizəm, -ēk-\ *n* -s *usu cap* **1 :** a characteristic feature of American English esp. as contrasted with British English (as *hydrant, lynch, cookie, prairie, frame house, woodchuck, I guess, catercorner, store* meaning "shop", *corn* meaning "maize") **2 :** attachment or allegiance to the traditions, interests, or ideals of the U.S. or of democracy as practiced in the U. S. 3 a : a custom peculiar to the U. S. or to America b : an American attitude or trait ⟨his frankness was considered an *Americanism*⟩ c : a socio-political principle or practice essential to American national culture ⟨the Declaration of Independence and the U. S. Constitution are fundamental to *Americanism*⟩ 4 : HECKERISM

amer·i·can·ist \-.nəst\ *n* -s *usu cap* 1 : a specialist in the languages or cultures of the aboriginal inhabitants of America 2 : a member of a nation other than the U. S. who is favorable to the policies of the U. S. or to cooperation with the U. S.

amer·i·can·is·tic \-ˌ-ˈnistik, -tēk\ *adj, usu cap* : relating to America as a subject of study

amer·i·can·ite \-ˈ-ˌnīt\ *n* -s *sometimes cap* [²*American* + *-ite*] : a glassy meteoritic mineral found in a large area of western So. America

amer·i·can·itis \-ˌ-ˈnīd·əs\ *n* -ES *usu cap* 1 : excessive nervous tension 2 : enthusiastic or aggressive advocacy of Americanism

american ivy *n, usu cap A* : VIRGINIA CREEPER

amer·i·can·i·za·tion \-ˌ-nəˈzāshən, -ˌnīˈz-\ *n* -s *usu cap* 1 : the act or process of americanizing 2 : instruction of foreigners (as immigrants) in the English language, in U. S. history and government, and in other studies to prepare them for life in the U. S. or to familiarize them with U. S. culture, institutions, and ideals

amer·i·can·ize \-ˈ-ˌnīz\ *vb* -ED/-ING/-S *often cap* [²*American* + *-ize*] *vt* 1 : to make American: a : to cause to acquire traits or characteristics distinctively or conceived as distinctively American b : to bring into close conformity with American national customs and institutions : change in behavior and attitude to suit the American way of life 2 : to bring into conformity with characteristically American spelling or pronunciation 3 : to bring (an area) under the political, cultural, or commercial influence of the U. S. ~ *vi* : to acquire American traits : integrate with or assimilate in spirit and culture to life in the U. S.

amer·i·can·iz·er \-zə(r)\ *n* -s *usu cap* 1 : one entrusted with or engaged in americanizing immigrants or resident aliens in the U. S. 2 : an ardent advocate of Americanism

american jade *n, usu cap A* : CALIFORNITE

american joy *n, usu cap A* : VIRGINIA CREEPER

american judas tree *n, usu cap A&J* : REDBUD

american jute *n, usu cap A* : INDIAN MALLOW 1

american language *n, usu cap A* : AMERICAN ENGLISH — usu. used with *the*

american lanner *n, usu cap A* : PRAIRIE FALCON

american larch *n, usu cap A* : a tamarack (*Larix laricina*)

american laurel *n, usu cap A* : MOUNTAIN LAUREL

american licorice *n, usu cap A* : WILD LICORICE 1

american lion *n, usu cap A* : COUGAR

american lobster *n, usu cap A* : the common lobster (*Homarus americanus*) of the northeastern coast of No. America

american lotus *n, usu cap A* : an aquatic plant (*Nelumbo lutea*) of the eastern U. S. with large usu. emerged leaves, very large yellow flowers, and deeply pitted fruits

amer·i·can·ly \-ˈ-ˌ-lē\ *adv, usu cap* : in a distinctively American way ⟨so able to meet anything that might come . . . so *Americanly* capable and sure of the event —Booth Tarkington⟩

american mandrake *n, usu cap A* : MAYAPPLE

american merganser *n, usu cap A* : a common No. American diving duck usu. considered a variety (*Mergus merganser americanus*) of the European goosander

american milk pea *n, usu cap A* : a prostrate herbaceous vine (*Galactia regularis*) of the southeastern U. S. having trifoliolate leaves and reddish purple racemose flowers

american mint *n, usu cap A* 1 : PEPPERMINT 1a 2 : CANADA MINT

american mistletoe *n, usu cap A* 1 : a small scaly leafless herb (*Arceuthobium pusillum*) that is parasitic on spruce and larch and has reddish brown stems, minute flowers, and berrylike fruits 2 : MISTLETOE 2a

american morse code *n, cap A & usu cap M* : the Morse code used on telegraphic landlines in the U.S. and Canada — see MORSE CODE table

american moss *n, usu cap A* : SPANISH MOSS

american mountain ash *n, usu cap 1st A* : a mountain ash (*Sorbus americana*) with leaves that become glabrous beneath, sticky winter buds, and fruit about ¼ inch in diameter

american nettle tree *n, usu cap A* : HACKBERRY 1

american nightshade *n, usu cap A* 1 : POKEWEED 2 : DITCH STONECROP

amer·i·ca·no \əˌmerəˈkä(ˌ)nō\ *also* **americano cocktail** *n* -s *usu cap A* [Sp *americano* American, fr. *América* + Sp *-ano* -an] : a cocktail made from sweet vermouth, bitters, and soda water

amer·i·can·oc·ra·cy \əˌmerəkəˈnäkrəsē\ *n* -ES *usu cap* [*American* + *-o-* + *-cracy*] : political and economic control of a country by the U. S.

amer·i·can·oid \-ˈ-ˌ-nȯid\ *adj, usu cap* : resembling or having the form of something American; *specif* : showing certain lexical or structural affinities with the American Indian languages — used of certain languages of northeastern Asia (as Yukaghir, Chukchi, and Koryak); compare PALEO-ASIATIC

american olive *n, usu cap A* : DEVILWOOD

american organ *n, usu cap A* : a reed organ in which the air is drawn in through the reeds by a suction bellows

american orpine *n, usu cap A* : a succulent herb (*Sedum telephioides*) of the eastern U. S. with thick fleshy leaves and pink flowers

american ostrich fern *n, usu cap A* : an ostrich fern (*Pteretis pennsylvanica*)

american pansy *n, usu cap A* : BIRD'S-FOOT VIOLET

american pasqueflower *n, usu cap A* : any of several American plants of the genus *Anemone*; *esp* : a hirsute perennial (*A. ludoviciana*) with long-petioled leaves and persistent plumose styles

american pellitory *n, usu cap A* : an alternate-leaved weed (*Parietaria pennsylvanica*) of eastern No. America having axillary green flowers

american perch *n, usu cap A* : YELLOW PERCH

american pintail *n, usu cap A* : a dabbling duck breeding in northwestern No. America and wintering along the southern part of both coasts southward to Panama usu. being considered indistinguishable from the Old World pintail

american plan *n, usu cap A* 1 : a hotel rate whereby guests are charged a fixed sum by the day, week, or other period for room and meals combined — contrasted with *European plan* 2 : the principle of direct dealing between employers and employees without the intervention of labor unions or their officials or through a company union

american plane *or* **american plane tree** *n, usu cap A* : SYCAMORE 3a

american plum *n, usu cap A* : any of various cultivated plums derived chiefly from native American plums (as from *Prunus americana*) — compare EUROPEAN PLUM

american pondweed *n, usu cap A* : WATERWEED

american poplar *n, usu cap A* 1 : AMERICAN ASPEN 2 : TULIP TREE

american redstart *n, usu cap A* : a fly-catching warbler (*Setophaga ruticilla*) chiefly of eastern No. America, the male being largely black with white belly and bright orange on sides, wings, and tail, the female being olivaceous with pale yellow markings

american robin *n, usu cap A* : ROBIN 1c

american rock brake *n, usu cap A* : a rock-inhabiting fern (*Cryptogramma acrostichoides*) of northern No. America

american ruby *n, usu cap A* : a garnet cut from pyrope found in Arizona and New Mexico

american russia leather *n, usu cap A&R* : calfskin or cowhide leather finished to resemble Russia leather

american sable *n, usu cap A* : a pine marten (*Martes americana*) or its fur — compare SIBERIAN SABLE

american saddle horse *n, usu cap A* : a 3-gaited or 5-gaited saddle horse of a breed developed chiefly in Kentucky from Thoroughbreds and native stock and distinguished by their slender clean-cut build, high clean action, and alert carriage of head and tail

american saffron *n, usu cap A* : SAFFLOWER 1

american saibling *n, usu cap A* : SUNAPEE TROUT

american sanicle *n, usu cap A* : either of two hairy greenish flowered herbs (*Heuchera americana* and *H. villosa*) of eastern No. America

american school *n, usu cap A* : the economists that adhered to the American system; *specif* : the American economists who rejected the Ricardian doctrine of rent and the Malthusian doctrine, advocated a protective tariff, accepted the labor theory of value but not its implication of a subsistence wage, and held that labor's lot continuously improves

american scoter *n, usu cap A* : a large No. American scoter (*Oidemia americana*), the male being coal black with a bright yellow protuberance at the base of the upper mandible, the female being dusky brown with whitish cheeks

american sea rocket *n, usu cap A* : a fleshy herb (*Cakile edentula*) with purplish flowers and jointed pods found on seabeaches

american senna *n, usu cap A* : a wild senna (*Cassia marilandica*)

american service tree *n, usu cap A* : MOUNTAIN ASH 1

american shad *n, usu cap A* : a shad (*Alosa sapidissima*)

american shield fern *n, usu cap A* : a woodland fern (*Dryopteris spinulosa intermedia*) of eastern No. America with pinnae bearing glandular hairs

american snowball *n, usu cap A* : a shrub (*Styrax grandifolia*) of the southeastern U. S. with large leaves and racemose white flowers appearing before or with the leaves

american spindle tree *n, usu cap A* : ²WAHOO 1a

american star grass *n, usu cap A* : a low grasslike herb (*Hypoxis hirsuta*) of eastern No. America with villous narrow leaves and yellow umbellate flowers

american sumac *n, usu cap A* 1 : STAGHORN SUMAC 2 : DIVI-DIVI 1

american surra *n, usu cap A* : INFECTIOUS ANEMIA

american system *n, cap A* : the policy of promoting industry in the U. S. by adoption of a high protective tariff and of developing internal improvements by the federal government (as advocated by Henry Clay from 1816 to 1828)

american tiger *n, usu cap A* : JAGUAR

american trotter *n, usu cap A* : a Standardbred horse

american trypanosomiasis *n, usu cap A* : CHAGAS' DISEASE

american valerian *n, usu cap A* : any of several American species of *Cypripedium*

american vegetable-tallow tree *n, usu cap A* : WAX MYRTLE

american vermilion *n, usu cap A* 1 : vermilion or a color resembling it (as imitation vermilion) 2 : a pigment usu. consisting of a lead molybdate or a basic lead chromate (as chrome red)

american vessel *n, usu cap A* : a vessel registered under the laws of the U. S. : a vessel owned by or chartered to Americans

american vetch *n, usu cap A* : a vetch (*Vicia americana*) with trailing or climbing stems, compound leaves, and racemose bluish purple flowers — called also *buffalo pea*

american walnut *n, usu cap A* : BLACK WALNUT 1

american watercress *n, usu cap A* : a weak perennial herb (*Cardamine rotundifolia*) found in cold springs in the eastern U. S. having undivided leaves and thin pods

american water spaniel *n, usu cap A* : a medium-sized spaniel of American origin with a thick curly chocolate or liver-colored coat

american wayfaring tree *n, usu cap A* : HOBBLEBUSH

american white avens *n, usu cap A* : a woodland herb (*Geum canadense*) of eastern No. America with hairy trifoliolate leaves, small white flowers, and bristly fruits

american white hellebore *n, usu cap A* : AMERICAN HELLEBORE

american white ipecac *n, usu cap A* : IPECAC SPURGE

american widgeon *n, usu cap A* : BALDPATE 2

american wine *n, usu cap A* : a U.S. wine made from grapes developed from or containing blood of an American wild grape (*Vitis labrusca*) and grown chiefly in the eastern or middle western part of the U. S.; *broadly* : any wine made in the U. S. — compare CALIFORNIA WINE

american wistaria *n, usu cap A* : a native woody vine (*Wisteria frutescens*) resembling the cultivated Japanese wistaria

american witch alder *n, usu cap A* : a shrub (*Fothergilla gardeni*) of the southeastern U. S. with hairy foliage and fruits and catkinlike spikes of apetalous flowers

american wormseed *n, usu cap A* : MEXICAN TEA

american wormseed oil *n, usu cap A* : CHENOPODIUM OIL

american yellow *n, usu cap A* : a variety of chrome yellow in the preparation of which alum and barium sulfate are used

american yew *n, usu cap A* : GROUND HEMLOCK

am·er·i·ci·um \ˌaməˈris(h)ēəm\ *n* -s [NL, fr. *America* + NL *-ium*] : a radioactive metallic element produced by bombardment of uranium with high-energy helium nuclei — symbol *Am*; see ELEMENT table

americo- — *comb form, cap* [*America*] 1 : relating to America or Americans ⟨*Americomania*⟩ 2 : American and ⟨*Americo-Liberian*⟩

amer·i·co-li·be·ri·an \əˈmerəˌkōˌlīˈbirēən\ *n, usu cap A&L* : a Liberian of American origin or descent

amerikani *often cap A, var of* AMERICANI

am·er·ind \ˈaməˌrind\ *n* -s *cap* [*American Indian*] : an individual of one of the native peoples of America : an American Indian or Eskimo — **am·er·in·di·an** \ˌ-ˈ-ˌ-ēən\ *adj, usu cap* — **am·er·in·dic** \-dik\ *adj, usu cap*

am·er·ism \ˈaməˌrizəm, (ˈ)āˈme,r-\ *n* -s [*ameristic* + *-ism*] : the quality or state of being ameristic

am·er·is·tic \ˌaməˈristik, ˌāˌmeˈr-\ *adj* [Gk *ameristos* undivided (fr. *a-* ²*a-* + *meristos* divided) + E *-ic* — more at MERISTEM] : UNDIFFERENTIATED — used of certain ferns having the prothallia not fully developed and lacking in meristematic tissue thus failing to produce archegonia

amero- — see AMER-

am·er·toy \ˈamə(r)ˌtȯi\ *n* -s [*Amer-* + *toy* (*terrier*)] : a small terrierlike dog of a breed of American origin having a short sleek satiny coat and attaining a weight of 6 to 10 pounds

amesace *var of* AMBSACE

ames·ite \ˈāmˌzīt\ *n* -s [alter. (influenced by *-ite*) of earlier *amesine*, fr. James *Ames fl* 1876 Am. mineowner + E *-ine*] : an apple-green chlorite mineral $(Mg,Fe)_4Al_4Si_2O_{10}(OH)_8$ occurring in foliated hexagonal plates

ame·tab·o·la \ˌāməˈtabələ\ *n pl, cap* [NL, fr. Gk *ametabolos* unchanged] : a group of insects that includes certain primitive orders (as Thysanura) that undergo an inconspicuous metamorphosis — **amet·a·bo·li·an** \ˌāˌmed·əˈbōlēən\ *adj*

amet·a·bo·lia \ˌāˌmed·əˈbōlēə\ *syn of* AMETABOLA

amet·a·bol·ic \ˌāˌmed·əˈbälik\ *or* **ame·tab·o·lous** \ˌāmeˈtabələs\ *adj* [²*a-* + *metabolic, metabolous*] : lacking metamorphosis

ame·tab·o·lism \ˌāməˈtabəˌlizəm\ *n* -s [Gk *ametabolos* + E *-ism*] : development without or with minimal metamorphosis (as in the Ametabola) — compare HOLOMETABOLISM

ameth·o·caine \əˈmethəˌkān\ *n* -s [perh. fr. Gk *amethystos* not intoxicating + *-ocaine* (as in *cocaine*)] : TETRACAINE

am·e·thyst \ˈaməthəst, -(ˌ)thi-\ *n* -s [ME *amatist, ametist*, fr. OF & L; OF *amatiste, ametiste*, fr. L *amethystus*, fr. Gk *amethystos* remedy against drunkenness, amethyst (so considered), fr. *amethystos* not drunk, not intoxicating, fr. *a-* ²*a-* + *-methystos* drunk (fr. *methyskein* to make drunk, fr. *methyein* to be drunk, fr. *methy* wine) — more at MEAD] 1 a : a clear purple or bluish violet variety of crystallized quartz much used as a jeweler's stone b : a deep purple variety of corundum — called also *Oriental amethyst* 2 *or* **amethyst violet** : a variable color averaging a moderate purple that is redder and duller than heliotrope (sense 4a) or manganese violet, bluer and duller than cobalt violet, and darker and slightly stronger than average lilac (sense 3a)

am·e·thys·tine \ˌ-ˈthistən, -ˌtīn, -ˌtēn\ *adj* [L *amethystinus*, fr. Gk *amethystinos*, fr. *amethystos* + *-inos* -ine] 1 : resembling, composed of, or containing amethyst 2 : of the color amethyst

am·e·trope \ˈaməˌtrōp\ *n* -s [back-formation fr. *ametropic*] : an ametropic person

am·e·tro·pia \ˌaməˈtrōpēə\ *n* -s [NL, fr. Gk *ametros* without measure (fr. *a-* ²*a-* + *-metros*, fr. *metron* measure) + NL *-opia* — more at MEASURE] : a condition of abnormal refractive ability of the eye in which visual images do not come to a focus upon the retina (as myopia, hypermetropia, or astigmatism) — **am·e·tro·pic** \ˌaməˈträpik, -ˈāp-\ *adj*

AMF *abbr* airmail field

amg *abbr* among

am·garn \ˈamˌgärn\ *n* -s [W, ferrule, fr. *am-* around + *carn* handle; akin to L *ambi-* on both sides, around and to Corn *karn* handle — more at AMBI-] : an ancient stone implement supposed to have served as a guard or ferrule for the shaft or butt of a spear

am ha·a·rez \ˌämˌ(ˌ)häˈäˌrets\ *n, pl* **am·me haarez** *or* **ame haarez** \ˈämə-\ [Heb *ʿam hā'āreṣ* the people of the land] 1 *cap A* : the inhabitants of Palestine as distinguished from the Israelites; *also* : the country people as distinguished from the inhabitants of Jerusalem 2 *often cap A, in rabbinic literature* : the Jews not ritually as strict as the Pharisees 3 *sometimes cap A* : IGNORAMUS : one who is ignorant of Jewish custom, law, or ethics

am·hara \amˈharə, -ˈärə\ *n, pl* **amharas** *or* **amhara** *usu cap* 1 : a Semitic-speaking people of northern Ethiopia 2 : a member of the Amhara people

¹**am·har·ic** \-ik\ *n* -s *cap* : the Semitic language of the central part of the Abyssinian plateau in Ethiopia that as the official language of Ethiopia is also used in government, education, and trade throughout the country

²**amharic** *adj, usu cap* : of, relating to, characteristic of, or composed in Amharic

am·herst·ia \amˈhərstēə, aˈmər-\ *n, cap* [NL, fr. Sarah, Countess *Amherst* †1838 & Sarah Elizabeth *Amherst* †1876 British amateur naturalists + NL *-ia*] : a genus of leguminous trees of India and Burma containing a single species (*A. nobilis*) of trees with immense pinnate leaves and pendent clusters of yellow-spotted vermilion flowers

am·herst·ite \ˈamərˌstīt\ *n* -s [*Amherst* co., Va., its locality + E *-ite*] : a plutonic syenodiorite rock whose feldspar is andesine-antiperthite

amherst pheasant *n, usu cap A* : LADY AMHERST'S PHEASANT

ami *or* **amy** \aˈmē, äˈ-\ *n, pl* **amis** *or* **amies** [ME, fr. OF *ami*, fr. L *amicus*] *law* : FRIEND — see PROCHEIN AMI

¹**amia** \ˈāmēə, ˈam-\ *n, cap* [NL, fr. Gk, a tunny] : a genus of ganoid fishes (order Cycloganoidei) including only the bowfin and being the type of a small otherwise extinct family

²**amia** \"\ [NL, fr. Gk, a tunny] *syn of* APOGON — a prior use that has been ruled invalid by the International Commission for Zoological Nomenclature

ami·a·bil·i·ty \ˌāmēəˈbilad·ē, -ətē, -i *also* -myəˈ-\ *n* -ES 1 : the quality of being amiable : genial disposition ⟨made everyone happy by his unfailing ~⟩ 2 : a manifestation or instance of being amiable ⟨the natives showed them every courtesy and ~⟩

ami·a·ble \ˈāmēəbəl *also* -myəb-\ *adj, sometimes* **amia·bler** \-blə(r)\ **amia·blest** \-bləst\ [ME, fr. MF, fr. LL *amicabilis* friendly, fr. L *amicus* friend + *-abilis* -able; akin to L *amare* to love — more at AMATEUR] 1 *archaic* : PLEASING, LOVELY, ATTRACTIVE ⟨how ~ are thy tabernacles —Ps 84:1 (AV)⟩ 2 a *obs* : AMOROUS ⟨lay an ~ siege to the honesty of this Ford's wife —Shak.⟩ b : generally agreeable : devoid of anything contentious or offensive : good-natured and well-intentioned ⟨he has no improper pride. He is perfectly ~ —Jane Austen⟩ c : friendly, sociable, and congenial : civil and urbane : not stiff, cold, haughty, or stubborn ⟨an ~ friend⟩ ⟨an ~ gathering⟩ d : praiseworthy esp. as mild, lovable, socially beneficent, or unaggressive ⟨an ~ character⟩ ⟨so ~ a virtue as moral honesty —Laurence Sterne⟩ e : ENJOYABLE : affording ready easy pleasure ⟨a genial comic swagger . . . very ~ to behold —Hilaire Belloc⟩

syn GOOD-NATURED, OBLIGING, COMPLAISANT: AMIABLE may suggest an easy congenial good humor, socially pleasant and unaggressive smoothness, or gracious acquiescence ⟨an *amiable* neighborhood character⟩ ⟨the women . . . seemed to find a great deal of time for *amiable* empty gabbling —Edna Ferber⟩ ⟨their manners were more engaging, their tempers more *amiable* —T.B.Macaulay⟩ ⟨he considered a passive attitude in love more feminine and preferred an *amiable* softness to a tragic intensity —Ellen Glasgow⟩ GOOD-NATURED suggests a good-humored willingness to help or cooperate, sometimes an undue compliance ⟨the crowd was *good-natured* and civil . . . all seemed desirous to welcome me with every sign of pleasure —C.B.Nordhoff & J.N.Hall⟩ ⟨"If you're sick of the job, I'll take her off your hands", said the *good-natured* Fred —Anthony Trollope⟩ ⟨when he is *good-natured* . . . he will often pay her more than he is legally obliged to —G.B.Shaw⟩ OBLIGING suggests ready accommodation of others' wishes, usu. with civility or friendliness ⟨Dr. Armstrong, whose name the *obliging* young lady at the office allowed me to read upon the counterfoil of Staunton's urgent message —A. Conan Doyle⟩ ⟨he always had the courtesy to answer me, for he was a most *obliging* fellow —Agnes N. Keith⟩ COMPLAISANT, less common than the others, suggests courteous amiability and willingness to accede, sometimes because of a weak lack of resistance ⟨even if Mrs. Smith had been *complaisant*, Andrew's plan could not have been carried out —Margaret Deland⟩ ⟨her importunity prevailed with me and I am extremely glad I was so *complaisant* —Mary W. Montagu⟩

ami·able·ness *n* -ES : the quality or state of being amiable

ami·a·bly \-blē, -i\ *adv* : in an amiable manner ⟨~ talkative —Jean Stafford⟩

am·i·an·thine \ˌamēˈan(t)thən, ˌthīn\ *adj* [*amianthus* + *-ine*] : of, relating to, or like amianthus

am·i·an·thoid \ˌ-ˈ-ˌthȯid\ *or* **am·i·an·thoid·al** \ˌ-ˌ-ˈthȯidəl, ˌ-ˈ-ˌ-\ *adj* [*amianthus* + *-oid, -oidal*] : resembling amianthus

am·i·an·thus \ˌamēˈan(t)thəs\ *or* **am·i·an·tus** \-ntəs\ *n* -ES [L *amiantus*, fr. Gk *amiantos*, fr. *amiantos* unpolluted, pure, fr. *a-* ²*a-* + *-miantos* (fr. *miainein* to pollute) — more at MIASMA] : fine silky asbestos

am·i·ca·bil·i·ty \ˌaməkəˈbilad·ē, -mēk-, -ətē, -i\ *n* -ES 1 : the quality of being amicable ⟨constant ~ existed between the two nations⟩ 2 : a manifestation or instance of amicableness ⟨much impressed by all these *amicabilities*⟩

am·i·ca·ble \ˈ-ˌkəbəl\ *adj* [ME, fr. LL *amicabilis* — more at AMIABLE] : characterized by or as if by friendship and goodwill : PEACEABLE : not quarrelsome ⟨consistently ~ discussions —F.D.Roosevelt⟩

syn NEIGHBORLY, FRIENDLY: AMICABLE stresses lack of quarreling, contention, bitterness, or hostility ⟨at the precise time when the feeling between the two countries was friendliest, and an *amicable* settlement of differences seemed likeliest —V.L.Parrington⟩ ⟨after more than thirty-two years of trading, *amicable* relations with the Indians were severed by the Indian wars —*Amer. Guide Series: Maine*⟩ NEIGHBORLY suggests either complete goodwill or sociable helpfulness and interest befitting a neighbor ⟨the only encirclement sought is the encircling bond of good old-fashioned *neighborly* friendship —F.D.Roosevelt⟩ ⟨a lover of men, the most *neighborly* soul in the world, mingling freely with all classes, and although quite properly proud of a visit from the governor or other great person, never above chatting with the carpenter, or doing a kindness to an old nurse —V.L.Parrington⟩ FRIENDLY may suggest warm intimacy, kindly benevolence, or amiable lack of ill will ⟨continually thanking Father John for his *friendly* visit, saying how kind it was of him to come and sit with an old man like him —Anthony Trollope⟩ Sometimes it indicates only an appearance of these qualities ⟨we must keep smiling faces and be *friendly* with him no matter how repulsive it may be —Jack London⟩

amicable action *n* : an action commenced and prosecuted by amicable consent of the parties for the purpose of obtaining a decision of the court on some matter of law ⟨*amicable action*, in the sense in which these words are used in courts of justice, presupposes that there is a real dispute between the parties concerning some matter of right . . . The amity consists in the manner in which it is brought to issue before the court. And such *amicable actions*, so far from being objects of censure, are always approved and encouraged—49 U.S. 251, 255⟩

am·i·ca·ble·ness *n* -ES : the quality or state of being amicable

amicable number *n* : either of two numbers each of which is equal to the sum of all the submultiples of the other

am·i·ca·bly \-kəblē, -li\ *adv* : in an amicable manner ⟨a Presbyterian elder and a Methodist parson who rode in ~ together one April afternoon —Green Peyton⟩

am·ic acid \ˈamˈik-\ *n* [*amide* + *-ic*] : a compound (as carbamic acid) that is both an amide and an acid

am·i·cal \ˈaməkəl\ *adj* [L *amicalis*, fr. *amicus* friend + *-alis* -al] : FRIENDLY

1am·ice \ˈaməs\ *n* -s [ME *amyse*, prob. fr. MF *amis* amices, pl. of *amit* amice, fr. ML *amictus*, fr. L, cloak, fr. *amictus*, past part. of *amicire* to wrap around, clothe, fr. *am-*, *amb-* around + *-icire* (fr. *jacere* to throw) — more at AMBI-, JET] **:** a liturgical vestment consisting of an oblong piece of cloth usu. of white linen, worn about the neck and shoulders and partly under the alb

1 amice

2amice \"\ *n* -s [ME *amisse*, fr. MF *aumuce*, fr. ML *almucia, almutia*] **:** ALMUCE

ami·ci prism \əˈmēchē-\ *n, usu cap A* [after G. B. *Amici* †*ab*1863 It. astronomer] **:** a composite prism used in direct-vision spectroscopes and made by combining alternate flint and crown glass components with their refracting edges in opposite directions and with prism angles so chosen that nonhomogeneous light passing through the prism is dispersed into a spectrum, the beam as a whole undergoing no net deviation — compare ACHROMATIC PRISM

ami·cron \(ˈ)āˈmī,krän *sometimes* -mi- *or* -ˌkrən\ *n* -s [ISV *2a-* + *micron*, orig. formed as G *amikron*] **:** one of the smallest particles detectable with the ultramicroscope (about 1×10^{-7} cm in diameter)

ami·cro·nu·cle·ate \ˌā¦==¦=-\ *adj* [*2a-* + *micronucleate*] **:** lacking a micronucleus

amic·tic \əˈmiktik, (ˈ)ā¦-\ *adj* [Gk *amiktos* unmixed (fr. *a-* *2a-* + *miktos* mixed) + E *-ic*] **1 :** incapable of being fertilized **:** PARTHENOGENETIC **:** producing eggs that develop without fertilization — used of female rotifers **2 :** produced by an amictic female ⟨~ egg⟩

ami·cus cu·ri·ae \əˈmēkə'skyüre,ī\ *n, pl* **ami·ci curiae** \-ē(ˌ)kē'ky-\ [NL, lit., friend of the court] **:** a bystander that suggests or states some matter of law for the assistance of a court; *specif* **:** a lawyer that files a printed brief or makes an oral argument before an appellate court on behalf of a person affected by or interested in a pending case but not actually a party to it

amid \əˈmid\ *or* **amidst** \-idzt,-idst,-itst\ *prep* [*amid* fr. ME *amidde*, fr. OE *onmiddan*, fr. *on* + *middan*, dat. sing. masc. of *midde*, adj., middle, mid; *amidst* fr. ME *amiddes*, fr. *amidde* + *-s* — more at MID] **1 a :** in or into the middle of ⟨burst like a bombshell *amidst* the contemporary complacency —Isaac Goldberg⟩ ⟨*amid* such a world, if anywhere, our ideals henceforth must find a home —Bertrand Russell⟩ **b :** surrounded or encompassed by **:** AMONG ⟨*amidst* a patch of snow-covered firs, a sixth cart waited —F.V.W.Mason⟩ ⟨*amid* bulging wicker and pasteboard suitcases and bundles done up in cloth sat elderly men —Andy Logan⟩ **2 a :** in the course of **:** DURING ⟨*amidst* all the fighting there still remained a steady hope for peace⟩ **b :** with the accompaniment of — used to indicate that two or more specified conditions or occurrences are linked in time, cause, or circumstance ⟨he completed the feat *amidst* cheers —*Time*⟩ ⟨the buffaloes, who reproduced so rapidly *amidst* the favorable environment —R.A.Billington⟩

amid- *or* **amido-** *comb form* [ISV, fr. *amide*] **1 :** containing the group NH_2 characteristic of amides united to a radical of acid character ⟨*amido*sulfuric⟩ — distinguished from *amin-* **2 :** AMIN- ⟨*amido*phenol⟩ **3 :** containing the radical –CONH– characteristic of polyamides, peptides, and proteins

ami·dah \əˈmē(ˌ)də, ä'-, -(ˌ)dä; ˌämēˈdō\ *n, pl* **ami·doth** *or* **ami·dot** \-ˌdōs, -ˌdōt; -ˈdōt\ *or* **amidahs** *usu cap* [Heb *ʽămīdhāh* standing] **:** a benediction recited while standing during the main section of the daily Jewish liturgy and at the additional service on Sabbaths and holy days

am·i·dase \ˈamə,dās, -āz\ *n* -s [ISV *amid-* + *-ase*] **:** an enzyme that hydrolyzes acid amides usu. with the liberation of ammonia

am·i·date \-,dāt\ *vt* -ED/-ING/-S [*amid-* + *-ate*] **1 :** to convert into an amide **2 :** AMINATE — **am·i·da·tion** \ˌaməˈdāshən\ *n* -s

am·ide \ˈa,mīd, ˈaməd, *in compounds often* ə,mīd *or* ˌəməd\ *n* -s [G *amid* (fr. *ammoniak* ammonia — fr. F or L— + *-id* -ide) or F *amide*, fr. *ammoniaque* ammonia + *-ide* — more at AMMONIAC] **1 :** any of a class of crystalline compounds derived from ammonia by replacement of one hydrogen atom by a metal ⟨lithium ~ $LiNH_2$⟩ ⟨calcium ~ $Ca(NH_2)_2$⟩ — called also *metallic amide* **2 :** any of a class of compounds (as acetamide, sulfamide) derived from ammonia or an amine by replacement of ammoniacal hydrogen by an acid radical (as an acyl radical) — called also *acid amide;* compare IMIDE; see SULFONAMIDE

amid·ic \əˈmidik, a'-\ *adj* [*amid-* + *-ic*] **:** of or relating to an amide

am·i·dine \ˈamə,dēn, -ˌdən\ *n* -s [ISV *amid-* + *-ine*] **:** any strong monobasic compound containing an amino and an imino group attached to the same carbon atom, having the general formula $RC({=}NH)NH_2$, and formed by the action of ammonia on nitriles or by reaction of ammonia with imido esters

am·i·di·no \ˌaməˈdē(ˌ)nō\ *adj* [*amidino-*] **:** containing the group $-C({=}NH)NH_2$

amidino- *comb form* [ISV, fr. *amidine* + *-o-*] **:** containing the univalent group $-C({=}NH)NH_2$ characteristic of an amidine ⟨*amidino*pyridine⟩

am·i·dism \ˈamə,dizəm\ *n* -s *usu cap* [Jap *Amida* the Buddha Amitabha (fr. Chin *a*[4] *-mi*[2] *-t'o*[2] *-fu*[2], fr. Skt *Amitābha*, a Mahayana Buddha, worshiped as the Buddha of boundless light, life, and mercy, lit., of boundless light, fr. *amita* boundless, unmeasured — fr. *a-* *2a-* + *mita* measured — + *ābhā* light, fr. *ā* towards + *-bhā*, akin to *bhāti* it shines) + E *-ism;* akin to Skt *māti* he measures — more at ACHARYA, FANCY, MEASURE] **:** the Buddhist cult of Amitabha that promises rebirth in paradise to its followers and emphasizes salvation by faith — see PURE LAND

1am·i·dist \-ˌdəst\ *adj, usu cap* [Jap *Amida* + E *-ist*] **:** of or relating to Amidism

2amidist \"\ *n* -s *usu cap* **:** a member of the cult of Amitabha

ami·do \əˈmē(ˌ)dō, ˈamə,dō\ *adj* [*amid-*] **1 :** relating to or containing the group NH_2 or a substituted group NHR or NR_2 united to a radical of acid character — distinguished from *amino* **2 :** AMINO — now less used than formerly

amido black green B *n, often cap A&B&G* **:** an acid azo dye — see DYE table I (under *Acid Green 20*)

ami·do·gen \əˈmēdəjən, -ˌjen\ *n* -s [*amid-* + *-gen*] **:** the radical NH_2 derived from ammonia esp. as detected in the free state — compare AMIDO, AMINO

am·i·dol \ˈamə,dōl, -ōl\ *n* -s [G, fr. *Amidol*, a trademark] **:** a colorless crystalline salt $C_6H_3(NH_2)_2OH.2HCl$ used chiefly as a photographic developer; the dihydrochloride of 2,4-diamino-phenol

ami·do naph·thol red \əˈmēdō¦=,=-, ¦amə,dō¦-\ *n, often cap A&N&R* [*amid-* + *naphthol*] **:** either of two acid azo dyes — see DYE table I (under *Acid Red 1* and *Acid Violet 7*)

am·i·done \ˈamə,dōn\ *n* -s [ISV dimethyl*amino-* + *d*iphenyl + heptan*one;* prob. orig. formed as G *amidon*] **:** METHADONE

ami·do·phos·phor·ic acid \əˈmēdō¦=¦==-, ¦amə,dō¦-\ *n* [*amid-* + *phosphoric*] **:** an acid $PONH_2(OH)_2$ derived from phosphoric acid by replacement of one hydroxyl group by an amido group — called also *phosphamic acid, phosphoramidic acid*

ami·do·py·rine \ə,mēdōˈpī,rēn, ˌamə,dō'-, -ˌrən\ *n* -s [*amid-* + *pyrine*] **:** AMINOPYRINE

am·i·dos·to·mum \ˌaməˈdästəməm\ *n, cap* [NL, fr. Gk *amid-*, *amis* chamber pot + NL *-o-* + *-stomum*] **:** a genus of strongyloid nematodes including destructive parasites of the gizzard wall of ducks and geese

amidoth *or* **amidot** *pl of* AMIDAH

am·i·dox·ime \ˌaməˈdäk,sēm, -ˌsəm\ *n* -s [ISV *amid-* + *oxime;* orig. formed as G *amidoxim*] **:** the oxime of an amide having the general formula $RC({=}NOH)NH_2$

amido yellow E *n, often cap A&Y* **:** an acid dye — see DYE table I (under *Acid Orange 3*)

1amidships *also* **amidship** \=ˈ=,=\ *adv* [*amidships* fr. *amid* + *ship* + *-s* (gen. ending); *amidship*, alter. of *amidships*] **1 a :** in or toward that part of a ship midway between the bow and the stern **b :** in or toward that part of a ship midway between the sides **2 :** in or toward the middle

2amidships *also* **amidship** \"\ *adj* **:** of, relating to, or situated in the middle part of a ship ⟨an ~ cabin⟩

amidst *var of* AMID

amidstream \=ˈ=,=\ *adv* **:** in midstream

amies *pl of* AMY

ami·go \əˈmē(ˌ)gō, ä'-\ *n* -s [Sp, fr. L *amicus;* akin to L *amare* to love — more at AMATEUR] **:** FRIEND

amil \ˈäməl, -ˌmil\ *var of* AUMIL

amil·dar \ˈämәl,där\ *var of* AUMILDAR

amil·le·nar·i·an \ˌā-\ *n* -s [*2a-* + *millenarian*] **:** one who holds the doctrine of amillennialism

amil·len·ni·al \ˌā=ˈ=-\ *adj* **1 :** of or relating to amillennialism **2** [*2a-* + *millenial*] **:** not expecting a literal millennium

amil·len·ni·al·ism \ˌā-\ *n* -s [*2a-* + *millenialism*] **:** the denial that an earthly millennium of universal righteousness and peace will either precede or follow the second advent of Jesus Christ — compare POSTMILLENNIALISM, PREMILLENNIALISM

amil·len·ni·al·ist \ˌā-\ *n* -s **:** AMILLENARIAN

amim·ia \(ˈ)āˈmimēə\ *n* -s [NL, fr. *2a-* + Gk *mimos* actor, mime + NL *-ia* — more at MIME] **1 :** loss or impairment of the power of communicating thought by gestures, due to cerebral disease or injury **2 :** loss of the power to give facial expression to emotion (as the inability to smile) because of paralysis of the facial muscles

a·min *var of* AMEEN

amin- *or* **amino-** *comb form* [ISV, fr. *amine*] *now usu amino-* **:** containing the group NH_2 characteristic of primary amines united to a radical other than an acid radical ⟨*amino*acetanilide⟩ ⟨*amino*guanidine⟩ — distinguished from *amid-*

am·i·nase \ˈamə,nās\ *n* -s [*amin-* + *-ase*] **:** any of a group of enzymes capable of promoting assimilation of ammonia

1am·i·nate \-,nāt\ *n* -s [*amin-* + *-ate*] **:** a compound with an amine

2aminate \"\ *vt* -ED/-ING/-S [*amin-* + *-ate*] **:** to introduce the amino group into **:** convert into an amine — **am·i·na·tion** \ˌaməˈnāshən\ *n* -s

amine \əˈmēn, ˈamən\ *n* -s [ISV *ammonium* + *-ine*] **1 :** any of a class of basic compounds derived from ammonia by replacement of hydrogen by one or more univalent hydrocarbon radicals or other nonacidic organic radicals, being classed as primary, secondary, or tertiary according as one, two, or three atoms of ammoniacal hydrogen have been replaced — distinguished from *imine;* compare QUATERNARY AMMONIUM COMPOUND **2 :** a compound (as a chloramine) containing one or more halogen atoms attached to nitrogen

amin·ic \əˈmēnik, -in-, a'-\ *adj* [*amin-* + *-ic*] **:** of or relating to an amine or the amino group

am·in·ize \ˈamə,nīz; əˈmē,-, a'-\ *vt* -ED/-ING/-S [*amin-* + *-ize*] **:** AMINATE

ami·no \əˈmē(ˌ)nō, a'-; ˈamə,nō\ *adj* [*amin-*] **:** relating to or containing the group NH_2 or a substituted group NHR or NR_2 united to a radical other than an acid radical — distinguished from *amido*

ami·no·ace·tic acid \=¦===¦=-, ¦==¦=¦==\ *n* [*amin-* + *acetic*] **:** GLYCINE

amino acid *n* **:** an organic acid in which a portion of the nonacid hydrogen has been replaced by one or more amino groups and which therefore shows both basic and acidic properties; *esp* **:** one of the more than 20 alpha-amino acids, most of which have the general formula $RCH(NH_2)COOH$, that are synthesized in plant and animal tissues, that are considered the building blocks of proteins, from which they can be obtained by hydrolysis, and that play an important role in metabolism, growth, maintenance, and repair of tissue — see ESSENTIAL AMINO ACID, PEPTIDE

amino alcohol *n* **:** a compound (as ethanolamine) that is both an alcohol and an amine — called also *alcamine, hydroxy amine*

ami·no·azo \=¦=+a(ˌ)zō, ¦==,=-\ *adj* [*aminoazo-*] **:** containing both the amino and azo groups

aminoazo- *comb form* [ISV, fr. *amin-* + *az-*] **:** containing both the amino and azo groups esp. in compounds formed by rearrangement of diazoamino compounds

ami·no·azo·benzene \"+\ *n* [ISV *aminoazo-* + *benzene*] **:** a solvent dye $C_6H_5N{=}NC_6H_4NH_2$ — see DYE table I (under *Solvent Yellow 1*)

ami·no·azo·toluene \"+\ *n* [*aminoazo-* + *toluene*] **:** a solvent dye — see DYE table I (under *Solvent Yellow 3*)

ami·no·ben·zo·ate \=,==-, ¦==¦=-\ *n* -s [*amin-* + *benzoate*] **:** a salt or ester of an aminobenzoic acid, esp. of the para isomer

ami·no·ben·zo·ic acid \=¦==¦=¦==-, ¦==¦=¦==-\ *n* [ISV *amin-* + *benzoic*] **:** any of three crystalline monoamino derivatives $NH_2C_6H_4COOH$ of benzoic acid: as **a :** the colorless or yellowish para-substituted acid that is found as a component of the vitamin B complex and of the folic acids but is usu. made synthetically, that is antagonistic to many sulfa drugs in their action on bacteria, and that is used in local anesthesia in the form of some of its esters (as butacaine, procaine) — called also *PABA, p-aminobenzoic acid, para-aminobenzoic acid* **b :** ANTHRANILIC ACID

am·i·nol·y·sis \ˌaməˈnäləsəs\ *n, pl* **aminoly·ses** \-ə,sēz\ [NL, fr. *amin-* + *-lysis*] **1 :** ammonolysis or any analogous decomposition in which an amine takes the place of ammonia **2 :** hydrolytic deamination (as the conversion of an amino acid into a hydroxy acid) — **ami·no·lyt·ic** \əˈmēnō¦lid·ik, a¦-; ¦amə,nō¦-\ *adj*

ami·no·meth·yl·a·tion \ə¦mēnō,methəˈlāshən, a¦-; ¦amə,nō,-\ *n* -s [*aminomethyl* (fr. *amin-* + *methyl*) + *-ation*] **:** introduction of the amino-methyl group NH_2CH_2– into a compound

amino nitrogen *n* **:** nitrogen occurring as a constituent of the amino group

ami·no·pep·ti·dase \=,==ˈpeptə,dās, ¦===-\ *n* -s [*amin-* + *peptide* + *-ase*] **:** an enzyme (as an enzyme found in the duodenum) that hydrolyzes peptides, esp. polypeptides, by splitting off the amino acids containing free amino groups

ami·no·phe·nol \-ˈ=,=\ *n* -s [ISV *amin-* + *phenol;* orig. formed in G] **1 :** any of three crystalline compounds $NH_2C_6H_4OH$ derived from phenol, distinguished as *ortho*-aminophenol, *meta*-aminophenol, and *para*-aminophenol, and used as dye intermediates, the para compound being also used as a fur and hair dye and as a photographic developer **2** *usu* **amino phenol :** any amino derivative of a phenol

am·i·noph·er·ase \ˌaməˈnäfə,rās\ *n* -s [*amin-* + *pher-* + *-ase*] **:** TRANSAMINASE

ami·no·phyl·line \ə,mēnōˈfi,lēn, ˌamə,nō'-; ˌaməˈnäfə,-\ *n* -s [*amin-* + *theophylline*] **:** a white or slightly yellow granular compound $(C_7H_8N_4O_2)_2.C_2N_4(NH_2)_2.2H_2O$ of theophylline and ethylenediamine that has an ammoniacal odor and bitter taste and is used in medicine similarly to theophylline

ami·no·plast \ˈ==,plast, ˈ==,=-\ *n* -s [by shortening] **:** AMINO PLASTIC

amino plastic *or* **amino resin** *n* **:** a plastic or synthetic resin (as a urea-formaldehyde resin) made from amino or amido compounds usu. excluding the polyamides

ami·no·pol·y·pep·ti·dase \=¦==,päləˈpeptə,dās, ¦==,=-\ *n* -s [*amin-* + *polypeptide* + *-ase*] **:** an aminopeptidase that acts on polypeptides

am·i·nop·ter·in \ˌaməˈnäptərən\ *n* -s [*aminopter*oylglutamic + *-in*] **:** a yellow crystalline compound $C_{19}H_{20}N_8O_5.2H_2O$ used clinically as an antagonist to folic acid in the treatment of certain leukemias — called also *4-aminopteroylglutamic acid*

ami·no·py·rine \ə,mēnōˈpī,rēn, a,-, -ˌrən; ˌamə,nō'-\ *n* -s [ISV dimethyl*amino-* + anti*pyrine*] **:** a white crystalline compound $C_{13}H_{17}N_3O$ derived from pyrazolone and used as an anodyne and antipyretic — called also *amidopyrine*

a minor \ˈāˈmīnə(r)\ *n, usu cap A* **:** the minor musical key having neither sharps nor flats in its signature

a mi·no·re \ˌämēˈnōrē, ˌäm-; ¦ā,mīˈ-\ *adj* [L, from the lesser] **:** of or relating to an ionic foot beginning with two short syllables

ami·no·sal·i·cyl·ic acid \=¦==¦=¦==-, ¦==¦=¦==-\ *n* [*amin-* + *salicylic*] **:** any of four isomeric monoamino derivatives $NH_2C_6H_3(OH)COOH$ of salicylic acid; *esp* **:** the white crystalline para-substituted acid made synthetically and used in the treatment of tuberculosis usu. as an adjunct to streptomycin or dihydrostreptomycin

ami·no·thi·a·zole \=¦==-¦==-\ *n* -s [*amin-* + *thiazole*] **:** a light yellow crystalline heterocyclic amine $H_2NC_3H_2NS$ made by condensing thiourea and chloro-acetaldehyde and used esp. in the manufacture of sulfathiazole — called also *2-aminothiazole*

am·i·oi·dei \ˌamēˈȯidē,ī\ [NL, fr. *1Amia* + *-oidei*] *syn of* CYCLOGANOIDEI

amir *var of* EMIR

amis *pl of* AMI

1amish \ˈämish, -ēsh *also* ˈam- *sometimes* ˈām-\ *adj, usu cap* [prob. fr. G *amisch*, fr. Jacob *Amman* or *Amen* *fl* 1693 Swiss Mennonite bishop, the founder of the sect + G *-isch* -ish] **:** of, belonging, or relating to a strict sect of Mennonite followers of Amman that settled in America

2amish \"\ *n, cap* **:** the Amish people

amish·go \əˈmish(ˌ)gō\ *n, usu cap* **:** AMUSGO

am·ish·man \ˈämishmən, ˈam-,ˈām-, -ēsh-\ *n, pl* **amishmen** *cap* **:** an Amish Mennonite

1amiss \əˈmis\ *adv* [ME *amis*, fr. *1a-* + *mis* mistake, wrong — more at MISS] **1 a :** in a mistaken way **:** WRONGLY ⟨if you think he is guilty, you judge ~⟩ **b :** out of the right way **:** ASTRAY ⟨something had gone ~ —Van Wyck Brooks⟩ **2 :** in a faulty way **:** IMPERFECTLY ⟨Miss Bennet would not play at all ~ if she practiced more —Jane Austen⟩ **3 a :** in a reprehensible way ⟨no doubt he got his money ~⟩ **b :** in an uncalled-for way ⟨a crude fellow, forever speaking ~⟩

2amiss \"\ *adj* [ME *amis*, fr. *amis*, adv.] **1 :** not in accordance with right order **:** WRONG ⟨undue provincialism is ~ —D.G. Mandelbaum⟩ **2 :** FAULTY, IMPERFECT ⟨whether his general health had been previously at all ~ —Charles Dickens⟩ **3 a :** deserving blame **:** REPREHENSIBLE ⟨could prove nothing ~ —Hartzell Spence⟩ **b :** out of place under given circumstances **:** uncalled for — usu. used with a negative ⟨a few expurgated excerpts may not be ~ —R.B.Merriman⟩; usu. used predicatively

3amiss *n* -ES [ME *amis*, fr. *amis*, adj. & adv.] *obs* **:** FAULT, MISDEED

amis·si·bil·i·ty \ə,misəˈbiləd·ē\ *n* -ES [prob. fr. NL *amissibilitas*, fr. LL *amissibilis* amissible + L *-itas* -ity] **:** capability of being lost **:** likelihood of being lost

amis·si·ble \əˈmisəbəl\ *adj* [LL *amissibilis*, fr. L *amissus* (past part. of *amittere* to lose, send away, fr. *a*, *ab* from + *mittere* to send) + *-ibilis* -able — more at OF, SMITE] **:** capable of being lost **:** likely to be lost

amission *n* -s [F or L; F, fr. L *amission-*, *amissio*, fr. *amissus* + *-ion-*, *-io* -ion] *obs* **:** LOSS

amit *vt* [L *amittere*] *obs* **:** LOSE ⟨a loadstone fired doth presently ~ its proper virtue —Sir Thomas Browne⟩

am·i·tate \ˈamə,tāt -ˌtət\ *n* -s [L *amita* paternal aunt + E *-ate*] **1 :** a special relationship obtaining among some peoples between a niece and her paternal aunt **2 :** authority of a woman over her brother's children and the rights and responsibilities associated therewith — compare AVUNCULATE

ami·to·sis \ˌā,mīˈtōsəs, ˌamə'-\ *n, pl* **amito·ses** \-ō,sēz\ [NL, fr. *2a-* + *mitosis*] **:** cell division in which there is first a simple cleavage of the nucleus without differentiation (as of chromosomes or spindle) followed by the division of the cytoplasm — called also *direct cell division;* opposed to *mitosis*

ami·tot·ic \ˌā,mīˈtäd·ik, ¦amə¦-\ *adj* [fr. NL *amitosis*, after such pairs as NL *hypnosis:* E *hypnotic*] **:** of, relating to, or involving amitosis — **ami·tot·i·cal·ly** \-ək(ə)lē\ *adv*

am·i·ty \ˈaməd·ē, -ətē, -i\ *n* -ES [ME *amite*, fr. MF *amité, amitié*, fr. ML *amicitas*, fr. L *amicus* friend, friendly + *-itas* -ity; akin to L *amare* to love — more at AMATEUR] **:** friendship and goodwill esp. as characterized by mutual acceptance and toleration of potentially antagonistic standpoints or aims ⟨so the two women kept up an elaborate pretense of warm ~ —Scott Fitzgerald⟩; *specif* **:** friendly relations between large groups ⟨nations striving for lasting ~⟩

am·i·u·rus \ˌa,mīˈyürəs\ *syn of* AMEIURUS

amix·ia \(ˈ)āˈmiksēə\ *n* -s [NL, fr. Gk, purity, lack of intercourse, fr. *amiktos* unmixed, pure, unsociable (fr. *a-* *2a-* + *miktos* mixed, fr. *meignynai* to mix) + *-ia* — more at MIX] *biol* **:** absence of interbreeding (as that resulting from geographical isolation)

am·i·zil·ia \ˌaməˈzilyə\ *n, cap* [NL] **:** a genus of large hummingbirds chiefly of Central America of which two species (*Amizilia tzacal* and *A. yucatanensis chalconota*) range as far north as southern Texas

am·la \ˈämlə\ *n* -s [Hindi *āmlā*, fr. Skt *āmalaka*] **:** EMBLIC

amlah *var of* AMALA

amm- *or* **ammo-** *comb form* [*ammo-*, fr. Gk, fr. *ammos* sand — more at SAND] **:** sand ⟨*ammo*philous⟩

am·man \ˈa,man, ˈä,män\ *adj, usu cap* [fr. *Amman*, Jordan] **:** of or from Amman, the capital of Jordan **:** of the kind or style prevalent in Amman

am·man·ite \ˈamə,nīt\ *n* -s *usu cap* [Jacob *Ammann* or *Amen* *fl* 1693 Swiss Mennonite bishop + E *-ite*] **:** an Amish Mennonite

amme haarez *pl of* AM HAAREZ

am·me·ter \ˈa(m),mēd·ə(r), -ētə- *sometimes* ˈamə-\ *n* -s [*ampere* + *-meter*] **:** an instrument for measuring electric current in amperes by an indicator activated by the movement of a coil in a magnetic field or by the longitudinal expansion of a wire carrying the current — compare GALVANOMETER, MICROAMMETER, MILLIAMMETER, VOLTAMETER

am·mi \ˈa,mī\ *n, cap* [NL, fr. L *ammi*, *ami*, a plant (prob. *Carum copticum*), fr. Gk] **:** a small genus (the type of the family Umbelliferae) of branched annual herbs of the Mediterranean region and the No. Atlantic islands with pinnate or pinnatifid leaves and compound umbels — see BISHOP'S WEED

am·mi·a·ce·ae \ˌaməˈāsē,ē\ *n pl, cap* [NL, fr. *Ammi*, type genus + *-aceae*] *in some classifications* **:** a family of plants coextensive with Umbelliferae — **am·mi·a·ceous** \ˌaməˈāshəs\ *adj*

am·mine \ˈa,mēn, ˈamən; əˈmēn, a'-\ *n* -s [ISV *ammonia* + *-ine*] **1 :** a molecule of ammonia as it exists in a coordination complex ⟨hex-*ammine*-cobalt chloride $[Co(NH_3)_6]Cl_3$⟩ **2 :** any compound with ammonia or sometimes with an amine regarded as a coordination complex ⟨metal ~s⟩ — compare AMMONIATE

am·mi·no \ˈamə,nō; əˈmē(ˌ)nō, a'-\ *adj* [*ammino-*] **:** of, relating to, or characteristic of an ammine

ammino- *comb form* [prob. fr. G, fr. *ammin* ammine] **:** ammine ⟨*ammino*chloride⟩

am·mo \ˈa(ˌ)mō\ *n* -s [by shortening & alter.] **:** AMMUNITION ⟨a GI carrying enough ~ to fight a week⟩

am·mo·bi·um \əˈmōbēəm, a'-\ *n* [NL, fr. *amm-* + *-bium* (fr. Gk *bios* life)] **1** *cap* **:** a small genus of Australian herbs (family Compositae) with yellow flowers and silvery foliage — see WINGED EVERLASTING **2** -s **:** a plant of the genus *Ammobium*

am·mo·coe·tes \ˌaməˈsēd·ēz\ *also* **am·mo·coete** \ˈamə,sēt\ *n, pl* **am·mo·coetes** \ˌaməˈsēd·ēz, ˈamə,sēts\ [NL *Ammocoetes*, former genus consisting of the ammocoetes, fr. *amm-* + *-coetes* (fr. Gk *koitē* bed, fr. *keisthai* to lie) — more at CEMETERY] **:** the larva of any of various lampreys — **am·mo·coe·tid** \ˌaməˈsēd·əd\ *n or adj* — **am·mo·coe·toid** \-ˈsē,tȯid\ *adj*

am·mo·dyte \ˈamə,dīt\ *n* -s [NL *Ammodytes*] **:** SAND LAUNCE

am·mo·dy·tes \ˌaməˈdīd·ēz\ *n, cap* [NL, fr. Gk *ammodytēs*, a snake, lit., sand burrower, fr. *amm-* + *dytēs* diver, fr. *dyein* to enter, get into, sink] **:** a genus (the type of the family Ammodytidae) of percomorph fishes containing the typical sand launces — **am·mo·dy·toid** \ˌamə¦dī,tȯid\ *adj*

am·mo·nal \ˈamə,nal\ *n* -s [ISV *ammonium* + *aluminum;* prob. orig. formed in G] **:** an explosive containing chiefly ammonium nitrate, trinitrotoluene, and powdered aluminum

1am·mo·nate \ˈamə,nāt\ *vb* -ED/-ING/-S [*ammonia* + *-ate*] **:** to combine with ammonia to form only one product without decomposition (as in ammonolysis) of the ammonia — **am·mo·na·tion** \ˌaməˈnāshən\ *n* -s

2ammonate *var of* AMMONIATE

am·mo·nea \ˌaməˈnēə\ [NL, by shortening] *syn of* AMMONOIDEA

ammoni- *or* **ammonio-** *comb form* [ISV, fr. *ammonium*] **:** containing ammonia or ammonium ⟨*ammonio*cupric sulfate⟩

am·mo·nia \əˈmōnyə *also* -nēə\ *n* -s [NL, fr. L (*sal*) *ammoniacus* sal ammoniac, lit., salt of Ammon, fr. *ammoniacus* of Ammon, fr. Gk *ammōniakos*, fr. *Ammōn*, an Egyptian deity identified by the Greeks with Zeus, fr. Egypt *Amōn;* fr. its having been prepared near a temple of Ammon in Egypt] **1 :** a colorless gaseous alkaline compound of nitrogen and hydrogen NH_3 that is lighter than air, of extremely pungent smell and taste, and very soluble in water, that can easily be condensed by cold and pressure to a liquid and for this reason is much used in producing artificial cold by the absorption of heat that takes place when the liquid ammonia evaporates, that was formerly made from nitrogenous organic matter (as horn, hoofs) but is now produced as a by-product of the gas and coke industry, that forms ammonium salts by combination with acids and forms many organic derivatives (as amines, amino acids, amides, alkaloids), and that is used both free and combined in medicine, the arts, and industry (as in making fertilizers and explosives) — see LIQUID AMMONIA, SYNTHETIC AMMONIA PROCESS **2 :** AMMONIA WATER

ammonia alum *n* **:** ALUM 1b

am·mo·ni·ac \ə'mōnē,ak\ *or* **am·mo·ni·a·cum** \,amə'nīəkəm\ *n* -s [ME & L; ME *ammonyak*, fr. L *ammoniacum* ammoniac, fr. Gk *ammōniakon*, fr. neut. of *ammōniakos* of Ammon; prob. fr. its occurrence in plants growing near a temple of Ammon in Egypt] **1 :** the aromatic gum resin of the ammoniac plant that occurs in commerce in the form of yellowish tears or lumps with a bittersweet somewhat nauseous and acrid taste and that is used as an expectorant and stimulant and in the formation of certain plasters — called also *gum ammoniac, Persian ammoniac* **2 :** a dark-colored gum resin derived from a northern African plant (*Ferula brevifolia*) — called also *African ammoniac*

am·mo·ni·a·cal \;amə'nīəkəl\ *or* **am·mo·ni·ac** \ə'mōnē,ak\ *adj* [*ammoniacal* fr. *ammoniac*, n. + *-al*; *ammoniac* fr. ME (*sal*) *ammoniac*, fr. L *sal ammoniacus* — more at AMMONIA] **:** of or relating to ammonia **:** containing or having the properties of ammonia

ammoniac plant *n* **:** a tall Persian herb (*Dorema ammoniacum*) of the family Umbelliferae whose milky juice yields ammoniac

ammonia dynamite *n* **:** DYNAMITE 1c

ammonia gelatin *n* **:** an explosive of the gelatin dynamite class containing ammonium nitrate

ammonia liquor *or* **ammoniacal liquor** *n* **:** AMMONIA WATER; *esp* **:** the impure solution obtained as a by-product in destructive distillation (as of coal, tar, and bones)

am·mo·ni·an \ə'mōnēən, -nyən\ *adj, usu cap* [*Ammonius*, 3d cent. Alexandrian Christian philosopher + E *-an*] **:** of or relating to Ammonius of Alexandria, reputed author of a harmony of the Gospels and a work on the agreement of the teachings of Moses and Jesus

ammonia nitrogen *n* **:** nitrogen combined in the form of ammonia or ammonium

ammonia soda *n* **:** soda made by the ammonia soda process

ammonia soda process *n* **:** a process for making soda from common salt by using ammonia and carbon dioxide; *specif* **:** SOLVAY PROCESS

[1]**am·mo·ni·ate** \ə'mōnē,āt, *usu* -ād.+V\ *vt* -ED/-ING/-S [*ammonia* + *-ate*] **1 :** to combine or impregnate with ammonia or an ammonium compound ⟨*ammoniated* superphosphate⟩ **2 :** AMMONIFY

[2]**ammoniate** \"\ *also* **am·mo·nate** \'amə,nāt\ *n* -s [*ammonia* + *-ate*] **1 :** a compound with ammonia regarded as analogous to a hydrate ⟨calcium chloride hexa-*ammoniate* $CaCl_2.6NH_3$⟩ — compare AMMINE **2 :** any organic material (as tankage or hoof and horn) from which nitrogen can be obtained in the form of ammonia — used chiefly commercially

ammoniated mercury *n* **:** a heavy white odorless amorphous compound NH_2HgCl obtained by treating a solution of mercuric chloride with excess of ammonia and used in external treatment of skin diseases and to destroy lice — called also *white precipitate*

am·mo·ni·a·tion \ə,mōnē'āshən\ *n* -s **:** the act or process of ammoniating

am·mo·ni·a·tor \ə'mōnē,ād·ə(r)\ *n* -s **:** an apparatus for introducing ammonia into a compound or for impregnating a substance with ammonia

ammonia water *or* **ammonia solution** *n* **:** a solution of ammonia in water — called also *aqua ammonia, aqueous ammonia, spirit of hartshorn;* compare AMMONIUM HYDROXIDE, HOUSEHOLD AMMONIA

am·mo·ni·fi·ca·tion \ə,mōnəfə'kāshən, -mä-\ *n* -s [*ammonia* + *-ification*] **1 :** AMMONIATION **2 :** decomposition with production of ammonia or ammonium compounds esp. by the action of bacteria on nitrogenous organic matter (as in soils)

am·mo·ni·fi·er \=ˈ==,fī(ə)r\ *n* -s **:** a bacterium that produces ammonia from organic matter containing nitrogen

am·mo·ni·fy \ə'mōnə,fī, -mä-\ *vb* -ED/-ING/-ES [*ammonia* + *-fy*] *vt* **:** to subject to ammonification ~ *vi* **:** to produce or undergo ammonification

ammonio- — see AMMONI-

am·mo·ni·o·bo·rite \ə,mōnē(,)ō-\ *n* -s [*ammoni-* + *borite*] **:** a mineral consisting of hydrous ammonium borite $(NH_4)_2B_{10}O_{16}.5H_2O$ found at Larderello, Italy

am·mo·ni·o·ja·ro·site \=ˈ==(,)=-\ *n* -s [*ammoni-* + *jarosite*] **:** a member of the jarosite group of minerals in which ammonium replaces potassium

[1]**am·mo·nite** \'amə,nīt, *usu* -īd.+V\ *n* -s [NL *ammonites*, fr. *ammon-* (fr. L *cornu Ammonis* ammonite, lit., horn of Ammon, Egyptian deity represented with ram's horns, fr. *cornu* horn + *Ammonis*, gen. of *Ammon*, fr. Gk *Ammōn*) + *-ites* -ite — more at AMMONIA] **1 :** any of numerous fossil shells of cephalopods of the order Ammonoidea having the form of a flat spiral similar to that of the nautilus and esp. abundant in the Mesozoic age, some being 3 feet or more in diameter **2 :** one of the Ammonoidea — **am·mo·nit·ic** \;amə;nid·ik\ *adj*

[2]**am·mo·nite** \"\ *n* -s [*ammon-* (in *ammonium nitrate*) + *-ite*] **:** a nitrogenous animal product of rendering works consisting largely of dried meat residues and used as a fertilizer

[3]**am·mon·ite** \"\ *n -s usu cap* [LL *Ammonites*, fr. Heb *'Ammōn*, people of the Ammonites + L *-ites* -ite] **1 :** a member of a people who in Old Testament times lived east of the Jordan between the Jabbok and the Arnon **2 :** the Semitic language of the Ammonites, closely allied to Hebrew

[4]**am·mon·ite** \"\ *adj, usu cap* **:** of or relating to the Ammonites

am·mo·ni·tes \,amə'nīd·ēz\ *n, cap* [NL, fr. *ammonites* ammonite] **1** *in former classifications* **:** a genus of ammonites **2 :** a group of ammonites comprising forms known only from fragments too imperfect to allow accurate identification — used as a generic name

am·mo·ni·ti·cone \,amə'nīd·ə,kōn, -ni-\ *n* -s [[1]*ammonite* + *-i-* + *cone*] **:** [1]AMMONITE 1

am·mo·ni·ti·da \,amə'nīd·əd·ə\ [NL, fr. *Ammonites* + *-ida*] *syn of* AMMONOIDEA

am·mo·nit·if·er·ous \;amə,nīd·;if(ə)rəs\ *adj* [[1]*ammonite* + *-i-* + *-ferous*] **:** containing ammonites

[1]**am·mon·it·ish** \'amə,nīd·ish\ *adj, usu cap* [[3]*Ammonite* + *-ish*] **:** [4]AMMONITE

[2]**ammonitish** \"\ *n, usu cap* **:** [3]AMMONITE 2

am·mo·nit·oid \;amə'nīd·,ȯid, ə'mänə,tȯid\ *adj* [[1]*ammonite* + *-oid*] **:** resembling an ammonite

am·mo·nit·oi·dea \,amə,nīd·'ȯidēə\ [NL, fr. *Ammonites* + *-oidea*] *syn of* AMMONOIDEA

am·mo·ni·um \ə'mōnēəm, -nyəm\ *n* -s [NL, fr. *ammonia* + *-ium*] **:** an ion NH_4^+ or radical NH_4 derived from ammonia by combination with a hydrogen ion or atom and known in compounds (as salts formed by reaction of dry or aqueous ammonia with acids) that resemble in properties the compounds of the alkali metals and known also in organic compounds (as quaternary ammonium compounds) in which one or more of the hydrogen atoms attached to the nitrogen are substituted by organic radicals

ammonium alum *or* **ammonium aluminum sulfate** *n* **:** ALUM 1b

ammonium bicarbonate *n* **:** a white crystalline salt NH_4HCO_3 made by passing carbon dioxide through an aqueous ammonia solution and used chiefly in baking powders and in fire-extinguishing compositions — called also *ammonium acid carbonate, ammonium hydrogen carbonate*

ammonium bromide *n* **:** a colorless crystalline salt NH_4Br used in photography and in medicine as a sedative

ammonium carbamate *n* **:** a salt NH_2COONH_4 found in commercial ammonium carbonate and formed as an intermediate in the manufacture of urea by reaction of ammonia and carbon dioxide

ammonium carbonate *n* **:** a ammonium salt of carbonic acid: as **a :** the normal carbonate $(NH_4)_2CO_3$ that readily decomposes into the bicarbonate and ammonia **b :** AMMONIUM BICARBONATE **c :** a white crystalline mixture of ammonium bicarbonate and ammonium carbamate obtained commercially by subliming an ammonium salt with calcium carbonate and used chiefly in medicine, in smelling salts, in baking powders, in fire-extinguishing compositions, and in scouring and dyeing preparations

ammonium chloride *n* **:** a white crystalline volatile salt NH_4Cl that occurs naturally esp. as a product of volcanic action or is manufactured and that is used chiefly as an electrolyte in dry cells and as an expectorant for bronchitis — called also *sal ammoniac*

ammonium cyanate *n* **:** a white crystalline salt NH_4OCN that changes into urea on standing or on heating in an aqueous solution

ammonium hydrosulfide *n* **:** AMMONIUM SULFIDE b

ammonium hydroxide *n* **:** a weak base NH_4OH formed when ammonia dissolves in water and existing only in solution

ammonium molybdate *n* **:** a white crystalline salt used in analytical chemistry as a precipitant of phosphoric acid with which it forms a yellow precipitate of ammonium phosphomolybdate

ammonium nitrate *n* **:** a colorless crystalline salt NH_4NO_3 made usu. by the union of ammonia and nitric acid and used chiefly in explosives and fertilizers

ammonium perchlorate *n* **:** a crystalline salt NH_4ClO_4 used chiefly as an oxidizer in explosives, in fireworks, and solid propellant systems for rockets

ammonium persulfate *n* **:** a colorless crystalline salt $(NH_4)_2S_2O_8$ used as an oxidizing agent and for improving dense photographic negatives

ammonium phosphate *n* **:** a phosphate of ammonium made by reaction of ammonia and phosphoric acid: as **a :** the white crystalline primary phosphate $NH_4H_2PO_4$ or sometimes a commercial mixture of this with ammonium sulfate, used chiefly as a fertilizer and as a fire retardant — called also *ammonium dihydrogen phosphate, monoammonium phosphate, monobasic ammonium phosphate* **b :** the white crystalline secondary phosphate $(NH_4)_2HPO_4$ similarly used — called also *diammonium phosphate, dibasic ammonium phosphate*

ammonium picrate *n* **:** a yellow or red salt of picric acid $NH_4OC_6H_2(NO_2)_3$ used as an explosive, its resistance to impact, shock, and friction permitting its use in armor-piercing projectiles

ammonium sulfamate *n* **:** a white crystalline salt $NH_4SO_3NH_2$ used chiefly as a fire retardant and as a weed killer

ammonium sulfate *n* **:** a colorless crystalline salt $(NH_4)_2SO_4$ occurring in nature as mascagnite and made usu. by reaction of sulfuric acid with ammonia and used chiefly as a fertilizer

ammonium sulfide *n* **:** a sulfide of ammonium: as **a :** the unstable colorless to yellow crystalline normal sulfide $(NH_4)_2S$ **b :** the white crystalline hydrosulfide NH_4HS used in aqueous solution chiefly in the textile industry

ammonium thiocyanate *n* **:** a colorless crystalline salt NH_4SCN made by reaction of ammonia and carbon disulfide and used chiefly in textile printing, as a rust inhibitor, and as a weed killer and defoliant

ammonium thioglycolate *n* **:** a colorless crystalline salt NH_4OOCH_2SH used in setting cold waves

am·mo·no \ə'mō(,)nō\ *adj* [*ammono-*] **:** of or relating to compounds considered as bearing to ammonia relations analogous to those that certain other compounds bear to water ⟨lithium amide $LiNH_2$ is an ~ base⟩ — compare AQUO

ammono- *comb form* [ISV, fr. *ammonia*] **1 :** ammonia ⟨*ammonolysis*⟩ **2 :** derived from ammonia — in names of chemical compounds ⟨*ammono*carbonic acid $HN{=}C(NH_2)_2$⟩ — compare AQUO- 2

am·mo·noid \'amə,nȯid\ *n* -s [NL *Ammonoidea*] **:** one of the Ammonoidea **:** AMMONITE

am·mo·noi·dea \,amə'nȯidēə\ *n pl, cap* [NL, irreg. fr. *Ammonites* + *-oidea*] **:** an order of extinct chiefly Mesozoic Tetrabranchia comprising cephalopods having an external chambered shell that is either straight or variously curved or coiled — see [1]AMMONITE — **am·mo·noi·de·an** \;amə;nȯidēən\ *adj or n*

am·mo·nol·y·sis \,amə'näləsəs\ *n, pl* **ammonoly·ses** \-ə,sēz\ [NL, fr. *ammono-* + *-lysis*] **:** any chemical reaction analogous to hydrolysis in which ammonia plays a role similar to that of water, one or more atoms of hydrogen in the ammonia being replaced by other atoms or radicals ⟨the ~ of organic esters yields acid amides⟩ — often distinguished from *ammonation* — **am·mo·no·lyt·ic** \ə;mōnə;lid·ik, a;-; ;amənō;-\ *adj*

am·mo·no·lyze \ə'mōnᵊl,īz, a'-\ *vt* -ED/-ING/-S [fr. NL *ammonolysis*, after such pairs as E *analysis: analyze*] **:** to subject to ammonolysis

am·mon's law \'ämənz-, 'am-; 'ä,mȯnz-\ *n, usu cap A* [after Otto *Ammon* †1916 Ger. anthropologist] **:** a generalization in anthropology: the cephalic index varies inversely as the stature

[1]**am·moph·i·la** \ə'mäfələ, a'-\ *n, cap* [NL, fr. *amm-* + *-phila*] **:** a small genus of coarse perennial grasses growing on sandy shores and dunes and having awnless flowers crowded into a long spikelike panicle — see BEACH GRASS, MARRAM GRASS

[2]**ammophila** \"\ [NL, fr. *amm-* + *-phila*] *syn of* SPHEX

[3]**ammophila** \"\ *n* -s **:** a sand wasp of the genus *Sphex*

am·moph·i·lous \-ləs\ *adj* [*amm-* + *-philous*] **:** living or growing in the sand or in dry sandy places ⟨~ grasses⟩

ammos *pl of* AMMO

[1]**am·mu·ni·tion** \,amyə'nishən, *chiefly in substand speech* ,amə'-\ *n* -s [obs. F *amunition, amonition*, fr. MF, alter. (influenced by MF *amonition* admonition) of *munition*] **1** *obs* **:** general military supplies **2 a :** the various projectiles together with their fuzes, propelling charges, and primers that are fired from guns **b :** explosive military items (as grenades, bombs, and pyrotechnical matériel) **c :** any item or material that is thrown in fight or play (as spears or snowballs) **3 :** resources for attack or defense often in a contention or struggle in which one must engage ⟨~ to support sweeping changes —T.W.Arnold⟩

[2]**ammunition** \"\ *vb* -ED/-ING/-S **:** to supply with ammunition **:** LOAD ⟨the gunners were fast in firing and ~*ing*⟩

ammunition scuttle *n* **:** an opening through a ship door or bulkhead to permit the passing of ammunition

amn *abbr* ammunition

am·ne·sia \am'nēzhə, aam-\ *n* -s [NL, fr. Gk *amnēsia* forgetfulness, prob. alter. of *amnēstia*] **1 :** loss of memory sometimes including the memory of personal identity due to brain injury, shock, fatigue, repression, or illness or sometimes induced by anesthesia ⟨suffering from ~ and unable to identify himself⟩ ⟨a period of ~ after the wreck⟩ **2 :** a gap in one's memory ⟨an ~ concerning his high-school years⟩

am·ne·si·ac \-z(h)ē,ak\ *also* **am·ne·sic** \-zik, -sik, -ēk\ *n* -s [*amnesia* + *-ac* (as in *maniac*, n.) or *-ic*] **:** a sufferer from amnesia

am·ne·sic \(')am;nēzik, -aam-, -sik, -ēk\ *also* **am·ne·si·ac** \-z(h)ē,ak\ *adj* [NL *amnesia* + E *-ic* or *-ac* (as in *maniac*, adj.)] **:** of or relating to amnesia **:** suffering from or caused by amnesia ⟨an ~ patient⟩ ⟨an ~ trauma⟩

am·nes·tic (')=;nestik, -ēs-\ *adj* [Gk *amnēstia* forgetfulness + E *-ic*] **:** AMNESIC

[1]**am·nes·ty** \'amnəstē, 'aam-, -ti *also* -,nes-\ *n* -ES [Gk *amnēstia* forgetfulness, amnesty, fr. *amnēstos* forgotten (fr. *a-* [2]*a-* + *-mnēstos*, fr. *mnasthai* to remember) + *-ia* -y — more at MIND] **1** *archaic* **:** the voluntary overlooking of an offense by the one offended **2 :** the act of an authority (as a government) by which general pardon of an offense is granted often before trial or conviction esp. to a large group of individuals ⟨an ~ for war criminals⟩ **syn** see PARDON

[2]**amnesty** \"\ *vt* -ED/-ING/-ES **:** to grant amnesty to

amnia *pl of* AMNION

am·ni·ac \'amnē,ak\ *adj* [*amnion* + *-ac* (as in *cardiac*)] **:** AMNIOTIC

am·ni·col·i·dae \,amnə'kälə,dē\ [NL, fr. *Amnicola*, type genus (fr. L, that dwells by a river, fr. *amnis* river + *-cola*, fr. *colere* to dwell) + *-idae*] *syn of* BULIMIDAE

am·ni·o- *comb form* [NL, fr. *amnion*, fr. Gk] **1 :** amnion ⟨*amnio*tome⟩ **2 :** amniotic and ⟨*amnio*allantoic⟩

am·nio·car·di·ac vesicle \;amnē(,)ō;=-\ *n* **:** one of the paired infolding portions of the vertebrate embryonic coelom that give rise to the pericardial cavity

am·ni·o·cho·ri·on \;==(,)=ˈ-\ *n* -s [NL, fr. *amnio-* + *chorion*] **:** the amnion and chorion acting as a functional unit

am·ni·o·gen·e·sis \,==(,)=ˈ-\ *n* [NL, fr. *amnio-* + L *genesis*] **:** amnion formation

am·ni·on \'amnē,än, -,ən\ *n, pl* **amnions** \-nz\ *or* **am·nia** \-ēə\ [NL, fr. Gk, caul, prob. fr. dim. of *amnos* lamb — more at YEAN] **1 :** a thin membranous fluid-filled sac surrounding the embryo (of reptile, bird, or mammal) that is typically formed together with the chorion through growth about the embryo of the amniotic folds, these folds completely enclosing the embryo, fusing at their line of final contact, and then splitting across the line of fusion to separate an inner amnion immediately enclosing the embryo and an outer chorion **2 :** a membrane resembling an amnion and enclosing the embryos of many insects and other invertebrates

am·ni·on·ic \;amnē;änik\ *also* **am·nic** \'amnik\ *adj* [NL *amnion* or *amnion* + E *-ic*] **:** AMNIOTIC

am·ni·os \'amnē,äs\ *n, pl* **amnios** [NL, fr. Gk, alter. of *amnion*] **:** AMNION

am·ni·o·ta \,amnē'ōd·ə\ *n pl, cap* [NL, irreg. fr. *amnion*] **:** the group of vertebrates that develop an amnion in embryonic life — **am·ni·ote** \'amnē,ōt\ *adj or n*

am·ni·ot·ic \;amnē;äd·ik\ *adj* [*amnio-* + *-otic*] **1 :** of or relating to the amnion **2 :** characterized by the development of an amnion

amniotic band *n* **:** a band of fibrous tissue extending between the embryo and amnion and often associated with faulty development of the fetus

amniotic fluid *n* **:** the serous fluid in which the embryo is suspended within the amnion

amniotic fold *n* **:** one of the folds consisting of ectoderm and the outer layer of mesoderm that arises from the extraembryonic blastoderm first at the head, then at the tail, and finally on each side and that gives rise to the amnion and much of the chorion

amn't \'ànt *sometimes* 'a(a)nt *or* 'amənt *or* 'a(a)m(p)t\ [by contr.] *dial* **:** am not

am·o·bar·bi·tal \,a(,)mō'-\ *n* -s [*amyl* + *-o-* + *barbital*] **:** a crystalline compound $C_{11}H_{18}N_2O_3$ used as a sedative and hypnotic with its sodium salt being used similarly; 5-ethyl-5-isoamyl-barbituric acid

am·o·di·a·quin \-'dīə,kwin\ *also* **am·o·di·a·quine** \-,kwēn\ *n* -s [*amino-* + *di*hydrochloride + connective *-a-* + *-quin* (fr. *quinoline*) or *-quine*] **:** a compound $C_{20}H_{22}ClN_3O$ derived from quinoline and used in the form of its dihydrochloride as an antimalarial

amoe·ba \ə'mēbə\ *n* [NL, fr. Gk *amoibē* change, fr. *ameibein* to change — more at MIGRATE] **1 a** *cap* **:** a large genus of naked rhizopod protozoans with lobose and never anastomosing pseudopodia and without permanent organelles or supporting structures and that are widely distributed in fresh and salt water and moist terrestrial situations **b** *also* **ameba** \"\ *pl* **amoebas** \-bəz\ *or* **amoe·bae** \-(,)bē\ **:** any protozoan of this or a related genus **c** *also* **ameba** *pl* **amoebas** *or* **amoebae :** an amoeboid unicellular individual (as the amoeboid stage of a flagellate or of a sporozoan) **2** -s **:** a contour (as of a table top) of irregular curves

amoeba (magnified) showing *1* nucleus, *2* contractile vacuole, *3* food vacuole

amoeba disease *n* **:** a disease of adult honeybees caused by an amoeba (*Vahlkampfia mellifica*)

[1]**am·oe·baea** \,amē'bēə, -mə'-\ *n pl, cap* [NL, fr. *Amoeba*] *in some classifications* **:** a subclass of Sarcodina comprising the Amoebina and Testacea

[2]**amoebaea** \"\ [NL, fr. *Amoeba*] *syn of* AMOEBINA

am·oe·be·an verse \;amē;bēən-, -mə;-\ *n* [L *amoebaeus* alternate, fr. Gk *amoibaios* interchanging (fr. *amoibē* change) + E *-an*] **:** poetry written in the form of a dialogue between two speakers — compare STICHOMYTHIA

amoebiasis *var of* AMEBIASIS

amoe·bic *also* **ame·bic** \ə'mēbik, -ēk\ *or* **amoe·ban** *or* **ame·ban** \-bən\ *or* **amoe·bous** *or* **ame·bous** \-bəs\ *adj* [NL *amoeba, ameba* + E *-ic* or *-an* or *-ous*] **1 :** resembling or relating to an amoeba **2** *usu amebic* **:** caused by amoebas or amoebalike organisms

amoebicide *var of* AMEBICIDE

amoe·bid *also* **ame·bid** \-bəd\ *n* -s [NL *amoeba, ameba* + E *-id*] **:** an amoeba or amoebalike animal

amoe·bi·form \-bə,fȯrm\ *adj* [NL *amoeba, ameba* + E *-iform*] **1** *also* **ame·bi·form** \"\ **:** AMOEBOID **2 :** having an amoeba contour ⟨an ~ swimming pool⟩

am·oe·bi·na \,amē'bīnə, -mə'-, -ēnə\ *n pl, cap* [NL, fr. *Amoeba* + *-ina*] **:** an order of naked rhizopods that are commonly clearly differentiated into endoplasm and ectoplasm, form lobopodia, and include the common amoebas of soil and water and some parasitic forms — see ENDAMOEBIDAE

amoe·bo·bac·ter \ə'mēbō,baktə(r)\ *n* [NL, fr. *Amoeba* + *-o-* + *-bacter*] **1** *cap* **:** a genus of purple sulfur bacteria (family Thiorhodaceae) having spherical or elongated cells that are aggregated in amoeboid colonies without an enclosing capsule and that occur in mud and stagnant water **2** -s **:** any organism of the genus *Amoebobacter*

amoe·bo·cyte *also* **ame·bo·cyte** \ə'mēbə,sīt\ *n* -s [NL *amoeba, ameba* + E *-o-* + *-cyte*] **:** a cell having amoeboid form or movements: as **a :** a wandering cell of blood or tissues of many invertebrate animals that acts as a phagocyte and aids in assimilation and excretion **b :** LEUKOCYTE

amoe·bo·ge·ni·ae \ə,mēbō'jenē,ē\ [NL, fr. *Amoeba* + *-o-* + *-gen* + *-iae* (pl. of *-ia*)] *syn of* NEOSPORIDIA

amoe·boid *also* **ame·boid** \ə'mē,bȯid\ *adj* [ISV *amoeb-, ameb-* (fr. NL *amoeba, ameba*) + *-oid*] **1 :** like an amoeba specif. in moving or changing in shape by means of protoplasmic flow brought about by sequential changes in the protoplasmic colloidal system **2 :** AMOEBIFORM 2

amoe·bo·tae·nia \ə,mēbō'tēnēə\ *n, cap* [NL, fr. *amoeba* + *-o-* + *Taenia*] **:** a genus of tapeworms (family Dilepididae) parasitic in the intestines of poultry

amoe·bu·la *also* **ame·bu·la** \ə'mēbyələ\ *n, pl* **amoebulas** \-ləz\ *or* **amoebu·lae** \-,lē\ [NL, dim. of *amoeba, ameba*] **1 :** a small amoeba **2 :** any small organism or cell resembling an amoeba in form (as certain stages in the life cycles of myxomycetes or of gregarines)

[1]**amok** \ə'mək *also* -äk\ *or* **amuck** \ə'mək\ *n* -s [Malay *amok* furious attack, charge (as in *mĕngamok* he runs amok, *pĕngamok* one that runs amok] **1** *archaic* **:** a Malay that goes into a murderous frenzy and attacks people at random **2 :** a murderous frenzy that occurs chiefly among Malays ⟨an inflexible, confined, and unpermissive environment is the essence of ~ —J.M.Van der Kroef⟩

[2]**amok** \"\ *or* **amuck** \"\ *adv* [Malay *amok*] **1 :** in a murderously frenzied manner **2 a :** in a violently raging manner ⟨the North Sea ran ~ —Joseph O'Connor⟩ **b :** in an undisciplined manner **:** NEEDLESSLY ⟨an era which seems to have run ~ with its love for the strange —E.P.Hanson⟩

[3]**amok** \"\ *or* **amuck** \"\ *adj* [Malay *amok*] **:** possessed with a murderous or violently uncontrollable frenzy ⟨an ~ soldier⟩

amol·der·ing \ə'mōld(ə)riŋ\ *adj* [[1]*a-* + *moldering*, gerund of *molder*] **:** in a decaying condition ⟨~ in the grave⟩

amo·le \ə'mōlē, -,lā\ *n* -s [Sp, fr. Nahuatl *amolli* soap, prob. fr. *atl* water + *molli* stew, confection] **1 :** any part of a plant possessing detergent properties and used as a substitute for soap **2 :** any of a number of plants utilized as a source of soap: as **a :** SOAP PLANT a **b :** any of various Mexican amaryllidaceous plants of the genera *Manfreda* (as *M. brachystachys*), *Agave* (as *A. heteracantha*), and *Prochnyanthes* whose rootstock when pounded to a pulp readily produces a lather when moistened

amo·mis \ə'mōməs\ *n, cap* [NL, fr. L, a plant similar to amomum, fr. Gk *amōmon*] **:** a genus of aromatic tropical American trees (family Myrtaceae) with large leathery leaves and small axillary flowers

amo·mum \ə'mōməm\ *n* [NL, fr. L, an aromatic shrub, fr. Gk *amōmon*] **1** *cap* **:** a large genus of herbs (family Zingiberaceae) found in tropical regions of the Old World and differing from members of the genus *Zingiber* only in having the anther cells divergent and the connective between them not long-spurred **2** -s **:** a plant of the genus *Amomum* **3** -s **:** the fruit or root of an amomum plant

among \ə'məŋ\ *or* **amongst** \-ŋzt,-ŋ(k)st\ *prep* [among fr. ME, fr. OE *on gemonge, on gemange*, fr. *on* + *gemonge, gemange*, dat. of *gemong, gemang* mingling, crowd, fr. *ge-* (collective prefix) + *-mong, -mang* (akin to OE *mengan* to mix, mingle); *amongst*, alter. of ME *amonges*, fr. *among* + *-es* -s — more at CO-, MINGLE] **1 a :** surrounded by **:** in the midst of **:** intermingled with ⟨~ the celebrity-packed audience at each opening were seven men —*Time*⟩ **b :** through the midst of ⟨he passed ~ the crowd⟩ **2** *among, obs* **:** DURING **:** in the course of **3 a :** in or to the locality of ⟨he lived ~ us for a few days⟩ **b :** in company with **:** in association with **:** WITH ⟨living ~ a group of artists⟩ **4 a :** with or by the generality of ⟨a characteristic activity ~ pioneer Norwegian congregations —*Amer. Guide Series: Minn.*⟩ — used to indicate the group agent of an activity or the group source of an attribute **b :** in a widening circle throughout ⟨discontent spreads ~ the ignorant⟩ **c :** in the opinion or estimation of ⟨an author held, ~ a large part of our reading public, as superior⟩ **5 :** outstanding in the category of ⟨an actor ~ actors⟩ **6 :** in the number or class of ⟨~ their good qualities is a high regard for tolerance⟩ **:** in or from the group of **:** from the number of ⟨~ so many only a few can survive⟩ ⟨choose ~ us⟩ **7 a :** in separate and usu. equal shares to each of ⟨the property was divided ~ the four survivors⟩ **b :** for distribution to **:** to be shared by ⟨there's not enough food ~ a crowd like this⟩ ⟨that leaves five dollars ~ us⟩ **8 a :** through the reciprocal acts of ⟨fighting ~ themselves⟩ **b :** by the joint action of esp. so as to produce a separable effect ⟨they earned a fortune ~ themselves⟩

amon·til·la·do \ə,mäntə'lä(,)dō, -tə(l)'yä(,)thō\ *n* -s [Sp, fr. *a-* (fr. L *ad-*) + *montilla* + *-ado* (fr. L *-atus* -ate) — more at MONTILLA] **:** a pale dry sherry

amor \'ä,mō(ə)r\ *n* -s [L, fr. *amare* to love — more at AMATEUR] **:** CUPID, CHERUB 3

amo·ra \ə'mōrə\ *n, pl* **amo·ra·im** \,ämō'rä,im\ *often cap* [Heb *āmōrā'* (pl. *āmōrā'īm*) speaker, interpreter, fr. Aram *āmōrā*] **:** one of a group of rabbis (A.D. 250–500) who discussed the Mishnaic law in the law schools of Palestine and Mesopotamia and whose discussions are recorded in the Palestinian and Babylonian Talmuds — compare SABORA, TANNA

amo·ra·ic \,ämō¦räik\ *adj, often cap* **:** of or relating to the amoraim ⟨the ~ period⟩

amor·al \(')ā¦-, (')a¦-\ *adj* [²*a-* + *moral*] **1 a :** neither moral nor immoral **:** NONMORAL; *specif* **:** outside the bounds of that to which moral distinctions or judgments apply ⟨science as such is completely ~ —W.S.Thompson⟩ **b :** without moral sensibility ⟨infants are ~⟩ **2 a :** outside or beyond the moral order or any specific traditional code of morals ⟨~ customs⟩ **b :** ethically neutral **:** not entailing moral norms or ideals ⟨~ metaethical statements⟩ **3 :** refraining from making value judgments **:** OBJECTIVE ⟨an ~ historian⟩ — **amor·al·ly** *adv*

amor·al·ism \(')ā'-, (')a'-\ *n* -s **1 :** a doctrine that repudiates ordinary moral distinctions as invalid ⟨the ~ professed by many students of human affairs —Ernest Nagel⟩ **2 :** an amoral state, condition, or attitude **:** AMORALITY

amor·al·ist \(')ā'-, (')a'-\ *n* -s **1 :** one who professes the doctrine of amoralism **2 :** one who lives amorally

amor·al·is·tic \¦=¦==¦==\ *adj* **:** of, relating to, or professing amoralism

amo·ral·i·ty \¦ā-, ¦a-\ *n* -ES **:** the state of being amoral **:** amoral procedure ⟨power politics in an atmosphere of ~⟩

amo·ret·to \,amə'red·(,)ō, ,äm-\ *n, pl* **amoret·ti** \-d·(,)ē\ *or* **amorettos** *also* **amorettes** [It, dim. of *amore* cupid] **:** CUPID, CHERUB 3

am·o·reux·ia \,amə'rüksēə, -zh(ē)ə\ *n, cap* [NL, fr. Pierre Joseph *Amoreux* †1824 Fr. physician + NL *-ia*] **:** a genus of herbs or undershrubs (family Cochlospermaceae) of the southwestern U.S. and Mexico having palmate leaves and large flowers

amo·ri·no \,amə'rē(,)nō, ,äm-\ *n, pl* **amori·ni** \-(,)nē\ *also* **amorinos** [It, dim. of *amore* cupid, fr. L *Amor*, god of love, fr. *amor* love] **:** CUPID, CHERUB 3

am·or·ist \'amərəst\ *also* **am·our·ist** \", ə'mür-, a'-,ä-\ *n* -s [L *amor* + E *-ist*] **1 :** a devotee of love, esp. sexual love **:** GALLANT **2 :** one that writes romantically about love — **am·or·is·tic** \¦amə¦ristik\ *adj*

¹**am·o·rite** \'amə,rīt, *usu* -īd·+V\ *n* -s *usu cap* [Heb *ĕmōrī* + E *-ite*] **1** *in the Bible* **a :** a member of a pre-Israelite people of Palestine that dwelt in the hill country of Canaan and also east of the Jordan between the Moabites and the Ammonites — distinguished from *Canaanite* **b :** any pre-Israelite inhabitant of Palestine **:** CANAANITE **2 a :** a member of an ancient Semitic people that settled in Mesopotamia, Syria, and Palestine as early as the 3d millennium B.C. and established a kingdom, with its capital at Mari on the middle Euphrates, which was at the height of its power approximately from 2200 to 1700 B.C. **b :** the Semitic language spoken by this people, known only from proper names in Akkadian texts **3 :** ¹CANAANITE 3

²**amorite** *adj, usu cap* **:** of or belonging to any of the peoples known as Amorites

¹**am·o·rit·ic** \¦amə¦rid·ik\ *adj, usu cap* [¹*Amorite* + *-ic*] **1 :** ²AMORITE **2 :** of, belonging to, or characteristic of the language Amorite **3 :** ¹CANAANITIC 2—compare ¹AMORITE 2b

²**amoritic** *n, usu cap* **1 :** ¹AMORITE 2b **2 :** ²CANAANITIC

¹**am·o·rit·ish** \¦amə¦rīd·ish\ *adj, usu cap* [¹*Amorite* + *-ish*] **:** ²AMORITE

²**amoritish** *n* -ES *usu cap* **1 :** ¹AMORITE 2b **2 :** ¹CANAANITE 3

amornings *adv* [ME *amorninges*, fr. ¹*a-* + *morninges*, gen. of *morning*] *obs* **:** in the morning

am·o·ros·i·ty \,amə'räsəd·ē\ *n* -ES [ME *amorouste, amorositie*, fr. *amorous* + *-te* -ty, *-itie* -ity] **:** AMOROUSNESS

amo·ro·so \¦ämə¦rō(,)sō, ¦am-\ *adv (or adj)* [It, amorous, fr. ML *amorosus*] **:** with tenderness — used as a direction in music

am·o·rous \'am(ə)rəs, 'aamr-\ *adj* [ME, fr. MF, fr. ML *amorosus*, fr. L *amor* love (fr. *amare* to love) + *-osus* -ose — more at AMATEUR] **1 :** strongly moved by love, esp. sexual love **:** given to lovemaking ⟨a prey for ~ women —H.S.Canby⟩ **2 :** in love **:** ENAMORED — usu. used with *of*, formerly with *on* ⟨he is ~ of the girl⟩ ⟨naturally ~ of all that is beautiful —Sir Thomas Browne⟩ **3 a :** manifesting love **:** indicative of love ⟨black swans on the lake twine their necks in ~ play —James McAuley⟩ **b :** produced by or productive of love **c :** of or relating to love ⟨an ~ novel⟩ **4 a :** warmly affectionate **:** FOND, LOVING ⟨the ~ care with which Tom drew a volume from the bookcase —Arnold Bennett⟩ **b :** characterized by warmth and passion ⟨~ music or poetry⟩ ⟨an ~ outburst of lyricism⟩ — **am·o·rous·ly** *adv* — **am·o·rous·ness** *n* -ES

amorph \'ā,mȯrf, ə'mȯ(ə)rf\ *n* -s [²*a-* + *-morph*] **:** a gene without a determinable effect

amorph- *or* **amorpho-** *comb form* [Gk *amorph-*, fr. *amorphos*] **:** amorphous ⟨*amorph*ism⟩ ⟨*amorpho*phyte⟩

amor·pha \ə'mȯrfə\ *n* [NL, fr. Gk *amorphē*, fem. of *amorphos* shapeless] **1** *cap* **:** a genus of American herbs or shrubs (family Leguminosae) with odd-pinnate leaves and purplish spicate flowers, the corolla being reduced to one petal — see FALSE INDIGO, LEADPLANT **2** -s **:** a plant of the genus *Amorpha*

amor·phic \-fik\ *adj* [²*a-* + *-morphic*] **:** AMORPHOUS

amor·phin·ism \(')ā'-\ *n* -s [²*a-* + *morphinism*] **:** the condition caused by depriving an addict of morphine

amor·phism \ə'mȯr,fizəm\ *n* -s [G *amorphismus*, fr. *amorph* amorphous + *-ismus* -ism] **:** the quality or state of being amorphous

amor·pho·phal·lus \ə,mȯrfə'faləs\ *n* [NL, fr. *amorph-* + *phallus*] **1** *cap* **:** a genus of tropical East Indian aroids having a mottled flowering spathe in advance of the large compound leaf and often attaining a height of several feet — see KRUBI **2** -ES **:** a plant of the genus *Amorphophallus*

amor·pho·phyte \=¦==,fīt\ *n* -s [ISV *amorph-* + *-phyte*] **:** a plant producing irregular or anomalous flowers

amor·phous \ə'mȯrfəs, -ō(ə)f-\ *also* **amor·phose** \-,fōs\ *adj* [Gk *amorphos*, fr. *a-* ²a- + *morphē* form — more at FORM] **1 a :** without definite form or shape **:** FORMLESS ⟨an ~ cloud of dust⟩ ⟨an ~ mass⟩ **b :** without clearly drawn limits **:** not precisely indicated or established ⟨an ~ boundary⟩ **c :** without definite nature or character **:** not allowing clear classification or analysis **:** UNCLASSIFIABLE ⟨cities have swollen into ~ agglomerations —Siegfried Giedion⟩ ⟨that indefinite ~ thing called the consuming public —John Dewey⟩ **d :** without organization **:** without cohesion **:** lacking unity ⟨an ~ mass of frightened fugitives —J.W.Aldridge⟩ ⟨an ~ style of writing⟩ **e :** without a clearly defined direction, purpose, or controlling influence ⟨lifeless and ~ routine —Phyllis Ackerman⟩ ⟨growth is not ~, but restricted by a limited number of physical laws —Herbert Read⟩ **2 a (1) :** without real or apparent crystalline form **:** UNCRYSTALLIZED — used esp. of supercooled liquids (as glasses) and colloidal substances ⟨~ sulfur⟩ ⟨~ wax⟩ **(2) :** without crystal structure ⟨an ~ mineral⟩ **b :** without division in parts such as that effected by stratification or cleavage **c :** without developed organization — used chiefly of the lower forms of life — **amor·phous·ly** *adv* — **amor·phous·ness** *n* -ES

amor·phus \-,fəs\ *n, pl* **amor·phi** \-,fī, -,fē\ *or* **amorphuses** [NL, fr. Gk *amorphos*, adj.] **:** a fetus without head, heart, or limbs

amor·phy \'ā,mȯrfē, ə'm-\ *n* -ES [Gk *amorphia* shapelessness, fr. *amorph-* + *-ia* -y] **:** AMORPHISM

amors *pl of* AMOR

amort \ə'mȯrt\ *adj* [short for *all-a-mort*, taken as an adjectival phrase beginning with ²*all*] **1** *archaic* **:** at the point of death ⟨I felt benumbed, ~ —Llewelyn Powys⟩ **2** *archaic* **:** OBLIVIOUS ⟨all ~ save to St. Agnes —John Keats⟩ **3** *archaic* **:** utterly cast down with discouragement **:** DEJECTED

amor·tis·seur \ə¦mȯrd·ə¦sər, +V -ər-\ *or* **amortisseur winding** *n* -s [F *amortisseur*, fr. *amortir* to deaden — more at AMORTIZE] **:** DAMPER WINDING

am·or·tiz·a·ble \'amə(r),tīzəbəl, *sometimes* ə'mȯr,- *or* 'a,mȯr,- *or* -mō(ə),-\ *adj* **:** capable of being amortized

am·or·ti·za·tion \,amə(r)d·ə'zāshən, -tə'- *also* ə,mȯ(r)- *or* ,a,mō(r)- *or* -ō,,ī'z- *or* -),tī'z-\ *n* -s [ML *admortization-, admortizatio*, fr. *admortizatus* (past part. of *admortizare*) + L *-ion-, -io* -ion] **1 :** the act or process of amortizing **2 :** the result of amortizing

am·or·tize \'amə(r),tīz *sometimes* ə'mȯr,- *or* 'a,mȯr,- *or* -mō(ə),-\ *also* **am·or·tise** \"\ *vt* -ED/-ING/-s [ME *amortisen*, modif. (influenced by ML *amortizare* to amortize, fr. OF *amortir* + LL *-izare* -ize) of MF *amortiss-*, stem of *amortir*, fr. (assumed) VL *admortire* to deaden, fr. L *ad-* + (assumed) VL-*mortire*, fr. *mort-, mors* death — more at MURDER] **1** *law* **:** to alienate in mortmain ⟨*amortized* the estate⟩ **2** *accounting* **a :** to provide for the gradual extinguishment of (an obligation, as a mortgage or bond issue) by payment of a part of the principal or by contribution to a sinking fund usu. with or at the time of each periodic interest payment **b :** to write down gradually to extinguishment the cost of (an asset) by periodic charges to expense or profit and loss — usu. applicable to intangible assets (as patents, bond premiums)

am·or·tize·ment \¦amə(r)¦tīzmənt; ə'mȯ(r)d·əzm-, -ȯsm-\ *n* -s [modif. (influenced by *amortize*) of F *amortissement*, fr. OF, fr. *amortiss-* (stem of *amortir*) + *-ment*] **1 :** AMORTIZATION **2 a :** the sloping top of a projecting pier (as a buttress) **b :** a crowning architectural member in an edifice

am·o·site \'amə,sīt, -,z-\ *n* -s [Asbestos *Mine* of *South Africa* + E *-ite*] **:** a mineral that is an iron-rich variety of anthophyllite occurring in long fibers and much used as a type of asbestos

amo·tion \a'mōshən, ə'-\ *n* -s [L *amotion-, amotio* removal, fr. *amotus* (past part. of *amovēre* to remove) + *-ion-, -io* -ion — more at AMOVE] **1 a :** removal of a specified object from a place or position **b :** OUSTING; *specif* **:** removal of a corporate officer from his office — distinguished from *disfranchisement* **2 :** deprivation of possession of property

¹**amount** \ə'maunt\ *vi* -ED/-ING/-s [ME *amounten*, fr. OF *amonter, amounter*, fr. *amont* upward, fr. *a-* (fr. L *ad-*) + *mont* mountain — more at MOUNT] **1** *obs* **:** ASCEND **2 :** to add up **:** reach a total — used with *to* ⟨the bill ~*ed* to 10 dollars⟩ ⟨total casualties ~*ing* to over a thousand⟩ **3 :** to be really or practically equivalent **:** attain in effect or significance — used with *to* ⟨anxiety that almost ~*ed* to agony —Mary W.Shelley⟩ ⟨an act that ~*ed* to treason⟩

²**amount** \"\ *n* -s **1 a :** the total number or quantity **:** AGGREGATE ⟨the ~ of the fine is doubled⟩ **:** SUM, NUMBER ⟨add the same ~ to each column⟩ ⟨the ~ of the policy is 10,000 dollars⟩ **b :** the sum of individuals ⟨the unique ~ of worthless IOUs collected during each day's business —R.L.Taylor⟩ **c :** the quantity at hand or under consideration ⟨only a small ~ of trouble involved⟩ ⟨a surprising ~ of patience⟩ **2 :** the whole or final effect, significance, or import ⟨the ~ of his remarks is that we are hopelessly beaten⟩ **3** *accounting* **:** a principal sum and the interest on it **syn** see SUM

amount at risk : the difference between the face amount of a life-insurance policy and its reserve value

amount limit *n* **:** a fixed quantity of work assigned in a test with the object of measuring either the time required by an individual to finish that amount or the total he can do in unlimited time — contrasted with *time limit*

amount subject *n* **:** any value estimated by an underwriter to be the expected loss as a result of a fire or casualty, variable according to the risk involved

amour \ə'mu̇(ə)r, a'-,ä'-, -üə\ *n* -s [ME, fr. OF *amour, amor*, fr. OProv *amor*, fr. L., fr. *amare* to love — more at AMATEUR] **1** *obs* **:** close attachment **:** intimate friendship **2 a :** LOVEMAKING, COURTSHIP — usu. used in pl. ⟨passing the hours in tender ~s⟩ **b :** a love affair esp. when illicit ⟨rushing from one ~ to another⟩ **3 :** LOVE; *esp* **:** sexual love ⟨the film explores various aspects of ~⟩ ⟨an almost endless chain of exploits in ~ —H.L.Mencken⟩ **4 a :** one that is loved **b :** MISTRESS **:** LOVER ⟨she was his newest ~⟩

am·ou·rette \¦amə¦ret\ *n* -s [F, fr. OF, fr. *amour* + *-ette*] **1 :** a trifling or ephemeral love affair **2 :** a woman involved in a trifling love affair

am·ou·rist *var of* AMORIST

amour pro·pre \a,mu̇(ə)r'prōp(rᵊ), ¦ä,-, -üə'p-, -rōp-\ *n* [F *amour-propre*, lit., love of oneself, fr. *amour* love + *propre* own, proper — more at PROPER] **1 :** self-love characterized by sensitive regard for one's rights, dignity, and honor as an individual and in relationship with one's fellows **:** SELF-RESPECT, SELF-ESTEEM ⟨offensive to a wife's *amour propre* —H.L.Mencken⟩ **2 :** exaggerated self-love **:** VANITY ⟨his *amour propre* would not tolerate criticism⟩ **syn** see CONCEIT

amov·a·bil·i·ty \(,)a,müvə'biləd·ē, ə,m-\ *n* -ES **:** capability of being removed from a given position; *specif* **:** liability to amotion

amov·a·ble \='==bəl\ *adj* [alter. of earlier *amovible*, fr. F, fr. L *amovēre* to remove + F *-ible*] **:** REMOVABLE; *specif* **:** liable to amotion

¹**amove** *vt* -ED/-ING/-s [ME *amoven, ameven*, fr. MF *amovoir* to incite (fr. L *admovēre* to bring to, put to, apply to, fr. *ad-* + *movēre* to move) & *esmovoir* to set in motion, stir up emotionally (fr. L *exmovēre, emovēre* to move away, remove, fr. *ex*, e out of, from + *movēre* to move) — more at EX-, MOVE] *obs* **:** to cause to be agitated (as with excitement); *specif* **:** to stir up emotionally

²**amove** \a'müv, ə'-\ *vt* -ED/-ING/-s [ME *amoven, ameven*, modif. (influenced by ME *amoven, ameven* to stir up emotionally) of L *amovēre*, fr. *a-* (fr. *ab-*) + *movēre* to move — more at MOVE] **:** REMOVE; *esp* **:** to dismiss from an office or position

¹**amoy** \(')ä¦mȯi, (')a¦-\ *adj, usu cap* [fr. *Amoy*, China] **:** of or from Amoy, China **:** of the kind or style prevalent in Amoy

²**amoy** \"\ *n, usu cap* **:** the dialect of Chinese spoken in and near Amoy in southeastern China

amoy·ese \¦ä,mȯi¦ēz, ¦a,-, -ēs, =¦=,=\ *n, pl* **amoyese** *usu cap* **1 :** a native or inhabitant of Amoy, China **2 :** AMOY

amp \'amp, 'aa-,'ai-\ *abbr or n* -s amperage; ampere

am·pa·la·ya \¦ämpəl¦äyə\ *n* -s [Tag *ampalayá*] *Philippines* **:** BALSAM APPLE

am·pan·ga·be·ite \,äm,pän'gäbē,īt\ *n* -s [F *ampangabéite*, fr. *Ampangabé*, Madagascar, its locality + F *-ite*] **:** a mineral consisting of a tantalo-niobate (as of yttrium, erbium, or uranium) occurring in reddish brown rectangular prisms

am·pa·ro \äm'pä(,)rō\ *n* -s [Sp, lit., protection, fr. *amparar* to protect, fr. (assumed) VL *anteparare*, fr. L *ante* before + *parare* to prepare — more at ANTE-, PARE] **1** *Spanish law* **:** a preliminary certificate issued to a claimant of land as a protection to his claim until a survey can be had and the full title vested **2** *Spanish law* **:** a proceeding analogous to habeas corpus

amparo blue \"-\ *n* **:** a strong blue to brilliant purplish blue

amparo purple *n* **:** a moderate purple that is redder and paler than heliotrope (sense 4a) and bluer, lighter, and stronger than average amethyst or cobalt violet

ampel- *or* **ampelo-** *comb form* [NL *ampel-*, fr. Gk *ampel-*, *ampelo-*, fr. *ampelos*] **:** grapevine ⟨*ampel*opsis⟩ ⟨*ampelog*raphy⟩

am·pe·lite \'ampə,līt\ *n* -s [L *ampelitis*, fr. Gk, fr. *ampelos* vine] **1 :** a black earth rich in pyrites used by the ancients to kill insects on vines **2 :** carbonaceous schist **:** CANNEL COAL — **am·pe·lit·ic** \¦ampə¦lid·ik\ *adj*

am·pe·lop·sis \,ampə'läpsəs\ *n* [NL, fr. *ampel-* + *-opsis*] **1** *cap* **:** a genus of woody climbers (family Vitaceae) closely related to *Vitis* and distinguished by the separate petals and the absence of adhesive disks on the tendrils **2** *pl* **ampelopsis :** a plant of the genus *Parthenocissus*: as **a :** BOSTON IVY **b :** VIRGINIA CREEPER

am·per \'ampə(r)\ *n* -s [ME *ampre*, fr. OE *ompre* swelling, varicose vein] **1** *now dial Eng* **:** SWELLING, BLOTCH **2** *now dial Eng* **:** PUS, MATTER

am·per·age \'amp(ə)rij, 'aam-, -ēj *also* -,pir-\ *n* -s [ISV *ampere* + *-age*] **:** the strength of a current of electricity expressed in amperes

am·pere \'am,pi(ə)r, 'aam-, -iə\ *n* -s [after André M. *Ampère* †1836 Fr. physicist] **1 :** the practical mks unit of electric current that is equivalent to a flow of one coulomb per second or to the steady current produced by one volt applied across a resistance of one ohm and that is taken as the standard in the U.S. **:** 1/10 abampere **2 :** a unit of electric current equal to .99985 ampere and formerly taken as the standard — called also *international ampere*

ampere-hour \'==¦=\ *n* **:** a unit quantity of electricity, being the quantity carried past any point of a circuit in one hour by a steady current of one ampere, one ampere-hour equaling 3600 coulombs

am·pere·me·ter \-,mēd·ə(r)\ *n* [ISV *ampere* + *-meter*] **:** AMMETER

ampere's law *n, usu cap A* **:** either of two laws in electromagnetism: (1) the magnetic field resulting from an electric current in a circuit element and at any point perpendicular to the plane passing through the circuit element and the point, appears clockwise to an observer looking along the element in the direction of the current flow, is directly proportional to the product of the current multiplied by the length of the component of the element perpendicular to the line joining it to the point, and is inversely proportional to the square of the length of this line; or (2) the work done in carrying a magnetic pole around any closed path is proportional to the electric current flowing through the area bounded by the closed path

ampere-turn \'=,=¦=\ *n* **:** the mks unit of magnetomotive force equal to the magnetomotive force around a path that links with one turn of wire carrying an electric current of one ampere, one ampere-turn being equal to 0.4π or 1.257 gilberts

am·per·o·met·ric \¦am,pirə¦me·trik\ *adj* [*ampere* + *-o-* + *-metric*] *of chemical titration* **:** based on the measurement of the electric current that flows when a potential is applied between two electrodes in a solution for the purpose of detecting the end point — compare POLAROGRAPHIC

am·per·om·e·try \,ampə'rämə·trē, -,pi'r-\ *n* -ES [*ampere* + *-o-* + *-metry*] **:** the process of performing an amperometric titration

am·per·sand \'ampə(r),sand, 'aam-, -aand *also* -,z-\ *also* **am·per·zand** \-,z-\ *n* -s [alter. of *and* (&) *per se and*, lit., (the character) & by itself (is the word) *and*] **:** a single character (typically & or &) standing for the word *and* — called also *short and*

amph *abbr* amphibian; amphibious

am·phe·rot·o·kous \¦amfə¦räd·əkəs\ *adj* [*ampherotoky* + *-ous*] **:** of or relating to ampherotoky

am·phe·rot·o·ky \,amfə'räd·əkē\ *or* **am·phit·o·ky** \am'fid·əkē\ *also* **am·phot·er·ot·o·ky** \(,)am,fäd·ə'räd·əkē\ *n* -ES [*ampherotoky* irreg. fr. Gk *amphoteros* both + *tokos* offspring + E *-y*; *amphitoky* fr. *amphi-* + Gk *tokos* + E *-y*; *amphoterotoky* fr. Gk *amphoteros* + *tokos* + E *-y*] **:** parthenogenesis in which both male and female offspring are produced — compare ARRHENOTOKY, THELYTOKY

am·phet·a·mine \am'fed·ə,mēn, -,mən\ *n* -s [ISV *alpha-methyl-phenethyl* + *amine*] **:** a substance $C_9H_{13}N$ used as an inhalant and in solution as a spray in head colds and hay fever or in the form of its sulfate or phosphate as a stimulant for the central nervous system; racemic alpha-methyl-phenethylamine

amphi- *or* **amph-** *prefix* [L *amphi-* around, on both sides, fr. Gk *amphi-, amph-*, fr. *amphi* — more at AMBI-] **1 :** around ⟨*amphi*spermous⟩ **2 :** on both sides **:** of both kinds **:** both ⟨*amphi*carpic⟩ ⟨*amphi*vorous⟩ **3** *usu amphi-, chem, usu ital* **:** having substituents in positions 2 and 6 in two fused 6-membered rings (as in naphthalene)

am·phi·ap·o·mict \¦amfē'apə,mikt\ *n* -s [*amphi-* + *apo-* + Gk *miktos* blended] **:** an organism reproducing both sexually and asexually

am·phi·ar·thro·di·al \¦amfē,är¦thrōdēəl\ *adj* [*amphi-* + *arthrodial*] **:** characterized by amphiarthrosis

am·phi·ar·thro·sis \,==,='=sōsəs\ *n* [NL, fr. *amphi-* + *arthrosis*] *anat* **:** articulation admitting slight motion and including symphysis and syndesmosis

am·phi·as·ter \'==,astə(r)\ *n* -s [NL, fr. *amphi-* + *-aster*] **1 :** a spicule stellate at both ends (as in some sponges) **2 :** the achromatic figure, esp. of animal cells, in which well-defined asters are commonly formed — compare MITOSIS — **am·phi·as·tral** \¦==¦=trəl\ *adj*

am·phib \(')am¦fib, -aam-\ *n* -s [by shortening] **1 :** ²AMPHIBIAN 3 **2 amphibs** *pl* **:** amphibious forces

am·phib·a·lus \am'fibələs\ *n, pl* **amphiba·li** \-,lī, -,lē\ [ML, fr. LL *amphibalus, amphibalum* cloak, prob. irreg. fr. Gk *amphiballein* to put around, throw around — more at AMPHIBOLE] **:** CHASUBLE; *also* **:** a vestment resembling the chasuble worn by the Gallican clergy prior to the 9th century

am·phib·ia \am'fibēə, aam-\ *n pl, cap* [NL, fr. *amphibia*, pl. of *amphibium* amphibious being, fr. Gk *amphibion*, fr. neut. of *amphibios* leading a double life, amphibious — more at AMPHIBIOUS] **1 :** a class of Vertebrata comprising forms (as the frogs, toads, newts, and salamanders) that are intermediate in many respects between fishes and reptiles, all being cold-blooded with nucleated red blood cells and a 3-chambered heart; having limbs that, when present, terminate in digits that are unlike fins, two occipital condyles, ribs not attached to the sternum, and a moist skin without scales, feathers, or hair; developing without forming either amnion or allantois; being in most cases oviparous, passing through an aquatic larval stage in which they are provided with gills, afterwards undergoing a more or less marked metamorphosis usu. losing the gills and breathing by means of lungs or, when these are lacking, as in certain salamanders, through the skin or mucous membrane of the mouth; and feeding chiefly on insects and other small invertebrates, some forms being important destroyers of insects — see CAUDATA, GYMNOPHIONA, SALIENTIA **2 :** the members of the class Amphibia **:** AMPHIBIANS

¹**am·phib·i·an** \(')=¦=ēən\ *adj* [Gk *amphibios* + E *-an*] **1 :** AMPHIBIOUS **2** [NL *Amphibia* + E *-an*] **:** of, relating to, or belonging to the class Amphibia **3** [²*amphibian* (vehicle)] **:** of or relating to an amphibian (sense 3)

²**amphibian** \"\ *n* -s **1 a :** an animal or plant accustomed or adapted to life both on land and in the water (as certain snakes) **b :** any animal of the class Amphibia (as a frog or newt) **2 :** an airplane designed to take off from and land on either land or water ⟨an ~ . . . is perhaps the most difficult of all airplane types to build and design —T.A.Dickinson⟩ **3 :** a flat-bottomed vehicle that moves on tracks having finlike extensions by means of which it is propelled on land or water and that is typically used for landing assault troops

am·phi·bich·nite \,amfə'bik,nīt\ *n* -s [*amphibian* + *ichnite*] **:** the fossil track of an extinct amphibian

am·phi·bi·e·ty \,amfə'bīed·ē\ *n* -ES **:** the quality or state of being amphibious

am·phib·i·o·log·i·cal \am¦fibēə¦läjəkəl\ *adj* **:** of or relating to amphibiology

am·phib·i·ol·o·gist \am,fibē'äləjəst\ *n* -s **:** a specialist in amphibiology

am·phib·i·ol·o·gy \-jē\ *n* -ES [NL *Amphibia* + E *-o-* + *-logy*] **:** the branch of zoology that deals with the Amphibia

am·phib·i·on \ˌ=ˈ=ēən, -ē,än\ *n* -S [Gk, amphibious being, fr. neut. of *amphibios* leading a double life, amphibious] **:** an amphibian aircraft

am·phib·i·on·tic \am¦fibē¦äntik, ¦am,f-\ *adj* [Gk *amphibiont-, amphibion* + E *-ic*] **:** LITTORAL a, b

am·phi·bi·ot·ic \¦amfə,bī¦äd·ik\ *adj* [ISV *amphi-* + *-biotic*] **:** terrestrial in the adult stage but aquatic as a larva or nymph

am·phib·i·ous \(ˈ)amˈfibēəs, -aam-\ *adj* [Gk *amphibios* leading a double life, amphibious, fr. *amphi-* + *bios* life — more at QUICK] **1 :** able to live both on land and in water ⟨frogs, crocodiles and beavers are ~⟩ ⟨~ plants⟩ **2 a :** belonging to, adapted for, or consisting of both land and water ⟨the ~ character of an island people⟩ ⟨~ activities in a lakeside village⟩ ⟨an ~ swampy country⟩ **b** (1) **:** executed by coordinated action of land, sea, and air forces organized for invasion from the sea, usu. employing warships, assault boats, landing barges, assault troops, aircraft carriers, and covering aircraft (2) **:** trained or organized for participation in such action ⟨skill in ~ warfare⟩ ⟨an ~ corps⟩ **3 :** having or combining two lives, positions, or qualities ⟨an ~ existence, both mental and physical⟩ — **am·phib·i·ous·ly** *adv* — **am·phib·i·ous·ness** *n* -ES

am·phi·blas·tic \¦amfə¦blastik\ *adj* [*amphi-* + *-blastic*] **:** segmenting unequally — used of telolecithal eggs with complete segmentation

am·phi·blas·tu·la \¦amfə+\ *n, pl* **amphiblastu·lae** [NL, fr. *amphi-* + *blastula*] **:** a free-swimming larva of certain sponges that is essentially a blastula with small flagellated cells in one hemisphere and large nonflagellated cells in the other

am·phib·o·la \amˈfibələ\ *n, cap* [NL, fr. LL, fem. of *amphibolus*] **:** a genus of marine snails common in New Zealand having a rough turbinate shell and being unique among Pulmonata in possessing a well-developed operculum

am·phi·bole \ˈamfə,bōl\ *n* -S [F, fr. LL *amphibolus* fr. Gk *amphibolos* ambiguous, doubtful, fr. *amphiballein* to throw round, doubt, fr. *amphi-* + *ballein* to throw; fr. its many varieties — more at DEVIL] **1 :** HORNBLENDE **2 a :** a mineral or mineral variety belonging to the amphibole group

amphibole group *n* **:** a group of minerals (as anthophyllite, tremolite, actinolite, and hornblende) with essentially like crystal structures involving a silicate chain $[OH(Si_4O_{11})]n$ and generally containing three groups of metal ions, the large ions being sodium and calcium, the intermediate being chiefly bivalent iron, magnesium, and manganese, and the small ions chiefly silicon with some aluminum and rarely ferric iron, the general formula for the group being $A_2B_5(Si,Al)_8O_{22}(OH)_2$

am·phi·bo·lia \,amfəˈbōlēə, -lyə\ *n, pl* **amphiboli·ae** \-ōlē,ē\ [LL — more at AMPHIBOLOGY] **:** AMPHIBOLOGY

am·phi·bol·ic \¦amfə¦bälik\ *adj* [*amphiboly* + *-ic*] **1 :** AMPHIBOLOGICAL **2** *zool* **:** capable of being directed either forward or backward ⟨the ~ outer toe of a fish hawk or owl⟩ **3** *med* **:** UNCERTAIN, IRREGULAR — used of stages in fevers or the critical period of disease when prognosis is uncertain

am·phi·bol·if·er·ous \-(,)bō¦lif(ə)rəs\ *adj* [*amphibole* + *-i-* + *-ferous*] **:** containing or producing amphibole

am·phib·o·lips \amˈfibə,lips\ *n, cap* [NL, fr. Gk *amphibolos* ambiguous, doubtful + *ips* woodworm — more at AMPHIBOLE] **:** a genus of gall wasps including forms responsible for many of the large oak-apple galls

am·phib·o·lite \amˈfibə,līt, ˈamfə,bō,l-\ *n* -S [F, fr. *amphibole* + *-ite*] **:** a usu. metamorphic rock consisting essentially of amphibole — **am·phib·o·lit·ic** \¦am,fibə¦lid·ik, am¦f-, ¦amfə(,)bō¦l-\ *adj*

am·phib·o·li·tize \amˈfibələ,tīz, ,amfəˈbōlə-\ *vt* -ED/-ING/-S **:** to convert (rock) to amphibolite

am·phib·o·li·za·tion \am,fibələˈzāshən, ,amfə,bōlə-\ *n* -S [*amphibole* + *-ization*] **:** a metasomatic process whereby a preexisting dark mineral has been converted to amphibole

am·phib·o·log·i·cal \¦am,fibə¦läjəkəl, am¦f-\ *adj* **:** characterized by the ambiguity found in an amphibology **:** AMBIGUOUS **:** EQUIVOCAL — **am·phib·o·log·i·cal·ly** \-k(ə)lē\ *adv*

am·phi·bol·o·gy \,amfəˈbäləjē\ *n* -ES [ME *amphibologie*, fr. LL *amphibologia*, alter. (influenced by L *-logia* -logy) of *amphibolia*, fr. Gk, fr. *amphibolos* ambiguous + *-ia* -y — more at AMPHIBOLE] **1 :** ambiguity in language **2 :** a phrase or sentence susceptible of more than one interpretation by virtue of an ambiguous grammatical construction — contrasted with *equivocation*

am·phib·o·lous \(ˈ)amˈfibələs\ *adj* [LL *amphibolus*, fr. Gk *amphibolos*] **:** capable of two meanings; *specif* **:** manifesting amphibology

am·phib·o·ly \amˈfibəlē\ *n* -ES [LL *amphibolia*] **:** AMPHIBOLOGY

am·phi·brach \ˈamfə,brak\ *n* -S [L *amphibrachys*, fr. Gk, lit., short at both ends, fr. *amphi-* + *brachys* short — more at BRIEF] **:** a trisyllabic foot consisting of a long syllable between two short syllables in quantitative verse or of a stressed syllable between two unstressed syllables in accentual verse ⟨the word *romantic* is an accentual ~⟩ — **am·phi·brach·ic** \¦=¦=ˈbrakik\ *adj*

amphibs *pl of* AMPHIB

am·phi·car·pa \,amfəˈkärpə\ *n, cap* [NL, fr. *amphi-* + *-carpa* (fr. Gk *karpos* fruit)] **:** a genus of No. American and Asiatic vines (family Leguminosae) having trifoliate leaves and small white or violet flowers and bearing both aerial and hypogeous pods

am·phi·car·pic \¦=¦=ˈ=pik\ *or* **am·phi·car·pous** \-pəs\ *adj* [*amphi-* + *-carpic* or *-carpous*] **:** producing fruit of two kinds, either as to form or time of ripening

am·phi·car·pi·um \,=¦=ˈ=pēəm\ *n, pl* **amphicar·pia** \-ēə\ [NL, fr. *amphi-* + Gk *karpos* + NL *-ium*] **:** an archegonium that persists after fertilization to form a fruit envelope

am·phi·car·pog·e·nous \¦amfə,kär¦päjənəs\ *adj* [*amphi-* + *carpogenous*] **:** producing fruit aboveground which becomes buried before the time of ripening ⟨the peanut is ~⟩

am·phi·cen·tric \¦amfə¦-\ *adj* [*amphi-* + *-centric*] **:** converging at both ends — used of a plexus of blood vessels having one afferent and one efferent trunk

am·phi·chrome \ˈamfə,krōm\ *n* -S [*amphi-* + *-chrome*] **:** a plant that produces flowers of different colors on the same stalk (as certain of the sweet williams) — **am·phi·chro·my** \-mē\ *n* -ES

am·phi·coe·lia \,amfəˈsēlēə\ *n pl, cap* [NL, fr. LGk *amphikoilos* + NL *-ia*] *in some classifications* **:** an order of extinct crocodilians comprising Mesozoic forms with amphicoelous or amphiplatyan presacral vertebrae

am·phi·coe·li·an \¦amfə¦sēlēən\ *adj* [LGk *amphikoilos* + E *-ian*] **:** AMPHICOELOUS

am·phi·coe·lous *also* **am·phi·ce·lous** *or* **am·phy·coe·lous** \-¦sēləs\ *adj* [LGk *amphikoilos* doubly concave, fr. Gk *amphi-* + *koilos* hollow — more at CAVE] **:** BICONCAVE — used of vertebrae (as those of certain reptiles) having both the anterior and posterior surfaces of the centrum concave

am·phi·con·dy·lous \¦=¦kändələs\ *adj* [*amphi-* + *condyle* + *-ous*] **:** provided with two condyles

am·phi·cra·nia \,amfəˈkrānēə\ *n* -S [NL, fr. *amphi-* + *-crania*] **:** pain affecting both sides of the head — opposed to *hemicrania*

am·phi·crib·ral \¦=¦=ˈkribrəl\ *adj* [*amphi-* + *cribral*] **:** having the phloem surrounding the xylem — used of certain concentric vascular bundles; compare AMPHIVASAL

am·phic·ty·on \amˈfiktēən, -ē,än\ *n* -S [back-formation fr. *Amphictyons*, pl., fr. L *Amphictyones*, fr. Gk *Amphiktyones, Amphiktiones*, lit., neighbors, fr. *amphi-* + *-ktyones, -ktiones* (fr. *ktizein* to found); akin to Skt *kṣeti* he dwells, *kṣiti* abode, Av *shitish* dwelling, Arm *šen* inhabited, cultivated] **:** a deputy to an amphictyonic council

am·phic·ty·on·ic \¦am,fiktē¦änik, am¦f-\ *adj* [Gk *amphiktyonikos, amphiktionikos*, fr. *Amphiktyones, Amphiktiones* + *-ikos* -ic] **:** relating to an amphictyony or to the amphictyons

am·phic·ty·o·ny \amˈfiktēənē\ *n* -ES [Gk *amphiktyonia, amphiktionia*, fr. *Amphiktyones, Amphiktiones* + *-ia* -y] **:** an association of neighboring states or tribes in ancient Greece orig. established to defend a common religious center and later developing into a league with certain legislative and judicial functions; *broadly* **:** any association of neighboring states banded together for their common protection and interest

am·phic·y·on \amˈfisē,än, -ēən\ *n, cap* [NL, fr. *amphi-* + Gk *kyōn* dog] **:** a genus (the type of the family Amphicyonidae) of Miocene and Pliocene Carnivora intermediate between the dogs and the bears — see BEAR DOG

am·phi·cyr·tic \¦amfə¦sərd·ik\ *adj* [LL *amphicyrtos* (fr. Gk *amphikyrtos*—fr. *amphi-* + *kyrtos* curved, bent—) + E *-ic*; akin to Gk *korōnos* curved — more at CROWN] **:** having both sides convex — used of angles between curves

am·phi·cyt·u·la \,amfəˈsichələ\ *n, pl* **amphicytu·lae** \-,lē\ [NL, fr. *amphi-* + *cytula* fertilized egg cell, fr. *cyt-* + *-ula*] *embryol* **:** a zygote capable of holoblastic unequal cleavage

am·phid \ˈamfəd\ *n* -S [Gk *amphidea* anything that is bound around] **:** one of a pair of circular depressions situated laterally at the anterior end of aquatic nematodes and believed to be chemoreceptors

am·phi·des·mous \¦amfə¦dezməs\ *adj* [*amphi-* + Gk *desmos* bond + E *-ous* — more at DIADEM] **:** provided with two ligaments

am·phi·det·ic \¦=¦=ˈded·ik\ *adj* [Gk *amphidetos* tied all around (fr. *amphidein* to tie around, fr. *amphi-* + *dein* to tie) + E *-ic* — more at DIADEM] **:** extending both before and behind the beak — used of the ligament of certain bivalves; compare OPISTHODETIC, PROSODETIC

am·phid·i·al \(ˈ)amˈfidēəl\ *adj* **:** of or relating to an amphid

¹am·phi·dip·loid \¦amfə¦di,plȯid\ *adj* [*amphi-* + *diploid*] *of an interspecific hybrid* **:** having a complete diploid chromosome set from each parent strain as a result of chromosome doubling in the first hybrid generation — **am·phi·dip·loi·dy** \¦amfəˈdi,plȯidē\ *n* -ES

²amphidiploid \"\ *n* -S **:** an amphidiploid individual or strain

am·phi·dis·coph·o·ra \,amfə(,)diˈskäfərə\ *n pl, cap* [NL, fr. *Amphidiscus*, genus of sponges (fr. *amphi-* + *-discus*) + *-o-* + *-phora*] **:** an order of Hyalospongiae comprising sponges with an anchoring root tuft and with amphidisks but no hexasters among the spicules

am·phi·disk *or* **am·phi·disc** \ˈamfə,disk\ *n* -S [*amphi-* + *disk, disc*] **:** a spicule having a stellate disk at each end found in the reproductive bodies of freshwater sponges of the genus *Spongilla* and in some of the Hyalospongiae

am·phi·drom·ic \¦=¦=ˈdrämik\ *adj* [Gk *amphidromos* running both ways (fr. *amphi-* + *dromos* course, racecourse) + E *-ic* — more at DROMEDARY] **:** relating to a system of tidal action in which the tide wave progresses around a point or center of little or no tide ⟨~ point⟩ ⟨~ region⟩

am·phid·ro·mous \(ˈ)amˈfidrəməs\ *adj* [*amphi-* + *-dromous*] *of fishes* **:** migrating from fresh to salt water or from salt to fresh water at some stage of the life cycle other than the breeding period

am·phi·erot·ic \¦amfē+\ *adj* [*amphi-* + *erotic*] **:** of, relating to, or manifesting amphierotism

am·phi·erotism \¦amfē+\ *n* -S [*amphi-* + *erotism*] **:** capacity of erotic reaction toward either sex

¹am·phi·gae·an *or* **am·phi·ge·an** \¦amfə¦jēən\ *adj, often cap* [*amphi-* + *-gaean, -gean* (fr. Gk *gaia* earth + E *-an*)] **1** *of a plant or animal* **:** found in both hemispheres **:** COSMOPOLITAN **2** *of a plant* **:** having flowers arising from the rootstock

²amphigaean *also* **amphigean** \"\ *adj, often cap* [NL *Amphigaea* (fr. *amphi-* + *-gaea*) temperate So. America + E *-an*] **:** occurring in temperate parts of So. America

am·phi·gas·tri·um \-ˈgastrēəm\ *n, pl* **amphigas·tria** \-rēə\ [NL, fr. *amphi-* + *gastr-* + *-ium*] **:** one of the small appressed stipulelike leaves on the ventral side of the stem in certain liverworts — compare JUNGERMANNIALES

am·phi·gas·tru·la \¦amfə+\ *n, pl* **amphigastru·lae** [NL, fr. *amphi-* + *gastrula*] *embryol* **:** a gastrula developed from an amphicytula

am·phi·gene \ˈamfə,jēn\ *n* -S [F *amphigène*, fr. *amphi-* + *-gène* -gene] **:** LEUCITE

am·phi·gen·e·sis \,amfə+\ *n, pl* **amphigene·ses** [NL, fr. *amphi-* + *genesis*] **:** AMPHIGONY — **am·phi·ge·net·ic** \¦=¦=ˈ=¦=\ *adj*

am·phig·e·nous \(ˈ)amˈfijənəs\ *adj* [*amphi-* + *-genous*] **1 a** *of the fruiting bodies of parasitic fungi* **:** occurring on both surfaces of the leaves of an infected plant **b** *of the oogonium of fungi of the family Pythiaceae* **:** growing through an encircling antheridium **2 :** given to or marked by sexual attraction to members either of the same or of the opposite sex — **am·phig·e·nous·ly** *adv*

am·phi·gon·ic \¦amfə¦gänik\ *or* **am·phig·o·nous** \(ˈ)amˈfigənəs\ *adj* **:** reproducing sexually — used esp. of female insects

am·phig·o·ny \amˈfigənē\ *n* -ES [*amphi-* + *-gony*] **:** sexual reproduction

am·phi·go·ry \ˈamfə,gōrē, amˈfigərē\ *also* **am·phi·gou·ri** \,amfə(,)güˈrē\ *n, pl* **amphigories** *also* **amphigouris** [F *amphigouri*] **:** a nonsense verse or composition **:** a rigmarole with apparent meaning which proves to be meaningless

am·phi·kar·y·on \,amfəˈkarē,än, -ēən\ *n* -S [ISV *amphi-* + *karyon*; orig. formed in G] **:** a cell nucleus containing two haploid groups of chromosomes — opposed to *hemikaryon*; compare DIPLOKARYON — **am·phi·kar·y·ot·ic** \¦=¦=¦=ē¦äd·ik\ *adj*

am·phil·i·na \amˈfilənə\ *n, cap* [NL, fr. Gk *amphilinos* bound with flaxen thongs] **:** a genus (the type of the family Amphilinidae) comprising the cestodarian worms with flat leaflike body and an anterior extensible proboscis — compare GYROCOTYLE — **am·phil·i·nid** \-nəd, -,nid\ *adj or n*

am·phim·a·cer \amˈfiməsə(r), ˈamfə,mās-\ *n* -S [L *amphimacrus*, fr. Gk *amphimakros*, lit., long at both ends, fr. *amphi-* + *makros* long — more at MEAGER] **:** a trisyllabic foot consisting of a short syllable between two long syllables in quantitative verse or of an unstressed syllable between two stressed syllables in accentual verse ⟨the word *runaway* is an accentual ~⟩ — called also *cretic*

am·phi·mict \ˈamfə,mikt\ *n* -S [*amphi-* + Gk *miktos* blended, fr. *mignynai* to mix — more at MIX] **:** an individual produced by or reproducing by sexual means

am·phi·mic·tic \¦=¦=ˈmiktik\ *or* **am·phi·mic·ti·cal** \-tәkəl\ *adj* [ISV *amphi-* + Gk *miktos* + ISV *-ic, -ical*] **:** capable of interbreeding freely and of producing fertile offspring — **am·phi·mic·ti·cal·ly** \-tək(ə)lē\ *adv*

am·phi·mix·is \,=¦=ˈmiksəs\ *n, pl* **amphimix·es** \-k,sēz\ [NL, fr. *amphi-* + Gk *mixis* mingling, fr. *mignynai*] **1 :** the union of germ cells in sexual reproduction — compare AUTOMIXIS **2 :** INTERBREEDING **3 :** the combining of pregenital, anal, and urethral eroticism in the development of genital sexuality

am·phi·neu·ra \-ˈn(y)u̇rə\ *n pl, cap* [NL, fr. *amphi-* + *-neura*] **:** a class of bilaterally symmetrical marine mollusks sometimes considered an order of Gastropoda, comprising the chitons and their related forms, having two lateral and two ventral nerve cords, and being commonly divided into the Polyplacophora and the Aplacophora — **am·phi·neu·ran** \-rən\ *n* — **am·phi·neu·rous** \¦=¦=ˈrəs\ *adj*

am·phi·nu·cle·us \,amfə+\ *n* [NL, fr. *amphi-* + *nucleus*] **:** a cell nucleus that contains a large karyosome

amph·ion \ˈam(p)fīən *also* -ī,än\ *n* -S [*amphi-* + *ion*] **:** DIPOLAR ION — **amph·ion·ic** \¦=¦=¦änik\ *adj*

am·phi·ox·ea \,amfēˈäksēə, -ē(,)äkˈsēə\ *n* -S [NL, fr. *amphi-* + *oxea*] **:** a slightly curved needlelike sponge spicule

am·phi·oxi \-ˈäk,sī\ [NL, pl. of *amphioxus*] *syn of* CIRROSTOMI

am·phi·ox·i·dae \-ˈäksə,dē\ [NL, fr. *Amphioxus*, type genus + *-idae*] *syn of* BRANCHIOSTOMIDAE

am·phi·ox·i·des \-,dēz\ *n, cap* [NL, fr. ¹*Amphioxus* + Gk *-idēs* (patronymic suffix)] **:** a formerly recognized genus of pelagic lancelets mistakenly based on larvae of the genus *Asymmetron*

am·phi·ox·id·i·dae \-(,)äkˈsidə,dē\ [NL, fr. *Amphioxides*, type genus + *-idae*] *syn of* BRANCHIOSTOMIDAE

¹am·phi·ox·us \-ˈäksəs\ [NL, irreg. fr. *amphi-* + Gk *oxys* sharp] *syn of* BRANCHIOSTOMA

²amphioxus \"\ *n, pl* **am·phi·oxi** \-ˈäk,sī\ *or* **amphioxuses** **:** a lancelet of the genus *Branchiostoma*, typically being a small transparent marine animal pointed at both ends, having an oral opening just below the anterior end surrounded by cirri, dorsal and anal fins but no limbs, a notochord, a dorsally situated nerve cord but no definite brain, a system of blood vessels but no heart, eyes represented by a medium pigment spot, and an olfactory but no auditory organ

am·phi·phlo·ic \¦amfə¦flōik\ *adj* [*amphi-* + *phloem* + *-ic*] **:** having phloem both internal and external to the xylem — used of the siphonostele of certain vascular plants; compare ECTOPHLOIC

am·phi·plat·y·an \-ˈplad·ēən\ *adj* [*amphi-* + Gk *platys* flat + E *-an*] **:** flat at both ends — used of vertebrae having both anterior and posterior surfaces of the centrum flat

am·phi·pleu·ra \,amfəˈplu̇rə\ *n, cap* [NL, fr. *amphi-* + *-pleura*] **:** a genus of diatoms (family Naviculaceae) that includes one species (*A. pellucida*) which is distinguished by a finely striate and punctate frustule often used to test the resolving power of microscope lenses

¹am·phi·ploid \ˈ=ˈ=,plȯid\ *adj* [*amphi-* + *-ploid*] *of an interspecific hybrid* **:** having at least one complete diploid set of chromosomes derived from each ancestral species — compare AMPHIDIPLOID — **am·phi·ploi·dy** \-ōidē\ *n* -ES

²amphiploid \"\ *n* -S **:** an amphiploid individual or strain

am·phi·pneus·tic \¦amfə¦n(y)üstik, -,fip¦n-\ *adj* [*amphi-* + Gk *pneustikos* of or for breathing, fr. (assumed) Gk *pneustos* (verbal of Gk *pnein* to breathe) + Gk *-ikos* -ic — more at SNEEZE] **1** *of some amphibians* **:** having both gills and lungs throughout life **2** *of an insect larva* **:** having the first and last pair of spiracles functional

am·phip·no·us \amˈfipnəwəs\ *n, cap* [NL, irreg. fr. *amphi-* + Gk *pnoē* breath, fr. *pnein* to breathe] **:** a genus of teleost fishes (order Symbranchii) comprising the cuchia

¹am·phi·pod \ˈamfə,päd\ *or* **am·phip·o·dal** \(ˈ)amˈfipəd°l\ *or* **am·phip·o·dan** \-ədən\ *or* **am·phip·o·dous** \-ədəs\ *adj* [*amphipod* fr. NL *Amphipoda*; *amphipodal, amphipodan, amphipodous* fr. NL *Amphipoda* + E *-al* or *-an* or *-ous*] **:** of or relating to the Amphipoda

²amphipod \"\ *or* **amphipodan** \"\ *n* -S **:** one of the Amphipoda

am·phip·o·da \amˈfipədə\ *n pl, cap* [NL, fr. *amphi-* + *-poda*] **:** a large group, usu. an order, of malacostracan crustaceans (division Peracarida) comprising the beach fleas and related forms; being mostly of small size with laterally compressed body, four anterior pairs of thoracic limbs directed forward, and three posterior pairs directed backward and upward, the thoracic limbs bearing gills; being usu. aquatic in fresh or salt water, and a few (as the whale louse) being parasitic

am·phi·pod·i·form \¦amfə¦pädə,fȯrm\ *adj* **:** resembling an amphipod

¹am·phi·pro·style \,amfəˈprō,stī(ə)l\ *adj* [L *amphiprostylos*, fr. Gk, fr. *amphi-* + *prostylos* having pillars in front — more at PROSTYLE] **:** marked by columniation consisting of free columns in porticoes at both ends of the structure and across the full ends — see COLUMNIATION illustration

²amphiprostyle \"\ *n* -S **:** an amphiprostyle building

am·phi·pro·tic \¦amfə¦prōd·ik\ *adj* [*amphi-* + *proton* + *-ic*] **:** AMPHOTERIC

am·phi·rhi·na \,amfəˈrīnə\ *n pl, cap* [NL, fr. *amphi-* + *-rhina* (fr. Gk *rhin-, rhis* nose)] *in some classifications* **:** a primary division of Vertebrata having double nasal chambers and including all vertebrates except the lancelets and cyclostomes — **am·phi·rhi·nal** \¦=¦=ˈrīn°l\ *adj* — **am·phi·rhine** \ˈ=ˈ=,rīn\ *adj*

am·phi·sar·ca \,=ˈ=ˈsärkə\ *n* -S [NL, fr. *amphi-* + *-sarca* (fr. Gk *sark-, sarx* flesh) — more at SARCASM] **:** a many-celled and many-seeded indehiscent fruit that is pulpy within and has a hard or woody rind (as the melon or the calabash)

am·phis·bae·na \,amfəsˈbēnə\ *n* [L, fr. Gk *amphisbaina*, fr. *amphis* on both sides (fr. *amphi* around) + *-baina* (fr. *bainein* to walk, go) — more at BY, COME] **1** *pl* **amphisbae·nae** \-(,)nē\ *or* **amphisbaenas :** a serpent in classical mythology having a head at each end and being capable of moving in either direction **2** *cap* [NL, fr. L] **:** a genus (the type of the family Amphisbaenidae) of harmless limbless lizards having concealed eyes and ears and short blunt tail and living in warm or tropical countries — **am·phis·bae·ni·an** \¦=¦=ˈnēən\ *adj or n* — **am·phis·bae·nic** \-nik\ *adj* — **am·phis·bae·noid** \-,nȯid\ *adj* — **am·phis·bae·nous** \-,nəs\ *adj*

am·phis·ci·ans \amˈfish(ē)ənz\ *or* **am·phis·cii** \-shē,ī\ *n pl* [*amphiscians* fr. LL *amphiscius* one who dwells in the tropics (fr. Gk *amphiskios*, fr. the adj., throwing a shadow both ways, fr. *amphi-* + *skia* shadow) + E *-an* + *-s*; *amphiscii* fr. LL, pl. of *amphiscius* — more at SCENE] *archaic* **:** the inhabitants of the tropics

am·phi·sex·u·al \¦amfə¦-\ *adj* [*amphi-* + *sexual*] **:** possessing the potentiality for development of the characters specific to each sex

am·phis·i·le \amˈfisə,lē\ [NL] *syn of* CENTRISCUS

am·phi·sil·i·dae \,amfəˈsilə,dē\ [NL, fr. *Amphisile*, type genus + *-idae*] *syn of* CENTRISCIDAE

am·phi·spore \ˈ=ˈ=,-\ *n* -S [ISV *amphi-* + *spore*] **:** a modified urediniospore that is characteristic of certain rusts of arid regions and that functions as a resting spore

am·phi·sto·ma·ta \,amfəˈstōməd·ə\ *n pl, cap* [NL, fr. *amphi-* + *-stomata*] *in some classifications* **:** a suborder of Digenea comprising trematodes somewhat conical in form with a highly developed posterior acetabulum — **am·phis·to·mate** \amˈfistə,māt, -,mət\ *adj* — **am·phi·stome** \ˈamfə,stōm\ *adj or n*

am·phi·sto·mat·ic \¦amfəstō¦mad·ik\ *adj* [*amphi-* + *stomatic*] **:** having stomata on both surfaces ⟨~ leaves⟩

am·phis·to·mous \(ˈ)amˈfistəməs\ *adj* [NL *amphistomus*, fr. Gk *amphistomos* with a double mouth, fr. *amphi-* + *-stomos* (fr. *stoma* mouth) — more at STOMACH] *zool* **:** having a sucker at each extremity

am·phi·sty·lar \¦amfə¦stīlə(r)\ *adj* [*amphi-* + *-stylar*] **:** marked by columniation consisting of free columns in porticoes either at both ends or at both sides of the structure and across the full ends or sides — see COLUMNIATION illustration

am·phi·sty·lic \-lik\ *adj* [*amphi-* + *-stylic*] **:** having the upper jaw partly free from the brain case and braced by the hyomandibular cartilage (as in certain primitive sharks) — compare AUTOSTYLIC, HYOSTYLIC

am·phi·tene \ˈamfə,tēn\ *n* -S [ISV *amphi-* + *-tene*; orig. formed as F *amphitène*] **:** ZYGOTENE

am·phi·the·a·ter \ˈam(p)fə,-, ˈaam-, ÷-mpə-, ,=ˈ=ˈ-\ *n* -S [L *amphitheatrum*, fr. Gk *amphitheatron*, fr. *amphi-* + *theatron* theater — more at THEATER] **1 :** an oval, circular, or semicircular building with rising tiers of seats about a central open space used in ancient Rome for spectacles and contests ⟨Marcus Aurelius could sit for hours in the ~, bored and distrait . . . but with unmoved serenity —Agnes Repplier⟩ **2 :** something felt to resemble an amphitheater: **a :** a large auditorium used esp. for conventions, stock shows, sports events, and indoor circuses ⟨an exposition held in the International *Amphitheater* in Chicago⟩ **b :** a large room (as in a hospital) with a rising gallery of seats from which doctors and medical students may observe surgical operations **c :** a semicircular rising gallery in a modern theater **d :** a land form characterized by steep slopes rising abruptly from a somewhat semicircular flat or gently sloping area ⟨laid out the prisoners' camp in a sort of ~ among knolls —Kenneth Roberts⟩ **3 :** a place of public contests or games **:** ARENA

am·phi·the·a·tral \¦=¦=ˈthēə·trəl\ *adj* [L *amphitheatralis*, fr. *amphitheatrum* + *-alis* -al] **:** AMPHITHEATRIC

am·phi·the·at·ric \¦=¦=thē¦a·trik\ *or* **am·phi·the·at·ri·cal** \-rəkəl\ *adj* [L *amphitheatricus*, fr. *amphitheatrum* + *-icus* -ic, -ical] **1 :** performed in an amphitheater **2 :** resembling an amphitheater or its arrangement of seats — **am·phi·the·at·ri·cal·ly** \-rək(ə)lē\ *adv*

am·phi·the·cial \¦amfə¦thēsh(ē)əl, -sēəl\ *adj* [NL *amphithecium* + E *-al*] **:** of or relating to the amphithecium

am·phi·the·ci·um \,=ˈ=ˈs(h)ēəm\ *n, pl* **amphithe·cia** \-ēə\ [NL, fr. *amphi-* + *-thecium*] **1 :** the external layer of cells surrounding the sporogenous tissue in the sporangium of a moss **2 :** the inner layer of the perithecium next to the hymenium in certain lichens

am·phith·y·ron \amˈfithə,rän\ *n, pl* **amphithy·ra** \-ərə\ [LGk, fr. Gk, hall, fr. neut. of *amphithyros* having a door on both sides, fr. *amphi-* + *thyra* door — more at DOOR] **:** a veil or curtain before the doors of the iconostasis in the Eastern Church

am·phit·o·ky *var of* AMPHEROTOKY

am·phi·tri·aene \¦amfə¦trī,ēn\ *n* -S [*amphi-* + *triaene*] **:** a sponge spicule with three divergent rays at each end — see TRIAENE

am·phit·ri·chous \(ˈ)amˈfi·trəkəs\ *adj* [*amphi-* + *-trichous*] **:** having flagella at both ends

am·phi·tri·te \ˈamfə,trīd·ē, ,==ˈ==\ *n, cap* [NL, fr. *Amphitrite,* wife of Neptune and goddess of the sea, fr. L, fr. Gk *Amphitritē*] **:** a genus of tube-inhabiting marine annelid worms having branching gills and many tentacles anterior to the mouth

am·phit·ro·pous \(ˈ)amˈfi·trəpəs\ *adj* [*amphi-* + *-tropous*] **:** having the ovule inverted but with the attachment near the middle of one side — compare ANATROPOUS

am·phi·uma \,amfēˈyümə\ *n, cap* [NL, prob. irreg. fr. *amphi-* + Gk *pneuma* breath, fr. *pnein* to breathe] **:** a genus (coextensive with the family Amphiumidae) of amphibians including only the congo snakes

am·phi·va·sal \ˌamfə;-\ *adj* [*amphi-* + *vasal*] **:** having the xylem surrounding the phloem — used of certain concentric vascular bundles; compare AMPHICRIBRAL

am·phiv·o·rous \(ˈ)amˈfiv(ə)rəs\ *adj* [*amphi-* + *-vorous*] **:** eating both animal and vegetable food

ampho- *comb form* [NL, fr. Gk *amphō* — more at AMBI-] **:** both ⟨*ampho*philic⟩

am·pho·gen·ic \ˌamfəˌjenik\ *adj* [*ampho-* + *-genic*] **:** producing approximately equal numbers of male and female offspring — **am·phog·e·ny** \amˈfäjənē\ *n* -ES

am·pho·lyte \ˈamfə,līt\ *n* -s [*amphoteric* + *electrolyte*] **:** an amphoteric electrolyte — **am·pho·lyt·ic** \ˌamfəˌlid·ik\ *adj*

am·pho·phil·ic \ˌ==ˈfilik\ *also* **am·pho·phil** \ˈ==,fil\ *or* **am·phoph·i·lous** \(ˈ)amˈfäfələs\ *adj* [*ampho-* + *-philic, -phil, -philous*] **:** staining with both acid and basic dyes **:** NEUTROPHILIC

am·pho·ra \ˈamfərə, ˈaam-\ *n, pl* **ampho·rae** \-,rē\ *or* **amphoras** [L, modif. of Gk *amphoreus* jar with two handles, alter. of *amphiphoreus,* fr. *amphi-* + *phoreus* bearer, fr. *pherein* to bear — more at BEAR] **1 a :** an ancient Greek jar or vase having a large oval body, narrow cylindrical neck, and two handles that rise almost to the level of the mouth: (1) **:** a jar usu. undecorated and pointed at the bottom, used esp. for holding or storing wine, oil, honey, or grain (2) **:** a decorated vase with a disk-shaped base, used esp. as an ornament or a prize (as in athletic contests) **b :** a 2-handled vessel shaped like an amphora **2 :** an ancient unit of capacity: **a :** a Greek unit equal to 10.3 gal (39 liters) **b :** a Roman unit equal to 6.7 gal (25.5 liters)

amphora 1a (1)

am·phor·ic \(ˈ)amˈfórik\ *adj* [NL *amphoricus,* fr. L *amphora* + *-icus* -ic] **:** resembling the sound made by blowing across the mouth of an empty bottle ⟨~ breathing⟩ — **am·pho·ric·i·ty** \,amfəˈrisəd·ē\ *n* -ES

am·pho·ris·kos \,amfəˈriskəs\ *n, pl* **amphoris·koi** \-,kòi\ [Gk, dim. of *amphoreus* jar with two handles — more at AMPHORA] **:** a small amphora typically four inches high

am·pho·ter·ic \ˌamfəˌterik\ *adj* [ISV *amphoter-* (fr. Gk *amphoteros* each of two, fr. *amphō* both) + *-ic* — more at AMBI-] **:** partly one and partly the other; *specif* **:** capable of reacting chemically either as an acid or as a base

am·phot·er·ism \amˈfäd·ə,rizəm\ *n* -s **:** the property of being amphoteric

am·phot·er·ite \-,rīt\ *n* -s [Gk *amphoteros* + E *-ite*] **:** a meteorite consisting essentially of olivine and bronzite with minor amounts of iron sulfide and metal

amphoterotoky *var of* AMPHETEROTOKY

amphycoelous *var of* AMPHICOELOUS

am·ple \ˈampəl, ˈaim-\ *adj* **ampler** \-p(ə)lə(r)\ **amplest** \-p(ə)ləst\ [MF, fr. L *amplus;* prob. akin to L *ampla* handle and perh. to Skt *amatra* vessel, drinking bowl; basic meaning: grasping] **1 :** marked by extensive or more than adequate size, volume, space, or room ⟨two celebrated palaces, each with an ~ garden —T.B.Macaulay⟩ ⟨it is doubtful that the Fathers in 1783 contemplated expansion across the empty continent beyond the ~ boundaries set down —S.F.Bemis⟩ **2 a :** marked by more than adequate measure in strength, force, scope, effectiveness, or influence ⟨the light they yielded was more than ~ for the purpose —Thomas Hardy⟩ ⟨a government entrusted with such ~ powers —John Marshall⟩ **b :** marked by more than adequate measure in number or amount ⟨possessing ~ means they entertained generously —C.A.Dinsmore⟩ ⟨supplies were ~ for three days —Dorothy Sayers⟩ **3 a :** marked by generous plenty or by abundance **:** more than adequate **:** not scant or niggard ⟨an ~ picnic basket —Dixon Wecter⟩ **b :** COPIOUS, VOLUMINOUS, FULL ⟨an ~ biography⟩ **4 :** satisfying wants or desires more than adequately ⟨~ comfort⟩ **5 :** BUXOM, PORTLY ⟨an imposing creature, tall and stout, with an ~ bust —W.S.Maugham⟩

syn SPACIOUS, CAPACIOUS, COMMODIOUS: AMPLE always means considerably more than adequate or sufficient. Applied to what can be measured or counted, it suggests size, scope, space, or fullness and contrasts with *scant, sparse,* or *narrow* ⟨an *ample* sum—one sufficient to supply those wants of hers —Thomas Hardy⟩ ⟨"Do you want me to miss this train?" But he knew that the margin of time was *ample* —Arnold Bennett⟩ ⟨the plan, which Julius had designed for a lengthy campaign and *ample* forces, failed when it was put into execution in a hurry with inadequate troops —John Buchan⟩ Applied to persons' figures it suggests stoutness ⟨a plump, maternal-looking woman, with an *ample* figure, which did not conform to the wasp waist of the period —Ellen Glasgow⟩ ⟨genial clergy of *ample* girth, stuffed with the buttered toast of a refectory tea —S.B.Leacock⟩ In other matters it may indicate unstinted copiousness or generosity ⟨the work . . . is of *ample* proportions. There will be six volumes altogether —Dumas Malone⟩ SPACIOUS stresses great space, area, or scope ⟨white villas, gray convents, church spires, villages, towns . . . were scattered upon this *spacious* map —Nathaniel Hawthorne⟩ ⟨the great chilly unused drawing room whose *spacious* ceremoniousness seemed to embrace and envelope her —J.C. Powys⟩ In more figurative senses it may suggest breadth, expanse, and freedom from constriction ⟨in his lordly way — for he always talked, and unfortunately acted, in a *spacious* manner —Osbert Sitwell⟩ ⟨frequent visits to Europe, with grouse shooting in Scotland and swimming on the Riviera, were part of the *spacious* life of the wealthy —H.W.Baehr⟩ CAPACIOUS suggests ability to hold or contain a great deal, a wealth of freely available space ⟨a *capacious* old house with big rooms⟩ It is often used with humorous suggestion ⟨was very stout . . . he wore a *capacious* waistcoat —Samuel Butler⟩ ⟨a man of *capacious* mind, seeing that he could draw much wider conclusions without evidence than could be expected of his neighbors —George Eliot⟩ COMMODIOUS stresses roominess and freedom from constriction, from being limited or pent in ⟨we passed a large inlet . . . it appeared to be the entrance to a safe and *commodious* harbor —C.B.Nordhoff & J.N.Hall⟩ It may have added suggestions of convenience and comfort ⟨my mother's room is very *commodious* . . . large and cheerful looking . . . the most comfortable apartment in the house — Jane Austen⟩ **syn** see in addition PLENTIFUL

am·plec·tic \(ˈ)amˈplektik\ *adj* [L *amplecti* to embrace, surround + E *-ic*] **:** of or relating to amplexus

am·ple·ness *n* -ES **:** the quality or state of being ample

am·plex·i·cau·date \ˌam,pleksə;-, amˌp-\ *adj* [ISV *amplexi-* (fr. L *amplexus,* past part. of *amplecti*) + *caudate*] **:** having the whole tail included in the interfemoral web — used of various bats

am·plex·i·caul \amˈpleksə,kòl\ *adj* [NL *amplexicaulis,* fr. L *amplexus* (past part. of *amplecti* to entwine, embrace) + *-i-* + *caulis* stem, cabbage — more at COLE] *of a leaf* **:** sessile with the base or with stipules surrounding the stem from which it arises — compare PERFOLIATE

am·plex·i·fo·li·ate \ˌam,pleksə;-, amˌp-\ *adj* [ISV *amplexi-* (fr. L *amplexus,* past part. of *amplecti*) + *foliate*] **:** having amplexicaul leaves

am·plex·us \amˈpleksəs\ *n, pl* **amplexus** \"\ [L, lit., embrace, fr. *amplexus,* past part. of *amplecti*] **:** the mating embrace of the frog or toad during which eggs are shed into the water and there fertilized

am·pli·ate \ˈamplēət, -ē,āt\ *adj* [L *ampliatus,* past part. of *ampliare* to make wider, enlarge, fr. *amplior,* compar. of *amplus* wide, large — more at AMPLE] **1 :** WIDENED, ENLARGED **2 :** having the outer edge prominent — used of insects' wings

am·pli·a·tion \,amplēˈāshən\ *n* -s [MF, fr. LL *ampliation-, ampliatio,* fr. L, postponement of the decision of a cause, fr. *ampliatus* (past part of *ampliare* to enlarge, postpone the decision of) + *-ion-, -io* -ion] **1** *archaic* **:** ENLARGEMENT, AMPLIFICATION **2** [L *ampliation-, ampliatio*] **:** a postponement of the decision of a cause in civil law

am·pli·a·tive \ˈamplē,ād·iv\ *adj* [ML *ampliativus,* fr. L *ampliatus* + *-ivus* -ive] *logic* **:** adding in the predicate something not contained in the meaning of the subject term **:** SYNTHETIC ⟨an ~ proposition⟩ — opposed to *explicative*

ampliative inference *n* **:** BACONIAN INDUCTION

am·pli·dyne \ˈamplə,dīn\ *n* -s [*amplifier* + *-dyne* (fr. Gk *dynamis* power) — more at DYNAMIC] **:** a direct-current generator that by the use of compensating coils and a short circuit across two of its brushes precisely controls a large power output whenever a small power input is varied in the field winding of the generator

am·pli·fi·ca·tion \,ampləfəˈkāshən, ,aam-\ *n* -s [L *amplification-, amplificatio,* fr. *amplificatus* (past part. of *amplificare* to amplify, enlarge) + *-ion-, -io* -ion — more at AMPLIFY] **1 :** an act, example, or product of amplifying **:** ENLARGEMENT, EXTENSION ⟨a few final remarks may be added in defense and ~ of this account —R.J.Hirst⟩ ⟨~ of radio signals⟩ **2 a :** matter by which a statement or idea is expanded **b :** an expanded statement ⟨he offered no ~ of his pleasure —Clemence Dane⟩

amplification factor *n* **:** the ratio of the changes in plate and grid voltage that cause equal changes in the plate current of an electron tube

am·pli·fi·er \ˈ==,fī(ə)r, -īə\ *n* -s **:** one that amplifies; *specif* **:** an electronic circuit usu. employing vacuum tubes and used to obtain amplification of voltage, current, or power

am·pli·fy \ˈamplə,fī, ˈaam-\ *vb* -ED/ -ING/ -ES [ME *amplifien,* fr. MF *amplifier,* fr. L *amplificare,* fr. *amplus* ample + *-ficare* -fy — more at AMPLE] *vt* **1 :** to enlarge, expand, or extend (a statement or other expression of idea in words) by addition of detail or illustration or by logical development **2 a** *obs* **:** to enlarge in size or capacity **b :** to increase or extend (as in amount, importance, or intensity) ⟨~ knowledge⟩ ⟨~ the jurisdiction of a court⟩ **c** *archaic* **:** OVERSTRESS, EXAGGERATE **3 :** to utilize (an input of voltage, current, or power) so as to obtain an output of greater magnitude through the relay action of a transducer ~ *vi* **:** to explain in greater detail or expand or extend one's remarks or ideas ⟨~ on his remarks⟩ **syn** see EXPAND

am·pli·stat \ˈamplə,stat\ *n* -s [*amplifier* + *-stat*] **:** a magnetic amplifier for the regulation of voltage

am·pli·tude \ˈamplə,tüd, ˈaam-, -lə-,tyüd\ *n* -s [L *amplitudo,* fr. *amplus* + *-tudo* -tude] **1 :** the quality or state of being ample **:** extent esp. of surface or space **:** largeness of dimensions **:** SIZE **2 :** largeness of scope **:** BREADTH, ABUNDANCE, FULLNESS: **a :** extent of mental capacity or intellectual power **b :** extent esp. of means, resources, dignity, or splendor **3** *navigation* **a :** the arc of the horizon between the true east or west point and the foot of the vertical circle passing through any star or object — compare AZIMUTH **b :** the arc of the horizon between the magnetic east or west point and a heavenly body — called also *magnetic amplitude* **4 :** the extent of a vibratory movement or of an oscillation **:** the maximum numerical value of a periodically varying quantity (as an alternating current, a radio wave, the air pressure in a sound-wave field, or the angular displacement of a pendulum) measured from its normal or equilibrium value taken as zero **5 :** ARGUMENT 6b **6 :** the range of ecological adaptability of a kind or group of organisms (as of a species, genus, or family)

amplitude-modulated \ˈ==,=;==,==\ *adj* **:** operating by amplitude modulation

amplitude modulation *n* **:** modulation of the amplitude of a radio carrier wave in accordance with the strength of the audio or other signal; *also* **:** a broadcasting system using such modulation — abbr. *AM;* compare FREQUENCY MODULATION

amplitude of accommodation : the difference between the refracting power of the eye when adjusted for vision at the far point and when adjusted for vision at the near point

am·plo·some \ˈamplə,sōm\ *n* -s [L *amplus* large, ample + E *-o-* + *-some* — more at AMPLE] **:** a body of endomorphic build **:** an endomorphic or pyknic individual

am·ply \ˈamp(ə)lē, ˈaam-,ˈaim-, -li\ *adv* **:** in an ample manner

am·pongue \ˈam,pòŋ\ *n* -s [native name in Madagascar] **:** WOOLLY LEMUR

amps *pl of* AMP

am·pul \ˈam·,pyül, ˈaam- *sometimes* -,pùl *or* -,pəl\ *also* **am·pule** \-,pyül\ *or* **am·poule** \-,pyül *sometimes* -,pül\ *n* -s [*ampul* fr. ME *ampulle* flask, fr. OE & OF; OE *ampulle* & OF *ampole, ampoule,* fr. L *ampulla; ampule, ampoule* fr. F *ampoule*] **1 :** a small bulbous glass vessel hermetically sealed and used to hold a solution for hypodermic injection **2 :** a vessel or vial resembling an ampul

am·pul·la \amˈpùlə, -ˈpə-, aam-\ *n, pl* **ampul·lae** \-,lē, -ī\ [ME, fr. OE, fr. L, dim. of *amphora* — more at AMPHORA] **1 :** a flask of glass or earthenware having a somewhat globular body and two handles and used esp. by the ancient Romans to hold ointment, perfume, or wine **2 a :** a vessel in which holy oil is kept ⟨the ~ ordered for the coronation of Charles II —L.G.W.Legg⟩ **b :** a cruet in which wine or water for ecclesiastical use is kept **3** [NL, fr. L] **a :** one of the small bladders attached to the submerged parts of plants of *Utricularia* and related genera **b :** one of the flask-shaped swellings on the hyphae of certain fungi **4** [NL, fr. L] **:** a flasklike dilatation or sac: as **a :** the dilatation containing a patch of sensory epithelium at one end of each semicircular canal of the ear **b :** one of the muscular vesicles of the water vascular system of echinoderms by the contraction of which the suckers are protruded **c :** one of the dilatations of the lactiferous tubules of the mammary glands that serve as reservoirs for milk **d :** the middle portion of the fallopian tube

ampulla 1

am·pul·la·ceous \ˌ=pəˌlāshəs, -,pù-, -,pə-\ *adj* [L *ampullaceus,* fr. *ampulla* + *-aceus* -aceous] **:** resembling an ampulla **:** shaped like a flask or bladder

ampulla of va·ter \-ˈfätə(r), -ät-\ *usu cap V* [trans. of G *Vatersche ampulle,* after Abraham *Vater* †1751 Ger. anatomist] **:** a trumpet-mouthed dilatation of the duodenal wall at the opening of the fused pancreatic and common bile ducts

am·pul·lar \(ˈ)amˈpùlə(r), -ˌpə\ *also* **am·pul·la·ry** \-ləré; ˈampə,lerē\ *adj* **:** resembling or relating to an ampulla

am·pul·lar·ia \,ampəˈla(a)rēə\ [NL, fr. L *ampulla* + NL *-aria*] *syn of* PILA

ampullar sense *n* **:** the sense for rotation for which the end organs are in the ampullae of the semicircular canals

am·pul·late \(ˈ)amˈpùlət, -ˌpə-; ˈampələt, -,lāt\ *or* **am·pul·lat·ed** \ˈampə,lād·əd\ *adj* **:** having an ampulla **:** shaped like a flask

am·pul·li·form \amˈpùlə,fórm, -ˈpə-\ *adj* **:** shaped like a flask **:** DILATED

am·pul·lu·la \amˈpùlyələ, -ˈpə-\ *n, pl* **ampullu·lae** \-,lē, -,lī\ [NL, fr. LL, dim. of L *ampulla*] *anat* **:** a minute ampulla (as of the lymphatics or lacteals)

am·pu·tate \ˈampyə,tāt, ˈaam-, *usu* -ād.+V\ *vt* -ED/ -ING/ -S [L *amputatus,* past part. of *amputare* to cut around, prune, fr. *am-, amb-* around + *putare* to cut, prune — more at AMBI-, PAVE] **1 :** to cut or lop off **:** PRUNE ⟨*amputating* data from its cultural context —S.E.Hyman⟩ ⟨a dimension has been *amputated* from man's political existence —Irving Kristol⟩ **2 :** to cut off (a limb or portion of a limb or a projecting part of the body) — compare EXCISE

am·pu·ta·tion \,==ˈtāshən\ *n* -s [L *amputation-, amputatio,* fr. *amputatus,* + *-ion-, -io* -ion] **1 a :** a cutting, pruning, or lopping off ⟨bare thorny stumps and slanting marks of ~ — Kathleen Fruman⟩ ⟨a deliberate ~ of freedom —*Time*⟩ **b :** excision (as of letters, words, or sentences) from writing ⟨confusion follows too drastic an ~ —Creighton Peet⟩ **2 :** an act, process, or instance of amputating a body part whether occurring immediately after an injury or delayed until inflammation and suppuration are present — called also respectively *primary amputation, secondary amputation;* see CONGENITAL AMPUTATION, SPONTANEOUS AMPUTATION

am·pu·ta·tor \ˈ==,tād·ə(r), -ātə\ *n* -s **:** one that amputates

am·pu·tee \ˌ==ˈtē *also* -tā\ *n* -s [prob. modif. of F *amputé,* fr. past part. of *amputer,* fr. L *amputare*] **:** one that has had a limb amputated ⟨a quadruple ~⟩

am·pyx \ˈam(,)piks\ *n, cap* [NL, fr. Gk, woman's diadem, prob. fr. *am-* (fr. *ana-*) + *-pyx* (akin to Gk *pykazein* to cover closely, surround, crown); akin to Av *pusā-* diadem] **:** a genus of small blind Ordovician trilobites with a long spine at the anterior end of the head

am·ra \ˈəm(,)rä, ˈämrə\ *n* -s [Hindi *amrā, amṛā, ambāṛā* — more at AMBARELLA] **:** a hog plum (*Spondias mangifera*) of India

am·rad gum \ˈäm,räd-\ *n* [Bengali *āmrāt* hog plum] **:** an inferior usu. colored gum arabic obtained chiefly in India from the babul

am·ra·tian \(ˈ)amˈrāshən\ *adj, usu cap* [El-*Amra,* site near Abydos, Egypt, its type station + E *-atian* (as in *Alsatian*)] **:** of or belonging to an aeneolithic culture of Upper Egypt characterized by semisubterranean dwellings, working of raw gold, the use of copper and ivory, and the wearing of linen

am·ri \ˈäm(,)rē\ *adj, usu cap* [fr. *Amri,* town in Sind province, Pakistan, its type station] **:** of or belonging to the earliest known stone-using and shell-using culture of the Indus river system which extends also into the Sind and southern Baluchistan and is characterized by a distinctive pottery

am·rit \ˈamrət\ *or* **am·ri·ta** \amˈrēd·ə\ *n* -s [Panjabi & Skt; Panjabi *amṛt,* lit., immortal, fr. Skt *amṛta,* fr. *a-* ²*a-* + *mṛta* dead, death — more at MURDER] **:** a sweetened water used by the Sikhs as a sacred drink and as baptismal water

¹**am·rit·sar** \(ˈ)amˈritsə(r), ˌəmˈ-\ *adj, usu cap* [fr. *Amritsar,* India] **:** of or from Amritsar, India **:** of the kind or style prevalent in Amritsar

²**amritsar** \"\ *n* -s *usu cap* [fr. *Amritsar,* where it is made] **:** a large-sized machine-made Indian carpet

AMs *pl of* AM

-ams *pl of* -AM

am·sinck·ia \amˈsiŋkēə\ *n, cap* [NL, fr. Wilhelm *Amsinck* †1831 Ger. botanist + NL *-ia*] **:** a genus of rough annual herbs (family Boraginaceae) with oblong leaves and scorpioid-spicate yellow flowers, at least the lowest being leafy-bracted — see FIDDLE-NECK 2

am·so·nia \amˈsōnēə, -nyə\ *n* [NL, fr. Charles *Amson fl* 1760 Am. physician + NL *-ia*] **1** *cap* **:** a genus of herbs (family Apocynaceae) having a milky juice, alternate entire leaves, and showy bluish flowers in terminal cymes, one species (*A. tabernaemontana*) being common in the southeastern U.S. **2** -s **:** an herb of the genus *Amsonia*

am·ster·dam \ˈamztə(r),dam, -mstə-, ˈaam...da(ə)m\ *adj, usu cap* [fr. *Amsterdam,* Netherlands] **:** of or from Amsterdam, the capital of the Netherlands **:** of the kind or style prevalent in Amsterdam

am·ster·dam·er *or* **am·ster·dam·mer** \-mə(r)\ *n* -s *cap* [D, *Amsterdammer,* fr. *Amsterdam* + D *-er*] **:** a native or inhabitant of Amsterdam

amt \ˈam(p)t, ˈä-\ *n* -s [Dan, fr. G, fr. OHG *ambaht* service — more at EMBASSY] **:** a magistracy or administrative district in some countries of Teutonic origin

amt *abbr* amount

am·trac *or* **am·track** \ˈam·,trak\ *n* -s [*amphibious* + *tractor*] **:** AMPHIBIAN

AMU *abbr, often not cap* atomic mass unit

amuck *var of* AMOK

amue·sha \ämˈwāshə\ *n, pl* **amuesha** *or* **amueshas** *usu cap* [Sp, of AmerInd origin] **1 a :** a people of central Peru **b :** a member of such people **2 :** a language of the Amuesha people of uncertain but perhaps Arawakan affinity

amu·guis *also* **amu·gis** \äˈmü(,)gēs\ *n* -ES [Tag *amugis*] **1 :** a timber tree (*Koordersiodendron pinnatum*) of the family Anacardiaceae found in the Philippines, Celebes, and New Guinea **2 :** the light-colored reddish water-resisting and ant-resisting wood of the amuguis

am·u·la \ˈamyələ\ *n, pl* **amu·lae** \-,lē, -ī\ *or* **amulas** [LL *amula, hamula,* fr. L, water bucket, dim. of *ama, hama* bucket — more at AMA] **:** a vessel for eucharistic wine offered by the people in the early Christian church

am·u·let \ˈamyələt *also* -,let, *usu* -d.+V\ *n* -s [L *amuletum*] **:** a charm (as an ornament, gem, or relic) often inscribed with a spell, magic incantation, or symbol and believed to protect the wearer against evil (as disease or witchcraft) or to aid him (as in love or war)

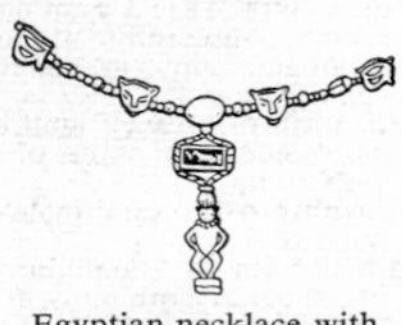

Egyptian necklace with amulets

am·u·let·ic \ˌamyəˌled·ik\ *adj* **:** functioning as an amulet

amur cork \(ˈ)äˌmù(ə)r-, əˈm-\ *n, usu cap A* [fr. *Amur* river, NE Asia, where it grows] **:** a medium-sized tree (*Phellodendron amurense*) with corky bark and pinnate leaves native to eastern Asia but used as an ornamental elsewhere

amur maple *n, usu cap A* [fr. *Amur* river] **:** a graceful shrub (*Acer ginnala*) of eastern Asia used in cultivation and having 3-lobed leaves and yellow paniculate flowers

amur privet *or* **amur river privet** *n, usu cap A* [fr. *Amur* river] **:** a shrub (*Ligustrum amurense*) of eastern Asia cultivated for its persistent foliage, white flowers, and black fruit

amuse \əˈmyüz\ *vb* -ED/-ING/-S [MF *amuser* to cause to waste time, amuse, bemuse, deceive, fr. OF, fr. *a-* (fr. L *ad-*) + *muser* to muse — more at MUSE] *vt* **1** *archaic* **:** to divert the attention of (as from the truth or one's real intent) **:** DECEIVE, DELUDE, BEMUSE **2** *obs* **a :** to occupy or engage the attention of **:** plunge in deep thought **:** ABSORB **b :** DISTRACT, BEWILDER **3 a :** to entertain or occupy in a pleasant manner **:** DIVERT ⟨he ~*s* himself by reading⟩ ⟨~ the child with a story⟩ ⟨~ his friends⟩ **b :** to while away ⟨~ leisure time⟩ ~ *vi, obs* **:** MUSE

syn DIVERT, ENTERTAIN, RECREATE: AMUSE means to engage the attention in a way to keep one interested or engrossed esp. in a laugh-provoking, usu. light or frivolous way ⟨I write because it *amuses* me —Rose Macaulay⟩ ⟨he has something to say that will either *amuse* or help his audience —W.J.Reilly⟩ DIVERT, in this comparison, stresses the distraction of the attention, esp. from worry and routine occupations, and usu. the inducing of relaxation or gaiety ⟨a series of *diverting* and sometimes mildly harrowing adventures —*Current Biog.*⟩ ⟨when idle moments occur during the day, fill them in quickly by *diverting* yourself with an absorbing book —*Better Homes & Gardens*⟩ ⟨only men of leisure have the need for beautiful women to *divert* them —Pearl Buck⟩ ENTERTAIN implies the activity of others to provide amusement or diversion and usu. suggests formal or specially contrived methods ⟨his prose has been described as lucid, *entertaining,* and, at times, inspired —*Current Biog.*⟩ ⟨the radio keeps them informed and *entertained* —Harold Griffin⟩ ⟨a party of Frenchmen . . . *entertained* the friendly natives aboard their boats —*Amer. Guide Series: La.*⟩ RECREATE, an infrequent verb in this sense, implies a change of occupation or an indulgence in diversions for the sake of relaxation or refreshment of mind or body ⟨*recreating* herself in the housekeeper's room —Jane Austen⟩

amused *adj* **1 :** pleasantly diverted ⟨~ spectators⟩ **2 :** expressing amusement ⟨an ~ look on his face⟩ — **amus·ed·ly** \-zədlē, -li\ *adv*

amuse·ment \-zmənt\ *n* -s *often attrib* [F, fr. MF, fr. *amuser* + *-ment*] **1** *obs* **a :** BEWILDERMENT **b :** diversion of the attention (as from the truth or one's real intent) **:** DISTRACTION **2 a :** a means of amusing or entertaining ⟨what are your favorite ~*s*⟩ **b :** the condition of being amused ⟨his ~ knew no bounds⟩ **c :** pleasurable diversion **:** ENTERTAINMENT ⟨he plays the piano for his own ~⟩

amusement park *n* **:** a commercially operated park having various devices for entertainment (as a merry-go-round and roller coaster) and usu. booths for the sale of food and drink

amuses *pres 3d sing of* AMUSE

am·u·sette \ˌamyəˌzet\ *n* -s [F, lit., plaything, diversion, fr. *amuser* + *-ette*] **:** an obsolete light rifled fieldpiece

amus·go \əˈmüs,gō, -üz-\ *n, pl* **amusgo** *or* **amusgos** *usu cap* [Sp, of AmerInd origin] **1 a :** a people of the coast of Oaxaca and Guerrero, Mexico **b :** a member of such people **2 :** a Mixtecan language of the Amusgo people

amu·sia \(ˈ)āˈmyüzēə\ *n* -s [NL, fr. Gk *amousia* lack of harmony, fr. *a-* ²a- + *mousia* music, song] **:** a condition marked by an inability to produce music or to comprehend it — called also respectively *motor amusia, sensory amusia;* compare APHASIA

amusing *adj* **:** giving amusement **:** pleasantly entertaining **:** DIVERTING ⟨an ~ story⟩ — **amus·ing·ly** *adv*

amus·ive \əˈmyüziv, -siv\ *adj* **:** tending to amuse or to tickle the fancy or excite mirth **:** AMUSING — **amus·ive·ly** *adv*

amy *var of* AMI

am·y·da \ˈamədə\ [NL, fr. ²a- + *-myda* (fr. Gk *mydos* dampness)] *syn of* TRIONYX

amyd·ri·caine \əˈmidrə,kān\ *n* -s [²a- + *mydriatic* + *-caine* (as in *cocaine*)] **:** a local anesthetic $C_{16}H_{26}N_2O_2$ that is usu. administered in the form of its bitter crystalline hydrochloride and that unlike cocaine is not mydriatic

amy·e·lin·ic \ˌā,mīəˈlinik, ˌāˌm-\ *adj* [²a- + *myelinic*] **:** NONMEDULLATED — used of nerve fibers

amy·e·lon·ic \-ˈlänik\ *adj* [²a- + *myelonic*] **1 :** lacking a spinal cord **2 :** lacking marrow

amygdal- *or* **amygdalo-** *comb form* [L *amygdal-*, fr. *amygdala*] **1 :** almond **:** almond family ⟨*amygdal*ase⟩ ⟨*amygdali*ferous⟩ **2** [NL, fr. *amygdala*] **a :** tonsil ⟨*amygdalo*tomy⟩ **b :** tonsillar and ⟨*amygdalo*-uvular⟩

amyg·da·la \əˈmigdələ\ *n, pl* **amygda·lae** \-ˌlē, -ˌī\ [NL, fr. L, almond — more at ALMOND] **1 :** one of the tonsils of the pharynx **2 :** one of the rounded prominences of the lower surface of the lateral hemispheres of the cerebellum **3 :** AMYGDALOID NUCLEUS

amyg·da·la·ce·ae \ə,≈≈ˈlāsē,ē\ *n pl, cap* [NL, fr. *Amygdalus*, type genus + *-aceae*] *in some esp. former classifications* **:** a family of trees and shrubs comprising those plants of the family Rosaceae (as the plum, peach, and almond) that have a single pistil with united carpels and a characteristic drupe — **amyg·da·la·ceous** \-ˈ≈≈shəs\ *adj*

amyg·da·lin \əˈ≈≈lən\ *n* -s [*amygdal-* + *-in*] **:** a white crystalline glucoside $C_6H_5CH(CN)OC_{12}H_{21}O_{10}$ that occurs in the kernels of the bitter almond and certain other plants of the genus *Prunus* and that on complete hydrolysis yields benzaldehyde, hydrogen cyanide, and glucose

amyg·da·line \ˈ", -ˌlīn\ *adj* [L *amygdalinus* of almonds, fr. Gk *amygdalinos*, fr. *amygdalē* almond + *-inos* -ine — more at ALMOND] **1 :** of, relating to, or resembling an almond **2 :** of or relating to a tonsil

amyg·da·loid \-ˌlȯid\ *n* -s [*amygdal-* + *-oid*] **:** an igneous and usu. volcanic rock orig. containing small cavities produced before solidification by expansion of steam and afterward filled with deposits of different minerals (as chalcedony, quartz, calcite, or zeolites)

amyg·da·loi·dal \ə,≈≈ˈlȯidᵊl\ *also* **amyg·da·loid** \əˈ≈≈,≈\ *adj* **:** having the characteristics of amygdaloid

amygdaloid nucleus *n* **:** an almond-shaped mass of gray matter in the anterior extremity of the temporal lobe

amyg·da·lus \əˈ≈≈ləs\ *n, cap* [NL, fr. LL, almond tree, fr. Gk *amygdalos*] *in some esp. former classifications* **:** a small genus of Asiatic trees and shrubs including those plants of the genus *Prunus* (as the peach and almond) that have numerous stamens, an often velvety exocarp, and a deeply grooved stone

amyg·dule \əˈmig,d(y)üi, ˈamig-\ *also* **amyg·dale** \-,dā(ə)l\ *n* -s [irreg. fr. *amygdal-* + *-ule*] **:** one of the rounded nodules occurring in an amygdaloid

am·yl \ˈamᵊl *also* ˈām-\ *n* -s [blend of *amyl-* and *-yl*] **1 :** PENTYL **2 :** either of two mixtures of pentyl radicals: **a :** the radicals derived from amyl alcohol (sense 2a) — called also *isoamyl* **b :** the radicals derived from amyl alcohol (sense 2b)

amyl- *or* **amylo-** *comb form* [LL *amyl-*, fr. L *amylum*, fr. Gk *amylon*, fr. neut. of *amylos* not ground at the mill, fr. *a-* ²a- + *mylos, mylē* mill — more at MEAL] **:** starch ⟨*amyl*ase⟩ ⟨*amyl*emia⟩ ⟨*amylo*meter⟩

am·y·la·ceous \ˌaməˈlāshəs\ *adj* [*amyl-* + *-aceous*] **:** of, relating to, or having the characteristics of starch **:** STARCHY

amyl acetate *n* **:** an acetic ester $CH_3COOC_5H_{11}$ of pentyl alcohol: as **a :** the ester obtained from a commercial amyl alcohol as a water-insoluble liquid with a strong fruity odor and used as a solvent (as for cellulose nitrate lacquers) and in artificial fruit essences and perfumes — called also *banana oil, pear oil* **b :** ISOAMYL ACETATE

amyl alcohol *n* **1 :** PENTYL ALCOHOL **2 :** either of two commercially produced mixtures of pentyl alcohols used chiefly in making esters and as solvents: **a :** the optically active mixture consisting of isopentyl alcohol and active amyl alcohol obtained from fusel oil — called also *fermentation amyl alcohol, isoamyl alcohol* **b :** the optically inactive mixture consisting of seven pentyl alcohols obtained by chlorination of pentanes from natural-gas gasoline or petroleum followed by hydrolysis — called also *synthetic amyl alcohol*

am·y·lase \ˈamə,lās\ *n* -s [ISV *amyl-* + *-ase*] **1 :** any of the enzymes that accelerate the hydrolysis of starch and glycogen or their intermediate products of hydrolysis — called also *diastase* **2 a :** an enzyme that is found esp. in malt, in certain molds and bacteria, and in saliva and pancreatic juice and that acts chiefly on starch and glycogen with the formation of dextrins as intermediate products and sugars as final products — called also *alpha-amylase, dextrinogenic enzyme* **b :** an enzyme that is found esp. in grains, malt, and vegetables (as sweet potatoes) and that acts on starch, glycogen, and some dextrins with the formation of maltose — called also *beta-amylase, saccharifying enzyme*

am·yl·ene \-,lēn\ *n* -s [ISV *amyl* + *-ene*] **:** any of several low-boiling olefin hydrocarbons C_5H_{10}: as **a :** a flammable liquid $CH_3CH{=}C(CH_3)_2$ obtained from fusel oil by dehydration; 2-methyl-2-butene — called also *beta-isoamylene, trimethylethylene* **b :** PENTENE

amylene hydrate *n* **:** TERTIARY AMYL ALCOHOL — used chiefly in pharmacy

amyl ether *n* **:** any symmetrical ether $(C_5H_{11})_2O$ derived from amyl alcohol; *esp* **:** a mixture of normal pentyl ether and isopentyl ether obtained as a by-product in the preparation of amyl alcohol (sense 2a) and used as a solvent

amyl·i·dene \ˈamilə,dēn, aˈ-\ *n* -s [ISV *amyl* + *-idene*] **:** PENTYLIDENE

am·y·lif·er·ous \ˌaməˈlif(ə)rəs\ *adj* [*amyl-* + *-i-* + *-ferous*] **:** bearing or producing starch

amyl nitrate *n* **:** the nitric ester $C_5H_{11}ONO_2$ of commercial amyl alcohol used as a liquid additive to diesel fuel for raising the cetane number

amyl nitrite *n* **:** a pale yellow pungent flammable liquid ester $C_5H_{11}ONO$ of commercial amyl alcohol and nitrous acid that is used chiefly in medicine as a vasodilator esp. in angina pectoris — called also *isoamyl nitrite*

am·y·lo \ˈamə,lō\ *adj* [*amyl-*] **:** of or relating to starch

amylo- — see AMYL-

am·y·lo·dex·trin \ˌ≈≈(ˌ)≈ˈdekstrən\ *n* -s [ISV *amyl-* + *dextrin*] **:** an intermediate product of the hydrolysis of starch that is soluble in water and gives a blue color with iodine — compare LIMIT DEXTRIN

am·y·lo·gram \ˈamələ,gram\ *n* -s [*amyl-* + *-gram*] **:** the record made by an amylograph

am·y·lo·graph \-,graf\ *n* -s [*amyl-* + *-graph*] **:** an instrument that measures and records the gelatinization temperature and viscosity of pastes of starch and flour

¹am·y·loid \ˈamə,lȯid\ *or* **amy·loi·dal** \ˌ≈≈ˈ≈dᵊl\ *adj* [ISV *amyl-* + *-oid, -oidal*] **1 :** like or containing amylum **:** like starch **2 :** relating to or marked by the production of amyloid (sense 3)

²amyloid \ˈ"\ *n* -s **1 :** a nonnitrogenous starchy food **:** a starchlike substance **2 a :** a gelatinous hydrated cellulose produced by the action of moderately concentrated sulfuric acid on cellulose (as in making parchment paper) **b :** a gummy substance found in the seeds of the nasturtium and other plants **3 :** a waxy translucent substance related to protein and deposited in some animal organs under abnormal conditions probably a disturbance of protein metabolism

amyloid degeneration *n* **:** AMYLOIDOSIS

am·y·loi·do·sis \ˌamə,lȯiˈdōsəs\ *n, pl* **amyloido·ses** \-ō,sēz\ [NL, fr. ISV ²*amyloid* + NL *-osis*] **:** a condition characterized by the deposition of amyloid in organs or tissues of the animal body either as a primary disease of unknown cause or secondary to chronic disease (as tuberculosis or osteomyelitis)

am·y·lo·leu·cite \ˌamə(ˌ)lōˈlü,sīt\ *n* -s [ISV *amyl-* + *leucite*] **:** LEUCOPLAST

am·y·lol·y·sis \ˌaməˈläləsəs\ *n, pl* **amyloly·ses** \-ə,sēz\ [NL, fr. *amyl-* + *-lysis*] **:** the conversion of starch into soluble products (as dextrins and sugars) esp. by the action of enzymes — **amy·lo·lyt·ic** \ˌamə(ˌ)lōˈlid·ik\ *adj*

am·y·lo·pec·tin \ˌamə(ˌ)lōˈpektən\ *n* -s [ISV *amyl-* + *pectin*] **:** a component of starch that comprises about four fifths of cornstarch, that is separated from amylose by precipitation of the amylose from a dilute starch solution, and that is characterized by the lack of tendency of its aqueous solutions to gel, by the red color it gives with iodine, and by its high molecular weight and branched structure made up in some cases of as many as 2000 glucose units

am·y·lo·plast \ˈ≈≈(ˌ)≈,plast\ *also* **am·y·lo·plas·tid** \ˌ≈≈(ˌ)≈ˈplastəd\ *or* **am·y·lo·plas·tide** \ˈ", -ˌstīd\ *n* -s [ISV *amyl-* + *-plast, plastid, plastide*] **:** a starch-forming leucoplast

am·y·lop·sin \ˌaməˈläpsən, ˌ≈≈ˈ≈≈\ *n* -s [*amyl-* + *-psin* (as in *trypsin, pepsin*)] **:** the amylase of the pancreatic juice

am·y·lose \ˈamə,lōs\ *n* -s [ISV *amyl-* + *-ose*] **1 :** any of various polysaccharides (as starch or cellulose) **2 :** a component of starch that comprises about one fifth of cornstarch, that is separated from amylopectin by precipitation from a dilute starch solution with butyl or amyl alcohol, and that is characterized by the tendency of its aqueous solutions to set to a stiff gel at room temperature, by the blue color it gives with iodine, and by its moderately high molecular weight and linear structure made up of hundreds of glucose units **3 :** any of various compounds (as dextrin) $(C_6H_{10}O_5)_x$ obtained by the hydrolysis of starch

amyl salicylate *n* **:** the salicylic ester $C_6H_4(OH)COOC_5H_{11}$ of commercial amyl alcohol that is a liquid of lasting pleasant odor used chiefly as an ingredient of perfumes and soaps — called also *isoamyl salicylate*

am·y·lum \ˈaməlәm\ *n* -s [L — more at AMYL-] **:** STARCH

amylum body *n* **:** a starch grain

amylum center *n* **:** PYRENOID

amylum grain *n* **:** a laminated starch body formed by the leucoplasts

amylum star *n* **:** a star-shaped propagative body densely filled with starch and formed about the lower nodes of certain stoneworts

amyn·o·don \əˈminə,dän\ *n, cap* [NL, fr. Gk *amynein* to ward off + NL *-odon*] **:** a genus of Eocene perissodactyls related to the rhinoceros but hornless and having the canines developed into curved tusks — **amyn·o·dont** \-nt\ *n or adj*

amy·o·to·nia \ˌā,mīəˈtōnēə\ *n* -s [NL, fr. ²a- + *myotonia*] **:** deficiency of muscle tone

amyotonia con·gen·i·ta \-kənˈjenəd·ə\ *n* [NL, congenital amyotonia] **:** a congenital disease of infants characterized by flaccidity of the skeletal muscles resulting in an inability to move freely or maintain upright posture

amy·o·tro·phia \ˌā,mīəˈtrōfēə\ *or* **amy·ot·ro·phy** \-ˈīˈä·trəfē\ *n, pl* **amyotrophias** *or* **amyotrophies** [NL *amyotrophia*, fr. ²a- + *my-* + *-trophia*] **:** atrophy of a muscle

amy·o·troph·ic \ˌā,mīəˈträfik, ˌāˌm-, -ōf-\ *adj* **:** relating to or marked by amyotrophy

am·y·ral·dism \ˌaməˈral,dizəm\ *n* -s *usu cap* [Moses *Amyraldus* (Moïse Amyraut) †1664 Fr. Protestant theologian + E *-ism*] **:** a liberal form of Calvinism distinguished by its doctrines of universal atonement and universal salvation

am·y·rin \ˈamərən\ *n* -s [ISV *amyr-* (fr. NL *Amyris*) + *-in*] **:** either of two crystalline isomeric triterpenoid alcohols $C_{30}H_{49}OH$ found esp. in Manila elemi and dandelion roots and distinguished as alpha-amyrin and beta-amyrin

am·y·ris \ˈamərəs\ *n, cap* [NL, prob. irreg. fr. Gk *amyros* not watery, prob. fr. *a-* (akin to *hama* together) + *myron* sweet oil, unguent; fr. the oily quality of the plant] **:** a genus of tropical American trees and shrubs (family Rutaceae) with compound leaves and white flowers

amyris oil *n* **:** an oil distilled from the wood of a torchwood (*Amyris balsamifera*) and used in perfumery

amy·root \ˈāmē,-\ *n* -s [origin unknown] **:** INDIAN HEMP 1

Am·y·tal \ˈamə,tȯl *also* -al\ *trademark* — used for amobarbital

¹an \ən, *after some consonants often* ᵊn, *esp emphatic or hesitating or after a pause* (ˈ)an; *see usage note below*\ *indefinite article* [ME, fr. OE *ān* one — more at ONE] **:** ²A — in standard speech and writing used (1) invariably before words beginning with a vowel letter and sound ⟨*an* oak⟩; (2) invariably before *h*-initial words in which the *h* is silent when the words are pronounced in isolation ⟨*an* honor⟩ ⟨*an* herb⟩ (*but a herb* with speakers who pronounce the *h* in *herb*); (3) frequently before *h*-initial words which have an initial \h\ sound when pronounced in isolation, whose first syllable has weaker than primary and usually weaker than secondary stress, and which may or may not in pronunciation have an \h\ sound after the \n\ ⟨*an* historian⟩ ⟨*an* hypertrophied heart⟩; (4) sometimes (less often now than formerly and most often in England) before words like *union* and *European*, whose initial letter is a vowel and whose initial sounds are \yü\ or \yu̇\ or in some dialects \iü\ or \iu̇\

²an *or* **an'** *conj* [ME *an*, alter. of *and*] **1** *the spelling without "d" is substand but the pronunciation without* d *is not* — *see* ¹AND\ *substand* **:** AND ⟨he would sit ~ let on to be learning —Wright Morris⟩ **2** \(ˈ)an, ən, ᵊn\ *archaic* **:** IF ⟨~ thou dalliest, then I am thy foe —Ben Jonson⟩

an- — see ²A-

¹-an *or* **-ian** *also* **-ean** *n suffix* -s [*-an* & *-ian* fr. ME *-an, -ian, -ien*, fr. OF & L; OF *-ien*, fr. L *-ianus*, fr. *-i-* + *-anus*, fr. *-anus*, adj. suffix; *-ean* fr. such words as *Mediterranean, European*] **1 :** one that is of or belonging to ⟨American⟩ ⟨Bostonian⟩ **2 :** one skilled in or specializing in — esp. in derivatives from nouns ending in *-ic* or *-ics*, in the latter case with loss of *-s* ⟨dialectician⟩ ⟨phonetician⟩ ⟨statistician⟩ **3 :** one belonging to a (specified) zoological group ⟨crustacean⟩ ⟨mammalian⟩ ⟨crocodilian⟩

²-an *or* **-ian** *also* **-ean** *adj suffix* [*-an* & *-ian* fr. ME *-an, -ian, -ien*, fr. OF & L; OF *-ien*, fr. L *-ianus*, fr. *-i-* + *-anus; -ean* fr. such words as *Mediterranean, European*] **1 :** of or belonging to ⟨American⟩ ⟨Floridian⟩ ⟨Wesleyan⟩ **2 :** characteristic of **:** resembling ⟨Mozartean⟩ ⟨Proustian⟩ ⟨Shavian⟩ **3 :** of or belonging to a (specified) geologic period, epoch, or series ⟨Cambrian⟩

³-an *n suffix* -s [ISV *-an, -ane*, alter. of *-ene, -ine*, & *-one*] **1 :** unsaturated carbon compound ⟨tolan $C_6H_5C{\equiv}CC_6H_5$⟩ ⟨urethan⟩ — esp. in names of heterocyclic compounds ⟨furan⟩ ⟨alloxan⟩; compare -ANE **2 a :** anhydride representing a polymer of a carbohydrate — usu. replacing final *-ose* of the carbohydrate name ⟨xylan⟩ ⟨dextran⟩, less often replacing final *-e* ⟨pentosan⟩ **b :** intramolecular anhydride of a carbohydrate — replacing final *-e* of the carbohydrate name ⟨β-glucosan⟩

an *abbr* **1** [L *anno*] in the year; [L *annum; annus*] year **2** anonymous

AN *abbr* **1** *often not cap* above-named **2** army-navy **3** arrival notice

¹ana \ˈanə\ *adv* [ME, fr. ML, fr. Gk, to the amount of, at the rate of, lit., up] **:** of each an equal quantity — used in prescriptions ⟨wine and honey ~ two ounces⟩; usu. written ĀĀ or Ā

²ana \ˈanə, ˈä-,ˈā- *also* ˈā-\ *n, pl* **ana** *or* **anas** [*-ana*] **1 a :** a collection of the memorable sayings or table talk of a person ⟨his chatty autobiographic sketches are a notable ~⟩ **b :** a collection of anecdotes or interesting or curious information about a person or a place ⟨the ~ of the graduate dormitories⟩ **2 :** an item in or suitable for a collection of table talk or anecdotes ⟨a secretarial corps was employed to examine and list the ~ —S.H.Adams⟩

³ana *var of* ANNA

ana- *or* **an-** *prefix* [ML, fr. L *ana-* & LL *an-*, fr. Gk *ana-, an-*, fr. *ana* up, on — more at ON] **1 :** up **:** upward ⟨*an*ode⟩ ⟨*Ana*cardium⟩ **2 :** back **:** backward ⟨*an*anym⟩ **3 :** again **:** anew ⟨*ana*genesis⟩ **4** *usu* **ana-**, *chem, usu ital* **:** having substituents in positions 1 and 5 in two fused 6-membered rings (as in naphthalene, quinoline)

-ana \ˈanə, ˈä-,ˈā- *also* ˈā-\ *or* **-i·ana** \ēˈ-\ *n pl suffix* [NL, collected quotations from, fr. L, neut. pl. of *-anus* -an & *-ianus* -ian] **:** collected items of information esp. anecdotal or bibliographical concerning ⟨Americana⟩ ⟨Johnsoniana⟩ ⟨Burnsiana⟩ ⟨collegiana⟩ — chiefly in derivatives from personal names and place names

an'a \əˈnȧ, -nō\ [by alter.] *Scot* **:** and all

an·a·bae·na \ˌanəˈbēnə\ *n* [NL, fr. Gk *anabainein* to go up, shoot up, fr. *ana-* + *bainein* to go — more at COME] **1** *cap* **:** a genus of freshwater blue-green algae (family Nostocaceae) having cells in beadlike filaments and often contaminating reservoirs **2** -s **:** an alga of the genus *Anabaena*

an·a·ban·tid \ˌanəˈbantəd\ *adj* [NL *Anabantidae*, fr. *Anabant-*, *Anabas*, type genus + *-idae*] **:** of or relating to the genus *Anabas* or the family Anabantidae

an·a·bap·tism \ˌanəˈ-\ *n* -s [NL *anabaptismus*, fr. LGk *anabaptismos* rebaptism, fr. *anabaptizein* + Gk *-ismos* -ism] **1** *usu cap* **:** the doctrine or practices of the Anabaptists **2 :** REBAPTISM; *esp* **:** the baptism of adults formerly baptized as infants practiced by Anabaptists

¹an·a·bap·tist \ˌanəˈ-\ *n* -s *usu cap* [NL *anabaptista*, fr. LGk *anabaptizein* + L *-ista* -ist] **:** an adherent of a religious sect which arose in Zurich in 1523, which advocated the restoration of a primitive Christianity, and which specif. held that infant baptism was scripturally unwarranted, that there should be no union of church and state, and that Christians should renounce private possessions and practice a religious communalism

²anabaptist \ˈ"\ *or* **an·a·bap·tis·tic** \ˌ≈≈≈ˈ≈≈\ *adj, usu cap* **:** of, relating to, or characteristic of the Anabaptists or their doctrine and practice — **an·a·bap·tis·ti·cal·ly** \-tək(ə)lē\ *adv*

an·a·bap·tize \ˌ≈≈ˈ≈, ˌ≈≈ˈ≈ˌ≈, ˈ≈≈ˌ≈ˌ≈\ *vt* -ED/-ING/-S [LGk *anabaptizein* to rebaptize, fr. *ana-* + *baptizein* to baptize — more at BAPTIZE] **:** to baptize over again **:** RECHRISTEN

an·a·bas \ˈanəbəs, -ˌbas\ *n, cap* [NL, fr. Gk, aorist part. of *anabainein*] **:** a genus (the type of a family Anabantidae) comprising small perchlike freshwater spiny-finned fishes of southeastern Asia and Africa and often being placed with a few related fishes in a separate suborder of the Percomorphi — see CLIMBING PERCH

anab·a·sine \əˈnabə,sēn, -sən\ *n* -s [NL *Anabasis* (genus name of *Anabasis aphylla*) + E *-ine*] **:** an insecticidal liquid alkaloid $(C_5H_4N)\ C_5H_{10}N$ related to nicotine and found in tobacco and in a nearly leafless subshrub (*Anabasis aphylla*) of southeastern Russia; 2-(3-pyridyl)-piperidine

anab·a·sis \əˈnabəsəs\ *n* [Gk, act of going up, expedition up from the coast into Asia, increasing period of a disease, fr. *anabainein* to go up, to go up from the coast — more at ANABAENA] **1** *pl* **anaba·ses** \-ə,sēz\ **:** a going or marching up **:** ADVANCE ⟨~ or slump —Wallace Stevens⟩; *esp* **:** a military advance ⟨the Russian ~ and katabasis of Napoleon —Thomas De Quincey⟩ **2** [NL, fr. L, a plant, fr. Gk] *cap* **:** a genus of small woody or herbaceous perennials (family Chenopodiaceae) native to the Caucasus and nearby regions and having jointed stems and opposite fleshy often reduced leaves **3** [so called fr. the fact that a famous retreat of Greek mercenaries from the Euphrates to the Black sea is described in the *Anabasis*, historical work by Xenophon †*ab*355 B.C. Greek historian & essayist] *pl* **anabases :** a difficult and dangerous military retreat

anab·a·ta \əˈnabəd·ə\ *n* -s [NGk, fr. ML *anabata, anabala*, prob. modif. of Gk *anabolē* cloak, fr. *anaballein* to put on (also, to lift or throw up, delay), fr. *ana-* + *ballein* to throw — more at DEVIL] **:** a hooded cope worn esp. in outdoor processions in the Eastern Church

ana·bath·mos \ˌanəˈbathˌmȯs\ *n, pl* **anabath·moi** \-ˈmē\ [MGk, fr. Gk. flight of steps, "song of steps", fr. *anabainein* to go up — more at ANABAENA] **:** one of the gradual psalms in the Eastern Church

an·a·bat·ic \ˌanəˈbad·ik\ *adj* [LGk *anabatikos* (influenced in meaning by Gk *anabasis* going up, ascension), fr. Gk, skilled in mounting, fr. *anabainein* to go up, mount, ascend] **:** upward-moving ⟨an ~ wind⟩

an·a·be·ro·ga \ˌanəbəˈrōgə\ *n* -s [Malay *anabiroga*, fr. *anak* child + (*ayam*) *biroga* jungle fowl] **:** a root disease and collar rot of the areca palm attributed to a pore fungus (*Fomes lucidus*)

an·a·bib·a·zon \ˌanəˈbibə,zän\ *n* -s [Gk *anabibazōn*, pres. part. act. of *anabibazein* to raise, mount, fr. *ana-* + *bibazein* to lift, fr. *bainein* to go — more at COME] **:** the ascending node of the moon's orbit with the ecliptic

ana·bi·o·sis \ˌanə,bīˈōsəs\ *n, pl* **anabio·ses** \-ō,sēz\ [NL, fr. Gk *anabiōsis* return to life, fr. *anabioun* to return to life, fr. *ana-* + *bioun* to live, fr. *bios* life — more at QUICK] **:** a state of suspended animation induced in organisms (as rotifers) by desiccation and ending on return of moisture in resumption of normal life

ana·bi·ot·ic \ˌanə,bīˈäd·ik\ *adj* [fr. NL *anabiosis*, after such pairs as E *narcosis: narcotic*] **:** of or related to anabiosis

an·a·blep·id \ˌanəˈblepəd\ *adj* [NL *Anablepidae*, family of fishes, fr. *Anableps*, type genus + *-idae*] **:** of or belonging to *Anableps* or to the four-eyed fishes

an·a·bleps \ˈanə,bleps\ *n, cap* [NL, fr. Gk *anableps-*, stem of *anablepein* to look up, fr. *ana-* + *blepein* to look] **:** a genus of tropical American saltwater and freshwater fishes comprising the four-eyed fishes, being closely related to the topminnows but constituting a separate family, and having the eyes divided into an upper and lower division by the growth of two processes of the iris across the pupil and a band of conjunctiva across the cornea, the upper part serving to see objects in the air, the lower part to see objects under water

an·a·bo·hit·site \ˌanəˈbōˈhit,sīt\ *n* -s [F *anabohitsite*, fr. *Anabohitsy*, Madagascar, its locality + F *-ite*] **:** a variety of olivine-pyroxenite rock containing hypersthene, hornblende, and about 30 percent of ilmenite and magnetite

an·a·bol·ic \ˌanəˈbälik\ *adj* [ISV *ana-* + *-bolic* (as in *metabolic*)] **1 :** relating to or characterized by anabolism **2 :** of, relating to, or exhibiting anaboly

anab·o·lism \əˈnabə,lizəm, aˈ-\ *n* -s [ISV *ana-* + *-bolism* (as in *metabolism*)] **:** constructive metabolism — opposed to *catabolism*

anab·o·lite \-,līt\ *also* **anab·o·lin** \-lən\ *n* -s [*anabolism* + *-ite* or *-in*] **:** a product of an anabolic process — **anab·o·lit·ic** \əˌnabəˈlid·ik\ *adj*

anab·o·lize \əˈ≈≈,līz\ *vi* -ED/-ING/-S [fr. *anabolism*, after such pairs as E *hypnotism: hypnotize*] **:** to perform anabolism

anab·o·ly \əˈnabəlē\ *n* -ES [modif. of Gk *anabolē* anything thrown up, prelude, act of delaying, ascent, fr. *anaballein* to throw or lift up, delay, put on — more at ANABATA] **:** evolutionary differentiation involving the addition of new terminal stages to the ancestral pattern of morphogenesis

an·a·branch \ˈanə,branch\ *n* -ES [*ana-* + *branch*] **:** a diverging branch of a river which reenters the main stream or which loses itself in sandy soil

ana·ca·hui·ta \ˌanəkəˈwēd·ə\ *or* **ana·ca·hui·te** \ˈ", -ē,tā\ *n* -s [Sp, fr. Nahuatl *amacuahuitl* — more at AMATE] **:** a small aromatic tree (*Cordia boissieri*) found in Texas and Mexico, having yellowish white flowers, and used medicinally

an·a·can·thine \ˌanəˈkan(t)thən, -n,thīn\ *adj* [NL *Anacanthini*] **:** of or belonging to the Anacanthini

an·acan·thi·ni \ˌanəˈkan(t)thə,nī\ *n pl, cap* [NL, fr. Gk *anakanthos* without a spine, without thorns (fr. *an-* + *akanthos* spine, thorn) + NL *-ini*] **:** an order or suborder of teleost fishes having all the rays of the median and pelvic fins soft and jointed, the pelvic fins thoracic or jugular in position, and the air bladder, when present, usu. without a duct, and comprising the codfishes, hakes, and their related forms and formerly sometimes including the flounders and soles — **an·acan·thous** \ˌ≈≈ˈ≈thəs\ *adj*

an·a·car·di·a·ce·ae \ˌanə,kärdēˈāsē,ē\ *n pl, cap* [NL, fr. *Anacardium*, type genus + *-aceae*] **:** a widely distributed family of trees and shrubs (order Sapindales) comprising the sumacs, cashews, and related plants and having compound leaves, small regular dioecious or perfect flowers, and drupaceous fruits — **an·a·car·di·a·ceous** \ˌ≈≈ˌ≈≈ˈāshəs\ *adj*

an·a·car·dic acid \ˌanəˈkärdik-\ *n* [ISV *anacardic* (fr. NL *Anacardium* + ISV *-ic*) + *acid*; orig. formed as G *anakardsäure*] **:** a brown crystalline vesicant phenolic acid found as the principal constituent of cashew nutshell liquid, held to consist of a mixture of unsaturated derivatives of salicylic acid, and converted to cardanol by decarboxylation

an·a·car·di·um \ˌanəˈkärdēəm\ *n* [NL, fr. *ana-* + Gk *kardia* heart + NL *-ium*; fr. the heartlike shape of the top of the fruit stem] **1** *cap* **:** a small genus of tropical American trees (the type of the family Anacardiaceae) having kidney-shaped fruit borne at the apex of a fleshy receptacle — see CASHEW **2** *pl* **anacar·dia** \-dēə\ : a plant of the genus *Anacardium*

anacardium nut *n* : CASHEW NUT

anach·a·ris \ə'nakərəs\ [NL, fr. *ana-* + Gk *charis* grace] *syn of* ELODEA

an·a·chop·ter·is \,anə'käptərəs\ *n, cap* [NL, fr. LGk *anachoē* eruption + NL *-pteris*] : a genus (the type of the family Anachopteridaceae) of fossil ferns characterized by pinnately divided leaves having all leaflets in the same plane and sporangia on the flattened margins of the ultimate segments

anachoret *var of* ANCHORITE

an·a·chro·ma·sis \,anə'krōməsəs\ *n, pl* **anachroma·ses** \-ə,sēz\ [NL, fr. *ana-* + *chrom-* + connective *-a-* + *-sis*] : the mitotic nuclear transformations leading to formation of the metaphase plate — compare KATACHROMASIS

an·a·chron·ic \¦anə¦kränik\ *or* **an·a·chron·i·cal** \-nəkəl\ *or* **anach·ro·nous** \ə'nakrənəs\ *adj* [*anachronism* + *-ic, -ical,* or *-ous*] : ANACHRONISTIC — **an·a·chron·i·cal·ly** \¦anə¦kränək(ə)lē\ *adv* — **anach·ro·nous·ly** \ə'nakrənəslē\ *adv*

anach·ro·nism \ə'nakrə,nizəm\ *n* -s [prob. fr. MGk *anachronismos,* fr. *anachronizesthai* to be an anachronism, fr. LGk *anachronizein* to be late, fr. Gk *ana-* + *chronizein* to spend time, continue, linger, fr. *chronos* time + *-izein* -ize] **1** : an error in chronology; *esp* : a chronological misplacing of persons, events, objects, or customs in regard to each other ⟨two of the rulers mentioned . . . are otherwise unknown but there is no glaring ~ in the names that can be tested —F.M.Stenton⟩ **2** : a person or a thing that is chronologically out of place; *esp* : one that belongs to a former age and is incongruous if found in the present ⟨born a thousand years . . . too late and an ~ in this culminating century of civilization —Jack London⟩ ⟨felt . . . that an absolute monarchy was an ~ for a civilized country —Kenneth Lawson⟩

anach·ro·nis·tic \ə,nakrə¦nistik, -ēk\ *also* **anach·ro·nis·ti·cal** \-təkəl, -ēk-\ *adj* [*anachronism* + *-istic, -istical*] : characterized by or involving anachronism : chronologically out of place — **anach·ro·nis·ti·cal·ly** \-tək(ə)lē, -ēk-, -li\ *adv*

an·acid·i·ty \¦anə'sidəd·ē\ *n* -ES [*an-* + *acidity*] : ACHLORHYDRIA

anac·la·sis \ə'nakləsəs\ *n, pl* **anacla·ses** \-ə,sēz\ [NL, fr. Gk *anaklasis* act of bending back, reflection, fr. *anaklan* to bend back, reflect (fr. *ana-* + *klan* to break) + *-sis* — more at GLADIATOR] : an exchange of place between a short syllable and a preceding long one that is frequent in ionic rhythms

an·a·clas·tic \¦anə¦klastik\ *adj* [Gk *anaklastos* bent back, reflected (fr. *anaklan* to bend back, reflect, fr. *ana-* + *klan* to break, deflect) + E *-ic*] **1** : capable of springing back ⟨the bottom of an ~ glass springs out or in when air is forced into or drawn from the glass⟩ **2** : relating to or constituting anaclasis

an·a·cli·nal \¦anə¦klīnᵊl\ *adj* [*ana-* + *-clinal*] : descending in a direction opposite to that of the dip of the strata ⟨an ~ river⟩ — opposed to *cataclinal*

an·a·clit·ic \¦anə¦klid·ik\ *adj* [Gk *anaklitos* for reclining (fr. *anaklinein* to lean upon, fr. *ana-* + *klinein* to lean) + E *-ic* — more at LEAN] : characterized by dependence: **a** : characterized by dependence of libido on a nonsexual instinct (such as the hunger drive) **b** : of, relating to, or characterized by the direction of libido toward a pregenital love object (as the mother)

an·a·co·lu·thia \,anəkə'lüthēə\ *n* -s [NL, alter. of LL *anacoluthon*] : ANACOLUTHON

an·a·co·lu·thic \¦anəkə¦lüthik\ *adj* [*anacoluthon* + *-ic*] : of or relating to anacoluthon — **an·a·co·lu·thi·cal·ly** \-thək(ə)lē\ *adv*

an·a·co·lu·thon \,anəkə'lü,thän\ *n, pl* **anacolu·tha** \-,thə\ *or* **anacoluthons** [LL, fr. LGk *anakolouthon* inconsistency in logic, fr. Gk, neut. of *anakolouthos* inconsistent, fr. *an-* + *akolouthos* following — more at AKOLUTHIA] : syntactical inconsistency or incoherence within a sentence; *esp* : the shift from one construction, left incomplete, to another, sometimes for rhetorical effect (as "you really ought — well, do it your own way")

an·a·con·da \,anə'kändə\ *n* -s [prob. modif. of Singhalese *henakandayā* green whip snake (*Dryophis mycterizans*), understood to be a name for the python, lit., lightning stem, fr. *hena* lightning + *kanda* stem (prob. fr. Skt, bulbous root, perh. of Dravidian origin; akin to Tamil *kaṇṭa* bulbous root, Tulu *kaṇde*) + *-yā* (nominal suffix)] **1** *archaic* : a python of Ceylon **2** : a large arboreal snake (*Eunectes murinus*) of the boa family of tropical So. America having a double row of large black spots along the back, being semiaquatic in its habits, capturing its food by lying in wait in trees at watering places chiefly at night for animals that come to drink, and being powerful enough to crush in its coils a small deer though subsisting mostly on smaller animals and waterfowl **3** *broadly* : any large constricting snake

¹anac·re·on·tic \ə,nakrē¦äntik\ *n* -s *sometimes cap* [L *Anacreonticus,* adj.] **1** : a poem in imitation of or in the manner of Anacreon : a drinking song or light lyric **2** *in Greek prosody* : a verse having the cadence analyzed as two ionics a minore with anaclasis and supplement or as iambic dimeter catalectic with anapestic opening

²anacreontic \"\ *adj, usu cap* [L *Anacreonticus,* fr. *Anacreont-, Anacreon* †ab488B.C. Greek poet noted for his gay songs of love and drinking (fr. Gk *Anakreont-, Anakreōn*) + L *-icus* -ic] **1 a** : of or relating to Anacreon **b** : like the poetry of Anacreon in structure, style, or theme **2** : relating to the praise of love and wine : gay, convivial, or amatory in tone or theme ⟨Adrian waxed now and then *Anacreontic* in his compliments —George Meredith⟩ — **anacreontically** *adv*

an·a·cri·sis \,anə'krīsəs\ *n, pl* **anacri·ses** \-ī,sēz\ [Gk *anakrisis* examination of the parties concerned in a lawsuit fr. *anakrinein* to examine, interrogate, fr. *ana-* + *krinein* to choose, determine, separate — more at CRISIS] : an investigation of truth in a civil law case in which the interrogation and inquiry are often accompanied by torture

an·a·crog·y·nae \,anə'kräjə,nē\ *n pl, cap* [NL, fr. *an-* + *Acrogynae*] *in some classifications* : a group of liverworts including all the thalloid members of the Jungermanniaceae — compare ACROGYNAE

an·a·crog·y·nous \¦anə¦kräjənəs\ *adj* [ISV *an-* + *acrogynous*] **1** : having the archegonia arising below the apex of the stem and not involving the apical cell **2** : having indeterminate growth of the gametophyte

anac·ro·my·o·di·an \¦a,nakrə,mī¦ōdēən, a¦n-\ *adj* [*ana-* + *acromyodian*] : having the intrinsic syringeal muscles inserted on the dorsal ends of the bronchial semirings

an·a·cru·sis \,anə'krüsəs\ *n, pl* **anacru·ses** \-ü,sēz\ [NL & Gk; NL *anacrusis,* fr. Gk *anakrousis* act of pushing back, beginning of a song, fr. *anakrouein* to push back, begin a song (fr. *ana-* + *krouein* to strike, push) + *-sis* — more at RUE] **1** *also* **an·a·krou·sis** \-'krüsəs\ : one or more syllables at the beginning of a line of poetry that are regarded as preliminary to and not a part of the metrical pattern of that line **2** *also* **anakrousis** : UPBEAT; *specif* : one or more notes or tones preceding the first downbeat of a musical phrase — called also *pickup* **3** : a preparatory gesture leading into an accented or climactic dancing movement

an·a·cul·ture \'anə,-\ *n* -s [ISV *ana-* + *culture;* prob. orig. formed in F] : a mixed bacterial culture; *esp* : a culture containing various strains of pathogenic bacteria used in the preparation of autogenous vaccines

an·a·cy·clus \,anə'sikləs, -īk-\ *n, cap* [NL, fr. *ana-* + Gk *kyklos* ring, circle] : a small genus of annual herbs (family Compositae) of the Mediterranean region having dissected leaves and white or yellow flowers

an·a·dem \'anə,dem, -,dəm\ *n* -s [L *anadema,* fr. Gk *anadēma,* fr. *anadein* to wreathe, fr. *ana-* + *dein* to bind — more at DIADEM] : a wreath for the head : GARLAND, CHAPLET

an·a·di·plo·sis \,anədə'plōsəs\ *n, pl* **anadiplo·ses** \-ō,sēz\ [LL, fr. Gk *anadiplōsis,* lit., repetition, fr. *anadiploun* to double, reduplicate (fr. *ana-* + *diploun* to double) + *-sis* — more at DIPLOMA] : repetition of a prominent word, usu. the last in a phrase, clause, sentence, or verse, at the beginning of the next phrase, clause, sentence, or verse (as "rely on his honor — honor such as his?")

anad·ro·mous \ə'nadrəməs, a'n-\ *adj* [Gk *anadromos* running upward, fr. *anadramein* to run upward, fr. *ana-* + *dramein* to run — more at TREAD] **1** *of fish* : ascending rivers from the sea at certain seasons for breeding ⟨salmon and shad are ~⟩ — compare CATADROMOUS **2** *also* **an·a·drom·ic** \¦anə¦drämik\ [*anadromic* fr. Gk *anadromos* + E *-ic*] : having the first set of veins arising on the upper side of the midrib toward the tip — used of the pinnae of a fern frond

anaemia *var of* ANEMIA

an·aer·obe \'anə,rōb; (')a'na(a)(ə),rōb, -ne(ə),-, -nāə,-\ *n* -s [ISV *an-* + *aerobe;* orig. formed as F *anaérobie*] : an organism (as a bacterium) that does not require air or free oxygen for maintaining life— compare AEROBE; FACULTATIVE, OBLIGATE

¹an·aer·o·bi·an \¦anə¦rōbēən; ¦a,na(a)(ə)¦r-, ¦a,ne(ə)¦r-, ¦a,nāə¦r-\ *adj* [*anaerobe* + *-ian*] : ANAEROBIC

²anaerobian \"\ *n* -s : ANAEROBE

an·aer·o·bic \¦anə¦rōbik; ¦a,na(a)(ə)¦r-, ¦a,ne(ə)¦r-, ¦a,nāə¦r-\ *also* **an·er·o·bic** \¦anə¦r-\ *adj* [*anaerobe* + *-ic*] **1** : living or active in the absence of free oxygen **2** : relating to or induced by anaerobes ⟨~ fermentation⟩ — **an·aer·o·bi·cal·ly** \-bək(ə)lē\ *adv*

an·aer·o·bi·on \,=='=bē,än, ,=,=(=)=b-, -ēən\ *n, pl* **anaero·bia** \-bēə\ [NL, fr. ISV *anaerobe* + NL *-ion*] : ANAEROBE

an·aer·o·bi·ont \-bē,änt, ¦anə,rō'bī,ä-, ¦a,na(a)rō'bī,ä-\ *n* -s [blend of *anaerobe* and *-biont*] : ANAEROBE

an·aer·o·bi·o·sis \,anə,rō,bī'ōsəs, ¦a,na(a)rō,b-\ *n, pl* **anaerobio·ses** \-ō,sēz\ [NL, fr. *an-* + *aer-* + *biosis*] : life in the absence of air or free oxygen

an·aer·o·bi·ot·ic \¦anə,rō,bī¦äd·ik, ¦a,na(a)rō,b-\ *adj* : ANAEROBIC — **an·aer·o·bi·ot·i·cal·ly** \-ək(ə)lē\ *adv*

an·aer·o·bi·um \,anə'rōbēəm, ,a,na(a)'r-\ *n, pl* **anaero·bia** \-ēə\ [NL, fr. ISV *anaerobe* + NL *-ium*] : ANAEROBE

an·aes·the·si·a *var of* ANESTHESIA

anaesthetic *var of* ANESTHETIC

anag *abbr* anagram

an·a·ga·lac·tic \¦anəgə¦laktik\ *adj* [Gk *ana-* (alter. of *an-*) + E *galactic*] : EXTRAGALACTIC

an·a·gal·lis \,anə'galəs\ *n* [NL, fr. L, a plant (prob. pimpernel or chickweed), fr. Gk, pimpernel] **1** *cap* : a genus of 15 species of chiefly Old World herbs (family Primulaceae) having mostly opposite leaves and small axillary 5-parted rotate flowers — see PIMPERNEL 2 **2** -ES : a plant of the genus *Anagallis*

an·a·gen·e·sis \,anə'-\ *n, pl* **anageneses** [NL, fr. *ana-* + L *genesis*] : REPRODUCTION, REGENERATION ⟨~ of tissue⟩ —**an·a·ge·net·ic** \¦anə=¦==\ *adj*

an·a·gig·nos·kom·e·na \,anə,gignə'skämənə\ *n pl* [NGk *anagignōskomena,* fr. Gk, neut. pl. of pres. pass. part. of *anagignōskein,* to know, acknowledge, read, fr. *ana-* + *gignōskein* to know, recognize — more at KNOW] *Eastern Church* : the Old Testament Apocrypha

an·a·glyph \'anə,glif\ *n* -s [LL *anaglyphus* wrought in low relief, embossed, fr. Gk *anaglyphos,* fr. *anaglyphein* to emboss, fr. *ana-* + *glyphein* to carve — more at CLEAVE] **1** : any sculptured, chased, or embossed ornament worked in low relief (as a cameo) **2** : a stereoscopic motion or still picture in which the right component of a composite image usu. red in color is superposed upon the left component in a contrasting color (as bluish green) to produce a three-dimensional effect when viewed through correspondingly colored filters in the form of spectacles

an·a·glyph·ic \¦==¦=ik\ *also* **an·a·glyph·i·cal** \-əkəl\ *adj* : relating to anaglyphs or anaglyphy — opposed to *diaglyphic*

an·a·glyph·ics \,anə'glifiks\ *n pl but sing in constr* [*anaglyph* + *-ics*] : ANAGLYPHY 1

an·a·glyph·o·scope \-fə,skōp\ *n* -s [ISV *anaglyph* + *-o-* + *-scope*] : a pair of spectacles for viewing an anaglyph

anag·ly·phy \ə'nagləfē, 'anə,glifē\ *n* -ES [*anaglyph* + *-y*] **1** : art of carving, chasing, or embossing in relief **2** : work done in relief

an·a·glyp·tic \¦anə¦gliptik\ *also* **an·a·glyp·ti·cal** \-təkəl\ *adj* [LL *anaglypticus,* fr. L *anaglyptus* wrought in bas-relief (fr. Gk *anaglyptos, anaglyphos*) + *-icus* -ic — more at ANAGLYPH] : ANAGLYPHIC

an·a·glyp·tics \,=='=tiks\ *n pl but sing in constr* : ANAGLYPHY

an·a·glyp·to·graph \-ptə,graf\ *n* -s [Gk *anaglyptos* + E *-graph*] : an instrument for the mechanical execution from any embossed object of an engraving giving the proper appearance of relief — **an·a·glyp·tog·ra·phy** \-,glip'tägrəfē\ *n* -ES

an·a·glyp·ton \,anə'glip,tän, -,tən\ *n* -s [Gk, neut. of *anaglyptos*] : ANAGLYPH

an·ag·no·ri·sis \,a,nag'nōrəsəs\ *n, pl* **anagnori·ses** \-ə,sēz\ [Gk *anagnōrisis,* fr. *anagnōrizein* to recognize, fr. *ana-* + *gnōrizein* to make known, become acquainted (fr. *gnōrimos* well-known) + *-sis* — more at GNORIMOSCHEMA] : RECOGNITION 1g

an·ag·nost \'a,nag,näst\ *or* **an·ag·nos·tes** \,=,='näs,tēz\ *n, pl* **anagnosts** \-sts\ *or* **anagnos·tae** \-,stī, -ē\ [LGk *anagnōstēs,* fr. Gk, reader, slave trained to read, secretary, fr. *anagignōskein* to read, fr. *ana-* + *gignōskein* to know — more at KNOW] : a cleric in the first of the minor orders of the Eastern Church who reads lessons aloud from the Epistles or the Old Testament in the liturgy

an·a·go·ge \'anə,gōjē *sometimes* -gäjē *or* ,=='==\ *or* **an·a·go·gy** \'==,==\ *n, pl* **anagoges** *or* **anagogies** [LL, fr. LGk *anagōgē,* fr. *anagein* to spiritualize, fr. Gk, to lead up, bring up, lift up, fr. *ana-* + *agein* to lead, drive — more at AGENT] : literary interpretation that seeks to extract from language a spiritual significance; *specif* : exegesis that stresses what is taken to be a secret heavenly meaning in scriptural texts or a hidden reference to a future life in heaven

an·a·gog·ic \,anə¦gäjik, -ēk\ *or* **an·a·gog·i·cal** \-jəkəl\ *adj* [*anagogic* fr. ME, fr. ML *anagogicus,* fr. LL *anagoge* + L *-icus* -ic; *anagogical* fr. *anagogic* + *-al*] **1** : of, exemplifying, or based on anagoge; *specif* : having a spiritual meaning or a sense referring to the heavenly life ⟨the final or ~ meaning that transformed the symbolic object into a spiritual truth —Malcolm Cowley⟩ **2 a** : relating to or arising from the striving of inner psychic forces toward progressive or lofty ideals ⟨an ~ image⟩ **b** : relating to the psychotherapeutic interpretation of dreams and with emphasis on anagogic striving ⟨~ methods⟩ — **an·a·gog·i·cal·ly** \-jək(ə)lē, -ēk-, -li\ *adv*

¹an·a·gram \'anə,gram, -aa(ə)m\ *n* -s [prob. fr. MF *anagramme,* fr. NL *anagramma,* modif. of Gk *anagrammatismos,* fr. *anagrammatizein* to transpose letters, fr. *ana-* + *grammat-, gramma* letter + *-izein* -ize — more at GRAMMAR] **1 a** : the change of one word or phrase into another by the transposition of its letters **b** : the word or phrase made by transposing the letters of another word or phrase ⟨*rebate* is an ~ of *beater*⟩ **2** *obs* : MUTATION, TRANSPOSITION **3 anagrams** *pl but sing in constr* : a game in which words are formed by rearranging the letters of other words or by arranging letters taken at random (as printed blocks from a stock)

²anagram \"\ *vt* **anagrammed; anagrammed; anagramming; anagrams 1** : ANAGRAMMATIZE **2** : to rearrange (the letters of a text) in order to discover a hidden message **3** : to attack (a transposition cipher) by moving a set of letters presumed to have related encipherments (as successive letters presumed to be from the same column of the transposition rectangle, or the letters from the same position in a number of messages) into position next to another such set, forming a tentative set of plaintext polygraphs, a promising juxtaposition being recognized by the formation of many common polygraphs and a probably wrong juxtaposition by the formation of improbable polygraphs

an·a·gram·mat·ic \¦anəgrə¦mad·ik, -atik, -ēk\ *or* **an·a·gram·mat·i·cal** \-ad·əkəl, -atək-, -ēk-\ *adj* [*anagram* + *-matic, -matical* (as in *grammatic, grammatical*)] : of, relating to, containing, or making an anagram — **an·a·gram·mat·i·cal·ly** \-ək(ə)lē, -ēk-, -li\ *adv*

an·a·gram·ma·tism \,anə'gramə,tizəm\ *n* -s [F *anagrammatisme,* fr. Gk *anagrammatismos* — more at ANAGRAM] : the formation of anagrams

an·a·gram·ma·tist \-məd·əst, -mətə-\ *n* -s : a maker of anagrams

an·a·gram·ma·tize *or* **anagrammatise** \-mə,tīz\ *vt* -ED/-ING/-S [Gk *anagrammatizein* — more at ANAGRAM] : to transpose (as letters in a word) so as to form an anagram

ana·gua \ə'nägwə\ *n* -s [MexSp *anacua, anagua*] : a tree (*Ehretia elliptica*) of Mexico and southern Texas that is sometimes planted for shade

an·a·gy·ris \,anə'jīrəs\ *n, cap* [NL, fr. Gk, alter. of *anagyros* bean trefoil, fr. *ana-* + *gyros* ring] : a small genus of shrubs (family Leguminosae) of the Mediterranean region having trifoliolate leaves, yellow flowers, and narrow compound pods — see BEAN TREFOIL 1

ana·hau *also* **ana·hao** \ä'nä,haù\ *n* -s [Tag & Hiligaynon *anahaw*] : a tall Philippine palm (*Livistona rotundifolia*) yielding a valuable wood used for golf clubs, a fiber used for bowstrings, and leaves used for thatching and for hats and fans

an·a·heim disease \'anə,hīm-\ *n, usu cap A* [fr. *Anaheim,* Calif.] : PIERCE'S DISEASE

an·a·kim \'anə,kim\ *n pl, usu cap* [Heb *'ănāqīm,* pl. of *'ănāq*] : aboriginal giants reported in the Old Testament to have inhabited southern Palestine before the Hebrews entered the land and virtually annihilated them

anakrousis *var of* ANACRUSIS

¹anal \'ānᵊl\ *adj* [*anus* + *-al*] **1** : of, relating to, or situated near the anus **2 a** : of, relating to, or characterized by the phase of psychosexual development following the oral stage and during which a child is largely concerned with the products of alimentation, and his parents with his toilet training **b** : of, relating to, or characterized by those personality traits that are believed to develop from overconcentration on this phase of maturation — see ANAL CHARACTER — **anal·i·ty** \ā'naləd·ē\ *n* -ES — **anal·ly** \-ᵊlē, -ᵊli\ *adv*

²anal \"\ *n* -s : an anal structure (as an anal fin or plate)

anal *abbr* **1** analogous; analogy **2** analysis; analytic

ana·la·bos \ä'näla,bòs\ *n* -ES [LGk, fr. Gk *ana-* + *-labos* (fr. *lambanein* to take) — more at LATCH] : a cloak decorated with crosses worn by monks in the Eastern Church

anal angle *n* : the angle between the outer and inner margins of an insect's wing

anal area *n* : the posterior part of usu. the hind wing of many insects that bears the anal veins

anal canal *n* : the terminal section of the rectum

anal character *n* : a personality type characterized by a predilection for anal eroticism or by its symbolic manifestations (as excessive neatness, acquisitiveness, miserliness, self-discipline, pedantry, and obstinacy)

anal·cime \ə'nal,sēm, -īm\ *n* -s [F, fr. Gk *analkimos* weak, fr. *an-* + *alkimos* strong, fr. *alkē* strength, defense] : a white or slightly colored zeolite $NaAlSi_2O_6.H_2O$ occurring in certain igneous rocks massive or in isometric crystals

analcime basalt *n* : a variety of basalt consisting of augite, olivine, magnetite, analcite, and usu. a little feldspar

anal·ci·mite \ə'nalsə,mīt\ *n* -s [It, fr. *analcimo* analcime (fr. F *analcime*) + *-ite*] **1** : a rock occurring in the Cyclades that orig. was probably a nephelite-syenite but is now altered and contains over 50 percent of analcime **2** : ANALCITITE

anal·cite \ə'nal,sīt\ *n* -s [alter. (influenced by *-ite*) of *analcime*] : ANALCIME

anal·ci·tite \-sə,tīt\ *n* -s [*analcite* + *-ite*] : olivine-free analcime basalt — called also *analcimite*

an·a·lects \'anᵊl,ek(t)s\ *also* **an·a·lec·ta** \,anə'lektə\ *n pl* [L *analecta,* fr. Gk *analekta,* neut. pl. of *analektos* select, choice, fr. *analegein* to collect, fr. *ana-* + *legein* to gather, speak — more at LEGEND] **1** : leftovers from a feast ⟨I delight in the *analecta* . . . of the preceding day's dinner —Sir Walter Scott⟩ **2** : selected miscellaneous written passages : literary gleanings : COLLECTANEA ⟨the *Analects* of Confucius⟩

an·a·lem·ma \,anə'lemə\ *n, pl* **analemmas** \-məz\ *or* **ana·lemma·ta** \-məd·ə\ [L, sundial on a pedestal, showing latitude and meridian, fr. Gk *analēmma* sundial, construction, support, fr. *analambanein* to take up, fr. *ana-* + *lambanein* to take — more at LATCH] **1** : an archaic astronomical instrument of wood or brass on which an orthographic projection of the sphere is made with a movable horizon or cursor **2** : a graduated scale shaped like a figure 8 and showing the sun's declination and the equation of time for each day of the year usu. constituting part of a sundial and often shown on terrestrial globes

an·a·lep·sis \,anə'lepsəs\ *n, pl* **analep·ses** \-(,)sēz\ [LGk *analēpsis,* fr. Gk, act of taking up, fr. *ana-* + *lēpsis* act of taking, fr. *lambanein* to take — more at LATCH] *Eastern Church* : the feast of Christ's ascension into heaven

¹an·a·lep·tic \¦anə¦leptik\ *adj* [Gk *analēptikos* restorative, fr. (assumed) *analēptos* (verbal of *analambanein* to take up, regain, fr. *ana-* + *lambanein* to take, seize) + *-ikos* -ic] : of, relating to, or acting as an analeptic

²analeptic \"\ *n* -s : a restorative agent; *esp* : a drug that acts as a stimulant on the central nervous system

anal erotic *adj* : marked by or related to anal eroticism

anal eroticism *or* **anal erotism** *n* : the experiencing of pleasurable sensations or sexual excitement associated with or symbolic of stimulation of the anus — compare ANAL CHARACTER

anal fin *n, in fishes* : a median unpaired fin on the lower posterior part of the body behind the vent and sometimes confluent with the caudal fin—see FISH illustration

an·al·ge·sia \,anᵊl'jēzēə, -ēzhə\ *n* -s [NL, fr. Gk *analgēsia,* fr. *an-* + *algēsis* sense of pain + *-ia*] : insensibility to pain without loss of consciousness

¹an·al·ge·sic \¦anᵊl¦jēzik, -ēs- *sometimes* -es-\ *adj* [ISV *analges-* (fr. NL *analgesia*) + *-ic*] : relating to, characterized by, or producing analgesia

²analgesic \"\ *n* -s : an agent for producing analgesia

analgesic balm *n* : an ointment containing methyl salicylate and menthol used as a rubefacient

¹an·al·ge·sid \ə'naljəsəd, ,anᵊl'jesəd\ *adj* [NL *Analgesidae*] : of or relating to the Analgesidae

²analgesid \"\ *n* -s : a mite of the family Analgesidae

an·al·ges·i·dae \,anᵊl'jesədē\ *n pl, cap* [NL, fr. *Analges,* type genus (fr. Gk *analgēs* painless, fr. *an-* + *-algēs,* fr. *algos* pain) + *-idae*] : a large family of small soft-bodied blind mites that live on birds esp. on the feathers

an·al·get·ic \¦anᵊl¦jed·ik\ *n or adj* [Gk *analgētos* without pain (fr. *an-* + (assumed) *algētos,* verbal of *algein* to suffer pain) + E *-ic* — more at ALGESIA] : ANALGESIC

anal gland *n* : any of numerous glands, occurring solitary or in pairs or groups, near the anus and sometimes opening into the rectum: as **a** : either of the paired glands of a skunk that produce an offensive secretion **b** : a gland in mollusks of the genus *Murex* that secretes a purple substance used in dyeing **c** : INK SAC

an·al·lan·to·ic \¦a,nalən¦tōik, -a,lan-, a¦na-\ *adj* [*an-* + *allantoic*] : not having or not developing an allantois

an·al·lan·toi·dea \¦a,nalən'tòidēə, -na,lan'-\ *n pl, cap* [NL, fr. *an-* + *allantois* + *-idea*] : the division of Vertebrata, including amphibians, fishes, and cyclostomes, in which no allantois, or at most a rudimentary one, is developed — compare AMNIOTA — **an·al·lan·toi·de·an** \-¦tòidēən\ *adj or n*

an·al·lo·bar \(')a'nalə,bär\ *n* -s [*ana-* + *allobar*] : an area over which barometric pressure has increased

anal margin *n* : the inner margin of an insect's wing

anal membrane *n* : the membranous partition occluding the fetal anus : PROCTODAEUM

analog *var of* ANALOGUE

anal·o·gate \ə'nalə,gāt, -,gət\ *n* -s [*analogue* + *-ate*] : a thing, term, or concept analogized : ANALOGUE ⟨the First Being is the prime ~⟩

an·a·log·i·cal \,anᵊl¦äjəkəl, -ēk-\ *also* **an·a·log·ic** \¦==¦=ik, -ēk\ *adj* [*analogy* + *-ical, -ic*] **1 a** : of, relating to, or based on analogy ⟨~ reasoning⟩ **b** : expressing or implying an analogy ⟨when a country which has . . . colonies is termed the mother country the expression is *analogical* —J.S.Mill⟩ **2** *archaic* : having analogy : ANALOGOUS — **an·a·log·i·cal·ly** \-jək(ə)lē, -ēk-, -li\ *adv*

ana·lo·gi·on \¦änə¦lō'yē,ōn, -ə'lō,yōn\ *n, pl* **analo·gia** \-,lō'yē-,ä-, -'lō,yä\ *or* **analogions** [Gk *analogeion* reading desk, fr. *analegesthai* to read through, fr. *ana-* + *legein* to gather, speak — more at LEGEND] : a stand on which choir singers in the Eastern Church keep their books

anal·o·gism \ə'nalə,jizəm\ *n* -s [*analogy* + *-ism*] : reasoning by analogy ⟨investigates the philosophy of Aristotle and . . . rejects it as ~ —L.A.Foley⟩

anal·o·gist \-jəst\ *n* -s [*analogy* + *-ist*] **1** : one who searches for or reasons from analogies **2** : an adherent of the view held by certain Greek grammarians of the 2d century B.C. that language is based on correspondence between word and idea — opposed to *anomalist*

anal·o·gize \-,jīz\ *vb* -ED/-ING/-S [*analogy* + *-ize*] *vi* **1** : to make use of analogy esp. in reasoning ⟨~s effectively in debate⟩ **2** : to show analogy ~ *vt* : to make analogous : bring into analogy ⟨~s nature to the crafts —Austin Warren⟩

anal·o·gon \-ˌgän, -ˌgən\ *n, pl* **analo·ga** \-ˌgə\ [Gk, fr. neut. of *analogos*] : ANALOGUE

anal·o·gous \əˈnaləgəs\ *adj* [L, fr. Gk *analogos* according to a due ratio, proportionate, fr. *ana-* + *logos* ratio, thought, word, fr. *legein* to gather, speak — more at LEGEND] **1** : showing an analogy or a likeness permitting one to draw an analogy : susceptible of comparison either in general or in some specific detail ⟨the doctrines of symbolism were . . . ~ to the doctrines of romanticism —Edmund Wilson⟩ **2 a** : having a similar function but differing in structure and origin ⟨the wings of a bird and those of an airplane are ~⟩ **b** *in commerce* : showing similar characteristics (as bulk, weight, or value) ⟨~ articles likewise given special handling⟩ **3** *of colors* : having a close relationship with respect to hue **syn** see LIKE

analogously *adv* : by or according to analogy

analogous pole *n* : the pole of a crystal that becomes positively electrified when the crystal is heated

an·a·logue \ˈanᵊlˌȯg *also* -ˌäg\ *also* **an·a·log** \"\ *n* -S [F *analogue*, fr. *analogue* analogous, fr. Gk *analogos*] **1** : anything that is analogous or similar to something else : PARALLEL ⟨he would relate the poem to earlier sources and ~*s* —C.W. Shumaker⟩ **2 a** : an organ similar in function to an organ of another animal or plant but different in structure and origin ⟨the gill of a fish is the ~ of the lung of a cat⟩ — distinguished from *homologue* **b** : a species in one group corresponding in some particular characters with a member of another group **c** : a species or genus in one country that is closely related to a species of the same genus or a genus of the same group in another country **3** : a previous weather chart that in its main features resembles the current weather chart

analogue computer *n* : a type of calculating machine that operates with numbers represented by directly measurable quantities (as voltages, resistances, or rotations)

anal·o·gy \əˈnaləjē, -ji\ *n* -ES [prob. fr. Gk *analogia* mathematical proportion, correspondence, fr. *analogos* proportionate + *-ia* -y] **1 a** : mathematical proportion or ratios (as in a statement of the form $a \times b = c \times d$ where the values of *a*, *b*, and *c* are given, so that *d* may be calculated) **b** : a proposition or a statement that embodies such an analogy **2 a** : similarity of ratios or of properties **b** : inference that if two or more things agree with one another in one or more respects they will prob. agree in yet other respects ⟨scholasticism distinguished between *analogies* of proportionality, *analogies* by attribution, and *analogies* by metaphor⟩ **3** : resemblance in some particulars between things otherwise unlike : SIMILARITY, CORRESPONDENCE, PARALLELISM ⟨mathematicians have . . . appealed to the arts in order to find some ~ to their own work —Havelock Ellis⟩ ⟨enameled bowls . . . show *analogies* . . . with late twelfth century English illumination —O. Elfrida Saunders⟩ **4 a** : ANALOGUE **b** : a figure of speech embodying an extended or elaborate comparison between two things or situations : SIMILITUDE **5** : correspondence between the members of pairs or sets of linguistic forms that is taken as a basis for the creation of another form (as *reindeers*, plural of *reindeer*, created on the basis of such pairs as *bear, bears* or *dog, dogs; cows*, plural of *cow*, replacing earlier *kine* and *kye*, on the basis of such pairs as *bough, boughs; glided*, past tense of *glide*, replacing earlier *glode* and *glid*, on the basis of such pairs as *guide, guided; a deck of cigarettes*, standing in the same synonymous relationship to *a pack of cigarettes* as *a deck of cards* does to *a pack of cards*) **6** [F *analogie*, fr. Gk *analogia*] : correspondence in function between organs or parts of different structure and origin — distinguished from *homology*

analogy test *n* : a reasoning test requiring a person examined to supply a final term in a proportion (as to supply *darkness* in the proportion *day: light:: night: . . .*)

an·al·pha·bet \(ˈ)aˈnalfəˌbet *also* -ˌbət\ *n* -S [Gk *analphabētos* not knowing the alphabet, fr. *an-* + *alphabētos* alphabet — more at ALPHABET] : one who cannot read : ILLITERATE

¹an·al·pha·bet·ic \ˌaˌnalfəˈbed·ik, aˌn-\ *adj* [*analphabet* + *-ic*] **1** : ILLITERATE **2** [*an-* + *alphabetic*] : not alphabetic; *specif, of a system of phonetic transcription* : representing each sound by a set of three symbols indicating respectively the articulating organs, place of articulation, and size and form of aperture

²analphabetic \"\ *n* -S : one who cannot read : ILLITERATE ⟨these . . . humble ~*s* . . . have left us no record —Norman Douglas⟩

an·al·pha·bet·ism \(ˈ)aˈnal-\ *n* -S : an analphabetic phonetic system

anal pit *n* : the posterior terminal depression of the primitive streak of the embryo

anal plate *n* **1 a** : one of the posterior plates of the plastron of a turtle **b** : the large scale in front of the anus of most snakes **2** : the fused plate of early embryonic ectoderm and endoderm through which the anus later ruptures

anal proleg *n* : either of the pair of false legs occurring on the 10th abdominal segment of caterpillars

anals *pl of* ANAL

anal sadism *n* : a level of personality development characterized by preoccupation with pleasant sensations arising from fecal retention or by its symbolic manifestations (as power and cruelty) — compare ANAL CHARACTER

anal–sadistic \ˌ==ˈ=ˌ==\ *adj* : relating to anal sadism

anal sphincter *n* : either of two sphincters controlling the closing of the vertebrate anus: **a** : an outer sphincter of striated muscle extending from the coccyx to the central tendinous part of the perineum and surrounding the anus immediately beneath the skin — called also *external anal sphincter* **b** : an inner sphincter formed by thickening of the circular smooth muscle of the rectum — called also *internal anal sphincter*

anal vein *n* : one of the three posterior veins of the wing of a primitive insect

anal·y·sand \əˈnaləˌsand, -ˌza-\ *n* -S [*analyse* + *-and* (as in *multiplicand*)] : one that is analyzed; *specif* : one who is undergoing psychoanalysis

anal·y·san·dum \ə,==ˈ=əm\ *n, pl* **analysan·da** \-ə\ [NL, fr. *analysis* + L *-andum* (gerundive suffix)] : something that is to be analyzed or defined

anal·y·sans \ə'==ˌsanz, -ˌza-\ *n, pl* **analysans** [NL, fr. *analysis* + L *-ans* (part. suffix)] : something that serves to analyze or define

¹an·a·lyse *chiefly Brit var of* ANALYZE

²analyse *n* -S [F, fr. Gk *analysis*] *obs* : ANALYSIS

anal·y·sis \əˈnaləsəs\ *n, pl* **analy·ses** \-əˌsēz\ [NL, fr. Gk, fr. *analyein* to dissolve (fr. *ana-* + *lyein* to loosen, dissolve) + *-sis* — more at LOSE] **1** : separation or breaking up of a whole into its fundamental elements or component parts ⟨his problem defied ~⟩ **2 a** : a detailed examination of anything complex (as a novel, an organization, a race) made in order to understand its nature or to determine its essential features : a thorough study ⟨the ~ . . . of the structure of a poem can be a form of literary criticism —James Thorpe⟩ **b** : the presentation, usu. in writing, of such an analysis ⟨each chapter of the book is an ~ of a well-known painting⟩ **3** : the use of function words (as prepositions, pronouns, and auxiliary verbs) instead of inflectional forms as a highly frequent and characteristic device in the structure of a language (as English *I have seen* contrasted with Latin *vidi* or English *of the room* tending to replace *the room's* or *does he know that?* replacing *knows he that?*) — contrasted with *synthesis* **4 a** : the separation of compound substances into their constituents by chemical processes **b** : the determination, which may or may not involve actual separation, of one or more ingredients of a substance either as to kind or amount; *also* : the tabulated result of such a determination — see GRAVIMETRIC ANALYSIS, PROXIMATE ANALYSIS, QUALITATIVE ANALYSIS, QUANTITATIVE ANALYSIS, ULTIMATE ANALYSIS **c** : a statement of the amount or percent of each functional ingredient present in a mixture (as a vitamin solution or an animal feed); *often* : a statement of the percentage of nitrogen expressed as N, phosphoric acid as P_2O_5, and potash as K_2O in a fertilizer — called also *fertilizer analysis, fertilizer grade* **5 a** : the practice of proving a mathematical proposition by assuming the result and reasoning back to the data or to already established principles **b** : the investigation of a problem by the methods of algebra **c** : any proof based on considerations of number and the theory of limits, as opposed to geometric intuition **d** : the differential and integral calculus **6 a** : the resolution of knowledge into its fundamental factors or original principles and the tracing or reduction of physical, phenomenal, or abstract entities to their source or elements **b** : the elucidation, clarification, and explication of expressions and statements through a determination of their meaning or logical use **7** : the process of ascertaining the name of a species in biology or its place in a system of classification by means of an analytical table or key **8** : PSYCHOANALYSIS **9** : BOWLING ANALYSIS — **in the final analysis** *or* **in the last analysis** : everything having been taken into consideration ⟨it is the individual who is responsible, *in the last analysis*, for all additions to culture —L.A.White⟩ ⟨the lower grades of glue, while they may give satisfactory results, may not always be the cheapest *in the final analysis* —*Bindery Glues*⟩

analysis si·tus \-ˈsīd·əs, -ˈsē-\ *n* [NL, analysis of situation] : TOPOLOGY 3

an·a·lyst \ˈanᵊləst\ *n* -S [prob. fr. *analyze*, after such pairs as E *Latinize: Latinist*] : a person who analyzes or who is skilled in analysis: as **a** : one whose occupation is the making of analyses of the chemical, physical, or other properties of a substance or product **b** : a columnist or commentator who specializes in interpreting social and political developments **c** : PSYCHOANALYST **d** : STATISTICIAN

¹an·a·lyt·ic \ˌanᵊlˈid·ik, -itik, -ēk\ *adj* [LL *analyticus*, fr. Gk *analytikos*, fr. (assumed) *analytos* (verbal of *analyein*) + *-ikos* -ic] **1** : of or relating to analysis or analytics; *esp* : separating or breaking up a whole or a compound into its component parts or constituent elements ⟨an ~ experiment⟩ ⟨~ reasoning⟩ **2** : skilled in or using analysis ⟨a keenly ~ man⟩ **3** *logic* : of or relating to a truth, a proposition, or a statement that is true in all possible worlds, that is true independently of any facts by reference to meanings alone, or that is logically true or definitionally reducible to logical truth **4** : characterized by analysis (sense 3) rather than inflection ⟨English is an ~ language⟩ — contrasted with *synthetic;* compare ISOLATING **5** : PSYCHOANALYTIC **6** : treated by the methods or represented by the symbolism of algebra or calculus ⟨~ statics⟩ — distinguished from *graphic*

²analytic \"\ *n* -S **1** : something that is analytic **2** : ANALYTICAL ENTRY

an·a·lyt·i·cal \-ə̇kəl, -ēk-\ *adj* [LL *analyticus* + E *-al*] **1** : ANALYTIC **2** *of cubist art* : involving the breakdown of a natural subject into component planes and geometric forms — **an·a·lyt·i·cal·ly** \-ə̇k(ə)lē, -ēk-, -lī\ *adv*

analytical balance *n* : a balance of precision used esp. in quantitative chemical analysis

analytical chemistry *n* : the branch of chemistry that deals with analysis

analytical entry *n* : an entry in a library catalog that locates a specific part of a more general work or collection (as the treatment of one specific subject in a book)

analytical jurisprudence *n* : the study and examination of law in terms of its logical structure

analytical note *n* : the information at an analytical entry that locates the source of that analytical entry

analytical table *n* : KEY 3c

4 2 3 4 1 5 6 6

analytical balance: *1* handle to move rider, *3*, on beam, *2; 4, 4* knife edges; *5* pointer; *6, 6* scalepans

analytic geometry *n* : a branch of mathematics that studies geometric properties by means of arithmetic and algebraic operations upon symbols defined in terms of a coordinate system — called also *coordinate geometry*

an·a·ly·tic·i·ty \ˌanᵊləˈtisəd·ē\ *n* -ES : the nature, character, or property of being analytic

analytic judgment *n, logic* : a judgment in which what is predicated is already implied in the subject of the predication — opposed to *synthetic judgment*

analytic mechanics *n* : theoretical mechanics esp. as treated by the methods of infinitesimal calculus

analytic psychology *n* **1** : the analysis and classification of mental data (as sensations and feelings) esp. by introspection — contrasted with *experimental psychology* **2** : a modification of psychoanalysis that adds to the concept of the personal unconscious by postulating a racial or collective unconscious, that objects to a narrowly sexual interpretation of libido, and that advocates that psychotherapy be conducted in terms of the patient's present-day conflicts and maladjustments rather than in terms of his early psychosexual development

an·a·lyt·ics \ˌanᵊlˈid·iks, -iti-\ *n pl but sing in constr* : the science of analysis esp. as a subdivision of logic

analytic trigonometry *n* : the branch of trigonometry that treats of the relations and properties of the trigonometrical functions

an·a·lyz·a·ble \ˈanᵊlˌīzəbəl\ *adj* : admitting or capable of being analyzed ⟨the . . . data into which he believed things are ~ —Ernest Nagel⟩

an·a·ly·za·tion \ˌanᵊləˈzāshən, -ˌīˈz-\ *n* -S : ANALYSIS

an·a·lyze \ˈanᵊlˌīz\ *vb* -ED/-ING/-S *see -ize in Explan Notes* [prob. irreg. fr. *analysis* + *-ize*] *vt* **1 a** : to ascertain the components of or separate into component parts : determine carefully the fundamental elements of (as by separation or isolation) for close scrutiny and examination of constituents or for accurate resolution of an overall structure or nature ⟨in the laboratory . . . we were required to ~ specimens —V.G. Heiser⟩ : subject to analysis **b** : to determine by mental discernment the nature, significance, and relationship of the various parts, elements, aspects, or qualities of (whatever is under consideration) ⟨Balzac . . . *analyzed* a society in which human existence was no longer possible —P.F.Drucker⟩ **2** : to weigh or study (various aspects, factors, or elements) in order to arrive at an answer, result, or solution ⟨constantly tries to ~ the motives for his own behavior —*Midwest Jour.*⟩ **3 a** : to determine one or more chemical ingredients of : examine by chemical analysis ⟨~ cast iron for phosphorus⟩ **b** : to show or yield on chemical analysis ⟨a slag that ~*s* 25 percent silica⟩ **4** : to divide (as a sentence) into parts and indicate the relation of each part to the other parts or to the whole **5** : to make an analytical entry for **6** : PSYCHOANALYZE ~ *vi* : to engage in analysis

syn RESOLVE, BREAK (*down*), DISSECT, ANATOMIZE: ANALYZE is likely to suggest ascertainment of components, sometimes by physical separation of those components, in the interests of determining a thing's nature or structure or the relationship of its parts ⟨he would make a plate or a fork or a bell, set it to ringing by a blow, and *analyze* the combination of musical notes which it emitted —K.K.Darrow⟩ It may suggest a scientific or objective attitude ⟨a cultured person, therefore, regards Nature with what might be called a Goethean, rather than a Newtonian, eye. He trains himself to see and to feel, rather than to *analyze* or to explain —J.C.Powys⟩ In more complex matters it involves ascertainment and individual scrutiny of aspects, traits, characteristics, qualities ⟨Gard was much struck. It never occurred to him to *analyze* the people that he loved —Mary Austin⟩ RESOLVE is likely to stress the fact of change of form, of metamorphosis, rather than necessarily indicating division into components, through some process or chain of effects ⟨one inseparable drop, crystallized beyond change . . ., nor *resolved* by any alchemy —W.H. Hudson⟩ ⟨labor measures the value not only of that part of price which *resolves* itself into labor, but of that which *resolves* itself into rent, and of that which *resolves* itself into profit —Adam Smith⟩ ⟨nothing but death was strong enough to shatter that inherited restraint and *resolve* it into tenderness —Ellen Glasgow⟩ BREAK (*down*) suggests classifying, itemizing, subgrouping, or other treatment of specific, individual component items for clarity or convenience ⟨an overall figure of 1,623,404. There was no attempt to *break* this *down* into dead, wounded, and missing —*N.Y.Times*⟩ DISSECT suggests laying bare parts, pieces, or relationships under consideration or actually severing them for individual scrutiny, as with a scalpel ⟨when I speak of *dissecting* atoms or *dissecting* matter, I refer to the fact that we can draw negative electricity out of every substance which there is —K.K.Darrow⟩ ⟨to understand Elizabethan drama it is necessary to study a dozen playwrights at once, to *dissect* with all care the complex growth —T.S.Eliot⟩ ⟨a complicated record must be *dissected*, the narratives of witnesses, more or less incoherent and unintelligible, must be analyzed —B.N.Cardozo⟩ ANATOMIZE differs from DISSECT chiefly in suggesting even more meticulous innate scrutiny, often of character traits ⟨his colleagues also are vividly described and *anatomized* — with a few brush strokes to show us their outsides, and a few scalpel thrusts to expose their insides —Robert Halsband⟩ ⟨Thoreau could *anatomize* the professional reformer as amusingly as Dickens —Laurence Stapleton⟩

an·a·lyz·er \-zə(r)\ *n* -S : one that analyzes: as **a** : the part of a polariscope that receives the light after polarization and exhibits the properties of light **b** : a combined ammeter, voltmeter, and ohmmeter designed for testing electronic equipment **c** : the part of an absorption or gas refrigeration apparatus in which the ammonia vapor escapes from the recently heated solution and passes on to be liquefied in the condensing coils — compare ABSORPTION SYSTEM

an·a·mir·ta \ˌanəˈmərd·ə\ *n, cap* [NL, prob. fr. *an-* + Skt *amṛta*, a plant (slightly different from *Anamirta*), fr. *amṛta* immortal] : a genus of East Indian woody vines (family Menispermaceae) having dioecious flowers and very numerous stamens — see COCCULUS INDICUS

an·a·mite \ˈanəˌmīt\ *n* -S [origin unknown] : TWINE 5

an·am·ne·sis \ˌanəmˈnēsə̇s, ˌaˌnam-\ *n, pl* **anamne·ses** \-ēˌsēz\ [NL, fr. Gk *anamnēsis*, fr. *anamimnēskein* to remind (fr. *ana-* + *mimnēskein* to remind) + *-sis* — more at MIND] **1** : a recalling to mind : REMINISCENCE ⟨in only one sense is *B.F.'s Daughter* a departure from the author's previous *anamneses* —John Woodburn⟩ **2** : information concerning a medical or psychiatric patient and his background for use in analyzing his condition — compare CATAMNESIS, FOLLOW-UP **3** *often cap* : the eucharistic prayer recalling the sacrifice of Christ and ending with the words "Do this in remembrance of me"

an·am·nes·tic \ˌ=(ˌ)=ˈnestik\ *adj* [Gk *anamnēstikos* easily recalled, fr. *anamnēstos* capable of being recalled (fr. *anamimnēskein*) + *-ikos* -ic] : of or relating to anamnesis — **an·am·nes·ti·cal·ly** \-tə̇k(ə)lē\ *adv*

anamnestic reaction *n* : renewed rapid production of an antibody following second or later contact with the provoking antigen or with related antigens

an·am·ni·on·ic \(ˌ)aˌnamnēˈänik, aˌn-\ *adj* [*an-* + *amnionic*] : not developing an amnion

an·am·ni·o·ta \-nēˈōd·ə\ *also* **an·am·nia** \(ˈ)aˈnamnēə\ *or* **an·am·ni·a·ta** \ˌaˌnamnēˈād·ə, aˌn-, -ˈäd·ə\ *or* **an·am·ni·o·na·ta** \-nēəˈnād·ə, -ád·ə\ *n pl, cap* [*Anamniota*, NL, fr. *an-* + *Amniota; Anamnia*, NL, fr. *an-* + *amnia*, pl. of *amnion; Anamniata, Anamnionata*, NL fr. *an-* + *amnion* + *-ata*] : vertebrates that develop no amnion regarded as a natural group — **an·am·ni·ote** \(ˈ)aˈnamnēˌōt\ *adj or n* — **an·am·ni·ot·ic** \ˌaˌnamnēˈäd·ik, aˌn-\ *adj*

an·a·mor·pha \ˌanəˈmȯrfə\ *n pl, cap* [NL, fr. *ana-* + *-morpha*] : a division (commonly considered a subclass) of Chilopoda comprising the centipedes whose number of body segments increases as the animals mature, the young hatching with 7 pairs of legs and the adults having 15 pairs — compare EPIMORPHA, NOTOSTIGMA, PLEUROSTIGMA

an·a·mor·phic \ˌ==ˈ=fik\ *adj* [*anamorphism* + *-ic*] **1** : characterized by progressive complexity or changing to a form of greater complexity : exhibiting or relating to anamorphosis **2** : producing or having different magnification of the image in each of two perpendicular meridians — used of an optical device or the image formed by one

anamorphic zone *n* : the zone within the earth in which simple mineralogical compounds become changed by silication, decarbonization, and deoxidation to more complex ones

an·a·mor·phism \ˌ==ˈ=ˌfizəm\ *n* -S [*ana-* + *-morphism*] **1** : ANAMORPHOSIS 2 **2** : the group of changes that rocks undergo in the anamorphic zone or the group of processes that effect the change — compare KATAMORPHISM, METAMORPHISM

an·a·mor·pho·scope \-ˌfəˌskōp\ *n* -S [*anamorphosis* + *-scope*] : an optical device consisting usu. of a cylindrical mirror or lens that restores to its normal proportions an image distorted by anamorphosis

an·a·mor·phose \-ˌfōz, -ōs\ *vt* -ED/-ING/-S [back-formation fr. *anamorphosis*] : to represent by anamorphosis

an·a·mor·phos·er \-ˌfōzər, -ˌfōs-, -fōs-\ *n* -S : an optical device used to form a sharply defined image having a different magnification in each of two perpendicular meridians, usu. vertical and horizontal

an·a·mor·pho·sis \ˌanəˈmȯrfəsə̇s *sometimes* -ˌmȯrˈfō-\ *n, pl* **anamorpho·ses** \-ˌsēz\ [MGk *anamorphōsis*, fr. LGk *anamorphoun* to transform (fr. Gk *ana-* + *morphoun* to form, fr. *morphē* shape) + Gk *-sis* — more at FORM] **1 a** : an image produced by a distorting optical system or by some other method that renders the image unrecognizable unless viewed by the proper restoring device **b** : the process of making such distorted images **2** : a gradually ascending progression or change of form from one type to another in the evolution of a group of animals or plants; *esp* : the acquisition in certain arthropods of additional body segments after hatching

an·a·mor·phote lens \ˌanəˈmȯrˌfōt-\ *n* [LGk *anamorphōtēs* transforming, fr. *anamorphoun* to transform] : a distorting lens used to produce anamorphosis — compare ANAMORPHOSCOPE

an·a·mor·phot·ic \-ˌmȯrˈfäd·ik\ *adj* [LGk *anamorphōtēs* transforming + E *-ic*] : ANAMORPHIC

anan \əˈnan\ *dial var of* ²ANON

ana·nas \ˈanəˌnas, əˈnanəs; *in sense 1* ˌanəˈnäs *or* ˈän-\ *n* [F or Sp; F, fr. Sp *ananás*, fr. Pg, modif. of Guarani *naná*] **1** *cap* : a small genus of tropical American plants (family Bromeliaceae) having basal sword-shaped leaves, terminal racemose flowers, and large syncarpous fruits — see PINEAPPLE **2** *also* **ana·na** \ˌanəˈnä, ˈän-\ *pl* **ananas** \-ˈnäz\ : any of several plants of the family Bromeliaceae: as **a** : PINEAPPLE **b** : PINGUIN

an·a·ni·as \ˌanəˈnīəs\ *n* -ES *usu cap* [after *Ananias*, an early Christian who, according to Acts 5:1–11, was struck dead for lying to the Apostle Peter] : LIAR

ana·ni·no \ˈanəˈnyēˌnō, -änə-\ *adj, usu cap* [fr. *Ananino*, town in the Kirov region, U.S.S.R., its type station] : of or belonging to a culture of east central Europe transitional between the Bronze and Iron ages and possibly ancestral to the culture of the early Volga Finns

an·an·ism \ˈanəˌnizəm, əˈnäˌn-\ *n* -S *usu cap* [*Anan* ben David, 8th cent. Jewish religious leader in Persia + E *-ism*] : Karaism as taught by Anan ben David

an·an·kas·tic *also* **an·an·cas·tic** \ˌanənˈkastik, ˌaˌnanˈ-, ˈaˌnanˈ-\ *adj* [Gk *anankastikos* compulsory, fr. *anankastos* forced (fr. *anankē*) + *-ikos* -ic] : of, relating to, or arising from compulsion esp. in an obsessive or compulsive neurosis

anan·ke \əˈnaŋ(ˌ)kē, -an,kē\ *n* -S *usu cap* [Gk *Anankē*, fr. *anankē* necessity; akin to OIr *écen* necessity, need, W *angen*, Corn & Bret *anken*] *Greek relig* : a personification of compelling necessity or ultimate fate to which even the gods must yield

an·a·nym \ˈanəˌnim\ *n* -S [*ana-* + *-nym* (as in *anonym*)] : a pseudonym consisting of the real name written backwards ⟨*Elberp* is the ~ of *Preble*⟩

anapa·ite \əˈnäpəˌīt\ *n* -S [G *anapait*, fr. *Anapa*, seaport on Black sea, U.S.S.R., its locality + G *-it* -ite] : a calcium ferrous iron hydrous phosphate occurring in pale-green transparent triclinic crystals and in columnar massive forms (hardness 3–4, sp. gr. 3.81)

an·a·pest *or* **an·a·paest** \ˈanəˌpest, *esp Brit* -ēst\ *n* -S [L *anapaestus*, fr. Gk *anapaistos*, lit., struck back (whence LGk *anapaistos* a dactyl reversed), fr. (assumed) *anapaiein* to strike back (whence LGk *anapaiein*), fr. *ana-* + *paiein* to strike] **1** : a metrical foot of three syllables the first two being unstressed and the last being stressed (as in Lord Byron's "and his cohorts were gleaming in purple and gold") or the first two being short and the last being long (as in classical prosody) : a trisyllabic rising cadence — symbol ⏑⏑– or oóó; compare DACTYL **2 a :** a verse written in anapests

¹an·a·pes·tic *or* **an·a·paes·tic** \¦==¦=tik\ *adj* [LL *anapaesticus*, fr. Gk *anapaistikos*, fr. *anapaistos* + *-ikos* -ic] **:** relating to or consisting of anapests — **an·a·pes·ti·cal·ly** \-tək(ə)lē\ *adv*

²anapestic *or* **anapaestic** *n* -s **:** an anapestic foot or line

anaph·a·lis \ə'nafələs\ *n, cap* [NL] **:** a genus of herbs (family Compositae) of north temperate regions having canescent foliage and small discoid heads of dioecious flowers — see PEARLY EVERLASTING

an·a·phase \'anə,fāz\ *n* -s [ISV *ana* + *phase*; orig. formed in G] **:** the stage of mitosis in which the chromosome halves move towards the poles of the spindle — **an·a·phas·ic** \¦==¦=zik\ *adj*

anaph·o·ra \ə'naf(ə)rə, *in sense 2* " *or* ,anəfə'rä\ *n* -s [LL, fr. LGk, fr. Gk, act of carrying up, ascent, offering, fr. *anapherein* to carry up, fr. *ana-* + *pherein* to carry — more at BEAR] **1 a :** repetition of a word or words at the beginning of two or more successive clauses or verses esp. for rhetorical or poetic effect **b :** use of a grammatical substitute to refer to a preceding word or group of words (as use of *does* in place of *dances* in "Mary dances better than June does") **2** [LGk, fr. Gk, offering] *often cap, Eastern Church* **a :** a eucharistic prayer of consecration in the divine liturgy **b :** the portion of the liturgy in which the eucharistic elements are offered as an oblation **c :** the eucharistic oblation — **anaph·o·ral** \ə'naf(ə)rəl\ *adj*

an·a·phor·ic \¦anə¦fórik, -är-\ *adj* [*anaphora* + *-ic*] **:** referring to a preceding word or group of words ⟨the ~ pronoun *one* in "I prefer a big bun to a little one"⟩ ⟨the ~ verb *do* in "act as we do"⟩ — **an·a·phor·i·cal·ly** \-rək(ə)lē\ *adv*

anaph·o·thrips \ə'nafə,thrips\ *n, cap* [NL] **:** a widely distributed genus of thrips including species destructive to many wild and cultivated grasses

an·aph·ro·di·sia \¦a,nafrə'dizh(ē)ə, a,n-\ *n* -s [NL, fr. *an-* + *aphrodisia*] **:** absence or impairment of sexual desire

¹an·aph·ro·dis·i·ac \¦a,nafrə¦dizē,ak, a¦n-\ *adj* [*an-* + *aphrodisiac*] **:** of, relating to, or causing anaphrodisia

²anaphrodisiac \"\ *n* -s **:** an anaphrodisiac agent

an·a·phy·lac·tic \¦anəfə¦laktik\ *adj* [fr. NL *anaphylaxis*, after such pairs as NL *prophylaxis*: E *prophylactic*] **:** of, relating to, affected by, or accompanying anaphylaxis — **an·a·phy·lac·ti·cal·ly** \-tək(ə)lē\ *adv*

anaphylactic shock *n* **:** a state of shock in an anaphylactic animal resulting from injection or more rarely ingestion of sensitizing antigen or hapten and due mainly to contraction of smooth muscle and increased capillary permeability caused by release in the tissues and circulation of histamine, heparin, and perhaps acetylcholine and serotonin

an·a·phy·lac·tin \,anəfə'laktən\ *n* -s [*anaphylactic* + *-in*] **:** an antibody held to produce anaphylaxis — called also *sensibilisin*

an·a·phy·lac·to·gen \-təjən\ *n* -s [ISV *anaphylactic* + *-o-* + *-gen*] **:** any substance capable of producing a condition of anaphylaxis — **an·a·phy·lac·to·gen·ic** \¦===,=tə¦jenik\ *adj*

an·a·phy·lac·toid \¦===¦=,tòid\ *adj* [ISV *anaphylactic* + *-oid*] **:** resembling anaphylaxis

an·a·phyl·a·tox·in \,anə,filə'täksən\ *n* -s [ISV *anaphyla-* (fr. NL *anaphylaxis*) + *toxin*] **:** a hypothetical substance formerly regarded as responsible for the symptoms of anaphylaxis

an·a·phy·lax·is \,anəfə'laksəs\ *n, pl* **anaphylax·es** \-k,sēz\ [NL, fr. *ana-* + *-phylaxis* (as in *prophylaxis*)] **1 :** hypersensitivity (as to foreign proteins or drugs) that is marked by a tendency to intense systemic reaction and that results from specific sensitization following one or more usu. parenteral contacts with a sensitizing agent and seen chiefly in experimental animals but manifested in man in acute serum sickness and in severe or fatal reactions to second or later administrations of certain drugs (as penicillin) **2 :** ANAPHYLACTIC SHOCK

an·a·pla·sia \,anə'plāzh(ē)ə\ *n* -s [NL, fr. *ana-* + *-plasia*] **:** reversion of cells or tissues to a more primitive, embryonic, or undifferentiated form often with increased capacity for multiplication (as in a malignant tumor) — **an·a·plas·tic** \¦==¦plastik\ *adj*

an·a·plasm \'anə,plazəm\ *n* -s [NL *anaplasma*] **:** ANAPLASMA 2; *specif* **:** a marginal body

an·a·plas·ma \,anə'plazmə\ *n* [NL, fr. *ana-* + *-plasma*] **1** *cap* **:** a genus of microorganisms that are found in the red blood cells of ruminants, resemble small masses of chromatin without cytoplasm, are transmitted by ticks and other biting arthropods, cause anaplasmosis, and are now usu. considered to constitute a family of rickettsias though sometimes esp. formerly considered sporozoans related to *Babesia* **2** *pl* **anaplasma·ta** \-məd·ə\ *or* **anaplasmas :** an organism of the genus *Anaplasma*

an·a·plas·mo·sis \,==,='mōsəs\ *n, pl* **anaplasmo·ses** \-ō,sēz\ [NL, fr. *Anaplasma* + *-osis*] **:** infection with organisms of the genus *Anaplasma*; *specif* **:** a disease of cattle transmitted by ticks and showing symptoms like those of Texas fever except that blood does not tinge the urine

an·a·pol·y·sis \,anə'päləsəs\ *n, pl* **anapoly·ses** \-ə,sēz\ [NL, fr. *an-* + *apolysis*] **:** the retention of ripe proglottids throughout life (as in most pseudophyllidean tapeworms) — compare APOLYSIS — **an·apo·lyt·ic** \(')a¦napə¦lid·ik, ¦anəp-\ *adj*

an·ap·o·phys·i·al \¦a,napə¦fizēəl, a¦n-\ *adj* [NL *anapophysis* + E *-al*] **:** of or relating to an anapophysis

an·a·poph·y·sis \,anə'päfəsəs\ *n, pl* **anapophy·ses** \-ə,sēz\ [NL, fr. *ana-* + *apophysis*] **:** a small process arising at the dorsal side of the base of the transverse process of the lumbar vertebrae in man and many other mammals

an·a·pro·tas·pis \,anəprō'taspəs\ *n, pl* **anaprotas·pes** \-ta,spēz\ [NL, fr. *ana-* + *protaspis*] **:** an early protaspis with but six segments all of which are incorporated in the cephalon of the adult trilobite

an·ap·sid \ə'napsəd\ *adj* [NL *Anapsida*] **:** of, belonging to, or like that of the Anapsida

an·ap·si·da \-sədə\ *n pl, cap* [NL, fr. *an-* + *-apsida* (fr. Gk *apsid-*, *apsis* mesh, loop, net)] **:** a subclass of Reptilia comprising primitive forms in which the skull lacks temporal openings and including chiefly Permian forms with the turtles as its only present representatives

an·ap·to·mor·phus \ə,naptə'mȯrfəs, a,-\ *n, cap* [NL, fr. *an-* + Gk *haptein* to bind + NL *-o-* + *-morphus* -morphous] **:** a genus (the type of the family Anaptomorphidae) of extinct short-skulled large-eyed lemurs from the Eocene of No. America sometimes regarded as near the ancestral line of the anthropoids

an·ap·tyc·tic \¦anap¦tiktik, ¦a,nap-\ *also* **an·ap·tyc·ti·cal** \-ktəkəl\ *adj* [fr. NL *anaptyxis*, after such pairs as LL *syntaxis* syntax: E *syntactic*, *syntactical*] **:** relating to or resulting from anaptyxis ⟨development of an ~ vowel⟩

an·ap·tyx·is \,a=(,)='tiksəs\ *n, pl* **anaptyx·es** \-k,sēz\ [NL, fr. Gk *anaptyxis* act of unfolding, fr. *anaptyssein* to unfold, fr. *ana-* + *ptyssein* to fold] **:** vowel epenthesis

ana·qua \ə'näkwə\ *n* -s [MexSp *anacua, anagua*] **:** a tree (*Ehretria elliptica*) of Mexico and southern Texas that is sometimes planted for shade

an·ar·ces·tes \,anär'se,stēz, ,a,när-\ *n, cap* [NL, fr. *an-* + *Arcestes*, genus of mollusks] **:** a genus of primitive early Devonian ammonoids from central Europe

an·arch \'a,närk, -ák *sometimes* 'anə(r)k\ *n* -s [back-formation fr. *anarchy*] **1 :** a leader or advocate of revolt **:** REBEL, ANARCHIST **2 :** DESPOT, TYRANT ⟨imperial ~s doubling human woes —Lord Byron⟩

anarch- *or* **anarcho-** *comb form* [ML *anarch-*, fr. Gk, fr. *anarchos*] **1 :** without government ⟨*anarch*ical⟩ **2 a :** anarchism and ⟨*anarcho*pacifism⟩ **b :** anarchist and ⟨*anarcho*-individualist⟩

an·ar·chic \(')a¦närkik, ə'n-, -nák-, -kēk\ *also* **an·ar·chi·cal** \-əkəl, -ēk-\ *or* **an·ar·chi·al** \-kēəl\ *adj* [*anarchy* + *-ic*, *-ical* or *-ial*] **:** of, relating to, or tending toward anarchy **:** LAWLESS, REBELLIOUS ⟨thought is ~ and lawless, indifferent to authority —Bertrand Russell⟩ — **an·ar·chi·cal·ly** \-kək(ə)lē, -kēk-, -li\ *adv*

an·ar·chism \'anə(r),kizəm *also* -,när,- *or* -,ná,-\ *n* -s [*anarchy* + *-ism*] **1 :** a political theory opposed to all forms of government and governmental restraint and advocating voluntary cooperation and free association of individuals and groups in order to satisfy their needs — compare NIHILISM **2 :** the advocacy or practice of anarchistic principles ⟨stood for the divine character of established authority against the ~ of free and critical thought —A.L.Guérard⟩

an·ar·chist \'anə(r)kəst\ *n* -s *often attrib* [*anarchy* + *-ist*] **1 :** one who rebels against any authority, established order, or ruling power ⟨the drawing-room ~, the literary rebel, the artistic iconoclast lay down the law for all of us —C.H.Grandgent⟩ **2 :** one who believes in, advocates, or promotes anarchism or anarchy; *esp* **:** one who uses violent means to overthrow the established order ⟨I feel like an ~! I want to blow up the whole town —Sinclair Lewis⟩

an·ar·chis·tic \¦anə(r)¦kistik, -tēk\ *adj* **:** of, relating to, or tending toward anarchism or the acts or principles of anarchists ⟨an almost ~ distrust of government —J.H.Plumb⟩

an·ar·cho–syn·di·cal·ism \a¦när(,)kō'-, ə¦n-, ¦anər,kō'-\ *n* **:** SYNDICALISM

an·ar·cho–syn·di·cal·ist \"-\ *n* **:** SYNDICALIST

an·ar·chy \'anə(r)kē, -ki *sometimes* -,närk-, -,nák-\ *n* -ES [ML *anarchia*, fr. Gk, fr. *anarchos* rulerless (fr. *an-* + *archos* ruler) + *-ia* -y — more at ARCHI-] **1 a :** absence of government ⟨society finds its highest perfection in the union of order with ~ —B.R.Tucker⟩ **b :** a state of lawlessness or political disorder due to the absence of governmental authority ⟨an ~ as absolute as that . . . during the terror —W.C.Brownell⟩ **c :** a Utopian society having no government and made up of individuals who enjoy complete freedom ⟨looks forward to the establishment of ~ . . . the absence of a master and the rule of law —J.H.Hallowell⟩ **2 a :** absence or denial of any authority, established order, or ruling power ⟨for our people liberty so often means only license and ~ —C.L.Sulzberger⟩ **b :** absence of order **:** CONFUSION ⟨have managed to achieve complete ~ in their electrical fixtures —Richard Joseph⟩ **3 :** ANARCHISM ⟨society defending itself against heretical ~ from within —Hilaire Belloc⟩

an·ar·gy·ros \ä'näryē,rōs\ *n, pl* **anargy·roi** \-(,)rē\ [LGk, fr. Gk, adj., without money, not accepting money, fr. *an-* + *argyros* silver, money — more at ARGENT] *Eastern Church* **:** one of thirteen saints who were mostly physicians said to have assisted the suffering and needy without accepting payment

an·a·rith·mia \,anə'rithmēə, -ith-\ *n* -s [NL, fr. *an-* + Gk *arithmos* number + NL *-ia* — more at ARITHMETIC] **:** loss of the ability to count (as resulting from a brain lesion)

an·ar·thria \a'närthrēə\ *n* -s [NL, fr. Gk *anarthros* inarticulate + NL *-ia*] **:** inability to articulate remembered words as a result of brain lesion — compare APHASIA — **an·ar·thric** \(')a¦närthrik\ *adj*

an·ar·throus \(')a¦närthrəs\ *adj* [Gk *anarthros* not differentiated, strengthless, inarticulate, without the article, fr. *an-* + *arthron* joint, article — more at ARTHR-] **1** *of a Greek substantive* **:** used without the article **2** *zool* **:** without distinct joints — **an·ar·throus·ly** *adv*

¹an·ar·ya \(,)ə'näryə\ *adj* [Skt *anārya*, fr. *an-* + *ārya* Aryan — more at ARYAN] *India* **:** not Aryan

²anarya \"\ *n* -s [Skt *anārya*] *India* **:** one that is not Aryan

¹anas *pl of* ANA

²an·as \'anəs\ *n, cap* [NL, fr. L, duck; akin to OE *æned* duck, OS *anad*, OHG *enit, anut*, ON *önd*, Lith *ántis*, and perh. to Gk *nassa, nēssa* duck, and perh. to Skt *āti* aquatic bird] **:** the type genus of Anatidae comprising a large number of widely distributed freshwater ducks (as the mallard and black duck)

an·a·sa \'anəsə\ *n, cap* [NL] **:** a genus of coreid bugs including the squash bugs

an·a·sar·ca \,anə'särkə\ *n* -s [NL, fr. *ana-* + *-sarca* (fr. Gk *sark-*, *sarx* flesh) — more at SARCASM] **:** edema characterized by the accumulation of serum in the connective tissue of the body — called also *dropsy*

an·a·sar·cous \¦==¦=kəs\ *adj* [NL *anasarca* + E *-ous*] **:** characterized or affected by anasarca **:** DROPSICAL

¹ana·sa·zi \¦anə¦säzē, ,an-\ *n, pl* **anasazi** *or* **anasazis** *usu cap* [Navaho *'a-naa-sází* alien ancient one] **:** one of the people who produced the Anasazi culture **:** a Basket Maker or a Pueblo

²anasazi \¦==¦==\ *adj, usu cap* **:** of or belonging to the Basket Maker-Pueblo culture of the plateau area of northern Arizona, New Mexico, and adjacent areas of Colorado and Utah contemporaneous with the Hohokam to the south

an·a·schist·ic \¦anə¦shistik, -¦ski-\ *adj* [*ana-* + *schistic*] **:** dividing longitudinally — used esp. of normal meiotic chromosomes; compare DIASCHISTIC

anas·pa·lin \ə'naspələn\ *n* -s [origin unknown] *pharmacy* **:** a mixture of wool fat and petrolatum; *also* **:** impure wool fat

an·as·pid \ə'naspəd\ *n* -s [NL *Anaspida*] **:** one of the Anaspida

an·as·pi·da \-pədə\ *n pl, cap* [NL, fr. *an-* + *-aspida* (fr. Gk *aspid-*, *aspis* shield)] **:** a class or other division of primitive fishlike ostracoderms having a heterocercal tail and a covering of small elongated scales and known from Silurian-Devonian transition beds of Europe and America

an·as·pi·da·cea \ə,naspə'dāshēə, (,)a,n-\ *n pl, cap* [NL, fr. *Anaspides*, genus of crustaceans (fr. *an-* + *-aspides*, fr. Gk *aspid-*, *aspis* shield) + *-acea*] **:** an order of crustaceans (Malacostraca) like shrimp that have mostly biramous thoracic limbs and deposit their eggs among water plants or under stones

an·a·state \'anə,stāt\ *n* -s [*anabolism* + *-state*] **:** ANABOLITE

an·a·stat·ic \¦anə¦stad·ik\ *adj* [*ana-* + Gk *statikos* causing to stand — more at STATIC] **1 :** relating to a process of printing from a zinc plate on which a transferred design is left in relief by the etching out of the rest of the surface **2** [*anastate* + *-ic*] **:** ANABOLIC

an·a·stat·i·ca \,==¦stad·əkə\ *n, cap* [NL, fr. *ana-* + *-statica* (fr. Gk *statikos*)] **:** a genus of Arabian herbs (family Cruciferae) having a taproot, a dislike crown, and axillary white flowers

an·as·tig·mat \(')a'nastig,mat, ,anə'stig,-\ *n* -s [G, back-formation fr. *anastigmatisch* anastigmatic] **:** an anastigmatic lens

an·a·stig·mat·ic \¦anə(,)stig¦mad·ik, ¦a,nast-, a¦nast-, -naast-, -a(a)stēg-, -matik, -ēk\ *also* **an·as·tig·mat** \(')a¦nastig,mat, ¦anə¦stig,-\ *adj* [*anastigmatic*, ISV, fr. *an-* + *astigmatic*; *anastigmat* fr. *anastigmat*, n.] **:** not astigmatic — used esp. of lenses that are able to form approximately point images of object points

anas·to·mose \ə'nastə,mōz, -ōs\ *vb* -ED/-ING/-S [prob. fr. F, anastomosis, fr. Gk *anastomōsis*] *vt* **:** to connect or join by anastomosis ~ *vi* **1 :** to communicate by anastomosis **:** INOSCULATE **2 :** to divide, subdivide, and reunite repeatedly ⟨an *anastomosing* stream⟩

anas·to·mo·sis \ə,nastə'mōsəs, ,anəs-\ *n, pl* **anastomo·ses** \-ō,sēz\ [LL, fr. Gk *anastomōsis* opening, fr. *anastomoun* to furnish with a mouth, to open (fr. *ana-* + *stoma* mouth, opening) + *-sis* — more at STOMACH] **1 :** an act or instance of joining, intercommunicating, or inosculating: **a :** the union of artery and vein or the rejoining of branches of a common vascular trunk to form a network by which the circulation of a part is maintained when the usual channel is obstructed (as by ligature or a thrombus) **b :** similar joining of the parts of other branched systems (as the veins of a leaf or streams in a swamp) **c :** the surgical union of parts, esp. of hollow tubular parts ⟨~ of the ureter and colon is surgically practicable⟩ **2 :** a product of anastomosis; *esp* **:** a network (as of channels or branches) produced by anastomosis

anas·to·mot·ic \ə¦nastə¦mäd·ik, ¦anəs-\ *also* **anas·to·mat·ic** \-mad·ik\ *adj* [*anastomosis* + *-otic* or *-atic*] **:** of, relating to, or exhibiting anastomosis

an·as·tral \(')a¦nastrəl\ *adj* [*an-* + *astral*] **:** lacking asters — used of achromatic figures

anas·tre·pha \ə'nastrəfə\ *n, cap* [NL, fr. Gk *anastrephein* to turn upside down, fr. *ana-* + *strephein* to turn — more at STROPHE] **:** a genus of tropical American fruit flies (family Trypetidae) including a number of destructive pests of citrus

anas·tro·phe \ə'nastrə(,)fē\ *n* -s [ML, fr. Gk *anastrophē*, lit., turning back, fr. *anastrephein* to turn back, fr. *ana-* + *strephein* to turn — more at STROPHE] **:** inversion of the usual syntactical order of words for rhetorical effect

an·a·stro·phia \,anə'strōfēə\ *n, cap* [NL, fr. Gk *anastrophē* + NL *-ia*] **:** a genus of costate subglobular Silurian and Devonian brachiopods

an·a·sty·lo·sis \,anə,stī'lōsəs\ *n, pl* **anastylo·ses** \-ō'sēz\ [NL, fr. *ana-* + Gk *stylōsis* colonnade, fr. *styloun* to prop with pillars (fr. *stylos* pillar) + *-sis* — more at STEER] **:** the reconstruction of a monument from fallen parts

anat *abbr* anatomical; anatomy

an·a·tase \'anə,tās\ *n* -s [F, fr. Gk *anatasis* extension, fr. *anateinein* to extend, fr. *ana-* + *teinein* to stretch — more at THIN] **:** a tetragonal form of titanium dioxide used esp. as a white pigment in paints and printing inks

an·a·tec·tic \¦anə¦tektik\ *adj* [fr. NL *anatexis*, after such pairs as LL *syntaxis* syntax: E *syntactic*] **:** of or relating to anatexis

an·a·tex·is \,anə'teksəs\ *n, pl* **anatex·es** \-k,sēz\ [NL, fr. Gk *anatēxis* act of melting, thawing, fr. *anatēkein* to melt, thaw (fr. *ana-* + *tēkein* to thaw) + *-sis* — more at THAW] **:** any process by which plutonic rocks are dissolved and again converted into magmas

¹an·a·the·ma \,anə'thēmə, ə'nathəmə\ *n, pl* **anathemas** \-məz\ *or* **anathem·a·ta** \,anə'themәd·ə, ə'nathəməd·ə\ [LL, fr. Gk *anathēma*, lit., anything set up, fr. *anatithenai*] **:** a thing consecrated to divine use **:** a votive offering

²anath·e·ma \ə'nathəmə\ *n* -s [LL, fr. Gk, anything devoted, anything devoted to evil, curse, fr. *anatithenai* to set up, dedicate, fr. *ana-* + *tithenai* to place, set — more at DO] **1 a :** a ban or curse solemnly pronounced by ecclesiastical authority and accompanied by excommunication ⟨the third letter to Nestorius . . . contained the ~s —R.M.French⟩ **b :** the denunciation of anything as accursed ⟨continued openly . . . to flaunt their beauties in spite of the ~s from the pulpits —P.I.Wellman⟩ **c :** a vigorous denunciation **:** IMPRECATION, CURSE ⟨the direst critical ~s —James Hinton⟩ **2 a :** one that is cursed by ecclesiastical authority ⟨the encyclical . . . declared the society ~ —C.W.Ferguson⟩ **b :** one that is intensely disliked or loathed ⟨he was ~ to the moderates —S.H.Adams⟩ ⟨changing a law is ~ to many people —S.L.Payne⟩

anath·e·mat·ic \ə,nathə¦mad·ik\ *or* **anath·e·mat·i·cal** \-əkəl\ *adj* [Gk *anathemat-*, *anathema* + E *-ic*, *-ical*] **:** HATEFUL, LOATHSOME ⟨however *anathematic* the principle may be — *Life*⟩ — **anath·e·mat·i·cal·ly** \-ək(ə)lē\ *adv*

anath·e·ma·tism \ə'==mə,tizəm\ *n* -s [LL, fr. LGk *anathematismos*, fr. Gk *anathematizein* + *-ismos* -ism] **:** ²ANATHEMA

anath·e·ma·ti·za·tion \ə,==məd·ə'zāshən, -mə,tī'z-\ *n* -s [ML *anathematisation-*, *anathematisatio*, fr. LL *anathematizatus* (past part. of *anathematizare*) + L *-ion-*, *-io* -ion] **:** ²ANATHEMA

anath·e·ma·tize *also* **anathematise** \ə'==mə,tīz\ *vt* -ED/-ING/-S [LL *anathematizare*, fr. Gk *anathematizein*, fr. *anathemat-*, *anathema* anything devoted to evil + *-izein* -ize — more at ANATHEMA] **:** to pronounce an anathema upon **:** CURSE, DENOUNCE ⟨*anathematized* the leader of the Kentist insurgents —F.M.Stenton⟩ **syn** see EXECRATE

anath·e·mize \-,mīz\ *vt* -ED/-ING/-S [²*anathema* + *-ize*] **:** ANATHEMATIZE

an·a·tid \'anətəd, ə'nad·əd\ *n* -s [NL *Anatidae*] **:** one of the Anatidae

anat·i·dae \ə'nad·ə,dē\ *n pl, cap* [NL, fr. *Anat-*, *Anas*, type genus + *-idae*] **:** a large family of chiefly aquatic birds (order Anseriformes) having relatively heavy bodies, short legs, webbed feet, a bill with a hard horny nail at the tip and transverse toothlike ridges on the biting edges and including the ducks, geese, swans, and related forms

an·a·ti·na·cea \,anətə'nāshēə\ *n pl, cap* [NL, fr. *Anatina*, genus of mollusks (fr. L *anat-*, *anas* duck + NL *-ina*) + *-acea*] **:** a suborder of Eulamellibranchia of worldwide distribution comprising mollusks that have separate orifices for the ovaries and testes, a small foot, and the hinge of the shell without teeth

an·a·tine \'anə,tīn\ *adj* [L *anatinus* of a duck, fr. *anat-*, *anas* duck + *-inus* -ine] **:** of or belonging to the surface-feeding ducks of *Anas* and closely related genera

anat·i·pes·ti·fer infection \ə¦nad·ə¦pestəfə(r)-\ *n* [NL *anatipestifer*, fr. L *anat-*, *anas* duck + NL *-i-* + L *pestifer* pestiferous — more at PESTIFEROUS] **:** an acute infectious disease of domestic ducks caused by a bacterium (*Pasteurella anatipestifer* or *Pfeifferella anatipestifer*) and marked by sluggishness, greenish diarrhea, and respiratory symptoms with death commonly resulting in 6 to 12 hours

anatman *var of* ANATTA

anato *var of* ANNATTO

anat·o·cism \ə'nad·ə,sizəm\ *n* -s [L *anatocismus*, fr. Gk *anatokismos*, fr. *ana-* + *tokismos* usury, fr. *tokizein* to lend on interest (fr. *tokos* interest, offspring, fr. *tiktein* to beget) + *-ismos* -ism — more at THANE] **:** COMPOUND INTEREST **:** the taking of compound interest

¹an·a·to·li·an \¦anə¦tōlēən, -lyən\ *adj, usu cap* [*Anatolia* Asia Minor + E *-an*] **1 :** of, relating to, or characteristic of Anatolia, the country east of the Bosporus, roughly coincident with Asia Minor **2 :** of, relating to, or characteristic of the inhabitants of Anatolia or their languages **3 :** ARMENIAN

²anatolian \"\ *n* -s *cap* **1 :** a native or inhabitant of Anatolia, specif. of the western plateau lands of Turkey in Asia **2 a :** a southern dialect or group of dialects of Turkish **b :** a group of extinct languages of ancient Anatolia sometimes considered a branch of the Indo-European language family — see INDO-EUROPEAN LANGUAGES table **3 :** any rug or carpet woven in Anatolia

an·a·tol·ic \¦anə¦tälik\ *adj, usu cap* [*Anatolia* + E *-ic*] **:** ANATOLIAN

an·a·tom·ic \¦anə¦tämik, -ēk\ *or* **an·a·tom·i·cal** \-əkəl, -ēk-\ *adj* [*anatomic* fr. F *anatomique*, fr. MF, fr. LL *anatomicus*, fr. Gk *anatomikos*, fr. *anatomē* dissection + *-ikos* -ic; *anatomical* fr. MF *anatomique* + E *-al* — more at ANATOMY] **1 :** of or relating to anatomy ⟨*anatomical* knowledge⟩ **2 :** STRUCTURAL 2 ⟨an *anatomic* obstruction⟩ — opposed to *functional* — **an·a·tom·i·cal·ly** \-ək(ə)lē, -ēk-, -li\ *adv*

anatomical age *n* **:** the age of an individual in terms of his anatomical development

anatomical dead space *n* **:** the air-bearing portion of the respiratory system in which no significant gaseous exchange takes place and which includes the air-conveying ducts from the nostrils to the terminal bronchioles

anatomical position *n* **:** the normal position of activity ⟨the upright posture is man's *anatomical position*⟩

an·a·tom·i·co·path·o·log·ic \,anə'tämə,kō¦==¦==\ *or* **an·a·tom·i·co·path·o·log·i·cal** \-¦==¦===\ *adj* [*anatomic* + *-o-* + *pathologic* or *pathological*] **:** of or relating to anatomy and pathology or to pathological anatomy

anat·o·mist \ə'nad·əməst, -atəm-\ *n* -s [MF *anatomiste*, fr. *anatomie* + *-iste* -ist] **1 :** a student of anatomy; *specif* **:** one skilled in the art of dissection **2 :** one who examines and analyzes minutely and critically ⟨an ~ of urban society⟩

anat·o·mi·za·tion \ə,==mə'zāshən, -,mī'z-\ *n* -s **:** DISSECTION

anat·o·mize *also* **anatomise** \ə'==,mīz\ *vt* -ED/-ING/-S [MF *anatomiser*, fr. *anatomie* anatomy (fr. LL *anatomia*) + *-iser* -ize] **1 :** to cut (an animal or plant body) in pieces in order to display or examine the structure and use of the several parts **:** DISSECT **2 :** to separate minutely or thoroughly the parts, aspects, or components of in order to permit detailed scrutiny or meticulous examination **:** ANALYZE ⟨the novel . . . written to ~ adequately this moment of our history —R.P. Warren⟩ **syn** see ANALYZE

anat·o·my \ə'nad·əmē, -atəm-, -mi\ *n* -ES [LL *anatomia* dissection, fr. Gk *anatomē* dissection (fr. *anatemnein* to dissect, fr. *ana-* + *temnein* to cut) + L *-ia* -y — more at TOME] **1 a :** the branch of morphology that deals with the structure of animals — see HISTOLOGY **b :** the branch of morphology that deals with the structure of plants, esp. the internal structure as revealed by the microscope **:** PHYTOTOMY **2 :** a treatise on anatomic science or art **3 :** the art of artificially separating the different parts of an animal or plant in order to ascertain their position, relations, structure, and function **:** DISSECTION **4** *obs* **a :** a body dissected or to be dissected **b :** a representation of a dissected body (as in plaster) **5 :** the structural makeup, esp. of an organism or any of its parts ⟨the peculiar ~ of the duckbill⟩ **6 :** a separating or dividing into parts, aspects, or components in order to make a thorough study **:** detailed examination **:** ANALYSIS ⟨an attempt at an ~ of modern . . . conservatism —Clinton Rossiter⟩ ⟨the ~ of melancholy⟩ **7 a :** one that has been or appears to have been anatomized or dissected: (1) **:** SKELETON (2) **:** a corpse dried to skin and bone (3) **:** a withered or emaciated person **b :** the human body ⟨in what vile part of this ~ doth my name lodge —Shak.⟩

an·a·to·no·sis \,anətə'nōsəs\ *n, pl* **anatono·ses** \-ō,sēz\ [NL, fr. *ana-* + Gk *tonōsis* strengthening] **:** the process of adjustment of intracellular osmotic pressure of plant cells by variation of the sugar content of the vacuolar sap

an·a·tox·in \,anə'täksən\ *n* -s [ISV *ana-* + *toxin*] **:** TOXOID

an·a·tri·aene \,anə'trī,ēn\ *n* -s [*ana-* + *triaene*] **:** a triaene with downcurved cladi

anat·ro·pous \ə'na·trəpəs\ *adj* [*ana-* + *-tropous*] **:** having the ovule inverted at an early period in its development so that the micropyle is bent down to the funiculus to which the body of the ovule is united — compare AMPHITROPOUS, CAMPYLOTROPOUS, ORTHOTROPOUS

[1]**an·at·ta** \ˌənəˈtä\ *or* **an·at·man** \(ˌ)əˈnätmən\ *n* -s [Pali & Skt; Pali *anatta*, fr. Skt *anātman*, lit., having no soul] **:** a basic Buddhist doctrine affirming the nonexistence of a soul, essence, or any other enduring substantial entity underlying any form of phenomenal existence

[2]**anatta** *or* **anatto** *var of* ANNATTO

an·au·dia \aˈnȯdēə, əˈ-\ *n* -s [NL, fr. Gk, fr. *anaudos* without voice (fr. *an-* + *audē* voice) + *-ia*; akin to Gk *audein* to sing — more at ODE] **:** loss of voice **:** inability to articulate

an·aun·ters \əˈnantə(r)z\ *conj* [ME *anaunter* (fr. *an* — fr. OE, var. of *on* — + *aunter*, var. of *aventure* adventure) + *-s* — more at ADVENTURE] *now dial Eng* **:** on the chance that **:** LEST

an·aux·ite \əˈnȯkˌsīt\ *n* -s [G *anauxit*, fr. Gk *anauxēs* not increasing (fr. *an-* + *-auxēs*, fr. *auxein* to increase) + G *-it* -ite] **:** a mineral consisting of hydrous aluminum silicate, occurring as interstratified layers of silica Si_8O_{16} and kaolin $Al_4Si_4O_{10}(OH)_8$ with the latter predominant, and being a constituent of certain clays

an·ax·ag·o·re·an \ˌaˌnakˌsagəˈrēən, ˌanək-\ *adj, usu cap* [*Anaxagoras* †428 B.C. Greek philosopher + E *-ean*] **:** of or relating to the philosophy of Anaxagoras who taught that the world is composed of many qualitatively different substances that developed from homogeneous particles under the impetus of nous

an·ax·i·al \(ˈ)aˈnaksēəl\ *adj* [*an-* + *axial*] **:** having no distinct axis or axes **:** irregular in form

anax·i·man·dri·an \əˈnaksəˈmandrēən\ *adj, usu cap* [*Anaximander* †547 B.C. Greek astronomer and philosopher + E *-ian*] **:** of or relating to the philosophy of Anaximander who taught that the first principle is an infinite indeterminate matter out of which arise the elementary contraries, warm and cold, moist and dry, that evolve the universe

an·ax·o·nia \ˌaˌnakˈsōnēə\ *n pl, usu cap* [NL, fr. *an-* + *Axonia*] **:** the organisms that have no distinct axis regarded as a group — opposed to *Axonia*

an·ba \ˈambə\ *or* **am·ba** \ˈ"\ *n* -s [Ar, fr. Copt *apa, abba*, fr. Syr *abbā* father] **:** FATHER — used as a title of a Coptic clergyman or saint

an·bury \ˈanbərē, ˈam-, -ˌbe-\ *n* -ES [prob. alter. of (assumed) earlier E *angberry*, fr. *ang-* (fr. OE, narrow, painful) + *berry* — more at AGNAIL] **1 :** ANGLEBERRY **2 :** CLUBROOT

anc *abbr* ancient

ance \ˈan(t)s\ *adj or adv or conj or n* [ME (northern dial.) *anes*, var. of *ones* — more at ONCE] *chiefly Scot* **:** ONCE

-ance \ən(t)s, ᵊn(t)s\ *n suffix* -s [ME, fr. OF, fr. L *-antia*, fr. *-ant-*, *-ans* -ant + *-ia* -y] **1 :** action or process ⟨attend*ance*⟩ ⟨deliver*ance*⟩ ⟨further*ance*⟩ **:** instance of an action or process ⟨appear*ance*⟩ ⟨perform*ance*⟩ **2 :** quality or state ⟨resembl*ance*⟩ ⟨temper*ance*⟩ **:** instance of a quality or state ⟨protuber*ance*⟩ **3 :** amount or degree ⟨conduct*ance*⟩ ⟨transmitt*ance*⟩

an·ce·ra·ta \ˌansəˈrädə, -ädə\ [NL, irreg. fr. *an-* + Gk *kerat-*, *keras* horn — more at CEREBRAL] *syn of* TYLOPODA

[1]**an·ces·tor** \ˈanˌsestə(r), ˈaan-, *Brit usu & US sometimes* -ˌsəs-\ *n* -s [ME *ancestre*, *ancessour*, fr. OF *ancestre* (fr. LL *antecessor*, nom.), *ancessour* (fr. LL *antecessorem*, acc.), fr. LL *antecessor* predecessor, fr. L, one that goes in front, fr. *antecessus* (past part. of *antecedere* to go before, fr. *ante-* ante- + *cedere* to go) + *-or* — more at CEDE] **1 :** one from whom a person is descended and who is usu. more remote in the line of descent than a grandparent; *specif* **:** one from whom an estate has descended, at the common law being orig. only a person in the line of ascent and later also of descent, but under the statutes including any person of lineal or collateral relationship from whom the property has been derived by descent — compare HEIR **2 :** something belonging to a relatively early developmental period of a contemporary or fully developed object or phenomenon **:** FORERUNNER, PROTOTYPE ⟨modern scholarly ideas and their classic Greek *~s*⟩ ⟨the *~s* of today's station wagon —Mildred B. Smith⟩ **3 :** a progenitor (as one living in an earlier geological period) of a more recent or existing species or group ⟨species descended from a 5-chromosome ~ —E.B.Babcock⟩

syn PROGENITOR, FOREFATHER, FOREBEAR (or FORBEAR): ANCESTOR implies lineal descent through father or mother but may apply to kinship through collaterals or race, never, however, being applied except humorously to a relation within family memory ⟨have *ancestors* in British royal families⟩ ⟨generation after generation adding its part . . . to what their *ancestors* had begun —Manès Sperber⟩ ⟨we have a better chance of living far beyond 55, and even well beyond 65, than our *ancestors* had —W.J.Reilly⟩ PROGENITOR can include parents or grandparents as well as ancestors though it generally involves no family or racial feeling, usu. suggesting a reference to heredity or the transmission of characters ⟨the Finlayson family, whose *progenitors* came to America from Scotland in 1800 —*Amer. Guide Series: Fla.*⟩ ⟨the wild relatives of the goat include the pasang [which is] generally regarded as the true *progenitor* of all our modern domesticated breeds —V.A. Rice & F.N.Andrews⟩ FOREFATHER is more common than ANCESTOR in rhetorical or poetic context, usu. emphasizing family feeling or family or group unity ⟨political beliefs for which our *forefathers* gladly fought and died⟩ FOREBEAR is interchangeable with though more neutral than ANCESTOR, being generally devoid of associations with feeling ⟨one of his *forebears* fought under Washington in the Revolutionary War —*Current Biog.*⟩ ⟨carnivals, in which the members impersonate their primal *forbears* —*Amer. Guide Series: Oregon*⟩ ⟨this male specialization in strength must indeed . . . have been inherited from our ape *forebears* —Weston La Barre⟩

[2]**ancestor** \ˈ"\ *vt* -ED/-ING/-S **:** to provide with ancestors ⟨the biographer finally gets his subject *~ed* and born⟩ **:** be the ancestor of ⟨the man who *~ed* many of the residents of this place⟩

ancestor cult *n* **:** a ritualistic system of veneration, honor, and propitiation of the spirits of dead ancestors for the purpose of avoiding evil consequences and securing good fortune

an·ces·to·ri·al \ˌanˌseˈstōrēəl, ˌaan-, -ˌsəˈ-, -ȯr-\ *adj* **:** ANCESTRAL — **an·ces·to·ri·al·ly** \-əlē\ *adv*

an·ces·tral \(ˈ)anˈsestrəl, -aan-\ *adj* [earlier *auncestrell*, fr. MF *ancestrel*, fr. *ancestre* + *-el* -al] **1 a :** of or belonging to an ancestor or ancestors ⟨~ portraits⟩ ⟨~ ideas no longer valid⟩ **b :** inherited or derived from an ancestor or ancestors ⟨~ estates⟩ **2 :** being, serving as, or of the nature of a forerunner, prototype, or precursor ⟨an ~ language⟩ ⟨a second pre-Phoenician alphabet is clearly not ~ to the Phoenician —A.L. Kroeber⟩ — **an·ces·tral·ly** *adv*

an·ces·tress \ˈanˌsestrəs, ˈaan-, -ˌsəs-\ *n* -ES **:** a female ancestor

an·ces·tri·al \(ˈ)anˈsestrēəl\ *adj* [by alter.] *archaic* **:** ANCESTRAL

an·ces·tri·an \-ēən\ *adj* [*ancestry* + *-an*] *archaic* **:** ANCESTRAL

an·ces·tru·la \anˈsestrələ, aan-\ *n, pl* **ancestru·lae** \-ˌlē\ *or* **ancestrulas** [NL, fr. E *ancestor* + NL *-ula*] **:** the primary or first zooid of a bryozoan colony from which secondary individuals are formed by budding — **an·ces·tru·lar** \(ˈ)ˌ≈ˈ≈lə(r)\ *adj*

an·ces·try \ˈanˌsestrē, ˈaan-, -ri, *Brit usu & US sometimes* -ˌsəs-\ *n* -ES [ME *ancestrie*, modif. (influenced by ME *ancestre* ancestor) of MF *ancesserie*, fr. OF, fr. *ancessour* ancestor + *-ie* -y — more at ANCESTOR] **1 a :** line of descent **:** genealogical succession **:** LINEAGE ⟨a Mexican proud of his pure Spanish ~⟩; *specif* **:** good birth **:** honorable, noble, or aristocratic descent ⟨an upstart society without breeding or ~⟩ **b :** persons initiating or comprising a line of descent **:** ANCESTORS ⟨farmers still using methods employed by their colonial ~⟩ **2 a :** material inception (as of an object or phenomenon) ⟨a mountain of volcanic ~⟩ **b :** developmental process **:** HISTORY ⟨radical politics had a far longer ~ than most people had thought —*Times Lit. Supp.*⟩

syn ANCESTRY, LINEAGE, PEDIGREE are often used interchangeably to designate one's progenitors or their total quality or character, often distinguished or notable. ANCESTRY, however, usu. connotes the treelike family branchings and ramifications as symbolized on a chart showing one's relation to progenitors through parental lines ⟨came of distinguished Scotch, Welsh, and Huguenot *ancestry* settled in the Carolinas before the Revolution —Allan Westcott⟩ LINEAGE stresses descent in line, suggesting an order of persons descending from a single ancestor, though each may have a different ancestry ⟨a family which traced its *lineage* from a Cavalier who came to America —*Americana Annual*⟩ ⟨his mother . . . traced her *lineage* to Miles Standish, John and Priscilla Alden, and George Soule, of the Mayflower group —C.J.Kraemer⟩ PEDIGREE implies a known and recorded ancestry, usu. distinguished or notable ⟨accustomed when making his marriage alliances to seek out *pedigree* as well as fortune in his wives —L.G.Pine⟩ ⟨son of a local baronet with a bank balance that makes up for lack of *pedigree* —Richard Harrison⟩ ⟨a champion show dog with a champion's *pedigree*⟩

an·chi·e·tea \ˌaŋkēˈeshēə, ˌanchē-, -ˈēd·ēə\ *n, cap* [NL, after José de *Anchieta* †1597 Port. Jesuit missionary in Brazil] **:** a genus of So. American climbing shrubs (family Violaceae) with white clustered flowers and thin capsules

an·chi·eu·tec·tic \ˈaŋkēyüˈtektik\ *adj* [ISV *anchi-* (fr. Gk *anchi* near) + *-eutectic* (fr. Gk *eutēktos* easily melted + ISV *-ic*); orig. formed as G *anchi-eutektisch*] **:** having minerals in practically eutectic proportions

an·chi·mono·min·er·al \-ˌmänōˈmin(ə)rəl\ *adj* [ISV *anchi-* + *mono-* + *mineral*; orig. formed as G *anchi-monomineralisch*] **:** composed essentially of a single-mineral species

an·chis·tea \ˌaŋkiˈstēə, aŋˈkis-\ *n, cap* [NL, fr. Gk *anchisteia* close kinship, fr. *anchistos* nearest, superl. of *anchi* near; fr. its relationship with another genus (*Woodwardia*); akin to Gk *anchein* to strangle — more at ANGER] *in some classifications* **:** a genus of ferns (family Polypodiaceae) of eastern No. America including only the chain fern — compare WOODWARDIA

an·chi·there \ˈaŋkəˌthi(ə)r\ *n* -s [NL *Anchitherium*] **:** a member of the genus *Anchitherium*

an·chi·the·ri·um \ˌaŋkəˈthirēəm\ *n, cap* [NL, fr. Gk *anchi* near + NL *-therium*] **:** a genus of extinct Miocene and Pliocene perissodactyl mammals related to the modern horse from which they differ in dentition and esp. in the limbs, having a complete ulna and fibula and three functional toes of which the middle one is much the largest

[1]**an·chor** \ˈaŋkə(r), ˈaiŋ-\ *n* -s *often attrib* [ME *anker, ancre*, fr. OE *ancer, ancor*, fr. L *ancora, anchora*, fr. Gk *ankyra*; akin to Gk *ankos* bend, hollow, glen — more at ANGLE] **1 a :** a device usu. of metal (as steel) attached to a ship or boat by a cable and cast overboard to hold the vessel in a particular place by means of a fluke that digs into the bottom ⟨the trawler dropped ~ in the inner harbor⟩ — see [1]STOCK 6a **b :** any device (as a stone or piece of concrete) used in the manner of an anchor to hold a boat in place **2 :** a reliable support (as in danger) **:** a source of confidence ⟨we have this as a sure and steadfast ~ of the soul — Heb 6:19 (RSV)⟩ **3 :** something that serves to hold an object firmly: **a :** a contrivance to hold the end of a bridge cable **b :** an arrangement of timber for holding a dam fast **c :** an escapement piece on which the pallets of a timepiece are formed or to which they are attached **d :** CHAPLET 4 **e** (1) **:** a device (as a metal tie) for giving stability to one part of a structure by making it fast to another (as a beam to a wall, one wall to another, or a stone facing to rough masonry behind it) (2) **:** a tie rod with visible ends, decorated or plain **f :** the loop of a rope used by mountain climbers that is made fast to some fixed object (as a piton or tree) **g :** a boss to which one end of each brake shoe in an internal brake is pivoted to prevent its being dragged around by the drum **4 :** an object shaped like a ship's anchor: as **a :** the dart an egg-and-dart molding **b :** SPICULE ⟨the *~s* in certain holothurians⟩ **5 a :** the rear man on either side in a tug-of-war contest **b** *or* **anchor man :** the member of a team who competes last ⟨the ~ on a relay team⟩ ⟨the ~ of a bowling team⟩ — **at anchor :** being anchored (as to the bottom by an anchor or to a buoy secured to the bottom) ⟨a ship riding *at anchor* in the bay⟩ — used also in law of a vessel moored to a dock

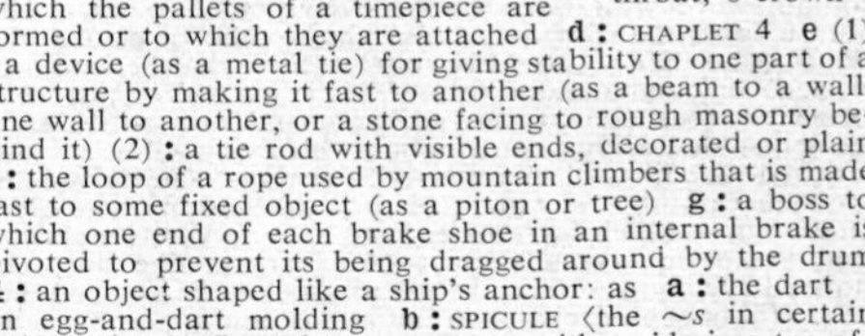

anchor 1a: *1* ring; *2* stock; *3* shank; *4* bill; *5* fluke, or palm; *6* arm; *7* throat; *8* crown

[2]**anchor** \ˈ"\ *vb* **anchored; anchored; anchoring** \-k(ə)riŋ\ **anchors** [ME *ancren*, prob. fr. *anker, ancre*, n.] *vt* **1 :** to hold in place in the water by an anchor ⟨~ a dinghy with a grapnel⟩ — compare MOOR 1 **2 :** to secure firmly **:** fasten in a stable condition **:** FIX ⟨~ a post in concrete⟩ ⟨~ the roof of a house⟩ ⟨~ papers on a desk by a paperweight⟩ ⟨the railroad car on the siding was *~ed* when the hand brakes were set⟩ ⟨he was *~ed* to his home⟩ **3 :** to serve or act as an anchor for ⟨the loveliness of the Loire Valley might fail to ~ the attention of the hurried traveler —Isolde Farrell⟩ ⟨*~ed* the Japanese women's relay team —*Time*⟩ **4** *psychol* **:** to relate to a point or frame of reference (as to a person, a situation, an object, or a conceptual scheme) ~ *vi* **1 :** to cast anchor **:** come to anchor ⟨the ship *~ed* in the stream⟩ **2 :** to become fixed **:** FIX, REST, STOP ⟨his attention *~s* on his friend⟩

[3]**anchor** *n* -s [ME *anker, ancre*, fr. OE *ancor, ancra*, fr. OIr *anchara*, fr. LL *anachoreta* — more at ANCHORITE] *obs* **:** ANCHORITE, HERMIT

[4]**anchor** *n* -s *obs* **:** ANKER

[1]**an·chor·age** \ˈaŋk(ə)rij, ˈaiŋ-, -ēj\ *n* -s [[1]*anchor* + *-age*] **1** *obs* **:** a toll or duty for anchoring a ship (as in a harbor) **2** *obs* **:** the set of anchors used to hold a ship **3 a :** the act or action of anchoring a ship **b :** condition of lying at anchor ⟨room for the ~ of many ships⟩ ⟨pay duty for ~⟩ **c** *also* **anchorage ground :** a place where vessels anchor or a place suitable for anchoring ⟨the inner harbor is an ~ used only in the hurricane season⟩ **d :** bottom for holding a ship's anchor ⟨fine sand offers poor ~ in rough weather⟩ **4 :** a means of security **:** a ground of trust **:** a resting place for the mind or feelings **:** a source of emotional reassurance ⟨this ~ of Christian hope —T.O.Wedel⟩ ⟨a deep and healing sense of ~ —Adria Langley⟩ **5 :** the provision of a secure hold for something **:** that which provides a secure hold ⟨~ supplied for a dental plate⟩ ⟨~ for the second coat of paint⟩ ⟨erosion caused by lack of forest ~⟩ ⟨the importance of roof ~ during hurricanes⟩ ⟨*~s* for suspension cables⟩ **6** *psychol* **:** a point or frame of reference

[2]**anchorage** \ˈ"\ *n* -s [[3]*anchor* + *-age*] **:** the dwelling place of an anchorite

anchor and collar *n* **:** a hinge (as for heavy gates or doors) having the socket attached to or made with an anchor which is embedded in the masonry

an·chor·ate \-kərət, -ˌrāt\ *adj* [[1]*anchor* + *-ate*] *of a sponge spicule* **:** having one or more processes like the fluke of an anchor

anchor ax *n* **:** a crescent-shaped stone weapon once used in Brazil

anchor ball *n* **1 :** a projectile with grappling hooks attached used in the lifesaving service to fire into the rigging of wrecked vessels **2 :** a black ball displayed in the rigging between bow and foremast by a vessel at anchor in or near a channel

anchor bar *n* **:** a handspike with an ironshod wedge-shaped end used in prying (as an anchor into or out of its place)

anchor bed *n* **:** [1]BILLBOARD

anchor bend *n* **:** FISHERMAN'S BEND

anchor bolt *n* **:** a bolt for securing a machine, structure, or part to masonry or other material — called also *anchor rod*

anchor box *n* **:** ANCHOR SPACE

anchor buoy *n* **:** a buoy attached to or marking the position of an anchor

anchor chock *n* **1 :** a reinforcing piece of wood let into an anchor stock where worn **2 :** a chock or a wooden block used to hold a stowed anchor steady

anchor dart *n* **:** the arrowhead part of an egg-and-dart molding

anchor drag *n* **:** DRAG 3a(1)

anchored *adj, of the object balls in billiards* **:** situated so close together (as on the rail or in a corner of the table) that a number of caroms can be made with little or no disturbance of position

anchor escapement *n* **:** a clock escapement employing an anchor-shaped pallet piece which causes the escape wheel to recoil slightly upon the locking action of each arm of the anchor

an·cho·ress \ˈaŋk(ə)rəs, ˈaiŋ-\ *or* **an·cress** \-kr-\ *n* -ES [ME *ankeresse, ancresse*, fr. *anker, ancre* hermit + *-esse* -ess — more at ANCHOR] **:** a female anchorite

[1]**anchor-hold** \ˈ≈ˌ≈\ *n* [[1]*anchor* + *hold* (grasp)] **1 a :** the grip of an anchor **b :** the bottom that an anchor grips **2 :** firm hold **:** SECURITY

[2]**anchor-hold** \ˈ"\ *n* [[3]*anchor* + *hold* (shelter)] **:** the cell of an anchorite

anchor hoy *n* **:** a lighter equipped for raising or handling anchors and chains

anchor ice *n* **:** ice formed below the surface of a body of water (as a stream or lake) and attached to the bottom or to submerged objects — called also *ground ice*

anchoring *pres part of* ANCHOR

[1]**an·cho·rite** \ˈaŋkəˌrīt, ˈaiŋ-\ *also* **an·cho·ret** \-ˌret\ *n* -s [ME *ancorite*, fr. ML *anchorita*, alter. (prob. influenced by L *anchora* anchor) of LL *anachoreta*, (assumed) LL *anachorita*, fr. LGk *anachōrētēs*, fr. Gk *anachōrein* to withdraw, retire, fr. *ana-* + *chōrein* to make room, give way, fr. *chōros* place; akin to Gk *chēros* left, bereaved — more at HEIR] **:** one that renounces the world to live in seclusion usu. for religious reasons **:** HERMIT, RECLUSE

[2]**an·chor·ite** \ˈ"\ *n* -s [fr. *Anchor* Inn, Caldecote, Nuneaton, England, its locality + E *-ite*] **:** a variety of diorite mottled with dark mafic segregations and light feldspathic veins

an·cho·rit·ess \-ˌrīd·əs\ *n* -ES [[1]*anchorite* + *-ess*] **:** ANCHORESS

an·cho·rit·ic \ˌ≈≈ˈrid·ik\ *also* **an·cho·ret·ic** \-red·ik\ *adj* [[1]*anchorite* + *-ic*] **:** relating to, belonging to, or suggestive of an anchorite ⟨~ devotions⟩

an·cho·rit·ism \ˈ≈≈ˌrīd·ˌizəm\ *n* -s [[1]*anchorite* + *-ism*] **:** the practice or mode of life of an anchorite

an·chor·less \ˈaŋkə(r)ləs, ˈaiŋ-\ *adj* [[1]*anchor* + *-less*] **:** UNSETTLED, DRIFTING ⟨~ people perpetually riding the crest of their emotions —William Phillips b.1907⟩

anchor lift *n* **:** a grappling device to raise a grouser

anchor light *n* **:** the light shown at night by a vessel at anchor

anchor lining *n* **:** a protection of planks or sheathing on a ship's side to prevent the anchor from injuring the side

anchor log *n* **:** a wooden, concrete, or metal bar buried in the earth to hold a guy rope firmly — called also *deadman*

anchor man *n* **:** [1]ANCHOR 5b

anchor nurse *n* **:** a nurse in billiards in which the two object balls are kept anchored

anchor plant *n* [so called fr. the shape of the branches] **:** a So. American shrub (*Colletia cruciata*) with flattened branches and creamy-white flowers

anchor plate *n* **:** a wooden or metal plate attached to or embedded in a support and used as an anchor (as for supporting cables)

anchor point *n* **:** a point on an archer's face (as the chin) up to which he brings his drawing hand in order to stabilize his aim before release of the arrow

anchor ring *n* **:** the surface formed by rotating a circle around a line that lies in the plane of the circle but does not intersect the circle — called also *torus*

anchor rocket *n* **:** a rocket with flukes like an anchor used in the lifesaving service in carrying a line to a wrecked vessel

anchor rod *n* **:** ANCHOR BOLT

anchors *pl of* ANCHOR, *pres 3d sing of* ANCHOR

anchor shackle *n* **:** a shackle to secure a chain to the ring of an anchor **:** BENDING SHACKLE

anchor shot *n* **1 :** GRAPPLE SHOT **2** *or* **anchor stroke :** a shot in billiards made with the object balls anchored

anchor space *n* **:** any of eight spaces in balkline billiards seven inches square lying along a cushion and bisected transversely by a balkline in which object balls are treated as in balk — called also *anchor box*

anchor tooth *n* **:** ABUTMENT 2c

anchor watch *n* **:** a detail of one or more men who keep watch on deck at night when a vessel is at anchor

anchor well *n* **:** a well for anchors in the forward overhang of a ship

an·chory \-k(ə)rē, -ri\ *adj* [prob. modif. (influenced by [1]*anchor*) of F *ancré*] **:** ANCRÉE

an·cho·ve·ta *or* **an·cho·vet·ta** \ˌanchōˈved·ə\ *n* -s [Sp *anchoveta*, dim. of *anchova*] **:** a small anchovy (*Cetengraulis mysticetus*) common along the Pacific coast of No. America and often used as bait

an·cho·vy \ˈanˌchōvē, anˈchō-, ˈanchə-, (ˈ)aan-, -vi\ *n, pl* **anchovies** *or* **anchovy** [Sp *anchova, anchoa*, prob. fr. It dial. (Genoa) *ancioa*, fr. (assumed) VL *apjua*, fr. Gk *aphyē* small fry (of any of several fishes)] **:** any of a number of small herringlike fishes (family Engraulidae); *esp* **:** a common Mediterranean form (*Engraulis encrasicholus*) esteemed for its rich and peculiar flavor and caught in vast numbers for preserving and for making sauces and relishes

anchovy pear *n* [so called fr. its use as an hors d'oeuvre] **1 :** the fruit of a West Indian tree (*Grias cauliflora*) of the family Lecythidaceae often eaten as a pickle **2 :** the tree that bears anchovy pears

an·chu·sa \aŋˈkyüsə, -üzə\ *n* [NL, fr. L, alkanet, fr. Gk *anchousa*] **1** *cap* **:** a large genus of rough-hairy Old World herbs (family Boraginaceae) with one-sided clusters of trumpet-shaped flowers — see BUGLOSS **2** -s **:** a plant of the genus *Anchusa*

anchyl- *or* **anchylo-** — see ANKYL-

anchylose *var of* ANKYLOSE

anchylosis *var of* ANKYLOSIS

anchylostomiasis *var of* ANCYLOSTOMIASIS

anchylotic *var of* ANKYLOTIC

anciency *n* -ES [alter. of ME *anciente*, fr. MF *ancienté*, fr. *ancien* + *-té* -ty] *archaic* **:** ANTIQUITY

an·cien ré·gime \äⁿsyaⁿrāzhēm\ *n, pl* **anciens régimes** \-m(z)\ [F, lit., old regime] **1 :** the political and social system of France before the Revolution of 1789 **2 :** a system or mode no longer prevailing

[1]**an·cient** \ˈānshənt, ˈānch- *also* ˈāŋ(k)sh-\ *adj, often* -ER/-EST [ME *ancien*, fr. MF, fr. (assumed) VL *anteanus*, fr. L *ante* before + *-anus* -an — more at ANTE-] **1 :** having had an existence of many years **:** OLD: **a :** AGED ⟨a strangely dressed ~ man⟩ **b** *archaic* **:** of long standing in some capacity or relation ⟨an ~ champion still defending his title⟩ **c :** existing from a long-past date or period **:** of early origin ⟨an ~ landmark⟩ ⟨the ~ rights of freemen⟩ **d :** having had an uninterrupted existence of 20 or 30 or more years — used of various things the continued existence of which for such a period gives rise to a presumption of legal validity in aid of the defect in proof due to lapse of memory, absence of witnesses, or loss of documents **2 :** belonging or relating to a remote period, to a time early in history, or to those who lived in such a period or time; *specif* **:** belonging or relating to the historical period beginning with the earliest known civilizations and extending to the fall of the western Roman Empire A.D.476 — compare MEDIEVAL, MODERN **3 :** having the qualities of age or long existence: **a** *of a person* (1) **:** VENERABLE (2) **:** adept by reason of long experience **:** WISE **b :** OLD-FASHIONED, ANTIQUE ⟨dressed in ~ garb⟩ **4** *obs* **:** FORMER, BYGONE, SOMETIME **syn** see OLD

[2]**ancient** \ˈ"\ *n* -s **1 :** an aged living being: **a :** a patriarchal or venerable man or woman ⟨a dignified ~⟩ **b** (1) *obs* **:** one older in age **:** SENIOR — usu. used with the possessive (2) *archaic* **:** an elder in his capacity as dignitary **2** *obs* **:** ANCESTOR **3 :** one who lived in ancient times: **a ancients** *pl* **:** the civilized peoples of antiquity; *esp* **:** those of the classical nations — usu. used with *the* ⟨the religions of the *~s*⟩ **b :** one of the classical authors ⟨Plutarch and other *~s*⟩ **4** *archaic* **:** one of the senior members forming the governing body of the Inns of Court or of Chancery **5 :** an ancient coin

[3]**ancient** \ˈ"\ *n* -s [alter. (influenced by [1]*ancient*) of *ensign*] **1** *archaic* **:** an ensign, standard, or flag **2** *or* **ancient bearer** *obs* **:** the bearer of an ensign ⟨my ~, a man he is of honesty and trust —Shak.⟩

ancient demesne *n* **:** demesne held from ancient times; *specif* **:** the demesne belonging to the English crown at the time of the settlement of the Norman Conquest as recorded in the Domesday Book

ancient history *n* **:** knowledge or information (as of something in the recent past) that is widespread and has lost its initial freshness or importance **:** common knowledge ⟨this may be *ancient history,* but it still makes fascinating reading —Leland Stowe⟩

ancient light *n* **:** a window or other opening that has been used 20 or more years without interruption and is therefore protected at common law against obstruction by an adjoining holder

an·cient·ly *adv* **1 :** in ancient times **:** long ago **2** *obs* **:** FORMERLY

ancient murrelet *n* [so called fr. its having a form known fr. the Pleistocene] **:** a murrelet (*Synthliboramphus antiquum*) of the No. Pacific that is chiefly dark slate above and white below

ancientness *n* -ES **1 :** the quality or state of being ancient **2** *obs* **:** PRIORITY, SENIORITY

ancient regime *prond as English*\\ *n* [part trans.] **:** ANCIEN RÉGIME

an·cient·ry \\-rē\\ *n* -ES **1** *obs* **:** old people **:** ELDERS **2 a :** ANCIENTNESS, ANTIQUITY ⟨a custom drawn from the ~ of the East —John Buchan⟩ **b :** old-fashioned style ⟨married with great state and ~ —Rudyard Kipling⟩ **3** *obs* **:** ancient lineage **:** ANCESTRY **4 :** ancient times ⟨legends of ~⟩

-ancies *pl of* -ANCY

an·ci·le \\ăn'kē,lā, an'sīlē\\ *n, pl* **ancil·ia** \\ăn'kilēə, an'si-\\ [L, prob. fr. *ancidere* to cut around, fr. *an-* (var. of *ambi-* around) + *-cidere* (fr. *caedere* to cut) — more at AMBI-, CONCISE] **:** any of 12 sacred shields of the ancient Romans that were thought to guarantee the preservation of the city

an·cil·la \\an'silə\\ *n, pl* **ancil·lae** \\-i(,)lē\\ [L, female servant, dim. of (assumed) *ancula* (whence *Ancula,* a goddess who ministered to the gods), fem. of (assumed) *anculus* (whence *Anculus,* a ministering god), fr. *an-* (var. of *ambi-* around) + *-culus* circulating (akin to *colere* to cultivate, dwell — formerly, to circulate) — more at AMBI-, WHEEL] **1 :** an adjunct esp. to something large or significant **:** ACCESSORY ⟨a mere ~ to architecture⟩ **2 :** an aid in achieving or mastering something difficult, complex, or obscure **:** HELPER ⟨a most necessary ~ to literary appreciation —George Saintsbury⟩

¹an·cil·lary \\'ansə,lerē, 'aan-, -nts-, -ri, *US also & Brit usu* an'silər- *or* aan-\\ *adj* [L *ancillaris* of a maidservant, fr. *ancilla* + *-aris* -ar] **:** SUBORDINATE, SUBSIDIARY ⟨the main factory and its ~ plants⟩ **:** AUXILIARY ⟨surgery and ~ treatment⟩ **:** RELATED ⟨mathematics and ~ subjects⟩ **:** SUPPLEMENTARY ⟨the need for ~ evidence⟩; *specif* **:** subordinate or auxiliary to a primary or principal legal document, proceeding, office, or officer ⟨~ letters of administration⟩ ⟨~ action⟩ ⟨~ administrator⟩

²ancillary \\"\\ *n* -ES **1** *Brit* **:** one who assists or serves another person ⟨the bill proposed no more than a three-year experiment in training and employing *ancillaries* under the direction of the General Dental Council —*Lancet*⟩ **2** *Brit* **:** APPURTENANCE, ACCESSORY ⟨development of aircraft, aircraft engines, and *ancillaries* —*Manchester Guardian Weekly*⟩

an·cip·i·tal \\(')an¦sipəd°l\\ *or* **an·cip·i·tous** \\-d·əs\\ *adj* [L *ancipit-, anceps* two-headed, two-edged (fr. — assumed — *ambicipit-, ambiceps,* fr. *ambi-* + *-ceps,* fr. *caput* head) + E *-al* or *-ous* — more at HEAD] **:** DOUBLE-EDGED — used of flattened stems (as of certain grasses)

an·ci·pi·tis usus \\an'sipəd·əs'yüsəs, äŋ'kipəd·ə'süsəs\\ *adj* [L] **:** of twofold use — used esp. of an article (as coal) that can be utilized for commercial as well as belligerent purposes and hence raises the question of whether or not it is justifiable contraband of war

an·cis·troc·la·dus \\,an,sis'träkləḍəs\\ *n, cap* [NL, fr. Gk *ankistron* fishhook + *klados* branch; akin to Gk *ankos* glen — more at ANGLE, GLADIATOR] **:** a genus of climbing shrubs (order Parietales) of the East Indies and Africa constituting a distinct family and having hooked branches and panicled flowers with 10 stamens and a single pistil that are followed by nutlike fruits

an·cis·tro·don \\an'sistrə,dän\\ *syn of* AGKISTRODON

an·cis·troid \\an'si,strȯid, 'ansi,s-\\ *adj* [Gk *ankistroeidēs,* fr. *ankistron* fishhook + *-eidēs* -oid] **:** shaped like a hook **:** resembling a hook

an·cis·tro·syrinx \\an¦sistrō +\\ *n* [NL, fr. Gk *ankistron* fishhook + *syrinx* shepherd's pipe — more at SYRINX] **1** *cap* **:** a small genus (family Turritidae) of gastropod mollusks that occur in warm deep seas and have delicate steeply shouldered pale shells ringed with upward-curving spines **2** *pl* **ancistrosyringes :** any mollusk or shell of the genus *Ancistrosyrinx*

an·cle *Brit var of* ANKLE

an·co·bar \\'aŋkō,bär\\ *n* -S *usu cap* [*Ancona* + *barred Plymouth Rock*] **:** any of an autosexing strain or breed of chickens developed by crossing Anconas and barred Plymouth Rocks

an·co·dont \\-,dänt\\ *n* -S [NL *Ancodonta*] **:** an animal or fossil of the division Ancodonta

an·co·don·ta \\,aŋkō'däntə\\ *n pl, cap* [NL, fr. Gk *ankos* bend, hollow + NL *-odonta*] **:** a division of Artiodactyla comprising the hippopotamuses and extinct related forms and with the Suina and certain extinct related forms forming the suborder Suiformes

¹an·con \\'aŋ,kän\\ *also* **an·cone** \\-kōn\\ *n, pl* **an·cones** *as pl of "ancon",* aŋ'kōnēz; *as pl of "ancone",* 'aŋ,kōnz\\ [L *ancon,* fr. Gk *ankōn* elbow] **:** a bracket, elbow, or console used as an architectural support (as for the cornice over a doorway) **:** CROSSETTE 1, MODILLION

²ancon *usu cap, var of* ANCON SHEEP

³an·con \\'aŋ,kōn, -än, (')äŋ¦kȯn\\ *adj, usu cap* [fr. *Ancón,* near Lima, Peru, its type station] **:** of or belonging to an early, middle, or late period of the Chavin civilization of Peru characterized by distinct pottery types

¹an·co·na \\aŋ'kōnə\\ *n* -S *usu cap* [fr. *Ancona,* Italy] **:** a domestic fowl of a breed of the Mediterranean class resembling the Leghorns in build and having mottled black-and-white plumage

²ancona \\"\\ *n, pl* **anco·ne** \\-nē\\ *or* **anconas** [It, prob. modif. (prob. influenced by *Ancona,* seaport on Adriatic coast, Italy) of Gk *eikona,* acc. of *eikōn-, eikōn* image — more at ICON] **:** ALTARPIECE; *specif* **:** one composed of one or more paintings in an elaborate architectural framework

an·co·nal \\(')aŋ¦kōn°l\\ *also* **an·co·ne·al** \\-nēəl\\ *adj* [NL *ancon* elbow (fr. Gk *ankōn*) + E *-al, -eal*] **:** of, relating to, or belonging to the elbow ⟨~ pain⟩

an·co·ne·us \\aŋ'kōnēəs\\ *n, pl* **anco·nei** \\-ē,ī\\ [NL, fr. *ancon* + L *-eus* -eous] **:** a small triangular extensor muscle superficially situated behind and below the elbow joint

an·co·noid \\'aŋkə,nȯid\\ *adj* [NL *ancon* + E *-oid*] **:** resembling an elbow

an·con sheep \\'aŋkən-, -,kän-\\ *also* **ancon** *n* -S *usu cap A* [NL *ancon;* fr. their short, crooked legs] **:** a short-legged achondroplastic sheep; *esp* **:** such a sheep of an extinct strain or breed formerly maintained in Massachusetts

ancony *n* -ES [origin unknown] *archaic* **:** a piece of iron wrought into the shape of a bar in the middle and left rough at the ends

an·cred \\'aŋkə(r)d\\ *adj* [prob. modif. of F *ancré*] **:** ANCRÉE

an·crée \\aŋ·,krā\\ *adj* [F *ancré,* fr. *ancre* anchor (fr. L *ancora, anchora*) + *-é* (fr. L *-atus* -ate) — more at ANCHOR] *of a cross* **:** having the end of each arm divided into two recurving points like the flukes of an anchor — usu. used postpositively; often distinguished from *moline*

ancress *var of* ANCHORESS

anct *abbr* ancient

-an·cy \\ənsē, -si\\ *n suffix* -ES [L *-antia* — more at -ANCE] **1 :** quality or state ⟨buoyancy⟩ ⟨pliancy⟩ **2 :** instance of a quality or state ⟨expectancy⟩

ancyl- *or* **ancylo-** — see ANKYL-

an·cyl·i·dae \\aŋ'kilə,dē, an'si-\\ *n pl, cap* [NL, fr. *Ancylus,* type genus + *-idae*] **:** a cosmopolitan family of small thin-shelled conical pulmonate snails related to the Planorbidae — compare FRESHWATER LIMPET

an·cy·lite \\'ansə,līt\\ *n* -S [prob. fr. Dan *ankylit,* fr. *ankyl-* + *-it* -ite] **:** a mineral $Sr_3Ce_4(CO_3)_7(OH)_.3H_2O$ consisting of hydrous basic carbonate of strontium and cerium

an·cy·loc·er·as \\,ansə'läsərəs\\ *n, cap* [NL, fr. *ankyl-* + *-ceras*] **:** a genus of ammonoids having a partly uncoiled shell and the aperture of the living chamber directed toward the coiled part

an·cy·loc·la·dus \\-ükləḍəs\\ [NL, fr. *ankyl-* + Gk *klados* branch] *syn of* WILLUGHBEIA

an·cy·lo·dac·ty·la \\¦ansə(,)lō'daktələ\\ [NL, fr. *ankyl-* + *-dactyla* (fr. Gk *daktylos* finger)] *syn of* ANCYLOPODA

an·cy·lop·o·da \\,ansə'läpədə\\ *n pl, cap* [NL, fr. *ankyl-* + *-poda*] *in some classifications* **:** a division of fossil Miocene and Pliocene ungulates of both the Old and the New World having clawed feet resembling those of the edentates

ancylose *var of* ANKYLOSE

ancylosis *var of* ANKYLOSIS

an·cy·los·to·ma \\,aŋkə'lästəmə, -kē'- *also* ,ansə'-\\ *n, cap* [NL, fr. *ankyl-* + *-stoma*] **:** the type genus of Ancylostomatidae comprising hookworms that have buccal teeth resembling hooks and are parasites in the intestines of man and various mammals — compare NECATOR

an·cy·lo·sto·mat·i·dae \\¦=,=(,)lōstō'mad·ə,dē, ,==,lästə'm-\\ *n pl, cap* [NL, fr. *Ancylostomat-, Ancylostoma,* type genus + *-idae*] **:** a family of strongyloid nematodes containing the hookworms

an·cyl·o·stome \\aŋ-'kilə,stōm *also* an'si-\\ *or* **an·kyl·o·stome** \\aŋ-'ki-\\ *n* -S [NL *Ancylostoma*] **:** a hookworm of the genus *Ancylostoma*

an·cy·lo·sto·mi·a·sis \\,aŋkə(,)lōstō'mīəsəs, -kē-, ,==,lästə'm- *also* ¦ansə- *or* ,ansə-\\ *also* **an·ky·lo·sto·mi·a·sis** *or* **an·chy·lo·sto·mi·a·sis** \\¦aŋk-, ,aŋk-\\ *n, pl* **ancylostomia·ses** \\-ə,sēz\\ [NL, fr. *Ancylostoma* + *-iasis*] **:** infestation with or disease caused in man or animals by hookworms; *specif* **:** a condition in man marked by lethargy, severe anemia, and relative eosinophilia due to loss of blood through the feeding of hookworms in the small intestine — called also *hookworm disease*

an·cy·lo·stom·i·dae \\¦aŋkə(,)lō'stämə,dē, -kē- *also* ¦ansə-\\ [NL, fr. *Ancylostoma,* type genus + *-idae*] *syn of* ANCYLOSTOMATIDAE

an·cy·los·to·mum \\,=='lästəməm\\ [NL, fr. *ankyl-* + *-stomum*] *syn of* ANCYLOSTOMA

ancylotic *var of* ANKYLOTIC

an·cy·lus \\'aŋkələs, -kē-, 'ansəl-\\ *n, cap* [NL, fr. Gk *ankylos* curved — more at ANKYL-] **:** the type genus of Ancylidae

ancyroid *var of* ANKYROID

¹and \\ən(d), (')an(d); *usu* °n(d) *after* t, d, s, *or* z *as in "hit and run", often* °m *after* p *or* b *as in "up and down", sometimes* °ŋ *after* k *or* g *as in "lock and key"; in rapid speech sometimes* n *(as in one pronunciation,* ,bəd·ə(r)'negz, *of "butter and eggs") or sometimes* m *(as in one pronunciation,* bīm'bī, *of "by and by");* *sometimes* (')aa(ə)n(d); *sporadically* (')en(d)\\ *conj* [ME, fr. OE *and, ond, end;* akin to OFris *anda, enda* and, OHG *anti, enti, unti, inti,* ON *enn* and, but, and perh. to Oscan *ant* up to, Toch B *entwe* then, therefore, and perh. to OE *in* — more at IN] **1 a :** along with or together with ⟨he ~ his son were here⟩ **b :** added to or linked to ⟨a thousand ~ one nights⟩ ⟨I have a hundred ~ one things to do⟩ ⟨cream ~ sugar with your coffee⟩ **c :** as well as ⟨he took aspirin ~ bicarbonate of soda⟩ **d :** again then again ⟨the dog barked ~ barked⟩ **e :** also at the same time ⟨they walked ~ talked⟩ **f :** THEN ⟨they drove five miles ~ stopped to eat⟩ **g :** in addition to being ⟨secretary ~ treasurer⟩ **h :** but not less truly **:** YET ⟨an entertaining ~ scholarly book⟩ — symbol *&;* used as a function word to (1) express the general relation of connection or addition, esp. accompaniment, participation, combination, contiguity, continuance, simultaneity, sequence or (2) conjoin word with word ⟨bread ~ butter⟩ or phrase with phrase ⟨over the river ~ through the woods⟩ or clause with clause ⟨said that he would be nominated ~ that he would be elected⟩ or combinations thereof (as adjectival or adverbial elements of different types, adjective and substantive complements, or various constructions involving ellipsis) ⟨dissatisfied ~ with still unanswered questions⟩ ⟨he solved the problem carefully ~ without error⟩ ⟨allegations heretofore unuttered ~ which force us to take action⟩ ⟨he is a shrewd man ~ apt to take advantage of a bargain like this⟩ ⟨he stopped speaking ~ then the awful shock — he slapped me⟩ or (3) fill in expletively (as in initial position in a sentence or between completely disparate elements) ⟨~ it came to pass in those days⟩ ⟨when that I was ~ a little tiny boy —Shak.⟩ **2** — used as a function word to express (1) repetition ⟨they rode two ~ two⟩ ⟨hundreds ~ hundreds⟩ or (2) variation or difference ⟨there are women ~ women⟩ or (3) logical or semantic modification of one notion by another as when (a) two elements are joined so that the second logically qualifies the first ⟨your fair ~ outward character⟩ ⟨in poverty ~ distress⟩ or (b) two adjectives are joined so that the first becomes equivalent to an adverb modifying the second ⟨nice ~ warm⟩ ⟨good ~ ready⟩ or (c) one finite verb (as *go, come, try, write*) is joined with another so that it becomes logically equal to an infinitive of purpose ⟨go ~ call him⟩ ⟨come ~ see me⟩ ⟨try ~ stop me⟩ ⟨write ~ tell me⟩ or (d) two verbs are joined so that the first represents a position or state and the second represents an attendant action that may also be expressed by a participle ⟨he sat ~ smoked⟩ ⟨to sit ~ wait⟩ or (4) a consequence or sequel ⟨I said go ~ he went⟩ ⟨one step further ~ he is a dead man⟩ or (5) contrary action, incongruous outcome, or antithesis ⟨he promised to come ~ didn't⟩ ⟨he sailed for Florida ~ landed in Cuba⟩ or (6) reference to either or both of two alternatives ⟨choose between him ~ me⟩ esp. in legal language when also plainly intended to mean *or* ⟨bequeathed to a person ~ her bodily issue⟩ ⟨property taxable for state ~ county purposes⟩ or (7) supplementary explanation or restriction often with climactic emphasis in an appended phrase ⟨he ~ he alone could control it⟩ ⟨living in one room ~ that room a cellar⟩ or (8) at the point of junction or intersection ⟨Main Street ~ First Avenue⟩ **3** *obs* **:** as if **:** IF, THOUGH ⟨they will set an house on fire, ~ it were but to roast their eggs —Francis Bacon⟩ — see ²AN **4** — used in logic as a sentential or propositional connective that produces a compound proposition true only if both compounds are true ⟨symbolically *p·q* is true if ~ only if neither *p* nor *q* is false⟩ — see CONJUNCTION — **and how** \\(')an(d)'hau̇\\ — used to emphasize the preceding idea ⟨Congress is fully restored to its position as a separate branch of the government — *and how* —*Barron's*⟩ — **and interest :** with an amount equal to all interest accrued to the date of payment to be added to the price of a bond being purchased — compare ³FLAT 4 — **and so forth** \\=¦=,= *also* =¦=¦=\\ **:** and others or more of the same or similar kind ⟨pamphlets, books, *and so forth*⟩ **:** further in the same or similar manner ⟨afterward she screamed and cried *and so forth*⟩ **:** and the rest ⟨he moved his furniture, clothes, *and so forth*⟩ **:** and other things (as ingredients) ⟨milk, eggs, flour, *and so forth*⟩ — **and so on** \\=¦=,= *also* =¦=¦=\\ **:** and so forth

²and *conj* [ME, prob. modif. (influenced by ¹*and*) of ON *an, enn,* fr. Runic Norse *than* — more at THAN] *obs* **:** ¹THAN 1a

³and \\'and *sometimes* 'aa(ə)nd, *sporadically* 'end\\ *n, pl* **ands** \\-n(d)z\\ [¹*and*] **:** an added particular or condition ⟨I want to hear no ifs or ~s about it⟩

and *abbr* andante

an·da \\an'dä\\ *or* **an·da–as·su** \\an'dä(,)sü\\ *n* -S [*anda* fr. Pg, fr. Tupi; *anda-assu* fr. Pg, fr. Tupi *andá-açu,* fr. *anda* + *açu* big] **:** a Brazilian timber tree (*Joannesia princeps*) of the family Euphorbiaceae having light soft wood

an·da·ki *or* **an·da·qui** \\¦ändə¦kē, ¦an-\\ *n, pl* **andaki** *or* **andakis** *or* **andaqui** *or* **andaquis** *usu cap* [Sp *andaquí,* of AmerInd origin] **1 a :** a Chibchan people of southern Colombia **b :** a member of such people **2 :** the language of the Andaki people — **an·da·qui·an** \\-ēən\\ *adj, usu cap*

¹an·da·lu·sian \\¦andə¦lüzhən, ¦aan-\\ *adj, usu cap* [*Andalusia* (Sp *Andalucía*), region of southern Spain + E *-an*] **1 :** of, relating to, or characteristic of Andalusia ⟨*Andalusian* music⟩ **2 :** of, relating to, or characteristic of the people of Andalusia

²andalusian \\"\\ *n* -S **1** *usu cap* **:** a native or inhabitant of Andalusia **2** *often cap* **:** a domestic fowl of a Mediterranean breed similar to the Leghorn **3** *cap* **:** the dialect of Spanish spoken in Andalusia

an·da·lu·site \\,==¦=,sīt\\ *n* -S [F *andalousite,* fr. *Andalousie* Andalusia, region in Spain where it was discovered + F *-ite*] **:** a silicate of aluminum Al_2SiO_5 usu. in thick nearly square orthorhombic prisms of various colors used in making refractory porcelains

an·da·man \\'andəmən, -,man\\ *also* **an·da·man·ese** \\¦andəmə¦nēz, -ēs\\ *adj, usu cap* [*Andaman* fr. *Andaman* islands, Bay of Bengal, India; *Andamanese* fr. *Andaman* islands + E *-ese*] **1 a :** of, relating to, or characteristic of the Andaman islands **b :** of, relating to, or characteristic of the people of the Andaman islands **2 :** of, relating to, or characteristic of the Andamanese language

andamanese \\"\\ *n, pl* **andamanese** *usu cap* **1** *or* **an·da·man** \\'andəmən, -,man\\ *usu cap* **:** a Negrito native to the Andaman islands — called also *Andaman Islander* **2 :** an agglutinative language of the Andamanese which is unconnected with any known language family

andaman marble *or* **andaman marblewood** *n, usu cap A* **:** MARBLEWOOD

andaman padauk *n, usu cap A* **1 :** a tree (*Pterocarpus dalbergioides*) of the Andaman islands with reddish or red-brown wood like mahogany **2 :** the wood of the Andaman padauk tree

andaman redwood *n, usu cap A* **:** AMBOYNA

¹an·dan·te \\(')an¦dantē, -aan¦daa-; än'dän,tā, än'dän-, (')=¦=,tē\\ *adv (or adj)* [It, lit., going, pres. part. of *andare* to go, prob. fr. (assumed) VL *amlare* — more at ALLEY] **1** *in 18th century musical notation* **:** in strict time **2 :** moderately slow and in tempo between larghetto and allegretto ⟨a cello passage in an ~ section⟩ — often used as a direction in music

²andante \\"\\ *n* -S **:** a musical piece or movement in andante tempo

¹an·dan·ti·no \\,=,='tē(,)nō\\ *adj (or adv)* [It, fr. *andante* + *-ino* -ine (fr. L *-inus*)] **:** rather quicker in tempo than andante; *sometimes* **:** somewhat slower than andante — often used as a direction in music

²andantino \\"\\ *n* -ES **:** a musical piece or movement in andantino tempo; *also* **:** a short andante

an·de·an \\'andēən, 'aan-, =¦==\\ *adj, usu cap* [*Andes* + E *-an*] **:** of, relating to, or characteristic of the Andes mountain system ⟨the *Andean* wolf⟩ ⟨*Andean* Indians⟩

-an·der \\,andə(r), ,aan-\\ *n comb form* -S [NL *-andrus,* fr. Gk *-andros* having (such or so many) men — more at -ANDROUS] **:** one having (such or so many) stamens — in words denoting members of Linnaean botanical classes in *-andria* ⟨hexander⟩

an·der·son·ite \\'andə(r)sə,nīt\\ *n* -S [Charles A. *Anderson* b1902 Am. geologist + E *-ite*] **:** a mineral consisting of a secondary hydrous sodium calcium uranium carbonate $Na_2Ca(UO_2)(CO_3)_3.6H_2O$ found in the uranium districts of the western U.S.

an·des berry \\'an(,)dēz-, 'aan-\\ *n, usu cap A* [fr. *Andes* mts.] **:** a bramble (*Rubus glaucus*) of tropical American highlands having dark purple fruit like raspberries

an·de·sine \\'andə,zēn\\ *n* -S [G *andesin,* fr. *Andes,* mountain system in So. America, where it is found + G *-in* -ine] **:** a triclinic feldspar intermediate between albite and anorthite that is an ingredient of andesite — **an·de·sin·ic** \\¦andə¦zinik\\ *adj*

an·de·si·nite \\'andəzə,nīt\\ *n* -S [*andesine* + *-ite*] **:** a leucocratic rock composed essentially of andesine

an·de·site \\'andə,zīt\\ *n* -S [G *andesit,* fr. *Andes,* its locality + G *-it* -ite] **:** an extrusive usu. dark grayish rock consisting essentially of oligoclase or andesine feldspar with augite, hornblende, hypersthene, or biotite — **an·de·sit·ic** \\¦andə¦zid·ik\\ *adj*

an·dhra \\'ändrə\\ *n* -S *usu cap* [fr. *Andhra,* India] **:** the Dravidian language of the Andhra region of southern India

an·dhran \\'ändrən\\ *n* -S *usu cap* [fr. *Andhra,* India + E *-an*] **:** a native or inhabitant of the Andhra region or of Andhra Pradesh, southern India

an·di \\'āndē\\ *n* -S *usu cap* **:** a north Caucasic language — **an·di·an** \\-ēən\\ *adj, usu cap*

an·dine \\'an,dēn, -,dīn\\ *adj, usu cap* [Sp *andino,* fr. *Andes* mountains + Sp *-ino* (fr. L *-inus* -ine)] **:** ANDEAN

¹an·di·no \\an'dē(,)nō\\ *n* -S *usu cap* [Sp, adj. & n.] **:** a native or inhabitant of the Andes

²andino \\"\\ *adj, usu cap* [Sp, Andean] **:** of or belonging to the middle period of the ancient Tiahuanaco culture of coastal Peru

an·di·ra \\an'dērə, -dirə\\ *n, cap* [NL, fr. Pg, angelim, fr. Tupi] **:** a genus of tropical American trees (family Leguminosae) characterized by large odd-pinnate leaves, fragrant showy rose to purplish flowers in terminal clusters, and a fruit resembling a drupe

an·di·ro·ba \\,andə'rōbə\\ *n* -S [AmerSp *andiroba* or Pg *andiroba, jandiroba,* fr. Tupi *andiróba, nandiroba*] **:** ¹CRABWOOD

and·iron \\'an,dī(ə)rn, 'aan-,-īən\\ *n* -S [ME *aundiren,* modif. (influenced by ME *iren* iron) of OF *andier,* fr. (assumed) Gaulish *anderos* young bull; akin to W *anner* heifer, MIr *ainder* young woman; fr. the figures used as ornamentation] **:** one of a pair of metal supports for firewood used on a hearth and consisting of a horizontal bar mounted on short legs, one in the rear and two in front, an often ornamented vertical shaft usu. surmounting the front end

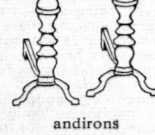

andirons

an·do·ke \\an'dōkē\\ *n, pl* **andoke** *or* **an·dokes** *usu cap* **1 a :** a people of southern Colombia **b :** a member of such people **2 :** the language of the Andoke people, of uncertain relationship

and/or \\'and¦ȯr, -ō(ə)\\ *conj* — used as a function word to indicate that words are to be taken together or individually ⟨men *and/or* women means men *and* women or men *or* women⟩

an·dor·ite \\'andə,rīt\\ *n* -S [G *andorit,* fr. *Andor* von Semsey †1923 Hungarian nobleman + G *-it* -ite] **:** a mineral consisting of a compound of silver, lead, antimony, and sulfur $PbAgSb_3S_6$ occurring in dark gray or black prisms

an·dor·ra \\(')an¦dȯrə, -ärə\\ *adj, usu cap* [fr. *Andorra,* state in the Pyrenees between France and Spain] **:** of or from the republic of Andorra **:** of the kind or style prevalent in Andorra **:** ANDORRAN

¹an·dor·ran \\-rən\\ *adj, usu cap* [*Andorra* + *-an*] **:** of, relating to, or characteristic of Andorra

²andorran \\"\\ *n* -S *cap* **:** a native or inhabitant of Andorra

an·do·ver green \\'an,dōvə(r)-, 'aan-, -,dəv-\\ *n, often cap A* [prob. fr. *Andover,* Mass.] **:** a grayish olive green that is greener and paler than average ivy green and yellower and paler than bronze green

andr- *or* **andro-** *comb form* [MF *andro-,* fr. L *andr-, andro-,* fr. Gk, fr. *andr-, anēr* man (male person); akin to OIr *nert* strength, Oscan *ner* man (male person), Skt *nṛ*] **1 :** man ⟨*androcentric*⟩ ⟨*androphagous*⟩ **:** of or belonging to a man or men ⟨*androcracy*⟩ ⟨*androphobia*⟩ **:** having the characteristics of a man and ⟨*androtauric*⟩ **2 :** male ⟨*androgenesis*⟩ **:** male and ⟨*androgynous*⟩ **3 :** stamen **:** anther ⟨*androecium*⟩

-an·dra \\'andrə, 'aan-\\ *n comb form* — NL, fem. of *-andrus* -androus] **:** one having (such) a stamen — in generic names of plants ⟨*Calliandra*⟩ ⟨*Pachysandra*⟩

an·dra·dite \\an'drä,dīt\\ *n* -S [José B. de *Andrada* e Silva †1838 Brazilian geologist and statesman + E *-ite*] **:** a garnet $Ca_3Fe_2(SiO_4)_3$ of any of various colors ranging from yellow and green to brown and black

an·dre·ae·a·les \\,andrē'ēə,lēz\\ *n pl, cap* [NL, fr. *Andreaea* genus of mosses (after G. R. *Andreae* Ger. botanist) + *-ales*] **:** an order of Musci comprising a single genus of brown or blackish alpine mosses with a capsule that dehisces by four longitudinal slits

an·drea·sen method \\?an'dräz°n-\\ *n, usu cap A* [fr. the name *Andreasen*] **:** a method of estimating particle size of ceramic clay by sedimentation

an·dre·na \\an'drēnə\\ *n, cap* [NL, prob. irreg. fr. Gk *anthrēnē* hornet, wasp — more at ATHEROMA] **:** a genus (the type of the family Andrenidae) of burrowing solitary short-tongued bees including important pollinators of economic plants

an·dre·nid \\-ēnəd\\ *n* -S [NL *Andrenidae*] **:** a bee of the family Andrenidae

an·dren·i·dae \\-renə,dē, -ēn-\\ *n pl, cap* [NL, fr. *Andrena,* type genus + *-idae*] **:** a large family of short-tongued bees which are solitary in habit and most of which burrow in the ground

an·drews·ite \\'an(,)drü,zīt\\ *n* -S [Thomas *Andrews* †1885 Ir. chemist + E *-ite*] **:** a mineral consisting of a hydrous phosphate of copper and iron $(Cu,Fe^{II})_3Fe_6^{III}(PO_4)_4(OH)_{12}$

-an·dria \\'andrēə, 'aan-\\ *n pl comb form* [NL, fr. Gk, fact or condition of having (such or so many) men — more at -ANDRY] **:** plants having (such or so many) stamens — in names of Linnaean botanical classes ⟨*Polyandria*⟩

an·dri·as \\'andrēəs\\ *n, cap* [NL, fr. Gk, image of a man, fr. *andr-, anēr* man; fr. the fact that the first specimen found was believed to be the remains of a man destroyed by the Deluge] **:** a genus of large fossil Miocene salamanders scarcely distinct from the recent genus *Cryptobranchus*

an·dric \ˈandrik\ *adj* [Gk *andrikos*, fr. *andr-* + *-ikos* -ic] **:** of or belonging to a male person — contrasted with *gynic*

an·dri·cus \anˈdrīkəs\ *n, cap* [NL] **:** a genus of cynipid gall wasps chiefly affecting various oaks

-andries *pl of* -ANDRY

an·drite \ˈan,drīt\ *n* -S [origin unknown] **:** a meteorite composed essentially of augite with a little olivine and troilite

andro- *in pronunciations below*, ¦== = ¦andrə *or* ¦aan- *or* -drō *sometimes* -,drō\ — see ANDR-

an·dro·cen·tric \¦==¦==\ *adj* [*andr-* + *-centric*] **:** centering or centered on or in the male **:** dominated by or emphasizing masculine interests or point of view ⟨an ~ society⟩ — contrasted with *gynecocentric*

an·dro·co·ni·um \,==ˈkōnēəm\ *n, pl* **an·dro·co·nia** \-ēə\ [NL, fr. *andr-* + Gk *konis* dust + NL *-ium* — more at INCINERATE] **:** any of certain modified scales associated with glandular structures on the fore wings of the male of some butterflies and moths and concerned with the production of an odor attractive to members of the opposite sex

an·droc·ra·cy \anˈdräkrəsē\ *n* -ES [*andr-* + *-cracy*] **:** political and social supremacy of men — contrasted with *gynecocracy*; compare PATRIARCHY — **an·dro·crat·ic** \¦andrə¦krad·ik\ *adj*

an·dro·cyte \ˈ==,sīt\ *n* -S [*andr-* + *-cyte*] **:** a cell in bryophytes that by modification becomes a sperm cell — compare SPERMATID, SPERMATOCYTE

an·dro·di·oe·cious *or* **an·dro·di·ecious** \¦==,=¦==\ *adj* [*andr-* + *dioecious, diecious*] **:** having perfect and staminate flowers on different plants — **an·dro·di·oe·cism** \-,dīˈē,sizəm\ *n* -S

an·droe·ci·um \anˈdrēs(h)ēəm\ *n, pl* **androe·cia** \-)ēə\ [NL, fr. *andr-* + Gk *oikion*, dim. of *oikos* house — more at VICINITY] **1 :** the aggregate of microsporophylls in the flower of a seed plant **:** stamens and their appendages **2 :** the male inflorescence of a liverwort

an·dro·gam·one \,==ˈga,mōn\ *n* -S [*andr-* + *gamone*] **:** a gamone in a male cell

an·dro·gen \ˈ==jən, -,jen\ *n* -S [ISV *andr-* + *-gen*] **:** a sex hormone (as androsterone or testosterone) produced esp. in the testes and adrenal cortex and usu. characterized by its ability to stimulate the development of sex characteristics in the male; *also* **:** a synthetic compound (as methyltestosterone) having similar biological activity — compare ESTROGEN — **an·dro·gen·ic** \¦==¦jenik\ *adj*

an·dro·gen·e·sis \,==ˈjenəsəs\ *n* [NL, fr. *andr-* + *-genesis*] **:** male parthenogenesis **:** development in which the embryo contains only paternal chromosomes due to failure of the egg nucleus to participate in fertilization — compare GYNOGENESIS — **an·dro·ge·net·ic** \¦==jə¦net·ik\ *adj* — **an·dro·ge·net·i·cal·ly** *adv* — **an·drog·e·nous** \(ˈ)anˈdräjənəs\ *adj*

an·dro·gen·ic·i·ty \¦==jəˈnisəd·ē\ *n* -ES [*androgen* + *-icity*] **:** the property of producing physiological reactions similar to those produced by androgens

an·drog·e·ny \anˈdräjənē\ *n* -ES [*andr-* + *-geny*] **:** ANDROGENESIS

androgen zone *or* **androgenic zone** *n* **:** the portion of the adrenal cortex believed to secrete male hormones or steroids resembling male hormones

an·dro·gone \ˈ==,gōn\ *n* -S [*andr-* + *gone*] **:** ANDROGONIUM

an·dro·go·ni·al \¦==¦gōnēəl\ *adj* [NL, fr. *androgonium* + E *-al*] **:** of or relating to an androgonium

an·dro·go·nid·i·um \,==gōˈnidēəm\ *n, pl* **androgonid·ia** \-ēə\ [NL, fr. *andr-* + *gonidium*] **1 :** one of the male cells whose subsequent divisions produce spermatozoids in members of the genus *Volvox* **2 :** ANDROSPORE 1

an·dro·go·ni·um \-ˈgōnēəm\ *n, pl* **androgo·nia** \-ēə\ [NL, fr. *andr-* + *-gonium*] **:** one of the group of cells that divide to produce androcytes and eventually spermatozoids (as in mosses and ferns)

an·drog·ra·phis \anˈdrägrəfəs\ *n, cap* [NL, fr. *andr-* + Gk *graphis* stylus, pencil, paintbrush, fr. *graphein* to write; fr. the form of the filaments — more at CARVE] **:** a genus of Indian plants (family Acanthaceae) with entire leaves, small tubular flowers, and dry capsular fruits — see CREAT

an·dro·gyne \ˈ==,jīn\ *also* **an·dro·gyn** \-,jin\ *n* -S [MF, fr. L *androgynus*, fr. Gk *androgynos*, fr. *andr-* + *-gynos* -gynous] **1 :** HERMAPHRODITE **2** *archaic* **:** an effeminate man

an·dro·gy·ne·i·ty \¦==jəˈnēəd·ē, -jīˈ-\ *n* -ES [*androgyne* + *-ity*] **:** ANDROGYNY

an·drog·y·nism \anˈdräjə,nizəm\ *n* -S [*androgynous* + *-ism*] **:** the quality or state of being androgynous **:** HERMAPHRODITISM

an·drog·y·nous \(ˈ)anˈdräjənəs\ *adj* [*androgyne* + *-ous*] **1 :** having the characteristics of both sexes **:** being at once both male and female **:** HERMAPHRODITIC **2** *archaic* **:** sometimes hot and sometimes cold — used of planets **3 a :** bearing both staminate and pistillate flowers in the same cluster with the male flowers uppermost — compare GYNAECANDROUS **b** *of fungi* **:** bearing both antheridium and oogonium on the same hypha

an·drog·y·ny \anˈdräjənē\ *n* -ES [*androgynous* + *-y*] **:** the quality or state of being androgynous **:** HERMAPHRODITISM, EFFEMINACY

[1]**an·droid** \ˈan,drȯid\ *also* **an·droi·des** \anˈdrȯi(,)dēz\ *n, pl* **androids** *or* **androides** [LGk *androeidēs* manlike, fr. Gk *andr-* + *-oeidēs* -oid] **:** an automaton of human form

[2]**android** \"\ *adj* [LGk *androeidēs* manlike] *of the pelvis* **:** having the angular form and narrow outlet typical of a well-built man ⟨a disproportionate number of difficult labors occur in women with ~ pelves⟩ — compare GYNECOID

an·drom·e·da \anˈdrämədə\ *n* [NL, fr. *Andromeda*, mythological Ethiopian princess (daughter of Cepheus) fastened to a rock for a sea monster to devour but rescued by Perseus, fr. L, fr. Gk] **1** *cap* **:** a small genus of low evergreen boreal or arctic shrubs (family Ericaceae) with revolute coriaceous leaves and drooping white or pinkish flowers in terminal umbels — see BOG ROSEMARY **2** -S **:** a plant of the genus *Andromeda* **3** -S **:** JAPANESE ANDROMEDA

an·drom·edo·tox·in \an¦drämə(,)dōˈtäksən\ *n* [ISV *andromed-* (fr. NL *Andromeda*) + *-o-* + *toxin*; orig. formed in G] **:** a toxic crystalline compound $C_{31}H_{50}O_{10}$ that exists in various ericaceous plants (as members of the genus *Andromeda*) and that taken in small doses lowers the blood pressure of animals

an·dro·me·rog·o·ny \¦an(,)drōməˈrägənē\ *n* -ES [*andr-* + *merogony*] **:** development of an embryo from a fertilized enucleated egg or egg fragment which shows only male characters **:** ANDROGENESIS

an·dro·mi·met·ic \¦==,=¦==\ *adj* [*androgen* + *mimetic*] **:** simulating the effect of androgen

an·dro·mo·noe·cious *also* **an·dro·mo·ne·cious** \¦==¦==¦==\ *adj* [*andr-* + *monoecious, monecious*] **:** having perfect and staminate flowers on the same plant — **an·dro·mo·noe·cism** \-ˈnē,sizəm\ *n* -S

an·dro·phil·ic \¦==ˈfilik\ *adj* [*andr-* + *-philic*] **:** showing preference for males or for men as distinguished from animals ⟨an ~ mosquito⟩

an·dro·pho·bia \,==ˈfōbēə\ *n* -S [NL, fr. *andr-* + *-phobia*] **:** an abnormal dread of men **:** repugnance to the male sex — **an·dro·pho·bic** \¦==¦fōbik *also* -äb-\ *adj*

an·dro·phore \ˈ==,fō(ə)r\ *n* -S [F, fr. *andr-* + *-phore*] **1 :** the stalk or column supporting the stamens in certain flowers **2 :** a branch bearing antheridia in fungi **3 :** a generative bud or modified medusa in coelenterates in which only male elements are developed **:** a male gonophore

an·droph·o·rous \(ˈ)anˈdräf(ə)rəs\ *adj* [*andr-* + *-phorous*] **:** bearing male sexual organs or zooids

an·dro·po·gon \,==ˈpō,gän\ *n, cap* [NL, fr. *andr-* + *-pogon*] **:** a large and important genus of almost cosmopolitan grasses with spikelike racemes having the flowers in pairs, one sterile and one fertile — see BLUESTEM, BROOM SEDGE

an·dros·a·ce \anˈdräsə,kē, -əsē\ *n, cap* [NL, alter. of L *androsaces*, a plant or zoophyte, fr. Gk *androsakes*, a sea plant (prob. a species of *Acetabularia*)] **:** a genus of usu. tufted herbs (family Primulaceae) native to the northern hemisphere having basal tufted leaves, small terminal white or pink flowers, and capsular fruits — see ROCK JASMINE

an·dro·sin \ˈandrəsən, -,sin\ *n* -S [ISV *andros-* (fr. NL *androsaemifolium* — specific epithet of *Apocynum androsaemifolium* — , fr. *andr-* + *saemi-* semi- + L *folium* leaf) + *-in*] **:** a crystalline glucoside $C_{15}H_{20}O_8$ that is found in an herb (*Apocynum androsaemifolium*) and that yields glucose and acetovanillone on hydrolysis

an·dro·spo·ran·gi·um \¦==-\ *n, pl* **androsporan·gia** [NL, fr. *andr-* + *sporangium*] **:** a sporangium for androspores

an·dro·spore \ˈ==,spō(ə)r\ *n* -S [NL *androsporus*, fr. *andr-* + *spora* spore] **1 :** a zoospore characteristic of members of the algal family Oedogoniaceae that gives rise to a small male plant that produces true spermatozoids — called also *androgonidium* **2 :** MICROSPORE

an·dro·stane \ˈ==,stān\ *n* -S [*androsterone* + *-ane*] **:** a crystalline saturated steroid hydrocarbon $C_{19}H_{32}$ obtainable from androsterone by reduction

an·dros·te·rone \anˈdrästə,rōn, aan-\ *n* -S [ISV *andr-* + *sterol* + *-one*; orig. formed as G *androsteron*] **:** an androgenic hormone that is much less active than testosterone and that is a hydroxy ketone $C_{19}H_{30}O_2$ found esp. in human male urine and obtained synthetically from cholesterol

an·drot·o·my \anˈdräd·əmē\ *n* -ES [*andr-* + *anatomy*] **:** ANTHROPOTOMY

an·dro·type \ˈ==,tīp\ *n* -S [*andr-* + *type*] **:** a designated male type specimen

-an·drous \¦andrəs, ¦aan-\ *adj comb form* [NL *-andrus*, fr. Gk *-andros* having (such or so many) men, fr. *andr-*, *anēr* man (male person) — more at ANDR-] **:** having (such or so many) stamens ⟨mon*androus*⟩

-an·dry \,andrē, ,aan-, -ri\ *n comb form* -ES [NL *-andria*, fr. Gk, fact or condition of having (such or so many) men, fr. *-andros* + *-ia* -y] **:** possession of (such or so many) stamens ⟨hetero*andry*⟩

an·dry·a·la \anˈdrīələ\ *n, cap* [NL] **:** a genus of hardy perennial composite herbs with milky sap and alternate leaves that are native to the Mediterranean region and occas. cultivated for their heads of bright yellow ligulate flowers

ands *pl of* AND

andy over *var of* ANTONY OVER

ane \ˈān\ *adj or n or pron* [ME (northern dial.) *an*, fr. OE *ān* — more at ONE] *chiefly Scot* **:** ONE

-ane \,ān\ *n suffix* -S [ISV *-an, -ane*, alter. of *-ene, -ine*, & *-one*] **1 :** [3]-AN 1 ⟨*urethane*⟩ **2 :** saturated or completely hydrogenated carbon compound — in names of hydrocarbons and some parent heterocyclic compounds ⟨*methane*⟩ ⟨*cholestane*⟩ ⟨*dioxane*⟩; distinguished from *-ene, -yne*

[1]**anear** \əˈ-\ *vt* [[1]*a-* + *near*, v.] *archaic* **:** to come near to **:** NEAR

[2]**anear** \"\ *adv* [[1]*a-* + *near*, adv.] **1** *archaic* **:** NEARLY, ALMOST ⟨the lady shrieks and well ~ does fall —Shak.⟩ **2** *archaic* **:** CLOSE, NEAR ⟨timidly the women drew ~ —William Morris⟩

[3]**anear** \"\ *prep, now chiefly dial* **:** NEAR **:** close to ⟨sat ~ me⟩

aneath \əˈnēth, -neth\ *prep* [[1]*a-* + *beneath*] *dial Brit* **:** BENEATH

an·ec·dot·age \ˈanik,dōd·ij\ *n* -S **1 :** ANECDOTES ⟨something of the interest in ~ common to the time —Bernard Smith⟩ **2** [blend of *anecdote* and *dotage*] **:** advanced age that is accompanied by a strong tendency to reminisce and tell anecdotes ⟨some kindly, garrulous old gentleman who was in his ~ —*Amer. Jour. of Pub. Health*⟩ — compare DOTAGE

an·ec·dot·al \¦anik¦dōd·ᵊl, -ōtᵊl\ *adj* **1 :** relating to, characteristic of, or containing anecdotes ⟨~ conversation⟩ **2** *of a painting or sculpture* **:** representing an incident that implies earlier or later action or dramatizes a situation of human interest ⟨an ~ painting of a dejected girl leaving a post office⟩ — **an·ec·dot·al·ism** \-,lizəm\ *n* -S — **an·ec·dot·al·ist** \-ləst\ *n* -S — **an·ec·dot·al·ly** \-ᵊlē, -li\ *adv*

an·ec·dote \ˈanik,dōt *also* -nək-; *usu* -ōd-+V\ *n, pl* **anecdotes** \-ts\ *or* **anecdo·ta** \,==ˈdōd·ə, -ōtə\ *see numbered senses* [F & Gk; F, fr. Gk *anekdotos* unpublished, fr. *an-* + *ekdotos* given out, fr. *ekdidonai* to give out, publish, fr. *ek* out, out of + *didonai* to give — more at EX-, DATE] **1** *pl* **anecdota** *also* **anecdotes :** items of unpublished or secret history or biography **2** *pl* **anecdotes :** a usu. short narrative of an interesting, amusing, or curious incident often biographical and generally characterized by human interest — **an·ec·dot·ism** \ˈ==,dōd-,izəm, -ō,tiz-\ *n* -S — **an·ec·dot·ist** \-ōd·əst, -ōtə-\ *n* -S

an·ec·dot·ic \¦anik¦däd·ik, -ätik, -ēk\ *or* **an·ec·dot·i·cal** \-əkəl, -ēk-\ *adj* [prob. fr. F *anecdotique*, fr. *anecdote* + *-ique* -ic] **1 :** ANECDOTAL **2 :** given to or ready at telling anecdotes ⟨at his most ~⟩ — **an·ec·dot·i·cal·ly** \-ək(ə)lē, -ēk-, -li\ *adv*

an·echo·ic \¦anə¦kōik, -(,)ne-\ *adj* [*an-* + *echoic*] **:** free from echoes and reverberations — used of rooms with sound-absorbent walls esp. designed for acoustic measurements; compare DEAD 10

an·ei·le·ma \,a,nīˈlēmə, ,anə-\ *n, cap* [NL, fr. Gk *aneilēma* act of rolling up, fr. *aneilein* to roll up, fr. *ana-* + *eilein* to roll, wind; akin to Gk *eilyein* to enfold, enwrap — more at VOLUBLE] **:** a large genus of widely distributed chiefly tropical trailing or creeping perennial herbs (family Commelinaceae) that have slender evergreen leaves and blue flowers usu. in small panicles and are sometimes cultivated in the cool greenhouse

an·elas·tic \¦an=¦==\ *adj* [*an-* + *elastic*] **:** having no single-valued relation between stress and strain in the elastic region of the stress-strain curve — **an·elas·tic·i·ty** \¦an=\ *n*

anele \əˈnē(ə)l\ *vt* -ED/-ING/-S [ME *anelen*, fr. *an* (fr. OE, var. of *on*) + *elen* to anoint, fr. *ele* oil, fr. OE *ele*, fr. L *oleum* — more at OIL] *archaic* **:** to anoint esp. in giving extreme unction

an·elec·tro·ton·ic \¦anə¦lek-trə¦tänik\ *adj* **:** relating to anelectrotonus

an·elec·trot·o·nus \¦anə,lekˈträtᵊnəs\ *n* -ES [NL, fr. *ana-* + *electrotonus*] **:** the condition of decreased irritability of a nerve in the region of a positive electrode or anode on the passage of a current of electricity through it — compare CATELECTROTONUS

an·el·y·trous \(ˈ)a¦ne-\ *adj* [*an-* + *elytrous*] **:** without elytra

anem- *or* **anemo-** *comb form* [prob. fr. F *anémo-*, fr. Gk *anem-*, *anemo-*, fr. *anemos* — more at ANIMATE] **1 :** wind ⟨*anemosis*⟩ ⟨*anemometer*⟩ **2 :** inhalation ⟨*anemopathy*⟩

ane·ma·tize \əˈnemə,tīz\ *vt* -ED/-ING/-S **:** to affect with anemia **:** induce anemia in

anemi *var of* ANIMÉ

[1]**ane·mia** *also* **anae·mia** \əˈnēmēə, *esp Brit* -myə\ *n* -S [NL, fr. Gk *anaimia*, fr. *an-* + *-aimia* -emia] **1 a :** a condition in which the blood is deficient in red blood cells, hemoglobin, or both or deficient in total volume (as from hemorrhage) — see HYPOCHROMIC ANEMIA, PERNICIOUS ANEMIA **b :** ISCHEMIA **2 :** lack of vitality **:** BLOODLESSNESS, LIFELESSNESS, EMPTINESS ⟨intellectual ~ —John Fischer⟩ ⟨the New England tradition had died of ~ —Malcolm Cowley⟩

[2]**anemia** \"\ *n, cap* [NL, fr. Gk *aneimōn* unclad (fr. *an-* + *-eimōn* clad, fr. *heima* garment) + NL *-ia*; fr. the naked sporangia; akin to Gk *hennynai* to clothe — more at WEAR] **:** a genus of ferns (family Schizaeaceae) found in warm regions having pinnatifid almost skeletonlike fronds with sporangia borne in a close single row on either side of the pinnules

ane·mic *also* **anae·mic** \əˈnēmik, -mēk\ *adj* [ISV *anem-*, *anaem-* (fr. NL *anemia, anaemia*) + *-ic*] **1 :** relating to or affected with anemia **2 :** lacking vitality **:** BLOODLESS ⟨pale and ~ interpretations of Mozart —A.E.Wier⟩ — **ane·mi·cal·ly** \-mək(ə)lē, -ēk-, -li\ *adv*

an·e·mo·bi·a·graph \¦anə(,)mōˈbīə,graf\ *n* -S [*anem-* + Gk *bia* force + E *-graph*] **:** a pressure-tube anemometer that records wind speed

anem·o·chore \əˈnemə,kō(ə)r\ *n* -S [*anem-* + *-chore*] **:** a plant that has seeds or spores adapted (as by pappi) to distribution by wind — **anem·o·cho·ry** \-ōrē\ *n* -ES

an·e·mo·clas·tic \¦anəmō¦klastik\ *adj* [*anem-* + *clastic*] **:** formed by wind action — used of clastic rocks

ane·mo·gen·ic \ə¦nēmə¦jenik\ *adj* [*anem-* + *-genic*] **:** causing anemia

anem·o·gram \əˈnemə,gram\ *n* -S [*anem-* + *-gram*] **:** a record made by an anemograph

anem·o·graph \-,graf\ *n* -S [*anem-* + *-graph*] **:** a recording anemometer — **anem·o·graph·ic** \=¦==¦=ik\ *adj* — **anem·o·graph·i·cal·ly** \-ək(ə)lē\ *adv*

an·e·mo·log·i·cal \¦anəmə¦läjəkəl\ *adj* **:** of or relating to anemology

an·e·mol·o·gy \,anəˈmäləjē\ *n* -ES [*anem-* + *-logy*] **:** the study of winds

an·e·mom·e·ter \,anəˈmäməd·ə(r), -ətə(r)\ *n* -S [*anem-* + *-meter*] **:** an instrument for measuring and indicating the force or speed of the wind **:** WIND GAUGE

anemometer

an·e·mo·met·ric \¦anəmō¦me·trik\ *also* **an·e·mo·met·ri·cal** \-rəkəl\ *adj* **:** of or relating to anemometry

an·e·mo·met·ro·graph \,anəmōˈme·trə,graf\ *n* -S [*anemometer* + *-o-* + *-graph*] **:** ANEMOGRAPH; *esp* **:** one that records simultaneously the pressure, speed, and direction of the wind — **an·e·mo·met·ro·graph·ic** \,anəmō,me·trə¦grafik\ *adj* — **an·e·mo·met·ro·graph·i·cal·ly** \-ək(ə)lē\ *adv*

an·e·mom·e·try \,anəˈmämə·trē\ *n* -ES [*anem-* + *-metry*] **:** the act or process of ascertaining the force, speed, and direction of wind

anem·o·ne \əˈnemənē, -ni *also* -,nē\ *n* [L, fr. Gk *anemōnē*, perh. by folk etymology (influence of *anemos* wind) fr. a word of Sem origin; akin to Heb *Na'ămān*, epithet of Adonis] **1** -S **:** a plant or flower of the genus *Anemone* **2** *cap* [NL, fr. L] **:** a genus of herbs (family Ranunculaceae) widely distributed in temperate and subarctic regions that have lobed or divided often involucral leaves and showy flowers that lack petals but have showy sepals **3** -S **:** SEA ANEMONE **4** -S **:** a pale reddish purple that is redder, stronger, and slightly lighter than dusty orchid

wood anemone

anemone dahlia *n* **:** any of a class of dahlias having flower heads with only one row of rays and with the disk flowers elongated and forming an effect like a pincushion

anem·o·nin \əˈnemənən\ *n* -S [G, fr. NL *Anemone* (genus name of *Anemone pulsatilla*) + G *-in*] **:** an acrid poisonous crystallizable dilactone obtained from certain plants esp. of the genera *Ranunculus* and *Anemone*

anemony *n* -ES [by alter.] *archaic* **:** ANEMONE

an·e·moph·i·lous \,anəˈmäfələs\ *adj* [*anem-* + *-philous*] **:** normally wind-pollinated ⟨~ flowers⟩ — compare ENTOMOPHILOUS — **an·e·moph·i·ly** \,anəˈmäfəlē\ *n* -ES

an·e·mop·sis \,anəˈmäpsəs\ *n, cap* [NL, fr. *anem-* (fr. *Anemone*) + *-opsis*; fr. its resemblance to an anemone] **:** a small genus of herbs (family Saururaceae) found in southwestern No. America having long-stalked entire leaves and minute flowers in a terminal bracted spike

anem·o·scope \əˈnemə,skōp\ *n* -S [prob. fr. F *anémoscope* (fr. *anémo-* anem- + *-scope*)] **:** a contrivance for indicating or for indicating and recording the direction of the wind; *also* **:** a device intended to foretell changes in the weather

an·e·mo·sis \,anəˈmōsəs\ *n, pl* **anemo·ses** \-ō,sēz\ [NL, fr. *anem-* + *-osis*] **:** WIND SHAKE

an·e·mo·tax·is \,anəmōˈtaksəs\ *n, pl* **anemotax·es** \-k,sēz\ [NL, fr. *anem-* + *-taxis*] **:** ANEMOTROPISM

an·e·mo·trop·ic \¦anəmō¦träpik\ *adj* [*anem-* + *-tropic*] **:** relating to anemotropism

an·e·mot·ro·pism \,anəˈmä·trə,pizəm\ *n* -S [*anem-* + *tropism*] **:** a tropism in which a current of air is the orienting factor (as in flies poised facing the wind)

an·en·ce·pha·lia \¦a,nensəˈfālyə\ *n* -S [NL, fr. *an-* + *-encephalia*] **:** ANENCEPHALY

an·en·ce·phal·ic \¦a,nensə¦falik\ *or* **an·en·ceph·a·lous** \¦anənˈsefələs, ¦a,nen-\ *adj* [*anencephalic* fr. *an-* + *encephalic*; *anencephalous* fr. Gk *anenkephalos* having no brain, fr. *an-* + *-enkephalos* -encephalous] **:** characterized by partial or total absence of the brain

an·en·ceph·a·lus \,anənˈsefələs, ,a,nen-\ *n, pl* **anencepha·li** \-,lī\ [NL, fr. *an-* + *-encephalus*] **:** a fetus characterized by anencephaly

an·en·ceph·a·ly \-lē\ *n* -ES [*an-* + *-encephaly*] **:** congenital absence of all or a major part of the brain

an end *adv* [ME *an ende*, *on ende*, fr. *an* (alter. of *on*), *on* + *ende* end] **1** *archaic* **:** to the end **:** CONTINUOUSLY **2** *obs* **:** UPRIGHT, ENDWAYS **3 :** directly ahead **:** LENGTHWISE

anenst \əˈnenzt, -en(t)st\ *prep* [ME, alter. of *anentes*, alter. (influenced by *-es* -s, adv. ending) of *anent*] *dial chiefly Brit* **:** ANENT

anent \əˈnent\ *prep* [ME *anent*, *onevent*, fr. OE *onemn*, *on efen* alongside, together (akin to OS *an eban*), fr. *on* + *efen* even — more at EVEN] **1** *now dial Brit* **:** on a line or level with **:** BESIDE **2** *archaic* **:** TOWARD, AGAINST **3** *chiefly dial* **:** over against **:** OPPOSITE **:** close to ⟨the house is ~ the church⟩ **4 :** in reference to **:** ABOUT, CONCERNING ⟨thoughts ~ the proper dissemination of religion —F. Tennyson Jesse⟩

an·en·ter·ous \(ˈ)a¦nentərəs\ *adj* [*an-* + *enterous*] **:** having no stomach or intestine

aner \ˈanər, äˈne(ə)r\ *n* -S [Gk *anēr* man, male animal — more at ANDR-] **:** a male insect; *esp* **:** a male ant

an·er·gic \(ˈ)a¦nərjik\ *adj* **:** exhibiting or marked by anergy

an·er·gy \ˈa,nərjē, ˈanər-\ *n* -ES [NL *anergia*, fr. *an-* + Gk *ergon* work + NL *-ia* — more at WORK] **:** a condition in which the body fails to react to an injected allergen or antigen (as tuberculin)

anerobic *var of* ANAEROBIC

an·er·oid \ˈanə,rȯid\ *adj* [F *anéroïde*, fr. *a-* [2]*a-* + LGk *nēron* water (fr. Gk *nearon*, neut. of *nearos* fresh, new) + F *-oïde* -oid; akin to L *noverca* stepmother, Arm *nor* new, Gk *neos* new — more at NEW] **:** containing no liquid or actuated without the use of liquid ⟨an ~ mechanism⟩ ⟨~ manometer⟩

aneroid barometer *also* **aneroid** *n* -S **:** a barometer in which the action of atmospheric pressure in bending the thin corrugated top of a closed and partially exhausted metallic box or in distorting a thin-walled bent tube of metal is made to move a pointer

aneroid barometer: *1*, exhausted box; *2*, spring attached to box and connected by lever, *3*, with rocking bar, *4*, which is connected by chain, *5*, with spindle of pointer, *6*

an·er·oid·o·graph \¦==ˈ=də,graf\ *n* -S [*aneroid* + *-o-* + *-graph*] **:** an aneroid barometer with a mechanism for recording automatically and continuously the atmospheric pressure

[1]**anes** \ˈān(t)s, ˈänz\ *adv* [ME (northern dial.), var. of *ones* — more at ONCE] *chiefly Scot* **:** ONCE

[2]**anes** *pl of* ANE

-anes *pl of* -ANE

an·e·sone \ˈanə,sōn\ *n* -S [origin unknown] **:** an anise-flavored liqueur often added to black coffee

an·es·the·sia *also* **an·aes·the·sia** \,anəsˈthēzhə\ *n* -S [NL, fr. Gk *anaisthēsia* insensibility, fr. *an-* + *aisthēsis* feeling, perception (fr. *aisthanesthai* to perceive, feel) + *-ia* — more at AUDIBLE] **1 a :** loss of sensation esp. to touch usu. resulting from a lesion in the nervous system or from some other abnormality — see GLOVE ANESTHESIA **b :** loss of sensation and usu. of consciousness without loss of vital functions artificially produced by the administration of one or more agents that block the passage of pain impulses along nerve pathways to the brain **2 :** temporary dullness of perception or sensitiveness ⟨feeling the ~ of exhaustion —Norman Mailer⟩

Anes·the·sin \əˈnesthəsən, aˈ-\ *trademark* — used for benzocaine

an·es·the·si·ol·o·gist \,anəs,thēzēˈäləjəst *also* -thēsē-\ *n* -S **:** ANESTHETIST; *specif* **:** a physician specializing in anesthesiology

an·es·the·si·ol·o·gy \-jē, -ji\ *n* -ES [ISV *anesthesio-* (fr. NL *anesthesia*) + *-logy*] **:** a branch of medical science dealing with anesthesia and anesthetics

[1]**an·es·thet·ic** *also* **an·aes·thet·ic** \¦anəs¦thed·ik, -etik, -ēk\ *adj* [Gk *anaisthētos* without sense or feeling, unfelt, imper-

ceptible (fr. *an-* + *aisthētos* sensible, perceptible, fr. *aisthanesthai* to perceive, feel) + E *-ic* — more at AUDIBLE] **1 a :** capable of producing anesthesia ⟨~ agents⟩ **b :** involving or connected with anesthesia ⟨~ effect⟩ ⟨~ symptoms⟩ **2 a :** lacking perceptive sensitiveness ⟨the young girls are in a state of possession, blind, deaf, and ~ —Joyce Cary⟩ **b :** OBTUSE — used with *to* ⟨persons ~ to new ideas⟩ — **an·es·thet·i·cal·ly** *adv*

²anesthetic *also* **anaesthetic** \"\ *n* -s **1 :** a substance that produces anesthesia **2 :** something that brings relief (as from pain, worry, uneasiness) **:** PALLIATIVE ⟨Vienna's most effective mass ~ against our time is the coffeehouse —Frederic Morton⟩

anes·the·tist *also* **anaes·the·tist** \ə'nesthəd·əst, a'-, -thətə-, *Brit usu* -nēs-\ *n* -s [*anesthetize, anaesthetize* + *-ist*] **:** one who administers anesthetics — compare ANESTHESIOLOGIST

anes·the·ti·za·tion *also* **anaes·the·ti·za·tion** \ə,ˌthəd·ə'zāshən, -ətə'-, -ə,tī'z-\ *n* -s **:** the process of anesthetizing or state of being anesthetized

anes·the·tize *also* **anaes·the·tize** \ə'nesthə,tīz, a'-, *Brit usu* -nēs-\ *vt* -ED/-ING/-S [²*anesthetic, anaesthetic* + *-ize*] **:** to subject to anesthesia esp. by the use of an anesthetic

anes·thyl \-thəl\ *also* **anes·tile** \-tᵊl, -,tīl\ *n* -s [NL *anesthesia* + E *-yl* or *-ile*] **:** a mixture of ethyl and methyl chlorides used for the production of local anesthesia by spraying

an·es·trous \(')a¦nestrəs, *esp Brit* -ēs-\ *also* **an·es·tric** \-rik\ *or* **an·oes·trous** \-rəs\ *adj* [NL *anestrus, anoestrus* + E *-ous* or *-ic*] **:** of or relating to anestrus

an·es·trus \(')ˌ'ˌstrəs\ *also* **an·es·trum** \-rəm\ *or* **an·oes·trus** \-rəs\ *or* **an·oes·trum** \-rəm\ *n, pl* **anes·tri** \-,strī\ *or* **anes·tra** \-,strə\ [NL, fr. *an-* + *estrus, estrum, oestrus, or oestrum*] **:** the period of sexual quiescence between two periods of sexual activity in cyclically breeding mammals — compare ESTRUS

aneth \ə'neth\ *Scot var of* ANEATH

an·e·thole \'anə,thōl\ *also* **an·e·thol** \-ōl,-ōl\ *n* -s [ISV *aneth-* (fr. L *anethum*) + *-ole, -ol;* prob. orig. formed as G *anethol*] **:** an ether $CH_3OC_6H_4C_3H_5$ obtained esp. from the oils of anise and fennel in the form of soft shining scales and used in flavoring and in cosmetics **:** *para*-propenyl-anisole — called also *anise camphor*

ane·thum \ə'nēthəm\ *n* [NL, fr. L, dill, fr. Gk *anēthon*] **1** *cap* **:** a small genus of Asiatic herbs (family Umbelliferae) with dissected foliage and yellow flowers — see DILL **2** *pl* **ane·tha** \-thə\ *or* **anethums :** the dried ripe fruit of an herb (*Anethum graveolens*) that is used in medicine as a carminative and stomachic

aneuch \ə'n(y)ük\ *adj or adv or n* [ME, var. of *enogh* — more at ENOUGH] *Scot* **:** ENOUGH

¹an·eu·ploid \'a(,)nyü,plȯid, 'anyə,-, (')a'nyü,-\ *adj* [*an-* + *euploid*] **:** having or being a chromosome number that is not a multiple of the monoploid number — compare EUPLOID, HETEROPLOID, HYPERPLOID — **an·eu·ploi·dy** \'a(,)nyü,plȯidē, 'anyə,-\ *n* -ES

²aneuploid \"\ *n* -s **:** an organism having an aneuploid chromosome number

aneu·ri·lem·mic \ˌā,ˌˌˌ'ˌˌ\ *adj* [²*a-* + NL *neurilemma* + E *-ic*] **:** having no neurilemma

an·eu·rin \'anyərən, (')ā'nyür-\ *also* **an·eu·rine** \-,rēn\ *n* -s [ISV ²*a-* + *neur-* + *-in*] **:** THIAMINE

aneu·ro·gen·ic \ˌā,nürə¦jenik, -ür-\ *adj* [²*a-* + *neur-* + *-genic*] *of embryonic parts* **:** developing without the normal neural component ⟨a grafted limb bud is ~⟩

an·eu·rysm *also* **an·eu·rism** \'anyə,rizəm\ *n* -s [Gk *aneurysma*, fr. *aneurynein* to dilate, fr. *ana-* + *eurynein* to stretch, fr. *eurys* wide — more at EURY-] **:** a localized abnormal dilatation of a blood vessel (as an artery) filled with fluid or clotted blood, usu. forming a pulsating tumor, and resulting from disease of the vessel wall

an·eu·rys·mal *also* **an·eu·ris·mal** \¦anyə¦rizməl\ *adj* **:** relating to or affected by an aneurysm ⟨an ~ dilatation⟩ — **an·eu·rys·mal·ly** \-məlē\ *adv*

anew \ə'n(y)ü\ *adv* [ME *anewe*, of *newe*, fr. OE *of nīwe*, fr. *of* + *nīwe* new — more at NEW] **1 :** for an additional time ⟨each day raises ~ the possibility —*N.Y.Times*⟩ **:** as if a new start were being made and without reference to or observance of past acts or actions **:** AFRESH ⟨men chosen ~ on each occasion —S.G.Morley⟩ **2 :** in a new form

ane·zeh *or* **aney·ze** \ə'nāzə\ *n, pl* **anezeh** *or* **anezehs** *or* **aneyze** *or* **aneyzes** *usu cap* **1 :** an Arab people of the Syrian desert **2 :** a member of the Anezeh people

an·frac·tu·os·i·ty \(,)an,frakchə'wäsəd·ē\ *n* -ES [MF *anfractuosité*, fr. LL *anfractuosus* + MF *-ité* -ity] **1 :** the quality or state of being anfractuous **2 :** a winding channel, course, or passage; *esp* **:** an intricate path or process (as of the mind) ⟨the history of mathematics . . . is one of quirks and *anfractuosities* —Norbert Wiener⟩

an·frac·tu·ous \(')an¦frakchəwəs\ *adj* [F *anfractueux*, fr. LL *anfractuosus*, fr. L *anfractus* coil, crook (fr. *anfractus* crooked, fr. *an-* — fr. *ambi-* around — + *fractus*, past part. of *frangere* to break) + *-osus* -ose — more at AMBI-, BREAK] **:** full of windings and esp. intricate turnings **:** TORTUOUS, SINUOUS ⟨~ cliffs —T.H.White b. 1906⟩ ⟨these ~ times —Richard Eberhart⟩

ang- *comb form, usu ital* [*angular*] **:** angular (sense 5)

ang *abbr* angular

an·gai·té \ˌaŋ,gī'tā\ *n, pl* **angaité** *or* **angaités** *usu cap* [Sp, of AmerInd origin] **1 :** an Indian people of Paraguay **2 :** a member of the Angaité people

an·ga·kok *also* **an·ge·kok** \'aŋgə,käk\ *n, pl* **angakoks** *also* **angekoks** \-,käks\ [Esk] **:** an Eskimo medicine man or shaman

an·ga·mi \an'gämē\ *also* **angami-na·ga** \-'nägə\ *n, pl* **angami** *or* **angamis** *also* **angami-naga** *or* **angami-nagas** *usu cap A&N* **1 a :** a people of Assam, India **b :** a member of such people **2 :** the language of the Angami

an·gar·a·lite \an'garə,līt\ *n* -s [G *angaralith*, fr. *Angara* river, U.S.S.R., its locality + G *-lith* -lite] **:** a mineral $Mg_2(Al,Fe)_{10}Si_6O_{29}$ consisting of a magnesium aluminum iron silicate and occurring in thin black plates (sp. gr. 5.6)

an·gar·ia \an'ga(a)rēə, an'-\ *n* [LL, fr. Gk *angareia*, fr. *angaros* royal (Persian) courier — more at ANGEL] **1** *in Roman and civil law* **:** a compulsory service exacted by the government, a lord, or the church **2** *in maritime law* **:** the forcible seizure of a ship for public service **3** *in international law* **:** ANGARY **4** *in feudal law* **:** a troublesome or vexatious service exacted by a lord of his tenant

an·ga·ry \'aŋgərē\ *n* [LL *angaria*] **:** the right in international law of a belligerent to seize, use, or destroy property of neutrals, or to take over use of neutral ships in case of necessity

-ange \ˌanj, ˌaa(ə)nj\ *n comb form* -s [NL *-angium*] **:** -ANGIUM

¹an·gel \'ānjəl\ *n* -s [ME *angel*, fr. OF *angele*, fr. LL *angelus*, fr. Gk *angelos* (trans. of Heb *mal'ākh*), lit., messenger, prob. of Iranian origin; akin to the source of Gk *angaros* imperial Persian courier; perh. akin to Skt *aṅgiras* one of a group of luminous divine beings] **1 a :** a supernatural spirit esp. in Persian, Jewish, Christian, and Islamic theologies that is commonly depicted as being winged and serving as God's messenger and divine intermediary and as special guardian of an individual or nation **b :** a member of any order of the heavenly hierarchy, esp. of the lowest order — see CELESTIAL HIERARCHY **2** *obs* **:** one of the fallen spirits regarded as former angels of God **3 :** one bearing a divine message (as a preacher or prophet) **4 :** BISHOP, PASTOR ⟨to the ~ of the church in Ephesus —Rev 2:1 (RSV)⟩ **5 :** an attendant spirit or guardian — often used without implication of belief in its supernatural character ⟨my good ~⟩ **6 :** a person deceased and regarded as received into heaven **7 a** *or* **angel-noble** \'ˌˌ'ˌˌ\ **:** an English gold coin issued 1465–1634 that was similar in device to the Anglo-Gallic angelot and at first valued at *6s 8d*, but later at *7s 6d*, then at *8s*, and after 1553 at *10s* **b :** a corresponding unit of value ⟨half an ~⟩ **c** *obs* **:** a bill of public credit for 10 shillings issued in the Massachusetts Colony in 1713 **8 :** a white-robed winged figure of human form in fine art **9 :** MESSENGER, HARBINGER ⟨the ~ of the spring, the nightingale —Ben Jonson⟩ **10 :** a person (as a woman or a child) felt to resemble an angel (as in innocence or loveliness) **11** *Christian Science* **:** a message originating from God in his aspects of Truth and Love **12** *slang* **:** one who aids or supports with money or influence (as a backer of a theatrical venture) — sometimes used derogatively to refer to a wealthy man easily separated from his money **13 :** ANGELFISH ⟨a black ~⟩ **14 :** a member of a religious cult called Father Divine's Peace Mission

²angel \"\ *vt* -ED/-ING/-S *slang* **:** to support or back with contributions of money ⟨~*ed* several musicals⟩

angel bed *n* [trans. of F *lit d'ange*] **:** a bed without posts but with a small canopy

angel cake *or* **angel food** *or* **angel food cake** *n* [so called fr. its pure white color] **:** a white sponge cake made of flour, sugar, and whites of eggs

an·ge·le·no *also* **an·ge·le·ño** \ˌanjə'lē(,)nō *also* -lān(,)yō\ *n* -s *cap* [AmerSp *angeleño*, fr. Los *Angeles*, Calif. + Sp *-eño* (suffix added to place names to form names of inhabitants)] **:** a native or resident of Los Angeles, Calif.

an·gel·et \'ānjə¦let\ *n* -s [ME, fr. MF, fr. OF, little angel, fr. OF *angele* angel + *-et* — more at ANGEL] **:** an English gold coin issued 1470–1619 that was worth half an angel

angeleyes \'ˌˌ,ˌ\ *n pl* **:** BLUETS

angelfish \'ˌˌ,ˌ\ *n* [so called fr. its appearance, suggesting in sense 1 the wings, in other senses the splendor and delicacy, of an angel] **1 :** MONKFISH 1 **2 :** any of several compressed bright-colored teleost fishes of warm seas of the family Chaetodontidae — called also *butterfly fish;* see BLACK ANGELFISH, BLUE ANGELFISH **3 :** SPADEFISH **4 :** SCALARE

an·gel·hood \-,hu̇d\ *n* **1 :** the nature or status of an angel **2 :** an angelic being

an·gel·ic \(')an¦jelik, aan-, -ēk\ *or* **an·gel·i·cal** \-əkəl, -ēk-\ *adj* [*angelic* fr. MF *angelique*, fr. LL *angelicus*, fr. Gk *angelikos*, fr. *angelos* angel + *-ikos* -ic; *angelical* fr. *angelic* + *-al*] **:** of, relating to, or proceeding from angels ⟨~ forms⟩ **:** resembling, characteristic of, or having the nature of an angel ⟨~ innocence⟩ ⟨~ beneficence⟩ **:** HEAVENLY, SAINTLY — **an·gel·i·cal·ly** \-ək(ə)lē, -ēk-, -li\ *adv*

an·gel·i·ca \an'jelәkə, aan-, -ēkə\ *n* [NL, fr. ML, angelica plant, fr. LL, fem. of *angelicus* angelic; fr. the supposed medicinal properties] **1** *cap* **:** a genus of herbs (family Umbelliferae) found in the temperate zone and New Zealand and having decompound leaves, mostly white flowers, and prominently dorsal-ribbed fruit **2** *also* **an·ge·lique** \ˌanjə¦lēk, ¦aan-\ -s [*angelique* fr. F *angélique*] **:** any plant of the genus *Angelica; esp* **:** a biennial cultivated herb (*A. archangelica*) having rootstalks that are candied and roots and seeds that yield a flavoring oil — see ANGELICA OIL **3** -s *usu cap* [MexSp *angélica*, fr. fem. of *angélico* angelic, fr. LL *angelicus*] **:** a sweet straw-colored or amber-colored dessert wine produced in California **4** *or* **angelique** -s [*angelica* prob. fr. It, prob. fr. F *angélique*, fr. *angélique* angelic; *angelique* prob. fr. F *angélique*] **:** a lute with approximately 16 strings tuned scalewise — called also *angelot*

an·gel·ic acid \(')an¦jelik-\ *n* [NL *Angelica*] **:** an unsaturated crystalline acid $CH_3CH{=}C(CH_3)COOH$ obtained from angelica and some other plants; *cis*-*α*-methyl-crotonic acid — compare TIGLIC ACID

angelica lactone *n* **:** either of two lactones $C_5H_6O_2$ related to angelic acid

angelica oil *n* **:** either of two essential oils that have a musky odor and are obtained usu. from the roots but sometimes from the fruits of angelica and are used chiefly in making liqueurs

angelica tree *n* **:** HERCULES'-CLUB 3

an·gel·i·co \an'jelə,kō\ *n* -s [prob. alter. of *angelica*] **:** NONDO

an·gel·i·fy \an'jelə,fī\ *vt* -ED/-ING/-ES [¹*angel* + *-ify*] **:** to make into or like an angel **:** ANGELIZE

an·ge·lim \ˌanjə¦lim\ *or* **an·ge·lin** \-in\ *n* -s [Pg *angelim*, fr. Tamil *anjili-maram, anjali-maram*] **:** any of several chiefly tropical American trees of the genus *Andira; esp* **:** CABBAGE BARK

angeling *pres part of* ANGEL

an·ge·lique \ˌanjə¦lēk, ¦aan-\ *n* -s [F *angélique*, fr. MF *angélique* angelica (plant of the genus *Angelica*), fr. *angélique* angelic — more at ANGELIC] **1 a :** the wood of a So. American timber tree (*Dicorynia paraensis*) **b :** the tree that produces angelique **c :** ANGELICA 2 **2 :** a liqueur flavored with angelica oil and other flavoring agents (as coriander and oil of bitter almonds) **3 :** ANGELICA 4

an·gel·ism \'ānjə,lizəm\ *n* -s **:** the regarding of human affairs from an unrealistically sanguine point of view, as though a man were an angel

an·gel·ize \-,līz\ *vt* -ED/-ING/-S **:** to raise to the state of an angel **:** render angelic

angel light *n* **:** a small triangular light between subordinate arches of window tracery (as in English perpendicular style)

angel-noble *n* **:** ANGEL 7a

an·gel·ol·o·gy \ˌānjə'läləjē\ *n* -ES [NL *angelologia*, fr. L *angelus* angel + NL *-o-* + *-logia* -logy — more at ANGEL] **:** the doctrine or theory of angels **:** beliefs concerning angels

an·ge·lón \ˌanjə¦lōn\ *n* -s [AmerSp, fr. Sp, large angel, aug. of *ángel* angel, fr. LL *angelus* — more at ANGEL] **:** a plant of the genus *Angelonia*

an·ge·lo·nia \ˌanjə'lōnyə\ *n, cap* [NL, fr. AmerSp *angelón* + NL *-ia*] **:** a genus of tropical American herbs (family Scrophulariaceae) having long racemes of light purple flowers

an·ge·lot \'anjə,lät, ¦ˌˌ¦lō\ *n* -s [MF, fr. OF, little angel, dim. of *angele* angel — more at ANGEL] **1** [so called fr. the device on the obverse, showing the archangel Michael slaying a dragon] **:** an Anglo-Gallic gold coin issued by Henry VI of England **2 :** ANGELICA 4 **3 :** a small rich cheese made in Normandy

angel pie *n* **:** a dessert consisting of a baked shell of meringue filled with crushed fruit (as strawberries) and whipped cream

angel red *n* **:** COLCOTHAR 2

angels *pl of* ANGEL, *pres 3d sing of* ANGEL

angel's hair *n* **:** spun-glass strands used for Christmas-tree decoration

angel shark *n* [so called fr. its wing-shaped pectoral fins] **:** a shark of the family Squatinidae **:** MONKFISH 1

angel skin *n* [trans. of F *peau d'ange*] **:** PEAU D'ANGE

angel's kiss *n* **:** a cocktail made from crème de cacao and cream and occas. brandy and an additional liqueur and so poured into a glass that each ingredient forms a layer — compare POUSSE-CAFÉ 2

angel sleeve *n* **:** a very long wide sleeve usu. hanging loose from the shoulder often used on robes and gowns

angels on horseback : oysters wrapped in bacon and skewered, broiled, and served on toast

angel's seat *n, slang* **:** a raised observation seat in a railroad caboose

angel's–trumpet \'ˌˌ,ˌˌ\ *n, pl* **angel's–trumpets :** either of two So. American plants of the genus *Datura* (*D. suaveolens* and *D. arborea*) cultivated for their large and fragrant trumpet-shaped blossoms

angel's wing *or* **angel wing** *n* **:** a boring mollusk of the family Pholadidae **:** PIDDOCK

an·ge·lus \'anjələs, 'aan-\ *n* -ES *usu cap* [ML, fr. LL, angel; fr. the first word of the opening versicle — more at ANGEL] **1 :** a form of devotion that commemorates the Incarnation and is said in the morning, at noon, and at night by Roman Catholics usu. at the sounding of a bell **2 :** the bell announcing the time for the Angelus

angel-wing begonia *n* **:** any of several begonias having prominent basal leaf lobes that suggest the form of the upper part of the wing of an angel or bird

an·gen·e·sis \an'jenəsəs\ *n, pl* **angene·ses** \-ə,sēz\ [NL, fr. *ana-* + *genesis*] **:** regeneration esp. of tissues

¹an·ger \'aŋgə(r), 'aiŋ-\ *n* -s [ME, affliction, anger, fr. ON *angr* grief, sorrow; akin to OE *enge* narrow, OHG *engi*, ON *öngr*, Goth *aggwus*, L *angor* strangling, anguish, *angere* to strangle, distress, Gk *anchein* to strangle, Skt *aṁhas* anxiety] **1** *now dial Eng* **:** inflammation esp. of a wound or sore **2 a :** a strong feeling of displeasure and usu. of antagonism ⟨an outburst of ~⟩ **3 :** a cause or manifestation of anger ⟨or if thy mistress some rich ~ shows —John Keats⟩ **4 :** something resembling the state, appearance, or behavior of an angry person ⟨the ~ of sea and sky⟩ ⟨the monstrous ~ of the guns —Wilfred Owen⟩

syn IRE, RAGE, FURY, INDIGNATION, WRATH: ANGER is the most general of these terms, merely indicating the emotional reaction of extreme displeasure and suggesting no definite degree of intensity ⟨boys and girls come to the hospitals full of fear and, sometimes, *anger* —J.N.Bell⟩ ⟨his *angers*, his personal spites reached metaphysical proportions —Lionel Abel⟩ IRE is literary, usu. suggesting a somewhat greater emotional turmoil than ANGER ⟨it turns the people's *ire* from local abuses —Stanley Ross⟩ ⟨undismayed by the dark flush of *ire* he kindled —George Meredith⟩ ⟨concealed his resentful *ire* —Jane Austen⟩ RAGE usu. adds to ANGER the idea of loss of control, of usu. strong outward display presumably reflecting an intense inner frustration, revengefulness, or temporary derangement ⟨his curses of *rage* and frustration tore the air and made the soldiers cringe —Allen Churchill⟩ ⟨hurled themselves at the spot, jaws snapping, trembling with violent *rage* —William Beebe⟩ FURY usu. indicates extreme overmastering rage; sometimes it applies to a violent and indignant anger kept barely under control ⟨the *fury* and devastation of World War II —*Lamp*⟩ ⟨phrases could move crowds to *fury* or pity —Arnold Bennett⟩ ⟨his anger deepened into *fury* —Agnes Repplier⟩ ⟨to watch in a cold *fury*⟩ INDIGNATION implies anger of no specified intensity or outward display but provoked by what one considers mean, shameful, unworthy, or outrageous ⟨the crime of aggression arouses their moral *indignation* —A.O. Wolfers⟩ ⟨the colonies were aflame with *indignation* —H.E. Scudder⟩ WRATH may imply either rage or indignation, usu. also implying a grievance and a desire to revenge or punish in return ⟨violent outbursts of *wrath* and summary chastisements do occur —Margaret Mead⟩ ⟨in *wrath* he had a widening glower that enveloped the offender — yet his eye seemed to stab — a flash shot from its center to transfix and pierce —G.D.Brown⟩ ⟨the *wrath* of God⟩

²anger \"\ *vb* **angered; angered; angering** \-g(ə)riŋ\ **angers** [ME *angren* to distress, anger, fr. ON *angra*, fr. *angr*] *vt* **1 :** to excite to anger **:** make angry ⟨her helplessness ~*ed* her —Robert Grant †1940⟩ **2** *chiefly dial* **:** to cause to smart **:** INFLAME ⟨the continued exertion ~*ed* his wound⟩ ~ *vi* **:** to become angry ⟨a man who ~*s* easily⟩

an·ger·ly *adv* [*anger* + *-ly*] *archaic* **:** ANGRILY

an·gers \(')äⁿ¦zhā\ *adj, usu cap* [fr. *Angers*, France] **:** of or from the city of Angers, France **:** of the kind or style prevalent in Angers

-anges *pl of* -ANGE

¹an·ge·vin \'anjəvən, 'aan-\ *also* **an·ge·vine** \", -,vēn, -,vīn\ *adj, usu cap* [F, fr. OF, fr. ML *andegavinus*, fr. *Andegavia* Anjou, former province of France (fr. *Andegavum* Angers, former capital of Anjou) + L *-inus* -ine] **1 :** of, relating to, or characteristic of Anjou, France **2 :** of, relating to, or characteristic of the natives or inhabitants of Anjou **3 :** of, relating to, or characteristic of the Plantagenets **4 :** of or relating to the period of English history from the accession of Henry II in 1154 to the loss of Anjou in 1204 or to the division of the Plantagenets into the houses of Lancaster and York in 1399

²angevin \"\ *also* **angevine** \"\ *n* -s *cap* [F, fr. OF, fr. *angevin*, adj.] **1 :** a native or inhabitant of Anjou **2 :** any of the Plantagenet kings or their kinsmen or retainers

angi- *or* **angio-** *comb form* [NL, fr. Gk *angei-, angeio-* vessel, blood vessel, fr. *angeion*, dim. of *angos* vessel; perh. akin to L *angulus* angle — more at ANGLE] **1 a :** blood or lymph vessel ⟨*angioid*⟩ ⟨*angiolith*⟩ ⟨*angiosis*⟩ **b :** angiomatous ⟨*angiofibroma*⟩ **:** angiomatous and ⟨*angiocavernous*⟩ **2 :** seed vessel ⟨*angiocarpous*⟩

-angia *pl of* -ANGIUM

an·gi·co \an'jē(,)kü, -kō\ *n* -s [Pg] **:** any of various So. American trees of the family Leguminosae (esp. *Piptadenia rigida*) that yields a brown gum used in tanning

an·gi·i·tis \ˌanjē'īd·əs\ *n, pl* **angiit·i·des** \-ē'id·ə,dēz\ [NL, fr. *angi-* + *-itis*] **:** inflammation of a blood or lymph vessel or duct

angild *n* -s [OE *āngilde, āngylde*, fr. *ān* one + *-gilde, -gylde* (akin to *gieldan* to pay for, reward, serve, punish) — more at ONE, YIELD] **:** a compensation in Anglo-Saxon times made in a single payment at a fixed valuation for a given injury to person or property

an·gi·na \an'jīnə, aan- *also* 'a(a)njənə\ *n* -s [L, quinsy, fr. L *angere* to strangle, distress, — more at ANGER] **:** a disease marked by spasmodic attacks of intense suffocative pain: as **a :** a severe inflammatory or ulcerated condition of the mouth or throat ⟨diphtheritic ~⟩ — compare LUDWIG'S ANGINA **b :** ANGINA PECTORIS — **an·gi·nal** \(')a(a)n¦jīnᵊl,'a(a)njənᵊl\ *adj*

angina pec·to·ris \-'pektərəs, *chiefly substand* -,pek'tōr-\ *n* [NL, lit., quinsy of the chest] **:** a disease characterized by paroxysmal attacks of substernal pain of short duration that is usu. associated with a sense of apprehension or fear of impending death, precipitated by effort or emotion, and relieved quickly by rest or administration of nitroglycerin — compare CORONARY INSUFFICIENCY, HEART FAILURE, MYOCARDIAL INFARCTION

an·gi·noid \'anjə,nȯid, an'jī-\ *adj* [*angina* + *-oid*] **:** resembling angina

an·gi·nose \'anjə,nōs, an'jī,-\ *or* **an·gi·nous** \(')an¦jīnəs, 'anjən-\ *adj* [*angina* + *-ose, -ous*] **:** relating to angina or angina pectoris

angio- *in pronunciations below*, ¦ˌˌˌ = ¦anjēō *or* ¦aan- *or* -ēə *or* -ē,ō\ — see ANGI-

an·gi·o·blast \'ˌˌˌ,blast\ *n* -s [*angi-* + *-blast*] **:** one of the extraembryonic mesenchyme cells that differentiate into the endothelium of the embryonic blood vessels — **an·gi·o·blas·tic** \¦ˌˌˌ¦stik\ *adj*

an·gi·o·car·di·o·gram \¦ˌˌˌ-\ *n* -s [*angi-* + *cardiogram*] **:** a roentgenogram of the heart and its blood vessels after injection of a radiopaque substance

an·gi·o·car·di·o·graph·ic \¦ˌˌˌ,ˌˌˌ¦ˌˌ\ *adj* **:** of or by means of angiocardiography

an·gi·o·car·di·og·ra·phy \¦ˌˌˌ-\ *n* -ES [*angi-* + *cardiography*] **:** the roentgenographic visualization of the heart and its blood vessels after injection of a radiopaque substance

an·gi·o·car·pous \¦ˌˌˌ¦kärpəs\ *or* **an·gi·o·car·pic** \-pik\ *adj* [*angi-* + *-carpous, -carpic*] **1 :** having or being fruit enclosed within an external covering ⟨the acorn in its cupule is an ~ fruit⟩ — compare PYRENOCARPIC **2 :** having the hymenium enclosed or immersed in the thallus — used of some lichens and fungi; compare GYMNOCARPOUS — **an·gi·o·car·py** \'ˌˌˌ,kärpē\ *n* -ES

an·gi·o·cho·li·tis \¦ˌˌˌ-\ *n* -ES [NL, fr. *angi-* + *chol-* + *-itis*] **:** inflammation of the gall ducts **:** CHOLANGITIS

an·gi·o·cyst \'ˌˌˌ,sist\ *n* -s [*angi-* + *cyst*] *anat* **:** a pouch of mesothelial tissue having blood-forming properties

an·gi·o·ede·ma \¦ˌˌˌ-\ *n, pl* **angioedemas** *or* **angioede·ma·ta** [NL, fr. *angi-* + *edema*] **:** ANGIONEUROTIC EDEMA

an·gi·o·gen·e·sis \¦ˌˌˌ-\ *n, pl* **angiogene·ses** [NL, fr. *angi-* + *genesis*] **:** the formation and differentiation of blood vessels; *esp* **:** the development of the vessels of the embryo from mesenchyme

an·gi·o·gen·ic \¦ˌˌˌ¦jenik\ *adj* [*angi-* + *-genic*] **:** of or relating to the development of the embryonic circulatory system

an·gi·o·gram \'ˌˌˌ,gram\ *n* -s [*angi-* + *-gram*] **:** a roentgenogram of the blood vessels after injection of a radiopaque substance

an·gi·og·ra·phy \ˌanjē'ägrəfē\ *n* -ES [*angi-* + *-graphy*] **:** the roentgenographic visualization of the blood vessels after injection of a radiopaque substance

an·gi·oid \'anjē,ȯid\ *adj* [*angi-* + *-oid*] **:** resembling a blood vessel or lymph vessel

an·gi·ol·o·gy \ˌanjē'äləjē\ *n* -ES [*angi-* + *-logy*] **:** a science dealing with the blood vessels and lymphatics

an·gi·o·ma \ˌanjē'ōmə\ *n, pl* **angiomas** *also* **angioma·ta** \-məd·ə\ [NL, fr. *angi-* + *-oma*] **:** a tumor composed chiefly of blood vessels or lymph vessels: as **a :** HEMANGIOMA **b :** LYMPHANGIOMA

an·gi·o·ma·to·sis \ˌanjē,ōmə'tōsəs\ *n, pl* **angiomato·ses** \-ō,sēz\ [NL, fr. *angiomat-, angioma* + *-osis*] **:** a condition characterized by the formation of multiple angiomas

an·gi·om·a·tous \ˌanjē¦äməd·əs, -ōm-\ *adj* [NL *angiomat-, angioma* + E *-ous*] **:** of, relating to, or having an angioma

an·gi·o·neu·rot·ic edema \¦ˌˌ(,)ˌ¦ˌ-\ *n* [ISV *angi-* + *neurotic*] **:** a condition characterized by patches of circumscribed swelling of the skin, mucous membranes, and sometimes viscera and believed to be an expression of allergy

an·gi·op·ter·is \ˌanjē'äptərəs\ *n, cap* [NL, fr. *angi-* + *-pteris*] **:** a genus of tree ferns (family Marattiaceae) having sporangia closely arranged in two rows forming linear sori surrounded by a false indusium of fringed scales

an·gi·o·sco·to·ma \¦===-\ *n, pl* **angioscotomas** *also* **angio·scoto·ma·ta** [NL, fr. *angi-* + *scotoma*] **:** a blind spot or defect in the visual field produced by dilated retinal vessels that is esp. prevalent in persons long exposed to high altitudes

an·gi·o·sco·tom·e·try \¦===skō'tämə·trē\ *n* -ES [blend of NL *angioscotoma* and E *-metry*] **:** the charting of scotomas, esp. angioscotomas

an·gi·o·spasm \'===,spazəm\ *n* -S [*angi-* + *spasm*] **:** spasmodic contraction of the blood vessels with increase in blood pressure — **an·gi·o·spas·tic** \¦===¦spastik\ *adj*

an·gi·o·sperm \'===,spərm\ *n* -S [NL *Angiospermae*] **:** a plant of the class Angiospermae

an·gi·o·sper·mae \,===ˈspər,mē\ *n pl, cap* [NL, fr. *angi-* + *-spermae*] **:** a class of Pteropsida or in some classifications a subdivision of Spermatophyta comprising seed plants (as orchids or roses) that produce seeds enclosed in an ovary, including the vast majority of seed plants, and being divided into the subclasses Dicotyledoneae and Monocotyledoneae — compare FILICINEAE, GYMNOSPERMAE

an·gi·o·sper·mous \¦===¦məs\ *or* **an·gi·o·sper·mal** \-məl\ *also* **an·gi·o·sper·ma·tous** \-məd·əs\ *or* **an·gi·o·sper·mic** \-mik\ *adj* [*angi-* + *-spermous, -spermal, -spermatous, -spermic*] **:** of, relating to, or characteristic of the class Angiospermae; *often* **:** having ovules and seeds enclosed in an ovary — contrasted with *gymnospermous* — **an·gi·o·sper·my** \'===,=mē\ *n* -ES

an·gi·os·to·my \,anjē'ästəmē\ *n* -ES [*angi-* + *-stomy*] **:** the surgical establishment of an opening into a blood vessel esp. through a cannula

an·gi·o·tome \'===,tōm\ *n* -S [*angi-* + *-tome*] **:** a segment or unit of the vascular system in the embryo

an·gi·o·ton·ic \¦===¦tänik\ *adj* [*angi-* + *tonic*] **:** inducing or involving increased tonus in the wall of a blood vessel ⟨an ~ substance⟩ ⟨~ spasm⟩

an·gi·o·to·nin \,===ˈtōnən\ *n* -S [*angiotonic* + *-in*] **:** HYPERTENSIN

-an·gi·um \'anjēəm, 'aan-\ *n comb form, pl* **-an·gia** \-ēə\ [NL, fr. Gk *angeion* — more at ANGI-] **:** vessel **:** receptacle ⟨gamet*angium*⟩ ⟨gon*angium*⟩

ang·ka \'aŋkə\ *n pl, usu cap* **:** a people in northern Assam, India

ang-khak \'aŋ,kak\ *n* -S [prob. fr. a Chin dial. phrase akin to Chin (Canton) *hung kuk* red rice, Chin (Peking) *hung² ku³*] **:** RED RICE 1

angklung *var of* ANKLONG

angl *abbr, often cap* **1** [L *Anglice*] in English **2** anglicized

¹an·glaise \(ˈ)äŋ¦glāz, (ˈ)aŋ-,(ˈ)äⁿ¦-\ *n* -S [F, fr. fem. of *anglais* English, of Gmc origin; akin to OE *englisc* English — more at ENGLISH] **1 :** an old English country-dance **2 :** a lively musical dance form in duple time esp. as an optional member of the classical suite

²anglaise \"\ *adj* [F (*à la*) *anglaise* in the English manner; *anglaise*, fem. of *anglais* English] **1 :** boiled and served without sauce ⟨potatoes ~⟩ **2 :** BREADED ⟨cutlets ~⟩

¹an·gle \'aŋgəl, 'aiŋ-\ *n* -S *usu cap* [L *Angli*, pl., of Gmc origin; akin to OE *Engle*, pl., Angles] **:** a member of a Germanic people that entered and conquered England with the Saxons and Jutes in the 5th century A.D. and merged with them to form the Anglo-Saxon peoples

²angle \"\ *n* -S [ME *angel*, fr. OE *angel, angul*, fr. *anga* hook; akin to OHG *angul* fishhook, *ango* hook, ON *öngull* fishhook, L *uncus* hook, Gk *onkos* barbed hook, *ankos* hollow, glen, Skt *aṅka* bend, hook] **1** *archaic* **:** FISHHOOK **2** *archaic* **:** fishing line, hook, and bait with or without rod

³angle \"\ *vb* **angled; angled; angling** \-g(ə)liŋ\ **angles** [ME *angelen*, fr. *angel*, n.] *vi* **1 :** to fish with a hook ⟨the fish one ~s for⟩ **2 :** to use artful bait or wily means **:** SCHEME ⟨~ for an invitation to the party⟩ **~** *vt* **:** FISH ⟨~ a stream⟩

⁴angle \"\ *n* -S [ME, fr. MF, fr. L *angulus*; akin to OE *anclēow* ankle, OHG *anchlāo, anchal, enchil*, ON *ökkla*, Gk *angos* pail, Skt *aṅga* limb, OE *angel, ongul* fishhook — more at ANGLE (fishhook)] **1 a** *archaic* **:** a corner or area near a corner **b** *archaic* **:** an out-of-the-way place ⟨into the utmost ~ of the world —Edmund Spenser⟩ **:** NOOK **2 a :** the figure formed by two lines diverging from the same point or by two surfaces diverging from the same line **b :** a representation of such a figure or space **3 :** one of the four astrological houses at the cardinal points of the compass **4 :** a projecting corner (as of a stone or building) **:** a pointed form or sharp fragment **5** *math* **:** a measure of the amount of rotation of either of two intersecting lines necessary to produce coincidence with the other, the rotation being in the plane of the lines and about the point of intersection; *also* **:** a measure based on this for indicating the divergence of two nonintersecting nonparallel lines, two intersecting planes, or two intersecting curves **6 a** (1) **:** the direction from which an object is viewed **:** POINT OF VIEW ⟨a camera ~⟩ **:** ASPECT, PHASE ⟨to discuss all ~s of a question⟩ (2) **:** the point of view or special interest or emphasis controlling a presentation (as of a story, article, or speech) or the phase of a presentation that is of interest to or bears upon a certain group or point of view **b** *slang* **:** SCHEME **:** a slick knowledge of method esp. in criminal activities **:** a method for illegal gain **7 :** a curving direction given a ball (as by a stroke or kick) ⟨put ~ on a tennis return⟩ **8 :** ANGLE IRON **syn** see PHASE

E A F E′ F′ E″ F″ C D B G

angles: *ABD* and *ABC* right angles; *FBD, F′BD, F″BD* acute angles; *EBD, E′BD, E″BD* obtuse angles; *CBD* straight angle; *GBD* reflex angle; *B* vertex

⁵angle \"\ *vb* **angled; angled; angling** \-g(ə)liŋ\ **angles** *vt* **1 a :** to turn, bend, move, or direct at an angle ⟨I *angled* a look behind me — *Think*⟩ **b :** to hit at an angle **:** strike or kick (a ball) toward the sidelines ⟨~ a tennis return⟩ **2 :** to adjust at an angle ⟨~ a camera⟩ **3 a :** to present the material of (as a news story, article, or speech) from a particular point of view or favorable to the interests of a particular group **b :** to warp (such a presentation) by emphasis or implication to favor a particular person, class, group, or race **~** *vi* **1 :** to change direction by making an angular turn or turns ⟨the road ~s up the hill⟩ **2 :** to go at an angle ⟨~ across the road⟩

angle bar *n* **1 :** ANGLE IRON **2 :** one of two bars used to splice the joint of two railroad rails

angle bead *n* **:** a corner bead set vertically at the meeting of two walls

angle beam *n* **:** a beam in which one part (as a flange) is at an angle with another

an·gle·ber·ry \'aŋgəl,berē\ *n* [prob. fr. (assumed) earlier E *angberry* — more at ANBURY] **:** a papilloma or warty growth of the skin or mucous membranes of cattle and sometimes horses often occurring in great numbers and thought to be caused by a filterable virus

angle brace *n* **1 :** a brace across two pieces that meet at an angle — called also *angle tie* **2 :** a boring brace for use in cramped places (as in a corner)

angle bracket *n* **1 :** a bracket in an angle or corner of a molded cornice **2 :** BRACKET 4b

angle brick *n* **:** a brick of oblique shape (as for use at a salient angle)

angle capital *n* **:** the capital of a corner column; *esp* **:** a capital modified from the ordinary form so as to face on both sides of the corner (as in the Ionic order)

angle chair *n* **:** a corner chair or desk chair

angle clip *n* **:** a short piece of angle iron for connecting structural parts (as plates) at angles

angled *adj* [⁴*angle* + *-ed*] **1 :** having an angle or angles — used of a geometric figure **:** having an angular outline ⟨an ~ sail⟩ **:** set or placed at angles rather than parallel **2 :** placed so that a part of the pool cushion at a pocket prevents a direct shot at an object ball ⟨the cue ball was ~⟩ **:** marked by such a situation **:** having to play with the cue ball so placed

angled draft *n* **:** a method of drawing cloth in which alternate twilling to left and right produces a herringbone

angle divider *n* **:** a square for bisecting or dividing angles

angledog \'==,=\ *n* [²*angle* + *dog*] *dial* **:** EARTHWORM

An·gle·doz·er \'aŋgəl,dōzə(r)\ *trademark* — used for a tractor-driven pusher and scraper with the blade at an angle for pushing material to one side or the other (as for clearing land or leveling runways)

angle float *n* **:** a plasterer's trowel having flat surfaces meeting at an angle used for finishing corners of plastered walls

angle gear *n* **:** a gear with teeth at an angle to its axis (as a bevel gear)

angle iron *n* **1 :** an iron or steel cleat or brace used to hold together two parts whose faces are at an angle **2** *also* **angle** -S **:** a piece of structural steel rolled with an L-shaped section

angle iron 1

angle meter *n* **:** an instrument for measuring angles; *esp* **:** CLINOMETER

angle of action : the angle of revolution of either of two wheels in gear during which any particular tooth continues in contact

angle of altitude : ANGLE OF ELEVATION 1

angle of approach : the angle turned through by either of a pair of wheels in gear from the first contact of a pair of teeth until the pitch points of these teeth fall together

angle of attack : the acute angle between the direction of the relative wind and a reference line (as the geometric chord) fixed in an airfoil

angle of bank : ANGLE OF ROLL

angle of climb : the angle between the horizontal and the flight path of a climbing airplane

angle of contact *physics* **:** the angle between the meniscus and the containing walls of a column of liquid measured from the vertical wall below the surface of the liquid to the position of the tangent to the meniscus at its point of contact with the wall

angle of declination 1 : the angle made by a descending line or plane with a horizontal plane **2 :** the angle between the direction indicated by a magnetic needle and the true meridian — called also *magnetic declination*

angle of departure : the vertical angle between the line of departure of a projectile and the line of site of the gun

angle of depression 1 : the angle that a descending line makes with a horizontal plane **2 :** the angle of elevation when the line of elevation of a gun falls below the horizontal

angle of elevation 1 : the angle that an ascending line makes with a horizontal plane **2 :** the vertical angle between the line of elevation and the line of site of a gun

angle of fall : the vertical angle between the horizontal and the tangent to the trajectory of a projectile at the point of fall —called also *striking angle*

angle of incidence 1 : ANGLE OF ATTACK **2 :** the angle that a line (as a ray of light) falling on a surface makes with a perpendicular to the surface at the point of incidence — see GLANCING ANGLE **3 :** the angle between the chord of an airplane wing section and the longitudinal axis of the airplane, being positive when the leading edge is higher than the trailing edge

angle of lag 1 : the angle through which the brushes of a commutator of a direct-current motor or generator must be shifted from the neutral plane on account of the armature reaction **2 :** the angle by which the current in an alternating-current circuit lags behind the electromotive force

angle of lead \-'lēd\ **:** the angle by which the current in an alternating-current circuit leads the electromotive force

angle of obliquity *or* **angle of pressure :** the angle that the line of pressure or of action of two gear teeth in contact makes with the tangent at the point of contact of the two pitch circles

angle of pitch : the angle between two planes one of which includes the lateral axis of an airplane and the direction of the relative wind and the other of which includes the lateral and the longitudinal axes that in normal flight is measured between the longitudinal axis and the direction of the relative wind and that is positive when the nose of the airplane rises

angle of position : ANGLE OF SITE

angle of recess : the angle turned through by either of a pair of wheels in gear from the coincidence of the pitch points of a pair of teeth until the last point of contact of the teeth

angle of reflection : the angle between a reflected ray and the normal drawn at the point of incidence to a reflecting surface — called also *specular angle*

angle of refraction : the angle between a refracted ray and the normal drawn at the point of incidence to the interface at which refraction occurs — called also *refraction angle*

angle of repose 1 *physics* **:** the angle that the plane of contact between two bodies makes with the horizontal when the upper body is just on the point of sliding **:** the angle whose tangent is the coefficient of friction between the two bodies **2** *or* **angle of rest :** the angle of maximum slope at which a heap of any loose solid material (as earth) will stand without sliding — compare ANGLE OF SLIDE

angle of roll : the angle through which an airplane must be rotated about its longitudinal axis to bring its lateral axis into a horizontal plane, being positive when the left wing is higher than the right — called also *angle of bank*

angle of site : the vertical angle between the line of site of a gun and the horizontal — called also *angle of position*

angle of slide : the angle of minimum slope usu. measured from the horizontal at which any loose solid material (as earth) will flow — compare ANGLE OF REPOSE

angle of the mandible *or* **angle of the jaw :** the angle formed by the junction of the ramus and the body of the human mandible

angle of thread : the angle between the sides of a screw thread measured in an axial plane

angle of torsion *or* **angle of twist :** the angle through which a radial section of a body (as a wire or a shaft) deflects from its normal position when the body is subjected to torque

angle of view : the angle in a lens between lines drawn from opposite edges of the image to the second nodal point of the lens

angle of yaw : the angle between the direction of the relative wind and the plane of symmetry of an airplane, being positive when the airplane turns to the right

angle of zero lift : ZERO-LIFT ANGLE

angle plate *n* **:** a plate having an L-shaped or angular section; *specif* **:** one of two such plates used to clamp and hold work in a shaper or other metalworking machine — compare ANGLE IRON

anglepod \'==,=\ *n* [⁴*angle* + *pod*] **:** any of several plants (genus *Gonolobus*) that have angled pods (as *G. gonocarpos*)

an·gler \'aŋglə(r), 'aiŋ-\ *n* -S [³*angle* + *-er*] **1 :** one that angles **2 a :** a European and American marine fish (*Lophius piscatorius*) of the order Pediculati that reaches a length of from three to five feet, has a large broad depressed head and large mouth, and lies partly buried on the bottom enticing other fishes within its reach by movements of a lure on its head and fleshy appendages around its mouth **b :** any of several closely related fishes (family Lophiidae)

angler (*Lophius piscatorius*)

angle rafter *n* **:** a rafter at the angle of a roof: as **a :** HIP RAFTER **b :** the principal rafter under the hip rafter

anglerfish \'==,=\ *n* **:** ANGLER 2

angle rib *n* **1 :** one of the great diagonal ribs that divide each rectangle of a Gothic vaulting and form the main part of the structure **2 :** a group of moldings ornamenting an angle in decorative work

angles *pl of* ANGLE, *pres 3d sing of* ANGLE

angle set *n* **1** *mining engin* **:** a timber set containing an angle brace **2** *mining engin* **:** one of a series of sets making angles with one another (as in a curving shaft or tunnel)

an·gle·sey \'aŋgəlsē, -si\ *adj, usu cap* [fr. *Anglesey*, island and county in Wales] **:** of or from the island or county of Anglesey, Wales **:** of the kind or style prevalent in Anglesey

angle shaft *n* **:** an enriched corner bead often having a capital or base or both

angle shear *n* **:** a machine for shearing or cutting angle irons

angle shot *n* **1 :** a picture taken with the camera pointed at an angle from the horizontal **2 :** a motion-picture shot duplicating or continuing the action of the previous shot but from a different position

an·gle·site \'aŋgəl,sīt, -glə,-\ *n* -S [F *anglesite*, fr. *Anglesey* island, Wales, its locality + F *-ite*] **:** a common secondary mineral consisting of lead sulfate $PbSO_4$ and formed by the oxidation of galena

anglesmith \'==,=\ *n* [⁴*angle* + *smith*] **1 :** one who bends and welds metal to form angular shapes (as angle irons or brackets) **2 :** a furnaceman who shapes steel structural members esp. for use in shipbuilding and repair — called also *slabman*

angle steel *n* **:** steel in rolled bars of L section

angle tie *n* **1 :** ANGLE BRACE 1 **2 :** a tie to prevent displacement of building elements due to thrust

an·gle·ton grass \'aŋgəltən-, -tᵊn-\ *n* [prob. fr. *Angleton*, Texas, where it was introduced] **:** a grass (*Andropogon nodosus*) native to the Old World tropics and introduced in the West Indies having one or two racemes with the spikelets closely overlapping

an·gle·twitch \'aŋ(g)əl-,twich\ *also* **an·gle·touch** \-l,təch\ *n* -ES [ME *angeltwicche, angeltwacche*, fr. OE *angeltwæcce, angeltwicce*, fr. *angel* hook + *-twæcce, -twicce* (fr. *twiccian* to pluck, catch hold of) — more at ANGLE, TWITCH] *now dial Eng* **:** EARTHWORM

angle valve *n* **:** a valve with intake and exit ports at right angles

anglewing \'==,=\ *n* [⁴*angle* + *wing*] **:** one of numerous butterflies (including members of the genera *Polygonia, Nymphalis*, and *Anaea*) having the outer edge of the fore wings more or less notched or angular

anglewise \'==,=\ *adv* [⁴*angle* + *-wise*] **:** ANGULARLY

angleworm \'==,=\ *n* [²*angle* + *worm*] **:** EARTHWORM

¹an·gli·an \'aŋglēən, 'aiŋ-\ *adj, usu cap* [L *Angli* Angles + E *-an* — more at ANGLE] **1 :** of, relating to, or constituting the Angles or Anglian **2 :** East Anglian

²anglian \"\ *n* -S *usu cap* **1 :** ¹ANGLE **2 :** ²EAST ANGLIAN 1 **3 a :** the Old English dialects of Mercia and Northumbria **b :** ²EAST ANGLIAN 2

¹an·glic \-lik\ *adj, usu cap* [ML *Anglicus* English] **:** ANGLIAN

²anglic \"\ *n, usu cap* [ML *Anglicus*] **:** a proposed international language devised by R.E.Zachrisson †1937 Swedish philologist, and consisting of English written according to a system of simplified spelling without the introduction of any new letters

¹an·gli·can \'aŋglәkən, 'aiŋ-, -ēk-\ *adj, usu cap* [ML *Anglicanus*, fr. *Anglicus* English (fr. *Angli* English people, fr. L, Angles) + L *-anus* -an — more at ANGLE] **1 :** relating to or connected with the Church of England and churches in communion with it **2 :** of or relating to England or the English nation

²anglican \"\ *n* -S *usu cap* **:** one who acknowledges the faith and order common to the Anglican Communion

anglican chant *n, usu cap A* **:** a harmonized chant consisting of two strains of three and four measures respectively, the first measure of each containing a single reciting note and the remaining measures a cadence sung in strict rhythm

anglican communion *n, cap A&C* **:** a body of churches including the Church of England and those churches that hold essentially the same faith, order, and worship with it and are therefore in communion with each other (as the Church of Ireland, the Church in Wales, the Scottish Episcopal Church, the Protestant Episcopal Church in the U.S., the Anglican churches in the British dominions and colonies, and other kindred organizations)

an·gli·can·ism \-,nizəm\ *n* -S *cap* **1 :** the faith and order of the Anglican churches; *also* **:** adherence to the Anglican faith and order **2** *usu cap* **:** adherence or attachment to English attitudes and ways ⟨an extremely civilized literary and theatrical *Anglicanism* —John Gassner⟩

an·gli·ce \'aŋglә(,)sē, 'aiŋ-, -əsi\ *adv, usu cap* [ML, adv. of *Anglicus*] **:** in English; *esp* **:** in readily understood English ⟨the city of Livorno, *Anglice* Leghorn⟩

an·gli·cism \-,sizəm\ *n* -S *often cap* [ML *Anglicus* + E *-ism*] **1 a :** a characteristic feature of English occurring in another language **b :** a trend toward linguistic borrowing from English **2 :** the quality or qualities distinctive of the English **3 :** a partiality for English customs, manners, or ideas

an·gli·cist \-,səst\ *n* -S *usu cap* [ML *Anglicus* + E *-ist*] **:** a specialist in the English language or in English literature

an·gli·ci·za·tion \,===sə'zāshən, -,sī'z-\ *n* -S *often cap* **:** the process or the result of anglicizing or being anglicized

an·gli·cize *or* **an·gli·cise** \-,sīz\ *vb* -ED/-ING/-S *often cap* [ML *Anglicus* + E *-ize, -ise*] *vt* **1 :** to make English in quality or characteristics **:** cause to become adapted in customs, manners, speech, or outlook to the culture of the English-speaking world and often esp. to the culture distinctive of England ⟨an *anglicized* Indian princess⟩ **2 :** to adapt (a foreign word or phrase) to English usage: as **a :** to alter to a characteristically English form, sound, or spelling (as *indexes* from Latin *indices*) **b :** to change to an English equivalent (as *John* for *Giovanni*) **c :** to borrow into English without alteration of form or spelling and with or without change in pronunciation (as *bona fide, soprano, kindergarten, matinee*) **3 :** to adapt to the characteristics of English meter or rhythm **~** *vi* **:** to take on English characteristics in conduct, speech, or outlook ⟨the immigrants gradually *anglicized*⟩

an·gli·fy \-,fī\ *vt* -ED/-ING/-ES *sometimes cap* [ML *Angli* English people (fr. L, Angles) + E *-fy* — more at ANGLE] **:** ANGLICIZE

an·gling \'aŋgliŋ, 'aiŋ-\ *n* -S [ME, fr. gerund of *angelen* to angle] **:** the act of one who angles; *esp* **:** the action or art of fishing with hook and line

an·glist \-gləst\ *n* -S *usu cap* [G, fr. ML *Angli* English people (fr. L, Angles) + G *-ist* — more at ANGLE] **:** ANGLICIST

an·glis·tics \aŋ'glistiks, aiŋ-\ *n pl but sing in constr, usu cap* [modif. of G *anglistik*, fr. *anglist* + *-ik* -ics] **:** the study of the English language or of literature composed in English

an·glo \'aŋ,glō, 'aiŋ-\ *n* -S *cap* [short for *Anglo-American*] *Southwest* **:** an Anglo-American as distinguished from a Spanish-American or a Mexican

an·glo- *in pronunciations below*, ¦== = ¦aŋ(,)glō *or* ¦aiŋ- *or* -ŋglə\ *comb form, usu cap* [NL, fr. ML *Angli* English people, fr. L, Angles — more at ANGLE] **1 :** English: **a :** of or belonging to England ⟨*Anglo*-Norman⟩ **b :** of English origin, descent, or culture ⟨*Anglo*-Indian⟩ ⟨*Anglo*-Irish⟩ **2 :** English and ⟨*Anglo*-Japanese⟩ ⟨*Anglo*-Russian⟩

anglo-american \¦===¦===\ *n, cap both As* [*Anglo-* + *American*] **1 :** a citizen of the U.S. of English origin or descent **2 :** a North American whose native language is English and whose culture is of English origin as distinguished from one whose language and culture are of non-English origin

anglo-arab \¦==¦==\ *n, usu cap both As* [*Anglo-* + *Arab* (horse)] **:** a horse produced by interbreeding Arab and Thoroughbred horses

anglo-burman \¦==¦==\ *n, cap A&B* [*Anglo-* + *Burman*] **1 :** a minority ethnic group in Burma deriving from intermarriage between British and Burmese **2 :** a member of the Anglo-Burman group

anglo-catholic \¦==ˈ=(=)=\ *n, usu cap A&C* [*Anglo-* + *Catholic*] **:** one who professes the tenets of Anglo-Catholicism **:** HIGH CHURCHMAN — compare LAUDIAN, TRACTARIAN

anglo-catholicism \¦==-\ *n, cap A&C* **:** the doctrines and practices of those in the Anglican Communion who maintain (1) that Catholicity is inherent in a church whose episcopate can trace its line of descent from the apostles and whose faith is agreed by all Catholics to be revealed truth and (2) that any church of the Anglican Communion is such a church, its method of church government and its doctrine remaining unchanged by the Reformation

anglo-french \¦==¦=\ *n, cap A&F* [*Anglo-* + *French*] **:** the French language used in medieval England: **a :** the French of Normandy used in England in the 11th and 12th centuries **b :** the French resulting from admixture of Norman and central French used from the 12th to the 15th centuries

an·glo·gae·an \¦==¦jēən\ *adj, usu cap* [NL *Anglogaea* Nearctica (fr. *Anglo-* + *-gaea*) + E *-an*] **:** NEARCTIC

anglo-gallic \¦==¦==\ *adj, usu cap A&G* [*Anglo-* + *Gallic*] **:** of or relating to one of the coins issued by English rulers from Henry II to Henry VIII in their territory in France

an·glo·hel·ve·ti·um \¦==,hel'vēshēəm\ *n* [NL, fr. *Anglo-* + *Helvetia* + *-ium*] **:** element 85 — a name superseded by *astatine*

¹anglo-indian \¦==¦-\ *adj, usu cap A&I* [*Anglo-* + *Indian* (of India)] **1 :** of, relating to, or characteristic of British India or the English in India **:** of or concerning the English and the

Indian peoples **2 :** of or belonging to the language of the English in India

[2]**anglo-indian** \"\ *n, cap A&I* **1 :** an Englishman living in India **2** *India* **:** a person of European (as British) and Indian ancestry — called also *Eurasian* **3 :** the terms adopted into English from the languages of India

anglo-irish \¦==ˈ-\ *n pl, cap A&I* [*Anglo-* + *Irish*] **1 :** persons of English origin or descent living in Ireland **2 :** persons of mixed English and Irish ancestry

anglo-israelism \¦==ˈ-\ *n, usu cap A&I* [*Anglo-* + *Israel* + E *-ism*] **:** the theory that the Anglo-Saxon peoples are descendants of the 10 lost tribes of Israel

anglo-israelite *n, usu cap A&I* **:** a believer in Anglo-Israelism

anglo-latin \¦==ˈ-\ *n, cap A&L* [*Anglo-* + *Latin*] **:** Medieval Latin as used in England

an·glo·ma·nia \ˌ==ˈmānēə, -nyə\ *n, often cap* [NL, fr. *Anglo-* + *mania*] **:** excessive fondness for what is English (as English customs and institutions) on the part of a foreigner

an·glo·ma·ni·ac \ˌ==ˈmānē,ak\ *n, usu cap* [*Anglo-* + *maniac*] **:** one affected with anglomania — **an·glo·ma·ni·a·cal** \¦==_mə¦nīəkəl\ *adj, usu cap*

anglo-norman \¦==¦==\ *n, cap A&N* [*Anglo-* + *Norman*] **1 :** one of the Normans who lived in England after the Conquest or any of their descendants **2 :** the form of Anglo= French used by Anglo-Normans

anglo-nubian \¦==ˈ===\ *n, usu cap A&N* [*Anglo-* + *Nubian* (goat)] **:** a British breed of goats developed by interbreeding native British goats with Nubians

an·glo·phile \ˈ==,fīl\ *also* **an·glo·phil** \-,fil\ *n* -s *often cap* [F *anglophile*, fr. *anglo-* Anglo- + *-phile* -phile, -phil] **:** one who esp. admires or is partial to England or English ways

an·glo·phil·ia \ˌ==ˈfilēə, -lyə\ *n* -s *often cap* [NL, fr. *Anglo-* + *-philia*] **:** particular unreasoned admiration of or partiality for England or English ways — **an·glo·phil·i·ac** \¦==¦filē,ak\ *or* **an·glo·phil·ic** \-lik\ *adj, often cap*

an·glo·phobe \ˈ==,fōb\ *n* -s *often cap* [prob. fr. F, fr. *anglo-* Anglo- + *-phobe*] **:** one who has anglophobia

an·glo·pho·bia \ˌ==ˈfōbēə\ *n* -s *often cap* [NL, fr. *Anglo-* + *-phobia*] **:** intense dislike or distrust of England, the English, or English ways — **an·glo·pho·bi·ac** \¦==¦fōbē,ak\ *or* **an·glo·pho·bic** \¦==¦fōbik *also* -äb-\ *adj, often cap*

anglos *pl of* ANGLO

an·glo-saxon \¦==¦saksən\ *n, cap A&S* [NL *Anglo-Saxones*, pl., alter. of ML *Angli Saxones*, fr. L *Angli* Angles + LL *Saxones* Saxons — more at ANGLE, SAXON] **1 a :** an Angle, Saxon, or Jute who came to England in the 5th century A.D. **b :** a descendant of one of these Anglo-Saxons **2 :** ENGLISHMAN; *broadly* **:** a person of English ancestry descended from the Anglo-Saxons **:** a white gentile whose native tongue is English **3 :** the language of the Anglo-Saxon people **:** OLD ENGLISH — see INDO-EUROPEAN LANGUAGES table **4 :** the Germanic element present in the English language since the emergence of the latter as a separate entity **5 a :** forthright direct plain English **b :** English employing words considered crude or vulgar ⟨the word-of-mouth version, which has come through generations of army men, is more bluntly *Anglo-Saxon* —Roger Butterfield⟩

anglo-saxon alphabet *n, usu cap 1st A&S* **:** the Latin alphabet as modified for writing Old English by the addition of the four characters æ or ę, edh, thorn, and wen — called also *Old English alphabet*

an·glo-sax·on·ism \¦==ˈ==,nizəm\ *n* -s *usu cap A&S* **1 :** a word or idiom that strongly suggests Anglo-Saxon origin **2 a :** the quality, qualities, traits, or outlook regarded as distinctive of the English or of the people of English descent **b :** the belief in the superiority of Anglo-Saxon characteristics or of the Anglo-Saxon people

an·glo-sax·on·ize \-,nīz\ *vt, sometimes cap A&S* **:** to inculcate with characteristics considered Anglo-Saxon or English

anglo-saxon word *n, usu cap A&S* **:** any of a group of monosyllabic English words whether or not of Anglo-Saxon origin that are considered vulgar and unacceptable in polite use — compare FOUR-LETTER WORD

anglo-vernacular \¦===¦===\ *adj, usu cap A&V* [*Anglo-* + *vernacular*] **:** using both English and a local vernacular — used esp. of schools in India, Burma, and Ceylon during the period of British rule

[1]**an·go·la** \aŋˈgōlə, aiŋˈ-, anˈ-, aanˈ- *attrib* (ˈ)=¦==\ *n* -s *sometimes cap* [by alter.] **:** ANGORA

[2]**angola** *adj, usu cap* [fr. *Angola*, colony in southwestern Africa] **:** of or relating to Angola **:** of the kind or style prevalent in Angola

angola cloth *n, sometimes cap A* **1 :** a clothing fabric of plain or twill weave with cotton warp and wool weft **2 :** a cotton fabric with diaper pattern used for embroidery

angola grass *n, usu cap A* [fr. *Angola* (Port. West Africa), its place of origin] **:** PARA GRASS 1

an·go·lan \(ˈ)=¦gōlən\ *n* -s *cap* [*Angola*, Africa + E *-an*] **:** a native or inhabitant of Angola — **angolan** *adj, usu cap*

angola pea *n, usu cap A* [fr. *Angola*, Africa] **:** PIGEON PEA

an·go·lar \¦aŋgō¦lär\ *n, pl* **angola·res** \ˌ==ˈlärēz\ [Pg, lit., of Angola, fr. *Angola* + Pg *-ar*] **1 :** the basic monetary unit of Angola established in 1928 and equal to the Portuguese escudo **2 :** a currency note representing one angolar

an·go·lese \¦aŋgō,lēz, ¦aiŋ-, -gə-, -ēs\ *n, pl* **angolese** *usu cap* [*Angola*, Africa + E *-ese*] **1 :** a member of any of the Bantu peoples of Angola **2 :** the Bantu language of the Angolese people

an·go·ni \aŋˈgōnē, anˈ-\ *n* -s *cap* [fr. *Angoni*land, plateau region in southwestern Nyasaland, Africa] **:** an animal of an eastern African native strain of zebu cattle

[1]**an·go·ra** \aŋˈgōrə, aiŋˈ-,anˈ-,aanˈ-, -ȯrə, *attrib also* ˈ=,==\ *n* -s [prob. trans. of G *angorakaninchen* or F *lapin angora*, fr. *Angora* (Ankara), Turkey; prob. fr. the view that it originated in Asia Minor] **1** *also* **angora wool :** the hair of the Angora rabbit or the Angora goat **2 :** a yarn of Angora rabbit hair used esp. for knitting **3** *usu cap* **a :** ANGORA CAT **b :** ANGORA GOAT **c :** ANGORA RABBIT

[2]**angora** \"\ *adj* **:** of or relating to a mutant coat form in mammals characterized by great increase in length and silkiness of the hairs as compared with the wild type

angora cat *n, usu cap A* **1 :** a long-haired domestic cat with narrow pointed head and long slim body, tail, and limbs that prob. originated in the interior of Turkey and is nearly or wholly extinct as a pure breed in the U.S. — called also *coon cat, Maine cat* **2 :** a long-haired domestic cat

angora goat *n, usu cap A* **:** a breed or variety of the domestic goat reared for its long silky hair which is the true mohair of commerce and differs from the wool of the sheep in not felting

angora rabbit *n, usu cap A* **:** a long-haired rabbit usu. white with red eyes of a domestic breed raised for fine wool

an·gos·tu·ra bark \¦aŋgə¦st(y)u̇rə-, ¦aiŋ-, -ürə\ *also* **angostura** *n* -s [prob. trans. of AmerSp *corteza de Angostura*, lit., bark of Angostura, fr. *Angostura* (now Ciudad Bolívar), river port in Venezuela] **:** an aromatic bitter bark used as a tonic and antipyretic and obtained from either of two So. American trees (*Galipea officinalis* and *Cusparia trifoliata*) of the family Rutaceae, the latter yielding Brazilian angostura bark

an·gou·mois grain moth *also* **angoumois moth** \¦än-,güm¦wä-\ *n, often cap A* [fr. *Angoumois*, former province of France] **:** a small tineid moth (*Sitotroga cerealella*) of which the larva is a destructive pest of stored grain feeding in the interior of the kernels of various cereals

an·grae·cum \aŋˈgrēkəm\ *syn of* ANGRECUM

an·gre·cum \aŋˈgrēkəm\ *n, cap* [NL, modif. of Malay *anggĕrek* orchid] **:** a genus of epiphytic orchids found in tropical regions of the Old World with 2-ranked leaves and in several species grotesque showy flowers

an·gri·ly \ˈaŋgrəlē, ˈaiŋ-, -li\ *adv* [ME, fr. *angry* + *-ly*] **:** in an angry manner **:** with anger

an·gri·ness \-rēnəs, -rin-\ *n* -ES **:** the state of being angry

an·grite \ˈaŋ,grīt\ *n* -s [*Angra* dos Reis, town near Rio de Janeiro, Brazil + E *-ite*] **:** a meteoritic stone consisting essentially of titanaugite and having no chondrules

an·gry \ˈaŋgrē, ˈaiŋ-, -ri, *chiefly substand* -ŋr-\ *adj, often* -ER/-EST [ME, fr.[1]*anger* + *-y*] **1 :** feeling some degree of anger **:** showing vexation or hot resentment **:** WRATHFUL, IRATE ⟨~ with anyone who dislikes the Cockney manner —*Times Lit. Supp.*⟩ ⟨~ at the weather⟩ **2 a :** indicative of anger **:** proceeding from anger ⟨~ words⟩ **b :** seeming to show anger **:** threatening or seeming to threaten angrily ⟨an ~ sky⟩ ⟨a scorpion with wide ~ nippers —Robert Browning⟩ **3 :** inflamed and painful — used of a sore **4 a** *archaic* **:** habitually irascible and bad-tempered **b :** appearing or being naturally fierce or feral ⟨by ~ wolf —John Keats⟩ **5 :** having some characteristic associated with anger; *esp* **:** having a hue that suggests anger ⟨an ~ red⟩

syn MAD, IRATE, INDIGNANT, WRATHFUL, WROTH, ACRIMONIOUS: Although one may occasionally be inwardly and secretly ANGRY, the word commonly implies excited displeasure outwardly expressed ⟨she wanted somebody to be *angry* with, somebody to abuse —George Meredith⟩ Often but not always the word may imply a justifiable cause for displeasure ⟨he hardly ever gets *angry*, doesn't half stand up for his rights —Margaret Mead⟩ MAD is a close equivalent to ANGRY but lacks implications about expression ⟨Old Rough and Ready was getting *mad* . . . no official thanks for the victories had reached him —Bernard De Voto⟩ IRATE stresses vehement irascible expression of displeasure ⟨the men were getting more cautious and at the same time more *irate* and violent in their language —Anthony Trollope⟩ INDIGNANT always suggests some justification for wrath, some righteousness of anger ⟨he . . . grows very hot and *indignant* when he thinks of the disrespectful treatment he received —Rudyard Kipling⟩ ⟨the natives, *indignant* at the insult offered their laws . . ., made a dash at the rioters —Herman Melville⟩ WRATHFUL and the less common WROTH may express the vehemence of IRATE and the justification of INDIGNANT ⟨Mr. Seddon winced. Then he became *wrathful* in a dry legal fashion. "That", he said, "is a most improper question" —Agatha Christie⟩ ⟨eyes more wild than those of Moses when, at the sight of the golden calf and the dancing, his heart waxed *wroth* within him —L.P.Smith⟩ ACRIMONIOUS implies bitter feeling, rising temper, and caustic expression ⟨no modern subject, probably, has brought forth so much lyric liturgy and *acrimonious* debate —M.R.Cohen⟩ ANGRY and MAD are more common than the other words in reference to animals ⟨an *angry* hornet⟩ ⟨a *mad* bull⟩ and ANGRY and WRATHFUL are the most commonly used in the group in reference to raging or ominous natural phenomena ⟨*angry* storm clouds⟩ ⟨*wrathful* lightning⟩

angst \ˈäŋzt, ˈaŋ-, -ŋ(k)st\ *n, pl* **äng·ste** \ˈeŋztə, -ŋ(k)stə\ [Dan & G; Dan, fr. G, fr. OHG *angust;* akin to MLG *angest* dread, MD *anxt*, OFris *ångost* dread, OHG *engi* narrow — more at ANGER] **:** a feeling of anxiety **:** DREAD, ANGUISH

ang·ster \ˈäŋzte(r), -ŋ(k)st-\ *n* -s [G, fr. MHG, fr. ML *angustus* thin, fr. L, narrow — more at ANGUISH] **:** an old Swiss minor coin of copper coined in various cantons from the 15th to the 19th centuries

ang·strom \ˈaŋztrəm, ˈaiŋ-, -ŋst- *sometimes* ˈȯŋ-\ *or* **angstrom unit** *n* -s [after Anders J. *Ångström* †1874 Swedish physicist] **:** either of two units of wavelength: **a :** one ten= billionth of a meter — called also *absolute angstrom* **b :** the wavelength of the red spectrum line of cadmium divided by 6438.4696 — called also *international angstrom*

an·gu·clast \ˈaŋgyü,klast\ *n* -s [*angu*lar + pheno*clast*] **:** an angular phenoclast

an·gui·dae \ˈaŋgwə,dē\ *n pl, cap* [NL, fr. *Anguis*, type genus + *-idae*] **:** a family of lizards some of which are limbless and all of which are entirely harmless and useful as destroyers of slugs, worms, and insects — compare BLINDWORM

an·gui·form \-,fȯrm\ *adj* [L *anguis* snake + E *-form*] *archaic* **:** having the form of a snake

an·guil·la \aŋˈgwilə\ *n, cap* [NL, fr. L, eel] **:** a genus (the type of the family Anguillidae) of fishes that includes the common eel and certain related forms and has the dorsal and anal fins continuous with the reduced caudal and pectoral fins

an·guil·lar·ia \ˌaŋgwəˈla(a)rēə\ *n, cap* [NL, fr. Luigi *Anguillara* †1570 Ital. botanist + NL *-ia*] **:** a small genus of herbs (family Melanthaceae) natives of Australia and Tasmania with sessile lilylike flowers

an·guil·li·form \aŋˈgwilə,fȯrm\ *adj* [L *anguilla* eel + E *-iform*] *archaic* **:** having the form of an eel

an·guil·lu·la \aŋˈgwilyələ\ [NL, fr. L *anguilla* eel + NL *-ula*] *syn of* TURBATRIX

an·guil·lu·li·na \(ˌ)aŋ,gwilyəˈlīnə, -ēnə\ *n, cap* [NL, fr. *anguillula* (dim. of L *anguilla* eel) + NL *-ina*] *in some classifications* **:** a genus of widely distributed phasmid nematodes including free-living forms and a number of important plant pathogens and being approximately equal to *Tylenchus* and *Anguina* of other classifications

an·gui·mor·pha \ˌaŋgwəˈmȯrfə\ *n pl, cap* [NL, fr. *Anguis* + *-morpha*] **:** a section of the saurian division Autarchoglossa comprising the Anguidae and certain related families and characterized by simple clavicles, a smooth or papillate tongue, flounced hemipenes, and teeth that are usu. conical, pointed, or recurved — **an·gui·mor·phine** \¦==¦=,fīn, -fən\ *adj*

an·gui·na \aŋˈgwīnə, anˈ-, -ēnə\ *n, cap* [NL, fr. L, fem. of *anguinus*] **:** a genus of plant-parasitic phasmid nematodes (family Tylenchidae) including several serious pests of cultivated crops and typically forming galls on leaves, stems, or roots — compare ANGUILLULINA; see TYLENCHUS

an·guine \ˈaŋ,gwīn\ *adj* [L *anguinus*, fr. *anguis* snake + *-inus* -ine — more at ANGUIS] *archaic* **:** of, relating to, or suggestive of a snake

an·guin·e·ous \(ˈ)aŋ¦gwinēəs\ *adj* [L *anguineus*, fr. *anguin-*, *anguen* snake (fr. *anguis*) + *-eus* -eous] *archaic* **:** having the nature or appearance of a snake

an·guin·i·dae \aŋˈgwinə,dē\ [NL, fr. *Anguin-*, *Anguis*, type genus + *-idae*] *syn of* ANGUIDAE

an·gui·ped \ˈaŋgwə,ped\ *adj* [L *anguiped-*, *anguipes*, fr. *anguis* + *ped-*, *pes* foot — more at FOOT] **:** having legs in the form of serpents — used esp. of a statue

an·guis \ˈaŋgwəs\ *n, cap* [NL, fr. L, snake; akin to OE & OHG *igil* hedgehog, OHG *unc* snake, L *anguilla* eel, Gk *enchelys* eel, *echidna* viper, *echinos* hedgehog, *ophis* snake, Skt *ahi*] **:** the type genus of Anguidae including only the limbless blindworm

[1]**an·guish** \ˈaŋgwish, ˈaiŋ-, -ēsh *also* -əsh\ *n* -ES [ME *angwisshe*, fr. OF *angoisse* anguish, narrowness, restraint, fr. L *angustia* narrowness, difficulty, distress, fr. *angustus* narrow, difficult; akin to OE *enge* narrow — more at ANGER] **:** extreme pain either of body or mind **:** excruciating distress — usu. used in sing. ⟨the keenest of all ~, self-reproach —Jane Austen⟩ ⟨his whole frame quivering with ~ as kick followed kick in rapid succession —Charles Dickens⟩ **syn** see SORROW

[2]**anguish** \"\ *vb* -ED/-ING/-ES [ME *angwisshen*, fr. MF *angoissier*, fr. LL *angustiare* to distress, fr. L *angustia*] *vi* **:** to distress oneself **:** suffer intense pain or sorrow ⟨his heart *~ed* within him —Edith Sitwell⟩ ~ *vt* **:** to cause to suffer anguish **:** distress severely ⟨a heart that had been *~ed* with sorrow⟩

anguished *adj* [ME *angwisshed*, fr. past. part. of *angwisshen*] **:** produced, affected, or accompanied by anguish **:** TORMENTED ⟨an ~ conscience⟩ **:** AGONIZED ⟨an ~ shriek⟩

[1]**an·gu·lar** \ˈaŋgyələ(r), ˈaiŋ-\ *adj* [MF or L; MF *angulaire*, fr. L *angularis*, fr. *angulus* angle, corner + *-aris* -ar — more at ANGLE] **1 :** having an angle or angles **:** forming an angle or corner **:** sharp-cornered ⟨an ~ brick structure —*Amer. Guide Series: Maine*⟩ **2 :** of or relating to the 1st, 4th, 7th, and 10th mundane houses of a horoscope **3 :** measured by an angle ⟨~ distance⟩ **4 a :** sharp and stiff in character or manner **:** lacking in smoothness ⟨a rough, ~, explosive poetry —*Saturday Rev.*⟩ **b :** having the bones prominent from lack of plumpness ⟨an ~ youth⟩ **5 :** relating to or having a chemical structure in which a ring or group is so joined as to form an angle and not a straight alignment ⟨an ~ methyl group⟩ **6** *anat* **:** relating to or situated near an angle ⟨the ~ head of the quadratus labii superioris⟩; *specif* **:** relating to or situated near the inner angle of the eye **syn** see LEAN

[2]**angular** \"\ *n* -s [NL *angulare*, fr. L, neut. of *angularis*, adj.] **:** a membrane bone in the lower posterior part of the lower jaw of most vertebrates except mammals

angular acceleration *n* **:** the time rate of change of angular velocity

angular aperture *n* **:** the angle subtended at the principal focus of an optical system by the diameter of its entrance pupil

angular artery *n* **:** the terminal part of the facial artery that passes up alongside the nose to the inner angle of the orbit

angular capital *n* **:** an Ionic capital with volutes on four faces, those of adjacent faces meeting and projecting diagonally under each corner of the abacus

angular convolution *or* **angular gyrus** *n* **:** one of the convolutions of the posterior part of the external surface of the parietal lobe of the cerebrum

angular cutter *n* **:** a tool-steel cutter for finishing surfaces at other than 90 degrees with its axis of rotation

angular displacement *n* **:** a definite amount of rotation (as of a disk) about a specified axis

an·gu·la·re \ˌaŋgyəˈlärē, -la(a)rē\ *n, pl* **angula·ria** \-ärēə, -a(a)rēə\ [NL, fr. L, neut. of *angularis* angular — more at ANGULAR] **:** ANGULAR

angular frequency *n* **:** frequency of a periodic process (as electric oscillation or sound vibration) expressed in radians per second, equivalent to frequency in cycles multiplied by 2π

angular impulse *n* **:** the product of a torque and its time of duration being equal to the change in angular momentum of a body free to rotate — compare IMPULSE 4a

an·gu·lar·i·ty \ˌaŋgyəˈlarəd·ē, ˌaiŋ-, -ətē, -i *also* -er-\ *n* -ES **1 :** the quality of being angular ⟨an almost impressionistic ~ —Robert Evett⟩ **2 a :** an ungainly appearance (as in dress or manner) **b :** lack of suaveness **:** CRANKINESS ⟨the ~ of his disposition⟩ **3 angularities** *pl* **:** angular outlines **:** sharp corners ⟨*angularities* of handwriting⟩

an·gu·lar·i·za·tion \ˌ==_lərəˈzāshən, -ˌrīˈz-\ *n* -s **:** the act, process, or result of angularizing

an·gu·lar·ize \ˈ===,rīz\ *vt* -ED/-ING/-S [[1]*angular* + *-ize*] **:** to make angular; *esp* **:** to transform by changing curved lines into angular lines

angular leaf spot *also* **angular spot** *n* **:** a disease of plants in which the leaf spots have angular and usu. sharply limited outlines (as that of cotton caused by the bacterium *Xanthomonas malvacearum* and that of cucumber caused by the bacterium *Pseudomonas lachrymans*) — see BLACKFIRE

an·gu·lar·ly *adv* **:** in an angular manner

angular magnification *n* **:** the ratio of the angle subtended at the eye by the image formed by an optical instrument to that subtended at the eye by the object when not viewed through the instrument

angular milling *n* **:** the process of milling flat surfaces that are at an angle to the axis of the milling-machine spindle

angular momentum *n* **:** a vector quantity measuring the intensity of rotational motion and being equal in classical physics to the product of the angular velocity of a rotating body and its moment of inertia with respect to the rotation axis — called also *moment of momentum*

angular motion *n* **:** ROTATION 1a

angular position *n* **:** the orientation of a body or figure with respect to a specified reference position as expressed by the amount of rotation necessary to change from one orientation to the other about a specified axis

angular process *n* **:** any of the processes terminating the supraorbital arches of the frontal bone

angular speed *n* **:** the speed element of angular velocity

angular vein *n* **:** a vein that runs obliquely down at the side of the upper part of the nose and is continued across the cheek as the anterior facial vein

angular velocity *n* **:** the time rate of angular displacement usu. expressed in radians per second or in revolutions per second or per minute being a vector whose direction and sense are such that the motion appears clockwise to one looking in the direction of the vector

angular-winged katydid \ˈ===,wiŋd-\ *n* **:** a common large green long-horned grasshopper (*Microcentrum retinerve*) of the eastern U. S.

[1]**an·gu·late** \ˈaŋgyələt, ˈaiŋ-, -,lāt *usu* -d·+V\ *adj* [L *angulatus*, fr. *angulus* angle, corner + *-atus* -ate] **:** formed with corners **:** ANGLED ⟨~ leaves⟩ — **an·gu·late·ly** *adv*

[2]**an·gu·late** \-,lāt *usu* -d·+V\ *vb* -ED/-ING/-S [ME *angulaten*, fr. L *angulatus*] *vt* **:** to make angulate ~ *vi* **:** to become angulate

an·gu·la·tion \ˌ==ˈlāshən\ *n* -s [[1]*angulate* + *-ion*] **1 :** the action of making angulate **2 a :** an angular formation or shape **b** *med* **:** an abnormal bend or curve in an organ **3 :** the measurement of angles (as in surveying)

an·gu·la·tor \ˈ==,lād·ə(r)\ *n* -s **:** a mechanical device for converting angles measured in an oblique plane to their projections on a horizontal plane and used esp. in surveying

anguli *pl of* ANGULUS

anguli- *or* **angulo-** *comb form* [prob. fr. NL, fr. L *angulus* angle — more at ANGLE] **1 :** angle ⟨*angulo*meter⟩ **:** angular ⟨*anguli*nerved⟩ **2 :** of or belonging to the angular and ⟨*angulo*splenial⟩

an·gu·lif·er·ous \¦aŋgyə¦lif(ə)rəs\ *adj* [*anguli-* + *-ferous*] *of a gastropod shell* **:** having the last whorl angular

an·gu·loa \ˌaŋgyəˈlōə, aŋˈgyüləwə\ *n, cap* [NL, after Francisco de *Angulo* 18th cent. Span. naturalist] **:** a small genus of So. American orchids with large plicate leaves cultivated for their showy irregular flowers

[1]**an·gu·lo·sple·ni·al** \¦aŋgyə(ˌ)lō¦-\ *adj* [*angulo-* + *splenial*] *anat* **:** of or relating to both the angular and the splenial

[2]**angulosplenial** \¦==(=)ˈ-\ *n* -s **:** the angulosplenial bone forming most of the inner and lower part of the mandible of amphibians

an·gu·lous \ˈaŋgyələs\ *also* **an·gu·lose** \-,lōs\ *adj* [F *anguleux*, fr. L *angulosus*, fr. *angulus* angle + *-osus* -ous, -ose] *archaic* **:** having angles or corners **:** ANGULAR

an·gu·lus \-_ləs\ *n, pl* **angu·li** \-,lī, -,lē\ [L — more at ANGLE] *anat* **:** ANGLE; *also* **:** an angular part or relationship

[1]**an·gus** \ˈaŋgəs, ˈaiŋ-\ *adj, usu cap* [fr. *Angus*, county in Scotland] **:** of or from the county of Angus, Scotland **:** of the kind or style prevalent in Angus

[2]**angus** \"\ *n, usu cap* [fr. *Angus*, county where the breed originated] **:** ABERDEEN ANGUS

angusti- *comb form* [prob. fr. L, fr. *angustus* — more at ANGUISH] **:** narrow ⟨*angusti*foliate⟩ ⟨*angusti*rostrate⟩

an·gus·ti·ros·trate \¦aŋ¦gəstə¦-\ *adj* [*angusti-* + *rostrate*] **:** having a narrow rostrum or snout

an·gus·ti·sel·late \¦=¦==¦-\ *adj* [*angusti-* + *sellate*] *paleontol* **:** having sutures in which there are a prominent ventral saddle, deep lateral lobes, and deep umbilical saddles — used of a stage in the development of the ammonoid shell

ang·wan·ti·bo \aŋˈ(g)wäntə,bō\ *n* -s [Efik] **:** a small lemur (*Arctocebus calabarensis*) of western Africa having a rather long snout and a rudimentary tail

anh *abbr* anhydrous

an·ha·lo·ni·um alkaloid \ˌan(h)əˈlōnēəm-\ *n* [NL *Anhalonium*, genus of cacti, fr. Gk *an-* + *halōnion* small threshing floor (equated with NL *areola* areole, fr. L, small open space, dim. of *area* piece of level ground, threshing floor), dim. of *halōn* threshing floor; fr. the belief that the areoles were lacking — more at HALO] **:** any of a group of alkaloids (as hordenine, mescaline) that are found in mescal buttons and that are used as cerebral stimulants and motor depressants — called also *cactus alkaloid*

an·har·mon·ic \¦an,=¦==\ *adj* [F *anharmonique*, fr. *an-* + *harmonique* harmonic, fr. L *harmonicus*] **:** not harmonic — **an·har·mo·nic·i·ty** \¦an,härməˈnisəd·ē\ *n* -ES

an·he·do·nia \¦anhēˈdōnēə\ *n* -s [NL, fr. *an-* + Gk *hēdonē* pleasure + NL *-ia* — more at HEDONIC] **1 :** insensitiveness to pleasure **2 :** incapacity for experiencing happiness — compare ANALGESIA — **an·he·don·ic** \¦==¦dänik\ *adj*

an·he·dral \(ˈ)an¦hēdrəl\ *adj* [*an-* + *-hedral*] **:** ALLOTRIOMORPHIC

an·hi·dro·sis *or* **an·hy·dro·sis** \ˌanhiˈdrōsəs\ *also* **an·idro·sis** \ˌaniˈ-\ *n, pl* **anhidro·ses** *or* **anhydro·ses** \-ō,sēz\ [NL, fr. *an-* + *hidrosis, hydrosis*] **:** abnormal deficiency or absence of sweating

[1]**an·hi·drot·ic** *or* **an·hy·drot·ic** *also* **an·idrot·ic** \¦== ¦dräd·ik\ *adj* [*an-* + *hidrotic, hydrotic*] **:** tending to check sweating

[2]**anhidrotic** *or* **anhydrotic** \"\ *also* **anidrotic** \"\ *n* -s **:** an anhidrotic agent

anhi·ma \anˈhīmə; əˈnēmə, aˈ-\ *n* [NL, fr. Pg, fr. Tupi] **1** -s **:** HORNED SCREAMER **2** *cap* **:** a genus of birds that includes only the horned screamer and is the type of the family Anhimidae

an·him·i·dae \anˈhimə,dē\ *n pl, cap* [NL, fr. *Anhima*, type genus + *-idae*] **:** a family (coextensive with the suborder Anhimae of the order Anseriformes) of large stout-billed birds having spurred wings and more or less webbed feet and comprising the screamers of So. America

an·hin·ga \an'hiŋgə\ *n* [Pg, fr. Tupi] **1** -s : an American snakebird **2** *cap* [NL, fr. Pg] : a genus of aquatic birds related to the gannets and cormorants and consisting of the snakebirds

an·his·tous \(')an¦histəs\ *also* **an·his·tic** \-tik\ *adj* [*an-* + *hist-* + *-ous* or *-ic*] : not differentiated into tissues : NONCELLULAR ⟨~ matrix⟩ ⟨~ intercellular cement⟩

anhungered *adj* [ME *anhungred*, alter. of ME *ahungred* ahungered] **1** *obs* : HUNGRY **2** *archaic* : eagerly longing

anhungry *adj* [alter. of earlier *ahungry*] *obs* : HUNGRY

anhydr- *or* **anhydro-** *comb form* [modif. (influenced by *hydr-*, *hydro-*) of Gk *anydr-*, fr. *anydros* — more at ANHYDROUS] **1 a** : waterless ⟨*anhydremia*⟩ **b** : lacking fluid ⟨*anhydromyelia*⟩ **2** : anhydride of ⟨*anhydroglucose*⟩

an·hy·drase \an'hī,drās\ *n* -s [*anhydr-* + *-ase*] : an enzyme (as carbonic anhydrase) promoting a specific dehydration reaction and the reverse hydration reaction

an·hy·drate \-,drāt, *usu* -ād·+V\ *vt* -ED/-ING/-S [*an-* + *hydrate*] : DEHYDRATE; *esp* : to dehydrate quickly in food processing — **an·hy·dra·tion** \,an,hī'drāshən\ *n* -s — **an·hy·dra·tor** \an'hī,drād·ə(r)\ *n* -s

an·hy·dre·mia *also* **an·hy·drae·mia** \,an,hī'drēmēə\ *n* -s [NL, fr. *anhydr-* + *-emia*] : an abnormal reduction of water in the blood — **an·hy·dre·mic** *also* **an·hy·drae·mic** \¦==¦drēmik\ *adj*

an·hy·dride \an'hī,drīd, -,drəd\ *n* -s [ISV *anhydr-* + *-ide*] : a compound derived from another compound (as an acid) by removal of the elements of water ⟨benzoic ~ $(C_6H_5CO)_2O$⟩

an·hy·drid·i·za·tion \(,)an,hīdrədə'zāshən, -,dī'z-\ *or* **an·hy·dri·za·tion** \(,)an,hīdrə'z-\ *n* -s : the process of anhydridizing or the state of being anhydridized

an·hy·drid·ize \an'hīdrə,dīz\ *or* **an·hy·drize** \-,drīz\ *vt* -ED/-ING/-S : to convert into an anhydride

an·hy·drite \an'hī,drīt\ *n* -s [G *anhydrit*, fr. *anhydr-* + *-it* -ite] : a mineral consisting of an anhydrous calcium sulfate $CaSO_4$ occurring rarely in orthorhombic crystals usu. massive and white or slightly colored (hardness 3–3.5, sp. gr. 2.90–2.99) — compare GYPSUM

an·hy·dro \an'hī(,)drō\ *adj* [*anhydr-*] : of or relating to an anhydride ⟨~ sugars⟩ — compare DEHYDRO

anhydro base *n* : a dehydration product (as ammonia or an imine) of a base, usu. an oxygen-containing nitrogen base (as ammonium hydroxide or the color base of certain triphenylamine dyes)

an·hy·dro·bi·o·sis \(,)an,hydrōbī'ōsəs\ *n*, *pl* **anhydrobio·ses** \-ō,sēz\ [NL, fr. *anhydr-* + *biosis*] **1** *of a usu aquatic organism* : life away from water **2** : ANABIOSIS

an·hy·dro·hy·droxy·pro·ges·ter·one \an¦hīdrō,hī¦dräksē-prō'jestə,rōn\ *n* -s [*anhydr-* + *hydroxy-* + *progesterone*] : ETHISTERONE

an·hy·drous \(')an'hīdrəs\ *adj* [modif. (influenced by *hydr-*, *hydro-*) of Gk *anydros* waterless, fr. *an-* + *-ydros* (fr. *hydōr* water) — more at WATER] : destitute of water — used of water of crystallization, dissolved or combined water, adsorbed water

anhydrous hydrofluoric acid *n* : HYDROGEN FLUORIDE

an·hys·ter·et·ic \¦an,histə¦red·ik, an¦h-\ *adj* [*an-* + *hysteretic*] : not subject to hysteresis

ani \ä'nē, ə'-\ *n* -s [Sp *ani* or Pg *ani*, fr. Tupi *ani*, *anú*] : any of several black cuckoos (genus *Crotaphagus*) with arched laterally compressed bills found mostly in tropical America but occasionally (as the common ani *C. ani*) northward to the southern limits of the U. S.

ani·ba \ə'nībə, -ēbə\ *n*, *cap* [NL, prob. fr. Tupi *anhoaiba*, *anhuhyba*] : a genus of tropical American trees of the family Lauraceae with aromatic foliage, inconspicuous flowers, and succulent fruit, the seeds of some having tonic properties

an·i·can·o·don·ta \,anə,kanə'däntə\ [NL, fr. Gk *anikanos* insufficient + NL *-odonta*] *syn of* PILOSA

anic·ca \ə'nikə\ *n* -s [Pali, fr. Skt *anitya* not eternal, fr. *²a-* + *nitya* eternal] *Buddhism* : evanescence or impermanence of existence

an·icon·ic \¦a,nī¦känik\ *adj* [*an-* + *iconic*] **1** : symbolic or suggestive rather than literally representational : not made or designed as a likeness ⟨trees, boulders, and other ~ objects of primitive worship⟩ ⟨an ~ image⟩ **2** : without idols or images : opposed to the use of idols or images ⟨an ~ religion⟩

an·icon·ism \(')a'nīkən,izəm\ *n* -s [*an-* + *iconism*] **1** : worship of an aniconic object **2** : opposition to the use of idols

an·ic·ter·ic \¦an(,)ik¦terik\ *adj* [ISV *an-* + *icteric*] : not accompanied or characterized by jaundice ⟨~ hepatitis⟩

an·i·cut *or* **an·ni·cut** \'anə̇,kət\ *n* -s [Tamil *aṇaikkaṭṭu*, fr. *aṇai* dam + *kaṭṭu* building, structure] : a dam made in a stream for maintaining and regulating irrigation

an·id·i·an \(')a'nidēən\ *adj* [*an-* + Gk *eidos* form + E *-ian*] *of an embryo or fetus* : FORMLESS : lacking differentiation

anidrosis *var of* ANHIDROSIS

anidrotic *var of* ANHIDROTIC

an·i·el·li·dae \,anē'elə,dē\ *syn of* ANNIELLIDAE

an if *conj* [*²an*] *archaic* : provided that : IF ⟨these be fine things *an if* they be not sprites —Shak.⟩

¹anigh *prep* [*¹a-* + *nigh*] *archaic* : NIGH

²anigh *adv* -ER/-EST [*¹a-* + *nigh*] *archaic* : NIGH

anight *or* **anights** *adv* [ME, fr. OE *on niht*, fr. *on* + *niht* night — more at NIGHT] *archaic* : at night

an·il \'anᵊl\ *n* -s [ISV, fr. *aniline*] : a Schiff base derived from an aromatic amine; *esp* : one derived from aniline ⟨the ~ $C_6H_5CH{:}NC_6H_5$ of benzaldehyde⟩

ani·lao *or* **ani·lau** \ä'nē,lau̇\ *or* **ani·lo** \-(,)lō\ *n* -s [Tag] **1** : a shrub (*Columbia serratifolia*) of the family Tiliaceae yielding a strong bast fiber that is found chiefly in the Philippines **2** : any of several shrubs or trees of the genus *Grewia* yielding a cordage fiber

an·ile \'a,nīl, 'ā,-, - īəl\ *adj* [L *anilis*, fr. *anus* old woman + *-ilis* -ile; akin to OHG *ano* grandfather, male ancestor, Gk *annis* grandmother, Arm *han*, and perh. to L *senex* old man — more at SENIOR] : of or like a doddering old woman; *esp* : FLIGHTY ⟨pathetic questions which showed an ~ loss of time sense —R.O.Bowen⟩

anil·ic \ə'nilik, a'-\ *adj* [ISV *anil* + *-ic*] : of or relating to aniline or anil

anilic acid \ə'==-\ *or* **an·i·lid·ic acid** \¦anᵊl¦idik-\ *n* : a compound [as phthalanilic acid $C_6H_4(CONHC_6H_5)COOH$] that is both an anilide and an acid

anil·i·dae \ə'nilə,dē\ *syn of* ANILIIDAE

an·i·lide \'anᵊləd, -,līd\ *n* -s [G *anilid*, fr. *anil* + *-id* -ide] **1** : an amide (as acetanilide) in which hydrogen of the amido group is replaced by phenyl : an *N*-acyl derivative of aniline **2** : ARYLIDE

an·i·li·id \,anᵊl'īəd\ *n* -s [NL *Aniliidae*] : a snake of the family Aniliidae

an·i·li·idae \-īə,dē\ *n pl*, *cap* [NL, fr. *Anilius*, type genus (irreg. fr. L *anulus* ring) + *-idae*] : a small family of tropical nonvenomous burrowing snakes with vestigial pelvis and vestigial hind legs

¹an·i·line \'anᵊlən *sometimes* -,līn *or* -,ēn\ *also* **an·i·lin** \-ən\ *n* -s [G *anilin*, fr. *anil* indigo, (fr. F, fr. Pg, fr. Ar *an-nīl* the indigo plant, fr. Skt *nīlī* indigo, fr. fem. of *nīla* dark blue) + *-in* -ine, -in] : an oily liquid poisonous amine $C_6H_5NH_2$ colorless when pure and obtainable by destructive distillation (as of indigo or coal) but now usu. made by the reduction of nitrobenzene or by the high-pressure reaction of chlorobenzene and ammonia and used chiefly in organic synthesis (as of dyes, pharmaceuticals, rubber chemicals, and explosives) and as a solvent; amino-benzene

²aniline \"\ *adj* : relating to aniline : made from or by the use of aniline or a chemically related compound

aniline black *n* : a black dye produced on fiber (as cotton) by the oxidation of aniline oil or aniline hydrochloride and noted for its fastness, intensity of color, and resistance to greening — see DYE table I (under *Oxidation Base 1* and *Pigment Black 1*)

aniline blue *n* : any of the soluble blue dyes used as a biological dye

aniline dye *n* : a dye made by the use of aniline : any of various chemically related dyes; *broadly* : any synthetic organic dye — compare COAL-TAR DYE

aniline-formaldehyde resin *n* : a synthetic usu. thermoplastic resin made from aniline and formaldehyde

aniline hydrochloride *n* : a white crystalline salt $C_6H_5NH_3Cl$ made from aniline and hydrochloric acid and used chiefly in the manufacture of dyes and in the production of aniline black

aniline ink *n* : a quick-drying printing ink usu. made with an alcohol as vehicle and with an organic or inorganic pigment

aniline oil *n* : ANILINE — used chiefly commercially; see DYE table I (under *Oxidation Base 1*)

aniline point *n* : the lowest temperature at which aniline and a solvent (as gasoline) are completely miscible and which serves as an indication of the type of hydrocarbons present in the solvent, the content of aromatics being higher according as the temperature is lower

aniline printing *also* **aniline process** *n* : a process in which nonabsorbent surfaces are printed with aniline inks

aniline salt *n* : ANILINE HYDROCHLORIDE — used chiefly commercially; see DYE table I (under *Oxidation Base 1*)

ani·lin·gus \,ānə'liŋgəs\ *or* **ani·linc·tus** \-ŋ(k)təs\ *n* -ES [NL, fr. *anus* + *-i-* + *-lingus*, -linctus (as in *cunnilingus*, *cunnilinctus*)] : erotic stimulation achieved by contact between mouth and anus

an·i·lin·ism \'anᵊlə,nizəm\ *n* -s [ISV *aniline* + *-ism*] : poisoning from fumes inhaled in the manufacture of aniline

an·i·li·no- \¦anᵊl¦ēnō, -nə\ *comb form* [ISV, fr. *aniline* + *-o-*] : containing the univalent radical $C_6H_5NH_2$— derived from aniline ⟨*anilino*phenol $C_6H_5NHC_6H_4OH$⟩

anil·i·ty \ə'nilәd·ē, a'-\ *n* -ES [L *anilitas*, fr. *anilis* + *-tat-*, *-tas* -ty] **1** : the state of being an old woman **2** : an objectionable quality (as flightiness) felt to be typical of a doddering old woman ⟨the utter ~ of their political views⟩

anilo *var of* ANILAO

anils *pl of* ANIL

an·i·ma \'anəmə\ *n* -s [L — more at ANIMATE] **1 a** : SOUL, LIFE; *specif* : the passive or animal soul **b** : an individual's true inner self reflecting archetypal ideals of conduct — used esp. in contrast with *persona* in the analytic psychology of Carl Gustav Jung; compare ARCHETYPE 5 **2** [NL, fr. L, soul] *old pharmacy* **a** : the active ingredient of an animal or vegetable drug **b** : a dried plant juice or an aqueous extract

an·i·mad·ver·sion \,anə,mad'vərzhən, -,məd-, -ərl,-əil\ *also* |sh-\ *n* -s [L *animadversion-*, *animadversio*, fr. *animadversus* (past part. of *animadvertere*) + *-ion-*, *-io* -ion — more at ANIMADVERT] **1 a** : criticism that is usu. adverse and prompted by some degree of hostility : CENSURE : a censorious remark or observation ⟨his ~ upon his old acquaintance and pupil —James Boswell⟩ ⟨the customary ~s of a reviewer —R.B. Gottfried⟩ **b** : an observation, remark, or commentary that is usu. based on careful analysis and impartial judgment ⟨illuminating and scholarly ~s⟩ **2** *archaic* : judicial cognizance and punishment of an offense

an·i·mad·vert \¦==(,)=¦vərt, -ət,-əit\ *vb* -ED/-ING/-S [L *animadvertere*, fr. *animus* mind, soul + *advertere* to advert — more at ANIMATE, ADVERT] *vt*, *archaic* : NOTICE, OBSERVE ~ *vi* : to make an animadversion ⟨~*ing* on a wide variety of things they disliked⟩ ⟨she ~*ed* upon her closest interests⟩

animae mundi *pl of* ANIMA MUNDI

¹an·i·mal \'anəməl\ *n* -s [L, fr. *animale*, neut. of *animalis* animate, fr. *anima* breath, soul, + *-alis* -al — more at ANIMATE] **1** : an organism of the kingdom Animalia being characterized by a requirement for complex organic nutrients including proteins or their constituents which are usu. digested in an internal cavity before assimilation into the body proper and being distinguished from typical plants by lack of chlorophyll and inability to perform photosynthesis, by cells that lack cellulose walls, and usu. by greater mobility with some degree of voluntary locomotor ability, by greater irritability commonly mediated through a more or less centralized nervous system, and by the frequent presence of discrete complex sense organs **2 a** : one of the lower animals : a brute or beast as distinguished from man : any creature except a human being — compare DOMESTIC ANIMAL, FERAE NATURAE **b** : a mammal as distinguished from a bird, reptile, or other nonmammal **c** *North* : a male bovine : BULL **3 a** : a human being considered chiefly from the aspect of his animal nature and animal qualities ⟨a majestic ~ of a man —*Newsweek*⟩ **b** : a human being considered from a speculative or abstract viewpoint : PERSON, BEING, CREATURE ⟨women wonder so often about this strange creature, the male ~ —Theodor Reik⟩ **c** : THING — a counterword ⟨the theater, obviously, is an entirely different ~ —Arthur Miller⟩ **4** : animal nature : ANIMALITY ⟨unable to control the ~ in himself⟩

²animal \"\ *adj* **1 a** : of, relating to, resembling, or having the qualities of animals ⟨~ instincts⟩ ⟨~ behavior⟩; *esp* : more like a brute animal than a man ⟨the butler . . . betrayed a sullen and almost ~ affection for his master —G.K.Chesterton⟩ **b** : derived from animals as distinguished from vegetable or mineral sources ⟨furs and other ~ products⟩ **2** : of or relating to the physical or sentient ⟨the savage, when he first began to lift his thoughts above the satisfaction of his merely ~ wants —J.G.Frazer⟩ — contrasted with *intellectual*, *rational*, *spiritual* **3** : GROSS, CARNAL ⟨an ~ hunger for every pleasure⟩ **4** : physically relaxing or soothing : pleasurable to the senses ⟨the ~ looseness of their summer home clothes —D.C.Peattie⟩ **5** : of or relating to the animal pole of an egg or to that part of an egg from which ectoderm normally develops — compare VEGETAL **syn** see CARNAL

animal black *n* : a black pigment made by carbonizing animal matter: as **a** : BONE BLACK **b** : DROP BLACK **c** : IVORY BLACK

animal cellulose *n* : a substance like cellulose occurring in the test of certain tunicates

animal charcoal *n* : a charcoal of animal origin; *esp* : BONE BLACK

animal cracker *n* : a small semisweet animal-shaped cracker

an·i·mal·cu·lar \¦anə¦malkyələ(r)\ *also* **an·i·mal·cu·line** \-kyə,līn, -,lən\ *or* **an·i·mal·cu·lous** \-,ləs\ *adj* : of, relating to, or resembling animalcules

an·i·mal·cule \,anə'mal(,)kyül\ *or* **an·i·mal·cu·lum** \-kyələm\ *n*, *pl* **animalcules** \-kyülz\ *or* **animalcu·la** \-kyələ\ *also* **animalcu·lae** \-kyə,lē, -,lī\ [NL *animalculum*, dim. of L *animal*] **1** *archaic* : a tiny animal (as a fly) **2** : a minute usu. microscopic organism — compare INFUSORIA

an·i·mal·cu·lism \-,kyə,lizəm\ *n* -s **1** : a former theory in biology: various obscure physiological and pathological phenomena are caused by the activities of minute invisible animals **2** : a former theory in biology: the spermatozoon contains the whole embryo in miniature — compare OVISM

an·i·mal·cu·list \-,ləst\ *n* -s **1** : a specialist in animalcules **2** : one that accepts animalculism

animal dance *n* : a stylized dance (as among American Indians) imitating or suggestive of the movements of an animal or bird (as a bear or owl) often marked by the use of masks

animal electricity *n* : electricity generated in the bodies of animals (as through friction); *specif* : electricity generated by specially adapted organs of some fishes (as the electric eel) and apparently used chiefly in attack or defense

animal faith *n* : instinctive belief without rational foundation — used esp. in the philosophy of George Santayana

animal flower *n* : an animal (as a hydroid) resembling a flower

animal glue *n* : an adhesive, sizing agent, and protective colloidal material that is obtained by hydrolysis of proteins of the skins, bones, connective tissues, and tendons of cattle, sheep, goats, horses, and other animals

animal heat *n* : heat produced in the body of a living animal by functional chemical and physical activities — called also *body heat*; compare TEMPERATURE 5b

animal husbandman *n* **1** : a specialist in animal husbandry **2** : one that keeps or tends livestock

animal husbandry *n* : a branch of agriculture concerned with the production and care of domestic animals; *specif* : scientific study of the problems of animal production (as breeding and feeding)

animal hypnosis *n* : CATAPLEXY

an·i·ma·lia \,anə'mālyə, -lēə\ *n pl*, *often cap* [NL, fr. L, pl. of *animal*] : that one of the basic groups of living things that comprises either all the animals or all the multicellular animals — compare ANIMAL KINGDOM, PLANTAE, PROTISTA

an·i·mal·ic \¦anə¦malik\ *also* **an·i·ma·li·an** \-mālyən, -lēən\ *adj* : of or relating to animals or animalism

an·i·mal·ier \¦anəma¦li(ə)r\ *n* -s [F, fr. *animal* + *-ier* -er] : a sculptor or painter of animal subjects — compare ANIMALIST 2

an·i·mal·ism \'anəmə,lizəm\ *n* -s **1 a** : the aggregate of physical qualities felt to be typical of animals; *esp* : buoyant health and vitality and the uninhibited satisfaction of physical drives ⟨the joyous ~ of ancient Greece⟩ **b** : extreme preoccupation with the satisfaction of physical drives (as toward sex or food) sometimes accompanied by cruelty and brutality ⟨soldiers who passionately hated their enemies could revert to ~ —Webster Schott⟩ **2** : a theory according to which human beings are basically brutes and little or nothing more ⟨a growing ~ that has accompanied the attempt to make social planning the be-all and end-all of human existence —R.M.Weaver⟩

an·i·mal·ist \-ləst\ *n* -s **1 a** : one that follows animalism (sense 1b) as a mode of living : SENSUALIST **b** : one that accepts the theory of animalism **2** : a painter, sculptor, or writer that deals with animal subjects — compare ANIMALIER

an·i·mal·is·tic \¦anəmə¦listik\ *adj* **1** : of, relating to, or having the qualities of animals or animalism ⟨an ~ approach to life⟩ **2** : resembling or suggestive of an animal ⟨an ~ door knocker⟩

an·i·mal·i·tar·i·an·ism \,anə,malə'terēə,nizəm\ *n* -s [*¹animal* + *-itarianism* (as in *humanitarianism*)] : the view that animals are more natural, happier, and admirable than human beings

an·i·mal·i·ty \,anə'maləd·ē, -ətē, -i\ *n* -ES [F *animalité*, fr. *animal* + *-ité* -ity] **1** : animal healthiness, vitality, and absence of inhibitions : ANIMALISM ⟨the freedom of primitive sensuous ~ —John Dewey⟩ **2 a** : the state of being an animal **b** : animal nature esp. when not conferring of itself the faculty of reason ⟨that mental life which is characteristically human and above the level of sheer ~ —Susanne K. Langer⟩ **c** : a characteristic function or expression of animal nature ⟨the rude ~ of eating —R.L.Taylor⟩ **3 a** : animal life as distinguished from plant life ⟨the relationship of vegetable life and ~⟩ **b** : ANIMAL KINGDOM ⟨gradations of ~ that include a wide variety of creatures⟩

an·i·mal·iv·o·ra \,anəmə'liv(ə)rə\ [NL, fr. L *animal* + NL *-i-* + *-vora*] *syn of* MICROCHIROPTERA

an·i·mal·i·vore \,anə'malə,vō(ə)r\ *n* -s [NL *Animalivora*] : MICROCHIROPTERAN — **an·i·mal·iv·o·rous** \¦anəmə¦liv(ə)rəs\ *adj*

an·i·mal·i·za·tion \,anəmələ'zāshən, -,lī'z-\ *n* -s **1** : the act of animalizing or state of being animalized **2** : regional distribution of animals by number and species : animal population

an·i·mal·ize \'anəmə,līz\ *vb* -ED/-ING/-S *vt* **1 a** : to represent in animal form ⟨the Egyptian god Sebek *animalized* as a crocodile⟩ **b** *fine art* : to endow (a human figure) with animal features : distort (human features) to make animallike : emphasize human features of animallike appearance ⟨a man's *animalized* head, adorned with ram's horns⟩ **2** : to convert into animal matter ⟨*animalizing* food through digestion⟩ **3 a** : to reduce to the state of a lower animal : BRUTALIZE ⟨men that were *animalized* by war⟩ **b** : SENSUALIZE ⟨*animalized* by passion⟩ **4** : to alter (vegetable fibers or synthetic fibers) by chemical treatment so as to cause to react like wool toward dyes **5** : to cause (vegetal embryonic cells) to exhibit animal characteristics ~ *vi*, *of vegetal embryonic cells* : to exhibit animal characteristics

animal kingdom *n* : the one of the three basic groups of natural objects that comprises all living and extinct animals and includes about a million described species — compare MINERAL KINGDOM, PLANT KINGDOM

an·i·mal·like *adj* : having characteristics of an animal

an·i·mal·ly \-əlē, -li\ *adv* : in an animal manner

animal magnetism *n* **1 a** : a spiritlike force alleged by the Austrian physician Franz Anton Mesmer (1734–1815) to reside within himself and to be active in his use of therapeutical hypnosis — compare MESMERISM **b** : a spiritlike force held to reside in some individuals by the emanation of which a strong quasi-hypnotic influence can assertedly be exerted over others **2** *Christian Science* : ERROR, MORTAL MIND

animal mechanics *n* : the laws of equilibrium and motion in the animal body

animal mound *n* : EFFIGY MOUND

animal oil *n* : an oil obtained from animal substances; *specif* : BONE OIL 1

animal pole *n* : the point on the surface of an egg marking the center of the most active part of the protoplasm or the part containing least yolk, being in most animals whose embryology has been studied the point where the polar bodies are segmented off and where the protoplasm about it forms the ectoderm — opposed to *vegetal pole*; see BLASTULA illustration

animal protein factor *n* : vitamin B_{12} or a concentrate containing this vitamin and usu. antibiotics obtained esp. in the fermentation production of vitamin B_{12} and chlortetracycline and used as a supplement in some animal and poultry feeds

animal psychology *n* : the psychological behavior of animals other than man

animal rouge *n* : CARMINE 2

animals *pl of* ANIMAL

animal size *or* **animal sizing** *n* **1** : an animal glue or gelatin used for surface-sizing the higher grades of paper **2** : a solution or other preparation of animal size

animal-sized \'==¦=\ *adj* : sized with animal size

animal soul *n* **1** : the soul that in the scholastic tradition is characteristic of an animal and has sensitive, appetitive, and locomotive faculties and controls a more developed form of vital activity than the lower vegetable soul but has no independent existence apart from the body and is distinguished thereby from the higher rational soul — compare RATIONAL SOUL, VEGETABLE SOUL **2** *theosophy* : the center of animal passions

animal spirits *n pl* [L *animalis* animate — more at ANIMAL] **1** *sometimes* **animal spirit** *obs* : the nervous energy that is the source of physical sensation and movement **2** [influenced in meaning by *¹animal*] : vivacity arising from physical health and energy ⟨gay, full of contagious *animal spirits* —W.P.Eaton⟩

animal starch *n* : GLYCOGEN

animal step *n* : a dance step (as a fox trot, duck walk) named after and usu. imitative of a beast, bird, or fish

animal unit *n* : a unit expressing the feed requirements of different kinds of domestic animals on a common scale usu. based on the average or theoretical requirements of a mature cow ⟨100 hens equal one *animal unit*⟩

an·i·ma mun·di \,anəmə'mən,dī, -mün(,)dē\ *n*, *pl* **ani·mae mundi** \-,mē'mə-, -,mī'mü-\ [ML, vital force of the world] : a vital force or principle conceived of as permeating the world — compare ARCHEUS, WORLD SOUL

ani·man·do \,änə'män(,)dō, ,ānə-\ *adj* (*or adv*) [It, animating, fr. L *animandum*, gerund of *animare*] : becoming animated — used as a direction in music

animas *pl of* ANIMA

¹an·i·mate \'anəmət, *sometimes* -,māt, *usu* -d·+V\ *adj* [ME *animat*, fr. L *animatus*, past part. of *animare* to quicken, enliven, endow with breath or soul, fr. *anima* breath, soul; akin to OE *ōthian*, *ēthian* to breathe, OFris *omma* breath, ON *önd*, gen. *andar* breath, life, soul, Goth *uzanan* to breathe one's last, expire, L *animus* soul, mind, Gk *anemos* breath, wind, Skt *aniti* he breathes] **1** : possessing life : ALIVE, LIVING ⟨primitive worship of ~ and inanimate objects⟩ **2 a** : of, relating to, or associated with animal life as opposed to plant life ⟨the vast range of ~ and inanimate life⟩ **b** : marked by movement belonging to or suggesting the movement of animal life : MOVING : not static ⟨the swiftly flowing river was the only thing ~ in the valley⟩ **3** : full of life : possessing to an intensive degree the qualities of a living being or suggesting such qualities : VIVACIOUS, ANIMATED, SPIRITED, LIVELY ⟨her happy laughter and the ~ sparkle of her eyes⟩ **4** *of a grammatical gender* : referring typically to living things or to things considered as living — opposed to *inanimate* — **an·i·mate·ly** *adv* — **an·i·mate·ness** *n* -ES

²an·i·mate \-,māt, *usu* -ād·+V\ *vt* -ED/-ING/-S **1** : to give spirit and support to : stimulate to courage and perseverance : encourage or cheer up ⟨*animating* the tired men with a kind word⟩ **2 a** : to give life to : make alive : bring to life : fill with life ⟨the mysterious vital force that ~s the cells of the body⟩ **b** : to permeate deeply in such a way as to stimulate and enliven ⟨the forward-reaching spirit of inquiry which *animated* the study of logic —R.W.Southern⟩ **c** : to give vigor and vitality to : impart zest and color to : add sharply heightened interest and life to : brighten up ⟨an unusual gaiety . . . *animated* her conversation and actions —Osbert

Sitwell⟩ ⟨a smile *animated* his face⟩ **3 :** to move to action **:** MOTIVATE, PROMPT, INCITE **:** stir up ⟨all this apparatus of research *animated* the young historians —Van Wyck Brooks⟩ **4 :** to make, build, equip, or design in such a way that automatic, apparently spontaneous, and often lifelike movement is effected ⟨a miniature city of the future, completely *animated* —*Ford Times*⟩ ⟨*animated* puppets⟩ **5 a :** to produce in the form of an animated cartoon or of an animation ⟨three of the scenes in the musical will be *animated* by a New York studio⟩ **b :** to contribute to (the production of an animated cartoon or of an animation) by drawings or photographic work ⟨West Coast artists will ~ the last part of the film⟩ **syn** see QUICKEN

animated *adj* **1 a :** vibrantly alive ⟨she became intensely, rigidly ~ —Willa Cather⟩ **b :** full of the bustle and activity of life ⟨an ~ city street⟩ **c :** full of vigor and spirit **:** VIVACIOUS, LIVELY ⟨plunged into an ~ discussion —Dorothy Sayers⟩ **2 :** having the appearance of something alive **:** LIFELIKE ⟨an unusually ~ piece of sculpture⟩ **3 :** made in the form of an animated cartoon or of an animation ⟨the ~ sequences of the film are hilarious⟩ ⟨~ cutaways to show how the motors work⟩ **syn** see LIVELY

animated cartoon *n* **1** *also* **animated drawing a :** a series of drawings each of which shows a successive position of a figure or other object, the drawings being photographed on film or made directly on film so that projection of the film produces a picture in which the objects drawn seem to move in a lifelike and realistic manner **b :** a series of drawings similar to those of a film or tape animated cartoon but made on or transferred to a sequence of pages so that rapid flipping of the pages produces an illusion of movement in the objects drawn **2 :** ANIMATION 2a

an·i·mat·ed·ly \ˌanəˈmādədlē, -ātə-, -li\ *adv* **1 :** in a vivacious manner **:** with sparkling enthusiasm ⟨speaking ~ of vacation plans⟩ **2 :** with driving conviction often accompanied by a somewhat impatient vehemence **:** HEATEDLY ⟨the pros and cons were ~ argued⟩

animated oat *n* **:** an oat grass (*Avena sterilis*) marked by movements of the spikelets caused by twisting of the awns through changes in moisture

an·i·ma·tion \ˌanəˈmāshən\ *n* -s [L *animation-, animatio*, fr. *animatus* + *-ion-, -io* -ion] **1 a :** the act of animating or the state of being animate or animated ⟨cheerful words meant for the ~ of the discouraged⟩ **b :** the quality of being full of spirit and vigor **:** brightness of appearance or manner **:** VIVACIOUSNESS ⟨talking with great ~ —Dorothy Sayers⟩ **2 a :** a motion picture made by photographing successive positions or poses of puppets and other inanimate objects so that projection of the film produces a picture in which the puppets or other objects seem to move in a lifelike and realistic manner **b :** ANIMATED CARTOON 1 **c :** an inanimate object or group of objects designed for exhibit and illustration and usu. having movable and often automatically moving parts **3 :** production of an animation or animated cartoon

an·i·mat·ism \ˈanəməˌtizəm, -məd-,iz-\ *n* -s [¹*animate* + *-ism*] **:** attribution of consciousness and personality but not of individual spirit to such natural phenomena as thunderstorms and earthquakes and to such objects as plants and stones — compare ANIMISM — **an·i·ma·tis·tic** \¦==məˈtistik, -məd-¦is-\ *adj*

ani·ma·to \ˌanəˈmä(ˌ)tō, ˌän-, -ˈäd-(ˌ)ō\ *adj (or adv)* [It, fr. L *animatus*, past part. of *animare* to animate — more at ANIMATE] **:** with animation — used as a direction in music

an·i·mat·o·graph \ˌanəˈmadəˌgraf\ *n* -s [²*animate* + *-ograph* (as in *cinematograph*)] **:** an early form of motion-picture projector

an·i·ma·tor *also* **an·i·ma·ter** \ˈanəˌmād·ə(r), -ātə-\ *n* -s **:** one that contributes to the production of an animated cartoon or animation (as by making drawings)

¹**ani·mé** \əˈnēmē, ˌanəˈmā\ *or* **ane·mi** *or* **ani·mi** \əˈnēmē\ *n* -s [F *animé*, fr. Sp or Pg *anime*, fr. Tupi *ananim, oananim, oanani* resin] **:** any of various resins or oleoresins: as **a :** COPAL; *esp* **:** ZANZIBAR COPAL **b :** ELEMI

²**ani·mé** \ˌanəˈmā\ *adj (or adv)* [F, animated, past part. of *animer* to animate, fr. L *animare*] **:** ANIMATO — used as a direction in music

anim·i·ke·an \əˈnimə¦kēən\ *or* **anim·i·ki** \əˈnimə(ˌ)kē\ *adj, usu cap* [Chippewa *animiki*] **:** of or relating to the series of Proterozoic rocks that underlies the Keweenawan

anim·i·kite \əˈniməˌkīt\ *n* -s [Chippewa *animiki* thunder (intended as trans. of *Thunder Bay*, inlet in northwestern Lake Superior, Ontario, Canada, near which it was discovered) + E *-ite*] **:** a mineral consisting of a silver antimonide occurring in white or gray granular masses

an·i·mism \ˈanəˌmizəm\ *n* -s [G *animismus*, fr. L *anima* soul + G *-ismus* -ism — more at ANIMATE] **1 :** a doctrine according to which the immaterial soul is the vital principle responsible for every organic development **2 :** attribution of conscious life and a discrete indwelling spirit to every material form of reality (as to such objects as plants and stones and to such natural phenomena as thunderstorms and earthquakes) often including belief in the continued existence of individual disembodied spirits capable of exercising a benignant or malignant influence — compare ANIMATISM

an·i·mist \-məst\ *n* -s *often attrib*: one who accepts the doctrine of animism — **an·i·mis·tic** \¦==ˈmistik\ *adj*

an·i·mos·i·ty \ˌanəˈmäsəd·ē, -ətē, -i\ *n* -ES [ME *animosite*, fr. MF or LL; MF *animosité*, fr. LL *animositat-, animositas*, fr. L *animosus* courageous, spirited (fr. *animus* soul, spirit + *-osus* -ose) + *-itat-, -itas* -ity — more at ANIMATE] **:** ill will or resentment tending toward hostile action **:** smoldering enmity **:** a feeling of antagonism ⟨growling, snarling ~ toward public officials —*New Republic*⟩ **syn** see ENMITY

an·i·mo·so \ˌanəˈmō(ˌ)sō, ˌän-\ *adj (or adv)* [It, spirited, fr. L *animosus*] **:** ANIMATO — used as a direction in music

an·i·mus \ˈanəməs\ *n* -ES [L, mind, soul — more at ANIMATE] **1 a :** INTENTION, OBJECTIVE ⟨his ~ is not to overlook the progress made⟩ ⟨the ~ that led to the expansion of the machine was narrowly utilitarian —Lewis Mumford⟩ **b :** effort or tendency as directed toward a definite, often inevitable, but not always clearly or consciously recognized end ⟨the ~ of war is to enforce uniformity —Lewis Mumford⟩ ⟨youthful ~ toward happiness⟩ **c :** pervading and characteristic approach or treatment **:** dominant tone **:** ideological attitude **:** governing spirit ⟨other novelists of the same political ~ —*Partisan Rev.*⟩ ⟨the curious ~ of that philosophy⟩ **d :** breadth of vision esp. as a vitalizing and creative force **:** INSPIRATION ⟨too simple and too little charged with ~ —F.R.Leavis⟩ ⟨an important writer with a really interesting ~ —Donald Barr⟩ **2 :** life-giving spirit **:** animating principle of life; *specif* **:** the active or rational soul ⟨that spiritual ~ so universally needed —Mary B. Eddy⟩ **3 :** ill will, antagonism, or hostility usu. controlled but deep-seated and sometimes virulent **:** ANIMOSITY ⟨a large school of thought cherishes a curious ~ against what it calls intellectualism —W.R.Inge⟩ ⟨calmly and without ~⟩ ⟨an ~ against the plaintiff⟩ ⟨the antimodernistic ~ (whatever is, is wrong) —R.B.Heilman⟩ **syn** see ENMITY

an·ion \ˈaˌnīən *also* -ˌīˌän\ *n* -s [Gk, neut. of *aniōn*, pres. part. of *anienai* to go up, fr. *ana-* + *ienai* to go — more at ISSUE] **1 :** a negatively charged ion (as a hydroxide, chloride, or acetate ion) — opposed to *cation* **2 a :** the ion in an electrolyzed solution that migrates to the anode and is there discharged and liberated or deposited **b :** a negative gaseous ion

anion–active *adj* **:** ANIONIC 2

anion exchange *n* **:** a chemical process in which anions are exchanged or removed: **a :** ion exchange in which one anion (as chloride or hydroxide) is substituted for one or more other anions (as sulfate) **b :** a process in which anions in the form of acids are adsorbed by a basic substance

anion exchanger *n* **:** an anion-exchange agent that can exchange its anion with the anion or anions of a solution passed through it or that can adsorb anions in the form of acids; *esp* **:** an insoluble basic synthetic organic resin usu. containing amine groups or quaternary ammonium groups

an·ion·ic \ˌaˌnīˈänik\ *adj* **1 :** relating to or consisting of anions **2 :** *of a chemical compound* **:** characterized by an active anion, esp. a surface-active anion (as a large hydrophobic organic acid group) ⟨~ emulsifying agent⟩ ⟨~ surface-active agent⟩

anionic detergent *n* **:** any of a class of synthetic detergents usu. consisting essentially of an alkali metal salt or an ammonium salt of a strong acid containing 12 to 24 carbon atoms together with an inorganic salt (as sodium sulfate) and, for heavy-duty laundering, a builder (as sodium tripolyphosphate): as **a :** an alkyl aryl sulfonate (as sodium dodecylbenzene-sulfonate $C_{12}H_{25}C_6H_4SO_3Na$) **b :** a salt (as sodium lauryl sulfate $C_{12}H_{25}SO_4Na$) of a sulfated alcohol

an·ion·oid \(ˈ)aˈnīəˌnȯid\ *adj* [*anion* + *-oid*] **:** NUCLEOPHILIC

an·ion·o·trop·ic \ˌaˌnīˌänəˈträpik\ *adj* **:** of, relating to, or marked by anionotropy

an·ion·ot·ro·py \ˌaˌnīəˈnä·trəpē\ *n* -ES [*anion* + *-o-* + *-tropy*] **:** tautomerism involving migration of an anion (as chloride, hydroxyl, or acetate), the best-known type being allylic rearrangement — distinguished from *cationotropy* and *prototropy*

an·irid·ia \ˌaˌnīˈridēə\ *n* -s [NL, fr. *an-* + Gk *irid-, iris* iris + NL *-ia* — more at IRIS] **:** congenital absence or defect of the iris

anis *pl of* ANI

¹**anis-** *or* **aniso-** *comb form* [NL, fr. Gk, fr. *anisos*, fr. *an-* + *isos* equal — more at IS-] **:** unequal ⟨*aniso*dont⟩ ⟨*aniso*sthenic⟩

²**an·is-** *or* **a·ni·so-** *comb form* [L *anisum* anise] **:** anise ⟨*anis*ic⟩ **:** anisic acid ⟨*anis*oyl⟩

an·is·al·de·hyde \ˌanəˈsaldəˌhīd\ *n* -s [ISV ²*anis-* + *aldehyde*] **:** a liquid aldehyde $CH_3OC_6H_4CHO$ obtained by mild oxidation of anethole, having a characteristic hawthorn odor, and used in making perfumes — called also *aubepine*

an·is·ate \ˈanəˌsāt, -sət\ *n* -s [ISV *anisic* + *-ate*] **:** a salt or ester of anisic acid

an·ise \ˈanəs\ *n, pl* **anises** *also* **anise** *often attrib* [ME *anis*, fr. OF, fr. L *anisum, anesum*, fr. Gk *anison, anēson*] **1 :** an herb (*Pimpinella anisum*) growing naturally in Egypt and cultivated in many lands for its carminative and aromatic seeds **2 :** the fruit or seeds of anise **:** ANISEED

anise alcohol *or* **anisic alcohol** *n* **:** ANISYL ALCOHOL

anise camphor *n* **:** ANETHOLE

an·i·seed *also* **an·ise·seed** \ˈanə(s)ˌsēd\ *n* -s [ME *anis seed*, fr. *anis* anise + *seed*] **:** the seed of anise often used as a flavoring in cordials and in cooking

aniseed star *n* **:** the fruit of the star anise

aniseed tree *n* **:** STAR ANISE

anise hyssop *n* [prob. so called fr. the aromatic nature of its seeds] **:** a No. American herb (*Agastache foeniculum*) with an odor like fennel

an·is·ei·ko·nia \ˌaˌnīˌsīˈkōnēə\ *n* -s [NL, fr. ¹*anis-* + Gk *eikōn* image + NL *-ia* — more at ICON] **:** a defect of binocular vision in which the two retinal images of the same object are of unequal size — **an·is·ei·kon·ic** \-¦känik\ *adj*

anise oil *or* **aniseed oil** *n* **1 :** a colorless or pale yellow essential oil obtained from the dried fruits of anise and used as a flavoring agent and as a carminative **2 :** STAR ANISE OIL

anise plant *n* **:** an herb (*Seseli harveyanum*) that has an aroma like anise and that is found chiefly in Australia

aniseroot \ˈ==ˌ=\ *n* -s [so called from the taste and odor of its root] **:** SWEET CHERVIL

an·is·ette \ˌanəˈset, -ˈzet\ *n* -s [F, fr. *anis* anise + *-ette* — more at ANISE] **:** a sweet usu. colorless liqueur with a flavor like licorice derived from aniseed and used as a cocktail ingredient and after-dinner drink

anis·ic acid \əˈnisik, (ˈ)aˈn- *also* -nī- *sometimes* -nē-\ *n* [ISV *anise* + *-ic*; orig. formed as F *anisique*] **:** a crystalline acid $CH_3OC_6H_4COOH$ obtained by oxidizing anethole or anisaldehyde — called also *para-anisic acid*

anisic aldehyde *n* **:** ANISALDEHYDE

anis·i·dine \əˈnisəˌdēn, -dən\ *n* -s [F, fr. *anis-* ²*anis-* + *-ide* + *-ine*] **:** any of one of three isomeric bases $CH_3OC_6H_4NH_2$ that are amino derivatives of anisole and are used in the manufacture of guaiacol and of azo dyes

aniso- — see ANIS-

an·iso·car·pic \ˌaˌnīsə¦kärpik, a¦n-\ *or* **an·iso·car·pous** \-pəs\ *adj* [¹*anis-* + *-carpic, -carpous*] *of flowers* **:** having fewer members in the whorl of carpels than in any of the other floral whorls — compare ISOCARPIC

an·iso·cer·cal \-¦sarkəl\ *adj* [¹*anis-* + *-cercal*] **:** not isocercal

an·iso·che·la \-ˈkēlə\ *n, pl* **anisochelas** \-ləz\ *or* **anisochelae** \-ˌlē\ [NL, fr. ¹*anis-* + *chela*] **:** a chelate sponge spicule having the ends dissimilar

an·iso·co·ria \-ˈkōrēə\ *n* -s [NL, fr. ¹*anis-* + Gk *korē* pupil of the eye + NL *-ia*] **:** inequality in the size of the pupils of the eyes

an·iso·cy·to·sis \-ˌsīˈtōsəs\ *n, pl* **anisocyto·ses** \-ōˌsēz\ [NL, fr. ¹*anis-* + *cyt-* + *-osis*] **:** variation in size of cells, esp. of the red blood cells (as in pernicious anemia) — **an·iso·cy·tot·ic** \-¦täd·ik\ *adj*

an·iso·dac·ty·lous \-¦daktələs\ *adj* [¹*anis-* + *-dactylous*] **:** having unequal toes — used esp. of passerine and picarian birds having three toes turned forward and one backward

an·iso·ga·mete \-gə¦mēt, -ˈgaˌmēt\ *n* -s [¹*anis-* + *gamete*] **:** HETEROGAMETE — **an·iso·ga·met·ic** \-gə¦med·ik\ *adj*

an·isog·a·mous \ˌaˌnīˈsägəməs\ *adj* [¹*anis-* + *-gamous* or *-gamic*] *also* **an·iso·gam·ic** \ˌaˌnīsə¦gamik\ **1** *of sexual reproduction* **a :** characterized by fusion of unlike gametes or individuals usu. differing chiefly in size — used esp. of processes in lower organisms; see HETEROGAMOUS; compare OOGAMOUS **b :** HETEROGAMOUS **a 2 :** having anisogamous reproduction — **an·isog·a·my** \ˌaˌnīˈsägəmē\ *n* -ES

an·isog·e·nous \ˌaˌnīˈsäjənəs\ *adj* **:** of, relating to, or marked by anisogeny

an·isog·e·ny \ˌaˌnīˈsäjənē\ *n* -ES [¹*anis-* + *-geny*] **:** the property of exhibiting different inheritance in reciprocal crosses because of consistent differences in the male and female gametes of the parents

an·isog·na·thism \ˌaˌnīˈsägnəˌthizəm\ *n* -s [¹*anis-* + *gnath-* + *-ism*] **:** the property of having the teeth in the two jaws unlike — **an·isog·na·thous** \ˌaˌnīˈsägnəthəs\ *adj*

an·is·ole \ˈanəˌsōl\ *n* -s [F *anisol*, fr. *anis-* ²*anis-* + *-ol* -ole] **:** a colorless liquid ether $C_6H_5OCH_3$ of pleasant odor obtained by distilling anisic acid or by the action of dimethyl sulfate and alkali on phenol and used chiefly in perfumery; methyl phenyl ether

an·isom·e·les \ˌaˌnīˈsäməˌlēz\ *n, cap* [NL, fr. ¹*anis-* + *-meles* (fr. Gk *melē* cup); fr. the lack of uniformity in the anthers] **:** a small genus of herbs (family Labiatae) of tropical Asia and Australia with purplish cymose flowers

an·isom·er·ism \ˌaˌnīˈsäməˌrizəm\ *n* -s [*an-* + *isomere* + *-ism*] **:** the tendency of the primitive polyisomeres of an organism to become differentiated so that more highly evolved organisms do not consist of a linear series of similar and equivalent parts

an·iso·met·ric \ˌaˌnīsə¦me·trik, a¦n-\ *adj* [F *anisométrique*, fr. *an-* + *isométrique* isometric] **1 :** not isometric **:** having unsymmetrical parts — used of crystals with three unequal axes **2 :** of or relating to a rock of granular texture but with constituents of unequal size ⟨~ granite⟩ **3 :** not having equal or corresponding poetic meters

an·iso·me·tro·pia \-ˌmə·ˈtrōpēə\ *n* -s [NL, fr. Gk *anisometros* of unequal measure + NL *-opia*] **:** unequal refractive power in the two eyes — **an·iso·me·trop·ic** \-¦träpik\ *adj*

an·iso·my·ar·ia \-ˌmīˈa(a)rēə\ *n pl, cap* [NL, fr. ¹*anis-* + *-myaria*] *in some classifications* **:** an order of Lamellibranchia comprising bivalve mollusks having the anterior adductor muscle highly developed and the posterior muscle only slightly developed — **an·iso·my·ar·i·an** \-¦a(a)rēən\ *adj or n*

an·iso·my·o·di·an \-ˌmīˈōdēən\ *or* **an·iso·my·o·dous** \-¦mīədəs\ *adj* [¹*anis-* + Gk *myōdēs* muscular + E *-ian* or *-ous* — more at MYODES] **:** having the syringeal muscles inserted unequally either in the middle of the bronchial half rings or only upon the dorsal or ventral ends of the bronchial half rings — used of certain passerine birds

an·iso·mys \aˈnīsəˌmis\ *n, cap* [NL, fr. ¹*anis-* + *-mys*] **:** a genus of giant rats of New Guinea and Papua

an·iso·phyl·lous \ˌaˌnīsə¦filəs, a¦n-\ *adj* [F *anisophylle*, fr. ¹*anis-* + *-phylle* -phyllous] **1 :** having leaves of two or more shapes and sizes ⟨some conifers and many aquatic plants are ~⟩ **2 :** having the leaves of a pair different in shape and size — compare ISOPHYLLOUS — **an·iso·phyl·ly** \(ˈ)aˈnīsəˌfilē\ *n* -ES

an·iso·ploid \(ˈ)a¦nīsəˌplȯid\ *adj* [¹*anis-* + *-ploid*] **:** having a chromosome number (as triploid, pentaploid) that is an odd multiple of the basic number with consequent genetic incapability of sexual reproduction — **an·iso·ploi·dy** \(ˈ)aˈnīsəˌplȯidē\ *n* -ES

an·iso·pol·y·ploid \ˌaˌnīsə¦päləˌplȯid, a¦n-\ *adj* [¹*anis-* + *polyploid*] **:** ANISOPLOID — **an·iso·pol·y·ploi·dy** \-ˈpäləˌplȯidē\ *n* -ES

an·isop·tera \ˌaˌnīˈsäptərə\ *n pl, cap* [NL, fr. ¹*anis-* + *-ptera*] **:** a suborder of Odonata comprising the dragonflies that are larger stouter members of the order, hold the wings horizontally in repose, and have rectal gills during the naiad stage — compare ZYGOPTERA

an·iso·spore \(ˈ)aˈnīsəˌspō(ə)r\ *n* -s [¹*anis-* + *spore*] **:** a sexual spore exhibiting sexual dimorphism esp. of size — opposed to *isospore*

an·iso·tre·mus \(ˌ)aˌnīsəˈtrēməs\ *n, cap* [NL, fr. ¹*anis-* + *-tremus* (fr. Gk *trēma* perforation, aperture)] **:** a genus of tropical American grunts (family Pomadasidae) including a number of food and game species (as the porkfish, the pompon, and the sargo)

an·iso·trop·ic \ˌaˌnīsə¦träpik, a¦n-\ *also* **an·isot·ro·pous** \ˌaˌnīˈsä·trəpəs\ *adj* [*an-* + *isotropic, isotropous*] **1** *physics* **:** exhibiting properties (as velocity of light transmission, conductivity of heat or electricity, compressibility) with different values when measured along axes in different directions **:** AEOLOTROPIC **:** not isotropic ⟨an ~ crystal⟩ **2** *bot* **:** assuming different positions in response to the action of external stimuli **3 :** having a predetermined axis or axes — used of the eggs of certain animals — **an·iso·trop·i·cal·ly** \(ˌ)aˌnīsə¦träpək(ə)lē, a¦n-\ *adv*

anisotropic liquid *n* **:** LIQUID CRYSTAL

an·isot·ro·py \ˌaˌnīˈsä·trəpē\ *or* **an·isot·ro·pism** \-ˌpizəm\ *n, pl* **anisotropies** *or* **anisotropisms** [*anisotropic* + *-y* or *-ism*] **:** the quality or property of being anisotropic

ani·sum \əˈnīsəm, -ēs-\ *n* -s [L *anisum, anesum* — more at ANISE] **:** ANISE

an·i·syl alcohol \ˈanəˌsil-\ *n* [ISV ²*anis-* + *-yl*] **:** a colorless liquid alcohol $CH_3OC_6H_4CH_2OH$ having an odor like hawthorn and used in perfumery; *para*-methoxy-benzyl alcohol — called also *anise alcohol*

anith·er \əˈnithər\ *Scot var of* ANOTHER

ani·to \əˈnē(ˌ)tō\ *n* -s [Sp, fr. Tag] *Philippines* **:** a spirit esp. of an ancestor

an·jan \ˈanjən, -ˌjan\ *n* -s [native name in India] **1 :** a timber tree (*Hardwickia binata*) of India **2 :** the very hard dark red or purplish wood of the anjan tree

an·ka·ra \ˈaŋkərə, ˈaiŋ-,ˈäŋ-,ˈäŋ-\ *adj, usu cap* [fr. *Ankara*, Turkey] **:** of or from Ankara, the capital of Turkey **:** of the kind or style prevalent in Ankara

an·ka·ra·mite \ˌaŋkəˈräˌmīt\ *n* -s [F, fr. *Ankaramy*, Madagascar + F *-ite*] **:** a melanocratic basaltic rock with a feldspar content greater than picrite and less than basalt and differing from picrite in containing more augite than olivine

an·ka·ra·trite \-ˈä-ˌtrīt\ *n* -s [F *ankaratrite*, fr. *Ankaratra* mts., Madagascar, its locality + F *-ite*] **:** a melanocratic nephelite-basalt containing some feldspar, phenocrysts of olivine, microlites of titanaugite, and from 10 to 15 percent nephelite

an·ker \ˈäŋkər, ˈa-\ *n* -s [D, prob. fr. ML *ancheria, anceria*] **1 :** a unit of capacity: **a :** an old Dutch and German liquid measure used in various countries of Europe esp. for spirits and equal to about 9 to 10.5 U.S. gallons (30 to 40 liters) **b :** a U.S. unit equal to 10 gallons (37.85 liters) **c :** a unit of So. Africa equal to 7½ imperial gallons (34.10 liters) **2 :** a cask or keg having a capacity of one anker

an·ker·ite \ˈaŋkəˌrīt\ *n* -s [G *ankerit*, fr. M. J. *Anker* †1843 Austrian mineralogist + G *-it* -ite] **:** a variety of dolomite $Ca(Fe,Mg,Mn)(CO_3)_2$ containing much iron (sp. gr. 2.95–3.1)

ankh \ˈaŋk, ˈä-\ *n* -s [Egypt *ˁnḫ*] **:** a figure like a cross having a loop instead of an upper vertical arm used esp. in ancient Egypt as an attribute or sacred emblem symbolizing life—called also *ansate cross, crux ansata, handled cross, key of life*

ankh

an·king \ˈänˌkiŋ\ *adj, usu cap* [fr. *Anking*, China] **:** of or from the city of Anking, China **:** of the kind or style prevalent in Anking

¹**an·kle** \ˈaŋkəl, ˈai-\ *n* -s [ME *ankel, anclowe*, fr. OE *anclēow*; akin to OHG *anchlāo, anchal, enchil* ankle, ON *ǫkkla*, L *angulus* angle, Gk *angos* pail, Skt *aṅga* limb — more at ANGLE] **1 a :** the joint between the foot and the leg corresponding to the wrist in the arm, the hock of a horse, and what is often called the knee of a bird and constituting in man a ginglymus joint between the tibia and fibula above and the talus below **b :** the joint between the cannon bone and pastern in certain hoofed quadrupeds (as horses) **:** FETLOCK JOINT **2 :** the region of this joint **:** TARSUS; *broadly* **:** this region together with the lower part of the leg below the calf

²**ankle** *vi* **ankled; ankled; ankling** \-k(ə)liŋ\ **ankles** *slang* **:** to move esp. by walking ⟨*ankling* down the street⟩

anklebone \ˈ==ˌ=\ *n* [ME *anclebone*, fr. *ancle* ankle + *bone*] **:** TALUS

ankle boot *n* **1 :** a boot reaching only to the ankle **2 :** a protective covering for a horse's ankle

ankle–deep \ˈ==¦=\ *adj* **:** of depth sufficient to reach the ankles ⟨a street *ankle-deep* in mud⟩

ankle jerk *n* **:** a reflex downward movement of the foot due to a spasmodic contraction of the muscles of the calf caused by sudden extension of the leg or by striking the Achilles' tendon above the heel

ankle strap *n* **:** a single or multiple strap attached to a shoe to hold it on the foot or having a purely ornamental function and passing either above the instep near the arch or around the ankle

an·klet \ˈaŋklət, ˈai-\ *n* -s [*ankle* + *-let*] **1 a :** a bracelet or similar ornament worn around the ankle **b :** a brace that supports the ankle **c :** a fetter attached to the ankle **d :** ANKLE STRAP **2 a :** a short sock usu. extending only slightly above the ankle **b :** a knitted or woven band designed for protection from cold (as one attached to the bottom of a trouser leg or pajama leg) **3 :** a woman's or child's low shoe having one or more ankle straps

anklet 3

an·klong \ˈaŋˌklōŋ\ *or* **an·klung** *or* **ang·klung** \-ˌkləŋ\ *n* -s [Malay *aṅkluṅ*] **:** a Malayan musical instrument made of suspended bamboo tubes

an·ko·le *also* **an·ko·li** \aŋˈkōlē\ *n, usu cap* [fr. *Ankole*, plateau region in Uganda, its native habitat] **:** an African breed of long-horned humpless cattle

an·kus \ˈaŋkəs, ˈəŋkəsh\ *also* **an·ku·sha** \ˈəŋkəshə\ *n, pl* **ankus** *also* **ankusha** *or* **ankuses** *also* **ankushas** [Hindi *aṅkus*, fr. Skt *aṅkuśa*; akin to Skt *aṅka* bend, hook — more at ANGLE (hook)] **:** an elephant goad used in India having a sharp spike and hook and resembling a short-handled boat hook

ankyl- *or* **ankylo-** *also* **anchyl-** *or* **anchylo-** *or* **ancyl-** *or* **ancylo-** *comb form* [NL, fr. Gk *ankyl-, ankylo-*, fr. *ankylos*; akin to Gk *ankos* glen — more at ANGLE] **1 :** crooked **:** curved ⟨*Ancylo*stoma⟩ **2** [NL, fr. Gk *ankyl-, ankylo-*, fr. *ankylōsis*] **a :** stiff, immobile, constricted, or closed because of adhesion ⟨*ankylo*glossia⟩ ⟨*ankyl*urethria⟩ **b :** ankylosis ⟨*ankylo*phobia⟩

an·ky·lo·saur \ˈaŋkəlōˌsȯ(ə)r\ *n* -s [NL *Ankylosauria*, fr. *ankyl-* + *-sauria*] **:** any of a suborder (Ankylosauria) of heavily armored more or less dorsoventrally flattened Cretaceous dinosaurs somewhat resembling immense horned toads in shape

an·ky·lose *also* **an·chy·lose** \ˈaŋkəˌlōs, ˈai-, -kē,-, -ōz\ *or* **an·cy·lose** \"; ˈansə,-, ˈaa-\ *vb* -ED/-ING/-S [irreg. fr. NL *ankylosis, anchylosis, ancylosis*] *vt* **:** to unite or consolidate so as to make a more or less rigid and inflexible joint **:** cause to grow together into one **:** produce ankylosis in ⟨*ankylosed* bones⟩ ⟨a joint *ankylosed* by surgery⟩ ~ *vi* **:** to form a more or less rigid and inflexible joint **:** grow together into one **:** undergo ankylosis

an·ky·lo·sis *also* **an·chy·lo·sis** *or* **an·cy·lo·sis** \ˌ==ˈlōsəs\ *n, pl* **ankylo·ses** *also* **anchylo·ses** *or* **ancylo·ses** \-ōˌsēz\ [NL, fr. Gk *ankylōsis* stiffening, tongue-tie, adhesion of the eyelids, fr. *ankyloun* to crook, stiffen (fr. *ankylos* crooked) + *-ōsis* -osis — more at ANGLE] **1 :** stiffness or fixation of a

joint by disease or surgery **:** formation of a stiff joint through obliteration of the joint space by fibrous or bony tissue **2 :** union of two or more separate bones or other hard parts to form a single bone or part without intervening soft tissues
an·ky·los·to·ma \¦,==ˈlästəmə\ *or* **an·ky·los·to·mum** \-məm\ [NL, fr. *ankyl-* + *-stoma, -stomum*] *syn of* ANCYLOSTOMA
ankylostome *var of* ANCYLOSTOME
ankylostomiasis *var of* ANCYLOSTOMIASIS
an·ky·lot·ic *also* **an·chy·lot·ic** *or* **an·cy·lot·ic** \¦==¦läd·ik\ *adj* [fr. NL *ankylosis, ancylosis*, after such pairs as E *narcosis: narcotic*] **:** of, relating to, or marked by ankylosis **:** STIFFENED
an·ky·roid \aŋˈkī,rȯid, ˈaŋkə,-\ *also* **an·cy·roid** \anˈsī,-, ˈansə,-\ *adj* [Gk *ankyroeidēs* anchor-shaped, fr. *ankyra* anchor + *-oeidos* -oid — more at ANCHOR] *anat* **:** shaped like a hook
anl *abbr* **1** animal **2** anneal
an·lace \ˈanləs, -,läs\ *n* -s [ME *anlas, anelas*, fr. OF *alenaz, alesnaz*, aug. of *alesne* awl, of Gmc origin; akin to OHG *alasna, alansa* awl, fr. *āla* — more at AWL] **:** a tapering medieval dagger
an·la·ge \ˈän,lägə, ˈan,lā-, *G* ˈän,lä̈ä-\ *n, pl* **anla·gen** \-gən\ *also* **anlages** *sometimes cap* [G, fr. MHG *anlāge* request, ambush, fr. *ane* on, at (fr. OHG *ana*) + *lāge* act of laying, position, fr. OHG *lāga* laying; akin to OHG *ligen* to lie — more at ON, LIE] **:** the foundation or basis of a subsequent development **:** RUDIMENT; *specif* **:** the first accumulation of cells in an embryo recognizable as the commencement of a developing part or organ
an·laut \ˈän,lau̇t\ *n, pl* **anlau·te** \-au̇d·ə,-au̇tə\ *also* **anlauts** [G, fr. *an* on, at (fr. OHG *ana*) + *laut* sound, fr. OHG *lūt*; akin to OE *hlūd* loud — more at ON, LOUD] *phonetics* **:** initial sound or position of a word or syllable — compare AUSLAUT, INLAUT
ann \ˈan\ *or* **an·nat** \ˈa,nat, ˈanət\ *n* -s [Sc, fr. ML *annata* annates — more at ANNATES] *Scots law* **:** a half-year's stipend over and above what is owing for the incumbency due to a deceased minister's executors

anlace

ann *abbr* **1** annals **2** annealed **3** [L *anni*] years **4** annual **5** annuity
an·na *also* **ana** \ˈänə, ˈa-\ *n* -s [Hindi *ānā*] **1 a :** a former unit of value in Pakistan, India, and Burma equal to 1/16 rupee **b :** one sixteenth ⟨a 4-*anna* crop⟩ **2 :** a coin representing one anna unit
an·na·berg·ite \ˈanə,bər,gīt\ *n* -s [*Annaberg*, Saxony, Germany, its locality + E *-ite*] **:** a mineral consisting of a hydrous nickel cobalt arsenate $(Ni,Co)_3(AsO_4)_2.8H_2O$ occurring in apple-green masses or capillary crystals and isomorphous with erythrite
annal *n* -s [back-formation fr. *annals*] *archaic* **:** ANNALS; *esp* **:** annals of a single year, locale, or people
an·nal·ist \ˈanᵊləst\ *n* -s [F *annaliste*, fr. MF, fr. *annales* annals (fr. L) + *-iste* -ist] **:** a writer of annals **:** HISTORIAN
an·nal·is·tic \¦anᵊl¦istik, -ēk\ *adj* **:** of or relating to annals or an annalist; *esp* **:** peculiar to annals or an annalist ⟨a book with an ~ approach⟩ — **an·nal·is·ti·cal·ly** \-ək(ə)lē,-li\ *adv*
an·nals \ˈanᵊlz\ *n pl* [L *annales*, fr. pl. of *annalis* yearly, fr. *annus* year + *-alis* -al — more at ANNUAL] **1 :** a record of events arranged in yearly sequence usu. without comment or interpretation by the compiler **2 :** historical records; *specif* **:** any of several histories of Roman times written by contemporary authors ⟨the ~ of Tacitus⟩ **3** *sometimes sing in constr* **:** records of the activities of an organization, usu. published ⟨the ~ of a welfare society⟩
¹an·nam·ese \¦anə¦mēz, -ēs\ *or* **an·nam·ite** \ˈ==,mīt\ *adj, usu cap* [*Annam*, eastern section of Indochina + E *-ese* or *-ite*] **1 a :** of, relating to, or characteristic of Annam **b :** of, relating to, or characteristic of the Annamese people **2 :** of, relating to, or characteristic of the Annamese language
²annamese \"\ *n, pl* **annamese** *usu cap* **1 a :** a Mongolian people that occupies mainly Cochin China and the coast regions of Annam and Tonkin in eastern Indochina, being the dominant ethnic group among the Vietnamese **b** *or* **annamite** \"\ -s **:** a member of such people **2** *or* **annamite :** the language of the Annamese people **:** VIETNAMESE
an·nam–muong \(ˈ)a¦nam¦wȯŋ,ə¦n-\ *n, usu cap A&M* [*Annamese* + *Muong*] **:** a language group of problematical status and relationship containing Annamese and Muong and perhaps related to Mon-Khmer or Thai
an·nam ulcer \(ˈ)a¦nam, ə¦n-\ *n, usu cap A* [fr. *Annam*, Indochina] **:** TROPICAL ULCER 2
an·nap·o·lis \əˈnap(ə)ləs\ *adj, usu cap* [fr. *Annapolis*, Md.] **:** of or from Annapolis, the capital of Maryland **:** of the kind or style prevalent in Annapolis
an·na·pol·i·tan \,anəˈpälətᵊn\ *n* -s *cap* [*Annapolis*, Maryland + E *-itan* (as in *Neapolitan, metropolitan*)] **:** a native or resident of Annapolis, Md.
an·na's hummingbird \ˈanəz-\ *also* **anna hummingbird** *n, usu cap A* [after *Anna fl*1829 duchess of Rivoli] **:** a rather large hummingbird (*Calypte anna*) of western Mexico and California, the male being chiefly metallic bronze-green with rose-red forehead, crown, and throat and a dusky blackish tail, the female bronzy green above and dull gray below
annat *var of* ANN
an·nates \ˈa,nāts, ˈanəts\ *n pl* [ML *annata*, fr. L *annus* year — more at ANNUAL] **:** the first-fruits of an ecclesiastical benefice paid to the one presenting the benefice
an·nat·to *also* **ana·to** *or* **anat·to** \əˈnä\d·(,)ō, əˈna\,äˈnä\, \d·ə, \(,)tō,\ ,tə\ *or* **anat·ta** \d·ə,\ ,tə\ *or* **ar·nat·ta** *or* **ar·nat·to** \ärˈn-,äˈn-\ *or* **ar·not·ta** *or* **ar·not·to** \-nä\ *n* -s [of Cariban origin; akin to Galibi *annoto* annatto tree] **1 a :** a red or yellowish red dyestuff containing bixin prepared from the pulp surrounding the seeds of the annatto tree and used esp. for coloring oils, butter, and cheese **b :** ANNATTO TREE **2 a :** a moderate yellowish pink that is yellower and less strong than coral pink and duller and slightly yellower than peach pink — called also *terra orellana* **b :** SALMON 4
annatto tree *n* **:** a tropical American tree (*Bixa orellana*) having cordate leaves and spinose capsules filled with seeds that yield annatto
anncr *abbr* announcer
¹an·neal \əˈnēl, -ēəl\ *vt* -ED/-ING/-S [ME *anelen*, fr. OE *onǣlan*, fr. *on* on + *ǣlan* to set on fire, burn, bake, fr. *āl* fire; akin to ON *eldr* fire, OE *ād* funeral pyre — more at EDIFY] **1 :** to heat (as glass) in order to fix laid-on colors **2 a :** to heat and then cool usu. for softening and rendering less brittle, gradual cooling being required for some materials (as steel and glass) but not for others (as copper and brass) — compare TEMPER **b :** to process (structural-clay products) by slow cooling after subjection to heat in order to prevent checking, cracking, and warping ⟨~*ed* paving brick⟩ **3 :** STRENGTHEN, TOUGHEN ⟨a man rocklike in endurance, rocklike in insensibility, ~*ed* by a simple, rigorous religion —Lionel Trilling⟩
²anneal \"\ *n* -s **:** the act, process, or result of annealing
an·neal·er *n* -s **:** one that anneals
an·nec·tent *also* **an·nec·tant** \əˈnektənt, aˈ-\ *adj* [L *annectent-, annectens*, pres. part. of *annectere* to tie to, fr. *ad-* + *nectere* to tie, fasten together — more at ANNEX] *biol* **:** CONNECTING, LINKING — used esp. of species or groups having characters intermediate between those of two other species or groups
an·ne·la·ta \,anᵊlˈäd·ə, -ād·ə\ [NL, fr. F *annelés*, subdivision of invertebrates + NL *-ata*] *syn of* ANNELIDA
¹an·ne·lid \ˈanᵊləd\ *adj* [F *annélide*, adj. & n., fr. NL *Annelida*] **:** of or relating to the Annelida
²annelid \"\ *n* -s **:** an animal of the phylum Annelida
an·nel·i·da \əˈnelədə, aˈ-\ *n pl, cap* [NL, fr. F *annelés*, subdivision of invertebrates proposed 1801 by Lamarck, lit., ringed ones (fr. pl. of *annelé*, past part. of *anneler* to furnish or adorn with a ring or rings, fr. MF, fr. *annel-*, fr. OF, fr. *anel, annel* ring, fr. L *anellus* small ring, dim. of *anus* ring) + NL *-ida* — more at ANUS] **:** a phylum of typically elongated metameric animals having a voluminous true coelom, a closed vascular system usu. containing hemoglobin-bearing blood, a double ventral nervous system with anterior cerebral ganglion and esophageal ring, paired nephridia in one or many segments, and appendages that when present are not jointed as in arthropods — **an·nel·i·dan** \-dən, -dᵊn\ *adj or n*
an·nel·i·des \-,dēz\ *or* **an·nel·la·ta** \,anᵊlˈäd·ə, -ād·ə\ [NL, irreg. fr. F *annelés*] *syn of* ANNELIDA
an·ne·loid \ˈanᵊl,ȯid\ *n* -s [F *annelé* ringed + E *-oid*] **:** an animal resembling an annelid
an·ne·ro·dite \,anəˈrō,dīt\ *n* -s [Sw *ånnerödit*, fr. *Ånnerød*, town near Moss, Norway, its locality + Sw *-it* -ite] **:** SAMARSKITE
¹an·nex \əˈneks, (ˈ)a¦n-\ *vt* -ED/-ING/-ES [ME *annexen*, fr. MF *annexer*, fr. OF, fr. *annexe* joined, fr. L *annexus*, past part. of *annectere, adnectere* to bind to, fr. *ad-* + *nectere* to tie, bind, alter. (prob. influenced by L *plectere* to plait) of a prehistoric form akin to L *nodus* knot — more at NET, PLY] **1 a :** to attach as a proper attribute or as a distinctive quality ⟨many privileges were ~*ed* exclusively to royalty⟩ **b :** to attach as a necessary consequence ⟨happiness is not always ~*ed* to wealth⟩ ⟨I would enjoy the pleasures of the table and of wine, but stop short of the pains inseparably ~*ed* to an excess —Earl of Chesterfield⟩ **c :** to add or join as a condition ⟨only one requirement is ~*ed* to this job⟩ **2 a** *archaic* **:** to add or join as an essential part **b** *archaic* **:** to add or join as a subordinate and accessory part ⟨this mansion, to which were ~*ed* a tennis court, a bowling green, and a wilderness —T.B. Macaulay⟩ **3 a :** to add at the end of something written or spoken **:** SUBJOIN, APPEND ⟨a protocol ~*ed* to the treaty—E.C. Helmreich⟩ ⟨a declaration with a promise ~*ed*—W.F.Hambly⟩ **b :** to affix as an authoritative sanction ⟨~*ing* his signature to the letter⟩ ⟨the president ~*ed* his seal to the document⟩ **4 a :** to join in a closely united but subordinate capacity **:** take possession or control of **:** assume rights or jurisdiction over; *specif* **:** to incorporate (a country or other territory) within the sovereign domain of a state ⟨a move was made to ~ Texas by a treaty —Dorothy B. Goebel⟩ **b :** to include (an area) within the limits of a governmental unit ⟨outlying districts were ~*ed* by the city⟩ **5 a :** GET, OBTAIN ⟨we ~*ed* a local guide —Thomas Barbour⟩ ⟨~*ing* all the prizes in the dog show⟩ **b :** to appropriate esp. by highhanded or ethically questionable methods **:** get hold of **:** make off with; *often* **:** STEAL ⟨criminals trying to ~ the miners' gold —Julian Dana⟩ ⟨she did not like to see him ~*ed* by another woman —Joseph Conrad⟩
²annex \ˈa,neks, ˈani-,ˈanē-\ *n* -ES *often attrib* [MF *annexe*, fr. *annexe* joined] **:** something annexed or appended: as **a :** an added stipulation or statement; *esp* **:** an appendix of or codicil to a legislative document or international agreement ⟨the upper house approved two ~*es* in the treaties —*Time*⟩ **b :** SUPPLEMENT; *esp* **:** a collection of supplementary matter ⟨this appendix is a worthwhile ~ to the book⟩ ⟨anthropology was included as an ~ to the regular curriculum⟩ **c :** a subsidiary supplementary structure either part of or separate from a main structure ⟨the new college wing was used as a science ~⟩ **d :** a subsidiary district **:** SUBURB ⟨the big city and its ~*es*⟩ **e** *Scots law* **:** FIXTURE, APPURTENANCE
an·nex·a *var of* ADNEXA
an·nex·a·tion \,a,nekˈsāshən, ,anə-, ,anē-\ *n* -s [*annex* + *-ation*] **1 :** the act of annexing or state of being annexed ⟨the possibility of cultural ~⟩ **2 :** something that is annexed ⟨defended their ~s with fire and sword —G.B.Shaw⟩ **3 :** the union of property with a freehold so as to become a fixture
an·nex·a·tion·al \¦=(,)=¦==¦l\ *adj* **1 :** of or relating to annexation **2 :** favoring annexation
an·nex·a·tion·ism \,=(,)=ˈ=shə,nizəm\ *n* -s **:** the policy or advocacy of annexing territory
an·nex·a·tion·ist \-,nəst\ *n* -s **:** one who favors annexation
an·nexe \ˈa,neks, ˈani-\ *chiefly Brit var of* ²ANNEX
an·nex·ion \əˈnekshən, aˈ-\ *n* -s [LL *annexion-, annexio*, fr. L *annexus* + *-ion-, -io* -ion — more at ANNEX] **:** ANNEXATION
an·nex·ion·ist \-əst\ *n* -s **:** ANNEXATIONIST
an·nex·ive \əˈneksiv, (ˈ)a¦n-\ *adj* **:** COPULATIVE 1a, 1b
annexment *n* -s **1** *archaic* **:** ANNEXATION **2** *archaic* **:** ANNEX
an·nex·ure \əˈnekshə(r), (ˈ)a¦n-\ *n* -s **1** *chiefly Brit* **:** ANNEXATION **2** *chiefly Brit* **:** ANNEX
an·ni·cut *var of* ANICUT
an·ni·el·li·dae \,anēˈelə,dē\ *n pl, cap* [NL, fr. *Anniella*, type genus (irreg. fr. Sp *aniello, anillo* ring, fr. L *anellus* small ring) + *-idae* — more at ANNELIDA] **:** a family of degenerate wormlike California lizards apparently closely related to the Anguidae
an·nie oak·ley \¦anēˈōklē, -li\ *n, pl* **annie oakleys** *usu cap A&O* [after *Annie Oakley* †1926 Am. markswoman; fr. the resemblance of a punched pass to a playing card with bullet holes through the spots] *slang* **:** a free ticket (as to a theater)
annie over *sometimes cap A, var of* ANTONY OVER
an·ni·hi·la·ble \əˈnīələbəl *sometimes* -īhə-\ *adj* [*annihilate* + *-able*] **:** capable of being annihilated
¹an·ni·hi·late \-lət, -,lāt\ *adj* [ME *adnichilat*, fr. LL *annihilatus*] *archaic* **:** ANNIHILATED
²an·ni·hi·late \-,lāt, *usu* -ād·+V\ *vt* -ED/-ING/-S [LL *annihilatus*, past part. of *annihilare*, fr. L *ad-* + *nihil* nothing — more at NIL] **1 a :** to cause to be of no effect **:** NULLIFY, ABROGATE ⟨a right to freedom that cannot be *annihilated*⟩ **b :** to destroy the substance or force of **:** totally weaken ⟨fear ~*s* wit—Harvey Breit⟩ **2 :** to look upon as nothing **:** regard as of no consequence **:** make light of ⟨laughing at the past and *annihilating* its endeavors⟩ **3 a :** to do away with entirely so that nothing remains **:** reduce to nothing **:** cause to cease to exist **:** destroy totally **:** blot out entirely ⟨matter cannot be *annihilated*⟩ ⟨are we to suppose that I can ~ so substantial an object simply by shutting my eyes —C.H. Whitely⟩ **b :** to strip of power and influence **:** check the activity of **:** neutralize the operations of ⟨*annihilating* the government's functions⟩ **c :** to destroy the interest and relevance of ⟨towering scenic backgrounds that *annihilated* the tiny figure on the stage⟩ ⟨a low building rightly placed will pull together surrounding high buildings instead of being *annihilated* by them —John Dewey⟩ **4 a :** to destroy a considerable part of **:** DECIMATE ⟨the army was *annihilated*⟩ ⟨little remained of the *annihilated* city⟩ **b :** to vanquish completely **:** CRUSH, ROUT ⟨the visiting football team was *annihilated*⟩ **syn** see ABOLISH
annihilating *adj* **:** CRUSHING, WITHERING ⟨a master of witty and ~ rudeness —Edgar Johnson⟩ ⟨afire with ~ invective —*Time*⟩
an·ni·hi·la·tion \=,==ˈlāshən\ *n* -s [LL *annihilation-, annihilatio*, fr. *annihilatus* + L *-ion-, -io* -ion] **1 :** the act of annihilating or state of being annihilated ⟨the ~ of the individual is the worst perversity of man —W.L.Sullivan⟩ **2 :** cessation of being **:** NOTHINGNESS ⟨sentient beings are doomed to complete ~ —C.R.Darwin⟩ **3 :** the process whereby an electron and a positron unite and consequently lose their identity as particles transforming themselves into short gamma rays — see ANNIHILATION RADIATION
an·ni·hi·la·tion·ism \-shə,nizəm\ *n* -s **:** the theological doctrine that the wicked will cease to exist after this life
an·ni·hi·la·tion·ist \-,nəst\ *n* -s **:** one who accepts annihilationism
annihilation radiation *n* **:** radiation produced by the mutually annihilating coalescence of an electron and a positron from which two radiation quanta travel in opposite directions with a wavelength corresponding to that of very short gamma rays, being approximately 0.024 angstrom
an·ni·hi·la·tive \əˈ==,lād·iv, -,ləd-\ *adj* **:** producing annihilation **:** DESTRUCTIVE ⟨an explosion that could be ~ of nearly all life⟩
an·ni·hi·la·tor \-,lād·ə(r), -ātə-\ *n* -s **:** one that annihilates
an·ni·hi·la·to·ry \-,lə,tōrē\ *adj* **:** ANNIHILATIVE
anni mirabiles *pl of* ANNUS MIRABILIS
an·ni·ver·sa·ry \,anəˈvərs(ə)rē, -vəs-,-vəis-, -ri\ *n* -ES *often attrib* [ME *anniversarie*, fr. ML *anniversaria, anniversarium*, fr. fem. & neut. of L *anniversarius*, fr. *annus* year + *versus* (past part. of *vertere* to turn) + *-arius* -ary — more at ANNUAL, WORTH] **1 a :** the annual recurrence of a date marking an event or occurrence of notable importance ⟨the ~ of the Declaration of Independence⟩ ⟨the ~ of the founding of a publishing house⟩ ⟨a wedding ~⟩ **b :** the celebration or commemoration of an anniversary **2** *Roman Catholicism* **:** a mass said periodically for the soul of someone deceased
anniversary clock *n* **:** a clock with a slow torsion pendulum that enables it to run as long as 400 days on a single winding — called also *four-hundred-day clock*
anniversary day *n, usu cap A&D* **:** AUSTRALIA DAY
¹an·no dom·i·ni \¦a(,)nōˈdämənē *also* ¦ä- *or* -ōm- *or* -,nē *or* -,nī\ *adv, often cap A, usu cap D* [ML, in the year of the Lord (i.e., Jesus Christ)] — used to indicate that a time division falls within the Christian era, usu. being placed before the year ⟨*anno Domini* 1980⟩ and after other time divisions ⟨in the 8th century *anno Domini*⟩ ⟨within the 1st millennium *anno Domini*⟩; abbr. *A.D.* often printed in small capitals
²anno domini \"\ *n, usu cap A&D* **:** advancing years **:** old age ⟨*Anno Domini* softens even the cynics —*Atlantic*⟩
anno he·gi·rae \-,hēˈjī(,)rē, -ˈhejə,rē\ *adv, often cap A&H* [NL, in the year of the Hegira] — used to indicate that a time division falls within the Muslim era; abbr. *A.H.* often printed in small capitals
annoint *var of* ANOINT
an·no lu·cis \-ˈlüsəs, -ük-\ *adv, often cap A&L* [NL, in the year of light; fr. the conception that God's word creating light in Gen 1:3 marks the beginning of creation] — used by many Freemasons with a year to indicate the number of years elapsed since 4000 B.C., 4000 being added to the usual computation of the year ⟨A.D. 1980 is *Anno Lucis* 5980⟩; abbr. *A.L.* often printed in small capitals
an·no·na \əˈnōnə\ *n, cap* [NL, fr. Sp *anona, anón* annona, fr. Taino *anon*] **:** a large genus of trees and shrubs (family Annonaceae) chiefly tropical American but widely cultivated having leathery leaves, solitary nodding flowers, and compound usu. edible fruit — see CUSTARD APPLE, SOURSOP, SWEETSOP
an·no·na·ce·ae \,anəˈnāsē,ē\ *n pl, cap* [NL, fr. *Annona*, type genus + *-aceae*] **:** a family of mostly tropical trees or shrubs (order Ranales) comprising the custard apples and related plants that have alternate leaves, flowers with three sepals and six petals, and fleshy fruits — **an·no·na·ceous** \¦anə¦nāshəs\ *adj*
an·no·tate \ˈanə,tāt, -nō-, *usu* -ād·+V\ *vb* -ED/-ING/-S [L *annotatus*, past part. of *annotare*, fr. *ad-* + *notare* to mark — more at NOTE] *vi* **:** to make or furnish esp. critical or explanatory notes usu. on a literary work or subject ⟨he was always reading or *annotating*⟩ **~** *vt* **:** to make or furnish esp. critical or explanatory notes on (a literary work or subject) ⟨she asked me to ~ and introduce her book —W.B.Yeats⟩
an·no·ta·tion \,==ˈtāshən\ *n* -s [ME *annotacioun*, fr. L *annotation-, annotatio*, fr. *annotatus* + *-ion-, -io* -ion] **1 :** the act of annotating **2 a :** a note added by way of comment or explanation ⟨~*s* on the text of an author⟩ **b :** an informational and descriptive note esp. about a book ⟨~*s* on the newest acquisitions of the public library⟩ **3 :** a rescript in reply to a private citizen
an·no·ta·tor *also* **an·no·tat·er** \ˈ==,tād·ə(r), -ātə\ *n* -s [L *annotator*, fr. *annotatus* + *-or*] **:** one that makes annotations
an·no·ta·to·ry \ˈanə,tād·ərē, -,tə,tōrē; əˈnōd·ə,tōrē\ *adj* **:** of or belonging to an annotator or annotation
an·not·i·nous \əˈnät°nəs, aˈ-\ *adj* [L *annotinus*, fr. *annus* year — more at ANNUAL] *biol* **:** one year old
an·not·to \əˈnäd·(,)ō, äˈ-, -d·ə\ *n* -s [Galibi *annoto*] **:** ANNATTO
an·nounce \əˈnau̇n(t)s\ *vb* -ED/-ING/-S [ME *announcen*, fr. MF *annoncer*, fr. L *annuntiare, adnuntiare*, fr. *ad-* + *nuntiare* to report, relate, fr. *nuntius* messenger] *vt* **1 a :** to give public notice of **:** make known officially or publicly **:** deliver news of **:** PROCLAIM ⟨the government *announced* a cut in taxes⟩ **b :** to state or declare often with some degree of self-importance or pomposity ⟨the child *announced* that the picnic had been fun⟩ **c :** to cause (an individual) to be known in a specified role, capacity, or condition — usu. used with *as* ⟨was *announced* as a sponsor⟩ ⟨was *announced* as chief of cavalry —Eben Swift⟩ ⟨she could not live without *announcing* herself to him as his mother —Thomas Hardy⟩ **2 a :** to give notice of the arrival, presence, or readiness of ⟨~ dinner⟩ **b :** to point to or indicate in advance **:** declare beforehand **:** FORETELL ⟨the invention of the printing press *announced* the diffusion of knowledge⟩ ⟨in 1926 Malraux was *announcing* the historical downfall of Europe —Ignazio Silone⟩ **3 :** to give evidence of esp. without oral communication ⟨his earlier work *announced* a lyric talent of the first order —Louise Bogan⟩ **:** indicate by action, appearance, or condition **:** make obvious by furnishing support for an inferrible conclusion ⟨loud shrieks *announced* his discovery —T.B.Costain⟩ **4 :** to serve as an announcer of ⟨he ~*s* three programs a week⟩ ⟨he ~*s* the biggest football games⟩ **~** *vi* **1 :** to serve as an announcer ⟨he ~*s* for a national network⟩ **2 a :** to declare one's candidacy — usu. used with *for* to specify the office sought ⟨12 days after he *announced* for governor —John Gunther⟩ **b :** to give one's support or allegiance — used with *for* to specify the recipient **syn** see DECLARE
an·nounce·ment \-mənt\ *n* -s **1 :** the act of announcing or of being announced ⟨during the long ~ the crowd stirred restlessly⟩ **2 a :** public notification **:** official statement ⟨the governor will soon make a new ~⟩ ⟨the college's ~ of summer courses⟩ **b :** a usu. more or less formal declaration of an approaching or already realized event ⟨an ~ of marriage⟩ **c :** a message delivered on radio or television **3 :** REMARK, OBSERVATION, STATEMENT ⟨every new ~ of hers was greeted with shouts of laughter⟩ **4 :** a piece of formal stationery or a formal card designed for social or business purposes
an·nounc·er \-ə(r)\ *n* -s **1 :** one that introduces television or radio programs, often acts as master of ceremonies, makes commercial announcements, reads news summaries and sports reviews, gives station identification, and signals the control room for the switching of network broadcasts **2 :** one that comments on sports events (as baseball games) to television spectators or describes them to a radio audience
¹annoy *n* -s [ME *anoi*, fr. OF *anoi, enui*, fr. *anoier, enuier*] **1** *archaic* **:** a feeling of discomfort or vexation **:** ANNOYANCE **2** *obs* **:** something that is a source of annoyance or trouble
²an·noy \əˈnȯi\ *vb* -ED/-ING/-S [ME *anoien*, fr. OF *anoier, enuier*, fr. LL *inodiare* to make loathsome, fr. L *in odio* in hatred, odious, fr. *in* + *odio*, abl. of *odium* hatred — more at IN, ODIUM] *vt* **1 :** to irritate with a nettling or exasperating effect esp. by being a continuous or repeatedly renewed source of vexation **:** PROVOKE, VEX ⟨by living together they ~*ed* the rest of the family even more than they irritated each other —William Thornton⟩ ⟨often puzzled and sometimes ~*ed* by the ways of other peoples who are strange to us —W.A. Parker⟩ **2 a :** to harass esp. by quick and brief attacks ⟨dogs ~*ing* a cornered bear⟩ ⟨infiltrating behind the lines so as to ~ the enemy replacements⟩ **b** *obs* **:** to injure slightly **3** *obs* **:** to interfere with **:** affect detrimentally **~** *vi* **:** to be a source of annoyance ⟨some personalities antagonize; others simply ~⟩
syn VEX, IRK, BOTHER, WORRY: ANNOY suggests disturbed or irritated loss of composure, placidity, or patience through enduring affliction, molestation, slight, or discomfort ⟨Richard's absence *annoyed* him. The youth was vivacious, and his enthusiasm good fun —George Meredith⟩ ⟨*annoy* you with unnecessary details —P.B.Kyne⟩ ⟨Hopkinson *annoyed* the British in Philadelphia with a satirical ballad —*Amer. Guide Series: Pa.*⟩ VEX, somewhat stronger than ANNOY in implying a deep effect, applies to what provokes, disturbs, or perplexes ⟨the faulty translation that so *vexes* teachers —C.H. Grandgent⟩ ⟨you take delight in *vexing* me. You have no compassion on my poor nerves —Jane Austen⟩ ⟨Mr. Hudson, in his *La Plata*, has *vexed* himself with similar problems —Norman Douglas⟩ IRK now often applies to angering or provoking into a rejoinder; its older meaning of wearying and boring is becoming less common ⟨the supervision of the ubiquitous secret-service men *irked* his nerves —S.H.Adams⟩ ⟨the overiterated becomes the monotonous, and the monotonous *irks* and bores —J.L.Lowes⟩ BOTHER applies to whatever distracts, upsets, frets, or discomposes so that one cannot be placid or intent ⟨she is also a little *bothered*, I think, because the servant is going to leave —Arnold Bennett⟩ ⟨Jack and Ethel *bothered* him, they might think he'd quit on them —Oliver La Farge⟩ WORRY indicates suffering with fretting care or anxiety ⟨half sick and *worried* by debts⟩ ⟨one who has *worried* over governmental problems all of his mature life —Felix Frankfurter⟩ ⟨I'm to have my peace of mind destroyed — I'm to be *worried* into my grave —Douglas Jerrold⟩ **syn** see in addition WORRY
an·noy·ance \-ȯiən(t)s\ *n* -s [ME *anoiaunce*, fr. MF *anoiance, enuiance*, fr. OF, fr. *anoier, enuier* + *-ance*] **1 :** the act of an-

noying or of being annoyed ⟨her constant ~ of her grandmother⟩ **2 :** the state or feeling of being annoyed **:** VEXATION, IRRITATION ⟨he gave up the search and went on with rising ~ to find the address —Ethel Wilson⟩ **3 :** a source of vexation or irritation **:** bothersome disturbance **:** NUISANCE ⟨these attacks had proved to be an ~ rather than a menace —C.E.Black & E.C.Helmreich⟩ ⟨plaster cracks and other ~s —J.R.Dalzell⟩

annoying *adj* [ME *anoiing*, fr. pres. part. of *anoien* to annoy] **:** IRRITATING, VEXING — **an·noy·ing·ly** *adv*

¹**an·nu·al** \ˈanyə(wə)l\ *adj* [ME *annuel, annual*, fr. MF & LL; MF *annuel*, fr. LL *annualis*, blend of L *annuus* yearly (fr. *annus* year) and L *annalis* yearly (fr. *annus* year + *-alis* -al); akin to Goth *athnam* (dat. pl.) years, Skt *atati* he walks, goes] **1 a :** reckoned by the year ⟨~ value of coffee exports⟩ **b :** covering the period of a year **:** based on a year ⟨an ~ total⟩ ⟨~ statistics⟩ ⟨~ rainfall⟩ **2 :** occurring, appearing, made, done, or acted upon every year or once a year ⟨an ~ event⟩ ⟨an ~ magazine⟩ ⟨an ~ visit⟩ **3 :** completing the life cycle in one growing season **:** lasting one year or growing season ⟨an ~ plant⟩ — compare BIENNIAL, PERENNIAL — **an·nu·al·ly** \-)lē, -i\ *adv*

²**annual** \"\ *n* -s **1 a :** a publication appearing yearly and often treating of matters of interest in a year just past ⟨editor of the high-school ~⟩; *specif* **:** a publication appearing as one of a series published to meet a yearly seasonal market ⟨a children's Christmas ~⟩ **b :** GIFTBOOK 2 **2 :** a yearly event; *specif* **:** an annual exhibition of paintings or sculpture **3 :** something that lasts one year or season; *specif* **:** a plant that completes its growth in one growing season

annual bluegrass *or* **annual meadowgrass** *n* **:** an annual European grass (*Poa annua*) of wide distribution introduced into No. America where it is often a weed esp. in lawns

annual epact *n* **:** EPACT 1a

annual improvement factor *n* **:** a provision in a labor contract calling for an annual increase in the hourly wage rates of the workers so as to provide a constantly rising standard of living

an·nu·al·ist \-əst\ *n* -s [²*annual* + *-ist*] **:** one who writes for an annual

an·nu·al·i·za·tion \ˌanyə(wə)lə̇ˈzāshən, -ˌlīˈz-\ *n* -s **:** the act of annualizing or the state of being annualized

an·nu·al·ize \ˈanyə(wə)ˌlīz\ *vt* -ED/-ING/-S [¹*annual* + *-ize*] **:** to compute for periods of less than a year on a basis corresponding to that applicable to a full year ⟨*annualized* income⟩

annual leave *n* **:** free time granted annually to a jobholder

annual meeting *n* **:** a meeting (as of the stockholders of a business concern) held annually for reviewing developments of the year just past, electing new officers, and voting on major organizational policies

annual parallax *n* **:** HELIOCENTRIC PARALLAX

annual phlox *n* **:** any of various phloxes derived from an herb (*Phlox drummondii*) with erect stems usu. less than 18 inches high, leaves 1 to 3 inches long, the upper ones alternate, and flowers in close clusters — compare PERENNIAL PHLOX

annual rent *n* **1** *Scots law* **:** GROUND ANNUAL **2** *Scots law* **:** INTEREST

annual ring *n* **1** *of a woody plant* **:** the layer of wood produced by the growth of a single year and appearing in cross section as a ring or rings surrounding previously produced similar rings — called also *growth ring* **2 :** one of the markings or ridges on the scales of some fishes that correspond with a year's growth — called also *annulus*

3
2
1
4

transverse section of a twig of the tulip tree: *1* pith; *2* wood, showing three annual rings; *3* bark; *4* wood rays

annual sage *n* **1 :** CHIA 1 **2 :** THISTLE SAGE

annual variation *n* **:** the yearly change in a star's mean right ascension or declination produced by precession of the equinoxes and proper motion of the star

annual wage *n* **:** GUARANTEED ANNUAL WAGE

an·nu·ary \ˈanyəˌwerē\ *n* -ES [F *annuaire*, fr. LL *annuarius*, fr. L *annuus* yearly + *-arius* -ary — more at ANNUAL] **:** YEARBOOK, ANNUAL

an·nu·a·tion \ˌanyəˈwāshən\ *n* -s [L *annuus* yearly + E *-ation* — more at ANNUAL] **1 :** annual variation in the presence or absence or the abundance of particular members of a plant community usu. relatable to annual climatic variation — compare ASPECTION **2 :** ecological observations made over a period of years

an·nu·i·tant \əˈn(y)üəd·ənt, -ətənt *also* aˈ- *or* -əˈt°nt\ *n* -s [*annuity* + *-ant*] **:** one that receives benefits or payments from an annuity or that is entitled to receive such benefits

an·nu·i·ty \-əd·ē, -ətē, -i\ *n* -ES *often attrib* [ME *annuite*, fr. MF *annuité*, fr. ML *annuitat-, annuitas*, fr. L *annuus* yearly + *-itat-, -itas* -ity — more at ANNUAL] **1 :** an amount payable yearly or at other regular intervals (as quarterly) for a certain or uncertain period (as for years, for life, or in perpetuity) **2 :** the grant of or the right to receive an annuity ⟨his will included *annuities* for several old servants⟩ **3 :** a contract or agreement under which one or more persons receive annuities in return for prior set payments made by themselves or another (as an employer) ⟨bought an ~ to take care of his parents⟩

annuity certain *n, pl* **annuities certain :** an annuity payable in any event for a term of years

annuity due *n, pl* **annuities due :** an annuity providing for the first payment at the beginning rather than at the end of the first period

an·nul \əˈnəl\ *vt* **annulled; annulled; annulling; annuls** [ME *annullen*, fr. MF *annuller*, fr. LL *annullare, adnullare* to destroy (trans. of Gk *exoudenein, exoudenoun*), fr. L *ad-* + LL *-nullare* (fr. L *nullus* none) — more at NULL] **1 a :** to cause to cease to exist **:** reduce to nothing **:** blot out **:** OBLITERATE ⟨*annulling* every memory⟩ **b :** to check effectively **:** make inoperative (as by an opposite influence or force) **:** NEUTRALIZE, CANCEL ⟨she stood very still, as if by her stillness to ~ the small leaden sound the key had made —Dorothy Baker⟩ **2 a :** to declare (a marriage) legally invalid ⟨he may then have the marriage *annulled* —S.G.Kling⟩ **b :** to make legally void **:** declare to be no longer of legal effect **:** ABOLISH **syn** see NULLIFY

an·nu·lar \ˈanyələ(r)\ *adj* [MF or L; MF *annulaire*, fr. L *annularis, anularis*, fr. *annulus, anulus* ring — more at ANNULUS] **1 a :** of or relating to a ring **:** forming a ring **:** shaped like a ring ⟨~ growths in the trunk of a tree⟩ **b** *chem* **:** CYCLIC **2 :** banded, marked, or thickened in circles ⟨an ~ cell of a plant⟩ — **an·nu·lar·ly** *adv*

annular auger *n* **:** a ring-shaped boring tool that cuts a circular channel leaving the center intact

annular budding *n* **:** budding in which a ring of bark is removed from the stock and replaced with one containing a bud of the desired species or variety

annular eclipse *n* **:** a solar eclipse in which a thin outer ring of the sun's disk is not covered by the apparently smaller dark disk of the moon

annular finger *n* **:** RING FINGER

annular gear *n* **:** INTERNAL GEAR

an·nu·lar·ia \ˌanyəˈla(a)rēə\ *n, cap* [NL, fr. L *annulus* + NL *-aria*] **:** a large genus of fossil pteridophytic plants of the order Equisetales having annuli formed by the basal sheaths of the leaf whorls

an·nu·lar·i·ty \-ˈlarəd·ē\ *n* -ES **:** annular state or form

annular ligament *n, anat* **:** a ringlike ligament or band of fibrous tissue encircling a part: **a :** any of the transverse bands holding in place the extensor and flexor tendons of the wrist and ankle **b :** a strong band of fibers surrounding the head of the radius and retaining it in the radial notch of the ulna — called also *orbicular ligament* **c :** any of certain strengthening bands of the tendon sheaths of the digits **d :** a ring attaching the base of the stapes to the fenestra vestibuli

annular solid *n, math* **:** a solid generated by a closed curve when rotated about a straight line lying in the plane of the curve and not intersecting the curve (as a torus)

annular vault *n* **:** a vault rising from two walls that are circular in plan (as above the walls of an ambulatory)

an·nu·lary \ˈanyəˌlerē\ *n* -ES [short for earlier *annulary finger*, fr. obs. E *annulary* of a ring (fr. L *annularius*) + *finger* — more at ANNULAR] **:** RING FINGER

¹**an·nu·la·ta** \ˌanyəˈläd·ə, -ād·ə\ [NL, fr. L, neut. pl. of *annulatus*] *syn of* ANNELIDA

²**annulata** \"\ *n pl, cap* [NL, fr. L] *in some classifications* **:** a major division of Invertebrata comprising bilaterally symmetrical animals with true metamerism and including the annelids, arthropods, and a few related forms

¹**an·nu·late** \ˈanyələt, -ˌlāt, *usu* -d·+V\ *or* **an·nu·lat·ed** \-ˌlād·əd\ *adj* [L *annulatus, anulatus*, fr. *annulus, anulus* ring + *-atus* -ate — more at ANNULUS] **1 :** having rings, ringlike structures, or ringlike characteristics **2 :** ANNULAR **3** [NL *Annulata*] **:** of or relating to the Annulata

²**annulate** \"\ *n* -s **:** an animal of the division Annulata

annulated column *or* **annulated shaft** *n* **:** a column made up of a cluster of shafts seemingly held together by an annular band at intervals but commonly worked on an interposed stone plate whose edge slightly projects and often found in clustered piers of Gothic churches

an·nu·la·tion \ˌanyəˈlāshən\ *n* -s **1 :** the formation of rings **2 :** a ringlike structure

an·nule \ˈa(ˌ)nyül\ *n* -s [L *annulus*] **:** ANNULUS; *specif* **:** a circular band formed by two transverse grooves in the cuticle of some nematodes with consequent apparent segmentation

an·nu·let \ˈanyələt, -ˌlet\ *n* -s [modif. (influenced by L *annulus, anulus* ring) of MF *annelet, anelet*, dim. of *anel*, fr. L *anellus* little ring, dim. of *annulus, anulus* ring — more at ANNULUS] **1 :** a little ring **2** *heraldry* **:** a ring-shaped charge that when borne as a cadency mark represents position as a 6th son or descendant of a 6th son **3** *archit* **:** a small molding or ridge forming a ring (as a list, fillet, or cincture); *esp* **:** one of the fillets used at the lower part of the Doric capital **4** *zool* **:** a narrow circle of some distinct color on a surface or around an organ

annulet 2

annuli *pl of* ANNULUS

an·nu·lism \-ˌlizəm\ *n* -s [*annulus* + *-ism*] **:** annulated state or structure

annulled *past of* ANNUL

an·nul·ler \əˈnələ(r)\ *n* -s **:** one that annuls

annulling *pres part of* ANNUL

an·nul·ment \əˈnəlmənt\ *n* -s **:** the act of annulling or of being annulled **:** NULLIFICATION; *specif* **:** a judicial pronouncement declaring the invalidity of a marriage — distinguished from *divorce* and *separation*

an·nu·lo·sa \ˌanyəˈlōsə, -ōzə\ *n pl, cap* [NL, fr. L *annulus* ring + *-osa* (neut. pl. of *-osus*) -ose] *in some classifications* **:** a subkingdom of animals including forms with articulate bodies and a double ventral chain of ganglia and comprising the annelid worms and the arthropods — **an·nu·losan** \-s°n, -z°n\ *n* -s — **an·nu·lose** \ˈanyəˌlōs\ *adj*

annuls *pres 3d sing of* ANNUL

an·nu·lus \ˈanyələs\ *n, pl* **annu·li** \-ˌlī\ *also* **annuluses** [L *annulus, anulus* ring, dim. of *anus* ring, circle, anus — more at ANUS] **1 :** a ringlike part, structure, or marking **2** *anat* **:** any of certain ringlike parts (as the abdominal ring) **3 :** ANNULET 3 **4 :** the plane space between two concentric circles one within the other **5 a** *of fungi* **:** a membranous or fleshy ring that surrounds the stipe of certain agarics after the expansion of the pileus **:** the remnant of the veil **b** *of a moss* **:** an elastic ring of cells between the operculum and the mouth of the capsule **c** *of a fern* **:** a line of cells partly or entirely surrounding the sporangium and each having inner tangential and radial walls thickened and outer wall thin and by its contraction bringing about rupture of the sporangium and assisting in spore discharge **d :** the fleshy rim of the corolla in some asclepiads (as of the genus *Stapelia*) **e :** the calyxlike whorl at the base of the strobilus of some horsetails (genus *Equisetum*) **6 a :** one of the ringlike but not truly segmented parts of the body of some annelids (as leeches) **b :** ANNUAL RING 2

an·nun·ci·ate \əˈnən(t)sēˌāt *also* aˈ-\ *vt* -ED/-ING/-S [L *annuntiatus, adnuntiatus*] **:** ANNOUNCE

an·nun·ci·a·tion \ə,ˌ==ˈāshən\ *n* -s [ME *annunciacioun*, fr. MF *anunciation, annonciation*, fr. LL *annuntiation-, annuntiatio*, fr. L *annuntiatus, adnuntiatus* (past part. of *annuntiare, adnuntiare* to announce) + *-ion-, -io* -ion — more at ANNOUNCE] **1 :** the act of announcing or of being announced **:** ANNOUNCEMENT ⟨~ of the good news⟩ **2** *also* **annunciation day** *usu cap A&D* **:** the 25th of March on which many Christian churches commemorate the announcement of the Incarnation related in Luke 1:28–35 — called also *Lady Day*

annunciation lily *n, usu cap A* [so called fr. its use by painters in pictures of the Annunciation] **1 :** MADONNA LILY **2 :** BERMUDA LILY

an·nun·ci·a·tor \əˈ==ˌād·ə(r), -ātə-\ *n* -s [LL, fr. L *annuntiatus* + *-or*] **1 :** one that annunciates **:** ANNOUNCER **2 :** a device for giving audible or visible directives or information: as **a :** an electrically controlled signaling apparatus for indicating which of the connecting lines is calling (as the rooms calling a hotel desk or the floors at which people are signaling for an elevator to stop) **b :** a device for transmitting speed orders to the engine room of a ship

an·nun·ci·a·to·ry \-ə,tōrē\ *adj* **:** serving to announce ⟨a condition ~ of what was to follow⟩

an·nus mi·ra·bi·lis \ˌanəsməˈrabələs, -rab-; ˈänəsməˈrä-\ *n, pl* **an·ni mirabi·les** \ˈaˌnīməˈrabəˌlēz, -rab-; ˈäˌnēməˈräbəˌlās\ *sometimes cap A&M* [L] **:** wonderful year — used of any esp. notable year ⟨1776 — an *annus mirabilis* in American history⟩

¹**ano-** *prefix* [NL, fr. Gk *anō* upward, above, fr. *ana* up, on — more at ON] **1 :** upward ⟨anogenic⟩ ⟨anoopsia⟩ **2 :** upper ⟨anocarpous⟩

²**ano-** *comb form* [NL, fr. L *anus*] **:** anus ⟨anoscopy⟩ **:** anal and ⟨anococcygeal⟩

anoa \əˈnōə\ *n* -s [native name in the Celebes] **:** a small wild ox of Celebes (*Anoa depressicornis*) related to the buffalo but having nearly straight horns

ano·bi·id \əˈnōbēəd\ *adj* [NL *Anobiidae*] **:** of or belonging to the Anobiidae

an·o·bi·i·dae \ˌanəˈbīəˌdē\ *n pl, cap* [NL, fr. *Anobium*, type genus + *-idae*] **:** a family of small hard-bodied beetles with 5-jointed tarsi and generally serrate clubbed antennae that feed on dry vegetable material and include destructive pests of stored foods and tobacco — see DRUGSTORE BEETLE

anobing *var of* ANUBING

ano·bi·um \əˈnōbēəm\ *n, cap* [NL, fr. ¹*ano-* + *-bium*] **:** a genus (the type of the family Anobiidae) of small beetles including a number of forms that bore in dry wood — compare FURNITURE BEETLE, POWDER-POST BEETLE

an·ode \ˈaˌnōd\ *n* -s [Gk *anodos* way up, rise, fr. *ana-* + *hodos* road; fr. the belief that the electric current passes from east to west — more at CEDE] **1 :** the electrode at which electrons leave a device to enter the external circuit — opposed to *cathode* **2 a :** the positive terminal of an electrolytic cell **b :** the negative terminal of a primary cell or of a storage battery that is delivering current **c :** the electron-collecting electrode of an electron tube **:** PLATE

anode current *n* **:** PLATE CURRENT

anode ray *n* **:** any of the streams of positively charged particles emitted by the metallic anode of a discharge tube or by impurities on the surface of the anode

an·od·ic \(ˈ)aˈnädik, -ōd-, əˈnä-\ *adj* [Gk *anodos* road up (fr. *ana-* + *hodos* road) + E *-ic*] **1 :** ASCENDING **2** *bot* **:** turned toward — used only of that half of a leaf which is turned toward the course of the genetic spiral; compare CATHODIC **3** [*anode* + *-ic*] **a :** of, at, or relating to an anode — opposed to *cathodic* **b :** *of a chemical element* **:** tending to form an anode in an electrochemical cell in relation to another element, often hydrogen ⟨zinc is ~ to copper⟩ **4 :** produced by or involving a process in which a metal is made to serve as the anode in an electrolytic cell (as for coating the metal with an oxide for protection) ⟨~ coating⟩ ⟨~ finish⟩ ⟨~ treatment⟩ — **an·od·i·cal·ly** \(ˈ)aˈnädək(ə)lē, -ōd-, əˈnä-\ *adv*

anodic coating *n* **:** the process of anodizing

an·od·ize *or* **an·od·ise** \ˈa(ˌ)nōˌdīz, ˈanə,-\ *vt* -ED/-ING/-S [*anode* + *-ize*] **:** to subject (a metal) to electrolytic action by making (it) the anode of a cell before coating with a protective or decorative film

an·o·do·lu·mi·nes·cence \ˌanəˌdō-\ *n* -s [*anode* + *-o-* + *luminescence*] **:** luminescence excited by anode rays

¹**an·o·don** \ˈanəˌdän\ [NL, fr. Gk *anodōn* toothless, fr. *an-* + *odōn* tooth — more at TOOTH] *syn of* ANODONTA

²**anodon** \"\ *n* -s **:** a freshwater mussel of the genus *Anodonta*

an·o·don·ta \ˌanəˈdäntə\ *n, cap* [NL, fr. Gk *anodont-, anodōn* toothless] **:** a large genus of freshwater mussels (family Unionidae) having the hinge teeth rudimentary or wanting and the shell usu. thin and fragile

an·o·don·tia \ˌanōˈdänch(ē)ə\ *n* -s [NL, fr. *an-* + *-odontia*] **:** an esp. congenital absence of teeth

¹**an·o·dyne** \ˈanəˌdīn, -nō,-\ *adj* [L *anodynos*, fr. Gk *anōdynos*, fr. *an-* + *odynē* pain; akin to Arm *erkn* birth pains, Lith *ėdžiótis* to hurt, OE *etan* to eat — more at EAT] **1 :** serving to assuage pain **:** SOOTHING ⟨the ~ properties of certain drugs⟩ **2 :** serving or intended to soothe the mind or feelings **:** inducing forgetfulness, oblivion, or unconcern **:** RELAXING ⟨his pleasant voice and pious, ~ opinions making of his sentences so many gentle opiates —F.M.Ford⟩ ⟨all that doughy, woolly, ~ writing that exists merely to fill a gap of leisure —Aldous Huxley⟩ **3 :** marked by an absence of power of stimulation **:** BLAND ⟨~ translations from Homer and Sophocles in . . . sleepy prose —George Santayana⟩; *sometimes* **:** designedly weakened or softened (as by qualification or expurgation) ⟨read the ~ and doctored accounts of the transactions that had cost them their savings —*New Republic*⟩

²**anodyne** \"\ *n* -s [LL *anodynon*, fr. Gk *anōdynon*, fr. neut. of *anōdynos*] **1 :** a drug that allays pain (as an opiate or narcotic) **2 :** something that soothes, calms, or comforts ⟨the ~ of work⟩ ⟨old wounds heal; new friendships and associations come as ~s —Nevil Shute⟩ ⟨an escape, a distraction, an ~ —J.C.Powys⟩ — **an·o·dyn·ic** \ˌ==ˈdinik, -ēk\ *adj*

anodyne necklace *n* **1 :** a necklace usu. of henbane roots used in the 18th century esp. by teething children as a charm against illness **2 :** a hangman's noose

an·o·dyn·ia \ˌ==ˈdinēə, -dīn-\ *n* -s [NL, fr. Gk *anōdynia*, fr. *anōdynos* + *-ia*] **:** absence of pain

an·od·y·nous \aˈnäd°nəs; ˈanəˌdīnəs, -nō,-\ *adj* [L *anodynos*] **:** ANODYNE

an·o·e·sia \ˌanōˈēzh(ē)ə\ *n* -s [NL, fr. Gk *anoēsia* want of understanding, fr. *a-* ²*a-* + *noēsis*] **:** ANOIA

an·o·e·sis \ˌanōˈēsə̇s\ *n, pl* **anoe·ses** \-ˌsēz\ [²*a-* + *noesis*] **:** consciousness that is pure passive receptiveness without understanding or intellectual organization of the materials presented

anoestrous [*an-* + *oestrous*] *var of* ANESTROUS

anoestrous *or* **anoestrum** *var of* ANESTRUS

an·o·et·ic \ˈanōˈed·ik\ *adj* [²*a-* + *noetic*] **:** relating to or characterized by anoesis

ano·gra \əˈnōgrə\ *n cap* [NL anagram of *Onagra* (syn. of *Oenothera*) — more at ONAGRA] **:** a genus of herbs (family Onagraceae) found in the southern part of No. America and having alternate leaves and flowers with four notched petals

anoia \əˈnȯi(y)ə\ *n* -s [NL, fr. Gk *anoia* lack of understanding, fr. *a-* ²*a-* + *noos, nous* sense, mind, understanding + *-ia*] **:** mental deficiency; *esp* **:** IDIOCY

ano·ine \ˈanōˌīn, -ˌən\ *adj* [*anoa* + *-ine*] **:** of or relating to the anoa

anoint \əˈnȯint\ *vt* -ED/-ING/-S [ME *anointen, enointen*, fr. MF *enoint* (past part. of *enoindre*, fr. L *inunguere*), fr. L *inunctus*, past part. of *inunguere*, fr. *in-* + *unguere, ungere* to smear, anoint — more at OINTMENT] **1 :** to rub over with oil or an oily substance ⟨~*ing* his boat —Herman Melville⟩ ⟨heron fat . . . was used by fishermen to ~ their lines —*Irish Digest*⟩ ⟨that road to ruin for which extravagant habits . . . were plentifully ~*ing* their wheels —George Eliot⟩ **:** RUB —used with *with* ⟨~*ing* one another with suntan oil⟩ ⟨drew the cork and ~*ed* his head with the lotion⟩ **2** *also* **an·noint** \"\ **a :** to apply oil to or pour oil upon as a sacred rite esp. for consecration ⟨they ~*ed* David king —2 Sam 2:4 (RSV)⟩ **b :** to choose by or as if by divine election **:** designate as if through the rite of anointment **:** CONSECRATE ⟨he has ~*ed* me to preach good news to the poor —Lk 4:18 (RSV)⟩ ⟨the elect and ~*ed* of God⟩ ⟨regarded by all as his ~*ed* successor⟩ **3** *chiefly dial* **:** BEAT, THRASH, CHASTISE

anoint·ment \-mənt\ *n* -s [ME, fr. *anointen* + *-ment*] **1 :** the action of anointing or state of being anointed **2** *archaic* **:** OINTMENT

ano·le \əˈnōlē\ *also* **ano·li** \"\ *n* -s [F *anolis*, fr. Island Carib *anoli*] **:** a lizard of the genus *Anolis*

ano·lis \əˈnōlə̇s, ˈanə-\ *n, cap* [NL, fr. F *anolis*] **:** a genus of small American pleurodont lizards (family Iguanidae) comprising the New World chameleons that have the power of changing color like the true chameleons of the Old World

an·o·lyte \ˈanəˌlīt, -nō,-\ *n* -s [*anode* + electro*lyte*] **:** that portion of the electrolyte in the immediate vicinity of the anode in an electrolytic cell — opposed to *catholyte*

anom- *or* **anomo-** *comb form* [NL, fr. Gk *anom-* lawless, fr. *anomos*, fr. *a-* ²*a-* + *nomos* law, fr. *nemein* to distribute — more at NIMBLE] **:** unusual **:** abnormal **:** irregular ⟨*anomite*⟩ ⟨*anomocarpous*⟩

anomal- *or* **anomali-** *or* **anomalo-** *comb form* [L *anomal-*, fr. Gk, fr. *anōmalos* uneven, irregular — more at ANOMALOUS] **:** anomalous **:** irregular ⟨*anomali*florous⟩ ⟨*anomal*ism⟩ ⟨*anomalo*cephalus⟩

anom·a·la \əˈnäməla\ *n, cap* [NL, fr. LL, fem. of *anomalus* anomalous] **:** a genus of beetles (family Scarabaeidae) having grubs that feed mainly on the roots of plants and including several pests of cultivated grasses — see ORIENTAL BEETLE

anomalies *pl of* ANOMALY

anom·a·li·ped \əˈnäməlaˌped\ *or* **anom·a·li·pod** \-ˌpäd\ *adj* [F *anomalipède*, fr. *anomal-* + *-pède* -ped] **:** having more or less of the digits united ⟨the kingfisher and the kangaroo are ~⟩ **:** SYNDACTYLIC

anom·a·lism \əˈnäməˌlizəm\ *n* -s [*anomal-* + *-ism*] **1 :** the quality of being anomalous **2 :** ANOMALY

anom·a·list \-ləst\ *n* -s [perh. fr. G, fr. *anomal-* + *-ist*] **:** an adherent of the view held by certain Greek grammarians of the 2d century B.C. that in language the connection between the word and the idea is arbitrary and based on convention alone — opposed to *analogist*

anom·a·lis·tic \əˌnäməˈlistik, -ēk\ *also* **anom·a·lis·ti·cal** \ˌ=ˌ==ˈ=əkəl\ *adj* [*anomaly* + *-istic*] **1** *astron* **:** relating to the anomaly (sense 1a) **2** [*anomalist* + *-ic*] **:** of or relating to the anomalists **3 :** ANOMALOUS — **anom·a·lis·ti·cal·ly** \-ək(ə)lē, -li\ *adv*

anomalistic month *n* **:** the mean time of the moon's revolution from perigee to perigee again, being approximately 27.554550 days

anomalistic year *n* **:** the time of the earth's revolution from perihelion to perihelion again, being 365 days, 6 hours, 13 minutes, and 53.1 seconds

anom·a·lops \əˈnäməˌläps\ *n, cap* [NL, fr. *anomal-* + *-ops*] **:** a genus of fishes (order Berycomorphi) having a luminous organ beneath each eye filled with light-producing bacteria and known from warm seas of the southwestern Pacific and about Puerto Rico

anom·a·lop·ter·yx \əˌnäməˈläptəˌriks\ *n, cap* [NL, fr. *anomal-* + *-pteryx*] **:** a genus of moas of slender build and a height of three or four feet

anom·a·lo·scope \əˈnäməlaˌskōp\ *n* -s [*anomal-* + *-scope*] **:** an optical device designed to test color vision by matching a yellow light which may be varied in intensity with a combination of red and green lights of constant intensity

anom·a·lous \əˈnäməlas\ *adj* [LL *anomalus*, fr. Gk *anōmalos* lit., uneven, irregular, fr. *an-* + *homalos* even, level, fr. *homos* same, common — more at SAME] **1** *archaic* **:** UNCONFORMABLE, DISSIMILAR — used with *to* **2 :** deviating from a general rule, method, or analogy **:** ABNORMAL, IRREGULAR ⟨an ~ verb⟩ ⟨in nature, the ~ or lawless systems often are most interesting and instructive —Otto Glasser⟩ ⟨any hereditary peculiarity — as a supernumerary finger, or an ~ shape of feature —Nathaniel Hawthorne⟩ **3 :** not conformable to established or accepted conceptions of fitness or harmonious combination:

a : out of keeping with its recognized nature, characteristics, surroundings, or conditions of occurrence ⟨a person on a heath in raiment of modern cut and colors has more or less an ~ look —Thomas Hardy⟩ ⟨an ~ figure in the world of politics⟩ ⟨an ~ remark, coming from him⟩ **b** : exhibiting or containing incongruous or often contradictory elements ⟨the ~ position of the free Negro in the slave states —E.T.Price⟩ ⟨in the ~ position of being ranked second nationally . . . but first in the world —*New Yorker*⟩

anomalous dispersion *n* : dispersion of light in some refraction spectra in which the normal order of the separation of components is reversed in the vicinity of certain wavelengths

anomalous indorser *n* : a person other than the maker, payee, or holder of a negotiable bill or note who indorses it for some purpose other than to transfer it

anom·a·lous·ly *adv* : in an anomalous manner

anomalous plea *n, law* : a plea partly affirmative and partly negative, the one part being used to show that the other does not defeat the rights of the pleader

anomalous trichromatism *n* : a slight defect of color vision in which the proportions of the three primary colors required in color mixture deviate from the normal — compare COLOR 1

anom·a·lure \ə'nämə,lu̇(ə)r\ *n* -s [NL *Anomalurus*] : a member of the genus *Anomalurus* : SCALETAIL

anom·a·lu·rus \ə,nämə'lu̇rəs\ *n, cap* [NL, fr. *anomal-* + *-urus*] : a genus (the type of the family Anomaluridae) of sciuromorph rodents comprising the scaletails and resembling flying squirrels but having scaly tails used in climbing

anom·a·ly \ə'näməlē, -li\ *n* -ES [L *anomalia*, fr. Gk *anōmalia*, fr. *anōmalos* + *-ia*] **1** : the state or fact of being out of place, out of true, or out of a normal or expected position : INEQUALITY, UNEVENNESS: as **a** : the angular distance of a planet from its perihelion as seen from the sun **b** (1) : the difference between the mean of any meteorological element or phase of that element over a given time at a particular place and the mean of the same element or phase over the same time for all other points on the same parallel of latitude (2) : the difference between the current value of a meteorological element and its long-term average **c** : a deviation of optical properties of a crystal from its apparent symmetry as expressed in its external form — usu. used in the phrase *optical anomaly* **2** : deviation from the common rule : IRREGULARITY ⟨that supreme triumph of British ~, the unreformed House of Lords —R.W.Chapman⟩ **3** : something anomalous : something irregular or abnormal: as **a** : a word form, set of inflectional forms, construction, or idiom analogous to few or no others (as the conjugation of the verb *to be* or *stood*, past tense of *stand*) **b** *biol* : a deviation in excess of normal variation from the form characteristic of a natural group **c** *geol* : a local departure from the general regional conditions (as of gravity, magnetism, radioactivity, or topography) **4** : something out of keeping esp. with established or accepted notions of fitness or order ⟨her religion was no ~ but perfectly natural —George Santayana⟩

an·o·mer \'anəmər\ *n* -s [[1]*ano-* + *-mer*] : a cyclic stereoisomer in the carbohydrate series with isomerism involving only the arrangement of atoms or groups at the aldehyde or ketone position (as in *alpha*-D-glucose and *beta*-D-glucose) — **an·o·mer·ic** \¦anə¦merik\ *adj*

ano·mia \ə'nōmēə\ *n, cap* [NL, fr. Gk *anomos* lawless + NL *-ia* — more at ANOM-] : a genus (the type of the family Anomiidae) of thin-shelled bivalve mollusks comprising the saddle oysters, having the right valve deeply notched for passage of the byssus, and forming with a few related forms a suborder of Filibranchia

anom·ic \ə'nämik, (,)ā¦n-; -nō-\ *adj* [*anomie* + *-ic*] : relating to or characterized by anomie

anomic aphasia *n* : loss of the power to use or understand words denoting objects

an·o·mie \'anə,mē\ *also* **ano·mia** \ə'nōmēə, ā'n-, ,anə'mēə\ *or* **an·o·my** \'anəmē, -mi\ *n* -s [*anomie, anomy* fr. F *anomie*, fr. Gk *anomia, anomiē* lawlessness; *anomia* fr. Gk — more at ANOMY] : a state of normlessness or lawlessness: **a** : a state of society in which normative standards of conduct and belief have weakened or disappeared **b** : a similar condition in an individual commonly characterized by personal disorientation, anxiety, and social isolation

an·o·mite \'anə,mīt\ *n* -s [ISV *anom-* + *-ite;* orig. formed as G *anomit*] : a variety of biotite differing optically from the ordinary kind

anomo- — see ANOM-

an·o·mo·coe·lous \¦anə(,)mō¦sēləs\ *adj* [*anom-* + *coelous*] : concave in front — used of a vertebra in which the anterior surface of the centrum is hollowed out while the posterior surface is flat or convex

[1]an·o·mo·dont \'anə(,)mō,dänt\ *adj* [NL *Anomodontia*] : of or belonging to Anomodontia

[2]anomodont \"\ *n* -s : an anomodont reptile

[1]an·o·mo·don·tia \,anə(,)mō'dänsh(ē)ə\ [NL, fr. *anom-* + *-odontia*] *syn of* PELYCOSAURIA

[2]anomodontia \"\ [NL, fr. *anom-* + *-odontia*] *syn of* DICYNODONTIA

[1]an·o·moe·an \,anə'mēən\ *also* **an·o·moi·an** \-mȯiən\ *n* -s *usu cap* [LGk *Anomoios* (fr. Gk *anomoios*, adj., unlike, fr. *an-* + *homoios* similar, fr. *homos* same) + E *-an* — more at SAME] : a member of an extreme division of Arians of the 4th century A.D. who declared that since the son of God is a created being he is unlike God in essence — called also EUNOMIAN

[2]anomoean \¦==¦==\ *adj, usu cap* : of, relating to, or belonging to the Anomoeans

an·o·mu·ra \,anə'm(y)u̇rə\ *also* **an·o·mou·ra** \-'mu̇-\ *n pl, cap* [NL, fr. *anom-* + *-ura*] : a tribe or other division of Reptantia including decapod crustaceans with the abdomen more or less reduced and usu. permanently flexed (as the hermit crabs), being in some classifications placed in Macrura or treated as a separate suborder intermediate between Macrura and Brachyura — **an·o·mu·ral** \¦==¦m(y)u̇rəl\ *adj* — **an·o·mu·ran** \-¦m(y)u̇rən\ *adj or n* — **an·o·mu·rous** \-¦m(y)u̇rəs\ *adj*

[1]an·o·my \'anəmē, -mi\ *n* -ES [Gk *anomia, anomiē* lawlessness, fr. *anomos* + *-ia, -iē* -y] **1** *obs* : the state of being without law or order or esp. without natural law or uniformity **2** : an act or phenomenon that can be ascribed to the operation of no known law : MIRACLE

[2]anomy *var of* ANOMIE

[1]anon \ə'nän\ *adv* [ME *anon, onon*, fr. OE *on ān* in one, continually, immediately, fr. *on* in, on + *ān* one — more at ON, ONE] **1** *archaic* : at once : IMMEDIATELY, FORTHWITH ⟨he that heareth the word and ~ with joy receiveth it —Mt 13:20 (AV)⟩ — used esp. to express prompt response to a request or a summons **2** : in a little while: **a** : SOON, PRESENTLY ⟨thou dost me yet but little hurt; thou wilt ~ —Shak.⟩ **b** : LATER ⟨but more of that ~⟩ **3** : at another time : AGAIN, THEN ⟨on hill sometimes, ~ in shady vale —John Milton⟩ ⟨ever and ~⟩ ⟨now and ~⟩

[2]anon \"\ *interj, dial* — used to express failure to hear or understand something spoken or sometimes to express impatience or surprise

[3]anon \ä'nōn, ə'n-\ *n, pl* **ano·nes** \-(,)nes, -ās\ [Sp *anón*, fr. Taino *anon*] : SWEETSOP 2

anon *abbr* anonymous

ano·na \ə'nōnə\ *syn of* ANNONA

ano·na·ce·ae \,anō'nāsē,ē\ *syn of* ANNONACEAE

ano·nang \ə'nō,näŋ\ *n* -s [Tag] : a Philippine tree (*Cordia myxa*) the inner bark of which furnishes a cordage fiber; *also* : the fiber itself

anon·cil·lo \,ä(,)nōn'sēl,yō\ *n* -s [AmerSp, dim. of Sp *anón*] : the fiber yielded by the bark of various Venezuelan trees of the genus *Annona*

an·o·nych·ia \,anə'nikēə\ *n* -s [NL, fr. *an-* + *-onychia*] *med* : congenital absence of the nails

an·o·nym *also* **an·o·nyme** \'anə,nim\ *n* -s [F *anonyme*, fr. *anonyme* anonymous, fr. LL *anonymus*] **1 a** : one that retains anonymity or is of unknown name ⟨the essential if vaguely defined role of the recording director seems to be played by complete ~*s* —R.D.Darrell⟩ ⟨the party is an omnipotent and all-present ~ —Sergey Levitsky⟩ **b** : an anonymous book **2** : an idea that has no exact term to express it **3** : PSEUDONYM

anon·y·ma \ə'nänəmə *also* a'-\ *n, pl* **anony·mae** \-,mē, -,mī\ *or* **anonymas** [NL fr. LL, fem. of *anonymus*] : the innominate artery

an·o·nym·i·ty \,anə'nimədē, -ətē, -i\ *n* -ES **1** : the quality or state of being anonymous (as through absence or lack of identification, individuality, or personality) : ANONYMOUSNESS ⟨made it a rule not to debate important issues with men who . . . hide behind ~ —Norman Thomas⟩ ⟨the vast and kindly ~ of London life —James Hilton⟩ **2** : someone or something that is anonymous ⟨*anonymities* made "immortal" by their chance mention in a diary or a letter —*New Republic*⟩

anon·y·mous \ə'nänəməs *also* (')a¦n-\ *adj* [LL *anonymus*, fr. Gk *anōnymos*, fr. *an-* + *onoma* name — more at NAME] **1** : having or giving no name : of a name or with the name unknown or unrevealed : NAMELESS ⟨an ~ author⟩ ⟨giant corporations responsible to distant ~ owners⟩ ⟨the perfect type of the ~ assistant⟩ ⟨the ~ mass of mankind⟩ **2 a** : of unknown or unnamed source or origin (as authorship, donorship, workmanship) ⟨an ~ book⟩ ⟨~ furniture⟩ ⟨an ~ gift⟩ ⟨a bottle of imported but ~ claret⟩ **b** *of a coin or token* : bearing no indication (as name or insignia) of the issuer **3** : not having or not imparting a sense of clearly marked individuality or personality : producing an effect of being without name or identity ⟨a sea of ~ faces⟩ ⟨a district of brown ~ houses —Sinclair Lewis⟩ ⟨its characters are both static and lifeless; they have names but they remain ~ —Bernard De Voto⟩ ⟨the bodies are ~ in their cotton khaki clothes —Harry Brown⟩ ⟨an ~ fear, the fear of forces rather than of men —Roger Burlingame⟩ **4** : reported without the names of the persons involved — **anon·y·mous·ly** *adv* — **anon·y·mous·ness** *n* -ES

anon·y·mun·cule \ə,nänə'məŋ·,kyül\ *n* -s [blend of *anonymous* and *homuncule* "homuncle", fr. L *homunculus*] : an insignificant anonymous writer

an·o·op·sia \,anō'äpsēə\ *or* **anop·sia** \ə'näp-\ *n* -s [NL, fr. [1]*ano-* + *-opsia*] *med* : upward strabismus

anoph·e·les \ə'näfə,lēz, -nō-\ *n, cap* [NL, fr. Gk *anōphelēs* useless, hurtful, fr. *an-* + *-ōphelēs* (fr. *ophelos* advantage, help) — more at OPHELIMITY] : a genus of mosquitoes that differ from most other mosquitoes in having the palpi slender and nearly as long as the beak, in holding the body and beak in a straight line pointed at the substratum when at rest, and in lacking a caudal breathing siphon in the larva and that includes all the mosquitoes capable of transmitting the malaria parasite to man —compare CULEX

[1]anoph·e·line \ə'näfə,līn, -ˌlən\ *adj* [NL *Anopheles* + E *-ine*] : of, involving, or affecting mosquitoes of *Anopheles* or a closely related genus (as *Chagasia*) — compare CULICINE

[2]anopheline \"\ *n* -s : an anopheline mosquito

anoph·e·lism \-fə,lizəm\ *n* -s [NL *Anopheles* + E *-ism*] : infestation of a locality with anopheline mosquitoes

an·oph·thal·mia \,anəf'thalmēə\ *n* -s [NL, fr. *an-* + *-ophthalmia*] : congenital absence of the eyes

an·oph·thal·mos \-məs\ *n* -ES [NL, fr. MGk, without eyes] **1** : ANOPHTHALMIA **2** : an individual born without eyes

an·oph·thal·mus \"\ *n, cap* [NL, fr. MGk *anophthalmos* without eyes, fr. Gk *an-* an- + *ophthalmos* eye — more at OPHTHALMIA] : a genus of blind cave-inhabiting beetles (family Carabidae) of No. America

an·o·phyte \'anə,fīt\ *n* -s [[1]*ano-* + *-phyte*] : BRYOPHYTE

an·o·pis·tho·graph·ic \¦anə,pisthə¦==\ *adj* [*an-* + *opisthographic*] : having writing or printing on one side only — **an·o·pis·tho·graph·i·cal·ly** \-ək(ə)lē\ *adv*

anopl- *or* **anoplo-** *comb form* [NL, fr. Gk *anoplos*, fr. *an-* + *-hoplos* (fr. *hoplon* tool, weapon) — more at HOPLITE] : unarmed — chiefly in names of zoological taxa ⟨*Anopl*anthus⟩ ⟨*anoplo*cephalic⟩

an·o·pla \'anəplə\ *n pl, cap* [NL, fr. Gk *anoplos*] : a class or other division of Nemertea comprising forms in which the mouth is posterior to the brain and the proboscis lacks stylets and including the orders Palaeonemertea and Heteronemertea

an·o·pleu·ra \,anə'plu̇rə\ *syn of* ANOPLURA

an·op·lo·ceph·a·la \,anə(,)plō'sefələ\ *n, cap* [NL, fr. *anopl-* + *-cephala* (fem. of *-cephalus*)] : a genus of taenioid tapeworms including certain parasites of horses that may be pathogenic when present in large numbers

an·op·lo·ce·phal·ic \¦==(,)=sə¦falik\ *adj* [*anopl-* + *cephalic*] *zool* : lacking hooks on the scolex ⟨~ tapeworms⟩

an·op·lo·ceph·a·lid \,==(,)='sefələd\ *adj* [NL *Anoplocephalidae*] : of or belonging to the Anoplocephalidae

an·op·lo·ce·phal·i·dae \-sə'falə,dē\ *n pl, cap* [NL, fr. *Anoplocephala*, type genus + *-idae*] : a family of taenioid tapeworms with unarmed scolices that live as adults in the intestines of various herbivores and pass their larval stages in certain free-living mites

an·op·lo·nem·er·ti·ni \-,nemər'tī,nī\ [NL, fr. *anopl-* + *Nemertini*] *syn of* ANOPLA

an·op·lo·the·ri·um \-'thirēəm\ *n, cap* [NL, fr. *anopl-* + *-therium*] : a genus of hornless artiodactyl mammals with a long tail and weak canine teeth that is the type of a family (Anoplotheriidae) of the lower Oligocene of Europe

an·o·plu·ra \,anə'plu̇rə\ *n pl, cap* [NL, fr. *anopl-* + *-ura*] : an order of Insecta comprising the sucking lice and in some classifications the bird lice — compare MALLOPHAGA; see LOUSE 1a — **an·o·plu·ri·form** \¦==¦plu̇rə,fȯrm\ *adj*

anopsia *var of* ANOOPSIA

anor *abbr* another

an·o·rak \'anə,rak, 'änō,räk\ *n* -s [Greenland Esk *ánorâq*] : PARKA

an·or·chism \ə'nȯr,kizəm, a'n-\ *n* -s [NL *anorch*us + E *-ism*] : congenital absence of one or both testes

an·or·chous \-ˌkəs\ *adj* [NL *anorchus*, fr. Gk *anorchos*, fr. *an-* + *orchis* testicle — more at ORCHIS] : having no testes

an·or·chus \"\ *n, pl* **anorchi** \-,kī\ [NL, fr. *anorchus*, adj.] : one without testes or whose testes have not descended

ano·rectal \¦anō¦-\ *adj* [[2]*ano-* + *rectal*] : of, relating to, or involving both the anus and rectum ⟨~ surgery⟩

[1]an·o·ret·ic \¦anō¦red·ik, -nə-\ *also* **an·o·rec·tic** \-rek-\ *adj* [*anoretic* alter. of *anorectic; anorectic* fr. Gk *anorekt*os without appetite (fr. *an-* + *orektos* longed for, desired, stretched out, fr. *oregein*) + E *-ic*] : lacking appetite ⟨an ~ patient⟩ : causing loss of appetite ⟨an ~ drug⟩

[2]anoretic \,=='red-\ *n* -s : an anoretic agent

an·o·rex·ia \-'reksēə\ *n* -s [NL, fr. Gk, fr. *an-* + *orexis* desire, appetite, fr. *oregein* to stretch out, reach after — more at RIGHT] **1** : loss of appetite esp. when prolonged **2** : ANOREXIA NERVOSA

anorexia ner·vo·sa \-(,)nər'vōsə, -zə\ *n* [NL, nervous anorexia] : pathological loss of appetite from psychic causes typically accompanied by deficiency symptoms, emaciation, and wasting and atrophic changes

ano·rex·i·ant \,anō'reksēənt, -nə-\ *n* -s [NL *anorexia* + E *-ant*] : ANORETIC

ano·rex·i·gen·ic \¦==,reksə¦jenik\ *adj* [NL *anorexia* + E *-genic*] : causing loss of appetite ⟨an ~ drug⟩ : ANORETIC

an·or·gan·ic \¦an=¦==\ *adj* [*an-* + *organic*] : INORGANIC

anor·mal \(')ā¦==\ *adj* [F, fr. ML *anormalis*, fr. L *a-* [2]a- + LL *normalis* according to rule — more at NORMAL] : not normal — used in distinction from the positive emphasis of *abnormal* — **anor·mal·i·ty** \¦ā(,)='===\ *n* -ES

an·or·o·gen·ic \¦a,nȯ(,)rō¦jenik\ *also* **an·or·o·ge·net·ic** \¦=,=(,)=jə¦ned·ik\ *adj* [*an-* + *orogenic, orogenetic*] *geol* : free from mountain-making disturbance ⟨an ~ period⟩

an·or·thic \(')a¦nȯrthik, ə¦n-\ *adj* [*an-* + *orth-* + *-ic*] *mineralogy* : having unequal oblique axes : TRICLINIC

an·or·thite \ə'nȯr,thīt\ *n* -s [F, fr. *an-* + Gk *orthos* straight + F *-ite;* fr. its oblique crystals — more at ORTH-] : a white, grayish, or reddish mineral consisting of feldspar of oblique triclinic crystallization, composed of calcium aluminum silicate $CaAl_2Si_2O_8$, and occurring in many igneous rocks (hardness 6–6.5, sp. gr. 2.74–2.76) — **an·or·thit·ic** \¦a(,)nȯr¦thid·ik\ *adj*

anorthite-basalt *n* : a rock consisting of a basic variety of basalt with anorthite instead of labradorite

an·or·thi·tite \ə'nȯrthə,tīt\ *n* -s [*anorthite* + *-ite*] : a leucocratic differentiation rock of the gabbro family consisting almost entirely of anorthite

an·or·tho·clase \ə'nȯrthə,klās, -āz\ *n* -s [ISV *an-* + *orthoclase;* orig. formed as G *anorthoklase*] : a feldspar of chiefly sodium potassium aluminum silicate that is closely related to orthoclase but triclinic

an·or·tho·pia \,a(,)nȯr'thōpēə\ *n* -s [NL, fr. *an-* + *orth-* + *-opia*] : distorted vision in which straight lines appear bent or curved

an·or·those \ə'nȯr,thōs\ *n* -s [F, fr. *an-* + Gk *orthos* straight] : ANORTHOCLASE

an·or·tho·site \-ˌthə,sīt\ *n* -s [*anorthose* + *-ite*] : a granular plutonic igneous rock composed almost exclusively of a soda-lime feldspar (as labradorite) — **an·or·tho·sit·ic** \=¦==¦sid·ik\ *adj*

ano·scope \'ānə,skōp\ *n* -s [[2]*ano-* + *-scope*] : an instrument for facilitating visual examination of the anal canal — **anos·co·py** \ā'näskəpē\ *n* -ES

ano·sia \ə'nōzh(ē)ə\ [NL, fr. Gk *anosos* harmless, healthy (fr. *a-* [2]a- + *nosos* sickness) + NL *-ia*] *syn of* DANAUS

an·os·mat·ic \¦a(,)näz¦mad·ik, -ˌnəz¦-\ *adj* [*an-* + *osmatic*] **1** : having the organs of smell rudimentary — used esp. of toothed cetaceans **2** : lacking the sense of smell

an·os·mia \ə'näzmēə, -äs-, a'n-\ *n* -s [NL, fr. *an-* + Gk *osmē* smell (fr. *ozein* to smell) + NL *-ia* — more at ODOR] : loss or impairment of the sense of smell — **an·os·mic** \ə'n-, (')a¦n-\ *adj*

an·os·phre·sia \,anəs'frēzh(ē)ə, -(,)näs-\ *also* **an·os·phra·sia** \-'frā-\ *n* -s [NL, fr. *an-* + *-osphresia, -osphrasia*] : ANOSMIA

an·os·tra·ca \ə'nästrəkə\ *n pl, cap* [NL, fr. *an-* + *-ostraca*] : an order of small aquatic crustaceans (subclass Branchiopoda) lacking a carapace, having stalked eyes and 11 to 19 pairs of thoracic appendages, and including *Artemia* and similar freshwater forms — **an·os·tra·can** \-kən\ *adj or n*

[1]an·oth·er \ə'nəthə(r), a'n-\ *adj* [ME, fr. *an* + *other*] **1** : different or distinct from the one first named or considered ⟨the same scene viewed from ~ angle⟩: as **a** : altered or diametrically opposed ⟨it is ~ thing to ask us to affirm the reality of things we know to be illusions —G.F.Kennan⟩ **b** : changed in quality or behavior though the same in substance or identity ⟨a dog asleep was one thing, a dog very much awake and filled with active antagonism was ~ thing altogether —Jack McLaren⟩ ⟨since his illness he has been ~ man⟩ ⟨tomorrow is ~ day⟩ **c** : some other : LATER ⟨reserve this for ~ occasion⟩ ⟨~ time don't be so hasty⟩ **d** : FORMER, PAST ⟨the splendors of ~ age⟩ **2 a** : being one more in addition to one or a number of the same kind : ADDITIONAL, SECOND ⟨have ~ slice of cake⟩ ⟨this wall needs ~ coat of paint⟩ ⟨it will take ~ two years to finish the building⟩ **b** : not different or not significantly differing from the first named or considered or from others — used often with *just* ⟨just ~ mishap in a long series of mishaps that day⟩ **c** : patterned after or equal to ⟨he fancies himself as ~ Napoleon⟩ : NEW, FRESH ⟨bring me ~ cup, this one is chipped⟩

[2]another \"\ *pron* [ME, fr. *another*, adj.] **1** : an additional one of the same kind : one more ⟨one copy to send out, ~ for the files⟩ — often used after *one* and in distinction to *the other* to indicate more than one other ⟨one carried a gun, ~ a knife⟩ **2** : one other than oneself ⟨living subject to the will of ~⟩ : one that is different, separate, or in contrast to the first or present one ⟨peace is one thing but peace with dishonor is ~⟩ — often used reciprocally with *one* esp. of more than two ⟨and they said one to ~⟩; compare ONE ANOTHER **3** : one of a set or group of unspecified or indefinite things ⟨in one way or ~⟩ ⟨for one reason or ~⟩

another-guess *adj* [earlier *anothergets, anothergates*, fr. [1]*another* + *gates*, gen. of *gate* (way)] *archaic* : of another sort ⟨I should behave to him in *another-guess* manner —Henry Fielding⟩

an·ou·ra \ə'nu̇rə, -nau̇-\ [NL, fr. *an-* + *-oura* (var. of *-ura*)] *syn of* SALIENTIA

anourous *var of* ANUROUS

an·o·üs \'anəwəs\ *n, cap* [NL, fr. Gk *anoos, anous* silly, fr. *a-* [2]a- + *noos, nous* mind] : a genus of terns with a short tail and dark plumage found in warm countries — see NODDY 2a

an·o·vu·la·to·ry \(')a¦nōvyələ,tōrē, -näv-\ *adj* [*an-* + *ovulatory*] : without ovulation ⟨an ~ menstrual cycle⟩

an·ox·e·mia *also* **an·ox·ae·mia** \,a(,)näk'sēmēə\ *n* -s [NL, fr. *an-* + *ox-* + *-emia, -aemia*] : a condition of subnormal oxygenation of the arterial blood — called also *anoxic anoxia* — **an·ox·e·mic** *also* **an·ox·ae·mic** \¦=(,)=¦sēmik, -em-\ *adj*

an·ox·ia \a'näksēə, ə'n-\ *n* -s [NL, fr. *an-* + *ox-* + *-ia*] : hypoxia esp. of such severity or duration as to result in permanent damage to the affected individual or part

an·ox·ic \(')a¦näksik, ə'n-\ *adj* [NL *anox*ia + E *-ic*] **1** : of, relating to, or marked by anoxia ⟨a severe ~ state⟩ **2** *of anoxia* : caused by inadequate oxygenation of the blood — see ANOXEMIA

an·ox·i·da·tive \(')a¦näksə,dād·iv, ə'n-\ *adj* [*an-* + *oxidative*] : not characterized by oxidation

an·ox·y·bi·o·sis \a,näksə,bī'ōsəs, ə'n-\ *n* [NL, fr. *an-* + *oxy-* (oxygen) + *-biosis*] : ANAEROBIOSIS

an·ox·y·bi·ot·ic \=¦==,=¦äd·ik\ *adj* [*an-* + *oxy-* + *-biotic*] : of or relating to anoxybiosis

an·quera \an'kerə, aŋ-\ *n* -s [MexSp] *Southwest* : a tailpiece of leather for a stock saddle cut in the form of a crescent and attached to the base of the cantle from which it extends back to cover the rump and flanks of the horse

anr *abbr* another

-ans *pl of* -AN

ans *abbr* answer

ANS *abbr* autograph note signed

an·sa \'ansə\ *n, pl* **an·sae** \-,sē\ [NL, fr. L, handle; akin to MLG *öse* eye for a hook, loop, ON *æs* shoestring hole, Lith *ąsà* pot handle, OPruss *ansis* kettle hook] **1** : part of a celestial body having the appearance of a handle (as the projecting part of Saturn's rings) **2** *anat* : a loop or a structure resembling a loop

an·sar \'an,sär, ='=\ *n pl* [Ar *ansār*, pl. of *nāṣir* helper] *often cap* : the citizens of Medina who received and supported Muhammad following the hegira

an·sar·ie \an'sa(a)rēə\ *or* **an·sar·i·yah** \-rē(y)ə\ *n, pl* **ansarie** *or* **ansaries** *or* **ansariyah** *usu cap* [Ar *an-Nuṣayrīyah* the Nusairis] : NUSAIRI

an·sate \'an,sāt, -ˌsət\ *or* **an·sa·ted** \-,sād·əd\ *adj* [L *ansatus*, fr. *ansa* + *-atus* -ate, -ated] : having a handle or handle-shaped part

ansate cross *n* : ANKH

an·sa·tion \an'sāshən\ *n* -s : the making or providing of handles

an·schau·ung \'än,shau̇əŋ, -au̇·(,)u̇ŋ\ *n, pl* **an·schau·ung·en** \-ŋən\ *usu cap* [G, fr. MHG *aneschouwunge* contemplation, fr. *aneschouwen* to look at, contemplate (fr. OHG *anascouwōn*, fr *ana* on, at + *scouwōn* to look) + *-unge* (fr. OHG *-unga* -ing) — more at ON, SHOW] **1** : INTUITION; *specif* : sense intuition **2** : the element in knowledge that is directly given in sense awareness; *also* : sense perception or sense presentation : apprehension or immediate perception that involves fewest elements of rational insight

an·schluss \'än,shlu̇s\ *n* -ES *often cap* [G, lit., joining (after *anschliessen* to join), fr. *an* on, at (fr. OHG *ana*) + *schluss* closing, fr. MHG *sluz;* akin to OHG *sliozan* to close — more at ON, CLOSE] : UNION; *esp* : political or economic union of one government or territory with another ⟨some Austrians favored ~ with Germany⟩ ⟨the German-Austrian ~⟩ ⟨New Delhi then strongly protested against this forced ~ of Tibet —*New Republic*⟩ ⟨a campaign to effect an economic ~ of the notoriously jealous twin cities —*Newsweek*⟩

ansd *abbr* answered

anse de pa·nier \'äⁿsdə(,)pȧn'yā\ *n* [F, lit., basket handle] *archit* : a broadly elliptical or 3-centered curve

an·sel·mi·an \(')an¦selmēən\ *or* **an·sel·mic** \-mik\ *adj, usu cap* [St. *Anselm* of Canterbury †1109 Eng. scholastic philosopher + E *-ian* or *-ic*] : of or relating to the scholastic philosopher St. Anselm of Canterbury (1033–1109) ⟨the *Anselmian* logic⟩

an·ser \'an(t)sə(r), 'aan-\ *n, cap* [NL, fr. L, goose — more at GOOSE] : a genus of birds (family Anatidae) comprising the typical geese with large strongly serrated bills, rather simple plumage patterns, and comparatively short necks — compare BRANTA; see CHEN

an·ser·es \'==,rēz\ *n pl, cap* [NL, fr. L, pl. of *anser* goose] : a suborder of Anseriformes usu. being coextensive with the family Anatidae and including the ducks, geese, swans, and mergansers or in old classifications including most or all of the web-footed swimming birds and ranking as an order

an·ser·i·form \-ˌrə,fȯrm\ *adj* [NL *Anseriformes*] : of or belonging to the Anseriformes

an·ser·i·for·mes \ˌ⸗⸗⸗ˈfȯrˌmēz\ *n pl, cap* [NL, fr. *Anser* + *-iformes*] **:** an order of birds comprising the ducks, geese, swans, and mergansers and the screamers — see ANSERES

¹an·ser·ine \ˈ⸗⸗ˌrīn, -ˌrən\ *adj* [L *anserinus*, fr. *anser* goose + *-inus* -ine — more at GOOSE] **1 a :** of, relating to, or resembling a goose ⟨~ characteristics⟩ **b :** STUPID, SILLY ⟨ridiculous ~ behavior⟩ **2 :** of or belonging to the Anseres ⟨the ~ birds⟩

²an·ser·ine \ˈ⸗⸗ˌrēn, -ˌrən\ *also* **an·ser·in** \-ˌrən\ *n* -s [ISV *anser-* (fr. L *anser* goose) + *-ine*] **:** a crystalline base $C_{10}H_{16}N_4O_3$ found in the muscles of birds; methyl-carnosine

anserine skin *n* **:** GOOSE FLESH

an·ser·ous \ˈ⸗⸗rəs\ *adj* [L *anser* goose + E *-ous*] **:** like a goose **:** STUPID, SILLY — compare ¹ANSERINE

an·shan \ˈänˌshän\ *adj, usu cap* [fr. *Anshan*, Manchuria] **:** of or from the city of Anshan, Manchuria **:** of the kind or style prevalent in Anshan

an·si·form \ˈan(t)səˌfȯrm, ˈaan-\ *adj* [L *ansa* handle + E *-iform* — more at ANSA] **:** having a shape like a loop

an·su \ˈänˌsü, -zü\ *n* -s [Jap *anzu*, prob. fr. Chin *hsing⁴ tzu³* apricot, fr. *hsing⁴* apricot + *tzu³*, diminutive suffix] **1 :** APRICOT 1 **2 :** an apricot (*Prunus armeniaca ansu*) that is native to Korea but is cultivated also in Japan

¹an·swer \ˈan(t)sə(r), ˈaan-, ˈain-, ˈȧn-\ *n* -s [ME *answer*, *andswere*, fr. OE *andswaru* (akin to OFris *ondser*, OS *antswōr*, ON *andsvar*), fr. *and-* against + *-swaru* (fr. the root of OE *swerian* to swear) — more at ANTE-, SWEAR] **1 a :** something spoken or written in reply **:** a response to a question, call, summons, or appeal **:** a rejoinder to a remark, argument, or objection **:** letter sent in return for one received **:** REPLY ⟨an honest ~ to a fair question⟩ ⟨a soft ~ turns away wrath —Prov 15:1 (RSV)⟩ ⟨I called him but he gave no ~ —Song of Sol 5:6 (RSV)⟩ ⟨sent him five letters without receiving a single ~⟩ **b :** a correct response to a question intended to test knowledge (as one asked as part of an examination or one implied in a topic assigned for discussion) ⟨knew the ~s to only 3 of the 10 questions⟩ **2 a :** a reply to a charge or accusation **:** DEFENSE ⟨at my first ~ no man stood with me —2 Tim 4:16 (AV)⟩ **b** *common law* **:** a counterstatement of facts in a course of pleadings; *esp* **:** the counterstatement made by the defendant in an equity case by way of reply to the charges made by the complainant in his bill — distinguished from *demurrer* **c** *modern statutory law* **:** the defendant's pleading made in either law or equity often including a demurrer or any other pleading whereby an issue is made or tendered by the defendant (as where a statute provides that judgment by default may be entered if no answer is filed) **d** *English law* **:** the plaintiff's reply to a defendant's plea setting up circumstances in defense **3 :** something done or given in response or in return for something else **:** a reply made through action ⟨its publication . . . comes as the ~ to an acute demand —*Survey Graphic*⟩ ⟨the Western ~ to this move was the use of planes to supply food⟩ ⟨his only ~ was to take his hat and walk out⟩; *also* **:** responsive action ⟨received a slap by way of ~⟩ ⟨men from the neighboring villages gathered in ~ to the warning⟩ ⟨in ~ to your request⟩ **4 :** a solution of a problem: **a :** a solution resulting from mathematical operation or other similar exercise of the reasoning power ⟨the ~ to a chess problem⟩ ⟨the ~ to a cryptogram⟩ **b :** a solution of any intricate problem **:** explanation of a perplexing or difficult situation offered or accepted as correct and as furnishing a guide to procedure ⟨the world situation is not one to which there is an easy ~ —Dean Acheson⟩ ⟨the search for an ~ to life⟩ **5** *of a fugue* **:** the imitation or exact transposition of the subject by a different voice usu. at the interval of a fifth above or a fourth below

²answer \"\ *vb* **answered; answered; answering** \-s(ə)riŋ\ **answers** [ME *answeren*, *andsweren*, fr. OE *andswarian*, *andswerian*, fr. *andswaru*, n.] *vi* **1 a :** to speak or write in reply to something said or written by another **:** REPLY, RESPOND, REJOIN ⟨too nervous to ~ effectively⟩ ⟨~*ed* well in all his examinations except one⟩ ⟨refused to ~ on grounds of possible self-incrimination⟩ ⟨should give the . . . organizations attacked by him a chance to ~ through public hearings —S.H.Slichter⟩ ⟨think carefully before ~*ing*⟩ **b :** to serve or file an answer (sense 2) **2 a :** to be or make oneself responsible or accountable **:** undertake responsibility **:** give assurance or guaranty — used with *for* ⟨stood ready to ~ for the conduct of his children⟩ ⟨unless immediate reforms are made, we cannot ~ for the consequences⟩ ⟨no one can ~ for the future⟩ **b :** to meet or suffer the consequences of responsibility **:** make amends **:** ATONE, PAY — used with *for* ⟨a crime for which he ~*ed* with his life⟩ ⟨someday you will ~ for this⟩ **3 :** to be in conformity or correspondence in size, shape, position, character, or quality **:** be similar or equivalent **:** CORRESPOND — usu. used with *to* ⟨as in water face ~*s* to face, so the mind of man reflects the man —Prov 27:19 (RSV)⟩ ⟨a result that did not ~ to expectations⟩ ⟨the boundless ocean of prairie vanishing into the far horizon, and above it the ~*ing* disk of sky —Meridel Le Sueur⟩ ⟨~*ed* perfectly to the description we had been given of it⟩ **4 :** to make a responsive sound (as of an echo) **5 :** to act in response to a request, a signal, a controlling action or instrument, or any action performed elsewhere or by another esp. in obedience or sympathy or suitably in return ⟨we rang several times but no one ~*ed*⟩ ⟨if you make the sign of the Man then she will ~ with the sign of the Fox —Lafcadio Hearn⟩ ⟨underground treasures . . . seldom ~ clearly when they are queried by the geologist's instruments —*Time*⟩ ⟨a flashing light ~*ed* on the leading destroyer —Wirt Williams⟩ **6 :** to serve the purpose **:** be adequate or sufficient **:** SERVE, DO ⟨in teaching the young to think hard, any subject will ~ —C.W.Eliot⟩ — often used with *for* ⟨a sofa that was quite often made to ~ for a bed⟩ **7 :** to repeat or imitate a musical theme stated by a preceding voice ⟨the second voice ~*s* in the dominant⟩ ~ *vt* **1 :** to speak or write in response to **:** reply to ⟨~ me when I speak to you⟩ ⟨you have not ~*ed* my question⟩ ⟨wrote him several letters which he did not ~⟩ ⟨a job which he secured by ~*ing* an advertisement⟩; *also* **:** to say or write by way of reply ⟨~*ed* that they would be happy to come⟩ ⟨~*ed* the first thing that came into his head⟩ **2 :** to reply to by way of rebuttal, justification, or satisfactory explanation **:** meet successfully in opposition ⟨an argument that is not easily ~*ed*⟩ ⟨the only faith that can immediately and finally ~ communism —Stephen Spender⟩ **3 :** to reply to in defense (as a charge, accusation, or complaint) **:** make a defense against ⟨was held in bail to ~ a charge of petty larceny⟩ **4 :** to act or be in correspondence to: **a :** to give back in kind or in retaliation **:** return esp. suitably or commensurately ⟨~*ing* blow with blow⟩ ⟨~*ed* the enemy's fire shell for shell⟩ **b :** to correspond or conform to **:** agree with **:** FIT, SUIT ⟨if thy appearance ~ loud report —John Milton⟩ ⟨a man exactly ~*ing* the description broadcast by the police⟩ ⟨all work must ~ the specifications laid down⟩ **c :** to correspond to in position ⟨the subtle antiphonal effects that come from curve ~*ing* curve, angle echoing angle —Hunter Mead⟩ ⟨parts that ~ each other on a blueprint⟩ **5 :** to fulfill, satisfy, or meet (as an obligation, requirement, expectation) ⟨studies day and night to ~ all the debt he owes unto you —Shak.⟩ **:** be sufficient for **:** SERVE ⟨a first-aid kit designed to ~ all common emergencies⟩ ⟨if peace did not serve his purposes, war might ~ them —Francis Hackett⟩ **6 :** to reply favorably to (as a petition) ⟨our prayers were ~*ed*⟩ **7** *obs* **:** to atone or make amends for **:** suffer the consequences of ⟨a grievous fault, and grievously hath Caesar ~*ed* it —Shak.⟩ **8 :** to act in or by way of response to ⟨a word of protest would be ~*ed* by a blow from a scimitar —C.S.Forester⟩ ⟨a call for 1000 bottles of blood was ~*ed* promptly —Irene Kuhn⟩ ⟨the ship was listing heavily and wouldn't ~ her rudder⟩ ⟨three fire companies ~*ed* the alarm⟩ ⟨the phone is ringing but nobody ~*s* it⟩ **9 :** to solve or offer a solution for ⟨can you ~ this riddle⟩ ⟨tried not only to ~ problems but to anticipate them⟩

syn RESPOND, REPLY, REJOIN, RETORT: ANSWER is the most general term of this group and is used without especial suggestion for any action of saying, writing, or doing something called for in return ⟨to *answer* a question⟩ ⟨to *answer* the telephone⟩ It may suggest full or ample return ⟨he could assert, produce arguments, opinions, and information but he couldn't meet or *answer* arguments —Rose Macaulay⟩ RESPOND may suggest a ready, willing, or immediate answering; it is used in connection with various stimuli, ANSWER being more limited ⟨*responding* to that appeal, many men and women went forth into the foreign field —Elmer Davis⟩ ⟨they were all quick to learn and *respond* to ethical values —Frances G. Patton⟩ ⟨*responding* to the threat of death with behavior that is a degradation of the human spirit —*Time*⟩ REPLY may focus attention on the act of answering in the same way, covering the same ground, giving an appropriate return ⟨to *reply* to a charge⟩ ⟨to *reply* to a salute⟩ ⟨"if anything starts, we are lost, sir", observed the first lieutenant again. "I'm perfectly aware of it", *replied* the captain, in a calm tone —Frederick Marryat⟩ ⟨three deep throaty blasts announce the approaching ship, to which the bridge *replies* with a like number of shrill signals —*Amer. Guide Series: Minn.*⟩ REJOIN means merely making an answer but may apply to a sharp or pointed reply to an ill-taken comment ⟨"he can't sleep comfortably on that ship", she said. "In his present state", *rejoined* Andrew, "he might not sleep comfortably anywhere" —L.C.Douglas⟩ RETORT applies to a retaliatory countering answer to some criticism, charge, rebuke, or argument ⟨the plundering soldier in Georgia who *retorted* to Sherman's sermon with "you can't expect all the cardinal virtues for thirteen dollars a month" —D.W. Brogan⟩ ⟨"you wouldn't let me send you a book or two just as a friendly memento?" she cried, incredulous. "I don't take anything from anybody", he *retorted* —S.H.Adams⟩ **syn** see in addition SATISFY

— **answer back :** to reply impertinently **:** RETORT — **answer to a name of :** to have as one's name

an·swer·a·bil·i·ty \ˌ⸗s(ə)rəˈbilədˌē, -ətē, -i\ *n* -ES **:** the quality or state of being answerable

an·swer·a·ble \ˈ⸗s(ə)rəbəl\ *adj* **1 :** liable to be called to account **:** ACCOUNTABLE, RESPONSIBLE ⟨was no one ~ for the grim despair of that half-starved wretch —Anthony Trollope⟩ ⟨a legislative body politically ~ to the people⟩ **2** *archaic* **:** able to serve a purpose or fill a need: **a :** SUITABLE, FITTING ⟨attended with an ~ train, in rich liveries —Anthony Wood⟩ **b :** EQUAL, EQUIVALENT, ADEQUATE ⟨had the valor of his soldiers been ~, he had reached that year . . . the utmost bounds of Britain —John Milton⟩ **3** *archaic* **:** in conformity **:** ACCORDANT, CORRESPONDING ⟨this revelation . . . was ~ to that of the apostle to the Thessalonians —John Milton⟩; *esp* **:** corresponding in quantity or degree ⟨render your future progress ~ to your past improvement —Joshua Reynolds⟩ **4 :** capable of being answered or refuted **:** admitting a satisfactory answer ⟨an ~ argument⟩ ⟨an interrogation confined to questions supposedly ~ in one word⟩ **syn** see RESPONSIBLE

answered *past of* ANSWER

an·swer·er \ˈ⸗s(ə)rə(r)\ *n* -s **:** one that answers **:** RESPONDENT

answering *pres part of* ANSWER

an·swer·ing·ly \ˈ⸗s(ə)riŋlē, -li\ *adv* [ME, fr. *answering* (pres. part. of *answeren*) + *-ly*] **1 :** in answer **2 :** CORRESPONDINGLY

answering pennant *n* **:** a red and white vertically striped pennant with the fly red used in the International Signal Code primarily for the reply "signal is received and understood"

an·swer·less \ˈ⸗sə(r)ləs\ *adj* **:** without an answer: as **a :** giving no answer **:** UNANSWERING **b :** having received no answer **c :** impossible to be answered **:** UNANSWERABLE — **an·swer·less·ly** *adv*

answer print *n* **:** the first print of a motion-picture film in the form intended for release

answers *pl of* ANSWER, *pres 3d sing of* ANSWER

ant \ˈant, ˈaa-, ˈai- *rarely* ˈä-\ *n* -s *often attrib* [ME *ante*, *amete*, *emete*, fr. OE *ǣmette* (akin to OHG *āmeiza*), fr. *ǣ-* (fr. *of* from, off) + *-mette* cutter; akin to OHG *meizan* to cut — more at OF, MITE] **:** an insect of the family Formicidae (order Hymenoptera) all having a complex social organization, living in colonies with various castes performing special duties, usu. burrowing in the ground or in wood and making chambers and passages in which they store their food and raise their young, the adult males being winged and short-lived, the fertile females usu. temporarily winged, and the remainder of the colony made up of wingless sterile females called workers — compare CASTE, QUEEN TERMITE, VELVET ANT — **ants in one's pants :** a usu. obvious and excessive eagerness for action **:** RESTLESSNESS, IMPATIENCE

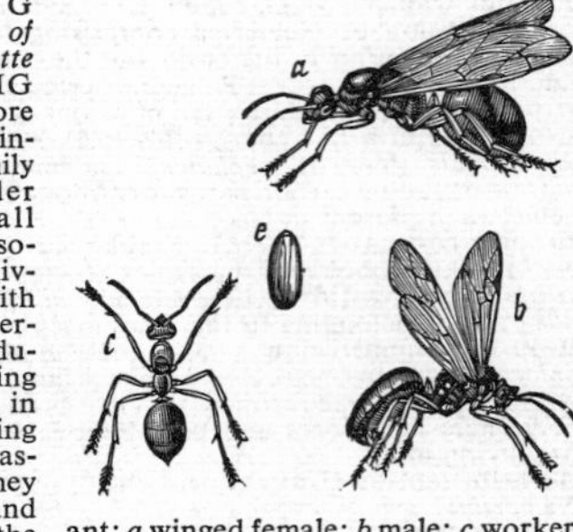

ant: *a* winged female; *b* male; *c* worker; *e* pupa

ant- — see ¹ANTI-

¹-ant \ənt, ᵊnt\ *n suffix* -s [ME, fr. OF, fr. *-ant*, pres. part. suffix, fr. L *-ant-*, *-ans*, pres. part. suffix of first conjugation, fr. *-a-* (vowel of first conjugation) + *-nt-*, *-ns*, pres. part. suffix; akin to OE *-nde*, pres. part. suffix, OHG *-nti*, ON *-ndi*, Goth *-nds*, Gk *-nt-*, *-n*, pres., fut., & aor. part. suffix, Skt *-nt*, pres., fut., & aor. act. part. suffix] **1 a :** one that performs (a specified action) **:** personal or impersonal agent ⟨assist*ant*⟩ ⟨claim*ant*⟩ ⟨cool*ant*⟩ ⟨deodor*ant*⟩ ⟨result*ant*⟩ **b :** thing that promotes (a specified action or process) ⟨expector*ant*⟩ **2 :** person or thing connected with ⟨annuit*ant*⟩ ⟨chemotherapeut*ant*⟩ **3 :** thing that is acted upon (in a specified manner) ⟨inhal*ant*⟩ ⟨ingest*ant*⟩ **4 :** thing that is used (for a specified purpose) ⟨disinfect*ant*⟩

²-ant \"\ *adj suffix* [ME, fr. OF, fr. *-ant*, pres. part. suffix] **1 :** performing (a specified action) or being (in a specified condition) ⟨denud*ant*⟩ ⟨propell*ant*⟩ ⟨somnambul*ant*⟩ **2 :** promoting (a specified action or process) ⟨expector*ant*⟩

ant *abbr* **1** antenna **2** anticipated **3** antiquarian; antiquity **4** antonym

¹an't \(ˈ)ant\ [by contr.] **:** an it **:** if it — compare ²AN 2

²an't *var of* AIN'T

¹an·ta \ˈantə\ *n, pl* **antas** \-əz\ *or* **an·tae** \-ˌtē, -ˌtī\ [L; akin to ON *önd* anteroom, Skt *ātā* doorframe, Arm *dr-and* doorjamb] **:** a pier produced by thickening a wall at its termination

²an·ta \", ˈän-\ *n* -s [Pg, tapir, elk, fr. Sp *anta* elk, modif. of Ar *lamṭ*] **:** TAPIR

³an·ta \"\ *n, pl* **anta** *or* **antas** \-əz\ *usu cap* [Pg, of AmerInd origin] **1 a :** a Tupian people dwelling west of the lower Tocantins river in northern Brazil — called also *Tapirana* **b :** a member of this people **2 :** the Tupian language of the Anta people

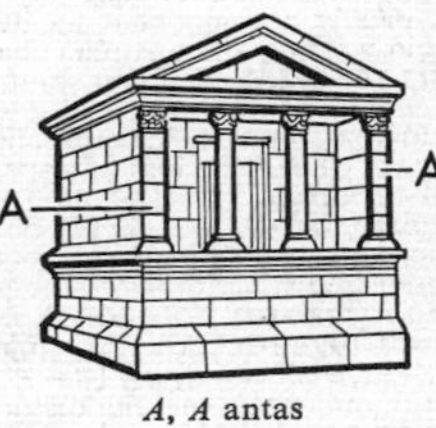

A, A antas

Ant·a·bus \ˈantəˌbyüs\ *trademark* — used for tetraethylthiuram disulfide

an·ta·cea \anˈtāsēə\ [NL] *syn of* CHONDRICHTHYES

¹ant·ac·id \(ˈ)ant-ˈ⸗⸗, (ˈ)aan-, (ˈ)ain-\ *also* **an·ti·ac·id** \ˌ⸗ˌtī-ˈ⸗⸗, -ˌtē-, -tə-\ *adj* [*anti-* + *acid*] **:** counteractive of acidity

²antacid \"\ *also* **antiacid** \"\ *n* -s **:** an agent that counteracts or neutralizes acidity (as an alkali or absorbent)

antae *pl of* ¹ANTA

an·tae·an \(ˈ)an-ˈtēən\ *adj, usu cap* [*Antaeus*, a mythical Libyan giant, son of Poseidon and Gaea (earth), who was long invincible because his strength was renewed by contact with the earth (fr. L, fr. Gk *Antaios*) + E *-an*] **:** possessed of superhuman strength with earthiness ⟨an ~ figure⟩

an·tag·o·nism \anˈtagəˌnizəm, aan-\ *n* -s [F *antagonisme*, fr. LGk *antagōnisma*, fr. Gk *antagōnizesthai* to contend with — more at ANTAGONIZE] **1 a :** actively expressed opposition, hostility, or antipathy ⟨~ between factions⟩ ⟨a yokel's ~ to city people⟩ **b :** opposition or contrariety of a conflicting activity, cause, or principle ⟨the ~ of democracy to dictatorship⟩ **:** contrariety of conflicting forces or tendencies ⟨alleged ~ between religion and science⟩ **2 :** opposition in physiological action: **a :** contrariety in the effect of contraction of muscles (as the extensors and flexors of a part) **b :** interaction of two or more substances such that the action of any one of them on living cells or tissues is modified (as by interference with the uptake or by an opposing physiological reaction) — opposed to *synergism* **3 :** the sum of the mutual interference between dissimilar organisms occupying or attempting to occupy the same ecological niche **syn** see ENMITY

an·tag·o·nist \-ˌnəst\ *n* -s [LL *antagonista*, fr. Gk *antagōnistēs*, fr. *antagōnizesthai*] **1 a :** one that contends with or opposes another (as in a fight, conflict, or other contest) **:** OPPONENT, ADVERSARY ⟨completely vanquishing his ~⟩ **b :** the principal opponent or foil of the main character in a drama or narrative ⟨the gangster leader was the ~ to the detective hero⟩ — opposed to *protagonist* **2 :** an agent that acts in physiological opposition ⟨contact between a tooth and its ~ in the opposing jaw⟩: as **a :** a muscle that contracts with and limits the action of an agonist with which it is paired **b :** a drug that opposes the action on the organism of another drug by a physiological, chemical, or competitive mechanism

an·tag·o·nis·tic \ˌ;⸗⸗ˈnistik, ⸗;⸗-, -ēk\ *also* **an·tag·o·nis·ti·cal** \-tәkәl, -ēk-\ *adj* **1 :** characterized by or resulting from antagonism **:** marked by or arising from opposition, hostility, antipathy, or discord ⟨slaves ~ to their master⟩ ⟨~ criticisms⟩ **:** marked by counter tendencies **:** OPPOSING ⟨monopoly and free trade are ~⟩ **2** *of colors* **:** complementary or nearly so **syn** see ADVERSE

an·tag·o·nis·ti·cal·ly \-ək(ə)lē, -ēk-, -li\ *adv* **:** in an antagonistic way **:** with antagonism

antagonistic cooperation *n* **:** the suppression of minor differences by two or more persons or groups to achieve a major common interest

antagonistic symbiosis *n* **:** PARASITISM 2

an·tag·o·nize *or* **an·tag·o·nise** \anˈtagəˌnīz, aan-\ *vb* -ED/-ING/-S [Gk *antagōnizesthai*, fr. *anti-* ¹anti- + *agōnizesthai* to struggle, fr. *agōn* contest — more at AGONY] *vt* **1 a** *archaic* **:** to contend with **:** OPPOSE ⟨stormed the castle and *antagonized* the enemy in pitched battle⟩ **b :** COUNTERACT ⟨the coldness of the air *antagonizing* the warmth of the metal⟩ **:** act in opposition to ⟨these effects are *antagonized* by atropine —Ernest Bueding & Harry Most⟩ **2 :** to make antagonistic **:** incur or provoke the hostility of ⟨~ his friends by open criticism of their actions⟩ ~ *vi* **:** to arouse antagonism against oneself ⟨a personality that ~*s* almost immediately⟩ **syn** see CONTEST

antaimerina *usu cap, var of* ANTIMERINA

ant·ambulacral \ˌant-, ¦aant-+\ *adj* [ˈ*anti-* + *ambulacral*] **:** situated away from the ambulacral region

an·ta·nan·a·ri·vo \ˌantəˌnanəˈrē(ˌ)vō\ *adj, usu cap* [fr. *Antananarivo* (Tananarive), Madagascar] **:** TANANARIVE

ant·apex \(ˈ)⸗+\ *n, pl* **antapexes** *or* **antapices** [ˈ*anti-* + *apex*] **:** the point of the celestial sphere from which the solar system is moving — compare SOLAR APEX

an·ta·ra \anˈtarə\ *n* -s [AmerSp, fr. Quechua *antára*] **:** a Peruvian panpipe

ant·arc·ta·lian \ˌant-¦ärkˈtālyən, -lēən *also* -n-¦tär-\ *adj, usu cap* [NL *Antarctalia*, the antarctic marine realm (fr. L *antarcticus* antarctic + NL *-alia*) + E *-an*] **:** of, relating to, or being the marine biogeographic realm that comprises all regions south of a line at which mean temperatures approximate 44° F

ant·arc·tic \(ˈ)ant-, (ˈ)aant- +¦- *also* -n-¦tä- *or* -n-¦tā-\ *adj, often cap* [alter. (influenced by L *antarcticus*) of earlier *antartic*, fr. ME *antartik*, fr. ML *antarticus*, alter. of L *antarcticus*, fr. Gk *antarktikos*, fr. *anti-* ¹anti- + *arktikos* arctic] **1 :** opposite to the north pole **:** relating to the south pole or to the region near it **2** *obs* **:** ANTIPODAL, OPPOSED, CONTRADICTORY

ant·arc·ti·ca \(ˈ)ant-¦ärktəkə *also* -n-¦tä-\ *adj, usu cap* [fr. *Antarctica*, the continent, fr. fem. of L *antarcticus*] **:** of or relating to the continent of Antarctica **:** ANTARCTIC

antarctic beech *n* **:** any of various plants of the genus *Nothofagus*; *esp* **:** an evergreen tree (*N. antarctica*) common in rainy regions of extreme southern So. America

antarctic circle *n, often cap A&C* **:** a small circle of the earth parallel to its equator approximately 23° 27′ from the south pole — see ZONE illustration

ant·arc·to·gae·an *or* **ant·arc·to·ge·an** \(ˈ)ant-¦ärktəˈjēən *also* -n-¦tär-\ *adj, usu cap* [NL *Antarctogaea*, *Antarctogea*, a biogeographic realm (fr. L *antarcticus* + NL *-o-* + *-gaea*, *-gea*) + E *-an*] **:** of, relating to, or being a biogeographic realm that comprises New Zealand and the Antarctic continent and islands — compare NOTOGAEAN

antas *pl of* ANTA

ant bear *n* **1 :** a So. American mammal (*Myrmecophaga jubata*) of the order Edentata that is about four feet in length exclusive of the long tail, has long shaggy gray fur with a black breast band and white stripe on the shoulder, and is toothless but has a long slender tongue with which it licks up ants and powerful claws with which it tears up logs and anthills — called also *great anteater*, *tamanoir*; see ANTEATER **2 :** AARDVARK

ant·bird \ˈ⸗ˌ⸗\ *n* **:** any of numerous birds believed to feed largely on ants; *esp* **:** a member of the family Formicariidae of the forest regions of tropical America that is small or medium sized, often black-and-white or brown, and of retiring habits — called also *ant thrush*

ant cattle *n pl* **:** plant lice or aphids tended by ants for the sake of their honeydew

ant cow *n* **:** an aphid from which ants obtain honeydew

¹an·te \ˈantē, ˈaan-\ *adv or prep* [*ante-*] **:** BEFORE

²ante \"\ *n* -s **1 :** a poker stake usu. arbitrarily fixed and usu. put up before the deal to build the pot ⟨the dealer called for a dollar ~⟩ **2 :** an amount paid in advance esp. as a share in a joint financial venture **:** amount charged each entrant or participant **:** PRICE ⟨the ~ of these shareholders —*Atlantic*⟩ ⟨considerations that tend to raise the ~ —*Amer. Fabrics*⟩

³ante \"\ *vb* **anted; anted; anteing; antes** [²*ante*] *vt* **:** to put up (an ante) **:** PAY, PRODUCE ⟨~*ing* dollar bills for the next hand⟩ — often used with *up* ⟨they *anted up* $1,000,000 to build a pilot plant —*Newsweek*⟩ ⟨~ up ideas in a general conversation —George Biddle⟩ ~ *vi* **:** to pay up — usu. used with *up* ⟨~ up or move into the street —*Time*⟩

an·te- \¦ante, ¦aan-, -tə\ *prefix* [ME, fr. L, fr. *ante* before, in front, in front of; akin to OE *and-*, *on-* against, OHG *ant-*, *int-*, ON *and-*, Goth *anda-*, *and-*, Gk *anti* before, against, Skt *anti* in the presence of, Hitt *hanti* in front — more at END] **1 a :** prior **:** precedent **:** earlier ⟨*ante*nati⟩ ⟨*ante*past⟩ ⟨*ante*type⟩ **b :** anterior ⟨*ante*room⟩ **:** forward ⟨*ante*flexion⟩ ⟨*ante*version⟩ **2 a :** prior to **:** earlier than ⟨*ante*classical⟩ ⟨*ante*natal⟩ ⟨*ante*partum⟩ **b :** in front of ⟨*ante*orbital⟩ ⟨*ante*temple⟩

anteater \ˈ⸗ˌ⸗⸗\ *n* **1 :** any of several mammals that feed largely or entirely on ants: as **a :** any of certain edentates or related animals with the mouth modified for this purpose and having a long narrow snout, a long tongue with which they lick up the insects, and enormously developed salivary glands (as the ant bear, the tamandua, and the pangolins) **b :** ECHIDNA **c :** BANDED ANTEATER **d :** AARDVARK **2 :** ANTBIRD

an·te·bel·lum \ˌantēˈbeləm, -tə-, ¦aan-\ *adj* [L *ante bellum* before the war] **:** existing before the war ⟨the four ~ years from 1936 to 1939 —Otto Springer⟩ or esp. the Civil War (1861–65)

an·te·brach·i·al \¦antə¦-, -tē-\ *or* **an·ti·brach·i·al** \"\ *adj* [NL *antebrachium*, *antibrachium* + E *-al*] **:** of or relating to the antebrachium

an·te·bra·chi·um \ˌ⸗⸗ˈ⸗⸗⸗\ *or* **an·ti·bra·chi·um** \"\ *n, pl* **antebrachia** *or* **antibrachia** [NL, fr. *ante-*, ²*anti-* + *brachium*] **:** the part of the arm or forelimb between the brachium and the carpus **:** FOREARM

an·te·cab·i·net \ˈantə,-, -tē-\ *n* [*ante-* + *cabinet*] **:** an antechamber to a private audience room

antecardium *var of* ANTICARDIUM

an·te·cede \ˌantəˈsēd, ¦aan-\ *vb* -ED/-ING/-S [L *antecedere*, fr. *ante-* + *cedere* to go, yield — more at CEDE] *vt* **:** to go before in time or place **:** PRECEDE ⟨thinkers who *anteceded* the rise of capitalism —Sidney Hook⟩ ~ *vi, obs* **:** to come before

an·te·ced·ence \ˌ⸗⸗ˈsēdᵊn(t)s\ *n* -s [L *antecedentia*] **1 :** PRIORITY, PRECEDENCE ⟨the ~ of certain institutions⟩ **2 :** a postulated sequence of erosional and orogenic events resulting in the development of an antecedent river or drainage system

an·te·ced·en·cy \-ᵊnsē, -si\ *n* -ES [L *antecedentia*, neut. pl. of *antecedent-, antecedens*, pres. part. of *antecedere* to go before — more at ANTECEDE] **1** : the condition of being antecedent : PRIORITY **2 antecedencies** *pl* : antecedent events

¹an·te·ced·ent \ˌantəˈsēdᵊnt, ˌaan-\ *n* -S [ME, fr. ML & L; ML *antecedent-, antecedens* grammatical antecedent, logical antecedent, fr. L *antecedent-, antecedens* logical antecedent, lit., one that goes before, fr. neut. of *antecedent-, antecedens*, pres. part. of *antecedere*] **1 a** : a substantive word, phrase, or clause referred to by a pronoun, typically by a following pronoun (as *John* in "I saw John and spoke to him" or *that he is ill* in "I hear that he is ill and it worries me") **b** : any word or group of words replaced and referred to by a substitute (as *at the meeting* in "I looked for him at the meeting but he wasn't there") **2** *logic* **a** (1) : the conditional element in a proposition (as *if A* in the proposition "if A, then B") (2) : either premise in a categorical syllogism **b** : the condition upon which truth depends **3** : the first term of a mathematical ratio (as *a* in the ratio *a* : *b*) **4 a** : an event, condition, situation, circumstance, or complex preceding and often influencing or conditioning an occurrence or issue — usu. used in pl. ⟨~*s* and consequences of the war⟩ **b antecedents** *pl* : the significant events, conditions, principles, traits, or activities of one's earlier life **5 a** : a predecessor in a series; *esp* : one that may serve as a model or stimulus for later developments in the series ⟨a stringed instrument believed to be an ~ of the banjo⟩ **b antecedents** *pl* : ANCESTORS, FOREFATHERS, PARENTS ⟨of English and Scotch-Irish ~*s*⟩ **6 a** *in canon and fugue* : the subject or opening theme restated by the consequent **b** : a proposing phrase or section of a musical passage as distinguished from the following responding phrase or section **syn** see CAUSE

²antecedent \ˈ≈≈ˈ≈≈\ *adj* [ME, fr. L *antecedent-, antecedens*, pres. part. of *antecedere*] **1** : existing or occurring before in time or order often with consequential effects : PRIOR, ANTERIOR, PRECEDING ⟨a synthesis of much ~ thought —H.O. Taylor⟩ ⟨rights ~ to government —*Time*⟩ **2** *logic* : prior to investigation, further knowledge, or setting up of conditions : a priori : PRESUMPTIVE ⟨an ~ probability⟩ **3** : established before the deformation of a surface and persisting after the deformation has taken place and in spite of it — used of drainage, a stream, or a valley; compare ²CONSEQUENT 5 — **an·te·ced·ent·ly** *adv*

an·te·ce·den·tal \ˈ≈≈ˌsēˈdentᵊl\ *adj* : of or relating to an antecedent

an·te·ces·sor \ˈ≈≈ˌsesə(r), -ntē-\ *n* -S [ME *antecessour*, fr. L *antecessor* — more at ANCESTOR] **1** : one that goes before (as in office or the possession of property) : previous incumbent or owner : PREDECESSOR **2** *obs* : ANCESTOR, PROGENITOR

an·te·cham·ber \ˈantē-, ˈaan-, -tə-\ *n* [alter. (influenced by *ante-*) of earlier *antichamber*, fr. F *antichambre*, fr. MF (part trans. of It *anticamera*, fr. *anti-* — fr. L *ante-* ante- — + *camera* room), fr. It *anti-* + MF *chambre* room — more at CHAMBER] : a room or foyer placed before and leading into a chief apartment and serving as a waiting room

an·te·chap·el \ˈ≈≈ˌ≈\ *n* [*ante-* + *chapel*] : a vestibule or anteroom to a chapel

ant·echi·no·mys \ˌant-ēˈkīnəˌmis\ *n*, *cap* [NL, fr. ¹*anti-* + *Echinomys*] : a genus of small insectivorous marsupials (family Dasyuridae) comprising the Australian jerboa pouched mice

ant·echi·nus \-ˈkīnəs\ *n*, *cap* [NL, fr. ¹*anti-* + L *echinus* hedgehog, sea urchin — more at ECHINUS] : a genus of Australian marsupial mice

an·te·choir \ˈantē-, ˈaan-, -tə-\ *n* [*ante-* + *choir*] **1** : a space enclosed or reserved for the clergy and choristers at the entrance to a choir **2** : the division of a divided choir that is farther away from the sanctuary

an·te·church \ˈ≈≈ˌ≈\ *n* [*ante-* + *church*] : a portico or narthex at the main entrance of a church

an·te·clyp·e·us \ˌ≈≈ˈ≈\ *n*, *pl* **anteclyp·ei** [NL, fr. *ante-* + *clypeus*] : the lower or anterior portion of the clypeus of certain insects

an·te·col·ic \ˈ≈≈ˈ≈≈\ *adj* [*ante-* + *colic*] : situated in front of the colon

an·te-com·mun·ion \ˈ≈≈≈ˈ≈≈\ *n*, *usu cap A&C* [*ante-* + *communion*] : the part of the Anglican or Episcopal service of Holy Communion up to or including the prayer for the whole state of Christ's church that is used separately with a blessing when there is no Communion

an·te·con·se·quent \ˈ≈≈ˈ≈≈≈\ *adj* [*ante-* + *consequent*] : consequent in the earlier and antecedent in the later stages of erosional history ⟨an ~ river⟩

an·te·con·so·nan·tic \ˈ≈≈ˌ≈≈ˈ≈≈\ *adj* [*ante-* + *consonantic*] : immediately preceding a consonant : PRECONSONANTAL

an·te·cor·nu \ˈ≈≈ˌ≈\ *n* [NL, fr. *ante-* + *cornu*] : the anterior cornu of either lateral ventricle of the brain

an·te·cos·ta \ˈantə-, -tē-\ *n*, *pl* **antecos·tae** *or* **antecostas** [NL, fr. *ante-* + *costa*] : the internal ridge that is externally manifested as a groove, that appears near the anterior margin of the typical dorsal or ventral plate of the primitive segment of an arthropod, and that provides attachment for the longitudinal muscles

an·te·cu·bi·tal \ˈ≈≈ˈ≈\ *adj* [*ante-* + *cubital*] : of or relating to the inner or front surface of the forearm

anted *past of* ANTE

¹an·te·date \ˈantəˌdāt, ˈaan-, -tē-\ *n* [earlier *antidate*, prob. fr. MF, fr. *anti-* ²anti- + *date*] : a prior date; *esp* : a date assigned to an event or affixed to a document that is earlier than the actual date of the event or document ⟨recognition of prior military service to establish the ~ of seniority in certain civilian categories⟩

²antedate \", ˌ≈ˈ≈, *usu* -ad-+V\ *vt* [earlier *antidate*, prob. fr. MF *antidater*, fr. *antidate*, n.] **1 a** : to date (as a check or deed) as of a time prior to that of execution **b** : to assign (an event) to a date prior to that of actual occurrence ⟨archeological discoveries may show that the coming of man to this continent has not been *antedated*⟩ **2 a** : to transfer to an earlier date or period **b** : to cause to occur earlier than expected : ACCELERATE **3** *archaic* : ANTICIPATE **4** : to precede in time : come before in date ⟨his death *antedated* his brother's⟩

¹an·te·di·lu·vi·an \ˌantēdəˈlüvēən ˌaan-, -tēd-, -ˌdī-, -vyən\ *also* **an·te·di·lu·vi·al** \-vēəl, -vyəl\ *adj* [*antediluvian* fr. *ante-* + L *diluvium* flood + E *-an*; *antediluvial* fr. *ante-* + *diluvial* — more at DELUGE] **1** : of or relating to the period before the flood described in the Bible ⟨~ man⟩ **2** : ANTIQUATED : made, evolved, or developed a long time ago ⟨an ~ automobile⟩ **syn** see OLD

²antediluvian \"\ *n* -S **1** : one that lived before the Flood described in the Bible **2** : one that is very old or behind the times

an·te·don \anˈtēdᵊn, -ˌdän\ *n*, *cap* [NL, perh. irreg. fr. Gk *Anthēdōn*, nymph associated with the ancient city Anthedon on the northern coast of Boeotia] : a large genus of recent and fossil comatulid crinoids having 10 or more arms

an·te·fix \ˈantəˌfiks, -tē-\ *n* -ES [L *antefixum*, fr. neut. of *antefixus*, past part. of *antefigere* to fasten before, fr. *ante-* + *figere* to fasten — more at DIKE] **1** *classical archit* : an ornament at the eaves concealing the ends of the joint tiles of the roof **2** *classical archit* : an ornament of the cymatium of a classic cornice that is sometimes pierced for the escape of water — **an·te·fix·al** \ˈ≈≈ˈfiksəl\ *adj*

antefix 2

an·te·fixa \ˌ≈≈ˈfiksə\ *n pl* [L, pl. of *antefixum*] : ANTEFIXES

an·te·flex·ion \ˌ≈≈ˈ≈\ *n* [ISV *ante-* + *flexion*] : a displacement forward of an organ (as the uterus) so that its axis is bent upon itself

an·te·fur·ca \ˌ≈≈ˈ≈\ *n*, *pl* **antefurcae** [NL, fr. *ante-* + *furca*] : a forked chitinous process projecting into the thoracic cavity from the sternal wall of the anterior thoracic segment of certain insects — **an·te·fur·cal** \ˈ≈≈ˈ≈\ *adj*

ant egg *n* : one of the white egglike pupae or cocoons of ants that are often dried and sold for food for captive turtles, fish, and birds

an·te·hy·poph·y·sis \ˌantē-, -tə-\ *n*, *pl* **antehypophyses** [NL, fr. *ante-* + *hypophysis*] : the anterior lobe of the pituitary body

anteing *pres part of* ANTE

an·te·ju·ra·men·tum \ˌantē-, -tə-\ *n*, *pl* **antejuramenta** [ML, fr. L *ante-* + *juramentum* oath — more at JURAMENT] : the preliminary oath required of the accuser and accused in a trial by compurgation

an·te·la·bi·um \ˌ≈≈ˈ≈\ *n*, *pl* **antelabia** [NL, fr. *ante-* + L *labium* lip — more at LIP] : the exterior or protruding margin of a lip

an·te·lope \ˈantᵊlˌōp, ˈaan-, -təˌlōp\ *n*, *pl* **antelope** *or* **antelopes** [ME, fabulous beast represented in heraldic devices, prob. fr. MF *antelop* savage animal with sawlike horns believed to live near the Euphrates, fr. ML *anthalopus*, fr. LGk *antholop-*, *antholops*] **1 a** : any of various Old World ruminant mammals of the family Bovidae that are esp. abundant in Africa, that differ from the true oxen by lighter racier build, horns directed upward and backward, and great variability in size, and that range from the ox-sized eland to forms scarcely larger than rabbits — see ADDAX, BLACK BUCK, DIK-DIK, GAZELLE **b** : any of various ruminant mammals chiefly of the family Bovidae that in appearance or behavior resemble true antelopes — compare PRONGHORN **2** : leather made from the hide of an antelope **3** : DUST 11

antelope brush *or* **antelope bitterbrush** *n* [so called fr. its use as browse] : BITTERBRUSH

antelope horn *n* : a spreading perennial (*Asclepidora decumbens*) of the family Asclepiadaceae resembling milkweed and having greenish white flowers and curved greenish pods — usu. used in pl.

antelope jack rabbit *n* : a very large pale jack rabbit (*Lepus alleni*) of the Arizona and western Mexican deserts having long ears and whitish sides suggesting the antelope's white rump when in motion

antelope squirrel *also* **antelope chipmunk** *n* : a small ground squirrel (*Citellus leucurus*) of the western U.S. having a white undersurface of the tail that when displayed over the back suggests the white rump of the American antelope; *also* : any of several similar and closely related rodents

an·te·lo·pi·an \ˈ≈≈ˈpēən\ *or* **an·te·lo·pine** \-pən, -ˌpīn\ *adj* : resembling or relating to antelopes

an·te·lu·can \ˌantəˈlükən\ *adj* [L *antelucanus*, fr. *ante-* + *luc-*, *lux* light + *-anus* -an — more at LIGHT] *archaic* : before dawn ⟨~ worship⟩

antemask *var of* ANTIMASQUE

an·te·me·rid·i·an \ˌantēməˈridēən, -tə-\ *adj* [L *antemeridianus*, fr. *ante-* + *meridianus* of noon — more at MERIDIAN] : occurring before noon : of or relating to the forenoon ⟨~ chores⟩ ⟨at 9 o'clock ~⟩ — compare ANTE MERIDIEM

an·te me·rid·i·em \-ˈridēəm, -ēˌem\ *adj* [L, before noon] : being before noon — abbr. *A.M.* or *a.m.*

an·te·mor·tem \-ˈmȯrtəm\ *adj* [L] : before death ⟨~ diagnosis⟩

an·te·na·tal \ˌantēˈ-, -tə-\ *adj* [*ante-* + *natal*] : of or relating to an unborn child ⟨~ injury⟩ : occurring during pregnancy ⟨~ care⟩ — compare INTRANATAL, NEONATAL, POSTNATAL

an·te·na·tus \ˌ≈≈ˈnādəs\ *n*, *pl* **antena·ti** \-ˌāˌtī\ [ML, firstborn son, ancestor, predecessor, fr. L *ante-* + *natus*, past part. of *nasci* to be born — more at NATION] : a person born before a certain time or event esp. with reference to the existence of political rights (as a person born in one of the 13 American colonies before the Declaration of Independence) — usu. used in pl. ⟨eligibility of *antenati* to hold office⟩; opposed to *postnatus*

an·te·nave \ˈantē-, -tə-\ *n* [*ante-* + *nave*] : a church porch leading into the nave only or a part of a porch that leads directly into the nave

an·te-ni·cene \ˈ≈≈ˈ≈\ *also* **an·te-ni·cae·an** \ˈ≈≈ˈ≈\ *adj*, *usu cap N* [*ante-* + *Nicene*, *Nicaean*] : of or relating to the Christian church or era before the first council of Nicaea (A.D. 325)

an·ten·na \anˈtenə, aan-\ *n*, *pl* **anten·nae** \-(ˌ)nē *also* -ˌnī\ *or* **antennas** [ML, fr. L *antemna, antenna* sail yard] **1** : one of the paired movable sensory appendages of the preoral segments of the head of certain arthropods (two pairs being present in most crustaceans, one in insects and myriapods) consisting typically of basal scape, intermediate pedicel, and elongated multisegmented terminal flagellum, the last often much specialized and bearing numerous sensilla that function chiefly as touch and olfactory receptors — called also *feeler* **2** : an organ on certain lower invertebrates (as rotifers) that is similar to the antenna of arthropods **3** *pl usu antennas* : a usu. metallic device (as a rod, wire, or arrangement of wires) for radiating or receiving radio waves

antennae of insects: *1* setaceous, *2* filiform, *3* moniliform, *4* serrate, *5* pectinate, *6* clavate, *7* capitate, *8* lamellate

antenna array *n* : a radio antenna consisting of numerous parallel wires arranged to transmit or receive substantially more in some directions than in others — called also *beam antenna*

antenna circuit *n* : the complete electric circuit of which the radio antenna is a part

antennae sword *n* : a sword of the late Bronze Age or early Iron Age whose hilt ends in a pair of ornaments suggesting antennae

antenna inductance *n* **1** : the inductance of an antenna, its value varying at different frequencies as evidenced by the current distribution **2** : the inductor or loading coil in an antenna circuit

an·ten·nal \(ˈ)anˈtenᵊl, (ˈ)aan-\ *adj* : of or relating to an antenna ⟨~ senses of insects⟩

antennal gland *n* : GREEN GLAND

an·ten·nar·ia \ˌan·teˈna(a)rēə\ *n*, *cap* [NL, fr. ML *antenna* + NL *-aria*; fr. the resemblance of the pappus of the staminate flowers to the antennae of certain insects] : a genus of woolly or hoary herbs (family Compositae) that are natives mostly of temperate regions and have small whitish discoid flower heads and a pappus formed of club-shaped bristles — see CAT'S-FOOT

an·ten·na·ri·i·dae \anˌtenəˈrīəˌdē\ *n pl*, *cap* [NL, *Antennarius*, type genus (fr. ML *antenna* + L *-arius* -ary) + *-idae*; fr. the antennary process on the head] : a family of fishes (order Pediculati) that have an elongated somewhat compressed body, a short head deeper than broad, a large nearly vertical mouth with protrusible premaxillaries, rather large pectoral fins with elongated carpal bones forming a wrist, a first dorsal fin consisting of separate spines of which the first is usu. elongated and provided with a membranous flap that projects forward over the mouth and functions as a bait, that scramble about among seaweeds, and that include the frogfishes and sargassum fishes — compare ANGLER

an·ten·na·ry \(ˈ)anˈtenərē, -ri\ *adj* : of, relating to, or like an antenna : bearing antennae ⟨the ~ segment of the head of an insect⟩

antennary gland *n* : GREEN GLAND

antenna switch *n* : LIGHTNING SWITCH

an·ten·na·ta \ˌantəˈnādə\ *n pl*, *cap* [NL, fr. ML *antenna* + NL *-ata*] *in some classifications* : a primary division of Arthropoda comprising the arthropods with antennae or less broadly the true insects and the myriapods

an·ten·nate \anˈtenət, -(ˌ)nāt\ *adj* : having antennae

an·ten·ni·fer \anˈtenəfə(r)\ *n* -S [NL, fr. ML *antenna* + NL *-i-* + *-fer*] *zool* : the pivotal process that supports the base of an antenna — **an·ten·nif·er·ous** \ˌan·teˈnif(ə)rəs\ *adj*

an·ten·ni·form \anˈtenəˌfȯrm\ *adj* : shaped like antenna

an·ten·nu·la \anˈtenyələ\ *n*, *pl* **antennu·lae** \-ˌlē, -ˌī\ [NL, dim. of ML *antenna*] : ANTENNULE

an·ten·nu·lar \(ˈ)anˈtenyələ(r)\ *or* **an·ten·nu·lary** \-ˌlerē\ *adj* : of, relating to, or bearing antennules

an·ten·nule \anˈte(ˌ)nyül\ *n* -S [F, dim. of *antenne* antenna, fr. ML *antenna* — more at ANTENNA] : a small antenna or similar appendage; *specif* : one of the anterior pair of antennae of crustaceans

an·te·num·ber \ˈantē-, -tə-\ *n* [*ante-* + *number*] : a number immediately preceding another

an·te·nup·tial \ˈ≈≈ˈ≈\ *adj* [*ante-* + *nuptial*] : preceding marriage ⟨an ~ contract⟩

an·te·o·per·cu·lum \ˌantēōˈpərkyələm\ *also* **an·te·o·per·cle** \-ˈpərkəl\ *n*, *pl* **anteopercu·la** \-lə\ *or* **anteoperculums** *also* **anteopercles** [NL *anteoperculum*, fr. *ante-* + *operculum*] : PREOPERCLE

an·te·or·bit·al \ˈ≈≈ˈ≈\ *adj* [*ante-* + *orbital*] *anat* : situated in front of the eye or orbit

ante over *sometimes cap A*, *var of* ANTONY OVER

an·te·pag·ments \ˌantēˈpagmənts, -tə-\ *or* **an·te·pag·men·ta** \-ˌpagˈmentə\ *n pl* [L *antepagmenta*, pl. of *antepagmentum*, fr. *ante-* + *pag-* (stem of *pangere* to make fast) + *-mentum* -ment — more at FANG] : trimmings added to a building esp. on the jambs of a door; *also* : a jamb so trimmed

an·te·pal·a·tal \ˈ≈≈ˈ≈\ *adj* [*ante-* + *palatal*] : articulated against the front half of the palate as a whole : articulated against the hard palate : PALATAL

an·te·par·tum \ˈ≈≈ˈpärd·əm\ *adj* [L *ante partum* before birth, fr. *ante* before + *partum*, acc. of *partus* birth, fr. *partus*, past part. of *parere* to bear offspring — more at ANTE-, PARE] : relating to the period before parturition : before childbirth ⟨~ infection⟩

an·te·past \ˈantəˌpast, -tē-\ *n* -S [*ante-* + *-past* (as in *repast*)] *archaic* : FORETASTE; *specif* : a first course to whet the appetite

an·te·pen·di·um *also* **an·ti·pen·di·um** \ˌantəˈpendēəm, ˌantē-\ *n*, *pl* **antependiums** *or* **antepen·dia** *also* **antipendia** \-dēə\ [ML *antependium*, fr. (assumed) *antependēre* to hang in front, fr. L *ante-* + *pendēre* to hang — more at PENDANT] : a hanging for the front of an altar, pulpit, or lectern

an·te·pe·nult \ˌ≈≈ˈ≈\ *also* **an·te·pe·nul·ti·ma** \ˌ≈≈-\ *n* -S [LL *antepaenultima*, fem. of *antepaenultimus* preceding the next to last, fr. L *ante-* + *paenultimus* next to last — more at PENULTIMATE] : the third syllable of a word counting from the end : the syllable preceding the next-to-last syllable (as *cu* in *accumulate*)

¹an·te·pe·nul·ti·mate \ˈ≈≈≈ˈ≈\ *adj* [*ante* + *penultimate* (after LL *antepaenultimus*)] **1** : of or relating to an antepenult **2** : coming before the next to last in any series

²antepenultimate \"\ *n* -S : something that is antepenultimate; *specif* : an antepenultimate syllable

ant·ep·ir·rhe·ma \(ˌ)antˌepəˈrēmə\ *n* [Gk *antepirrhēma*, fr. *anti-* ¹anti- + *epirrhēma* — more at EPIRRHEMA] : a continuation of an epirrhema following an antistrophe

anteport *n* [alter. (influenced by *ante-*) of earlier *antiport*, fr. It *antiporta*, fr. *anti-* ²anti- (fr. L) + *porta* gate, fr. L — more at PORT (gate)] *obs* : an outer port, gate, or door

an·te·po·si·tion \ˈantə(ˌ)-, -tē-\ *n* [fr. L *anteponere* to place before, after such pairs as L *ponere* to place: E *position* — more at POSITION] : the placing of one word or word group before another or esp. before one which by usual usage would precede it (as in *fiddlers three*)

an·te·post \ˈantəˌpōst\ *adj* [*ante-* + *post*] *Brit*, *of a horse-racing bet* : made before the racers' numbers are posted

an·te·predicament \ˈ≈≈+\ *n* [*ante-* + *predicament*] : a prerequisite to a clear understanding of philosophical predicaments or categories (as the definition of equivocal, univocal, and denominative terms) — **an·te·predicamental** \"+\ *adj*

an·te rem \ˌantēˈrem, ˌän-\ *or* **ante res** \-ˈrās\ *adv* [ML, lit., before the thing] : prior in reality or existence to particulars ⟨philosophical disputes over the proposition that universals exist *ante rem*⟩ — see AVICENNISM

an·te·rev·o·lu·tion·ary \ˌantēˌ≈≈ˈ≈≈\ *adj* [*ante-* + *revolutionary*] : of or relating to the time before a revolution (as the American Revolution)

ant·er·gic \(ˈ)anˈtərjik\ *adj* [¹*anti-* + *-ergic* (as in *synergic*)] *of muscles* : ANTAGONISTIC — **ant·er·gism** \ˈantərˌjizəm, anˈt-\ *n* -S

an·te·ri·ad \anˈtirēˌad\ *adv* [*anterior* + *-ad*] : toward the anterior part of the body

an·te·ri·or \(ˈ)anˈtirēə(r), -tēr-, (ˈ)aan-\ *adj* [L, comp. of *ante* before — more at ANTE-] **1 a** : situated toward the front : before in place — opposed to *posterior* **b** : relating to or situated near or toward the head or in headless animals the end most nearly corresponding **c** *bot* : ABAXIAL, INFERIOR **2 a** : before in time : ANTECEDENT **b** : logically prior or antecedent **3** *anat* : VENTRAL — used in ref. to man because of his upright position — **an·te·ri·or·ly** *adv*

anterior crural nerve *n* : FEMORAL NERVE

anterior horn *n* **1** : either of the ventral gray columns of the spinal cord **2** : the cornu of the lateral ventricle that curves outward and forward

anterior inferior spine *n* : the forward lower projection of the iliac crest

an·te·ri·or·i·ty \(ˌ)anˌtirēˈȯrəd·ē\ *n* -ES [prob. fr. F *antériorité*, fr. ML *anterioritat-*, *anterioritas*, fr. L *anterior* + *-itat-*, *-itas* -ity] : the quality or state of being anterior : PRIORITY

anterior lingual gland *n* : any of the nonserous or mixed glands near the tip of the tongue secreting mucus

anterior nasal spine *n* : the nasal spine formed by the union of processes of the two premaxillaries and projecting upward between the anterior nares

anterior superior spine *n* : the forward upper projection of the iliac crest

anterior tibial nerve *n* : PERONEAL NERVE

antero- *comb form* [NL, fr. L *anterior*] : anterior ⟨*antero*parietal⟩ : anterior and ⟨*antero*lateral⟩ : from front to ⟨*antero*posterior⟩

an·ter·o·grade \ˈantə(ˌ)rō,-, -ˌrə-\ *adj* [*antero-* + *grade*] : effective for a period immediately following a shock or seizure; *sometimes* : effective for and in effect during the period from the time of seizure to the present — used esp. of amnesia

an·te·room \ˈantē-, -tə-, ˈaan-\ *n* [*ante-* + *room*] **1** : a room placed before or forming an entrance to another and often used as a waiting room **2** *Brit* : a sitting room in an officers' mess

¹an·tes \ˈanˌtēz\ *n pl* : ANTAE

²antes *pl of* ANTE, *pres 3d sing of* ANTE

an·te·script \ˈantēˌskript\ *n* -S [*ante-* + *-script* (as in *postscript*)] : a passage (as a note affixed to a letter) written before or above — opposed to *postscript*

an·te·ster·num \ˌ≈≈ˈ≈\ *n*, *pl* **antesterna** [NL, fr. *ante-* + *sternum*] : the median underpart of an insect's prothorax

an·te·tem·ple \ˈ≈≈ˌ≈\ *n* [*ante-* + *temple*] : NARTHEX

an·te·type \ˈ≈≈ˌ≈\ *n* [*ante-* + *type*] : an earlier type : PROTOTYPE

an·te·ver·sion \ˌ≈≈ˈ≈\ *n* -S [*ante-* + *version* (condition of the uterus)] : the condition of being anteverted — used esp. of the uterus

an·te·vert \ˈ≈≈ˌvərt, ˌ≈≈ˈ≈\ *vt* -ED/-ING/-S [L *antevertere*, *anteverti* to come before, prevent, prefer, fr. *ante-* + *vertere* to turn — more at WORTH] : to displace (a body organ) so that the whole axis is directed farther forward than normal

an·te·vo·cal·ic \ˈ≈≈(ˌ)≈ˈ≈≈\ *adj* [*ante-* + *vocalic*] : immediately preceding a vowel : PREVOCALIC

¹anth- *or* **antho-** *comb form* [L *anth-*, fr. Gk *anth-*, *antho-*, fr. *anthos* — more at ANTHOLOGY] **1** : flower ⟨*anth*ecology⟩ ⟨*antho*cyanin⟩ **2** : flowerlike ⟨*Antho*zoa⟩

²anth- — see ¹ANTI-

anth *abbr* anthology

ant heap *n* : ANTHILL

ant·he·li·on \(ˈ)antˈhēlyən, (ˈ)anˈthē-, -lēən\ *n*, *pl* **anthe·lia** \-yə,-ēə\ *or* **anthelions** [Gk *anthēlion*, fr. neut. of *anthēlios*, alter. of *antēlios* opposite the sun, fr. *anti-* ¹anti- + *hēlios* sun — more at SOLAR] : the brightish white halolike spot appearing occas. on the parhelic circle opposite the sun — called also *antisun*, *countersun*

anthelix *var of* ANTIHELIX

1an·thel·min·tic \ˌant,helˈmintik, ˌan,thel-\ *also* **anthel·min·thic** \-nthik\ *adj* [*anti-* + Gk *helminth-, helmins* worm + E *-ic*] **:** expelling or destroying parasitic worms esp. of the intestine

2anthelmintic \"\ *also* **anthelminthic** \"\ *n* -s **:** an anthelmintic drug

an·them \ˈan(t)thəm, ˈaan-\ *n* -s [alter. of ME *antem, antefn*, fr. OE *antefn*, fr. LL *antiphona, antefana*, fr. LGk *antiphōna*, pl. of *antiphōnon*, fr. Gk, neut. of *antiphōnos* concordant, responsive, fr. *anti-* 1anti- + *-phōnos* (fr. *phōnē* sound, voice) — more at BAN] **1 a :** a psalm or hymn sung antiphonally or responsively **b :** a sacred vocal composition with words usu. from the Scriptures that is usu. sung by a church choir **2 a :** a song or hymn of praise or gladness; *typically* **:** a patriotic song **b :** NATIONAL ANTHEM

2anthem \"\ *vt* -ED/-ING/-S **:** to praise with or as if with an anthem

-an·the·ma \ˌanˈthēmə\ *n comb form, pl* **-anthe·ma·ta** \-ēməd·ə, -em-\ *or* **-anthemas** \-ēməz\ [LL, fr. Gk *-anthēma*; akin to Gk *anthos* flower — more at ANTHOLOGY] **:** eruption **:** rash ⟨*enanthema*⟩

an·the·mi·on \anˈthēmēən, -ē,än\ *n, pl* **anthe·mia** \-ēə\ [Gk, lit., flower, dim. of *anthemon*, fr. *anthos* flower — more at ANTHOLOGY] **:** an ornament consisting of floral or foliated forms arranged in a radiating cluster but always flat (as in relief sculpture or in painting) — called also *honeysuckle ornament*

anthemion

an·the·mis \ˈan(t)thəmə̇s\ *n* [NL, fr. L, chamomile, fr. Gk, fr. *anthos*] **1** *cap* **:** a large genus of Old World herbs (family Compositae) with pinnatifid leaves and daisylike heads in which the disk flowers are perfect and the ray flowers pistillate or neutral — see CHAMOMILE **2** -ES **:** the dried flower heads of a common chamomile (*Anthemis nobilis*) used as a bitter tonic and stomachic

-an·the·mum \ˈan(t)thəməm, ˈaan-\ *n comb form* [L, fr. Gk *anthemon* flower, fr. *anthos*] **:** plant having (such) a flower — in generic names ⟨*Helianthemum*⟩ ⟨*Xeranthemum*⟩

anthemwise \ˈ==,=\ *adv* [1anthem + *-wise*] **:** ANTIPHONALLY

an·ther \ˈan(t)thə(r), ˈaan-\ *n* -s [NL *anthera*, fr. L, medicine made from flowers, fr. Gk *anthēra*, fr. fem. of *anthēros* flowery, fr. *anthos* flower — more at ANTHOLOGY] **:** the part of the stamen in seed plants that consists of microsporangia, develops and contains pollen, and though sometimes sessile is usu. borne on a stalk — see FILAMENT, STAMEN — **an·ther·al** \-rəl\ *adj*

A A A

anthers, *A*

-an·the·ra \ˈan(t)thərə, ˈaan-; a(a)nˈthirə, -ērə\ *n comb form* [NL, fr. *anthera*] **:** plant having (such) an anther — in generic names ⟨*Adenanthera*⟩ ⟨*Pyxidanthera*⟩

an·the·raea \ˌan(t)thəˈrēə\ *n, cap* [NL, prob. irreg. fr. Gk *anthēros* flowery] **:** a genus of large moths (family Saturniidae) including the American polyphemus moth and several Asiatic species with larvae that produce silk of high quality — see TUSSAH

anther cell *or* **anther sac** *n* **:** POLLEN SAC

an·ther·i·cum \anˈtherə̇kəm\ *n, cap* [NL, irreg. fr. Gk *antherikos* asphodel; akin to Gk *athēr* beard of grain — more at ATHEROMA] **:** a genus of mainly African plants (family Liliaceae) with rootstocks like tubers, narrow leaves, and racemes of small white flowers with a rotate perianth

an·ther·id·i·al \ˌan(t)thəˈridēəl\ *adj* [NL *antheridium* + E *-al*] **:** relating to or characterized by an antheridium

antheridial cell *n* **:** a cell that remains after one or more vegetative or prothallial cells are cut off from the microspore and that gives rise to tube and generative cells of the male gametophyte of gymnosperms

an·ther·id·i·o·phore \ˌan(t)thəˈridēə,fō(ə)r\ *n* -s [NL *antheridium* + E *-o-* + *-phore*] **:** a gametophore bearing antheridia only (as in certain mosses and liverworts)

an·ther·id·i·um \-ˈridēəm\ *n, pl* **antherid·ia** \-ēə\ [NL, fr. *anthera* anther + *-idium*] **1** *in cryptogamous plants* **:** the male reproductive organ within which the male sexual cells are organized — compare ANTHEROZOID, SPERM, SPERMATOZOID **2** *in seed plants* **:** a minute structure of only a few cells developed within the microspore or pollen grain

an·ther·less *adj* **:** lacking anthers

-an·ther·ous \ˌan(t)thərəs, ˈaan-\ *adj comb form* [prob. fr. NL *-antherus*, fr. *anthera* anther] **:** having (such) an anther or (such or so many) anthers ⟨*decantherous*⟩ ⟨*phaenantherous*⟩

an·ther·o·zo·id \ˌan(t)thərəˈzōəd\ *n* -s [*anther* + *-o-* + *-zoid*] **:** a motile male gamete **:** SPERMATOZOID — **an·ther·o·zo·i·dal** \-ōdᵊl\ *adj*

anther smut *n* **:** a smut fungus (*Ustilago violacea*) that attacks certain plants of the pink family and forms spores instead of pollen in the anthers

-an·thery \ˈan(t)thərē, ˈaan-,ˈain-, -ri\ *n comb form* -ES **:** possession of anthers, esp. as indicated ⟨*phaenanthery*⟩

-an·thes \ˌanˌthēz, ˈaan-, ˈain-, -n(t)ˌthēz\ *n comb form* [NL, fr. Gk *-anthēs* blooming, flowered, fr. *anthos* flower — more at ANTHOLOGY] **:** plant having (such) a flower — in generic names ⟨*Achyranthes*⟩ ⟨*Polianthes*⟩ ⟨*Zephyranthes*⟩

an·the·sis \anˈthēsə̇s\ *n, pl* **anthe·ses** \-ē,sēz\ [NL, fr. Gk *anthēsis* bloom, fr. *anthein* to flower (fr. *anthos* flower) + *-sis*] **:** the action or period of opening of a flower **:** full bloom

an·thid·i·um \anˈthidēəm\ *n* [NL, fr. 1anth- + *-idium*] **1** *cap* **:** a genus of solitary bees that use resin as a cement in building their nests **2** *pl* **anthid·ia** \-ēə\ **:** a bee of the genus *Anthidium*

-anthies *pl of* -ANTHY

ant·hill \ˈ=,=\ *n* [ME *ante hil*, fr. *ante* ant + *hil* hill] **1 :** a mound thrown up by ants or by termites in digging their nest **2 :** a community congested with busy people unceasingly on the move ⟨the human ~ —H.G.Wells⟩

an·thine \ˈan,thīn, -,thə̇n\ *adj* [NL *Anthus* + E *-ine*] **:** of or belonging to the genus *Anthus*

antho- — see 1ANTH-

an·tho·car·pous \ˌan(t)thəˈkärpəs, -(ˌ)thō-\ *adj* [1anth- + *-carpous*] **1 :** having accessory parts ⟨~ fruits⟩ **2 :** composed chiefly of the enlarged and altered perianth or torus ⟨the ~ fruit of the wintergreen and the strawberry⟩

an·tho·cau·lus \ˌ==ˈkȯləs\ *n, pl* **anthocau·li** \-,lī\ [NL, fr. 1anth- + Gk *kaulos* stem] **:** the stalklike basal portion of the zooid in certain solitary corals from which the oral portion is pinched off to form a new zooid

an·thoc·er·os \anˈthäsərəs\ *n, cap* [NL, fr. 1anth- + *-ceros* (fr. Gk *keras* horn) — more at HORN] **:** a genus of liverworts (family Anthocerotaceae) having slender hornlike or awllike 2-valved capsules, the thallus more than one cell thick, and the involucre covering only the base of the sporangium

an·thoc·er·o·ta·ce·ae \an,thäsə(ˌ)rōˈtāsē,ē, -ˌrə-\ *n pl, cap* [NL, fr. *Anthocerot-, Anthoceros*, type genus + *-aceae*] **:** a family of liverworts (order Anthocerotales) having the gametophyte without definite pores and with irregular or dichotomous lobing or branching

an·thoc·er·o·ta·les \-ˈtā(,)lēz\ *n pl, cap* [NL, fr. *Anthocerot-, Anthoceros* + *-ales*] **:** an order of liverworts (class Hepaticae) having a thalloid gametophyte, green cells with one or occas. two chloroplasts, and rhizoids smooth or punctate

an·thoc·er·ote \anˈthäsə,rōt\ *n* -s [NL *Anthocerotaceae* & *Anthocerotales* & *Anthocerotes*] **:** one of the Anthocerotaceae or of the Anthocerotales or Anthocerotes — **an·thoc·er·o·te·an** \ˌ=ˌ==ˈrōd·ēən\ *adj*

an·thoc·er·o·tes \ˌ=ˌ==ˈrōd·(ˌ)ēz\ *n pl, cap* [NL, fr. *Anthocerot-, Anthoceros*] *in some classifications* **:** a class of plants coextensive with the order Anthocerotales

an·tho·co·di·um \ˌan(t)thəˈkōdēəm, -(ˌ)thō-\ *or* **an·tho·co·dia** \-dēə\ *n, pl* **anthoco·dia** \-ēə\ *or* **anthocodi·ae** \-dē,ē\ [NL, fr. 1anth- + *-codium* (fr. Gk *kōdeia* head of a plant)] **:** the free oral end of an anthozoan polyp the basal portion of which is united with other zooids in a common mass

an·tho·cor·i·dae \-ˈkȯrə,dē\ *n pl* [NL, fr. *Anthocoris*, type genus (fr. 1anth- + Gk *koris* bug) + *-idae*] **:** a family of small active bugs including a number predacious on other insects

an·tho·cy·an·i·din \-,sīˈanədə̇n\ *n* -s [ISV 1anth- + *cyanidin*] **:** a plant pigment (as cyanidin, delphinidin, or pelargonidin) formed by the hydrolysis of an anthocyanin and characterized by the same ring structure as the flavones and flavonols but having no ketone group

an·tho·cy·a·nin \-ˈsīənə̇n\ *also* **an·tho·cy·an** \-ˈsīən\ *n* -s [*anthocyanin* fr. *anthocyan* + *-in*; *anthocyan* fr. 1anth- + Gk *kyanos* dark blue] **:** any of a class of soluble glycoside pigments that are responsible for most of the blue to red colors in leaves, flowers, and other plant parts and differ from the plastid pigments in usu. being dissolved throughout the cell sap, that are reddish in an acid medium and violet or blue in an alkaline medium, and that yield anthocyanidins and sugars on hydrolysis

an·tho·cy·a·thus \-ˈsīəthəs\ *n, pl* **anthocya·thi** \-,thī\ [NL, fr. 1anth- + *cyathus*] **:** the oral disk that is pinched off from the basal portion in some solitary corals (as members of the genus *Fungia*) and that enlarges to become a new zooid

an·tho·di·um \anˈthōdēəm\ *n, pl* **antho·dia** \-dēə\ [NL, fr. Gk *anthōdēs* flowerlike (fr. *anth-* 1anth- + *-eidēs* -oid) + NL *-ium*] **1 :** the capitulum in plants of the family Compositae, the involucre simulating a calyx and the rays when present resembling petals **2 :** the involucre in the Compositae

an·tho·ecology \ˌan(t)(ˌ)thō+\ *n* -ES [1anth- + *ecology*] **:** the study of flowers as related to their environment

an·thog·ra·phy \anˈthägrəfē\ *n* -ES [1anth- + *-graphy*] **:** the description of flowers

an·thoin·ite \anˈthȯi,nīt\ *n* -s [F, fr. Raymond *Anthoine*, 20th cent. Belgian mining engineer + F *-ite*] **:** a mineral $Al(WO_4)(OH).H_2O$ consisting of a hydrous basic aluminum tungstate

an·tho·log·i·cal \ˌan(t)thəˈläjə̇kəl, ˈaan-, -ēk-\ *adj* **:** resembling or having the characteristics of an anthology — **an·tho·log·i·cal·ly** \-jə̇k(ə)lē, -ēk-, -li\ *adv*

an·thol·o·gist \anˈthäləjə̇st, aan-\ *n* -s **:** a maker of an anthology

an·thol·o·gize *or* **an·thol·o·gise** \-,jīz\ *vt* -ED/-ING/-S **1 :** to compile in an anthology **:** treat in an anthology ⟨~ American poetry⟩ **2 :** to publish (as a poem or piece of music) in an anthology ⟨the story has often been *anthologized*⟩

an·thol·o·gy \anˈthäləjē, aan-, -ji\ *n* -ES [NL *anthologia* collection of epigrams, fr. MGk, fr. Gk, flower-gathering, fr. *anthos* flower + *logia*, *logeia* collecting, fr. *legein* to collect, speak; akin to Skt *andha* herb, soma plant, and perh. to Alb *ënde* blossom — more at LEGEND] **:** a usu. representative collection of selected literary pieces or passages ⟨an ~ of 19th century poetry⟩ or of selected pieces in any art form (as songs or recordings, paintings, or sculpture) ⟨a huge ~ of paintings, sculpture, and models for architecture⟩; *also* **:** something felt to resemble such a collection ⟨his performance was an ~ of hilarity⟩

an·thol·y·sis \anˈthäləsə̇s\ *n, pl* **antholy·ses** \-,sēz\ [NL, fr. 1anth- + *-lysis*] **:** a metamorphosis of flower organs in which they become more or less foliaceous

an·tho·ly·za \an(t)thəˈlīzə\ *n* [NL, irreg. fr. 1anth- + Gk *lyssa* rage, rabies; fr. the gaping perianth, felt to resemble the open jaws of a rabid dog — more at LYSSA] **1** *cap* **:** a genus of southern African bulbous plants (family Iridaceae) with sword-shaped leaves and red and yellow flowers in 2-sided spikes **2** -s **:** a plant of the genus *Antholyza*

an·tho·me·du·sae \ˌan(ˌ)thōˈ=(ˌ)=, -(t)ˌthə-\ *n pl, cap* [NL, fr. 1anth- + *medusae* (pl. of *medusa*)] **:** a suborder of Hydroida that is sometimes regarded as a separate order of Hydrozoa and that includes hydrozoans, that has the hydranths and reproductive zooids unprotected by thecae, and that sometimes has medusae which bear the gonads in the manubrium and lack lithocysts — **an·tho·me·du·san** \ˌ=(ˌ)=ˈ=ˈ==\ *adj or n*

1an·tho·my·iid \ˌan(t)thəˈmīyə̇d\ *adj* [NL *Anthomyiidae*] **:** of or relating to the Anthomyiidae ⟨an ~ fly⟩

2anthomyiid \"\ *n* -s **:** one of the Anthomyiidae

an·tho·my·i·i·dae \-ˈmīyə,dē\ *n pl, cap* [NL, fr. *Anthomyia*, type genus (fr. 1anth- + *-myia*) + *-idae*] **:** a large family of two-winged flies closely related to the houseflies but usu. distinguished by a bristly abdomen and bristleless pleura and including a number of species of economic importance because of their plant-eating larvae (as the onion maggot, wheat bulb fly, and cabbage maggot)

an·thon·o·mus \anˈthänəməs\ *n, cap* [NL, fr. Gk *anthonomos* feeding on flowers, fr. 1anth- + *-nomos* (fr. *nemein* to pasture) — more at NIMBLE] **:** a large genus of weevils (family Curculionidae) including a number of destructive pests of cultivated plants — see BOLL WEEVIL

anthony over *sometimes cap A, var of* ANTONY OVER

an·thoph·a·gous \(ˈ)anˈthäfəgəs\ *adj* [1anth- + *-phagous*] **:** feeding on flowers ⟨~ larvae —*Biol. Abstracts*⟩

an·thoph·a·gy \-əjē\ *n* -ES [1anth- + *-phagy*] **:** the practice of feeding on flowers

an·thoph·i·la \-ələ\ [NL, fr. 1anth- + *-phila*] *syn of* APOIDEA

an·thoph·i·lous \anˈthäfələs\ *also* **an·tho·phil·i·an** \ˌan(t)thəˈfilēən, -(ˌ)thō-\ *adj* [*anthophilous* ISV 1anth- + *-philous*; *anthophilian* fr. 1anth- + *-phil* + *-ian*] **1 :** feeding upon or living among flowers ⟨~ insects⟩ **2** [NL *Anthophila* + E *-ous* or *-ian*] **:** of or belonging to the Anthophila

an·thoph·o·ra \anˈthäfərə\ *n, cap* [NL, fr. 1anth- + *-phora*] **:** a genus of solitary wood-boring bees (family Megachilidae)

an·tho·phore \ˈan(t)thə,fō(ə)r\ *n* -s [Gk *anthophoros* flower-bearing, fr. *anth-* 1anth- + *-phoros* (fr. *pherein* to bear) — more at BEAR (carry)] **:** a stalklike extension of the receptacle on which the pistil and corolla are borne (as in the pinks) — compare GYNOPHORE, STIPE

an·thoph·o·rous \anˈthäfərəs\ *adj* [Gk *anthophoros*] **:** flower-bearing **:** FLORIFEROUS ⟨~ plants⟩

an·tho·phyl·lite \ˌan(ˌ)thōˈfi,līt, -(t)ˌthə-, -ˈthäfə,-\ *n* -s [G *anthophyllit*, fr. NL *anthophyllum* (fr. *anth-* 1anth- + *-phyllum*, fr. Gk *phyllon* leaf) + G *-it* -ite] **:** an orthorhombic mineral $(Mg,Fe)_7Si_8O_{22}(OH)_2$ of the amphibole group that is often clove brown in color and lamellar or fibrous and is essentially a magnesium ferrous silicate — **an·tho·phyl·lit·ic** \ˌan(ˌ)thōfəˈlidik, (t)ˌthə-\ *adj*

a

section of flower of pink showing anthophore, *a*

an·thoph·y·ta \anˈthäfəd·ə, an(t)thəˈfīd·ə\ *n pl, cap* [NL, fr. 1anth- + *-phyta*] *in some classifications* **:** a division including all the flowering plants

an·tho·sper·mum \ˌan(ˌ)thōˈspərməm, -(t)ˌthə-\ *n, cap* [NL, fr. 1anth- + *-spermum*] **:** a genus of herbs and shrubs (family Rubiaceae) found in Africa and Madagascar and having small tubular flowers

-an·thous \ˈan(t)thəs, ˈaan-, ˈain-\ *adj comb form* [prob. fr. NL *-anthus*, fr. Gk *anthos* flower — more at ANTHOLOGY] **:** -flowered ⟨*gymnanthous*⟩ ⟨*monanthous*⟩ — **-an·thy** \ˌan(t)thē, ˌaan-, ˌain-, -thi\ *n comb form* -ES

an·tho·xan·thin \ˌan(ˌ)thōˈzanthə̇n, -(t)ˌthə-\ *n* -s [1anth- + Gk *xanthos* + E *-in*] **:** any of a group of ivory to yellow or orange crystalline pigments that are similar to anthocyanins in their solubility in plant cell sap but are derived in most cases from flavone or flavonol

an·tho·xan·thum \-thəm\ *n, cap* [NL, fr. 1anth- + *-xanthum* (fr. Gk *xanthos* yellow) — more at XANTHIC] **:** a genus of European grasses (family Poaceae) with contracted panicles, the spikelets consisting of one fertile floret and two sterile glumes below it — see SWEET VERNAL GRASS

an·tho·zoa \ˌan(ˌ)thōˈzōə, -(+)ˌthə-\ *n pl, cap* [NL, fr. 1anth- + *-zoa*] **:** a class of marine coelenterates comprising the corals, sea anemones, and related forms all of which lack medusa generation and are distinguished by polyps with radial partitions or mesenteries projecting from the body wall into the gastrovascular cavity — see ALCYONARIA, ZOANTHARIA — **an·tho·zo·an** \ˌ=(ˌ)=ˈzōən\ *adj or n* — **an·tho·zo·ic** \-ˈzōik\ *adj*

an·tho·zo·on \ˌ==ˈzō,än, -ən\ *n, pl* **anthozoa**

an·tho·zo·oid \-ˈzō,ȯid\ *n* -s [1anth- + *zooid*] **:** an individual zooid of a compound anthozoan

anthr- *or* **anthra-** *comb form* [ISV *anthracene*] **:** anthracene nucleus ⟨*anthrol*⟩ ⟨*anthragallol*⟩

anthrac- *or* **anthraco-** *comb form* [L *anthrac-*, fr. Gk *anthrak-*, *anthrako-* charcoal, carbuncle, fr. *anthrak-*, *anthrax* — more at ANTHRAX] **1 :** coal **:** carbon ⟨*anthracosis*⟩ ⟨*anthracolithic*⟩ ⟨*Anthracosaurus*⟩ **2 :** carbuncle ⟨*anthracnose*⟩ **:** anthrax ⟨*anthracoid*⟩ ⟨*anthracocide*⟩

an·thra·cene \ˈan(t)thrə,sēn, ˈaan-\ *n* -s [ISV *anthrac-* + *-ene*] **:** a crystalline tricyclic hydrocarbon $C_6H_4(CH)_2C_6H_4$ that is white with violet fluorescence when pure and is obtained in the last stages of the distillation of coal tar and used esp. in coatings (as for absorbing ultraviolet light) and as a luminescent material (as in scintillation counters) — see ANTHRAQUINONE; compare STRUCTURAL FORMULA

8 9 1 7 2 6 3 5 10 4

anthracene

anthracene blue *n, often cap A&B* **:** any of various blue mordant or acid anthraquinone dyes — see DYE table I

anthracene brown *n* **:** ANTHRAGALLOL

anthracene dye *n* **:** any of several mordant azo dyes — see DYE table I

anthracene oil *n* **:** a heavy green oil that distills over from coal tar above 270° C and is the principal source of anthracene, phenanthrene, and carbazole

anthraces *pl of* ANTHRAX

an·thra·cif·er·ous \ˌan(t)thrəˈsif(ə)rəs, ˌaan-\ *adj* [*anthracite* + *-ferous*] **:** containing or yielding anthracite ⟨~ strata⟩

an·thra·cite \ˈan(t)thrə,sīt, ˈaan-\ *or* **anthracite coal** *n* -s [L *anthracites* a kind of bloodstone, fr. Gk *anthrakitēs*, fr. *anthrak-*, *anthrax* coal + *-itēs* -ite — more at ANTHRAX] **:** a hard compact natural coal of high luster differing from bituminous coal in containing only a small amount of volatile matter and burning with a nearly smokeless flame

ANTHRACITE COAL SIZES AS SORTED IN THE U.S.

Name of size	Will pass through	Will not pass through
Broken	4⅜ in. round mesh	3¼–3 in. round mesh
Egg	3¼–3 " " "	2 7/16 " " "
Stove	2 7/16 " " "	1⅝ " " "
Chestnut	1⅝ " " "	13/16 " " "
Pea	13/16 " " "	9/16 " " "
Buckwheat		
No. 1	9/16 " " "	5/16 " " "
" No. 2 (Rice)	5/16 " " "	3/16 " " "
" No. 3 (Barley)	3/16 " " "	3/32 " " "
" No. 4	3/32 " " "	3/64 " " "
" No. 5	3/64 " " "	

anthracite silt *n* **:** minute particles of anthracite too fine to be used in ordinary combustion

an·thra·cit·ic \ˌ==ˈsid·ik, -itik, -ēk\ *adj* **:** of, belonging to, or resembling anthracite

an·thra·cit·i·za·tion \ˌ==,sīd·ə̇ˈzāshən, -ītə̇ˈ-\ *n* -s **:** the natural change of bituminous coal into anthracite by pressure or heat

an·thra·cit·ous \ˈan(t)thrə,sīd·əs, -ītəs, ˈaan-\ *adj* **:** containing anthracite

an·thrac·nose \anˈthrak,nōs\ *n* -s [F, fr. *anthrac-* + *-nose* (fr. Gk *nosos* disease)] **1 :** any of numerous plant diseases caused by imperfect fungi chiefly of the order Melanconiales, characterized by the formation of blisters, lesions like ulcers, or cankers often sunken and dark and with a brownish or purplish margin, and found destructive to important crop plants (as potatoes, melons, and cane fruits) **2 :** BITTER ROT

anthraco- — see ANTHRAC-

an·thrac·o·cide \(ˈ)anˈthrakə,sīd\ *adj* [*anthrac-* + *-cide*] **:** capable of destroying the bacteria of anthrax

an·thra·coid \ˈan(t)thrə,kȯid\ *adj* [ISV *anthrac-* + *-oid*] **1 :** resembling anthrax **2 :** resembling the carbuncle (sense 1) **3 :** resembling charcoal or carbon

an·thra·co·lith·ic \ˌ==kəˈlithik, -(ˌ)kō-\ *adj* [ISV *anthrac-* + *-lithic*] **:** containing anthracite or graphite

an·thra·co·mar·ti \ˌ==(ˌ)=ˈmärd·,ī\ *n pl, cap* [NL, fr. *Anthracomartus*, type genus, irreg. fr. *anthrac-*] **:** an order of carboniferous arthropods related to the spiders — **an·thra·co·mar·tian** \ˌ=ˈ==(ˌ)=ˈmärshən\ *adj or n*

an·thra·co·saur \ˈ==(ˌ)=ˌsȯ(ə)r\ *n* -s [NL *Anthracosaurus*] **:** a member of *Anthracosaurus* or a closely related genus of labyrinthodonts — **an·thra·co·sau·roid** \ˌ==(ˌ)=ˈsȯ,rȯid\ *n* -s

an·thra·co·sau·rus \ˌ==(ˌ)=ˈsȯrəs\ *n, cap* [NL, fr. *anthrac-* + *-saurus*] **:** a genus of labyrinthodonts from the coal measures of England perhaps in the direct ancestral line of the reptiles

an·thra·co·sil·i·co·sis \ˌ==(ˌ)=,=\ *also* **an·thra·sil·i·co·sis** \ˌ==-\ *n* \-,sēz\ [NL, fr. *anthrac-* + *silicosis*] **:** massive fibrosis of the lungs marked by shortness of breath from inhalation of carbon and quartz dusts — called also *miner's phthisis*

an·thra·co·sis \ˌan(t)thrəˈkōsə̇s\ *n, pl* **anthraco·ses** \-,sēz\ [NL, fr. *anthrac-* + *-osis*] **:** a benign deposition of coal dust within the lungs from inhalation of sooty air — compare ANTHRACOSILICOSIS — **an·thra·cot·ic** \ˌ=ˈ=ˈkäd·ik\ *adj*

an·thra·co·the·ri·um \ˌan(t)thrə(ˌ)kōˈthirēəm, -ˌkə-\ *n, cap* [NL, fr. *anthrac-* + *-therium*] **:** a genus of Tertiary artiodactyl mammals of Asia and Europe related to the pigs but sometimes as large as the rhinoceros

an·thra·fla·vic acid \ˌ==ˈflāvik-, -av-\ *n* [ISV *anthr-* + *flavic*] **:** a yellow crystalline compound $C_{14}H_6O_2(OH)_2$; 2,6-dihydroxy-anthraquinone

an·thra·fla·vin \ˌ==ˈflāvə̇n, -av-\ *n* -s [ISV *anthr-* + *flavin*] **:** ANTHRAFLAVIC ACID

anthraflavone GC *n, usu cap* **:** a vat dye — see DYE table I (under *Vat Yellow 2*)

an·thra·gal·lol \-ˈga,lōl, -lȯl\ *n* -s [ISV *anthr-* + *gallic* + *-ol*] **:** an orange crystalline compound $C_{14}H_5O_2(OH)_3$ used as a brown mordant dye; 1,2,3-trihydroxy-anthraquinone — called also *alizarine brown, anthracene brown*; see DYE table I (under *Mordant Brown 42*)

anthra green B *n, usu cap A&G* **:** a vat dye — see DYE table I (under *Vat Green 9*)

an·thra·lin \ˈan(t)thrələn\ *n* -s [*anthr-* + *-al* + *-in*] **:** a yellowish brown crystalline triphenol $C_{14}H_7(OH)_3$ used in the treatment of skin diseases

an·thran·i·late \ˌanˈthranə,lāt, -lə̇t, ˈan(t)thrə-\ *n* -s [ISV *anthranilic* + *-ate*] **:** a salt or ester of anthranilic acid

an·thra·nil·ic acid \ˌan(t)thrəˈnilik-\ *n* [ISV *anthr-* + *anilic*] **:** a white to pale yellow crystalline acid $NH_2C_6H_4COOH$ orig. obtained by fusing indigo with alkali, now made chiefly from phthalimide, and used as an intermediate in the manufacture of dyes (as indigo), pharmaceuticals, and perfumes; *ortho*-aminobenzoic acid

an·thra·nol \ˈan(t)thrə,nōl, -ȯl— *n* -s [ISV *anthracene* + *-ol*] **:** an unstable brown-yellow alkali-soluble fluorescent solid phenol $C_{14}H_9OH$ formed from anthrone by alkaline treatment and changing to anthrone on standing — called also *9-anthrol*

an·thran·o·yl \anˈthranə,wil\ *n* -s [*anthranilic* + *-o-* + *-yl*] **:** the radical $NH_2C_6H_4CO$— of anthranilic acid; *ortho*-aminobenzoyl

an·thra·pur·pu·rin \ˌan(t)thrəˈpərp(y)ərə̇n\ *n* -s [ISV *anthr-* + *purpurin*] **:** an orange crystalline compound $C_{14}H_5O_2(OH)_3$ found in commercial synthetic alizarin and also made separately; 1,2,7-trihydroxy-anthraquinone

an·thra·qui·none \-kwəˈnōn, -ˈkwi,nōn\ *n* -s [prob. fr. F, fr. *anthr-* + *quinone*] **:** a yellow crystalline diketone $C_6H_4(CO)_2C_6H_4$ obtained by oxidation of anthracene or by reaction of phthalic anhydride with benzene and used esp. in the manufacture of an important class of dyes

anthraquinone dye *n* **:** any of a large class of dyes (as mordant, acid, acetate, and vat dyes) derived from anthraquinone and noted for their fastness — see DYE table I

an·thra·qui·no·nyl \-,kwəˈnō,nil\ *n* -s [*anthraquinone* + *-yl*] **:** either of two univalent radicals $C_{14}H_7O_2$ derived from anthraquinone

an·thra·ru·fin \-ˈrüfə̇n\ *n* -s [ISV *anthr-* + L *rufus* red + ISV *-in*] **:** a yellow crystalline compound $C_{14}H_6O_2(OH)_2$ used in dye manufacture; 1,5-dihydroxy-anthraquinone

anthrasilicosis *var of* ANTHRACOSILICOSIS

an·thrax \ˈan,thraks, ˈaan-\ *n, pl* **anthra·ces** \-nthrə,sēz\ [ME *antrax* carbuncle, fr. L *anthrax*, fr. Gk, coal, charcoal, carbuncle; perh. akin to Arm *ant'el* glowing coal] **1** *archaic* **:** a carbuncle or malignant pustule **2 :** an infectious disease of warm-blooded animals (as cattle and sheep) caused by a spore-forming bacterium (*Bacillus anthracis*), transmissible from animals to man esp. by the handling of infected animal products (as hair), and characterized by external ulcerating nodules or by lesions in the lungs **3 :** the bacterium causing anthrax (sense 2)

an·thrax·o·lite \an'thraksə,līt\ *n* -s [Gk *anthrax* coal + E *-o-* + *-lite*] **:** a bituminous substance like coal that occurs in veins and masses in sedimentary rocks

an·thrax·y·lon \-sə,län\ *n* -s [NL, blend of Gk *anthrax* and *xylon* wood — more at XYL-] **:** the glossy jet-black constituent of banded bituminous coal including clarain and vitrain

-an·threne \'an,thrēn, 'aan-,'ain-\ *n comb form* -s [ISV *anthracene*] **:** substance related to anthracene ⟨phen*anthrene*⟩ ⟨methylchol*anthrene*⟩

an·thre·nus \an'thrēnəs\ *n, cap* [NL, irreg. fr. Gk *anthrēnē* hornet, wasp — more at ATHEROMA] **:** a genus of small beetles (family Dermestidae) having hairy larvae very destructive to woolen goods, fur, or other organic materials and including the carpet beetles and small gray and brown museum pests (*A. varius* and *A. musaeorum*) that destroy botanical and zoological specimens

an·thrib·i·dae \an'thribə,dē\ *n pl, cap* [NL, fr. *Anthribus*, type genus + *-idae*] **:** a small family of chiefly tropical short-snouted weevils mostly living and feeding on woody fungi or decaying wood

an·thris·cus \an'thriskəs\ *n, cap* [NL, fr. L, chervil, fr. Gk *anthriskos*; prob. akin to Gk *athēr* beard of grain — more at ATHEROMA] **:** a genus of Eurasian herbs (family Umbelliferae) with finely dissected leaves and short-beaked fruit

an·throne \'an,thrōn, ⁼'⁼\ *n* -s [ISV *anthr-* + *-one*] **:** a pale yellow alkali-insoluble crystalline ketone $C_{14}H_{10}O$ formed by partial reduction of anthraquinone and used in sulfuric⁼ acid solution as a colorimetric reagent for carbohydrates

anthrop- *or* **anthropo-** *comb form* [L *anthropo-*, fr. Gk *anthrōp-*, *anthrōpo-*, fr. *anthrōpos*, perh. irreg. fr. *andr-*, *anēr* man (male person) + *-ōpos* (fr. *ōps* face) — more at ANDR-, OPTIC] **:** human being ⟨*anthrop*oid⟩ ⟨*anthropo*genesis⟩

an·thro·pe·ic \,an(t)thrə'pēik, ,aan-\ *adj* [Gk *anthrōpikos* human, fr. *anthrōp-* anthrop- + *-ikos* -ic] **:** ANTHROPOGENIC

an·throp·ic \an'thräpik, -ēk, aan-\ *also* **an·throp·i·cal** \-əkəl\ *adj* [Gk *anthrōpikos*, fr. *anthrōpos* + *-ikos* -ic, -ical] **:** having to do with mankind or with the period of man's existence on earth ⟨~ gods⟩; *often* **:** ANTHROPOGENIC ⟨~ vegetation⟩

an·thro·pism \'⁼(t)thrə,pizəm, -(,)thrō-\ *n* -s [*anthrop-* + *-ism*] **:** ANTHROPOCENTRICISM

an·thro·po·cen·tric \,an(t)thrə,pō'sentrik, -ēk, -(,)thrō-, -,pə-, ,aan-\ *adj* [*anthrop-* + *-centric*] **:** centering in man: **a :** considering man to be the central or most significant fact of the universe **b :** assuming man to be the measure of all things **c :** interpreting or regarding the world in terms of human values and experiences — **an·thro·po·cen·tric·al·ly** \-ək(ə)lē, -ēk-, -li\ *adv* — **an·thro·po·cen·tric·i·ty** \,⁼(,)⁼(,)⁼'trisəd·ē; -ətē, -i\ *n* -ES

an·thro·po·cen·tri·cism \-'sentrə,sizəm\ *or* **an·thro·po·cen·trism** \-'sen,trizəm\ *n* -s **:** an anthropocentric theory or outlook

an·thro·po·chore \'⁼(,)⁼(,)⁼,kō(ə)r\ *n* -s [*anthrop-* + *-chore*] **:** a plant that is regularly distributed by man whether deliberately (as crop plants) or accidentally (as weeds) — **an·thro·po·cho·rous** \,⁼(,)⁼(,)⁼'kōrəs\ *adj*

an·thro·po·dermic \,⁼(,)⁼(,)⁼'⁼⁼\ *adj* [*anthrop-* + *dermic*] **:** consisting of human skin

an·thro·po·gen·e·sis \-'⁼⁼⁼\ *n, pl* **anthropogene·ses** [NL, fr. *anthrop-* + L *genesis*] **:** the study of the ontogenetic or phylogenetic origin and development of man — **an·thro·po·ge·net·ic** \,⁼(,)⁼(,)⁼⁼'⁼⁼\ *adj*

an·thro·po·gen·ic \,⁼(,)⁼(,)⁼'jenik, -ēk\ *adj* [*anthrop-* + *-genic*] **1 :** of or relating to anthropogenesis **2 :** involving the impact of man on nature **:** induced or altered by the presence and activities of man ⟨~ effects on vegetation⟩

an·thro·pog·e·ny \,⁼(,)⁼'päjənē\ *n* -ES [*anthrop-* + *-geny*] **:** ANTHROPOGENESIS

an·thro·po·ge·og·ra·phy \,an(t)thrə,pō-, -(,)thrō-, -,pə-, ,aan-\ *n* -ES [ISV *anthrop-* + *geography*; orig. formed as G *anthropogeographie*] **:** the study of man's geographic distribution — compare ETHNOGEOGRAPHY

an·thro·po·gon·ic \,⁼(,)⁼(,)⁼'gänik\ *adj* **:** relating to anthropogony

an·thro·pog·o·ny \,⁼(,)⁼'pägənē\ *n* -ES [*anthrop-* + *-gony*] **:** ANTHROPOGENESIS

an·thro·pog·ra·phy \-'pägrəfē\ *n* -ES [*anthrop-* + *-graphy*] **:** a branch of anthropology dealing with the distribution of the human race in its different divisions as distinguished by physical character, language, institutions, and customs — compare ANTHROPOLOGY, ETHNOGRAPHY

¹an·thro·poid \'an(t)thrə,pȯid, -thrō-, 'aan-; *sometimes* an'thrō-\ *adj* [Gk *anthrōpoeidēs*, fr. *anthrōp-* anthrop- + *-eidos* -oid] **1 a :** resembling man — used esp. of the apes of the family Pongidae including the gibbons, chimpanzee, orangutan, and gorilla **b :** shaped like a man ⟨~ mummy cases⟩ **2** *anat* **:** like that of an ape ⟨an ~ pelvis⟩ **3 :** resembling or suggesting an ape in ugliness, brute strength, brutality, or lack of perception and appreciation ⟨~ mobsters⟩

²anthropoid \"\ *n* -s **1 :** a person resembling an ape either in stature and gait or in lack of knowledge, perception, and appreciation **2 :** an anthropoid ape

an·thro·poi·dal \,⁼⁼'pȯidᵊl\ *adj* **:** resembling or being an anthropoid

an·thro·poi·dea \,⁼⁼'pȯidēə\ *n pl, cap* [NL, fr. *anthrop-* + *-oidea*] **1 :** the suborder of Primates including the monkeys, apes, and man, all being distinguished from the Lemuroidea by the larger cerebrum, more nearly enclosed orbit with the lachrymal gland opening within it, undivided uterus, and always pectoral mammae **2** *in some classifications* **:** HOMINOIDEA 1 — **an·thro·poi·de·an** \,⁼⁼⁼'dēən\ *adj*

an·thro·pol·a·try \,⁼(,)⁼'pälə·trē, -tri\ *n* -ES [*anthrop-* + *-latry*] **:** the worship of a human **:** deification of a man

an·thro·po·lith \⁼'thrōpə,lith, -'thrä-, '⁼(t)thrə-\ *or* **an·thro·po·lite** \-,līt\ *n* -s [ISV *anthrop-* + *-lith*, *-lite*] **:** a petrified human body or portion of it — **an·thro·po·lith·ic** \,⁼thrəpə¦lithik\ *or* **an·thro·po·lit·ic** \-¦lid·ik\ *adj*

an·thro·po·log·i·cal \,an(t)thrəpə'läjəkəl, (,)thrō-, -,pō-, -ēk-, aan-\ *also* **an·thro·po·log·ic** \-jik, -ēk\ *adj* **:** of or relating to anthropology — **an·thro·po·log·i·cal·ly** \-ək(ə)lē, -li\ *adv*

an·thro·pol·o·gist \,⁼(,)⁼'päləjəst, -lō-\ *n* -s **:** a specialist in anthropology

an·thro·pol·o·gy \-jē, -ji\ *n* -ES [NL *anthropologia*, fr. *anthrop-* + *-logia* -logy] **1 :** a study of man: as **a :** the study of body and mind and their interrelationships **b :** the study combining human anatomy and physiology **c :** ANTHROPOMETRY **d :** the study considering man's physical character, historical and present geographical distribution, racial classification, group relationships, and cultural history, the latter often limited to primitive stages **2 :** religious teaching about the origin, nature, and destiny of man from the perspective of his relation to God; *specif* **:** the branch of systematic theology dealing with anthropology

an·thro·po·man·cy \'⁼(,)⁼(,)⁼,mansē\ *n* -ES [*anthrop-* + *-mancy*] **:** divination from the entrails of a human being

an·thro·pom·e·ter \,⁼(,)⁼'pämad·ə(r)\ *n* -s [ISV *anthrop-* + *-meter*] **:** an instrument used for making anthropometric measurements and consisting of four hollow graduated tubes that fit into one another to form a rigid rod

an·thro·po·met·ric \,⁼(,)⁼(,)⁼'me·trik, -ēk\ *also* **an·thro·po·met·ri·cal** \-rəkəl, -ēk-\ *adj* **:** involving or based on anthropometry ⟨~ examination⟩ — **an·thro·po·met·ri·cal·ly** \-rək(ə)lē, -li, -ēk-\ *adv*

an·thro·pom·e·trist \,⁼(,)⁼'pämətrəst\ *n* -s **:** a specialist in anthropometry

an·thro·pom·e·try \-mətrē\ *n* -ES [F *anthropométrie*, fr. *anthrop-* + *-métrie* -metry] **:** the science of measuring the human body and its parts and functional capacities esp. as an aid to the study of human evolution and variation

an·thro·po·morph \'an(t)thrəpə,mȯrf, -(,)thrō-, -(,)pō-, 'aan-\ *n* -s [LL *anthropomorphus* of human shape — more at ANTHROPOMORPHOUS] **1 :** a representation of the human figure — used esp. of conventionalized primitive art **2** [NL *Anthropomorpha*] **:** a member of the Anthropomorpha

an·thro·po·mor·pha \,⁼(,)⁼(,)⁼'mȯrfə\ *n pl, cap* [NL, fr. Gk *anthrōpomorpha*, neut. pl. of *anthrōpomorphos* of human form] *in some former classifications* **:** a group of primates comprising the anthropoid apes and being equivalent to the family Pongidae; *broadly* **:** HOMINOIDEA 2

an·thro·po·morph·ic \,⁼(,)⁼(,)⁼'mȯrfik, -ēk\ *also* **an·thro·po·morph·i·cal** \-fəkəl, -ēk-\ *adj* [LL *anthropomorphus* + E *-ic*, *-ical*] **1 :** described or conceived in a human form or with human attributes **:** represented with human characteristics or under a human form **:** ascribing human characteristics to nonhuman things **:** crudely human or man-centered in character ⟨an ~ concept of God⟩ ⟨~ figurines⟩ ⟨crude ~ supernaturalism⟩ ⟨~ terms used in describing the activities of ants⟩ ⟨an ~ picture of the universe⟩ **2 :** derived from or having a human form ⟨an ~ monument⟩ ⟨geometric, zoomorphic, and ~ ornament⟩ — **an·thro·po·morph·i·cal·ly** \-fək(ə)lē, -li, -ēk-\ *adv*

an·thro·po·morph·i·dae \-fə,dē\ *n pl, cap* [NL, fr. *Anthropomorpha*, type genus (fr. LL, of human shape) + *-idae*] *syn of* PONGIDAE

an·thro·po·morph·ism \-,fizəm\ *n* -s [LL *anthropomorphus* + E *-ism*] **:** an interpretation of what is not human or personal in terms of human or personal characteristics **:** HUMANIZATION ⟨the language of ~ in saying that God sees, hears, knows, and loves⟩ **;** ANTHROPOCENTRICISM ⟨when a scientist speaks of force, he uses an ~ drawn from the act of will —W.L.Sullivan⟩ **:** PERSONIFICATION ⟨more of this ~: ". . . this was the mountain's first joyous cry as it awoke" —Joseph Braddock⟩

an·thro·po·morph·ist \-,fəst\ *n* -s **:** a believer in anthropomorphism — **an·thro·po·mor·phis·tic** \,⁼(,)⁼(,)⁼,⁼'fistik, -ēk\ *adj*

an·thro·po·mor·phite \,⁼(,)⁼(,)⁼'mȯr,fīt\ *n* -s [LL *anthropomorphita*, fr. LGk *anthrōpomorphitēs*, fr. *anthrōpomorphos* + *-itēs* -ite] **:** ANTHROPOMORPHIST

an·thro·po·mor·phi·za·tion \-,mȯrfə'zāshən\ *n* -s **:** the act or process of anthropomorphizing

an·thro·po·mor·phize *or* **an·thro·po·mor·phise** \-'mȯr,fīz\ *vb* -ED/-ING/-S [*anthropomorphous* + *-ize*, *-ise*] *vt* **:** to attribute a human form or personality to (as an animal or inanimate object) ⟨children ~ cats —Elmer Davis⟩ ~ *vi* **:** to attribute human form or personality to animals or things ⟨imaginative primitives ~ freely⟩

an·thro·po·mor·phol·o·gy \-,mȯr'fäləjē, -ji\ *n* -ES [*anthropomorphic* + *morphology*] **:** the use of anthropomorphic language esp. in application to God or a god

an·thro·po·mor·pho·sis \-'mȯrfəsəs *sometimes* -,mȯr'fō-\ *n, pl* **anthropomorpho·ses** \-,sēz\ [*anthropomorphic* + *-osis* (as in *metamorphosis*)] **:** metamorphosis into human form

an·thro·po·mor·phous \,⁼(,)⁼(,)⁼'mȯrfəs\ *adj* [LL *anthropomorphus*, fr. Gk *anthrōpomorphos*, fr. *anthrōp-* anthrop- + *-morphos* -morphous] **:** ANTHROPOMORPHIC — **an·thro·po·mor·phous·ly** *adv*

an·thro·pon·y·my \,an(t)thrə'pänəmē, -(,)thrō-, ,aan-\ *n* -ES [ISV *anthrop-* + *-onymy*] **:** a branch of onomastics that consists of the study of personal names

an·thro·po·path·ic \,⁼(,)⁼(,)pō¦pathik, -,pə¦p-, -ēk\ *adj* [*anthrop-* + *-pathic*] **:** ascribing human feelings to something that is not human ⟨~ writing⟩ — **an·thro·po·path·i·cal·ly** \-thək(ə)lē, -li, -ēk-\ *adv*

an·thro·pop·a·thism \,⁼(,)⁼'päpə,thizəm\ *n* -s [*anthropopathy* + *-ism*] **:** the ascription of human feelings to something that is not human

an·thro·pop·a·thite \-'päpə,thīt\ *n* -s [*anthropopathy* + *-ite*] **:** one who ascribes human feelings to something not human

an·thro·pop·a·thy \-'päpəthē\ *n* -ES [LGk *anthrōpopatheia* humanity, possession of human feelings, fr. Gk *anthrōpopathēs* having human feelings (fr. *anthrōp-* anthrop- + *-pathēs* -path) + *-ia*] **:** ANTHROPOPATHISM

an·thro·poph·a·gin·i·an \,⁼(,)⁼,päfə'jinēən\ *n* -s [*anthropophagus* + *-inian* (as in *Carthaginian*)] **:** CANNIBAL 1

an·thro·poph·a·gite \-'päfə,jīt\ *n* -s [NL *anthropophagus* + E *-ite*] **:** CANNIBAL 1

an·thro·poph·a·gous \,⁼(,)⁼'päfəgəs\ *adj* [L *anthropophagus*] **:** feeding on human flesh **:** man-eating **:** CANNIBAL — **an·thro·poph·a·gous·ly** *adv*

an·thro·poph·a·gus \"\ *n, pl* **anthropopha·gi** \-ə,jī\ [L, adj. & n., fr. Gk *anthrōpophagos*, fr. *anthrōp-* anthrop- + *-phagos* -phagous] **:** MAN-EATER, CANNIBAL

an·thro·poph·a·gy \-'päfəjē\ *n* -ES [NL *anthropophagia*, fr. Gk *anthrōpophagia*, fr. *anthrōpophagos* + *-ia*] **:** the eating by man of human flesh **:** CANNIBALISM

an·thro·po·phil·ic \,an(t)thrə,pō¦filik, -ēk, -(,)thrō-, -,pə-, ,aan-\ *also* **an·thro·poph·i·lous** \,⁼(,)⁼'päfələs\ *adj* [*anthrop-* + *-philic*, *-philous*] **:** attracted to man esp. as a source of food ⟨~ mosquitoes⟩; *sometimes* **:** indicating relative attraction to man ⟨~ indices of certain forest insects⟩ — **an·thro·poph·i·lism** \-'päfə,lizəm\ *n* -s

an·thro·poph·u·ism \,⁼(,)⁼'päfyü,izəm\ *n* -s [irreg. fr. *anthrop-* + Gk *phyē* growth, nature, character (fr. *phyein* to bring forth, arise) + E *-ism* — more at BE] **:** ascription of human nature to God or a god — **an·thro·poph·u·is·tic** \,⁼(,)⁼,⁼⁼'istik\ *adj*

¹an·thro·po·pi·the·cus \,an(t)thrə,pōpə'thēkəs, ,aan-, -'pithikəs\ [NL, fr. *anthrop-* + *-pithecus*] *syn of* ⁷PAN

²anthropopithecus \"\ *n, pl* **anthropopithe·ci** \-,sī\ *sometimes cap* [NL, fr. *anthrop-* + *-pithecus*] **:** a hypothetical mammal or group of mammals intermediate in character between man and apes

an·thro·po·psy·chic \,⁼(,)⁼(,)⁼,⁼'⁼\ *adj* [*anthrop-* + *psychic*] **:** relating to anthropopsychism — **an·thro·po·psy·chi·cal·ly** *adv*

an·thro·po·psy·chism \,⁼(,)⁼,⁼'⁼\ *n* -s [*anthrop-* + *psychism*] **:** ascription of a soul like that of man to nature or to something that governs natural processes

an·thro·po·scop·ic \,⁼(,)⁼,⁼¦skäpik\ *adj* **:** involving or based on anthroposcopy ⟨~ method⟩ — **an·thro·po·scop·i·cal·ly** \-ək(ə)lē\ *adv*

an·thro·pos·co·py \,⁼(,)⁼'päskəpē\ *n* -ES [*anthrop-* + *-scopy*] **:** determination of human bodily characteristics by inspection as opposed to exact measurements — compare ANTHROPOMETRY

an·thro·po·so·ci·ol·o·gy \,an(t)thrə,pō,-, -thrō-, ,aan-\ *n* -ES [*anthrop-* + *sociology*] **:** the sociological study of race by anthropological methods (as in the theories of Lapouge) as a means of establishing the social superiority of dolichocephalic peoples

an·thro·po·soph·i·cal \-¦säfəkəl\ *also* **an·thro·po·soph·ic** \-fik\ *adj* **:** relating to anthroposophy

an·thro·pos·o·phy \,⁼⁼'päsəfē\ *n* -ES [*anthrop-* + *-sophy*] **1 a :** knowledge of the nature of man **b :** human wisdom **2 :** a spiritual and mystical doctrine that grew out of theosophy and derives mainly from the philosophy of Rudolf Steiner, Austrian social philosopher (1861–1925)

an·thro·po·the·ism \,an(t)thrə,pō'-, -thrō-, -,pə-, ,aan-\ *n* -s [*anthrop-* + *-theism*] **:** the doctrine that the gods originated as men or are essentially human in their nature

an·thro·po·tom·i·cal \,⁼(,)⁼(,)⁼¦tämәkəl\ *adj* **:** relating to anthropotomy

an·thro·pot·o·mist \,⁼(,)⁼'päd·əməst\ *n* -s **:** a specialist in anthropotomy **:** ANATOMIST

an·thro·pot·o·my \-'pad·əmē\ *n* -ES [*anthrop-* + *anatomy*] **:** anatomy of the human body

-an·thro·pus \'an(t)thrəpəs, ,an'thrōpəs, -aan-,-ain-\ *n comb form* [NL, fr. Gk *anthrōpos* — more at ANTHROP-] **:** man — in generic names of primates ⟨Pithec*anthropus*⟩ ⟨Sin*anthropus*⟩

an·thryl \'an,thril, -ēl\ *n* -s [ISV *anthr-* + *-yl*] **:** any of three univalent radicals $C_{14}H_9$ derived from anthracene

an·thry·lene \'an(t)thrə,lēn\ *n* -s [*anthryl* + *-ene*] **:** any of several bivalent radicals $C_{14}H_8$ derived from anthracene

an·thu·ri·um \an'th(y)urēəm\ *n* [NL, fr. ¹*anth-* + *-urium* (fr. Gk *oura* tail); akin to Gk *orrhos* backside — more at ASS] **1** *cap* **:** a genus of tropical American plants (family Araceae) with large often highly colored leaves, a cylindrical spadix, and a colored spathe **2** -s **:** a plant of the genus *Anthurium*

an·thus \'an(t)thəs\ *n, cap* [NL, fr. L, a bird, prob. the yellow wagtail, fr. Gk *anthos*] **:** a genus of singing birds (family Motacillidae) comprising the typical pipits

-an·thus \'an(t)thəs, 'aan-,'ain-\ *n comb form* [NL, fr. Gk *anthos* flower — more at ANTHOLOGY] **:** organism having or resembling (such) a flower — in generic names in botany ⟨Cycl*anthus*⟩ ⟨Schiz*anthus*⟩ and zoology ⟨Oec*anthus*⟩

-anthy — see -ANTHOUS

an·thyl·lis \an'thiləs\ *n, cap* [NL, fr. L, a plant, fr. Gk] **:** a genus of Old World plants (family Leguminosae) with often yellowish red flowers and a pod enclosed in the calyx — see KIDNEY VETCH

¹an·ti \'an,tī, -,tē, 'aan-,'ain-\ *n* -s [¹*anti-*] **:** one who is opposed (as to a practice, law, policy, or movement) ⟨the division of the country into pros and ~s is widely deplored —*Atlantic*⟩

²anti \"\ *adj* [¹*anti-*] **1 :** opposed esp. to a proposal or policy ⟨the ~ group⟩ **2 :** TRANS — opposed to *syn*; compare ¹ANTI- 7

³anti \"\ *prep* [¹*anti-*] **:** in opposition or enmity to **:** AGAINST ⟨he has always been ~ sales tax⟩

⁴an·ti \'än(,)tē\ *n, pl* **anti** *or* **antis** *usu cap* [Sp, of AmerInd origin] **:** CAMPA

¹an·ti- *in pronunciations below*, ¦⁼(,)⁼ = ¦an,tī *or* ¦an,tē *or* ¦antə (-tə *occurring chiefly before consonants*) *or* ¦aan-*or* ¦ain-\ *or* **ant-** *or* **anth-** *prefix* [*anti-* fr. ME, fr. OF & L; OF, fr. L, against, fr. Gk, fr. *anti*; *ant-* fr. ME, fr. L, against, fr. Gk, fr. *anti*; *anth-* fr. L, against, fr. Gk, fr. *anti* — more at ANTE-] **1 a :** one opposing the claims of **:** rival **:** spurious ⟨*anti*christ⟩ ⟨*anti*king⟩ ⟨*anti*pope⟩ **b :** of the same kind but situated opposite, exerting energy in the opposite direction, or pursuing an opposite policy ⟨*anti*apex⟩ ⟨*ant*arctic⟩ ⟨*anti*cline⟩ ⟨*anti*school⟩ ⟨*anti*volition⟩ **c :** one that is opposite in kind to ⟨*anti*climax⟩ ⟨*anti*hero⟩ ⟨*anti*religion⟩ — *anti-* before consonants other than *h* and sometimes *ant-* before vowels and *anth-* before *h* (which is not repeated), but more frequently *anti-* even before *h* or a vowel **2 a :** opposing or hostile to in opinion, sympathy, or practice ⟨*anti*capitalist⟩ ⟨*anti*democratic⟩ ⟨*anti*romantic⟩ ⟨*anti*slavery⟩ ⟨*anti*union⟩ **b :** opposing in effect or activity **:** inhibiting **:** preventing **:** counteracting ⟨*ant*acid⟩ ⟨*anth*elminthic⟩ ⟨*anti*aging⟩ ⟨*anti*-Comintern⟩ ⟨*anti*enzyme⟩ ⟨*anti*fat⟩ ⟨*anti*fogging⟩ ⟨*anti*-inflationary⟩ ⟨*anti*slip⟩ ⟨*anti*trust⟩ **3 :** not ⟨*anti*grammatical⟩ ⟨*anti*logical⟩ **4 :** serving to prevent, cure, or alleviate (a pathological condition) ⟨*anti*arthritic⟩ ⟨*anti*spasmodic⟩ **5 a :** opposing or neutralizing another substance ⟨*anti*body⟩ ⟨*anti*serum⟩ **b :** substance that opposes or neutralizes (another substance); *esp* **:** substance that is an antibody to (a specified antigen) ⟨*anti*toxin⟩ **6 :** combating **:** destroying **:** defending against ⟨*anti*aircraft⟩ ⟨*anti*mine⟩ ⟨*anti*tank⟩ **7** *anti-* **:** TRANS- 3 — esp. in names of chemical structures in which the opposed atoms or groups are attached to carbon-to-nitrogen or nitrogen-to-nitrogen double bonds ⟨sodium *anti*-benzene-diazoate⟩; opposed to *syn-*; see BENZALDOXIME

²anti- *prefix* [MF & ML, fr. L *ante-*] **:** ANTE- — now little used because of possible confusion with ¹*anti-*

antiacid *var of* ANTACID

an·ti·air \¦⁼(,)⁼ *at* ¹ANTI- + ¦⁼\ *adj* [by shortening] **:** ¹ANTIAIRCRAFT

¹an·ti·air·craft \¦⁼(,)⁼¦⁼-\ *adj* [¹*anti-* + *aircraft*] **:** designed for or concerned with defense against air attack ⟨~ battery⟩ ⟨~ shell⟩ ⟨~ training⟩

²antiaircraft \"\ *n* -s **1 :** an antiaircraft weapon or weapons **2 :** the organizations that serve antiaircraft weapons, lights, and pointing devices **3 :** the flight and burst of antiaircraft shells

an·ti·air·craft·er \¦⁼(,)⁼¦⁼,⁼ə(r)\ *n* -s **:** ANTIAIRCRAFTSMAN

an·ti·air·crafts·man \¦⁼(,)⁼'⁼,⁼smən\ *n* **:** a member of an antiaircraft unit

an·ti·al·co·hol·ism \¦⁼(,)⁼¦⁼-\ *n* -s [¹*anti-* + *alcohol* + *-ism*] **:** opposition to immoderate use of alcohol

an·ti·an·a·phy·lax·is \¦⁼(,)⁼,⁼-\ *n, pl* **antianaphylax·es** [NL, fr. ¹*anti-* + NL *anaphylaxis*] **1 :** a condition in which an anaphylactic reaction is not obtained because of the presence of free antibodies in the blood **2 :** the state of desensitization to an antigen

an·ti·a·ne·mic \¦⁼(,)⁼⁼¦⁼⁼\ *adj* [¹*anti-* + *anemic*] **:** effective in or relating to the prevention or correction of anemia ⟨~ agent⟩ ⟨~ potency⟩

antianemic factor *or* **antianemic principle** *n* **:** a substance having antianemic activity; *esp* **:** VITAMIN B_{12}

an·ti·ar \'antē,är\ *n* -s [Jav *antjar* upas tree] **1 :** a poisonous gum resin from the upas tree **2 :** an arrow poison prepared from antiar

an·ti·arch \'antē,ärk\ *n* -s [NL *Antiarcha*] **:** one of the Antiarcha

an·ti·ar·cha \,⁼⁼'ärkə\ *n pl, cap* [NL, fr. ¹*anti-* + *-archa* (fr. Gk *archos* anus); fr. the contrast in the location of the anus with that of the Urochorda] **:** a subclass or other division of Placodermi comprising small Devonian freshwater ostracoderms having complex bony armor on the anterior part of the body and a pair of pectoral appendages resembling paddles

an·ti·ar·chi \-'är,kī\ [NL, fr. ¹*anti-* + *-archi* (fr. Gk *archos*)] *syn of* ANTIARCHA

an·ti·a·rin \'antēərən\ *n* -s [ISV *antiar* + *-in*] **:** either of two crystalline glycosides $C_{29}H_{42}O_{11}$ that are obtained from antiar and are powerful cardiac poisons

an·ti·a·ris \,antē'a(a)rəs\ *n, cap* [NL, fr. Jav *antjar*] **:** a genus of East Indian trees (family Moraceae) with axillary clustered flowers and fleshy purple fruits — see UPAS

¹an·ti·bac·chic \¦⁼(,)⁼ *at* ¹ANTI- + ¦⁼⁼\ *adj* [LL *antibacchius* + E *-ic*] **:** relating to or composed of antibacchii

²antibacchic \"\ *n* -s **1 :** ANTIBACCHIUS **2 :** an antibacchic cadence

an·ti·bac·chi·us \¦⁼(,)⁼-\ *n, pl* **antibac·chii** [LL, fr. LGk *antibakcheios*, fr. Gk *anti-* ¹anti- + *bakcheios* bacchius — more at BACCHIUS] **:** a metrical foot of three syllables the first two having either primary or intermediate stress and the last being unstressed (as in accentual poetry) or the first two being long and the last short (as in classical prosody)

¹an·ti·bac·te·ri·al \¦⁼(,)⁼(')-\ *adj* [ISV ¹*anti-* + *bacterial*] **:** inimical to bacteria

²antibacterial \"\ *n* -s **:** an antibacterial agent

an·ti·bal·loon·er \,⁼(,)⁼-\ *n* [¹*anti-* + *balloon* + *-er*] **:** SEPARATOR 3a(2)

an·ti·bi·ont \¦⁼(,)⁼ *at* ¹ANTI + 'bī,änt\ *n* -s [¹*anti-* + *symbiont*] **:** an organism participating in antibiosis

an·ti·bi·o·sis \,⁼(,)⁼,bī'ōsəs\ *n, pl* **antibio·ses** \-ō,sēz\ [NL, fr. ¹*anti-* + *-biosis*] **:** antagonistic association between organisms to the detriment of one of them or between one organism and a metabolic product of another (as that existing between certain bacteria and penicillin)

¹an·ti·bi·ot·ic \¦antē,bī¦äd·ik, -ätik, -ēk, -tə-, ,-bē-, ¦aan-, ¦ain-; -,tī,bī-\ *adj* [prob. fr. NL *antibioticus*, fr. ¹*anti-* + Gk *biōtikos* of life — more at BIOTIC] **1 :** tending to prevent, inhibit, or destroy life **2 :** of or relating to antibiosis **3 :** of, with, or relating to an antibiotic — **an·ti·bi·ot·i·cal·ly** \-ək(ə)lē, -li\ *adv*

²antibiotic \"\ *n* -s **:** a substance produced by a microorganism (as a bacterium or a fungus) and in dilute solution having the capacity to inhibit the growth of or kill another microorganism (as a disease germ)

an·ti·blas·tic \¦⁼(,)⁼ *at* ¹ANTI- + ¦blastik\ *adj* [¹*anti-* + *-blastic*] *biol* **:** antagonistic to growth; *esp* **:** of or relating to substances in the body of a host that interfere with normal metabolism of a parasite

an·ti·body \'anti,bädē, -ädi, -tē-, 'aan-, 'ain-\ *n* -ES [¹*anti-* + *body*; trans. of G *antikörper*] **:** any of various body globulins normally present or produced in response to infection or administration of suitable antigens or haptens that combine specifically with antigens (as bacteria, toxins, or foreign red blood cells) and neutralize toxins, agglutinate bacteria or cells, and precipitate soluble antigens — see AGGLUTININ, ANTITOXIN, PRECIPITIN

antibrachium *var of* ANTEBRACHIUM

an·ti·burgh·er \'an,tī,-, -,tē-, -,tə-; *Scot* 'änti-\ *n* -s *usu cap* [¹*anti-* + *burgher*] **:** a member of the party of the Scottish Secession Church that held that its members could not conscientiously take the burgess oath — compare BURGHER 2

¹an·tic \'antik, 'aan-, -ēk\ *n* -s [It *antico* ancient thing or person, fr. *antico*, adj.] **1 :** an instance of grotesquely ludicrous or other unusual or unpredictable behavior **:** CAPER — usu. used in pl. ⟨the wondrous ~s of the financial community —C.J.Rolo⟩ ⟨blackbirds fill the air with their ~s —D.C.Peattie⟩ **2** *archaic* **a :** GROTESQUE **b :** a fantastic sculptured human figure or face; *esp* **:** one serving as an architectural support **3** *archaic* **:** one who performs a grotesque or ludicrous part (as in a play) **:** BUFFOON, MERRY⁼

ANDREW **4** *obs* **:** one of the people of ancient times **:** ANTIQUE 2a **5** *obs* **:** a grotesque pageant

[2]**antic** \"\ *also* **an·ti·cal** \-tə̇kəl, -ēk-\ *adj* [It *antico* ancient, fr. L *antiquus* — more at ANTIQUE] **1** *archaic* **:** having incongruous ornament of grotesque design **:** BIZARRE ⟨walls overlaid with ~ work⟩ **2 a :** characterized by ludicrous or clownish extravagance or absurdity ⟨the first specific instance of Hamlet's assumed ~ disposition —Harold Goddard⟩ **b :** fantastic in a light gay fashion **:** FROLICSOME ⟨music gives a humorous lift to the ~ words —Douglas Watt⟩ **syn** see FANTASTIC

[3]**antic** \"\ *vb* **anticked** *also* **antickt; anticked** *also* **antickt; antick·ing** \-tə̇kiŋ, -ēk-\ **antics** [[1]*antic*] *vt, obs* **:** to make appear like a buffoon ~ *vi* **:** to perform antics ⟨minced, strode, and *anticked* in a parody of life and manners —Nora Waln⟩

antica *pl of* ANTICUM

an·ti·car·di·ac \ˌantē¦kärdē,ak, -tə̇- *sometimes* -ˌtī-\ *adj* [NL *anticardium* + E *-ac* (as in *cardiac*)] **:** belonging or relating to the anticardium

an·ti·car·di·um \-ˈkärdēəm\ *or* **an·te·car·di·um** \ˈantē, -tə̇-\ *n, pl* **anticar·dia** *or* **antecar·dia** \-dēə\ [NL, fr. [2]*anti-* or *ante-* + *-cardium*] **:** the pit of the stomach **:** EPIGASTRIUM

an·ti·cat·a·lyst \¦=(ˌ)= *at* [1]ANTI- + ¦=-\ *n* -s [[1]*anti-* + *catalyst*] **1 :** NEGATIVE CATALYST **2 :** a catalytic poison

an·ti·cath·ode \¦=(ˌ)='-\ *n* -s [ISV [1]*anti-* + *cathode*] **:** the target in an electron tube, esp. an X-ray tube

an·ti·cen·ter \¦=(ˌ)='-\ *n* -s [[1]*anti-* + *center*] **:** the direction in the sky opposite to that toward the center of the Milky Way galaxy

an·ti·chance \¦=(ˌ)='-\ *n* -s [[1]*anti-* + *chance*] **:** factors in evolution regarded as vitalistic and nonmaterialistic

an·ti·chlor \¦=(ˌ)='klō(ə)r\ *n* -s [[1]*anti-* + *chlorine*] **:** a substance used in removing the excess of chlorine or bleaching liquor left in paper pulp or textile fibers after bleaching

[1]**an·ti·cho·lin·er·gic** \¦=(ˌ)=ˌ=-\ *adj* [[1]*anti-* + *cholinergic*] **:** opposing or annulling the physiologic action of acetylcholine

[2]**anticholinergic** \"\ *n* -s **:** a substance having an anticholinergic action

an·ti·cho·lin·es·ter·ase \¦=(ˌ)=ˌ=-\ *n* -s [[1]*anti-* + *cholinesterase*] **:** a substance that inhibits a cholinesterase by combination with it: as **a :** a drug (as physostigmine or neostigmine) useful as a cholinergic stimulant whose effect on a cholinesterase is reversible **b :** a nerve poison; *esp* **:** an organic phosphate derivative (as tetraethyl pyrophosphate or parathion) useful as an insecticide whose effect on a cholinesterase is irreversible or only partially reversible

an·ti·chre·sis \ˌantə̇ˈkrēsə̇s\ *n, pl* **antichre·ses** \-ēˌsēz\ [NL, fr. Gk, fr. *anti-* [1]anti- + *chrēsis* use, fr. *chrēsthai* to use, need — more at CHRESTOMATHY] **:** a mortgage contract by which the mortgagee takes possession of the mortgaged property and has its fruits or profits in lieu of interest — **an·ti·chret·ic** \-ed·ik, -ēd·ik\ *adj*

an·ti·christ \'=(ˌ)= *at* [1]ANTI- + ˌkrīst\ *n* -s *often cap A, sometimes cap C with hyphen* [ME *anticrist, antecrist*, fr. OF & LL; OF *antecrist, anticrist*, fr. LL *Antichristus*, fr. Gk *Antichristos*, fr. [1]*anti-* + *Christos* Christ — more at CHRIST] **:** one who denies or opposes Christ

[1]**an·ti·chris·tian** \¦=(ˌ)¦-\ *adj* [[1]*anti-* + *Christian*] **1 :** of or relating to an antichrist **2 :** opposed to or rejecting Christ or Christianity — **an·ti·chris·tian·ism** \¦=(ˌ)='-\ *n* -s

[2]**antichristian** \"\ *n* -s **1** *obs* **:** a follower of an antichrist **2 :** one who is opposed to or rejects Christ or Christianity

antichristianity *n* -ES [[1]*anti-* + *christianity*] *obs* **:** the system or rule of an antichrist

antichronism *n* -s [Gk *antichronismos* use of one tense for another, fr. *anti-* [1]anti- + *chronos* time + *-ismos* -ism] *obs* **:** ANACHRONISM

an·tich·thon \an'tik,thän, -ˌthōn, -ˌthən\ *n, pl* **antichtho·nes** \-ˌthəˌnēz\ [LL, fr. Gk *antichthōn* counterearth, southern hemisphere, fr. *anti-* [1]anti- + *chthōn* earth — more at HUMBLE] **1 :** COUNTEREARTH **2** [L *antichthones*, pl., fr. Gk, pl. of *antichthōn*] *obs* **:** an inhabitant of the antipodes — usu. used in pl.

[1]**an·tic·i·pant** \an'tisəpənt, aan-\ *adj* [L *anticipant-, anticipans*, pres. part. of *anticipare*] **:** ANTICIPATING, EXPECTANT — usu. used with *of* ⟨~ of gaining support⟩

[2]**anticipant** \"\ *n* -s **:** one that anticipates ⟨he remains an ~ to the end —J.M.Grant⟩

an·tic·i·pate \an'tisəˌpāt, aan-, *usu* -ād·+V\ *vb* -ED/-ING/-S [L *anticipatus*, past part. of *anticipare* to anticipate, fr. *anti-* [2]ante- + *-cipare* (fr. *-cipere*, fr. *capere* to take) — more at HEAVE] *vt* **1 :** to consider in advance **:** give advance thought, discussion, or treatment to ⟨the author had *anticipated* the question in a preceding chapter⟩ **2 :** to cause to occur prematurely ⟨it is impossible for the bank to ~ payment —J.A. Todd⟩ **:** meet (an obligation) before a due date **3 a :** to deal with in advance **:** counter, guard against, or forestall by prior action ⟨*anticipating* the action of the enemy and taking due precautions⟩ **b :** to foresee and satisfy or fulfill beforehand ⟨*anticipating* the customers' demands⟩ **4 :** to realize or actualize before an expected or plausible time ⟨*anticipating* the happiness of heaven⟩ **5 :** to use or expend in advance of actual possession ⟨*anticipating* his salary and buying many clothes⟩ **6 :** to act before (another) often with the intent or effect of checking or countering ⟨*anticipating* his opponent and protecting the threatened area⟩ **7 :** look forward to as certain ⟨to ~ the stormy weather⟩ ~ *vi* **1 :** to come before the expected time — usu. used of medical symptoms **2 :** to speak or write in a way conditioned by knowledge or expectation of what will be treated later **syn** see FORESEE, PREVENT

an·tic·i·pa·tion \=ˌ==ˈpāshən\ *n* -s [ME *anticipacioun*, fr. L *anticipation-, anticipatio*, fr. *anticipatus* + *-ion-, -io* -ion] **1 :** the use or spending of money before it is due or available: as **a :** the taking or alienation (as by assignment) of the income of a trust estate before it is due **b :** a discount for advance payment of a bill for goods or services where no cash discount is specified in the terms of sale **2 a :** intuitive preconception **:** a priori knowledge **:** INTUITION **b** *obs* **:** formation of an opinion before all the facts are known **:** PREJUDICE, PREPOSSESSION **3 :** a prior action that takes into account, deals with, or prevents the action of another **4 a :** occurrence before the normal or expected time **b :** assignment to or observance at a time earlier than the correct one; *specif* **:** regressive assimilation **c :** prior recognition, realization, invention, or accomplishment ⟨a species of early competitors or ~s of pocket watches —A.L.Kroeber⟩ **d :** the act of looking forward **:** EXPECTATION ⟨a mass meeting held in ~ of the visit —R.M.Lovett⟩; *specif* **:** pleasurable expectation ⟨look forward with ~ to his book —*Encounter*⟩ **5 :** the entry of one or more tones of a succeeding chord or the entire chord as a rhythmic upbeat to the tone or tones anticipated **6 :** a convention of bridge that a player making an opening suit-bid of one promises to rebid if his partner bids a different suit

an·tic·i·pa·tive \='==ˌpād·iv, -ātiv, -ˌpətiv, -ēv\ *adj* **:** given to anticipation **:** ANTICIPATING — **an·tic·i·pa·tive·ly** *adv*

an·tic·i·pa·tor \-ˌpād·ə(r), -ātə(r)\ *n* -s [L, fr. *anticipatus* + *-or*] **:** one that anticipates

an·tic·i·pa·to·ri·ly \=¦==ˌpəˈtōrəlē, -ōr-, -li\ *adv* **:** in an anticipatory manner

an·tic·i·pa·to·ry \='==pəˌtōrē, -ōrē, -ri, *or chiefly Brit* -ˌpātə-\ *adj* **1 :** characterized by anticipation ⟨could scarcely repress the ~ shiver —Mary Austin⟩ **:** ANTICIPATING ⟨an elder who has given a child a gift and waits, ~, for delighted thanks —J.H.Wheelwright⟩ **2 :** standing as formal subject or object in place of a following word or word group esp. when it is the logical subject or object ⟨*it* in *it is customary to kiss the bride* and *it* in *he found it necessary to tell us*⟩ or French *c'* in *c'est à vous que je parle* "it is to you that I am speaking" or German *es* in *es ist möglich, dass er kommen wird* "it is possible that he will come" are ~⟩

anticked *also* **antickt** *past of* ANTIC

anticking *pres part of* ANTIC

an·ti·clas·tic \¦=(ˌ)= *at* [1]ANTI- + ¦klastik\ *adj* [[1]*anti-* + Gk *klastos* (fr. *klan* to break) + E *-ic*] **:** having opposite curvatures at a given point; *specif* **:** curved convexly along a longitudinal plane section and concavely along the perpendicular section — used of a surface; opposed to *synclastic*

[1]**an·ti·cler·i·cal** \¦=(ˌ)=¦-\ *adj* [[1]*anti-* + *clerical*] **:** opposed to clericalism or to the interference or influence of the clergy in secular affairs — **an·ti·cler·i·cal·ism** \¦=(ˌ)=¦-\ *n* -s

[2]**anticlerical** \"\ *n* -s **:** a believer in anticlerical principles

an·ti·cli·mac·tic \¦=(ˌ)=¦==\ *also* **an·ti·cli·mac·ti·cal** \-¦==\ *adj* [fr. *anticlimax*, after E *climax: climactic, climactical*] **:** relating to, attended by, or manifesting anticlimax — **an·ti·cli·mac·ti·cal·ly** \-¦=¦tə̇k(ə)lē, -li\ *adv*

an·ti·cli·max \¦=(ˌ)=¦-\ *n* -ES [[1]*anti-* + *climax*] **1 :** the usu. sudden transition in writing or speaking from an idea of significance or dignity to an idea trivial or ludicrous by comparison esp. at the close of a series, sentence, or passage (as *a love of God, justice, and sports cars*); *also* **:** an instance of such transition **2 a :** an event or occurrence (as the last of a series) that is strikingly or ludicrously less important, significant, or dignified than what has preceded it **b :** a disappointment of expectation ⟨the ~ of his later years⟩

[1]**an·ti·cli·nal** \¦=(ˌ)=¦klīnᵊl\ *adj* [[1]*anti-* + *clin-* (fr. Gk *klinein* to lean) + E *-al* — more at LEAN] **:** inclining in opposite directions: **a** *geol* **:** having or relating to a fold in which the sides dip from a common line or crest — compare SYNCLINAL **b** *bot* **:** occurring at right angles to the surface or circumference of an organ — **an·ti·cli·nal·ly** \-īnᵊlē, -i\ *adv*

[2]**anticlinal** \"\ *n* -s **:** an anticlinal structure, fold, or axis

anticlinal theory *n* **:** a theory in geology: petroleum and natural gas migrate to the most elevated portions of permeable beds and so will usu. be found in anticlines

anticlinal valley *n* **:** a valley excavated by erosion along the axial portion of an anticlinal fold

anticlinal vertebra *n* **:** one of the dorsal vertebrae in many animals that has an upright spine toward which the spines of the neighboring vertebrae are inclined

an·ti·cline \'=(ˌ)=ˌklīn\ *n* -s [back-formation fr. [1]*anticlinal*]

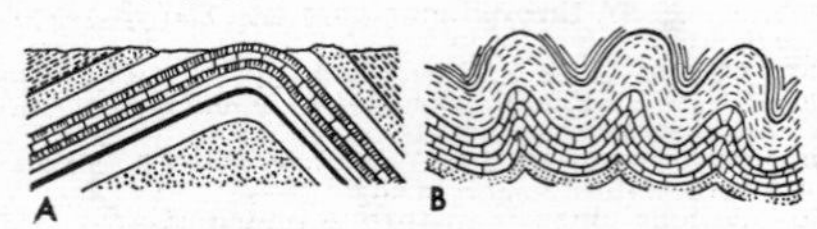

A, cross section of anticline 1; *B*, anticlinorium

1 : an upfold or arch of stratified rock in which the beds or layers bend downward in opposite directions from the crest or axis of the fold — compare SYNCLINE **2** *bot* **:** an anticlinal wall

an·ti·cli·no·ri·um \ˌ=(ˌ)=ˌklīˈnōrēəm\ *n, pl* **anticlino·ria** \-rēə\ [NL, fr. ISV *anticline* + NL *-orium*] **:** a series of anticlines and synclines so grouped that taken together they have the general outline of an arch — opposed to *synclinorium*; see ANTICLINE illustration

an·ti·clock·wise \¦=(ˌ)=¦-\ *adj* (*or adv*) [[1]*anti-* + *clockwise*] **:** COUNTERCLOCKWISE

anticly *adv* [[2]*antic* + *-ly*] **:** in an antic manner

antic masque *n* [by alter.] *obs* **:** ANTIMASQUE

an·tic·ne·mi·on \ˌantik'nēmēˌän, -ˌōn, -ˌən\ *n* -s [Gk *antiknēmion*, fr. *anti-* [1]anti- + *knēmion* small leg, dim. of *knēmē* leg, shank — more at HAM] **:** the front of the leg

[1]**an·ti·co·ag·u·lant** \¦=(ˌ)= *at* [1]ANTI- + (ˌ)=¦-\ *adj* [[1]*anti-* + *coagulant*] **:** hindering coagulation esp. of blood

[2]**anticoagulant** \"\ *n* -s **:** a substance (as a drug) that hinders coagulation or clotting of blood

an·ti·co·ag·u·lin \¦=(ˌ)=¦-\ *n* -s [[1]*anti-* + *coagulate* + *-in*] **:** a substance present esp. in the saliva of blood-sucking insects that prevents or retards coagulation of vertebrate blood

an·ti·co·in·ci·dence \¦=(ˌ)='-\ *n* -s [[1]*anti-* + *coincidence*] **:** the indication of the passage of an ionizing particle through one counting tube only in a set, the circuit having been designed so that coincidences will not be registered

an·ti·co·mo·der·no \än¦tē(ˌ)kōmə¦der(ˌ)nō\ *adj* [It, artist that combines ancient and modern style, fr. *antico* ancient + *moderno* modern, fr. LL *modernus* — more at ANTIC, MODERN] **:** of, relating to, or being modern imitations of antiques

an·ti·com·ple·men·ta·ry \¦=(ˌ)= *at* [1]ANTI- + ˌ=='-\ *adj* [[1]*anti-* + *complementary*] *immunol* **:** having the power to remove or inactivate complement nonspecifically

an·ti·cor \'=(ˌ)=ˌkȯ(ə)r\ *n* -s [NL, fr. [1]*anti-* + L *cor* heart — more at HEART] **:** an inflammatory swelling in the front of the chest of a horse caused by pressure or friction of the harness

an·ti·creep·er \'=(ˌ)=ˌ-\ *n* [[1]*anti-* + *creeper*] **:** a device attached to a railroad rail to keep it from moving longitudinally

an·ti·cre·pus·cu·lar ray \¦=(ˌ)==¦=-\ *n* [[1]*anti-* + *crepuscular*] **:** any of the extensions of the crepuscular rays that seem to converge to the antisolar point

an·ti·cro·tal·ic \¦=(ˌ)=(')=¦-\ *adj* [[1]*anti-* + *crotalic*] **:** effective against rattlesnake bites — used chiefly of antivenin serums

an·ti·cryp·tic \¦=(ˌ)=¦-\ *adj* [[1]*anti-* + *cryptic*] **:** of or relating to resemblance to surroundings that renders an animal less conspicuous to its prey — compare AGGRESSIVE 3a

antics *pl of* ANTIC, *pres 3d sing of* ANTIC

an·ti·cum \an'tīkəm\ *n, pl* **anti·ca** \-kə\ [*ante-* + *-icum* (as in *posticum*)] **:** a front porch — compare POSTICUM

an·ti·cus \an'tīkəs\ *adj* [L, fr. *ante* before + *-icus* -ic — more at ANTE-] **:** ANTERIOR

an·ti·cy·clo·gen·e·sis \¦=(ˌ) *at* [1]ANTI- + ¦sīklō¦jenəsə̇s\ *n* [NL, fr. E *anticyclone* + L *genesis*] **:** the formation or development of an anticyclone

an·ti·cy·clol·y·sis \¦=(ˌ)=ˌsī¦klälə̇sə̇s\ *n, pl* **anticycloly·ses** \-əˌsēz\ [NL, fr. E *anticyclone* + NL *-lysis*] **:** the destruction or weakening of an anticyclone

an·ti·cy·clone \'=(ˌ)=-\ *n* [[1]*anti-* + *cyclone*] **:** a system of winds that rotates about a center of high atmospheric pressure clockwise in the northern hemisphere, counterclockwise in the southern, that usu. advances at 20 to 30 miles per hour, that often brings cool dry weather, and that usu. has a diameter of 1500 to 2500 miles — **an·ti·cy·clon·ic** \¦=(ˌ)=¦-\ *adj*

an·ti·dac·tyl \'=(ˌ)=ˌ-\ *n* [LL *antidactylus*, fr. Gk *antidaktylos*, fr. *anti-* [1]anti- + *daktylos* dactyl — more at DACTYL] **:** reversed dactyl **:** ANAPEST

an·ti·de·riv·a·tive \¦=(ˌ)=¦==\ *n* [[1]*anti-* + *derivative*] **:** the inverse of a given mathematical function which can be obtained by differentiating the inverse ⟨$F(x)$ is the ~ of $f(x)$⟩

an·ti·det·o·nant \¦=(ˌ)=¦detᵊnᵊnt\ *n* -s [[1]*anti-* + *detonate* + *-ant*] **:** ANTIKNOCK

[1]**an·ti·diph·the·rit·ic** \¦=(ˌ)=ˌ=¦-\ *adj* [ISV [1]*anti-* + *diphtheritic*] **:** preventing diphtheria esp. by immunization ⟨immunization with ~ toxoid⟩

[2]**antidiphtheritic** \"\ *n* -s **:** an agent that prevents or modifies the course of diphtheria ⟨antitoxin is an ~⟩

[1]**an·ti·di·u·ret·ic** \¦=(ˌ)=ˌ=¦-\ *adj* [[1]*anti-* + *diuretic*] *med* **:** tending to check or oppose excretion of urine

[2]**antidiuretic** \"\ *n* -s **:** an antidiuretic agent or substance ⟨some hormones are ~s⟩

an·ti·dor·cas \ˌantē'dȯrkəs, -ˌtī-\ *n, cap* [NL, fr. Gk *anti-* similar to, like (fr. *anti* against, instead of, equivalent to) + *dorkas* gazelle — more at ANTI-, DORCAS GAZELLE] **:** a genus of antelopes including only the springbok

an·ti·do·ron \-'dōˌrän, -ōn, -ˌrən\ *n, pl* **antido·ra** \-rə\ [LGk *antidōron* return gift, fr. Gk *anti-* [1]anti- + *dōron* gift, fr. *didonai* to give — more at DATE] **:** bread blessed but not consecrated and eaten in the Eucharist of the Eastern Church but instead distributed after the service as a sign of their participation in the blessing to worshipers who did not communicate **:** bread of fellowship — called also *eulogia*

an·ti·dot·al \ˌantə̇¦dōdᵊl, -ōtᵊl, ¦aan-\ *adj* **:** consisting of, suited for, or acting as an antidote — **an·ti·dot·al·ly** \-ᵊlē, -ᵊli\ *adv*

antidotary *n* -ES [ML *antidotarius*, fr. L *antidotum, antidotus* + *-arius* -ary] *obs* **:** a book of antidotes

[1]**an·ti·dote** \'antə̇ˌdōt, *usu* -ōd·+V\ *n* -s [ME *antidot, antidotum*, fr. L *antidotum, antidotus*, fr. Gk *antidoton, antidotos*, fr. neut. & fem. of (assumed) *antidotos*, verbal of *antididonai* to give in return, give as an antidote, fr. *anti-* [1]anti- + *didonai* to give — more at DATE (point of time)] **1 :** a remedy to counteract the effects of poison ⟨an ~ for arsenic⟩ ⟨an ~ against several dangerous drugs⟩ **2 :** something that relieves, prevents, or counteracts ⟨an ~ to complacency⟩ ⟨a soothing ~ for throats parched by a pungent Mexican repast —Green Peyton⟩

[2]**antidote** \"\ *vt* -ED/-ING/-S **1 :** to counteract or neutralize by giving or taking an antidote ⟨*antidoted* the poison with quick medication⟩ **2 :** to provide with an antidote ⟨kept whiskey to ~ himself against snake bite⟩

an·ti·drom·ic \ˌantə̇¦drämik\ *or* **an·tid·ro·mal** \(')an¦tidrəməl\ *adj* [[1]*anti-* + *drom-* + *-ic* or *-al*] **:** proceeding or conducting on a course opposite in direction to the usual — used esp. of a nerve impulse or fiber — **an·ti·drom·i·cal·ly** \ˌantə̇¦drämə̇k(ə)lē\ *adv*

antient *archaic var of* ANCIENT

an·ti·en·zyme \¦=(ˌ)= *at* [1]ANTI- + '=ˌ=\ *n* [[1]*anti-* + *enzyme*] **:** a substance that inhibits enzyme action; *esp* **:** an inhibitor (as antitrypsin) produced normally by animal and plant cells or following injection of an enzyme

an·ti·ep·i·cen·ter \¦=(ˌ)=¦=-\ *n* -s [[1]*anti-* + *epicenter*] **:** the point at which a straight line drawn through the epicenter of an earthquake and the earth's center would emerge on the opposite side of the globe

An·ti·fe·brin \¦=(ˌ)=¦fēbrə̇n, -fe-\ *trademark* — used for acetanilide

an·ti·fed·er·al·ist \¦=(ˌ)=¦-\ *n* -s *usu cap F* [[1]*anti-* + *Federalist*] **:** a member of the group that opposed the adoption of the U.S. Constitution

an·ti·fer·ro·mag·net \¦=(ˌ)=ˌ-\ *n* [[1]*anti-* + *ferromagnet*] **:** a substance that exhibits antiferromagnetism

an·ti·fer·ro·mag·net·ic \¦=(ˌ)=¦-\ *adj* [[1]*anti-* + *ferromagnetic*] **:** of, relating to, or showing antiferromagnetism

an·ti·fer·ro·mag·net·ism \¦=(ˌ)=ˌ-\ *n* [[1]*anti-* + *ferromagnetism*] **:** magnetic behavior characteristic of certain feebly magnetic substances (as manganese monoxide and chromium sesquioxide) thought to have two oppositely directed electron spins not quite neutralizing each other with the result that the magnetic susceptibility at first increases and then decreases as the substance is heated

an·ti·fi·bri·nol·y·sin \¦=(ˌ) =ˌ-\n -s [[1]*anti-* + *fibrinolysin*] **:** an antibody in the blood of persons convalescent from infection with hemolytic streptococci that specifically opposes fibrinolysins produced by these organisms and is used chiefly in certain diagnostic tests

an·ti·fi·bri·nol·y·sis \¦=(ˌ)=ˌ-\ *n, pl* **antifibrinoly·ses** [NL, fr. [1]*anti-* + *fibrinolysis*] **:** the action of an antifibrinolysin in opposing streptococcal fibrinolysis

an·ti·flash \¦=(ˌ)=¦-\ *adj* [[1]*anti-* + *flash*, n.] **:** capable of withstanding or minimizing the effects of flash or heat, esp. the intense heat encountered in fire fighting

an·ti·foam \'=(ˌ)=ˌ-\ *n* -s [[1]*anti-* + *foam*] **:** a substance that reduces or prevents the formation of foam

an·ti·fog·gant \'=(ˌ)=¦=ənt\ *n* -s [[1]*anti-* + *fog* + *-ant*] **:** a reagent added to an emulsion, developer, or other photographic solution to reduce or prevent fog

an·ti·fog·mat·ic \¦=(ˌ)=ˌ=¦mad·ik\ *n* -s [[1]*anti-* + *fog* + *-matic* (as in *rheumatic*)] **:** a drink of liquor taken to counteract the effect of fog or dampness

an·ti·for·eign·ism \¦=(ˌ)=¦-\ *n* -s [[1]*anti-* + *foreignism*] **:** aversion or opposition to foreigners

an·ti·foul·ing \¦=(ˌ)=¦==\ *adj* [[1]*anti-* + *fouling*] **:** intended to prevent fouling of underwater structures (as the bottoms of ships) ⟨~ paint⟩

an·ti·freeze \'=(ˌ)=ˌ-\ *n* -s [[1]*anti-* + *freeze*, v.] **:** a substance (as alcohol) added to a liquid (as the coolant in an automobile, tractor, or airplane engine) to lower its freezing point

an·ti·fric·tion \¦=(ˌ)=¦==\ *adj* [[1]*anti-* + *friction*] **:** reducing friction; *specif* **:** having rolling contact instead of sliding contact ⟨~ ball bearing⟩

an·ti·gen \'antə̇jən, -ˌjen, -in\ *n* -s [ISV [1]*anti-* + *-gen*] **1 :** a usu. protein or carbohydrate substance (as a toxin, enzyme, or any of certain constituents of blood corpuscles or of other cells), that when introduced into the body stimulates the production of an antibody **2 :** a substance that reacts in complement fixation with an antibody to bind complement, the antigen and antibody usu. being specific — **an·ti·gen·ic** \¦=='jenik\ *adj* — **an·ti·gen·i·cal·ly** \-ə̇k(ə)lē\ *adv* — **an·ti·genicity** \-jə¦nisəd·ē\ *n* -ES

[1]**an·ti·god·lin** \ˌantə̇¦gädlə̇n, -gōd,lēn\ *or* **an·ti·gog·lin** \-¦gäglə̇n\ *adj* [origin unknown] *chiefly Midland* **:** out of line **:** ASKEW

[2]**antigodlin** \"\ *or* **antigoglin** \"\ *adv, chiefly Midland* **:** at angles **:** CROSSWISE ⟨he went ~ across the field⟩

an·tig·o·non \an'tigəˌnän\ *n, cap* [NL, fr. Gk *anti-* similar to, like (fr. *anti* against, instead of, equivalent to) + *-gonon*, fr. *polygonon* knotgrass (*Polygonum aviculare*) — more at ANTI-, POLYGONUM] **:** a genus of tropical American tendril-climbing herbs (family Polygonaceae) having apetalous flowers with brightly colored petaloid sepals — see CORALVINE

an·tig·o·rite \an'tigəˌrīt\ *n* -s [G *antigorit*, fr. *Antigorio* valley, Piedmont, Italy, its locality + G *-it* -ite] **:** a brownish green lamellar variety of the mineral serpentine $Mg_3Si_2O_5(OH)_4$ — **an·tig·o·rit·ic** \(')=¦=ə¦rid·ik\ *adj*

an·ti·grop·e·los \ˌantə̇'gräpələs, -ˌläs, -ˌlōs\ *n, pl* **antigropelos** \", -ˌlōz\ [perh. irreg. fr. Gk *anti-* [1]anti- + *hygros* wet + *pēlos* mud — more at HYGR-, SQUALOR] **:** waterproof leggings

an·ti-g suit \¦=(ˌ)= *at* [1]ANTI- + ¦jē,-\ *n, usu cap G* [[1]*anti-* + *G suit*] **:** G SUIT

[1]**an·ti·guan** \(')an¦tēg(w)ən, -ig-\ *adj, usu cap* [*Antigua*, island in West Indies + E *-an*] **1 :** of, relating to, or characteristic of the island of Antigua **2 :** of, relating to, or characteristic of Antiguans

[2]**antiguan** \"\ *n* -s *cap* **:** a native or inhabitant of Antigua

an·ti·ha·la·tion \¦=(ˌ)= *at* [1]ANTI- + =¦==\ *adj* [[1]*anti-* + *halation*] **:** preventing halation

an·ti·ha·lo \'=(ˌ)=-\ *adj* [[1]*anti-* + *halo*] **:** preventing halation ⟨film with ~ backing⟩

an·ti·he·lix \'=(ˌ)=ˌ-\ *also* **anthelix** \(')ant¦hē-, -¦thē-\ *n, pl* **antihelices** *or* **antihelixes** [[1]*anti-* + *helix*] *anat* **:** the curved elevation of cartilage within or in front of the helix

an·ti·his·ta·mine \¦=(ˌ)='-\ *or* **an·ti·his·ta·min·ic** \-ˌhistəˈminik, -ēk\ *n* -s [[1]*anti-* + *histamine*] **:** any of various compounds used for treating certain allergic reactions and cold symptoms and presumably effective by inactivating histamine — **an·ti·his·ta·min·ic** \¦=(ˌ)=ˌ==¦==\ *adj*

an·ti·hor·mone \¦=(ˌ)=¦-\ *n* -s [[1]*anti-* + *hormone*] **:** a fraction of blood globulin that is capable of rendering ineffective a protein-containing heterologous hormone when the latter is administered over a period of time and that is now generally considered to be a true antibody formed in response to the presence of foreign protein

an·ti·ic·er \¦=(ˌ)=ˌ-\ *n* -s [[1]*anti-* + *ice* + *-er*] **:** a device serving to prevent ice formation esp. on an airplane (as a slinger ring, a windshield sprayer, a pump forcing alcohol and glycerin into the throat of a carburetor, or a thermal device supplying the leading edges of wings and tail with heated air

an·ti·in·tel·lec·tu·al·ism \¦=(ˌ)=ˌ-\ *n* -s [[1]*anti-* + *intellectualism*] **1 :** the philosophic attitude or doctrine that assigns intellect or reason to a subordinate place or denies the power of intellect to grasp the true nature of things — compare BERGSONISM **2 :** hostility toward or suspicion of intellectuals **:** hostility toward inquiring, speculative, or academic habits of thought ⟨reflected trends toward *anti-intellectualism* by cutting the university's budget —Richard Schickel⟩

an·ti·in·tel·lec·tu·al·ist \¦=(ˌ)=ˌ-\ *n* -s **:** one given to anti-intellectualism

an·ti·jac·o·bin \¦=(ˌ)=¦-\ *n, usu cap J* [[1]*anti-* + *Jacobin*] **:** an opponent of the Jacobins — **an·ti·jac·o·bin·ism** \¦=(ˌ)=¦-\ *n* -s *usu cap J*

an·ti·knock \'=(ˌ)=ˌ-\ *n* -s [[1]*anti-* + *knock*] **:** a substance used as a fuel or fuel additive to prevent detonation in the combustion process of an internal-combustion engine

an·ti·lar·val \¦=(ˌ)=¦-\ *adj* [[1]*anti-* + *larval*] **:** directed against larvae — used of insect control measures designed to destroy larval insects, esp. disease-transmitting mosquitoes

an·ti·lea·guer \'=(ˌ)=ˌlēgə(r)\ *n, often cap L* [[1]*anti-* + *League* (*of Nations*) + *-er*] **:** one opposed to the League of Nations or to the entrance of the U.S. into it

an·ti·le·gom·e·na \ˌ=(ˌ)=lə¦gämənə\ *n pl, often cap* [Gk, fr. neut. pl. of *antilegomenos*, pres. part. pass. of *antilegein* to speak against, fr. *anti-* [1]anti- + *legein* to speak — more at LEGEND] **:** the books of the New Testament whose canonicity was for a time in dispute — compare HOMOLOGOUMENA

[1]**an·til·le·an** \ˌantə̇¦lēən, ¦aan-, (')=¦tilēən\ *adj, usu cap* [*Antilles*, islands in the West Indies + E *-an*] **1 :** of, relating to, or characteristic of the Antilles **2 :** of, relating to, or characteristic of Antilleans **3 :** of, relating to, or being the biogeographic subregion of the Greater and Lesser Antilles

[2]**antillean** \"\ *n* -s *cap* **:** a native or inhabitant of the Antilles

an·ti·lo·bi·um \ˌ=(ˌ)=ˈlōbēəm\ *n, pl* **antilo·bia** \-bēə\ [NL, fr. Gk *antilobion,* fr. *anti-* ¹anti- + *lobion,* dim. of *lobos* lobe, pod — more at SLEEP] : TRAGUS

an·ti·lo·ca·pra \ˌantə(ˌ)lōˈkaprə\ *n, cap* [NL, fr. *antilo-* (fr. *Antilope*) + *Capra*] : a genus of ruminants (the type of the family Antilocapridae) consisting of the pronghorn — **an·ti·lo·cap·rid** \ˌ==(ˌ)=ˈkaprəd\ *adj or n*

an·ti·log·a·rithm \ˌ=(ˌ)at ¹ANTI- +ˌ-\ *n* [¹*anti-* + *logarithm*] : the number corresponding to a logarithm ⟨in the common system, the ~ of 2 is 100, since the logarithm of 100 is 2⟩ —abbr. *antilog*

an·til·o·gism \anˈtiləˌjizəm\ *n* -s [LGk *antilogismos,* fr. Gk *anti-* ¹anti- + *logismos* calculating, reasoning, fr. *logizesthai* to calculate, fr. *logos* word, computation — more at LEGEND] : an inconsistent triad of propositions in logic of which two are premises of a valid syllogism while the third is the contradictory of its conclusion — **an·til·o·gis·tic** \(ˈ)=ˌ==ˈjistik\ *adj* — **an·til·o·gis·ti·cal·ly** \-tək(ə)lē\ *adv*

an·til·o·gous pole \(ˈ)anˈtiləgəs-\ *n* [Gk *antilogos* contradictory, fr. *anti-* ¹anti- + *logos* word — more at LEGEND] : the pole of a crystal that becomes negatively electrified when the crystal is heated

an·til·o·gy \anˈtiləjē\ *n* -ES [Gk *antilogia,* fr. *anti-* ¹anti- + *-logia* -logy] : a contradiction in terms or ideas

an·ti·lo·pe \anˈtiləˌpē\ *n, cap* [NL, prob. fr. obs. E *antilope,* fr. ME *antilope, antelope* fabulous beast represented in heraldic devices — more at ANTELOPE] : a genus of antelopes comprising the Indian black buck

an·ti·lu·et·ic \ˌ=(ˌ)= at ¹ANTI- +=ˌ==\ *n* -s [¹*anti-* + *luetic*] : ANTISYPHILITIC

an·ti·ly·sin \ˈ=(ˌ)=ˌ-\ *n* [¹*anti-* + *lysin*] : a substance antagonistic to a lysin and serving to protect the cells from the attacks of the lysin

an·ti·ly·sis \ˈ=(ˌ)=ˌ-\ *n, pl* **antily·ses** [NL, fr. ¹*anti-* + *-lysis*] : action of an antilysin — **an·ti·lyt·ic** \ˌ=(ˌ)=ˌ-\ *adj*

an·ti·ma·cas·sar \ˌantēməˈkasə(r), -tə-, ˌaan . . . ˈkaas-\ *n* -s [¹*anti-* + *Macassar (oil)*] : a cover to protect the back or arms of furniture from Macassar oil or other hair preparations : TIDY

an·ti·mag·ma·tist \ˌ=(ˌ)= at ¹ANTI- + ˈmagmətəst\ *n* -s [¹*anti-* + NL *magmat-, magma* + E *-ist*] : one that believes that granite and other similar igneous rocks are formed in situ by a process called granitization rather than intruded as magma

an·ti·mag·net·ic \ˌ=(ˌ)=ˌ=ˌ-\ *adj* [¹*anti-* + *magnetic*] *of a watch* : having a balance unit composed of alloys that will not remain magnetized thus reducing the extremes of error resulting from magnetism

¹**an·ti·ma·lar·i·al** \ˌ=(ˌ)==ˌ-\ *adj* [¹*anti-* + *malarial*] : serving to prevent, check, or cure malaria

²**antimalarial** \"\ *n* -s : an antimalarial drug

an·ti–ma·son \ˌ=(ˌ)=ˌ-\ *n, often cap A&M* [¹*anti* + *mason*] : one opposed to Freemasonry — used esp. of a member of an American political party — **an·ti–ma·son·ic** \-=ˌ==\ *adj, often cap A&M* — **an·ti–mason·ry** \-ˌ===\ *n, often cap A&M*

an·ti·masque *or* **an·ti·mask** *also* **an·te·mask** \ˈantē,-, -tə-\ *n* -s [²*anti-* or *ante-* + *masque, mask*] : an additional masque usu. preceding the main masque and introduced for comic or grotesque contrast

an·ti·mas·quer *or* **an·ti·mask·er** \ˈ==,-\ *n* -s : a performer in an antimasque

an·ti·mat·ter \ˈ=(ˌ)= at ¹ANTI- + ˌ==\ *n* -s [¹*anti-* + *matter*] : matter composed of the counterparts of ordinary matter, antiprotons instead of protons, positrons instead of electrons, and antineutrons instead of neutrons

an·ti·mech·a·nized \ˌ=(ˌ)=ˌ-\ *adj* [¹*anti-* + *mechanized*] : employed in defense against armored combat vehicles ⟨~ weapons⟩ ⟨~ firing⟩

an·ti·men·si·on \ˌantəˈmensēˌän, -tē-, -ōn, -ən\ *or* **an·ti·men·si·um** \-sēəm\ *or* **an·ti·mins** \-ˌminz\ *or* **an·ti·min·si·on** \-ˈminsēˌän, -ōn, -ən\ *n, pl* **antimensia** *or* **antiminsia** \-sēə\ [ML *antimensium,* fr. MGk *antimension, antimēsion,* prob. fr. Gk *anti-* ¹anti- + L *mensa* table + Gk *-ion* -ium — more at MENSA] *Eastern Church* : a consecrated piece of silk or linen cloth containing relics consecrated by a bishop and kept on the altar

an·ti·mere \ˈ==ˌmi(ə)r\ *n* -s [¹*anti-* + *-mere*] **1** *zool* : one of opposite corresponding parts symmetrical with respect to a main axis (as the halves of bilaterally symmetrical animals) : one half of a metamere **2** *zool* : any of the segments essentially similar to an antimere into which a radially symmetrical animal can be divided — **an·ti·mer·ic** \ˌ==ˈmerik\ *adj*

an·ti·me·ri·na \ˌ==məˈrēnə\ *also* **an·tai·me·ri·na** \ˌanˌtī-\ *n, pl* **antimerina** *or* **antimerinas** *also* **antaimerina** *or* **antaimerinas** *usu cap* : HOVA

an·ti·mes·o·me·tri·al \ˌ=(ˌ)=ˌ-\ *adj* [¹*anti-* + *mesometrium* + *-al*] *anat* : of or relating to the front or ventral mesometrium

an·ti·me·tab·o·lite \ˌ=(ˌ)= at ¹ANTI- + =ˈ==ˌ=\ *n* -s [¹*anti-* + *metabolite*] : a substance that inhibits the utilization of a metabolite (as by antagonistic action) — compare ANTIVITAMIN

an·ti·mi·cro·bi·al \ˌ=(ˌ)=ˌ=ˈ==\ *also* **an·ti·mi·cro·bic** \-ˌ=ˈ=\ *adj* [¹*anti-* + *microbial, microbic*] : inimical to microbes

an·ti·mis·sion \ˌ=(ˌ)ˈ-\ *adj* [¹*anti-* + *mission*] : opposed to foreign religious missions ⟨an ~ Baptist⟩

an·ti·mo·nate \ˈantəməˌnāt, ˌnət\ *also* **an·ti·mo·ni·ate** \ˌ==ˈmōnēˌāt, -ēˌət\ *n* -s [ISV *antimony* + *-ate*] : a salt [as potassium antimonate $KSb(OH)_6$] containing pentavalent antimony and oxygen in the anion

¹**an·ti·mo·ni·al** \ˌantəˈmōnēəl, -tē-, -nyəl, ˌaan-\ *adj* [*antimony* + *-al*] : of, relating to, or containing antimony

²**antimonial** \"\ *n* -s : an antimonial compound or preparation

antimonial lead *n* : lead containing antimony; *specif* : a hard alloy of lead containing 4 to 10 percent antimony used for the framework of storage-battery plates and tank linings — compare GRID METAL, HARD LEAD

antimonial powder *n* : a powder consisting of one part oxide of antimony and two parts phosphate of calcium that has been used as a diaphoretic, emetic, and cathartic — called also *James's powder*

an·ti·mon·ic \ˌ==ˈmänik, -ēk, -mō-\ *adj* [*antimony* + *-ic*] : of, relating to, or derived from antimony — used esp. of compounds in which antimony is pentavalent

an·ti·mo·nide \ˈ==məˌnīd ˌnəd\ *n* -s [*antimony* + *-ide*] : a binary compound of antimony with a more positive element

an·ti·mo·nif·er·ous \ˌ===ˈnif(ə)rəs\ *adj* [ISV *antimony* + *-ferous*] : bearing antimony

an·ti·mo·ni·ous \ˌ==ˈmōnēəs\ *also* **an·ti·mo·nous** \ˈ==mənəs\ *adj* [*antimony* + *-ous*] : of, relating to, or derived from antimony — used esp. of compounds in which antimony is trivalent

antimonious oxide *n* : ANTIMONY TRIOXIDE

an·ti·mo·nite \ˈ==məˌnīt\ *n* -s [G *antimonit,* fr. *antimon* antimony + *-it* -ite] : STIBNITE

an·ti·mo·ni·um \ˌ=ˈmōnēəm\ *n, pl* **antimo·nia** \-nēə\ [ML] : ANTIMONY

an·ti·mo·ny \ˈantəˌmōnē, ˈaan-, -ni, *US also & Brit usu* -mən-\ *n* -ES [ME *antimonie,* fr. ML *antimonium,* perh. modif. of Ar *ithmid,* of Hamitic origin; akin to Egypt *sdm* antimony, Copt *stēm*] **1** : STIBNITE **2** : a trivalent and pentavalent metalloid element that is commonly metallic silvery white, crystalline, and brittle yet rather soft but is known also in black amorphous, unstable yellow, and explosive forms, that occurs in the free state but more often combined in minerals (as stibnite, kermesite, valentinite, and cervantite) and in ores of other metals (as lead), that is prepared chiefly from stibnite usu. by roasting and smelting, and that is used esp. as a constituent of alloys (as antimonial lead, type metals, and bearing metals) — symbol *Sb;* see ELEMENT table

antimony blende *n* : KERMESITE

antimony bloom *n* : VALENTINITE

antimony chloride *n* : either of two chlorides of antimony: **a** : the trichloride $SbCl_3$ obtained as a colorless hygroscopic caustic crystalline solid from antimony and chlorine and used chiefly in coloring metals (as iron, zinc), as a catalyst, and as a mordant — called also *butter of antimony* **b** : the pentachloride $SbCl_5$ obtained as a colorless to reddish yellow caustic oily liquid with an offensive odor and used chiefly as a chlorine carrier in organic synthesis and as a catalyst

antimony cinnabar *n* : ANTIMONY VERMILION

antimony crocus *n* : CROCUS OF ANTIMONY

antimony crude *n* : ANTIMONY SULFIDE

antimony glance *n* : STIBNITE

antimony hydride *n* : STIBINE

an·ti·mo·nyl \-məˌnil, -ēl\ *n* -s [ISV *antimony* + *-yl*] : a univalent radical SbO composed of antimony and oxygen held by some to exist in the molecules of tartar emetic and some basic salts of antimony

antimony ocher *n* : native antimony oxide; *esp* : CERVANTITE

antimony oxide *n* : an oxide of antimony; *esp* : ANTIMONY TRIOXIDE

antimony potassium tartrate *n* : TARTAR EMETIC

antimony regulus *n* : impure antimony made by smelting antimony ore

antimony salt *n* : a double salt of antimony fluoride (as with sodium fluoride or ammonium sulfate) used as a mordant — often used in pl.

antimony sulfide *n* : either of two sulfides of antimony: **a** *also* **antimony trisulfide** : the trisulfide Sb_2S_3 occurring native as stibnite, obtained synthetically as an orange-red precipitate, and used chiefly as a pigment (as in camouflage paints), in percussion primer compositions, and in fireworks — compare ANTIMONY VERMILION **b** *also* **antimony pentasulfide** : the pentasulfide Sb_2S_5 obtained as an orange-yellow precipitate and used chiefly as a pigment, in coloring and vulcanizing rubber, and in fireworks — called also *golden antimony sulfide*

antimony trioxide *n* : a white crystalline compound Sb_2O_3 or Sb_4O_6 occurring native as valentinite and senarmontite, formed when antimony burns, and used chiefly as a source of other antimony compounds and as a pigment esp. in fire-retardant paints — called also *antimonious oxide*

antimony vermilion *n* : a vermilion pigment made by treating a soluble antimony compound (as antimony trichloride) with a thiosulfate or hydrogen sulfide and consisting of antimony trisulfide or oxysulfide — called also *antimony cinnabar*

antimony white *n* : antimony trioxide used as a pigment

antimony yellow *n* **1** : any of several yellow pigments containing antimony: as **a** : NAPLES YELLOW **b** : MÉRIMÉE'S YELLOW **2** : a moderate orange yellow that is paler than ocher yellow and yellower and less strong than deep chrome yellow — called also *sunray*

an·ti·morph \ˈ=(ˌ)= at ¹ANTI- + ˌmȯrf\ *n* -s [¹*anti-* + *-morph*] : a gene producing an effect opposite to that of the wild-type gene of the same locus — **an·ti·morph·ic** \ˌ=(ˌ)=ˈmȯrfik\ *adj*

an·ti·my·cin A \ˌ=(ˌ)=ˈmīsᵊnˈā\ *n* [¹*anti-* + *-mycin*] : a crystalline antibiotic $C_{28}H_{40}N_2O_9$ produced by an actinomycete (a species of *Streptomyces*) that is active against various fungi and insects

an·ti·neu·rit·ic \ˌ=(ˌ)==ˈ==\ *adj* [¹*anti-* + *neuritic*] : preventing or relieving neuritis ⟨an ~ vitamin⟩

an·ti·neu·tri·no \ˌ=(ˌ)=-\ *n* -s [¹*anti-* + *neutrino*] : an elementary particle which is identical to the neutrino in mass but opposite to it in electric and magnetic properties and whose encounter with a neutrino results in mutual annihilation

an·ti·neu·tron \ˌ=(ˌ)=ˌ-\ *n* -s [¹*anti-* + *neutron*] : an uncharged particle of mass equal to that of the neutron but having a magnetic moment in the opposite direction

ant·ing \ˈan(t)iŋ\ *n* -s [¹*ant* + *-ing*] *of certain birds* : the deliberate placing of living ants or other small invertebrates among the feathers

an·tin·i·al \(ˈ)anˈtinēəl\ *adj* : relating to the antinion

an·tin·i·on \anˈtinēən, -ēˌän\ *n* -s [¹*anti-* + Gk *inion* back of the head — more at INION] : the farthest projection of the forehead, opposite to the inion

an·ti·node \ˈantəˌnōd, -tē-\ *n* -s [ISV ¹*anti-* + *node*] : a region of maximum amplitude (as one of the vibrating segments of a musical string) situated between adjacent nodes in a field of wave interference — compare LOOP 4b, STANDING WAVE

an·ti·nome \-ˌnōm\ *n* -s [back-formation fr. *antinomy*] : a contradictory such as occurs in antinomy

¹**an·ti·no·mi·an** \ˌantəˈnōmēən, -tē-, -ˌtī-\ *adj* [ML *antinomus* (fr. L *anti-* ¹anti- + Gk *nomos* law) + E *-an* — more at NIMBLE] : relating to, proceeding from, or influenced by antinomianism

²**antinomian** \"\ *n* -s : an adherent of antinomianism

an·ti·no·mi·an·ism \ˌ=(ˌ)=ˈ==əˌnizəm\ *n* -s : the theological doctrine that by faith and God's gift of grace through the gospel a Christian is freed not only from the Old Testament law of Moses and all forms of legalism but also from all law including the generally accepted standards of morality prevailing in any given culture

an·ti·nom·ic \ˌ=(ˌ)=ˈnämik, -nō-\ *or* **an·ti·nom·i·cal** \-ˈnäməkəl\ *adj* : characterized by or involving antinomy — **an·ti·nom·i·cal·ly** \-mək(ə)lē, -li\ *adv*

an·tin·o·my \anˈtinəmē, -mi\ *n* -ES [L *antinomia,* fr. Gk, fr. *anti-* ¹anti- + *-nomia* (fr. *nomos* law) — more at NIMBLE] **1** : opposition of one law or rule to another law or rule : contradiction within a law **2** *obs* : an opposing law or rule of any kind : a law that contradicts itself **3** [G *antinomie,* fr. L *antinomia*] **a** : a contradiction between two philosophical principles each of which is taken to be true or between inferences correctly drawn from such principles; *esp* : a conflict or opposition between the products of reason and of experience **b** : a statement embodying an antinomy : PARADOX **4** : an apparent or real opposition, contradiction, conflict, or contrast

antinous release \anˈtanəs-\ *n* [perh. after *Antinous,* a Bithynian youth noted for his beauty, fr. L, fr. Gk *Antinoos*] : CABLE RELEASE

an·ti·nu·cle·on \ˈ=(ˌ)= at ¹ANTI- + ˌ-\ *n* -s [¹*anti-* + *nucleon*] : a particle of the same mass as a nucleon but differing from it in the sign of its electrical charge or the direction of its magnetic moment and capable of coalescing with the nucleon with the resultant annihilation of both

¹**an·ti·o·chene** \anˈtīəˌkēn, ˌantēˈä)ˌkēn\ *adj, usu cap* [LL *Antiochenus,* fr. *Antiochia* Antioch, ancient capital of Syria (now *Antakya,* Turkey) + L *-enus* -ene] : of or belonging to Antioch or to the theological doctrines associated with the Christian church at Syrian Antioch in the 4th and 5th centuries A.D. characterized by concern for the human and historical and by inductive and rationalistic method — compare ALEXANDRIAN SCHOOL 3

²**antiochene** \"\ *n* -s *usu cap* : a member of the church at Syrian Antioch or an adherent of its theological doctrines

¹**an·ti·och·i·an** \ˌantēˈäkēən, -ōk-\ *adj, usu cap* [*Antiochus,* name of thirteen kings of Syria who reigned from 280–64 B.C. + E *-ian*] : of or belonging to the Seleucidan kings of Syria who bore the name Antiochus

²**antiochian** \"\ *adj, usu cap* [*Antioch* + E *-ian*] : of, relating to, or characteristic of Antioch, esp. Syrian Antioch

³**antiochian** \"\ *n* -s *cap* : a native or inhabitant of Antioch, esp. Syrian Antioch

an·ti·o·dont \ˈantēəˌdänt, (ˈ)anˈtīə-\ *adj* [¹*anti-* + *-odont*] *zool* : relating to or being lophodont dentition in which the crests of opposing teeth meet

¹**an·ti·ox·i·dant** \ˈ=(ˌ)= at ¹ANTI- + ˌ-\ *n* -s [¹*anti-* + *oxidant*] : a substance that opposes oxidation or inhibits reactions promoted by oxygen or peroxides, many of these substances (as the tocopherols) being used as preservatives in various products (as in fats, oils, food products, and soaps for retarding the development of rancidity, in gasoline and other petroleum products for retarding gum formation and other undesirable changes, and in rubber for retarding aging)

²**antioxidant** \"\ *adj* : of or relating to an antioxidant

an·ti·ox·y·gen \ˌ=(ˌ)=ˌ-\ *n* -s [¹*anti-* + *oxygen*] : ANTIOXIDANT — **an·ti·ox·y·gen·ic** \ˌ=(ˌ)=ˌ==ˈ==\ *adj*

antipaedobaptism *often cap, var of* ANTIPEDOBAPTISM

an·ti·par·a·be·ma \ˌ=(ˌ)=ˌ-\ *n, pl* **antiparabema·ta** [¹*anti-* + *parabema*] : either of the two chapels opposite the parabemata in Byzantine architecture

an·ti·par·al·lel \ˌ=(ˌ)=ˌ-\ *adj* [¹*anti-* + *parallel*] *physics* : parallel but oppositely directed — used esp. of vectors

an·ti·pas·cha \ˌantēˈpaskə, -tə-\ *or* **an·ti·pasch** \-ˌpask\ *n* -s *usu cap* [MGk *antipascha,* fr. LGk, week immediately following Easter week, fr. Gk *anti-* ¹anti- + LGk *pascha* Easter — more at PASCH] *Eastern Church* : the first Sunday after Easter : LOW SUNDAY

an·ti·pas·to \ˌantēˈpastō, ˌän...ˈpä-, -tə-\ *n, pl* **antipas·ti** \-stē\ *or* **antipastos** [It, fr. *anti-* ²anti- (fr. L *ante-*) + *pasto* food, fr. L *pastus,* fr. *pastus,* past part. of *pascere* to feed — more at FOOD] : HORS D'OEUVRE

an·ti·pa·thar·ia \ˌantēpəˈtha(a)rēə, -tə-\ *n pl, cap* [NL, fr. *Antipathes* genus of antipatharian corals (fr. Gk *antipathes* black coral, lit., remedy for suffering, fr. neut. of *antipathēs* in exchange for suffering, of opposite feelings) + *-aria*] : an order or suborder of Anthozoa comprising the black or thorny corals, all having a usu. brown or black axial skeleton that is much branched and horned and with polyps with few mesenteries or tentacles — **an·ti·pa·thar·i·an** \ˌ===ˌ==ən\ *adj or n*

an·ti·pa·thet·ic \ˌantəpəˈthed·ik, ˌaan-, -tēp-, -etik, -ēk, *also* anˌtip- *or* aan-\ *also* **an·ti·pa·thet·i·cal** \-ə̇kəl, -ēk-\ *adj* [L *antipathia* antipathy + E *-etic, -etical* (as in *pathetic, pathetical*)] **1** : having a natural opposition or constitutional aversion ⟨~ variation of minerals in sedimentary rocks⟩ ⟨forces ~ to the spread of literacy —Helen Sullivan⟩ **2 a** : arousing antipathy ⟨mountains, which are most remote from the sea, are ~ to me —Havelock Ellis⟩ ⟨the really disliked Sir Theodosius, who was in every way ~ to him —Gabrielle Long⟩ **b** : instinctively averse — **an·ti·pa·thet·i·cal·ly** \-ə̇k(ə)lē, -ēk-, -li\ *adv*

an·ti·path·ic \ˌantəˈpathik\ *adj* [F *antipathique,* fr. *antipathie* antipathy + *-ique* -ic] : ANTIPATHETIC

an·ti·path·i·da \ˌantəˈpathədə\ [NL, fr. *Antipathes* genus of antipatharian corals + *-ida* — more at ANTIPATHARIA] *syn of* ANTIPATHARIA

an·tip·a·thist \anˈtipəthə̇st, aan-\ *n* -s : one who has an antipathy

antipathize *vi* -ED/-ING/-s *archaic* : to feel or show antipathy

an·tip·a·thy \anˈtipəthē, aan-, -thi\ *n* -ES [L *antipathia,* fr. Gk *antipatheia,* fr. *antipathēs* of opposite feelings (fr. *anti-* ¹anti- + *-pathēs* -path) + *-ia* -y] **1** *obs* : opposition in feeling : natural incompatibility **2** : settled aversion or dislike : REPUGNANCE, DISTASTE ⟨some deep and secret ~ —Mary R. Rinehart⟩ ⟨*antipathies* against particular nations —George Washington⟩ ⟨Tolstoy's mounting ~ to the university —E.J. Simmons⟩ ⟨~ toward other persons or groups —E.A.Hoebel⟩ **3** : an object of aversion ⟨evil is the greatest ~ of human nature —John Norris⟩ **syn** see ENMITY

an·ti·pa·tri·ot·ic \ˌ=(ˌ)= at ¹ANTI- +\ *adj* [¹*anti-* + *patriotic*] : tending to undermine patriotism ⟨~ propaganda⟩ ⟨~ activities⟩

an·ti·pe·dal \ˌ=(ˌ)= at ¹ANTI- + ˈpēdᵊl\ *adj* [¹*anti-* + *pedal*] : opposite to the foot — used of parts of the body of a mollusk

an·ti·pe·do·bap·tism *also* **an·ti·pae·do·bap·tism** \ˌ=(ˌ)=ˌpēdōˈbapˌtizəm\ *n* -s *often cap* [¹*anti-* + *pedobaptism, paedobaptism*] : the doctrine that infant baptism is scripturally unwarranted and inefficacious

an·ti·pe·do·bap·tist *or* **an·ti·pae·do·bap·tist** \ˌ=(ˌ)=ˌpēdōˈbaptəst\ *n* -s [¹*anti-* + *pedobaptist, paedobaptist*] **1** *usu cap* : one of a sect of Anabaptists opposed to infant baptism **2** : an opponent of infant baptism

antipendium *var of* ANTEPENDIUM

¹**an·ti·pe·ri·od·ic** \ˌ=(ˌ)=ˌ-\ *adj* [ISV ¹*anti-* + *periodic*] : preventive of periodic returns of paroxysms or exacerbations of disease (as in intermittent fevers)

²**antiperiodic** \"\ *n* -s : an antiperiodic agent

an·ti·per·i·stal·sis \ˌ=(ˌ)=ˌ-\ *n* [NL, fr. ¹*anti-* + *peristalsis*] : reversed peristalsis

an·ti·per·i·stal·tic \ˌ=(ˌ)=ˌ==ˈ==\ *adj* [¹*anti-* + *peristaltic*] **1** : opposed to or checking peristaltic motion **2** : relating to antiperistalsis

an·ti·pe·ris·ta·sis \ˌ=(ˌ)=pəˈristəsə̇s\ *n, pl* **antiperista·ses** \-təˌsēz\ [Gk, fr. *anti-* ¹anti- + *peristasis* act of standing around, fr. *periistanai* to make stand around (fr. *peri-* + *histanai* to cause to stand) + *-sis* — more at STAND] *archaic* : resistance or reaction roused by opposition or by the action of an opposite principle or quality

an·ti·per·ni·cious anemia factor \ˌ=(ˌ)=-\ *n* [¹*anti-* + *pernicious*] : VITAMIN B_{12}

an·ti·per·son·nel \ˌ=(ˌ)=ˌ=ˌ=\ *adj* [¹*anti-* + *personnel*] : designed to destroy, maim, or obstruct military personnel ⟨~ bomb⟩ ⟨~ mine⟩ ⟨~ weapons⟩

an·ti·per·spi·rant \ˌ=(ˌ)=ˈpərspərənt, -ˈpəs- *sometimes* -ˌpə(r)ˈspīrənt\ *n* -s [¹*anti-* + *perspiration* + *-ant*] : a cosmetic preparation used to check excessive perspiration by astringent action when applied to the skin

an·ti·perth·ite \ˌ=(ˌ)=ˈpərˌthīt\ *n* -s [ISV ¹*anti-* + *perthite*] : a feldspar rock consisting of plagioclase containing lamellae of orthoclase — **an·ti·per·thit·ic** \ˌ=(ˌ)=ˌ=ˈthid·ik\ *adj*

an·ti·pet·al·ous \ˌ=(ˌ)=ˌ-\ *adj* [¹*anti-* + *petalous*] : having stamens opposite the petals

an·ti·phage \ˈ=(ˌ)=ˌfāj\ *adj* [¹*anti-* + *phage*] : inimical to phages

¹**an·ti·phlo·gis·tic** \ˌ=(ˌ)=-\ *adj* [¹*anti-* + *phlogistic*] **1** : opposed to the doctrine of phlogiston **2** : counteracting inflammation

²**antiphlogistic** \"\ *n* -s : an antiphlogistic agent

an·ti·phon \ˈantəfən, ˈaan-, -ˌfän\ *n* -s [LL *antiphona* — more at ANTHEM] **1 a** : a devotional verse sung responsively as a part of a liturgy by two choirs usu. by men's voices alternating with boys' or women's voices; *specif* : one of three of the chants of the mass: introit, offertory, and communion **b** : a liturgical verse or series of verses chanted responsively before the psalms or other hymns **2** : RESPONSE, ANSWER ⟨deputies shrilled a dissenting ~ —*Time*⟩

¹**an·tiph·o·nal** \anˈtifənᵊl, aan-\ *n* -s : ANTIPHONARY

²**antiphonal** \(ˈ)=ˈ===\ *adj* **1** : relating to or resembling an antiphon **2** : answering or alternating (as in antiphony) — **an·tiph·o·nal·ly** \-ᵊnᵊlē, -li\ *adv*

antiphonal organ *n* : an enclosed division of a pipe organ situated some distance from the main enclosure and permitting answering or antiphonal effects

¹**an·tiph·o·nary** \anˈtifəˌnerē, aan-, -ri\ *also* **antiphoner** *n, pl* **antiphonaries** *also* **antiphoners** [ME *antiphonary, antiphonarium,* fr. ML *antiphonarium,* fr. neut. of *antiphonarius*] : a book containing a collection of antiphons; *specif* : the book in which the choral parts of the breviary are contained

²**antiphonary** \(ˈ)=ˈ-\ *adj* [ML *antiphonarius,* fr. LL *antiphona* antiphon + L *-arius* -ary — more at ANTHEM] : ANTIPHONAL

antiphone *archaic var of* ANTIPHON

an·tiph·o·net·ic \anˌtifəˈned·ik\ *adj* [*antiphon* + *-etic* (as in *phonetic*)] : RHYMING

an·ti·phon·ic \ˌantəˈfänik ˌaan-, -ēk\ *adj* [*antiphon* + *-ic*] : ANTIPHONAL — **an·ti·phon·i·cal·ly** \-nə̇k(ə)lē, -ēk-, -li\ *adv*

an·tiph·o·ny \anˈtifənē, aan-, -ni\ *n* -ES [Gk *antiphōnos* concordant, responsive + E *-y* — more at ANTHEM] **1 a** : musical response **b** : antiphonal chanting or singing; *broadly* : any alternation of voices **2 a** : an anthem, psalm, or musical composition sung alternately by divisions of a choir or congregation **b** : ANTIPHON 1 **3** *Greek music* : accompaniment or response in the octave **4** : responsive movement between two dancers or groups of dancers

an·tiph·ra·sis \anˈtifrəsə̇s\ *n, pl* **antiphra·ses** \-əˌsēz\ [LL, fr. Gk, fr. *anti-* ¹anti- + *phrasis* diction — more at PHRASE] : the use of words in senses opposite to the generally accepted meanings or the use of a word in this way usu. for humorous or ironical purposes (as, a giant of three feet, four inches) — **an·ti·phras·tic** \ˌantəˈfrastik\ *adj* — **an·ti·phras·ti·cal·ly** \-tə̇k(ə)lē, -li\ *adv*

an·ti·plas·tic \ˈ=(ˌ)= at ¹ANTI- + ˌ-\ *adj* [¹*anti-* + *plastic*] : preventing or checking the process of healing or granulation

an·ti·plum·ming \ˌ=(ˌ)=ˌ-\ *adj* [¹*anti-* + *plumming*] : preventing or reducing the tendency to undergo plumming ⟨an ~ agent in a photographic emulsion⟩

an·ti·pneu·mo·coc·cus \ˌ=(ˌ)=ˌ=ˌ-\ *or* **an·ti·pneu·mo·coc·cic** \ˌ=(ˌ)=ˌ-\ *also* **an·ti·pneu·mo·coc·cal** \ˌ=(ˌ)=ˌ-\ *adj* [¹*anti-* + *pneumococcus, pneumococcic, pneumococcal*] : inimical to pneumococci

¹**an·tip·o·dal** \(ˈ)anˈtipədᵊl, (ˈ)aan-\ *also* **an·ti·pod·ic** \ˌ=ˈpädik, -ēk\ *adj* [*antipode* + *-al* or *-ic*] **1** : of or relating to the antipodes; *specif* : situated at the opposite side of the earth ⟨~ latitudes⟩ ⟨~ to our region⟩ **2** : diametrically opposite ⟨~ points on opposite sides of a sphere⟩ **3** : OPPOSED : widely different ⟨nothing so ~ to his nature as this man's cold, unimaginative sagacity —Nathaniel Hawthorne⟩ ⟨have often marveled at the friendship of these two ~ men —W.H.Wright⟩ **syn** see OPPOSITE

²**an·tip·o·dal** \"\ *or* **antipodal cell** *n* -s : any of three cells in the female gametophyte of most angiosperms that are grouped at the end of the embryo sac farthest from the micropyle and

that usu. degenerate after fertilization but sometimes survive as part of the embryo
an·tip·o·dal·ly \(ˈ)=¦=d°lē, -li\ *adv* **:** in an antipodal position or manner
an·ti·pode \ˈantə,pōd\ *n, pl* **an·tip·o·des** \an·tipə,dēz *sometimes* ˈantə,pōdz *by those aware that there is a singular "antipode"*\ [back-formation fr. *antipodes*, pl., fr. ME, fr. L, fr. Gk, fr. pl. of *antipod-, antipous* with the feet opposite, fr. *anti-* ¹anti- + *pod-, pous* foot — more at FOOT] **1** *antipodes pl, archaic* **a :** persons dwelling at a directly opposite point on the globe of the earth **b :** those who are felt in some way to resemble such persons **2** *antipodes pl, sometimes cap* **:** the parts of the earth diametrically opposite — often used of Australia, New Zealand, and contiguous areas ⟨the churches of the ~*s* — *Christian Century*⟩; sometimes used in sing. ⟨the South Pole is the ~ of the North Pole —Irving Fisher & O.M.Miller⟩ **3 :** the exact opposite or contrary ⟨virtue is the ~ of self-love —G.P.Fisher⟩ — often used in pl. ⟨the very ~*s* of scholarly humanism —A.L.Guérard⟩ **4 :** a chemical compound having an exact opposite configuration of its atoms in space — compare ENANTIOMORPH 2 **5** *antipodes pl* **:** antipodal points
¹**an·tip·o·de·an** \an·¦tipə¦dēən, ¦an-,t-, aan-, ¦aan-\ *adj* [*antipode* + *-an*] **1 :** ANTIPODAL **2** *sometimes cap, Brit* **:** AUSTRALIAN **syn** see OPPOSITE
²**antipodean** \"\ *n* -s **1 :** one living at the antipodes **2** *sometimes cap, Brit* **:** AUSTRALIAN
an·ti·pole \ˈantə̇pōl, -tē-, ˈaan-\ *n* -s [¹*anti-* + *pole*] **:** the opposite pole **:** ²OPPOSITE
an·ti·po·lo \,äntēˈpōlō\ *n* -s [Tag] *Philippines* **:** BREADFRUIT 1
an·ti·pope \ˈantē,pōp, -tə̇-, -tī-, ˈaan-\ *n* [alter. of earlier *antipape*, fr. MF, fr. ML *antipapa*, fr. *anti-* ¹anti- + *papa* pope] **:** one elected or claiming to be pope in opposition to the pope canonically chosen
an·ti·pros·tate \ˈantē,-, -tə̇-\ *n* -s [²*anti-* + *prostate*] **:** COWPER'S GLAND
an·ti·pro·throm·bic \¦=(,)= *at* ¹ANTI- + ,=¦==\ *adj* **:** of or like that of an antiprothrombin
an·ti·pro·throm·bin \ˈ=(,)=(,)=¦==\ *n* -s [¹*anti-* + *prothrombin*] **:** a substance that interferes with the conversion of prothrombin to thrombin — compare ANTITHROMBIN, HEPARIN
an·ti·pro·ton \ˈ=(,)=¦-\ *n* -s [¹*anti-* + *proton*] **:** a particle equal in mass but opposite in electrical charge to a proton
¹**an·ti·pru·rit·ic** \¦=(,)=¦==\ *adj* [¹*anti-* + *pruritic*] **:** tending to check or alleviate itching
²**antipruritic** \"\ *n* -s **:** an antipruritic agent
an·ti·py·re·sis \,=(,)=,pīˈrēsə̇s\ *n* [NL, fr. E *antipyretic*, after such pairs as E *genetic*: L *genesis*] **:** treatment of fever by use of antipyretics
¹**an·ti·py·ret·ic** \,=(,)=,-\ *n* -s [¹*anti-* + *pyretic*] **:** an antipyretic agent
²**antipyretic** \¦=(,)=,-\ *adj* **:** preventing, removing, or allaying fever
an·ti·py·rine \,=(,)=ˈpī,rēn, -,rə̇n\ *also* **an·ti·py·rin** \-,rə̇n\ *n* -s [fr. G *antipyrin*, fr. *Antipyrin*, a trademark] **:** a white crystalline compound $C_{11}H_{12}N_2O$ derived from pyrazolone and used as an antipyretic, analgesic, and antirheumatic
¹**an·ti·quar·i·an** \,antə̇ˈkwerēən, ,aan-, -wa(a)r-,-wär-\ *n* -s [L *antiquarius* antiquary + E *-an*] **1 :** ANTIQUARY **2 :** a size of paper (as for drawing) 31 x 53 inches
²**antiquarian** \¦==¦==\ *adj* **1 a :** of or belonging to antiquaries, the study of antiquities, or old times **b :** connected with a dilettante interest in old things or former times **2 :** dealing in old and rare books or in secondhand books ⟨~ booksellers⟩
an·ti·quar·i·an·ism \,=ˈ=o,nizəm\ *n* -s **:** antiquarian interests or research **:** study or love of antiquities
¹**an·ti·quary** \ˈ==,kwerē, -ri\ *n* -ES [L *antiquarius* student of antiquities, fr. *antiquarius*, adj.] **1** *archaic* **:** an official custodian of antiquities **2 :** one who studies the relics of antiquity **:** one who collects or studies antiquities
²**antiquary** \"\ *adj* [L *antiquarius*, fr. *antiquus* ancient — more at ANTIQUE] **:** belonging to or suggestive of antiquity
¹**antiquate** *adj* [LL *antiquatus*] *archaic* **:** ANTIQUATED
²**an·ti·quate** \ˈantə̇,kwāt, -tē-, ˈaan-, *usu* -ād· + V\ *vt* -ED/-ING/-S [LL *antiquatus*, past part. of *antiquare* to make obsolete, fr. L *antiquus* old — more at ANTIQUE] **1 a :** to make old or obsolete ⟨new appliances ~ millions of old wiring systems — *Better Homes & Gardens*⟩ **b :** to make void or abolish as out of date ⟨the Copernican system . . . *antiquated* an astronomic theory —Jacob Taubes⟩ **2 :** to make antique **:** ANTIQUE
an·ti·quat·ed \ˈ==,kwād·ə̇d, -ātə̇d\ *adj* **1 :** fallen into disuse or lack of esteem because of age **:** OBSOLETE ⟨a calendar becomes ~ —A.L.Kroeber⟩ **2 :** of long standing **:** DEEP-ROOTED, INVETERATE ⟨every royal master had whims of his own — ~ prejudices, family ties, fragments of knowledge —A.J.P. Taylor⟩ **3 :** surviving from or imitating the past **:** OLD-FASHIONED ⟨~ legal ideas —Felix Frankfurter⟩ **4 :** advanced in age **:** OLD **syn** see OLD
an·ti·qua·tion \,==ˈkwāshən\ *n* -s [LL *antiquation-, antiquatio*, fr. L *antiquatus* + *-ion-, -io* -ion] **:** the act of making antiquated **:** the state of being antiquated
¹**an·tique** \(ˈ)an¦tēk, (ˈ)aan-\ *adj* [MF, fr. L *antiquus, anticus*, fr. *ante* before — more at ANTE-] **1 :** existing since ancient or former times **:** among the oldest of its class ⟨~ nations⟩ **2 :** of or belonging to earlier periods **:** ANCIENT ⟨an ~ philosopher⟩ ⟨~ legends⟩ ⟨ruins of an ~ city⟩ **3 :** exhibiting the style or fashion of ancient or former times **:** OLD-FASHIONED, ARCHAIC ⟨~ manners⟩ ⟨a mirror of ~ design⟩ **4** *of fabric* **:** having an indistinct design woven, printed, or watered in imitation of ancient silks **5 a :** embossed or impressed without ink, foil, or gold ⟨an ~ book cover⟩ **:** BLIND 6d **b :** having the appearance of age **:** suggesting the crafts of an older period ⟨~ decorations⟩ **syn** see OLD
²**antique** \"\ *n* -s **1 a :** a relic or object of ancient times or of an earlier period than the present **b :** a work of art, piece of furniture, or decorative object made at a much earlier period than the present and according to U.S. customs laws at least 100 years old **2 a** *obs* **:** a man of ancient times **b :** a person belonging to an older generation ⟨a handsome ~ —Wolcott Gibbs⟩ **3 :** SYRUP 3 **4 :** a paper having a rough finish and often relatively great bulk — compare EGGSHELL
³**antique** \"\ *vt* **an·tiqued; an·tiqued; an·tiqu·ing; antiques 1 :** to finish or refinish in antique style **:** give an appearance of age to **2 :** to emboss or impress (lettering) without ink, foil, or gold ⟨a book with *antiqued* backbone⟩
antique brass *n* **:** a light to light grayish olive color
antique bronze *n* **:** a moderate yellowish brown that is redder and lighter than bronze, very slightly stronger than Bismarck brown, slightly yellower and very slightly stronger than cinnamon brown, and darker and very slightly yellower than maple sugar
antique brown *n* **:** a moderate brown that is yellower, lighter, and stronger than auburn, lighter, stronger, and slightly yellower than chestnut brown, and lighter, stronger, and slightly redder than coffee — called also *cigarette*
antique crown *n, heraldry* **:** a figure of a crown composed of a circular band with an indefinite number of pointed rays rising from it — called also *eastern crown*
antique drab *n* **:** FOX 5
antique gold *n* **1 :** a variable color averaging a dark yellow that is greener, lighter, and stronger than mustard (sense 3a) **2 :** a strong yellowish brown that is redder, stronger, and slightly lighter than buckthorn brown and yellower and paler than orange rust

antique crown

antique green *n* **:** a grayish to moderate green
an·tique·ly \(ˈ)=¦=lē, -li\ *adv* **:** in an antique manner
an·tique·ness *n* -ES **:** the quality or state of being antique
an·tiqu·er \=ˈtēkə(r)\ *n* -s [²*antique* + *-er*] **1 :** a collector of antiques ⟨this is a book for ~*s* alone —*N.Y.Herald Tribune*⟩ **2** [³*antique* + *-er*] **:** one that antiques new furniture
antique red *n* **:** a dark reddish orange that is yellower and paler than average lacquer red and redder and paler than ocher red or burnt sienna — called also *canna, chaudron, Rembrandt's madder*
antique rose *n* **:** a grayish red that is yellower and darker than appleblossom and bluer and duller than bois de rose or Pompeian red
antiques and horribles *n pl* **:** fantastic impersonations forming part of a parade

an·tiqu·ing \=ˈtēkiŋ, -kēŋ\ *n* -s [²*antique* + *-ing*] **:** the collecting of antiques
an·tiq·ui·tar·i·an \(,)an-,tikwəˈterēən\ *n* -s [*antiquity* + *-arian* (as in *humanitarian*)] **:** one who is attached to the opinions or practices of antiquity
an·tiq·ui·ty \anˈtikwəd·ē, aan-, -ətē, -i\ *n* -ES [ME *antiquite*, fr. MF *antiquité*, fr. L *antiquitat-, antiquitas*, fr. *antiquus* ancient + *-itat-, -itas* -ity — more at ANTIQUE] **1 :** ancient times **:** times long since past **:** former ages esp. when before the middle ages ⟨Greek ~⟩ ⟨Christian ~⟩ **2 :** the quality of being ancient **:** great age **:** ANCIENTNESS ⟨a castle of great ~⟩ ⟨he had an air of ~ about him⟩ **3 antiquities** *pl* **a :** relics or monuments of ancient times (as coins, statues, or buildings) **b :** matters relating to the life or culture of ancient times ⟨the study of Germanic *antiquities*⟩ **4 :** the people of ancient times ⟨the records left by ~⟩ **5** *obs* **a :** old age **b :** an old man ⟨you are a shrewd ~, neighbor —Ben Jonson⟩
an·ti·rab·ic \¦=(,)= *at* ¹ANTI- + ¦==\ *adj* [¹*anti-* + *rabic*] **:** tending to prevent or control rabies
an·ti·rac·er \ˈ=(,)=,-\ *n* [¹*anti-* + *racer*] **:** a device to prevent the racing of a ship's propeller
¹**an·ti·ra·chit·ic** \¦=(,)==¦-\ *adj* [¹*anti-* + *rachitic*] **:** opposing or preventing the development of rickets ⟨an ~ vitamin⟩
²**antirachitic** \"\ *n* -s **:** an antirachitic agent
an·ti·re·flec·tion film \¦=(,)==¦-\ *or* **antireflection coating** *n* [¹*anti-* + *reflection*] **:** a transparent film applied to a transparent optical surface (as glass) of such thickness and refractive index as to reduce the intensity of reflected light almost to zero
an·ti·re·mon·strant \,=(,)=-\ *n, usu cap* [¹*anti-* + *Remonstrant*] **:** one of the Dutch Calvinistic party that opposed the Remonstrants or Arminians
an·ti·rent \ˈ=(,)=,-\ *adj, usu cap* [¹*anti-* + *rent*] **:** of or relating to a political party (1839–47) in the state of New York that supported those tenants resisting collection of rents by patroons — **an·ti·rent·er** \¦=(,)=¦-\ *n* -s *usu cap*
an·ti·res·o·nance \¦=(,)=¦-\ *n* -s [¹*anti-* + *resonance*] **:** the state of adjustment of the components of an alternating current or acoustic network that produces for a given frequency minimum amplitude and intensity of current or acoustic flux — **an·ti·res·o·nant** \¦=(,)=¦-\ *adj*
an·ti·re·tic·u·lar cytotoxic serum \¦=(,)==¦-\ *n* [ISV ¹*anti-* + *reticular*] **:** a serum prepared from blood of horses inoculated with cells of normal human spleen and bone marrow and claimed to have restorative and regenerative effects on certain reticular tissues in humans
an·tir·rhi·num \,antə̇ˈrīnəm, -tē-\ *n* [NL, fr. L, snapdragon, fr. Gk *antirrhinon*, fr. *anti-* similar to, like (fr. *anti* against, instead of, equivalent to) + *-rrhinon* (fr. *rhin-, rhis* nose, snout); fr. the resemblance of the flower to a calf's snout] **1** *cap* **:** a genus of herbs (family Scrophulariaceae) of the northern hemisphere with brightly colored irregular flowers distinguished from those of *Linaria* by the absence of a spur — see SNAPDRAGON **2** -s **:** any plant of the genus *Antirrhinum*
antis *pl of* ANTI
anti-sabbatarian *n* [¹*anti-* + *sabbatarian*] **:** one who denies any obligation for observing the Sabbath day
antiscion *n, pl* **antiscia** [Gk *antiskion*, fr. *anti-* ¹anti- + *-skion* (fr. *skia* shadow) — more at SCENE] *archaic* **:** either of any two signs of the zodiac equally distant from Cancer and Capricorn on opposite sides
¹**an·ti·scor·bu·tic** \¦=(,)= *at* ¹ANTI-+,=¦==\ *adj* [¹*anti-* + *scorbutic*] **:** counteracting scurvy ⟨the ~ vitamin is vitamin C⟩
²**antiscorbutic** \"\ *n* -s **:** a remedy for scurvy
an·ti·se·le·ne \,=(,)=səˈlēnē\ *n* -s [NL, fr. *anti-* ¹anti- + Gk *selēnē* moon — more at SELEN-] **:** a white luminous spot like a halo occurring rarely at the same elevation as the moon and in the opposite azimuth
an·ti-sem·ite \,=(,)=ˈ-\ *n, usu cap S* [¹*anti-* + *Semite*] **:** one who is hostile to Jews or who practices anti-Semitism
an·ti-se·mit·ic \¦=(,)=¦==\ *adj, often cap S* [¹*anti-* + *Semitic*] **:** relating to or characterized by anti-Semitism
an·ti-sem·i·tism \,=(,)=ˈ-\ *n, usu cap S* **1 :** hostility toward Jews as a religious or racial minority group often accompanied by social, economic, and political discrimination — compare RACISM **2 :** opposition to Zionism **:** sympathy with opponents of the state of Israel
an·ti·sep·sis \,antəˈsepsə̇s, ,aan-\ *n, pl* **an·ti·sep·ses** \-p,sēz\ [NL, fr. E *antiseptic*, after such pairs as E *septic*: NL *sepsis*] **:** the process of inhibiting the growth and multiplication of microorganisms **:** the prevention or treatment of sepsis by antiseptic means — compare ASEPSIS, DISINFECTION, STERILIZATION
¹**an·ti·sep·tic** \¦==¦septik, -ēk\ *adj* [¹*anti-* + Gk *sēptikos* putrefying — more at SEPTIC] **1 a :** opposing sepsis, putrefaction, or decay **:** having the properties of an antiseptic **:** preventing or arresting the growth or action of microorganisms esp. on or in living tissue — compare DISINFECTANT **b :** acting like an antiseptic **:** CLEANSING, PURIFYING ⟨the ~ effect of sturdy criticism —*New Republic*⟩; *also* **:** BRACING ⟨smelling the crisp ~ air —Berton Roueché⟩ **c :** giving protection from what is contaminating ⟨new settlements a safe number of ~ miles from Johannesburg's whites —*Time*⟩ **2 :** relating to or characterized by the use of antiseptics ⟨~ treatment⟩ — compare ASEPTIC **3 a :** free from living microorganisms **:** characterized by scrupulous cleanliness, sterilization, exclusion of bacteria **:** ASEPTIC ⟨a technician in an ~ white jacket —*Monsanto Mag.*⟩ **b** (1) **:** suggestive of a hospital or operating room (as in cleanliness or orderliness) ⟨abstract art's ~ charm —Lewis Mumford⟩ ⟨the ~ world of interstellar mathematics —*Time*⟩ (2) **:** excessively neat, well-ordered, or severe ⟨the room itself was bare, almost ~ —Nicholas Blake⟩ (3) **:** lacking warmth or vitality ⟨a conception that was much too meek and ~ —Joseph Katz⟩ (4) **:** DULL, VAPID, UNIMAGINATIVE ⟨main building of ~ institutional Georgian —Nathaniel Burt⟩ **c :** free or protected from what is contaminating ⟨lyrics that were ~ as Sunday school —*Saturday Rev.*⟩ ⟨two romances of a lively but ~ nature —Wolcott Gibbs⟩ **d :** marked by objectivity or detachment; *esp* **:** coldly impersonal ⟨gave the score an ~ reading —Horst Koegler⟩ ⟨~, dehumanized procedures of science —Lewis Mumford⟩ — **an·ti·sep·ti·cal·ly** \-tə̇k(ə)lē, -ēk-, -li\ *adv*
²**antiseptic** \"\ *n* -s **:** a substance that opposes sepsis, putrefaction, or decay **:** one that prevents or arrests the growth or action of microorganisms either by inhibiting their activity or by destroying them — used esp. of agents applied to living tissue; compare DISINFECTANT, GERMICIDE
an·ti·sep·ti·cize \¦==ˈstə,sīz\ *vt* -ED/-ING/-S **:** to make antiseptic
an·ti·se·rum \ˈ=(,)= *at* ¹ANTI-+,==\ *n* [ISV ¹*anti-* + *serum*] **:** a serum containing antibodies that is obtained from the blood of an animal subjected to repeated sublethal doses of a microorganism or a specific toxin and that is used in treatment of the disease caused by the respective microorganism or toxin (as diphtheria or tetanus) — compare ANTITOXIN
an·ti·si \ˈäntē,sē\ *also* **an·ti·si·ans** \,==ˈsēənz\ *n pl, usu cap* [modif. of Sp *antis*, of AmerInd origin] **:** the Indian peoples of the eastern slopes of the Andes
an·ti·si·der·ic \¦=(,)= *at* ¹ANTI- + ¦==\ *n* -s [¹*anti-* + Gk *sidēros* iron + E *-ic*] **:** a pharmaceutical agent that counteracts the physiological action of iron
an·ti·si·phon \,=(,)=¦-\ *adj* [¹*anti-* + *siphon*] **:** designed to prevent the emptying of a sanitary trap because of difference of pressure
an·ti·si·phon·al \¦=(,)=¦-\ *adj* [¹*anti-* + *siphonal*] **:** opposite the siphuncle or siphon — used esp. of an unpaired lobe of the suture on the dorsal side of a cephalopod
an·ti·skid plate \¦=(,)=¦-\ *n* [¹*anti-* + *skid*] **:** a piece of sheet iron roughed on both sides by punching holes through it alternately on each side, and placed between piled boxes or other objects to prevent sliding (as in a freight car)
an·ti·skin·ning \¦=(,)=¦-\ *adj* [¹*anti-* + *skinning*, gerund of *skin*] **:** serving to prevent the formation of skin (as on paint)
an·ti·slav·ery *n, often attrib* [¹*anti-* + *slavery*] **:** opposition to slavery
an·ti·so·cial \¦=(,)=¦-\ *adj* [¹*anti-* + *social*] **1 a :** tending to interrupt or destroy social intercourse **b :** hostile to the well-being of society **c :** characterized by markedly deviating behavior ⟨~ actions⟩ ⟨crime is ~⟩ ⟨~ persons⟩ **2 :** averse to the society of others or to social intercourse **:** MISANTHROPIC ⟨stand-offish and ~ —Hamilton Basso⟩ — **an·ti·so·ci·al·i·ty** \,=(,)=,-\ *n* -ES — **an·ti·so·cial·ly** \¦=(,)=¦-\ *adv*
an·ti·so·lar \¦=(,)=¦-\ *adj* [¹*anti-* + *solar*] **:** directly opposite the sun on the celestial sphere
an·ti·spa·dix \¦=(,)=¦-\ *n* [¹*anti-* + *spadix*] **:** the four modified tentacles opposite the spadix in mollusks of the genus *Nautilus*
¹**an·ti·spas·mod·ic** \,=(,)=,-\ *n* -s [¹*anti-* + *spasmodic*] **:** an antispasmodic agent
²**antispasmodic** \¦=(,)=,-\ *adj* **:** tending or having the power to prevent or relieve spasms or convulsions **:** SPASMOLYTIC
an·ti·spast \ˈantē,spast, -tə̇-\ *n* -s [LL *antispastus*, fr. Gk *antispastos* drawn in the contrary direction, fr. *antispan* to draw in the contrary direction, fr. *anti-* ¹anti- + *span* to draw — more at SPAN] **:** a metrical foot or system of four syllables in which an iambic cadence is followed by a trochaic
an·ti·spas·tic \¦==¦spastik\ *adj* [LL *antispasticus*, fr. Gk *antispastikos*, fr. *antispastos* + *-ikos* -ic] **:** relating to, consisting of, or containing antispasts
an·ti·squa·ma \,==ˈ-\ *or* **an·ti·squame** \,==ˈ-\ *n, pl* **antisqua·mae** *or* **antisquames** [NL *antisquama*, fr. ¹*anti-* + *squama*] **:** a scalelike lobe between the base of the wing and the squama of various two-winged flies
an·tis·tes \anˈtis,tēz\ *n, pl* **antis·ti·tes** \-tə,tēz\ [LL, priest, bishop, fr. L, overseer, high priest, fr. *ante-* + *-stes* (fr. *stare* to stand) — more at STAND] **1 :** a presiding officer in the church **:** PRESBYTER **2 :** a Moravian bishop
an·ti·stokes line \¦=(,)= *at* ¹ANTI- + ˈstōks-\ *n, usu cap S* [¹*anti-* + *Stokes'* (*law*) + *line*] **:** a spectrum line of radiation not conforming to Stokes' law (sense 1)
an·ti·strep·to·ly·sin \¦=(,)=¦-\ *n* -s [¹*anti-* + *streptolysin*] **:** an antibody against a streptolysin produced by the body of an individual injected with a streptolysin-forming streptococcus
an·tis·tro·phe \anˈtistrə(,)fē, -,fi\ *n* -s [LL, fr. Gk *antistrophē*, fr. Gk *anti-* ¹anti- + *strophē* turning, movement of the chorus in Greek drama — more at STROPHE] **1** *in the Greek choral dance* **a :** the returning of the chorus exactly answering to a previous strophe **b :** the part of a choral song corresponding to this returning **2** *archaic* **:** an inverse relation or correspondence — **an·ti·stroph·ic** \¦antə̇¦sträfik *also* -ōf-\ *adj* — **an·ti·stroph·i·cal·ly** \-fə̇k(ə)lē\ *adv*
antistrophon *n* -s [Gk, neut. of *antistrophos* turned about or against, fr. *anti-* ¹anti- + *strephein* to turn — more at STROPHE] *obs* **:** an argument that is or may be turned against its user
an·ti·sub·ma·rine \¦=(,)= *at* ¹ANTI- + \ *adj* [¹*anti-* + *submarine*] **:** designed or waged to destroy submarines ⟨~ warfare⟩
an·ti·sun \ˈ=(,)= *at* ¹ANTI- + ,=\ *n* [¹*anti-* + *sun*] **:** ANTHELION
an·ti·sym·met·ric \¦=(,)==¦-\ *adj* [¹*anti-* + *symmetric*] *of a square matrix or a tensor* **:** having the sign of every element or component changed by the interchange of any two indices of that element or component
an·ti·sym·pa·tho·mi·met·ic \¦=(,)=,==(,)=(,)=¦-\ *adj* [¹*anti-* + *sympathomimetic*] **:** SYMPATHOLYTIC
¹**an·ti·syph·i·lit·ic** \¦=(,)=,==¦-\ *adj* [¹*anti-* + *syphilitic*] **:** effective against syphilis ⟨~ treatment⟩
²**antisyphilitic** \"\ *n* -s **:** an agent effective against syphilis
an·ti·tank \¦=(,)=¦=\ *adj* [¹*anti-* + *tank*] **:** designed to destroy or check tanks ⟨an ~ gun⟩
an·ti·the·nar \¦antə̇ˈthēnər, -tē-, -,när, (ˈ)an¦tithə-\ *adj* [ISV ¹*anti-* + Gk *thenar* palm of the hand; akin to OHG *tenar* palm of the hand — more at DEN] **1 :** situated opposite to the palm or sole **2 :** HYPOTHENAR
an·tith·e·sis \anˈtithəsə̇s, aan-\ *n, pl* **antithe·ses** \-ə,sēz\ [LL, fr. Gk, lit., opposition, fr. *antithe-* (stem of *antitithenai* to set against, oppose, fr. *anti-* ¹anti- + *tithenai* to set) + *-sis* — more at DO] **1 a :** the rhetorical opposing or contrasting of ideas by means of grammatically parallel arrangements of words, clauses, or sentences (as *action*, not *words* or they *promised freedom* and *provided slavery*); *broadly* **:** a balanced contrast formed by a pair or several pairs of objects or concepts, each member in a pair being the opposite of the other in essence or in particulars ⟨the ~ of prose and verse⟩ **b** (1) **:** the second of the two opposing constituents of an antithesis ⟨~ opposed to thesis⟩ (2) **:** an object or concept that counteracts or contradicts another ⟨that mystic faith in unseen powers which is the ~ of materialism —Rose Macaulay⟩ **:** the direct opposite **:** CONTRARY ⟨his temperament is the very ~ of mine⟩ **2 :** a philosophical proposition opposed to a given thesis: **a** *Kantianism* **:** the negative member of one of the antinomies of reason **b** *Hegelianism* **:** the negative moment in the movement of thought that denies the thesis and is in turn transcended in the synthesis **syn** see COMPARISON
antithet *n* -s [L, fr. Gk, fr. neut. of *antithetos*, fr. *antitithenai*] *archaic* **:** ANTITHESIS 1
an·ti·thet·i·cal \¦antə̇¦thed·ə̇kəl, ¦aan-, -etə̇k-, -ēk-\ *or* **an·ti·thet·ic** \-ik,-ēk\ *adj* [LL *antitheticus*, fr. LGk *antithetikos*, fr. Gk *antithetos* placed in opposition (fr. *antitithenai*) + *-ikos* -ical, -ic] **1 :** constituting or resembling antithesis **:** containing or marked by antithesis ⟨~ symbolism of ice and flame—Leslie Rees⟩ **2 :** marked by direct opposition **:** exactly opposite **:** COUNTER, OPPOSING ⟨respective ways of life which looked to wholly *antithetic* ends —H.J.Laski⟩ **syn** see OPPOSITE
an·ti·thet·i·cal·ly \-ə̇k(ə)lē, -ēk-, -li\ *adv* **:** with antithesis in an antithetical manner
antithetic theory *n* **:** a theory in botany: the sporophyte and gametophyte in plants are fundamentally distinct, the gametophyte representing the primitive ancestral phase and the sporophyte being a new structure evolved as a result of increasingly retarded zygotic reduction — compare HOMOLOGOUS THEORY
an·ti·throm·bic \¦=(,)= *at* ¹ANTI- + ¦thrämbik\ *adj* **:** of or like that of an antithrombin
an·ti·throm·bin \¦=(,)=¦-\ *n* [ISV ¹*anti-* + *thrombin*] **:** a substance in blood that inactivates thrombin and prevents conversion of fibrinogen to fibrin — compare HEPARIN
an·ti·thy·roid \¦=(,)=¦-\ *adj* [¹*anti-* + *thyroid*] **:** tending or having power to counteract thyroid overactivity ⟨~ drugs⟩
an·ti·torque rotor \¦=(,)=¦-\ *n* [¹*anti-* + *torque*] **:** a small rotor mounted on the tail of a helicopter that balances the torque reaction of the main lifting rotor and thus permits the craft to maintain a desired heading
an·ti·tox·ic \¦=(,)=¦-\ *adj* [¹*anti-* + *toxic*] **1 :** counteracting poison **2 :** of, relating to, or being an antitoxin
an·ti·tox·in \,=tēˈtäksə̇n, -təˈ-\ *n* [ISV ¹*anti-* + *toxin*] **:** an antibody formed in the body as a result of the introduction of a toxin and capable of neutralizing the specific toxin that stimulated its production, being produced for medical purposes by injection of animals (as horses) with gradually increased doses of a toxin or toxoid (as of diphtheria, tetanus, or botulism), the resulting serum being used to counteract the same toxin in other individuals — compare ANTIVENIN
an·ti·trades \ˈ=(,)=,=\ *n pl* [¹*anti-* + *trades* (trade winds)] **:** the prevailing westerly winds of middle latitudes **:** the westerly winds above the trade winds
an·ti·trag·i·cus \,antēˈtrajə̇kəs, -ntə̇-\ *n, pl* **antitragi·ci** \-jə,sī\ [NL, fr. *antitragus* + L *-icus* -ic] **:** a small muscle arising from the outer part of the antitragus and inserted into the antihelix
an·ti·tra·gus \¦==¦trāgəs\ *n, pl* **antitra·gi** \-ā,jī, -ā,gī\ [NL, fr. Gk *antitragos*, fr. *anti-* ¹anti- + *tragos* he-goat, part of the inner ear] **:** a prominence on the lower posterior portion of the concha of the external ear opposite the tragus
an·ti·tro·chan·ter \-trōˈkantər\ *n* [¹*anti-* + *trochanter*] **:** an articular surface on the ilium of birds against which the great trochanter of the femur plays
an·ti·trope \ˈantē,trōp, -tə̇-\ *n* -s [¹*anti-* + *-trope*] *zool* **:** an antitropic part or appendage — opposed to *syntrope*
an·ti·trop·ic \¦==¦träpik\ *or* **an·ti·trop·i·cal** \-pə̇kəl\ *adj* [*antitropic* fr. ¹*anti-* + *-tropic; antitropical* fr. *antitropic* + *-al*] **1 :** SINISTRORSE **2 :** repeated and reversed symmetrically ⟨the corresponding limbs on the right and left sides of a vertebrate are ~⟩ — opposed to *syntropic* — **an·ti·trop·i·cal·i·ty** \,==,pəˈkaləd·ē\ *n*
an·tit·ro·py \anˈti·trəpē\ *n* -ES [¹*anti-* + *-tropy*] **:** the condition or quality of being antitropic
an·ti·trust \¦=(,)= *at* ¹ANTI- + ¦=\ *adj* [¹*anti-* + *trust*] **:** of or relating to opposition to trusts or combinations; *specif* **:** consisting of federal and state laws and their enforcement for the protection of trade and commerce from unlawful restraints and monopolies or unfair business practices
an·ti·tryp·sin \ˈ=(,)=,tripsə̇n\ *n* -s [ISV ¹*anti-* + *trypsin;*

orig. formed in G] : a substance (as one obtained from pancreatic extracts or from soybeans) that inhibits the action of trypsin — **an·ti·tryp·tic** \¦=(,)=¦triptik\ *adj*
an·ti·tus·sive \¦=(,)=¦-\ *adj* [¹*anti-* + *tussive*] : tending or having the power to control or prevent cough
an·ti·twi·light \'antē,-, -tī-\ *or* **antitwilight arch** *n* [¹*anti-* + *twilight*] : the pink or purplish glow in the eastern sky after sunset
an·ti·type \'antə,tīp, -tē- *also* -(,)tī-, 'aan-\ *n* [LL *antitypus* (fr. LGk *antitypos*) or NL *antitypum*, fr. LGk *antitypon*; both fr. Gk, masc. & neut. of *antitypos* repelled by a hard body, corresponding to a die, fr. *antitypoun* to strike against, fr. *anti-* ¹anti- + *typoun* to stamp, fr. *typos* blow, mark of a blow, mold — more at TYPE] **1 a** : something that corresponds to or is foreshadowed in a type **b** : an opposite type **2** : ANTISTROPE
an·ti·typ·i·cal \¦=(,)=¦tipəkəl, -ēk-\ *or* **an·ti·typ·ic** \-¦tipik, -ēk\ *adj* **1** : of or relating to an antitype **2** : ANTITROPIC 2 — **an·ti·typ·i·cal·ly** \-ək(ə)lē, -li, -ēk-\ *adv*
an·tit·y·py \an'tidəpē, -pi, -titə-\ *n* -ES [Gk *antitypia*, fr. *antitypos* + *-ia*] : resistance offered esp. by matter to penetrative force, alteration, or change
an·ti·ven·in \¦=(,)= at ¹ANTI- + ¦venən, ¦vē-\ *also* **an·ti·venene** \-və¦nēn, -¦ve,nēn, -¦vē,-\ *n* -S [ISV ¹*anti-* + *venin, venene*] : an antitoxin to a venom; *also* : an antiserum containing such an antitoxin
an·ti·viral \¦=(,)=¦-\ *adj* [¹*anti-* + *viral*] : acting to make a virus ineffective
an·ti·vi·rot·ic \¦=(,)=,vī¦räd·ik, -ätik, -ēk\ *n* -S [¹*anti-* + *virus* + *-otic*] : an antibiotic effective against viruses
an·ti·vi·ta·min \¦=(,)=¦-\ *n* [¹*anti-* + *vitamin*] : a substance that renders a vitamin ineffective either by converting it into a compound of different structure or by making it unavailable through combination with it — compare ANTIMETABOLITE
an·ti·viv·i·sec·tion·ist \¦=(,)=¦-\ *n* -S [¹*anti-* + *vivisection* + *-ist*] : a person opposed to animal experimentation
an·ti·xe·roph·thal·mic vitamin \¦=(,)=,zirəf¦thalmik-\ *n* [¹*anti-* + *xerophthalmia* + *-ic*] : VITAMIN A
an·ti·zi·on·ism \,=(,)='-\ *n* -S *usu cap Z* [¹*anti-* + *Zionism*] : opposition to the establishment or support of the state of Israel
an·ti·zo·ea \,antē,zō'ēə, -tə-\ *n, pl* **antizoe·ae** \-'ē,ē, -'ē,ī\ [NL, fr. ²*anti-* + *zoea*] : an early stomatopod larva
ant·ler \'antlə(r), 'aan-\ *n* -S [ME *aunteler*, fr. MF *antoillier*, fr. (assumed) VL *anteoculare*, fr. neut. of *anteocularis* located before the eye, fr. L *ante-* + *oculus* eye + *-aris* -ar — more at EYE] : a horn of an animal of the deer family being typically present only in the male and differing from the horns of other ruminants in being a solid generally branched bony outgrowth that is shed and renewed annually; *sometimes* : a branch of an antler — see BEAM; compare VELVET
ant·lered crab \-lə(d)-\ *n* : an Australian deepwater crab (*Latreillopsis petterdi*) with a tuberculated carapace and an antler-shaped spine over each eye
ant·ler·ite \lə,rīt\ *n* -S [*Antler* Mine, Arizona, its locality + E *-ite*] : a mineral $Cu_3SO_4(OH)_4$ consisting of a basic copper sulfate, occurring in green crystals, and interlaced aggregates of needlelike crystals

antler: *a* brow antler, *b* bay antler, *c* royal antler, *d* sur-royal antler

antler lichen *n* : a fruticose antler-shaped lichen (*Evernia cladonia*)
antler moth *n* : a brownish white-marked European moth (*Charaeas graminis*) whose larva devastates grasslands
antler sponge *n* : any of several branching erect calcareous sponges suggesting an antler in form
ant lion *n* : an insect of *Myrmeleon* or related genera (order Neuroptera), most having a larva that digs a small conical pit in sandy soil in the bottom of which it lies buried with its long jaws protruding to catch any insects (as ants) which fall into the pit
antney over *sometimes cap A, var of* ANTONY OVER
an·toe·ci \an'tē,sī\ *also* **an·toe·cians** \-shənz\ *n pl* [*antoeci* fr. LL, fr. Gk *antoikoi*, fr. *anti-* ¹anti- + *oikos* house; *antoecians* fr. LL *antoeci* + E *-an* + *-s* — more at VICINITY] : those who live under the same meridian but on opposite parallels of latitude equidistant north and south of the equator
an·to·nine \'antə,nīn\ *also* **an·to·nin·i·an** \¦antə¦ninēən, -ninyən\ *adj, usu cap* [*Antonine* fr. *Antoninus* Pius † A.D. 161 and Marcus Aurelius *Antoninus* † A.D. 180 Roman emperors; *Antoninian* fr. *Antoninus* + E *-ian*] : characteristic of the Roman emperors Antoninus Pius and Marcus Aurelius Antoninus or their rule
an·to·nin·i·a·nus \,antə,ninē'ānəs\ *n, pl* **antoninia·ni** \-'ā,nī\ [LL, lit., of Antoninus, fr. Marcus Aurelius *Antoninus* Caracalla † A.D. 217 Roman emperor who introduced it + L *-ianus* -ian] : an ancient Roman coin orig. worth two denarii
an·ton·o·ma·sia \(,)an,tänə'māzh(ē)ə\ *n* -S [L, fr. Gk, fr. *antonomazein* to name instead (fr. *anti-* instead, against + *onomazein* to name, fr. *onoma* name) + *-ia* — more at ANTI-, NAME] **1** : the substitution of another designation for a common, obvious, or normal one: as **a** : the use of an official title or an epithet in place of a proper name (as *his honor* for *Judge Doe*) or ordinary appellative (as *chief executive* for *the president*) **b** : the use of a proper name to designate a member of a class (as a *Solomon* for a *wise ruler*); *also* : the making of a common noun or verb from a proper name (as *pasteurize* from *Pasteur*) **2** : the giving of a proper name (as to a character in fiction) that names or suggests a leading quality (as Squire *Allworthy*, Doctor *Sawbones*)
an·to·nym \'antə,nim, 'aan-, -tᵊn,im\ *n* -S [¹*anti-* + *-onym*] : a word of opposite meaning ⟨the usual ~ of *good* is *bad*⟩ — opposed to *synonym* — **an·ton·y·my** \an'tänəmē, aan-, -mi\ *n* -ES
an·ton·y·mous \(')=¦tänəməs\ *adj* : being an antonym : indicating an opposite significance : OPPOSING, CONTRADICTING **syn** see OPPOSITE
an·to·ny over \'ant(ᵊ)nē'-, 'aan-,'ain-\ *or* **an·dy over** \'andē-, 'aan-\ *or* **an·nie over** \'anē-, -ni\ *also* **an·te over** \'antē-, 'aan-,'ain-, -ti\ *or* **an·tho·ny over** *like* ANTONY OVER; *or, sometimes*, -thən-\ *or* **ant·ney over** *or* **an·ty over** *n* -S *sometimes cap A* [origin unknown] : a game played by two teams (as of schoolboys) in which a ball is tossed back and forth over any small building or bounced against its side
ant·or·bi·tal \¦ant·¦=-\ *adj* [¹*anti-* + *orbital*] : situated in front of the orbit
ant plant *n* : MYRMECOPHYTE
antr- *or* **antro-** *comb form* [NL, fr. LL *antrum* cavity in the body — more at ANTRUM] **1** : antrum ⟨*antritis*⟩ **2** : antral and ⟨*antronasal*⟩
antra *pl of* ANTRUM
an·tral \'antrəl, 'aan-, 'ain-\ *adj* : of or relating to an antrum
an·tre \'antə(r)\ *n* -S [F, fr. L *antrum* — more at ANTRUM] : CAVE 1
an·trim \'an·trəm\ *adj, usu cap* [fr. *Antrim*, county of Ireland] : of or from County Antrim, Northern Ireland : of the kind or style prevalent in Antrim
an·trin \'äntrən\ *adj* [fr. past part. of Sc *anter* to adventure, to chance on, fr. ME *auntren, aventuren* — more at ADVENTURE] *Scot* : RARE, OCCASIONAL ⟨he comes around at ~ times⟩
an·trorse \'an,trȯrs, ='=\ *adj* [NL *antrorsus*, irreg. fr. *antero-* + *-orsus* (as in *dextrorsus* toward the right) — more at DEXTRORSE] : directed forward or upward — compare RETRORSE — **an·trorse·ly** *adv*
an·tros·to·mus \an'trästəməs\ *n, cap* [NL, fr. *antro-* (fr. L *antrum* cave) + *-stomus*] *in some classifications* : a genus of birds including the whippoorwill and chuck-will's-widow
an·tros·to·my \-təmē\ *n* -ES [*antr-* + *-stomy*] : the operation of opening an antrum (as for drainage); *also* : the opening made in such an operation
an·trot·o·my \an'träd·əmē\ *n* -ES [ISV *antr-* + *-tomy*] : ANTROSTOMY
an·trum \'an·trəm\ *n, pl* **an·tra** \-rə\ [LL, cavity in the body, fr. L, cave, fr. Gk *antron*; perh. akin to Gk *anemos* wind — more at ANIMATE] : the cavity of a hollow organ or a sinus ⟨the ~ of the Graafian follicle⟩
antrum of high·more \-'hī,mō(ə)r\ *usu cap H* [after Nathaniel *Highmore* †1685 Eng. physician who first described it] : MAXILLARY SINUS
an·trus·tion \an'trəschən\ *n* -S [ML *antrustion-, antrustio*, of Gmc origin; akin to OHG *ant-, int-* against and OHG *trōst* help, comfort — more at ANTE-, TRUST] : a follower usu. in the bodyguard of Frankish princes of the 5th to 7th centuries
An·try·cide \'antrə,sīd\ *trademark* — used for a white crystalline compound derived from quinoline and used in the control of trypanosomiasis in cattle
ants *pl of* ANT
ant·shrike \'ant,shrīk\ *n* [*ant*bird + shrike] : any of numerous tropical American antbirds (family Formicariidae) resembling shrikes
ant's-wood *n, pl* **ant's-woods** : SAFFRON PLUM; *broadly* : BUCKTHORN 2
antsy \'an(t)sē, 'aan-, 'ain-\ *adj, usu* -ER/-EST [*ants* (pl. of ¹*ant*) + *-y*] *slang* : EAGER, IMPATIENT, RESTLESS; *sometimes* : CONCUPISCENT
ant thrush *n* **1** : ANTBIRD **2** : PITTA 2
ant tree *n* : any of several So. American trees of the genus *Triplaris* having hollow stems inhabited by venomous ants which repel intruders
ANTU \'an,tü\ *abbr or n* -S *sometimes not cap* [alpha-naphthyl*thiourea*] : a chemical $C_{10}H_7NHCSNH_2$ produced as a gray powder for use as a rat poison; alpha-naphthylthiourea
an·tung \'än-,tůŋ, -,důŋ\ *adj, usu cap* [fr. *Antung*, Manchuria] : of or from the city of Antung, Manchuria : of the kind or style prevalent in Antung
ant·werp \'ant-,wərp, 'aan-, 'ain-, -,wōp, -,wə(r)p\ *adj, usu cap* [fr. *Antwerp*, Belgium] : of or from the city of Antwerp, Belgium : of the kind or style prevalent in Antwerp
antwerp *or* **antwerp pigeon** *n* -S *usu cap A* [fr. *Antwerp*, Belgium] : one of a Belgian variety of homing pigeons
antwerp blue *n, usu cap A* **1** : any of various iron-blue pigments (as one containing alumina or a zinc compound) **2** : a moderate blue that is greener and duller than average copen and greener and deeper than azurite blue, Dresden blue, or pompadour — called also *Harlem blue, mineral blue*
antwerp brown *n, often cap A* : CONGO 4
antwerp red *n, often cap A* : ²BOLE 3
antwren \'=¦=\ *n* [¹*ant* + *wren*] : any of various small antbirds having short tails like wrens
anty over *sometimes cap A, var of* ANTONY OVER
anu \'ä,nü, -,nyü, 'a-\ *also* **an·yu** \-,nyü\ *n* -S [AmerSp *añú*, fr. Quechua *añu*] **1** : a So. American herb (*Tropaeolum tuberosum*) cultivated for its edible tubers **2** : the tuber produced by the anu
anu·bing \'änü,biŋ, ,==¦=\ *also* **anu·bin** \-,bēn\ *or* **ano·bing** \-nō,biŋ\ *n* -S [Tag *anubing*] **1** : any of several trees of the genus *Artocarpus* **2** : the wood of the anubing
anu·bis baboon \ə'n(y)übəs-\ *n* [after *Anubis*, a jackal god in ancient Egyptian religion the pictorial representation of which the animal was thought to resemble, fr. L, fr. Gk *Anoubis*, fr. Egypt *Anpu, Anp*] : a rather rare Sudanese baboon (*Papio doguera*)
anucleate *also* **anucleated** \(')ā+\ *adj* [²*a-* + *nucleate, nucleated*] : lacking a nucleus
a number 1 \'ā¦=='wən\ *adj, cap A* : A1 (sense 2)
an·un·der \ə'nən(d)ə(r)\ *prep* [ME, fr. *an, on* on + *under*] *chiefly dial* : UNDER
an·u·ra \ə'n(y)ürə, a'-\ *n pl* [NL, fr. *an-* + *-ura*] *syn of* SALIENTIA
an·u·ran \-'n(y)ürən\ *adj or n* [NL *Anura* + E *-an*] : SALIENTIAN
an·u·re·sis \,anyə'rēsəs, -nə'-\ *n, pl* **anure·ses** \-ē,sēz\ [NL, fr. *an-* + *uresis*] : retention of urine in the urinary bladder : failure or inability to void urine — compare ANURIA — **an·u·ret·ic** \¦=¦=¦red·ik\ *adj*
an·u·ria \ə'n(y)ürēə, a'-\ *n* -S [NL, fr. *an-* + *-uria*] : absence or defective excretion of urine — compare ANURESIS — **an·u·ric** \-ürik\ *adj*
an·u·rous \ə'n(y)ürəs, a'-\ *or* **an·our·ous** \-'nürəs\ *adj* [*an-* + *-urous, -ourous*] *zool* : having no tail ⟨~ toads⟩ ⟨~ frogs⟩
an·u·ry \'anyərē, -ri\ *n* -ES [*an-* + Gk *oura* tail + E *-y*] *zool* : absence of a tail ⟨the inheritance of ~ in mice⟩
anus \'ānəs\ *n, pl* **anuses** *also* **ani** \'ā(,)nī\ [L, ring, anus; akin to OIr *āinne* and perh. to Arm *anur* necklace, ring] : the posterior opening of the alimentary canal
an·us·va·ra \,anəs'värə, ,än-\ *n* -S [Skt *anusvāra*] **1** : a Sanskrit postvocalic nasal sound or group of sounds occurring in the interior of a morpheme only before *ś, ṣ, s*, or *h* and at the end of a morpheme only before an initial consonant of a following morpheme **2** : a sign used in writing Sanskrit to represent the anusvara sound or sounds and in some manuscripts and editions certain other postvocalic nasal sounds — see ALPHABET table
¹an·vil \'anvəl, 'aan- *sometimes* -(,)vil\ *n* -S [alter. of ME *anfilt, anfelt*, fr. OE *anfealt, anfilt* (akin to OHG *anafalz*, G dial. *änefilt*, MD *anvilt*), fr. *an* on + *-fealt, -filt* (akin to Sw dial. *filta* to beat) — more at ON, FELT] **1 a** : a heavy usu. steel-faced iron block on which metal is shaped (as by hand hammering or forging)

anvil 1a

b : a machine part that serves a similar purpose — compare SNARLING IRON **2** : something that resembles an anvil in shape or use ⟨bold imagination, able thought, and discussion . . . are the ~ of public policy —A.E.Stevenson b.1900⟩ : as **a** : INCUS **b** : the metal structure of a cartridge against which the percussion composition is exploded by the blow of the firing pin upon the head of the primer **c** : the lower contact of a telegraphic key **d** : the fixed jaw in a measuring instrument (as a micrometer caliper) **e** : a musical percussion instrument consisting of a steel bar that when struck with a hammer sounds like an anvil — **on the anvil** *adv (or adj)* : under discussion or in preparation
²anvil \"\ *vt* **anvilled; anvilled; anvilling; anvils** *obs* : to shape on an anvil : hammer out
anvil bat *n* : EPAULET BAT
anvil block *n* : the anvil for a power hammer
anvil chisel *n* : HARDIE
anvil cloud *n* : the anvil-shaped top of a cumulonimbus
anx·i·ety \aŋ'zīəd·ē, aiŋ-, -ətē, -i\ *n* -ES [L *anxietas*, fr. *anxius* + *-tas* -ty] **1 a** (1) : a state of being anxious or of experiencing a strong or dominating blend of uncertainty, agitation or dread, and brooding fear about some contingency : UNEASINESS ⟨your ~ about the child's health . . . is . . . unfounded —Agnes Repplier⟩ (2) : the cause for such a state ⟨there was no escaping his *anxieties*, and plagued as he was by them, he sought solitude —Jean Stafford⟩ **b** : a strong concern about some imminent development or a strong desire, mixed with doubt and fear, for some event or issue ⟨~ to succeed had dragged her out of her capable and mechanical indifference —Arnold Bennett⟩ **2 a** : an abnormal and overwhelming sense of apprehension and of fear often marked by such physical symptoms as tension, tremor, sweating, palpitation, and increased pulse rate **b** (1) : an unpleasant feeling of helplessness and isolation sometimes accompanied by physiological manifestations of fear, consciously accounted for by the anticipation of pain, death, or some unknown catastrophe but without sufficient objective justification, and explained on the basis of repressed libidinal expression resulting from parental apprehension and rejection (2) : a condition experimentally produced in laboratory animals and manifested by the physiological changes that in man accompany fear **3** *existentialism* : a state of mind that is deeply troubled or distressed; *esp* : one that results from apparently being confronted with nothingness (as in a situation involving the need or the responsibility to make valuations and decisions and to take actions without the guidance of tradition or society) **syn** see CARE
anxiety attack *n* : an acute psychobiologic reaction manifested by anxiety or panic and by the physiologic changes characteristically accompanying fear
anxiety equivalent *n* : a spontaneous attack in which an intense somatic symptom (as palpitation of the heart) replaces fear
anxiety hysteria *n* : a psychoneurotic disorder with features of both conversion reaction and anxiety neurosis
anxiety neurosis *or* **anxiety reaction** *or* **anxiety state** *n* : a psychoneurotic disorder characterized by diffuse anxiety often accompanied by somatic manifestations of fear
anx·ious \'aŋ(k)shəs, 'aiŋ-\ *adj* [L *anxius*, fr. *angere* to strangle, distress — more at ANGER] **1** : characterized by extreme uneasiness of mind about some contingency : experiencing a sense of brooding fear : APPREHENSIVE, WORRIED ⟨wounded by the disapproval of . . . her friends and ~ for the future —R.M.Lovett⟩ ⟨a timid young woman, not used to cities, ~ about small things —Leslie Rees⟩ **2** : characterized by, resulting from, or causing anxiety : WORRYING ⟨two ~ days followed while the ship was being loaded —T.B. Costain⟩ ⟨bid my ~ fears subside —William Williams⟩ **3** : characterized by strong earnest desire : ardently wishing ⟨a kindhearted landlord ever ~ to ameliorate the condition of the poor —Anthony Trollope⟩ **syn** see AFRAID, EAGER
anxious bench *or* **anxious seat** *n* **1** : a seat near the pulpit reserved at some revival meetings for persons esp. concerned about their spiritual condition — called also *mourners' bench* **2** : a state of worry or anxiety caused by uncertainty ⟨everybody was kept on the *anxious seat* by this system of perpetual probation —Alva Johnston⟩
anx·ious·ly *adv* : in an anxious manner
anx·ious·ness *n* -ES : the state of being anxious
¹any \'enē, -ni *sometimes* ən- *or, after* t *or* d, ᵊn-\ *adj* [ME *any, eny*, fr. OE *ǣnig* (akin to OFris *ēnig*, OHG *einag*, ON *einigr* anyone, no one), fr. *ān* one + *-ig* -y — more at ONE] **1** : one indifferently out of more than two : one or some indiscriminately of whatever kind: **a** : one or another : this, that, or the other — used as a function word esp. in interrogative and conditional expressions to indicate one that is not a particular or definite individual of the given category but whichever one chance may select ⟨did you experience ~ trouble⟩ ⟨if ~ defect appears⟩ ⟨ask ~ man you meet⟩ **b** : one, no matter what one : EVERY — used as a function word esp. in assertions and denials to indicate one that is selected without restriction or limitation of choice ⟨~ child would know that⟩ ⟨forbidden to enter ~ house⟩ **c** : one or some of whatever kind or sort; *esp* : one or some however imperfect — used as a function word to indicate one that is selected with indifference to quality ⟨~ plan is better than no plan⟩ **2** : one, some, or all indiscriminately of whatever quantity: **a** : one or more : not none — used as a function word to indicate a positive but undetermined number or amount ⟨I can't find ~ stamps⟩ ⟨have you ~ money⟩ **b** : ALL — used as a function word to indicate the maximum or whole of a number or quantity ⟨give me ~ letters you find⟩ ⟨he needs ~ help he can get⟩ **c** : a or some no matter how great or small — used as a function word to indicate what is considered despite its quantity or extent ⟨determined to win at ~ cost⟩ ⟨it is good of you to pay ~ attention to him⟩ **3 a** : great, unmeasured, or unlimited in amount, quantity, number, time, or extent : up to whatever measure may be needed or desired ⟨the falls can produce ~ quantity of water power⟩ ⟨could have seen him ~ time last week⟩ **b** : appreciably or at all large, prolonged, or extended in amount, quantity, time, or extent — used with a preceding negative ⟨could not endure it ~ length of time⟩ ⟨could not walk ~ distance without falling⟩
²any \"\ *pron, pl* **any** [ME *any, eny* fr. OE *ǣnig*, fr. *ǣnig*, adj.] **1** : one or more indiscriminately from all those of a kind: **a** : any person or persons : ANYBODY ⟨asked if there were ~ present who had remembered⟩ ⟨~ of them could answer the question⟩ **b** : any thing or things : any part, quantity, or number ⟨promised not to lose ~ of the books⟩ ⟨a scene as effective as ~ in modern drama⟩ ⟨no money and no prospect of ~⟩ **2** *now dial Eng* : one of two : EITHER
³any \"\ *adv* [ME *any, eny*, fr. *any, eny*, adj.] : to any extent : in any degree : at all ⟨he won't be ~ happier there⟩ ⟨he could not walk ~ farther⟩ ⟨you certainly aren't helping me ~⟩
an·yath·i·an \(')än¦yathēən\ *adj, usu cap* [Burmese *ăn-ya-thā* native of upper Burma + E *-ian*] : of or belonging to a lower Paleolithic culture of Burma and Thailand characterized by distinctive chopping tools
¹any·body \'enē,bädē, -(,)bədē, -ni..di\ *pron* [¹*any* + *body*] : a person out of an indefinite number : any person : ANYONE ⟨is ~ home⟩ ⟨had forgotten to ask ~ to come⟩
²anybody \"\ *n* : a person of some importance ⟨everybody who was ~ at all was at the dance⟩
anyhow \'==,=\ *adv* **1 a** : in any manner whatever : ANYWISE ⟨wheat may be sown almost ~ —Adrian Bell⟩ **b** : without order or arrangement : HAPHAZARDLY ⟨untidy scrambles of bed linen . . . flung ~ over balustrades —Richard Llewellyn⟩ **2** : in any case : at any rate : in any event ⟨and ~ it was very much better for the generals to go on with the military operations —Sir Winston Churchill⟩
anymore \¦==¦=\ *adv* [³*any* + *more*] : at the present time : NOWADAYS, CURRENTLY, NOW — used only in a negative context ⟨I am not lucky ~ —Ernest Hemingway⟩ or a statement with negative implication ⟨he rarely comes here ~⟩ except in dial. ⟨used to be I had to . . . carry my own whiskey out of the Hollow, but ~ I'm such a good customer they tote it up here . . . for me —Charley Robertson⟩ ⟨every time I even smile at a man ~ the papers have me practically married to him —Betty Grable⟩
any·one \'==(,)wən\ *pron* [ME *any on, eny on*, fr. *any, eny* + *on* one] : any person indiscriminately : ANYBODY ⟨~ on the lookout for good prose —J.W.Beach⟩ ⟨did ~ care for her opinion —Hugh Walpole⟩
anyplace \'==,=\ *adv* [¹*any* + *place*] : in any place : ANYWHERE ⟨wouldn't let you work ~ else —Edmund Wilson⟩
any-quantity rate *n* : a freight rate with the charge per unit the same regardless of the quantity offered for shipment — abbr. *AQ*
anys·ti·dae \ə'nistə,dē\ *n pl, cap* [NL, fr. *Anystis*, type genus + *-idae*] : a family of predatory mites having no median groove in the cephalothorax and the last joint of the first pair of legs not swollen though usu. long
¹any·thing \'enē,thiŋ, -ni,-, *often* -,thiŋ *or* -,thēŋ *when another word follows without pause*\ *pron* [ME *anything, enything* fr. OE *ǣnig thing*, fr. *ǣnig* any + *thing*] : any thing whatever : something or other : AUGHT ⟨does not include ~ he does not need —E.R.Bentley⟩ ⟨don't bother to do ~ about it —W.J. Reilly⟩
²anything \"\ *adv* [ME, fr. OE *ǣngi thinga* to any extent, inst. of *ǣnig thing* anything] : in any measure : to any extent : at all ⟨if the remaining books . . . are ~ up to the standard of those already published —*Times Lit. Supp.*⟩
³anything \"\ *n* [¹*anything*] : thing of whatever kind : thing of any sort ⟨my horse, my ox, my ass, my ~ —Shak.⟩
any·thing·ar·i·an \,=(,)=¦erēən\ *n* -S [¹*anything* + *-arian* (as in *unitarian*)] : one that holds no particular creed or dogma
anything but *adv* : not at all : by no means : in no respect ⟨it was *anything but* clear . . . what the political democracy . . . would be like —John Strachey⟩
anything like *adv* : in any way : to any extent : at all ⟨give *anything like* an adequate image of the phonetic facts —R.M.S. Heffner⟩
anytime \'==¦=\ *adv* [¹*any* + *time*] : at any time whatever : under any circumstances ⟨can get a job anywhere ~ —Jack Kerouac⟩
anyu *var of* ANU
anyway *adv* [¹*any* + *way*] **1** : in any way whatever : ANYWISE ⟨told him to do the job ~ he wanted⟩ **2** : at all events : in any case : ANYHOW ⟨~ he would not forget⟩
anyways \'==,=\ *adv* [¹*any* + *-ways*] **1 a** *archaic* : in any manner or respect : ANYWISE **b** *dial* : to any degree at all ⟨it didn't look ~ good for him⟩ **2** *chiefly dial* : in any case
anywhen \'==¦=\ *adv* [³*any* + *when*] *chiefly dial* : at any time ⟨will vote ~ and anywhere —William Faulkner⟩
¹any·where \'==,(h)we(ə)r, -eə, -,(h)wa(ə)r\ *adv* [ME *anywhere, enywhere*, fr. *any, eny* + *where*] **1** : at, in, or to any place or point ⟨could sail ~ along the coast⟩ **2** : at all : to any extent ⟨do not rank ~ near the other species —J.B.Robson⟩ **3** — used as a function word to indicate limits of variation ⟨~ from 10 to 30 minutes⟩ ⟨~ from 40 to 60 students⟩
²anywhere \"\ *n* [ME, fr. *anywhere*, adv.] : any place ⟨will flock to the cities, to the new world, to ~ where it can have a full life —*Irish Statesman*⟩ ⟨welcomes visitors from ~⟩
any·wheres \-rz, -əz, -,(h)wərz, -wēz\ *adv* [*anywhere* + *-s*] *chiefly dial* : ANYWHERE

any which way *adv* **:** in any way or direction at all **:** HAPHAZARDLY ⟨the . . . fence lay *any which way* between the bare black yard and the broken sidewalk —Marcia Davenport⟩

anywhither \ˈ==,==\ *adv* [¹*any* + *whither*] *archaic* **:** in any direction whatever ⟨rivers ran ~ —J.B.Cabell⟩

any·wise \ˈ==,wīz\ *adv* [ME *anywise, enywise,* fr. OE (*on*) *ǣnige wīsan* in any wise, fr. *ǣnige* (acc. fem. of *ǣnig*) + *wīsan,* acc. of *wīse* wise, way — more at WISE] **:** in any way or manner whatever **:** at all ⟨nor was it ~⟩

an·zac \ˈan,zak, ˈaan-\ *n* -s *cap* [*A*ustralian and *N*ew *Z*ealand *A*rmy *C*orps] **:** an Australian or New Zealander ⟨the burly *Anzac* saw his chance and merely kept the ball in play —J.R. Tunis⟩; *specif* **:** a soldier from Australia or New Zealand

anzac day *n, usu cap A&D* **:** April 25 observed as a legal holiday in Australia and New Zealand in celebration of the anniversary of the landing of Australian and New Zealand forces at Gallipoli in 1915

an·zan·ite \ˈanzə,nīt\ *n* -s *usu cap* [*Anzan* (*Anshan*), region of ancient Persia + E *-ite*] **:** ELAMITE

AO *abbr, often not cap* **1** account of **2** among others **3** and others

AOL *abbr* absent over leave

aonach *var of* AENACH

A1 \ˈā¦wən\ *adj* [¹*a*] **1 :** having the highest possible classification — used as a symbol by Lloyd's Register of Shipping to designate the characteristics of a ship **2 :** of the highest quality **:** FIRST-CLASS, FIRST-RATE, SUPERIOR ⟨an *A1* man of music as well as an *A1* man of the orchestra —Virgil Thomson⟩

ao·ni·an \(ˈ)ā¦ōnēən, -nyən\ *adj, usu cap* [*Aonia,* district of ancient Greece (fr. L, fr. Gk) + E *-an*] **:** of or relating to Aonia or to the Muses ⟨to waste and spoil the sweet *Aonian* fields —Christopher Marlowe⟩

ao·nid·i·el·la \,āə,nidēˈelə\ *n, cap* [NL] **:** a genus of widely distributed chiefly tropical armored scales including several pests of cultivated plants (as the red scale of citrus)

aor \ˈaů(ə)r\ *n* -s *usu cap* **:** one of a group of related peoples inhabiting the Naga hills in eastern Assam along the Burma frontier

ao·rist \ˈāərəst, ˈa(a)r-\ *n* -s [LL & Gk; LL *aoristos,* fr. Gk, fr. *aoristos* undefined, fr. *a-* ²a- + *horistos* definable, fr. *horizein* to define — more at HORIZON] **:** a set or one of a set of inflectional forms of a verb typically denoting simple occurrence of an action without reference to its completeness or incompleteness, duration, or repetition and typically without reference to its position in time but sometimes (as in the indicative mood in Greek and Sanskrit) with reference to past time — used first in Greek grammar and later in the grammar of Sanskrit and various other languages ⟨most dialects prefer the ~ as the narrative tense —K.H.Menges⟩

ao·ris·tic \¦āə¦ristik, (ˈ)a(ə)¦r-\ *adj* [MGk *aoristikos,* fr. *aoristos* + *-ikos* -ic] **1 :** of or belonging to the aorist **:** like the aorist **2 :** INDEFINITE, INDETERMINATE — **ao·ris·ti·cal·ly** \-tək(ə)lē\ *adv*

aort- *or* **aorto-** *comb form* [NL, fr. *aorta*] **:** aorta ⟨*aort*itis⟩ ⟨*aorto*lith⟩

aor·ta \āˈȯr\|d·ə, -ō(ə)\|, \|tə\ *n, pl* **aortas** \-əz\ *or* **aor·tae** \\|,tē\ [NL, fr. Gk *aortē,* fr. *aeirein, airein* to lift, heave; perh. akin to Alb *vjer* I hang up] **1 :** the chief arterial trunk of the vertebrate body that carries blood from the heart to be distributed to all parts of the body reached by the systemic circulation, being divided in lower vertebrates and embryos of higher forms into an ascending portion arising from the ventricle of the heart and a descending or dorsal portion continuous with the former through the aortic arches but in birds and mammals arising from the left ventricle and continuing over the root of the lung through the single remaining aortic arch then passing posteriorly beside the spinal column to bifurcate into the common iliac arteries after having given off various branches to the head, forelimbs, and trunk **2 :** a large dorsal blood vessel in various invertebrates; *esp* **:** the anterior prolongation of the heart of an insect or other arthropod

diagram of the heart showing *a* aorta, *l* left ventricle, *r* right ventricle

aor·tic \(ˈ)ā¦ȯr\|d·ik, -ō(ə)-, \|tik, -ēk\ *or* **aor·tal** \\|d·ᵊl,\|tᵊl\ *adj* [*aort-* + *-ic* or *-al*] **:** of or relating to the aorta

aortic arch *n* **:** one of the branches that arise from the ascending aorta in pairs in fishes and the embryos of higher vertebrates and pass to the gill clefts of either side and thence round the esophagus to fuse into the dorsal aorta and that are reduced in adult higher forms, one pair persisting in most amphibians and reptiles and a single arch, forming the base of the aortic trunk, in warm-blooded vertebrates, in birds the right and in mammals the left

aortic incompetence *or* **aortic insufficiency** *n* **:** incomplete closure of the aortic valve resulting in return of blood to the left ventricle during diastole

aortic murmur *n* **:** a heart murmur originating at the aortic valve

aortic stenosis *n* **:** a condition usu. the result of disease in which the aorta, esp. its orifice, is abnormally narrow

aortic valve *n* **:** the semilunar valve separating the aorta from the left ventricle

aor·ti·tis \,ā,ȯ(r)ˈtīd·əs\ *n* -ES [NL, fr. *aort-* + *-itis*] **:** inflammation of the aorta

aorto- — see AORT-

aor·tog·ra·phy \,ā,ȯ(r)ˈtägrəfē\ *n* -ES [ISV *aort-* + *-graphy*] **:** arteriography of the aorta

ao·tes \āˈōd·ēz, -ō,tēz\ *n, cap* [NL, prob. irreg. fr. Gk *aōtos* without ears, fr. *a-* ²a- + *ōt-, ous* ear — more at EAR] **:** a genus of tropical American nocturnal monkeys (family Cebidae) having long nonprehensile tails, projecting lower incisors, and very large eyes and comprising the douroucoulis

ao·tus \āˈōd·əs\ [NL, fr. Gk *aōtos*] *syn of* AOTES

aou·dad *also* **au·dad** \ˈaů,dad\ *n* -s [F *aoudad,* fr. Berber *audad*] **:** a wild sheep (*Ammotragus lervia*) of No. Africa thought to be the chamois of the Old Testament — called also *arui, maned sheep*

aoudad (*Ammotragus lervia*)

¹aoul \ˈaů(ə)l\ *n* -s *cap* [Nepali *aul* marsh, fever] **:** a member of any of several small peoples living in the malarial terai districts of Nepal

²aoul \"\ *n* -s [native name in Ethiopia] **:** an Abyssinian gazelle (*Gazella soemmerringii soemmerringii*)

à ou·trance \¦ä,üˈträⁿs\ *also* **à l'ou·trance** \¦ä,lü-\ *adv* [F] **:** to the utmost **:** to the death **:** UNSPARINGLY ⟨planned in secrecy and waged *à outrance* —E.M. Earle⟩

ao·ya·ma's fluid \aůˈyäməz-\ *n, usu cap A* [after Fumio *Aoyama,* 20th cent. Jap. anatomist] **:** a solution of cadmium chloride and neutral formalin used for fixing tissues prior to osmic acid impregnation of the Golgi apparatus

¹ap- — see AD-

²ap- — see APO-

ap *abbr* **1** apostle **2** apothecaries' **3** [L *apud*] according to or in the works of

AP *abbr* **1** above proof **2** account paid **3** accounts payable **4** additional premium **5** advanced post **6** advice of payment **7** airplane **8** airplane pilot **9** antipersonnel **10** armor-piercing **11** as purchased **12** assessment paid **13** assumed position **14** authority to pay **15** authority to purchase **16** author's proof

apa \əˈpä\ *n* -s [Pg, fr. Tupi, fr. Galibi] **:** WALLABA

apa·bhram·sa \,əpəˈbrəmshə\ *n* -s *usu cap* [Skt *apabhraṁśa,* lit., fall] **:** a stage of an Indic language characterized by linguistic changes not found in a more conservative stage that serves as a standard of correctness: **a :** non-Sanskrit linguistic forms in Indic speech prior to approximately the 3d century A.D. **b :** an Indic language spoken in approximately the 3d to the 5th centuries A.D. and differing from the literary Prakrit **c :** an Indic language that was used as a vehicle for poetry from approximately the 6th to the 12th centuries and that shows linguistic changes not found in Prakrit

apace \əˈpās\ *adv* [ME *apas, apace* step by step, slowly, rapidly, prob. fr. MF *à pas,* fr. *à* to, at, on (fr. L *ad*) + *pas* step — more at AT, PACE] **:** at a quick pace **:** SPEEDILY, SWIFTLY, FAST ⟨the concentration of corporate wealth has proceeded ~ —G.B.Hurff⟩

apache *in senses 1 & 2 & prob 4* əˈpachē *or* -chi *sometimes* -pä- *or* -pà-; *in sense 3* əˈpash *or* -paa- *or* -pai- *or* -pä- *or* -pà-\ *n, pl* **apache** *or* **apaches** [Sp, prob. fr. Zuñi *Ápachu,* lit., enemy] **1** *usu cap* **a :** an Athapaskan people of Arizona, New Mexico, Texas, and northern Mexico **b :** a member of such people **2** *usu cap* **:** any of the Athapaskan languages of the Apache people **3** [F, fr. *Apache* Apache Indian, prob. fr. E] **a** *sometimes cap* **:** a member of a gang of criminals esp. in Paris noted for their crimes of violence **b :** RUFFIAN **4 :** SIENNA BROWN

apach·e·an \-chēən\ *adj, usu cap* **:** of or relating to the Apache people or their languages

apache dance \-sh¦d-\ *n* **1 a :** a violent duet dance of the Parisian underworld **b :** a subdued version of such a dance in vaudeville, burlesque, and revues **2 :** a ballroom dance with close contact, jerks, and spins

apache devil dance \-chē¦d-\ *n, usu cap A* **:** a dance of the Apache Indian gahe in which the performer crouches with arms in angular position and the knees turned outward and jumps in even rhythm with both feet at the same time or at intervals with one leg extended and a jumping movement on the other foot

apache pine \-chē-\ *n, usu cap A* **:** a 3-leaved pine (*Pinus latifolia*) of Arizona and New Mexico resembling the ponderosa pine but having very long leaves when young

apache plume \-chē-\ *n, usu cap A* **:** an evergreen shrub (*Fallugia paradoxa*) of the family Rosaceae of the southwestern U. S. and Mexico having showy plumed fruits

apach·ite \əˈpa,chīt\ *n* -s [G *apachit,* fr. *Apache* mts., Texas, its locality + G *-it* -ite] **:** a phonolitic rock containing abundant amphibole and aenigmatite associated with the pyroxene and microperthite as the feldspar

apa·da·na \,apəˈdänə, ,äp-\ *n* -s [OPer *apadāna* palace, fr. *apa-* away + *dāna* container, receptacle, fr. *dā* to put, make, create; akin to Av & Skt *apa* away and to Av *dadāiti* he puts, gives, Skt *dadhāti* — more at OF, DO] **:** the great hall in ancient Persian palaces

ap·a·go·ge \,apə,gōjē *sometimes* -gäjē *or* ,==ˈ==\ *n* -s [Gk *apagōgē,* lit., act of leading away, fr. *apo-* + *agōgē* leading, carrying away, fr. *agein* to lead, drive, act, do — more at AGENT] **1 :** ABDUCTION 3a **2 :** argument by the reductio ad absurdum

ap·a·gog·ic \¦apə¦gäjik\ *or* **ap·a·gog·i·cal** \-jəkəl\ *adj* **:** of, relating to, or involving an apagoge; *esp* **:** proceeding by the method of disproving the proposition that contradicts the one to be established — **ap·a·gog·i·cal·ly** \-jək(ə)lē\ *adv*

apagogic reduction *n* **:** INDIRECT REDUCTION

apaid *adj* [ME *apayed, apaid,* fr. past part. of *apayen, apaien* to satisfy, please, requite — more at APPAY] *archaic* **:** SATISFIED, PLEASED, REWARDED

ap·a·lach·ee *also* **ap·a·lachi** \,apəˈlachē\ *n, pl* **apalachee** *or* **apalachees** *also* **apalachi** *or* **apalachis** *usu cap* [prob. fr. Choctaw *apelachi* helper, ally] **1 a :** a Muskogean people of northwestern Florida **b :** a member of such people **2 :** the language of the Apalachee people

ap·a·lach·i·co·la \,apə,lachəˈkōlə\ *n, pl* **apalachicola** *or* **apalachicolas** *usu cap* [Hitchiti *Apolachicoli* or Muskogee *Apalachicolo,* lit., people of the other side] **1 :** a Muskogean people of Georgia, Alabama, and Florida **2 :** a member of the Apalachicola people — compare CREEK

apa·lai \¦apə¦lī\ *n, pl* **apalai** *or* **apalais** *usu cap* [Pg, of AmerInd origin] **1 a :** a Cariban people of the north bank of the mouth of the Amazon **b :** a member of such people **2 :** the language of the Apalai people

apanage *var of* APPANAGE

ap·an·drous \(ˈ)a¦pandrəs\ *adj* [*apo-* + *-androus*] *bot* **:** having functionless male organs ⟨~ fungi⟩ — **ap·an·dry** \ˈa,pandrē\ *n* -ES

apan·te·les \əˈpantᵊl,ēz\ *n, cap* [NL, fr. ²a- + Gk *pantelēs* altogether complete, fr. *pan-* + *-telēs* (fr. *telos* end, completion); fr. the lack of a caudal appendage — more at WHEEL] **:** a genus of small wasps (family Braconidae) parasitic as larvae on caterpillars and used in the biological control of certain destructive caterpillars

ap·an·te·sis \,apənˈtēsəs\ *n, cap* [NL, perh. fr. Gk *apantēsis* encounter, fr. *apantan* to meet, fr. *apo-* + *antan* to meet face to face, fr. *anta* face to face; akin to Gk *anti* against — more at ANTE-] **:** a genus of tiger moths frequently having the fore wings velvety black with branching light colored stripes and the hind wings red, pink, or yellow with black spots

apan·to \əˈpan·,tō\ *n, pl* **apanto** *or* **apantos** *usu cap* [Pg, of AmerInd origin] **1 a :** a Tupian people of northern Brazil **b :** a member of such people **2 :** the language of the Apanto people

apar \əˈpär\ *n* -s [Pg or AmerSp, fr. Tupi *tatuapára* rolled armadillo, fr. *tatu* armadillo + *iapáre* to roll] **:** the three-banded armadillo (*Tolypeutes tricinctus*) of So. America

apa·raph·y·sate \¦āpə¦rafəsət, -,sāt\ *adj* [²*a-* + *paraphysate*] **:** destitute of paraphyses

apa·re·jo \,apəˈrā(,)ō, ,äp-, -ā,hō\ *n* -s [AmerSp, fr. Sp, preparation, equipment, fr. *aparejar* to prepare, fr. (assumed) VL *appariculare* — more at APPAREL] **:** a packsaddle of stuffed leather or canvas

¹apart \əˈpärt, -pȧt, *usu* -d·+V\ *adv* [ME, fr. MF *a part,* lit., at the side, to the side, fr. (assumed) VL *ad partem,* fr. L *ad* at, to + LL *partem,* accus. of *pars* side, fr. L, part — more at AT, PART] **1 :** to or at one side **:** at a little distance ⟨the kitchen stood ~ from the house⟩ **2 :** separately in space or time **:** away from one another ⟨towns five miles ~⟩ ⟨children born two years ~⟩ **3 :** as a separate or distinct object of thought **:** INDEPENDENTLY, INDIVIDUALLY ⟨viewed ~, his arguments were unsound⟩ **4 :** excluded from consideration **:** ASIDE ⟨these things ~, I have been working steadily —H.J.Laski⟩ **5 :** in or into two or more parts **:** to pieces **:** ASUNDER ⟨was showing signs of coming ~ at the seams —Milton Hindus⟩ **6 :** aside from common use **:** above the general level ⟨the elite were definitely set ~ from the mass —A.N.Christensen⟩

²apart \"\ *adj* **1 :** having its own particular characteristics **:** unlike all others **:** REMOVED ⟨had been preserved because they inhabited a place ~ —W.H.Hudson †1922⟩ **2 :** holding different opinions **:** in disagreement **:** DIVERGENT ⟨the allies are still ~ —*Time*⟩

apart from *prep* **:** aside from **:** other than **:** BESIDES ⟨*apart from* his legal avocations his only interest was music —H.W.H. Knott⟩

apart·heid \əˈpär,t¦āt, -pȧ,t¦, ¦īt, -ärt,h¦, -ȧt,h¦\ *n* -s [Afrik, lit., separateness, fr. D, fr. *apart* separate (fr. F *à part*) + *-heid* -hood — more at APART] **:** separation of the races **:** racial segregation; *specif* **:** a policy of segregation and political and economic discrimination against non-European groups in the Republic of So. Africa

apart·ment \əˈpärtmənt, -pȧt-\ *n* -s *often attrib* [F *appartement,* fr. It *appartamento* (trans. of Sp *apartamiento,* lit., separation), fr. *appartare* to put aside, separate (fr. *a parte* aside, separately, lit., at the side, to the side, fr. assumed VL *ad partem*) + *-mento* -ment (fr. L *-mentum*)] **1 :** a room or a set of rooms used as a dwelling and located in a private house, a hotel, or a building containing only such rooms or suites with necessary passages and hallways **:** FLAT **2** *obs* **a :** a separate or special abode **:** a dwelling place ⟨came down from my ~ in the tree —Daniel Defoe⟩ **b :** COMPARTMENT **3 :** any room in a building ⟨the dining room at the hall was not a cheerful ~ —Osbert Lancaster⟩ **4 :** a building made up of individual dwelling units ⟨these new ~s have intensified the parking problem⟩ — **a·part·men·tal** \ə¦pärt¦mentᵊl, ¦a,p-, -pȧt-\ *adj*

apartment building *or* **apartment house** *n* **:** a building containing a number of separate residential units and usu. having conveniences (as heat and elevators) in common

apartment hotel *n* **:** an apartment house containing suites equipped for housekeeping purposes and in addition furnished rooms and dining service for transient and permanent guests

apart·ness \əˈpärtnəs, -pȧt-\ *n* -ES [²*apart* + *-ness*] **:** the quality or state of being apart **:** ALOOFNESS, ISOLATION ⟨our own . . . grandiose ~ and air of exclusive ease . . . threatened to defeat us —W.H.Hale⟩

apas *pl of* APA

apast \əˈp-\ *adv or prep* [¹*a-* + *past*] *chiefly Midland* **:** PAST

ap·as·tron \(ˈ)a¦pastrən, -,strän\ *n, pl* **apas·tra** \-strə\ [NL, fr. *apo-* + Gk *astron* star — more at STAR] **:** the point in the orbit of one star of a binary where it is farthest from the other — compare PERIASTRON

apa ta·ni \,apəˈtänē\ *n, pl* **apa tani** *or* **apa tanis** *usu cap A&T* **1 :** an Assamese people of the eastern outer Himalaya mountain region **2 :** a member of the Apa Tani people

ap·a·tet·ic \¦apə¦ted·ik\ *adj* [Gk *apatētikos* fallacious, fr. *apatan* to deceive, cheat, fr. *apatē* deceit — more at APATITE] *zool* **:** imitative in color or form

ap·a·theia \,apəˈthīə\ *or* **apath·ia** \əˈpathēə\ *n* -s [Gk — more at APATHY] **:** freedom or release from emotion or excitement

ap·a·thet·ic \¦apə¦thed·ik, -etik, -ēk\ *adj* [*apathy* + *-etic* (as in *pathetic*)] **1 :** having or showing little or no feeling or emotion **:** SPIRITLESS, IMPASSIVE ⟨rare women who . . . become active instead of ~ as they grow older —Ellen Glasgow⟩ **2 :** having or showing little or no interest or concern **:** INDIFFERENT ⟨not that the people were ~ . . . for they were . . . curious about everything —L.C.Stevens⟩ **syn** see IMPASSIVE

ap·a·thet·i·cal·ly \-ək(ə)lē, -ēk-, -li\ *adv* **:** in an apathetic manner

apath·o·gen·ic \¦ā,patho¦jenik, ā¦p-\ *adj* [²*a-* + *pathogenic*] **:** not capable of causing disease **:** NONPATHOGENIC

ap·a·thy \ˈapəthē, -thi\ *n* -ES [Gk *apatheia, apathia,* fr. *apathēs* without feeling (fr. *a-* ²a- + *pathos* feeling, suffering) + *-ia* -y — more at PATHOS] **1 :** release or freedom from passion, excitement, or emotion ⟨this attitude of calm is the Epicurean counterpart of the Stoic ~ —Frank Thilly⟩ **2 a :** absence or lack of feeling or emotion **:** UNFEELINGNESS, IMPASSIVENESS ⟨the dull ~ of despair —Oscar Wilde⟩ **b :** absence or lack of interest or concern **:** LISTLESSNESS, INDIFFERENCE ⟨an alarming degree of ~ among the party's rank and file —G.C.Wright⟩

ap·a·tite \ˈapə,tīt\ *n* -s [G *apatit,* fr. Gk *apatē* deceit (perh. fr. *apo-* + *patos* path) + G *-it* -ite; fr. its being taken for other minerals — more at FIND] **:** any of a group of calcium phosphate minerals containing other elements or radicals (as fluorine, chlorine, hydroxyl, or carbonate), having the approximate general formula $Ca_5(F,Cl,OH,\frac{1}{2}CO_3)(PO_4)_3$, and occurring variously as hexagonal crystals, as granular masses, or in fine-grained often impure masses as the chief constituent of phosphate rock and of most or all bones and teeth; *specif* **:** FLUORAPATITE — see CARBONATE-APATITE, CHLORAPATITE, HYDROXYLAPATITE

ap·a·tor·nis \,apəˈtȯrnəs\ *n, cap* [NL, fr. Gk *apatē* + NL *-ornis*] **:** a genus of toothed birds from the Cretaceous of Kansas related to *Ichthyornis*

ap·a·to·sau·rus \,apətōˈsȯrəs\ *n, cap* [NL, fr. *apato-* (fr. Gk *apatē*) + *-saurus*] **:** a genus of American Jurassic herbivorous dinosaurs (order Sauropoda) that reached a length of over 65 feet and a height of 12 feet and are thought to have attained a weight of up to 30 tons

apaumé *var of* APPAUMÉ

apa·yao \¦äpə¦yaů\ *n, pl* **apayao** *or* **apayaos** *usu cap* [Sp, fr. native name in northern Luzon] **1 a :** a predominantly pagan people of northern Luzon, Philippines **b :** a member of such people **2 :** the Austronesian language of the Apayao people

APC *abbr* **1** aspirin, phenacetin, caffeine **2** autographed presentation copy

¹ape \ˈāp\ *n* -s [ME, fr. OE *apa;* akin to OS *apo,* OHG *affo,* ON *api*] **1 a :** MONKEY — used esp. of the larger tailless Old World forms **b :** a member of the family Pongidae **2 :** one that imitates or copies **:** MIMIC ⟨be his duplicate but not his ~ —Earl of Chesterfield⟩ ⟨the ~s of fashion —Malcolm Cowley⟩ **3** *obs* **:** DUPE, FOOL **4 :** one that is felt to resemble an ape esp. in appearance and manners **:** a large uncouth person ⟨didn't know who the big ~ was —Edwin Corle⟩

²ape *vt* -ED/-ING/-S **:** to follow as a pattern or example **:** IMITATE, COPY, MIMIC ⟨had *aped* the styles of various authors —Van Wyck Brooks⟩ **syn** see COPY

³ape \ˈä(,)pā\ *n* -s [Hawaiian *ˈape*] **1 :** any of several herbaceous aroids (as *Alocasia macrorrhiza* and some members of the genus *Xanthosoma*) having large heart-shaped blades rising on long petioles from short trunks and being cultivated as ornamentals esp. in Hawaii **2 :** APE-APE

apeak \əˈpēk\ *adv (or adj)* [alter. (influenced by *peak*) of earlier *apike,* prob. fr. ¹*a-* + *pike* (mountain)] **:** in a vertical position **:** held vertically ⟨the oars were all ~ —W.J.Dakin⟩

ape-ape \¦äpē¦äpē\ *n* -s [Hawaiian *ˈapeˈape*] **:** a rhizomatous perennial herb (*Gunnera petaloidea*) of Hawaiian uplands having a branched inflorescence and bluntly heart-shaped leaves several feet in diameter that rise from a short fleshy crown

ape fissure *n* **:** SULCUS LUNATUS

ape hand *n* **:** a wasting deformity of the hand seen in muscular dystrophy

apei·ron \əˈpī,rän, -pā-\ *n, pl* **apei·ra** \-,rə, -,rä\ [Gk, fr. neut. of *apeiros* endless, infinite, fr. *a-* ²a- + *-peiron* (fr. *peirat-, peirar* end, conclusion); akin to *peri* around — more at FAR] **:** the unlimited, indeterminate, and indefinite ground, origin, or primal principle of all matter postulated esp. by Anaximander

ape·let \ˈāplət\ *or* **ape·ling** \ˈāpliŋ, -lēŋ\ *n* -s **:** a little ape

ape-man \ˈ=¦=\ *n, pl* **ape-men :** a primate (as a member of the genera *Pithecanthropus, Australopithecus,* and *Sinanthropus*) intermediate in character between true man (*Homo sapiens*) and the higher apes

ap·en·nine \ˈapə,nīn\ *adj, usu cap* [L *Appenninus, Apenninus,* a chain of mountains in Italy] **:** of or relating to the Apennines

¹ap·er \ˈāpə(r)\ *n* -s [²*ape* + *-er*] **:** one that apes ⟨~s of the nobility⟩

²aper \ˈäpə(r), ˈä-\ *n* -s [L; akin to OE *eofor* wild boar, OS *ebur,* OHG *ebur,* ON *jöfurr* prince, chieftain, Umbrian *apruf, abrof* wild boar (acc. pl.), OSlav *veprĭ,* Lith *vepris*] **:** the European wild boar

aper·çu \¦apə(r)¦sü, *F* àpersüē\ *n* -s [F, fr. *aperçu,* past part. of *apercevoir* to perceive, fr. OF, fr. *a-* (fr. L *ad-*) + *perceveir* to perceive, fr. L *percipere* — more at PERCEIVE] **1 :** a brief glimpse or immediate impression; *esp* **:** an intuitive insight ⟨the many brilliant ~s that illustrate and illuminate the main theme —D.W.Brogan⟩ **2 :** a brief survey or sketch **:** OUTLINE ⟨if reduced to . . . two pages it would be the profoundest ~ of the universe that I ever have read —O.W.Holmes †1935⟩ **syn** see COMPENDIUM

ape·rea \,apəˈrēə\ *or* **pe·rea** \,perēˈä\ *n* -s [Sp & Pg *apereá, aperea,* fr. Tupi *apereá*] **:** a wild cavy (*Cavia porcellus*) possibly ancestral to the domesticated guinea pig

¹ape·ri·ent \əˈpirēənt\ *adj* [L *aperient-, aperiens,* pres. part. of *aperire* to uncover, open — more at APERTURE] **:** gently moving the bowels **:** LAXATIVE

²aperient \"\ *n* -s **:** an aperient agent

aperies *pl of* APERY

ape·ri·od·ic \¦ā,pirē¦ädik, ā¦p-\ *adj* [²*a-* + *periodic*] **1 :** of irregular occurrence **:** not periodic ⟨~ floods⟩ **2 :** not having periodic vibrations **:** nonoscillatory and hence capable of moving steadily to a position of equilibrium **3** *cryptology* **:** not repeating or not repeating with a short or easily discoverable period ⟨an ~ key⟩ — **ape·ri·od·i·cal·ly** \-dək(ə)lē\ *adv* — **ape·ri·o·dic·i·ty** \¦ā,pirēə¦disəd·ē\ *n* -ES

aper·i·tif \ä,perəˈtēf, -rē-; ä¦==,=, ə¦-\ *n* -s [F *apéritif* aperitif, aperient, fr. MF *aperitif,* adj., aperient, fr. ML *aperitivus,* irreg. fr. L *aperire* to open + *-ivus* -ive — more at APERTURE] **1 :** an alcoholic drink (as a cocktail or appetizer wine) often taken before a meal **:** APPETIZER **2** *also* **aperitif wine :** an appetizer wine that is chiefly of French or Italian origin, flavored with herbs and other substances, and used as an appetizer or cocktail ingredient

¹aper·i·tive \əˈperəd·iv\ *adj* [ML *aperitivus*] **1 :** APERIENT **2** [F *apéritif* aperient, stimulating the appetite, fr. MF *aperitif* aperient] **:** stimulating the appetite

²aperitive \"\ *n* -s **1 :** APERIENT **2** [F *apéritif*] **:** APERITIF

apert *adj* [ME, fr. OF, fr. L *apertus,* fr. past part. of *aperire* to open] **1** *archaic* **:** OPEN, MANIFEST, EVIDENT **2** *obs* **:** BOLD, STRAIGHTFORWARD, OUTSPOKEN — **apertly** *adv, archaic*

apertion *n* -s [L *apertion-, apertio,* fr. *apertus* (past part. of

aperire to open) + *-ion-*, *-io* -ion — more at APERTURE] **1** *obs* **:** the act of opening **2** *obs* **:** an opening or aperture
ap·er·tom·e·ter \ˌapə(r)ˈtäməd·ə(r)\ *n* -s [*aperture* + *-o-* + *-meter*] **:** an instrument for measuring the numerical aperture of objectives (as those of a microscope)
ap·er·tur·al \ˈapə(r)ˌchu̇rəl\ *adj* **:** of, relating to, or like an aperture
apertural canal *n* **:** the basal extension of the aperture affording lodgment for the siphon in univalve shells
ap·er·ture *R* ˈapə(r)ˌchu̇(ə)r, -ˌchər; -*R* -pəˌchu̇ə, -pəchə\ *n* -s [ME, fr. L *apertura*, fr. *apertus* open (fr. past part. of *aperire* to open, uncover, prob. fr. *ap-* — akin to L *ab* from — + — assumed — *verire* to cover) + *-ura* -ure — more at OF, WEIR] **1** *obs* **:** the act or process of opening **2 :** an opening or open space (as between parts or sections of solid matter) **:** HOLE, GAP, CLEFT, CHASM, SLIT ⟨the only light . . . came through the narrow ~ between the stone lips —Willa Cather⟩ **3 a :** an opening that restricts a beam of radiation or a stream of particles; *specif* **:** the opening in a photographic lens that admits the light passing through, the size often being controlled by an iris diaphragm **b :** the diameter of the entrance pupil of an optical system **4 :** the opening of a univalve shell
ap·er·tured \-ˌchu̇(ə)rd, -u̇əd, -ˌchə(r)d\ *adj* **:** having an aperture
aperture plate *n* **:** a smooth plate that establishes the film plane in a motion-picture camera or projector and that has a rectangular opening defining the margins of the picture area as recorded or projected
aperture ratio *n* **:** RELATIVE APERTURE
aperture vignette *n* **:** MASK 2d (1)
ap·ery \ˈāpərē, -ri\ *n* -ES [¹*ape* + *-ery*] **:** the act or practice of aping **:** MIMICRY
apes *pl of* APE, *pres 3d sing of* APE
apes–earring \ˈ=ˈ=(ˌ)=\ *n* **:** MANILA TAMARIND
apet·a·lae \(ˈ)āˈped·ᵊlˌē\ *n pl*, *cap* [NL, fr. ²*a-* + *-petalae*] *in some classifications* **:** a group of the Archichlamydeae comprising plants whose flowers have no petals — compare CHORIPETALAE
apet·al·ous \(ˈ)āˈped·ᵊləs\ *adj* [²*a-* + *-petalous*] **1 :** of, relating to, or characteristic of the Apetalae; *often*, *of flowers* **:** having no petals **2 :** not petaloid; *specif* **:** lacking the petallike expansion of the ambulacra ⟨~ sea urchins⟩ — **apet·aly** \(ˈ)=ˈ=ᵊlē\ *n* -ES
à pe·tits fers \ˌäp(ə)ˌtēˈfe(ə)r, ˌap-\ *adv* [F, lit., with small tools] **:** made up of small decorative elements ⟨a book binding with a design *à petits fers*⟩
¹**apex** \ˈāˌpeks\ *n*, *pl* **apexes** \-ksəz\ *or* **api·ces** \ˈāpəˌsēz *also* ˈap-\ [L, summit, small rod at top of flamen's cap; prob. akin to L *aptus* fastened, attached — more at APT] **1 a :** the highest or uppermost point **:** SUMMIT, TOP, PEAK ⟨the ~ of the mountain⟩: as (1) **:** the vertex of an angle, a cone, or a pyramid (2) **:** the point of the heavens toward which a celestial body is moving at a given time ⟨solar ~⟩ **b :** the pointed end **:** TIP ⟨the ~ of the tongue⟩ **2 :** the highest or culminating point **:** CLIMAX, ACME, CULMINATION ⟨the ~ of his career⟩ ⟨the ~ of an era⟩ **3 :** the end, edge, or crest of a vein of mineral nearest the surface **4** *in palmistry* **:** a triangle formed by capillary lines on the pads of the fingers and the mounts **5 a :** the narrow somewhat conical upper part of a lung extending into the root **b :** the lower pointed end of the heart situated in man opposite the space between the cartilages of the fifth and sixth ribs on the left side **c :** the extremity of the root of a tooth

a apex (1b) of a leaf

²**apex** \"\ *vi* -ED/-ING/-ES *of a vein of mineral* **:** to form an apex **:** present an upper edge
apex beat *n* **:** the pulsation made by the apex of the left ventricle of the heart read or felt at the fifth left intercostal space
apexed \ˈāˌpekst\ *adj* **:** having an apex
apex stone *n* **:** the top stone in a gable end — called also *saddle stone*
APF *abbr* animal protein factor
aph- — see APO-
aphaer·e·sis *or* **apher·e·sis** \əˈferəsəs, aˈ-, -fir-\ *n*, *pl* **aphaere·ses** *or* **aphere·ses** \-əˌsēz\ [LL, fr. Gk *aphairesis*, lit., taking off, fr. *aphairein* to take away (fr. *apo-* + *hairein* to take) + *-sis* — more at HERESY] **1 :** the loss of one or more sounds or letters at the beginning of a word (as in *round* for *around*, *coon* for *raccoon*, baby talk *'top* for *stop*) — compare APHESIS 1, APOCOPE, SYNCOPE 2a **2 :** the omission of one or more syllables at the beginning of a member or verse — used esp. in ref. to Greek and Latin prosody; compare PROSTHESIS
aph·ae·ret·ic *or* **aph·er·et·ic** \ˌafəˈred·ik\ *adj* [Gk *aphairetikos* fit for taking away, fr. *aphairein*] **:** of or relating to aphaeresis **:** formed by aphaeresis **:** consisting of aphaeresis
apha·gia \əˈfāj(ē)ə, aˈ-\ *n* -S [NL, fr. ²*a-* + *-phagia*] **1 :** loss of the ability to swallow **2 :** an inability to feed — used of the state of certain insect imagos (as mayflies) in which the adult is dependent on reserves stored during larval life and takes no food
apha·kia \əˈfākēə, aˈ-\ *also* **apha·cia** \-āsh(ē)ə\ *n* -S [NL, fr. ²*a-* + Gk *phakos* lentil + NL *-ia* — more at BEAN] **:** absence of the crystalline lens of the eye; *also* **:** the anomalous state of refraction resulting therefrom — **apha·kic** \-ākik\ *adj or n*
aphan- *or* **aphano-** *comb form* [F *aphan-*, fr. Gk *aphanēs*, fr. *a-* ²*a-* + *-phanēs* (fr. *phainesthai* to appear) — more at PHENOMENON] **:** invisible **:** obscure ⟨*aphanite*⟩ ⟨*Aphanomyces*⟩
aph·a·nap·ter·yx \ˌafəˈnaptəˌriks\ *n*, *cap* [NL, fr. *aphan-* + *Apteryx*] **:** a genus comprising a large long-billed flightless rail of Mauritius that has been exterminated by man
aph·a·nip·tera \ˌafəˈniptərə\ [NL, fr. *aphan-* + *-i-* + *-ptera*] *syn of* SIPHONAPTERA
aph·a·ni·sia \ˌafəˈnizh(ē)ə, -nēzh-\ *n* -S [NL, fr. Gk *aphanisis* disappearance + NL *-ia*] **:** early normal development of a vestigial organ followed by regression — compare RUDIMENTATION
aph·a·nite \ˈafəˌnīt, *usu* -d·+V\ *n* -S [F, fr. *aphan-* + *-ite*] **:** a dark rock of such close texture that its separate grains are invisible to the naked eye — **aph·a·nit·ic** \ˌafəˈnid·ik\ *adj* — **aph·a·nit·ism** \ˈafəˌnīd·ˌizəm; əˈfanəˌtiz-, ˈaˈ-\ *n* -S
aph·a·no·my·ces \ˌafənōˈmīˌsēz\ *n*, *cap* [NL, fr. *aphan-* + *-myces*] **:** a genus of fungi (order Saprolegniales) characterized by slender zoosporangia with but one row of zoospores and occurring as parasites in algae and roots of higher plants
aphan·o·phyre \əˈfanəˌfī(ə)r, aˈ-\ *n* -S [*aphan-* + *-phyre*] **:** a porphyry with aphanitic groundmass
aph·a·no·zy·gous \ˌafəˈnōˈzīgəs\ *adj* [*aphan-* + *-zygous*] **:** CRYPTOZYGOUS
apha·ryn·gent \ˌāfəˈrinjənt\ *adj* [²*a-* + *pharyng-* + *-ent*] **:** lacking a pharynx
apha·sia \əˈfāzh(ē)ə\ *n* -S [NL, fr. Gk, fr. *a-* ²*a-* + *-phasia*] **:** the loss or impairment of the power to use words as symbols of ideas that results from a brain lesion — see AUDITORY APHASIA, MOTOR APHASIA
¹**apha·sic** \-āzik\ *adj* [NL *aphasia* + E *-ic*] **:** of, relating to, or affected by aphasia
²**aphasic** \"\ *n* -S **:** an aphasic person **:** one suffering from aphasia
aphas·mid·ia \ˌāˌfazˈmidēə\ *n pl*, *cap* [NL, fr. ²*a-* + *Phasmidia*] *in many classifications* **:** a subclass of Nematoda comprising worms in which phasmids are lacking or greatly reduced, deirids are absent, and amphids are usu. modified while sensory organs are often setose — compare PHASMIDIA
aph·e·lan·dra \ˌafəˈlandrə\ *n*, *cap* [NL, fr. Gk *aphelēs* simple, lit., smooth + NL *-andra*; fr. the one-celled anthers] **:** a genus of tropical American plants (family Acanthaceae) having quadrangular spikes of red 2-lipped flowers
aph·e·len·chi·dae \ˌafəˈleŋkəˌdē\ *n pl*, *cap* [NL, fr. *Aphelenchus*, type genus + *-idae*] **:** a family of soil-dwelling and plant-parasitic nematodes (superfamily Rhabditoidea) sometimes regarded as constituting a distinct superfamily nearly related to Tylenchoidea — see APHELENCHOIDES
aph·e·len·choi·des \ˌafəˌleŋˈkȯi(ˌ)dēz\ *n*, *cap* [NL, fr. *Aphelenchus* + *-oides*] **:** a large cosmopolitan genus of nematodes (family Aphelenchidae) including free-living forms, insect parasites, and a number of serious plant pathogens that attack the leaves and buds of various cultivated plants
aph·e·len·chus \ˌafəˈleŋkəs\ *n*, *cap* [NL, fr. Gk *aphelēs* simple, lit., smooth + *enchos* spear; fr. the absence of basal knobs on the stylet] **:** a genus of rhabditoid nematode worms that is the type of the family Aphelenchidae and that includes several important plant pathogens
aph·e·li·nid \ˌafəˈlīnəd, -ēn-, -in-\ *n* -S [NL *Aphelinidae*] **:** an insect of the family Aphelinidae
aph·e·lin·i·dae \ˌafəˈlinəˌdē\ *n pl*, *cap* [NL, fr. *Aphelinus*, type genus + *-idae*] **:** a family of small narrow-winged hymenopterous flies closely related to the chalcid flies and parasitic as larvae on plant lice and scales
aph·e·li·nus \ˌafəˈlīnəs, -ēn-\ *n*, *cap* [NL, fr. Gk *aphelēs* smooth (fr. *a-* ²*a-* + *-phelēs*, fr. *phelleus* stony ground) + L *-inus* -ine; prob. akin to L *follis* bellows — more at BLOW] **:** a genus of hymenopterous flies that is the type of the family Aphelinidae and that includes a species (*A. mali*) important in the biological control of the woolly apple aphid
aph·e·lion \(ˈ)aˈfēlyən, (ˈ)afˈhē-, (ˈ)apˈhē-, -lēən\ *n*, *pl* **aphe·lia** \-yə, -ēə\ [NL, alter. (influenced by Gk words in *-ion*, dim. suffix) of *aphelium*, fr. *apo-* + *-helium* (fr. Gk *hēlios* sun) — more at SOLAR] **:** the point of a planet's or comet's orbit most distant from the sun — opposed to *perihelion*

diagram of earth's orbit (actually an ellipse): position of the earth in July, *A;* in January, *P;* sun, *S;* minor axis, *aa;* major axis, *AP;* aphelion distance, *AS;* perihelion distance, *PS*

aph·e·li·o·trop·ic \ˌafˌhēlēəˈträpik, ˌaˌfē-, ˌapˌhē-\ *adj* [*apo-* + *heliotropic*] **:** characterized by apheliotropism — **aph·e·li·o·trop·i·cal·ly** \-pək(ə)lē\ *adv*
aph·e·li·ot·ro·pism \ˌ=ˌ==ˈä·trəˌpizəm\ *n* -S [*apo-* + *heliotropism*] **:** negative heliotropism (as in certain roots that turn away from the sun)
aph·e·lops \ˈafəˌläps\ *n*, *cap* [NL, fr. Gk *aphelēs* smooth + *ōps* face; fr. the absence of a horn — more at OPTIC] **:** a genus of fossil rhinoceroses of very robust build and with very short legs found in the Miocene and Pliocene of America
aphe·mia \əˈfēmēə\ *n* -S [NL, fr. ²*a-* + *-phemia*] **:** MOTOR APHASIA — **aphe·mic** \-mik\ *adj*
apheresis *var of* APHAERESIS
aph·e·sis \ˈafəsəs\ *n*, *pl* **aphe·ses** \-əˌsēz\ [NL, fr. Gk, release, dismissal, fr. *aphienai* to let go, dismiss (fr. *apo-* + *hienai* to let go, send, throw, hurl, cast) — more at JET] **1 :** aphaeresis consisting of the loss of a short unaccented vowel at the beginning of a word (as in *lone* for *alone*) **2 :** APHAERESIS 1
aph·e·ta \ˈafəd·ə\ *n* -S [NL, fr. Gk *aphetēs* heavenly body determining the vital quadrant, fr. *aphienai* to send forth, fr. *apo-* + *hienai* to send — more at JET (to spout)] *in astrology* **:** the ruler or giver of life in a nativity
aphet·ic \əˈfed·ik, (ˈ)aˌf-\ *adj* [Gk *aphetos* let loose (fr. *aphienai*) + E *-ic*] **:** produced by aphesis or aphaeresis ⟨the ~ form *dobe* for *adobe*⟩ — **aphet·i·cal·ly** \-d·ək(ə)lē\ *adv*
aph·e·tize \ˈafəˌtīz\ *vt* -ED/-ING/-S [*aphetic* + *-ize*] **:** to shorten by aphesis ⟨*esquire* was *aphetized* to *squire*⟩ **:** produce by aphesis ⟨the *aphetized* form *down*, from *adown*⟩
aph·e·to·hy·oi·dea \ˌafəˌtōˌhīˈȯidēə\ [NL, fr. Gk *aphetos* let loose, free + NL *-hyoidea* (fr. Gk *hyoeidēs* shaped like an upsilon, fr. *hy*, *y* upsilon + *-oeidēs* -oid)] *syn of* PLACODERMI
aph·e·to·hy·oi·de·an \-ēən\ *n* -S [NL *Aphetohyoidea* + E *-an*] **:** PLACODERM
aphi·cid·al \ˌāfəˈsīdᵊl *also* ˌaf-\ *adj* [*aphid* + *-cidal*] **:** toxic to or used for killing aphids
aphi·cide \ˈ=fəˌsīd\ *n* -S [*aphid* + *-cide*] **:** a substance used to kill aphids
aphid \ˈāfəd *also* ˈaf-\ *n* -S [NL *Aphid-*, *Aphis*] **:** any of numerous small sluggish homopterous insects (superfamily Aphidoidea) that suck the juices of plants thereby causing wilting, distorted growth, or gall formation, serve as vectors of certain important virus diseases of plants, and excrete as a by-product of their metabolism a sweet liquid very attractive to ants — see PHYLLOXERA, PLANT LOUSE, WOOLLY APPLE APHID; compare APHIDIDAE, APHIS
aphi·dae \ˈ=fəˌdē\ *syn of* APHIDIDAE
aphides *pl of* APHIS
aphid·i·dae \əˈfidəˌdē, āˈ-, aˈ-\ *n pl*, *cap* [NL, fr. *Aphid-*, *Aphis*, type genus + *-idae*] **:** a large family of Homoptera comprising small soft-bodied plant lice that are usu. somewhat pear-shaped with wings if present held vertically over the back when at rest, well-developed antennae, and a pair of prominent wax-secreting cornicles on the posterior part of the abdomen from which the covering of white waxy filaments typical of many species is produced and that have a complex life cycle in which resistant fertilized eggs produced in the fall hatch out parthenogenetic females in the spring that give birth to repeated generations of winged or wingless parthenogenetic females on the same or other kinds of host plants, finally producing a generation of winged males and winged or wingless females that mate and produce the fertilized eggs
aphid·iv·o·rous \ˌāfəˈdivərəs *also* ˌaf-\ *adj* [*aphid* + *-i-* + *-vorous*] **:** APHIDOPHAGOUS
aphid lion *n* **:** APHIS LION
aphi·doi·dea \ˌāfəˈdȯidēə *also* ˌaf-\ *n pl*, *cap* [NL, fr. *Aphid-*, *Aphis* + *-oidea*] **:** a superfamily of Homoptera comprising the aphids and now usu. divided into a number of families (as Aphididae, Eriosomatidae, and Phylloxeridae)
aphid·ol·o·gist \-ˈdäləjəst\ *n* -S [*aphid* + *-ologist* (as in *biologist*)] **:** one specializing in the study of aphids
aphid·oph·a·gous \ˌāfəˈdäfəgəs *also* ˌaf-\ *adj* [*aphid* + *-o-* + *-phagous*] **:** feeding on aphids ⟨~ syrphus fly larvae⟩
aphid·oph·i·lous \-ˌdäfələs\ *adj* [*aphid* + *-o-* + *-philous*] **:** of or relating to certain ants that nurture aphids in return for the honeydew they obtain from them
aphi·doz·er \ˈ==ˌdōzə(r)\ *n* -S [blend of *aphid* and *hopper-dozer*] **:** a device consisting of a hopper and revolving brushes used to brush off and collect aphids from cultivated crops
aphis \ˈāfəs *also* ˈaf-\ *n* [NL, perh. irreg. fr. Gk *apheidēs* unsparing, lavish, fr. *a-* ²*a-* + *-pheidēs* (fr. *pheidesthai* to spare); prob. akin to L *findere* to split — more at BITE] **1** *cap* **:** the type genus of Aphididae comprising many aphids injurious to fruit trees and vegetables **2** *pl* **aphi·des** \-fəˌdēz\ **a :** an insect of the genus *Aphis* **b :** APHID
aphis lion *n* **:** a larval lacewing that is usu. vigorously predaceous on aphids; *also* **:** any of certain other insect larvae (as of the ladybird and syrphus fly) that feed on aphids
aphle·bia \(ˈ)āˈflēbēə, -leb-\ *n* -S [NL, fr. Gk *aphlebos* without veins, fr. *a-* ²*a-* + *phleb-*, *phleps* vein — more at PHLEB-] **:** one of the imperfect pinnae found in certain fossil ferns of the Carboniferous age
aph·o·dal \ˈafədᵊl\ *adj* [NL *aphodus* + E *-al*] **:** of or relating to an aphodus **:** having aphodi
apho·di·us \əˈfōdēəs\ *n*, *cap* [NL, fr. Gk *aphodos* excrement, fr. *apo-* + *hodos* way, road — more at CEDE] **:** a large genus of small somewhat elongated dung beetles commonly placed in the family Scarabaeidae — see PASTURE COCKCHAFER
aph·o·dus \ˈafədəs\ *n*, *pl* **apho·di** \-ˌdī, -ˌdē\ [NL, fr. Gk *aphodos* going away, fr. *apo-* + *hodos* way — more at CEDE] **:** a short canal in rhagon sponges leading from a flagellated chamber to an excurrent canal
apho·nia \(ˈ)āˈfōnēə, əˈ-\ *n* -S [NL, fr. Gk *aphōnia*, fr. *aphōnos* voiceless, (fr. *a-* ²*a-* + *phōnē* sound, voice) + *-ia*] — more at BAN] **:** loss of voice and of all but whispered speech as a result of hysteria, disease, or overuse of the vocal cords
aphon·ic \(ˈ)āˈfänik\ *adj* [²*a-* + *phonic*] **1 a :** having no sound or pronunciation **:** SILENT, NOISELESS **b** *phonetics* **:** VOICELESS **2 :** of, relating to, or characterized by aphonia
aph·o·rism \ˈafəˌrizəm\ *n* -S [MF *aphorisme*, fr. LL *aphorismus*, fr. Gk *aphorismos* definition, short, pithy sentence, fr. *aphorizein* to mark off by boundaries, set aside, cast out, define (fr. *apo-* + *horizein* to separate, part) + *-ismos* -ism — more at HORIZON] **1 :** a concise statement of a principle **2 :** a terse and often ingenious formulation of a truth or sentiment usu. in a single sentence **:** ADAGE, MAXIM ⟨one must reverse the ~ "the style is the man" —Emily Genauer⟩
aph·o·ris·mat·ic \ˌafəˌrizˈmad·ik\ *adj* **:** APHORISTIC
aph·o·ris·mic \ˌafəˈrizmik\ *adj* **:** APHORISTIC
apho·ris·mos \ˌäfōrēzˈmōs\ *n*, *pl* **aphoris·moi** \-ˈmē\ [LGk (influenced in meaning by *aphorizein* to excommunicate, fr. Gk, to cast out), fr. Gk, definition, short, pithy sentence] *Eastern Church* **:** temporary excommunication
aph·o·rist \ˈafərəst\ *n* -S **:** one who formulates or repeats aphorisms
aph·o·ris·tic \ˌafəˈristik\ *adj* [Gk *aphoristikos* delimiting, aphoristic, fr. (assumed) *aphoristos* (verbal of *aphorizein*) + *-ikos* -ic] **1 :** of, resembling, or characterized by aphorisms **:** TERSE, PITHY ⟨the suggestive virtues of the ~ style —Douglas Bush⟩ **2 :** given to the use of aphorisms ⟨do not be brilliant and ~ —J.B.Cabell⟩ — **aph·o·ris·ti·cal·ly** \-tək(ə)lē\ *adv*
aph·o·rize \ˈafəˌrīz\ *vi* -ED/-ING/-S [fr. *aphorism*, after such pairs as E *baptism*: *baptize*] **:** to write or speak in or as if in aphorisms **:** express terse general opinions
aphos·pho·ro·sis \ˌāˌfäsfəˈrōsəs\ *n*, *pl* **aphosphoro·ses** \-ōˌsēz\ [NL, fr. ²*a-* + *phosphor-* + *-osis*] **:** a deficiency disease esp. of domestic cattle caused by inadequate intake of dietary phosphorus and marked by inappetence, unthriftiness, lameness, and scouring and in affected animals commonly by depraved appetite and the avid devouring of bones and other materials containing phosphates — compare LAMSIEKTE, PICA
aphos·pho·rot·ic \ˌ=ˌ==ˈräd·ik, =ˌ==ˈ-\ *adj* [²*a-* + *phosphor-* + *-otic*] **:** characterized or accompanied by aphosphorosis
apho·tic \(ˈ)āˈfōd·ik\ *adj* [²*a-* + *photic*] **:** without light ⟨~ depths⟩
aphotic region *n* **:** the lightless biogeographic region of deep water where organisms directly dependent on photosynthesis cannot exist
apho·to·tax·is \ˌāˌfōd·əˈtaksəs, (ˈ)āˈ==ˌ==\ *n*, *pl* **aphototax·es** \-kˌsēz\ [NL, fr. ²*a-* + *phototaxis*] **:** absence of phototaxis
apho·to·trop·ic \ˌāˌfōd·əˈträpik, āˌf-\ *adj* [²*a-* + *phototropic*] **:** turning away from the source of light ⟨~ roots⟩ — **apho·tot·ro·pism** \ˌāfōˈtä·trəˌpizəm\ *n* -S
aphr- *or* **aphro-** *comb form* [G *aphr-*, fr. Gk *aphr-*, *aphro-*, fr. *aphros*; perh. akin to L *imber* rain — more at IMBRICATE] **:** foam ⟨*aphrite*⟩ ⟨*aphrometer*⟩
aphra·sia \əˈfrāzh(ē)ə, aˈ-\ *n* -S [NL, fr. ²*a-* + *-phrasia*] **1 :** an inability to utter words in intelligible order **2 :** pathological refusal to speak — **aphra·sic** \-āzik\ *adj*
aph·rite \ˈaˌfrīt\ *n* -S [G *aphrit*, fr. *aphr-* foam + G *-it* -ite] **:** a foliated or chalky variety of calcite that is pearly in luster
aph·ro·di·sia \ˌafrəˈdizh(ē)ə\ *n* -S [NL, irreg. fr. Gk, pl., sexual pleasures, fr. neut. pl. of *aphrodisios* of Aphrodite, of sexual love, fr. *Aphroditē*] **:** sexual desire esp. when violent
¹**aph·ro·dis·i·ac** \ˌ=ˌ=ˈdizēˌak\ *or* **aph·ro·di·si·a·cal** \-ˌdiˈsīəkəl, -ˌzī-\ *adj* [Gk *aphrodisiakos* sexual, fr. *aphrodisia*] **:** provocative of or exciting sexual desire ⟨the labored unreserve of ~ novels —C.E.Montague⟩ ⟨hatches *aphrodisiacal* schemes . . . when confronted with temptations of the flesh —*Time*⟩
²**aphrodisiac** \"\ *n* -S **:** an aphrodisiac agent ⟨odors and . . . other chemical stimuli which are ~s —A.C.Kinsey⟩ ⟨the reputation of cantharides as an ~ —C.H.Thienes⟩
aph·ro·di·te \ˌafrōˈdīd·ē, -rəˈ-, -ītē, -i\ *n* [NL, after *Aphrodite*, Greek goddess of love, fr. Gk *Aphroditē*] **1** *cap* **:** a genus (the type of the family Aphroditidae) of large marine polychaetous annelids covered with long lustrous golden hairlike setae — compare SEA MOUSE **2** -S *sometimes cap* [NL (specific epithet of *Argynnis aphrodite*), after *Aphrodite*, goddess] **:** a brown black-spotted butterfly (*Speyeria aphrodite*) of the U.S. with silver spots on the underside **3** -S *often cap* [after *Aphrodite*, goddess] **:** a light bluish green that is greener and deeper than average aqua green (sense 1) or robin's-egg blue (sense 2) and greener and darker than average turquoise green
aph·ro·lite \ˈafrōˌlīt\ *n* -S [alter. of earlier *aphrolith*, fr. *aphr-* + *-lith*] **:** AA
aph·ro·sid·er·ite \ˌafrōˈsidəˌrīt\ *n* -S [G *aphrosiderit*, fr. *aphr-* + *siderit* siderite] **:** a mineral consisting of a hydrous silicate of the chlorite group
aph·tha \ˈafthə, ˈapthə *also* **ap·tha** \ˈap-\ *n*, *pl* **aph·thae** \-ˌthē\ [NL, back-formation fr. LL *aphthae*, pl., fr. Gk *aphthai*, pl. of *aphtha*, perh. fr. *haptein* to fasten, seize, set on fire — more at HAPTO-] **1 :** a speck, flake, or blister on the mucous membranes (as in the mouth or gastrointestinal tract or on the lips) characteristic of some diseases (as thrush) **2 :** one of the vesicles filled with clear serous fluid that occur in the mouth, on the udder, and in the spaces between the digits of cloven-footed animals in certain diseases — usu. used in pl. **3 :** a disease characterized by aphthae (as foot-and-mouth disease) — **aph·thic** \-ˌthik\ *adj*
aph·thar·to·do·ce·tae \afˌthärd·ōdōˈsēd·ē, apˌth-, -sē(ˌ)tē\ *n pl*, *usu cap* [NL, pl., fr. LGk *aphthartodokētai*, pl. of *aphthartodokētēs*, fr. Gk *aphthartos* incorruptible (fr. *a-* ²*a-* + *phthartos* destructible, fr. *phtheirein* to corrupt, defile) + *-dokētēs* (fr. *dokein* to think) — more at PHTHIRIASIS, DECENT] **:** a 6th century Monophysitic sect that taught that from the moment of the union with the divine nature the body of Christ was incorruptible — compare PHTHARTOLATRAE
aph·thar·to·do·ce·tism \-sēd·ˌizəm, -ēˌtiz-\ *n* -S *usu cap* **:** the doctrines of the Aphthartodocetae
aph·thar·to·do·ce·tist \-sēd·əst\ *n* -S *usu cap* **:** a member of the Aphthartodocetae
aph·thit·a·lite \afˈthid·ᵊlˌīt, apˈth-\ *n* -S [Gk *aphthitos* indestructible (fr. *a-* ²*a-* + — assumed — *phthitos*, verbal of *phthiein* to waste away) + *hal-*, *hals* salt + E *-lite* — more at PHTHISIS, SALT] **:** a mineral $(K,Na)_3Na(SO_4)_2$ consisting of potassium sodium sulfate occurring massive or in white rhombohedral crystals
aph·thoid \ˈafˌthȯid, ˈapˌ-\ *adj* [NL *aptha* + E *-oid*] **:** having the characteristics of aphthae; *specif* **:** resembling thrush
aph·tho·sis \afˈthōsəs\ *n*, *pl* **aphtho·ses** \-ōˌsēz\ [NL, fr. *aphtha* + *-osis*] **:** a condition characterized by the formation of aphthae
aph·thous \ˈafthəs, ˈapth-\ *adj* [NL *aphtha* + ISV *-ous*] **:** of, relating to, or characterized by aphthae
aphthous fever *n* **:** FOOT-AND-MOUTH DISEASE
aph·y·dro·trop·ic \ˌafˌhīˈ==, ˌaˌfī-, =ˈ==ˈ==\ *also* **ap·o·hy·dro·trop·ic** \ˌapōˌhīˈ=ˈ==\ *adj* [*apo-* + *hydrotropic*] **:** turning away from or shunning moisture ⟨an ~ plant⟩ — **aph·y·drot·ro·pism** \ˌafˌhīˈdrä·trəˌpizəm, ˌaˌfī-, ˌapˌhī-\ *n* -S
aphyl·lous \(ˈ)āˈfiləs\ *adj* [Gk *aphyllos*, fr. *a-* ²*a-* + *phyllon* leaf — more at BLADE] **:** destitute of foliage leaves — **aphyl·ly** \ˈāˌfilē\ *n* -ES
aphyr·ic \(ˈ)āˈfirik, -fīr-\ *adj* [ISV ²*a-* + *-phyric*; orig formed as G *aphyrisch*] **:** not porphyritic
aphy·tal zone \(ˈ)āˈfīd·ᵊl-\ *n* [²*a-* + Gk *phyton* plant + E *-al*] **:** APHOTIC REGION; *esp* **:** the plantless depths of a lake floor
api- *comb form* [L, fr. *apis*] **:** bee ⟨*apiculture*⟩ ⟨*apiphobia*⟩
api·a·ca \ˌapēˈäkä, ˌäp-\ *n*, *pl* **apiaca** *or* **apiacas** *usu cap* [Pg *apiacá*, of AmerInd origin] **1 a :** a Cariban people living near the mouth of the Tocantins river, Brazil **b :** a member of such people **2 a :** a Tupi-Guaranian people living on the Tapajoz river, Mato Grosso, Brazil **b :** a member of such people **3 :** the language of the Tupi-Guaranian Apiaca people
api·a·ce·ae \ˌāpēˈāsēˌē, ˌap-\ [NL, fr. *Apium*, type genus + *-aceae*] *syn of* UMBELLIFERAE
api·a·ceous \ˌāpēˈāshəs, ˌap-\ *adj* [NL *Apiaceae* + E *-ous*] **:** UMBELLIFEROUS
a pia·ce·re \ˌäpyäˈchārē, -erē\ *adv* [It] **:** at pleasure **:** ad libitum — used in ref. to a musical performance
api·an \ˈāpēən\ *adj* [L *apianus*, fr. *apis* + *-anus* -an] **:** of or relating to bees
api·ar·i·an \ˌāpēˈerēən, -ˈa(a)r-, -ˈär-\ *adj* **:** of or relating to beekeeping or bees
api·a·rist \ˈāpēərəst\ *n* -S **:** BEEKEEPER
api·ary \ˈāpēˌerē, -ri\ *n* -ES [L *apiarium*, fr. *apis* bee + *-arium* -ary] **:** a place where bees are kept; *esp* **:** a collection of hives or colonies of bees kept for their honey
apic- *or* **apici-** *or* **apico-** *comb form* [prob. fr. NL, fr. L *apic-*, *apex*] **1 :** apex **:** tip esp. of an organ ⟨*apicad*⟩ ⟨*apicifixed*⟩ ⟨*apicoectomy*⟩ **2 :** apical and ⟨*apicodental* consonant⟩
ap·i·cad \ˈapəˌkad, ˈāp-\ *adv* [*apic-* + *-ad*] **:** toward the apex
¹**ap·i·cal** \ˈapəkəl, ˈāp-, -ēk-\ *adj* [prob. fr. NL *apicalis*, fr. *apic-* + L *-alis* -al] **1 :** of or belonging to an apex, tip, or summit **2** *phonetics* **:** of, relating to, or formed with the participation of the tip of the tongue — **ap·i·cal·ly** \-k(ə)lē, -li\ *adv*
²**apical** \"\ *n* -S **:** an apical speech sound
apical cap *n* **:** one of a series of bands resembling collars formed at the ends of the cells of green algae of the genus *Oedogonium* as a result of cell divisions

apical cell *n* **:** the single cell that terminates the vegetative axis in many cryptogamous plants **:** the initial point of longitudinal growth

apical dominance *n* **:** inhibition of the growth of lateral buds by the terminal bud of a shoot that is believed to be effected principally or at least in part by auxins produced by the terminal bud

apical meristem *n* **:** a meristem located at the apex of a root or shoot and responsible for increase in length of the organ — compare INTERCALARY MERISTEM, LATERAL MERISTEM

apical plate *n* **:** a group of specialized cells of nervous and sensory function at the anterior end of the trochophore larva of certain invertebrates

apices *pl of* APEX

api·cian \ə'pishən\ *adj, usu cap* [L *Apicianus*, fr. Marcus Gavius *Apicius fl* A.D. 14–37 Roman epicure + L *-anus* -an] **:** befitting Apicius; *specif* **:** EPICUREAN

ap·i·ci·fixed \'apəsə,fikst\ *adj* [*apic-* + *fixed*] **:** attached by the apex

apick·a·back \ə'-\ *archaic var of* PIGGYBACK

ap·i·co·bas·al \ˌapə(ˌ)kō¦-, ¦āp-\ *adj* [*apic-* + *basal*] **:** of or relating to apex and base ⟨an ~ axis⟩

apic·u·late \ə'pikyələt, ā'-, -ˌlāt, *usu* -d·+V\ *also* **apic·u·lat·ed** \-ˌlād·əd\ *adj* [NL *apiculus* + E *-ate*, *-ated*] **:** ending abruptly in a small distinct point ⟨an ~ leaf⟩

api·cu·la·tion \=ˌ==ˈlāshən\ *n* -s **:** APICULUS

api·cul·tur·al \¦āpə¦-\ *adj* **:** of, relating to, or affecting apiculture

api·cul·ture \'āpə¦-\ *n* -s [prob. fr. F, fr. *api-* + *culture*] **:** beekeeping esp. when pursued on a large scale

api·cul·tur·ist \¦āpə¦-\ *n* -s **:** one who specializes in the breeding and culture of bees **:** BEEKEEPER

apic·u·lus \ə'pikyələs, ā'-\ *n, pl* **apicu·li** \-ˌlī, -ˌlē\ [NL, dim. of L *apic-, apex* summit] **:** a small acute point or tip

ap·i·dae \'apəˌdē\ *n pl, cap* [NL, fr. *Apis*, type genus + *-idae*] **:** a family of social bees having the glossa and basal joints of the labial palpi elongate and including the common honeybees and the stingless bees, in some classifications also the bumblebees and some solitary bees, and formerly all the bees

apiece \ə'pēs\ *adv* [ME *a pece*, fr. ²*a* (for each) + *pece* piece — more at PIECE] **:** for each person or thing **:** for each one **:** EACH, INDIVIDUALLY, SEVERALLY ⟨available at a dollar ~⟩ ⟨took an hour ~ to work the problems⟩

apieces *adv* [¹*a-* + *pieces*] *archaic* **:** in or to pieces

api·gen·in \ˌāpə'jenən, ˌap-\ *n* -s [ISV *apiin* + *-gen* + *-in*] **:** a yellowish crystalline compound $C_{15}H_{10}O_5$ occurring usu. as glycosides (as apiin) in various plants; 4′,5,7-trihydroxy= flavone

api·in \'āpēən, 'ap-\ *n* -s [ISV *api-* (fr. L *apium* parsley, celery) + *-in* — more at APIUM] **:** a crystalline glycoside $C_{26}H_{28}O_{14}$ obtained from parsley

api·ko·res *or* **api·ko·ros** \ˌäpē'kōrəs\ *n, pl* **apikor·sim** \-rsəm\ [Yiddish & Heb; Yiddish *apikurus*, fr. Heb *apiqōrōs*, fr. Gk *Epikouros* Epicurus — more at EPICURE] **:** a Jew who is lax in observing Jewish law or who does not believe in Judaism; *also* **:** SKEPTIC, ATHEIST

api·na·yé \ˌäpē(ˌ)nä'yā\ *n, pl* **apinayé** *usu cap* [Pg, of Amer-Ind origin] **1 a :** a Gesan people of north central Brazil **b :** a member of such people **2 :** the language of the Apinayé people

aping *pres part of* APE

apio \'äpēˌō\ *n* -s [AmerSp, fr. Sp, celery, fr. L *apium* — more at APIUM] **:** ARRACACHA

api·ole \'āpēˌōl, 'ap-\ *also* **api·ol** \-ˌōl, -ˌȯl\ *n* -s [ISV *api-* (fr. L *apium* parsley, celery) + *-ole*, *-ol* — more at APIUM] **1 a :** a colorless crystalline diether $C_{14}H_{14}O_4$ of the aromatic series found esp. in the plant and fruit of parsley — called also *parsley camphor* **b :** an isomeric liquid ether from certain dill oils — called also *dill apiole* **2 :** an oleoresin from parsley fruit used as an emmenagogue and antiperiodic

api·ol·o·gy \ˌāpē'äləjē\ *n* -ES [*api-* + *-logy*] **:** the scientific study of honeybees

api·on \'āpēˌän\ *n, cap* [NL, fr. Gk, pear; fr. the shape of the beak — more at PEAR] **:** a large cosmopolitan genus of small long-beaked weevils including a number of serious pests of cultivated plants

api·os \'āpēˌäs\ *n, cap* [NL, fr. Gk, pear tree; fr. the shape of the tubers — more at PEAR] **:** a widely distributed genus of trailing or climbing herbs (family Leguminosae) having tuberous roots, compound leaves, small racemose flowers, and linear pods — see GROUNDNUT

api·ose \'āpēˌōs, 'ap-\ *n* -s [*apiin* + *-ose*] **:** a branched-chain pentose $(HOCH_2)_2C(OH)CHOHCHO$ obtained as a syrup by hydrolyzing apiin

api·o·so·ma \ˌāpēō'sōmə, ˌap-\ [NL] *syn of* BABESIA

apis \'āpəs\ *n, cap* [NL, fr. L, bee] **:** the type genus of Apidae including brownish social bees lacking spurs but having scopae on the hind tibiae and including the common honeybee

ap·ish \'āpish, -ēsh\ *adj* **:** like an ape: as **a :** given to servile imitation **b :** extremely silly or affected ⟨the ~ gallantry of a fantastic boy —Sir Walter Scott⟩ — **ap·ish·ly** *adv*

apish·a·more \ə'pishəˌmō(ə)r\ *n* -s [modif. of Ojibwa *apishamon* something to lie down on] **:** a saddle blanket usu. of buffalo hide

apis·to·gram·ma \əˌpistə'gramə\ *n, cap* [NL, perh. fr. Gk *apistos* untrustworthy (fr. *a-* ²*a-* + *pistos* trustworthy) + *gramma* letter] **:** a genus of small cichlid fishes including a species (*A. agassizi*) commonly kept in the tropical aquarium

api·tong \ə'pēˌtȯŋ\ *n* -s [Tag] **1 :** any of several trees of the genus *Dipterocarpus*; *esp* **:** an important Philippine timber tree (*D. grandiflorus*) yielding a resin used as an illuminant or varnish or for calking boats **2 :** the reddish brown wood of an apitong tree

api·um \'āpēəm, 'ap-\ *n, cap* [NL, fr. L, parsley, celery; perh. akin to Skt *ap-* water — more at ABKAR] **:** a genus of Eurasian herbs of the carrot family having pinnate leaves and white or yellowish flowers in compound umbels — see CELERY

apiv·o·rous \(ˈ)ā¦pivərəs\ *adj* [prob. fr. F *apivore*, fr. *api-* + *-vore* -vorous] **:** bee-eating ⟨~ birds⟩

ap·john·ite \'apˌjäˌnīt\ *n* -s [G *apjohnit*, fr. James *Apjohn* †1886 Ir. chemist who first examined it + G *-it* -ite] **:** a mineral $MnSO_4.Al_2(SO_4)_3.22H_2O$ consisting of manganese aluminum sulfate containing water and occurring in crusts or fibrous masses

apl- — see HAPL-

apla·cen·tal \¦ā=¦==\ *adj* [²*a-* + *placental*] **:** having or developing no placenta

apla·coph·o·ra \¦āˌpla'käfərə, ˌaplə'-\ *n pl, cap* [NL, fr. ²*a-* + *plac-* + *-phora*] **:** an order of Amphineura comprising wormlike mollusks in which the body is without calcareous plates but the mantle bears numerous calcified spicules over its entire surface — **apla·coph·o·ran** \¦=(ˌ)=¦==rən\ *adj or n* — **apla·coph·o·rous** \-rəs\ *adj*

ap·la·nat \'apləˌnat, *usu* -ad·+V\ *n* -s [G, back-formation fr. *aplanatisch*, fr. E *aplanatic*] **:** an aplanatic lens

ap·la·nat·ic \¦aplə¦nad·ik\ *adj* [irreg. fr. Gk *aplanētos* that cannot go astray (fr. *a-* ²*a-* + *planētos* wandering) + E *-ic* — more at PLANET] **:** free from or corrected for spherical aberration ⟨an ~ lens⟩ — **ap·la·nat·i·cal·ly** \-d·ək(ə)lē\ *adv*

aplan·a·tism \ā'planəˌtizəm, ə'-; 'apləˌnad·ˌizəm\ *n* -s **:** freedom from spherical aberration

aplan·e·tism \ā'planəˌtizəm, ə'-\ *n* -s [Gk *aplanētos* that cannot go astray + E *-ism*] **:** the state of producing nonmotile asexual spores

aplano- *comb form* [prob. fr. NL, fr. Gk *aplanēs* not wandering, fixed, fr. *a-* ²*a-* + *-planēs* wandering, fr. *planasthai* to wander — more at PLANET] **:** nonmotile ⟨*Aplanobacter*⟩ ⟨*aplanospore*⟩

aplan·o·bac·ter \(ˈ)ā'planəˌbaktə(r)\ [NL, fr. *aplano-* + *-bacter*] *syn of* ¹BACILLUS

aplan·o·ga·mete \(ˈ)ā'planəgəˌmēt, ˌāˌplanəgə'm-, ¦āˌplanə'gaˌm-\ *n* -s [*aplano-* + *gamete*] **:** a nonmotile gamete (as in certain lower algae) — compare PLANOGAMETE

apla·nog·a·mous \¦āˌpla¦nägəməs, ¦aplə'-\ *adj* [*aplano-* + *-gamous*] **:** having nonmotile gametes — **apla·nog·a·my** \-'nägəmē\ *n* -ES

aplan·o·spore \(ˈ)ā'planəˌspō(ə)r\ *n* -s [*aplano-* + *spore*] **1 :** a nonmotile asexual spore formed by rejuvenescence in certain algae and distinguished from an akinete by developing a new cell wall distinct from that of the parent cell — compare HYPNOSPORE, ZOOSPORE **2 :** a nonmotile asexual spore produced within the sporangium in certain fungi (as Mucoraceae)

apla·sia \ə'plāzh(ē)ə, (ˈ)ā'p-,(ˈ)a'p-\ *n* -s [NL, fr. ²*a-* + *-plasia*] **:** the incomplete or faulty development of an organ or part

aplas·tic \(ˈ)ā¦-\ *adj* [²*a-* + *plastic*] **1 a :** not plastic **:** not easily molded **b :** not exhibiting growth or change in structure **2 :** of, relating to, or exhibiting aplasia

aplastic anemia *n* **:** anemia characterized by defective function of the blood-forming organs (as the bone marrow) and believed to be caused by toxic agents

¹**aplen·ty** \ə'-\ *adj* [¹*a-* + *plenty*] **:** in plenty or abundance **:** enough and to spare **:** ABUNDANT ⟨money ~ for all our needs⟩ — used postpositively or predicatively

²**aplenty** \"\ *adv* [¹*a-* + *plenty*] **1 :** in abundance **:** PLENTIFULLY ⟨history pours forth~through the tale—*Time*⟩ **2 :** very much **:** EXTREMELY ⟨scared ~ —Booth Tarkington⟩

³**aplenty** \"\ *n* -ES [¹*aplenty*] **:** an abundance or a plenty ⟨wished now to get ~ while they were getting —*Nation*⟩

ap·lite \'aˌplīt\ *also* **hap·lite** \'ha-\ *n* -s [ISV *hapl-* + *-ite*; prob. orig. formed as G *aplit*] **:** a fine-grained light-colored differentiation rock; *specif* **:** a differentiate of granite consisting almost entirely of quartz and feldspar and generally occurring in dikes — **ap·lit·ic** \(ˈ)a¦plid·ik\ *adj*

aplo- — see HAPL-

ap·lo·chei·lus \ˌaplō'kīləs\ *n, cap* [NL, fr. *hapl-* + Gk *cheilos* hand] **:** a genus of tropical killifishes including the panchaxes

ap·lo·di·no·tus \ˌa(ˌ)plōdə'nōd·əs\ *n, cap* [NL, fr. *hapl-* + Gk *dinōtos* round] **:** a genus of freshwater fishes (family Scaenidae) including the freshwater drum or sheepshead (*A. grunniens*) widely distributed in larger rivers and lakes of No. America

ap·lo·don·tia \ˌaplō'dänch(ē)ə\ *n, cap* [NL, fr. *hapl-* + *-odontia*] **:** a genus (the type of the family Aplodontiidae) of rodents comprising the mountain beavers — **ap·lo·don·ti·id** \¦aplō¦dänchēəd\ *adj or n*

ap·lo·don·toi·dea \ˌaplōˌdän'tȯidēə\ *n pl, cap* [NL, fr. *Aplodontia* + *-oidea*] **:** a superfamily of primitive rodents represented among modern forms by the mountain beaver

ap·lo·gran·ite \¦aplō¦granət\ *n* -s [*hapl-* + *granite*] **:** a rock of granitic texture consisting of alkali-feldspar and quartz with some biotite

aplomb \ə'pläm, -əm *also* -ōm *or* -ȯm; *F* äplōⁿ\ *n* -s [F, lit., perpendicularity, fr. MF, fr. *a plomb* perpendicularly, lit., according to the plummet, fr. *a* to, at, according to (fr. L *ad* to, at) + *plomb* lead, plummet — more at AT, PLUMB] **1 :** complete confidence or assurance in oneself **:** SELF-POSSESSION, POISE ⟨summed up the situation with his usual ~ —John Marks⟩ ⟨few of them, however, possess the ~ to order a martini before lunch —Edward Newhouse⟩ **2 :** the perpendicular position **:** PERPENDICULARITY **3** *of a ballet dancer* **:** the perfect equilibrium required to maintain stability in a pose or movement

ap·lome \'aˌplōm\ *n* -s [F, fr. *hapl-* + *-ome*] **:** a dark brown or green variety of andradite containing manganese — compare GARNET

ap·lo·pap·pus \ˌaplō'papəs\ *syn of* HAPLOPAPPUS

ap·lo·per·i·stom·a·tous \¦aplōˌperə'stäməd·əs, -ōm-\ *adj* [*hapl-* + NL *peristomat-, peristoma* + E *-ous*] *of a moss* **:** having in the peristome a single row of teeth or none

aplus·tre \ə'plästrē\ *n, pl* **aplus·tria** \-rēə\ *or* **aplus·tras** \-rəs\ [L, prob. fr. an Etruscan word borrowed fr. Gk *aphlaston*] **:** the curved ornamented stern of an ancient Greek or Roman ship

aply·sia \ə'plizh(ē)ə\ [NL, fr. Gk, a kind of sponge, fr. *aplytos* unwashed (fr. *a-* ²*a-* + *plytos* washed) + *-ia*; akin to *plynein* to wash, *plein* to sail, float, swim — more at FLOW] *syn of* TETHYS

ap·ly·si·i·dae \ˌaplə'sīəˌdē\ [NL, fr. *Aplysia*, type genus + *-idae*] *syn of* TETHYIDAE

ap·nea *or* **ap·noea** \'apnēə, ap'n-\ *n* -s [NL, fr. ²*a-* + *-pnea*, *-pnoea*] **1 :** transient cessation of respiration whether normal (as in hibernating animals) or abnormal (as that caused by certain drugs) **2 :** ASPHYXIA — **ap·ne·ic** *or* **ap·noe·ic** \(ˈ)ap¦nēik\ *adj*

apneu·mo·na \(ˈ)ā'n(y)ümənə, ap'n-\ *or* **apneu·mo·nes** \-məˌnēz\ *n pl, cap* [NL, fr. ²*a-* + *-pneumona*, *-pneumones* (fr. Gk *pneumon-, pneumōn* lung) — more at PNEUMONIA] **:** a formerly recognized division of Holothurioidea comprising forms lacking an internal respiratory apparatus — compare PNEUMONOPHORA — **apneu·mo·nous** \(ˈ)ā¦n-,(ˈ)ap¦n-\ *adj*

apneu·mo·no·mor·phae \=ˌ==nō'mȯrˌfē\ *n pl, cap* [NL, fr. *Apneumona* + *-o-* + *-morphae*] *in some classifications* **:** a suborder of Arachnida comprising the arachnomorph spiders that lack book lungs

ap·neu·sis \ap'n(y)üsəs\ *n, pl* **apneu·ses** \-üˌsēz\ [NL, fr. ²*a-* + Gk *pneusis* breathing, fr. *pnein* to breathe — more at SNEEZE] **:** sustained tonic contraction of the respiratory muscles resulting in the prolonged inspiration characteristic of many lower vertebrates

ap·neus·tic \(ˈ)=¦=ˌstik\ *adj* [²*a-* + Gk *pneustikos* of or for breathing, fr. (assumed) Gk *pneustos* (verbal of *pnein* to breathe) + Gk *-ikos* -ic] **1** *of an insect larva* **:** having all the spiracles absent or closed **2 :** exhibiting apneusis

apo- *or* **ap-** *or* **aph-** *prefix* [*apo-* fr. ME, fr. MF & L; MF, fr. L, fr. Gk, fr. *apo*; *ap-* fr. Gk, fr. *apo*; *aph-* fr. LL, fr. Gk, fr. *apo* — more at OF] **1 :** away from **:** off ⟨*apastron*⟩ ⟨*aphelion*⟩ **2 :** detached **:** separate ⟨*apocarpous*⟩ **3 :** formed from **:** related to — in names of chemical compounds ⟨*apocodeine*⟩; *apo-* before consonants other than *h* and sometimes *ap-* before vowels and *aph-* before *h* (which is not repeated) but frequently *apo-* even before *h* or a vowel

apo *abbr* apogee

APO *abbr* army post office

apo·at·ro·pine \ˌapō'-\ *n* [ISV *apo-* + *atropine*] **:** a bitter crystalline poisonous alkaloid $C_{17}H_{21}NO_2$ occurring naturally in belladonna root or prepared synthetically by the action of nitric acid on atropine and having no mydriatic effect

apoc·a·lypse \ə'päkəˌlips\ *n* -s [ME *apocalipse* Revelation of St. John (book of the New Testament), revelation, vision, fr. LL *apocalypsis*, fr. Gk *apokalypsis*, lit., uncovering, revelation, fr. *apokalyptein* to uncover, reveal (fr. *apo-* + *kalyptein* to cover, conceal) + *-sis* — more at HELL] **1 :** a writing professing to reveal the future; *esp* **:** such a pseudonymous writing in Jewish or early Christian circles between about 200 B.C. and A.D. 150 predicting the future shape of eschatological events by means of a symbolism understandable to the faithful but hidden from others **2 :** something viewed as a revelation **:** DISCLOSURE

¹**apoc·a·lyp·tic** \əˌpäkə¦liptik *also* ¦aˌpäkə- *sometimes* ¦apəkə-\ *also* **apoc·a·lyp·ti·cal** \-təkəl, -ēk-\ *adj* [LGk *apokalyptikos*, fr. Gk *apokalyptein* + *-ikos* -ic, -ical] **1 a :** of or relating to an apocalypse **b :** resembling or having the characteristics of an apocalypse **2 :** forecasting or predicting the ultimate destiny of the world in the shape of future events **:** PROPHETIC, REVELATORY **3 :** foreboding imminent disaster or final doom **:** TERRIBLE **4 :** wildly unrestrained **:** GRANDIOSE **5 :** CLIMACTIC **:** ultimately decisive — **apoc·a·lyp·ti·cal·ly** \-tək(ə)lē, -ēk-, -li\ *adv*

²**apocalyptic** \"\ *n* -s **:** literature resembling or having characteristics of an apocalypse

apoc·a·lyp·ti·cism \əˌpäkə'liptəˌsizəm *also* ˌaˌpäk- *sometimes* ˌapək-\ *or* **apoc·a·lyp·tism** \ə¦päkə¦lipˌtiz-, ˌaˌpäkə'l-, ˌapəkə'l-\ *n* -s **:** apocalyptic expectation; *esp* **:** a doctrine distinguished by the expectation of an imminent end of the present temporal world, the final destruction of the unrighteous in a purging holocaust engulfing the earth, and the resurrection of the righteous to a purified world of bliss

apoc·a·lyp·tist \ə¦päkə¦liptəst, ˌaˌpäkə'l-, ˌapəkə'l-\ *n* -s **:** the writer of an apocalypse

ap·o·car·pous \¦apə¦kärpəs\ *adj* [*apo-* + *-carpous*] **:** having the carpels of the gynoecium separate ⟨the buttercup is ~⟩ — opposed to *syncarpous*

ap·o·car·py \'apəˌkärpē\ *n* -ES [*apocarpous* + *-y*] **:** the state of being apocarpous

ap·o·ca·tas·ta·sis *or* **ap·o·ka·tas·ta·sis** \¦apəkə'tastəsəs\ *n, pl* **apocatasta·ses** *or* **apokatasta·ses** \-əˌsēz\ [NL, fr. LL, fr. Gk *apokatastasis*, lit. restitution, recovery, fr. *apo-* + *katastasis* restoration, condition — more at CATASTASIS] **:** RESTITUTION, RESTORATION; *esp* **:** the doctrine of the final restoration of all sinful beings to God and to the state of blessedness — compare UNIVERSALISM — **ap·o·cat·a·stat·ic** \¦apəˌkad·ə¦stad·ik\ *adj*

ap·o·cen·ter \'apə¦-\ *n* -s [*apo-* + *center, centre*] **:** the point of an orbit farthest from the center of attraction

ap·o·cen·tric \¦==¦-\ *adj* [*apo-* + *centric*] *biol* **:** deviating from the archetype — opposed to *archecentric* — **ap·o·cen·tric·i·ty** \ˌapəˌsen·'trisəd·ē, -ˌsən-\ *n* -ES

ap·o·cha \'apəkə\ *n, pl* **apo·chae** \-ˌkī, -ˌkē\ [LL, fr. Gk *apochē* receipt] *Roman & civil law* **:** a written receipt for the payment of money

apocha tri·um an·no·rum \-¦trēəmə'nōrəm, -¦trīə-\ *n, pl* **apochae trium annorum** [NL, lit., three year receipt] *Scots law* **:** a written receipt for a debt due (as rent or interest) for three consecutive separate yearly or periodical payments from which the payment of the preceding installments is presumed

ap·o·chro·mat \¦apəkrōˌmat, ˌapə'krōˌm-, *usu* -ad·+V\ *n* -s [G, back-formation fr. *apochromatisch* apochromatic] **:** an apochromatic lens

ap·o·chro·mat·ic \¦apəkrō¦mad·ik\ *adj* [ISV *apo-* + *chromatic*] **:** free from chromatic and spherical aberration — used of a lens in which rays of three or more colors are brought to the same focus, the degree of achromatism thus obtained being more nearly complete than where two rays only are thus focused

apoc·o·pate \ə'päkəˌpāt, *usu* -ād·+V\ *vt* -ED/-ING/-S [*apocope* + *-ate*] **:** to shorten by apocope — **apoc·o·pa·tion** \əˌpäkə'pāshən\ *n* -s

apoc·o·pe \ə'päkə(ˌ)pē\ *n* -s [LL, fr. Gk *apokopē*, lit., cutting off, fr. *apokoptein* to cut off, fr. *apo-* + *koptein* to strike, cut off — more at CAPON] **:** the loss of one or more sounds or letters at the end of a word (as in *sing* from Old English *singan*, *my* from Old English *mīn*, or *tho* for *though*) — compare APHAERESIS, SYNCOPE

ap·o·crine \'apəkrən; -ˌkrin, -ˌīn,-ˌēn\ *adj* [ISV *apo-* + *-crine* (fr. Gk *krinein* to separate)] **:** producing a secretion that involves breaking off of the part of the cytoplasm of the secreting cells above the nucleus **:** produced by an apocrine gland — compare ECCRINE, MEROCRINE

apocrine gland *n* **:** any of the large sweat glands that produce both a fluid and an apocrine secretion, are restricted in man to hairy regions of the body, and are lined by a single layer of tall columnar cells with acidophile cytoplasm — compare ECCRINE GLAND

ap·o·cri·si·ar·i·us \ˌapəˌkriz(h)ē'a(a)rēəs\ *also* **ap·o·cri·si·ary** \-'kriz(h)ēˌerē, -zhərē\ *n, pl* **apocrisiar·ii** \-a(a)rēˌī, -rēˌē\ *or* **apocrisiar·ies** [LL *apocrisiarius, apocrisarius*, fr. LGk *apokrisis* message (fr. Gk, answer, fr. *apokrinesthai* to answer — fr. *apokrinein* to separate, choose, fr. *apo-* + *krinein* to separate, distinguish, decide — + *-sis*) + L *-arius* -ary — more at RIDDLE (sieve)] **:** a plenipotentiary delegate formerly representing a power and residing at a foreign capital; *esp* **:** a papal nuncio serving at the imperial court in Constantinople during the early centuries of the medieval era

apoc·ri·ta \ə'päkrəd·ə\ [NL, fr. Gk *apokrita*, neut. pl. of *apokritos* separated, fr. *apokrinein* to separate] *syn of* CLISTOGASTRA

ap·o·cryph \'apəˌkrif\ *n* -s [ME *apocrife*, fr. MF, fr. ML *apocrypha*] **:** an apocryphal writing

apoc·ry·pha \ə'päkrəfə\ *n pl but sometimes sing in constr, often cap* [ML, fr. neut. pl. of LL *apocryphus* secret, uncanonical (said of writings not to be read to the congregation), fr. LGk *apokryphos*, fr. Gk, hidden, fr. *apokryptein* to hide away, fr. *apo* + *kryptein* to hide — more at CRYPT] **1 :** quasi= scriptural noncanonical or deuterocanonical books of doubtful authorship and authority ⟨the Old Testament *Apocrypha*⟩ ⟨in these ~ we find Confucius being regarded as a superhuman being —Yu-lan Feng⟩ **2 :** writings or statements of doubtful or spurious authorship ⟨his early rise is shrouded in ~ —E.S.Turner⟩

apoc·ry·phal \-fəl\ *adj* **1** *often cap* **:** similar to the Apocrypha **2 :** not canonical **:** of doubtful authenticity **:** FICTITIOUS, MYTHICAL, SPURIOUS, UNTRUSTWORTHY ⟨noting which works are regarded as authentic and which ~ —L.J.Thro⟩ **3** *archaic* **:** COUNTERFEIT, IMITATIVE, SHAM ⟨a ring with ~ diamonds⟩ **syn** see FICTITIOUS

apoc·ry·phal·ly \-fəlē, -li\ *adv* **:** in an apocryphal manner **:** without authenticity

apoc·ry·phon \-ˌfän\ *sing of* APOCRYPHA

ap·o·cy·a·nine \¦apə¦-\ *n* -s [ISV *apo-* + *cyanine*] **:** any of a class of cyanine dyes in whose structure the two heterocyclic rings are directly attached to each other by a double bond

apoc·y·na·ce·ae \əˌpäsə'nāsēˌē, ˌapəsə'-, -əˌsī'-\ *n pl, cap* [NL, fr. *Apocynum*, type genus + *-aceae*] **:** a family of chiefly tropical herbs, shrubs, or trees (order Gentianales) having a milky juice, simple entire leaves, often showy flowers, and a fruit consisting of two follicles or drupes — compare DOGBANE, OLEANDER, PERIWINKLE — **apoc·y·na·ceous** \=¦=¦=¦nāshəs, ¦==(ˌ)=¦-\ *adj*

apoc·y·nin \ə'päsənən\ *n* -s [ISV *apocyn-* (fr. NL *Apocynum*) + *-in*] **:** ACETOVANILLONE

apoc·y·num \-sənəm\ *n, cap* [NL, fr. L, dogbane, fr. Gk *apokynon*, fr. *apo-* + *-kynon* (fr. *kyn-, kyōn dog*) — more at HOUND] **:** a genus of chiefly American perennial herbs (family Apocynaceae) with opposite leaves and small white or pink flowers in corymbose cymes — see INDIAN HEMP 1

ap·o·cyte \'apəˌsīt\ *n* -s [ISV *apo-* + *-cyte*] **:** a multinucleate cell

ap·o·da \'apədə\ *n pl, cap* [NL, fr. Gk, neut. pl. of *apod-, apous* footless] **:** any of several different groups of animals that have been so named from their lacking limbs or feet: as **a :** an order of slender wormlike holothurians that lack tube feet and radial ambulacral vessels — compare HOLOTHURIOIDEA **b :** a group of fishes without pelvic fins **c :** CAECILIANS **d :** an order or suborder of parasitic segmented cirripedes **e :** worms without appendages (as the leeches)

¹**ap·o·dal** \'apəd°l\ *also* **ap·o·dan** \-dən, -d°n\ *or* **ap·o·dous** \-dəs\ *adj* [Gk *apod-, apous* + E *-al* or *-an* or *-ous*] **1 :** having no feet **:** FOOTLESS **2 :** lacking appendages ⟨eels and some insect larvae are ~⟩ **3** [NL *Apodes* & *Apoda* + E *-al* or *-an* or *-ous*] **:** of or relating to the Apoda or Apodes

²**apodal** \"\ *also* **apodan** \"\ *n* -s **:** an apodal animal

apodeictic *var of* APODICTIC

apo·deip·non \ä'pōdēpˌnōn\ *n, pl* **apodeip·na** \-ˌnä\ *often cap* [MGk, fr. Gk *apo-* + *deipnon* meal] **:** the last part of the divine office in the Eastern Church — compare COMPLINE

apod·e·mal \ə'padəməl, ¦apə¦dēm-\ *adj* **:** of, relating to, or functioning as an apodeme

ap·o·deme \'apəˌdēm\ *also* **apod·e·ma** \ə'pädəmə\ *n, pl* **apodemes** \-ēmz\ *also* **apodemas** \-əməz\ *or* **apodem·a·ta** \ˌapə'demədə\ [NL *apodema*, fr. *apo-* + *-dema* (fr. Gk *demas* body, bodily build); akin to Gk *demein* to build — more at TIMBER] **:** one of the internal ridges or ingrowths from the exoskeleton of most arthropods that support the internal organs, provide points of attachment for the muscles, and constitute the endoskeleton of the animal

ap·o·de·mus \ˌapə'dēməs\ *n, cap* [NL, fr. Gk *apodēmos* abroad, fr. *apodēmein* to go abroad, be abroad, fr. *apo-* + *dēmos* country, people — more at DEMOCRACY] **:** a genus consisting of the Old World field mice

¹**ap·o·des** \'apəˌdēz\ *n pl, cap* [NL, fr. Gk, masc. & fem. pl. of *apod-, apous* footless] **1 :** a group of soft-finned, elongated, and probably degenerate fishes consisting of the eels, often including the morays and in old classifications also many others having no pelvic fins, and being now commonly treated as an order but sometimes as including several orders or, formerly, made a division of the Physostomi **2 :** any of several groups of animals lacking appendages; *specif* **:** APODA a, c

²**apodes** *pl of* APUS

ap·o·di \'apəˌdī, -ˌdē\ *n pl, cap* [NL, fr. Gk *apodoi*, pl. of *apous* footless, fr. *a-* ²*a-* + *-pous* (fr. *pous* foot) — more at FOOT] **:** a suborder of Apodiformes that comprises the swifts

apo·dia \ā'pōdēə, a'-,ə'-\ *n pl, cap* [NL, fr. Gk, fr. *apod-, apous* + *-ia*] **:** APODA a

ap·o·dic·tic \¦apə¦diktik\ *also* **ap·o·dic·ti·cal** \-təkəl\ *also* **ap·o·deic·tic** \-¦dīktik\ *adj* [L, fr. Gk *apodeiktikos*, fr. *apodeiktos* demonstrable, fr. *apodeiknynai* to point out, demonstrate (fr. *apo-* + *deiknynai* to show) + *-ikos* -ic, -ical — more at TOKEN] **1 :** expressing necessary truth **:** absolutely certain ⟨categories of human action . . . are ~ and absolute and do not admit of any gradation —Alfred Sherrard⟩ **2 :** capable of clear and certain demonstration ⟨an ~ theory⟩ — **ap·o·dic·ti·cal·ly** \-tək(ə)lē\ *adv*

¹apod·i·dae \ə'pädə,dē\ [NL, fr. *Apod-, Apus* (syn. of *Triops*), type genus + *-idae* — more at APUS] *syn of* TRIOPIDAE

²apodidae \"\ *n pl, cap* [NL, fr. *Apod-, Apus,* type genus + *-idae* — more at APUS] **:** a widely distributed family of birds (order Apodiformes) comprising the swifts and having flat skulls and all toes pointing forward but being swallowlike in appearance and behavior

apod·i·form \ə'pädə,fórm\ *adj* [NL *Apodiformes*] **:** of or relating to the Apodiformes

apod·i·for·mes \ə,pädə'fór,mēz\ *n pl, cap* [NL, fr. *Apod-, Apus* + *-iformes*] **:** an order of birds with long narrow wings and weak feet that comprises the swifts and the humming birds

apod·o·sis \ə'pädəsəs\ *n, pl* **apodo·ses** \-ə,sēz\ [NL, fr. Gk, restitution, definition, apodosis, fr. *apodidonai* to restore, define, make an apodosis (fr. *apo-* + *didonai* to give) + *-sis* — more at DATE (point of time)] **1 :** CONCLUSION 7 — contrasted with *protasis* **2 :** the last day of a festival period in the Eastern Church comparable to the last day of an octave in the Western Church except in the variable duration of the period

ap·o·dy·te·ri·um \,apə,dī'tirēəm\ *n, pl* **apodyte·ria** \-rēə\ [L, fr. Gk *apodytērion,* fr. *apodyein* to strip off, fr. *apo-* + *dyein* to dive in, put on (clothes) — more at ADYTUM] **:** a dressing room in an ancient Greek or Roman bath or palaestra

ap·o·en·zyme \,apō,-\ *n* -s [ISV *apo-* + *enzyme*] **:** any protein that forms an active enzyme system by combination with a coenzyme and that determines the specificity of this system for any one substrate

ap·o·fer·ri·tin \,apō,-\ *n* -s [ISV *apo-* + *ferritin*] **:** a colorless crystalline protein capable of storing iron in the cells of the body — compare FERRITIN

ap·o·gae·ic \,apə¦jēik\ *or* **ap·o·ga·ic** \-¦gāik\ *adj* [NL *apogaeum* & Gk *apogaion* apogee + E *-ic*] **:** APOGEAN

ap·o·ga·lac·te·um \,apəgə'laktēəm, -kshēəm; -,ga,lak'tē-\ *n* -s [NL, fr. *apo-* + *-galacteum* (fr. Gk *galakt-, gala* milk) — more at GALAXY] **:** the point of the hypothetical orbit of the sun or another star at which it is most remote from the galactic nucleus

ap·o·gam·ic \,apə¦gamik\ *or* **ap·o·ga·met·ic** \-,ga¦med·ik\ *or* **apog·a·mous** \ə'pägəməs, a'-\ *adj* **:** of or relating to apogamy — **ap·o·gam·i·cal·ly** \,apə¦gamək(ə)lē\ *adv* — **apog·a·mous·ly** \ə'pägəməslē, a'-\ *adv*

apog·a·my \ə'pägəmē, (')a¦p-\ *n* -ES [ISV *apo-* + *-gamy*] **1** *biol* **:** interbreeding within a segregated group not having any common differentiating character — compare HOMOGAMY **2** *bot* **:** development of the sporophyte from the gametophyte without fertilization — used esp. of a form of apomixis in seed plants wherein an embryo arises from a cell or cells other than the egg and without fertilization

ap·o·ge·an \,apə¦jēən\ *also* **ap·o·ge·al** \-ēəl\ *or* **ap·o·ge·ic** \-ēik\ *adj* **:** of or connected with the apogee ⟨~ tides that occur when the moon is at the apogee of its orbit⟩

ap·o·gee \'apə(,)jē, -əji\ *n* -s [It & Gk & F & NL; It *apogeo* & F *apogée* & NL *apogaeum,* fr. Gk *apogeion, apogaion,* fr. neut. of *apogeios, apogaios* far from the earth, fr. *apo-* + *-geios, -gaios* (fr. *gē* earth)] **1 :** the point in the orbit of a satellite of the earth (as the moon or an artificial body) at the greatest distance from the center of the earth **2 :** the farthest or highest point **:** APEX ⟨the ~ of Renaissance art —*Time*⟩

apog·e·nous \ə'päjənəs, (')a¦p-\ *adj* [*apo-* + *-genous*] **:** relating to or causing apogeny

apog·e·ny \ə'päjənē, a'-\ *n* -ES [*apo-* + *-geny*] *bot* **:** loss of the reproductive function

ap·o·ge·o·trop·ic \,apə¦==¦==\ *adj* [*apo-* + *geotropic*] **:** bending up or away from the ground ⟨the short ~ roots of the mangrove⟩ — **ap·o·ge·o·trop·i·cal·ly** \¦==,==¦=pək(ə)lē\ *adv*

ap·o·ge·ot·ro·pism \,apə¦====\ *n* -s [*apo-* + *geotropism*] *bot* **:** the state of being apogeotropic **:** negative geotropism

apo·gon \ə'pō,gän, ā'-\ *n, cap* [NL, fr. MGk *apōgōn* beardless, fr. Gk *a-* ²a- + *pōgōn* beard — more at -POGON] **:** a genus of large-headed marine percoid fishes having the body oblong and compressed and comprising the cardinal fishes — see APOGONIDAE

apo·gon·id \ə'pōgənəd, ā'-; ,apə'gän-\ *n* -s [NL *Apogonidae*] **:** a fish of the genus *Apogon* or family Apogonidae

ap·o·gon·i·dae \,apə'gänə,dē\ *n pl, cap* [NL, fr. *Apogon,* type genus + *-idae*] *in many classifications* **:** a family (type genus *Apogon*) of bright-colored tropical marine percoid fishes many of which incubate the eggs in the mouth

apogon iris *n, usu cap A* **:** BEARDLESS IRIS

ap·o·graph \'apə,graf\ *n, pl* **apog·ra·pha** \ə'pägrəfə, a'-\ [L *apographon,* fr. Gk, fr. neut. of *apographos* copied, fr. *apo-* + *-graphos* -graph] **:** COPY, TRANSCRIPT — **apog·ra·phal** \ə'pägrəfəl, (')a¦p-\ *adj*

ap·o·hy·al \,apə¦hīəl\ *n* -s [*apo-* + *hyoidal*] **:** CERATOBRANCHIAL

apohydrotropic *var of* APHYDROTROPIC

ap·oid \'a,pȯid, 'ā,-\ *adj* [NL *Apoidea*] **:** of or relating to the Apoidea **:** resembling one of the Apoidea or some part of one of these insects ⟨~ mouth parts⟩

apoi·de·a \ə'pȯidēə, ā'p-,a'p-\ *n pl, cap* [NL, fr. *Apis* + *-oidea*] **:** a superfamily of Hymenoptera comprising the true bees — compare APIDAE, SPHECOIDEA

apoise \ə'-\ *adj* [¹*a-* + *poise* (v.)] **:** in readiness **:** POISED ⟨bridesmaids were ~ to resume their places —Edith Wharton⟩

ap·o·jove \'apə,jōv\ *n* -s [NL *apojovium,* fr. *apo-* + *-jovium* (fr. *Jovis* Jupiter) — more at JOVE] **:** the point farthest from the planet Jupiter in the orbit of each of its satellites

apokatastasis *var of* APOCATASTASIS

apo koi·nou \,ä(,)pō,kȯi'nü, ä,p-\ *n, pl* **apo koinous** \-nüz\ [Gk, lit., in common] **:** the occurrence of one and the same word or word group, not repeated, in two constructions (as *three crows* in "there were three crows sat on a tree")

apo·lar \(')ā¦-\ *adj* [²*a-* + *polar*] **:** having no poles — used esp. of nerve cells formerly believed to lack processes

ap·o·laus·tic \,apə¦lȯstik\ *adj* [Gk *apolaustikos,* fr. *apolaustos* enjoyed, enjoyable (fr. *apolauein* to enjoy, benefit from, fr. *apo-* + *-lauein,* akin to *leia* booty, prey) + *-ikos* -ic — more at LUCRE] **:** devoted to enjoyment ⟨a learned, ~ buffoon who loved good food —James Stern⟩

ap·o·le·gam·ic \,apələ¦gamik\ *adj* [Gk *apolegein* to pick out (fr. *apo-* + *legein* to gather) + E *-gamic* — more at LEGEND] *biol* **:** relating to selection — used specif. of mating based on sexual selection

apo·lis·ta \,äpə'lēstə\ *n, pl* **apolista** *or* **apolistas** *usu cap* [Sp, of AmerInd origin] **1 a :** a people of the Apolo river valley, Bolivia **b :** a member of such people **2 :** the language of the Apolista people

apo·lit·i·cal \¦ā+¦===\ *adj* [²*a-* + *political*] **1 :** having an aversion for or no interest or involvement in political affairs **2 :** without political significance

¹apol·li·nar·i·an \ə¦pälə¦na(a)rēən\ *adj, usu cap* [L *Apollinaris* (fr. *Apollin-, Apollo* + L *-aris* -ary) + E *-an*] **:** relating to or in honor of Apollo

²apollinarian \"\ *adj, usu cap* [LL *Apollinarianus,* fr. LGk *Apollinarianos,* fr. *Apollinaris* of Laodicea †*ab* A.D. 390 Syrian teacher & theologian + Gk *-anos* -an] **:** relating to Apollinaris of Laodicea or to the doctrine held by Apollinarians

³apollinarian \"\ *n* -s *usu cap* **:** an adherent of the Christological doctrine that asserted that in Jesus Christ a perfect divine nature in the form of the divine Logos assumed an imperfect human body with the Logos taking the controlling place ordinarily held by the mind

apol·line \ə'pälən, -,līn\ *adj, usu cap* [L *Apollineus,* fr. *Apollin-, Apollo* + *-eus* -eous] **:** of or relating to Apollo or his worship ⟨~ serenity⟩ ⟨~ choruses⟩

ap·ol·lin·i·an \,apə¦linēən *also* ¦a,pä¦-\ *adj, usu cap* [L *Apollineus* of Apollo + E *-ian*] **:** ¹APOLLONIAN

apol·lo \ə'pä(,)lō\ *n* -s *usu cap* [after *Apollo,* Graeco-Roman god of manly beauty, of poetry and music, and of the wisdom of oracles, fr. L, fr. Gk *Apollōn*] **1 :** a man of graceful beauty esp. when young **2** *or* **apollo butterfly** [*apollo,* NL, specific epithet of *Parnassius apollo,* after *Apollo,* the god] **:** a European alpine butterfly (*Parnassius apollo*), largely white with eyelike markings; *also* **:** a related but darker butterfly (*P. mnemosyne*)

¹ap·ol·lo·ni·an \¦apə¦lōnēən, -nyən *also* ¦a,pä¦-\ *also* **ap·ol·lon·ic** \-¦länik\ *or* **apol·lo·nis·tic** \ə¦pälə¦nistik\ *adj, usu cap* [Gk *Apollōn* + E *-ian* or *-ic* or *-istic*] **1 :** of, relating to, or resembling the god Apollo **2** [trans. of G *apollonisch*] **:** harmonious, measured, ordered, or balanced in character **:** of a rational or nomothetic nature fundamentally temperate, restrained, or meditative — contrasted with *dionysian*

²apollonian \"\ *adj, usu cap* [*Apollonius* of Perga, 3d cent. B.C. Greek mathematician & *Apollonius* of Tyana, 1st cent. A.D. Greek philosopher + E *-an*] **:** of or named after Apollonius, esp. Apollonius of Perga or Apollonius of Tyana

³apollonian *n* -s *usu cap* **:** one that has a well-developed Mount of Apollo and a long and large finger of Apollo and that is usu. held by palmists to be characterized by health, versatility, and an attractive personality

apollonian problem *n, usu cap A* [²*Apollonian,* after *Apollonius* of Perga] **:** the problem in geometry of the construction of a circle touching three given circles

apol·lyon \ə'pälyən, -lēən\ *n* -s *usu cap* [after *Apollyon,* "the angel of the bottomless pit" (Rev 9:11)] **:** DEVIL 1

ap·o·lo·gete \ə'pälə,jēt\ *n* -s [back-formation fr. *apologetic*] **:** one skilled in apologetics **:** APOLOGIST

¹apol·o·get·ic \ə¦pälə¦jed·ik, -etik, -ēk\ *adj* [prob. back-formation fr. *apologetical,* fr. LL *apologeticus* formal apology or justification + E *-al*] **1 :** defending by discourse ⟨modern tolerance often listens benevolently to many ~ pleas —G.G. Coulton⟩ **:** said, written, or done in defense or by way of apology ⟨her little ~ titter —Audrey Barker⟩ **2 :** regretfully excusing or acknowledging ⟨an ~ essay⟩ — **apol·o·get·i·cal·ly** \-ək(ə)lē, -ēk-, -li\ *adv*

²apologetic \"\ *n* -s [LL *apologeticus,* fr. *apologeticus* suitable for defense, fr. Gk *apologētikos,* fr. *apologeisthai* to speak in defense, defend oneself verbally, fr. *apo-* + *-logeisthai* (fr. *logos* speech) — more at LEGEND] **1 :** a formal apology or justification ⟨a type of ~ for natural laissez-faire and the pursuit of narrow individual self-interest —P.H.Douglas⟩ **2 :** APOLOGETICS; *esp* **:** the systematic defense and exposition of the Christian faith addressed primarily to non-Christians

apol·o·get·i·cal \-ökəl\ *archaic var of* APOLOGETIC

apol·o·get·ics \-iks\ *n pl but usu sing in constr* **1 :** systematic argumentative tactics or discourse in defense (as of a doctrine, a historical character, or particular actions) **2 :** that branch of theology devoted to the defense of a religious faith and addressed primarily to criticism originating from outside the religious faith; *esp* **:** such defense of the Christian faith

ap·o·lo·gia \,apə'lōj(ē)ə, ə,pōlə'jēə\ *n, pl* **apologias** \-əz\ *also* **apologi·ae** \,apə'lōjē,ē, ə,pōlə'jē,ā\ [LL — more at APOLOGY] **1 :** an apology or a defense ⟨the present volume is no ~, on the contrary, it is the pugnacious self-vindication of an . . . able man —*Times Lit. Supp.*⟩ **2 :** justification of the acts of a person's life ⟨*En Miroir* turns out to be an ~, suffering from all the faults of self-justification —*Times Lit. Supp.*⟩ **syn** see APOLOGY

apol·o·gist \ə'päləjəst *sometimes* ,apə'lōj-\ *n* -s [F *apologiste,* fr. *apologie* apology + *-iste* -ist] **1 :** one who makes an apology or defense **:** one who speaks or writes in defense of a faith, a cause, or an institution; *esp* **:** one who makes a systematic defense of Christianity **2** *usu cap* **:** one of a number of 2d century church fathers who wrote treatises in defense of the Christian faith

apol·o·gize *also* **apol·o·gise** \ə'pälə,jīz\ *vi* -ED/-ING/-S [¹*apology* + *-ize*] **1 :** to offer a defense or excuse **2 :** to acknowledge a fault or offense with expression of regret by way of amends ⟨when he gives an assignment to a reporter it seems he is doing all but ~ for troubling him —Stanley Walker⟩ ⟨the least you can do is ~⟩ — **apol·o·giz·er** \-zə(r)\ *n* -s

ap·o·logue \'apə,lȯg *also* -äg\ *n* -s [alter. of earlier *apology,* modif. (influenced by *apology*) of F *apologue,* fr. L *apologus,* fr. Gk *apologos,* fr. *apo-* + *logos* word — more at LEGEND] **:** an allegorical narrative (as a beast fable) usu. intended to convey a moral ⟨Aesop was the master of the ~⟩ **syn** see ALLEGORY

apol·o·gy \ə'päləjē\ *n* -ES [MF or LL; MF *apologie,* fr. LL *apologia,* fr. Gk, fr. *apo-* + *-logia* (fr. *logos* speech) — more at LEGEND] **1 :** something said or written in defense or justification of what appears to others to be wrong or of what may be liable to disapprobation ⟨an ~ for a country's foreign policy⟩ **2 :** an attempt to justify or excuse ⟨a convenient ~ for their ruthlessness in Darwinian philosophy —J.D. Hicks⟩ **3 :** an acknowledgment intended as an atonement for some improper or injurious remark or act **:** an admission to another of a wrong or discourtesy done him accompanied by an expression of regret ⟨an ~ to a hostess for being late⟩ **4 :** something that serves as an excuse for the absence of something **:** a poor specimen or substitute **:** MAKESHIFT ⟨devising *apologies* for window curtains —Charles Dickens⟩

syn APOLOGIA, EXCUSE, PLEA, PRETEXT, ALIBI: APOLOGY in today's English usu. indicates either a frank regretful admission that one has been wrong or a defense involving mitigating or extenuating circumstances ⟨an *apology* for the offense⟩ ⟨traffic congestion was their *apology* for being so late⟩ Sometimes, like the word APOLOGIA, it is used without suggestions of guilt or error simply to indicate an explanation for a course or belief ⟨Justin Martyr, a native of Samaria, who wrote one of the more famous of the *apologies* for Christianity, and who won his sobriquet by his death for the faith —K.S.Latourette⟩ ⟨the preface to Mirsky's book on Lenin contains his *apologia* for his shift of allegiance to the Soviet power —Edmund Wilson⟩ EXCUSE indicates an explanation offered to escape censure or blame ⟨it matters not that some uncontrollable impulse, the product of mental disease, may have driven the defendant to the commission of the murderous act. The law knows nothing of such *excuses* —B.N.Cardozo⟩ PLEA usu. involves an appeal for understanding, sympathy, or clemency ⟨old Hepzibah's scowl could no longer vindicate itself entirely on the *plea* of nearsightedness —Nathaniel Hawthorne⟩ PRETEXT suggests a subterfuge, an offer of an untrue reason or motive ⟨he made my health a *pretext* for taking all the heavy chores, long after I was as well as he was —Willa Cather⟩ ⟨the hypocrisy that covers gainful exploitation by the *pretext* of a civilizing mission, concerned with the elevation of the native population —J.A.Hobson⟩ ALIBI, legally a plea that one was elsewhere than at the place at which a crime was committed, may be applied to a mitigating or placating explanation ⟨the *alibis* of many churches for their failure to provide qualified chaplains —Scott Hershey & Harry Tennant⟩ ⟨federal taxes are already being used as an *alibi* for cuts in local school budgets —H.M.Groves⟩

apo·lou·sis *or* **apo·lu·sis** \ä'pōlü,sēs, ,apə'lüsəs\ *n* [MGk *apolousis,* fr. Gk, act of washing off, fr. *apolouein* to wash off, fr. *apo-* + *louein* to wash — more at LYE] **:** the ceremony in the Eastern Church of washing away the baptismal chrism performed by a priest on the eighth day after baptism

¹apo·ly·sis \ä'pōlē,sēs\ *n* [LGk, fr. Gk, loosening, dismissal, fr. *apolyein* to loose from, release, dismiss (fr. *apo-* + *lyein* to loosen, free, destroy) + *-sis* — more at LOSE] **:** the prayer of dismissal used at the conclusion of a service in the Eastern Church

²apol·y·sis \ə'päləsəs\ *n, pl* **apoly·ses** \-ə,sēz\ [NL, fr. *apo-* + *-lysis*] **:** the shedding of ripe proglottids during life (as in most tapeworms) — compare ANAPOLYSIS

apo·ly·ti·kion \,ä,pōlē'tē,kyōn\ *n, pl* **apolyti·kia** \-yä\ [MGk, alter. of *apolytikon,* fr. neut. of *apolytikos* absolving, dismissing, fr. Gk *apolytos* freed, dismissed (fr. *apolyein* to dismiss) + *-ikos* -ic] **:** the concluding hymn sung in the Eastern Church at the end of offices (as matins and vespers) and varying from day to day according to the calendar

ap·o·mei·o·sis \,apə,mī¦ōsəs\ *n, pl* **apomeio·ses** \-ō,sēz\ [NL, fr. *apo-* + *meiosis*] **:** imperfect or suppressed meiosis, a characteristic of the life cycle of many higher polyploids

ap·o·mei·ot·ic \-ī¦äd·ik\ *adj* [fr. NL *apomeiosis,* after such pairs as NL *hypnosis:* E *hypnotic*] **:** relating to or marked by apomeiosis **:** formed without meiosis

ap·o·mict \'apə,mikt\ *n* -s [prob. back-formation fr. ISV *apomictic,* fr. *apo-* + Gk *miktos* mixed] *biol* **:** an individual or species produced by or reproducing by apomixis — **ap·o·mic·tic** \,apə¦miktik\ *or* **ap·o·mic·ti·cal** \-təkəl\ *adj* — **ap·o·mic·ti·cal·ly** \-tək(ə)lē\ *adv*

ap·o·mix·is \,apə'miksəs\ *n, pl* **apomix·es** \-k,sēz\ [NL, fr. *apo-* + *-mixis*] **1** *biol* **:** reproduction involving the specialized generative tissues but not dependent upon fertilization (as apogamy or parthenogenesis) **2** *biol* **:** APOMIXY

ap·o·mixy \'apə,miksē\ *n* -ES [*apo-* + *-mixy* (as in *panmixy*)] **:** the total absence or great limitation of interbreeding restricting the possibility of genetic exchange — opposed to *panmixia*

ap·o·mor·phine \,apə¦-\ *n* [ISV *apo-* + *morphine*] **:** an artificial crystalline alkaloid $C_{17}H_{17}NO_2$ obtained from morphine by dehydration and having a powerful emetic action when injected hypodermically usu. in the form of its hydrochloride

ap·o·neu·ro·sis \,apənə'rōsəs, -n(y)ü'-\ *n, pl* **aponeuro·ses** \-ō,sēz\ [NL, fr. Gk *aponeurōsis,* fr. *aponeurousthai* to pass into a tendon (fr. *apo-* + *neuron* sinew, nerve) + *-sis* — more at NERVE] **:** any of the thicker and denser of the deep fasciae that cover, invest, and form the terminations and attachments of certain muscles and differ from tendons in being flat and thin

ap·o·neu·rot·ic \¦===¦räd·ik\ *adj* [fr. NL *aponeurosis,* after NL *neurosis:* E *neurotic*] **:** of or relating to an aponeurosis

ap·o·no·ge·ton \,apə(,)nō'jē,tän\ *n* [NL, fr. *apono-* (prob. fr. L *Aponus,* hot mineral spring near Padua in northeastern Italy) + Gk *geitōn* neighbor] **1** *cap* **:** a genus (coextensive with the family Aponogetonaceae) of 25 species of Old World aquatic herbs (order Naiadales) with oblong often skeletonized leaves and small spicate flowers — see LATTICE PLANT **2** -s **:** a plant of the genus *Aponogeton* — **ap·o·no·ge·to·na·ceous** \,apə(,)nō,jēd·ə'nāshəs\ *adj*

apoop \ə'püp\ *adv (or adj)* [¹*a-* + *poop*] **:** ASTERN

ap·o·pemp·tic \,apə¦pem(p)tik\ *adj* [LGk *apopemptikos,* fr. Gk *apopemptos* dismissed (fr. *apopempein* to send off, dismiss, fr. *apo-* + *pempein* to send) + *-ikos* -ic — more at POMP] *archaic* **:** sung or addressed to one departing **:** VALEDICTORY ⟨~ hymns⟩

ap·o·pet·al·ous \,apə¦-\ *adj* [*apo-* + *-petalous*] *bot* **:** POLYPETALOUS

ap·o·phan·tic \,apə'fantik\ *n* -s [Gk *apophantikos,* adj., categorical, declaratory, fr. *apophantos* declared (fr. *apophainein* to declare, display, fr. *apo-* + *phainein* to show) + *-ikos* -ic — more at FANCY] *logic* **:** the doctrine of predicative judgment

ap·o·phon·ic \,apə¦fanik\ *adj* **:** of or relating to ablaut **:** cognate in a manner explainable in terms of apophony

apoph·o·ny \ə'päfənē, a'-\ *n* -ES [*apo-* + *-phony;* trans. of G *ablaut*] **:** ABLAUT

ap·o·pho·rom·e·ter \,apəfə'rämәd·ə(r)\ *n* -s [Gk *apophora* act of carrying away, absorption (fr. *apopherein* to carry away, fr. *apo-* + *pherein* to carry) + E *-o-* + *-meter* — more at BEAR] **:** an apparatus for identifying minerals by sublimation

apophthegm *var of* APOTHEGM

apoph·y·ge \ə'päfə(,)jē\ *n* -s [Gk *apophygē,* lit., escape, fr. *apo-* + *phygē* flight, fr. *pheugein* to flee — more at BOW (to bend)] **:** the small hollow curvature given to the top (as in a Doric column) or bottom (as in an Ionic or Corinthian column) of the shaft of a column where it expands to meet the edge of the fillet — compare CONGÉ 4, SCAPE

ap·o·phyl·lite \,apə'fi,līt, ə'päfə,l-\ *n* -s [F, fr. *apo-* + *phyllite*] **:** a mineral $KCa_4Si_8O_{20}(F,OH).8H_2O$ composed of a hydrous potassium calcium silicate related to the zeolites and usu. occurring in transparent square prisms or white or grayish masses (hardness 4.5-5, sp. gr., 2.3-2.4)

ap·o·phyl·lous \,apə¦filəs\ *adj* [*apo-* + *-phyllous*] *bot* **:** having the parts distinct — used of a whorl of the perianth

apoph·y·sal \ə'päfəsəl\ *adj* [NL *apophysis* + E *-al*] *geol* **:** of or relating to an apophysis

apoph·y·sate \-sət,-,sāt\ *adj* [ISV *apophys-* (fr. NL *apophysis*) + *-ate*] *bot* **:** having an apophysis

apoph·y·se·al \ə¦päfə¦sēəl, -¦zē- *also* ¦apə¦fizē-\ *also* **ap·o·phys·i·al** \¦apə¦fizēəl\ *or* **apoph·y·sary** \ə'päfə,serē\ *adj* [*apophyseal* alter. of *apophysial; apophysial* fr. *apophysis* + *-al; apophysary* fr. *apophysis* + *-ary*] **:** of or relating to an apophysis

apoph·y·sis \ə'päfəsəs\ *n, pl* **apophy·ses** \-ə,sēz\ [NL, fr. Gk, offshoot, process of a bone, fr. *apo-* + *-physis* (fr. *phyein, phyesthai* to grow, produce) — more at BE] **1 :** a process of a bone (as a vertebra) **2 :** a swelling of the seta at the base of the capsule of certain mosses often provided with many stomata and functioning as the chief assimilative part of the sporogonium **3 :** a swelling on the cone scale of certain conifers **4** *of certain fungi* **:** a swollen part of the filament or a swelling of the stalk (as in certain members of the genus *Geaster*) **5 :** an expansion or swelling of the hypha (as that below the sporangium in *Mucor*) **6 :** an offshoot from an intrusive body of igneous rock **7 :** a process of the exoskeleton of an insect (as an apodeme or an external spur)

ap·o·plec·tic \,apə¦plektik, -ēk\ *also* **ap·o·plec·ti·cal** \-təkəl, -ēk-\ *adj* [*apoplectic* fr. F or LL; F *apoplectique,* fr. LL *apoplecticus,* fr. Gk *apoplēktikos,* fr. *apoplēssein* to cripple by a stroke; *apoplectical* prob. fr. LL *apoplecticus* + E *-al* — more at APOPLEXY] **:** of, relating to, or causing apoplexy ⟨~ stroke⟩ **:** affected with, inclined to, or symptomatic of apoplexy ⟨an ~ person⟩ — **ap·o·plec·ti·cal·ly** \-tək(ə)lē, -ēk-, -li\ *adv*

ap·o·plec·ti·form \¦==¦=tə,fórm\ *also* **ap·o·plec·toid** \¦==¦=,tȯid\ *adj* [*apoplectic* + *-iform* or *-oid*] **:** resembling apoplexy

apoplectiform septicemia *n* **:** a highly infectious disease of gallinaceous birds caused by a bacterium (*Streptococcus gallinarum*) and characterized by depression, listlessness, and a staggering gait usu. followed by prostration and death

¹apoplex *n* -ES [LL *apoplexis*] *obs* **:** APOPLEXY

²ap·o·plex \'apə,pleks\ *vt* -ED/-ING/-ES *archaic* **:** to strike with apoplexy

ap·o·plexy \'apə,pleksē, -si\ *n* -ES [ME *apoplexie,* fr. MF & LL; MF *apoplexie,* fr. LL *apoplexia, apoplexis,* fr. Gk *apoplēxia, apoplēxis,* fr. *apoplēssein* to cripple by a stroke, fr. *apo-* + *plēssein* to strike — more at PLAINT] **1 a :** a sudden loss of consciousness followed by paralysis caused by hemorrhage into the brain from rupture of an artery or by sudden anemia of a part of the brain from obstruction of its artery either by a blood clot or by the lodgment of an embolus — called also *stroke;* compare CEREBRAL HEMORRHAGE, CEREBRAL THROMBOSIS **b :** gross hemorrhage into a cavity or into the substance of an organ ⟨abdominal ~⟩ ⟨adrenal ~⟩ **2** [so called fr. the rapid drying of the vine] *bot* **:** BLACK MEASLES

ap·o·pyle \'apə,pīl\ *n* -s [*apo-* + Gk *pylē* gate — more at PYLON] *zool* **:** one of the openings by which the water passes out of a radial canal or flagellated chamber of a sponge

apor·al \(')ā¦pōrəl, (')a¦-\ *adj* [irreg. fr. ¹*ab-* + *poral*] **:** located farther from a pore than another structure ⟨on the ~ side of the ovary⟩

ap·o·ret·ic \,apə¦red·ik\ *also* **ap·o·re·mat·ic** \-,rə¦mad·ik\ *adj* [Gk *aporētikos, aporēmatikos,* fr. *aporein* to doubt] **:** SKEPTICAL

ap·o·rhy·o·lite \,apə¦rīə,līt\ *n* -s [*apo-* + *rhyolite*] **:** a rock consisting of a felsite whose structure shows it to have been orig. vitreous like some rhyolites

apo·ria \ə'pōrēə, -ȯr-\ *n, pl* **aporias** \-ēəz\ *or* **apori·ae** \-ē,ē\ [NL, fr. LL, doubt, perplexity, fr. Gk, difficulty, perplexity, fr. *aporos* impassable, difficult (fr. *a-* ²a- + *poros* passage, path) + *-ia* — more at FARE] **1 :** a problem or difficulty arising from an awareness of opposing or incompatible views on the same theoretic matter; *esp* **:** one giving rise to philosophically systematic doubt **2 :** a passage in speech or writing incorporating or presenting a difficulty or doubt

ap·o·rid·ea \,apə'ridēə\ *n pl, cap* [NL, fr. Gk *aporos* + NL *-idea*] *in some classifications* **:** an order of Cestoda including a single genus (*Nematoparataenia*) of unsegmented tapeworms parasitic in swans

ap·o·ro·sa \,apə'rōsə, ,ap-, -ōzə\ *n pl, cap* [NL, fr. ²*a-* + *Porosa* (syn. of *Perforata*), fr. ML, neut. pl. of *porosus* porous — more at POROUS] **:** a division of corals (order Madreporaria) having the corallum solid — opposed to *Perforata* — **apo·rose** \(')ā¦pō,rōs, 'apə,rōs\ *adj*

ap·or·phine \'a,pȯr,fēn, 'apər,-; (')a'pȯr,-\ *n* -s [ISV *apo-* + *morphine*] **:** a synthetic alkaloid $C_{17}H_{17}N$ regarded as the parent from which morphine, bulbocapnine, and related alkaloids are derived

ap·or·rha·is \,apə'rāəs\ *n, cap* [NL, fr. Gk, a shellfish (perh. a species of *Aporrhais*)] **:** a genus of small solid long-spired marine snails related to *Strombus* but having the foot broad and flat — **ap·or·rha·oid** \-ā,ȯid\ *adj*

aporrhoea *n* -s [NL, fr. *apo-* + *-rrhoea*] *obs* **:** EFFLUVIUM, EMANATION

aport \ə'-\ *adv (or adj)* [*a-* + *port* (left side)] **:** on or toward the left side of a ship — used esp. of the helm
apos *abbr* apostrophe
ap·o·se·mat·ic \ˌapəsəˈmad·ik\ *adj* [*apo-* + *sematic*] *zool* **:** CONSPICUOUS, WARNING — used of colors or structures indicative of special means of defense against enemies (as in the skunk and certain actinians and insects) — **ap·o·se·mat·i·cal·ly** \-d·ək(ə)lē\ *adv*
ap·o·seme \ˈapəˌsēm\ *n* -s [*apo-* + *-seme*] *zool* **:** a group distinguished by possession of similar aposematic coloration
ap·o·sep·al·ous \ˌapəˈ-\ *adj* [*apo-* + *-sepalous*] *bot* **:** POLYSEPALOUS
ap·o·si·o·pe·sis \ˌapəˌsīəˈpēsəs\ *n, pl* **aposiope·ses** \-ēˌsēz\ [LL, fr. Gk *aposiōpēsis*, fr. *aposiōpan* to be quite silent, fr. *apo-* + *siōpan* to be silent, fr. *siōpē* silence] **:** the leaving of a thought explicitly incomplete in writing or speaking often by a sudden breaking off and shifting of grammatical construction for rhetorical purposes (as *his behavior was — but I blush to mention that*) or by the use of *etc.* — **ap·o·si·o·pet·ic** \ˌapəˌsīəˈped·ik\ *adj*
ap·o·so·ro \ˌapəˈsōr(ˌ)ō\ *n* -s [prob. native name in Africa] **:** POTTO
ap·o·spor·ic \ˌapəˈspōrik\ *or* **ap·o·spor·ous** \ˌapəˈspōrəs; əˈpäspər-, aˈ-\ *adj* **:** of or relating to apospory
ap·o·spor·i·cal·ly \ˌapəˈspōrək(ə)lē\ *adv* **:** in an aposporic manner
ap·o·spo·rog·o·ny \ˌapəˌ‧‧‧\ *n* -ES [*apo-* + *sporogony*] *biol* **:** suppression of sporogony
ap·o·spory \ˈapəˌspōrē; əˈpäspərē, aˈ-\ *n* -ES [*apo-* + *-spory*] **:** production of gametophytes directly from somatic cells of the sporophytes without spore formation (as in certain ferns and mosses)
apos·ta·cize *or* **apos·ta·size** \əˈpästəˌsīz *also* -ȯs-\ *vi* -ED/-ING/-S **:** APOSTATIZE
apos·ta·cy \-sē\ *archaic var of* APOSTASY
apos·ta·sy \əˈpästəsē, -si *also* -ȯs-\ *n* -ES [ME *apostasie*, fr. LL *apostasia*, fr. Gk, lit., revolt, defection, fr. *aphistanai* to remove, cause to revolt, fr. *apo-* + *histanai* to cause to stand — more at STAND] **1 :** the renunciation of a religious faith **2 :** an abandonment of what one has voluntarily professed **:** a total desertion or departure (as from one's principles or party) ⟨*apostasies* of disciples who refused to accept Freud's theories —*Time*⟩
¹apos·tate \əˈpäˌstāt, -ˌstət *also* -ȯˌs-; *usu* -d·+V\ *n* -s [ME, fr. MF & LL; MF *apostate*, fr. LL *apostata*, fr. Gk *apostatēs*, lit., deserter, rebel, fr. *aphistanai*] **1 :** one who has renounced or forsaken his religious faith or given up his moral allegiance ⟨a Church decree . . . excommunicated as ~*s* all . . . "who profess . . . the materialistic and anti-Christian doctrine" —H.L.Matthews⟩ **2 :** one who has given up the principles or party to which he adhered **:** RENEGADE ⟨that incomparable ~ from intelligence, George Moore —H.J.Laski⟩
²apostate \"\ *adj* [ME, fr. *apostate*, n.] **1 :** relating to or characterized by apostasy ⟨the child of an ~ . . . Catholic —*Time*⟩ **:** faithless to moral allegiance **:** RENEGADE ⟨so spoke the ~ angel —John Milton⟩ **2 :** abandoning or involving the abandonment of any form of allegiance ⟨an ~ and unnatural connection with any foreign power —George Washington⟩
ap·o·stat·ic \ˌapəˈstad·ik\ *or* **ap·o·stat·i·cal** \-d·əkəl\ *adj* **:** APOSTATE — **ap·o·stat·i·cal·ly** \-d·ək(ə)lē\ *adv*
apos·ta·tize \əˈpästəˌtīz *also* -ȯs-\ *vi* -ED/-ING/-S [MF or LL; MF *apostatiser*, fr. LL *apostatizare*, fr. L *apostata* + *-izare* -ize] **:** to commit apostasy **:** to renounce one's faith, party, or principles ⟨the church had *apostatized* and gone against the commandment —Edson Jessop⟩
ap·o·stax·is \ˌapəˈstaksəs\ *n, pl* **apostax·es** \-kˌsēz\ [NL, fr. Gk *apostaxis* drippings, fr. *apostazein* to drip off, fr. *apo-* + *stazein* to drip — more at STAGNATE] *bot* **:** an abnormal exudation
aposteme *n* -s [ME, fr. MF, fr. L *apostema*, fr. Gk *apostēma* abscess, distance, fr. *aphistanai* to remove — more at APOSTASY] *obs* **:** a swelling filled with purulent matter **:** ABSCESS
a pos·te·ri·o·ri \ˌäˌpäˌstirēˈōrˌī, -ˈōˌrī; ˌäˌpäˌsterēˈōr(ˌ)ē, ˌāˌ-, -ˈō(ˌ)rē, -i\ *adj* [L, lit., from the latter] **1 :** of or relating to the kind of reasoning that derives propositions from the observation of facts or that by generalizations from facts arrives at principles ⟨*a posteriori* demonstration⟩ — contrasted with *a priori* **2 :** of or relating to what cannot be known except from experience **:** proved by induction from facts obtained by observation or experiment ⟨*a posteriori* truth⟩
apos·til *or* **apos·tille** \əˈpästəl\ *n* -s [MF *apostille*, fr. *apostiller* to annotate, fr. *a-* (fr. L *ad-*) + *postiller* to annotate — more at POSTIL] *archaic* **:** a marginal note **:** ANNOTATION
apos·tle \əˈpäsəl *also* -ȯs-\ *n* -s [ME *apostle*, *apostel*, fr. OF & OE; OF *apostle* & OE *apostol*, fr. LL *apostolus*, fr. Gk *apostolos*, lit., messenger, fr. *apostellein* to send away, fr. *apo-* + *stellein* to send — more at STALL] **1 a :** one who is sent forth **:** MESSENGER; *specif* **:** one of the 12 disciples of Christ **b :** one of certain early Christian missionaries (as Paul and Barnabas) or in Eastern orthodoxy one of the 70 disciples of Jesus **2 a :** the first or the first prominent Christian missionary in any part of the world **:** one who has extraordinary success as a missionary or reformer ⟨St. Boniface, ~ to Germany⟩ **b :** one who initiates a great moral reform or first advocates any important belief or system **3 :** the highest ecclesiastical official in some church organizations (as in the Church of God in Christ and in the New Apostolic Church of No. America) **4 apostles** *pl, civil & admiralty law* **:** a brief letter dimissory sent by a court appealed from to the superior court, stating the case **:** papers sent up on appeal, equivalent to the record in a case at law **5 :** one of a council or quorum of 12 men in the Mormon Church acting principally as administrators **6 apostles** *pl* **:** bollards and bitts in a sailing ship
apostle bird *n, Austral* **:** a bird that goes about in small flocks: **a :** BABBLER; *esp* **:** GRAY-CROWNED BABBLER **b :** a loud-voiced gray crowlike bird (*Struthidea cinerea*) with brown wings and black legs and bill
apos·tle·hood \-ˌhu̇d\ *n* [ME *apostlehed*, *apostlehod*, fr. OE *apostolhād*, fr. *apostol* + *-hād* -hood] **:** the office or status of an apostle
apostle jug *n* **:** a jug with raised figures of apostles on it
apostle plant *or* **apostle flower** *n* **:** an irislike plant (*Neomarica gracilis*) of the family Iridaceae having flat leaflike stems, ribbonlike leaves, and flowers with the outer perianth members white with basal brown and yellow marking or blotching and inner members blue and strongly reflexed
apos·tle·ship \-ˌship\ *n* **:** the status, rank, or office of an apostle
apostle spoon *n* **:** a silver spoon with the handle terminating in the figure of an apostle formerly often presented by sponsors at baptism to the godchild
apos·to·late \əˈpästəˌlāt, -ˌlət *also* -ȯs-; *usu* -d·+V\ *n* -s [LL *apostolatus*, fr. *apostolus* + L *-atus* -ate] **1 :** the office or mission of an apostle **:** APOSTLESHIP ⟨fulfillment of an ~ to the world⟩ **2 :** an association of persons dedicated to the propagation of a religious faith or doctrine
apos·to·li \-ˌlī, -ˌlē\ *n pl* [L, pl. of *apostolus*, fr. Gk *apostolos* messenger — more at APOSTLE] *civil law* **:** letters dimissory from an inferior court to a superior court
¹ap·os·tol·ic \ˌapəˈstälik, -ēk *sometimes* əˌpäˈ- *or* əˌpȯˈ-\ *also* **ap·os·tol·i·cal** \-ləkəl, -ēk-\ *adj* [*apostolic* fr. ME *apostolik*, fr. LL *apostolicus*, fr. Gk *apostolikos*, fr. *apostolos* apostle + *-ikos* -ic; *apostolical* fr. ME, fr. *apostolik* + *-al*] **1 :** of, relating to, or resembling an apostle or the apostles, their times, or their spirit ⟨~ fervor⟩ **2 a :** according to the doctrine of the apostles **:** taught by or in the tradition of the apostles **b :** genuine and authoritative ⟨~ faith⟩ **3** *Roman Catholicism* **:** PAPAL ⟨~ indulgences⟩ **4** *usu cap* **:** of or relating to one of various Christian religious bodies usu. with the term *Apostolic* included in the official name that seek to bring doctrine and practice into close accord with that of the first Christian apostles and usu. distinguished from other organized forms of Christianity by their emphasis on evangelistic methods, the doctrines of entire sanctification and the direct operation of the Holy Spirit, a fundamentalistic theology, and such practices as foot washing, the gift of tongues, divine healing, and spirit baptism — **ap·os·tol·i·cal·ly** \-lək(ə)lē, -ēk-, -li\ *adv*
²apostolic \"\ *n* -s *cap* **:** a member of an Apostolic church
apostolic church *n* **1** *usu cap A&C* **:** the Christian church as founded by the apostles **2 :** a church founded by an apostle
apostolic delegate *n* **:** an ecclesiastical plenipotentiary representing a church in a country that has no formal diplomatic relations with the church's headquarters
apostolic father *n, usu cap A&F* **:** one of the authors of a collection of 2d century A.D. writings of religious significance
ap·os·tol·i·ci \ˌapəˈstäləˌsī\ *n pl, usu cap* [LL, fr. pl. of *apostolicus* apostolic] **:** members of various ascetic sects of the 3d and 4th centuries A.D. in Phrygia, Cilicia, and Pamphylia who sought apostolic purity of life by renouncing marriage and private property — called also *Apotactici, Apotactites*
apos·to·lic·i·ty \əˌpästəˈlisəd·ē, -ətē, -i *also* əˌpȯs- *sometimes* ˌapəs-\ *n* -ES **:** the quality or character of being apostolic
apostolic see *n* **1 :** a see established by an apostle (as Jerusalem, Antioch, or Rome) **2** *usu cap A, Roman Catholicism* **:** the Roman see
apostolic succession *n* **:** the succession or descent believed to be uninterrupted from the apostles and perpetuated by successive ordinations of bishops, held (as by Roman Catholics, Anglicans, and Eastern Orthodox) to be necessary for valid administration of the sacraments and the transmission of orders
apostolize *vb* -ED/-ING/-S [LL *apostolus* + E *-ize*] *vt, obs* **:** PROCLAIM ~ *vi, obs* **:** to act as an apostle
apos·to·los \əˈpästəˌläs, -ōstəˌlōs\ *n, pl* **aposto·loi** \-ˌlȯi, -ˌlē\ *cap* [LGk, fr. Gk, apostle] *Eastern Church* **:** EPISTLE 1a
¹apos·tro·phe \əˈpästrə(ˌ)fē *also* -ȯs-\ *n* -s [L, fr. Gk *apostrophē*, lit., turning away, fr. *apo-* + *strophē* turning — more at STROPHE] **1 :** the addressing of a person usu. not present or of a thing usu. personified for rhetorical purposes ⟨an ~ to Shakespeare⟩ **2 :** the arrangement of chloroplasts along the lateral walls of leaf cells — called *positive* when caused by intense light and *negative* when by prolonged darkness
²apostrophe \"\ *n* -s [MF & LL; MF *apostrophe*, fr. LL *apostrophus*, fr. Gk *apostrophos*, fr. *apostrophos* turned away, fr. *apostrephein* to turn away, fr. *apo-* + *strephein* to turn — more at STROPHE] **:** the mark ' or ' used to indicate omission of one or more letters or figures (as in *can't* for *cannot, judg'd* for *judged, wish'd* for *wished, mascara'd* for *mascaraed,* '76 for *1776*), to mark the possessive case of English nouns and of certain English pronouns (as in *Bill's, Moses', women's, boys', anyone's*) or the plural of letters (as in *two a's*) or of figures (as in *three 7's*) and sometimes of words that are not normally nouns (as in *no if's or but's*), to set off an inflectional or derivational suffix from a word that is pronounced by uttering the name of each of its letters (as in *their IQ's, he OK's it, GOP'er*), or to constitute a terminal quotation mark
¹ap·os·troph·ic \ˌapəˈsträfik *also* ˌaˌpäˈ- *or* ˌaˌpȯˈ- *or* -ōfik\ *adj* [¹*apostrophe* + *-ic*] **:** of or characteristic of apostrophe ⟨a passage of ~ grandeur⟩ ⟨an ~ manner of writing⟩; *also* **:** given to the use of apostrophe ⟨an ~ writer⟩
²apostrophic \"\ *adj* [²*apostrophe* + *-ic*] **:** associated with or including the mark called an apostrophe ⟨the ~ possessive ending⟩ **:** being an apostrophe
¹apos·tro·phize \əˈpästrəˌfīz *also* -ȯs-\ *vb* -ED/-ING/-S [¹*apostrophe* + *-ize*] *vt* **:** to address by or in apostrophe ⟨~ the spirit of freedom⟩ ~ *vi* **:** to express an apostrophe ⟨~ in a speech⟩
²apostrophize \"\ *vt* -ED/-ING/-S [²*apostrophe* + *-ize*] **:** to shorten by omitting a letter **:** mark with an apostrophe
apos·tro·phus \-fəs\ *n, pl* **apostro·phi** \-ˌfī\ [LL — more at APOSTROPHE] **1 :** ²APOSTROPHE **2 :** the symbol Ɔ of the ancient Roman numeral system used for indicating the number 500 — see NUMBER table
ap·o·tac·ti·ci \ˌapəˈtaktəˌsī\ *n pl, cap* [LL or ML, pl. of *Apotacticus*, fr. LGk *Apotaktikos*, lit., renouncer, fr. *apotaktikos* disposed to renounce, fr. Gk *apotassein* to set apart, fr. *apo-* + *tassein* to put in order, arrange — more at TACTICS] **:** APOSTOLICI
ap·o·tac·tites \-kˌtīts\ *n pl, cap* [ML *Apotactitae*, fr. LGk *Apotaktitai*, fr. Gk *apotaktos* set apart (fr. *apotassein* to set apart, fr. *apo-* + *tassein* to arrange, put in a certain order) + *-itai* (pl. of *-itēs* -ite) — more at TACTICS] **:** APOSTOLICI
apotelesm *n* -s [LL *apotelesma* effect, effect of the stars on human destiny, fr. Gk, fr. *apotelein* to complete, fr. *apo-* + *telein* to complete, fr. *telos* goal — more at WHEEL] *archaic* **:** the casting of a horoscope
apotelesmatic *adj* [Gk *apotelesmatikos*, productive, astrologically influential, fr. *apotelesmat-*, *apotelesma* + *-ikos* -ic] *archaic* **:** of or relating to the casting of horoscopes
apothecaries' measure *or* **apothecary measure** *n* **:** the series of liquid units of capacity (gallon, pint, fluid ounce, fluid dram, minim) that are used by pharmacists
apothecaries' weight *or* **apothecary weight** *n* **:** the series of units of weight, including the pound of 12 ounces, the dram of 60 grains, and the scruple, used chiefly by pharmacists in compounding medical prescriptions — see MEASURE table
apoth·e·cary \əˈpäthəˌkerē, -ri\ *n* -ES [ME *apotecarie*, fr. ML *apothecarius*, fr. LL, shopkeeper, warehouseman, fr. L *apotheca* warehouse (fr. Gk *apothēkē*, fr. *apotithenai* to put away, fr. *apo-* + *tithenai* to put, place) + *-arius* -ary — more at DO] **1 :** one who prepares and sells drugs or compounds for medicinal purposes — now usu. called *druggist, pharmacist* **2 :** PHARMACY
apothecary jar *n* **:** a wide-mouthed covered usu. ceramic and ornamented jar (as for drugs, herbs, or bathroom and kitchen supplies)
ap·o·the·cial \ˌapəˈthēsh(ē)əl, -sēəl\ *adj* [NL *apothecium* + E *-al*] **:** of or relating to an apothecium
ap·o·the·ci·um \-ēs(h)ēəm\ *n, pl* **apothe·cia** \-s(h)ēə\ [NL, fr. L *apotheca* storehouse + NL *-ium*] **:** a spore-bearing structure in many lichens and ascomycetous fungi consisting of a disklike, saucer-shaped, or cuplike body bearing asci in an extended layer (the hymenium) on the exposed flat or concave surface

apothecary jars

ap·o·thegm *or* **ap·o·phthegm** \ˈapəˌthem\ *n* -s [Gk *apophthegma*, fr. *apo-* + *phthegma* voice, saying, word, fr. *phthengesthai* to speak out] **:** a short, pointed, and instructive saying **:** a short usu. pointedly concise formulation of a truth or precept **:** a terse aphorism
ap·o·theg·mat·ic \ˌapəˌthegˈmad·ik\ *or* **ap·o·theg·mat·i·cal** \-d·əkəl\ *also* **ap·o·phtheg·mat·ic** *or* **ap·o·phtheg·mat·i·cal** \ˌapəˌth-\ *adj* [Gk *apophthegmatikos*, fr. *apophthegmat-*, *apophthegma* + *-ikos* -ic] **:** relating to or characteristic of apothegms **:** given to apothegms **:** characterized by apothegms — **ap·o·theg·mat·i·cal·ly** \-d·ək(ə)lē\ *adv*
ap·o·them \ˈapəˌthem\ *n* -s [ISV *apo-* + *-them* (fr. *thema* that which is laid down, proposition) — more at THEME] **:** the perpendicular from the center to one of the sides of a regular polygon

regular polygon showing *A* center; *BD* side; *C* midpoint of *BD*; *AC* apothem

apoth·e·ose \əˈpäthēˌōz, -ōs\ *vt* -ED/-ING/-S [back-formation fr. *apotheosis*] *archaic* **:** APOTHEOSIZE
apoth·e·o·sis \əˌpäthēˈōsəs, ˌapəˈthēəs- *also* (ˌ)aˌpäthēˈōs- *sometimes* ˌapəthēˈōs-\ *n, pl* **apotheo·ses** \-ˌsēz\ [LL, fr. Gk *apotheōsis*, fr. *apotheoun* to deify (fr. *apo-* + *theos* god) + *-sis* — more at THEISM] **1 :** the elevation of a human to the rank of a god **:** the raising of a person or thing to divine status **:** DEIFICATION **2 :** the culmination or highest development of a thing **:** the ultimate, quintessential, or final form ⟨she is the ~ of womanhood⟩ ⟨the ~ of brute force and vulgarity⟩ **3 a :** the exaltation of a person or a thing to a final state of triumph or glory **b :** the ascension of a person or a thing from earthly existence to heavenly glory
ap·o·the·o·size \ˌapəˈthēəˌsīz, əˈpäthēə-\ *vt* -ED/-ING/-S **:** DEIFY **:** raise to an apotheosis **:** elevate to divine status **:** GLORIFY
apot·o·me \əˈpäd·ə(ˌ)mē\ *n* -s [Gk *apotomē*, lit., cutting off, fr. *apotemnein* to cut off, fr. *apo-* + *temnein* to cut — more at CONTEMN] *in Greek music* **:** the interval of a semitone in the Pythagorean scale that is slightly greater than half a whole tone and is equal to the difference between the tetrachord and two whole tones
ap·o·tra·che·al \ˌapəˈ-\ *adj* [*apo-* + *tracheal*] **:** not associated or contiguous with vessels or vascular tracheids ⟨~ parenchyma⟩ — compare METATRACHEAL, PARATRACHEAL, VASICENTRIC
ap·o·tro·pa·ic \ˌapətrəˈpāik\ *adj* [Gk *apotropaios* (fr. *apotropein* to turn away, fr. *apo-* + *tropein* to turn) + E *-ic* — more at TROPE] **:** designed to avert or turn aside evil ⟨an ~ ritual —J.H.Moulton⟩
ap·o·tro·pa·ism \ˌ‧‧‧ˈ‧ˌizəm\ *n* -s **:** the performance of magic ritual or incantatory formulas with the purpose of averting or overcoming evil
ap·o·type \ˈapəˌtīp\ *n* -s [*apo-* + *type*] **:** HYPOTYPE
ap·o·typ·ic \ˌapəˈtipik\ *adj, biol* **:** varying or departing from a type
a power supply \ˈā-\ *n, usu cap A* [¹*A*] **:** a battery or transformer supplying electric power to heat the cathode in an electron tube — compare B POWER SUPPLY, C POWER SUPPLY; A BATTERY
ap·o·zem \ˈapəˌzem\ *also* **apoz·e·ma** \əˈpäzəmə\ *n* -s [*apozem* prob. fr. F *apozème*, fr. L *apozema*, fr. Gk, fr. *apozein* to boil till the scum is thrown off, fr. *apo-* + *zein* to boil; *apozema* fr. L — more at YEAST] *pharmacy* **:** DECOCTION — **ap·o·zem·i·cal** \ˌapəˈzeməkəl\ *adj*
ap·o·zy·mase \ˌapəˈ-\ *n* [*apo-* + *zymase*] **:** the protein portion of a zymase
app *abbr* **1** apparatus **2** apparent **3** appeal; appellate **4** appended; appendix **5** applied **6** appointed **7** apprentice
¹ap·pa·la·chian \ˌapəˈlāchən, *southeastern U.S. usu* -achən *also* -āchēən *or* -achēən *or* -āshən *sometimes* -āshēən\ *adj, usu cap* [prob. irreg. fr. *Apalachee* + E *-an*] **1 :** of or relating to a system of mountains in the eastern U.S. or to the region where they are found **2 :** of or relating to the mountain-making movements in No. America in or near the Pennsylvanian period — see GEOLOGIC TIME table
²appalachian \"\ *n* -s *usu cap* **:** APALACHEE
appalachian tea *n, usu cap A* **1 :** the leaves of either of two shrubs (*Ilex glabra* and *I. vomitoria*) of the eastern U.S. locally used as a tea **2 :** any plant that yields Appalachian tea **3 :** WITHE ROD
ap·pall *also* **ap·pal** \əˈpȯl\ *vb* **appalled; appalled; appalling; appalls** *also* **appals** [ME *appallen*, *apallen*, fr. MF *appalir*, *apalir* to grow pale, make pale, fr. OF fr. *a-* (fr. L *ad-*) + *palir* to grow pale, fr. L *pallescere*, incho. of *pallēre* to be pale — more at FALLOW] *vi, obs* **:** to become pale, faint, or weak **:** FAIL ⟨therewith her wrathful courage gan ~ —Edmund Spenser⟩ ~ *vt* **:** to overcome with consternation or horror **:** fill with fear, astonishment, or amazement **:** DISMAY, SHOCK ⟨~*ed* at the deadly nature of the duel —R.W.Thorp⟩ **syn** see DISMAY
appalling *adj* **:** tending to appall **:** capable of appalling **:** inspiring dismay **:** SHOCKING ⟨an ~ accident⟩ — often used to show intense displeasure ⟨eating the most ~ food — stew, mostly, made of old mutton or goat —Oliver La Farge⟩
syn see FEARFUL
appallingly *adv* **:** in an appalling manner
ap·pa·loo·sa \ˌapəˈlüsə, ˌäp-\ *n* -s *usu cap* [prob. after the *Palouse* Indians] **:** one of a breed of rugged saddle horses developed in western No. America from stock of Spanish origin and distinguished by a mottled skin, vertically striped hoofs, and a patch of white hair over the rump and loins that is blotched or dotted with darker color
¹ap·pa·nage *also* **ap·a·nage** \ˈapənij\ *n* -s [F *apanage*, fr. OF, fr. *apaner* to make suitable provision for a younger son or a daughter (fr. OProv *apanar* to feed, support, fr. *a-* — fr. L *ad-* — + *-panar*, fr. *pan* bread, fr. L *panis*) + *-age* — more at FOOD] **1 a :** a grant (as of lands, offices, state revenues, or money) made by a sovereign or a legislative body for the support of dependent members of the royal family or of the ruler's principal liegemen **b :** a property or a privilege appropriated to or by a person as his share or perquisite ⟨religious supremacy became a kind of ~ to the civil sovereignty —H.H.Milman⟩ **2 :** a customary or rightful endowment or adjunct ⟨beauty which is the natural ~ of happiness —C.K.D.Patmore⟩ **3 a :** a territory or province held in possession as an appanage **:** PRINCIPALITY **b :** a territory subject to outside rule **:** DEPENDENCY **syn** see RIGHT
²appanage *also* **apanage** *vt* -ED/-ING/-S **:** to provide or endow with an appanage
ap·pa·rat \ˈapəˌrat, ˈäpəˌrät, ˌ‧‧ˈ‧\ *n* -s [Russ, fr. G, lit., apparatus, prob. fr. G, fr. L *apparatus*] **:** the political machine of the Communist party ⟨no other book throws so much light on the inside story of Joseph Stalin's ~ . . . , secret police, and rise to absolute power —B.D.Wolfe⟩
ap·pa·ra·tchik \ˌäpəˈrächik\ *n, pl* **apparatchiks** \-iks\ *or* **apparatchi·ki** \-ˈrächəkē\ [Russ, fr. *apparat* + *-chik* (agent suffix)] **:** a Communist secret agent ⟨after her return to Germany began work as an ~ —J.H.Lichtblau⟩
ap·pa·rat·us \ˌapəˈrad·əs, -ˈā|, |təs *sometimes* -ä| \ *n, pl* **apparatus** *or* **apparatuses** [L, preparation, equipment, fr. *apparatus*, past part. of *apparare* to prepare, fr. *ad-* + *parare* to make ready — more at PARE] **1** *obs* **:** a preparation for action **2 a :** a collection or set of materials, instruments, appliances, or machinery designed for a particular use ⟨the ~ of art —Arnold Bennett⟩: as (1) **:** scholarly resources used in the critical study of documents and texts (2) **:** FIRE APPARATUS (3) **:** gymnastic equipment (as parallel bars) ⟨worked out on the ~ for an hour⟩ **b :** any compound instrument or appliance designed for a specific mechanical or chemical action or operation **:** MACHINERY, MECHANISM **c :** a system or group of physical organs that unite in a common function ⟨the respiratory ~⟩ **3 :** the complex of instrumentalities and processes by means of which an organization functions or a systematized activity is carried out: **a :** the machinery of government **b :** the organization of a political party or of an underground movement **syn** see EQUIPMENT, MACHINE
apparatus crit·i·cus \ˌ‧‧ˈ‧‧ˈkrid·ikəs, -it|, |ēk-\ *n* [NL, critical apparatus] **:** supplementary data (as variant readings) provided as part of an edition of a text as a basis for critical study
¹ap·par·el \əˈparəl *also* -er-\ *vt* **appareled** *or* **apparelled; appareled** *or* **apparelled; appareling** *or* **apparelling; apparels** [ME *appareillen*, fr. OF *apareillier* to prepare, fr. (assumed) VL *appariculare*, irreg. fr. L *apparare*] **1** *obs* **:** to make or get ready **:** prepare or prepare for **2 :** DRESS, CLOTHE **:** ATTIRE ⟨~*ed* like circuit riders in Missouri —Frederick O'Brien⟩ **3** *archaic* **:** to furnish (as a ship) with apparatus **:** fit out **:** EQUIP ⟨how are such ships . . . rigged and ~*ed* —Alan Moore⟩ **4 :** to clothe with ornaments **:** cover with something ornamental **:** ADORN, DECK, EMBELLISH ⟨the work is magnificently printed and tastefully ~*ed* —E.E.Noth⟩
²apparel \"\ *n* -s [ME *appareil*, fr. OF *appareil* preparation, provision, furniture, fr. *apareillier*] **1 a** *obs* **:** material designed for a particular use **:** APPARATUS **b :** the equipment of a ship (as masts, sails, rigging, and anchors) **2 a :** a person's clothing **:** DRESS, ATTIRE, RAIMENT ⟨his daily ~ was rough and shabby —Willa Cather⟩ **b :** something that clothes or adorns as if with garments ⟨the gay ~ of spring⟩ **3** *archaic* **:** outward appearance **:** ASPECT, GUISE ⟨so correct that she had puzzled the acutest hinters without the ~ of being circumspect —Lord Byron⟩ **4 :** an oblong piece of embroidery on certain ecclesiastical vestments (as on an alb or amice)
ap·par·en·cy \əˈparənsē, -si *also* -aar- *or* -er-\ *n* -ES [L *apparentia*, fr. *apparent-*, *apparens* + *-ia* -y] **1** *obs* **:** APPEARANCE, SEMBLANCE **2 :** the quality or state of being apparent **3 :** the position of being heir apparent ⟨the bare right of ~ carried certain privileges with it —John Erskine †1951⟩
¹ap·par·ent \-rənt\ *adj* [ME *apparaunt*, *apparent*, fr. OF *aparant*, *aparent* (pres. part. of *aparoir* to appear), fr. L *apparent-*, *apparens*, pres. part. of *apparēre* to appear — more at APPEAR] **1 :** capable of easy perception: as **a :** readily perceptible to the senses, esp. sight **:** open to ready observation or full view **:** unobstructed and unconcealed ⟨an ~ change⟩ ⟨the flaw in the metal was ~⟩ ⟨deposits of transported material left by the retreating ice are perhaps the most widely ~ results of the glaciation —*Amer. Guide Series: N. H.*⟩ **b :** capable of being readily perceived by the sensibilities or understanding as certainly existent or present ⟨a face in which a strange strife . . . was ~ —Thomas Hardy⟩ ⟨"you see — my wife — " he let it go at that because it was ~ that they understood —John Steinbeck⟩ **2 :** readily manifest to senses or mind as real or true and supported by credible evidence of genuine existence but possibly distinct from or contrary to reality or truth ⟨the states are very jealous of any even ~ encroachment by the

federal government —Stephen Duggan〉 〈to this end his ~ digressions eventually return —H.O.Taylor〉 — distinguished from *actual* **3** *obs* **:** LIKELY, PROBABLE 〈as well the fear of harm as harm ~ . . . ought to be prevented —Shak.〉 **4 :** entitled (as by right of birth) to inherit (as property) or succeed (as to a throne) in the ordinary course of events — see HEIR APPARENT; compare PRESUMPTIVE

syn SEEMING, OSTENSIBLE, ILLUSORY: APPARENT may imply only distinctness from reality or truth 〈most children have periods of *apparent* stagnation . . . but probably throughout these periods there is progress in ways that are not easily perceptible —Bertrand Russell〉 It may also describe a semblance contrary to truth and actuality, a likeness dissipated by close scrutiny or consideration of all facts 〈the high mineral content is the reason why irrigation often produces bumper crops from *apparent* deserts —Stuart Chase〉 It usu. does not suggest a reprehensible intent to deceive 〈the long corridor . . . carpeted with a narrow bordered carpet whose parallel lines increased its *apparent* length —Arnold Bennett〉 SEEMING stresses a close resemblance to reality detected only by correcting faulty observation or analysis 〈John had doubtless no wish to be entangled in a long quarrel . . . and the Archbishop's mediation allowed him to withdraw with *seeming* dignity —J.R.Green〉 It is not derogatory in suggesting deception 〈the whole of Burns' song has an air of straight dealing . . . but these *seeming* simplicities are craftily charged —C.E.Montague〉 OSTENSIBLE applies to what is explicitly declared or avowed or to what one would naturally and logically assume from what appears 〈it is by no means true that every law is void which may seem . . . unsuited to its *ostensible* end —O.W.Holmes †1935〉 It often applies to differences between such declarations or appearances and a true or actual end, aim, purpose, or character 〈natives . . . whose *ostensible* business was the repair of broken necklaces . . . but whose real end seemed to be to raise money for angry Maharanees —Rudyard Kipling〉 It often applies to conscious deception 〈the first time that he had been *ostensibly* frank as to his purpose while really concealing it —Thomas Hardy〉 ILLUSORY definitely states that the described impressions of truth or actuality are illusions based on deceptive semblances, formed through faulty observation or analysis, or warped by emotional forces 〈the multiplication of wants, real or *illusory* —Lewis Mumford〉 〈we need a deeper reality to take the place of these early beliefs which the growth of intelligence necessarily shows to be *illusory* —Havelock Ellis〉 〈but hopes may be *illusory* or ill-founded — they may even attach to what is demonstrably impossible —M.R.Cohen〉 **syn** see in addition EVIDENT

²apparent \"\ *n* -s [by shortening] *obs* **:** HEIR APPARENT

³ap·par·ent \ə'pa(a)rənt, a'-, -per- *sometimes* -pär-\ *vt* -ED/-ING/-S [*ad-* + L *parent-, parens* parent, relative — more at PARENT] **:** to bring into close relationship **:** connect (as by way of descent or derivation) 〈Islam, the universal church through which . . . Syriac society came . . . to be ~*ed* to the Iranic and Arabic societies —A.J.Toynbee〉

ap·par·en·ta·tion \ˌ=ˌ=ən'tāshən, ˌa,p-\ *n* -s **:** the process of apparenting **:** AFFILIATION

apparent authority *n* **:** the authority that an agent appears to have by reason of his actual agency or by such acts or conduct of the principal as estop the latter from denying the authority

apparent candle power *n* **:** the candle power of an extended source of light that is equal to the candle power of a point source of light which if located at the extended source would produce an equivalent illumination at the distance specified

apparent danger *n* **:** danger that appears from overt actual demonstration (as by conduct and acts indicative of a design to take life or inflict great personal injury) to make homicide appear necessary to self-preservation

apparent easement *or* **apparent servitude** *n* **:** an easement that involves (as in its nature or as a means of its enjoyment) some permanent visible sign of its existence (as the bed of a stream, an overhanging roof, or a water pipe)

ap·pa·rente·ment \àpàrä"tmä"\ *n* -s [F, lit., alliance by marriage, fr. *apparenter* to ally by marriage (fr. OF *aparenter* to take or treat as a relative, fr. *a-* — fr. L *ad-* — + *parent* relative, parent) + *-ment* — more at PARENT] **:** an alliance of French political parties formed during an election

apparent expansion *n* **:** the thermal expansion of a liquid as measured in a graduated container without allowance for the expansion of the container

apparent horizon *n* **:** the somewhat irregular boundary between the sky and the land or water surface of the earth as viewed from any given point — called also *visible horizon*

ap·par·ent·ly \ə'par(ə)ntlē, -li *also* -aar- *or* -er-\ *adv* [¹*apparent* + *-ly*] **:** in an apparent manner **:** SEEMINGLY, EVIDENTLY

apparent magnitude *n* **:** the observed or apparent brightness of a celestial body expressed on the magnitude scale and varying in accordance with the spectral sensitivity of the means of observing (as the eye, a photographic material, or an instrument)

apparent motion *or* **apparent movement** *n* **:** an optical illusion in which stationary objects viewed in quick succession or in relation to moving objects appear to be in motion

apparent noon *n* **:** the instant of transit of the sun's center over the meridian at any particular place — compare APPARENT TIME

apparent photosynthesis *n* **:** the rate of photosynthesis less the rate of respiration

apparent power *n* **:** the product of the effective electromotive force and the effective current in an alternating-current circuit

apparent time *or* **apparent solar time** *n* **:** the time of day at any particular place indicated by the hour angle of the apparent or true sun or by a simple sundial and differing from mean time by the equation of time

apparent variable *n* **:** BOUND VARIABLE — opposed to *real variable*

apparent volume *n* **:** the result obtained by subtracting from the volume of a binary solution the volume of the pure solvent entering into it at the same temperature, being in general somewhat less than the volume of the pure solute

apparent weight *n* **:** the weight of a body as affected by the buoyancy of a fluid (as air) in which it is immersed, being the true weight minus the weight of the displaced fluid — compare ARCHIMEDES' PRINCIPLE

apparent wind *n* **:** the wind as observed aboard a moving vessel, being the vectorial combination of the true wind and the wind due to the ship's motion

ap·pa·ri·tion \ˌapə'rishən\ *n* -s [ME *appariciounn*, fr. LL *apparition-, apparitio* appearance, epiphany (trans. of Gk *epiphaneia*), fr. L *apparitus* (past part. of *apparēre* to appear) + *-ion-, -io* -ion — more at APPEAR] **1 a :** someone or something unusual or unexpected that appears **:** PHENOMENON 〈Shakespeare is an ~ as genius forever is —W.L.Sullivan〉 **b :** a supernatural appearance **:** GHOST, PHANTOM, SPECTER 〈was never allowed to hear of a goblin or ~ or scarcely to be told of bad men —Charles Lamb〉 **2 a :** the act of becoming visible **:** APPEARANCE 〈I was recalled to the present by the ~ of my adversary riding his pony toward me —R.H.Davis〉 **b** (1) **:** the first appearance of a planet, comet, star, or other luminary after being invisible or obscured (2) **:** the period during which such a body is visible **3** *obs* **:** SEMBLANCE, ASPECT **4** *usu cap*, *obs* **:** EPIPHANY

ap·pa·ri·tion·al \ˌapə'rishən°l, -shnəl\ *adj* **:** of, relating to, or being a phantom **:** SPECTRAL

ap·par·i·tor \ə'parəd·ə(r)\ *n* -s [L, fr. *apparitus* (past part. of *apparēre* to appear) + *-or* — more at APPEAR] **1 :** one that attends or serves an officer or authority: **a :** an officer who executed the orders of a Roman magistrate **b :** an officer who executed the orders and decrees of an ecclesiastical court esp. by serving summonses **c :** an officer formerly present to execute the order of the magistrate or judge of a civil court **2** *obs* **:** one that announces the approach of **:** HERALD

ap·pas·si·o·na·ta·men·te \ə¦päsēə¦näd·ə'mentē, -as-, -syə,-, ə,pashə,n-\ *adv* [It, fr. *appassionato*] **:** with passion — used as a direction in music

¹ap·pas·si·o·na·to \=¦=(=)=¦näd·(ˌ)ō\ *or* **ap·pas·si·o·na·ta** \-äd·ə\ *adj* [It *appassionato* (masc.) & *appassionata* (fem.), past part. of *appassionare* to impassion, fr. *ap-* (fr. L, fr. *ad-*) + *passionare* to impassion, fr. *passione* passion, fr. LL *passion-, passio* — more at PASSION] **:** deeply emotional **:** IMPASSIONED — used as a direction in music

²appassionato \"\ *n* -s [It, fr. *appassionato*, past part.] **:** a musical movement or piece marked *appassionato*

ap·pau·mé *or* **ap·pau·mée** *also* **apau·mé** \ˌa(ˌ)pō¦mā\ *adj* [F *appaumé*, fr. *ap-* (fr. L, fr. *ad-*) + *-paumé* (fr. *paume* palm of the hand) — more at PALM] *heraldry* **:** opened out so as to show the palm of the hand

appay *vt* [ME *apaien*, fr. OF *apaier*, fr. *a-* (fr. L *ad-*) + *paier* to pacify, fr. L *pacare* — more at PAY] **1** *obs* **:** SATISFY, CONTENT **2** *obs* **:** REPAY, REQUITE

appd *abbr* approved

appeach *vb* -ED/-ING/-ES [ME *apechen*, fr. (assumed) AF *apecher, anpecher*, fr. LL *impedicare* to entangle — more at IMPEACH] *vt* **1** *obs* **:** to bring a charge against **:** ACCUSE **2** *obs* **:** to cast aspersions on ~ *vi*, *obs* **:** to bring accusation

¹ap·peal \ə'pēl, -ēəl\ *n* -s [ME *appel, apel*, fr. OF *apel*, fr. *apeler*] **1 a :** a legal proceeding by which a case is brought from a lower to a higher court for rehearing — compare WRIT OF ERROR **b :** a request for such an appeal **c :** the right to such an appeal **d :** a case so appealed **2 :** a formal accusation of a felony or heinous crime made against a person by another who demands punishment for the private injury rather than for the public offense **3** *obs* **:** a challenge to defend oneself (as by a duel) against a charge **4 :** an application or reference (as to a recognized authority) for corroboration, vindication, or decision 〈an ~ to his superiors〉 〈an ~ to the umpire〉 〈an ~ to reason〉 **5 :** an earnest plea or request (as for help or support) **:** ENTREATY 〈~*s* for current support from alumni —T.L.Hungate〉 **6 :** the power or property of arousing a sympathetic response **:** ATTRACTION 〈the great ~ of a freighter crossing is . . . its . . . informality —Richard Joseph〉 **syn** see PRAYER

²appeal \"\ *vb* -ED/-ING/-S [ME *appelen, apelen* to appeal, accuse, fr. MF *apeler*, fr. L *appellare* to address, entreat, appeal to, accuse, summon, call by name, fr. *appellere* to drive to, fr. *ad-* + *pellere* to drive, strike — more at PULSE] *vt* **1 :** to charge with a crime **:** ACCUSE; *specif* **:** to institute a private criminal prosecution against for a felony or heinous crime **2 :** to take proceedings for the removal of (a case) from a lower to a higher court for rehearing **3** *archaic* **:** CHALLENGE 〈man to man I will ~ the Norman to the lists —Sir Walter Scott〉 **4** *obs* **:** to call to witness **:** INVOKE ~ *vi* **1 :** to apply for the removal of a case from a lower to a higher court for rehearing **2 :** to call upon or refer to another as a recognized authority for corroboration, vindication, or decision 〈to what sources of information do I ~ —B.N.Cardozo〉 〈Burke's teaching . . . ~*ed* from the spoken to the unspoken rules of freedom —Michael Polanyi〉 **3 :** to plead seriously **:** make an earnest request 〈both contestants ~*ed* for the ballots of the . . . electors —M.M.Quaife〉 〈~*ed* to the president for aid〉 **4 :** to have a particular interest or attraction **:** arouse a sympathetic response 〈the idea of a European federation has ~*ed* to many statesmen —Vera M. Dean〉 〈educational questions . . . ~ to their sense of duty —J.B.Conant〉

ap·peal·a·bil·i·ty \ə,pēlə'biləd·ē\ *n* -ES **:** the quality or state of being appealable 〈on the question of ~ the court relied entirely on United States v. Snyder —*Harvard Law Rev.*〉

ap·peal·a·ble \ə'pēləbəl\ *adj* **:** capable of being appealed esp. to a higher tribunal 〈decisions . . . ~ to the head of the agency —*New Republic*〉

ap·peal·er \-ēlə(r)\ *n* -s **:** APPELLANT

ap·peal·ing \-ēliŋ, -lēŋ\ *adj* **1 :** having appeal **:** ATTRACTIVE, PLEASING 〈he added an ~ and memorable figure to popular American mythology —Vincent Starrett〉 **2 :** PLEADING, IMPLORING 〈the ~ and frightened look worn by a domestic dog when injured —James Stevenson-Hamilton〉 — **ap·peal·ing·ly** *adv* — **ap·peal·ing·ness** *n* -ES

appeals *pl of* APPEAL, *pres 3d sing of* APPEAL

appeal to the country : a British general election after a government measure has been defeated and parliament dissolved

ap·pear \ə'pi(ə)r, -iə\ *vi* -ED/-ING/-S [ME *apperen, aperen*, fr. OF *aparoir* (3d pers. pl. pres. indic. *aperent*), fr. L *apparēre*, fr. *ad-* + *parēre* to come forth, be visible; akin to Gk *peparein* to display] **1 a :** to come into view (as from a distance or a place of concealment) **:** become visible 〈sandbars which ~ in the river bed at low water —P.E.James〉 **b :** to be in sight **:** be visible 〈a faint but courteous smile occasionally ~*ed* upon the veteran's lips —E.H.Collis〉 **2 :** to come formally before an authoritative body 〈I ~*ed* before the committee in executive session —R.M.Lovett〉; *specif* **:** to present oneself formally as plaintiff, defendant, or counsel 〈was instructed to ~ in court the next morning〉 **3 :** to be taken as **:** LOOK, SEEM 〈a spirit of tolerance which allows the expression of all opinions, however heretical they may ~ —J.B.Conant〉 **4 a :** to be clear to the mind **:** be obvious or evident 〈it perpetually ~*s* throughout history that one man achieves and is the true creator of a capital event —Hilaire Belloc〉 **b :** to reveal itself to an observer or reader **:** be manifest 〈his range of interest ~*s* also in his books —Allan Westcott〉 **5 :** to come before the public or into public view 〈thank the delegates for the great honor they have done me in inviting me to ~ before them —D.D. Eisenhower〉**:** **a :** to come before the public as an actor 〈he first ~*ed* on Broadway last year〉 **b :** to come before the public as an author 〈he ~*ed* in print for the first time〉 **c :** to come out in published form 〈his papers ~*ed* in various scientific journals〉**:** be out 〈a new recording of the symphony ~*ed* last week〉 **6 :** to come into existence 〈primitives may very well ~ at any stage of a country's development —Bernard Smith〉**:** become created, developed, discovered, founded, or invented 〈the sources whence civilization flowed westward centuries before Greece and Rome ~ —Edward Clodd〉

ap·pear·ance \ə'pirən(t)s\ *n* -s [ME *apperaunce*, alter. (influenced by *apperen* to appear) of *apparaunce, apparence*, fr. MF *aparance, apparence*, fr. LL *apparentia*, fr. L *apparent-, apparens* (pres. part. of *apparēre* to appear) + *-ia* -y] **1 :** the act, action, or process of appearing: as **a :** the act or action of coming into view or being visible 〈the sudden ~ of enemy troops〉 〈the unexpected ~ of smoke on the horizon〉 **b :** the act or action of coming before the public or into public view 〈his last ~ on the London stage〉 〈financially secure since the ~ of his last novel〉 **c :** the action or process of coming into existence (as by development, discovery, or invention) 〈within a few years after the ~ of the . . . canal boat —*Amer. Guide Series: N.Y.*〉 **d :** the act or action of coming formally before an authoritative body 〈his ~ before the board〉 **e** (1) **:** the coming into court of either of the parties to a suit (2) **:** the coming into court of a party summoned in an action or his attorney (3) **:** the act or proceeding by which a party proceeded against places himself before the court and submits to its jurisdiction (as by making the proper entry in the court records and remaining within reach of its process) **2 a :** the state or form in which one appears **:** ASPECT, LOOK, MIEN 〈his whole ~ was markedly different from that of the guests usually to be seen —Archibald Marshall〉 **b** (1) **:** an outward state of appearing as opposed to an actual state **:** external show or pretense **:** SEMBLANCE 〈traders, though hostile to the settlement, had to preserve an ~ of neutrality —B.K.Sandwell〉 (2) **appearances** *pl* **:** outward show intended esp. to conceal a real or fancied disgrace or to avoid a social lapse 〈they spent their lives trying to keep up ~*s* and to make his salary do more than it could —Willa Cather〉 **c appearances** *pl* **:** outward indications, circumstances, or events 〈to all ~*s* he was guilty〉 **d** (1) **:** a sense impression of a thing as distinguished from its true nature or real existence 〈the blue of distant hills is only an ~〉 (2) **:** a sensation of an object as produced or modified by the character of the sense organs or by particular circumstances 〈the different ~*s* of a penny viewed from different angles〉 **e :** the phenomenal as opposed to the real: (1) **:** something given in sensation or impression as contrasted with something subject to rational verification (2) **:** the sum total of human or finite experience as contrasted with the reality of the absolute 〈that philosophic legerdemain which, with only experience for its datum, would condemn this experience to the status of ~ and disclose a reality more edifying —C.I.Lewis〉 **3 a :** something that appears: (1) **:** PHENOMENON 〈a great observer of natural ~*s* —William Cowper〉 (2) *archaic* **:** APPARITION 〈this ~ passed for as real a thing as the blazing star itself —Daniel Defoe〉 **b :** an instance of appearing **:** OCCURRENCE 〈the first ~ of that word in English〉 **4** *obs* **:** a gathering or company **:** ATTENDANCE 〈an innumerable ~ of gallants —John Evelyn〉

syn APPEARANCE, LOOK, ASPECT, SEMBLANCE can mean, in common, the outward show or image presented by a person or thing. APPEARANCE usu. suggests no more than the meaning common to the group 〈the *appearance* of the house has been unfortunately altered by the addition of an upper gallery —*Amer. Guide Series: La.*〉 〈his long, flowing beard, whitening with the years, gave to his countenance a patriarchal *appearance* —H.A.Bridgman〉 but can suggest a dissembling or pretense 〈giving highway robbery the *appearance* of legality —H.W.Carter〉 〈going into debt to keep up an *appearance* of prosperity〉 LOOK usu. carries the meaning common to the group but often (generally in the plural) suggests a more objective condition than APPEARANCE, stressing the concrete details of outward appearance 〈he's wearing a queer kind of knickerbocker suit. He hasn't the *look* of a journalist —John Buchan〉 〈did not care for the *looks* of Labrador —Russell Lord〉 〈nor has she lost her dark, good *looks* —*Irish Digest*〉 ASPECT is like LOOK in stressing the features, usu. suggesting a characteristic or habitual appearance, esp. facial expression, but most commonly is applied to nonconcrete things 〈his voice and *aspect* were quite friendly —George Meredith〉 〈this was the dreariest evening *aspect* of the sea he had ever seen —Joseph Conrad〉 〈such is the lot of the man who writes upon the subject of the day; the *aspect* of affairs changes in an hour or two —William Cowper〉 〈"Democracy," he says, "has different *aspects* in different lands" —C.L.Sulzberger〉 SEMBLANCE can signify an outward seeming, an approximation, without suggesting falseness or hypocrisy, but generally implies a difference between outward appearance and inner reality 〈it is the *semblance* which interests the painter, not the actual object —*Times Lit. Supp.*〉 〈this mission has recently been restored to some *semblance* of its former grandeur —*Amer. Guide Series: Texas*〉 〈giving defeat the *semblance* of victory —H.A.Overstreet〉 〈a regime with efficient instruments of terror must cloak its power so as to give it a *semblance* of legitimacy —Julian Towster〉

appeared *past of* APPEAR

appearing *pres part of* APPEAR

ap·pear·ing·ly *adv, now dial* **:** APPARENTLY

appears *pres 3d sing of* APPEAR

ap·peas·a·ble \ə'pēzəbəl\ *adj* **:** capable of being appeased **:** PLACABLE

ap·pease \ə'pēz\ *vt* -ED/-ING/-S [ME *appesen, apesen*, fr. OF *apaisier*, fr. *a-* (fr. L *ad-*) + *-paisier* (fr. *pais* peace) — more at PEACE] **1 :** to bring to a state of peace or quiet **:** CALM, SETTLE 〈instead of *appeasing* the quarrel the government's action intensified it —J.H.Plumb〉 **2 :** to cause to subside **:** ALLAY, ASSUAGE 〈the man had *appeased* his great hunger —Elizabeth M.Roberts〉 〈the same kind of supposition which had *appeased* Mrs. Bennet's curiosity —Jane Austen〉 **3 a :** to bring to a state of ease or content **:** CONCILIATE, SATISFY 〈when he has once tasted the blood of popular applause, he is a tiger, nevermore to be *appeased* —C.H.Grandgent〉 **b :** to conciliate or buy off (a potential aggressor) by political or economic concessions usu. at the sacrifice of principles 〈the attempt to ~ the Nazis at Munich〉 **syn** see PACIFY

ap·pease·ment \-mənt\ *n* -s [ME *appesement*, fr. MF *apaisement*, fr. OF, fr. *apaisier* + *-ment*] **1 a :** the act or action of appeasing **:** PACIFICATION 〈one tribe may go in for the ~ of local ghosts —W.D.Howells〉 **:** CONCILIATION 〈that we should accept wrong and call it right . . . would be ~ at its most cowardly —A.L.Guérard〉 **b :** the state of being appeased **:** SATISFACTION 〈an experience from which he derived little ~〉 **2 :** a policy of appeasing a potential aggressor 〈some defensible reasons for the ~ which London and Paris practiced in the thirties —D.F.Fleming〉

ap·peas·er \-zə(r)\ *n* -s **:** one that appeases

¹ap·pel·lant \ə'pelənt\ *adj* [ME, fr. MF *apelant* (pres. part. of *apeler* to appeal), fr. L *appellant-, appellans*, pres. part. of *appellare* to appeal to — more at APPEAL] **:** relating to an appeal **:** APPEALING, APPELLATE 〈~ jurisdiction〉

²appellant \"\ *n* -s **1 a :** one that accuses another of treason or felony **b** *obs* **:** one that challenges another to combat esp. to prove treason or felony **2 :** one that appeals; *specif* **:** one that appeals from a judicial decision or decree — opposed to *appellee*

ap·pel·late \ə'pelət, *outside the legal profession sometimes* 'apə,lāt *or* 'apələt; *usu* -d·+V\ *adj* [L *appellatus*, past. part. of *appellare* to appeal to, call by name — more at APPEAL] **:** of, relating to, or taking cognizance of appeals; *specif* **:** having the power to review and affirm, reverse, or modify the judgment or decision of another tribunal 〈an ~ court〉

ap·pel·la·tion \ˌapə'lāshən\ *n* -s [ME *appellacioun*, fr. L *appellation-, appellatio*, fr. *appellatus* + *-ion-, -io* -ion] **1** *obs* **:** the act of appealing esp. to a higher court or authority **2** *archaic* **:** the act of calling by a name **3 :** a name or title by which a person, thing, or clan is called and known **:** DESIGNATION 〈he had received the added ~ of Jerry —Charles Dickens〉 〈none of us was well acquainted with the road; indeed, I could see nothing which was fairly entitled to that ~ —George Borrow〉

¹ap·pel·la·tive \ə'peləd·iv, -ətiv\ *adj* [ME, fr. LL *appellativus*, fr. L *appellatus* + *-ivus* -ive] **1 :** designating a being or thing of which more than one specimen exists **:** being a common noun **:** dealing with common nouns **2 :** of, relating to, or inclined to the giving of names 〈the ~ faculty of children〉 — **ap·pel·la·tive·ly** *adv*

²appellative \"\ *n* -s **1 :** COMMON NOUN **2 :** APPELLATION 3

ap·pel·lee \ˌapə¦lē\ *n* -s [MF *appelé, apelé*, fr. past part. of *appeler, apeler* to appeal — more at APPEAL] **:** one against whom an appeal is taken **:** the respondent to an appeal — opposed to *appellant*

ap·pel·lor \ˌapə¦lȯ(ə)r, ə'pelər\ *n* -s [ME *appellour, apellour*, fr. AF *apelour*, fr. L *appellator* appellant, fr. *appellatus* (past part. of *appellare* to address, appeal to) + *-or* — more at APPEAL] **:** APPELLANT 1a

ap·pend \ə'pend *also* a'-\ *vt* -ED/-ING/-S [F *appendre*, fr. LL *appendere*, fr. L, to weigh, fr. *ad-* + *pendere* to weigh — more at PENDANT] **1 :** to hang or suspend (as by a string) **:** ATTACH 〈a seal ~*ed* to a document〉 **2 :** to add as something secondary or subordinate 〈the final summary of his views which he enjoyed ~*ing* to his long-winded discourses —I.V.Morris〉; *specif* **:** to add as a supplement or appendix 〈notes ~*ed* to a chapter〉

append- *or* **appendo-** *or* **appendic-** *or* **appendico-** *comb form* [NL, fr. *appendic-, appendix*, fr. L, appendage, supplement] **:** vermiform appendix 〈*append*ectomy〉 〈*append*icitis〉 〈*appendico*stomy〉 〈*appendo*tome〉

ap·pend·age \ə'pendij, -dēj *also* a'-\ *n* -s **1 :** something accompanying or appended to another thing and usu. subordinate or not essential to it **:** ADJUNCT, APPURTENANCE 〈most factories are an accumulation of ~*s* — something tacked on here, something tacked on there —G.S.Perry〉 〈music . . . had been treated for the most part as a kind of decorative ~ to life —H.A.Overstreet〉 〈the vermiform appendix is a small tubular ~ of the cecum〉 **2 :** a person accompanying or in constant attendance on another usu. as a subordinate **:** HANGER-ON 〈occupation forces and their civilian ~*s* constantly traveling about on cut-rate military tickets —*N.Y.Times*〉 **3 :** LIMB 2a; *broadly* **:** any peripheral extension of an animal body esp. when functioning as a limb (as a seta or cirrus)

ap·pend·aged \-jd\ *adj* **:** having an appendage

ap·pend·ance \-dən(t)s\ *or* **ap·pend·an·cy** \-dənsē, -si\ *n, pl* **appendances** *or* **appendancies** [MF *apendance*, fr. OF, fr. *apendre* to be attached, depend, belong, append (fr. LL *appendere* to suspend) + *-ance*] **:** the quality or state of being appendant

¹ap·pend·ant \-dənt\ *adj* [ME *appendaunt, apendaunt*, fr. MF *apendant*, fr. OF, pres. part. of *apendre*] **1 :** associated as an attendant circumstance or consequence 〈as they have transmitted the benefit to us, it is but reasonable we should suffer the ~ calamity —Jeremy Taylor〉 **2 :** annexed or belonging as a right — used in English law of certain ancient immemorial rights in land (as an advowson or common) that are annexed to the land of the persons claiming them **3 :** attached as an appendage **:** ANNEXED 〈the governor of a colony has jurisdiction within the ~ protectorate — Martin Wight〉 〈a seal ~ to a document〉

²appendant \"\ *n* -s **1 :** an appendant inheritance or right **2 :** APPENDAGE

ap·pen·dec·to·my \ˌapən'dektəmē, -mi, ˌaˌpen-\ *n* -ES [*append-* + *-ectomy*] **:** surgical removal of the vermiform appendix

appended *past of* APPEND

ap·pen·di·ceal \ˌapən'dishəl, ˌaˌpen-; əˌpendə'sēəl, ˌaˌp-\ *also* **ap·pen·di·cal** \ə'pendəkəl, (ˈ)aˌp-, -dēk-\ *or* **ap·pen·di·cial** \ˌapən'dishəl, ˌaˌpen-\ *adj* [*appendic-* + *-eal, -al, -ial*] **:** of, relating to, or involving the vermiform appendix

ap·pen·di·cec·to·my \əˌpendə'sektəmi, (ˌ)aˌp-\ *n* -ES [ISV *appendic-* + *-ectomy*] *Brit* **:** APPENDECTOMY

appendices *pl of* APPENDIX

ap·pen·di·ci·tis \əˌpendə'sīdəs\ *n* -ES [NL, fr. *appendic-* + *-itis*] **:** inflammation of the vermiform appendix characterized by usu. right-sided abdominal pain and sometimes by nausea and vomiting

ap·pen·di·cle \ə'pendəkəl\ *n* -S [F or L; F *appendicule*, fr. L *appendicula*, fr. *appendic-, appendix* + *-ula*] **:** a small appendage

appendico- — see APPEND-

ap·pen·dic·u·lar \ˌapən'dikyələ(r), ˌaˌpen-\ *adj* [L *appendicula* + E *-ar*] **:** of or relating to an appendage: **a :** of or relating to a limb or limbs ⟨the ~ skeleton⟩ **b :** APPENDICEAL ⟨~ inflammation⟩

¹ap·pen·dic·u·lar·ia \ˌ=(ˌ)=ˌ==ˈla(a)rēə\ *n, cap* [NL, fr. L *appendicula* appendicle + NL *-aria*] **:** a genus of small free-swimming pelagic tunicates shaped somewhat like a tadpole and remarkable for resemblances to the larvae of other tunicates

²appendicularia \"\ *or* **ap·pen·dic·u·lar·i·ae** \-rēˌē\ [NL, fr. L *appendicula* + NL *-aria, -ariae*] *syn of* LARVACEA

¹ap·pen·dic·u·lar·i·an \ˌ=(ˌ)=ˌ==ˈeən\ *adj* [NL *²Appendicularia* + E *-an*] **:** of or relating to the Larvacea

²appendicularian \"\ *n* -S **:** a tunicate of the order Larvacea

ap·pen·dic·u·la·ta \ˌ=(ˌ)=ˌ==ˈlād·ə, -ād·ə\ *n pl, cap* [NL, fr. L *appendicula* + NL *-ata*] *in some classifications* **:** a group that together with the Chaetopoda and Rotifera is nearly equivalent to the Arthropoda

ap·pen·dic·u·late \ˌ=ˈ==ˌlət, -ˌlāt, *usu* -d·+V\ *also* **ap·pen·dic·u·lat·ed** \-ˌlād·əd\ *adj* [L *appendicula* + E *-ate, -ated* — more at APPENDICLE] **:** having appendages ⟨~ corolla⟩ **:** forming an appendage

appending *pres part of* APPEND

¹ap·pen·dix \ə'pendiks, -ēks\ *n, pl* **appendixes** \-ksəz\ *or* **appendi·ces** \-dəˌsēz\ [L *appendic-, appendix*, fr. *appendere* to attach — more at APPEND (attach)] **1 :** APPENDAGE ⟨the principle of official management was invented . . . as a natural ~ to political dictatorship —N.S.Timasheff⟩ **2 :** matter added to a book but not essential to its completeness (as a bibliography or a series of tables usu. following the text) **3 :** a supplementary part or process attached to another part; *specif* **:** VERMIFORM APPENDIX **4 :** the tube that is located at the bottom of a balloon and used in inflation and deflation

²appendix \"\ *vt* -ED/-ING/-ES **:** to add as an appendix **:** APPEND ⟨~*ed*, indexed, and footnoted the book in bang-up scholarly fashion —*New Yorker*⟩

appendix dig·i·ti·for·mis \-ˌdijəd·ə'fȯrməs\ *n* [NL, finger-shaped appendix] **:** the finger-shaped anal gland in elasmobranchs

appendo- — see APPEND-

appends *pres 3d sing of* APPEND

ap·pen·zell \'apənˌzel, 'äpəntˌsel\ *n* -S *sometimes cap* [fr. *Appenzell*, canton and commune in Switzerland, where it is made] **:** a fine hand or machine embroidery of Swiss origin usu. worked in pale blue thread on white cloth

ap·per·ceive \ˌapə(r)'sēv\ *vt* -ED/-ING/-S [ME *apperceiven, aperceiven*, fr. OF *aperceivre*, fr. *a-* (fr. L *ad-*) + *perceivre* to perceive — more at PERCEIVE] **1** *obs* **:** PERCEIVE, OBSERVE **2** *philos* **:** to possess apperception of **3** *psychol* **:** to understand (as a new percept) in terms of previous experience — compare APPERCEPTIVE MASS

ap·per·cep·tion \ˌapə(r)'sepshən\ *n* -S [F *apperception*, fr. *apercevoir* to apperceive, perceive (after F *percevoir: perception*), fr. OF, to perceive, fr. *a-* (fr. L *ad-*) + *percevoir* to perceive, fr. L *percipere* — more at PERCEIVE] **1** *philos* **a** *in Leibnitz* **:** a mental act in which the mind becomes aware or has knowledge of itself as it perceives **b** *in Kant* (1) **:** consciousness of oneself as a changing phenomenon with a variable content — called also *empirical apperception* (2) **:** consciousness of the persisting identity of oneself, irrespective of changing representations, as a necessary prerequisite to any experience — called also *pure apperception, transcendental apperception* **2 :** mental perception **:** RECOGNITION **3** *psychol* **a :** the process of understanding (as of a new percept) in terms of one's previous experience — compare APPERCEPTIVE MASS, ASSIMILATION 5 **b :** the perception of meaning

ap·per·cep·tion·ism \ˌ=ˈ==ˌnizəm\ *n* -S **:** the theory that mental development is determined chiefly by apperception rather than by association — opposed to *associationism*

ap·per·cep·tion·ist \-n̩əst\ *n* -S **:** one who believes in apperceptionism — **ap·per·cep·tion·is·tic** \ˌ=ˌ==ˈnistik\ *adj*

ap·per·cep·tive \ˌ==ˈ=tiv\ *adj* [*apperception* + *-ive*] **:** relating to, involved in, or produced by apperception **:** capable of apperceiving — **ap·per·cep·tive·ly** *adv*

apperceptive mass *n, psychol* **:** the whole of a person's previous experience that is used in understanding a new percept or idea — called also *apperceiving mass, apperception mass*

¹ap·per·cip·i·ent \ˌapə(r)'sipēənt\ *adj* [fr. *apperception*, after E *perception: percipient*] **:** possessing apperception **:** APPERCEPTIVE

²appercipient \"\ *n* -S **:** one who apperceives

apperil *n* -S [*ad-* + *peril*] *obs* **:** PERIL

ap·per·son·ate \a'pərsᵊnˌāt, ə'-\ *vt* -ED/-ING/-S [back-formation fr. *appersonation*] **:** to subject to appersonation

ap·per·son·a·tion \(ˌ)aˌpərsᵊn'āshən, əˌp-\ *n* -S [*ad-* + *personation*; part trans. of G *appersonierung*] **:** the incorporation of characteristics of external objects or persons through a process of ego extension

ap·per·tain \ˌapə(r)'tān\ *vi* -ED/-ING/-S [ME *apperteinen, apertenen, apertenen*, fr. MF *apartenir*, fr. (assumed) VL *appartenēre*, alter. (influenced by L *part-, pars* part) of LL *appertinēre*, fr. L *ad-* + *pertinēre* to reach to, belong — more at PERTAIN] **:** to belong either as something appropriate or as a part, possession, right, or attribute **:** PERTAIN ⟨he will grow into an adult with the privileges and obligations ~*ing* thereto —Richard Joseph⟩ ⟨islands which have been determined by the President to ~ to the U. S. —E.D.Dickinson⟩

appertinent *adj* [ME *apertinent* — more at APPURTENANT] *archaic* **:** APPURTENANT 2

ap·pe·stat \'apəˌstat\ *n* -S [*appetite* + *-stat*] **:** a neural center in the hypothalamus believed to regulate appetite

ap·pe·ten·cy \'apəd·ənsē, |tən-, -si *also* |tᵊn-\ *or* **ap·pe·tence** \-n(t)s\ *n, pl* **appetencies** *or* **appetences** [L *appetentia*, fr. *appetent-, appetens* + *-ia*] **1 :** a strong ingrained desire **:** APPETITE, CRAVING ⟨the object of life is to satisfy as many *appetencies* as possible —Granville Hicks⟩ **2 :** a natural affinity of a substance or inanimate object for another ⟨the ~ of substance for oxygen⟩ **3 :** an instinctive inclination or propensity in animals to perform certain actions **syn** see DESIRE

ap·pe·tent \-nt\ *adj* [ME, fr. L *appetent-, appetens*, pres. part. of *appetere*] **:** marked by eager desire **:** LONGING ⟨the crash and scramble of that big rich ~ Western city —Willa Cather⟩

ap·pet·i·bil·i·ty \(ˌ)aˌped·ə'biləd·ē, əˌp-; ˌapəd·ə-\ *n* -ES **:** the quality or state of being appetible ⟨beauty is the ~ of truth —*Liturgical Arts*⟩

ap·pet·i·ble \a'ped·əbəl, ə'-; 'apəd·əbəl\ *adj* [L *appetibilis*, fr. *appetere* to strive after, long for + *-ibilis* -ible — more at APPETITE] **:** worthy of desire **:** DESIRABLE

ap·pe·tite \'apəˌtīt, *usu* -īd·+V\ *n* -S [ME *appetit, apetit*, fr. MF *apetit*, fr. L *appetitus*, fr. *appetitus*, past part. of *appetere* to strive after, long for, fr. *ad-* + *petere* to go to, head for — more at FEATHER] **1 :** a natural desire **:** one of the instinctive desires necessary to keep up organic life; *esp* **:** the immediate desire to eat when food is present **2 a :** an inherent or habitual desire or propensity for gratification or satisfaction ⟨an ~ for life, a robust reaching out to life —V.S.Pritchett⟩ ⟨an insatiable ~ for the acquisition of more territory —A.J.Toynbee⟩ **b :** TASTE, LIKING, PREFERENCE ⟨a faculty for idleness implies a catholic ~ —R.L.Stevenson⟩ ⟨the cultural ~s of the time —J.D.Hart⟩ **c** *obs* **:** APPETENCY 2 **3** *archaic* **:** an object of desire ⟨power being the natural ~ of princes —Jonathan Swift⟩ **syn** see DESIRE

ap·pe·ti·tion \ˌapə'tishən\ *n* -S [L *appetition-, appetitio*, fr. *appetitus* + *-ion-, -io* -ion] **:** a longing for or seeking after something **:** DESIRE ⟨something which creates an informed ~ for the good —R.M.Weaver⟩

ap·pe·ti·tious \ˌapə'tishəs\ *adj, archaic* **:** suited to appetite ⟨thick slabs of ~ meat —William Sansom⟩

ap·pet·i·tive \(ˈ)aˌped·əd·iv, əˈp-\ *adj* [MF *appetitif*, fr. ML *appetitivus*, fr. L *appetitus* appetite + *-ivus* -ive] **:** belonging or relating to appetite ⟨~ needs⟩ ⟨~ behavior⟩

ap·pe·tit·ost \'äpəˌtēd·ˌu̇st\ *n* -S [Dan, fr. *appetit* appetite (fr. G, fr. MHG, fr. MF *apetit*) + *ost* cheese; akin to OSwed *ōster* cheese, ON *ostr* — more at JUICE] **:** a soft Danish cheese made from sour buttermilk

ap·pe·tiz·er *also* **ap·pe·tis·er** \'apəˌtīzə(r)\ *n* -S **1 :** a food or drink that stimulates the appetite and is usu. served before a meal (as a canapé, hors d'oeuvre, aperitif, or cocktail) **2 :** something that stimulates a desire for more ⟨the street events are but an ~ to the carnival —Louise Gerdts⟩ ⟨a mere ~ for the more formidable pleasure of reading the whole —*New Yorker*⟩ ⟨the preliminaries were an effective ~ for the main bout⟩

appetizer wine *n* **:** an extra-dry to semisweet fortified wine (as sherry or vermouth) usu. served before a meal or used as a cocktail ingredient

ap·pe·tiz·ing *also* **ap·pe·tis·ing** \-ˌīziŋ, -zēŋ\ *adj* **:** appealing to the appetite esp. in appearance ⟨~ fruit⟩ ⟨an ~ newcomer from Hollywood —Wolcott Gibbs⟩ ⟨an expert at preparing ~ dishes⟩ **syn** see PALATABLE

ap·pe·tiz·ing·ly *adv* **:** in an appetizing manner

ap·pin·ite \'apəˌnīt\ *n* -S [*Appin*, Loch Linnhe, Scotland, its locality + E *-ite*] **:** any of a group of melanocratic hornblende-rich syenite, monzonite, or diorite rocks

appl *abbr* **1** appeal **2** applied; applicable

ap·pla·nate \'apləˌnāt, (ˈ)a'plāˌn-\ *adj* [ML *applanatus*, past part. of *applanare* to flatten, fr. L *ad-* + LL *planare* to flatten, fr. L *planus* even — more at FIELD] **:** flattened or horizontally expanded ⟨the ~ thallus of certain liverworts and lichens⟩

ap·plaud \ə'plȯd\ *vb* -ED/-ING/-S [MF or L; MF *applaudir*, fr. L *applaudere*, fr. *ad-* + *plaudere* to beat, clap, applaud] *vi* **:** to express approval esp. by clapping the hands repeatedly and usu. loudly ⟨the audience ~*ed* vigorously⟩ ~ *vt* **1 :** to express approval of **:** PRAISE, COMMEND ⟨the only foreign policy which a democratic public opinion can ~ —A.J.P.Taylor⟩ **2 :** to show approval of esp. by clapping the hands ⟨everywhere on the streets there were Romans who ~*ed* the passing troops —Eric Linklater⟩ ⟨spectators ~*ing* his performance⟩

ap·plaud·a·ble \-dəbəl\ *adj* **:** worthy of being applauded — **ap·plaud·a·bly** \-dəblē, -li\ *adv*

ap·plaud·ing·ly *adv* **:** in an applauding manner

ap·plause \ə'plȯz\ *n* -S [ML *applausus*, fr. L, clashing noise, fr. *applausus*, past part. of *applaudere*] **:** approval publicly expressed (as by clapping the hands) **:** marked commendation ⟨long and vociferous ~ —A.R.Williams⟩ ⟨the kind of ~ every really creative writer wants —Robert Tallant⟩

ap·plaus·ive \ə'plȯziv, a'-, -ȯs-\ *adj* [ML *applausivus*, fr. *applausus* + L *-ivus* -ive] **1** *obs* **:** APPLAUDABLE **2** *archaic* **:** expressing approval or applause — **ap·plaus·ive·ly** *adv*

ap·ple \'apəl\ *n* -S *often attrib* [ME *appel*, fr. OE *æppel*; akin to OHG *apful, afful*, ON *apall, epli*, Crimean Goth *apel*, OIr *ubull*, OSlav *abl'ŭko, jablŭko*] **1 a :** the pome fruit of any tree of the genus *Malus* being important economically esp. in No. America, Europe, and Australasia and markedly variable but usu. round in shape and red, yellow, or greenish in color ⟨~ dumpling⟩ **b :** any fruit or other vegetable production that resembles the apple ⟨balsam ~⟩ ⟨oak ~⟩ ⟨thorn ~⟩ **2 a :** a tree of the genus *Malus* **:** APPLE TREE **b :** the wood of the apple tree **3 :** something that resembles an apple esp. in shape (as a baseball) or color ⟨~ cheeks⟩ **4 :** APPLE OF ONE'S EYE **5** *Austral* **:** any of several trees: as **a :** a eucalypt (*Eucalyptus stuartiana*) with pendulous branches and soft whitish bark **b :** any tree of a genus of the myrtle family having opposite leaves and flowers in corymbose panicles

apple anthracnose *n* **:** a disease of the apple, pear, and quince in the Pacific coast region of northwestern America caused by a fungus (*Neofabraea malicorticis*) producing limb cankers and esp. after storage a rot of the fruit — called also *black spot*

apple aphid *n* **:** an aphid that infests the apple; *specif* **:** a bright-green aphid (*Aphis pomi*) that feeds on and causes curling of apple leaves — called also *green apple aphid*; see ROSY APPLE APHID, WOOLLY APPLE APHID

apple banana *n* [so called fr. its applelike flavor] **:** a banana (*Musa sapientum cubensis*) having fruit much smaller than that of the common banana and with a very thin skin

apple bee *n* **:** a bee at which apples are prepared for drying

ap·ple·ber·ry \'==ˌ=- — *see* BERRY\ *n* **1 :** an Australian woody vine (*Billardiera scandens*) with showy flowers **2 :** the pleasant subacid fruit of the appleberry

apple blight *n* **1 :** any of various plant lice attacking the apple; *esp* **:** WOOLLY APPLE APHID **2 :** FIRE BLIGHT

appleblossom \'==ˌ==\ *or* **appleblossom pink** *n* **:** a grayish red that is bluer, less strong, and slightly lighter than bois de rose, bluer and slightly less strong than Pompeian red, and bluer, lighter, and stronger than livid brown

apple blossom weevil *n* **:** a European weevil (*Anthonomus pomorum*) that is related to the American boll weevil and that feeds as an adult on the leaves of apple and lays its eggs in the young flower buds where the developing larva feeds and causes the bud to turn brown and fail to open

apple blotch *n* **:** BLOTCH 2a

apple box *n, Austral* **:** any of several trees of the genus *Eucalyptus* with gray bark (as *E. bicolor* and *E. baueriana*)

apple brandy *n* **:** brandy that is distilled from fermented apple juice

apple bucculatrix *n* **:** a small tineid moth (*Bucculatrix pomifoliella*) having a yellowish green brown-headed larva that feeds upon apple leaves

apple butter *n* **:** a spread made of apples stewed down with sugar and spices usu. in cider

apple canker *n* **:** any of several diseases of the apple tree that produce cankers (as bark canker, bitter rot, black rot, blister canker, European canker, fire blight, or perennial canker)

applecart \'==ˌ=\ *n* [*apple* + *cart*] **:** a plan, scheme, system, undertaking, or situation that is or may be overturned or disrupted often unexpectedly — used esp. with *upset* ⟨upset the whole Darwinian ~ —Julian Huxley⟩ ⟨we might make a wrong move and upset somebody's ~ —*Survey Graphic*⟩

apple cheese *n* **:** the cake of apple pomace from a cider press

apple curculio *n* **:** a small weevil (*Tachypterellus quadrigibbus*) the larva of which feeds about the core in the fruits of apple and pear

apple essence *n* **:** apple oil (sense 2) esp. when in alcohol solution

apple family *n* **:** MALACEAE

apple flea weevil *n* **:** a minute dull-black weevil (*Rhynchaenus pallicornis*) that feeds as an adult on the undersurface of apple and cherry leaves, the larvae burrowing and feeding within the leaves

apple fly *n* **:** FRUIT FLY

apple geranium *n* **:** NUTMEG GERANIUM

apple grain aphid *n* **:** a yellowish green aphid (*Rhopalosiphum fitchii*) with dark bands on the abdomen that produces its fertilized eggs on apple and related trees and feeds on their leaves in early spring but passes most of the growing season on various small grains and grasses

apple green *n* **1 :** a moderate yellow green that is greener, lighter, and stronger than average moss green or mosstone and lighter and stronger than average pea green or spinach green **2 :** a light yellowish green that is greener and deeper than ocean green, pistachio, or crayon green

apple grunt *n, chiefly New Eng* **:** a dessert made with apples and pie crust; *esp* **:** a deep-dish apple pie

apple gum *n* **:** an Australian timber tree (*Eucalyptus stuartiana*) resembling the apple tree

apple haw *n* **:** MAYHAW

apple head *n* **:** a domed or rounded skull typical of certain toy dogs — **ap·ple-head·ed** \'==ˌ==\ *adj*

apple honey *n* **:** a clarified condensation of apple syrup used as a sweetening agent in the food industry

ap·ple·jack \-ˌjak\ *n* [*apple* + *jack* (man)] **1 :** APPLE BRANDY **2 :** an alcoholic beverage consisting of the central unfrozen portion of a container (as a keg) of frozen hard cider; *also* **:** HARD CIDER

applejohn *n, often cap* [*apple* + *John*, the name; prob. fr. St. John's Day, when it was said to get ripe] *archaic* **:** a variety of apple the flavor of which is said to be improved by drying

apple knocker *n* **1** *slang* **:** an apple picker **:** fruit picker **2** *slang* **:** HICK, RUBE **3** *slang* **:** one beginning a new job **:** BEGINNER, GREENHORN

apple leafhopper *n* **:** a small greenish leafhopper (*Empoasca maligna*) that injures the foliage of apple trees and many other plants; *also* **:** a related Australian insect (*Typhlocyba frogatti*)

apple leaf skeletonizer *n* **:** a small dark-brownish moth (*Psorosina hammondi*) having a brownish green caterpillar that feeds on the interveinal tissue of apple leaves

apple-leaf trumpet miner *n* **:** a leaf-mining caterpillar (*Tischeria malifoliella*) that injures the leaves of apple trees by excavating trumpet-shaped burrows

apple maggot *n* **:** the larva of a dark brown and yellowish trypetid fly (*Rhagoletis pomonella*) with dark-marked wings that burrows in and feeds on apples or sometimes other fruits and is a vector of a bacterial rot of this fruit — called also *railroad worm*

apple mealybug *n* **:** a mealybug (*Phenacoccus aceris*) common on apple trees in parts of Canada

apple mildew *n* **1 :** a disease of the apple caused by a powdery mildew (*Podosphaera leucotricha*) **2 :** the fungus that causes apple mildew

apple mint *n* **:** a European mint (*Mentha rotundifolia*) naturalized in the U. S.

apple moss *n* **:** a moss of the genus *Bartramia* having spherical capsules

apple moth *n* **:** a moth whose larva feeds on apple trees or fruits; *specif* **:** a pale brownish moth (*Tortrix postvittana*) of which the larvae feed on the leaves and fruit of apples and many other cultivated plants in Australia, New Zealand, and various Pacific islands

applenut \'==ˌ=\ *n* **:** the apple-shaped nut of an ivory palm (*Coelococcus amicarum*) — called also *ivory nut*

apple of discord [trans. of LL *malum Discordiae*; fr. the golden apple inscribed "for the fairest" which was thrown into an assembly of the gods by the goddess Discord (L *Discordia*, Gk *Eris*) and claimed by Hera, Athena, and Aphrodite] **:** a subject of contention and envy ⟨the chief *apple of discord* was western lands —T.A.Bailey⟩

apple of one's eye [obs. *apple of the eye* pupil of the eye] **:** something highly cherished ⟨his daughter is the *apple of his eye*⟩

apple of pe·ru \-pə'rü, -pē'-\ *usu cap P* [fr. *Peru*, country in So. America] **1 :** a coarse herb (*Nicandra physalodes*) bearing pale blue flowers and a bladderlike fruit enclosing a dry berry **2 :** JIMSONWEED

apple of sod·om \-'sädəm\ *usu cap S* [fr. *Sodom*, biblical city destroyed by God (Gen 10)] **1 a :** a fruit described by ancient writers as externally of fair appearance but dissolving into smoke and ashes when plucked — called also *Dead Sea apple* **b :** an empty mockery ⟨had seen the fruits of victory turn into *apples of Sodom* —R.M.Lovett⟩ **2 a :** the small yellow tomato-like fruit of a prickly shrub (*Solanum sodomeum*) **b :** a spiny herb (*Solanum carolinense*) that bears yellow and orange berries

apple oil *n* **1 :** the essential oil of apples **2 :** an artificially prepared oil (as amyl isovalerate) used to imitate the odor or flavor of apples

apple pandowdy *n* **:** PANDOWDY

apple paring *n* **:** APPLE BEE

apple-pie \'==ˌ=\ *adj* **:** PERFECT, EXCELLENT, FIRST-RATE — used esp. in the phrase *apple-pie order*

apple-pie bed *n* **:** a bed in which as a joke the sheets are doubled like the cover of an apple turnover to prevent anyone from stretching at full length between them

apple-pol·ish \'==ˌ==\ *vi* **:** to attempt to ingratiate oneself **:** TOADY ⟨this called for some extra *apple-polishing* by employees —M.S.Davis⟩ ~ *vt* **:** to curry favor with (as by flattery or services) ⟨he hopes to pass the course by *apple-polishing* the instructor⟩ — **apple-polisher** \'==ˌ===\ *n*

apple pox *n* **:** BLISTER CANKER

apple red *n* **:** a vivid red that is yellower and slightly lighter and stronger than carmine, duller and slightly bluer than Castilian red, yellower and paler than madder crimson, bluer and duller than pimento, and bluer and slightly deeper than scarlet

apple red bug *n* **:** a small plump reddish bug (*Lygidea mendax*) that feeds on young apple foliage and developing fruits causing russeting, dwarfing, and catfacing of the mature apples

apple rose *n* **:** a rose (*Rosa pomifera*) of central Europe often cultivated for its showy scarlet fruits that are about an inch in diameter

apple rust *n* **1 :** any of several diseases caused by fungi of the genus *Gymnosporangium*; *esp* **:** a destructive fungous disease esp. of the apple but also attacking pears and quinces that is caused by a rust (*G. juniperi-virginianae*) having its pycnial and aecial stages on the leaves and fruit of the apple and the telial stage on species of *Juniperus*, esp. a common red cedar (*J. virginiana*) **2 :** the fungus causing apple rust — called also *cedar apple rust, cedar rust*; compare CEDAR APPLE

apples *pl of* APPLE

applesauce \'==ˌ=\ *n* **1 :** a relish or dessert made of apples sweetened and stewed to a pulp **2** *slang* **:** an insincere expression of opinion **:** an assertion that is patently absurd and usu. phrased in exaggerated terms **:** BUNK, BALONEY ⟨I know ~ when I hear it —Ring Lardner⟩

apple sawfly *n* **:** a sawfly (*Hoplocampa testudinea*) native to Europe but now established in the eastern U.S. that lays its eggs singly in the calyx or receptacle of the apple flower, the larva feeding in the core of the developing fruit

apple scab *n* **:** a widespread destructive disease caused by a fungus (*Venturia inaequalis*) producing dark or sooty blotches on the leaves and blackish scurfy or scablike lesions on the fruit and sometimes on the young twigs

apple scald *n* **:** a brown discoloration of apples in storage

apple scale *n* **:** any scale infesting the apple tree; *esp* **:** OYSTER-SHELL SCALE

apple-seed chalcid *n* **:** a chalcid fly (*Torymus varians*) whose larva feeds on the seed of the apple

apple shell *n* **:** the apple snail or its shell

apple skin worm *n* **:** a larval moth (*Argyrotaenia franciscana*) that is related to the red-banded leaf roller and that feeds on the surface of the developing fruits of apple and a number of other cultivated fruits

apple snail *n* **:** any of a number of large rounded smooth-shelled freshwater snails of the family Pilidae — see PILA

apple-squire *n, obs* **:** a kept gallant **:** PIMP

apple sucker *n* **:** a small jumping plant louse (*Psylla mali* or *Psyllia mali*) the larva of which feeds in and injures developing apple blossoms in Europe and eastern No. America

ap·ple·ton layer \'apəltən-, -tᵊn-\ *n, usu cap A* [after Sir Edward *Appleton* †1965 Eng. physicist] **:** F LAYER

apple tree *n* **1 :** any tree that bears apples **2** *Austral* **:** APPLE GUM **3 :** an Australian tree (*Angophora subvelutina*) that yields kino

apple tree borer *n* **:** a beetle having larvae that bore in apple trees: **a :** FLATHEADED APPLE TREE BORER **b :** a larger beetle (*Saperda candida*) brown striped with white above and dull white beneath that is esp. destructive to apple and other fruit trees — called also *roundheaded apple tree borer*

apple tree canker *n* **:** APPLE CANKER

apple twig borer *n* **:** a small brown cylindrical beetle (*Amphicerus bicaudatus*) that bores into the twigs of esp. fruit trees

apple weevil *n* **:** any of several weevils that feed chiefly on apple, the adults on the foliage, the larvae in the fruit

applewife \'==ˌ=\ *n, pl* **applewives** **:** a woman who sells apples

applewood \'==ˌ=\ *n* **:** the wood of an apple tree esp. of the genus *Malus*

apple worm *n* **:** an insect larva that burrows in the interior of apples; *esp* **:** the larva of the codling moth

ap·pli·a·ble \ə'plīəbəl\ *adj* [ME, fr. *applien* to apply + *-able* — more at APPLY] **1** *obs* **:** COMPLIANT **2 :** APPLICABLE — **ap·pli·a·bly** \-əblē\ *adv*

ap·pli·ance \ə'plīən(t)s\ *n* -S [*apply* + *-ance*] **1 :** the act of applying or using **:** APPLICATION ⟨when schoolboys were punished by ~ of the birch⟩ **2 :** something applied to a purpose or use: as **a** archaic **:** DEVICE, MEASURE, STRATAGEM **b :** a piece of equipment for adapting a tool or machine to a special purpose **:** ACCESSORY, FIXTURE, ATTACHMENT **c :** a tool, instrument, or device specially designed for a particular use **:** APPARATUS ⟨fire-fighting ~s⟩ **d :** a household or office utensil, apparatus, instrument, or machine that utilizes a power supply, esp. electric current (as a vacuum cleaner, a refrigerator, a toaster, an air conditioner) **3** obs **:** obedient service **:** COMPLIANCE **syn** see IMPLEMENT, MACHINE

ap·pli·ca·bil·i·ty \ˌapləkəˈbiləd·ē, -lēk-, -ətē, -i sometimes əˌplik- or aˌplik-\ n -ES **:** the quality or state of being applicable

ap·pli·ca·ble \ˈapləkəbəl, ˈaplēk-,ˈaˌplik- sometimes əˈplik- or aˈplik-\ adj [F, fr. appliquer to apply (fr. L applicare to attach to, devote to) + -able] **1 :** capable of being applied **:** having relevance ⟨a basic technique of musical rendition that is ~ to any piece —Virgil Thomson⟩ **2 :** fit, suitable, or right to be applied **:** APPROPRIATE ⟨prosecuted in any ~ court —U.S. Code⟩ **syn** see RELEVANT

ap·pli·ca·ble·ness n -ES **:** APPLICABILITY

applicable surfaces n pl, math **:** two surfaces that may be deformed one into the other without stretching or tearing

ap·pli·ca·bly \-blē,-bli\ adj **:** in an applicable manner

ap·pli·cant \ˈapləkənt, -lēk-\ n -S [L applicant-, applicans, pres. part. of applicare] **:** one who applies for something **:** one who makes a usu. formal request esp. for something of benefit to himself ⟨an ~ for a job⟩ ⟨an ~ for a scholarship⟩

applicate adj [L applicatus, past part. of applicare] archaic **:** put to use **:** APPLIED ⟨those ~ sciences that extend the power of man over the elements —Isaac Taylor †1865⟩

ap·pli·ca·tion \ˌapləˈkāshən\ n -S [ME applicacioun, fr. ML application-, applicatio, fr. L, inclination, fr. applicatus (past part. of applicare to attach) + -ion-, -io -ion — more at APPLY] **1 :** the act of applying: **a :** the bringing to bear (as of one general statement upon another) by way of elucidation ⟨the ~ of a theory to a case⟩ **b :** employment as a means **:** specific use ⟨the ~ of certain new techniques⟩ **c :** the act of laying on or of bringing into contact ⟨the ~ of a dressing to the wound⟩ **d :** the act of fixing one's mind closely or attentively **:** assiduous attention ⟨learn by intense ~⟩ **2** in astrology **:** approach (as of one planet to another) **3 :** APPEAL, REQUEST, PETITION ⟨an ~ for a position⟩ ⟨an ~ to an underwriter for insurance⟩ **4 :** something applied or used in applying: as **a** (1) **:** the part of a discourse in which principles stated previously are applied to practical uses (2) **:** the moral lesson or inference to be derived from a moral tale; esp **:** the explicit formulation of this often given at the end of the tale **b :** something applied to the body locally as a remedial device (as a tourniquet, ointment, or poultice) **5 :** capacity of being practically applied or used **:** RELEVANCY ⟨words of varied ~⟩ **6 :** the denotation of a term in logic

¹ap·pli·ca·tive \ˈapləˌkād·iv, -ˌkəd·-; əˈplikəd·-, aˈ-\ adj [obs. E applicate + E -ive] **1 :** APPLICABLE **2 :** put to use **:** APPLIED — **ap·pli·ca·tive·ly** adv

²applicative \"\ n -S **:** QUANTIFIER

ap·pli·ca·tor \ˈapləˌkād·ə(r), -ātə-\ n -S [obs. E applicate to apply (fr. L applicatus) + E -or] **1 :** a device (as a cotton-tipped rod, a pad, or a nozzle) for applying substances (as medicine, cosmetics, polish, or chemical foam) **2 :** one that applies substances ⟨urges that ~s avoid using sprays during windy weather —Country Gentleman⟩

ap·pli·ca·to·ry \ˈapləkəˌtōrē, əˈplik-\ adj [obs. E applicate + E -ory] **:** capable of being applied

ap·plied \əˈplīd\ adj **1 :** put to practical use **:** engaged in for a utilitarian or contributory purpose **:** concerned with concrete problems or data rather than with fundamental principles ⟨~ mathematics⟩ ⟨~ psychology⟩ ⟨technical problems in medicine, engineering, economics, and other ~ disciplines —Sidney Hook⟩ — contrasted with pure; compare ABSTRACT, THEORETICAL **2** of art **:** employed in the decoration, design, or execution of useful objects **3 :** APPLIQUÉD

applied music n **:** vocal or instrumental musical performance subject to instruction in college or school as contrasted with musical theory and literature — called also practical music

applied ornament n **:** appliquéd ornament **:** APPLIQUÉ

ap·pli·er \əˈplī(ə)r, -īə\ n -S **:** one that applies

¹ap·pli·qué \ˌapləˌkā\ n -S often attrib [F appliqué (past part. of appliquer to put on), fr. L applicatus, past part. of applicare to attach — more at APPLY] **:** a cutout decoration of a material laid on and fastened to a larger piece of the same or different material: **a :** a design composed of various fabric shapes stitched, embroidered, or sometimes pasted onto a surface (as of a quilt, skirt, or tablecloth) **b :** a lace motif made separately and attached to a ground of net or lace **c :** a shaped piece of wood or metal attached as a decoration to furniture **d :** something usu. of metal applied decoratively (as a wall sconce)

²appliqué \"\ vt **appliquéd**; **appliquéd**; **appliquéing** \-kāiŋ\ **appliqués :** to apply (as a decoration or ornament) **:** OVERLAY — used esp. of fabrics ⟨of finest percale with appliquéd designs —New Yorker⟩

ap·pli·quer \ˌapləˌkāə(r)\ n -S **:** one that appliqués; esp **:** a worker who stitches monograms or ornamental patches to knitted garments

appln abbr application

ap·plo·sion \əˈplōzhən, (ˈ)aˌp-\ n -S [ad- + -plosion (as in explosion, implosion)] phonetics **:** interruption and compression of the breath in the production of a stop

ap·plot \əˈplät, aˈ-\ vt -ED/-ING/-S [ad- + plot] archaic **:** to divide into parts **:** APPORTION — **ap·plot·ment** \-mənt\ n -S archaic

ap·ply \əˈplī\ vb -ED/-ING/-ES [ME applien, aplien, fr. MF aplier, fr. L applicare to apply, attach, devote, fr. ad- + plicare to fold, twist together — more at PLY] vt **1 a :** to make use of as suitable, fitting, or relevant ⟨~ the rule to each situation⟩ ⟨~ an epithet to a person⟩ ⟨~ a word to a new idea⟩ **b :** to put to use esp. for some practical purpose ⟨~ knowledge⟩ **:** to use for a particular purpose or in a particular case ⟨~ money to the payment of a debt⟩ **c :** to bring into action ⟨he applied his brakes quickly⟩ **d :** to put into effect **:** IMPOSE ⟨~ an embargo⟩ **e** (1) **:** to place in contact ⟨~ an antiseptic to a cut⟩ **:** lay or spread on **:** OVERLAY ⟨sand the wood before ~ing the varnish⟩ (2) **:** SUPERPOSE ⟨~ one triangle upon another⟩ **2 :** to devote or employ diligently or with close attention ⟨~ oneself to a task⟩ ⟨~ your wits to this problem⟩ **3** obs **:** PRACTICE **:** carry on **:** PLY ~ vi **1 a :** to be in contact **:** ADHERE, FIT ⟨nails ~ in prebored holes⟩ **b :** to have a valid connection, agreement, or analogy **:** have a bearing **:** be pertinent ⟨the argument applies to the case⟩ **2 a** obs **:** to be adapted **:** SUIT **b :** to devote oneself **:** attend closely ⟨the more you ~ the quicker you will learn⟩ **3 :** to make an appeal or a request esp. formally and often in writing and usu. for something of benefit to oneself ⟨~ to an employer for a job⟩ ⟨~ to a bank for a loan⟩ **syn** see DIRECT, USE

appmt abbr appointment

ap·pog·gia·tu·ra \əˌpäjəˈtu̇rə, -tü-\ n -S [It, lit., support, fr. appoggiare to lean, rest, fr. (assumed) VL appodiare, fr. L ad- + (assumed) VL -podiare (fr. L podium balcony) — more at PEW] **:** an accessory embellishing note or tone preceding an essential melodic note or tone and usu. written as a note of smaller size — see LONG APPOGGIATURA, SHORT APPOGGIATURA

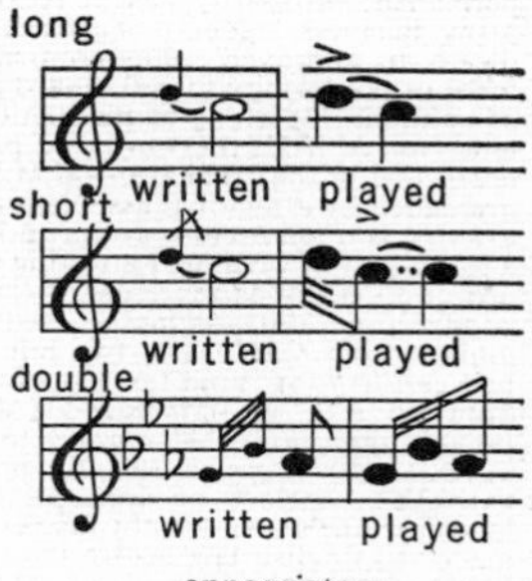

appoggiatura

ap·point \əˈpȯint\ vb -ED/-ING/-S [ME appointen, apointen, fr. MF apointier to arrange, settle, equip, fr. OF, fr. a- (fr. L ad-) + -pointier (fr. point) — more at POINT] vt **1 a** (1) **:** to fix by a decree, order, command, resolve, decision, or mutual agreement **:** ORDAIN, PRESCRIBE (2) **:** to establish with power or firmness **:** mark out **b** (1) **:** to designate (the person) in whom shall be vested an estate subject to a power of appointment (2) **:** to direct or determine the disposition of (an estate) by designating the person or persons in whom it shall vest by virtue of a power of appointment **c :** to assign, designate, or set apart by authority ⟨~ each man to his position⟩: (1) archaic **:** DESTINE, ASSIGN, DEVOTE ⟨sheep ~ed to be slain⟩ (2) **:** DESIGNATE ⟨~ an officer⟩⟨~an official⟩ **:** place in an office or post ⟨~ a superintendent⟩ ⟨~ a committee⟩ **d** (1) archaic **:** to arrange for a meeting with (a person) (2) archaic **:** to fix the time and place of ⟨~ the meeting, even at his father's house —Shak.⟩ (3) **:** to fix (the time) for an event ⟨in our places at the ~ed hour⟩ **2 :** to provide with necessary equipment **:** FURNISH, EQUIP **:** fit out ⟨beautifully ~ed public rooms —N.Y. Times Mag.⟩ ~ vi **1** obs **:** SETTLE, ARRANGE **2** obs **:** ORDAIN, DETERMINE **3** archaic **:** to make an engagement **:** arrange a meeting with a person **syn** see DESIGNATE, FURNISH

ap·poin·tee \əˌpȯin·ˈtē also ˌaˌp- sometimes əˌpȯint·ˈē or əˈ=(ˌ)=\ n -S [appoint + -ee] **1 :** one that is appointed (as to an office) **2 :** one to whom an estate is appointed

ap·point·ive \əˈpȯintiv, -ēv also -əv\ adj **1 :** of or relating to the act or power of appointing ⟨the president's ~ powers⟩ **2 :** subject to appointment ⟨an ~ office⟩

ap·point·ment \əˈpȯintmənt\ n -S [ME appointement, apointement, fr. MF apointement, fr. apointier to arrange + -ment — more at APPOINT] **1 :** act of appointing: **a** obs **:** the act of coming to terms of capitulation **b :** designation by virtue of a vested power of a person to enjoy an estate or other specific property subject to that power **c :** designation of a person to hold a nonelective office or perform a function ⟨exercise the right of ~⟩ **2 a** obs **:** terms made with an opponent (as for surrender) **:** CAPITULATION, AGREEMENT **b** archaic **:** ORDINANCE, DISPENSATION ⟨the merciful ~ of Providence⟩ **c** (1) **:** OFFICE, POSITION ⟨he received the ~ of ambassador⟩ (2) archaic **:** a monetary allowance esp. to a public officer **:** PERQUISITE — usu. used in pl. **3 :** an arrangement for a meeting **:** ENGAGEMENT ⟨an ~ for an interview⟩ ⟨broke his ~ with the dentist⟩ **4 :** equipment or furnishings esp. for a hotel or a ship **:** ACCOUTERMENTS — usu. used in pl. ⟨~s for a soldier or a horse⟩ ⟨famous for the luxury and comfort of its ~s⟩ ⟨the coat of arms appeared on the ~s of the knight and his mount⟩ **syn** see ENGAGEMENT

ap·poin·tor \əˌpȯin·ˈtȯ(ə)r also ˌaˌp- or əˈpȯintər sometimes əˌpȯint·ˈȯ(ə)r or əˈpȯin·ˌtȯ- or əˈpȯint·ˌȯ-\ n -S **:** one that appoints an estate under a power of appointment

appoints pres 3d sing of APPOINT

¹ap·port \əˈpō(ə)rt, aˈ-, -ȯ(ə)rt\ n -S [ME aport, apport, alter. (influenced by ME aport, apport offering, contribution, fr. MF aport, fr. OF, fr. aporter to bring, fr. L apportare) of port — more at PORT] **1** obs **:** BEARING, PORT **2** [F, lit., action of bringing, thing brought, fr. apporter to bring, fr. L apportare] **:** motion or production of an object by a spiritualist medium without apparent physical agency; also **:** the object so produced

²apport \"\ vt -ED/-ING/-S [prob. fr. F apporter, lit., to bring, fr. L apportare, fr. ad- + portare to carry — more at PORT] **:** to produce (a material object) at a spiritualist séance without any apparent physical means

ap·por·tion \əˈpōrshən, -ȯrsh-,-ōəsh-,-ȯ(ə)sh- also aˈ-\ vt **apportioned**; **apportioned**; **apportioning** \-sh(ə)niŋ\ **apportions** [MF apportionner, fr. a- (fr. L ad-) + portionner to portion — more at PORTION] **:** to divide and assign in proportion **:** divide and distribute proportionately **:** make an apportionment of **:** portion out **:** ALLOT ⟨~ time among various employments⟩; specif **:** to assign (a capitation or other direct federal tax) among the states in proportion to population as provided in the U.S. Constitution

syn PORTION, PARCEL, RATION, PRORATE: APPORTION applies to distribution on an equitable, or suitable basis ⟨representatives shall be apportioned among the several states according to their respective numbers, counting the whole number of persons in each —U. S. Constitution⟩ ⟨he will be a brave man who will apportion responsibility for Britain's attitude between parties and classes —Roy Lewis & Angus Maude⟩ ⟨nature seems to have apportioned the voices of many of her creatures with sensitive regard for their environment —William Beebe⟩ PORTION may apply to distribution of more or less equal shares ⟨firing 270 rounds portioned equally among pistols of three calibers —Time⟩ PARCEL, usu. used with out, may indicate division into many small pieces, lots, or units for subsequent delivery, claim, or execution ⟨being compelled to parcel out its inadequate combat resources sparingly between the many vulnerable points —Herbert Feis⟩ ⟨Mother would parcel out her year: three months with Herbert and Mabel, three with Carrie and Roland —Victoria Sackville-West⟩ RATION may apply to division by authority, presumably equitably, on some such basis as need ⟨where capital is short, it must be rationed intelligently, in the same way as gasoline and sugar were rationed in wartime —A.B.Lans⟩ ⟨he rationed his time, told visitors he could give them three minutes —Time⟩ PRORATE suggests equitable proportional distribution according to authority or common agreement ⟨the entire field was to be put in truck crops, and the yield prorated to the workers —Russell Lord⟩ **syn** see in addition ALLOT

apportionate vt -ED/-ING/-S [ML apportionatus, past part. of apportionare, fr. MF apportionner] obs **:** APPORTION

ap·por·tion·ment \-shənmənt\ n -S [prob. fr. MF apportionnement, fr. apportionner + -ment] **1 :** the act or result of apportioning ⟨the ~ of lands among settlers⟩ **2 :** the division of rights or liabilities among several persons entitled or liable to them in accordance with their respective interests (as where a contractor is given part payment in return for part performance or where rents are divided according to some scale of interest) **3 :** the apportioning of representatives or taxes to the several states according to U. S. law

apportionment clause n **:** a clause in an insurance policy that prescribes the method of determining the insurer's portion of liability for loss where property is covered by other insurance

ap·pose \aˈpōz\ vt -ED/-ING/-S [MF aposer, fr. OF, fr. a- (fr. L ad-) + poser to put, place — more at POSE] **1** archaic **:** to place opposite or before **:** apply (one thing) to another ⟨~ a seal to a document⟩ **2 :** to place in juxtaposition or proximity ⟨chromosomes . . . with their transverse bands exactly apposed —Discovery⟩

ap·po·site \ˈapəzət sometimes əˈpäz- or aˈpäz-\ adj [L appositus, fr. past part. of apponere to place near, apply to, fr. ad- + ponere to put — more at POSITION] **:** highly pertinent or appropriate **:** RELEVANT, APT ⟨examples more or less ~ to one subject —Edward Clodd⟩ ⟨~ illustrations may be found in recent statutes —B.N.Cardozo⟩ ⟨her use of anecdote is ~ — Carl Van Vechten⟩ **syn** see RELEVANT

ap·po·site·ly adv **:** in an apposite manner **:** RELEVANTLY

ap·po·site·ness n -ES **:** the quality or state of being apposite **:** APTNESS

ap·po·si·tion \ˌapəˈzishən\ n -S [ME apposicioun, fr. ML apposition-, appositio, fr. LL, act of setting before, fr. L appositus (past part. of apponere) + -ion-, -io -ion] **1 a :** a grammatical construction that consists of two nouns or noun equivalents referring to the same person or thing, standing in the same syntactical relation to the rest of the sentence without being joined to each other by a coordinating conjunction, and typically adjacent to each other (as the poet and Burns in "a biography of the poet Burns", my sister and Jane in "this is my sister Jane", John and a bashful child in "John, a bashful child, was afraid of strangers", or the fact and that he is rich in "the fact that he is rich is obvious") **b :** the relation of one of such a pair of nouns or noun equivalents to the other, esp. of the second to the first **2** [F fr. LL apposition-, appositio] **a** archaic **:** the application of one thing to another (as a seal to a document) **b :** the placing of things in juxtaposition or proximity; specif **:** deposition of successive layers upon those already present (as in cell walls) — compare INTUSSUSCEPTION **3 :** the state of being in juxtaposition or proximity (as in the drawing together of cut edges of tissue in healing)

ap·po·si·tion·al \ˌ==ˌ=shənᵊl, -shnəl\ adj **:** relating to or being in apposition — **ap·po·si·tion·al·ly** \-shənᵊlē,-shnəlē, -li\ adv

apposition beach n **:** one of a series of beaches successively formed on the seaward side of an older beach

apposition eye n **:** a compound eye that is characteristic of diurnal insects and in which entering light reaches the retina of each ommatidium as a single spot and the image is a composite of all the spots — compare SUPERPOSITION EYE

¹ap·pos·i·tive \əˈpäzəd·iv, -ətiv also aˈ-\ adj [apposition + -ive] **1 :** standing in grammatical apposition ⟨an ~ noun⟩ **:** being a grammatical apposition ⟨an ~ construction⟩ **2** of an adjective or adjective equivalent **:** standing in a relation to its noun like that of the second noun or noun equivalent to the first in an apposition (as shy and embarrassed in "the child, shy and embarrassed, said nothing") — compare ADHERENT 4, ATTRIBUTIVE 1a, ¹PREDICATE 2 — **appositively** adv

²appositive \"\ n -S **:** an appositive noun, noun equivalent, adjective, or adjective equivalent

appr abbr apprentice

ap·prais·al \əˈprāzəl, aˈ-\ also **ap·praise·ment** \-zmənt\ n -S [appraise + -al or -ment] **1 :** an act of estimating or evaluating (as quality, status, or character) esp. by one fitted to judge ⟨a more realistic ~ of the difficulties inherent in the undertaking —J.B.Conant⟩ ⟨a swift ~ by shrewd eyes —George Whiting⟩; also **:** the stated result of such an act ⟨an over-generous ~ of his worth⟩ ⟨a detailed ~ of a program⟩ **2 :** a valuation of property by the estimate of an authorized person; specif **:** the valuation of imported goods according to methods set forth in the tariff laws of a country

appraisal clause n **:** the provision in fire and certain other insurance policies for a procedure to be followed in determining the amount of loss when the insurer and insured cannot agree

ap·praise \əˈprāz, aˈ-\ vt -ED/-ING/-S [ME appreisen, modif. (influenced by preisen to set a value on) of MF aprisier — more at APPRIZE] **1 :** to set a value on (as goods, lands, or the estate of a deceased person) **:** estimate the amount of (as a loss by fire) **2 :** to judge and analyze the worth, significance or status of; esp **:** to give a definitive expert judgment of the merit, rank, or importance of ⟨~ recent American poetry⟩ ⟨~ a political trend⟩ ⟨~ the cost of an objective in terms of human life —O.N.Bradley⟩ **syn** see ESTIMATE

ap·prais·er \-zə(r)\ n -S **1 :** one that appraises (as real estate for determining tax rates or sales prices, imported articles for the assessing of tariff duties, damaged goods for salvage, or the property of bankrupt businesses for auction-sale value of assets) **2 :** one that estimates status, excellence, or potentiality; specif **:** one that as a guide to the establishment of new businesses or advertising contracts studies a neighborhood to appraise its buying power, class of goods used, or services desired **3 :** one that determines the authenticity of works of art by means of X ray and other scientific methods of examination

appraiser's store n **:** a storeroom or building where goods are held by U.S. customs officials for appraisal

ap·prais·ing·ly adv **:** in an appraising manner ⟨looked about him ~ —Erle Stanley Gardner⟩

ap·prais·ive \-āziv\ adj **:** forming an appraisal ⟨both aesthetic and ethical discourse . . . are treated as primarily ~ in their mode of signifying —P.B.Rice⟩ **:** APPRAISING ⟨so many harshly ~ eyes fixed upon her —I.S.Cobb⟩

apprecate vt -ED/-ING/-S [L apprecatus, past part. of apprecari, fr. ad- + precari to pray — more at PRAY] obs **:** to pray for — **apprecation** n -S obs — **apprecatory** adj, obs

ap·pre·cia·ble \əˈprēshəbəl sometimes -rishəb- or -rēshēəb-\ adj [F appréciable, fr. MF appreciable, fr. apprecier, aprecier to appraise (fr. LL appretiare) + -able] **:** capable of being perceived and recognized or of being weighed and appraised ⟨seldom capable of any ~ color change —W.H.Dowdeswell⟩ ⟨voters were unable to exert any ~ influence upon the selection of the candidates put forward by their party —F.A.Ogg & P.O.Ray⟩ **syn** see PERCEPTIBLE

ap·pre·cia·bly \-əblē, -li\ adv **:** to an appreciable extent or degree **:** NOTICEABLY

ap·pre·ci·ate \əˈprēshēˌāt sometimes -rishē- rarely -rēsē-, usu -ād·+V\ vb -ED/-ING/-S [ML & LL; ML appretiatus (past part. of appretiare to value, esteem), fr. LL, past part. of appretiare to appraise, put a price on, fr. L ad- + pretium price, value — more at PRICE] vt **1 a** (1) **:** to evaluate highly or approve warmly often with expressions or tokens of liking ⟨to be loved, to be appreciated, to be admired and highly valued —Theodor Reik⟩ (2) **:** to judge or evaluate the worth, merit, quality, or significance of **:** comprehend with knowledge, judgment, and discrimination ⟨incapable of appreciating the difference between right and wrong —B.N.Cardozo⟩ ⟨appreciated that a new era was beginning —David Fairchild⟩ ⟨my power of appreciating your many charms and my desire that you should become my wife —Samuel Butler †1902⟩ **b :** to judge with heightened perception or understanding: (1) **:** to be critically and emotionally aware of delicate subtle aesthetic or artistic values ⟨he could not ~ artistic quality⟩ (2) **:** to be fully sensible of often through or as if through personal experience ⟨must be experienced to be appreciated —Rudyard Kipling⟩ **c :** to esteem highly and express thanks or gratitude for ⟨I ~ your kindness but I should be much happier alone —Louis Bromfield⟩ **2 :** to raise the value of **:** increase the market price of ⟨from 1820 onwards gold was mainly appreciated —J.A.Todd⟩ — opposed to depreciate ~ vi **:** to rise in value or quantity ⟨apples appreciated 2 to 5 cents per box —Wall Street Jour.⟩ ⟨the calving and lambing season is good and numbers greatly ~ —James Stevenson-Hamilton⟩

syn VALUE, PRIZE, TREASURE, CHERISH: APPRECIATE connotes recognition of worth or merit through wise judgment, analytical perception, and keen insight ⟨the author appreciates the historical development of the Roman law and the character of its various sources —H.O.Taylor⟩ ⟨he liked to be near people and have his talent as a whittler appreciated —Sherwood Anderson⟩ It is rarely used without these notions, although in less precise use it may carry added notions of warm hearty approval or full or delicate enjoyment ⟨attach herself to someone who knew how to appreciate the fullness of her ardor —Morley Callaghan⟩ ⟨youth appreciates that sort of recognition which is the subtlest form of flattery age can offer —Joseph Conrad⟩ In this series VALUE is less rich in suggestion than the others. It may suggest judgment blending the analytic and the subjective ⟨she only valued rest to herself when it came in the midst of other people's labor —Thomas Hardy⟩ ⟨suddenly Gard was smitten by the tragedy of plain women; to be valued, but not loved —Mary Austin⟩ PRIZE stresses high evaluation, often subjective; it may suggest a sense of pride in acquisition or possession and reluctance to lose or be deprived of the thing in question ⟨his grandfather's two prized standing cups —T.B.Costain⟩ ⟨we had prized our solitude when we had to fight for it —Virginia D. Dawson & Betty D. Wilson⟩ ⟨what is freedom and why is it prized? —John Dewey⟩ TREASURE, used with things considered or felt to be of extreme value, stresses notions of storing or of jealous guarding against loss or theft, notions of cleaving to and preserving ⟨that the volumes I write will be treasured up with the utmost care for ages —William Cowper⟩ ⟨ecstatic moments for him, to be treasured and conned over —T.B.Costain⟩ ⟨if . . . I have your friendship, I shall treasure it —Edna S. V. Millay⟩ CHERISH, rich in affective suggestion, adds the idea of deep-seated, perhaps tacit affection or intimate fond reflection on ⟨he cherished a painfully nostalgic memory of his childhood sweetheart —Saxe Commins⟩ ⟨troubled by the conflict of many ideas in his fruitful mind, and ardently cherishing those he thought true and good —Carl Van Doren⟩ ⟨cherish their allegiance to Christ in solitude and silence —Katharine F. Gerould⟩ **syn** see in addition UNDERSTAND

appreciated surplus n **:** a surplus due to increase in the book value of the capital assets of a corporation

ap·pre·ci·a·tion \əˌprēshēˈāshən also -rēsē'- sometimes -rishē'- — -ēsē- is more freq in "appreciation" than in "appreciate", as a result of sh- dissimilation\ n -S [F & LL; F appréciation, fr. MF apreciation, prob. fr. aprecier to appraise + -ation; LL appretiation-, appretiatio valuation, fr. appretiatus + L -ion-, -io -ion — more at APPRECIABLE] **1 a :** recognition through the senses esp. with delicacy of perception ⟨an ~ of fine shades of meaning⟩; specif **:** sensitive awareness of worth or esp. aesthetic value ⟨his fine ~ of painting⟩ **b :** ESTIMATION, JUDGMENT ⟨~ of quality or character⟩; specif **:** a written or spoken critical estimate esp. when favorable ⟨write a brief ~ of a book⟩ **c :** expression of gratification and approval, of gratitude, or of aesthetic satisfaction ⟨in ~ of your work⟩ ⟨we offer this small token by way of ~⟩ **d :** recognition of aesthetic values that is cultivated in students esp. through courses emphasizing enjoyment and discrimination rather than historical background or scholarly method **2 :** increase in exchangeable value (as of money, goods, or property) — opposed to *depreciation*

ap·pre·cia·tive \ə'prēshə|d·iv, |tiv *sometimes* -rishə| *or* -rēshē,ā| *or* -rēshēə|\ *also* **ap·pre·cia·to·ry** \ə'prēshə,tōrē, -tȯ-, -ri *sometimes* -rishə,- *or* -rēshēə,-\ *adj* **:** having or showing appreciation ⟨an ~ audience⟩ ⟨~ of a beautiful landscape⟩ — **ap·pre·cia·tive·ly** *adv* — **ap·pre·cia·tive·ness** *n* -ES

ap·pre·ci·a·tor \ə'prēshē,ād·ə(r), -ātə- *sometimes* -rishē- *rarely* -rēsē-\ *n* -S **:** one that appreciates ⟨the artist and his ~*s* —Hunter Mead⟩

ap·pre·hend \¦aprə̇¦hend, -rē¦-\ *vb* -ED/-ING/-S [ME *apprehenden*, fr. L *apprehendere* to grasp mentally, seize, fr. *ad-* + *prehendere* to seize — more at PREHENSILE] *vt* **1 a** *obs* **:** to come to know **:** LEARN **b :** to lay hold of with the understanding **:** recognize the existence or meaning of **c** *obs* **:** to sense emotionally **:** APPRECIATE **d :** to anticipate esp. with anxiety, dread, or fear **e :** to become aware of through the senses ⟨~ the flame of a candle⟩ **f :** to view or consider as being of a certain description ⟨~ eternal truths⟩ **2 a** *obs* **:** to take possession of **:** take hold of **b :** to take (a person) in legal process **:** ARREST, SEIZE ⟨~ a thief⟩ **~** *vi* **:** to receive knowledge or grasp notions **syn** see FORESEE

ap·pre·hen·si·bil·i·ty \,==,hen(t)sə'biləd·ē\ *n* -ES **:** the quality or state of being apprehensible

ap·pre·hen·si·ble \¦==¦hen(t)səbəl\ *adj* [LL *apprehensibilis*, fr. L *apprehensus* (past part. of *apprehendere*) + *-ibilis* -ible] **:** capable of being apprehended or conceived — **ap·pre·hen·si·bly** \-blē, -i\ *adv*

ap·pre·hen·sion \,=='henchən\ *n* -S [ME *apprehensioun*, fr. LL *apprehension-*, *apprehensio*, fr. L *apprehensus* (past part. of *apprehendere*) + *-ion-*, *-io* -ion] **1 a** *obs* **:** the act of learning **b :** the faculty of grasping with the intellect **:** UNDERSTANDING ⟨a man of dull ~⟩ **c :** the act of grasping with the intellect **:** INTELLECTION, PERCEPTION **d** (1) **:** the result of apprehending mentally **:** OPINION, CONCEPTION ⟨according to popular ~⟩ (2) **:** NOTION, SENTIMENT, IDEA ⟨to mistrust one's own ~*s*⟩ **e** *philos* **:** the act of mentally grasping or of bringing before the mind; *specif* **:** a perception that is comparatively simple, direct, and immediate and has as its object something considered to be directly and nondiscursively understandable; *broadly* **:** an intellectual awareness **:** a relatively simple or unreflective idea, opinion, or belief **f** *in traditional logic* **:** that one of the three operations of thought by which one grasps what is expressed by a term or name — contrasted with *judgment* and *reasoning* **g** *psychol* **:** the observing of an object as a whole without distinguishing its parts **2 :** the taking by legal, esp. criminal, process **:** ARREST ⟨~ of a felon⟩ **3 :** anticipation esp. of unfavorable things **:** suspicion or fear esp. of future evil

syn FOREBODING, MISGIVING, PRESENTIMENT: APPREHENSION may refer to a fear, sometimes vague, that obsesses and keeps one anxious about the future ⟨peasants who have survived a famine will be perpetually haunted by memory and *apprehension* —Bertrand Russell⟩ ⟨daily *apprehension* lest the wholesome sons and daughters whom they commit to a college return to them as brazen fools without culture —W.L.Sullivan⟩ FOREBODING applies to oppressive anticipatory fear, often ill-grounded, ill-defined, or superstitious ⟨my wife was curiously silent throughout the drive and seemed oppressed with *forebodings* of evil —H.G.Wells⟩ ⟨there was a sadness and constraint about all persons that day, which filled Mr. Esmond with gloomy *forebodings* —W.M.Thackeray⟩ MISGIVING applies to sudden uneasy fear and worried doubt rather than due anxiety or dread ⟨a *misgiving* arose within him that such dread experiences would revive the old danger —Charles Dickens⟩ ⟨his self-confidence had given place to a *misgiving* that he had been making a fool of himself —G.B.Shaw⟩ PRESENTIMENT indicates a shadowy, almost mystical, intuitive perception of some coming event, often unpleasant and fearful ⟨this unfortunate accident has upset me. I have a horrible *presentiment* that something of the kind may happen to me —Oscar Wilde⟩

ap·pre·hen·sive \¦==¦hen(t)siv, -ēv *also* -əv\ *adj* [ME, fr. ML *apprehensivus*, fr. L *apprehensus* + *-ivus* -ive] **1** *archaic* **:** serving for apprehension **2 :** capable of apprehending or quick to do so **:** APT, DISCERNING ⟨a kind and ~ friend —Nathaniel Hawthorne⟩ **3 :** having apprehension **:** KNOWING, CONSCIOUS, COGNIZANT ⟨~ of one's youthful folly⟩ **4 :** anticipative of something unfavorable **:** fearful of what may be coming **:** in dread of possible evil or harm ⟨~ of danger⟩ ⟨~ for one's life⟩ **5 :** relating to the faculty of apprehension ⟨judgment is implied in every ~ act —William Hamilton †1856⟩ — **ap·pre·hen·sive·ly** *adv* — **ap·pre·hen·sive·ness** *n* -ES

[1]**ap·pren·tice** \ə'prentə̇s\ *n* -S *often attrib* [ME *apprentis*, *aprentis*, fr. MF *aprentis*, fr. OF, fr. *aprendre* to learn, fr. L *apprendere* to grasp mentally, seize, contr. of *apprehendere* — more at APPREHEND] **1 a :** one who is bound by indentures or by legal agreement to serve another person for a certain time with a view to learning an art or trade in consideration of instruction therein and formerly usu. of maintenance by the master **b :** one who is learning by practical experience under skilled workers a trade, art, or calling usu. for a prescribed period of time and at a prescribed rate of pay ⟨~ bricklayer⟩ ⟨actor's ~⟩ ⟨~ teacher⟩ **2 a** *English law, archaic* **:** a barrister-at-law of less than 16 years' standing and ranking below a serjeant-at-law **b :** an enlisted man in the U.S. Navy who has completed recruit training at a training center ashore but who has not been promoted to seaman or airman **c :** a jockey who has yet to win 40 races or has ridden less than a year **d :** the lowest rank in the exploring program of the Boy Scouts of America **3 :** one not well versed in a subject **:** an inexperienced person **:** TYRO, NOVICE ⟨an ~ in suffering and humiliation —Saul Bellow⟩ **syn** see NOVICE

[2]**apprentice** \"\ *vt* -ED/-ING/-S **:** to bind by contract or indenture; *also* **:** to set at work as an apprentice ⟨at the age of sixteen he was *apprenticed* to a blacksmith —H.U.Faulkner⟩

apprenticeage *n* -S [MF *aprentissage*, fr. *aprentis* apprentice + *-age*] *obs* **:** APPRENTICESHIP

apprenticehood *n* -S [ME *apprentishod*, *aprentishod*, fr. *apprentis*, *aprentis* apprentice + *-hod* -hood] *obs* **:** APPRENTICESHIP

ap·pren·tice·ship \-tə̇(sh),ship *also* -tə̇s,sh-\ *n* -S **1 :** service or status as an apprentice or novice ⟨begin one's ~⟩ ⟨his early intellectual ~ —Paul Willen⟩ **2 :** the time during which an apprentice or novice serves ⟨the customary three years of ~ —*Current Biog.*⟩ ⟨a writer with a long ~ in reporting the inner and outer lives of the maladjusted —R.N.Denney⟩

ap·pressed \ə'prest, (')a¦p-\ *or* **ad·pressed** \(')ad¦p-\ *adj* [L *appressus*, *adpressus* (past part. of *apprimere*, *adprimere*, fr. *ad-* + *primere* to press) + E *-ed* — more at PRESS] **:** pressed close to or lying flat against something ⟨closely ~ to the lower surface of the much larger dorsal lobe —D.H.Campbell⟩ ⟨igneous rocks . . . folded and closely ~ by this force —L.V.Pirsson⟩

ap·pres·sion \a'preshən\ *n* -S **:** the state of being appressed

ap·pres·so·ri·al \¦aprə¦sōrēəl\ *adj* [NL *appressorium* + E *-al*] **:** belonging or relating to an appressorium

ap·pres·so·ri·um \,apre'sōrēəm\ *n, pl* **appresso·ria** \-rēə\ [NL, fr. L *appressus* + NL *-orium*] **:** the flattened, thickened, or tuftlike tip of a hyphal branch by which certain parasitic fungi are attached to their hosts, giving rise to either haustoria or infection hyphae

ap·prise *also* **ap·prize** \ə'prīz, a'-\ *vt* -ED/-ING/-S [F *appris* (fem. *apprise*), past part. of *apprendre* to learn, teach, inform, fr. OF *aprendre* to learn, teach — more at APPRENTICE] **1 :** to give oral or written notice to (a person) **:** INFORM ⟨Mrs. Berry came in to ~ Lucy that she was wanted —George Meredith⟩ ⟨Emily was fairly *apprised* of the situation —Mary Austin⟩ **2 :** to give notice of (a thing) **syn** see INFORM

ap·priz·al *also* **ap·pris·al** \-zəl\ *n* -S **:** APPRAISAL

ap·prize *also* **ap·prise** \-īz\ *vt* -ED/-ING/-S [ME *apprisen*, *aprisen*, fr. MF *aprisier*, fr. OF, fr. *a-* (fr. L *ad-*) + *prisier* to value, appraise — more at PRIZE] **1** *obs* **:** to put a value upon **:** APPRAISE **2 :** to value or appreciate ⟨learn to ~ knowledge for the sake of knowledge —*U.S. Daily*⟩ **3** *Scots law, obs* **:** to make a judicial sale of (a heritable estate) for the benefit of a creditor — compare ADJUDGE 5

ap·prize·ment *also* **ap·prise·ment** \-mənt\ *n* -S [ME *apprisement*, fr. MF *aprisement*, fr. *aprisier* + *-ment*] *archaic* **:** APPRAISAL

ap·priz·er \-zə(r)\ *n* -S **1** *archaic* **:** APPRAISER **2** *Scots law* **:** a creditor who had an apprizing made

appro *abbr* **1** approbation **2** approval

[1]**ap·proach** \ə'prōch\ *vb* -ED/-ING/-ES [ME *approchen*, *aprochen*, fr. OF *aprochier*, fr. LL *appropiare*, fr. L *ad-* + LL *-propiare* (fr. L *prope* near); akin to L *pro* before, for — more at FOR] *vt* **1 a :** to come or go near or nearer to in place or time **:** draw nearer to ⟨we ~*ed* the city⟩ ⟨~ the hour of departure with dread⟩ **b :** to come or go near or nearer to in character or quality ⟨~ manhood⟩ ⟨a performance that ~*es* perfection⟩ or quantity ⟨an error that ~*es* zero as a limit⟩ **2 :** to bring near or nearer ⟨he ~*ed* the drill to the work⟩ **3 :** to address tentatively or make an overture to esp. in order to create a desired point of view or result: **a :** to take preliminary steps toward accomplishment or full knowledge or experience of ⟨~ a task⟩ ⟨~ a problem⟩ ⟨~ an author's works⟩ **b :** to begin discussion of ⟨having discussed crime, they ~*ed* its elimination⟩ **c** (1) **:** to make advances to **:** SOLICIT (as a prospective purchaser or contributor) (2) **:** to attempt to bribe or influence ⟨~ a member of the legislature⟩ **~** *vi* **1 a :** to come or go near or nearer in place or time **:** to draw nearer ⟨the sound ~*ed* more rapidly⟩ ⟨as daylight ~*es*⟩ **b :** to come or go near or nearer in character or quality ⟨~ to or recede from a line⟩ **2 :** to make a golfing approach ⟨he spoils his game by ~*ing* badly⟩ **syn** see MATCH

[2]**approach** \"\ *n* -ES [ME *approche*, fr. *approchen*, v.] **1 a :** a drawing near in space or time ⟨the rapid ~ of a tornado⟩ ⟨the ~ of summer⟩ **b :** a coming or being near in quality or character ⟨the ~ of dictatorship was foreshadowed by certain events⟩ ⟨in this fine work he made his closest ~ to true greatness⟩ **2 a** *obs* **:** ability to approach **:** opportunity of approaching **b :** a way of gaining access (as to the understanding of a subject) ⟨this book provides a good ~ to nuclear physics⟩ **3 a approaches** *pl, obs* **:** advances or maneuvers toward one **b** (1) **:** the taking of tentative or introductory steps for a particular purpose (as full accomplishment, discussion, acquaintance, or solicitation) ⟨his method of ~ to the subject repels most readers⟩ ⟨new lines of ~⟩ (2) **:** a particular manner of taking such steps ⟨her ~ was obviously friendly⟩ **4 a** (1) **:** a way, passage, or avenue by which a place or a building can be approached ⟨the ~ to the park⟩ (2) **approaches** *pl* **:** the means of approaching an area ⟨air ~*es* between the continental U.S. and outlying bases⟩ **b approaches** *pl* **:** means of approach (as zigzag trenches) prepared by besiegers in advancing toward fortifications **c :** an embankment, trestle, or other construction that provides access at either end of a bridge or tunnel **d :** a portion of railroad track along which a train passes before entering an area controlled by a signal **5** *also* **approaching :** APPROACH GRAFT **6 a :** a golfing stroke from the fairway for the green **b** (1) **:** the steps and motion of a bowler before he delivers the ball (2) **:** the part of the alley in front of the foul line from which a bowler delivers the ball **7 :** descent of an airplane toward a landing strip

ap·proach·a·bil·i·ty \ə,prōchə'biləd·ē\ *n* -ES **:** the quality or state of being approachable

ap·proach·a·ble \-əbəl\ *adj* **:** capable of being approached ⟨a squalid place ~ from a complicated branch of the Niger —H.H.Johnston⟩ ⟨the tales ... seem more ~ than his more difficult novels —F.B.Millett⟩; *specif* **:** easy to meet, converse with, or do business with ⟨a friendly ~ person —C.H. Voss⟩

approach bid *n* **:** a bid in auction bridge or contract bridge in a particular suit on a hand that would justify either a suit bid or a no-trump bid

approach-forcing system \='=,==-\ *n* **:** CULBERTSON SYSTEM

approach graft *n* **:** a plant graft made by joining stock and scion laterally at an intermediate point but leaving both rooted and uncut until firm union is established when the stock is cut above and the scion below the union

approach light *n* **:** one of a group of usu. green lights placed outside a landing area and arranged to indicate to the pilot of an approaching airplane the direction and termination of a runway or landing strip

ap·proach·ment \-mənt\ *n* -S [MF *aprochement*, fr. *aprochier* to approach + *-ment* — more at APPROACH] **:** [2]APPROACH 1a

approach signal *n* **:** DISTANT SIGNAL

approach trench *n* **:** a trench providing protected passage between the front and rear elements of a defensive position

ap·pro·bate \'aprə,bāt\ *vt* -ED/-ING/-S [ME *approbaten*, fr. L *approbatus*, past part. of *approbare* — more at APPROVE (sanction)] **1 :** to express approval of formally or legally **:** sanction officially ⟨a certificate *approbating* the hotel⟩: **a :** to certify (a person) as officially licensed to preach ⟨an *approbated* minister⟩ **b** *Scots law* **:** to accept as legal or valid (as part of a deed) — used esp. in the phrase *approbate and reprobate* ⟨a deed cannot be both *approbated* and reprobated⟩ **2 :** to have a favorable opinion of **:** approve of ⟨everyone ~*s* him⟩

ap·pro·ba·tion \,aprə'bāshən\ *n* -S [ME *approbacioun*, fr. MF *approbation*, fr. L *approbation-*, *approbatio*, fr. *approbatus* (past part. of *approbare* to approve, prove) + *-ion-*, *-io* -ion — more at APPROVE] **1** *obs* **:** PROOF, ATTESTATION, CONFIRMATION **2 a :** act of approving formally or authoritatively **:** SANCTION ⟨without the previous ~ of any public officer —T.B.Macaulay⟩; *specif* **:** official certification that a person is authorized to perform the functions of an ecclesiastic **b :** an assenting to anything usu. with some degree of pleasure or satisfaction **:** COMMENDATION ⟨one of his early books . . . received the ~ of scholars —*Current Biog.*⟩ ⟨deportment that wins ~ —George Meredith⟩ ⟨the pleasure of social ~ —Bertrand Russell⟩ **3** *obs* **:** PROBATION, NOVITIATE, TRIAL

ap·pro·ba·tive \'aprə,bād·iv, -,bəd--; ə'prōbəd--, ə'präb-\ *adj* [F *approbatif*, fr. ML *approbativus* proving, fr. LL, giving a reason, fr. L *approbatus* + *-ivus* -ive] **:** FAVORABLE ⟨once criticism of the plan took a favorable turn, it remained ~⟩

ap·pro·ba·to·ry \'aprəbə,tōrē, ə'prōb-,ə'präb-\ *adj* [*approbate* + *-ory*] **:** expressing approbation **:** COMMENDATORY

ap·proof \a'prüf, ə'-\ *n* -S [fr. [1]*approve*, after E *prove*: *proof*] **1** *archaic* **:** TRIAL, PROOF, TEST **2** *archaic* **:** APPROVAL

ap·pro·pin·quate \,aprə'piŋ·,kwāt\ *vi* -ED/-ING/-S [L *appropinquatus*, past part. of *appropinquare* to approach, fr. *ad-* + *propinquare* to approach, fr. *propinquus* near — more at PROPINQUITY] *archaic* **:** APPROACH — **ap·pro·pin·qua·tion** \,aprə,piŋ·'kwāshən\ *n* -S

ap·pro·pin·qui·ty \,aprə'piŋkwəd·ē\ *n* -ES [*ad-* + *propinquity*] **:** NEARNESS, PROPINQUITY

ap·pro·pri·a·ble \ə'prōprēəbəl, *chiefly substand* (*by* r-*dissimilation*) ə'pōprē-\ *adj* [*appropriate* + *-able*] **:** capable of being appropriated

[1]**ap·pro·pri·ate** \-ē,āt, *usu* -ād·+V\ *vt* -ED/-ING/-S [ME *appropriaten*, fr. LL *appropriatus*, past part. of *appropriare*, fr. L *ad-* + *propriare* to appropriate, fr. *proprius* own — more at PROPER] **1 :** to annex (a benefice) to a spiritual corporation to its perpetual use — distinguished from *impropriate* **2** *archaic* **:** to assign or attribute as specially belonging **3 a :** to make peculiarly the possession of someone ⟨~ goods to the lord⟩ ⟨~ the money to himself⟩ **b :** to claim or use as if by an exclusive or preeminent right ⟨let no man ~ a common benefit⟩ **4** *archaic* **:** to make suitable **:** SUIT ⟨terms so exquisitely *appropriated* to the character he draws —E.V.Lucas⟩ **5 :** to set apart for or assign to a particular purpose or use in exclusion of all others ⟨~ money for the navy⟩ ⟨~ the building for storage⟩ **6 :** to take without permission **:** PILFER, PURLOIN ⟨he *appropriated* my notebook —R.M.Lovett⟩

syn PREEMPT, USURP, ARROGATE, CONFISCATE: these verbs all mean to seize or take over more or less dictatorially. In the order APPROPRIATE, PREEMPT, USURP, ARROGATE, CONFISCATE they may be said to form an ascending scale of highhandedness. APPROPRIATE has the common meaning of to set aside for a special purpose ⟨it would not be easy to induce the town to *appropriate* money for improvements —*Amer. Guide Series: Maine*⟩ but it signifies more generally to take over or acquire without authority or with questionable authority, usu. also implying a conversion to one's own use of the thing taken over ⟨to the natives, it is sacrilegious . . . for the white men to *appropriate* the sacred watering places —Rex Ingamells⟩ ⟨the winners *appropriated* all of the best jobs —Charlton Laird⟩ PREEMPT adds to APPROPRIATE the idea of beforehandedness and suggests a stronger action, as a seizure, esp. of something desired by others ⟨*preempt* a lion's share of the profits⟩ ⟨the Hindu Maharajah . . . *preempted* the country's entire public motor transport —Faubion Bowers⟩ ⟨tall, modern apartments *preempt* Washington Square West —*Amer. Guide Series: N. Y. City*⟩ USURP stresses more the idea of the unlawfulness or unwarranted nature of the action and more frequently has as its object rather powers, rights, or offices taken by strong-arm methods than tangible goods seized by force ⟨new rulers have to prove that they have not *usurped* their title, but possess some higher right to govern than the mere fact of having grabbed power —Aldous Huxley⟩ ⟨the executive officer of the *Caine* who *usurps* command from Captain Queeg in the midst of the typhoon —H.W.Baldwin⟩ ⟨legislative assemblies have *usurped* the powers which rightfully belong to the executive branch —H.J.Morgenthau⟩ ⟨the persistence with which certain birds *usurped* and clung to favorite perches —William Beebe⟩ ARROGATE stresses an extreme highhandedness, as of presumption or insolence, and usu. has as its object a right, power, or function ⟨a ruthlessness that *arrogates* to them sole control of local political life —T.H.White⟩ ⟨not only did he reconstitute himself the final court of appeals, but he gradually *arrogated* to himself the function of all the courts —G.W.Johnson⟩ ⟨the artist's productivity pretends to be creation, that is, it *arrogates* to man what is the privilege of God —Hannah Arendt⟩ ⟨the clique which had *arrogated* to itself the function of dictating to Ireland in all things literary —M.P.Linehan⟩ CONFISCATE stresses stongly the idea of unwarranted seizure itself, suggesting often rather a display of power or control than any conversion of the thing seized to one's own purpose ⟨they *confiscated* Tory property worth a million dollars —*Amer. Guide Series: N. C.*⟩ ⟨eight were banished from the United States and their property *confiscated* —H.S.Canby⟩ ⟨pots and pans *confiscated* from the kitchen —R.M.Lovett⟩

[2]**ap·pro·pri·ate** \-ēə̇t *sometimes* -ē,āt; *usu* -d·+V\ *adj* [ME *appropriat*, fr. LL *appropriatus*] **1 :** specially suitable **:** FIT, PROPER ⟨sit down anywhere and the ~ waiter comes up —P.E. Deutschman⟩ ⟨gift packages are likewise ~ for the girls you regularly remember —*Phoenix Flame*⟩ ⟨by any means ~ to our use —George Meredith⟩ **2 :** belonging peculiarly **:** SPECIAL ⟨an ~ symbol of that swanky and luxurious town —Virgil Thomson⟩ ⟨the pupil lacks the qualities ~ to the master's style —David Sylvester⟩ **3** *obs* **:** attached as an accessory possession **syn** see FIT

ap·pro·pri·ate·ly *adv* **:** in an appropriate manner

ap·pro·pri·ate·ness *n* -ES **:** the quality or state of being appropriate

ap·pro·pri·a·tion \=,=='āshən\ *n* -S [ME *appropriacioun*, fr. MF or LL; MF *appropriation*, fr. LL *appropriation-*, *appropriatio*, fr. *appropriatus* + L *-ion-*, *-io* -ion] **1 a :** the act of appropriating to oneself or another person or to a particular use ⟨he was punished for his ~ of their belongings⟩ **b :** something that has been appropriated; *specif* **:** a sum of money set aside or allotted by official or formal action for a specific use (as from public revenue by a legislative body that stipulates the amount, manner, and purpose of items of expenditure) ⟨~ bill⟩ ⟨an annual ~ for flood control⟩ **2** [ML, fr. LL] *ecclesiastical law* **:** transference of a benefice with its spiritual or temporal interests to a spiritual corporation, provision for the service of the church being made in return; *also* **:** the benefice so transferred **3** *obs* **:** a special attribute or application **4 :** a taking over of a reaction pattern or activity by members of one species (as of birds) or group from those of another group with which the former is associated **:** imitative behavior

ap·pro·pri·a·tive \='==,ā|d·iv, -,ə|, |tiv\ *adj* **:** relating to appropriation **:** APPROPRIATING

ap·pro·pri·a·tor \-,ād·ə(r), -,ātə-\ *n* -S **1 :** one that appropriates **2** *ecclesiastical law* **:** a religious corporation that owns an appropriated benefice

ap·prov·a·bil·i·ty \ə,prüvə'biləd·ē *also* a,-\ *n* -ES **:** the quality or state of being approvable

ap·prov·a·ble \='=vəbəl\ *adj* [ME, fr. *approven* + *-able*] **:** capable of being approved — **ap·prov·a·bly** \-əblē\ *adv*

ap·prov·al \-vəl\ *n* -S **1 :** the act of approving **:** APPROBATION, SANCTION ⟨a procedure likely to meet with the ~ of the circumspect —S.H.Adams⟩ **2 :** certification as to acceptability (as of a request for capital expenditure) ⟨these ~*s* are usually indicated on the invoice before the voucher is prepared —H.S.Noble⟩ — **on approval** *adv* (*or adj*) **:** subject to a prospective purchaser's decision to accept or refuse ⟨goods sent out *on approval*⟩

approval book *n* **:** a set of small approval sheets in book form

approval sheet *n* **:** a sheet of paper on which postage stamps are mounted for sending on approval to purchasers

ap·prov·ance \-vən(t)s\ *n* -S [[1]*approve* + *-ance*] *archaic* **:** APPROVAL

[1]**ap·prove** \ə'prüv *also* a'-\ *vb* -ED/-ING/-S [ME *approven*, *aproven*, fr. OF *aprover*, fr. L *approbare* to approve, prove, fr. *ad-* + *probare* to approve, prove — more at PROVE] *vt* **1 a** *obs* **:** to demonstrate the truth or correctness of **:** establish as fact or as being sound **b** *archaic* **:** CORROBORATE, AUTHENTICATE **c** *obs* **:** CONVICT ⟨*approved* in this offense —Shak.⟩ **2** *obs* **a :** TEST, TRY **b :** EXPERIENCE **3** *archaic* **a :** to make or show to be worthy of approbation or acceptance — used reflexively with *to* ⟨the first care and concern must be to ~ himself to God —John Rogers⟩ **b :** to offer proof of by active demonstration **:** manifest or display actually or practically **:** EXHIBIT ⟨his behavior under fire *approved* him a man of courage⟩ **4 :** to judge and find commendable or acceptable **:** think well of **:** have or express a favorable opinion or judgment of ⟨a friend, whom he liked, but whose conduct he could not ~ —Osbert Sitwell⟩ ⟨Jane secretly *approved* his discernment —Rose Macaulay⟩ **5 a :** to express often formally agreement with and support of or commendation of as meeting a standard ⟨the governor *approved* the project⟩ ⟨one of the first hospitals in the state to be *approved* by the organization⟩ **b :** to vote into effect **:** pass formally ⟨the legislature *approved* the bill⟩ **~** *vi* **:** to have or express a favorable opinion **:** judge favorably — usu. used with *of* ⟨she wants to teach him not to fight; she doesn't ~ of fighting —Margaret Mead⟩

syn SANCTION, ENDORSE, ACCREDIT, CERTIFY: APPROVE applies to a feeling or expression of commendation or of agreement with, but it may suggest a judicious attitude involved ⟨fools admire, but men of wits *approve* —Joseph Furphey⟩ ⟨the discomfiture . . . of doing, as he must, what he did not fully *approve* —J.G.Cozzens⟩ SANCTION adds to APPROVE notions of permission, countenancing, authorization, encouragement by something or someone in an authoritative position ⟨the court has also *sanctioned* recently some federal efforts to protect Negroes in the South from violence —Alan Barth⟩ ⟨"Come! Give me your authority . . . For his daughter's sake . . ." "In her name, then, let it be done; I *sanction* it" —Charles Dickens⟩ ENDORSE or INDORSE (see note at ENDORSE) suggests vouching for, supporting, or explicitly expressing approval of and is often used in reference to things needing promotion or publicity ⟨the Kentucky Republicans *endorsed* him for the presidential nomination —E.M.Coulter⟩ ⟨the view that increasing money wages is the only road to permanent prosperity has in recent years been *endorsed* by many business leaders —*Fortune*⟩ ACCREDIT is likely to indicate an approved status confirmed by some authoritative force or conformity to a standard officially vouched for ⟨few of us think of turning to the dictionary before writing a sentence to see if all the words we propose to use are properly *accredited* in the language —M.M.Mathews⟩ ⟨institutions not *accredited* by a regional association —*Bull. of Bates College*⟩ CERTIFY is often a close synonym for ACCREDIT; it may stress a formal act of writing or attesting to conformity with a standard or to being as represented ⟨labels by which brain merit is advertised and *certified* — medals, honors, degrees —Virginia Woolf⟩ ⟨the nearly two billion that these utilities have had *certified* for rapid tax write-off —*New Republic*⟩

[2]**approve** \"\ *vt* -ED/-ING/-S [ME *approven*, *aproven*, *approuen*, *aprouen*, fr. MF *aprouer* to cause to profit, fr. OF, fr. *a-* (fr. L *ad-*) + *-prouer* (fr. *prou* profit, advantage) — more at PROW] **:** to enclose or appropriate (wasteland or common land) for one's own benefit (as permitted esp. to the lord of a manor in English law before the Enclosure acts)

approved school *n, Brit* **:** a school for juvenile delinquents

[1]**ap·prove·ment** \-vmənt\ *n* -S [ME *approvement*, *approuement*, fr. MF *approuement*, *aprouement*, fr. OF, fr. *aprouer* + *-ment*] *English law* **:** the act of approving lands

[2]**approvement** \"\ *n* -S [[1]*approve* + *-ment*] **1** *obs* **:** APPROBA-

TION, APPROVAL **2** *Old English law* **:** the act of one that when appealed of a felony confessed his guilt and appealed another as an accomplice of the same crime to obtain his own pardon

[1]ap·prov·er \-və(r)\ *n* -s [AF *aprouour*, fr. MF *aprouer* to cause to profit + *-our* -or — more at APPROVE] *English law, obs* **:** BAILIFF, STEWARD, AGENT

[2]approver \"\ *n* -s [[1]*approve* + *-er*] *Old English law* **:** one that makes an approvement

approves *pres 3d sing of* APPROVE

ap·prov·ing·ly *adv* **:** in an approving manner

ap·prox·i·mal \ə'präksəməl, (')a¦p-\ *adj* [*ad-* + L *proximus* nearest, next + E *-al*] **:** CONTIGUOUS ⟨~ surfaces of teeth⟩

[1]ap·prox·i·mate \ə'präksəmət, *usu* -əd·+V\ *adj* [LL *approximatus*, past part. of *approximare* to come near, fr. L *ad-* + *proximare* to come near — more at PROXIMATE] **1 :** nearly resembling ⟨doing such ~ justice as we could —W.A.White⟩ **2 :** near to correctness or accuracy **:** nearly exact ⟨a sketch map with ~ topography —C.B.Hitchcock⟩ ⟨an ~ idea of the agricultural area —J.M.Mogey⟩ ⟨at the ~ center of the state⟩ **3 :** located very close together ⟨leaves that are ovate and ~⟩

[2]ap·prox·i·mate \-ˌmāt, *usu* -ād·+V\ *vb* -ED/ -ING/ -S *vt* **1 a :** to bring near or close to **:** cause to approach **:** make approximate ⟨the closer the performing conditions for Sebastian Bach's concerted music are *approximated* to those of early eighteenth century provincial Germany —Virgil Thomson⟩ **b** *med* **:** to bring together (cut edges of tissue) **2 :** to come near to **:** APPROACH ⟨the candidate's memory should closely ~ a hypothetical norm —H.G.Armstrong⟩ ⟨nothing *approximating* a history of American letters was printed —H.M.Jones⟩ **3 :** to set by hasty and crude calculation **:** ESTIMATE ⟨maybe the map is just *approximated* when it comes to precise distances —A.R.Marcus⟩ **~** *vi* **:** to come close ⟨to make the effects of poetry ~ to those of music —Edmund Wilson⟩

ap·prox·i·mate·ly \-ˌmətlē, -li\ *adv* **:** reasonably close to **:** NEARLY, ALMOST, ABOUT

ap·prox·i·ma·tion \əˌpräksə'māshən\ *n* -s **1 :** the action of coming or bringing near or close together ⟨effectively prevents ~ of viable parietal and visceral tissues —*Surgical Forum*⟩ **2 :** the state of being near ⟨an ~ to the truth⟩ **:** an approach esp. to a correct estimate, calculation, or conception or to a given quantity or quality ⟨to deal with crude ~*s* and somewhat meaningless generalities —W.A.Noyes⟩ **3** *math* **a :** a continual approach to a correct result ⟨solve an equation by successive ~⟩ **b :** a value that is nearly but not exactly correct

ap·prox·i·ma·tive \⸗'⸗⸗ˌmād·iv, -ˌməd·-\ *adj* **:** APPROACHING, APPROXIMATE — **ap·prox·i·ma·tive·ly** *adv*

appt *abbr* appoint; appointment

apptd *abbr* appointed

ap·pulse \ə'pəls, a'p-, 'aˌp- *also* -lts\ *n* -s [L *appulsus* driving forward, approach, fr. *appulsus*, past part. of *appellere* to drive toward, strike against, fr. *ad-* + *pellere* to drive, beat, push — more at FELT] **1 :** a driving or running toward (as a place) **:** act of striking against (as a point) ⟨the days have passed when national differences could be settled by the ~ of small professional armies —R.S.Ellery⟩ **2 :** the apparent very near approach of one celestial body to another **:** a coming into conjunction — see LUNAR APPULSE

ap·pur·te·nance \ə'pərt(ᵊ)nən(t)s, -pōt-,-pəit-\ *n* -s [ME *appurtenaunce*, *apurtenaunce*, fr. AF *apurtenance*, alter. (prob. influenced by OF *pour*, *pur* for) of OF *apartenance*, fr. *apartenir* to belong + *-ance* — more at APPERTAIN, PURCHASE] **1 :** an incidental property right or privilege (as to a right of way, a barn, or an orchard) belonging to a principal right and passing in possession with it **2 :** a subordinate part, adjunct, or accessory ⟨an ~ to his own vast vanity —Donn Byrne⟩ — usu. used in pl. ⟨the swashbuckling ~*s* of the historical novel⟩ **3 appurtenances** *pl* **:** accessory objects used in any function **:** APPARATUS, GEAR ⟨from cameras and lenses to all the ~*s* of the darkroom —J.T.Soby⟩ ⟨all the ~*s* of their daily existence —Marcia Davenport⟩

[1]ap·pur·te·nant \-ənt\ *adj* [ME *appurtenaunt*, *apurtenaunt*, alter. (prob. influenced by ME *appurtenaunce*) of *appertenant*, *apertenant*, *apertinent*, fr. MF *apertenant*, *apartenant*, fr. OF, pres. part. of *apartenir*] **1 a :** annexed or belonging legally to some more important thing ⟨a right-of-way ~ to land or buildings⟩ **b :** incident to and passing in possession with real estate — used of certain profits or easements; compare APPENDANT 2 **2 :** BELONGING, APPROPRIATE, ACCESSORY ⟨all other necessary ~ equipment —*Military Engineer*⟩ ⟨compressor station facilities ~ to this line —*Annual Report of Cities Service Co.*⟩

[2]appurtenant \"\ *n* -s **:** APPURTENANCE

appx *abbr* appendix

aprac·tic \(')ā¦praktik\ *or* **aprax·ic** \-aksik\ *adj* [*apractic* fr. Gk *apraktos* not taking part in action, fr. *a-* [2]a- + *-praktos* (fr. *prattein*, *prassein* to do, carry out); *apraxic* fr. NL *apraxia* + E *-ic*] **:** of, relating to, or marked by apraxia

aprax·ia \ā'praksēə\ *n* -s [NL, fr. Gk, inaction, fr. *a-* [2]a- + *praxis* action (fr. *prattein*, *prassein* to do, carry out + *-sis*) + *-ia* — more at PRACTICAL] **:** loss or impairment of ability to execute movements (as in manipulating objects) without muscular paralysis

après \ä'prā\ *adv* [F, fr. LL *ad pressum* near, fr. L *ad* to, at + *pressum*, accus. neut. of *pressus*, past part. of *premere* to press — more at AT, PRESS] **:** AFTER, AFTERWARD — used specif. in the game of rouge et noir to announce a refait

aprick·le \ə'-\ *adj* [[1]*a-* + *prickle* (*v.*)] **:** PRICKLY

apricock *archaic var of* APRICOT

apri·cot \'aprəˌkät, āp-, *usu* käd·+V; 'ap- *is more freq than* 'āp- *in N*, 'āp- *is much more freq than* 'ap- *in S*\ *n* -s [alter. (prob. influenced by L *apricum* sunny place and MF *abricot* apricot) of earlier *abrecock*, prob. fr. obs. Catal *abercoc*, fr. Ar *al-birqūq* the apricot, fr. *al-* the + *birqūq* apricot, prob. fr. Gk *praikokion*, fr. L *praecocia* (in *persica praecocia*, lit., early ripening peaches), neut. pl. of *praecox* early ripening — more at PRECOCIOUS] **1 a :** the oval orange-colored fruit of a temperate-zone tree (*Prunus armeniaca*) resembling both peach and plum in flavor **b :** any tree that bears apricots **2 :** a variable color averaging a moderate orange that is yellower, less strong, and slightly lighter than honeydew, yellower and paler than Persian orange, and paler and slightly yellower than ocher brown

apricot-kernel oil *n* **:** either of two oils obtained from apricot kernels and very similar in properties and uses to the true almond oils: **a :** a colorless or straw-colored nondrying fatty oil obtained by expression — called also *persic oil* **b :** a colorless to yellow aromatic toxic essential oil obtained by steam distillation — called also *bitter almond oil*

apricot palm *n* **:** a small Brazilian palm (*Cocos eriospatha*) that bears apricot-flavored fruit and is cultivated in California

apricot plum *n* **1 :** a Chinese tree (*Prunus simonii*) yielding an inferior fruit but used in hybridizing **2 :** the slightly astringent fruit of the apricot plum

apricot vine *n* **:** MAYPOP 1

apricot yellow *n* **:** a light to moderate yellow that is redder than amber yellow, snapdragon, or primrose yellow (sense 2)

april \'āprəl *sometimes* -(ˌ)pril\ *n* -s *usu cap, often attrib* [ME *April*, *Averil*, *Aperil*, fr. OF & L; OF *avrill*, fr. L *Aprilis*, prob. of Etruscan origin; akin to Etruscan *apru* April, perh. fr. Gk *Aphrō*, short for *Aphroditē* Greek goddess of love, perh. orig. a goddess of the underworld] **1 :** the fourth month of the Gregorian calendar — abbr. *Apr.;* see MONTH table **2 :** the season of spring ⟨something fresh and full of hope, an *April* of the spirit —Alzada Comstock⟩

april fool *n, usu cap A* **1 :** the butt or victim of a joke or trick played on April Fools' Day; *also* **:** such a joke or trick **2 :** PASQUEFLOWER

april fools' day *n, usu cap A&F&D* **:** April 1st, when practical jokes are played on the unwary — called also *All Fools' Day*

april·i·an \(')ā¦prilēən\ *adj, usu cap* [*April* + *-ian*] **:** of, relating to, or like April

[1]a pri·o·ri \¦āprē¦ōrē, ¦ä-, ¦a-, ¦à-, -ȯr-, -ri; ¦āˌprī¦ōrˌī, -ȯˌrī, -ōrē, -ȯrē, -ri\ *adv* [L, lit., from the former] **1 :** by reasoning from definitions formed or principles assumed **:** DEDUCTIVELY **2 :** without examination or analysis **:** PRESUMPTIVELY **3 :** independently of experience **:** INTUITIVELY

[2]a priori \"\ *adj* **1 a :** marked by reasoning or by deducing consequences from definitions formed or principles assumed **:** DEDUCTIVE ⟨an *a priori* argument⟩ ⟨an *a priori* order of propositions⟩ **b** (1) **:** of or relating to something that can be known by reason alone ⟨*a priori* geometrical propositions⟩ (2) **:** of or relating to reasoning from mere examination of ideas alone **:** marked by being knowable by reasoning from what is considered self-evident and therefore without appeal to the particular facts of experience **c :** of or relating to something that is presupposed by experience in general **:** considered as antecedently necessary in order that experience in general should be intelligible — used in Kantianism **d :** true or false by definition or convention alone **:** ANALYTIC ⟨*a priori* statements⟩ **e :** arbitrarily or conventionally postulated for formalization or axiomatization — contrasted with *a posteriori* **2 :** without examination or analysis **:** PRESUMPTIVE ⟨*a priori* acceptance of the greatness of a book —Norman Cousins⟩

[3]a priori \"\ *n, pl* **a prioris :** something that is a priori; *esp* **:** an a priori conception or proposition ⟨the *a priori* coextensive with the formal —W.S.Sellars⟩

apri·o·rism \ˌ⸗(ˌ)⸗'ōrˌizəm, -'ȯˌri-\ *n* -s [prob. trans. of D *apriorisme*] **1 :** belief in a priori principles or reasoning; *specif* **:** the doctrine that knowledge rests upon principles that are self-evident to reason or are presupposed by experience in general **2 a :** an a priori principle **:** ASSUMPTION **b :** an example of a priori reasoning **c :** a statement that makes evident a belief in a priori principles

apri·o·rist \-'ōrəst, -'ȯr-\ *n* -s **:** one who believes in a priori principles or seeks to establish his position by a priori reasoning

apri·o·ris·tic \¦⸗ˌprēˌōr¦istik, -ˌprīˌ-, -ˌȯ¦ris-; ¦⸗ˌprīə¦ri-\ *adj* **:** based upon a priori principles **:** A PRIORI ⟨~ positivism⟩ — **apri·o·ris·ti·cal·ly** \-tək(ə)lē\ *adv*

apri·or·i·ty \ˌ⸗ˌprē'ȯrəd·ē, ¦⸗ˌprī'-, -'ärə-\ *n* -ES **1 :** the quality or state of being a priori **2 :** the character in a proposition of following from principles that are a priori

apris·mo \ä'prēz(ˌ)mō\ *n* -s *usu cap* [AmerSp, fr. *Apra*, Peruvian political party (fr. *Alianza Popular Revolucionaria Americana* American Popular Revolutionary Alliance) + Sp *-ismo* -ism] **:** the political philosophy and policies advocated by Apristas

apris·ta \ä'prēstə\ *n* -s *usu cap* [AmerSp, fr. *Apra* + Sp *-ista* -ist] **:** a member or adherent of any of various Latin-American socialist parties advocating division of landed estates, domestic social reform, and cooperation among Latin-American countries

aproc·ta \(')ā'präktə\ [NL, fr. [2]*a-* + *-procta*] *syn of* TURBELLARIA

aproc·tous \(')ā¦präktəs\ *adj* [[2]*a-* + *-proctous*] **:** without an anal orifice

[1]apron \'āprən, *less often in stand than in substand speech* -pə(r)n\ *n* -s *often attrib* [ME, alter. (resulting from incorrect division of *a napron*) of *napron*, fr. MF *naperon*, dim. of *nape* cloth, tablecloth, modif. of L *mappa* napkin — more at MAP] **1 a :** an article made of cloth, plastic, leather, or other material, usu. worn on the front of the body and tied around the waist with strings, and used to protect the clothing, to cover the body, or to adorn a costume **b :** a part of certain official costumes ⟨the ~ and gaiters of a bishop —Donn Byrne⟩ **2 :** a horizontal or vertical cover appended to a structure for protection and often serving also as a brace or decoration: as **a :** an extension of a building material (as trim or flashing) along another surface for the purpose of decorating, hiding unfinished surfaces, or protecting against impact or the elements; *specif* **:** the lower member under the sill of the interior casing of a window **b** (1) **:** a downward extension of the frame of a piece of furniture (as immediately below a table top or chair seat) (2) **:** an upward or downward vertical extension of a sink or lavatory **c** (1) **:** a strip of planking along the side of a boat (2) **:** a reinforcing piece of timber behind the stempost of a boat **d :** a swinging part of a gun shield **e** (1) **:** a piece of waterproof cloth or other material spread out (as before the seat of a vehicle) as a protection from rain or mud (2) **:** a horizontal or vertical metal shield extending across the front of an automobile below the radiator **f :** a covering or casing (as of sheet metal) for protecting parts of machinery **g :** a strip of leather forming part of the upper of an oxford shoe and extending from the shank over the waist and instep **h :** a canvas jacket fitted over the back of a hen turkey to prevent injury during mating **3 a :** a device or mechanism serving to move or guide material into or retain it in a desired position: as (1) **:** an endless belt for carrying material of any kind — called also *traveling apron* (2) **:** a receptacle for conveying material (as rock) by a cableway and trolley (3) **:** a revolving canvas for conveying cut grain (as wheat) to the binding mechanism of a harvester **:** a platform or elevator canvas (4) **:** a flap on which paper pulp is led from the strainer **b** (1) **:** a moving lattice for feeding loose fibers to a machine (as in a cotton picker) (2) **:** a leather or composition belt operating in conjunction with other devices to draft, rub, or condense roving in preparatory and spinning processes (3) **:** a means (as a fabric) for attaching warp threads to the cloth roller in weaving **c** (1) **:** a flat plate or lip serving as a chute or deflector in mining engineering (2) **:** a copper plate coated with amalgam used outside a stamp battery in gold mining — called also *apron plate* (3) **:** the canvas-covered frame used in a gold miner's cradle to deflect material washed and to catch the fine gold **d** (1) **:** the vertical front plate of a lathe carriage that bears the mechanism by which the carriage is moved (2) **:** the piece to which the cutting tool of a planer is clamped — called also *tool apron* **e** (1) **:** a metal strip used in turpentining to support the cup and to guide the crude turpentine into it (2) **:** a piece of leather or board for conducting loose material (as grain) past an opening (as in a separator) **f :** a broad shallow vat used for evaporating **g :** a strip of often embossed plastic material used to separate the turns of a film rolled up for development in a tank **4 :** an anatomical structure that resembles an apron: as **a :** HOTTENTOT APRON **b** (1) **:** the diaphragm or midriff of an animal (2) **:** a thick transverse fold of skin on the fore part of the breast or lower part of the neck of a ram (3) **:** the fat skin covering the belly of a goose or duck (4) **:** the infolded abdomen of a crab (5) **:** a frill of esp. long hair on the lower throat and chest of a long-haired dog **5 :** an extensive usu. unconsolidated alluvial, glaciofluvial, eolian, or marine deposit spread outward from an identifiable source **:** a piedmont alluvial plain **:** ALLUVIAL FAN **:** OUTWASH PLAIN **6 a :** the part of the stage in front of the proscenium arch and the curtain **:** FORESTAGE ⟨stepped to the ~ of the stage and took the bow —Bennett Cerf⟩ **b :** the part of the boxing-ring floor that extends beyond the ropes **c :** the part of a golf course immediately surrounding a green **7 a :** a flat steel plate between a railroad locomotive and tender used as a standing place by the fireman **b** (1) **:** the area along the waterfront edge of a pier or wharf used for the direct transfer of cargo between ship's hold and railroad cars (2) **:** a bridge structure supporting railroad tracks that connects a car ferry with the tracks extending to land **8 a :** a shield (as of concrete, planking, or brushwood) along the bank of a river, along a sea wall, or below a dam **b** (1) **:** a cover (as of concrete or metal) that protects an inclined surface of a fortification (2) **:** a strip of barbed-wire entanglements **c** (1) **:** the extensive paved part of an airport located immediately adjacent to the terminal area or hangars and used for loading, unloading, and parking aircraft (2) **:** an extensive usu. hard-surfaced area; *esp* **:** such an area used for stopping or parking automobiles **9 :** a sheet attached to or a space on an invoice for notations or facts relative to payment

[2]apron \"\ *vt* -ED/-ING/-S **:** to put an apron on **:** cover with or as if with an apron

apron conveyor *n* **:** a chain conveyor having plates attached to the chain for carrying material — compare APRON 3a(1)

apron feeder *n* **:** an apron conveyor so operated as to control the rate of delivery of material to be processed by a machine

apron lining *n* **:** the casing of the apron piece that forms part of the finish of a staircase

apron man *n, obs* **:** a man who wears an apron **:** WORKMAN, TRADESMAN

apron piece *n* **:** a beam supporting a landing or a series of winders in a staircase

apron stage *n* **:** the flat wide part of the Elizabethan stage projecting into the audience and used as the main acting area

apron string *n* **:** the string of an apron — usu. used in pl. as a symbol of complete dependence on or domineering control by a wife or mother ⟨succeeds . . . in tying him to her *apron strings* forever —J.H.Lawson⟩

apron wall *n* **:** SPANDREL 3

[1]ap·ro·pos \¦aprə¦pō\ *adv* [F *à propos*, lit., to the purpose] **1 :** at an opportune time **:** SEASONABLY, FITLY ⟨your letter comes ~ as usual —O.W.Holmes †1935⟩ **2 :** by the way **:** INCIDENTALLY ⟨~, are there any cases of women being held captive by the sirens —Norman Douglas⟩

[2]apropos \"\ *adj* **:** to the point **:** APPROPRIATE, PERTINENT, RELEVANT ⟨have some ~ comments —Dorothy Barclay⟩ **syn** see RELEVANT

[3]apropos \"\ *prep* **:** with respect to **:** CONCERNING, REGARDING ⟨~ the return of young Americans to lyricism —Peter Viereck⟩ — often used with *of* ⟨his remark to Emerson ~ of diplomas —H.S.Canby⟩

apros·cop·i·nous \¦āˌprä¦skäpənəs\ *adj* [[2]*a-* + *proscopinous*] **:** lacking the supraorbital ridge — **apros·cop·i·ny** \-'skäpənē\ *n* -ES

apros·ex·ia \¦āˌprä'seksēə\ *n* -s [NL, fr. Gk, want of attention, fr. *a-* [2]a- + *-prosexia* (fr. *prosechein* to turn something, as one's mind or attention, to, fr. *pros* toward + *echein* to hold — more at SCHEME] **:** abnormal inability to sustain attention

aprot·er·o·dont \(')ā¦prädərəˌdänt, ¦āprō¦terə,-\ *adj* [[2]*a-* + *proter-* + *-odont*] **:** having the intermaxillaries toothless

apro·tic \(')ā¦prōd·ik\ *adj* [[2]*a-* + *proton* + *-ic*] **:** incapable of acting as a proton acceptor or proton donor or as an acid or a base ⟨~ solvent⟩

aprowl \ə'-\ *adj* [[1]*a-* + *prowl*, v.] **:** in a state of activity or motion **:** on the prowl ⟨battleships and cruisers were ~ —J.A.Michener⟩

apse \'aps\ *n* -s [ML & L; ML *apsis*, *absis* apse of a church, fr. L, vault, arch, orbit of a heavenly body — more at APSIS] **1 :** a projecting part of a building (as a church) usu. semicircular in plan and vaulted; *specif* **:** the bishop's seat or throne in ancient churches usu. in the apse at the eastern end of the choir — see BASILICA illustration **2** [NL, fr. L] **:** APSIS 2

apse aisle *n* **:** an aisle or ambulatory continuing a choir aisle around an apse or chevet

ap·si·dal \'apsədᵊl\ *adj* [L *apsid-*, *apsis* + E *-al*] **1 :** of or relating to the apsides of an orbit ⟨~ motion⟩ **2** [ML *apsid-*, *apsis* + E *-al*] **:** of or relating to the apse of a church — **ap·si·dal·ly** \-dəlē *also* -dᵊlē\ *adv*

apsides *pl of* APSIS

ap·sid·i·ole \ap'sidēˌōl\ *also* **ab·sid·i·ole** \ab's-\ *n* -s [F *absidiole*, fr. *abside* apse (fr. ML *absid-*, *absis*) + *-i-* + *-ole* — more at APSE] **:** a small apse; *specif* **:** one of the smaller or secondary apses in a church having several apses

ap·sis \'apsəs\ *n, pl* **apsi·des** \-psəˌdēz, ap'sī(ˌ)dēz\ [L *apsis*, *absis*, fr. Gk *apsid-*, *apsis*, *hapsid-*, *hapsis* loop, wheel, arch, orbit, fr. *haptein* to fasten; perh. akin to Gk *oiphein* to copulate with, Skt *yabhati* he copulates with] **1** *obs* **:** CIRCUMFERENCE, ORBIT **2** [NL, fr. L] **:** the point in an orbit at which the distance of the body from the center of attraction is either greatest or least (as the apogee or perigee of the moon or the aphelion or perihelion of a planet) **3** [ML, fr. L] **:** APSE 1

apsis 2

[1]apt \'apt\ *adj, usu* -ER/-EST [ME, fr. L *aptus* fastened, attached, suitable, fr. past part. of *apere* to fasten; akin to L *apisci* to reach, attain, *apud* near, Skt *āpta* fit, *āpnoti* he reaches] **1 :** having the necessary qualifications **:** unusually fitted or qualified **:** READY, PREPARED ⟨tall was he, slim, made ~ for feats of war —William Morris⟩ **2 a :** having an habitual tendency or inclination **:** LIKELY ⟨the fish is ~ to be lighter in shallower water —Francesca R. La Monte⟩ **b :** ordinarily disposed **:** GIVEN, INCLINED, PRONE ⟨are ~ to believe what we like to believe —John Mason Brown⟩ **3 :** suited to its purpose **:** FITTING, SUITABLE ⟨picking out every term or figure ~ for literary use —C.E.Montague⟩; *specif* **:** to the point **:** APPOSITE, APPROPRIATE, PAT ⟨words were ~ and well chosen —Osbert Sitwell⟩ ⟨~ quotations from classical Arabic travelers —W.L.Wright⟩ **4 :** keenly intelligent **:** mentally alert **:** QUICK-WITTED, QUICK ⟨an ~ student⟩ ⟨an ~ wit —Samuel Johnson⟩ ⟨the boy was observant and ~ to learn —J.G.Cozzens⟩ **syn** see FIT, QUICK

[2]apt *vt* -ED/ -ING/ -S [L *aptare*, fr. *aptus*] *obs* **:** to make fit or suitable **:** DISPOSE

apt *abbr* apartment

ap·tal \'apˌtal\ *n* -s *usu cap* **:** a member of a Gypsy people of northern Syria

ap·te·no·dy·tes \ˌapˌtēnə'dīd·ēz, -īˌtēz\ *n, cap* [NL, fr. *apteno-* (fr. Gk *aptēn* wingless, fr. *a-* [2]a- + *-ptēn*, fr. *ptēnos* winged) + *-dytes;* akin to Gk *petesthai* to fly — more at FEATHER] **:** a genus of large penguins including the king penguin and emperor penguin

[1]ap·tera \'aptərə\ *n pl, cap* [NL, fr. Gk, neut. pl. of *apteros*] **1** *in former classifications* **:** an order comprising various wingless arthropods (as spiders, centipedes, and certain insects) **2** *in some modern classifications* **a :** an order of insects coextensive with Entotrophi **b :** an order of insects coextensive with Apterygota — **ap·ter·an** \-rən\ *adj or n*

[2]aptera \"\ *n, pl* **apter·ae** \-əˌrē\ [NL, fr. Gk *apterē*, fem. of *apteros*] **:** a wingless parthenogenetic female aphid that lives on the definitive host plants producing other generations of like aphids and later a generation of alates

ap·ter·al \'aptərəl\ *adj* [Gk *apteros* + E *-al*] **1 :** APTEROUS, WINGLESS **2 :** marked by columniation consisting of a portico at one or both ends but no lateral columns — see COLUMNIATION illustration

ap·te·ri·al \(')ap¦tirēəl\ *adj* [NL *apterium* + E *-al*] **:** of or relating to an apterium

ap·te·ri·um \ap'tirēəm\ *n, pl* **apte·ria** \-ēə\ [NL, fr. *a-* [2]a- + *pter-* + *-ium*] **:** one of the bare spaces between the feathered areas on the body of a bird

ap·ter·ous \'aptərəs\ *adj* [Gk *apteros*, fr. *a-* [2]a- + *-pteros* (fr. *pteron* wing) — more at FEATHER] **1 :** lacking wings ⟨an ~ insect⟩ **2 :** lacking winglike expansions ⟨~ petioles⟩ ⟨an ~ seed⟩

ap·tery \-rē\ *n* -ES [[2]*a-* + *pter-* + *-y*] *zool* **:** the state of being wingless

ap·ter·y·ges \ap'terəˌjēz\ [NL, fr. pl. of *Apteryg-*, *Apteryx*] *syn of* APTERYGIFORMES

ap·ter·yg·ial \¦aptə¦rij(ē)əl\ *adj* [[2]*a-* + Gk *pterygion* fin, lit., little wing + E *-al* — more at PTERYGIUM] **:** without paired fins or limbs (as of the cyclostomes)

ap·ter·yg·i·for·mes \ˌaptəˌrijə'fȯrˌmēz\ *n pl, cap* [NL, fr. *Apteryg-*, *Apteryx* + *-iformes*] **:** an order of flightless ground birds (superorder Palaeognathae) having vestigial wings, long bills, and small eyes and being coextensive with a family (Apterygidae) that includes the New Zealand kiwis and extinct related birds of Australia and New Zealand — see APTERYX

ap·ter·y·go·ge·nea \apˌterə(ˌ)gō'jēnēə\ [NL, fr. [2]*a-* + *pteryg-* + *-genea* (fr. Gk *genos* race, kin) — more at KIN] *syn of* APTERYGOTA

ap·ter·y·go·ta \(ˌ)apˌterə'gōd·ə, ¦āˌte-\ *n pl, cap* [NL, fr. [2]*a-* + *Pterygota*] **:** a subclass of Insecta comprising primitive insects that are presumed never to have developed wings and have no conspicuous metamorphosis — compare PTERYGOTA

ap·ter·y·gote \(')ap¦terəˌgōt, (')ā¦te-\ *or* **ap·ter·y·go·tous** \¦apˌterə¦gōd·əs, ¦āˌte\ *adj* [*apterygote* fr. NL *Apterygota;* *apterygotous*, fr. NL *Apterygota* + E *-ous*] **:** of or relating to the subclass Apterygota

ap·ter·y·la \(')ap¦terələ, (')ā¦te-\ *n, pl* **aptery·lae** \-ˌlē, -ˌlī\ [NL, fr. [2]*a-* + *pteryla*] **:** one of the spaces between the feather tracts of birds

ap·ter·yx \'aptə(ˌ)riks\ *n* [NL, fr. [2]*a-* + *-pteryx*] **1** *cap* **:** a genus (the type of the family Apterygidae) of flightless birds comprising the kiwis and including all surviving members of the order Apterygiformes **2** -ES **:** KIWI

aptest *superlative of* APT

aptha *var of* APHTHA

apt·i·an \'aptēən, -psh(ē)ən\ *adj, usu cap* [F *aptien,* fr. *Apt,* commune near Avignon, France + F *-ien* -ian] **:** of or relating to a subdivision of the European Lower Cretaceous — see GEOLOGIC TIME table

ap·ti·ana \,aptē'anə, -'ä-,-'ā- *also* -'ā-\ *n, cap* [NL, fr. ISV *Aptian*] **:** a genus of fossil plants of the Lower Cretaceous of England said to represent one of the earliest known ancestors of existing angiosperms

apting *pres part of* APT

ap·ti·tude \'aptə,tüd, -ptə-,tyüd\ *n* -s [ME, fr. ML *aptitudo,* fr. LL, fitness, fr. L *aptus* fit + *-i-* + *-tudo* -tude — more at APT] **1 :** a tendency, capacity, or inclination to learn or understand **:** mental alertness **:** QUICK-WITTEDNESS, APTNESS ⟨boys of real ability with an ~ for classics —A.C.Benson⟩ **2 a :** a natural inclination or disposition ⟨beavers have an ~ for building dams⟩ **b :** a natural or acquired capacity or ability ⟨she was endowed mentally with a stubborn ~ for facing facts —Ellen Glasgow⟩ **3 :** a general fitness or suitableness **:** APPROPRIATENESS ⟨that sociable and helpful ~ which God implanted between man and woman —John Milton⟩ **4** *obs* **:** ATTITUDE 1 **5 :** any constellation of measurable characteristics known to predispose to the learning of certain skills **syn** see GIFT

aptitude test *n* **:** a standardized test designed to predict an individual's ability to learn certain skills — compare INTELLIGENCE TEST

ap·ti·tu·di·nal \¦==¦=dᵊnəl\ *adj* [ML *aptitudin-, aptitudo* + E *-al*] **:** of or relating to aptitude — **ap·ti·tu·di·nal·ly** \-əlē, -li\ *adv*

apt·ly \'aptlē, -li, *rap.* -pl-\ *adv* **1 :** in an apt manner **:** APPROPRIATELY, FITTINGLY, READILY **2** *archaic* **:** with exact adjustment or correspondence

apt·ness \'ap(t)nəs\ *n* -ES **:** the quality or state of being apt: **a :** FITNESS, SUITABLENESS ⟨the universal ~ of a religious system —A.W.Kinglake⟩ **b :** habitual tendency or inclination **:** LIKELIHOOD ⟨the ~ of iron to rust⟩ **:** PROPENSITY, PRONENESS ⟨the ~ of men to sin⟩ **c :** APPROPRIATENESS, APPOSITENESS ⟨this last metaphor has a peculiar ~ —F.R.Leavis⟩ **d :** mental alertness **:** QUICK-WITTEDNESS, APTITUDE ⟨his ~ in illustration was as charming as it was effective —Broadus Mitchell⟩

apts *pres 3d sing of* APT

apty·a·lism \(')ā'tīə,lizəm\ *also* **apty·a·lia** \,ā,tī'ālyə, -lēə\ *n* -s [*aptyalism,* fr. ²*a-* + *ptyalism; aptyalia,* NL, fr. ²*a-* + *ptyal-* + *-ia*] **:** absence of or deficiency in secretion of saliva

ap·ty·chus \'aptəkəs\ *n, pl* **apty·chi** \-,kī\ [NL, fr. ²*a-* + Gk *ptychē* fold — more at PTYCH-] **:** a shelly plate usu. of two pieces found in ammonites and regarded as an operculum

¹**apu·lian** \ə'pyülēən, -lyən\ *adj, usu cap* [*Apulia* (It *Puglia*), compartimento of southeastern Italy + E *-an*] **:** of or relating to Apulia or the Apulians

²**apulian** \"\ *n* -s *cap* **:** a native or inhabitant of Apulia

apulian pottery *n, usu cap A* **:** a kind of ancient pottery found in Apulia; *esp* **:** a species of vase or stamnos having red designs on a lustrous black surface

a pun·ta d'ar·co \ä¦püntə'där(,)kō\ *adv* [It] **:** with or at the point of the bow — used as a direction for players of stringed instruments

apur·pose \ə'-\ *adv* [¹*a-* + *purpose*] *dial* **:** on purpose **:** DELIBERATELY

¹**apus** \'āpəs, 'ä-\ *n, cap* [NL, fr. L *apod-, apus* swallow supposed to be footless, fr. Gk *apod-, apous* sand-martin, swift, fr. *apod-, apous* footless, fr. *a-* ²*a-* + *pod-, pous* foot — more at FOOT] **:** a genus of birds containing the typical Old World swifts

²**apus** \"\ [NL, fr. Gk *apod-, apous* footless] *syn of* TRIOPS

³**apus** \"\ *n, pl* **apuses** \-əsəz\ *or* **ap·o·des** \'apə,dēz\ [NL ²*Apus*] **:** a crustacean of the genus *Triops* certain tropical forms of which are destructive pests of young rice

apx *abbr* appendix

ap·y·rase \'apə,rās\ *n* -s [adenyl*pyr*ophosphat*ase*] **:** any enzyme that hydrolyzes adenosine triphosphate with the liberation of phosphate — compare ADENOSINE TRIPHOSPHATASE

apy·rene \(')ā¦pī,rēn\ *adj* [ISV ²*a-* + *-pyrene* (fr. Gk *pyrēn* stone of a fruit) — more at FURZE] **:** lacking a nucleus ⟨~ spermatozoa⟩

apy·ret·ic \¦ā,pī¦red·ik, ¦apə¦r-\ *adj* [²*a-* + *pyretic*] **:** without fever **:** AFEBRILE

apy·rex·ia \¦ā,pī'reksēə, ,apə'r-\ *also* **apy·rexy** \(')ā'pī-,reksē, 'apə,r-\ *n, pl* **apyrexias** *also* **apyrexies** [NL *apyrexia,* fr. Gk, fr. *a-* ²*a-* + *-pyrexia* (fr. *pyressein* to be feverish, fr. *pyr* fire) — more at FIRE] **:** absence or intermission of fever — **apy·rex·i·al** \¦ā,pī¦reksēəl, ¦apə¦r-\ *adj*

apy·rous \(')ā¦pīrəs\ *adj* [Gk *apyros* without fire, fr. *a-* ²*a-* + *pyr* fire] **:** NONCOMBUSTIBLE

aq *abbr* aqua; aqueous

AQ *abbr* accomplishment quotient; achievement quotient

aq bull *abbr* [L *aqua bulliens*] boiling water

aq dest *abbr* [NL *aqua destillata*] distilled water

aq ferv *abbr* [L *aqua fervens*] warm water

aq font *abbr* [L *aqua fontana*] spring water

aq·ua \'akwə; 'äkwə, 'á- *sometimes* -(,)kwä; *sometimes* 'ākwə\ *n, pl* **aq·uae** \'a(,)kwē, 'a,kwī; 'ä,kwī, 'á-\ *or* **aquas** [L — more at ISLAND] **1** *pl aquae* **:** WATER: **a** (1) *in old chem* **:** LIQUID (2) **:** a solution esp. in water **b :** an indefinite usu. infinitely large amount of water — used in abbreviated form in chemical formulas ⟨$CaCl_2$.*aq*⟩ **2** *pl aquas* **:** a variable color averaging a light greenish blue that is greener and paler than average robin's-egg blue (sense 1), paler and slightly bluer than average turquoise (sense 2a), paler and very slightly bluer than average turquoise blue, and greener and slightly deeper than average aqua blue

aqua- — see AQUI-

aqua am·mo·nia \-ə'mōnēə, -nyə\ *or* **aqua am·mo·ni·ae** \-nē,ē\ *n, pl* **aquae am·mo·ni·ae** \-nē,ē\ [NL] **:** AMMONIA WATER; *esp* **:** a solution of ammonia containing 10 percent of ammonia by weight

aqua ar·o·mat·i·ca \-,arə'mad·əkə\ *n, pl* **aquae ar·o·mat·i·cae** \-ə,kē,sē\ [NL] **:** AROMATIC WATER

aq·ua·belle \'akwə,bel, 'ä-\ *n* -s [prob. fr. *aquacade* + *belle*] **:** an attractive young woman in a bathing suit

aqua blue *n* **:** a variable color averaging a light greenish blue that is greener and paler than average robin's-egg blue (sense 1), bluer and slightly paler than average aqua, and bluer and paler than average turquoise blue

aq·ua·cade \¦akwə¦kād, ¦äk-\ *n* -s [after *Aquacade,* a water entertainment spectacle at the Cleveland, O. Great Lakes Exposition of 1937 and the New York World's Fair of 1939-40] **:** a water spectacle that consists usu. of exhibitions of swimming and diving with musical accompaniment

aqua cam·pho·rae \-'kam(p)fə,rē\ *n, pl* **aquae camphorae** [NL, water of camphor] **:** CAMPHOR WATER

aquaculture *var of* AQUICULTURE

Aq·ua·dag \'akwə,dag\ *trademark* — used for a substance that consists of a colloidal suspension of fine particles of graphite in water and is used esp. as a lubricant

aqua des·til·la·ta \-,destə'läd·ə\ *n, pl* **aquae destilla·tae** \-ä,tē\ [NL] **:** DISTILLED WATER

aq·uae·duc·tus \,akwə'dəktəs, -wē'-\ *n, pl* **aquaeduc·ti** \-,tī,-,tē\ [L, lit., conveying of water, aqueduct — more at AQUEDUCT] **:** the right in law to lead or conduct water over the land of another

aq·uae·haus·tus \-'hȯstəs, -haùs-\ *n, pl* **aquaehaus·ti** \-ȯ,stī, -aù,stē\ [L *aquae haustus* drawing of water, fr. *aquae* (gen. of *aqua* water) + *haustus* act of drawing, fr. *haustus,* past part. of *haurire* to draw — more at ISLAND, EXHAUST] **:** the right in law to draw water from a well, spring, or stream on another's land

aquae im·mit·ten·dae \-,imə'ten,dē, -,dī — *see* AQUA\ *n pl but sing in constr* [L, waters to be thrown out] **:** the right in law to throw water from one's windows on a neighbor's buildings or soil

aquafer *var of* AQUIFER

aq·ua·flo·ri·um \,akwə'flōrēəm, ,äk-, -ȯr-\ *n* -s [NL, fr. L *aqua* water + *flor-, flos* flower + NL *-ium* — more at ISLAND, BLOSSOM] **:** an inverted glass bowl resting on a base and containing a flower or flowers submerged in water

aq·ua·for·tis \-'fȯrd·əs\ *n* -ES [NL *aqua fortis,* lit., strong water, fr. L *aqua* water + *fortis* strong — more at FORT] **1 :** NITRIC ACID **2 :** etching in which nitric acid is used as a mordant

aq·ua·for·tist \-rd·əst\ *n* -s [prob. fr. F *aquafortiste,* irreg. fr. NL *aqua fortis* + F *-iste* -ist] **:** one who uses aquafortis in etching

aqua gray *n* **:** a variable color averaging a pale blue that is greener and paler than average powder blue, Sistine, or average cadet gray

aqua green *n* **1 :** a variable color averaging a light bluish green that is bluer, lighter, and stronger than robin's-egg blue (sense 2), greener, lighter, and stronger than Eton blue, and slightly paler and very slightly greener than turquoise (sense 2 b) **2 :** a light yellowish green that is greener, stronger, and slightly lighter than pistachio, yellower and paler than apple green (sense 2), greener and deeper than ocean green, and deeper than crayon green

aqua green tint *n* **:** a variable color averaging a very pale green that is paler and slightly bluer than tourmaline and bluer and duller than emerald tint or celadon tint

aquake \ə'-\ *adj* [¹*a-* + *quake* (v.)] **:** QUAKING

aq·ua·lung·er \-,ləŋə(r)\ *n* -s [fr. *Aqualung,* a trademark] **:** an underwater swimmer who uses a breathing device (as a cylinder of compressed air and a watertight face mask)

aq·ua·ma·ni·le \,akwəmə'nī(,)lē, ,äkwəmə'nēlē\ *n, pl* **aqua·mani·les** \-ī(,)lēz, -ē,lās\ *or* **aquamanil·ia** \-'nilēə\ [LL, alter. of L *aquae manale,* fr. *aquae* (gen. of *aqua* water) + *manale* ewer, fr. neut. of *manalis* flowing, fr. *manare* to flow + *-alis* -al — more at EMANATE] **:** a water vessel or ewer; *specif* **:** a basin used by the priest for washing his hands during the celebration of Mass

aq·ua·ma·rine \,akwəmə'rēn *also* ,äk- *or* ,ák-; *attrib* ¦==¦=\ *n* -s *often attrib* [NL *aqua marina,* fr. L, sea water, fr. *aqua* water + *marina,* fem. of *marinus* of the sea — more at MARINE] **1 :** a transparent variety of beryl that is blue, blue-green, or green in color **2 :** a pale blue to light greenish blue

aquamarine chrysolite *n* **:** a beryl of a greenish yellow color

aquamarine topaz *n* **:** a topaz shading to green

aquameter *var of* AQUOMETER

aquam·e·try \ə'kwämə·trē\ *n* -ES [*aqua* + *-metry*] **:** determination of amount of water esp. by means of the Karl Fischer reagent

aqua mi·ra·bi·lis \-mə'räbələs, -rab-\ *n, pl* **aquae mirabi·les** \-äbə,lēz, -,lās; -abə,lēz\ [NL, wonderful water] **:** a distilled cordial of old pharmacy made of spirits, sage, betony, balm, and other aromatic ingredients

¹**aq·ua·plane** \'akwə,plān *also* 'äk- *or* 'ák-\ *n* [L *aqua* water + E *plane* (surface) — more at ISLAND] **:** a board on which a person stands and which when towed behind a speedboat planes on the surface of the water

²**aquaplane** \"\ *vi* -ED/-ING/-S **:** to ride on an aquaplane

aq·ua·plan·er \-,plānə(r)\ *n* -s **:** one that aquaplanes

aqua pu·ra \-'pyürə, 'pùrə\ *n, pl* **aquae pu·rae** \-ē'pyü(,)rē, -ī'pù,rī — *see* AQUA\ [L] **:** pure water

aquardiente *var of* AGUARDIENTE

aqua re·gia \-'rēj(ē)ə\ *n, pl* **aquae regi·ae** \-jē,ē\ [NL, lit., royal water; fr. its ability to dissolve gold] **:** a very corrosive fuming yellow liquid made by mixing nitric and hydrochloric acids usu. in the proportion of one volume of nitric to three or four of hydrochloric and used in dissolving metals (as gold or platinum) and in etching — called also *nitrohydrochloric acid*

aq·ua·relle \¦akwə¦rel, ¦äk- \ *n* -s [F, fr. obs. It *acquarella* (now *acquerello*), fr. *acqua* water, fr. L *aqua*] **1 a :** drawing or painting in watercolor, esp. transparent water color — compare GOUACHE **b :** a watercolor drawing or painting esp. when executed in transparent colors **2 :** a picture produced by printing from a key plate and then with brushes applying water colors through stencils placed over the print — **aq·ua·rel·list** \¦==¦reləst\ *n* -s

aquar·i·an \ə'kwa(a)rēən, -wer-, -wär-\ *n* -s *usu cap* [LL *Aquarius* (fr. L *aqua* + *-arius* -ary) + E *-an*] **:** a member of any of certain sects in the early church (as the Encratites) that used water instead of wine in the Eucharist

aquar·ii \-rē,ī, -rē,ē\ *n pl, usu cap* [LL, pl. of *Aquarius*] **:** AQUARIANS

aquar·ist \-rəst\ *n* -s [*aquarium* + *-ist*] **:** one who keeps an aquarium

aquar·i·um \-rēəm\ *n, pl* **aquariums** \-ēəmz\ *or* **aquar·ia** \-ēə\ [L, watering place for cattle, fr. neut. of *aquarius* of water, fr. *aqua* + *-arius* -ary — more at ISLAND] **1 :** a glass bowl or globe, a tank usu. having glass sides, or an artificial pond in which living aquatic animals or plants are kept **2 :** a place or establishment in which aquatic collections are kept and exhibited

aquarium

aquar·i·us \-rēəs\ *n, pl* **aquar·ii** \-ē,ī, -ē,ē\ *or* **aquariuses** *usu cap* [ME, fr. L (trans. of Gk *Hydrochoos*), lit., water carrier, fr. *aqua* + *-arius* -ary] **:** the 11th sign of the zodiac — see SIGN table; ZODIAC illustration

aquas *pl of* AQUA

Aq·ua·stat \'akwə,stat *also* 'äk-\ *trademark* — used for an automatic device for regulating the temperature of water heated by a boiler or furnace

aqua system *n* **:** a system for storing fuel oil or gasoline in tanks having the lower part filled with water upon which the lighter oil rests, water being pumped in from below to maintain the pressure as oil is withdrawn

aquate \ə'kwāt\ *vt* -ED/-ING/-S [back-formation fr. *aquation*] **:** to subject to aquation **:** combine with water (as in the formation of coordination complexes, esp. ions) — compare HYDRATE

aq·ua·terrarium \¦akwə, ¦äk-+\ *n* [*aqua* + *terrarium*] **:** a box or aquarium adapted for water and a sloping bank of earth and rocks in which to culture snails and other amphibious animals

¹**aquat·ic** \ə'kwä\|d·ik, -wal, \|tik, -ēk\ *adj* [MF *aquatique,* fr. L *aquaticus,* fr. *aqua* water] **:** of or relating to water **:** WATER: **a** (1) **:** living wholly or chiefly in or on water ⟨porpoises and seals are ~ animals⟩ (2) **:** growing in or on water ⟨~ plants⟩ (3) **:** living near or frequenting water ⟨gulls and herons are ~ birds⟩ **b :** engaged in or performed in or on water ⟨~ sports⟩ — **aquat·i·cal·ly** \-ək(ə)lē, -ēk-, -li\ *adv*

²**aquatic** \"\ *n* -s **1 :** an aquatic animal or plant **2 :** one given to bathing or swimming or to taking part in aquatic sports **3 aquat·ics** \-ks\ *pl but sometimes sing in constr* **:** water sports

aquatic plant *n* **:** a plant that grows in water (as the water lily, floating heart, or lattice plant) whether rooted in the mud (as a lotus) or floating without anchorage (as the water hyacinth)

¹**aq·ua·tile** \'akwə,tīl\ *adj* [L *aquatilis,* fr. *aqua*] **:** AQUATIC

²**aquatile** *n* -s *obs* **:** an aquatic animal or plant

¹**aq·ua·tint** \'akwə,tint, 'äk-\ *n* -s [It *acqua tinta* dyed water] **1 :** a process of etching in which the plate is grained by an application of powdered rosin and subjected to a series of bitings between some of which certain areas are stopped out, the resulting print resembling a water color made with flat washes of different strengths **2 :** an engraving produced by the aquatint process

²**aquatint** \"\ *vt* -ED/-ING/-S **:** to etch by aquatint

aq·ua·tin·ta \¦==¦tintə\ *adj* [It *acqua tinta* dyed water] **:** in aquatint ⟨~ engravings⟩

aqua·tion \ə'kwāshən\ *n* -s [L *aquation-, aquatio* act of fetching water, fr. *aquatus* (past part. of *aquari* to bring or fetch water, fr. *aqua* water) + *-ion-, -io* -ion] **:** the replacement by water molecules of a coordinated atom or group in a coordination complex

aq·ua·ti·za·tion \,akwəd·ə'zāshən, -wə,tī'z-\ *n* -s [*aquate* + *-ization*] **:** AQUATION

aq·ua·tone \'akwə,tōn, 'äk-\ *n* -s [*aqua* + *tone*] **:** an offset printing method utilizing a gelatin-coated zinc plate hardened and sensitized to print type, line illustrations, and fine-screen halftones **2 :** a print produced by aquatone

à qua·tre mains \,äkatrəmaⁿ\ *adj* [F, lit., for four hands] **:** to be played as a duet at one keyboard — used as a direction in music

aq·ua·vit *also* **ak·va·vit** \'äkwə,vēt, 'ak-; 'äk(,)vä-, 'ák(,)vá-; *also* -,vit *or* ,==¦vēt\ *n* -s [Sw, Dan & Norw *akvavit,* fr. ML *aqua vitae*] **:** a colorless or slightly yellow alcoholic liquor produced in the Scandinavian countries by redistilling neutral spirits (as grain, potato, or wood spirits), flavored with caraway seeds, and often taken neat as an aperitif

aqua vi·tae \-'vīd·ē, -ī,tē\ *n* [ME *aqua vite,* fr. ML *aqua vitae,* lit., water of life; prob. fr. the use of brandy as a medicine] **1 :** ALCOHOL; *esp* **:** alcohol obtained by distilling vinous liquids **2 :** a strong liquor (as brandy or whiskey)

aq·ue·duct \'akwə,dəkt\ *n* -s [L *aquaeductus,* fr. *aquae* (gen. of *aqua* water) + *ductus* leading, conducting — more at ISLAND, DUCT] **1 a :** a conduit or artificial channel for conveying water; *esp* **:** one for carrying a large quantity of water which flows by gravitation **b** *or* **aqueduct bridge :** a structure for conveying a canal over a river or hollow **2 :** a canal or passage in a part or organ

aqueduct of fal·lo·pi·us \-fə'lōpēəs\ *usu cap F* [trans. of NL *aquaeductus Fallopii,* after Gabriel *Fallopius* — more at FALLOPIAN TUBE] **:** FACIAL CANAL

aqueduct of syl·vi·us \-'silvēəs\ *usu cap S* [trans. of NL *aquaeductus Sylvii,* after *Sylvius* (Jacques Dubois) †1555 Fr. anatomist] **:** a channel connecting the third and fourth ventricles of the brain

aque·ous \'ākwēəs, 'ak-\ *adj* [ML *aqueus,* fr. L *aqua* + *-eus* -eous] **1 a :** of, relating to, or having the characteristics of water **:** WATERY ⟨the ~ vapor of the air —John Tyndall⟩ **b :** made from, with, or by means of water ⟨~ solutions⟩ **c :** produced by the action of water ⟨~ deposits⟩ **2 :** of or relating to the aqueous humor — **aque·ous·ly** *adv*

aqueous ammonia *n* **:** AMMONIA WATER

aqueous extract *n* **:** an extract prepared by evaporating a watery solution of the soluble principles of a vegetable drug (as licorice) to a semisolid or solid consistency

aqueous humor *n* **:** a limpid fluid occupying the space between the crystalline lens and the cornea of the eye

aqueous meteor *n* **:** a meteor consisting of rain, hail, snow, or dew

aqueous rock *n* **:** a sedimentary rock deposited by or in water — compare EOLIAN

aqui- *also* **aqua-** *comb form* [L *aqui-,* fr. *aqua* — more at ISLAND] **:** water ⟨*aqui*culture⟩ ⟨*aqui*ferous⟩ ⟨*aqua*cade⟩

aq·ui·clude \'akwə,klüd, 'äk-\ *n* -s [*aqui-* + L *cludere, claudere* to close, shut up, block up — more at CLOSE] **:** a geologic formation or stratum that confines water in an adjacent aquifer

aq·ui·cul·tur·al \¦akwə¦-\ *adj* **:** of, relating to, or involving the methods of aquiculture

aq·ui·cul·ture \"==,-\ *or* **aq·ua·cul·ture** \"\ *n* -s [*aqui-* or *aqua-* + *-culture* (as in *agriculture*] **1 a :** the art of cultivating the natural produce of water **b :** the raising or fattening of fish in enclosed ponds **2 :** HYDROPONICS

aq·ui·fer *also* **aq·ua·fer** \'akwəfə(r)\ *n* -s [NL, fr. L *aqui-* or *aqua* + *-fer*] **:** a water-bearing bed or stratum of permeable rock, sand, or gravel capable of yielding considerable quantities of water to wells or springs — **aquif·er·ous** \ə'kwifərəs\ *adj*

aquifer spring *n* **:** a spring whose water rises from an aquifer

aq·ui·fo·li·a·ce·ae \,akwə,fōlē'āsē,ē\ *n pl, cap* [NL, fr. *Aquifolium,* type genus (fr. L, holly tree, fr. *aqui-* — fr. *acer* sharp — + *folium* leaf) + *-aceae* — more at EDGE, BLADE] **:** a family of widely distributed shrubs and trees (order Sapindales) having alternate simple often evergreen leaves, small dioecious flowers usu. in axillary clusters, and berrylike drupes — see ILEX — **aq·ui·fo·li·a·ceous** \¦==,==¦āshəs\ *adj*

aq·ui·fuge \'==,fyüj\ *n* -s [prob. fr. *aqui-* + *-fuge* (as in *refuge*)] **:** AQUICLUDE

aq·ui·la \'akwələ\ *n, cap* [NL, fr. L, eagle] **:** a cosmopolitan genus of eagles including a number of typical forms with the legs feathered to the toes (as the golden eagle)

aq·ui·la·ria \,akwə'la(a)rēə\ *n, cap* [NL (prob. approximate trans. of F *bois d'aigle* agalloch), fr. L *aquila* + NL *-aria* — more at EAGLEWOOD] **:** a genus of Asiatic trees (family Thymelaeaceae) having lanceolate leaves and nearly sessile umbels of flowers — see AGALLOCH

aq·ui·lege \'==,lēj\ *n* -s [NL *aquilegia*] **:** COLUMBINE 1

aq·ui·le·gia \,==¦lēj(ē)ə\ *n* [NL, fr. *aquilegia, aquileia* columbine] **1** *cap* **:** a genus of herbs (family Ranunculaceae) having irregular showy spurred flowers — see COLUMBINE **2** -s **:** COLUMBINE 1

aquil·i·an \ə'kwilēən\ *adj, usu cap* [L *Aquilianus,* fr. C. *Aquilius* Gallus 1st cent. B.C. Roman jurist + L *-anus* -an] **:** arising from or governed by a statute of the Roman republic with respect to wrongful damage to property — used of a fault or liability in civil and Roman law

aquilian stipulation *n, usu cap A* **:** a stipulation in civil and Roman law whereby an obligation can be reduced to a stipulation and then discharged by an acceptilation

aq·ui·line \'akwə,līn, -,lən\ *adj* [L *aquilinus,* fr. *aquila* eagle + *-inus* -ine — more at EAGLE] **1 :** of, belonging to, or like an eagle **2 :** curving or hooked like an eagle's beak **:** PROMINENT ⟨an ~ nose⟩ ⟨the ~ profile of a Roman senator —Ellen Glasgow⟩ — **aq·ui·lin·i·ty** \,==¦linəd·ē, -ətē, -i\ *n* -ES

aqui·li·no \,äkwə'lēnō\ *n* -s [It, fr. *aquila* eagle, fr. L] **:** any of several silver coins having the device of an eagle and issued by various Italian states; *esp* **:** the one first issued by Padua in the 13th century

aqui·nist \ə'kwīnəst\ *n* -s *usu cap* [Thomas *Aquinas* †1274, It. scholastic philosopher + E *-ist*] **:** a follower of or specialist in the study of St. Thomas Aquinas **:** THOMIST

¹**aq·ui·ta·ni·an** \¦akwə¦tānēən, -nyən\ *adj, usu cap* [*Aquitania,* Roman division of southwestern Gaul + E *-ian*] **1 :** of or relating to Aquitania **2 :** of or relating to a subdivision of the European Oligocene

²**aquitanian** \"\ *n* -s *cap* **1 :** a native or inhabitant of Aquitania **2 :** the Aquitanian geologic stage

aquiv·er \ə'-\ *adj* [¹*a-* + *quiver,* v.] **:** QUIVERING, TREMBLING

aq·uo \'a(,)kwō, 'ä-\ *adj* [*aquo-*] **:** of or relating to compounds derived from water ⟨lithium hydroxide LiOH is an ~ base⟩ — compare AMMONO

aquo- *comb form* [ISV, fr. L *aqua* water + ISV *-o-*] **1 :** containing a molecule of water as part of a coordination complex ⟨hexa*aquo*cobalt(III) chloride $[Co(H_2O)_6]Cl_3$⟩ **2 :** derived from water — in names of chemical compounds ⟨*aquo*carbonic acid $OC(OH)_2$⟩; compare AMMONO- 2

aquo ion *n* **1 :** a complex ion containing one or more water molecules **2 :** an ion formed by aquation

aq·uo·me·ter *also* **aq·ua·me·ter** \'akwə,mēd·ə(r), ə'kwä-məd·-\ *n* [*aquometer* fr. L *aqua* water + E *-o-* + *-meter; aquameter* fr. *aqua-* + *-meter*] **:** PULSOMETER

aquos·i·ty \ə'kwäsəd·ē, ä'-\ *n* -ES [LL *aquositas,* fr. L *aquosus* aqueous (fr. *aqua* + *-osus* -ose) + *-itas* -ity] **:** the quality or state of being moist or wet **:** WATERINESS

aq·uo·ti·za·tion \,akwəd·ə'zāshən, -wə,tī'z-\ *n* -s **:** AQUATION

aq·uo·tize \'akwə,tīz\ *vi* -ED/-ING/-S [*aquo-* + connective *-t-* + *-ize*] **:** to undergo aquotization

ar \'är, 'á\ *n* -s [ME] **:** the letter *r*

-ar \ə(r) *sometimes* ,är *or* ,á\ *adj suffix* [ME *-ar, -er,* fr. OF & L; OF *-er,* fr. L *-aris,* alter. (after bases containing *l*) of *-alis* -al] **:** of or belonging to ⟨linear⟩ ⟨molecular⟩ ⟨nuclear⟩ ⟨polar⟩ **:** being ⟨spectacular⟩ ⟨triangular⟩ **:** resembling ⟨annular⟩ ⟨oracular⟩ — chiefly in words containing *l* and often accompanied by change of final postconsonantal *-le* of the base word to *-ul-* ⟨angular⟩ ⟨muscular⟩ ⟨titular⟩

ar *abbr* **1** area **2** argent; argentum **3** aromatic **4** arrival; arrive

AR *abbr* **1** account receivable **2** acknowledgment of receipt **3** all rail **4** all risks **5** analyzed reagent **6** [L *anno regni*] in the year of the reign **7** annual return **8** army regulation **9** autonomous republic

Ar *symbol* **1** argon **2** aryl

¹**ara** \'a(a)rə, 'ärə\ *n, cap* [NL, prob. modif. of Tupi *arara* macaw] **:** a genus of macaws containing the blue-and-yellow macaw and the military macaw

²**ara** \"\ *n* -s [origin unknown] **:** TEXTILE SCREW PINE

¹**ar·ab** \'arəb *also* 'er-; *usual or frequent in sense 2, chiefly old-fash in other senses* 'ā,rab *or* 'ā,raa(ə)b\ *n* -s [ME, fr. L *Arabus, Arabs,* fr. Gk *Arab-, Araps,* fr. Ar *'Arab*] **1** *cap* **a :** a member of the Semitic people of the Arabian peninsula, orig. of the Bedouin tribes in the north of the peninsula and east of Palestine **:** ²ARABIAN 1 **b :** a member of any Arabic-speaking people **c :** a tent-dwelling nomadic Arab as distinguished from the oasis or town dweller **2** *sometimes cap* **a :** STREET ARAB **b** *dial* **:** a street peddler or house-to-house peddler of fruits and vegetables **3** *usu cap* **:** a horse of the stock used

by the natives of Arabia, adjacent regions of Asia, and parts of northern Africa; *specif* **:** a horse of a breed noted for its graceful build, speed, intelligence, and spirit and often used as sires to improve or modify other stocks — compare THOROUGHBRED 1 **4** *also* **arab brown** *often cap A* **:** a strong brown that is yellower, less strong, and slightly lighter than average russet and yellower and paler than average copper brown — called also *rugby tan*

²**arab** \"\ *adj, usu cap* **:** of, relating to, or characteristic of the Arabs **:** ARABIAN

arab- *or* **arabo-** *comb form* [ISV, fr. *arabinose*] **1 :** related to arabinose ⟨*arabo*ascorbic acid⟩ **2** *arabo-, usu ital* **:** having the stereochemical arrangement of atoms or groups found in arabinose ⟨D-*arabo*-3-hexulose⟩

¹**ara·ba** \ˈarəbə\ *also* **aro·ba** \"\ *or* **ar·ba** \ˈärbə\ *n* -s [Russ & Turk; Russ *arba*, fr. Turk *araba*] **:** a carriage (as a cab or coach) used in Turkey and neighboring countries

²**ar·a·ba** \ˈarəbə\ *n* -s [Pg, prob. fr. Tupi] **:** a So. American howler monkey (*Alouatta straminea*)

ar·a·ban \ˈarəˌban\ *n* -s [*arab-* + *-an*] **:** a pentosan yielding arabinose on hydrolysis

ar·a·bel·la \ˌarəˈbelə\ *n, cap* [NL] **:** a common genus of slender cylindrical polychaete worms

¹**ar·a·besque** \ˌarəˈbesk *also* ˌer-\ *adj* [F, fr. It *arabesco*, fr. *arabesco* Arabic, made or done in the Arabic fashion, fr. *Arabo* Arab (fr. L *Arabus*) + *-esco* -esque — more at ARAB] **:** relating to or exhibiting the style of ornament called arabesque ⟨~ frescoes⟩

²**arabesque** \"\ *n* -s **1 a :** an ornament or a style of ornamentation found in painting, low-relief carving, mosaic, and textile design that employs flower, foliage, or fruit and sometimes animal and figural outlines or forms so as to produce an intricate pattern of interlaced lines sometimes geometric and angular in character (as in Islamic art) and sometimes curviform and flowing (as in Renaissance decoration) **b :** a linear design motif of the kind occurring in arabesque ornament **2 :** musical embellishment; *specif* **:** a passage of music suggestive of an arabesque **3 :** a posture (as in ballet dancing) in which the body is bent forward from the hip on one leg with the corresponding arm extended forward and the other arm and leg backward in a line parallel to the floor

arabesque 1

³**arabesque** \"\ *vt* -ED/-ING/-S [²*arabesque*] **:** to ornament with or in the style of arabesques

arabesque spin *n* **:** a forward or backward skating spiral done in arabesque position

¹**ara·bi·an** \əˈrābēən *also* -byən\ *adj, usu cap* [*Arabia*, peninsula in southwestern Asia + E *-an*] **:** of, relating to, or characteristic of Arabia or Arabians ⟨*Arabian* nomads⟩

²**arabian** \"\ *n* -s *cap* **1 :** a native or inhabitant of Arabia **2 :** ARAB 3

arabian baboon *n, usu cap A* **:** SACRED BABOON

arabian brown *n, often cap A* **:** a moderate to strong brown that is redder and slightly darker than oak and darker than Vassar tan

arabian camel *n, usu cap A* **:** the one-humped camel (*Camelus dromedarius*) of western Asia and northern Africa — called also *dromedary*

arabian coffee *n, usu cap A* **:** a large evergreen shrub or small tree (*Coffea arabica*) native to tropical Africa but widely cultivated in a number of horticultural varieties in tropical and subtropical regions for its seeds which form most of the coffee of commerce

arabian gum *n, usu cap A* **:** KORDOFAN GUM

arabian horse *n, usu cap A* **:** ARAB 3

arabian hyrax *n, usu cap A* **:** SYRIAN HYRAX

arabian jasmine *or* **arabian jessamine** *n, usu cap A* **:** an East Indian vine (*Jasminum sambac*) cultivated for its profuse fragrant white flowers

arabian red *n, often cap A* **:** INDIA RED

arabian senna *n, usu cap A* **:** an Arabian form of senna derived from a shrub (*Cassia acutifolia*)

arabian tea *n, usu cap A* **:** KAT

¹**ar·a·bic** \ˈarəbik *also* ˈer-\ *adj, usu cap* [ME *arabik*, fr. MF *arabic*, fr. L *Arabicus*, fr. *Arabus* Arab + *-icus* -ic — more at ARAB] **1 :** of, relating to, or characteristic of Arabia **2 :** of, relating to, or characteristic of the Arabs **3 :** of, relating to, characteristic of, or constituting the language Arabic **4 :** of, relating to, constituting, or written in the Arabic alphabet

²**arabic** \"\ *n* -s *cap* [ME *arabik*, fr. MF *arabic*, fr. *arabic*, adj.] **:** a Semitic language orig. of the Arabs of the Hejaz and Nejd that is now the prevailing speech of Arabia, Jordan, Lebanon, Syria, Iraq, Egypt, and parts of northern Africa and that has numerous dialects but in the written form usu. conforms to the classical standards of the Koran — see AFRO-ASIATIC LANGUAGES table

arab·i·ca coffee *also* **arabica** \əˈrabəkə\ *n, often cap A* [NL *arabica* (specific epithet of *Coffea arabica*), fr. L, fem. of *Arabicus*] **:** coffee (sense 2) produced from Arabian coffee — compare MOCHA

arabic alphabet *n, usu cap 1st A* **:** the alphabet of 28 letters derived from the Aramaic which is used for writing Arabic and also with adaptations for numerous other languages of Asia, Africa, and Europe of peoples professing the Muslim religion — see ALPHABET table

arabic architecture *n, usu cap 1st A* **:** the Saracenic architecture of the Arab dominions established in Syria and Egypt during the 1st century after the hegira (A.D. 622-722)

arab·i·cism \əˈrabəˌsizəm\ *n* -s *usu cap* [*arabic* + *-ism*] **:** ARABISM 1

arab·i·cize \-ˌsīz\ *vt* -ED/-ING/-S *often cap* [*arabic* + *-ize*] **1 :** to adapt (a language or elements of language) to the phonetic or structural pattern of Arabic **2 :** ARABIZE 1

arabic numeral *or* **arabic figure** *n, often cap A* **:** one of the number symbols 0, 1, 2, 3, 4, 5, 6, 7, 8, 9 conventionally so written for enumeration and for arithmetical computation — called also *Hindu numeral;* see NUMBER table

ar·a·bi·dopsis \ˌarəbəˈdäpsəs\ *n, cap* [NL, fr. *Arabid-*, *Arabis* + *-opsis*] **:** a small genus of annual or biennial herbs (family Brassicaceae) of north temperate regions with basal rosettes of petioled leaves, cauline leaves short-petioled or clasping, and flowers having white, purplish, or sometimes yellow petals — see MOUSE-EAR CRESS

ar·a·bil·i·ty \ˌarəˈbiləd-ē, -ətē, -i *also* ˌer-\ *n* -ES **:** the state of being arable

arab·i·nose \əˈrabəˌnōs, ˈarəb-\ *n* -s [ISV *arabin*, the solid principle in gum arabic (fr. — *gum* — *arabic* + *-in*) + *-ose*] **:** a crystalline aldose sugar $C_5H_{10}O_5$ of the pentose class obtained in the dextrorotatory L-form esp. from cherry-tree gum or mesquite gum or prepared synthetically in the levorotatory D-form from D-glucose — **arab·i·nos·ic** \əˌrabəˈnōsik, ˌarəb-\ *adj*

ar·a·bin·o·side \ˌarəˈbinəˌsīd\ *n* -s [*arabinose* + *-ide*] **:** a glycoside that yields arabinose on hydrolysis

ar·a·bis \ˈarəbəs\ *n, cap* [NL, fr. Gk *arabid-*, *arabis*, a brassicaceous plant, prob. fr. *Arab-*, *Araps* Arab; fr. its ability to grow in rocky or sandy soil] **:** a large genus of herbs (family Cruciferae) with white or purple flowers and flat siliques with nerved valves — see SICKLEPOD, TOWER MUSTARD

ar·ab·ism \ˈarəˌbizəm\ *n* -s *usu cap* [²*Arab* + *-ism*] **1 :** a characteristic feature of Arabic occurring in another language **2 :** devotion to Arab interests, customs, culture, ideas, or ideals

ar·ab·ist \-bəst\ *n* -s *usu cap* [²*Arab* + *-ist*] **:** a specialist in the Arabic language or in the culture of the Arabic-speaking peoples

arab·i·tol \əˈrabəˌtōl, -ōl\ *n* -s [*arab-* + *-itol*] **:** a sweet crystalline pentahydroxy alcohol $C_5H_7(OH)_5$ obtained by the reduction of arabinose

ar·ab·i·za·tion \ˌarəbəˈzāshən\ *n* -s *usu cap* **:** the act or process of arabizing or of being arabized ⟨linguistic *Arabization* —George Antonius⟩

ar·ab·ize \ˈarəˌbīz\ *vt* -ED/-ING/-S *often cap* [²*arab* + *-ize*] **1 a :** to cause to acquire Arab customs, manners, speech, or outlook **b :** to modify (a racial or national stock) by an admixture of Arab blood **2 :** ARABICIZE 1

¹**ar·a·ble** \ˈarəbəl *also* ˈer-\ *adj* [MF or L; MF *arable*, fr. L *arabilis*, fr. *arare* to plow + *-abilis* -able — more at EAR] **1 a :** capable of being plowed **:** fit for tillage and crop production ⟨~ land⟩ **b** *Brit* **:** engaged in or involving the production of cultivated crops ⟨~ farmer⟩ ⟨~ farming⟩ **c** *Brit, of crops* **:** requiring cultivation; *esp* **:** seeded and grown annually rather than from the regrowth of an established sod ⟨small grains or other ~ crops⟩ **2** *Brit, of livestock* **:** fed on cultivated crops (as roots) ⟨the ~ ewe going back on to the rough grazing —S.J.Watson⟩

²**arable** \"\ *n* -s **1 :** land that is tilled or tillable **2** *Brit* **:** TILLAGE

arabo- — see ARAB-

ar·a·bo·galactan \ˌarəˌbō+\ *n* -s [*arab-* + *galactan*] **:** a gummy substance that is found esp. in the wood of the western larch and that yields arabinose and galactose on hydrolysis

ar·a·bon·ic acid \ˌarəˈbänik-\ *n* [ISV *arab-* + *-onic*] **:** a crystalline acid $HOCH_2(CHOH)_3COOH$ obtained by oxidation of arabinose, dextrose, or levulose and used in synthesizing riboflavin

ar·a·ça \ˌarəˈsä\ *n* -s [Pg *araçá*, fr. Tupi] **:** a Brazilian timber tree (*Terminalia januarensis*) suggesting birch in its working properties

ar·a·can·ga \ˌarəˈkaŋgə\ *n* -s [Pg, fr. Tupi *araracanga*] **:** SCARLET MACAW

ara·ca·ri \ˌärəˈsärē\ *n* -s [Pg *araçari*, fr. Tupi] **:** any of several brilliantly colored tropical American toucans

ara·ce·ae \əˈrāsēˌē\ *n pl, cap* [NL, fr. *Arum*, type genus + *-aceae* — more at ARUM] **:** a family of plants (order Arales) chiefly of tropical distribution distinguished by having the flowers on a fleshy spadix subtended by a leafy spathe — **ara·ceous** \-shəs\ *adj*

arach *abbr* ARACHNOLOGY

ar·a·chide \ˈarəˌkīd, -ˌkəd\ *n* -s [F, fr. NL *Arachid-*, *Arachis*] **:** PEANUT 1

ar·a·chid·ic acid \ˌarəˈkidik-\ *also* **arach·ic acid** \əˈrakik-\ *n* [ISV *arachid-* or *arach-* (fr. NL *Arachid-* *Arachis*) + *-ic*] **:** a white crystalline saturated fatty acid $CH_3(CH_2)_{18}COOH$ found in the form of esters esp. in vegetable fats and oils (as peanut oil) — called also *eicosanoic acid*

ar·a·chi·don·ic acid \ˌarəkəˈdänik-\ *n* [ISV *arachidic* + *-onic*] **:** a liquid unsaturated acid $C_{19}H_{31}COOH$ occurring in most animal fats (as in the phosphatides of beef adrenal glands and the lipides of the liver) and considered essential in animal nutrition

ar·a·chin \ˈarəkən\ *n* -s [ISV *arachic* + *-in*] **:** a globulin constituting the chief protein of the peanut

ar·a·chis \-kəs\ *n* [NL, perh. modif. of Gk *arakis* chickling vetch, dim. of *arakos* chickling vetch; perh. akin to L *arinca*, a cereal grain] **1** *cap* **:** a small genus of mostly Brazilian herbs (family Leguminosae) with yellow flowers and pods that ripen underground — see PEANUT **2** -ES **:** a plant of the genus *Arachis*

arachis oil *n* **:** PEANUT OIL

arachn- *or* **arachno-** *comb form* [NL & Gk; NL, fr. Gk, fr. *arachnē*; perh. akin to L *aranea* spider, Gk *arkys* net] **1 :** spider ⟨*arachn*ism⟩ ⟨*arachno*dactyly⟩ ⟨*arachno*logy⟩ **2 :** arachnoid membrane ⟨*arachn*itis⟩

ar·ach·nac·tis \ˌaˌrakˈnaktəs\ *n, pl* **arach·nac·ti·nes** \əˌrakˌnakˈtī(ˌ)nēz\ [NL, fr. *arachn-* + Gk *aktis* ray — more at ACTIN-] **:** a free-swimming larva of certain actinians

arach·ne·an \əˈraknēən, ¦aˌrak¦nēən\ *adj* [*arachn-* + *-ean*] **:** having the lightness or fineness of texture of a spider's web **:** GOSSAMER

arach·ni·cide \əˈraknəˌsīd\ *n* -s [*arachnid* + *-cide*] **:** a substance that kills arachnids (as mites)

arach·nid \əˈraknəd\ *n* -s [NL *Arachnida*] **:** one of the Arachnida

arach·ni·da \-nədə\ *n pl, cap* [NL, fr. *arachn-* + *-ida*] **1 :** a large class of arthropods including scorpions, spiders, mites, and related forms all lacking wings and free first antennae and having highly modified prehensile second antennae and most being also air-breathing by means of tracheae or book lungs and having head and thorax fused to form a cephalothorax that bears six pairs of appendages consisting of four pairs of walking legs, a pair of pedipalpi variously specialized in different groups, and a pair of buccal chelicerae often provided with poison glands **2** *in former classifications* **:** a more extensive group including the Arachnida together with the king crabs, tongue worms, sea spiders, water bears, and sometimes the extinct eurypterids

arach·nid·ism \-nəˌdizəm\ *n* -s [*arachnid* + *-ism*] **:** poisoning caused by the bite or sting of an arachnid (as a spider, tick, or scorpion); *esp* **:** a syndrome marked by extreme pain and muscular rigidity due to the bite of a black widow spider

ar·ach·nid·i·um \ˌaˌrakˈnidēəm\ *n, pl* **arachnid·ia** \-ēə\ [NL, fr. *Arachnida* + *-ium*] **:** the apparatus by which a spider's web is produced consisting of the silk glands and their ducts and the spinnerets

arach·nid·ol·o·gy \əˌrakˈnīˈdäləjē\ *n* -ES [*arachnid* + *-ology*] **:** ARACHNOLOGY

ar·ach·ni·tis \ˌaˌrakˈnīd-əs\ *n* -ES [NL, fr. *arachn-* + *-itis*] **:** ARACHNOIDITIS

arach·no·dac·ty·ly \əˌraknōˈdaktəlē\ *n* -ES [*arachn-* + *-dactyly* (fr. NL *-dactylia*)] **:** a hereditary abnormality characterized by excessive length of the long bones (as of the fingers and toes) and usu. associated with other abnormalities

¹**arach·noid** \əˈrakˌnȯid\ *n* -s [NL *arachnoides*, fr. Gk *arachnoeidēs* cobweblike, fr. *arachn-* + *-eidēs* -oid] **:** a thin membrane of the brain and spinal cord that lies between the dura mater and the pia mater

²**arachnoid** \"\ *adj* **:** of or relating to the arachnoid membrane

³**arachnoid** \"\ *adj* [*arachn-* + *-oid*] **:** of, relating to, or characterizing the Arachnida **:** like arachnids

⁴**arachnoid** \"\ *n* -s **:** ARACHNID; *broadly* **:** any of various invertebrate animals that resemble or are related to arachnids

⁵**arachnoid** \"\ *adj* [Gk *arachnoeidēs*] **:** resembling a spider's web; *specif* **:** covered with or composed of soft loose hairs or fibers — used esp. of plants ⟨an ~ leaf⟩

ar·ach·noi·dal \ˌaˌrak¦nȯidᵊl\ *also* **ar·ach·noi·de·an** \-dēən\ *adj* **:** ²ARACHNOID

¹**ar·ach·noi·dea** \ˌaˌrakˈnȯidēə\ [NL, fr. Gk *arachnoeidēs*] *syn of* ARACHNIDA

²**arachnoidea** \"\ *n* -s [NL, alter. of *arachnoides* — more at ARACHNOID] **:** ¹ARACHNOID

arachnoid granulation *n* **:** PACCHIONIAN BODY

arach·noid·ism \əˈrakˌnȯiˌdizəm\ *n* -s [⁴*arachnoid* + *-ism*] **:** ARACHNIDISM

arach·noid·i·tis \əˌrakˌnȯiˈdīd-əs\ *n* -ES [NL, fr. *arachnoides* or *arachnoidea* + *-itis*] **:** inflammation of the arachnoid membrane

ar·ach·nol·o·gist \ˌaˌrakˈnäləjəst\ *n* -s **:** a specialist in arachnology

ar·ach·nol·o·gy \-jē\ *n* -ES [ISV *arachn-* + *-logy*] **:** the branch of zoology that deals with spiders and other arachnids

arach·no·ly·sin \əˌraknōˈlīsᵊn\ *n* -s [ISV *arachn-* + *-lysin*] **:** a hemolysin secreted by certain spiders

arach·no·morph \əˈraknōˌmȯrf\ *adj* [NL *Arachnomorphae*] **:** of or relating to the Arachnomorphae

arach·no·mor·phae \ə¦=ˈmȯrˌfē\ *n pl, cap* [NL, fr. *arachn-* + *-morphae*] *in some classifications* **:** a suborder of Araneida including the great majority of spiders and distinguished by having the poison fangs moving in and out and the venom glands extending beyond the base of the fangs

ar·ach·noph·a·gous \ˌaˌrakˈnäfəgəs\ *adj* [*arachn-* + *-phagous*] **:** feeding on spiders

ar·ach·no·pia \-ˈnōpēə\ *n* -s [NL, fr. *arachn-* + *pia* (membrane)] **:** PIA-ARACHNOID

ar·a·did \ˈarədəd, -ˌdid\ *n* -s [NL *Arididae*] **:** one of the Aradidae

arad·i·dae \əˈradəˌdē\ *n pl, cap* [NL, fr. *Aradus*, type genus (perh. fr. Gk *arados* disturbance) + *-idae*] **:** a family of small flat narrow-headed bugs usu. living under bark and including a So. American species capable of inflicting severe bites

arae·o·style \əˈrēəˌstīl\ *or* **are·o·style** \", ˈareō-\ *n* -s [earlier *areostylos*, fr. L *araeostylos*, adj., having such an intercolumniation, fr. Gk *araiostylos*, fr. *araios* thin, weak, intermittent + *stylos* pillar — more at STEER] **:** an intercolumniation of usu. four or more diameters — see INTERCOLUMNIATION illustration

araeo·systyle \ə¦rēə+\ *or* **areo·systle** \", ˈarē(ˌ)ō+\ *n* -s [F *aréosystyle*, fr. Gk *araios* + F *systyle*, fr. L *systylos* — more at SYSTYLE] **:** an intercolumniation that is alternately a systyle and an araeostyle

ar·a·go·ne·sa \ˌarəgōˈnāsə, -āzə\ *n* -s *often cap* [Sp (*jota*) *aragonesa* Aragonese jota; *aragonesa*, fem. of *aragonés*] **:** a Spanish couple folk dance from Aragon — called also *jota aragonesa*

¹**ar·a·go·nese** \ˌarəgə¦nēz, -ēs\ *adj, usu cap* [Sp *aragonés*, fr. *Aragón* Aragon, region and ancient kingdom in northeastern Spain + Sp *-és* -ese (fr. L *-ensis*)] **:** of or relating to the Aragon region and former kingdom of northeastern Spain or to its inhabitants

²**aragonese** \"\ *n, pl* **aragonese** *cap* **1 :** a native or inhabitant of Aragon **2 :** the dialect of Spanish spoken in Aragon

arag·o·nite \əˈragəˌnīt, ˈarəgəˌnīt\ *n* -s [G *aragonit*, fr. *Aragon*, its locality + G *-it* -ite] **:** a mineral consisting like calcite of calcium carbonate $CaCO_3$ but differing from calcite esp. in its orthorhombic crystallization, greater density, and less distinct cleavage and occurring most commonly in beds of gypsum and of iron ore (hardness 3.5-4, sp. gr. 2.93-2.95)

ar·a·gon spar \ˈarəˌgän-\ *n* -s *usu cap A & sometimes cap S* **:** ARAGONITE

ara·gua·nay *also* **ara·gua·ne** *or* **ara·gua·ney** \ˌärəgwäˈnā\ *n* -s [AmerSp *araguaney*] **:** any of several trees of the genus *Tecoma*

ara·gua·to \ˌärəˈgwäˌdō\ *n* -ES [modif. of F *araguate*, of Cariban origin — more at ALOUATTE] **:** URSINE HOWLER

arahat *or* **arahant** *often cap, var of* ARHAT

¹**arain** \ˈärən\ *n* -s [ME *arain*, *irain*, *aran*, fr. MF & L; MF *araigne*, *iraigne*, fr. L *aranea* — more at ARACHN-] *now dial* **:** SPIDER

²**arain** \əˈrīn\ *n* -s *usu cap* **1 :** a Muslim people of the Punjab region in India **2 :** a member of the Arain people

araire \əˈre(ə)r\ *n* -s [F, fr. Prov, fr. L *aratrum*, fr. *arare* to plow — more at EAR] **:** a primitive plow used in southern Europe

araise *vt* -ED/-ING/-S [ME *araisen*, *areisen*, fr. *a-* (perfective prefix) + *raisen*, *reisen* to raise — more at ABEAR, RAISE] *obs* **:** to raise esp. from the dead

arak *var of* ARRACK

ar·a·ka·nese \ˌarəkə¦nēz, -ēs\ *n, pl* **arakanese** *usu cap* [*Arakan*, division of Lower Burma + E *-ese*] **1 a :** a Burmese people of the western Arakan coastlands of Burma who have been strongly influenced by contact with Muslim culture in India **b :** a member of such people **2 :** the language of the Arakanese

ara·ka·wa·ite \ˌärəˈkäwəˌīt\ *n* -s [*Arakawa* mine, Akita prov., Japan, its locality + E *-ite*] **:** VESZELYITE

arake \əˈrāk\ *adj* [¹*a-* + *rake*] **:** inclined from the perpendicular **:** RAKED

ara·les \əˈrāˌlēz\ *n pl, cap* [NL, fr. *Arum* genus of araceous plants + *-ales* — more at ARUM] **:** an order of monocotyledonous woody or herbaceous plants that are usu. sympodial with cyclic flowers on a spadix — see ARACEAE, LEMNACEAE

ara·lia \əˈrālēə, -lyə\ *n* [NL] **1** *cap* **:** a large genus (the type of the family Araliaceae) of widely distributed often aromatic herbs, shrubs, and trees with compound leaves and umbellate flowers — see HERCULES'-CLUB, SPIKENARD 2 **2** -s **:** a plant of the genus *Aralia* **3 :** the dried rhizome and roots of a plant (*Aralia racemosa*) used as a diaphoretic and aromatic

ara·li·a·ce·ae \əˌrālēˈāsēˌē\ *n pl, cap* [NL, fr. *Aralia*, type genus + *-aceae*] **:** a widely distributed family of plants (order Umbellales) with flowers typically pentamerous and umbellate and fruit a drupe or berry — compare GINSENG, HEDERA

ara·li·a·ceous \ə¦rālē¦āshəs\ *adj* [NL *Araliaceae* + E *-ous*] **:** of or belonging to the Araliaceae

ara·li·ad \əˈrālēˌad\ *n* -s [NL *Aralia* + E *-ad*] **:** an araliaceous plant

ar·al·i·phat·ic \ˌaˌraləˈfad-ik\ *adj* [*aryl* + *aliphatic*] **:** of or relating to an essentially aliphatic compound containing one or more aryl groups ⟨~ amines⟩

ar·al·koxy \ˌarəl¦käksē\ *adj* [*aralkoxy-*, fr. *aralkyl* + *oxy-*] **:** of, relating to, or containing a univalent radical composed of an aralkyl group united with one atom of oxygen

ar·al·kyl \aˈralˌkil\ *n* -s [ISV *aryl* + *alkyl*] **:** an aryl-substituted alkyl radical ⟨benzyl is the best-known ~⟩

ar·al·kyl·ate \ˌaˈralkəˌlāt, -lət, *usu* -d·+V\ *vt* -ED/-ING/-S **:** to introduce aralkyl into (a compound)

¹**ar·a·mae·an** *also* **ar·a·me·an** \ˌarə¦mēən\ *adj, usu cap* [L *Aramaeus* (fr. Gk *Aramaios*, fr. Heb *'Ărām* Aram, ancient name for Syria) + E *-an*] **1 :** of, relating to, or characteristic of ancient Aram or the Aramaeans **2 :** ARAMAIC

²**aramaean** *also* **aramean** \"\ *n, pl* **aramaeans** *or* **arameans** *usu cap* **1 :** a member of a Semitic people that settled in the second millennium B.C. in Syria and Upper Mesopotamia, where they established a number of city-states and came to be engaged extensively in overland trade **2 :** ARAMAIC

¹**ar·a·ma·ic** \ˌarə¦māik\ *adj, usu cap* [Gk *Aramaios* + E *-ic*] **:** of, relating to, characteristic of, or composed in Aramaic

²**aramaic** \"\ *n* -s *cap* **:** a Semitic language of which documents are known from as early as the 9th century B.C., orig. the speech of the Aramaeans but later used extensively in southwest Asia as a commercial lingua franca and governmental language and adopted as their customary speech by various non-Aramaean peoples including the Jews among whom it replaced Hebrew after the Babylonian exile, developing into an eastern and a western type, each having various dialects some of which are often regarded as separate languages, but ultimately being largely displaced by Arabic as a consequence of the Muslim conquests, only neo-Syriac of the eastern group and Modern Western Aramaic of the western group being still spoken

aramaic alphabet *n, usu cap 1st A* **1 :** an extinct North Semitic alphabet dating from the 9th century B.C. which was for several centuries the commercial alphabet of southwest Asia and was the parent of the Syriac, Arabic, and numerous other alphabets **2 :** the square Hebrew alphabet as distinguished from the early Hebrew alphabet

ar·a·ma·ism \ˌarəˈmāˌizəm, ˈarə(ˌ)mā-\ *also* **ar·a·ma·i·cism** \ˌarəˈmāəˌsizəm\ *n* -s *usu cap* [¹*aramaic* + *-ism*] **:** a characteristic feature of Aramaic occurring in another language

ar·a·ma·ize \-ˌīz\ *vt* -ED/-ING/-S *often cap* [¹*aramaic* + *-ize*] **1 :** to tincture with Aramaisms ⟨*aramaized* Greek⟩ **2 :** to cause to become Aramaean in culture or Aramaic in language ⟨all Syria and a great part of Mesopotamia became thoroughly *Aramaized* —David Diringer⟩

ar·a·may·o·ite \ˌarəˈmīəˌwīt\ *n* -s [F. A. *Aramayo*, 20th cent. mine director in Bolivia + E *-ite*] **:** a black metallic mineral consisting of silver antimony bismuth sulfide $Ag(Sb,Bi)S_2$ related in crystal structure to galena

ara·mi·na \ˌarəˈmēnə\ *n* -s [Pg, dim. of *arame* wire, fr. LL *aeramen* copper, fr. L *aes* copper, ore — more at ORE] **:** the fiber of the Caesar weed — called also *Congo jute*

ara·ña \əˈrānyə\ *n* -s [AmerSp, fr. Sp, spider, fr. L *aranea* — more at ARACHN-] **:** a Mexican 2-wheeled horse-drawn cab

araña del mar \-ˌdelˈmär\ *n* [Sp, lit., spider of the sea] **:** ARROW CRAB

aranda *or* **aranta** *usu cap, var of* ARUNTA

ara·nea \əˈrānēə\ *n, cap* [NL, fr. L, spider — more at ARACHN-] **:** a genus of orb-weaving spiders (family Argiopidae) including the common garden spiders

ara·ne·ae \-nēˌē\ [NL, fr. pl. of *Aranea*] *syn of* ARANEIDA

araneae ther·a·pho·sae \-ˌtherəˈfōˌsē\ *n pl, cap A* [NL, theraphose *Araneae*] *in some classifications* **:** a division of spiders that comprises those with vertically articulated chelicerae and is equivalent to the Liphistiomorphae plus the Mygalomorphae

araneae ve·rae \-ˈviˌrē\ *n pl, cap A* [NL, lit., true spiders] *in some classifications* **:** a division of spiders that comprises those with laterally articulated chelicerae and is equivalent to the Apneumonomorphae, Dipneumonomorphae, and Hypochilomorphae

ara·ne·id \əˈrānēəd, -ˌid\ *n* -s [NL *Araneida*] **:** SPIDER 1

ar·a·ne·i·da \ˌarəˈnēədə\ *n pl, cap* [NL, fr. *Aranea* + *-ida*] **:** the order of Arachnida consisting of the spiders, all having the body divided into a cephalothorax and a short usu. unsegmented abdomen, the chelicerae modified into poison fangs, leglike pedipalpi, simple eyes, a web-spinning apparatus at the end of the abdomen, and respiratory lung sacs or tracheae in the abdomen — **ar·a·ne·i·dal** \¦==¦=əd°l\ *adj* — **ar·a·ne·i·dan** \-əd°n\ *adj or n*

ar·a·ne·i·form \¦==¦=ə,fȯrm\ *adj* [L *aranea* + E *-iform*] **:** like a spider

ar·a·ne·i·for·mes \,==,=='fȯr,mēz\ *also* **araneifor·mia** \-,mēə\ *n pl, cap* [*Araneiformes* fr. NL, fr. L *aranea* spider + NL *-iformes*; *Araneiformia* fr. NL, prob. alter. of *Araneiformes*] *in old classifications* **:** PYCNOGONIDA

ara·ne·i·na \ə,rā,nē'īnə\ *or* **ara·ne·oi·dea** \-'ȯidēə\ [NL, fr. *Aranea* + *-ina* or *-oidea*] *syn of* ARANEIDA

ara·ne·ol·o·gist \-'äləjəst\ *n* -S **:** a specialist in the study of spiders

ara·ne·ol·o·gy \-jē, -i\ *n* -ES [F *aranéologie*, fr. L *aranea* + F *-o-* + *-logie* -logy] **:** the branch of zoology that deals with spiders

ara·ne·o·morph \ə'rānēə,mȯrf\ *adj* [NL *Araneomorphae*] **:** ARACHNOMORPH

ara·ne·o·mor·phae \=,===='mȯr,fē\ [NL, fr. *araneo-* (fr. *Aranea*) + *-morphae*] *syn of* ARACHNOMORPHAE

ara·ne·ous \ə'rānēəs\ *also* **ara·ne·ose** \-,ōs\ *adj* [*araneous* prob. modif. (influenced by L *araneus* of a spider, fr. *aranea* spider) of L *araneosus*, fr. *aranea* spider + *-osus* -ose; *araneose* fr. L *araneosus*] **:** [5]ARACHNOID

ara·ne·us \-əs\ [NL, fr. L, of a spider, fr. *aranea* spider] *syn of* ARANEA

aran·ga \ə'räŋgə\ *n* -S [Tag] **1** *Philippines* **:** a tree of the genus *Homalium* (esp. *H. luzoniense*) **2** *Philippines* **:** the hard reddish wood of aranga

aran·ya·ka \ä'rənyəkə\ *n* -S *usu cap* [Skt *āraṇyaka*, lit., forest treatise] **:** one of a group of sacred Hindu writings composed between the Brahmanas and the Upanishads and used in Vedic ritual

ara·ona \,arə'ōnə\ *or* **ara·una** \,arə'ünə\ *n, pl* **araona** *or* **araonas** *or* **arauna** *or* **araunas** *usu cap* [Sp *araona* & Pg *araúna*, of AmerInd origin] **1 a :** a Tacanan people of northwest Bolivia and adjacent parts of Brazil **b :** a member of such people **2 :** the language of the Araona people

arap·a·hite \ə'rapə,hīt\ *n* -S [*Arapaho* + E *-ite*; fr. its discovery on land owned by Arapahos] **:** a basic basalt rock containing bytownite, augite, over 50 percent of magnetite, and abundant apatite

arap·a·ho *or* **arap·a·hoe** \ə'rapə,hō\ *n, pl* **arapaho** *or* **arapahos** *or* **arapahoe** *or* **arapahoes** *usu cap* [perh. fr. Crow *aa=raxpé-ahu*, lit., tattoo, fr. *aa-* with + *raxpé* skin + *-ahu* lots, many] **1 a :** an Algonquian people ranging over the plains region from southern Saskatchewan and Manitoba to New Mexico and Texas **b :** a member of such people **2 :** the Algonquian language of the Arapaho people

ar·a·pai·ma \,arə'pīmə\ *n* [NL, fr. Pg & Sp, pirarucu, of Tupian origin; akin to Mura *uarapáinu*] **1** *cap* **:** a genus of Osteoglossidae comprising the pirarucu **2** -S [Pg & Sp] **:** PIRARUCU

ar·a·pesh \'arə,pesh\ *n, pl* **arapesh** *or* **arapeshes** *usu cap* **1 :** a Papuan people inhabiting the Sepik district, Territory of New Guinea **2 :** a member of the Arapesh people

ar·a·pho·ros·tic \¦arəfə¦rästik\ *or* **ar·a·phos·tic** \¦==¦fästik\ *adj* [irreg., fr. Gk *arrhaphos* (fr. *a-* [2]a- + *-rhaphos*, fr. *rhaptein* to sew) + E *-ic* — more at RHAPSODY] **:** lacking seams **:** UNSEWED ⟨an ~ shoe⟩

ar·a·pon·ga \,arə'päŋgə\ *n* -S [Pg] **:** BELLBIRD a

ara·ri·ba \¦arərē¦bä\ *n* -S [Pg *araribá*, fr. Tupi] **1 :** any of several trees of the genus *Centrolobium* (family Leguminosae); *esp* **:** a Brazilian tree (*C. robustum*) — called also *zebrawood* **2 :** any of several trees of the genus *Sickingia* usu. with heavy dark red wood **3 :** the wood of an arariba tree

ara·ro·ba \,arə'rōbə\ *n* -S [Pg, of Tupian origin; akin to Tupi *araribá*] **1 :** GOA POWDER **2 :** ARARIBA

arastra *var of* ARRASTRA

ar·a·tin·ga \,arə'tiŋgə\ *n* [NL, fr. Pg] **1** *cap* **:** a genus of rather large chiefly green parrakeets of tropical America **2** -S **:** a parrakeet of the genus *Aratinga* **:** CONURE

arau \ä'raů\ *n, pl* **arau** *or* **araus** *usu cap* **1 :** a Papuan people of western New Guinea **2 :** a member of the Arau people

arauá \¦arə¦wä\ *n, pl* **arauá** *or* **arauás** *usu cap* [Sp *araua*, *arauá*, *aragua*, of AmerInd origin] **1 a :** a group of Indian peoples of western Brazil **b :** a member of one of these peoples **2 :** the language of the Arauá people considered by some Americanists to constitute an independent language family and by others to be a branch of Arawakan

arau·ca·na \ə,raů'kānə\ *n* -S *usu cap* [AmerSp, fr. fem. of *araucano* of Arauco, fr. *Arauco*, district in Chile + Sp *-ano* -an] **:** a chicken of a So. American breed distinguished by lack of tail feathers, by bushy tufts of feathers on each side of the head, and by the production of blue eggs

[1]**arau·ca·nian** \ə,raů'kānēən, -kā-, -nyən; ,a,rȯ'kān-\ *also* **arau·can** \ə'raůkən\ *or* **arau·ca·no** \ə,raů'kä(,)nō\ *n, pl* **araucanians** *also* **araucan** *or* **araucans** *or* **araucano** *or* **araucanos** *usu cap* [Sp *araucano*, fr. *Arauco*, locality (now a province) in Chile (fr. Araucan *ragh, raq, rau* clay + *ko, co* water) + *-ano* -an] **1 :** a member of a group of Indian peoples of south central Chile and adjacent regions of Argentina **2 :** the language of the Araucanian people, constituting an independent language family

[2]**araucanian** \"\ *adj, usu cap* **:** of or relating to Araucanian or Araucanians

ar·au·car·ia \,a,rȯ'ka(a)rēə\ *n* [NL, fr. *Arauco*, locality in Chile + NL *-aria*] **1** *cap* **:** a small genus of tall So. American or Australian trees (family Pinaceae) with branches usu. in whorls, stiff broad scalelike leaves, large cones, and edible seeds — see MONKEY PUZZLE, NORFOLK ISLAND PINE **2** -S **:** a plant of the genus *Araucaria* — **ar·au·car·i·an** \-ēən\ *adj*

ar·au·car·i·a·ce·ae \-,ka(a)rē'āsē,ē\ *n pl, cap* [NL, fr. *Araucaria*, type genus + *-aceae*] *in some classifications* **:** a family of plants comprising *Araucaria* and *Agathis* and often included in the Pinaceae

ar·au·car·i·ox·y·lon \-,ka(a)rē'äksə,län, -,lən\ *n* [NL, fr. *Araucaria* + *-o-* + *-xylon*] **1** *cap* **:** a genus of widely distributed fossil conifers of late Paleozoic to late Mesozoic time having a wood structure resembling that of modern araucarias **2 :** any of several fossil woods having a structure like that of modern araucarias

arau·jia \ə'rōjēə, -raůj-\ *n, cap* [NL, fr. Antônio de *Araujo* de Azevedo †1817 Port. statesman + NL *-ia*] **:** a small genus of So. American vines (family Asclepiadaceae) sometimes cultivated in greenhouses for their white or pink flowers

arauna *var of* ARAONA

ara·wa \'ärəwə\ *n, pl* **arawa** *or* **arawas** *cap* [Maori] **:** a Maori people of New Zealand

ar·a·wak \'arə,wäk, -,wak\ *n, pl* **arawak** *or* **arawaks** *usu cap* **1 a :** an Indian people or peoples of the Arawakan group formerly occupying most of the Greater Antilles but now scattered in small numbers along the coast of British Guiana **b :** a member of such people **2 :** the language of the Arawak people **3 :** ARAWAKAN

[1]**ar·a·wak·an** \¦==¦=kən\ *adj, usu cap* **:** of or belonging to Arawakan or the Arawakan peoples

[2]**arawakan** \"\ *n, pl* **arawakan** *or* **arawakans** *usu cap* **1 a :** a group of Indian peoples of Bolivia, Brazil, Colombia, Guiana, Paraguay, Peru, Venezuela, and, formerly, the West Indies whose languages constitute a large language family **b :** a member of such peoples **2 :** the language family of the Arawakan peoples

arba *var of* ARABA

ar·ba·cia \är'bāsēə\ *n* [NL, fr. *Arbaces* †*ab*848 B.C. king of Media + NL *-ia*] **1** *cap* **:** a genus of sea urchins (order Centrechinoida) having the ambulacral plates with three pairs of pores, the periproct covered by four triangular plates, the test rather low and stout, and the spines short with those near the mouth having enameled flattened tips **2** -S **:** a sea urchin of the genus *Arbacia*

ar·ba kan·foth *or* **arba kan·fot** \¦ärbə'känfəs, -,fōs, -,fōt\ *n* [Heb *arbaʽ kanphōth* four corners] **:** a rectangular strip of cloth that has fringes fastened to its four corners and has an opening for the head and is worn under the ordinary clothes by orthodox male Jews — compare TALLITH

ar·ba·lest \'ärbələst, -,lest\ *also* **ar·ba·list** \-,ləst, -,list\ *n* -S [ME *arbelast, arblast*, fr. OE *arblast*, fr. OF *arbaleste*, fr. LL *arcoballista, arcuballista*, fr. L *arcu-* (fr. *arcus* bow) + *ballista* — more at ARROW, BALLISTA] **:** CROSSBOW; *esp* **:** one used as a military weapon in medieval and early modern times often having a steel bow and sometimes used to throw balls or stones as well as quarrels

ar·ba·lest·er \'==,lestə(r)\ *also* **ar·ba·les·tri·er** \,=='lestrēə(r)\ *or* **ar·ba·list·er** \'==,listə(r)\ *n* -S [ME *arbalaster, arblaster*, fr. OF *arbalestier*, fr. LL *arcuballistarius*, fr. *arcuballista* + L *-arius* -ary] **:** a user of an arbalest **:** CROSSBOWMAN

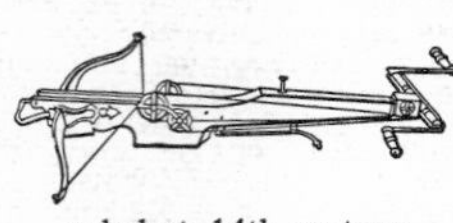
arbalest, 14th century

ar·bi·ter \'ärbə̇d·ər, 'åbə̇d·ə, |tə(r) *sometimes* ÷ -,bī|\ *n* -S [ME *arbitre, arbitour*, fr. MF *arbitre*, fr. L *arbiter* (akin to Umbrian *ařputrati* according to judgment), perh. fr. *ad-* + *-biter* (fr. *baetere* to go)] **1 :** a person having the authority to decide a matter in dispute **:** JUDGE; *esp* **:** one chosen by parties or appointed in their behalf by a court to determine a controversy between them ⟨whenever a political body controls arbitration-machinery, appoints ~s, and enforces rulings —*Christian Science Monitor*⟩ **2 :** a person or agency having absolute power of judging, determining, or ruling or one whose decisions are accepted as final ⟨she . . . became the supreme ~ of skating fashions —Maribel Y. Vinson⟩ ⟨the market, overseas and at home, will be the final ~ —*Economist*⟩

arbiter ele·gan·ti·ae \-,elə'ganshē,ē\ *or* **arbiter eleganti·a·rum** \-,ganshē'a(a)rəm\ *n* [L, judge of elegance] **:** a person who prescribes, rules on, or is a recognized authority on matters of social behavior and taste

ar·bith *or* **ar·bit** \är'bēt, '=,=; 'ärvəs\ *n* -S [Heb *ʽarbīth*] **:** MAARIB

ar·bi·tra·ble \'ärbə·trəbəl, (')är¦bi·tr-\ *adj* [L *arbitrari* to judge + E *-able* — more at ARBITRATE] **:** subject to decision by arbitration **:** referable to an arbitrator or arbiter ⟨the issues were not ~ according to the contract⟩

[1]**ar·bi·trage** *in sense 2* 'ärbə,träzh *or* ,==¦=; *in sense 1 possibly* 'ärbə·trij\ *n* -S [ME, fr. MF, fr. OF, fr. *arbitrer* to render judgment (fr. L *arbitrari*) + *-age*] **1** *archaic* **:** judgment by an arbiter **:** authoritative determination **:** ARBITRATION **2 :** simultaneous purchase and sale of the same or equivalent security, commodity contract, insurance, or foreign exchange on the same or different markets in order to profit from price discrepancies — compare ARBITRATION OF EXCHANGE

[2]**ar·bi·trage** \-äzh\ *vi* -ED/-ING/-S **:** to practice arbitrage ⟨~ in stock rights⟩

ar·bi·trag·er \-äzhər\ *also* **ar·bi·tra·geur** \¦==·(,)trä¦zhər\ *n* -S [F *arbitrageur*, fr. *arbitrage* + *-eur* -or] **:** one that practices arbitrage

ar·bi·tra·gist \¦==¦träzhəst\ *n* -S [F *arbitragiste*, fr. *arbitrage* + *-iste* -ist] **:** ARBITRAGER

ar·bi·tral \'ärbə·trəl, 'åb-\ *adj* [ME, fr. MF, fr. LL *arbitralis*, fr. L *arbitr-, arbiter* + *-alis* -al — more at ARBITER] **:** of or concerning arbiters or arbitration ⟨the ~ adjustment of controversial legal questions —S.F.Bemis⟩

ar·bit·ra·ment *also* **ar·bit·re·ment** \är'bi·trəmənt, å'b-\ *n* -S [ME, fr. MF *arbitrement*, fr. *arbitrer* to render judgment (fr. L *arbitrari*) + *-ment* — more at ARBITRATE] **1** *archaic* **:** the right or power of deciding, directing, or controlling ⟨thou seest thy life . . . at my ~ —Christopher Marlowe⟩ **2 :** the act of deciding as an arbiter **:** authoritative decision **:** ARBITRATION ⟨submit a case to the ~ of the judges⟩ **3 :** the judgment given by an arbitrator **:** DECISION

ar·bi·trar·i·ly \¦ärbə¦trerəlē, ¦åb-, -li\ *adv* **:** in an arbitrary manner **:** at will ⟨the genus will here be rather ~ described as though it were one man —W.S.White⟩ ⟨inflexible rules, ~ ordained—Havelock Ellis⟩⟨~set the lunch hour at one o'clock⟩

ar·bi·trar·i·ness *n* -ES **:** the quality or state of being arbitrary

arbitrarious *adj* [L *arbitrarius*] *obs* **:** ARBITRARY — **ar·bi·trar·i·ous·ly** *adv, obs*

[1]**ar·bi·trary** \'ärbə,trerē, 'åb-, -ri\ *adj* [ME, fr. MF or L; MF *arbitraire*, fr. L *arbitrarius*, fr. *arbitr-, arbiter* judge + *-arius* -ary — more at ARBITER] **1 :** depending on choice or discretion; *specif* **:** determinable by decision of a judge or tribunal rather than defined by statute ⟨an ~ decision⟩ ⟨~ punishment⟩ **2 a** (1) **:** arising from unrestrained exercise of the will, caprice, or personal preference **:** given to expressing opinions that arise thus (2) **:** selected at random or as a typical example ⟨such ~ items as clothing, room furnishings, travel —*Official Register of Harvard Univ.*⟩ **b :** based on random or convenient selection or choice rather than on reason or nature ⟨an ~ symbol⟩ ⟨~ division of historical studies into watertight compartments —A.J.Toynbee⟩ **c** *Brit, of a printing character* **:** not usu. found in the ordinary type font **3 a :** given to will-ful irrational choices and demands **:** IMPERIOUS ⟨a man of iron will and ~ decision⟩ **b :** characterized by absolute power or authority **:** DESPOTIC, TYRANNICAL ⟨~ rule⟩ ⟨an ~ governor⟩ **syn** see ABSOLUTE

[2]**arbitrary** \"\ *n* -ES **1 :** something that is arbitrary ⟨the . . . conception of cosmic rule, into which an element of the ~ had found its way —S.F.Mason⟩ **2 a :** a fixed sum allowed a carrier in making or dividing a through rate **b :** an amount added to or deducted from a basic transportation rate, fare, or charge (as an increment for abnormal services or features); *also* **:** a payment to employees for work other than regular duties

arbitrary constant *n, math* **:** a symbol to which various values may be assigned but which remains unaffected by the changes in the values of the variables of the equation

arbitrary function *n* **:** a symbol that may be considered to represent any one function of a set of functions

ar·bi·trate \-·,trāt, *usu* -ād·+V\ *vb* -ED/-ING/-S [L *arbitratus*, past part. of *arbitrari* to render judgment, consider as, fr. *arbitr-, arbiter* judge — more at ARBITER] *vi* **:** to act as arbitrator or judge ⟨~ upon several reports⟩ ⟨~ between parties to a suit⟩ ~ *vt* **1 :** to act as arbiter upon (a disputed question) ⟨political leaders deem themselves competent to ~ scientific disputes —Martin Gardner⟩ ⟨the commission *arbitrated* boundaries between the countries⟩ **2 :** to submit or refer for decision (as a quarrel) to an arbiter ⟨she was invariably right when we *arbitrated* our dispute —Ernest Beaglehole⟩ **3** *archaic* **:** to make authoritative decisions concerning **:** DECIDE, DETERMINE ⟨decides that which long process could not ~ —Shak.⟩

ar·bi·tra·tion \,=='trāshən\ *n* -S [ME *arbitracioun*, fr. MF *arbitration*, fr. L *arbitration-, arbitratio*, fr. *arbitratus* + *-ion-, -io* -ion] **:** the act of arbitrating; *esp* **:** the hearing and determination of a case between parties in controversy by a person or persons chosen by the parties or appointed under statutory authority instead of by a judicial tribunal provided by law ⟨~ of a dispute between management and labor⟩

ar·bi·tra·tion·al \¦==¦=shən°l, -shnəl\ *adj* **:** relating to or resulting from arbitration ⟨an ~ settlement⟩

ar·bi·tra·tion·ist \,=='sh(ə)nəst\ *n* -S **:** a person in favor of arbitration

arbitration of exchange : simultaneous purchase and sale of foreign exchanges in two or more markets to profit from discrepancies in quotations — compare ARBITRAGE

ar·bi·tra·tive \'==,trād·iv\ *adj* **:** of or relating to arbitration **:** having the authority to arbitrate ⟨an ~ board⟩ **:** done by arbitration

ar·bi·tra·tor \-·,trād·ə(r), -ātə-\ *n* -S [ME *arbitratour*, fr. MF, fr. LL *arbitrator*, fr. L *arbitratus* (past part. of *arbitrari* to render judgment) + *-or* — more at ARBITRATE] **1 :** a person or one of two or more persons chosen to settle by arbitration the differences between two parties in controversy **:** CONCILIATOR — distinguished from *mediator* **2 :** one with absolute power of deciding **:** ARBITER ⟨made himself the ~ of his own destiny —Geoffrey Clive⟩

arbitrement *var of* ARBITRAMENT

arbitrer *n* -S [ME *arbitrour*, fr. OF *arbitreor*, fr. LL *arbitrator*] *obs* **:** ARBITRATOR

ar·bi·tress \'ärbə·trəs, 'åb-\ *n* -ES [ME *arbitres*, fr. MF *arbitresse*, fem. of *arbitre* judge — more at ARBITER] **:** a female arbiter

arblast *archaic var of* ARBALEST

ar·bo·lo·co \,ärbə'lō(,)kō\ *n* -ES [AmerSp, fr. Sp *árbol* tree (fr. L *arbor*) + *loco* mad — more at ARBOR, LOCO] **:** a Colombian tree (*Montanoa lehmannii*) of the family Compositae whose wood is used esp. for making billiard cues

[1]**ar·bor** \'ärbər, 'åbə\ *n* -S *see -or in Explan Notes* [ME *erber, herber* plot of grass, herb garden, shady bower, fr. OF *erbier, herbier* plot of grass, fr. *herbe* herb, grass — more at HERB] **1 :** a bower formed of vines or branches or of latticework covered with climbing shrubs or vines **:** a shaded retreat **2** *obs* **:** a shaded or covered walk

arbor 1

[2]**ar·bor** \"\ *n* [L, tree, beam; perh. akin to L *arduus* steep, high — more at ARDUOUS] **1** -S **:** a principal supporting rod or bar: as **a :** a spindle or axle of a wheel (as in a clock or watch) **b :** a metal shaft or axis on which a revolving cutting tool (as a circular saw) is mounted; *sometimes* **:** a spindle or bar on a cutting machine that holds the work to be cut — compare MANDREL **c :** the central bar or support of a mold core **2** *pl* **ar·bo·res** \'ärbə,rēz, 'åb-\ **:** a tree as distinguished from a shrub

ar·bo·ra·ceous \¦ärbə¦rāshəs, ¦åb-\ *or* **ar·bo·ral** \'=b(ə)rəl\ *adj* [[2]*arbor* (tree) + *-aceous* or *-al*] **:** ARBOREAL

ar·bo·rary \'=bə,rerē\ *adj* [L *arborarius*, fr. *arbor* tree + *-arius* -ary] **:** ARBOREAL

arbor day *n, usu cap A&D* **:** a day in April or May designated in most states as a tree-planting day

ar·bo·re·al \(')är¦bōrēəl, (')å¦b-, -ȯr-\ *also* **ar·bo·re·an** \-ēən\ *adj* [L *arboreus* + E *-al* or *-an*] **1 :** of or relating to a tree **:** resembling a tree **2 :** inhabiting or frequenting trees ⟨~ animals⟩ — **ar·bo·re·al·ly** \-ēəlē, -li\ *adv*

ar·bored \'ärbərd, 'åbəd\ *adj* [[1]*arbor* + *-ed*] **:** furnished with an arbor **:** lined with trees **:** having trees **:** EMBOWERED ⟨an ~ walk⟩

ar·bo·re·ous \(')är¦bōrēəs, (')å¦b-, -ȯr-\ *adj* [L *arboreus* of a tree, fr. *arbor* + *-eus* -eous] **1 :** abounding in trees **:** WOODED ⟨an ~ landscape⟩ **2 :** having the form, duration of life, or structure of a tree in distinction from an herb or shrub **3 :** ARBOREAL 2

ar·bor·er \'ärbərər, 'åbərə\ *n* -S [[2]*arbor* + *-er*] **:** a jewelry worker who shapes rings on an arbor

ar·bo·res·cence \,=='res°n(t)s\ *n* -S **:** the state of being arborescent **:** treelike form or appearance (as in minerals)

ar·bo·res·cent \¦==¦=°nt\ *adj* [L *arborescent-, arborescens*, pres. part. of *arborescere* to become a tree, fr. *arbor*] **1 :** resembling a tree in growth, structure, or appearance; *esp* **:** branching like a tree **2 :** having crystallizations disposed like the branches and twigs of a tree ⟨~ frost-growths —F.C. Phillips⟩ — **ar·bo·res·cent·ly** *adv*

arborescent appendage *n* **:** any branched accessory vascular structure in the gill chamber of certain fishes that leave the water (as the climbing perch) by which they are enabled to breathe air

ar·bo·resque \¦==¦resk\ *adj* [[2]*arbor* (tree) + E *-esque*] **:** like a tree

ar·bo·ret \¦==¦ret\ *n* -S [L *arbor* tree + E *-et*] **:** a small tree **:** SHRUB

ar·bo·re·tum \,ärbə'rēd·|əm, ,åb-, -ēt|\ *n, pl* **arboretums** \|əmz\ *also* **arbore·ta** \|ə\ [NL, fr. L, a place grown with trees, fr. *arbor* + *-etum*] **:** a place where trees, shrubs, and herbaceous plants are cultivated for scientific and educational purposes **:** a botanic garden of trees

ar·bor·i·cal \(')är¦bȯrəkəl\ *adj* [[2]*arbor* (tree) + *-ical*] **:** ARBOREAL 1

ar·bor·i·cole \=¦=rə,kōl\ *also* **ar·bo·ric·o·lous** \¦ärbə¦rikələs\ *adj* [F, fr. L *arbor* tree + F *-i-* + *-cole* -colous] **:** inhabiting trees ⟨certain mollusks are ~⟩

ar·bo·ri·cul·tur·al \¦ärbərə¦- är¦bȯrə¦-\ *adj* **:** of or relating to arboriculture

ar·bo·ri·cul·ture \'ärbərə,-, är'bȯrə,-\ *n* -S [[2]*arbor* (tree) + *-iculture* (as in *agriculture*)] **:** the cultivation of trees and shrubs esp. for ornamental purposes — compare SILVICULTURE — **ar·bo·ri·cul·tur·ist** \,===¦-, =,==-\ *n* -S

ar·bo·ri·form \'ärbərə,fȯrm, är'bȯrə-\ *adj* [[2]*arbor* (tree) + *-iform*] **:** resembling a tree in shape or appearance

ar·bo·rist \'ärbərəst\ *n* -S [L *arbor* tree + E *-ist*] **:** a specialist in planting and transplanting, pruning, and diagnosing the ailments of trees and in tree surgery and tree maintenance

ar·bo·ri·za·tion \,==rə'zāshən, -,rī'z-\ *n* -S **1 :** formation of or into a figure or arrangement resembling a tree or shrub **:** RAMIFICATION ⟨the extent of the ~ of axons and dendrites⟩ **2 :** a treelike figure or arrangement of branching parts: as **a :** an outline or impression of a tree or plant in fossils **b :** DENDRITE 1 **c :** a treelike process of a nerve cell ⟨the terminal ~ of an axon⟩

ar·bo·rize \'ärbə,rīz\ *vb* -ED/-ING/-S [F *arboriser*, fr. L *arbor* tree + F *-iser* -ize] *vt* **:** to give a treelike appearance to ~ *vi* **:** to assume a treelike appearance ⟨the nerve fibers *arborized*⟩

ar·bo·rous \-,rəs\ *adj* [L *arbor* tree + E *-ous*] **:** of, relating to, or formed by trees ⟨an ~ roof⟩

arbor por·phy·ri·ana \-(,)pȯr,firē'anə\ *n, sometimes cap A & usu cap P* [prob. fr. ML — more at TREE OF PORPHYRY] **:** TREE OF PORPHYRY

arbor press *n* [[2]*arbor*] **1 :** MANDREL PRESS **2 :** a light press commonly operated by a hand lever

ar·bor·vi·tae \¦ärbər'vīd·|ē, ¦åbə'v-, -īt|, |ī\ *n* -S [NL *arbor vitae*, lit., tree of life] **1 :** a tree or shrub of the genus *Thuja* or the closely related *Thujopsis* — see AMERICAN ARBORVITAE, ORIENTAL ARBORVITAE; TREE illustration **2 :** any of several plants of the genus *Libocedrus* **3** *usu* **arbor vitae :** a treelike structure or arrangement (as of nervous tissue in the cerebellum)

arborvitae leaf miner *n* **:** the larva of a small moth (*Argyresthia thuiella*) that mines in the leaves of the arborvitae

arborway \'==,=\ *n* [[1]*arbor* + *way*] **:** an arbored passage or walk

arbour *chiefly Brit var of* ARBOR

arbtrn *abbr* arbitration

ar·bus·cle \'är,bəsəl\ *or* **ar·bus·cu·la** \är'bəskyələ\ *n* -S [L *arbuscula*, dim. of *arbor* tree] **:** a dwarf tree or treelike shrub

ar·bus·cu·lar \(')är¦bəskyələr\ *adj* **:** of or relating to an arbuscule

ar·bus·cule \=¦=(,)kyül\ *n* -S [L *arbuscula*] **1 :** a tuft of hairs or cilia **2 :** a branched treelike organ; *specif* **:** one of the treelike haustorial organs in certain mycorhizal fungi

ar·bus·tum \är'bəstəm\ *n, pl* **arbus·ta** \-tə\ [L, fr. *arbor* tree] **:** a plantation of shrubs or small trees **:** COPSE, ORCHARD

arbute *n* -S [L *arbutus*] *archaic* **:** a tree of the genus *Arbutus* — **arbutean** *adj, archaic*

ar·bu·tin \är'byüt°n, 'ärbyətən\ *n* -S [ISV *arbut-* (fr. NL *arbutus*) + *-in*] **:** a crystalline glucoside $C_{12}H_{16}O_7$ found in the leaves of the bearberry and in other plants and sometimes used as a urinary antiseptic

ar·bu·tus \är'byüd·əs, å'b-, -ütəs\ *n* [NL, fr. L, strawberry tree] **1** *cap* **:** a genus of evergreen shrubs or trees (family Ericaceae) of southern Europe and western No. America with white or pink flowers and many-seeded scarlet berries — see STRAWBERRY TREE **2** -ES **:** a tree of the genus *Arbutus* **3** -ES **:** a trailing plant (*Epigaea repens*) of eastern No. America with oblong hairy leaves and fragrant pink or white spring-blooming flowers with a 5-parted salver-shaped corolla — called also *ground laurel, mayflower, trailing arbutus* **4** -ES **:** a deep pink to purplish pink that is paler than France rose

arbutus pink *n* **:** a moderate pink that is bluer and paler than blossom pink, bluer, lighter, and stronger than chalk pink, and bluer and stronger than hydrangea pink

[1]**arc** \'ärk, 'åk\ *n* -S [ME *ark*, fr. MF *arc*, fr. L *arcus* bow, arc — more at ARROW] **1 :** the apparent path described above and below the horizon by the sun or other celestial body **2 :** something that is arched or curved **:** an arched or curved shape or figure ⟨with eyebrows raised in a quizzical ~⟩ ⟨he bent the twig into an ~⟩: as **a** *obs* **:** ARCH ⟨triumphal ~s —John Milton⟩ **b :** a geologic or topographic feature repeated along a curving line on the earth's surface ⟨island ~s . . . so well developed in the western Pacific —F.P.Shepard⟩ ⟨volcanic ~s⟩ **c** (1) **:** a sustained brilliantly luminous glow sometimes having the appearance of a curved line of flame that is formed under certain conditions when a break is made in an electric circuit

arcs 3

(2) **:** a spotlight or lamp that uses an electric arc as the light source **d :** one of the curved stripes that close the open angle at the bottom or top of certain chevrons on military uniforms **e :** the quarter circle enclosing the service box on a squash rackets court **3 :** a continuous portion of a curved line or path (as part of a circle or an ellipse) **4 :** angular measure — used chiefly in the phrase *of arc* ⟨11 minutes 3 seconds of ∼⟩

²**arc** \"\ *vi* **arced** \-kt\ **arced** \"\ **arcing** \-kiŋ\ **arcs** **1 :** to form an electric arc **2 :** to follow or describe a curving course resembling the form of an arc ⟨waterfalls ∼ outward into . . . white plumes —C.H.Baker⟩ ⟨the meandering Kum river, ∼*ing* around Taejon —*Newsweek*⟩

ar·ca \'ärkə\ *n* [NL, fr. L, chest, box — more at ARK] **1** *pl* **ar·cae** \-,kī, -,sē\ [L] **:** a chest or strong box used in ancient times as a receptacle for money or valuables and also by primitive Christians for reserving the consecrated bread of the Eucharist **2** *cap* **:** a genus (the type of the family Arcidae) of bivalve mollusks comprising the ark shells and blood clams

ar·ca·cea \är'kāshēə\ *n pl, cap* [NL, fr. *Arca* + *-acea*] **:** a suborder of the order Filibranchia including the ark shells and related forms

ar·cade \(')är¦kād, (')å¦k-\ *n* -s [F, fr. (assumed) It dial. (northern) *arcada*, fr. It *arco* arch, bow, arc (fr. L *arcus*) + *-ada* -ade (fr. LL *-ata*) — more at ARROW] **1 a** *obs* **:** an arched or vaulted place **:** an arched opening with its structural parts **b :** a long arched building or gallery **2 a :** an arched or curved passageway or avenue **b :** a covered passageway along which rows of shops are located **3 :** a series of arches with the columns or piers that support them, the spandrels above, and other necessary appurtenances, sometimes open and serving as an entrance or to give light, sometimes closed at the back and forming a decorative feature **4** *anat* **a :** a structure comprising a series of arches **b :** DENTAL ARCH

arcade 3

ar·cad·ed \-ādəd\ *adj* **:** having arcades **:** lined with arcades ⟨∼ streets⟩ **:** formed in, furnished, or decorated with arches or arcades ⟨a chair with an ∼ back design⟩ ⟨an ∼ courtyard⟩

ar·ca·dia \är'kādēə, å'k-\ *also* **ar·ca·dy** \'ärkədē, 'åk-, -di\ *n, pl* **arcadias** *also* **arcadies** *often cap* [fr. *Arcadia*, pastoral region of ancient Greece regarded as a rural paradise, fr. L, fr. Gk *Arkadia*] **:** a usu. idealized region or scene of simple pleasure, rustic innocence, and uninterrupted quiet ⟨Jefferson . . . with his dream of . . . an 18th century rural ∼ —W.H. Hale⟩

¹**ar·ca·di·an** \är'kādēən, å'k-\ *n* -s [*Arcadia* + E *-an*] **1** *often cap* **:** a person who lives a life of simple pleasure, rustic innocence, and untroubled quiet **2** *cap* **:** a native or inhabitant of Arcadia, a region of ancient Greece **3** *cap* **:** a dialect of ancient Greek used in Arcadia

²**arcadian** \(')ˌ=¦===\ *adj, sometimes cap* **1 :** of, belonging to, or characteristic of the idealized representations of pastoral life in literature **2 :** idyllically pastoral; *esp* **:** idyllically innocent, simple, or untroubled ⟨in retrospect the past sometimes seems ∼⟩ **3 a** *usu cap* **:** of or relating to Arcadia or to the Arcadians **b :** of or relating to Arcadian

ar·ca·di·an·ism \=ˈ===,nizəm\ *n* -s *often cap* **1 :** adoption or affectation of conduct or dress imitative of or suggestive of that depicted in arcadian literature **2 :** the use of arcadian literary conventions in writing

ar·cad·ing \=ˈkādiŋ, -dēŋ\ *n* -s **:** the series of arches or arcades used in the construction or decoration of a building or other object ⟨the ∼ of the walls is in two stories —Ian Finlay⟩

arcana *pl of* ARCANUM

ar·cane \(')är¦kān\ *adj* [L *arcanus* — more at ARCANUM] **:** being or resembling an arcanum **:** SECRET, MYSTERIOUS ⟨what is ∼ to them is lucid to Dr. Leavis —*Times Lit. Supp.*⟩ — **ar·cane·ly** *adv*

ar·ca·nist \'ärkānəst\ *n* -s [*arcanum* + *-ist*] **:** a workman having knowledge of a secret process of manufacture (as of the manufacture of porcelain)

ar·ca·nite \-,nīt, 'ärkə,-\ *n* -s [G *arkanit*, fr. NL *arcanum (duplicatum)*, lit., double arcanum + G *-it* -ite] **:** POTASSIUM SULFATE

ar·ca·num \är'kānəm *sometimes* -an- *or* -än-\ *n, pl* **arca·na** \-nə\ [L, fr. neut. of *arcanus* closed, secret, fr. *arca* chest — more at ARK] **1 :** a secret or mysterious knowledge or information known only to the initiate ⟨an ∼ of prosodic theory which is the province of specialists —P.F.Baum⟩ ⟨certain *arcana* . . . which you must with the utmost care conceal, and never seem to know —Earl of Chesterfield⟩ **2** [NL, fr. L] **:** an extract of the vital nature of something **:** a powerful natural agent **:** ELIXIR ⟨the search of the alchemists for the grand ∼⟩

arcanum ar·ca·no·rum \-nə,märkə'nōrəm\ *n* [NL] **:** the mystery of mysteries; *specif* **:** the one ultimate secret supposed to lie behind all astrology, alchemy, and magic

ar·ca·to \är'käd·(,)ō\ *adj (or adv)* [It, fr. *arco* bow (fr. L *arcus* bow, arc) + *-ato* (fr. L *-atus* -ate) — more at ARROW] **:** COLL'ARCO — usu. used as a direction in music

ar·ca·ture \'ärkə,chü(ə)r, -,chər\ *n* -s [F, prob. irreg. fr. *arcade* + *-ure*] **1 :** a small arcade (as in a balustrade) **2 :** a blind arcade; *esp* **:** one that is decorative rather than structural

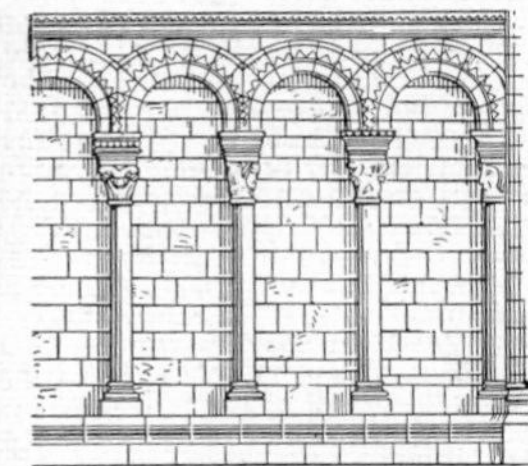
arcature 2

arc–back \'=,=\ *n* **:** failure of a gas-filled or mercury-vapor rectifier to suppress the current during the inverse-voltage half of a cycle due to overheating of the anode or to other causes

arc–bou·tant \årbütäⁿ\ *n, pl* **arcs–boutants** \-äⁿ(z)\ [F, fr. MF *arc boutant*, lit., thrusting arch, fr. *arc* arch, bow, arc (fr. L *arcus*) + *boutant*, pres. part. of *bouter* to thrust — more at ARROW, BUTT] **:** FLYING BUTTRESS

arc chute *n* **:** a set of insulating barriers on a circuit breaker arranged to confine the arc and prevent it from causing damage

arc cosecant *n* **:** the inverse function to the cosecant ⟨if *y* is the cosecant of *θ*, then *θ* is the *arc cosecant of y*⟩ — called also *inverse cosecant*

arc cosine *n* **:** the inverse function to the cosine ⟨if *y* is the cosine of *θ*, then *θ* is the *arc cosine of y*⟩ — called also *inverse cosine*

arc cotangent *n* **:** the inverse function to the cotangent ⟨if *y* is the cotangent of *θ*, then *θ* is the *arc cotangent of y*⟩ — called also *inverse cotangent*

arc de tri·omphe \,ärkdə(,)trē'ōⁿf\ *n, pl* **arcs de triomphe** \-k(s)d-\ [F] **:** TRIUMPHAL ARCH

arced *past of* ARC

ar·cel·la \är'selə\ *n* [NL, fr. L *arca* box, chest + NL *-ella*] **1** *cap* **:** the type genus of Arcellidae comprising protozoans resembling amoebas and provided with a chitinous shell suggesting an umbrella **2** -s **:** a protozoan of the genus *Arcella*

ar·cel·li·dae \-ə,dē\ *n pl, cap* [NL, fr. *Arcella*, type genus + *-idae*] **:** a cosmopolitan family of soil and freshwater protozoans related to the amoebas but commonly enclosed in a test — see ARCELLA

ar·ceu·tho·bi·um \,ärsyə'thōbēəm, ,ar,sü'-\ *n, cap* [NL, fr. Gk *arkeuthos* juniper + NL *-bium*; fr. its parasitism on conifers; perh. akin to Gk *arkys* net — more at ARACHN-] **:** a genus of chiefly American plants (family Loranthaceae) parasitic on various conifers and having 4-angled branches, scalelike leaves, dioecious flowers, and fleshy stalked berries — see AMERICAN MISTLETOE

arc furnace *n* **:** an electric furnace in which the heat is provided by an arc formed between two electrodes — compare INDUCTION FURNACE

¹**arch** \'ärch, 'åch\ *n* -ES [ME *arche*, fr. OF, fr. (assumed) VL

arches: *1* round (*ext* extrados, *int* intrados, *imp* impost, *k* keystone, *sp* springer, *v* voussoir); *2* horseshoe; *3* lancet; *4* ogee; *5* trefoil; *6* basket-handle; *7* Tudor

arca, fr. L *arcus* arch, bow, arc — more at ARROW] **1** *archaic* **:** a part of a curve **:** ARC **2 :** a typically curved structural member spanning an opening and serving as a support (as for the wall or other weight above the opening) by resolving vertical pressure into horizontal thrust, sometimes consisting of a framed structure similar in construction to a truss, sometimes made up of wedge-shaped solids with their joints at right angles to the curve **3 :** a structure or other object having the form of an arch or resembling an arch in form or function: as **a :** either of two vaulted portions of the bony structure of the foot that impart elasticity to and cushion the foot against shock (as in walking, running, leaping): (1) **:** a longitudinal arch supported posteriorly by the basal tuberosity of the calcaneus and anteriorly by the heads of the metatarsal bones (2) **:** a transverse arch consisting of the metatarsals and 1st row of tarsals and resulting from elevation of the central anterior portion of the median longitudinal arch **b :** one of the fire chambers of a brick kiln; *also* **:** the fire chamber in certain kinds of furnaces and ovens **c :** the arched top of a furnace or gas retort **d :** a round transverse bar shaped like an inverted U whose ends form the wheel axles of a row-crop cultivator, the arch providing clearance for the plants as they are cultivated **e :** a fingerprint in which all the ridges run from side to side and make no backward turn — compare LOOP, WHORL **f :** a natural bridge resulting from erosion **g** *geol* **:** an upward flexure of sedimentary rocks ⟨the Cincinnati ∼⟩ **:** a broad anticline **h :** an arch formed in dancing by raised and joined hands, kerchiefs, or swords by a couple, a pair, or a row of couples for the passage of a soloist or the remaining couples in line **i :** the lengthwise frame piece of a loom beneath which the warp travels and the cloth is woven **j :** the semicircular side plates of a carding machine **k :** a derricklike device consisting of a metal frame and fairlead mounted on the rear of a tractor or on separate wheels or tracks and used for lifting log ends clear of the ground so as to facilitate their skidding — compare SULKY **4 a :** a curvature having or approximating the form of an arch ⟨a slight ∼ to her eyebrows⟩ ⟨an ∼ in the cat's back⟩ **b :** the perpendicular distance from the master leaf of a leaf spring to a line drawn through the centers of the spring eyes **5 :** a place covered by an arch **:** ARCHWAY

²**arch** \"\ *vb* -ED/ -ING/ -ES [ME *archen*, fr. *arche*, n.] *vt* **1 :** to cover or provide with an arch or arches **:** span with an arch ⟨a bridge ∼*es* the stream⟩ ⟨the high blue heaven that ∼*es* our continent —D.C.Peattie⟩ **2 :** to form or bend into the shape of an arch **:** CURVE ⟨∼ her eyebrows⟩ ⟨∼ the ball a trifle higher —W.L.Hughes⟩ ∼ *vi* **1 :** to form into an arch **:** take the shape of an arch ⟨trees ∼ above the promenade —*Amer. Guide Series: Maine*⟩ **2 :** to follow or take an arch-shaped path or course ⟨the ball ∼*ed* toward the basket⟩ ⟨the meteor ∼*ed* across the sky⟩ **3** *dancing* **a :** to form an arch by joining hands with the dance partner or neighbor **b :** to place the toe of the free foot against the arch of the supporting foot

³**arch** \"\ *adj* [¹*arch-*] **1 :** most important or outstanding **:** PRINCIPAL, CHIEF — used attributively usu. with a hyphen ⟨an *arch*-villain⟩ ⟨the life of Thoreau as an ∼ Yankee —H.S. Canby⟩ **2** [¹*arch-*; fr. its use as an intensifying prefix in such compounds as *archrogue, archwag*, whereby some of the semantic range of *rogue* and *wag* was extended to the prefix] **a :** characterized by clever or sly alertness ⟨that ∼ eye of yours! it sees through everything —Jane Austen⟩ **b :** playfully saucy **:** ROGUISH ⟨an ∼ look⟩ **:** having an exaggerated often forced or artificial playfulness ⟨simpering expressions and ∼ posturing —Osbert Lancaster⟩

⁴**arch** *n* -ES *obs* **:** one that is preeminent **:** CHIEF

¹**arch-** \¦ärch, ¦åch, *but* ¦ärk *or* ¦åk *in "archangel" and derivatives*\ *prefix* [ME *arche-, arch-*, fr. OE & OF; OE *arce-, erce-*, fr. LL *arch-* & L *archi-*, fr. Gk *arch-, archi-*; OF *arch-, arche-*, fr. LL *arch-* & L *archi-* — more at ARCHI-] **1 :** chief **:** principal ⟨*arch*angel⟩ ⟨*arch*bishop⟩ ⟨*arch*diocese⟩ ⟨*arch*duke⟩ ⟨*arch*pillar⟩ **2 :** preeminent **:** extreme **:** most fully embodying the qualities of his or its kind ⟨*arch*antiquary⟩ ⟨*arch*capitalist⟩ ⟨*arch*fool⟩ ⟨*arch*infamy⟩ ⟨*arch*philosopher⟩ ⟨*arch*puritan⟩ ⟨*arch*rogue⟩ **3 :** first in time ⟨*arch*father⟩ **:** primitive ⟨*arch*form⟩

²**arch-** — see ARCHI-

¹**-arch** \,ärk, ,åk, *alternatively* -ə(r)k *in a few common words (as "monarch") in which the preceding syllable has stress*\ *n comb form* -s [ME *-arke, -arche*, fr. OF & LL & L; OF *-arche*, fr. LL *-archa*, fr. L *-arches, -archus*, fr. Gk *-archēs, archos* — more at ARCHI-] **:** ruler **:** leader ⟨matri*arch*⟩ ⟨nom*arch*⟩

²**-arch** \,ärk, ,åk\ *adj comb form* [prob. fr. G, fr. Gk *archē* beginning — more at ARCHI-] **:** having (such) a point or (so many) points of origin ⟨end*arch*⟩ ⟨pent*arch*⟩

arch *abbr* **1** archaic **2** *often cap* archbishop **3** archery **4** archipelago **5** architecture **6** archive

archabbey \'=¦==\ *n* [¹*arch-* + *abbey*] **:** a chief Benedictine abbey

archabbot \'=¦==\ *n* [¹*arch-* + *abbot*] **:** the superior of an archabbey

archae- *or* **archaeo-** *also* **archeo-** *in pronunciations below*, ¦==(,)= = ¦ärkē(,)ō *or* ¦åk- *or* -ēə, =¦== = är¦kēō *or* å¦k- *or* -ēə\ *comb form* [Gk *archaio-*, fr. *archaios* ancient, fr. *archē* beginning — more at ARCHI-] **1 :** antiquity ⟨*archaeo*graphy⟩ **2 :** ancient **:** primitive ⟨*archae*craniate⟩ ⟨*archaeo*lithic⟩ ⟨*archeo*zoic⟩

archaean *usu cap, var of* ARCHEAN

ar·chae·cra·ni·ate \¦ärkē¦-\ *adj* [*archae-* + *craniate*] **:** of, relating to, or having a primitive type of skull (as that of Amphibia) — opposed to *syncraniate*

archaei *pl of* ARCHAEUS

ar·chaeo·calamites \¦==(,)= *or* =¦== *at* ARCHAE- +\ *n, cap* [NL, fr. *archae-* + *Calamites*] **:** a genus of fossil plants related to *Calamites*, found in the oldest Carboniferous strata, and having large repeatedly dichotomous leaves and a strobilus like an equisetum

ar·chaeo·cete \'=== *or* =ˈ== *at* ARCHAE- + ,sēt\ *adj or n* [NL *Archaeoceti*] **:** ZEUGLODON

ar·chaeo·ce·ti \,=== *or* =,== *at* ARCHAE- + 'sē,tī\ [NL, fr. *archae-* + *ceti*, pl. of L *cetus* whale — more at CETE] *syn of* ZEUGLODONTIA

ar·chaeo·cy·a·tha \,=== *or* =,== *at* ARCHAE- + 'sīathə\ *n pl, cap* [NL, fr. *Archaeocyathus*] *in some classifications* **:** a phylum of extinct animals of uncertain systematic relations represented by fossils of the genus *Archaeocyathus*

ar·chaeo·cy·a·thus \-thəs\ *n, cap* [NL, fr. *archae-* + L *cyathus* cup — more at CYATHUS] **:** a genus of Cambrian fossils with characteristics of both sponges and corals that is included among the pleosponges or placed in Archaeocyatha

ar·chaeo·cyte *also* **ar·cheo·cyte** \'=== *or* =ˈ== *at* ARCHAE- + ,sīt\ *n* -s [*archae-* + *-cyte*] **:** an indifferent commonly amoeboid interstitial cell; *specif* **:** any of certain amoebocytes of sponges that have large nuclei and blunt pseudopods, are believed to be persistent undifferentiated embryonic cells, and develop into the sex cells

ar·chaeo·gastropod \¦==(,)= *or* =¦== *at* ARCHAE- + \ *n* -s [NL *Archaeogastropoda*] **:** one of the Aspidobranchia

ar·chaeo·gastropoda \¦==(,)= *or* =¦== *at* ARCHAE- + \ [NL, fr. *archae-* + *Gastropoda*] *syn of* ASPIDOBRANCHIA

ar·chaeo·geology \"\ *n* -ES [*archae-* + *geology*] **:** the geology of the most ancient periods

ar·chaeo·hippus \¦==(,)= *or* =¦== *at* ARCHAE- + 'hipəs\ *n, cap* [NL, fr. *archae-* + *-hippus*] **:** a genus of small No. American Miocene horses ancestral to modern horses

ar·chae·ol·a·try \,ärkē'äla·trē\ *n* -ES [*archae-* + *-latry*] **:** the worship of archaism

ar·chae·o·log·i·cal *or* **ar·che·o·log·i·cal** \¦ärkēə¦läjəkəl, ¦åk-, -jēk-\ *also* **ar·chae·o·log·ic** *or* **ar·che·o·log·ic** \-jik, -ēk\ *adj* **:** of, belonging to, or relating to archaeology; *also* **:** dealing with or devoted to archaeology

ar·chae·o·log·i·cal·ly *or* **ar·che·o·log·i·cal·ly** \-ək(ə)lē, -ēk-, -li\ *adv* **:** in or according to archaeology **:** from an archaeological standpoint ⟨an ∼ rich country⟩

ar·chae·ol·o·gist *or* **ar·che·ol·o·gist** \,=ˈ==äləjəst\ *n* -s **:** a specialist in archaeology

ar·chae·ol·o·gy *or* **ar·che·ol·o·gy** \-jē, -i\ *n* -ES [LL *archaeologia* antiquarian lore, fr. Gk *archaiologia*, fr. *archaio-* archae- + *-logia* -logy] **1** *archaic* **:** ancient history **2** [F *archéologie*, fr. LL *archaeologia*] **:** the scientific study of extinct peoples or of past phases of the culture of historic peoples through skeletal remains, fossils, and objects of human workmanship (as implements, artifacts, monuments, or inscriptions) found in the earth **3 :** remains of the culture of a people **:** ANTIQUITIES ⟨the ∼ of the Incas⟩ ⟨the museum displayed Aztec ∼⟩

ar·chaeo·pithecus \¦==(,)= *or* =¦== *at* ARCHAE- + \ *n, cap* [NL, fr. *archae-* + *-pithecus*] **:** a genus of extinct So. American Eocene mammals once supposed to be ancestral to Pithecanthropus but now recognized as notoungulates

ar·chaeo·op·ter·is \,ärkē'äptərəs\ *n, cap* [NL, fr. *archae-* + *-pteris*] **:** a genus of fossil plants esp. characteristic of the Devonian that were formerly regarded as ferns but are now generally included in the order Cycadofilicales

ar·chae·op·ter·yg·i·for·mes \,ärkē,äptə,rijə'fōr,mēz\ *n pl, cap* [NL, fr. *Archaeopteryg-, Archaeopteryx* + *-iformes*] **:** an order of extinct toothed birds including the genera *Archaeopteryx* and *Archaeornis*

ar·chae·op·ter·yx \,ärkē'äptə(,)riks\ *n* [NL, fr. *archae-* + *-pteryx*] **1** *cap* **:** a genus of primitive reptilelike birds (subclass Archaeornithes) known from only a few specimens from the Upper Jurassic of Europe and having a long slender tail with feathers along each side **2** -ES **:** a bird or fossil of the genus *Archaeopteryx* or of the subclass Archaeornithes

ar·chae·or·nis \,ärkē'ōrnəs\ *n* [NL, fr. *archae-* + *-ornis*] **1** *cap* **:** a genus of Upper Jurassic birds (subclass Archaeornithes) having a long feathered tail, showing reptilian characteristics in the absence of a bill, presence of teeth in the jaws, and on the wings three free digits with claws **2** -ES **:** a bird or fossil of the genus *Archaeornis*

ar·chae·or·ni·thes \-'ōrnə,thēz, -,ōr'nī(,)thēz\ *n pl, cap* [NL, fr. *archae-* + *-ornithes*] **:** a subclass of Aves comprising the earliest and most primitive of fossil birds, retaining distinctive reptilian characters, and including the two genera *Archaeornis* and *Archaeopteryx*

archaeozoic *usu cap, var of* ARCHEOZOIC

archaeus *var of* ARCHEUS

archai *pl of* ARCHE

ar·cha·ic \(')är¦kāik, (')å¦k-\ *adj* [F or Gk; F *archaïque*, fr. Gk *archaïkos* old-fashioned, fr. *archaios* ancient + *-ikos* -ic — more at ARCHAE-] **1 :** relating to, belonging to, or having the characteristics of an earlier and often more primitive time **:** OLD-FASHIONED, ANTIQUATED ⟨many procedures of the law have long seemed ∼ to laymen —W.O.Douglas⟩ **2 a :** having the characteristics of the language of the past and surviving in the present chiefly in legal language (as *malice aforethought*), in biblical or ecclesiastical language (as *thou art, brethren, saith*), or in the language of poetry, imaginative prose, and esp. historical fiction (as *belike, methinks, in sooth*)

☞ In this dict. the label *archaic* is affixed to words and senses relatively common in earlier times but infrequently used in present-day English

b : current without restriction in the present stage of a language but surviving from an earlier stage or from a parent language ⟨verbs like *sing-sang-sung* which form their past and past participle by vowel change are an ∼ feature of English⟩ **c** *of a writer or literary work* **:** characterized by the intentional use of old-fashioned language **3 :** of or belonging to an early or formative stage or period in the development of an artistic style, esp. a period immediately preceding one of fully realized expression ⟨the ∼ Greek art of the 6th century B.C.⟩ **4 :** surviving essentially unchanged from an earlier period ⟨∼ usages govern his conduct toward all the crucial issues of life —Norman Lewis⟩; *specif* **:** typical of a previously dominant evolutionary stage ⟨sphenodon is an ∼ reptile⟩ **5 :** having the characteristics of primitive man and his animal forebears esp. as represented in the unconscious and appearing in behavior as manifestations of the unconscious **6** *usu cap* **:** of or belonging to a prehistoric period to which has been assigned the earliest known culture or cultures of a particular area **syn** see OLD

ar·cha·i·cal·ly \-āək(ə)lē, -li\ *adv* **:** in an archaic manner or form **:** with archaic characteristics

ar·cha·i·cism \=ˈ=ə,sizəm\ *n* -s **:** ARCHAISM

archaic smile *n* **:** a facial expression determined by prominent cheekbones and upturned mouth corners and resembling a smile — used esp. in ref. to archaic Greek sculpture

ar·cha·ism \'ärkē,izəm, 'åk-, -kā-\ *n* -s [NL *archaismus*, fr. Gk *archaïsmos* use of obsolete expressions, fr. *archaios* ancient + *-ismos* -ism — more at ARCHAE-] **1 :** the use of obsolete or old-fashioned diction, idiom, or style in writing or speaking or of the style of an earlier period in painting or other arts; *also* **:** old-fashionedness in diction and style ⟨by 1377 the idiom of 1311 was . . . an ∼ already withering into anachronism —*Bull. of Inst. of Historical Research*⟩ **2 :** an instance of archaic usage **:** an archaic word, idiom, or style occurring in such usage ⟨the ∼ *thou art*⟩ **3 :** something archaic: as **a** *biol* **:** a survivor from a past period distinguished by retained characteristics out of keeping with its present surroundings **b :** an outmoded or inefficient custom, method, or way of thinking that survives from a past era ⟨we must discard the ∼*s* that retard our culture⟩ **c :** the preference for standards, customs, or behavior characteristic of a past era ⟨∼ — the referring of everything to the infallible authority of antiquity —*Times Lit. Supp.*⟩

ar·cha·ist \-,əst\ *n* -s [*archaism* + *-ist*] **:** ANTIQUARY; *also* **:** one who archaizes

ar·cha·is·tic \¦=ˈ=¦istik, -(,)kā-, -tēk\ *adj* **1 :** imitative of archaic style, form, manner ⟨∼ writing⟩ ⟨∼ pottery⟩ **:** using or affecting archaisms ⟨an ∼ writer⟩ ⟨∼ behavior⟩ **2 :** ARCHAIC ⟨an ∼ word⟩ ⟨an ∼ fear of foreigners⟩ **:** characterized by archaism ⟨an ∼ taste in manners and speech⟩ **3 :** tending to preserve or return to the methods, customs, art, or culture of the past ⟨∼ or culturally reactionary tendencies⟩ — **ar·cha·is·ti·cal·ly** \-tək(ə)lē, -ēk-, -li\ *adv*

ar·cha·ize \'=,kē,īz, -,kā-\ *vb* -ED/-ING/-S [Gk *archaïzein*, fr. *archaios* + *-izein* -ize] *vt* **:** to make appear archaic or antique ⟨∼ the styles⟩ ∼ *vi* **:** to use archaisms ⟨conscious *archaizing* of the language by the translator⟩

ar·chal·lax·is \,ärkə'laksəs\ *n, pl* **archallax·es** \-k,sēz\ [NL, fr. *archi-* + Gk *allaxis* exchange, barter, fr. *allassein* to exchange, fr. *allos* other — more at ELSE] *biol* **:** the early deviation from an ancestral developmental pattern eliminating recapitulation

¹**arch·angel** \'ärk-, 'åk-+,-; (')=+'-\ *n* -s [ME, fr. OF or LL; OF *archangele*, fr. LL *archangelus*, fr. Gk *archangelos*, fr. Gk *arch-* ¹arch- + *angelos* angel — more at ANGEL] **1 :** an angel of high rank **2 :** a being in the heavenly hierarchy ranking above an angel — see CELESTIAL HIERARCHY **3 a :** ANGELICA 2 **b :** any of several plants of the mint family: as (1) **:** BLACK HOREHOUND (2) **:** RED ARCHANGEL (3) **:** WHITE DEAD NETTLE

²**archangel** \'=,==\ *or* **ar·khan·gelsk** \är'kan,gelsk\ *adj, usu cap* [fr. *Archangel* or *Arkhangelsk*, U.S.S.R.] **:** of or from the city of Archangel, U.S.S.R. **:** of the kind or style prevalent in Archangel

arch·angelic \¦ärk-, ¦åk- + ,=¦==\ *or* **arch·angelical** \+,=¦===\ *adj* [LL *archangelicus*, fr. LGk *archangelikos*, fr. Gk *archangelos* + *-ikos* -ic] **:** of or relating to archangels **:** being or resembling an archangel ⟨a face with a look of ∼ power⟩

arch·an·gel·i·ca \¦ärk-,an'jeləkə\ [NL, fr. *archi-* + *Angelica*] *syn of* ANGELICA

arch·an·thro·pi·nae \¦ärk-'anthrə'pī(,)nē\ *n pl, cap* [NL, fr. *archi-* + *anthrop-* + *-inae*] **:** an anthropological subdivision of

Hominidae regarded as comparable to a subfamily and including *Pithecanthropus* and related forms distinguished by extreme development of the occipital torus — compare NEOANTHROPINAE, PALEOANTHROPINAE

arch·an·thro·pine \ärk·ˈanthrə,pīn\ *n* -s *usu cap* [NL *Archanthropinae*] **:** a member of the Archanthropinae

ar·cha·rios \är'kärēōs\ *n* -ES [LGk, fr. Gk *archē* beginning + *-arios* (fr. L *-arius* -ary) — more at ARCHI-] **:** a novice in a monastic community of the Eastern Orthodox Church

archband \ˈ=,=\ *n* -s [ˡ*arch* + *band*] **:** a strip of masonry connected with an arch surface: as **a :** ARCHIVOLT **b :** the part of an arch or rib visible below the vaulting surface

arch bar *n* **:** a bar of arched shape: as **a :** a curved bar in a window sash **b :** an iron bar arching over an ashpit

arch·bishop \(ˈ)ärch,(ˈ)äch+\ *n* [ME *erchebishop, archebishop*, fr. OE *ærcebiscop, arcebiscop*, fr. LL *archiepiscopus*, fr. LGk *archiepiskopos*, fr. Gk *archi-* + *episkopos* bishop — more at BISHOP] **:** a chief bishop **:** a prelate at the head of an ecclesiastical province or one of equivalent honorary rank with duties and dignities variously comprised in the titles of exarch, patriarch, metropolitan, or primate

arch·bishopric \(ˈ)=+ˈ-\ *n* -s [ME *archebischopric*, fr. OE *arcebiscoprice*, fr. *arcebiscop* + *-rice* -ric] **1 :** the jurisdiction or office of an archbishop **2 :** the see or province over which an archbishop exercises authority

archbp *abbr, often cap* archbishop

arch brace *n* **:** a curved brace in a wooden truss

arch brick *n* **1 :** a wedge-shaped brick used in the building of an arch — compare COMPASS BRICK **2 :** brick that has been overburned through being placed in contact with the fire in the arch of a kiln **:** CLINKER BRICK; *also* **:** one such brick

arch bridge *n* **:** a bridge in which the main supporting elements are arches

arch buttress *n* **:** FLYING BUTTRESS

arch center *n* **:** a temporary structure supporting a concrete or masonry arch during construction

arch·confraternity \ˈärch+\ *n* -ES [ˡ*arch-* + *confraternity*; trans. of It *arciconfraternita*] *Roman Catholicism* **:** a confraternity canonically empowered to affiliate with and confer its privileges and indulgences on other confraternities with similar purposes

archd *abbr, often cap* **1** archdeacon **2** archduke

arch dam *n* **:** a dam built in a gorge in the form of a horizontal arch having the convex side upstream and abutting against the side walls

arch·deacon \(ˈ)ärch,(ˈ)äch+ˌ-\ *n* [ME *erchedeken, archedeken*, fr. OE *ærcediacon, arcediacon*, fr. LL *archidiaconus*, fr. LGk *archidiakonos*, fr. Gk *archi-* + *diakonos* deacon — more at DEACON] **1 :** a chief deacon **:** an ecclesiastical dignitary next in rank below a bishop or in most Eastern Orthodox churches below an archpriest **2 :** a priest in the Episcopal Church who supervises an archdeaconry or who superintends the missionary work of a district

arch·deaconate \(ˈ)=+ˈ-\ *n* -s **:** the position of archdeacon

arch·deaconry \(ˈ)=+ˈ-\ *n* -ES **:** the office, tenure, or state of an archdeacon **:** the district or residence of an archdeacon

arch·dean \ˈärch-,ˈäch+ˌ-\ *n* [ME *archdene*, fr. ˡ*arch-* + *dene* dean] **:** a chief dean **:** one who supervises other deans

arch·diocesan \ˌärch,ˌäch+,=ˈ===\ *adj* **:** of or relating to an archdiocese

arch·diocese \(ˈ)=+\ *n* [ˡ*arch-* + *diocese*] **:** the diocese of an archbishop

arch·ducal \(ˈ)=+ˈ==\ *adj* [earlier *archiducal*, fr. F, fr. *archiduc* archduke + *-al*] **:** of, belonging to, or befitting an archduke or archduchy

arch·duchess \ˈ=+ˌ==\ *n* [F *archiduchesse*, fem. of *archiduc* archduke, fr. MF *archeduc*] **1 :** the wife or widow of an archduke **2 :** a woman who holds an archducal title in her own right; *specif* **:** a princess of the imperial family of Austria

arch·duchy \ˈ=+ˌ==\ *n* -ES [F *archeduché* (now *archiduché*), fr. MF, fr. *arche-* ˡarch- + *duché* duchy — more at DUCHY] **:** the territory of an archduke or archduchess

arch·duke \ˈ=+ˌ-\ *n* [MF *archeduc*, fr. *arche-* ˡarch- + *duc* duke — more at DUKE] **:** a sovereign prince; *specif* **:** a prince of the imperial family of Austria

arch·dukedom \ˈ=+ˌ=\ *n* -s **:** ARCHDUCHY

ar·che \ˈär,kē; ärˈkā, -ˈkē\ *n, pl* **ar·chai** \-kī\ [Gk *archē*, lit., beginning — more at ARCHI-] **:** something that was in the beginning **:** a first principle: **a** *in early Greek philosophy* **:** a substance or primal element **b** *in Aristotle* **:** an actuating principle (as a cause)

arche- *prefix* [L, fr. Gk, fr. *archein* to begin — more at ARCHI-] **:** primitive **:** original ⟨*arche*centric⟩ ⟨*arche*spore⟩

ˡ**ar·che·an** *or* **ar·chae·an** \(ˈ)ärˈkēən, ˈär,k-\ *adj, usu cap* [Gk *archaios* ancient + E *-an* — more at ARCHAE-] **:** of, belonging to, or contemporary with the oldest known group of rocks, usu. with the earlier portion of the Precambrian; *sometimes* **:** PRECAMBRIAN — see GEOLOGIC TIME table

²**archean** *or* **archaean** \"\ *n* -s *usu cap* **:** the Archean era or system of rocks

archean protaxis *n, usu cap A* **:** the area or mass of Archean rocks in any continent that throughout post-Archeozoic time remained a land area

ar·che·bi·o·sis \ˌärkē,bīˈōsəs\ *n* [NL, fr. *arche-* + *-biosis*] **:** abiogenesis esp. as relating to the initial formation of living matter on earth

ar·che·centric \ˌ==+ˌ-\ *adj* [*arche-* + *centric*] **:** of, relating to, or designating an archetype (sense 3a) — opposed to *apocentric*

arched \ˈärcht, ˈächt\ *adj* **:** made with or formed in an arch or arches ⟨an ~ beam⟩ **:** covered with an arch ⟨an ~ door⟩

ar·che·dic·ty·on \ˌärkəˈdiktē,än\ *n* -s [NL, fr. *arche-* + Gk *diktyon* net, fr. *dikein* to throw] **:** a fine veinlike network on the wings of primitive insects esp. of some extinct groups

arched squall *n* **:** a violent thunder squall advancing broadside, its front seeming to form an arch

ar·che·gone \ˈärkə,gōn\ *n* -s [F, fr. NL *archegonium*] **:** ARCHEGONIUM

archegonia *pl of* ARCHEGONIUM

ar·che·go·ni·al \ˌärkəˈgōnēəl\ *adj* [NL *archegonium* + E *-al*] **:** of or relating to an archegonium **:** ARCHEGONIATE

archegonial chamber *n* **:** a cavity above the archegonium in the female gametophyte of some gymnosperms (as ginkgo and the cycads)

ar·che·go·ni·a·ta \ˌärkəˌgōnēˈäd·ə, -ˈād·ə\ [NL, fr. *archegonium* + *-ata*] *syn of* ARCHEGONIATAE

ar·che·go·ni·a·tae \-nēˈā,tē, -ˈä,-\ *n pl, cap* [NL, fr. *archegonium* + *-atae* (fr. fem. pl. of L *-atus* -ate)] *in some classifications* **:** a primary division of the plant kingdom coextensive with the subkingdom Embryophyta and containing all the plants that produce archegonia (as the mosses, ferns, horsetails, and club mosses)

ˡ**ar·che·go·ni·ate** \ˌ==ˈgōnēət, -ē,āt\ *adj* [NL *archegonium* + E *-ate*] **:** bearing archegonia

²**archegoniate** \"\ *n* -s **1 :** a plant bearing archegonia **2** [NL *Archegoniatae*] **:** a plant belonging to the division Archegoniatae

ar·che·go·ni·o·phore \ˌ==ˈgōnēə,fō(ə)r\ *n* -s [NL *archegonium* + E *-o-* + *-phore*] **:** the stalk or other outgrowth of a prothallium upon which archegonia are borne (as in liverworts of the genus *Marchantia*) — compare CARPOCEPHALUM

ar·che·go·ni·um \ˌärkəˈgōnēəm\ *n, pl* **archego·nia** \-nēə\ [NL, fr. Gk *archegonos* original, primal (fr. *arche-* + *-gonos*, akin to *gignesthai* to be born) + NL *-ium* — more at KIN] **:** the flask-shaped female sex organ in mosses and ferns and some gymnosperms

ar·che·go·sau·rus \ˌärkēgōˈsȯrəs\ *n, cap* [NL, fr. Gk *archēgos* primary, originating (fr. *archē* beginning + *-ēgos*, akin to Gk *agein* to lead, drive) + NL *-saurus* — more at ARCHI-, AGENT] **:** a genus of extinct long-snouted aquatic labyrinthodont amphibians from the Lower Permian of Europe

ar·chel·o·gy \ärˈkeləjē\ *n* -ES [NL *archelogia*, fr. Gk *archē* beginning, element + L *-logia* -logy] **:** the science of first principles

ar·che·lon \ˈärkə,län\ *n, cap* [NL, prob. irreg. fr. *archi-* + Gk *chelōnē* tortoise; akin to Gk *chelys* tortoise — more at CHELYS] **:** a genus of very large extinct marine turtles from the Cretaceous of So. Dakota having a well-developed plastron but poorly developed carapace

ˡ**arch·en·ceph·a·la** \ˌärk·,enˈsefələ\ *n pl, cap* [NL, fr. *archi-* + *encephala* (pl. of *encephalon*) — more at ENCEPHALON] **:** man regarded as constituting a separate subclass of Mammalia — not now regarded as an acceptable taxonomic concept

²**archencephala** *pl of* ARCHENCEPHALON

arch·en·ce·phal·ic \ˌärk·,ensəˈfalik\ *adj* [NL *archencephalon* + E *-ic*] **:** of or relating to the archencephalon

arch·encephalon \ˌärk·+,-\ *n, pl* **archencephala** [NL, fr. *archi-* + *encephalon*] **:** the primitive forebrain of the early embryo

arch·enemy \ˈärˌchen-\ *n* -ES [ˡ*arch-* + *enemy*] **:** a principal enemy **:** a great enemy

arch·en·ter·ic \ˌärk·,enˈterik, ˌärkən-\ *adj* [NL *archenteron* + E *-ic*] **:** of or relating to the archenteron

archenteric pouch *n* **:** one of the paired pouches budded off the dorsolateral aspect of the archenteron of amphioxus and some other chordates giving rise to the anterior somites and coelomic mesoderm

arch·en·ter·on \(ˈ)ärk·ˈentə,rän\ *n, pl* **archen·tera** \-tərə\ [NL, fr. *archi-* + Gk *enteron* intestine] **:** the cavity formed by the invagination or ingrowth of cells of the gastrula stage of the embryo (as that of the frog)

archeo- — see ARCHAE-

archeocyte *var of* ARCHAEOCYTE

archeology *var of* ARCHAEOLOGY

ˡ**ar·cheo·zo·ic** *also* **ar·chaeo·zo·ic** \ˌärkēəˈzōik *sometimes* ärˌk-\ *adj, usu cap* [*archae-* + *-zoic*] **:** of, belonging to, or relating to the earliest era of geological history, the era of the Archean rocks — see GEOLOGIC TIME table

²**archeozoic** *also* **archaeozoic** \"\ *n* -s *usu cap* **:** the Archeozoic era or system of rocks

archepiscopal *var of* ARCHIEPISCOPAL

arch·er \ˈärchər, ˈächə\ *n* -s [ME, fr. OF *archier, archer*, fr. LL *arcarius*, alter. of *arcuarius*, fr. *arcuarius* of a bow, fr. L *arcus* bow + *-arius* -ary — more at ARROW] **1 :** one skilled in the use of the bow and arrow **:** BOWMAN **2 :** ARCHERFISH **3 :** a shoe worker who operates a machine for shaping the arch or shank of outsoles and insoles

archerfish \ˈ==,=\ *n* **:** a small fish (*Toxotes jaculator*) of the East Indies that ejects drops of water from its mouth at insects resting on objects over the water causing them to fall so that it can capture them; *also* **:** any of several other closely related fishes of similar habits

archerfish (*Toxotes jaculator*)

arch·ery \ˈärch(ə)rē, ˈäch-, -ri\ *n* -ES [ME *archerie*, fr. MF, fr. OF, fr. *archier*, *archer* + *-ie* -y] **1 :** the use of bow and arrows (as in battle or as a sport) **:** the art, practice, or skill of shooting with bow and arrow ⟨he excels in ~⟩ **2 :** an archer's weapons (as bows and arrows) ⟨the troops were supplied with new ~⟩ **3 :** a body of archers (as a company or corps) ⟨the order was given for the ~ to advance⟩

arches *pl of* ARCH, *pres 3d sing of* ARCH

ar·che·spore \ˈärkə,spō(ə)r\ *or* **ar·che·spo·ri·um** \ˌ==ˈspōrēəm\ *n, pl* **arche·spores** \-rz\ *or* **archespo·ria** \-ōrēə\ [NL *archesporium*, fr. *arche-* + *-sporium*] **:** the cell or group of cells from which spore mother cells develop (as those from which the microspores develop in the pollen sac or the megaspore in the ovule) — **ar·che·spo·ri·al** \ˌ==ˈspōrēəl\ *adj*

ar·che·tis·ta \ˌärkəˈtistə\ *n pl, cap* [NL] **:** a hypothetical assemblage of primitive organisms comprising viruses, bacteriophages, and supposed free-living related viroids

ar·che·typ·al \ˌärkəˈtīpəl, ˌäk-\ *or* **ar·che·typ·i·cal** \-ˈtipəkəl, -ēk-\ *adj* **:** of, relating to, or representing an archetype or archetypes ⟨~ patterns and images⟩ **:** constituting a model either actual or ideal ⟨~ figures and characters⟩ — **ar·che·typ·al·ly** \-īpəlē, -li\ *or* **ar·che·typ·i·cal·ly** \-ipək(ə)lē, -ēk-, -li\ *adv*

ar·che·type \ˈärkə,tīp, ˈäk-\ *n* -s [L *archetypum*, fr. Gk *archetypon*, fr. neut. of *archetypos* molded first as a model, exemplary, fr. *arche-* + *typos* impression of a seal, mold, replica — more at TYPE] **1 :** the original model, form, or pattern from which something is made or from which something develops ⟨in . . . oral ballads, variation has gone so far that it is impossible to reconstruct the exact words of the ~ —M.J.C.Hodgart⟩ ⟨the House of Commons, the ~ of all the representative assemblies which now meet —T.B.Macaulay⟩ **2 a** *in Platonism* **:** one of the ideas of which existent things are imitations — compare IDEA 1 **b** *in scholastic philosophy* **:** the idea in the divine intellect that determines the form of a created thing **c** *in Locke* **:** one of the external realities with which our ideas and impressions to some extent correspond **3 a :** a primitive generalized plan of structure deduced from the characters of the members of a natural group of animals or plants and assumed to be the type from which they have been modified **b :** the original ancestor of a group of animals or plants **4 :** a manuscript usu. no longer extant from which others were copied **5** *in the psychology of C.G.Jung* **:** an inherited idea or mode of thought derived from the experiences of the race and present in the unconscious of the individual **6 a :** a perfectly typical example **:** a perfect example of a particular type ⟨the ~ of his profession — stocky, thick-chested, bull-necked —*New Yorker*⟩ **:** the most extreme example ⟨the ~ of the stuffy aesthetic reactionary —*N.Y. Herald Tribune*⟩ **b :** an abstract or ideal conception of a type ⟨the various . . . ideals or ~s; the gentleman, the scholar . . . the go-getter . . . the captain of industry —Walter Moberly⟩

ar·che·us *also* **ar·chae·us** \ärˈkēəs\ *n, pl* **ar·chei** *also* **ar·chaei** \-ē,ī\ [NL, fr. Gk *archos* ruler — more at ARCHI-] **:** the vital principle that according to Paracelsians directs and maintains the growth and continuation of living beings

archfiend \ˈärchˌfēnd, ˈäch-\ *n* -s [ˡ*arch-* + *fiend*] **:** a chief fiend; *esp* **:** SATAN

arch-gravity dam *n* [ˡ*arch*] **:** an arch dam having also sufficient mass and breadth of base to provide gravity stability

archi- *or* **arch-** *prefix* [MF & It & L; MF *archi-* & It *arci-*, fr. L *archi-*, fr. Gk *arch-, archi-*; akin to Gk *archein* to begin, *archē* beginning, *archos* ruler] **1 :** chief **:** principal ⟨*archi*episcopal⟩ — *archi-* before consonants, *arch-* or more frequently *archi-* before vowels **2 :** primitive **:** original **:** primary ⟨*arch*enteron⟩ ⟨*archi*blast⟩ ⟨*archi*carp⟩ ⟨*archi*continent⟩ ⟨*archi*pterygium⟩

ar·chi·acanthocephala \ˌärkē+\ *n pl, cap* [NL, fr. *archi-* + *Acanthocephala*] **:** an order of Acanthocephala comprising parasites of terrestrial vertebrates having the proboscis hooks arranged in concentric circles and lacking trunk spines

ar·chi·annelida \ˌ==+\ *n pl, cap* [NL, fr. *archi-* + *Annelida*] **:** a group, usu. a class, of small primitive or secondarily simplified annelid worms lacking external segmentation and resembling polychaete larvae — compare POLYGORDIUS

ar·chi·a·ter \ˈärkē,ād·ər, ˌ==ˈ==\ *n* -s [LL *archiater, archiatrus*, fr. Gk *archiatros*, fr. *archi-* + *iatros* physician — more at IATRO-] **:** a chief physician orig. of the court of a Hellenistic king or a Roman emperor

ar·chi·benthic *also* **ar·chi·benthal** \ˌärkē+ˌ-\ *adj* [*archi-* + *benthic, benthal*] **:** of, relating to, or being the upper part of the benthic region that includes the continental shelf and extends from the sublittoral to the abyssal

ar·chi·benthos \ˌärkē+\ *n* [NL, fr. *archi-* + *benthos*] **:** MESOBENTHOS

ar·chi·blast \ˈärkə,blast\ *n* -s [*archi-* + *-blast*] **1 :** the active protoplasmic components of the egg in contrast to the stored yolk and other reserves **2 :** EPIBLAST

ar·chi·blas·tic \ˌ==ˈblastik\ *adj* **:** of, relating to, or derived from the archiblast

ar·chi·blastula \ˌärkē+ˌ-\ *n* -s [NL, fr. *archi-* + *blastula*] **:** COELOBLASTULA

ar·chi·carp \ˈärkē,kärp\ *n* -s [*archi-* + *-carp*] **:** the female reproductive organ in ascomycetous fungi; *specif* **:** one consisting of a carpogonium and a trichogyne

ar·chi·cephalic \ˌärkē+=ˈ==\ *adj* [NL *archicephalon* + E *-ic*] **:** of or relating to the archicephalon

ar·chi·ceph·a·lon \ˌ==ˈsefə,län\ *n* [NL, fr. *archi-* + *cephalon*] **:** the primitive head region in insects consisting of the preoral segments and probably equivalent to the prostomium of annelid worms

ar·chi·cerebellum \ˌärkē+\ *n* [NL, fr. *archi-* + *cerebellum*] **:** the part of the cerebellum related to labyrinthine sense and comprising the flocculus, nodulus, and part of the vermis — compare NEOCEREBELLUM, PALEOCEREBELLUM

ar·chi·cerebrum \ˌärkē+\ *n* [NL, fr. *archi-* + *cerebrum*] **:** the supra-esophageal ganglia of invertebrates

ar·chi·chla·myd·e·ae \ˌärkēkləˈmidē,ē\ *n pl, cap* [NL, fr. *archi-* + *-chlamydeae* (fr. Gk *chlamyd-, chlamys* cloak, mantle)] **:** a group of Dicotyledoneae comprising plants in which the petals of the flowers are separate or absent — compare METACHLAMYDEAE; see APETALAE, CHORIPETALAE — **ar·chi·chla·myd·e·ous** \ˌ===ˈ=ēəs\ *adj*

ar·chi·cleistogamous \ˌärkē+,=ˈ===\ *adj* **:** of or relating to archicleistogamy

ar·chi·cleistogamy \ˌärkē+,=ˈ===\ *n* -ES [*archi-* + *cleistogamy*] **:** permanent cleistogamy

ar·chi·coele *also* **ar·chi·coel** \ˈärkē,sēl\ *n* -s [*archi-* + *-coele, -coel*] **:** the segmentation cavity in some forms persisting as a body cavity between the ectoderm and endoderm

ar·chi·continent \ˌärkē+ˈ-\ *n* [*archi-* + *continent*] **:** a continental nucleus that has persisted throughout the recorded portion of geologic time

ar·chi·diaconal \ˌärkē+,=ˈ===\ *adj* [LL *archidiaconus* archdeacon + E *-al* — more at ARCHDEACON] **:** of or relating to an archdeacon or his office ⟨~ visitation⟩

ar·chi·diaconate \ˌärkē+\ *n* -s [ML *archidiaconatus*, fr. LL *archidiaconus* + L *-atus* -ate] **:** the office or order of an archdeacon

ar·chi·did·as·ca·li·an \ˌärkē,didəˈskālēən, -lyən\ *or* **ar·chi·di·das·ca·line** \-dəˈdaskələn, -ˌdīˌd-, -ˌlīn\ *adj* **:** of or relating to an archididascalos

ar·chi·di·das·ca·los \ˌ==dəˈdaskə,läs, -ˌdīˈd-, -ləs\ *or* **ar·chi·di·das·ca·lus** \-ləs\ *n, pl* **archididasca·li** \-,lī\ [LGk *archididaskalos*, fr. Gk *archi-* + *didaskalos* teacher, fr. *didaskein* to teach — more at DOCILE] **:** a chief teacher (as a headmaster in a school)

ar·chid·i·um \ärˈkidēəm\ *n, cap* [NL] **:** a genus of acrocarpous mosses related to *Dicranum* but having sessile capsules and sometimes made type of a separate family

ar·chie \ˈärchē\ *n* -s *often cap* [prob. fr. *Archie*, nickname for *Archibald*] *slang* **:** ANTIAIRCRAFT

ar·chi·episcopacy \ˌärkē, ˌäkē+\ *n* [LL *archiepiscopus* archbishop + E *-acy* — more at ARCHBISHOP] **1 :** the form of episcopacy in which the chief power is in the hands of archbishops **2 :** ARCHIEPISCOPATE

ar·chi·episcopal \ˌ+=ˈ===\ *also* **arch·episcopal** \ˌärk, ˌäk+=ˈ===\ *adj* [ML *archiepiscopalis*, fr. LL *archiepiscopus* + L *-alis* -al] **:** of or relating to an archbishop ⟨an ~ see⟩ — **ar·chi·episcopally** *adv*

archiepiscopal cross *n* **:** PATRIARCHAL CROSS

archiepiscopal staff *n* **:** CROSS-STAFF 1a

ar·chi·episcopate \ˌärkē, ˌäkē+\ *n* [ML *archiepiscopatus*, fr. LL *archiepiscopus* + L *-atus* -ate] **:** the office, tenure, or state of an archbishop **:** ARCHBISHOPRIC

archi-episcopal cross

-archies *pl of* -ARCHY

ar·chi·gas·ter \ˈärkē,gastə(r), ˌ==ˈ==\ *n* -s [*archi-* + *gaster*] **:** ARCHENTERON

ar·chi·gastrula \ˌärkē+ˈ-\ *n* [NL, fr. *archi-* + *gastrula*] **:** a gastrula formed by simple invagination

ar·chi·gen·e·sis \ˌärkē+\ *n* [NL, fr. *archi-* + *genesis*] **:** ARCHEBIOSIS

ar·chi·ge·tes \ˌärkəˈjēd·ēz, ärˈkijə,tēz\ *n, cap* [NL] **:** a genus of pseudophyllidean tapeworms living as neotenic larvae in the coelom of aquatic oligochaete worms, some being reported to develop into typical caryophyllid worms when the host is ingested by a suitable fish — compare CARYOPHYLLAEIDAE

ar·chil \ˈärchəl\ *also* **or·chil** \ˈȯr-\ *or* **ar·chil·la** \ärˈchilə\ *n* -s [ME *orchell*, prob. fr. OIt *oricello*] **1 :** a violet dye obtained as a pasty mass from certain lichens of the genera *Roccella* and *Lecanora* by fermentation with alkali (as ammonia) — compare CUDBEAR, LITMUS **2 :** a plant that yields archil **3 :** any of the colors imparted by the dye archil varying from moderate red to dark purplish red according as the dye bath is acid or alkaline — called also *corcir*

ˡ**ar·chi·lo·chi·an** \ˌärkəˈlōkēən\ *adj, usu cap* [*Archilochus*, 7th cent. B.C. Greek poet (fr. L, fr. Gk *Archilochos*) + E *-ian*] **1 a :** of or relating to Archilochus **b :** TRENCHANT, SARCASTIC, BITTER **2 :** marked by use of Archilochians or of Archilochian strophes

²**archilochian** \"\ *n* -s *usu cap* **:** a verse form ascribed to Archilochus: as **a :** a line composed of a dactylic tetrapody followed by a trochaic tripody — called also *greater Archilochian* **b :** a dactylic tripody catalectic — sometimes called also *lesser Archilochian* **c :** a dactylic tetrapody with spondee or trochee as the fourth foot **d :** a dicolon composed of a complete prosodiac followed by an ithyphallic

archilochian strophe *n* **1 :** a dactylic hexameter followed by a lesser Archilochian **2 :** a dactylic hexameter followed by an iambelegus **3 :** an iambic trimeter followed by an elegiambus **4 :** a greater Archilochian followed by an iambic trimeter catalectic

archilowe *n* -s [origin unknown] *Scot* **:** the return that one who has been treated in an inn makes to the company

ar·chi·mage \ˈärkə,māj\ *n* -s [NL *archimagus*, fr. LGk *archimagos*, fr. Gk *archi-* + *magos* magus, wizard — more at MAGIC] **:** a great magician, wizard, or enchanter

ar·chi·man·drite \ˌärkəˈman,drīt\ *n* -s [LL *archimandrites, archimandrita*, fr. LGk *archimandritēs*, fr. Gk *archi-* + LGk *mandra* monastery, fr. Gk, fold, pen] **1** *Eastern Church* **:** the superior or abbot of a larger monastery — compare HEGUMEN **2** *Eastern Church* **:** an honorary title bestowed by a patriarch, catholicos, or bishop (as upon heads of a number of monasteries or prominent hieromonks)

ar·chi·me·de·an \ˌärkəˈmēdēən, ˌäk- *also* -məˈd-\ *adj, usu cap* [*Archimedes* (fr. Gk *Archimēdēs*) †212 B.C. Greek mathematician & inventor + E *-an*] **:** of, relating to, or invented by Archimedes **:** constructed on the principle of or invented by Archimedes ⟨~ drill⟩ ⟨~ lever⟩

archimedean solid *n, usu cap A* **:** one of 13 possible solids each of which has plane faces that are all regular polygons though not all of the polygons are of the same species and each of which has all its polyhedral angles equal

archimedean spiral *n, usu cap A* **:** a plane curve generated by a point moving away from or toward a fixed point at a constant rate while the radius vector from the fixed point rotates at a constant rate

ar·chi·me·des \ˌärkəˈmē(ˌ)dēz\ *n* [NL, fr. *Archimedes* †212 B.C.; fr. the screwlike axis] **1** *cap* **:** a genus of extinct colonial bryozoans having a spiral screwlike axis and being typical of Mississippian formations but known also from Pennsylvanian and Permian rocks **2** *pl* **archimedes :** any bryozoan or fossil of the genus *Archimedes*

archimedes *a* zoarium, *b* axis

ar·chi·me·des' principle \-dēzˈp-\ *n, usu cap A & sometimes cap P* **:** a law of fluid mechanics: a body while wholly or partly immersed in a fluid apparently loses weight by an amount equal to that of the fluid displaced

archimedes' problem *n, usu cap A* **:** the mathematical problem of bisecting the volume of a hemisphere by means of a plane parallel to the base insoluble by Euclidean methods

archimedes' screw *n, usu cap A* **:** a device consisting of a tube bent spirally around an axis or of a broad-threaded screw encased by a hollow open cylinder and used to raise water by rotating the apparatus when partly immersed in a slantwise direction

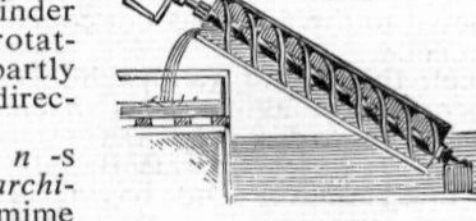

archimedes' screw

ar·chi·mime \ˈärkə,mīm\ *n* -s [L *archimimus*, fr. Gk *archimimos*, fr. *archi-* + *mimos* mime — more at MIME] **:** the chief performer in the Roman mime

ar·chi·my·ce·tes \ˌärkə,mīˈsēd·ēz\ *n pl, cap* [NL, fr. *archi-* + *-mycetes*] **1** *in some classifications* **:** a subclass or order of

Phycomycetes coextensive with Chytridiales **2** *in some classifications* **:** a class of primitive fungi comprising the Chytridiales and certain related forms

archin *or* **archine** *var of* ARSHIN

ar·chi·nephridium \ˌärkē+ₑ¦ₑₑₑ\ *n* [NL, fr. *archi-* + *nephridium*] **:** the primitive nephridium found paired in each segment of certain annelid larvae

arch·ing \ˈärchiŋ, ˈȧch-, -ēŋ\ *n* -s [fr. gerund of [2]*arch*] **:** the arched part of a structure **:** a system of arches

ar·chi·oligochaeta \ˌärkē+ˌₑₑₑ¦ₑₑ\ *n pl, cap* [NL, fr. *archi-* + *Oligochaeta*] *in some classifications* **:** a division of Oligochaeta comprising relatively small aquatic worms of few segments that reproduce vegetatively by fission as well as by sexual means (as members of the genera *Aeolosoma, Nais,* and *Dero*) — compare LIMICOLAE, MICRODRILI — **ar·chi·oligo·chaete** \+¦-\ *adj or n*

ar·chi·pallial \¦ärkē+¦-\ *adj* [NL *archipallium* + E *-al*] **:** of or relating to the archipallium

ar·chi·pallium \+¦-\ *n* -s [NL, fr. *archi-* + *pallium*] **:** the olfactory part of the pallium comprising the hippocampus and part of the hippocampal gyrus and evolved earlier than the neopallium

ar·chi·pe·lag·ic \¦ärkəpə¦lajik, -rchə-\ *also* **ar·chi·pe·la·gian** \-¦lāj(ē)ən\ *adj* [*archipelago* + *-ic* or *-ian*] **:** of, relating to, or located in an archipelago ⟨an ~ war —*New Republic*⟩

ar·chi·pel·a·go \ˌärkəˈpeləˌgō, ˌärchə-, ˌȧk-, ˌȧch-; *the Italian source word "Arcipelago" (see etymology) is pronounced* ˌärch-\ *n, pl* **archipelagoes** *or* **archipelagos** [*Archipelago* Aegean sea, fr. It *Arcipelago*] **1 :** a sea or other expanse of water having many scattered islands **2 :** a group or cluster of islands

ar·chi·phoneme \¦ärkē, -kə̇+¦-\ *n* -s [ISV *archi-* + *phoneme*] **:** a class of phonemes consisting usu. of a pair sharing all distinctive features except one (as *d* and *t* share all distinctive features except that *d* is voiced and *t* is voiceless); *esp* **:** a structurally descriptive category in which a sound may be placed when it occurs in a position where it may belong to any of two or more phonemes because of neutralization or suspension of the usual contrast between them (as German *t* in final position where it may correspond either to medial *t* or to medial *d*)

ar·chi·plasm \ˈärkəˌplazəm\ *n* -s [G *archiplasma*, fr. *archi-* + *-plasma* -plasm] **1 :** a hypothetical primitive undifferentiated protoplasm **2 :** ARCHOPLASM — **ar·chi·plas·mic** \¦ₑₑ¦plazmik\ *adj*

archipresbyter *var of* ARCHPRESBYTER

archipresbyterate *var of* ARCHPRESBYTERATE

ar·chips \ˈärˌkips\ *n, cap* [NL, fr. *archi-* + Gk *ips* woodworm] **:** a large genus of tortricid moths including a number with larvae that are serious pests of economically important plants, feeding on and webbing the leaves and causing defoliation — compare UGLY-NEST CATERPILLAR

ar·chip·te·ryg·i·al \¦ärˌkiptəˈrij(ē)əl, ä¦k-\ *adj* [NL *archipterygium* + E *-al*] **:** of or relating to archipterygium

ar·chip·te·ryg·i·um \(ˌ)ₑˌₑₑˈₑjēəm\ *n* [NL, fr. *archi-* + Gk *pterygion* little wing, fin — more at PTERYGIUM] **:** a primitive form of fin having a long segmented axis (as that of *Neoceratodus*)

ar·chi·sper·mae \ˌärkəˈspərˌmē\ *n pl, cap* [NL, fr. *archi-* + *-spermae;* fr. their presumed antiquity] *in some classifications* **:** a class equivalent to Gymnospermae

ar·chis·tia \ärˈkistēə\ *n pl, cap* [NL, fr. *archi-* + *-istia* (as in *Cladistia*)] **:** an order of primitive Paleozoic ganoid fishes of moderate size superficially resembling modern herrings but having heterocercal tails, the maxilla expanded over the cheek, and a true clavicle in the pectoral girdle

ar·chi·stome \ˈärkəˌstōm\ *n* -s [*archi-* + *-stome*] **:** BLASTOPORE

[1]**ar·chi·tect** \ˈärkəˌtekt, ˈȧk-\ *n* -s [MF *architecte*, fr. L *architectus, architecton*, fr. Gk *architektōn* chief artificer, master builder, fr. *archi-* + *tektōn* workman, carpenter — more at TECHNICAL] **1 :** a person skilled in the art of building **:** a professional student of architecture or one who makes it his occupation to form plans and designs of and to draw up specifications for buildings and to superintend their execution — compare LANDSCAPE ARCHITECT, MARINE ARCHITECT **2 :** one that plans and achieves esp. an objective that is felt to be the product of painstaking construction ⟨the . . . ~s of Portugal's . . . empire in the Far East —S.E.Morison⟩ ⟨the great ~ of the military victory —*Time*⟩

[2]**architect** \"\ *vt* -ED/-ING/-S **:** to plan and contrive as an architect ⟨the book is not well ~ed —*Times Lit. Supp.*⟩

ar·chi·tec·ton·ic \¦ärkəˌtek¦tänik, ¦ȧk-\ *adj* [L *architectonicus* of architecture, fr. Gk *architektonikos* of a master builder, fr. *architekton-, architektōn* + *-ikos* -ic] **1 :** of, related to, or in accordance with the technical principles of architecture **:** ARCHITECTURAL ⟨~ feature⟩ ⟨~ purposes⟩ **2 a :** having the organized structural and rational qualities of architecture ⟨severe and ~ landscape —Osbert Sitwell⟩ ⟨make his book a series of essays rather than an ~ whole —D.W.Petegorsky⟩ **b :** giving, creating, or tending to give the quality of structural unity or order ⟨creative energy . . . is . . . ~, and it imposes upon the lyric impulse an ordered sequence and an organic unity —J.L.Lowes⟩

ar·chi·tec·ton·i·ca \ˌₑₑˌₑˈₑnə̇kə\ *n, cap* [NL, fr. L, fem. of *architectonicus*] **:** a genus of tropical marine snails having a depressed conical shell the umbilicus of which is wide so that the upper whorls can be seen in it

ar·chi·tec·ton·i·cal·ly \¦ₑₑˌₑ¦ₑnə̇k(ə)lē\ *adv* **:** with respect to or in terms of architectonics ⟨regarded not ~, but as a loose collective⟩

ar·chi·tec·ton·ics \ˌₑₑˌₑˈₑniks\ *n pl but sing in constr, also* **ar·chi·tec·ton·ic** \-ik\ **1 :** the science of architecture **2** *philos* **a :** the doctrine of pure method or of the abstract systematization of knowledge **b :** the abstract scheme or plan or the purely formal elucidation of something **3 a :** the structural design that imposes order, balance, and unity upon a work or an entity **:** the element of form that relates the parts to each other and to the whole ⟨good novels . . . have rhythm, ~, focus —*New Republic*⟩ ⟨drawing is the ~, . . . the living skeleton of painting —George Biddle⟩ **b :** system of structure **:** plan of order ⟨Dante's . . . ~ of the relationships of authority and obedience —Israel Knox⟩

architector *n* -s [MF *architecteur*, fr. L *architectus, architecton* + MF *-eur* -or — more at ARCHITECT] *obs* **:** ARCHITECT

architects' scale *n* **:** a scale or rule usu. of triangular section made of boxwood and having a variety of graduations on its edges, one edge usu. being graduated in inches and sixteenths of an inch, the other edges graduated in twelfths and fractions thereof for lengths of 3 inches, 1½ inches, and 1 inch so that dimensions of reduced-scale drawings may be measured directly in feet and inches

ar·chi·tec·tur·al \¦ärkə¦tekchərəl, ¦ȧk-, -ksh(ə)rəl\ *adj* **1 :** of, resembling, or relating to architecture **:** characteristic of architecture **:** conforming to the rules of architecture ⟨~ effects⟩ ⟨~ quality⟩ **2 :** used for construction and esp. for ornamentation in architecture ⟨~ bronze⟩ ⟨~ glass⟩ **3 :** having features, ornaments, or motifs characteristic of some style of architecture ⟨~ canopy⟩ — **ar·chi·tec·tur·al·ly** \-kchərəlē, -ksh(ə)rəlē, -li\ *adv*

architectural concrete *n* **:** concrete used for the exterior or interior ornamentation or finish of a building or structure, often being cast integral with the reinforced concrete frame

architectural engineering *n* **:** the art and science of engineering and construction as practiced in regard to buildings as distinguished from architecture as an art of design

architectural furniture *n* **:** furniture designed to match or to accord with the architectural features of the rooms for which it is intended

architectural projected window *n* **:** a better grade of projected window for use in buildings where the architectural effect is important

ar·chi·tec·ture \ˈärkəˌtekchər, ˈȧkəˌtekchə, -ksh-\ *n* -s [MF, fr. L *architectura*, fr. *architectus* architect + *-ura* -ure — more at ARCHITECT] **1 :** the art or science of building; *specif* **:** the art or practice of designing and building structures, esp. habitable structures, in accordance with principles determined by aesthetic and practical or material considerations **2 :** formation or construction whether the result of conscious act or of growth or of random disposition of the parts ⟨~ and function of the cerebral cortex⟩ ⟨the fountains blow their ~ of slender pillars —Aldous Huxley⟩ ⟨the careful ~ of *Tom Jones* in the innumerable subplots which give the book the proportions of life, the personal story of Jones taking its place in the general orchestration —Graham Greene⟩ **3 :** the exercise or an instance of the exercise of the art or science of architecture ⟨building must go beyond mere building for shelter to become ~ —T.E.Sanford⟩ **:** architectural product **:** architectural work ⟨the mansions which comprise the entire ~ of the Square —Blake Ehrlich⟩ **4 :** a method or style of building characterized by certain peculiarities of structure or ornamentation ⟨many other ~s besides Gothic —John Ruskin⟩

ar·chi·teu·this \ˌärkəˈt(y)üthə̇s\ *n, cap* [NL, fr. *archi-* + *Teuthis*] **:** a genus of gigantic squids containing the largest mollusks known, some being 40 feet long inclusive of the long arms

ar·chit·o·my \ärˈkid·əmē\ *n* -ES [*archi-* + *-tomy*] **:** reproduction by fission followed by bodily reorganization (as in certain annelids) — compare PARATOMY

ar·chi·trave \ˈärkəˌtrāv, ˈȧk-\ *n* -s [MF, fr. OIt, fr. *archi-* (fr. L *archi-*) + *trave* beam, fr. L *trabs* — more at THORP] **1 :** the lowest division of an entablature resting (as in classical architecture) immediately on the capital of the column — see ENTABLATURE illustration **2 :** the molded band, group of moldings, or other architectural member around a door or other opening esp. if rectangular in form

ar·chi·traved \-vd\ *adj* **:** furnished with an architrave

ar·chi·val \(ˈ)är¦kīvəl, (ˈ)ȧ¦k-; ˈₑ̩kə̇vəl\ *adj* [[1]*archive* + *-al*] **:** of, relating to, contained in, or constituting archives or records

ar·chi·va·lia \ˌärkə̇ˈvālēə, -lyə\ *n pl* [NL, fr. L *archivum* + NL *-alia*] **:** material preserved in or suitable for preservation in archives **:** ARCHIVE 2

[1]**ar·chive** \ˈärˌkīv, ˈȧˌk-\ *n* -s [F & L; obs. F *archive* (now *archives*, pl.), fr. L *archivum, archium*, fr. Gk *archeion* government house, *archeia* (pl. of *archeion*) archives, fr. *archē* beginning, first place, government — more at ARCHI-] **1** *usu pl* **a :** a place in which public or institutional records (as minutes, correspondence, reports, accounts) are systematically preserved **b :** a repository for any documents or other materials esp. of historical value (as diaries, photographs, private correspondence) ⟨the Trotsky ~s at Harvard⟩ **c :** any repository or collection esp. of information ⟨the ~s of memory⟩ **2 :** public or institutional records, historic documents, and other materials that have been preserved — usu. used in pl.

[2]**archive** \"\ *vt* -ED/-ING/-S **:** to file or collect (as records or documents) in an archive or other repository ⟨methods for *archiving* languages of the world —*Linguistic Institute*⟩

ar·chi·vism \ˈärkə̇ˌvizəm\ *n* -s **:** the process of archiving

ar·chi·vist \ˈärkə̇və̇st, -ˌkīv-, ˈȧ(ˌ)k-\ *n* -s [prob. fr. F *archiviste*, fr. *archives* + *-iste* -ist] **:** one who is in charge of archives **:** one responsible for the collection, cataloging, and preservation of archives

ar·chi·vis·tic \¦ärkə̇¦vistik, ¦ȧk-, -tēk\ *adj* **:** of or relating to archives

ar·chi·volt \ˈärkəˌvōlt, ˈȧk-\ *n* -s [It *archivolto*, fr. ML *archivoltum*, prob. modif. (influenced by ML *archi-* bow, fr. L *arqui-, arci-*, fr. *arcus*) of OF *arvolt, arcvolt* arch, arcade, fr. *arc* arch (fr. L *arcus*) + *volt* curved, fr. (assumed) VL *volvitus*, past part. of L *volvere* to roll — more at ARROW, VOLUBLE] **1 :** the architectural member or members forming the inner surface of an arch **2 a :** the usu. ornamental band or molding surrounding an arch and corresponding to the architrave of a rectangular opening **b :** the molding or other ornaments on the wall face of the voussoirs

archivolt 2a

ar·chi·zo·ic \¦ₑₑ¦zōik\ *adj* [*archi-* + *-zoic*] **:** of or relating to the earliest forms of life

arch·lute \ˈärch¦lüt\ *n* [F or It; F *archiluth*, fr. It *arciliuto, arcileuto*, fr. *arci-* archi- + *liuto, leuto* lute, fr. Ar *al-ʽūd* the lute, the wood] **:** a large lute **:** CHITARRONE, THEORBO

arch·ly \ˈärchlē, ˈȧch-, -li\ *adv* [[3]*arch* + *-ly*] **:** in an arch manner **:** with playful slyness or roguishness

arch·ness \-nə̇s\ *n* -ES [[3]*arch* + *-ness*] **:** the quality of being arch **:** playful slyness or roguishness

arch of corti *usu cap C* [after Alfonso *Corti* †1876 Ital. anatomist] *anat* **:** any of the series of arches composing the tunnel of Corti — compare ORGAN OF CORTI

arch of the fauces : PILLAR OF THE FAUCES

ar·chol·o·gy \ärˈkäləjē\ *n* -ES [*archi* + *-ology*] **:** the doctrine of origins

ar·chon \ˈärˌkän, -̩kən\ *n* -s [L, fr. Gk *archōn*, fr. pres. part. of *archein* to rule, begin — more at ARCHI-] **1 :** a chief magistrate in ancient Athens; *esp* **:** one of nine chief magistrates in Athens after 683 B.C. with executive, judicial, religious, military, legislative, and administrative functions **2 :** a magistrate of any of the Jewish communities of the Diaspora in the Greco-Roman period **3 :** a ruler, high official, presiding officer, or leader ⟨George Ripley, ~ of the Farm, built Brook Farm in the image of his belief —Tom Brooks⟩ **4** [MGk, fr. Gk] *Eastern Church* **a :** an ecclesiastical official who directs special services of a cathedral **b :** an ecclesiastic who administers various business matters of the churches of a patriarchate

ar·chon·tate \ˈₑ̩kənˌtāt\ *n* -s [F *archontat*, fr. *archonte* archon (fr. L *archont-, archon*) + *-at* -ate] **:** an archon's term of office

ar·chon·tia \ärˈkänch(ē)ə\ *n pl, cap* [NL, fr. Gk *archont-, archōn*, pres. part. of *archein*] **:** ARCHENCEPHALA

ar·cho·plasm \ˈärkəˌplazəm\ *also* **ar·cho·plas·ma** \ˌₑₑˈplazmə\ *n* -s [NL *archoplasma*, fr. *archo-* (fr. Gk *archōn* ruler) + *-plasma* — more at ARCHON] **:** supposedly specialized protoplasm formerly held to constitute the achromatic figure but now usu. regarded as an optical artifact indicative of changes in colloidal state occurring during mitosis — **ar·cho·plas·mic** \¦ₑₑ¦plazmik\ *adj*

arch order *n* **:** the system in classical architecture of framing arches with columns and entablatures — called also *Roman order*

ar·cho·sau·ria \ˌärkəˈsȯrēə\ *n pl, cap* [NL, fr. *archo-* (fr. Gk *archōn*) + *-sauria*] **:** a large subclass of Reptilia comprising the dinosaurs, pterosaurs, and crocodilians all distinguished by possessing temporal openings separated from each other by a postorbitosquamosal arch — **ar·cho·sau·ri·an** \¦ₑₑ¦ₑrēən\ *adj or n*

arch–poet \ˈärch, ˈȧch +¦-\ *n* [[1]*arch-* + *poet*] **:** a chief poet ⟨*arch-poet* in the king's court⟩

arch·presbyter \(ˈ)ärch +¦-\ *or* **ar·chi·presbyter** \¦ärkē +¦-\ *n* [LL *archipresbyter* — more at ARCHPRIEST] **:** ARCHPRIEST

arch·presbyterate \¦ärch+\ *or* **ar·chi·presbyterate** \¦ärkē +\ *n* [ML *archipresbyteratus*, fr. LL *archipresbyter* + L *-atus* -ate] **1 :** a district or part of a medieval diocese under an archpriest **2 :** a rural deanery

arch press *n* **:** a punch press having an arch-shaped frame giving greater width at the bolster plate and permitting operations on wider work at the expense of strength and rigidity in the frame

arch·priest \ˈärch¦prēst, ˈȧch-\ *n* [ME *archeprest*, fr. MF *archeprestre*, fr. LL *archipresbyter*, fr. L *archi-* + LL *presbyter* priest — more at PRIEST] **1 :** a chief priest **:** a priest who formerly acted as the chief assistant or as the vicar of a bishop in a cathedral particularly in liturgical functions — later called *dean* **2 :** a priest who formerly supervised the clergy of a town other than an episcopal city and the surrounding rural area — later called *rural dean* **3** *Eastern Church* **:** the highest title of honor given a member of the secular clergy

arch ring *n* **:** the curved member which is the main supporting element in an arched structure

-archs *pl of* -ARCH

arch·see \ˈärch¦sē\ *n* [[1]*arch-* + *see*] **:** an archbishop's see

arch spring *n* **:** the upward curve in the shank of a shoe or last measured from a straight line drawn from the ball to the heel

arch stone *also* **arch solid** *n* **:** VOUSSOIR

arch support *n* **:** a corrective device worn in the shoe and so molded as to provide support for the natural arch of the foot

archt *abbr* architect

arch·type \ˈärchˌtīp\ *n* [alter. of *archetype*] **:** ARCHETYPE 6

archway \ˈₑˌₑ\ *n* **:** a way or passage under an arch; *also* **:** an arch over a passage

-ar·chy \ˌärkē, ˌȧkē, -ki, *alternatively* -̩ə(r)kē *or* -ki *in a few common words (as "monarchy") in which the preceding syllable has stress*\ *n comb form* -ES [ME *-archie*, fr. MF, fr. L *-archia*, fr. Gk, fr. *-archēs* [1]-arch + *-ia* -y] **:** rule **:** government ⟨dy*archy*⟩ ⟨squire*archy*⟩

ar·ci·dae \ˈärsəˌdē\ *n pl, cap* [NL, fr. *Arca*, type genus + *-idae*] **:** a large family of chiefly tropical lamellibranch mollusks (order Filibranchia) with ribbed equivalve shell having a strong toothed hinge — see ARK SHELL

ar·cif·era \ärˈsif(ə)rə\ *n pl, cap* [NL, fr. L *arci-* (fr. *arcus* bow) + NL *-fera* (neut. pl. of *-fer* -ferous) — more at ARROW] **:** a division of the amphibian suborder Linguata including most of the frogs of the world and characterized by having the epicoracoids of the two sides overlapping each other — **ar·cif·er·al** \(ˈ)ₑ¦ₑ(ₑ)rəl\ *or* **ar·cif·er·ous** \-rəs\ *adj*

ar·ci·fin·i·ous \¦ärsə¦fineəs\ *adj* [L *arcifinius*, prob. fr. *arcēre* to hold off, enclose + *-i-* + *finis* boundary — more at ARK, FINAL] **1** *law* **:** having a natural boundary ⟨an ~ estate bounded by a river⟩ **2** *of a nation* **:** having a frontier forming a natural defense

ar·ci·form \ˈärsəˌfȯrm\ *adj* [L *arci-* (fr. *arcus* bow) + E *-form*] **:** having the form of an arch **:** CURVED

arcing *pres part of* ARC

arcing contact *n* **1 :** one of the readily replaceable parts (as of a circuit breaker) on which the arc, because of the opening of an electric circuit, is drawn after the main contacts have opened **2 :** BREAK JAW

arc lamp *n* **:** an electric lamp that produces light by means of an arc made when a current passes between two incandescent carbon or metal electrodes, the gas about the electrodes being at atmospheric pressure — see ENCLOSED ARC LAMP

arc light *n* **:** ARC LAMP; *also* **:** the light from an arc lamp

ar·co \ˈär(ˌ)kō\ *adv (or adj)* [It, bow, fr. L *arcus* — more at ARROW] **:** with the bow — usu. used as a direction in music for players of stringed instruments; compare PIZZICATO

ar·co·cen·trum \¦ärkō¦sen·trəm\ *n* [NL, fr. *arco-* (fr. L *arcus* bow) + *centrum*] **:** a centrum of a vertebra formed of basal parts or segments of the neural and hemal arches more or less modified and fused together — compare CHORDACENTRUM

arc of action : the arc made up in gearing of the arcs of approach and recess

arc of approach : the part of the arc of contact of toothed gearing along which the flank of the driving wheel touches the face of the driven wheel

arc of contact : the portion of a circular surface that is in contact with another surface (as that between a belt and a pulley); *specif* **:** the arc on a toothed gear between the point where the teeth first make contact with another gear wheel and the point where that contact ends

arc of lo·witz \-ˈlōˌvits\ *usu cap L* [after J. T. *Lowitz fl* 1794 Russ. astronomer] **:** a rare halo extending obliquely downward and inward from a 22 degree parhelion

arc of meridian 1 : a portion of a great circle of a sphere — used esp. with reference to the earth or the celestial sphere **2 :** a portion of a meridian curve

arc of recess *or* **arc of recession :** the part of the arc of contact in toothed gearing in which the face of the driving wheel touches the flank of the driven wheel

[1]**ar·co sal·tan·do** \¦är(ˌ)kōˌsälˈtän(ˌ)dō\ *n* [It, jumping bow] **:** a rapid staccato in which the bow rebounds from the string at each tone

[2]**arco saltando** \"\ *adv (or adj)* **:** with arco saltando **:** SALTATO, SAUTILLÉ, SPICCATO

arcose *var of* ARKOSE

ar·co·so·li·um \ˌärkəˈsōlēəm\ *n, pl* **arcoso·lia** \-lēə\ [NL, fr. *arco-* (fr. L *arcus* bow) + L *solium* seat, sarcophagus, fr. *sedēre* to sit — more at ARROW, SIT] **:** an arched cell in a Roman catacomb; *esp* **:** one designed to receive a sarcophagus

arc–over \ˈₑˌₑₑ\ *n* -s **:** an undesired arc following the opening of a switch or a breakdown of insulation

arcs *pl of* ARC, *pres 3d sing of* ARC

arc secant *n* **:** the inverse function to the secant ⟨if y is the secant of θ, then θ is the *arc secant* of y⟩ — called also *inverse secant*

arc sine *n* **:** the inverse function to the sine ⟨if y is the sine of θ, then θ is the *arc sine* of y⟩ — called also *inverse sine*

arc spectrum *n* **:** the spectrum of a substance that is vaporized by introducing it into an electric arc — compare SPARK SPECTRUM

arct- *or* **arcto-** *comb form* [L *arct-*, fr. Gk *arkt-, arkto-*, fr. *arktos* bear, Ursa Major, north — more at ARCTIC] **1 :** north **:** arctic ⟨*Arct*alia⟩ ⟨*Arcto*gaea⟩ **2 :** bear ⟨*Arct*oidea⟩ ⟨*Arcto*staphylus⟩

arc·ta·lian \(ˈ)ärk¦tālyən, -lēən\ *adj, usu cap* [NL *Arctalia* northern biogeographic realm (fr. *arct-* + *-alia*) + E *-an*] **:** of, relating to, or being the biogeographic realm that comprises all northern seas and extends southward as far as floating ice occurs

arct·american \¦ärkt+ₑ¦ₑₑₑ\ *adj, usu cap* [*arct-* + *American*] **:** NEARCTIC

arc tangent *n* **:** the inverse function to the tangent ⟨if y is the tangent of θ, then θ is the *arc tangent* of y⟩ — called also *inverse tangent*

[1]**arc·tic** \ˈärktik, ˈärd·ik, ˈärtik, ˈȧkt-, ˈȧd·-, ˈȧt-, -ēk — *the pronunciation without the first* k *is the original one in English (see etymology) and has centuries of oral tradition behind it*\ *adj* [alter. (influenced by L *arcticus*) of earlier *artic*, fr. ME *artik*, fr. ML *articus*, alter. of L *arcticus*, fr. Gk *arktikos*, fr. *arktos* bear, Ursa Major, north + *-ikos* -ic; akin to MIr *art* bear, L *ursus*, Skt *ṛkṣa*] **1** *sometimes cap* **:** of, in, characteristic of, or used in the region around the north pole to approximately 65° N ⟨~ nights⟩ ⟨~ waters⟩ ⟨~ clothing⟩ **2 a :** bitter cold **:** FRIGID ⟨~ temperatures⟩ **b :** cold in temper or mood ⟨an ~ smile⟩ **3** *usu cap* **:** of or belonging to an early Stone Age culture of northwestern Europe or to a culture based on the hunting of sea mammals on the islands of Bering strait **4** *usu cap* **:** of, relating to, or being a biogeographic realm or zone that comprises the tundra and treeless grounds lying north of timberline in the northern hemisphere or this together with more southerly areas that are above timberline — compare ALPINE BOREAL — **arc·ti·cal·ly** \-t¦ə̇k(ə)lē, -d·¦, ¦ēk-, li\ *adv*

[2]**arctic** \"\ *n* -s **:** a fabric-lined rubber overshoe reaching to the ankle or above and having a fastening device (as a buckle or zipper)

arctic

arctic air *n* **:** an air mass characterized by cold dry air from the arctic region — compare POLAR AIR

arctic–alpine \¦ₑₑ¦ₑ(ˌ)ₑ\ *adj, usu cap both A's* **:** NEARCTIC

arctic birch *n* **:** a low shrub (*Betula nana*) having small roundish leaves and found in northern boreal regions

arctic bluebell *n* **:** an arctic or alpine harebell (*Campanula uniflora*) with a solitary blue flower and narrow leaves

arctic chamomile *n* **:** a white-flowered herb (*Matricaria ambigua*) with dissected foliage found in northern Canada and Alaska

arctic charr *n* **:** a charr (*Salvelinus alpinus*) known from lakes and streams of arctic No. America but probably circumpolar in distribution — called also *arctic trout*

arctic circle *n, often cap A&C* **:** a small circle of the earth parallel to its equator approximately 23° 27′ from the north pole and circumscribing the frigid zone — see ZONE illustration

arctic dog disease *n, usu cap A* **:** a destructive disease of dogs in northwestern No. America related to or possibly identical with rabies

arctic fox *n, often cap A* **:** a small fox (*Alopex lagopus*) of the arctic regions of both hemispheres having valuable fur that is blue-gray or brownish in summer and white in winter — see BLUE FOX

arctic front *n* **:** the boundary between an arctic and a polar air mass

arctic grass *n* **:** RESCUE GRASS

arctic grayling *n, often cap A* **:** a grayling (*Thymallus signifer*)

ARCHITECTURE

Historic Styles	Types and Examples	Characteristic Features
EGYPTIAN		Mass, solidity, colossal size; source of the columnar orders and of lotiform ornament
OLD KINGDOM: B.C. 2980–2475	*Pyramids* at Giza	Simplicity of geometrical form; highly finished stonework
MIDDLE KINGDOM: B.C. 2160–1788	*Tombs* at Beni Hasan	Hewn in cliffs; open porticoes with columns, some of proto-Doric type
EMPIRE: B.C. 1580–1090	*Temple* at Der-el-Bahri	Terraced courts with colonnades; ascent by ramp
	Great temples, Karnak (Thebes)	Pylons, peristylar forecourts, hypostyle hall, and sanctuary; clerestory lighting; obelisks; colossi
	Temple at Elephantine	Exterior peristyle
PTOLEMAIC and ROMAN: B.C. 324–A.D. 330	*Temples* at Edfu and Philae	Rich elaboration and variety of detail; screen walls; Hathor-headed capitals
MESOPOTAMIAN		Massive brick construction with arches; terraced roofs; colored tile ornament; ziggurats
OLD BABYLONIAN KINGDOM: B.C. 2100–1750	*Houses* and *temples* at Babylon	Square open court, arched doorways, battlemented walls
ASSYRIAN EMPIRE: B.C. 885–607	*Palaces* at Khorsabad and Nineveh	Complex plan with interior courts; fortified walls with flanking towers, barbicans, etc.; doorways flanked with winged bulls; continuous friezes of sculpture
NEW BABYLONIAN KINGDOM: B.C. 612–538	*Temples* and *palaces* at Babylon	Great ziggurat, or "Tower of Babel"; vaulted substructure of "Hanging Gardens"
PERSIAN		Derivative forms from Egypt, Assyria, and Greece; native columnar forms with bull capitals
B.C. 550–330	*Palaces* and *tombs* at Persepolis	Propylaea and throne rooms, or apadanas, with slender columns
GREEK		Simplicity, symmetry; column and lintel construction in masonry
MINOAN: B.C. 3000–1400	*Palaces* at Knossos	Complex plan with terraced roofs, courts and light wells, stories and staircases
MYCENAEAN: B.C. 1500–1100	*Palaces* at Mycenae and Tiryns	Megaron with gabled roof and vestibule in antis; propylaea
	Beehive tombs at Mycenae	Circular chamber with pointed corbel vault
ARCHAIC: B.C. 776–480	*Doric temples* at Selinus and Akragas	Long narrow cella with exterior peristyle and gable roof; stout columns
TRANSITIONAL: B.C. 480–460	*Temple* of Zeus at Olympia	Broader cella divided by longitudinal colonnades; sculptured pediments
PERICLEAN: B.C. 460–400	*Temples,* Theseum, Parthenon, Erechtheum, Wingless Victory, at Athens	Subtle design and execution in marble; sculptured pediments and continuous friezes; delicate optical refinements; entasis and inclinations; Ionic order (of Asian origin) attains its established form
FOURTH CENTURY: B.C. 400–330	*Mausoleum* at Halicarnassus	High basement supporting peristyle crowned by pyramid; many friezes
	Tholos at Epidaurus	Circular cella with outer and inner peristyles, latter of the Corinthian order
HELLENISTIC: B.C. 330–146	*Altar* at Pergamum	Vast flight of steps leading to Ionic colonnade above basement with colossal sculptured frieze
	Pharos at Alexandria	Lighthouse tower of diminishing stages, square, octagonal, and circular
GRECO-ROMAN: B.C. 146–A.D. 330	*Temple* of Olympian Zeus at Athens	Colossal columns of the Corinthian order
ROMAN		Greek orders with arched construction; civil buildings for varied uses
ETRUSCAN: B.C. 500–300	*Tombs; temples; sewers,* Cloaca Maxima; *Gateway* at Perugia	Molded arch ring in stone, ample abutment
REPUBLICAN: B.C. 300–50	*Basilicas, bridges, aqueducts, theaters; temples,* "Fortuna Virilis"	Cella with engaged columns at sides and rear
IMPERIAL: B.C. 50–A.D. 330	*Fora; thermae,* Diocletian; *basilicas,* Constantine; *commemorative arches* and *columns; palaces* and villas; *amphitheaters,* Colosseum	Axial planning with vaulted interiors in groupings over extended areas; massive concrete cores with incrustation of marble
MEDIEVAL	The basilican *church*	Arched construction functionally used; freedom of craftsmanship
EARLY CHRISTIAN: 325–525	*Basilicas,* Santa Maria Maggiore, St. Paul beyond the Walls, Rome; *baptisteries*	T plan; light walls and wooden truss roofs; mosaic decoration
BYZANTINE: in Eastern Europe, 525–1453	*Domed churches,* St. Sophia, Constantinople; St. Mark's, Venice	Domed basilica, or Greek-cross plan, the dome placed over a square by means of pendentives; construction without centering; incised carving; mosaics
ROMANESQUE: in Western Europe, about 775–1200	*Churches,* esp. *monastic; castles*	Vaulted basilica; massive stone construction; round arched openings
Italian:	Sant' Ambrogio, Milan	Ribbed groined vaults with compound piers; arcaded and corbel cornices
	Cathedral, baptistery, and Leaning Tower at Pisa	Wooden-roofed basilica; exterior arcading in multiplied stories; optical refinements
French:	*Abbeys* of Cluny, Clairvaux, and Citeaux; Saint-Martin, Tours; Saint-Sernin, Toulouse	Experiments in vaulting, culminating in Île de France with Gothic system; Latin-cross plan; chevet with apse aisle and radiating chapels; west front with twin towers
English ("Norman"):	Durham Cathedral	Roofs mostly wooden, permitting high clerestory
German ("Rhenish"):	*Cathedrals* of Worms, Mainz, and Speyer	Double-ended church with two transepts and many turrets; triconch plans
Spanish:	Santiago de Compostela	Profusion of sculptured decoration
GOTHIC: 1160–1530	*Cathedrals; castles,* Coucy, Pierrefonds; *colleges,* Christ Church, Oxford; *town* and *guild halls,* Cloth Hall, Louvain	Ribbed vaulting, pointed arches, vertical lines; concentrated and balanced thrusts, making possible substitution for walls of large windows with tracery and stained glass; effects of complexity and mystery; scientific fortification
French: 12th Century:	Notre-Dame, Paris	Solution of structural problems; sexpartite vaults; relative solidity
13th Century:	Amiens; Reims; Sainte-Chapelle, Paris	Greater slenderness and height; quadripartite vaults; rose windows; vertical effect
14th Century:	Transept of Notre-Dame; Saint-Ouen, Rouen	Extremely thin geometrical lines
"Flamboyant": 1450–1530	Saint-Maclou, Rouen; N spire of Chartres	Flowing or flaming lines in tracery; profuse decoration
English:	*Abbeys,* Fountains, Ripon	Lancet-shaped windows without mullions; naves of great length
Early English "Lancet": 1180–1250	Salisbury Cathedral	Square east end
"Decorated" or "Geometric": 1250–1380	Lichfield Cathedral, "Angel Choir" of Lincoln	Multiple ribs and liernes; tracery at first geometric, then flowing or curvilinear; rich floral decoration
"Perpendicular": 1380–1530	King's College Chapel; St. George's, Windsor; Henry VII Chapel, Westminster	Fan vaulting with tracery and pendants; four-centered arches; perpendicular mullions with horizontal transoms
German:	Strasbourg and Ulm cathedrals	Nave and aisles sometimes of equal height; vault ribs fancifully curved
Italian:	*Cathedrals* of Florence, Siena, Orvieto	Relatively large wall surfaces with smaller windows; surface decoration of marble, mosaic, and painting
RENAISSANCE	*Palaces, villas, churches*	Revival and adaptation of classic orders and Roman types
ITALIAN: Early Renaissance: 1420–1500	Church of San Lorenzo, Pazzi Chapel, Riccardi Palace, Florence; Loggia, Verona	Reversion to basilican type with columns and wooden roof; dome over square, polygonal, and Greek-cross plans; delicate arabesque ornament
"High Renaissance": 1500–1540	Sant' Andrea, Mantua; Cancelleria Palace, St. Peter's, Vatican, Rome; Library of St. Mark's, Venice	Facades with superposed orders; classic proportions and detail with little decorative carving; repetition of uniform self-sufficient elements; calm serenity of horizontal lines and harmonious proportions
SPANISH: 1480–1570	Town Hall, Seville; Palace of Charles V, Granada	Plateresque ornament, Mudejar style with Moorish elements
FRENCH: 1495–1590	*Châteaux,* Blois, Chambord; Court of the Louvre, Paris	Classic ornaments on northern body; steep roofs, dormers, high chimneys; pavilions
ENGLISH: 1520–1625	*Country houses,* Longleat, Kirby	E and H plans; hall with tall mullioned windows, plaster ceilings, oak wainscot
GERMAN: 1520–1600	*Castles,* Heidelberg; *town halls,* Cologne	Fanciful arabesque decoration on northern body; stepped gables and dormers
ACADEMIC and BAROQUE 1540–1780	*Royal palaces, churches*	Strict classic proportions of the orders; plastic freedom of composition in mass and space
ITALIAN:	Colonnades of St. Peter's; Sant' Agnese, Rome; Santa Maria della Salute, Venice; *villas*	Dynamic opposition of unbalanced masses and lines; rustic columns, broken pediments; union of building and environment; terraced gardens
FRENCH:	Palace of Versailles; Colonnade of the Louvre	Stately formal exteriors with rich interior decoration culminating in rocaille ornament; plan with cour d'honneur
SPANISH:	Escorial; Town Hall of Salamanca	Somber walls with concentrated adornment of entrance; churriguerresque ornament
ENGLISH:	Banqueting House, Whitehall; St. Paul's Cathedral; *country houses*	Sober monumental treatment on Palladian models; adoption of Roman elements; garden temples of classic design
GERMAN:	Zwinger, Dresden	Lavish use of baroque forms
MODERN		Influence of historical and natural science, pure and applied
CLASSIC REVIVAL: 1760–1830	*Churches,* Madeleine, Paris; *government buildings; monuments*	Literal imitation of classic buildings, first Roman, then Greek; supremacy of abstract form over practical convenience
GOTHIC REVIVAL: 1750–1870	*Churches; college buildings;* Houses of Parliament, London	Imitation of medieval forms; revival of handicraft
ECLECTICISM: 1820–1900	*Theaters* and *opera houses,* Opera, Paris; *government buildings; libraries*	Free choice between the historic styles according to supposed appropriateness to use or to national and local traditions
FUNCTIONALISM: 1860–	*Railroad stations, factories, office buildings, exposition buildings;* Reliance Building, Chicago	Expression of use and material; exploitation of new materials (as iron and steel, glass, concrete)
INTERNATIONAL: 1920–	*Public buildings; residences; commercial structures;* Salvation Army building, Paris	Expression of contemporary techniques and design philosophies liberated from the limitations of historic or local influence

that is widely distributed in northern No. America and represented more southerly by two varieties, the Montana grayling and the Michigan grayling

arctic hare *n, usu cap A* : POLAR HARE

arctic hysteria *n* : a form of individual and mass hysteria that is peculiar to Arctic peoples and is characterized by compulsive mimicry

arc·ti·cize \-tə,sīz, -d-ə,-\ *vt* -ED/-ING/-S : to acclimate to or make suitable for arctic conditions

arctic moss *n, often cap A* : REINDEER MOSS

arctic owl *n, often cap A* : SNOWY OWL

arctic penguin *n, often cap A* : GREAT AUK

arctic poppy *n* : ICELAND POPPY

arctic seal *n, often cap A* : rabbit fur processed to simulate seal

arctic sea smoke *also* **arctic smoke** *or* **arctic mist** *n* : a fog that forms in arctic regions when very cold air flows over warmer waters

arctic skua *n, often cap A* : PARASITIC JAEGER

arctic tern *n, sometimes cap A* : a tern (*Sterna paradisaea*) resembling the common tern but breeding in the northern circumpolar regions and migrating to southern Africa and So. America

arctic timothy *n, sometimes cap A* : a grass (*Alopecurus alpinus*) used by the Eskimos for padding, insulation, and in a variety of other ways

arc·tic·tis \ärk'tiktəs\ *n, cap* [NL, fr. *arct-* + Gk *iktis* yellow-breasted marten] : the genus of aeluroid mammals (family Viverridae) consisting of the binturong

arctic trout *n* : ARCTIC CHARR

arctic willow *n, sometimes cap A* : a low shrub (*Salix arctica*) with pale foliage and stalked catkins found in arctic America and Asia

arctic wolf *n, often cap A* : a wolf of the arctic regions having white fur and a black-tipped tail and being perhaps a variety (*Canis lupus tundrarum*) of the timber wolf

arc·ti·id \'ärktēəd, -kshē-\ *adj* [NL *Arctiidae*] : of or relating to the Arctiidae

arc·ti·i·dae \ärk'tīə,dē\ *n pl, cap* [NL, fr. *Arctia*, type genus (fr. Gk *arktos* bear + NL *-ia*) + *-idae*; fr. the furry appearance — more at ARCTIC] : a large and variously delimited family of moths typically having stout bodies and broad wings often conspicuously striped or spotted, the larvae being usu. hairy caterpillars — see TIGER MOTH, WOOLLY BEAR

arc·tis·ca \ärk'tiskə\ [NL, fr. Gk *arktos* bear] *syn of* TARDIGRADA

arc·ti·um \'ärkshēəm, -ktēəm\ *n, cap* [NL, fr. Gk *arktion*, a plant, prob. fr. *arktos* bear] : a genus of Old World coarse biennial herbs (family Compositae) distinguished by the bristly receptacle of the flower heads and by the hooked involucral bracts — see BURDOCK

arcto- — see ARCT-

arc·to·ceph·a·lus \,ärk(,)tō'sefələs\ *n, cap* [NL, fr. *arct-* + *-cephalus*] : the genus containing the fur seals of the southern hemisphere

arc·to·cy·on·i·dae \;=(,)=,sī'änə,dē\ *n pl, cap* [NL, fr. *Arctocyon*, type genus (fr. *arct-* + Gk *kyōn* dog) + *-idae*] : a family of primitive generalized early Tertiary mammals that may belong to the direct ancestral line of the Carnivora

arc·to·gae·an *or* **arc·to·ge·an** \,ärktə'jēən\ *also* **arc·to·gae·al** *or* **arc·to·ge·al** \-ēəl\ *adj, usu cap* [NL *Arctogaea*, *Arctogea*, a biogeographic realm (fr. *arct-* + *-gaea*, *-gea*) + E *-an*] : of, relating to, or being a biogeographic realm that comprises the Holarctic, Ethiopian, and Oriental regions

¹arc·toid \'ärk,tȯid\ *adj* [NL *Arctoidea*] : of, relating to, or like the Arctoidea : URSINE

²arctoid \"\ *n* -S : an animal of the superfamily Arctoidea

arc·toi·dea \ärk'tȯidēə\ *n pl, cap* [NL, fr. *arct-* + *-oidea*] : a superfamily of Carnivora comprising bears, raccoons, weasels, and related forms and now but not formerly including the dogs — **arc·toi·de·an** \(')=;=dēən\ *adj*

arc·to·mys \'ärktə,mis\ [NL, fr. *arct-* + *-mys*] *syn of* MARMOTA

arc·to·nyx \-,niks\ *n, cap* [NL, fr. *arct-* + Gk *onyx* talon, claw — more at NAIL] : the genus that consists of the hog-nosed badgers

arc·to·staph·y·los \,ärk(,)tō'stafələs, -,läs\ *n* [NL, irreg. fr. *arct-* + Gk *staphylē* bunch of grapes — more at STAPHYLE] **1** *cap* : a genus of chiefly No. American woody plants (family Ericaceae) with alternate evergreen leaves, nodding flowers, and drupaceous fruits **2** -ES : a plant of the genus *Arctostaphylos* — see BEARBERRY

arc·to·tis \ärk'tōd·əs\ *n, cap* [NL, irreg. fr. *arct-* + Gk *ōt-*, *ous* ear; fr. the earlike pappus scales — more at EAR] : a genus of African herbs (family Compositae) having white woolly foliage and long-stalked flower heads — see AFRICAN DAISY 2

arc triangulation *n* : a triangulation that follows approximately the arc of a great circle on the earth's surface in order to tie in two distant control points — compare AREA TRIANGULATION, CONTROL 3c

ar·cu·al \'ärkyəwəl\ *adj* [L *arcus* bow, arc + E *-al* — more at ARROW] : of or relating to an arc

ar·cu·a·le \,ärkyə'wā(,)lē\ *n, pl* **arcua·lia** \-lēə\ [NL, fr. L *arcus* bow + *-ale* (neut. of *-alis* -al)] : any of the primitive cartilages or structural elements of which a typical vertebra is formed, there being four pairs, two dorsal and two ventral, usu. combined with various dorsal and ventral accessory elements

ar·cu·ate \'ärkyəwət, -,wāt\ *adj* [L *arcuatus*, past part. of *arcuare* to bend like a bow, fr. *arcus* bow] : bent or curved in the form of a bow ⟨~ veins in a leaf⟩ — **ar·cu·ate·ly** *adv*

ar·cu·at·ed \-,wād·əd\ *adj* [L *arcuatus* + E *-ed*] **1** : ARCUATE **2** *archit* : having arches

ar·cu·a·tion \,=;='wāshən\ *n* -S [L *arcuation-*, *arcuatio* arch, fr. *arcuatus* + *-ion-*, *-io* -ion] **1** : an arching or curving : INCURVATION ⟨the ~ of the face of a cliff⟩ **2** *archit* : the employment of arches; *also* : a system of arches

arcubalist *n* -S [LL *arcoballista*, *arcuballista* — more at ARBALEST] *obs* : ARBALEST

arcubalister *n* -S [LL *arcoballista*, *arcuballista* + E *-er*] *obs* : ARBALESTER

ar·cus \'ärkəs\ *n* -ES [NL, fr. L, bow, arch, arc — more at ARROW] **1** : a whitish ring-shaped or bow-shaped deposit sometimes seen in the cornea **2** : an arch-shaped cloud that sometimes accompanies a cumulonimbus

arc weld *n* : a weld made by arc welding

arc-weld \'=;=\ *vt* : to join by means of a form of fusion welding in which the heat for fusion is supplied by an electric arc formed between a metal or carbon electrode and the part being welded or between two separate electrodes or between the two separate pieces being welded — **arc welding** *n*

-ard \ə(r)d *or, in a few loan words from French (as "communard")*, ¦ärd *or* ¦äd\ *also* **-art** \ə(r)t\ *n suffix* -S [ME, fr. OF, of Gmc origin; akin to OHG *-hart* (in personal names such as *Gērhart* Gerard); akin to OE *heard* hard — more at HARD] : one that is characterized by performing some action, possessing some quality, or being associated with some thing esp. conspicuously or excessively ⟨*braggart*⟩ ⟨*drunkard*⟩ ⟨*dullard*⟩ ⟨*pollard*⟩ ⟨*sluggard*⟩ ⟨*stinkard*⟩ ⟨*wizard*⟩ : a large one of its kind ⟨*staggard*⟩

ar·da \'är(,)dä\ *n* -S *usu cap* [Sp, of AmerInd origin] : an extinct language family of southeastern Colombia

ar·dea \'ärdēə\ *n, cap* [NL, fr. L, heron; akin to ON *arta* garganey, Gk *erōdios* heron] : the type genus of Ardeidae including a number of large strong-flying New and Old World herons

ar·de·ae \'ärdē,ē\ *n pl, cap* [NL, fr. L, pl. of *ardea* heron] : the suborder of Ciconiiformes comprising the herons

ar·de·al·ite \,ärdē'ä,līt\ *n* -S [G *ardealit*, fr. *Ardeal* Transylvania, region of Romania + G *-it* -ite] : a mineral Ca_2H-$(PO_4)(SO_4).4H_2O$ consisting of a hydrous acid calcium phosphate-sulfate

ar·deb \'är,deb\ *also* **ar·dab** \-,dab\ *n* -S [colloq. Ar *ardabb* (class. Ar *irdabb*), fr. Gk *artabē*] : any of a number of Egyptian units of capacity; *esp* : the customs unit equal to 5.44 imperial or 5.619 U.S. bushels

ar·de·id \'ärdēəd\ *adj* [NL *Ardeidae*] : of or belonging to the Ardeidae

ar·de·i·dae \är'dēə,dē\ *n pl, cap* [NL, fr. *Ardea*, type genus + *-idae*] : a family of long-legged and long-necked migratory wading birds (order Ciconiiformes) comprising the herons and bitterns

ar·del·la \är'delə\ *n, pl* **ardel·lae** \-'delē\ [NL, perh. fr. Gk *arda* dirt (perh. fr. *ardein* to water) + NL *-ella*; akin to Skt *vari* water] : any of the small dust-resembling apothecia of certain lichens

ar·den·cy \'ärdᵊnsē, 'äd-, -si\ *n* -ES : the quality or state of being ardent : ARDOR, WARMTH ⟨the spirituality of Channing was enriched in Parker by the ~ of his loving nature —V.L. Parrington⟩

ar·dennes \(')är¦den(z)\ *n, pl* **ardennes** *usu cap* [fr. the *Ardennes* region in France and Belgium, where it originated] : a strong rugged medium-sized horse of draft type esp. popular in Sweden and Russia

ar·den·nite \'är'de,nīt\ *n* -S [G *ardennit*, fr. *Ardennes* region, Belgium, its locality + G *-it* -ite] : a mineral $Mn_5Al_5(VO_4)$-$(SiO_4)_5(OH)_2.2H_2O$ consisting of a hydrous silicate vanadate and arsenate of manganese and aluminum

¹ar·dent \'ärdᵊnt, 'äd-\ *adj* [ME *ardaunt*, *ardent*, fr. MF *ardant*, *ardent*, fr. L *ardent-*, *ardens*, pres. part. of *ardēre* to burn — more at ARDOR] **1 a** : characterized by warmth or heat of emotion, feeling, or sentiment : WARM, PASSIONATE ⟨a faint influence of his ~ spirit reached the West —R.W.Southern⟩ ⟨has left me a less ~ lover than I should perhaps otherwise have been —Samuel Butler †1902⟩ **b** : characterized by intensity : very strong or great : EXTREME ⟨gave constant proofs of his ~ longing for an education —R.B.Merriman⟩ ⟨glanced with ~ loathing at Mrs. Follansbee —Jean Stafford⟩ **c** (1) : extremely enthusiastic : EAGER, ZEALOUS ⟨an ~ naturalist⟩ (2) : extremely loyal : DEVOTED, FAITHFUL ⟨an ~ supporter of Gladstone —H.D.Jordan⟩ **2** : burning or causing a sensation of burning : FIERY, HOT ⟨an ~ fever⟩ ⟨the ~ sun⟩ **3** : INFLAMMABLE, COMBUSTIBLE — now used only in the phrase *ardent spirits* **4** : having the appearance of fire : GLOWING, SHINING ⟨from rank to rank she darts her ~ eyes —Alexander Pope⟩ **syn** see IMPASSIONED

²ardent \"\ *n* -S : ARDENT SPIRITS — used with *the* ⟨a man extremely fond of the ~⟩

ar·dent·ly *adv* [ME *ardauntly*, *ardently*, fr. *ardaunt*, *ardent* + *-ly*] : in an ardent manner

ar·dent·ness *n* -ES : the quality or state of being ardent

ardent spirits *n pl* : strong alcoholic liquors (as brandy, rum, whiskey) obtained by distillation : spirituous liquors

arder *n* -S [prob. fr. ON *arthr* plow; akin to *erja* to plow — more at EAR (to plow)] **1** *obs* : plowing or fallowing **2** *obs* : land left fallow

ar·dha·ma·ga·dhi \,ärdə'mägədē\ *n* -S *usu cap* : a Prakrit language of north India used in a large part of the Jain canon

ar·dis·ia \är'dizh(ē)ə\ *n* [NL, fr. Gk *ardis* point of an arrow + NL *-ia*; fr. the shape of the lobes of the corolla; perh. akin to OIr *aird* point, height] **1** *cap* : a genus of tropical evergreen shrubs and trees (family Myrsinaceae) having panicled flowers and drupaceous fruits **2** -S : a plant of the genus *Ardisia*

ar·doise \är'dwäz\ *n* [F, fr. lit., slate] : a grayish purple that is stronger than telegraph blue, bluer and deeper than mauve gray, and bluer and paler than average rose mauve

ar·dor *or* **ar·dour** \'ärdər, 'ädə(r)\ *n* -S [ME *ardour*, fr. MF & L; MF *ardour*, fr. L *ardor*, fr. *ardēre* to burn; akin to OHG *essa* forge, ON *arinn* hearth, L *arēre* to be dry, *aridus* dry, Gk *azein* to parch, Skt *āsa* ashes, dust] **1 a** : warmth or heat of emotion, feeling, or sentiment ⟨enough ~ in his tone to melt a heart of ice —Joseph Conrad⟩ : SPIRIT ⟨impressed the House as much by candor as by ~ —S.E.Morison⟩ : PASSION ⟨gave him love potions and herb teas to increase his ~ —Willa Cather⟩ **b** : extreme vigor, force, or energy : INTENSITY ⟨its ~ was the greater for being so long delayed —V.L.Parrington⟩ **c** (1) : intense enthusiasm or eagerness : FERVOR, ZEAL ⟨his ~ cooled off in the course of the war —Edmund Wilson⟩ ⟨desired it with an ~ that far exceeded moderation —Mary W. Shelley⟩ (2) : deep-seated devotion : FIDELITY, LOYALTY ⟨loving this country with that extra ~ of the immigrant —John Mason Brown⟩ **2** : strong or burning heat : FIRE, FLAME ⟨the ~ of the noonday sun⟩ **3** : an instance or an expression of an ardent emotion ⟨the stress of unbridled ~*s* —H.M.Parshley⟩ **syn** see PASSION

ar·dor uri·nae \'är,dȯryu̇'rī,nē, -,nī, -,dər-, -yə-\ *n* [NL, lit., heat of urine] : a scalding sensation during urination

ard·ri *also* **ard·righ** \ȯr'drē, är'-, '=,=\ *n* -S [IrGael *ārdrī*, fr. *ārd* high, noble (fr. OIr *ard*) + *rī* king, fr. OIr — more at ARDUOUS, RICH] : the high king in ancient Ireland — compare ⁹RIG

-ards *pl of* -ARD

ar·du·i·nite \,ärdə'wē,nīt, är'düə,n-\ *n* -S [Giovanni *Arduino* †1795 Ital. geologist + E *-ite*] : MORDENITE

ar·du·ous \'ärjəwəs, 'ä|, *Brit usu & US sometimes* |dyəw-\ *adj* [L *arduus* high, steep, difficult; akin to ON *ǫrthigr*, *ǫrthugr* high, steep, bold, OIr *ard* high, tall, Toch A *orto* up, Av *ərədva* high] **1 a** : hard to accomplish or achieve : DIFFICULT, ONEROUS ⟨building a college curriculum . . . is a long, ~, and difficult task —J.P.Leonard⟩ **b** : marked by great labor or effort : STRENUOUS, EXACTING ⟨determined to save him from a life of ~ toil —A.C.Cole⟩ **2** : hard to climb : STEEP, LOFTY ⟨those ~ paths they trod —Alexander Pope⟩ **3** : hard to endure : full of difficulties and hardships : TRYING ⟨your willingness after these six ~ days to remain here —F.D.Roosevelt⟩ **syn** see HARD

ar·du·ous·ly *adv* : in an arduous manner

ar·du·ous·ness *n* -ES : the quality or state of being arduous

¹are [ME *are*, *arne*, fr. OE *aron*, *earun*; akin to ON *eru* (they) are, *erum* (we) are, OE *is* — more at IS] *pres 2d sing or pres pl of* BE

²are \'a(a)(ə)r, 'e(ə)r, 'är\ *n* -S [F, fr. L *area*] : a metric unit of area equal to the area of a square 10 meters long on each side : 100 square meters — see METRIC SYSTEM table

ar·ea \'arēə, 'er-,'aar-,'ār-\ *n* -S [L, piece of level ground, threshing floor, fr. *arēre* to be dry; fr. its use as a place to dry grain, or fr. the vegetation's having been burned off — more at ARDOR] **1 a** : a level or relatively level piece of unoccupied or unused ground : a clear or open space of land ⟨plants his crops on any ~ he can find —P.E.James⟩ **b** : a definitely bounded piece of ground set aside for a specific use or purpose ⟨the state has provided several picnic ~*s* along the new highway⟩ ⟨a free parking ~ in the center of town⟩ **2** : the superficial contents of any figure : superficial extent : the surface included within any set of lines; *specif* : the number of squares, each with a side one unit long, that exactly cover a surface (as in certain rectangles) when it can be covered in such a manner or a number that is equally acceptable as a measure of the surface (as in spheres or circles) when it cannot be covered in this manner **3 a** : the enclosed space or site on which a building stands **b** : AREAWAY ⟨went down the steps into the ~ of a house —James Joyce⟩ **4 a** : a clear or open space within a building ⟨the communion table should be removed from the middle of the ~ —David Hume †1776⟩ **b** : a definitely bounded part or section of a building set aside for a specific use or purpose ⟨the house has a large kitchen ~⟩ **5** : any particular extent of space or surface: as **a** : a part of the surface of the human body ⟨if the ethyl fluid should come in contact with the skin, wash the ~ immediately —H.G.Armstrong⟩ **b** : an expanse or tract of the earth's surface ⟨a large ~ outside the marshes is submerged —Wilfred Thesiger⟩ **c** : a section, district, or zone of a town or city ⟨the shopping ~⟩ ⟨the residential ~⟩ **d** : a region or territory including and surrounding a city, consisting of a large part of a state or country or several states or countries, or embracing an entire continent or parts of more than one continent ⟨the Chicago ~⟩ ⟨the West Virginia mining ~⟩ ⟨the Caribbean ~⟩ ⟨Europe . . . was considered the chief danger ~ —A.O.Wolfers⟩ **e** : the territory assigned to a military unit ⟨the battalion's new ~ was on the fringe of the town —Bill Davidson⟩ **f** : CULTURE AREA **6 a** : the range or extent covered by or included in some thing or concept : the sphere or scope of operation or action : FIELD ⟨the whole ~ of foreign policy⟩ ⟨the novel has steadily widened the ~*s* of experience it will deal with —Bernard De Voto⟩ **b** : a system or sphere of intellectual activity or study; *specif* : a major section of a curriculum ⟨courses in the ~ of the humanities⟩ **7** : a part of the cerebral cortex regarded as having a particular function — see ASSOCIATION AREA, MOTOR AREA, SENSORY AREA **syn** see SIZE

COMMON AREA FORMULAS

FIGURE	FORMULA	MEANING OF LETTERS
rectangle	A=ab	a=base; b=height
square	A=a²	a=a side
triangle	$A=\frac{ab}{2}$	a=base; b=height
trapezoid	$A=\frac{h(a+b)}{2}$	h=height; a=the longer parallel side; b=the shorter side
parallelogram	A=ab	a=base; b=height
regular pentagon	A=1.720a²	a=a side
regular hexagon	A=2.598a²	a=a side
regular octagon	A=4.828a²	a=a side
circle	A=πr²	r=radius; π=3.1416

area am·ni·ot·i·ca \-,amnē'äd·əkə, -ēkə\ *n* [NL, amniotic area] : the transparent part of the mammalian blastodisc corresponding approximately to the area pellucida

area bombing *n* : air bombardment in which all attacking aircraft release their bombs in a fairly large target area instead of attempting to hit one specific target — called also *carpet bombing*, *pattern bombing*, *saturation bombing*; compare PRECISION BOMBING

aread *or* **areed** \ə'rēd\ *vt* **ared** \ə'red\ **ared; areading** *or* **areeding; areads** *or* **areeds** [ME *areden*, fr. OE *ārǣdan*, fr. *ā-* (perfective prefix) + *rǣdan* to advise, explain, read — more at ABEAR, READ] **1** *obs* : to make known : DECLARE, TELL **2** *archaic* : to explain the meaning of : INTERPRET ⟨rightly he *ared* the maid's intent —Robert Southey⟩ **3** *obs* : to give counsel to : ADVISE **4** *archaic* : ADJUDGE, DECREE ⟨did plain *areed* that unto him the horse belonged —Edmund Spenser⟩

ar·e·al \-ēəl\ *adj* [*area* + *-al*] : of, relating to, or involving an area; *specif* : of or belonging to the school of areal linguistics : interpreted in the manner of the school of areal linguistics

areal linguistics *also* **area linguistics** *n* : a school of historical and comparative linguistics that denies the existence of phonetic laws without exceptions, questions the value of attempts to trace individual languages back to a common ancestral language, and chiefly emphasizes the study of the transmission through space of linguistic innovations which is considered as taking place quite readily even between languages that are not of common origin — called also *neolinguistics*

ar·e·al·ly \-ēəlē, -li\ *adv* : in or according to area

area of langerhans *usu cap L* : ISLET OF LANGERHANS

area opa·ca \-ō'pākə\ *n* [NL, opaque area] : the peripheral opaque area surrounding the area pellucida of vertebrate embryos with discoidal cleavage

area pel·lu·ci·da \-pə'lüsədə\ *n* [NL, pellucid area] : the pellucid central area immediately surrounding the embryo in vertebrates with discoidal cleavage

area pla·cen·ta·lis \-,plasən'tāləs\ *n* [NL, placental area] : the part of the trophoblast in early placental vertebrate embryos that lies in immediate contact with the uterine mucosa

¹arear *vt* -ED/-ING/-S [ME *arearen*, *areren*, fr. OE *ārǣran* (akin to Goth *urraisjan*), fr. *ā-* (perfective prefix) + *rǣran* to rear, raise — more at ABEAR, REAR] *obs* : to raise up: as **a** : to set up : ERECT **b** : to raise in rank or status

²arear \ə'-\ *adv* ['*a-* + *rear* (n.)] : in or to the rear ⟨went ~ for rest and rehabilitation⟩

area research *n* : interdisciplinary research (as in the social sciences) in a distinct geographic, sociocultural, or political area aimed at a scientific understanding of the area as an entity and at relating it to other areas

areas *pl of* AREA

area study *n* : a study of a political or geographical area including its history, geography, language, and general culture

area target *n* : a target most profitably attacked by area bombing or for which the tactical or strategic situation demands area bombing

area triangulation *n* : triangulation extending in various directions from a control point and covering the region surrounding it — compare ARC TRIANGULATION, CONTROL 3c

area vas·cu·lo·sa \-,vaskyə'lōsə\ *n* [NL, vascular area] : the inner portion of the area opaca in which blood and blood-vessel formation is initiated

area vector *n* : the vector of a plane surface whose magnitude is the area of the figure and whose direction is that of a perpendicular to the plane of the figure

area vit·el·li·na \-,vid·ə'līnə, -,vī-\ *n* [NL, vitelline area] : the outer nonvascular portion of the area opaca

area wall *n* : a retaining wall surrounding an areaway

ar·ea·way \'==,=\ *n* : an open subsurface space adjacent to a building for affording access to or for lighting or ventilating a basement

are·ca \ə'rēkə, 'arəkə\ *n* [NL, fr. Pg *areca* betel palm, fr. Malayalam *aṭekka*, *aṭakka*] **1** *cap* : a small but important genus of pinnate-leaved palms of tropical Asia and the Malay archipelago characterized by the thick-rinded fruits — see BETEL PALM **2** -S : a palm of the genus *Areca* or of any of several genera related to *Areca* (as *Chrysalidocarpus lutescens*)

ar·e·ca·ce·ae \,arə'kāsē,ē\ *n pl, cap* [NL, fr. *Areca*, type genus + *-aceae*] *in some classifications* : a family of palms that is coextensive with Palmae or restricted to forms closely related to the areca palm

areca nut *n* : BETEL NUT

areca palm *n* : a palm of the genus *Areca*

are·co·line \ə'rēkə,lēn, -,lən\ *n* -S [ISV *arec-* (fr. NL *Areca*) + *-ol* + *-ine*] : a colorless oily toxic alkaloid $C_8H_{13}NO_2$ that is a derivative of nicotinic acid and constitutes the active principle of betel nuts

are·cu·na *or* **are·ku·na** \,ärə'künə\ *n, pl* **arecuna** *or* **arecunas** *or* **arekuna** *or* **arekunas** *usu cap* [Sp, of AmerInd origin] **1 a** : a Cariban people dwelling on the headwaters of the Caroni river in southeastern Venezuela **b** : a member of such people **2** : the language of the Arecuna people

ared *past of* AREAD

areed *var of* AREAD

a·re·flex·ia \¦ārə'fleksēə\ *n* -S [NL, fr. ²*a-* + ISV *reflex* + NL *-ia*] : absence of reflexes — **a·re·flex·ic** \¦=;=(,)==ik\ *adj*

aregenerative \¦ā + =;==(,)==\ *adj* [²*a-* + *regenerative*] : not regenerating after disease or injury

arei·to \ə'rā,tō\ *n* -S [Sp, fr. Taino *areyto* historical poem, song, dance] : a ceremonial dance among the Indians of Spanish America; *also* : the songs and masks associated with the dance

a-religious \¦ā + =;==\ *adj* [²*a-* + *religious*] : noncommittal or professedly neutral concerning religious matters

are·na \ə'rēnə\ *n* -S [L *harena*, *arena* sand, sandy place, arena] **1** : the area in the central part of a Roman amphitheater where gladiatorial combats and other spectacles took place **2 a** : a central area or open space within an enclosure used for public entertainment ⟨the circus elephants were led into the ~⟩ ⟨the livestock ~ had once been a small auto race track⟩ ⟨the side ~ seats in Madison Square Garden were full⟩ **b** : a building containing an arena used esp. for indoor sports ⟨the wrestling ~ burned to the ground⟩ **3** : a sphere or field of interest, activity, or controversy : SCENE ⟨left in undisputed control of the political ~ —H.S.Commager⟩

arenaceo- *comb form* [perh. fr. F *arénacéo-*, fr. L *arenaceus*] : arenaceous and ⟨*arenaceo*-argillaceous⟩

ar·e·na·ceous \,arə'nāshəs\ *adj* [L *harenaceus*, *arenaceus*, fr. *harena*, *arena* + *-aceus* -aceous] **1** : resembling, made of, or containing sand or sandy particles : SANDY ⟨~ limestone⟩ ⟨the ~ elytra of a beetle⟩ **2** : growing in sandy places

ar·e·nar·ia \,=='na(a)rēə\ *n, cap* [NL, fr. LL *harenaria*, *arenaria*, fem. of *harenarius*, *arenarius* of sand] : a genus of widely distributed chiefly low-tufted herbs with sessile leaves (family Caryophyllaceae) — see THYME-LEAVED SANDWORT

ar·e·nar·i·ous \,=='=ēəs\ *adj* [LL *harenarius*, *arenarius*, fr. L *harena*, *arena* + *-arius* -ary] : ARENACEOUS

arena theater *n* **1** : a theater having the acting area in the center of the auditorium with the audience seated on all sides of the stage — called also *theater-in-the-round* **2** : the style or method of staging plays in an arena theater

aren·dal·ite \ə'rendᵊl,īt\ *n* -S [G *arendalit*, fr. *Arendal*, Norway, its locality + G *-it* -ite] : a variety of epidote

ar·ene \'a,rēn, ≠'≠\ *n* -s [*ar*omatic + *-ene*] **:** an aromatic hydrocarbon (as benzene, toluene, naphthalene)

aren·ga \ə'reŋgə, -eŋgə\ *n, cap* [NL, fr. Jav *arén*] **:** a genus of tropical Asiatic and Malaysian palms having pendent branching spadices and large berrylike fruits — see GOMUTI

ar·e·nic·o·la \,arə'nikələ\ *n, cap* [NL, fr. L *hareni-, areni-* (fr. *harena, arena* sand) + *-cola* inhabitant — more at -COLOUS] **:** a genus of stout-bodied burrowing polychaete worms comprising the lugworms — **ar·e·nic·o·lid** \-ələd\ *adj or n*

ar·e·nic·o·lite \-ə,līt\ *n* -s [NL *Arenicola* + E *-ite*] **:** a marking found on certain stratified rocks generally regarded as the trail of a mollusk or crustacean though formerly supposed to represent arenicolous worm burrows or trails

ar·e·nic·o·lous \¦≠≠¦≠ələs\ *adj* [L *arena, harena* sand + E *-i-* + *-colous*] **:** inhabiting or burrowing in sand **:** growing in sand soil

are·nig \ə'rānig\ *adj, usu cap* [fr. *Arenig* mountains, Wales] **:** of or relating to a subdivision of the European Ordovician — see GEOLOGIC TIME table

ar·e·nite \'arə,nīt, ə'rē,-\ *n* -s [L *arena, harena* sand + E *-ite*] **:** medium-grained detrital rock (as sandstone, graywacke, arkose, and orthoquartzite) — **ar·e·nit·ic** \¦arə¦nid·ik\ *adj*

aren't \="*are not*", (¦)ärnt, (¦)ånt *also* (*esp when emphatic or sentence-final*) ¦ärənt *or* ¦årənt; = "*am not*" (*most often in the speech of r-droppers*), (¦)ånt, (¦)ärnt\ [by contr.] **1 :** are not ⟨they *aren't* going⟩ **2 :** am not — used in questions ⟨the thing is, Sidney, *aren't* I ever to know you?—Elizabeth Bowen⟩

areo- *comb form* [Gk *Arēs* Ares (god of war), Mars (planet)] **:** the planet Mars ⟨*areo*centric longitude⟩ **:** of or belonging to the planet Mars ⟨*areo*graphy⟩

1**ar·e·og·ra·phy** \,a(a)rē'ägrəfē\ *n* -ES [*areo-* + *-graphy*] **:** description of the surface of the planet Mars

2**areography** \"\ *n* -ES [*area* + *-o-* + *-graphy*] **:** descriptive biogeography

are·o·la \ə'rēələ\ *n, pl* **areolae** \-ə,lē, -lī\ *or* **areolas** [NL, fr. L, small open space, dim. of *area* piece of level ground — more at AREA] **:** a small area: as **a :** an interstice or small space (as between the veins of leaves, between the cracks of the surface in certain crustaceous lichens, between the fibers composing organs or vessels that interlace, or between the nervures of an insect's wing) **b :** the colored ring around the nipple or around a vesicle or pustule **c :** the portion of the iris that borders the pupil of the eye

are·o·lar \-ələ(r)\ *adj* **1 :** of, relating to, or like an areola **:** filled with interstices **2 :** of, relating to, or consisting of areolar tissue

areolar tissue *n* **:** fibrous connective tissue having the fibers loosely arranged in a net or meshwork

are·o·late \-ələt, -,lāt\ *also* **are·o·lat·ed** \-ə,lād·əd\ *adj* [NL *areola* + E *-ate, -ated*] **:** divided into or marked by areolae

areolate mildew *n* **:** a leaf spot of cotton caused by an imperfect fungus (*Ramularia areola*)

are·o·la·tion \ə,rēə'lāshən, ,a(a)rē-\ *n* -s **1 :** division into areolae **2 :** an areola or space marked by areolae

ar·e·ole \'a(a)rē,ōl\ *n* -s [F *aréole*, fr. L *areola*] **1 :** AREOLA **2 a :** one of the thinner areas arranged in characteristic pattern in the siliceous deposit on the wall of diatoms — compare PUNCTA **b :** a small pit or cavity (as that from which the spines arise in cacti)

are·o·let \ə'rēələt, 'a(a)rēə,let\ *n* -s [blend of NL *areola* and E *-let*] **:** a small areola

ar·e·ol·o·gy \,arē'äləjē, -ji\ *n* -ES [*areo-* + *-logy*] **:** the scientific study of the planet Mars

ar·e·om·e·ter \,arē'ämǝd·ə(r)\ *n* -s [prob. fr. F *aréomètre*, fr. Gk *araios* thin + F *-mètre* -meter] **:** HYDROMETER — **ar·e·o·met·ric** \¦≠≠ə¦me·trik\ *or* **ar·e·o·met·ri·cal** \-trəkəl\ *adj* — **ar·e·o·met·ri·cal·ly** \-ək(ə)lē\ *adv*

ar·e·op·a·gite \,arē'äpə,jīt, -,gīt\ *n* -s *usu cap* [L *Areopagites*, fr. Gk *Areopagitēs*, fr. *Areiopagos* + *-itēs* -ite] **:** a member of the tribunal of the Areopagus

ar·e·op·a·git·ic \¦≠≠,≠≠¦jid·ik\ *adj, usu cap* [LL *Areopagiticus*, fr. Gk *Areopagitikos*, fr. *Areopagitēs* + *-ikos* -ic] **:** of or relating to the Areopagus

ar·e·op·a·gus \,arē'äpəgəs\ *n* -ES *usu cap* [L, fr. Gk *Areiopagos*, alter. of *Areios pagos*, lit., hill of Ares (a hill in Athens where the supreme tribunal met), fr. *Areios* of Ares (fr. *Arēs* Ares, Greek god of war) + *pagos* rock, rocky hill, frost — more at PAGOSCOPE] **1 :** the supreme tribunal of Athens **2 :** any tribunal or group of persons whose judgments are decisive or authoritative

areostyle *var of* ARAEOSTYLE

areosystyle *var of* ARAEOSYSTYLE

are·re \ə'rerē\ *n* -s [native name in Africa] **:** OBECHE

ares *pl of* ARE

ar·e·ta·ics \,arə'tāiks\ *n pl but sing in constr* [irreg. fr. Gk *aretē* + E *-ics*] **:** science of virtue — contrasted with *eudaemonics*

ar·e·tal·o·gy \,arə'taləjē\ *n* -ES [Gk *aretalogia*, fr. *aretē* virtue + *-logia* -logy] **:** a narrative of the miraculous deeds of a god or hero

1**arête** \ə'rāt, a'-\ *n* -s [F, ridge, fishbone, beard of grain, fr. LL *arista* fishbone, fr. L, beard of grain] **:** a sharp-crested ridge in rugged mountains commonly present in those (as the Alps) that have been sculptured by glaciers

2**ar·e·te** \,arə'tā, -tē\ *n* -s [Gk *aretē*, fr. *areskein* to appease, please, satisfy; akin to *arariskein* to fit — more at ARM] **:** the sum of good qualities that make character **:** EXCELLENCE, VALOR, VIRTUE, MANLINESS

ar·e·thu·sa \,arə'th(y)üzə, -sə\ *n* [NL, fr. L *Arethusa*, fountain nymph of Elis transported to Sicily to escape from the pursuit of the river god Alpheus, fr. Gk *Arethousa*] **1** *cap* **:** a genus of bog orchids having small bulbs with a single linear leaf and a solitary purple-fringed flower that appears in late spring **2** -s **:** a plant of the genus *Arethusa*

ar·e·tin·i·an \¦≠≠¦tinēən, -tē-\ *adj, usu cap* [It *aretino* of Guido d'Arezzo †*ab* 1050 Ital. monk and musician, lit., of Arezzo, city in Tuscany, Italy, where he lived (fr. L *Arretinus*, fr. *Arretium* Arezzo + *-inus* -ine) + E *-ian*] **:** GUIDONIAN

arf·ved·son·ite \'ärvədsə,nīt\ *n* -s [J.A.*Arfvedson* †1841 Swedish chemist + E *-ite*] **:** a silicate of sodium, calcium, and iron, approximately $Na_{2\text{-}3}(Fe,Mg,Al)_5Si_8O_{22}(OH)_2$, of the amphibole group occurring in black monoclinic strongly pleochroic prisms in certain igneous rocks

arg *abbr* **1** argent; argentum **2** argument

1**ar·gal** \'ärgəl\ *adv* [alter. of *ergo*] **:** THEREFORE — used chiefly to imply that the reasoning is specious or absurd

2**argal** *var of* ARGOL

ar·ga·li \'ärgəlē, -li\ *n, pl* **argali** *or* **argalis** [Mongolian] **1 :** a large wild sheep (*Ovis ammon*) having immense horns, widely distributed in mountainous central and eastern Asia, and being probably not on the direct ancestral line of domesticated sheep though some authorities regard certain of its races as an ancestor of the fat-tailed sheep **2 :** any of several large wild sheep (as the bighorn or the aoudad) **3 :** HAIR BROWN

argali (*Ovis ammon*)

ar·gand burner \'är,gan(d)-, -än(d)-, -gən(d)-\ *n, usu cap A* [after Aimé *Argand* †1803 Swiss physicist and inventor] **:** a burner for an Argand lamp or a gas burner applying the principle of that lamp

argand diagram *n, usu cap A* [after Jean Robert *Argand* †1825 Fr. mathematician] **:** a conventional diagram or graph in which the complex number $x + iy$ is represented by the point whose rectangular coordinates are x and y

argand lamp *n, usu cap A* [after Aimé *Argand*] **:** a lamp with a tubular wick that admits a current of air inside as well as outside of the flame

ar·gan oil \'ärgən-, -,gan-\ *n* **:** a fatty oil obtained from the seeds of the argan tree and used in cooking

ar·gan·ti·dae \är'gantə,dē\ [NL, fr. *Argant-, Argas*, type genus + *-idae*] *syn of* ARGASIDAE

ar·gan tree *n* [Ar *arjān*] **:** a tall Moroccan tree (*Argania sideroxylon*) of the family Sapotaceae bearing fruits like olives that are used as a cattle food and seeds that yield argan oil

ar·gas \'ärgəs, -,gas\ *n, cap* [NL, perh. irreg. fr. Gk *argos* idle, fr. *a-* 2a- + *-ergos* (fr. *ergon* work) — more at WORK] **:** a genus (the type of the family Argasidae) of ticks including the cosmopolitan chicken tick (*A. persicus*), a serious enemy of poultry in warmer countries

ar·ga·sid \'≠gəsəd\ *adj* [NL *Argasidae*] **:** of or relating to the Argasidae

ar·gas·i·dae \är'gasə,dē\ *n pl, cap* [NL, fr. *Argas*, type genus + *-idae*] **:** a family of ticks that includes a number of medically and economically important ticks all of which lack a scutum and exhibit no marked sexual dimorphism — see ARGAS, ORNITHODOROS

1**ar·ge·an** \(')är¦jēən\ *adj, usu cap* [*Argo*, ship in which the Argonauts sailed, constellation in the southern hemisphere (fr. Gk *Argō*) + E *-ean*] **:** relating to the ship or the constellation Argo

2**argean** \"\ *adj, usu cap* [*Argeia* or *Argos*, district of ancient Greece (fr. Gk) + E *-an, -ean*] **:** of or relating to the district of Argeia or Argos or its inhabitants

ar·gel \'ärgəl, -,gel\ *n* -s [EgyptAr *ḥargel*] **:** either of two related African plants (*Solenostemma argel* and *Asclepias fruticosus*) whose leaves have been used to adulterate senna

ar·ge·lan·der's method \'ärgə,landərz-, -län-\ *n, cap A* [after F.W.A. *Argelander* †1875 Ger. astronomer] **:** a method of visual photometry that determines the magnitude of a star or the extent of changes in brightness of a variable star by comparisons with a sequence of neighboring stars of slightly different magnitudes

ar·gem·o·ne \är'jemənē; 'ärjə,mōnē, ,≠≠'≠≠\ *n* [NL, fr. L, wind rose (*Papaver argemone*), fr. Gk *argemōnē*] **1** *cap* **:** a genus of American herbs (family Papaveraceae) having yellow sap, prickly leaves, and showy white or yellow flowers — see PRICKLY POPPY **2** -s **:** a plant of the genus *Argemone*

argemone oil *n* **:** a semidrying fatty oil obtained from the prickly poppy

1**ar·gent** \'ärjənt, 'äj-\ *n* -s [ME, fr. MF & L; MF *argent*, fr. L *argentum;* akin to OIr *arggat* silver, L *arguere* to make clear, Gk *argyros* silver, *argos* white, Skt *rajata* silver, whitish] **1** *archaic* **a :** the metal silver **b :** WHITENESS ⟨the polished ~ of her breast —Alfred Tennyson⟩ **2** *obs* **:** silver coin **:** MONEY **3 :** a metal tincture used in heraldry and conventionally supposed to be represented by silver but in practice represented by either silver or white **4 :** SILVER 6b

2**argent** \"\ *adj* **1 :** made of or resembling silver **:** SILVERY **2 :** shining like silver **:** silvery white ⟨the prophet was already erect with ~ garments and uplifted hands —G.K.Chesterton⟩ **3 :** of the heraldic metal argent — abbr. *arg.*

argent- *or* **argenti-** *or* **argento-** *comb form* [MF *argent-*, fr. L, fr. *argentum*] **:** silver ⟨*argent*amide⟩ ⟨*argenti*nitrate⟩ ⟨*argento*metry⟩

argenta dei *pl of* ARGENTUM DEI

ar·gen·taf·fin \är'jentəfən\ *or* **ar·gen·taf·fine** \", -ə,fēn\ *adj* [prob. back-formation fr. *argentaffinity*, fr. *argent-* + *affinity*] **1 a :** depositing reduced silver from ammoniated silver hydroxide solutions — used of certain cell granules containing phenols or polyamines **b :** of, relating to, or being a cell type of the gastrointestinal tract that is postulated to have a role in the production of intrinsic factor **2 :** ARGENTOPHIL — **ar·gen·taf·fin·i·ty** \≠,≠ə'finəd·ē\ *n*

ar·gen·taf·fi·no·ma \är,jentəfə'nōmə, ,är,jən,tafə'-\ *n* -s [NL, fr. E *argentaffin* + NL *-oma*] **:** CARCINOID

ar·gen·tal mercury \(')är¦jent°l-\ *n* [part trans. of F *mercure argental; argental*, fr. *argent* silver + *-al* — more at ARGENT] **:** a native silver amalgam

ar·gen·tan \'ärjən,tan\ *n* -s *usu cap* [fr. *Argentan*, commune in France where it is made] **:** a needlepoint lace of the Alençon type with bold designs

ar·gen·tate \'ärjən,tāt\ *adj* [L *argentatus* silver-plated, fr. *argentum* silver + *-atus* -ate — more at ARGENT] **:** SILVERY

ar·gen·te·ous \(')är¦jentēəs, (')å¦j-\ *adj* [L *argenteus*, fr. *argentum* + *-eus* -eous] **:** SILVERY

ar·gen·te·um \-tēəm\ *n* -s [NL, fr. L, neut. of *argenteus*] **:** a layer of connective tissue containing microscopic crystals of guanine that forms a reflecting surface in the skin of many fishes and is the source of pearl essence

ar·gen·tian \(')är¦jenchən\ *adj* [*argent-* + *-ian*] **:** containing silver ⟨~ galena⟩

ar·gen·tic \(')är¦jentik, -ēk, (')å¦j-\ *adj* [*argent-* + *-ic*] **:** of, relating to, or containing silver — used esp. of compounds in which this element is bivalent; compare ARGENTOUS

ar·gen·tif·er·ous \¦≠jən¦tif(ə)rəs\ *adj* **:** producing or containing silver

1**ar·gen·ti·na** \¦ärjən¦tēnə, ¦åj-\ *adj, usu cap* [fr. *Argentina*, country in So. America] **:** of or from Argentina **:** of the kind or style prevalent in Argentina **:** ARGENTINE

2**argentina** \", -īnə\ *n, cap* [NL, fr. *argent-* + *-ina* (fr. L, fem. of *-inus* -ine)] **:** the type genus of the family Argentinidae

3**argentina** \"\ *n* -s *often cap* [prob. fr. *Argentina*, country in So. America] **:** ART BROWN

1**ar·gen·tine** \'≠≠,tīn *also* -tən *or* -,tēn\ *adj* [ME, fr. MF *argentin*, fr. OF, fr. *argent* silver + *-in* -ine — more at ARGENT] **:** relating to, containing, or resembling silver **:** SILVERY

2**argentine** \"\ *n* -s **1 :** SILVER; *also* **:** any of various materials resembling it (as plate metal) **2 :** any of various small silvery-scaled marine fishes: as **a :** PEARLSIDES **b :** any of various fishes of the genera *Argentina* or *Myctophum* **3 :** a pearly variety of calcite with undulating lamellae

3**argentine** \-,tēn, -īn\ *adj, usu cap* [Sp *argentino*, adj. & n., fr. *Argentina*, country in So. America] **:** of or relating to Argentina

4**argentine** \"\ *n* -s [Sp *argentino*] **1** *cap* **:** a native or inhabitant of Argentina **2 :** a ballroom dance similar to the tango but distinguished by low dips, scissors, and twisting steps on the toes

1**ar·gen·tin·e·an** *or* **ar·gen·tin·i·an** \¦ärjən¦tinēən, ¦åj-, -¦tē-, -nyən\ *adj, usu cap* [*Argentina* + E *-ean* or *-ian*] **:** 3ARGENTINE

2**argentinean** *or* **argentinian** \"\ *n* -s *cap* **:** 4ARGENTINE 1

argentine ant *n, usu cap 1st A* [3*Argentine*] **:** a small brown ant (*Iridomyrmex humilis*) introduced from So. America into the southern and western U.S., Australia, southern Africa, and other warm regions where it has become a household and orchard pest

ar·gen·tin·i·dae \,ärjən'tinə,dē\ *n pl, cap* [NL, fr. *Argentina*, type genus + *-idae*] **:** a family of small silvery marine fishes related to the salmons and trouts and including the capelins and a few other fishes and formerly the true smelts

ar·gen·ti·no \-'tē(,)nō\ *n* -s [Sp — more at ARGENTINE] **1** *cap* **:** 4ARGENTINE 1 **2 :** a gold coin of Argentina worth five pesos and issued between 1880 and 1914

ar·gen·tite \'ärjən,tīt\ *n* -s [G *argentit*, fr. *argent-* + *-it* -ite] **:** a sectile mineral Ag_2S consisting of native silver sulfide, having a metallic luster and dark lead-gray color, occurring in isometric crystals and in masses and coatings, and constituting a valuable ore of silver (hardness 2–2.5, sp. gr. 7.20–7.36)

argento- — see ARGENT-

ar·gen·to·cyanide \är,jentō +\ *n* [*argent-* + *cyanide*] **:** any of a series of complex salts (as sodium argentocyanide $Na[Ag(CN)_2]$ formed in the cyanide process for silver) made by the union of silver cyanide with another cyanide

ar·gen·to·jarosite \≠,≠≠+\ *n* [*argent-* + *jarosite*] **:** a mineral $AgFe_3(SO_4)_2(OH)_6$ consisting of basic silver ferric sulfate resembling jarosite but with silver replacing potassium

ar·gen·tom·e·ter \,ärjən'tämǝd·ə(r)\ *n* -s [*argent-* + *-meter*] **:** an instrument for measuring the amount of silver salt in a solution (as by finding the specific gravity or by photoelectric means)

ar·gen·to·met·ric \(')är¦jentə¦me·trik\ *adj* [*argent-* + *-metric*] **:** relating to or making use of argentometry — **ar·gen·to·met·ri·cal·ly** \-trək(ə)lē\ *adv*

ar·gen·tom·e·try \,ärjən'tämə·trē\ *n* -ES [*argent-* + *-metry*] **:** chemical analysis involving the use of silver compounds; *esp* **:** a volumetric method employing a silver salt solution

ar·gen·ton \är'jent°n\ *n* -s [modif. of L *argentum* silver — more at ARGENT] **:** an alloy of nickel, copper, and zinc first used for coins by the Swiss in 1850

ar·gen·to·phil \(')är¦jentə,fil\ *or* **ar·gen·to·phile** \-,fīl\ *or* **ar·gen·to·phil·ic** \≠¦≠≠¦filik\ *adj* [*argent-* + *-phil, -phile, -philic*] **:** having an affinity for silver — used of certain cells, structures, or tissues that selectively reduce silver salts to metallic silver

ar·gen·to·pro·te·i·num \är¦jentō,prōtē'īnəm\ *n* -s [NL, fr. *argent-* + ISV *protein*] **:** SILVER PROTEIN

ar·gen·tose \'ärjən,tōs, är'jen-\ *n* -s [*argent-* + *-ose*] **:** a compound of silver and a nucleoprotein used like silver nitrate as an astringent antiseptic

argen·tous \(')är¦jentəs\ *adj* [*argent-* + *-ous*] **:** of, relating to, or containing silver — used esp. of compounds in which this element is univalent; compare ARGENTIC

ar·gen·tum \är'jentəm\ *n* -s [L — more at ARGENT] **:** SILVER — symbol *Ag*

ar·gen·tum dei \-'dē,ī, -'dā,ē\ *n, pl* **argen·ta dei** \-tə-\ *usu cap D* [ML, lit., God's silver] **:** GOD'S PENNY

argh \'ärf, 'ärk\ *adj* [ME, cowardly, lazy, slow, wretched, fr. OE *earg;* akin to OFris *erg* evil, bad, OHG *arg, arag* cowardly, worthless, stingy, ON *argr* evil, homosexual, effeminate, Av *ərəgant-* evil, repulsive, Lith *aržùs* sensual, lustful] *dial Eng* **:** TIMID, COWARDLY

ar·ghan \'ärgən\ *n* -s [origin unknown] **:** PITA 1c

ar·ghool *also* **ar·ghoul** \är'gül\ *n* -s [Ar *arghūl*] **:** an Egyptian musical reed instrument

ar·gi·dae \'ärjə,dē\ *n pl, cap* [NL, fr. *Arge*, type genus (perh. fr. Gk *argēs* bright) + *-idae;* akin to Gk *argos* white — more at ARGENT] **:** a family of sawflies having 3-jointed antennae

ar·gil \'ärjəl\ *n* -s [ME *argil, argilla*, fr. L *argilla*, fr. Gk *argillos;* akin to Gk *argos* white] **1 :** CLAY; *esp* **:** POTTER'S CLAY **2 :** ALUMINA

argill- *or* **argilli-** *or* **argillo-** *comb form* [ME *argill-*, fr. L, fr. *argilla*] **1 :** clay ⟨*argilli*ferous⟩ ⟨*argill*oid⟩ **2 :** argillaceous and ⟨*argillo*arenaceous⟩

argillaceo- *comb form* [*argillaceous*] **:** argillaceous and ⟨*argillaceo*calcareous⟩

ar·gil·la·ceous \¦ärjə¦lāshəs\ *adj* [L *argillaceus*, fr. *argilla* + *-aceus* -aceous] **:** of, relating to, or containing clay or clay minerals **:** CLAYEY ⟨~ rocks⟩

ar·gil·lic \(')är¦jilik\ *adj* [*argill-* + *-ic*] **:** of or relating to clay or clay minerals **:** ARGILLACEOUS ⟨~ alteration⟩

ar·gil·lif·er·ous \¦ärjə¦lif(ə)rəs\ *adj* [*argill-* + *-ferous*] **:** producing or abounding in clay

ar·gil·lite \'ärjə,līt\ *n* -s [*argill-* + *-ite*] **:** a compact argillaceous rock differing from shale in being cemented by silica and from slate in having no slaty cleavage — **ar·gil·lit·ic** \¦≠≠¦lid·ik\ *adj*

ar·gil·loid \'≠≠,lȯid\ *adj* [ISV *argill-* + *-oid*] **:** like clay

ar·gil·lous \(')är¦jiləs\ *adj* [ME *argillose, argillous*, fr. L *argillosus*, fr. *argilla* + *-osus* -ose] **:** ARGILLACEOUS

ar·gi·nase \'ärjə,nās\ *n* -s [ISV *argin*ine + *-ase*] **:** a crystalline enzyme obtained esp. from liver that converts naturally occurring arginine into ornithine and urea

ar·gi·nine \-,nēn, -nən\ *n* -s [ISV *argin-* (perh. fr. Gk *arginoeis* bright, white) + *-ine;* orig. formed as G *arginin*] **:** a crystalline basic amino acid $C_5H_{13}N_4COOH$ that is essential in the nutrition of rats, is derived from guanidine, is obtained esp. from certain vegetable tissues and from the decomposition of protamines and proteins, and is also made synthetically — see ORNITHINE

ar·gi·ope \är'jīə(,)pē\ *n, cap* [NL, fr. Gk *Argiopē*, nymph who was mother of the mythical bard Thamyris] **:** a small genus (the type of the family Argiopidae) of orb-weaving spiders including the common black and gold garden spider (*A. aurantia*)

ar·gi·op·i·dae \,är,jī'äpə,dē, -jē-\ *n pl, cap* [NL, fr. *Argiope*, type genus + *-idae*] **:** a cosmopolitan family of orb-weaving spiders with eight similar eyes, legs hairy or spiny, and no stridulating organs and including many well-known large or brightly colored garden spiders

1**ar·give** \'är,jīv, -gīv\ *adj, usu cap* [L *Argivus*, adj. & n., fr. (assumed) Gk *Argeiwos* (whence Gk *Argeios*) lit., of Argos, fr. *Argos* city-state of ancient Greece + (assumed) Gk *-eiwos* (whence Gk *-eios* -ive)] **:** of or relating to the Greeks or Greece, esp. the Achaean city of Argos or the surrounding territory of Argolis

2**argive** \"\ *n* -s *cap* [L *Argivus*] **:** GREEK; *esp* **:** a Greek of Argos

ar·gle \'ärgəl\ *dial var of* ARGUE

ar·gle-bar·gle \'ärgəl'bärgəl\ *n* -s [redupl. of *argle*] *chiefly Scot* **:** ARGY-BARGY

ar·gob·ba \är'gäbə\ *n* -s *usu cap* **:** a Semitic language closely related to Amharic and spoken in east-central Ethiopia

1**ar·gol** *or* **ar·gal** \'ärgəl\ *n* -s [ME *argoile*, prob. fr. AF *argoil*] **:** a grayish or reddish crystalline crust deposited in wine casks during aging

2**argol** \"\ *n* -s [Mongolian] **:** dry dung (as of camels or cattle) used as fuel esp. in Central Asia

ar·gon \'är,gän, 'åg-\ *n* -s [Gk, neut. of *argos* idle, lazy, fr. *a-* 2a- + *ergon* work — more at WORK] **:** a colorless odorless inert gaseous element that occurs in the air to the extent of 0.94 percent by volume and in volcanic gases, is obtained by separating from liquid air, and is used chiefly as a protecting atmosphere during fabrication and arc welding of metals and as a filler for electric incandescent and fluorescent bulbs, for gas-filled electron tubes, and for Geiger-Müller counters — symbol *A* or *Ar;* see ELEMENT table

ar·go·naut \'ärgə,nȯt, 'åg-\ *n* -s [L *Argonauta, Argonautes*, fr. Gk *Argonautēs*, fr. *Argō*, ship in which the Argonauts sailed + Gk *nautēs* sailor — more at NAUTICAL] **1 a** *usu cap* **:** one of the legendary heroes who sailed with Jason on the ship Argo in quest of the Golden Fleece **b :** *often cap* **:** an adventurer or traveler engaged in a particular quest; *specif* **:** one of those who went to California in 1849 in search of gold **2 :** PAPER NAUTILUS

ar·go·nau·ta \,≠≠'nȯd·ə\ *n, cap* [NL, fr. L, *Argonaut*] **:** a genus of cephalopods (order Dibranchia) including a single recent form, the paper nautilus (*A. argos*), related to the octopus and like it having eight arms two of which in the female are expanded at the tips to clasp the thin fragile unchambered shell — compare NAUTILUS

ar·go·nau·tic \¦≠≠¦nȯd·ik\ *adj, usu cap* [L *Argonauticus*, fr. Gk *Argonautikos*, fr. *Argonautēs* + *-ikos* -ic] **:** of or relating to the Argonauts

ar·go·nau·ti·dae \,≠≠'nȯd·ə,dē\ *n pl, cap* [NL, fr. *Argonauta*, type genus + *-idae*] **:** a family of cephalopods now represented solely by the genus *Argonauta*

ar·go·sy \'ärgəsē, 'åg-, -si\ *n* -ES [alter. of earlier *ragusye*, fr. It *ragusea* Ragusan vessel, fr. *Ragusa*, port of Dalmatia (now Dubrovnik, Yugoslavia)] **1 :** a large ship; *esp* **:** a richly laden merchant ship ⟨three of your *argosies* are . . . come to harbor —Shak.⟩ **2 :** a fleet of ships or of anything likened to ships ⟨white clouds sailed in splendid *argosies* across the sea of the sky —B.A.Williams⟩ **3 :** a rich store or supply **:** STOREHOUSE ⟨an ~ of railway folklore for all time —F.P.Donovan⟩

ar·got \'ärgət, 'åg-, -(,)gō *sometimes* -,gät; *usu* -əd· *or* -äd· + V\ *n* -s [F] **1 :** a special vocabulary and idiom used by a particular underworld group esp. as a means of private communication ⟨the ~ of pickpockets⟩ **2 :** the special vocabulary and idiom (as slang) of a particular social group or class ⟨the ~ of sport⟩ ⟨the ~ of teen-agers⟩ **3 :** SLANG 2 — used esp. of French **syn** see DIALECT

ar·gu·a·ble \'ärgyəwəbəl, 'åg-\ *adj* **:** capable of being argued **:** open to argument, dispute, or question ⟨~ matters of policy still undecided⟩

ar·gu·a·bly \-blē, -i\ *adv* **:** as may be shown by argument

ar·gue \'är(,)gyü, 'åg-, -gyə, *often* -gyəw+V\ *vb* **argued; argued; arguing; argues** [ME *arguen*, fr. MF *arguer* to accuse, reason & L *arguere* to accuse, assert, make clear; MF *arguer*, fr. L *argutare* to prate, fr. *argutus*, past part. of *arguere* — more at ARGENT] *vi* **1 :** to give or provide reasons for or against a matter under discussion or in dispute **:** make statements or present facts in support of or in opposition to a proposal or opinion ⟨three considerations . . . ~ against increasing the fee —T.L.Hungate⟩ ⟨am not *arguing* for an emotional art —H.S.Langfeld⟩ ⟨by *arguing* thus he showed that he had missed my meaning completely⟩ **2 :** to contend or disagree in words **:** DISPUTE, DEBATE ⟨you can always come and ~ with me about it —C.B.Flood⟩ ⟨they have been *arguing* for the past hour⟩ ~ *vt* **1** *obs* **:** to bring evidence against **:** accuse or convict **2 :** to give evidence of **:** suggest strongly **:** imply clearly **:** INDICATE, SHOW ⟨the presence of a large population in a restricted area generally ~*s* long occupancy —Edward Sapir⟩ **3 :** to give reasons for or against **:** consider the pros and cons of **:** DISCUSS ⟨cadets should be allowed to ~ any question that troubles the world —J.M.Burns⟩ **4 :** to prove or try to prove by giving reasons **:** MAINTAIN, CONTEND ⟨*argued* that this would jeopardize the Monroe Doctrine —Vera M. Dean⟩ **5** *obs* **:** to give as a reason **:** ADDUCE **6 :** to persuade by giving reasons **:** INDUCE ⟨~*s* an elderly rabbi . . . into holding services frequently —*Saturday Rev.*⟩ **syn** see DISCUSS, INDICATE

argue away *vt* **:** to get rid of by argument or by giving reasons ⟨*argue away* the fact that he had not kept his promises⟩

ar·gu·en·do \ˌärgyəˈwen(ˌ)dō\ *adv* [L, abl. of *arguendum*, gerund of *arguere*] **:** in the course of the argument

ar·gu·er \ˈärgyəwə(r)ˌ ˈȧgyəwə(r)\ *n* -S [ME, fr. *arguen* + *-er*] **:** one that argues

ar·gu·fi·er \-yəˌfī(ə)r, -fīə\ *n* -S **:** one that argufies

ar·gu·fy \-ˌfī\ *vb* -ED/-ING/-ES [*argue* + *-fy*] *vt* **1 :** to persuade by argument **:** prevail on ⟨~ a judge —Adria Langley⟩ **2 :** DISPUTE, DEBATE ⟨ready to ~ the point⟩ ~ *vi* **1 :** to argue obstinately **:** WRANGLE ⟨like lawyers in a murder case they stoutly ~ —Carl Sandburg⟩ **2** *archaic* **:** to be of consequence **:** be of use **:** MATTER

ar·gu·lus \ˈärgyələs\ *n* [NL, fr. *Argus*, mythological being + NL *-ulus* — more at ARGUS] **1** *cap* **:** a common genus of fish lice including forms highly destructive to goldfish and related forms **2** *pl* **argu·li** \-ˌlī\ **:** a fish louse of the genus *Argulus* **:** CARP LOUSE

ar·gu·ment \ˈärgyəmənt, ˈȧg-\ *n* -S [ME, fr. MF, fr. L *argumentum*, fr. *arguere* to make clear + *-mentum* -ment] **1** *obs* **:** an outward sign **:** EVIDENCE, INDICATION ⟨it is no addition to her wit nor no great ~ of her folly —Shak.⟩ **2 a :** a reason given for or against a matter under discussion **:** a statement made or a fact presented in support of or in opposition to a proposal or opinion ⟨paper was a party organ providing usable facts and ~*s* in terse paragraphs —Helen C.Boatfield⟩; *specif* **:** the middle term of a syllogism **b :** a form of rhetorical expression intended to convince or persuade ⟨the textbook contained good examples of exposition and ~⟩ **3 a :** the act or process of arguing, reasoning, or discussing **:** ARGUMENTATION, DISPUTATION ⟨reiteration is not ~ —C.M.Fuess⟩ **b :** a coherent series of reasons, statements, or facts intended to support or establish a point of view **:** a discussion often involving a controversial topic ⟨the plaintiff has made his closing ~ —W.E. Sedgwick⟩ ⟨keep to the single thread of my ~ —E.R.Bentley⟩ **c :** an instance of arguing **:** a difference of opinion **:** DISAGREEMENT, DISPUTE, QUARREL ⟨the ~ . . . will not be settled by any showdown —*Saturday Rev.*⟩ **4 :** an abstract or summary esp. of a poem, play, or part of a literary work ⟨a later editor added the ~ to the poem⟩ **5 :** the subject matter, plot, or central idea esp. of a novel, poem, or speech ⟨the ~ of the book is as simple as you could wish for —Robert Parris⟩ **6** *math* **a :** one of the independent variables upon whose value that of a function depends **b :** the angle that fixes the direction of a complex number — compare ARGAND DIAGRAM **syn** see REASON

ar·gu·men·tal \ˌ==ˈment³l\ *adj* [LL *argumentalis*, fr. L *argumentum* + *-alis* -al] **:** ARGUMENTATIVE

ar·gu·men·ta·tion \ˌ==ˌmanˈtāshən, -ˌmen-\ *n* -S [ME *argumentacioun*, fr. L *argumentation-, argumentatio*, fr. *argumentatus* (past part. of *argumentari* to bring forward proof, fr. *argumentum*) + *-ion-, -io* -ion] **1 a :** the act of forming reasons, making inductions, drawing conclusions, and applying them to the case in discussion **:** the operation of inferring propositions not known or admitted as true from facts or principles known, admitted, or proved to be true **b :** a process of reasoning **:** the result of an argument **:** a series of arguments **:** a reasoning process ⟨ingenious ~*s*⟩ **2 a :** discussion esp. of a controversial topic **:** DEBATE **b :** ARGUMENT 2b

ar·gu·men·ta·tive \ˌ==ˈmentəd·iv, -ətiv\ *or* **ar·gu·men·tive** \-ntiv\ *adj* **1 :** consisting of or characterized by argument **:** containing a process of reasoning **:** CONTROVERSIAL ⟨an ~ discourse⟩ **2 :** PRESUMPTIVE, INDICATIVE, SUGGESTIVE ⟨his silence is ~ of guilt⟩ **3 :** given to or fond of argument **:** CONTENTIOUS, DISPUTATIOUS ⟨~ to the point of being cantankerous —J.S.Clarke⟩ — **ar·gu·men·ta·tive·ly** *adv*

ar·gu·men·ta·tor \ˈ==ˌmənˌtād·ə(r), -ˌmen-\ *n* -S [LL, fr. L *argumentatus* + *-or*] **:** one who engages in argument **:** CONTROVERSIALIST

argument from design : an argument for the existence of God based on the hypothesis of an ultimate design, intention, or purpose in the universe

ar·gu·men·tize *vi* -ED/-ING/-S *obs* **:** ARGUE

ar·gu·men·tum \ˌ==ˈmentəm\ *n, pl* **argumen·ta** \-tə\ [L — more at ARGUMENT] **:** an argument, proof, or appeal to reason — used as the first term in many technical phrases designating forms both of sound and of fallacious reasoning ⟨~ ad hominem⟩ ⟨~ ad captandum⟩; compare AD CAPTANDUM, AD HOMINEM

¹ar·gus \ˈärgəs, ˈȧg-\ *n* -ES [after *Argus*, mythological being with many eyes some of which were always open, known as a zealous watchman, fr. L, fr. Gk *Argos*] **1** *usu cap* **:** a very watchful person **:** a vigilant guardian **2** *or* **argus pheasant** [NL, fr. L; fr. the many eyelike spots, likened to the eyes of Argus] **:** any of several large brilliantly patterned East Indian pheasants chiefly of the genus *Argusianus* that are closely related to the peacocks **3 :** any of several butterflies esp. of the family Satyridae with numerous circular eyespots on the wings

²argus \"\ [NL, after *Argus*, mythological being] *syn of* ARGAS

³argus \"\ [NL, after *Argus*, mythological being] *syn of* ARGUSIANUS

argus brown *n* [¹*argus* (pheasant)] **:** a moderate brown that is yellower, stronger, and slightly darker than bay, redder, stronger, and slightly lighter than coffee, and deeper and slightly redder than chestnut brown — called also *cochin, Mars brown, moccasin*

argus-eyed \ˈ==ˌ=\ *adj, often cap A* [¹*argus*] **:** vigilantly observant **:** SHARP-SIGHTED

argusfish \ˈ==ˌ=\ *n* [after *Argus*, mythological being; fr. its eyelike spots] **:** a small spotted scaly-finned fish (*Ephippus argus*) from brackish waters of India

ar·gu·si·a·nus \ˌärˌgyüzēˈānəs, -üsē-\ *n, cap* [NL, irreg. fr. ³*Argus* + L *-ianus* -ian] **:** a genus of East Indian pheasants (family Phasianidae) including the typical argus pheasants

argus shell *n* [after *Argus*, mythological being; fr. its spots] **:** a tropical marine gastropod shell (*Cypraea argus*) having ocellate spots

argus tortoise beetle *n* [after *Argus*, mythological being; fr. its spots] **:** a reddish tortoise beetle (*Chelymorpha cassidea*) spotted with black

ar·gute \(ˈ)ärˈgyüt\ *adj* [L *argutus*, fr. past part. of *arguere* to make clear — more at ARGUE] **1 :** characterized by shrewdness, acuteness, or sagacity ⟨an ~ critic⟩ **2 :** SHRILL ⟨a rich but too ~ guitar —W.S.Landor⟩ **3 :** sharply serrate — **argute·ly** *adv* — **ar·gute·ness** *n* -ES

¹ar·gy-bar·gy \ˈärgēˈbärgē\ *vi* -ED/-ING/-ES [redupl. of Sc & E dial. *argy*, alter. of *argue*] *chiefly dial* **:** to engage in argument **:** WRANGLE, HAGGLE

²argy-bargy \"\ *n* -ES **1** *chiefly dial* **:** ARGUMENT, DISPUTE **2** *chiefly dial* **:** a lively discussion

ar·gyle *also* **ar·gyll** \ärˈgīl, ˈä,g-, ==ˈ=\ *n* -S [after *Argyle, Argyll*, branch of the Scottish clan of Campbell, from whose tartan the design was adapted] **1** *often cap* **a :** any of various geometric knitting patterns that are balanced patterns of varicolored diamond figures in solid and outline shapes on a single background color **b :** a sock knit in such a pattern **2** [prob. after a duke of *Argyle*] **:** a serving vessel for gravy or sauce having either an outer compartment for holding hot water or an inner one for a heated iron to keep the contents warm

argyle 1a

argyle purple *n, often cap A* **:** a pale to grayish reddish purple that is stronger than crocus (sense 3a)

ar·gyll-rob·ert·son pupil \ärˌgīlˈräbərtsən-\ *n, usu cap A&R* [after D. *Argyll-Robertson* †1909 Scot. physician] **:** a pupil that fails to react to light but still reacts in accommodation to distance, characteristic of neurosyphilis

ar·gyll·shire \ärˈgīlˌshi(ə)r, -shə(r)\ *or* **ar·gyll** \ˈ=ˌ=, =ˈ=\ *adj, usu cap* [fr. *Argyllshire* or *Argyll*, county in western Scotland] **:** of or from Argyllshire **:** of the kind or style prevalent in Argyllshire

ar·gyn·nis \ärˈjinəs\ *n, cap* [NL, prob. fr. Gk *Argynnis*, epithet of Aphrodite as worshiped in the Boeotian town Argynnos] **:** a genus of nymphalid butterflies mostly fulvous above with small black spots or markings and with silvery spots on the underside of the hind wings — see FRITILLARY

argyr- *or* **argyro-** *comb form* [NL, fr. Gk, fr. *argyros* — more at ARGENT] **:** silver ⟨*argyr*ite⟩ ⟨*argyro*cephalous⟩

ar·gyr·ia \ärˈjirēə\ *n* -S [NL, fr. *argyr-* + *-ia*] **:** permanent dark discoloration of the skin due to absorption following overuse of medicinal silver preparations

ar·gyr·ic \(ˈ)ärˈjirik\ *adj* [Gk *argyrikos* of silver, fr. *argyros* + *-ikos* -ic] **:** ARGENTIC

ar·gyr·o·dite \=ˈjirəˌdīt\ *n* -S [ISV *argyrod-* (fr. Gk *argyrōdēs* rich in silver, fr. *argyros* silver + *-ōdēs* -ode) + *-ite*; orig. formed as G *argyrodit*] **:** a steel-gray mineral Ag_8GeS_6 consisting of silver, germanium, and sulfur

ar·gy·ro·pel·e·cus \ˌärjə(ˌ)rōˈpeləkəs\ *n, cap* [NL, fr. *argyr-* + Gk *pelekys* ax; fr. the shape — more at PELICAN] **:** a genus of small deep-sea fishes (order Stomiatoidea) having short deep bodies with a silvery sheen and luminous spots

ar·gyr·o·phil \ˈärjərəˌfil, ˌrə-\ *or* **ar·gyr·o·phile** \-ˌfīl\ *also* **ar·gyr·o·phil·ic** \ˌ==(ˌ)=ˈfilik\ *or* **ar·gyr·oph·i·lous** \ˌ==ˈräfələs\ *adj* [*argyr-* + *-phil, -phile, -philic, -philous*] **:** ARGENTOPHIL — **ar·gyr·o·phil·ia** \ˌ==(ˌ)rōˈfilēə, -rə-\ *n* -S

ar·gy·ro·sis \ˌärjəˈrōsəs\ *n, pl* **argyro·ses** \-ōˌsēz\ [NL, fr. *argyr-* + *-osis*] **:** ARGYRIA

ar·gyr·o·tae·nia \ˌ==(ˌ)rōˈtēnēə, -ˌrə-\ *n, cap* [NL, fr. *argyr-* + *taenia*] **:** a genus of tortricid moths including a number having larvae that are serious leaf-rolling pests of economic plants — compare ORANGE TORTRIX, RED-BANDED LEAF ROLLER

ar·har \ˈärˌhär\ *n* -S [Hindi *arhar, arhar*, perh. fr. Skt *ādhakī* (*Cajanus indicus*)] **:** PIGEON PEA

ar·hat \ˈär(ˌ)hət\ *also* **ar·a·hat** \ˈarə(ˌ)hət\ *or* **ar·a·hant** \-ˌhant\ *n* -S *often cap* [Skt *arhat*, lit., deserving respect, fr. *arhati* he deserves; akin to Gk *alphein* to gain, Av *arəzhaiti* it is worth, Lith *algà* wage, salary] **:** a Buddhist monk who has attained Nirvana

ar·hat·ship \ˈ=(ˌ)=ˌship\ *n* -S *sometimes cap* **:** the state of being an arhat ⟨trying to attain ~⟩

ar·hua·co \ärˈwä(ˌ)kō\ *or* **aro·a·co** \ˌäroˈä-\ *or* **aru·ac** \ˈärüˌäk\ *n, pl* **arhuaco** *or* **arhuacos** *or* **aroaco** *or* **aroacos** *or* **aruac** *or* **aruacs** *usu cap* [Sp, of AmerInd origin] **1 :** a Chibchan people of northern Colombia **2 :** a member of the Arhuaco people

arhyn·chob·del·li·da \ˌāˌriŋˌkäbˈdelədə\ *n pl, cap* [NL, fr. ²*a-* + *rhynch-* + *-bdellida* (fr. *-bdella* + *-ida*)] *in some classifications* **:** an order or other division of leeches comprising the Gnathobdellida and Pharyngobdellida

arhythmia *var of* ARRHYTHMIA

arhythmicity \ˌā+,=ˈ===\ *n* -ES [²*a-* + *rhythm* + *-icity*] *ecol* **:** a condition characterized by the absence of some rhythm of behavior or physiology that might be expected to be present

¹aria \ˈärēə, ˈar- *also* ˈa(a)r- *or* ˈer- *or* ˈär-\ *n, pl* **ari·as** \-ēəz *also* **arie** \-ēˌā\ [It, lit., atmospheric air, fr. L *aera* (accus. of *aer*), fr. Gk *aera*, accus. of *aēr* — more at AIR] **:** AIR, MELODY, TUNE; *specif* **:** an accompanied, extended, and usu. elaborate melody sung by a single voice (as in an opera or oratorio) — compare RECITATIVE

²aria \əˈrēə\ *n* -S [NL, fr. Gk, a kind of tree] **:** WHITEBEAM

¹-aria *pl of* -ARIUM

²-ar·ia \ˈa(a)rēə, ˈer-, ˈär-\ *n suffix* [NL, fr. L, fem. sing. & neut. pl. of *-arius* -ary] **:** one or ones like or connected with — esp. in biological taxonomic names ⟨Campanul*aria*⟩ ⟨Madrepor*aria*⟩ ⟨Utricul*aria*⟩

aria da ca·po \ˈärēədəˈkä(ˌ)pō\ *n, pl* **arias da capo** \-ēəzd-\ *also* **arie da capo** \-ēˌäd-\ [It, air from the beginning] **:** an aria in 3-part musical form comprising a theme, a secondary contrasting part, and a repetition of the first part

aria d'i·mi·ta·zi·o·ne \-ˌdēmə,tätsēˈō,nā\ *n, pl* **arias d'imitazione** \-ēəz,d-\ *also* **arie d'imitazione** \-ē,ä,d-\ [It, air of imitation] **:** an aria in which the voice or accompaniment imitates sounds of nature or is otherwise descriptive

¹ar·i·an \ˈa(a)rēən, ˈer-, ˈär-\ *n* -S *usu cap* [LL *Arianus*, adj. & n., fr. *Arius* †A.D.336 Alexandrian Greek theologian + L *-anus* -an] **:** one adhering to or supporting Arianism

²arian \"\ *adj, usu cap* [LL *Arianus*] **:** of or relating to Arius, the Arians, or Arianism

³arian *usu cap, var of* ARYAN

-ar·i·an \ˈ===\ *n suffix* -S [L *-arius* -ary + E ¹*-an*] **1 :** believer ⟨necessit*arian*⟩ **:** advocate ⟨latitudin*arian*⟩ **2 :** producer ⟨platitudin*arian*⟩ ⟨tract*arian*⟩

ar·i·an·ism \ˈ==əˌnizəm\ *n* -S *usu cap* [²*arian* + *-ism*] **1 :** a theological movement initiated by Arius in opposition to Sabellianism that won strong support during the 4th century A.D. chiefly in the Eastern churches but that was condemned in general councils at Nicaea (A.D.325) and Constantinople (A.D.381), the doctrine being marked by the following principles: (1) God is absolutely alone, unknowable, and separate from every created being; (2) the Christ, the Logos or Son of God, preexistent but not eternally real, is a created being and so not God in the fullest sense, though as maker of all other creatures he may be regarded and worshiped as a secondary divinity; (3) in the incarnation the Logos assumed a body but not a human soul, and so Jesus Christ was neither truly God nor truly man — compare ANOMOEAN, HOMOEAN **2 a :** Arian doctrine **b :** adherence to or advocacy of Arian doctrine

ar·i·an·is·tic \ˌ===ˈnistik\ *or* **ar·i·an·is·ti·cal** \-tәkəl\ *adj, usu cap* [ML *Arianista* (fr. LL *Arianus* + L *-ista* -ist) + E *-ic, -ical*] **:** of, relating to, or characterized by Arianism

aria par·lan·te \-ˌpärˈlän,tā\ *n, pl* **arias parlante** \-ēəz,p-\ *also* **arie parlan·ti** \-ē,ä,pärˈlän(ˌ)tē\ [It, speaking air] **:** an aria characterized by a declamatory melodic style

ari·bo·fla·vin·o·sis \ˌāˌrībəˌflāvəˈnōsəs *also* -rib- *or* -lav-\ *n, pl* **ariboflavino·ses** \-ōˌsēz\ [NL, fr. ²*a-* + ISV *riboflavin* + NL *-osis*] **1 :** a deficiency disease due to inadequate intake of riboflavin that is marked by cheilosis, scaling around the nose, and sensitivity to light **2 :** CURLED-TOE PARALYSIS

aricara *usu cap, var of* ARIKARA

aricuri *var of* OURICURY

ar·id \ˈarəd *also* ˈer-\ *adj, sometimes* -ER/-EST [F or L; F *aride*, fr. L *aridus* — more at ARDOR] **1 :** without moisture **:** excessively dry **:** parched and barren; *specif* **:** having insufficient rainfall to support agriculture, usu. less than 10 to 15 inches annually ⟨~ miles of brushland —Green Peyton⟩ **2 :** devoid of interest and life **:** dry and monotonous **:** JEJUNE ⟨the dullest and most ~ documents —J.L.Lowes⟩ **syn** see DRY

arid cycle *n* **:** the cycle of erosion in an arid region as contrasted with that in a humid region

arid·i·ty \əˈridədē, aˈ-,eˈ-, -ətē, -i\ *n* -ES [L *ariditas*, fr. *aridus* + *-itas* -ity] **1 :** the quality or state of being arid **:** DRYNESS ⟨the ~ of desert sands⟩ **2 :** unavailability of water present in a habitat to organisms occupying that habitat whether caused by inability of the organisms to remove the water or to the ability of the soil to withhold it

ar·id·ly *adv* **:** in an arid manner **:** DRILY, MONOTONOUSLY

ar·id·ness *n* -ES **:** ARIDITY

ar·i·e·gite \ˌarēˈä,zhīt\ *n* -S [F *ariégite*, fr. Dept. *Ariège*, France, its locality + F *-ite*] **:** a rock consisting of granular pyroxenite with dark green spinel and pyrope and sometimes biotite or hornblende

¹ar·i·el \ˈa(a)rēəl, ˈer-,ˈär-\ *n* -S [prob. fr. *Ariel*, an airy spirit in Shakespeare's *Tempest*] **:** an Australian flying phalanger of the genus *Petaurus*

²ariel \"\ *or* **ariel gazelle** *n* -S [Ar *aryal*, var of *ayyil* stag] **:** a gazelle (*Gazella arabica*) of Arabia and adjacent regions

ari·es \ˈa(a)rēˌēz, ˈer-,ˈär-, -rēz\ *n, usu cap* [L, lit., ram; akin to Umbrian *erietu*, acc., ram, Gk *eriphos* kid, OIr *heirp* doe, female goat, *erb* cow, Arm *or-oj* lamb] **:** the 1st sign of the zodiac — see SIGN table; ZODIAC illustration

-aries *pl of* -ARY

ar·i·et·ta \ˌarēˈed·ə, ˌär-\ *also* **ar·i·ette** \ˌ==ˈet\ *n* -S [*arietta* fr. It, dim. of *aria*; *ariette* fr. F, fr. It *arietta*] **:** a short aria

aright \əˈrīt\ *adv* [ME, fr. OE *ariht*, fr. ¹*a-* + *riht* right (n.) — more at RIGHT] **:** RIGHTLY, CORRECTLY ⟨if I remember ~⟩

ari·id \əˈrīəd\ *adj* [NL *Ariidae*] **:** belonging to the Ariidae

ari·i·dae \əˈrīəˌdē\ *n pl, cap* [NL, fr. *Arius*, type genus (prob. fr. Gk *areios* warlike, devoted to Ares, fr. *Arēs* Ares, god of war) + *-idae*] **:** a family of marine fishes (order Ostariophysi) comprising the sea catfishes and usu. having a bony buckler from the skull to the dorsal spine — compare CRUCIFIX FISH

arik·a·ra *also* **aric·a·ra** \əˈrikərə\ *n, pl* **arikara** *or* **arikaras** *also* **aricara** *or* **aricaras** *usu cap* [Skidi Pawnee *Arikara*, lit., horns, fr. pl. of *ariki* horn; fr. their hair style with hornlike bones inserted] **1 a :** a Caddo people west of the Missouri river in the Dakotas **b :** a member of such people **2 :** the language of the Arikara people

ariki *or* **arii** *var of* ALII

ar·il \ˈarəl\ *n* -S [prob. fr. NL *arillus*, fr. ML, raisin, grape seed] **:** an exterior covering or appendage of certain seeds that develops after fertilization as an outgrowth from the funiculus and envelops the seed — see ARILLODE

ar·il·late \ˈarəˌlāt, -ə,lət\ *or* **ar·il·lat·ed** \-əˌlād·əd\ *or* **ar·iled** *or* **ar·illed** \ˈarəld\ *adj* [*aril* + *-ate, -ated* or *-ed*] **:** having an aril

ar·il·lode \ˈarəˌlōd\ *or* **ar·il·lo·di·um** \ˌarəˈlōdēəm\ *n* -S [*arillode* fr. *aril* + *-ode*; *arillodium* fr. NL, fr. *arillus* + *-odium* (fr. *-odes* -ode — fr. Gk *-ōdēs* — + *-ium*)] **:** a false aril **:** an aril originating from tissue in the region of the micropyle instead of from the funicle or chalaza of the ovule

ar·il·loid \ˈarəˌlȯid\ *adj* [*aril* + *-oid*] **:** resembling an aril

aril·lus \əˈriləs\ *n, pl* **aril·li** \-ˌrī,lī, -i(ˌ)lē\ *or* **arilluses** [NL — more at ARIL] **:** ARIL

ar·i·masp \ˈarəˌmasp\ *or* **ar·i·mas·pi·an** \ˌ==ˈmaspēən\ *n, pl* **arimasps** *or* **arimaspians** *also* **arimas·pi** \ˌ==ˈmaˌspī, -(ˌ)spē\ *often cap* [*Arimasp* fr. L *Arimaspus*, fr. Gk *Arimaspos*; *Arimaspian* fr. L *Arimaspus* + E *-ian*] **:** one of a mythical race of one-eyed men of Scythia represented in ancient art as in constant strife with griffins for gold guarded by the griffins — **arimaspian** \ˌ==ˈmaspēən\ *adj, often cap*

ari·o·car·pus \ˌarē(ˌ)ōˈkärpəs, -rēəˈk-\ *n, cap* [NL, fr. *ario-* (fr. *Aria* section of *Sorbus* once considered a separate genus of Malaceae, fr. Gk *aria* holm oak) + *-carpus*] **:** a genus of spineless cacti found in Texas and adjacent Mexico consisting of spirally arranged triangular horny tubercles

ari·on \əˈrīən\ *n, cap* [NL, fr. *Arion*, 7th cent. B.C. semilegendary Greek poet, fr. L, fr. Gk *Ariōn*] **:** a genus of slugs including a common European black slug (*A. ater*)

ari·ose \ˈärēˌōs, ˈar-\ *adj* [It *arioso*, fr. *aria* + *-oso* -ose (fr. L *-osus*)] **:** like an aria **:** characterized by melody — distinguished from *recitative*

¹ari·o·so \ˈärēˈō(ˌ)sō, ˈar-, -(ˌ)zō\ *adj* [It] **:** like an aria: as **a** *of a vocal passage* **:** involving a mixture of free recitative and metrical song **b** *of an instrumental passage* **:** resembling an accompanied recitative or aria

²arioso \"\ *adv* **:** in arioso style — used as a direction in music

³arioso \"\ *n, pl* **ariosos** *also* **ario·si** \-(ˌ)sē\ **:** an arioso composition or passage

ari·ot \əˈ-\ *adj* [¹*a-* + *riot*, v.] **:** running riot ⟨vines ~ everywhere⟩

arip·ple \əˈ-\ *adj* [¹*a-* + *ripple*, v.] **:** RIPPLING ⟨the lake was quiet, its waters ~⟩

aris *var of* ARRIS

ar·i·sae·ma \ˌarəˈsēmə\ *n, cap* [NL, fr. L *aris* arum (fr. Gk) + Gk *haima* blood; fr. the red-spotted leaves of some species; akin to Gk *aron* arum — more at ARUM, HEM-] **:** a genus of herbs (family Araceae) of temperate and subtropical regions having flowers without perianth that are borne at the base of the spadix which is prolonged into a fleshy tip — see GREEN DRAGON, JACK-IN-THE-PULPIT

arisaid *n* -S [Sc, fr. earlier *arisad, arrisat*] **:** a full robe or skirt of tartan gathered and girdled at the waist

ari·sa·ka *or* **arisaka rifle** \ˌarəˈsäkə, ˌär-\ *n* -S *usu cap A* [after Col. Nariaka *Arisaka fl* 1896 Jap. army officer & superintendent of Tokyo arsenal] **:** any of a series of bolt-action rifles of about .30 caliber that were standard issue to Japanese forces from about 1905 until 1945

¹arise \əˈrīz\ *vi* **arose** \-rōz\ **arisen** \-riz³n\ **arising**; **arises** [ME *arisen*, fr. OE *ārīsan* (akin to OS *arīsan*, OHG *irrīsan*, Goth *urreisan*), fr. *ā-* (perfective prefix) + *rīsan* to rise — more at ABEAR, RISE] **1 a :** to rise from a fallen position ⟨he *arose* slowly, brushing the dust of the street from his clothes⟩ **b :** to get up from a lying, sitting, or kneeling position ⟨when they finally stood up to look at the finished table, Millie *arose* too —J.M.MacDonald⟩ **c :** to shake off a state of inactivity **:** pursue a less tranquil way of living or course of procedure; *esp* **:** to rise belligerently, hostilely, or in rebellion ⟨~ from your torpor and taste life⟩ ⟨every group or institution ~*s* in defense of an ideal —*Encounter*⟩ ⟨no rival native house *arose* to dispute the throne —Kemp Malone⟩ **2 a :** to rise from sleep or rest ⟨*arising* early in the morning⟩ **b :** to return from death to life ⟨they firmly believed that the dead ~⟩ **3 :** to become violently active (as of the sea, the wind, or a deep emotion) **4 a :** to originate from a specified source ⟨a historical precedent for it *arising* out of the period of English rule —G.G. Weigend⟩ **b :** to come into being ⟨no poets, no historians had *arisen* —Van Wyck Brooks⟩ ⟨local cultures *arose* which were distinguished for fine pottery —Angélica Mendoza⟩ **c :** to become operative esp. in such a way as to attract attention ⟨a group of enthusiastic naturalists had *arisen* —H.A. Pilsbry⟩ **5 a :** to appear above the horizon (as of the sun) **b :** to move upward physically **:** MOUNT, ASCEND ⟨a heavy mist *arose* and hung over the city⟩ **6** *of circumstances and occurrences* **a :** to come about **:** come up **:** take place ⟨a situation almost unique in the world has *arisen* —L.D.Stamp⟩ **b :** to become apparent in such a way as to demand attention ⟨various claims in the economic sphere which *arose* at the end of World War II —G.W.Hoffman⟩ ⟨important problems which ~ when two different groups having diverse languages and cultures meet —T.A.Sebeok⟩ **7 :** to become audible **:** become heard ⟨a storm of protest immediately *arose* —*Current Biog.*⟩ **8** *obs* **:** to attain a higher rank **:** come into greater eminence **syn** see RISE, SPRING

²arise *n* -S *obs* **:** RISING ⟨his morning's next ~ —Christopher Marlowe⟩

aris·ings \əˈrīziŋz, -zēŋz\ *n pl* **:** surplus products or salvageable leftover materials (as in manufacturing)

aris·ta \əˈristə\ *n, pl* **aris·tae** \-(ˌ)stē, -ˌstī\ *or* **aristas** [NL, fr. L, beard of grain] **:** the bristlelike structure near or at the tip of the antenna of many two-winged flies

aristapedia *var of* ARISTOPEDIA

ar·is·tarch \ˈarəˌstärk\ *n* -S *sometimes cap* [after *Aristarchus* †*ab* 145B.C. Greek grammarian and critic] **:** a severe critic

aris·tate \əˈriˌstāt, -ˌstət\ *adj* [L *aristatus* having beards of grain, fr. *arista* + *-atus* -ate] *biol* **:** having a slender sharp or spinelike tip **:** having an arista

aris·ti·da \əˈristədə\ *n, cap* [NL, irreg. fr. L *arista* beard of grain] **:** a genus of grasses with one-flowered spikelets and hard sharp-pointed lemma terminating in three awns — see DOGTOWN GRASS

aris·to \əˈri(ˌ)stō, F ärēstō\ [F, short for *aristocrate*] **:** ARISTOCRAT

aris·to- *in pronunciations below*, =ˈ=(ˌ)==əˈri(ˌ)stō *or* -stə *sometimes* aˈ-\ *comb form* [MF & LL; MF, fr. LL, fr. Gk, fr. *aristos*; akin to Gk *ararískein* to fit — more at ARM] **1 :** best ⟨*aristo*genesis⟩ **2 :** aristocracy and ⟨*aristo*democracy⟩ **:** aristocratic and ⟨*aristo*democratic⟩

ar·is·toc·ra·cy \ˌarəˈstäkrəsē, -si *also* ˌer-\ *n* -ES [MF & LL; MF *aristocratie*, fr. LL *aristocratia*, fr. Gk *aristokratia*, fr. *aristo-* + *-kratia* -cracy] **1 :** government by the best individuals or by a relatively small privileged class **2 a :** a form of government in which the power is vested in a minority consisting of those felt to be best qualified to rule **b :** a state having such a government **3 :** a governing body made up of those felt to be outstanding citizens, esp. nobles or others of high rank **:** an upper class usu. made up of an hereditary nobility **:** a patrician order **4 :** the aggregate of those felt to be superior (as in rank, wealth, or intellect)

aris·to·crat \əˈristəˌkrat *sometimes* aˈ- *or* eˈ-, *Brit usu & US sometimes* ˈaris-; *usu* -ad·+V\ *n* -S [F *aristocrate*, back-formation fr. *aristocratie* & *aristocratique*] **1 :** a high-ranking or otherwise superior individual **:** a member of an aristocracy; *esp* **:** NOBLE **2 :** one who has the bearing and viewpoint typical of a ruling, privileged, or otherwise superior class; *sometimes* **:** one who favors aristocracy

aris·to·crat·ic \əˌristəˈkrad·ik, -atik, -ēk *sometimes* aˌ- *or* eˌ-, *Brit usu & US sometimes* ˌa(ˌ)ris- *or* ˌarəs-\ *also* **aris·to·crat·i·cal** \-ȧkəl, -ēk-\ *adj* [*aristocratic* fr. MF *aristocratique*, fr. ML *aristocraticus*, fr. Gk *aristokratikos*, fr. *aristo-* + *-kratikos* -cratic; *aristocratical* fr. MF *aristocratique* + E *-al*] **1 :** belonging to, having the qualities of, or favoring aristocracy ⟨an ~ government⟩ **2 :** socially exclusive ⟨an ~ neighborhood⟩; *sometimes* **:** SNOBBISH ⟨an essentially ~ movement — superior, sniffish, and antidemocratic —H.L.Mencken⟩ — **aris·to·crat·i·cal·ly** \-ȯk(ə)lē, -ēk-, -li\ *adv*

ar·is·toc·ra·tism \ˌarəˈstäkrəˌtizəm, əˈristəˌkradˌiz-\ *n* -s [*aristocrat* + *-ism*] **:** the principles or practices of aristocracy

aristo·genesis \ˌ=ˌ=(ˌ)= *at* ARISTO- +\ *n, pl* **aristogeneses** [*aristo-* + *genesis*] **:** a theory now not widely accepted in biology: evolution is the product of a continuous orderly creative faculty innate in living matter and manifested in response to external stimuli at such a rate that perfection of an adaptation anticipates the need of that adaptation — **aristo·genetic** \(ˈ)=ˌ=(ˌ)==ˈ=\ *adj* — **aris·to·gen·ic** \(ˈ)=ˌ=(ˌ)=ˈjenik, -ēk\ *adj*

ar·is·toi \ˈarəˌstȯi\ *n pl* [Gk, fr. pl. of *aristos* best, noblest — more at ARISTO-] **1 :** ARISTOCRATS ⟨every country has its bourgeois and its ~⟩ **2** *usu sing in constr* **:** aristocratic class

aris·to·lo·chia \=ˌ=(ˌ)= *at* ARISTO- + ˈlōkēə\ *n, cap* [NL, fr. L, birthwort, fr. Gk *aristolocheia*, fr. *aristo-* + *locheia* childbirth; akin to *lechos* bed — more at LIE] **:** a large genus (the type of the family Aristolochiaceae) of mostly tropical herbs or woody vines with pungent aromatic rootstocks and very irregular flowers — see BIRTHWORT, DUTCHMAN'S-PIPE, PELICAN FLOWER

aris·to·lo·chi·a·ce·ae \=ˌ=(ˌ)=ˌlōkēˈāsēˌē\ *n pl, cap* [NL, fr. *Aristolochia*, type genus + *-aceae*] **:** a family of erect or climbing herbs or shrubs (order Aristolochiales) having alternate petioled leaves and apetalous flowers with a petaloid calyx and stamens adnate to the style — see ARISTOLOCHIA —**aris·to·lo·chi·a·ceous** \(ˈ)=ˌ=(ˌ)=ˌ==ˈāshəs\ *adj*

aris·to·lo·chi·a·les \=ˌ=(ˌ)=ˌ==ˈāˌlēz\ *n pl, cap* [NL, fr. *Aristolochia* + *-ales*] **:** an order of metachlamydeous dicotyledonous plants embracing the families Aristolochiaceae, Rafflesiaceae, and Hydnoraceae and distinguished by the tubular petaloid perianth, inferior ovary, and numerous stamens free from the perianth

aris·to·pe·dia *also* **aris·ta·pe·dia** \əˌristəˈpēdēə\ *n* -s [NL, fr. *aristo-* (fr. *arista*), *arista* + *ped-* + *-ia*] *of insects* **:** the replacement of an antennal arista by a more or less perfect leg, a not uncommon developmental aberration in drosophilas

¹ar·is·to·phan·ic \ˈarəstəˈfanik, ˈaˌris-\ *adj, usu cap* [LL *Aristophanicus*, fr. *Aristophanes* (Gk *Aristophanēs*) †*ab* 380 B.C. Athenian comic dramatist + L *-icus* -ic] **:** of, relating to, or characteristic of Aristophanes or his dramas

²aristophanic \"\ *n* -s **:** PHERECRATIC

aristos *pl of* ARISTO

¹ar·is·to·te·lian *also* **ar·is·to·te·lean** \ˌarəstəˈtēlyən, ˈaˌris-, -lēən *also* ˈer- *or* ˌaˈris-\ *or* **ar·is·to·tel·ic** \-ˈtelik\ *adj, usu cap* [L *Aristoteles* Aristotle †322 B.C. Greek philosopher (fr. Gk *Aristotelēs*) + E *-ian, -ean, -ic*] **:** of or relating to Aristotle or his philosophy

²aristotelian \"\ *n* -s *usu cap* **:** a follower of Aristotle or adherent of Aristotelianism

ar·is·to·te·lian·ism \-ˌnizəm\ *also* **ar·is·tot·e·lism** \ˈarəˌstädᵊlˌizəm, -ätᵊl- *also* ˈer- *or* ˌ==ˈ==ˌ==\ *n* -s *usu cap* **1 :** the philosophy of Aristotle that elaborates the fundamental principles of formal logic esp. through the doctrine of the syllogism and holds that all reality is of particular things each of which is the union of matter and a form which is characteristic of its kind except that God is pure actuality, being the unmoved mover and unchanging cause of all change, and except that prime matter is pure potentiality — compare CATEGORY, CATHARSIS, CAUSE, FORM, MATTER, PREDICABLE **2 :** a philosophy incorporating essential features of that of Aristotle with usu. the inclusion of factors stemming from later ideological traditions ⟨a mystical *Aristotelianism* also got into parts of the Jewish Cabala —S.P.Lamprecht⟩

aristotelian logic *n, usu cap A* **:** the logic of Aristotle: **a :** the total organon of Aristotle including his theories of the predicables and categories, of definition and syllogistic **b :** the traditional formal logic inaugurated by Aristotle — compare TRADITIONAL LOGIC

ar·is·tot·le's dictum \ˈarəˌstädᵊlz-, -ätᵊlz- *also* ˈer-\ *n, usu cap A* **:** DICTUM DE OMNI ET NULLO

aristotle's lantern *n, usu cap A* [*lantern*, trans. of Gk *lamptēr*; fr. a passage in Aristotle where the shape of a sea urchin is said to resemble the frame of a lantern] **:** the protrusible 5-sided masticatory apparatus of a sea urchin, each side being made up of a tooth with its supporting ossicles and the muscles that activate it

ari·ta ware *or* **arita porcelain** \əˈrēd·ə-, äˈr-\ *n, usu cap A* [fr. *Arita*, Japan] **:** Japanese porcelain produced in and about Arita on Kyushu Island and including blue-and-white and enamel-decorated ware (as Imari and Kakiemon wares)

ar·ith·log paper \ˈarəthˌlȯg-, -äg-\ *n* [*arith*metic + *log*arithm] **:** semilogarithmic coordinate paper

¹arith·me·tic \əˈrithməˌtik\ *n* -s [alter. (influenced by Gk *arithmētikē*) of earlier *arithmetrik*, fr. ME, alter. (influenced by L *arithmetica* or Gk *arithmētikē*) of *arsmetrike*, modif. (influenced by L *ars* art & L *metricus* of measurement) of OF *arismetique*, fr. L & Gk; L *arithmetica*, fr. Gk *arithmētikē*, fr. fem. of *arithmētikos* arithmetical, fr. *arithmein* to count, fr. *arithmos* number — more at ARITHMO-, ART, METRIC] **1 a :** the branch of mathematics that treats of the properties and relationships of real numbers and of computations with them involving chiefly addition, subtraction, multiplication, and division **b :** a textbook or treatise on the principles of arithmetic **2 :** application of arithmetic **:** COMPUTATION, CALCULATION, RECKONING ⟨your ~ is pretty bad⟩ ⟨he jogged himself into an ~ of the number of nips of liquor he had taken —George Meredith⟩

²ar·ith·met·ic \ˈa(ˌ)rithˈmed·ik, -ˌrəth-, -etik, -ēk *also* ˈe-\ *or* **ar·ith·met·i·cal** \-ȯkəl, -ēk-\ *adj* **1 :** of or relating to arithmetic **:** in agreement with the rules or methods of arithmetic **2 :** proceeding by an arithmetic progression; *esp* **:** having equal spacing between divisions corresponding to successive positive or negative integers ⟨~ scale⟩ — **ar·ith·met·i·cal·ly** \-ȯk(ə)lē, -li\ *adv*

arithmetical discount *n* **:** the interest discounted in advance on a note and computed on the principal of the note ⟨the *arithmetical discount* on a $1000 note for one year at 5% is $47.62⟩ — called also *true discount;* compare BANK DISCOUNT

arithmetical sum *n* **:** the sum of two or more positive quantities ⟨the *arithmetical sum* of 2, 8, and 1 is 11⟩ — compare ALGEBRAIC SUM

arithmetic graph *or* **arithmetic chart** *n* **:** a graph on which both coordinates are plotted on arithmetic scales

arith·me·ti·cian \əˌrithməˈtishən *sometimes* ˌaˌri- *or* ˌeˌri-\ *n* -s [MF *arithmeticien*, fr. *arithmetique* arithmetic (alter. — influenced by L *arithmetica* or Gk *arithmētikē* — of *arismetique*) + *-ien* -ian] **:** one skilled in arithmetic

arithmetic mean *n* **:** a quantity formed by adding quantities together in any order and dividing by their number ⟨the *arithmetic mean* of 6, 4, and 5 is 5⟩

arithmetic progression *n* **:** a sequence of numbers (as 3, 5, 7, 9 etc.) in which the difference between any number of the sequence and the number immediately preceding it is always the same

arith·me·ti·za·tion \əˌrithməd·əˈzāshən, -əˌtīˈz-; ˌa(ˌ)rithˌməd·əˈz-\ *n* -s **:** the treatment of various branches of higher mathematics by methods involving only the fundamental concepts and operations of arithmetic

arithmo- *comb form* [prob. fr. NL, fr. LGk, fr. Gk *arithmos;* akin to Gk *arariskein* to fit — more at ARM] **:** number ⟨*arithmograph*⟩ ⟨*arithmomania*⟩

ar·ith·moc·ra·cy \ˌa(ˌ)rithˈmäkrəsē\ *n* -ES [*arithmo-* + *-cracy*] **:** rule of the majority

ar·ith·mom·e·ter \-ˈmäməd·ə(r)\ *n* -s [F *arithmomètre*, fr. *arithmo-* + *-mètre* -meter] **:** an early type of adding machine

-ar·i·um \ˈa(a)r-,ˈär-, ˈerēəm\ *n suffix, pl* **-ariums** *or* **-aria** [L, fr. neut. of *-arius* -ary] **:** thing or place belonging to or connected with ⟨*aquarium*⟩ ⟨*planetarium*⟩

ar·i·vai·pa \ˌarəˈvīpə\ *n, pl* **arivaipa** *or* **arivaipas** *usu cap* [perh. fr. Pima *aarivapa*, lit., girls] **:** SAN CARLOS

ar·i·zo·na \ˌarəˈzōnə *also* ˈer-\ *adj, usu cap* [fr. *Arizona*, state in the southwestern U. S., fr. AmerSp, region in southern Arizona and northern Mexico, prob. fr. Papago *arizonac*, lit., few springs, small springs] **:** of or from the state of Arizona **:** of the kind or style prevalent in Arizona **:** ARIZONAN

arizona ash *n, usu cap 1st A* **:** an ash (*Fraxinus velutina*) of the southern U. S. and Mexico having leaves with 3 to 5 leaflets and fruit less than an inch long

arizona cardinal *n, usu cap A* **:** a rather large pale cardinal bird (*Richmondena cardinalis superba*) that ranges from Arizona to Mexico

arizona crested flycatcher *n, usu cap A* **:** a rather large crested flycatcher (*Myiarchus tyrannulus magister*) of the southern Arizona desert

arizona cypress *n, usu cap A* **:** a timber tree (*Cupressus arizonica*) with bluish silvery foliage found chiefly in Arizona

arizona gourd *n, usu cap A* **:** CALABAZILLA

arizona hooded oriole *n, usu cap A* **:** a hooded oriole (*Icterus cucullatus nelsoni*) that breeds in the extreme southwestern U.S. and winters in Mexico

arizona jay *n, usu cap A* **:** a blue and gray crestless jay (*Aphelocoma ultramarina arizonae*) of Arizona and New Mexico

arizona longleaf pine *n, usu cap A* **:** APACHE PINE

¹ar·i·zo·nan \ˌ==ˈzōnən\ *also* **ar·i·zo·ni·an** \-nēən, -nyən\ *n* -s *cap* [*Arizona* + E *-an, -ian*] **:** a native or resident of the state of Arizona

²arizonan \ˈ==ˈ==\ *also* **arizonian** \ˈ==ˈ=(=)=\ *adj, usu cap* **:** of, relating to, or characteristic of Arizona or Arizonans

arizona pine *n, usu cap A* **:** a timber tree (*Pinus arizonica*) of Arizona and adjacent regions with leaves clustered in groups of three, four, or five and tufted at the ends of branches

arizona ruby *n, usu cap A* **:** a ruby-colored pyrope garnet of igneous origin from the southwestern U. S.

arizona sycamore *n, usu cap A* **:** a medium-sized tree (*Platanus wrightii*) of Arizona and adjacent regions with deeply lobed leaves and collective fruits in groups of from three to five

arizona walnut *n, usu cap A* **:** a short stout tree (*Juglans major*) with a thin-shelled edible nut found in the southwestern U. S. and adjacent Mexico

arizona white oak *n, usu cap A* **:** an oak (*Quercus arizonica*) of Arizona and Mexico with entire oblong to obovate leaves and a hemispherical cup around the acorn

ar·i·zo·nite \ˌarəˈzōˌnīt\ *n* -s [*Arizona*, its locality + E *-ite*] **:** a mineral $Fe_2Ti_3O_9$ consisting of ferric titanium oxide found in irregular metallic steel-gray masses

ar·jun *also* **ar·jan** \ˈärjən\ *n* -s [Hindi *arjun*, fr. Skt *arjuna*, lit., white; akin to L *argentum* — more at ARGENT] **:** either of two trees of the genus *Terminalia* (*T. arjuna* and *T. glabra*) found in tropical Asia and characterized by astringent bark that is used in tanning — called also *kumbuk*

ark \ˈärk, ˈȧk\ *n* -s [ME, fr. OE *arc, earc;* akin to OHG *arahha* ark, ON *örk*, Goth *arka*, all fr. a prehistoric Gmc word borrowed fr. L *arca;* akin to L *arcēre* to hold off, enclose, Gk *arkein* to ward off, defend, Lith *rāktas* key, Hitt *ḫark-* to have, hold and perh. to ME *rail*, OHG *rigil;* basic meaning: protecting, locking in] **1** *now chiefly dial* **a :** a chest, coffer, covered basket, or other closed receptacle **b :** BIN, HUTCH **c** *Brit* **:** a small movable poultry house having the shape of an inverted V **2 a :** a boat or ship felt to resemble in some way that in which according to Gen 6 Noah and his family together with pairs of animals were preserved from the Deluge **b :** a large flatboat formerly used on American rivers to carry produce and stock to market — called also *broadhorn* **c :** a wanigan on a log raft **d :** something that affords protection and safety ⟨many look to the U. S. as an ~ of refuge⟩ **3 :** an ornamental somewhat elevated closet or recess traditionally built into or placed against the wall of a synagogue on the side nearest Jerusalem and serving as a repository for the scrolls of the Torah used in public worship **4 :** a storage vat for potter's clay slip **5 :** ARK SHELL

¹ar·kan·san \ärˈkanzən, ȧˈk=, -kaan- *sometimes* -n(t)sən\ *also* **ar·kan·si·an** \-zēən, -(t)sēən\ *n* -s *cap* [²*Arkansas* + E *-an, -ian*] **:** a native or resident of the state of Arkansas

²arkansan \(ˈ)=ˈ==\ *also* **arkansi·an** \(ˈ)=ˈ===\ *adj, usu cap* **1 :** of, relating to, or characteristic of the state of Arkansas **2 :** of, relating to, or characteristic of Arkansans

¹ar·kan·sas \ˈärkənˌsȯ, ˈȧk-, *rap. also* -kᵊnˌ-\ *n, pl* **arkansas** \-ȯ(z)\ *usu cap* [F (recorded in the 17th cent. also as *Acansa, Acansas*), of AmerInd origin] **:** QUAPAW

²arkansas \"\ *adj, usu cap* [fr. *Arkansas*, state in the south central U. S., fr. ¹*arkansas*] **:** of or from the state of Arkansas **:** of the kind or style prevalent in Arkansas

arkansas goldfinch *n, usu cap A* **:** a small goldfinch (*Spinus psaltria psaltria*) of southwestern No. America from Colorado and New Mexico south into Mexico, the adult males being black-backed, the females somewhat greenish

arkansas kingbird *n, usu cap A* **:** a kingbird (*Tyrannus verticalis*) appearing widely in the western U. S. and having the head and back pale gray, the underparts yellowish, and the tail black narrowly bordered with white — called also *western kingbird*

arkansas soft pine *n, usu cap A* **:** the lumber of any of several soft pines: as **a :** LOBLOLLY PINE 1 **b :** SHORTLEAF PINE 1

arkansas stone *n, usu cap A* **1 :** a superior variety of novaculite found in the Ouachita mountains in Arkansas **2 :** a whetstone made of Arkansas stone

arkansas toothpick *n, usu cap A* **1 :** BOWIE KNIFE **2 :** a long pointed often double-edged sheath knife used esp. as a weapon

ar·kan·saw·yer \ˈärkənˌsȯyər, ˈäk . . . yə(r), ˌ==ˈ=ˌ=\ *n* -s *usu cap* [*Arkansaw* (older spelling of *Arkansas*) + *-yer* (as in *sawyer*)] **:** ARKANSAN — used as a nickname

ar·kar \ˈärˌkär\ *n, pl* **arkars** *also* **arkar** [origin unknown] **:** ARGALI

arkhangelsk *usu cap, var of* ARCHANGEL

ar·kie \ˈärkē, ˈȧkē, -ki\ *n* -s *usu cap* [*Arkansas* + *-ie*] **:** an itinerant agricultural worker; *esp* **:** such a worker from Arkansas — compare OKIE

¹ar·kite \ˈärˌkīt\ *n* -s *usu cap* [Heb *ʽArqī* + E *-ite*] **1 :** a member of an ancient Canaanite people **2 :** a member of the Arkite people

²arkite \"\ *n* -s [*Ark*ansas, its locality + E *-ite*] **:** a porphyritic leucite rock consisting of pseudoleucite, orthoclase, nepheline, diopside, aegirite, and garnet

ark of the law *n, often cap A&L* **:** ARK 3

ar·kose *also* **ar·cose** \ˈärˌkōs *also* -ōz\ *n* -s [F *arkose*] **:** a sandstone derived from the rapid disintegration of granite or gneiss and characterized by feldspar fragments

ar·ko·sic \(ˈ)ärˈkōsik *also* -ōz-\ *adj* **:** of or relating to arkose

ark shell *n* [so called fr. the boat-shaped interior of the shell] **:** a marine bivalve mollusk of the family Arcidae

ar·leng \ˈärˌleŋ\ *n, pl* **arleng** *or* **arlengs** *usu cap* **:** MIKIR

arles \ˈär(ə)lz\ *n pl* [ME *erles*, modif. of OF *erres* (pl.) — more at EARNEST] *chiefly Scot* **:** EARNEST MONEY

¹arm \ˈärm, ˈȧm\ *n* -s [ME, fr. OE *arm, earm;* akin to OHG *aram* arm, ON *armr*, Goth *arms*, L *armus* shoulder, Gk *harmos* joint, Skt *īrma* arm, L *arma* tools, weapons, *art-, ars* skill, Gk *arariskein* to fit; basic meaning: joining, fitting] **1 a** (1) **:** a human upper limb (2) **:** the part of an arm between the shoulder and the wrist; *sometimes* **:** the part of an arm above the elbow **b :** the corresponding part of any other vertebrate **c :** HUMERUS ⟨a broken ~⟩ **2 a :** a limb or a locomotive or prehensile organ of an invertebrate animal: as (1) **:** a ray of a starfish or brittle star (2) **:** a brachium of a brachiopod or crinoid **b :** either of the two portions of a chromosome that lie lateral to the centromere **3 a :** an inlet of water from the sea or from some other body of water **:** an often long and relatively narrow bay in the shoreline of a body of water **b :** a tributary or branch of a river or stream **4 a :** a narrow extension of a larger area, mass or region ⟨Baja California, the long, narrow ~ of western Mexico —Marion Wilhelm⟩ ⟨the spiral ~*s* of the Milky Way —George Gamow⟩ ⟨an ~ of the population⟩ **b :** a ridge or elevation extending from a mountain **:** SPUR ⟨two enormous parallel ~*s* with a high plateau between —Forrest Morgan⟩ **c :** an extension of a building or of a group of buildings **:** WING ⟨a cruciform church with three equilateral ~*s*⟩ **5 a :** POWER, MIGHT ⟨the ~ of the law⟩ **b :** STRENGTH, SUPPORT ⟨the governor relied on diplomacy and his own capable ~⟩ **6 a :** BRANCH ⟨the sheltering ~*s* of the great birches and maples —John Burroughs⟩ **b :** a lateral shoot (as of the grape, hop, or other plants); *specif* **:** a main division of the trunk of a grapevine **7 :** a support for the elbow and forearm ⟨his elbow resting on the left ~ of the chair⟩ **8 :** a projecting part of a machine or mechanical appliance that often moves up and down or rotates ⟨the ~*s* of a windmill⟩ ⟨a long derrick ~ —E.S.Gardner⟩ **9 a :** a lateral and usu. horizontally extended attachment or device ⟨a metal ~ to support a wall rack⟩ **b :** one of two or more lateral and usu. horizontally extended parts ⟨the ~*s* of a candelabrum⟩ ⟨the ~*s* of a pair of eyeglasses⟩ **c** (1) **:** the end of a yard (as of a ship) (2) **:** the part of an anchor from the crown to the fluke — see ANCHOR illustration **10 :** SLEEVE ⟨both ~*s* of the shirt were torn⟩ **11** *baseball* **:** ability to throw or pitch ⟨to lose one's ~⟩ **12 :** an extension, division, or supplement of a specified group or activity esp. when viewed as accomplishing a functional and operative aim of the group or activity ⟨the logistical ~ of the air force⟩ ⟨because it is an ~ of merchandising, the sales finance company is under a special incentive to promote consumer goodwill —C.W.Phelps⟩ ⟨making literature serve utilitarian and ulterior ends as an ~ of propaganda —C.I.Glicksberg⟩ **13 :** TONE ARM ⟨use of a properly adjusted professional-type pickup ~ with diamond styli —R.D.Darrell⟩ **14 :** a shoulder cut of meat containing a small round bone and cross sections of three to five ribs — see BEEF illustration **syn** see POWER — **arm in arm :** with arms linked together ⟨they walked down the street *arm in arm*⟩ — **in arms :** extremely young and unable to walk independently **:** requiring to be carried ⟨still a babe *in arms*⟩ — **in the arms of morpheus** *usu cap M* **:** ASLEEP

²arm \"\ *vb* -ED/-ING/-s *vt* **1** *obs* **:** EMBRACE **2 :** to take or hold by the arm (as in guiding) ⟨~*ing* her friend along through the town⟩ ~ *vi* **:** to develop lateral shoots or branches (as of the hop or pole bean)

³arm \"\ *vb* -ED/-ING/-s [ME *armen*, fr. OF *armer*, fr. L *armare*, fr. *arma* (pl.) tools, weapons] *vt* **1 :** to furnish or equip with weapons ⟨~*ing* the soldiers for battle⟩ **2 :** to furnish or equip with something that adds strength, force, security, or efficiency ⟨an animal ~*ed* with a protective shell⟩ ⟨~*ed* with a good meal⟩ ⟨the divers were ~*ed* with cameras and collecting gear —T.A.Manar⟩ **3 :** to prepare for struggle or resistance by some means other than physical **:** fortify morally ⟨~*ed* only with knowledge —J.F.Golay⟩ **4 :** to equip, fit out, or ready for action or operation: as **a :** to free the plunger of (a percussion fuze) from the wire, pin, or other safety device so as to allow the plunger to be driven against the cap **b :** to apply grease or tallow to the socket at the end of (a sounding lead) so as to bring up a specimen of the sea bottom ⟨~ your lead with soap and sound all around the boat —H.A.Calahan⟩ **c :** to make an adjustment in (a bomb, torpedo, or grenade) so that all safety devices are released and the mechanism is in such condition that it will function under predetermined conditions (as impact, pressure, proximity, preset time) ~ *vi* **:** to prepare oneself (as with weapons) for struggle or resistance ⟨~*ing* for the fight⟩ **syn** see FURNISH

⁴arm \"\ *n* -s [back-formation fr. *arms*, pl., fr. ME *armes*, fr. OF, fr. L *arma*] **1 a :** a means of offense or defense **:** WEAPON ⟨air power today is the dominant ~ in war —Donald Armstrong⟩ ⟨he had been found to be in possession of a prohibited ~ —F.M.Ford⟩; *esp* **:** FIREARM ⟨an ~*s* manufacturer⟩ — often used in pl. ⟨taking up ~*s* to defend themselves⟩ **b :** a combat branch (as of an army) ⟨the coast artillery is an important ~ of the military⟩ **c :** an organized branch of national defense (as the navy) **2 arms** *pl* **a :** the hereditary ensigns armorial of a family consisting of figures and colors borne (as on shields or banners) as marks of dignity and distinction **b :** heraldic devices adopted by governments as a symbol of authority or official dignity and used esp. on seals and documents **c :** heraldic devices granted to or adopted by towns, corporations, and others as a badge or trademark **3 arms** *pl, archaic* **:** defensive covering **:** ARMOR ⟨clothed in brilliantly polished ~*s*⟩ **4 arms** *pl* **:** active hostilities **:** WARFARE ⟨the call to ~*s*⟩ **5 arms** *pl* **:** military service **:** a military career ⟨choosing ~*s* as his profession⟩ **syn** see WEAPON — **in arms :** ARMED **:** in a state of hostility — **under arms 1 :** in battle order **2 :** enrolled for military service — **up in arms :** aroused and ready to undertake hostilities

arm *abbr* **1** armature **2** armament

ar·ma·da \ärˈmädə, ȧˈmä- *also* -ādə *sometimes* -adə\ *n* -s [Sp, fr. ML *armata* army, fleet, fr. L, fem. of *armatus*, past part. of *armare*] **1 a :** a fleet of warships **b :** a large number of ships **:** FLEET **c :** a large force, body, or number of things, esp. moving things (as vehicles) ⟨an ~ of planes⟩ ⟨an ~ of buses⟩ **2 :** an arrangement of two tiers of fixed guns simultaneously fired and used in Mexico for the mass shooting of duck

ar·ma·dil·li·di·i·dae \ˌärməˌdiləˈdīəˌdē\ *n pl, cap* [NL, fr. *Armadillidium*, type genus (fr. ²*Armadillo* + *-idium*) + *-idae;* fr. the habit of rolling the body up into a ball when touched] **:** a cosmopolitan family (type genus *Armadillidium*) of terrestrial isopods having arched bodies that can be rolled into a ball and including all the pill bugs

¹ar·ma·dil·lo \ˌärməˈdi(ˌ)lō, ˌȧm-, -dilə *sometimes* -dē(ˌ)(y)ō\ *n, pl* **armadillos** *also* **armadilloes** [Sp, dim. of *armado* armed one (past part. of *armar* to arm), fr. L *armatus*] **:** any of several burrowing chiefly nocturnal mammals (family Dasypodidae) having body and head encased in an armor of small bony plates in which many of them can curl up into a ball presenting the armor on all sides when attacked, being widely distributed in warmer parts of the Americas and in some areas esteemed as food — see PEBA, PELUDO

armadillo (*Dasypus sexcinctus*)

²armadillo \"\ [NL, fr. Sp] *syn of* ARMADILLIDIUM; see ARMADILLIDIIDAE

armado *obs var of* ARMADA

ar·ma·ged·don \ˌärməˈgedᵊn, ˌȧm-\ *n* -s *usu cap* [LL *Armagedon*, scene of a battle between good and evil to take place on Judgment Day according to Rev 16:14–16, fr. Gk *Armageddōn, Harmagedōn*] **1 a :** final and conclusive conflict between the forces of good and evil **:** an apocalyptic battle **b :** the site or time of Armageddon **2 :** a widespread annihilating war **:** a vast conflict that is marked by great slaughter and widespread destruction and that is usu. so decisive as to make further or renewed conflict impossible

ar·magh \(ˈ)ärˈmä\ *adj, usu cap* [fr. *Armagh*, county in Ireland] **1 :** of or from the urban district of Armagh, Ireland **:** of the kind or style prevalent in Armagh **2 :** of or from County Armagh **:** of the kind or style prevalent in County Armagh

ar·ma·gnac \ˈärmənˌyak\ *n* -s *often cap* [F, fr. *Armagnac*, region in southwest France] **:** a brown dry brandy from the department of Gers in southern France distilled from grape wine and aged in oak barrels

ar·ma·ment \ˈärməmənt, ˈȧm-\ *n* -s *often attrib* [modif. (influenced by L *armamenta* utensils) of F *armement*, partly fr. *armer* to arm + *-ment*, partly fr. LL *armamentum* arms, fr. L, utensil, fr. *arma* weapons, tools + *-mentum* -ment — more at ARM] **1 :** an army, air, or naval force **:** a combat or defense unit **:** a military detachment ⟨the vast ~ sent by the Roman emperor crossed the sea⟩ **2** *often pl* **a :** the aggregate of a nation's military strength **:** military, air, and naval personnel, their weapons and equipment, and full manpower of a nation when organized for war or defense together with essential industry, raw materials, and stockpiles of manufactured goods ⟨a small nation that is determined to have adequate ~*s*⟩ **b :** arms and accessory equipment of a combat or defense unit ⟨planes with the newest ~⟩ **c :** means of protection or defense **:** ARMOR ⟨a rosebush well protected by thorns, its natural ~⟩ **3 :** the process of readying or equipping for war (as through building up an army or stockpiling) ⟨the country's ~ will take years⟩

ar·ma·men·tar·i·um \ˌärməˌmenˈterēəm, -ˌmən-\ *n, pl* **armamentaria** \-ēə\ *also* **armamentariums** [L, armory, arsenal, fr. *armamentum* + *-arium* -ary] **1 :** the total store of available resources: **a :** the equipment (as drugs or instruments) and methods used in an activity or profession, esp. in medicine ⟨new medicines that are a welcome addition to the ~ of the medical profession⟩ ⟨the whole ~ of science is being marshaled to increase our understanding of life —J.R.Killian⟩ **b :** factual, experimental, and speculative data ⟨adding to the ~ of knowledge⟩ **2 :** array (as of materials) : COLLECTION ⟨an immense ~ of new antibiotics —*Newsweek*⟩ **3** : essential components : APPARATUS ⟨the ~ used in producing intelligible speech⟩

ar·man·gite \ˈär'man,gīt, -aŋ,-; ˈärmən,gīt\ *n* -s [*ar*senite of *mang*anese + *-ite*] : a mineral $Mn_3(AsO_3)_2$ consisting of a manganese arsenite occurring in black rhombohedral crystals

ar·mar·i·um \är'ma(a)rēəm\ *n, pl* **armar·ia** \-ēə\ *or* **ar·mariums** [L — more at AMBRY] : AMBRY

ar·ma·ta \är'mäd·ə, -ād·ə\ [NL, fr. L, neut. pl. of *armatus*] *syn of* ECHIUROIDEA

ar·ma·ture \ˈärmə,chu̇(ə)r, -,chər, -,tu̇(ə)r, -,tyu̇(ə)r; ˈämə-,chu̇ə, -,chə, -,tu̇ə, -,tyu̇ə\ *n* -s [L *armatura*, fr. *armatus* (past part. of *armare* to arm) + *-ura* -ure — more at ARM] **1** : ARMOR **2** : iron bars or framing employed for the consolidation of a building (as in sustaining slender columns, holding up canopies, stiffening glass windows) **3** : an organ or structure having a protective function ⟨the ~ of armadillos⟩; *sometimes* : an organ or structure used for attack ⟨a small animal having sharp teeth for its ~⟩ **4** : any of various spinous or sclerotized processes on insects; *esp* : the corneous parts of the genitalia **5** [NL *armatura*, fr. L] **a** : a piece of soft iron or steel that connects the poles of a magnet or of adjacent magnets to preserve the intensity of magnetization, produce signals (as in the telegraph), or do mechanical work by its motions to and from the magnet **b** : the part of a dynamoelectric machine carrying the conductors whose relative movement through the magnetic field between the pole pieces causes an electric current to be induced in the conductors (as in the dynamo) or which by having a current passed through them are caused by electromagnetic induction to move through this field (as in the motor) **c** : the movable part of an electromagnetic device (as a relay, buzzer, loudspeaker, or pickup) **6** : a skeleton or framework used by a sculptor to support a figure being modeled in a plastic material

armature reaction *n* : a magnetomotive force set up by the current induced in the armature of a dynamo that results in altering as to both magnitude and direction the flux due to the field magnet

armband \ˈ=,=\ *n* -s [¹*arm* + *band*] : a band of cloth or other material usu. worn round the upper part of a sleeve esp. in mourning or for identification

arm bar *n* : ¹BAR 11

arm board *n* [so called fr. its being strapped to the worker's arm] : a graining board used in leatherworking and made from the outer bark of the cork oak

¹**armchair** \ˈ=,=\ *n* [¹*arm* + *chair*] : a chair with armrests

²**armchair** \ˈ=,=\ *adj* **1** : characterized by comfort, ease, and lazy inactivity ⟨an atmosphere of relaxation, almost of ~ leisure —M.A.C.Gorham⟩ **2** : remote from the necessity of dealing directly with the solution of problems : given to a purely speculative approach to the demands of reality : theoretical rather than practical : lacking firsthand knowledge and experience ⟨an ~ strategist⟩ ⟨~ authorities, whose concern is with contemplation, not action —F.C.Neff⟩ ⟨from ~ speculation to empirical investigation —P.H.Odegard⟩ **3** : sharing vicariously in another's experiences (as through reading) ⟨an ~ traveler⟩

armd *abbr* armored

arme blanche \ˈärm'blä^nsh, *F* ärməbläⁿsh\ *n, pl* **armes blanches** \-m(z)'b-, *F* ärməbläⁿsh\ [F, lit., white weapon] : a cutting or thrusting weapon (as a sword or lance) as distinguished from a firearm

armed \ˈärmd, ˈämd\ *adj* [ME, fr. past part. of *armen* to arm] **1 a** : furnished with weapons of offense or defense : FORTIFIED, EQUIPPED ⟨~ forces⟩ **b** : furnished with something that provides security, strength, or efficacy ⟨~ with letters of recommendation⟩ **c** : furnished with organs or structures esp. adapted to defense or attack ⟨the mandibles of the ~ soldier ants⟩ ⟨rosebushes and other ~ shrubs⟩ **2** *heraldry* **a** : BLAZONED **b** : represented with horns, beak, or talons or having them of a specified tincture — used of beasts and birds of prey ⟨an eagle gules, ~ or⟩ **3** : marked by the maintenance of armed forces in readiness for possible conflict ⟨~ peace⟩ ⟨an ~ truce⟩

armed forces *n pl* : the combined military, naval, and air forces of a nation or a group of nations

armed guard *n* : a naval detachment aboard a merchant ship in wartime

armed neutrality *n* : the position taken by a neutral country during war in which it is prepared to maintain its neutral rights against the belligerents by force if necessary

armed reconnaissance *n* **1** : reconnaissance by aircraft to locate and attack targets of opportunity in a general area rather than to attack predesignated targets **2** : air reconnaissance to locate and gather intelligence on targets in areas where lack of air superiority makes it necessary for the aircraft to fight its way in and out again

armed tapeworm *n* : a tapeworm with a spiny rostellum (as the pork tapeworm)

¹**ar·me·nian** \(ˈ)är'mēnēən, -ā'm-, -nyən\ *adj, usu cap* [*Armenia* (fr. L, fr. Gk) ancient country in western Asia, now divided among U.S.S.R., Turkey, & Iran + E *-an*] : of or relating to Armenia, Armenians, or the language of Armenians

²**armenian** \"\ *n* -s *cap* **1** : a member of a people dwelling chiefly in Armenia but also dispersed throughout the Middle East and emigrated to the New World **2** : the Indo-European language of the Armenians — see INDO-EUROPEAN LANGUAGES table **3** *usu cap* : a member of the Armenian Church which was established about A.D. 302 by St. Gregory the Illuminator as the earliest national Christian church and which professes a modified Monophysitism but otherwise agrees doctrinally with the Eastern Orthodox Church

armenian alphabet *n, usu cap 1st A* : the alphabet of 38 letters in which Armenian is written and of which the invention is ascribed to the bishop Mesrob in the early 5th century A.D.

armenian blue *n, often cap A* [prob. fr. *Armenian* (*stone*), n.] : ULTRAMARINE

armenian bole *n, often cap A* **1** : a soft clayey bright red earth found chiefly in Armenia and Tuscany and used esp. as a coloring material **2** : ²BOLE 3

armenian catholic *n, usu cap A&C* : an Eastern-rite Armenian united with the Roman Catholic Church — see UNIATE

armenian red *n, often cap A* : a strong brown that is yellower and stronger than average russet, stronger and slightly yellower and lighter than average copper brown, and yellower and deeper than rust

armenian stone *n, often cap A* [*Armenian stone*, n., "lapis lazuli", source of blue pigment] : AZURITE BLUE

ar·men·ic \(ˈ)=ˈmenik\ *adj, cap* [*Armenia* + *-ic*] : of or relating to the Armenian language or tongues of the same stock

ar·me·nite \är'mē,nīt, ˈärmə,-\ *n* -s [F *arménite*, fr. *Arménie* Armenia + *-ite*] : a mineral $BaCa_2Al_6Si_8O_{28}.2H_2O$ consisting of a hydrous calcium barium aluminosilicate

ar·me·noid \är'mē,nȯid, ˈärmə,n-\ *n* -s *usu cap* [²*Armenian* + *-oid*] : one having the physical characters of the eastern branch of the Alpine subrace chiefly characterized by dark skin, prominent nose, and broad short skull often flat in the back with a sloping forehead

ar·me·no-turk·ish \är'mē(,)nō'-\ *n, cap A&T* [*Armeno-* (fr. ¹*Armenian*) + *Turkish*] : Turkish as used by Armenians in Turkey with an admixture of Armenian words

ar·me·ria \är'mirēə\ *n, cap* [NL] : a genus of evergreen tufted herbs or subshrubs (family Plumbaginaceae) formerly included in *Limonium* but distinguished by narrow often linear leaves and flowers in dense globular heads — see THRIFT

ar·me·ri·a·ce·ae \(,)är,mirē'āsē,ē\ [NL, fr. *Armeria*, type genus + *-aceae*] *syn of* PLUMBAGINACEAE

armes blanches *pl of* ARME BLANCHE

armes par·lantes \ärməpärlä^nt\ *n pl* [F, lit., speaking arms] *heraldry* : punning arms : canting arms

ar·met \ˈärmət\ *n* -s [MF, modif. (influenced by *arme* arm, weapon) of OSp *almete*, fr. OF *helmet* — more at HELMET] : a late and perfected medieval helmet of many light parts closing neatly round the head by means of hinges following the contour of chin and neck

arm·ful \ˈärm,fu̇l, ˈäm-\ *n, pl* **armfuls** \-lz\ *or* **arms·ful** \-mz,fu̇l\ : as much as the arm can hold ⟨a huge ~ of red roses —L.C.Douglas⟩

arm garter *n* : GARTER 1c

armguard \ˈ=,=\ *n* [¹*arm* + *guard*] : a covering to protect the arm; *specif* : ¹BRACER

armhole \ˈ=,=\ *n* [ME, fr. ¹*arm* + *hole*] **1** *obs* : ARMPIT **2** : an opening for the arm in the body of a garment **3** : ARMSCYE

armies *pl of* ARMY

ar·mi·ger \ˈärməjər\ *n, pl* **armigers** \-rz\ *also* **armig·eri** \är'mijə,rī\ [ML, squire, fr. L, armor-bearer, fr. *armiger* armor-bearing, fr. *arma* weapons, armor + *-i-* + *-ger* -gerous — more at ARM] **1** : ARMOR-BEARER, SQUIRE ⟨~ of a knight⟩ **2** : one entitled to armorial bearings — **ar·mig·er·al** \(ˈ)är'mijərəl\ *adj*

ar·mig·er·ous \(ˈ)är'mijərəs\ *adj* [L *armiger* armor-bearing + E *-ous*] : bearing heraldic arms ⟨the ~ part of the population —Thomas De Quincey⟩

ar·mil *or* **ar·mill** \ˈärməl, -(,)mil\ *n* -s [ME *armille* bracelet, fr. MF, fr. L *armilla*] **1** : ARMILLA 1, 3 **2** [earlier *armilla*, fr. ML, fr. L] : an ancient astronomical instrument for determining equinoxes and solstices by the shadows cast by the sun

ar·mil·la \är'milə\ *n, pl* **armil·lae** \-i(,)lē, -,lī\ *or* **armillas** [L, bracelet, iron ring, fr. *armus* shoulder, arm — more at ARM] **1** : BRACELET; *esp* : a gold coronation bracelet **2** [NL, fr. L] : the annular ligament of the wrist **3** : a stole similar to the ecclesiastical stole and used in the British coronation ceremony

ar·mil·lar·ia \,ärmə'la(a)rēə\ *n, cap* [NL, fr. L *armilla* + NL *-aria*; fr. the ring-shaped veil] : a genus of edible agarics having white spores, an annulus, decurrent gills, and blue juice — see HONEY MUSHROOM, SHOESTRING FUNGUS

ar·mil·lary sphere \ˈärmə,lerē, är'milərē\ *n* [MF *armillaire*, fr. ML *armilla* + MF *-aire* -ary] : an ancient astronomical instrument composed of an assemblage of rings, designed to represent the positions of important circles of the celestial sphere, and turning on its polar axis within a meridian and horizon

armillary sphere

arming \ˈärmiŋ, ˈäm-\ *n* -s [ME, fr. gerund of *armen* to arm] : something that arms or that is used to arm; *specif* : tallow or grease used in arming a sounding lead

arming press *n* : a press for stamping a design on a book cover

¹**ar·min·ian** \(ˈ)är'minēən, -nyən\ *adj, usu cap* [Jacobus *Arminius* (Jacob Harmensen or Hermansz) †1609 Dutch Protestant theologian + E *-ian*] : of or relating to the theologian Arminius, his followers, or their doctrines — see ARMINIANISM

²**arminian** \"\ *n* -s *usu cap* : a follower of Arminius : a believer in Arminianism

arminian baptist *n, usu cap A&B* **1** : GENERAL BAPTIST **2** : a Baptist holding Arminian doctrinal principles

ar·min·ian·ism \-,nizəm\ *n* -s *usu cap* : the doctrines or teachings of Arminius who opposed the absolute predestination taught by Calvin and maintained the real possibility of salvation for all — compare CALVINISM

ar·mip·o·tent \(ˈ)är'mipəd·ənt\ *adj* [ME, fr. L *armipotent-*, *armipotens*, fr. *arma* arms + *potent-*, *potens* powerful — more at ARM, POTENT] *archaic* : powerful in arms : mighty in battle

ar·mi·stice \ˈärməstəs, ˈäm-, *rapid* -mstəs; är'mis- *and* ä'mis-, *often heard immediately after the 1918 armistice, is now chiefly substand*\ *n* -s [F or NL; F *armistice*, fr. NL *armistitium*, fr. L *armi-* (fr. *arma* weapons) + *-stitium* (as in *solstitium* solstice) — more at ARM] : temporary suspension of hostilities as agreed upon by those engaged in the hostilities : a truce either localized or general

armistice day *n, usu cap A&D* : November 11, observed as a legal holiday in the U.S. and Canada in commemoration of the end of hostilities in 1918 and 1945 — used before the official adoption of *Veterans Day* in 1954; called also *Remembrance Day*

ar·mi·tas \är'mēd·əz\ *n pl* [MexSp, pl. of *armita*, dim. of Sp *arma* weapon, fr. L, weapons — more at ARM] : ankle-length divided leather aprons tying around waist and knees formerly worn by cowboys

arm·less \ˈärmləs, ˈäm-\ *adj* : lacking arms

arm·let \ˈärmlət, ˈäm-\ *n* -s [¹*arm* + *-let*] **1** : a band of cloth, metal, or other material worn around the upper arm for ornament, identification, or protection **2** : a small arm (as of the sea)

armload \ˈ=,=\ *n* : as much as an arm can carry ⟨~s of firewood⟩

armlock \ˈ=,=\ *n* [¹*arm* + *lock*] : HAMMERLOCK

ar·moire \ˈärmər, ˈämə(r\ *n* -s [MF, alter. of OF *armaire*, fr. L *armarium* — more at AMBRY] : a usu. large and ornate cupboard, wardrobe, or clothespress

armonica *n* -s [It, fem. of *armonico* harmonious, fr. L *harmonicus* musical — more at HARMONIC] : GLASS HARMONICA

¹**ar·mor** \ˈärmər, ˈämə(r\ *n* -s *see -or in Explan Notes* [ME *armour*, alter. of *armure*, fr. OF, fr. L *armatura* — more at ARMATURE] **1** : defensive covering for the body: **a** : the usu. metal defensive covering worn in combat in the medieval period ⟨suits of ~⟩ — see MAIL 1 **b** : the defensive covering (as that made of resin-treated glass-fiber cloth) used esp. in modern warfare ⟨troops with body ~ and helmets⟩ **c** : the watertight pressure-resistant gear of a diver (as in deep-sea diving) **2** : a quality or circumstance that affords protection ⟨the ~ of courage⟩ ⟨the ~ of prosperity⟩ **3** : steel or iron plating designed to resist gunfire and used esp. to protect ships, tanks, and aircraft **4** : a more or less hard and rigid protective covering of an animal or plant; *esp* : the vegetable tissue enveloping the ligneous interior of certain fossil tree trunks — see BENNETTITALES **5 a** : a protective sheathing on wire, cordage, or hose **b** : a metal sheath commonly of woven wire or spiraled tape covering the insulation of an electrical conducting cable and serving both as a mechanical protection and as a shield against electrostatic or electromagnetic induction **6** : armored forces and vehicles (as mechanized artillery and tanks) ⟨night attacks with ~ —V.G. Gilbert⟩

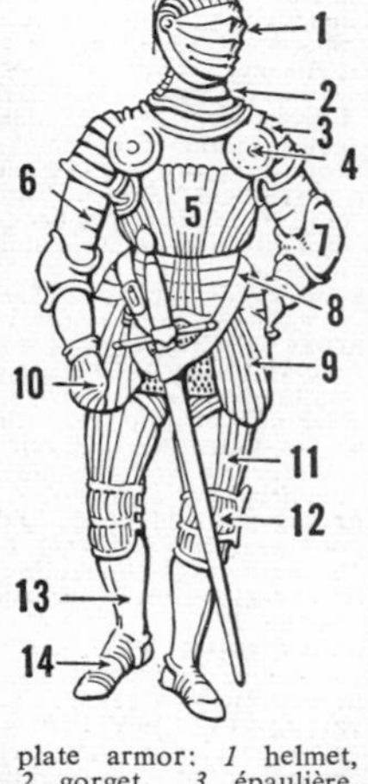

plate armor: *1* helmet, *2* gorget, *3* épaulière, *4* pallette, *5* breastplate, *6* brassard, *7* cubitière, *8* skirt of tasses, *9* tuille, *10* gauntlet, *11* cuisse, *12* knee piece, *13* jambeau, *14* solleret

²**armor** \"\ *vt* **armored; armored; armoring** \-m(ə)riŋ\ **armors** : to equip with armor ⟨four divisions were being ~*ed*⟩

armor-bearer \ˈ=,=,=\ *n* : one that bears armor; *specif* : SQUIRE

¹**armor-clad** \ˈ=,=\ *adj* [¹*armor* + *clad*] : sheathed in or protected by armor

²**armor-clad** \ˈ=,=\ *n* -s : a ship (as a warship) protected by armor

armored *adj* **1** : equipped with armor ⟨an ~ ship⟩ ⟨~ concrete⟩ **2** : marked by the use of armor ⟨an ~ attack⟩ **3** : of or relating to an armored force ⟨an ~ training center⟩

armored cable *n* : an electrical conducting cable with a wrapping of metal (as tape or wire) — compare ¹ARMOR 5b

armored car *n* **1** : an armored wheeled vehicle (as an automobile) often mounting machine guns and light cannon — compare TANK **2** : a railroad car protected by armor

armored catfish *n* : any of certain So. American catfishes chiefly of the family Loricariidae having the body covered by rough and often interlocking bony plates

armored scale *n* : any of numerous scales constituting the family Diaspididae and having a firm covering of wax best developed in the female that is secreted from special glands — compare SOFT SCALE

ar·mor·er \ˈärmərər, ˈämərə\ *n* -s [ME *armourer*, alter. (influenced by ME *armour* armor) of *armurer*, fr. MF *armurier*, fr. OF, fr. *armure* armor — more at ARMOR] **1** : one that makes armor or arms ⟨a sword made by a British ~⟩ **2** : an attendant to assist in the donning of a suit of armor ⟨the knight's young ~⟩ **3** : one that repairs, assembles, and tests firearms: as **a** : an enlisted man having charge of the repair and maintenance of the small arms of his unit **b** : a member of a ground crew charged with repair and service of aircraft armament including bombs and machine guns

¹**ar·mo·ri·al** \(ˈ)är'mōrēəl, -ā'm-, -ȯr-\ *adj* [²*armory* + *-al*] : belonging to or bearing heraldic arms — **ar·mo·ri·al·ly** \-ēəlē, -li\ *adv*

²**armorial** \"\ *n* -s **1** : a book of heraldic arms **2** : ⁴ARM 2a

armorial bearing *n* : ⁴ARM 2a — usu. used in pl.

¹**ar·mor·i·can** \(ˈ)är'mȯrəkən, -mär-\ *also* **ar·mor·ic** \-rik\ *adj, usu cap* [*armorican* fr. L *Armoricae* (pl.) Armorica, region comprising the coast of Gaul between the Seine and Loire rivers + E *-an*; *armoric* prob. fr. L *armoricus* (akin to *Armoricae*, n. pl.)] **1 a** : of or relating to the region in northwest France between the Seine and Loire rivers; *esp* : of or relating to Brittany **b** : of or relating to the people of that region **c** : of or relating to the language of the Armorican people **2** : HERCYNIAN

²**armorican** \"\ *also* **armoric** \"\ *n* -s *cap* **1** : a native or inhabitant of Armorica (now Brittany) : BRETON **2** : the language of the Armoricans

ar·mo·ried \ˈärm(ə)rēd\ *adj* [²*armory* + *-ed*] : decked with armorial bearings

ar·mor·ist \ˈärmərəst\ *n* -s : one skilled in the study of coat armor or heraldry

armor-piercing \ˈ=,=,=\ *adj* : capable of or used for piercing armor — used esp. of rifle bullets, artillery projectiles, and antitank grenades

armor-plated \ˈ=,=\ *adj* : covered with or protected by plating of armor ⟨the barge had *armor-plated* sides⟩

armors *pl of* ARMOR, *pres 3d sing of* ARMOR

¹**ar·mo·ry** \ˈärm(ə)rē, ˈäm-, -ri\ *n* -ES [ME *armourie*, alter. (influenced by ME *armour* armor) of *armurie*, fr. *armure* armor + *-ie* -y — more at ARMOR] **1 a** *archaic* : ARMOR : defensive and offensive arms **b** *archaic* : protective trappings : defensive gear **c** : ensemble of arms for defense or attack : array of weapons ⟨an important weapon in the antiaircraft ~⟩ **d** : the storehouse of resources : repository of usable material : collection of available data ⟨within the ~ of the artist⟩ ⟨a whole ~ of intellectual tools —Sidney Hook⟩ ⟨his ~ of mythological lore —Dudley Fitts⟩ **2** : a place where arms and military equipment are deposited, often being a large building including also a drill hall and offices **3** : a usu. government-owned building or site where arms (as rifles, pistols, bayonets, and swords) are manufactured

²**armory** \"\ *n* -ES [MF *armoierie*, fr. OF, fr. *armoier* to blazon (fr. *armes* arms, coat of arms) + *-erie* -ery — more at ARM] **1** : the art of blazoning arms : HERALDRY **2** : ⁴ARM 2a **3 a** : a branch of heraldry that treats of coat armor **b** : the use and display of coat armor **c** : a book of coats of arms arranged in the order of the bearers' names — compare ORDINARY

armour \ˈärmə(r\ *chiefly Brit var of* ARMOR

ar·mo·zeen *or* **ar·mo·zine** \,ärmə'zēn\ *n* -s [prob. fr. It *ermesino*, fr. *Harmozia* (now *Hormuz*, *Ormuz*), ancient town on coast of Persia] : a heavy generally black taffeta-weave silk used for clerical robes and mourning

armpit \ˈ=,=\ *n* [ME, fr. ¹*arm* + *pit*] : the hollow beneath the junction of the arm and shoulder : AXILLA

armrack \ˈ=,=\ *n* [⁴*arm* + *rack*] : a frame for holding pistols or other small arms

armrest \ˈ=,=\ *n* : a support for the arm (as on a chair)

arms *pl of* ARM, *pres 3d sing of* ARM

arm·scye \ˈärm,sī, -,zī\ *also* **arms·eye** \-,zī\ *n* -s [*armscye* fr. ¹*arm* + E dial. *scye*, *sey* armhole; *armseye* prob. by folk etymology fr. *armscye*] : ARMHOLE; *specif*, *in tailoring and dressmaking* : the shape or outline of the armhole

armsful *pl of* ARMFUL

arm's length *n* : a distance preventing or excluding personal contact, familiarity, or intimacy ⟨pompous and ornate and keeps us stiffly at *arm's length* —Virginia Woolf⟩; *specif* : the condition or fact that the parties to a transaction or negotiation are independent and that one does not dominate the other ⟨sale at *arm's length*⟩ ⟨*arm's-length* bargaining⟩

arms of adoption *heraldry* : arms taken by a stranger in blood in compliance with the will of a testator

arms of affection *heraldry* : arms assumed out of gratitude to a benefactor and borne quartered with one's paternal arms

arms of alliance **1** *heraldry* : arms taken up by the issue of heiresses to show their maternal descent **2** *heraldry* : arms acquired by marriage

arms of augmentation *heraldry* : armorial bearings additional to those already possessed and conferred by special grant for distinguished services to the state

arms of community *heraldry* : arms of corporate and other bodies (as bishops' sees, abbeys, universities, and towns)

arms of dominion *also* **arms of sovereignty** *heraldry* : national arms borne by a sovereign

arms of office *heraldry* : arms borne by virtue of tenancy of an office or dignity ⟨a bishop's *arms of office*⟩

arms of pretension *heraldry* : arms of a sovereignty or other rank that are assumed to denote a claim to a realm or rank by one not in possession of it (as the fleurs-de-lis of France borne on the shield of England from 1340 to 1801)

arms of succession *heraldry* : arms denoting inheritance

arm spread *n* : SPAN 1b

arm stake *n* : ¹STAKE 9

armt *abbr* armament

ar·mure \ˈär,myu̇(ə)r, -,myər\ *n* -s [F, lit., armor — more at ARMOR] : a pebbly-surfaced fabric made from various fibers or combinations of fibers and used for clothing and interior decoration, the usual armure pattern being an allover one of small conventional motifs flocked on a twilled or rep ground

ar·my \ˈärmē, ˈäm-, -mi\ *n* -ES [ME *armee*, fr. MF *armée*, fr. ML *armata* army, fleet — more at ARMADA] **1 a** : a large organized body of men armed and trained for war and destined chiefly for land service **b** : a unit organized to be capable of independent action and consisting conventionally of a headquarters, two or more corps, and auxiliary troops **c** *often cap* : the complete military organization of a nation for land warfare ⟨the ~ of the U.S.⟩ **2** : a great number : vast multitude : ARRAY ⟨an ~ of skilled technicians would be necessary⟩ **3** : a body of persons organized for the advancement of a cause ⟨an ~ of dedicated doctors⟩ ⟨the Salvation *Army*⟩

army ant *n* [so called fr. its moving in large groups] : any of a number of nomadic social ants constituting a subfamily (Dorylinae) of the Formicidae, ranging and foraging freely, and establishing temporary bivouacs rather than permanent nests — compare DRIVER ANT, LEGIONARY ANT

army aviation *n* : aircraft with necessary personnel and equipment organically a part of the army rather than the air force

army brat *n, often cap A, slang* : the son or daughter of a regular-army officer or enlisted man

army brown *n* : a light brown that is darker and slightly yellower than blush and redder and darker than cork — called also *rosario*

army corps *n* : CORPS 1b

army cutworm *n* [so called fr. its moving in large groups] : a cutworm (*Chorizagrotis auxiliaris*) destructive mainly to forage crops and small grains

army group *n* : a primarily tactical organization that consists of two or more armies (sense 1b)

army of occupation : an army sent to hold and exercise a military government in the territory of the enemy after his subjugation in war usu. to ensure compliance with peace terms

armyworm \ˈ=,=\ *n* **1** : any of a number of larval noctuid moths that often travel in great multitudes from field to field destroying grass, grain, and other crops; *esp* : the common armyworm (*Pseudaletia unipuncta*) of the northern U.S. — see BEET ARMYWORM, FALL ARMYWORM **2** : one of the larvae of certain small two-winged flies (genus *Sciara*) that march in large companies in regular order

arn \ˈärn\ *n* -s [earlier *alryne*, *alrone*, fr. ME *alloren*, *allerne* of alder, fr. OE *ælren*, fr. *aler*, *alor* alder + *-en* — more at ALDER] *Scot* : the alder tree

ar·na \ˈär,nä\ *n* -s [Hindi *arnā*; akin to Skt *araṇya* forest, fr. *araṇa* foreign, distant; akin to Av *auruna-* wild and perh. to L *alius* other — more at ELSE] : a wild water buffalo

arnatta *or* **arnatto** *var of* ANNATTO
ar·naut \'är,naůt, =ˈ=\ *n* -s *usu cap* [Turk *arnavut* Albanian, perh. fr. MGk *Arbanitēs*, alter. of *Albanitēs*, fr. *Albania* (fr. ML) + Gk *-itēs* -ite] **:** an inhabitant of Albania and neighboring mountainous regions; *esp* **:** an Albanian serving in the Turkish army
ar·ne·bia \är'nēbēə, ,ärnə'bēə\ *n, cap* [NL, fr. Ar *arnabīyah*] **:** a genus of Asiatic and northern African herbs (family Boraginaceae) having alternate leaves and yellow or violet flowers that change color in age — see PROPHET FLOWER
ar·nee \'är,nē\ *n* -s [Hindi *arnī*, fem. of *arnā* — more at ARNA] **:** ARNA; *esp* **:** the female arna
ar·neth index \'är,net·'-, -ed·'-\ *n, cap A* [after Joseph *Arneth* †1955 Ger. physician] **:** an age classification of blood granulocytes, specif. neutrophils, based on the number of lobes of the nucleus, increasing lobulation being regarded as a criterion of increasing age — compare SCHILLING INDEX, SHIFT TO THE LEFT, SHIFT TO THE RIGHT
arn·hem \'ärnəm, -n,hem\ *adj, usu cap* [fr. *Arnhem*, Netherlands] **:** of or from Arnhem, Netherlands **:** of the kind or style prevalent in Arnhem
ar·ni·ca \'ärnikə, -nē-, *dial* -nəkē\ *n* [NL] **1 a** *cap* **:** a large genus of herbs (family Compositae) of the northern hemisphere having opposite leaves and flower heads that are discoid or have bright yellow rays — see LEOPARD'S BANE 2 **b** -s **:** a plant of the genus *Arnica* **2** -s **a :** the dried flower head of an herb (*Arnica montana*) and other plants of the genus *Arnica* used for stimulant and local irritant effect esp. in the form of the tincture as an embrocation for bruises, sprains, and swellings **b :** the tincture made from arnica
arnica bud *n* [*arnica*, fr. the appearance of its leaves] **:** FALL DANDELION
ar·nim·ite \'ärnə,mīt\ *n* -s [G *arnimit*, fr. von *Arnim*, name of the German family owning a mine near Planitz, Germany, its locality + G *-it* -ite] **:** a mineral $Cu_5(SO_4)_2(OH)_6.3H_2O$ consisting of a basic copper carbonate
ar·nold·ist \'ärnᵊldəst\ *n* -s *cap* [*Arnold* of Brescia (Arnaldo da Brescia) †1155 Ital. political reformer + E *-ist*] **:** one of the followers of Arnold of Brescia, who preached against clerical riches and corruption and instigated the Romans to rebel against the temporal power of the pope
ar·nold's ganglion \'ärnᵊl(d)z-\ *n, usu cap A* [after Friedrich *Arnold* †1890 Ger. anatomist] **:** OTIC GANGLION
ar·nold sterilizer \-nᵊl(d)'st-\ *n, usu cap A* [after Julius *Arnold* †1915 Ger. pathologist] **:** a sterilizer used for fractional sterilization at 212°F by the free circulation of steam at atmospheric pressure
arnotta *or* **arnotto** *var of* ANNATTO
aroaco *cap, var of* ARHUACO
aroar \ə'-\ *adj* [¹*a-* + *roar*, v.] **:** ROARING
aroba *var of* ARABA
aro·ei·ra \,arə'wārə\ *n* -s [Pg] **:** any of several So. American resin-yielding timber trees of the genera *Schinus* and *Astronium* of the family Anacardiaceae
¹ar·oid \'a(a),rȯid\ *or* **aroi·de·ous** \(')=ˈ=dēəs, ə'rȯid-\ *adj* [*aroid* fr. NL *Arum* + E *-oid*; *aroideous* fr. ²*aroid* + *-eous*] **:** belonging to the family Araceae **:** ARACEOUS
²aroid \"\ *n* -s **:** a plant of the family Araceae
aroint \ə'rȯint\ *vb* [origin unknown] *v imper* **:** BEGONE — used with reflexive *thee* ⟨~ thee, witch —Shak.⟩ ~ *vt* -ED/-ING/-S **:** to drive away by or as if by an exclamation or curse ⟨the . . . church duly ~*ed* witches —D.C.Peattie⟩
aro·li·um \ə'rōlēəm\ *n, pl* **aro·lia** \-ēə\ [NL, fr. ML, roll of cloth] **:** a padlike lobe projecting between the tarsal claws of many insects
arol·la \ə'rälə, -ōlə,-ȯlə\ *or* **arolla pine** *n* -s [F dial. (Valais canton, Switzerland) *arolla*, prob. of non-IE origin; akin to G dial. (Switzerland) *arve* Swiss pine] **:** SWISS PINE
¹aro·ma \ə'rōmə\ *n* -s [alter. (influenced by L *aroma*) of earlier *aromat*, fr. ME, fr. OF, fr. L *aromat-, aroma*, fr. Gk *arōmat-, arōma*] **1** *obs* **:** SPICE — usu. used in pl. **2 a** (1) **:** a distinctive pleasing odor **:** FRAGRANCE ⟨the ~ of fresh coffee⟩ ⟨the ~ of a wood fire⟩ (2) **:** the fragrance of a wine derived from the particular variety of grape used **:** BOUQUET **b :** any smell or odor ⟨the gruesomely strong ~ of the old dog —Christopher Morley⟩ **3 :** a distinctive pervasive quality, characteristic, or atmosphere **:** FLAVOR ⟨ancient capitals around which hang an ~ and mystery —Lin Yutang⟩ ⟨the ~ and fragrance of new thought were perceptible —Nathaniel Hawthorne⟩ **syn** see SMELL
²aro·ma \"\ *or* **aro·mo** \-(,)mō\ *n* -s [AmerSp, fr. Sp *aroma* flower of the huisache, lit., fragrant plant product, fr. L, spice] **:** any of several spiny shrubs and trees (as the huisache)
aro·ma·den·drene \ə,rōmə'den,drēn\ *n* -s [ISV ¹*aroma* + *dendr-* + *-ene*] **:** a sesquiterpenoid hydrocarbon $C_{15}H_{24}$ occurring as a major constituent of oils from several eucalyptus trees
aro·mal \ə'rōməl\ *adj* [¹*aroma* + *-al*] **:** AROMATIC
¹ar·o·mat·ic \,arə¦mad·ik, -atik, -ēk *also* ¦er-\ *adj* [ME *aromatyk*, fr. MF *aromatique*, fr. LL *aromaticus*, fr. Gk *arōmatikos*, fr. *arōmat-, arōma* + *-ikos* -ic] **1 :** of, relating to, or having aroma **:** as **a :** having a distinctive pleasing odor **:** sweet-smelling **:** FRAGRANT ⟨the ~ breath of spruce and pine —Willa Cather⟩ ⟨an ~ blend of domestic and imported tobaccos⟩ **b :** having a strong smell or odor ⟨steerage accommodations . . . were at best congested and strikingly ~ —Robert Rice⟩ **c :** having a distinctive pervasive quality or atmosphere ⟨all the places with ~ names —John Woodburn⟩ **2 a :** of, relating to, or characterized by the presence of at least one benzene ring — used of a large class of monocyclic, bicyclic, and polycyclic hydrocarbons and their derivatives (as benzene, toluene, naphthalene, phenol, aniline, salicylic acid); distinguished from *alicyclic, aliphatic, heterocyclic*; *see* CARBOCYCLIC; compare BENZENOID **b :** similar in chemical properties to the benzene ring or to compounds containing it — used esp. in relation to some unsaturated heterocyclic compounds (as thiophene and pyridine) — **ar·o·mat·i·cal·ly** \-ək(ə)lē, -ēk-, -li\ *adv* — **ar·o·mat·ic·ness** \-iknəs, -ēk-\ *n* -ES
²aromatic \"\ *n* -s **1 :** a plant, drug, or medicine characterized by a fragrant smell and usu. by a warm pungent taste (as ginger, cinnamon, and spices) **2 :** an organic compound of the aromatic class
aromatical [¹*aromatic* + *-al*] *archaic var of* AROMATIC
aromatic bitters *n* **:** bitters that contain aromatic oils but little tannin
ar·o·ma·tic·i·ty \,arəmə'tisəd·ē, ə,rōm-\ *n* -ES **1 :** aromatic quality **2 :** the quality of being or resembling a member of the aromatic class of chemical compounds
aromatic spirit of ammonia *n* **:** a solution of ammonia and ammonium carbonate in alcohol and distilled water perfumed with the oils of lemon, lavender, and nutmeg and used as a stimulant, carminative, and antacid
aromatic sulfuric acid *n* **:** a mixture of sulfuric acid, tincture of ginger, oil or spirit of cinnamon, and alcohol formerly used as a tonic and astringent
aromatic vinegar *n* **:** a solution of acetic acid highly flavored with fragrant substances and used as smelling salts
aromatic water *n* **:** a saturated aqueous solution of a volatile oil or other volatile substance prepared either by distillation or by dissolving the substance
aromatic wintergreen *n* **:** WINTERGREEN 2a
aro·ma·ti·tes \ə,rōmə'tīd·ēz\ *n, pl* **aromati·tae** \-ī,tē\ [L, fr. Gk *arōmatitēs*, fr. *arōmatitēs* aromatic, fr. *arōmat-, arōma* + *-itēs* -ite — more at AROMA] **:** a precious stone of ancient Arabia and Egypt
aro·ma·ti·za·tion \ə,rōməd·ə'zāshən, -mədə-, -mə,tī'z-\ *n* -s **1 :** the act or process of making aromatic or the quality or state of being aromatic **2 a :** chemical conversion into one or more aromatic compounds **b** *in petroleum refining* **:** conversion of aliphatic or alicyclic hydrocarbons into aromatic hydrocarbons by cyclization or dehydrogenation or both (as heptane into toluene or cyclohexane into benzene) — see HYDROFORMING
aro·ma·tize \ə'rōmə,tīz\ *vt* -ED/-ING/-S [MF *aromatiser*, fr. LL *aromatizare*, fr. Gk *arōmatizein*, fr. *arōmat-, arōma* + *-izein* -ize] **1 :** to make aromatic (as with herbs) **:** give a fragrant scent to **:** FLAVOR **2 :** to subject to chemical aromatization
aromo *var of* AROMA
ar·o·mor·pho·sis \,arə'mȯrfəsəs *sometimes* -,mȯr'fō-\ *n, pl* **aromorpho·ses** \-,sēz\ [NL, fr. *aro-* (fr. Gk *ara, ar* there and then, straightway; also, interrogative and connective particle) + *morphosis*; akin to Lith *ir̃* and, also, *ar̃*, interrogative particle] **:** biological evolution marked by general increase in degree of organization without sharp specialization — compare ALLOMORPHOSIS
aro·nia \ə'rōnēə\ *n, cap* [NL, fr. Gk *arōnia* medlar tree] **:** a small genus of shrubs (family Rosaceae) comprising the chokeberries and having white or pink flowers in terminal compound cymes
aroon \ə'rün\ *n* -s [IrGael *a rūn* oh darling, fr. *a* oh + *rūn* darling, lit., secret, fr. OIr — more at RUNE] *Irish* **:** DARLING
aroosha *var of* ARUSHA
aro·ras \ə'rōrəz\ *n pl, usu cap* [native name in India] **:** a prosperous mercantile caste of Hindus of the Punjab region of the Indian subcontinent
arose *past of* ARISE
¹around \ə'raůnd\ *adv* [ME, prob. fr. ¹*a-* + *round*, n.] **1 a :** in a circle or in circumference **:** ROUND ⟨the wheel kept going ~⟩ ⟨the track is a mile ~⟩ **b :** in a course making a circle or part of a circle ⟨waltz your partner ~ again⟩ ⟨the wind has gone ~ to the south⟩ **c :** by a circuitous route **:** in a roundabout way ⟨the road goes ~ by the lake⟩ **2 a :** on every side **:** in all or various directions from a fixed point ⟨the water of this well is famous for miles ~⟩ **b :** in close from all sides so as to surround, confine, or envelop **:** close about ⟨the old house is hemmed ~ by new apartments⟩ ⟨people crowded ~ to look at the wreck⟩ **c :** in or near one's present situation ⟨you have time to stay ~ a while⟩ **3 a :** here and there at random **:** at, in, or to various places **:** from one place to another **:** all about ⟨for a year he traveled ~ from state to state⟩ ⟨the news soon got ~⟩ **b :** to a particular place either specified or understood ⟨invited him to come ~ for supper⟩ **c :** into a situation permitting doing or attending — used with *to* ⟨it was a long time before he got ~ to reading the book⟩ ⟨we'll get ~ to the work in the morning⟩ **4 a :** in rotation or succession **:** in turn ⟨another winter has come ~⟩ ⟨he passed the candy ~ to his guests⟩ **b :** from beginning to end **:** THROUGH ⟨the region has a mild climate the year ~⟩ **c :** in order ⟨the other way ~⟩ **d :** to a customary condition (as of health or consciousness) **:** to an improved state ⟨medicines that will bring the invalids ~⟩ **5 :** somewhere close by **:** in the vicinity or neighborhood **:** NEARBY ⟨all he could do was stand ~ and wait⟩ **6 a :** in the reverse or opposite direction **:** to the rear ⟨suddenly he turned ~⟩ **b :** from one opinion, belief, or point of view to another **:** to an altogether different position or attitude ⟨the public's reaction soon brought the legislators ~⟩ **7 :** in the neighborhood of **:** APPROXIMATELY, ABOUT ⟨the book runs to ~ 500 pages⟩ ⟨he comes at ~ the same time every day⟩ —**been around :** undergone many varied experiences **:** become worldly-wise or sophisticated ⟨what most of them need is just a little advice from somebody who's *been around* —W.L. Gresham⟩
²around \"\ *prep* [ME, fr. *around*, adv.] **1 a :** along the outer edge or boundary of **:** on all sides of ⟨a neat yard with a fence ~ it⟩ **:** so as to encircle or enclose **:** ABOUT ⟨threw her arm ~ his neck⟩ ⟨several people seated ~ the table⟩ **b :** so as to make the circuit of ⟨~ the world in 80 days⟩ or partial circuit of ⟨a voyage ~ Cape Horn⟩ **:** so as to follow the curving course of ⟨coming ~ the bend of the river⟩ **c :** so as to avoid or get past ⟨leaping over fences and dodging ~ boulders⟩ **2 a :** in the neighborhood of **:** NEAR ⟨the fields ~ the village⟩ **:** in the same region with ⟨the country ~ the source of the Nile⟩ **b :** close to ⟨only the men ~ the president knew of his illness⟩ **3 a :** in all directions outward from ⟨stood looking ~ him⟩ **b :** so as to have a center or basis in ⟨primitive societies which are organized ~ kinship ties —Weston La Barre⟩ **4 a :** here and there at random in or throughout **:** ABOUT, OVER ⟨constantly traveling ~ the country⟩ **b :** from one part to another of ⟨wandering restlessly ~ the house⟩
³around \"\ *adj* [¹*around*] **1 :** going or moving about **:** ASTIR ⟨he has been up and ~ for two days⟩ **2 :** in existence **:** ALIVE, LIVING, PRESENT ⟨one of the most alertly intelligent of the artists ~ today —R.M.Coates⟩ ⟨the troubles arising out of lack of money have been ~ for a long time —Murray Illson⟩
around-the-clock \=¦==¦=\ *adj* **:** being in effect, continuing, or lasting 24 hours a day **:** UNCEASING, CONSTANT ⟨an *around-the-clock* operation⟩
aroura *or* **arura** \ə'rùrə\ *n, pl* **arourae** *or* **arurae** \-,rē\ [Gk *aroura*, lit., tilled or arable land, fr. *aroun* to plow — more at EAR (to plow)] **:** an ancient Egyptian unit of land measure equal to 0.677 acres (27.4 ares)
arous·al \ə'raůzəl\ *n* -s **:** the act of arousing **:** the state of being aroused
arouse \ə'raůz\ *vb* -ED/-ING/-S [*a-* (perfective prefix) + *rouse* — more at ABEAR] *vt* **1 a :** to awake from or as if from sleep **:** wake up ⟨ran to the flaming house and *aroused* the old man⟩ **b :** to rouse to action or readiness for action from a state of inactivity ⟨the new force stirred and *aroused* the people —Sherwood Anderson⟩ **2 :** to give rise to **:** EXCITE, STIMULATE **:** stir into activity ⟨the book and the play . . . *aroused* debate within the navy —H.W.Baldwin⟩ ~ *vi* **:** to awake from or as if from sleep **:** STIR ⟨a soldier would ~ and turn his body to a new position —Stephen Crane⟩ **syn** see STIR
arous·er \-zə(r)\ *n* -s **:** one that arouses
a ro·ve·scio \,ärō've(,)shō, -eshē,ō\ *also* **al rovescio** \,älr-\ *adv* [It, upside down, backwards] **:** in contrary motion — used as a direction in music indicating imitation by reversion or by inversion
arow \ə'rō\ *adv (or adj)* [ME *arewe, arowe*, fr. ¹*a-* + *rewe, rowe* row, line — more at ROW] **:** in a row, line, or rank
aroxy \(')a¦räksē\ *adj* [*aroxy-*, fr. *aryl* + *oxy-*] **:** ARYLOXY
ar·o·yl \'arəwəl, -,wēl\ *n* -s [*aromatic* + *-yl*] **:** an aromatic acid radical (as benzoyl)
ARP *abbr* air raid precautions
ar·peg·gian·do \(,)är,pejē'än(,)dō, ¦ärpe¦jä-\ *adv* [It, playing an arpeggio, verbal of *arpeggiare* to play an arpeggio, play on the harp] **:** in arpeggio
ar·peg·gi·at·ed \är'pejē,ād·əd\ *adj* [It *arpeggiato* (past part. of *arpeggiare*) + E *-ed*] **1** *of a chord* **:** played as an arpeggio **2** *of a passage* **:** consisting of or played as arpeggios
ar·peg·gi·a·tion \(,)är,pejē'āshən\ *n* -s **:** arpeggio playing or writing
ar·peg·gia·to \(,)är,pejē'äd·(,)ō, ¦ärpe¦jä-\ *adj* [It] **:** in arpeggios **:** ARPEGGIATED
ar·peg·gio \är'pej(ē),ō, -e(,)jō\ *n, pl* **arpeggios** \-ōz\ *or* **arpeg·gi** \-e(,)jē\ [It, fr. *arpeggiare* to play on the harp, fr. *arpa* harp, of Gmc origin; akin to OHG *harpha* harp — more at HARP] **1 :** production of the tones of a chord in succession and not simultaneously **2 a :** a chord played in arpeggio

arpeggio 2

ar·peg·gioed \-ōd\ *adj* **:** ARPEGGIATED
ar·peg·gio·ne \(,)är,pejē'ōnē, ,ärpe'jō-\ *n* -s [G, fr. It *arpeggio*] **:** a cellolike bowed instrument of the early 19th century having frets and drone strings
ar·pent \'ärpənt, -,pänt\ *also* **ar·pen** \-,pən, -,päⁿ\ *n* -s [MF *arpent*, fr. (assumed) VL *arependis*, prob. alter. of L *arepennis*, fr. Gaulish; akin to MIr *airchenn*, a measure of land area; both fr. a prehistoric Celtic compound whose first and second constituents respectively are akin to Gaulish *are* by, in front of (akin to OHG *furi* for, in front of) and to OIr *cenn* head, end, W *pen* — more at FOR] **1 :** any of various old French units of land area; *esp* **:** a unit still used in certain French sections of Canada and the U. S. equal to about 0.85 acre **2 :** a unit of length equal to one side of a square constituting one arpent
arquebus *var of* HARQUEBUS
ar·que·rite \'ärkə,rīt\ *n* -s [F *arquérite*, fr. *Arqueros*, Chile, its locality + F *-ite*] **:** a mineral consisting of a soft malleable variety of amalgam
arr \'er, 'är\ *n* -s [ME *erre, arre*, of Scand origin; akin to ON *err, örr* scar, OSw *ær, ar*, Dan *ar, arr*; akin to MLG *are* scar, G dial. *arbe*, Skt *aru* wound and perh. to ON *rögg* long hair, long wool — more at RUG] *now dial Brit* **:** ²SCAR
arr *abbr* **1** arranged; arrangement **2** arrival; arrive
ARR *abbr* [L *anno regni regis* or *reginae*] in the year of the king's or queen's reign
ar·ra·ca·cha \,arə'kachə, ,ärə'kä-, '==,==\ *also* **ar·ra·cach** \,==ˈkach, '==,=\ *n, pl* **arracachas** *also* **arracaches** [Sp *arracacha, aracacha*, fr. Quechua *rakkácha*] **:** a tropical American perennial herb (*Arracacia xanthorrhiza* or *A. esculenta*) that is related to the carrot and is cultivated in the uplands of northern and western So. America for its edible root — called also *apio, Peruvian carrot*
ar·ra·ca·cia \,arə'kāsh(ē)ə\ *n, cap* [NL, fr. Sp *arracacha*] **:** a genus of chiefly Mexican herbs (family Umbelliferae) having compound leaves, white flowers in umbels without an involucre, and a distinct stylopodium — see ARRACACHA
ar·rack *also* **ar·ak** *or* **ar·rak** \'arək, 'a,rak\ *n* -s [Ar *'araq* sweet juice, liquor] **:** an alcoholic beverage from the Far East or Near East; *esp* **:** a liquor of high alcoholic content resembling rum in taste and distilled in the Far East from the fermented juice of the coconut palm or from a fermented mash of rice and molasses
arrack punsch *or* **arrack punch** *n* [Sw *arrakpunsch*, fr. *arrak* arrack (fr. E *arrack*) + *punsch* punch, fr. E *punch* — more at PUNCH] **:** SWEDISH PUNSCH
ar·rah \'arə\ *interj* [IrGael *ara*] *Irish* — used to express surprise or excitement
¹ar·raign \ə'rān *also* a'-\ *vt* -ED/-ING/-S [ME *arreinen*, fr. MF *araisnier* to speak to, arraign, fr. OF, fr. *a-* (fr. L *ad-*) + *raisnier* to speak, fr. (assumed) VL *rationare*, fr. L *ration-, ratio* reason, reasoning — more at REASON] **1 :** to call (a prisoner) to the bar of a court to answer to the charge of an indictment **:** ACCUSE, CHARGE **2 :** to accuse of wrong, inadequacy, or imperfection **:** find fault with **:** DENOUNCE ⟨St. Peter Damiani . . . ~*s* the monks for teaching grammar rather than things spiritual —H.O.Taylor⟩ **syn** see ACCUSE
²arraign \"\ *vt* -ED/-ING/-S [AF *arrainer*, alter. of *arramer*, irreg. fr. ML *adhramire, arramire* to promise to perform a juridical act, to arraign, fr. L *ad-* + ML *-hramire*, of Gmc origin; akin to OE *hremman* to hinder, ON *hremma* to clutch, Goth *hramjan* to crucify; akin to Russ *kromy* (pl.) loom] **:** to appeal to **:** DEMAND
ar·raign·er \-nə(r)\ *n* -s **:** one that arraigns
ar·raign·ment \-nmənt\ *n* -s [ME *arreinement*, fr. MF *araisnement* action of speaking to, fr. OF, fr. *araisnier* + *-ment*] **:** the act of arraigning or the state of being arraigned **:** ACCUSATION, DENUNCIATION ⟨the wholesale ~ of existing educational standards —F.N.Robinson⟩
ar·rame \ə'rām\ *vt* -ED/-ING/-S [ML *arramire* to arraign (as in *arramire assisam* to hold an assize) — more at ARRAIGN] *law* **:** COMMENCE ⟨~ the assize⟩
arrand *var of* ARAIN
ar·range \ə'rānj *also* a'-\ *vb* -ED/-ING/-S [ME *arangen, arengen*, fr. MF *arangier, arengier*, fr. OF, fr. *a-* (fr. L *ad-*) + *rengier* to set in a row — more at RANGE] *vt* **1 :** to put in correct, convenient, or desired order **:** adjust properly **:** DISPOSE, PLACE ⟨the girl carefully *arranged* her hair⟩ ⟨minerals *arranged* according to the Dana classification⟩ **2 :** to put in order beforehand **:** make preparations for **:** PLAN ⟨would be grateful to them for *arranging* her few remaining years —Victoria Sackville-West⟩ **3 :** to effect usu. by consulting **:** come to an agreement or understanding about **:** SETTLE ⟨decided as a matter of wisdom to ~ a truce —C.B.Hitchcock⟩ ⟨the date of the marriage was finally *arranged*⟩ **4 a :** to adapt (a musical composition) by rescoring to voices or instruments other than those for which orig. written **b :** ORCHESTRATE ⟨~ a folk melody⟩ ~ *vi* **1 :** to come to an agreement, understanding, or settlement ⟨*arranged* with the travel agent for a June passage⟩ **2 :** to make preparations **:** PLAN ⟨the band *arranged* for a series of concerts⟩ **syn** see ORDER
ar·range·ment \-jmənt\ *n* -s [F, fr. MF *arengement*, fr. *arengier* + *-ment*] **1 a :** the act or action of arranging or putting in correct, convenient, or desired order ⟨there was time only for the quickest ~ of mind —Jane Austen⟩ **b :** the quality or state of being arranged or put in order **2 :** the style, manner, or way in which things are arranged **:** ORDER, SYSTEM ⟨was shocked at the helter-skelter ~ of the papers —Jean Stafford⟩ **3 :** a preliminary step or measure **:** PREPARATION, PLAN — usu. used in pl. ⟨when the emigration to America was decided upon, he was one of four to complete the ~*s* —R.G.Usher⟩ **4 a :** a structure or combination of things arranged in a particular way or for a specific purpose **:** COMBINATION ⟨this does not prevent his paintings from being handsome aesthetic ~*s* —*Encounter*⟩ ⟨the church was decorated with ~*s* of roses and snapdragons⟩ **b :** CONTRIVANCE, AFFAIR, THING ⟨the machine was powered by a man who pumped a bicycle ~⟩ **5 a :** adaptation by rescoring of a musical composition to voices or instruments for which it was not orig. written **b :** a piece so adapted ⟨an orchestral ~ of a song⟩ **6 a :** a settlement or adjustment esp. of a dispute or claim ⟨I'm in a very delicate position but I'll fall in with any ~ Thespis may propose —W.S.Gilbert⟩ **b** (1) **:** a mutual agreement or understanding (as between persons or nations) ⟨nothing . . . precludes the existence of regional ~*s* or agencies —Vera M. Dean⟩ (2) **:** an agreement between a debtor and his creditors modifying his obligations to them **7 :** PERMUTATION 3
ar·rang·er \-jə(r)\ *n* -s **1 :** one that arranges **2 :** one that transcribes music for voices or instruments for which it was not orig. written or adapts it to a style suitable to a particular group of performers — called also *adapter*
ar·rant \'arənt *also* 'er-\ *adj* [alter. of *errant*] **1 :** wandering or roving about **:** ITINERANT, VAGRANT ⟨an ~ thief⟩ **2 a :** OUT-AND-OUT, THOROUGHGOING, CONFIRMED, EXTREME ⟨~ individualists pursuing separate courses —C.M.Smith⟩ ⟨his own perilous air of ~ omniscience —C.E.Montague⟩ **b :** notoriously or outstandingly bad **:** SHAMELESS ⟨is an ~ coward and shows the white feather at the slightest display of pluck in his antagonist —John Burroughs⟩ — **ar·rant·ly** *adv*
¹ar·ras \'arəs *also* 'er- *sometimes* -,ras *or* -aa(ə)s\ *n, pl* **arras** [ME, fr. *Arras*, city in northern France] **1 a :** a high-warp tapestry of 14th and 15th century Flemish origin having rich pictorial designs and being used for wall hangings and curtains **b :** any tapestry of similar design **2 :** a wall hanging or hanging screen of tapestry ⟨behind the ~ I'll convey myself —Shak.⟩
²ar·ras \'ä,räs\ *n pl* [Sp, fr. LL *arrae*, fr. L, pl. of *arra* earnest — more at EARNEST] *Spanish law* **:** a gift made by a husband to his wife upon marriage
ar·ra·sene \,arə'sēn, '==,=\ *n* -s [¹*arras* + *-ene* (as in *damascene*)] **:** a silk or wool embroidery cord resembling chenille
ar·ras·tra \ə'rästrə\ *or* **ar·ras·tre** \-,strā\ *or* **aras·tra** \ə'rästrə\ *n* -s [modif. of MexSp *arrastre*, fr. Sp, haulage, dragging, fr. *arrastrar* to drag, fr. *a-* (fr. L *ad-*) + *rastrar* to drag, fr. *rastro* rake, harrow, fr. L *rastrum* rake — more at RASTER] **:** a rude drag-stone mill for pulverizing ores (as those containing free gold)
ar·ras·tre \ə'rä,strā\ *n* -s [PhilSp, fr. Sp, haulage, dragging] **1** *Philippines* **:** the operation of receiving, conveying, and loading or unloading merchandise on piers or wharves **2** [Sp, lit., dragging] **:** the act or process of dragging a dead bull from the ring after a bullfight
ar·rau \'ä,raů, ə'raů, ə'räü\ *n* -s [AmerSp & Pg, fr. Maipure *arráu*] **:** a large turtle (*Podocnemis expansa*) of the group Pleurodira found in the Amazon river and valued for its edible eggs and as a source of oil
arrawak *usu cap, var of* ARAWAK
¹ar·ray \ə'rā, a'-\ *vt* -ED/-ING/-S [ME *arayen, arrayen*, fr. OF *areer, arayer*, fr. (assumed) VL *arredare* to arrange, fr. L *ad-* + (assumed) VL *redare* to provide, of Gmc origin; akin to Goth *garaiths* arranged — more at READY] **1 a :** to set or place in order **:** draw up **:** MARSHAL ⟨time to ~ his men at the town-ward wall —A.C.Whitehead⟩ ⟨served only to ~ public sentiment . . . against the owners —W.J.Ghent⟩ **b :** to set or set forth in order (as a jury) for the trial of a cause **:** call (as a jury) man by man **2 :** to clothe or dress esp. in splendid or impressive attire **:** dress up **:** deck out **:** ADORN ⟨did she not ~ herself in what seemed unbelievably beautiful clothes —Sherwood Anderson⟩
²array \"\ *n* -s [ME *aray, array*, fr. OF *arrai, arroi, aroi* order, arrangement, dress, fr. *areer, arayer*] **1 a :** a regular and imposing grouping or arrangement **:** ORDER ⟨tending to place the great geographical interests in hostile ~ —U.B.Phillips⟩ **b :** military order ⟨with horse and chariots ranked in loose ~ —John Milton⟩ **c** (1) **:** an orderly listing of jurors impaneled (2) **:** JURY **d :** a group of individuals or kinds of individuals that has a definite modal point forming a center of variations ⟨an interesting ~ of halophiles⟩ **2 a :** CLOTHING, ATTIRE

⟨clad in white ~⟩ **b :** rich or beautiful apparel : FINERY ⟨my silks and fine ~ —William Blake⟩ **3 a :** the summoning of a military force **b :** a body of soldiers : MILITIA ⟨the rule was established that foreign wars should be conducted by the feudal ~ —Edward Jenks⟩ **4 a :** an imposing group of company or persons : large number ⟨such an ~ of attorneys —Sinclair Lewis⟩ **b :** an impressive list, series, or group of things : SUPPLY, DISPLAY ⟨it revives the past as no ~ of facts can do —H.C.Perkins⟩ ⟨this rather bewildering ~ of records and playing equipment —Herbert Kupferberg⟩ **5 a :** a number of mathematical elements arranged in rows and columns ⟨a square determinant ~⟩ ⟨a rectangular ~⟩ **b :** a series of statistical observations or data arranged in classes in order of magnitude : a statistical distribution **6 :** ANTENNA ARRAY **syn** see DISPLAY

ar·ray·al \-āəl\ *n* -s **1 :** the act or process of arraying **2 :** something that is arrayed

ar·ra·yán \,ärə'yän, '==,=\ *n* -s [MexSp, fr. Sp, myrtle, fr. Ar *ar-raiḥān*, any fragrant plant] **1 :** any of several Mexican trees or shrubs of the genera *Psidium, Myrtus, Gaultheria, Pernettya*, and *Rapanea* **2** [AmerSp, fr. Sp] *in the West Indies* **a :** WAX MYRTLE **b :** any of several plants of the genus *Ardisia* **3** [AmerSp, fr. Sp] **a :** an ornamental shrub (*Eugenia apiculata*) of Chile **b :** a shrub (*Eugenia arayan*) of Colombia and Ecuador

ar·ray·er \ə'rāə(r), a'-\ *n* -s : one that arrays

ar·ray·ment \-āmənt\ *n* -s [ME *arayment, arrayment*, fr. MF *arraiement, areement*, fr. OF, fr. *areer, arayer* + *-ment*] **1 :** the act of arraying or the quality or state of being arrayed ⟨then in ~ close . . . rush to war —William Morris⟩ **2 :** CLOTHING, DRESS ⟨titled ladies in fine ~⟩

ar·rear \ə'ri(ə)r, -iə *also* a'-\ *n* -s [obs. *arrear*, adv., behindhand, fr. ME *arrere* behind, backward, fr. MF, fr. OF *ariere, arriere, arere*, fr. (assumed) VL *ad retro* backward, fr. L *ad* to + *retro* backward, behind — more at AT, RETRO-] **1 :** the state of being behind in the discharge of duties, obligations, or responsibilities — usu. used in pl. ⟨he is in ~s with his payments⟩ **2** *archaic* **:** the rear part (as of a procession) **3** *usu pl* **a :** an obligation that has not been met on time or duty that is unfinished ⟨set about the ~s of work that had piled up —Nevil Shute⟩ **b :** an unpaid and overdue debt; *esp* **:** a remainder or balance due ⟨after securing to the present incumbents all ~s in salary —C.G.Bowers⟩ **4** *archaic* **:** something that is held back or in reserve **syn** see DEBT

ar·rear·age \-rij, -ēj\ *n* -s [ME *arrerage*, fr. MF, fr. OF, fr. *arrere* + *-age*] **1 :** the condition of being in arrears **2 :** something that is in arrears; *esp* **:** something that remains unpaid and overdue after previous payment of a part — often used in pl. ⟨a formal demand for the payment of ~s —Washington Irving⟩ **3** *archaic* **:** something that is held back or in reserve **syn** see DEBT

ar·rect \(')a¦rekt\ *adj* [L *arrectus*, past part. of *arrigere* to raise up, fr. *ad-* + *-rigere* (fr. *regere* to direct, guide) — more at RIGHT] **1 :** rigidly erect : lifted up : RAISED ⟨a rabbit with ears ~⟩ **2 :** ATTENTIVE, ALERT ⟨God speaks . . . to the vigilant and ~ —George Smalridge⟩

ar·rec·tor \a'rektə(r)\ *n, pl* **arrecto·res** \,a,rek'tōr(,)ēz\ *or* **arrectors** [NL, fr. L *arrectus* + *-or*] : ERECTOR a

arrenotokous *var of* ARRHENOTOKOUS

ar·rent \a'rent, ə'-\ *vt* -ED/-ING/-S [ME *arenten*, fr. MF *arenter*, fr. OF, fr. *a-* (fr. L *ad-*) + *-renter* (fr. *rente* income from a property) — more at RENT] **:** to let or farm out at a rent; *specif* **:** to permit the enclosure of (forest lands) with a low hedge and a ditch under a yearly rent — **ar·ren·ta·tion** \,a,ren'tāshən\ *n* -s

¹ar·rest \ə'rest *also* a'-\ *vt* -ED/-ING/-S [ME *aresten*, fr. MF *arester*, fr. (assumed) VL *arrestare*, fr. L *ad-* + *restare* to stay back, remain — more at REST] **1 a :** to bring to a stop or halt the motion, course, or progress of : halt or prevent the development of ⟨the girl was caught in a pine tree which ~*ed* her fall —Willa Cather⟩ ⟨the physician cannot ~ the coming on of age —J.A.Froude⟩ **b :** to check, hinder, or slow down the course or progress of : moderate the force of ⟨various expedients to ~ fierce willful human nature in its outward course —J.H.Newman⟩ **c :** to bring to a standstill or state of inactivity ⟨~*ed* tuberculosis⟩ ⟨~*ed* labor⟩ **2 :** to catch or take hold of : SEIZE, CAPTURE; *specif* **:** to take or keep in custody by authority of law ⟨they ~*ed* him for speeding⟩ **3 a :** to catch and hold (as the senses or intellectual faculties) ⟨the racial difference that at once ~s attention is skin color —Ruth Benedict⟩ **b :** to seize or hold in focus the attention, thought, or consideration of ⟨an easy beauty of style which ~s even the least prepared reader —T.S. Eliot⟩

syn CHECK, INTERRUPT : ARREST indicates a stopping or holding fixed in the midst of motion, progress, development, or course with suddenness and with such power, force, or decisiveness that some sort of release is needed for resumed advance or motion ⟨he had gone from task to task until this last attack of blackwater fever had *arrested* his activities —H.G.Wells⟩ ⟨thought was *arrested* by utter bewilderment —George Eliot⟩ CHECK may suggest a quite sudden stopping, perhaps with force, with no implication at all about possible resumption of advance or activity in question ⟨Lucian . . . seemed about to speak but *checked* himself —G.B.Shaw⟩ ⟨while making a tour of his northern provinces he was *checked* by the information that the Penobscot Indians . . . were about to go on the warpath —*Encycl. Americana*⟩ INTERRUPT indicates some sort of breaking in and stopping smooth continuation of action under way; it stresses the fact of breaking in and is usu. used in situations in which a resumption of activity by the performer, doer, or speaker is possible ⟨he entered the Lawrence Scientific School . . . where his studies in chemistry and natural history were *interrupted* by the Civil War —F.H.Garrison⟩ ⟨Emily could never have suspected that she had *interrupted* Mrs. Hetherington on the point of establishing an emotional mastery over the situation —Mary Austin⟩

²ar·rest \"\ *n* -s [ME *arest, areste*, fr. MF, fr. OF, fr. *arester*] **1 a :** the act of stopping or restraining (as from further motion) : CHECK, STAY, STOPPAGE ⟨in my attempt to explain the ~ of the scientific spirit among the Greeks —Benjamin Farrington⟩ **b :** the condition of being stopped ⟨since the heart was in complete ~, massage was immediately started⟩ **2 a :** the act of seizing or taking hold of : SEIZURE ⟨the first ~s of sleep —Charles Lamb⟩ **b** (1) **:** the taking or detaining of a person in custody by authority of law (2) **:** legal restraint of the person : CUSTODY, IMPRISONMENT (3) **:** seizure or detention of chattels under process of law, esp. of vessels in admiralty cases or of movable obligations in a proceeding in Scots law analogous to garnishment **3** *obs* **:** a JUDGMENT, DECREE, SENTENCE : ARRET **4 :** a device for arresting motion (as one for checking the swinging of the beam or pans of a balance) — **under arrest :** in legal custody : ARRESTED

ar·res·ta·tion \,a,re'stāshən\ *n* -s [F, fr. MF *arestation*, fr. *arester* + *-ation*] : ARREST: **a :** STOPPING ⟨the sudden ~ of life under the magic spell —E.V.Lucas⟩ **b :** apprehension by legal authority ⟨the ~ of the criminal⟩

arrested *adj* **:** showing cessation of growth or activity ⟨~ tuberculous activity⟩ ⟨~ development⟩

ar·rest·ee \,a,re'stē, ə're,stē, a'-\ *n* -s [¹*arrest* + *-ee*] **1** *Scots law* **:** the person who holds property attached by arrestment **2 :** one who is under arrest ⟨follow the ~s to city hall and the magistrate's court —Saul Bellow⟩

ar·rest·er *or* **ar·res·tor** \ə'restə(r), a'-\ *n* -s [ME *arester*, fr. *aresten* + *-er*] : one that arrests: as **a :** one that arrests by legal authority **b :** LIGHTNING ARRESTER **c :** SPARK ARRESTER

arrester hook *n* **:** a retractable hook on the underside of the tail of a carrier-based airplane extended in landing to engage an arresting-gear cable on the deck of the carrier

arresting *adj* **:** catching or holding the attention, thought, or feelings : GRIPPING, STRIKING, INTERESTING ⟨a cryptic and ~ personality that compels attention —Geoffrey Bruun⟩ ⟨an ~ and sensitively written contribution to the still slim literature of undersea warfare —Walter Millis⟩ **syn** see NOTICEABLE

arresting gear *n* **:** a series of rather widely spaced parallel wire cables held taut by strong springs and extending across the flight deck of an aircraft carrier, one such cable by being caught by the arrester hook of an airplane in the process of landing halting the forward motion of the plane within a limited space

ar·rest·ing·ly *adv* **:** in an arresting manner

ar·res·tive \ə'restiv, a'-, -ēv\ *adj* **:** tending to arrest or catch the attention or interest : STRIKING

ar·rest·ment \-s(t)mənt\ *n* -s [ME *arestment*, fr. MF *arestement*, fr. OF, fr. *arester* + *-ment*] **1 a :** the arrest of a person or the seizure of his personal property to secure his presence at a trial or the satisfaction of any judgment against him **b** *Scots law* **:** a process secured by a second creditor whereby a debtor is prohibited from making payment or delivery of movable property to one of his creditors until that creditor's debt to the second creditor is settled or secured — compare EQUITABLE ATTACHMENT, GARNISHMENT, TRUSTEE PROCESS **c** *Scots law* **:** a process whereby the movable property of one domiciled outside of Scotland is seized in order to give jurisdiction against him — called also *arrestment jurisdictionis fundae causa* **2 a :** the action of stopping or checking **b :** a stoppage or check

arrest of judgment : the staying or stopping of a judgment after verdict for legal cause

arrests *pres 3d sing of* ARREST, *pl of* ARREST

ar·ret \a're, -rā\ *n* -s [F *arrêt* decision of a court, act of stopping, fr. MF *arest* — more at ARREST] : a judgment, decision, or decree of a court or sovereign

ar·re·tine \'arə,tīn, -ēn\ *adj, usu cap* [L *Arretinus*, fr. *Arretium* (now *Arezzo*), ancient city of Italy + L *-inus* -ine] : of or relating to the ancient Arretium

arretine ware *n, usu cap A* **:** red terracotta ware usu. decorated in relief made at Arretium and elsewhere in Italy from about 100 B.C. to about A.D. 100 — called also *Samian ware, terra sigillata*

arrgt *abbr* arrangement

ar·rha \'arə\ *n, pl* **arrhae** \-(,)rē\ [L *arra, arrha* — more at EARNEST] : EARNEST MONEY — **ar·rhal** \'arəl\ *adj*

ar·rhe·nath·er·um \,arə'nathərəm\ *n, cap* [NL, fr. Gk *arrhen-, arrhēn* male + *ather-, athēr* awn; fr. the awned staminate lemma; akin to Skt *arṣati* it flows, *ṛṣabha* bull, L *ros* dew — more at RORIC] : a genus of Eurasiatic grasses that have 2-flowered spikelets, the first floret staminate and awned from the back and are naturalized in cooler parts of No. America — see TALL OAT GRASS

ar·rhe·nite \'arə,nīt\ *n* -s [Sw or G *arrhenit*, fr. Col. Carl A. *Arrhenius*, 19th cent. Swedish army officer + Sw or G *-it* -ite] : an altered variety of fergusonite

ar·rhe·no·blas·to·ma \,arə,nō,bla'stōmə, ə,rē,-\ *n, pl* **arrhenoblastomas** *also* **arrhenoblasto·ma·ta** \-məd·ə\ [NL, fr. Gk *arrhen-, arrhēn* male + NL *-o-* + *blastoma*] : a sometimes malignant tumor of the ovary that by the secretion of male hormone induces development of secondary male characteristics

ar·rhe·no·kar·y·ot·ic \¦arə,nō,karē¦ad·ik, ə¦rē,-\ *adj* [Gk *arrhen-, arrhēn* male + E *-o-* + *kary-* + *-otic*] : of or relating to a blastomere possessing only chromosomes of paternal origin

ar·rhe·not·o·kous *also* **ar·re·not·o·kous** \¦arə¦näd·əkəs\ *adj* [Gk *arrhenotokos* bearing male children] : of, relating to, or involving arrhenotoky

ar·rhe·not·o·ky *also* **ar·re·not·o·ky** \,==¦näd·əkē\ *n* -ES [LGk *arrhenotokia* act of bearing male children, fr. Gk *arrhenotokos* bearing male children (fr. *arrhenotokein* to bear male children, fr. *arrhen-, arrhēn* male + *tokein* to bear) + *-ia* -y] : parthenogenesis in which only male offspring are produced — compare THELYTOKY

ar·rho·stia \ə'rōstēə\ *n* -s [NL, fr. Gk *arrhōstia* sickness, weakness, fr. *arrhōstos* sickly, weak (fr. *a-* ²a- + *-rhōstos*, fr. *rhōsis* strength) + *-ia* -y] : an evolutionary product or trend that appears to be more or less pathological (as the immense size attained by certain dinosaurs) — **ar·rhos·tic** \ə'rästik\ *adj*

ar·rhyth·mia *also* **ar·ryth·mia** \ā'rithmēə, a'r- *also* -th-\ *n* -s [NL, fr. Gk, lack of rhythm, fr. *arrhythmos* unrhythmical (fr. *a-* ²a- + *rhythmos* rhythm) + *-ia* — more at RHYTHM] : an alteration in the rhythm of the heartbeat either in time or force that is of functional or organic origin — compare BRADYCARDIA, TACHYCARDIA; FIBRILLATION

ar·rhyth·mic \(')=¦=mik\ *or* **ar·rhyth·mi·cal** \-məkəl\ *adj* [Gk *arrhythmos* + E *-ic, -ical*] : lacking rhythm or regularity — **ar·rhyth·mi·cal·ly** \-mək(ə)lē\ *adv*

ar·ric·cio \ə'rē(,)chō\ *n* -s [It, fr. *arricciare* to bristle up, curl, groove (a plastered wall), fr. *a-* (fr. L *ad-*) + *riccio* hedgehog, curl, fr. L *ericius* hedgehog — more at URCHIN] : the rough first coat of plaster in fresco painting — compare INTONACO

ar·ride \a'rīd, ə'-\ *vt* -ED/-ING/-S [L *arridēre*, fr. *ad-* + *ridēre* to laugh — more at RIDICULOUS] **1** *obs* **:** to smile or laugh at **2 :** PLEASE, GRATIFY, DELIGHT ⟨I . . . was greatly *arrided* . . . by what I saw —William Hardman⟩ **syn** see PLEASE

ar·ridge \'arij\ *n* -s [alter. (influenced by *ridge*) of *arris*] *dial Brit* : ARRIS

ar·rie \'arē\ *n* -s [prob. native name in the Aleutians] : MURRE

ar·rière-ban \'arē,er'bän\ *n* -s [F, fr. OF *arriereban*, alter. (influenced by *ariere, arriere* behind) of *herban* proclamation to serve in the army, of Gmc origin; akin to OHG *heri* army and to OHG *ban* proclamation — more at HARRY, BAN] **1 :** a proclamation of a king (as of France) calling to arms his immediate feudatories and their vassals **2 :** the body of vassals summoned to military service

ar·ri·ere fee *or* **arriere fief** \'arē,er-\ *n* [MF *arriere fie, arriere fief*, fr. OF *ariere fief*, fr. *ariere, arriere* behind + *fief* fee — more at ARREAR, FEE] : a fee or fief dependent on a fee : a fee held of a feudatory : SUBFIEF

arrière-pen·sée \-,pän'sā\ *n* -s [F, fr. MF *arriere pensee*, fr. *arriere* behind + *pensee* thought, fr. fem. of *pensé*, past par of *penser* to think — more at PENSIVE] : an undisclosed thought or intention : mental reservation

arrière-vous·sure \-,vü'sü(ə)r\ *n* -s [F, lit., rear arching, fr. *arrière* rear, behind + *voussure* arching, bend of an arch, fr. (assumed) VL *volsura*, fr. *volsus* (past part. of L *volvere* to roll) + L *-ura* -ure — more at VOLUBLE] **1 :** an inner or rear arch in a thick wall that carries the inner part of that wall; *esp* **:** such an arch over a door or window frame **2 :** a relieving arch behind the face of a wall

ar·rie·ro \,arē'e(,)rō\ *n* -s [Sp, fr. *arre* get up!, giddap!] : MULETEER

ar·rie·ros \-ōz,-ōs\ *n pl* [MexSp (*baile de los*) *arrieros* the muleteers' dance] : Mexican men's fiesta dances that follow two local patterns, one portraying a muleteers' camp and the other including votive flagellation and hymns — compare PENITENTE

ar·ris *also* **ar·is** \'arəs *also* 'er-\ *n, pl* **arris** *or* **arrises** *also* **aris** *or* **arises** [prob. modif. of MF *areste* arris, fishbone, beard of grain, fr. LL *arista* fishbone, fr. L, beard of grain] : the sharp edge or salient angle formed by the meeting of two surfaces whether plane or curved — used esp. of the edges in moldings and of the raised edges separating the flutings in a Doric column

arris fillet *n* **:** a triangular piece of wood used to raise the slates of a roof against a chimney or wall to shed the rain

arris gutter *n* **:** a V-shaped gutter at the eaves of a building

ar·rish \'arish\ *n* -ES [alter. of *eddish*] **1** *dial Eng* **:** the stubble of wheat or grass **2** *dial Eng* **:** STUBBLE FIELD

arris rail *n* **:** a rail (as of wood) of triangular section

ar·ris·ways \'arə,swāz\ *also* **ar·ris·wise** \-wīz\ *adv* **:** with the angle or edge presented

ar·riv·al \ə'rīvəl\ *n* -s [ME *arivaille*, fr. MF, fr. *ariver*] **1 :** the act of arriving: as **a :** the act of reaching a destination or of coming to the end of a journey ⟨bad weather delayed our ~⟩ **b :** the act of making an appearance or of coming upon the scene ⟨his ~ brought complete silence to the room⟩ **c :** the attainment or reaching of an end, a state of mind, or a position esp. by conscious effort ⟨his ~ at this conclusion was the result of much thought⟩ **d :** the attainment of or coming to a stage of development esp. by the passage of time ⟨on his ~ at thirty he began to work harder⟩ **2 :** one that is arriving or has arrived ⟨the beach was crowded with recent ~s⟩

arrival draft *n* **:** a draft drawn in foreign trade payable upon receipt of the goods by the buyer

ar·riv·ance \-vən(t)s\ *n* -s [¹*arrive* + *-ance* (as in *entrance*)] *now dial* : ARRIVAL

¹ar·rive \ə'rīv\ *vb* -ED/-ING/-S [ME *ariven*, fr. OF *ariver*, fr. (assumed) VL *arripare* to land, come to shore, fr. L *ad-* + (assumed) VL *-ripare* (fr. L *ripa* bank, shore) — more at RIVE] *vi* **1 a :** to reach a destination : come to the end of a journey ⟨they *arrived* by plane at midnight⟩ **b :** to make an appearance : come upon the scene ⟨the crowd became silent when the officers *arrived*⟩ **2 a :** to gain or achieve an end esp. by conscious effort : attain or reach a state of mind or a position — used with *at* ⟨many attempts to ~ at an understanding —C.L.Jones⟩ **b :** to reach or come to a stage of development esp. by the passage of time : ATTAIN — used with *at* ⟨moved out to the suburb last year when their eldest child was *arriving* at school age —F.L.Allen⟩ **3 a** *archaic* **:** to come to pass : HAPPEN, OCCUR ⟨any such event may ~ to a woman —Henry Fielding⟩ **b :** to be near or at hand in time : COME ⟨the time to go finally *arrived*⟩ **4 :** to achieve success or gain recognition : be successful ⟨believed that a man who has not arrived by forty will never ~ —Catherine D. Bowen⟩ ~ *vt* **1** *obs* **:** to cause to arrive : BRING, CONVEY ⟨and made the sea-trod ship ~ them near —George Chapman⟩ **2** *archaic* **:** to come to : REACH ⟨ere he ~ the happy isle —John Milton⟩

²ar·ri·vé \¦a(,)rē¦vā\ *n* -s [F, fr. past part. of *arriver* to arrive, fr. OF *ariver*] : one who has arrived; *specif* **:** one who has risen rapidly to success, power, or fame ⟨the upstart or ~ who has made his fortune in trade —*Fortnightly Rev.*⟩

ar·riv·er \ə'rīvə(r)\ *n* -s : one that arrives

ar·ri·vism \¦a(,)rē¦vēzəm, -viz-\ *n* -s [F *arrivisme*, fr. *arriviste* + *-isme* -ism] : the practice or conduct of an arriviste ⟨middle-class ~⟩

ar·ri·viste *also* **ar·ri·vist** \¦a(,)rē¦vēst, -vist\ *n* -s [F *arriviste*, fr. *arriver* + *-iste* -ist] : one who employs any means however questionable or unscrupulous to achieve success : an aggressive pushing person : PARVENU, UPSTART ⟨an impoverished family of high breeding and training sneers self-consolingly at vulgar ~s —John Hersey⟩

ar·ro·ba \ə'rōbə\ *n* -s [Sp & Pg, fr. Ar *ar-rub'* the quarter (of the weight *al-qinṭār*)] : a unit of weight: **a :** an old Spanish unit equal to about 25 pounds now used locally in certain Spanish-American countries **b :** an old Portuguese unit equal to about 32 pounds now used locally in Brazil

ar·ro·gance \'arəgən(t)s *also* 'er- *sometimes* -rē- *or* -ri-\ *n* -s [ME *arrogaunce*, fr. MF *arrogance*, fr. L *arrogantia*, fr. *arrogant-, arrogans* + *-ia* -y] : a genuine or assumed feeling of superiority that shows itself in an overbearing manner or attitude or in excessive claims of position, dignity, or power or that unduly exalts one's own worth or importance : overbearing pride ⟨all his words and actions had an irritating ~; he was always right —O.E.Rölvaag⟩

ar·ro·gan·cy \-gənsē, -si\ *n* -ES [L *arrogantia* — more at ARROGANCE] : the quality or state of being arrogant

ar·ro·gant \-gənt\ *adj* [ME, fr. L *arrogant-, arrogans*, pres. part. of *arrogare*] **1 :** having a feeling of superiority that shows or is inclined to show itself in an overbearing attitude or in claiming more consideration than is due to one's position, dignity, or power : exaggerating or disposed to exaggerate one's own worth or importance : overbearingly haughty ⟨he was ~, overbearing, conceited, and passionate — without any rank which could excuse pride —Anthony Trollope⟩ **2 :** proceeding from or characterized by arrogance ⟨his administration had been ~ and despotic —Willa Cather⟩ **syn** see PROUD

ar·ro·gant·ly *adv* **:** in an arrogant manner

ar·ro·gant·ness *n* -ES : ARROGANCE

ar·ro·gate \-rə,gāt, *usu* -ād·+V\ *vt* -ED/-ING/-S [L *arrogatus*, past part. of *arrogare* to appropriate to oneself, fr. *ad-* + *rogare* to ask — more at RIGHT] **1 a :** to claim or seize as one's right (something one is not entitled to) : APPROPRIATE ⟨the sweeping powers the federal government would ~ . . . over a domain that had always hitherto been under the states —T.H.White⟩ **b :** to make undue claims to the possession of : maintain without reason that one has : ASSUME ⟨the unwarranted importance *arrogated* to themselves by public men —Kenneth Roberts⟩ **2 :** to lay claim to on behalf of another : ASCRIBE, ATTRIBUTE ⟨a proposal which would have *arrogated* to the four general staff sections all the functions of a headquarters⟩ **3 :** to adopt (as a person sui juris and independent) in the form and under the special circumstances permitted under the Roman law — see ARROGATION; compare POTESTAS **syn** see APPROPRIATE

ar·ro·ga·tion \,=='gāshən\ *n* -s [L *arrogation-, arrogatio*, fr. *arrogatus* + *-ion-, -io* -ion] **1 :** the act of arrogating or the state of being arrogated ⟨an ~ by Congress of a role that belongs to the courts —*New Republic*⟩ **2** *Roman law* **:** the adoption of a person sui juris and independent, the person adopted losing his independence and together with his children and his property becoming subject to the paternal power of the adopting father

ar·ro·ja·dite \,arə'jä,dīt\ *n* -s [Pg *arrojadita*, fr. Miguel *Arrojado* Lisbôa 20th cent. Brazilian geologist + Pg *-ita* -ite] : a mineral $Na_2(Fe,Mn)_5(PO_4)_4$ consisting of a phosphate of sodium, iron, and manganese occurring in Brazil as dark green monoclinic masses

ar·ron·di \,a,rōⁿ'dē\ *adj* [F, past part. of *arrondir*] : CURVED, ROUNDED ⟨~ arm posture or leg movement in ballet dancing⟩

ar·ron·disse·ment \ə'rändəsmənt, ,arən'dēsmənt, ,a'rändē,smäⁿ, *F* ärōⁿdēsmäⁿ\ *n, pl* **arrondissements** \-ənts,-äⁿz, *F* -äⁿ\ [F, fr. MF, action of making round, fr. *arrondiss-* (stem of *arrondir* to make round, fr. OF *arondir, areondir*, fr. *a-* — fr. L *ad-* — + *-rondir, -reondir*, fr. *reont, roont* round) + connective *-e-* + MF *-ment* — more at ROUND] **1 :** the largest administrative subdivision of a French department **2 :** a ward or administrative district of some large cities of France ⟨Paris is subdivided into 20 ~s⟩

¹ar·row \'a(,)rō, 'arə *also* 'e-; *often* -,rəw+V\ *n* -s *often attrib* [ME *arewe, arwe*, fr. OE *arwe, earh*; akin to ON *ǫr* arrow, Goth *arhwazna*, L *arcus* bow, arc] **1 :** a missile weapon shot from a bow and usu. consisting of a straight slender shaft that has a point or sharp head of stone or metal, feathers or vanes fastened near the butt, and a nock to be fitted to a bowstring **2 :** something felt to resemble an arrow esp. in shape: as **a :** a mark (as on a map or signboard) to indicate direction **b :** the inflorescence of the sugarcane or the shoot that develops into the inflorescence **c :** a surveyor's marking pin used to mark the ground at each chain's length — called also *chain pin*

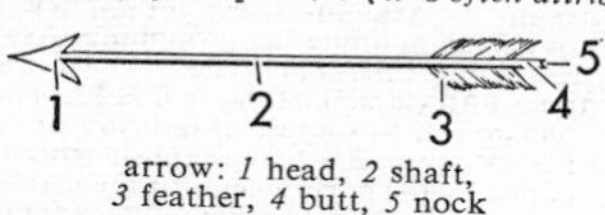

arrow: *1* head, *2* shaft, *3* feather, *4* butt, *5* nock

²arrow \"\ *vi* -ED/-ING/-S **1 :** to move fast and straight like an arrow in flight : DART ⟨the wild geese could not ~ through the storm —S.V.Benét⟩ **2** *of sugarcane* **:** to develop arrows : FLOWER

³arrow \'arə\ *adj* [by folk etymology fr. *e'er a*] *dial Eng* **:** ever a

arrow arum *n* **:** a plant of the genus *Peltandra* (as *P. virginica*)

arrow-back chair *n* **:** a chair having a back with vertical balusters that are broadened and flattened near one end

arrow crab *n* **:** a brilliantly colored crab (*Stenorhynchus seticornis*) that is widely distributed in the southern Atlantic

ar·rowed \'a(,)rōd, 'e-, -,rəd\ *adj* **:** shaped like or furnished with an arrow

arrow grass *n* [so called fr. the shape of the burst capsules] **1 :** a plant of the genus *Triglochin*; *esp* **:** an herb (*T. maritima*) that sometimes poisons livestock **2 :** any of several grasses of the genus *Aristida* (as *A. purpurascens*) **3 :** PORCUPINE GRASS 1

arrow-grass family *n* **:** SCHEUCHZERIACEAE

arrow·head \'=(,)=+,=\ *n* [ME *arewe hed*, fr. *arewe* arrow + *hed* head] **1 :** the striking end of an arrow usu. separate from the shaft, shaped like a thin wedge, and having a barb or barbs **2 :** something resembling an arrowhead: as **a :** a stroke or mark (as on a drawing) to limit a dimension line or indicate a note **b :** the dart of an egg-and-dart molding **c :** a triangular decoration or reinforcement consisting of intercrossed satin stitches used on tailored garments **3 :** a plant of the genus *Sagittaria*

arrowhead 2c

arrow horn *n* **:** a wedge usu. of horn or fiber set in the butt of an arrow shaft and containing a nock

arrow·leaf \ˈ=(,)=+,=\ *n* **:** ARROWHEAD 3

arrow·plate \"+,=\ *n* **:** an inlaid strip (as of ivory) set in a bow where the arrow crosses it when shot or released and designed to prevent wear

arrow·point \"+,=\ *n* **:** a stone arrowhead

arrow rest *n* **:** a shoulder of horn or metal used on some bows to support the arrow

arrow·root \ˈ=(,)=+,=\ *n* [prob. so called fr. its use by American Indians to heal wounds from poisoned arrows] **1 a :** a tropical American plant of the genus *Maranta* (as the widely cultivated *M. arundinacea*) **b :** a plant or root yielding arrowroot starch **2 a :** a nutritive starch obtained from the rootstock of the arrowroot (*M. arundinacea*) that is used esp. in foods prepared for children and invalids **b :** any of various starches used as substitutes for arrowroot and obtained from other plants of the genus *Maranta* or from plants of other genera (as *Zamia, Curcuma, Tacca, Canna,* and *Musa*) — see PORTLAND ARROWROOT

arrowroot family *n* **:** MARANTACEAE

arrow·stone \ˈ=(,)=+,=\ *n* **:** BELEMNITE

arrow straightener *n* **:** an instrument used by the Eskimo consisting of a piece of bone, horn, ivory, or wood having at one end a hole through which a heated shaft (as of an arrow) is drawn for straightening — compare BATON 5

arrow–toothed halibut \ˈ=(,)=,tütht- *sometimes* -üthd-\ *or* **arrowtooth halibut** *or* **arrowtooth sole** *n* **:** a flatfish (*Atheresthes stomias*) of the northern Pacific coasts of America

arrow·weed \ˈ=(,)=+,=\ *n* **:** ARROWWOOD 1b

arrow·wood \"+,=\ *n* **1 :** any of several shrubs having tough pliant shoots formerly used to make arrows: as **a :** any of various plants of the genus *Viburnum* (as *V. dentatum*) **b :** a low composite shrub (*Pluchea sericea*) of the southwestern U.S. and Mexico **c :** OCEAN SPRAY **d :** ALDER BUCKTHORN **2 :** BURROBRUSH

arrow·worm \"+,=\ *n* **:** a worm of the class Chaetognatha — see SAGITTA

arrowworm: *1* spines, *2* mouth, *3* jaws, *4* alimentary canal, *5* ventral ganglion, *6* ovary, *7* oviduct, *8* anus, *9* vas deferens, *10* seminal vesicle, *11* fins, *12* testis

ar·rowy \ˈarəwē, ˈer-, -wi\ *adj* **1 :** consisting of or full of arrows **2 :** like an arrow or arrows (as in appearance, motion, or effect) **:** SWIFT, DARTING, PIERCING ⟨that frail ~ figure was invariably clothed in black —Norman Douglas⟩ ⟨fish darting in an ~ rush⟩ ⟨deflates tower and university with one ~ pun —Florence B.Lennon⟩

ar·royo \əˈrȯi(y)ə, -rō(,)yō, -rȯi(,)(y)ō\ *also* **ar·roya** \-rȯi(y)ə\ *n* -s [Sp *arroyo*, prob. of non-IE origin; akin to the source of L *arrugia* gallery in a mine] **1 :** BROOK, CREEK, STREAM **:** WATERCOURSE ⟨around all of these lakes are extensive flood lands, and stemming from each are brooks or ~s which drain into other lakes —A.R.Holmberg⟩ **2 :** a water-carved gully or channel **:** DRY WASH, RAVINE ⟨he rode out of a deep ~ between bare mountainsides —S.H.Adams⟩

arroyo grape *n* **:** CHICKEN GRAPE

arroyo willow *n* **:** a shrubby willow (*Salix lasiolepis*) of the western U.S.

arroz \äˈrōth, -ōs\ *n* [Sp, fr. Ar *ar-ruzz* the rice] **:** RICE

arroz con po·llo \-ōth(,)kōnˈpōl(,)yō, -ō(s)(,)kōnˈpō(,)yō\ *n* [Sp, lit., rice with chicken] **:** rice and chicken cooked together and seasoned usu. with saffron, garlic, and other condiments

arrs *pl of* ARR

arrythmia *var of* ARRHYTHMIA

ars *pl of* AR

ars- *comb form* [ISV, fr. ¹*arsenic*] **:** arsenic ⟨*arsine*⟩ ⟨*arsphenamine*⟩

ars *abbr* arsenal

¹**ar·sac·id** \ärˈsasəd, ˈärsəs-\ *n, pl* **arsacids** \-dz\ *or* **arsacidae** \ärˈsasə,dē\ *or* **arsac·ides** \ärˈsasədz; ˈärsəsədz, -,sīdz\ *usu cap* [L *Arsacides*, fr. *Arsaces* I *fl ab* 250 B.C. king of Parthia, founder of the dynasty (fr. Gk *Arsakēs*) + L *-ides* (patronymic suffix) — more at -IDAE] **:** a member of a dynasty of Parthian rulers established in revolt against the Seleucids about 250 B.C. and overthrown by the Persian Sassanids A.D. 226

²**arsacid** \(ˈ)ärˈsasəd, ˈärsəs-\ *adj, usu cap* **:** of or relating to the empire of the Arsacids

ars·anil·ic acid \ˌärsəˈnilik-\ *n* [*ars-* + *aniline* + *-ic*] **:** any of three poisonous crystalline isomeric acids $NH_2C_6H_4AsO(OH)_2$; amino-benzene-arsonic acid; *esp* **:** the para isomer analogous to sulfanilic acid used in making organic arsenical drugs

ars an·ti·qua \ˌär,san·ˈtēkwə, -r,za-\ *n* [ML, old art] **:** the style of musical composition before about 1300 and esp. of the 13th century — contrasted with *ars nova*

ars ar·ti·um \ärˈsärd-ēəm, ˈärs-ˈär-, (ˈ)ärˈzärshēəm\ *n* [ML, lit., art of arts] **:** LOGIC 1

¹**arse** *var of* ASS

²**arse** \ˈärs, ˈäs\ *n* -s [¹*arse*] **:** the bottom end of a wooden pulley block in which is the score for the rope strap

ar·se·dine \ˈärsə,dēn, -dīn\ *n* -s [ME *assady, assadyn, assaden*] **:** an alloy of copper and zinc made into very thin sheets like gold leaf and used in decoration

ar·sem furnace \ˈärsəm,-\ *n, usu cap A* [after William C. *Arsem b*1880, Am. chemical engineer] **:** an electric furnace usu. of the vacuum type heated by electrical resistance

arsen- *or* **arseno-** *comb form* [ISV, fr. *arsenic*] **:** arsenic; *specif* **:** containing the grouping —As=As— analogous to the azo group ⟨*arsenobenzene*⟩

ar·se·nal \ˈärs(ᵊ)nəl, ˈäs-\ *n* -s [It *arsenale*, modif. of Ar *dār ṣināʽah* court or house of industry or manufacture] **1** *archaic* **:** DOCKYARD **2 a :** an establishment often operated and maintained by the government for the manufacture, repair, storage, or issue of arms and other military equipment **b :** a storehouse or source of supply for arms, ammunition, or other military equipment ⟨we must be the great ~ of democracy —F.D. Roosevelt⟩ **c :** a stock or collection of weapons ⟨Wild Bill added one item to his usual ~ of two revolvers and bowie knife —S.H.Holbrook⟩ **3 :** STORE, STOREHOUSE **:** SUPPLY, REPERTORY ⟨this was the ~ of learning from which he drew —Van Wyck Brooks⟩ ⟨will have occasion to use her full ~ of charm, clear thinking, and equanimity —Robert Rice⟩

ar·se·nate \ˈärs(ᵊ)nət, ˈäs-, -sᵊn,āt, *usu* -d·+V\ *n* -s [earlier *arseniate*, prob. fr. F *arséniate*, fr. *arsenic* + *-ate*] **:** a salt or ester of an arsenic acid

ar·se·nian \ärˈsēnēən, -nyən\ *adj* **:** containing arsenic

¹**ar·se·nic** \ˈärs(ᵊ)nik, ˈäs-, -ēk — see ²ARSENIC\ *n* -s [ME *arsenic, arsenicum*, fr. MF & L; MF *arsenic*, fr. L *arsenicum*, fr. Gk *arsenikon, arrhenikon* yellow orpiment, by folk etymology (influence of Gk *arsenikos, arrhenikos* male, virile, fr. *arsen-, arrhen-, arsēn, arrhēn* male + *-ikos* -ic) fr. Syr *zarnīg*, of Iranian origin; akin to Av *zaranya* gold, OPer *daraniya;* akin to Skt *hiranya* gold, *hari* yellowish — more at ARRHENATHERUM, YELLOW] **1 :** a trivalent and pentavalent metalloid element commonly metallic steel-gray, crystalline, and brittle but known also in other forms (as black amorphous and yellow crystalline forms), that occurs in the free state (as in tarnished granular or kidney-shaped masses having a sp. gr. of 5.73) and also combined in minerals (as arsenopyrite, orpiment, realgar, arsenolite) and in ores of other metals (as copper, gold) from which it is usu. separated as a by-product in the form of arsenic trioxide, and that is used in small amounts in alloys (as an alloy with lead for shot) and in the form of its compounds chiefly as poisons (as insecticides), in pharmaceutical preparations, and in glass — symbol *As;* see ELEMENT table **2 :** ARSENIC TRIOXIDE — used chiefly commercially

²**ar·sen·ic** \(ˈ)ärˈsenik, (ˈ)äˈs-, -ēk; *in names of compounds below beginning with "arsenic", the usu pronunc in "arsenic acid" is that found here, the usu pronunc in other cases is that found at* ¹ARSENIC\ *adj* **:** of, relating to, or containing arsenic — used esp. of compounds in which this element is pentavalent

arsenic acid *n* **1 :** any of three acids derived from arsenic pentoxide analogous to the phosphoric acids; *esp* **:** the ortho acid obtained as the white crystalline hemihydrate $H_3AsO_4·½H_2O$ **2 :** ARSENIC PENTOXIDE — not used scientifically

¹**ar·sen·i·cal** \(ˈ)ärˈsenəkəl, (ˈ)äˈs-, -ēk-\ *adj* [¹*arsenic* + *-al*] **:** of, relating to, or containing arsenic ⟨~ vapor⟩ ⟨~ wallpapers⟩

²**arsenical** \"\ *n* -s **:** a compound or preparation containing arsenic

arsenical antimony *n* **:** ALLEMONTITE

ar·sen·i·cal·ism \=ˈ===,lizəm\ *n* -s **:** chronic arsenic poisoning

arsenical pyrites *n* **:** ARSENOPYRITE

arsenic antidote *n* **:** a preparation of ferric hydroxide and magnesia that envelops or occludes arsenic thus rendering it inert

ar·sen·i·cate \ärˈsenə,kāt\ *vt* -ED/-ING/-S **:** to combine, treat, or impregnate with arsenic

arsenic bloom *n* **:** ARSENOLITE

arsenic disulfide *or* **arsenic monosulfide** *n* **:** an orange, red, or black compound As_4S_4, As_2S_2, or AsS occurring native as realgar, also prepared artificially, and used esp. in fireworks and formerly as a pigment

arsenic oxide *n* **:** an oxide of arsenic: as **a :** ARSENIC TRIOXIDE **b :** ARSENIC PENTOXIDE

arsenic pentoxide *n* **:** a white amorphous deliquescent compound As_2O_5 or As_4O_{10} usu. made by oxidizing arsenic trioxide and used in making arsenates

arsenic trichloride *n* **:** a colorless oily liquid $AsCl_3$ obtained by burning arsenic in chlorine and used in making organic arsenicals and in ceramics

arsenic trioxide *n* **:** a white or transparent glassy extremely poisonous compound As_2O_3 or As_4O_6 that occurs naturally as arsenolite and claudetite, that is obtained usu. from the flue dusts from smelters roasting arsenic-containing ores, and that is used esp. as a decolorizing agent chiefly in making insecticides, weed killers, pigments, and glass — called also *arsenious oxide, white arsenic*

arsenic trisulfide *n* **:** a yellow compound As_2S_3 or As_4S_6 occurring native as orpiment, also prepared artificially, and used in fireworks and as a pigment — called also *king's yellow*

ar·se·nide \ˈärsᵊn,īd\ *n* -s [F, fr. *arsen-* + *-ide*] **:** a binary compound of arsenic with a more positive element

ar·se·nif·er·ous \ˌärsᵊnˈif(ə)rəs\ *adj* [*arsen-* + *-i-* + *-ferous*] **:** yielding arsenic

ar·se·ni·llo \ˌärsəˈnē(,)(y)ō\ *n* -s [AmerSp] **:** powdered or granulated atacamite

ar·se·ni·o·ple·ite \ärˌsēnē(,)ōˈplē,īt\ *n* -s [ISV *arsenio-* (fr. *arsenic*) + Gk *pleiōn* more + ISV *-ite;* orig. formed as G *arseniopleit*] **:** a mineral consisting of a basic arsenate of manganese, calcium, iron, and other metals occurring in brownish red cleavable masses

ar·se·ni·o·sid·er·ite \-ˈsīdə,rīt\ *n* -s [F *arsénio-sidérite*, fr. *arsénio-* + *sidérite* siderite, fr. G *siderit*] **:** a mineral $Ca_3Fe_4(AsO_4)_4(OH)_6·4H_2O$ consisting of a basic iron calcium arsenate occurring as yellowish brown concretions

ar·se·ni·ous \(ˈ)ärˈsēnēəs, (ˈ)äˈs- *also* -nyəs\ *also* **ar·se·nous** \ˈ=s(ᵊ)nəs\ *adj* [F *arsénieux*, fr. *arsenic* + *-eux* -ous] **:** of, relating to, or containing arsenic — used esp. of compounds in which this element is trivalent

arsenious acid *n* **1 :** an acid (as ortho-arsenious acid H_3AsO_3) derived from arsenic trioxide known only in solution and esp. in the form of salts (as sodium arsenite) **2 :** ARSENIC TRIOXIDE

arsenious anhydride *or* **arsenious oxide** *n* **:** ARSENIC TRIOXIDE

ar·se·nite \ˈärsə,nīt\ *n* -s [F *arsénite*, fr. *arsén-* arsen- + *-ite*] **:** a salt or ester of an arsenious acid

ar·se·ni·um \ärˈsēnēəm\ *n* -s [NL, fr. *arsen-* + *-ium*] **:** ARSENIC

ar·sen·iu·ret·ted *or* **ar·sen·iu·ret·ed** \ärˈsenyə,red·əd, -sēn-\ *adj* [*arseniurete*, old name for *arsenide* (fr. F *arséniure*, fr. *arsenic* + *-ure* -uret) + *-ed*] **:** combined with arsenic

arseniuretted hydrogen *n* **:** ARSINE 1

arseno- — see ARSEN-

ar·se·no·benzene \ˌärs(ᵊ)nō, ärˌsenō+\ *n* [*arsen-* + *benzene*] **:** a pale yellow crystalline compound $C_6H_5As:AsC_6H_5$, derivatives of which are used in medicine — see ARSPHENAMINE

ar·se·no·bismite \"+\ *n* -s [*arsen-* + *bismite*] **:** a mineral consisting of a hydrous bismuth arsenate occurring in yellowish green aggregates

ar·se·no·cla·site \"+ˈklā,sīt, -,zīt\ *n* -s [ISV *arsen-* + Gk *klasis* breaking, fracture + ISV *-ite;* orig. formed as Sw or G *arsenoklasit*] **:** a mineral $Mn_5As_2O_4(OH)_4$ consisting of a basic manganese arsenate

ar·se·no·lite \ärˈsenᵊl,īt\ *n* -s [*arsen-* + *-lite*] **:** a mineral As_2O_3 consisting of a native arsenic trioxide usu. occurring as a white bloom or crust — compare CLAUDETITE

ar·se·no·pyrite \ˌärs(ᵊ)nō, ärˌsenō+\ *n* -s [*arsen-* + *pyrite*] **:** a mineral FeAsS consisting of a hard tin-white or grayish iron sulfarsenide occurring in prismatic orthorhombic crystals or in masses or grains, found chiefly in crystalline rocks, and constituting the principal ore of arsenic (hardness 5.5–6, sp. gr. 5.9–6.2) — called also *arsenical pyrites, mispickel*

ar·se·no·so \ˌärsᵊnˈō(,)sō\ *adj* [*arsenoso-*] **:** relating to or containing the radical —AsO

arsenoso- \"\ *comb form* [ISV, fr. *arsen-* + *-oso-* (as in *ferroso-*)] **:** containing the univalent radical —AsO composed of arsenic and oxygen ⟨*arsenoso*phenol⟩

ar·se·no·therapy \ˌärs(ᵊ)nō, ärˌsenō+\ *n* -ES [ISV *arsen-* + *therapy*] **:** treatment of disease with any form of arsenic

ar·se·nous *var of* ARSENIOUS

ar·sen·oxide \ˌärsᵊn+\ *n* [ISV *arsen-* + *oxide*] **:** an organic arsenoso compound RAsO; *specif* **:** oxophenarsine hydrochloride — used chiefly in pharmaceutical names

arses *pl of* ARSIS *or of* ARSE

arse·smart \ˈ=,=\ — *see* ASS\ *n* -s [*arse* + *smart*, v.] *dial* **:** a plant of the genus *Polygonum; esp* **:** SMARTWEED

ar·shin *or* **ar·shine** *or* **ar·chin** *or* **ar·chine** \ärˈshēn\ *n* -s [Russ, of Turkic origin; akin to Turk *arşın*, Kazan Tatar *aršyn*, Jagatai *aršun*] **:** a Russian unit of length equal to 28 inches

ar·sine \ärˈsēn, ˈär,s-\ *n* -s [ISV *ars-* + *-ine*] **1 :** a colorless extremely poisonous gas AsH_3 having an odor like garlic, burning with a bluish flame, and made by reaction of an arsenide (as zinc arsenide) with an acid and in other ways — see MARSH TEST **2 :** any of a class of very poisonous organic compounds derived from arsine that are analogous to the amines and phosphines — compare DIPHENYLCHLOROARSINE, LEWISITE

ar·sin·ic acid \(ˈ)ärˈsinik-\ *n* [ISV *arsine* + *-ic*] **1 :** any of a series of organic acids (as cacodylic acid) having the general formula RR′AsOOH and obtainable by oxidizing disubstituted organic arsines [as dimethyl-arsine $(CH_3)_2AsH$] **2 :** ARSONIC ACID 1

arsino- *comb form* [ISV, fr. *arsine* + *-o-*] **:** arsine **:** containing the univalent radical AsH_2

ar·si·noi·the·ri·um \ˌärsə,nȯiˈthirēəm\ *n, cap* [NL, irreg. fr. *Arsinoë* II †271B.C. queen of Egypt + NL *-therium*] **:** a genus of extinct mammals (order Embrithopoda) of the Oligocene of Egypt having limbs resembling those of the elephant and a pair of large horns

ar·sis \ˈärsəs, ˈäs-\ *n, pl* **ar·ses** \-,sēz\ [LL & Gk; LL, accented syllable of a metrical foot, fr. Gk, unaccented syllable of a metrical foot, lifting of the foot in beating time, irreg. fr. *aeirein* to lift + *-sis* — more at AORTA] **1 a :** the lighter or shorter part of a poetic foot esp. in quantitative verse **b :** the accented or longer part of a poetic foot esp. in accentual verse **2 :** the weak or unaccented part of a musical measure **:** UPBEAT — compare THESIS

ar·sle \ˈärsəl\ *vi* -ED/-ING/-S [¹*arse* + *-le*] *dial* **:** to move backward

ars mag·na \ˈärs·ˈmägnə, ˈärz-, -ag-\ *n, usu cap A&M* [ML, lit., great art] **:** a logistic system designed to function as a universal science that would be basic to all others; *specif* **:** the combinative method orig. designed by Raymond Lully

ars no·va \-ˈnōvə\ *n* [ML, new art] **:** the style of musical composition of the late middle ages and esp. of the 14th century — contrasted with *ars antiqua*

ar·so·ite \ˈär(,)sō,īt\ *n* -s [G *arsoit*, fr. *Arso*, town on the island of Ischia, Italy + G *-it* -ite] **:** a dark gray porous rock consisting of trachyandesite containing phenocrysts of andesine, sanidine, diopside, and a little olivine in a trachytic groundmass of sanidine, a little oligoclase, much diopside, and magnetite

arson- *or* **arsono-** *comb form* [ISV, fr. *arsonic*] **:** containing the radical $—AsO(OH)_2$ characteristic of the arsonic acids ⟨*arsonate*⟩ ⟨*arsono*acetic acid⟩

ar·son \ˈärsᵊn, ˈäs-\ *n* -s [obs. F, fr. OF, fr. *ars*, past part. of *ardre* to burn, fr. L *ardēre* — more at ARDOR] **:** the willful and malicious burning of or attempt to burn any building, structure, or property of another (as a house, a church, or a boat) or of one's own usu. with criminal or fraudulent intent

¹**ar·so·nate** \ˈärsᵊn,āt, -,ət\ *n* -s [*arsonic* + *-ate*] **:** a salt or ester of an arsonic acid

²**arsonate** \-,āt\ *vt* -ED/-ING/-S [*arson-* + *-ate*] **:** to introduce the arsono group into **:** convert into an arsonic acid or derivative—**ar·so·na·tion** \ˌ==ˈāshən\ *n* -s

ar·son·ic acid \(ˈ)ärˈsänik-, -sō-\ *n* [ISV *arson*ium + *-ic*] **1 :** any of a series of organic acids (as the arsanilic acids) having the general formula $RAsO(OH)_2$ and obtainable by oxidizing monosubstituted organic arsines (as phenyl-arsine $C_6H_5AsH_2$) **2 :** ARSINIC ACID 1

ar·son·ist \ˈärs(ᵊ)nəst, ˈäs-\ *n* -s **:** one who commits arson **:** INCENDIARY, FIREBUG

ar·so·ni·um \ärˈsōnēəm\ *n* -s [*ars-* + *ammonium*] **:** a univalent radical AsH_4 containing arsenic analogous to ammonium and known in the form of organic derivatives (as tetramethyl-arsonium iodide $As(CH_3)_4I$) — compare QUATERNARY AMMONIUM COMPOUND

ar·so·no \ärˈsō(,)nō\ *adj* [*arsono-*] **:** containing the radical $—AsO(OH)_2$ — compare ARSON-

ars·phen·a·mine \ärsˈfenə,mēn, -,mən\ *n* -s [ISV *ars-* + *phenamine*] **:** a light-yellow toxic hygroscopic powder $C_{12}H_{12}As_2N_2O_2.2HCl.2H_2O$ derived from arsenobenzene that was formerly used in the treatment of spirochetal diseases (as syphilis, relapsing fever) — see NEOARSPHENAMINE

ars po·et·i·ca \ˈärs(,)pōˈed·əkə, ˈärz-, -etə-, -ēkə\ *n, pl* **ars poeticas** [L *Ars Poetica* The Art of Poetry, poetic epistle by Horace †8 B.C. Roman poet] **:** a treatise on the art of literary and esp. poetic composition

¹**ar·sy–var·sy** \ˌärsēˈvärsē\ *or* **ar·sy–ver·sy** \-ˈvər-\ *adv* [redupl. (prob. influenced by L *versus*) of *arsy*, fr. ¹*arse* + *-y*] **:** backside forward **:** head over heels **:** TOPSY-TURVY ⟨knocked him *arsy-varsy*⟩

²**arsy–varsy** *or* **arsy–versy** \ˌ==ˈ==\ *adj* **:** upside down **:** TOPSY-TURVY

¹**art** [ME *art, ert,* fr. OE *eart;* akin to ON *est, ert,* (thou) art, Goth *is,* L *es,* Gk *essi,* Skt *asi,* OE *is* is — more at IS] *archaic pres 2d sing of* BE

²**art** \ˈärt, ˈät, *usu* -d·+V\ *n* -s *often attrib* [ME, fr. OF, fr. L *art-, ars* — more at ARM] **1 a :** the power of performing certain actions esp. as acquired by experience, study, or observation **:** SKILL, DEXTERITY ⟨there's an ~ to tightrope walking⟩ **b** (1) **:** skill in the adaptation of things in the natural world to the uses of human life **:** human contrivance or ingenuity ⟨are these chipped stones the product of ~⟩ (2) *obs* **:** technical skill often as though aided by magic **2 a :** a branch of learning: **a :** one of the humanities traditionally including history, philosophy, literature, languages, and the fine arts ⟨the College of *Arts* and Sciences⟩ **b arts** *pl* **:** the liberal arts ⟨bachelor of *arts*⟩ **c** *archaic* **:** LEARNING, SCHOLARSHIP **3 a :** an occupation or business requiring knowledge or skill **:** CRAFT **b :** an organization of men practicing a craft or trade ⟨the ~ of Wool, that is, . . . the corporation of the dealers in wool —C.E.Norton⟩ **c :** the general principles of any branch of learning or of any developed craft **:** a system of rules or of organized modes of operation serving to facilitate the performance of certain actions ⟨the ~ of building⟩ ⟨the ~ of engraving⟩ ⟨the ~ of navigation⟩ **d :** systematic application of knowledge or skill in effecting a desired result **4 a :** application of skill and taste to production according to aesthetic principles **:** the conscious use of skill, taste, and creative imagination in the practical definition or production of beauty **b :** the product of skill and taste applied according to aesthetic principles **:** expression of beauty **:** works of art ⟨an ~ gallery⟩ **5 a** *archaic* **:** a skillful plan or device ⟨employed every ~ to soothe the discontented —T.B.Macaulay⟩ **b :** CUNNING, ARTIFICE ⟨I swear I use no ~ at all —Shak.⟩ ⟨she owes her wavy hair to ~ rather than to nature⟩ **c :** artificial and studied behavior ⟨~s that allure, the magic nod and wink —Robert Browning⟩ **6 a :** the craft of the artist; *specif* **:** the technical devices used by a painter regarded esp. as a subject of study **b :** a method or device that produces an artistic effect or is used for decorative purposes ⟨~ needlework⟩ **7 a :** FINE ARTS **b :** one of the fine arts **c :** a plastic art **d :** a graphic art **e :** PAINTING **8 :** decorative or illustrative elements in printed matter as distinguished from the text or other parts printed from standard alphabetic types; *esp* **:** the illustrative material of a newspaper or periodical

syn SKILL, CUNNING, ARTIFICE, CRAFT, ART can mean, in common, the faculty, usu. expert, of performing or executing what is planned or devised. SKILL stresses technical knowledge, proficiency, or expertness ⟨a first-rate specimen of the composer's art, the interpreter's *skill* and the engineer's craft —Herbert Weinstock⟩ ⟨dentistry as a *skill* alone is limited at present largely to repair and restoration —J.B. Conant⟩ ⟨varying *skill* and thoroughness in the detection of crime —Havelock Ellis⟩ ⟨a *skilled* toolmaker⟩ CUNNING may emphasize special, often tricky, inventive or creative power ⟨the *cunning* and consummate artistry by which he has achieved certain effects —J.D.Adams⟩ ⟨his unerring eye and his incomparable *cunning* of hand . . . a most able painter —Laurence Binyon⟩ ⟨a scout whose *cunning* exceeded that of the Indian —*Amer. Guide Series: Ariz.*⟩ ARTIFICE can stress skill or intelligence in contriving or devising, but usu. stresses at the same time a certain lack of true creative power, a certain artificiality ⟨what amazing *artifice* is found under that apparently straightforward tale —A.T.Quiller-Couch⟩ ⟨no matter what skill is displayed toward objectifying fiction, the omniscience of the author is naturally assumed . . . but such is *artifice* that it attempts to conceal this basic convention —Robert Humphrey⟩ ⟨he heightened the *artifice* of this style — its inversions, its verbal encrustation, its complexity of syntax, yet combined it with the natural speech rhythms and homely idioms —C.D.Lewis⟩ CRAFT can suggest ingenuity and subtlety in workmanship or trickery or guile; applied to a skilled pursuit or vocation, it may suggest a lower type of skill or inventive power joined with mastery of materials and technique but lacking true creative force or quality ⟨professional writers who take their *craft* seriously —M.D.Geismar⟩ ⟨small teams of dressmakers, each of them a mistress of her *craft* —*Choice of Careers: Dressmaking*⟩ ⟨no great artist but a master of his *craft*⟩ ART is the most variable of these words in meaning, often interchangeable with, often contrasting with, the others: its significant weight can fall upon recondite, inventive, or creative power ⟨the rare *art* of the alchemist or witch doctor⟩ It can, like SKILL, suggest proficiency or expertness ⟨the shoemaker's *art*⟩ ⟨*arts* such as medicine, husbandry —Benjamin Farrington⟩ or, like CRAFT, or, rarely, like ARTIFICE, can point to skill, ingenuity, and inventiveness in contriving even though the act or result lacks any true creative force or quality ⟨handmade tools, utensils, and furniture of the premachine age, . . . are interesting as *art* because of skillful handling of materials —*Amer. Guide Series: Mich.*⟩ ⟨practicing their *arts* as masons, brickmakers, carpenters, leather dressers —*Amer. Guide Series: Md.*⟩ ⟨to gain an end by one art or another⟩ But more frequently and in its most distinct sense ART contrasts with SKILL, ARTIFICE, and CRAFT in putting stress upon something more, in implying a personal, unanalyzable creative force that transmits and raises the art or product beyond a skill, artifice, or craft though it may involve the essential elements of all of these ⟨to turn from the mere skill of figurine making to the *art* of sculpture⟩ ⟨most of the symbolic details are examples of artifice rather than of *art* —R.M. Kain⟩ ⟨so much English acting which is very fine . . . is so satisfactory and so limited as *art* —H.E.Clurman⟩

³**art** \"\ *adj* **1 :** composed or created with conscious artistry — opposed to *folk* ⟨an ~ ballad⟩ ⟨an ~ song⟩ **2 :** designed for decorative purposes or to produce an artistic effect ⟨~ pottery⟩

-art — see -ARD

art *abbr* **1** article **2** artificial **3** artillery **4** artist

artal *or* **artel** [Ar *arṭāl*, pl. of *raṭl* rotl] *pl of* ROTL — sometimes used as sing.

¹art and part \ˌärtᵊnˈpärt\ *n* [ME; *art*, prob. fr. OF *hart* segment (in the expression *ne hart ne part* nothing at all), branch, willow withe, noose, of Gmc origin; perh. akin to OE *heordan* hurds — more at HURDS] *Scots law* **:** indirect participation in a crime by instigating, counseling, or assisting the actual perpetrator

²art and part *adv, Scots law* **:** by being an accessory before the fact or an accomplice in a crime ⟨pronounced guilty *art and part*⟩

art brown *n* **:** a dark brown that is darker than leafmold — called also *Argentina, mirador*

art director *n* **1 :** one who directs the artistic features of a theatrical production (as scenic, costume, and lighting effects) **2** *also* **art editor :** one who executes, supervises, or coordinates designs, illustrations, and layouts to be used in printed matter

artefact *or* **artefac** *var of* ARTIFACT

¹artel *var of* ARTAL

²ar·tel \ärˈtel(ʸ)\ *n* -S [Russ *artel'*, fr. It *artieri*, pl. of *artiere* artisan, fr. *arte* art, fr. L *art-, ars* — more at ARM] **:** the traditional Russian association of laborers for collective work **:** a cooperative craft society

ar·te·mia \ärˈtēmēə\ *n* [NL, irreg. fr. *Artemis*, Greek goddess of forests and hills (fr. L, fr. Gk) + NL *-ia*] **1** *cap* **:** a genus of crustaceans (order Anostraca) found in salt lakes and the brines of saltworks **2** -S **:** any crustacean of the genus *Artemia* **:** BRINE SHRIMP

ar·te·mis·ia \ˌärdəˈmizh(ē)ə, -rtə'-, -izēə, -is-\ *n* [NL *Artemisia*, fr. L *artemisia* mugwort, fr. Gk, prob. irreg. fr. *Artemid-, Artemis* + *-ia*] **1** *cap* **:** a genus of shrubs and herbs (family Compositae) widely distributed in temperate and cool regions and having strongly scented foliage and small rayless flower heads **2** -S **:** any plant of the genus *Artemisia*, abundant in the western U.S.

artemisia green *n* **:** a greenish gray that is slightly yellower and stronger than cabbage green

ar·te·mon \ˈärdəˌmän\ *n, pl* **artem·o·nes** \ärˈteməˌnēz\ [LL, foresail, fr. Gk *artemōn*] **1 :** a mast in ancient sailing ships forward of the foremast and raking forward **2 :** the sail set on an artemon

ar·ten·kreis \ˈärtᵊnˌkrīs\ *n, pl* **artenkrei·se** \-īzə\ *or* **ar·tenkreis·es** \-īsəz\ *usu cap* [G, lit., cycle of species, fr. *arten* (pl. of *art* species, kind, type, nature, fr. MHG) + *kreis* cycle, circle, fr. OHG *kreiz*; akin to MLG *kreit, krēt* circle, enclosed dueling space, OHG *krizzōn* to scratch in (as letters), *krazzōn* to scratch — more at ARTICLE, SCRATCH] **:** a group of species that replace one another in geographic sequence, presumably trace ultimately to a common ancestral form, and are equivalent as a group to a subgenus

ar·ter \ˈärdər, ˈȧd-ə(r)\ *dial var of* AFTER

ar·te·re·nol \ˌärdəˈrēˌnȯl, -rtə'-, -ōl\ *n* -S [fr. *Arterenol*, a trademark] **:** NOREPINEPHRINE

arteri- *or* **arterio-** *comb form* [MF, fr. LL, fr. Gk *artēri-*, *artērio-*, fr. *artēria* — more at ARTERY] **1 :** artery ⟨*arteri*ectasia⟩ ⟨*arterio*logy⟩ **2 :** arterial and ⟨*arterio*venous⟩

ar·te·ria \ärˈtirēə\ *n, pl* **arteri·ae** \-ēˌē\ [L — more at ARTERY] **:** ARTERY

¹ar·te·ri·al \(ˈ)ärˈtirēəl, (ˈ)ȧ'-, -tēr-\ *adj* [MF *arterial, arteriel*, fr. (assumed) ML *arterialis*, fr. L *arteria* + *-alis* -al] **1 a :** of or relating to an artery or arteries ⟨the ~ system⟩ **b :** relating to the bright red blood present in most arteries and a few veins that has been oxygenated and arterialized during passage through lungs or gills — compare PULMONARY VEIN, VENOUS **2 :** of, relating to, or constituting through-traffic facilities ⟨newly widened ~ avenues —Duncan Aikman⟩ ⟨its tributaries form the ~ system of the continent —W.W.Huggett⟩ — **ar·te·ri·al·ly** \-rēəlē, -li\ *adv*

²arterial \"\ *n* -S **:** a through street or arterial highway

arterial bulb *n* **:** BULBUS ARTERIOSUS

arterial gland *n* **:** any of certain small masses of vascular and chromaffin tissue found in several parts of the body (as the carotid and coccygeal glands)

ar·te·ri·al·i·za·tion \ärˌtirēələˈzāshən, -ˌlī'-\ *n* -S **:** the process of arterializing

ar·te·ri·al·ize \ärˈtirēəˌlīz\ *vt* -ED/-ING/-S **:** to transform (venous blood) into arterial blood by exposure to oxygen in lungs or other respiratory organs, oxygen being taken up and carbon dioxide given off **:** make blood arterial

ar·te·ri·o·gram \ärˈtirēəˌgram, -rēō-,-\ *n* -S [ISV *arteri-* + *-gram*] **:** a roentgenogram of an artery made by arteriography

ar·te·ri·o·graph·ic \ˌ⸗⸗⸗ˈgrafik\ *adj* [ISV *arteriography* + *-ic*] **:** of, by, or relating to arteriography ⟨~ and histological studies have shown that circulation in bone follows particular rules —M.J.Dallemagne⟩

ar·te·ri·og·ra·phy \ärˌtirēˈägrəfē\ *n* -ES [ISV *arteri-* + *-graphy*] **:** the roentgenographic visualization of an artery after injection of a radiopaque substance

ar·te·ri·o·lar \ärˌtirēˈōlər\ *adj* **:** of, relating to, or involving an arteriole ⟨associated with arterial and ~ disease —*Jour. Amer. Med. Assoc.*⟩

ar·te·ri·ole \ärˈtirēˌōl\ *n* -S [F or NL; F *artériole*, prob. fr. NL *arteriola*, fr. L *arteria* artery + *-ola* -ole] **:** one of the small terminal twigs of an artery that joins the artery to its capillary bed

ar·te·ri·o·lop·a·thy \ärˌtirēəˈläpəthē, -rē(ˌ)ō'-\ *n* -ES [*arteriole* + *-o-* + *-pathy*] **:** disease of the arterioles

ar·te·ri·o·lo·sclerosis \⸗ˌ⸗⸗ˌōlō, ⸗ˌ⸗⸗ˌəˌlō + ⸗ˌ⸗⸗\ *n, pl* **arterioloscleroses** [NL, fr. *arteriola* + *-o-* + *sclerosis*] **:** thickening of the intima of arterioles by hyaline and fatty deposits resulting in reduction of the lumen with obstruction to blood flow, seen chiefly in the kidneys (as in hypertension) but occurring also in other tissues and organs

ar·te·ri·o·sclerosis \⸗ˌ⸗⸗(ˌ)ō, -ˌə+\ *n, pl* **arterioscleroses** [NL, fr. *arteri-* + *sclerosis*] **:** a chronic disease of the arteries characterized by abnormal thickening and hardening of the vessel walls resulting in loss of elasticity — compare ATHEROSCLEROSIS

¹ar·te·ri·o·scle·rot·ic \⸗ˌ⸗⸗(ˌ)⸗skləˈrädˌik\ *adj* [fr. NL *arteriosclerosis*, after such pairs as NL *hypnosis*: E *hypnotic*] **:** of, relating to, or affected by arteriosclerosis

²arteriosclerotic \"\ *n* -S **:** an arteriosclerotic individual

ar·te·ri·ot·o·my \ärˌtirēˈädəmē\ *n* -ES [LL *arteriotomia*, fr. Gk *artēriotomia*, fr. *artēri-* arteri- + *-tomia* -tomy] **:** the surgical incision of an artery

ar·te·ri·ous \(ˈ)ärˈtirēəs\ *adj* [*arteri-* + *-ous*] *archaic* **:** ARTERIAL

ar·te·ri·o·venous \ärˈtirē(ˌ)ō, -rēˌə+ˈ⸗⸗\ *adj* [ISV *arteri-* + *venous*] **:** of, relating to, or connecting the arteries and veins ⟨an ~ fistula⟩

ar·te·ri·tis \ˌärdəˈrīdəs, ˌärtə-, -ītəs\ *n* -ES [NL, irreg. fr. *arteri-* + *-itis*] **:** inflammation of an artery

ar·tery \ˈär|dərē, ˈȧ|, |tə-, -ri *sometimes* |tre or -i\ *n* -ES [ME *arterie*, fr. L *arteria* windpipe, artery, fr. Gk *artēria*; akin to Gk *aortē* aorta — more at AORTA] **1 a :** one of the tubular branching vessels that carry blood from the heart to the various parts and organs of the body and have thicker more muscular and elastic walls than veins, the outer coating being in smaller arteries increasingly reduced until the ultimate capillaries connecting them with the veins possess only the innermost endothelial layer, blood in the arteries being under pressure and flowing in waves due to beats of the heart — compare ADVENTITIA, INTIMA, MEDIA; PULMONARY ARTERY, SYSTEMIC; CIRCULATION **b :** an often contractile vessel distributing blood to the tissues of an invertebrate animal **2** *obs* **:** TRACHEA 1 **3 a :** the main waterway of a river system ⟨he had stood at the confluence of the Monongahela and the Allegheny and seen the great ~ of the Ohio flow out of them —Roger Burlingame⟩ **b :** a channel of transportation or communication; *esp* **:** the principal channel in a branching system ⟨~ of trade⟩ ⟨through many *arteries* — publications, radio and television programs, movies, lectures —J.H.Baker⟩ **c :** a principal street or road ⟨they issue from a side road into a main ~ —Green Peyton⟩ **syn** see WAY

ar·te·sian \(ˈ)ärˈtēzhən, (ˈ)ȧ'-\ *adj* [F *artésien*, lit., of Artois, fr. OF, fr. *Arteis* Artois, region of northern France + OF *-ien* -ian; fr. the wells of this type bored in Artois in the 18th century] **:** involving, relating to, or supplied by the upward movement of water under hydrostatic pressure in rocks or unconsolidated material beneath the earth's surface ⟨~ spring⟩ ⟨~ water⟩ ⟨~ pressure⟩ — distinguished from *subartesian*

artesian well *n* **1 :** a usu. deep and narrow well made by boring until water is reached that will flow upward through artesian pressures **2 :** any deep-bored well

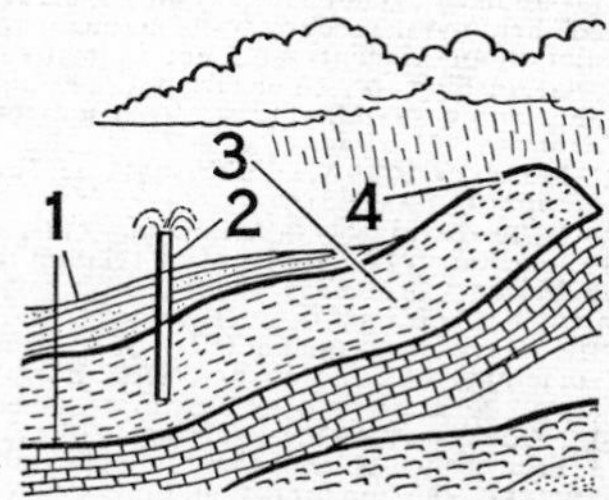

section of an artesian well: *1* impervious layers, *2* well, *3* inclined water-bearing strata, *4* catchment area

art film *n* **:** a motion picture produced as an artistic or experimental venture; *specif* **:** a film documentary depicting works of art or artists at work

art form *n* **1 a :** a recognized form in which artistic expression is cast (as a sonnet or a symphony) **b :** a recognized medium of artistic expression (as writing or painting) **2 :** an unconventional form or medium in which expression regarded as artistic may be cast ⟨fireworks are an *art form* of the Mexican provinces⟩ ⟨baseball is a popular American *art form*⟩ **3 a :** a production that is regarded as a work of art **b :** a production outside the realm of painting and sculpture in which are discerned elements in some way comparable with those involved in artistic creation ⟨a snuffbox valued as an *art form* by connoisseurs⟩

art·ful \ˈärtfəl, ˈȧt-\ *adj* [²*art* + *-ful*] **1 a :** performed with, characterized by, or exhibiting art or skill ⟨so ~ is the choice of detail that the reader is given the illusion of having lived through every painful minute of the lengthy trial —Howard Haycraft⟩ **b :** produced by art **:** ARTIFICIAL ⟨the wording a shade too clever, the vowel-patterns too ~ —*Times Lit. Supp.*⟩ **c** (1) **:** ingeniously designed ⟨~ vases and pitchers —*N.Y.Times*⟩ (2) **:** craftily deceptive ⟨she hit upon an ~ conjecture —George Meredith⟩ **2 a :** using art or skill **:** DEXTEROUS, SKILLFUL ⟨something more than the mere ~ prose stylist he is so often considered —David Daiches⟩ **b :** adroit in taking advantage usu. unfairly **:** CRAFTY, DECEITFUL ⟨many an ~ shipmaster who thought the barristers were fools . . . has seen his nautical evidence torn to shreds by a lawyer who had never been to sea —*N.Y.Herald Tribune*⟩ **syn** see SLY

art·ful·ly \-fəlē, -li\ *adv* **:** in an artful manner **:** with art, dexterity, or craft

art·ful·ness \-fəlnəs\ *n* -ES **:** the quality or state of being artful

art glass *n* **:** articles of glass designed primarily for decorative purposes; *esp* **:** novelty glassware

art gray *n* **:** a purplish gray that is bluer and lighter than crane, bluer and less strong than dove gray, and bluer than cinder gray — called also *Quaker, sea mist*

art green *n* **:** a moderate yellow green to olive green that is greener and less strong than woodbine green

art house *n* **:** ART THEATER

arthr- *or* **arthro-** *comb form* [L *arthr-*, fr. Gk *arthr-, arthro-*, fr. *arthron*; akin to Gk *arariskein* to fit — more at ARM] **:** joint ⟨*arthr*algia⟩ ⟨*arthro*pathy⟩

arthra *pl of* ARTHRON

ar·thral \ˈärthrəl\ *adj* [*arthr-* + *-al*] **:** of or relating to a joint

ar·thral·gia \ärˈthralj(ē)ə\ *n* -S [NL, fr. *arthr-* + *-algia*] **:** neuralgic pain in one or more joints esp. accompanying systemic infections (as scarlet fever)

¹ar·thrit·ic \(ˈ)ärˈthrid·ik, (ˈ)ȧ'-, -itik, -ēk\ *also* **ar·thrit·i·cal** \-ə̇kəl, -ēk-\ *adj* [*arthritic* alter. (influenced by L *arthriticus*) of earlier *artetic, arthetic*, fr. ME *artetyk, arthretik*, fr. MF *artetique*, modif. of L *arthriticus*, fr. Gk *arthritikos*, fr. *arthritis* + *-ikos* -ic; *arthritical* alter. (influenced by L *arthriticus*) of earlier *artetical*, fr. *artetic* + *-al*] **1 :** of, relating to, or affected with arthritis **2 :** creaky esp. with age ⟨enough singable songs have been produced to take the place of the present ~ repertory —*New Yorker*⟩ — **ar·thrit·i·cal·ly** \-ə̇k(ə)lē, -ēk-, -li\ *adv*

²arthritic \"\ *n* -S **:** a person affected with arthritis

ar·thri·tis \ärˈthrīdəs, ȧ'-, -ītəs\ *n, pl* **ar·thrit·i·des** \-ˈthridəˌdēz, -itə-\ [L, fr. Gk, fr. *arthron* joint + *-itis*] **:** inflammation of one or more joints due to infectious, metabolic, or constitutional causes — compare DEGENERATIVE ARTHRITIS, GOUT, RHEUMATOID ARTHRITIS

arthritis de·for·mans \-dēˈfȯrˌmanz\ *n* [NL, deforming arthritis] **:** a chronic arthritis marked by deformation of affected joints

arthro- *in pronunciations below*, ˈ⸗(ˌ)⸗⸗ ˈär(ˌ)thrō *or* ˈȧ(ˌ)thr- *or* -thrə\ — see ARTHR-

ar·thro·bac·ter \ˈ⸗(ˌ)⸗ˌbaktə(r)\ *n, cap* [NL, fr. *arthr-* + *-bacter*] **:** a genus of soil bacteria comprising cellulolytic forms that resemble and are often considered to be members of *Corynebacterium*

ar·thro·branch \ˈ⸗(ˌ)⸗ˌbraŋk\ *also* **ar·thro·bran·chia** \ˌ⸗(ˌ)⸗ˈbraŋkēə\ *n, pl* **arthrobranchs** *also* **arthrobranchi·ae** \-kēˌē\ [NL *arthrobranchia*, fr. *arthr-* + *-branchia*] **:** a gill attached to the articular membrane between the body and the basal joint of a leg of a crustacean

ar·thro·derm \ˈ⸗(ˌ)⸗ˌdərm\ *n* -S [*arthr-* + *-derm*] **:** the external covering of an arthropod

ar·thro·dese \ˈ⸗⸗ˌdēz, ˌ⸗⸗ˈ⸗\ *vt* -ED/ -ING/ -S [back-formation fr. *arthrodesis*] **:** IMMOBILIZE ⟨a hip *arthrodesed* by polio⟩

ar·throd·e·sis \ärˈthrädəsə̇s\ *n, pl* **arthrode·ses** \-əˌsēz\ [NL, fr. *arthr-* + *-desis*] **:** the surgical operation of immobilizing a joint by removing the cartilaginous surfaces so that the bones grow solidly together **:** artificial ankylosis

ar·thro·dia \ärˈthrōdēə\ *n, pl* **arthrodi·ae** \-dēˌē\ [NL, fr. Gk *arthrōdia*, fr. *arthrōdēs* articulated (fr. *arthron* joint + *-ōdēs* -ode) + *-ia*] **:** a gliding joint **:** a diarthrosis in which the articular surfaces glide upon each other without axial motion — **ar·thro·di·al** \(ˈ)⸗ˈ⸗dēəl\ *adj* — **ar·throd·ic** \-ˈthrädik\ *adj*

ar·thro·di·ra \ˌ⸗⸗ *at* ARTHRO- + ˈdīrə\ *n pl, cap* [NL, fr. *arthr-* + *-dira* (fr. Gk *deirē* neck); akin to Latvian *grīva* mouth of a river, OSlav *griva* mane, Skt *grīvā* neck, L *vorare* to devour — more at VORACIOUS] **:** a group of Devonian fishes forming a subclass of Placodermi or esp. formerly an order of Ostracodermi or a separate class and having the forepart of the body protected by bony plates and with an imperfectly ossified internal skeleton — see COCCOSTEIDAE, DINICHTHYS — **ar·thro·di·ran** \ˌ⸗⸗ˈdīrən\ *adj or n* — **ar·thro·dire** \ˈ⸗⸗ˌdī(ə)r\ *n* -S — **ar·thro·di·rous** \-ˈdīrəs\ *adj*

ar·thro·gastra \ˌ⸗⸗ˈgastrə\ *n pl, cap* [NL, fr. *arthr-* + *-gastra* (fr. Gk *gastr-, gastēr* stomach) — more at GASTRIC] *in some classifications* **:** a primary division of the Arachnida comprising those which have the abdomen segmented (as the scorpions) — **ar·thro·gas·tran** \ˌ⸗⸗ˈgastrən\ *adj or n*

ar·throg·e·nous \(ˈ)ärˈthräjənəs\ *adj* [*arthrospore* + *-genous*] **:** developing vegetative resting cells (as arthrospores) that function as spores ⟨~ algae⟩ ⟨~ fungi⟩

ar·thro·gram \ˈ⸗⸗ *at* ARTHRO- + ˌgram\ *n* -S [ISV *arthr-* + *-gram*] **:** a roentgenogram of a joint made by arthrography

ar·throg·ra·phy \ärˈthrägrəfē\ *n* -ES [ISV *arthr-* + *-graphy*] **:** the roentgenographic visualization of a joint after the injection of an opaque substance

ar·thro·lite \ˈ⸗⸗ *at* ARTHRO- + ˌlīt\ *n* -S [*arthr-* + *-lite*] **:** a cylindrical concretion with transverse joints occas. found in clays or shales

ar·thro·mere \ˈ⸗⸗ˌmi(ə)r\ *n* -S [*arthr-* + *-mere*] **:** one of the body segments of jointed animals — **ar·thro·mer·ic** \ˌ⸗⸗ˈmerik\ *adj*

ar·thron \ˈärˌthrän\ *n, pl* **ar·thra** \-ˌthrə\ [NL, fr. Gk] **:** ARTICULATION, JOINT

ar·throp·a·thy \ärˈthräpəthē\ *n* -ES [ISV *arthr-* + *-pathy*] **:** a disease of a joint

ar·thro·plas·ty \ˈ⸗⸗ *at* ARTHRO- + ˌplastē\ *n* -ES [ISV *arthr-* + *-plasty*] **:** plastic surgery of a joint **:** the operative formation or restoration of a joint

ar·thro·ple·o·na \ˌ⸗⸗ˈplēənə\ *n pl, cap* [NL, fr. *arthr-* + *-pleona* (fr. Gk *plein* to swim, float) — more at FLOW] **:** a suborder of Collembola including most of the springtails and characterized by an elongate body and distinct abdominal segmentation — compare SYMPHYPLEONA

ar·thro·pleure \ˈ⸗⸗ˌplu̇(ə)r\ *also* **ar·thro·pleu·ra** \ˌ⸗⸗ˈplu̇rə\ *n, pl* **arthropleures** \ˈ⸗⸗ˌplu̇(ə)rz\ *also* **arthropleu·rae** \ˌ⸗⸗ˈplu̇ˌrē\ [NL *arthropleura*, fr. *arthr-* + *pleura*] **:** the lateral or limb-bearing portion of an arthromere

¹ar·thro·pod \ˈ⸗⸗ˌpäd\ *adj* [NL *Arthropoda*] **:** of or belonging to the Arthropoda

²arthropod \"\ *n* -S **:** one of the Arthropoda

ar·throp·o·da \ärˈthräpədə\ *n pl, cap* [NL, fr. *arthr-* + *-poda*] **:** a phylum comprising articulate invertebrate animals with jointed limbs, the body divided into metameric segments, the brain dorsal to the alimentary canal and connected with a ventral chain of ganglia, and the body generally covered with a chitinous shell that is molted at intervals and including the crustaceans, insects, and spiders and related forms as well as several less prominent groups (as the millepedes and onychophores), often the trilobites, and sometimes the tongue worms, sea spiders, and water bears — **ar·throp·o·dal** \(ˈ)⸗ˈ⸗pədᵊl\ *adj* — **ar·throp·o·dan** \-dən\ *adj* — **ar·throp·o·dous** \-dəs\ *adj*

ar·thro·po·ma·ta \ˌ⸗⸗ *at* ARTHRO- + ˈpōmədə, -ämˌ-, -ətə\ [NL, fr. *arthr-* + *-pomata* (fr. Gk *pōmat-, pōma* lid) — more at POMACENTRIDAE] *syn of* ARTICULATA 2

ar·thro·pom·a·tous \ˌ⸗⸗ˈpämədˌəs, -ōm-, -ətəs\ *adj* [NL *Arthropomata* + E *-ous*] **:** of or relating to the Arthropomata

ar·throp·ter·ous \(ˈ)ärˈthräptərəs\ *adj* [ISV *arthr-* + *-pterous*] **:** having jointed fin rays ⟨most fishes are ~⟩

ar·thro·sis \ärˈthrōsə̇s\ *n, pl* **arthro·ses** \-ōˌsēz\ [NL, fr. Gk *arthrōsis*, fr. *arthroun* to articulate (fr. *arthron* joint) + *-ōsis* -osis] **:** an articulation or suture uniting two bones

ar·thro·spore \ˈ⸗⸗ *at* ARTHRO- + ˌspō(ə)r\ *n* -S [*arthr-* + *spore*] **1 a :** a thick-walled vegetative resting cell formed by segmentation of the filament in certain blue-green algae esp. of the genus *Nostoc* **b :** an oidium in fungi **2 :** a refractile body other than an endospore encountered in bacterial cultures and variously regarded as degenerate cells, as resistant vegetative forms, or as forms associated with a sexual cycle — **ar·thro·spor·ic** \ˌ⸗⸗ˈspōrik\ *adj* — **ar·thro·spor·ous** \-ˈspōrəs, (ˈ)⸗ˈthräspərəs\ *adj*

ar·thro·stome \ˈ⸗⸗ˌstōm\ *n* -S [*arthr-* + *-stome*] **:** a mouth with complex jointed mouthparts that are modified segmental appendages — used typically of the Arthropoda

ar·thros·tra·ca \ärˈthrästrəkə\ *n pl, cap* [NL, fr. *arthr-* + *-ostraca*] *in some classifications* **:** a division of Crustacea comprising the orders Amphipoda, Isopoda, and usu. Tanaidacea in which both thorax and abdomen are segmented and there are seven pairs of thoracic appendages

ar·throus \ˈärthrəs\ *adj* [*arthr-* + *-ous*] **:** ARTHRAL, JOINTED

ar·thro·zoa \ˌ⸗⸗ˈzōə\ *n pl, cap* [NL, fr. *arthr-* + *-zoa*] **:** a primary division of Invertebrata in which the Arthropoda and certain worms were formerly grouped — **ar·thro·zo·an** \ˌ⸗⸗ˈzōən\ *adj or n* — **ar·thro·zo·ic** \-ˈzōik\ *adj*

ar·thu·ri·an \(ˈ)ärˈthu̇rēən, (ˈ)ȧ'-, -ir-\ *adj, usu cap* [fr. *Arthur*, semilegendary 6th cent. king of the Britons + E *-ian*] **:** of, relating to, or characteristic of the legends or romances built around King Arthur and his knights ⟨the ~ legend⟩

ar·thu·ri·ana \(ˌ)⸗ˌ⸗ˈanə, -ˈä-, -ˈā- *also* -ˈā-\ *n pl, usu cap* [NL, fr. *Arthur* + *-i-* + *-ana*] **:** Arthuriana and other materials concerning the Arthurian story

ar·thus phenomenon \ˈärthəs-, *F* ärtüēs-\ *n, usu cap A* [prob. trans. of F *phénomène d'Arthus*, after Nicholas M. *Arthus* †1945 Fr. bacteriologist] **:** a reaction following injection of an antigen into an animal in which hypersensitivity has been previously established involving infiltrations, edema, sterile abscesses, and in severe cases gangrene

ar·ti·ad \ˈärdēˌad, -rshē-\ *n* -S [Gk *artios* even + E *-ad*] **1 a** *obs* **:** an element or radical of even valence **b :** an element of even atomic number — contrasted with *perissad* **2 :** one of the Artiodactyla

artic *obs var of* ARCTIC

ar·ti·choke \ˈär|dəˌchōk, ˈȧ|, |tə-\ *n* -S [It dial. (Lombardy) *articiocco*, fr. Ar *al-khurshūf* the artichoke] **1 :** a tall herb (*Cynara scolymus*) that resembles a thistle and has coarse pinnately incised leaves **2 :** the flower head of the artichoke having large oval involucral bracts with fleshy bases that with the receptacle are cooked as a vegetable — called also *globe artichoke* **3 :** JERUSALEM ARTICHOKE

artichoke flower head

artichoke green *n* **:** a grayish yellow green that is yellower and paler than palmetto or average sage green and yellower and lighter than mermaid or celadon

artichoke thistle *n* **:** CARDOON

¹ar·ti·cle \ˈär|də̇kəl, ˈȧ|, |tə-, -ēk-\ *n* -S [ME, fr. OF, fr. L *articulus* division, part, joint, dim. of *artus* joint; akin to OE *eard* condition, fate, MHG *art* innate character, nature, ON *einarthr* firm, single, L *art-, ars* skill, Gk *artyein* to arrange, prepare, Skt *ṛta* fit, right — more at ARM] **1 a :** a distinguishable and usu. separately marked section (as of a creed, statute, indictment, treaty, legacy, or other writing consisting of two or more such sections) ⟨an ~ of the constitution⟩ **b :** a distinct and separate point, count, charge, or clause ⟨an explanation of the statute in six ~s⟩ **c :** a condition or stipulation esp. in a contract or a creed — often used in pl. ⟨sign ship's ~s⟩ ⟨~s of indenture⟩ ⟨~s of agreement⟩ ⟨~s of faith⟩ **d :** a paragraph, section, or other distinct part of a document ⟨mentioned in the next ~⟩ **e :** a generally short nonfictional prose composition usu. forming an independent portion of a publication (as a newspaper, magazine, or encyclopedia) ⟨write an ~ for a magazine⟩ ⟨have you seen the ~ in the morning newspaper⟩ **2** *archaic* **:** a particular juncture, point of time, or moment — used esp. in the phrase *article of death* **3 a :** a particular item of business **:** MATTER ⟨a very great revolution that has happened in this ~ of good breeding —Joseph Addison⟩ **b :** a distinct detail or particular (as of an action or proceeding) ⟨each ~ of human duty —William Paley⟩ **4 :** any of a usu. small set of words or affixes used with substantives (as nouns) to limit, individualize, or give definiteness or indefiniteness to their application (as *a, an, the*) — traditionally considered an adjective; compare ¹DEFINITE 3a, ¹INDEFINITE **5 a :** one of a class of material things ⟨an ~ of living-room furniture⟩ **b :** piece of goods **:** COMMODITY ⟨a tax on such ~s as playing cards⟩ **6 a :** a thing of a particular class or kind as distinct from a thing of another class or kind ⟨this disclaimer to any resemblance between a real cowhand and the Hollywood ~ —M.C.Boatright⟩ **b :** one who is adept or practiced ⟨as a professional gambler was about the slickest ~ in his line —H.E.Fosdick⟩ **c :** PERSON ⟨the second clerk . . . was a fairly smooth ~ —Frederick Way⟩ **7 a** *obs* **:** a joint of the body **b :** an articulated segment of a plant or of an arthropods

²article \"\ *vb* **articled; articled; articling** \-k(ə)liŋ\ **articles** [ME *articlen*, fr. *article*, n.] *vt* **1** *archaic* **a :** to set forth in distinct particulars **:** SPECIFY **b :** to set forth or charge someone with (offenses) **2 a** *obs* **:** to stipulate esp. in a treaty **b :** to bind by articles (as of apprenticeship) ⟨*articled* at seventeen to a well-known London architect —J.D.Beresford⟩ ~ *vi* **1** *archaic* **:** to bring a particularized charge or accusation **2** *archaic* **:** to make an arrangement or agreement **:** STIPULATE

articled *adj* **:** bound by articles of apprenticeship **:** APPRENTICED

articles of association 1 : a written agreement embodying the purposes or other terms and conditions of the association of a number of persons for the prosecution of a joint enterprise; *specif* **:** a written agreement duly executed and filed so as to have the force of a charter under general incorporation laws **2 :** a written agreement that in England under the Companies Act may accompany the memorandum of association of a company with a liability limited by shares, that must accompany that of a company with a liability limited by guarantee or unlimited, and that prescribes the regulations for the government of the company

ar·tic·u·la·ble \ärˈtikyələbəl, ȧ'-\ *adj* [*articulate* + *-able*] **:** capable of being articulated

ar·tic·u·la·cy \-ləsē\ *n* -ES [¹*articulate* + *-cy*] **:** the quality or state of being articulate

ar·tic·u·la·men·tum \ärˌtikyələˈmentəm\ *n, pl* **articulamen·ta** \-tə\ [NL, fr. L, articulation of the limbs, joint, fr.

articulare to divide into joints + *-mentum* -ment — more at ARTICULATE] **:** the inner layer of a plate of a chiton projecting anteriorly and articulating with the plate in front — compare TEGUMENTUM

[1]**ar·tic·u·lar** \är'tikyələr, ȧ'tikyələ(r)\ *adj* [ME *articuler*, fr. L *articularis*, fr. *articulus* joint + *-aris* -ar, -ary — more at ARTICLE] **1** *also* **ar·tic·u·lary** \-ˌlerē\ **:** of or relating to a joint or joints ⟨~ disease⟩ ⟨an ~ condyle⟩ **2** [LL *articularis*, fr. L] **:** being an article **:** accompanied by an article ⟨the ~ infinitive in Greek⟩ **:** characteristic of an article ⟨~ use of a former demonstrative adjective⟩

[2]**articular** \"\ *also* **articulary** \"\ *or* **ar·tic·u·lare** \⸗ˌ⸗⸗ 'lärē, -la(a)rē\ *n, pl* **articulars** \-ə(r)z\ *also* **articularies** \-erēz\ *or* **articula·ria** \-ärēə,-a(a)rēə\ [NL *articulare*, fr. L, neut. of *articularis*] **:** a bone in the base of the lower jaw of most vertebrates except mammals by which the jaw usu. articulates with the quadrate bone — compare MECKEL'S CARTILAGE

articular cartilage *n* **:** cartilage that covers the articular surfaces of bones

articular disk *n* **:** a cartilage interposed between two articular surfaces and partially or completely separating the joint cavity into two compartments

articular lamella *n* **:** the layer of compact bone to which the articular cartilage is attached

articularly *adv, obs* **:** in separate items

articular membrane *n* **:** a region of flexible unsclerotized cuticle between areas of sclerotization in the exoskeleton of an arthropod that functions as a joint permitting movement of the body or its parts

ar·tic·u·la·ta \är,tikyə'läd·ə, -ād·ə\ *n pl, cap* [NL, fr. neut. pl. of *articulatus* jointed, fr. L, uttered distinctly, past part. of *articulare*] **1 :** one of the four subkingdoms in the classification of Cuvier comprising invertebrates having the body composed of a series of ringlike segments (as arthromeres, somites, or metameres) **2 :** a class or other division of Brachiopoda comprising forms with the valves hinged and usu. bearing teeth — compare INARTICULATA

[1]**ar·tic·u·late** \är'tikyələt, ȧ'- *sometimes* -ˌlāt; *usu* -d·+V\ *adj* [NL *articulatus*, fr. L, past part. of *articulare* to divide into joints, utter distinctly, fr. *articulus* division, part, joint] **1** *obs* **:** expressed in separate items or particulars **2 a :** segmented into syllables or esp. into words meaningfully arranged **:** constituting intelligible speech ⟨an ~ cry⟩ **b :** possessing the faculty or power of speech **c :** expressing oneself readily **:** not reserved **:** not reticent ⟨too ~ to be trusted with a secret⟩ **:** expressed readily ⟨gratitude is one of the least ~ of the emotions —*Survey Graphic*⟩ **d :** expressing oneself clearly and effectively enough to gain attention; *also* **:** expressed in such a manner ⟨the primitive poet . . . was used by the community to make its spiritual needs ~ —C.D.Lewis⟩ **3 a :** jointed on **:** consisting of segments united by joints **:** JOINTED ⟨~ animals⟩ ⟨~ plants⟩ **b :** distinctly marked off **:** formulated in clearly distinguished parts **:** DISTINCT ⟨an ~ period of history⟩ ⟨the way in which an ~ system blinds the thinker —Irwin Edman⟩ **syn** see VOCAL

[2]**articulate** \-ˌlāt, *usu* -ād·+V\ *vb* -ED/-ING/-S *vt* **1** *obs* **:** to draw up or write in separate articles **:** SPECIFY, PARTICULARIZE **2 a** (1) **:** to make (the breath stream) articulate ⟨speech is *articulated* air⟩ (2) **:** to pronounce distinctly (a syllable, word, or speech sound) **b :** to give clear and effective utterance to ⟨~ the dumb, deep want of the people —Thomas Carlyle⟩ **3 a** (1) **:** to unite by means of a joint **:** put together with joints or at the joints ⟨*articulated* mastodon remains —*Jour. of Geol.*⟩ (2) **:** to join together permanently or semipermanently by means of a pivot connection for operating separate forms, frames, or segments as a unit ⟨*articulated* locomotive⟩ ⟨*articulated* railroad car⟩ **b :** to form or fit into a systematically related whole **:** interrelate systematically **:** coordinate coherently ⟨the high schools have been *articulated* with the state university⟩ ⟨the problem is to ~ the ideas —E.D. Canham⟩ **4 :** to arrange (artificial teeth) on an articulator ~ *vi* **1** *obs* **:** to make or come to terms **2 a :** to utter articulate sounds or utter intelligible speech **:** speak distinctly ⟨too frightened to ~⟩ **b :** to manipulate the vocal organs so as to produce a speech sound **3 a :** to become jointed **:** become united or connected by means of a joint ⟨bones that ~ with each other⟩ **b :** to be united or connected in a systematic interrelation ⟨at the beginning of the 19th century there were a number of school units in existence, none of which *articulated* with the others —J.D.Russell & C.H.Judd⟩

[3]**articulate** \-ˌlət, -ˌlāt, *usu* -d·+V\ *n* -S [NL *Articulata*] **:** one of the Articulata

articulated train *n* **:** a railroad train whose cars are permanently or semipermanently joined together for operation as a unit as distinguished from one whose cars may be readily uncoupled and operated in other trains

ar·tic·u·late·ly \-ˌlətlē, -li\ *adv* **:** in an articulate manner

ar·tic·u·late·ness *n* -ES **:** the quality or state of being articulate

ar·tic·u·la·tion \(ˌ)är,tikyə'lāshən, (ˌ)ȧ,t-\ *n* -S [F, fr. MF, fr. L *articulatus* + F *-ion*] **1 a :** the action or manner of jointing or interrelating ⟨a sketch showing the ~ of the limbs⟩ ⟨try to show them the inner structure, the ~ of the parts —M.J.Adler⟩ **b :** the state of being jointed or systematically interrelated into a whole ⟨~ of the detail with the central thought —Gilbert Highet⟩ ⟨the potency of movies depends upon the quality of their dramatic ~ —Bosley Crowther⟩; *specif* **:** interrelation of different levels of education (as elementary education, secondary education, higher education) for ensuring continuous advancement in learning **c :** the clarification of an architectural design by emphasizing certain parts of the structure (as stairs, corridors, or floors) **2 a** (1) **:** a joint or juncture between bones or cartilages in the skeleton of a vertebrate, being immovable when the bones are directly united, slightly movable when they are united by an intervening substance, or more or less freely movable when the articular surfaces are covered with smooth cartilage and surrounded by a fibrous capsule lined with synovial membrane — see AMPHIARTHROSIS, DIARTHROSIS, SYNARTHROSIS (2) **:** a movable joint between rigid parts of any animal (as between the segments of an insect appendage) **b** (1) **:** a joint or connection between two parts capable of spontaneous separation (as the base of a leafstalk or of the peduncle of a flower) (2) **:** a node or thickened portion of a stem or the interval between two such points **3 a** (1) **:** the act or manner of articulating (2) **:** an articulated utterance or sound; *specif* **:** CONSONANT **b :** a measure of the extent to which a transmission system is capable of reproducing the original speech **c :** the manner of sounding or uttering the separate notes or phrases that make up a melodic line in music **4 a** (1) **:** the act of properly arranging artificial teeth (2) **:** an arrangement of artificial teeth **b :** OCCLUSION 2a

articulation index *n* **:** an indication based on a test consisting of the utterance of nonsense words or syllables of the percentage of speech sounds that would be heard correctly without contextual help

ar·tic·u·la·tion·ist \-nəst\ *n* -S **:** one who uses or favors the oral method of teaching the deaf

ar·tic·u·la·tive \⸗'⸗⸗ˌlə|d·iv, -ˌlā|, |tiv, -ēv\ *adj* **:** of or relating to articulation

ar·tic·u·la·tor \-ˌlād·ə(r), -ātə-\ *n* -S **1 :** one that speaks distinctly **2 :** a movable vocal organ (as the tongue) — compare POINT OF ARTICULATION **3 :** an apparatus used in dentistry for obtaining correct articulation in artificial teeth

ar·tic·u·la·to·ri·ly \⸗¦⸗⸗ˌlə¦tōrəlē, -ȯr-, -li\ *adv* **:** in an articulatory manner

ar·tic·u·la·to·ry \⸗'⸗⸗lə,tōrē, -ȯr-, -ri\ *adj* **:** of or relating to articulation

ar·tic·u·lite \är'tikyə,līt\ *n* -S [L *articulus* joint + E *-ite* — more at ARTICLE] **:** ITACOLUMITE

ar·tic·u·lus \-ˌləs\ *n, pl* **articu·li** \-ˌlī\ [NL, fr. L, joint — more at ARTICLE] **:** the hinge including the hinge plate, teeth, and ligament in bivalve mollusks

artier *comparative of* ARTY

artiest *superlative of* ARTY

ar·ti·fact *or* **ar·te·fact** \'är|d·ə,fakt, 'ȧ|, |tə-, -ē,f-\ *also* **ar·te·fac** \-ak\ *n* -S [*artifact* alter. (prob. influenced by *artifice*) of *artefact*, fr. L *arte* by skill (abl. of *art-, ars* skill) + *factum* something done, fr. neut. of *factus*, past part. of *facere* to do, make; *artefac* alter. of *artefact* — more at ARM, DO] **1 :** a usu. simple object (as a tool or ornament) showing human workmanship or modification as distinguished from a natural object **2 a :** a product of artificial character due to extraneous (as human) agency; *specif* **:** an appearance in a fixed tissue or cell held in microscopy to be an inconstant product of manipulation or reagents and not indicative of actual structural relationships **b :** an electrocardiographic and electroencephalographic wave that arises from sources other than the heart or brain

ar·ti·fac·ti·tious \¦⸗⸗,fak¦tishəs\ *adj* [*artifact* + *-itious* (as in *factitious*)] **:** ARTIFACTUAL

ar·ti·fac·tu·al \¦⸗⸗¦fakch(əw)əl, -ksh-; -kshwəl\ *adj* [*artifact* + *-ual* (as in *factual*)] **:** of or relating to an artifact

ar·ti·fice \'är|d·əfəs, 'ȧ|, |tə-\ *n* -S [MF, fr. L *artificium*, fr. *artific-, artifex* artificer, fr. *arti-* (fr. *art-, ars* skill) + *-fic-, -fex* (fr. *facere* to do, make)] **1 a** *obs* **:** production or making of something esp. in arts or crafts **b** *archaic* **:** artistic skill or style **2 a :** a wily or artful stratagem **:** TRICK, TRICKERY **b :** GUILE, INSINCERITY ⟨a master of ~⟩ **3 :** an ingenious or skillful device or expedient **:** clever skill **:** INGENUITY, INVENTIVENESS ⟨the sum total of all this ~, melodrama, and incredible behavior is a warm, witty, profoundly tragic portrait —*Time*⟩ **syn** see ART, TRICK

ar·ti·ficed \-fəst\ *adj* **:** fashioned with artifice ⟨a plot too ingeniously ~ to be the inevitable outcome of the characters' motivation —Frederic Morton⟩

ar·tif·i·cer \är'tifəsər, ȧ'tifəsə(r) *sometimes* 'är|d·əf- *or* 'ȧ| *or* |təf-\ *n* -S [ME *artificier, artificer*, fr. (assumed) AF *artificier*, fr. MF *artifice* + *-ier* -er] **1 a :** a skilled or artistic worker **:** a mechanic or craftsman whose handicraft requires skill or knowledge of a special kind (as a silversmith) **b :** an enlisted man or noncommissioned officer in the army or navy with specialized technical duties **:** ARMORER ⟨Royal Navy engine⸗room ~⟩ ⟨U.S. Army small arms ~⟩ **2 :** one that makes or contrives **:** DEVISER, INVENTOR, FRAMER ⟨the grand ~ of the national life —L.P.Curtis⟩ **3** *obs* **:** a cunning or artful fellow ⟨these base and illiterate ~*s* —Robert Burton⟩

[1]**ar·ti·fi·cial** \¦är|də¦fishəl, ¦ȧ|, |tə-\ *adj* [ME, fr. MF or L; MF *artificial, artificiel*, fr. L *artificialis* according to the rules of art, fr. *artificium* artifice + *-alis* -al] **1 :** contrived through human art or effort and not by natural causes detached from human agency **:** relating to human direction or effect in contrast to nature: **a :** formed or established by man's efforts, not by nature ⟨the people do not resort to ~ irrigation —J.G. Frazer⟩ **b :** produced or effected by man's skill to imitate nature **:** SIMULATED ⟨whether Milly's bloom was natural, as it appeared, or ~, as Victoria suspected —Ellen Glasgow⟩ ⟨the use of live bait versus ~ flies in angling⟩ ⟨an ~ limb replacing the amputated leg⟩ **:** made esp. by chemical process to resemble a raw material or something derived from it **:** SYNTHETIC ⟨~ silk⟩ ⟨~ cotton⟩ ⟨~ diamonds⟩ **c :** of, relating to, or produced by artificial insemination ⟨~ daughters of all breeds of cattle⟩ ⟨first ~ breeding association formed in U.S. —*New England Homestead*⟩ **2 a :** characteristic of human social, economic, or legal organization or structure and devoid of or contrary to actual existence in nature as detached from man **b :** taking form from an exceptional legalistic, economic, or social situation **:** palpably unnatural **:** FABRICATED ⟨the empire must be felt not as an ~ novelty but as the natural extension of the republican tradition —John Buchan⟩ ⟨most of the inequalities in the existing world are ~ —Bertrand Russell⟩ **3** *obs* **a :** displaying skill **:** SKILLFUL **b :** ARTFUL, CUNNING, CRAFTY **c :** of or according to fine or practical art **4 a :** not genuinely and spontaneously felt or experienced **:** seemingly not genuine **:** achieved through effort, not naturally **:** FEIGNED, ASSUMED, SPURIOUS ⟨the common tone was ~, was unreal —C.E.Norton⟩ ⟨none of that ~ shamefacedness which her husband mistook for delicacy — W.M.Thackeray⟩ **b :** AFFECTED, SHALLOW, CONVENTIONALIZED, STILTED **:** not natural, spontaneous, or free ⟨so affected, so fussy, so ~ —Kenneth Roberts⟩ ⟨to disregard the ~ rules of somewhat emptied rhetoric —H.O. Taylor⟩ **c :** IMITATION, SHAM ⟨a training army which has not been equipped with guns and artillery and tanks uses ~ guns and masquerading trucks —John Steinbeck⟩ **5 :** of or relating to a bid or bidding system in contract bridge intended to inform one's partner as to the nature of the hand held but not necessarily to show strength in the suit named or willingness to undertake the contract named

syn SYNTHETIC, FACTITIOUS: ARTIFICIAL and SYNTHETIC are often interchangeable when applied to fabrication ⟨rayon is called *artificial* silk and is spoken of as a *synthetic* fabric⟩ ARTIFICIAL contrasts with *natural* ⟨*artificial* and natural silks⟩ ⟨*artificial* and natural heat⟩ ⟨the miner must work by *artificial* light even though the sun be shining outside: still further down in the seams, he must work by *artificial* ventilation, too —Lewis Mumford⟩ SYNTHETIC is likely to connote chemical combination or similar processes ⟨*synthetic* flavors or dyes⟩ ⟨synthesis always means synthesis. *Synthetic* camphor and *synthetic* quinine mean just that —H.L.Fisher⟩ ARTIFICIAL may apply to anything existing in human but not in natural affairs ⟨a corporation is an *artificial* being, invisible, intangible and existing only in contemplation of law —John Marshall⟩ ⟨now magicians or medicine men appear to constitute the oldest *artificial* or professional class in the evolution of society —J.G.Frazer⟩ ARTIFICIAL, FACTITIOUS, and SYNTHETIC may all describe the forced, constrained, simulated, fabricated, or unnatural in matters social or personal; they all indicate a lack of the natural or spontaneous ⟨the strained *artificial* romanticism of Kotzebue's lugubrious dramas —J.W.Krutch⟩ ⟨at her best she is *artificial* . . . one can always feel the heavily conscious performer —G.J.Nathan⟩ ⟨in the degree in which decorative effect is achieved in isolation, it becomes empty embellishment, *factitious* ornamentation — like sugar figures on a cake —John Dewey⟩ ⟨emotional depths which till now had seemed to him unreal, theatrical, *factitious* —B.A.Williams⟩ ⟨an esoteric jargon which did not even have the authentic ring of American slang. It was purely *synthetic* —Stanley Walker⟩ ⟨the usually *synthetic* obscenities of the popular joke, the remote glamor of the embraces of moving-picture stars —Lewis Mumford⟩ FACTITIOUS is less common than ARTIFICIAL; SYNTHETIC is more recent in this use and more likely to suggest technological fabrication.

[2]**artificial** \"\ *n* -S **1 :** an imitation of a natural object ⟨there are many live-bait fishermen but the advocates of ~*s* are agreed on one thing —Eddie Finlay⟩; *specif* **:** an artificial flower **2 artificials** *pl, chiefly Brit* **:** artificial manure **:** chemical fertilizer ⟨this crop grows easily on poor soil and although it responds to lime it does not like ~*s* —*Farming*⟩

artificial accession *n* **:** INDUSTRIAL ACCESSION

artificial asphalt *n* **:** the solid residuum from the refining of certain kinds of petroleum

artificial bitter almond oil *n* **:** BENZALDEHYDE

artificial fever *n* **:** FEVER THERAPY

artificial harmonic *n* **:** a harmonic produced on a stopped string on a stringed instrument — compare NATURAL HARMONIC

artificial heart *n* **:** MECHANICAL HEART

artificial horizon *n* **1 :** HORIZON 1b (4) **2 :** an aeronautical instrument based upon a gyroscope and designed to furnish a surface constantly perpendicular to the vertical and therefore parallel to the horizon

artificial insemination *n* **:** introduction of semen into the uterus or oviduct by other than natural means either in order to increase the probability of conception or to extend the usefulness of a valued and prepotent male

ar·ti·fi·ci·al·i·ty \,⸗⸗,fishē'aləd·ē, -ətē, -i *sometimes* -(ˌ)fi'shal-\ *n* -ES **:** the quality or state of being artificial **:** the appearance of being artificial **:** something that is artificial

ar·ti·fi·cial·ize \,⸗⸗'fishə,līz\ *vt* -ED/-ING/-S **:** to make artificial ⟨~ sport for profit —A.S.Leopold⟩ ⟨a singularly *artificialized* life —*Harper's*⟩

artificial key *n* **:** a key used to determine the name of a plant or animal and based on convenient differential morphological characters that do not necessarily indicate natural relationships

artificial kidney *n* **:** an apparatus designed to do the work of the kidney in instances of temporary stoppage of kidney function

artificial language *n* **:** a language devised by an individual or a small group of individuals and proposed for an international language or for some more specific purpose (as aptitude testing) but not functioning as the native speech of its users — compare NATURAL LANGUAGE

ar·ti·fi·cial·ly \¦⸗⸗¦⸗shəlē, -li, *rap.* -shl-\ *adv* **:** in an artificial manner

ar·ti·fi·cial·ness *n* -ES **:** ARTIFICIALITY

artificial nucleation *n* **:** a process in which a cloud of liquid-water droplets at below-freezing temperature is converted to an ice crystal-cloud by artificial means

artificial person *n* **:** JURISTIC PERSON

artificial radioactivity *n* **:** radioactivity produced in a substance by bombardment with high-speed particles (as protons or neutrons) — called also *induced radioactivity*

artificial respiration *n* **:** the restoration or initiation by manual or mechanical means of breathing that has failed or that has never begun consisting essentially of forcing air into and out of the lungs to establish the rhythm of inspiration and expiration — compare ELECTROPHRENIC RESPIRATION, IRON LUNG, RESPIRATOR

artificial selection *n* **:** the process of modifying organisms by selection in breeding controlled by man

artificial system *n* **:** a system of classification based on characters that do not indicate natural relationship; *specif* **:** LINNAEAN CLASSIFICATION

artificial ultramarine *n* **:** FRENCH BLUE

artificial vagina *n* **:** a device for collecting semen for artificial insemination

artificious *adj* [prob. fr. MF *artificieux*, fr. L *artificiosus*, fr. *artificium* artifice + *-osus* -ose, -ous — more at ARTIFICE] *obs* **:** displaying skill or artifice — **artificiously** *adv*

ar·til·ler·ist \är'til(ə)rəst, ȧ'-\ *n* -S **:** one skilled in artillery **:** GUNNER, ARTILLERYMAN

ar·til·lery \är'til(ə)rē, ȧ'-, -ri, *attrib* (')⸗¦⸗(⸗)⸗\ *n* -ES *often attrib* [ME *artilrie, artillerie*, fr. MF *artillerie*, fr. OF, fr. *artillier* to furnish with implements esp. for warfare (prob. fr. *art* skill) + *-erie* -ery — more at ART] **1 a** *archaic* **:** munitions of war **:** implements for offensive and defensive warfare **b :** weapons (as bows, slings, arbalests, and catapults) for discharging missiles **c :** crew-served carriage-mounted firearms used in modern warfare that are of caliber greater than that of small arms **:** ordnance (as guns or howitzers) with its equipment **:** CANNON **d** *slang* **:** personal weapons **:** SMALL ARMS **2 a** (1) **:** the missiles discharged by the weapons of war, esp. from modern ordnance (2) **:** the massed fire of artillery weapons **b :** means of arguing or persuading ⟨his own high-powered conversational ~ —*Newsweek*⟩ **3** *obs* **:** the practice of archery **4 :** the branch or analogous organization of an army that is armed with artillery and whose primary missions are furnishing close-fire support to forward combat units, supplying counterbattery fire and fire directed against the enemy's rear areas, and using antiaircraft weapons against enemy planes **5 :** CARTHAMUS RED

ar·til·lery·man \⸗'⸗(⸗)⸗mən\ *n, pl* **artillerymen :** a soldier who belongs to the artillery **:** a person who manages or serves a piece of artillery

artillery plant *n* **:** a tropical American herb (*Pilea microphylla*) that discharges its pollen explosively

artillery wheel *n* **:** a heavily built dished wheel with a long axle box used on gun carriages and usu. having 14 spokes and 7 fellies

art·i·ly \'ärd·|ᵊlē, 'ȧd·|, -t|, |ə̇lē, -li\ *adv* [*arty* + *-ly*] **:** in an arty manner

art·i·ness \|ēnəs, |in-\ *n* -ES **:** the quality or state of being arty ⟨substitute ~ for taste⟩

ar·ti·nite \är'tē,nīt, 'ärtᵊn,īt\ *n* -S [It *artinite*, fr. Ettore *Artini* †1928 Ital. mineralogist + It *-ite*] **:** a hydrous magnesium carbonate $Mg_2(CO_3)(OH)_2.3H_2O$ occurring in white orthorhombic crystals and fibrous aggregates

[1]**ar·ti·o·dac·tyl** \¦ärd·ēə¦daktᵊl, -rshē-\ *or* **ar·ti·o·dac·tyle** \", -ˌtīl\ *adj* [NL *Artiodactyla*] **:** of, relating to, or belonging to the Artiodactyla **:** even-toed

[2]**artiodactyl** \"\ *or* **artiodactyle** \"\ *n* -S **:** one of the Artiodactyla

ar·ti·o·dac·ty·la \,⸗⸗⸗'daktələ\ *n pl, cap* [NL, fr. neut. pl. of *artiodactylus* having an even number of toes, fr. Gk *artios* complete, even, even-numbered + *daktylos* finger, toe; akin to L *artus* joint — more at ARTICLE, DACTYL] **:** an order of ungulate mammals including the ox, sheep, goat, antelope, deer, giraffe, camel, hippopotamus, pig, and related forms all having the functional toes of the hind feet and forefeet even in number and the 3d digit of each foot symmetrical with and paired with the 4th digit — compare PERISSODACTYLA

ar·ti·o·dac·ty·lous \¦⸗⸗⸗¦daktələs\ *adj* [NL *Artiodactyla* + E *-ous*] **:** ARTIODACTYL

ar·ti·san *also* **ar·ti·zan** \'är|d·əzən, 'ȧ|, |tə-, -əsən *sometimes* -ˌzan *or* -aa(ə)n, *Brit usu* ¦ȧti¦zan\ *n* -S [MF, fr. OIt *artigiano*, fr. *arte* art, fr. L *art-, ars* skill — more at ARM] **1** *obs* **:** one who practices an art **:** ARTIST **2 :** one trained to manual dexterity or skill in a trade **:** HANDICRAFTSMAN **3 :** the second rank earned by members of a Horizon Club, senior program of the Camp Fire Girls — compare JOURNEYMAN

ar·ti·san·al \'⸗⸗ˌzənᵊl, -sən-\ *adj* [F, fr. *artisan* + *-al*] **:** of or relating to artisans

ar·ti·san·ship \-ˌzən,ship, -ˌsən-, -¦zan, -aan-\ *or* **ar·ti·san·ry** \'⸗⸗ˌzənrē, -sən-, -ri\ *n, pl* **artisanships** *or* **artisanries :** the work or workmanship of an artisan

art·ist \'är|d·əst, 'ȧ|, |tə-\ *n* -S [MF *artiste* artist, artisan, learned man, fr. ML *artista* student or master of the liberal arts, fr. L *art-, ars* art, skill + *-ista* -ist] **1 a :** one who professes and practices an art in which conception and execution are governed by imagination and taste **b :** a person skilled in one of the fine arts; *esp* **:** PAINTER **2a :** a performer of music in public (as a singer, pianist, or conductor) **b :** a theatrical performer ⟨a dramatic ~⟩; *broadly* **:** a usu. adept or skillful public performer or entertainer ⟨a trapeze ~⟩ **:** ARTISTE **3 a** *obs* **:** one skilled or versed in learned arts — used esp. of philosophers, savants, physicians or surgeons, astrologers, or alchemists **b** *archaic* **:** one skilled in some technical or mechanical art or trade (as a cobbler, miner, surveyor, or seaman) **:** ARTISAN **4 :** one who is adept esp. at deception, fraud, artifice, or stratagem **:** one who is expert esp. at something dubious or reprehensible ⟨an ~ with loaded dice⟩ ⟨a short-weight ~ in the coal business⟩ **5 :** one whose vocation involves drawing, painting, designing, or layout work ⟨landscape ~⟩ **syn** see EXPERT

ar·tiste \är'tēst, ȧ'-\ *n* -S [F, artist, skilled performer or workman] **1 :** a skilled adept performer, often a woman; *specif* **:** a musical or theatrical entertainer **2 :** a skillful and pleasing worker (as a cook or milliner) **syn** see EXPERT

ar·tis·tic \(')är¦tistik, (')ȧ¦-, -ēk\ *also* **ar·tis·ti·cal** \-ə̇kəl, -ēk-\ *adj* **1 :** relating to, suitable for, or characteristic of art or artists ⟨certain subjects are considered ~ subjects —Bernard Smith⟩ **2 :** characterized by taste, discrimination, and judgment or by art and skill ⟨you may have an ~ interior or you may have a museum —Herbert Spencer⟩ **3 a :** produced by human art ⟨for Plato ~ production is but an imitation of an imitation —A.E.Vassilion⟩ **b :** appropriate for or relevant to a fine-arts presentation ⟨~ subjects⟩ **:** associated with the arts **:** compatible with an artist's attitudes or intentions **:** not material, objective, or moralistic ⟨the difference between mechanical or purely objective construction and ~ production —John Dewey⟩ **c :** suggestive often speciously of art or artists **:** seemingly frequented by artists **:** BOHEMIAN ⟨the people who came to this Soho restaurant because it was notoriously so ~ —Aldous Huxley⟩

syn AESTHETIC: ARTISTIC may stress the viewpoint or suggest the aspirations of the artist as the producer of beautiful things, and AESTHETIC the appreciative attitude of one who views with enjoyment the resulting product or situation ⟨we have no word in the English language that unambiguously includes what is signified by the two words *artistic* and *aesthetic*. Since *artistic* refers primarily to the act of production and *aesthetic* to that of perception and enjoyment, the absence of a term designating the two processes taken together is unfortunate —John Dewey⟩ ⟨the intensity of the *artistic* process, the pressure . . . under which the fusion takes place —T.S.Eliot⟩ ⟨the artist's work in life is full of struggle and toil; it is only the spectator of morals who can assume the calm *aesthetic* attitude —Havelock Ellis⟩ Sometimes this distinction is not followed ⟨an *artistic* satisfaction in the contemplation of evil —W.S. Maugham⟩ ⟨that loveliness which is the creation of the *aesthetic* human spirit —John Galsworthy⟩

ar·tis·ti·cal·ly \-ə̇k(ə)lē, -ēk-, -li\ *adv* **:** in an artistic manner

artist lithography *n* : AUTOLITHOGRAPHY

art·ist·ry \ˈärd·əstrē, ˈä|, |tə-, -ri\ *n* -ES **1** : artistic quality of effect or workmanship ⟨the ~ of this first chapter —G.H. Genzmer⟩ **2** : artistic ability ⟨to be on the winning side in every argument requires an ~ not always fully appreciated —Julian Dana⟩

artist's proof *n* : one of the first and therefore best proofs printed from an engraved plate

art·less \ˈärtləs, ˈät-\ *adj* **1 a** : lacking art, skill, or knowledge : IGNORANT, UNSKILLFUL ⟨to be ~ is to be dehumanized —E.A. Hoebel⟩ **b** : devoid of artistic quality or taste : UNCULTURED ⟨the land vaguely realizing westward but still unstoried, ~ —Robert Frost⟩ **2** : free from the artificial : easy, natural, and not contrived ⟨its atmosphere of something we call an ~ charm pervades through the narrative —H.V.Gregory⟩ **3** : made or contrived without skill or art : CRUDE, INARTISTIC ⟨marred by an ~ summerhouse in the garden⟩ **4** : marked by freedom from calculated craft, guile, and duplicity and by sincerity, simplicity, and genuineness ⟨open, candid, ~, guileless, with affections strong, but simple, forming no pretensions, and knowing no disguise —Jane Austen⟩ **syn** see NATURAL

art·less·ly *adv* : in an artless manner : without art, skill, or guile : UNAFFECTEDLY

art·less·ness *n* -ES : the quality or state of being artless

art marble *n* : a cast stone made of crushed marble with the exposed surface highly polished to resemble natural marble

art music *n* : music composed by the trained musician as contrasted with folk music and often with popular music

art nou·veau \ˌär,nü'vō\ *n, often cap A&N* [F, lit., new art] : a late 19th century and early 20th century decorative style characterized by organic foliate forms, sinuous lines, and nongeometric curves

arto- *comb form* [L, fr. Gk, fr. *artos*; perh. akin to Gk *ararískein* to fit — more at ARM] : bread ⟨*Artocarpus*⟩

art object *n* [by trans.] : OBJET D'ART

ar·to·car·pus \ˌärd·ə'kärpəs\ *n* [NL, fr. *arto-* + *-carpus*] **1** *cap* : a large genus of tall evergreen milky-juiced trees (family Moraceae) orig. Asiatic but now grown throughout the tropics having large alternate entire or lobed leaves and flowers in catkinlike clusters with the pistillate ones in crowded heads that produce a multiple fleshy fruit **2** -ES : a plant of the genus *Artocarpus* : BREADFRUIT, JACKFRUIT

art of self-defense 1 : BOXING **2** : FENCING

art·o·gra·vure \ˌärd·əgrə'vyü(ə)r\ *n* -S [²*art* + *-o-* + *gravure*] : the process of preparing silk-screen stencils photographically by sensitizing the silk and printing the image on it

ar·to·pho·ri·on \-'fōrē,än\ *n, pl* **artopho·ria** \-rē.ə\ [MGk, fr. Gk, bread basket, fr. *arto-* + *-phorion* (akin to *pherein* to carry) — more at BEAR] : a container for the reserved sacrament in the Eastern Church

ar·to·type \ˈärd·ə,tīp\ *n* -S [²*art* + *-o-* + *type*] : COLLOTYPE

ar·to·ty·rite \ˌärd·ə'tī,rīt\ *n* -S *usu cap* [LL *Artotyrita*, fr. LGk *Artotyritēs*, fr. Gk *artotyros* bread and cheese (fr. *arto-* + *tyros* cheese) + *-itēs* -ite — more at TYR-] : one of a Montanist sect that according to its opponents used bread and cheese in the celebration of the Lord's Supper

art paper *n* **1** *Brit* : coated paper **2** : heavy colored paper used esp. by students for art or craft projects — compare CONSTRUCTION PAPER

arts *pl of* ART

-arts *pl of* -ART

arts and crafts *n pl* : the arts of decorative design and handicraft (as bookbinding, weaving, and needlework) that are concerned with objects of use

arts college *n* : a college in which the liberal arts are the only or the principal studies

artsman *n, pl* **artsmen** *obs* : a man skilled in an art

arts master *n, obs* : a teacher or master of art or of an art

art song *n* : a song that is lyric in character with melody and accompaniment usu. through-composed by a trained musician — see LIED; compare FOLK SONG

art square *n* : a patterned rectangle of carpet woven in one piece for a rug

art theater *n* : a theater that specializes in the presentation of artistic dramatic productions and esp. foreign films

art union *n* : any of several 19th century American associations for promoting the arts esp. through the distribution of paintings and prints by lottery

artware \ˈ=,=\ *n* : merchandise (as knickknacks) that is aesthetic as well as utilitarian

artwork \ˈ=,=\ *n* **1 a** : the making of decorative or artistic objects by hand **b** : the decoration of artistic objects so made **2** : artistic work produced in quantity; *specif* : 19th century factory-made objects **3** : ART 8

arty \ˈärd·ē, ˈä|, |tē, -i\ *adj* -ER/-EST **1** : imitative often unsuccessfully of art : having some of the showier characteristics of art ⟨no ~ or pretentious line ever got into his daily cartoon —James Thurber⟩ **2** : aspiring often unsuccessfully to be artistic : showing dilettante interests : marked by concern with accidental rather than essential characteristics of art ⟨his ~ but beautiful wife —V.P.Hass⟩

arty *abbr* artillery

arty–crafty \ˈ===ˈ==\ *also* **arty–and–crafty** \ˈ====ˈ==\ *or* **artsy–craftsy** \ˈärtsē¦kraf(t)sē\ *adj* [irreg. fr. *arts and crafts*] **1 a** : simultaneously arty and somewhat useless, novel, and often expensive and uncomfortable ⟨*arty-crafty* lawn furniture⟩ **b** : marked by pretension esp. to artlessness or simplicity ⟨*arty-crafty* street terminology that garden suburbs have lately made their own —*Architectural Rev.*⟩ **2** : ARTY 2 ⟨a free-thinking, *arty-crafty* little sculptress —Eleazar Lipsky⟩

arua \ˌärə¦wä\ *n, pl* **arua** *or* **aruas** *usu cap* [Pg *aruá*, of Amer Ind origin] **1 a** : an Arawakan people of French Guiana and Brazil **b** : a member of such people **2** : the language of the Arua people

aruac *usu cap, var of* ARHUACO

arui \ˈärü,ē\ *n* -S [native name in eastern Africa] : AOUDAD

aru·ke \ˈärü,kā\ *n* -S [Maori *aruhe*] *New Zeal* : the starchy rhizome of the brake (*Pteridium aquilinum*)

ar·um \ˈa(a)rəm, ˈer-, ˈär-\ *n* [NL, fr. L, arum, fr. Gk *aron*; perh. akin to L *arundo* reed] **1** *cap* : a genus (the type of the family Araceae) of herbs of Europe and Asia with usu. heart-shaped leaves and a large spathe with edges involute at the base **2** -S : any of several plants of the family Araceae, esp. of the genus *Arum* — see CUCKOOPINT **3** -S : a sagolike starch obtained from cuckoopint root : PORTLAND ARROWROOT

arum family *n* : ARACEAE

arum lily *n* : CALLA LILY

arun·cus \ə'rəŋkəs\ *n, cap* [NL, fr. L, beard of a goat, fr. (assumed) Gk (Dor) *aryngos*; akin to Gk (Attic) *ēryngos*] : a small genus of herbs (family Rosaceae) found in No. America and Japan and having compound leaves and a showy branched cluster of white flowers — see GOATSBEARD

arun·del \ə'rəndᵊl\ *adj, usu cap* [fr. Anne Arundel county, Md.] : of or relating to a subdivision of the Lower Cretaceous

arun·di·na·ceous \ə¦rəndə¦nāshəs\ *adj* [L *arundinaceus*, *harundinaceus* reedlike, fr. *arundin-*, *arundo*, *harundin-*, *harundo* reed + *-aceus* -aceous] : of or relating to a reed : resembling reed or cane

arun·di·nar·ia \ə,rəndə'na(a)rēə\ *n, cap* [NL, fr. L *arundin-*, *arundo*, *harundin-*, *harundo* reed + NL *-aria*] : a genus of large woody bamboo grasses that are natives of Asia and America and have terete culms, persistent leaf sheaths with stiff scabrous bristles, and flower spikelets arranged in racemes or panicles — compare CANEBRAKE, GIANT CANE, SMALL CANE

arun·do \ə'rən(,)dō\ *n, cap* [NL, fr. L *arundo*, *harundo* reed] : a small genus of coarse tall grasses found in most warm countries and having conspicuous 2-ranked long leaves and an erect panicle up to 2 feet or more in length — see GIANT REED

arun·ta \ə'rəntə\ *or* **aran·da** \-əndə, -än-\ *or* **aran·ta** \-antə, -än-\ *n, pl* **arunta** *or* **aruntas** *or* **aranda** *or* **arandas** *or* **aranta** *or* **arantas** *usu cap* **1 a** : an aboriginal people in central Australia **b** : a member of such people **2** : the language of the Arunta people

arura *var of* AROURA

aru·sa \ə'rüshə\ *n* -S [modif. of Hindi *arus*, perh. fr. Skt *aṭaruṣa*] **1** : a small shrub (*Adhatoda vasica*) found in India **2** : a yellow dye derived from arusa leaves

aru·sha *also* **aroo·sha** \ə'rüshə\ *n* -S [perh. fr. Skt *aruṣa* red] : an Indian shrub (*Callicarpa cana*) yielding a flaxlike fiber

aruspex *var of* HARUSPEX

arv *abbr* arrive

¹ar·val *also* **ar·vel** \ˈärvəl\ *n* -S [ME *arvell*, of Scand origin; akin to ON *erfiöl* funeral feast, fr. *erfi* inheritance, funeral feast + *öl* ale, drinking bout, banquet; akin to ON *arfi* inheritance — more at ORPHAN, ALE] *dial Brit* : a funeral feast

²arval \"\ *adj, usu cap* [L *arvalis*, lit., of cultivated field, fr. *arvum* cultivated field + *-alis* -al] : relating to a body of ancient Roman priests who presided over an annual fertility festival in May

ar·ver·ni \är'vər,nī\ *n pl, usu cap* [L] : a powerful and civilized people of southern Gaul that were conquered by Caesar in his Gallic wars

¹ar·vic·o·la \-'vikələ\ *n, cap* [NL, fr. LL *arvi-* (fr. L *arvum* cultivated field, fr. neut. of *arvus* arable) + L *-cola* inhabitant; akin to L *arare* to plow — more at EAR, -COLOUS] : a genus of rodents consisting of the water voles

²arvicola \"\ [NL, fr. LL *arvi-* + L *-cola*] *syn of* MICROTUS

ar·vi·cole \ˈärvə,kōl\ *n* -S [NL *Arvicola*] : a member of the genus *Arvicola*

ar·vi·cul·ture \-,kəlchər *also* ,==ˈ==\ *n* -S [prob. fr. F, fr. LL *arvi-* + F *culture*] : the cultivation of field crops : the science and art of growing field crops

ARW *abbr* air raid warden

ary \ˈarē, ˈer-, ˈaar-, -ri *S also* ˈar *or* ˈaə\ *adj* [alter. of *e'er a*, fr. *e'er* + ²*a*] *dial* : ANY, A ⟨was there ~ thing I could do —Marjorie K. Rawlings⟩

¹-ary *US*: ,erē, ,eri, *infrequently* ,ər- *or* r-, *S also* ,ār-, *when an unstressed syllable precedes*; ər- *also* r-, *in a few words* ,er- *S also* ,ār-, *when a stressed syllable precedes. Brit: whatever the preceding stress, usu* ,əri, *alternatively often* ri *when a vowel or semivowel does not immediately precede*\ *n suffix* -ES [ME *-arie*, fr. OF & L; OF *-arie*, *-aire*, fr. L *-arius*, *-aria*, *-arium*, fr. *-arius*, adj. suffix] : one that belongs to or is connected with: **a** : thing belonging to or connected with; *esp* : place of ⟨avi*ary*⟩ ⟨besti*ary*⟩ ⟨herb*ary*⟩ ⟨semin*ary*⟩ ⟨termit*ary*⟩ **b** : person belonging to, connected with, or engaged in ⟨function*ary*⟩ ⟨sedition*ary*⟩

²-ary \"\ *adj suffix* [ME *-arie*, fr. MF & L; MF *-aire*, fr. L *-arius*] : of or belonging to or connected with ⟨budget*ary*⟩ ⟨discretion*ary*⟩ ⟨parliament*ary*⟩ ⟨unit*ary*⟩

ar·ya *like next without* n\ *n, pl* **aryas** *also* **arya** *usu cap* [Skt *ārya*] : ARYAN

¹ar·yan *also* **ar·ian** \ˈa(a)rēən, ˈer-, ˈär- *sometimes* ˈärēən *or* ˈäryən *or* ˈarē- *or* ˈäy-\ *adj, usu cap* [Skt *ārya*, adj. & n., noble, Aryan, member of the upper castes, prob. fr. *ari* stranger, enemy; akin to Av *airyō* Aryan, OPer *ariya*, and prob. to L *alius* other — more at ELSE] **1** : of or relating to the Indo-European family of languages or to their hypothetical prototype **2** : of or relating to speakers of Indo-European languages **3 a** : of or relating to a hypothetical ethnic type illustrated by or descended from early speakers of Indo-European languages **b** : NORDIC **4** : of or relating to the Indo-Iranians or their speech

²aryan *also* **arian** \"\ *n* -S *usu cap* [Skt *ārya*] **1** : a member of the Indo-European-speaking people one branch of which early occupied the Iranian plateau while another branch entered India and conquered and amalgamated with the earlier non-Indo-European inhabitants : INDO-IRANIAN **2 a** : member of the people that spoke the language from which the Indo-European languages are derived **b** : an individual of any of those peoples who have spoken these languages since prehistoric times : INDO-EUROPEAN **c** : NORDIC **d** : GENTILE **3** : a member of the Indo-European-speaking modern peoples of India as opposed to the Dravidian-speaking ones

ar·yan·ism \-,nizəm\ *n* -S *usu cap* **1** : the doctrine popularized by Nazism that the so-called Aryan peoples possess superior capacities for government, social organization, and civilization **2** : the belief in the doctrine of Aryanism and acceptance of its social and ethical implications often accompanied by suppression of the so-called non-Aryan peoples (as the Jews) — compare NORDICISM

ar·yan·ist \-nəst\ *n* -S *usu cap* : one who makes a special study of the facts bearing on the Aryan race as a homogeneous group; *specif* : one who argues the existence of the Aryan race or credits the hypothetical Aryans with racially superior capacities or traits

ar·yan·i·za·tion \,=(=)=nə'zāshən, -,nī'z-\ *n* -S *usu cap* : the act or process of aryanizing

ar·yan·ize \ˈ=(=)=,nīz\ *vt* -ED/-ING/-S *often cap* **1** : to make Aryan in speech characteristics or culture **2** : to clear of non-Aryan (as Semitic) personnel, control, or influence

ar·y·bal·los *or* **ar·y·bal·lus** \,arə'baləs\ *n* -ES [Gk *aryballos* bag, purse, aryballos, perh. fr. *ary-* (fr. *aryein* to draw — water) + *-ballos* (fr. *ballein* to throw) — more at DEVIL] : a flask or bottle that has a short neck, single handle, small orifice with a flaring lip, and globular body often elaborately decorated and that is used for holding oils or ointments — compare ALABASTRUM

aryballos

ar·y·epiglottic \¦arē + ¦==¦==\ *adj* [Gk *ary-* (fr. *aryein* to draw — water) + E *epiglottic*] : ARYTENOEPIGLOTTIC

ar·yl \ˈarəl\ *n* -S [ISV *aromatic* + *-yl*; prob. orig. formed in G] **1** : a univalent aromatic radical (as phenyl or tolyl) derived from an arene by removal of one hydrogen atom from a carbon atom of the nucleus — compare ARALKYL **2** : a compound of one or more aryl radicals with a metal ⟨sodium ~s⟩

ar·yl·amine \,arəl+\ *n* -S [ISV *aryl* + *amine*] : an amine (as aniline) containing aryl attached to amino nitrogen

ar·yl·a·mi·no \¦=s=ə¦mē(,)nō, -¦amə,nō\ *adj* [ISV *arylamino-*, fr. *arylamine*] : of, relating to, or containing an arylamine

ar·yl·ate \ˈarə,lāt\ *vt* -ED/-ING/-S [ISV *aryl* + *-ate*] : to introduce one or more aryl groups into (a compound)

ar·yl·a·tion \,==ˈlāshən\ *n* -S : the act or process of arylating

ar·yl·ene \ˈarə,lēn\ *n* -S [ISV *aryl-* + *-ene*] : a bivalent radical (as phenylene) derived from an aromatic hydrocarbon by removal of a hydrogen atom from each of two carbon atoms of the nucleus

ar·yl·ide \-,līd\ *n* -S [*aryl* + *amide*] : a usu. acid amide (as an anilide) in which hydrogen of the amido group is replaced by aryl (as phenyl)

ar·yl·oxy \-,läksē\ *adj* [*aryloxy-*, fr. *aryl* + *oxy-*] : of, relating to, or containing a univalent radical ArO (as phenoxy) composed of an aryl radical united with oxygen

¹ar·yo–dravidian \,a(a)rē,ō, ¦er-, ¦är- *sometimes* ˈärē,ō *or* ˈär(,)yō *or* ˈarē,ō *or* ˈä(,)yō+\ *adj, usu cap A&D* [*Aryo-* (fr. ¹*Aryan*) + *Dravidian*] : of, relating to, or characteristic of the Indian people having a mixture of Aryan and Dravidian blood that constitute the chief population of northern India between the Punjab and Bengal and of the southern half of Ceylon

²aryo–dravidian \"+\ *n* -S *cap A&D* : one of the Aryo-Dravidian people

aryo–indian \"+\ *n, cap A&I* : a person of a native race in India having an Aryan element in his ancestry

ar·y·te·no·epiglottic \¦arə¦tē(,)nō, ə¦ritᵊn(,)ō+\ *or* **ar·y·te·no·epiglottidean** \"+\ *adj* [*aryteno-* fr. NL *arytenoides*) + *epiglottic* or *epiglottidean*] : relating to or linking the arytenoid cartilage and the epiglottis ⟨~ folds⟩

¹ar·y·te·noid \,arə'tē,nȯid, ə'ritᵊn,ȯid\ *also* **ar·y·te·noi·dal** \,arə(,)tē¦nȯidᵊl, ə¦ritᵊn¦ȯi-\ *adj* [*arytaenoid* fr. NL *arytenoides*, fr. Gk *arytainoeidēs*, lit., ladle-shaped, fr. *arytaina* ladle (fr. *aryein* to draw —water—, prob. fr. a prehistoric Gk compound whose first and second constituents are akin respectively to Skt *vār* water and to L *haurire* to draw) + *-oeidēs* -oid; *arytenoidal* fr. ²*arytenoid* + *-al* — more at URINE, EXHAUST] **1** : relating to or being either of two small cartilages to which the vocal cords are attached and which are situated at the upper back part of the larynx **2** : relating to or being either of a pair of small muscles or an unpaired muscle of the larynx

²arytenoid \"\ *n* -S [NL *arytaenoides*, fr. Gk *arytainoeidēs*, adj.] : an arytenoid cartilage or muscle

arz·ru·nite \ˈärz'rü,nīt, ˈärts'-\ *n* -S [G *arzrunit*, fr. Andreas *Arzruni* †1898 Ger. mineralogist who first recognized it + G *-it*] : a mineral consisting of a basic copper sulfate with copper chloride occurring as bluish green incrustations

¹as \əz, (ˈ)az\ *adv* [ME *as*, *alse*, *alswa*, adv. & conj., fr. OE *alswā*, *ealswā*, *ælswā* just as, likewise — more at ALSO] **1** : to the same degree or amount : to such an extent : EQUALLY — used to modify an adjective or an adverb ⟨I haven't found any new poems ~ good as my old favorites —Randall Jarrell⟩ ⟨neither of them wrote ~ well after the experience as before it —Van Wyck Brooks⟩ ⟨nowhere else in the world is there a people ~ intelligent or ~ perceptive of humor —F.P.Adams⟩ **2** : for instance : by way of example : THUS — usu. used to introduce illustrative details ⟨high-pitched sounds come to suggest spatial height, ~ in bird songs —Thomas Munro⟩

²as \"\ *conj* [ME *as*, *alse*, *alswa*] **1** : to which (degree or amount) : in which (degree or extent) : in or to the same degree in which — usu. used as a correlative after an adjective or adverb modified by adverbial *as* or *so* and often followed by a noun or pronoun representing an incomplete clause whose verb would be the same as that of the main clause ⟨the position of this science is as honorable ~ it is secure —L.A.White⟩ ⟨no general presentation . . . can interest the children as much ~ the learning of the foreign language —Ruth Mays⟩ ⟨his dull red hair was snow-powdered nearly as white ~ that of a British grenadier⟩ **2** : in the same way or manner that : in the form or condition in which ⟨his hair is brown ~ are his eyes⟩ ⟨studied the simile ~ Horner used it⟩ — sometimes followed by a noun or pronoun representing an incomplete clause whose verb would be the same as that of the main clause ⟨during his stay on the island he lived ~ an islander⟩ **3** : according to what : in accordance with that which or the way in which ⟨~ he said, the stream was full of trout⟩ ⟨his criticisms, ~ I remember, were coldly received⟩ ⟨he is really quite good ~ boys go⟩ **4** : as if ⟨were saying farewell to each other ~ to their childhood —Edith Sitwell⟩ ⟨this mechanical thought is crushing ~ with an iron roller all that is organic —W.B.Yeats⟩ **5** : during or at the same time that : WHILE, WHEN ⟨promptly opened fire again ~ he turned away —C.S.Forester⟩ ⟨~ he paced back and forth the idea occurred to him⟩ ⟨you will see the tower ~ you cross the bridge⟩ **6** : notwithstanding the degree to which : THOUGH ⟨some see in him, Gael ~ he was, the earliest Protestant —Gilbert Highet⟩ **7** : in a manner or degree befitting or having equal certainty with the fact, belief, or hope that ⟨this swears he, ~ he is a prince, is just and ~ I am a gentleman, I credit him —Shak.⟩ ⟨~ I live, I cannot believe it⟩ **8** : for the reason that : BECAUSE, SINCE ⟨remained in great loneliness and considerable privation ~ he had no income —W.L.Sullivan⟩ **9** *dial* : THAN — used in comparisons ⟨he better not be later ~ midnight —T.B.Costain⟩ **10 a** : that the result is : THAT — used with preceding *so* or *such* ⟨so clearly guilty ~ to leave no doubt of his conviction⟩ ⟨and such a son ~ all men hailed me happy —John Milton⟩ **b** : THAT — used to introduce a noun clause and now dial. except in certain negative expressions with *know*, *say*, or *see* that have wide usage in informal speech ⟨he said ~ he would come⟩ ⟨I don't know ~ it makes any difference⟩ **c** *dial* : in so far as : THAT — used to introduce an adverbial clause ⟨he hasn't come out again ~ I've seen⟩ — **as is** \(ˈ)a'ziz, ,ə'z-\ : in its present condition : without any repairs, improvements, or alterations being made ⟨the car was priced at $1000 *as is*⟩ — **as it were** : as if it were so : in a manner of speaking ⟨her triumph, *as it were*, did not last long⟩ — **as new** : practically new : in the best secondhand condition ⟨the clothes offered for sale were all prewar and all *as new*⟩ — **as you were** — a military command used (1) to cancel another command that has not yet been executed or (2) to direct troops to return to the position occupied before the last command

³as \"\ *pron* **1 a** : THAT, WHO, WHICH — used to introduce an adjectival clause and having *same* or *such* as antecedent ⟨their children should grow up in the same intellectual culture ~ they have enjoyed —G.B.Jeffery⟩ ⟨tears such ~ angels weep burst forth —John Milton⟩ **b** *now dial* : THAT, WHO, WHICH — used to introduce an adjectival clause and having a noun or pronoun as antecedent ⟨a lot of things happened . . . ~ never ought to —Richard Llewellyn⟩ ⟨was going to tell the gospel to them ~ had ears —R.P.Warren⟩ **2** : a fact that : THAT ⟨he is a foreigner, ~ is evident from his accent⟩ ⟨I have used thee, filth ~ thou art, with humane care —Shak.⟩

⁴as \"\ *prep* [¹*as*] **1** : after the manner of : the same as : LIKE ⟨had seen strong men become ~ weaklings when they were faced with . . . being shipwrecked —H.A.Chippendale⟩ ⟨his face was ~ a mask of gauze through which nothing was quite clearly visible —Max Beerbohm⟩ **2 a** : in the character, role, function, capacity, condition, or sense of ⟨more interested in . . . attitudes ~ attitudes than he is in their definition and embodiment in aesthetic forms —Mark Schorer⟩ ⟨eager for power ~ power⟩ ⟨his appearance ~ Hamlet⟩ ⟨his appointment ~ instructor⟩ **b** : in a way or of a nature constituting ⟨he comes home at six ~ a rule⟩ ⟨~ a result of the trip he was exhausted⟩ **c** : for consideration or considered in a specified form or relation — usu. used before prepositions and participles (as *against*, *between*, *distinguished*, and *opposed*) ⟨his argument ~ against yours⟩ ⟨my opinion ~ distinguished from theirs⟩

⁵as \ˈas\ *n, pl* **as·ses** \ˈa(,)sēz, -səz\ [L — more at ACE] **1** : LIBRA 2 **2 a** (1) : a bronze coin of the ancient Roman republic varying in weight from 1 as, or 12 ounces, to ½ ounce (2) : one of several similar coins issued by some of the Roman emperors **b** : a unit of value equivalent to an as coin

Roman as, showing head of Janus

⁶as *sing of* AESIR

⁷as \ˈas\ *also* **as nas** \-nȧs\ *n* [Per] : a Persian card game similar to poker and by some thought to be its progenitor

¹as- — see AD-

²as- *also* **asym-** *comb form, usu ital* [ISV *asymmetric*] : asymmetric — in names of organic compounds ⟨*as*-dichloro-ethylene⟩

-as *pl of* -A

AS *abbr* **1** account sales **2** after sight **3** air service **4** air speed **5** alongside **6** [ML *anno salutis*] in the year of redemption **7** antisubmarine **8** applied science **9** apprentice seaman **10** at sight

As *symbol* arsenic

a's *or* **as** *pl of* A

asa·do \ə'sä(,)dō\ *n* -S [AmerSp, fr. Sp, roast meat, fr. *asado* (past part. of *asar* to roast), fr. L *assatus*, past part. of *assare* to roast, fr. *assus* roasted; akin to L *ardēre* to burn — more at ARDOR] : BARBECUE

asa dul·cis \¦asə'dəlsəs, ¦äs-\ *n* [NL, lit., sweet gum] : BENZOIN 1

as·a·fet·i·da *or* **as·a·foet·i·da** *or* **as·sa·fet·i·da** *or* **as·sa·foet·i·da** \,asə'fid·ədē, -fed·ə-,-fetə-, as'f-; -fid·ədə, -fetədə\ *also* **as·fet·i·da** \as'f-,aas'f-,ais'f-\ *n* -S [ME *asafetida*, fr. ML *asafoetida*, fr. *asa* gum (of Iranian origin; akin to Per *azā* mastic) + L *foetida*, fem. of *foetidus* fetid] : the fetid gum resin of various Persian and East Indian plants of the genus *Ferula* (esp. *F. assafoetida*, *F. foetida*, or *F. narthex*) occurring in the form of tears and dark-colored masses, having a strong odor and taste, and formerly used in medicine as an antispasmodic

asa·hi·ka·wa \¦äsəhē¦käwə\ *adj, usu cap* [fr. *Asahikawa*, city on Hokkaido island, Japan] : of or from Asahikawa, Japan : of the kind or style prevalent in Asahikawa

¹asak *var of* ASOKA

²as·ak \ˈasək\ *n* -S [Hindi *asok* — more at ASOKA] : MAST TREE

¹asa·na \ˈäsənə\ *n* -S [Skt *āsana*, fr. *āste* he sits; akin to Gk *hēsthai* to sit, Av *āstē* he sits, Hitt *es-* to sit] : manner of sitting (as in the practice of yoga) : POSTURE

²asa·na \ˌäsə'nä\ *n* -S [PhilSp *asand*, fr. Tag *asanā*] : NARRA

asante *usu cap, var of* ASHANTI

asaph·ic \(ˈ)ā¦safik\ *adj, usu cap* [*Asaph*, 10th cent. B.C. Levite and musician mentioned in 1 Chron 16:5, 25:1–2 + E *-ic*] : of or relating to Asaph, chief musician of the sanctuary in the time of David, or to the hereditary musical guild founded by him ⟨*Asaphic* psalms⟩

asaph·ite \ˈā,sa,fīt\ *n* -S *usu cap* [*Asaph* + E *-ite*] : a descendant of the Levite Asaph

as·a·phus \'asəfəs\ *n, cap* [NL, irreg. fr. Gk *asaphēs* indistinct, dim, fr. *a-* ²a- + *saphēs* distinct, clear] : a genus of trilobites occurring abundantly in the Ordovician of northern Europe and having subequal cephala and pygidia

as·a·ra·bac·ca \,asərə'bakə\ *n* -s [alter. of earlier *asarabacara*, prob. fr. Sp *asarabácara*, irreg. fr. *ásaro* asarabacca (fr. L *asarum* hazelwort) + *bácara* clary (*Salvia sclarea*), fr. L *baccaris*, a plant with an aromatic root, fr. Gk *bakkaris*] : a plant of the genus *Asarum*

asa·rah b'te·bet \ä'sō,rōbə'tā(,)ves\ *n* -s *usu cap A&T* [Heb *'ăsārāh bĕṭēbhēth*] : a Jewish fast day observed on the 10th day of Tebet to mark the beginning of the siege of Jerusalem by Nebuchadnezzar in 586 B.C.

asarh \'ä,sär\ *n* -s *usu cap* [Skt *Āṣāḍha*] : a month of the Hindu year — see MONTH table

as·a·ron \'asə,rän\ *also* **as·a·rone** \-,rōn\ *n* -s [ISV *asar-* (fr. NL *Asarum*) + *-on, -one*] : a crystalline phenolic ether $C_{12}H_{16}O_3$ found in the oils of a number of plants esp. of the genus *Asarum* —called also *asarum camphor*

as·a·ro·tum \,asə'rōd·əm\ *n, pl* **asaro·ta** \-ōd·ə\ [L, fr. Gk *asarōton*, neut. of *asarōtos* paved in mosaic resembling an unswept floor, lit., unswept, fr. *a-* ²a- + *sarōtos*, verbal of *saroun* to sweep, fr. *saron* broom; prob. akin to L *turba* disturbance, tumult — more at TURBID] : ancient Roman painted pavement

as·a·rum \'asərəm\ *n* [NL, fr. L, hazelwort, fr. Gk *asaron*] **1** *cap* : a genus of acaulescent herbs (family Aristolochiaceae) native to north-temperate regions and having pungent aromatic roots and dull-colored flowers — see WILD GINGER **2** -s : the dried rhizome and roots of wild ginger used as an aromatic bitters and flavoring agent

asarum camphor *n* : ASARON

as·best \'as,best, ⸗'⸗ *also* (')az-\ *n* -s *archaic* : ASBESTOS

as·bes·tic \(')as'bestik, -z'b-\ *n* -s : a fibrous sand formed by mixing second-grade asbestos and serpentine and used when crushed and mixed with lime to form a fireproof wall plaster

as·bes·ti·form \as'bestə,fórm, az-\ *adj* [¹*asbestos* + *-iform*] : having the form or appearance of asbestos

as·bes·tine \(')⸗'⸗,stən, ⸗'⸗,stēn\ *or* **as·bes·tous** \(')⸗'⸗stəs\ *or* **as·bes·tic** \(')⸗'⸗stik\ *adj* [*asbestos* + *-ine* or *-ous* or *-ic*] : of, relating to, or having the characteristics of asbestos : INCOMBUSTIBLE

Asbestine \⸗'⸗,stēn, -stən\ *trademark* — used for a finely fibrous variety of talc used esp. as a filler for rubber and paper and as an extender and white pigment in paints

as·bes·toid \⸗'⸗,stóid\ *or* **as·bes·toi·dal** \;⸗;⸗'stóidᵊl\ *adj* [¹*asbestos* + *-oid, -oidal*] : resembling asbestos

¹**as·bes·tos** *also* **as·bes·tus** \as'bestəs *also* az'- *or* əs'- *or* əz'-\ *n* -ES [ME *asbestus* mineral supposed to be inextinguishable when set on fire, alter. (influenced by L & Gk *asbestos*) of *albestron*, prob. fr. MF, alter. (prob. influenced by L *albus* white) of *abeston*, fr. ML *asbeston*, alter. of L *asbestos*, fr. Gk, unslaked lime, fr. *asbestos* inextinguishable, unextinguished, fr. *a-* ²a- + (assumed) *sbestos*, verbal of *sbennynai* to quench, extinguish; akin to Lith *gesti* to be extinguished, Skt *jasate* he is exhausted and perh. to OHG *quist* annihilation, Goth *qistjan* to destroy, Toch B *käs-* to pass out of existence] **1** : a mineral (as chrysotile, tremolite, or actinolite) that readily separates into long flexible fibers suitable for uses where incombustible, nonconducting, or chemically resistant material is required **2 a** : a mineral fiber usu. long, smooth, and white **b** *or* **asbestos yarn** : a yarn usu. made of asbestos or of asbestos and other fibers **3** *or* **asbestos curtain** : a fireproof curtain made of asbestos or other material and used in a theater to close the proscenium opening in case of fire

²**asbestos** \"\ *adj* : made of, containing, or resembling asbestos

asbestos cement *n* : a hardened mixture of asbestos fibers, portland cement, and water used in relatively thin slabs for shingles, wallboard, and siding

as·bes·to·sis \,as,be'stōsəs, ,az-\ *n, pl* **asbesto·ses** \-ō,sēz\ [NL, fr. L *asbestos* + NL *-osis*] : a form of pneumoconiosis caused by the inhalation of fine particles of asbestos

as·bo·lite \'azbə,līt, 'as-\ *also* **as·bo·lan** \-,lan\ *or* **as·bo·lane** \-,lān\ *n* -s [*asbolite*, modif. (influenced by *-ite*) of G *asbolan*, fr. Gk *asbolos* soot + G *-an* -an, -ane; *asbolan*, *asbolane* fr. G *asbolan*; perh. akin to Goth *azgo* ash — more at ASH] : an earthy mineral aggregate containing manganese and cobalt oxides

asc- *or* **asci-** *or* **asco-** *comb form* [NL, fr. *ascus*] : bladder : ascus ⟨ascula⟩ ⟨ascigerous⟩ ⟨ascospore⟩

as·ca·la·bo·ta \,askələ'bōd·ə\ *n pl, cap* [NL, fr. *Ascalabotes*, type genus, fr. Gk *askalabōtēs* spotted lizard] *zool* : a division of Lacertilia comprising the Gekkones, Iguania, and Rhiptoglossa

as·ca·laph·i·dae \,askə'lafə,dē\ *n pl, cap* [NL, fr. *Ascalaphus*, type genus (fr. Gk *askalaphos*, a kind of owl) + *-idae*] : a family of rather large nocturnal insects (order Neuroptera) superficially resembling dragonflies but having long club-tipped antennae

as·caph·i·dae \ə'skafə,dē\ *n pl, cap* [NL, fr. *Ascaphus*, type genus + *-idae*] *in some classifications* : a family of western No. American toads — see ASCAPHUS

as·ca·phus \'askəfəs\ *n, cap* [NL, fr. Gk *askaphos* not dug about, fr. *a-* ²a- + *-skaphos* (fr. *skaptein* to dig); akin to L *capo* capon — more at CAPON] : a genus of western No. American toads including only the bell toad which is distinguished by a taillike copulatory organ in the male cloaca and which is sometimes isolated in a separate family (Ascaphidae) but usu. included in the Liopelmidae

ascared \ə'-\ *adj* [*a-* (as in *afraid*) + *scared*] *chiefly dial* : AFRAID

as·ca·ri·a·sis \,askə'rīəsəs\ *n, pl* **ascaria·ses** \-ə,sēz\ [NL, fr. *Ascaris* + *-iasis*] : infestation with or disease caused by ascarids; *specif* : infestation of the human intestine by the large roundworm (*Ascaris lumbricoides*) usu. accompanied by colicky pains and diarrhea

as·car·i·cid·al \ə¦skarə¦sīdᵊl\ *adj* : capable of destroying ascarids

as·car·i·cide \ə'skarə,sīd\ *n* -s [F, fr. *ascaride* ascarid + *-cide*] : an agent destructive of ascarids

as·ca·rid \'askərəd, -,rid\ *n, pl* **asca·rids** \-dz\ *also* **as·car·i·des** \ə'skarə,dēz\ [LL *ascarid-*, *ascaris* intestinal worm — more at ASCARIS] : a roundworm of the family Ascaridae

as·car·i·dae \ə'skarə,dē\ *n pl, cap* [NL, fr. *Ascarid-*, *Ascaris* type genus + *-idae*] : a large family of nematode worms (superfamily Ascaridoidea) usu. parasitic in the intestines of vertebrates, of large size, and having three well-developed lips and a simple cylindrical esophagus — see ASCARIDIA, ASCARIS

as·car·i·da·ta \ə,skarə'däd·ə, -ād·ə\ [NL, fr. *Ascarid-*, *Ascaris* + *-ata*] *syn of* ASCARIDINA

ascarides *pl of* ASCARID *or of* ASCARIS

as·ca·rid·ia \,askə'ridēə\ *n, cap* [NL, fr. LL *ascarid-*, *ascaris* intestinal worm + NL *-ia*] : a genus of nematode worms (family Ascaridae) including an important intestinal parasite (*A. galli*) of chickens and other domestic fowls and being distinguished from other ascarids by the presence of a preanal sucker — **as·ca·rid·i·al** \;⸗⸗;⸗dēəl\ *adj*

as·car·i·di·a·sis \ə,skarə'dīəsəs\ *also* **as·ca·rid·i·o·sis** \,askə,ridē'ōsəs\ *n, pl* **ascaridia·ses** \-ə,sēz\ *also* **ascaridio·ses** \-ō,sēz\ [NL, fr. *Ascarid-*, *Ascaris* + *-iasis* or *-iosis* (fr. *-i-* + *-osis*)] : ASCARIASIS

as·car·i·di·na \ə,skarə'dīnə\ *n pl, cap* [NL, fr. *Ascarid-*, *Ascaris* + *-ina*] : a suborder of Rhabditida comprising comparatively large nematode worms without a stylet and parasitic in arthropods, mollusks, and vertebrates including man — compare ASCARIDATA

as·car·i·doi·dea \ə'dóidēə\ *n pl, cap* [NL, fr. *Ascarid-*, *Ascaris* + *-oidea*] : a superfamily of Ascaridina comprising polymyarian nematodes (as *Ascaris* and *Heterakis*) with cervical papillae and the esophagus highly muscular

as·car·i·dole \ə'skarə,dōl\ *also* **as·car·i·dol** \-,dól, -ōl\ *n* -s [ISV *ascarid* + *-ole, -ol*] : a liquid terpenoid peroxide $C_{10}H_{16}O_2$ constituting the active anthelmintic and toxic principle of chenopodium oil, made by addition of oxygen to alpha-terpinene, and used as a catalyst in promoting polymerization reactions

as·ca·ris \'askərəs\ *n* [NL, fr. LL *ascaris* intestinal worm, fr. Gk *askaris*; akin to Gk *skairein* to gambol — more at CARDINAL] **1** *cap* : the type genus of Ascaridae comprising nematode worms having a 3-lipped mouth, including the common roundworm (*A. lumbricoides*) parasitic in the human intestines and like an earthworm in size and superficial appearance, and including also many other species that infest animals **2** *pl* **ascar·i·des** \ə'skarə,dēz\ : ASCARID

as·ca·roid \'askə,róid\ *adj* [NL *Ascaroidea*] : of or belonging to the Ascaridoidea

as·ca·roi·dea \,askə'róidēə\ [NL, fr. *Ascaris* + *-oidea*] *syn of* ASCARIDOIDEA

as·ca·rops \'askə,räps\ *n, cap* [NL, fr. LL *ascaris* intestinal worm + NL *-ops*] : a genus of nematode worms (family Spiruridae) that includes a common reddish stomach worm (*A. strongylina*) of wild and domestic swine and is sometimes made type of a separate family

as·cend \ə'send *also* a'-\ *vb* -ED/-ING/-S [ME *ascenden*, fr. L *ascendere, adscendere*, fr. *ad-* + *-scendere* (fr. *scandere* to climb) — more at SCAN] *vi* **1 a** : to move upward : go up sometimes by stages with gradual motion : become raised ⟨~*ed* to Mistover by a circuitous and easy incline —Thomas Hardy⟩ ⟨~ to the roof of her dwelling house —Lafcadio Hearn⟩ **b** : to appear above the horizon and approach the zenith ⟨higher yet that star ~*s* —John Bowring⟩ **c** : to attain height through growth or construction : rise up : TOWER ⟨the city ~*ed* . . . taking the firmness of its foundation for granted —Frederic Beck⟩ ⟨the redwood trees ~ over the others⟩ **d** : to slope upward : lie along a rising slope ⟨the paths ~ through pine woods to the mountain lake⟩ **2 a** : to go up or upward from a lower level or degree : RISE ⟨when man ceases to wander he will cease to ~ in the scale of being —A.N.Whitehead⟩ ⟨doomed always to ~ to power under the worst possible objective conditions —Arthur Koestler⟩ **b** : to go back in time or in order of genealogical succession ⟨female kin in the ~*ing* generations are excluded —Mary Tew⟩ **c** *of a sound* : to rise in pitch ~ *vt* **1** : to go or move up, upon, along, to the top of, or over : CLIMB, MOUNT ⟨began to ~ the vale towards Mistover —Thomas Hardy⟩ ⟨~*ed* the river farther than any white man had been before —L.H.Bolander⟩ **2** : to come to hold or occupy : succeed to ⟨~*ed* the throne on the death of his father⟩

syn MOUNT, CLIMB, SCALE: ASCEND, a general term, lacks vivid connotation; it suggests merely upward movement, often with gradual or steady motion ⟨to *ascend* a mountain⟩ ⟨an *ascending* elevator⟩ MOUNT, in its transitive uses particularly, implies getting up on something raised, something above the ground ⟨to *mount* a horse⟩ ⟨the speaker *mounting* the platform⟩ ⟨the condemned king *mounting* the scaffold⟩ Intransitively, MOUNT is a close synonym for ASCEND ⟨as he proceeded south, his crossness seemed to *mount* with the temperature —Osbert Sitwell⟩ CLIMB may suggest sustained effort to reach a height or to go over something; it is esp. likely to be used in situations involving clambering or scrambling ⟨*climbing* out of the gulch⟩ ⟨*climbing* up the rigging⟩ ⟨*climbing* into the window⟩ SCALE is likely to add to CLIMB notions of dexterity and adroitness, as of an alpinist, athlete, or esp. trained ladderman ⟨*scaling* the highest peaks⟩ ⟨the baron's men *scaling* the ramparts⟩ ⟨a fireman *scaling* the wall⟩ **syn** see in addition RISE

as·cend·ance *also* **as·cend·ence** \ə'sendən(t)s *also* a'-\ *n* -s : ASCENDANCY, LEADERSHIP, DOMINATION

as·cend·an·cy *or* **as·cend·en·cy** \-dənsē, -si\ *n* -ES : the quality or state of being in the ascendant : controlling influence : governing power : DOMINATION ⟨dominant castes seek to retain their ~ —Bertrand Russell⟩ ⟨the growing ~ of brains and skills over capital power —Bud Wilson⟩ ⟨would not patiently submit to the ~ of France —T. B. Macaulay⟩

¹**as·cend·ant** *also* **as·cend·ent** \-dənt\ *n* -S [ME *ascendent*, fr. ML *ascendent-*, *ascendens*, fr. L, pres. part. of *ascendere* to ascend] **1** : the point of the ecliptic or degree of the zodiac that rises above the eastern horizon at any moment (as that of one's birth) **2** : the quality, state, or position of being supreme, dominant, or in power : the point of highest development or influence : PREEMINENCE, SUPERIORITY ⟨men who want the president to fight for this program now appear to be in the ~ —E.K.Lindley⟩ ⟨conservatism was in the ~ —C.L. Jones⟩ **3** : a lineal or collateral relative in the ascending line : one that precedes in genealogical succession : ANCESTOR ⟨nearly the whole of a man's heredity must be supplied by his immediate ~*s* —Havelock Ellis⟩

²**ascendant** *also* **ascendent** \"\ *adj* [ME *ascendent*, fr. L *ascendent-*, *ascendens*] **1 a** : moving or tending upward : RISING ⟨rooted and ~ strength like that of foliage —John Ruskin⟩ **b** : directed upward ⟨an ~ stem⟩ ⟨an ~ leaf⟩ ⟨an ~ inflorescence⟩ **2 a** : in a supreme, dominant, or powerful position : SUPERIOR, PREEMINENT, CONTROLLING ⟨the proletariat, the ~ class —Granville Hicks⟩ **b** : inclined to dominate : DOMINANT ⟨the chief difference between the ~ and nonascendant child was in the amount of self-confidence —K.C.Garrison⟩

as·cend·er \-də(r)\ *n* -s : one that ascends: as **a** : the part of a lowercase letter that exceeds x height (as in "b" or "t") **b** : an ascending letter or character ⟨Aldus used only one size of capitals but they did not reach the height of the lowercase ~*s* —J.C.Oswald⟩

as·cend·ing \(')a¦sendiŋ, ə's-\ *adj* **1** : that ascends : mounting up or sloping upward : RISING **2** : rising upward usu. from a more or less prostrate base or point of attachment ⟨the ~ stems of chickweed⟩ — **as·cend·ing·ly** *adv*

ascending aorta *n* : the part of the aorta from its origin to the beginning of the arch

ascending diphthong *n* : RISING DIPHTHONG

ascending frontal convolution *n* : a frontal convolution lying immediately behind the precentral sulcus

ascending node *n, astron* : the node passed as the body goes north

ascending rhythm *n* : RISING RHYTHM

ascending series *n* **1** : a mathematical series arranged according to the ascending powers of a quantity **2** : a mathematical series in which each term is greater than the preceding

ascends *pres 3d sing of* ASCEND

as·cen·sion \ə'senchən *also* a'-\ *n* -s [ME *ascencioun*, fr. MF & L; MF *ascension* ascension of Jesus into heaven, fr. LL *ascension-*, *ascensio*, fr. L, ascent, fr. *ascensus* (past part. of *ascendere* to ascend) + *-ion-*, *-io* -ion] **1** : the act or process of ascending ⟨balloon ~⟩ ⟨thin ~*s* of smoke from the breached roof —Ambrose Bierce⟩ **2 a** *often cap* : the ascending of Jesus to heaven on the 40th day after his resurrection **b** *usu cap* : ASCENSION DAY **3** *archaic* : DISTILLATION, EVAPORATION

as·cen·sion·al \-chənᵊl, -chnəl\ *adj* : of or relating to ascension or ascent : tending upward

ascension day *n, usu cap A&D* : the Thursday 40 days after Easter on which is commemorated Christ's ascension after his resurrection — called also *Holy Thursday*

as·cen·sion·ist \-ch(ə)nəst\ *n* -s **1** : one that makes ascensions or ascents ⟨a balloon ~⟩ **2** *often cap* : one of a group of 19th century Christians that prepared for the coming of Christ, the end of the world, and the ascension of the faithful; *specif* : MILLERITE

ascensiontide \⸗'⸗⸗,⸗\ *n, usu cap* [*ascension* + *tide*] : the period of 10 days from Ascension Day to Whitsunday

as·cen·sive \(')a¦sen(t)siv, ə's-\ *adj* [*ascension* + *-ive*] **1** : rising or tending to rise : ASCENDING **2** : INTENSIVE 2b

as·cen·sor \ə'sen(t)sə(r), a'-\ *n, pl* **ascenso·res** \,a,sen'sōr,(,)ēz\ [Sp, fr. L, one that ascends, fr. *ascensus* (past part. of *ascendere* to ascend) + *-or* — more at ASCEND] : a nearly vertical funicular railway used on very steep ascents

as·cent \ə'sent *also* a'-\ *n* -s [fr. *ascend*, after E *descend*: *descent*] **1 a** : the act of ascending or rising : a moving or mounting upward ⟨the ~ of vapors from the earth⟩ **b** : a going, traveling, or climbing up (as to the top of a hill or the source of a river) ⟨their ~ of the mountain⟩ ⟨his ~ of the river in a canoe⟩ **c** : the way or means of ascending : an upward slope or rising grade : ACCLIVITY ⟨the ~ by which he goes up on to the roof of the house to get in at the window of his workshop —R.F.Kilvert⟩ **d** : the degree of elevation or upward slope : INCLINATION, GRADIENT ⟨the road has an ~ of six degrees⟩ **2** : a rising or ascending from a lower level or degree : advancement esp. in social status, intellectual achievement, or reputation : PROGRESS ⟨the ~ from the working class to the middle class —Liam O'Flaherty⟩ ⟨the long ages of struggle and ~ —B.N.Cardozo⟩ **3** : a going back in time or upward in order of genealogical succession ⟨any person in the line of ~ from the claimant to the common ancestor —Morris Ploscowe⟩

as·cer·tain \¦asə(r)¦tān, ,aas-\ *vt* -ED/-ING/-S [ME *acertainen*, fr. MF *acertainer, acertener*, fr. OF *acertener*, fr. *a-* (fr. L *ad-*) + *-certener* (fr. *certain*) — more at CERTAIN] **1 a** *obs* : to make (a person) certain, sure, or confident : ASSURE ⟨but how shall I be ~*ed* that I also shall be entertained —John Bunyan⟩ **b** *archaic* : to make (a thing) certain : establish as a certainty : determine with certainty ⟨but who shall exactly ~ to us what superstition is —George Horne †1792⟩ **c** *obs* : to make certain the possession of : SECURE ⟨no diligence can ~ success —Samuel Johnson⟩ **d** *obs* : to bring or deliver (a person) certainly : DESTINE ⟨would ~ us into a possession of all the promises —Jeremy Taylor⟩ **e** *archaic* : to make (a thing) certain, exact, or precise : SETTLE, FIX ⟨some effectual method for correcting, enlarging, and ~*ing* our language —Jonathan Swift⟩ **2** : to find out or learn for a certainty (as by examination or investigation) : make sure of : DISCOVER ⟨a sensitive instrument for ~*ing* the people's ideas and wishes —A.R.Williams⟩ ⟨had ~*ed* . . . that his son-in-law was among the living prisoners —Charles Dickens⟩ **syn** see DISCOVER

as·cer·tain·a·ble \-nəbəl\ *adj* : capable of being ascertained ⟨~ facts⟩ — **as·cer·tain·a·bly** \-əblē, -li\ *adv*

as·cer·tain·ment \,⸗⸗'⸗mənt\ *n* -s : the act of ascertaining: **a** *archaic* : a reducing to certainty : exact determination ⟨that a period might be put and some ~ made and a time fixed —Oliver Cromwell⟩ **b** : a finding out (as by investigation) : DISCOVERY ⟨his work . . . was the ~ of historical truth —Arnold Bennett⟩

as·ce·sis \ə'sēsəs, a'-\ *or* **as·ke·sis** \-'skēsəs\ *n, pl* **asce·ses** *or* **aske·ses** \-ē,sēz\ [LL or Gk; LL, fr. Gk *askēsis*, lit., exercise, fr. *askein* to work, exercise + *-ēsis* -esis] : rigorous training, self-discipline, or self-restraint : ASCETICISM

¹**as·cet·ic** \ə'sed·ik, a'-, -etik\ *also* **as·cet·i·cal** \-ə̇kəl, -ēk-\ *adj* [Gk *askētikos*, lit., laborious, fr. *askētēs* one that exercises, hermit (fr. *askein* to work, exercise) + *-ikos* -ic, -ical] **1** : extremely strict in religious exercises : religiously austere ⟨the monastic profession was then a little more than a vow of celibacy and his devotion took no ~ turn —J.R.Green⟩ **2** : refraining from self-indulgence : SELF-DENYING, SELF-DISCIPLINED, AUSTERE ⟨the severely ~ life and cold personality of the celebrated scholar —Dorothy C. Fisher⟩ **syn** see SEVERE

²**ascetic** \"\ *n* -s **1 a** : one who devotes himself to a life of solitude and contemplation and practices such methods of self-discipline as celibacy, fasting, and self-mortification ⟨the desert was often the abode of the ~*s*⟩ **b** : one who is rigorously strict in religious exercises ⟨his predecessor, Ignatius, a zealous and devout ~ . . . allowed himself to be used by the extremists —R.M.French⟩ **2** : one who leads a life of self-denial, rigorous self-discipline, or austerity ⟨he is no ~ — he loves food and drink and friendly talk —Katherine Simonds⟩

as·cet·i·cal·ly \-ə̇k(ə)lē, -ēk-, -li\ *adv* : in an ascetic manner

ascetical theology *n* : the branch of Roman Catholic theology that deals with the practice of virtue and the means of attaining holiness and perfection

as·cet·i·cism \-ə,sizəm\ *n* -s **1 a** : the condition, practice, or mode of life of an ascetic : rigorous abstention from self-indulgence ⟨his direction toward a life of ~ and contemplation was already clear —W.P.Clancy⟩ **b** : a disciplinary course of conduct in which certain actions (as contemplation and fasting) are performed for their intellectual, moral, or religious effect ⟨for the Catholic ~ of poverty the Protestant substituted the ~ of work —Stringfellow Barr⟩ **2** : the doctrine that through the renunciation of the desires of the flesh and of pleasure in worldly things and through self-mortification or self-denial one can subdue his appetites and discipline himself so as to reach a high spiritual or intellectual state ⟨the Greek ideal was far removed from ~ —G.L.Dickinson⟩

aschaf·fite \ə'sha,fīt\ *n* -s [G *aschaffit*, fr. *Aschaffenburg*, Bavaria, Germany, its locality + G *-it* -ite] : a lamprophyric dike rock that is related to the quartz-diorites and contains phenocrysts of quartz, plagioclase, and biotite

as·cham \'askəm\ *n* -s [after Roger *Ascham* †1568 Eng. scholar, author of a treatise on archery] : a tall narrow locker or box in which bows and arrows are kept

asc·hel·min·thes \,ask,hel'min,thēz, ,a,skel-\ *n pl, cap* [NL, fr. *asc-* + *Helminthes*] *in some classifications* : a phylum of pseudocoelomate animals including the Rotifera, Gastrotricha, Kinorhyncha, Nematoda, Nematomorpha, and sometimes the Acanthocephala all of which are sometimes regarded as independent phyla — compare ENTOPROCTA

asch·er·so·nia \,ashə(r)'sōnyə\ *n, cap* [NL, fr. Paul F. A. *Ascherson* †1913 Ger. botanist + NL *-ia*] : a genus of imperfect fungi (family Phyllostictaceae) parasitic on whiteflies and soft scales and characterized by development of characteristic often highly colored stromata in which conidia and occas. later ascospores of the perfect stage are produced

asch·heim-zon·dek test \'ä,shīm'z¦ändik-, 'ash,hīm-, -m'ts|,|ōn-, -dek-\ *n, usu cap A&Z* [after Selmar *Aschheim* b1878 and Bernhard *Zondek* b1891 Ger. gynecologists] : a test used (1) to determine human pregnancy in its early stages on the basis of the effect of a subcutaneous injection of the patient's urine on the ovaries of an immature female mouse or (2) to diagnose the presence in a man or woman of a tumor containing embryonic elements (as choriocarcinoma)

aschistic \(')ā+¦⸗⸗\ *adj* [²*a-* + *schistic*] *of rock* : not differentiated — opposed to *diaschistic*

aschi·za \ə'skīzə\ *n pl, cap* [NL, fr. ²*a-* + Gk *schiza* splinter] : a group of cyclorrhaphous Diptera comprising two-winged flies (as syrphus flies) that lack a lunule and do not suck blood

aschoff body *or* **aschoff nodule** \'ä,shóf-\ *n, usu cap A* [after Ludwig *Aschoff* †1942 Ger. pathologist] : one of the tiny lumps consisting of swollen collagen, cells, and fibrils found in the heart muscle and typical of rheumatic heart disease; *also* : one of the similar but larger lumps found under the skin esp. in rheumatic fever or polyarthritis

asci *pl of* **ascus**

asci- — see ASC-

as·ci·an \'ash(ē)ən\ *n* -s [L *ascius* (fr. Gk *askios*, fr. *a-* ²a- + *skia* shadow) + E *-an* — more at SCENE] : one that has no shadow; *specif* : an inhabitant of the torrid zone where the sun is vertical at noon for a few days every year

ascidi- *or* **ascidio-** *comb form* [NL, fr. ²*Ascidia* & *ascidium*] : ascidian ⟨ascidiozooid⟩ : ascidium ⟨ascidiferous⟩

¹**as·cid·ia** \ə'sidēə, a'-\ *n, cap* [NL, fr. Gk *askidion* little wineskin + NL *-ia* — more at ASCIDIUM] : a genus of simple ascidians now restricted to a few typical species or replaced by *Phallusia* but formerly including all the simple Ascidiacea

²**ascidia** \"\ [NL, fr. Gk *askidia*, pl. of *askidion*] *syn of* UROCHORDA

as·cid·i·a·cea \⸗,⸗⸗'āshēə\ *n pl, cap* [NL, fr. ¹*Ascidia* + *-acea*] : an order of tunicates comprising simple ascidians, compound ascidians that reproduce by budding and remain connected together embedded in a common test, and certain atypical pelagic compound ascidians (as of the genus *Pyrosoma*)

as·cid·i·ae \⸗'⸗dē,ē\ [NL, fr. pl. of ¹*Ascidia*] *syn of* ASCIDIACEA

as·cid·i·an \-ēən\ *n* -s [NL ²*Ascidia* + E *-an*] : a simple or compound tunicate of the order Ascidiacea suggesting as a larva a minute active tadpole with an elongated tail that contains a distinct notochord and dorsal nerve chord showing obvious relationship to the vertebrates but as an adult lacking the tail and being reduced to a sessile saclike form with an anterior branchial opening through which water passes to a branchial sac having perforated walls which strain microscopic food into the digestive tract before the water emerges by way of an atrium and dorsal atrial opening; *broadly* : TUNICATE

as·cid·i·ar·i·um \⸗,⸗dē'a(a)rēəm\ *n, pl* **ascidiar·ia** \-ēə\ [NL, fr. *ascidi-* + *-arium*] : an entire compound ascidian

¹**as·cid·i·ate** \⸗'⸗dēət, -ē,āt\ *adj* [*ascidi-* + *-ate*] : resembling an ascidian

²**ascidiate** \"\ *adj* [NL *ascidium* + E *-ate*] : having ascidia

as·ci·dic·o·lous \,asə'dikələs\ *adj* [*ascidi-* + *-colous*] : commensal with or parasitic in an ascidian

as·cid·i·form \ə'sidə,fórm, a'-\ *adj* [ISV *ascidi-* + *-form*] **1** : shaped like a pitcher ⟨an ~ leaf⟩ **2** : shaped like an ascidian or an ascidium

as·cid·i·oi·da \ə,sidē'óidə, a,-\ *or* **as·cid·i·oi·dea** \-dēə\ [NL, fr. *ascidi-* + *-oida, -oidea*] *syn of* ASCIDIACEA

as·cid·i·ol·o·gy \-ˈälәjē\ *n* -ES [*ascidi-* + *-logy*] **:** a branch of zoology that deals with the Ascidiacea or broadly the Urochorda

as·cid·i·o·zoa \-dēәˈzōә\ [NL, fr. *ascidi-* + *-zoa*] *syn of* UROCHORDA

as·cid·i·o·zo·oid \⸗,⸗⸗⸗ˈzōȯid\ *n* -S [*ascidi-* + *zooid*] **:** one of the individual zooids of a compound ascidian

as·cid·i·um \әˈsidēәm, aˈ-\ *n, pl* **ascid·ia** \-ēә\ [NL, fr. Gk *askidion* little wineskin, fr. *askos* wineskin + *-idion* -idium] **:** a pitcher-shaped or flask-shaped organ or appendage of a plant (as the leaf of the pitcher plant)

as·cig·er·ous \aˈsijәrәs\ *also* **as·cif·er·ous** \aˈsifәr-\ *a* [*asc-* + *-gerous* or *-ferous*] **:** bearing or associated with asci ⟨an ~ fruit⟩

as·ci·tes \әˈsīd·ēz, aˈ-\ *n, pl* **ascites** [ME *aschytes*, fr. LL *ascites*, fr. Gk *askitēs*, fr. *askos* wineskin, bladder, belly — more at ASCUS] **:** the abnormal accumulation of serous fluid in the abdominal cavity — called also *hydroperitoneum;* compare EDEMA — **as·cit·ic** \-ˈsid·ik\ *adj*

as·ci·ti·tious \ˌasәˈtishәs\ *var of* ADSCITITIOUS

¹as·cle·pi·ad \әˈsklēpēˌad, aˈ-, -ēˌad\ *n* -S *usu cap* [Gk *asklēpiadeios*, fr. *asklēpiadeios* asclepiadean, fr. *Asklēpiadēs* Asclepiades, 3d cent. B.C. Greek poet] **:** a Greek lyric verse that extends a glyconic base by repetition of the choriambic cadence (1) once before the final iambus (as ‒‒‒∪∪‒‒∪∪‒∪‒) or (2) twice (as ‒‒‒∪∪‒‒∪∪‒‒∪∪‒∪‒) — called also respectively (1) *lesser asclepiad, minor asclepiad;* (2) *greater asclepiad, major asclepiad*

²asclepiad \"\ *n* -S [NL *Asclepiad-, Asclepias*] **:** a plant of the family Asclepiadaceae

as·cle·pi·a·da·ce·ae \⸗,⸗⸗әˈdāsēˌē\ *n pl, cap* [NL, fr. *Asclepiad-, Asclepias*, type genus + *-aceae*] **:** a widely distributed family of herbs or shrubs (order Gentianales) mostly with milky juice and with umbellate flowers that have a prominent corona between corolla and stamens — see MILKWEED — **as·cle·pi·a·da·ceous** \⸗¦⸗⸗⸗¦⸗shәs\ *adj*

¹as·cle·pi·a·de·an \⸗¦⸗⸗әˈdēәn\ *or* **as·cle·pi·ad·ic** \-ˈadik\ *adj, usu cap* [LL *asclepiadeus, asclepiadius* asclepiadean (fr. Gk *asklēpiadeios*) + E *-an* or *-ic*] **1 :** relating to the Greek poet Asclepiades of Samos **2 :** relating to, containing, or consisting of asclepiads

²asclepiadean \"\ *or* **asclepiadic** \"\ *n* -S *usu cap* **1 :** ASCLEPIAD **2 :** a distich or strophe constructed with asclepiads

as·cle·pi·as \әˈsklēpēәs, aˈ-\ *n* [NL, fr. L, swallowwort (*Cynanchum vincetoxicum*), fr. Gk *asklēpias*, fr. *Asklēpios*, physician-hero of Greek myth sometimes worshiped as god of healing] **1** *cap* **:** a genus (the type of the family Asclepiadaceae) of perennial herbs found chiefly in No. America with flowers having a corona of five concave hoods each of which bears a slender horn — see BUTTERFLY WEED, MILKWEED **2** -ES **:** a plant of the genus *Asclepias* **3** -ES **a :** the dried root of the butterfly weed formerly used as a diaphoretic and expectorant — called also *pleurisy root* **b :** the root of the swamp milkweed used similarly

as·cle·pi·o·do·ra \⸗,⸗⸗әˈdōrә\ *n, cap* [prob. irreg. fr. *Asclepias*] **:** a genus of American plants (family Asclepiadaceae) with alternate leaves and a crest on each hood of the corona

asco- — see ASC-

as·co·carp \ˈaskәˌkärp\ *n* -S [*asc-* + *-carp*] **:** the mature fruiting body of an ascomycetous fungus; *broadly* **:** such a body including the enclosed asci, spores, and paraphyses — see ASCOMA; compare APOTHECIUM, PERITHECIUM — **as·co·car·pous** \ˌ⸗⸗¦kärpәs\ *adj*

as·coch·y·ta \aˈskäkәd·ә\ *n, cap* [NL, fr. *asc-* + *-chyta* (prob. fr. Gk. *chytos* poured, verbal of *chein* to pour) — more at FOUND] **:** a form genus of imperfect fungi (order Sphaeropsidales) with hyaline 2-celled pycnospores formed in pycnidia located in discolored spots in leaves, stems, or fruits

as·cog·e·nous \aˈskäjәnәs\ *adj* [*asc-* + *-genous*] **:** of, relating to, or producing asci

as·co·go·ni·al \ˌaskәˈgōnēәl\ *adj* [NL *ascogonium* + E *-al*] **:** of or relating to an ascogonium

as·co·go·ni·um \ˌ⸗⸗ˈgōnēәm\ *also* **as·co·gone** \ˈ⸗⸗ˌgōn\ *n, pl* **ascogo·nia** \-ˈgōnēә\ *also* **ascogones** [NL *ascogonium*, fr. *asc-* + *gonium*] **:** the female sexual organ in many ascomycetous fungi consisting of a single cell or a group of cells — compare ARCHICARP

as·co·li·chen \ˌaskōˈlīkәn\ *n* -S [NL *Ascolichenes*] **:** a lichen of the group Ascolichenes — compare BASIDIOLICHEN

as·co·li·che·nes \¦⸗⸗ˌlīˈkē(ˌ)nēz\ *n pl, cap* [NL, fr. *asc-* + *Lichenes*] **:** a group of lichens comprising all those in which the fungous component is an ascomycete — compare BASIDIOLICHENES, DISCOLICHEN, PYRENOLICHEN

as·co·ma \aˈskōmә\ *n, pl* **ascoma·ta** \-mәd·ә\ [NL, fr. Gk *askōma* leather lining protecting the aperture for the oar, fr. *askos* wineskin — more at ASCUS] **:** an ascocarp having the hymenium on a broadly expanded or disklike receptacle esp. characteristic of the order Helvellales; *specif* **:** the simple type of fruiting body made up of an undifferentiated mass of tissue on or in which the asci are borne

as·co·my·cete \ˌaskōˈmīˌsēt, -ˌmīˈsēt\ *n* -S [NL *Ascomycetes*] **:** a fungus of the class Ascomycetes

as·co·my·ce·tes \-ˌmīˈsēd·ēz\ *n pl, cap* [NL, fr. *asc-* + *-mycetes*] **:** a large class of higher fungi distinguished by having septate hyphae and spores formed in asci and comprising the two subclasses Hemiascomycetes and Euascomycetes and in some classifications also the subclass Protoascomycetes and many orders, mainly in the Euascomycetes — **as·co·my·ce·tous** \¦⸗⸗,⸗¦sēd·әs\ *adj*

¹as·con \ˈaˌskän\ *n* -S [NL, fr. Gk *askos* wineskin] **:** a sponge or sponge larva having incurrent canals that lead directly to the paragaster — compare LEUCON, SYCON — **as·co·noid** \ˈaskәˌnȯid\ *adj or n*

²ascon \äskōⁿ\ *n* -S [origin unknown] **:** a Haitian voodoo fetish made of a gourd entwined with snake vertebrae and beads and shaken to summon the gods

¹as·co·nes \aˈskō(ˌ)nēz\ [NL, fr. pl. of ¹*ascon*] *syn of* ASCONOSA

²ascones \"\ *n pl* [NL, pl. of ¹*ascon*] **1 :** the ascon sponges **2** *cap* **:** a suborder of Homocoela

as·co·no·sa \ˌaskәˈnōsә\ *n pl, cap* [NL, fr. ¹*ascon* + *-osa* (neut. pl. of L *-osus* -ose)] **:** an order of Calcispongiae comprising simple asconoid sponges and others derived from this type — compare LEUCETTA

3 1 2 4

diagram of canal system of an ascon type of sponge: *1* gastral layer, *2* dermal layer, *3* osculum, *4* gastral cavity

a-scope \ˈāˌskōp\ *n, usu cap A* [¹*A* + *-scope*] **:** a radarscope on which signals appear as displacements of the trace and indicate only range of the target — compare B-SCOPE

as·co·phore \ˈaskәˌfō(ә)r\ *n* -S [prob. fr. F, fr. *asc-* + *-phore*] **1 :** an ascus-bearing hypha **2 :** ASCOCARP

as·coph·o·rous \(ˈ)a¦skäfәrәs\ *adj* **:** ASCOGENOUS

as·co·phyl·lum \ˌaskәˈfilәm\ *n, cap* [NL, fr. *asc-* + *-phyllum*] **:** a genus of brown algae (family Fucaceae) distinguished by clavate, compressed, or somewhat inflated branchlets scattered along the axis and constituting with *Fucus* the bladder⸗bearing rockweeds of the northern Atlantic coast of which some species are used in the kelp industry

ascor·bate \äˈskȯrbәt\ *n* -S [*ascorbic* + *-ate*] **:** a salt of ascorbic acid

ascor·bic acid \әˈskȯrbik-\ *n* [²*a-* + NL *scorbutus* scurvy + E *-ic* — more at SCORBUTIC] **1 :** a crystalline water-soluble vitamin $C_6H_8O_6$ that occurs esp. in fruits (as citrus fruits, tomatoes), vegetables (as leafy vegetables, new potatoes), and fresh tea leaves, that is usu. obtained commercially from sorbitol by a series of synthetic steps, that is a strong reducing agent and is reversibly oxidized to dehydroascorbic acid, and that is used chiefly in the prevention and cure of scurvy and in antioxidants for food; an enolic lactone of a 2- or 3-keto aldonic acid related to xylose — called also *L-ascorbic acid, vitamin C, L-xylo-ascorbic acid* **2 :** any of several enolic lactones of keto aldonic acids that are stereoisomers of ascorbic acid

as·co·spore \ˈaskәˌspō(ә)r\ *n* -S [prob. fr. F *ascospore*, fr. *asc-* + *spore*] **:** one of the spores contained in an ascus and upon germination usu. producing mycelium upon which sexual organs are developed — **as·co·spor·ic** \ˌ⸗⸗¦spōrik\ *adj* — **as·co·spor·ous** \ˌaskә¦spōrәs, (ˈ)a¦skäspәr-\ *adj*

as·cot \ˈaskәt, ˈaas-, -ˌskät\ *n* -S *often attrib* [fr. *Ascot* Heath, fashionable racetrack near Ascot, village in Berkshire, England; fr. the neckwear worn by men of fashion there] **1 :** a broad necktie whose usu. square ends are tied in a knot, crossed diagonally, and then pinned **2 :** a broad neck scarf that is looped under the chin and sometimes secured by a pin

ascot 2

as·co·tho·rac·i·ca \ˌaskōthәˈrasәkә\ *n pl, cap* [NL, fr. *asc-* + *Thoracica*] **:** a minor order or suborder of small hermaphrodite barnacles that live enveloped in a soft mantle and partly buried in other animals (as black corals)

ascot tan *n, often cap A* **:** COCONUT 4

as·crib·a·ble \әˈskrībәbәl *also* aˈ-\ *adj* **:** capable of being ascribed **:** ATTRIBUTABLE ⟨punctuation errors ~ to careless proofreading⟩

as·cribe \әˈskrīb *also* aˈ-\ *vt* -ED/-ING/-S [ME *ascriben*, alter. (influenced by L *ascribere*) of *ascriven*, fr. MF *ascrivre*, fr. L *ascribere, adscribere* to ascribe, add to, fr. *ad-* + *scribere* to write — more at SCRIBE] **1 :** to refer esp. to a supposed cause, source, or author **:** ASSIGN, ATTRIBUTE ⟨it is conventional to ~ this mastery to the development of scientific method —P.W.Bridgman⟩ ⟨in so far as we can ~ those changes to individuals —Christopher Hollis⟩ **2** *obs* **:** to add in writing **:** SUBSCRIBE **3** *obs* **:** INSCRIBE, DEDICATE

syn ATTRIBUTE, ASSIGN, REFER, CREDIT, ACCREDIT, IMPUTE, CHARGE: ASCRIBE may suggest tentative, conjectural, inferential, or accustomed indication of cause or characteristic ⟨they have *ascribed* their victories — in superstitious terms — to the operations of fortune —A.J.Toynbee⟩ ⟨disinclined to *ascribe* to her more than an indiscreet friendship with Wildeve —Thomas Hardy⟩ ATTRIBUTE may imply less of the tentative than ASCRIBE; in its suggestion it falls between ASCRIBE and ASSIGN ⟨this knowledge was partly communicated by visions and revelations, to which St. Paul *attributed* some importance —W.R.Inge⟩ ⟨the French had then given up their conventional trick of *attributing* Eleanor's acts to her want of morals —Henry Adams⟩ ASSIGN may suggest the certainty and definiteness of cause, characterization, or placement that comes with deliberate consideration ⟨more than one rejoinder declared that the importance I here *assigned* to criticism was excessive —Matthew Arnold⟩ ⟨they bore a strong likeness to the poems of Henry Vaughan the Silurist, and he concluded that they must be *assigned* to Vaughan —A.T.Quiller-Couch⟩ REFER, now less frequent in this sense, suggests explaining or characterizing by adducing an ultimate cause of major significance or by subsuming in a comprehensive group ⟨I am convinced that at least one half of their bad manners may be *referred* to their education —A.T.Quiller-Couch⟩ CREDIT and ACCREDIT usu. suggest favorable ascription bringing credit, although they may be used in unfavorable situations ⟨I am sure both parties *credited* them with too much idealism and too little plain horse sense —Rose Macaulay⟩ ⟨literary style . . . is *credited* with being a mysterious preservative for subject matter which no longer interests —T.S.Eliot⟩ ⟨several Bangor houses have been *accredited* to Bulfinch —*Amer. Guide Series: Maine*⟩ IMPUTE is likely to be used with discreditable ascription ranging from accusation to implication ⟨you *imputed* mean motives to them for giving such advice and cowardice to me for listening to them —Oscar Wilde⟩ ⟨no one should . . . find it necessary to *impute* to the critic . . . a puritanic way —F.R. Leavis⟩ Unlike IMPUTE, CHARGE always suggests unfavorable ascription, usu. in direct accusation ⟨the tyrannies . . . *charged* upon the New England oligarchy —V.L.Parrington⟩ ⟨crimes as base as any *charged* on me —William Cowper⟩

as·crip·tion \әˈskripshәn *also* aˈ-\ *n* -S [LL *ascription-, ascriptio*, fr. L, written addition, fr. *ascriptus* (past part. of *ascribere* to ascribe, add in writing) + *-ion-, -io* -ion] **1 :** the act of ascribing ⟨the common ~ of special religiousness to the middle ages —G.C.Sellery⟩ **2 :** a statement or declaration that ascribes ⟨"most gracious" as an ~ applied to the king first appears in the litany in 1559 —F.H.A.Micklewright⟩; *specif* **:** a form of prayer ascribing praise to God spoken by a minister usu. after the sermon **3 :** the quality or state of being adscript

ascrip·tive \әˈskriptiv *also* aˈ-\ *adj* [L *ascriptivus, adscriptivus*, fr. *ascriptus, adscriptus* + *-ivus* -ive] **:** relating to or involving ascription; *specif* **:** entailing elements that attribute or impute rather than factually describe ⟨some ethical statements have a noncognitive function in the sense of being emotive or ~⟩

as·cu·la \ˈaskyәlә\ *n, pl* **ascu·lae** \-ˌlē, -ˌlī\ [NL, fr. *asc-* + *-ula*] **:** OLYNTHUS

as·cus \ˈaskәs\ *n, pl* **as·ci** \ˈaˌsī, ˈaˌskē\ [NL, fr. Gk *askos* wineskin, bladder, belly; prob. akin to Skt *atka* garment] **:** the membranous oval or tubular spore sac in fungi of the class Ascomycetes that is produced either directly from the fertilized ascogonium or from ascogenous hyphae produced therefrom and that bears within it, following nuclear fusion, ascospores, typically eight in number — compare APOTHECIUM, ASCOCARP, PERITHECIUM

ascy·phous \(ˈ)ā¦sīfәs\ *adj* [²*a-* + NL *scyphus*] **:** having no scyphi

as·cy·rum \әˈsīrәm, ˈasәrәm\ *n, cap* [NL, fr. Gk *askyron* St.-John's-wort] **:** a genus of American subshrubs (family Hypericaceae) having short leafy branches, yellow flowers, and one-celled capsular fruit — see SAINT-PETER'S-WORT

as·dic \ˈazˌdik\ *n* -S [*Anti-Submarine Detection Investigation Committee*] **:** SONAR

-ase \ˌās\ *n suffix* -S [F, fr. *diastase*] **:** enzyme **:** destroying substance ⟨aureomycin*ase*⟩ ⟨prote*ase*⟩ ⟨ure*ase*⟩

a-sea \әˈ-\ *adv* [¹*a-* + *sea*] **:** at sea **:** SEAWARD

aseel *or* **asil** \әˈsē(ә)l\ *n* -S *often cap* [prob. native name in India] **:** MALAY 3

aseethe \әˈ-\ *adj* [¹*a-* + *seethe*, v.] **:** SEETHING

aseismatic \ˌā+,⸗¦⸗⸗\ *adj* [²*a-* + Gk *seismat-, seisma* shaking + E *-ic* — more at SEISMATICAL] **:** withstanding or mitigating the effects of earthquake shocks

aseismic \(ˈ)ā+¦⸗⸗\ *adj* [ISV ²*a-* + *seismic*] **1 :** not subject to earthquakes ⟨an ~ region⟩ **2 :** resisting the destructive forces of earthquakes — **aseismicity** \ˌā+,-\ *n* -ES

ase·i·ty \āˈsēәd·ē, әˈ-\ *also* **ase·i·tas** \-ēәˌtas\ *n, pl* **asei·ties** \-әd·ēz\ *also* **aseita·tes** \(ˌ)⸗,⸗әˈtād·ēz\ [ML *aseitas*, fr. L *a se* from oneself (fr. *a, ab* from + *se* oneself) + *-itas* -ity — more at OF, SUICIDE] **:** the quality or state of being self-derived or self-originated; *specif* **:** the absolute self-sufficiency, independence, and autonomy of God

asel·late \(ˈ)ā¦selәt, (ˈ)āˈseˌlāt\ *adj* [²*a-* + L *sella* saddle + E *-ate* — more at SETTLE] *paleontol* **:** without saddles — used specif. of the simplest known ammonoid suture

asel·li·dae \әˈselәˌdē\ *n pl, cap* [NL, fr. *Asellus*, type genus + *-idae*] **:** a family of chiefly freshwater isopod crustaceans having terminal biramous uropods and a single shieldlike plate covering the abdomen

asel·lus \әˈselәs\ *n* [NL, fr. L, small ass, dim. of *asinus* ass — more at ASS] **1** *cap* **:** the type genus of Asellidae **2** *pl* **asel·li** \-ˌlī, -ˌlē\ **:** an isopod of the genus *Asellus* or of the family Asellidae

asepsis \(ˈ)ā+\ *n, pl* **asepses** [NL, fr. ²*a-* + *sepsis*] **1 :** the quality or state of being aseptic — compare ANTISEPSIS **2 :** the methods of making or keeping aseptic

aseptate \(ˈ)ā+\ *adj* [²*a-* + *septate*] **:** not septate

aseptic \(ˈ)ā+¦-\ *adj* [ISV ²*a-* + *septic*] **1 :** preventing or not involving infection ⟨an ~ wound⟩; *specif* **:** free or freed from pathogenic microorganisms by special methods ⟨~ surgery⟩ ⟨instruments sterilized by heat are ~⟩ — compare ANTISEPTIC **2 a :** lacking vitality, emotion, or warmth ⟨the bureaucrat's world is prim and proper and ~ —R.M.Weaver⟩ **b :** DETACHED, OBJECTIVE ⟨the more ~ idealism of the social philosopher —H.L.Smith⟩ **c :** CLEANSING, PURIFYING ⟨~ laughter to cut through . . . fears —*Saturday Night*⟩ — **aseptically** *adv*

asexual \(ˈ)ā+\ *adj* [²*a-* + *sexual*] **:** not sexual: **a :** having no sex or functional sexual organs **b :** produced without sexual action or differentiation ⟨an ~ spore⟩ **c :** not relating to sex — **asexually** \(ˈ)ā+¦-\ *adv*

asexual generation *n* **:** the generation that reproduces only by asexual processes — used of plants or animals exhibiting alternation of generations; compare SEXUAL REPRODUCTION

asexuality \ˌā+\ *n* -ES [ISV *asexual* + *-ity*] **:** absence of sex

asexualization \ˌā+\ *n* -S [²*a-* + *sexualization*] **:** the act or process of rendering incapable of reproduction **:** STERILIZATION, CASTRATION

asexual reproduction *n* **:** a process of reproduction (as cell division, spore formation, fission, or budding) that does not involve or directly follow the union of individuals or germ cells of two different sexes — compare ALTERNATION OF GENERATIONS

asexual spore *n* **:** a spore produced by cell division or encystment and capable of developing without conjugation into a new individual (as the spores developed by a sporophyte)

as far as *conj* **:** to the degree or extent that ⟨*as far as* I know, he can come⟩

asfetida *var of* ASAFETIDA

as for \ˈazfә(r), ˌәzfә(r)\ *prep* **:** with reference to **:** CONCERNING ⟨*as for* me, give me liberty —Patrick Henry⟩

asgd *abbr* assigned

¹ash \ˈash, ˈaa(ә)sh, ˈaish\ *n* -ES [ME *asshe*, fr. OE *æsc;* akin to OHG *ask* ash, ON *askr*, L *ornus* wild mountain ash, Gk *oxyē* beech, Lith *uosis* ash] **1 :** a tree of the genus *Fraxinus* — see TREE illustration **2 :** the wood of ash which is tough and elastic and is used esp. to make tool handles, skis, and bats **3 :** any of numerous Australian trees of various genera (as *Acronychia, Alphitonia, Cupania, Elaeocarpus, Eucalyptus, Flindersia, Litsea, Malaisia, Panax*, and *Schizomeria*) having tough strong wood — see BLACK ASH, BLUE ASH, MOUNTAIN ASH **4** [OE *æsc*, name of the corresponding runic letter] **:** the ligature æ used in Old English to represent a low front vowel

²ash \"\ *adj* **1 :** of or relating to the ash **2 :** made of ash wood

³ash \"\ *n* -ES *often attrib* [ME *asshe*, fr. OE *asce, æsce;* akin to OHG *asca* ash, ON *aska*, Goth *azgo*, L *arēre* to be dry — more at ARDOR] **1 a :** the earthy or mineral residue that remains after combustible substances (as coal) have been thoroughly burned — usu. used in pl. ⟨carried the ~*es* from the cellar to the alley⟩ **b :** the solid residue of nonvolatile oxides or salts of metals (as sodium, calcium, magnesium, iron) or of nonmetallic atoms (as silica) or of pure metal (as platinum) left when combustible substances (as plants, foods) have been thoroughly oxidized (as by nitric acid or some other wet oxidizing agent) and frequently used in quantitative analysis as a measure of the mineral-matter content of the original material **c :** fine particles of mineral matter ejected from a volcanic vent during an explosive eruption ⟨lava may be blown out as fragments by explosions of steam, to fall as dust, ~, and cinders —L.V.Pirsson⟩ **d :** SODA ASH — used chiefly commercially **2 ashes** *pl* **:** the ruins or remains of anything that has been destroyed esp. by fire **:** the last traces ⟨a new city was built on the ~*es* of the old⟩ **3 ashes** *pl* **a :** whatever remains after the cremation or disintegration of the human body ⟨having collected from the funeral pile the ~*es* of her lover —Lafcadio Hearn⟩ **b :** man or his body as mortal or subject to decay ⟨we are ~*es* and dust —Alfred Tennyson⟩ **4 ashes** *pl* **:** something that symbolizes grief, repentance, or humiliation ⟨there was room for an innocent mistake but he cast ~*es* on his head that it should have happened to Mr. Tibbets —John Buchan⟩ **5 a ashes** *pl* **:** deathlike pallor ⟨the lip of ~*es* and the cheek of flame —Lord Byron⟩ **b ashes** *pl but sing in constr* **:** a light brownish gray that is paler than slate gray and redder and darker than silver gray **c :** ASH GRAY **6 ashes** *pl* **:** the mythical symbol of supremacy contested for in Australia-versus-England cricket test matches ⟨England . . . retains the ~*es* —*Australian Weekly Rev.*⟩

⁴ash \"\ *vt* -ED/-ING/-ES **1 :** to sprinkle with ashes ⟨the corn was ~*ed* to keep away weevils⟩ **2 :** to convert into ash **:** burn to ashes ⟨the bones were ~*ed* in a furnace⟩ **3 :** to buff or scour with a wet paste of pumice or other abrasive

ashake \әˈ-\ *adj* [¹*a-* + *shake*, v.] **:** SHAKING ⟨their long manes ~ —W.B.Yeats⟩

ashamed \әˈshāmd\ *adj* [ME, fr. OE *āscamod*, past part. of *āscamian* to shame, fr. *ā-* (perfective prefix) + *scamian* to shame — more at ABEAR, SHAME] **1 a :** feeling shame **:** humiliated or disconcerted by feelings of guilt, disgrace, or impropriety about something discreditable or indecorous ⟨rather ~ that on my first appearance I had stayed so late —Scott Fitzgerald⟩ — usu. used predicatively **b :** ill at ease or subdued by feelings of inferiority or unworthiness ⟨they can't afford the stalls and are ~ to be seen in the gallery —G.B. Shaw⟩ **2 :** restrained by anticipation of feelings of shame **:** reluctant or unwilling to undertake an action likely to involve shame ⟨he looked at his own shabby person and was ~ to enter —Sherwood Anderson⟩ **3** *chiefly Midland* **:** TIMID, BASHFUL

syn MORTIFIED, CHAGRINED: MORTIFIED and CHAGRINED also apply to feelings and situations involving embarrassment and humiliation. ASHAMED stresses regretful feelings of guilt, discredit, or disgrace at one's own or another's shameful or discreditable actions, behavior, or condition ⟨you were *ashamed* because you had gone against the community judgment —Mary Austin⟩ ⟨the hunter, who is *ashamed* if he does not hit his quarry in the appointed, difficult, and honorable spot —Margaret Mead⟩ ⟨Catherine, recollecting herself, grew *ashamed* of her eagerness —Jane Austen⟩ ⟨I have been *ashamed* of your moroseness there! Your manners have been of that silent and sullen and hangdog kind —Charles Dickens⟩ MORTIFIED suggests sorry or resentful hurt pride at being put into a false and embarrassing but not necessarily shameful position ⟨*mortified* at finding the house shut —Harriet Martineau⟩ CHAGRINED stresses the feeling of vexation at a rebuff or disappointment ⟨"you've done your best, Blundell, but I think we had better hand the thing over . . . to Scotland Yard. . .". Mr. Blundell looked *chagrined* —Dorothy Sayers⟩ ⟨Tony, somewhat *chagrined* at his mistake, said he should like to see the other pictures —Archibald Marshall⟩

ashamed·ly \-mәdlē, -li\ *adv* **:** in an embarrassed manner

ashamed·ness \-mәdnәs, -m(d)n-\ *n* -ES **:** the quality or state of being ashamed

ashan·go \әˈshaŋ(ˌ)gō\ *n, pl* **ashango** *or* **ashangos** *usu cap* **1 :** a pygmy people of central Africa **2 :** a member of the Ashango people

ashan·ti \әˈshantē, -aan-,-ain-,-än-,-än-; aˈshan-, -aan-,-ain-; äˈshän-; äˈshän-\ *also* **asan·te** \-ˈsantē, -saan-,-sain-,-sän-, -sän-\ *n, pl* **ashanti** *or* **ashantis** *also* **asante** *or* **asantes** *usu cap* [Ashanti *Asanˈteˈ*] **1 :** a West African people that are divided into various tribes organized as a kingdom in Ghana and that are skilled in cotton weaving, goldbeating and gold casting, and agriculture **2 :** a dialect of Akan spoken by the Ashanti people

ashanti pepper *n, usu cap A* **:** AFRICAN CUBEB

ash·ʽa·rite *or* **ash·a·rite** \ˈashәˌrīt\ *n* -S *cap* [Ali al-*Ashʽari* †935 Muslim theologian + E *-ite*] **:** an adherent of the doctrine of al-Ashʽari, who reconciled a dialectic method with orthodox beliefs to form a scholasticism of primary importance in Islam

a sharp \ˈā+ˈ-\ *n, usu cap A* **1 :** the keynote of A-sharp minor **2 :** the tone a half step above A

a-sharp minor \ˈ⸗,⸗ˈ⸗⸗\ *n, usu cap A* **:** the minor musical key having a signature of seven sharps

ash-blonde \ˈ⸗¦⸗\ *adj* [³*ash*] *of hair* **:** light in color without reddish tint or tinge **:** pale blonde

ash borer *n* [¹*ash*] **:** any of various insect larvae that bore in the wood of ash trees; *esp* **:** a larval clearwing (*Podosesia syringae fraxini*) of eastern and central No. America

ashcake \ˈ⸗,⸗\ *n* [³*ash* + *cake*] *South & Midland* **:** a cake of corn meal baked in hot ashes

ash can *n* [³*ash*] **1 :** a metal receptacle for refuse (as ashes) — see CAN illustration **2** *slang* **:** DEPTH CHARGE

ashcan \ˈ⸗,⸗\ *adj, often cap* **:** relating to the street life of a city, esp. to its unidealized or seamy aspects; *specif* **:** depicting or working to depict genre scenes of city life realistically — used esp. of an early 20th century school of American artists

ash cone *n* [³*ash*] **:** a conical accumulation of volcanic ash around a vent

ash dump *n* [³*ash*] **:** an opening in the bottom of a fireplace or furnace leading to an ashpit below

¹ash·en \ˈashәn, ˈaa-,ˈai-\ *adj* [ME *asshen*, fr. *asshe* ash (tree) + *-en*] **:** ²ASH

²ashen \"\ *adj* [ME *asshen*, fr. *asshe* ash (residue of combustion) + *-en*] **1 :** consisting of or resembling ashes **2 a :** of the color of ashes **b :** of the color ash gray **3 :** deadly pale **:** BLANCHED, PALLID ⟨his face was ~ with rage and apprehension —P.B.Kyne⟩

ashe·rah \ə'shirə\ *n, pl* **ashe·rim** \-rəm\ *or* **asherahs** *usu cap* [Heb *ăshērāh*] **:** a sacred wooden post, pole, or pillar that stood near the altar in various Canaanite high places and that symbolized the goddess Asherah

ash·er·ite \'ashə,rīt\ *n* -s *usu cap* [*Asher*, Jacob's 8th son (Gen 30:12-13) + E *-ite*] **:** a member of the Hebrew tribe of Asher **:** a descendant of Asher

ash·ery \'ashərē, 'aa-, 'ai- -ri\ *n* -ES [³*ash* + *-ery*] **:** a place where potash is made ⟨the burnt trees as they stood and took them to *asheries* —H.W.Thompson⟩

ashes *pl of* ASH, *pres 3d sing of* ASH

ashes of rose *or* **ashes of roses** **1 :** a variable color averaging a light grayish red that is yellower and very slightly darker than livid violet — called also *rose gray* **2** *of textiles* **:** a grayish purplish red that is redder and slightly darker than tourmaline pink

ash·et \'ashət\ *n* -s [F *assiette* — more at ASSIETTE] *chiefly Scot* **:** PLATTER

ashfall \'⸗,⸗\ *n* [³*ash* + *fall*] **:** a deposit of volcanic ash — called also *ash shower*

ash field *n* [³*ash*] **:** a thick widespread deposit of volcanic ash — called also *ash plain*

ash furnace *n* [³*ash*] **:** a furnace or oven for fritting materials for glassmaking — called also *ash oven*

ash gray *n* [³*ash*] **:** a light greenish gray that is yellower, lighter, and stronger than French gray and yellower than lichen green

ashier *comparative of* ASHY

ashiest *superlative of* ASHY

ashim·mer \ə'⸗\ *adj* [¹*a-* + *shimmer*, v.] **:** SHIMMERING

ashine \ə'⸗\ *adj* [¹*a-* + *shine*, v.] **:** SHINING

ashing *pres part of* ASH

ash·ip·board \ə'⸗\ *adv* [¹*a-* + *shipboard*] **:** on shipboard

ashiv·er \ə'⸗\ *adj* [¹*a-* + *shiver*, v.] **:** SHIVERING

ash·ke·na·zi \,ashkə'nazē, ,äshkə'nä-, -zi\ *n, pl* **ashkena·zim** \-(,)zim\ *also* **ashkenazi** *usu cap* [Heb *Ashkĕnāzī*] **:** a member of one of the two great divisions of Jews comprising the eastern European Yiddish-speaking Jews — compare SEPHARDI

ash·ke·naz·ic \¦⸗⸗¦⸗zik\ *or* **ash·ke·na·zi** \-zē, -zi\ *adj, usu cap* **:** of, belonging to, or characteristic of the Ashkenazim — compare SEPHARDIC

ashkh·a·bad \'ashkə,bad\ *adj, usu cap* [fr. *Ashkhabad*, city in southern U.S.S.R.] **:** of or from Ashkhabad, Turkmen S.S.R., U.S.S.R. **:** of the kind or style prevalent in Ashkhabad

ash·ko·ko \ash'kō(,)kō, 'ashkə,kō\ *n* -s [Amharic *askoko*] **:** ²HYRAX

¹**ash·lar** *also* **ash·ler** \'ashlə(r), 'aa-,'ai-\ *n* -s *often attrib* [ME *asheler*, fr. MF *aissilier* crossbeam, fr. OF, fr. *ais* board, plank, fr. L *axis*, by folk etymology (influence of L *axis* axle) fr. *assis* — more at ACE, AXIS] **1 a :** hewn or squared stone **:** masonry of such stone **b :** a thin squared and dressed stone for facing a wall of rubble or brick **2 :** one of the short upright studs between the floor beams and the rafters of a garret cutting off the sharp side angles

²**ashlar** \"\ *vt* -ED/-ING/-S **:** to cover with ashlar

ashlar brick *n* **:** a brick with the faces rough-hackled to resemble stone

ashlar facing *n* **:** sawed or dressed squared stones used in facing masonry walls

ashlaring *n* -s **1 :** ASHLAR MASONRY **2 :** ASHLAR 2

ashlar line *n* **:** the outer line of an exterior wall above any projecting base

ashlar masonry *n* **:** masonry made of sawed, dressed, tooled, or quarry-faced stone with proper bond

ash–leaved maple \'⸗,⸗-\ *n* [¹*ash*] **:** BOX ELDER

ash·lu·slay \,äshlü'slī\ *n, pl* **ashluslay** *usu cap* **1 a :** a Matacan people of southwestern Paraguay **b :** a member of such people **2 :** the language of the Ashluslay people

ash·man \'⸗,⸗\ *n, pl* **ashmen** [³*ash*] **:** a worker who removes ashes — called also *cinderman*

ash·o·chi·mi \,ashə'chēmē\ *n, pl* **ashochimi** *or* **ashochimis** *usu cap* **:** WAPPO

ashore \ə'⸗\ *adv (or adj)* [¹*a-* + *shore*] **:** on or to the shore **:** on or to land ⟨the troops came ~ at midnight⟩ ⟨the captain was ~ for two hours⟩

ash oven *n* [³*ash*] **:** ASH FURNACE

as how *conj* **1** *dial* **:** ³THAT ⟨seeing *as how* the captain had been hauling him over the coals —Frederick Marryat⟩ **2** *dial* **:** IF, WHETHER ⟨I don't know *as how* this will be any better⟩

ashpan \'⸗,⸗\ *n* [³*ash* + *pan*] **:** a pan under a grate for collecting and removing ashes

ashpit \'⸗,⸗\ *n* [³*ash* + *pit*] **:** a pit for ashes esp. under a grate

ash plain *n* **:** ASH FIELD

ashplant \'⸗,⸗\ *n* [¹*ash* + *plant*] **1 :** an ash sapling **2 :** a walking stick; *esp* **:** one made from an ash sapling

ashraf \ä'shräf\ *n pl, often cap* [Ar *ashrāf*, pl. of *sharīf* noble] **:** descendants of the prophet Muhammad regarded as of noble lineage and preeminence in Islam — compare SAYYID, SHARIF

ashram \'äshrəm\ *n* -s [Skt *āśrama*, fr. *ā* towards, near to + *śrama* fatigue, exertion, religious exercise; akin to Skt *śrāmyati*, *klāmyati*, *klāmati* he gets tired, OIr *clam* leprous, W *claf* ill, Bret *klañv*, *klañ*, Corn *claf* ill, leprous — more at ACHARYA] **1** *India* **:** HERMITAGE **2** *India* **:** a religious retreat for a colony of disciples

ashra·ma *also* **asra·ma** \'äshrəmə\ *n* -s [Skt *āśrama*] **1** *India* **:** ASHRAM **2 :** any one of the four stages of the Brahmanic scheme of life — compare BRAHMACHARYA, GRIHASTHA, SANNYASI, VANAPRASTHA

ashra·mite \'äshrə,mīt\ *n* -s **:** a member of an ashram

ashre \ä'shrā\ *n, pl* **ashre** [Heb *ashrē* happy, the first word of the first two verses (Psalms 84:4 & 144:15) of the recital] **:** a recital in the daily liturgy of the Jews of the two verses from Psalms 84 and 144 followed by the recitation of Psalm 145

ash rock *n* [³*ash*] **:** rock consisting of volcanic ash

ash rose *n* [³*ash*] **:** a variable color averaging a grayish red that is bluer and paler than bois de rose, bluer and less strong than appleblossom or Pompeian red, and bluer, lighter, and stronger than livid brown

ash rust *n* [¹*ash*] **:** a rust disease of ash trees caused by a fungus (*Puccinia peridermiospora*)

ash sawfly *n* **:** any of various sawflies (esp. *Tomostethus multicinctus* and *Tethida cordigera*) having larvae that feed on and defoliate ash trees

ash shower *or* **ash spread** *n* **:** ASHFALL

ashstone \'⸗,⸗\ *n* [³*ash* + *stone*] **:** a rock composed of particles of volcanic ash less than 0.06 millimeter in greatest dimension

ash–throated flycatcher \'⸗,⸗⸗-\ *n* [³*ash*] **:** a common flycatcher (*Myiarchus cinerascens*) of the western U.S. and northern Mexico that resembles the crested flycatcher but has the throat and chest ashy to white and the outer web of the outer tail feather white

ashtray \'⸗,⸗\ *n* [³*ash* + *tray*] **:** a receptacle for tobacco ashes and for cigar and cigarette butts

¹**ashu·ra** \ə'shürə\ *n* -s *often cap* [Ar *'ashūrā*, fr. *'asharah* ten] **:** a Muslim voluntary fast day observed on the 10th day of Muharram and esp. sacred to Shiites

²**ashura** \"\ *n, usu cap* [Jap] **:** a Japanese breed of medium-sized game fowls

ash wednesday *n, usu cap A & W* [ME *Asshe Wednesday*, fr. *asshe* ash + *Wednesday*] **:** the first day of Lent in Western Christendom

ashy \'ashē, 'aa-,'ai-, -i\ *adj* -ER/-EST [ME *asshy*, fr. *asshe* ash (residue of combustion) + *-y*] **1 :** composed of, covered with, or resembling ashes ⟨the carpet would be dim with a gray ~ dust from the tobacco —Elizabeth M. Roberts⟩ ⟨all these things ~ to his taste —J.L.Liebman⟩ **2 :** like ashes in color **:** deadly pale **:** ASHEN ⟨some return of color to the ~ cheeks —Bram Stoker⟩ **3** *chiefly Midland* **:** ANGRY, ENRAGED ⟨he argued awhile and then he began to get ~⟩

ASI *abbr* air-speed indicator

asia \'āzhə *also* -shə *sometimes* -zhēə\ *adj, usu cap* [fr. *Asia*, largest continent in the world] **:** of or from the continent of Asia **:** of the kind or style prevalent in Asia **:** ASIAN

asia·go \,äsē'ä(,)gō, ,äsyä-\ *n* -s [fr. *Asiago*, commune in province of Vicenza, Italy, where it originated] **:** a sweet-curd semicooked Italian cheese with pungent aroma

¹**asian** \'āzhən *also* -shən *sometimes* -zhēən *or* -shēən *or (esp Brit)* -syən *or* -siən\ *adj, usu cap* [L *asianus*, adj. & n., fr. Gk *asianos*, fr. *Asia* + *-anos* -an] **1 :** of, relating to, or characteristic of the continent of Asia **2 :** of, relating to, or characteristic of the people of Asia

²**asian** \"\ *n* -s *cap* [L *asianus*] **:** a native or inhabitant of Asia

asi·an·ic \¦āzhē¦anik *also* -shē-\ *adj, usu cap* [*Asian* + *-ic*] **1 :** ASIAN **2 :** of, belonging to, or constituting a group of non-Indo-European languages not admitted by many linguists to be demonstrably or even plausibly of common origin, spoken in Asia Minor or in southwestern Asia and southern Europe before the coming of the Indo-Europeans, and perhaps including Lycian, Lydian, Etruscan, and the languages ancestral to Basque and some Caucasian languages

asian influenza *n, usu cap A* **:** influenza caused by a mutant strain of the influenza virus

asi·arch \'āzhē,ärk *also* -shē-\ *n* -s *usu cap* [LL *Asiarcha*, fr. Gk *Asiarchēs*, fr. *Asia* Asia, Roman province in western Asia Minor + *-archēs* -arch] **:** one of a group of civil and priestly officials in the Roman province of Asia who presided over the public games and religious rites

¹**asi·at·ic** \¦āzhē¦ad·ik, -atik, -ēk *also* ¦āzē- *or* ¦āshē- *sometimes* ¦āsē-\ *adj, usu cap* [L *Asiaticus*, adj. & n., fr. Gk *Asiatikos*, fr. *Asia*] **1 :** ASIAN — now often taken to be offensive **2 :** tending to excessive ornamentation or emotionalism in literary or oratorical style **:** FLORID

²**asiatic** \"\ *n* -s *cap* [L *Asiaticus*] **1 :** ASIAN — now often taken to be offensive **2** *Africa* **:** one of Indian descent

asiatic beetle *n, usu cap A* **:** ORIENTAL BEETLE

asiatic bronze *n, often cap A* **:** BRONZE BROWN

asiatic cholera *n, usu cap A* **:** an acute infectious epidemic and endemic disease of man esp. in Asia involving the small intestine, characterized by severe effortless diarrhea with rice-water stools, vomiting, and muscle cramps, marked by toxemia, dehydration, and collapse, caused by a bacterium (*Vibrio comma*), and spread by contaminated food and water

asiatic class *n, usu cap A* **:** a group of breeds of domestic fowls supposed to have originated in eastern Asia and containing the Brahmas, Cochins, and Langshans, all consisting of large heavy birds that have feathered legs and red ear lobes and lay brown-shelled eggs — compare MEDITERRANEAN CLASS

asiatic cockroach *n, usu cap A* **:** ORIENTAL COCKROACH

asiatic garden beetle *n, usu cap A* **:** a small brown beetle (*Maladera castanea*) resembling the related Oriental beetle in appearance and habits and like the latter introduced into eastern No. America from Asia

asi·at·i·cism \,⸗⸗'⸗ə,sizəm\ *n, usu cap* **:** a literary, oratorical, or architectural style characterized by excessive ornamentation or emotionalism **:** FLORIDITY

asi·at·i·cize \-ə,sīz\ *also* **asi·a·tize** \'⸗⸗ə,tīz; ,⸗⸗'ad·,īz -'a,tīz\ *vt* -ED/-ING/-S *often cap* **:** to make Asian or partially Asian in customs or ideas

asiatic sweetleaf *n, usu cap A* **:** an eastern Asian shrub (*Symplocos paniculata*) cultivated for its fragrant white flowers and bright blue fruits

asiatic white pine *n, usu cap A* **:** HIMALAYAN PINE

¹**aside** \ə'⸗\ *adv* [ME, fr. ¹*a-* + *side*] **1 a :** to or toward one side ⟨draw ~ the curtains⟩ **b :** SIDEWISE, ASLANT, OBLIQUELY ⟨practiced to lisp and hang the head ~ —Alexander Pope⟩ **2** *now dial* **:** by the side **:** ALONGSIDE — usu. used with following *of* ⟨he sat down ~ of me⟩ **3 a :** out of the way **:** away from a group **:** in or into privacy **:** APART ⟨had been taken ~ by his father —Rex Ingamells⟩ **b :** away from oneself ⟨he threw his coat ~⟩ **c :** away from one's thought or use **:** out of consideration ⟨all such protests were brushed ~ as purely superficial —Osbert Lancaster⟩ **d** *archaic* **:** away from the correct or right way **:** ASTRAY ⟨they are all gone ~ —Ps 14:3 (AV)⟩ **4 :** set to one side ⟨matters which, exceptional cases ~, no investor can settle with the foreign government —M.A.Heilperin⟩ **5 :** on each side **:** to a side ⟨a football match in the High Street with 50 or 60 ~ —G.G.Carter⟩

²**aside** \"\ *prep* **1** *obs* **:** BEYOND, PAST ⟨the kind prince . . . hath rushed ~ the law —Shak.⟩ **2** *dial* **:** BESIDE, NEAR ⟨was always at the wheel with the little boy ~ him —Karlton Kelm⟩

³**aside** \"\ *n* -s **1 a :** words spoken aside or in a low tone so as to be inaudible to some person or persons present ⟨after a few parting ~s to Mrs. Wales she led Cecily into the house —Hamilton Basso⟩ **b (1) :** words spoken by a character in a play that are heard by the audience but are supposedly not heard by other characters on stage **(2) :** a stage convention using such words **2 :** a departure from the subject or principal theme (as of an essay or lecture) **:** DIGRESSION, PARENTHESIS ⟨the author frequently stops the narrative for caustic ~s and remarks on a wide variety of subjects —R.A.Cordell⟩

aside from *prep* **1 :** in addition to **:** BESIDES ⟨*aside from* being a plane stop, [it] is the most important station for the river steamers —Tom Marvel⟩ **2 :** except for **:** apart from ⟨they were farmers almost to a man, *aside from* a few mechanics —Van Wyck Brooks⟩

asid·en \ə'sīdᵊn\ *adv* [prob. fr. ME *asidenhand* aside, aslant, fr. *aside* + *hand*] *now dial Eng* **:** SIDEWISE, AWRY

asien·to *or* **as·sien·to** \,asē'en(,)tō, ,äs-\ *n* -s [Sp *asiento* seat, meeting place of a tribunal, treaty, contract, fr. *asentar* to seat, make an agreement, fr. *a-* (fr. L *ad-*) + *sentar* to seat] **:** a contract or convention between Spain and another power or company or individual for furnishing Negro slaves for the Spanish dominions in America

¹**as if** *conj* **:** as it would be if ⟨it was *as if* he had lost his last friend⟩ **:** as one would do if ⟨he ran *as if* ghosts were chasing him⟩ **:** THAT ⟨it seemed *as if* the day would never end⟩

²**as if** *n* **:** ALS OB

asigmatic \¦ā+;⸗¦⸗⸗\ *adj* [²*a-* + *sigmatic*] *of a tense* **:** formed without the addition of *s* to the root — opposed to *sigmatic*

asil *often cap, var of* ASEEL

¹**asi·lid** \ə'sīləd, -il-\ *adj* [NL *Asilidae*] **:** of or relating to the Asilidae

²**asilid** \"\ *n* -s **:** one of the Asilidae **:** ROBBER FLY

asil·i·dae \ə'silə,dē\ *n pl, cap* [NL, fr. *Asilus*, type genus + *-idae*] **:** a family of rather large usu. slender two-winged flies with strong legs and wings and the proboscis a hardened beak used for sucking the body fluids of other insects which they capture on the wing — compare ROBBER FLY

asi·lus \ə'sīləs\ *n, cap* [NL, fr. L, gadfly] **:** the type genus of Asilidae

asim·i·na \ə'simənə\ *n, cap* [NL, fr. AmerF *assimine* papaw, modif. of Illinois *rassimina*, fr. *rassi* divided lengthwise into equal parts + *mina* seeds] **:** a small genus of eastern No. American shrubs and small trees (family Annonaceae) having aromatic alternate leaves and flowers with 3 to 15 stamens and carpels — see PAPAW

asim·mer \ə'⸗\ *adj* [¹*a-* + *simmer*, v.] **:** SIMMERING ⟨the stuff and nonsense long ~ in their noddles —Robert Browning⟩

asin \'äsən\ *n* -s *usu cap* [Skt *Āśvina*] **:** a month of the Hindu year — see MONTH table

asinego *n* -ES [alter. of earlier *asinico*, modif. (influenced by L *asinus*) of Sp *asnico*, dim. of *asno* ass, fr. L *asinus*] **1** *obs* **:** a little ass **2** *obs* **:** FOOL

as·i·nine \'asᵊn,īn, 'aas- *sometimes* 'az-\ *adj* [L *asininus*, fr. *asinus* ass + *-inus* -ine — more at ASS] **1 :** of, relating to, or resembling an ass or asses ⟨this interesting animal is definitely horselike although it has ~ characteristics as well —R.S. Summerhays⟩ **2 :** UNINTELLIGENT, STUPID, SILLY, OBSTINATE ⟨a man so ~ that he looks for gratitude in this world —H.L. Mencken⟩ ⟨a polite smile at what he thought an ~ joke —Dashiell Hammett⟩ **syn** see SIMPLE

as·i·nin·i·ty \,⸗⸗'ninəd·ē, -ətē, -i\ *n* -ES **1 :** the quality or state of being asinine ⟨capable of an ~ that can snatch defeat from the very jaws of victory —G.W.Johnson⟩ **2 :** something that is asinine ⟨that sickening list of *asininities* —Max Ascoli⟩

¹**asiphonate** \(')ā+¦-\ *adj* [²*a-* + *siphonate*] **:** having no siphon ⟨an ~ oyster⟩

²**asiphonate** \"\ *n* -s **:** an asiphonate mollusk

¹**ask** \'ask, 'aa(ə)-,'ai-,'á-, *chiefly substand* -st\ *vb* **asked** \-s(k)t, *before a word (esp consonant-initial) following without pause, often* -sk\ **asked** \"\ **asking** \-skiŋ, *chiefly substand* -stiŋ *or* -stən\ **asks** \-sks, *chiefly substand* -s(t)s\ [ME *asken*, *axen*, fr. OE *āscian*, *ācsian* to ask, demand; akin to OFris *āskia* to demand, OS *ēscon*, OHG *eiscōn* to ask, L *aeruscare* to beg, Gk *himeros* longing, Skt *icchati* he seeks, desires] *vt* **1 a :** to call upon for an answer or informative response **:** put a question to **:** inquire of ⟨he ~*ed* him about his trip⟩ **b :** to seek to be informed about **:** put a question about **:** inquire concerning ⟨the two or three people of whom I ~*ed* his whereabouts —Scott Fitzgerald⟩ **c :** to speak or utter (a question or a request for information) ⟨he never ~s foolish questions⟩ **2 a :** to make a request of **:** BEG, PETITION ⟨they ~*ed* him to be quiet⟩ **b :** to make a request for **:** seek by words to obtain ⟨she ~*ed* help from her teacher⟩ ⟨he ~*ed* advice of several friends⟩ **3 :** to call for **:** NEED, REQUIRE ⟨it ~s some strenuous agility to keep them both in the mind together —Donald Davie⟩ **4** *archaic* **:** to make known publicly **:** PUBLISH ⟨the day when I shall ~ the banns —Shak.⟩ **5 :** to set as a price **:** DEMAND, EXPECT ⟨the dealer ~*ed* $2000 for the car⟩ **6 :** to extend an invitation to **:** INVITE ⟨we ~*ed* him to come to lunch⟩ ~ *vi* **1 :** to seek information **:** make inquiries **:** INQUIRE ⟨he ~*ed* about your job⟩ ⟨he ~*ed* for the owner⟩ ⟨he ~*ed* after the old man's health⟩ **2 :** to make a request **:** SEEK, PETITION ⟨they ~*ed* for food and lodging⟩ **3 :** to seek or invite punishment or retaliation ⟨if you do that you're just ~*ing* for trouble⟩ — often used with following phrase *for it* ⟨the Nazis and the Fascists have ~*ed* for it and they are going to get it —F.D.Roosevelt⟩

syn INQUIRE, QUERY, QUESTION, INTERROGATE, EXAMINE, QUIZ, CATECHIZE: ASK is a general and colorless term suggesting mainly the placing of a single question in order to gain information. It may verge onto connoting seeking or requesting ⟨where lies the land to which your ship must go . . . yet still I *ask*, what haven is her mark? —William Wordsworth⟩ ⟨an increasing number were *asking* many things from philosophy —H.O.Taylor⟩ INQUIRE in this sense is likely to indicate an honest request for information, a question asked solely to lead to enlightening the questioner on the matter ostensibly under primary consideration ⟨my literary conscience . . . *inquires* if ideas were really free at Oxford —Ellen Glasgow⟩ QUERY indicates asking for an answer which clarifies, substantiates, removes doubt from the questioner's mind ⟨the anthropologist, on the other hand, might *query* the statement —J.F.Embree⟩ QUESTION heightens the implication that the questioner finds an assertion or notion doubtful, unconvincing, and perhaps incorrect ⟨*Newsweek's* incoming mail sacks bulge. Some letters *query*, others *question* facts —*Newsweek*⟩ ⟨even today *questioning* a statement made by a person is often taken by him as a reflection upon his integrity, and is resented —John Dewey⟩ To QUESTION a person is to keep asking him searching questions ⟨*question* the committee about the deficit⟩ INTERROGATE may suggest systematic and thorough questions; it implies, however, a simple search for facts and indicates nothing about the attitude of the questioner ⟨he had landed on the Arno and *interrogated* the natives with the help of an interpreter —John Dos Passos⟩ EXAMINE, in reference to things, is a synonym for *inspect* rather than for QUESTION; in reference to persons, it may suggest either detailed questions intended to discover the correctness of a person's conduct or beliefs or the scope of his knowledge or abilities, the examiner often having knowledge of the correct or preferred answers ⟨where he had himself *examined* for three days by the learned and wise king of Naples —R.A.Hall b.1911⟩ QUIZ suggests the asking of a series of questions by one knowing the answers in order to test another's knowledge; it may suggest a lighter, more casual, less significant procedure than EXAMINE ⟨*quizzed* by feature writers in magazines —G.A. Miller⟩ CATECHIZE, which often pertains to matters religious, may suggest systematic, rapid questioning, often calling for answers by rote, to verify accuracy, correctness, or orthodoxy of another's notions, and to trip him up if possible ⟨the awkward situation in which you found yourself on receiving a visit from an authoress whose works though presented to you . . . you had never read. . . . I hope she *catechized* you well —William Cowper⟩

syn ASK, REQUEST, SOLICIT mean, in a common application, to try to obtain by making one's wants known. ASK implies little more than the statement of the desire ⟨*ask* the cooperation of all concerned⟩ ⟨what more can be *asked* of books than that they provoke laughter, more reading, discussion, a pilgrimage —D.S.Davis⟩ REQUEST implies more formality, greater display of courtesy, and anticipation of affirmative response ⟨*request* the cooperation of neighboring towns in the control of Dutch elm disease⟩ ⟨*request* a meeting to discuss common problems and the possibility of mutual help⟩ ⟨*requesting* that Italy be given the trusteeship of that territory —*Collier's Yr. Bk.*⟩ ⟨16 nations *requesting* aid under the European Recovery Program —*Current Biog.*⟩ SOLICIT, in modern use and in this connection, commonly means no more than calling attention to one's wants or desires ⟨*solicit* trade or patronage by advertisement⟩ ⟨*solicit* funds for flood relief⟩ ⟨our interest is *solicited* by the characters themselves rather than by anything that they do —A.J.Ayer⟩

²**ask** \'ask\ *n* -s [ME *aske*, *ascre*, fr. OE *āthexe* (akin to OHG *egidehsa*, OS *egithassa*, MD *haghedisse*), fr. *ā-* (perh. akin to Gk *ophis* snake) + *-thexe* (perh. akin to MHG *dehse* spindle) — more at ANGUIS] *dial Brit* **:** WATER NEWT

¹**askance** \ə'skan(t)s, -aa(ə)n-,-ain- *also* -ȧn-\ *adv* [origin unknown] **1 :** with a side glance **:** SIDEWAYS, OBLIQUELY ⟨did not now turn quite all the way back but looked at me ~ with her bright steady eyes —Edmund Wilson⟩ **2 :** with disapproval or distrust **:** SUSPICIOUSLY, ⟨one trained in . . . the basic sciences may look ~ at this process —D.H.K. Lee⟩

²**askance** \"\ *adj* **:** turned askance **:** SIDEWAYS ⟨her eyes with their misted ~ look —Elizabeth Bowen⟩

¹**askant** \-ant, -aa(ə)nt,-aint\ *adv* [prob. alter. (influenced by *aslant*) of ¹*askance*] **:** ASKANCE ⟨and I saw ~ the armies —Walt Whitman⟩

²**askant** \"\ *adj* [alter. of ²*askance*] **:** ASKANCE ⟨oil lamps with their wick ~ in the socket —George Meredith⟩

as·kar \'askə(r)\ *n, pl* **askar** [Ar *'askar* soldier] **:** a native infantryman in the army of Morocco or any other Arabic-speaking country

as·ka·rel \¦askə¦rel\ *n* -s [origin unknown] **:** a synthetic electrically insulating liquid that is noncombustible

as·ka·ri \'askərē; ə'skärē, a's-\ *n, pl* **askaris** [Ar *'askarī*] **1 :** a native soldier esp. of eastern Africa in the service of a European power **2 :** a native policeman, guard, or watchman esp. of eastern Africa

asked *past of* ASK

askeletal \(')ā+¦-\ *adj* [²*a-* + *skeletal*] **:** without a skeleton — used esp. of sponges

¹**ask·er** \'askə(r), 'aa-,ai-,ȧ-\ *n* -s [ME, fr. *asken* + *-er*] **:** one that asks: **a :** one that asks questions **:** INQUIRER **b :** one that asks favors, gifts, or alms **:** SUPPLIANT, BEGGAR

²**as·ker** \'askə(r)\ *n* -s [ME *ascre* — more at ASK (n.)] *dial Eng* **:** WATER NEWT

askesis *var of* ASCESIS

¹**askew** \ə'skyü\ *adv* [prob. fr. ¹*a-* + *skew*] **1 :** out of line **:** to one side **:** AWRY, OBLIQUELY ⟨something has gone seriously ~ with the show —Angelica Gibbs⟩ ⟨the gate hung ~ —Agatha Christie⟩ **2 :** with contempt or disdain **:** SCORNFULLY ⟨the ladies looked somewhat ~ at his tipsy, giggling wife⟩

²**askew** \"\ *adj* **:** made or standing out of line **:** set or turned to one side **:** AWRY, SKEW ⟨leaning against an ~ lamppost to light a cigarette —R.P.Warren⟩

asking *pres part of* ASK

asking bid *n* **:** an artificial bid in contract bridge that asks for certain information from the bidder's partner

ask·ing·ly *adv* **:** in an entreating or inquiring manner

asking price *n* **:** the price at which something is offered for sale ⟨he refused to haggle with the clerk and paid the *asking price*⟩

asklent \ə'sklent\ *dial Scot var of* ASLANT

asks *pres 3d sing of* ASK, *pl of* ASK

aslake \ə'slāk\ *vt* -ED/-ING/-S [ME *aslaken*, fr. OE *āslacian* to become or make slack, diminish, loosen, fr. *ā-* (perfective prefix) + *slacian* to slacken — more at ABEAR, SLAKE] *archaic* **:** to cause to abate or diminish ⟨waits for the prey . . . its hunger to ~ —Robert Southey⟩

¹**aslant** \ə'slant, -aa(ə)nt,-aint,-ȧnt\ *adv* [ME *aslante*, *aslonte*, *aslunte*, prob. fr. ¹*a-* + the root of ME *slente* slope — more at SLANT (n.)] **:** in a slanting or sloping direction **:** toward one side **:** OBLIQUELY ⟨the sun shone ~ across his face —Elizabeth M. Roberts⟩

²**aslant** \"\ *prep* **:** over or across in a slanting direction **:** ATHWART ⟨there is a willow grows ~ a brook —Shak.⟩

³aslant \"\ *adj* : SLANTING, OBLIQUE ⟨with head ~⟩

¹asleep \ə'slēp\ *adj* [ME *aslepe*, adj. & adv., fr. ¹*a-* + *slepe* sleep] **1** : in a state of sleep : SLEEPING ⟨he has been ~ since noon⟩ **2** : in the sleep of death : DEAD ⟨we would not have you ignorant . . . concerning those who are ~ —1 Thess 4:13 (RSV)⟩ **3** : in a state of numbness : lacking sensation or feeling : NUMB ⟨my arm is ~⟩ **4** : in a state of mental or physical inactivity, sluggishness, or indifference : not alert : INACTIVE, DORMANT ⟨a weak, timid, lethargic government usually ~ —Sir Winston Churchill⟩ ⟨the sea ~ and at peace —Thomas Wood †1950⟩ **5** *of a sail* : MOTIONLESS, UNRUFFLED — **asleep at the switch** : not alert to a duty or opportunity

²asleep \"\ *adv* [ME *aslepe*] **1** : into a state of sleep ⟨he fell ~ at noon⟩ **2** : into the sleep of death : DEAD ⟨God will bring with him those who have fallen ~ —1 Thess 4:14 (RSV)⟩ **3** : into a state of inactivity, sluggishness, or indifference ⟨the falling ~ of the critical faculty —R.W. Southern⟩

as long as *conj* : inasmuch as : SINCE ⟨*as long as* you are going, I'll go too⟩

¹aslope \ə'slōp\ *adj* [ME, adj. & adv.] : SLOPING, SLANTING

²aslope \"\ *adv* [ME] : in a sloping or slanting direction : SLOPINGLY ⟨he was leaning ~ against the building⟩

asm *abbr* assembly

as·ma·ra \azmärə, as'-, -marə\ *adj, usu cap* [fr. *Asmara*, Eritrea] : of or from Asmara, the capital of Eritrea : of the kind or style prevalent in Asmara

asmoke \ə'-\ *adj* [¹*a-* + *smoke*, v.] : SMOKING

asmonaean *or* **asmonean** *usu cap, var of* HASMONAEAN

asmt *abbr* assortment

as much *pron* : nearly the same

as much as *adv* : in effect : ALMOST ⟨he *as much as* admitted the whole story⟩

as nas *var of* ⁷AS

asocial \(')ā+\ *adj* [²*a-* + *social*] **1** : inconsiderate of or hostile to the needs, desires, or customs of others : SELFISH ⟨a defensory wall of ~ behavior —F.H.Allport⟩ **2** : withdrawn from society and from normal social intercourse : unable or unwilling to conform to social demands — sometimes distinguished from *antisocial* ⟨a vast difference between an acceptable social attitude and an ~ or reclusive attitude —A.T.Weaver⟩ — **asocialism** \(')ā+\ *n* -s — **asociality** \,ā+\ *n* -ES

as of \,aza(v)\ *prep* : at or on (a specific time or date) ⟨the rule takes effect *as of* July 1⟩

aso·ka \ə's(h)ōkə\ *also* **as·ak** *or* **as·ok** \'asək\ *n* -s [Hindi *asok*, fr. Skt *aśoka*] : a showy tree (*Saraca indica*) of the family Leguminosae of tropical Asia that is cultivated for its orange scarlet flowers and is used to decorate temples

aso·kan column \ə's(h)ōkən-\ *n, usu cap A* [*Asoka* the Great †232 B.C. king of Magadha, ancient kingdom of India, at whose behest they were erected + E *-an*] : a stone column found in India and usu. of considerable height on which Buddhist inscriptions were cut — compare ²LAT

aso·ma·tog·no·sia \,ā,sōmə,täg'nōzh(ē)ə\ *n* [NL, fr. ²*a-* + *somat-* + *-gnosia*] : ignorance of paralysis as a result of brain damage

asomatophyte \,ā+\ *n* -s [²*a-* + *somat-* + *-phyte*] : a plant in which body and reproductive cells are not distinct and which lacking permanent tissue loses none of its capacity to grow and multiply — compare SOMATOPHYTE

aso·ma·tous \(')ā¦sōməd·əs\ *adj* [LL *asomatus*, fr. Gk *asōmatos*, fr. *a-* ²*a-* + *-sōmatos* (fr. *sōmat-*, *sōma* body) — more at -SOMA] : INCORPOREAL, IMMATERIAL

asonant \(')ā+\ *adj* [²*a-* + *sonant*] : not sonant

as·or \'a,sȯ(ə)r\ *n* -s [Heb *'āsōr*, fr. *'āsār* ten] : an ancient Hebrew zitherlike instrument having 10 strings and played with a plectrum

¹asp \'asp, 'aa(ə)-,'ai- *also* 'å-\ *n* -s [ME *aspe* — more at ASPEN] : ASPEN

²asp \"\ *n* -s [ME *aspis*, fr. L, fr. Gk] : a small venomous snake of Egypt variously identified as the horned viper or a small African cobra (*Naja haje*) — see URAEUS

as·pal·a·thus \a'spaləthəs\ *n* [L, fr. Gk *aspalathos*] **1** -ES : a biblical shrub yielding a fragrant oil and generally believed to be a member of the genus *Alhagi* or of the genus *Convolvulus* **2** [NL, fr. L] *cap* : a genus of southern African shrubs (family Fabaceae) with heathlike often tufted leaves and yellow or rarely purple flowers

aspar \ə'spär\ *adv* [¹*a-* + *spar*] *chiefly Scot* : wide apart : spread out ⟨he stood with legs ~⟩

as·pa·rag·i·nase \,aspə'rajə,nās, -āz\ *n* -s [*asparagine* + *-ase*] : an enzyme obtained esp. from liver extracts that hydrolyzes asparagine to aspartic acid and ammonia

as·par·a·gine \ə'sparə,jēn, -jən\ *n* -s [F, fr. L *asparagus* + F *-ine*] : a white crystalline amino acid $H_2NOCCH_2CH(NH_2)COOH$ found in most plants (as asparagus and leguminous plants) and used in culture media for some bacteria (as lactobacilli and tubercle bacilli); α-amino-succinamic acid

as·pa·rag·i·nyl \,aspə'rajənəl, -nēl\ *n* -s [*asparagine* + *-yl*] : the univalent acyl radical $H_2NCOCH_2CH(NH_2)CO$— of asparagine

as·par·a·gus \ə'sparəgəs *also* -er-\ *n* [in sense 1, fr. NL, fr. L, asparagus (plant), fr. Gk *asparagos, aspharagos;* in other senses, fr. L, asparagus (plant); akin to Gk *spargan* to swell — more at SPARK] **1** *cap* : a genus of Old World perennial herbs (family Liliaceae) having erect much-branched stems, minute scalelike leaves, and linear cladophylls often mistaken for leaves **2** -ES **a** : any plant of the genus *Asparagus; esp* : a plant (*A. officinalis*) widely cultivated for its tender edible young shoots **b** : the root of cultivated asparagus formerly used as a diuretic

asparagus bean *n* : a So. American bean (*Vigna sesquipedalis*) having very long succulent pods

asparagus bed *n* : a military obstacle consisting of series of steel, wood, or concrete uprights planted in the ground

asparagus beetle *n* : either of two small dark-colored but brightly marked beetles (*Crioceris asparagi* and *C. duodecimpunctata*) of which both the adult and larva feed on the asparagus

asparagus broccoli *n* : CALABRESE

asparagus fern *n* : a feathery cultivated asparagus (*A. plumosus*) resembling a fern

asparagus lettuce *n* : a variety (*Lactuca sativa angustana*) of the common lettuce grown for its thick edible stem

asparagus pea *n* : GOA BEAN

asparagus stone *n* : a variety of apatite occurring in yellow-green crystals

as·par·tase \ə'spär,tās, -āz\ *n* -s [*aspartic* + *-ase*] : an enzyme that occurs in various bacteria, yeasts, and higher plants and that catalyzes the conversion reaction of aspartic acid to fumaric acid by the removal of ammonia and also the reverse reaction of the addition of ammonia to fumaric acid

as·par·tate \-,tāt\ *n* -s [ISV *aspartic* + *-ate*] : a salt or ester of aspartic acid

as·par·tic acid \-,tik-\ *n* [ISV *aspar-* (fr. L *asparagus*) + connective *-t-* + *-ic*] : a crystalline amino dicarboxylic acid $HOOCCH_2CH(NH_2)COOH$ that is found esp. in many plants (as young sugar cane) and is obtained by hydrolysis of asparagine and proteins, that takes part in transamination reactions in the living organism, and that is used in bacteriological culture media; amino-succinic acid

as·par·to·yl \-tə,wil\ *also* **as·par·tyl** \-rd·ᵊl, -r,tēl\ *n* -s [*aspartic* + *-oyl, -yl*] : the bivalent radical $—OCCH_2CH(NH_2)CO—$ of aspartic acid; amino-succinyl

¹as·pect \'a,spekt, 'aa- *sometimes* -,spēkt *or* -,spikt\ *n* -s [ME, fr. L *aspectus*, fr. *aspectus*, past part. of *aspicere, adspicere* to look at, fr. *ad-* + *-spicere* (fr. *specere* to look) — more at SPY] **1 a** (1) : the position of planets or stars with respect to one another held by astrologers to exert an influence upon human affairs : the joint look of planets or stars upon each other or upon the earth ⟨the shepherd's issue at whose birth heaven did afford a gracious ~ —Christopher Marlowe⟩ (2) : the effect of this position ⟨astrologers call the evil influences of the stars evil ~*s* —Francis Bacon⟩ **b** *archaic* : the direction in which influence is brought to bear **c** (1) : a position facing or fronting a particular direction : a position in relation to the points of the compass : EXPOSURE ⟨the house has a southern ~⟩ (2) : a view of a plane from a given direction : the manner of presentation of a plane to a fluid (as the air) through which it is moving or to a current (3) : orientation of a slope in respect to the compass : exposure to sunlight ⟨lands are planted with vines where soil and ~ permit⟩ **d** : the part of an object in a particular position ⟨a sandbag placed over the dorsal ~*s* of the feet will prevent them from slipping —*Med. Radiography & Photography*⟩ **2 a** (1) *obs* : CONSIDERATION, RESPECT (2) : appearance to the eye or mind ⟨the ~ of affairs —T.B.Macaulay⟩ (3) : a particular status or phase in which anything appears or may be regarded ⟨a question having many ~*s*⟩ ⟨in other ~*s* of our living conditions —W.C.Allee⟩ **b** (1) : a particular appearance of the face : COUNTENANCE, MIEN, AIR ⟨serious in ~ —John Dryden⟩ (2) : the apparent position of a body in the solar system with reference to the sun including conjunction, quadrature, and opposition (3) : the appearance of a fixed railroad signal as viewed from the direction of an approaching train or the appearance of a cab signal as viewed by an observer in the cab **c** : the distinctive seasonal appearance of a plant community ⟨spring ~⟩ — see ASPECTION **3** *archaic* **a** : act of looking or gazing : GAZE ⟨his ~ was bent on the ground —Sir Walter Scott⟩ **b** : GLANCE, LOOK **4** [trans. of Russ *vid*] **a** : a set of inflectional forms of a verb that indicate the nature of the action or the manner in which the action is regarded esp. with reference to its beginning, duration, completion, or repetition and without reference to its position in time — used first of the Slavic languages, later of many others; compare COMPLETIVE, IMPERFECTIVE, INCHOATIVE, ITERATIVE, PERFECTIVE **b** : the nature of the action of a verb or the manner in which that action is regarded esp. with reference to its beginning, duration, completion, or repetition and without reference to its position in time, whether indicated by a set of inflectional forms (as in sense 4a), by the meaning of the verb itself (as in *find*, expressing momentary or completed action, by contrast with *seek*, expressing continuing action), by an adverbial modifier (as in *sit down*, meaning "get into a sitting position", by contrast with *sit there till the doctor is ready*, where *sit* means "remain in a sitting position"), by such devices as the so-called progressive tenses in English (as *was eating*, which expresses continuing action, by contrast with *left*, which expresses momentary or completed action, in "he left while I was eating"), or by some other means **5** *in the Midwestern system for American archaeology* : a unit of classification constituting a group of foci that have an approximate majority of determinant types in common — see PHASE; compare COMPONENT, PATTERN **syn** see APPEARANCE, PHASE

²as·pect \", a'spekt\ *vt* -ED/-ING/-S [L *aspectare*, fr. *aspectus*, past part. of *aspicere*] **1** *astrol, of a planet or constellation* : to look upon (a person, house, or another planet) in a particular aspect ⟨when badly ~*ed* the subjects of Scorpio are, however, most destructive —W.T.&Kate Pavitt⟩ **2** *obs* : to look at : BEHOLD

as·pect·a·ble \a'spektəbəl, 'a,spek-\ *adj* [L *aspectabilis*, fr. *aspectare* to look at + *-abilis* -able] *archaic* : capable of being seen : VISIBLE

as·pec·tion \a'spekshən\ *n* -s [L *aspection-, aspectio*, fr. L *aspectus* (past part. of *aspicere*) + *-ion-, -io* -ion] **1** *archaic* : VIEWING **2** : seasonal variation in the appearance or makeup of a plant community usu. relatable to seasonal climatic variation — compare ANNUATION

aspect ratio *n* **1** : the ratio of span to mean chord of an airfoil **2** : the ratio of the width of a television image to its height **3** : the ratio of the longer to the shorter dimension of the cross section of an air duct opening in an air-conditioning system

as·pec·tu·al \a'spekchəwəl, a's-\ *adj* [L *aspectus* aspect + E *-al*] : of or belonging to an aspect (as aspect of a verb)

¹as·pen \'aspən, 'aas-, 'ais- *also* 'ås- *or* -pin\ *adj* [ME, fr. *aspe*, n. + *-en*] **1 a** : of, relating to, or resembling the aspen **b** : made of the wood of the aspen **2** : quivering like the leaves of the aspen : TREMULOUS, QUAKING

²aspen \"\ *n* -s [alter. (influenced by ¹*aspen*) of ME *aspe*, fr. OE *æspe, æpse;* akin to OHG *aspa* aspen, ON *ösp*, Latvian *apsa*, Russ *osina*] : any of several poplars (esp. *Populus tremula* of Europe and *P. tremuloides* and *P. grandidentata* of No. America) the leaves of which flutter in the lightest wind on account of their flattened petioles

aspen poplar *n* : WHITE POPLAR 1b

aspen tortrix *n* : a tortricid moth (*Archips conflictana*) having a larva that feeds on and may seriously defoliate various species of aspen esp. in parts of Canada

¹asper *adj* [ME *aspre, asper*, fr. MF & L; MF *aspre*, fr. L *asper*, lit., rough] *obs* : HARSH, BITTER, STERN

²as·per \'aspə(r)\ *n* -s [ME, fr. MF *aspre* or It *aspro*, fr. MGk *aspron*, fr. neut. of *aspros* white, fr. L *asper* rough, newly minted] **1** : any one of several small silver coins circulating in the eastern Mediterranean area from the 12th to the 17th centuries: **a** : a coin issued by the Comneni of Trebizond **b** : a coin issued by the Knights of Rhodes equivalent to the denier of western Europe **c** : a Turkish coin first issued in the 14th century **2** : a Turkish unit of value that continued in use after the disappearance of the Turkish asper at one time equivalent to the 120th part of a piaster

¹as·per·ate \'asp(ə)rət\ *adj* [L *asperatus*, past part. of *asperare* to make rough, fr. *asper* rough] *archaic* : somewhat rough or harsh to the touch : ASPEROUS

²as·per·ate \-,rāt\ *vt* -ED/-ING/-S [L *asperatus*] *archaic* : to make rough or harsh

as·perge \ə'spərj, a'-\ *vt* -ED/-ING/-S [MF *asperger*, fr. L *aspergere* — more at ASPERSE] : to sprinkle esp. with holy water

as·per·ges \-(,)jēz\ *n, sometimes cap* [L, thou wilt sprinkle, 2d pers. sing. fut. indic. of *aspergere*] : the ceremony of sprinkling altar, clergy, and people with holy water

as·per·gil·la·ce·ae \,aspərjə'lāsē,ē\ *n pl, cap* [NL, fr. *Aspergillus*, type genus + *-aceae*] : a family of fungi (order Eurotiales) including the common molds of the genera *Aspergillus* and *Penicillium* and the fungus *Thielavia basicola* which is the cause of root rot or black root rot of numerous hosts

as·per·gil·la·les \-ā(,)lēz\ [NL, fr. *Aspergillus* + *-ales*] *syn of* EUROTIALES

as·per·gil·li·form \,aspər¦jilə,fȯrm\ *adj* [ISV *aspergill-* (fr. NL *aspergillus*) + *-iform*] : like a brush; *specif* : resembling the sporophore of *Aspergillus* ⟨an ~ stigma⟩

as·per·gil·lin \-lən\ *n* -s [ISV *aspergill-* (fr. NL *Aspergillus*) + *-in*] **1** : an amorphous black pigment found in the spores of various fungi of the genus *Aspergillus* **2** : an antibacterial substance obtained from cultures of two molds (*Aspergillus flavus* and *A. fumigatus*) reported to possess activity against both gram-positive and gram-negative bacteria

as·per·gil·lo·sis \,aspər,jə'lōsəs\ *n, pl* **aspergillo·ses** \-ō,-sēz\ [NL, fr. *Aspergillus* + *-osis*] : infection with or disease caused by molds of the genus *Aspergillus*: **a** : a severe respiratory disease of birds caused by a mold (*A. fumigatus* or rarely *A. niger*) and marked by unthriftiness, emaciation, and pulmonary calcification resembling that of tuberculosis or in young chickens and turkeys taking the form of an acute rapidly fatal pneumonia — called also *brooder pneumonia* **b** : a disease of man usu. occurring in agricultural workers, hair or fur cleaners and others exposed to inhalation of spores (esp. *A. fumigatus*) and characterized by formation of lumps in the skin, ears, sinuses, and respiratory organs

as·per·gil·lum \,aspə(r)'jiləm\ *or* **as·per·gil** *or* **as·per·gill** \'aspə(r),jil\ *n, pl* **as·per·gil·la** \-'jilə\ *or* **aspergil·lums** \-'jiləmz\ *or* **aspergils** *or* **aspergills** \-,jilz\ [NL *aspergillum*, fr. L *aspergere* to sprinkle] : a short-handled brush or a perforated globe holding a sponge used for sprinkling holy water

aspergillum

as·per·gil·lus \,aspə(r)'jiləs\ *n* [NL, alter. of *aspergillum*] **1** *pl* **aspergil·li** \-,lī\ : ASPERGILLUM **2** *cap* : a genus (the type of the family Aspergillaceae) of fungi including besides common molds species pathogenic to plants and animals and characterized by spores borne in chains on numerous simple or branched usu. bottle-shaped sterigmata that radiate from the upper part or the whole of the swollen tip of the conidiophore — see ASPERGILLOSIS

as·per·i·fo·li·ate \¦aspərə¦fōlēət, -ē,āt\ *or* **as·per·i·fo·li·ous** \-ēəs\ *adj* [fr. NL *asperifoliate* fr. NL *asperifolius* + E *-ate; asperifolious* fr. NL *asperifolius*, fr. L *asper* rough + *-i-* + *-folius* (fr. *folium* leaf) — more at BLADE] : rough-leaved

as·per·i·ty \a'sperəd·ē, ə'-, -ətē, -i\ *n* -ES [alter. (influenced by MF *asperité* — fr. L *asperitat-, asperitas*, fr. *asper* rough + *-itat-, -itas* -ity — or by L *asperitas*) of ME *asprete*, fr. OF *aspreté*, fr. *aspre* rough (fr. L *asper*) + *-té* -ty] **1** : a characteristic making for hardship : RIGOR, SEVERITY ⟨the path of beauty is not soft and smooth, but full of harshness and ~ —Havelock Ellis⟩ **2 a** (1) : roughness of surface (as of a leaf) : UNEVENNESS (2) **asperities** *pl* : rough places : EXCRESCENCES ⟨ultramicroscopic *asperities* . . . upon the solid surface —J.W.McBain⟩ **b** *obs* : roughness to the taste : SOURNESS, TARTNESS **c** : roughness or harshness of sound : RAUCOUSNESS ⟨the elderly ladies in his audience had been shocked by the *asperities* of the new style in music —Aaron Copland⟩ **3** : a characteristic making for bitterness : roughness of manner or of temper ⟨he repented of his ~, however, when he saw Shiloh droop his head and wither visibly into sadness —Elinor Wylie⟩ ⟨it caused him a passing ~ to observe her lay places for three —A.J.Cronin⟩ : SEVERITY ⟨the portrait . . . on the wall, whose painted eyes, it seemed, were now inhumanly surveying them . . . with some little ~ —Walter de la Mare⟩ : TARTNESS ⟨a little ~ was in her voice —George Meredith⟩ **syn** see MALIGN

aspermatism \(')ā+\ *n* -s [ISV ²*a-* + *spermatism*] : ASPERMIA

asper·mia \ā'spərmēə\ *n* -s [NL, fr. ²*a-* + *-spermia*] : inability to produce or ejaculate semen — compare AZOOSPERMIA — **asper·mic** \(')ā¦spərmik\ *adj*

as·per·ous \'asp(ə)rəs\ *adj* [L *asper* rough + E *-ous*] : ROUGH, SCABROUS — **as·per·ous·ly** *adv*

aspers *pl of* ASPER

as·perse \ə'spərs, a'-, -əs, -əis\ *vt* -ED/-ING/-S [L *aspersus*, past part. of *aspergere, adspergere* to sprinkle, fr. *ad-* + *-spergere* (fr. *spargere* to strew, scatter) — more at SPARK] **1 a** *archaic* (1) : to besprinkle (a person or thing) with a liquid or with dust (2) : to sprinkle (as water or dust) upon anybody or anything **b** (1) : to baptize by sprinkling ⟨use of sprinkling and *aspersing* was made in old times but only exceptionally and in the case of dying and dangerously sick persons —C.N.Callinicos⟩ (2) : to sprinkle with holy water **2** : to attack with foul reports or false and injurious charges : utter damaging charges or implications against in order to hurt the reputation of ⟨~ a man's character⟩ **syn** see MALIGN

as·pers·er \-sə(r)\ *n* -s : one that asperses

as·per·sion \ə'spərzhən, -ə̇zh-, -əizh- *also* a's-, *Brit usu & US also* -shən\ *n* -s [L *aspersion-, aspersio*, fr. *aspersus* + *-ion-, -io* -ion] **1 a** : a sprinkling with water esp. in religious ceremonies (as some forms of baptism) ⟨~*s* of holy water —F.B.Artz⟩ **b** *archaic* : SHOWER, SPRAY **2 a** : the act of calumniating : DEFAMATION ⟨groundless ~ of his wife's fidelity⟩ **b** : a calumnious or defamatory expression or reflection ⟨some of his more detailed ~*s* seem trigger-happy —P.H.Nowell-Smith⟩ ⟨greets you by casting ~*s* on your honesty —E.W.Lumsden⟩

as·per·so·ri·um \,aspər'sōrēəm, -sȯrē-\ *n, pl* **asperso·ria** \-ēə\ *or* **aspersoriums** [ML, fr. L *aspersus* + *-orium*] **1** : a stoup, basin, or other vessel for holy water **2** : ASPERGILLUM

as·per·so·ry \a'spərsərē, ə'-\ *n* -ES [ML *aspersorium*] : ASPERGILLUM

as·per·u·la \a'sper(y)ələ, ə'-\ *n, cap* [NL, fr. fem. of *asperulus*] : a genus of Old World herbs (family Rubiaceae) with small flowers and whorled leaves — see WOODRUFF

as·per·u·late \-,lāt,-lət\ *adj* [NL *asperulus* + E *-ate*] *bot* : delicately roughened

as·per·u·lous \-ləs\ *adj* [NL *asperulus*, fr. L *asper* rough + *-ulus*] *bot* : slightly rough

¹as·phalt \'a,sfȯlt, 'aa-, *Brit usu & US sometimes* -falt, *sporadic & old-fash* -felt\ *or* **as·phal·tum** \-'ɵtəm\ *also* **as·phalte** *like* ASPHALT\ *n* -s *often attrib* [alter. (prob. influenced by LL *asphaltus*, fr. Gk *asphaltos*) of earlier *aspaltum*, alter. (prob. influenced by assumed ML *aspaltum*, alter. of LL *aspaltus*) of ME *aspaltoun, aspalt*, fr. (assumed) ML *aspaltum* & LL *aspaltus*, fr. Gk *asphaltos, asphalton*, perh. fr. *a-* ²*a-* + *-sphaltos, -sphalton* (akin to Gk *sphallein* to cause to fall); fr. its possible use as a binding agent in stone walls — more at SPELL] **1** : a brown to black bituminous substance found native around the Dead sea, in Trinidad, and elsewhere and also obtained as a residue from certain petroleums, coal tar, and lignite tar consisting chiefly of a mixture of hydrocarbons, varying from hard and brittle to plastic in form, melting on heating, being insoluble in water but soluble in gasoline, and used esp. for paving and roofing, in paints and varnishes, and because light renders certain grades insoluble in oil of turpentine for photomechanical work **2 a** : a composition of ground asphalt rock and bitumen, of bitumen, lime, and gravel, or even of coal tar, lime, and sand used for forming pavements and as a waterproof cement (as for bridges and roofs) **b** : a surface (as a path or roadway) paved with asphalt **3 a** : SMOKE BROWN **b** *asphaltum* : CONGO 4

²asphalt \"\ *vt* -ED/-ING/-S **1** : to cover or pave with asphalt or a mixture containing asphalt ⟨the road itself was magnificently ~*ed* from side to side —Max Beerbohm⟩ **2** : to impregnate (as paper) with asphalt ⟨~*ed* bags, placed between the outer case and the packaged food —*Science News Letter*⟩

asphalt-base \'=,=¦=\ *adj* : containing relatively large amounts of asphalt-forming substances : yielding asphaltic residues on refining — used esp. of crude petroleum; compare NAPHTHENE-BASE, PARAFFIN-BASE

asphalt cement *n* : a refined asphalt free from water and coarse foreign material and containing less than one percent of ash

as·phal·tene \-'=,tēn\ *n* -s [F *asphaltène*, fr. *asphalte* asphalt + *-ène* -ene] : any of the components of a bitumen (as asphalt) that are soluble in carbon disulfide but not in paraffin naphtha and that are held to constitute the solid dispersed particles of the bitumen and to consist chiefly of high-molecular-weight hydrocarbons — compare CARBENE

as·phal·tic \(')=¦=tik, -ēk\ *adj* : of or containing asphalt

asphaltic felt *n* : a roofing and waterproofing material consisting of saturated asbestos or rag felt cemented together with asphalt or tar pitch

as·phal·tite \='=,tīt, '=,=¦=\ *n* -s [Gk *asphaltitēs*, fr. *asphaltos* + *-itēs* -ite] : a native asphalt occurring in vein deposits below the surface of the ground

asphalt lamination *n* : lamination (as of kraft papers) in which asphalt is used as the adhesive

asphalt macadam *n* : a pavement similar to tarmacadam but having asphaltic binder in place of tar

asphalt mastic *n* : a mixture of asphalt and other material (as sand, crushed rock, or asbestos) used like cement

asphalt paper *n* : paper that is impregnated, coated, or laminated with asphalt

asphalt process *n* : BITUMEN PROCESS

asphalt rock *n* : rock (as sandstone or limestone) impregnated naturally with asphalt

asphaltum *var of* ASPHALT

asphaltus *n* [LL — more at ASPHALT] *obs* : ASPHALT

aspheric \(')ā+¦-\ *or* **aspherical** \(')ā+¦=\ *adj* [²*a-* + *spheric, spherical*] **1** : departing slightly from the spherical form — used of an optical surface **2** : free from spherical aberration

as·pho·del \'asfə,del, 'aas-\ *n, pl* **asphodel** *also* **asphodels** [L *asphodelus*, fr. Gk *asphodelos*] : any of various Old World usu. perennial herbs of the family Liliaceae and chiefly of the genera *Asphodelus* and *Asphodeline* that bear their flowers in long erect racemes — see FALSE ASPHODEL

asphodel green *n* : a moderate yellow green that is greener and paler than average moss green, yellower and less strong than average pea green, and yellower and paler than spinach green

as·pho·del·i·ne \,asfə'delə,nē\ *n, cap* [NL, fr. Gk *asphodelinē*, fem. of *asphodelinos* of asphodel, fr. *asphodelos*] : a genus of asphodels native to the Mediterranean region that have usu. yellow or white flowers in long bracted racemes

as·phod·e·lus \a'sfädᵊləs\ *n, cap* [NL, fr. L] : a genus of asphodels native to southern Asia and the Mediterranean region that have white, pink, or yellow flowers and clustered fleshy roots

as·phyx·ia \a'sfiksēə, ə's-, -kshə\ *n* -s [NL, fr. Gk, stopping of the pulse, fr. *a-* ²*a-* + *-sphyxia* (fr. *sphyzein* to throb)] : local or systemic deficiency of oxygen and excess of carbon dioxide in living tissues usu. as a result of interruption of respiration; *broadly* : ANOXIA — compare SUFFOCATION

as·phyx·i·al \-ksēəl\ *adj* [NL *asphyxia* + E *-al*] : marked by or relating to asphyxia

as·phyx·i·ant \-ksēənt\ *n* -s [*asphyxia*te + *-ant*] : an agent (as a gas) capable of causing asphyxia

as·phyx·i·ate \-ē,āt, *usu* -ād.+V\ *vb* -ED/-ING/-S [NL *asphyxia* + E *-ate*] *vt* **:** to cause asphyxia in **:** kill, suspend animation in, or make unconscious through want of adequate oxygen, presence of noxious agents, or other obstruction to normal breathing ⟨*asphyxiated* by carbon monoxide in the garage⟩ ~ *vi* **:** to suffer asphyxia **:** die, be overcome, or faint typically because of noxious gas or want of adequate oxygen ⟨the rescue squad almost *asphyxiated*⟩ **syn** see SUFFOCATE

as·phyx·i·a·tion \(,)a,sfiksē'āshən, ə,s-\ *n* -S **1 :** act of causing asphyxia **:** a state of asphyxia **:** SUFFOCATION **2 :** a physiological disorder of plants caused by shortage of air and characterized by failure of seeds to germinate or by yellowing or blighting of established plants

as·phyx·i·a·tor \a'sfiksē,ād·ə(r), ə's-\ *n* -S **:** one that asphyxiates: as **a :** an asphyxiating agent **b :** a device for killing animals by asphyxiation

as·phyxy \a'sfiksē, ə's-, 'a,s-\ *n* -ES [F *asphyxie*, fr. NL *asphyxia*] **:** ASPHYXIA

¹as·pic \'aspik, 'aas-,'ais-, -ēk\ *n* -S [MF, fr. OF, alter. of *aspe*, fr. L *aspis* — more at ASP] *obs* **:** the venomous asp

²aspic \"\ *n* -S [F, fr. MF, modif. of OProv *espic* head (of grain), spike, fr. L *spica* — more at SPIKE] **:** a European lavender (*Lavandula spica*) that produces a volatile oil — compare SPIKE LAVENDER

³aspic \"\ *n* -S [F, lit., asp] **:** a savory jelly made from fish or meat stock thickened with gelatin and seasoned and used cold to garnish meat or fish or to make a mold of meat, fish, or vegetables

aspiculate \(')ā+¦-\ *or* **aspiculous** \(')ā+¦-\ *adj* [²*a-* + *spiculate, spiculous*] **:** without spicules ⟨~ sponges⟩

aspid- *or* **aspido-** *comb form* [NL, fr. Gk, fr. *aspid-, aspis*; perh. akin to Gk *aspidēs* vast, broad, L *spatium* space — more at SPEED] **:** shield ⟨*Aspidosperma*⟩

as·pid·i·nol \a'spidᵊn,ōl, -ōl\ *n* -S [ISV *aspidin* $C_{25}H_{32}O_8$ (fr. *aspid-* — fr. NL *Aspidium* — + *-in*; orig. formed in G) + *-ol*; orig. formed in G] **:** a yellow crystalline compound $C_{12}H_{16}O_4$ found in the rhizome of the male fern

as·pid·i·o·tus \(,)a,spidē'ōd·əs\ *n, cap* [NL, modif. of Gk *aspidiōtēs* one bearing a shield, fr. *aspid-, aspis* shield] **:** a genus of armored scales including the San Jose scale and several others that are very destructive to orchard trees

as·pi·dis·tra \,aspə'distrə, ,aas-\ *n* [NL, irreg. fr. Gk *aspid-, aspis* shield] **1** *cap* **:** a genus of Asiatic herbs (family Liliaceae) with large handsome basal leaves and tetramerous flowers borne close to the ground — see CAST-IRON PLANT **2** -S **:** any plant of the genus *Aspidistra*

¹as·pid·i·um \a'spidēəm\ [NL, fr. Gk *aspidion* small shield, dim. of *aspid-, aspis*] *syn of* DRYOPTERIS

²aspidium \"\ *n* [NL, fr. Gk *aspidion*] **1** *cap, in some classifications* **:** a genus of ferns including those otherwise divided among the genera *Dryopteris, Polystichum*, and *Tectaria* **2** *pl* **aspidia** \-ēə\ **:** any fern belonging to the genus *Dryopteris, Polystichum*, or *Tectaria* **3** *pl* **aspidia :** a drug consisting of the rhizome and stipes esp. of the male fern used as the oleoresinous extract for the expulsion of tapeworms

as·pi·do·both·ria \,aspə,dō'bäthrēə\ *or* **aspidoboth·rii** \-rē,ī\ [NL, fr. *aspid-* + *-bothria, -bothrii* (fr. *bothrium*)] *syn of* ASPIDOGASTREA

as·pi·do·bran·chia \-'braŋkēə\ *n pl, cap* [NL, fr. *aspid-* + *-branchia*] **:** an order of Streptoneura comprising marine gastropods having the nervous system only slightly concentrated, usu. exhibiting clear traces of ancestral bilateral symmetry, with two kidneys and two auricles, and including the limpets and other primitive forms — **as·pi·do·bran·chi·ate** \-'braŋkēət, -ē,āt\ *adj or n*

as·pi·do·ceph·a·li \-'sefə,lī\ [NL, fr. *aspid-* + *-cephali*] *syn of* CEPHALASPIDA

as·pi·do·chi·ro·ta \-,kī'rōd·ə\ *n pl, cap* [NL, fr. *aspid-* + Gk *-cheirōta* (neut. pl. of *-cheirōtos*, fr. *cheir* hand) — more at CHIR-] **:** an order of chiefly tropical holothurians having tube feet and having the branches of the tentacles confined to the tip where they form a more or less circular shield-shaped terminal disk

as·pi·do·co·tyl·ea \-kə'tilēə, -,käd·ᵊl'ēə\ [NL, fr. *aspid-* + *-cotylea* (fr. Gk *kotylē* anything hollow)] *syn of* ASPIDOGASTREA

as·pi·do·gas·trea \-'gastrēə\ *n pl, cap* [NL, fr. *aspid-* + *-gastrea* (fr. Gk *gastr-, gastēr* stomach) — more at GASTRIC] **:** a small subclass of Trematoda comprising flukes with large complex ventral sucking disks that are intermediate in some respects between monogenetic and digenetic trematodes and are internal or external parasites of aquatic animals, sometimes having alternation of hosts though completely lacking sexual reproduction — **as·pi·do·gas·trid** \-'gastrəd\ *adj or n*

as·pi·do·sper·ma \-'spərmə\ *n* [NL, fr. *aspid-* + *-sperma*] **1** *cap* **:** a genus of tropical American trees or rarely shrubs (family Apocynaceae) having alternate leaves, small flowers, follicular fruits, and peltate compressed seeds with a flat papery wing — see PADDLEWOOD, QUEBRACHO **2** -S **:** the dried bark of the white quebracho used as a respiratory sedative in dyspnea and in asthma

as·pi·do·sper·mine \-'spər,mēn, -,mən\ *n* -S [ISV *aspidosperm-* (fr. NL *Aspidosperma*) + *-ine*] **:** a bitter crystalline alkaloid $C_{22}H_{30}N_2O_2$ obtained from quebracho bark, its sulfate having been used formerly as a respiratory stimulant and antispasmodic and as an antipyretic in typhoid fever

aspinose \(')ā+ *adj* [²*a-* + *spinose*] *zool* **:** without a spine

¹as·pi·rant \'asp(ə)rənt, 'aas- *also* ə'spīr-\ *n* -S [L *aspirant-, aspirans*, pres. part. of *aspirare* to aspire] **:** one who aspires **:** one who is ambitious of advancement or attainment ⟨any ~, whoever he may be, can try his hand at writing —James Britton⟩ ⟨~*s* to medicine and philosophy —Benjamin Farrington⟩

²aspirant \"\ *adj* [L *aspirant-, aspirans*] **:** ASPIRING ⟨good American historical writing is the work of professors and of ~ professors —*Times Lit. Supp.*⟩

as·pi·ra·ta \,aspə'räd·ə, -ād·ə\ *n, pl* **aspira·tae** \-ä,tē, -ä,tī, -ā,tē\ [NL, fr. L, fem. of past part. of *aspirare* to aspirate] **:** ROUGH STOP

¹as·pi·rate \'asp(ə)rət, 'aas-, *usu* -əd.+V\ *adj* [L *aspiratus*, past part. of *aspirare*, lit., to breathe upon — more at ASPIRE] **1 :** ASPIRATED **2 :** silent but not preceded by liaison or elision — used of *h* in modern French

²as·pi·rate \-pə,rāt, *usu* -ād.+V\ *vt* -ED/-ING/-S [L *aspiratus*] **1 a :** to pronounce or to mark so as to be pronounced (a vowel or word) with an *h*-sound as the initial element (as in ancient Greek) **b :** to pronounce (a stop consonant) with an immediately following *h*-sound in a syllable in which the *h* is not usu. represented (as in English) **2 a :** to draw by suction ⟨a new charge is simultaneously being *aspirated* by the lower cylinder by way of inlet ports —G.G.Smith⟩ **b :** to remove (material) by aspiration ⟨the portal vein is exposed and blood is *aspirated* with a 50-ml. syringe —*Biol. Abstracts*⟩ ⟨mucus *aspirated* from the bronchus by bronchoscopy⟩ **c :** INHALE ⟨~ food particles⟩

³as·pi·rate \-p(ə)rət, *usu* -əd.+V\ *n* -S [¹*aspirate*] **1 :** \h\ as an independent sound or a character representing it (as the letter *h* or the rough breathing symbol in Greek) — compare BREATHING 2 **2 :** a consonant having as its final element aspiration in the same syllable; *broadly* **:** a combination of letters of which the last is *h* or the sound of such a combination **3 :** material removed by aspiration ⟨parasites may be more readily found in ~*s* from the spleen —K.F.Maxcy⟩

aspirating stroke *n* **:** SUCTION STROKE

as·pi·ra·tion \(,)aspə'rāshən, ,aas- *sometimes* -(,)spī'- *or* -,spē'-\ *n* -S [ME *aspiracioun*, fr. L *aspiration-, aspiratio* breathing, blowing, aspiration, fr. *aspiratus* + *-ion-, -io* -ion] **1 a :** the act of aspirating **:** addition of an aspirate sound **:** pronunciation of an aspirate **b :** an aspirated sound (as \h\) **:** a breathed sound in Greek **2 a :** act of breathing, esp. breathing in, sometimes audibly **b** (1) **:** the withdrawal esp. by means of suction of fluids or friable tissue from the body (2) **:** the operation of making such a withdrawal — compare ASPIRATOR 2 **3** [ML *aspiration-, aspiratio* aspiration, desire, fr. L] **a :** a strong desire for realization (as of ambitions, ideals, or accomplishment) ⟨the ~ of America is still upward, toward a better job —Bernard De Voto⟩ ⟨the religious ~ which raised the first Gothic cathedrals —O. Elfrida Saunders⟩ ⟨the only independent institution of learning of any size with liberal ~*s* is the university —Green Peyton⟩ **b :** an end or goal aspired to **:** a condition strongly desired ⟨the democratic ideal . . . was the common ~ of men —W.A.White⟩ ⟨flying is her ~ and her passion —E.A.Weeks⟩

as·pi·ra·tion·al \¦=(,)=¦shənᵊl, -shnəl\ *adj* **:** of or relating to aspiration ⟨an accepted moral and ~ life —K.L.Patton⟩

aspiration biopsy *n* **:** biopsy by means of aspiration

aspiration pneumonia *n* **:** pneumonia resulting from inhalation of foreign bodies (as food particles)

as·pi·ra·tor \'aspə,rād·ə(r), 'aas-, -ātə-\ *n* -S [G, fr. L *aspiratus* + *-or*] **1 :** an apparatus for moving gases, liquids, or granular substances by suction ⟨grain ~*s* probe the holds of a . . . merchantman with long tentaclelike tubes and discharge her cargo into canalboats —D.S.Boyer⟩ **2 a :** an instrument for collecting material by suction; *specif* **:** a hollow needle or cannula connected with a reservoir in which a partial vacuum can be created and used for the removal of foreign bodies, or the collection of secretions or tissue from the body esp. for diagnostic purposes **b :** any of various devices for producing suction; *esp* **:** a device in which a fluid at high velocity passes an orifice thus creating a partial vacuum behind the orifice **3 :** RESPIRATOR

aspire \ə'spī(ə)r, -īə *also* a'-\ *vb* -ED/-ING/-S [ME *aspiren*, fr. MF or L; MF *aspirer*, fr. L *aspirare, adspirare*, lit., to breathe upon, fr. *ad-* + *spirare* to breathe — more at SPIRIT] *vi* **1 :** to be ambitious **:** YEARN, LONG **:** seek to attain or accomplish something, esp. something high or great — used often with *to* or *after* ⟨souls will still live and will ~ —W.L.Sullivan⟩ ⟨Romans who *aspired* to philosophy —Benjamin Farrington⟩ ⟨self-realization to which they *aspired* —G.L.Dickinson⟩ ⟨the perfect lyrist should ~, if not to epics, at least to odes —Herbert Read⟩ ⟨dictatorships that ~ to control the economy —Peter Wiles⟩ **2 :** RISE, ASCEND, TOWER, SOAR ⟨a tall thin flame that *aspired* —J.B.Cabell⟩ ⟨here still an aged elm ~*s* —Philip Freneau⟩ ~ *vt* **1** *obs* **:** to mount to **:** ATTAIN ⟨our souls ~ celestial thrones —Christopher Marlowe⟩ **2** *archaic* **:** to long for

aspi·ré *or* **aspi·rée** \,aspə'rā, -pē-\ *adj* [F, lit., aspirated, fr. masc. & fem. respectively of pres. part. of *aspirer* to aspirate, breathe] *of h in French* **:** initial in the orthography of a word before which elision and liaison do not occur — compare MUET

aspir·er \ə'spīrə(r) *also* a'-\ *n* -S **:** one that aspires

as·pi·rin \'asp(ə)rən, 'aas- *also* -pərn\ *n, pl* **aspirin** *or* **aspirins** [ISV, acetyl + *spir-* (fr. *spiraeic acid*, old name for salicylic acid (fr. ISV *spirae-* — fr. NL *Spiraea* — + *-ic* + *acid*; orig. formed as G *spirsäure*) + *-in*; orig. formed in G] **1 a :** a white crystalline compound $CH_3COOC_6H_4COOH$ of salicylic acid used esp. in tablet form as an antipyretic and analgesic like the salicylates but producing fewer undesirable effects — called also *acetylsalicylic acid* **2 :** a tablet of aspirin

as·pis \'aspəs, 'aas-\ *n, cap* [NL, fr. L, asp, viper, fr. Gk] **:** a genus of vipers including the horned viper and related hornless forms

-as·pis \"\ *n comb form* [NL, fr. Gk *aspis* shield — more at ASPID-] **:** one having (such) a shield — in generic names in zoology and paleontology ⟨Cephal*aspis*⟩ ⟨Odont*aspis*⟩

asp·ish \'aspish, 'aas-,'ais-, -ēsh\ *adj* [²*asp* + *-ish*] **:** like that of an asp ⟨~ venom⟩ — **asp·ish·ly** *adv*

asplanchnic \(')ā+¦-\ *adj* [Gk *asplanchnos* without bowels (fr. *a-* ²*a-* + *-splanchnos*, fr. *splanchnon* entrail) + E *-ic* — more at SPLANCHNO-] **:** having no alimentary canal

as·ple·ni·oid \a'splēnē,ȯid\ *adj* [ISV *aspleni-* (fr. NL *Asplenium*) + *-oid*] **:** of or resembling ferns of the genus *Asplenium*

as·ple·ni·um \-ēəm\ *n, cap* [NL, alter. of L *asplenum* spleenwort, fr. Gk *asplēnon*, irreg. fr. *splēn* spleen — more at SPLEEN] **:** a widely distributed genus of ferns (family Polypodiaceae) having linear or oblong sori borne obliquely on the upper side of a veinlet and comprising the spleenworts — see EBONY SPLEENWORT, WALL RUE

asporogenous \¦ā+¦=¦===\ *or* **asporogenic** \¦ā+,==¦==\ *adj* [ISV ²*a-* + *sporogenous, sporogenic*] **:** not spore-bearing **:** not producing spores — used esp. of yeasts

asporous \(')ā+¦-\ *adj* [ISV ²*a-* + *sporous*] **:** without true spores

as·por·ta·tion \,aspə(r)'tāshən\ *n* -S [ME *asportacioun*, fr. L *asportation-, asportatio*, fr. *asportatus* (past part. of *asportare* to carry off, fr. *as-* — fr. *abs, ab* away — + *portare* to carry) + *-ion-, -io* -ion — more at OF, PORT] **:** a carrying away; *specif* **:** felonious removal of goods

asporulate \(')ā+¦-\ *adj* [²*a-* + *sporulate*, v., taken as an adj.] **:** not sporulating

asprawl \ə'-\ *adv (or adj)* [¹*a-* + *sprawl*, v.] **:** in or into a sprawling position ⟨landed ~ on the floor⟩ ⟨with legs ~⟩

aspre *var of* ¹ASPER

aspread \ə'-\ *adj* [¹*a-* + *spread*, v.] **:** spread out **:** SPREADING

aspre·do \a'sprē(,)dō\ *n, cap* [NL, fr. L, roughness, fr. *asper* rough] **:** a genus of So. American catfishes the females of which carry their eggs attached to the skin of the lower surface of the body until hatched

asps *pl of* ASP

asquat \ə'-\ *adj* [¹*a-* + *squat*, v.] **:** SQUATTING

asquint \ə'-\ *adv (or adj)* [ME] **:** with the eye directed to one side, obliquely, or squintingly as if with distorted vision or as if to peer or glance furtively or slyly ⟨when he . . . speaks falsely, the eye is muddy and sometimes ~ —R.W.Emerson⟩

asquirm \ə'-\ *adj* [¹*a-* + *squirm*, v.] **:** SQUIRMING

asram \'äs(h)rəm\ *n* -S [Skt *āśrama* — more at ASHRAM] **:** ASHRAM

asrama *var of* ASHRAMA

as regards *or* **as respects** *prep* **:** in regard to **:** with respect to **:** CONCERNING ⟨*as regards* his suggestions I was noncommittal⟩

¹ass \'as, 'aa(ə)s,'ais *also* 'äs *in NE & Brit esp* (*in Brit at least*) *in sense 2*\ *n* -ES [ME *asse*, fr. OE *assa*, perh. fr. OIr *asan*, fr. L *asinus*, prob. fr. a language of Asia Minor; akin to the source of Gk *onos* ass] **1 :** any of several mammals of the genus *Equus* that is smaller than the horse, with a shorter mane and shorter hair on the tail, with long ears, and without callosities on the inner surface of the hind limbs, that are hardy and gregarious sure-footed natives of Asia and No. Africa, and of which one species (*E. asinus*) is the domestic ass, a rugged, patient, but somewhat stubborn beast of burden, made a popular symbol of obstinacy and stupidity — see KIANG, MULE **2 :** one that is utterly silly **:** a simple-minded fool often marked by stubbornness or stolidity ⟨when they make ~*es* of themselves they do it in the grand style —Leonard Bacon⟩

wild ass

²ass \"\ *vi* -ED/-ING/-ES **:** to act like an ass **:** to play the ass ⟨~*ing* along . . . as though we were still back in the nineteen-twenties —Margery Allingham⟩

³ass \'as\ *Scot var of* ³ASH

⁴ass *or* **arse** \ *in the U S* 'as, 'aa(ə)s, 'ais *also* 'äs, *and sometimes* 'ärs *euphemistically by speakers who have preconsonantal r and who are aware that there is a spelling "arse"*; 'äs *in standard Brit and* 'a(r)s *or* 'ärs *or* 'ȧrs *or* 'ers *in Brit and Scot dialect; in the US the pronunc* 'äs *occurs chiefly in NE and is there prob more often associated with the spelling "ass" than with "arse"*\ *n* -ES [ME *ars, ers*, fr. OE *ærs, ears*; akin to OHG & ON *ars* buttocks, Gk *orrhos*, Arm *or*, Hitt *arraš*, OIr *err* tail] **1 a :** BUTTOCKS, RUMP — often considered vulgar **b :** ANUS — often considered vulgar **2** *dial Brit* **:** the lower or rear end of anything **:** BOTTOM **3 :** sexual intercourse — usu. considered vulgar

ass *abbr* **1** assembly **2** assistant **3** association

as·sa·cu \,asə'kü\ *n* -S [Pg *assacú*, fr. Tupi] **:** SANDBOX TREE

assafetida *or* **assafoetida** *var of* ASAFETIDA

assagai *var of* ASSEGAI

¹as·sai \ä'sī, -sīē\ *adv* [It, fr. (assumed) VL *ad satis* enough — more at ASSET] **:** VERY — used with tempo direction in music ⟨allegro ~⟩

²as·sai *also* **as·sa·hy** \ä¦sä¦ē\ *n, pl* **assa·is** *or* **assa·hies** [Pg *assaí*, fr. Tupi] **1** *or* **assai palm :** a slender pinnate-leaved palm (*Euterpe edulis*) of Brazil and British Guiana having dark purple fleshy fibrous edible fruit **2 a :** a nutritious Brazilian drink made by infusion from the fruit of the assai palm with the addition of cassava **b :** a flavor (as for desserts or ice cream) made from the assai fruit

¹as·sail \ə'sāl *also* a'-\ *vt* -ED/-ING/-S [ME *assailen*, fr. OF *asaillir*, fr. (assumed) VL *assalire*, alter. (influenced by *salire*) of L *assilire, adsilire* to leap upon, fr. *ad-* + *salire* to leap — more at SALLY] **1 :** to attack with violence or vehemence **:** ASSAULT ⟨~ a man with blows⟩ ⟨~ a city⟩ ⟨the noise ~*ed* his ears⟩ **2 :** to attack forcefully or violently by nonphysical means (as with words) ⟨the adherents of the new learning were ~*ed* with every sort of ridicule —G.G.Coulton⟩ **:** beset strongly with or as if with intent to overcome ⟨~*ed* by a cloud of disturbing thoughts —T.B.Costain⟩ **3** *archaic* **:** WOO ⟨~ her with tenderness⟩ **4 :** to encounter or confront (as an obstacle) in order to prevail over ⟨~ the slope below the cliff⟩ **5 :** to make an impact upon ⟨the faint smell of copper ~*ed* my nostrils —Amy Lowell⟩ **syn** see ATTACK

²assail \"\ *n* -S [ME, fr. *assailen*] *archaic* **:** ATTACK

as·sail·a·ble \-əbəl\ *adj* **:** capable of being assailed

¹as·sail·ant \-ənt\ *n* -S [MF *assaillant*, fr. *assaillant*, pres. part. of *assaillir*] **1 :** one who assails or attacks ⟨met by ~*s* and in the scuffle one worker was killed —*Current Biog.*⟩ **2 :** an aggressive opponent in controversy ⟨an ~ of the religious belief of the day —Leslie Stephen⟩

²assailant \"\ *adj* [MF *assaillant*, pres. part. of *assaillir*, fr. OF *asaillir*] *archaic* **:** ASSAILING

as·sail·ment \-mənt\ *n* -S **:** act of assailing **:** ATTACK, ASSAULT

assai palm *n* [²*assai* + *palm*] **:** ²ASSAI 1

as·sam \ə'sam, a'-, -saa(ə)m, 'a,s-\ *also* **assam tea** *n* -S *usu cap A* [fr. *Assam*, state of northeastern India] **:** tea from Assam

¹as·sam·ese \,asə'mēz, -ēs\ *n, pl* **assamese** *cap* [*Assam* + *-ese*] **1 :** a native or inhabitant of Assam, India **2 :** the language of Assam the alphabet of which is the same as that of Bengali with one additional letter for the sound of *w*

²assamese \¦=¦=¦=\ *adj, usu cap* **1 a :** of, relating to, or characteristic of Assam **b :** of, relating to, or characteristic of the natives or inhabitants of Assam **2 :** of, relating to, or characteristic of the Assamese language

assam rubber *n, usu cap A* **:** a rubber obtained from a rubber tree (*Ficus elastica*) **:** RAMBONG RUBBER

as·sa·pan \'asə,pan\ *also* **as·sa·pan·ic** \,==¦nik\ *n* -S [of Virginian origin; akin to Sac & Fox *äsepäna* raccoon, Ojibwa *assânogo* grey squirrel] **:** the American flying squirrel

¹as·sart \ə'särt\ *also* **es·sart** \ə'-\ *vi* -ED/-ING/-S [MF *essarter*, fr. OF, fr. *essart*] *English law* **:** to grub up trees and bushes to make land arable

²assart \"\ *also* **essart** \"\ *n* -S [MF *essart*, fr. OF, fr. LL *exartum*, fr. (assumed) VL *exsartum*, neut. of *exsartus*, past part. of *exsarire* to weed out, fr. L *ex* out + *sarire* to hoe, weed; akin to OHG *sarf* sharp, L *sarpere* to prune, Gk *harpagē* hook, rake, Skt *sṛṇi* sickle — more at EX-] **1** *English law* **:** act of grubbing up trees or bushes usu. in converting forest land into arable land **2** *English law* **:** a piece of land cleared

¹as·sas·sin \ə'sasᵊn, -saas- *sometimes* -sin\ *n* -S [ML *assassinus*, fr. Ar *ḥashshāshīn*, pl. of *ḥashshāsh* one addicted to hashish, fr. *ḥashīsh* hemp, hashish] **1** *usu cap* **:** one of a secret order of Muslims that at the time of the Crusades terrorized Christians and other enemies by secret murder committed under the influence of hashish **2 :** MURDERER; *esp* **:** one that murders either for hire or from fanatic adherence to a cause

²assassin *vt* -ED/-ING/-S *obs* **:** ASSASSINATE

¹assassinate *n* -S [MF *assassinat*, fr. ML *assassinatus*, fr. *assassinatus*, past part. of *assassinare*] **1** *obs* **:** ASSASSINATION **2** *obs* **:** ASSASSIN

²as·sas·si·nate \ə'sasᵊn,āt, -saas-, *usu* -ād.+V\ *vt* -ED/-ING/-S [ML *assassinatus*, past part. of *assassinare*, fr. *assassinus*] **1 :** to murder (a usu. prominent person) violently **2** *obs* **:** to assail with murderous intent **3 :** to injure, wound, or destroy usu. unexpectedly and treacherously ⟨he was *assassinating* a man's character —*Atlantic*⟩ **syn** see KILL

as·sas·si·na·tion \ə,=='nāshən\ *n* -S **1 :** act of assassinating **:** killing by treacherous violence **2 :** destruction esp. of reputation

assassin bug *n* **:** a predaceous bug of the family Reduviidae living mostly on other insects though a few attack mammals and even man **:** CONENOSE

assassin fly *n* **:** ROBBER FLY

as·sa·tion \a'sāshən\ *n* -S [F, fr. MF, fr. L *assatus* (past part. of *assare* to roast, fr. *assus* roasted, fr. *ardēre* to burn) + MF *-ion* — more at ARDOR] *archaic* **:** the act of baking or roasting

¹as·sault \ə'sȯlt\ *n* -S [ME *assaut*, fr. OF *asaut, assaut*, fr. (assumed) VL *assaltus*, fr. *assaltus*, past part. of *assalire* to assail — more at ASSAIL] **1 :** a violent attack with physical means (as blows or weapons): as **a :** a military charge or onslaught esp. against a walled or defended position **b :** the phase of an attack in which the attacker moves forward and by means of close combat seeks to eliminate enemy resistance and establish control of the objective **c :** a part of an offensive action in which close firing develops or may be expected to develop ⟨an ~ on beaches⟩ ⟨~ troops⟩ ⟨~ guns⟩ **2 :** a violent attack with nonphysical weapons (as words, arguments, or appeals) ⟨an ~ upon science —W.L.Sullivan⟩ ⟨an ~ on his character⟩ **3 a :** an apparently violent attempt or a willful offer with force or violence to do hurt to another without the actual doing of the hurt threatened (as by lifting the fist or a cane in a threatening manner) — compare ASSAULT AND BATTERY, BATTERY 2b(2) **b :** RAPE **:** indecent attack or overture forcibly effected **4 :** a bout with foils, broadswords, or similar weapons

²assault \"\ *vb* -ED/-ING/-S [ME *assauten*, fr. MF *assauter*, fr. (assumed) VL *assaltare*, fr. *assaltus*] *vt* **1 a :** to make an assault upon **:** rush violently and hostilely against **:** attack with strong violent onslaught ⟨the soldiers were ~*ing* the castle⟩ **b :** to attack (a person) typically with brutal violence ⟨a policeman ~*ed* by the mob⟩ **c :** to commit rape upon **:** subject to indecent attack **2** *obs* **:** TEMPT **3 :** to attack violently by nonphysical means (as words, arguments, or unfriendly measures) **:** ASSAIL ⟨~ the Constitution —J.B.Oakes⟩ **4 :** to strike against violently ⟨we ~ our eyes with colors unknown in the natural world —T.F.Hamlin⟩ **:** impinge upon ⟨an ounce of fact is ~*ed* by a ton of footnotes —L.Ruth Middlebrook⟩ ~ *vi* **:** to make an assault ⟨within 50 yards of their objective, they ~*ed* —Mack Morriss⟩ **syn** see ATTACK

as·sault·a·ble \-əbəl\ *adj* **:** exposed to assault

assault and battery *n* **:** assault (sense 3a) combined with the actual doing of an injury — compare BATTERY 2b (2)

assault-at-arms \=¦=¦=¦=\ *n, pl* **assaults-at-arms** *Brit* **:** a public team contest in which individual boxers, wrestlers, and fencers of various weights and classes are matched

assault boat *n* **:** a small portable boat used in an amphibious military attack or in land warfare for crossing rivers or lakes

assault fire *n* **:** fire delivered by infantry in the assault esp. with rifles fired from the hip or rapidly from the shoulder

as·sault·ive \ə'sȯltiv\ *adj* **:** inclined toward or disposed to committing assault ⟨viciously ~ even to the point of homicide —Richard Warden⟩ — **as·sault·ive·ness** *n* -ES

¹as·say \'a,sā, a'sā\ *n* -S [ME, fr. ONF *assai*, alter. (influenced by *a* to, fr. L *ad*) of OF *essai* — more at AT, ESSAY] **1 a** *archaic* (1) **:** trial in order to test **:** TESTING (2) **:** EXPERIMENT (3) **:** TRIAL, AFFLICTION **b :** examination and determination as to characteristics (as weight, measure, or quality) ⟨an ~ merely of the technical operations of the poem —*Amer. Scholar*⟩ ⟨~ of the historical role of the individual —Jerome Nathanson⟩ ⟨microbiological ~ methods —*U. S. Dept. Agric. Report on Experiment Stations*⟩ ⟨under the ~ conditions employed —*Biol. Abstracts*⟩: (1) **:** a chemical test to determine the presence or absence or more often the quantity of one or more components of a material (as an ore, alloy, drug, antibiotic, or dietary substance) (2) *archaic* **:** a testing by taste **:** TASTING (3) *obs* **:** the usu. complimentary or courteous act of tasting food or drink before offering it to a person (4) *obs* **:** testing as to compliance with a standard (as of weights, measures, or foodstuffs) **c :** tested purity, value, or character ⟨of high poetic ~ —Roland Gelatt⟩ **d** (1) **:** a substance to be tested or being tested ⟨the blowpipe test was made on the ~⟩ (2) **:** the reported result of such testing **:** measurable quantity ⟨the town always had a fairly high ~ of Nazis —Paul Moor⟩ **2 a** *archaic* **:** ASSAULT, ATTACK

⟨the men . . . strove vainly at the first ~ by dint of climbing on other men's shoulders to storm the platform —*Century Mag.*⟩ **b** *obs* **:** initial or tentative effort **3 a** *archaic* **:** an effort to accomplish **:** ENDEAVOR, ATTEMPT ⟨two brief ~*s* at teaching —*Americana Annual*⟩ — now rarely used in this sense; compare ESSAY **b** *archaic* **:** best effort or maximum exertion — **at all assays 1** *obs* **:** at or for any emergency **2** *obs* **:** in any case **:** ALWAYS

²as·say \a'sā *also* 'a,sā *sometimes* ə'sā\ *vb* -ED/-ING/-S [ME *assayen*, fr. ONF *assayer*, fr. *assai*] *vt* **1 :** TRY, ATTEMPT, ESSAY ⟨here we have two authors ~*ing* that task once more —Oscar Lewis⟩ ⟨has ~*ed* to penetrate a field that by its very nature requires consummate skill —J.W.Chase⟩ **2** *obs* **:** to learn from experience **3** *obs* **a :** to taste (food or drink) before serving (as to a person of rank) **b :** to practice experimentally **c :** to subject to the trial of afflictions or temptations **4 a :** to analyze (an impure substance or mixture) for one or more valuable components — used esp. of determinations in mining, metallurgy, pharmacy, food chemistry **b :** to analyze and judge the significance, worth, or status of ⟨~ a play⟩ ⟨~ an event⟩ ⟨~ the various intellectual changes which the great reformers within and without the Catholic Church accomplished —J.H.Randall⟩ ~ *vi* **:** to show or prove to be of a particular nature by means of an assay ⟨the ore ~*s* high in silver⟩ **syn** see ESTIMATE

as·say·a·ble \(')a¦sāəbəl\ *adj* **:** capable of being assayed

assay bar *n* **:** a bar of pure or nearly pure gold or silver manufactured by the government as a standard

as·say·er \a'sāə(r), 'a,s-, ə's-\ *n* -S [ME, fr. *assayen* + *-er*] **:** one that assays; *specif* **:** a chemist who assays the value and amount of metals in ores and alloys

assay office *n* **:** a government or commercial office and laboratory in which assays are made (as of precious metals)

assay ton *n* **:** a unit of weight of ore taken for assay equal to 29166⅔ milligrams, the number of milligrams of precious metal in this amount of ore being equal to the number of troy ounces per 2000-pound ton

¹ass-backward \'ˌ=ˌ=\ *adj* [*²ass* + *backward*] **:** ludicrously disordered **:** showing an arrangement grotesquely counter to the usual or workable ⟨incompetents doing their work in an *ass-backward* way⟩

²ass-backward *or* **ass-backwards** \'ˌ=ˌ=\ *adv* **:** in an ass-backward way ⟨an inexperienced assistant filing everything *ass-backward*⟩

assce *abbr* assurance

assd *abbr* **1** assessed **2** assigned **3** assured

asse \'as\ *n* -S [prob. native name in southern Africa] **:** a fox of southern Africa (*Vulpes chama*)

¹as·se·gai *or* **as·sa·gai** \'asə,gī, ,=ˌ='=\ *n* -S [prob. fr. MF *azagaie*, fr. OSp *azagaya*, Ar *az-zaghāya* the assegai, fr. Ar *al-* the + *zaghāya*, fr. Berber] **1 :** a slender hardwood spear or light javelin usu. tipped with iron and used by tribes in southern Africa **2 :** a southern African tree (*Curtisia faginea*) of the dogwood family, whose wood may be used in making assegais

assegai

²assegai *or* **assagai** \"\ *vt* -ED/-ING/-S **:** to pierce with an assegai

asselar man \'asə,lär-\ *n, usu cap A* [fr. *Asselar*, Fr. garrison near Tombouctou, Fr. West Africa, near where it was found] **:** a post-Paleolithic negroid type of man known from a single tall dolichocephalic skeleton from the southern Sahara having points of resemblance to both Boskop and Grimaldi man

as·self \a'self\ *vt* -ED/-ING/-S [*ad-* + *self*] *archaic* **:** to take to oneself **:** APPROPRIATE

as·sem·blage \ə'semblij, -ēj\ *n* -S [F, fr. MF, fr. *assembler* + *-age*] **1 a :** a collection of individuals or of particular things **:** AGGREGATION ⟨a strange ~ of human beings —Bertrand Russell⟩ ⟨the ~ of forms of mosquitoes formerly included in the species —G.S.Carter⟩ ⟨a slow but general southward migration of the various plant ~*s* —C.O.Dunbar⟩ **b :** a group of organisms or fossils sharing a common situation (as a microhabitat) essentially by chance **2 a :** the act of assembling ⟨building became the ~ of accurately measured elements —Lewis Mumford⟩ **:** ASSEMBLY **b :** the state of being assembled ⟨a motion-picture theater or other place of public ~⟩ **3 :** AGGREGATE 5 **4 :** the cost of bringing two or more parcels of land under a single ownership **:** PLOTTAGE ⟨the entire Dodge ~ designated by (B) on the map is $1,140,000 for land and $1,270,000 for land and buildings —*N. Y. Herald Tribune*⟩ **5 :** the total of related culture traits and artifacts associated with any one archaeological manifestation

as·sem·blance \-blən(t)s, a's-\ *n* -S [MF, fr. *a-* (fr. L *ad-*) + *semblance* — more at SEMBLANCE] *archaic* **:** SEMBLANCE, APPEARANCE

¹as·sem·ble \ə'sembəl\ *vb* **assembled**; **assembled**; **assembling** \-b(ə)liŋ\ **assembles** [ME *assemblen*, fr. OF *assembler*, fr. (assumed) VL *assimulare*, fr. L *ad-* + (assumed) VL *-simulare* (fr. L *simul* together, at the same time) — more at SAME] *vt* **1 :** to bring or summon together into a group, crowd, company, assembly, or unit ⟨even after a new crew had, at great pains, been *assembled* —V.G.Heiser⟩ ⟨hold all planes until a striking force could be *assembled* —H.L. Merillat⟩ **2 :** to bring together: as **a :** to put or join together usu. in an orderly way with logical selection or sequence ⟨~ statistics⟩ ⟨evaluating the data *assembled*⟩ ⟨he *assembled* a large library⟩ **b :** to fit together various parts of so as to make into an operative whole ⟨~ a radio set⟩ ⟨airplanes being *assembled*⟩ ~ *vi* **:** to come or meet together in a group, company, assembly, or unit often purposively, sometimes formally ⟨the right of the people peaceably to ~ —*U. S. Constitution*⟩ ⟨help drill Federal volunteers then *assembling* about Washington —Robert Bruce⟩ ⟨~ at one of the taverns for convivial purposes —*Amer. Guide Series: N. H.*⟩ **syn** see GATHER

²as·sem·blé \äsäⁿblā\ *n* -S [F, fr. *assemblé*, past part. of *assembler*] **:** a figure of two successive movements in ballet dancing in the first of which one leg is extended outward in any direction from the hip while the other leaps from the floor and in the second both feet come to rest crossed and with toes turned outward in fifth position

as·sem·bler \ə'semblə(r)\ *n* -S **1 :** one that assembles: as **a :** a worker who assembles component parts of an item of manufacture **b :** a middleman who buys mainly farm products from small and scattered producers and prepares them for shipment in economical quantities to the city markets **2** *obs* **:** one of an assembly

assembling *n* -S **:** the act or action of those that assemble: as **a :** the gathering of the males of certain moths over considerable distances in response to odors produced by sexually receptive females **b :** the concentrating of goods or the achieving of control of goods to facilitate sales or purchases

as·sem·bly \ə'semblē, -li\ *n* -ES *often attrib* [ME *assemblee*, fr. MF, fr. OF, fem. of *assemblé*, past part. of *assembler*] **1 :** a company of persons collected together in one place usu. for some common purpose (as deliberation and legislation, worship, or entertainment): **a** *usu cap* **:** a legislative body; *specif* **:** the lower house of a legislature ⟨the *Assembly* of New York State⟩ ⟨the National *Assembly* of France⟩ — compare GENERAL ASSEMBLY, HOUSE OF ASSEMBLY, LEGISLATIVE ASSEMBLY **b** *usu cap* **:** the highest judiciary or governing board in any of various religious denominations ⟨the General *Assembly* of the Presbyterian Church⟩ **c :** a formal social gathering (as a subscription ball) **d :** a local congregation or religious association similar to a church **e :** a scheduled meeting of the whole student body and usu. the faculty of a school or college either for purposes of administrative routine or for educational or recreational programs **2 :** the act of coming together **:** the state of being assembled ⟨prohibits unlawful ~⟩ **3 :** ASSEMBLAGE 1b **4 a :** a signal given by drum, bugle, trumpet, or all field music for troops to assemble or fall in **b :** the collection of the elements of a military command into a given locality **5 a :** the act or process of building up a complete unit (as a motor vehicle) using parts already in themselves finished manufactured products ⟨to work on the ~ line⟩ **b :** a collection of parts so assembled as to form a complete machine, structure, or unit of a machine ⟨a hub ~⟩ ⟨a dome ~⟩ **6 :** a hall or room in which an assembly is held

assembly district *n* **:** an election district in some states of the U. S. (as New York) that returns a member to the state legislature

assembly line *n* **1 :** an arrangement of machines, equipment, and workers so that work passes from operation to operation in direct line until the product is assembled **2 :** a process for turning out a finished product in an efficient impartial often cursory manner ⟨war criminals . . . rolling off the Allied amnesty *assembly line* —*Nation*⟩

as·sem·bly·man \-mən\ *n, pl* **assemblymen 1 :** a member of an assembly, esp. of a legislative assembly **2 :** one that assembles components usu. in a manufacturing process to produce finished goods **:** ASSEMBLER

assembly mark *or* **assembling mark** *n* **:** one of a number of marks placed on the parts of a machine or structure to define the position or order in which the parts are to be assembled

¹as·sent \ə'sent *also* a'-\ *vi* -ED/-ING/-S [ME *assenten*, fr. OF *assenter*, fr. L *assentari*, fr. *assentire*, *adsentire*, fr. *ad-* + *sentire* to feel, think — more at SENSE] **1 :** to give or express one's concurrence, acquiescence, or compliance **:** CONSENT ⟨he at once ~*ed* to my wishes — W.F.DeMorgan⟩ **2 :** to admit as true **:** express one's agreement or concession ⟨we see and immediately ~ to the beauty of an object —Joseph Addison⟩

syn CONSENT, ACCEDE, ACQUIESCE, AGREE, SUBSCRIBE: ASSENT indicates a concurring, either a positive agreeing or more passive conceding, without expressed doubts or objections ⟨I fully *assent* to the proposition that here as elsewhere the distinctions of the law are distinctions of degree —O.W. Holmes †1935⟩ ⟨"Yes, of course", said the lady, vaguely, evidently *assenting* to the doctor's remark rather than expressing a conviction of her own —G.B.Shaw⟩ CONSENT indicates a complying, granting, or yielding, willing or reluctant, to request or demand ⟨whatever you ask of me I will *consent* to —George Meredith⟩ ⟨at first Mary would not wed the white man, but in the end *consented* to do so in order to help forward conversions among her people to the Christian faith —I.B. Richman⟩ ACCEDE may heighten suggestions of conceding or yielding to something proposed, with or without pressure or importunity ⟨he suggested that they go to his room and talk it over. She *acceded* without demur —S.H.Adams⟩ ⟨Mr. Bennet could have no hesitation in *acceding* to the proposal before him —Jane Austen⟩ ACQUIESCE stresses the fact of compliance without effective opposition or resistance ⟨it seemed mad and stupid to Ripton's sense of reason, but he was a bondsman and bound to *acquiesce* —George Meredith⟩ ⟨he was obliged to *acquiesce* in the repression of his individuality —Van Wyck Brooks⟩ AGREE may suggest an according or concurring, often one arrived at after settling differences and points at issue ⟨it might make a bad impression. Myles had to *agree* with that, if reluctantly —J.F.Powers⟩ ⟨whatever answers the philosophers of history might eventually *agree* on —C.E. Black & E.C.Helmreich⟩ ⟨the United States has tacitly *agreed* to Russia's occupation of the Kurile islands —Vera M. Dean⟩ SUBSCRIBE may indicate a ready willingness not only to concur in but to endorse and maintain ⟨those scientists who *subscribe* to the current program in its entirety, who would follow blindly, who could produce a synthetic enthusiasm even if they retained doubts —Vannevar Bush⟩ ⟨Russia declared war on Japan and *subscribed* to the terms presented to Tokyo by its three great allies —Vera M. Dean⟩

²assent \"\ *n* -S [ME, fr. OF, fr. *assenter*] **1 a** *archaic* **:** ACQUIESCENCE, COMPLIANCE, CONSENT **b** *obs* **:** common accord **:** general approval **c :** concurrence with approval **:** SANCTION ⟨~ to ratification would be by simple majority —F.A.Ogg & P.O.Ray⟩ — compare ROYAL ASSENT **2 :** the accepting as true or certain of something (as a doctrine or conclusion) proposed for belief ⟨rational ~ may arrive late, intellectual conviction may come slowly —T.S.Eliot⟩ **3 :** agreement with a statement or proposal esp. in a matter of minor importance or one detached from personal concern **:** mere acquiescence ⟨give a nod of ~⟩ — distinguished from *consent*

as·sen·ta·tion \,asᵊn·'tāshən, ,a,sen-'t-\ *n* -S [L *assentation-*, *assentatio*, fr. *assentatus* (past part. of *assentari*) + *-ion-*, *-io* -ion] **:** ready assent esp. when insincere or obsequious ⟨a tame and banal ~ —George Saintsbury⟩

assented *or* **assenting** *adj, of securities* **:** subject to deposit under an agreement by which the owners assent to some proposed change affecting or affected by amount, nature, or status of the securities

as·sent·ing·ly *adv* **:** in an assenting manner **:** so as to give or express assent

as·sen·tor \ə'sentə(r), a'-\ *n* -S *English law* **:** one of the voters in addition to the proposer and seconder required to endorse the nomination of a candidate for election (as to Parliament)

as·sert \ə'sərt, -ət,-əit *also* a'-; *usu* -d·+V\ *vt* -ED/-ING/-S [L *assertus*, *adsertus*, past part. of *asserere*, *adserere* to assert, lay claim to, liberate, fr. *ad-* + *serere* to join — more at SERIES] **1 :** to state or affirm positively, assuredly, plainly, or strongly ⟨I am far from ~*ing* it was the actual way —Havelock Ellis⟩ **2 a :** to demonstrate the existence of (an attribute) **:** SIGNIFY ⟨~ his manhood —James Joyce⟩ **b :** to demand and compel recognition of ⟨he was never able to ~ himself sufficiently⟩ **c :** to postulate or to affirm the existence of ⟨by again ~*ing* God as an active force in history —*Time*⟩ **3** *archaic* **a :** to lay claim to as a possession or attribute **b :** to take a stand with or for **:** CHAMPION, DEFEND ⟨I will ~ it from the scandal —Jeremy Taylor⟩

syn DECLARE, PROFESS, AFFIRM, AVER, PROTEST, AVOUCH, AVOW, PREDICATE, WARRANT: ASSERT puts stress on the fact of positive statement; it may imply noteworthy assuredness or force on the speaker's part or lack of proof for the statement ⟨we dissect and study and describe a language in modern times on the basis of a structural analysis, and then *assert* what its usage is —Joshua Whatmough⟩ ⟨as early as 1808 Jefferson's cabinet *asserted* that the United States had a common interest with the revolutionists in excluding European influence —A.P.Whitaker⟩ ⟨hill-dwellers, whose language, it is *asserted*, resembles Elizabethan English —*Amer. Guide Series: Ark.*⟩ DECLARE is sometimes used in reference to explicit, open, public statement, perhaps formal ⟨almost without exception, the New Jersey press daily *declares* its independence from its metropolitan rivals —*Amer. Guide Series: N. J.*⟩ ⟨the law in many states *declared* mixed marriages illegal—Oscar Handlin⟩ PROFESS may refer to open declaration, perhaps repeated, esp. of one's own inclinations or capacities, sometimes hypocritical ⟨if judicial critics do not learn modesty from the past they *profess* to esteem, it is not from lack of material —John Dewey⟩ ⟨an orthodox Communist leader who *professed* to speak for the submerged masses —Allan Murray⟩ ⟨enjoyment in occasionally *professing* opinions which in fact are not your own —Jane Austen⟩ AFFIRM may suggest delivery of a statement with an earnest appearance of truth and conviction, sometimes a factitious appearance ⟨*affirmed* that he took no part in this black deed —W.H.Hudson †1922⟩ ⟨it will be *affirmed* that much learning deadens or perverts poetic sensibility —T.S.Eliot⟩ ⟨politicians more often *affirm* their desire for retirement than they state that they really mean it —*Times Lit. Supp.*⟩ AVER may suggest confidence and genuine belief in the truth of a statement that might be questioned ⟨Sedgwick *averred* that he had wasted two years' work through adhering to Werner's notions —S.F.Mason⟩ ⟨*averring* that leniency would be a mistake in the case of the confirmed young criminal —*Current Biog.*⟩ PROTEST may indicate forceful declaration in the face of doubt or contradiction ⟨Streicher *protesting* he'd never hurt a soul —*Current Biog.*⟩ ⟨we tend to suspect that a man who *protests* that his aim is the production of beauty and goodness is something of a charlatan —T.D.Weldon⟩ AVOUCH, less used than others in this group, may apply to statements substantiated by certain personal knowledge or by irrefutable authority ⟨as anyone who is familiar with Communist tactics can *avouch* —W.R.Kintner⟩ AVOW stresses open, frank declaration, with full personal acknowledgment and responsibility ⟨communists, fascists, and other *avowed* enemies of parliamentarism —F.Ogg & H.Zink⟩ ⟨"as to the great service," said Carton, "I am bound to *avow* to you, when you speak of it in that way, that it was mere professional claptrap" —Charles Dickens⟩ PREDICATE in this sense may indicate an affirming of something as a quality, attribute, or concomitant ⟨to *predicate* of diabolic agencies, which are gifted with angelic intellects, the highly ridiculous activities which are so characteristic of poltergeist visitations —J.McCarthy⟩ ⟨logic works by *predicating* of the single instance what is true of all its kind —William James⟩ WARRANT may apply to assured statement made without brooking contradiction, with or as if with one's personal guarantee ⟨I'll *warrant* he's as good a gentleman as any —John Buchan⟩ **syn** see in addition MAINTAIN

as·sert·a·tive \-d·əd·iv, -tətiv\ *adj* [by alter.] **:** ASSERTIVE

as·sert·ed·ly *adv* **:** by positive and usu. unsubstantiated assertion **:** ALLEGEDLY ⟨a lens . . . for goggles which would ~ protect the eyes from atomic glare —*Newsweek*⟩

as·sert·i·ble \-d·əbəl, -təb-\ *adj* **:** capable of being asserted or affirmed **:** NONCONTRADICTORY

as·ser·tion \ə'sərshən, -ōsh-, -əish- *also* a'-\ *n* -S [ME *assercioun*, fr. MF or LL; MF *assertion*, fr. LL *assertion-*, *assertio*, fr. L, formal declaration of free or servile status, fr. *assertus* + *-ion-*, *-io* -ion] **1 :** the act of asserting or something that is asserted: as **a** *archaic* **:** a defense from attack ⟨the ~ of a friend's character⟩ **b :** insistent and positive affirming, maintaining, or defending (as of a right or attribute) ⟨an ~ of ownership⟩ **c :** a declaration that something is the case (as that a proposition is true or that a formula is a theorem in an axiomatized system)

as·ser·tion·al \-shənᵊl, -shnəl\ *adj* **:** of or relating to assertion

assertion of the consequent : AFFIRMATION OF THE CONSEQUENT

as·ser·tive \ə'sərd·iv, -ōt-,-əit-, -ēv *also* a'-\ *adj* [*assertion* + *-ive*] **1 :** resembling, suited to, or characterized by assertion **2 :** disposed to make assertions **:** characterized by self-confidence, determination, and boldness in asserting opinions or in otherwise making one's presence or influence felt **syn** see AGGRESSIVE

as·ser·tive·ly *adv* **:** in an assertive manner **:** with assertion

as·ser·tive·ness *n* -ES **:** the quality or state of being assertive

as·ser·tor \ə'sərd·ə(r), -tə(r)\ *n* -S **:** one that asserts something

as·ser·to·ri·al \¦asə(r)¦tōrēəl, -ór-\ *adj* **:** ASSERTORIC — **as·ser·to·ri·al·ly** \-ēəlē\ *adv*

as·ser·to·ric \-¦tōrik, -ór-, -är-\ *adj* **:** of or relating to assertion — **as·ser·tor·i·cal·ly** \-ək(ə)lē\ *adv*

as·ser·to·ry \ə'sərd·ərē *also* a'-\ *adj* **:** ASSERTORIC, ASSERTIVE

as·ser·tum \ə'sərd·əm *also* a'-\ *n, pl* **asser·ta** \-d·ə\ [NL, fr. LL, assertion, fr. L, neut. of *assertus*] **:** something that is asserted

asses *pl of* AS *or of* ASS

asses' bridge *n* [trans. of NL *pons asinorum*; prob. fr. the similarity of the geometrical construction demonstrating it to the trusses of a bridge and fr. its being considered a difficulty for poor students of geometry] **:** the fifth proposition of the first book of Euclid: the angles at the base of an isosceles triangle are equal to one another ⟨a schoolboy, stammering out his *asses' bridge* —Frederic Harrison⟩

as·sess \ə'ses, (')a¦ses\ *vt* -ED/-ING/-ES [ME *assessen*, prob. fr. ML *assessus*, past part. of *assidēre*, fr. L, to sit beside, assist in the office of judge — more at ASSIZE] **1 :** to determine the rate or amount of (as a tax, charge, or fine) ⟨~ damages after an accident⟩ **2 a :** to determine the amount of and impose (as a tax, charge, or fine) according to an established rate or apportionment ⟨the tax to be ~*ed* upon all retail sales⟩ **b :** to subject to a tax, charge, or levy so determined ⟨each member will be ~*ed* $25⟩ **3 :** to make an official valuation or estimate of (property) esp. for the purposes of taxation **4 :** to analyze critically and judge definitively the nature, significance, status, or merit of **:** determine the importance, size, or value of ⟨~ men as leaders⟩ ⟨properly ~*ing* the financial needs of individual students —J.B.Conant⟩ **syn** see ESTIMATE

as·sess·a·ble \-'=əbəl\ *adj* **:** capable of being assessed

as·sess·ee \,a,se¦sē, ə,se'sē; ə'se,sē, a'-\ *n* -S **:** one upon whom a payment is assessed

as·ses·sion \ə'seshən, a'-\ *n* -S [L *assession-*, *assessio*, fr. *assessus* (past part. of *assidēre* to sit beside) + *-ion-*, *-io* -ion] **1** *archaic* **:** SESSION **2** [prob. fr. *assess* + *-ion*] **:** the assessing or renting of a lord's demesnes in the duchy of Cornwall — **as·ses·sion·a·ble** \-sh(ə)nəbəl\ *adj* — **as·ses·sion·al** \-shənᵊl,-shnəl\ *adj*

as·sess·ment \ə'sesmənt *also* a'-\ *n* -S **1 a :** a valuation of property usu. for the purpose of taxation **b :** a valuation and an adjudging of the sum to be levied on property **2 :** the act of assessing **:** the act of apportioning or determining an amount to be paid ⟨an ~ of damages⟩ **3 :** an appraisal or evaluation (as of merit) ⟨a critical ~ of the composer's work⟩ **4 a :** a specific charge or tax determined upon by assessing **:** amount assessed **b :** the entire plan or scheme fixed upon for charging or taxing **5 a** (1) **:** an apportionment of an amount subscribed for stock into successive installments (2) **:** one of these installments **b :** a demand by a company for payment of the remainder or part of the remainder of the price of stock not yet fully paid for — called also *call* **c** (1) **:** a demand made under various statutory provisions upon holders of stock in a bank for proportional contribution to make good capital losses (2) **:** a similar demand on holders of other kinds of stock **d :** a levy variable in amount collected by insurance companies from certificate or policy holders in order to meet their obligations **e :** a levy made by an American political party on appointive officers for campaign expenses **f :** a levy made on members of an organization (as a club or union) for a special purpose not covered by dues

assessment company *n* **:** a company that issues assessment insurance

assessment insurance *n* **:** insurance providing for the payment of claims in whole or in part from the proceeds of assessments levied upon the members of an association for that purpose

assessment work *n* **:** the annual work upon an unpatented mining claim on the public domain necessary under the U. S. law for the maintenance of the possessory title thereto

as·ses·sor \ə'sesə(r) *also* a'-\ *n* -S [ME *assessour*, fr. MF or L; MF *assesseur*, fr. L *assessor* assistant, judge's assistant, fr. *assessus* (past part. of *assidēre* to sit beside, assist in the office of judge) + *-or*] **1 :** one appointed or elected to assist a judge or magistrate; *esp* **:** one with special knowledge of the subject to be decided ⟨legal ~*s*⟩ ⟨nautical ~*s*⟩ **2** [ML, fr. L] **:** one that assesses; *specif* **:** one that is authorized to assess property for taxation **3** *archaic* **:** one that sits by another as next in dignity or as an assistant and adviser **:** an associate in office **4** *Brit* **:** INSURANCE ADJUSTER

as·ses·so·ri·al \ə,se'sōrēəl, ¦a,se¦s-, ¦asə¦s-, -ór-\ *adj* **:** of or relating to an assessor or a court of assessors

as·ses·sor·ship \ə'sesə(r),ship *also* a'-\ *n* -S **:** the position of assessor

as·set \'a,set, 'aa,- *sometimes* -sət; *usu* -d·+V\ *n* -S [back-formation fr. *assets*, sing., sufficient property to pay debts and legacies, fr. AF *asetz*, fr. OF *asez*, *assez* enough, fr. (assumed) VL *ad satis*, fr. L *ad* to + *satis* enough — more at AT, SAD] **1 assets** *pl* **a** (1) **:** the property of a deceased person that in the hands of his heir or executor is sufficient to pay his debts and legacies (2) **:** the property of a deceased person subject by law to the payment of his debts and legacies **b :** the entire property of all sorts of an insolvent or bankrupt or of a person, association, corporation, or estate applicable or subject to the payment of his or its debts **2 :** a quality, condition, or entity that serves as an advantage, support, resource, or source of strength ⟨wit, a good deal of shrewd classical allusion, and a Voltairean satire are the book's ~*s* —Edmund Fuller⟩ ⟨a college degree is considered a valuable ~ for the beginner —A.W.McCain⟩ ⟨he was a most useful ~ when it came to practical affairs —J.D.Beresford⟩ **3 a :** an item of value owned **b assets** *pl* **:** the series of items on a balance sheet representing the book values at a given date of resources, rights, or items of property owned grouped under appropriate headings according to their nature — see CAPITAL ASSETS, CASH ASSETS, CURRENT ASSETS, FIXED ASSETS, NET ASSETS; ²INTANGIBLE, ²TANGIBLE

asset currency *n* **:** currency secured exclusively by the general assets of the issuing bank as distinguished from that secured by special deposits (as of government bonds or commercial paper)

assets by descent *or* **assets per descent :** assets descending to the heir and rendering him liable to their extent for specialty debts of his ancestor — used in the older law of the administration of estates

assets en·tre main \ˌäⁿ·trə'māⁿ\ [AF *asetz entre maines*] : ASSETS IN HAND

assets in hand [trans. of AF *asetz entre maines*] : assets going directly to the executor or other trustee to satisfy the claims against him as such — used in the older law of the administration of estates; called also *assets entre main*

as·sev·er \ə'sevə(r), a'-\ *vt* **assevered; assevered; assever·ing** \-v(ə)riŋ\ **assevers** [L *asseverare*] *archaic* : ASSEVERATE

as·sev·er·ate \ə'sevəˌrāt, a'-, *usu* -ād·+V\ *vt* -ED/-ING/-S [L *asseveratus, adseveratus,* past part. of *asseverare, adseverare,* fr. *ad-* + *-severare* (fr. *severus* serious, severe) — more at SEVERE] : to affirm or aver positively or earnestly ⟨admit or ~ the necessity and inevitability of almost everything that follows —S.C.Pepper⟩ **syn** see SWEAR

as·sev·er·a·tion \ə,ˌ≈'rāshən\ *n* -S [L *asseveration-, asseveratio,* fr. *asseveratus* + *-ion-, -io* -ion] : the act of asseverating : positive or emphatic affirmation or assertion : solemn declaration ⟨a simple factual account of the author's ~*s* —Muna Lee⟩

as·sev·er·a·tive \ə'sevəˌrād·iv, a'-, -ˌrəd·iv\ *adj* : characterized by asseveration : ASSEVERATING

asshead \'≈,≈\ *n* [¹*ass* + *head*] : BLOCKHEAD, ASS

as·si \'asē\ *n* -S [Creek *ássi,* short for *ássi-lupútski* small leaves] : YAUPON

as·sib·i·late \ə'sibəˌlāt, a'-, *usu* -ād·+V\ *vb* -ED/-ING/-S [*ad-* + *sibilate*] *vt* **1** : to introduce a sibilant sound after or less often before ⟨*z* was an *assibilated d* in primitive Greek — either \dz\ or \zd\⟩ **2** : to convert to or replace by a sibilant sound or a sound of which a sibilant is one constituent (as when the pronunciation \'indyən\ for *Indian* becomes \'injən\; \j\ = \d\ + \zh\) ~ *vi* : to change by introducing a sibilant sound ⟨(noninitial) Indo-European *ti* (unless preceded by *s*) ~*s* (through palatalization) to *si* —G.U.Bonfante⟩

as·sib·i·la·tion \≈,≈'lāshən\ *n* -S : the development of a sound into a sibilant or into an affricate whose second element is a sibilant

as·si·de·an *or* **as·si·dae·an** \ˌasə'dēən\ *or* **has·i·de·an** *or* **has·i·dae·an** *also* **has·si·de·an** *or* **has·si·dae·an** \ˌhas-\ *n* -S *usu cap* [Gk *Asidaioi,* pl. (fr. Heb *ḥăsīdhīm* pious ones) + E *-an* — more at HASID] : HASID 1

as·si·du·i·ty \ˌasə'd(y)üəd·ē, ˌaas-, -ətē, -i\ *n* -ES [L *assiduitas,* fr. *assiduus* assiduous + *-itas* -ity] **1** : the quality or state of being assiduous : constant or close application or attention esp. to some business or enterprise : DILIGENCE **2** *obs* : frequent repetition **3** : solicitous or obsequious attention to a person : persistent personal attention — often used in pl. ⟨vanquish her coldness . . . by my *assiduities* —Tobias Smollett⟩

as·sid·u·ous \ə'sijəwəs, a'-\ *adj* [L *assiduus,* fr. *assidēre* to sit beside, take care of — more at ASSIZE] **1** : marked or characterized by constant unremitting attention or by persistent energetic application ⟨an ~ servant⟩ ⟨~ labor⟩ **2** : SOLICITOUS, OBSEQUIOUS **syn** see BUSY

as·sid·u·ous·ly *adv* : in an assiduous manner : with assiduity ⟨tried ~ to make the sale⟩

as·sid·u·ous·ness *n* -ES : ASSIDUITY

assiege *vt* -ED/-ING/-S [ME *asegen, assegen,* fr. MF *assegier,* fr. OF, prob. fr. *a-* (fr. L *ad-*) + *sege* seat, siege — more at SIEGE] *obs* : BESIEGE — **assiegement** *n* -S *archaic*

assiento *var of* ASIENTO

as·si·ette \"\ *n* -S [F, fr. MF, seating of guests at table, course (of a meal), fr. OF, assessment (of a tax), fr. (assumed) VL *assedita* action of seating or placing, fr. fem. of *asseditus,* past part. of *assedēre* to seat, place — more at ASSIZE] **1 a** : PLATE 3c **b** : hors d'oeuvres or cold cuts served on one plate **2** : a mixture of bole, bloodstone, and galena used as a gilding surface (as by bookbinders)

¹as·sign \ə'sīn *also* a'-\ *vt* -ED/-ING/-S [ME *assignen,* fr. OF *assigner,* fr. L *assignare, adsignare,* fr. *ad-* + *signare* to mark, mark out, designate — more at SIGN] **1** : to transfer to another in writing (one's title to or interest in property, esp. intangible property) ⟨~ a bond by an endorsement⟩; *specif* : to transfer (property) to another in trust or for the benefit of creditors ⟨the bankrupt must also ~ all of his patents to the receiver⟩ **2 a** : to appoint (one) to a post or duty ⟨she was ~*ed* to the laboratory and school —*Current Biog.*⟩ ⟨though ~*ed* only menial tasks —B.L.Robinson⟩; *specif* : to order (an individual or unit) to serve more or less permanently as an organic member of a particular military organization — distinguished from *attach* **b** : PRESCRIBE ⟨carbines are ~*ed* for guard duty⟩ ⟨the teacher ~*ed* the next 20 pages of the text⟩ **3** : SPECIFY, SELECT, DESIGNATE : fix authoritatively or exactly ⟨~ a limit⟩ ⟨~ counsel⟩ ⟨~ a day for trial⟩ **4 a** : to give, adduce, or allege by way of explanation or cause esp. after deliberation ⟨financial difficulties . . . were ~*ed* as the probable cause of his suicide —G.S.Bryan⟩ **b** : to think of after deliberation as characterizing or being possessed as indicated : ALLOT, ENDOW ⟨by ~*ing* to a nation energy and honesty as its chief spiritual characteristics —Matthew Arnold⟩ **c** : to regard as done by or during : reckon as composed, made, or executed as indicated ⟨the temple of Baal Lebanon, which is ~*ed* to the eleventh century B.C. —Edward Clodd⟩ **5** *archaic* : to point out : SHOW ⟨the dwarf the way to her ~*ed* —Edmund Spenser⟩ **syn** see ALLOT, ASCRIBE, PRESCRIBE

²assign \"\ *n* -S [ME *assigne,* fr. MF *assigné* — more at ASSIGNEE] **1** : ASSIGNEE b **2** *obs* : ASSIGNEE a

as·sign·a·bil·i·ty \ə,sīnə'biləd·ē, -ətē, -i\ *n* -ES : the quality of being assignable

as·sign·a·ble \ə'≈əbəl\ *adj* : capable of being assigned ⟨definite, ~ reasons —William James⟩ ⟨the bill of exchange is par excellence an ~ debt —W.M.Dacey⟩ — **as·sign·a·bly** \-əblē, -li\ *adv*

as·sig·nat \'asig,nat, F äsēnʸä\ *n* -S [F, fr. L *assignatus,* past part. of *assignare* to assign] : one of the bills issued as currency by the Revolutionary government of France (1790-95) and based on the security of the lands that had been appropriated by the state

as·sig·na·tion \ˌasig'nāshən, ˌasēg-\ *n* -S [ME *assignacion,* fr. MF, fr. L *assignation-, assignatio,* fr. *assignatus* + *-ion-, -io* -ion] **1** *obs* : authoritative order **2 a** *obs* : assignment of funds : ALLOWANCE **b** : something assigned (as a sum of money) **c** *obs* : a piece of paper currency **3 a** : a making over by transfer of title : ASSIGNMENT **b** : an assigning by allotment : APPORTIONMENT **4** : an appointment of time and place for a meeting esp. for illicit sexual relations ⟨known places of ~ —E.A.Armstrong⟩ ⟨returned from an ~ with his mistress —W.B.Yeats⟩ **5** : ATTRIBUTION, ASCRIPTION ⟨the ~ to Mark Twain of "everybody talks about the weather, but nobody does anything about it" —*Saturday Rev.*⟩ **syn** see ENGAGEMENT

assigned risk *n* : a risk that qualified underwriters of workmen's compensation or automobile liability insurance would reject under applicable standards but accept so as to permit compliance with state law, the insurance being handled through a pool of insurers and assigned to companies in turn

as·sign·ee \ə,sī'nē, ¦a,sī¦nē; ə'sī(,)nē, a'sī(,)nē, -ˌni; *Brit usu* ¦asə¦nē\ *n* -S [ME *assigne,* fr. MF *assigné,* past part. of *assigner* to assign — more at ASSIGN] : one to whom an assignment is made: as **a** : one appointed to act for another : AGENT, REPRESENTATIVE **b** : one to whom a right or property is legally transferred — **as·sign·ee·ship** \-,ship\ *n* -S

as·sign·er \ə'sīnə(r) *also* a'-\ *n* -S : one that assigns or makes an assignment

as·sign·ment \-nmənt\ *n* -S [ME *assignement,* fr. MF, fr. OF, fr. *assigner* to assign + *-ment*] **1** : the act of assigning: as **a** : ALLOTMENT ⟨the ~ of land to veterans⟩ **b** : a pointing out or specifying ⟨~ of error in proceedings for review⟩ **c** : ALLEGEMENT, STATEMENT ⟨the ~ of these reasons⟩ **d** : ATTRIBUTION ⟨his ~ of different functions to different parts⟩ **2 a** : a position, post, or office to which one is assigned : APPOINTMENT ⟨his ~ as vice-consul in Liverpool⟩ ⟨his ~ as minister of two rural churches⟩ **b** : a specified amount of work or a definite task or mission assigned by authority or undertaken as though so assigned ⟨an ~ of 10 arithmetic problems⟩ ⟨the reporter's ~ was to interview the congressman⟩ **3 a** : the transfer to another of one's legal interest or right; *esp* : the transfer of property to be held in trust or to be used for the benefit of creditors **b** : the document by which such an interest or right is transferred **syn** see TASK

as·sign·or \ə'sīnər, a'-, -,nȯ(ə)r; ə,sī'nȯ(ə)r, ¦a,sī¦nȯ(ə)r; *Brit usu* ¦asə¦nȯ(ə)\ *n* -S : one that makes an assignment; *esp* : one that transfers to another a legal interest or right

assigt *abbr* assignment

as·sim·i·la·bil·i·ty \ə,simələ'biləd·ē, -ətē, -i\ *n* -ES : the quality or state of being assimilable ⟨the ~ of new immigrants⟩

as·sim·i·la·ble \ə'≈≈≈bəl\ *adj* : capable of being assimilated

¹as·sim·i·late \ə'siməˌlāt, *usu* -ād·+V\ *vb* -ED/-ING/-S [ML *assimilatus,* past part. of *assimilare,* fr. L *assimulare, assimilare, adsimulare, adsimilare* to make similar, compare, fr. *ad-* + *simulare, similare* to make similar, simulate — more at SIMULATE] *vt* **1 a** : to appropriate and transform or incorporate into the substance of the assimilator : take in and appropriate as nourishment : absorb into the system ⟨the body ~*s* digested food into its protoplasm⟩ **b** : to take in and absorb as one's own : receive into the mind and consider and thoroughly comprehend ⟨the wide range of influences . . . which he *assimilated* in his years of apprenticeship —Herbert Read⟩ ⟨an amazing amount of scientific information which he had *assimilated* —V.G.Heiser⟩ **2 a** : to make similar or alike : cause to resemble — usu. used with *to* or *with* ⟨~ our law in this respect to the law of Scotland —John Bright⟩ ⟨stains, and vegetation, which ~ the architecture with the work of nature —John Ruskin⟩ **b** : to alter by the process of assimilation ⟨the prefix *im-* is an *assimilated* form of *in-*⟩ **c** : to absorb into the cultural tradition of a population or group ⟨the community *assimilated* persons of many nationalities⟩ **3** : to represent as similar or alike : COMPARE, LIKEN ⟨*assimilated* the career of a conqueror to that of a simple robber —W.E.H.Lecky⟩ — usu. used with following *to* or *with* **4** *archaic* : to bring into conformity : ADAPT ~ *vi* **1 a** : to become of the same substance : become absorbed or incorporated into the system ⟨some foods ~ more readily than others⟩ **b** : to become absorbed ⟨cannot ~ with the Church of England —J.H. Newman⟩ **2 a** : to be or become similar or alike : RESEMBLE — usu. used with following *to* or *with* ⟨~*s* with the character of English scenery⟩ **b** : to become altered by the process of assimilation ⟨the sound *m* often ~*s* before a following *n*⟩ **c** : to become culturally assimilated : undergo cultural assimilation **3** *archaic* : to become adapted : CONFORM

²as·sim·i·late \-ˌlət, -ˌlāt, *usu* -d·+V\ *n* -S : something that is assimilated

as·sim·i·la·tion \≈,≈≈'lāshən\ *n* -S [prob. fr. ML *assimilation-, assimilatio* physiological assimilation, fr. L *assimulatio, assimilatio* similarity, fr. *assimulatus, assimilatus* (past part. of *assimulare, assimilare* to make similar) + *-ion-, -io* -ion] **1 a** : the act or process of assimilating ⟨this creative ~ of what is handed down constitutes the great conservative force in poetry —J.L.Lowes⟩ **b** : the quality or state of being assimilated ⟨some writings had to be translated many times before reaching their final ~ —G.A.L.Sarton⟩ **2 a** : the conversion or incorporation of nutritive material into the fluid or solid substance of the body and being the last stage or series of stages in the process of nutrition following after digestion and absorption or occurring with the latter **b** : the incorporation of foreign blastematous material into the organized pattern of an embryo or blastema (as in certain experimental transfers of tissue) **c** (1) : the incorporation of food materials into the protoplasm : photosynthesis together with root absorption (2) : PHOTOSYNTHESIS — used esp. in England **3** : the process in which the chemical composition of molten magmas is changed by the fusion of the country rock with which they come in contact **4** : partial or total adaptation of the position or type of articulation of a particular sound (as a consonant) to that of an adjacent or neighboring sound — compare UMLAUT ⟨in the word *cupboard* the \p\ sound of the word *cup* has undergone complete ~⟩ ⟨in *conduct* the \m\ of the prefix *com-* shows ~⟩ **5** : the process of receiving new facts or responding to new situations in conformity with what is already available to consciousness — compare APPERCEPTION **6** : sociocultural fusion wherein individuals and groups of differing ethnic heritage acquire the basic habits, attitudes, and mode of life of an embracing national culture — distinguished from *acculturation*

as·sim·i·la·tion·ist \-əst\ *n* -S : one that believes in or advocates a policy of assimilation of differing racial or cultural groups, sometimes specif. of the Jews

as·sim·i·la·tive \≈'≈≈ˌlād·iv, -ˌləd·-\ *adj* [ML *assimilativus,* lit., making similar, fr. L *assimulatus, assimilatus* + *-ivus* -ive] : tending to, characterized by, or causing assimilation : ASSIMILATING ⟨an ~ pattern⟩ ⟨an ~ process⟩

as·sim·i·la·tor \-ˌlād·ə(r)\ *n* -S : one that assimilates

as·sim·i·la·to·ry \-ləˌtōrē, -ˌtȯr-\ *adj* : ASSIMILATIVE

as·sim·i·nea \ə,simə'nēə\ *n, cap* [NL] : a genus (the type of the widely distributed family Assimineidae) of small conical operculate pulmonate snails (order Pectinibranchia) of brackish water including a species (*A. lutea*) sometimes serving as an intermediate host of the lung fluke

as·sin·i·boin *also* **as·sin·i·boine** \ə'sinəˌbȯin\ *n, pl* **assiniboin** *or* **assiniboins** *also* **assiniboine** *or* **assiniboines** *usu cap* [Ojibwa *úsini-üpwäwᵃ,* lit., one who cooks by use of stones, fr. *úsini* stone + *üpwäwᵃ* he cooks by roasting] **1 a** : a Siouan people of the area between the upper Missouri and middle Saskatchewan rivers **b** : a member of such people **2** : a dialect of Dakota spoken by the Assiniboin people

¹as·sis \a'sē\ *adj* [F, past part. of *asseoir* to seat — more at ASSIZE] : sitting down — used of animals in heraldry

²assis *pl of* ASSI

as·sise \a'sēz\ *n* -S [F, fr. *assise,* fem. of *assis*] : a succession of two or more paleontologic zones bearing typical fossils of the same species or genera

as·si·si \ə'sē(,)sē, ə'sēzē *also* ə'sisē *or* ə'sizē\ *n* -S [fr. *Assisi,* commune, Perugia province, Italy, where it was originally made] : an embroidery with unworked designs outlined by a solid background of cross-stitch

¹as·sist \ə'sist\ *vb* -ED/-ING/-S [MF or L: MF *assister* to help, be present, fr. L *assistere, adsistere* to help, stand by, fr. *ad-* + *sistere* to cause to stand, stand; akin to L *stare* to stand — more at STAND] *vi* **1** : to give support or aid : HELP ⟨refused to ~ in the campaign⟩ ⟨waited to see if he could ~ in any way⟩ **2** : to be present as a spectator ⟨unwilling to ~ at an interview between Amy and Amy's mistress —Arnold Bennett⟩ **3 a** *in euchre* : to order the dealer when he is the partner to take up the turned trump **b** *in bridge* : RAISE ~ *vt* **1 a** : to give support or aid to esp. in some undertaking or effort : AID ⟨diligently endeavored to ~ his search for a mate —George Meredith⟩ ⟨~*ed* the boy with his lessons⟩ **b** : to perform some service for : HELP ⟨a good and faithful helpmate ~*ed* me much by attending the shop —Benjamin Franklin⟩ ⟨~*ed* the old man up the stairs⟩ **2** *obs* : to take one's place with : JOIN, ATTEND **syn** see HELP

²assist \" *sometimes* 'a,s- *in sense 2*\ *n* -S **1** : an act of assistance : AID ⟨without any ~ from her brother . . . she has written . . . a breezy novel —Bernard Kalb⟩ **2 a** : the act of a player who by handling the ball (as in baseball) or passing the puck (as in hockey) enables a teammate to make a put-out or score a goal **b** : the official credit given a player for making such a play **3** : an act or circumstance that helps to bring about a decisive result ⟨the winning candidate got an ~ from his opponent's inept tactics⟩

as·sist·ance \ə'sistən(t)s\ *n* -S [ME *assistence* (fr. ML *assistentia,* fr. L *assistent-, assistens* + *-ia* -y) & *assistance,* fr. MF, fr. *assister* + *-ance*] **1 a** : the act or action of assisting ⟨might from time to time require the ~ of a mild digestive —Dorothy Sayers⟩ **b** : the help supplied or given : SUPPORT ⟨economic ~ to several countries⟩; *specif* : aid (often financial) to the needy ⟨a program of public ~⟩ **2** *archaic* **a** : PRESENCE, ATTENDANCE **b** : AUDIENCE

¹as·sist·ant \-tənt\ *adj* [ME *assistant* (fr. MF, pres. part. of *assister*) & *assistent,* fr. L *assistent-, assistens,* pres. part. of *assistere*] **1** : giving aid or support : HELPFUL, AUXILIARY ⟨the guilty trade and the innocent manufacture were mutually ~ in more ways than one —G.M.Trevelyan⟩ **2** : acting as a subordinate to another : having a subordinate position or rank ⟨an ~ editor⟩ ⟨an ~ minister⟩

²assistant \"\ *n* -S [alter. (influenced by MF *assistant*) of ME *assistent,* fr. L *assistent-, assistens*] **1** *archaic* : one who is present : SPECTATOR **2 a** : one who assists : HELPER ⟨my close associate and invaluable ~ throughout the struggle⟩ **b** : one who acts as a subordinate to another or as an official in a subordinate capacity ⟨accepted a post as resident ~ in a large hospital⟩ ⟨was elected ~ and was for three years the only other officer —R.G.Usher⟩ **c** : a member of a college or university faculty of the lowest rank of a college or university faculty whose duties may include grading papers, supervising laboratories, or teaching classes ⟨was appointed ~ in English⟩ **3** : a means of help : AUXILIARY ⟨rhyme is an ~ to memory⟩ **4** : a substance that aids in the processing of textile fibers; *esp* : a substance (as sodium sulfate) added to a dyebath for helping fix the dye or mordant to the yarn or fabric, for promoting level dyeing, or for promoting exhaustion of the dyebath

assistant professor *n* : a member of a college or university faculty who ranks immediately above an instructor and immediately below an associate professor

as·sist·ant·ship \-,ship\ *n* : the position of assistant at a college or university often given to a graduate student working for an advanced degree ⟨an ~ in chemistry⟩

as·sist·er \ə'sistə(r)\ *n* -S **1** *archaic* : one that is present **2** : one that assists

as·sist·ive \-tiv\ *adj* : giving aid : HELPFUL

¹as·size \ə'sīz *also* a'-\ *n* -S [ME *assise,* fr. OF, session, settlement, assessment, fr. fem. of *assis,* past part. of *asseoir* to seat, place, fr. (assumed) VL *assedēre,* alter. (influenced by L *sedēre*) of L *assidēre, adsidēre* to sit beside, assist in the office of judge, fr. *ad-* + *sedēre* to sit — more at SIT] **1** : an instruction, decree, or enactment made or issued at a legislative sitting or assembly : EDICT, ORDINANCE ⟨the *Assize* of Clarendon⟩ ⟨the *Assize* of Arms⟩ **2 a** : a statute or ordinance regulating weights and measures or the weight, measure, proportions of ingredients, or price of articles sold in the market ⟨the *Assize* of Weights and Measures⟩ **b** : the regulation of the price of bread or ale by the price of grain **3** : a fixed or customary standard (as of quantity, quality, or price) **4 a** : a trial or hearing in the nature of an inquest or recognition before sworn jurymen or assessors : judicial inquest **b** : an action to be decided by such a hearing, the writ for instituting it, or the verdict or finding rendered by the jury **5 a** : the periodical sessions of the judges of the superior courts in every county of England for the purpose of administering justice in the trial and determination of civil and criminal cases — usu. used in pl. **b** : the time or place of holding such a court, the court itself, or a session of it — usu. used in pl. **c** *Scot* (1) : a jury trial (2) : JURY, PANEL **6** : a cylinder-shaped block of stone forming part of a column or of a layer of stone in a building

²assize *vt* -ED/-ING/-S [ME *assisen,* fr *assise,* n.] *obs* : to regulate or fix (as a price) according to an ordinance or standard

as·siz·er \-zə(r)\ *n* -S [ME *assisour,* fr. AF, fr. OF *assise* + *-our* -or] **1** : a member of an assize : JURYMAN **2** : an officer appointed to execute the provisions of various assizes (sense 2a)

assmt *abbr* assessment

assn *abbr* association

as·so·cia·bil·i·ty \ə,sōsh(ē)ə'biləd·ē, -ōsēə-, -lətē, -i *also* a,s-\ *n* -ES : the quality or state of being associable

as·so·cia·ble \≈'≈(≈)≈bəl\ *adj* [ISV ¹*associate* + *-able*] : capable of being associated, joined, or connected in thought ⟨a word . . . easily ~ with collective nouns —Yakov Malkiel⟩

¹as·so·ci·ate \ə'sōs(h)ēˌāt, *usu* -ād·+V\ *vb* -ED/-ING/-S [ME *associat* (3d pers. sing. past indic.), fr. L *associatus,* past part. of *associare*] *vt* **1 a** : to join often in a loose relationship as a partner, fellow worker, colleague, friend, companion, or ally ⟨was *associated* with him in a large law firm⟩ ⟨were closely *associated* with each other during the war⟩ **b** : to elect as an associate ⟨was *associated* to the Royal Academy —Robert Southey⟩ **2** *obs* : to keep company with : ATTEND ⟨friends should ~ friends in grief and woe —Shak.⟩ **3** : to join (things) together or connect (one thing) with another : COMBINE ⟨particles of gold *associated* with heavy minerals⟩ **4** : to join or connect in any of various intangible or unspecified ways (as in general mental, legendary, or historical relationship, in unspecified causal relationship, or in unspecified professional or scholarly relationship) ⟨surrealism has been *associated* with psychological and intellectual atmosphere common to periods of war —Bernard Smith⟩ ⟨she wished to ~ him with her unusual mood —J.C.Powys⟩ **5** : to submit to public identification (as with a principle or sentiment) ⟨the House will ~ itself with these expressions —Sir Winston Churchill⟩ ⟨I should wholeheartedly ~ myself with the general libertarian views —Felix Frankfurter⟩ **6** *chem* : to join in loose combinations — see ASSOCIATION 7 ~ *vi* **1** : to come together as partners, fellow workers, colleagues, friends, companions, or allies ⟨my father's conviction that they were too lowly to ~ with me —G.B.Shaw⟩ **2** : to combine or join with another or others as component parts : UNITE ⟨protons and neutrons with their encircling electrons ~ together to form atoms —G.W.Gray⟩ **3** : to engage in free association ⟨the patient *associated* freely about his childhood⟩ — see FREE ASSOCIATION **syn** see JOIN

²as·so·ciate \-s(h)ēət, -shət, -shēˌāt, -sēˌāt, *usu* -d·+V\ *adj* [ME *associat,* fr. L *associatus, adsociatus,* past part. of *associare, adsociare* to join, unite, fr. *ad-* + *sociare* to join, share, fr. *socius* companion — more at SOCIAL] **1** : closely connected, joined, or united with another (as in interest, function, activity, or office) : sharing in responsibility or authority ⟨descent through darkness . . . to my ~ powers —John Milton⟩ ⟨an ~ judge⟩ **2** : closely related esp. in the mind : ALLIED, ACCOMPANYING ⟨they want some ~ sounds to make them harmonious —Samuel Johnson⟩ **3** : admitted to some but not to all rights and privileges : having a secondary or subordinate status ⟨admitted to ~ membership in the society⟩

³associate \"\ *n* -S **1** : one associated with another: as **a** : one who shares with another an enterprise, business, or action : a fellow worker : PARTNER ⟨the chemist and his ~*s* finally completed their experiment⟩ **b** : one who shares with another an office or position of authority : COLLEAGUE ⟨they were ~*s* on the bench for 20 years⟩ **c** : one who is frequently in company with another : COMPANION, COMRADE ⟨his most intimate ~ during his college years⟩ **2** : something that is closely connected with or that usu. accompanies another : ACCOMPANIMENT, CONCOMITANT; *esp* : a word or concept linked to another by association ⟨no sooner at any time comes into the understanding but its ~ appears with it —John Locke⟩ **3 a** : an officer of the superior common-law courts in England **b** : a member of a learned society or academy ranking below a fellow ⟨an ~ of the Royal Academy⟩ **c** : a research worker or teacher affiliated with a college, university, or some other professional organization or institution and ranking below a professor or full member ⟨research ~ in anthropology⟩ ⟨~ in German⟩ ⟨~ in medicine⟩ **4** *often cap* **a** : a degree conferred by a junior college upon its graduates ⟨~ in arts⟩ **b** : a degree or title granted by some colleges and universities to students who finish a course that is complete in itself but shorter than that leading to a bachelor's degree

associated state *n, often cap A&S* [trans. of F *état associé*] : a semi-independent state within the French Union bound to France by special treaties ⟨most of the *associated states* were once protectorates⟩

associate professor *n* : a faculty member in a college or university who ranks immediately below a professor and above an assistant professor

as·so·ci·a·tion \ə,sōsē'āshən, -ōshē- — -ōsh- *is somewhat less freq in this than in the other associ- words, by reason of* sh-*dissimilation*\ *n* -S [MF or ML; MF *association,* fr. ML *association-, associatio,* fr. L *associatus* (past part. of *associare* to join, unite) + *-ion-, -io* -ion — more at ASSOCIATE] **1 a** : the act or action of associating ⟨there is no such thing as criminal guilt by ~ in Anglo-American law —Sidney Hook⟩ ⟨the house dog's intimate ~ with people —J.W.Cross⟩ **b** : the quality or state of being associated : COMPANIONSHIP, PARTNERSHIP, CONNECTION, COMBINATION ⟨my four years of close ~ with Alec —Sidney Lovett⟩ ⟨the cerebrospinal fluid, due to its intimate ~ with the central nervous system —H.G.Armstrong⟩ ⟨flint implements in ~ with the remains of the extinct prehistoric cave bear —R.W.Murray⟩ **2** *archaic* : a written pledge to carry out an undertaking ⟨the six men had forged the ~⟩ **3** : an organization of persons having a common interest : SOCIETY, LEAGUE, UNION ⟨the Modern Language *Association* of America⟩: as **a** (1) : a voluntary union of neighboring self-governing local churches of the same denomination ⟨~ of the Baptists⟩ (2) : a stated meeting of the clergymen and other appointed delegates of such churches

b : a body of persons organized for the prosecution of some purpose, having no charter from the state, but having the general form and mode of procedure of a corporation — distinguished from *corporation* **4 a :** a feeling, thought, or recollection linked in the mind or associated in the memory with a thing or person **:** CONNOTATION, OVERTONE ⟨words stir our feelings . . . through their enveloping atmosphere of ~*s* —J.L.Lowes⟩ ⟨each new hearing yields some new richness in tonal ~ —Richard Eberhart⟩ **5 a :** the mental connection or bond existing between any sensations, perceptions, ideas, or feelings that to a subject or observer have a relational significance with one another ⟨the laws of ~⟩ **b :** the process of forming mental connections or bonds between sensations, perceptions, ideas, or feelings — compare LEARNING 1a(2) **c :** FREE ASSOCIATION **6** [short for *association football*] *Brit* **:** SOCCER **7** *chem* **:** aggregation to form loosely bound complexes; *esp* **:** the formation of polymers in the liquid and solid states by molecules (as of water or ammonia) by means of hydrogen bonds — called also *molecular association* **8 a :** a major unit often taken to be the fundamental unit in ecological community organization that is characterized by essential uniformity in physiognomy, composition, and structure and has usu. two or more dominant species of a particular life form or habit **b :** such a unit when considered a major subdivision of a formation or biome **c :** a group of organisms usu. of similar life form associated in a given environment and distinguishable as a group from neighboring groups of like nature **9** *sociol* **:** a formal or secondary social group expressly organized to satisfy the specific intents and purposes of its members **10 :** a group of defined and named soils usu. having different characteristics and regularly associated in a geographic pattern

as·so·ci·a·tion·al \ə¦sō-sēˈāshənᵊl, -shnəl\ *adj* **:** of or relating to association, associationism, or an association

as·so·ci·a·tion·al·ism \-ˈsēˈāshənᵊl,izəm, -shnə,li-\ *n* -s **:** ASSOCIATIONISM

as·so·ci·a·tion·al·ist \-əst\ *n* -s **:** an adherent of associationalism

association area *n* **:** an area of the cerebral cortex considered to function in linking and coordinating the projection areas

association book *n* **:** a copy of a book prized for its association with some prominent person

association center *n* **:** a nervous center of an invertebrate concerned with the coordination and distribution of stimuli from sensory receptors

association fibers *n pl* **:** nerve fibers connecting different parts of the brain; *specif* **:** fibers connecting different areas within the cortex of each cerebral hemisphere

association football *n* **:** SOCCER

as·so·ci·a·tion·ism \-ˈāshə,nizəm\ *n* -s [prob. fr. F *associationnisme*, fr. *association* + *-isme* -ism] **:** a theory that attempts to account for ideas or the content of consciousness in terms of the combination of sensory and perceptual elements known chiefly through introspective analysis — opposed to *apperceptionism;* compare MENTAL CHEMISTRY

¹as·so·ci·a·tion·ist \-sh(ə)nəst\ *n* -s [prob. fr. F *associationiste*, fr. *association* + *-iste* -ist] **:** an adherent of associationism

²associationist \ ... \ *also* **as·so·ci·a·tion·is·tic** \ ... ¦shə¦nistik\ *adj* **:** of or relating to associationists or associationism

association psychology *or* **association theory** *n* **:** ASSOCIATIONISM

association test *n* **:** WORD ASSOCIATION TEST

as·so·cia·tive \əˈsōs(h)ē,ād·iv, -ōshəd·iv,-ōs(h)ēəd·iv\ *adj* **1 :** tending to, inducing, or characterized by association esp. of ideas or images ⟨an ~ symbol⟩ **2 a :** dependent on or characterized by association ⟨an ~ reaction⟩ **b :** acquired by a process of learning ⟨an ~ reflex⟩ **3 :** *of a mathematical operation* **:** involving a number of elements (as terms or factors) and being such that the result of the operation is independent of the grouping of the elements — **as·so·cia·tive·ly** *adv* — **as·so·ci·a·tiv·i·ty** \ə,sōs(h)ēəˈtivəd·ē\ *n* -ES

associative anamnesis *n* **:** history taking by the method of free association

associative law *n* **:** a law indicating immateriality in the grouping of variables; *specif* **:** any law of the form $(\phi R\chi)R\psi = \phi R(\chi R\psi)$ where ϕ, χ, ψ are variables and R a dyadic operator [as $(a+b)+c=a+(b+c)$ in arithmetic or $(pvq)vr' .=. pv(qvr)$ in the propositional calculus] — called also *principle of association*

associative learning *n* **:** the mental process whereby discrete ideas and percepts become linked with one another

as·so·ci·a·tor \əˈsōs(h)ē,ād·ə(r), -,ātə-\ *n* -s **:** ASSOCIATE, CONFEDERATE

as·so·ci·a·to·ry \əˈsōs(h)ēə,tōrē, -ōshə,-\ *adj* **:** ASSOCIATIVE

as·so·ci·es \əˈsōsē,ēz\ *n, pl* **associes** [NL, prob. irreg. fr. L *associare*] **:** an impermanent nonclimax biotic community similar in scope to an association

as·soil \əˈsȯi(ə)l, aˈ-\ *vt* -ED/-ING/-S [ME *assoilen*, fr. OF *assoldre, assoudre* (1st pers. sing. pres. indic. *assoil*), fr. L *absolvere* — more at ABSOLVE] **1 a** *archaic* **:** to absolve or set free from sin **:** PARDON, FORGIVE ⟨the work of our brother in Christ and St. Francis . . . whom God ~ —Mary Austin⟩ **b** *obs* **:** to absolve or set free from an ecclesiastical punishment **c** *archaic* **:** to set free **:** RELEASE, DELIVER ⟨till from her bands the spright ~*ed* is —Edmund Spenser⟩ **2** *obs* **:** to clear up (a doubt or problem) **:** RESOLVE, SOLVE **3** *archaic* **:** to acquit of a criminal charge **:** CLEAR ⟨thou art ~*ed* of man-slaying —Gilbert Murray⟩ **4** *archaic* **:** to atone for **:** EXPIATE ⟨let each act ~ a fault —Edwin Arnold⟩

as·soil·ment \-mənt\ *n* -s *archaic* **:** ABSOLUTION ⟨a station of purification and ~ —Thomas De Quincey⟩

as·soil·zie \əˈsȯil(y)ē\ *vt* -ED/-ING/-S [ME (Scots dial.) *assoilyen, assolyen*, fr. MF *assoudre* (1st pers. sing. pres. indic. *assoil*, 3d pers. sing. pres. subj. *assoille*)] *Scot* **:** ASSOIL; *specif* **:** to acquit by sentence of court

as·so·nance \ˈasᵊnən(t)s, ˈaas-\ *n* -s [F, fr. L *assonare* + F *-ance*] **1 :** resemblance of sound in words or syllables ⟨notice the ~ in *ring* and *hild* —George Saintsbury⟩ **2 a :** relatively close juxtaposition of similar sounds esp. of vowels **b :** repetition of vowels without repetition of consonants (as in *cálamo* and *plátano*) used as an alternative to rhyme in verse — called also *vowel rhyme* **3 :** incomplete correspondence **:** RESEMBLANCE ⟨~ between facts seemingly remote —J.R. Lowell⟩ — compare CONSONANCE

¹as·so·nant \-ənt\ *adj* [F or L; F *assonant*, fr. L *assonant-, assonans, adsonant-, adsonans*, pres. part. of *assonare, adsonare* to answer with the same sound, fr. *ad-* + *sonare* to sound — more at SOUND] **:** relating to or marked by assonance

²assonant \"\ *n* -s **:** a word or syllable that is assonant with another word or syllable

as·so·nan·tal \¦...¦antᵊl\ *also* **as·so·nan·tic** \-tik\ *adj* **:** ASSONANT

as·so·nate \ˈ...,āt\ *vi* -ED/-ING/-S [L *assonatus, assonitus*, past part. of *assonare*] **:** to correspond in sound esp. by assonance ⟨syllables that ~⟩

as·so·nia \əˈsōnēə\ [NL, fr. I. J. de Asso y del Río †1814 Span. naturalist + NL connective *-n-* + *-ia*] *syn of* DOMBEYA

as soon as *conj* **:** immediately at or just after the time that ⟨*as soon as* he came, the meeting began⟩

as·sort \əˈsȯ(ə)rt, -ȯ(ə)t, *usu* -d+V\ *vb* -ED/-ING/-S [MF *assortir*, fr. *a-* to (fr. L *ad-*) + *-sortir* (fr. *sorte* sort, kind) — more at SORT] *vt* **1 :** to separate and distribute into groups of a like kind, quality, or purpose **:** CLASSIFY, SORT ⟨her mind was busily ~*ing* and grouping the faces before her —Ellen Glasgow⟩ **2 :** to supply with a suitable assortment or variety (as of goods) ⟨helped to balance and ~ that month's listings —*Atlantic Bull.*⟩ **3 :** to place in the same group with others **:** associate in a class **:** CLASS ⟨~ this fiction with the short stories and novelettes⟩ ~ *vi* **1 :** to fall into a class or place **:** agree in sort or kind **:** become adapted or suited **:** MATCH, HARMONIZE ⟨the donkey trail ~*ed* oddly with the house —D.C.Peattie⟩ **2 :** to keep company **:** ASSOCIATE, CONSORT ⟨I could abide to ~ with fisher-swains —Charles Lamb⟩

as·sort·a·tive \əˈsȯ(r)d·əd·iv, -ȯ(ə)|, |tətiv\ *also* **as·sort·ive** \əˈsȯr|d·iv, -ȯ(ə)|, |tiv, -ēv\ *adj* **1 :** ASSORTING **2 :** of or relating to selection on the basis of likeness — **as·sor·ta·tive·ly** *adv*

assortative mating *n* **:** nonrandom mating: as **a :** mating between the more similar individuals of a population esp. when regarded as a factor in evolutionary differentiation within a population **b :** selective mating between individuals whose choice of marriage partners is determined by similarity of social environment — see HOMOGAMY

as·sort·ed \əˈsȯr|d·əd, -ȯ(ə)|, |təd\ *adj* **1 a :** consisting of selected kinds or sorts ⟨a box of ~ chocolates⟩ **b :** consisting of various kinds or sorts **:** MISCELLANEOUS, HETEROGENEOUS ⟨the hotel was full of ~ British and American accents —Arnold Bennett⟩ **2 :** MATCHED, SUITED, FITTED ⟨the doctor and his wife . . . had been a curiously ~ pair —Alan Hynd⟩

as·sort·er \-d·ə(r), -tə(r)\ *n* -s **:** one that assorts; *specif* **:** a garment worker who matches pieces or bundles garments

as·sort·ment \əˈsȯrtmənt, -ȯ(ə)t-\ *n* -s **1 a :** the act of assorting **:** arrangement into kinds and sorts ⟨Harnwell's household goods got mingled in the roadway with those appertaining to the Fishers and their ~ . . . was a task —Arthur Morrison⟩ **b :** the quality or state of being assorted **:** VARIETY ⟨the absence of quantity and ~ in his wares —W.D.Howells⟩ **2 :** an assorted group or collection: as **a :** a selected group or collection consisting of one sort **b :** a collection containing a variety of sorts adapted to various wants, demands, or purposes ⟨an ~ of tools⟩ **c :** a miscellaneous group or collection consisting of various sorts ⟨canoes . . . loaded with an ~ of yabbering, singing natives, whining dogs, cooked reptiles and fish —Francis Birtles⟩ **3 :** the separation and segregation of homologous genes at meiosis — compare MENDEL'S LAW

ass's-ear \ˈ...\ *n, pl* **ass's-ears :** a slender tropical abalone (*Haliotis asinina*) common in the Pacific islands and northern Australia

asst *abbr* assistant

asstd *abbr* **1** assented **2** associated **3** assorted

as·suage \əˈswāj\ *vb* -ED/-ING/-S [ME *aswagen*, fr. OF *assouagier*, fr. (assumed) VL *assuaviare, adsuaviare*, fr. L *ad-* + (assumed) VL *-suaviare* (fr. L *suavis* sweet) — more at SWEET] *vt* **1 :** to reduce the intensity of **:** make less severe or violent **:** ALLAY, MITIGATE, EASE ⟨stroking her right wrist with her left hand as though to ~ the ache —Jean Stafford⟩ ⟨forgetting her own sorrow in her effort to ~ his —B.A. Williams⟩ **2 :** to reduce to a state of peace, calm, or quiet **:** MOLLIFY, PACIFY ⟨she found herself . . . pleasantly *assuaged* by the sense of anonymity which enveloped her —Helen Howe⟩ **3 :** to put an end to by satisfying **:** APPEASE, QUENCH ⟨surrounded with more than enough to ~ its hunger —F.G. Kay⟩ **4** *obs* **:** to reduce esp. in size **:** DIMINISH ~ *vi, archaic* **:** to grow less **:** ABATE, SUBSIDE ⟨God made a wind to pass over the earth and the waters *assuaged* —Gen 8:1 (AV)⟩ **syn** see RELIEVE

as·suage·ment \-mənt\ *n* -s **1 a :** the act of assuaging **:** ALLEVIATION, RELIEF ⟨the ~ of their hunger by a few more mouthfuls than usual —Glenway Wescott⟩ **b :** the quality or state of being assuaged ⟨the founts whereat my soul . . . may cool ~ find —Selwyn Image⟩ **2 :** something that assuages **:** ALLEVIATIVE ⟨his social . . . inadequacies led him to the ~*s* of anti-Semitism and a superpatriotism —*Time*⟩

as·sua·sive \ə, a+\ *adj* [*ad-* + *suasive*] **:** having a pleasantly soothing quality or effect **:** CALMING ⟨she feels the earth under him germinating in the spring night, the sweet ~ air —Norman Mailer⟩

assubjugate *vt* -ED/-ING/-S [*ad-* + *subjugate*] *archaic* **:** to reduce to subjugation

assuefaction *n* -s [F, fr. OF, fr. L *assuefactus* (past part. of *assuefacere* to accustom, fr. *assuetus* + *facere* to make, do) + OF *-ion* — more at DO] *obs* **:** HABITUATION, USE

as·sue·tude \ˈaswə,tüd, -ē,tyüd\ *n* -s [L *assuetudo*, fr. *assuetus*, past part. of *assuescere* to be accustomed, fr. *ad-* + *suescere* to become accustomed; akin to L *suus* one's own — more at SUICIDE] **:** ACCUSTOMEDNESS, HABIT

as·sum·a·ble \əˈsüməbəl\ *adj* **:** capable of being assumed

as·sum·a·bly \-blē, -li\ *adv* **:** as may be assumed **:** PRESUMABLY

as·sume \əˈsüm\ *vb* -ED/-ING/-S [ME *assumen*, fr. L *assumere, adsumere*, fr. *ad-* + *sumere* to take, fr. *sub* under + *emere* to buy, obtain — more at SUB-, REDEEM] *vt* **1 :** to take up or into **:** RECEIVE, ACCEPT: **a :** to receive into heaven ⟨in what wise the Mother of God had been *assumed* into her place in Heaven —William James⟩ **b :** to take into partnership, employment, or use **:** receive as an associate ⟨revealed religion ~*s* them into her service —R.C.Trench⟩ **2 :** to take to or upon oneself **:** UNDERTAKE: **a :** to invest oneself with (a form, attribute, or aspect) ⟨anxious in this lecture not to ~ the role of a Christian apologist —W.R.Inge⟩ ⟨visits of inspection often ~ a dramatic character —C.L.Jones⟩ **b :** to put on (an article of clothing) **:** DON ⟨had *assumed* her bonnet and shawl —Arnold Bennett⟩ **c :** to invest oneself formally with (an office or its symbols) **:** enter upon the duties of ⟨at the age of 40 he *assumed* the presidency of the college⟩ **d :** to take upon oneself (to do or perform) **:** UNDERTAKE — used chiefly in law and with following infinitive ⟨did ~ to carry his horse . . . over the water of Humber sound —William Fulbecke⟩ **3 :** to take as one's right or possession **:** ARROGATE, SEIZE, USURP ⟨the king *assumed* to himself the right of filling up the chief municipal offices —T.B.Macaulay⟩ **4 :** to take in appearance only **:** pretend to have or be **:** FEIGN ⟨she felt, without knowing why, that the gaiety was *assumed* —Ellen Glasgow⟩ **5 :** to take for granted **:** accept arbitrarily or tentatively **:** SUPPOSE ⟨we simply *assumed* that we were going to be married —R.P.Warren⟩ **6 :** to take as an assumption or premise in logic **7 :** to take over as one's own (the debts of another) **:** make oneself formally liable for ⟨the public debt which the incorporators *assumed* —W.P.Webb⟩ ~ *vi* **:** to claim more than is due **:** be pretentious ⟨in the absence of proof history has no right to ~ —Hilaire Belloc⟩

syn AFFECT, PRETEND, SIMULATE, FEIGN, COUNTERFEIT, SHAM: ASSUME may apply to putting on a false or deceptive appearance through either pardonable or blameworthy motives ⟨by *assuming* an air of cheerfulness we become cheerful in reality —William Cowper⟩ ⟨an elderly "buck" with an air of *assumed* juvenility —W.S.Gilbert⟩ ⟨the defense counsel *assumes* great friendliness and the inexperienced witness assumes that this friendliness may be genuine —Paul Wilson⟩ ⟨*assume* a meek look⟩ AFFECT indicates making a false show of possessing, using, feeling, or preferring ⟨Gayerson, a Bengal Civilian, who *affected* the customs—as he had the heart—of youth —Rudyard Kipling⟩ ⟨Elizabeth could but just *affect* concern in missing him; she really rejoiced at it —Jane Austen⟩ ⟨a tramp cyclist, *affecting* turtleneck sweaters and gray flannel bags —P.G.Wodehouse⟩ PRETEND may suggest sustained profession of or adherence to what is false ⟨I shall find myself *pretending* that I am so full of resources that I do not require any outside help to enjoy a holiday in a lovely place —O.S.J.Gogarty⟩ ⟨absurd to *pretend* that the young men of Europe ever wanted to hunt each other into holes in the ground and throw bombs into the holes to disembowel one another —G.B.Shaw⟩ ⟨they had high critical standards; even their clowns had to be learned or to *pretend* learning —Gilbert Highet⟩ SIMULATE indicates factitiously appearing or imitating for a purpose ⟨Tibetan women do not like to appear sunburnt, even powdering their faces to *simulate* a fair complexion —Heinrich Harrer⟩ ⟨since few cannon were available, trees hewn to *simulate* formidable artillery pieces were dragged into position all along the ramparts —*Amer. Guide Series: La.*⟩ ⟨casting myself face downwards on the earth, . . . *simulating* death —W.H.Hudson †1922⟩ FEIGN, often interchangeable with SIMULATE, may suggest calculated intent and artful execution ⟨a clever young man who had evaded conscription by *feigning* epilepsy —Eric Linklater⟩ ⟨Bouquet, *feigning* retreat, drew the Indians forward to receive a flanking fire from companies ambushed for the purpose —S.J.Buck⟩ COUNTERFEIT may imply imitation that copies very closely ⟨*counterfeit* coins⟩ ⟨many noblemen gave the actor-manager access to their collections of armor and weapons in order that his accouterment should exactly *counterfeit* that of a Norman baron —G.B. Shaw⟩ SHAM may apply to deception so obvious that it deceives only the gullible ⟨when the curtain falls there are more actors *shamming* dead upon the stage than actors upright —H.A.L.Craig⟩ **syn** see in addition PRESUPPOSE

as·sumed \-ümd\ *adj* **1 :** taken as one's right or possession **:** APPROPRIATED, USURPED ⟨bearing evidence in an ~ capacity⟩ **2 a :** MAKE-BELIEVE, PRETENDED, FEIGNED ⟨an ~ cheerfulness⟩ **b :** FICTITIOUS, FALSE ⟨an ~ name⟩ **3 :** taken for granted **:** SUPPOSED ⟨the ~ reason for his absence⟩ — **as·sum·ed·ly** \-mədlē, -li\ *adv*

assumed bond *n* **:** a bond issued by one corporation and assumed by another

assumed position *n* **:** the position at which a craft is assumed to be located for the determination of a line of position

as·sum·er \-mə(r)\ *n* -s **:** one that assumes

assuming *adj* **:** taking too much upon oneself **:** PRETENTIOUS, PRESUMPTUOUS ⟨upon a subject like this . . . it would be altogether too ~ for a single individual to decide —Herman Melville⟩ — **as·sum·ing·ly** *adv*

as·sump·sit \əˈsəm(p)sət, aˈ-\ *n* -s [NL, he undertook, 3d pers. sing. perf. indic. act. of *assumere* to undertake, fr. L, to take up — more at ASSUME] **1 a :** a form of common-law action on the case not now used in which the plaintiff alleged a breach of agreement by the defendant from which the plaintiff had suffered legal damage **b :** an action on contract to recover damages for a breach or nonperformance of a contract or promise express or implied, oral or in writing, and formerly not under seal — see NON ASSUMPSIT **2 :** a promise or contract not under seal on which an action of assumpsit may be brought

assumpt *vt* -ED/-ING/-S [L *assumptus*, past part. of *assumere*] *obs* **:** ASSUME

as·sump·tion \əˈsəm(p)shən\ *n* -s [ME, fr. LL *assumption-, assumptio*, fr. L, reception, taking up, adoption, fr. *assumptus* (past part. of *assumere* to take up) + *-ion-, -io* -ion] **1** *usu cap* **a :** the bodily taking up of a person into heaven ⟨the dogma of the *Assumption* of the Virgin Mary⟩ **b :** the church feast commemorating the Assumption of the Virgin Mary that is observed on August 15 — compare FALLING ASLEEP **2** *archaic* **:** the taking into association or union **:** ADOPTION, INCORPORATION **3 a :** the act of taking to or upon oneself an attribute, form, duty, or office ⟨his meek ~ of innocence⟩ ⟨a delay in the ~ of his new position⟩ **b :** the act of laying claim to or taking possession of **:** APPROPRIATION, USURPATION ⟨the Nazi ~ of power in 1934⟩ **4 :** unwarranted pretentiousness **:** ARROGANCE ⟨his usual air of haughty ~ —Sir Walter Scott⟩ **5 a :** the act of taking for granted or supposing that a thing is true ⟨the structural characteristics of the order and the fallacies in ~ —R.E.Montgomery⟩ **b :** something that is taken for granted **:** SUPPOSITION ⟨it was, like all societies, built on certain ~*s* —M.C.Hollis⟩ **6 :** the taking over of debts or obligations by another; *specif* **:** the adoption by the federal government of the states' debts incurred during the American Revolution **7 a :** the proposition, axiom, postulate, or notion assumed **b :** the minor or second premise in a categorical syllogism

as·sump·tion·ist \-shənəst\ *n* -s **1 :** one who favored the taking over by the federal government of the states' debts incurred during the American Revolution **2** *usu cap* **:** AUGUSTINIAN OF THE ASSUMPTION

assumption of risk : a rule of common law that an employee entering upon employment assumes risks of injury incident to such employment

as·sump·tious \əˈsəm(p)shəs\ *adj* [*assumption* + *-ous*] **:** ASSUMING

as·sump·tive \-(p)tiv\ *adj* [prob. fr. (assumed) NL *assumptivus*, fr. L *assumptus*, past part. of *assumere* + *-ivus* -ive] **:** ASSUMED, ASSUMING: as **a :** taken as one's own ⟨upstarts with their ~ arms⟩ **b :** taken for granted or inclined to take for granted ⟨~ beliefs⟩ ⟨the ~ habits of her mind⟩ **c :** making undue claims ⟨an ~ person⟩

as·sur·ance \əˈshürən(t)s, aˈ-\ *n* -s [ME *assuraunce*, fr. MF *assurance*, fr. OF *aseürance*, fr. *aseürer* + *-ance*] **1 a :** the act of assuring **:** PLEDGE, GUARANTEE ⟨can tell you . . . with my most solemn ~ that it's true —Richard Joseph⟩ **b** *archaic* **:** a guarantee or pledge of peace and safety — usu. used in pl. ⟨angry that ~*s* had been given the enemy⟩ **2 :** something that inspires or tends to inspire confidence ⟨~*s* of support came pouring in daily —T.B.Macaulay⟩ **3 a :** the quality or state of being sure or certain **:** freedom from doubt **:** CERTAINTY ⟨said with as much ~ as is ever brought to human affairs —*Time*⟩ **b :** assuredness of divine grace or of forgiveness and salvation **:** consciousness of personal fellowship with God ⟨blessed ~, Jesus is mine —Fanny J.Crosby⟩ **4 :** the quality or state of being sure or safe **:** SECURITY, SAFETY ⟨the king's ascent to the crown and ~ therein —Thomas Keightley⟩ **5 :** the act of conveying or the instrument or other legal evidence of the conveyance of real property — called also *common assurance* **6** *now chiefly Brit* **:** INSURANCE **7 :** confidence of manner **:** freedom from timidity **:** SELF-CONFIDENCE, SELF-RELIANCE ⟨to face a good orchestra with inward and outward authority and ~ —J.N.Burk⟩ **8 :** excessive or presumptuous boldness **:** IMPUDENCE, AUDACITY ⟨no experience so far served to reveal the whole offensiveness of the man's ~ —Mary Austin⟩

as·sure \əˈshü(ə)r, aˈ-, -üə\ *vt* -ED/-ING/-S [ME *assuren*, fr. MF *assurer*, fr. OF *aseürer*, fr. ML *assecurare*, fr. L *ad-* + ML *-securare* (fr. L *securus* secure) — more at SECURE] **1 :** to make safe (as from risks or against overthrow) **:** INSURE, SECURE ⟨an international organization capable of *assuring* the security of all nations —Vera M. Dean⟩ **2 :** to give confidence to **:** REASSURE, ENCOURAGE, STRENGTHEN ⟨a pure man forgives or pleads for mercy or ~*s* the penitent —F.W.Robertson⟩ **3 :** to make sure or certain **:** put beyond all doubt **:** CONVINCE ⟨glancing backward . . . to ~ himself that neither of his late antagonists was returning —C.G.D.Roberts⟩ **4 :** to inform positively **:** tell earnestly **:** declare confidently to ⟨Constance *assured* her that the doctor would have nothing new to advise —Arnold Bennett⟩ ⟨I can ~ you of his reliability⟩ **5** *obs* **a :** to give a pledge or guarantee of **:** PROMISE ⟨*assuring* the king perpetual love —John Smith †1631⟩ **b :** to state with assurance ⟨about which neither . . . could ~ anything —Isaac Barrow⟩ **c :** to make sure the possession of **:** secure the title of ⟨and with my proper blood ~ any soul to be great Lucifer's —Christopher Marlowe⟩ **6 :** to make certain the coming or attainment of **:** ENSURE ⟨spent the better part of a year in painstaking research to ~ accuracy —A.W.Barkley⟩ **syn** see ENSURE

¹as·sured \-ü(ə)rd, -üəd\ *adj* [ME, fr. past part. of *assuren*] **1 a :** characterized by certainty or security **:** SURE ⟨deluded into believing that we can ever have completely ~ lives —C.C. Furnas⟩ **b :** beyond doubt or question **:** UNQUESTIONABLE, CERTAIN ⟨beliefs that were ~ became doubtful —C.W. de Kiewiet⟩ **c :** GUARANTEED, INSURED ⟨a tiny but ~ income for the rest of his life —Elinor Wylie⟩ **2** *obs* **:** ENGAGED, PLEDGED; *specif* **:** BETROTHED **3 a :** characterized by self-assurance **:** CONFIDENT, SELF-POSSESSED ⟨most ~ of all in appearance was the commissary of prisoners —Kenneth Roberts⟩ ⟨an art so ~ as to appear casual —Margery Bailey⟩ **b :** characterized by undue or excessive self-confidence **:** SELF-SATISFIED ⟨with an air of ~ ignorance —Isaac Watts⟩ **4 :** satisfied as to the certainty or truth (of a matter) **:** CONVINCED ⟨so ~ was Augustus of the merits of his plan —John Buchan⟩ **syn** see CONFIDENT

²assured \"\ *n, pl* **assured** *or* **assureds 1 :** the person in whose favor an insurance policy stands **2 :** the person who is insured

as·sur·ed·ly \-ürədlē, -li\ *adv* **1 :** without a doubt **:** CERTAINLY, SURELY **2 :** with assurance **:** CONFIDENTLY

as·sur·ed·ness *n* -ES **:** the quality or state of being assured

as·sur·er *or* **as·sur·or** \-ürə(r)\ *n* -s **:** one that assures; *specif* **:** one that gives or underwrites an insurance policy

as·sur·gen·cy \əˈsərjənsē\ *n* -ES [*assurgent* + *-cy*] **:** the tendency to rise

as·sur·gent \-jənt\ *adj* [L *assurgent-, assurgens, adsurgent-, adsurgens*, pres. part. of *assurgere, adsurgere* to rise, fr. *ad-* + *surgere* to rise — more at SURGE] **:** ASCENDING, RISING: as **a** *heraldry* **:** rising from the sea ⟨a sea horse ~⟩ **b :** ASCENDANT 1b

assuring *adj* **:** that assures or tends to assure **:** giving confidence — **as·sur·ing·ly** *adv*

asswage *obs var of* ASSUAGE

assy *abbr* assembly

¹as·syr·i·an \əˈsirēən *also* aˈ-\ *adj, usu cap* [*Assyria*, ancient empire of Western Asia + E *-an*] **1 a :** of, relating to, or characteristic of Assyria, an ancient empire of western Asia **b :** of, relating to, or characteristic of the Assyrians **2 :** of, relating to, or characteristic of the Assyrian language

²**assyrian** \"\ *n* -s *cap* **1 a :** a member of an ancient Semitic race forming the Assyrian nation and characterized physically by a muscular frame, brachycephaly, a tawny complexion, and a prominent hooked nose **b :** a Babylonian Semite **2 :** the Semitic language of the Assyrians, a dialect of Akkadian — see AFRO-ASIATIC LANGUAGES table **3 :** a member of a brunette Caucasian ethnic group in Asia Minor and Iraq whose language is neo-Syriac — compare CHALDEAN

assyrian plum *n, usu cap A* **:** SEBESTEN

as·syr·i·ol·o·gist \ə¦sirē'äləjəst\ *n* -s *usu cap* **:** a specialist in Assyriology

as·syr·i·ol·o·gy \-jē, -i\ *n* -ES *usu cap* [*Assyria* + E *-o-* + *-logy*] **:** the science or study of the history, language, and antiquities of ancient Assyria and Babylonia

¹**as·syro-babylonian** \ə¦si(,)rō, a¦s-+¦==¦=(=)=\ *adj, usu cap A&B* [*Assyro-* (fr. *Assyria*) + *Babylonian*] **:** of, relating to, or characteristic of Assyria and Babylonia or their common culture

²**assyro-babylonian** *n, usu cap A&B* **:** AKKADIAN 3a

assythment *n* -s [Sc *assythe* to compensate, satisfy (fr. ME *assithen, assethen,* fr. *assith, asseth,* n., satisfaction, reparation, fr. MF *asseit,* back-formation fr. *assez* enough) + E *-ment* — more at ASSET] *Scot law* **:** indemnification for injury; *specif* **:** the satisfaction formerly demandable by the family of a person slain but now superseded by damages recoverable by an action — compare MANBOTE

¹**ast** \'ast, aa(ə)-,ai-,â-\ *dial var of* ASK

²**ast** \"\ **:** ASKED — used esp. in written dialogue to represent a supposed dialect or substandard speech

-ast \,ast, ,aa(ə)-, ,əst\ *n suffix* -s [ME *-aste,* fr. L *-astes,* fr. Gk *-astēs* (akin to *-istēs* -ist)] **:** one connected with ⟨ecdysiast⟩ ⟨hypochondriast⟩

AST *abbr* Atlantic standard time

as·ta·cid·ea \,astə'sidēə\ [NL, fr. *Astacus* + *-idea*] *syn of* ASTACURA

as·ta·cin \'astəsən\ *also* **as·ta·cene** \-,sēn\ *n* -s [ISV *astac-* (fr. NL *Astacus*) + *-in* or *-ene*] **:** a red carotenoid ketone pigment $C_{40}H_{48}O_4$ found esp. in crustaceans (as in boiled lobster shell) and obtained by oxidation of astaxanthin

as·ta·cu·ra \,astə'kyu̇rə\ *n pl, cap* [NL, fr. *Astacus* + *-ura*] *zool* **:** a tribe of Reptantia that includes the freshwater crayfishes and the true lobsters both formerly placed in the suborder Macrura — **as·ta·cu·ran** \¦==¦=rən\ *adj or n*

as·ta·cus \'astəkəs\ *n, cap* [NL, fr. L, crab, fr. Gk *astakos, ostakos* lobster, crayfish; akin to Gk *osteon* bone — more at OSSEOUS] **:** a genus (the type of the family Astacidae) of crustaceans containing the freshwater crayfishes of Europe and related species of western No. America

a-stage resin \'ā,-\ *n, usu cap A* [¹*a*] **:** RESOLE

a star \'ā-\ *n, usu cap A* [¹*a*] **:** a star of spectral type A — see SPECTRAL TYPE table

astar·board \ə'-\ *adv* [¹*a-* + *starboard*] **:** over toward or on the starboard side of a ship — usu. used of the helm ⟨put the helm hard ~⟩

astare \ə'-\ *adj* [¹*a-* + *stare,* v.] **:** STARING ⟨the round face . . . high-collared and ~ —Maurice Hewlett⟩ ⟨with eyes ~⟩

astart \ə'-\ *adv* [¹*a-* + *start* (to move convulsively)] **:** with a start **:** SUDDENLY

as·tar·te \ə'stärd·ē, a'-\ *n* [NL, fr. L *Astarte,* principal goddess of Tyre and Sidon (often identified with Aphrodite by the Greeks), fr. Gk *Astartē,* of Sem origin; akin to Heb *'Ashtōreth,* Phoenician and Canaanite goddess] **1** *cap* **:** a genus (the type of the family Astartidae) comprising marine bivalve mollusks (order Eulamellibranchia) with thick equivalved shells often concentrically ridged and with well-developed hinge teeth **2** -s **:** any member of the genus *Astarte*

asta·sia \ə'stāzh(ē)ə\ *n* -s [NL, fr. Gk, unsteadiness, fr. *astatos* unsteady (fr. *a-* ²a- + *statos* standing, fr. *histanai* to cause to stand) + *-ia* — more at STAND] *med* **:** muscular incoordination in standing — compare ABASIA

asta·sia-abasia \"+\ *n* -s [NL, fr. *astasia* + *abasia*] *med* **:** inability to stand and walk resulting from muscular incoordination

astatic \(')ā+¦-\ *adj* [²*a-* + *static*] **1 :** not static **:** not stable or steady **2** *physics* **:** having little or no tendency to take a fixed or definite position or direction — **astatically** *adv* — **astat·i·cism** \(')ā'stad·ə,sizəm\ *n* -s

astatic galvanometer *n* **:** a galvanometer having two needles with opposite polarities that reduce the effect of the earth's magnetism

astatic pair *n* **:** two small coplanar magnets of equal moment rigidly attached at right angles to a stiff wire with their moments oppositely directed and forming a system that experiences no directive influence when suspended in a uniform magnetic field

as·ta·tine \'astə,tēn, -,tən\ *n* -s [Gk *astat*os unsteady, unstable + E *-ine*] **:** a radioactive element belonging to the halogens discovered by bombarding bismuth with helium nuclei and also formed by radioactive decay — symbol *At;* see ELEMENT table

as·ta·tize \-,tīz\ *vt* -ED/-ING/-s [*astatic* + *-ize*] **:** to render astatic

as·ta·xanthin \¦astə+\ *n* -s [NL *Astacus* + E *xanthin*] **:** a violet crystalline carotenoid pigment $C_{40}H_{52}O_4$ found combined (as with proteins) esp. in the shells of crustaceans and the feathers of birds

astay \ə'stā\ *adj* [¹*a-* + *stay* (rope)] *of an anchor being hove in* **:** having its cable parallel to one of the ship's stays

ast·bury \'as(t)b(ə)rē, -ri\ *or* **ast·bur·y·ware** \'=(=)=,=\ *n* -s *usu cap* [after John *Astbury* †1743 Eng. potter] **:** 18th century English pottery including red stoneware with sprigged or molded ornamentation and mottled lead-glazed earthenware figures

asteep \ə'-\ *adj* [¹*a-* + *steep,* v.] **:** undergoing steeping

asteer \ə'stēr\ *Scot var of* ASTIR

aste·lic \(')ā¦stēlik\ *adj* [²*a-* + *-stelic*] **:** lacking a stele or having the cylindrical arrangement of the vascular bundles discontinuous or disrupted — **aste·ly** \'ā,stēlē\ *n* -ES

as·ter \'astə(r), 'aas-\ *n* [in senses 1 and 2, fr. NL, fr. L, aster, fr. Gk *aster-, astēr* star, aster; in sense 3, fr. NL, fr. LL, star, fr. Gk *aster-, astēr;* in sense 4, fr. MGk *aster-, astēr,* fr. Gk, star — more at STAR] **1** *cap* **:** a large genus of chiefly fall-blooming leafy-stemmed herbaceous plants (family Compositae) native of temperate regions and having discoid and usu. daisylike radiate heads, a multiseriate involucre, and a pappus of a single series of capillary bristles — see MICHAELMAS DAISY **2** -s **a :** any plant of the genus *Aster* or its immediate related forms **b :** any of a number of plants derived from the China aster **3** -s *biol* **:** a system of gelated cytoplasmic rays (aster rays) typically arranged radially about a centrosome at either end of the mitotic spindle and sometimes persisting between mitoses — called also *cytaster* **4** *Eastern Church* **:** ASTERISK 2

aster- *or* **astero-** *comb form* [Gk, fr. *aster-, astēr*] **:** star ⟨*aster*oid⟩ ⟨*Astero*lepis⟩

¹**-as·ter** \,astə(r), ¦aas-\ *n suffix* -s [ME, fr. L, suffix denoting partial resemblance] **:** one that is inferior, worthless, or not genuine ⟨critic*aster*⟩ ⟨poet*aster*⟩

²**-aster** \¦==\ *n comb form* -s [NL, fr. Gk *astēr*] **:** star — in structural and generic names in biology ⟨di*aster*⟩ ⟨*Geaster*⟩

as·ter·a·ce·ae \,astə'rāsē,ē\ [NL, fr. *Aster,* type genus + *-aceae*] *syn of* COMPOSITAE

as·ter·a·ceous \¦==¦rāshəs\ *adj* [NL *Asteraceae* + E *-ous*] **:** COMPOSITE b

as·ter·a·les \,==¦rā(,)lēz\ *n pl, cap* [NL, fr. *Aster* + *-ales*] *in some classifications* **:** an order of flowering plants coextensive with the superfamily Compositae and now usu. included in Campanulales

aster cloth *n* **:** a fine-mesh cotton fabric used to shade growing plants and to exclude insects — compare TOBACCO CLOTH

as·ter·el·la \,astə'relə\ [NL, fr. L *aster* star + NL *-ella*] *syn of* REBOULIA

astereognosis \(')ā+\ *n, pl* **astereognoses** [NL, fr. *a-* ²a- + *stereognosis*] *med* **:** loss of the ability to recognize the shapes of objects by handling them

aster family *n* **:** COMPOSITAE

¹**as·te·ria** \a'stirēə\ *n* -s [L, a precious stone, perh. the star sapphire, fr. Gk, fem. of *asterios* starry, fr. *aster-, astēr* star] **:** a gem stone cut so as to show asterism

²**asteria** *pl of* ASTERION

as·te·ri·al \(')a¦stirēəl\ *adj* [L *aster* or Gk *aster-, astēr* star + E *-ial*] **:** of or relating to stars **:** like a star

as·te·ri·as \a'stirēəs\ *n, cap* [NL, fr. Gk, starred, fr. *aster-, astēr*] **:** a genus of echinoderms formerly comprising nearly all starfishes and ophiurans but now restricted to certain typical starfishes including the common littoral forms of Europe and eastern No. America

as·te·ri·at·ed \='==,ād·əd\ *adj* [Gk *asterios* starry, of a star + E *-ate* + *-ed* — more at ASTERIA] **:** exhibiting asterism

as·te·ri·i·dae \,astə'rīə,dē\ *n pl, cap* [NL, fr. *Asterias,* type genus + *-idae*] **:** a large and important family of starfishes including the common species of No. America and Europe and having *Asterias* as its type and best-known genus

as·ter·in·i·dae \-'rinə,dē\ *n pl, cap* [NL, fr. *Asterina,* type genus (fr. Gk *aster-, astēr* star, starfish + NL *-ina*) + *-idae*] **:** a widely distributed family of usu. pentagonal quite flat starfishes

¹**as·te·ri·oid** \a'stirē,ȯid\ *adj* [NL *Asterioidea*] **:** ASTEROID 2

²**asterioid** \"\ *n* -s **:** ASTEROID 2

as·te·ri·oi·dea \,==='ȯidēə\ [NL *Asterias* + *-oidea*] *syn of* ASTEROIDEA

as·te·ri·on \a'stirē,än\ *n, pl* **aste·ria** \-ēə\ [NL, fr. Gk, neut. of *asterios* starry] **:** the point behind the ear where the parietal, temporal, and occipital bones meet — see CRANIOMETRY illustration — **as·te·ri·on·ic** \(')=¦==¦änik\ *adj*

as·te·ri·o·nel·la \,===ə'nelə\ *n* [NL, fr. Gk *asterion* (neut. of *asterios* starry) + NL *-ella*] **1** *cap* **:** a small genus of narrowly linear diatoms (family Fragilariaceae) arranged in stellate free-floating colonies and often causing geraniumlike or fishy odors in public water supplies **2** -s **:** a diatom of the genus *Asterionella*

¹**as·ter·isk** \'astə,risk, 'aas-\ *n* -s [LL *asteriscus,* fr. Gk *asteriskos,* lit., little star, dim. of *aster-, astēr* star] **1 :** the character * used in printing as the first in series of the reference marks, to indicate the omission of letters or words, in linguistic works to mark hypothetical forms belonging to a reconstructed ancestral language, and in various arbitrary uses — called also *star* **2** *also* **as·te·ris·kos** \,astə'rē,skȯs\ -ES *Eastern Church* **:** a star-shaped liturgical utensil used to cover the eucharistic elements lying in a paten and to guard them from contact with the first veil

²**asterisk** \"\ *vt* -ED/-ING/-s **:** to mark with an asterisk **:** STAR

as·ter·ism \-,rizəm\ *n* -s [Gk *asterismos,* fr. *asterizein* to arrange in constellations, fr. *aster-, astēr* star + *-izein* -ize] **1 a :** CONSTELLATION **b :** a small group of stars **2 :** the optical phenomenon of a star-shaped figure exhibited by some crystals by reflected light (as in a star sapphire) or by transmitted light (as in some mica) **3 :** three asterisks arranged in the form of an inverted or upright pyramid (as *⁎* or ⁎*⁎) esp. in order to direct attention to a following passage

as·ter·is·mal \¦==¦rizməl\ *adj* **:** of or relating to asterisms or constellations

aster leafhopper *n* **:** SIX-SPOTTED LEAFHOPPER

¹**astern** \ə'-\ *adv* [¹*a-* + *stern* (n.)] **1 :** behind a ship or aircraft **:** in the rear ⟨we were sailing due east and the setting sun was now directly ~⟩ ⟨~, the sea gulls wheeled and dipped⟩ **2 :** at or toward the stern of a ship or aircraft ⟨it ended ~ in a clumsy-looking bulge that was closed by a pair of huge clamshell doors —W.F.Jenkins⟩ ⟨he paused ~, gazing over the rail at the wake of the ship⟩ **3 :** stern foremost **:** to the rear **:** BACKWARD ⟨rang full ~ on the telegraph⟩ ⟨maneuvers that involve going ~ should never be taken until the dinghy line is shortened —W.P.Moore⟩

²**astern** \"\ *adj* **1 :** placed or situated astern **2 :** directing astern **:** signaling motion astern

asternal \(')ā+¦-\ *adj* [²*a-* + *sternal*] *anat* **:** not sternal: **a :** unattached to the sternum ⟨the floating ribs are ~⟩ **b :** having no sternum

astero- — see ASTER-

as·tero·calamites \¦astə(,)rō+\ [NL, fr. *aster-* + *Calamites*] *syn of* ARCHAEOCALAMITES

¹**as·tero·coc·cus** \,astərō'käkəs\ [NL, fr. *aster-* + *-coccus*] *syn of* MYCOPLASMA

²**asterococcus** \"\ *n, pl* **asterococ·ci** \-ä,kī, -äkē, -äk,sī, -äksē\ [NL, fr. *aster-* + *-coccus*] **1 :** an organism of the genus *Mycoplasma* **2 :** a disk-shaped developmental form of an asterococcus

¹**as·ter·oid** \'astə,rȯid, 'aas-\ *n* -s [Gk *asteroeidēs* starlike] **1 :** a celestial body resembling a star in appearance; *specif* **:** one of thousands of small planets most of which have orbits between those of Mars and Jupiter, approximating on the average the orbit at 2.8 astronomical units assigned by Bode's law, and ranging in size from a fraction of a mile in largest dimension to nearly 500 miles in diameter — called also *minor planet, planetoid* **2** [NL *Asteroidea*] **:** one of the Asteroidea **:** STARFISH

²**asteroid** \"\ *adj* [ISV, fr. Gk *asteroeidēs* starlike, fr. *aster-, astēr* star + *-oeidēs* -oid] **1 :** like a star **2** [NL *Asteroidea*] **:** of or resembling a starfish **3** [NL *Aster* + E *-oid*] **:** resembling or belonging to the genus *Aster*

as·ter·oi·dal \¦==¦rȯid°l\ *adj* **:** of or belonging to an asteroid or the asteroids

as·ter·oi·dea \,=='rȯidēə\ *n pl, cap* [NL, fr. *Asterias* + *-oidea*] **:** the class of echinoderms comprising the starfishes, all being unattached, having (1) a star-shaped or pentagonal body, the rays or arms (usu. 5 in number) hollow and containing prolongations of the coelom and alimentary and other viscera, (2) a skeleton of calcareous plates and ossicles somewhat loosely united, often allowing the arms great freedom of movement, and (3) a mouth on the lower surface without jaws or teeth, an aboral madreporic plate, and the anus often wanting or functionless (undigested matter being thrown out at the mouth), and moving by means of the arms or of long spines on the sides of the arms or by rows of tube feet that occur in a furrow on the lower surface of each arm — **as·ter·oi·de·an** \¦==¦dēən\ *adj or n*

as·tero·lecanium \¦astə(,)rō+\ *n, cap* [NL, fr. *aster-* + *Lecanium*] **:** a large genus of chiefly tropical scales including some that are pests of oaks and ornamental plantings in California — compare PIT SCALE

as·ter·ol·e·pis \,astə'räləpəs\ *n, cap* [NL, fr. *aster-* + *-lepis*] **:** a genus of Middle Devonian ostracoderms (subclass Antiarcha) with greatly developed pectoral spines

as·tero·phyl·li·tes \,astə(,)rōfə'līd·ēz\ *n, cap* [NL, fr. *aster-* + Gk *phyllon* leaf + NL *-ites* -ite — more at BLADE] **:** a form genus of fossil plants abundantly represented in the coal measures, having a starlike disposition of the leaves, and considered now to be branches of *Calamites*

as·tero·spon·dy·li \-'spändə,lī\ *n pl, cap* [NL, fr. *aster-* + *-spondyli*] *in some classifications* **:** an order of Elasmobranchii comprising forms having asterospondylic vertebrae and including most of the present sharks and dogfishes

as·tero·spon·dyl·ic \¦==(,)=,spän¦dilik\ *or* **as·tero·spon·dy·lous** \-¦spändələs\ *adj* [*aster-* + *spondylic, spondylous*] **1 :** having the vertebral centra strengthened by longitudinal calcified plates radiating outward from a central cylinder surrounding the notochord — compare CYCLOSPONDYLIC **2** [NL *Asterospondyli* + E *-ic* or *-ous*] **:** of or relating to the Asterospondyli

as·tero·the·ca \,==(,)='thēkə\ *n, cap* [NL, fr. *aster-* + *-theca*] **:** a form genus of Paleozoic fossil ferns based on the sporangia which are grouped in a circular sorus

as·ter·oxy·la·ce·ae \,astə,räksə'lāsē,ē\ *n pl, cap* [NL, fr. *Asteroxylon,* type genus (fr. *aster-* + *-xylon*) + *-aceae*] **:** a family of Paleozoic plants (order Psilophytales) having a xylem that is star-shaped in cross section

as·ter·oxy·lon \,-'räksə,län\ *n, cap* [NL, fr. *aster-* + *-xylon*] **:** a genus of Paleozoic plants (family Asteroxylaceae) having a single star-shaped vascular strand in the shoot

as·tero·zoa \,astərə'zōə\ *n pl, cap* [NL, fr. *aster-* + *-zoa*] *in some classifications* **:** a subphylum of echinoderms comprising the starfishes (Asteroidea) and brittle stars (Ophiuroidea)

aster purple *n* **:** a deep purplish red that is bluer and deeper than American beauty, redder and duller than magenta (sense 2a), and bluer and less strong than hollyhock

aster ray *n* **:** one of the rays making up an aster (sense 3)

asters *pl of* ASTER

-asters *pl of* -ASTER

aster yellows *n pl* **:** a widespread virus disease of the aster and many other plants characterized by yellowing and dwarfing and a greenish tinge to the flower heads and transmitted by leafhoppers

asthen- *or* **astheno-** *comb form* [Gk, fr. *asthenēs* weak, fr. *a-* ²a- + *-sthenēs* (fr. *sthenos* strength); perh. akin to Skt *saghnoti* he takes upon himself, is a match for] **:** weak ⟨*asthenopia*⟩ **:** weakness ⟨*astheno*logy⟩

as·the·nia \as'thēnēə, əs- *also* ,asthə'nēə\ *n* -s [NL, fr. Gk *astheneia,* fr. *asthenēs* + *-ia*] **:** lack or loss of strength **:** DEBILITY **:** deficient vitality

as·then·ic \(')as¦thenik, əs'th-\ *adj* [fr. Gk *asthenikos,* fr. *astheneia* + *-ikos* -ic] **1 :** belonging to or characterized by asthenia **:** WEAK, DEBILITATED **2 :** characterized by slender build and slight muscular development **:** ECTOMORPHIC — compare ATHLETIC, PYKNIC

as·the·no·bi·o·sis \¦asthə(,)nō,bī'ōsəs\ *n, pl* **asthenobio·ses** \-ō,sēz\ [NL, fr. *asthen-* + *-biosis*] **:** a state of reduced activity that precedes pupation in the larvae of certain insects

as·then·o·lith \as'thenə,lith, əs-\ *n* -s [*asthen-* + *-lith*] **:** the material in the asthenosphere

as·the·no·pia \,asthə'nōpēə\ *n* -s [NL, fr. *asthen-* + *-opia*] **:** weakness or rapid fatigue of the eyes often accompanied by pain and headache — **as·the·nop·ic** \¦==¦näpik, -ōp-\ *adj*

as·theno·sphere \as'thenə,sfi(ə)r, əs'th-\ *n* -s [*asthen-* + *-sphere*] **:** a hypothetical earth-circling shell or zone which lies from 30 to 75 miles below the earth's surface and within which the material not necessarily molten is believed to yield more readily to persistent stresses than the rigid crust above or the solid nucleus below — called also *tectosphere, zone of mobility, zone of weakness;* compare SIMA, ZONE OF FLOW

asth·ma \'azmə, *Brit usu & US rarely* 'asmə\ *n* -s [alter. (influenced by Gk *asthma*) of earlier *asma,* fr. ME, fr. ML, modif. of Gk *asthma;* perh. akin to Gk *aēnai* to blow — more at WIND] **:** labored breathing either continuous or paroxysmal accompanied by wheezing, a sense of constriction in the chest, and often by attacks of coughing or gasping caused by conditions that interfere with the normal inflow and outflow of air in the lungs (as swelling of the mucous membrane of the bronchi or constriction of the bronchial or bronchiolar walls with resultant narrowing of the lumen) — see BRONCHIAL ASTHMA; compare CARDIAC ASTHMA

asthma herb *n* **:** a tropical weed (*Euphorbia hirta*) reputed in Australia to be effective in the treatment of asthma

asthma paper *n* **:** paper impregnated with saltpeter whose fumes when burned are sometimes inhaled as an alleviative for asthma

¹**asth·mat·ic** \(')az¦mad·ik, -atik, -ēk\ *also* **asth·mat·i·cal** \-ə̇kəl, -ēk-\ *adj* [L *asthmaticus,* fr. Gk *asthmatikos,* fr. *asthmat-, asthma* + *-ikos* -ic] **1 :** caused by or affected with asthma ⟨an ~ cough⟩ ⟨an ~ patient⟩ **:** relating to asthma **2 :** suggesting the breathing of an asthmatic person **:** WHEEZY ⟨traveling in ancient and ~ cars⟩ **:** PANTING, SHORT-BREATHED ⟨the coarse tone and ~ phrasing of Bach's oboe —Ralph Vaughan Williams⟩ — **asth·mat·i·cal·ly** \-ək(ə)lē, -ēk-, -li\ *adv*

²**asthmatic** \"\ *n* -s **:** an asthmatic person

asthmatic cigarette *n* **:** a medicated cigarette smoked for the relief of spasmodic asthma

asth·ma·toid \'azmə,tȯid\ *adj* [ISV *asthmat-* (fr. Gk *asthmat-, arthma*) + *-oid*] **:** resembling asthma ⟨an ~ wheeze⟩

asthma weed *n* **:** INDIAN TOBACCO

asth·mo·gen·ic \¦azmə¦jenik\ *adj* [ISV *asthmo-* (fr. *asthma*) + *-genic*] **:** causing asthmatic attacks

asthore \as'thō(ə)r\ *n* -s [IrGael *a stōr* oh treasure, fr. *a* oh + *stōr* treasure] *Irish* **:** TREASURE — a term of endearment

as though *conj* **:** as if ⟨the Charter makes "aggression" synonymous with "wrongdoing" but drops the matter there, *as though* everyone understood the nature of sin —E.B.White⟩

as·ti·chous \'astəkəs\ *adj* [²*a-* + *-stichous*] *bot* **:** not arranged in rows

as·tig·mat \'astig,mat, ə'stig-\ *n* -s [short for *astigmatic*] **:** an astigmatic person

as·tig·mat·ic \¦astig¦mad·ik, -tēg-, -atik, -ēk\ *also* **as·tig·mat·i·cal** \-ə̇kəl, -ēk-\ *adj* [²*a-* + Gk *stigmat-, stigma* spot, mark + E *-ic, -ical*] **1 :** affected with or relating to astigmatism ⟨~ eyes⟩ **:** correcting astigmatism ⟨~ lenses⟩ **2 :** having or showing an inability or unwillingness to observe, discriminate, or evaluate closely or in accordance with fact ⟨~, flabby, and bemused writing about the Civil War —Bernard De Voto⟩ ⟨an ~ fanaticism, a disregard for the facts —*N.Y. Herald Tribune*⟩ — **as·tig·mat·i·cal·ly** \-ək(ə)lē, -ēk-, -li\ *adv*

astig·ma·tism \ə'stigmə,tizəm, a'-\ *n* -s [*astigmatic* + *-ism*] **1** *physics* **:** a defect of an optical system (as a lens or mirror) in consequence of which rays from a single point of an object fail to meet in a single focal point thus causing the image of a point to be drawn out into a line and the images of lines having a certain direction to be less distinct than those of lines transverse to that direction **2 :** a defect of vision due to astigmatism of the refractive system of the eye commonly caused by irregular conformation of the cornea **3 :** distorted mental perception suggestive of the blurred vision of a person affected with astigmatism of the eyes **:** want of true discernment or appreciation esp. when resulting from prejudice or deliberate obtuseness ⟨foreign travelers . . . whose subjective observations were highly colored by their own mental ~, provincialism, and an absurd moral rectitude —E.J.Simmons⟩ ⟨swayed . . . by his ~ and his hates —H.L.Ickes⟩

astig·ma·tiz·er \-,tīzə(r)\ *n* -s **:** a device used for drawing out a point of light into a line (as in a range finder)

astig·mia \-mēə\ *n* -s [NL, fr. ²*a-* + Gk *stigma* spot, mark + NL *-ia* — more at STIGMA] **:** ASTIGMATISM

as·tig·mom·e·ter \,a(,)stig'mäməd·ə(r), ,astēg-\ *or* **astig·ma·tom·e·ter** \ə,stigmə'täməd·ə(r), a,s-\ *n* -s [ISV *astigmo-, astigmato-* (fr. *astigmatism*) + *-meter;* orig. formed as F *astigmomètre*] **:** an apparatus for measuring the degree of astigmatism — **as·tig·mom·e·try** \,astig'mämətrē, -i\ *n* -ES

astil·be \ə'stil(,)bē\ *n* [NL, fr. ²*a-* + Gk *stilbē,* fem. of *stilbos* glistening — more at STILBUM] **1** *cap* **:** a genus of chiefly Asiatic perennials (family Saxifragaceae) with ample ternately compound leaves and large terminal panicles composed of spikes and small white flowers — see FALSE GOATSBEARD **2** -s **:** any plant of the genus *Astilbe* ⟨the feathery charm of the ~s⟩

¹**astipulate** *vb* -ED/-ING/-s [L *astipulatus,* past part. of *astipulari,* fr. *ad-* + *stipulari* to stipulate — more at STIPULATE] *vi, obs* **:** AGREE, ASSENT ~ *vt, obs* **:** to agree to — **astipulation** *n* -s

²**astipulate** \(')ā+¦-\ *adj* [²*a-* + *stipulate*] *bot* **:** EXSTIPULATE

astir \ə'stər, +V -ər-; ə'stə, +V -ər- *also* -ər\ *adj* [prob. alter. of Sc *asteer,* fr. ¹*a-* + *steer,* var. of *stir*] **1 :** STIRRING **:** in a state of activity or motion ⟨a fresh and more vigorous spirit was plainly ~ —Van Wyck Brooks⟩ ⟨hundreds of men moved restlessly, so that the whole hill was ~ —Kenneth Roberts⟩ — often used with *with* ⟨streams ~ with trout⟩ ⟨the ship was ~ with agitated passengers —Ngaio Marsh⟩ **2 :** out of bed **:** UP

as·tite \ə'stīt\ *adv* [ME, fr. *as* + *tite*] *dial Brit* **:** as soon **:** RATHER

as to *prep* [ME, fr. *as* + *to*] **:** with reference to **:** in regard to **:** as regards: **a :** ABOUT, CONCERNING, RESPECTING ⟨a matter *as to* which opinions might differ⟩ ⟨stopped short of their objective *as to* production⟩ ⟨felt somewhat at a loss *as to* how to begin —*Life*⟩ ⟨*as to* my own views, they will be mentioned later⟩ ⟨uncertain *as to* what to do next⟩ **b :** according to **:** BY ⟨classified and graded *as to* size and color⟩

as·to·gen·ic \¦astə¦jenik\ *adj* **:** relating to or marked by astogeny

as·tog·e·ny \a'stäjənē\ *n* -ES [prob. fr. Gk *astos* inhabitant of a city (fr. *asty* city) + E *-geny*] **:** a more or less marked change in size or form shown by all the zooids in colonial animals (as graptolites) as the colony grows older

astomatal \(')ā+¦-\ *adj* [²*a-* + *stomatal*] **:** without stomata — used of green plants or their parts ⟨an ~ leaf⟩

astomatous \(')ā+¦-\ *adj* [²*a-* + *stomatous*] **1 :** having no mouth; *esp* **:** lacking a cytostome ⟨~ ciliates⟩

as·to·mous \'astəməs\ *adj* [²*a-* + *-stomous*] **1 :** ASTOMATAL **2 :** having a capsule that bursts irregularly and is not dehiscent by an operculum — used of certain mosses

as·ton dark space \'astən-\ *n, usu cap A* [after Francis W. *Aston* †1945 Eng. chemist and physicist] **:** a nonluminous layer between the cathode surface and the cathode glow in a vacuum tube

astonied *past of* ASTONY

as·ton·ish \ə'stänish, -ēsh, *esp in pres part* -əsh\ *vt* -ED/-ING/-ES [prob. fr. *astony* + *-ish* (as in *abolish*)] **1** *obs* **:** to render senseless (as by a blow) **:** STUN, PARALYZE, DEADEN ⟨enough, Captain; you have ~*ed* him —Shak.⟩ **2** *obs* **:** to stupefy the mind of **:** BEWILDER, DAZE, CONFUSE ⟨had his wits ~*ed* with sorrow —Philip Sidney⟩ ⟨blind, ~*ed*, and struck with superstition as with a planet —John Milton⟩ **3** *obs* **:** to strike with sudden fear or dismay ⟨that with the very shaking of their chains they may ~ these fell-lurking curs —Shak.⟩ **4 :** to strike with a sudden sense of surprise or wonder esp. through something unexpected or difficult to accept as true or reasonable **:** surprise greatly **:** AMAZE ⟨was ~*ed* to find a thick forest where in 1915 I had mowed thick grass with a scythe —S.H. Holbrook⟩ ⟨~*ed* by the vastness and majesty of the cathedral⟩ ⟨a gross desire to ~ his friends with his sudden wealth⟩ ⟨the customs of non-European groups were treated as curios with which to ~ the uninformed —Ralph Linton⟩ **syn** see SURPRISE

astonishable *adj, obs* **:** ASTONISHING

as·ton·ished·ly \-shtlē\ *adv* **:** in an astonished manner **:** with astonishment

astonishing *adj* **:** causing or tending to cause astonishment esp. by surpassing expectation or ready belief **:** SURPRISING, AMAZING ⟨the longbow and the arrow which whizzed from it with ~ power —Hardiman Scott⟩ ⟨an ~ success story⟩ ⟨an ~ eye for seeing sermons in stones —C.D.Lewis⟩ — **as·ton·ish·ing·ly** *adv* — **as·ton·ish·ing·ness** *n* -ES

as·ton·ish·ment \ə'stänishmənt, -ēsh-\ *n* -S **1 :** the state of being astonished or of one who is astonished: as **a** *obs* **:** PARALYSIS, NUMBNESS **b** *obs* **:** STUPOR, BEWILDERMENT **c** *archaic* **:** DISMAY, CONSTERNATION ⟨~ though not in itself fear is nevertheless a good stage towards it —T.L.Peacock⟩ **d :** great surprise or wonder **:** AMAZEMENT ⟨saw ~ giving place to horror on the faces of the people —H.G.Wells⟩ ⟨children watching with ~ and delight⟩ ⟨in his first ~ he had stopped dead short —Joseph Conrad⟩ ⟨sincere women sometimes express their ~ over the exaggerated sense of romance . . . which many men show —Theodor Reik⟩ **2 :** one that astonishes; *esp* **:** a cause of amazement or wonder ⟨a never-ending ~ to his parents⟩ ⟨my first meeting with Oscar Wilde was an ~ —W.B.Yeats⟩ ⟨the book races on from one ~ to the next —Dan Wickenden⟩

as·tony \ə'stänē\ *vt* -ED/-ING/-S [ME *astonien*, alter. of *astonen*, modif. of OF *estoner*, fr. (assumed) VL *extonare*, fr. L *ex-* + *tonare* to thunder — more at THUNDER] **1** *obs* **:** STUN, PARALYZE **2** *archaic* **:** DAZE, DISMAY, AMAZE ⟨then Daniel was *astonied* for one hour —Dan 4:19 (AV)⟩ ⟨I rent my garment and my mantle . . . and sat down *astonied* —Ezra 9:3 (AV)⟩ ⟨and I *astonied* fell and could not pray —Elizabeth B. Browning⟩

astoop \ə'-\ *adj* [¹*a-* + *stoop* (act of stooping)] **:** in an inclined position **:** TILTED, STOOPING

¹**as·to·ri·an** \a'stōrēən, ə'-, -ȯr-\ *n* -S *usu cap* [*Astoria*, former trading post in Oregon (now site of Astoria, Oregon) founded 1811 by John J. Astor †1848 Am. merchant + E *-an*] **:** a fur trader of the Astoria trading post

²**astorian** \"\ *adj, usu cap* **:** relating to the Astoria trading post or to its activities

¹**as·tound** \ə'staůnd\ *adj* [ME *astouned*, *astoned*, fr. past part. of *astounen*, *astonen* to stun, astound — more at ASTONY] *archaic* **:** ASTOUNDED ⟨dizzy and ~, as sudden ruin yawned around —Sir Walter Scott⟩

²**astound** \"\ *vb* -ED/-ING/-S [partly fr. ¹*astound*, partly back-formation fr. *astounded*, fr. ME, alter. of *astoured*] **1** *obs* **:** STUN, STUPEFY **2 :** to stun with bewildered or incredulous wonder **:** overwhelm with astonishment or amazement ⟨Constance was ~*ed* at her sister's self-control, which entirely passed her comprehension —Arnold Bennett⟩ ⟨it was naval disasters or failures that ~*ed* and angered the man in the street —D.W.Brogan⟩ **syn** see SURPRISE

astounding *adj* **:** calculated to astound **:** causing or capable of causing wonder and surprise in high degree **:** AMAZING ⟨the look of a man who has come up against ~ things but always with the determination not to be astounded —Mary Austin⟩ ⟨a fascinating account of an ~ epoch⟩ ⟨an ~ recovery⟩ — **astound·ing·ly** *adv*

as·tound·ment \-n(d)mənt\ *n* -S *archaic* **:** the state of being astounded **:** AMAZEMENT, ASTONISHMENT

astr- *or* **astro-** *comb form* [ME *astro-*, fr. OF, fr. L *astr-*, *astro-*, fr. Gk, fr. *astron* star — more at STAR] **1 :** star ⟨*astr*oid⟩ ⟨*astro*meter⟩ **:** the heavens ⟨*astro*graphy⟩ ⟨*astro*nautics⟩ **:** astronomical ⟨*astro*physics⟩ **2 :** astrological ⟨*astro*diagnosis⟩ **:** astrological and ⟨*astro*medical⟩ **3 :** aster in cells ⟨*astro*sphere⟩

astrachan *often cap, var of* ASTRAKHAN

¹**astrad·dle** \ə'-\ *adv* [¹*a-* + *straddle* (v.)] **:** ASTRIDE ⟨sit ~ on the horse⟩ **:** on or above and extending onto both sides ⟨the battle was fought ~ of the road⟩

²**astraddle** \"\ *prep* **:** with one leg on each side of **:** ASTRIDE ⟨seated ~ a horse⟩ ⟨with one foot in either hemisphere, ~ longitude 0 —C.S.Forester⟩

¹**as·trae·an** \a'strēən\ *adj* [NL *Astraea*, genus of corals (fr. Gk *astraios* starry, fr. *astr-*, *astēr* star) + E *-an* — more at STAR] **:** of or relating to the star corals

²**astraean** \"\ *n* -S **:** STAR CORAL

as·traeo·spon·gia \ˌastrē(ˌ)ō'spənjēə, -pän-\ *n, cap* [NL, fr. *astraeo-* (fr. Gk *astraios* starry, fr. *aster-*, *astēr* star) + *-spongia* — more at STAR] **:** a genus of saucer-shaped Silurian fossil sponges having 6-rayed stellate spicules and important as Paleozoic index fossils

as·tra·gal \'astrəgəl\ *n* -S [L *astragalus*, fr. Gk *astragalos* vertebra, anklebone, molding, milk vetch; prob. akin to Gk *osteon* bone — more at OSSEOUS] **1 :** a small convex molding of rounded surface generally from half to three quarters of a circle: as **a :** a projecting strip on the edge of folding doors **b :** BAR 1d(3) — compare BEAD 5 **2 :** a molding encircling a cannon near the muzzle **3** [prob. fr. NL *astragalus*, fr. Gk *astragalos*] **:** TALUS

astragal- *or* **astragalo-** *comb form* [Gk, fr. *astragalos*] **1 :** dice ⟨*astragalo*mancy⟩ **2** [NL *astragalus*, fr. Gk *astragalos*] **a :** the bone astragalus ⟨*astragal*ectomy⟩ **b :** astragalar and ⟨*astragalo*calcaneal⟩

as·trag·a·lar \ə'stragələ(r), a'-\ *adj* **:** of or relating to the astragalus

as·trag·a·lo·man·cy \-lō,man(t)sē\ *n* -ES [*astragal-* + *-mancy*] **:** divination by means of small bones or dice

as·trag·a·lus \-ləs\ *n* [prob. NL, fr. Gk *astragalos*] **1** *pl* **astraga·li** \-ˌlī, -ˌlē\ **:** one of the proximal bones of the tarsus of the higher vertebrates supposed to represent the united tibiale and intermedium of many lower vertebrates — usu. called in man *talus* or *anklebone*; see TALUS **2** *cap* [NL, fr. L, milk vetch, fr. Gk *astragalos*] **:** a large genus of herbs and shrubs (family Leguminosae) characterized by the narrow standard of the corolla, the blunt keel, and the fleshy or papery uninflated pod — see LOCOWEED, MILK VETCH, TRAGACANTH **3** *pl* **astragali** *or* **astragaluses** [L, fr. Gk *astragalos*] **:** ASTRAGAL 1

astrain \ə'-\ *adj* [¹*a-* + *strain* (v.)] **:** STRAINING ⟨with all his senses ~, afraid to move a step —Arnold Bennett⟩

as·tra·kan·ite *or* **as·tra·khan·ite** \'astrəkəˌnīt\ *n* -S [G *astrakanit*, irreg. fr. *Astrakhan*, region in U.S.S.R., its locality + G *-it* -ite] **:** a variety of the mineral bloedite

¹**as·tra·khan** \'astrəkən, 'aas-, -ˌkan, -ˌkaa(ə)n\ *adj, usu cap* [fr. *Astrakhan*, U.S.S.R.] **:** of or from the city or region of Astrakhan, U.S.S.R. **:** of the kind or style prevalent in Astrakhan

²**astrakhan** \"\ *also* **as·tra·chan** \"\ *n* -S *often cap* **1 :** the fur or skin of a karakul lamb of Russian breeding — now seldom used because of confusion resulting from varied and conflicting application within the fur trade **2 :** a lustrous cloth of wool or of cotton and wool made with a curled and looped pile often cut to imitate astrakhan fur

¹**as·tral** \'astrəl, 'aas-\ *adj* [LL *astralis*, fr. L *astrum* star (fr. Gk *astron*) + *-alis* -al — more at STAR] **1 a :** of or relating to the stars ⟨~ myths⟩ ⟨~ imagery⟩ **:** coming or thought of as coming from the stars ⟨~ beams⟩ ⟨~ influences⟩ **b :** consisting of stars **:** like stars ⟨~ showers⟩ **:** STARRY ⟨an ~ gleam⟩ **2** *biol* **:** of or relating to an aster ⟨~ rays⟩ **3** *theosophy* **:** consisting of, belonging to, or being a supersensible substance supposed to be next above the tangible world in refinement **4 :** suggestive of the remoteness of the stars (as from common concerns or values): as **a :** VISIONARY, UNWORLDLY ⟨an ~ and most impractical thinker⟩ **b :** EXALTED ⟨the most ~ circles of society⟩ — **as·tral·ly** \-əlē, -li\ *adv*

²**astral** \"\ *n* -S **1 :** ASTRAL LAMP **2** *theosophy* **:** an astral body or spirit

astral body *n, theosophy* **:** a subtle counterpart of the physical human body accompanying but not usu. separated from it in life and surviving its death — compare KAMARUPA

astral crown *n* **1 :** CELESTIAL CROWN **2 :** a figure of a coronet having along the rim 8 low points from every other one of which arises a 6-pointed star between 2 wings — used in heraldry esp. to symbolize association with aviation

astral lamp *n* **:** an Argand lamp so constructed that no interruption of the light upon the table is made by the flattened ring-shaped reservoir containing the oil

astral spirit *n* **1 :** one of various celestial intelligences (as the souls of dead men, demons, or spirits originating in fire) formerly thought to live in and control the movements of stars and planets **2** *theosophy* **:** a spirit composed of astral substance

astrand \ə'-\ *adj* [¹*a-* + *strand* (v.)] **:** STRANDED

as·tran·tia \ə'stranch(ē)ə, -ntēə\ *n, cap* [NL] **:** a small genus of Eurasian herbs (family Umbelliferae) having aromatic roots, palmate leaves, and showy flowers in starlike bracted umbels — see MASTERWORT b

as·tra·po·there \'astrəpəˌthi(ə)r\ *n* -S [NL *Astrapotheria*] **:** an animal or fossil of the Astrapotheria

as·tra·po·the·ria \ˌ≈≈≈'thirēə\ *n pl, cap* [NL, fr. Gk *astrapo-* (fr. *astrapē* lightning) + NL *-theria*; akin to Gk *aster-*, *astēr* star — more at STAR] **:** an order of extinct So. American ungulates that may have diverged from primitive notoungulates in the Paleocene, flourished in the Oligocene and Miocene, and were distinguished by large size with marked disproportion between the powerful forequarters and feebly developed hindquarters, cowlike incisors accompanied by immense persistently growing canines and huge molars, and probably an elephantine proboscis

astray \ə'strā\ *adv (or adj)* [ME *astray*, *astrayey*, fr. MF *estraié* wandering, masterless, fr. *estraier* to roam about without a master — more at STRAY] **1 :** out of the right way **:** off the right path or route ⟨mark the trail so travelers will not go ~⟩ **:** away from native or familiar surroundings **:** lost or wandering ⟨some circus juggernaut ~ from winter quarters —A.T.Lougee⟩ **2 :** into a wrong or mistaken way of thinking or acting **:** in or into error **:** WRONG ⟨the desire to escape from subjectivity . . . has led some modern philosophers ~ —Bertrand Russell⟩ ⟨his calculations were ~⟩ **:** away from a proper or desirable course or development ⟨originality gone ~, seduced . . . by the mania for novelty —J.L.Lowes⟩ **3 :** wandering in mind or fancy **:** lost in thought ⟨her thoughts had been entirely ~ during . . . family devotions —W.M.Thackeray⟩

astray freight *n* **:** freight marked for destination but separated from the waybill

astre *n* -S [ME *aster*, *ayster*, fr. MF *astre*, *aistre* hearth, fr. ML *astracus*, *ostracus* pavement of potsherds, pavement, fr. Gk *ostrakon* pot, potsherd, hard shell — more at OYSTER] **:** HEARTH, HOME — compare ASTRER

¹**astream** \ə'-\ *adj* [¹*a-* + *stream*, v.] **:** STREAMING ⟨glorious the northern lights ~ —Christopher Smart⟩

²**astream** \"\ *adv* [¹*a-* + *stream*, n.] **:** in line with the stream ⟨swinging ~ of the tide⟩

astrer *or* **astrier** *n* -S [*astrer* fr. *astre* + *-er*; *astrier*, alter. of *astrer*] *old English law* **:** one belonging to the hearth or home — used of various persons having certain rights or disabilities by reason of their residence or holding of tenements

ast·rex \'aˌstreks\ *n* -ES *usu cap* [blend of *Astrakhan* and *rex*] **:** a rex rabbit of a variety characterized by curled or wavy fur that suggests broadtail

as·trict \ə'strikt\ *vt* -ED/-ING/-S [L *astrictus*, past part. of *astringere* to bind fast] **1 :** to bind up **:** CONFINE, CONSTRICT; *sometimes* **:** CONSTIPATE **2 :** to bind by a moral or legal obligation **:** CONSTRAIN, RESTRICT, LIMIT ⟨trade unions were illegal and peasants were ~*ed* to the soil⟩

as·tric·tion \ə'strikshən\ *n* -S [ML *astriction-*, *astrictio* restriction, obligation, fr. L, astringency, fr. *astrictus* (past part. of *astringere*) + *-ion-*, *-io* -ion] **1 :** the act of binding or the state of being bound **:** CONSTRICTION, RESTRICTION **2 :** CONSTIPATION

as·tric·tive \ə'striktiv\ *adj or n* **:** ASTRINGENT — **as·tric·tive·ly** *adv*

¹**astride** \ə'-\ *adv* [¹*a-* + *stride* (n.)] **1 :** with one leg on each side ⟨women seldom rode ~⟩ **2 :** with the legs stretched wide apart ⟨standing ~ with arms folded⟩

²**astride** \"\ *prep* **1 :** on or above and with one leg on each side of **:** BESTRIDING ⟨~ a horse⟩ **:** STRADDLING ⟨her little baby ~ her hips —William Beebe⟩ **2 :** placed or lying on both sides of ⟨established frontier provinces along or ~ the river —W.G.East⟩ ⟨an enemy roadblock ~ his regiment's supply route —*N. Y. Times*⟩ **3 :** extending or stretching over or across (as from one limit to another) **:** SPANNING, BRIDGING ⟨no single individual stands more firmly ~ the history of England from 1906 onwards —*Times Lit. Supp.*⟩ ⟨stands ~ two worlds — our own and the utterly alien world of the Greenland Eskimos —Jeannette Mirsky⟩

as·trild \'aˌstrild\ *n* -S [Afrik] **:** a southern African waxbill (*Estrilda astrild*) often kept as a cage bird

as·tringe \ə'strinj\ *vt* -ED/-ING/-S [L *astringere*, *adstringere* to bind fast, fr. *ad-* + *stringere* to bind tight — more at STRAIN] **:** to bind together **:** cause (tissue) to draw together **:** CONSTRICT, COMPRESS

as·trin·gence \ə'strinjən(t)s\ *n* -S **:** ASTRINGENCY ⟨the first tartness of fall, the ~ of winter —Marc Brandel⟩

as·trin·gen·cy \-jənsē, -si\ *n* -ES **:** the quality or state of being astringent ⟨pungency is a sensation of the gums . . . a roughness or ~ in the mouth —W.H.Ukers⟩ ⟨the soldier's traditional bluntness, and also an ~ of phrases —*Saturday Rev.*⟩

¹**as·trin·gent** \-jənt\ *adj* [prob. fr. MF, fr. L *astringent-*, *astringens*, pres. part. of *astringere*] **1 :** having the property of drawing together the soft organic tissues **:** CONTRACTING, CONSTRICTING ⟨~ cosmetic lotions⟩ ⟨the air was so ~ with pine scent that it tightened the nostrils —Grace Campbell⟩: **a :** tending to shrink mucous membranes or raw or exposed tissues **:** checking discharge (as of serum or mucus) **:** STYPTIC **b :** tending to pucker the tissues of the mouth ⟨~ fruits and wines⟩ ⟨green persimmons are strongly ~⟩ ⟨he remembered the musty ~ taste of his own cup of tea —Elinor Wylie⟩ **2 :** suggestive of an astringent effect upon tissue **:** free of slackness or expansiveness **:** SEVERE, AUSTERE ⟨his own writing has an ~ quality which often matches the sharp, clear outlines of the Greek landscape —*Spectator*⟩ **:** SHARP, TONIC ⟨there was something ~ and bracing about that man's mind —William McFee⟩ **:** STERN, STRICT ⟨made enemies by his ~ honesty —*Time*⟩ — **as·trin·gent·ly** *adv*

²**astringent** \"\ *n* -S **:** an astringent agent or substance: as **a :** a medicine for checking the discharge of mucus or serum by causing shrinkage of tissue **b :** a liquid cosmetic for cleansing the skin and contracting the pores

astringent bitters *n pl* **:** bitters containing tannin but little aromatic oil

astringent clay *n* **:** a clay containing an astringent salt (as alum)

astringent root *n* **:** SPOTTED CRANESBILL

as·tro- *in pronunciations below*, ¦≈(ˌ)≈ = ¦a(ˌ)strō *or* ¦aa- *or* -ˌstrə\ — see ASTR-

as·tro·blast \'≈≈ˌblast\ *n* -S [*astr-* + *-blast*] *anat* **:** a primordial astrocyte — **as·tro·blas·tic** \¦≈≈¦blastik\ *adj*

as·tro·car·y·um \ˌ≈≈'ka(a)rēəm\ *n, cap* [NL, fr. *astr-* + *-caryum* (fr. Gk *karyon* nut); prob. fr. the radiating arrangement of the pores on the kernel of the fruit — more at CAREEN] **:** a genus of very spiny pinnate-leaved tropical American palms (family Palmae), some with edible fruit, others grown for ornament

as·tro·chronological \¦≈(ˌ)≈+\ *adj* [*astr-* + *chronological*] **:** relating to the chronology of heavenly bodies

as·tro·compass \'≈≈+ˌ-\ *n* -S [*astr-* + *compass*] **:** a device that by mechanically solving the astronomical triangle reveals the bearing of any recognized celestial body to a navigator and is used esp. near the earth's magnetic pole where magnetic compasses are not reliable

as·tro·cyte \'astrəˌsīt\ *n* -S [ISV *astr-* + *-cyte*] *anat* **:** a star-shaped cell: as **a :** any comparatively large much-branched neuroglial cell **:** MOSSY CELL, SPIDER CELL **b :** OSTEOBLAST

as·tro·cy·to·ma \ˌ≈≈sī'tōmə\ *n, pl* **astrocytomas** \-məz\ *or* **astrocyto·ma·ta** \-məd·ə\ [NL, fr. ISV *astrocyte* + NL *-oma*] **:** a nerve-tissue tumor composed of astrocytes

as·tro·diagnosis \¦≈≈+\ *n* [*astr-* + *diagnosis*] **:** diagnosis by means of horoscopy and palmistry

as·tro·dome \'astrəˌdōm\ *n* -S [ISV *astr-* + *dome*] **:** a transparent dome-shaped projection in the upper surface of an aircraft from within which the navigator makes celestial observations

as·tro·gate \-ˌgāt\ *vb* -ED/-ING/-S [*astr-* + *-gate* (as in *navigate*)] *vt* **:** to guide (as a spaceship or rocket) in interplanetary flight ~ *vi* **:** to navigate in space

as·tro·ga·tion \ˌ≈≈'gāshən\ *n* -S [*astr-* + *-gation* (as in *navigation*)] **:** the science or art of navigating a spaceship **:** space navigation

as·tro·ga·tor \'≈≈ˌgād·ə(r)\ *n* -S [*astr-* + *-gator* (as in *navigator*)] **1 :** one that is qualified in the science or skilled in the art of astrogation **2 :** the pilot of a spaceship

as·trog·lia \a'sträglēə, ˌastrə'glīə\ *n* -S [NL, fr. *astro-* (as in ISV *astrocyte*) + *-glia* (as in *neuroglia*)] **:** neuroglia tissue composed of astrocytes

as·trog·no·sy \a'strägnəsē\ *n* -ES [*astr-* + *-gnosy*] **:** a branch of astronomy having to do with the fixed stars

as·tro·gon·ic \¦≈≈ *at* ASTRO- + ¦gänik\ *adj* **:** of or relating to astrogony

as·trog·o·ny \a'strägənē\ *n* -ES [*astr-* + *-gony*] **:** stellar cosmogony

as·tro·graph \'astrōˌgraf\ *n* -S [ISV *astr-* + *-graph*] **1 :** a photographic telescope designed for use in mapping the heavens **2 :** a now little used navigational instrument for projecting star-altitude curves from film directly onto a Mercator chart of proper scale

as·tro·graph·ic \¦≈≈¦grafik\ *adj* **:** relating to or used in astrography ⟨~ camera⟩

as·trog·ra·phy \a'strägrəfē\ *n* -ES [*astr-* + *-graphy*] **:** description or mapping of the heavens

¹**as·troid** \'aˌstrȯid\ *adj* [Gk *astroeidēs* starlike, fr. *astr-* + *-oeidēs* -oid] **:** shaped like a star

²**astroid** \"\ *n* -S [*astr-* + *-oid*] **:** a hypocycloid of four cusps, the radius of the rolling circle being one fourth that of the fixed circle

A B C D E F G

AB = ¼ *AC*; *DEFG* astroid

astroite *n* -S [L *astroītes* asteriated gem, fr. (assumed) Gk *astroitēs*, fr. Gk *astron* star + *-itēs* -ite — more at STAR] *obs* **:** a radiated or star-shaped mineral or fossil

as·tro·labe \'astrəˌlāb, 'aas- *sometimes* -lab *or* -laa(ə)b\ *n* -S [ME *astrolabe*, *astrolabie*, fr. MF & ML; MF *astrolabe*, fr. ML *astrolabium*, fr. LGk *astrolabion*, dim. of Gk *astrolabos*, fr. *astr-* + *-labos* (fr. *lambanein* to take) — more at LEMMA] **1 :** a compact instrument for observing the positions of the celestial bodies, among the ancients often having been essentially the armillary sphere, in the 18th century a graduated circle for taking altitudes at sea, and now having been superseded by the sextant — see PRISMATIC ASTROLABE **2 :** a stereographic projection of the sphere on the plane of a great circle (as the equator or meridian) **:** PLANISPHERE

as·tro·lab·i·cal \¦≈≈¦labəkəl, -ab-\ *adj* **:** of or relating to an astrolabe

as·trol·a·ter \ə'strälad·ə(r)\ *n* -S [fr. *astrolatry*, after E *idolatry*: *idolater*] **:** one that practices astrolatry

as·trol·a·try \-ə·trē, -i\ *n* -ES [*astr-* + *-latry*] **:** worship of the heavenly bodies

as·tro·lithology \¦astrō+\ *n* -ES [*astr-* + *lithology*] **:** the science dealing with meteoritic stones

as·trol·o·ger \ə'sträləjə(r)\ *n* -S [ME, astronomer, prob. modif. (influenced by *-er*) of MF *astrologien*] **1** *obs* **:** one that studies the stars **:** ASTRONOMER **2 :** one that practices astrology

¹**as·tro·lo·gian** \ˌastrə'lōj(ē)ən\ *n* -S [ME *astrologien*, fr. MF, fr. *astrologie* astrology] **:** ASTROLOGER

²**astrologian** *adj, obs* **:** ASTROLOGICAL

as·tro·log·i·cal \¦≈≈¦läjəkəl, -ēk-\ *also* **as·tro·log·ic** \-jik, -ēk\ *adj* [*astrological* fr. LL *astrologicus* of astrology (fr. Gk *astrologikos* of astronomy, fr. *astrologos* astronomer + *-ikos* -ic) + E *-al*; *astrologic* fr. LL *astrologicus*] **:** of or belonging to astrology **:** professing astrology — **as·tro·log·i·cal·ly** \-jək(ə)lē, -ēk-, -li\ *adv*

as·trol·o·gist \ə'sträləjəst\ *n* -S **:** ASTROLOGER

as·trol·o·gis·tic \ə¦≈≈¦jistik\ *adj* **:** using astrology

as·trol·o·gize \ə'≈≈ˌjīz\ *vb* -ED/-ING/-S *vt* **:** to apply astrology to ~ *vi* **:** to study or practice astrology

as·trol·o·gous \-ləgəs\ *adj* [*astrology* + *-ous*] **:** ASTROLOGICAL

as·trol·o·gy \ə'sträləjē, -ji\ *n* -ES [ME *astrologie* astronomy, applied astronomy, fr. MF, fr. L *astrologia* astronomy, fr. Gk, fr. *astrologos* astronomer (fr. *astr-* + *logos* speech, discourse) + *-ia* -y — more at LEGEND] **1 :** divination that treats of the supposed influences of the stars upon human affairs and of foretelling terrestrial events by their positions and aspects — see JUDICIAL ASTROLOGY, NATURAL ASTROLOGY; compare HOROSCOPE **2** *obs* **:** ASTRONOMY

as·tro·meteorological \ˌastrō+\ *adj* **:** relating to astrometeorology

as·tro·meteorologist \"+\ *n* -S **:** a specialist in astrometeorology

as·tro·meteorology \"+\ *n* -ES [*astr-* + *meteorology*] **:** investigation of the supposed relation between the celestial bodies and the weather

as·tro·met·ric \ˌastrō¦me·trik\ *or* **as·tro·met·ri·cal** \-rəkəl\ *adj* **:** of or relating to astrometry

as·trom·e·try \ə'strämə·trē\ *n* -ES [*astr-* + *-metry*] **:** a branch of astronomy that deals with measurements of the celestial bodies, esp. those made to determine their positions and movements

as·tro·naut \'astrəˌnȯt, -ät\ *n* -S [*astr-* + *-naut* (as in *aeronaut*)] **1 :** a traveler in interplanetary space **2 :** a student, devotee, or advocate of astronautics

as·tro·nau·ti·cal \¦≈≈¦nȯd·əkəl, -nä-\ *adj* [*astr-* + *-nautical* (as in *aeronautical*)] **:** of or belonging to astronautics or to astronauts — **as·tro·nau·ti·cal·ly** \-d·ək(ə)lē\ *adv*

as·tro·nau·tics \ˌ≈≈'≈d·iks\ *n pl but usu sing in constr* [ISV *astr-* + *-nautics* (as in *aeronautics*)] **1 :** the science that treats of the construction and operation of vehicles designed for travel in interplanetary or interstellar space **2 :** ASTROGATION

as·tro·navigation \ˌastrō+\ *n* [*astr-* + *navigation*] **:** CELESTIAL NAVIGATION

as·tron·o·mer \ə'strānəmə(r)\ *n* -S [ME, alter. of *astronomien*, fr. MF, fr. LL *astronomus* (fr. Gk *astronomos*) + MF *-ien* -ian] **1** *obs* **:** ASTROLOGER **2 :** one skilled in astronomy **:** one having a knowledge of the laws and phenomena of the celestial bodies **:** one that makes observations of celestial phenomena

astronomer royal *n, pl* **astronomers royal** *usu cap A&R* **:** the director of one of the royal observatories of Great Britain

astronomer's staff *n* **:** ALMUCANTAR STAFF

as·tro·nom·i·cal \-məkəl, -ēk-\ *or* **as·tro·nom·ic** \¦astrə¦nämik, ¦aas-, -mēk\ *adj* [*astronomical* fr. L *astronomicus* + E *-al*; *astronomic* fr. L *astronomicus*, fr. Gk *astronomikos*, fr. *astronomos* astronomer + *-ikos* -ic] **1 :** of or belonging to astronomy **2 :** suggestive of astronomy or of the magnitude of the forces and phenomena treated of or the quantities used by the astronomer ⟨the change must come, if come it did, with ~ slowness, like the cooling of the sun —W.B.Yeats⟩; *esp* **:** enormously or inconceivably large or great in extent or degree ⟨300[1600], a truly ~ number —G.A.Miller⟩ ⟨voted ~ sums for rearmament⟩ ⟨inflation on an ~ scale —Bruce Bliven b. 1889⟩

astronomical clock *n* **1 :** a high-precision clock (as a

Riefler clock or a quartz-crystal clock) used in an astronomical observatory to time the movements of celestial bodies or assist in locating them or to serve as the basis of standard time **2 :** a clock with mechanism and dials for indicating various astronomical phenomena (as phases of the moon, movements of the planets)

astronomical coordinate *n* **:** CELESTIAL COORDINATE

astronomical geography *n* **:** the part of mathematical geography that treats of the earth in its relation to the other celestial bodies

astronomical latitude *n* **:** the angle between the plane of the earth's equator and the plumb line (direction of gravity) at a given point on the earth's surface — compare TERRESTRIAL LATITUDE

as·tro·nom·i·cal·ly \\-mək(ə)lē, -ēk-, -li\\ *adv* **1 :** in accordance with the methods or principles of astronomy **2 :** in or to a degree suggestive of the quantities and measurements used in astronomy ⟨an ~ costly system of government⟩ ⟨prices in this field have risen ~⟩ **:** in or to an astronomical degree

astronomical telescope *n* **:** a telescope that is designed for observing celestial bodies and that requires no image-erecting system — compare TERRESTRIAL TELESCOPE

astronomical time *n* **:** time reckoned in mean solar time units continuously through the 24 hours beginning either at noon or since 1925 at midnight of each civil day — compare GREENWICH TIME

astronomical triangle *n* **:** a triangle on the celestial sphere whose vertices are the pole, the zenith, and the observed body

astronomical twilight *n* **:** the period after sunset or before sunrise ending or beginning when the sun is about 18 degrees below the horizon

astronomical unit *n* **:** a unit of length used in astronomy equal to the mean radius of the earth's orbit or about 93 million miles

as·tron·o·mize \\ə'stränə,mīz\\ *vi* -ED/-ING/-S [*astronomy* + *-ize*] **1 :** to study or practice astronomy **2 :** to discourse on astronomy **:** talk astronomically

as·tron·o·my \\-mē, -i\\ *n* -ES [ME *astronomie*, fr. OF, fr. L *astronomia*, fr. Gk, fr. *astronomos* astronomer (fr. *astr-* + *nomos* law) + *-ia* -y — more at NIMBLE] **1 :** the science that treats of the celestial bodies, of their positions, magnitudes, motions, distances, constitution, physical condition, mutual relations, history, and destiny — formerly used as synonymous with *astrology* **2 :** a treatise on this science

as·tro·pec·ten \\,astrō'pektən\\ *n, cap* [NL, fr. *astr-* + L *pecten* comb — more at PECTINATE] **:** a large genus of chiefly tropical starfishes of shallow water that are markedly stellate in form with the disk and arms flat, the largest species being a foot or more across

astrophic \\(')ā+\\ *adj* [[2]*a-* + *strophic*] **1** *of stanzas or stanzaic structure* **:** arranged in series without regular repetition of stanzaic units **:** irregular in arrangement **2 :** not arranged or divided into strophes or stanzas **:** not stanzaic

as·tro·phile \\'astrə,fīl\\ *or* **as·tro·phil** \\-,fil\\ *n* -S [*astr-* + *-phile, -phil*] **:** one fond of star lore **:** an amateur astronomer ⟨go for its members into the ranks of the amateurs and ~*s* —Harlow Shapley⟩

as·tro·photograph \\,== *at* ASTRO-+\\ *n* [ISV *astr-* + *photograph*] **:** a photograph of a celestial body or any astronomical phenomenon

as·tro·photographic \\¦==+\\ *adj* [ISV *astr-* + *photographic*] **:** relating to or used in astrophotography ⟨~ telescope⟩

as·tro·photography \\,==+\\ *n* [ISV *astr-* + *photography*] **:** the application of photography to astronomical investigations

as·tro·phyl·lite \\,astrə'fi,līt\\ *n* -S [ISV *astr-* + Gk *phyllon* leaf + ISV *-ite;* orig. formed as G *astrophyllit* — more at BLADE] **:** a mineral $(K,Na)_2(Fe,Mn)TiSi_4O_{14}(OH)_2$ consisting of a basic silicate of potassium or sodium, iron or manganese, and titanium

as·tro·physical \\¦== *at* ASTRO-+¦-\\ *adj* [*astr-* + *physical*] **:** of or relating to astrophysics

as·tro·physicist \\,==+\\ *n* **:** a specialist in astrophysics

as·tro·physics \\"+\\ *n pl but usu sing in constr* [ISV *astr-* + *physics;* orig. formed as G *astrophysik*] **:** a branch of astronomy dealing principally with the physical and chemical natures of the heavenly bodies and their origin and evolution

as·troph·y·ton \\a'sträfə,tän\\ *n, cap* [NL, fr. *astr-* + Gk *phyton* plant — more at PHYT-] **:** a genus of ophiuroids having complexly branching arms and including many of the basket stars

as·tro·sclereid \\,== *at* ASTRO-+\\ *n* -S [*astr-* + *sclereid*] **:** a sclereid having its cell wall drawn out into lobes or arms to form a more or less stellate body (as those in the leaves and stems of certain xerophytes)

as·trose \\'a,strōs\\ *adj* [*astr-* + *-ose*] *of a sponge spicule* **:** STELLATE

as·tro·sphere \\'== *at* ASTRO-+,-\\ *n* -S [ISV *astr-* + *-sphere*] **1 :** the central mass of the aster exclusive of the rays **:** CENTROSPHERE **2 :** the entire aster exclusive of the centrosome — compare ASTER 3

as·tro·stereogram \\¦==+\\ *n* -S [*astr-* + *stereogram*] **:** a pair of stereoscopic photographs of a celestial body

astrut \\ə'strət\\ *adj* [ME *astrout, astrut*, fr. [1]*a-* + *strout, strut* strut — more at STRUT] **:** puffed up (as with conceit)

-asts *pl of* -AST

as·tu·cious \\ə'st(y)üshəs, a'-\\ *adj* [F *astucieux*, fr. MF, fr. *astuce* astuteness (fr. L *astutia*, fr. *astutus* astute + *-ia* -y) + *-ieux* -ious] **:** ASTUTE — **as·tu·cious·ly** *adv*

as·tu·ci·ty \\-üsəd·ē\\ *n* -ES [fr. *astucious*, after such pairs as E *ferocious: ferocity*] **:** the quality of being astute **:** ASTUTENESS ⟨they had been fools (to put it mildly), while the M'gai had been devils of ~ and treachery —John Masefield⟩

as·tur \\'astə(r)\\ *n* [NL, fr. *astur*, a hawk (prob. a 16th cent. insertion in the MS of a LL writer), prob. fr. Romansh, hawk, fr. L *accipiter* — more at ACCIPITER] **1** *cap* **:** a genus consisting of the goshawks and sometimes considered a subgenus of *Accipiter* **2** -S **:** GOSHAWK

[1]**as·tu·ri·an** \\a'st(y)ůrēən, ə'-\\ *adj, usu cap* [Sp *asturiano*, adj. & n., fr. *Asturias*, region in northwestern Spain + Sp *-ano* -an (fr. L *-anus*)] **1 :** of, relating to, or characteristic of Asturias, now the province of Oviedo, in Spain **2 :** belonging to a late Mesolithic culture of northern Spain characterized by picks chipped from cobblestones and by subsistence on shellfish

[2]**asturian** \\"\\ *n* -S *cap* [Sp *asturiano*] **:** a native or inhabitant of Asturias

as·tute \\ə'st(y)üt, a'-, *attrib sometimes* 'a,s-; *usu* -üd·+V\\ *adj* [L *astutus*, fr. *astus* craft, cunning] **1 :** having or displaying shrewd discernment and sagacity ⟨an ~ and trustworthy observer of the political scene⟩ ⟨one of the most ~ field workers in American anthropology⟩ ⟨an ~ study of a complex subject⟩ **2 :** CRAFTY, CUNNING, WILY ⟨sold . . . on the basis of clever packaging and ~ advertising —Lewis Mumford⟩ **syn** see SHREWD

as·tute·ly *adv* **:** in an astute manner **:** SHREWDLY, CLEVERLY

as·tute·ness *n* -ES **:** the quality or state of being astute

as·ty·a·nax \\ə'stīə,naks, a'-\\ *n, cap* [NL, fr. *Astyanax*, young son of Hector and Andromache of Troy, fr. L, fr. Gk] **:** a genus of small brightly colored So. and Central American fishes (order Ostariophysi) including a silvery black-spotted species (*A. bimaculatus*) with orange-red fins and tail that is popular in the tropical aquarium

asty·lar \\(')ā¦stīlə(r)\\ *adj* [[2]*a-* + Gk *stylos* pillar + E *-ar*] *archit* **:** without columns or pilasters

asty·lo·spon·gia \\¦ā,stīlə'spənjēə, -pän-\\ *n, cap* [NL, fr. *astyl-, astylo-* (fr. [2]*a-* + *styl-*) + *-spongia*] **:** a genus of small pear-shaped siliceous fossil sponges including important index fossils occurring in Middle Silurian strata

asud·den \\ə'-\\ *adv* [[1]*a-* + *sudden*] **:** SUDDENLY

asun·ci·ón *or* **asun·ci·on** \\ə¦sün(t)sē¦ōn, ä¦s-, -sůn-,-sən-, -ē¦än, -ē¦ōn\\ *adj, usu cap* [fr. *Asunción*, capital of Paraguay] **:** of or from Asunción, the capital of Paraguay **:** of the kind or style prevalent in Asunción

asun·der \\ə'səndə(r)\\ *adv* (*or adj*) [ME *asonder, asunder*, fr. OE *onsundran, onsundrum*, fr. *on* + *sundran, sundrum* apart, fr. *sunder, sundor* apart, separate — more at SUNDER] **1 :** into parts **:** into different pieces ⟨the American constitutional fabric would be torn ~ —H.S.Commager⟩ **2 :** apart from each other in position ⟨as wide ~ as pole and pole —J.A. Froude⟩ **3 :** distinct from each other in kind, quality, or nature ⟨I do not know their faces ~ —Thomas Gray⟩ ⟨their philosophies are poles ~⟩

asu·ra \\'əsərə, (,)ə'sůrə\\ *n* -S *usu cap* [Skt — more at AESIR] **1 :** one of a class of beneficent celestial spirits of early Vedic and Zoroastrian mythology higher than men but lower than gods **2 :** one of a class of demons or titans in later Hinduism and Buddhism, the enemies of the gods

asu·ri \\-(,)rē\\ *n, usu cap* **:** a dialect of the Munda group of languages in central India

asu·ri·ní \\¦äsərə¦nē\\ *n, pl* **asuriní** *or* **asurinís** *usu cap* [Pg, of AmerInd origin] **1 a :** a Tupi-Guaranian people of the southern part of the state of Mato Grosso, Brazil **b :** a member of such people **2 :** the language of the Asuriní people

aswang \\ä'swäŋ\\ *also* **asu·wang** \\,äsə'w-\\ *or* **asuang** \\ä'swäŋ\\ *n* -S [Tag *asuwáng, aswáng*] *Philippines* **:** WITCH **:** evil spirit

aswarm \\ə'-\\ *adj* [[1]*a-* + *swarm*, v.] **:** SWARMING ⟨boulevards and cafés ~ with people⟩

asway \\ə'-\\ *adj* [[1]*a-* + *sway*, v.] **:** SWAYING ⟨buzz of bees in blooms ~ —G.F.Savage-Armstrong⟩

asweat \\ə'-\\ *adj* [[1]*a-* + *sweat*, v.] **:** SWEATING, SWEATY ⟨all the stone vault ~ with steam —Robinson Jeffers⟩

aswell \\ə'-\\ *adj* [[1]*a-* + *swell*, v.] **:** SWELLING ⟨with sails ~⟩

as well *adv* **:** in addition **:** BESIDES, ALSO, TOO ⟨there were other features *as well*⟩

as well as *prep* **:** in addition to **:** BESIDES ⟨a real scholar *as well as* . . . a composer of the highest integrity —Norman Demuth⟩

aswim \\ə'-\\ *adj* [[1]*a-* + *swim*, v.] **:** SWIMMING

aswing \\ə'-\\ *adj* [[1]*a-* + *swing*, v.] **:** SWINGING

aswirl \\ə'-\\ *adj* [[1]*a-* + *swirl*, v.] **:** SWIRLING

aswoon \\ə'swün\\ *adj* [ME *aswoue, aswoune, aswone*, fr. OE *geswōgen*] **:** SWOONING

as yet *adv* **:** up to the present time **:** so far ⟨he has not *as yet* arrived⟩

asyl·la·bia \\,āsə'lābēə\\ *n* -S [NL, fr. [2]*a-* + L *syllaba* syllable + NL *-ia* — more at SYLLABLE] **:** aphasia in which the patient can recognize letters but cannot form their sounds into syllables

asyllabic \\¦ā+=¦==\\ *also* **asyl·lab·i·cal** \\¦ā+=¦===\\ *adj* [[2]*a-* + *syllabic, syllabical*] **:** not syllabic

asy·lum \\ə'sīləm\\ *n, pl* **asy·lums** \\-ləmz\\ [ME *asilum*, fr. L *asylum*, fr. Gk *asylon*, neut. of *asylos* exempt from spoliation, inviolable, fr. *a-* [2]a- + *sylon* right of seizure] **1 a :** a place of refuge and protection (as a temple, altar, or statue of a god or in later times a Christian church) where criminals and debtors found shelter and from which they could not be forcibly taken without sacrilege **:** SANCTUARY **b** *international law* **:** a place exempted by custom or convention from the territorial jurisdiction of a state within which it is so that refugees may not be followed to or taken from it except by the consent of the state enjoying the immunity **2 :** a place of retreat and security **:** SHELTER ⟨the land of the free and the ~ of the downtrodden —G.W.Pierson⟩ ⟨the ideal world . . . is an ~ in which he takes refuge from the troubles of existence —John Dewey⟩ **3 a :** the protection or inviolability afforded by an asylum **:** REFUGE ⟨the right to seek and to enjoy in other countries ~ from persecution —*U.N. Declaration of Human Rights*⟩ ⟨fled to England, where he requested and has received political ~ —*Encounter*⟩ ⟨he can, if he wishes, seek ~ from present tumults in a past period of history —Reinhold Niebuhr⟩ **b :** the act or the custom of affording shelter or protection to one under or in danger of persecution ⟨the controversial custom of ~ —*Time*⟩ ⟨for the United States diplomatic ~ is not a principle of international law —Alona Evans⟩ **4 :** an institution for the protection or relief of some class of destitute, afflicted, or otherwise unfortunate persons ⟨an orphan ~⟩ ⟨an ~ for the deaf and dumb⟩; *esp* **:** an institution for the care of the insane

asym- — see AS-

asym·bo·lia \\,ā,sim'bōlēə\\ *n* -S [NL, fr. [2]*a-* + L *symbolus, symbolum* symbol + NL *-ia* — more at SYMBOL] **:** loss of power to understand previously familiar symbols and signs usu. in consequence of brain lesion

asymbolic \\¦ā+,=¦==\\ *also* **asymbolical** \\¦ā+,=¦===\\ *adj* [[2]*a-* + *symbolic*] **:** not symbolic

asymmetric \\¦ā, ¦a+=¦==\\ *or* **asymmetrical** \\"+=¦===\\ *adj* [*asymmetry* + *-ic, -ical*] **:** not symmetrical ⟨an ~ face⟩ ⟨~ growth or development⟩ ⟨a strikingly ~ architectural design⟩: **a** *bot* (1) **:** not isobilateral (2) **:** ZYGOMORPHIC ⟨an ~ flower⟩ ⟨an ~ corolla⟩ **b :** relating to derivatives in which groups are substituted unsymmetrically in the molecule ⟨~ dichloroethylene $CH_2{=}CCl_2$⟩ ⟨~ or 1,2,4-trinitro-benzene⟩ **c :** relating to or characterized by asymmetry in spatial arrangement or in the placement of parts or components **d :** of, belonging to, or designating the crystallographic system having no plane of symmetry or the group of this system having no plane, axis, or center of symmetry **e :** so constituted as never to hold when related arguments are interchanged (as in the relation *x* is the father of *y*) — **asymmetrically** *adv*

asymmetric carbon atom *n* **:** a carbon atom in union with four atoms or groups no two of which are alike, compounds containing such a carbon atom being capable of existing in two optically active forms which are distinguished by being respectively levorotatory and dextrorotatory and also in some cases by having enantiomorphous crystal forms

asymmetric carbon atom: the two tetrahedrons illustrate the two ways in which four different atoms or groups, *a, b, c, d*, may be arranged in mirror-image relationship about a carbon atom assumed to be at the center of each tetrahedron

asymmetric synthesis *n, chem* **:** a process that directly produces an optically active compound (as one containing an asymmetric carbon atom) from symmetrically constituted molecules without requiring resolution of a racemic mixture

asym·me·tron \\ā'simə·,trän\\ *n, cap* [NL, fr. Gk, neut. of *asymmetros*] **:** a genus of lancelets (family Epigonichthyidae) differing from *Branchiostoma* in having asymmetrical metapleura and but one series of gonads, the right — compare AMPHIOXUS

asymmetry \\(')ā, (')a+\\ *n* -ES [Gk *asymmetria* incommensurability, lack of proportion, fr. *asymmetros* incommensurable, ill-proportioned (fr. *a-* [2]a- + *symmetros* commensurate, suitable, symmetrical) + *-ia* -y — more at SYMMETRY] **1** *math* **a** *obs* **:** INCOMMENSURABILITY **b :** SKEWNESS **2 :** lack or absence of symmetry ⟨the ideal of nonmetrical rhythm, like that of atonality, is ~ —Virgil Thomson⟩ ⟨the *Art Nouveau's* wriggling *asymmetries* —T.H.Robsjohn-Gibbings⟩: as **a :** lack of proportion between the parts of a thing; *esp* **:** want of bilateral symmetry ⟨~ in the development of the two sides of the brain⟩ **b :** lack of coordination of two parts acting in connection with one another ⟨~ of convergence of the eyes⟩ **3 :** want of symmetry in spatial arrangement of atoms and groups in a molecule (as similar to two nonsuperimposable mirror images) which may result from the presence of an asymmetric atom (as carbon, nitrogen, or sulfur) or if none is present in molecules with rigid structures (as in certain allenes, spirans, or cycloparaffin) or in molecules with restricted rotation about single bonds (as in certain biphenyls) — called also *molecular asymmetry;* see OPTICAL ISOMERISM

asymptomatic \\(')ā+\\ *adj* [[2]*a-* + *symptomatic*] **:** SYMPTOMLESS **:** presenting no subjective evidence of disease — **asymptomatically** *adv*

as·ymp·tote \\'asəm(p),tōt, *usu* -ōd·+-V\\ *n* -S [prob. fr. (assumed) NL *asymptotus*, fr. Gk *asymptōtos*, fr. *asymptōtos* not meeting, fr. *a-* [2]a- + *symptōtos*, verbal of *sympiptein* to meet, fall together — more at SYMPTOM] *math* **:** a straight line associated with a curve such that as a point P moves out along an infinite branch of the curve the distance from the point P to the line approaches zero and the slope of the curve at P approaches the slope of the line ⟨not all curves have ~*s*⟩ ⟨the hyperbola has two ~*s* while the parabola has none⟩

asymptotes to the hyperbola

as·ymp·tot·ic \\¦==¦täd·ik\\ *also* **as·ymp·tot·i·cal** \\-d·əkəl\\ *adj* **:** of, relating to, or of the nature of an asymptote — **as·ymp·tot·i·cal·ly** \\-d·ək(ə)lē\\ *adv*

asymptotic curve *or* **asymptotic line** *n* **:** a curve on a surface whose osculating plane at each point coincides with the tangent plane to the surface at that point

asymptotic developable *n* **:** the developable surface generated by the tangent planes of a ruled surface whose rulings are supposed not to be minimal lines

asymptotic formula *n* **:** a formula that approaches perfect accuracy as the independent variable increases indefinitely

asynapsis \\,ā+\\ *n, pl* **asynapses** [NL, fr. [2]*a-* + *synapsis*] **:** failure of synapsis or pairing of homologous chromosomes in meiosis — compare DESYNAPSIS, SYNAPSIS — **asynaptic** \\¦ā+=¦==\\ *adj* — **asynaptically** *adv*

asynartetic \\(')ā+\\ *adj* [*asynartete* asynartetic verse (fr. Gk *asynartētos* asynartetic, fr. *a-* [2]a- + — assumed — *synartētos*, verbal of Gk *synartan* to join together, fr. *syn-* + *artan* to fasten, hang) + *-ic;* perh. akin to Gk *aeirein* to lift — more at AORTA] *of a line of verse* **:** containing disparate or unconnected rhythmic units: as **a :** with unhomogeneous rhythms in the two members distinguished by the caesura **b :** with diaeresis, hiatus, or syllaba anceps at the caesura so that a quasi independence of the two members is effected

asynchronism \\(')ā+\\ *or* **asynchrony** \\(')ā+\\ *n, pl* **asynchronisms** *or* **asynchronies** [[2]*a-* + *synchronism, synchrony*] **:** the quality or state of being asynchronous **:** absence or lack of concurrence in time

asynchronistic \\(')ā+\\ *adj* [[2]*a-* + *synchronistic*] **:** ASYNCHRONOUS

asynchronous \\(')ā+¦-\\ *adj* [[2]*a-* + *synchronous*] **:** not simultaneous **:** not concurrent in time — opposed to *synchronous* — **asynchronously** *adv*

asyndesis \\(')ā+\\ *n, pl* **asyndeses** [NL, fr. [2]*a-* + *syndesis*] **:** ASYNAPSIS

[1]**asyn·det·ic** \\¦asən¦ded·ik, ¦ās-, -(,)sin-\\ *adj* [ISV *asyndeton* + *-ic*] **:** characterized by asyndeton ⟨the ~ and not altogether logical sequence of thought —Norah K. Chadwick⟩ — **asyn·det·i·cal·ly** \\-ək(ə)lē\\ *adv*

[2]**asyndetic** \\"\\ *adj* [NL *asyndesis* + E *-etic*] **:** ASYNAPTIC ⟨~ hybrids . . . where the satellite chromosomes do not conjugate —*Biol. Abstracts*⟩ — **asyn·det·i·cal·ly** \\-ək(ə)lē\\ *adv*

asyn·de·ton \\ə'sində-,tän, -,tən\\ *n, pl* **asynde·tons** \\-nz\\ *or* **asynde·ta** \\,dətə\\ [LL, fr. Gk, fr. neut. of *asyndetos* unconnected, fr. *a-* [2]a- + *syndetos* bound together, verbal of *syndein* to bind together, fr. *syn-* + *dein* to bind — more at DIADEM] **:** omission of the conjunctions that ordinarily join coordinate words or clauses (as in *I came, I saw, I conquered*)

asy·ner·gia \\,āsi'nərj(ē)ə\\ *also* **asyn·er·gy** \\ā'sinərjē\\ *n, pl* **asynergias** *also* **asynergies** [NL *asynergia*, fr. [2]*a-* + *synergia* synergy] *med* **:** lack of coordination (as of muscles) ⟨~ results in jerkiness, overaction and imperfect muscle control —C.H.Best & N.B.Taylor⟩ — **asy·ner·gic** \\¦āsi¦nərjik\\ *adj*

asyn·tac·tic \\¦ā+(,)=¦==\\ *also* **asyntactical** \\¦ā+(,)=¦===\\ *adj* [Gk *asyntaktikos*, fr. *a-* [2]a- + *syntaktikos* syntactic, syntactical — more at SYNTACTIC] **:** not syntactic ⟨an ~ narrative⟩ ⟨an ~ compound such as *star-spangled*, with a structure differing from that of the phrase *spangled with stars*⟩

asystole \\(')ā+\\ *n* -S [[2]*a-* + *systole*] *physiol* **:** a condition of weakening or cessation of systole — **asystolic** \\¦ā+\\ *adj* — **asys·to·lism** \\(')ā'sistə,lizəm\\ *n* -S

[1]**at** \\ət, (')at, *usu* -d·+V\\ *prep* [ME, fr. OE *æt;* akin to OHG *az* at, to, ON & Goth *at*, L *ad*, OIr *ad-*] **1** — used as a function word to indicate presence in, on, or near: as (1) presence or occurrence in a particular place ⟨lying ~ the bottom of the sea⟩ ⟨staying ~ a hotel⟩ ⟨road ~ the edge of the woods⟩ ⟨enter ~ the south gate⟩ ⟨walk ~ my side⟩; used dial. with a point of the compass to designate an area of the country ⟨transportation to cities ~ the South⟩; (2) attendance as a spectator ⟨~ the wedding⟩ or attendance as a participant or as one connected with an activity ⟨been ~ college since September⟩; (3) location of a feeling, quality, or condition ⟨sick ~ heart⟩ ⟨out ~ the elbows⟩ **2 a** — used as a function word to indicate that which is the goal of an action or that toward which an action or motion is directed ⟨aimed the arrow ~ the target⟩ ⟨snatched ~ the purse but missed⟩ ⟨laughed ~ him⟩ ⟨hinted ~ the answer⟩ ⟨angry ~ his brother⟩ **b** (1) **:** in personal contact with **:** into the presence of ⟨hard to get ~ the president⟩ (2) **:** in active or aggressive pursuit of or contact with ⟨creditors are ~ him again⟩ **3** — used as a function word to indicate that with which one is occupied or employed ⟨a student ~ work on his experiment⟩ ⟨the pilot ~ the controls⟩ ⟨an expert ~ chess⟩ **4** — used as a function word to indicate situation in an active or passive state or condition ⟨two nations ~ war⟩ ⟨negotiations ~ a standstill⟩ ⟨a criminal ~ liberty⟩ ⟨the people ~ rest⟩ **5** — used as a function word to indicate means, agency, cause, source, or manner ⟨sell the goods ~ auction⟩ ⟨laughed ~ his joke⟩ ⟨angry ~ his reply⟩ ⟨the child jumped ~ his command⟩ ⟨suffered ~ his hands⟩ ⟨act ~ your own discretion⟩ **6** — used as a function word to indicate (1) rate, degree, or position in a scale or series ⟨proceed ~ 20 miles an hour⟩ ⟨the temperature ~ 90⟩ ⟨a bargain ~ five dollars⟩ ⟨a crowd estimated ~ 10,000⟩ or (2) relative order or value ⟨the news came ~ first as a terrific shock⟩ ⟨the performance was ~ its best mediocre⟩ **7** — used as a function word to indicate age or position in time ⟨retire ~ 65⟩ ⟨ready for college ~ 18⟩ ⟨awoke ~ midnight⟩ ⟨president of the company ~ his death⟩ ⟨was serving on four committees ~ this time⟩ **8** — used substand. as an intensive with *where* ⟨don't know where they are ~⟩ — **at after** *now dial Eng* **:** AFTER, AFTERWARD — **at and from** *insurance* **:** covering a ship at the port of departure as well as on the voyage — **at it :** busily engaged in some particular activity (as work, play, or fighting) ⟨he was up and *at it* before breakfast⟩ ⟨the neighbors are *at it* again⟩ — **at law :** under or within the provisions of the law **:** as required by law **:** according to law practice ⟨enforceable *at law*⟩ ⟨*at* common *law*⟩ — see ATTORNEY-AT-LAW — **at that 1 :** without further effort, argument, or consideration **:** as matters now stand ⟨we'll let it go *at that*⟩ **2 :** over and above what is expected or bargained for **:** BESIDES ⟨an interesting experience but a painful one *at that*⟩ **3 :** even so **:** notwithstanding that ⟨*at that*, you can still make a good profit⟩

[2]**at** \\ət, *usu* əd·+V\\ *conj* [ME, alter. of *that*] *now dial* **:** THAT

[3]**at** \\(')at, *usu* (')ad·+V\\ *pron* [ME, alter. of *that*] *now dial* **:** THAT

[4]**at** *var of* ATT

[5]**at** \\'ät, 'at\\ *n, pl* **at** [Siamese] **:** a subsidiary unit of value of Laos from 1955 equal to 1/100 kip

at- — see AD-

at *abbr* **1** airtight **2** atmosphere; atmospheric **3** atomic **4** attorney

AT *abbr* **1** American terms **2** ampere-turn **3** antitank **4** assay ton

At *symbol* astatine

[1]**ata** *var of* [1]ATTA

[2]**ata** \\'äd·ə, -d·,ä\\ *n, pl* **ata** *or* **atas** *usu cap* **1 a :** a predominantly pagan people near Mount Apo in central Mindanao, Philippines **b :** a member of such people **2 :** an Austronesian language of the Ata people

-a·ta \\'ä|d·ə, 'ā|, 'å|, |tə — *in the pronunc of words containing this suffix, usu only the first two variants are shown*\\ *n pl suffix* [NL, fr. L, neut. pl. of *-atus* -ate] **:** ones characterized by having (such a feature) — in names of zoological groups ⟨Coelenter*ata*⟩ ⟨Vertebr*ata*⟩ ⟨Chord*ata*⟩ ⟨Branchi*ata*⟩

at·a·bal \\'ad·ə,bal, -äl, ,=='=\\ *n* -S [Sp, fr. Ar *aṭ-ṭabl* the drum] **1 :** an Arabian kettledrum **2 :** a small So. American drum

ata·beg \\'ad·ə,beg, 'äd·ə-, ,=='=\\ *or* **ata·bek** \\-,bek\\ *n* -S [Russ, of Turkic origin; akin to Jagatai *atabäg*, Turk *atabey*, fr. *ata* father + *bäg, bey* prince — more at BEY] **1 :** a Seljuk provincial governor **2 :** any of various Turkish high officials (as a vizier or prime minister)

at about *adv* **:** nearly at **:** ABOUT ⟨who were arriving *at about* the same time —Thomas Pyles⟩ ⟨paid *at about* that rate —Anthony Trollope⟩ ⟨*at about* the western border —Bernard De Voto⟩ ⟨*at about* five o'clock —Florette Henri⟩

At·a·brine \\'ad·əbrən, 'atə-, -,brēn *also* -īn\\ *trademark* — used for quinacrine

ata·ca·me·ñan \\¦ad·əkə¦mānyən, ¦äd·ə-\\ *adj, usu cap* **1 :** relating or belonging to the Atacameño people **2 :** of or relating to the language of the Atacameño people

ata·ca·me·ño \ˌ=ˌ=ˈmān(ˌ)yō\ *or* **at·a·ca·ma** \ˌ=ˌ=ˈkämə\ *n, pl* **atacameño** *or* **atacameños** *or* **atacama** *or* **atacamas** *usu cap* [Sp, fr. the *Atacama* desert, northern Chile, their locality] **1 a :** a So. American Indian people of the Atacama desert in northern Chile **b :** a member of such people **2 :** the language formerly spoken by the Atacameño people

at·a·cam·ite \ˌad·əˈkaˌmīt, əˈtakəˌm-\ *n* -s [F, fr. *Atacama* desert, its locality + F *-ite*] **:** a mineral $Cu_2Cl(OH)_3$ consisting of a basic copper chloride that is transparent or translucent and of various shades of green and occurs usu. in prismatic orthorhombic crystals but also in crystalline aggregates or massive (hardness 3–3.5, sp. gr. 3.75–3.77)

atac·tic \(ˈ)āˈtaktik, -ēk\ *adj* [Gk *ataktos* not ordered (fr. *a-* ²a- + *taktos* ordered, fr. *tassein* to arrange, put in order) + E *-ic* — more at TACTICS] **1 :** lacking regularity or coordination; *specif* **:** ATAXIC **2 :** having no syntactic connection

atac·ti·form \(ˈ)āˈtaktəˌfȯrm\ *adj* [*atact-* (fr. NL *ataxia*) + *-iform*] **:** resembling ataxia

ataghan *var of* YATAGHAN

ata·jo \əˈtä(ˌ)hō, -ta-, -tä-\ *n* -s [Sp, fr. *atajar* to intercept, cut off, take a short cut, fr. *a-* (fr. L *ad-*) + *tajar* to divide, slice, fr. (assumed) VL *taliare* — more at TAILOR] **1** *chiefly Southwest* **:** a drove of mules or horses **2** *chiefly Southwest* **:** an expedient of any kind **:** SHORT CUT

ata·ka·pa *or* **at·ta·ca·pa** \əˈtakəpə, -äk-, -ˌpä,-ˌpȯ\ *n, pl* **atakapa** *or* **atakapas** *or* **attacapa** *or* **attacapas** *usu cap* [F *Atac-Apa*, fr. Choctaw *hatak-apa* cannibal, fr. *hatak* man + *apa* eats] **1 a :** an Indian people of the Gulf coast of Louisiana and Texas **b :** a member of such people **2 :** the language of the Atakapa people

ata·ka·pan *or* **at·ta·ca·pan** \-ˌpən,-ˌpän,-ˌpȯn\ *n, pl* **atakapan** *or* **atakapans** *or* **attacapan** *or* **attacapans** *usu cap* **:** a language family of the Gulf phylum in Louisiana and Texas comprising the Atakapa language

ata·la·lá \ˌad·ələˈlä\ *n, pl* **atalalá** *or* **atalalás** *usu cap* [Sp, of AmerInd origin] **1 :** a people of the Vilela group **2 :** a member of the Vilela people

ata·lán \ˌad·ᵊlˈän\ *n, pl* **atalán** *or* **ataláns** *usu cap* [Sp *atalán*, of AmerInd origin] **:** a language family of Ecuador

at all \əˈtȯl *also* ad·əˈȯl\ *adv (or adj)* **:** in any way or respect **:** to even the least extent or degree **:** under any circumstances — used chiefly for emphasis esp. in negative, conditional, or interrogative sentences or phrases ⟨he has no ambition *at all*⟩ ⟨not *at all* likely⟩ ⟨wherever an *at all* Catholic culture exists —R.G.Davis⟩

at·a·man \ˈad·əˈman\ *n* -s [Russ, fr. ORuss *vatamanŭ*] **:** HETMAN

at·a·mas·co lily \ˌad·əˈma(ˌ)skō-\ *also* **atamasco** *n* [Virginia *attamusco*, lit., it is red] **:** a plant of the genus *Zephyranthes* (esp. *Z. atamasco* and *Z. longifolia*)

at·ap *or* **at·tap** \ˈaˌtap\ *n* -s [Malay *atap* roof, thatch] **1 :** NIPA PALM **2 :** the leaves of the nipa palm used esp. for thatching in Malayan countries **3 :** a thatched roof often made with the leaves of the nipa palm

atar *var of* ATTAR

¹at·a·rac·tic \ˌad·əˈraktik\ *adj* [Gk *ataraktos* + E *-ic*] **1 :** tending to tranquilize — used of drugs for the treatment of anxiety and tension states or mental diseases **2 :** of or relating to mental tranquillity ⟨~ effect⟩

²ataractic \"\ *or* **at·a·rax·ic** \-raksik\ *n* -s [*ataractic* fr. ¹*ataractic*; *ataraxic* fr. *ataraxy* + *-ic*] **:** an ataractic drug

at·a·raxy \ˈad·əˌraksē\ *also* **at·a·rax·ia** \ˌ=ˌ=ˈraksēə\ *n, pl* **ataraxies** *also* **ataraxias** [MF & Gk; MF *ataraxie*, fr. Gk *ataraxia*, fr. *ataraktos* undisturbed (fr. *a-* ²a- + *taraktos*, verbal of *tarattein, tarassein* to disturb, stir) + *-ia* -y — more at DREG] **:** calmness untroubled by mental or emotional disquiet **:** intellectual detachment **:** IMPERTURBABILITY

ataroi *usu cap, var of* ATORAI

atas *pl of* ATA

ataunt \əˈtȯnt, -änt\ *or* **ataun·to** \-(ˌ)tō\ *adj* [*ataunt* fr. ME, as much as possible, fr. MF *autant* as much, as much as possible, fr. OF *altant, autant* as much, fr. *al, el* other, other thing (fr. assumed VL *ale*, alter. of L *aliud*, neut. of *alius* other) + *tant* so much, fr. L *tantum*, neut. of *tantus* so great; *ataunto*, alter. of *ataunt* — more at ELSE, TANTAMOUNT] **1 :** fully rigged; *esp* **:** with all light upper spars hoisted and rigged **2 :** completely in order **:** SHIPSHAPE

at·a·vic \ˈad·ə(ˌ)vik, ˈatə-; əˈtav-, (ˈ)aˈt-\ *adj* [prob. fr. F *atavique*, fr. L *atavus* ancestor + F *-ique* -ic] **:** ATAVISTIC

at·a·vism \ˈad·əˌvizəm, ˈatə,-\ *n* -s [F *atavisme*, fr. L *atavus* ancestor, grandfather's or grandmother's great-grandfather (perh. fr. *atta* daddy + *avus* grandfather) + F *-isme* -ism] **1 :** recurrence in an organism or in any of its parts of a form typical of ancestors more remote than the parents usu. due to recombination of ancestral genes **2 :** an individual or character manifesting atavism **:** THROWBACK, REVERSION ⟨he was a magnificent ~, a man so purely primitive —Jack London⟩

at·a·vist \-vəst\ *n* -s [*atavism* + *-ist*] **:** one that is marked by atavism

at·a·vis·tic \ˌ=ˌ=ˈvistik, -ēk\ *adj* **:** of, relating to, tending to, or marked by atavism ⟨from some ~ inheritance of the cave dweller he always disliked people on first acquaintance —W.S. Maugham⟩ ⟨called his work uncultured and ~⟩ — **at·a·vis·ti·cal·ly** \-tək(ə)lē, -ēk-, -li\ *adv*

at·a·vus \ˈad·əvəs\ *n, pl* **ata·vi** \-ˌvī, -ˌvē\ [L] **:** an ancestor or ancestral type from which a character is assumed to be inherited

atax·aphasia \əˌtaks +\ *or* **ataxi·aphasia** \əˌtaksē +\ *n* -s [NL, fr. *ataxia* + *aphasia*] **:** aphasia marked by inability to order words into sentences

atax·ia \əˈtaksēə\ *also* **ataxy** \əˈtaksē, ˈaˌt-\ *n, pl* **ataxias** *also* **ataxies** [Gk *ataxia*, fr. *ataktos* disorderly (fr. *a-* ²a- + *taktos* ordered, verbal of *tattein, tassein* to put in order) + *-ia* -y — more at TACTICS] **1 :** lack of order **:** CONFUSION ⟨their political ~ . . . kept them unaware of themselves and unaware of each other —Waldo Frank⟩ **2** [NL, fr. Gk] **:** an inability to coordinate voluntary muscular movements that is symptomatic of any of several disorders of the nervous system; *specif* **:** such an abnormality in sheep associated with inadequate intake of copper and common in parts of Australia

atax·i·a·gram \əˈtaksēəˌgram\ *n* -s [NL *ataxia* + E *-gram*] **:** a record obtained with an ataxiameter

atax·i·am·e·ter \əˌtaksēˈaməd·ə(r)\ *or* **atax·i·a·graph** \=ˈ=ˌ=ˌgraf\ *n* -s [NL *ataxia* + E *-meter* or *-graph*] **:** an instrument for measuring involuntary tremor and unsteadiness (as the swaying of the whole body in the erect posture)

atax·ic \əˈtaksik\ *adj* **1 :** marked or caused by ataxia **2 :** of or relating to unstratified ore deposits — opposed to *eutaxic*

atax·ite \əˈtakˌsīt, āˈ-\ *n* -s [ISV *atax-* (fr. Gk *ataxia* disorder) + *-ite*; orig. formed as G *ataxit* — more at ATAXIA] **1 :** a taxitic rock whose components have no definite arrangement, simulating a breccia **2 :** an iron meteorite lacking the structure of either hexahedrites or octahedrites — **atax·it·ic** \ˌāˌtakˈsid·ik\ *adj*

ataxonomic \(ˈ)ā + ˌ=ˈ=ˈ=\ *adj* [²a- + *taxonomic*] **:** not concerned with classification or systematic botany and zoology — compare TAXONOMY

atayal *usu cap, var of* TAYAL

atbash *var of* ATHBASH

at bat \ˈ=ˈ=\ *n, pl* **at bats 1 :** a turn at attempting to hit a ball thrown by a baseball or softball pitcher **2 :** an official time at the plate charged to the batter except when he walks, sacrifices, is hit by a pitched ball, or is interfered with by the catcher ⟨the shortstop made three hits in five *at bats*⟩

atdt *abbr* attendant

¹ate *past of* EAT

²ate \ˈād·ē, ˈä-; ˈäˌtā, ˈāˌtē\ *n* -s [Gk *atē*; prob. akin to Latvian *vâts* wound] **:** blind impulse, reckless ambition, or excessive folly that drives men to ruin

¹-ate \ət, ˌāt, *usu* -d-+V\ *n suffix* -s [ME *-at*, fr. OF, fr. L *-atus* (nom. sing. masc.), *-atum* (nom. sing. neut.), fr. *-atus*, past part. ending of 1st conj. verbs] **1 :** one acted upon (in a specified way) ⟨advoc*ate*⟩ ⟨centrifug*ate*⟩ ⟨duplic*ate*⟩ ⟨mand*ate*⟩ ⟨vulcaniz*ate*⟩ **2** [NL *-atum*, fr. L, neut. of *-atus*] **:** chemical compound or complex anion derived from a (specified) compound or element ⟨alcohol*ate*⟩ ⟨ferr*ate*⟩; *esp* **:** salt or ester of an acid with a name ending in *-ic* and not beginning with *hydro-* ⟨acet*ate*⟩ ⟨carbon*ate*⟩ — compare STOCK SYSTEM

²-ate \"\ *n suffix* -s [ME *-at*, fr. OF, fr. L *-atus*, fr. *-atus*, past part. ending of 1st conj. verbs] **:** office **:** function **:** rank **:** state **:** group of persons holding a (specified) office or rank, having a (specified) function, or being in a (specified) state ⟨episcop*ate*⟩ ⟨pontific*ate*⟩ ⟨professor*ate*⟩ ⟨rabbin*ate*⟩

³-ate \"\ *adj suffix* [ME *-at*, fr. L *-atus*, past part. ending of 1st conj. verbs, fr. *-a-* (thematic vowel of 1st conj.) + *-tus*, past part. ending — more at -ED] **1 :** acted upon (in a specified way) **:** brought into or being in a (specified) state ⟨consumm*ate*⟩ ⟨degener*ate*⟩ ⟨inanim*ate*⟩ ⟨Italianate⟩ ⟨temper*ate*⟩ **2 :** characterized by having ⟨branchi*ate*⟩ ⟨chord*ate*⟩ ⟨foli*ate*⟩

⁴-ate \ˌāt, *usu* ˌād·+V\ *vb suffix* -ED/-ING/-S [ME *-aten*, fr. L *-atus*, past part. ending of 1st conj. verbs] **:** to act (in a specified way) ⟨negoti*ate*⟩ ⟨pontific*ate*⟩ **:** act upon (in a specified way) ⟨assassin*ate*⟩ ⟨vener*ate*⟩ **:** cause to be modified or affected by ⟨camphor*ate*⟩ ⟨hyphen*ate*⟩ ⟨pollin*ate*⟩ **:** cause to become ⟨activ*ate*⟩ ⟨domestic*ate*⟩ ⟨fraction*ate*⟩ **:** furnish with ⟨capacit*ate*⟩ ⟨substanti*ate*⟩

A·te·brin \ˈad·əbrən, ˈatə-, *also* -ˌbrēn\ *trademark* — used for quinacrine

atef \ˈäˌtef\ *n* -s [alternate transliteration of Egypt ʾ*tf*] **:** a tall crown with a long feather on each side shown in the art of ancient Upper Egypt as worn by Osiris

atel- *or* **atelo-** *comb form* [NL, fr. Gk *atel-* imperfect, incomplete, fr. *atelēs*, fr. *a-* ²a- + *-telēs* (fr. *telos* end) — more at WHEEL] **:** defective ⟨*atel*ectasis⟩ ⟨*atelo*myelia⟩

at·e·lec·ta·sis \ˌad·ᵊlˈektəsəs\ *n, pl* **atelecta·ses** \-əˌsēz\ [NL, fr. *atel-* + Gk *ektasis* extension — more at ECTASIS] **:** collapse of the expanded lung; *also* **:** defective expansion of the pulmonary alveoli at birth — **at·e·lec·tat·ic** \ˌ=ˌ=ˌlekˈtad·ik\ *adj*

at·e·les \ˈad·ᵊlˌēz\ *n, cap* [NL, fr. Gk *atelēs*; fr. the absence or rudimentary development of the thumb] **:** a genus comprising the spider monkeys

at·e·les·tite \ˌad·ᵊlˈeˌstīt\ *n* -s [G *atelestit*, fr. Gk *atelestos* unaccomplished (fr. *a-* ²a- + *telestos* accomplished, fr. *telein* to accomplish, fr. *telos* end) + G *-it* -ite] **:** a mineral consisting of basic bismuth arsenate occurring in minute yellow crystals (sp. gr. 6.82)

atel·ic \(ˈ)āˈtelik\ *adj* [²a- + *telic*] **:** IMPERFECTIVE 2 — contrasted with *telic*

ate·lier \ˈad·ᵊlˌyā, ˌatᵊl- *also* aˈtelˌyā *or* əˈt-\ *n* -s [F, fr. MF *astelier* woodpile, construction yard, workshop, fr. *astele* splinter, chip of wood, fr. LL *astella* splinter, alter. (influenced by L *-ella*) of L *astula*, alter. of *assula*, dim. of *assis* board — more at ACE] **1 a :** an artist's studio or workroom **b :** a studio in which students of art or architecture receive instruction **2 :** WORKSHOP: **a :** an artist's studio or workshop in which several assistants or apprentices contribute toward the execution of a work bearing a master's signature ⟨Rubens's ~⟩ **b :** a workshop in which several people are employed at artisans' tasks **3 :** a business establishment devoted to the design and execution of women's fine clothing ⟨a showing of summer models at a Paris ~⟩

atel·i·o·sis \əˌtelēˈōsəs, -tē-\ *also* **atel·ei·o·sis** \", -lī-\ *n, pl* **atelio·ses** *also* **ateleio·ses** \-ˈōˌsēz\ [NL, fr. Gk *ateleia* incompleteness (fr. *atelēs* incomplete) + NL *-osis*] **:** incomplete development **:** INFANTILISM; *esp* **:** dwarfism associated with anterior pituitary deficiencies and marked by essentially normal intelligence and proportions though often retarded sexual development — compare ACHONDROPLASIA — **atel·i·ot·ic** \əˌtelēˈäd·ik, -tēl-\ *also* **atel·ei·ot·ic** \", -lī-\ *adj*

atel·lan \əˈtelən\ *also* **atel·lane** \", -ˌlān\ *adj, usu cap* [L *Atellanus* of Atella, fr. *Atella*, ancient Oscan town in southern Italy where the Roman farce originated + L *-anus* -an] **:** of, relating to, or having the characteristics of a Roman genre of farce developed from impromptu rustic plays of country life and adopted for interludes and afterpieces during the Republic and up to the time of Tiberius

atelomitic \ˌā + ˌ=ˈ=ˈ=\ *adj* [²a- + *telomitic*] **:** NONTERMINAL ⟨the ~ centromeres and spindle attachment of certain chromosomes⟩

ate·moya \ˌad·əˈmȯiə, ˌa-, -tə-\ *n* -s [*ates* + *cherimoya*] **:** a white-pulped tropical fruit produced by crossing the sweetsop and the cherimoya

a tempo \ä +\ *adv (or adj)* [It] **:** in time — used as a direction in music to return to the original rate of speed of a piece after any change in the tempo

atentaculata \ˌā +\ *n, pl, cap* [NL, fr. ²a- + *Tentaculata*] *syn of* NUDA

a ter·go \äˈter(ˌ)gō\ *adv* [L] **:** from behind ⟨assisted him out *a tergo* with his own footwear —H.W.Thompson⟩

ate·ri·an \əˈtirēən\ *adj, usu cap* [F *atérien*, fr. Bir el-*Ater* (Constantine), Algeria + F *-ien* -ian] **:** of or belonging to a derived Mousterian culture of northern Africa which has in addition to the usual European Mousterian traits tanged and winged arrow points and leaf-shaped spearheads and which may be said to carry on the Mousterian tradition into upper Paleolithic times

à terre \äˈte(ə)r, *F* ätɛr\ *adv (or adj)* [F] *ballet* **:** on the ground **:** PAR TERRE

¹ates *pl of* ATE

²ates \ˈäˌtes\ *n, pl* **ates** [Tag] **:** SWEETSOP

-ates *pl of* -ATE, *present 3d sing of* -ATE

¹ates·tine \əˈtesˌtən, -ˌtīn\ *adj, usu cap* [L *atestinus*, fr. *Ateste*, city in northeastern Italy + L *-inus* -ine] **:** of or belonging to the early Roman Iron Age culture of Ateste related to the Villanova culture but later influenced by the Etruscans

²atestine \"\ *n* -s *usu cap* **:** one of the people of Ateste (modern Este, Italy) esp. of the period 800-400 B.C.

at·fa·la·ti \atˈfälədˌē\ *n, pl* **atfalati** *or* **atfalatis** *usu cap* [perh. fr. Kalapooia *Tfalati*, fr. Shahaptian *Twalatin*, lit., river people, fr. *wala* river + *tin* people] **1 :** a people of the northern dialectic branch of the Kalapooian language family **2 :** a member of the Atfalati people

at fault *adj, of a hunting dog* **:** coming to check

ath *abbr* athletic

athabascan *or* **athabaskan** *usu cap, var of* ATHAPASKAN

athal·a·mous \(ˈ)āˈthaləməs\ *adj* [²a- + L *thalamus* marriage bed, bedroom (fr. Gk *thalamos* bedroom, room) + E *-ous*; akin to Gk *tholos* rotunda — more at DALE] **1 :** lacking a torus or receptacle ⟨~ flowers⟩ **2 :** without apothecia, beds, or shields for spores ⟨~ lichens⟩

¹ath·a·na·sian \ˌathəˈnāzhən, -nāsh-\ *adj, usu cap* [*Athanasius* the Great †373 Greek church father & patriarch of Alexandria + E *-an*] **:** of or relating to Athanasius, who advocated the homoousian doctrine against Arianism

²athanasian \"\ *n* -s *usu cap* **:** an adherent of Athanasius or of his teachings

ath·a·na·sian·ism \ˌ=ˌ=ˈ=ˌnizəm\ *n* -s *usu cap* **:** the theological doctrine of Athanasius; *esp* **:** the doctrine that the Son is of the same substance with the Father — opposed to *Arianism*

ath·a·nor \ˈathəˌnȯ(ə)r\ *n* -s [ME, fr. (assumed) ML, fr. Ar *at-tannūr* the oven, fr. Aram *tannūr* oven] **:** a self-feeding digesting furnace that maintained a uniform and durable heat and was used by alchemists

ath·a·pas·kan *or* **ath·a·pas·can** \ˌathəˈpaskən\ *or* **ath·a·bas·can** *or* **ath·a·bas·kan** \-ˈba-\ *n* -s *usu cap* [*Athapaska, Athapasca, Athabasca, Athabaska* an Athapaskan people (fr. Cree *Athap-askaw*, lit., grass or reeds here and there) + E *-an*] **1 :** a language stock of the Na-dene phylum in No. America consisting of the three groups Apachean, Pacific Athapaskan, and Déné or Northern Athapaskan **2 a :** a people speaking an Athapaskan language **b :** a member of any such people

athar *var of* ATTAR

ath·bash \ˈatˌbash, ˈäth-, ˈ=ˌ=\ *also* **at·bash** \ˈat-, ˈ=ˌ=\ *n* -ES [Heb *athbash*, a word formed from the first, last, second, and next-to-last letters of the Hebrew alphabet] **:** a cipher used in Jewish mystical and allegorical writing in which each letter of a word is replaced by that letter which stands as many places from the end of the Hebrew alphabet as the letter replaced stands from the beginning — compare ALBAM

athe·cae \əˈthēˌ(ˌ)sē\ *n pl, cap* [NL, fr. fem. pl. of (assumed) NL *athecus* having no cover, fr. NL ²a- + (assumed) NL *-thecus* (fr. L *theca* cover, sheath) — more at TICK] **:** a division usu. made a suborder of Testudinata comprising turtles with the carapace separate from the internal skeleton and usu. with greatly reduced ossification and represented among recent forms by the marine leatherback — **athe·can** \-ēkən\ *adj or n*

ath·e·ca·ta \ˌathəˈkäd·ə, -ād·ə\ [NL, fr. ²a- + *thec-* + *-ata*] *syn of* ANTHOMEDUSAE

athe·cate \(ˈ)āˈ-; *in sense 2 also* ˈathəˌkāt, -ˌkət\ *adj* **1** [²a- + *thecate*] **:** lacking a theca **2** [NL *Athecata*] **:** of or belonging to the gymnoblastic hydroids

ath·e·coi·dea \ˌathəˈkȯidēə\ [NL, fr. ²a- + *thec-* + *-oidea*] *syn of* ATHECAE

athe·ism \ˈāthēˌizəm\ *n* -s [MF *athéisme*, fr. *athée* atheist (fr. Gk *atheos* godless, not believing in the existence of gods, fr. *a-* ²a- + *theos* god) + *-isme* -ism — more at THEISM] **1 a :** disbelief in the existence of God or any other deity **b :** the doctrine that there is neither God nor any other deity — compare AGNOSTICISM **2 :** godlessness esp. in conduct **:** UNGODLINESS, WICKEDNESS

¹athe·ist \-ˌəst\ *n* -s [MF *athéiste*, fr. *athée* + *-iste* -ist] **:** one who subscribes to, advocates, or practices atheism **syn** see AGNOSTIC

²atheist \"\ *adj* **:** ATHEISTIC ⟨~ radicalism⟩

athe·is·tic \ˌāthēˈistik, -ēk\ *also* **athe·is·ti·cal** \-tək əl, -ēk-\ *adj* **:** relating to, characterized by, or given to atheism **:** GODLESS, IMPIOUS, IRREVERENT — **athe·is·ti·cal·ly** \-tək(ə)lē, -ēk-, -li\ *adv* — **athe·is·tic·ness** *n* -ES

athe·ize \ˈāthēˌīz\ *vt* -ED/-ING/-S [*atheist* + *-ize*] **:** to make atheistic

ath·el·ing *also* **aeth·e·ling** \ˈathəliŋ, -th-\ *or* **eth·e·ling** \ˈe-\ *n* -s *often cap* [ME, fr. OE *ætheling* (akin to OHG *adalung, adaling*, OS *ethiling*, ON *ǫthlingr*), fr. *æthelu* nobility, family, nature + *-ling*; akin to OHG *adal* family, noble family, nobility, OS *athal*, ON *athal* nature, disposition, offspring, OE *ōthel* property, inheritance, OHG *uodal*, ON *ōthal*] **:** an Anglo-Saxon prince or nobleman; *esp* **:** the heir apparent or a prince of the royal family

athel tree \ˈathəl-\ *also* **athel tamarisk** *or* **athel** *n* -s [Ar *athlah*] **:** a small drought-resistant evergreen tree (*Tamarix aphylla*) native to southern and western Asia but now widely planted as an ornamental or shelter-belt tree in warm dry regions (as of the southwestern U. S. and Australia); *broadly* **:** any of several other trees or shrubs of the genus *Tamarix*

athematic \ˌā + ˌ=ˈ=\ *adj* [²a- + *thematic*] **1** *of a verb or class of verbs* **:** having no thematic vowel ⟨Sanskrit *as-ti* "he is", Greek *es-ti*, Latin *es-t* are ~ verbs⟩ **2** *music* **:** not based on the repetition or elaboration of themes ⟨an ~ style⟩

ath·e·nae·um *or* **ath·e·ne·um** \ˌathəˈnēəm\ *n* -s [L *Athenaeum*, a school in ancient Rome for the study of the arts, fr. Gk *Athēnaion*, a temple of Athena in Athens where poets read their works, fr. *Athēna, Athēnē*, major Greek deity, goddess of war, fertility, arts, and wisdom] **1 :** a literary or scientific association or club **2 :** a building or a room in which books, periodicals, and newspapers are kept for use **:** READING ROOM, LIBRARY

¹athe·ni·an \əˈthēnēən, -nyən\ *adj, usu cap* [L *Atheniensis*, adj. & n., fr. *Athenae* Athens (fr. Gk *Athēnai*) + L *-iensis* -ian] **:** of, relating to, or having the characteristics of Athens or its ancient civilization

²athenian \"\ *n* -s *cap* [L *Atheniensis*] **:** a native or inhabitant of Athens, esp. Athens, Greece

¹ath·ens \ˈathənz\ *n* -ES *cap* [fr. *Athens*, city-state and cultural center of ancient Greece, fr. L *Athenae*, fr. Gk *Athēnai*] **:** a city regarded as a center of culture and intellectual achievement ⟨Boston has often been called the *Athens* of America⟩

²athens *adj, usu cap* [fr. *Athens*, Greece] **:** of or from Athens, the capital of Greece **:** of the kind or style prevalent in Athens **:** ATHENIAN

atheology \ˌā + \ *n* -ES [²a- + *theology*] **:** opposition to theology

athe·ous \ˈāthēəs\ *adj* [Gk *atheos* without god, fr. *a-* ²a- + *theos* god — more at THEISM] **1** *obs* **:** ATHEISTIC **2 :** neither accepting nor denying the existence of God

ath·e·ric·era \ˌathəˈrisərə\ *n pl, cap* [NL, fr. Gk *athēr* barb, awn + NL *-cera*] *in some classifications* **:** a group of two-winged flies part of the suborder Cyclorrhapha and having three basal joints to the antennae and a bristle arising from the base of the third — **ath·e·ric·er·an** \ˌ=ˌ=ˈ=ˌrən\ *adj or n* — **ath·e·ric·er·ous** \-rəs\ *adj*

ath·er·i·na \ˌathəˈrīnə\ *n* [NL, fr. Gk *atherinē* smelt] **1** *cap* **:** the type genus of Atherinidae **2** -s **:** a fish of the genus *Atherina*

ath·er·ine \ˈ=ˌ=ˌrīn, -ˌrən\ *n* -s [NL *Atherina*] **:** any of numerous small fishes of the family Atherinidae; *esp* **:** a European food fish (*Atherina presbyter*)

ath·er·in·id \ˌathəˈrinəd, -rī-\ *n* -s [NL *Atherinidae*] **:** a fish of the family Atherinidae **:** SILVERSIDES 1

ath·er·in·i·dae \ˌ=ˌ=ˈrinəˌdē\ *n pl, cap* [NL, fr. *Atherina*, type genus + *-idae*] **:** a family of small spiny-finned fishes of both salt and fresh water, all having a silvery band along the sides sometimes underlaid by black pigment — see SILVERSIDES

athe·ri·o·gae·an *or* **athe·ri·o·ge·an** \əˌthirēōˈjēən\ *adj, usu cap* [NL *Atheriogaea, Atheriogea* Antarctogaea (fr. ²a- + Gk *thērion* wild animal, animal — dim. of *thēr* beast of prey, wild animal — + NL *-gaea, -gea*) + E *-an* — more at FIERCE] **:** ANTARCTOGAEAN

ather·mal·ize \ˌāˈthərməˌlīz, -thə-\ *vt* -ED/-ING/-S [²a- + *thermal* + *-ize*] **:** to render (as an optical system) independent of temperature or of thermal effects

ather·man·cy \ˌ=ˈ=ˌmənsē\ *n* -ES [²a- + *-thermancy* (as in *diathermancy*)] **:** inability to transmit infrared radiation — compare DIATHERMANCY

ather·ma·nous \ˌ=ˈ=mənəs\ *adj* [²a- + *-thermanous* (as in *diathermanous*)] **:** not transmitting infrared radiation — compare DIATHERMANOUS

athermic \ˌā+ˈ=ˌ=\ *adj* [²a- + *thermic*] **:** HEATLESS ⟨an ~ motor⟩

athero- *comb form* [NL, fr. *atheroma*] **:** atheroma ⟨*athero*genesis⟩

ath·er·o·ma \ˌathəˈrōmə\ *n, pl* **atheromas** *also* **atheroma·ta** \-ˈrōməd·ə\ [NL, fr. L, a tumor containing gruellike matter, fr. Gk *athērōma*, fr. *atherē, athēra* gruel, fr. *ather-, athēr* beard of grain, point of a lance, barb; akin to Gk *antherix* beard of grain, stalk, *antheréōn* chin, *anthryskion* chervil, *anthrēnē* hornet, wasp] **:** a disease characterized by fatty degeneration of the inner coat of the arteries

ath·er·o·ma·to·sis \ˌ=ˌ=ˌmōˌməˈtōsəs\ *n, pl* **atheromato·ses** \-ōˌsēz\ [NL, fr. *atheromat-, atheroma* + *-osis*] **:** a disease characterized by more or less generalized atheromatous degeneration of the arteries

ath·er·om·a·tous \ˌ=ˌ=ˈrämədəs, -ōm-\ *also* **ath·er·o·mat·ic** \-(ˌ)rōˈmad·ik\ *adj* [NL *atheromat-, atheroma* + E *-ous* or *-ic*] **:** of, relating to, or having the characteristics of atheroma

ath·er·o·sclerosis \ˌathə(ˌ)rō+\ *n, pl* **atheroscleroses** [NL, fr. *athero-* + *sclerosis*] **:** a degenerative disease of the arteries that is a stage of arteriosclerosis and is characterized by the deposition of fatty substances in and the fibrous thickening of the intima, resulting in the narrowing of the vessel passages and ultimately hardening and loss of elasticity — **ath·er·o·sclerotic** \ˌ=ˌ=(ˌ)= + ˌ=ˈ=ˌ=\ *adj*

ath·e·ru·rus \ˌathəˈrürəs\ *n, cap* [NL, fr. Gk *athēr* barb, awn + NL *-urus*] **:** a genus of long-bodied Old World porcupines having the tail scaly except at its spiny tip and comprising the brush-tailed porcupines

ath·e·te·sis \ˌathəˈtēsəs\ *n, pl* **athete·ses** \-ēˌsēz\ [Gk *athetēsis* art of setting aside, abolition, annulling, fr. *athetos* + *-ēsis* -esis] **:** the rejecting or marking of a passage (as in a poem) as spurious

ath·e·tize \ˈ=ˌ=ˌtīz\ *vt* -ED/-ING/-S [Gk *athetein* (fr. *athetos* set aside, not fixed, fr. *a-* ²a- + *thetos* placed, fr. *tithenai* to place) + E *-ize* — more at DO] **:** to reject or mark (a passage) as spurious ⟨the *athetized* lines of the Iliad⟩

¹ath·e·toid \ˈathəˌtȯid\ *adj* [ISV *athet-* (fr. NL *athetosis*) + *-oid*] **:** exhibiting or characteristic of athetosis ⟨~ children⟩ ⟨~ movements⟩

²athetoid \"\ *n* -s **:** an athetoid individual

ath·e·to·sis \ˌathəˈtōsəs\ *n, pl* **atheto·ses** \-ōˌsēz\ [NL, fr. Gk *athetos* + NL *-osis*] **:** a nervous disorder seen chiefly in children that is marked by continual slow movements esp. of the extremities and is usu. due to a brain lesion

ath·e·tot·ic \ˌ=ˌ=ˈtäd·ik\ *or* **ath·e·to·sic** \-ˈtōsik\ *adj* [*athetotic* fr. NL *athetosis*, after such pairs as NL *hypnosis*: E *hypnotic*; *athetosic* fr. NL *athetosis* + E *-ic*] **:** relating to athetosis **:** ATHETOID

athey wheel \'athē-\ *n, usu cap A* [origin unknown] : a crawler wheel assembly used on trailers for moving heavy loads over soft terrain (as in logging operations)

athing \'ȯ(,)thiŋ, 'ä-\ *n* -s [[7]*a* + *thing*] *Scot* : EVERYTHING

athi·o·rho·da·ce·ae \ā,thīə,rō'dāsē,ē\ *n pl, cap* [NL, fr. [2]*a-* + *thi-* + *rhod-* + *-aceae*] : a family of small motile sulfur bacteria having polar flagella and red to brown coloration due to various combinations of bacteriochlorophyll and carotenoid pigments

athirst \ə'thərst, -ə̄st,-əist\ *adj* [ME *athirst, athurst*, fr. OE *ofthyrst, ofthyrsted*, past part. of *ofthyrstan* to suffer from thirst, fr. *of-* overcoming, destroying (fr. *of* off, from) + *thyrstan* to thirst — more at OF, THIRST] : THIRSTY: **a** : suffering from or experiencing thirst ⟨and when thou art ~ go unto the vessels and drink —Ruth 2:9 (AV)⟩ **b** : having a strong desire or yearning : EAGER, LONGING ⟨these that gather in mid-Manhattan . . . ~ for merriment —R.L.Shayon⟩ **syn** see EAGER

ath·lete \'ath,lēt, *chiefly substand* -thə,l-; *usu* -ēd·+V\ *n* -s [ME, fr. L *athleta*, fr. Gk *athlētēs, aethlētēs*, fr. *athlein, aethlein* to contend for a prize, fr. *athlos, aethlos* contest, or *athlon, aethlon* prize, contest; perh. akin to L *vad-, vas* bail, security — more at WED] **1** : one who competed for a prize in the public games of ancient Greece and Rome **2 a** : one who is trained to compete either professionally or as an amateur in exercises, sports, or games requiring physical strength, agility, or stamina **b** : one who has a natural aptitude for or is reasonably skilled in physical exercises, sports, or games **3** : one who takes part in or is capable of taking part in exercises or activities requiring mental agility, endurance, or strength ⟨nor does the world cheer the natural ~*s* of the mind —J.M.Barzun⟩

athlete's foot *n* : ringworm of the feet characterized by softening and cracking of the skin between the toes, accompanied by painful itching, and caused by infection with any of several fungi and occasionally by unrelated organisms

athlete's heart *n* : a supposed hypertrophic dilated heart attributed to the effects of repeated overexertion (as on the part of professional athletes) — not used technically

ath·let·ic \(')ath¦led·ik, -etik, -ēk, *chiefly substand* ¦athə¦l-\ *adj* [L *athleticus*, fr. Gk *athlētikos*, fr. *athlētēs* + *-ikos* -ic] **1** : of or relating to athletes or athletics ⟨the college ~ association⟩ **2** : having the characteristics of or befitting an athlete : STRONG, MUSCULAR, ROBUST, VIGOROUS, AGILE, ACTIVE ⟨an ~ build⟩ ⟨a powerful and ~ mind⟩ **3** : characterized by heavy frame, large chest, and powerful muscular development : MESOMORPHIC — compare ASTHENIC, PYKNIC **4** : designed or suitable for use or wear by athletes ⟨a new ~ dormitory⟩ ⟨~ shorts⟩ — **ath·let·i·cal·ly** \-ə̇k(ə)lē, -ēk-, -li\ *adv*

ath·let·i·cism \ath'led·ə,sizəm, -letə-\ *n* -s **1 a** : an intense interest in athletics ⟨you carry your disdain of ~ too far —Christopher Isherwood⟩ **b** : an ardent participation in athletics **c** : a zealous encouragement of athletics **2** : intense energy or activity : STRENUOSITY ⟨an objective and healthy, almost happy ~ about his later works such as the *Third Symphony* —Aaron Copland⟩

ath·let·ics \ath'led·iks, -etiks, -ēks\ *n pl* **1** *sometimes sing in constr* **a** : the physical exercises, sports, or games engaged in by athletes ⟨intercollegiate ~⟩ **b** *Brit* : track-and-field sports **2** *usu sing in constr* **a** : the practice of athletic activities **b** : the principles of athletic activities and training

ath·o·dyd \'athə,did\ *n* -s [*a*ero- + *th*ermo*dy*namic + *d*uct] : a jet engine consisting essentially of a continuous duct or tube of varying diameter which admits air at the forward end, adds heat to it by the combustion of fuel, and discharges it from the after end

athole brose *or* **atholl brose** \'athəl'brōz\ *n, usu cap A* [fr. *Athole, Atholl*, district in Scotland] *Scot* : whiskey mixed with honey or meal

at home \ət'hōm, *Brit sometimes* ə'tōm\ *n* : a reception given at one's home ⟨if you are serving tea and chocolate and a variety of food . . . call it an *at home* —Emily Post⟩

at-home·ness \"+nə̇s\ *n* -ES : the quality or state of being at home ⟨his complete *at-homeness* in Chopin's music —Virgil Thomson⟩

[1]**atho·nite** \'athə,nīt\ *adj, usu cap* [L *Athon-, Athos* Athos, mountain in northeastern Greece (fr. Gk *Athōs* — acc. sometimes *Athōn*) + E *-ite*] : of or relating to Mount Athos, an important monastic center of the Eastern Orthodox Church

[2]**athonite** \"\ *n* -s *usu cap* : a monk of Mount Athos, Greece

athort \ə'thȯrt\ *Scot var of* ATHWART

athrep·sia \ə'threpsēə, ā'-\ *n* -s [NL, fr. [2]*a-* + Gk *threpsis* nourishing + NL *-ia*] : MARASMUS — **athrep·tic** \ə'threptik, (')ā¦-\ *adj*

athrill \ə'-\ *adj* [[1]*a-* + *thrill* (v.)] : in a state of thrill : EXCITED ⟨his whole being was ~ with excitement —O.E.Rölvaag⟩

athrob \ə'-\ *adj* [[1]*a-* + *throb* (v.)] : THROBBING

ath·ro·cyte \'athrə,sīt\ *n* -s [ISV *athro-* (fr. Gk *athroos* collected) + *-cyte*] : a cell (as a Kupffer cell) having the property of picking up extraneous material and storing it in granular form in its cytoplasm — compare PHAGOCYTE — **ath·ro·cy·to·sis** \,==,sī'tōsə̇s\ *n, pl* **athrocytoses**

ath·ro·gen·ic \¦athrə¦jenik\ *adj* [F *athrogénique*, fr. Gk *athroos, hathroos* together, collected + F *-génique* -genic; akin to Skt *sādhati* he comes to his goal, Av *āsna* successful, Gk *ithys* straight] : of or relating to clastic rocks of igneous origin

[1]**athwart** \ə'-\ *adv* [ME, adv. & prep., fr. [1]*a-* + *thwart*] **1 a** : from side to side : across esp. in an oblique direction : TRANSVERSELY ⟨the line of probable advance runs ~ to the high chains of mountains —W.V.Pratt⟩ **b** : at right angles to the center line (of a ship) **2** : in opposition to the right or expected course : CROSSWISE, AWRY ⟨and quite ~ goes all decorum —Shak.⟩

[2]**athwart** \"\ *prep* [ME] **1 a** : from side to side of : transversely over : ACROSS ⟨a row of steppingstones set ~ the creek —Eden Phillpotts⟩ **b** : from side to side of the length, direction, or course of (a ship) : ACROSS ⟨a fleet standing ~ our course⟩ **2** : in opposition to : contrary to ⟨a procedure directly ~ the New England prejudices —R.G.Cole⟩

athwart·hawse \" + ,-\ *adv (or adj)* : across the cable or stem (of another ship) — used with following *of*

athwart·ship \"+,-\ *adj* : across the ship from side to side ⟨this vessel has two watertight ~ bulkheads in the middle portion —E.L.Attwood⟩ — opposed to *fore-and-aft*

athwart·ships \-,ships\ *adv* [*athwart* + *ship* + *-s*] : across the ship from side to side ⟨the boilers were installed ~⟩

athwart·wise \-t·,wīz\ *adv (or adj)* : CROSSWISE

athy·re·o·sis \ā,thīrē'ōsə̇s\ *n, pl* **athyreo·ses** \-ō,sēz\ [NL, fr. [2]*a-* + *thyreo-* + *-osis*] : an abnormal condition caused by absence or functional deficiency of the thyroid gland — **athy·re·ot·ic** \=¦==¦äd·ik\ *adj*

ath·y·ris \'athərə̇s\ *n, cap* [NL, fr. [2]*a-* + Gk *thyris* valve, opening] : a genus of smooth biconvex extinct brachiopods having the plates of the brachidium prolonged into spirally rolled laterally directed processes

athyr·i·um \ə'thirēəm\ *n, cap* [NL, irreg. fr. Gk *athoros* without sperm (fr. *a-* [2]a- + *thoros* semen) + NL *-ium;* akin to MIr *dairim* I leap upon, Skt *dhārā* stream] : a genus of ferns (family Polypodiaceae) differing from *Asplenium* (in which it is often included) in having curved or lunate sori — compare LADY FERN

[1]**athyroid** \'athə,rȯid\ *adj* [NL *Athyris* + E *-oid*] : belonging to or characteristic of the genus *Athyris*

[2]**athyroid** \"\ *n* -s : a brachiopod of the genus *Athyris* — see BRACHIOPOD illustration

ati \'äd·ē\ *n, pl* **ati** *or* **atis** *usu cap* [Hiligaynon] **1** : a predominantly pagan Negritoid people on Panay, Philippines **2** : a member of the Ati people

at·i·ko·ka·nia \ad·ə̇(,)kō'kānēə, -nyə\ *n, cap* [NL, fr. *Atikokan* river, Ontario, Canada + NL *-ia*] : a genus of Precambrian fossils possibly of siliceous sponges and if actually such the only fossil animal known from this early period

atilt \ə'-\ *adj (or adv)* [[1]*a-* + *tilt*, v.] **1** : in a tilting position ⟨huge trees dangerously ~ were still falling —G.S.Perry⟩ **2** : with lance in hand (as in a tourney) ⟨run ~ at men —Samuel Butler †1680⟩

-ating *pres part of* -ATE

atin·gle \ə'-\ *adj* [[1]*a-* + *tingle*, v.] : TINGLING

-a·tion \'āshən\ *n suffix* -s [ME *-acioun*, fr. OF *-ation*, fr. L *-ation-, -atio*, fr. *-atus* -ate + *-ion-, -io* -ion] : action or process ⟨comput*ation*⟩ ⟨flirt*ation*⟩ ⟨visit*ation*⟩ : something connected with an action or process ⟨civiliz*ation*⟩ ⟨discolor*ation*⟩

a·tip·toe \ə'-\ *adv (or adj)* [[1]*a-* + *tiptoe*] **1** : on the tip of one's toes ⟨stood ~ by the terrace wall watching the barges —Anne Green⟩ **2** : in a state of expectancy : alert and expectant ⟨it was disquieting news and the ordnance . . . is ~ —*Nation*⟩

[1]**atis** \ə'tēs\ *n* -ES [Hindi *atīs*] **1** : a monkshood (*Aconitum heterophyllum*) found in the Himalayas **2** : any of several trees of the genus *Annona; esp* : SWEETSOP

[2]**atis** *pl of* ATI

ati·u·an \,äd·ē'üən\ *adj, usu cap* [*Atiu*, one of the Cook islands in the So. Pacific + E *-an*] : of or concerning the island of Atiu

-a·tive *When the preceding syllable has a stress (as in "purgative")* əd·iv *or* ətiv *or, sometimes in some words (as "rotative") answering to paroxytone disyllabic verbs in "-ate",* ,ād·iv *or* ,ātiv *or* -ēv *also* -əv; *when the preceding syllable is noninitial and unstressed (as in "legislative" or "nominative")* ,ā- *or* ,ə-; *in some words (as "elative") answering to oxytone verbs in "-ate",* 'ā-\ *adj suffix* [ME, fr. MF *-atif*, fr. L *-ativus*, fr. *-atus* -ate + *-ivus* -ive] : of, relating to, or connected with ⟨authorit*ative*⟩ ⟨consult*ative*⟩ ⟨norm*ative*⟩ ⟨quantit*ative*⟩ : tending to ⟨fix*ative*⟩ ⟨form*ative*⟩ ⟨lax*ative*⟩ ⟨talk*ative*⟩

atjeh·nese \,achə'nēz, ,ä-, -ēs\ *n, pl* **atjehnese** *usu cap* [*Atjeh*, part of Sumatra + E *-nese* (as in *Japanese*)] **1** : a Muslim Indonesian people of northern Sumatra **2** : a member of the Atjehnese people

at·ka mackerel *also* **atka fish** \'atkə-, 'ät-\ *n, usu cap A* [fr. *Atka* Island, Alaska, its locality] : a valuable marine food fish (*Pleurogrammus monopterygius*) of the family Hexagrammidae of Alaska and adjacent regions

atlant- *or* **atlanto-** *comb form* [NL *atlant-, atlas*] **1** : atlas (sense 3) ⟨*atlant*ad⟩ **2** : atlantal and ⟨*atlanto*axial⟩ ⟨*atlanto*=odontoid⟩

[1]**at·lan·ta** \ət'lantə, at-\ *n, cap* [NL, prob. irreg. fr. L (*mare*) *Atlanticum* Atlantic ocean, fr. *Atlanticum*, neut. of *Atlanticus* Atlantic] : a cosmopolitan genus (the type of the small family Atlantidae) comprising small transparent heteropod mollusks with a sharply keeled spiral shell

[2]**at·lan·ta** \ət'lantə, -aan-\ *adj, usu cap* [fr. *Atlanta*, Ga.] : of or from Atlanta, the capital of Georgia ⟨an *Atlanta* businessman⟩ : of the kind or style prevalent in Atlanta

at·lan·tad \-,tad\ *adv* [NL *atlant-, atlas* + E *-ad*] *anat* : toward the atlas

at·lan·tal \ət'lantᵊl, (')at¦-\ *adj* [NL *atlant-, atlas* + E *-al*] **1** *anat* : of or relating to the atlas **2** *anat* : ANTERIOR, CEPHALIC

[1]**at·lan·tan** \ət'lantᵊn, -ntən\ *or* **at·lan·ti·an** \-ntēən\ *adj, usu cap* [*Atlanta*, Georgia + E *-an, -ian*] **1** : of, relating to, or characteristic of Atlanta, the capital of Georgia **2** : of, relating to, or characteristic of the people of Atlanta

[2]**atlantan** \"\ *or* **atlantian** \"\ *n* -s *cap* : a native or resident of Atlanta

[1]**at·lan·te·an** \¦at,lan¦tēən, -,lən-; ət'lant-, (')at¦lant-\ *adj, usu cap* [L *Atlante*us (fr. *Atlant-, Atlas*) + E *-an*] : of, relating to, or resembling Atlas : STRONG ⟨my *Atlantean* shoulders are bent beneath the load of the firmament —L.P.Smith⟩

[2]**atlantean** \"\ *adj, usu cap* [*Atlanti*s, legendary sunken continent in the Atlantic ocean, mentioned by Pliny and Plato (fr. L, fr. Gk, prob. fr. *Atlantis* Atlantic ocean) + E *-ean*] : of or relating to Atlantis or its hypothetical culture

atlantes *pl of* ATLAS

at·lan·tic \ət'lantik, -aan-, -ēk\ *adj* [L *Atlanticus*, fr. Gk *Atlantikos*, fr. *Atlantis* Atlantic ocean (fr. *Atlant-, Atlas*, the Titan or the Atlas mountains in southern Mauretania, named after him) + *-ikos* -ic] **1** *usu cap* **a** : of, relating to, or found in, on, or near the Atlantic ocean ⟨the author's picture is fundamentally valid for our *Atlantic* civilization as a whole —H.M.Parshley⟩ **b** : of, relating to, or found on or near the east coast of the U.S. ⟨the chief *Atlantic* ports⟩ ⟨the middle=*Atlantic* states⟩ **2** [NL *atlant-, atlas* + E *-ic*] *anat* : of or relating to the atlas

atlantic bonito *n, usu cap A* : an oily-fleshed bonito (*Sarda sarda*) of the western Atlantic that is marked with oblique dark stripes, is highly regarded as a sport fish, but is little used for food — compare CHILE BONITO, PACIFIC BONITO

atlantic brant *n, usu cap A* : AMERICAN BRANT

atlantic croaker *n, usu cap A* : a small but important food fish (*Micropogon undulatus*) of the Gulf coast and the Atlantic coast south of Cape Cod

atlantic flyway *n, usu cap A* : the easternmost of the American flyways extending northward between the Atlantic ocean and the Appalachians and dividing northerly into a western branch through West Virginia and Pennsylvania, a central up the Hudson river to Canada, and a northeasterly across New England

atlantic halibut *n, usu cap A* : the halibut (*Hippoglossus hippoglossus*) of the No. Atlantic

atlantic kittiwake *n, usu cap A* : a kittiwake (*Rissa tridactyla*) of the No. Atlantic coasts largely pure white with pale gray mantling and black wing tips and feet — compare PACIFIC KITTIWAKE

atlantic puffin *n, usu cap A* : a puffin (*Fratercula arctica*) of the No. Atlantic largely white below but with the upper parts blackish

atlantic sailfish *n, usu cap A* : a sailfish (*Istiophorus americanus*) common in the warmer parts of the Atlantic and the Gulf of Mexico that is highly esteemed as a sport fish and whose smoked flesh is considered a delicacy

atlantic salmon *n, usu cap A* : SALMON 1a

atlantic time *or* **atlantic standard time** *n, cap A* : the time of the 4th time zone west of Greenwich based on the 60th meridian and used in Nova Scotia, New Brunswick, Prince Edward Island, and eastern Quebec, Canada

at·lan·tite \ət'lan,tīt\ *n* -s [ISV *Atlanti*c + *-ite;* orig. formed as G *atlantit;* fr. its occurrence in the Atlantic petrographic province] : a melanocratic nephelite-basalt rock consisting of plagioclase, augite, and olivine phenocrysts in a groundmass predominantly nephelite

atlanto- — see ATLANT-

at·lan·to·sau·rus \ət,lantə'sȯrəs\ [NL, fr. L *Atlant-, Atlas* (fr. Gk) + NL *-o-* + *-saurus*] *syn of* CAMARASAURUS

[1]**at·las** \'atləs\ *n* -ES *see sense 4* [after *Atlas*, a Titan of Greek mythology often represented as bearing the heavens on his shoulders, fr. L *Atlant-, Atlas*, fr. Gk] **1** *usu cap* : one who bears a heavy burden : chief supporter : MAINSTAY **2** [fr. NL *Atlas*, title of a cartographical work (published in 1595) by Gerhardus Mercator (Gerhard Kremer) †1594 Flemish geographer; prob. fr. the fact that the title pages of cartographical works of this period often had a representation of Atlas bearing the heavens] **a** : a bound collection of maps ⟨a glance at the ~ showed that the city is near the coast⟩ **b** : a bound collection of tables, charts, or plates illustrating any subject ⟨an ~ of peripheral nerve injuries⟩ ⟨a chromosome ~⟩ ⟨an ~ of climatic charts⟩ **3** [NL, fr. Gk, after *Atlas*, the Titan] : the first cervical vertebra articulating immediately with the skull and thus sustaining the globe of the head **4** *pl usu* **at·lan·tes** \ət'lan(,)tēz, at'-, -aan-\ [Gk, after *Atlas*, the Titan] : a figure or half figure of a man used as a column to support an entablature — called also *telamon;* compare CARYATID

atlas 4: one of the atlantes from Theater of Bacchus, Athens

[2]**atlas** \"\ *n* -ES [Ar *aṭlas*] : a rich satin made in the Far East

atlas beetle *n, usu cap A* : a very large shining mahogany=colored grotesquely horned beetle (*Chalcosoma atlas*) of the Old World tropics

atlas cedar *n, usu cap A* : an Algerian evergreen tree (*Cedrus atlantica*) much planted for ornament esp. in some of its horticultural bluish-foliaged forms

atlas moth *n, usu cap A* **1** : a giant silk moth (*Attacus atlas*) widespread and often abundant in Asia that is cultured for silk in some places **2** : any of several giant silk moths of the East Indies and southern Asia

at·latl \'at,latᵊl, ät,lä-\ *n* -s [of Uto-Aztecan origin; akin to Nahuatl *atlatl* spear thrower] : THROWING-STICK; *specif* : the spear thrower of ancient Mexico

at·le *or* **at·lee** \'atlē\ *n* -s [Ar *athlah* tamarisk] : ATHEL TREE

atlo- *comb form* [*atlas*] : atlantal and ⟨*atlo*axoid⟩

at·loid \'at,lȯid\ *or* **at·loi·de·an** \ət'lȯidēən, (')at¦-\ *adj* [F *atloïde*, fr. NL *atlas* + F *-oïde* -oid] : ATLANTAL

atloido- *comb form* [F *atloïdo-*, fr. *atloïde*] : atlantal and ⟨*atloido*axoid⟩

atm- *or* **atmo-** *comb form* [NL *atmo-* vapor, fr. Gk *atm-, atmo-*, fr. *atmos;* akin to Gk *aēnai* to blow — more at WIND] : vapor ⟨*atm*iatry⟩ : air ⟨*atmo*genic⟩

atm *abbr* atmosphere

at·man \'ätmən\ *n* -s *often cap* [Skt *ātman* breath, self, soul, Universal Self, Supreme Spirit; akin to OHG *ātum* breath] *Hinduism* : the innermost essence of each individual; *often* : the supreme universal self

atmid- *or* **atmido-** *comb form* [ISV, fr. Gk, fr. *atmid-, atmis*, fr. *atmos*] : steam : vapor ⟨*atmid*albumin⟩ ⟨*atmido*meter⟩

at·mo·clas·tic \¦atmə¦klastik\ *adj* [*atm-* + *clastic*] : disintegrated by atmospheric action and consolidated or cemented without transportation — used of rock

at·mo·gen·ic \-¦jenik\ *adj* [*atm-* + *-genic*] : of atmospheric origin by condensation, wind action, or deposition from volcanic vapors ⟨~ glacial ice⟩ — used chiefly of rocks and minerals

at·mol·y·sis \ət'mäləsə̇s, at-\ *n, pl* **atmoly·ses** \-ə,sēz\ [NL, fr. *atm-* + *-lysis*] : the act or process of separating mingled gases of unequal diffusibility by transmission through porous substances

at·mom·e·ter \-'mämәd·ə(r), -ətə-\ *n* -s [*atm-* + *-meter*] : an instrument for measuring the evaporating capacity of the air

at·mo·phile \'atmə,fīl\ *or* **at·mo·phil** \-,fil\ *adj* [*atm-* + *-phile, -phil*] : found in, attracted to, or having a tendency to occur in the atmosphere — used esp. of chemical elements or compounds

[1]**at·mo·sphere** \'atmə,sfi(ə)r, -iə\ *n* -s [NL *atmosphaera*, fr. Gk *atm-* + L *sphaera* sphere — more at SPHERE] **1 a** : a gaseous mass enveloping a heavenly body (as a planet or satellite) ⟨the ~ of Mars⟩ **b** : the whole mass of air surrounding the earth **c** : a gaseous envelope or medium ⟨an inert ~⟩ **2** : a supposed medium around various bodies : any surrounding envelope ⟨the ~ of electrons⟩ **3** : the air of a given place or locality esp. as affected by a particular characteristic (as heat, moisture, wholesomeness, or unwholesomeness) ⟨the close ~ of the schoolroom⟩ ⟨the fetid swamp ~⟩ ⟨a refreshing mountain ~⟩ **4 a** : a conditioning surrounding influence : mental or moral environment : physical milieu viewed as having a mental or moral influence ⟨an ~ of war, of blood, of excitement —Stuart Cloete⟩ ⟨the Sunday-school ~ of conventional religiosity —Havelock Ellis⟩ **b** : the typical environment of a given locality or period, class of people, or way of life : characteristic background or setting ⟨the ~ of a New England college town —C.G.Poore⟩ **5** : a unit of pressure equal to 101,325 newtons per square meter and very nearly equal to the pressure exerted by a vertical column of mercury 760 millimeters high at a temperature of 0°C under standard gravity **6 a** : the pervasive strongly dominant mood of a creative work (as a painting, symphony, or poem) evoked by and dependent on the successful suggestion, delineation, and heightening of elements vital to the desired effect ⟨the brooding ~ of *Macbeth*⟩ **b** : overall aesthetic effect of a creative work (as of art) that succeeds in producing a sense of intimate contact with and sharing in its physical or psychic environment ⟨a novel rich in ~⟩ **c** : color, interest, and appeal : FASCINATION : individual or exotic tone or effect ⟨a tiny inn that was full of ~⟩ **d** : intriguing effect esp. when arising from exotic, bizarre, or other beguilingly unusual qualities ⟨the languorous, bewitching ~ of a pagan island⟩ **7** : a brownish pink that is slightly redder and duller than nude — called also *mauve blush* **8** : an effect of slight haziness or mistiness (as that caused by particles of dust or moisture suspended in the air and leading to the diffusion of light rays); *specif* : such an effect in a painting

[2]**atmosphere** \"\ *vb* -ED/ -ING/ -S *vt* : to provide with atmosphere or an atmosphere ⟨the play needs to be *atmosphered*⟩ ~ *vi* : to be accessible to the atmosphere : VENT ⟨a water tank with a single pipe for *atmosphering*⟩

at·mo·spher·ic \¦==¦sfirik, -er-, -ēk\ *also* **at·mo·spher·i·cal** \-rə̇kəl, -ēk-\ *adj* **1 a** : of or relating to the atmosphere ⟨favorable ~ conditions⟩ **b** : like the atmosphere : AIRY ⟨fine lace with an ~ lightness⟩ **c** : occurring in or actuated by the atmosphere ⟨~ disturbances⟩ ⟨~ moisture⟩ **2** : having, marked by, or contributing atmosphere or an atmosphere ⟨an engaging ~ book⟩ ⟨tales handled in a poetic ~ way⟩ ⟨~ music⟩ **3** : having an effect of haziness ⟨~ subdued colors⟩ — **at·mo·spher·i·cal·ly** \-rə̇k(ə)lē, -ēk-, -li\ *adv*

atmospheric absorption *n* : absorption of radio waves by the atmosphere

atmospheric electricity *n* : electricity involved in such natural phenomena as lightning, St. Elmo's fire, or the aurora borealis

atmospheric perspective *n* : AERIAL PERSPECTIVE

atmospheric pressure *n* : the pressure exerted in every direction at any given point by the weight of the atmosphere

at·mo·spher·ics \,atmə'sfiriks, -er-, -ēks\ *n pl* **1 a** : disturbances produced in radio receiving apparatus by atmospheric electrical phenomena (as electrical storms) : STATIC **b** : atmospheric electrical phenomena **2** : ATMOSPHERE 6 ⟨midnight, rain-swept, graveyard ~ —W.T.Scott⟩

atmospheric tide *n* : one of the tidal movements of the atmosphere resembling those of the ocean but produced mainly by diurnal temperature changes

ato \'äd·ō\ *n, pl* **atos** *or* **ato** [Bontok] : a political division of a Bontok village

ato·cha \ə'tōchə, ä'-\ *n* -s [Sp] : ESPARTO 1

ato·kan \ə'tōkən\ *adj, usu cap* [*Atoka* county, Okla. + E *-an*] : of or relating to a subdivision of the Pennsylvanian geologic period — see GEOLOGIC TIME table

atoke \'a,tōk, 'ā-\ *n* -s [Gk *atokos* without offspring, fr. *a-* [2]a- + *tokos* childbirth, offspring; akin to Gk *teknon* child — more at THANE] : the anterior sexless part of certain polychaete worms from which grows the sexual portion — compare EPITOKE — **at·o·kous** *also* **at·o·cous** \'ad·əkəs\ *or* **at·o·kal** \-kəl\ *adj*

ato·le \ə'tō(,)lā\ *n* -s [Sp, fr. Nahuatl *atolli*] : corn meal that is cooked and eaten as mush or that is drunk as a thin gruel

at·oll \'a,tȯl, -äl, -ōl *also* 'ā- *sometimes* a't- *or* ə't-\ *n* -s [native name in the Maldive islands] : a coral reef appearing above the sea as a low ring-shaped coral island or as a chain of closely spaced coral islets around a shallow lagoon that may vary in diameter from less than a mile to 80 or more

at·om \'ad·əm, 'atəm\ *n* -s *often attrib* [ME *atome*, fr. L *atomus*, fr. Gk *atomos*, fr. *atomos* indivisible, fr. *a-* [2]a- + *tomos*, verbal of *temnein* to cut — more at TOME] **1** *philos* **a** : one of the minute, indivisible, discrete, and concrete particles of which according to ancient materialism the universe is composed; *often* : a similar particle considered as being of the stuff of which the mind is composed **b** : one of the various final irreducible or basic units or constituents of which according to different theories the universe is ultimately constructed (as minute things or processes in physicalistic theories and presentations or sense qualia in phenomenalistic theories); *often* : a logical construct that is formed from such basic units **c** : a particular or an element that is considered to be ultimate or unanalyzable for the purposes of a given system **2 a** : a tiny particle : MOTE, BIT ⟨~*s* of dust dancing in the sunlight⟩ ⟨the glass bowl was smashed to ~*s*⟩ **b** : the smallest possible part : minute fragment : tiny portion or quantity ⟨not an ~ of water to drink⟩ ⟨without an ~ of common sense⟩ **c** : a very small creature or object : MITE ⟨brilliant hummingbirds, flashing ~*s* of color⟩ **d** : a small individual unit usu. viewed as a relatively independent member of a group ⟨every man is a social ~⟩ **3 a** *according to the atomic theory* : the smallest particle of an element that can exist either alone or in combination with similar particles of the same or of a different element : the smallest particle of an element that enters into the composition of molecules — see ATOMIC THEORY 2 **b** : a group of such particles constituting the smallest quantity of a radical ⟨an ~ of ammonium⟩ **c** : MOLECULE — used esp. in earlier literature **d** : a quantity proportional to the atomic weight : the atomic weight in grams : GRAM ATOM **4** : the atom considered as a source of vast potential destructive or constructive energy ⟨attempts to use the ~ in peacetime projects⟩; *esp* : the atom as the core nucleus of the fission bomb ⟨trying to defend our cities against the ~⟩

at·om·ate \-,māt, -,mət\ *adj, bot* : sprinkled with small particles

atom beam *or* **atomic beam** *n* : a beam of molecular rays composed of the monatomic molecules of a vaporized metal

atom bomb *or* **atomic bomb** *n* **1** : a bomb whose violent explosive power is due to the sudden release of atomic energy resulting from the splitting of nuclei of a heavy chemical element (as plutonium or uranium) by neutrons in a very rapid chain reaction — called also *fission bomb;* contrasted with *fusion bomb* **2** : any bomb whose explosive power is due to the release of atomic energy

atom-bomb \ˈ==,=\ *vt* : to bomb with an atom bomb **~** *vi* : to drop an atom bomb

atomic \əˈtämik, -ēk *also* aˈ-\ *also* **atomical** \-mə̇kəl, -ēk-\ *adj* **1** : of, relating to, or concerned with atoms **2** : marked by acceptance of the theory of atomism **3** : MINUTE : divided into minute particles **4** : being ultimate, logically simple, unanalyzable, or noncompound either actually or taken as such within a given universe of discourse ⟨"this is red" may be considered an ~ proposition⟩; *specif* : without sentential connectives and variables — compare MONADIC **5** *of a chemical element* : in the state of separate atoms : not combined with itself or with other elements ⟨~ hydrogen⟩ **6** : of, relating to, or utilizing changes in the nucleus of an atom: **a** : utilizing atomic energy ⟨~ power⟩ ⟨~ weapons⟩ **b** : utilizing or resulting from an atom bomb ⟨~ armaments⟩ ⟨~ warfare⟩ ⟨an ~ explosion⟩ — **atom·i·cal·ly** \-mə̇k(ə)lē, -ēk-, -li\ *adv*

atomic clock *n* : a precision clock that depends for its operation on an electrical oscillator (as a quartz crystal) regulated by the natural vibration frequencies of an atomic system (as a beam of cesium atoms or of ammonia molecules)

atomic cocktail *n* : a radioactive substance (as sodium iodide) administered orally in water to patients with cancer

atomic constant *n* : any one of certain fundamental constants (as the electronic charge *e*, the electronic mass *m*, and the Planck constant *h*) relating to all atoms

atomic energy *n* : energy that can be liberated by changes in the nucleus of an atom (as by fission of a heavy nucleus or fusion of light nuclei into heavier ones with accompanying loss of mass)

atomic furnace *n* : REACTOR

atomic heat *n* : the thermal capacity per gram atom of any element, being the specific heat in calories per degree per gram multiplied by the atomic weight — compare DULONG AND PETIT'S LAW, MOLECULAR HEAT

atomic hydrogen welding *n* : arc welding that utilizes an alternating-current arc between two metal electrodes to dissociate hydrogen from a surrounding stream so that when the hydrogen atoms recombine into molecules at the surface of the part being welded they supply to the surface for fusion the heat that was absorbed in the arc during dissociation

at·o·mic·i·ty \,adəˈmisəd·ē, ,atə-, -ətē, -i\ *n* -ES [ISV *atomic* + *-ity*] **1 a** : VALENCE **b** : the number of atoms in the molecule of an element **c** : the number of replaceable atoms or groups in the molecule of a compound **2** : the state of consisting of atoms **3** *philos* : the nature, character, or property of being atomic

atomic mass *n* : the mass of any species of atom usu. expressed in atomic mass units

atomic mass unit *n* : a unit of mass for expressing masses of atoms, molecules, or nuclear particles equal to ¹⁄₁₂ of the atomic mass of the most abundant carbon isotope, $_6C^{12}$, which is about 1.66043×10^{-27} kilogram or in terms of equivalent energy to about 9.31478×10^8 electron volts — called also *mass unit*

atomic number *n* : a number characteristic of an element and taken to represent the positive charge on the nucleus of an atom of the element, being equal to the number of protons in the nucleus and in a neutral atom to the number of electrons outside the nucleus, an atomic number as determined experimentally by X-ray spectra being assigned to each element and determining its place in the periodic table and its properties except those depending on atomic weight — symbol *Z;* abbr. *at. no.;* see ELEMENT table; ISOTOPE, PERIODIC TABLE

atomic pile *n* : REACTOR

atom·ics \əˈtämiks, -ēks *also* aˈ-\ *n pl but sing in constr* : the science of atoms esp. as applied in the development and utilization of atomic energy for bombs or power

atomic spectrum *n* : a spectrum of radiation due to electron transitions within atoms and consisting mainly of series of spectrum lines characteristic of the element

atomic theory *n* **1** : ATOMISM 1 **2** *also* **atomic hypothesis** : a theory of the nature of matter: all material substances are composed of minute particles or atoms of a comparatively small number of kinds, all the atoms of the same kind being uniform in size, weight, and other properties **3** : any of several theories of the structure of the atom, most modern ones, based on experimentation and theoretical considerations, holding that the atom is composed essentially of a small positively charged comparatively heavy nucleus surrounded by a comparatively large arrangement of electrons — compare THOMSON'S HYPOTHESIS, RUTHERFORD ATOM, LEWIS-LANGMUIR THEORY, BOHR THEORY, SCHRÖDINGER ATOM

atomic volume *n* : the quotient obtained by dividing the atomic weight of an element by its specific gravity

atomic weight *n* : the average relative weight of an element as it occurs in nature referred to some element taken as a standard, hydrogen sometimes being assigned an atomic weight of 1 but oxygen with an atomic weight of 16 or carbon with an atomic weight of 12 usu. being taken as a basis — abbr. *at. wt.;* see ELEMENT table, PERIODIC TABLE; compare ATOMIC MASS, ISOTOPE

at·om·ism \ˈadə,mizəm, ˈatə-\ *n* -S **1** : a doctrine according to which either the physical universe or the physical and mental universe is composed of simple, indivisible, and minute particles or atoms: as **a** : the theory formulated in pre-Socratic times by Leucippus and Democritus who taught that all phenomena are to be explained by the incessant movement of atoms differing only in shape, order, and position **b** : one of the various modern philosophical theories treating atoms as composed either of sense elements or as matter of which the mind is made up — compare NEUTRAL MONISM, PANPSYCHISM, PHENOMENALISM **2 a** : ATOMIC THEORY 3 **b** : ATOMICITY **3** : the psychological doctrine that perceptions, thoughts, and all mental processes are built up by the combination of simple elements **4 a** : division of society into individual units or groups ⟨the caste ~ of India⟩ **b** : a theory or doctrine holding that the individual is the only objective unit of analysis **c** : a tendency toward individualism; *esp* : mutually opposed or antagonistic action of the members of a group or society

at·om·ist \-məst\ *n* -S : an adherent of atomism

at·om·is·tic \,adəˈmistik, ,atə-, -ēk\ *also* **at·om·is·ti·cal** \-tə̇kəl, -ēk-\ *adj* **1** : of or relating to atoms **2 a** : relating to, based on, or characterized by atomism **b** : viewing the content of consciousness or the succession of ideas or mental experiences as the primary concern of psychology (as among structuralists and existentialists) rather than the integrated conscious self (as among holists and personalists) **3** : characterized by a structure made up of sharply distinct and independent individuals or units ⟨an ~ society⟩ ⟨an ~ economy⟩ : tending toward atomism or individualism ⟨~ social structure⟩ — **at·om·is·ti·cal·ly** \-tə̇k(ə)lē, -ēk-, -li\ *adv*

at·om·is·tics \,==ˈmistiks, -ēks\ *n pl but sing in constr* : a branch of science dealing with the atom : the art of applied use of atomic energy

at·om·i·za·tion \,adəmə̇ˈzāshən, ,atəm-, -,mīˈz-\ *n* -S : the act or process of atomizing

at·om·ize \ˈ==,mīz\ *vt* -ED/-ING/-S *see -ize in Explan Notes* **1** : to reduce to minute particles ⟨the TNT *atomized* the bridge⟩ **2** : to convert (a liquid or solid) to a fine spray, minute particles, or light dust ⟨*atomized* fuel oil⟩ ⟨*atomized* soft coal⟩ ⟨an *atomized* medicated powder⟩ **3 a** : to divide in atomistic multiplicity ⟨alone in an unsympathetic *atomized* society⟩ **b** : to view or treat as made up of discrete or atomistic units rather than as an organismic whole ⟨*atomizing* human behavior⟩ **4** : to subject (a place) to an atomic attack : devastate by atomic bombing **5** : to individualize or cause to lose social cohesion ⟨contacts with Europeans have *atomized* some native cultures⟩

at·om·iz·er \-zə(r)\ *n* -S **1** : one that atomizes **2** : an instrument for atomizing; *esp* : an instrument that atomizes a perfume or disinfectant

atomizer

atoms *pl of* ATOM

atom smasher *n* : ACCELERATOR 1g

¹**at·o·my** \ˈad·əmē, ˈatə-, -mi\ *n* -ES [irreg. fr. L *atomi*, pl. (taken as sing.) of *atomus* atom — more at ATOM] **1** : a tiny particle : MOTE, ATOM ⟨specks of dust, swirling *atomies*⟩ **2** : a tiny and often contemptible creature or object ⟨the army was still so far distant that it seemed a mere swarm of *atomies*⟩

²**atomy** \"\ *n* -ES [for *anatomy* (*an-* being taken as the indefinite article)] **1** : a body used in anatomy; *often* : SKELETON **2** : an extremely gaunt emaciated body : a living skeleton ⟨hunger made them waste away to *atomies*⟩

aton·a·ble *also* **atone·a·ble** \əˈtōnəbəl\ *adj* : able to be atoned for

aton·al \(ˈ)āˈtōnᵊl, (ˈ)a¦- *also* əˈ-\ *adj* [²*a-* + *tonal*] : characterized by avoidance of traditional tonality — **aton·al·ly** \-ᵊlē, -i\ *adv*

aton·al·ism \(ˈ)=ˈ=ᵊl,izəm\ *n* -S **1** : the avoidance of traditional tonality as a principle of musical composition **2** : musical composition in atonal style **3** : the theory of atonal composition

aton·al·ist \-ᵊləst\ *n* -S : one who advocates or practices atonalism — **aton·al·is·tic** \(ˈ)ā¦tōnᵊl¦istik, (ˈ)a¦-, -ēk\ *adj*

ato·nal·i·ty \¦ātō¦nalədē, ¦a-, -təˈn-, -lətē, -i\ *n* -ES : a style of composition in which the musical material is organized without reference to key or tonal center and in which the tones of the chromatic scale are used impartially

at once *adv* [ME *at ones*, fr. *at* + *ones* once] **1 a** : at the same time : SIMULTANEOUSLY ⟨the two events happened *at once*⟩ **b** : IMMEDIATELY ⟨don't delay; do your work *at once*⟩ **2** : in one and the same way, manner, degree, or condition ⟨a plan that is *at once* stupid and dangerous⟩

at one *adv* [ME *at on*, fr. *at* + *on* one] **1 a** : in a state of unity of feeling : in harmony : in a closely united friendly relationship ⟨the poet felt *at one* with nature⟩ **b** *archaic* : into peaceful agreement : into harmony — used esp. with *bring*, *make*, or *set* ⟨bringing the quarreling men *at one*⟩ **2** : of an identical or sympathetic frame of mind : of the same opinion : in a state of agreement ⟨on these points we are *at one*⟩ **3** *obs* : TOGETHER ⟨they walked along *at one*⟩

atone \əˈtōn\ *vb* -ED/-ING/-S [ME *atonen*, fr. *at on*] *vt* **1** *obs* : to bring from a state of enmity or opposition to a state of friendliness, toleration, or harmony : RECONCILE ⟨trying to ~ the two countries⟩ **2 a** *archaic* : to make reparation to : PROPITIATE, CONCILIATE ⟨they *atoned* the emperor for their lack of courtesy⟩ **b** : to make reparation or supply satisfaction for : EXPIATE — used in the passive voice with *for* ⟨the crime must be *atoned* for⟩; passive use without *for* and active use are archaic ⟨his errors were quickly *atoned*⟩ ⟨*atoning* her thoughtlessness⟩ **~** *vi* **1** *obs* : to enjoy a peaceful harmonious relationship : AGREE ⟨nations once at war now gladly ~⟩ **2** : to make amends — used with *for* ⟨colorful description ~s for the story's lack of cohesion⟩

atone·ment \-mənt\ *n* -S **1** *obs* : restoration of friendly relations : RECONCILIATION ⟨making an ~ between the king and his subjects⟩ **2** *sometimes cap* : a theological doctrine concerning the reconciliation of God and man esp. as effected by the saving and redeeming work of Jesus Christ **3** : reparation (as for an offense or injury) : SATISFACTION ⟨she accepted his self-reproach as sufficient ~ for his cruelty⟩ **4** *Christian Science* : the exemplifying of man's oneness with God

¹**aton·ic** \(ˈ)ā¦tänik, (ˈ)a¦-, əˈ-, -ēk\ *adj* [prob. fr. F *atonique*, fr. Gk *atonos* + F *-ique* -ic (fr. L *-icus*)] **1** : characterized by atony ⟨an ~ bladder⟩ **2** : uttered without accent (sense 2) ⟨an ~ word⟩ ⟨an ~ syllable⟩

²**atonic** \"\ *n* -S : a word or syllable uttered without accent or written without accent mark

ato·nic·i·ty \¦atəˈnisəd·ē, ¦at-, -tō-, -ətē, -i\ *n* -ES : lack of normal tension or tonus ⟨intestinal ~ as a cause of constipation⟩

at·o·ny \ˈatᵊnē, -ni\ *also* **ato·nia** \əˈtōnēə, āˈ-\ *n, pl* **atonies** *also* **atonias** [LL *atonia*, fr. Gk, fr. *atonos* slack, without tone (fr. *a-* ²*a-* + *tonos* tone) + *-ia* -y — more at TONE] **1** : lack of tonus or vital energy : weakness esp. of a contractile organ **2** *phonetics* : lack of stress or accent

¹**atop** \əˈ-\ *also* **atop of** *prep* [¹*a-* + *top*] : on top of ⟨standing ~ the tall building⟩ ⟨a cottage *atop of* the hill⟩

²**atop** \"\ *adv, archaic* : to or at the top

³**atop** \"\ *adj* : on or at the top — used postpositively ⟨tall trees with clusters of coconuts ~⟩

ato·pen \ˈadəpən, -,pen\ *n* -S [*atopic allergen*] : an agent inducing atopic allergy

atop·ic \(ˈ)ā¦täpik, (ˈ)a¦-, əˈ-, -ēk\ *adj* [in sense 1, fr. ²*a-* + Gk *topos* place + E *-ic;* in sense 2, fr. *atopy* + *-ic* — more at TOPIC] **1** *of an organ of the body* : not in the usual place **2** : relating to or characterized by atopy ⟨~ dermatitis⟩

at·o·pite \ˈad·ə,pīt\ *n* -S [ISV *atop-* (fr. Gk *atopos* out of the way, unusual, fr. *a-* ²*a-* + *topos* place) + *-ite;* prob. orig. formed as Sw *atopit*] : a yellow or brown variety of romeite

atopognosis \¦ā+\ *n* [NL, fr. ²*a-* + *topognosis*] : absence or loss of the power of topognosia

at·o·py \ˈad·əpē, -pi\ *n* -ES [Gk *atopia* unusualness, fr. *atopos* out of the way, unusual + *-ia* -y] **1** : clinically evident hypersensitivity in man having a basis of hereditary predisposition **2** : hypersensitivity in which reagin is formed in place of the usual precipitins or agglutinins

-a·tor \ˌād·ə(r), ¦āt̬ə(r) *sometimes* ¦ā,tȯ(ə)r *or* -,tȯ(ə)\ *n suffix* -S [ME *-atour*, fr. OF & L; OF *-atour*, *-ator*, fr. L *-ator*, fr. *-atus* -ate + *-or*] : one that does ⟨calorizator⟩ ⟨totalizator⟩

ato·rai \¦äd·ə¦rī\ *also* **ata·roi** \¦äd·ə¦rȯi\ *n, pl* **atorai** *or* **atorais** *also* **ataroi** *or* **ataròis** *usu cap* [Sp & Pg, of AmerInd origin] **1 a** : an Arawakan people of the headwaters of the Essequibo river in British Guiana **b** : a member of such people **2** : the language of the Atorai people

-a·to·ry \ə,tōrē, -tȯr-, -ri; *esp Brit* ətəri *or* ə·tri *or sometimes when an unstressed syllable precedes* ¦ātəri *or* ¦ā·tri\ *adj suffix* [ME, fr. L *-atorius*, fr. *-atus* -ate + *-orius* -ory] : of, belonging to, or connected with ⟨perspir*atory*⟩ : serving or tending to ⟨amend*atory*⟩

atos *pl of* ATO

atour \əˈtōr\ *adv or prep* [ME (northern dial.), fr. ¹*at* + (northern dial.) *our*, alter. of *over*] *Scot* : OVER

atox·yl \əˈtäksəl, āˈ-, -ēl\ *n* -S [ISV ²*a-* + *toxic* + *-yl;* orig. formed in G] : a white crystalline compound $C_6H_7AsNNaO_3.4H_2O$ formerly used in the treatment of syphilis and sleeping sickness, its use frequently causing blindness : the monosodium salt of *para*-arsanilic acid

ATP *abbr* adenosine triphosphate

at·ra·bi·lar·i·ous \ˌa·trəbə̇¦la(a)rēəs\ *adj* [NL *atrabilarius*, fr. L *atra bilis* black bile (fr. *atra* — fem. of *ater* black — + *bilis* bile) + *-arius* -ary — more at BILE] *archaic* : ATRABILIOUS

at·ra·bil·iar \-¦bilēə(r), -lyə(r)\ *adj* [NL *atrabiliarius*] : ATRABILIOUS

at·ra·bil·i·ous \-¦bilyəs, -lēəs\ *adj* [L *atra bilis* + E *-ous*] **1** : given to or marked by melancholy : GLOOMY ⟨an ~ outlook on life⟩ **2** : ILL-NATURED, PEEVISH ⟨an ~ scowl⟩

atracheate \(ˈ)ā+¦-\ *adj* [²*a-* + *tracheate*] : without tracheae

at·rac·tas·pis \ˌa·trakˈtaspə̇s\ *n, cap* [NL, fr. Gk *atraktos* spindle, arrow + L *aspis* asp — more at TORTURE, ASP] : a genus of slender African burrowing oviparous vipers having large head shields like harmless snakes of the region but provided with long poison fangs

atrag·e·ne \əˈtrajə,nē\ *n* [NL, modif. of Gk *athragenē* traveler's-joy] **1** *cap* : a small genus of perennial vines (family Ranunculaceae) with small spatulate petals **2** -S : a plant of the genus *Atragene*

at·ra·ment \ˈa·trəmənt\ *n* -S [ME, fr. L *atramentum*, fr. (assumed) L *atrare* to make black (fr. L *atr-*, *ater* black) + L *-mentum* -ment — more at ATROCIOUS] **1** *obs* : INK ⟨writing with ~⟩ **2** : a very dark substance — usu. used of liquids ⟨a puff of ~ emitted by the octopus⟩

at·ra·men·tous \,==ˈmentəs\ *adj* : black as ink : INKY

atraumatic \¦ā+,=¦==\ *adj* [²*a-* + *traumatic*] *med* : specially designed or planned to minimize injurious effects ⟨~ suture⟩

atraumatically \¦ā+,=¦==(=)=\ *adv* : in a way that is marked by the use of atraumatic methods or instruments ⟨surgery performed as ~ as possible⟩

¹**atrem·a·ta** \əˈtremədə, -trē-, āˈ-\ *n pl, cap* [NL, fr. ²*a-* + *-tremata*] : an order of inarticulate Brachiopoda having the peduncle emerging freely from between the valves

²**atremata** \"\ [NL, fr. ²*a-* + *-tremata*] *syn of* LARVACEA

atrem·ate \əˈtremət\ *n* -S [NL ¹*Atremata*] : a brachiopod of the order Atremata

atrem·a·tous \əˈtremədəs, (ˈ)ā¦-\ *adj* [NL ¹*Atremata* + E *-ous*] : of or belonging to the Atremata

atrem·ble \əˈt-\ *adj* [¹*a-* + *tremble* (v.)] : TREMBLING, QUIVERING — usu. used postpositively or predicatively ⟨~ like an aspen leaf —Seyril Schochen⟩

atre·sia \əˈtrēzh(ē)ə\ *n* -S [NL, fr. ²*a-* + *-tresia*] **1** *med* : absence or closure of a natural passage of the body : IMPERFORATION ⟨~ of the small intestine⟩ **2** *med* : involution of a part (as of an ovarian follicle not destined to produce a functional ovum)

atre·sic \-zik, -sik\ *adj* [NL *atresia* + E *-ic*] : ATRETIC

atretic \-ˈtred·ik\ *adj* [NL *atresia* + E *-etic*] : of, relating to, or marked by atresia

atri- *or* **atrio-** *comb form* [NL *atrium*, fr. L] **1** : atrium (sense 3, 4) ⟨*atrial*⟩ ⟨*atrio*pore⟩ **2** : atrial and ⟨*atrio*coelomic⟩ ⟨*atrio*ventricular⟩

atria *pl of* ATRIUM

atri·al \ˈā·trēəl\ *adj* [*atrium* + *-al*] : of or relating to an atrium — often used in combination ⟨sino*atrial*⟩

atrich·ia \ā¦trikēə, əˈ-\ *n* -S [NL, fr. ²*a-* + *-trichia*] : congenital or acquired baldness : ALOPECIA

atrich·ic \-kik\ *adj* [Gk *atrichos* + E *-ic*] : HAIRLESS

atrichosis \,ā,trə̇ˈkōsə̇s\ *n, pl* **atrichoses** \-ō,sēz\ [NL, fr. Gk *atrichos* hairless + NL *-osis*] : ATRICHIA

at·ri·chous \ˈa·trəkəs, (ˈ)ā¦trik-\ *adj* [Gk *atrichos* hairless, fr. *a-* ²*a-* + *trich-*, *thrix* hair — more at TRICH-] : having no flagellum

atrio \ˈä·trē,ō\ *n* -S [It, fr. L *atrium*] : the valley between two cones of a volcano

atri·o·pore \ˈā·trēə,pō(ə)r\ *n* -S [*atri-* + *-pore*] *zool* : the opening of an atrium : an atrial pore (as in amphioxus)

atri·o·ventricular \¦ā·trē(,)ō+,=¦===\ *adj* [*atri-* + *ventricular*] **1** : of, relating to, or between an atrium and ventricle ⟨an ~ valve⟩ **2** : of, involving, or being the atrioventricular node

atrioventricular bundle *n* : a slender bundle of modified cardiac muscle that passes from the atrioventricular node in the right atrium to the right and left ventricles by way of the septum and that conducts the wave of excitation from the right atrium to the ventricles, thus maintaining the normal sequence of the heartbeat — see PURKINJE'S NETWORK

atrioventricular node *n* : a small mass of tissue lying in the wall of the right auricle adjacent to the septum between the auricles, being structurally and functionally related to the sinoatrial node, passing impulses received from the latter by way of the atrioventricular bundles, and in certain pathological states replacing the sinoatrial node as pacemaker of the heart

atrip \əˈtrip\ *adj* [¹*a-* + *trip* (v.)] **1** : hove just clear of the ground — used of an anchor **2** : sheeted home, hoisted taut up, and ready for trimming — used of sails **3** : hoisted up and ready to be swayed across — used of light yards **4** : with the fid out and ready for lowering — used of upper masts

at·ri·plex \ˈa·trə,pleks\ *n, cap* [NL, fr. L, orache — more at ORACHE] : a widely distributed genus of herbs or subshrubs (family Chenopodiaceae) with small diclinous flowers and utricular fruit enclosed in two bracts — see ORACHE

atri·um \ˈā·trēəm *also esp in senses 1 & 2* ˈä·-\ *n, pl* **atria** \-ēə\ [L] **1** : the central hall of a Roman house **2 a** : the open court leading to a basilica or dwelling having a covered way on three or (as in a cloister) on all four sides **b** : a square hall from which other rooms open and which is used as a sitting room in a modern house **3** [NL, fr. L] : CAVITY, CHAMBER: as **a** : the main chamber of either auricle of the heart as distinct from the auricular appendix **b** : the whole auricle **c** : the main part of the tympanic cavity **4** [NL, fr. L] : ENTRANCE, PASSAGE : an external chamber in tunicates and lancelets that receives water from the gills : a vestibule in various insects from which one or more tracheae extend into the body

atro- *comb form* [L *atr-*, *ater* black + E *-o-*] : black and ⟨*atro*castaneous⟩

at·ro·cha \ˈa·trəkə\ *n* -S [NL, fr. ²*a-* + *-trocha* (fr. Gk *trochos* wheel) — more at -TROCH] : a chaetopod larva lacking the preoral circle of cilia and having most of the body uniformly ciliated — **at·ro·chal** \-kəl\ *adj*

atro·cious \əˈtrōshəs\ *adj* [L *atroc-*, *atrox* gloomy, cruel, atrocious (fr. *atr-*, *ater* black + *-oc-*, *-ox* looking, appearing — akin to L *oculus* eye) + E *-ious;* akin to Arm *airem* I set on fire, Av *ātar-* fire, and perh. to W *odyn* kiln — more at EYE] **1** : marked by or given to extreme wickedness ⟨leading an ~ life⟩ ⟨an ~ criminal⟩ **2 a** : marked by or given to extreme brutality or cruelty : grossly inhumane ⟨his ~ treatment in prison —Hugh Byas⟩ ⟨an ~ dictatorship⟩ **b** : OUTRAGEOUS : violating the bounds of common decency : UNCIVILIZED, BARBARIC ⟨the ~ exploitation of human beings in mines and mills —M.R.Cohen⟩ **3 a** : extremely painful : marked by intense distress : GRIEVOUS ⟨he had known long and ~ sufferings from wounds in the war —Rebecca West⟩ **b** : marked by extreme violence : savagely fierce : MURDEROUS ⟨~ assault and battery⟩ **4** : of such a kind as to fill with fright or dismay : APPALLING, TERRIBLE ⟨the ~ truth blazed in the night like lightning —Elinor Wylie⟩ ⟨an ~ accident⟩ **5 a** : utterly revolting : ABOMINABLE ⟨~ weather⟩ ⟨~ working conditions⟩ **b** : markedly inferior in quality ⟨an ~ speller⟩ ⟨~ manners⟩

syn see OUTRAGEOUS

atro·cious·ly *adv* : in an atrocious manner

atro·cious·ness *n* -ES : ATROCITY

atroc·i·ty \əˈträsəd·ē, -ətē, -i, *rap. also* -stē, -i\ *n* -ES [MF *atrocité*, fr. L *atrocitat-*, *atrocitas*, fr. *atroc-*, *atrox* + *-itat-*, *-itas* -ity] **1 a** : the quality or state of being atrocious ⟨the tyrant's ~ in dealing with the prisoners⟩ **b** : something that is atrocious: as (1) : an execrable situation or circumstance ⟨having to put up with the *atrocities* of living in a narrow-minded society⟩ (2) : a gross departure from social correctness or good taste ⟨drunken guests committing one ~ after another⟩ ⟨a hat that was an utter ~⟩ **2** : a savagely brutal or cruel deed; *esp* : an act violating the code of humane restrictions morally imposed on belligerents ⟨accused of war *atrocities*⟩

à trois \äˈtrwä, *F* åtrwå\ *adj* [F] : designed for or shared among three individuals — usu. used postpositively ⟨a pleasant little dinner *à trois*⟩ ⟨a discussion *à trois*⟩

at·ro·pa \ˈa·trəpə\ *n, cap* [NL, fr. Gk *Atropos*, that one of the three mythological Fates who severs the thread of life] : a genus of Eurasian and African herbs (family Solanaceae) with leaves entire, calyx, and corolla, the fruit being a berry subtended by the enlarged calyx lobes — see BELLADONNA 1

at·ro·pa·ceous \¦a·trə¦pāshəs\ *adj* [NL *Atropa* + E *-aceous*] : of or relating to the genus *Atropa*

atro·phia \əˈtrōfēə\ *n* -S [LL] : ATROPHY

atroph·ic \əˈträfik, (ˈ)a¦t-, -trō-, -ēk\ *adj* : relating to or characterized by atrophy

atrophic arthritis *n* : RHEUMATOID ARTHRITIS

atrophied *adj* : affected with atrophy : SHRUNKEN, WASTED, EMACIATED

¹**at·ro·phy** \ˈa·trəfē, -fi\ *n* -ES [LL *atrophia*, fr. Gk, fr. *atrophos* ill fed (fr. *a-* ²*a-* + *trophos* feeder, fr. *trephein* to nourish, curdle) + *-ia* -y; akin to Gk *thremma* nursling, *trophis* fat, *thrombos* clot, curd, and perh. to Skt *drapsa* drop] **1** : decrease in size of a part or tissue after full development has been attained : a wasting away of tissue (as from disuse, old age, injury, or disease) ⟨senile ~⟩ ⟨muscular ~⟩ **2** : a stoppage of development of a part or organ incidental to the normal development or life of an animal or plant often followed by diminution in size or of complete disappearance of the part or organ **3** : a wasting away or progressive decline : DEGENERATION ⟨the ~ of freedom⟩ ⟨the ~ of an empire⟩

²**atrophy** \"\ *vb* -ED/-ING/-ES *vi* : to undergo atrophy ⟨the inactive muscles *atrophied*⟩ **~** *vt* : to cause to undergo atrophy ⟨disuse *atrophied* the arm⟩

atro·pia \ə'trōpēə\ *n* -s [NL, fr. *Atropa* + *-ia*] : ATROPINE

atrop·i·dae \ə'träpə,dē\ *n pl, cap* [NL, fr. *Atropos*, type genus (fr. Gk *Atropos*) + *-idae*; fr. the belief that the ticking sound made by some species of book lice forebodes a death] : a widely distributed family of wingless insects (order Corrodentia) that include most book lice and that feed on organic debris and often damage processed foods, book bindings, herbarium specimens, and similar stored products

at·ro·pine \'a·trə,pēn, -,pən\ *n* -s [G *atropin*, fr. NL *Atropa* (genus name of *Atropa belladonna*) + G *-in* -ine] : a poisonous white crystalline alkaloid $C_{17}H_{23}NO_3$ extracted from the belladonna and other plants of the family Solanaceae and used esp. in the form of its sulfate to relieve spasms, to diminish secretions, to relieve pain, and to dilate the pupil of the eye; racemic hyoscyamine

at·ro·pin·ize \-pə,nīz\ *vt* -ED/-ING/-S : to bring under the influence of atropine

at·ro·pous \'a·trəpəs\ *adj* [Gk *atropos* not to be turned, fr. *a-* [2]*a* + *-tropos* -trope] *bot* : not inverted : ORTHOTROPOUS

at·ro·scine \-,sēn,-,sən\ *n* -s [ISV *atro-* (fr. NL *Atropa*) + hyo*scine*] : racemic scopolamine

atry \ə'trī\ *adj* [[1]*a-* + *try* ("to lie to")] : kept bow on to the sea by a balance of sails

atry·pa \ə'trīpə\ *n, cap* [NL, fr. [2]*a-* + Gk *trypa* hole — more at TRYPA] : a genus of extinct Silurian and Devonian plicate-shelled or costate-shelled brachiopods having the plates of the brachidium produced into spirally rolled processes with the apices usu. directed toward the plane of symmetry of the valve

[1]**atry·poid** \-,pȯid\ *adj* [NL *Atrypa* + E *-oid*] : belonging to or characteristic of the genus *Atrypa*

[2]**atrypoid** \"\ *n* -s : a brachiopod of the genus *Atrypa* — see BRACHIOPOD illustration

ats *pl of* [4]AT

ats *abbr* at the suit of

atsara *var of* ACHARA

at·si·na \at'sēnə\ *n, pl* **atsina** *or* **atsinas** *usu cap* [Blackfoot, lit., good people] **1 a** : an Indian people in Montana and southern Saskatchewan that are part of the Arapaho **b** : a member of such people **2** : a dialect of Arapaho

at·su·ge·wi \,atsü'gäwē\ *n, pl* **atsugewi** *or* **atsugewis** *usu cap* [Atsugewi] **1 a** : an Indian people of the Pit river valley in northern California **b** : a member of such people **2** : a Shastan language of the Atsugewi people

att \'ät\ *n* -s [Siamese] **1** : an old subsidiary coin of Siam worth 1/64 of a tical issued before 1868 in pewter and after that up to 1906 in copper **2** : a unit of value corresponding to the att ⟨2-*att* postage stamp⟩ ⟨½-*att* coin⟩

att *abbr* **1** attaché **2** attached **3** attention **4** *often cap* attorney

[1]**at·ta** \'ä,tä\ *n* -s [Hindi *āṭā*] *India* : unsorted wheat flour or meal

[2]**at·ta** \'ad·ə\ *n, cap* [NL] : a New World genus of typical leaf-cutting chiefly tropical ants often very destructive to crops

at·ta·boy \'ad·ə,bȯi, 'atə-, ,==ˈ=\ *interj* [alter. of *that's the boy*] — used to express encouragement, approval, or admiration

attacapa *usu cap, var of* ATAKAPA

at·tac·ca \ə'täkə, -akə\ *v imper* [It, lit., attack, imper. sing. of *attaccare* to attack — more at ATTACK] : attack at once — used as a direction in music at the end of a movement to begin the next without pause

at·tac·co \ə'tä(,)kō, -ta-\ *n* -s [It, lit., attachment, connection, fr. *attaccare* to attach, attack] : a motive or short phrase in music presented in contrapuntal imitation and introduced in the course of a composition as development or as the feature of a fugue exposition

at·tach \ə'tach\ *vb* -ED/-ING/-ES [ME *attachen*, fr. MF *attacher*, fr. OF *atachier*, alter. (influenced by *a* to, fr. L *ad*) of *estachier*, fr. *estache* stake, of Gmc origin; akin to OE *staca* stake — more at AT, STAKE] *vt* **1** : to take by legal authority: **a** : to arrest by writ and bring before a court (as to answer for a debt or a contempt) — now applied chiefly to a taking of the person by a civil process **b** : to seize or take (property) by virtue of a writ or precept to hold the same to satisfy a judgment that may be rendered in the suit — compare ATTACHMENT 1 **2** *obs* **a** : INDICT, ACCUSE ⟨~ a person of murder⟩ **b** : to lay hold of : SEIZE ⟨be ~*ed* by an illness⟩ ⟨~ the food hungrily⟩ **3 a** : CONNECT : place so as to belong : APPOINT ⟨consider to what branch of the law to ~ himself⟩ **b** : to fasten (itself) — used reflexively ⟨a figure of universal fame, of a kind that scarcely ~*es* itself to anyone in this age —Osbert Sitwell⟩ **c** : to order (an individual or unit in the military) to serve more or less temporarily with another organization **d** : to place (an individual or unit in the military) under the control of another organization for specific purposes (as for rations, quarters, or training) — distinguished from *assign* **4** : to bind by personal ties (as of affection or sympathy) : win to affection or devotion — used with *to* ⟨she undertakes to ~ him to her by strong ties: a child, or marriage —H.M. Parshley⟩ **5** : make fast or join (as by string or glue) : BIND, FASTEN, TIE ⟨~ price tags on each article⟩ **6** : to connect by attribution : ASCRIBE — used with *to* ⟨the fetish worshiper ~*es* magical potency to stones —M.R.Cohen⟩ **7** : to associate as a property or adjunct ⟨to this treasure a curse is ~*ed* —Bayard Taylor⟩ ~ *vi* **1** : to fix or fasten itself : ADHERE ⟨the suspicion that he is guilty ~*es* upon his strange actions⟩ ⟨all the advantages that ~ to the office⟩ **2** : to come into legal operation : VEST ⟨an ancient law ~*ed* in this case⟩ **syn** see FASTEN

at·tach·a·ble \-əbəl\ *adj* **1** : liable to arrest or legal seizure ⟨goods that are ~ for debt⟩ **2 a** : capable of being fastened or added to something ⟨a handle ~ by two bolts⟩ **b** : capable of being attributed as an adjunct ⟨complete cooperativeness was not ~ to his actions⟩

at·ta·ché \,ad·ə'shā, ,atə'shā, ,a,ta'shā *also* ə,ta'shā *sometimes* ad·,a'shā, *Brit usu & US sometimes* ə'ta(,)shā *or* ə't-\ *n* -s [F, past part. of *attacher* to attach] : one attached to another person or to a group; *specif* : an expert (as in science or aviation) on duty with the diplomatic representative of his country at a foreign capital ⟨a military ~⟩ — see COMMERCIAL ATTACHÉ

at·ta·ché case \ə'tashē-, -aash-,-aish-, -(,)shā, *less often one of the other pronunciations at* ATTACHÉ, *sometimes* ə'tachə-\ *n* **1** : a traveling case like a suitcase but smaller **2** : BRIEFCASE

attaché case

attached *adj* **1** : permanently fixed when adult ⟨an ~ barnacle⟩ ⟨an ~ oyster⟩ **2** *archit* : ENGAGED

at·tach·ment \ə'tachmənt\ *n* -s [ME *attachement*, fr. MF, fr. OF *atachement*, fr. *atachier* to attach + *-ment* — more at ATTACH] **1 a** : a seizure or taking into custody (of persons or property) by virtue of a legal process **b** : the writ or precept commanding such seizure — compare GARNISHMENT **2 a** : the state of being attached (as by affection, sympathy, or self-interest) : FIDELITY ⟨~ to a friend⟩ ⟨~ to a cause⟩ **b** : a feeling (as affection) that binds a person : REGARD ⟨sense a growing ~ for a person⟩ **3** : a device that is attached (as to a machine) esp. for doing special work ⟨~*s* for a vacuum cleaner⟩ **4** : the physical connection by which one thing is attached to another : FASTENING ⟨cut the ~*s* of a muscle to a bone⟩ **5** : an attaching by physical connection ⟨the ~ of a recording device to a telephone⟩

syn AFFECTION, LOVE: ATTACHMENT implies strong liking, devotion, or loyalty ⟨the *attachment* which they all so obviously felt for him —W.S.Maugham⟩ ⟨are not to lose their *attachment* to the land —*Farmer's Weekly (So. Africa)*⟩ ⟨strong party *attachments*⟩ ⟨an *attachment* to a lost cause⟩ AFFECTION, usu. having as its object a sentient thing, implies warmth and tenderness of sentiment, usu. settled and regulated ⟨a vast amount of quiet, restrained *affection*, of mutual confidence and respect, even of tenderness —Arnold Bennett⟩ ⟨*affection* for a dog⟩ ⟨widespread American *affection* for France and respect for her very special culture —E.B.George⟩ ⟨heightened *affection* for the memory of the dead —W.D.Howells⟩ LOVE implies a feeling stronger and more intense than AFFECTION, often connoting passion ⟨a *love* of parent for child⟩ ⟨a *love* of man for woman⟩ ⟨a *love* of God⟩ ⟨a *love* of painting⟩

attachment disk *n* : the holdfast of an alga

attachment plug *n* : a plug consisting usu. of a screw-shell body and cap and connecting a flexible conductor to a lamp holder or receptacle

[1]**at·tack** \ə'tak, *chiefly substand* -kt\ *vb* **attacked** \-kt, *chiefly substand* -ktəd\ **attacked**; **attacking**; **attacks** [MF *attaquer*, fr. OIt *attaccare* to attach, attack, alter. (influenced by *a* to, fr. L *ad*) of (assumed) OIt *estaccare* to attach, fr. (assumed) OIt *stacca* stake, of Gmc origin; akin to OE *staca* stake — more at AT, STAKE] *vt* **1 a** : to set upon or work against forcefully ⟨~ a man without warning⟩ ⟨if we study any modern river we note how determinedly it ~*s* its banks —W.E.Swinton⟩ : assail esp. with force and weapons ⟨~ the enemy positions⟩ : ASSAULT **b** : to set upon forcibly with sexual intent : subject to indecent assault : RAPE, RAVISH **2** : to threaten (a piece in chess) with immediate capture ⟨the rook is ~*ing* the queen⟩ **3** : to assail with unfriendly or bitter words : begin a controversy with : attempt to overthrow or bring into disrepute (as by criticism or satire) **4** : to begin to affect : seize upon ⟨the kidneys are ~*ed* by an embryonic tumor —H.R.Litchfield & L.H.Dembo⟩ ⟨~*ed* by a fever⟩ **5 a** : to begin to injure, damage, or eat ⟨worms ~*ed* the cabbage plants⟩ **b** : to act upon destructively : DECOMPOSE ⟨the acid ~*s* the metal cup⟩ **6** : to set to work upon (as a problem or an investigation) esp. vigorously : TACKLE ⟨a plan which ~*s* the four basic problems —*Collier's Yr. Bk.*⟩ ~ *vi* : to make an attack ⟨waiting for the enemy to ~⟩ ⟨they ~*ed* furiously in an effort to score the tying goal⟩

syn ATTACK, ASSAIL, ASSAULT, BOMBARD, STORM mean to make a more or less violent onslaught upon, literally or figuratively. ATTACK means to move against with more or less violent intent, implying aggression in any sense and the initiative in the onset ⟨the infantry and air force *attacked* the town in coordinated waves⟩ ⟨he and other union leaders were physically *attacked* —*Current Biog.*⟩ ⟨erosion *attacked* the range and began its relentless work of reducing the land to sea level once more —*Amer. Guide Series: N.Y.*⟩ ASSAIL suggests repeated blows in an attack, as with or as if with shells or sword thrusts ⟨the expedition . . . *assailed* by a fleet of fifty-four war canoes —Tom Marvel⟩ ⟨the rain *assailed* him and thorns tore him —H.G.Wells⟩ ⟨*assailed* by doubts⟩ ASSAULT stresses attack at close quarters, the use of brute strength, suddenness, and violence ⟨pilots hammered a rail marshaling yard, bombing twenty boxcars, while other aircraft *assaulted* supply buildings —*N.Y.Times*⟩ ⟨adult ears are not to be *assaulted* by the sudden screams of childish exuberance —Richard Joseph⟩ BOMBARD means to assail with bombs, suggesting by extension an unremitting importuning or pestering with a series of similar things ⟨naval artillery *bombarded* the shore fortifications⟩ ⟨magazine editors are *bombarded* with manuscripts —L.D.Robin⟩ ⟨he and his office associates were *bombarded* with requests for box seats —*New Yorker*⟩ STORM stresses a violence, rush, and effectiveness of assault that usu. and summarily clears all opposition out of the way ⟨the waves of light tanks *stormed* the infantry positions —S.L.A.Marshall⟩ ⟨a group of soldiers in the International Brigade *stormed* the jail —*Current Biog.*⟩

[2]**attack** \"\ *n* -s **1** : the act of falling on with force or violence : ONSET, ASSAULT, OFFENSE ⟨retreat before the infantry ~⟩ — opposed to *defense* **2 a** : an offensive or antagonistic movement or action of any kind ⟨television was used in many parts of the country as an instrument of ~, rather than of argument —Gilbert Seldes⟩ ⟨the team launched an ~ that carried deep into enemy territory⟩ **b** : RAPE, INDECENT ASSAULT **3 a** : an assault with unfriendly or bitter words ⟨her vocal ~*s* are less savage than they once were —*Newsweek*⟩ **b** : the beginning of corrosive, decomposing, or destructive action by a chemical agent **4 a** : the setting to work upon some undertaking : beginning or method of procedure ⟨the solution in each problem calls for a different ~⟩ **b** : an often extraordinary Salvationist effort to make converts **5** : the act or manner of beginning a musical tone or phrase: as **a** : unanimity of entrance of several performers ⟨a ragged ~⟩ **b** : suddenness or gradualness of beginning a tone **c** : the initial precision of pitch and quality esp. in singing **6** : the initiation or onset of the articulation of a speech sound **7** : a series of aggressive moves in chess usu. for positional advantage; *also* : a threat to capture an opponent's man **8** : cricket bowling (esp. as contrasted with batting); *also* : the bowlers of a cricket team **9** : an effort to hit in fencing — used also as a word of command **10** : any of three lacrosse positions or players between out home and center — called respectively in their order from the opponents' goal *first attack*, *second attack*, *third attack* **11** : the setting in or the duration of a depressive or destructive process: as **a** : an access of disease : fit of sickness ⟨an ~ of bronchitis⟩ **b** : a period of being strongly affected by some particular desire or mood ⟨an ~ of melancholy⟩

[3]**attack** \"\ *adj* [[2]*attack*] : designed, planned, or employed for initiating, supporting, or carrying out a military attack ⟨an ~ formation⟩ ⟨an ~ bomber⟩

at·tack·a·ble \-əbəl\ *adj* : that can be attacked esp. with some prospect of success

attack cargo ship *n* : a naval ship with specially trained boat crews for landing material in an amphibious assault

attack plane *n* : a military airplane designed and armed for attacking the enemy's ground forces

attack transport *n* : a naval ship with specially trained boat crews for landing troops in an amphibious assault

at·ta·cus \'ad·əkəs\ *n* [LL, fr. Gk *attakos*] **1** -ES : an edible insect mentioned in Lev 11:22(DV) — called *bald locust* in the Authorized and Revised Standard versions **2** *cap* [NL, fr. LL] : a widely distributed genus of large chiefly tropical moths (family Saturniidae) that include the Asiatic Atlas moth

at·tain \ə'tān\ *vb* -ED/-ING/-S [ME *atteynen*, *ateignen*, fr. OF *ataign-*, stem of *ataindre*, fr. (assumed) VL *attangere*, alter. (influenced by L *tangere*) of L *attingere*, fr. *ad-* + *tangere* to touch, reach — more at TANGENT] *vt* **1** : REACH, GAIN, ACHIEVE, ACCOMPLISH ⟨difficult to ~ a realistic effect⟩ ⟨~ repose⟩ ⟨~ his goal⟩ **2** *obs* : to get at the knowledge of : ASCERTAIN ⟨~ the meaning of a statement⟩ **3** : to come into possession of : OBTAIN ⟨~ a kingdom⟩ ⟨~ preferment⟩ **4** *obs* : OVERTAKE : get at : CATCH **5** : to reach or come to by progression or motion : arrive at ⟨~ the top of the hill⟩ ⟨~ a ripe old age⟩ ~ *vi* : to come or arrive by motion, growth, or effort toward a place, object, or state : REACH ⟨to his stature we . . . may in time ~ —C.W.Eliot⟩ — usu. used with *to* or *unto* ⟨this plant ~*s* to a height of 10 feet⟩ ⟨knowledge no man has ~*ed* unto⟩ **syn** see REACH

at·tain·a·bil·i·ty \ə,tānə'biləd·ē, -ətē, -i\ *n* -ES : the quality or state of being attainable

at·tain·a·ble \ə'tānəbəl\ *adj* : capable of being attained

at·tain·a·ble·ness *n* -ES : ATTAINABILITY

at·tain·der \ə'tāndə(r)\ *n* -S [ME *attaynder*, fr. MF *ataindre* to accuse, convict, attain] **1** : the act of attainting or state of being attainted : extinction of the civil rights and capacities of a person consequent upon sentence of death or outlawry ⟨an act of ~⟩ ⟨no ~ of treason shall work corruption of blood or forfeiture except during the life of the person attainted —*U.S. Constitution*⟩ **2** *obs* **a** : dishonoring accusation : SENTENCE ⟨a criminal pursued by the ~*s* of his victims⟩ **b** : the stain of dishonor ⟨to live his life free from all ~⟩

at·tain·ment \ə'tānmənt\ *n* -S **1** : the act of attaining : the condition of being attained ⟨the ~ of her life ambition⟩ ⟨notions difficult of ~⟩ **2** : something that is attained or attained to (as a mental acquirement or social accomplishment) ⟨famous for his scientific ~*s*⟩

[1]**at·taint** \ə'tānt, a'-\ *vt* **attainted**; **attainted** *or archaic* **attaint**; **attainting**; **attaints** [ME *attaynten*, fr. MF *ataint*, past part. of *ataindre*] **1** *obs* : to prove guilty **2** *obs* : to find guilty : CONVICT — used esp. of a jury on trial for giving a false verdict **3** : to subject (a person) to the legal condition formerly resulting from a sentence of death or outlawry for treason or felony : affect by attainder **4** *obs* **a** : to affect or infect esp. with disease **b** : to taint esp. with corruption or poison **5** *archaic* : to charge with a crime or a dishonorable act : ACCUSE **6** *archaic* : SULLY **syn** see CONTAMINATE

[2]**attaint** \"\ *n* -S [MF *atainte*, fr. fem. of *ataint*] **1 a** : a legal proceeding or process formerly instituted by writ after judgment to inquire and try by a grand jury whether a trial jury has given a false verdict **b** : the convicting of the jury so tried **c** : ATTAINDER **2** *obs* : TOUCH — used specif. in tilting **3** *obs* : a stain esp. upon honor or purity : DISGRACE

at·taint·ment \-mənt\ *n* -S : ATTAINDER

attainture *n* -S **1** *obs* : ATTAINDER **2** *obs* : an imputation of disgrace : STAIN

at·ta·lea \ə'tālēə\ *n, cap* [NL, after *Attalus* I †197 B.C. king of Pergamum] : a genus of tropical American pinnate-leaved palms with ringed stems and immense leaves — see COQUILLA NUT, PIASSAVA

at·ta·lid \'ad·əlᵊd, -,id\ *n, pl* **attalids** \-dz\ *or* **attal·i·dae** \ə'talə,dē, a'-\ *cap* [*Attalus* I †197 B.C. king of Pergamum, victor in a decisive battle with the Gauls of Asia Minor and first of his line to bear the title of king + E *-id*] : a member of a Hellenistic dynasty that ruled Pergamum from about 283 to 133 B.C.

attap *var of* ATAP

at·ta·pul·gite \,ad·ə'pəl,jīt\ *n* -S [*Attapulgus*, Ga. + E *-ite*] : a fibrous clay mineral typically $(OH_2)_4MgSi_8O_{20}(OH)_2 \cdot 4H_2O$

at·tar *also* **at·ar** \'ad·ə(r), 'atə-, 'a,tär, 'a,tȧ(r *also* 'ä|d·ə(r) *or* 'ä| *or* |tə-\ *or* **ath·ar** \'athə(r\ *or* -,thär, -,thȧ(r\ *or* **ot·tar** \'äd·ə(r), 'ätə-, 'ä,tär, 'ä,tȧ(r\ *or* **ot·to** \'äd·(,)ō, 'ä(,)tō\ *n* -S [Per *'aṭir* perfumed, fr. *'iṭr* perfume, fr. Ar] : a perfume obtained from flowers; *specif* : ATTAR OF ROSES

attar of roses : a fragrant essential oil obtained by distillation from petals esp. of damask rose and with geraniol and citronellol as its principal odorous constituents : ROSE OIL

attas *pl of* ATTA

attask *vt* -ED/-ING/-S [[1]*a-* + *task*] *obs* : to take to task : BLAME

at·tem·per \ə'tempə(r), a'-\ *vt* -ED/-ING/-S [ME *attempren*, fr. MF *atemprer*, fr. L *attemperare* to adjust, accommodate, fr. *ad-* + *temperare* to temper — more at TEMPER] **1** *obs* : REGULATE, CONTROL, ORDER ⟨as God the good governor *attempereth* —Geoffrey Chaucer⟩ **2** *archaic* **a** : SOFTEN, MITIGATE **b** : SOOTHE, APPEASE ⟨~ an angry crowd⟩ **3** *archaic* **a** : to reduce, modify, or moderate by mixture **b** : to modify the temperature of : make (as air) warmer or colder **4** *archaic* : to make suitable : ACCOMMODATE, ADAPT **5** *archaic* : to bring into harmony : ATTUNE **syn** see MODERATE

at·tem·per·a·ment \-p(ə)rəmənt\ *n* -S [fr. *attemper*, after E *temper*: *temperament*] : a mixing in proper proportion

at·tem·per·ate \-pə,rāt, *usu* -ād·+V\ *vt* -ED/-ING/-S [L *attemperatus*, past part. of *attemperare*] : ATTEMPER 3b — **at·tem·per·a·tion** \=,==ˈrāshən\ *n* -S

at·tem·per·a·tor \-ād·ə(r), -ātə-\ *n* -S : one that attempers; *specif* : a coil of pipe through which hot or cold water may be run for regulating temperature

[1]**at·tempt** \ə'tem(p)t *also* a'-\ *vb* -ED/-ING/-S [L *attemptare*, fr. *ad-* + *temptare* to touch, try — more at TEMPT] *vt* **1** : to make an effort to do, accomplish, solve, or effect ⟨~ to swim⟩ ⟨~ a problem⟩ — often used in venturous or experimental situations sometimes with implications of failure ⟨I doubted at first whether I should ~ the creation of a being like myself —Mary W.Shelley⟩ **2 a** *archaic* : to try to win over by temptations : TEMPT **b** : to try to seduce or ravish **3** *obs* **a** : to try to get or win (as by tempting) ⟨~ a woman's love⟩ **b** : to try to persuade : seek to influence (as by entreaty or reasoning) ⟨~ a friend that he stay to dinner⟩ **4** *archaic* : to try to subdue, overcome, or take by force : ATTACK, ASSAIL ~ *vi, obs* : to make an attempt — used with *on* or *upon* **syn** see TRY

[2]**attempt** \"\ *n* -S **1** : the act of attempting : ESSAY, TRIAL, ENDEAVOR, UNDERTAKING; *esp* : an unsuccessful effort **2** *archaic* : an effort to achieve something by force: as **a** : ATTACK ⟨the enemy's ~ against our lines⟩ **b** : an assault esp. upon a person's life or a woman's honor **3** *obs* : the thing attempted : AIM

at·tempt·a·ble \-əbəl\ *adj* : capable of being attempted

at·tend \ə'tend *also* a'-\ *vb* -ED/-ING/-S [ME *attenden*, fr. OF *atendre*, fr. L *attendere* to stretch, apply the mind to, fr. *ad-* + *tendere* to stretch — more at THIN] *vt* **1** *archaic* : to direct the attention to : fix the mind upon : give heed to : listen to ⟨~ the warning of the soothsayer⟩ ⟨~ my words⟩ **2** : to look after : take charge of : watch over the working of ⟨the prisoners were ~*ed* by guards⟩ **3** *archaic* **a** : to wait for (as a person or the arrival of a person) ⟨the committee ~*ed* the arrival of the president⟩ **b** : to be in store for ⟨the state that ~*s* all men after this —John Locke⟩ **4** : to go or stay with as a companion, nurse, or servant : visit professionally as a physician : accompany in order to do service : ESCORT : wait on ⟨fawning ministers who ~ the king⟩ **5** *obs* : to follow up : CONJOIN, ASSOCIATE **6** : to be present with : ACCOMPANY : be united or consequent to ⟨the immense amount of work that has ~*ed* the creation of these lists —C.C.Fries & A.A. Traver⟩ ⟨what cares must then ~ the toiling swain —John Dryden⟩ **7** : to be present at ⟨~ a meeting⟩ ~ *vi* **1** : to direct one's energies : apply oneself ⟨~ to your work⟩ ⟨~ strictly to business⟩ **2** : to apply the mind or pay attention with a view to perceiving, understanding, or complying : pay regard : HEED, LISTEN — usu. followed by *to* ⟨one is lucky to meet six or seven people who know how to ~; the rest have fidgety ears —J.M.Barzun⟩ ⟨~ to the voice of my supplications —Ps 86: 6(AV)⟩ **3** : to be present or near at hand in pursuance of duty ⟨the good lord was dismissed, and has not ~*ed* in the drawing room since —Mary W. Montagu⟩ : be ready for service : wait or be in waiting — often used with *on* or *upon* ⟨ministers who ~ upon the king⟩ **4** *obs* : WAIT, STAY, DELAY — often used with *for* **5** : to direct one's care : SEE — used with *to* ⟨producers should ~ to the following important aspects of marketing —*Farmer's Weekly (So. Africa)*⟩

at·tend·ance \ə'tendən(t)s\ *n* -S [ME *attendaunce*, fr. MF *atendance*, fr. OF, fr. *atendre* to attend + *-ance*] **1** : the act or fact of attending: as **a** : the act or state of being in waiting : service esp. at court or at a hospital ⟨a physician in ~⟩ **b** : a being present : PRESENCE ⟨~ at a play⟩ **2** : the persons attending: as **a** *obs* : a body of attendants : RETINUE ⟨the king, with his ~ of court officials⟩ **b** : the persons or number of persons present (as at a public performance or a session of school) ⟨the broadcasting of plays . . . does not seem to diminish the ~*s* at original performances —Joseph Trenaman⟩

attendance area *n* : the territory served by a given public school

attendance officer *n* : one employed by a public-school system to investigate the continued absences of pupils — called also *truant officer*

attendancy *n* -ES *obs* : ATTENDANCE

[1]**at·tend·ant** \ə'tendənt\ *adj* [ME, fr. MF *atendant*, pres. part. of *atendre*] **1** : accompanying, waiting upon, or following in order to perform service ⟨the defensive responsibilities of the fleet's ~ aircraft —S.L.A.Marshall⟩ — often used with *on* or *upon* ⟨Cherub and Seraph . . . ~ on their Lord —John Milton⟩ **2** *law* : owing duty or service : DEPENDING — used with *on* or *to* ⟨the widow ~ to the heir⟩ **3** : accompanying, connected with, or immediately following as consequential : CONSEQUENT ⟨the raising of silkworms and . . . its ~ occupation, the culture of mulberry trees —Tom Marvel⟩ — often used with *on* or *upon* ⟨the disadvantages ~ upon being jealous —F.R.Leavis⟩

[2]**attendant** \"\ *n* -S **1** *law* : one owing duty or service to or depending on another **2** : one who attends or accompanies another in order to render a service (as a companion, servant, keeper, or agent) ⟨the bride's ~*s* at the wedding⟩ ⟨ward ~*s* in a hospital⟩; *esp* : an employee who waits on customers ⟨a gasoline-station ~⟩ **3** : something that accompanies as a circumstance : ACCOMPANIMENT, CONCOMITANT ⟨the love of luxury and its literary and artistic ~*s* —*Encyc. Americana*⟩ **4** : one who is present on a given occasion or at a given place ⟨~*s* at the festival⟩

attendant term *n* : a mortgage or long lease kept in force in form to protect the title of the owner of an English estate

attended *past of* ATTEND

at·tend·ee \ə,ten'dē, ,a,t-; ə'ten,dē\ *n* -S : ATTENDANT 4

[1]**attending** *pres part of* ATTEND

[2]**attending** *adj* : serving as a physician on the staff of a teaching hospital ⟨~ surgeon⟩ ⟨a large ~ staff⟩

attends *pres 3d sing of* ATTEND

at·ten·si·ty \a'ten(t)səd·ē, ə'-\ *n* -ES [attributive + *-tensity* (as in *protensity*)] : sensory clearness (as in differentiating between a sensation that is in the center of attention and one that is not)

at·ten·tat \(,)a,tän'tä, (,)a,täⁿ't-, -'tȧ\ *n, pl* **attentats** \-äz,-ȧz\ [F] : an attempt to commit a crime of violence — usu. used of an unsuccessful attempt at a political crime

attentate *n* -s [F *attentat*, fr. MF *attentat, attemptat*, fr. *attenter, attempter* to attempt (fr. L *attentare, attemptare*) + *-at* -ate — more at ATTEMPT, -ATE (office)] *obs* **:** any step wrongly innovated or attempted in a suit by an inferior judge pending an appeal or after inhibition

at·ten·tion \ə'tenchən *also* a'-; *as a command in sense 5* (ə)ˌten'shən *or* (a)ˌ-, *with prolongation of* -ten-\ *n* -s [ME *attencioun*, fr. L *attention-, attentio*, fr. *attentus* (past part. of *attendere* to attend) + *-ion-* *-io* -ion — more at ATTEND] **1 :** the act or state of attending **:** the application of the mind to any object of sense or thought ⟨the magnitude of his literary output . . . engaged his undivided ~ —H.W.H.Knott⟩ **:** CONSIDERATION, NOTICE ⟨gain worldwide ~ for a contribution to science⟩ **:** mental power of attending ⟨call ~ to an error⟩ ⟨fix ~ on a moving light⟩ **2 :** consideration with a view to action **:** observant care ⟨call this to the manager's ~⟩ **3 :** an act of civility or courtesy **:** care for the wishes, comfort, or pleasure of others **:** ATTENTIVENESS ⟨she loved her children, but did not . . . spoil them . . . with injudicious ~s —Rose Macaulay⟩; *specif* **:** interest and concern expressed in courtship ⟨she would now marry Voldi whose constant ~s . . . were unmistakable —L.C.Douglas⟩ **4 a :** an organismic condition of selective awareness or perceptual receptivity; *specif* **:** the complex of neuromuscular adjustments that permit maximum excitability or responsiveness to a given class of stimuli **b :** the process of focusing consciousness to produce greater vividness and clarity of certain of its contents relative to others **5 :** a position assumed by a soldier with heels together at a 45 degree angle, body erect, arms and hands hanging naturally at the sides and eyes to the front — often used as a command

attention 5

at·ten·tion·al \ə'tenchənᵊl, -chnəl *also* a'-\ *adj* **:** of or relating to attention ⟨~ factors in reaction time —*Psychological Abstracts*⟩

attention line *n* **:** a line usu. placed above the salutation in a business letter directing the letter to a specific individual, office, or department esp. when the name of the person to whom the letter should go is unknown

attention span *n* **:** the length of time during which an individual is able to concentrate

at·ten·tive \ə'tentiv, -ēv *also* a'- *or* -əv\ *adj* [ME *attentif*, fr. MF *atentif*, fr. *atente* expectation (fr. OF, fr. fem. of assumed *atent*, past part. of OF *atendre* to attend, direct the attention to) + *-if* -ive — more at ATTEND] **1 :** regarding with care or attention **:** HEEDFUL, OBSERVANT, INTENT ⟨certain of an ~ ear and reasonable counsel —W.S.Maugham⟩ **2 :** heedful of the comfort of others **:** COURTEOUS, POLITE ⟨his behavior to us . . . was more than civil; it was really ~ —Jane Austen⟩ **3 :** paying attentions (as in courting) — **at·ten·tive·ly** \-əvlē, -li\ *adv*

at·ten·tive·ness *n* -ES **:** the quality or state of being attentive

¹at·ten·u·ate \ə'tenyəˌwāt *also* a'-; *usu* -ād·+V\ *vb* -ED/-ING/-S [L *attenuatus*, past part. of *attenuare* to make thin, fr. *ad-* + *tenuare* to make thin, fr. *tenuis* thin — more at THIN] *vt* **1 :** to make thin or slender (as by mechanical or chemical action) ⟨glass . . . may be *attenuated* into the finest of fibers —M.F.Brooke⟩ **2 :** to lessen the amount, force, or value of **:** make less complex **:** WEAKEN ⟨he refuses to ~ human life —Hardin Craig⟩ ⟨a cloudburst will ~ UHF signals —*RCA Review*⟩ **3 :** to reduce the severity of (a disease) or the virulence or vitality of (a pathogenic agent) **4** *archaic* **:** to break into finer parts (as the humors of the body) **5 :** to make thin in consistency **:** render less viscid or dense **:** RAREFY ⟨~ oil by heating it⟩ ~ *vi* **:** to become thin, fine, or less **:** LESSEN ⟨the vividness of a memory ~s with time⟩ **syn** see THIN

²at·ten·u·ate \-yəwət, -ˌwāt, *usu* -d·+V\ *adj* [L *attenuatus*] **1 :** attenuated esp. in thickness, density, or force **:** SLENDER, THIN ⟨the ~ limbs of a starving person⟩ **2** *bot* **:** tapering gradually often into a long slender point ⟨narrow ~ leaves⟩ **3 :** thin in consistency **:** RAREFIED, FINE, REFINED ⟨ an ~ kind of beauty⟩

at·ten·u·a·tion \⸗ˌ⸗⸗'wāshən\ *n* -s [L *attenuation-, attenuatio*, fr. *attenuatus* + *-ion-*, *-io* -ion] **1 :** the act or process of attenuating ⟨the treble can stand a little ~ —P.H.Lang⟩ **:** the state of being attenuated ⟨the city of Duluth shows an . . . ~ between Lake Superior and the uplands —C.L.White & G.T.Renner⟩: as **a :** diminution of thickness **:** THINNING, EMACIATION ⟨the patient shows the ~ characteristic of that disease⟩ **b :** diminution of density ⟨~ of a country's population⟩ **c :** diminution of force or intensity **:** WEAKENING ⟨~ of the volume of sound⟩ **2 :** a decrease in the pathogenicity or vitality of a microorganism or in the severity of a disease **3 :** the diminution of density of wort resulting from its fermentation **4 :** the decrease in amplitude of a wave or current with increasing distance from the source of transmission

attenuation constant *n* **:** DECAY CONSTANT

attenuation factor *n* **:** TRANSMISSION 1a

at·ten·u·a·tor \⸗'⸗⸗ˌwād·ə(r), -ātə-\ *n* -s **:** a device for reducing the amplitude of an alternating-current wave without introducing appreciable distortion

at·ter \'ad·ər\ *n* -s [ME, fr. OE *ātor;* akin to OHG *eitar* poison, OS *ettar*, ON *eitr*, OHG *eiz* pustule, boil, Gk *oidos* swelling, tumor, OSlav *jadŭ* poison, and perh. to Skt *indrastrong*, fr. and perh. to OE *āte* oat] *chiefly Scot* **:** corrupt matter from a sore

at·ter·cop \'ad·ərˌkäp\ *dial Eng var of* ETTERCAP

at·ter·mine \ə'tərmən, a'-\ *vt* -ED/-ING/-S [ME *atermynen*, fr. MF *aterminer*, fr. LL *atterminare*, fr. L *ad-* + *terminare* to limit — more at TERMINATE] **:** to fix the term or limit of; *esp* **:** to put off payment of (a debt) until an appointed date — **at·ter·mine·ment** \-mənmənt\ *n* -s

atterrate *vt* -ED/-ING/-S [It *atterrato*, past part. of *atterrare*, fr. *a-* (fr. L *ad-*) + *terra* earth, fr. L — more at TERRACE] *obs* **:** to fill up with alluvium or other earth—**atterration** *n* -s *obs*

¹at·test \ə'test, a'-\ *vb* -ED/-ING/-S [MF *attester*, fr. L *attestari*, fr. *ad-* + *testari* to be a witness — more at TESTAMENT] *vt* **1 a :** to bear witness to **:** affirm to be true or genuine **:** CERTIFY; *specif* **:** to witness and authenticate by signing as a witness **b :** to authenticate officially (as the truth of a writing) **c** *Brit* **:** to authenticate officially the freedom of (livestock) from a specified disease ⟨an ~*ed* herd⟩ **2 :** to establish or verify the usage of ⟨*railroad* is ~*ed* earlier than *railway*—by one year—R.A.Hall b. 1911⟩ **3 :** to be or stand as proof of **:** MANIFEST ⟨the ruins of Palmyra ~ its ancient magnificence⟩ **4** *obs* **:** to call to witness **:** INVOKE **5 :** to put on oath or solemn declaration **6 :** to enroll for military service ⟨the day on which the recruits were ~*ed*⟩ ~ *vi* **1 :** to bear witness **:** TESTIFY — often used with *to* ⟨~ to the truth of the statement⟩ **2 :** to enroll oneself for service in the armed forces ⟨the day on which the recruits ~*ed*⟩ **syn** see INDICATE

²attest *n* -s *obs* **:** TESTIMONY, WITNESS

at·test·a·ble \-əbəl\ *adj* **:** capable of being attested

at·test·ant \-stənt\ *n* -s [L *attestant-, attestans*, pres. part. of *attestari* to bear witness] **:** one who attests

at·tes·ta·tion \ˌaˌte'stāshən, ˌad·ə'stā-, ˌatə's-, əˌte's-\ *n* -s [MF, fr. LL *attestation-, attestatio*, fr. L *attestatus* (past part. of *attestari*) + *-ion-*, *-io* -ion] **1 :** the act of attesting **2 :** the proof or evidence by which something is attested ⟨the . . . volumes . . . stand, like a solid ~ of the victory —Edmund Wilson⟩ **3 :** the formal authentication of an act or instrument by a subscribing witness or an official **4** *Brit* **:** the giving of an oath (as the taking of an oath by an army recruit)

at·tes·ta·tive \ə'testəd·iv, a'-\ *adj* [*attestation* + *-ive*] **:** of or relating to attestation

at·tes·ta·tor \ə'teˌstād·ə(r), a'-, 'ad·əˌs-\ *n* -s [L *attestatus* + E *-or*] **:** one that attests

at·test·er \ə'testə(r), a'-\ *or* **at·tes·tor** \" *also* -ˌstȯr *or* -ˌstó(ə)\ *n* -s **:** one that attests

at·tes·tive \-ˌstiv\ *adj* **:** ATTESTING

¹at·tic \'ad·ik, 'atik, -ēk\ *adj, usu cap* [L *Atticus*, adj. & n., fr. Gk *Attikos*, fr. *Attikē* (Attica), region of ancient Greece] **1 a :** GREEK **b :** ATHENIAN **2 :** marked by simplicity, purity, and refinement ⟨*Attic* taste⟩ ⟨an *Attic* style⟩

²attic \"\ *n* -s *cap* [L *Atticus*] **1 :** GREEK; *specif* **:** ATHENIAN **2 :** a dialect of ancient Greek that was originally used in Attica and became the literary language of the entire Greek-speaking world

³attic \"\ *n* -s [F *attique*, fr. *attique* Attic, of Attica, fr. L *Atticus;* fr. the use of pilasters in the Attic style] **1 a :** a low story or wall above the main order or orders of a façade in the classical styles **b :** a room or rooms behind an attic **c :** the part of a building immediately below the roof and wholly or partly within the roof framing **:** a garret or storage space under the roof **2 :** the small upper space of the tympanic cavity

attic base *n, usu cap A* **:** a molded base consisting of an upper and lower torus separated by a scotia and two narrow fillets and assumed to be the typical form of base for the Ionic and Corinthian orders

at·ti·cism \'ad·əˌsizəm, 'atə-\ *n* -s *often cap* [L *Atticismus*, fr. Gk *Attikismos*, fr. *Attikos* + *-ismos* -ism] **1 :** a favoring of or attachment to the Athenians **2 :** a characteristic feature of Attic Greek occurring in another language or dialect **3 :** a concisely witty or well-turned phrase or sentence **4 a :** a style like that of Attic writers or orators **b :** adherence to or practice of Attic manner or style

at·ti·cist \-ˌsəst\ *n* -s *usu cap* [Gk *Attikistēs*, fr. *Attikos* + *-istēs* -ist] **:** one who affects Atticisms

at·ti·cize \-ˌsīz\ *vb* -ED/-ING/-S *often cap* [¹*Attic* + *-ize*, after Gk *attikizein*, fr. *Attikos* + *-izein* -ize] *vt* **:** to make conformable to Athenian or Greek language or customs ~ *vi* **1 :** to favor or side with the Athenians **2 :** to speak or write in Attic

at·ti·co·mastoid \ˌad·ə(ˌ)kō+ˌ-\ *adj* [³*attic* + *-o-* + *mastoid*] *anat* **:** of or relating to the attic and the mastoid

attic order *n* [³*attic*] **:** an order (as of pilasters) adorning the front of an attic

attic salt *or* **attic wit** *n, often cap A* [¹*Attic*] **:** poignant delicate wit

attic story *n* [³*attic*] **:** the space enclosed by the attic **:** the top story of a house

at·tid \'ad·əd\ *adj or n* [NL *Attidae*] **:** SALTICID

at·ti·dae \'ad·əˌdē\ [NL, fr. *Attus*, type genus (prob. fr. L *atta* one that walks on tiptoes) + *-idae*] *syn of* SALTICIDAE

at·tine \'aˌtīn\ *adj* [NL *Atta* + E *-ine*] **:** of or relating to the genus *Atta* or to the ants constituting this genus

attinge *vt* **attinged; attinged; attinging; attinges** [L *attingere*, fr. *ad-* + *-tingere* (fr. *tangere* to touch) — more at TANGENT] **1** *obs* **:** TOUCH **:** come in contact with **2** *obs* **:** INFLUENCE, AFFECT

at·tin·gent \ə'tinjənt, a'-\ *adj* [L *attingent-, attingens*, pres. part. of *attingere*] *archaic* **:** in contact **:** TOUCHING

¹at·tire \ə'tī(ə)r, a'-, -īə\ *vt* -ED/-ING/-S [ME *attiren*, fr. OF *atirier*, fr. *a-* (fr. L *ad-*) + *-tirier* (fr. *tire* order, rank, of Gmc origin; akin to OE *tīr* glory, OHG *ziari* adorned, ON *tīrr* glory); akin to Lith *dyrėti* to gaze, Toch A *tiri* manner, L *deus* god — more at DEITY] **1 :** to put garments on **:** DRESS, ARRAY ⟨a shabby look, common to all thus *attired*⟩ ⟨*attired* himself in a gray business suit⟩ **2 :** to clothe with fancy or rich garments **:** ADORN ⟨*attired* in the huge black cloak and the large black hat which he always affected —Osbert Sitwell⟩

²attire \"\ *n* -s [ME, fr. *attiren* to attire] **1** *obs* **:** DRESS, CLOTHING, CLOTHES ⟨the usual ~ of a gentleman —W.M. Thackeray⟩ ⟨his unfashionable ~ and clumsy manners —A.C. Cole⟩; *esp* **:** splendid or decorative clothing ⟨the king in his royal ~⟩ **2 :** the antlers or antlers and scalp of a stag or buck **3** *obs* **:** DRESS, GARMENT, HEADDRESS, ORNAMENT — usu. used in pl. **4 :** something felt to dress or adorn ⟨the sparkling ~ of trees after a snowstorm⟩

at·tired \-ī(ə)rd, -īəd\ *adj* [ME, past part. of *attiren* to attire] **:** emblazoned with antlers ⟨a stag argent ~ sable⟩

at·tire·ment \-ī(ə)rmənt, -īəm-\ *n* -s **:** ATTIRE

at·ti·tude \'ad·əˌtüd, 'atə-, -əˌtyüd *also* -d·ē- *or* -tē-\ *n* -s [F, fr. It *attitudine* (influenced in meaning by It *atto* act, action, fr. L *actus* act), fr. *attitudine* aptitude, natural tendency, fr. LL *aptitudin-, aptitudo* fitness — more at APTITUDE, ACT] **1 a :** the arrangement of the parts of a sculptured or painted figure **b :** the posture of a figure in a sculpture or a painting **2 a :** a posture or bearing as indicating action, feeling, or mood ⟨a firm ~⟩ **b :** the feeling or mood itself ⟨one's ~ regarding vivisection⟩ **3 a :** the posture or position of a person, an animal, or an inanimate object or the manner in which the parts of the body are disposed ⟨toys lying in tumbled ~s on the nursery floor⟩ **b :** a position assumed to serve a purpose ⟨strike a threatening ~⟩ **4 a :** behavior representative of feeling or conviction **b :** a disposition that is primarily grounded in affect and emotion and is expressive of opinions rather than belief **c :** an organismic state of readiness to act that is often accompanied by considerable affect and that may be activated by an appropriate stimulus into significant or meaningful behavior **d :** a persistent disposition to act either positively or negatively toward a person, group, object, situation, or value **5** *geol* **:** the position of a bed, fault plane, or other planar body or surface with respect to a horizontal plane **6 a :** any posture held momentarily in dancing **b :** a variation of the arabesque used in ballet with the lifted leg bent sharply at the knee, the body held upright, the corresponding arm usu. raised forward, and the opposite arm extended to the side **7 :** the position or orientation of an aircraft in the air as seen by an observer stationary on the earth determined and expressed mathematically by the inclination of the axes of the aircraft to three fixed axes on the earth that form a frame of reference

attitude gyro *n* **:** an instrument that indicates continuously the attitude of an airplane in flight in relation to a horizontal plane

attitude of flight : inclination of the three principal axes of an airplane in flight to the relative wind

attitude scale *n* **:** a measure of the relative quantity of an attitude possessed by an individual as contrasted with a reference group

at·ti·tu·di·nal \ˌ⸗⸗'⸗dᵊnəl\ *adj* [*attitude* + *-inal* (as in *aptitudinal*)] **:** relating to, based on, or expressive of personal attitudes or feelings ⟨~ judgment⟩

at·ti·tu·di·nar·i·an \ˌ⸗⸗ˌ⸗⸗'ererēən\ *n* -s [*attitude* + *-inarian* (as in *valetudinarian*)] **:** one who attitudinizes **:** POSTURER — **at·ti·tu·di·nar·i·an·ism** \-rēəˌnizəm\ *n* -s

at·ti·tu·di·nize \ˌ⸗⸗'⸗dᵊnˌīz\ *vi* -ED/-ING/-S *see -ize in Explan Notes* [*attitude* + *-in-* (fr. L, suffixal element of oblique cases of nouns ending in *-udo*) + *-ize*] **:** to assume or practice attitudes **:** strike an attitude **:** pose for effect ⟨below the conventional *attitudinizing* a man lies hid —H.S.Bennett⟩

at·ti·wan·da·ronk \ˌad·ə'wändəˌräŋk\ *n* -s *usu cap* **:** an Indian of the Neutral people

attn *abbr* attention

at·torn \ə'tərn\ *vb* -ED/-ING/-S [ME *attournen*, fr. MF *atorner* to direct, dispose, attorn, fr. OF, fr. *a* to (fr. L *ad*) + *torner* to turn — more at AT, TURN] *vi* **1** *feudal law* **:** to turn or transfer homage and service from one lord to another **:** render homage and service to a lord **2** *modern law* **:** to agree to become tenant to one as owner or landlord of an estate previously held of another **:** recognize one expressly or by implication as landlord or the person in whose behalf one holds something — see ATTORNMENT 2 ~ *vt* **:** TRANSFER

at·tor·ney \ə'tərnē, -tōn-, -təin-, -ni\ *n* -s [ME *attourney*, fr. MF *atorné*, past part. of *atorner*] **:** one who is legally appointed by another to transact any business for him; *specif* **:** a legal agent qualified to act for suitors and defendants in legal proceedings — **at·tor·ney·ship** \⸗'⸗⸗ˌship\ *n* -s

attorney-at-law \⸗ˌ⸗⸗⸗'⸗\ *n, pl* **attorneys-at-law :** a practitioner in a court of law who is legally qualified to prosecute and defend actions in such court on the retainer of clients — compare ADVOCATE, BARRISTER, LAWYER, PROCTOR, SOLICITOR

attorney general *n, pl* **attorneys general** *or* **attorney generals :** the chief law officer of a state who is empowered to act in all litigation in which the government is a party and to advise the chief executive whenever required — **attorney generalship** *n*

attorney-in-fact \⸗ˌ⸗⸗⸗'⸗\ *n, pl* **attorneys-in-fact 1 :** a person appointed by another by a letter or power of attorney to transact any business for him out of court — compare ATTORNEY-AT-LAW **2 :** an agent employed in any business or to do any act in pais for another

at·torn·ment \ə'tərnmənt\ *n* -s [MF *atornement*, fr. OF, fr. *atorner* + *-ment*] **1 :** the act of a feudatory, vassal, or tenant by which he consents upon the alienation of an estate to receive a new lord or superior and transfers to him his homage and service **:** the agreement or acknowledgment by a tenant that he holds his tenement of a new person as landlord **2 :** the acknowledgment by a bailee that he holds a property on behalf of a new party

at·tour \ə'tȯr\ *var of* ATOUR

at·tract \ə'trakt\ *vb* -ED/-ING/-S [ME *attracten*, fr. L *attractus*, past part. of *attrahere*, fr. *ad-* + *trahere* to draw — more at DRAW] *vt* **1** *obs* **:** to draw or draw in esp. by suction or pulling **:** INHALE **2 :** to influence and draw to or cause to approach or adhere: as **a :** to pull together or towards **:** cause or expedite union, compounding, adhering, or approach **:** resist separation or decomposition of ⟨cathode rays are ~*ed* by a positive charge —K.K.Darrow⟩ **b :** to call forth or compel (as interest in or appreciation of) ⟨often ~s admiring glances⟩ ⟨her agitation at a steeplechase . . . ~s her husband's notice —Matthew Arnold⟩ **c :** to invite or draw by exposure or openness to or by some natural appeal for ⟨a swarm in the tree for weeks, ~*ed* by some secretion —Richard Jefferies⟩ ⟨~ bitter criticism⟩ **d :** to draw or entice to one by an aesthetic or emotional appeal ⟨clad in a pale buff frock . . . she ~*ed* every eye —John Galsworthy⟩ **e :** to interest and lead to consideration of, participation in, or attendance at ⟨the talent which the organization ~*ed*⟩ ~ *vi* **:** exercise attraction ⟨her voice has the power to ~⟩ ⟨opposites ~⟩

syn ALLURE, CAPTIVATE, FASCINATE, BEWITCH, CHARM, ENCHANT, TAKE: of these words ATTRACT is at once the widest in its use and the least rich in connotation. It stresses the fact of one thing's being able to draw another to it in some way or other ⟨tempting summer, when song and shade and colour *attract* every one to the field —Richard Jefferies⟩ ⟨to Papa, who had begun to be *attracted* rather against his will —Virginia Woolf⟩ ⟨men could be *attracted* into these by higher pay or shorter hours —Bertrand Russell⟩ ALLURE may add the notion of the enticement of something good or enjoyable being offered or withheld ⟨new class of technicians, *allured* by their wide opportunities of service —Bernard Pares⟩ ⟨the beauty that *allured* men for pleasure had failed to hold them —Ellen Glasgow⟩ CAPTIVATE, like the succeeding words in this list, suggests an appeal irresistible and blocking rational consideration which might diminish its force. CAPTIVATE is less strong than the following words since it may be used for fleeting or short-lived impressions produced by an individual trait ⟨a serene expression upon her face which *captivated* almost all who saw her —Samuel Butler †1902⟩ ⟨the Republican State Convention . . . *captivated* by his address as temporary chairman, nominated him for governor —A.C.Flick⟩ FASCINATE, in older usage and sometimes in today's, implies a spell which irresistibly transfixes the victim ⟨the younger and weaker man was *fascinated* and helpless before the creeping approach of so monstrous a wrath —G.D.Brown⟩ It often indicates a compelling attraction or interest or enthusiasm ⟨James . . . carried the exploration of the technics of his craft into depths and recesses almost as *fascinating* as Leonardo da Vinci's abstruse, inspired-looking speculations about his —C.E.Montague⟩ BEWITCH suggests domination and absorption of interest or liking precluding any check and possibly against the subject's will ⟨if you suffer yourself to think how pretty they are, you are *bewitched* and vanquished —Lafcadio Hearn⟩ ⟨these small splinters of perfection in the art of letters would still *bewitch* us if they had no context at all —C.E.Montague⟩ CHARM suggests domination as by magic; it indicates pleasure on the subject's part and may be used with reference to sensuous or social traits that appeal ⟨she gave some attention to her flowers, but it was perfunctorily bestowed, for they no longer *charmed* her —Thomas Hardy⟩ ⟨a grace about him which *charmed*, and a hint of latent power which impressed —John Buchan⟩ ENCHANT is possibly the strongest word in the list; it may suggest a more complex appeal, its irresistibility, utter absence of thoughtful reservation, and sheer delight on the part of the subject ⟨a mature person . . . cannot be utterly *enchanted* by what he feels to be trivial or false —George Santayana⟩ ⟨man's power to *enchant* himself with his own dreams —Irving Babbitt⟩ TAKE, usu. used in the passive, is somewhat informal and has suggestions ranging from those of ATTRACT to those of CAPTIVATE ⟨he stared at her . . . the more he stared, the more *taken* was he —Rudyard Kipling⟩

at·tract·a·ble \-əbəl\ *adj* **:** capable of being attracted

at·tract·ance \-ən(t)s\ *also* **at·tract·an·cy** \-ənsē, -si\ *n, pl* **attractances** *also* **attractancies :** the tendency (as of an insecticide) to attract positively

at·tract·ant \-ənt\ *n* -s **:** something that attracts; *specif* **:** a substance used to attract insects or other animals

at·tract·ing·ly *adv* **:** in an attracting manner

at·trac·tion \ə'trakshən\ *n* -s [MF & ML; MF, attraction, fr. ML *attraction-, attractio* attraction, fr. L, contraction, fr. *attractus* (past part. of *attrahere* to attract, contract) + *-ion-*, *-io* -ion] **1 a :** a characteristic that elicits interest or admiration **:** an attracting quality — usu. used in pl. ⟨relationships between individual members are based primarily on spontaneous mutual ~s —*Jour. of Communication*⟩ **b :** personal magnetic charm ⟨unable to resist her mysterious ~s⟩ **2 :** a force acting between oppositely electrified bodies or oppositely magnetized bodies that tends to draw them together and resist their separation **3 a :** the action or power of drawing forth a response (as interest or affection) **:** attractive quality ⟨the career of the father came to have an ~ for the son⟩ **b (1) :** something that draws people by appealing to their desires and tastes **(2) :** a person, thing, or performance that attracts crowds ⟨another $100 dinner, with the presidential candidate as the main ~⟩ **4 :** grammatical agreement between two words usu. near each other that are not syntactically connected in a way that makes it normal for them to agree (as between *books* and *were* in "neither of the books were sold")

at·trac·tion·al·ly \-shənᵊlē, -shnəlē\ *adv* [*attraction* + *-al* + ²*-ly*] **:** by means of attraction

attraction cone *n* **:** ENTRANCE CONE

attraction sphere *n* **:** the central mass of the aster in mitotic cell division **:** CENTROSPHERE

¹at·tract·ive \ə'traktiv, -ēv *also* -əv\ *adj* [ME, fr. MF & LL; MF *attractif*, fr. LL *attractivus*, fr. L *attractus* + *-ivus* -ive] **1 a :** able to cause (a person or animal) to approach by influencing the will or appealing to the senses ⟨a sanctuary ~ to birds⟩ **b :** able to draw to itself objects not attached to it ⟨~ powers of a magnet⟩ **2 :** having qualities that arouse interest, pleasure, or affection in the observer **:** PLEASING ⟨an ~ personality⟩ ⟨goods ~ in price or quality⟩ **:** handsome or pleasing in appearance — **at·tract·ive·ly** \-təvlē, -li\ *adv* — **at·tract·ive·ness** \-tivnəs, -tēv- *also* -təv-\ *n* -ES

²attractive \"\ *n* -s [ME] *archaic* **:** ATTRACTION

attractive nuisance *n* **:** something (as a turntable or scaffold) unsafe and unprotected and often under construction that tempts children to risk injury by playing with, in, or on it

at·trac·tor \-ktə(r) *also* -ˌtō(ə)r *or* -ō(ə)\ *also* **at·tract·er** \-ktə(r)\ *n* -s **:** one that attracts

attracts *pres 3d sing of* ATTRACT

at·tra·hent \'a·trəhənt\ *n* -s [L *attrahent-, attrahens*, pres. part. of *attrahere* to attract — more at ATTRACT] **:** ATTRACTANT

at·trib·ut·a·ble \ə'tribyəd·əbəl, -yətə-\ *adj* **:** capable of being attributed

at·trib·u·tal \-yəd·ᵊl\ *adj* **:** DESCRIPTIVE

¹at·tri·bute \'a·trəˌbyüt, *usu* -üd·+V\ *n* -s [ME, fr. L *attributus*, past part. of *attribuere* to attribute, fr. *ad-* + *tribuere* to bestow — more at TRIBUTE] **1 :** a quality, character, or characteristic ascribed usu. commonly: **a :** a characteristic either essential and intrinsic or accidental and concomitant ⟨to endow her with all the ~s of a mythological paragon upon Olympus —Elinor Wylie⟩ **b :** a quality intrinsic, inherent, naturally belonging to a thing or person ⟨not in spiritual nor even in moral ~s —G.L.Dickinson⟩ **2 :** an object closely associated with and thought of as belonging to a specific person, thing, or office ⟨a scepter is the ~ of power⟩ ⟨all his ~s are here — ring, cigarette case, tiepin, cane —Osbert Sitwell⟩; *esp* **:** such an accessory object used for identification or association in painting or sculpture (as a club for Hercules) **3 a** *logic* **:** any quality or characteristic that may be predicated of some subject — compare PREDICATE **b** *philos* **:** a necessary or essential quality or characteristic of substance — compare CARTESIANISM, SPINOZISM **4 a :** a word ascribing a quality; *esp* **:** ADJECTIVE, ADJECTIVE EQUIVALENT **b :** that one of the two immediate constituents of an endocentric compound or construction that does not have the same grammatical function as the whole (as *this* in *this paper, completely* in *completely new, black* in *blackbird*) — opposed to *head* **5 :** any one of the ways (as intensity, duration, or quality) in which one sensation, image, or feeling can differ from another **syn** see QUALITY, SYMBOL

²at·trib·ute \ə'tribyət *also* -i(,)byüt, *chiefly substand* -,bət; *usu* -d.+V\ *vt* **attributed** \-yəd·əd,-yətəd\ **attributed** \"\ **attributing** \-yəd·iŋ,-yətiŋ\ **attributes** \-yəts *also* -yüts\ [L *attributus*] **1** *archaic* **:** to bestow as a right **2 :** to explain as caused or brought about by **:** regard as occurring in consequence of or on account of ⟨the collapse of the movement can be *attributed* to lack of morale⟩ **3 :** to regard as possessed, owned, originated, characterized, or described as indicated: as **a :** to reckon as a quality, characteristic, or trait possessed sometimes fitly or properly ⟨Delia reproached herself for *attributing* feelings of jealousy to her cousin —Edith Wharton⟩ **b :** to reckon as executed, made, originated, or achieved as indicated ⟨*attributed* the invention to a Russian⟩ **c :** CLASSIFY, DESIGNATE, DATE ⟨a manuscript *attributed* to the 10th century⟩ **syn** see ASCRIBE

at·tri·bu·tion \,a·trə'byüshən\ *n* -s [ME, fr. MF, fr. L *attribution-, attributio* assignment of a debt of money, fr. *attributus* (past part. of *attribuere* to attribute, assign) + *-ion-, -io* -ion] **1 :** the action of bestowing or assigning ⟨~ of a gift⟩ **2 :** the process of ascribing to someone or something ⟨the ~ of guilt to the accused⟩ **3 :** the ascribing of a work to an author, date, or place; *esp* **:** the ascribing of a work of art to a particular artist **4 :** the fact of being an attribute **:** the logical relation of an attribute to its subject

¹at·trib·u·tive \ə'tribyəd·iv, -yətiv\ *adj* [F *attributif*, fr. MF, fr. *attribution*, after such pairs as MF *distribution: distributif* distributive] **1 :** ATTRIBUTING **:** relating to or of the nature of attribution **2 :** expressing or assigning an attribute: as **a** *of an adjective or adjective equivalent* **:** joined directly to a modified noun without a copulative verb and in English usu. preceding the noun (as of *red* in *red hair, city* in *city streets, militant* in *the church militant*) but in some other languages (as French) typically following it (as *moderne* in *un roman moderne* "a modern novel") — compare ADHERENT 4, APPOSITIVE 2, PREDICATE 2 **b :** of or belonging to an attributive adjective or adjective equivalent ⟨~ position⟩ ⟨~ function⟩ **:** including an attributive adjective or adjective equivalent ⟨an ~ collocation⟩ **2 :** ADJECTIVAL — used of a term ⟨*redness* is abstract but *red* is ~⟩ **3 :** of an attributed or assigned nature or origin — used of the authorship of a work of art — **at·trib·u·tive·ly** \-əvlē, -li\ *adv*

²attributive \"\ *n* -s **:** an attributive word; *esp* **:** ADJECTIVE, ADJECTIVE EQUIVALENT

attrist *vt* -ED/-ING/-S [F *attrister*, fr. MF, fr. *a-* (fr. L *ad-*) + *-trister* (fr. *triste* sad, fr. L *tristis*) — more at TRISTE] *obs* **:** SADDEN

at·tri·tal \ə'trīd·ᵊl, a'-, -ītᵊ\ *adj* [L *attritus* + E *-al*] **:** of or relating to matter that has been worn by attrition ⟨~ coal⟩

at·trite \ə'trīt, a'-\ *adj* [L *attritus*, past part. of *atterere* to rub against, rub away, fr. *ad-* + *terere* to rub — more at THROW] **:** having attrition

at·trit·ed \ə'trīd·əd\ *adj* **:** worn by attrition

at·tri·tion \ə'trishən *also* a'-\ *n* -s [L *attrition-, attritio*, fr. *attritus* + *-ion-, -io* -ion] **1** [ME *attricioun*, fr. (assumed) ML *attrition-, attritio*, fr. L] **:** sorrow for one's own sins that arises from a motive considered lower than that of the love of God (as a fear of punishment or a sense of shame) **:** imperfect contrition — used in Roman Catholic theology **2 :** the act of rubbing together or wearing down **:** the condition of being worn down or ground down by friction ⟨withstand moisture, pressure, and ~ —*Farmer's Weekly (So. Africa)*⟩ ⟨tweeds that drag out into woolly knots and strings wherever there is ~ —H.G.Wells⟩ **3 :** the act of weakening to the point of exhaustion by constant harassment, use, or abuse ⟨the slow ~ of the soul by the conduct of life —Thornton Wilder⟩ **:** a breaking down or wearing down from repeated attacks or constant diminution ⟨war of ~⟩ ⟨the rate of ~ in some industries⟩ **:** gradual loss of strength from attrition **4 :** the wear of rock particles while being moved about by wind, stream currents, waves, or glaciers; *also* **:** the removal of ice from a glacier by melting or evaporation **5 :** the absence of a consonant sound (as of a sound no longer pronounced) **6 :** the portion of a maturing debt issue not turned in for exchange into new securities in a refunding **syn** see PENITENCE

at·tri·tion·al \-shənᵊl,-shnəl\ *adj* **:** relating to or caused by attrition

attrition mill *n* **:** a machine in which materials (as grain or spices) are pulverized between two toothed metal disks rotating in opposite directions

at·tri·tive \ə'trīd·iv, a'-\ *adj* [*attrition* + *-ive*] **:** causing attrition

at·tri·tus \ə'trīd·əs, a'-, -ītəs\ *n* -ES [NL, fr. L, act of rubbing against, rubbing away, fr. *attritus* past part. of *atterere* to rub against, rub away — more at ATTRITE] **:** matter pulverized or finely divided by attrition; *specif* **:** one of the constituents of durain consisting of a macerated plant debris including leaves, bark, cuticle, spore and pollen extines, resins, and mineral matter

atts *pl of* ATT

at·tune \ə'tün, ə'tyün *also* a-\ *vt* -ED/-ING/-S [*ad-* + *tune*] **1 :** to bring into harmony or accord, esp. musical harmony **:** make melodious **2 :** to put in tune **:** TUNE ⟨*attuned* the violin⟩

at·tune·ment \-mənt\ *n* -s **:** the act of attuning **:** the state of being attuned ⟨a delicate ~ to the written word —*Atlantic*⟩

atty *abbr* attorney

atua \ə'tüə\ *or* **akua** \-'küə\ *n, pl* **atua** *or* **atuas** *or* **akua** *or* **akuas** [Tahitian, Maori, or Samoan *atua*, Hawaiian *akua*] **:** a Polynesian supernatural being or spirit

atu·a·mi \,äd·ə'wämē\ *n, pl* **atuami** *or* **atuamis** *usu cap* **1 :** a Palaihnihan Indian people of Shastan stock **2 :** a member of the Atuami people

atule *var of* AKULE

atun \ä'tün\ *n* -s [Sp *atún*, fr. Ar *at-tūn, at-tunn* the tunny, fr. L *thunnus* — more at TUNNY] **:** TUNA

atwain \ə'twān\ *adv* [ME *atweyne*, fr. ¹*a-* + *tweyne* twain] *archaic* **:** in twain **:** in two parts **:** ASUNDER

atweel \ə'twēl\ *adv* [alter. of Sc (*I*) *wat weel* I well know] *Scot* **:** SURELY, TRULY

atween \ə'twēn\ *prep or adv* [ME *atwene*, fr. ¹*a-* + *-twene* (as in *betwene*)] *now dial* **:** BETWEEN

atwist \ə+\ *adv* [¹*a-* + *twist*, v.] **:** in a twisted manner **:** TWISTED

atwitter \ə+\ *adj* [¹*a-* + *twitter*, v.] **:** nervously concerned ⟨~ . . . thinking of her among all those Indians —Kenneth Roberts⟩ **:** EXCITED, TWITTERING ⟨Hollywood gossips ~ with speculation —*Time*⟩

atwixt \ə'twikst\ *prep* [ME, fr. ¹*a-* + *-twixt* (as in *betwixt*)] *dial* **:** BETWIXT, BETWEEN

atwo \ə'tü\ *adv* [ME *atwo, ato*, fr. OE *on twā, on tū*, fr. *on* + *twā, tū* two — more at TWO] *dial Brit* **:** in two **:** into two parts

a2–horizon \'ā'tü+\ *n, usu cap A* [¹*A*] **:** the often whitish gray or ash-gray portion of the A-horizon below the dark layer at the immediate surface

at·wood's machine \'at·,wüdz-\ *n, usu cap A* [after George *Atwood* †1807 Eng. mathematician, its inventor] **:** an apparatus for demonstrating the laws of accelerated motion by means of a light nearly frictionless pulley wheel over which passes a thread having at its ends fairly heavy masses whose slight difference in weight is the cause of the acceleration

a–type star \'ā,=-\ *n, usu cap A* [¹*A*] **:** A STAR

atyp·ia \(')ā'tipēə\ *n* -s [NL, fr. ²*a-* + L *typus* type + NL *-ia* — more at TYPE] **:** ATYPISM

atypical \(')ā+\ *adj* [²*a-* + *typical*] **:** not typical **:** unlike the type **:** IRREGULAR ⟨this sample is ~⟩ **:** ABNORMAL ⟨~ behavior . . . not the accepted type of response that we expect from children —G.E.Gardner⟩ — **atypically** *adv*

atyp·ism \(')ā'tī,pizəm\ *n* -s [²*a-* + *type* + *-ism*] **:** the condition of being uncharacteristic or lacking uniformity ⟨nuclear ~ of cells characterizes certain precancerous conditions⟩

AU *abbr* **1** *often not cap* [L *ad usum*] according to custom **2** angstrom unit **3** astronomical unit

Au [L *aurum*] *symbol* gold

a'u \'ä,ü\ *n* -s [Hawaiian] *Hawaii* **:** any of certain scombroid fishes: **a :** a member of the family Istiophoridae (as a sailfish or marlin) **b :** SWORDFISH 1a

au·bade \ō'bäd, -ad\ *n* -s [F, fr. MF, fr. (assumed) OProv *aubada*, fr. OProv *auba, alba* dawn — more at ALBA] **1 :** a song or poem greeting the dawn **:** a walking or rising song — called also *matin song* **2 a :** a morning love song **b :** a song or poem of lovers parting at daybreak **3 :** morning music — compare SERENADE, NOCTURNE

au·bain \ō'ban\ *n* -s [F, fr. OF *aubain, albain*, prob. fr. (assumed) OFrk *aliban* one belonging to another jurisdiction, fr. (assumed) OFrk *ali-* (akin to Goth *aljis* other) + OFrk *ban* jurisdiction — more at ELSE, BAN] **:** a resident alien subject to the droit d'aubaine

aubaine \"\ *n* [by shortening] **:** DROIT D'AUBAINE

aube \'ōb\ *n* -s [ME, fr. MF, fr. ML *alba* — more at ALB] **1** *archaic* **:** ALB 1 **2 :** ¹ALBA 1

au·be·pine \'ōbə,pēn, -bā-, -,pən, ,ōbā'pēn\ *n* -s [F *aubépine*, fr. OF *aubespin*, fr. (assumed) VL *albispina*, fr. (assumed) L *alba spina* (attested as *spina alba*), fr. L *alba* white (fem. of *albus*) + *spina* thorn — more at ELF, SPINE] **:** ANISALDEHYDE

au·berge \ō'berzh\ *n* -s [F, of Gmc origin; akin to OHG *heriberga* army encampment — more at HARBOR] **:** INN

au·ber·gine \'ōbər,zhēn, 'ō,ber-, -,jēn, ,=(,)='=\ *n* -s [F, fr. Catal *albergínia*, fr. Ar *al-bādhinjān* the eggplant — more at BRINJAL] **:** EGGPLANT

aubergine purple *n* **:** BISHOP'S PURPLE 1

au·brie·tia \ō'brēsh(ē)ə, ō'-\ *n* [NL, fr. Claude *Aubriet* †1742 Fr. painter of flowers and animals + NL *-ia*] **1** *cap* **:** a genus of Mediterranean herbs (family Cruciferae) often growing in dense mats and cultivated in rock gardens, and having showy purplish flowers **2** *also* **aubretia** -s **:** a plant of the genus *Aubrietia*

au·brite \'ō,brīt\ *n* -s [*Aubres*, commune near Nyons, Dept. Drôme, France, where a meteorite containing it fell in 1836 + E *-ite*] **:** an achondrite containing enstatite

¹au·burn \'ōbə(r)n\ *adj* [ME *aborne* blond, fr. MF *auborne*, fr. OF *auborne, alborne*, fr. ML *alburnus* whitish, fr. L *albus* white — more at ELF] **1 :** of the color auburn **2 :** having reddish brown hair

²auburn \"\ *n* -s **:** a moderate brown that is yellower and duller than toast brown, lighter and slightly yellower than tobacco, paler and slightly yellower than bay, redder and slightly lighter and stronger than chestnut brown, and redder, lighter, and slightly stronger than coffee — called also *cashew lake, gorevan, tulipwood, Zuñi brown*

¹au·bus·son \'ōbə,sōⁿ, ,=='=\ *n* -s *usu cap* [fr. *Aubusson*, France, where it was made] **1 :** a tapestry woven orig. in the 16th century, noted for its figure and scenic designs, and used for wall hangings and upholstery **2 :** a fine usu. wool or silk rug with ornate floral, scroll, and medallion designs woven without pile to resemble the tapestry Aubusson; *also* **:** any rug with similar designs usu. in pastel colors

²aubusson \"\ *n* -s **:** a dark red that is less strong and slightly yellower and darker than cranberry and bluer and paler than average garnet or average wine

AUC *abbr* **1** [L *ab urbe condita*] from the founding of the city **2** [L *anno urbis conditae*] in the year from the founding of the city

au·ca \'aùkə, -,kä *also* 'ōkə\ *n* -s [Sp., fr. Araucanian, lit., enemy, fr. Quechua *áukka* enemy, rebel] **1** *sometimes cap* **:** a primitive Indian of western or southern So. America **2** *usu cap* **:** ARAUCANIAN

au·can \'aùkən, 'ōk-\ *also* **au·ca·ni·an** \(')=¦kānēən, -nyən\ *n* -s *usu cap* [*Aucan* fr. Sp *aucano*, fr. *auca* + *-ano* -an; *Aucanian* fr. Sp *aucano* + E *-ian*] **:** ARAUCANIAN

au·can·er *or* **au·kan·er** \'ōkənər\ *n* -s *usu cap* **:** one of the Bush Negroes dwelling on the upper Cormotibo river in Dutch Guiana

au·che·nia \ō'kēnēə\ [NL, fr. Gk *auchēn* neck + NL *-ia*] *syn of* ²LAMA 1

aucht \'äkt, 'ō-\ *var of* AUGHT

auchten *pres part of* AUGHT

auchts *pres 3d sing of* AUGHT

auck·land \'ōklənd\ *adj, usu cap* [fr. *Auckland*, New Zealand] **:** of or from the city or provincial district of Auckland, New Zealand **:** of the kind or style prevalent in Auckland

au cou·rant \,ō,kü'räⁿ\ *adj* [F, lit., in the current] **1 a :** marked by keen awareness of latest developments and trends **:** fully informed ⟨people who consider themselves to be *au courant* and indisputably advanced — J.T.Farrell⟩ ⟨he seemed to be *au courant* of everything —Arnold Bennett⟩ **b :** UP-TO-DATE, ABREAST ⟨keeping its public *au courant* with recent significant work —Dwight Macdonald⟩ ⟨the book stays *au courant* by constant revision⟩ **2 :** fully familiar (as with a given object of knowledge or experience) **:** ACQUAINTED, CONVERSANT ⟨very *au courant* with the little things that gave life its color and texture —Margaret Evans⟩ **3 :** not lacking knowledge **:** COGNIZANT ⟨she was *au courant* of what had happened⟩

¹auc·tion \'ókshən\ *n* -s [L *auction-, auctio*, lit., increase, fr. *auctus* (past part. of *augēre* to increase) + *-ion-, -io* -ion — more at EKE] **1 :** a public sale of property to the highest bidder (as by successive increased bids) ⟨going to an ~ of household goods⟩ ⟨two cows bought at the ~⟩ — sometimes used with *at* ⟨sell at ~⟩ **2** *in card games* **a :** the act or process of bidding (as in auction bridge) **b :** the final declaration **:** CONTRACT **c :** any game (as auction pinochle) marked by bidding with the exception of contract bridge; *esp* **:** AUCTION BRIDGE ⟨playing a game of ~⟩ **3 :** an organization of wholesale dealers who make offers in a year-round competitive selling system marked by leisurely bidding ⟨some poultrymen sell eggs through an egg ~⟩

²auction \"\ *vt* **auctioned; auctioned; auctioning** \-sh(ə)niŋ\ **auctions :** to sell at auction — often used with *off* ⟨all the books were ~*ed off*⟩

auction bridge *n* **:** a bridge game differing from contract bridge in that tricks made in excess of the contract are scored toward game

¹auc·tion·eer \,ókshə¦ni(ə)r, -iə\ *n* -s [¹*auction* + *-eer*] **:** one who conducts the sale of goods at public auction usu. as an agent on commission

²auctioneer \"\ *vt* -ED/-ING/-S **:** AUCTION

auction forty-fives *n pl but sing or pl in constr, also* **auction forty-five :** a card game that is a variant of spoil five and forty-five

auction market *n* **:** a trading center operating without set prices, terms and transactions being arranged between sellers offering lowest prices and buyers offering highest

auction pinochle *n* **1 :** a pinochle game usu. for four players, sometimes for three or five, only three being active on each deal, active players being dealt 15 cards each and bidding for the privilege of using the 3-card widow, melding, designating the trump, and leading to the first trick **2 :** any pinochle game in which the players bid for the privilege of designating the trump

auction pitch *n* **:** an all-fours game in which the players bid for the privilege of leading a card of the suit that is to be the trump — called also *setback*

auction pool *n* **:** a betting pool in which selections (as of starters in a horse race) are sold at auction, the auctioneer usu. retaining a percentage of the pool

auc·tor \'ók,tó(ə)r, 'aùk-\ *n, pl* **auctors** \-rz\ *also* **aucto·res** \='tō,rēz\ [L, author — more at AUTHOR] **:** the author or source (as a vendor or assignor) of a right or title **:** PRINCIPAL

auc·to·ri·al \(')ók¦tōrēəl, (')aùk-\ *adj* [L *auctor* + E *-ial*] **:** of, coming from, or typical of an author **:** AUTHORIAL ⟨~ flights of imagination⟩ ⟨~ comment⟩

au·cu·ba \'ókyəbə\ *n* [NL, fr. Jap *aokoba* aucuba, fr. *ao* green + *ki, ko* tree + *ba* leaf] **1** *cap* **:** a genus of shrubs (family Cornaceae) native to eastern Asia and having persistent often mottled foliage, small purple flowers in terminal panicles, and red berries **2** -s **:** a plant of the genus *Aucuba*

aucuba green *n* **:** a light olive that is greener and stronger than citrine, deeper and slightly greener than grape green, and greener and very slightly lighter than old moss green — called also *oak green, sea moss*

aucuba mosaic *n* **:** a mosaic of the potato and other plants of the family Solanaceae, the leaves of affected plants resembling the normal leaves of the Japanese laurel (*Aucuba japonica*)

aud *abbr* **1** audible **2** audit; auditor

au·da·ce \aù'dä,chā, -,chē\ *adj* [It, fr. L *audac-, audax*] **:** BOLD, SPIRITED — used as a direction in music

¹au·da·cious \(')ó¦dāshəs\ *adj* [MF *audacieux*, fr. *audace* audacity, fr. L *audacia*, fr. *audac-, audax* bold (fr. *audēre* to dare) + *-ia* -y; akin to L *avidus* greedy — more at AVID] **1 a :** marked by spirited fearless daring **:** intrepidly adventurous ⟨~ visions of the total conquest of space⟩ **b :** recklessly venturesome **:** presumptuously bold **:** RASH ⟨an ~ disregard for physical limitations⟩ **2 a :** manifesting defiance of or contempt for the restrictions of law, religion, social codes, or tradition **:** arrogantly rebellious **:** INSOLENT ⟨~ individualists in love with absolute freedom⟩ **b :** marked by originality and verve **:** untrammeled by formalistic restraint **:** free of cautionary inhibitions ⟨making life an ~ experiment⟩ **syn** see BRAVE

²au·da·cious \", (')aù(t)¦d-\ *adv, dial Eng* **:** EXTREMELY, VERY ⟨~ cold weather⟩

au·da·cious·ly \(')ó¦d-\ *adv* [¹*audacious* + *-ly*] **:** in an audacious manner

au·da·cious·ness \ó'd-\ *n* -s **:** AUDACITY

au·dac·i·ty \ó'dasəd·ē, -aas-, -ətē, -i *sometimes* ə'-\ *n* -ES [ME *audacite*, fr. L *audac-, audax* + ME *-ite* -ity] **1 :** the quality or state of being audacious **:** daring boldness with assurance, presumption, or open disdain of restraint ⟨an innovating ~ for the form is unrelated to any traditional model —J.E. Gloag⟩ **2 :** an instance of audacity **:** an audacious act — usu. used in pl. ⟨my mind kindled at the thought of these *audacities* —L.P.Smith⟩ **syn** see TEMERITY

audad *var of* AOUDAD

au·dae·an \ó'dēən\ *or* **au·di·an** \'ódē-\ *n* -s *usu cap* [*Audaeus* or *Audius*, 4th cent. A.D. Mesopotamian religious reformer + E *-an*] **:** a member of an anthropomorphistic Christian sect founded by Audius in Asia in the 4th century A.D.

au·di·ber·tia \,ódə'bersh(ē)ə, ,ó-\ *n, cap* [NL, fr. Urbain *Audibert* †1846 Fr. botanist + NL *-ia*] **:** a genus of low shrubs (family Labiatae) of the western U.S. and adjacent Mexico with often hoary or canescent foliage and small spicate flowers — see BLACK SAGE 5

au·di·bil·i·ty \,ódə'biləd·ē, -ətē, -i\ *n* -ES **:** the quality or state of being audible; *specif* **:** the degree of intensity of a received radio signal estimated as the ratio of the current in the telephone receiver to that producing a signal that is sufficiently audible to permit the differentiation of telegraphic dot and dash elements of letters

audibility meter *n* **:** an instrument for measuring the intensity of radio signals that consists essentially of a variable resistor and a telephone receiver

au·di blade \'ó,dē-\ *n, usu cap A* [origin unknown] **:** an implement found in early Aurignacian cultural levels that is a development of a Mousterian flake tool

au·di·ble \'ódəbəl\ *adj* [LL *audibilis*, fr. L *audire* to hear + *-ibilis* -ible; akin to Gk *aiein* to hear, *aisthanesthai* to perceive, Skt *āvis* evidently, Av *āviš*, OSlav *avě, javě* evident] **:** capable of being heard **:** actually heard ⟨he spoke in an ~ whisper⟩ — **au·di·ble·ness** *n* -ES

audible control *n* **:** remote supervisory radio control that uses audible signals in conveying information or instructions

au·di·bly \-blē, -i\ *adv* **:** in such a way as to be audible ⟨expressed their disapproval ~⟩

au·di·ence \'ódēən(t)s, 'äd-, *Brit often & US sometimes* -dyən-\ *n* -s *often attrib* [ME, fr. MF, fr. L *audientia*, fr. *audient-, audiens* (pres. part. of *audire* to hear) + *-ia* -y] **1 a :** the act of hearing; *esp* **:** attention to that which is heard, usu. to words ⟨give me ~ and heed what I say⟩ **b** *archaic* **:** the state of hearing **:** the condition of being within hearing distance **:** HEARING ⟨he said this in the ~ of all⟩ **2 a :** formal hearing **:** formal interview (as with a sovereign or the head of a government) — often used with *with*, sometimes with *of* ⟨an ~ with the king⟩ ⟨they were received in the royal ~ chamber⟩ **b :** an opportunity of being heard ⟨he would succeed if he were once given an ~⟩ **3 a :** a group or assembly of listeners ⟨the lecturer spoke to a large ~⟩ ⟨the pianist had a very appreciative ~⟩ ⟨a nationwide radio ~⟩ **b :** a group or assembly of spectators ⟨a varied ~ attended the science exhibit⟩ ⟨a tremendous ~ of sports enthusiasts⟩ **c :** those attending a stage or film production or viewing a televised program ⟨the play met with favorable ~ reaction⟩ **d :** the public reached by books, newspapers, magazines, or other similar media ⟨influencing an ~ of millions through his books⟩ **4 :** those interested in, responsive to, or otherwise supporting an individual (as a writer), an ideology (as liberalism), an art form (as poetry), or other object of public interest **:** FOLLOWING ⟨developing an enthusiastic ~ for the free expression of ideas⟩

audience court *n* **:** the court held by an archbishop

audience flow *n* **:** the flux in audience size from one television or radio program to the next

au·di·en·cia \,aùdē'en(t)sēə, -nch(ē)ə\ *n* -s [Sp, lit., hearing, fr. L *audientia*] **1 a :** a tribunal in which the sovereign of Spain gave his personal attention to matters of justice **b :** a Spain ecclesiastical or secular court representing the king of Spain **2 :** a high court of justice in a Spanish colony frequently exercising military power as well as judicial and political functions **3 :** a provincial or territorial high court in modern Spain **4 :** the jurisdiction of an audiencia

au·di·ent \'ódēənt, 'äd-, -dyənt\ *n* -s [L *audient-, audiens*] **1 :** HEARER **2** *in the early Christian Church:* **a :** one permitted to attend services in the narthex but dismissed after the sermon **b :** a catechumen in the early stages of instruction for admission to the church but not yet an applicant for baptism

¹au·dile \'ó,dīl\ *n* -s [L *audire* to hear + E *-ile* — more at AUDIBLE] **:** one whose mental imagery is auditory rather than visual or motor — compare MOTILE, VISUALIZER

²audile \"\ *adj* [L *audire* + E *-ile*] **1 a :** AUDITORY **b :** of or relating to an audile **2 :** relating to or transmitted by the cochlear nerves and auditory tracts

aud·ing \'ódiŋ\ *n* -s [L *audire* + E *-ing*] **:** the process of hearing, listening to, recognizing, and interpreting spoken language

¹au·di·o \'ódē,ō\ *adj* [*audio-*] **1 :** of or relating to acoustic, mechanical, or electrical frequencies in the range of audible sound ⟨~ signal⟩ ⟨~ amplifier⟩ ⟨~ transformer⟩ **2 a :** of, relating to, or dealing with sound ⟨~ waves⟩ ⟨~ research⟩ ⟨a new ~ book⟩ **b :** relating to or used in the reproduction of sound (as in high-fidelity equipment) ⟨an ~ set⟩ **c :** relating to or used in the transmission or reception of sound (as in radio or television) ⟨~ components of a television set⟩ — compare VIDEO **3 a :** marked by special interest in and usu. a technical knowledge of the mechanics of sound, esp. its transmission, reception, and reproduction ⟨~ experts⟩ ⟨~ enthusiasts⟩ **b :** specializing in the manufacture, distribution, sale, or promotion of audio equipment ⟨an ~ supply house⟩ ⟨an ~ fair⟩ **4 :** of or relating to high fidelity ⟨a disc that pleases any ~ connoisseur⟩ ⟨a tape meeting exacting ~ standards⟩

²audio \"\ *n* -s **1 :** the transmission, reception, or reproduction of sound esp. in high fidelity **2 a :** the section of television equipment used to supply sound **:** electronic equipment primarily designed to handle signals of an audible frequency **b :** the part of an electric or acoustic signal that falls in the audible frequency spectrum

audio- *comb form* [L *audire* to hear + E *-o-*] **1 :** hearing ⟨*audio*logy⟩ ⟨*audio*meter⟩ **2 :** sound **:** frequencies in the range of audible sound ⟨*audio*genic⟩ **3 :** auditory and ⟨*audio*visual

audio frequency *n* **:** the frequency of any normally audible sound wave; *also* **:** any frequency in the range approximately between 15 and 20,000 cycles per second

au·di·o·gen·ic \¦ódē(,)ō¦jenik, -dēə¦-\ *adj* [*audio-* + *-genic*] **:** produced by frequencies corresponding to sound waves — used esp. of epileptoid responses ⟨~ seizures⟩

au·di·o·gram \'==(,)=,gram\ *n* -s [*audio-* + *-gram*] **:** a graphic representation of the relation of vibrational frequency and the auditory minimal threshold

au·di·ol·o·gist \,=='äləjəst\ *n* -s **:** a specialist in audiology

au·di·ol·o·gy \-'äləjē\ *n* -ES [*audio-* + *-logy*] **:** the branch of science dealing with hearing; *specif* **:** therapy of individuals having impaired hearing — distinguished from *otology*

au·di·om·e·ter \-'ämət·ə(r)\ *n* -s [*audio-* + *-meter*] **:** an instrument used in measuring the acuity of hearing in the individual ear for sounds of various frequencies esp. with a view to detecting departures from normal hearing

au·di·o·metric \¦ȯdē(ˌ)ō, -dēə + ¦==\ *adj* [*audio-* + *metric*] : of or relating to audiometry : marked by the use of audiometry

au·di·o·metrically \"+¦==(=)=\ *adv* : through the use of audiometry : in a manner marked by audiometric theory or methods ⟨testing prospective air pilots ~⟩

au·di·om·e·trist \ˌȯdē'ämətrəst\ *n* -S : a specialist in audiometry

au·di·om·e·try \-'ämətrē\ *n* -ES [*audio-* + *-metry*] : the testing and measurement of hearing acuity for variations in sound intensity and pitch and for tonal purity

Au·di·on \'ȯdēən, -ˌän\ *trademark* — used for a 3-electrode tube

au·di·o·phile \'ȯdēō,fīl, -ēə,-\ *n* -S [*audio-* + *-phile*] : an audio enthusiast

au·di·o·spectrograph \¦ȯdē(ˌ)ō +\ *n* -S [*audio-* + *spectrograph*] : an instrument that measures sound and records the measurement on a record sheet

audio spectrometer *n* : an instrument that records the relative intensities in a complex sound over a succession of equal frequency ranges

au·dio·visual \¦ȯdē(ˌ)ō + ¦-\ *adj* [*audio-* + *visual*] **1** : of or relating to both hearing and sight **2** : designed to aid in learning and teaching by making use of both hearing and sight ⟨an ~ education program⟩ ⟨an extensive ~ department of films and recordings⟩

au·di·phone \'ȯdə,fōn\ *n* -S [*audi-* (fr. L *audire* to hear) + *-phone*] : an instrument consisting of a diaphragm or plate that is placed against the teeth and conveys sound vibrations to the inner ear enabling persons with certain types of deafness to hear more or less distinctly

1au·dit \'ȯdət, *usu* -dəd·+V\ *n* -S [ME, fr. L *auditus* hearing, fr. *auditus*, past part. of *audire* to hear — more at AUDIBLE] **1 a** : a formal or official examination and verification of books of account (as for reporting on the financial condition of a business at a given date or on the results of its operations for a given period) **b** : a methodical examination and review of a situation or condition (as within a business enterprise) concluding with a detailed report of findings : a rendering and settling of accounts **2** : the final report following a formal examination of books of account : an account as adjusted by auditors : final statement of account **3** *archaic* : a judicial examination (as in a court) **4** : AUDIT ALE **5** : a check of publishers' records to verify claims as to the extent of a publication's circulation

2audit \"\ *vb* -ED/-ING/-S *vt* **1** : to examine and verify (as the books of account of a company or a treasurer's accounts) **2** : to attend (a course esp. in a college or university) without working for or expecting to receive formal credit ~ *vi* : to make an audit **syn** see SCRUTINIZE

audit- *or* **audito-** *comb form* [ME *audit-*, fr. MF & L; MF *audit-*, fr. L, fr. *auditus*, past part. of *audire* to hear] **1** : hearing : sound ⟨*audit*ize⟩ **2** : auditory and ⟨*audito*psychic⟩ ⟨*audito*sensory⟩

audit ale *n* [so called fr. its original use on the day of audit] : a strong ale brewed at some English universities, esp. at Cambridge and Oxford

au·di·ta que·re·la \aů¦dēd·əkwə'rālə\ *n* [L, the complaint having been heard] : a largely disused or abolished common-law writ lying for a party against whom judgment is recovered but to whom facts constituting a good basis for discharge have subsequently accrued or become possible that could not have been availed of to prevent such judgment

auditing *n* -S [fr. gerund of *2audit*] : a branch of accounting that deals with the examination and verification of accounts or books of account and with making the final reports

1au·di·tion \ȯ'dishən\ *n* -S [MF or L; MF, fr. L *audition-*, *auditio*, fr. *auditus* + *-ion-*, *-io* -ion] **1** : the power or sense of hearing : ability to hear **2** : the act of hearing **3** : the act of listening to intently : a critical hearing ⟨an ~ of new recordings⟩ **4** : a trial performance to appraise an entertainer's merits

2audition \"\ *vb* **auditioned**; **auditioned**; **auditioning** \-sh(ə)niŋ\ **auditions** *vt* : to try out in an audition ⟨the producer ~*ed* the choreography group⟩ ~ *vi* : to give a trial performance ⟨she ~*ed* for the leading role⟩

au·di·tive \'ȯdəd·iv, -ətiv\ *adj* [F *auditif*, fr. MF, fr. *audition*, after such pairs as MF *attraction: attractif* attractive] : AUDITORY

au·di·tor \'ȯdəd·ə(r), -ətə(r)\ *n* -S [ME *auditour*, fr. MF & ML; MF *auditeur* hearer, judge's assistant & ML *auditor* one that audits accounts, fr. L *auditor* hearer, fr. *auditus* + *-or*] **1** : one that hears or listens; *specif* : one that is part of an audience ⟨~*s* and viewers of radio and television programs⟩ **2 a** : one that audits **b** : one authorized to examine and verify accounts **c** : one skilled in the technique of auditing **3** : DISCIPLE, CATECHUMEN ⟨the elect were a class above the ~*s* or novices —G.P.Fisher⟩ **4** : one that hears judicially: as **a** : the presiding official of a court of inquiry in criminal cases in some European countries **b** : a judicial assessor to courts-martial in some countries **c** : one of the lowest rank of special members of the French Council of State **d** : a referee appointed by a court in a civil action in some jurisdictions; *esp* : one designated to take an account and report to the court **5** : one that audits a course of study esp. in a college or university

auditor-general *n*, *pl* **auditors-general** : a chief auditorial officer

au·di·to·ri·al \¦ȯdə¦tōrēəl\ *adj* : of or relating to an audit or an auditor of accounts

au·di·to·ri·um \ˌȯdə'tōrēəm, -ȯr-\ *n*, *pl* **auditoriums** \-ēəmz\ *also* **audito·ria** \-ēə\ [L, fr. *auditus* (past part. of *audire* to hear) + *-orium*] **1** : the part of a usu. public building (as a theater) assigned to the audience : a place of assemblage of spectators and listeners **2** : a room, hall, or entire building specially designed for stage and film presentations, concerts, recitals, lectures, and audio-visual features and activities ⟨a magnificent civic ~⟩ ⟨a school ~⟩

1au·di·to·ry \'ȯdə,tōrē, -ȯr-, -ri\ *n* -ES [ME *auditorie*, fr. L *auditorium* auditorium] **1** *archaic* : an assemblage of listeners and spectators : AUDIENCE **2** *archaic* : AUDITORIUM

2auditory \"\ *adj* [LL *auditorius*, fr. L *auditus* + *-orius* -ory] **1** : of or relating to hearing **2** : attained, produced, or experienced through hearing ⟨~ images⟩ ⟨the enjoyment of ~ rhythm⟩ **3** : marked by great or sometimes extreme susceptibility to impressions and reactions produced by acoustic stimuli : AUDILE ⟨an ~ type of individual⟩

auditory aphasia *n* : inability to understand spoken words

auditory area *or* **auditory center** *n* : a sensory area in the temporal cortex associated with the organ of hearing

auditory capsule *also* **auditory vesicle** *n* : OTIC VESICLE

auditory cell *n* : a hair cell of the organ of Corti

auditory ganglion *n* : ACOUSTIC TUBERCLE

auditory meatus *or* **auditory canal** *n* : either of two passages of the ear — in human anatomy sometimes called *acoustic meatus;* compare EXTERNAL AUDITORY MEATUS, INTERNAL AUDITORY MEATUS; see EAR illustration

auditory nerve *also* **auditory** *n* : either of the 8th pair of cranial nerves being a sensory nerve composed of two parts: (1) a part arising in the spiral ganglion of the cochlea and serving to conduct sensory stimuli from the organ of hearing to the brain and (2) a part arising from the vestibular ganglion of the internal auditory meatus and serving to conduct stimuli having to do with the maintenance of bodily equilibrium, the two entering the brain together through the lateral wall of the medulla — called also respectively (1) *cochlear nerve*, (2) *vestibular nerve;* see EAR illustration

auditory pit *n* : the indentation of thickened surface ectoderm to form the embryonic ear

auditory placode *n* : either of the anterior lateral areas of ectoderm that invaginate and sink beneath the body surface to form the internal ear structures of vertebrate embryos

auditory point *n* : the lowest part of the notch between the incurved rim of the outer ear and the tragus

auditory tube *n* : EUSTACHIAN TUBE

au·di·tress \'ȯdə·trəs\ *n* -ES [*auditor* + *-ess*] : a female auditor

audits *pl of* AUDIT, *pres 3d sing of* AUDIT

au·di·vise \'ȯdə,vīz\ *vb* -ED/-ING/-S [back-formation fr. *audivision*] : to transmit or receive by audivision

au·di·vi·sion \'ȯdə,vizhən *sometimes* ,=='==\ *n* -S [*audi-* (fr. L *audire* to hear) + *vision* — more at AUDIBLE] : the transmission or reception of a succession of images with accompanying sounds over wire or wireless circuits by electrical means

au·du·bon's caracara \'ȯdəbənz-, -,bänz *sometimes* 'ȯdyə- *or* 'ȯjə-\ *n*, *usu cap A* [after J. J. *Audubon* †1851 Am. ornithologist] : a No. American caracara (*Polyborus cheriway audubonii*) that is widespread from the southern U. S. through Mexico to Central America and is rusty black above with a bright bare face, a small black crest, and the breast and tail white marked with black

audubon's shearwater *n*, *usu cap A* : a small dark-footed shearwater (*Puffinus lherminieri* or *Procellaria lherminieri*) chiefly of the West Indies and the Florida coast

audubon warbler *also* **audubon's warbler** *n*, *usu cap A* : a common warbler (*Dendroica auduboni*) of western No. America resembling the myrtle warbler but more extensively yellow on the breast

aue *or* **au·we** \aů'wā\ *interj* [Maori, Hawaiian, Tahitian, Marquesan, & Samoan *auē*, *auwē*] — used in Polynesia to express an emotional reaction (as sorrow, surprise, or affection)

auer·bach's plexus \'aů(ə)r,bäks-\ *n*, *usu cap A* [G *Auerbachscher plexus*, after Leopold *Auerbach* †1897 Ger. anatomist] : a network of nerve fibers and ganglia between the longitudinal and circular muscular layers of the intestine — called also *myenteric plexus*

au·e·tö \ˌaůə'tō\ *n*, *pl* **auetö** *or* **auetös** *usu cap* [G *Auetö*, of AmerInd origin] **1 a** : a Tupian people of the upper Xingú river basin in the state of Mato Grosso, Brazil **b** : a member of such people **2** : the language of the Auetö people

auf *or* **awf** \'ȯf\ *n* -S [prob. fr. ON *alfr* elf — more at ELF] **1** *now dial Eng* : CHANGELING **2** *now dial Eng* : SIMPLETON

au fait \ō'fā\ *adj* [F, lit., to the point] **1** : fully competent : up to the mark : CAPABLE ⟨he is remarkably *au fait* in business⟩ ⟨quite *au fait* at playing tennis⟩ **2** : FAMILIAR : fully informed : in touch : au courant ⟨they are always *au fait* on the latest events⟩ ⟨putting her *au fait* with what had happened⟩ **3** : socially correct : PROPER : in good form ⟨a somewhat unusual piece of interior decoration, but really quite *au fait*⟩

au·fait \"\ *n* -S [prob. alter. (influenced by *1au fait*) of *parfait*] : brick ice cream in layers with frozen candied fruit between the layers

auf·ga·be \'aůf,gäbə\ *n*, *pl* **aufga·ben** \-bən\ *usu cap* [G (influenced in meaning by *aufgeben* to assign), fr. MHG *ūfgābe* act of handing over, fr. *ūf* up, on (fr. OHG) + *gābe* gift; akin to OHG *geban* to give — more at UP, GIVE] : a task esp. when assigned experimentally or as a test (as in psychology) : EXERCISE

auf·klä·rung \'aůf,klārəŋ, -ler-, -laar-, -(ˌ)růŋ\ *n* -S *usu cap* [G, fr. *aufklären* to enlighten, clear up (fr. *auf* up — fr. OHG *ūf* — + *klären* to clear, explain, fr. MHG *klæren*, fr. *klār* clear, fr. MD *claer*, fr. L *clarus*) + *-ung* -ing (fr. OHG *-unga*) — more at UP, CLEAR] : ENLIGHTENMENT 2

au fond \ō'fōⁿ\ *adv* [F, lit., at the bottom] : at bottom : FUNDAMENTALLY, ESSENTIALLY

auf·takt \'aůf,täkt\ *n* -S [G, fr. *auf* up + *takt*] : UPBEAT

auf·tak·tig·keit \'aůf,täktik,kīt\ *n* -S [G, fr. *auftakt*] : a principle in music: all musical phrases begin on an upbeat

auf wie·der·sehen \aůf'vēdər,zā(ə)n\ *interj*, *usu cap W* [G, trans. of F *au revoir*] : GOOD-BYE

aug *abbr* augmentative; augmented

au·ga·nite \'ȯgə,nīt\ *n* -S [*aug*ite + *an*desite] : an olivine-free basaltic rock whose essential minerals are calcic plagioclase and augite

1auge *n* -S [MF, fr. Ar *awj* top, summit] **1** *obs* : APSIS 1 **2** *obs* : APOGEE

2au·ge \'aůgə\ *n*, *pl* **au·gen** \-gən\ [G, lit., eye, fr. OHG *ouga* — more at EYE] : an elliptical or lens-shaped aggregate produced by the squeezing of the constituents of certain metamorphic rocks into an eyelike form

au·ge·an \(')ȯ¦jēən\ *adj*, *usu cap* [*Augeas* legendary king of Elis whose immense stable, left unclean for 30 years, was cleaned by Hercules (fr. L, fr. Gk *Augeias*) + E *-an*] : extremely difficult and usu. very distasteful ⟨an *Augean* task⟩

augean stable *n*, *usu cap A* : a condition or place marked by a staggering accumulation of corruption and filth ⟨every government ought to attend to cleaning its own *Augean stables*⟩

au·ge·lite \'ȯjə,līt, -gə-\ *n* -S [ISV *auge-* (fr. Gk *augē* brightness) + *-lite;* prob. orig. formed as G *augelith;* akin to Alb *agój* to dawn, OSlav *jugŭ* south; basic meaning: brightness] : a mineral $Al_2(OH)_3PO_4$ consisting of a colorless or white basic aluminum phosphate (sp. gr. 2.7)

au·gend \'ȯ,jend\ *n* -S [L *augendum*, neut. of *augendus*, gerundive of *augēre* to increase — more at EKE] : the quantity to which an addend is added

au·gen·phi·lo·lo·gie \'aůgən,fēləlō'gē, -_fə,lōl-\ *n* -S [G, lit., philology of the eyes, fr. *augen* (pl. of *auge* eye) + *philologie* philology] : linguistics that misrepresents the realities of speech because of overemphasis on writing

1au·ger \'ȯgə(r)\ *n* -S [ME, alter. (resulting from incorrect division of *a nauger*) of *nauger*, *navegar*, fr. OE *nafogār* (akin to OHG *nabugēr*, OS *nabugēr*, ON *nafarr*), fr. *nafu* nave (of a wheel) + *gār* spear — more at NAVE, GORE] **1** : a tool for boring holes in wood consisting of a shank with a crosswise handle for turning and having spiral channels that end in two spurs for marking the outline of the hole, a central tapered feed screw, and a pair of cutting lips **2** : any of various augerlike tools designed for boring into soil and used esp. for such purposes as prospecting, drilling for oil or water, and digging postholes **3** : a large spiral bit used to mix a material and force it through a die (as in a brickmaking machine or a meat grinder) **4** : the rotating helical member of a screw conveyor

screw auger

2auger \"\ *vt* -ED/-ING/-S : to move by use of an auger ⟨chopped and ~*ed* into silos —Ross Wurm⟩

auger beetle *n* : any of a number of elongated cylindrical beetles (family Bostrychidae) having the head protected by the heavy often spiny prothorax and boring in and feeding on wood

auger bit *n* : a wood-boring bit shaped like an auger but without a handle, one end of which usu. has a square tang to fit the chuck of a brace

auger conveyor *n* : CONVEYER 2a(8)

au·ger effect \(')ō¦zhā-\ *n*, *usu cap A* [after Pierre V. *Auger* *b*1899 Fr. physicist] : a process in which an atom singly ionized by emitting one electron with energy in the X-ray range instead of emitting the usual X-ray photon on recovery undergoes a transition in which a second electron is emitted

auger electron *n*, *usu cap A* [after P. V. *Auger*] : one of the electrons ejected from an atom as a result of the internal conversion of its own X rays in the Auger effect

auger shell \'ȯgə(r)-\ *n* : a gastropod mollusk of the family Terebridae with an elongated spiral shell; *also* : the shell itself

auger shower \(')ō¦zhā-\ *n*, *usu cap A* [after P. V. *Auger*] : an extensive air shower

auger stem \'ȯgə(r)-\ *n* : a long round bar of iron to which the bit and the rope socket or jars may be attached for oil-well drilling

1aught \'äkt, 'ȯ-\ *n* -S [ME *aught*, *aughte* property, possession, fr. OE *æht;* akin to OHG *ēht* property, ON *ātt*, *ætt* family, race, generation, Goth *aihts* property, possession, OE *āgan* to own — more at OWN] **1** *Scot* : OWNERSHIP, POSSESSION ⟨I am as weel worth looking at as ony book in your ~ —Sir Walter Scott⟩ **2** *Scot* : PROPERTY

2aught *also* **ought** \'ȯt, 'ät\ *pron* [ME *aught*, *awiht*, fr. OE *āwiht*, *ōwiht* (akin to OHG *eowiht*), fr. *ā*, *ō* ever + *wiht* creature, thing — more at AYE, WIGHT] **1** *archaic* : any least part : anything whatsoever ⟨go, my son, and see if ~ be wanting —Joseph Addison⟩ **2** : ALL ⟨for ~ he knew to the contrary, it might have been some quack —G.W. Johnson⟩

3aught \"\ *adv* [ME, fr. *2aught*] *archaic* : at all : in any degree : to any extent ⟨he doesn't care ~ for that⟩

4aught *or* **aucht** \'äkt, 'ȯ-\ *vt past* **aught** *or* **aucht** \"\ *pres part* **aught·ing** \-tən,-tiŋ\ *or* **aucht·en** \-tən\ *pres 3d sing* **aughts** *or* **aught** *or* **auchts** *or* **aucht** [ME *aghten*, *aughten*, *oughten* to be obliged to, to owe — more at OUGHT] **1** *Scot* : OWN **2** *Scot* : OWE

5aught \'äkt, 'ȯ-\ *adj* [ME *aghte*, *aughte*, *oughte* possessed, owned, owed, past & past part. of *aghen*, *aughen*, *awen* to possess, own, owe — more at OWE] *Scot* : possessed of

6aught \'äkt\ *adj* [ME *aghte*, *aughte*, var. of *eighte* — more at EIGHT] **1** *Scot* : EIGHT **2** *Scot* : EIGHTH

7aught \'ȯt, 'ät\ *n* -S [alter. (resulting from incorrect division of *a naught*) of *naught*] **1** : ZERO, CIPHER **2** *archaic* : NONENTITY, NOTHING

aught·lins \'äktlənz\ *var of* OUGHTLINS

au·gite \'ȯ,jīt, -gīt\ *n* -S [L *augites*, a precious stone, fr. Gk *augitēs*, fr. Gk *augē* brightness + *-ites* -ite — more at AUGELITE] **1** : a mineral principally $(Ca,Na)(Mg,Fe,Al)(Si,Al)_2O_6$ consisting of an aluminous usu. black or dark green variety of pyroxene occurring in igneous rocks such as basalt **2** : PYROXENE

au·git·ic \(')ȯ¦jid·ik\ *adj* : of or relating to augite

au·gi·tite \'ȯjəd·,īt, -gə-, -ə,tīt\ *n* -S [ISV *augite* + *-ite;* prob. orig. formed as G *augitit*] : an extrusive porphyritic rock consisting essentially of augite with small amounts of amphibole magnetite or ilmenite and apatite in a glassy groundmass

au·git·o·phyre \ȯ'jid·ə,fī(ə)r\ *n* -S [ISV *augite* + *-o-* + *-phyre*] : a porphyritic rock with augite phenocrysts in a groundmass of potash feldspar

1aug·ment \ȯg'ment, '=,=\ *vb* -ED/-ING/-S [ME *augmenten*, fr. MF *augmenter*, fr. LL *augmentare*, fr. *augmentum* increase, fr. L *augēre* to increase + *-mentum* -ment — more at EKE] *vi* : to become augmented : INCREASE ⟨as the morning advances, the din of labor ~*s* —Washington Irving⟩ ~ *vt* **1** : to enlarge or increase esp. in size, amount, or degree : make bigger : SWELL ⟨the army was ~*ed* by reinforcements⟩ ⟨rain ~*ed* the stream⟩ **2** : to make an augmentation to (a coat of arms) **3** : to add an augment to **4 a** : to increase by a half step (a perfect or a major interval in music) **b** : to double the note values in the development of (a theme in music) **syn** see INCREASE

2aug·ment \'ȯg,ment, *Brit usu* -_mənt\ *n* -S [ME, fr. MF, fr. LL *augmentum*] : a prefixed vowel (as epsilon in Greek, usu. short *a-* in Sanskrit) or a lengthening or diphthongization of the initial vowel in certain verb forms to indicate past time (as in Skt *asicat* "he poured" from *sic* "to pour", Gk *egrapse* "he wrote" from *graphein* "to write", Gk *ērche* "he began" from *archein* "to begin")

aug·men·ta·tion \ˌȯgmən·'tāshən, -ˌmen-\ *n* -S [ME *augmentacioun*, fr. MF *augmentation*, fr. LL *augmentation-*, *augmentatio*, fr. *augmentatus* (past part. of *augmentare*) + L *-ion-*, *-io* -ion] **1 a** : the act, action, or process of augmenting **b** : the process of becoming augmented : GROWTH, INCREASE **2** : the state of being augmented ⟨a general ~ of wealth and leisure⟩ **3** : something that augments : ADDITION ⟨a fleet of new jets was a notable ~ for the air force⟩ **4** : the device of modifying a musical subject or theme by repetition in tones of usu. twice the original length (as in polyphonic music) **5** *Scots law* : increase of stipend obtained by a parish minister **6** : an additional charge to a coat of arms given as an honor

1aug·men·ta·tive \(')ȯg¦mentəd·iv, -ətiv\ *adj* [MF or ML; MF *augmentatif*, fr. ML *augmentativus*, fr. LL *augmentatus* + L *-ivus* -ive] **1** : having the quality or power of augmenting **2** : indicating large size and sometimes awkwardness or unattractiveness — used of affixes and of words formed with them (as Italian *casone* "big house", from *casa* "house", and Italian *-one* in words like *casone*); contrasted with *diminutive*

2augmentative \"\ *n* -S : an augmentative word or affix

augmented *adj* : INCREASED, ENLARGED; *sometimes* : ENHANCED ⟨~ renown⟩ — **aug·ment·ed·ly** *adv*

augmented interval *n* : an interval in music greater by one half step than a major or perfect interval or greater by two half steps than a minor interval

augmented pedal *n* : the pedal division in an organ in which borrowing and unification are used

augmented triad *n* : a triad having a major third and an augmented fifth — see TRIAD illustration

aug·men·tor *also* **aug·ment·er** \ȯg'mentə(r), 'ȯg,m-\ *n* -S : one that augments; *specif* : a tube enclosing the exhaust jet of a jet engine to give more thrust — called also *thrust augmentor*

au gra·tin \ō'grätᵊn, ȯ'-, -rat-\ *adj* [F, lit., with the burnt particles left on the bottom of the pan] : browned under a flame or in a hot oven; *specif* : covered with bread crumbs, butter, and cheese and then browned ⟨potatoes *au gratin*⟩

augs·burg \'aůgz,bůrg, 'aůks,-, -rk; 'ȯgz,bərg\ *adj*, *usu cap* [fr. *Augsburg*, Germany] : of or from the city of Augsburg, Germany : of the kind or style prevalent in Augsburg

1au·gur \'ȯgə(r) *also* 'ȯgyə(r)\ *n* -S [L, prob. fr. *augēre* to increase — more at EKE] **1** : a member of the highest class of official diviners of ancient Rome **2** : one reputed to foretell events by omens : SOOTHSAYER, PROPHET

2augur \"\ *vb* -ED/-ING/-S [L *augurari*, *augurare*, fr. *augur*, n.] *vt* **1** : to predict or foretell esp. from signs or omens ⟨an unloved brother, of whom worse things had been ~*ed* —George Eliot⟩ — often used with *well* or *ill* ⟨he ~*ed* well for his plan⟩ **2** : to give promise of : give indirect evidence of : PORTEND, PRESAGE, BETOKEN ⟨their enthusiasm ~*s* continued success⟩ ⟨ominous delays that ~ the failure of the venture⟩ ~ *vi* : to predict the future (as from signs or omens) : make an augury ⟨she starts ~*ing* on the least pretext⟩ **syn** see FORETELL

au·gu·ral \'ȯg(y)ərəl\ *adj* [L *auguralis*, fr. *augur* + *-alis* -al] **1** : of or relating to an augur or augury **2** : signifying the future : ominous, portentous, or auspicious

augurate *vb* -ED/-ING/-S [L, *auguratus*, past part. of *augurare*, *augurari* to augur] *vt*, *obs* : to infer from signs or omens ~ *vi*, *obs* : to make an augury

au·gur·er \'ȯgərə(r) *also* 'ȯgyə-\ *n* -S [*2augur* + *-er*] **1** *obs* : AUGUR 1 **2** : AUGUR 2

au·gu·ry \'ȯgyərē, -ri *also* 'ȯgə-\ *n* -ES [ME *augurie*, fr. MF, fr. L *augurium*, fr. *augur*] **1 a** : divination by the interpretation of omens or portents (as inspection of the flight of birds or the entrails of sacrificed animals) or of chance phenomena (as the fall of lots) — see AUSPICE 1; compare SORTILEGE **b** : the rite or ceremony of divination followed by an augur **2** : a sign or omen taken as an indication of the future : PORTENT ⟨like an ~, the night was coming closer —Norman Mailer⟩ **3** : an indication of the future or of future events ⟨an exciting ~ of things to come —Bennett Cerf⟩

1au·gust \'ȯgəst\ *n* -S *usu cap* [ME, fr. OE, fr L *Augustus*, after *Augustus* Caesar †A.D. 14 1st Roman emperor] : the 8th month of the year in the Gregorian calendar — abbr. *Aug.;* see MONTH table

2au·gust \(')ȯ¦gəst *sometimes* ə'g- *or* 'ȯ_g-\ *adj*, *sometimes* -ER/-EST [L *augustus*, fr. *augēre* to increase — more at EKE] : of majestic dignity or grandeur : marked by stateliness or magnificence **syn** see GRAND

au·gus·ta \ȯ'gəstə, ə'-\ *adj*, *usu cap* [fr. *Augusta*, Maine] : of or from Augusta, the capital of Maine : of the kind or style prevalent in Augusta

au·gus·tal \ȯ'gəstᵊl, ə'-\ *or* **au·gus·ta·le** \ˌaůgə'stälē\ *or* **au·gus·ta·lis** \ˌȯgə'staləs\ *n*, *pl* **augustals** \-tᵊlz\ *or* **augusta·les** \ˌaůgə'stälēz, ˌȯgə'sta(ˌ)lēz\ [It & ML; It *augustale*, fr. ML *augustalis*, fr. *Augustalis* of Frederick II †1250 Holy Roman Emperor, bearing, like all Roman emperors, the surname *Augustus*, fr. L, of Caesar Augustus, fr. Caesar *Augustus* + L *-alis* *-al*] : a medieval Italian gold coin struck in the 13th century by Frederick II, patterned after the Roman aureus, and having on the obverse the emperor's bust draped in Roman garb

1au·gus·tan \(')ȯ¦gəstən, ə'-\ *adj*, *usu cap* [ML *Augustanus*, fr. L *Augusta* (Vindelicorum), Roman colony in Germany (now *Augsburg*) + L *-anus* -an] : of or relating to the town of Augsburg, Germany

2augustan \"\ *adj*, *usu cap* [L *Augustanus*, fr. *Augustus* + *-anus* -an] **1** : of, relating to, or characteristic of Augustus Caesar or his age **2** : of, relating to, or characteristic of any age felt to resemble that of Augustus Caesar (as the neoclassic period in England or specif. the reign of Queen Anne) — compare CLASSICAL 2

3augustan \"\ *n* -S *usu cap* **1** : an English Augustan writer ⟨Alexander Pope and Joseph Addison were *Augustans*⟩ **2** : a person of the Augustan period in England; *esp* : one sharing the neoclassic belief of the period ⟨an *Augustan* in spirit⟩

au·gus·tana lutheran \'ȯgə,stanə-\ *n*, *usu cap A&L* [NL *Augustana* (in *Confessio Augustana* Augsburg Confession, famous Lutheran document of 1530), fr. ML, fem. of *Augustanus* of Augsburg] : a member of the Augustana Evangelical

Lutheran Church organized chiefly by Swedish immigrants in the midwestern U. S. in 1860

au·guste \'au̇gəst\ *n* -s *often cap* [F, prob. fr. G *august*, fr. the name *August*] : a circus clown who appears in white makeup and follows a chiefly slapstick routine

augusti *pl of* AUGUSTUS

¹au·gus·tin·ian \ˌȯgəˈstinēən, -tēn-, -nyən\ *adj, usu cap* [St. *Augustine* (Aurelius Augustinus) †430 Numidian church father and philosopher, bishop of Hippo (ancient city near what is now Bône, Algeria) + E *-ian*] **1** : of or relating to St. Augustine or his doctrines (as the tenets of absolute predestination and the immediate efficacy of grace) **2** : of or relating to any of several orders deriving their name from St. Augustine

²augustinian \"\ *n* -s *usu cap* **1** : a follower of St. Augustine; *specif* : one who accepts the views of Augustine on predestination and grace **2** : a member of an Augustinian order

augustinian hermit *n, usu cap A & sometimes cap H* : HERMIT OF ST. AUGUSTINE

au·gus·tin·ian·ism \-ˌnizəm\ *also* **au·gus·tin·ism** \ȯˈgəstəˌni-, ə'-; ˈȯgəˌstēˌni-\ *n* -s *cap* : the philosophical or theological doctrine of or body of Christian teaching traceable to St. Augustine embodying a distinctive synthetic reconciliation of the doctrines of the fall, predestination, irresistible grace, and free will

augustinian of the assumption *usu cap both As* : a member of a religious congregation founded by D'Alzon in 1844 at Nimes — called also *Assumptionist*

au·gus·tin process \ˈau̇gəˌstēn-\ *n, usu cap A* [trans. of G *Augustinverfahren*, fr. the name *Augustin*] : a process for extracting silver by converting it into chloride by roasting, leaching with salt solution, and precipitating by metallic copper

august lily *n, usu cap A* [¹*August*] : PLANTAIN LILY

au·gust·ly \(ˈ)ȯ¦gəstlē, -li *sometimes* əˈg- *or* ˈȯˌg-\ *adv* : in an august manner

august meteor *n, usu cap A* [¹*August*] : one of the Perseids

au·gust·ness *n* -ES : the quality or state of being august

au·gus·tus \ȯˈgəstəs, ə'-\ *n, pl* **augus·ti** \-ˌstī, au̇ˈgu̇ˌstē\ *usu cap* [L, fr. *augustus* exalted, sacred — more at AUGUST] **1 a** : imperial majesty — a title conferred upon Gaius Julius Caesar Octavianus in 27 B.C. and assumed by subsequent Roman emperors **b** : one of the Roman emperors with the title *Augustus* **2** : one of the rulers of the Eastern and Western Roman empires (as Diocletian, A.D. 286)

au·jesz·ky's disease \ˈau̇ˌyeskēz-\ *n, usu cap A* [after Aladar *Aujeszky* †1933 Hungarian pathologist] : PSEUDORABIES

au jus \ōˈzhüs, ōˈjüs, F ōzhüe\ *adj* [F, lit., with juice] : served in the meat juice obtained from roasting ⟨roast beef *au jus*⟩

¹auk \ˈȯk\ *n* -s [Norw. or Icel. *alk, alka*, fr. ON *ālka*; akin to L *olor* swan, MIr *ela*, and perh. to Gk *elea* a marsh bird] : any of several black and white short-necked diving sea birds of the family Alcidae that breed in colder parts of the northern hemisphere, laying their eggs in the open on ledges of cliffs or sometimes in burrows — see GREAT AUK, RAZORBILL

²auk \ˈȯk, ˈau̇k\ *n, pl* **auk** *or* **auks** *usu cap* **1** : a Tlingit people on Stephens Passage and Douglas and Admiralty islands, Alaska **2** : a member of the Auk people

great auk

aukaner *usu cap, var of* AUCANER

auk·let \ˈȯklət\ *n* -s [¹*auk* + *-let*] : any of several small auks of the No. Pacific coasts — see CASSIN'S AUKLET

aul \ˈau̇(ə)l\ *n* -s [Russ, fr. Kazan Tatar & Kirghiz] **1** : a Caucasian mountain or desert settlement (as a village) **2** : a Central Asiatic tent made of felt or skins fastened over a circular wooden framework

aul- *or* **aulo-** *comb form* [NL, fr. Gk, fr. *aulos* — more at ALVEOLUS] : flute : pipe ⟨*aulophyte*⟩ ⟨*Aulacanthus*⟩ ⟨*Aulostomus*⟩

¹au·la \ˈau̇lə, ˈȯlə\ *n, pl* **aulas** \-əz\ *or* **au·lae** \ˈau̇ˌlī, ˈȯˌlē\ [G, fr. L, court, hall, fr. Gk *aulē*; prob. akin to *iauein* to rest, sleep, Arm *aganim* I spend the night, and perh. to OE *wērig* weary — more at WEARY] **1** : a hall or large room; *specif* : the assembly hall in a German school or university **2** [NL, fr. L] : the anterior part of the third ventricle of the brain leading to the lateral ventricles

²au·la \ˈau̇lə\ *n* -s [Marathi *āvḷā*, fr. Skt *āmalaka*] : EMBLIC

au·la·com·ni·um \ˌȯləˈkämnēəm\ *n, cap* [NL, fr. Gk *aulak-, aulax* furrow + NL *-o-* + *Mnium*] : a small genus (the type of the family Aulacomniaceae) of tufted mosses closely related to the genus *Mnium* with each leaf cell having a conical central papilla and the capsules being striate and with double peristomes

¹au·lar·i·an \(ˈ)ȯ¦la(a)rēən\ *adj, sometimes cap* [ML *aularius* (fr. L *aula* hall) + E *-an*] : of or belonging to a hall; *specif* : belonging to an English university hall

²aularian \"\ *n* -s : a member of an English university hall

auld \ˈȯl(d), ˈäl(d)\ *adj* -ER/-EST [ME (northern dial.), alter. of ME *auld* old — more at OLD] *chiefly Scot* : OLD

auld-far·rant *or* **auld-far·ran** \(ˈ)=¦farən, -ənt, -ənd\ *adj* [Sc *auld* + *farrant, farran*] *chiefly Scot* : wise beyond one's years : SAGACIOUS, CUNNING

auld kirk \ˈ=¦kirk\ *n* [fr. *Auld Kirk*, lit., old church, the established church of Scotland; prob. fr. the more lenient attitude toward strong drink of Auld Kirkers compared with dissenters] *Scot* : WHISKEY

auld kirk·er \ˈ=ˌkirkər\ *n, usu cap A&K* [*Auld Kirk* + E *-er*] : a member of the established church of Scotland

auld lang syne \ˌōlˌlaŋˈzīn, ˌōlˌlaŋ-, ˌōlˌdaŋ-, -aiŋ- *also* ¦ōl,dla- *or* ¦ōl- *or* ¦äl- *or* ¦äl- *or* -ˈsīn\ *n* [Sc, old long ago] : the good old times ⟨let's drink to *auld lang syne*⟩

auld licht \ˈōl,(d)likt, ˈäl-\ *n, usu cap A&L* [Sc, lit., old light] : a member of one of those parties in the Scottish Secession churches, both Burgher and Antiburgher, that continued to hold to the principle of the connection between church and state in opposition to the voluntaryism of the New Lichts

auld wife *n* **1** *Scot* : OLD WIFE **2** *Scot* : a fussy nervous person

au·lic \ˈȯlik, ˈau̇l\ *adj* [F *aulique*, fr. L *aulicus*, fr. Gk *aulikos*, fr.Gk *aulē* + *-ikos -ic*] **1** : of or relating to a court : COURTLY ⟨ecclesiastical wealth and ~ dignities —W.S.Landor⟩ **2** [NL *aula* + E *-ic*] *anat* : of or relating to the aula

aulo- — see AUL-

au·lo·phyte \ˈȯləˌfīt\ *n* -s [*aul-* + *-phyte*] : a plant that lives within the cavity of another plant but that is neither a symbiont nor a parasite

au·los \ˈȯˌläs\ *n, pl* **au·loi** \-ˌlȯi\ [Gk — more at ALVEOLUS] : a Greek woodwind musical instrument that is commonly called a flute but is in fact a reed instrument similar to an oboe

au·lo·sto·mat·i·dae \ˌȯləstəˈmad·əˌdē\ [NL, fr. *Aulostomat-, Aulostoma*, type genus (fr. *aul-* + *-stomat-, -stoma*) + *-idae*] *syn of* AULOSTOMIDAE

au·los·to·mi \ȯˈlästəˌmī, ə-, -ˌmē\ *n pl, cap* [NL, fr. *aul-* + *-stomi*] *in some classifications* : an order comprising the cornetfishes, bellows fishes, and shrimpfishes all having a tubelike snout with small terminal mouth

au·lo·stom·i·dae \ˌȯləˈstäməˌdē\ *n pl, cap* [NL *Aulostomus*, type genus + *-idae*] : a family (order Solenichthyes or Aulostomi) of elongated compressed small-scaled fishes of warm seas having a group of separate dorsal spines and a single barbel under the chin — see AULOSTOMUS

au·los·to·mus \ȯˈlästəməs, ə-\ *n, cap* [NL, fr. *aul-* + *-stomus*] : a genus of tropical marine fishes comprising the flutemouths and constituting the monotypic family Aulostomidae

auls *pl of* AUL

au·lu \ˈau̇(ˌ)lü, ˈäu̇,-\ *n* -s [Hawaiian] **1** : a Hawaiian tree (*Sideroxylon sandwicense*) the milky juice of which is used as birdlime **2** : a Hawaiian tree (*Sapindus oahuensis*) the fruit of which yields a native soap

¹aum \ˈōm\ *n* -s [D *aam*, fr. MD *āme*; akin to OE *ōme, ōma*, a liquid measure, MHG *ōme*, Icel *āma*; all fr. a prehistoric NGmc-WGmc word borrowed fr. L *ama* pail, fr. Gk *amē*; akin to L *sentina* bilge water, Lith *semti* to draw (water)] : an old Dutch and German unit of liquid capacity (as for wine) varying from 36 to 42 gallons

²aum *var of* OM

au·ma·ga \au̇ˈmägə\ *n* -s [Samoan *ˈaumāga*] : the village organization of untitled men in Samoa

aumakua \ˌau̇məˈküə\ *n, pl* **aumakua** [Hawaiian *'aumakua*] : a Hawaiian personal and family god

aumery *var of* AMBRY

au·mil \ˈōməl, -ˌmil\ *n* -s [Hindi *ˈāmil*, lit., worker, agent, fr. Ar] : a revenue collector under a local government in India

au·mil·dar \ˈōməlˌdär\ *n* -s [Hindi *ˈamaldār*, fr. Ar *ˈamal* work + Per *-dār* (agent suffix)] *India* : AGENT, FACTOR, MANAGER; *specif* : a revenue collector

au·mous \ˈämǝs, ˈō-\ *n, pl* **aumous** [ME (northern dial.) *almouse, almus, awmus* — more at ALMOUS] *chiefly Scot* : ALMS

aum·rie *or* **aum·ry** \ˈämri, ˈō-\ *var of* AMBRY 1b

AUN *abbr, often not cap* [L *absque ulla nota*] free from marking

au na·tu·rel \ˌōˌnad·əˈrel, ōˈnachərəl, ōˈnad·ərəl\ *adj* [F] **1 a** : in natural style or condition ⟨a remarkably *au naturel* attitude⟩ **b** : NUDE ⟨we went swimming *au naturel*⟩ **2 a** : cooked without dressing : cooked plainly ⟨oysters *au naturel*⟩ **b** : UNCOOKED

aun·cel \ˈȯnsəl, ˈä-\ *n* -s [ME, fr. AF *auncelle*, perh. alter. (resulting from incorrect division into definite article *l'* + noun) of (assumed) OF *lancelle*, fr. OIt *lancella* small balance, fr. *lance* balance (fr. L *lanc-, lanx* plate, scalepan) + *-ella* (fr. L) — more at BALANCE] : a medieval English balance for weighing or a weight used in medieval England

aune \ˈōn\ *n* -s [F, fr. OF *aulne* — more at ALNAGE] : any of various old French units of length for cloth corresponding to the English ell: as **a** : a Paris unit equal to 46.79 inches **b** : a unit used in Belgium and Switzerland and equal to 47.24 inches

aun·je·titz \ˈau̇nyəˌtits\ *adj, usu cap* [fr. *Aunjetitz*, village near Prague, Czechoslovakia] : of or belonging to an early Bronze Age culture of central Europe

aunt \ˈant, ˈaa(ə)-, ˈai-, ˈä-, ˈä-\ *n* -s [ME *aunte*, fr. OF *ante*, fr. L *amita* father's sister — more at AMATEUR] **1 a** : the sister of one's father or mother **b** : the wife of one's uncle — often used as a term of endearment for any woman (as an older one) who is regarded with benevolent affection **2** *obs* : an old crone or bawd

aunt·ie *or* **aunty** \-tē, -ti\ *n, pl* **aunties** : AUNT — often used as a term of endearment

aunt jer·i·cho \-ˈjerəˌkō, -rē,-\ *n, pl* **aunt jerichos** *usu cap A&J* [by folk etymology fr. NL *Angelica*] : a plant of the genus *Angelica*

auntly \ˈ=lē, -li\ *adj, sometimes* -ER/-EST : of, relating to, or suggesting an aunt ⟨an ~ interest in his welfare⟩

aunt sally \-ˈsalē, -li\ *n, pl* **aunt sallies** *also* **aunt sallys** *usu cap A&S* **1** : a representation (as an effigy or puppet figure) of a woman usu. with a pipe in her mouth **2** : a sport consisting in trying to break the pipe of an Aunt Sally or to knock the figure down by throwing sticks or balls

aunt·sary \=ˈserē\ *n* -ES [perh. alter. of *Aunt Sarah*] *Canad* : a catamaran turned up at both ends

au pair \(ˈ)ō¦pa(a)(ə)r, -pe(ə)r\ *adj* [F, lit., on equal terms] : consisting of an arrangement whereby one thing is exchanged for another of a similar nature ⟨an *au pair* tutoring post that enables one to learn a foreign language in return for English lessons⟩

au pied de la let·tre \ō¦pyādəlāˈletr(ᵊ), -et(rə)\ *adv* [F, lit., to the foot of the letter] : LITERALLY ⟨don't take everything I say *au pied de la lettre*⟩

aur *abbr* aurum

aur- *or* **auri-** *comb form* [L, fr. *auris* — more at EAR] **1** : ear ⟨*aural*⟩ ⟨*auriscope*⟩ **2** : aural and ⟨*aurinasal*⟩

au·ra \ˈȯrə\ *n, pl* **auras** \-əz\ *also* **au·rae** \-ˌrē\ [ME, fr. L, breeze, air, fr. Gk; akin to OE *weder* weather — more at WEATHER] **1 a** : a distinctive and often subtle sensory stimulus (as an aroma) ⟨an ~ of rosebuds filled the room⟩ **b** : a distinctive highly individualized atmosphere surrounding or attributed to a given source ⟨the warm earthy ~ of an old country inn, breathing friendliness and cheer⟩ **c** : distinctive appearance or impression : ASPECT ⟨everything they did had a smug ~ of respectability⟩ **2 a** : a luminous radiation : enveloping glow : NIMBUS ⟨she sparkled with vitality and seemed always to move in an ~ of brightness⟩ **b** : ASTRAL BODY **3** : a subjective sensation (as of voices, colored lights, or crawling and numbness) experienced before an attack of epilepsy, migraine, or certain other nervous disorders **4** *geol* : a zone of metamorphism surrounding an intrusive igneous body

au·ral \ˈȯrəl *also* ˈär-\ *adj* [L *auris* ear + E *-al* — more at EAR] **1** : of or relating to the ear ⟨an animal with a remarkably sensitive ~ apparatus⟩ **2** : of or relating to the sense of hearing ⟨a new musical with plenty of visual and ~ appeal⟩ — **au·ral·ly** *adv*

aural harmonic *n* : an overtone that is heard by the normal ear when a pure tone of suitable frequency and intensity is sounded and that is presumably due to the nonlinear response of the ear mechanism — compare COMBINATION TONE, DIFFERENCE TONE, SUMMATION TONE

au·ra·mine \ˈȯrəˌmēn, -ˌmən, ˌ==ˈmēn\ *also* **au·ra·min** \ˈ==ˌmən\ *n* -s [ISV *aur-* (fr. L *aurum* gold) + *amine*; orig. formed as G *auramin* — more at ORIOLE] : a bright yellow ketonimine dye $C_{17}H_{22}ClN_3$ of poor lightfastness and stability derived from diphenylmethane and used chiefly in coloring paper, in making pigments, in signal smokes, and as a fluorescent biological stain — called in full *auramine O*; see DYE table 1 (under *Basic yellow 2* and *Solvent yellow 34*)

au·ran·tia \ȯˈranch(ē)ə\ *n* -s [NL, fr. L *aurant-, aurans* (pres. part. of *aurare* to gild, fr. *aurum* gold) + NL *-ia* — more at ORIOLE] : a poisonous red-brown crystalline alcohol-soluble dye $C_{12}H_8N_8O_{12}$ used in biological staining, in desensitizing photographic plates, and in colored photographic filters; the ammonium salt of hexanitrodiphenylamine

au·ran·ti·a·ce·ae \əˌrantēˈāsēˌē\ [NL, fr. *Aurantium*, type genus (fr. L *aurant-, aurans*, pres. part. of *aurare* to gild + NL *-ium*) + *-aceae*] *syn of* RUTACEAE

au·ran·ti·a·ceous \=¦==ˈāshəs\ *adj* [in sense 1, fr. NL *aurantium* (specific epithet of *Citrus aurantium*) + E *-aceous*; in sense 2, fr. NL *Aurantiaceae* + E *-ous*] **1** : relating to or resembling the sour orange **2** : of or relating to the family Rutaceae

aurar *pl of* EYRIR

au·rate \ˈȯrˌāt, -ˌrāt\ *n* -s [*auric* + *-ate*] : a salt of auric acid

au·re·ate \ˈȯrēət *also* -ēˌāt; *usu* -d.+V\ *adj* [ME *aureat*, fr. ML *aureatus* decorated with gold, prob. blend of L *auratus* decorated with gold, gilded, golden (fr. *aurum* gold + *-atus* -ate) and L *aureus* golden (fr. *aurum* gold) — more at ORIOLE] **1 a** : golden in color ⟨her long ~ hair⟩ **b** : marked by a golden brilliance : RESPLENDENT ⟨the sea lay shimmering in ~ splendor⟩ **2** : marked by a style that is affected, grandiloquent, and heavily ornamental, that uses rhetorical flourishes excessively, and that often employs interlarded foreign words and phrases ⟨an early Renaissance poet using ~ language⟩

aurei *pl of* AUREUS

au·re·i·ty \ȯˈrēəd·ē\ *n* -ES [L *aureus* golden + E *-ity*] : the distinctive properties of gold

¹au·re·lia \ȯˈrēlyə, -lēə\ *n* -s [It & NL; NL, fr. It, fr. L *aurum* gold] : a chrysalis esp. of a lepidopterous insect

²aurelia \"\ *n* [NL, prob. fr. L *aurum*] **1** *cap* : a genus of large jellyfishes often studied as typical of the class Scyphozoa **2** -s : a jellyfish of *Aurelia* or of related genera

¹au·re·lian \(ˈ)ȯ¦rēlyən, -lēən\ *adj* [NL ¹*aurelia* + E *-an*] **1** : golden in color **2** : of or relating to an aurelia

²aurelian \"\ *n* -s [NL ¹*aurelia* + E *-an*] : a collector and breeder of moths and butterflies

³aurelian \"\ *adj* [NL ²*Aurelia* + E *-an*] : of or relating to *Aurelia* or related genera

au·rel·lia \ȯˈrelyə, -elēə\ *syn of* AURELIA 2a

au·rene \ˈȯrēn\ *n* -s [fr. *Aurene*, a trademark] : an early 20th century American iridescent glassware

¹au·re·ole \ˈȯrēˌōl\ *or* **au·re·o·la** \ȯˈrēələ, əˈ-\ *n, pl* **aureoles** \-ōlz\ *or* **aureolas** \-ələz\ *or* **aureo·lae** \-ˈrēə(ˌ)lē\ [ME & ML; ME *aureole, auriole*, fr. OF *auriole*, fr. ML *aureola*, fr. L, fem. of *aureolus* golden, fr. *aureus* golden] **1** *Roman Catholicism* : a special heavenly reward marked by a special degree of glory and given to those (as martyrs) who have practiced heroic virtue **2** *fine art* : an indication of radiant light around the head (as a nimbus) or body (as a vesica piscis) of a sacred personage **3** : a quality, condition, or circumstance that surrounds and glorifies a given object : RADIANCE ⟨the sweet ~ of youth⟩ **4 a** : the luminous area surrounding the sun or other bright light when seen through thin cloud, fog, or mist : CORONA, GLORY **b** : the inner portion of a corona : the whole of an incompletely developed corona **5** *geol* : a more or less ring-shaped contact zone surrounding a comparatively small igneous intrusion

²aureole \"\ *vt* -ED/-ING/-S : to surround with an aureole ⟨her head was *aureoled* with soft moonlight⟩

au·re·o·lin \ȯˈrēələn, ə-\ *n* -s [ISV *aureol-* (fr. L *aureolus* golden) + *-in*; prob. orig. formed in G] : COBALT YELLOW

au·re·o·lus trout \ȯˈrēələs-, ə-\ *n* [NL *aureolus* (specific epithet of the Sunapee trout *Salvelinus aureolus*), fr. L, golden] : SUNAPEE TROUT

Au·re·o·my·cin \ˌȯrē(ˌ)ōˈmīsᵊn, -ēəˈm-\ *trademark* — used for chlortetracycline

au·re·ous \ˈȯrēəs\ *adj* [L *aureus*] : golden in color

au·re·us \ˈȯrēəs\ *n, pl* **au·rei** \-rēˌī\ [L, lit., golden] : a gold coin of ancient Rome varying in weight from ¹⁄₅₀ libra to ¹⁄₇₀ libra

au re·voir \ˌōrəvˈwär, ˌȯr-, -wȧ, F ōrvwȧr *or* ōrəwȧȧr *or* ȯr- *or* ȯvwȧ(ȧr)\ *n* [F, lit., to the seeing again] : GOOD-BYE

¹auri- *comb form* [ME, fr. L, fr. *aurum* — more at ORIOLE] **1** : gold ⟨*auriferous*⟩ **2** : of, relating to, or containing trivalent gold : auric ⟨*auri-iodide*⟩ ⟨*auricyanide*⟩

²auri- — see AUR-

au·ric \ˈȯrik\ *adj* [L *aurum* gold + E *-ic*] : of, relating to, or like gold : derived from gold — used esp. of compounds in which this element is trivalent ⟨~ oxide Au_2O_3⟩

auric acid *n* : a weak acid $HAuO_2$ said to be obtained as a brown powder practically insoluble in water

au·ri·chal·cite \ˌȯrəˈkalˌsīt\ *n* -s [G *aurichalzit*, fr. L *aurichalcum* yellow copper ore (alter. — influenced by *aurum* gold — of *orichalcum*) + G *-it* -ite — more at ORICHALC] : a mineral $(Zn,Cu)_5(OH)_6(CO_3)_2$ consisting of a basic copper zinc carbonate found in pale green or pale blue crystalline incrustations

au·ri·chloride \ˌ==+\ *n* -s [¹*auri-* + *chloride*] : CHLOROAURATE

au·ri·cle \ˈȯrəkəl, -rēk-\ *n* -s [L *auricula*, dim. of *auris* ear — more at EAR] **1 a** : the pinna of the ear **b** [so called fr. a resemblance to the external ear of some quadrupeds] : the chamber or one of the two chambers of the heart by which the blood is received from the veins and forced into the ventricle or ventricles **c** : AURICULAR APPENDIX **2** : an angular or earlike lobe or process: as **a** : one of the plates of the jaw to which the jaw muscles are attached in certain sea urchins with jaws **b** : one of a pair of ciliated pitlike organs eversible for swimming in certain rotifers **c** : either of the wings at the hinged border of the shell in certain bivalve mollusks (as the scallop) **3** : an ear-shaped appendage (as that at the base of the leaf blade of many grasses)

¹au·ric·u·la \ȯˈrikyələ, ə-\ *n, pl* **auriculas** \-ləz\ *also* **au·ric·u·lae** \-ˌlē, -ˌlī\ [NL, fr. L, external ear] **1** : a yellow-flowered primrose (*Primula auricula*) native to the Alps and commonly cultivated — called also *bear's-ear* **2** : AURICLE; *esp* : the auricular appendix of the heart

²auricula \"\ [NL, fr. L] *syn of* ELLOBIUM

auricula purple *n* : a dark reddish purple that is redder and less strong than patriarch or amaranth and redder, stronger, and slightly lighter than raisin purple

¹au·ric·u·lar \(ˈ)ȯ¦rikyələ(r)\ *adj* [LL *auricularis*, fr. L *auricula* + *-aris* -ar] **1** : of, relating to, or using the ear or the sense of hearing **2** : told in the ear : told privately ⟨~ confession⟩ **3** : understood or recognized by the ear : known by the sense of hearing ⟨my apprehension of words is ~; I must hear what I read —George Santayana⟩ ⟨~ proof⟩ **4** : of, like, or relating to an auricle or auricula

²auricular \"\ *n* -s : one of the loose-webbed feathers overlying the opening of the ear of birds — usu. used in pl.

auricular appendix *or* **auricular appendage** *n* : an ear-shaped pouch projecting from each atrium of the heart

au·ric·u·lare \ȯˌrikyəˈla(a)rē, -ˈlärē\ *n, pl* **auricular·ia** \-a(a)rēə, -ˈärēə\ [NL, fr. LL, neut. of *auricularis*] : SUPRA-AURICULAR POINT

auricular fibrillation *n* : very rapid uncoordinated contractions of the auricles of the heart resulting in a lack of synchronism between heartbeat and pulse beat

auricular finger *n* [so called fr. the fact that it can be introduced into the ear passage] : LITTLE FINGER

auricular flutter *n* : an irregularity of the heartbeat in which the contractions of the auricle exceed in number those of the ventricle — compare AURICULAR FIBRILLATION

auricular height *n* **1** *anthrop* : cranial height as measured from the auditory point to the vertex **2** *anthrop* : the vertical section of the triangle formed by the distance between the poria and that from each porion to the bregma

¹au·ric·u·lar·ia \ȯˌrikyəˈla(a)rēə\ *n, cap* [NL, fr. L *auricula* + NL *-aria*] : the type genus of Auriculariaceae — see JEW'S-EAR

²auricularia \"\ *n, pl* **auricularias** \-əz\ *also* **auriculari·ae** \-rēˌē, -rēˌī\ [NL, fr. *auricula* + *-aria*] : a free-swimming holothurian larva of which the body has short blunt lobes

au·ric·u·lar·i·a·ce·ae \=ˌ==ˌ=rēˈāsēˌē\ *n pl, cap* [NL, fr. *Auricularia*, type genus + *-aceae*] : a family of basidiomycetous fungi (order Tremellales) with transversely septate basidia and gelatinous sporophores

au·ric·u·lar·i·a·les \=ˌ=ˌ=ˌ=rēˈāˌlēz\ *n pl, cap* [NL, fr. ¹*Auricularia* + *-ales*] *in some classifications* : an order of basidiomycetous fungi coextensive with the family Auriculariaceae

au·ric·u·lar·ian \ȯˈrikyəˈla(a)rēən, -ler-\ *adj* [NL ²*auricularia* + E *-an*] : of or relating to an auricularia

au·ric·u·la·ris \=ˌ==ˈla(a)rəs, -ˈlär-\ *n, pl* **auricula·res** \-ˌrēz\ [NL, fr. LL, of the ear] : any of three muscles attached to the cartilage of the external ear, one anterior, one superior, and one posterior in position — called also *auricular muscle*

auricular point *n, anthrop* : the center of the external auditory meatus — see CRANIOMETRY illustration

auricular witness *n* : one who witnesses to what he has heard

au·ric·u·late \(ˈ)ȯ¦rikyələt, -ˌlāt\ *also* **au·ric·u·lat·ed** \-ˌlād·əd\ *adj* [fr. (assumed) NL *auriculatus*, fr. LL, having ears, fr. L *auricula* + *-atus* -ate, -ated] : having ears or earlike appendages : having auricles : EARED ⟨an ~ leaf⟩

au·ri·cu·li·dae \ˌȯrəˈkyüləˌdē\ [NL, fr. ²*Auricula*, type genus + *-idae*] *syn of* ELLOBIIDAE

auriculo- *comb form* [prob. fr. NL, fr. *auricula* auricle of the heart, fr. L, external ear — more at AURICLE] **1** : of or belonging to an auricle of the heart and ⟨*auriculoventricular*⟩ **2** : aural and ⟨*auriculoparietal*⟩ ⟨*auriculotemporal*⟩

au·ric·u·lo-infraorbital plane \ȯ¦rikyəˌlō, -lə +\ *n* : the plane that passes through the auricular points and the lowest points of the orbits — see CRANIOMETRY illustration

auriculo-parietal angle \" + =¦===\ *n* [*auriculo-* + *parietal*] : PARIETAL ANGLE

auriculo-temporal nerve \" + ¦===-\ *n* [*auriculo-* + *temporal* (of the temple)] : the branch of the mandibular nerve that supplies sensory fibers to the skin of the external ear and temporal region and autonomic fibers from the otic ganglion to the parotid gland

auriculo-ventricular \" + (ˌ)=¦===\ *adj* [*auriculo-* + *ventricular*] : ATRIOVENTRICULAR

auriculoventricular valve *n* : a valve between an auricle and ventricle of the heart: **a** : MITRAL VALVE **b** : TRICUSPID VALVE

au·ri·cyanic acid \ˌȯrē, -ˌrī + (ˌ)=¦=\ *n* [¹*auri-* + *cyanic*] : CYANOAURIC ACID

au·rif·er·ous \(ˈ)ȯ¦rifərəs\ *adj* [L *aurifer*, fr. *auri-* ¹*auri-* + *-fer* -ferous] : gold-bearing — used of gravels and rocks ⟨~ quartz veins⟩

au·rif·ic \(ˈ)ȯ¦rifik\ *adj* [¹*auri-* + *-fic*] : producing gold

au·ri·fi·ca·tion \ˌȯrəfəˈkāshən\ *n* -s [¹*auri-* + *-fication*] : the act of working with or in gold

au·ri·form \ˈȯrəˌfȯrm\ *adj* [*aur-* + *-form*] : shaped like the human ear — used esp. of mollusk shells

au·ri·fy \ˈȯrəˌfī\ *vb* -ED/-ING/-ES [¹*auri-* + *-fy*] : to turn into gold

au·ri·gna·cian \¦ȯrənˈyāshən\ *adj, usu cap* [F *aurignacien*, fr. *Aurignac*, commune in Haute-Garonne dept., France, near which there are caves with paleolithic remains + F *-ien* -ian] : of or belonging to the epoch of the Upper Paleolithic period following the Mousterian and preceding the Solutrean that was characterized by stone artifacts some of Mousterian type but smaller and more finely made, figures and other artifacts of bone, and paintings and engravings on walls and bone

aurignacian man *n, usu cap A* **1** *or* **aurignacian race :** man (*Homo sapiens*) of the Aurignacian period: as **a :** COMBE-CAPELLE MAN **b :** CRO-MAGNON **2 :** an individual belonging to Aurignacian man

au·rin \'ȯrən\ *n* -s [prob. fr. G *aurin*, fr. *auri-* ¹auri- + -in] **:** a poisonous red dye $C_{19}H_{14}O_3$ derived from triphenylmethane often obtained commercially in impure yellowish brown lumps and used chiefly as a dye intermediate — called also *pararosolic acid, rosolic acid*

au·ri·nasal \ˌȯrə + ˈ==\ *adj* [*aur-* + *nasal*] **:** of or relating to the ear and nose

au·ri·phryg·i·ate \ˌȯrə¦frijēət, -jēˌāt\ *adj* [modif. (influenced by L *Phrygius* Phrygian) of ML *aurifrigiatus*, fr. *aurifrigium* orphrey + L -*atus* -ate — more at ORPHREY] **:** adorned with orphrey

au·ri·scope \'ȯrəˌskōp\ *n* -s [*aur-* + *-scope*] **:** OTOSCOPE

auro- *comb form* [ISV, fr. L *aurum* — more at ORIOLE] **1 a :** gold ⟨*auro*phobia⟩ **b :** gold and ⟨*auro*-plumbiferous⟩ **2 :** of, relating to, or containing univalent gold **:** aurous ⟨*auro*bromide⟩ ⟨*auro*thiosulfate⟩

au·rochs \'aůˌräks, 'ȯˌr-\ *also* **au·roch** \-äk\ *n, pl* **aurochs** *also* **aurochses** [G (now usu. *auerochs*), fr. OHG *ūrohso*, fr. *ūro* aurochs + *ohso* head of cattle, ox; akin to OE *ūr* aurochs, ON *ūrr*, Goth *uraz*, a runic name, and prob. to ON *ūr* drizzle — more at URINE, OX] **1 :** URUS **2 :** WISENT

au·ro·cyanide \ˌȯrō, -rə + \ *n* -s [ISV *auro-* + *cyanide*] **:** a complex salt (as sodium aurocyanide $Na[Au(CN)_2]$ formed in the cyanide process for gold) made by the union of aurous cyanide with another cyanide

au·ro·ra \ə'rȯrə, ȯ'-, -rōr-\ *n, pl* **auroras** *see senses 1 & 2* [L — more at EAST] **1** *pl also* **au·ro·rae** \-(ˌ)rē\ **:** the rising light of the morning **:** the dawn of day **:** the redness of the sky just before the sun rises **2** *pl also* **aurorae a :** AURORA BOREALIS **b :** AURORA AUSTRALIS **3** *or* **aurora orange :** a moderate reddish orange that is redder and paler than flamingo, crab apple, or burnt ocher — called also *orange aurora*

aurora aus·tra·lis \-(ˌ)ȯ'strāləs\ *n, pl* **aurorae aus·tra·les** \-(ˌ)lēz\ [NL, lit., southern aurora] **:** a phenomenon in the southern hemisphere corresponding to the aurora borealis in the northern

aurora bo·re·al·is \-ˌbȯrē'aləs, -bȯr- *also* -ē'āl-\ *n, pl* **aurorae bo·re·al·es** \-(ˌ)lēz\ [NL, lit., northern aurora] **:** a luminous phenomenon supposed to be of electrical origin that is visible only at night and is seen to best advantage in the arctic regions, usu. appearing in streamers ascending often in a fan shape from a dusky line or bank a few degrees above the northern horizon and on very rare occasions as an arch of light across the heavens from east to west — called also *northern lights*

aurora glory *n* **:** the corona of the aurora borealis

au·ro·ral \ə'rȯrəl, ȯ'-, -rȯr-\ *adj* **:** of, relating to, or resembling the dawn or the aurora borealis **:** ROSY, RADIANT ⟨a dim ~ glow⟩ ⟨a gorgeous ~ sunrise⟩

auroral line *n* **:** a prominent green line in the spectrum of the aurora borealis and aurora australis apparently due to the presence of oxygen in the upper atmosphere

aurora po·lar·is \-pə'larəs, -pō-\ *n, pl* **aurorae po·lar·es** \-(ˌ)rēz\ [NL, lit., polar aurora] **:** a high-latitude aurora borealis or aurora australis

aurora yellow *n* **:** CADMIUM YELLOW

¹au·rore \ə'rō(ə)r, ȯ'-, -rȯ(ə)r\ *n* -s [F, lit., dawn, fr. L *aurora*] **:** HYDRANGEA PINK

²aurore \"\ *adj* [F, fr. *aurore*, n.] **:** marked by or relating to a yellow or pink tint given a white sauce by the addition of egg yolks, tomato puree, or lobster coral

au·ro·re·an \-rōrēən, -rȯr-\ *adj* [*aurora* + *-ean*] **:** AURORAL

au·ro·thioglucose \ˌȯrō, -rə + \ *n* -s [*auro-* + *thi-* + *glucose*] **:** an organic compound of gold $C_6H_{11}AuO_5S$ injected intramuscularly in the treatment of active rheumatoid arthritis and nondisseminated lupus erythematosus

auro·thiosulfate \" +\ *n* -s [*auro-* + *thiosulfate*] **:** a complex salt containing gold in the anion $[Au(S_2O_3)]^{3-}$ and formed by the reaction of gold salts with thiosulfates

au·rous \'ȯrəs\ *adj* [prob. fr. F *aureux*, fr. LL *aurosus* goldlike, fr. L *aurum* gold + *-osus* -ous] **:** of, relating to, or containing gold — used esp. of compounds in which this element is univalent

au·rox \'aůˌräks, 'ȯˌr-\ *n, pl* **aurox** \"\ *or* **auroxes** \-ksəz\ *also* **aurox·en** \-ksən\ [part. trans. of G *aurochs* — more at AUROCHS] **:** AUROCHS

au·ru·lent \'ȯr(y)ələnt\ *adj* [LL *aurulentus*, fr. L *aurum* gold + *-ulentus* -ulent — more at ORIOLE] **:** golden in color

¹au·rum \'ȯrəm, 'aůr-\ *n* -s [L — more at ORIOLE] **1 :** GOLD — symbol *Au* **2 :** the color gold

²au·rum \'aůrəm\ *n* -s [fr. *Aurum*, a trademark] **:** a golden-colored Italian liqueur

au·rum po·ta·bi·le \ˌaůrəmpə'täbəlē, ¦ȯr . . . tab-\ *n* [NL, lit., drinkable gold] **:** a formerly used cordial or medicine consisting of some volatile oil in which minute particles of gold were suspended

¹aus \'aůs\ *n, pl* **aus** *usu cap* [Ar *Aws*] **:** one of an Arab people at Medina in the time of Muhammad

²aus *n, pl* **aus** \"\ [Hindi *āūs*] **:** short-stemmed rice grown in the dry season in India

aus·cul·tate \'ȯskəlˌtāt\ *vt* -ED/ -ING/ -S [back-formation fr. *auscultation*] **:** to examine by auscultation

aus·cul·ta·tion \ˌȯskəl'tāshən\ *n* -s [L *auscultation-, auscultatio*, fr. *auscultatus* (past part. of *auscultare* to listen, fr. *aus-* — akin to L *auris* ear — + *-cultare*, prob. akin to L *cluēre* to be named, be called) + *-ion-*, *-io* -ion — more at EAR, LOUD] **:** the act of listening to sounds arising within organs (as the lungs or heart) as an aid to diagnosis and treatment, the examination being made either by use of the stethoscope or by direct application of the ear to the body

aus·cul·ta·to·ry \ȯ'skəltəˌtȯrē\ *adj* [L *auscultatus* + E *-ory*] **:** of or relating to auscultation

au·shar \'aů(ˌ)shär\ *n, pl* **aushar** *or* **aushars** *usu cap* **:** AISSOR

aus·land·er \'aůsˌlandə(r), -len-; 'ȯˌslan-\ *n* -s [G *ausländer*, fr. MHG *ūzlender*, fr. *ūz* out (fr. OHG) + *-lender* (fr. *lend-* — mutated stem of *lant* land, province, fr. OHG *land* — + *-er*) — more at OUT, LAND] **:** OUTSIDER, FOREIGNER

aus·laut \'aůsˌlaůt, ˌaůs -d·+V\ *n, pl* **auslau·te** \-laůd·ə\ *or* **auslauts** [G, fr. *aus* out (fr. OHG *ūz*) + *laut* sound, fr. MHG *lūt*; akin to OE *hlūd* loud — more at OUT, LOUD] **:** final sound in a word or syllable **:** end position of a sound in a word or syllable — compare ANLAUT, INLAUT

au·so·nian \(')ȯ¦sōnēən, -nyən\ *adj, usu cap* [L *Ausonia* southern Italy, Italy + E *-an*] **:** ITALIAN — used in poetry

aus·pex \'ȯˌspeks, 'aů,-\ *n, pl* **auspi·ces** \-ˌspəˌsēz\ [L] **:** AUGUR

aus·pi·cate \'ȯspəˌkāt\ *vt* -ED/-ING/-S [L *auspicatus*, past part. of *auspicari* to take auspices, fr. *auspic-, auspex*] **1** *archaic* **:** to indicate in advance as though by an omen **:** PORTEND, AUGUR **2 :** to initiate or enter upon esp. under circumstances or with a procedure (as drinking a toast) calculated to ensure prosperity and good luck ⟨*auspicating* the trip with a cocktail⟩

aus·pice \'ȯspəs\ *n, pl* **auspic·es** \-əsəz *also* -əˌsēz\ [L *auspicium*, fr. *auspic-, auspex* bird seer, augur, fr. *au-* (fr. *avis* bird) + *-spic-, -spex* (fr. *spicere, specere* to look) — more at AVIARY, SPY] **1 :** observation (as in augury) esp. of the flight and feeding of birds intended to discover a sign of the future; *also* **:** an omen based on such observation **2 a :** any sign or portent apparently indicative of the future **:** prophetic token ⟨under these unpromising ~*s* the parting took place —Jane Austen⟩; *esp* **:** a sign taken as being a favorable indication of the future ⟨he took her gentle words as an ~ of happiness⟩ **b :** the interplay of events and circumstances esp. when favorable — usu. used in pl. ⟨with the right ~*s*, they will succeed⟩ **3 auspices** *pl* **:** patronage and kindly guidance **:** PROTECTION ⟨under the ~*s* of the United Nations⟩

auspices *pl of* AUSPEX *or of* AUSPICE

aus·pi·cious \(')ȯ¦spishəs\ *also* **aus·pi·cial** \-shəl\ *adj* [L *auspicium* + E *-ous* or *-al*] **1 :** affording an auspice **:** favorable auspice **:** favoring or conducive to success **:** PROPITIOUS ⟨an ~ beginning⟩ **2 :** attended by good auspices **:** FORTUNATE, PROSPEROUS **3** *archaic* **:** kindly disposed **syn** see FAVORABLE

aus·pi·cious·ly *adv* **:** in an auspicious manner

aus·pi·cious·ness \ˈ==ˌ==\ *n* -ES **:** the quality or state of being auspicious

aus·sa·ge test \'aůs,zägə-\ *n* [G *aussage* deposition, declaration, fr. *aussagen* to depose, declare, fr. MHG *ūzsagen*, fr. *ūz* out (fr. OHG) + *sagen* to say, fr. OHG *sagēn* — more at OUT, SAY] *psychol* **:** a test of reliability of testimony in which the subject is required to describe a situation or event familiar to the examiner

aus·sie \'ȯsē, 'ä-, -si\ *n* -s *cap, often attrib* [by shortening & alter.] **:** AUSTRALIAN

aus·tausch \'aůsˌtaůsh\ *n, pl* **austau·sche** \-shə\ [G, lit., exchange, fr. *austauschen* to exchange, fr. *aus* out (fr. OHG *ūz*) + *tauschen* to exchange, barter, fr. MHG *tūschen, tiuschen* to barter, deceive, mock, fr. MLG *tūschen*, lit., to tell a lie] **1 :** an effect of turbulent motion in the atmosphere that is manifested by an exchange of air and water vapor molecules, together with their momentum and heat energy, from one horizontal layer to another **2 :** the viscosity coefficient for horizontal flow in the atmosphere where it is affected by turbulence

aus·tem·per \ȯs-'tempə(r)\ *vt* -ED/-ING/-S [*austenite* + *temper*] **:** to quench (steel) from above the transformation temperature in a bath between 350° and 600° F and hold it there until transformation of austenite stops, for rendering it hard and tough

aus·ten·ite \'ȯstəˌnīt\ *n* -s [F, fr. Sir William C. Roberts-*Austen* †1902 Eng. metallurgist + F *-ite*] **:** a solid solution in gamma iron of carbon and sometimes other solutes that is characterized by face-centered cubic crystal structure (as in austenitic alloy steel)

aus·ten·it·ic \¦==¦nid·ik\ *adj* **:** composed principally of austenite ⟨~ stainless steel⟩

aus·ten·it·ize \'ȯstənəˌtīz\ *or* **aus·ten·ize** \-təˌnīz\ *vt* -ED/-ING/-S **:** to produce austenite of (a ferrous alloy) by heating above the transformation temperature

aus·tere \(')ȯ¦sti(ə)r, -iə\ *adj, sometimes* -ER/-EST [ME, fr. MF, fr. L *austerus*, fr. Gk *austēros*; akin to Gk *hauein* to parch, dry — more at SEAR] **1 a :** stern and unyielding in appearance and manner **:** forbiddingly severe ⟨~ Puritan colonists⟩ **b :** marked by a somber gravity and seriousness **:** UNSMILING ⟨the most ~ of critics—Virginia Woolf⟩ **2 :** characterized by an abstemious rigidly self-disciplined and sternly moral manner of living **:** ASCETIC ⟨an ~ old hermit⟩ **3** *archaic* **:** astringent to the taste and marked by sourness or bitterness **4 :** without ornamentation **:** UNEMBELLISHED, SIMPLE ⟨an uncomplicated, ~ style of architecture⟩ **syn** see SEVERE

aus·tere·ly *adv* **:** in an austere manner

aus·tere·ness *n* -ES **:** AUSTERITY

aus·ter·i·ty \ȯ'sterəd·ē, -ətē, -i\ *n* -ES [ME *austerite*, fr. MF *austerité*, fr. L *austeritat-, austeritas*, fr. *austerus* + *-itat-, -itas* -ity] **1 :** the quality or state of being austere **:** SEVERITY, STERNNESS, RIGOR **2 a :** an austere act, manner, or attitude **b :** an ascetic practice ⟨early Christian *austerities*⟩ **3 :** lack of luxuries **:** enforced or extreme economy esp. on a national scale ⟨live on an ~ diet⟩

austerity program *n* **:** a program of economic controls aimed at reducing current consumption so as to improve the national economy esp. by increased exports

¹aus·tin \'ȯstən, 'äs-\ *adj, usu cap* [ME *Austyn*, modif. of LL *Augustinus* Augustine †430 early Christian church father, bishop of Hippo in northern Africa] *chiefly Brit* **:** ¹AUGUSTINIAN

²austin \"\ *adj, usu cap* [fr. *Austin*, Texas] **:** of or from Austin, the capital of Texas **:** of the kind or style prevalent in Austin

aus·tin·i·an \(')ȯ¦stinēən, (')ä¦-\ *adj, usu cap* [John *Austin* †1859 Eng. jurist + E *-ian*] **:** of or relating to the theories of law and jurisprudence of Austin

aus·tin·ite \'ȯstəˌnīt, 'äs-\ *n* -s [*Austin* F. Rogers †1957 Am. mineralogist + E *-ite*] **:** a mineral $CaZn(AsO_4)(OH)$ consisting of a basic calcium zinc arsenate (hardness 4.5, sp. gr. 4.13)

¹austr- *or* **austro-** *comb form, usu cap* [ME *austr-*, fr. L, south, fr. *austr-, auster* south wind, south; akin to L *aurora* dawn — more at EAST] **1 :** south **:** southern ⟨*Austro*asiatic⟩ ⟨*Austro*riparian⟩ **2 :** Australian and ⟨*Austro*-Malayan⟩

²austr- *or* **austro-** *comb form, usu cap* [prob. fr. NL, fr. *Austria*] **1 :** Austrian and ⟨*Austro*-Hungarian⟩ **2 :** Austria ⟨*austr*ium⟩ ⟨*Austro*phobia⟩

¹aus·tral \'ȯstrəl\ *adj* [ME, fr. L *australis*, fr. *austr-, auster* + *-alis* -al] **1 :** SOUTHERN ⟨sailing the ~ seas⟩ **2** *usu cap* **:** of, relating to, or being a biogeographic zone extending across No. America between the transition and tropical zones **3** *usu cap* **:** AUSTRALIAN

²austral \"\ *n* -s *usu cap* **:** the language of the Austral islands

¹aus·tra·la·sian \ˌȯstrə¦lāzhən, -āsh-\ *adj, usu cap* [*Australasia* islands of the central and southern Pacific (fr. F *Australasie*) + E *-an*] **1 :** of or relating to the lands of the central and southern Pacific ocean (as Polynesia) **2 :** AUSTRALIAN — used in biogeographic description

²australasian \"\ *n* -s *cap* **:** a native or inhabitant of Australasian lands

austral english *n, cap A&E* **:** the language of most inhabitants of Australia and New Zealand — used esp. with the implication that it is a variety of English distinct from that used in Great Britain yet not so divergent as to be a separate language; compare AMERICAN ENGLISH, AUSTRALIAN ENGLISH, BRITISH ENGLISH

aus·tra·lia \ȯ'strālyə, ä's-, *US also & Australian appar usu* ə's-; *sometimes* -lēə\ *adj, usu cap* [fr. *Australia*, island continent of the southern Pacific] **:** of or from the continent or the commonwealth of Australia **:** of the kind or style prevalent in Australia **:** AUSTRALIAN

australia day *n, usu cap A&D* **:** a national holiday in Australia that commemorates the landing of the British under Arthur Phillip at Sydney Cove in 1788 and is observed on Jan. 26 when that date is a Monday, otherwise on the following Monday — called also *Anniversary Day*

¹aus·tra·lian \-lyən *sometimes* -lēən\ *n* -s *cap* [*Australia* + E *-an*] **1 :** an aborigine of Australia whose physical characters include dolichocephaly, dark brown skin, black often wavy hair, heavy beard, prominent brow ridges and marked prognathism, and medium stature **2 :** a native or inhabitant of the Australian commonwealth **3 :** AUSTRALIAN ENGLISH **4 :** the speech of the aboriginal inhabitants of Australia

²australian \"\ *adj, usu cap* **1 :** of or belonging to the continent or commonwealth of Australia, its inhabitants, or the languages spoken there **2 a :** of, relating to, or being a biogeographic region that comprises Australia and the islands north of it from Celebes eastward, Tasmania, New Zealand, and Polynesia **b :** of, relating to, or being the subregion of the Australian region that comprises Australia and Tasmania — compare AUSTROGAEAN **3 :** native to Australia — often used to indicate organisms with but superficial resemblance to those designated by the substantive

australian anteater *n, usu cap 1st A* **:** ECHIDNA

australian badger *n, usu cap A* **:** WOMBAT

australian ballot *n, usu cap A* **:** an official ballot printed at public expense on which the names of all the nominated candidates appear and which is distributed only at the polling place and marked in secret — see INDIANA BALLOT, MASSACHUSETTS BALLOT

australian banyan *n, usu cap A* **:** MORETON BAY FIG

australian baobab *n, usu cap A* **:** CREAM-OF-TARTAR TREE

australian bean tree *n, usu cap A* **1 :** a tall tree (*Castanospermum australe*) with pealike flowers and long pods **2 :** a tall spreading tree (*Bauhinia hookeri*) with broad flat pods

australian bear *n, usu cap A* **:** KOALA

australian beech *n, usu cap A* **:** a gum tree (*Eucalyptus polyanthemos*) with small flowers in many-flowered panicles

australian beech cherry *n, usu cap A* **:** a shrub or small tree (*Trochocarpa laurina*) with globular fruits

australian blackwood *n, usu cap A* **:** LIGHTWOOD 2a

australian bluebell *or* **australian bluebell creeper** *n, usu cap A* **:** a slender evergreen vine (*Sollya fusiformis*) with nodding blue flowers

australian bluegrass *n, usu cap A* **:** an Australian pasture grass (*Andropogon sericeus*) introduced into the West Indies

australian brake *n, usu cap A* **:** a bright green Australian fern (*Pteris tremula*) cultivated for its ornamental fronds

australian cat *n, usu cap A* **:** a variety of the Siamese cat developed in Australia

australian cattle dog *n, usu cap A* **:** a large-sized dog of a breed developed by crossing the dingo with the smooth-coated blue merle Scotch collie and having the face and ears black or red and the body dark blue evenly speckled with a lighter blue — called also *Australian heeler, blue heeler, merle*

australian cherry *n, usu cap A* **:** NATIVE CHERRY

australian cockroach *n, usu cap A* **:** a cockroach (*Periplaneta australasiae*) now widely distributed in warm countries

australian cranberry *n, usu cap A* **1 :** the edible berry of an Australian shrub (*Lissanthe sapida*) resembling the European cranberry **2 :** any plant that bears the Australian cranberry **3 :** a prostrate shrub (*Astroloma humifusum*) having cranberrylike leaves and nearly globular edible fruit

australian crawl *n, usu cap A* **:** a crawl stroke in swimming; *specif* **:** a 2-beat crawl

australian currant *n, usu cap A* **:** a shrub or small tree (*Leucopogon richei*) having oblong leaves, terminal spikes of small tubular flowers, and edible white fruits

australian desert kumquat *n, usu cap A* **:** DESERT LEMON

australian english *n, usu cap A&E* **:** the language of most inhabitants of Australia — used esp. with the implication that it is a variety of English distinct from that used in Great Britain yet not so divergent as to be a separate language; compare AMERICAN ENGLISH, AUSTRAL ENGLISH, BRITISH ENGLISH

australian football *n, usu cap A* **:** AUSTRALIAN RULES FOOTBALL

australian glasswort *n, usu cap A* **:** a leafless herb (*Salicornia australis*) with fleshy scaly branches

australian gourd *n, usu cap A* **:** STAR CUCUMBER — used of the plant when adventive in Australia

australian grass tree *n, usu cap A* **1 :** GRASS TREE 1 **2 :** a plant (*Kingia australis*) of western Australia that is variously assigned to Juncaceae or Liliaceae and has an erect black woody trunk crowned with long slender silvery leaves **3 :** a stout shrub (*Richea dracophylla*) with narrow leaves crowded at the ends of the branches and with dense terminal clusters of white or pink flowers

australian gum *n, usu cap A* **:** gum arabic from certain Australian wattles or acacias

australian heath *n, usu cap A* **:** any heathlike plant of the family Epacridaceae

australian heeler *n, usu cap A* **:** AUSTRALIAN CATTLE DOG

australian honeysuckle *n, usu cap A* **:** any of several plants of the genus *Banksia*; *esp* **:** a shrub or bushy tree (*B. integrifolia*) with silky foliage and cylindrical flower spikes

australian ironbark *n, usu cap A* **:** any of several trees of the genus *Eucalyptus*

aus·tra·lian·ism \-ˌnizəm\ *n* -s *usu cap* **1 :** a characteristic feature of Australian English esp. as contrasted with British English **2 :** patriotic or partisan feeling for Australia

aus·tra·lian·ize \-ˌnīz\ *vt* -ED/-ING/-S *often cap* **1 :** to cause to acquire traits distinctive of Australians **2 :** to cause to become devoted to Australia **3 :** to naturalize as an Australian

australian laurel *n, usu cap A* **1 :** NATIVE LAUREL 1 **2 :** AUSTRALIAN WALNUT

australian lilac *n, usu cap A* **:** AUSTRALIAN SARSAPARILLA

australian magpie *n, usu cap A* **:** PIPING CROW

australian mahogany *n, usu cap A* **1 :** JARRAH 1 **2 :** AUSTRALIAN ROSEWOOD 2

australian millet *n, usu cap A* **:** an Australian grass (*Panicum divaricatissimum*) with edible seeds

australian nettle tree *n, usu cap A* **:** any of several tall Australian trees of the genus *Laportea*

australian nut *n, usu cap A* **:** MACADAMIA 2

australian oak *n, usu cap A* **:** any of several Australian trees: as **a :** SILK OAK **b :** either of two mountain ashes (*Eucalyptus regnans* and *E. delagatensis*) having rather hard heavy durable pinkish or light brown wood that works and polishes well

australian oat *n, usu cap A* **:** RESCUE GRASS

australian opossum *n, usu cap A* **:** OPOSSUM 2

australian pea *n, usu cap A* **:** an evergreen partly woody vine (*Dolichos lignosus*) having 3-foliolate leaves, rose-purple or white flowers, and black seeds in a flat pod

australian pine *n, usu cap A* **1 :** any of several trees of the genus *Casuarina* **:** BEEFWOOD **2 :** a dark yellowish green that is yellower and paler than holly green (sense 1), lighter and stronger than deep chrome green, and yellower, lighter, and stronger than average hunter green

australian piripiri *n, usu cap A* **:** a silky herb (*Acaena ovina*) with flowers in an interrupted spike and prickly fruits

australian pitcher plant *n, usu cap A* **:** a scapose herb (*Cephalotus follicularis*) with leaves in a basal cluster and white flowers in a spike

australian plague locust *n, usu cap A* **:** a very destructive large migratory grasshopper (*Chortoicetes terminifera*) of the southern parts of Australia; *also* **:** a smaller form (*Austroicetes cruciata*) of similar habits

australian poker *n, usu cap A* **:** a British draw poker with blind opening

australian red snail *or* **australian snail** *n, usu cap A* **:** a brilliant red Australian pulmonate snail (*Lenameria dispar*) with red blood often kept as a scavenger in freshwater aquaria

australian rosewood *n, usu cap A* **1 :** BASTARD ROSEWOOD 2 **2 :** a tall tree (*Dysoxylum fraserianum*) of New South Wales having flowers with a united calyx

australian rules football *n, usu cap A&R* **:** a football game played on a field having 4 goalposts at each end between teams of 18 players of whom 3 play no fixed position, the players advancing the ball by kicking, underhand passing, and, provided it is bounced every 10 yards, running

australian salmon *n, usu cap A* **:** a common percoid fish (*Arripis trutta*) that occurs in schools along the coasts of New South Wales, Tasmania, and New Zealand and is fished with beach seines for food and bait

australian saltbush *n, usu cap A* **:** any of several Australian shrubs of the family Chenopodiaceae (as of the genus *Atriplex*) cultivated in the western U.S. as forage plants

australian sarsaparilla *n, usu cap A* **:** an Australian shrub (*Hardenbergia monophylla*) used as a substitute for sarsaparilla and often cultivated for ornament

australian sassafras *n, usu cap A* **1 :** a tall tree (*Doryphora sassafras*) of the family Monimiaceae with aromatic bark and leaves **2 :** a tree (*Atherosperma moschata*) of the family Monimiaceae with dark gray wood

australian sea holly *n, usu cap A* **:** a prostrate prickly herb (*Eryngium vesiculosum*) with a bracted flower cluster

australian shamrock *n, usu cap A* **:** MENINDIE CLOVER

australian sugar tree *n, usu cap A* [so called fr. its sweetish resin] **:** SUGAR TREE

australian swamp oak *n, usu cap A* **:** a small beefwood (*Casuarina glauca*) sometimes cultivated for ornament

australian tamarind *n, usu cap A* **:** a low tree (*Diploglottis cunninghamii*) yielding subacid fruits

australian teak *n, usu cap A* **:** any of several trees having teaklike timber: as **a :** a small tree (*Endiandra glauca*) of the family Lauraceae **b :** FLINDOSA

australian terrier *n, usu cap A* **:** a small rather short-legged wirehaired terrier of an Australian breed usu. grayish or bluish in color and with tan legs

australian turpentine tree *n, usu cap A* **1 :** BRUSH BOX **2 :** a medium-sized or large tree (*Syncarpia laurifolia*) of the family Myrtaceae with fibrous bark, opposite ovate thick leaves, and white flowers in dense round heads

australian walnut *n, usu cap A* **:** a timber tree (*Endiandra palmerstonii*) with brown to black and variegated wood

australian water lily *n, usu cap A* **:** an immense water lily (*Nymphaea gigantea*) with round leaves 18 inches wide and blue or purple-pink flowers nearly as large

australian water rat *n, usu cap A* **:** BEAVER RAT

australian willow *n, usu cap A* **:** WILGA

australian x-disease *also* **australian x encephalitis** *n, usu cap A&X* **:** X-DISEASE

aus·tra·lic \ȯ'stralik, ä's-,ə's-\ *adj, usu cap* [*Australia* + E *-ic*] **:** of or belonging to aboriginal Australians

aus·tra·lite \'ȯstrəˌlīt\ *n* -s [*Australia*, its locality + E *-ite*] **:** a natural meteoritic glass found in Australia

aus·tra·lo·an·thro·pus \ˌȯˌstrālō'an(t)thrəpəs, ä,-, -ˌan-'thrōpəs\ *n, cap* [NL, fr. *Australia* + NL *-o-* + *-anthropus*] *in some classifications* **:** a subgenus of *Homo* comprising the Australian aborigines and their extinct related forms, the Solo and Wadjak men

¹aus·tra·loid \'ȯstrəˌlȯid, 'äs-\ *also* **aus·tra·li·oid** \(')=-

¦strā̇lē,ȯid\ *adj, usu cap* [*Australia* + E *-oid*] **:** relating or belonging to an ethnic group including the Australian aborigines, the autochthonous Dravidians of southern India, and other peoples of southern Asia and Pacific islands sometimes including the Ainu

²australoid \"\ *n* -s *usu cap* **:** a person having the physical characteristics common to aboriginal Australians

aus·tra·lo·pith·e·ci·dae \ȯ,strā(,)lōpə'thēsə,dē, ä,-\ *n pl, cap* [NL, fr. *Australopithecus*, type genus + *-idae*] **:** the Australopithecinae regarded as a family of Hominoidea distinct from the Pongidae

aus·tra·lo·pith·e·ci·nae \-,pithə'sī(,)nē\ *n pl, cap* [NL, fr. *Australopithecus*, type genus + *-inae*] **:** a subfamily of Pongidae including extinct apes with near-human dentition and constituting *Australopithecus* and according to some authorities other genera all from southern Africa

¹aus·tra·lo·pith·e·cine \¦=¦==¦pithə,sīn, -,sēn\ *adj* [NL *Australopithecinae*] **:** of or belonging to Australopithecinae or the australopithecines

²aus·tra·lo·pith·e·cine \"\ *also* **aus·tra·lo·pithecid** \-pə'thēsəd, -'pithə,sid\ *or* **aus·tra·lo·pith** \=¦==,pith\ *n* -s [*australopithecine* fr. NL *Australopithecinae; australopithecid* fr. NL *Australopithecidae; australopith* fr. NL *Australopithecinae* or *Australopithecidae*] **:** an individual or fossil of the subfamily Australopithecinae

aus·tra·lo·pith·e·cus \=,=(,)=pə'thēkəs, -'pithikəs\ *n, cap* [NL, fr. L *australis* southern + NL *-o-* + *-pithecus* — more at AUSTRAL] **:** a genus of extinct generalized anthropoid apes (family Pongidae) known chiefly from skulls from the middle Pleistocene or possibly Upper Pliocene deposits of southern Africa which are all essentially apelike though showing advances towards the hominid condition in cranial capacity, in the form of the dental arch, and in dentition and that is usu. regarded as too recent to have been ancestral to man — see AUSTRALOPITHECINAE

aus·tral·or·bis \,ȯstrə'lȯrbəs, ¦äs-\ *n, cap* [NL, fr. L *australis* southern + *orbis* ring, circle] **:** a genus of New World pulmonate snails (family Planorbidae) including important So. and Central American intermediate hosts of the schistosome (*Schistosoma mansoni*)

aus·tral·orp \'==,lȯrp\ *n* -s *usu cap* [*Australian* + *Orpington*] **:** a utility type of black Orpington fowl developed in Australia and now a widely distributed and valued egg-producing breed, a white sport being less common

¹aus·tra·sian \(')ȯ¦strāzhən, -āsh-\ *adj, usu cap* [*Austrasia, Ostrasia*, eastern division of the Frankish dominions (fr. ML) + E *-an*] **1 :** of, relating to, or characteristic of Austrasia, the eastern part of the kingdom of the Franks **2 :** of, relating to, or characteristic of Austrasians

²austrasian \"\ *n* -s *cap* **:** a native or inhabitant of Austrasia

aus·tria \'ȯstrēə, 'äs-\ *adj, usu cap* [fr. *Austria*, country in central Europe] **:** of or from Austria **:** of the kind or style prevalent in Austria **:** AUSTRIAN

¹aus·tri·an \-ēən\ *adj, usu cap* [*Austria* + E *-an*] **1 a :** of, relating to, or characteristic of Austria **b :** of, relating to, or characteristic of the Austrians **2 :** of or relating to the Austrian school of economic theory

²austrian \"\ *n* -s **1** *cap* **a :** a native or inhabitant of Austria **b :** a native or inhabitant of Austria-Hungary **2** *usu cap* **:** a member of the Austrian school of economic theory

austrian brier *n, usu cap A* **:** a yellow rose (*Rosa foetida*) with an unpleasant odor

austrian copper *n, usu cap A* **:** a variety (*Rosa foetida bicolor*) of the Austrian brier rose with copper-colored petals

austrian fieldcress *or* **austrian cress** *n, usu cap A* **:** a perennial cress (*Rorippa austriaca*) with auricled stem leaves and fruiting pedicels three to four times the length of the ellipsoid fruit pods

austrian oak *n, usu cap A* **:** ENGLISH OAK

austrian pine *n, usu cap A* **:** a tall pine (*Pinus nigra*) of central Europe widely cultivated for ornament and having needles two in a cluster and grayish twigs

austrian school *n, usu cap A & sometimes cap S* **:** the proponents of and adherents to the economic theories developed by Karl Menger (1840-1921), Friedrich von Wieser (1851-1926), and Eugen Böhm-Bawerk (1851-1914) of Vienna, Austria, who originated a subjective theory of value that utilizes the doctrine of marginal utility rather than the Ricardian labor theory of value and who formulated a productivity theory of interest and capital that emphasizes the importance of the time element in production — compare MARGINAL UTILITY

austrian winter pea *n, usu cap A* **:** FIELD PEA

¹aus·tric \'ȯstrik, 'äs-\ *adj, usu cap* [*Austria* + E *-ic*] **:** AUSTRIAN

²austric \"\ *adj, usu cap* [¹*austr-* + *-ic*] **:** of, relating to, or belonging to the related Austronesian and Austroasiatic families of languages considered as subfamilies of a vast family of languages extending from northern India across the islands of the Pacific

austringer *n* -s [alter. of *ostreger* — more at OSTREGER] *obs* **:** one that keeps goshawks

¹austro- — see ¹AUSTR-

²austro- — see ²AUSTR-

aus·tro·asiatic \¦ȯ(,)strō, ¦ä-+,==¦==\ *adj, usu cap* [¹*austr-* + *Asiatic*] **:** of, relating to, or belonging to a family of languages once widespread over northeastern India and Indo-China and comprising (1) the older now almost extinct Malacca group in the Malay peninsula, including Semang, Sakai; (2) Khasi, including Nicobarese, Palaung, Wa, Khasi; (3) Mon-Khmer, including Mon, Khmer, Jakun; and (4) Munda, including Santali, Ho, Mundari, Korwa, Asuri, Korku, Kharia, Juang, Savara, Gadaba — see ²AUSTRIC

austro-columbian \"+\ *adj, usu cap A&C* [NL *Austro-Columbia*, the neotropical region (fr. ¹*austr-* + *Columbia* America) + E *-an*] **:** NEOTROPICAL

aus·tro·gae·an *or* **aus·tro·ge·an** \¦ȯstrō¦jēən, ¦äs-\ *adj, usu cap* [NL *Austrogaea, Austrogea*, a biogeographic region (fr. ¹*austr-* + *-gaea, -gea*) + E *-an*] **:** of, relating to, or being a biogeographic region that comprises the Australian region except Polynesia

¹aus·tro-hungarian \¦ȯ(,)strō, ¦ä-+,=¦==\ *adj, usu cap A&H* [²*Austr-* + *Hungarian*] **:** of or relating to the former dual monarchy of Austria-Hungary

²austro-hungarian \"\ *n, cap A&H* **:** a native or inhabitant of Austria-Hungary

austro-malayan \"+=¦==, ¦=,==\ *adj, usu cap A&M* [¹*austr-* + *Malayan*] **:** PAPUAN

¹aus·tro·ne·sian \¦ȯstrō¦nēzhən, ¦äs-, -ēsh-\ *adj, usu cap* [ISV, fr. NL *Austronesia*, islands of the southern Pacific + ISV *-an*; orig. formed as G *austronesisch*] **:** belonging or relating to a family of agglutinative languages spoken in the area extending from Madagascar in the west through the Malay peninsula and archipelago to Hawaii and Easter Island in the east and including practically all the native languages of the Pacific islands with exception of the Australian, Papuan, and Negrito languages — compare AUSTRIC 2, INDONESIAN

²austronesian \"\ *n* -s *usu cap* **:** the Austronesian language family

aus·tro·riparian \¦ȯstrō, ¦äs+(,)=¦===\ *adj, usu cap* [¹*austr-* + *riparian*] **:** of, relating to, or being the humid division of the Lower Austral life zone including the lower Mississippi valley and the greater part of the So. Atlantic and Gulf states from Virginia to eastern Texas

au·su \aù'sü\ *n* -s [Sp *ausú*] **:** any of several West Indian trees of the myrtle family; *esp* **:** BAYBERRY 1

au·su·bo \aù'sü(,)bō\ *n* -s [Sp] **1 a :** MASTIC TREE **b :** BUSTIC **2 :** the dark heavy strong and valuable wood of an ausubo

aut- *or* **auto-** *comb form* [Gk, fr. *autos*; perh. akin to L *aut* or — more at EKE] **1 a :** self **:** same one ⟨*autecology*⟩ ⟨*autism*⟩ ⟨*autobiography*⟩ ⟨*autogenetic*⟩ ⟨*autokinetic*⟩ ⟨*autolysis*⟩ **b** *usu auto-* **:** having similar genomes ⟨*autohexaploid*⟩ ⟨*autopolyploid*⟩ — opposed to *allo-* **2 :** automatic **:** self-acting **:** self-regulating ⟨*autoalarm*⟩ ⟨*autofeed*⟩ ⟨*autowind*⟩ **3** *auto-* **a :** of, by, affecting, or for the same individual ⟨*autohemagglutination*⟩ ⟨*autovaccine*⟩ **b :** self-caused **:** self-induced **:** occurring within one's own body sometimes pathologically ⟨*autointoxication*⟩ **c :** acting as an antibody on or produced as an antibody for a person's or animal's own antigens ⟨*autoagglutinin*⟩ ⟨*autohemolysin*⟩

au·ta·coid \'ȯd·ə,kȯid\ *n* -s [*aut-* + Gk *akos* remedy + E *-oid*; akin to OIr *hícc* healing, payment, W *iach* healthy, Corn *yogh*] **:** a specific organic substance formed by the cells of one part and transported in the body fluid or the sap of an organism and producing a specific effect on the activity of the cells of another part **:** an internal secretion (as a hormone or chalone) — **au·ta·coid·al** \¦==¦kȯidᵊl\ *adj*

aut·allotriomorphic \¦aùd·+=¦===¦==\ *adj* [*aut-* + *allotriomorphic*, fr. Gk *allotrios* strange (fr. *allos* other) + E *-morphic* — more at ELSE] **:** of, relating to, or like an aplitic texture of rock in which all of the constituents have crystallized simultaneously and mutually interfered

au·tarch \'ȯ,tärk\ *n* -s [Gk *autarchos*, fr. *autarchos* autocratic, fr. *aut-* self, independent, independently + *archos* ruler — more at ARCHI-] **:** AUTOCRAT, DESPOT

au·tar·chic \(')ȯ¦tärkik\ *or* **au·tar·chi·cal** \-rkəkəl\ *adj* **1 a :** of, relating to, or marked by autarchy ⟨an ~ government⟩ **b :** AUTARKIC **2 :** unaffected by adjacent genes — used of genes in mosaic tissues; compare HYPARCHIC **syn** see FREE

au·tar·chi·cal·ly \-rkək(ə)lē\ *adv* **:** in an autarchic manner

au·tar·chist \'=,=kəst\ *n* -s [by alter.] **:** AUTARKIST

au·tar·cho·glos·sa \ȯ,tärkō'gläsə, -ȯsə\ *n pl, cap* [NL, fr. Gk *autarchos* autocratic (fr. *aut-* + *-archos* -arch) + NL *-glossa*] **:** a division comprising all lizards except the Ascalabota

¹au·tar·chy \'ȯ,tärkē, -täk-, -ki *sometimes* 'ȯd·ə(r)k- *or* 'ȯtə-\ *n* -ES [Gk *autarchia*, fr. *autarchos* self-ruling + *-ia* -y] **:** absolute sovereignty **:** absolute or autocratic rule

²autarchy \"\ *n* -ES [by alter.] **:** AUTARKY

au·tar·kic \(')ȯ¦tärkik\ *or* **au·tar·ki·cal** \-rkəkəl\ *adj* **:** of, relating to, or marked by autarky **syn** see FREE

au·tar·ki·cal·ly \-rkək(ə)lē\ *adv* **:** in an autarkic manner

¹au·tar·kist \'=,=kəst\ *adj* **1 :** favoring autarky **2 :** AUTARKIC

²autarkist \"\ *n* -s **:** an advocate of autarky

au·tar·ky \'ȯ,tärkē, -täk-, -ki *sometimes* 'ȯd·ə(r)k- *or* 'ȯtə-\ *n* -ES [modif. of G *autarkie*, fr. Gk *autarkeia* personal self-sufficiency, fr. *autarkos* self-sufficient + *-eia* -y] **1 :** SELF-SUFFICIENCY, INDEPENDENCE; *specif* **:** national economic self-sufficiency and independence ⟨under a system of ~, trade between countries dwindled to almost nothing⟩ **2 :** a policy of establishing a national economy that is completely self-sufficient and independent of imports from other countries **3 :** an economically independent and self-sufficient region or nation

au·te \'aùd·ē\ *n* -s [Tahitian & Samoan *'aute*, or Maori *aute*] *in Tahiti & New Zealand* **:** PAPER MULBERRY

autecious *var of* AUTOECIOUS

aut·ecologic *or* **aut·ecological** \¦aùd·+\ *adj* **:** of, relating to, or involving autecology — **autecologically** *adv*

aut·ecology \,aùd·+\ *n* -ES [ISV *aut-* + *ecology*; orig. formed as G *autökologie*] **:** a branch of ecology dealing with the interrelations between individual organisms or individual kinds of organisms (as species) and their environment — compare SYNECOLOGY

auth *abbr* **1** authentic **2** author **3** authority; authorized

au·then·tic \ə'thentik, ȯ'-, -tēk\ *adj* [alter. (influenced by Gk *authentikos*) of earlier *autentyke*, fr. ME *autentik*, fr. MF *autentique*, fr. LL *authenticus*, fr. Gk *authentikos*, fr. *authentēs* murderer, master, doer (fr. *aut-* + *-hentēs* one that accomplishes) + *-ikos* -ic; akin to Gk *anyein, anein* to accomplish, *entea* (pl.) armor, Skt *sanoti* he gains] **1** *obs* **:** possessing authority that is not usu. open to challenge **:** AUTHORITATIVE **2 :** worthy of acceptance or belief by reason of conformity to fact and reality **:** not contradicted by evidence **:** TRUSTWORTHY, CREDIBLE, CONVINCING ⟨an ~ book on medieval customs⟩ ⟨an ~ portrayal⟩ **3 a :** vested with due formalities and legally attested **:** legally valid ⟨an ~ act⟩ **b** *obs* **:** properly qualified **:** AUTHORIZED **4 a :** not imaginary or specious **:** REAL, GENUINE ⟨~ joy over her return⟩ **b :** not copied **:** ORIGINAL ⟨an ~ manuscript⟩ ⟨an ~ Chippendale chair⟩ **5** *of a church mode* **:** ranging upwards from the keynote — distinguished from *plagal* **6 :** of an origin that cannot be questioned **:** indisputably proceeding from a given source that is avowed or implied **:** not spurious ⟨an ~ historical reference⟩ **7 a :** marked by conformity to widespread or long-continued tradition ⟨an ~ English custom⟩ **b :** marked by close conformity to an original **:** accurately and satisfyingly reproducing essential features ⟨an ~ portrait⟩ **8** *biol* **:** VALID

syn GENUINE, VERITABLE, BONA FIDE: AUTHENTIC stresses fidelity to actuality and fact, compatibility with a certain source or origin, accordance with usage or tradition, or complete sincerity without feigning or hypocrisy ⟨he told his grandfather that he had been in combat with a giant, and frightened his poor mother . . . with long, and by no means *authentic*, accounts of the battle —W.M.Thackeray⟩ ⟨an esoteric jargon which does not even have the *authentic* ring of American slang —Stanley Walker⟩ ⟨only the *authentic* Christian tradition has the answer to our present problems —*Times Lit. Supp.*⟩ ⟨an *authentic* passion for concrete detail, in the mind of the author himself —C.E.Montague⟩ GENUINE may stress definite origin from a certain source ⟨whose letter — *genuine* or counterfeited — had been so instrumental in hastening this outbreak —J.L.Motley⟩ GENUINE chiefly emphasizes a real actual character as contrasted with a fraudulent, deceptive appearance ⟨whether it is a *genuine* insight into the workings of his own mind or only a false explanation of them —C.D. Lewis⟩ ⟨sham motor bus companies which if *genuine* would have been very sensible and publicly useful investments —G.B.Shaw⟩ ⟨palming off paper imitations of all kinds of valuables on the simple-minded ghosts and gods, who take them in all good faith for the *genuine* articles —J.G.Frazer⟩ GENUINE may also describe emotions or mental states really experienced and not feigned ⟨that was no conventional expected shock that she had received. It was *genuine* unforeseen shock —Arnold Bennett⟩ In "a genuine authentic Gilbert Stuart portrait of Washington", GENUINE emphasizes certainty of ascription to Stuart and AUTHENTIC emphasizes the close similarity between portrait and subject. VERITABLE indicates a true existence or actual identity ⟨the ruffians were so utterly appalled, not only by the false powers of magic, but by *veritable* powers of majesty and eloquence —Charles Kingsley⟩ It may indicate a very close similarity and stress the suitability of a metaphor ⟨an old gray-haired lady, a *veritable* saint who had not been soured by her many deeds of charity —P.E.More⟩ BONA FIDE, often commercial or legal in suggestion, stresses good faith and lack of intent to deceive or the avoidance of equivocal casuistry ⟨*bona fide* residents who . . . maintained homes in no other places —*Harper's*⟩

authentical *archaic var of* AUTHENTIC

au·then·ti·cal·ly \-tək(ə)lē, -ēk-, -li\ *adv* **:** REALLY, GENUINELY, VALIDLY **:** with authority

au·then·ti·cate \-tə,kāt, *usu* -ād·+V\ *vt* -ED/-ING/-S [ML *authenticatus*, past part. of *authenticare*, fr. LL *authenticus* authentic] **:** to make authentic: **a :** to make authoritative **:** give authority to ⟨a book that is *authenticated* by the renown of those who contributed to it⟩ **b :** to make valid and effective by the proof, attestation, or formalities required by law ⟨an *authenticated* grant of land⟩ **c :** to make credible **:** make evident the reasonableness or logical necessity of ⟨authenticating a theory, assertion, or reputed fact⟩ ⟨*authenticating* her testimony by her obvious sincerity⟩ ⟨the date can be *authenticated* by documentary proof⟩ **d :** to establish convincingly as accurate, true, real, or genuine ⟨well-*authenticated* information⟩ ⟨an *authenticated* diamond⟩ **e :** to establish a conclusive basis for accepting as truly of an averred character, function, or position ⟨a diplomat *authenticating* himself and the object of his mission⟩ **f :** to verify the origin of **:** prove the authorship of ⟨a priceless and *authenticated* painting of Rembrandt⟩ **syn** see CONFIRM

au·then·ti·ca·tion \ə,thentə'kāshən, (,)ȯ,th-\ *n* -s **1 :** the action or process of authenticating **2 :** the state of being authenticated

au·then·ti·ca·tor \ə'thentə,kād·ə(r), ȯ'th-, -ātə-\ *n* -s **:** one that authenticates

authentic cadence *n* **:** a cadence consisting of the resolution of the dominant or the dominant seventh chord to the tonic

au·then·tic·i·ty \,ȯ,then'tisəd·ē, -ətē, -i *also* ,ȯthən-\ *n* -ES **:** the quality of being authentic **:** the quality of being authoritative, valid, true, real, or genuine ⟨a good adventure story with the added merit of complete ~ —Margaret B. Hexter⟩

au·thi·gen·e·sis \,ȯthə'jenəsəs\ *n, pl* **authigene·ses** \-ə,sēz\ [NL, fr. Gk *authi* + NL *genesis*] **:** the process by which minerals form in a sedimentary rock after its deposition

au·thi·gen·ic \,ȯthə'jenik\ *or* **au·thig·e·nous** \(')ȯ¦thijənəs\ *adj* [G *authigen* authigenic (fr. Gk *authigenēs* born in that place, native, fr. *authi* there + *-genēs* born) + E *-ic* or *-ous*; akin to Gk *au* again — more at EKE, -GEN] **:** formed where found — used of mineral particles of rocks formed by crystallization in the place they occupy; opposed to *allothogenic*

¹au·thor \'ȯthə(r)\ *n* -s [alter. of ME *autour, auctour*, fr. OF *autor, auctor*, fr. L *auctor*, fr. *auctus* (past part. of *augēre* to increase) + *-or* — more at EKE] **1** *archaic* **:** one that fathers **:** PROCREATOR, PARENT, ANCESTOR ⟨the ~ of his being was a shiftless, drunken, ill-tempered hack musician —H.W.Van Loon⟩ **2 a :** one that is the source of some form of intellectual or creative work ⟨the ~ of the theory of relativity⟩ ⟨the ~ of a beautifully designed mural⟩; *esp* **:** one that writes or otherwise composes a book, article, poem, play, or other work which involves literary composition and is intended for publication ⟨favorite American ~*s*⟩ ⟨~ of a textbook⟩ ⟨the ~*s* of a tariff law⟩ — compare COMPILER, EDITOR, TRANSLATOR **b :** one that compiles material (as for publication) in such a way that the finished compilation can be regarded as a relatively original work ⟨~ of an anthology of French poetry⟩ **c :** one (as an author's agent) having the right to make author's alterations **d :** a printer's customer **e :** a corporate author **3 a :** one that originates, makes, or gives existence **:** SOURCE, CREATOR; *esp* **:** GOD ⟨Eternal King . . . *Author* of all being —John Milton⟩ **b :** one that brings about or is the efficient cause of an action, event, circumstance, or condition ⟨the ~ of a plan for social improvement⟩ ⟨an ~ of world tension⟩ **c :** one that prompts to an action **:** INSTIGATOR ⟨~ of a mutiny⟩ **4** *obs* **:** one that is pointed out or appealed to as the source of an opinion **:** INFORMANT **5 authors** *pl but sing in constr, often cap* **:** a game played with special cards divided into sets or books, each set relating to a different author; *also* **:** this game played with standard playing cards **6 :** one that originally names and describes a particular taxon

²author \"\ *vt* **authored; authored; authoring** \-th(ə)riŋ\ **authors 1 :** to be the author of; *esp* **:** WRITE ⟨he ~*ed* a series of best sellers⟩ **2 :** MAKE, ORIGINATE, CREATE ⟨~*ing* a radically new fashion trend⟩

author catalog *n* **:** an alphabetical catalog in which titles are listed usu. under the names of authors only but sometimes also under the names of editors and compilers — compare DICTIONARY CATALOG

authorcraft \'==,=\ *n* **:** skill in or practice of authorship ⟨a man remarkable for his ~⟩

author entry *n* **:** a catalog entry of a writing under its author's name usu. with the surname placed first

au·thor·ess \'ȯthərəs *also* -thr-\ *n* -ES **:** a female author — now usu. replaced by *author*

au·tho·ri·al \(')ȯ¦thōrēəl, -ȯr-\ *adj* **:** AUCTORIAL

authorise *Brit var of* AUTHORIZE

¹au·thor·i·tar·i·an \ȯ,thȯrə'terēən, ə,th-, -,thȯr-, -'ta(a)r-, -'tär- *sometimes* ¦ȯthərə¦t-\ *adj* [*authority* + *-arian* (as in *humanitarian*)] **1 :** of, relating to, or favoring a principle of often blind submission to authority as opposed to individual freedom of thought and action ⟨a strict ~ hierarchy in which every man has his place, every class a defined function, a set of commands issuing from above, a group of subordinates below to be ordered ruthlessly about —Roy Lewis & Angus Maude⟩ **2 :** of, relating to, or favoring a political system that concentrates power in the hands of a leader or a small autocratic elite not constitutionally responsible to the body of the people — opposed to *democratic* ⟨an ~ regime⟩

²authoritarian \"\ *n* -s **:** one who advocates, supports, or furthers authoritarian principles and practices ⟨uncompromising ~*s*, contemptuous of the individual —B.R.Redman⟩

au·thor·i·tar·i·an·ism \-,nizəm\ *n* -s **:** an authoritarian system **:** authoritarian principles

au·thor·i·ta·tive \ə'thärə,tā|d·iv, -thȯr-, -,tə|, |tiv, -ēv *also* ȯ'th-\ *adj* [*authority* + *-ative*] **1 a :** of the nature of authority **:** marked by, possessing, or proceeding from authority **:** OFFICIAL ⟨an ~ decision⟩ **b :** exercising or assuming authority **:** having an air of authority; *sometimes* **:** demanding submission and conformity **:** PEREMPTORY, DICTATORIAL ⟨an ~ young officer⟩ **2 :** possessing recognized or evident authority that elicits acquiescence and acceptance **:** having qualities that mark as definitive **:** CONCLUSIVE, CONVINCING ⟨~ literature on the functioning of the human mind —Elspeth Mosscrop⟩ ⟨an ~ interpretation of the great composer⟩ ⟨a more sober and ~ view of the situation —D.W.Maurer & V.H.Vogel⟩ — **au·thor·i·ta·tive·ly** *adv* **au·thor·i·ta·tive·ness** *n* -ES

au·thor·i·ty \ə'thärəd·ē, -thȯr-, -ətē, -i *also* ȯ'th-\ *n* -ES [ME *autorite*, alter. of *auctorite*, fr. OF *autorité, auctorité*, fr. L *auctoritat-, auctoritas*, fr. *auctor* originator, author + *-itat-, -itas* -ity] **1 a :** a citation (as from a book) used in defense or support of one's actions, opinions, or beliefs; *also* **:** the source from which such a citation is drawn ⟨they used a brief passage from the book as their ~⟩ ⟨he quoted extensively from the Bible, his sole ~⟩ **b :** a conclusive statement or aggregate of statements (as an official decision of a court) **:** decisive declaration taken as a precedent; *also* **:** TESTIMONY ⟨they viewed the court's decision as an unquestionable ~ for their action⟩ ⟨heard on the best ~⟩ **c :** an individual (as a specialist in a given field) who is the source of conclusive statements or testimony **:** one who is cited or appealed to as an expert whose opinion deserves acceptance ⟨there was a long and fierce dispute between scholars who held that Cicero was an unchallengeable ~ —Gilbert Highet⟩ ⟨one should always be prepared to quote *authorities* in support of one's theories —Aldous Huxley⟩ **2 a :** power to require and receive submission **:** the right to expect obedience **:** superiority derived from a status that carries with it the right to command and give final decisions **:** DOMINION, JURISDICTION ⟨the ~ of parents over their children⟩ ⟨the ~ of the president⟩ ⟨the ~ of a judge⟩ **b :** delegated power over others **:** AUTHORIZATION ⟨he acted with the full ~ of the government⟩ **c :** freedom granted by one in authority **:** RIGHT ⟨do you have the ~ to leave when you want to⟩ **3 a :** power to influence thought and opinion **:** intellectual influence ⟨Voltaire had his enemies, but his ~ could not be denied⟩ **b :** power to influence the outward behavior of others **:** practical personal influence ⟨the ~ of fashion⟩ **4 a :** persons in command; *specif* **:** GOVERNMENT — now usu. used in pl. in the concrete ⟨the local *authorities* of each state⟩ and sing. in the abstract ⟨the public ~ is responsible for our protection⟩ **b :** a public administrative agency or corporation having quasi-governmental powers and authorized to administer a revenue-producing public enterprise ⟨the port ~⟩ ⟨the valley ~⟩ **5 :** justifying grounds **:** BASIS, WARRANT ⟨on what ~ can you act as you do⟩ **6 :** convincing force **:** WEIGHT ⟨his sincerity added much more ~ to the story⟩ **7 :** a combination of unstrained definitive masterfulness, clear-sighted ingenuity and skill, and economical attainment of an objective (as in a piece of writing or in a musical performance) ⟨a recording that is unequaled for its finesse and ~⟩ **8 :** AUTHOR 6 **syn** see INFLUENCE, POWER

authority to pay **:** LETTER OF CREDIT

authority to purchase **:** an instrument similar to a letter of credit under which drafts are drawn by the seller or exporter directly upon the buyer or importer rather than on a bank

au·tho·ri·za·tion \,ȯthərə'zāshən, -,rī'z-\ *n* -s **1 :** the act of authorizing **:** the state of being authorized **:** SANCTION, WARRANT **2 :** a grant of authority to the executive branch of a government to spend money for specified purposes or to contract for spending in the future

au·tho·rize \'ȯthə,rīz\ *vt* -ED/-ING/-S *see -ize in Explan Notes* [alter. of ME *autorisen*, fr. MF *autoriser*, fr. ML *auctorizare*, fr. L *auctor* + LL *-izare* -ize] **1 a :** to endorse, empower, justify, or permit by or as if by some recognized or proper authority (as custom, evidence, personal right, or regulating power) ⟨~ a new version⟩ **:** SANCTION ⟨idiom *authorized* by use⟩ ⟨he was not *authorized* to use my name⟩ ⟨I would on no account ~ in my girls the smallest degree of arrogance —Jane Austen⟩ **b** *archaic* **:** to furnish grounds for **:** JUSTIFY **2** *obs* **:** to vouch for **:** confirm the truth or reality of by alleging one's own or another's authority **3** *obs* **:** to give legality or effective force to (a power, instrument, order) **4 a :** to endow with authority or effective legal power, warrant, or right **:** appoint, empower, or warrant regularly, legally, or officially ⟨Congress has *authorized* the President to suspend the operation of a Statute —O.W.Holmes †1935⟩ ⟨before Ferdinand

and Isabella *authorized* the first voyage —*Times Lit. Supp.*› **b :** to grant or allot by proper authority ‹a million dollars *authorized* for the new bridge›

syn ACCREDIT, COMMISSION, LICENSE: AUTHORIZE indicates endowing formally with a power or right to act, usu. with discretionary privileges ‹a whipping post was erected and the keeper *authorized* to punish the convicts —Marjorie Freer› Sometimes it applies to the sanction of any force viewed as authoritative ‹an informality *authorized* by custom› ‹an agent *authorized* by the heirs› ‹a rite *authorized* by a church council› ACCREDIT may imply endowing or giving formal credentials or proof of authorization to ‹all ambassadors, ministers, and consuls *accredited* to foreign states —F.A.Ogg & Harold Zink› ‹the Association of American Railroads has had a competent mechanical engineer duly *accredited* to the Atomic Energy Commission —W.T.Faricy› COMMISSION may imply the conferring, usu. formal, of rank, office, or status, or specific instructions about duties and missions ‹Delaware, in *commissioning* its delegates, restrained them from assenting to any change in the "rule of suffrage" —E.K.Alden› ‹I *commissioned* a mutual friend . . . to break the matter to this gentleman as delicately as possible —W.M.Thackeray› LICENSE may indicate issuance of a formal legal document setting forth a particular permission or right ‹*licensed* to dispense narcotics› ‹he was *licensed* as a pilot› In other senses LICENSE may suggest a certain sanction in proceeding with what might be questioned or questionable ‹through the character of Huck, that disreputable, illiterate little boy . . . he [Mark Twain] was *licensed* to let himself go —Van Wyck Brooks›

authorized *or* **authorised** *adj* [alter. of ME *autorised*, fr. past part. of *autorisen*] **1** *archaic* **:** having authority **:** marked by authority **:** recognized as having authority **2 :** endowed with authority ‹an ~ representative› **3 :** sanctioned by authority **:** APPROVED ‹an ~ biography› ‹an ~ translation›

authorized capital *n* **:** the amount of capital stock that a corporation is authorized to issue under the terms of its charter

au·tho·riz·er \-zə(r)\ *n* -s **1 :** one that authorizes **2 :** a clerk who verifies the credit standing of customers and approves or disapproves charges against their accounts

au·thor·less \ˈȯthə(r)ləs\ *adj* **:** without an author; *specif* **:** ANONYMOUS

author number *also* **author mark** *n* **:** a character or characters representing an author's surname in a call number — see CUTTER NUMBER

authors *pl of* AUTHOR, *pres 3d sing of* AUTHOR

author's alteration *n* **:** a change or correction not of a printer's error ordered in a printer's proof by and customarily chargeable to an author — abbr. *AA*

author's correction *n* **:** AUTHOR'S ALTERATION — abbr. *AC*

author's edition *n* **:** an edition of a book for which the printing and publishing costs are borne by the author

au·thor·ship \ˈȯthə(r),ship\ *n* -s **1 a :** the profession of writing (as books, stories, or articles) **b :** the function or dignity of an author **2 a :** the origin of a literary production ‹the disputed ~ of the miracle plays› **b :** the state or act of creating or causing **:** INSTIGATION ‹the ~ of a crime›

au·tism \ˈȯ,tizəm, ˈȯd·,iz-\ *n* -s [NL *autismus*, fr. L *aut-* + *-ismus* -ism] **:** absorption in need-satisfying or wish-fulfilling fantasy as a mechanism of escape from reality

au·tis·tic \(ˈ)ȯ¦tistik\ *adj* **:** of, relating to, or marked by autism

¹au·to \ˈau̇|d·(,)ō, ˈȯ|, |(,)tō, *Pg* ˈau̇(,)tü\ *n* -s [Sp & Pg, fr. L *actus* act (of a play), act (in general) — more at ACT] **1 :** a short medieval play on a sacred or biblical subject (as a miracle or morality play) flourishing up to the middle of the 18th century and esp. popular among the Spanish and Portuguese **2 :** AUTO-DA-FÉ

²au·to \ˈȯd·(,)ō, ˈȯ,tō\ *n* -s [by shortening] **:** AUTOMOBILE

³auto \"\ *vi* -ED/-ING/-S **:** to drive an automobile or ride in one **:** MOTOR

⁴auto \"\ *adj or n* [by shortening] **:** AUTOMATIC

¹auto- *in pronunciations below*, ¦ᵊ(,)ᵊ = ¦ȯd·(,)ō *or* ¦ȯ(,)tō *also before consonants* -ə\ — see AUT-

²auto- \"\ *comb form* [¹*automobile*] **:** self-propelling **:** automotive ‹*autocab*› ‹*autocar*›

au·to·agglutination \¦ᵊ(,)ᵊ *at* ¹AUTO- +\ *n* -s [*aut-* + *agglutination*] **:** agglutination of an individual's red blood cells by cold agglutinins in his own serum usu. at lower than body temperature — called also *cold agglutination*

au·to·agglutinin \" +\ *n* -s [*aut-* + *agglutinin*] **:** an antibody that agglutinates the red blood cells of the individual that produces it — compare COLD AGGLUTININ

au·to·alarm \ˈᵊ(,)ᵊ + ᵊ,ᵊ\ *n* -s [*aut-* + *alarm*] **:** a radio receiving device used on ships that rings an alarm bell when a distress signal is received

au·to·antibody \" +\ *n* -ES [*aut-* + *antibody*] **:** an antibody against one of the constituents of the tissues of the individual that produces it — compare AUTOAGGLUTININ

au·to·asphyxiation \¦ᵊ(,)ᵊ + \ *n* -s [*aut-* + *asphyxiation*] **:** asphyxiation of an organism by the products of its own metabolism

au·to·bahn \ˈau̇d·ō,bän\ *n*, *pl* **autobahns** \-nz\ *also* **autobah·nen** \-nən\ *sometimes cap* [G (prob. trans. of It *autostrada*), fr. *auto-* ²auto- + *bahn* track, road, fr. MHG *ban, bane;* akin to G dial. (Westphalia) *baanen* to hammer out, OHG *bano* death, destruction — more at BANE] **:** a road in Germany with double traffic lanes in each direction separated by a parkway

au·to·basidii \¦ᵊ(,)ᵊ *at* ¹AUTO + bəˈsidē,ī\ *n pl*, *cap* [NL, fr. *aut-* + *basidii* (fr. *basidium*)] *in some classifications* **:** EUBASIDII

au·to·basidiomycetes \" +\ [NL, fr. *aut-* + *Basidiomycetes*] *syn of* AUTOBASIDII

au·to·basidium \"+\ *n*, *pl* **autobasidia** [NL, fr. *aut-* + *basidium*] **:** an undivided basidium typical of the higher basidiomycetes — compare HEMIBASIDIUM, PROMYCELIUM

au·to·bi·og·ra·pher \,ȯd·|ə,bīˈägrəfə(r), ,ȯt|, |ō- *also* -,bē-\ *n* -s [*aut-* + *biographer*] **:** one who writes his own biography

au·to·bi·o·graph·i·cal \ᵊ,bīə¦grafəkəl, -raif-, -fēk- *sometimes* -,bēə-\ *or* **au·to·bi·o·graph·ic** \-fik, -ēk\ *adj* **1 :** in the style of, suggestive of, or relating to an autobiography ‹a book based on personal incidents without being ~› of the nature of an autobiography ‹an ~ film› **2 :** of or relating to an autobiographer **:** marked by qualities associated with an autobiographer ‹the ~ impulse is normal in old age —Van Wyck Brooks› — **au·to·bi·o·graph·i·cal·ly** \-fək(ə)lē, -ēk-, -li\ *adv*

au·to·bi·og·ra·phist \,ᵊᵊ,bīˈägrəfəst *also* -,bē-\ *n* -s **:** AUTOBIOGRAPHER

au·to·bi·og·ra·phy \-fē, -fi\ *n* -ES [*aut-* + *biography*] **:** the biography of oneself narrated by oneself

au·to·boat \ˈᵊᵊ *at* ¹AUTO- + ,ᵊ\ *n* -s [²*auto-* + *boat*] **:** MOTORBOAT

au·to·bolide \" + ᵊ,ᵊ\ *n* -s [F, fr. *auto-* ²auto- + *bolide*] **:** an automobile designed to be projected through the air from a specially constructed track

au·to·bus \" + ,ᵊ\ *n*, *pl* **autobuses** *or* **autobusses** [²*auto-* + *bus*] **:** OMNIBUS 1

au·to·cade \ˈᵊᵊ + ¦kād\ *n* -s [²*auto* + *-cade* (as in *motorcade*)] **:** MOTORCADE

au·to·camp \ˈᵊᵊ + ,ᵊ\ *n* [²*auto* + *camp*] **:** a camping ground often provided with cabins or tents and designed for the accommodation of automobile tourists

au·to·car \" + ,ᵊ\ *n* [²*auto-* + *car*] **:** AUTOMOBILE — now usu. shortened to *auto* or *car*

au·to·carp \ˈᵊᵊ + ,kärp\ *n* -s [*aut-* + *-carp*] **1 :** a fruit resulting from self-fertilization **2 :** a fruit consisting of the ripened pericarp without adnate parts

au·to·car·pous \¦ᵊᵊ + ¦kärpəs\ *or* **au·to·car·pi·an** \-¦kärpēən\ *or* **au·to·car·pic** \-¦kärpik\ *adj* [*autocarpous, autocarpic* fr. *aut-* + *-carpous, -carpic; autocarpian* fr. *aut-* + *carp-* + *-an*] **:** consisting of the ripened pericarp with no adnate parts

au·to·car·py \ˈᵊᵊ + ,kärpē\ *n* -ES [*aut-* + *-carpy*] **:** the production of fruit by self-fertilization

au·to·catalysis \¦ᵊ(,)ᵊ +\ *n*, *pl* **autocatalyses** [NL, fr. *aut-* + *catalysis*] **:** SELF-CATALYSIS **:** catalysis of a reaction by one of its own products (as the reduction of silver oxide by the silver formed by reduction of a small portion of it or the activation of an enzyme precursor by the enzyme itself)

au·to·catalytic \" + ,ᵊᵊ¦ᵊᵊ\ *adj* [fr. NL *autocatalysis*, after NL *catalysis:* E *catalytic*] **:** relating to or proceeding by autocatalysis

au·to·ceph·a·lic·i·ty \" + ,sefəˈlisəd·ē\ *or* **au·to·ceph·a·lism** \-ˈsefə,lizəm\ *n*, *pl* **autocephalicities** *or* **autocephalisms** [*autocephalicity* fr. *autocephalous* + *-ic* + *-ity; autocephalism* fr. *autocephalous* + *-ism*] **:** AUTOCEPHALY

au·to·ceph·a·lous \¦ᵊᵊ + ¦sefələs\ *adj* [LGk *autokephalos*, fr. Gk *aut-* + *-kephalos* (fr. *kephalē* head) — more at CEPHALIC] *Eastern Orthodox Church* **:** INDEPENDENT, SELF-GOVERNING **:** not under the jurisdiction of another — used of a church that appoints its own chief bishop without outside sanction and enters into direct relations with other churches but is in communion with the ecumenical patriarch of Constantinople and thus with all other Orthodox churches

au·to·ceph·a·ly \ˈᵊ + ,sefəlē\ *n* -ES [LL *autocephalia*, fr. LGk *autokephalos* + L *-ia* -y] **:** the state of being autocephalous

au·to·chore \ˈȯd·ə,kō(ə)r\ *n* -s [*aut-* + *-chore*] **:** a plant that is the major agent in the distribution of its own seeds or spores (as by special ejecting organs) — **au·to·cho·rous** \¦ȯd·ə¦kōrəs\ *adj*

¹au·to·chrome \ˈᵊᵊ + ,krōm\ *n* -s [ISV *aut-* + *-chrome;* orig. formed in F] **:** a plate for additive color photography that uses a layer of minute grains of starch dyed red, green, and blue coated with a panchromatic emulsion

²autochrome \"\ *adj* **:** METACHROME

au·toch·thon \ȯˈtäkthən, -,thän\ *n*, *pl* **autochthons** \-nz\ *or* **autochtho·nes** \-,thə,nēz\ [modif. (influenced by Gk *autochthōn*) of L *autocthon*, fr. Gk *autochthon-, autochthōn*, fr. *aut-* + *chthon-, chthōn* earth — more at HUMBLE] **1 a :** one supposed to have risen or sprung from the ground of the region he inhabits **b :** one of the original inhabitants of a region **:** ABORIGINE **2 :** something that is autochthonous; *esp* **:** an indigenous plant or animal **3** *or* **au·toch·thone** \-,thōn\ **:** rock essentially in its place of origin in contrast to the adjacent rock of an allochthon

au·toch·tho·nism \-,thə,nizəm\ *n* -s **1 :** origin from the soil **2 :** the state of being aboriginal **:** the state of being native to a region

au·toch·tho·nous \(ˈ)ȯ¦täkthənəs\ *also* **au·toch·tho·nal** \-nᵊl\ *or* **au·toch·thon·ic** \ˌȯ,täkˈthänik\ *adj* **1 :** INDIGENOUS, NATIVE, ABORIGINAL — used esp. of floras and faunas **2 a :** formed or occurring in the place where found **:** AUTHIGENIC ‹~ rock› ‹~ minerals› **b :** indigenous to a region ‹~ fossils› **:** ENDEMIC ‹~ malaria› **:** not imported **:** NATIVE ‹~ culture› ‹~ literature› **3** *geol* **:** not displaced by overthrusting ‹an ~ zone› **4 :** originating in that part of the body where found — used chiefly of pathological conditions **syn** see NATIVE

autochthonous idea *n* **:** an abnormally dominating idea seeming to a psychiatric patient to have been thrust upon him and not to have developed out of his content of consciousness — compare FIXED IDEA

au·toch·tho·nous·ly \(ˈ)ȯ¦täkthənəslē\ *adv* **:** in an autochthonous manner

au·toch·tho·ny \ȯˈtäkthənē\ *n* -ES **:** autochthonous condition

autocinesis *var of* AUTOKINESIS

au·to·clastic \¦ᵊᵊ *at* ¹AUTO- + ¦ᵊᵊ\ *adj* [*aut-* + *clastic*] **:** broken in place — used of rocks having a broken or brecciated structure due to crushing in contrast to those of brecciated materials brought from a distance

¹au·to·clave \ˈᵊᵊ + ,klāv\ *n* -s [F, fr. *aut-* (fr. Gk) + L *clavis* key — more at CLAVICLE] **:** an airtight chamber that can be filled with steam under pressure or surrounded by another chamber for the steam and that is used for sterilizing, cooking, or other purposes requiring moist or dry temperatures above 212° F without boiling — compare PRESSURE COOKER

²autoclave \"\ *vt* -ED/-ING/-S **:** to subject to the action of an autoclave

autoclave cipher *n* [*aut-* + *-clave* (fr. L *clavis* key) — more at CLAVICLE] **:** AUTOKEY CIPHER

au·to·collimation \¦ᵊᵊ +\ *n* -s [*aut-* + *collimation*] **:** the process of collimating a telescope or other instrument having objective and cross hairs by directing it toward a plane mirror and adjusting the lens and cross hairs so that the latter coincide with their own reflected image

au·to·collimator \" +\ *n* -s [*aut-* + *collimator*] **:** a telescope with eyepiece adapted to the method of autocollimation either to collimate the instrument itself or to ensure that its axis is perpendicular to a reflecting surface

au·to·colony \" +\ *n* -ES [*aut-* + *colony*] *bot* **:** a daughter colony formed within one of the cells of a colony and duplicating in miniature the parent colony

au·to·copulation \" +\ *n* [*aut-* + *copulation*] **:** self-copulation that infrequently occurs in some hermaphroditic worms

au·to·cosm \ˈȯd·ō,käzəm\ *n* -s [*auto-* + *-cosm*] **:** a self-created microcosm **:** a private world

au·to·cos·mic \¦ᵊᵊ¦käzmik\ *adj* [*auto-* + *cosmic*] **:** of or relating to an autocosm **:** highly personalistic **:** AUTISTIC

auto court *n* [²*auto*] **:** MOTEL

au·toc·ra·cy \ȯˈtäkrəsē, -si\ *n* -ES [prob. fr. F *autocratie*, after such pairs as E *aristocrat: aristocracy*] **1 :** a form of government in which one person possesses unlimited power — compare ABSOLUTISM **2 :** the unlimited authority or rule of an autocrat **3 :** a community or state governed by autocracy **:** an autocratic community or state

au·to·crat \ˈȯd·|ə,krat, ˈȯt|, |ō-, *usu* -ad- + V\ *n* -s [F *autocrate*, fr. Gk *autokratēs* ruling by oneself, absolute, fr. *aut-* + *-kratēs* (fr. *kratos* strength, power) — more at HARD] **1 a :** a monarch ruling with unlimited authority **b :** a governor with absolute power **2 :** one who rules with undisputed sway in any relationship ‹he was the ~ of his household›

au·to·crat·ic \ˌȯd·|ə¦krad·ik, |ȯt|, |ō-, -atik, -ēk\ *also* **au·to·crat·i·cal** \-ᵊkəl, -ēk-\ *adj* **1 :** of the nature of or relating to an autocrat **:** having absolute and sole control **:** favoring autocracy **:** DESPOTIC ‹an ~ ruler› ‹those who have long been in the habit of exercising power become ~ and quarrelsome —Bertrand Russell› **2 :** of the nature of or relating to an autocracy **:** having the characteristics of an autocracy **:** marked by the exercising or favoring of absolute and sole control ‹an ~ government› ‹history of ~ political rule and economic backwardness —Vera M. Dean› **syn** see ABSOLUTE

au·to·crat·i·cal·ly \-ᵊk(ə)lē, -ēk-, -li\ *adv* **:** in an autocratic manner

au·toc·ra·tor \ȯˈtäkrəd·ə(r)\ *n* -s [Russ & LL; Russ *avtokrator* & LL *autocrator*, fr. Gk *autokratōr* absolute ruler, absolute, fr. *aut-* + *-kratōr* (fr. *kratein* to rule, fr. *kratos* power)] **:** AUTOCRAT

au·to·critical \¦ᵊᵊ *at* ¹AUTO- + ¦ᵊᵊᵊ\ *adj* [*aut-* + *critical*] **:** of or relating to autocriticism **:** disposed to or marked by the exercise of autocriticism ‹the ~ habit of mind indispensable to a genuine philosopher —David Gascoyne›

au·to·criticism \" +\ *n* -s [*aut-* + *criticism*] **:** criticism of oneself **:** searching self-examination

au·to·cytolysis \" +\ *n*, *pl* **autocytolyses** [NL, fr. *aut-* + *cyt-* + *-lysis*] **:** autolysis of cells

au·to-da-fé \¦au̇|d·ōdəˈfā, ¦ȯ|, |d·(,)ōd-,|təd-,|(,)tōd-\ *n*, *pl* **autos-da-fé** \əzd-, -ōzd-\ [Pg *auto da fé*, lit., act of the faith] **:** the ceremony accompanying the pronouncement of judgment by the Inquisition and followed by the execution of sentence by the secular authorities; *esp* **:** the burning of a person condemned as a heretic or of writings condemned as heretical

auto de fé \"\ *n*, *pl* **autos de fé** [Sp, fr. Pg *auto da fé*] **:** AUTO-DA-FÉ

au·to·di·dact \,ȯd·ōˈdī,dakt, -,dīˈd-, -,dəˈd-\ *n* -s [Gk *autodidaktos* self-taught, fr. *aut-* + *didaktos* taught, fr. *didaskein* to teach — more at DOCILE] **:** one who is self-taught

au·to·di·dac·tic \¦ᵊᵊ,dīˈdaktik, -,dəˈd-\ *adj* **:** of or relating to an autodidact **:** having the characteristics of an autodidact

au·to·digestion \¦ᵊ(,)ᵊ *at* ¹AUTO- +\ *n* -s [*aut-* + *digestion*] **:** AUTOLYSIS

au·to·dyne \ˈᵊᵊ + ,ᵊ\ *n* -s [ISV *aut-* + *dyne*] **:** a special heterodyne in which the auxiliary current is generated in the device used for rectification

¹au·toe·cious *also* **au·te·cious** \(ˈ)ȯ¦tēshəs, (ˈ)ȯd·¦ē-\ *adj* [*aut-* + *-oecious, -ecious* (fr. Gk *oikia* house + E *-ous*) — more at VICINITY] **:** passing through all the stages in its life history on the same host or on closely related hosts ‹certain parasitic fungi such as rusts are ~› — compare HETEROECIOUS — **au·toe·cious·ly** *also* **au·te·cious·ly** *adv* — **au·toe·cism** *also* **au·te·cism** \ȯˈtē,sizəm, ȯd·ˈē,-\ *n* -s

²autoecious *var of* AUTOICOUS

autoed *past of* AUTO

au·to·erotic \¦ᵊ(,)ᵊ *at* ¹AUTO- + ᵊ¦ᵊᵊ\ *adj* [*aut-* + *erotic*] **:** of, relating to, or marked by autoeroticism — **au·to·erotically** \" + ᵊ¦ᵊᵊ(ᵊ)ᵊ\ *adv*

au·to·erotism \¦ᵊᵊ+\ *also* **au·to·eroticism** \" +\ *n* -s [*aut-* + *erotism, eroticism*] **1 :** sexual gratification obtained through one's own organism without the participation or stimulus of another individual — contrasted with *alloerotism* **2 :** sexual feeling or desire arising endogenously without known external stimulation

au·to·ette \ˌȯd·(,)ōˈet, ¦ȯd·ə¦wet\ *n* -s [²*auto-* + *-ette*] **:** a 3-wheeled motorcycle provided usu. with a box or trunk for holding packages and used for light deliveries (as by parcel-post carriers)

au·to·focal \¦ᵊᵊ *at* ¹AUTO- + ¦ᵊᵊ\ *adj* [*aut-* + *focal*] **:** being a photographic enlarger that is automatically kept in focus as the enlarger head is moved up or down to secure the desired degree of enlargement

au·to·frettage \ˈᵊᵊ + ,ᵊᵊ\ *n* -s [prob. fr. F, fr. *aut-* + *frettage*] **:** the application of such interior pressure to the bore of a heavy ordnance gun as will deform the inner layers of steel beyond the elastic limit that would be reached by the explosion of any charge to be used subsequently in the gun

au·tog·a·mous \(ˈ)ȯ¦tägəməs, ə¦-\ *also* **au·to·gam·ic** \ˌȯd·ō¦gamik\ *adj* **:** relating to, or reproducing by autogamy

au·tog·a·my \ȯˈtägəmē, əˈ-\ *n* -ES [ISV *aut-* + *-gamy*] **:** SELF-FERTILIZATION; *esp* **:** pollination of a flower by its own pollen or, among protozoans and fungi, conjugation of two sister cells or sister nuclei

au·to·genesis \¦ᵊᵊ *at* ¹AUTO-+\ *n*, *pl* **autogeneses** [NL, fr. L *aut-* + *genesis*] **1 :** ABIOGENESIS **2 :** a concept that evolution is directed by innate orienting factors independent of the interaction of organism and environment

au·to·genetic \¦ᵊ(,)ᵊ+ᵊ¦ᵊᵊ\ *adj* [ISV, fr. NL *autogenesis*, after such pairs as E *antithesis: antithetic*] **1 :** SELF-GENERATED **2 :** of or relating to autogenesis **3** *geol* **:** determined by or developed under strictly local conditions **4** *of plankton* **:** originating where found — opposed to *allogenetic* — **au·to·geneti·cally** \" + ᵊ¦ᵊᵊ(ᵊ)ᵊ\ *adv*

autogenetic drainage *n* **:** drainage by streams whose courses have been determined solely by the conditions of the land surface over which they flow — compare EPIGENETIC DRAINAGE

au·to·gen·ic \ˌȯd·əˈjenik\ *adj* [*aut-* + *-genic*] **:** involving or resulting from biotic reaction — used chiefly in the phrase *autogenic succession*

au·to·genital \" + ¦ᵊᵊᵊ\ *adj* [*aut-* + *genital*] **:** of or relating to one's own genital organs

au·to·genotype \" + \ *n* -s [*aut-* + *genotype*] **:** a genotype specif. established in the original publication of a genus

au·tog·e·nous \(ˈ)ȯ¦täjənəs, ə¦-\ *also* **au·to·genic** \ˌȯd·ō¦jenik\ *adj* [Gk *autogenēs* self-produced (fr. *aut-* + *-genēs* -gen) + E *-ous* or *-ic*] **1 :** SELF-GENERATED **:** produced independently of external influence or aid **:** ENDOGENOUS **2** *anat* **:** ossifying from an independent center **3** *med* **:** of origin within or from oneself ‹~ skin graft› **4 :** AUTOGENETIC 3 **5 :** achieved without external aid — used esp. of a union of parts or surfaces without use of adhesives or solder ‹~ welding› ‹~ healing of a crack in asphalt paving› ‹~ tin-plating on sheet iron› **6** *biol* **a :** originating within the same individual **b :** caused by factors within the individual **:** not directly due to environmental influences ‹an ~ variation› — **au·tog·e·nous·ly** \(ˈ)ȯ¦täjənəslē, ə¦-\ *adv*

autogenous graft *n* **:** AUTOGRAFT

autogenous vaccine *n* **:** a vaccine prepared from cultures obtained from a specific lesion of the patient himself and used to immunize him against further spread and progress of the same organism

au·tog·e·ny \ȯˈtäjənē\ *n* -ES [alter. of earlier *autogony*, fr. G *autogonie*, fr. *aut-* + *-gonie* -gony] **:** SELF-GENERATION

au·to·geosynclinal \¦ᵊᵊ *at* ¹AUTO- +\ *adj* **:** of, relating to, or marked by the presence of an autogeosyncline

au·to·geosyncline \" + \ *n* -s [*aut-* + *geosyncline*] *geol* **:** an isolated basin which is relatively remote from uplifted source areas and in which fine clastic sediments, carbonate rocks, and evaporites are usu. deposited

au·to·gi·ro *also* **au·to·gy·ro** \ˌȯd·|ōˈjī(,)rō, ,ȯt|, |ə'-, 'ᵊᵊ,ᵊ(,)ᵊ\ *n* -s [fr. *Autogiro*, a trademark] **:** a rotating-wing aircraft that achieves slow flight and vertical takeoff by the use of a freely rotating rotor replacing or supplementing the wings but is driven forward by a conventional propeller

au·tog·no·sis \ˌȯd·əgˈnōsəs\ *n*, *pl* **autogno·ses** \-ō,sēz\ [NL, fr. *aut-* + *-gnosis*] **:** SELF-KNOWLEDGE; *esp* **:** an understanding of one's own psychodynamics

au·tog·nos·tic \¦ᵊᵊ¦nästik\ *adj* [fr. NL *autognosis*, after NL *-gnosis:* E *Gnostic*] **:** of, relating to, or characterized by autognosis

¹au·to·graft \ˈᵊᵊ *at* ¹AUTO- + ,ᵊ\ *n* -s [*aut-* + *graft*] **:** a tissue or organ that is transplanted from one part to another part of the same body

²autograft \"\ *vt* **:** to transplant as an autograft ‹~*ing* skin›

¹au·to·graph \ˈȯd·ə,graf, ˈȯtə-, -raa(ə)f,-raif,-råf\ *n* -s [LL *autographum*, fr. L, neut. of *autographus* written with one's own hand, fr. Gk *autographos*, fr. *aut-* + *-graphos* -graph] **1 :** something that is written with one's own hand **: a :** an original handwritten manuscript (as of an author's or composer's work) ‹valuable old ~*s* of Dickens› **b :** a person's handwritten signature ‹a book with the author's ~› ‹teenagers clamoring for the ~*s* of their favorite stars› **2 :** an autographic recorder **3 :** a print made by autography **4** *photog* **:** a representation or trace of an object produced with the object close to the emulsion or (as in the case of ions or elementary particles) with the object passing through the emulsion, the image being formed by mechanical, electrical, chemical, or radiation effects of the object itself and usu. being made visible by development — compare AUTORADIOGRAPH

²autograph \"\ *adj* **:** in the writer's own handwriting **:** not copied nor duplicated **:** ORIGINAL ‹an ~ letter› ‹an ~ will›

³autograph \"\ *vt* -ED/-ING/-S **1 :** to write with one's own hand **2 :** to write one's autograph or signature in or on

au·tog·ra·pher \ȯˈtägrəfə(r)\ *n* -s **:** one who copies the clef signs, key, title, instructions, and lyrics from original music manuscript to serve as a pattern for engravers

au·to·graph·ic \ˌȯd·ə¦grafik, ¦ȯtə-, -fēk\ *also* **au·to·graph·i·cal** \-fəkəl, -ēk-\ *adj* **1 :** of or relating to an autograph **:** of the nature of an autograph **:** written in the author's own handwriting ‹an unquestionably ~ document› **2 :** using or made by autography **3 a** *of an instrument* **:** SELF-RECORDING **b** *of a record* **:** produced by a self-recording instrument — **au·to·graph·i·cal·ly** \-fək(ə)lē, -ēk-, -li\ *adv*

au·tog·ra·phy \ȯˈtägrəfē\ *n* -ES [*aut-* + *-graphy*] **1 a :** the action of writing with one's own hand **:** one's own handwriting **:** AUTOGRAPH **b :** a collection of autographs **2 :** any process in which original copy is made on or transferred direct to the printing surface

Au·to·harp \ˈȯd·ō,härp\ *trademark* — used for a musical instrument which is somewhat like a zither and on which simple harmony is obtained by button-controlled dampers operating in sets that when depressed leave free the strings of the desired chord

au·to·hemorrhage \¦ᵊᵊ *at* ¹AUTO- +\ *n* -s [*aut-* + *hemorrhage*] **:** the voluntary exudation or ejection by certain insects of blood which is nauseous or poisonous and hence protective against enemies

au·to·hemotherapy \"+\ *n* -ES [ISV *aut-* + *hemotherapy;* orig. formed as F *autohémothérapie*] **:** treatment of disease with the patient's own blood either modified (as by irradiation) or introduced outside the blood stream (as by intramuscular injection)

au·toi·cous \(ˈ)ȯ¦tȯikəs, (ˈ)ȯd·¦ȯi-\ *also* **autoecious** *adj* [*aut-* + *-oicous, -oecious* (fr. Gk *oikos* dwelling + E *-ous*) — more at VICINITY] **:** having male and female organs on the same plant but on separate branches ‹certain mosses are ~› — compare DIOICOUS, PAROICOUS, SYNOICOUS

au·to·ignition \¦ᵊ(,)ᵊ *at* ¹AUTO- +\ *n* -s [*aut-* + *ignition*] **1 :** self-ignition in an internal-combustion engine cylinder either as a result of the heat of the compression alone or from this in combination with glowing carbon — compare PREIGNITION **2** : SPONTANEOUS COMBUSTION

au·to·immunization \"+\ *n* -s [ISV *aut-* + *immunization*] : production by an individual of antibodies against constituents of his own tissues that is a possible cause of a number of serious and apparently incurable diseases

au·to·infection \"+\ *n* -s [ISV *aut-* + *infection*] : reinfection (as through self-contamination) with larvae produced by parasitic worms already in the body — compare HYPERINFECTION

autoing *pres part of* AUTO

au·to·inoculability \"+\ *n* -ES : the condition of being autoinoculable

au·to·inoculable \"+⸗¦⸗⸗⸗⸗\ *adj* [*aut-* + *inoculable*] : capable of being transmitted by inoculation from one part of the body to another ⟨certain kinds of warts are ~⟩

au·to·inoculation \"+\ *n* -s [ISV *aut-* + *inoculation*] **1** : inoculation of an individual with vaccine prepared from material from his own body **2** : spread of infection from one part to other parts of the same body

au·to·intoxicated \"+⸗¦⸗⸗⸗⸗\ *adj* [*aut-* + *intoxicated*] : affected by autointoxication

au·to·intoxication \"+\ *n* -s [ISV *aut-* + *intoxication*; originally formed in F] **1** : a state of being poisoned by absorption of toxic substances produced within the body either by body cells or by microorganisms **2** : the act of arousing oneself psychologically to a state resembling drunkenness

au·to·ist \ˈȯd·əwə̇st, ˈȯd·ˌōə̇-\ *n* -s [²*auto* + *-ist*] : AUTOMOBILIST, MOTORIST

au·to·key cipher \ˈ⸗⸗ *at* ¹AUTO-+,⸗-\ *n* [*aut-* + *key*] : a cipher in which each letter serves as key for the next letter or for one at a constant interval

au·to·kinesis \¦⸗(,)⸗+\ *also* **autocinesis** \"+\ *n, pl* **autokineses** *also* **autocineses** [NL, fr. *aut-* + *kinesis*] : spontaneous movement; *esp* : apparent spontaneous movement of an actually stationary object

au·to·kinetic \"+⸗¦⸗⸗\ *adj* [*aut-* + *kinetic*] : of, relating to, or marked by autokinesis

autokinetic system *n* : a system of fire-alarm telegraphy so arranged that when one alarm is being transmitted no other alarm will be transmitted until after the first alarm has been disposed of

auto lift *n* [²*auto*] : a hydraulic machine by which automobiles are hoisted above the floor to give access to the underparts

au·to·lith \ˈ⸗⸗+,lith\ *n* -s [*aut-* + *-lith*] : a fragment of a previously crystallized portion of rock enclosed in material from the same magma which solidified later

¹**au·to·lithograph** \¦⸗⸗+\ *n* -s [*aut-* + *lithograph*] : a print made by autolithography

²**autolithograph** \"\ *vt* : to make (a print) by autolithography

au·to·lithographic \¦⸗⸗+\ *adj* : relating to or produced by autolithography

au·to·lithography \¦⸗(,)⸗+\ *n* [ISV *aut-* + *lithography*] : lithography in which an artist makes his original drawing direct on the printing surface — called also *artist lithography*

au·to·loader \ˈ⸗⸗+,⸗⸗\ *n* -s [*aut-* + *loader*] : an autoloading firearm

au·to·loading \¦⸗⸗+¦⸗⸗\ *adj* [*aut-* + *loading*] : SEMIAUTOMATIC — used of firearms

au·tol·o·gous \(ˈ)ȯ¦täləgəs\ *adj* [*aut-* + *-ologous* (as in *homologous*)] : derived from the same individual ⟨an ~ graft is taken from one part of the body and transplanted into another⟩ — compare HOMOLOGOUS

au·to·luminescence \¦⸗⸗ *at* ¹AUTO-+\ *n* -s [*aut-* + *luminescence*] : luminescence of a substance (as a radioactive material) due to energy originating within itself

au·to·luminescent \"+\ *adj* [*aut-* + *luminescent*] : of, relating to, or marked by autoluminescence

au·tol·y·sate \ȯˈtälə,sāt, -,sə̇t\ *n* -s [ISV *autolys-* (fr. NL *autolysis*) + *-ate*] : a product of autolysis

au·tol·y·sin \ȯˈtäləsə̇n, ,ȯd·əˈlīs-\ *n* -s [ISV *autolys-* (fr. NL *autolysis*) + *-in*] : any substance that produces autolysis (as certain proteolytic enzymes)

au·tol·y·sis \ȯˈtäləsə̇s\ *n* [NL, fr. *aut-* + *-lysis*] : self-digestion (as in fruit after picking, meat, or a diseased part of the body or one in which circulation has stopped) occurring in plant and animal tissues particularly after they have ceased to be a normal part of the organism to which they belong

au·to·lyt·ic \¦ȯd·ᵊl¦id·ik\ *adj* [fr. NL *autolysis*, after such pairs as ML *analysis*: E *analytic*] : of or relating to autolysis

au·tol·y·tus \ȯˈtäləd·əs\ *n, cap* [NL, fr. *aut-* + Gk *lytos* capable of being unfastened or dissolved, verbal of *lyein* to unfasten, dissolve, break up into parts — more at LOSE] : a genus of marine annelids (family Syllidae) that reproduce asexually by producing numerous new segments at a point near the posterior end, each of which develops into a new individual but remains attached for a time, a long chain of worms being thus formed

au·tol·y·zate \ȯˈtälə,zāt, -,zə̇t\ *n* -s [*autolyze* + *-ate*] : AUTOLYSATE

au·to·lyze \ˈȯd·ᵊl,īz\ *vb* -ED/-ING/-S [fr. NL *autolysis*, after such pairs as ML *analysis*: E *analyze*] *vi* : to undergo autolysis ~ *vt* : to subject to autolysis

au·to·mak·er \ˈ⸗⸗,⸗⸗\ *n* : a manufacturer of automobiles

au·to·mak·ing \ˈ⸗⸗,⸗⸗\ *n* : the manufacturing of automobiles

au·to·manual \¦⸗⸗ *at* ¹AUTO- + ¦⸗⸗⸗\ *adj* [*aut-* + *manual*] : of or relating to a railroad signal system in which the signals are operated manually but return to the danger position automatically after a train passes

Au·to·mat \ˈȯd·ə,mat, ˈȯtə-\ *service mark* — used for a cafeteria in which food is obtained esp. from coin-operated compartments

automat- *or* **automato-** *comb form* [Gk, self-acting, fr. *automatos* — more at AUTOMATON] : self-acting : self-regulating : automatic ⟨*automat*in⟩ ⟨*automato*graph⟩

automata *pl of* AUTOMATON

au·to·mate \ˈȯd·ə,māt, ˈȯtə-, *usu* -mād·+V\ *vt* -ED/-ING/-S [back-formation fr. *automation*] : to operate by automation : mechanize through automation : convert to largely automatic operation : make automatic : AUTOMATIZE ⟨*automated* business equipment⟩ ⟨*automating* a factory⟩

¹**au·to·mat·ic** \¦ȯd·ə¦mad·ik, ¦ȯtə-, -atik, -ēk\ *also* **au·to·mat·i·cal** \-ə̇kəl, -ēk-\ *adj* [Gk *automatos* self-acting + E *-ic*, *-ical* — more at AUTOMATON] **1 a** : involuntary either wholly or to a major extent so that any activity of the will is largely negligible : of a reflex nature : without volition ⟨the ~ blinking of the eyelids⟩ **b** : like or suggestive of an automaton : MECHANICAL ⟨the ~ smile of a tired store clerk⟩ **c** : performed without conscious awareness ⟨an unthinking ~ response⟩ **2** *archaic* : able to move and act in total independence of any outside cause : having the power of motion and action entirely within self **3** : having a self-acting or self-regulating mechanism that performs a required act at a predetermined point in an operation ⟨~ feed of a lathe⟩ ⟨~ record changer⟩ **4** : marked by spontaneous or apparently spontaneous action : marked by action that is unpremeditated and that arises as a really or apparently necessary reaction to or consequence of a given set of circumstances ⟨the ~ enthusiasm of the crowd over the returning heroes⟩ ⟨~ branding of the suspect as a traitor⟩ **5** *of a firearm* : marked by the use of either gas pressure or force of recoil and mechanical spring action for ejecting the empty cartridge case after the first shot, loading the next cartridge from the magazine, firing, ejecting the spent case, and repeating the above cycle as long as the pressure on the trigger is maintained and there is ammunition in the magazine or other loading device ⟨~ weapons⟩ — compare SEMIAUTOMATIC **syn** see SPONTANEOUS

²**automatic** \"\ *n* -s : a machine or apparatus that operates automatically; *esp* : an automatic or autoloading firearm

au·to·mat·i·cal·ly \-ə̇k(ə)lē, -ēk-, -li\ *adv* : in an automatic manner : without thought or conscious intention

automatic block signal *n* : a railroad signal at the entrance of a block actuated automatically by and governing the movement of trains entering and using the block

automatic coverage *n* : insurance that provides automatic adjustment of amount to correspond with fluctuating property values

automatic currency *n* : an elastic currency that adapts itself to business needs with little government intervention — contrasted with *managed currency*

automatic drill *n* : a straight brace for bits the shank of which consists of a screw of very coarse pitch sliding within a correspondingly threaded tube having a handle at the end, the tool being actuated by pushing the handle

automatic drive *n* : AUTOMATIC TRANSMISSION

au·to·ma·tic·i·ty \,ȯd·ə̇mə'tisəd·ē, ,ȯt¦, |ȯm-, -ətē, -i\ *n* -ES : the quality or state of being automatic ⟨the increasing ~ in industry⟩ ⟨the ~ of an habitual gesture⟩

automatic jointer *n* : a jointer that automatically assumes the proper position to turn under trash just before the plow turns over the furrow

automatic line finder *n* : a lever on a typewriter that when depressed disengages the line-spacing ratchet to allow writing between lines and when lifted returns the ratchet to place at the original line spacing

automatic machine *n* : a machine or machine tool (as a spinning machine or lathe) that after once being set operates automatically except for applying the power, lubricating, supplying material, and shutting off the power

automatic pilot *n* : a device for automatically steering ships and aircraft and automatically stabilizing aircraft

automatic pistol *n* : a pistol capable of automatic or semiautomatic fire

automatic premium loan *n* : an insurance policy loan made automatically to cover a premium due and unpaid at the end of the grace period

automatic progression *n* : the granting of advances in wages or salary on a scale between minimum and maximum strictly on a periodic basis

automatic reel *n* : a fly-fishing reel that retrieves line by a spring device

automatic reinstatement *n* : the reinstatement of the face value of an insurance policy after a loss has been incurred and paid for

automatic rifle *n* : a rifle capable commonly of either semiautomatic or full automatic fire and designed to be fired without a mount — compare MACHINE GUN

automatics *pl of* AUTOMATIC

automatic selling *n* : selling by vending machines or by self⸗service

automatic sequence *n* : the arrangement of a recording on successive sides of two or more phonograph discs so that the continuity of the recording is preserved when the discs are played on a record changer

automatic switch *n* : an electrical switch (as on a telephone) that is controlled from a central point

automatic transmission *n* : a usu. hydraulic or pneumatic mechanism whereby a motor vehicle automatically shifts gear according to actual car speed — called also *automatic drive*

automatic writing *n* : writing performed without conscious intention and sometimes without awareness as if of telepathic or spiritualistic origin

automating *pres part of* AUTOMATE

au·to·ma·tion \,ȯd·əˈmāshən, ,ȯtə-\ *n* -s [*automat-* + *-ion*] **1** : the technique of making an apparatus (as a calculating machine), a process (as of manufacturing), or a system (as of bookkeeping) operate automatically **2** : the state of being operated automatically **3** : automatically controlled operation of an apparatus, process, or system by mechanical or electronic devices that take the place of human organs of observation, effort, and decision

au·tom·a·tism \ȯˈtämə,tizəm *also* əˈt-\ *n* -s [F *automatisme*, fr. *automate* automaton + *-isme* -ism] **1 a** : the quality or state of being automatic **b** : an automatic action; *esp* : any action performed without the doer's intention or awareness **2** : a theory that views the body analogically as a machine and the mind or consciousness as a noncontrolling adjunct of the body **3** : the power or fact of moving without conscious control either without dependence on external stimulation (as in the beating of the heart) or more or less directly under the influence of external stimuli (as in the dilating or contracting of the pupil of the eye) **4** : suspension of the conscious mind to release subconscious images — used of technique in surrealist painting

au·tom·a·tist \-məd·ə̇st, -mətə̇-\ *n* -s **1** : one who accepts the theory of automatism **2 a** : one that performs automatic acts; *esp* : one that does automatic writing **b** : MEDIUM 7

au·tom·a·ti·za·tion \ȯ,tüməd·ə̇ˈzāshən, -mə,tīˈz- *also* ə,t-\ *n* -s : the action or process of automatizing : the state of being automatized : AUTOMATION

au·tom·a·tize \ȯˈtämə,tīz *also* əˈt-\ *vt* -ED/-ING/-S *see -ize in Explan Notes* [*automaton* + *-ize*] **1** : to make an automaton of **2** [*automat-* + *-ize*] : to make automatic : reduce (as an habitual action) to an automatic condition ⟨*automatized* responses⟩ **3** : AUTOMATE

automato- — see AUTOMAT-

au·to·mat·o·graph \,ȯd·əˈmad·ə,graf\ *n* -s [*automat-* + *-graph*] : AUTOSCOPE

au·tom·a·ton \ȯˈtämətən, -əd·ən, -ətᵊn *also* əˈtäm- *or* -mə,tän\ *n, pl* **automatons** \-nz\ *also* **automa·ta** \-mətə, -əd·ə *sometimes* -ə,tä *or* -ə,tȧ\ [L, fr. Gk, neut. of *automatos* self-acting, fr. *aut-* + *-matos* (akin to Skt *mata* thought) — more at MIND] **1** *archaic* : something that has within itself the principle of its movements **2 a** : a mechanism that is relatively self⸗moving **b** : a contrivance or figure that appears to imitate the motions of men or animals : ROBOT ⟨tiny wooden soldiers that could be wound with a key and that would then march stiffly along — wonderful little ~*s*⟩ **3** : a machine or a controlling mechanism designed to follow automatically a predetermined sequence of operations or respond to encoded instructions and correct errors or deviations occurring during operation **4** : a creature whose actions are fixed, routine, and mechanical with little or no indication of active intelligence ⟨dull unthinking human ~*s*⟩

au·tom·a·tous \-məd·əs\ *adj* [L *automatus*, fr. Gk *automatos*] : of, like, or suggestive of an automaton : AUTOMATIC, MECHANICAL ⟨the relentless ~ march of an army⟩

au·to·mechanism \ˈ⸗⸗ *at* ¹AUTO- +\ *n* -s [*aut-* + *mechanism*] : a machine or other device that works automatically or under servo control

au·to·metamorphic \¦⸗⸗ +\ *adj* [*aut-* + *metamorphic*] : of or relating to autometamorphism

au·to·metamorphism \" +\ *n* [*aut-* + *metamorphism*] : alteration of igneous rocks by their own residual solutions without introduction of extraneous matter

au·to·metasomatic \" +\ *adj* [*aut-* + *metasomatic*] : AUTOMETAMORPHIC

au·to·metasomatism \" +\ *n* [*aut-* + *metasomatism*] : AUTOMETAMORPHISM

au·to·mix·is \" + ¦miksə̇s\ *n, pl* **automix·es** \-k,sēz\ [NL, fr. *aut-* + *-mixis*] : parthenogenesis in which the chromosomes of a haploid gamete divide without nuclear division resulting in formation of a diploid restitution nucleus — called also *automictic parthenogenesis*; compare AUTOGAMY

au·tomne·sia \,ȯd·əmˈnēzh(ē)ə, ,ȯd·ōˈn-\ *n* -s [NL, fr. *auto-* + *-mnesia*] : memory of earlier experience without any apparent associative condition

¹**automobile** *like next*\ *adj* [F, fr. *aut-* + *mobile*] : AUTOMOTIVE

²**au·to·mo·bile** \,ȯd·əmōˈbēl, ,ȯtəm-, ˈ⸗⸗⸗,⸗ *also* ,⸗⸗ˈmō,bēl *or* ¦⸗⸗ mə¦bēl *sometimes* ¦⸗⸗¦bil *or* ,⸗⸗ˈmōbəl *or* ,⸗⸗ˈmō,bil\ *n* -s [F, fr. *automobile*, adj.] : a usu. 4-wheeled automotive vehicle designed for passenger transportation on streets and roadways and commonly propelled by an internal-combustion engine using a volatile fuel (as gasoline) — called also *car* or esp. Brit. *motorcar*

³**automobile** \"\ *vi* -ED/-ING/-S : to ride in or drive an automobile

automobile insurance *n* : insurance against loss arising from destruction of or damage to an insured motor vehicle; *also* : AUTOMOBILE LIABILITY INSURANCE

automobile liability insurance *n* : insurance against loss from or legal liability for damages arising out of ownership, maintenance, or operation of a motor vehicle

automobile sled *n* : AUTOSLED

automobile-weed \-,wēd\ *n* : a low European herb (*Tribulus terrestris*) having sharp stout spines on the fruits and occurring as a roadside weed in America

au·to·mo·bil·i·ana \,⸗⸗⸗,bēlē, -,bilē +\ *n pl* [*automobile* + *-i-* + *-ana*] : a collection of automobiles or of items relating to automobiles esp. of the early kinds

au·to·mo·bil·ism \-,lizəm\ *n* -s : the use of automobiles : MOTORING

au·to·mo·bil·ist \-,lə̇st\ *n* -s : one who uses an automobile : MOTORIST

au·to·mo·bil·i·ty \,⸗⸗mōˈbiləd·ē, -məb\ *n* -ES [²*automobile* + *-ity*] : use of automobiles : condition or capability of transportation by automobile

au·tom·o·lite \ȯˈtämə,līt\ *n* -s [Sw *automolit*, fr. Gk *automolos* deserter (fr. *aut-* + *-molos*, fr. *molein* to come, go, fr. aorist inf. of *blōskein*) + Sw *-it* -ite; akin to MIr *mell* hill, Slovenian *moliti* to stretch out, Alb *mal* mountain and perh. to Skt *mani* pearl; basic meaning: coming forth, going up] : a variety of gahnite

au·to·mor·phic \¦ȯd·ə¦mȯrfik\ *adj* [*aut-* + *-morphic*] **1** : patterned after self ⟨an ~ concept⟩ **2** [ISV *aut-* + *-morphic*; orig. formed as G *automorph*] : IDIOMORPHIC

automorphic-granular \"+¦-\ *adj, of a rock* : characterized by a texture whose constituents are all automorphic — called also *idiomorphic-granular*

au·to·mo·tive \¦ȯd·ə¦mōd·iv, ¦ȯtə¦mōtiv, -ēv *also* -əv\ *adj* [*aut-* + *motive*] **1** : containing within itself the means of propulsion : SELF-PROPELLING **2** : of, relating to, or concerned with vehicles or machines that propel themselves (as automobiles, trucks, airplanes, motorboats) ⟨~ principles⟩

au·to·narcosis \¦⸗(,)⸗ *at* ¹AUTO- +\ *n* [NL, fr. *aut-* + *narcosis*] : narcotization of members of a colony of insects by a chemical substance released by one or more of them

¹**au·to·nom·ic** \¦ȯd·ə¦nämik\ *also* **au·to·nom·i·cal** \-mə̇kəl\ *adj* [*autonomy* + *-ic*, *-ical*] **1** *archaic* : AUTONOMOUS **2 a** : acting independently of volition ⟨~ reflexes⟩ **b** : of, relating to, affecting, or controlled by the autonomic nervous system **3** *bot* : due to internal causes or influences : SPONTANEOUS ⟨~ movements⟩ — compare PARATONIC **4** *of a drug* : having an effect upon a tissue supplied by the autonomic nervous system — **au·to·nom·i·cal·ly** \¦⸗⸗¦⸗mə̇k(ə)lē\ *adv*

²**autonomic** \"\ *n* -s **1** : AUTONOMIC NERVOUS SYSTEM **2** : one of the parts (as a nerve or ganglion) of the autonomic nervous system

autonomic nervous system *n* **1** : a part of the vertebrate nervous system that innervates smooth and cardiac muscle and glandular tissues, governs actions that are more or less automatic (as secretion, vasoconstriction, or peristalsis), and consists of the sympathetic nervous system and the parasympathetic nervous system **2** : PARASYMPATHETIC NERVOUS SYSTEM

autonomic system *n* : AUTONOMIC NERVOUS SYSTEM

au·ton·o·mism \ȯˈtänə,mizəm, əˈ-\ *n* -s [*autonomous* + *-ism*] : the principle or system of independent self-government

au·ton·o·mist \-,mə̇st\ *n* -s : one who advocates autonomy

au·ton·o·mous \ȯˈtänəməs, əˈ-\ *adj* [Gk *autonomos* living under one's own laws, independent, fr. *aut-* + *nomos* law — more at NIMBLE] **1** : of, relating to, or marked by autonomy **2 a** : having the right or power of self-government : possessing a certain degree of political autonomy ⟨~ states⟩ **b** : undertaken or carried on without outside control : SELF-CONTAINED ⟨an ~ school system⟩ **c** : possessing individual autonomy : morally self-legislating ⟨an ~ will⟩ : self-directed in personality ⟨he is no mere conformist — he's ~⟩ **3** *biol* **a** : existing or capable of existing independently ⟨an ~ zooid⟩ : being a perfect whole : not forming a part (as does an embryo or seed) in the developmental sequence of an organism **b** : responding, reacting, or developing independently of the whole ⟨a tumor is an ~ growth⟩ **4** : AUTONOMIC 3 **5** : under control of the autonomic nervous system : AUTOMATIC **6** : issued by a political entity having the right of independent coinage ⟨ancient ~ coins minted by a subject city in the Roman Empire⟩ **7** : semi-independent and partially self-governing — used of some Eastern Orthodox churches **syn** see FREE

autonomous investment *n* : that portion of total investment not directly attributable to short-term changes in total output but correlated with the long-term growth of the economy — distinguished from *induced investment*

au·ton·o·mous·ly *adv* : in an autonomous manner : INDEPENDENTLY

au·ton·o·my \-mē, -mi\ *n* -ES [Gk *autonomia*, fr. *autonomos* + *-ia* -y] **1** : the quality or state of being independent, free, and self-directing : individual or group freedom ⟨the ~ of every individual should be respected⟩ **2 a** : the degree of self-determination or political control possessed by a minority group, territorial division, or political unit in its relations to the state or political community of which it forms a part and extending from local self-government to full independence (as in the dominions of the British Commonwealth) **b** : an autonomous body or community **3** : the sovereignty of reason in the sphere of morals : possession of moral freedom or self⸗determination : power of the individual to be self-legislating in the realm of morals — opposed to *heteronomy* **4** *biol* : independence from the organism as a whole in the capacity of a part for growth, reactivity, or responsiveness

au·ton·y·mous \(ˈ)ȯ¦tänəməs\ *adj* [*aut-* + *-onymous* (as in *anonymous*)] : naming or designating itself — used of symbols and expressions

auto-oxidation *var of* AUTOXIDATION

au·top·a·thy \ȯˈtäpəthē\ *n* -ES [Gk *autopatheia*, fr. *aut-* + *-patheia* -pathy] : IDIOPATHY

au·to·pelagic \¦⸗⸗ *at* ¹AUTO- +\ *adj* [*aut-* + *pelagic*] *of plankton* : strictly pelagic — compare SPANIPELAGIC

au·toph·a·gous \(ˈ)ȯ¦täfəgəs\ *adj* [Gk *autophagos*, fr. *aut-* + *-phagos* -phagous] : SELF-DEVOURING

au·to·pho·bia \,ȯd·əˈfōbēə\ *n* [NL, fr. *aut-* + *-phobia*] : morbid fear of solitude

au·to·phone \ˈ⸗⸗ *at* ¹AUTO- +,⸗\ *n* -s [Gk *autophōnos* self⸗sounding, fr. *aut-* + *-phōnos* (fr. *phōnē* sound) — more at PHONE] : IDIOPHONE — **autophonic** *adj*

au·to·phyte \" + ,fīt\ *n* -s [*aut-* + *-phyte*] : a plant capable of synthesizing its own food from simple inorganic substances — compare HETEROPHYTE, PARASITE, SAPROPHYTE — **au·to·phyt·ic** \¦⸗⸗¦fid·ik\ *adj* — **au·to·phyt·i·cal·ly** \-d·ə̇k(ə)lē\ *adv*

au·to·phytograph \,⸗⸗ +\ *n* -s [*aut-* + *phytograph*] : the outline or imprint produced upon a rock by the chemical action of a plant or plant fragment

au·to·phytography \" +\ *n* -ES [*aut-* + *phytography*] : the process by which an autophytograph is produced

au·to·pilot \ˈ⸗⸗ + ,⸗⸗\ *n* -s [*automatic pilot*] : AUTOMATIC PILOT

au·to·pistol \" + ,⸗⸗\ *n* -s [*automatic pistol*] : AUTOMATIC PISTOL

au·to·plastic \¦⸗⸗ + ¦⸗⸗\ *adj* **1** : of, relating to, or characterized by autoplasty ⟨~ transplant⟩ **2** : relating to or characterized by adaptation of oneself to one's environment ⟨~ evolution⟩ — contrasted with *alloplastic* — **au·to·plastically** \" + ¦⸗⸗(ə)⸗\ *adj*

autoplastic graft *n* : AUTOGRAFT

au·to·plasticity \¦⸗(,)⸗ +\ *or* **au·to·plas·ty** \ˈ⸗⸗ + ,plastē\ *n* -ES [*aut-* + *plasticity* or *-plasty*] : the capacity or tendency for intrapsychic molding of the mechanism for dealing with the external world — contrasted with *alloplasticity*

au·to·plas·ty \ˈ⸗⸗ + ,plastē\ *n* -ES [prob. fr. F *autoplastie*, fr. *aut-* + *-plastie* -plasty] : the repairing of lesions with tissue from the same body — compare GRAFT 2b

Au·to·plate \ˈ⸗⸗ + ,⸗\ *trademark* — used for a machine that casts, shaves, and cools curved stereotype plates

au·to·ploid \ˈ⸗⸗ + ,plȯid\ *n* -s [by contr.] : AUTOPOLYPLOID

au·to·ploidy \ˈ⸗⸗+ ,plȯidē\ *n* -ES [by contr.] : AUTOPOLYPLOIDY

au·to·pneumatolytic \¦⸗(,)⸗ +\ *adj* [*aut-* + *pneumatolytic*] : AUTOMETAMORPHIC

¹**au·to·polyploid** \" +\ *n* -s [*aut-* + *polyploid*] : an individual or strain exhibiting autopolyploidy

²**au·to·polyploid** \¦⸗⸗ + ¦⸗⸗,⸗\ *also* **au·to·polyploidic** \" +\ *adj* : exhibiting autopolyploidy : being an autopolyploid

au·to·polyploidy \" +\ *n* -ES [*aut-* + *polyploidy*] : the state of having more than two genomes, all being alike and derived from a single ancestral species — compare ALLOPOLYPLOIDY

au·to·pore \ˈ⸗⸗ +\ *n* -s [*aut-* + *-pore*] : ZOOECIUM

au·to·potamic \¦⸗⸗ *at* ¹AUTO- +\ *adj* [*aut-* + *potamic*] *of algae* : adapted to life in flowing streams — compare EUPOTAMIC, TYCHOPOTAMIC

au·top·sist \-səst — *see* ¹AUTOPSY\ *n* -s [*autopsy* + *-ist*] : one who performs an autopsy

¹**au·top·sy** \'ȯ,täpsē, 'ȯd·əp-, 'ȯtəp-, -si *sometimes* ȯ'täp- *or* ə'täp-\ *n* -ES [Gk *autopsia* seeing with one's own eyes, fr. *aut-* + *-opsia* (fr. *opsis* sight) — more at OPTIC] **1** : POSTMORTEM EXAMINATION, NECROPSY; *also* : permission to make such an examination ⟨~ was refused⟩ **2** : a critical analysis either hostile or dispassionate of a past event or a completed creative process ⟨history is at best ~ —F.L.Wright⟩

²**autopsy** \"\ *vt* -ED/-ING/-ES : to perform a postmortem examination upon

au·to·psychic \¦⸗⸗ *at* ¹AUTO- + ¦⸗⸗\ *adj* [*aut-* + *psychic*] : of or relating to one's own mind — contrasted with *allopsychic*

au·top·tic \(')ȯ¦täptik\ *adj* [Gk *autoptikos* of an eyewitness, fr. *aut-* + *optikos* of sight — more at OPTIC] : based on one's own observation ⟨an ~ report on the Far East⟩

au·to·radiograph \¦⸗⸗ *at* ¹AUTO- +\ *or* **au·to·radiogram** \" + \ *n* [ISV *aut-* + *radiograph* or *radiogram*] : an image produced on a photographic film or plate by the radiations from a radioactive substance in an object which is in close contact with the emulsion — called also *radioautograph* — **au·to·radiographic** \" + \ *adj*

au·to·radiography \" + \ *n* [*aut-* + *radiography*] : the process of making autoradiographs

au·to·rail \'⸗⸗ + ,⸗\ *or* **au·to·railer** \" + ,⸗⸗\ *n* -s [²*auto-* + *rail* or *railer*] : a self-propelled vehicle equipped with both flange wheels and pneumatic tires and thus adaptable to either railway or highway operation

au·to-rifle \'ȯd·ō,⸗⸗\ *n* -s [*automatic rifle*] : AUTOMATIC RIFLE

au·to roller \'ȯd·ō,-\ *n* [*automatic*] : a worker who feeds and operates an automatic machine for cutting wrapper leaves and rolling cigars

au·to·rotation \¦⸗(,)⸗ *at* ¹AUTO- + \ *n* -s [ISV *aut-* + *rotation*] : the turning of the rotor of an autogiro or a helicopter with resulting lift caused solely by the aerodynamic forces induced by motion of the rotor along its flight path — **au·to·rotational** \" + \ *adj*

autos *pl of* AUTO, *pres 3d sing of* AUTO

au·to·sau·ri \" + ¦sȯ,rī, -(,)rē\ *or* **au·to·sau·ri·a** \-¦sȯrēə\ [NL, fr. *aut-* + *-sauri* (pl. of *-saurus*) or *-sauria*] *syn of* LACERTILIA

au·to·sche·di·asm \,⸗⸗ + 'skēdē,azəm\ *n* -s [Gk *autoschediasma*, fr. *autoschediazein* to extemporize, fr. *aut-* + *schediazein* to improvise, do something offhand, fr. *schedios* casual; akin to Gk *schein*, *echein* to have, hold — more at SCHEME] : something that is done offhand : IMPROVISATION

au·to·sche·di·as·tic \¦⸗⸗ + ¦skēdē¦astik\ *adj* [Gk *autoschediastikos*, fr. *autoschediastos* extemporary (fr. *autoschediazein*) + *-ikos* -ic] : EXTEMPORARY, OFFHAND

au·to·scope \'⸗⸗ + ,skōp\ *n* -s [ISV *aut-* + *-scope*; prob. orig. formed as G *autoskop*] : a device for recording or magnifying small involuntary movements of the body

au·to·scopic \¦⸗⸗ + ¦⸗⸗\ *adj* : of, relating to, or marked by autoscopy

au·tos·co·py \ȯ'täskəpē\ *n* -ES [ISV *aut-* + *-scopy*; prob. orig. formed as G *autoskopie*] : visual hallucination of one's body image

autos-da-fé *pl of* AUTO-DA-FÉ

autos de fé *pl of* AUTO DE FÉ

au·to·sensitization \¦⸗(,)⸗ *at* ¹AUTO- + \ *n* -s [*aut-* + *sensitization*] : AUTOIMMUNIZATION

au·to·serum \'⸗⸗ + ,⸗⸗\ *n* -s [ISV *aut-* + *serum*] : a serum obtained from a patient for use in treating that patient

au·to·sexing \" + ,⸗⸗\ *adj* [*aut-* + *sexing*, pres. part. of *sex*] : showing characters that are differential for sex at birth or hatching — used esp. of domestic fowls crossbred for characteristic color or pattern differences in the two sexes

au·to·site \" + ,sīt\ *n* -s [F, fr. *aut-* + *-site* (as in *parasite*)] : that part of a double fetal monster that nourishes both itself and the parasitic twin

au·to·sit·ic \¦⸗⸗ + ¦sid·ik\ *adj* : of the nature of an autosite

au·to·skeleton \'⸗⸗ + ,⸗⸗⸗\ *n* -s [*aut-* + *skeleton*] : an internal skeleton; *specif* : the endoskeleton of sponges consisting of spicules or spongin fibers secreted by the cells — opposed to *pseudoskeleton*

au·to·sled \" + ,⸗\ *n* -s [²*auto-* + *sled*] **1** : a vehicle with four retractable runners and wheels that is driven by propeller blades and is capable of traveling on bare roads, packed snow, or ice **2** : a vehicle like an autosled but that has only the front wheels retractable and that is driven by the rear wheels

au·to·som·al \¦⸗⸗ + ¦sōməl\ *adj* : of, belonging to, located on, or transmitted by an autosome — used chiefly of genes

au·to·some \'⸗⸗ + ,sōm\ *n* -s [*aut-* + *-some*] : a chromosome other than a sex chromosome — called also *euchromosome*; compare ALLOSOME

au·to·spore \" + ,⸗\ *n* -s [*aut-* + *-spore*] : one of the daughter cells formed by the internal division of a single cell esp. in such unicellular algae as members of the order Chroococcales and duplicating in miniature the parent cell

au·to·spor·ic \¦⸗⸗ + ¦spōrik\ *adj* : of, relating to, or characterized by autospores

au·to·stability \" + \ *n* -ES [*aut-* + *stability*] : the ability (as of an airplane) to keep in steady poise either by virtue of its inherent shape and proportions or by a self-operative controlling mechanism

au·to·sty·lic \¦⸗⸗ + ¦stīlik\ *adj* [*aut-* + *-stylic*] : having the jaws connected directly with the cranium (as chimaeras, lungfishes, amphibians, and higher vertebrates) instead of indirectly by the hyoid arch — sometimes distinguished from *holostylic* to denote lack of fusion of the pterygoquadrate with the cranium; compare AMPHISTYLIC, HYOSTYLIC

au·to·sty·lism \" + ,stī,lizəm\ *or* **au·to·sty·ly** \'⸗⸗ + ,stīlē\ *n*, *pl* **autostylisms** *or* **autostylies** [*autostylic* + *-ism* or *-y*] : condition of being autostylic

au·to·suggestibility \¦⸗(,)⸗ + \ *n* -ES : the quality or state of being autosuggestible

au·to·suggestible \" + ⸗¦⸗⸗⸗\ *adj* [*autosuggestion* + *-ible*] : subject to autosuggestion

au·to·suggestion \" + \ *n* -s [ISV *aut-* + *suggestion*; orig. formed in G] : an influencing of one's own attitudes, behavior, or physical condition by mental processes other than conscious thought : SELF-HYPNOSIS

au·to·suggestive \" + ⸗¦⸗⸗\ *adj* [*autosuggestion* + *-ive*] : of, relating to, or marked by autosuggestion

au·to·synapsis \" + \ *n* [NL, fr. *aut-* + *synapsis*] : AUTOSYNDESIS

au·to·syndesis \" + \ *n* [NL, fr. *aut-* + *syndesis*] : pairing at meiosis of homologous chromosomes from the similar sets of an allopolyploid individual

au·to·syndetic \" + ⸗¦⸗⸗\ *adj* [*aut-* + *syndetic*] : of, relating to, or marked by autosyndesis — **au·to·syndetically** \" + ⸗¦⸗⸗(ə)lē\ *adv*

au·to·tel·ic \¦⸗⸗ + ¦telik\ *adj* [Gk *autotelēs* complete in itself (fr. *aut-* + *telos* end) + E *-ic*] : having an end or purpose in and not apart from itself ⟨poetry is ..., like mathematics, an ~ activity —Louis MacNeice⟩ — contrasted with *heterotelic*

au·to·tel·ism \,⸗⸗ + 'te,lizəm, -'tē,l- *also* ȯ'tēt°l,iz-\ *n* -s : the belief that a work of art, esp. a work of literature, is an end in itself or provides its own justification

au·to·tetraploid \¦⸗⸗ + \ *n* [*aut-* + *tetraploid*] : an individual or strain exhibiting autotetraploidy

au·to·tetraploidy \" + \ *n* -ES [*aut-* + *tetraploidy*] : the state of having four genomes due to doubling of the ancestral chromosome complement — compare C-MITOSIS

au·to·the·ism \'⸗(,)⸗ + (,)thē,izəm, ,⸗⸗'th-\ *n* -s [LGk *autotheos* very God (fr. Gk *aut-* + *theos* god) + E *-ism* — more at THEISM] **1** : the doctrine of the self-existence of God; *esp* : the doctrine that Christ is the self-existent God himself **2** : deification of oneself : SELF-WORSHIP

au·to·the·ist \'⸗(,)⸗ + ,thēəst, _thē,ist\ *n* -s : one who believes in or practices autotheism

au·to·theistic \¦⸗(,)⸗ + ¦⸗⸗\ *adj* : of, relating to, or marked by autotheism

au·to·therapy \¦⸗⸗ + ¦⸗⸗⸗\ *n* -ES [*aut-* + *therapy*] : medication of oneself or treatment of one's own disease without medical supervision or prescription

au·to·tomic \" + ¦tämik\ *or* **au·tot·o·mous** \ȯ'täd·əməs\ *adj* [*aut-* + Gk *tomos* cutting + E *-ic* or *-ous*] : of, relating to, or characterized by autotomy

au·tot·o·mize \ȯ'täd·ə,mīz\ *vb* -ED/-ING/-S *vt* : to effect autotomy of ~ *vi* : to undergo autotomy

autotomizer muscle *n* : a muscle that contracts in such a way as to cause autotomy (as in the limbs of a crayfish)

au·tot·o·my \ȯ'täd·əmē\ *n* -ES [ISV *aut-* + *-tomy*] : reflex separation of a part or limb from the body : division of the whole into two or more pieces (as in crustaceans, echinoderms, or worms)

au·to·toxemia *also* **au·to·toxaemia** \¦⸗(,)⸗ *at* ¹AUTO- + ⸗¦⸗⸗⸗\ *n* -s [NL, fr. *aut-* + *toxemia*, *toxaemia*] : AUTOINTOXICATION

au·to·toxin \" + ¦⸗⸗\ *n* -s [ISV *aut-* + *toxin*] : any toxin produced within the body

au·to·transformer \" + ⸗¦⸗⸗\ *n* -s [*aut-* + *transformer*] : a transformer in which the primary and secondary coils have part or all of their turns in common

au·to·transplant \" + ⸗¦⸗, ⸗¦⸗\ *vt* [*aut-* + *transplant*] : AUTOGRAFT

au·to·transplantation \" + ¦⸗⸗¦⸗⸗\ *n* -s : the action of autotransplanting or the condition of being autotransplanted

¹**au·to·triploid** \¦⸗⸗ + ¦⸗,⸗\ *adj* [*aut-* + *triploid*] : having a triploid set of chromosomes made up of like genomes — **au·to·triploidy** \ + ¦⸗,⸗⸗\ *n* -ES

²**autotriploid** \"\ *n* -s : an autotriploid individual

au·to·tron·ic \¦⸗⸗ + ¦tränik\ *adj* [fr. *Autotronic*, a trademark] : capable of automatically regulating the operation of banks of elevators in office buildings

au·to·troph \'⸗⸗ + ,träf, -ōf\ *also* **au·to·trophe** \-,trōf\ *n* -s [G, fr. *autotroph*, adj., autotrophic] : an autotrophic organism : AUTOPHYTE — **au·tot·ro·phy** \ȯ'tä·trəfē\ *n* -ES

autotroph hypothesis *n* : a hypothesis in biology: the most primitive first life was autotrophic — compare HETEROTROPH HYPOTHESIS

au·to·troph·ic \¦⸗⸗ + ¦träfik, -trō-\ *adj* [ISV *aut-* + *-trophic*; prob. orig. formed as G *autotroph*] **1** : capable of self-nourishment; *specif* : capable of using carbon dioxide or carbonates as a sole source of carbon and a simple inorganic nitrogen compound for metabolic synthesis — used of green plants and certain chemoautotrophic bacteria and protozoans; opposed to *heterotrophic*; see PHOTOAUTOTROPHIC **2** : not requiring a specified exogenous factor for normal metabolism — usu. used in combination ⟨strictly auxo*autotrophic*⟩ — **au·to·troph·i·cal·ly** \¦⸗¦⸗fək(ə)lē\ *adv*

au·to·truck \'⸗⸗ + ,⸗\ *n* -s [²*auto-* + *truck*] : a motor-driven truck

¹**au·to·type** \" + ,⸗\ *n* -s [*aut-* + *type*] **1** : FACSIMILE **2 a** : CARBON PROCESS **b** : a picture made by the carbon process **3 a** : HYPOTYPE **b** : AUTOGENOTYPE

²**autotype** \"\ *vt* -ED/-ING/-S : to make or copy by autotypy

au·to·typ·ic \¦⸗⸗ + ¦⸗⸗\ *adj* **1** : reproduced by the carbon process **2** : of, relating to, or of the nature of an autotype

au·to·typy \'⸗⸗ + ,tīpē; ȯ'täd·əpē\ *n* -ES : process of making autotypes (sense 2)

au·to·vaccine \'⸗⸗ + \ *n* -s [*autogenous vaccine*] : AUTOGENOUS VACCINE

auto wrench *also* **automobile wrench** *n* : a lightweight all-metal monkey wrench

au·tox·i·da·tion \ȯ,täksə'dāshən, ȯd·,äk-\ *also* **au·to-oxidation** \¦⸗⸗ *at* ¹AUTO- + ⸗⸗¦⸗⸗\ *n* [ISV *aut-* + *oxidation*] : oxidation by direct combination with oxygen (as in air) at ordinary temperatures ⟨the rancidity of fats and oils is caused by ~⟩

au·tox·i·da·tive \ȯ¦täksə¦dād·iv, ȯd·¦äk-\ *adj* : of, relating to, or caused by autoxidation

au·tox·i·diz·a·ble \⸗¦⸗⸗¦dīzəbəl\ *adj* : capable of undergoing autoxidation

au·tox·i·dize \⸗'⸗⸗,dīz\ *also* **au·to-oxidize** \¦⸗⸗ *at* ¹AUTO- + ¦⸗⸗,⸗\ *vi* [*aut-* + *oxidize*] : to undergo autoxidation

au·to·zooid \¦⸗⸗ *at* ¹AUTO- + ¦⸗,⸗\ *n* -s [*aut-* + *zooid*] : a fully formed alcyonarian zooid as distinguished from a siphonozooid

au·tre·fois ac·quit \¦ō·trəf,wä(,)a'kē\ *n* [AF, formerly acquitted] : a defendant's plea alleging previous trial and acquittal of the same offense

autrefois con·vict \-,kən'vikt\ *n* [AF, formerly convicted] : a defendant's plea alleging previous trial and conviction for the same offense

au·tumn \'ȯd·əm, 'ä|, |təm\ *n* -s *often attrib* [ME *autumpne*, fr. L *autumnus*] **1 a** : the season between summer and winter reckoned astronomically as extending from the September equinox to the December solstice **b** : the season comprising the months of September, October, and November — called also *fall* **c** *Brit* : the season comprising the months of August, September, and October **d** : the season reckoned astronomically in the southern hemisphere as extending from the March equinox to the June solstice **2** : time of full maturity or incipient decline : latter portion : third stage ⟨the ~ of life⟩ **3** : a moderate olive brown that is darker and very slightly greener than the typical or average olive brown

autumn adonis *n*, *usu cap 2d A* : PHEASANT'S-EYE 1

au·tum·nal \ȯ'təmnəl *sometimes* 'ȯ|d·əm- *or* 'ä| *or* |tə-\ *adj* [L *autumnalis*, fr. *autumnus* + *-alis* -al] **1** : of, belonging to, or peculiar to autumn ⟨mild, ~ sunshine —Nathaniel Hawthorne⟩ **2** : produced or gathered in autumn : maturing in autumn ⟨~ fruits⟩ **3** : characterized by qualities associated with or suggested by autumn ⟨a serene ~ mood⟩ — **au·tum·nal·ly** *adv*

autumnal tea *n* : a black tea grown during the autumn in certain Indian tea districts (as Assam, Darjeeling, Duars)

autumn blond *n* : FAWN 3

autumn brown *n* : a grayish to moderate brown that is yellower and darker than dark beaver

autumn crocus *n* : MEADOW SAFFRON

autumn elaeagnus *n*, *pl* **autumn elaeagnuses** : an Asiatic shrub (*Elaeagnus umbellata*) often escaped from cultivation esp. in the eastern U.S. with flowers in umbels and with the corolla tube much longer than the lobes

autumn glory *n* : a dark red to reddish orange that is slightly yellower and stronger than Moroccan

autumn green *n* : SPINACH GREEN

autumn leaf *n* [after F *feuille-morte*, lit., dead leaf] : FEUILLE MORTE

autumn mange *n* : a skin disease of domestic animals that is caused by the bites of chiggers, is characterized by papules and severe itching, and is most common in late summer and autumn

autumn oak *n* : LIVER 5

autumn snowflake *n* : a bulbous herb (*Leucojum autumnale*) with filiform leaves and the fall-blooming white flowers tinged with red — see SNOWFLAKE

autumn squill *n* : a hardy European bulbous garden plant (*Scilla autumnalis*) with persistent leaves that are produced after the naked raceme of pink flowers

autumn willow *n* : a bog shrub (*Salix serissima*) of northern No. America with shining dark-green leaves and fruits that persist until autumn

au·tun·ite \'ō'tə,nīt\ *n* -s [*Autun*, Dept. Saône-et-Loire, France, its locality + E *-ite*] : a radioactive lemon-yellow mineral composed of uranyl calcium phosphate $Ca(UO_2)_2(PO_4)_2.10\text{–}12H_2O$ occurring in tabular crystals with basal cleavage and in micalike scales (sp. gr. 3.05–3.19)

au·ver·gnat \¦ō,vern¦yä\ *n* -s *cap* [F, fr. *Auvergne*, region of south central France] : a native or inhabitant of Auvergne, France

au·wai \'au̇,wī\ *n* -s [Hawaiian *'auwai*] *Hawaii* : a watercourse or channel esp. for irrigation

au·we \'au̇(,)wā\ *var of* AUE

aux *abbr* auxiliary

auxano- *comb form* [ISV, fr. Gk *auxanein* to increase; akin to Gk *auxein* to increase — more at EKE] : growth ⟨*auxano*gram⟩ ⟨*auxano*logy⟩

aux·an·o·gram \ȯg'zanə,gram, ȯk'sa-\ *n* -s [*auxano-* + *-gram*] : a plate culture (as of bacteria) in which variable conditions are provided for growth that is used as a means of determining the effects of a particular condition or agent on the growth of a test organism

aux·an·o·graph·ic \⸗¦⸗⸗¦grafik\ *adj* : of, belonging to, or by means of auxanography — **aux·an·o·graph·i·cal·ly** \-fək(ə)lē\ *adv*

aux·a·nog·ra·phy \,ȯgzə'nägrəfē, ,ȯksə'-\ *n* -ES [*auxano-* + *-graphy*] : the study of growth-promoting or growth-inhibiting agents by means of auxanograms

aux·a·nom·e·ter \,⸗⸗'näməd·ə(r)\ *n* -s [ISV *auxano-* + *-meter*] : an instrument for determining and measuring the rate of growth in plants consisting essentially of a lever with a long and a short arm which is attached to the plant

-auxe \'ȯk(,)sē\ *n comb form*, *pl* **-auxae** [NL, fr. Gk *auxē* growth; akin to Gk *auxein* to increase — more at EKE] : enlargement : hypertrophy ⟨enter*auxe*⟩

aux·e·sis \ȯg'zēsəs, ȯk'se-\ *n*, *pl* **auxe·ses** \-ē,sēz\ [NL, fr. Gk *auxēsis* increase, fr. *auxanein*, *auxein* to increase + *-ēsis* -esis — more at EKE] **1** : GROWTH; *specif* : increase of cell size without cell division — compare MERISIS **2** : the process by which certain diatoms that have become small through repeated asexual divisions are restored to normal size, the protoplasts escaping from the cell wall and increasing to normal size or fusing to form auxospores or zygospores that then increase to normal size before new cell walls form

aux·et·ic \(')ȯg¦zed·ik, (')ȯk¦se-\ *adj* [Gk *auxētikos* growing, promoting growth, fr. *auxētos* increased, capable of being increased (fr. *auxanein*, *auxein* to increase) + *-ikos* -ic] **1** : characterized by auxesis **2** : inducing auxesis — **aux·et·i·cal·ly** \-d·ək(ə)lē\ *adv*

aux·il·i·an \ȯg'zilyən\ *n* -s [*auxiliary* + *-ian*] : a member of a hospital auxiliary group

auxiliar *adj or n* [L *auxiliaris*, fr. *auxilium* + *-aris* -ar] *archaic* : AUXILIARY

¹**aux·il·ia·ry** \(')ȯg¦zilyərē, əg'z-, ÷ -l(ə)r-, -ri *sometimes* -k¦s- *or* -k's- *or* -lē,er-\ *adj* [L *auxiliarius*, fr. *auxilium* help (akin to L *augēre* to increase) + *-arius* -ary — more at EKE] **1 a** : offering or providing help, assistance, or support esp. by interaction ⟨neither philosophy nor science has ever been more closely ~ to literature than at the moment —Wylie Sypher⟩ **b** : functioning in a subsidiary capacity ⟨an ~ branch of the state university⟩ **2** *of a verb* : accompanying a nonfinite verb form that expresses the main verbal meaning of its clause, expressing typically such things as person, number, mood, and tense, and finite in form unless accompanied by another auxiliary verb, in which case only one is finite (as *be*, *have*, *do*, *will*, *can*, in such expressions as "we were standing there", "I move the nominations be closed", "he has been informed", "where do they live?", "he will write", "I can swim", German *haben*, *sein*, *werden*, *dürfen*, or French *avoir*, *être*, *pouvoir*, *devoir*, in similar expressions) **3** : augmenting or available to augment a basic power, potential, or ability: as **a** : SUPPLEMENTARY ⟨with ~ instruments the new telescope has more power⟩ **b** : RESERVE ⟨the ~ police were called to the disaster area⟩ ⟨~ power plant⟩ **4** *of a boat* : equipped with an inboard engine to supplement the motive power of sails ⟨an ~ sloop⟩

²**auxiliary** \"\ *n* -ES **1** : one that helps : one that functions or serves in a supplementary often subordinate position **2 a** : an allied or foreign armed force in the service of a nation at war — usu. used in pl. **b** : a member of such a force **3** *or* **auxiliary bishop** : a titular bishop in the Roman Catholic Church who assists the ordinary of a diocese **4 a** : an auxiliary engine (as on a sailboat) **b** : an auxiliary boat (as a tanker, tender, or supply ship) — see NAVAL AUXILIARY **c** : a sailboat with an auxiliary engine **5** : a member of an auxiliary group (as of police or firemen) **6** : ASSISTANT 3 **7** : an auxiliary verb **8** : AUXILIARY INFLECTION **9 a** : an organization that is adjunct to one having a restricted membership; *esp* : an organization for wives and women relatives of such members ⟨the American Legion *Auxiliary*⟩ ⟨Women's *Auxiliary* of the State Medical Society⟩ **b** : an organization often of women that assists esp. by donations or volunteer services the work of a church, hospital, or charitable institution ⟨the Lutheran Home *Auxiliary*⟩

auxiliary cell *n* : a specialized cell in certain red algae often some distance from the carpogonium into which the diploid zygote nucleus migrates after fertilization sometimes by special threads called ooblasts and from which the carpospores eventually develop

auxiliary circle *n* : a circle described on the major or minor axis of an ellipse as diameter

auxiliary equation *n* : an equation obtained from the standard form of a linear differential equation by replacing the right member by zero

auxiliary goods *n pl* : PRODUCER GOODS

auxiliary inflection *n*, *paleontol* : any lateral lobe or saddle of the ammonoid suture added later than the first two or three pairs

auxiliary language *n* : a language (as Esperanto or pidgin English) used for communication between persons that do not understand each other's native language — compare INTERLANGUAGE

auxiliary rafter *n* : a rafter used to strengthen the principal rafter in a truss

auxiliary switch *n* : an electrical switch actuated by a main device (as a circuit breaker) for signaling or interlocking

auxiliary target *n* : a point of known location used as an adjusting point for subsequent fire on other targets

auxiliary tone *or* **auxiliary note** *n* : an unaccented nonharmonic tone approached from above or below by stepwise motion and returning to the original tone

aux·il·i·um \ȯg'zilēəm\ *n* -s [L] : an aid or tribute — compare AID 4

aux·i·mone \'ȯksə,mōn\ *n* -s [Gk *auximos* promoting growth + *-one* (as in *hormone*)] : any of certain substances considered necessary, though only in small quantities, for the vigorous growth of plants and occurring esp. in sphagnum peat decomposed by nitrogen bacteria — compare VITAMIN

aux·in \'ȯksən\ *n* -s [ISV *aux-* (fr. Gk *auxein* to increase) + *-in* — more at EKE] : any organic substance (as indoleacetic acid) characterized by its ability in low concentrations to promote growth of plant shoots along the longitudinal axis (as in the Avena test) and to produce various other effects (as root formation and bud inhibition) — compare PLANT HORMONE — **aux·in·ic** \(')ȯk¦sinik\ *or* **aux·in·i·cal** \-nəkəl\ *adj* — **aux·in·i·cal·ly** \-ək(ə)lē\ *adv*

aux·i·thal \'ȯksə,thal\ *n* -s [*auxi-* (fr. Gk *auxein* to increase) + *-thal* (fr. *thiamine* + *-al*)] : AUXIN

auxo- *comb form* [ISV, fr. Gk, fr. *auxein* to increase — more at EKE] **1** : growth ⟨*auxo*body⟩ ⟨*auxo*substance⟩ : increase ⟨*auxo*graph⟩ **2** : accelerating : stimulating ⟨*auxo*chrome⟩

aux·o·autotrophic \¦ȯk(,)sō¦⸗⸗¦⸗⸗\ *adj* [*auxo-* + *autotrophic*] *biol* : requiring no exogenous growth factors

aux·o·chrome \'ȯksə,krōm\ *n* -s [ISV *auxo-* + *-chrome*] : a salt-forming group (as hydroxyl or amino) that when introduced into a chromogen produces a dye — see CHROMOPHORE — **aux·o·chrom·ic** \¦⸗⸗¦krōmik\ *adj*

aux·o·cyte \'ȯksə,sīt\ *n* -s [*auxo-* + *-cyte*] *biol* : a gamete-forming cell (as an oocyte) or a sporocyte during its growth period

aux·o·drome \-,drōm\ *n* -s [*auxo-* + *drome*] : a plotted curve indicating the relative development of a child at any given age

aux·o·graph \'ȯksə,graf\ *n* -s [*auxo-* + *-graph*] : an instrument for the automatic recording of variations in volume of any body and orig. used to measure the swelling and shrinking of parts of plants — **aux·o·graph·ic** \¦⸗⸗¦grafik\ *adj*

aux·o·heterotrophic \¦ȯk(,)sō + ⸗⸗¦⸗⸗\ *adj* [*auxo-* + *heterotrophic*] *biol* : requiring exogenous growth factors or stimulants

aux·o·spore \'ȯksə,spō(ə)r\ *n* -s [ISV *auxo-* + *-spore*; prob. orig. formed in G] : a reproductive cell in diatoms usu. resulting from the union of two smaller cells or their contents and associated with rejuvenescence in cells that have become progressively smaller because of repeated divisions

aux·o·tonic \¦ȯksə¦tänik\ *adj* [ISV *auxo-* + *tonic*] *plant physiol* : determined or induced by growth rather than by external stimulus — opposed to *allassotonic*

av *usu cap*, *var of* AB

av *abbr* **1** avenue **2** average **3** aviation **4** avoirdupois

AV *abbr* **1** ad valorem **2** [L *annos vixit*] he lived (a given number of) years **3** audio-visual **4** average variability

ava *or* **ava'** \ə'vȧ, -vō\ *adv* [Sc *av* (alter. of E *of*) + ²*a*] **1** *Scot* : of all ⟨this pleased them warst ~ —Robert Burns⟩ **2** *Scot* : at all ⟨not like a gentleman ~⟩

'ava \'(')ävə\ *n* -s [Tahitian or Samoan *'ava*] *Central Polynesia* : KAVA

av·a·da·vat \'avədə,vat\ *also* **am·a·da·vat** \'amə-\ *n* -s [irreg. fr. *Ahmadabad*, city in India from which it was imported to Europe] : a very small weaverbird (*Estrilda aman-*

dava) native to southeast Asia but often kept as a cage bird, having the breeding male scarlet, darker above, and with white dots on wings and sides and the female and eclipse male olive brown above and grayish buff below — called also *strawberry finch*

ava·hi \ə'vä,hē\ *n* -s [native name in Madagascar] **:** WOOLLY LEMUR

¹avail \ə'väl, *esp bef pause or cons* -āəl\ *vb* -ED/-ING/-S [ME *availen*, prob. fr. *a-* (as in *abaten* to abate) + *vailen* to avail — more at VAIL] *vi* **1 :** to function effectively or advantageously in the accomplishment of an objective **:** be useful or beneficial for a specific purpose ⟨apparatus and pretension ~ nothing⟩ ⟨heroism could not ~ against the enemy fire⟩ ⟨the wall could not ~ to protect the town against cannon⟩ **2 :** to be of profit or value **:** serve to clarify or improve a situation ⟨no comparison would ~, he was one of a kind⟩ ⟨the forces of which judges avowedly ~ to shape the form and content of their judgments —B.N.Cardozo⟩ **~** *vt* **1 :** to be of service or advantage to **:** BENEFIT, PROFIT **2** *archaic* **:** to give (someone) a specific advantage or benefit — used with *of* ⟨~ Mr. Barclay of that fund —Thomas Jefferson⟩ **3 a :** to take advantage **:** make use — used with *of* ⟨far from resenting such tutelage I am only too glad to ~ myself of it —G.B.Shaw⟩ **b :** to use or apply to good advantage **syn** see USE

²avail \"\ *n* -s [ME, fr. *availen*, v.] **1** *obs* **:** PROFIT, BENEFIT, VALUE ⟨the ~ of a deathbed repentance —Jeremy Taylor⟩ **2 :** effective advantage toward attainment of a goal or purpose **:** USE — used chiefly after *of* or *to* and now usu. in negative contexts ⟨his effort was of no ~⟩ **3 avails** *pl, archaic* **:** profits or proceeds esp. from a business or from the sale of property ⟨I made it clear that none of my ~s were going to be dissipated —S.H.Adams⟩ **syn** see USE

avail·a·bil·i·ty \ə,välə'bilәd·ē, -ətē, -i\ *n* -ES **1 :** the quality or state of being available; *specif* **:** the calculated promise of a political candidate's success based chiefly on his personal popularity and appeal irrespective of ability or special fitness ⟨the emphasis has not been upon greatness in the candidate but upon ~ —D.D.McKean⟩ — compare AVAILABLE 5a **2 :** an available person or thing ⟨trying to furnish a house from local *availabilities*⟩

avail·a·ble \ə'väləbəl\ *adj* [ME, fr. *availen* + *-able*] **1 a** *obs* **:** capable of availing **:** having sufficient power or force to achieve an end **b** *archaic* **:** having a beneficial effect **2 :** VALID — used of a legal plea or charge ⟨all charges must be good and ~⟩ or of a taxonomic designation not currently preferred but properly published and not invalidated by other usages **3 :** such as may be availed of **:** capable of use for the accomplishment of a purpose **:** immediately utilizable ⟨the first thing to concentrate on was the sinking of the German navy on any ~ pretext —G.B.Shaw⟩ **4 :** that is accessible or may be obtained **:** personally obtainable (as for employment) ⟨physicist, industrial and academic experience, wants position, ~ late summer⟩ **:** at disposal esp. for sale or utilization ⟨~ in many colors and sizes⟩ ⟨latest readily ~ information⟩ **5 a :** having the requisite political associations and circumstantial qualifications for winning election to office — compare AVAILABILITY 1 **b :** willing to accept nomination for or election to an office ⟨he announced that he was ~ for the nomination⟩ **6 a :** present in such chemical or physical form esp. in the soil as to be capable of being utilized by a plant or animal ⟨~ nitrogen⟩ ⟨~ phosphorus⟩ ⟨~ water⟩ **b** *of a chemical element or compound* **:** in a reactive form ⟨~ alkali⟩ — **avail·a·ble·ness** *n* -ES — **avail·a·bly** *adv*

available assets *n pl* **:** assets available for use as collateral

available chlorine *n* **:** the amount of free chlorine that a substance (as bleaching powder) yields when treated with an acid in the presence of a chloride (as sodium chloride or calcium chloride), one atom of chlorine in a hypochlorite being thus computed as equivalent to a molecule of elemental chlorine

available energy *n, physics* **:** that part of the energy of bodies or systems which exists under such conditions that work may be theoretically derived from it — compare DEGRADATION OF ENERGY, ENTROPY, UNAVAILABLE ENERGY

aval \a'val\ *n* -s [F] *civil law* **:** a written engagement by one not a drawer, acceptor, or indorser of a note or bill of exchange that it will be paid at maturity

¹av·a·lanche \'avə,lanch, -aa(ə)n-,-ain-\ *n* -s *often attrib* [F, fr. F dial. (northwestern Alps) *avalantse*, alter. (influenced by F *avaler* to lower, go downstream) of F dial. (northwestern Alps) *lavantse*, prob. of non-IE origin; akin to the source of OProv *lavanca* avalanche, It *valanga*] **1 :** a large mass of snow, ice, earth, rock, or other material in swift motion down a mountainside or over a precipice **2 :** any sudden great or overwhelming rush or flood ⟨an ~ of water smashing on the decks —*Harper's*⟩ **3 :** an electric breakdown in a gas in which each electron released from its molecule acquires enough energy before collision with another molecule to cause the release of two or more other electrons thus initiating an electronic chain reaction — called also *electron avalanche, Townsend avalanche*

²avalanche \"\ *vb* -ED/-ING/-S *vi* **:** to rush or slide in or in the manner of an avalanche ⟨a pile of junk ~s out of the hall closet when you open the door⟩ **~** *vt* **:** to present or supply at one time with a superabundance of anything **:** OVERWHELM, FLOOD ⟨the office was *avalanched* with applications⟩

avalanche conduction *n* **:** conduction of the nervous impulse from one neuron through several others so as to converge on one point where the intensity of the discharge is increased by summation

avalanche lily *n* **:** a perennial herb (*Erythronium montanum*) having large white orange-marked flowers and commonly found near the snow line in the northwestern U. S.

avale *vb* -ED/-ING/-S [ME *avalen*, fr. MF *avaler*, fr. OF, fr. *aval* downward, fr. *a* to (fr. L *ad*) + *val* valley — more at AT, VALE] *vt* **1** *obs* **:** LOWER **:** let fall **2** *obs* **:** to bring low **:** ABASE **~** *vi* **1** *obs* **:** DESCEND, DISMOUNT **2** *obs* **:** to sink down **:** flow down

avalvular \(ˈ)ā+¦-\ *adj* [²*a-* + *valvular*] **1** *anat* **:** lacking valves **2** *anat* **:** not affecting valves

avant-corps \(¦)ä,vänt'kō(ə)r, -ō(ə)r\ *n* [F, fr. *avant* forward + *corps* body, fr. L *corpus* — more at AVAUNT, MIDRIFF] **:** a part which projects out from the main mass of a building (as a pavilion in front of the façade)

avant-courier \-¦ä,vänt+'-\ *n* -s [F *avant-courrier*, fr. *avant* + *courrier* courier — more at COURIER] **1 avant-couriers** *pl, archaic* **:** the scouts or advance guard of an army **2 :** one that goes or comes before another — called also *herald*

avant-garde \(¦)ä,vän(t)'gärd, ¦a,v-, ə,v-, (¦)å,v-, -vän 'g-, -vōn(t)'g-,-vōn 'g-, -gȧd\ *n* -s *often attrib* [F, vanguard] **1 :** those who create, produce, or apply new, original, or experimental ideas, designs, and techniques in any field, esp. in the arts — used usu. with *the* **2 :** a group (as of writers or artists) that is unorthodox and untraditional in its approach; *sometimes* **:** such a group that is extremist, bizarre, or arty and affected **3 :** advocates and admirers of the avant-garde

avant-gard·ism \-,dizəm\ *n* -s **:** predilection for or practice of intellectual or artistic experimentalism **:** participation in activity or effort associated with the avant-garde

avant-gard·ist \-,dəst\ *also* **avant-gar·diste** \-,gär'dēst, -,gȧ'd-\ *n* -s **:** a member of the avant-garde

avanturine *var of* AVENTURINE

avanyo *or* **avanyu** *var of* AWANYU

avar \'ä,vär\ *n* -s *usu cap* **1 :** a member of a people of Eastern origin now belonging to the Lezghian division of the peoples of the Caucasus prominent from the 6th to the 9th centuries at first in Dacia and later in Pannonia **2** *or* **avar·ish** \ä'värish\ **:** the No. Caucasic language of the Avars

ava·ram bark \'ävərəm,-\ *also* **avaram** *n* -s [Malayalam *āvīram*] **:** a tanbark from a bush or tree (*Cassia auriculata*) of India

avar·i·an \ä'värēən\ *or* **avar·ic** \-rik\ *adj, usu cap* **:** of or relating to the Avars

av·a·rice \'avərəs *rap.* -vr-\ *n* -s [ME, fr. OF, fr. L *avaritia*, fr. *avarus* avaricious, fr. *avēre* to covet, long for — more at AVID] **:** excessive or insatiable desire for wealth or gain **:** GREEDINESS, CUPIDITY ⟨they scrimped and stinted and starved themselves . . . out of ~ and the will-to-power —Lewis Mumford⟩ **syn** see CUPIDITY

av·a·ri·cious \¦avə¦rishəs\ *adj* [MF *avaricieux*, fr. OF, fr. *avarice*] **:** actuated by avarice **:** inordinately desirous of accumulating wealth, often in niggardly ways and merely in order to hoard it ⟨[they] were furtively ~; they couldn't help being stingy, since parsimony ran in their blood, but they were not frank about it —Victoria Sackville-West⟩ **syn** see COVETOUS

av·a·ri·cious·ly *adv* **:** in an avaricious manner

av·a·ri·cious·ness *n* -ES **:** AVARICE

avarish *usu cap, var of* AVAR

'avas *pl of* 'AVA

avascular \(ˈ)ā+¦-\ *adj* [²*a-* + *vascular*] **:** having few or no blood vessels ⟨the lens is a very ~ structure⟩ **:** lacking vascular tissue ⟨~ plants⟩ — **avascularity** *n* -ES

avast \ə'vast, -aa(ə)st,-aist,-ȧst\ *v imper* [perh. fr. D *houd vast* hold fast, stop, fr. *houd* (imp. of *houden* to hold, stop, fr. MD) + *vast* fast, fr. MD; akin to OHG *haltan* to hold and to OE *fæst* fast — more at HOLD, FAST] — a nautical command to stop or cease ⟨~ heaving⟩ ⟨~ lowering⟩

av·a·tar \'avə,tär, -tȧ(r, ,==ˈ=\ *n* -s [Skt *avatāra* descent, fr. *avatarati* he descends, fr. *ava* off, down + *tarati* he passes across or over (akin to L *trans* across, over) — more at TRANS-] **1** *or* **ava·ta·ra** \(,)əvə'tärə, -ärə\ **:** the descent and incarnation of a deity in earthly form — chiefly associated in Hinduism with the incarnations of Vishnu **2 a :** an incarnation or embodiment of another person — usu. used hyperbolically in comparisons ⟨here, one almost fancies, is an Eastern ~ of Mark Twain, telling fresh tales of Huckleberry Finn —*Times Lit. Supp.*⟩ **b :** a remarkably complete manifestation or embodiment usu. in a person, of a concept, philosophy, or tradition ⟨[he] is not merely a conservative, but the very archetype, the ~ of conservatism, since to him conservatism is a condition of existence —*N. Y. Herald Tribune*⟩ **3 :** a variant phase or version of a continuing basic entity sometimes implying no more than a change in name ⟨the privileges of the proprietary, whose current ~ was called the Company of the Indies —Bernard De Voto⟩

¹avaunt \ə'vȯnt, -änt,-ȧnt\ *vb* -ED/-ING/-S [ME *avaunten*, fr. MF *avanter*, fr. (fr. L *ad-*) + *vanter* to boast — more at VAUNT] *obs* **:** BOAST, VAUNT

²avaunt \"\ *adv* [ME, fr. MF *avant*, fr. L *abante* forward, before, fr. *ab* from, away + *ante* before — more at OF, ANTE-] *archaic* **:** HENCE 1 ⟨walks thrice round them, bidding malicious spirits ~ —J.G.Frazer⟩ ⟨~ thou very idiot —T.B.Costain⟩

³avaunt \"\ *n* -s *obs* **:** an order to be gone ⟨the devil tempted him but he gave him the ~ —William Barlow⟩

AVC *abbr* automatic volume control

avdp *abbr* avoirdupois

ave \'ä(,)vā, 'ā-, -,vē,-vi\ *n* -s [ME, fr. L *ave*, *have* hail, prob. fr. Punic *ḥwy* live!] **1 :** a salutation of greeting or of leave-taking **:** HAIL, FAREWELL — often used interjectionally **2** [short for *Ave Maria*] **a** *often cap* **:** AVE MARIA 1 ⟨saying *Aves* and Paternosters⟩ **b** *obs* **:** AVE MARIA 3

ave *abbr* avenue

AVE *abbr* automatic volume expansion

avel·lan \ə'velən, 'avəl-\ *or* **avel·lane** \-,lān\ *adj* [L *abellana, avellana* hazel nut, filbert, fr. fem. of *Abellanus, Avellanus* of Abella, fr. *Abella, Avella*, ancient town in Italy] **1 :** relating to the filbert or hazel **2** *of a cross* **:** having each of the four arms shaped like a conventional filbert — see CROSS illustration

ave·lla·ne·da \¦ävəzhə¦nāthə, ¦ävələ¦nādə\ *adj, usu cap* [fr. *Avellaneda*, Argentina] **:** of or from Avellaneda, Argentina **:** of the kind or style prevalent in Avellaneda

av·el·la·neous \¦avə¦lānēəs, -nyəs\ *adj* [L *abellana, avellana* + E *-eous*] **:** HAZEL

avel·la·no \,ävə'lä̈nō, ,a-, -vəl'yä-\ *n* -s [Sp, fr. *avellana* hazel nut, filbert, fr. L *abellana, avellana*] **:** a Chilean tree (*Gevuina avellana*) of the family Proteaceae with tough wood, evergreen foliage, and white flowers succeeded by red fruit containing oily edible seeds

ave ma·ria \¦=(,)= *as at* AVE + mə'rēə, -mä-,-mȧ-\ *also* **ave mary** \-'merē, -mār-,-ma(a)r-, -ri\ *n usu cap A&M* [ME *ave Maria*, fr. ML, hail, Mary!] **1 :** a salutation to the Virgin Mary combined as now used in the Roman Catholic Church with a prayer to her as mother of God **2 :** a particular time (as in Italy at the ringing of the bells about half an hour after sunset and also at early dawn) when the people repeat the Ave Maria **3 :** one of the small beads of a rosary by which Ave Marias are counted

ave·na \ə'vēnə\ *n, cap* [NL, fr. L, oats; akin to Lith *avižà* oats, Russ *oves*] **:** a genus of widely distributed grasses (family Gramineae) having a loosely paniculate inflorescence, lemmas 2-toothed and usu. awned near the apex, and deeply furrowed grains enclosed in the glumes and sometimes adherent to them — see OAT

avena test *n, usu cap A* [NL *Avena*] **:** a test of the growth-promoting or sometimes inhibiting value of a substance as judged by the reaction of a growing oat (genus *Avena*) coleoptile to which the substance is applied — see AUXIN

avenge \ə'venj\ *vb* -ED/-ING/-S [ME *avengen*, prob. fr. *a-* (as in *abaten* to abate) + *vengen* to avenge, fr. OF *vengier* — more at VENGEANCE] *vt* **1 :** to take vengeance for or on behalf of (oneself or another) ⟨~, O Lord, thy slaughtered saints —John Milton⟩ ⟨he *avenged* himself on his brother's killer⟩ **2 :** to exact satisfaction for (a wrong) by punishing the injurer ⟨though he always *avenged* an injury, he never bore malice for one —Charles Kingsley⟩ **~** *vi* **:** to take vengeance

syn AVENGE and REVENGE agree in meaning to punish a person who has wronged one or someone close to one. They are often used interchangeably but AVENGE more often suggests punishing a person when one is vindicating someone else than oneself or is serving the ends of justice, the suggestion of justice achieved being strong in any application of the word ⟨after all, if other people's children do not like him, he can always *avenge* himself by disliking them twice as much —Robert Lynd⟩ ⟨it was a son who would some day *avenge* his father —Charles Dickens⟩ ⟨his wife . . . entered the gubernatorial campaign to *avenge* her husband —*Amer. Guide Series: Texas*⟩ REVENGE more often applies to vindicating oneself and usu. suggests an evening up of scores or a personal satisfaction more than an achievement of justice, often connoting malice, spite, or vindictive retaliation ⟨the novelist obsessed with the errors of his past . . . is irresistibly drawn to *revenge* himself on his past by rewriting it —C.J.Rolo⟩ ⟨the hope of *revenging* himself on me was a strong inducement —Jane Austen⟩

avenge·ment \-mənt\ *n* -s [ME, fr. *avengen* + *-ment*] **:** act of taking vengeance

aveng·er \-njə(r)\ *n* -s **:** one that avenges

aveng·ing *adj* **:** that takes vengeance or treats revengefully — **aveng·ing·ly** *adv*

ave·nin \ə'vēnən, 'avən-\ *or* **ave·nine** \-,nēn\ *n* -s [ISV *aven-* (fr. L *avena* oats) + *-in, -ine*] **:** the glutelin of oats

av·ens \'avənz\ *n, pl* **avens** [ME *avence*, fr. OF] **:** a plant of the genus *Geum* — compare HERB BENNET, WATER AVENS

av·en·tail \'avən,tāl\ *n* -s [ME *aventaile*, prob. fr. (assumed) AF *aventaille*, alter. (resulting from incorrect division of *la ventaille* the aventail) of OF *ventaille* — more at VENTAIL] **:** VENTAIL

aventure *archaic var of* ADVENTURE

¹aven·tu·rine \ə'venchə,rēn,-,rən\ *also* **avan·tu·rine** \ə'van-\ *n* -s [F *aventurine*, fr. *aventure* chance; fr. its chance discovery — more at ADVENTURE] **1 :** glass containing opaque sparkling particles of foreign material, usu. (1) copper or (2) chromic oxide — called also respectively (1) *gold aventurine* or (2) *chrome aventurine, green aventurine* **2 :** a translucent quartz spangled throughout with scales of mica or other mineral

²aventurine \"\ *also* **avanturine** \"\ *adj* **:** having the brilliant spangled appearance of aventurine

av·e·nue \'avə,n(y)ü *also* 'aav-, *rapid sometimes* -v(,)nü *or* -vənyə\ *n* -s [MF, fr. fem. of *avenu*, past part. of *avenir* to come to, fr. L *advenire* — more at ADVENE] **1 :** an opening or passageway permitting actual approach or entry to a place — often followed by a prepositional phrase indicating a specific purpose ⟨the river is a great ~ of commerce⟩ ⟨a new ~ to India⟩ **2 :** a way or means by which an esp. intangible end may be pursued, approached, or accomplished ⟨an ~ of research⟩ ⟨new ~s to fame⟩ **3 a** *chiefly Brit* **:** the principal walk or driveway to a house situated off the main road **b :** a broad passageway bordered on either side by trees ⟨an ~ of poplars⟩ **4 :** a city street esp. when broad and attractive

¹aver \'ävər\ *now chiefly Scot var of* AIVER

²aver \ə'vər, +V -ər-; -vō, +V -ər- *also* -ōr\ *vt* **averred; averred; averring; avers** [ME *averren*, fr. MF *averer*, fr. ML *adverare* to confirm as authentic, fr. L *ad-* + ML *-verare* (fr. L *verus* true) — more at VERY] **1** *obs* **:** to acknowledge (a statement) as true **2** *archaic* **:** to acknowledge the existence of **:** admit as valid or real **3 a :** AVOUCH, VERIFY **b :** ASSERT, CLAIM, DECLARE **4 :** to affirm or declare in a positive confident manner **:** insist emphatically ⟨he had proudly *averred* that he needed no help⟩ **syn** see ASSERT

¹av·er·age \'av(ə)rij, -rēj\ *n* -s [modif. (influenced by E *-age*) of MF *avarie* damage to ship or cargo, port dues, fr. OIt *avaria* damage to ship or cargo, fr. Ar *'awārīyah* damaged merchandise, fr. *'awār* defect, damage, fr. *'ār* to harm] **1** *obs* **:** a tariff on goods transported by ship **2 a** *obs* **:** a charge payable by the owner or consignor in addition to the regular charge for freight of goods shipped **b :** sundry petty charges regularly and necessarily defrayed by the master (as port charges, pilotage) formerly borne partly by the ship and partly by the cargo but now usu. included in the freight **3** *marine insurance* **a :** a less than total loss sustained by a ship or cargo **b :** a charge arising from damage caused by sea perils customarily distributed equitably and proportionately among all chargeable with it **c :** an incidence of such loss or charge **4 :** ARITHMETIC MEAN **5 :** an estimate or approximate representation of an arithmetic mean ⟨students are expected to maintain a B ~ or better⟩ **6 :** something felt as representing an arithmetic average and hence typical of a group, class, or series ⟨the simple act of ringing doorbells while seeking votes introduced him to the ~ —John Mason Brown⟩ **7 :** a ratio expressing the average performance esp. of an athletic team or an athlete computed according to the number of opportunities for successful performance ⟨in a batting slump his ~ dropped from .303 to .261⟩ ⟨the team ~ so far this season⟩ **8 :** the average price of a group of securities or stocks (as industrials or railroads) used as a measure of changes in price levels — usu. used in pl. ⟨the current position of leading ~s⟩

syn AVERAGE, MEAN, MEDIAN, NORM, PAR can mean in common a number, quantity, or condition that represents a middle point between extremes. AVERAGE is chiefly an arithmetical term to indicate the figure arrived at by finding the sum of a given number of unequal figures and dividing by the number of figures ⟨the *average* of 10, 12, 14, 16, 18, and 20 is 15, that is, 90 divided by 6⟩ and is usu. computed as a means of getting a fair general estimate of something comprising a series of unequal but like things (as grades in school courses, depths of snowfall in successive years, weekly sales over a period of weeks). In certain applications, as in sports or gambling, an AVERAGE is usu. the proportion, expressed in a percentage, of successful performances (as hits achieved in a single baseball season by a ballplayer) to opportunities for or attempts at successful performance (as the total number of times a ballplayer goes to bat in a single baseball season); in other applications, as in statistical analysis, it may be, for example, the proportion, expressed in a percentage, of deaths in a given period for every 1000 citizens over 50 years old or automobile accidents in a given area over a given time for every 100 drivers. It may extend to designate a person who stands at a roughly estimated middle level in a scale presumably determining the intellectual or cultural capacity or quality of a group, esp. a society ⟨Dartmouth's Shattuck Observatory has been measuring snowfall since 1867, and the *average* at Hanover is six feet —R.S.Monahan⟩ ⟨only those renters are admitted whose incomes fall within certain fixed limits — limits which are, however, higher than the *average* of the people who formerly lived in the area —*Amer. Guide Series: Minn.*⟩ ⟨it is enough if we are of the same moral and mental stature as the "main" or "mean" part of men — that is to say as the *average* —Samuel Butler †1902⟩ ⟨the cleverest boys go to the École Normale Supérieure and do not mix any longer with the *average* —Bertrand Russell⟩ MEAN indicates a point midway between extremes, in an older sense signifying a point midway between any two extremes (as of condition, quality, or intensity) but today being confined chiefly to mathematics or statistics in which it may signify either an arithmetical or geometric midpoint, that is, a figure midway between two others (as a lowest and a highest figure in a series of temperature readings) or a figure arrived at by finding the square root of the product of two numbers or quantities ⟨a golden *mean* between extravagance and miserliness⟩ ⟨10 is the arithmetical *mean* of 4 and 16⟩ ⟨8 is the geometric *mean* of 4 and 16, that is, the square root of 64⟩ MEDIAN indicates a midpoint in position but is used chiefly in statistics to indicate the point below which there are as many instances as there are above ⟨a *median* of public opinion⟩ ⟨the average pay of five men earning respectively 10, 14, 20, 26, and 40 dollars a day is $22 but the *median* is only $20 since there are two men earning below and two above this⟩ NORM designates the sometimes computed sometimes estimated average performance or achievement or, often, average minimum performance or achievement, of a group, class, or category, set up as the standard for members ⟨demands made upon children of a certain age should be adjusted to the *norm* for children of that age group⟩ ⟨construction workers . . . protesting the imposition of a 10 percent increase in the working *norm* —*Newsweek*⟩ ⟨those which fall below the required level of academic decency are encouraged to bring their curricula and degrees up to the *norm* —W.L.Sperry⟩ PAR in this connection more frequently refers to the average performance or condition of an individual or established for an individual, analogous to a norm for a group, though sometimes and esp. in British use PAR may refer to an average in amount (as of barometric pressure) ⟨*par* for a fast typist in English: 120 words⟩ ⟨40 pounds a day is considered *par* for a Holstein —*New Yorker*⟩ ⟨while 200 pounds or slightly thereunder is *par* for him, he has a tendency toward fatness —E.J.Kahn⟩

— **on an average** *or* **on the average :** taking the mean of unequal numbers or quantities **:** taking the typical example of the group under consideration ⟨these are, *on the average*, a better class of article⟩

²average \"\ *adj* **1 :** equaling an arithmetic mean ⟨an ~ annual rainfall of 20 inches⟩ **2 a :** approximating or resembling an arithmetic mean specif. in being about midway between extremes **:** not out of the ordinary for members of the group under consideration ⟨served with ~ merit under Grant —H.E.Nettles⟩ ⟨a man of ~ height⟩ **:** TYPICAL, COMMON, ORDINARY ⟨not an ~ wind but a decidedly abnormal one⟩ ⟨typical of the middle class at its most ~ —*N.Y.Herald Tribune*⟩ **b** *of a color* **:** medial in value ⟨slightly redder than ~ mustard tan⟩ **3** *maritime law* **:** assessed according to the laws of average

³average \"\ *vb* -ED/-ING/-S *vi* **1 a :** to be, on an average or come to, on an average ⟨in these waters the fish ~ larger⟩ **:** amount to or come to, on an average ⟨losses will ~ 5000 dollars a year⟩ ⟨these poles ~ 10 feet in length⟩ — sometimes used with *out* ⟨the gain *averaged* out to 20 percent⟩ **b** *of a color* **:** to have a medial value of a specified color **2 :** to buy or sell additional shares or commodities when the price falls or rises so as to obtain a more favorable average price — often used with *up* or *to* **~** *vt* **1 :** to do, get, make, spend, have, on the average or as an average sum or quantity ⟨~s 20 inches a year rainfall⟩ ⟨~ two days a week on the golf course⟩ ⟨a writer who ~s three stories a month⟩ **2 :** to find the arithmetic mean of (a series of unequal quantities) **:** obtain an average of ⟨~ the hourly temperature readings⟩ **3 a :** to bring toward the average **:** reduce or level out to an average ⟨the *averaging* of tendencies, a movement toward a mean —John Dewey⟩ — sometimes used with *out* **b :** to divide among a number according to a given proportion ⟨~ a loss⟩

average agreement *n* **:** an arrangement by which penalties for failure to meet a requirement in certain instances (as in demurrage) may be offset by more than meeting it in others

average bond *n, marine insurance* **:** a bond required to procure delivery of goods and given by a consignee to the master of a ship for prompt payment of any chargeable general average when its amount is ascertained

average clause *n* **1 :** a clause in an insurance policy that restricts the amount payable to a sum not to exceed the value of the property destroyed and that bears the same proportion to the loss as the face of the policy does to the value of the property insured — compare COINSURANCE **2 :** a clause in a marine insurance policy that exempts the insurer from particular average and in respect of some things from all average

average due date *n* **:** a computed date on which with fairness to debtor and creditor one settlement in full may be made for all variously dated items in an account

average life *n, of a radioactive substance* **:** the average of the times required for the disintegration of all the atoms, being 1.443 times the half-life

av·er·age·ly *adv* **:** to a degree representative of some understood average or norm **:** MODERATELY, FAIRLY ⟨he was an ~ good barber — as good as could be expected —Robert Lynd⟩ ⟨a more than ~ happy marriage —Edward Sapir⟩

av·er·age·ness \-nəs\ *n* -ES **:** the quality or state of being average — often used to imply mediocrity or ordinariness

average out *vi* **:** to close out a stock or commodity transaction without loss or at a profit by averaging

average tare *n* **:** tare estimated from the weight of a number of packages selected from a large number of similar ones

aver·ment \ə'vərmənt, -vəm-\ *n* -S [ME *averrement*, fr. MF *averement*, fr. *averer* to verify + *-ment* — more at AVER] **1** *obs* **:** the establishment of a fact by evidence **2** *law* **:** a positive statement of facts **:** an allegation made with an offer to justify or prove what is alleged **:** VERIFICATION ⟨the ~ alleged negligence on the part of the defendant⟩ **3 a :** the act of making an averment **b :** a positive assertion **:** AFFIRMATION

aver·nal \ə'vərnᵊl\ *or* **aver·ni·an** \-nēən, -nyən\ *adj, sometimes cap* [*avernal* fr. L *Avernalis* of Avernus, fr. *Avernus*, lake near Pozzuoli, Italy (now *Lago Averno*), reputed because of its depth and stench to lead to the underworld, underworld + L *-alis* -al; *avernian* fr. *Avernus* + E *-ian*] **:** INFERNAL

averred *past of* AVER

av·er·rhoa \,avə'rōə, ə'verəwə\ *n, cap* [NL, fr. *Averroës*, *Averrhoës* †1198 Spanish-Arabian philosopher] **:** a genus of East Indian trees (family Oxalidaceae) with pinnate leaves — see BILIMBI, CARAMBOLA

averring *pres part of* AVER

aver·ro·ism \ə'verə,wizəm, a'v- *also* ,avə'rō,iz-\ *n* -S *usu cap* [*Averroës* + E *-ism*] **1 :** the doctrines of Averroës whose teachings were mainly written in the form of Neoplatonically influenced commentaries on Aristotle and differed from Avicennism in affirming that the whole world is created all at once by God directly, eternally, and continuously and that individual souls are not immortal except insofar as they participate in a universal intellect **2 :** any of numerous and widely diverse doctrines of Jewish and Christian teachers in the 13th and later centuries regarded by themselves or by their critics as followers of Averroes and repeatedly condemned esp. because of their real or supposed denial of human freedom and personal immortality

aver·ro·ist \-rəwəst, -rōəst\ *n* -S *usu cap* **:** an adherent to the doctrines of Averroism

aver·ro·is·tic \ə¦verə¦wistik, a¦v- *also* ¦avərō¦is-\ *adj, usu cap* **:** of, relating to, or characteristic of Averroism

averruncate *vt* -ED/-ING/-S [E *averruncate* (partly influenced in meaning by L *eruncare* to weed out), fr. L *averruncatus*, past part. of *averruncare* to avert, fr. *a*, *ab* from, away + *verruncare* to turn; perh. akin to L *verrere* to sweep — more at OF, WAR] **1** *obs* **:** to ward off or avert (as an evil) **2** *obs* **:** to weed out **:** UPROOT **:** cut away (as weeds) **:** REMOVE — **averruncation** *n* -S

avers *pres 3d sing of* AVER

aversation *n* -S [L *aversation-*, *aversatio*, fr. *aversatus* (past part. of *aversari* to turn away, fr. *aversus*) + *-ion-*, *-io* -ion] **1** *obs* **:** an act of turning away **:** ESTRANGEMENT **2** *archaic* **:** AVERSION

¹averse \ə'vərs, -vəs, -vəis\ *adj* [L *aversus*, past part. of *avertere* to avert] **1 :** having an active feeling of repugnance, dislike, or distaste for something and tending to avoid, spurn, or evade it as a result — used postpositively and predicatively, followed by *to* or chiefly Brit. *from* ⟨what cat's ~ to fish —Thomas Gray⟩ ⟨I am inveterately ~ from any sort of fuss —Max Beerbohm⟩ ⟨he is not ~ to a glass of wine or two with his friends —Green Peyton⟩ **2** *archaic* **:** turned backward or away **3** *archaic* **a :** ADVERSE **b :** OPPOSITE **4** *bot* **:** turned away from the stem or axis — opposed to *adverse* **syn** see DISINCLINED

²averse *vb* -ED/-ING/-S *obs* **:** to turn away

averse·ly \ə'vərslē, -vəs-, -vəis-, -li\ *adv* **:** in an averse manner, direction, or position

averse·ness *n* -ES **:** AVERSION

aver·sion \ə'vərzhən, -vəzh-, -vəizh- *also* a'v-; *Brit usu & US also* -shən\ *n* -S [L *aversion-*, *aversio*, fr. *aversus* + *-ion-*, *-io* -ion] **1** *obs* **:** the physical or mental act of averting ⟨an ~ of the eyes⟩ ⟨an ~ from goodness⟩ **2** [LL *aversion-*, *aversio*, fr. L] **a :** a feeling of revulsion and repugnance towards something usu. coupled with an intense desire to avoid or turn from it ⟨what had been terror and dislike before, was now absolute ~ —Jane Austen⟩ **b :** a firmly settled and vehement dislike **:** ANTIPATHY — used usu. with *to*, *for*, or *from* ⟨an ~ to crowds and crowd behavior —H.G.Wells⟩ ⟨he had the most unconquerable ~ for Tristram —Laurence Sterne⟩ ⟨a corpulency of the body, accentuated by an unhappy ~ from exercise —Ernest Barker⟩ **3** *archaic* **:** a person or thing that is the object of aversion ⟨Mrs. Susan Crosstitch, whom you know to be my utter ~ —Henry Fielding⟩ **4 :** antagonism (sense 3) between colonies of microorganisms **syn** see DISLIKE

aver·sive \-siv, -ziv\ *adj* [L *aversus* + E *-ive*] **1 :** showing aversion **:** characterized by aversion **2 :** tending to avert **:** for the purpose of averting ⟨~ magic to drive off evil⟩

avert \ə'vərt, -vət, -vəit *also* a'v-; *usu* -d+V\ *vb* -ED/-ING/-S [ME *averten*, fr. MF *avertir*, fr. L *avertere*, fr. *a*, *ab* from, away + *vertere* to turn — more at OF, WORTH] *vt* **1 :** to turn away or aside (one's face, eyes, thoughts) esp. in order to escape something dangerous, unpleasant, or disconcerting ⟨some mortar and dust came dropping down, while he ~*ed* his face to avoid —Charles Dickens⟩ ⟨he . . . ~*s* his attention from an uncomfortable topic as soon as possible —Walter Moberly⟩ **2 :** to cause to turn, change, or deviate **:** ESTRANGE, ALIENATE ⟨so many discordant and contrary opinions . . . ~ them from the church —Francis Bacon⟩ **3 :** to anticipate and ward off **:** prevent the occurrence or unfortunate, dangerous, and dire effects of ⟨war was ~*ed* by a timely peace mission⟩ ⟨many highway accidents can be ~*ed* by courtesy⟩ ~ *vi archaic* **:** to turn away — usu. used with *from* **syn** see PREVENT, TURN

averted *adj* **:** turned away esp. with the intention of avoiding ⟨she closed it, with ~ eyes, and pushed it away —Jane Austen⟩

Av·er·tin \'avərtən, ə'vərtᵊn\ *trademark* — used for tribromoethanol

¹aves *pl of* AVE

²aves \'ā(,)vēz\ *n pl, cap* [NL, fr. L, pl. of *avis* bird — more at AVIARY] **:** a class of Vertebrata derived from Reptilia and including all fossil and recent birds

¹aves·tan \ə'vestən\ *adj, usu cap* [*Avesta*, sacred books of the ancient Zoroastrian religion (fr. MPer *Avastāk*) + E *-an*] **:** of or relating to the Avesta or to Avestan

²avestan \"\ *or* **aves·tic** \-tik\ *n, cap* [*Avesta* + E *-an* or *-ic*] **:** one of the two ancient languages comprising Old Iranian and that in which the sacred books of the Zoroastrian religion were written — compare OLD PERSIAN

avg *abbr* average

av·gas \'av + ,-\ *n* [*aviation gasoline*] **:** gasoline produced for aircraft engines

avian \'āvēən\ *also* **avine** \-,vīn, -,vən\ *adj* [L *avis* bird + E *-ian* or *-ine*] **1 :** of, relating to, or characteristic of birds ⟨~ families⟩ ⟨~ studies⟩ **2 :** derived from a bird ⟨~ tubercle bacilli in a goat⟩

avian diphtheria *n* **:** FOWL POX b

avian encephalomyelitis *n* **:** an acute usu. fatal virus infection of young chickens characterized by ataxic gait and weakening of the legs and by tremor esp. of the head and neck

avi·an·ize \'āvēə,nīz\ *vt* -ED/-ING/-S **:** to modify (microorganisms) by repeated culture in the developing chick embryo; *specif* **:** to attenuate (a virus in the preparation of vaccines) by such means

avian leukosis complex *or* **avian lymphomatosis** *n* **:** the leukoses of fowls

avian monocytosis *n* **:** BLUE COMB

avian osteopetrosis *n* **:** OSTEOPETROSIS 2

avian pneumoencephalitis *n* **:** NEWCASTLE DISEASE

avian tuberculosis *n* **:** bird tuberculosis usu. caused by a bacterium (*Mycobacterium avium*); *also* **:** infection of mammals (as swine) by this species of *Mycobacterium*

avi·a·rist \'āvēərəst, -ē,er-\ *n* -S **:** one who keeps an aviary

avi·ary \'āvē,erē, *esp Brit* -vyər-\ *n* -ES [L *aviarium*, fr. *avis* bird + *-arium*; akin to Gk *aetos* eagle, Skt *vi* bird] **:** a house, enclosure, or large cage for confining live birds ⟨a glass-domed ~ . . . houses more than 500 birds —*Amer. Guide Series: Mich.*⟩

avi·ate \'āvē,āt, 'av-\ *vi* -ED/-ING/-S [back-formation fr. *aviation & aviator*] **:** to fly or navigate the air (as in an aircraft)

avi·a·tion \,āvē'āshən, ,av- — *the variant with* a *in 1st syll seems to be more frequent for* "aviation" *than for* "aviator"\ *n* -S *often attrib* [F, fr. *avi-* (fr. L *avis*) + *-ation*] **1 :** the operation of heavier-than-air aircraft **2 :** military aircraft ⟨carrier-based ~⟩ ⟨his ~ had sunk or damaged 52 Japanese vessels —*Newsweek*⟩ **3 :** aircraft manufacture, development, and design esp. of a particular group or nation ⟨advances in American ~⟩

aviation badge *n* **:** WINGS

aviation cadet *n* **:** a person in training to become an air-force officer with an aeronautical rating — abbr. *AC*

aviation engineer *n* **:** one who constructs runways or other field installations required for air operations

aviation insurance *n* **:** insurance against claims and losses arising from the ownership, maintenance, or use of aircraft, hangars, or airports including damage to aircraft, personal injury, and property damage

aviation medicine *n* **:** a branch of medicine including aeromedicine and space medicine and dealing with the study, prevention, alleviation, and cure of diseases and ailments connected with aviation

avi·a·tor \'āvē,ād·ə(r), 'av-, -,ātə- — *see* AVIATION\ *n* -S [F *aviateur*, fr. *avi-* (fr. L *avis*) + *-ateur* (as in *amateur*)] **1** *obs* **:** FLYING MACHINE **2 :** the operator or pilot of an airplane

avi·a·to·ri·al \¦==,ə¦tōrēəl\ *adj* **:** of or relating to aviation or an aviator

aviator's ear *n* **:** AERO-OTITIS MEDIA

avi·a·trix \,==¦ā·triks, -ēks\ *also* **avi·a·tress** \'==,ā·trəs\ *n, pl* **aviatrixes** \-ksəz\ *or* **aviatri·ces** \,==,ā·trə,sēz\ *also* **aviatresses** \'==,ā·trəsəz\ **:** a woman aviator

av·i·cen·nia \,avə'senēə\ *n, cap* [NL, fr. L *Avicenna* †1037 Arab physician and philosopher + NL *-ia*] **:** a small genus of tropical shrubs or trees (family Verbenaceae) having opposite evergreen leaves and terminal clusters of small flowers with five sepals, four petals, and a capsular fruit — see AVICENNIACEAE, BLACK MANGROVE, WHITE MANGROVE

av·i·cen·ni·a·ce·ae \,==,==¦āsē,ē\ *n pl, cap* [NL, fr. *Avicennia*, type genus + *-aceae*] *in some classifications* **:** a family coextensive with the genus *Avicennia*

avi·cen·nism \,avə'se,nizəm\ *n* -S *usu cap* [*Avicenna* + E *-ism*] **:** the doctrines of the philosopher Avicenna who taught a theory of emanation and a doctrine widely accepted in the middle ages that universals exist in rebus as the general characters of particulars but ante res only in the mind of God and post res only as abstractions in the human mind

avi·cide \'āvə,sīd, 'av-\ *n* -S [L *avis* bird + E *-cide* — more at AVIARY] **:** the killing of birds

avic·o·lous \ā'vikələs, ə'v-\ *adj* [L *avis* + E *-colous*] **:** living on birds ⟨~ bird lice⟩

avic·u·lar·ia \ə,vikyə'la(a)rēə\ *n, cap* [NL, fr. L *avicula* small bird (dim. of *avis* bird) + NL *-aria*] **:** a genus of large tropical spiders containing a number of typical bird spiders

avic·u·lar·i·an \¦=¦==¦rēən\ *adj* [NL *avicularium* + E *-an*] **:** of or relating to an avicularium or avicularia

avic·u·la·ri·idae \ə,vikyələ'rīə,dē\ [NL, fr. *Avicularia*, type genus + *-idae*] *syn of* THERAPHOSIDAE

avic·u·lar·i·um \ə,vikyə'la(a)rēəm\ *n, pl* **avicular·ia** \-ēə\ [NL, fr. L *avicula* + *-arium* -ary] **:** a small prehensile process resembling a bird's head with a movable mandible found on many bryozoans

av·i·cu·li·dae \,avə'kyülə,dē\ [NL, fr. *Avicula* (syn. of *Pteria*), type genus (fr. L *avicula* small bird) + *-idae*; fr. the winglike expansions of the hinge of some species] *syn of* PTERIIDAE

av·i·cul·tur·al \¦āvə¦kəlch(ə)rəl, ¦av-\ *adj* **:** of, relating, or devoted to the interests of aviculture ⟨an ~ society⟩

avi·cul·ture \'āvə,kəlchə(r), 'av-\ *n* -S [L *avis* bird + E *culture*] **:** the rearing and care of birds, esp. of wild birds in captivity — **avi·cul·tur·ist** \¦==¦ch(ə)rəst\ *n* -S

av·id \'avəd *sometimes* 'āv-\ *adj* [F or L; F *avide*, fr. L *avidus*, fr. *avēre* to long for; akin to Goth *awiliuth* thanks, Gk *enēēs* gentle, Skt *avati* he favors] **1 :** craving eagerly **:** desirous to the point of greed ⟨his ~ fondness for the limelight —*Time*⟩ — often used with *for*, sometimes with *of* ⟨convivial, bawdy, robustly ~ for pleasure —Scott Fitzgerald⟩ ⟨a powerful will . . . ~ of glory —H.A.Overstreet⟩ **2 :** characterized by enthusiasm, ardor, and vigorous pursuit ⟨an ~ reader⟩ ⟨an ~ gardener⟩ **syn** see EAGER

av·i·din \'avədən\ *n* -S [*avid* + *-in*; fr. its having an avidity for biotin] **:** a protein found in white of egg that combines with biotin, rendering it inactive and leading to egg-white injury

avid·i·ty \ə'vidəd·ē, -dətē, -i *also* a'v- *or* ā'v-\ *n* -ES [ME *avidite*, fr. MF or L; MF *avidité*, fr. L *aviditat-*, *aviditas*, fr. *avidus* + *-itat-*, *-itas* -ity] **1 :** the quality or state of being avid **:** great or extreme eagerness or enthusiasm ⟨he seized his opportunity with ~⟩ ⟨all the ~ of a love-hungered soul —Joseph Furphy⟩ **2 :** an intense desire for gain or profit **:** AVARICE **3** *chem* **a :** the strength of an acid or base dependent on its degree of dissociation **b :** AFFINITY 2b **4 a :** characteristic of antibodies (as antitoxins) that tends to enhance their rate of combination or firmness of combination with antigen

av·id·ly \'avədlē, -li *sometimes* 'āv-\ *adv* **:** in an avid manner

avi·dya \(,)ə'vid(,)yä\ *also* **avij·ja** \-i(,)jä\ *n* -S [Skt *avidyā*, lit., ignorance, fr. *a-* ²a- + *vidyā* knowledge — more at WIT] *Hinduism & Buddhism* **:** IGNORANCE; *specif* **:** blindness to ultimate truth

avi·fau·na \'āvə¦fōnə, ¦av-\ *n* -S [NL, fr. L *avis* bird + NL *fauna*] **:** the birds or the kinds of birds of a region, period, or environment — **avi·fau·nal** \¦==¦=nᵊl\ *adj* — **avi·fau·nal·ly** \-nᵊlē\ *adv* — **avi·fau·nis·tic** \¦===¦nistik\ *adj*

av·i·ga·tion \,avə'gāshən, ,āv-\ *n* -S [L *avis* bird + E *-gation* (as in *navigation*) — more at AVIARY] **:** navigation of aircraft

avi·gnon berry *or* **avignon grain** \ə'vinyən-\ *n, usu cap A* [fr. *Avignon*, France] **:** any of several buckthorn berries from France — called also *French berry*; compare PERSIAN BERRY

avi·gnon·ese \ə¦vinyə¦nēz, -ēs\ *adj, usu cap* [*Avignon* + E *-ese*] **:** of or belonging to Avignon or to the residence there of the popes during the period 1309–1377

avile *vt* -ED/-ING/-S [ME *avilen*, fr. OF *aviler*, fr. *a* to (fr. L *ad*) + *-viler* (fr. *vil* vile) — more at AT, VILE] *obs* **:** ABASE, DEBASE, VILIFY

a vin·cu·lo ma·tri·mo·nii \¦ä¦viŋkü(,)lō ,mä·trē'mōnē,ē, ā¦v . . . kyə . . . ,ma . . . nē,ī\ *also* **a vinculo** *adj* [NL, lit., from the bond of marriage] *of a divorce* **:** ABSOLUTE ⟨granted a decree *a vinculo*⟩

avine *var of* AVIAN

avion \àvyōⁿ\ *n* -S [F, fr. L *avis* bird — more at AVIARY] **:** AIRPLANE

avi·on·ic \¦āvē¦änik, ¦av-, -ēk\ *adj* [back-formation fr. *avionics*] **:** of, for, or relating to the field of avionics

avi·on·ics \,==¦niks\ *n pl* [*aviation electronics*] **:** the development and production of electrical and electronic devices for use in aviation, esp. of electronic control systems for aircraft and airborne weapons; *also* **:** the devices and systems so developed ⟨~ design and procurement⟩

avirulence \(')ā+\ *n* -S [²*a-* + *virulence*] **:** lack of virulence

avirulent \(')ā+\ *adj* [ISV ²*a-* + *virulent*] **:** not virulent — compare NONPATHOGENIC

avi·ta·min·o·sis \¦ā,vīd·əmə'nōsəs\ *n, pl* **avitamino·ses** \-ō,sēz\ [NL, fr. ²*a-* + ISV *vitamin* + NL *-osis*] **:** a disease in man and animals resulting from a deficiency of one or more vitamins — often used in combination to identify the vitamin involved ⟨~ A⟩ — **avi·ta·mi·not·ic** \-¦näd·ik\ *adj*

avizandum \,avi'zandəm\ *n* -S [ML, neut. of *avizandus*, gerundive of *avizare*, *avisare*, *advisare* to consider, fr. MF *aviser* — more at ADVISE] *Scots law* **:** private consideration

avn *abbr* aviation

avo \'ä(,)vü\ *n* -S [Pg] **:** a subsidiary unit of value in Portuguese Timor and in Macao that is worth ¹⁄₁₀₀ of a pataca ⟨bronze coins of 10 and 20 ~*s*⟩ ⟨postage stamp surcharged 6 ~*s*⟩

avo·ca·do \,avə'kä(,)dō, -'kā-, (*esp when* "pear" *follows*) -,də, *also* ,äv- *or* ,āv-\ *also* **avocado pear** *n, pl* **avocados** *also* **avocadoes** [modif. of Sp *aguacate*, fr. Nahuatl *ahuacatl*, short for *ahuacacuahuitl*, lit., testicle tree, fr. *ahuacatl* testicle + *cuahuitl* tree; fr. its use as an aphrodisiac] **1 :** the pulpy green or purple somewhat pear-shaped edible fruit of various tropical American trees of the genus *Persea*, esp. of cultivated varieties originating in the West Indies, Guatemala, and Mexico — called also *alligator pear* **2 :** a tree bearing avocados

av·o·ca·tion \,avə'kāshən\ *n* -S [L *avocation-*, *avocatio*, fr. *avocatus* (past part. of *avocare* to call away, fr. *a*, *ab* from, away + *vocare* to call, fr. *voc-*, *vox* voice) + *-ion-*, *-io* -ion — more at OF, VOICE] **1** *archaic* **:** a calling away **:** DIVERSION, DISTRACTION ⟨try, by every method of ~ and amusement, whether you cannot get the better of that dejection —Thomas Gray⟩ **2 :** a subordinate occupation pursued in addition to one's regular work esp. for enjoyment **:** HOBBY ⟨a lawyer by profession but painting has been his ~ for years⟩ — opposed to *vocation* **3 :** regular or customary work or employment **:** VOCATION — **av·o·ca·tion·al** \¦==¦=shənᵊl, -shnəl\ *adj*

av·o·cet \'avə,set\ *n* -S [F & It; F *avocette*, fr. It *avocetta*, *avosetta*] **:** any of several rather large long-legged shore birds (genus *Recurvirostra*) having webbed feet and a slender upwardly curved bill — compare STILT

European avocet

av·o·di·re \¦avədə-¦rā\ *n* -S [F *avodiré*] **1 :** the smooth-textured decorative whitish to pale yellow wood of a large tropical West African tree (*Turraeanthus africana*) of the mahogany family used for cabinetmaking **2 :** the tree that produces avodire

avo·ga·drite \,avə'gä,drīt, ,äv-\ *n* -S [It *avogadrite*, fr. Count Amedeo *Avogadro* †1856 Ital. chemist and physicist + It *-ite*] **:** a potassium and cesium fluoborate $(K,Cs)BF_4$ occurring in small crystals on Vesuvian lava

avo·ga·dro number *or* **avogadro constant** \¦==¦=(,)drō-\ *n, usu cap A* [after Count *Avogadro*] **:** the number of atoms in a gram atom or of molecules in a gram molecule of any substance (as for oxygen the number of atoms in 16 grams), its value being 6.023×10^{23} — compare AVOGADRO'S LAW

avogadro's law *or* **avogadro's hypothesis** *n, usu cap A* **:** a law in chemistry: equal volumes of all gases at the same temperature and pressure contain equal numbers of molecules — compare GAY-LUSSAC'S LAW 1

avo·gram \'avə-,gram\ *n* -S [*Avogadro* + *gram*] **:** a unit of mass and weight equal to one gram divided by the Avogadro number

avoid \ə'vȯid\ *vb* -ED/-ING/-S [ME *avoiden*, fr. OF *esvuidier*, fr. *es-* (fr. L *ex* out) + *vuidier* to empty — more at EX-, VOID] *vt* **1** *obs* **a :** VOID **b :** EXPEL **2** *archaic* **:** to depart or withdraw from **:** LEAVE **3** *law* **:** to make void **:** ANNUL, VACATE, DEFEAT, EVADE, INVALIDATE ⟨~ a plea⟩ **4 a :** to keep away from **:** stay clear of ⟨she was a professional do-gooder . . . and Horace Mann ~*ed* her —H.S.Commager⟩ **b :** to prevent the occurrence or effectiveness of ⟨be careful to ~ cracking the glass⟩ **:** SIDESTEP **:** BYPASS ⟨he is also a Puritan who does not smoke and drinks only to ~ an issue —*Amer. Fabrics*⟩ **:** refrain from ⟨they should ~ bringing out sensational books even if they promise to sell well —Lister Hill⟩ ~ *vi, obs* **:** RETREAT, WITHDRAW — usu. followed by a preposition ⟨David ~*ed* out of his presence —1 Sam 18:11 (AV)⟩ **syn** see ESCAPE

avoid·a·ble \-dəbəl\ *adj* **:** that can be avoided — **avoid·a·bly** \-blē, -li\ *adv*

avoid·ance \-dᵊn(t)s\ *n* -S [ME *avoidaunce*, fr. *avoiden* to avoid + *-aunce* -ance] **1** *obs* **a :** an action of emptying, vacating, or clearing away **b :** OUTLET **2 :** VACANCY — used esp. of an office or benefice ⟨the next ~ of an abbacy⟩ **3 :** the act of annulling or making void **:** ANNULMENT ⟨~ of a contract⟩ **4 :** an act or practice of avoiding something undesirable or unwelcome ⟨~ of danger⟩ ⟨the use of merger agreements . . . as a means of tax ~ —*Va. Law Rev.*⟩ **5 :** abstention from various types of social contact with persons of specified relationships, esp. with those of the opposite sex that are related by marriage (as a parent-in-law), a custom overtly signifying respect and difference in status and amounting to a taboo among some primitive peoples — compare JOKING RELATIONSHIP **6 :** the introduction of new material in pleading in order to avoid the effect of known and admitted facts presented in an adversary's former pleading ⟨a plea in ~⟩

avoiding reaction *n* **:** a reaction away from a stimulus **:** a negative tropism or taxis

¹av·oir·du·pois \,avə(r)də'pȯiz, '===,=\ *n* [alter. (influenced by F *du* of the) of earlier *averdepois*, *avoir de pois*, fr. ME *avoir de pois*, *aver de peis* goods sold by weight, fr. OF, lit., goods of weight, fr. *aver* property, goods + *de* of (fr. L *de* from) + *pois*, *peis* weight — more at AIVER, DE-, POISE] **1 :** AVOIRDUPOIS WEIGHT **2 :** WEIGHT, HEAVINESS; *specif* **:** personal weight **:** FATNESS, FAT ⟨the best advertisements for ~ since Santa Claus —Coulton Waugh⟩

²avoirdupois \"\ *adj* **:** expressed in avoirdupois weight ⟨~ units⟩ ⟨ounce ~⟩ — abbr. *av*, *avdp*, *avoir*

avoirdupois pound *n* **:** POUND 1b

avoirdupois weight *n* **:** the series of units of weight based on the pound of 16 ounces and the ounce of 16 drams — see MEASURE table

avond·bloem \'ävən,blüm\ *n* -S [obs. Afrik (now *aandblom*), fr. *avond* evening (fr. MD *āvont*, *āvent*) + *bloem* flower, fr. MD *bloeme*; akin to OHG *ābant* evening and to OHG *bluoma* flower — more at EVEN, BLOOM] **:** a southern African irislike bulbous plant (*Hesperantha falcata*) having claret-red flowers

avos *pl of* AVO

¹avouch \ə'vau̇ch\ *vb* -ED/-ING/-ES [ME *avouchen*, fr. MF *avochier* to summon, call to one's aid, fr. L *advocare* — more at ADVOCATE] *vt* **1** *obs* **:** to appeal to or cite as an authority for a statement **2 :** to declare as a matter of fact or as a thing that can be proved **:** AFFIRM ⟨~ the contrary⟩ ⟨unless Mr. Smith ~*es* and proves that she changed the spelling —Isabel Paterson⟩ **3 :** to maintain as just or true **:** vouch for **:** GUARANTEE ⟨~*ed* it for the law of God —John Milton⟩ **4 :** to acknowledge esp. as one's own **:** ACCEPT, CONFESS ⟨thou hast ~*ed* the Lord . . . to be thy God —Deut 26:17 (AV)⟩ **:** take responsibility for ⟨~ those unjust actions⟩ ~ *vi, archaic* **:** to give guarantee or assurance **:** VOUCH ⟨I cannot ~ for her reputation —Daniel Defoe⟩ **syn** see ASSERT

²avouch \"\ *n* -ES **:** the act of avouching

avouch·ment \-mənt\ *n* -S **:** the act of avouching **:** AFFIRMATION, ASSURANCE

avour·neen \ə'vu̇r,nēn\ *n* -S [IrGael *a mhuirnīn* oh, darling!, fr. *a* oh + *muirnīn* darling, fr. MIr *muirnīn*, dim. of *muirn* affection, joy] *Irish* **:** DARLING, SWEETHEART

¹avow \ə'vau̇\ *vt* -ED/-ING/-S [ME *avowen*, fr. OF *avouer*, fr. L *advocare* to summon, call to one's aid] **1** *obs* **:** to acknowledge (a person) as one's own **:** acknowledge with approval (an agent's actions) **2 a :** to assert or declare as a fact **:** CLAIM ⟨the modest procedure is not to ~ loudly . . . our love of truth —G.W.Sherburn⟩ ⟨I can . . . ~ him to be the best family a boy ever had —W.J.Locke⟩ **b :** to acknowledge and assert (an act, a purpose) with frankness and determination **:** declare openly, bluntly, and without shame ⟨the frankness to ~ poverty —G.B.Shaw⟩ **3** *law* **:** to acknowledge and justify (an act done); *specif* **:** to make an avowry of **syn** see ACKNOWLEDGE, ASSERT

²avow \"\ *n* -S [ME, fr. *avowen* to avow, to bind by a vow, fr. MF *avouer*, fr. *a-* (fr. L *ad-*) + *vouer* to vow — more at VOW] *archaic* **:** a solemn promise **:** VOW

avow·al \ə'vau̇(ə)l\ *n* -S [*avow* + *-al*] **:** an open declaration or frank acknowledgment ⟨an ~ of principle⟩

avow·ant \-au̇ənt\ *n* -S [MF *avouant*, pres. part. of *avouer* to avow] **:** the defendant in replevin who avows the distress of the goods and justifies the taking

avowed \-au̇d\ *adj* [ME, fr. past part. of *avowen* to avow, to declare openly] **:** openly acknowledged or declared **:** ADMITTED ⟨as an ~ Jeffersonian he has been . . . a guardian of constitutional checks and guarantees —*Current Biog.*⟩ ⟨~ aims⟩ **:** SWORN ⟨an ~ enemy⟩ — **avow·ed·ly** \-aủǝdlē, -li\ *adv*

avow·ry \-aủ(ǝ)rē, -ri\ *n* -ES [ME *avowrie*, fr. MF *avouerie* protection, patronage, fr. OF, fr. *avouer* to avow + *-erie* -ery] **1 a** *obs* **:** ADVOCACY, PATRONAGE, PROTECTION **b :** ADVOCATE, PATRON; *esp* **:** PATRON SAINT **2 :** the act of one who avows something; *esp* **:** the act of the distrainer of goods who in an action of replevin avows and justifies the taking in his own right — compare COGNIZANCE 5

avoy·el \ǝ'vȯiǝl, a'- *also* ȧvwȧ'(y)el\ *n, pl* **avoyel** *or* **avoyels** *usu cap* [F, of AmerInd origin] **1 :** a Natchesan people of central Louisiana **2 :** a member of the Avoyel people

avulse \ǝ'vǝls\ *vt* -ED/-ING/-S [L *avulsus*, past part. of *avellere* to tear off] **:** to pull off or tear away; *specif* **:** to separate by avulsion ⟨an *avulsed* ligament⟩

avul·sion \-lshǝn\ *n* -S [L *avulsion-, avulsio*, fr. *avulsus* (past part. of *avellere* to tear off, fr. *a, ab* from, away + *vellere* to pluck, pull) + *-ion-, -io* -ion — more at OF, VULNERABLE] **:** a forcible separation or detachment: as **a** *med* **:** a tearing away of a structure or part accidentally or surgically ⟨surgical ~ of a part of the phrenic nerve to rest a diseased lung⟩ **b :** a sudden cutting off of land by flood, currents, or change in course of a body of water; *esp* **:** one that separates a portion from one person's property and joins it to that of another

avun·cu·lar \ǝ'vǝŋkyǝlǝ(r)\ *adj* [L *avunculus* maternal uncle (dim. of *avus* grandfather) + E *-ar* — more at UNCLE] **1 :** of, being, or relating to an uncle, specif. a maternal uncle **2 :** acting or speaking with the familiarity, kindness, or indulgence of an uncle; *sometimes* **:** unduly benevolent and condescending ⟨then one evening he decided to join in. He became robust, ~, patronizing —Elizabeth Taylor⟩ — **avun·cu·lar·i·ty** \=,== 'larǝd·ē\ *n* -ES

avun·cu·late \=',== lǝt, -,lāt\ *n* -S [L *avunculus* + E *-ate*] **1 :** a special relationship obtaining among some tribal peoples between a nephew and his maternal uncle **2 :** authority of a man over his sister's family affairs but esp. over her children and the reciprocal rights and responsibilities associated therewith — compare AMITATE

avun·cu·lo·cal \ǝ,vǝŋkyǝ'lōkǝl\ *adj* [L *avunculus* + E *local*] **1 :** located at or centered around the residence of the husband's maternal uncle **2 :** belonging to a maternal uncle — compare MATRILOCAL, PATRILOCAL, NEOLOCAL

aw \'ȯ, 'ä\ *interj* — used to express mild remonstrance, incredulity, or disgust

AW *abbr* **1** above water **2** actual weight **3** aircraft warning **4** all water **5** all widths **6** articles of war **7** automatic weapon

[1]**awa** \ǝ'wȧ, -wȯ\ *adv* [by alter.] *Scot* **:** AWAY[1]

[2]**awa** \'ä(,)vä, -wä\ *n* -S [Hawaiian] **:** MILKFISH

[3]**awa** \'(?)ävǝ\ *n* -S [Hawaiian *'awa*] **:** KAVA

awa·bi \ǝ'wäbē\ *n, pl* **awabi** [Jap] **:** an abalone (*Haliotis gigantea*)

awa·dhi \'äwǝ(,)dē\ *n* -S *usu cap* [Hindi *Avadhī*] **:** a literary dialect of Eastern Hindi

[1]**await** \ǝ'wāt, *usu* -ād·+V\ *vb* -ED/-ING/-S [ME *awaiten*, fr. ONF *awaitier*, fr. *a-* (fr. L *ad-*) + *waitier* to watch — more at WAIT] *vt* **1** *obs* **:** to watch for esp. with hostile intent **:** lie in wait for ⟨your ill-meaning politician lords . . . appointed to ~ me thirty spies —John Milton⟩ **2 :** to wait for **:** stay for ⟨you must ~ the sequel —Walter de la Mare⟩ ⟨had decided to ~ me in the mountains —D.L.Busk⟩ **3 :** to be in store for **:** be ready or in waiting for ⟨a lavish Sunday dinner *~ing* them —Ellen Glasgow⟩ **~** *vi* **1** *obs* **:** to wait on someone **:** ATTEND ⟨on whom three hundred gold-capped youths ~ —Alexander Pope⟩ **2 :** to stay or be in waiting **:** WAIT ⟨the people *~ed* outside the building⟩ **3 :** to be in store ⟨marched . . . north to civilization where fame and fortune *~ed* —Tom Marvel⟩ **syn** see EXPECT

[2]**await** *n* -S [ME, fr. ONF, fr. *awaitier*] *obs* **:** a lying in wait or watching for with hostile intent **:** AMBUSH

[1]**awake** \ǝ'wāk\ **awoke** \-wōk\ *also* **awaked** \-wākt\ **awaked** \"\ *also* **awoke** \-wōk\ *or* **awok·en** \-wōkǝn\ **awaking; awakes** [ME *awaken* (fr. OE *awacan*, fr. [1]*a-* + *wacan* to awake, arise, be born) & *awakien*, fr. OE *awacian*, fr. [1]*a-* + *wacian* to be awake, watch — more at WAKE] *vi* **1 :** to emerge from sleep **:** regain consciousness after natural sleep **:** cease sleeping, dozing, or dreaming ⟨the elderly bellboy *awoke* from his dreams —Sinclair Lewis⟩ **2 a :** to emerge from a sleeplike state (as from inaction, indifference, or death) **:** bestir oneself ⟨cast off your bonds, ~, arise —William Wordsworth⟩ **b :** to become active again **:** be resurgent **3 :** to become conscious or aware — usu. used with following *to* ⟨unless the bar *~s* to its opportunity and power —B.N.Cardozo⟩ ⟨they *awoke* to their danger⟩ **~** *vt* **1 :** to arouse from sleep **:** bring back to consciousness after sleep ⟨the sound of heavy footsteps in the driveway *awoke* the watchdogs⟩ **2 a :** to arouse from a sleeplike state (as from inaction, indifference, or death) ⟨I was soon *awaked* from this disagreeable reverie —Oliver Goldsmith⟩ **b :** to incite to activity **:** make active **:** stir up ⟨certain of them *awoke* in me feelings of fear —Osbert Lancaster⟩

[2]**awake** \"\ *adj* [ME *awake, awaken*, past part. of *awaken*] **1 :** not asleep, dormant, or notably lethargic ⟨the boys sat in their chairs half asleep but Mack was ~ —John Steinbeck⟩ **2 a :** in a state of vigilance, arousal, or activity ⟨all the nationalistic elements now ~ on the African continent —J.M.Houston⟩ **b :** fully conscious or appreciative **:** AWARE — usu. used with following *to* ⟨was ~ to the dangers and disgrace of the existing maladministration —J.A.Froude⟩ **c :** brought back to consciousness **:** REACTIVATED, REANIMATED ⟨old memories suddenly ~ again⟩ **syn** see AWARE

awak·en \ǝ'wākǝn\ *vb* **awakened; awakened; awakening** \-k(ǝ)niŋ\ **awakens** [ME *awakenen*, fr. OE *awæcnian, onwæcnian*, fr. [1]*a-, on* + *wæcnian, wæcnan* to awake — more at WAKEN] *vi* **:** AWAKE ⟨the youth *~ed* slowly —Stephen Crane⟩ ⟨England . . . had *~ed* from its age-old isolation —Van Wyck Brooks⟩ ⟨old infirmities ~ under our skins —V.S.Pritchett⟩ ⟨we have *~ed* to this fact —G.W.Chapman⟩ **~** *vt* **:** AWAKE ⟨wondering what had *~ed* her —Ann Petry⟩ ⟨a rare gift of *~ing* the keen interest of his students —H.K.Barrows⟩ ⟨did more than any other to ~ the churches of this faith to the value of their heritage —C.A.Dinsmore⟩ **syn** see STIR

awak·en·er \-k(ǝ)nǝ(r)\ *n* -S **:** one that awakens

[1]**awakening** *n* -S **1 :** a rousing from sleep **2 a :** a rousing from inactivity, sloth, or indifference ⟨ancient and somnolent institutions were once again spared an ~ —E.B.George⟩ ⟨the most significant fact in the world today is the ~ that is going on in the East —Wendell Willkie⟩ **b :** a revival of interest in religion ⟨the later *~s* in Protestantism gave rise to novel movements in education and thought —K.S.Latourette⟩ **3 :** a coming into consciousness or awareness **:** REALIZATION, RECOGNITION — usu. used with following *to* ⟨a gradual ~ to the facts of the country's military position⟩

[2]**awakening** *adj* **:** AWAKING — **awak·en·ing·ly** *adv*

awak·en·ment \-kǝnmǝnt\ *n* -S **:** AWAKENING

awan \ǝ'wän\ *n* -S *usu cap* [native name in India] **:** a member of a people of the northwestern Indian subcontinent, mainly along the Indus

awant·ing \ǝ+\ *adj* [[1]*a-* + *wanting*] **:** WANTING ⟨jesters and jugglers were not ~ —Sir Walter Scott⟩

awanyu \ǝ'wän(,)yü\ *also* **avanyo** \-vän(,)yō\ *or* **avanyu** \-(,)yü\ *n* -S [Tewa] **:** a sacred plumed serpent in the mythology and art of the Tewa Indians

[1]**award** \ǝ'wȯ(ǝ)rd, -ō(ǝ)d\ *vt* -ED/-ING/-S [ME *awarden*, fr. ONF *eswarder*, fr. *es-* (fr. L *ex* out) + *warder* to observe, keep, guard; akin to OF *guarder, garder* to observe, keep, guard — more at EX-, GUARD] **1** *obs* **:** to determine after careful consideration **:** JUDGE, DECIDE ⟨shall then the testament ~ the right —John Dryden⟩ **2 :** to give by judicial decree **:** assign after careful judgment **:** ADJUDGE ⟨the arbitrators *~ed* heavy damages⟩ **3 :** to confer or bestow upon **:** GRANT, GIVE ⟨the university *~ed* him an honorary degree⟩ **syn** see GRANT

[2]**award** \"\ *n* -S [ME, fr. ONF *eswart*, fr. *eswarder*] **1 a :** a judgment, sentence, or final decision; *esp* **:** the decision of arbitrators in a case submitted to them ⟨following the arbitration ~ . . . he was retained as counsel by . . . the more important claimants —H.W.H.Knott⟩ **b :** the document containing the decision of arbitrators **2 a :** something that is conferred or bestowed upon a person **:** GRANT ⟨candidates for the *~s* in chemistry⟩ **b :** an emblem or medal symbolizing such an award ⟨the ~ is a blue-and-gold pin with an appropriate inscription⟩

[3]**award** *vt* -ED/-ING/-S [*a-* (perfective prefix) + *ward* — more at ABEAR] *obs* **:** to ward off

award clerk *n* **:** PROCUREMENT CLERK

award·ee \=,='dē, =',=dē\ *n* -S **:** one that receives an award

award·er \='=dǝ(r)\ *n* -S **:** one that awards

aware \ǝ'wa(a)(ǝ)r, -we(ǝ)r,-wa(a)ǝ,-weǝ\ *adj* [ME *iwar*, fr. OE *gewær*, fr. *ge-* (collective prefix) + *wær* wary — more at CO-, WARY] **1** *archaic* **:** on guard **:** WATCHFUL, VIGILANT ⟨are you all ~ of . . . talebearing and evil-speaking —John Wesley⟩ **2 a :** marked by realization, perception, or knowledge **:** CONSCIOUS, SENSIBLE, COGNIZANT ⟨he was never fully ~ of the extent of his failures —O.S.Nock⟩ ⟨Adams was ~ that the arrival of the tea ships might be used to precipitate a crisis —C.L.Becker⟩ **b :** showing heightened perception and ready comprehension and appreciation **:** INFORMED, KNOWING, ALERT ⟨the most intellectually ambitious and the most technically ~ of the novelists under thirty —W.S.Graham⟩

syn COGNIZANT, CONSCIOUS, SENSIBLE, ALIVE, AWAKE: AWARE may indicate either general information, wide knowledge, interpretative power, or vigilant perception ⟨few, so far as I am *aware*, now claim the free speech to call a knave a knave —T.S.Eliot⟩ ⟨more widely *aware* of the phenomena of biological chemistry —Sinclair Lewis⟩ ⟨Americans are becoming *aware* that American destiny can be pursued only in a world framework —Max Lerner⟩ COGNIZANT may imply the gradual impingement of knowledge or perception on one's consciousness or may connote special efforts to know ⟨Soapy's mind became *cognizant* of the fact —O.Henry⟩ ⟨through the servants, or from some other means, he had made himself *cognizant* of the projected elopement —Anthony Trollope⟩ It may imply arch knowingness ⟨"ah!" went the other eyeing Ripton in lordly *cognizant* style —George Meredith⟩ CONSCIOUS may indicate impingement on one's mind so that one recognizes the fact or existence of something ⟨dimly *conscious* that Hallward was speaking to him but not catching the meaning of the words —Oscar Wilde⟩ It may also indicate an extreme and dominating realization, even a preoccupation ⟨what makes a writer most acutely *conscious* of his place in time —T.S.Eliot⟩ SENSIBLE may apply to situations in which a thing is intuitively sensed and also to those in which it is rationally perceived, known, and admitted ⟨for my part, though deeply *sensible* of its influence, I cannot seize it —Nathaniel Hawthorne⟩ ⟨I am *sensible* that I write you short letters but I write you all I know —Horace Walpole⟩ It is often used to indicate awareness and acknowledgment of gratitude, pleasure, resentment, or pain ⟨I am *sensible* I may be indebted to you, sir —Charles Dickens⟩ ALIVE may suggest vivid awareness, certain keen perception ⟨Cromwell . . . was keenly *alive* to all that concerned England's honor and strength —A.T.Mahan⟩ ⟨these two had a certain cool judgment, and they were fully *alive* to the danger of thwarting Barbara —John Galsworthy⟩ AWAKE may suggest alert perception ⟨a large number of her [Britain's] leaders seem *awake* to the saving qualities of compromise —Leland Stowe⟩

aware·ness \-nǝs\ *n* -ES **:** the quality or state of being aware ⟨the crash of music broke into his ~ —Hamilton Basso⟩ ⟨their intelligence, social consciousness, and political ~ are of the highest degree —T.H.Fielding⟩

awa·ru·ite \ǝ'wä'rü,īt\ *n* -S [*Awarua*, South Island, New Zealand, its locality + E *-ite*] **:** a mineral consisting of a rare natural alloy of nickel and iron

awas *pl of* AWA

awash \ǝ+\ *adv (or adj)* [[1]*a-* + *wash*, v.] **1 a :** alternately covered and exposed by the waves or tide **:** washed by the sea ⟨two whales spouting close to the factory and lying carelessly ~ —R.B.Robertson⟩ ⟨a group of great islands almost ~ with the sea —C.O.Dunbar⟩ **b :** washing about **:** AFLOAT ⟨everything movable on deck was ~⟩ **c :** covered with water **:** FLOODED ⟨the street was ~ after the sudden storm⟩ **2 :** marked by an abundance **:** FULL, OVERFLOWING ⟨the resulting music is ~ with decayed Viennese romanticism —Herbert Weinstock⟩ ⟨here is the household ~ with children —Brendan Gill⟩

awave \ǝ+\ *adj* [[1]*a-* + *wave*, v.] **:** moving in or as if in waves **:** WAVING

[1]**away** \ǝ'wā\ *adv* [ME *away, on way*, fr. OE *aweg, onweg*, fr. [1]*a-, on* + *weg* way — more at WAY] **1 :** on the way **:** ONWARD, ALONG ⟨come ~ death —Shak.⟩ **2 :** from this or that place **:** HENCE, THENCE ⟨the lone and level sands stretch far ~ —P.B.Shelley⟩ ⟨go ~⟩ — sometimes used to indicate motion from a place with no expressed verb of motion or no expressed verb at all ⟨we must ~⟩ ⟨whither ~⟩ **3 a :** from contact or close association **:** ASIDE ⟨she folded her work and laid it ~ —H.W.Longfellow⟩ **b :** at a little distance **:** OFF ⟨he was a good boxer inside as well as ~ —A.J.Liebling⟩ **c :** in another direction; *esp* **:** in the opposite direction ⟨we've turned . . . hard ~ in a tight circle to port to get out of this area —Richard Dimbleby⟩ **4 :** from a condition of being **:** out of existence **:** to an end **:** to nothing ⟨tried to explain ~ the affair of the letter —H.E.Scudder⟩ ⟨a progressive twitching of the muscles with increasing weakness and wasting ~ —Morris Fishbein⟩ **5 :** from one's possession or use ⟨it is given ~ to a friend by the householder —J.G.Frazer⟩ **6 a :** onward in time **:** UNINTERRUPTEDLY, CONSTANTLY, ON ⟨a distinct compartment in one's mind that works ~ no matter what is going on —O.W. Holmes †1935⟩ **b :** without hesitation or delay **:** FORTHWITH, IMMEDIATELY ⟨the troops were ordered to fire ~⟩ **7 :** to a considerable degree **:** by a long distance or interval **:** FAR ⟨he is far and ~ the best player on the team⟩ ⟨the trouble began ~ back in 1910⟩

[2]**away** \"\ *adj* **1 a :** absent from a place **:** GONE ⟨he is ~ from home⟩ **b :** started on the way **:** OFF ⟨he was ~ at a gallop —Winston Churchill⟩ **2 :** distant in space or time **:** ⟨a lake 10 miles ~⟩ ⟨the opening of the season is only a week ~⟩ **3** *chiefly Scot* **:** gone out of or as if out of existence **:** dead, mad, or in a faint ⟨she was ~ in her head —Mary Deasy⟩ **4 a :** played on an opponent's home grounds ⟨league headquarters arranges the schedule of home and ~ games⟩ **b** *of a golf ball* **:** lying farthest from the cup and to be played first **c** *baseball* **:** OUT ⟨the home run came with two ~ in the 9th inning⟩

away-going crop \=',=-\ *n* **:** a crop that a tenant is under certain conditions entitled to remove after the end of his tenancy **:** EMBLEMENT

away·ness \ǝ'wānǝs\ *n* -ES **:** the quality or state of being out of the way **:** REMOTENESS ⟨it was the ~ of it that first attracted me to the place —Aldous Huxley⟩

[1]**awe** \'ȯ\ *n* -S [ME *awe, age, aghe*, fr. ON *agi*; akin to OE *ege* awe, fear, terror — more at AIL] **1** *obs* **:** intense fear **:** DREAD, TERROR ⟨waits for death with dread and trembling ~ —Edmund Spenser⟩ **2** *archaic* **:** the power to inspire fear or reverence ⟨you see, my lord, what an ~ you have upon me —John Dryden⟩ **3 :** fear mixed with dread, veneration, reverence, or wonder: as **a :** profound and reverent fear inspired by deity ⟨~ of the judgments of God —Daniel Defoe⟩ **b :** abashed reverence and fear inspired by authority or power ⟨nothing but an extreme ~ of your authority has hitherto prevented me from forcing my importunate attentions upon you —Dorothy Sayers⟩ **c :** veneration and latent fear inspired by something sacred, mysterious, or morally impressive ⟨jaguars were regarded with religious ~ and were the object of a cult —Alfred Métraux⟩ **d :** reverent wonder with a touch of fear inspired by the grand or sublime esp. in nature or art ⟨the bird was so beautiful that the vision of it . . . seemed to bring with it an overpowering sense of ~ —J.C.Powys⟩

[2]**awe** \"\ *vt* **awed; awed; awing** \'ȯ(·)iŋ\ **awes** [ME *awen*, fr. *awe*, n.] **1 :** to inspire with awe **:** FRIGHTEN, TERRIFY ⟨the exalted nature of the personage to whom she was being taken *awed* her —P.I.Wellman⟩ ⟨nature among the mountains is too fierce, too strong for man . . . and she *~s* him —Charles Kingsley⟩ **2 :** to influence, control, or check by inspiring with awe ⟨her pained reserve had no power to ~ them into decency —Joseph Conrad⟩

[3]**awe** \'ȯ, 'ȧ\ *n* -S [MF *auve, aube*, perh. fr. L *alapa* box on the ear; perh. akin to ON *lōfi* palm of the hand — more at GLOVE] **1 :** one of the boards or buckets against which the water acts in an undershot mill wheel **2 :** one of the sails of a windmill

awearied \ǝ+\ *adj* [[1]*a-* + *wearied*] **:** WEARIED

aweary \ǝ+\ *adj* [[1]*a-* + *weary*] **:** WEARY, TIRED

aweather \ǝ+\ *adv* [[1]*a-* + *weather*] **:** on or toward the weather or windward side — opposed to *alee*

awed \'ȯd\ *adj* **:** feeling or showing awe — **awed·ly** \'ȯ(ǝ)dlē, -li\ *adv* — **awed·ness** \'ȯ(ǝ)dnǝs\ *n* -ES

awee \ǝ'wē\ *adv* [[2]*a* + *wee*] *chiefly Scot* **:** a little while

aweel \ǝ'wēl, -wel\ *interj* [*ah* + Sc *weel*] *Scot* **:** well then

aweigh \ǝ'wā\ *adj* [[1]*a-* + *weigh* (to heave up)] *of an anchor* **:** just clear of the ground and hanging perpendicularly **:** ATRIP

awei·ko·ma \,äwä'kōmǝ\ *n, pl* **aweikoma** *or* **aweikomas** *usu cap* **:** CAINGANG

awe-inspiring \'=,==\ *adj* **:** that arouses awe ⟨*awe-inspiring* bravery⟩ ⟨an *awe-inspiring* cathedral⟩

awe·less *or* **aw·less** \'ȯlǝs\ *adj* [ME *awelesse, awlesse, ageless*, fr. *awe, age* + *-lesse* -less] **1 :** lacking awe: **a :** FEARLESS **b :** IRREVERENT **2** *obs* **:** inspiring no awe

awe·some \'ȯsǝm\ *adj* **1 :** expressive of awe **:** deeply reverent ⟨has paid ~ tribute to British soldiery —I.L.Salomon⟩ **2 :** causing awe **:** AWE-INSPIRING, DREADFUL, AWFUL ⟨one of the most ~ jungles in the world —John Hersey⟩ — **awe·some·ly** *adv* — **awe·some·ness** *n* -ES

awestricken \'=,==\ *adj* **:** AWESTRUCK ⟨in grim despair and ~ wonder —O.E.Rölvaag⟩

awe-strike \'=,=\ *vt, archaic* **:** to strike with awe

awestruck \'=,=\ *adj* **:** filled with awe ⟨his eyes had an ~ expression —Stephen Crane⟩

aweto \ä'wed·(,)ō, ä'fe-\ *n* -S [Maori] **:** a composite structure that occurs in New Zealand, that when dried and burned yields a useful black pigment, and that is made up of the mummified body of a caterpillar killed by the attack of a parasitic ascomycetous fungus (*Cordyceps robustus*) together with the elongated fruiting body of the fungus which projects from the neck of the mummy — called also *vegetable caterpillar*

awf *var of* AUF

[1]**aw·ful** \'ȯfǝl\ *adj, sometimes* **awfuller**; *sometimes* **awfullest** [ME *awful, aweful, ageful*, fr. *awe, age* + *-ful*] **1 :** inspiring awe: as **a :** causing dread or terror **:** APPALLING ⟨I am in fear — in ~ fear — and there is no escape for me —Bram Stoker⟩ **b :** commanding reverential fear or profound respect ⟨they may hold converse with some saint, their ~, kindly friend —Nathaniel Hawthorne⟩ **c :** solemnly impressive ⟨Westminster Hall . . . had an ~ majesty, so vast, so high, and so silent —E.W.Weeks⟩ **2 :** filled with awe: as **a** *obs* **:** terror-stricken ⟨great potentates do kneel with ~ fear —Christopher Marlowe⟩ **b :** deeply respectful ⟨towards the East our ~ greetings are wafted —John Keble⟩ **3 :** extremely unpleasant, disagreeable, or objectionable — often a generalized expression of disapproval ⟨she has an ~ voice⟩ ⟨an ~ person⟩ ⟨~ manners⟩ ⟨an ~ hat⟩ **4 :** very great — used as an intensive ⟨does an ~ lot of talking⟩ ⟨took an ~ chance⟩ **syn** see FEARFUL

[2]**awful** \"\ *adv* **:** AWFULLY, VERY, EXTREMELY ⟨my papa always said you were an ~ smart boy —Willa Cather⟩ — not often in formal use

aw·ful·ly *in senses 3 & 4* 'ȯflē *or* -li *also* -fǝl-, *in senses 1 & 2* 'ȯfǝl-\ *adv* [ME, fr. *awful* + *-ly*] **1 :** in a manner that inspires awe ⟨the drawing room in which New York's most chosen company was somewhat ~ assembled —Edith Wharton⟩ **2** *archaic* **:** with a feeling of awe ⟨and timorous passed and ~ withdrew —Alexander Pope⟩ **3 :** in an unpleasant, disagreeable, or objectionable manner — often a generalized expression of disapproval ⟨he of the red nightcap now commenced snoring ~ —George Borrow⟩ **4 :** EXCEEDINGLY, EXTREMELY, VERY — an intensive ⟨an ~ hard rain⟩ ⟨thanks ~⟩

aw·ful·ness \-fǝlnǝs\ *n* -ES **:** the quality or state of being awful

AWG *abbr* American wire gauge

awheel \ǝ+\ *adv (or adj)* [[1]*a-* (as in *afoot*) + *wheel*] **:** riding (as on a bicycle or in an automobile) ⟨a concourse of citizens ~ and afoot —Winston Churchill⟩ ⟨the lure of a spring holiday ~ —Bert Pierce⟩

awhile \ǝ+\ *adv* [ME *awhile, on while*, fr. [1]*a-, on* + *while*] **:** for a time ⟨the father of these girls . . . had settled ~ in Virginia —Dixon Wecter⟩ **:** for a brief period — often used for *a while* as the object of a preposition ⟨for ~ there is silence —Lord Dunsany⟩

awhirl \ǝ+\ *adj* [[1]*a-* + *whirl*, v.] **:** in a whirl **:** WHIRLING ⟨his head ~ with fantastic schemes⟩

awin \'ȯǝn\ [ME (northern dial.) *awen* to possess, own, owe — more at OWE] *Scot var of* [1]OWN

[1]**aw·ing** \'ȯ(·)iŋ\ *pres part of* AWE

[2]**awing** \ǝ'wiŋ\ *adv (or adj)* [[1]*a-* + *wing*] **:** on the wing **:** FLYING

awi·shi·ra \,äwǝ'sherǝ\ *n, pl* **awishira** *or* **awishiras** *usu cap* [Sp *avixira*, of AmerInd origin] **1 a :** an Indian people of northeastern Peru **b :** a member of such people **2 :** the language of the Awishira people

[1]**awk** *adj* [ME *awke*] **1** *obs* **:** turned or done the wrong way **2** *obs* **:** PERVERSE **3** *obs* **:** AWKWARD, CLUMSY

[2]**awk** *or* **awkly** *adv, obs* **:** in the wrong way

awk·ward \'ȯkwǝ(r)d\ *adj* -ER/-EST [ME *awkeward* in the wrong direction, upside down, fr. *awke* turned the wrong way, left-handed (fr. ON *öfugr* turned the wrong way) + *-ward*; akin to OHG *abuh* turned the wrong way, bad, evil, OS *abuh*, L *opacus* shady, obscure, OSlav *opaky* turned backward, Arm *haka-* toward] **1 a** *obs* **:** PERVERSE, FROWARD ⟨an ~ pride in my nature —Henry Fielding⟩ **b :** ADVERSE, UNFAVORABLE ⟨with ~ winds and with sore tempests driven —Christopher Marlowe⟩ **2 a :** lacking dexterity or skill esp. in the use of the hands or of instruments **:** CLUMSY ⟨she was too ~ with a needle to make her own clothes⟩ **b :** showing the result of inexpert handling or faulty craftsmanship **:** ILL-MADE ⟨the form of writing used . . . was extremely crude and was confined chiefly to expressing thoughts by means of ~ pictures —R.W.Murray⟩ **3 a :** lacking ease, grace, or deftness of movement **:** not graceful ⟨she had large feet and her walk was ~ and ungainly⟩ **b :** appearing ill-proportioned, outsize, or poorly fitted together **:** UNGAINLY ⟨how long, tall, quick, strong, or ~ in looks he was —Carl Sandburg⟩ **4 :** lacking ease, grace, or effectiveness of expression **:** CUMBERSOME ⟨an ~ piece of writing⟩ ⟨a title which is extremely ~ in English —R.A.Hall b.1911⟩ **5 a :** lacking social grace and assurance **:** feeling or showing embarrassment **:** ill at ease ⟨he hesitated, ~ and bashful, shifted his weight from one leg to the other —Jack London⟩ **b :** causing embarrassment **:** INCONVENIENT, DIFFICULT ⟨sometimes his quick brain runs him into ~ situations —John Ennis⟩ ⟨spared her from explanations and professions which it was exceedingly ~ to give —Jane Austen⟩ **6 :** inexpertly designed, placed, or organized **:** poorly adapted for use or handling ⟨attempts to combine . . . a single picture out of these ~ and contradictory tests —Havelock Ellis⟩ ⟨the dykes and drains make these roads so very ~ —Dorothy Sayers⟩ **7 :** requiring caution **:** somewhat dangerous ⟨the guide let himself down an ~ cliff⟩

syn CLUMSY, INEPT, MALADROIT, GAUCHE, UNGAINLY, LUMBERING, GAWKY: AWKWARD, CLUMSY, INEPT, MALADROIT, and GAUCHE denote lack of grace, ease, skill, or fitness in appearance or movement, action or speech, use or function; UNGAINLY, LUMBERING, and GAWKY denote a similar lack, usu. due to cumbersome build or ill-proportioned structure. AWKWARD may apply to a person who is lacking in muscular coordination or is deficient in poise ⟨you're as *awkward*, McGovery, as a bull calf —Anthony Trollope⟩ It often implies shyness and self-consciousness ⟨I, sitting in silence, felt *awkward*; but I was too shy to break into any of the groups that seemed absorbed in their own affairs —W.S.Maugham⟩ It may apply to an object that is not easily handled or dexterously managed ⟨*awkward* round boats⟩ to a situation or action likely to cause embarrassment or discomfiture ⟨an easy and welcome solution to an otherwise *awkward* problem —W.L. Sperry⟩ or to modes of expression that are cumbersome or confused ⟨an *awkward* sentence⟩ CLUMSY may denote a person or an animal that is blundering or lacking in skill or grace and often describes one who is grotesque and clattering from awkwardness, esp. as an inherent tendency ⟨a *clumsy* bear⟩ ⟨a *clumsy* and timid horseman —W.M.Thackeray⟩ It may also denote a person or object that is heavy or unwieldy ⟨the *clumsy* machinery of the plot —T.S.Eliot⟩ ⟨a *clumsy* horse⟩ INEPT, which applies to both persons and their actions or products, is the strongest word of those here compared, for it suggests total failure ⟨an *inept* mechanic⟩ ⟨an *inept* administrator⟩

⟨an *inept* translation⟩ and carries a suggestion of futility or absurdity ⟨by what *inept* logic must we bow to our creation if it be a machine and spurn it as "unreal" if it happens to be a painting or a poem? —Lewis Mumford⟩ MALADROIT may describe remarks or actions that are out of place, ill-timed, or tasteless and that cause embarrassment or resentment, or persons responsible for them ⟨Lloyd George, though a brilliant statesman, was often a *maladroit* politician —Malcolm Thomson⟩ GAUCHE also describes a person or something he says or does and often refers to a general tendency to be ill at ease from shyness, inexperience, or lack of breeding, and to increase one's discomfiture by inappropriate acts or remarks ⟨these *gauche* characters just don't know the rules of the game —John Farrelly⟩ ⟨that shy, rather *gauche* fellow, slinking nervously about the corridors —H.J.Laski⟩ UNGAINLY indicates marked physical gracelessness often due to excessive size ⟨she had long *ungainly* limbs and was very awkward in the use of them —Anthony Trollope⟩ LUMBERING describes one that is large and ponderous, formidable when at rest and moving, if at all, with real or apparent difficulty ⟨so that his slow *lumbering* plane would not be left behind by the faster bombers —H.L.Merillat⟩ GAWKY suggests graceless proportions and the self-consciousness often attendant on such an appearance ⟨one of these abrupt, rather *gawky* women, all hands and feet —Valentine Williams⟩

awkward age *n* **:** the age of early adolescence usu. characterized by awkwardness and shyness

awk·ward·ly *adv* **:** in an awkward manner: **a :** CLUMSILY **b :** EMBARRASSINGLY

awk·ward·ness \-nəs\ *n* -ES **1 :** the quality or state of being awkward: **a :** lack of dexterity or skill **:** CLUMSINESS ⟨a puppy's ~⟩ **b :** lack of ease or grace **:** INELEGANCE ⟨the ~ of his prose style⟩ **c :** lack of composure **:** EMBARRASSMENT ⟨the silence conveyed to neither any sense of ~ —Thomas Hardy⟩ **2 :** something that is awkward ⟨conscious of these minor ~*es* and disfigurements —Geoffrey Gorer⟩

awkward squad *n* **:** a group of inept recruits undergoing special drill

awl \ˈȯl\ *n* -S [ME *al*, fr. OE *æl*; akin to OHG *āla* awl, ON *alr*, (assumed) Goth *ela* (whence Lith *yla*), Skt *ārā*] **:** a pointed instrument for marking surfaces or piercing small holes (as in leather or wood), the blade being differently shaped and pointed for different uses

1 awl, *2* sewing awl

AWL *abbr* absent with leave

awless *var of* AWELESS

awl–shaped \ˈ=,=\ *adj* **:** shaped like an awl; *specif* **:** linear and tapering to a fine point ⟨an *awl-shaped* onion leaf⟩

awl·wort \ˈȯl,wərt, -ȯrt\ *n* -S [*awl* + *wort*] **:** a small aquatic plant (*Subularia aquatica*) of the family Cruciferae with tufted awl-shaped leaves and minute white flowers

aw·mous \ˈämәs, ˈȯm-\ *n, pl* **awmous** [ME (northern dial.) *almouse, almus, awmus* — more at ALMOUS] *Scot* **:** ALMS

¹awn \ˈȯn\ *n* -S [ME *awne*, fr. OE *agen* ear of grain, of Scand origin; akin to ON *ǫgn* chaff; akin to OE *egenu* chaff, Goth *ahana*, L *agna* ear of grain, Gk *akōn* javelin, Skt *aśani* arrowhead, missile, OE *ecg* edge, sword — more at EDGE] **1 a :** one of the slender bristles that terminate the glumes or bracts of the spikelet in barley, oats, some varieties of wheat, and other grasses **b :** a small pointed process (as that which terminates the anthers in members of the genus *Vaccinium*) **2 :** one of the barbed processes on the hemipenis of a reptile

²awn \"\ *vt* -ED/-ING/-S **:** to remove the awns from

³awn \ˈȯn\ [ME (northern dial.) *awen* to possess, own, owe — more at OWE] *chiefly Scot var of* OWN

⁴awn \ˈȯn\ *vt* -ED/-ING/-S [back-formation fr. *awning*] **:** to cover with or as if with an awning ⟨this green pavilion ~*ing* the moles —Daniel Sargent⟩

awned \ˈȯnd\ *adj* [¹*awn* + *-ed*] **:** furnished with an awn **:** BEARDED

awned wheatgrass *n* **:** BEARDED WHEATGRASS

awn·er \ˈȯnә(r)\ *n* -S **:** a machine for removing awns from grain

awn grass *n* **:** a tufted grass (*Chrysopogon aciculatus*) of tropical Asia and Pacific Islands with sharp-pointed seeds that penetrate clothing and sheep's wool

aw·ning \ˈȯniŋ, ˈän-, -nēŋ\ *n* -S [origin unknown] **1 :** a usu. canvas rooflike cover extended over or before any place as a shelter from the sun, rain, or wind (as over the deck of a ship or slanting outward before a window) **2 :** a shelter resembling an awning

awning cloth *or* **awning stripe** *n* **:** cloth suitable for awnings; *specif* **:** a heavy cotton duck or canvas with printed, painted, or woven stripes of bright colors

awning deck *n* **:** a light deck extending over the main deck from stem to stern — called also *hurricane deck*

aw·ninged \-ŋd\ *adj* **:** covered with an awning

awning window *n* **:** a window consisting of several top-hinged sections arranged in a vertical series, operated by one or more control devices that swing the bottom edges of the sections outward, and designed esp. to admit air while excluding rain

awning window

awn·less \ˈȯnləs\ *adj* **:** without awns

awnless bromegrass *n* **:** a drought-resistant perennial bromegrass (*Bromus inermis*) with awns lacking or very short that spreads by creeping rhizomes, is native to Europe, and is cultivated for forage and hay

awn·let \ˈȯnlәt\ *n* -S [*awn* + *-let*] **:** a small awn

awny \ˈȯnē, -i\ *adj* [¹*awn* + *-y*] **:** having awns **:** BEARDED

awoke *past of* AWAKE

awoken *past part of* AWAKE

¹awol \ˈā,wȯl, ˌā,dәbәl(,)yü,ō'el — *the first is prob more freq for the form "awol", the second for the form "AWOL"*\ *abbr or adj (or adv), often cap A & W & O & L* [*a*bsent *w*ithout *l*eave] **:** absent without leave ⟨an ~ private returning to barracks —Nelson Algren⟩ ⟨had gone *AWOL* from the British hospitals to get back into the fight —H.H.Martin⟩

²awol \"\ *n* -S *often cap A & W & O & L* **:** one who is absent without leave ⟨most of these *AWOLs* are soldiers on their first furlough —*Infantry Jour.*⟩

awork \ә+\ *adv (or adj)* [ME, fr. ¹*a-* + *work*, n.] **:** at work **:** in an active state

awry \әˈrī\ *adv (or adj)* [ME *on wry*, fr. *on* + *wry*] **1 :** turned or twisted toward one side **:** OBLIQUELY, OBLIQUE **:** not straight **:** ASKEW ⟨a dissipated-looking youth with a gorgeous red necktie all ~ —G.K.Chesterton⟩ **2 :** out of the right, expected, or hoped-for course **:** wide of the mark **:** WRONG, AMISS ⟨after three years of schooling in New York something went ~ in his education —S.H.Adams⟩

ax- *or* **axo-** *comb form* [ISV, fr. Gk *axōn* axle, axis — more at AXIS] **1 :** axis ⟨*axophyte*⟩ **2 :** axis cylinder ⟨*axite*⟩ ⟨*axodendrite*⟩

¹ax *or* **axe** \ˈaks\ *n, pl* **axes** [ME, fr. OE *æx, æces, acus*: akin to OHG *ackus, acchus* ax, ON *øx*, Goth *aqizi*, L *ascia*, Gk *axinē*, and perh. to OE *ecg* edge, sword — more at EDGE] **1 a :** a cutting tool or implement that consists of a relatively heavy edged head fixed to a handle, the edge or edges being parallel to the handle so as to be suited for striking, and that is used esp. for felling trees, chopping and splitting wood, and hewing timber **2 :** a hammer with a sharp edge for dressing or spalling stone **:** AXHAMMER **3 :** removal from office or release from employment **:** DISMISSAL, DISCHARGE — usu. used with *the* ⟨one of the leading candidates for the ~ when and if the expected purge comes —John Dean⟩ ⟨boys who had got the ~ —John McNulty⟩ — **ax to grind :** a selfish end to gain **:** an ulterior purpose to further

axes: *1* common ax; *2* double-bitted ax; *3* broadax; *4* section of 3; *5* fireman's ax

²ax \"\ *or* **axe** *vt* **axed; axed; axing; axes 1 a :** to shape, dress, or trim with an ax ⟨~ stone⟩ ⟨~ bricks⟩ **b :** to chop, cut, split, or sever with an ax ⟨~ branches from a tree⟩ **2 :** to relieve of office or employment **:** DISMISS, DISCHARGE ⟨columnists and correspondents were ~*ed* —*Time*⟩ **3 :** to put an end to, curtail, or impair ⟨congressmen who want to ~ the subsidy program —J.C.Cort⟩

³ax \"\ *vb* -ED/-ING/-ES [ME *axen* — more at ASK] *dial* **:** ASK

ax *abbr* **1** axiom **2** axis

axbreaker *or* **axebreaker** \ˈ=,==\ *n* -S **1 :** an Australian tree (*Notelaea longifolia*) with very hard wood **2 :** QUEBRACHO 1b

¹axe *var of* AX

²axe \ˈaks\ *n* -S [MF, fr. L *axis* — more at AXIS] *archaic* **:** AXIS

ax·el \ˈaksәl\ *n* -S *sometimes cap* [after *Axel* Paulsen *fl ab* 1890, its inventor] *figure skating* **:** a jump from the outer forward edge of one skate with 1½ turns taken in the air and a return to the outer backward edge of the other skate

axeman *var of* AXMAN

axen·ic \(ˈ)āˈzenik, -zēn-\ *adj* [²*a-* + *xen-* + *-ic*] **:** STERILE — used esp. of animals isolated from all other living things ⟨~ worms⟩ or of their environment ⟨~ conditions⟩

axes *pl of* AXIS *or of* AX, *pres 3d sing of* AX

axes of coordinates \ˈak,sēz-\ **1 :** two intersecting straight lines used as reference lines in plane Cartesian geometry **2 :** the three straight lines having a common point that are the intersections of the three coordinate planes of reference in three-dimensional Cartesian geometry

ax–grinder *or* **axe–grinder** \ˈ=,==\ *n* **:** one that has an ax to grind

ax–grinding *or* **axe–grinding** \ˈ=,==\ *n* **:** working for an ulterior purpose or toward a selfish end ⟨fulfills the . . . aims of its author with a minimum of *ax-grinding* —A.C.Danto⟩

axhammer \ˈ=,==\ *n* **:** an ax having two cutting edges or one cutting edge and one hammer face and used for dressing or spalling the rougher kinds of stone

axhead \ˈ=,=\ *n* **:** the head of an ax

axi- *comb form* [L, axle, axis, fr. *axis* — more at AXIS] **1 :** axis ⟨*axiform*⟩ **2 :** axis cylinder ⟨*axilemma*⟩

ax·i·al \ˈaksēәl\ *or* **ax·al** \-ksәl\ *adj* [*axi-, ax-* + *-al*] **1 a :** of or relating to an axis **b :** having the characteristics of or resembling an axis **2 a :** around an axis **:** in the direction of the axis **:** on or along the axis **b :** extending in a direction essentially parallel to the main axis of a cyclohexane or similar cyclic structure or characterized by bonds extending in this manner — distinguished from *equatorial* ⟨~ bonds⟩ ⟨~ hydrogen atoms⟩ — **ax·i·al·ly** \-ēәlē, -li\ *adv*

axial angle *n* **1 :** the angle between the two optic axes of a biaxial mineral **2 :** the angle between an axis of a plant and one of its appendages (as between a stem and a branch) — compare ABAXIAL, ADAXIAL

axial elements *n* **:** the angles between the crystallographic axes and the ratios of the unit-cell dimensions parallel to the axes of a crystal

axial feather *n* **:** a small feather between the primary and secondary wing feathers of some birds

axial filament *n* **:** a central often contractile filament of a flagellum **:** AXONEME

axial–flow \ˈ===,=\ *adj* **:** having the fluid or gas flowing parallel to the axis ⟨*axial-flow* turbine⟩ ⟨*axial-flow* pump⟩ — compare RADIAL-FLOW

axial gradient *n* **:** GRADIENT 4

ax·i·al·i·ty \ˌaksēˈalәdē\ *n* -ES **:** the quality or state of being axial

axial pencil *n* **:** a system of planes intersecting on a straight line

axial plane *n* **:** the imaginary plane bisecting the angle between the limbs of an anticline or syncline

axial skeleton *n* **:** the skeleton of the trunk and head — compare APPENDICULAR

ax·i·ate \ˈaksēәt, -ē,āt\ *adj* [*axi-* + *-ate*] **:** AXIAL

axiate gradient *n* **:** GRADIENT 4

ax·i·a·tion \ˌaksēˈāshәn\ *n* -S [*axi-* + *-ation*] **:** the development of polarity in an embryo or its parts

ax·if·era \akˈsifәrә\ [NL, fr. *axi-* + *-fera* (neut. pl. of *-fer*)] *syn of* GORGONACEA

ax·il \ˈaksәl, -(,)sil\ *n* -S [NL *axilla*, fr. L, armpit — more at AXIS] **:** the distal usu. upper angle or point of divergence between a branch or leaf and the axis from which it arises

ax·ile \ˈak,sīl\ *adj* [*ax-* + *-ile*] **:** belonging to or situated in the axis ⟨~ placentation⟩

ax·il·la \akˈsilә\ *n, pl* **axil·lae** \-i(,)lē, -i,lī\ *or* **axillas** [L] **1 :** the cavity beneath the junction of the arm or anterior appendage and shoulder or pectoral girdle containing the axillary artery and vein, a part of the brachial nerve plexus, many lymph nodes, and fat and areolar tissue **:** ARMPIT **2 :** SHOULDER

ax·il·lant \ˈaksәlәnt, (ˈ)akˈsilәnt\ *adj* [ISV *axil* + *-ant*] **:** forming, subtending, or growing in an axil

ax·il·lar \akˈsilә(r), ˈaksәl-\ *n* -S [*axilla* + *-ar*] **:** an axillary part (as a vein, nerve, or feather)

¹ax·il·lary \ˈaksә,lerē, -ri *also (esp in sense 1)* (ˈ)akˈsilәr-\ *also* **ax·il·lar** \ˈaksәl-*usu* (ˈ)akˈsilә(r) *in sense 1 and* ˈaksәl- *in sense 2*\ *adj* [prob. fr. F *axillaire*, fr. MF, fr. L *axilla* + MF *-aire* -ary] **1 :** of, near, or relating to the axilla ⟨an ~ nerve⟩ ⟨an ~ feather⟩ ⟨an ~ plate⟩ **2** [*axil* + *-ary, -ar*] **:** situated in, growing from, or related to an axil ⟨~ buds⟩

²axillary \"\ *n* -ES **:** AXILLAR: as **a :** one of a group of feathers arising from the axilla and closing the space between flight feathers and body when a bird is flying **b :** one of the small lateral sclerites of the thorax with which the wing of an insect articulates and flexes

axillary artery *n* **:** the part of the main artery of the arm that lies in the axilla and that is continuous with the subclavian above and the brachial below

axillary fossa *n* **:** AXILLA 1

axillary gland *n* **:** any of the lymph nodes of the axilla

axillary nerve *n* **:** a large nerve arising from the posterior cord of the brachial plexus and supplying the deltoid and teres minor muscles and the skin of the shoulder

axillary scale *n* **:** ACCESSORY SCALE

axillary vein *n* **:** the large vein passing through the axilla continuous with the basilic below and the subclavian above

ax·ine \ˈak,sīn\ *adj* [NL ²*Axis* + E *-ine*] **:** relating to or resembling the axis deer

axing *pres part of* AXE *or of* AX

ax·i·nite \ˈaksә,nīt\ *n* -S [F, fr. Gk *axinē* axhead, ax + F *-ite*; fr. its ax-shaped crystals] **:** a mineral $Ca_2(MnFe)Al_2BSi_4O_{15}OH$, consisting of borosilicate of aluminum and calcium with varying amounts of iron and manganese commonly in brown glassy sharp-edged triclinic crystals (hardness 6.5–7, sp. gr. 3.27–3.29)

ax·in·o·man·cy \ˈaksәnә,mansē, akˈsin-\ *n* -ES [L *axinomantia*, fr. (assumed) Gk *axinomanteia*, fr. Gk *axino-* (fr. *axinē* axhead, ax) + *manteia* divination — more at AX, -MANCY] **:** divination by means of the movement of an ax placed on a post

ax·i·o·lite \ˈaksēә,līt\ *n* -S [ISV *axi-* + *-o-* + *-lite*; orig. formed as G *axiolit*] **:** a spherulitic aggregate rock with grouping about a line or axis — **ax·i·o·lit·ic** \ˌ===ˈlid·ik\ *adj*

ax·i·o·log·i·cal \ˌ===ˈläjәkәl\ *adj* **1 :** of or relating to axiology ⟨~ investigations⟩ **2 a :** based on or involving intrinsic or fundamental values ⟨an ~ absolutism⟩ ⟨the ~ crisis⟩ **b :** making moral obligations dependent on values ⟨~ ethical theories⟩ — contrasted with *deontological* — **ax·i·o·log·i·cal·ly** \-jәk(ә)lē\ *adv*

ax·i·ol·o·gist \ˌaksēˈälәjәst\ *n* -S **1 :** a student of or specialist in axiology **2 :** a philosopher advocating an axiological theory of ethics — contrasted with *deontologist*

ax·i·ol·o·gy \-ˈälәjē\ *n* -ES [ISV *axio-* (fr. Gk *axios* worth, worthy) + *-logy*] **:** the theory or study of values, primarily of intrinsic values (as those in ethics, aesthetics, and religion) but also of instrumental values (as those in economics) particularly with reference to the manner in which they can be known or experienced, their nature and kinds, and their ontological status

ax·i·om \ˈaksēәm\ *n* -S [L *axioma*, fr. Gk *axiōma*, fr. *axioun* to think worthy, think fit, fr. *axios* worth, worthy, fit; akin to Gk *agein* to lead, drive, weigh as much as — more at AGENT] **1 a :** a proposition, principle, rule, or maxim that has found general acceptance or is thought worthy thereof whether by virtue of a claim to intrinsic merit ⟨the ~*s* of wisdom⟩ or on the basis of an appeal to self-evidence ⟨the ~*s* of euclidean geometry⟩ **b (1)** *Baconianism* **:** an empirical rule or generalization based on experience **(2)** *Kantianism* **:** an immediately certain synthetic a priori proposition **2 :** a self-consistent statement about the primitive terms or undefinable objects that form the basis for discourse **:** POSTULATE ⟨the statement that there is one and only one straight line passing through two given points is an ~⟩ **syn** see PRINCIPLE

ax·i·o·ma·ta me·dia \ˌaksēˈōmәdәˈmēdēә, -sēˈäm-\ *n pl* [NL, middle principles] **:** the general principles that are above simple empirical laws yet inferior to the highest generalizations or to those that are taken to be fundamental **:** middle principles

ax·i·o·mat·ic \ˌaksēәˈmad·ik, -matik, -ēk\ *also* **ax·i·o·mat·i·cal** \-ōkәl, -ēk-\ *adj* [MGk *axiōmatikos*, fr. Gk, dignified, honorable, fr. *axiōmat-, axiōma* honor, axiom + *-ikos* -ic] **:** of or relating to an axiom or axioms: as **a :** taken for granted **:** SELF-EVIDENT ⟨an ~ truth⟩ **b :** APHORISTIC ⟨~ wisdom⟩ **c :** POSTULATIONAL, HYPOTHETICO-DEDUCTIVE — **ax·i·o·mat·i·cal·ly** \-ōk(ә)lē, -ēk-, -li\ *adv*

ax·i·o·mat·i·cist \-d·әsәst, -tәsә-\ *n* -S **:** a student of or a specialist in axiomatics

ax·i·o·mat·ics \-d·iks, -tiks, -ēks\ *n pl but sing in constr* **1 :** a set of axioms **:** an axiomatized system **2 :** the study or a theory of axioms or axiom systems

ax·i·om·a·ti·za·tion \ˌaksē,ämәdәˈzāshәn, -mә,tīˈz-\ *n* -S **:** the act or process of axiomatizing — compare FORMALIZATION

ax·i·om·a·tize \ˌaksēˈämә,tīz\ *vt* -ED/-ING/-S [*axiomatic* + *-ize*] **1 :** to make axiomatic **2 :** to reduce to axioms or an axiom system

axiom of parallels : PARALLEL POSTULATE

axiom system *n* **:** a set of axioms together with formal rules for derivation of theorems — compare TRANSFORMATION RULE

¹ax·is \ˈaksәs\ *n, pl* **ax·es** \-k,sēz\ [L, axis, axle; akin to OE *eax* axis, axle, OHG *ahsa*, ON *öxull* axle, L *ala* wing, *axilla* armpit, Gk *axōn* axle, axis, Skt *akṣa* axle, axis, L *agere* to drive — more at AGENT] **1 a :** a straight line about which a body or a 3-dimensional figure rotates or may be supposed to rotate ⟨the earth's ~⟩ **b :** a straight line with respect to which a body, figure, or system of points is either radially or bilaterally symmetrical ⟨the ~ of a cone⟩ **c :** a straight line about which a line, curve, or plane figure is conceived to revolve in generating a solid of revolution ⟨the ~ of a hyperboloid⟩ **d :** one of the reference lines of a coordinate system ⟨the X ~ of a rectangular coordinate system⟩ **2** *archaic* **:** the axle of a wheel **3 a (1) :** the second vertebra of the neck of the higher vertebrates that is prolonged anteriorly within the foramen of the first vertebra and united with the odontoid process which serves as a pivot for the atlas and head to turn upon — called also *epistropheus* **(2) :** the first vertebra of amphibians **b :** any of various central, fundamental, or axial parts ⟨the cerebrospinal ~⟩ ⟨the skeletal ~⟩ **c :** AXILLA **4 :** the median lobe of a trilobite **5 :** the stem of a plant **:** the longitudinal support on which organs are arranged often including also the root, esp. a taproot **:** the hypothetical central line of any body or organ ⟨the ~ of a stem, petiole, or inflorescence⟩ **6 :** one of several imaginary lines assumed in describing the positions of the planes by which a crystal is bounded, the positions of atoms in the structure of the crystal, and the directions associated with vectorial and tensorial physical properties **7 :** a main line of direction, motion, growth, or extension ⟨the ~ of a city⟩ **8 a :** a line following the crest of a ridge or mountain range or the bottom of a depression in the earth's surface: as **(1) :** the crest line of an anticline ⟨anticlinal ~⟩ **(2) :** the trough line of a syncline ⟨synclinal ~⟩ **b :** the average direction of current at flood or ebb tide ⟨flood ~⟩ ⟨ebb ~⟩ **9 a** *in painting and sculpture* **:** an implied line through a composition to which elements in the composition are referred ⟨fruit and flowers arranged about a diagonal ~⟩ **b :** a line actually drawn and used as the basis of measurements in an architectural or other working drawing **10 :** any of three fixed lines of reference in an aircraft, usu. centroidal and mutually perpendicular, (1) one being the principal longitudinal line in the plane of symmetry, (2) one being perpendicular to this in the plane of symmetry, (3) one being perpendicular to the other two — called also respectively (1) *longitudinal axis*, (2) *normal axis*, (3) *lateral axis* **11** *dancing* **a :** the part of the body around which movements center and revolve **b :** the person, object, or imaginary line around which the dancers and dance patterns evolve or revolve **12 a :** an agreement entered into by two or more powers to demonstrate their solidarity of interest and to insure a common front and mutual support in foreign policies ⟨the Nazi-Fascist ~⟩ **b :** the countries adhering to such an agreement ⟨in the hope that either China or the London-Washington *Axis* . . . would listen —*Time*⟩ **13 :** any agreement of two or more in a common objective **:** PARTNERSHIP, ALLIANCE ⟨this unhealthy ~ . . . made it so difficult to bring any real democratic reform to the graft-ridden docks —Budd Schulberg⟩

²axis \"\ *n* [NL, fr. L, a wild animal of India] **1** *also* **axis deer** -ES **:** a deer (*Axis axis*) of India and other parts of southern Asia having rusine antlers and white-spotted body **2** *cap* **:** a genus of Cervidae containing the axis and hog deer

axis cylinder *n* **1 :** the central portion of a nerve fiber visibly divided into central and peripheral zones **2 :** the essential protoplasmic core of a medullated nerve fiber **:** AXON

axis cylinder process *n* **:** AXON

ax·ised \ˈaksәst\ *adj* **:** having an axis

axis of abscissas *in plane Cartesian coordinates* **:** the axis parallel to which abscissas are measured

axis of a curve : a straight line that bisects at right angles a system of parallel chords and divides the curve into two symmetrical portions (as in the parabola which has one such axis, the ellipse which has two, or the circle which has an infinite number)

axis of a lens : the common axis of symmetry of all the lens surfaces — compare OPTICAL AXIS

axis of an airfoil : a line perpendicular to an airfoil section

axis of ordinates *in plane Cartesian coordinates* **:** the axis parallel to which ordinates are measured

axis of rotation : the straight line through all fixed points of a rotating rigid body around which all other points of the body move in circles

axis of symmetry : the line about which a geometrical figure or drawing is symmetric

ax·i·symmetric \ˌaksә+\ *also* **ax·i·symmetrical** \" +\ *adj* [*axi-* + *symmetric, symmetrical*] **:** symmetric in respect to an axis

ax·ite \ˈak,sīt\ *n* -S [*ax-* + *-ite*] **1 :** AXON **2 :** any of the terminal branches of an axon

ax·le \ˈaksәl\ *n* -S [ME *axel-* (as in *axeltre* axletree) — more at AXLETREE] **1** *archaic* **:** AXIS ⟨the ~ of the earth⟩ **2 a :** the pin, bar, or shaft on which or with which a wheel or pair of wheels revolves — see DEAD AXLE, FLOATING AXLE, LIVE AXLE **b (1) :** the spindle of an axletree **(2) :** AXLETREE

axle bar *n* **:** an iron bar serving as an axletree

axle box *n* **1 :** a bushing in the hub of a wheel through which the axle passes **2** *Brit* **:** JOURNAL BOX

ax·led \ˈaksәld\ *adj* **:** having an axle

axle load *n* **:** the load of a vehicle applied through the wheels at both ends of an axle and equaling twice the wheel load

ax·le·tree \ˈaksәl,trē, -ltri\ *n* -S [ME *axeltre*, fr. ON *öxultrē*, fr. *öxull* axle + *trē* beam, tree — more at AXIS, TREE] **1 :** a fixed bar or beam having bearings at its ends upon which the wheels (as of a carriage, cart, or wagon) revolve **2** *obs* **:** AXIS

ax·man *or* **axe·man** \ˈaksmәn, -,man, -maa(ә)n\ *n, pl* **axmen** *or* **axemen :** one that wields an ax; *specif* **:** a worker who uses an ax to chop trees and logs for firewood or to clear away trees and brush

ax·master *or* **axe·master** \ˈaks + ,-\ *n* -S **1 :** BLACK IRONWOOD 1 **2 :** QUEBRACHO 1

ax·min·ster \ˈak,sminztә(r), -n(t)st-\ *n* -S *usu cap, often attrib* [fr. *Axminster*, England, its place of manufacture] **:** a machine-woven carpet having pile tufts of many types and colors inserted mechanically to form a variety of textures and patterns

axo- — see AX-

ax·o·den·drite \ˌaksō'denˌdrīt\ *n* -s [*ax-* + *dendrite*] **:** a nonmedullated process branching laterally from a nerve-cell axon

ax·og·a·my \ak'sägəmē\ *n* -ES [*ax-* + *-gamy*] **:** the condition of bearing sexual organs on a leafy stem

ax·oid \'akˌsȯid\ *or* **ax·oi·de·an** \(')ak¦sȯidēən\ *adj* [ISV *ax-* + *-oid*] **:** of or relating to the axis vertebra

ax·o·lotl \'aksəˌlätᵊl, -ätᵊl\ *n* -s [Nahuatl, lit., water doll, toy, fr. *atl* water + *xolotl* doll, toy, mythological personality] **:** any of several larval salamanders of the genus *Ambystoma* (as *A. tigrinum*) found in the mountain lakes of Mexico and the western U.S. ordinarily living and breeding in the larval condition but being capable when the pond it inhabits dries up of gradually losing the gills and fins while beginning to breathe air at the surface and of eventually emerging as an adult salamander — compare NEOTENY; see SIREDON

ax·om·e·ter \ak'sämәd·ə(r)\ *n* -s [ISV *ax-* + *-meter*] **:** an instrument used to locate the position of optical axes; *esp* **:** one used to adjust a pair of spectacles properly with respect to the axes of the eyes

ax·on \'akˌsän\ *also* **ax·one** \'akˌsōn\ *n* -s [NL *axon*, fr. Gk *axōn* axis, vertebra] **:** a nerve-cell process that is typically single and long, that terminates in short branches relatively far from the cell body, and that as a rule except in certain sensory neurones conducts impulses away from the cell body — called also *axis cylinder process, axite, neuraxis, neurite*

ax·o·nal \'aksənəl\ *or* **ax·on·ic** \(')ak¦sänik\ *adj* [NL *axon* + E *-al* or *-ic*] **:** of or relating to an axon

ax·o·neme \'aksəˌnēm\ *n* -s [*ax-* + *-neme*] **:** a central fibril or bundle of fibrils in a flagellum

axon hillock *n* **:** the prominence on a nerve-cell body from which an axon arises

ax·o·nia \ak'sōnēə\ *n pl, usu cap* [NL, fr. Gk *axōn* axis + NL *-ia*] **:** organisms having a distinct axis or axes — opposed to *Anaxonia*

axono- *comb form* [ISV, fr. Gk *axon-*, *axōn* axle, axis — more at AXIS] **:** axis ⟨*axono*metry⟩ ⟨*Axono*phora⟩

ax·o·nol·i·pa \aksə'näləpə\ *n pl, cap* [NL, fr. *axono-* + *-lipa* (irreg. fr. Gk *leipein* to leave, be lacking) — more at LOAN] **:** a suborder of Graptoloidea including all nondendroid forms lacking an axial support — **ax·o·nol·i·pous** \¦==¦=əpəs\ *adj*

ax·o·no·met·ric projection \¦aksə(ˌ)nō¦metrik-\ *n* [*axono-* + *-metric*] **:** the representation of objects by means of their perpendicular projections on a single plane (as the plane of the paper) so placed that a rectangular solid projected upon it would show three faces — compare OBLIQUE PROJECTION

ax·o·noph·o·ra \ˌaksə'näf(ə)rə\ *n pl, cap* [NL, fr. *axono-* + *-phora*] **:** a suborder of Graptoloidea in which the colony has a virgula — **ax·on·o·phore** \ak'sänəˌfō(ə)r\ *adj* — **ax·o·noph·o·rous** \¦aksə¦näf(ə)rəs\ *adj*

ax·on·o·pus \ak'sänəpəs\ *n, cap* [NL, fr. *axono-* + *-pus*] **:** a genus of American grasses with oblong one-flowered spikelets in one-sided spikelike racemes — see CARPET GRASS

ax·o·nost \'aksəˌnäst\ *n* -s [NL *axon* + E *-ost*] **:** any of the interspinal bones supporting the dorsal and anal fins of a fish

ax·o·plasm \-ˌplazəm\ *n* -s [ISV *ax-* + *-plasm*] **:** the protoplasm of an axon usu. visibly distinct from that of a nerve-cell body or a dendrite

ax·o·po·di·um \ˌaksə'pōdēəm\ *also* **ax·o·pod** \'aksəˌpäd\ *n, pl* **axopo·dia** \-'pōdēə\ *also* **axopods** [NL *axopodium*, fr. *ax-* + *-podium*] **:** a semipermanent pseudopodium that consists of an axial rod surrounded by an ectoplasmic sheath and that is typically present in Radiolaria and Heliozoa

ax·o·style \'aksə + ˌ-\ *n* -s [*ax-* + *-style*] **:** an axial rod present in many parasitic flagellates that is variously regarded as locomotor or supporting in function

ax·seed \'akˌsēd\ *n* **:** a European vetchlike herb (*Coronilla varia*) naturalized in the eastern U.S. and having umbels of pink-and-white flowers and sharp-angled pods — called also *crown vetch*

¹ax·um·ite *or* **ak·sum·ite** \'aksəˌmīt\ *adj, usu cap* [*Axum, Aksum*, ancient city of Ethiopia + E *-ite*] **:** of or relating to the ancient city of Aksum

²axumite *or* **aksumite** \"\ *n* -s *usu cap* **1 :** one of the Axumite people **2 :** the language of the Axumite people

ax·unge \'akˌsənj\ *n* -s [MF & LL; MF *axunge*, fr. LL *axungia*, fr. L axle grease, fr. *axis* axle + *-ungia* (fr. *ungere, unguere* to grease, anoint) — more at AXIS, OINTMENT] **:** fat or grease usu. of pigs or of geese; *esp* **:** lard prepared for medicinal use

¹ay *var of* AYE

²ay \'ī *sometimes* 'ā\ *interj* [MF *aymi* ay me] — usu. used with following *me* to express sorrow or regret ⟨~ me! I fondly dream —John Milton⟩

aya·ca·hui·te \ˌīyəkə'wēdˌā\ *or* **ayacahuite pine** *n* -s [Sp, fr. Nahuatl *ayacahuitl*, fr. *ayatl*, a kind of cloth + *cuahuitl* tree] **1 :** a large Mexican pine tree (*Pinus ayacahuite*) with long needles and extremely large yellowish red cones **2 :** the wood of ayacahuite

ayah \'īə, 'äyə\ *n* -s [Hindi *āyā, āya* (also in other languages of India), fr. Pg *aia* governess, nursemaid, fr. L *avia* grandmother] *India* **:** a native nurse or maid ⟨morning walks to the Bombay fruit market with my ~ —*N.Y.Times*⟩

aya·huas·co \ˌīyə'wä(ˌ)skō, -ˌskə\ *n* -s [AmerSp *ayahuasca*, fr. Quechua *ayawáskha*] **:** a So. American vine (*Banisteria caapi*) of the family Malpighiaceae having roots that yield a drink which produces a delirious psychosis that alternates with prolonged hallucinations and dreams

aya·pa·na \ˌīyə'pänə\ *n* -s [Sp & Pg; Sp *ayapaná*, fr. Pg *aiapana, aiapaina*, fr. Tupi *ayapana*] **:** a low spreading herbaceous Brazilian shrub (*Eupatorium aya-pana*) whose long narrow leaves are used to make a mildly stimulating decoction resembling tea

¹aye *also* **ay** \'ā, *in Brit dial* " *or* 'əi *or* 'ai\ *adv* [ME *aye, ai, agg*, fr. ON *ei*; akin to OE *ā, ō* always, OHG *eo, io*, Goth *aiws* time, eternity, L *aevum* age, lifetime, Gk *aiōn* age, eon, Skt *āyus* life] **:** for all time or for an indefinite time **:** FOREVER, EVER, ALWAYS, CONTINUALLY ⟨love that will ~ endure —W.S.Gilbert⟩ ⟨I ~ thought the quotations from him . . . most appetizing —John Buchan⟩ ⟨he's no a great one for speaking, but he ~ likes to be doing something —A.T.Cluness⟩

²aye *also* **ay** \'ī\ *adv* [earlier *I*, perh. fr. ME *yie*, alter. of *ye, ya* yes — more at YEA] **:** YES, CERTAINLY ⟨~, I mind him well —John Buchan⟩ — used as an affirmative response esp. in viva-voce voting, nautical language, and dialect speech; used reduplicatively in nautical language in response to an order or command ⟨*aye, aye*, sir means "I understand, sir, and I will do it"⟩

³aye *also* **ay** \'ī\ *n, pl* **ayes 1 :** an affirmative vote ⟨cast an ~ for all administration measures⟩ **2 :** one who votes affirmatively ⟨the ~s have it⟩

aye-aye \'īˌī\ *n* -s [F, fr. Malagasy *aiay*, of imit. origin] **:** a nocturnal lemur (*Daubentonia madagascariensis*) found in Madagascar that has incisor teeth like those of a rodent and long fingers with sharp nails

ayer·za's disease \ə'yerzəz-\ *n, usu cap A* [after Abel *Ayerza* †1918 Argentine physician] **:** a complex of symptoms marked esp. by cyanosis, dyspnea, polycythemia, and sclerosis of the pulmonary artery

ay·in *or* **'ay·in** *or* **ain** \'īən\ *n* -s [Heb *'ayin*] **1 :** the 16th letter of the Hebrew alphabet — symbol ע; see ALPHABET table **2 :** the letter of the Phoenician or of any of various other Semitic alphabets corresponding to Hebrew ayin

ayles·bury \'ālzbərē, -brē, -i\ *n* -s *usu cap* [fr. *Aylesbury*, England] **:** a breed of large white ducks somewhat similar to the Pekins

ayl·lu \'ī(ˌ)lü\ *n* -s [Quechua *áyllu*] **1 :** a sib or clan that constituted the basic socioeconomic unit of Inca society **2 :** a present-day Peruvian highland community of extended families that owns some land in common and that serves as an administrative unit

ay·ma·ra *also* **ai·ma·ra** \ˌīmə¦rä\ *n, pl* **aymara** *or* **aymaras** *also* **aimara** *or* **aimares** *usu cap* [Sp *aymará, aimará*, of AmerInd origin] **1 a :** an Indian people of Bolivia and Peru **b :** a member of such people **2 a :** the language of the Aymara people **b :** a language family of the Kechumaran stock comprising Aymara and formerly held to be an independent stock

aymara deformation *n, usu cap A* **:** a conoidal or oxycephalic head produced by binding the head of an infant with bands or with frontal pads and a band

ay·ma·ran \ˌīmə'rän\ *n* -s *usu cap* **:** AYMARA 2b

'ayn *or* **'ain** *or* **ain** \'īn, 'ān\ *n* -s [Ar *'ayn*] **:** the 18th letter of the Arabic alphabet — see ALPHABET table

ayont \ə'yänt\ *prep* [¹*a-* + *yont*] *dial* **:** BEYOND

ayous \ā'yüs\ *n* -ES [F, of African origin; akin to Yoruba *a²wu¹sa³* (*Monodora brevipes*)] **:** OBECHE

ayr *see* ¹AYRSHIRE\ *adj, usu cap* [fr. *Ayr*, burgh in Scotland] **1 :** of or from the burgh of Ayr, Scotland **:** of the kind or style prevalent in Ayr **2 :** AYRSHIRE

ayre *archaic var of* AIR 4

¹ayr·shire \'a(ə)(ə)rˌshi(ə)r, 'e(ə)r-; 'a(a)əˌshiə(r, 'eəˌ-; *also* -ˌshə(r); *sometimes by* r-*dissimilation* 'aˌshi(ə)r *or* 'aəˌ- *or* 'aiˌ-\ *or* **ayr** \'a(ə)(ə)r, 'e(ə)r, 'a(a)ə\ *adj, usu cap* [fr. *Ayrshire* or *Ayr*, county in Scotland] **:** of or from the county of Ayr, Scotland **:** of the kind or style prevalent in the county of Ayr

²ayrshire \"\ *n* -s *usu cap* **:** an animal of a breed of hardy dairy cattle that originated in Ayr, that vary in color from white to red or brown, and that are esp. adapted to market milk production

ayrshire rose *n, usu cap A* **:** any of certain formerly popular double often scentless garden roses derived from the species rose (*Rosa arvensis*)

ayr stone \'a(ə)(ə)r-, 'e(ə)r-\ *n, usu cap A* [fr. *Ayr*, Scotland] **:** a stone used as a whetstone and for surfacing and polishing

ayr·ton shunt \'a(ə)rtᵊn-, 'e(ə)r-\ *n, usu cap A* [after William E. *Ayrton* †1908 Eng. electrical engineer and inventor] **:** a shunt used to increase the range of a galvanometer — called also *universal shunt*

ay·thya \ī'thīə\ *n, cap* [NL, fr. Gk *aithyia*, a kind of diving bird] **:** a genus of diving ducks including the canvasback, redhead, pochard, and related forms

ayu \'ä(ˌ)yü, 'ī(ˌ)(y)ü\ *also* **ai** \'ī\ *n* -s [Jap *ayu, ai*] **:** a small salmonlike anadromous fish (*Plecoglossus altivelis*) of Japan that is highly esteemed as a food fish — called also *sweetfish*

ayun·ta·mien·to \īˌyün(ˌ)tämē'entō\ *n* -s [Sp, fr. OSp, fr. *ayuntar* to join, unite (fr. *a* to — fr. L *ad* — + *yuntar, juntar* to join, fr. L *junctus*, past part. of *jungere* to join) + *-miento* -ment (fr. L *-mentum*) — more at AT, YOKE] **1 :** the municipal council or governing body of a town or city in Spain or the former Spanish colonies **2 :** a town hall in Spain or the former Spanish colonies

ayur·ve·da \'äyərˌvādə\ *n* -s *usu cap* [Skt *āyurveda*, fr. *āyur* life, vital power + *veda* knowledge] **:** the traditional Hindu system of medicine based largely on homeopathy and naturopathy — **ayur·ve·dic** \-'dik\ *adj, usu cap*

ay·yub·id \ī'yübəd\ *also* **ay·yub·ite** \-üˌbīt\ *n* -s *usu cap* [*Ayyub* ibn -Shadhi †1173 Kurd general, father of the founder of the dynasty + E *-id* (patronymic suffix) or *-ite*] **:** a member of a Muslim dynasty founded in 1171 the separate branches of which flourished in Egypt, Syria, Palestine, Mesopotamia, and southern Arabia until the middle of the 13th century

az- *or* **azo-** *comb form* [ISV, fr. *azote*] **1 :** containing nitrogen ⟨*azo*litmin⟩ **2** *azo-* **:** containing the bivalent group —N=N— composed of doubly bonded nitrogen atoms united usu. on both sides to carbon ⟨*azo*methane $CH_3N{=}NCH_3$⟩ — compare DIAZ- 1

az *abbr* **1** azimuth **2** azure **3** *often cap A* nitrogen

aza- *or* **az-** *comb form* [ISV, fr. *az-* + *-a-*] **:** containing nitrogen in place of carbon, usu. the group —NH— for the group —CH_2— or a single nitrogen atom =N— for the group =CH— ⟨*aza*cyanine⟩ ⟨*aza*phenanthrene⟩ — compare OXA-, THIA-

aza·cyanine \ˌazə + \ *or* **azacyanine dye** *n* [*aza-* + *cyanine*] **:** any of a class of dyes differing from the cyanines in that the chain joining the heterocyclic rings contains one or more nitrogen atoms

azad·i·rach·ta \əˌzadə'raktə\ *n* -s [NL, fr. Per *āzād dirakht*, lit., free or noble tree] **:** MARGOSA

aza·fran \ˌäsə'frän, '==ˌ=\ *n* -s [Sp *azafrán*, fr. Ar *al-za'farān* the saffron] **:** SAFFRON

aza·lea \ə'zālyə *also* -lēə\ *n* [NL, fr. Gk, fem. of *azaleos* dry; fr. the supposition that it grows well in dry ground; akin to Czech *ozd* malt kiln, Gk *azein* to parch — more at ARDOR] **1** *cap, in some classifications* **:** a genus of shrubs or trees with deciduous leaves and funnel-shaped flowers now usu. considered a subgenus of *Rhododendron* **2** -s **:** any plant of the genus or subgenus *Azalea* **3** -s **:** a grayish red that is bluer than bois de rose, bluer, stronger, and slightly darker than Pompeian red, and stronger than appleblossom

aza·lea·mum \-(ˌ)məm\ *n* -s [*azalea* + chrysanthe*mum*] **:** any of various profusely flowering dwarf chrysanthemums

azan·de \ə'zandē\ *n, pl* **azande** *or* **azandes** *usu cap* **:** ZANDE

aza·ra's dog \ə'zärəz-\ *or* **azara's fox** *n, usu cap A* [trans. of NL *Canis Azarae*, after Félix de *Azara* †1821 Sp. soldier and naturalist] **:** a foxlike mammal (*Dusicyon gymnocercus* or *D. azarae*) of eastern and southern So. America

az·a·role \'azəˌrōl\ *n* -s [F *azerole*, fr. Sp *acerola*, fr. Ar *az-zu'rūr* the azarole] **1 :** the fruit of a shrub (*Crataegus azarolus*) of southern Europe **2 :** the shrub that bears azaroles

azed·a·rach \ə'zedəˌrak\ *n* -s [F *azédarac*, fr. Per *āzād dirakht*, lit., free or noble tree] **1 :** CHINABERRY 2 **2 :** the bark of the roots of the azedarach, formerly used as an emetic and anthelmintic

az·e·la·ic acid \¦azə¦lāik-\ *n* [*az-* + Gk *elaion* olive oil + E *-ic* — more at OIL] **:** a crystalline dicarboxylic acid HOOC$(CH_2)_7$COOH made usu. by the oxidation of oleic acid or the acids from castor oil (as with nitric acid or ozone) and used in the form of derivatives esp. in lubricants and as plasticizers

az·e·late \'azᵊlˌāt, -ˌət\ *n* -s [ISV *azelaic* + *-ate*] **:** a salt or ester of azelaic acid

aze·o·trope \ā'zēəˌtrōp\ *n* -s [ISV ²*a-* + Gk *zeo-* (fr. *zein* to boil) + *-trope* — more at YEAST] **:** a liquid mixture that is characterized by a constant minimum or maximum boiling point which is lower or higher than that of any of the components and that distills without change in composition

aze·o·trop·ic \¦āˌzēə¦träpik\ *adj* [ISV *azeotrope* + *-ic*] **1 :** being an azeotrope **:** relating to or having the characteristics of an azeotrope **2 :** involving an azeotrope or components that can form an azeotrope ⟨~ separation⟩

azeotropic distillation *n* **:** distillation involving the presence of a compound that forms an azeotrope with at least one of the components of a liquid mixture which can thereby be more readily separated because of the resulting increase in the difference between the volatilities of the components of the mixture

aze·ot·ro·pism \ˌāzē'ä·trəˌpizəm\ *n* -s [ISV *azeotrope* + *-ism*] **:** AZEOTROPY

aze·ot·ro·py \ˌāzē'ä·trəpē\ *n* -ES [ISV *azeotrope* + *-y*] **:** the phenomenon of being an azeotrope

azer·bai·ja·ni \ˌazə(r)ˌbī'jänē, ˌäz-\ *also* **azer·bai·ja·nese** \-ˌ¦bījə¦nēz, -ēs\ *or* **azer·bai·ja·ni·an** \-ˌbī'jänēən\ *n, pl* **azerbaijani** *or* **azerbaijanis** *also* **azerbaijanese** *or* **azerbaijanians** *usu cap* [fr. *Azerbaijan*, region of southwestern Asia comprised of Azerbaijan, province of Iran, and Azerbaidzhan, republic of the U.S.S.R.] **1 :** a member of a Turkic-speaking people of the Azerbaidzhan Soviet Socialist Republic or the province of Azerbaijan in northwestern Iran **2 :** the Turkic language of the Azerbaijani

az·ha·roth \ˌäz(h)ə'rōt, az-, -ōth,-ōs *also* ä'zō(ˌ)rōs\ *or* **az·ha·rot** \-ə'rōt,-ə'rōs\ *n pl, often cap* [Heb *azhārōth* warnings, exhortations] **:** Jewish liturgical poems containing exhortations to obedience to the religious commandments in the Torah

az·ide \'aˌzīd, 'ā-, -ˌzəd\ *n* -s [ISV *az-* + *-ide*] **:** a compound containing the azido group combined with an element or radical **:** HYDRAZOATE ⟨potassium ~ KN_3⟩ ⟨acid ~s⟩

az·i·do \'azə(ˌ)dō\ *adj* [*azido-*] **:** relating to or containing the group N_3

azido- \"\ *comb form* [ISV, fr. *azide* + *-o-*] **:** containing the univalent group N_3 derived from hydrazoic acid ⟨*azido*acetic acid⟩

azil·ian \ə'zēlyən, -zil-, -lēən\ *adj, usu cap* [Le Mas d' *Azil*, dept. Ariège, France, its type station + E *-ian*] **:** of or belonging to an early Mesolithic culture found primarily in France and characterized by stone and bone implements of degenerate Magdalenian type and esp. by pebbles painted with lines, dots, and geometric figures

az·i·muth \'azəməth\ *n* -s [ME *azimut, azimuth*, fr. (assumed) ML, fr. Ar *as-sumūt* the azimuth, pl. of *as-samt* the way, direction] **1 a :** an arc of the horizon measured between a fixed point (as true north) and the vertical circle passing through the center of an object, usu. in astronomy and navigation being measured clockwise from the north point through 360 degrees and in surveying clockwise from the south point ⟨the ~ of a star⟩ **b :** horizontal direction expressed as the angular distance between the direction of a fixed point (as the observer's heading) and the direction of the object **:** BEARING 7c **2 a :** the angle that the plane of polarization of polarized light makes with a specified reference plane **b :** a vectorial angle (as that defining the position of a particle in an orbit or of a point in an image field as measured around the instrumental axis) **3 :** a line or course **:** DIRECTION ⟨the ~ we must take to confirm the victories already won —F.R.Fogle⟩

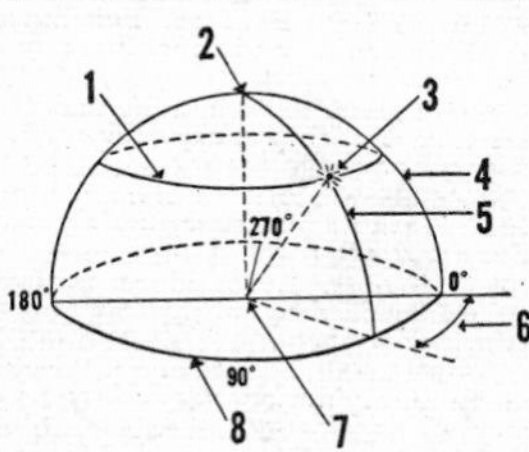

azimuth 1a: *1* almucantar, *2* zenith, *3* star, *4* meridian passing through north, *5* arc of vertical circle, *6* azimuth, *7* observer, *8* horizon

az·i·muth·al \¦azə¦məthəl, -myüth-\ *adj* **:** of or relating to azimuth **:** in azimuth — **az·i·muth·al·ly** \-əlē\ *adv*

azimuthal equidistant projection *n* **:** a map projection of the surface of the earth so centered at any given point that a straight line radiating from the center to any other point represents the shortest distance and can be measured to scale

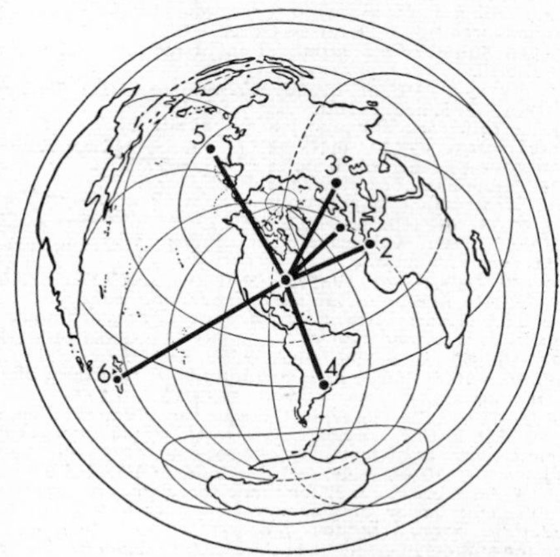

azimuthal equidistant projection centered on Washington, D.C.: *1* London, *2* Algiers, *3* Moscow, *4* Buenos Aires, *5* Tokyo, *6* Auckland

azimuthal quantum number *n* **:** an integer associated with the angular momentum of an atomic electron in any one of its possible stationary states, each state corresponding to a different integer — compare PRINCIPAL QUANTUM NUMBER, RADIAL QUANTUM NUMBER

azimuth circle *n* **1 :** one of the great circles of the celestial sphere intersecting each other in the zenith and nadir — called also *vertical circle;* compare MERIDIAN 2 **2 :** a horizontal graduated circle for indicating azimuth (as one having sight vanes and screens and attached to a compass to show magnetic azimuths or one having a telescope for accurate measurement of differences of azimuth)

azimuth compass *n* **:** a compass resembling the mariner's compass and having vertical sights used for taking the magnetic azimuth of a celestial body

azimuth dial *n* **:** a horizontal sundial whose gnomon is at right angles to the plane of the horizon

az·ine \'aˌzēn, 'ā-, -ˌzən\ *n* -s [ISV *az-* + *-ine*] **1 a :** any of a large class of organic compounds that is characterized by a 6-membered ring containing two or more atoms of nitrogen or at least one atom of nitrogen and one other hetero atom (as oxygen or sulfur) and that is subdivided according to the kind and number of hetero atoms (as diazines, triazines, oxazines, thiazines); *esp* **:** a paradiazine or analogous oxazine or thiazine **b :** AZINE DYE **2 :** a compound of the general formula RCH=NN=CHR or $R_2C{=}NN{=}CR_2$ formed by the action of hydrazine on aldehydes or ketones

azine dye *also* **azine** *n* -s **:** any of a class of acid quinonoid-type dyes containing a paradiazine ring fused to one or more aromatic rings and used esp. in dyeing wool, silk, paper, and leather and in coloring fats, oils, lacquers, and plastics; *also* **:** an oxazine or thiazine dye

az·lactone \az + \ *n* -s [*az-* + *lactone*] **:** a lactone of an unsaturated nitrogenous hydroxy acid (as the enol form $C_6H_5C(OH){=}NCH_2COOH$ of hippuric acid), some lactones being useful in the synthesis of alpha-amino acids

az·lon \'azˌlän\ *n* -s [*az-* + *-lon* (as in *nylon*)] **:** any of various textile fibers made from protein sources (as zein and casein)

azo \'a(ˌ)zō\ *adj* [*az-*] **:** relating to or containing the group —N=N— united at both ends to carbon usu. in two univalent organic radicals, esp. aryl radicals with the formation of solid compounds varying in color from yellow to red to violet and blue — see COUPLE *vi* 2b, DISAZO, TRISAZO; compare DIAZO

azo- — see AZ-

az·o·benzene \ˌazō, ˌā +\ *n* -s [ISV *az-* + *benzene*] **:** an orange-red crystalline compound $C_6H_5N{=}NC_6H_5$ obtained by reducing nitrobenzene and used as an insecticide esp. for spider mites in greenhouses

azo dye *n* **:** any of a very large class of dyes characterized by the presence of one or more azo groups, made by coupling an aromatic diazonium compound with a coupling component (as a phenol, an aromatic amine, or a pyrazolone), and noted for their versatility, being applied by various processes in dyeing or coloring a wide range of materials (as textile fibers, leather, plastics, foods, drugs, and cosmetics) and being used in making pigments and diazotypes — see DYE table I

az·o·fi·ca·tion \ˌazōfə'kāshən, ˌāz-\ *n* -s [*az-* + *-fication*] **:** nonsymbiotic fixation of atmospheric nitrogen in soil by bacteria

¹azo·ic \(')ā¦zōik, ə'z-\ *adj* [²*a-* + *-zoic*] **:** without life; *specif* **:** of or relating to the part of geologic time that antedates life — compare ARCHEAN

²azo·ic \(')a¦zōik *also* (')ā¦-, ə¦-\ *adj* [ISV *az-* + *-ic*; prob. orig. formed as F AZOIQUE] **:** AZO — now usu. restricted to insoluble dyes formed on the fiber

azoic dye *also* **azoic** *n* -s **:** any of a group of water-insoluble azo dyes formed by coupling of the components on the fiber — called also *ice color, ingrain dye;* see DYE table I

az·o·im·ide \ˌazō'iˌmīd, ˌāz-, -məd\ *also* **az·o·im·id** \-'iməd\ *n* -s [ISV *az-* + *imide;* orig. formed as G *azoimid*] **:** HYDRAZOIC ACID

az·ole \'aˌzōl, 'ā-\ *n* -s [ISV *az-* + *-ole*] **1 :** any of a large class of organic compounds that is characterized by a 5-membered ring containing two or more hetero atoms at least one of which is nitrogen and that is subdivided analogously to the azines (as diazoles, triazoles, thiazoles) **2 :** PYRROLE

az·o·lit·min \ˌazō'litmən, ˌā-\ *n* -s [ISV *az-* + *litmus* + *-in*] **:** a dark red nitrogenous coloring matter obtained from litmus and used as an acid-base indicator

azol·la \ə'zälə\ *n, cap* [NL] **:** a genus of minute water ferns (family Salviniaceae) having a sporophyte consisting of pinnately branching stems with small distichous 2-lobed leaves

az·o·methine \ˌazō, ˌā +\ *n* -s [*az-* + *methine*] **1 :** METHYLENIMINE **2** *or* **azomethine compound :** any of a class of compounds regarded as derivatives of methylenimine and characterized by the grouping −CH=N− or >C=N− **:** SCHIFF BASE — used esp. of dyes important in color photography

azon \'āˌzōn, -än\ *or* **azon bomb** *n* -s *often cap A* [*az*imuth *only*] **:** an aerial bomb that can be guided to the left or right by radio control — compare RAZON

azon·al \(')ā+\ *adj* [[2]*a-* + *zonal*] **:** not arranged in zones

azonal soil *n* **1 :** a major soil group often classified as a category of the highest rank and embracing soils that lack well-developed horizons because of immaturity or other factors that have prevented their development — compare INTRAZONAL SOIL, ZONAL SOIL **2 :** any soil belonging to the azonal soil group (as the rocky soils on steep slopes)

azo·osper·mia \āˌzōə'spərmēə, əˌz-\ *n* -s [NL, fr. Gk *azōos* lifeless (fr. *a-* [2]a- + *-zōos*, fr. *zōē* life) + NL *-spermia* — more at QUICK] **:** inability to produce spermatozoa — compare ASPERMIA

azo·protein \¦a(ˌ)zō+\ *n* -s [*az-* + *protein*] **:** any of various compounds made by coupling a protein (as serum albumin) with a diazotized amine (as histamine or sulfanilamide), and sometimes used as synthetic antigens

[1]**azor·e·an** \(')ā¦zōrēən, -ȯr- *also* ə'z-\ *adj, usu cap* [*Azore*s, islands in the No. Atlantic + E *-an*] **1 :** of, relating to, or characteristic of the Azores **2 :** of, relating to, or characteristic of Azoreans

[2]**azorean** \"\ *n* -s *cap* **:** a native or inhabitant of the Azores

azo ru·bine \ˌazō'rüˌbēn, ˌāz-, -ˌbən\ *n, usu cap A&R* [*az-* + L *rub*eus red + E *-ine* — more at RUBY] **:** a mordant acid azo dye that dyes wool bluish red — called also *carmoisin;* see DYE table I (under *Acid Red 14*)

az·o·sulfamide *also* **az·o·sulphamide** \ˌazō, ˌā- +\ *n* -s [*az-* + *sulfamide*] **:** a dark red crystalline azo compound $C_{18}H_{14}N_4Na_2O_{10}S_3$ of the sulfa class having antibacterial effect similar to that of sulfanilamide

az·ote \'aˌzōt, ə'z-\ *n* -s [F, fr. *a-* [2]a- (fr. Gk) + *-zote* (irreg. fr. Gk *zōē* life); fr. the observation that it cannot take the place of air in supporting life — more at QUICK] **:** NITROGEN

azo·tea \ˌazō'tāə\ *n* -s [Sp, fr. Ar *as- suṭayḥ* the azotea] **:** a flat roof or platform on the top of a house or other building

az·o·te·mia *also* **az·o·tae·mia** \ˌazə'tēmēə\ *n* -s [NL, fr. ISV *azote* + NL *-emia, -aemia*] **:** an excess of nitrogenous bodies in the blood as a result of kidney insufficiency associated with kidney disease or secondary to disease in other organs — compare AZOTURIA — **az·o·tem·ic** \¦==¦temik, -tē-\ *adj*

az·oth \'aˌzȯth, -ōth,-äth\ *n* -s [Ar *az-zā'ūq* the mercury] **1 :** mercury regarded by alchemists as the first principle of metals **2 :** the universal remedy of Paracelsus

azot·ic \(')a¦zäd·ik, ə'z-\ *adj* [F *azotique*, fr. *azote* + *-ique* -ic] **:** of or relating to azote **:** NITROGENOUS, NITRIC ⟨~ gas⟩ ⟨~ acid⟩

azo·to·bac·ter \a'zōd·əˌbaktə(r), ə'z-\ *n* [NL, fr. ISV *azote* + NL *-o-* + *-bacter*] **1** *cap* **:** a genus of large flagellated gram-negative rod-shaped or spherical nonsymbiotic bacteria (order Eubacteriales) occurring in soil and sewage that fix atmospheric nitrogen in the presence of carbohydrates and derive growth energy from oxidation of carbohydrates **2** -s *sometimes cap* **:** a bacterium of the genus *Azotobacter*

az·o·tom·e·ter \ˌazə'tämәd·ə(r)\ *n* -s [ISV *azote* + *-o-* + *-meter;* orig. formed in G] **:** NITROMETER

az·o·tu·ria \ˌazə'tu̇rēə, -ə·'tyu̇-\ *n* -s [NL, fr. ISV *azote* + NL *-uria*] **:** an excess of urea or other nitrogenous substances in the urine; *specif* **:** an acute disease of horses marked by passage of dark urine rich in nitrogenous compounds, stiffening and muscular paralysis, profuse sweating, and collapse that occurs in animals brought back to work after being heavily fed and inadequately exercised for several days — compare AZOTEMIA

az·oxy \(')a'zäksē, (')ā-\ *adj* [*azoxy-*] **:** relating to or containing the group −N(O)=N−

azoxy- *comb form* [ISV, fr. *az-* + *oxy-*] **:** containing the bivalent group −N(O)=N− composed of two nitrogen atoms and one oxygen atom united usu. on both sides to carbon ⟨*azoxy*naphthalene $C_{10}H_7N(O)=NC_{10}H_7$⟩

az·oxy·benzene \ˌa(ˌ)zäksē, ˌā- +\ *n* -s [ISV *azoxy-* + *benzene*] **:** a yellow crystalline compound $C_6H_5N(O)=NC_6H_5$ formed by reduction of nitrobenzene and yielding azobenzene on further reduction

azo yellow *n* **:** an acid dye — see DYE table I (under *Acid Yellow 63*)

az·ra·el \'azrāˌel\ *n* -s *usu cap* [Ar *'Azrā'īl*, fr. Heb *'Ăzar'ēl*, lit., God has helped] **:** the angel of death in Jewish and Islamic thought who watches over the dying and separates the soul from the body

az·tec \'azˌtek *sometimes* 'aˌstek\ *n* -s [Sp *azteca*, fr. Nahuatl, pl. of *aztecatl*, fr. *Aztlan*, *Aztatlan*, their legendary place of origin, lit., near the cranes (fr. *azta* — pl. of *aztatl* crane — + *tlan* near) + *-tecatl* (suffix denoting origin)] **1** *usu cap* **a :** a Nahuatl people that founded the Mexican empire conquered by Cortes in 1519 **b** (1) **:** a member of such people (2) **:** a member of any Nahuatl people or of any people under Aztec influence **2** *usu cap* **a :** the language of the Aztec people **b :** NAHUATL **3** *often cap* **:** a moderate to strong yellowish brown that is lighter and slightly redder than tobacco brown and slightly redder and darker than clay — called also *Indian tan*

az·te·ca \az'tākə, a'stā-\ *n, pl* **azteca** *or* **aztecas** *usu cap* [Sp] **:** AZTEC 1

az·tec·an \'azˌtekən *sometimes* 'aˌste-\ *adj, usu cap* **:** of or relating to the Aztec people or their language

aztec lily *n, usu cap A* **:** JACOBEAN LILY

aztec marigold *n, usu cap A* **:** AFRICAN MARIGOLD

aztec maroon *n, often cap A* **:** a grayish purplish red that is redder and deeper than average rose plum and redder and duller than tourmaline pink or daphne pink

azu·lene \'azhəˌlēn\ *n* -s [ISV *azul-* (fr. Sp *azul* blue, fr. OSp *azur, azul*) + *-ene* — more at AZURE] **1 a :** a liquid hydrocarbon $C_{15}H_{18}$ of intense blue color found in some essential oils (as oil of cubebs) and in lignite tar **b :** any of various blue to violet or green hydrocarbons closely related chemically to this hydrocarbon and occurring naturally in essential oils or formed from various colorless naturally occurring sesquiterpenes **2 :** a synthetic blue crystalline unsaturated bicyclic hydrocarbon $C_{10}H_8$ that resembles the isomeric naphthalene in some properties but is more active chemically and that is the parent compound of the azulenes; cyclo-penta-cyclo-heptene

azu·lite \-ˌlīt\ *n* -s [Sp *azul* blue + E *-ite*] **:** a mineral consisting of translucent pale blue smithsonite often found in Arizona and Greece in masses weighing over 20 pounds

[1]**azure** \'azhə(r), 'aizh-, *rare in stand speech in US at least* 'āzh-\ *n* -s [ME *asur*, fr. OF *azur*, prob. fr. OSp *azur, azul*, alter. of Ar *lāzaward, lāzuward* lapis lazuli, blue, fr. Per *lāzhuward*] **1** *archaic* **:** LAPIS LAZULI **2 :** the heraldic color blue **3 a :** the blue color of the clear sky **b :** any blue somewhat resembling that of the sky **4 :** the unclouded sky ⟨above, the crystal ~, perfect, pale —F.T.Palgrave⟩

[2]**azure** \"\ *adj* [ME *asur*, fr. *asur*, n.] **1 :** of the heraldic color blue **2 :** resembling the color of the unclouded sky **3 :** resembling the unclouded sky **:** CLOUDLESS, CLEAR **4 :** composed of horizontal parallel lines (as a tooled or stamped design on a book cover)

[3]**azure** \"\ *vt* -ED/-ING/-S **:** to make blue in color ⟨morning up the eastern stair marches, *azuring* the air —A.E.Housman⟩

azu·rean \¦azhə¦rēən; ə'zhu̇r-, a'-\ *adj* [*azure* + *-ean* (as in *cerulean*)] **:** [2]AZURE 2

azure blue *n* **1 :** [1]AZURE 3 **2 :** any of several blue pigments: as **a :** COBALT BLUE 1a **b :** SMALT 1 **3** *often cap A & B* **:** any of several dyes — see DYE table I (under *Acid Blue*)

azured *adj* **:** [2]AZURE 2

azure stone *n* **1 :** LAPIS LAZULI **2 :** LAZULITE

azur·ite \'azhəˌrīt\ *n* -s [F, fr. *azur* azure + *-ite*] **1 :** a mineral $Cu_3(OH)_2(CO_3)_2$ consisting of blue basic carbonate of copper, occurring in monoclinic crystals, massive, and in earthy form, being an ore of copper, and formerly used as a pigment (hardness 3.5–4, sp. gr. 3.77–3.83) — compare MALACHITE **2 :** a semiprecious stone derived from azurite when compact

azurite blue *n* **:** a moderate blue that is greener and duller than Dresden blue or average copen, greener and paler than smalt or bluebird, and greener and slightly duller than pompadour — called also *air blue, Armenian stone, bice blue, blue ashes, blue bice, blue verditer, cendre, ceramic, chessylite blue, copper blue, Hungarian blue, Lambert's blue, lime blue, mineral blue, mountain blue, stone blue, verditer blue*

az·ur·malachite \ˌazhər +\ *n* -s [*azur*ite + *malachite*] **:** azurite mixed with malachite, usu. occurring massive and concentrically banded, and used as ornamental stone

azury \'azhərē\ *adj* [[2]*azure* + *-y*] **:** azure or tinted with azure

azygo- *comb form* [ISV, fr. Gk *azygos*] **:** azygous ⟨*azygo*spore⟩

azygomatous \¦ā +\ *adj* [[2]*a-* + *zygomatous*] **:** without zygomatic arches

azy·go·spore \ā'zīgōˌspō(ə)r, ə'z-\ *n* -s [*azygo-* + *spore*] **:** a reproductive body found in certain fungi (class Phycomycetes) and in some algae that resembles a zygospore but is formed without gametic fusion

azygote \ā, ə +\ *n* -s [[2]*a-* + *zygote*] **:** an individual produced by haploid parthenogenesis

[1]**az·y·gous** *or* **az·y·gos** \'azəgəs\ *adj* [NL *azygos*, fr. Gk, fr. *a-* [2]a- + *-zygos* (fr. *zygon* yoke) — more at YOKE] **:** not one of a pair **:** ODD, SINGLE ⟨the ~ muscle of the uvula⟩

[2]**azygous** *or* **azygos** \"\ *n* -ES **:** an azygous part

azygous vein *n* **:** either of two large veins connecting the inferior and superior venae cavae, taking the place of these vessels in that part of the chest occupied by the heart and in obstructions of the inferior vena cava being the chief means of venous circulation — see HEMIAZYGOUS VEIN

azyme \'aˌzīm\ *also* **azym** \-zəm\ *n* -s [LL *azyma*, fr. L, neut. pl. of *azymus* unleavened, fr. Gk *azymos*, fr. *a-* [2]a- + *-zymos* (fr. *zymē* leaven); prob. akin to L *jus* broth — more at JUICE] **:** unleavened bread: **a :** such bread eaten by the Jews at the Passover **b :** such bread consecrated by Christians of the Western church in celebrating the Eucharist

az·zaz·a·me \ə'zazəmē\ *or* **az·zaz·i·mah** \-mə\ *n* -s *usu cap* [Ar *'Azāzamiyah*, colloq. Ar *'Az(z)āzme*] **1 :** an Arab people living chiefly in the Sinai peninsula but found scattered throughout the Arab world **2 :** a member of the Azzazame people

1b \ˈbē\ n, pl b's or bs \ˈbēz\ often cap, often attrib 1 a : the second letter of the English alphabet b : an instance of this letter printed, written, or otherwise represented c : a speech counterpart of orthographic b (as b in bib, baby, dabbed, or German bühne) 2 a : the keynote of B major or B minor b : the tone B 3 : a printer's type, a stamp, or some other instrument for reproducing the letter b 4 : someone or something arbitrarily or conveniently designated b esp. as the second in order or class ⟨A deeded land to B⟩ 5 a : a grade assigned by a teacher or examiner rating a student's work as good, better than average, but short of excellent ⟨the typical student begins at D, moves up steadily, and is doing C or B work at the finish —Philip Marsh⟩ b : one graded or rated with a B ⟨a B student⟩ c : a motion picture produced on a small budget and usu. shown as a supplement to the main feature of a program 6 : something having the shape of the capital letter B

2b abbr, often cap 1 bachelor 2 bacillus 3 back 4 bag 5 baht 6 balboa 7 bale 8 ball 9 ban 10 [ML bancus] bench 11 band 12 bar 13 barge 14 baron 15 base 16 bass 17 basso 18 bat 19 bath 20 battery 21 battle 22 Baumé 23 bay 24 bearing 25 [L beata (fem.) & beatus (masc.) — more at BEATIFY] blessed 26 before 27 bel 28 Bible 29 bid 30 bishop 31 bitch 32 black 33 blend 34 blue 35 boatswain 36 bogach 37 boils at 38 bolivar 39 boliviano 40 bomber 41 bond 42 book 43 born 44 bottom 45 bowled 46 brass 47 breadth 48 breezing 49 brick 50 brightness 51 British 52 British thermal unit 53 broadcast 54 broken 55 brotherhood 56 bulb 57 bulletin 58 bye

3b symbol, cap 1 boron 2 magnetic induction

ba \ˈbä\ n -s [alternate transliteration of Egypt bꜣ] : the living, immortal, eternal, and ultimately divine soul in Egyptian religious belief represented as a bird with a human head and believed to leave the body at death and return eventually to revivify the body if it is preserved

BA abbr or n -s Bachelor of Arts

Ba symbol barium

1baa or **ba** \ˈba, ˈbaa, ˈbä, ˈbȧ\ n -s [imit.] : the bleat of a sheep

2baa or **ba** \"\ vi -ED/-ING/-S : to cry baa : BLEAT ⟨the black goats and the dirty, gray-white sheep began slowly to amble down the slope, ~ing —Nora B. Kubie⟩

baal \ˈbā(ə)l\ n, pl **baa·lim** \ˈbā(ə)ləm, ˈbāə,lim\ or **baals** \-(ə)lz\ [Heb baʽal lord, name of a divinity] 1 often cap : any of a multitude of Canaanite and Phoenician chief deities worshiped individually rather than collectively at localized sanctuaries and commonly distinguished by name according to area or function (as Baal-peor, Baal of Peor) 2 : a false god : IDOL

baal–ha·bos var of BALABOS

baal·ism \ˈbā(ə),lizəm\ n -s often cap 1 : the worship of Baal 2 : IDOLATRY

baal·ist·ic \ˌbāəˌlistik, (ˈ)bāˌl-\ adj, often cap : of or relating to baalism

baal·ite \ˈbā(ə),līt\ n -s often cap : an adherent of or believer in baalism

baal·ize \ˈbā(ə),līz\ vi -ED/-ING/-S : to convert to or influence toward the worship of Baal or to some other form of idolatry

baal ko·re \bälˈkō(,)rā\ n [Heb baʽal qōrē, lit., reading master] : the person (as the cantor) who reads the weekly excerpt from the Torah during synagogue services

baal·shem also **bal·shem** \bälˈshäm\ n, often cap [Heb baʽal shēm one who possesses or works through the (divine) name] : one believed among Jews (as earlier Polish Jews) to work wonders by the use of the name of God

baas \ˈbäs, ˈbȧs\ n -ES [Afrik, fr. MD baes — more at BOSS] Africa : MASTER, BOSS — often used as a form of address

1ba·ba or **baba au rhum** \ˈbä,bäōˈrəm, F bȧbȧōrȯm\ n, pl **babas** or **babas au rhum** \-äzō-,-ȧzō-\ [baba fr. F, fr. Pol, lit., old woman; baba au rhum fr. F, baba with rum — more at BABUSHKA] : a rich yeast-leavened usu. fruited cake soaked in a rum and sugar syrup before serving

2ba·ba \ˈbä,bä\ n -s [Malay, colonial-born] in the southern part of the Malay peninsula : a Chinese or sometimes a European or Eurasian male born in Malacca, Penang, or the crown colony of Singapore

3baba \"\ n -s [Hindi bābā father, prob. fr. Ar; fr. the use in India of parent terms when addressing children] India : BABY, CHILD

ba·ba·coo·te \ˌbäbəˈküd·ē\ also **ba·ba·ko·to** \-kōd·(,)ō\ n -s [Malagasy babakoto] : a large Madagascan short-tailed lemur (Indri indri)

ba·ba·la \ˈbäbə,lä, -ˌlə\ n -s [Afrik] : PEARL MILLET

babasco var of BARBASCO

ba·bas·su \ˌbäbəˈsü\ n -s [Pg babaçú] : a tall pinnate-leaved palm (Orbignya speciosa or O. martiana) of northeastern Brazil with hard-shelled nuts yielding a valuable oil

babassu oil \"-\ also **ba·ba·çu oil** \"\ n : a fatty oil obtained from kernels of babassu nuts that is similar in properties and uses to coconut oil

ba·bay·lan or **ba·bai·lan** \ˌbäbīˈlän\ or **ba·bal·yan** \-bəlˈyän\ or **ba·ba·li·an** \-bəlēˈän\ n, pl **ba·bay·la·nes** \-ˈlˌnäs\ [of Philippine origin; akin to Tagbanuwa babalyan, fr. balyan mediumship, esoteric religious skill] in central and southern Philippines : a pagan priest, priestess, or medium

1bab·bitt also **bab·bit** \ˈbabət, usu -əd·+V\ n -s sometimes cap [(babbitt) metal] 1 : BABBITT METAL 2 : a babbitt-metal lining for a bearing

2babbitt \"\ also **babbit** adj, sometimes cap : made of or relating to babbitt metal

3babbitt \"\ vt -ED/-ING/-S : to line or furnish with babbitt metal

4babbitt \"\ also **babbit** n -s usu cap [after George F. Babbitt, stereotype Am. businessman portrayed in the novel Babbitt (1922) by Sinclair Lewis †1951 Am. novelist] : a person (as a business or professional man) who conforms unthinkingly and complacently to prevailing middle-class standards of respectability, who makes a cult of material success, and who is contemptuous of or incapable of appreciating artistic or intellectual values ⟨he was repelled by the prosperous and patronizing Babbitts⟩ — **bab·bitt·i·cal** \(ˈ)baˈbid·əkəl\ adj, usu cap — **bab·bitty** \ˈbabəd·ē\ adj, usu cap

bab·bitt·er \-əd·ə(r)\ n -s [3babbitt + -er] : a worker who applies babbitt metal to bearings or other surfaces

babbitting jig n [fr. pres. part. of 3babbitt] : a molding box in which bearings or bearing brasses are made while being babbitted

bab·bitt·ism \-əd·,izəm\ n -s often cap [George F. Babbitt + E -ism] : BABBITTRY

babbitt metal also **babbit metal** n, sometimes cap B [after Isaac Babbitt †1862 Am. inventor] : either of two alloys used for lining bearings: a : a tin-base alloy; esp : one containing 2 to 8 percent copper and 5 to 15 percent antimony b : a lead-base alloy containing 1 to 10 percent tin and 10 to 15 percent antimony with or without some arsenic

bab·bitt·ry also **bab·bit·ry** \-ətrē\ n -ES often cap [George F. Babbitt + E -ry] : the attitudes, beliefs, and conduct characteristic of Babbitts ⟨the obvious ~ and middle-class conventions are always being challenged on some level by the individual —Elizabeth Janeway⟩

bab·bla·tive \ˈbabləd·iv\ adj [1babble + -ative (as in talkative)] : GARRULOUS

1bab·ble \ˈbabəl\ vb **babbled**; **babbled**; **babbling** \-b(ə)liŋ\ **babbles** [ME babelen; prob. of imit. origin like ME babe, babie baby, LG babbeln to babble, ON babba, L babulus babbler, Gk barbaros foreign, LGk babazein to speak inarticulately, Skt balbalā stammering sound, barbara stammering] vi 1 a : to utter meaningless sounds as though talking ⟨a baby babbling in his crib⟩ b : to talk foolishly : PRATTLE ⟨~ about his responsibilities⟩ c : to talk excessively : CHATTER ⟨babbling about their plans for the coming holidays —Mabel C. Widdemer⟩ 2 a : to make sounds as though babbling ⟨the babbling of a mountain stream⟩ ⟨birds babbling in the hedge⟩ b of a hound : to bay before picking up the scent ~ vt 1 : to utter in an incoherent, inane, or meaningless repetitious manner ⟨why did the red-haired man ~ those excuses —Max Beerbohm⟩ 2 : to reveal (as a secret) by talking too freely or thoughtlessly ⟨before we could stop him he had babbled our plans to the group⟩

2babble \"\ n -s [ME bable, fr. babelen] 1 : foolish or idle talk : CHATTER, NONSENSE ⟨making ~ at an afternoon tea⟩ 2 : continuous meaningless vocal sounds ⟨the ~ of a baby in the next room⟩ : a murmur or a continuity of confused sounds ⟨the ~ of four or more voices going on at once —G.A.Miller⟩ ⟨the ~ of birds⟩; specif : the unwanted disturbing sounds in a telephone circuit resulting from cross-talk interference from a large number of other active circuits

bab·ble·ment \-bəlmənt\ n -s : 2BABBLE

bab·bler \ˈbab(ə)lə(r)\ n -s : one that babbles; specif : any of numerous birds esp. of the family Timaliidae having loud chattering notes

babbling n -s [ME babeling, fr. gerund of babelen] : idle talk or chatter : BABBLE ⟨her early love letters are almost childish ~s —Britain Today⟩

babbling·ly adv : in a babbling manner

babbling thrush n : any of several thrushlike babblers

bab·bly \ˈbab(ə)lē\ adj : CHATTERING, GARRULOUS

bab·by \ˈbabē\ dial var of BABY

bab·cock test \ˈbab,käk-\ n, usu cap B [after Stephen M. Babcock †1931 Am. agricultural chemist] : a test for determining the butter value of milk and milk products by treating with acid and whirling by means of a centrifugal apparatus in a bottle with a long graduated neck, the fat being brought to the top and its amount being read off directly

babe \ˈbāb\ n -s [ME — more at BABBLE] 1 a : INFANT, BABY ⟨a ~ in arms⟩ ⟨the book is not milk for ~s —Thomas Pyles⟩ b slang : GIRL, WOMAN ⟨the blond ~ who helps the gangster —P.T.Hartung⟩ 2 obs : DOLL 3 : an innocent, inexperienced, or ignorant person ⟨in the matter of handling money, he was just a ~⟩ — **babe in the woods** : an innocent trusting guileless person esp. in circumstances calling for sophistication or cunning ⟨made him an easy victim for the blandishments of tougher-minded men among whom he literally was a babe in the woods —A.L.Sachar⟩

ba·bel \ˈbābəl, ˈba-\ n -s often cap [fr. the Tower of Babel, biblical structure (Gen 11:4–9) that was erected for the purpose of reaching heaven and incurred the wrath of God, who as punishment made the builders' speech mutually unintelligible, fr. Assyr-Bab bāb-ilu gate of god] 1 a : a confusion or medley of sounds, voices, languages, or ideas ⟨such a ~! Everyone talking at once and nobody listening to anyone —Hugh Walpole⟩ ⟨a ~ of birds fills the nearby woods —Joseph Chiari⟩ ⟨a ~ of controversy —Gene Baro⟩ b : a place or scene of noise or confusion, esp. of mingled and confused noises ⟨all races and nationalities meet and talk in the streets to make the town a ~⟩ 2 a : a lofty or towering structure b : an excessively grandiose or visionary scheme or project ⟨the ~ of their ambitions must totter to the ground⟩ syn see DIN

ba·bel·ism \-,lizəm\ n -s sometimes cap : a confusion of sound or sense

ba·bel·i·za·tion \-ˌləˈzāshən, -ˌlīˈz-\ n -s often cap : the state of being babelized or the process of babelizing ⟨the ~ of this speech⟩ ⟨an approach to the problem of our ~ . . . let every man everywhere become at least bilingual —N.Y.Times⟩

ba·bel·ize \ˈ==,līz\ vt -ED/-ING/-S often cap [babel + -ize] : to confuse esp. through the mingling of markedly different languages and cultures : CONFOUND ⟨the mounting needs of intercourse between Babelized peoples —A.D.Sheffield⟩

ba·bes–ernst body or **babes–ernst granule** \ˈbä,beˈshərn(t)st-\ n, usu cap 1st B&E [after Victor Babeş †1926 Romanian bacteriologist and H.C.Ernst †1922 Am. bacteriologist] : a metachromatic granule in protoplasm

ba·be·sia \bəˈbēzh(ē)ə\ n [NL, fr. Victor Babeş + NL -ia] 1 cap : the type genus of Babesiidae 2 -s a : a protozoan of the genus Babesia b : PIROPLASM — **ba·be·sial** \-zh(ē)əl\ adj

bab·e·si·a·sis \ˌbabəˈzīəsəs, -ēˈz-\ n, pl **babesia·ses** \-ə,sēz\ [NL, fr. Babesia + -iasis] : infection with or disease caused by protozoans of the genus Babesia or the family Babesiidae : PIROPLASMOSIS

ba·be·si·el·la \bə,bēzēˈelə\ n, cap [NL, fr. Babesia + -ella] in some classifications : a genus of very small bacterialike piroplasms that are usu. included in Babesia

ba·be·si·el·lo·sis \-zēəˈlōsəs\ n, pl **babesiello·ses** \-ˈlō,sēz\ [NL, fr. Babesiella + -osis] : babesiasis caused by members of the genus Babesiella

ba·be·si·i·dae \ˌbabəˈzīə,dē, -zē-\ n, pl, cap [NL, fr. Babesia, type genus + -idae] : a family of Haemosporidia comprising minute parasites of the red blood cells of mammals that are transmitted from host to host by the bite of a tick intermediate host and cause certain destructive diseases of domestic animals — see BABESIA, PIROPLASM, THEILERIA

ba·be·si·o·sis \bə,bēzēˈōsəs\ n, pl **babesio·ses** \-ˈō,sēz\ [NL, fr. Babesia + -osis] : BABESIASIS

ba·bhan \ˈbäbən\ n -s usu cap [Bihari bābhan, fr. Skt brāhmana Brahman — more at BRAHMAN] : a Hindu of a high caste of the Aryo-Dravidian ethnic type that dwells mainly in Bihar

babi \ˈbä(,)bē\ n -s usu cap [after Bab, title of its founder — more at BABISM] 1 : a sect professing Babism 2 : an adherent of Babism

bab·i·a·na \ˌbabēˈanə, -ˈä-,-ˈā- also -ˈā-\ n [NL, fr. D babianer, fr. obs. D babiaen baboon (now baviaan), fr. MF babouin baboon; fr. the fact that its stems are eaten by baboons — more at BABOON] 1 cap : a genus of bulbous herbs (family Iridaceae) having showy red or yellow spicate flowers 2 -s : a plant of the genus Babiana

ba·biche \bəˈbēsh\ n -s [CanF, of Algonquian origin; akin to Micmac ababich cord, Ojibwa assababish thread] : thread or thong of sinew, gut, or rawhide

babied past of BABY

babier comparative of BABY

babies pl of BABY, pres 3d sing of BABY

babies'–feet \ˈ==,=\ n pl but sing or pl in constr [so called fr. its dainty pink blossoms] : GAYWINGS

babies'–slippers \ˈ==,=\ n pl but sing or pl in constr [so called fr. the shape of the pods] : BIRD'S-FOOT TREFOIL 1a

babiest superlative of BABY

babies'–toes \ˈ==,=\ n pl but sing or pl in constr : BABIES'-FEET

ba·bine \bəˈbēn\ n, pl **babine** or **babines** usu cap [F, lit., thick-lipped person, thick lip — more at BABOON] 1 : an Athapaskan people closely related to or a subdivision of the Carriers and living in central British Columbia 2 : a member of the Babine people

bab·ing·ton·ite \ˈbabiŋtə,nīt\ n -s [William Babington †1833 Eng. mineralogist + E -ite] : a greenish black mineral $Ca_2(Fe,Mn)Si_5O_{14}OH$ consisting of a silicate of iron and calcium occurring in triclinic crystals (hardness 5.5–6)

ba·bin·ski reflex or **babinski sign** \bəˈbinskē-\ also **babinski's reflex** or **babinski's sign** n, usu cap B [after J.F.F. Babinski †1932 Fr. neurologist] : a reflex movement in which when the sole is tickled the great toe turns upward instead of downward indicating an organic lesion in the brain or spinal cord

babion n -s [F, prob. alter. of babouin — more at BABOON] obs : BABOON

bab·i·ru·sa or **bab·i·rous·sa** or **bab·i·rus·sa** \ˌbabəˈrüsə, ˌbä-\ n -s [Malay bābīrūsa, fr. bābī hog + rūsa deer] : a large hoglike sometimes domesticated quadruped (Babirussa babyrussa) of the East Indies whose upper canine teeth in the male are large and recurved, coming out through the lips

babish adj [1baby + -ish] obs : like a baby : BABYISH

bab·ism \ˈbä,bizəm\ n -s usu cap [Bab, title of Ali Mohammed of Shiraz †1850 Persian religious leader, its founder + E -ism] : the doctrine and practice of a 19th century Iranian sect that affirmed the progressiveness of revelation, held that no revelation was final, and forbade concubinage and polygamy, mendicancy, the use of intoxicating liquors and drugs, and dealing in slaves

bab·ist \-bəst\ n -s usu cap : an adherent of Babism

ba·boen \ˈbä,bün\ n -s [D, short for baboen hoedoe, prob. native name in Surinam] : a tropical American timber tree (Myristica surinamensis) with reddish wood

ba·boon \(ˈ)baˈbün, Brit usu & US sometimes bəˈb-\ n -s [ME babewin, baboin, fr. MF babouin, fr. baboue grimace; akin to MF babine thick lip, babiller to babble, prob. of imit. origin like ME babelen to babble — more at BABBLE] 1 obs : a grotesque figure in architectural or decorative work 2 a : any of certain large African and Asiatic apes constituting the genus Papio and related genera and having doglike muzzles, large canine teeth, cheek pouches, usu. a short tail, and naked callosities on the buttocks — see CHACMA, 6DRILL, MANDRIL b : an uncouth, coarse, or ugly person; esp : one that combines the qualities of great physical strength, low intelligence, and brutish appearance ⟨a big ~ of a wrestler⟩

baboon (Papio leucophaeus)

ba·boon·ery \ˌ=ˈ=nərē\ n -ES [ME babwinrie, fr. babewin + -rie -ry] : conduct, activity, or attitudes that are brutish, degrading, or grotesquely humorous ⟨never . . . in the history of architecture has taste . . . descended to similar ~ —Architect & Building News⟩

ba·bouche \bəˈbüsh, bä-\ n -s [F, fr. Ar bābūj, bābūsh, fr. Per pāpūsh] : a chiefly oriental slipper made without heel or quarters

babouche

ba·bou·vism \bəˈbü,vizəm, bä-\ n -s usu cap [F babouvisme, fr. François Émile Babeuf or Babœuf †1797 Fr. revolutionary + F -isme -ism] : a social and political doctrine or movement advocating a program of egalitarianism and communism esp. as formulated by Babeuf

ba·bou·vist \-ˌvəst\ n -s usu cap [F babouviste, fr. F.E. Babeuf + F -iste -ist] : an advocate of Babouvism

bab·ra·cot \ˈbabrə,kät\ n -s [prob. native name in So. America] : a 3-legged or 4-legged wooden grating used by So. American Indians for the drying and smoking of meat and other foods

bab·root \ˈbab+,-\ n [origin unknown] : SAMPSON SNAKEROOT

ba·bu also **ba·boo** \ˈbä(,)bü\ n -s [Hindi bābū, bābu, lit., father] 1 : a Hindu gentleman — a form of address corresponding to Mr. or Esquire 2 a : an Indian clerk who writes English b : an Indian having some education in English — often used disparagingly

bab·u·i·na \ˌbabəˈwēnə\ n -s [NL, fr. F babouin baboon — more at BABOON] : a female baboon

ba·bul or **ba·bool** \bəˈbül\ or **ba·blah** \-ˈblä\ n -s [Per babūl; akin to Skt babbula, babbūla (Acacia arabica)] 1 a : an acacia tree (Acacia arabica) that is probably native to the Sudan but is widespread in northern Africa and across Asia through much of India and that is a source of gum arabic and of tannins and in part of its range of fodder and timber — compare AMRAD GUM b : the hard tough durable reddish woods of babul which is used esp. in India for agricultural implements, general construction, and carving 2 usu bablah : the pods and sometimes the bark of the babul that are rich in tannin and used in tanning and dyeing; also : the pods of any of several acacias that are similarly used

ba·bush·ka \ˈbäbəshkə, -,kä, in sense 2 usu bəˈbüshkə or bä- sometimes -ˈbü-\ n -s [Russ, grandmother, dim. of baba old woman; akin to Pol baba grandmother, old woman, Lith bóba old woman, Latvian bāba] 1 : GRANDMOTHER, GRANNY 2 a : a usu. triangular or triangularly folded kerchief worn over the head and usu. tied under the chin b : a head covering resembling a babushka

babushka 2a

1ba·by \ˈbābē, -bi\ n -ES [ME babie — more at BABBLE] 1 a (1) : an extremely young child; esp : one that is still in arms : INFANT (2) : the young of an animal ⟨of the nation's 640 full species of breeding birds, 170 raise their babies . . . along the Mexican border —W.F.Heald⟩ ⟨a ~ lamb⟩ b : the youngest member of a group, esp. of a family ⟨the ~ of the family⟩ ⟨the ~ member of the Eisenhower subcabinet —Drew Pearson⟩ c slang : something that is one's personal responsibility, achievement, or interest ⟨though other . . . detectives have helped out, the case is really the bomb squad's ~ —Joseph Carter⟩ ⟨the plan for a city-wide cleanup was the mayor's ~⟩ 2 a obs : DOLL b archaic : a diminutive reflection of oneself in the pupil of another's eye — used chiefly in the phrase to look babies in (another's) eyes 3 : one that is like a baby in character or conduct; esp : one that is petulant, dependent on another, or unable to endure even mild pain or deprivation 4 slang : GIRL, WOMAN, WIFE, SWEETHEART 5 slang : PERSON, THING ⟨this chap . . . is a tough ~ —D.G. Gerahty⟩ ⟨the young airman had sent a picture of the plane . . . with the notation, "This is the ~ I'm going to fly" —Springfield (Mass.) Daily News⟩

2baby \"\ adj -ER/-EST 1 : of or relating to a baby 2 : much smaller in size than is usual for a particular class of things : SMALL, DIMINUTIVE ⟨the Depot Commander had set forth in the babiest of baby cars —Blackwood's⟩ ⟨a ~ extension ladder —Training Manual for Auxiliary Firemen⟩ ⟨~ pine trees⟩

3baby \"\ vt -ED/-ING/-ES 1 a : to tend solicitously : make much of : gratify the whims of : HUMOR ⟨babied her strapping big son till he was thoroughly spoiled⟩ ⟨~ a sick husband⟩ b : to operate, handle, or treat with special or fond care ⟨~ the engine of a racing car⟩ ⟨windows, behind any one of which a German sniper might be hiding, ~ing his rifle —Irwin Shaw⟩ 2 : to hit (a ball) with a gentle stroke of the bat or racket (as in badminton) syn see INDULGE

baby beef n 1 : a fat young beef steer or heifer ready for market (as a yearling) 2 : meat from a baby beef

baby blue n 1 : a very pale blue that is greener, lighter, and stronger than pastel blue (sense 2) and stronger and slightly greener and darker than cloud blue 2 : a pale blue that is greener and paler than average powder blue, Sistine, or average cadet gray

baby blue–eyes \ˌ==ˈ=,=\ n pl but sing or pl in constr [so called fr. the eyelike spots] : a delicate California herb (Nemophila menziesii) having blue flowers marked with dark spots

baby bond n : a bond having a face value of $10, $25, $50, or $100 as distinguished from one of $500 or $1000 — called also small bond

baby carriage or **baby buggy** n : a 4-wheeled push carriage usu. with a folding top for a baby

baby carrier or **baby flattop** n : ESCORT CARRIER

baby coach n, chiefly North Midland : BABY CARRIAGE

baby eyes n pl but sing or pl in constr : a variety (Nemophila menziesii intermedia) of baby blue-eyes with white or pale blue flowers

baby face n : a usu. rounded face that gives the impression of extreme youth and innocence — **baby–faced** \ˈ==,=\ adj

baby farm n : a place where nursing and care of babies is provided for a fee — usu. used derogatorily — **baby farming** n

baby grand n : a small grand piano five to six feet in length

ba·by·hood \ˈ==,hu̇d\ n -s : INFANCY

ba·by·ish \ˈbābēish\ adj : resembling a baby : CHILDISH, INFANTILE ⟨a rounded face that gave her a peculiarly ~ appearance⟩ ⟨~ tears and petulance⟩ — **ba·by·ish·ly** adv

bab·y·lon \ˈbabələn also -ə,län sometimes -i,län or -ē,län\ n -s usu cap [fr. Babylon, ancient city of Babylonia noted for its luxurious living, fr. ME Babilon, Babiloine, fr. L Babylon, fr. Gk Babylōn, fr. Heb Bābhel] : a large city regarded as luxurious, wicked, or given to the gratification of the senses

1bab·y·lo·nian \ˌbabəˈlōnyən, -nēən\ n -s usu cap [Babylonia, ancient country of southwestern Asia + E -an] 1 : a native or resident of ancient Babylonia or of its capital city, Babylon 2 : the form of the Akkadian language that was used in ancient Babylonia and was also employed widely as a diplomatic language

2babylonian \ˌ==ˈ=(=)=\ adj, usu cap [Babylon or Babylonia, an ancient country of southern Mesopotamia, or its capital city, Babylon + E -an] 1 : of, relating to, or characteristic of Babylonia, an ancient country of southern Mesopotamia, or its capital city, Babylon 2 : of, relating to, or characteristic of the people of

Babylonia or Babylon **3 :** affording abundant or excessive gratification to the senses **:** LUXURIOUS, SUMPTUOUS, LAVISH **4 :** of, relating to, or characteristic of the Babylonian language **5** *obs* **:** ROMAN CATHOLIC

babylonian-assyrian *n, usu cap B&A* **:** 2AKKADIAN 3a

bab·y·lon·ic \¦babə¦länik\ *adj, usu cap* [*Babylonia* or *Babylon* + E *-ic*] **1 :** 2BABYLONIAN 1 **2 :** 2BABYLONIAN 3

bab·y·lon·ish \'babə,länish, ¦babə¦lōnish, 'babələnish\ *adj, usu cap* [*Babylonia* or *Babylon* + E *-ish*] **1 :** 2BABYLONIAN 1 — usu. used in the phrase *Babylonish captivity* **2 :** 2BABYLONIAN 3

baby louis heel *n, usu cap L* **:** a low Louis heel

baby–minder \'==,==\ *n, Brit* **:** BABY-SITTER

baby orchid *n* **:** a Guatemalan epiphytic orchid (*Odontoglossum grande*) that is often cultivated in the greenhouse for its large typically orange-yellow flowers which have a wavy-edged creamy lip and are blotched and barred with darker color and usu. chestnut brown

baby–pig disease *n* **:** an acute hypoglycemia of newborn pigs accompanied by weakness, loss of appetite, and diarrhea, and usu. fatal if untreated

baby pink *n* **:** a variable color averaging a light yellowish pink that is redder and deeper than average shell pink (sense 1) or petal pink and redder and stronger than opera pink

baby primrose *n* **1 :** a Chinese primrose (*Primula forbesii*) having numerous small pale lilac flowers **2 :** FAIRY PRIMROSE

baby rambler *n* **:** POLYANTHA

ba·by's breath *or* **ba·bies' breath** *n* [so called fr. its light fragrance and dainty blossoms] **1 :** a plant of the genus *Gypsophila:* as **a :** a tall much-branched perennial herb (*G. paniculata*) having clusters of small fragrant white or pink flowers **b :** an annual herb (*G. elegans*) with larger white or rosy flowers **2 :** any of several plants having delicately scented flowers: as **a :** GRAPE HYACINTH **b :** a bedstraw (*Galium sylvaticum*) with thin lanceolate leaves and white flowers

baby–sit \'==,=\ *vi* **:** to act or become employed as a baby-sitter ⟨ask her to *baby-sit* during church service⟩ ⟨I had to *baby-sit* with my grandchildren —Robert Frost⟩

baby–sitter \'==,==\ *n* **:** a person engaged usu. for pay and for relatively short periods of time to take care of a child or children while the parents are away from the home

baby spot *n* **:** a small usu. hooded spotlight used to concentrate light on an object or area (as on a stage) from a short distance

baby's tears *also* **baby tears** *n pl but sing or pl in constr* **:** a prostrate or creeping sparsely hairy Corsican herb (*Helxine soleirolii*) of the family Urticaceae often grown esp. as a house plant for its mosslike small round short-stalked leaves

baby talk *n* **1 a :** the syntactically imperfect speech or phonetically modified forms used by small children learning to talk **b :** the consciously imperfect or mutilated speech or prattle often used by adults in speaking to small children **2 a :** a deliberately oversimplified, ingenuous, or naïve talk or explanation ⟨indulge in intellectual *baby talk* —S.L.Payne⟩

baby tooth *n* **:** MILK TOOTH

baby walker *n* **:** WALKER

bac *abbr* [ML *baccalaureus*] bachelor

ba·ca·ba \bə'käbə\ *or* **bacaba palm** *n* -S [Pg *bacaba* fruit of the bacaba palm, fr. Tupi] **:** a palm of the genus *Oenocarpus* (esp. *O. bacaba* and *O. distichus*) the drupelike fruits of which yield oil used in soap manufacture

ba·ca·lao \¦bäkə¦laü, ¦ba-\ *n* -S [Sp] **1 :** CODFISH **2 :** any of various locally important marine food fishes

ba·ca·uan \bə'käwən\ *also* **ba·cao** \bə'kaü\ *n* -S [Tag *bakawan, bakaw*] *Philippines* **:** any of various Asiatic mangroves (as those of the genera *Rhizophora* and *Bruguiera*)

bac·ba·ki·ri *or* **back·bac·ki·ri** \,bakbə'kirē\ *n* -S [imit.] **:** BOKMAKIERIE

1**bac·ca** \'bakə\ *n, pl* **bac·cae** \-a,kē, -a,kī, -ak,sē, -ak,sī\ [L *baca, bacca* — more at BAY] **:** BERRY 1c

2**bac·ca** \'bakə\ *n* -S [by shortening & alter.] *slang* **:** TOBACCO

1**bac·ca·lau·re·ate** \,bakə'lȯrēət, -lär-\ *n* -S [ML *baccalaureatus*, fr. *baccalaureus* advanced student, bachelor (alter. — influenced by L *bacca* berry & *laureus* laurel — of *baccalarius* dependent farmer, tenant, young clerk, advanced student) + L *-atus* -ate — more at BACHELOR] **1 :** the degree of bachelor conferred by universities and colleges **2 a :** a religious or semireligious service held at many educational institutions the Sunday before commencement **b :** the sermon or address delivered at this service

2**baccalaureate** \"\ *adj* **:** of or relating to the degree of bachelor or to the ceremonies attending the conferral of that degree ⟨a ~ degree is required for many jobs⟩ ⟨the ~ service⟩ ⟨a ~ address⟩

bac·ca·rat *also* **bac·ca·ra** \'bäkə,rä, ,==¦= *also* -ak-\ *n* -S [F *baccara*] **1 :** a card game played in European casinos identical with chemin de fer except that in baccarat the dealer gives hands to each of two opponents and to himself **2 :** a hand counting zero in this game or in chemin de fer

baccarat glass \"-\ *n, usu cap B* [fr. *Baccarat*, a trademark] **:** fine blown, molded, and cut glass made at Baccarat, France, from 1765 to the present time

bac·cate \'bak,āt\ *adj* [L *baca, bacca* berry + E *-ate*] **1 :** pulpy throughout like a berry **2 :** bearing berries

bac·chae \'bak,ē, -k,ī\ *n pl, cap* [L, fr. Gk *Bakchai*, pl. of *Bakchē* maenad] **:** MAENADS

1**bac·cha·nal** \'bakənᵊl\ *adj* [L *bacchanalis* of Bacchus, irreg. fr. *Bacchus*, a name of Dionysus, god of fruits including esp. the grape (fr. Gk *Bakchos*, prob. of non-IE origin) + *-alis* -al — more at BAY] **:** BACCHANALIAN

2**bac·cha·nal** \¦bäkə¦näl, ¦bäkə¦nål, ¦bak-; ¦bakə¦nal\ *n* -S **1 :** a devotee of Bacchus; *esp* **:** one who celebrates the bacchanalian rites **:** REVELER, CAROUSER **2 a :** drunken revelry or carousal **:** excessive indulgence **:** BACCHANALIA **b :** a bacchanalian song or dance

bac·cha·nale \"\ *n* -S [F, back-formation fr. *bacchanales* bacchanalia, fr. L *bacchanalia*] **:** a ballet whose dances are marked by voluptuousness or pagan abandon

bac·cha·na·lia \,bakə'nālyə, -lēə\ *n, pl* **bacchanalia** *or* **bacchanalias** [L, fr. neut. pl. of *bacchanalis*] **:** a bacchanalian celebration **:** a drunken feast **:** ORGY

1**bac·cha·na·lian** \¦bakə¦nālyən, -lēən\ *adj* **:** of, relating to, or suggesting the ancient Roman religious rites marked by orgiastic revelry and drunkenness that were held in honor of Bacchus, the god of wine

2**bacchanalian** \"\ *n* -S **:** a bacchanalian reveler **:** 2BACCHANAL 1

1**bac·chant** \bə'kant, ba-, -aa(ə)nt; bə'kä-, ba-, -'kå-, bä'kä-, bå'kå-; 'bakənt\ *n, pl* **bacchants** \-n(t)s\ *or* **bac·chantes** *as at* BACCHANTE\ [L *bacchant-, bacchans*, pres. part. of *bacchari* to celebrate the festival of Bacchus, fr. *Bacchus*] **:** BACCHANALIAN

2**bacchant** \"\ *adj* **:** of or belonging to a bacchant

bac·chante \bə'kant(ē), ba-, -aa(ə)nt(ē); bə'kä-, ba-, -'kå-, bä'kä-,bå'kå-\ *n* -S [F, fr. L *bacchant-, bacchans*, pres. part.] **:** a priestess or female follower of Bacchus **:** MAENAD

bac·chan·tic \-ntik, -ēk\ *adj* **:** of, relating to, or like a bacchant

bac·cha·ris \'bakərəs\ *n, cap* [NL, fr. L *baccar, bacchar*, a plant having a fragrant root, fr. Gk *bakcharis* sowbread] **:** a genus of smooth and resinous or glutinous shrubs (family Compositae) having whitish or yellow flower heads in pyramidal panicles

bac·cha·roid \-,rȯid\ *adj* [NL *Baccharis* + E *-oid*] **:** belonging to or resembling the genus *Baccharis*

bac·chi·ac \bə'kīək, ba-; 'bakē,ak\ *adj* [Gk *bakcheiakos*, fr. *bakcheios* bacchius] **:** composed of or relating to bacchii

1**bac·chic** \'bakik, -ēk\ *adj* [L *Bacchicus*, fr. Gk *Bakchikos*, fr. *Bakchos* Bacchus + *-ikos* -ic] **:** BACCHANALIAN

2**bacchic** \"\ *adj* [L *bacchius* + E *-ic*] **:** relating to or composed of bacchii

3**bacchic** \"\ *n* -S **:** a bacchius or bacchic cadence

bac·chi·us \bə'kīəs, ba-\ *n, pl* **bac·chii** \-ī,ī\ [L, fr. Gk *Bakcheios*, fr. *Bakcheios*, adj., of Bacchus, fr. *Bakchos* Bacchus] **1** *in accentual prosody* **:** a metrical foot of three syllables, the first unstressed, the other two having either primary or intermediate stress **2** *in classical prosody* **:** a foot of three syllables, the first short, the other two long

bac·cif·er·ous \(')bak¦sif(ə)rəs\ *adj* [L *bacifer, baccifer* bearing berries (fr. *baca, bacca* berry + *-fer* -ferous) + E *-ous*] **:** bearing berries

baccubert *usu cap, var of* BACUBERT

bac·cy \'bakē\ *n* -ES [by shortening & alter.] *slang* **:** TOBACCO

1**bach** \'bach\ *n* -ES [by shortening] *slang* **:** BACHELOR

2**bach** *also* **batch** \"\ *vi* -ED/-ING/-ES *slang* **:** to live as a bachelor; *esp* **:** to keep house in the absence of a wife — often used with *it* ⟨while their wives were away the two men *~ed it* in a cabin by a lake and fished⟩

3**bach** \"\ *n* -ES [prob. fr. 1*bach*] *NewZeal* **:** a small house or weekend cottage

bache \'bach\ *n* -S [ME, fr. OE *bæce, bece* — more at BECK] *dial Eng* **:** the valley of a small stream — now used chiefly in place names

bach·e·lor \'bach(ə)lə(r)\ *n* -S [ME *bacheler*, fr. OF, young man, squire, fr. ML *baccalarius* dependent farmer, tenant, young clerk, advanced student, of Celt origin; akin to IrGael *bachlach* peasant, shepherd, fr. OIr *bachall* staff, fr. L *baculus, baculum* — more at BACTERIUM] **1 a :** a usu. young knight who was entitled to display his own pennon but who followed the banner of another **:** KNIGHT BACHELOR **b :** an apprentice or novice knight **2 :** a person who has received what is usu. the first or lowest degree conferred by a college or university or by some professional schools ⟨~ of letters⟩ ⟨~ of divinity⟩ ⟨~ of laws⟩ **3 a :** an unmarried person of marriageable age; *esp* **:** a man of marriageable age ⟨remained a ~ for seven years after his first wife's death⟩ ⟨a ~ girl⟩ **b :** a male animal; *specif* **:** a young male fur seal when without a mate during the breeding time **4 :** WHITE CRAPPIE — **bach·e·lor·dom** \-dəm\ *n* -S — **bach·e·lor·hood** \-,hu̇d\ *n* -S

bachelor dinner *n* **:** a party attended only by men and given by or for a man just prior to his wedding

bach·e·lor·ism \-lə,rizəm\ *n* -S **1 :** the state of being a bachelor **2 :** a peculiarity of a bachelor

bach·e·lor·ly \-lə(r)lē\ *adj* **:** of or like a bachelor

bachelor of arts *usu cap B&A* **1 :** the recipient of a bachelor's degree which usu. signifies that the recipient has passed a certain number of courses in the humanities — abbr. *B.A., A.B.* ⟨became a *Bachelor of Arts* after only three years of university attendance⟩ ⟨requires a year of Latin of the *Bachelors of Arts*⟩ **2 :** the degree making one a Bachelor of Arts — abbr. *B.A., A.B.* ⟨require a *Bachelor of Arts* of all high-school teachers⟩ ⟨get an *A.B.* in classics⟩ ⟨get a *B.A.* in history⟩

bachelor of science *usu cap B&S* **1 :** the recipient of a bachelor's degree which usu. signifies that the recipient has done the greater part of his course work in the sciences with some specialization in a particular science **2 :** the degree making one a Bachelor of Science — abbr. *B.S., B.Sc., S.B.* ⟨the degree of *Bachelor of Science* in agronomy⟩ ⟨a *B.S.* in chemical engineering⟩ ⟨a *B.Sc.* in architecture⟩

bachelor's–breeches \'=(=)=¦==\ *n pl but sing or pl in constr* **:** DUTCHMAN'S-BREECHES

bachelor's button \'=(=)=¦==\ *also* **bachelor button** \'=(=)=-,==\ *n, pl* **bachelor's buttons** *also* **bachelor buttons 1 :** any of numerous plants with flowers or flower heads that suggest buttons: as **a :** DAISY 1a **b :** ORANGE MILKWORT **c :** BLUE-EYED GRASS **d :** GLOBE AMARANTH **e :** BLUEBOTTLE 1a **2** *usu* *bachelor button* **:** a deep pink that is bluer than average coral (sense 3b) and bluer and duller than fiesta or begonia

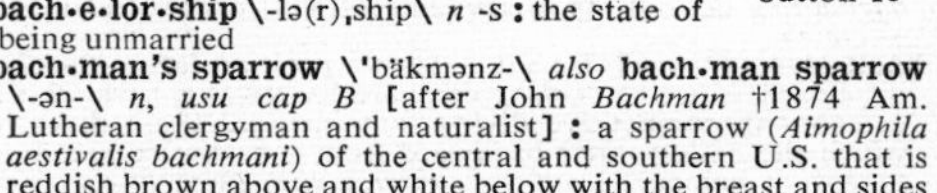

bachelor's button 1e

bachelor's chest *n* **:** a low chest of drawers with a pull-out slide for writing

bachelor's hall *n* **:** the residence of a bachelor or of a man whose wife is absent — usu. used in the phrase *to keep bachelor's hall*

bach·e·lor·ship \-lə(r),ship\ *n* -S **:** the state of being unmarried

bach·man's sparrow \'bäkmənz-\ *also* **bach·man sparrow** \-ən-\ *n, usu cap B* [after John *Bachman* †1874 Am. Lutheran clergyman and naturalist] **:** a sparrow (*Aimophila aestivalis bachmani*) of the central and southern U.S. that is reddish brown above and white below with the breast and sides washed with warm light brown

bach trumpet \'bäk, 'bä-, -k\ *n, usu cap B* [after Johann S. *Bach* †1750 Ger. composer and organist] **:** a trumpet of high pitch designed esp. for performing J.S.Bach's original trumpet parts

bachur *var of* BAHUR

bacill- *or* **bacilli-** *or* **bacillo-** *comb form* [NL *bacillus*] **:** bacillus ⟨*bacilliform*⟩ ⟨*bacilliculture*⟩ ⟨*bacillogenic*⟩

bac·il·la·ce·ae \,basə'lāsē,ē\ *n pl, cap* [NL, fr. *Bacillus*, type genus + *-aceae*] **:** a family comprising typically rod-shaped usu. gram-positive bacteria (order Eubacteriales) that produce endospores and including the genera *Bacillus* and *Clostridium*

bac·il·la·ri·a·ce·ae \,basə,lerē'āsē,ē\ *n pl, cap* [NL, fr. *Bacillaria*, type genus (fr. ML *bacillus* small rod + NL *-aria*) + *-aceae* — more at BACILLUS] *in some esp former classifications* **:** a family equivalent to Bacillariophyceae — **bac·il·la·ri·a·ceous** \¦==;=¦=¦āshəs\ *adj*

bac·il·la·ri·a·les \,basə,lerē'ā(,)lēz\ *n pl, cap* [NL, fr. *Bacillaria* + *-ales*] *in some esp former classifications* **:** an order equivalent to Bacillariophyceae

bac·il·la·ri·e·ae \-'ē,ē\ *n pl, cap* [NL, fr. *Bacillaria* + *-eae*] *in some classifications* **:** a group of algae comprising the diatoms and usu. regarded as a distinct class but sometimes esp. formerly treated as a subclass and included in the Zygophyceae

bac·il·lar·i·o·phy·ce·ae \-ə'fīsē,ē, -ə'fis-\ *n pl, cap* [NL, fr. *Bacillaria* + *-o-* + *-phyceae*] **:** a class of yellow-green algae (division Chrysophyta) comprising the diatoms

bac·il·la·ri·oph·y·ta \-'äfəd·ə\ *n pl, cap* [NL, fr. *Bacillaria* + *-o-* + *-phyta*] *in some classifications* **:** a division of plants coextensive with the class Bacillariophyceae

bac·il·lary \'basə,lerē, -ri *also* bə'silər-\ *or* **ba·cil·lar** \bə'silə(r), 'basəl-\ *adj* [ISV *bacill-* + *-ary, -ar*] **1 :** shaped like a rod **:** consisting of small rods or rodlike bodies **2 :** belonging to, resembling, produced by, or containing bacilli

bacillary dysentery *n* **:** SHIGELLOSIS

bacillary white diarrhea *n* **:** pullorum disease of the young bird

bac·il·le·mia \,basə'lēmēə\ *n* -S [NL, fr. *bacill-* + *-emia*] **:** BACTEREMIA

bacilli *pl of* BACILLUS

ba·cil·li·form \bə'silə,fȯrm, -fō(ə)m\ *adj* [NL *bacilliformis*, fr. *bacill-* + L *-formis* -form] **:** shaped like a rod **:** BACILLARY

ba·cil·lite \bə'si,līt\ *n* -S [L *bacillum* + E *-ite*] **:** a rodlike crystallite formed by a number of parallel longulites

bac·il·lo·sis \,basə'lōsəs\ *n, pl* **bacillo·ses** \-ō,sēz\ [NL, fr. *bacill-* + *-osis*] **:** a state of infection with bacilli

bac·il·lu·ria \,basə'lu̇rēə, -səl'yu̇-\ *n* -S [NL, fr. *bacill-* + *-uria*] **:** the passage of bacilli with the urine — **bac·il·lu·ric** \¦==¦=rik\ *adj*

1**ba·cil·lus** \bə'siləs\ *n* [NL, fr. ML *bacillus* small staff, alter. of L *baculum* — more at BACTERIUM] **1** *cap* **:** a large genus (the type of the family Bacillaceae) of aerobic rod-shaped bacteria producing endospores that do not thicken the rod, often forming long chains and rhizoid colonies, and as now restricted including (1) many saprophytes of soil, water, and comparable habitats that are important in the natural decay of organic matter and (2) a number of parasites (as *B. anthracis* the cause of anthrax, *B. larvae* of American foulbrood, and *B. popilliae* causing milky disease in the Japanese beetle) — compare CLOSTRIDIUM **2** *pl* **bacil·li** \-,lī, -ilē\ **a :** any member of the genus *Bacillus; broadly* **:** any straight rod-shaped bacterium — distinguished from *coccus* and *spirillum* **b :** BACTERIUM; *esp* **:** a disease-producing bacterium **syn** see MICROORGANISM

2**bacillus** \"\ *n, cap* [NL, fr. ML, small staff] **:** a genus of long slender wingless Old World stick insects commonly made type of a widely distributed family

bacillus cal·mette-gué·rin \-,kal'met(,)gā'raⁿ, -ran\ *n, usu cap C&G* [trans. of F *bacille Calmette-Guérin*, after Albert L.C.*Calmette* †1933 and Camille *Guérin* b1872 Fr. bacteriologists] **:** an attenuated strain of tubercle bacillus developed by repeated culture on a medium containing bile and used in preparation of tuberculosis vaccines — compare BCG VACCINE

ba·ci·roa \,basə'rōə\ *n, pl* **baciroa** *or* **baciroas** *usu cap* [Sp, of AmerInd origin] **1 :** a Taracahitian people in the state of Sonora, Mexico **2 :** a member of the Baciroa people

bac·i·tra·cin \,basə-'trāsᵊn\ *n* -S [NL *Bacillus* (genus name of *Bacillus subtilis*, the species producing the toxin) + Margaret *Tracy* b ab1936 Am. child in whose tissue it was found + E *-in*] **:** a water-soluble toxic polypeptide antibiotic or mixture of antibiotics isolated as a whitish powder from one strain of the hay bacillus, effective esp. against streptococci, staphylococci, pneumococci, and other gram-positive organisms, and administered chiefly topically

1**back** \'bak\ *n* -S [ME *bak, back*, fr. OE *bæc;* akin to OHG *bah* back, ON *bak*, OHG *bahho* side of bacon] **1 a** (1) **:** the rear part of the human body extending from the neck to the end of the spine, esp. the portion from shoulder to waist ⟨turned his ~ to the fire⟩ ⟨trudging down the road with a load on his ~⟩ (2) **:** the whole body considered as the wearer of clothing ⟨food for his belly and a fine blue uniform for his ~⟩ (3) **:** capacity esp. for labor, effort, or endurance ⟨imposing crushing burdens on the *~s* of the working class⟩ ⟨know where you desire to go in life and put your ~ into getting there —*Architect & Building News*⟩ **b :** the corresponding part of the body of vertebrates other than man **:** DORSUM ⟨ride on a horse's ~⟩ ⟨a bird with reddish coloring on ~ and wings⟩ ⟨an odd marking along the ~ of a snake⟩ **c :** the backbone or the muscles and ligaments of this part of the body ⟨break your ~⟩ ⟨strain her ~⟩ **d :** a surface analogous to this portion of a vertebrate ⟨riding the *~s* of waves⟩ **e :** the portion of a tanned leather hide resulting from cutting longitudinally down the backbone of the hide and trimming off the head and belly **f :** BACKBONE 3 **g** *in leapfrog* **:** the position of the player who is to be jumped over ⟨make a ~⟩; *also* **:** the player who is jumped over **2 a** (1) **:** the side or surface of something that is opposite to the side that is regarded as its front or face ⟨the ~ of the head⟩ or that is opposite to the more important, functional, or useful side ⟨scribbling his verses on the *~s* of old letters⟩ ⟨the dingy ~ of the hotel contrasting with its brilliant facade⟩ (2) **:** the side that is opposite to the side approached or seen ⟨the ~ of the mountain⟩ ⟨the ~ of the door⟩ (3) **:** the side or part of any object or space that is most remote from the observer or from its front or forward part ⟨the chorus was massed at the ~ of the stage⟩ ⟨moved to the ~ of the room⟩ ⟨a journey into the thinly settled ~ of the province⟩ **b** (1) **:** the upper, outer, or convex side or part of something as opposed to the inner, lower, or concave side or part ⟨rest a hand on the ~ of a handrail⟩ ⟨the ~ of an arch⟩ ⟨ ~ of a hoop⟩ (2) **:** the upper surface of a beam (3) **:** the side of a piece of printer's type opposite the belly — see TYPE illustration (4) **:** the roof, arch, or top surface of mine workings (5) **:** the mass of ore existing above a mine working — sometimes used in pl. (6) **:** a plane of cleavage in a coal seam **c :** the side or edge of something opposite to a side or edge designed for grasping, cutting, or striking ⟨the ~ of a knife⟩ ⟨the ~ of a saw⟩ ⟨the ~ of an ax⟩ **d :** the portion of a chair that supports the back of a sitter **e :** BACKING **f** (1) **:** the last few pages of a book (2) **:** the inside margin of a printed page **g :** the reverse of a currency note **h :** BACKYARD ⟨leave a bicycle in the ~⟩ **i :** the main or longest leaf of a leaf spring **j :** the upper part or convex portion of a saw tooth **3** *of a bird dog* **:** the action of backing **4 :** the part of the upper surface of the tongue behind the front and lying opposite the soft palate when the tongue is at rest **5 a :** a primarily defensive player (as in soccer or polo) with a position nearest his own goal — compare FORWARD **b :** a rugby player who is not a forward; *esp* **:** FULLBACK **c :** a primarily offensive player in football whose position is behind that of his linemen ⟨starred as a triple-threat ~⟩ — see FULLBACK, HALFBACK, QUARTERBACK — **at one's back :** close behind in support or pursuit ⟨in the battle the infantry stayed right *at our backs*⟩ — **behind one's back :** when one is not present **:** without one's knowledge **:** in secret ⟨make vicious remarks about you *behind your back*⟩ — **in back of** *prep* **:** BEHIND ⟨the tiny parlor *in back of* the store — John McNulty⟩ ⟨always been strongly *in back of* the venture —Thomas Wood b. 1910⟩ — **the back of beyond :** a place far out of the way **:** a remote region — **the back of one's hand :** a show of one's contempt — **the back of one's mind :** the remote or hidden part of one's thoughts ⟨the stranger's name hovered in *the back of his mind*⟩; *also* **:** the store of thoughts or memories that can be drawn upon on the appropriate occasion ⟨to keep someone's good advice in *the back of your mind* as a constant goad to activity⟩ — **with one's back to the wall :** at bay **:** in a position from which there is no retreat **:** CORNERED

2**back** \"\ *adv* [ME *bak*, fr. *bak*, n.] **1 a :** to or toward the rear **:** to or toward a place away from any place regarded as the front, center, or forward position ⟨move ~ from the front lines⟩ ⟨move ~ in a bus⟩ ⟨ask the crowd to move ~ from the scene of an accident⟩ **b :** at the rear or a position behind **:** at a place considered away from the front, center, or forward position ⟨a chapter beginning several pages ~⟩ ⟨left his friends two miles ~⟩ **c :** in or into the past ⟨to look ~ on his youth⟩ ⟨an event ~ in the last century⟩ **:** AGO ⟨several years ~⟩ ⟨met him in the street two days ~⟩ **d :** at an angle off the vertical ⟨banks slant evenly ~ from the highway⟩; *esp* **:** in a reclining position ⟨lying ~ in the boat —Frank Gallagher⟩ ⟨lie ~ on a couch⟩ **e** (1) **:** in a condition of check or restraint ⟨would have leaped if his friends had not held him ~⟩ ⟨poverty may hold a talented man ~⟩ ⟨hold ~ a laugh⟩ (2) **:** in a delayed or retarded condition **:** in a condition less advanced or advantageous than before — often used with *set* ⟨landslides set the construction job ~ many days⟩ ⟨unfortunate speculations set the firm ~⟩ **f :** in one's keeping or possession — usu. used of something that should be given up, yielded, or declared freely ⟨hold ~ part of the money⟩ ⟨keep ~ the truth⟩ **g :** in arrears ⟨he was ~ in payment of rent⟩ **h :** BACKSTAGE 1 **2 a :** to, toward, or in a place from which a person or thing came or was taken ⟨go ~ for something left behind⟩ ⟨go ~ home⟩ ⟨put a book ~⟩ **b :** to or toward a former condition **:** to or toward a former or original state (as of activity, consciousness, or productivity) ⟨go ~ to private life⟩ ⟨go ~ to barbarism⟩ ⟨needed two transfusions to bring him ~ —Bill Alcine⟩ ⟨good farming practices were needed to bring the fields ~⟩ **c** (1) **:** in repayment or return (as of a loan or favor) ⟨gave ~ the borrowed money⟩ (2) **:** in retaliation ⟨hit him right ~⟩ (3) **:** in reply usu. in the manner of a retort ⟨repressed a strong impulse to talk ~⟩ or a retraction ⟨refused to take ~ his charges⟩ or a withdrawal ⟨drew ~ from his earlier promise⟩ **3 :** OVER ⟨read your shorthand notes ~⟩

3**back** \"\ *adj* [ME *bak*, fr. *bak*, n.] **1 a :** being at the back or in the rear ⟨the ~ door⟩ ⟨the ~ porch⟩ ⟨a ~ alley⟩ **b :** distant from a center of population or habitation or off the main routes of travel ⟨~ settlements⟩ ⟨the near woodlands and ~ pastures afford good hunting —*Amer. Guide Series: Tenn.*⟩ ⟨a ~ river port⟩ ⟨~ roads and picturesque lanes⟩ **c** *comparative sometimes* **backer :** articulated at or toward the back of the oral passage ⟨the vowels \ü\ and \ä\ and \g\ in *go* are ~ sounds⟩ **2 a :** OVERDUE **:** in arrears ⟨pay ~ rent due for several months⟩ **b :** due for services performed prior to the latest pay period ⟨a retroactive increase results in ~ wages for workers⟩ **3 a :** moving or operating backward ⟨~ action with oars that drives a boat sternward⟩ **b :** moved or moving in a return direction ⟨pick up ~ cargo⟩ ⟨~ freight⟩ ⟨a ~ current⟩ **c :** constituting the second 9 holes of an 18-hole golf course ⟨play the ~ nine in record time⟩ **4** *of a publication* **:** not current ⟨a ~ number of a magazine⟩ ⟨a ~ issue⟩

4**back** \"\ *vb* -ED/-ING/-S [1*back*] *vt* **1 a :** to support or help by physical, moral, or financial assistance **:** UPHOLD **:** strengthen or encourage by aid or influence — often used with *up* ⟨~ a candidate for office⟩ ⟨~ up his son⟩; *specif* **:** to move into a position behind (a teammate) in order to assist in a play (as in stopping an offensive play in football or by retrieving a missed ball in baseball or cricket) **b :** to increase the persuasive or logical force of **:** SUBSTANTIATE — often used with *up* ⟨~ up an argument with forceful illustrations⟩ **c :** to bet on the success of ⟨~ a racehorse⟩ **d :** COUNTERSIGN, ENDORSE ⟨the warrant . . . had to be *~ed* or countersigned by a magistrate of the county to which the offender had fled —Edward Jenks & D.J.L.Davies⟩ ⟨~ a check⟩; *also* **:** to assume financial responsibility for **:** provide financial security for ⟨~ an enterprise⟩ ⟨~ a currency⟩ **e :** to supply the first stage of exhaustion in a pumping operation in connection with (another pump) ⟨a mechanical rotary pump ~ *ing* an oil diffusion pump⟩ **2 :** to get upon the back of **:** MOUNT ⟨~ a horse⟩; *esp* **:** to break (a horse) to the saddle **3 a :** to drive, force, or cause to move back, retreat, recede, or go in reverse — often used with *up* ⟨~ a car into a garage⟩ ⟨~ a car up⟩ ⟨~ a propeller at full speed⟩ **b :** to articulate (a sound) with the tongue further back **4 a :** to make or form a back for **:** furnish with a back **:** put a back to — often used with *up*, sometimes with *off* ⟨a row of hills ~*s* the town⟩ ⟨~ a skirt with stiff material⟩ ⟨~ up a bookcase with cardboard⟩ ⟨~ off a wall with bricks⟩ **b :** to be at the back of — often used with *up* ⟨a barn ~*ing* the house⟩ ⟨a row of garages ~ the building up⟩ **c** (1) **:** to print the second side of (a sheet with one printed side) **:** PERFECT, REITERATE; *esp* **:** to so print in close register — often used with *up* (2) **:** to fill (an electrotype shell) with molten metal to form a printing plate — often used with *up* (3) **:** to reinforce (a stereotype matrix) to enable to withstand molten-metal pressure in molding **d :** to widen the backbone of (an unbound book) by spreading the backs of the sections gradually from the center of the back thereby forming longitudinal ridges at each side in order to strengthen (the book) and facilitate attachment of the cover **e :** to provide (a film or plate) with a photographic backing **5** *dial* **:** to write an address on (an envelope) **6** *of a bird dog* **:** to assume pointing stance behind (another dog that has pointed a covey of birds) **7 :** to fasten a weight (as a second anchor) to the rear of (an anchor) to increase holding power **8 :** to brace (a sail) so that the wind presses upon the forward side thus checking headway or driving the bow over onto a new course ~ *vi* **1 :** to move backward ⟨~ up three paces⟩ ⟨~*ed* off in preparation for his leap⟩ ⟨~*ed* away from the door⟩ **2** *of a bird dog* **:** to stop and point behind another pointing dog **3** *of the wind* **:** to shift in a counterclockwise direction — opposed to *veer* **4 :** to have the back in the direction of and often close to something — used with *on, onto*, or *against* ⟨seaside resorts . . . seem to ~ onto the sea, instead of facing it —Stephen Potter⟩ ⟨house ~*s* onto a wall⟩ **syn** see RECEDE — **back and fill 1 :** to alternately back the sails and fill the sails of a ship so as to keep it clear of the shore and obstructions while the current of a river or channel carries it down **2 :** to take opposite positions alternately **:** alternately favor and disfavor **:** SHILLY-SHALLY ⟨he *backed and filled* and finally came to no decision at all⟩ **3 :** to maneuver esp. backward and forward ⟨turn the wheel to *back and fill* the car around⟩ ⟨the boar *backed and filled* as the dogs circulated and took nips —*Newsweek*⟩

⁵**back** \"\ *n* -S [D *bak*, fr. MD *bac*, fr. OF, fr. (assumed) VL *bacca* water vessel — more at BASIN] **:** a large shallow vat **:** a cistern, tub, or trough used (as by brewers, dyers, or gluemakers) esp. for mixing or cooling wort or holding water or hot glue

back *abbr* backwardation

backache \'=,=\ *n* **:** a pain in the lower back ⟨complains of ~*s*⟩

backache brake *or* **backache fern** \'=,=-\ *n* **:** LADY FERN

backaching \'=,==\ *adj* **:** demanding much physical exertion ⟨a ~ job⟩

back action *n* **:** action reversing the usual or direct action

back-alley *adj* **:** having a mean, furtive, or squalid character or air ⟨*back-alley* gossip⟩

back along *adv, dial* **:** some time back **:** in the past **:** some time ago ⟨a good old-timer dating *back along* —Robert Frost⟩

back and forth *adv* **:** backwards and forwards **:** to and fro ⟨a loose window shutter swinging *back and forth*⟩ ⟨to rock *back and forth* on his heels⟩

back answer *n* [³*back*] **:** a disrespectful retort ⟨hero-worshiping girl, absolutely dependent and submissive, with never a *back answer* —Richard Mallett⟩

back away *vi* **:** to withdraw or retreat gradually (as from a principle or a theoretical position) ⟨*back* slowly *away* from their insistence on repeal —Benjamin Rathbun⟩

backbackiri *var of* BACBAKIRI

back bacon *n* **:** CANADIAN BACON

backband \'=,=\ *n* **1 :** a band passing over a horse's neck and holding up the shafts of a vehicle **2 :** the outside molding of the trim around an opening (as a door or window)

backbar \'=;=\ *n* **1 :** a horizontal bar in the chimney of an open fireplace on which to hang a vessel over the fire **2 :** the shelf or counter space along the wall or backing of a bar area

back beam *n* **:** the cylinder of wood on a loom on which the warp is wound before the weaving process

back bench *n* **:** a row of seats occupied by backbenchers esp. in the British House of Commons ⟨told the meeting that . . . he would leave the shadow cabinet and return to the freedom of the *back benches*—Denis Healey⟩ — compare FRONT BENCH

backbencher \'=;==\ *n* -S **:** a rank-and-file member of a legislature; *esp* **:** such a member of the British House of Commons ⟨is cordially disliked by the ~*s* in Commons and some of the party intellectuals —M.H.Rubin⟩

backbend \'=,=\ *n* **:** a tumbling stunt in which from a standing position with the knees straight the body is arched backwards until the hands touch the floor over the head

back·ber·end *or* **back·ber·and** \'bak,berənd\ *or* **back·bear·ing** \'=,==\ *adj* [ME *bakberende*, fr. *bak* back + *berende*, pres. part. of *beren* to bear — more at BACK, BEAR] *law* **:** having in one's possession — used of a person carrying away stolen property

¹**back·bite** \'bak,bīt, *usu* -īd·+V\ *vb* [ME *bakbiten*, fr. *bak* back + *biten* to bite — more at BITE] *vt* **:** to say mean or spiteful things about (one absent) **:** SLANDER ⟨if a reader does not like what you have written, he ~*s* you to the editor, but if he is particularly pleased, he writes to you personally —Corra Harris⟩ ⟨had all *backbitten* and double-crossed each other while pretending to work together —Sir Winston Churchill⟩ ~ *vi* **:** to backbite a person

²**backbite** \"\ *n* **:** the act or an instance of backbiting ⟨manipulating a hundred and one strands of gossip and ~ —Eugene Walter⟩

back·bit·er \-īd·ə(r), -ītə-\ *n* -S [ME *bacbiter*, fr. *bakbiten* v.] **:** one that backbites

backbiting *n* -S [ME *bakbiting*, fr. *bak* back + *biting*] **:** the action of one who backbites or an instance of such action ⟨bickering and ~ —Margaret Stewart⟩ **syn** see DETRACTION

backblast \'=;=\ *n* **:** the rush of powder gases from the open or vented breech of a recoilless weapon

backblock \'=;=\ *n, Austral* **:** remote or sparsely settled country esp. far from a river or seacoast — usu. used in pl. ⟨he lived in the ~*s* of Queensland⟩ ⟨the difficulties of a ~*s* sheep farmer⟩

backboard \'=,=\ *n* **:** a board or other construction placed at or fastened to the back of some object (as a picture) or serving as the back (as of a wagon); *specif* **:** a rounded or rectangular board that is behind the basket on a basketball court and that serves to keep missed shots from going out of bounds and as a surface from which the ball can be made to rebound into the basket

back bond *n* [³*back*] *Scots law* **:** an instrument by which one apparently taking as absolute owner under another instrument acknowledges that he is only a trustee or mortgagee

backbone \'=;=\ *n* [ME *bakbon*, fr. *bak* back + *bon* bone] **1 :** SPINE, SPINAL COLUMN, VERTEBRAL COLUMN **2 a** (1) **:** the chief mountain ridge, range, or system of a country or region ⟨the broad uplands of the Pennines form . . . the ~ of England —L.D.Stamp⟩ ⟨down the small pod-shaped peninsula . . . runs a ~ of high mountains —J.B.P.Robinson⟩ (2) **:** the foundation or most substantial or sturdiest part of any material object ⟨a heavy length of wood . . . which forms the ~ of the boat —*Manual of Seamanship*⟩ ⟨saw the girders, the gaunt steel ~ of the building, rising in the air⟩ **b** (1) **:** the mainstay, principal support, or most substantial element or part of something ⟨the clothiers have been described as the ~ of the middle class —Roy Lewis & Angus Maude⟩ ⟨those branches of general medicine which form the ~ of aviation medicine —H.G. Armstrong⟩ ⟨corn is the ~ of our agriculture —P.C.Mangelsdorf⟩ (2) **:** firm and resolute character **:** strength of will ⟨she is dealing with a man who has ~ —Margaret Deland⟩ ⟨displayed ~ by his frank admission of guilt⟩ **3 :** the edge of a book along which the sections are secured together in binding **:** the part that shows as the book ordinarily stands on a shelf and that is often lettered with the title and the author's and publisher's names — called also *back, backstrip, shelfback, spine* **4 :** a rope attached fore and aft along the center of a ship's awning to support and strengthen it **5 :** a main railroad-yard track from which other tracks branch **syn** see FORTITUDE — **to the backbone** *adv* **:** THOROUGHLY, COMPLETELY ⟨O'Connor was Irish *to the backbone* —*Irish Digest*⟩

backboned \'=;=\ *adj* **:** having a backbone **:** VERTEBRATE

back·bone·less \'=;=ləs\ *adj* **:** without backbone or a backbone **:** SPINELESS, PLIANT ⟨a ~ submission to ill treatment⟩ — **back·bone·less·ness** \(')=;==nəs\ *n* -ES

backbreak \'=,=\ *n* -S **:** backbreaking labor ⟨a countryman tired of the ~ of a tenant farm —Hamilton Basso⟩

backbreaker \'=,==\ *n* -S **1 :** a backbreaking task **2 :** a refinery worker who breaks crust formed on the surface of the electrolytic bath in aluminum-reduction pots to free anode for lowering or raising during tapping

backbreaking \'=,==\ *adj* [*back* + *breaking*] **:** greatly taxing one's strength or endurance ⟨~ labor⟩ ⟨a ~ effort⟩

back bulb *n* **:** a pseudobulb on certain types of orchid plants that remains on the plant after the terminal growth has been removed and is used in the propagation of certain orchids

back-calving \'=,==\ *adj, Scot* **:** calving during the last part of the year

backcast \'=,=\ *n* -S [³*back* + *cast*] *dial Brit* **:** a relapse esp. during convalescence **:** REVERSAL

back center *n* **:** the center in the tailstock of a lathe

backchain \'=,=\ *n* **:** a chain attached to each side of a rudder and to a point under the counter to support the rudder in backing

backchat \'=,=\ *n* [³*back* + *chat*] **:** gossipy or bantering conversation **:** SMALL TALK ⟨~ that hardly went beyond tennis and dancing and cricket —Frank Sargeson⟩ **:** REPARTEE ⟨good humored ~ between audience and speaker —Alan Edwards⟩

back-check \'=,=\ *vb* [²*back*] *vt* **:** to check over (as a computation) ~ *vi* **:** to skate back towards one's own goal covering the rushes of opposing players in a hockey game

back choir *n* **:** RETROCHOIR

back cloth *n* **1 :** a piece of canvas secured to the after part of a topsail yard to stow the bunt of the topsail in **2** *or* **back gray :** an unfinished cloth used in cylinder printing of fabrics to absorb excess dye **3** *chiefly Brit* **:** BACKDROP

back comb *n* **:** an ornamental comb with a wide top and a few long teeth worn high at the back of the head

back comb

back·coun·try \'=;==\ *n* **1 :** a rural and relatively thinly settled and undeveloped area to the rear of a more densely peopled and developed region containing the main centers of population ⟨the antagonism between Tidewater and the ~ in colonial Virginia⟩ **:** farming area ⟨trucks daily bring in produce from the ~⟩ **2 :** the country to the rear of a settled district **:** a frontier area **:** BORDERLAND ⟨the first white men to set foot in that vast ~⟩

backcourt \'=,=\ *n* **1 :** the part of a tennis court between the service line and the base line **2 :** the space near or nearest the back boundary lines or back wall or walls of the playing area in net and wall games; *esp* **:** a basketball team's defensive half of the court

¹**backcross** \'=,=\ *vt* [²*back* + *cross*] **:** to cross (a first-generation hybrid) with one parent or with an individual of the same genetic composition as the parent

²**backcross** \"\ *n* -ES **:** an instance of backcrossing; *also* **:** an individual produced by backcrossing

³**backcross** \"\ *adj* [²*backcross*] **:** of, relating to, or produced by a backcross or by backcrossing

backdate \'=;=\ *vt* [²*back* + *date*] **:** PREDATE ⟨indicted for *backdating* tax returns to save interest and penalty payments —*Time*⟩

back dive *n* [³*back*] **1 :** a dive from a position facing the diving board — see CUTAWAY; compare BACKWARD DIVE **2 :** a category in competitive diving that includes those dives in which the body rotates backward from a backward standing takeoff — compare *front dive, reverse dive, twist dive*

back door *n* **1 a :** a door in the back or to the rear of something, esp. a habitation **b :** an entrance or approach (as to a country) regarded as at the back and usu. distant or geographically opposite the main route of approach ⟨but the richest area of all the peninsula was found . . . at the *back door* of Nome —*Encyc. Americana*⟩ ⟨the *back door* of Egypt —Hassoldt Davis⟩ **2 :** an indirect, surreptitious, underhanded, or illegal means or way ⟨the West entered America's popular literature through the *back door* of humor —J.D. Hart⟩ ⟨depends more and more on western *back doors* for essential war supplies —*Amerasia*⟩ ⟨a junk shop with a *back-door* trade in hides from illegally killed cattle —H.L.Davis⟩

backdoor trots *n pl but sing or pl in constr, dial* **:** DIARRHEA

back down *vi* **:** to retreat or withdraw from a previous commitment, position, or claim ⟨wished he had not undertaken the errand, but he was afraid to *back down* —Harold Sinclair⟩

backdown \'=,=\ *n* -S [*back down*] **:** the action or an instance of backing down on a stand or position ⟨a ~ on the explosive German question —*Newsweek*⟩

back draft *n* **:** an explosion of the gaseous products of incomplete combustion in admixture with air sometimes occurring during a fire (as in a building or mine) — called also *smoke explosion*

backdrop \'=,=\ *n* -S **1 a :** a cloth usu. painted or decorated in some way and hung across the rear of a stage or stage setting to mask the backstage area or to serve as scenic background **b :** a background used by a photographer consisting of a drapery or painted canvas stretched on a frame or hung from a support **2 :** BACKGROUND; *esp* **:** a background against which something is observed or stands out ⟨Indochina is the ~ for this tensely written story —*N.Y. Times*⟩

back drop *n* **:** a fundamental trampoline stunt in which from a bounce the performer lands on his back on the bed with head forward, hands in front of the body, and the legs at a 45 degree angle, then rebounds to an erect standing position

backed \'bakt\ *adj* [ME, having a back, fr. ¹*back* + *-ed*] **1** *of an archer's bow* **:** made of two or more strips glued together, one piece forming the back and another the belly — contrasted with *self* **2** *of cloth* **:** woven with a second set of threads in the warp or weft for additional weight or reversibility — see DOUBLE CLOTH **3** *of photographic film or plate* **:** coated on the side opposite the emulsion with a substance to absorb light and hence reduce halation

backed-blade \'=;=\ *n* **:** a prehistoric flint knife having one edge blunted

backed-off \'=;=\ *adj* **:** having metal removed from the back to provide clearance — used esp. of a milling cutter

back electromotive force *n* **:** COUNTER ELECTROMOTIVE FORCE

back·en \'bakən\ *vt* -ED/-ING/-S [³*back* + *-en*] *now dial* **:** to retard the progress of **:** DELAY ⟨cold weather will ~ the corn⟩

back end *n* **1 :** the rear end **2** *dial Brit* **:** the latter part of the year **:** the autumn and early winter

¹**back·er** \'bakə(r)\ *comparative of* BACK

²**backer** \"\ *n* -S **1 :** one that supports **2 :** a worker who works with backs or backing: as **a :** a slaughterhouse worker who removes the back, shoulders, and base of the tail of a hide from a carcass **b :** a worker who reinforces parts of shoes (as vamps, uppers, or straps) by pasting in pieces of lining material **c :** a worker who forms the ridges to which covers are hinged at the back of rounded book bodies **3 :** material used for backing; *specif* **:** a piece of canvas, flannel, or other material used to reinforce parts of linings or uppers of shoes **4 :** a strap usu. of sennit secured to a ship's yard and carrying a thimble through which an earing runs

³**backer** \"\ *n* -S [by shortening & alter.] *dial* **:** TOBACCO

backer-up \'=;=\ *n, pl* **backers-up :** one that backs up: as **a :** SPONSOR **b :** a linebacker in football **c :** a worker who mounts calendars between metal strips and staples calendar pads to metal

back·et \'bakət\ *n* -S [F *baquet*, dim. of *bac* tub — more at BACK] *Scot* **:** a shallow wooden box used esp. to carry fuel or ashes

backfall \'=,=\ *n* [³*back* + *fall*] **1** *obs* **:** a descending appoggiatura in music **2 :** the sloping surface in a beater or washing engine down which paper pulp passes on leaving the knives

back-fanged \'=;=\ *adj, of a snake* **:** having grooved venom-conducting teeth located posteriorly in the roof of the mouth — compare FRONT-FANGED, OPISTHOGLYPHA

back-feed *vt* **:** to put (as a paper) into a typewriter by inserting it bottom-first behind the top of a paper already in the machine and rolling the platen backward

back-fence \'=;=\ *adj* [*back fence*] **:** having an intimate informal but often malicious or slanderous character — used chiefly of conversation ⟨cheery *back-fence* chats⟩ ⟨vicious *back-fence* gossip⟩

back-field \'=,=\ *n* **:** the football players whose positions are behind the line of scrimmage; *also* **:** the positions themselves

back file *n* [³*back*] **:** a file of back numbers (as of a newspaper or documentary matter to be saved for use in the future)

¹**backfill** \'=,=\ *vt* [²*back* + *fill*] **:** to replace earth in (as a trench or the open space around a foundation wall); *also* **:** to refill (as an excavation) with any material

²**backfill** \"\ *n* -S **1 :** the refilling of a trench or other excavation or of the space around a foundation **2 :** the material used in backfilling

backfilled \'=;=\ *adj* [¹*back* + *filled*] *of an esp cotton fabric* **:** stiffened by applying size or finish to the back only

back·fill·er \'=,==\ *n* -S [¹*backfill* + *-er*] **1 :** a machine for backfilling **2 :** a worker who moves backfilling material

back fillet *n* **:** the edge or fillet by which a slightly projecting part (as a quoin or architrave) returns to the face of the wall — **back-filleted** \'=;===\ *adj*

back·fill·ing \'=,==\ *n* -S [³*back* + *filling*] **:** ²BACKFILL

¹**backfire** \'=,=\ *n* [³*back* + *fire*] **1 a :** a fire started counter to an advancing forest or prairie fire to check the latter by clearing an area **b :** a vigorous countermovement or activity ⟨delegates come under the influence of a strong ~ of opinion from the country —Allen Johnson⟩ **2 a :** an improperly timed explosion of fuel mixture in the cylinder of an internal-combustion engine; *esp* **:** one occurring when either the exhaust or intake valve is open and resulting in a loud detonation **b :** combustion in a fuel-supply line (as of a welding torch)

²**backfire** \"\ *vi* **1 a :** to make a backfire **b :** to make a sound like that of a backfire ⟨a big coffee urn *backfiring* with alarming pops and bangs —Frederick Way⟩ **2 :** to have or experience a backfire or backfires — used of an internal-combustion engine or a firearm **3 :** to light so that the flame proceeds from the internal gas jet instead of from the external jet of mixed gas and air — used of a Bunsen or similar air-fed burner **4 :** to have the reverse of the desired effect by causing loss or injury to the user or doer **:** BOOMERANG ⟨when the opposition publicized the lady candidate's photograph in a bathing suit, the strategy *backfired* —Emily T. Douglas⟩ **:** fail to have the desired effect **:** MISCARRY ⟨some of the marriages have been happy, some have badly *backfired* —Frank Gibney⟩ — **backfiring** *n* -S

back·fisch \'bäk,fish\ *n, pl* **back·fi·sche** \-shə\ [G, lit., fish for baking or frying, fr. *backen* to bake, fry (fr. OHG *backan*) + *fisch* fish, fr. OHG *fisc* — more at BAKE, FISH] **:** an adolescent immature girl ⟨his family . . . two grown-up gawky sons, and a ~ daughter —A.L.Mikhelson⟩

backflap \'=,=\ *n* **:** a flap that folds back or hangs down in back; *specif* **:** the part of a book jacket that folds over and onto the inside of the back cover

¹**backflash** \'=,=\ *n* -ES [³*back* + *flash*] **1 :** FLASHBACK **2 :** the act or an instance of backflashing **3 :** a groove formed around the outer portion of the flash to receive the metal squeezed through the flash in sinking an upper die — called also *gutter*

²**backflash** \"\ *vi* **1 :** to flash back (as of a gas) and burn at a point where combustion is not intended **2** *of a literary or dramatic work* **:** to introduce a flashback into the narrative ⟨the script ~*es* to a day in his life 10 years before⟩

¹**backflip** \'=;=\ *n* [³*back* + *flip*] **1 :** a backward somersault **2 :** a complete reversal of position or belief **:** VOLTE-FACE

²**backflip** \"\ *vi* **:** to do a backflip ⟨~ off a diving board⟩

backflow \'=,=\ *n* [³*back* + *flow*] **1 :** a flowing back or returning toward a source **2 :** the entrance of water or other liquid from any but the regular source of a potable water supply system — compare CROSS-CONNECTION

back focus *n* **:** the distance from the rear glass surface of a photographic lens to the focal plane when the lens is focused on a very distant object

back-formation \'=,=;==\ *n* **1 :** a word formed by subtraction of a real or supposed affix (as a suffix) from an already existing longer word (as *buttle* from *butler*, the final *-er* being taken as the suffix found in such words as *maker* or *player* or as *pea* from *pease*, the final *-se* \z\ being taken as a plural ending) **2 :** the formation of a back-formation

back-friend \'=,=\ *n* [perh. fr. ³*back* + *friend*] *archaic* **:** a seeming friend who is secretly an enemy

back-front \'=,=\ *n* **:** the rear facade of a building

backfurrow \'=;==\ *vb* [²*back* + *furrow*] **:** to plow by throwing or turning the soil from the first two furrows together, leaving clear furrows on the sides

backgame \'=,=\ *n* **:** a strategy in backgammon that aims at hindering the opponent's progress instead of advancing one's own men

¹**back·gam·mon** \'bak,gamən, === *sometimes* 'bagəmən *or* ba'gam- *or* bə'gam-\ *n* -S [perh. fr. ³*back* + *gammon*, alter. of ME *gamen* game, sport — more at GAME] **1 :** a game played with dice and counters on a board divided into two tables each marked with 12 points in which each player tries to move his own counters from point to point and off the board trying at the same time to block or capture those of his opponent — called also *tables* **2 :** the winning of a backgammon game before the loser has borne off any men and while one or more men remain on the winner's inner table or on the bar, the winner receiving triple score

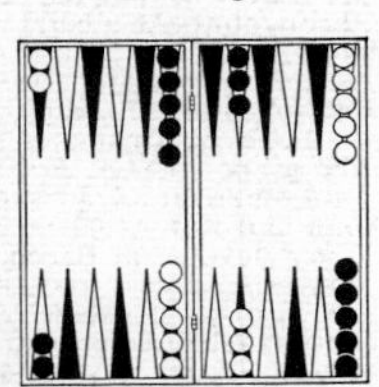

backgammon board with pieces arranged as at beginning of game

²**backgammon** \"\ *vt* -ED/-ING/-S **:** to beat (an opponent) in backgammon by scoring a backgammon

back gear *or* **back gearing** *n* **:** the gearing at the headstock of a lathe for reducing the speed of the spindle from that of the driving pulley — **back-geared** \'=;=\ *adj*

back gray *n* **:** BACK CLOTH 2

¹**background** \'=,=\ *n, often attrib* **1 a :** the ground, space, or its contents being or represented as being at the rear or behind the principal object or objects observed: as (1) **:** the rear part of a stage or its contents (as painted scenery) ⟨as the curtain rises, a rustic festival is in progress in the ~⟩ (2) **:** the space or ground and its contents shown in a pictorial representation as being at the rear of the principal figure or figures ⟨stands in a graceful pose against a ~ of peaceful stream and rolling hills⟩ **b :** the surface upon or against which the principal figures or parts of a two-dimensional representation or pattern are seen ⟨a study of white flowers against a solid black ~⟩ **2 :** a position away from that which holds the center of attention **:** an obscure, less prominent, or not readily noticed position or status ⟨the parents stayed in the ~ during the children's party⟩ ⟨pushed into the ~ by the brilliance and glamor of his rival⟩ **3 a** (1) **:** the natural, physical, or material conditions that form the setting within which something is viewed or experienced ⟨attractive private dwellings, all set in a ~ of tropical luxuriance —Tom Marvel⟩ ⟨a hum of distant street noises made a gentle ~ to the strident toughies of the big . . . American cars —Mollie Panter-Downes⟩ (2) **:** an harmonic or rhythmic accompaniment to a melodic line played or sung ⟨a violin duet with a bare viola and cello harmonic ~ —Ralph Hill⟩ **b** (1) **:** the conditions, circumstances, ideas, or events that stand in an antecedent, causal, or intimate relation to any phenomenon or development **:** SETTING, MILIEU ⟨made an exhaustive study of the ~ of the Crimean War⟩ ⟨the social and economic ~ of the Renaissance⟩ ⟨police probed into the ~ of the murder⟩ (2) **:** factual and circumstantial information that is essential to full understanding of a particular problem or situation ⟨take along a good standard book on British history to give you some ~ on what you'll be seeing —Richard Joseph⟩ **c** (1) **:** the environmental conditions or circumstances esp. of childhood and youth that form or contribute to the

formation of an individual's character, personality, and cultural makeup ⟨Lincoln's pioneer ~⟩ ⟨a family ~ of wealth, leisure, and cultivated tastes⟩ ⟨a German ~ on his mother's side⟩ (2) **:** the area or areas of past experience or concentration (as in training or employment) ⟨a ~ in sales promotion⟩ ⟨a ~ in medieval history⟩ ⟨a ~ of gold mining and prospecting for oil⟩ ⟨has unusual ~s of study and experience in international affairs —F.L.Mott⟩ (3) **:** an individual's life history or past career ⟨investigated the ~ of the suspect⟩ ⟨a ~ of success in all his varied enterprises⟩ **4 a :** intrusive often constant sound that confuses, distorts, or interferes with received or recorded electronic signals (as in radio reception or recording); *also* **:** adventitious flicks interfering with electronic instrument readings **b :** the more or less steady level of radiation or sound above which the effect (as radioactivity) being measured by an apparatus (as a Geiger counter) is detected

²**background** \"\ *vt* [¹*background*] **1 :** to form a background to ⟨elms that have ~*ed* memorable scenes in our history —Frank Thone⟩ **2 :** to provide with a background ⟨a richly ~*ed* study of a silent movie star —Hollis Alpert⟩

background music *also* **background** *n* **:** music performed esp. by unseen performers as an accompaniment to some activity essentially unrelated to it (as dining, shopping, or factory work); *specif* **:** music specially composed or arranged to accompany the dialogue or action (but not dancing or singing) of a motion picture or radio or television drama

background projection *n* **:** the projection of still or motion pictures onto a translucent screen that is then photographed from the opposite side and used as the background for live action sequences of a photoplay — called also *back projection, process projection*

¹**backhand** \ˈ⸗ˌ⸗ *sometimes* ˈ⸗ˈ⸗\ *n* [³*back* + *hand*] **1 a :** a stroke with the back of the hand turned in the direction of the movement ⟨a sharp ~ across the cheek⟩ **b :** a stroke (as in tennis) made from his left by a right-handed player or from his right by a left-handed player — opposed to *forehand* ⟨a good ~ in squash⟩ ⟨a good ~ game⟩ **2 :** handwriting whose up-and-down strokes slant at a downward angle from left to right ⟨to write a bold ~⟩ ⟨~ writing⟩

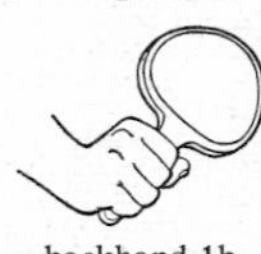
backhand 1b

²**backhand** \"\ *or* **back·hand·ed** *also* **back·hand·ed·ly** *adv* **1 :** using a backhand ⟨deliver a slap ~⟩ ⟨hit the tennis ball ~ on a tricky bounce⟩ **2** *of a catch in baseball* **:** with the glove hand across the body to the right in right-handed throwers or to the left in left-handed ones ⟨catch a long fly ~ on the run⟩

³**backhand** \"\ *vt* **:** to do or hit with the back of the hand or a backhand ⟨I ~*ed* the coffee right into the lap of the lippy guy —R.V.Williams⟩ ⟨he ~*ed* the man with a sharp slap across the cheek⟩ ⟨~ a tricky bounce on a tennis court⟩

back·hand·ed \ˈ⸗ˈ⸗⸗\ *adj* **1 :** using or consisting of backhand or a backhand ⟨~ writing⟩ ⟨a ~ slap in the face⟩ ⟨a ~ shot in tennis⟩ **2 :** HESITANT, DIFFIDENT ⟨not at all ~ in asking for second helpings⟩ **3 :** indirect, roundabout, or devious ⟨a ~, dishonest way of achieving his end⟩ — often used of an outcome opposed to the real or seeming intent of an act or statement ⟨attacks from that source amounted to a ~ compliment to the man's integrity⟩ ⟨the ~ censorship of providing information "channels" . . . actually aimed at hiding facts —Dale Kramer⟩ — compare LEFT-HANDED 3 **4** *of written letters of the alphabet* **:** inclining from upper left to lower right

backhanded rope *or* **backhand rope** *n* **:** LEFT-HANDED ROPE

back·hand·er \ˈ⸗ˌ⸗⸗ *also* ˈ⸗ˈ⸗⸗\ *n* -s [¹*backhand* + *-er*] **:** a backhanded blow, stroke, or catch

backhaul \ˈ⸗ˌ⸗\ *n* [³*back* + *haul*] **:** the return movement of a transportation vehicle from the direction of its principal haul esp. transporting a shipment back over part or all of the route

back-heel \ˈ⸗ˌ⸗\ *n* [³*back* + *heel*] **:** a method of tripping a wrestling opponent by getting a foot behind his heel and pushing him backward; *also* **:** a throw made in this way

backhoe \ˈ⸗ˌ⸗\ *n* [³*back* + *hoe*] **:** an excavating machine in which the bucket is rigidly attached to a hinged stick on the boom and is drawn toward the machine in operation — compare DRAGLINE

backhouse \ˈ⸗ˌ⸗\ *n* **:** PRIVY 2

back in *vi* **1** *in poker* **:** to bet after having passed at the first opportunity **2** *in bridge* **:** to overcall or double or to reopen the bidding after having passed in the first round

¹**backing** *pres part of* BACK

²**backing** *n* -s **1 :** something forming or used to form a back: as **a :** unsquared stone or rubble, brick, hollow tile, or concrete block used at the back of a wall in masonry or such supporting masonry itself **b :** a piece of cloth or other material serving as a foundation or used for stiffening ⟨a leather ~ on a cloth belt⟩ **c :** a thick layer of wood behind the armor of a warship **d :** the silvering on the back of a mirror **e :** a piece of scenery placed behind an opening (as a door or arch) in a stage setting to prevent the audience from seeing what lies behind it **f :** the metal portion of a dental crown, bridge, or similar structure to which a porcelain or plastic tooth facing is attached **g :** a light-absorbing coating either on the back of a photographic plate or film or between the emulsion and the base reducing interreflections between the surfaces and hence reducing halation **2 backings** *pl, Scot* **:** refuse of wool, flax, or cloth **3 a :** SUPPORT, AID ⟨his campaign had the solid ~ of the party leadership⟩ **:** the persons or elements providing support or aid ⟨his ~ includes all the substantial elements in the community⟩ **b :** endorsement esp. of a warrant by a magistrate **4 :** a secondary line attached to a casting line and wound onto the fishing reel spool before it

backing hammer *n* **:** a hammer with a broad claw at one end of the head and a flat head at the other end used in shaping the backbones of books

backing light *or* **backing lamp** *n* **:** BACKUP LIGHT

backing pump *n* **:** FOREPUMP

backing ring *n* **:** a metal ring used inside a butt-welded joint to reinforce the joint and to prevent weld metal from entering the pipe at the joint

backing strip *n* **:** long lighting units used for stage illumination (as behind doors, windows, or portholes)

backing yarn *n* **:** the yarn that holds the tufts and forms the skeleton of a pile fabric

backjoint \ˈ⸗ˌ⸗\ *n* **:** a rabbet or chase in masonry left to receive a permanent slab or other filling

backkick \ˈ⸗ˌ⸗\ *n* **:** KICKBACK

backland \ˈ⸗ˌ⸗\ *n* -s **1 :** BACKCOUNTRY, HINTERLAND — often used in pl. ⟨the remote ~s of the country⟩ **2 :** the part of a river floodplain separated from the river by a natural levee

¹**backlash** \ˈ⸗ˌ⸗\ *n* [³*back* + *lash*] **1 a :** a sudden often violent backward movement or recoil **b :** the clearance, slack, or play between adjacent movable parts (as in a train of cars or series of gears) or the jar or reaction often caused by such clearance when the parts are suddenly put in action or are in irregular action **c :** an action or reaction in a reverse direction suggesting such a backward movement or recoil **2 :** a snarl in that part of a fishing line which is wound on the spool of the reel caused by overrunning of the spool **3 :** a rearward movement of the trigger of a firearm past the position where hammer or firing pin is released **4 :** the small reverse phase of an imperfectly rectified alternating current resulting from positive ions produced in the gas of the rectifier tube by the impact of thermoelectrons

²**backlash** \"\ *vi* **:** to make or execute a backlash

back·less \ˈbakləs\ *adj* **:** not having a back

¹**backlight** \ˈ⸗ˌ⸗\ *n* [³*back* + *light*] **:** illumination falling upon an object from behind esp. throwing it into relief ⟨a feather floating white in the dazzling ~ of the sun —Ralph Ellison⟩

²**backlight** \"\ *vt* **:** to illuminate with a backlight or backlighting ⟨the sun dropped lower, ~*ing* the peaks —Douglass Wallop⟩ ⟨a ~*ed* camera shot⟩

backlighting *n* -s **:** controlled lighting of an object from the rear or from the side away from the camera for special photographic effects

backlining \ˈ⸗ˌ⸗⸗\ *n* -s [¹*back* + *lining*] **:** the material fastened to the backbone of a book or to the inside of the cover in the backbone area to provide strength and rigidity

back·lins \ˈbaklənz\ *adv* [ME (northern dial.) *bakling*, fr. *bak* back + *-ling*] *dial Brit* **:** BACKWARD

backlist \ˈ⸗ˌ⸗\ *n* **:** the books kept in print as distinguished from books newly published

back load *n* **:** a load or burden carried or suitable to be carried on the back ⟨a ~ of firewood⟩

¹**backlog** \ˈ⸗ˌ⸗\ *n* [³*back* + *log*] **1 :** a large log of wood forming the back of a campfire or hearthfire **2 :** a reserve that promises continuing work and profit ⟨a vast ~ of orders may soon make possible the greatest peacetime industrial activity that we have ever seen —H.S.Truman⟩ **3 :** an increasing accumulation of tasks unperformed or materials not processed ⟨eliminate the ~ of uncataloged books⟩ ⟨judges met . . . to discuss how to clear the ~ of 15,000 cases —*N.Y. Times*⟩

²**backlog** \"\ *vb* **:** to accumulate as a backlog

back loop jump *n* **:** a jump in figure skating executed from an outside backward loop and consisting of a full revolution of the body in the air landing on the same outside backward edge

back·lot·ter \ˈ⸗ˌlädər\ *or* **back·yard·er** \-ˌyärdər\ *n* [*back lot* or *back yard* + *-er*] **1 :** one who raises poultry or rabbits on a small lot, usu. a back lot **2 :** a breeder on a small scale

back marker *n, Brit* **:** one starting a handicapped race, game, or match with a high adverse handicap

back matter *n* **:** matter following the main text of a book — compare FRONT MATTER

back·most \ˈbak,mōst *esp Brit also* -məst\ *superlative of* BACK

back mutation *n* **:** atavistic biological mutation **:** mutation of a previously mutated gene to its former condition

back number *n* **1 :** an issue (as of a magazine) preceding the current one **2 :** something that is out of date ⟨the building has become a *back number* in construction and design —Lee Graham⟩

back of *prep* **1 :** BEHIND ⟨a hall *back of* the main staircase —*New Yorker*⟩ **2 :** beyond in past time **:** BEFORE ⟨the history of the islands goes far *back of* this —Nathaniel Burt⟩ ⟨two centuries *back of* the oldest complete Greek texts —I.M. Price⟩ **3 :** in a hidden causal or background relation to ⟨soon learned that the hardest kind of work was *back of* every success —Edward Bok⟩ ⟨wondered what was *back of* his strange remark⟩ **4 :** in support of ⟨*back of* the legislation stood those likely to gain by its passage⟩

back off *vt* **1 :** to reverse the direction of rotation of (a spindle) for a few turns in mule spinning so that the yarn between the nose of the cop and the point of the spindle may be uncoiled **2 a :** to remove metal from the back of (a cutting tool) to provide clearance from the work (as in cutting a screw thread) **b :** to remove (as part of a well casing) by unscrewing **3 :** to cut away or relieve on the back ⟨*back off* a cutter or drill to make a clearance⟩ ~ *vi* **:** to back down or back out

back office *n* **:** the inner private office or area of a business or institution

back order *n* **1 :** an unfulfilled order held for future completion or delivery **2 :** a new order made up of previously unavailable items of an old order

¹**back out** *vi* [⁴*back* + *out*] **:** to withdraw esp. from an agreement, commitment, or contest — often used with *of* ⟨*back out* of a fight⟩ ⟨agreed to come, then *backed out*⟩ ⟨*backed out* of their treaty obligations⟩

²**back out** *n* **:** the act or an instance of backing out of something ⟨a fight from which there was no chance of a *back out*⟩

¹**backpack** \ˈ⸗ˌ⸗\ *n* [¹*back* + *pack*] **1 :** a load carried on the back (as by knapsack) **2 :** a piece of equipment (as a fire extinguisher) designed for operation while being carried on the back

²**backpack** \"\ *vt* **:** to carry (food or equipment) on the back esp. in camping ⟨each wooden roof beam . . . had to be ~*ed* from the plain below up the steep trail —*Holiday*⟩ ⟨summer hikers who are ~*ing* all their equipment —K.A.Henderson⟩ ~ *vi* **:** to carry one's food or equipment on the back esp. in camping ⟨crampons would have been useful, but when ~*ing*, we hadn't considered their extra weight worth taking —*Appalachia*⟩

back-page \ˈ⸗ˌ⸗\ *adj* [*back page*] **:** of or relating to the back pages of a newspaper **:** of small news value — opposed to *front-page*

back-paint \ˈ⸗ˌ⸗\ *vt* **:** to paint the back or concealed portion of (as wood trim)

back-palm \ˈ⸗ˌ⸗\ *vt* **:** to conceal (as cards or coins) on the side of the hand away from the audience in sleight of hand

back parlor *n* **:** a private usu. second parlor in the back or the main living area of a house or inn

back-patting *n* -s **:** the act or an instance of complimenting or congratulating (as for merit or achievement) ⟨the time for *back-patting* is not yet —*Manufacturing Confectioner*⟩

backpedal \ˈ⸗ˌ⸗⸗\ *vi* [²*back* + *pedal*] **1 :** to press backward on the pedals of a bicycle to check the forward motion **2 a :** to retreat or back away esp. in boxing ⟨hamper . . . troops trying to ~ northward —*Newsweek*⟩ ⟨he sent several jolting hooks to the heart, forcing the defending champion to ~ —Nat Fleischer⟩ **b :** to back down from or reverse a previous opinion or stand ⟨a politician *backpedaling* on an earlier promise⟩

backpiece \ˈ⸗ˌ⸗\ *n* **:** a piece at the back or serving as a back; *esp* **:** a piece of armor designed to protect the back

back pitch *n* **:** the center-to-center distance between two parallel rows of rivets in riveted joints

backplaster \ˈ⸗ˌ⸗⸗\ *vt* **:** to apply plaster on the back of (lathing) or mortar on the back of (a masonry wall) — **back-plastering** *n* -s

back·plate \ˈ⸗ˌ⸗\ *n* **:** a metal piece in back or forming a back esp. of a suit of armor

back play *n, cricket* **:** batting in which the batsman steps back toward his wicket and plays the ball well behind the popping crease — contrasted with *forward play*

back pressure *n* **1 :** residual pressure on the exhaust side of a steam-engine piston against which the steam on the intake side must work **2 :** opposition to flow of a liquid or gas due to friction, inertia, gravity, or other cause

back pressure–arm lift method *n* **:** artificial respiration in which the operator kneels at the head of the victim, compresses the chest manually, then pulls up the elbows thereby expanding the lungs and repeats this sequence in a regular rhythm as long as considered necessary

back projection *n* **:** BACKGROUND PROJECTION

back-putty \ˈ⸗ˌ⸗⸗\ *vt* **:** to force putty into any space in a window sash that may be left between the edges of the rabbet and the glass

back-rake \ˈ⸗ˈ⸗\ *vt* [²*back*] **:** ²RAKE 4

back-reef \ˈ⸗ˈ⸗\ *adj* [*back reef*] **:** consisting of or belonging to a restricted lagoon behind barrier reefs ⟨a *back-reef* area⟩ ⟨*back-reef* geologic formations⟩

backrest *n* **:** a rest at the back: as **a :** a follow rest in a lathe **b** *Brit* **:** WHIP ROLL **c :** a grinding-machine rest that is fastened to the machine table to support the work

back room *n* **1 :** a room situated in the rear; *esp* **:** one accessible only to special or private groups ⟨in the *back room* of every tavern, clubs held meetings several times a week —Bernard Faÿ⟩ **2 :** the meeting place of a leadership or directing group (as of a political party) that wields its influence and authority in an informal, inconspicuous, and often indirect way reaching decisions through negotiation among its members and sometimes making use of dubious or underhanded methods ⟨the man in the *back room*, avoiding direct contacts, weaving a web of intrigue and influence —M.W. Straight⟩ ⟨delegates . . . were merely marking time until the real decisions were made in the *back rooms* —*Time*⟩

backroom boy \ˈ⸗ˈ⸗-\ *n, slang chiefly Brit* **:** a person engaged in scientific esp. secret research; *also* **:** an expert adviser or aide **:** BRAIN TRUSTER

backrope \ˈ⸗ˌ⸗\ *n* **1 :** a rope or chain extending aft on each side of a sailing ship from the lower end of the dolphin striker to the bows — see SHIP illustration **2 :** CAT BACK

back rubber *n* [¹*back*] **:** a device that automatically applies insecticide to cattle as they rub against it

back run *n* [³*back*] **:** the period in an industrial process in which the flow of materials (as of steam and gas in water-gas manufacture) is reversed

backs *pl of* BACK, *pres 3d sing of* BACK

back sail *n* **:** a sail upon which the wind pressure is on the forward side

backs and cutters *n pl* **:** any two main series of fractures that produce jointed rock structure by crossing each other at steep angles — used in quarrying

backsaw \ˈ⸗ˌ⸗\ *n* [so called fr. the stiffened back] **:** a short fine-toothed saw stiffened by a metal rib along its back edge

backsaw

backsawn \ˈ⸗ˌ⸗\ *adj* [²*back* + *sawn*] **:** sawed at right angles to the medullary rays ⟨~ wood⟩

backscatter \ˈ⸗ˌ⸗⸗\ *or* **backscattering** \ˈ⸗ˌ⸗⸗⸗\ *n* [²*back* + *scatter* or *scattering*] **:** the scattering of radiation (as X rays) in a direction approximately opposite to that of the incident radiation and due to reflection from particles of the medium traversed; *also* **:** the radiation so reversed in direction

backscattered *adj* **:** produced by backscatter

back score *n* **1 :** a line in curling drawn tangent to the parish and parallel with and midway between the sweeping score and the foot score — see CURLING illustration **2 :** a record in bridge of the number of points each player has won or lost in the course of the game

back scratcher *n* **:** a device shaped like a hand, mounted at the end of a stick, and used to scratch one's own back

back scratching *n* **:** the reciprocal exchange of favors, services, or assistance tending to the private advantage or interest of the parties to the exchange ⟨promotion becomes no longer a matter of merit but of log-rolling, *back scratching*, and of obsequious toadying —F.D.Roosevelt⟩ ⟨*back-scratching* alliances with . . . lobbies —*Progressive Labor World*⟩

backseat \ˈ⸗ˈ⸗\ *n* **:** a secondary, inferior, or inconspicuous position or status in relation to the position or status of something else — usu. used in the phrase *take a backseat* ⟨the poems were first-rate, but the comments didn't have to take a ~ —Harvey Breit⟩ ⟨foreign requirements for new freight cars will have to take a ~ to domestic needs —*Jour. of Commerce*⟩

backseat driver \ˈ⸗ˌ⸗-\ *n* **1 :** a person who directs or attempts to direct the actions of the driver of a car from the backseat (as by unsolicited advice or warnings) **2 :** any person esp. in a subordinate position who intervenes or tries to intervene in the direction or conduct of affairs that are not his proper concern or responsibility — **backseat driving** *n*

¹**backset** \ˈ⸗ˌ⸗\ *n* -s [³*back* + *set*] **1 :** SETBACK ⟨a ~ in his own personal finances —F.W.Crofts⟩ ⟨get out of bed too soon after an illness and suffer a ~⟩ **2 :** an eddy or countercurrent of water **3 :** the distance from the face of a lock to the center of the keyhole

²**backset** \"\ *vt* [²*back* + *set*] *West* **:** to plow again in the fall (prairie land broken up in the spring)

back-set bed \ˈ⸗ˌ⸗-\ *n* **:** a stratum deposited on the rear slope of a glacial apron or sand plain as the ice retreats and consequently dipping toward the retreating ice

backsetting *n* [fr. gerund of ²*backset*] *West* **:** newly broken prairie land after the second plowing of broken sod

backsey \ˈbak'sī\ *n* -s [³*back* + *sey*] *Scot* **:** a cut of meat usu. including all or most of the loin

back shaft *n* **1 :** a countershaft driven by a back gear **2 :** any shaft placed at the back of a machine

back·sheesh *or* **back·shish** \ˈbak,shēsh, ⸗ˈ⸗\ *var of* BAKSHEESH

backshift \ˈ⸗ˌ⸗\ *n* **:** the second shift of workers for the day in a mine

back shop *n* **1 :** a usu. private shop or area to the rear of the main shop or establishment; *specif* **:** the printing room of a newspaper or periodical **2 :** a locomotive repair shop

backshore \ˈ⸗ˌ⸗\ *n* **:** the part of the seashore between the foreshore and the coastline covered by water only during storms of exceptional severity

back shutter *n* **:** the backflap of a shutter

backside \ˈ⸗ˈ⸗\ *n* [ME *bakside*, fr. *bak* back + *side*] **1** *now dial Brit* **a :** the backyard of a house **b :** BARNYARD, FARMYARD **2 :** BUTTOCKS — often used in pl. **3 :** BACKSTRETCH

backsight \ˈ⸗ˌ⸗\ *n* **1** *surveying* **:** a reading of the leveling rod in its unchanged position when the leveling instrument has been taken to a new position **2** *surveying* **:** a sight directed backward to a previous station

back sinew *n* **:** the large flexor tendon at the back of the cannon bones of quadrupeds — called also *back tendon*

back slang *n* **:** a secret language in which each word is pronounced exactly or approximately as if spelled backwards (as *nam* for *man; nird* for *drink*) ⟨Cockney *back slang*⟩

¹**backslap** \ˈ⸗ˌ⸗\ *n* [¹*back* + *slap*] **1 :** a slap on the back esp. as an indication of good-fellowship ⟨the symbols . . . of quick liking and respect — the handshake, the ~ —James Thurber⟩ **2 :** a slap or blow caused by a sudden backward motion

²**backslap** \"\ *vt* **:** to slap on the back familiarly or approvingly; *also* **:** to make an excessive or effusive display of approval of ⟨many of the critics . . . tend to browbeat some authors as certainly as they can be guaranteed to ~ others —Vera Brittain⟩ ~ *vi* **:** to engage in backslapping **:** make a pronounced or excessive display of cheerfulness, cordiality, or good-fellowship ⟨would have puffed up and blustered and laughed and *backslapped* —T.W.Duncan⟩ — **back·slap·per** \-pə(r)\ *n*

¹**backslapping** *adj* **1 :** characterized by a tendency to backslap ⟨a jovial, backslapping, ~ type⟩ **2 :** having an excessively hearty or boisterous character ⟨the ~ jocosity that passes for humor here —Sinclair Lewis⟩

²**backslapping** *n* -s **:** the effusive display of approval, cordiality, or good-fellowship ⟨there has been much satisfied ~ over the presentation —Bosley Crowther⟩ ⟨a field where social drinking and hearty ~ had heretofore been prerequisites for success —Ralph de Toledano⟩

¹**backslide** \ˈ⸗ˌ⸗ *also* (ˈ)⸗ˈ⸗\ *vi* **backslid; backslid** *or* **backslidden; backsliding; backslides** [²*back* + *slide*] **:** to fall away or relapse from a previously adopted faith, position, or line of conduct ⟨when an earnest Christian encounters one who has *backslidden* —A.J.Russell⟩ ⟨had *backslid* so far as to bargain with the infidel —*Time*⟩ **:** revert to an earlier and worse condition **:** RETROGRESS, DECLINE ⟨a world that . . . had certainly *backslidden* in the ways of culture —V.L.Parrington⟩

²**backslide** \ˈ⸗ˌ⸗\ *n* **:** the act or an instance of backsliding ⟨a moral ~ —*New Republic*⟩

backslider \ˈ⸗ˌ⸗⸗\ *n* **:** one that backslides ⟨nor will a ~ be able to plead his former righteousness —W.L.Wardle⟩

backspace \ˈ⸗ˌ⸗\ *vi* [²*back* + *space*] **:** to move the carriage of a typewriter back one space with each depression of a key

back·spac·er \-sə(r)\ *n* **:** the typewriter key used for backspacing — called also *backspace key*

backspang \ˈ⸗ˌ⸗\ *n* -s [³*back* + *spang*] *chiefly Scot* **:** a trick or loophole that enables one to retreat from a bargain

backspin \ˈ⸗ˌ⸗\ *n* **:** a backward rotary motion imparted esp. to a ball (as a billiard or golf ball) that causes the ball on touching the ground or some other surface to recoil, bounce backward, stop dead, or roll forward only a short distance

backsplash \ˈ⸗ˌ⸗\ *or* **backsplasher** \-shə(r)\ *n* [³*back* + *splash* or *splasher*] **:** a plate or panel erected at the back of a fixture (as an electric range) usu. supporting control devices

backsplice \ˈ⸗ˌ⸗\ *n* [³*back* + *splice*] **:** a finish for the end of a rope that consists of a crown knot with the strands tucked over and under in the standing part

¹**backspread** \ˈ⸗ˌ⸗\ *vi* [²*back* + *spread*] **1** *in stock speculation* **:** to close the transactions previously made in a spreading operation **2** *in stock speculation* **:** to transfer a hedge from one market to another

²**backspread** \"\ *n* **:** an arbitrage operation like a spread but performed when the difference in price between the two markets is less than the normal one

backspring \ˈ⸗ˌ⸗\ *n* [³*back* + *spring*] **:** a spring hawser led at a forward angle to the wharf from the stern or midships

backstab \ˈ⸗ˌ⸗\ *vt* [¹*back* + *stab*] **:** to attack (a person) behind his back (as by making unfounded accusations) ⟨unscrupulous politicos ~*ing* opponents⟩

backstaff \ˈ⸗ˌ⸗\ *n* [¹*back* + *staff;* fr. the position of the observer, who has his back to the sun when using it] **:** an instrument similar to a cross-staff but fitted with a reflector and formerly used for taking the altitudes of heavy bodies

[1]backstage \'⸗'⸗\ *adv* [[2]*back* (used prepositionally by analogy with *upstage, downstage*) + *stage*] **1 :** in or to a backstage area ⟨changes of costume to be made ~ —Winifred Bambrick⟩ ⟨rushed ~ after the performance⟩ **2 :** in a backstage setting **:** SECRETLY, PRIVATELY ⟨officers of the convention were chosen ~⟩ ⟨working ~ to gain support for his plan⟩

[2]backstage \'⸗¦⸗\ *adj* **1 :** of, relating to, or occurring or carried on in a backstage ⟨~ voices and sounds to give the impression of a mob⟩ ⟨a ~ worker shifting scenery⟩ ⟨her ~ impersonations of the company's principal dancers —*Current Biog.*⟩ **2 :** of or relating to the private lives of actors, actresses, or theater people ⟨a ~ love affair⟩ or purporting to depict the private lives of theater people ⟨a ~ musical⟩ **3 :** of or relating to the hidden, inner, or behind-the-scenes workings or operations (as of an organization or institution) ⟨a key ~ figure in the new regime —*Newsweek*⟩ **:** concealed from public view ⟨~ deals and promises⟩

[3]backstage \'⸗¦⸗\ *n* [[3]*back* + *stage*] **:** the whole or any part of the area of a stage that is behind the proscenium; *specif* **:** the dressing rooms of a theater

back·stairs *also* **back·stair** \'⸗¦⸗\ *adj* [*back stairs*, n.] **1 :** characterized by a quality and air of secrecy and intrigue ⟨~ deals⟩ ⟨~ gossip⟩ **:** FURTIVE, DEVIOUS ⟨his low ~ cunning —A.L. Guérard⟩ **2 :** having a sordid or scandalous character ⟨~ intimacies —A.L.Kroeber⟩ ⟨cheap ~ fiction —E.A.Weeks⟩

[1]backstamp \'⸗¦⸗\ *vt* [[1]*back* + *stamp*] **:** to stamp on the back; *specif* **:** to stamp (a piece of mail) with the date of receipt and the name of the receiving post office along the transportation route

[2]backstamp \"\ *n* **:** a stamp (as a date stamp or postmark) on the back of a piece of mail

backstand \'⸗,⸗\ *n* **:** a device for regulating machinery belt tension

[1]backstay \'⸗,⸗\ *n* [[3]*back* + *stay*] **1 a :** a stay extending from the mastheads to the side of a ship and slanting a little aft — see SHIP illustration **b :** a supporting cable (as on a derrick) that prevents a falling forward of a more or less vertical part **2 :** any of various strengthening or supporting devices at the back or rear: as **a :** a rope or strap to prevent excessive forward motion (as of the carriage in a hand printing press) **b :** a spring used to keep the cutting edges of purchase shears in contact **c :** a bar topped with a glass rod running across a loom below the lowest motion of the warp yarns **d :** a rod extending from either end of the rear axle of a carriage to the reach **e :** a strip of leather covering and strengthening the back seam of a shoe

[2]backstay \"\ *vt* **:** to rig with backstays

backstay stool *n* **:** STOOL 6a

back·stein \'bäk,s(h)tīn\ *also* **back·stei·ner** \-nə(r)\ *n* -s *usu cap* [G *backsteinkäse*, lit., brick cheese, fr. *backstein* brick (fr. *backen* to bake — fr. OHG *backan* — + *stein* stone, fr. OHG) + *käse* cheese; akin to OHG *bahhan* to bake — more at BAKE, STONE] **:** a German cheese resembling limburger that is produced in brick shape

backstick \'⸗,⸗\ *n* **:** a large stick placed on or used as a backlog

[1]backstitch \'⸗,⸗\ *n* [[3]*back* + *stitch*] **:** a hand stitch resembling machine stitching that is made by inserting the needle a stitch length to the right and bringing it up an equal distance to the left

[2]backstitch \"\ *vb* **:** to sew with backstitches

back·stone \'bak,stōn, -,stən\ *dial Eng var of* BAKESTONE

back stool *n* **:** a stool with a back added for extra comfort **:** an early form of side chair

[1]back·stop \'bak,stäp\ *n* [[3]*back* + *stop*] **:** something serving as a stop behind something else: as **a :** a screen or fence (as that behind home plate in baseball or that behind the base line of a tennis court) intended to stop balls leaving the field of play **b :** a player (as the catcher in baseball or the wicket-keeper in cricket) whose position is behind the batter **c :** a stop (as a pawl) that prevents a backward movement (as of a wheel, elevator, or conveyor) beyond a certain point **d :** a dirt mound or other obstruction to catch the bullets going through or beyond the target in a rifle or pistol range

[2]backstop \'⸗,⸗\ *vt* **1 :** to serve as a backstop to ⟨barberry hedge . . . did its poor best to ~ errant baseballs —Philip Brady⟩ **2 :** to provide with backing or support **:** BOLSTER ⟨a lawyer, who ~*s* the president on problems involving national security —*Newsweek*⟩ ⟨no reserves except a British tank division which *backstopped* the line wherever it weakened —*Time*⟩

back straddle vault *n* **:** a gymnastics straddle vault in which the performer passes the left leg over the right side of the buck or horse and the right leg over the left side and clears the apparatus backward to land in a position the reverse of the starting position

back·strap \'⸗,⸗\ *n* **1 :** a pull strap attached to the top of the backstay of a shoe or boot **2 :** BACKBONE 3

back–strapped \'⸗,⸗\ *adj* [[2]*back*] *of a sailing ship* **:** forced by adverse winds or currents to leeward of a point to be weathered

back stream *n* **:** EDDY

back street *n* **:** a street away or far from the main thoroughfares

backstretch \'⸗¦⸗\ *n* **:** the far straightaway opposite the homestretch on an oval racecourse

back·strip \'⸗,⸗\ *n* [[1]*back* + *strip*] **:** BACKBONE 3

backstroke \'⸗,⸗\ *n* **1 :** a swimming stroke executed on the back and resembling an inverted crawl or inverted butterfly breaststroke but with more knee flexion and usu. six inverted crawl leg beats to an arm cycle **2 :** the bell ringer's pull on the rope that starts the bell down from its poised mouth-up position in full ringing — compare HANDSTROKE 2

backswamp \'⸗,⸗\ *n* **:** a swamp in a backland ⟨a ~ area⟩

back swath *n* **:** the swath that is next to the first one cut, that is usu. cut in the opposite direction, and that the tractor or horses have traveled over in cutting the first swath

back·swept \'⸗¦⸗\ *adj* [[2]*back* + *swept*] **:** swept, brushed, slanted, or slanting backward ⟨his gray ~ hair⟩ ⟨a full ~ skirt⟩; *specif* **:** characterized by or possessing sweepback ⟨a ~ airplane wing⟩

back swimmer *n* [[1]*back*] **:** an insect of the family Notonectidae characterized by swimming with the ventral surface uppermost

backswing \'⸗,⸗\ *n* [[3]*back* + *swing*] **:** the movement of a club, racket, or bat backward to the position from which the downward or forward stroke is made

backsword \'⸗,⸗\ *n* [[1]*back* + *sword*] **1 :** a sword with only one sharp edge **2 :** SINGLESTICK **3 :** *or* **back·sword·man** \-mən\ *pl* **backswordmen :** a fencer with the backsword

back·sword·ing \-diŋ\ *or* **back·sword** *n* -s **:** fencing with a backsword or singlestick

back talk *n* [[3]*back* + *talk* (after *talk back*, v.)] **:** an impudent, insolent, or argumentative reply esp. from a subordinate ⟨would take no *back talk* from his children⟩

back–tan \'⸗,⸗\ *vt* [[2]*back*] **:** to treat (dyed material) with tannin in order to fix the dye — **back–tanning** \'⸗,⸗⸗\ *n* -s

back taper *n* **:** a slight relief on a tap or drill causing it to have a larger diameter at the point than at the shank

back·tend·er \'⸗,⸗⸗\ *n* **:** a worker who tends the discharge end of an industrial machine: as **a :** one who tends the drier, calender, and slitting and rewinding sections of a paper machine **b :** a textile worker who rolls or folds cloth

back tendon *n* **:** BACK SINEW

back·ten·ter \'⸗,tentə(r)\ *Brit var of* BACKTENDER a

back–titrate \(')⸗¦⸗,⸗\ *vt, chem* **:** to titrate back to the end point after it has been passed — **back–titration** \¦⸗,⸗¦⸗⸗\ *n*

back to back *adj* **1 :** facing in opposite directions and often touching ⟨standing in a row *back to back*⟩ ⟨train seats *back to back*⟩ **2 :** dealt one in the hole and one face up — used of a pair in stud poker ⟨aces *back to back*⟩ **3 :** one after the other **:** CONSECUTIVE ⟨two home runs *back to back* in the third inning⟩ ⟨*back to back* telecasts⟩ **4** *of a letter of credit* **:** granted by a bank to an exporter to finance purchase of goods already covered by a letter of credit in his favor taken out by the importer

back–to–work \¦⸗⸗'⸗\ *adj* **:** urging or directing the return of strikers to their jobs ⟨a *back-to-work* movement⟩ ⟨a *back-to-work* injunction⟩

back track *n* [[3]*back* + *track*] **1 :** a return track or course **:** a track leading back to one's starting point; *also* **:** a retracing of one's steps ⟨took the *back track* through the woods⟩ ⟨beat a *back track* through the woods⟩ **2 :** a retreat from or reversal of a position or stand once taken ⟨after his assurance that he would help out, we did not expect so quick a *back track*⟩

backtrack \'⸗,⸗\ *vi* **1 :** to take or follow a back track **:** retrace one's steps ⟨when the trail became impassable, we ~*ed* to camp⟩ **2 :** to modify, retreat from, or reverse a position or stand once taken ⟨first thumping the table and laying down the law, then ~*ing* when the reaction sets in —*New Republic*⟩ ~ *vt* **:** to follow in the tracks of ⟨~*ed* many a Methodist circuit rider while educating himself in the mill towns of the Deep South —R.P.Ramsey⟩

back trail *n* **:** BACK TRACK

backtrail \'⸗,⸗\ *vb* [*back trail*] **:** BACKTRACK

back turn *n, music* **:** an inverted turn

back up *vi* **1** *of water checked by an obstruction* **:** to rise and flow backward or overflow adjacent areas ⟨clogged pipes caused drain water to *back up* into the house⟩ ⟨a dammed stream that *backs up* and floods a meadow⟩ **2** *of nonliquid objects* **:** to accumulate through lack of an outlet in undesirable or unmanageable excess or in a congested state ⟨supplies are ample, if not already *backing up* in the hands of the producers —*Biddle Survey*⟩ ⟨cars *back up* for blocks on either side of the Main Street traffic light —Louise Levitas⟩ **3** *cricket* **a** *of a batsman* **:** to move forward of one's crease in readiness to run **b** *of a nonstriker* **:** to so move as the ball is delivered ~ *vt* **:** to hold back (as a river) usu. causing an accumulation ⟨this dam . . . *backs up* billions of gallons of water to prevent floods —N.M.Clark⟩

backup \'⸗,⸗\ *n* -s [*back up*] **1 :** BACKING ⟨supported by military strength in being and strength in potential timely ~ —M.B.Ridgway⟩ ⟨a stiff ~ to the sheet so that it would not bend⟩ **2 :** an accumulation esp. as a result of the stoppage of a flow ⟨a ~ of sewage⟩ ⟨a ~ of cars before the intersection⟩ **:** RESERVE ⟨a ~ of material for emergency use⟩ **3 :** a backward movement **:** a retreat from a position ⟨asked Congress for a ~ on its policy and a repeal of the law⟩ **4 :** a ball that curves or fades to the right in bowling **5 :** a masonry backing to a wall **6 :** the presswork on the second side of a printed sheet

backup light *n* **:** a light mounted at the rear of a motor vehicle and so connected that it shines only when the vehicle is in reverse gear illuminating the road behind

backup relay *n* **:** a secondary relay to protect a power system against faults in the event of failure of the primary relay to function as desired

backup signal *n* **:** DWARF SIGNAL

backveld \'⸗,⸗\ *n* [[3]*back* + *veld;* prob. part trans. of Afrik *agterveld*] *Africa* **:** BACKCOUNTRY

back vent *n* **:** a ventilating pipe attached to a waste pipe on the sewer side of its trap to prevent siphonage — **back venting** *n*

[1]back·ward \'bakwə(r)d\ *or* **back·wards** \-dz\ *adv* [ME *bakward, bakwardes*, fr. *bak* back + *-ward, -wardes*] **1 a :** toward the back or rear ⟨throw the arms out and ~⟩ **b :** with the back in advance or foremost ⟨pull a chair ~ away from a table⟩ ⟨drive ~ up a driveway⟩ **2 a :** in the direction from which one came **:** in a reverse or contrary direction or way ⟨read ~⟩ ⟨do things ~⟩ ⟨turn a handle ~⟩ ⟨the tide ebbs ~ toward the sea —John DeMeyer⟩ **b :** toward the past ⟨lovers of romance who look fondly ~⟩ **c :** in a regressive direction ⟨under his administration the community was not only at a standstill but going ~⟩ **:** toward an earlier and worse state ⟨moving ~ culturally and morally⟩

[2]backward \"\ *adj* [ME *bakward*, fr. *bakward*, adv.] **1 a :** directed or turned backward ⟨a ~ glance⟩ ⟨a ~ movement of the train⟩ ⟨a ~ jerk of the arm —Wirt Williams⟩ ⟨a ~ slant to his handwriting⟩ **b :** done or executed backward ⟨a ~ twist of a handle⟩ **2** *archaic* **:** situated or placed toward or in the back or rear **3 :** RELUCTANT, DIFFIDENT, SHY ⟨a man hardly ~ in asserting himself⟩ ⟨a ~ suitor⟩ ⟨I have been ~ to begin my canvass —Edmund Burke⟩ **4 a :** slow to learn or dull of comprehension **:** mentally retarded ⟨a ~ child⟩ **b :** holding to outworn or traditional ideas, views, or principles **:** REACTIONARY, UNPROGRESSIVE ⟨a ~ person, imbued with strong and irrational prejudices⟩ **c :** in a relatively underdeveloped state esp. economically and socially ⟨technological assistance to the ~ areas of the world⟩ ⟨a ~ agrarian country⟩ ⟨desires to elevate the more ~ portions of the human family —Philip Mason⟩ **5 :** unsupported by a fellow pawn in chess and not readily movable to a position to be so supported — **back·ward·ly** *adv*

[3]backward \"\ *n* -s **:** the part behind or past ⟨the dark ~ . . . of time —Shak.⟩

back ward *n* **:** a ward where mentally ill patients whose prognosis is poor are housed and where patients typically receive only custodial care

back·ward·a·tion \,bakwə(r)'dāshən\ *n* -s [[1]*backward* + *-ation*] **1 :** the seller's postponement of delivery of stock or shares on the London Stock Exchange with the consent of the buyer upon payment of a premium to the latter **2 :** the premium paid in backwardation — compare CONTANGO

backward dive *n* **:** a dive in fancy diving from a position facing the board and keeping the back toward the water throughout — compare CUTAWAY

back·ward·ness \'bakwə(r)dnəs\ *n* -ES **:** the quality or state of being backward

backward pass *n* **:** a pass in football thrown at right angles to the direction of play or obliquely to the rear

[1]backwash \'⸗,⸗\ *n* [[3]*back* + *wash*] **1 a :** the motion of water or waves washed or thrown back (as by the propeller or oars of a boat) **b :** a backward flow or movement (as of air or matter) produced by and incidental or residual to some action or process ⟨the turbojet generates a ~ of such high velocity that the conventional wooden fences blow away —*Boeing Mag.*⟩ **2 :** a condition, movement, or event that is a reaction to or an extension, consequence, or by-product of some other event or development **:** SEQUEL, AFTERMATH, REPERCUSSION ⟨the ~ of English deism reached the shores of New England —V.L.Parrington⟩ ⟨Australians should have no fear of their ability to weather the ~ of an American recession —*Sydney (Australia) Bulletin*⟩ ⟨economic and social problems . . . are by no means the mere ~ of war and German occupation —Robert Strausz-Hupé⟩ **3 :** BACKWATER 4 ⟨an unspoiled rural paradise — called by some a ~ of eighteenth century manners and customs —*Amer. Guide Series: Del.*⟩

[2]backwash \"\ *vt* **1 :** to affect with backwash ⟨a steamer ~*ing* our small craft⟩ **2 :** to scour and dry (wool) in sliver form before or after combing **3 :** to clean (a water filter) by reversing the flow — **back·wash·er** \-shə(r)\ *n*

[1]backwater \'⸗,⸗⸗\ *n* [ME *bakwater*, fr. *bak* back + *water*] **1 a :** water turned back in its course (as in a sewer or river channel) by an obstruction, an opposing current, or the flow of the tide **b :** a body or accumulation of water resulting from this esp. when overflowing lowlands or forming a body fed by a side channel from the main current or sea **2 :** BACKWASH 1 **3 :** WHITE WATER 2 **4 :** an isolated, secluded, or backward place, section, or condition ⟨one of the cultural ~*s* of civilization⟩ ⟨the quiet ~ of a classroom —Anna M.Wells⟩ ⟨a rural New England ~ —R.F.Nichols⟩ **5 :** a large grayish or mottled Indo-Pacific ray (*Gymnura japonica*) esteemed for food

[2]backwater \"\ *vi* [[4]*back* + *water*, n.] **1 :** to reverse the usual forward rowing or paddling stroke usu. to check the forward motion of a boat or canoe or propel it backward **2 :** to retreat from a stand taken ⟨~ publicly on several issues⟩

backwearing \'⸗,⸗⸗\ *n* [[3]*back* + *wearing*] **:** erosion that causes an escarpment or mountain slope to retreat without changing its declivity

[1]backwind \'⸗¦⸗\ *n* [[3]*back* + *wind*] **:** a wind blowing onto the wrong side of a sail; *esp* **:** one directed upon a mainsail by a wrongly trimmed jib

[2]backwind \"\ *vt* **1 :** to direct a backwind upon ⟨a jib thus bellied is most apt to ~ the mainsail⟩ **2 :** to sail to windward of (another sailing ship) so as to blanket or interfere with the wind ⟨~ his opponent in a yacht race⟩

backwoods \'⸗¦⸗\ *n pl but sing or pl in constr, often attrib* **1 :** the wooded or outlying and only partly cleared areas on the frontier or in the backcountry ⟨the farmers who lived in the ~ and wrestled to clear the land —*Amer Guide Series: Ind.*⟩ **2 :** a rural area that is provincial or backward in culture or remote from the main centers of civilization ⟨a ~ newspaper⟩ ⟨the idiom of the East Texas ~ —G.S.Perry⟩

back·woods·er \-zə(r)\ *n* -s [*backwoods* + *-er*] **:** *chiefly Midland* **:** HICK, RUSTIC, BACKWOODSMAN

back·woods·man \'⸗¦⸗mən, ⸗'⸗mən\ *n, pl* **backwoodsmen** [*backwoods* + *man*] **1 :** one who lives in the backwoods **2** *Brit* **:** a member of the British House of Lords who takes little active part in the business of the house and rarely attends its meetings

back·woodsy \'⸗¦⸗ē, ⸗'⸗ē\ *adj* [*backwoods* + *-y*] **:** marked by plain, rustic, or uncouth speech, manners, or conduct ⟨five or six preachers . . . rough-cut and ~ —H.L.Davis⟩

back·wort \'bak,wərt, -wȯrt\ *n* -s [[1]*back* + *wort*] **:** COMFREY 1

backy \'bakē\ *n* -ES [by shortening & alter.] *dial* **:** TOBACCO

backyard \'⸗'⸗ *attrib* '⸗¦⸗\ *n, often attrib* **1 a :** an area often enclosed by a fence in the rear of a house or other habitation ⟨admired a lilac in his ~ —Nell G.Ahern⟩ ⟨a ~ shed⟩ **b :** an area or lot behind the main tent of a circus where property tents and dressing tents are located ⟨in the ~ . . . the equestrian director was given a dressing wagon —Hartzell Spence⟩ **2 :** an area that is close, easily accessible, and in a peculiarly intimate relation to a person, group, or another area ⟨right here in our own ~ we have some of the finest designers in the world —*New Englander*⟩ ⟨Latin America was the air ~ of the U.S. —A.P. de Seversky⟩

backyarder *var of* BACKLOTTER

ba·co·lod \bə'kō,lȯd\ *adj, usu cap* [fr. *Bacolod*, Philippines] **:** of or from the city of Bacolod, Philippines **:** of the kind or style prevalent in Bacolod

ba·con \'bākən *sometimes* -kᵊŋ\ *n* -s [ME *bacon, bacoun*, fr. MF *bacon*, of Gmc origin; akin to OHG *bahho* side of bacon — more at BACK] **1 :** a side of a pig after removal of spareribs and after being cured dry or in pickle and smoked **2** *obs slang* **:** HICK, RUSTIC **3** *South & Midland* **:** brine-cured bacon **:** SALT PORK — called also *white bacon*

bacon beetle *n* **:** LARDER BEETLE

bacon biliteral cipher \"-\ *n, cap 1st B* [after Francis *Bacon*, who proposed it] **:** a cipher that hides a message in a cover text by representing the letters of the plaintext by different combinations of two letter forms (as italic and roman) in each sequence of five letters of the cover text (as when "Spr*ing*-fie*l*d, Mass" hides the word CAB by the code xxxx*x*=A, xxx*xx*=B, xxxx*x*=C)

ba·con·er \'bākənə(r)\ *n* -s *Brit* **:** BACON HOG

bacon hog *also* **bacon pig** *n* **:** a hog raised for bacon or of a type fit to be made into bacon and other cured products **:** a meat-type hog

[1]ba·co·nian \(')bā¦kōnēən *also* bə'k- *or* -nyən\ *also* **ba·con·ic** \-känik\ *adj, usu cap* [Francis *Bacon* †1626 Eng. philosopher & author + E *-ian* or *-ic*] **1 a :** of or relating to Francis Bacon or his doctrines, esp. his belief in the inductive origin of valid ideas, the testing of ideas by controlled and scientific methods, and human progress and improvement by the control of nature through scientific knowledge ⟨their *Baconian* fear of speculative hypotheses —Sidney Ratner⟩ ⟨the *Baconian* principle of scientific investigation —C.W.Shumaker⟩ ⟨the *Baconian* theory of the experiential origin of all ideas to counter . . . intuitionism and absolutism —Willis Moore⟩ **b** *of a logical method* **:** consisting of the process of attaining general statements on the basis of observations, comparisons, and experiments through intermediate generalizations and with regard for negative as well as positive instances — compare INDUCTION **2 :** of or relating to the Baconians who believe that Francis Bacon was the author of the dramatic works usu. attributed to Shakespeare

[2]baconian \"\ *n* -s *usu cap* **:** one who supports or believes in Baconian doctrines

baconian induction *n, usu cap B* **:** the inductive method developed by Francis Bacon that consists in inferring that what has been observed or established in respect to a part, individual, or species may on the ground of analogy be affirmed or received of the whole to which it belongs — compare INDUCTION

ba·co·nian·ism \⸗'⸗(⸗)⸗,nizəm\ *n* -s *usu cap* **:** Baconian philosophy or scientific method

ba·con·ism \'bākə,nizəm\ *n, usu cap* [Francis *Bacon* + E *-ism*] **:** BACONIANISM

bacon square *n* **:** the jowl of a pig trimmed square, cured, and smoked

bacon type *n* **:** a type of hog adapted to producing the largest possible proportion of high-grade bacon

ba·con·weed \'⸗⸗,⸗\ *n* **:** LAMB'S-QUARTERS 1

ba·co·pa \bə'kōpə\ *n, cap* [NL, prob. fr. a native name in the Guianas] **:** a genus of chiefly tropical herbs (family Scrophulariaceae) with opposite leaves and small solitary flowers — see WATER HYSSOP

bac·so·ni·an \(')bak¦sōnēən\ *adj, usu cap* [*Bac-son*, locality in Tonkin, northern Vietnam, where the remains were found + E *-ian*] **:** of or relating to a Neolithic culture of southeast Asia characterized by unpainted pottery and polished stone implements

bact *abbr* **1** bacteriological; bacteriology **2** bacterium

-bac·ter \,baktə(r)\ *n comb form* [NL, fr. *bacterium*] **:** bacterial organism — in generic names ⟨Aero*bacter*⟩ ⟨Nitro*bacter*⟩

bac·te·re·mia \,baktə'rēmēə\ *or* **bac·te·ri·e·mia** *also* **bac·te·ri·ae·mia** \(,)bak,tirē'ēmēə\ *n* -s [*bacteremia*, NL, alter. of *bacteriemia, bacteriaemia; bacteriemia, bacteriaemia*, NL, fr. *bacteri-* + *-emia, -aemia*] **:** the usu. transient presence of bacteria or other microorganisms in the blood — compare SEPTICEMIA

bac·te·re·mic \¦baktə¦rēmik\ *adj* [NL *bacteremia* + E *-ic*] **:** being, relating to, or having bacteremia

bacteri- *or* **bacterio-** *comb form* [*bacterium*] **:** bacteria **:** bacterial ⟨*bacteri*form⟩ ⟨*bacterio*blast⟩ ⟨*bacterio*lysis⟩

bacteria *pl of* BACTERIUM

bac·te·ri·a·ce·ae \(,)bak,tirē'āsē,ē\ *n pl, cap* [NL, fr. *Bacterium*, type genus + *-aceae*] **1** *in some classifications* **:** a large family of rod-shaped usu. gram-negative bacteria (order Eubacteriales) that produce no spores and have a complex metabolism utilizing amino acids and generally carbohydrates **2** *in former classifications* **:** a family comprising all simple cylindrical bacteria lacking a sheath and including Bacteriaceae, *Bacillus*, and a number of other groups — **bac·te·ri·a·ceous** \(')⸗¦⸗⸗¦āshəs\ *adj*

bac·te·ri·a·cide \bak'tirēə,sīd\ *n* -s [by alter.] **:** BACTERICIDE

bac·te·ri·al \(')bak¦tirēəl, -tēr-\ *adj* [ISV *bacteri-* + *-al*] **:** belonging to, consisting of, resulting from, or caused by bacteria ⟨~ ooze⟩ ⟨~ decomposition⟩ ⟨~ wilt⟩ — **bac·te·ri·al·ly** \-rēəlē, -li\ *adv*

bacterial blight *n* **:** a blight of plants caused by bacteria: as **a :** HALO BLIGHT **b :** ANGULAR LEAF SPOT **c :** CELERY BLIGHT

bacterial canker *n* **:** any of various plant diseases caused by bacteria and characterized by the formation of cankers: as **a :** a disease of stone fruits (as plums and cherries) caused by bacteria of the genus *Pseudomonas* and marked by cankers on affected branches with copious exudation of gum and often severe dieback of affected areas **b :** TOMATO CANKER

bacterial nodule *n* **:** NODULE 2b(3)

bacterial speck *n* **:** a bacterial plant disease characterized by the production of small lesions — compare SPECK 3b

bacterial spot *n* **:** a bacterial plant disease characterized by spotting of the affected parts

bacterial vaccine *n* **:** BACTERIN

bacterial virus *n* **:** BACTERIOPHAGE

bacterial warfare *n* **:** BIOLOGICAL WARFARE

bac·te·ri·cid·al \(')bak¦tirə¦sīdᵊl\ *adj* **:** of or relating to a bactericide **:** destroying bacteria — **bac·te·ri·cid·al·ly** \-ᵊlē\ *adv*

bac·te·ri·cide \bak'tirə,sīd\ *n* -s [ISV *bacteri-* + *-cide*] **:** something that destroys bacteria

bac·te·ri·cid·in \bak¦tirə¦sīdᵊn\ *or* **bac·te·ri·o·cid·in** \bak,tirēə'sī-\ *n* -s [*bactericide* + *-in*] **:** an antibody that kills microorganisms against which it is active

bac·ter·id \'baktərəd\ *n* -s [*bacteri-* + *-id*] **:** a skin eruption associated with bacterial infection — compare ID

bacteriemia *also* **bacteriaemia** *var of* BACTEREMIA

bac·ter·in \'baktərən\ *n* -s [*bacteri-* + *-in*] **:** a suspension of killed or attenuated bacteria injected into a living body to stimulate the development of immunity to the same kind of bacteria

bacterio- — see BACTERI-

bac·te·rio·chlorophyll \bak¦tirēə+\ *n* -s [*bacteri-* + *chlorophyll*] **:** a pyrrole derivative in photosynthetic bacteria related to but not identical with the chlorophyll of higher plants

bac·te·rio·cid·al \(')bak¦tirēə¦sīdᵊl\ *adj* [*bacteri-* + *-cidal*] : BACTERICIDAL

bac·te·rio·cyte \bak'tirēə,sīt, -'tē-\ *n* -s [ISV *bacteri-* + *-cyte*] : a modified fat cell occurring in the fat body of certain insects and containing groups of bacterium-shaped rods that are believed to be symbiotic bacteria — compare MYCETOCYTE

bac·te·rio·fre·nic \bak¦tirēə¦frēnik\ *adj* [*bacteri-* + L *frenare* to curb, bridle (fr. *frenum* bridle) + E *-ic* — more at FRENUM] : checking the development of bacteria

bac·te·rio·gen·ic \-ə'jenik, -ēk\ *also* **bac·te·ri·og·e·nous** \-'äjənəs\ *adj* [*bacteri-* + *-genic, -genous*] : caused by bacteria

bacterioid *also* **bacterioidal** *var of* BACTEROID

bac·te·rio·log·ic \(')bak¦tirēə¦läjik, -tēr-, -jēk\ *or* **bac·te·rio·log·i·cal** \-jəkəl, -ēk-\ *adj* : of or belonging to bacteriology — **bac·te·ri·o·log·i·cal·ly** \-jək(ə)lē, -ēk-, -li\ *adv*

bacteriological warfare *n* : BIOLOGICAL WARFARE

bac·te·ri·ol·o·gist \(,)=,=='äləjəst\ *n* -s : one who specializes in the study of bacteria

bac·te·ri·ol·o·gy \(,)bak,tirē'äləjē, -tēr-, -ji\ *n* -ES [ISV *bacteri-* + *-logy*] **1** : a science that deals with the study of bacteria and with their relations to medicine, industry, and agriculture **2** : bacterial life and phenomena ⟨the ~ of a water supply⟩ ⟨the ~ of a disease⟩

bac·te·rio·ly·sin \bak,tirēə'līsᵊn\ *n* -s [ISV *bacteri-* + *lysin*] **1** : an antibody that acting together with its complement causes the solution of the microorganism against which it is directed **2** : an antibody that kills the microorganism against which it is active with or without lysis : BACTERICIDIN

bac·te·ri·ol·y·sis \(,)=,=='äləsəs\ *n, pl* **bacterioly·ses** \-ə,sēz\ [NL, fr. *bacteri-* + *-lysis*] : the destruction or dissolution of bacterial cells (as by antibodies)

bac·te·rio·lyt·ic \bak¦tirēə¦lid·ik\ *adj* [fr. NL *bacteriolysis,* after such pairs as E *analysis: analytic*] : of, belonging to, or producing bacteriolysis

bac·te·rio·phage \bak'tirēə,fāj\ *n* -s [ISV *bacteri-* + *-phage;* orig. formed in F] : any of various specific bacteriolytic viruses or bacteria-destroying agents that are normally present in sewage, in the intestinal tracts of man and animals esp. when recovering from a bacterial infection, and in blood, pus, urine, or other body products and that are of uncertain nature though possessing definite organization and certain other attributes of living matter — **bac·te·rio·phag·ic** \=¦===¦fajik\ *or* **bac·te·ri·oph·a·gous** \¦=,==¦äfəgəs\ *adj* — **bac·te·ri·oph·a·gy** \(,)=,=='==jē\ *n* -ES

bac·te·rio·purpurin \bak¦tirē(,)ō+\ *n* [*bacteri-* + *purpurin*] : a red coloring matter present in some bacteria that has the power of reducing highly oxidized compounds by absorption of certain rays of light; *broadly* : any of several bacterial photosynthetic pigments

bac·te·rio·scop·ic \bak¦tirēə¦skäpik\ *adj* : of, belonging to, or involving bacterioscopy

bac·te·ri·os·co·py \=,=='äskəpē\ *n* -ES [*bacteri-* + *-scopy*] : microscopic examination or investigation of bacteria

bac·te·rio·sis \(,)=,=='ōsəs\ *n, pl* **bacterio·ses** \-ō,sēz\ [NL, fr. *bacteri-* + *-osis*] : any bacterial disease of plants

bac·te·ri·osta·sis \bak,tirēō'stāsəs, -rē'ästəsəs,-rēō'stasəs\ *n, pl* **bacteriosta·ses** \-,sēz\ [NL, fr. *bacteri-* + *-stasis*] : inhibition of the growth of bacteria without destruction — **bac·te·rio·stat·ic** \=¦==ō¦stad·ik\ *adj* — **bac·te·rio·stat·i·cal·ly** \-d·ək(ə)lē\ *adv*

bac·te·rio·stat \bak'tirēō,stat\ *also* **bac·te·rio·stat·ic** \=,==='stad·ik\ *n* -s [*bacteri-* + *-stat* or *-static*] : an agent that causes bacteriostasis

bac·te·rio·tome \bak'tirēə,tōm\ *n* -s [*bacteri-* + *-tome*] : a mycetome containing bacteria

bac·te·rio·tox·in \=,==='täksən\ *n* [ISV *bacteri-* + *toxin*] : a specific substance that destroys or inhibits bacteria growth

bac·te·rio·trop·ic \=¦===¦träpik\ *adj* [ISV *bacteri-* + *-tropic*] : directed toward bacteria or affecting them in a specific way

bac·te·ri·ot·ro·pin \(,)=,=='ä·trəpən\ *n* -s [ISV *bacteri-* + *-trope* + *-in;* orig. formed in G] : any of certain constituents (probably antibodies) of serum that unite with bacteria and make them more susceptible to phagocytosis

bac·te·rit·ic \¦baktə¦rid·ik\ *adj* [*bacteri-* + *-itic*] : showing the presence of or caused by bacteria

bac·te·ri·um \bak'tirēəm, -tēr-\ *n* [NL, fr. Gk *baktērion* small staff, dim. of *baktēria* staff; akin to L *baculum* staff, Gk *baktron* stick] **1** *cap, in some classifications* : a more or less inclusive genus comprising straight rod-shaped bacteria with no flagella and (in modern usage) no spores and including a variable assemblage of species most of which are more commonly placed in other genera — compare ACETOBACTER, AEROBACTER, ALCALIGENES **2** *pl* **bacte·ria** \-rēə\ : any of a large group of microscopic plants constituting the class Schizomycetes, having round, rodlike, spiral, or filamentous single-celled or noncellular bodies that are often aggregated into colonies, are enclosed by a cell wall or membrane, usu. lack fully differentiated nuclei, and are often motile by means of flagella, reproducing by fission, by the formation of asexual resting spores or, in some higher forms, by conidia or by imperfectly understood sexual processes, living in soil, water, organic matter or the live bodies of plants and animals, and being autotrophic, saprophytic, or parasitic in nutrition and important to man because of their chemical effects (as in nitrogen fixation, putrefaction, and various fermentations) and as pathogens **syn** see MICROORGANISM

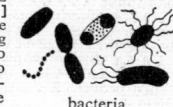

bacteria

bac·te·ri·uria \(,)=,=='yu̇rēə\ *n* -s [NL, fr. *bacteri-* + *-uria*] : BACILLURIA

bac·te·ri·za·tion \,baktərə'zāshən\ *n* -s : the act of bacterizing : the state of being bacterized

bac·te·rize \'baktə,rīz\ *vt* -ED/-ING/-S [*bacteri-* + *-ize*] : to subject to or modify by bacterial action ⟨*bacterized* peat⟩

1bac·te·roid \'baktə,ròid\ *or* **bac·te·roi·dal** \¦==¦ròidᵊl\ *also* **bac·te·ri·oid** \bak'tirē,òid\ *or* **bac·te·ri·oi·dal** \(')bak¦tirē¦òidᵊl\ *adj* [ISV *bacter-, bacteri-* (fr. NL *bacterium*) + *-oid, -oidal*] : resembling bacteria

2bacteroid \"\ *n* -s **1** : an enlarged branched bacterium (as the rhizobia found in the tubercles of leguminous plants) **2** : a symbiotic bacterium or an inclusion like a bacterium in the bacteriocytes of the fat body of certain insects

bac·te·roi·da·ce·ae \,baktə,ròi'dāsē,ē\ *n pl, cap* [NL, fr. *Bacteroides*, type genus + *-aceae*] : a family of extremely varied gram-negative bacteria (order Eubacteriales) that usu. live in the alimentary canal or on mucous surfaces of warm-blooded animals and are sometimes associated with acute infected processes — see BACTEROIDES

bacteroidal cell *n* : a peritoneal or coelomic cell in certain invertebrates that is packed with rodlike inclusions thought by some to be bacterial symbionts and by others excretory products

bac·te·roi·des \,baktə'ròi(,)dēz\ *n* [NL, fr. *bacterium* + *-oides*] **1** *cap* : a genus (the type of the family Bacteroidaceae) of gram-negative anaerobic bacteria having rounded ends, producing no endospores and no pigment, and living usu. in the normal intestinal tract **2** *pl* **bacteroides** : a bacterium of *Bacteroides* or a closely related genus

1bac·tri·an \'baktrēən\ *n* -s *usu cap* [L *Bactrianus*, adj. & n, fr. Gk *Baktrianos*, fr. *Baktria* Bactria, ancient country of southwestern Asia + Gk *-anos* -an] **1** : one of an ancient Iranian people located between the Hindu Kush and the Oxus **2** : the language of the Bactrians

2bactrian \"\ *adj, usu cap* [L *Bactrianus*] : of or relating to Bactria, a satrapy of ancient Persia

bactrian camel *also* **bactrian** *n, usu cap B* : the 2-humped camel

bac·tris \'baktrəs\ *n, cap* [NL, modif. of Gk *baktron* stick, staff — more at BACTERIUM] : a large genus of tropical American pinnate-leaved usu. spiny palms (family Palmae) with small fruit consisting of a fibrous pulp enclosing a hard, mostly oily, and sometimes edible nut

bac·tri·tes \bak'trīd·ēz\ *n, cap* [NL, fr. Gk *baktron* stick, staff + L *-ites* -ite] : a genus of Devonian ammonoids with straight tapering shells and simple sutures — **bac·tri·toid** \'baktrə,tòid\ *adj*

bac·trit·i·cone \bak'trid·ə,kōn\ *n* -s [NL *Bactrites* + E *-i-* + *cone*] : a straight ammonoid with simple sutures corresponding to the orthoceracone among the nautiloids

ba·cu·bert *also* **bac·cu·bert** \¦ba(,)kyü¦be(ə)r\ *n*, -s *usu cap* [F] : a semiceremonial sword dance of Dauphiné and Piedmont, France

bacula *pl of* BACULUM

baculi *pl of* BACULUS

bac·u·li·form \'bakyələ,fòrm; ba'kyül-, bə-\ *adj* [L *baculum* + E *-iform*] : shaped like a rod ⟨~ chromosomes⟩

bac·u·lite \'bakyə,līt\ *n* -s [NL *Baculites*] : an ammonoid of the genus *Baculites*

bac·u·li·tes \,bakyə'līd·ēz\ *n, cap* [NL, fr. L *baculum* + *-ites* -ite] : a genus of extinct Cretaceous ammonoids having the shell straight like a tapering rod — **baculitic** \¦==¦lid·ik\ *adj* — **baculoid** \'==,lòid\ *n* -s

bac·u·lit·i·cone \-'lid·ə,kōn\ *n* -s [*baculite* + *-i-* + *cone*] : any ammonoid (as a baculite) with a straight shell

bac·u·lum \'bakyələm\ *n, pl* **baculums** \-ləmz\ *or* **bacu·la** \-lə\ [NL, fr. L, staff, stick — more at BACTERIUM] : a slender bone reinforcing the penis in many mammals

bac·u·lus \-ləs\ *n, pl* **bacu·li** \-,lī, -,lē\ [LL; akin to L *baculum* staff] : a staff esp. one that is symbolic of authority (as the pastoral staff of a bishop)

ba·cu·ry *also* **ba·cu·ri** *or* **ba·ku·ri** \¦bäk(y)ə¦rē, ¦bak-\ *n, pl* **bacuries** *also* **bacuris** *or* **bakuris** [Pg *bacuri*, fr. Tupi] : a tropical So. American timber tree (*Platonia insignis*) valued for its yellowish brown wood and for its pleasantly perfumed edible fruits which yield an oil used in soapmaking

1bad *archaic past of* BID *or of* BIDE

2bad \'bad, -aa(ə)d,-aid\ *adj* **worse** \'wərs, -ōs,-əis\ *also sometimes* **badder** *also sometimes* **wors·er** \-sə(r)\ **worst** \'wərst, -ōst, -əist\ *also sometimes* **baddest** [ME *badde;* prob. akin to OE *bǣddel* hermaphrodite, *bǣdan* to defile] **1 a** : failing to come up to or achieve a certain standard : failing to display or attain the worth, quality, shape, or appearance proper or appropriate to its type or species : POOR, WORTHLESS, BLEMISHED ⟨a ~ car⟩ ⟨a ~ complexion⟩ ⟨a ~ book⟩ ⟨a ~ repair job⟩ **b** : unfavorable or derogatory in significance or tendency ⟨made a ~ impression on the examiners⟩ ⟨had ~ reports about his conduct⟩ ⟨youthful escapades gave him a ~ name⟩ : marked by unfavorable or unfortunate events, trends, or occurrences ⟨a ~ year for Rome —Robert Graves⟩ : contrary to expectations or hopes : INAUSPICIOUS ⟨the messenger brought ~ news⟩ ⟨regard the present as a ~ time to buy durable consumer goods —S.H.Slichter⟩ **c** : DECAYED, ROTTEN, SPOILED ⟨the meat has gone ~⟩ : DILAPIDATED : run-down ⟨a farmhouse in a ~ state⟩ **2 a** : having an evil, depraved, or vicious character or tendency ⟨a thoroughly ~ man, without a trace of feeling or conscience⟩ ⟨a ~ book, sowing harmful deluding ideas⟩ : IMMORAL ⟨gossip had it that she was a ~ girl⟩ **b** : MISCHIEVOUS, INTRACTABLE, DISOBEDIENT ⟨a ~ child⟩ **3 a** : inadequate or unsuited to its purpose : UNSATISFACTORY ⟨a ~ plan⟩ ⟨a ~ light to read by⟩ **b** : unsuccessful or unprofitable esp. on account of a lack (as of good judgment or skill) ⟨a ~ buy⟩ ⟨a ~ investment⟩ ⟨a ~ shot⟩ : displaying or revealing poor judgment or lack of skill ⟨a wild golf shot caused by ~ timing on the down stroke⟩ **4 a** (1) : offensive or painful to one's senses : DISAGREEABLE, DISPLEASING, UNPLEASANT ⟨a ~ smell⟩ ⟨a ~ taste⟩ (2) : causing or attended by sensations of discomfort or unease ⟨spent a few ~ minutes waiting for the jury's decision⟩ **b** *of language* : IMPROPER, BLASPHEMOUS ⟨scolded the boy for using ~ language⟩ **5 a** : inimical to welfare : INJURIOUS, DELETERIOUS, HARMFUL ⟨too close reading is often ~ for the eyes⟩ ⟨a climate ~ for the health⟩ **b** : severe or distressing esp. more so than is usual or customary ⟨a ~ cold⟩ ⟨a ~ shock⟩ **c** : DISASTROUS, CALAMITOUS ⟨a ~ train wreck⟩ ⟨a ~ forest fire⟩ **d** : causing or offering difficulty ⟨as languages go, I'd say Japanese isn't ~ —Bernard Bloch⟩ ⟨we went up the Elena Glacier . . . and found it as ~ as we had feared —D.L.Busk⟩ **6** : INCORRECT, FAULTY, SUBSTANDARD ⟨~ grammar⟩ ⟨conduct in the *worst* taste⟩ **7 a** : in pain or discomfort : ILL, SICK ⟨~ with fever⟩ ⟨the cold made him feel generally ~⟩ **b** : DISEASED, UNHEALTHY, DEFICIENT ⟨~ teeth⟩ ⟨a ~ constitution⟩ **8 a** : SORROWFUL, DOWNCAST, DEJECTED ⟨feel ~ at the death of a friend⟩ **b** : SORRY, REGRETFUL, REMORSEFUL ⟨feel ~ about slighting a friend⟩ **c** *of a person's character or disposition* : IRRITABLE, CROSS, SURLY ⟨everybody was in a ~ humor except the chief —Dashiell Hammett⟩ **9 a** : not legally good : INVALID, VOID ⟨a ~ claim⟩ **b** *of a debt* : not collectible **c** *of a check* : issued without sufficient funds in the bank to cover **d** *in games* : FOUL : not counted or counted against a player according to the rules ⟨a ~ tennis shot falling several feet outside the base line⟩

syn ILL, EVIL, WICKED, NAUGHTY: BAD, a very general term, applies to anything or anyone reprehensible, for whatever reason and to whatever degree ⟨Svengali walking up and down the earth seeking whom he might cheat, betray, exploit, borrow money from, make brutal fun of, bully if he dared, cringe to if he must — man, woman, child, or dog — was about as *bad* as they make 'em —George du Maurier⟩ ⟨that *bad* man in one of his raving outbursts threatened us with a terrifying increase in the numbers and activities of his U-boats . . . —Sir Winston Churchill⟩ ⟨she often stole little foods from the table and . . . ate them at odd hours of the night, with the pleased expression of a *bad* child —Sinclair Lewis⟩ ILL may imply vice or malevolence ⟨it was *ill* counsel had misled the girl —Alfred Tennyson⟩ ⟨the far results of an *ill* deed involve the innocent with the guilty —H.O.Taylor⟩ EVIL often adds the sinister to the reprehensible ⟨who attended him as his shadow and his *evil* genius — a confidential colleague who betrayed his confidence, mocked his projects, derided his authority —J.L.Motley⟩ ⟨the *evil* counselors who . . . abused his youth —J.R.Green⟩ ⟨an *evil* and treacherous folk, and they lied and murdered for gold —William Morris⟩ WICKED usually implies severe moral reprehensibility ⟨the *wicked* sorcerers who have done people to death by their charms —J.G.Frazer⟩ It may also suggest malevolence or malice ⟨this injury . . . has rankled in his *wicked*, scheming brain, and all his life he has longed for vengeance —A. Conan Doyle⟩ NAUGHTY generally applies to trivial misbehavior of children ⟨Charles never was a *naughty* boy. He never robbed birds' nests, or smoked behind the barn, or played marbles on Sunday —Margaret Deland⟩ Sometimes it suggests reprehensibility in a light and playful way ⟨can't I be a *naughty* little thing? —J.M.Cain⟩ ⟨the still popular, and still *naughty*, and perpetually profane Decameron —Gilbert Highet⟩

— **in a bad way** : having serious difficulty ⟨public schools are at the present time *in a bad way* —M.B.Smith⟩ ⟨the stricken man was *in* such *a bad way* he was immediately hospitalized⟩ — **too bad** : REGRETTABLE ⟨it is *too bad* that rewards often do not come to deserving men⟩

3bad \"\ *n* -s [ME *badde*, fr. *badde*, adj.] **1 a** : something that is bad ⟨the ~ or good I say of myself I say of them —Walt Whitman⟩ **b** : the bad part or portion of something ⟨the good in him was at constant variance with the ~⟩ **2** : an evil, unhappy, or degenerate state ⟨from ~ to worse⟩ ⟨he went to the ~ early in life⟩ — **in bad** *adv* : in or into disfavor ⟨lose a job by getting *in bad* with the boss⟩

4bad \"\ *adv* [2*bad*] **1** : BADLY ⟨want something ~ enough to fight for it⟩ ⟨the man was not doing so ~ despite handicaps⟩ ⟨the Americans didn't know how ~ off they were until daylight —E.J.Kahn⟩ **2** *substand* : SEVERELY, SERIOUSLY ⟨in the fight he was roughed up ~ and ended in the hospital⟩ ⟨mess up a plan real ~⟩ ⟨being ~ sick —James Jones⟩ ⟨put his fist through a window and cut it up ~⟩

bad actor *n* : an unruly, turbulent, or contentious individual : TROUBLEMAKER ⟨Nick's horse was a notorious *bad actor*, a kicker —D.M.Mankiewicz⟩ ⟨the boy became a *bad actor* early and ended in reform school⟩

ba·da·ga \bə'dägə\ *n, pl* **badaga** *or* **badagas** *usu cap* [Kanarese *baḍaga*, lit., northman] **1 a** : a Dravidian agricultural people of southern India **b** : a member of such people **2** : the dialect of Kanarese that is the language of the Badaga people

ba·dak \'bä,däk\ *n* -s [native name in Java] : a Javanese rhinoceros (*Rhinoceros sundaicus*) nearing extinction in most of its range

ba·dan \bə'dän, -an\ *n* -s [Russ] : a Siberian plant (*Saxifraga crassifolia*) whose roots are used as a tanning material

1ba·da·ri·an \bə'därēən\ *adj, usu cap* [*Badari*, village in Upper Egypt, where the discoveries were made + E *-an*] : of or belonging to an Egyptian predynastic neolithic culture dated about 5000 B.C. and characterized by fine handmade pottery (as black beakers with incised designs in white), flint tools, and polished stone axes

2badarian \"\ *n* -s *usu cap* : one of the ancient Egyptian people who produced the Badarian culture

badawi *often cap, var of* BEDAWI

bad blood *n* : RESENTMENT : ill feeling : BITTERNESS ⟨*bad blood* existing between Beaver Island Mormons and mainland fishermen —*Amer. Guide Series: Mich.*⟩

bad boy *n* : one who shocks or scandalizes by flouting or defying the moral or artistic conventions of a period ⟨the *bad boy* of English dramatic criticism —Leo Lerman⟩

bad books *n pl* : DISFAVOR ⟨got into the president's *bad books*⟩

bad·chan *or* **bad·han** *or* **bad·chen** \'bätkən, -ädk-\ *n, pl* **bad·cha·nim** *or* **bad·ha·nim** \='kònəm, -nēm *also* -kän-\ *or* **badchens** [Heb *badḥān*] : a professional jester and topical minstrel esp. at Jewish wedding celebrations

bad conduct discharge *n* : a discharge from one of the armed services given at the recommendation of a court-martial after conviction for an offense less serious than one leading to a dishonorable discharge

badde·ley·ite \'bad(ᵊ)lē,īt\ *n* -s [Joseph *Baddeley*, 19th cent. Englishman who brought the first specimens from Ceylon + E *-ite*] : a mineral ZrO_2 consisting of zirconium oxide occurring in colorless, yellow, brown, or black tabular crystals

bad delivery *n* : a tender of securities on a stock exchange that are not in proper transferable or negotiable form or not in compliance with the terms of a contract or the rules of an exchange

badder *comparative of* BAD

bad·der·locks \'badə(r),läks\ *n pl but sing in constr* [origin unknown] : a large brownish black seaweed (*Alaria esculenta*) often eaten as a vegetable in Europe — called also *henware, murlin*

baddest *superlative of* BAD

bad·die *or* **bad·dy** \'badē, 'baa-, 'bai-, -di\ *n, pl* **baddies** [2*bad* + *-ie, -y*] *slang* : a hoodlum or other malefactor; *esp* : a movie, radio, or TV villain or bad woman ⟨gathered together all the ace *baddies* of the West into one high-pressure action picture —*Argus*⟩

bad·dish \-dish,-dēsh\ *adj* : somewhat bad : INFERIOR ⟨a mediocre to ~ book⟩

bad doer *n* : a domestic animal that with normal care fails to develop or produce normally

bade *past of* BID *or of* BIDE

bad egg *n, slang* : a worthless, untrustworthy person : MALEFACTOR, CROOK, TROUBLEMAKER

bad·e·nite \'badᵊn,īt, bə'den,-\ *n* -s [prob. fr. F, fr. *Badeni*, near Botosani, Romania + F *-ite*] : a mineral consisting of cobalt, nickel, and iron bismuth-arsenide and occurring in metallic steel-gray masses

ba·de·ous *also* **ba·di·us** \'bādēəs\ *adj* [L *badius* brown, chestnut-colored — more at BAY] : of a bay color

1badge \'baj, -aa(ə)j\ *n* -s [ME *bagge, bage*, prob. fr. AF *bageys*] **1** : a distinctive or distinguishing mark, token, device, or sign esp. of membership in a society or group and usu. worn on the person ⟨a knight in armor wearing his lady's scarf as a ~⟩ ⟨a policeman's ~⟩ ⟨no ~ of authority such as a cap or uniform to distinguish them⟩ ⟨the yacht club ~ on the flag flying from the mainmast⟩ **2** : something so characteristic as to suggest or serve as a badge ⟨the black coat and green eyeshade that were the recognized ~ of his calling —Oscar Lewis⟩ ⟨higher education, or what passes for that, is neither a birthright nor a necessary ~ of respectability —Douglas Bush⟩ ⟨the contemporary ~*s* of boyhood — visor cap, short-pants suit, and black cotton stockings —Jack Alexander⟩ **3** : an emblem awarded for a particular accomplishment (as proficiency in marksmanship) ⟨a scout's merit ~⟩ ⟨combat infantryman's ~⟩ **syn** see SIGN

2badge \"\ *vt* -ED/-ING/-S [ME *baggen*, fr. *bagge*, n.] : to mark or distinguish with a badge

badge of ul·ster \-jə'vəlztə(r), -lst-\ *usu cap B&U, heraldry* : RED HAND

1badg·er \'bajə(r)\ *n* -s [ME *bagger*] **1** : a dealer licensed in former times to buy grain in one place and sell it in another **2** *now dial Eng* : an itinerant dealer in commodities used for food : HAWKER, HUCKSTER

2badger \"\ *n* -s [prob. fr. 1*badge* + *-er;* fr. the white mark on its forehead] **1 a** (1) : any of certain strong sturdily built burrowing mammals constituting two genera (*Meles* and *Taxidea*) of the family Mustelidae and being widely distributed in the northern hemisphere, represented in western No. America by a mammal (*T. taxus*) and in Europe and northern Asia by another (*M. meles*) (2) : the pelt or fur of one of these animals **b** : a related animal (as the teledu or ratel) **2** *Austral* **a** : WOMBAT **b** : BANDICOOT **3** *usu cap* : WISCONSINITE — used as a nickname **4** *or* **badgerweed** \'==,=\ : AMERICAN PASQUEFLOWER **5** : a bundle of sacks tied to the end of a rope and pulled through a line of drain tile as it is laid to clear away loose material

3badger \"\ *vt* **badgered; badgered; badgering** \-j(ə)riŋ\ **badgers** : to harass, pester, or bedevil persistently esp. in a manner likely or designed to confuse, annoy, or wear down ⟨~*ed* the witness out of her wits⟩ ⟨the mill foreman . . . taunted the workers . . ., ~*ed* them, and told them that they dared not quit —Sinclair Lewis⟩ **syn** see BAIT

badger baiting *or* **badger drawing** *n* : the former sport of setting dogs to pull a badger from an artificially made hole or from a barrel or box

badger bird *n* : MARBLED GODWIT

badger dog *n* [trans. of G *dachshund*] : DACHSHUND

badger game *n* [3*badger*] : an extortion racket in which a man is lured by a woman into a compromising position and is then confronted with and blackmailed by the woman's accomplice posing as her husband or brother

badg·er·ing·ly *adv* : in a badgering manner

badger skunk *n* : HOG-NOSED SKUNK

badhan *var of* BADCHAN

bad hat *n, slang Brit* : a disreputable dissolute person : BAD EGG ⟨the man is a *bad hat*, a swindler or worse —Joyce Cary⟩

ba·di·an \'bädēən, 'bad-\ *n* -s [F *badiane*, fr. Per *bādiān* anise] : the carminative fruit of the Chinese anise resembling true anise in flavor

1ba·di·geon \bə'dijən\ *n* -s [F] : a cement or paste (as of plaster and powdered freestone) used to fill holes or cover defects in wood or stone

2badigeon \"\ *vt* -ED/-ING/-S : to cover with badigeon

bad·i·nage \,badᵊn'äzh, -ȧzh, '==,=\ *n* -s [F, fr. *badiner* to joke (fr. MF, fr. *badin* joker, fool, fr. OProv, fr. *badar* to gape, fr. (assumed) VL *batare*) + MF *-age*] : light and playful repartee or wit : BANTER ⟨will read the deepest and eternal truths into your most topical ~ —Stella Campbell⟩ ⟨risen from the level of ~ to that of real grandiloquence —Frederic Prokosch⟩

ba·dis \'bādəs\ *n, cap* [NL] : a genus of small freshwater fishes (family Nandidae) including an Indian species (*B. badis*) that is yellowish brown with iridescent blue markings and a transparent tail and that is favored in tropical aquariums

badius *var of* BADEOUS

badjoo *or* **badju** *var of* BAJU

badland \'=,=\ *n* -s *often attrib* : a region characterized by the intricate and sharp erosional sculpture of generally weak rocks usu. forming nearly horizontal beds, generally developing in decomposed granite, loess, or other soft material, lacking or having only scanty vegetation, and consisting of steep, furrowed, or fantastically formed hills, labyrinthine drainage, and normally dry watercourses or arroyos ⟨the ~*s* of So. Dakota⟩ ⟨~ topography⟩

bad lot *n, slang* : a worthless, unreliable, immoral, or dishonest person : CROOK, TROUBLEMAKER ⟨decoyed by a thoroughly *bad lot* of a friend into helping him in a burglary —M.R.Ridley⟩

1bad·ly \'badlē, -aad-,-aid-, -li\ *adv* [ME *baddely*, fr. *badde* bad + *-ly*] **1** : in a bad manner: as **a** : POORLY, FAULTILY, DEFECTIVELY ⟨the car ran ~⟩ ⟨a picture ~ executed⟩ **b** : UNFAVORABLY ⟨the enterprise turned out ~ for the investors⟩ **c** : WRONGLY, EVILLY ⟨to steal is to act ~⟩ **d** : DISOBEDIENTLY, NAUGHTILY ⟨the child acted ~ in company⟩ **e** : INADEQUATELY, INCOMPLETELY, INEFFECTIVELY ⟨a picnic ~ planned⟩ ⟨provide ~ for emergencies⟩ **2 a** : very much : to a great or intense degree ⟨want something ~⟩ ⟨~ in need of help⟩ ⟨the cables of the Delei bridge had sagged ~ —Francis Kingdon-Ward⟩ ⟨the victim was not so ~ off⟩ ⟨the situation was ~ unbalanced —*Collier's Yr. Bk.*⟩ **b :** STRONGLY, COMPELLINGLY ⟨want something ~ enough to work hard for it⟩ **c :** SEVERELY ⟨so ~ frozen that . . . several fingers had to be amputated —*Amer. Guide Series: Minn.*⟩

²**badly** \"\ *adj* **1** *chiefly dial Brit* **:** SICK, UNWELL ⟨he has been ~ for a long time⟩ **2 :** BAD 8a, b ⟨feel ~ about a spiteful remark⟩ ⟨feel ~ about another's misfortune⟩

badly off *adv (or adj)* **1 :** in an unsatisfactory condition esp. in respect to money ⟨thanks to a private income, he's not *badly off*⟩ **2 :** suffering from a deficiency or shortage ⟨the company is *badly off* for experienced engineers⟩

badman \ˈ=,=\ *n, pl* **badmen :** OUTLAW, DESPERADO ⟨Jesse James, Missouri ~ —*Amer. Guide Series: Minn.*⟩ ⟨the classic western with its quick-drawing, dead-shot *badmen* and good men —*Time*⟩ ⟨a bunch of *badmen* who have kidnapped a blind girl —John McCarten⟩

bad·mash \ˈbəd,məsh\ *var of* BUDMASH

bad·min·ton \ˈbad,mintᵊn, -tən\ *n* **-s** [fr. *Badminton,* resi-

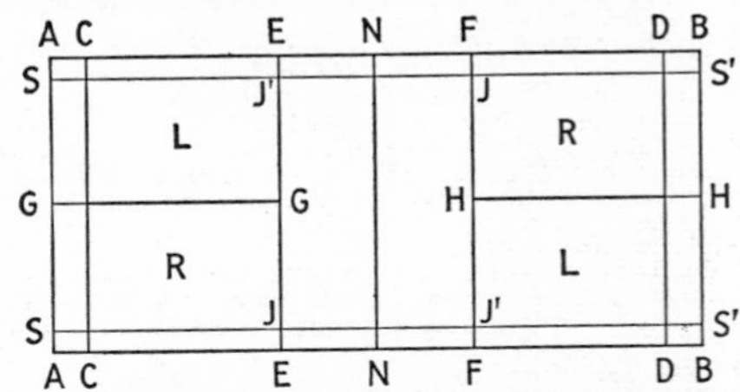

badminton court: *AA, BB* back boundary lines; *AB* doubles side boundary line; *SS'* singles side boundary line; *CC, DD* long-service lines (doubles only; the back boundary lines are long-service lines in singles); *EE, FF* short-service lines; *GG, HH* center lines; *R* right doubles service court; *L* left doubles service court; *GSJ'G, HS'J'H* left singles service courts; *GSJG, HS'JH* right singles service courts

dence of the duke of Beaufort, Gloucestershire, where it was first played in England] **:** a court game played by two or four persons with light long-handled rackets and a shuttlecock volleyed over a net suspended across the middle of the court surface — see RACKET illustration

bad·ness *n* **-ES :** the quality or state of being bad

bad·rans \ˈbadrənz, -at͟hr-\ *var of* BAUDRONS

bads *pl of* BAD

bad time *n* **:** the period of time that is not considered part of a serviceman's military service (as when he is AWOL or in prison for a military offense) and that must be made up before his release from duty

baeck·e·ol \ˈbākē,ōl, -ōl\ *n* **-s** [NL *Baeckea* (genus name of *Baeckea crenulata,* a species of myrtle that produces it) + E *-ol*] **:** a pale yellow crystalline phenolic ketone $C_{13}H_{18}O_4$ found in oils from various plants of various species of the myrtle family (esp. *Baeckea crenulata*)

baed *past of* BA

bae·de·ker \ˈbādəkə(r), -dēk-\ *n* **-s** *usu cap* [after Karl *Baedeker* †1859 Ger. publisher of guidebooks] **1 :** any one of a series of guidebooks devoted chiefly to European countries and cities ⟨seeing Paris with a *Baedeker*⟩ **2 :** GUIDEBOOK, HANDBOOK ⟨a *Baedeker* of contemporary arts⟩

bael *var of* BEL

baer·ia \ˈba(a)rēə\ *n, cap* [NL, fr. Karl E. von *Baer* †1876 Estonian naturalist + NL *-ia*] **:** a genus of annual herbs (family Compositae) having opposite hairy leaves and showy yellow flowers — see GOLD FIELDS

baer·mann apparatus \ˈba(a)rmən-\ *n, usu cap B* [fr. the name *Baermann*] **:** an apparatus consisting essentially of a funnel containing muslin filters for straining out larvae or worms from fecal or other specimens

baermann technique *also* **baermann method** *n, usu cap B* **:** isolation of nematode or other minute worms or larvae by means of the Baermann apparatus

bae·tyl \ˈbēdᵊl\ *or* **bae·tu·lus** \ˈbēchələs\ *or* **bae·ty·lus** \ˈbēdᵊləs\ *n, pl* **baetyls** \-ᵊlz\ *or* **baetu·li** \-chə,lī\ *or* **baety·li** \-dᵊ,lī\ [L *baetulus,* fr. Gk *baitylos,* a sacred meteorite] **:** a roughly shaped stone (as a meteorite) held sacred or worshiped as of divine origin — **bae·tyl·ic** \(ˈ)bēˈtilik\ *adj*

bae·yer strain theory \ˈbā(y)ə(r)-\ *n, usu cap B* [after Adolf von *Baeyer* †1917 Ger. chemist] **:** a theory in chemistry: the four valences of carbon are normally directed symmetrically in space making angles of 109° 28′ with one another and deflection of these directions produces strain in the molecule (as in the formation of rings)

ba·fa·ro \bəˈfä(,)rō\ *n* **-s** [Afrik, prob. fr. a native name in southern Africa] *Africa* **:** a stonebass (*Polyprion americanus*)

¹**baff** \ˈbaf, -aa(ə)f,-aif,-àf\ *n* **-s** [prob. of imit. origin] **1** *Scot* **:** BLOW, STROKE, THUD ⟨she struck him on the face with a resounding ~⟩ **2 :** a golf stroke in which the sole of the club hits the ground and drives the ball aloft

²**baff** \"\ *vt* **-ED/-ING/-S :** STRIKE; *specif* **:** to make a stroke with a golf club so that the sole of the club strikes the ground and lofts (the ball)

baffing spoon *n* [fr. pres. part. of ²*baff*] **:** BAFFY

¹**baf·fle** \ˈbafəl\ *vt* **baffled; baffled; baffling** \-f(ə)liŋ\ **baffles** [prob. alter. of ME (Scots dial.) *bawchillen, bachlen* to denounce or discredit publicly] **1** *obs* **a :** to subject to a disgraceful punishment or to infamy **b :** to subject to any disgrace or contumely **c :** CHEAT, TRICK **d :** to reduce to ineffectiveness **2 :** to defeat or check (as understanding, plans, efforts, actions) by confusing or puzzling **:** DISCONCERT, PERPLEX, FRUSTRATE ⟨with postwar verse, the . . . untutored reader is apt to admit himself quite *baffled* —C.D.Lewis⟩ ⟨the swiftness of his marches *baffled* alike flight and resistance —J.A.Froude⟩ **3 :** to check or break the force of **:** deflect or stop the flow of ⟨guard plates to ~ the steam⟩ **:** interfere with the free or straight motion of **:** disperse the effective force of ⟨the yawl was *baffled* by the changing winds⟩ **4 :** to equip with a baffle **5 :** to prevent (two or more sets of sound waves) from interfering with each other (as by introducing a partition between the front and back of a loudspeaker) **syn** see FRUSTRATE

²**baffle** \"\ *n* **-s 1 :** BAFFLEMENT, CONFUSION, UNCERTAINTY **2 :** something for deflecting, checking, or otherwise regulating flow: as **a :** a plate or wall for deflecting gases or other fluids (as in a steam-boiler flue, a reverberatory furnace, or a gasoline-engine muffler) **b :** a plate or grating in a channel or a pipe conveying fluid to check eddy currents and thus cause a uniform flow **c :** a device or structure (as a vane or partition) for preventing the passage of, deflecting, or regulating the intensity of light **d :** a device or structure for deadening, preventing the transmission of, or deflecting sound **3 :** a partition or cabinet used with the diaphragm of a loudspeaker to impede the exchange of sound waves between front and back

baffle gate *n* **:** a gate that permits passage in one direction only

baf·fle·ment \-fəlmənt\ *n* **-s 1 :** the action of baffling **:** the fact of being baffled ⟨their best efforts met with persistent ~⟩ **2 :** the state of being baffled **:** PERPLEXITY, CONFUSION ⟨she couldn't understand the meaning of all this and he gloated over her ~ —Adria Langley⟩

baffle painting *n* **:** camouflage of a ship to give it a deceptive appearance as to size, form, course, and speed

baffle plate *n* **:** a plate used as a baffle (sense 2)

baf·fler \ˈbaf(ə)lə(r)\ *n* **-s 1 :** one that baffles **2 :** BAFFLE 2

baffling *adj* **:** causing bafflement **:** PERPLEXING, CONFUSING ⟨a ~ problem⟩ ⟨a detective's most ~ case⟩ — **baf·fling·ly** *adv* — **baf·fling·ness** *n* **-ES**

baffling wind *n* **:** a light wind that frequently shifts from one point to another

baffy \ˈbafē, -aaf-,-aif-,-àf-, -fi\ *n* **-ES** [²*baff* + *-y*] **:** a short wooden golf club with a deeply lofted face

baft *adv* [ME *bafte, baften,* fr. OE *bæftan, beæftan* behind fr. *be-* + *æftan* from behind — more at AFT] *archaic* **:** ABAFT ASTERN

¹**bag** \ˈbag, -aa(ə)g,-aig\ *n* **-s** [ME *bagge,* fr. ON *baggi*] **1 :** a container made of paper, cloth, mesh, metal foil, plastic, or other flexible material and usu. closed on all sides except for an opening that may be closed (as by folding, pasting, tying, or sewing), being of sizes ranging from small to very large and being specially designed and treated for properly holding, storing, carrying, shipping, or distributing any material or product — compare POUCH, SACK **2 :** a bag for a particular purpose: as **a :** a bag to hold money **:** PURSE; *esp* **:** a woman's pocketbook **:** HANDBAG **b :** a bag for carrying game **:** GAME BAG ⟨several squirrels and a rabbit in his ~⟩ **c :** a silk pouch used to hold up the back hair (as of a powdered wig) **d :** MAILBAG **e :** TRAVELING BAG, VALISE, SUITCASE **3 :** something felt to resemble a bag (as in form or capaciousness): as **a :** a pouched or pendulous bodily part or organ: (1) **:** a sac or space containing a secretion or other fluid ⟨the poison ~ of a snake⟩ ⟨the honey ~ of a bee⟩ (2) **:** UDDER (3) *dial Brit* **:** BELLY (4) **:** a pendulous outpouching of flabby skin ⟨an aging face with ~*s* below the eyes⟩ (5) *slang* **:** SCROTUM **b :** a puffed out sag or bulge (as of cloth) suggestive of a bag ⟨~*s* at the knees of trousers⟩ ⟨the ~ in the sail of a ship⟩ **c bags** *pl, chiefly Brit* **:** SLACKS ⟨dressed with casual undergraduate elegance in sports coat, silk pullover, and flannel ~*s* —Christopher Isherwood⟩ **d :** a square white canvas container filled with sawdust that is fastened to the ground to mark the position of first, second, or third base in baseball **e :** PUNCHING BAG **f :** SLEEPING BAG **g :** any of the small upright chimneys inside a ceramic kiln through which the flames pass into the body of the structure **h :** a cavity filled with water or gas in a mine **4 :** something that is bagged: as **a :** the amount contained in a bag esp. when fixed (as by law) for a particular commodity and used as a unit of weight ⟨25 ~*s* to the ton⟩; *broadly* **:** a bag and its contents ⟨don't forget to get a ~ of potatoes⟩ **b :** a quantity of game taken during a particular hunt or during a particular period usu. by one person ⟨the ~ included an elephant, and a magnificent male tiger⟩; *often* **:** the amount of game permitted (as by law) to be taken by one hunter ⟨he got his ~ early and was home before lunch⟩ **c :** something likened to the bag taken by a hunter or fisherman esp. in being won, captured, seized, or otherwise taken by personal effort **:** TROPHY, SPOILS ⟨the flier finished the day with a ~ of four enemy planes⟩; *sometimes* **:** a group of persons or things **:** COLLECTION, ASSORTMENT ⟨a mixed ~ of bystanders —Ken Purdy⟩ ⟨a large ~ of special techniques—Greer Williams⟩ **5** *slang* **a :** PROSTITUTE **b :** WOMAN; *esp* **:** a slovenly unattractive woman — used chiefly in the phrase *old bag;* usu. used disparagingly — **in the bag 1 :** marked by evidence and surrounding circumstances that make the attainment of a given objective a virtual certainty **:** practically unquestionable **:** as good as already gained, acquired, or won **:** ASSURED, CERTAIN ⟨his nomination was *in the bag*⟩ — not often in formal use **2** *slang* **:** DRUNK ⟨was half *in the bag* and staggering slightly⟩

bag 2a

²**bag** \"\ *vb* **bagged; bagged; bagging; bags** [ME *baggen,* fr. *bagge,* n.] *vi* **1 a :** to swell out **:** BULGE ⟨the entire side of the tent *bagged* outward under the force of the gale⟩ **b :** to hang loosely (as of clothing) like a bag ⟨her dress *bagged* shapelessly about her⟩ **2** *of a milch animal* **:** to develop the udder — usu. used with *up* ⟨this heifer is *bagging up* well⟩ **~ vt 1 :** to cause to bulge or swell out ⟨the rush of air at once *bagged* and filled out the parachute⟩ **2 a :** to put into a bag ⟨*bagging* and shipping the sugar⟩ — often used with *up* ⟨don't sweep until you have *bagged* up the beans⟩ **b :** to cover (as plants) with bags so as to exclude insects or foreign pollen ⟨long rows of carefully *bagged* zinnias⟩ **3 a :** to take (animals) as game **:** to kill or capture (game) ⟨he *bagged* a fine 10-point buck⟩ **b :** to get possession of esp. by strategy or stealth **:** GAIN, ACQUIRE ⟨his shrewd business speculation helped him to ~ a fabulous fortune⟩; *also* **:** make off with **:** STEAL ⟨two little boys were caught *bagging* apples⟩ **c :** to win a victory over **:** get the mastery of **:** CAPTURE, SEIZE ⟨the police *bagged* the entire dope ring⟩; *also* **:** to shoot down **:** DESTROY ⟨his first day he *bagged* three enemy planes⟩ **syn** see CATCH

³**bag** \"\ *vt* **bagged; bagged; bagging; bags** [origin unknown] **:** to cut (as grain) with a heavy sickle and gather the cut produce into bundles

bag *abbr* baggage

ba·gac \bəˈgak\ *n* **-s** [native name in the Philippines] **:** APITONG

bag and baggage *adv* **:** with all one's belongings **:** COMPLETELY ⟨he got rid of all the visitors, *bag and baggage*⟩

ba·ga·ni \bəˈgänē\ *n* **-s** *often cap* **:** MAGANI

ba·gasse *also* **be·gass** *or* **be·gasse** \bəˈgas, -aa(ə)s,-ais,-ás\ *n, pl* **bagasses** *also* **begasses** [F *bagasse,* fr. Sp *bagazo,* fr. *baga* seed pod of flax, fr. L *baca, bacca* berry] **:** the crushed juiceless remains of sugar cane as it comes from the mill often used as fuel in the mill and sometimes commercially as a source of cellulose (as for papermaking) or as an ingredient in animal feeds; *sometimes* **:** similar plant residue remaining after extraction of a juice (as from sugar beets or grapes), an oil (as from olives), or a fiber (as from sisal)

bagasse disease *n* **:** an industrial disease characterized by cough, difficult breathing, chills, fever, and prolonged weakness and caused by the inhalation of the dust of bagasse

ba·gas·so·sis \,bagəˈsōsəs\ *n, pl* **bagasso·ses** \-ō,sēz\ [NL, fr. F *bagasse* + NL *-osis*] **:** BAGASSE DISEASE

bagataway *var of* BAGGATAWAY

bag·a·telle \,bagəˈtel\ *n* **-s** [F, fr. It *bagattella,* prob. fr. L *baca, bacca* berry] **1 :** a thing of little or no importance or value **:** a mere nothing **:** TRIFLE ⟨to him money was a ~⟩ **2 :** a game played with a cue and usu. nine balls on an oblong table having cups or both cups and arches at one end **3 :** a short piece of music or verse in a light style; *esp* **:** a short light piece for the piano

bagdad *usu cap, var of* BAGHDAD

bagdad boil [after *Baghdad, Bagdad,* Iraq] *n, usu cap 1st B* **:** ORIENTAL SORE

bag·di \ˈbägdē\ *n* **-s** *cap* [Bengali] **:** a member of a numerous caste of field laborers of Bengal

ba·gel \ˈbāgəl\ *n* **-s** [Yiddish *beygel,* fr. (assumed) MHG *böugel* (whence G dial. *beugel, bäugl*), dim. of MHG *boug-, bouc* ring, bracelet, fr. OHG *boug;* akin to OE *bēag, bēah* ring, bracelet — more at BEE] **:** a hard roll shaped like a doughnut that is made of raised dough and cooked by simmering in water and then baked to give it a glazed browned exterior over a firm white interior

bag filter *n* **:** a filter made of a cloth bag ordinarily about 30 feet long for recovery of metal oxides and other solid particles suspended in a gas (as from smelting or other furnaces)

bag fox *n* **:** a fox taken to a covert in a bag to be released before hounds

bag·ful \ˈbag,fu̇l, -aag-,-aig-\ *n, pl* **bagfuls** *also* **bagsful** \-g,fu̇lz, -gz,fu̇l\ [ME *baggeful,* fr. *bagge* bag + *-ful*] **:** the quantity held by a bag; *esp* **:** an indeterminate but usu. rather large quantity ⟨investors will come flocking in with ~*s* of money —Tom Fitzsimmons⟩

¹**bag·gage** \ˈbagij, -aig-, -gēj\ *n* **-s** [ME *bagage,* fr. MF, fr. *bague* bundle (perh. fr. ON *baggi* bag) + *-age*] **1 :** a group of traveling bags, trunks, or both esp. when packed and in transit **:** personal belongings of travelers either carried by hand or checked with a carrier **:** LUGGAGE ⟨the ~ was brought from the attic for packing⟩ ⟨since there were only a couple of small pieces, the traveler carried his own ~⟩ **2 :** equipment that is transported or that can be transported ⟨the ~ of an army⟩ **:** FURNISHINGS, APPARATUS ⟨the ~ of a science laboratory⟩ **3 a :** a combination of extraneous, superfluous, or intrusive things and circumstances that may impede free activity, progress, or the attainment of a specific goal ⟨smooth speech and writing depend very much upon freedom from purist grammar and from other linguistic ~⟩ **b :** theories, notions, or practices viewed as outmoded or as otherwise conflicting with and retarding desirable development ⟨cultural ~ which the Puritans brought from England to America in the seventeenth century —I.V.Brown⟩ ⟨mental ~ from bygone days —D.G. Haring⟩ **4** [prob. by folk etymology fr. MF *bagasse,* fr. OProv *bagassa*] **a :** a worthless or vile woman ⟨and it's wicked of me. You must think me a shameless ~ —Max Peacock⟩ ⟨a disreputable old ~, dealing in grass skirts and shrunken human heads —Wolcott Gibbs⟩ **:** a woman of loose morals **:** PROSTITUTE **b :** a young woman or girl; *esp* **:** a girl or young woman who is the object of affection, playfulness, usu. gentle criticism, or a somewhat patronizing attitude ⟨a toothsome blond ~ —*New Yorker*⟩ ⟨she's a pretty little ~ —Walter O'Meara⟩

²**baggage** \"\ *adj, obs* **:** WORTHLESS, TRASHY, RUBBISHY ⟨a ~ scoundrel⟩

baggage car *n* **:** a railroad car for passengers' baggage

bag·gage·man \-,man, -aa(ə)n *also* -,mən\ *n, pl* **baggagemen 1 :** a railroad employee who is in charge of the checked baggage of passengers during the run of a train and unloads it at the proper destination **2 :** a porter in a hotel who carries heavy luggage, arranges for receipt and shipment of baggage, sets up sample rooms, and supplies travel information **3 :** an employee at a bus terminal who takes care of the checking, loading, or release of travelers' baggage

baggagemaster \ˈ==,==\ *n* **1 :** a railroad employee in charge of a baggage car or baggage train **2 :** an employee on a ship who is responsible for the stowing, care, and removal of baggage **3 :** a bus company employee who traces and settles claims for baggage and other articles lost or damaged in shipment

baggage rack *n* **:** a shelf in a railroad passenger car or a bus for the accommodation of hand baggage and parcels

baggage-smasher \ˈ==,==\ *n, slang* **:** a person (as a baggageman) who handles the baggage of others esp. in a baggage car or steamship

baggage train *n* **:** a train of vehicles carrying baggage

bag·ga·la \ˈbəgə,lä, -lə\ *n* **-s** [Marathi *baglā, bagalā,* prob. fr. Pg *baixel,* fr. Catal *vaixell,* fr. L *vascellum* small vase — more at VESSEL] **:** a 2-masted trading vessel used in the Indian ocean

bag·gat·a·way *also* **ba·gat·a·way** \bəˈgad·ə,wā\ *n* **-s** [of Algonquian origin] **:** a Canadian Indian game from which lacrosse developed

bagged \ˈbagd, -aa(ə)gd,-aigd\ *adj* **1 :** hanging in bags **:** hanging loosely ⟨~ cheeks⟩ ⟨~ ropes⟩ **2 :** having a bag or bags ⟨she gave him an ugly look with her ~, spectacled eyes —Marcia Davenport⟩ **3** *slang* **:** DRUNK ⟨was so ~ he could hardly stand up⟩

bag·ger \-gə(r)\ *n* **-s** [²*bag* + *-er*] **:** one that bags: as **a :** one that fills bags with such goods as food, tobacco, and cement **b :** one that places stockings in bags to prepare them for dyeing — called also *batcher*

bag·gi·ly \-gəlē, -li\ *adv* **:** in a loose baggy way ⟨his clothes hung about him ~⟩

bag·gi·ness \-gēnəs, -gin-\ *n* **-ES** [*baggy* + *-ness*] **:** the quality or state of being baggy

¹**bag·ging** \-giŋ,-gēŋ\ *n* **-s** [¹*bag* + *-ing*] **1** *dial Eng* **:** food eaten between meals; *esp* **:** a midafternoon lunch **2 :** material for bags; *usu* **:** a coarse fabric (as burlap or gunny)

²**bagging** \"\ *n* **-s** [fr. gerund of ²*bag*] **:** filtration through a bag (as of sperm oil)

bag·git \ˈbagət\ *n* **-s** [Sc *baggit* pregnant, fr. ME *bagged,* fr. past part. of *baggen* to bag, swell — more at BAG] *Brit* **:** a female salmon just after spawning

bag·gy \ˈbagē, -aag-,-aig-, -gi\ *adj, usu* **-ER/-EST :** loose, puffed out, or hanging like a bag ⟨~ trousers⟩ ⟨~ cheeks⟩ ⟨round ~ shoulders —Thomas Wolfe⟩ ⟨~ generalities and shabby prejudices —H.J.Muller⟩

baggy crop *n* **:** PENDULOUS CROP

bag·gy·wrin·kle *also* **bagy·wrin·kle** \-,riŋkəl\ *n* **-s :** protective gear made from frayed out rope and used on ship rigging to prevent chafing

bag handle *vt* **:** to mar (as coins) by handling or storing in a bag or other container that allows the rubbing together of the contents ⟨gold coins that show evidence of having been *bag handled*⟩

bagh·dad *or* **bag·dad** \ˈbag,dad, ˈbag,daa(ə)d, ˈbaig,dad\ *adj, usu cap* [fr. *Baghdad* or *Bagdad,* Iraq] **:** of or from Baghdad, the capital of Iraq **:** of the kind or style prevalent in Baghdad

bagh·dadi \(ˈ)=ˈ=dē, -di\ *n* **-s** *cap* [fr. *Baghdad,* Iraq] **:** a native or inhabitant of Baghdad, Iraq

baghouse \ˈ=,=\ *n* **1 :** a building in which bag filters are used for filtering gas **2 :** BAG FILTER

ba·gio \,bägēˈō, bägˈyō\ *var of* BAGUIO

ba·gir·mi \bəˈgirmē\ *n, pl* **bagirmi** *or* **bagirmis** *usu cap* **1 a :** a Muslim people of a mixed Negroid stock living southeast of Lake Chad in the central Sudan **b :** a member of such people **2 :** a Central Sudanic language of the Bagirmi people

bagleaves \ˈ=,=\ *n pl but sing or pl in constr* **:** ORPINE

bag limit *n* **:** the maximum number of fish or game animals permitted by law to be taken by one person in a given period

bag·man \ˈbagmən, -aag-,-aig-\ *n, pl* **bagmen 1** *chiefly Brit* **:** TRAVELING SALESMAN ⟨*bagmen,* who did not in those days aspire to the title of commercial travelers —Hugh McCausland⟩ **2** *slang* **:** BAG FOX **3** *Austral* **:** TRAMP 1a, 1b **4 :** a person who collects or distributes money usu. illicitly on behalf of another (as in making payoffs or collecting bribes)

bag molding *n* **:** a technique or process in which plastic or plywood-plastic combinations are molded to curved forms by use of a rigid die within a flexible cover through which fluid pressure (as of steam, air, or vacuum) may act on the material to be molded

bag·net \ˈbag,net, ˈbāg-, -,nət\ *dial var of* BAYONET

bag net *n* **:** a bag-shaped net for catching fish

ba·gnio \ˈban(,)yō, ˈbän-\ *n* **-s** [It *bagno,* fr. L *balneum,* fr. Gk *balaneion;* akin to Gk *balaneus* bather, *blyein, blyzein* to gush forth, Skt *galati* it drips — more at DEVIL] **1** *obs* **:** an establishment providing Turkish baths **2** *obs* **:** PRISON **3 :** house of prostitution **:** BROTHEL

ba·go \ˈbä(,)gō\ *n* **-s** [Tag, Cebuan, & Bikol] **:** an evergreen Asiatic shrub (*Gnetum gnemon*) having edible young leaves and seeds

ba·go·bo \bəˈgō(,)bō\ *n, pl* **bagobo** *or* **bagobos** *usu cap* **1 a :** a predominantly pagan people inhabiting southern Mindanao, Philippines **b :** a member of such people **2 :** the Austronesian language of the Bagobo people

bag of bones : an extremely thin individual

bag of tricks : a supply of expedients or devices **:** stock of resources ⟨in their attempts to be original they have pretty well exhausted their *bag of tricks*⟩

bag of waters : the double-walled fluid-filled sac that encloses and protects the fetus in the mother's womb and breaks releasing its fluid during the birth process

bag of wind : WINDBAG 2

bag·o·net \ˈbag(ə),net, ˈbāg-, -,nət\ *dial var of* BAYONET

ba·go·ong \bäˈgō,ōŋ\ *n* **-s** [Tag] *Philippines* **:** a paste or sauce of small fish and prawns which have been salted and fermented that is much used as seasoning

bagpipe \ˈ=,=\ *n* [ME *baggepipe,* fr. *bagge* bag + *pipe*] **:** a musical instrument consisting of a double-reed melody pipe and one or more single-reed drone pipes that are sounded by air from a flexible bag which is in turn kept inflated either by a mouth tube or by an elbow-worked bellows — often used in pl.; compare MUSETTE; see CHANTER

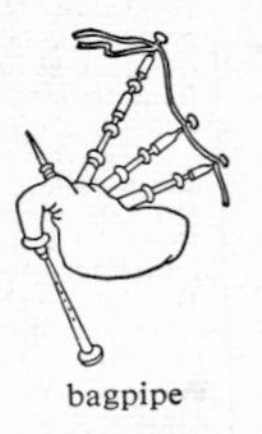
bagpipe

bag·pip·er \-ˌpīpə(r)\ *n* [ME *baggepiper,* fr. *baggepipe* + *-er*] **:** a player on a bagpipe **:** PIPER

bagpod \ˈ=,=\ *n* **:** an annual herb (*Glottidium vesicarium*) of the pea family having pinnate leaves with numerous leaflets, flowers in axillary clusters, and elliptic pods that taper at both ends — called also *bladderpod*

bag pudding *n* **:** a dessert pudding boiled or steamed in a bag

ba·gre \ˈbä(,)grā, ˈba-, -,grē,-grə\ *n* [Sp & Pg, fr. Ar *bāghir, baghār,* prob. fr. L *pagrus,* a bream — more at PARGO] **1 -s :** any of various catfishes esp. of Spanish-American waters **2** *cap* **:** the genus (family Ariidae) to which the gaff-topsail catfish belongs

bagreef \ˈ=,=\ *n* [²*bag* + *reef;* fr. its use in preventing a large sail from bagging] **1 :** the lower reef of fore-and-aft sails **2 :** a single reef in a square topsail

bags *pl of* BAG, *pres 3d sing of* BAG

bag table *n* : a small light worktable with one or two drawers the lower of which forms a frame from which is suspended a bag for needlework

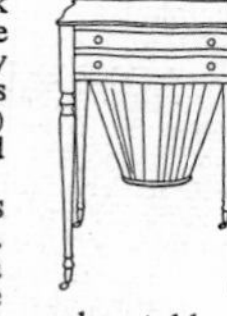
bag table

bag·ti·kan \bäg'tēkən\ *n* -s [native name in the Philippines] : the reddish gray heavy wood of either of two trees of the genus *Parashorea* (*P. malaanon* and *P. warburgii*) of the family Dipterocarpaceae — called also *Philippine mahogany*

ba·guette *also* **ba·guet** \ba'get, bai-\ *n* -s [F *baguette*, lit., rod, fr. It *bacchetta*, irreg. fr. L *baculum* — more at BACTERIUM] **1 a** : a small molding like but smaller than the astragal : BEAD **b** : a molding formerly placed along the angle between two planes of a hip roof **2** : a table-cut gem having the shape of a long, narrow, and sometimes tapered rectangle; *also* : the shape itself **3** : a very small narrow rectangular watch movement used esp. for bracelet and ring watches; *sometimes* : a wristwatch of which the movement is a baguette **4 a** : DRUMSTICK 1 **b** : the wooden part of a violin bow **c** : BATON 4

ba·guio \,bägē'ō, bäg'yō\ *n* -s [Sp, fr. Tag *bagyō*] *Philippines* : TROPICAL CYCLONE

bag–wall \'=,=\ *n* : a low wall inside a furnace or kiln against and over which the flame plays

bagwig \'=,=\ *n* : an 18th century wig with the back hair enclosed in a small silk bag

bagworm \'=,=\ *n* : a moth larva of the family Psychidae constructing and living in a silk case which is usu. covered with bits of plant debris; *esp* : an often destructive pest (*Thyridopteryx ephemeraeformis*) of trees and shrubs in the eastern U.S. — compare CASEWORM

bag·wyn \'bagwən\ *n* -s [origin unknown] : a fabulous beast like an antelope but having a goat's horns and a horse's tail

bagywrinkle *var of* BAGGYWRINKLE

bah \'bä, 'ba, 'bȧ, 'baa\ *interj* — used to express disdain or contempt

ba·ha·dur \bə'hȯdə(r), -'hä-,-'hā-\ *n* -s [Hindi *bahādur* hero, champion, fr. Per] *India* : a distinguished person — used as a title of respect

ba·hai \bä'hä·ē, bə-, -R sometimes -ärē\ *or* **ba·ha·ist** \-ä(,)ist, -ərəst\ *n* -s *usu cap* [Per *bahā'ī*, lit., of glory, fr. *bahā* glory, splendor, fr. Ar *bahā'*] : an adherent of Bahaism

ba·ha·ism \-ä,izəm, -ä,ri-\ *n* -s *usu cap* : the doctrine and practice of a sect founded in Iran in the 19th century that emphasizes the spiritual unity of mankind, advocates peace and universal education, and affirms the equality of men and women

ba·ha·ma \bə'hämə, -hā- (*pronunc in Bahamas*); -hā-\ *adj, usu cap* [fr. *Bahama* islands] : of or from the Bahama islands : of the kind or style prevalent in the Bahama islands

bahama duck *also* **bahama pintail** *n, usu cap B* [fr. the *Bahama* islands in the Atlantic southeast of Florida] : a pin-tailed duck (*Anas bahamensis*) with a white face and throat, red base to the bill, and pale buff tail that is widely distributed in the Caribbean islands and through much of So. America — called also *white-cheeked pintail*

bahama grass *n, usu cap B* : BERMUDA GRASS

bahama sisal *n, usu cap B* : SISAL 1a

¹ba·ha·mi·an \bə'hāmēən, -hä-,-hā-—*ä is used in this word by many Bahamians but apparently not in* "bahama(s)"\ *adj, usu cap* [*Bahama* islands + E -*ian*] **1** : of, relating to, or characteristic of the Bahama islands **2** : of, relating to, or characteristic of Bahamians

²bahamian \"\ *n* -s *cap* : a native or inhabitant of the Bahama islands

ba·hau \bə'hau̇\ *n, pl* **bahau** *or* **bahaus** *usu cap* **1** : a Dayak people of northern Borneo — see KAYAN, KENYA **2** : a member of the Bahau people

ba·he·ra \'bəhə,rä\ *n* -s [Hindi *baherā*] : an important East Indian tree (*Terminalia bellerica*) yielding an oil from its seed kernels, a dye and tanning extract from its fruits, and a gum from its bark — compare MYROBALAN

¹ba·hia \bə'hēə\ *n* -s *usu cap* [fr. *Bahia* (now Baía), state in Brazil] : Brazilian piassava

²bahia \"\ *adj, usu cap* [fr. *Bahia*, old name for Salvador, Brazil] : ²SALVADOR

ba·hia blan·ca *or* **ba·hía blan·ca** \bə¦hēə¦bläŋkə\ *adj, usu cap both Bs* [fr. *Bahia Blanca*, Argentina] : of or from the city of Bahía Blanca, Argentina : of the kind or style prevalent in Bahía Blanca

bahia grass *n, usu cap B* [fr. *Bahia*, state of Brazil] : a perennial tropical American grass (*Paspalum notatum*) used in the Gulf states as a pasture grass esp. in arid regions

bahia powder *n, usu cap B* [fr. *Bahia*, Brazil] : GOA POWDER

ba·his·ti \bə'hēstē\ *var of* BHEESTY

baho *var of* PAHO

bahr \'bär, 'bȧ(r\ *n* -s [Ar *baḥr*] : a body of water (as a lake, river, or sea)

bah·rain *or* **bah·rein** \'bä¦rān\ *adj, usu cap* [fr. *Bahrain*, country in the Persian Gulf] : of or from Bahrain : of the kind or style prevalent in Bahrain

¹bah·raini *also* **bah·reini** \bä'rānē\ *n, pl* **bahraini** *or* **bahrainis** *also* **bahreini** *or* **bahreinis** *cap* [modif. of Ar *baḥrāniy*, fr. *Baḥrayn* Bahrain] : a native or inhabitant of Bahrain

²bahraini *also* **bahreini** *adj, usu cap* : of or relating to Bahrain or its inhabitants

baht *or* **bat** \'bät\ *n, pl* **bahts** *also* **baht** *or* **bat** *also* **bats** [Thai *bāt*] **1** : TICAL 1 **2** : the basic monetary unit of Thailand; *also* : a coin or note representing one baht — see MONEY table

bahu \'bä(,)hü, 'bä·(,)ü, 'bau̇·\ *n* -s [Jav] : BOUW

ba·hur *or* **ba·chur** *also* **bo·chur** \'bȯkůr, 'bəkər\ *or* **bo·cher** \'bəkər\ *n, pl* **ba·hu·rim** *or* **ba·chu·rim** *also* **bo·chu·rim** \'bȯkůrəm, ,bəkər-, -rēm\ *or* **bo·che·rim** \'bəkər-\ [Heb *bāḥūr* youth] *in Jewish use* : a young unmarried man : YOUTH; *specif* : a student in a Talmudic academy — called also *yeshiva bocher*

ba·hut \bä,hüt, bə'hüt, -üt, *F* baüē\ *n* -s [F] **1** : a chest or cabinet; *esp* : one having a rounded top and used as furniture **2 a** : a low wall raised above the main cornice of a building and carrying the roof — compare ATTIC **b** : a parapet wall solid and generally not decorative; *often* : the rounded top course of masonry of such a wall

ba·hu·vri·hi \,bä(,)hüv'rēhē\ *n* -s [Skt *bahuvrīhi*, lit., having much rice (a compound of this type), fr. *bahu* much + *vrīhi* rice — more at PACHY-, RICE] : a class of compound words whose meanings follow the formula "(one) having a *B* that is *A*" where *A* stands for the first constituent of the compound and *B* for the second; *also* : a compound word belonging to this class (as *graybeard*, *blockhead*, *barefoot*) — see ¹POSSESSIVE 1b

ba·ian·ism \'bā(y)ə,nizəm\ *also* **ba·jan·ism** \", 'bäjə-\ *n* -s *usu cap* [F *baïanisme*, fr. *Baius* (Michel de Bay) †1589 Belgian theologian + F -*isme* -ism] : the doctrine of Baius according to which divine grace is neither gratuitous nor truly necessary, man's nature and actions are essentially evil through original sin, man's will is not really free, and the sacraments have a highly limited purpose and efficacy

baib grass \'bīb-\ *n* [prob. native name in India] : BHABAR 1

baidar *var of* BIDAR

baidarka *var of* BIDARKA

bai·dya \'bīdyə\ *n* -s *cap* [Skt *vaidya* lit., possessing knowledge, fr. *vidyā* knowledge — more at WIT] : a member of a high caste of eastern Bengal traditionally made up of physicians

bai·era \'bīərə\ *n* -s *cap* [NL, after J.J.*Baier* †1735 Ger. naturalist] : a genus of fossil gymnosperms (family Ginkgoaceae) that are known from the Trias to the Lower Cretaceous and are considered by some paleobotanists to be ancestors of the fossil and surviving ginkgoes

bai·ga \'bīgə\ *n, pl* **baiga** *or* **baigas** *usu cap* **1** : an aboriginal hill people living in the Central Provinces of India **2** : a member of the Baiga people

bai·gi·net \'bāg(ə),net, -,nət\ *Scot var of* BAYONET

bai·gnoire \bān'wär, '=,=\ *n* -s [F, lit., bathtub, fr. *baigner* to bathe, fr. LL *balneare*, fr. L *balneum* bath — more at BAGNIO] : a theater box having low partitions that is in the lowest tier

bai·kal·ite \bī'kä,līt, 'bīkə,l-\ *n* -s [G *baikalit*, fr. Lake *Baikal*, Siberia + G -*it* -ite] : a dark green variety of hedenbergite

bai·ker·in·ite \'bīkərə,nīt\ *n* -s [G *baikerinit*, blend of *baikerit* and -*in*] : a tarry hydrocarbon constituting about one third of baikerite

bai·ker·ite \'bīkə,rīt\ *n* -s [G *baikerit*, irreg. fr. Lake *Baikal* + G -*it* -ite] : a mineral wax apparently a mixture of ozokerite with other tarry, waxy, and resinous hydrocarbons

¹bail \'bāl, *esp bef pause or cons* -āəl\ *n* -s [ME *bail*, *baille*, fr. MF *bail*, fr. *baillier* to give, deliver, fr. L *bajulare* to bear a burden, keep in custody, fr. *bajulus* porter, load carrier] **1** *obs* : CUSTODY, JURISDICTION **2 a** *obs* : the custody of a prisoner or one under arrest by one who procures the release of the prisoner or arrested individual by giving surety for his due appearance **b** : the security or obligation given for the due appearance of a prisoner in order to obtain his release from imprisonment ⟨the man is out on ~⟩ **c** : the temporary delivery or release of a prisoner upon security for his due appearance **d** : one that agrees to assume legal liability for a money forfeit or damages if a prisoner released on bail fails to make his due appearance in court — compare MAINPRISE **e** : the process by which a person is released from custody

²bail \"\ *vt* -ED/-ING/-S **1** : to deliver (personal property) to another under an agreement express or implied that some special purpose be accomplished by the bailee with respect to the property and that at some time the property be returned to the bailor ⟨she ~*ed* the cloth to the tailor to be made into a dress⟩ **2** : to set free, deliver from arrest, or deliver out of custody on an undertaking of another to be responsible for the due appearance of the one so released ⟨the magistrate ~*ed* the prisoner⟩ **3** : to procure the release of by giving bail — often used with *out* ⟨his lawyer ~*ed* him out⟩ **4** : to set free from an unpleasant or difficult situation : come to the help of usu. through financial aid — used with *out*

³bail \"\ *n* -s [ME *bail*, *baile*, fr. OF, fortification, stake, perh. fr. L *bajulus* porter, load carrier] **1** : an outer wall of a feudal castle; *also* : the space enclosed by such a wall : COURT **2** : either of two crosspieces placed end to end on top of the stumps in cricket **3** *chiefly Brit* **a** : a bar, pole, or partition of suspended boards separating animals (as in an open stable or on shipboard) **b** : a frame for confining the head of a cow : STANCHION **c** : a movable open shed often on wheels that is used for milking and supplying concentrates to milch cows : MILKING PARLOR

⁴bail \"\ *vt* -ED/-ING/-S **1** *archaic* : CONFINE ⟨a lofty spirit ~*ed* by human limitation⟩ **2** *Brit* : to make fast with or in a bail — used with *up* ⟨~ a cow up for milking⟩ **3** *Austral* : to force to a halt : ACCOST, CHECK : detain esp. for purposes of robbery — used with *up* ⟨they were ~*ed* up by a gang of bushrangers —Bill Beatty⟩

⁵bail \"\ *n* -s [ME *baile*, *baille*, fr. MF *baille*, fr. (assumed) VL *bajula*, alter of L *bajulus*] : a bucket, dipper, or other container used to remove water that has entered a boat

⁶bail *also* **bale** \"\ *vb* -ED/-ING/-S *vt* **1** : to dip up and throw; *esp* : to clear (water) from a boat by dipping and throwing over the side — usu. used with *out* ⟨they spent half an hour ~*ing* out the rowboat⟩ ~ *vi* **1** : to dip up and throw out water from a boat ⟨they ~*ed* for hours but the water slowly deepened⟩ **2 a** : to parachute from an aircraft — used with *out* **b** : to escape from a predicament or avoid responsibility — used with *out*

⁷bail *also* **bale** \"\ *n* -s [ME *beil*, *baile*, prob. of Scand origin; akin to ON *beygja* to bend — more at BOW] **1 a** : a supporting half hoop or horseshoe-shaped strip (as for the cover of a delivery wagon or the canopy of a small boat) **b** : an iron yoke on a life car to suspend it from the hawser **c** : a yoke to the trunnions of a cannon to raise it from the carriage **d** : pivoted arched steel bow on a road scraper to which the motive power is attached **e** : either of the two metal clamps that hold a tympan sheet in place in a platen printing press **f** : a hinged bar for holding the paper against the platen of a typewriter **g** *angling* : an attachment of certain spinning reels that picks up the line for rewinding on the spool **2** : the usual arched handle of a kettle, pail, or similar vessel

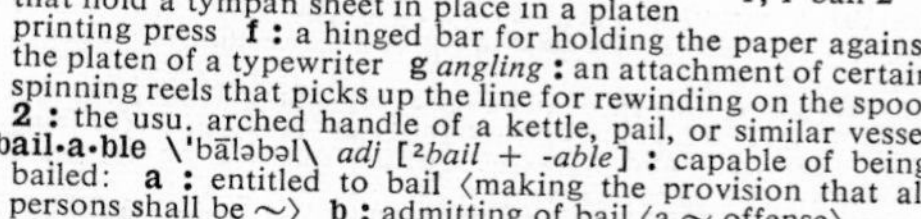

1, 1 bail 2

bail·a·ble \'bāləbəl\ *adj* [²*bail* + -*able*] : capable of being bailed: **a** : entitled to bail ⟨making the provision that all persons shall be ~⟩ **b** : admitting of bail ⟨a ~ offense⟩

bail above \¦==¦=\ *n* : bail given by a defendant after his appearance in court as a guarantee that he will satisfy the judgment of the court in damages, debt, or costs or failing to do so surrender himself in person to the court — called also *bail to the action, special bail*

bail below \¦==¦=\ *n* **1** : bail given by two sureties to the sheriff for the due appearance of the defendant **2** : a mere form with imaginary persons as sureties used as a method of entering the appearance of the defendant in civil actions — called also *common bail*

bail bond *n* [¹*bail*] : a bond by which bail is given

bai·le \'bī,lā\ *n* -s [Sp, fr. *bailar* to dance, fr. OSp, modif. of OProv *balar*, fr. LL *ballare* — more at BALL] *Southwest* : DANCE : a social gathering for dancing; *specif* : one at which Spanish or Mexican folk dances are performed

bailed *past of* BAIL

bail·ee \(')bā¦lē\ *n* -s [²*bail* + -*ee*] : the person to whom goods are committed in trust and who has a temporary possession and a qualified property in them for the purposes of the trust : one that receives goods under a contract of bailment

¹bail·er \'bālə(r)\ *var of* BAILOR

²bailer \"\ *n* -s [⁷*bail* + -*er*] : a worker who attaches handles to pails or buckets

³bailer \"\ *n* -s [³*bail* + -*er*] : a cricket ball bowled so that it hits and removes one or both bails

⁴bailer \"\ *n* -s [⁶*bail* + -*er*] : one that bails (as water); *esp* : a device used for bailing

bailer shell *also* **bailer** *n* -s [⁴*bailer*; fr. its capacity to hold water] : MELON SHELL

bai·ley \'bālē, -li\ *n* -s [ME *bailli*, fr. OF *balie*, var. of *baile* — more at BAIL (outer wall)] **1** : the outer wall of a medieval castle or any of the several walls surrounding the keep **2** : the space immediately within the external wall of a castle or fortress or between any two outer walls

bailey bridge \"-\ *n, usu cap 1st B* [After Sir Donald C. *Bailey* *b*1901 Eng. engineer who designed it] : a bridge designed for rapid construction from interchangeable latticed panels of high-tensile steel that are coupled with alloy steel pins set into ready-made holes to form girders and laid double or triple or superposed to suit the span and load

bai·lie \'bālē, -li\ *n* -s [ME] **1** *dial* : BAILIFF **2 a** : a onetime chief magistrate of a Scottish barony with duties similar to those of a sheriff **b** : a municipal magistrate in Scotland corresponding to the English alderman

bai·li·ery *also* **bai·li·ary** \'bālē,erē, -ri\ *n* -ES [ME *baillierie* fr. *baillie* + -*erie* -ery] : the jurisdicton of a bailie

bai·liff \'bāləf\ *n* -s [ME *bailif*, *bailiff*, *bailie*, fr. OF *baillif*, *bailliu*, *baillu*, fr. *bail* jurisdiction — more at BAIL] **1** : one deputed to exercise public administrative authority locally; *specif*, *chiefly Brit* : a sheriff's deputy — used formerly as a title of nearly any officer (as a mayor, sheriff, or chief officer of a hundred) in England nominated by the king; now used (1) as a title of the chief magistrate of some British towns and of a keeper of some royal castles and (2) as the English equivalent of the title of certain magistrates (as the Scottish bailie or the German landvogt) in countries other than England **2** : one having the custody and management of property for another: as **a** *Brit* : the agent of a lord (as for the collection of rents) **b** *chiefly Brit* : one that manages an estate or farm for another **3** : a court officer who seats witnesses and spectators, announces the entrance of the judge, and keeps order in the court — **bai·liff·ship** \-,ship\ *n* -s

bai·liff·ry \-rē\ *n* -ES : the office or jurisdiction of a bailiff : BAILIWICK

bailing *pres part of* BAIL

bai·li·wick \'bālē,wik, -lə-\ *n* -s [ME *baillifwik*, *bailliwik*, fr. *baillif*, *bailie* bailiff + *wik* wick] **1** *law* : office or jurisdiction esp. of a bailiff : range of authority **2 a** : the special province or domain in which one has superior aptitude, knowledge, or experience or in which one has a particular right to enjoy free activity, exercise authority, and command attention and respect ⟨a scientist intruding in a clergyman's ~⟩ **b** : field of activity : sphere of operations ⟨highly successful in the political ~⟩ **3** : surrounding territory : VICINITY, NEIGHBORHOOD ⟨the coastal areas in Florida's ~⟩ **syn** see FIELD

bail·li \bȧyē\ *n* -s [F, fr. OF *baillif* — more at BAILIFF] : a medieval officer representing the king or seignior and having wide judicial, financial, and military powers

bail·liage \bä'yäzh\ *n* -s [ME, fr. MF, fr. *baillir* to administer (fr. *bail* jurisdiction) + -*age* — more at BAIL] : a bailli's bailiwick

bail·ment \'bā(ə)lmənt\ *n* -s [MF *baillement*, fr. *baillier* to deliver + -*ment* — more at BAIL] **1** : the act of bailing a prisoner or a person accused **2** : a delivery of personal property by a bailor to a bailee for specific purposes under an express or implied agreement of the parties that when those purposes are accomplished the property will be returned to the bailor, kept until he reclaims it, or disposed of according to the agreement — compare MANDATE, PLEDGE

bailment for hire : a bailment for the mutual benefit of the bailor and bailee for compensation (as where one hires the use of another's property or agrees to keep it safely or to transport it or where one bestows care, labor, or attention upon it) — compare PLEDGE

bail·or \(')bā¦lȯ(ə)r, -ō(ə); 'bālə(r)\ *or* **bail·er** \'bālə(r)\ *n* -s [²*bail* + -*or*] : one that delivers goods or money to another in trust

bailout \'=,=\ *n* -s [⁶*bail* + *out*, v.] : an emergency departure and parachute descent from an aircraft aloft

bailpiece \'=,=\ *n* [¹*bail* + *piece*] **1** : a certificate formerly issued to the surety attesting his act of offering bail **2** : a warrant issued to the surety upon which he may arrest the person bailed by him

bails *pl of* BAIL, *pres 3d sing of* BAIL

bails·man \'bā(ə)lzmən\ *n, pl* **bailsmen** [fr. poss. of ¹*bail* + *man*] : one who gives bail for another : SURETY

bail to the action [¹*bail*] : BAIL ABOVE

ba·ly *dial var of* BAILIE

bai·ly's beads \'bālēz-, -liz-\ *n pl, usu cap 1st B* [after Francis *Baily* †1844 Eng. astronomer who described them] : the row of brilliant points of sunlight shining through valleys on the edge of the moon that are seen for a few seconds just before and after the central phase in an eclipse of the sun

¹bain \'bān\ *adj, usu* -ER/-EST [ME, fr. ON *beinn* straight, ready, hospitable] **1** *now dial Eng* **a** : WILLING, READY **b** : LITHE, SUPPLE **2** *dial Eng* : DIRECT, NEAR, SHORT ⟨the ~*est* way⟩

²bain \"\ *n* -s [ME, fr. MF, fr. L *balneum* — more at BAGNIO] *obs* : BATH

bain·bridge reflex \'bān(,)brij-\ *n, usu cap B* [after Francis A. *Bainbridge* †1921 Eng. physiologist] : a reflex mechanism adjusting the rate of the heartbeat to the bodily need and consisting of response by local stretch receptors of the great veins and auricles to increase in venous pressure with consequent acceleration of the heartbeat

baing *pres part of* BA

bai·ning \'bīniŋ\ *n, pl* **baining** *or* **bainings** *usu cap* **1 a** : a Papuan people of New Britain **b** : a member of such people **2** : the language of the Baining people

bain·ite \'bā,nīt\ *n* -s [Edgar C. *Bain* *b*1891 Am. physicist and metallurgist + E -*ite*] : a transformation product in solid steel developed from austenite at temperatures intermediate between those where pearlite and martensite form

bain–ma·rie \,baⁿmə'rē, bā'merē\ *n, pl* **bains–marie** \,baⁿm-, bā'm-\ [F, fr. ML, lit., bath (of) Mary, after *Mary* or *Miriam*, Moses' sister (Exod 15:20), to whom is ascribed a treatise on alchemy] **1** : WATER BATH **2** : STEAM TABLE

bai·noa \bī'nōə\ *n, pl* **bainoa** *or* **bainoas** *usu cap* [Sp, of AmerInd origin] **1** : an Arawakan people of Haiti and southwestern Santo Domingo **2** : a member of the Bainoa people

ba·ioc·co *or* **ba·joc·co** \bə'yō(,)kō\ *or* **ba·ioc** \bə'yōk\ *n, pl* **baioc·chi** \-ōkē\ *or* **baioccos** \-ō(,)kōz\ *or* **bajoc·chi** \-ōkē\ *or* **bajoccos** \-ō(,)kōz\ *or* **baiocs** \-ōks\ [It *baiocco*, prob. fr. ML *Baiocas* Bayeux, city in Normandy, France (appearing in inscriptions on certain Merovingian coins)] **1** : a minor billon or copper coin of the former Papal States equal to 1⁄100 scudo **2** : a unit of value equivalent to one baiocco coin ⟨coins worth 2 and 5 *baiocchi*⟩ ⟨postage stamps worth 6 and 8 *baiocchi* were issued⟩

baira *var of* BEIRA

bai·ram \(')bī¦räm\ *n* -s *usu cap* [Turk *bayram*] : either or both of two Muslim festivals held after Ramadan

baird's sandpiper \'ba(a)(ə)rdz-, 'be(ə)r-\ *n, usu cap B* [after Spencer F. *Baird* †1888 Am. zoologist] : a small migratory sandpiper (*Erolia bairdii*) chiefly of western No. America that breeds in the arctic tundras and winters in So. America and is mottled buff and gray with a dark rump and a short slender bill

bairn \'ba(a)(ə)rn,'be(ə)rn,'bärn\ *n* -s [ME *bern*, *barn*, fr. OE *bearn* & ON *barn*; akin to OS, OHG & Goth *barn* child, OE *beran* to bear — more at BEAR] *chiefly Scot* : CHILD

bairn·ie \-nē\ *n* -s *chiefly Scot* : a small child

bairn·ish \-nish\ *adj, chiefly Scot* : CHILDISH

bairn·ly \-nlē\ *adj* -ER/-EST *Scot* : CHILDISH

bairn's part *n* : LEGITIM

bairn·time \-n·,tīm\ *also* **bairn·team** \-ēm\ *n* -s [ME *bernteam*, *barnteam*, *barntime*, fr. OE *bearntēam*, fr. *bearn* child + *tēam* family, brood, team — more at BAIRN, TEAM] *Scot* : BROOD, OFFSPRING

bai·ru \'bī(,)rü\ *n, pl* **bairu** *or* **bairus** *usu cap* : a member of the peasant segment of the population of the kingdom of Ankole in Uganda — compare HERA, RUNDI

bai·sakh \'bī,säk\ *n* -s *usu cap* [Skt *Vaiśākha*] : a month of the Hindu year — see MONTH table

baise-mains \,bāz(ə)'maⁿ, ,bez-\ *n pl* [F, fr. *baiser* to kiss (fr. OF *baisier*, fr. L *basiare*) + *mains*, pl. of *main* hand, fr. L *manus*] : RESPECTS, COMPLIMENTS ⟨greeted the owners with curtsies and *baise-mains* —Natacha Stewart⟩

baist \'bāst\ *Brit var of* BASTE

¹bait \'bāt\ *vb* -ED/-ING/-S [ME *baiten*, fr. ON *beita*; akin to OE *bǣtan* to bait, worry, OHG *beizen*; causative fr. the root of E *bite* — more at BITE] *vt* **1 a** : to attack in speech or writing (as by derision or insult) usu. with malice : harass (an individual or group) in such a way as to wound the feelings or injure the reputation : PERSECUTE : gall or exasperate by repeated wanton attacks ⟨~*ing* minority groups in a cheap display of prejudice⟩ **b** : to nag at : goad in a carping way : HOUND ⟨his wife constantly ~*ed* him for not having more money⟩ **c** : to ruffle or rouse usu. in a playful good-natured way : TEASE ⟨she kept ~*ing* him about her other love affairs⟩ **2 a** : to harass (as a chained animal) by setting on dogs to worry and bite usu. as a sport ⟨the hunters captured a large bear and ~*ed* him⟩ **b** : to attack by biting and tearing : WORRY ⟨the dogs yapped with excitement as they ~*ed* the badger⟩ **3 a** : to furnish (as a hook or trap) with bait ⟨they sat along the riverbank, carefully ~*ing* the fish lines⟩ **b** : to place poisoned bait on or around (as a field or building) in order to kill pests ⟨he ~*ed* the crop for wireworms⟩; *also* : to provide or distribute bait for the consumption of (a pest) ⟨~ the rats for several days before putting out the poison⟩ **c** : to impale (bait) on or as if on a hook ⟨a ~*ed* earthworm⟩ **d** : to entice by or as if by bait ⟨~*ing* him by promises of a good job⟩ : lure esp. by trickery, duplicity, or strategy ⟨some planes were ~*ed* off course by false radio signals⟩ **4** *now dial* : to give a portion of food and drink to (an animal) esp. upon the road : FEED ⟨the travelers paused to ~ their horses⟩ **5** : to feed (a furnace) with fuel ~ *vi* **1** *archaic* **a** : to stop for food and drink (as when traveling) **b** : to make a brief halt **2** *archaic* : FEED ⟨the horses ~*ed* at the edge of the road⟩

syn RIDE, BADGER, HOUND, HECTOR, HECKLE, CHIVY: all these words indicate persistent harassing or annoying and are frequently interchangeable. BAIT may still be used in reference to wanton, malicious worrying or tormenting of a chained or tethered animal ⟨*baiting* the prisoner, terrorizing him —Liam O'Flaherty⟩ Common in politics today, it suggests any malicious or scornful attack, ridicule, calumny, esp. one goading a weak or defenseless opponent ⟨*baiting* these hapless citizens who had the gall to have Japanese parents —G.S. Schuyler⟩ RIDE in this sense suggests harassing by stringent unfair criticism, derision, or onerous imposition of tasks and charges ⟨the foreman *rides* him. They transfer him from one job to another —Lawrence Lader⟩ BADGER suggests bedeviling persistently with tactics calculated to confuse, madden, or enervate completely ⟨the mill foreman so taunted the workers, so *badgered* them —Sinclair Lewis⟩ ⟨she can't sit and think quietly anywhere else without being *badgered* —Nevil Shute⟩ HOUND implies persistent dogged pursuit and harassing ⟨how Grandfather was *hounded* out of his congregation because he couldn't hold her to their standards of behavior for a minister's wife —Mary Austin⟩ HECTOR suggests any sustained domineering esp. by bullying or scolding ⟨he will speak in a loud voice, and will *hector*, because he wishes to prove that he is "somebody" —F.A.Swinnerton⟩ HECKLE is esp. likely to suggest harassing of a speaker or spokesman by disconcerting tactics, although it may be used for other situations in which one is harried ⟨*heckling* the candidate with constant questions and interruptions⟩ CHIVY is now applicable to any situation involving persistent petty harassing and vexation ⟨having seen two successive wives of the delicate poet *chivied* and worried into their graves —Joseph Conrad⟩

²**bait** \"\ *n* -S [ME, fr. ON *beit* pasturage & *beita* food, bait; akin to OHG *beiza* corrosion, maceration, MLG *bēte*, ON *bīta* to bite — more at BITE] **1 a :** a lure (as a piece of meat) used to attract fish or other animals (as to a hook or trap) so that they can be caught **b :** the specific lure (as worms or an animal decoy) used in catching fish or other animals **c :** a poisonous material distributed where it will be eaten by pests (as rats or insects) **2 :** an attraction meant to win to or make compliant with an ulterior and often not immediately evident objective (as an objective that would otherwise be rejected or viewed with apathy); *also* **:** an enticement that is marked by trickery or duplicity ⟨asking harder work and holding up before them the ~ of higher commissions⟩ **3** *now dial* **a :** FOOD; *esp* **:** a light lunch or snack **b :** refreshment taken during a pause in a journey or during work **4** *obs* **:** a stopping (as for refreshment) in the course of traveling or other activity **5** *slang Brit* **:** a fit of temper **:** RAGE ⟨he'd be in an awful ~ if he knew⟩ **6** *chiefly South* **:** an indefinite but adequate amount **:** PLENTY ⟨a big ~ of pie⟩ ⟨a good ~ of firewood⟩ **7 a :** a preheated iron used for attaching one end of a gather of molten glass that is to be drawn into a cylindrical shape **b :** a device that is lowered into molten glass to start a drawing operation esp. of a sheet

³**bait** \"\ *dial Brit var of* ³BEET

⁴**bait** \"\ *archaic var of* BATE

bait bug *n* **:** a small crustacean of the genus *Emerita* found burrowing in sandy beaches and used for fish bait

bait casting *n* **:** the single-handed rod casting of a relatively heavy and usu. artificial bait which carries out with it the light and soft line from a free-spool reel

baited *past of* BAIT

baitfish \'=,=\ *n* **:** a fish suitable for or used for bait

baith \'bāth\ *adj or pron or conj* [ME (northern dial.) *bathe, baithe*, fr. ON *bāthir* — more at BOTH] *Scot* **:** BOTH

baiting *pres part of* BAIT

baits *pres 3d sing of* BAIT, *pl of* BAIT

bait set *n* **:** a baited trap — compare BLIND SET, WATER SET

bai·tsi \'bītsē\ *n, pl* **baitsi** *or* **baitsis** *usu cap* **1 a :** a Papuan people on Bougainville Island **b :** a member of such people **2 :** the language of the Baitsi people

bait·tle \'bāt³l\ *adj* [prob. of Scand origin; akin to ON *beiti* pasturage] *Scot* **:** RICH, NOURISHING — used of pasture

bai-u \(')bī¦ü\ *adj* [Jap, rain of the rainy season, fr. *bai* plum + *u* rain] **:** relating to the spring or early summer rainy season in China and Japan

bai·za \'bīzə\ *n -s sometimes cap* [colloq. Ar, fr. Hindi *paisā*] **1 :** a small copper coin of Muscat and Oman similar to the pice of India **2 :** a unit of value equivalent to a baiza coin ⟨5-*baiza* coins⟩

baize \'bāz\ *n* -S *often attrib* [MF *baies*, pl. (taken as sing.) of *baie* baize, fr. fem. of *bai* bay-colored — more at BAY] **1 :** a coarsely woven woolen or cotton fabric napped to imitate felt and dyed in solid colors **2 :** a baize drapery, table cover, or lining for furniture

ba·ja·da *also* **ba·ha·da** \bə'hädə\ *n* -S [Sp *bajada* slope, descent, fr. fem. of *bajado*, past part. of *bajar* to descend, fr. (assumed) VL *bassiare*, fr. LL *bassus* fat, short, low] **1** *Southwest* **:** a steep curved descending road or trail **2 :** a broad alluvial slope extending from the base of a mountain range out into a basin and formed by coalescence of separate alluvial fans

ba·jan \'bājən\ *var of* BEJAN

bajanism *usu cap, var of* BAIANISM

ba·jau \bə'jaü\ *n, pl* **bajau** *or* **bajaus** *usu cap* **1 :** a Malay people inhabiting coastal regions of Borneo and the southern Philippines — called also *orang laut* **2 :** a member of the Bajau people — called also *sea gypsy*

bajocco *var of* BAIOCCO

ba·jo·na·do \,bäkə'nä(,)dō\ *n* -S [Sp] **:** JOLTHEAD PORGY

ba·jou·ri \bə'jürē\ *n, pl* **bajouri** *or* **bajouris** *usu cap* **1 :** a Pathan people in the Afghan-Pakistan frontier region **2 :** a member of the Bajouri people

baj·ra \'bäjrə, -(,)rä\ *or* **baj·ri** *or* **baj·ree** \-(,)rē\ *n* -S [Hindi *bājrā, bājrī*] *India* **:** PEARL MILLET 1

ba·ju *also* **badjoo** *or* **badju** \'bä(,)jü\ *n* -S [Malay] **:** a Malay short jacket

ba·ka bomb *also* **baka** \'bäkə\ *n* -S [Jap *baka*, lit., fool, fr. *ba* horse + *ka* deer] **:** a Japanese rocket-propelled bomb-carrying airplane guided by a suicide pilot and used in World War II

ba·kau·an \bə'häwən\ *var of* BACAUAN

¹**bake** \'bāk\ *vb* **baked; baked** \-kt\ *or archaic* **bak·en** \-kən\ **baking; bakes** [ME *baken*, fr. OE *bacan*; akin to OHG *bahhan* to warm, *bahhan* to bake, ON *baka*, Gk *phōgein* to roast] *vt* **1 :** to prepare (as food) by a dry heat either in an oven or on heated metal or stone or under coals **2 :** to dry or harden by subjecting to heat ⟨the ground was *baked* by the hot sun⟩ ⟨*baked* bricks⟩ **3** *obs* **a :** to make into a hard or solid mass **b :** to harden by cold ~ *vi* **1 :** to prepare food by baking it **2 :** to undergo the process of baking ⟨the potatoes were *baking* in the oven⟩ **syn** see DRY

²**bake** \"\ *n* -S **1 :** the action or process of baking **:** subjection to or preparation by baking ⟨for best results a slow ~ at a moderate temperature is essential⟩ **2** *Scot* **:** a hard biscuit **3 a :** a meal or individual dish consisting largely of baked food ⟨a delicious vegetable ~⟩ **b :** a social gathering at which a baked specialty is served as the main dish; *esp* **:** CLAMBAKE **4 :** a batch of baked goods **:** production or total output of baked goods ⟨a bakery turning out a huge daily ~ of fresh bread⟩

bakeboard \'=,=\ *n, chiefly Brit* **:** a board on which dough is kneaded or rolled

baked alaska *n, often cap B & usu cap A* **:** a dessert consisting of cake topped with ice cream covered with meringue which then is quickly browned in an oven

baked-ap·ple \(')='==\ *or* **baked-apple berry** *also* **bakeapple** \'=,==\ *or* **bake-apple berry** *n* [so called fr. its wrinkly appearance] **:** CLOUDBERRY 2

baked beans *n pl* **:** beans softened by soaking and boiling and then baked usu. with salt pork and seasoning — see BOSTON BAKED BEANS

bakehead \'=,=\ *n, slang* **:** a locomotive fireman

bakehouse \'=,=\ *n* [ME *bakhous*, fr. *baken* to bake + *hous* house] **:** BAKERY

Bake·lite \'bākə,līt, -āk-,l-\ *trademark* — used for any of various synthetic resins and plastics

bakemeat *or* **baked meat** *n* [ME *bakemete*, fr. *baken* to bake + *mete* food — more at BAKE, MEAT] *obs* **:** cooked usu. baked food; *specif* **:** a meat pie

baken *archaic past part of* BAKE

Bake–Off \'=,=\ *service mark* — used for a public contest for amateur cooks in which contestants must prepare and bake their entries within a stated time

bakeout \'=,=\ *n* -S **:** protracted heating for the purpose of removing adsorbed substances (as gases)

¹**bak·er** \'bākə(r)\ *n* -S [ME, fr. OE *bæcere*, fr. *bacan* to bake + -*ere* -er — more at BAKE] **1 :** one that bakes: as **a :** one that specializes in the making of breads, cakes, cookies, and pastries **b :** an operator of equipment for the flaking, toasting, and cooling of cereals **c :** BURNER 1a(1) **2 a :** a utensil used for baking **b :** a food (as a meat, fruit, or vegetable) that is suitable for baking ⟨Idaho potatoes are esteemed as good ~s⟩ **3** *or* **baker bird** [so called fr. its ovenlike nest] **:** a So. American ovenbird (*Furnarius rufus*)

²**baker** \"\ *usu cap* — a communications code word for the letter *b*

ba·ker·ite \'bākə,rīt\ *n* -S [R.C.*Baker*, 20th cent. Englishman, its discoverer + E -*ite*] **:** a variety of the mineral datolite occurring in white fine-grained masses resembling marble, containing boron in place of some of the silicon, and having the probable formula $CaB_4(BO_4)(SiO_4)_3(OH)_3.H_2O$ (hardness 4.5)

baker's cheese *also* **bakers' cheese** *n* **:** soft uncooked cottage cheese

baker's dozen *n* **1 :** THIRTEEN ⟨a *baker's dozen* of eggs⟩ **2 :** a small unspecified number ⟨very few persons were there, and only a *baker's dozen* showed any real interest⟩

baker's itch *n* **:** GROCER'S ITCH

bakers' yeast *n* **:** a yeast (commonly *Saccharomyces cerevisiae*) used or suitable for use as leaven; *esp* **:** any yeast strain yielding maximum growth rather than high alcohol production — compare BREWERS' YEAST

bak·ery \'bāk(ə)rē, -ri\ *n* -ES [¹*bake* + -*ery*] **1** *archaic* **:** the work of a baker **2 :** a place in which baked products (as bread, cakes, cookies) are made **3 :** an establishment (as a retail shop) that sells baked products chiefly or exclusively

bakes *pres 3d sing of* BAKE, *pl of* BAKE

bakeshop \'=,=\ *n* **:** BAKERY

bake·stone \'bāk,stōn, -,stən\ *n* **:** a flat piece of stone or iron formerly used for baking (as of scones, cakes, or tarts)

bakeware \'=,=\ *n* **:** heat-resistant dishes (as of pottery) used for baking and serving food ⟨a set of ~⟩ ⟨this ~ is both durable and attractive⟩

bakh·tia·ri \,bäktē'ärē, bäk'tyä-\ *n, pl* **bakhtiari** *or* **bakhtiaris** *usu cap* [Per *Bakhtyārī*, perh. fr. *bakhtyār* fortunate, rich, fr. *bakht* fortune, prosperity] **1 :** a nomadic people ranging between Isfahan and Kermanshah, Iran **2 :** a member of the Bakhtiari people

ba·kie \'bāki\ *n* -S [ScGael *bacaid*, fr. (assumed) VL *bacca* water vessel — more at BASIN] *Scot* **:** a square wooden vessel; *esp* **:** one for carrying ashes or fodder

¹**baking** *n* -S [ME, fr. gerund of *baken*] **1 :** the action or process of baking **2 :** a quantity baked at or within a given time **:** BATCH ⟨served . . . wild turkey and deer and a week's ~ of mince and apple pies —Marjory S. Douglas⟩

²**baking** *adj* **1 :** designed for or used in baking ⟨a ~ utensil⟩ ⟨an essential ~ ingredient⟩ **2 :** marked by intense dry heat **:** SCORCHING ⟨the arid ~ sands of the desert⟩ — **baking·ly** *adv*

baking powder *n* **:** a powder used as a leavening agent in making baked goods (as quick breads or cake) and consisting essentially of a carbonate (as baking soda), an acid substance (as cream of tartar), and starch or flour so that when the mixture is moistened the carbonate and acid react, liberating carbon dioxide which raises the dough

baking soda *n* **:** SODIUM BICARBONATE

ba·kla·va *also* **ba·kla·wa** \'bäklə,vä, ,==='=\ *n* -S [Turk *baklava*] **:** a dessert of wafer-thin sheets of pastry put together with nuts and honey or a sugar syrup and cut usu. in diamond-shaped pieces for serving

bak·shaish \(')bäk¦shīsh\ *n* -ES *usu cap* [fr. *Bakhshis*, village in northwestern Iran] **:** a semiantique or antique Persian carpet with usu. angular designs

bak·sheesh *also* **bak·shish** *or* **bakh·sheesh** *or* **bakh·shish** \'bak,shēsh, ¦=\ *n, pl* **baksheesh** [Per *bakhshīsh*, fr. *bakhshīdan* to give, fr. MPer; akin to Av *baxshaiti* he has or gives a share, Gk *phagein* to eat, Toch A *pāk* part, OSlav *bogatŭ* rich, *bogŭ* god, Skt *bhakṣati* he enjoys, consumes, *bhajati* he allots, and perh. to OHG *backe, bahho* cheek; basic meaning: allot] *esp in northern Africa & southwestern Asia* **:** a gift of money (as for a favor or as a reward) **:** TIP ⟨knowing our porters could go no farther in their light clothes, we gave them their wages, plus liberal ~, and sent them back —Edmund Hillary⟩; *also* **:** ALMS ⟨assailed by hordes of homeless street waifs and their age-old wail of "~" —C.G.Pepper⟩

bak·tun \'bäk,tün\ *n* -S [Maya, fr. *bak* 400 + *tun* year of 360 days] **:** a period of 400 tuns in the Maya calendar — compare KATUN, PICTUN

¹**ba·ku** \'bä(,)kü\ *n* -S *sometimes cap* [native name in the Philippines] **1 :** a fine lightweight straw made of fibers from the talipot palm and marked by a dull finish **2 :** a hat made of baku straw

²**baku** \"\ *n* -S [of African origin; akin to Twi *abako* mahogany tree, *bakua* stalk of a plantain or banana tree] **1 :** either of two tropical African timber trees (*Mimusops heckelii* and *M. djave*) **2 :** the hard heavy wood of the baku trees

³**ba·ku** \(')bä¦kü *also* (')bə-\ *adj, usu cap* [fr. *Baku*, U.S.S.R.] **:** of or from the city of Baku, Azerbaidzhan S.S.R., U.S.S.R. **:** of the kind or style prevalent in Baku

⁴**baku** \"\ *n* -S *usu cap* **:** a fine western Caucasian rug with angular designs

ba·ku·la \'bəkələ\ *n* -S [Skt, perh. of Dravidian origin; akin to Kanarese *pagade*] **:** a tropical Asiatic tree (*Mimusops elengi*) with fragrant white flowers

ba·ku·nin·ism \bə'kün(y)ə,nizəm\ *n* -S *usu cap* [Mikhail A. *Bakunin* †1876 Russian anarchist and writer + E -*ism*] **:** a doctrine of revolutionary anarchism; *also* **:** its militant tenets

ba·ku·nin·ist \-ün(y)ənəst\ *also* **ba·ku·nist** \-ün(y)əst\ *n* -S *usu cap* [M.A.*Bakunin* + E -*ist*] **:** an advocate of Bakuninism

ba·ku·pa·ri \,bä(,)küpə'rē\ *n* -S [modif. of Pg *bacopari*, fr. Tupi] **:** a Brazilian tree (*Rheedia brasiliensis*) of the family Guttiferae with an edible fruit having snow-white slightly acid pulp

bakuri *var of* BACURY

¹**bal** \'bal\ *n* -S [Corn] *chiefly in Cornwall* **:** MINE

²**bal** \"\ *n* -S [by shortening] **:** BALMACAAN

³**bal** \"\ *n* -S [by shortening] **:** BALMORAL 1

bal *abbr* balance

BAL \"\ *abbr or n* -S [*British Anti-Lewisite*] **:** DIMERCAPROL

bala \'balə\ *adj, usu cap* [*Bala*, town in north Wales] **:** of or relating to a subdivision of the European Ordovician

ba·laam \'bāləm\ *n* -S [after *Balaam*, biblical prophet rebuked by his ass (Num 22–24); prob. fr. newspaper fillers being regarded as asinine] **1** *slang* **:** FILLER 1d(1) **2** *slang* **:** worthless or rejected newspaper or magazine copy ⟨could not prevent the publication of a certain amount of ~ —J.B.Hubbell⟩

bal·a·bos *or* **bal·ebos** \,bälə'bōs\ *or* **baal–ha–bos** \,bäl(h)ä'-\ *n, pl* **bal·a·ba·tim** *or* **baal–ha–ba·tim** \-'bātəm, -,tēm\ [Yiddish *balebos*, fr. Heb *ba'al habbayith*, lit., lord of the house] **:** a Jewish master of the house **:** a Jewish house owner or host

ba·la·bos·ta *or* **ba·le·bos·ta** \,bälə'bōstə\ *or* **baal–ha–bos·ta** \,bäl(h)ä-\ *n* -S [Yiddish *baleboste*, fr. *balebos*] **:** a Jewish mistress of the house; *esp* **:** an efficient or competent Jewish housewife or hostess

bal·a·cla·va \,balə'klävə, -avə, *attrib* ¦==¦==\ *or* **balaclava helmet** *n* -S [fr. *Balaclava* (now usu. *Balaklava*), village in the Crimea, U.S.S.R., where a battle of the Crimean War was fought on Oct. 25, 1854] **:** a hoodlike knitted cap covering the head, neck, and part of the shoulders and worn esp. by soldiers and mountaineers

bal·a·dine \,balə¦dēn\ *n* -S [MF *baladin*, fr. OProv, fr. *balar* to dance — more at BALLAD] *archaic* **:** a professional dancer esp. in a troupe of street entertainers

ba·lae·na \bə'lēnə\ *n, cap* [NL, fr. L, whale, modif. of Gk *phalaina, phallaina*; akin to Gk *phallos* penis — more at BLOW] **:** the genus consisting of the Greenland whale — compare RIGHT WHALE

ba·lae·ni·cip·i·tes \bə,lēnə'sipə,tēz\ *n pl, cap* [NL, fr. *Balaenicip-, Balaeniceps*, genus of Ciconiiformes (fr. L *balaena* whale + NL -*cip-*, -*ceps*, fr. L *caput* head) + -*ites* -ite — more at HEAD] **:** a suborder of Ciconiiformes constituted by the shoebill

ba·lae·nid \bə'lēnəd\ *n* -S [NL *Balaenidae*] **:** a whale of the family Balaenidae

ba·lae·ni·dae \bə'lēnə,dē\ *n pl, cap* [NL, fr. *Balaena*, type genus + -*idae*] **:** a family of whales comprising the right whales and extinct related forms

ba·lae·noid \-,nȯid\ *n* -S [NL *Balaenoidea*] **:** WHALEBONE WHALE — **bal·ae·noi·de·an** \¦balə¦nȯidēən\ *adj or n*

bal·ae·noi·dea \,balə'nȯidēə\ [NL, fr. *Balaena* + -*oidea*] *syn of* MYSTICETI

bal·ae·nop·tera \-'näptərə\ *n pl, cap* [NL, fr. *balaeno-* (fr. L *balaena* whale) + -*ptera*] **:** a genus (the type of the family Balaenopteridae) of whalebone whales that comprises the rorquals

bal·ae·nop·ter·i·dae \-(,)näp'terə,dē\ *n pl, cap* [NL, fr. *Balaenoptera*, type genus + -*idae*] **:** a family of whalebone whales that comprise the rorquals and humpbacks and are distinguished from the right whales by the dorsal fin, gular folds, and short whalebone

balafo *var of* BALAPHON

ba·la·ghat \¦bälə¦gȯt, -ät\ *n* -S [prob. fr. Hindi, fr. Per *bālā* above (fr. MPer) + Hindi *ghāṭ* pass — more at GHAT] *India* **:** tableland above mountain passes

ba·la·hi \bə'lähē\ *n, pl* **balahi** *or* **balahis** *usu cap* [Hindi *balāhī*] **1 :** an ethnic group among the untouchables inhabiting Madhya Pradesh state, India, who once were spinners and weavers but have become predominantly farm laborers for the cultivating castes **2 :** a member of the Balahi

bal·a·lai·ka \,balə'līkə\ *n* -S [Russ *balalaika, balabaika*; akin to Ukrainian *bałabajka* balalaika; perh. akin to Russ *balabolit'* to chatter, Czech *blaboliti* to murmur] **:** an instrument of the guitar kind used esp. in the U.S.S.R. and having a triangular wooden body and from two to four strings

balalaika

ba·lam \'bäləm\ *n* -S [Maya] **:** a supernatural being in Mayan religion that guards cornfields and villages ⟨the Mayas of Central America speak of *Balam* as a god of agriculture, describing him as an old fellow with a long head. He walks in the air and whistles as he goes — a much-dreaded nocturnal being —W.D.Wallis⟩

balan- *or* **balano-** *comb form* [NL, fr. Gk *balan-, balano-* acorn, fr. *balanos* acorn, glans penis — more at GLAND] **1 :** glans penis ⟨*balan*itis⟩ ⟨*balano*blennorrhea⟩ **2 :** acorn ⟨*Balan*ops⟩

¹**bal·ance** \'balən(t)s\ *n* -S [ME, fr. OF, modif. of (assumed) VL *bilancia*, fr. LL *bilanc-, bilanx* having two scalepans, fr. L *bi-* + *lanc-, lanx* plate, scalepan; akin to Gk *lekos* dish, Lith *uolektis* ell, OE *eln* ell — more at ELL] **1 a :** a device or apparatus designed esp. to measure the weight of an object: as (1) **:** a beam or lever supported by a fulcrum at the midpoint to form two equal arms, having a pan or tray suspended from each arm, one to hold an object of known weight and the other to hold an object to be weighed, and registering the weight of this object by the deflection of a pointer fastened to the beam and provided with a scale before which it swings (2) **:** a similar device but with unequal arms, the body to be weighed being suspended from the shorter arm while a sliding counterpoise is moved along the graduated scale that forms the other arm to produce equilibrium and indicate the body's weight (3) **:** a device using the elasticity of a spiral spring to measure weight (as of a body suspended from a spring) or force (as of a pull exerted upon the spring) by means of the extension produced in the coil to which is attached a pointer moving along a graduated scale — called also *spring balance* (4) **:** a measuring apparatus in which opposing phenomena (as forces or resistances) neutralize each other — compare NULL METHOD **b** *obs* **:** the tray or dish of a balance **:** SCALE ⟨a pair of ~s⟩ **2 a :** a means that judges or decides ⟨a nomination arrived at in the ~ of a free election⟩ — often used in pl. ⟨the peoples of Africa place insistently on the world's agenda matters of still greater weight in the ~s of human affairs —Alan Paton & H.R.Isaacs⟩ **b** *archaic* **:** the power to make authoritative judgments **3 :** an element, influence, or part that serves as a counterbalance or counterpart esp. to secure harmony, proportion, or symmetry **:** COUNTERPOISE ⟨the minstrel show . . . was soon introduced as a ~ to many heavy dramatic bills —*Amer. Guide Series: La.*⟩ **4 :** a vibrating wheel operating in conjunction with a hairspring to regulate the movement of a timepiece **5 a :** stability (as of an upright body) produced by even distribution of weight on each side of the vertical axis ⟨lose his ~ and fall⟩ **b :** equipoise produced between two contrasting or opposing elements whereby one neutralizes, makes up for, or offsets the other ⟨the benign ~ in him between science and humanism —Lucien Price⟩ ⟨the ~ we strike between security and freedom —Earl Warren⟩ **c :** equality between the totals of the two sides of an account **d :** the quality or state of having weight (as of a pulley or shaft) so distributed that (1) there will be no vibration when running or that (2) the body (as a shaft or a pulley mounted on a balanced shaft) will stand in any position in which it may be placed on a pair of knife-ways — called also respectively (1) *dynamic balance* or *running balance*, (2) *standing balance* or *static balance* **6 a** (1) **:** an aesthetically pleasing integration of elements (as in a work of art) achieved usu. by giving each element only its due prominence or significance and often by allowing one element to stand in contrast to, oppose, or otherwise be matched by another element **:** PROPORTION, HARMONY (2) **:** the juxtaposition in writing of two or more syntactically parallel constructions (as phrases or clauses) containing similar, contrasting, or opposing ideas (as "to err is human; to forgive, divine") **b :** the distribution of weight (as in an implement, device, or moving part of a mechanism) that promotes ease of handling or smoothness of performance **7 a :** physical equilibrium (as of an athlete) maintained before or returned to after a motion or series of motions that upsets the normal weight distribution of the body ⟨a gymnast with a fine sense of ~⟩ ⟨a fighter kept off ~ for a whole round⟩ **b** (1) **:** a controlled state in dancing of maintaining an erect posture (2) **:** a rocking shift from foot to foot esp. in ballroom dancing **8 a :** the weight that one side, faction, or element has in excess of another or others ⟨the ~ of the evidence lay on the side of the defendant⟩ **b :** something that is left over **:** REMAINDER ⟨answers will be given in the ~ of this chapter —R.W.Murray⟩ **c :** an excess or an amount in excess on either side of an account; *esp* **:** an amount in excess on the credit side of an account ⟨to have a comfortable ~ in the bank⟩ **9 a :** control of emotional bias and maintenance of the power of sober judgment esp. under stress **:** SANITY, COMMON SENSE **b :** normal psychological composure **:** EQUANIMITY ⟨I doubt that Thoreau would be thrown off ~ by the fantastic sights and sounds of the 20th century —E.B.White⟩ **10 a :** the relation in physiology between the intake of a particular nutrient and its excretion — used with *positive* when the nutrient is in excess of the bodily metabolic requirement ⟨a positive nitrogen ~⟩ and with *negative* when dietary inadequacy and withdrawal of bodily reserves is present ⟨a negative calcium ~⟩ **b :** the maintenance (as in laboratory cultures and natural habitats) of a population in about the same condition and level ⟨a ~ of biological life or of organic groups had been set up through the ages —*Science*⟩ **11 :** the point in the length of an object at which the moment of force on one side of the point equals that on the other ⟨a rifle with the ~ just two inches in front of the trigger guard⟩

balance 1a(1)

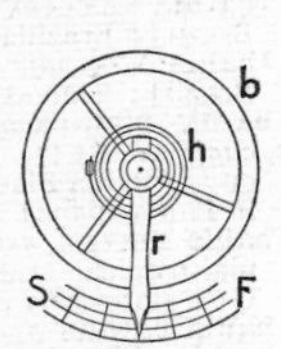

balance 4: *S* slow, *F* fast, *r* regulating lever, *h* hairspring, *b* balance

syn BALANCE, EQUILIBRIUM, EQUIPOISE, POISE, and TENSION can denote, in common, the stability or efficiency resulting from the equalization or exact adjustment of opposing forces. BALANCE suggests a steadiness that results when all parts are properly adjusted to each other, when no one part or constituting force outweighs or is out of proportion to another ⟨to keep her *balance* on an icy street⟩ ⟨to keep his emotional *balance* under stress⟩ ⟨the *balance* between civilian and military needs —*Collier's Yr. Bk.*⟩ ⟨establish an acceptable *balance* between satisfactions and frustrations —Abram Kardiner⟩ ⟨the inevitable outgrowth of the *balance* of character, theme, atmosphere, and structure —F.O.Baker⟩ EQUILIBRIUM, often interchangeable with BALANCE ⟨to keep her physical and emotional *equilibrium* under stress⟩, is more often restricted to a mechanically produced or producible property deriving from a thing's construction, support, or relation to external forces, often suggesting a tendency to return to an original position after disturbance ⟨a ship's *equilibrium*⟩ ⟨an *equilibrium* of opposing human impulses —Sinclair Lewis⟩ ⟨establishing an *equilibrium* between the Western forces and a possible aggressor —*Current History*⟩ ⟨a fundamental lack of *equilibrium* between different aspects of the constitutional distribution of power —R.M.Dawson⟩ EQUIPOISE suggests perfection of balance or stability of equilibrium ⟨to maintain . . . *equipoise* among contending interests —L.H.Butterfield⟩ ⟨the structure remains upright, a marvel of *equipoise* —Norman Douglas⟩ ⟨the *equipoise* of intellectual and pietistic interests in him —H.O.Taylor⟩ POISE denotes an equality of opposing or different things or forces, often designating the state or appearance of perfect balance or serenity, esp. of mind ⟨the condition of a *poise* between widely divergent impulses and emotions that produces a strange serenity —F.R.Leavis⟩ ⟨the main characteristic of their blond gray-eyed colleague is quiet *poise* that stands her in good stead in the exciting, high-pressure work —*Newsweek*⟩ TENSION, rare in this connection, implies strain, either a pull from both ends or an outward pressure in every direction, of such equality that there results a tautness without undue strain at any point; applied to a mental condition it implies an inner balanced vital opposition of moral or intellectual forces, powers, or qualities ⟨indolent as he was on all occasions which required *tension* of the mind, he was active and persevering in bodily exercise —T.B. Macaulay⟩ ⟨the whole *tension* of Gide's work is characterized in those sentences: the incessant dialectic of a man who knows no peace but the precarious equilibrium of opposites —*Times Lit. Supp.*⟩ ⟨in letting the whole physical system lose tone, for lack of the *tension* which gaiety imparts —W.C.Brownell⟩ — **in the balance** *or* **in balance** : in an uncertain critical position : with the fate or outcome about to be determined one way or the other ⟨some human being's right to life hangs *in the balance* —Lucius Garvin⟩ ⟨his . . . authority and his manly strength hesitating and hanging *in the balance* —Glenway Wescott⟩ — **on balance** *also* **in balance** : all things considered : in a final analysis ⟨economic aid has, *on balance*, been justified —H.C.Wolfe⟩ ⟨a . . . noble experiment which, *on balance*, has already proved itself an inexpensive insurance policy against social collapse —C.R.Decker⟩

²**balance** \"\ *vb* -ED/-ING/-S [prob. fr. ¹*balance*] *vt* **1 a** (1) : to compute the difference if any between the debits and credits of (an account) : arrange or prove (as an account or a book of accounts) so that the sum of the debits equals the sum of the credits ⟨~ the books of a company⟩ (2) : to pay the amount due on : SETTLE ⟨send a check to ~ her account⟩ (3) : to equalize the total debits and credits of (an account) **b** : to complete (an equation in chemistry) so that the same number of atoms of each kind appears on each side **2 a** : to set off : COUNTERBALANCE, COUNTERPOISE ⟨the pressures of business, labor, and farmers . . . manage to check and ~ each other —Max Ascoli⟩ ⟨~ one consideration against another⟩ ⟨a large expenditure *balanced* only by his large income⟩ — often used with *up* or *out* ⟨~ up the frustrations of their lives by . . . escapist types of recreation —Ernest & Pearl Beaglehole⟩ **b** : to equal or equalize in weight, number, form, or proportion : arrange in balance ⟨duties and pleasures *balanced* each other in his well-planned life⟩ **3 a** : to weigh (two things) in or as if in a balance : compare the relative weight, force, importance, or value of ⟨~ the profit and loss to see what had been gained⟩ **b** : to deliberate upon esp. by weighing opposing considerations : PONDER ⟨*balancing* the issues for hours on end with no decision ever reached⟩ **4 a** : to bring to a state or position of equipoise ⟨~ scales by adjusting the opposing weights⟩ **b** : to poise or arrange in or as if in balance ⟨a hat *balanced* precariously on his head⟩ ⟨~ a stick on his finger⟩ ⟨*balanced* a set of equations⟩ **c** : to adjust or apportion (as by even or due distribution of elements) to achieve proportion, harmony, or symmetry ⟨regulate your activities and ~ your diet⟩ ⟨~ the national economy⟩; *specif* : to bring (a body, as a flywheel) into balance by removing portions where the weight is excessive or by adding weight to lighter sections — see ¹BALANCE 5d ~ *vi* **1 a** : to become balanced or established in balance esp. in a position difficult to maintain ⟨~ on one hand on a diving board⟩ ⟨sit *balancing* on a porch rail⟩ ⟨an intellect that ~*s* between foolishness and genius⟩ **b** : to stay poised in dancing in an upright position that requires unusual control **2** : to be an equal counterpoise ⟨his periods of frenzy *balanced* with periods of cool meticulous deliberation⟩ **3** : FLUCTUATE, WAVER, HESITATE ⟨~ and temporize on all matters that demand action⟩ ⟨feel something like contempt for the mind that ~*s* and waits —P.E.More⟩ **4 a** : to move with a swaying or swinging motion; *esp* : to shift the weight lightly back and forth from foot to foot in dancing bending the body to the side on which the weight is placed **b** : to move in dancing toward a person or couple usu. with four steps and then back **5** : to bid in contract bridge on the assumption that one's partner must have a strong hand because the opponents have bid weakly **syn** see STABILIZE

³**ba·lan·cé** \bə'lä^n'sā, ˌba,lä^n'sā\ *adj* [F, past part. of *balancer* to balance, fr. *balance*, n.] : changing the weight in ballet lightly from foot to foot with knee flexion accompanied by closing in of the free foot and by body sway

balance beam *n* **1** : a beam used as a counterpoise (as to a drawbridge) **2** : a thin rail used for feats of balancing in gymnastics

balance cock *or* **balance bridge** *n* : the bridge that carries the top pivot of the balance staff in a watch

balance coil *n* : an iron-cored solenoid with a tap at the center or neutral point used to provide a neutral terminal in a three-wire system

balance crane *n* : a crane in which there is a counterbalancing wing opposite the load

balanced *adj* **1 a** : being in a state of balance : PROPORTIONATE, SYMMETRICAL, HARMONIOUS ⟨one of the notable early builders of the closed and ~ couplet —Douglas Bush⟩ ⟨the properly ~ classical symphonic orchestra —Ralph Hill⟩ ⟨a more sober and perhaps more ~ assessment of modern intellectual and cultural history —F.L.Baumer⟩ ⟨a ~ blend of Virginia and Oriental tobaccos —*Punch*⟩ ⟨prided herself on possessing a well-*balanced* mind —Dorothy Sayers⟩ ⟨the educated man shows a ~ development of all his powers —*Report: (Canadian) Royal Commission on Nat'l Development*⟩ **b** : having the physiologically active elements mutually counteracting ⟨a ~ solution⟩ **c** : possessing in proper proportions the living and nonliving elements necessary for the existence and continuation of an effective food chain ⟨a ~ pond⟩ ⟨a ~ aquarium⟩ **d** *of a diet or ration* : furnishing all needed nutrients in just the quantity, form, and proportion needed to support healthy growth and productivity ⟨a ~ chicken mash is essential for the first four to six weeks —*Farmer's Weekly (So. Africa)*⟩ ⟨low-cost ~ luncheons —*Current Biog.*⟩ **e** *of fishing tackle* : having rod, reel, line, and lure properly matched to provide maximum angling efficiency **f** : having players equally distributed on each side of the center — used of an offensive line or backfield formation in football; compare UNBALANCED **g** *of cards* : evenly distributed among the four suits **h** *of a budget* : having expenditures no greater than income ⟨insisted on a ~ budget and refused to permit government subsidies —*Collier's Yr. Bk.*⟩ **i** *of an electrical transmission line* : having equal impedance in each separate line and equal impedance from each line to ground **2 a** *of a fabric* : having the same type and number of yarns in weft and warp **b** *of twisted plied yarns* : that do not curl or kink

balanced anesthesia *n* : anesthesia produced by smaller doses of two or more agents considered safer than the usual large dose of a single agent

balanced fund *n* : a security portfolio comprising both bonds and stocks

balanced lethal *n* : a true-breeding heterozygous organism maintained in a stable state through the existence of different lethals on each of a pair of homologous chromosomes and resulting in loss of all homozygotes

balanced population *n* : a natural population in a particular land area or body of water that maintains itself year after year with little fluctuation in numbers of individuals in spite of regulated fishing or hunting

balanced rock *n* : an angular, subangular, or rounded rock of considerable size that rests more or less precariously on its base and is the result of weathering and erosion in situ — compare PERCHED BOULDER

balanced rudder *or* **balance rudder** *n* : a rudder hung with part of its area forward of the vertical axis to counterbalance the force of the water on the part abaft of the axis

balanced step *n* : any of a series of winders so arranged that their small ends are only a little narrower than the fliers

balanced ticket *n* : a political party ticket with a list of candidates designed to appeal to the major racial, national, and religious groups of the electorate

balance fish *n* : HAMMERHEAD 3a

balance frame *n* : the frame of a walking wheel cultivator having axles offset to the front to enable the weight of the machine to overcome the tendency of the tongue to fly upward when the gangs are hung up

balance gate *n* : a gate (as a floodgate) hung in the middle on a horizontal axis to facilitate turning

bal·an·celle \ˌbalən¦sel\ *n* -S [F, fr. It dial. (Genoa) *balanzella*] : a Mediterranean coasting and fishing boat with a single lateen sail

balance lugsail *n* : a lugsail not lowered in tacking and having the foot laced to a boom extending forward of the mast or with the tack fitted to travel on a horse set in the deck forward of the mast — see LUGSAIL illustration

balance of mind : emotional equilibrium : SANITY ⟨had taken her life when her *balance of mind* was disturbed⟩

balance of nature : a state of equilibrium in nature due to the constant interaction of the whole biotic and environmental complex, interference with this equilibrium (as by human intervention) being often extremely destructive — compare EROSION

balance of payments *also* **balance of international payments** : a summary of the international transactions of a country or region over a period of time including commodity and service transactions, capital transactions, and gold movements

balance of power : an equilibrium or adjustment of power (as between potentially opposing sovereign states) such that no one state is willing or able to upset the equilibrium by waging war or interfering with the independence of other states

balance of trade : the difference in value over a period of time between imports and exports of commodities or formerly of commodities and such transactions as services and remittances

balance piston *n* : a small piston moving in a steam cylinder and attached directly to a vertically reciprocating piece so as partly to balance its dead weight

bal·anc·er \'balən(t)sə(r)\ *n* -S : one that balances: as **a** (1) : ³HALTER (2) : a rodlike lateral protuberance of the head in certain larval salamanders **b** (1) : an electronic appliance (as a balancing condenser) used with a direction finder to improve the sharpness of the direction indication (2) : BALANCER SET

balance reef *n* **1** : the last reef used in a fore-and-aft sail and taken diagonally from the throat to the close-reef cringle of the leech **2** : the ordinary last reef or close reef used to steady a ship

balancer set *n* **1** : two or more similar direct-current machines directly coupled together and connected in series across the outer conductors of a multiple-wire system of distribution for the purpose of maintaining the potentials of the intermediate wires of the system, which are connected to the junction points between the machines — called also *compensator, equalizer set* **2** : reactors or transformers with their wires so interconnected as to equalize the voltages between the wires of a multiple-wire alternating-current system — called also *static balancer*

balance rudder *var of* BALANCED RUDDER

balances *pl of* BALANCE, *pres 3d sing of* BALANCE

balance screw *n* : one of the screws set into the rim of a watch balance or chronometer balance and used for regulating the poise of the balance and thereby the timekeeping rate — compare MEANTIME SCREW

balance sheet *n* **1** : a statement of the financial condition (as of a corporation) at a given date showing the equality of total assets to total liabilities plus net worth or of total liabilities to total assets plus deficit **2** : an accounting showing the relationship of counterpoised things (as profit and loss, achievement and lag, or activity and rest) ⟨a *balance sheet* of military government, showing its difficulties and achievements —Sigmund Neumann⟩ ⟨set up a *balance sheet* on each possible solution, stating your evidence for and against that course of action —W.J.Reilly⟩

balance spring *n* : HAIRSPRING

balance staff *n* : the pivoted arbor of a balance wheel

balance wheel *n* **1 a** : a wheel that regulates or stabilizes the motion of a mechanism (as a sewing machine or timepiece) — compare ¹BALANCE 4 **b** : FLYWHEEL **2** : something suggesting a balance wheel in acting as a regulating and stabilizing force ⟨George Washington . . . was the *balance wheel* of the convention —*World Today*⟩ ⟨a sense of humor that acts as a *balance wheel* in a man's life⟩

balancing *pres part of* BALANCE

balancing band *n* : a band fitted with a link or ring on each side of the shank at the balancing point of the ship's anchor — called also *gravity band*

balancing condenser *n* : a variable condenser used in an auxiliary way with a direction finder to make the indications of the instrument more precise — called also *compensating condenser*

balancing ring *n* : a ring attached to the balancing band of an anchor

ba·lan·gay \ˌbalən¦gī\ *also* **ba·ran·gay** \ˌbarən-\ *n* -S [*balangay* fr. Tag; *barangay* fr. Ilako or Bisayan] : a large swift canoe or boat of the Philippines

ba·lan·ic \bə'lanik\ *adj* [*balan-* + *-ic*] : of or relating to the glans of the penis or of the clitoris

¹**bal·a·nid** \'balənəd\ *adj* [NL *Balanidae*] : of or relating to the genus *Balanus*

²**balanid** \"\ *n* -S : a barnacle of the genus *Balanus*

ba·lan·i·dae \bə'lanə,dē\ *n pl, cap* [NL, fr. *Balanus*, type genus + *-idae*] : a family of highly evolved sessile barnacles comprising the acorn barnacles

bal·a·nite \'balə,nīt\ *n* -S [*balan-* + *-ite*] : a fossil balanoid shell

bal·a·ni·tes \ˌbalə'nīd·ēz\ *n, cap* [NL, fr. Gk *balanitēs* acorn-shaped, fr. *balan-* + *-itēs* -ite] : a small genus of Old World tropical trees of the family Zygophyllaceae distinguished by the one-seeded drupe

bal·a·ni·tis \-īd·əs\ *n* -ES [NL, fr. *balan-* + *-itis*] : inflammation of the glans penis

balano- — see BALAN-

bal·a·no·glos·sid \ˌbalə(ˌ)nō'gläsəd\ *n* -S [NL *Balanoglossida*] : ENTEROPNEUST

bal·a·no·glos·si·da \-sədə\ [NL, fr. *Balanoglossus* + *-ida*] *syn of* ENTEROPNEUSTA

bal·a·no·glos·sus \-səs\ *n, cap* [NL, fr. *balan-* + *-glossus* (fr. Gk *glōssa* tongue) — more at GLOSS] : a genus of marine burrowing wormlike animals that because of certain vertebrate-like characters are now usu. classed as chordates and made with certain closely related forms (as *Dolichoglossus*) to constitute an order (Enteropneusta) of the Hemichorda

¹**bal·a·noid** \'balə,nȯid\ *adj* [Gk *balanoeidēs* like an acorn, fr. *balan-* + *-eidēs* -oid] : of or relating to the acorn barnacles

²**balanoid** \"\ *n* -S : ACORN BARNACLE

bal·a·noph·o·ra \ˌbalə'näfərə\ *n, cap* [NL, fr. *balan-* + *-phora*] : a genus (typifying the family Balanophoraceae) of Asiatic parasitic plants having pistillate flowers without perianth and with one pistil

bal·a·noph·o·ra·ce·ae \ˌbalə,näfə'rāsē,ē\ *n pl, cap* [NL, fr. *Balanophora*, type genus + *-aceae*] : a family of yellow or red tropical root parasitic dicotyledonous plants related to and sometimes included among the Santalales — **bal·a·noph·o·ra·ceous** \¦=,=,=¦=shəs\ *adj*

bal·an·o·phore \bə'lanə,fō(ə)r, 'balənə,f-\ *adj* [NL *Balanophora*] : of or relating to the Balanophoraceae

bal·a·no·pos·thi·tis \¦balə(ˌ)nō(ˌ)päs'thīd·əs\ *n* -ES [NL, fr. *balan-* + *posthitis*] : inflammation of the glans penis and of the prepuce

bal·a·nops \'balə,näps\ *n, cap* [NL, fr. *balan-* + *-ops*] : a small genus (constituting the family Balanopsidaceae and order Balanopsidales) of tall little-known Australian dicotyledonous trees having large simple leaves, flowers in catkins, and a nutlike fruit enclosed in an involucre

ba·lante \bə'länt\ *also* **ba·lan·ta** \-ntə\ *n, pl* **balante** *or* **balantes** *also* **balanta** *or* **balantas** *usu cap* [*Balante* fr. F; *Balanta* fr. Pg] **1 a** : a Sudanese Negro people of French Senegal and Angola **b** : a member of such people **2** : the West-Atlantic language of the Balante people

bal·an·tid·i·al \¦balən¦tidēəl\ *or* **bal·an·tid·ic** \-dik\ *adj* [NL *Balantidium* + E *-al* or *-ic*] : of, relating to, or caused by protozoans of the genus *Balantidium*

bal·an·ti·di·a·sis \ˌbalən·tə'dīəsəs, bə,lan-\ *also* **bal·an·tid·i·o·sis** \ˌbalən,tidē'ōsəs\ *n, pl* **balantidia·ses** *also* **balantidio·ses** \-sēz\ [NL, fr. *Balantidium* + *-asis* or *-osis*] : infection with or disease caused by protozoans of the genus *Balantidium*

bal·an·tid·i·um \ˌbalən·'tidēəm\ *n* [NL, fr. Gk *balantidion* little bag, dim. of *balantion* bag, pouch, purse] **1** *cap* : a genus of large parasitic ciliate protozoans (order Heterotricha) having the peristome beginning near the anterior tip of the body and containing a species (*Balantidium coli*) that infests the intestines of swine and other mammals and may cause a chronic ulcerative dysentery in man **2** *pl* **balantid·ia** \-ēə\ : a protozoan of the genus *Balantidium*

bal·a·nus \'balənəs\ *n, cap* [NL, fr. L, acorn, fr. Gk *balanos* — more at GLAND] : a very large genus (the type of the family Balanidae) of barnacles comprising the sessile acorn barnacles and including littoral and deepwater forms some of which cause destructive fouling of ships and of underwater cables

ba·lao \bə'lau̇\ *n* -S [Sp] : HALFBEAK

bal·a·phon \'balə,fōn, -ăn\ *also* **balafo** \-,fō\ *n* -S [F & Bambara; F *balafon*, fr. Bambara *balafo* to play the xylophone, fr. *bala* xylophone] : a West African xylophone with gourd resonators

bal·as \'baləs\ *or* **balas ruby** *n* -ES [ME *baleis, balis, balas*, fr. MF *balais*, fr. Ar *balakhsh*, fr. *Badhakhshān, Balakhshān*, ancient region of Afghanistan] : a ruby spinel of a pale rose-red or orange

ba·la·ta \bə'läd·ə\ *n* -S [Sp, of Cariban origin; akin to Galibi *balata*] **1** : a hard substance produced by drying the milky juice of a bully tree (*Manilkara bidentata*) and that possess properties similar to those of gutta percha and is used chiefly in the manufacture of belting and golf balls — called also *gutta balata* **2** : any of certain tropical American trees of the genus *Manilkara* that yield balata; *esp* : a bully tree (*M. bidentata*)

ba·la·tong \'bälə,tȯŋ\ *n* -S [Tag] *Philippines* : MUNG BEAN

ba·latte \bə'lat\ *n* -S [origin unknown] : a cut slab of soft white limestone providing good reflective insulation owing to its natural white color

ba·laus·tre \bə'lau̇,strā\ *n* -S [AmerSp, fr. Sp *balaustre, balaústre* baluster, fr. It *balaustro* — more at BALUSTER] **1** : either of two So. American timber trees (*Centrolobium robustum* or *C. paraense*) with yellowish brown to purplish or rose-colored glossy wood **2** : the wood of the balaustre

ba·la·wa \bə'läwə\ *n, pl* **balawa** *or* **balawas** *usu cap* : a division of the Andamanese

bal·boa \bal'bōə\ *n* -S [Sp, after Vasco Núñez de *Balboa* †1517 Span. explorer] **1** : the basic monetary unit of Panama — see MONEY table **2** : a silver coin representing one balboa

bal·brig·gan \bal'brigən\ *n* -S [fr. *Balbriggan*, seaport town in Ireland where it was orig. manufactured] **1** : a plain-stitch knitted often tubular usu. cotton fabric used esp. for underwear, hosiery, or sweaters **2** : clothing (as pajamas) made of balbriggan — usu. used in pl.

bal·che *also* **bal·ché** \(')bäl¦chā\ *n* -S [AmerSp *balché*, fr. Maya] : a fermented drink prepared by the natives of Yucatan from the bark of a tree of the genus *Lonchocarpus* and honey

bal·co·net *or* **bal·co·nette** \¦balkə¦net\ *n* -S [*balcony* + *-et, -ette*] : a railing or balustrade on the outside of a window and in the form of a balcony

bal·co·nied \'balkənēd, -id\ *adj* : having balconies ⟨a ~ façade⟩ ⟨a spacious, turreted, ~ structure of dark, weather-beaten shingles —E.A.Weeks⟩

bal·co·ny \'balkənē, 'bau̇k-, -ni\ *n* -ES [It *balcone*, fr. OIt, scaffold, of Gmc origin; akin to OHG *balko, balcho* beam — more at BALK] **1 a** : a usu. unroofed platform projecting from the wall of a building, enclosed by a parapet or railing, and usu. resting on brackets or consoles **b** : an interior projecting gallery in a public building (as a theater); *specif* : such a gallery immediately above the main floor **2** : an elevated usu. railed platform similar to or suggesting a balcony (as on the side of a large cylinder printing press)

balcony 1a

syn GALLERY, LOGGIA, VERANDA, PIAZZA, PORCH, PORTICO, STOOP: these words often show considerable variation in use, esp. regional; the following comments bear on only those applications that appear to meet with approval in historical and architectural use. BALCONY in this comparison is applicable to any unroofed structure resting on brackets or corbels enclosed by balustrade or railing and extending along a side of a building. GALLERY applies to a long narrow structure roofed over and often enclosed. LOGGIA may apply to a balcony or gallery that is architecturally well integrated in a building's design. VERANDA applies to a roofed structure or area facilitating out-of-door activities. PIAZZA, orig. indicating an open square in a town, is interchangeable with, and may be a rather modish synonym for, VERANDA. PORCH orig. indicated a covered entrance affording protection but now is applicable to all but the largest verandas. PORTICO is likely to suggest a roofed gallery or gallerylike structure fronting a more or less large or imposing building. STOOP is applicable in regional speech to any relatively unpretentious construction outside an entrance, esp. to a small porch or to a flight of steps with a landing before a door

¹**bald** \'bȯld\ *adj* -ER/-EST [ME *balled*; akin to OE *bæl* fire, pyre, OHG *belihha* coot, ON *bāl* pyre, Dan *bældet* bald, Goth *bala* white-faced horse, L *fulica* coot, Gk *phalios* having a white spot, Skt *bhāla* forehead, luster] **1 a** : lacking all or a significant portion of the natural or usual covering of hair on the head or sometimes on other parts of the body ⟨his big head was ~ except for a wisp or two of brown hair —G.K.Chesterton⟩ ⟨comb the hair from the sides of the head across the top to disguise the fact that he is ~⟩ ⟨looking as ~ and hairless in a bathing suit as a plucked chicken⟩ ⟨a bearded or ~ face⟩ **b** : lacking some natural or expected covering (as of foliage, feathers, trees, soil, or nap) ⟨the trees were brown and ~ as in winter —George Borrow⟩ ⟨~, featureless, fire-blackened mountains —John Muir⟩ ⟨the banks rise suddenly, sometimes covered with timber and sometimes ~ —Anthony Trollope⟩ ⟨the ~ seat of his trousers⟩ **c** *of wheat* : lacking a beard **d** : not having a flange — used of a mechanical part **2** *archaic* : lacking merit, import, or effect : WORTHLESS, PALTRY **3 a** : lacking amplification, adornment, or decoration : SPARSE, PLAIN, MEAGER ⟨offered not a shred of evidence — nothing but ~ assertion —C.H.Grandgent⟩ ⟨a ~ statement of the facts⟩ ⟨only the ~ outlines of his legal career —George Bellairs⟩ ⟨the more poetic the theme, the ~*er*, or at least the briefer, its expression —W.C.Brownell⟩ **b** : UNDISGUISED, PATENT, PALPABLE, OUTRIGHT ⟨~ egotism —J.R.Lowell⟩ ⟨a ~ lie⟩ ⟨the ~, inaccurate . . . realism of the present theater —J.P.Marquand⟩ ⟨the present outcome is a ~ political compromise —*New Republic*⟩ **4** *of a horse* : having the face including the skin about the eyes and nostrils white **syn** see BARE

²**bald** \"\ *n* -S *chiefly Midland* : an often grassy mountain summit or other elevated area naturally bare of forest ⟨the grass-covered ~*s* of the Blue Ridge in North Carolina —*Fortune*⟩

³**bald** \"\ *vi* -ED/-ING/-S : to become bald ⟨was starting to ~ noticeably⟩ ⟨a young man as diplomats go, still under fifty, ~*ing* rapidly —J.P.O'Donnell⟩

bal·da·chin \'bȯldəkən, 'bal-\ *or* **bal·da·chi·no** *or* **bal·dac·chi·no** \,baldə'kē(,)nō\ *or* **bal·da·quin** \'bȯldəkən, 'bal-\ *n* -s [*baldachin, baldachino, baldacchino* fr. It *baldacchino,* fr. OIt, fr. *Baldacco* Bagdad, city in Iraq + OIt *-ino* (fr. L *-inus* -ine); *baldaquin* fr. MF *baldequin, baudequin,* fr. OF, fr. OIt *baldacchino*] **1 :** an embroidered fabric of silk and gold esp. for church vestments, ceremonial robes, and decorations **2 :** a cloth canopy fixed or carried over an important person or a sacred object often as a mark of honor **3 :** an ornamental canopy-like structure that projects from a wall, is suspended from above, or is supported by columns and that is used esp. over an altar or a seat of honor — compare CIBORIUM

baldachin 3

bald brant *n* **:** BLUE GOOSE
bald coot *n* **1 :** the Old World coot **2 :** FLORIDA GALLINULE **3 :** COOT 4
baldcrown \'=,=\ *n* **:** BALDPATE 2
bald cypress *n* [so called fr. the fact that it is deciduous] **1 :** either of two large swamp trees (*Taxodium distichum* and *T. ascendens*) of the southern states — see POND CYPRESS **2 :** the hard red wood of bald cypress much used for shingles
bald eagle *also* **bald–headed eagle** *n* **:** the common eagle (*Haliaeetus leucocephalus*) of No. America being entirely dark when young but having white feathers covering the head and neck when fully mature and also a white tail when old — see AMERICAN EAGLE
balder *comparative of* BALD
¹bal·der·dash \'bȯldə(r),dash, -aa(ə)sh,-aish\ *n* -ES [origin unknown] **1** *obs* **:** an odd and usu. objectionable mixture of drinks (as beer and milk or beer and wine) **2 :** NONSENSE, TRASH ⟨writers of this kind of sophomoric ~ —F.L.Mott⟩ ⟨poetry, some of it excellent, much of it ~ —J.D.Adams⟩
²balderdash \"\ *vt* -ED/-ING/-ES *archaic* **:** to make balderdash of ⟨wine ~*ed* with milk⟩ ⟨poetry . . . ~*ed* with false sentiment —Washington Irving⟩
baldest *superlative of* BALD
bald face *n* **1 :** a bald-faced horse **:** a bald horse **2** *obs slang* **:** raw or inferior whiskey
bald–faced \'=¦=\ *adj* **1 :** having a white face or a white mark on the face — usu. used of an animal (as a horse, cow, or stag) **2 :** BARE-FACED ⟨a plain, *bald-faced* case of highhanded graft —F.B.Gipson⟩ ⟨a *bald-faced* lie⟩ — compare BALD
bald–faced hornet *n* **:** WHITE-FACED HORNET
bald–faced widgeon *n* **:** BALDPATE 2
baldhead \'=,=\ *n* **1 :** a bald-headed person **2 a :** BALDPATE 2 **b :** a breed or color variety of domestic pigeon **3 :** an abnormality of seedlings esp. common among beans characterized by deformity, decay, or death of the growing point and the appearance of a bare stump above the cotyledons resulting from damage to the seed by mechanical, biological, or other factors; *also* **:** the stump itself
¹bald–headed \'=¦==\ *adj* **1 :** BALD **2** *of a schooner* **:** without topmasts
²bald–headed \'=,==\ *adv* [¹*bald-headed*] **:** in a rush without care or caution **:** PRECIPITATELY ⟨she came out *bald-headed* and accused me of having stolen the case —Valentine Williams⟩ ⟨the planes went *bald-headed* for the enemy squadron⟩
bal·die \'bȯldē\ *n* -s [prob. short for Giuseppe *Garibaldi* †1882 Ital. patriot] **:** a small double-ended fishing boat used on the east coast of Scotland
bald·ing \'bȯldiŋ, -ēŋ\ *adj* **:** getting bald ⟨a short stout ~ man —W.G.Smith⟩ ⟨a ~ head thinly sprinkled with grey hairs —Mervyn Wall⟩
bald·ish \'bȯldish, -ēsh\ *adj* **:** somewhat bald ⟨sixty years old now . . . gnarled and ~ —Stanley Walker⟩
bald locust *n* **:** ATTACUS 1
bald·ly \'bȯl(d)lē, -li\ *adv* **:** in a bald manner ⟨to put the case ~ without vain recrimination —Edith Wharton⟩ ⟨this evidence, which is only ~ summarized —Edward Clodd⟩ ⟨the appeal is simply and ~ to morbid curiosity —F.L.Mott⟩
baldmoney \"\ *n, pl* **baldmoneys** [by folk etymology fr. ME *baldemoine, baldemonie*] **1 :** any of several gentians (esp. *Gentiana amarella*) **2 :** SPICKNEL
bald·ness *n* -ES **:** the state of being bald
¹baldpate \'=,=\ *or* **bald–pated** \'=¦==\ *adj* [¹*bald* + *-pate* or *-pated*] **:** BALD-HEADED
²baldpate \"\ *n* **1 :** BALDHEAD 1 **2 :** a white-crowned widgeon (*Mareca americana* or *Anas americana*) with a short narrow bill that breeds in northwestern No. America and winters along both coasts of the U.S. and in Mexico
baldrib \'=,=\ *n, dial Eng* **:** a lean piece of pork cut from nearer the rump than the sparerib
bal·dric *also* **bal·drick** \'bȯldrik, -ēk\ *n* -s [ME *baudry, baudrik,* prob. modif. of OF *baudré*] **1 :** an often richly ornamented belt worn over one shoulder, across the breast, and under the opposite arm to support a sword or bugle **2 :** a belt resembling a baldric worn about the waist

baldric 1

bald rush *n* **:** an American sedge of the genus *Psilocarya*
balds *pres 3d sing of* BALD, *pl of* BALD
bald tire *n* **:** a flangeless steel tire shrunk or bolted to a locomotive drive wheel —called also *blind tire, flangeless tire, plain tire*
bald·win hoe \'bȯldwən-\ *n, usu cap B* [prob. after Henry I. *Baldwin b*1896 Am. research forester] **:** a heavy hoe with a long narrow blade used in planting small forest trees
baldwin spot *n, usu cap B* [fr. *Baldwin,* a variety of winter apple, after Col. Loammi *Baldwin* †1807 Am. civil engineer & soldier who developed it] **:** BITTER PIT
baldy \'bȯldē, -i\ *n* -ES **1** *slang* **:** one that is bald **2 :** a white-headed pigeon (*Columba norfolciensis*) of Australia that feeds on fruits and seeds
¹bale \'bāl, *esp bef pause or cons* -āəl\ *n* -s [ME, fr. OE *bealu, balu;* akin to OHG *balo* evil, ON *bǫl,* Goth *balwawesei* malice, Old Cornish *bal* plague, OBulg *bolŭ* sick man] **1 :** great evil **:** a malign pernicious influence **:** HARM, DISASTER ⟨gave him a final look, in which Reith read nothing but ~ —D.C. Peattie⟩ ⟨the day would come when the thunderous shout "Nika!" would mean ~ and woe to her —P.I.Wellman⟩ **2 :** pain or mental suffering **:** TORMENT, WOE, SORROW ⟨let . . . your bliss be turned into ~ —Edmund Spenser⟩
²bale \"\ *n* -s [ME, fr. OE *bæl* flame, pyre; akin to ON *bál* flame, pyre — more at BALD] *archaic* **:** a great fire; *esp* **:** a signal fire
³bale \"\ *n* -s [ME, fr. OF, of Gmc origin; akin to OHG *balla* ball — more at BALL] **1 a :** a large bundle of goods for storage or transportation; *specif* **:** a large closely pressed package of merchandise bound with cord, wire, or hoops and usu. protected by a wrapping (as of burlap) ⟨a ~ of paper⟩ ⟨a ~ of hay⟩ **b :** the amount contained in a bale esp. when fixed for a certain commodity and sometimes used as a unit of measure (as in the U. S. 500 pounds of cotton) **2** *archaic* **:** a set usu. of three — used of dice
⁴bale \"\ *vt* -ED/-ING/-S [³*bale*] **:** to make up into a bale ⟨loose pulp is *baled* in units measuring about 18x23x43 inches —H.R.Mauersberger⟩ ⟨spend an afternoon *baling* hay⟩
⁵bale *var of* BAIL
bale·age \'bālij, -ēj\ *n* -s [³*bale* + *-age*] **:** the total number of bales (as of cotton produced)
bal·e·ar·ic \,balē¦arik, -ēk, *also* -¦er- *sometimes* bə'lir-\ *adj, usu cap* [L *Balearicus, Balearicus* of the Balearic islands, fr. Gk *Baliarikos,* fr. *Baliareis* Balearic islands + *-ikos* -ic] **:** of or belonging to a group of islands in the Mediterranean sea off the coast of Spain including esp. Majorca, Minorca, and Iviza
bal·e·ar·i·ca \,balē'arəkə\ *n, cap* [NL, fr. L, fem. of *Balearicus*] **:** the genus comprising the crowned cranes
balearic crane *n, usu cap B* **:** a crowned crane (*Balearica pavonina*) of Africa
balebos *var of* BALABOSS
baleboste *var of* BALABOSTA
bale breaker *n* [³*bale*] **:** a breaker for baled material (as cotton)
bale cubic *n* [³*bale*] **:** the space available for cargo in a ship's hold that is measured in cubic feet to the inside of the cargo battens and to the underside of the beams
ba·leen \bə'lēn\ *n* -s [ME *baleine* whale, baleen, fr. OF, fr. L *balaena* whale — more at BALAENA] **:** a horny substance growing in the mouth of whales of the suborder Mysticeti that is esp. developed in the right whale and grows in dependent plates from 2 to 12 feet long attached in 2 ranks along the upper jaw forming a fringelike sieve to collect and retain food — called also *whalebone*

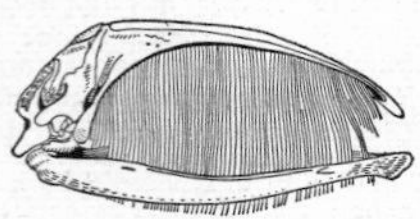
skull of right whale showing plates of baleen

baleen whale *n* **:** WHALEBONE WHALE
bale·fire \'bā(ə)l,fī(ə)r\ *n* [ME, fr. OE *bælfȳr* funeral fire, fr. *bǣl* pyre + *fȳr* fire — more at BALE, FIRE] **:** a large outdoor fire: **a :** a funeral pyre **b :** a signal fire **:** BEACON **c :** BONFIRE 2
bale·ful \'bālfəl\ *adj* [ME, fr. OE *bealuful, baluful,* fr. *bealu, balu* bale + *-ful* — more at BALE] **1 :** marked by a deadly, malign, or pernicious influence or effect **:** MALEFICENT ⟨the ~ arts of sorcerers —J.G.Frazer⟩ ⟨their pale and ghastly features, more ghastly in that ~ and malignant light —T.L. Peacock⟩ ⟨the grating supervision of one particularly ~ sergeant —Byron Bentley⟩ **2 :** foreboding evil **:** OMINOUS ⟨the . . . company, despite the ~ economic outlook, decided to seek national distribution of its products —D.C.Morrill⟩ ⟨a man full of gloom and ~ predictions⟩ — **bale·ful·ly** \-fəlē, -li\ *adv* — **bale·ful·ness** *n* -ES
bale·less \'bā(ə)lləs\ *adj* **:** being without a bale
bal·er \'bālə(r)\ *n* -s [⁴*bale* + *-er*] **:** one that bales (as a machine that bales hay, straw, cotton, and similar products or a person who operates such a machine)
baler bag *or* **baler sack** *n* **:** a large sack of cloth or multiply paper designed to hold a number of smaller filled bags or boxes under little or no compression
bale rope *n* [³*bale*] **:** a heavy unpolished twine esp. for bales
bales *pl of* BALE, *pres 3d sing of* BALE
bale sling *n* [³*bale*] **:** a length of rope with its ends spliced together that is used as a loading sling by being passed under an object (as a bale or barrel) so that its two loops meet on top with one being drawn under the other and placed over the hook of a hoisting block
ba·les·tra \bə'lestrə\ *n* -s [It, lit., crossbow, fr. L *ballista* — more at BALLISTA] **:** a jump forward in fencing followed by a lunge
ba·le·te *also* **ba·li·ti** \bə'lēd·ē\ *n* -s [Tag *baliti*] **:** any of several Philippine figs with aerial roots (as *Ficus indica* and *F. palawanensis*) used for rope making
balewort \'=,=\ *n* -s [¹*bale* + *wort*] **:** OPIUM POPPY
bal·four pine \'bal,fȯr-, -ùr-,-ȯr-\ *n, usu cap B* [after John H. *Balfour* †1884 Scottish botanist] **:** FOXTAIL PINE
balge yellow *pronunc unknown*\ *n* [origin unknown] **:** SUNFLOWER YELLOW
ba·li aga \,bälē'ägə\ *n, pl* **bali aga** *or* **bali agas** *usu cap B&A* **1 :** a people inhabiting the interior of the island of Bali, Indonesia **2 :** a member of the Bali Aga
ba·li·an \'bälēən\ *n, pl* **balian** *or* **balians** [Malay *bĕlian* medium, shaman] **:** a Malaysian medium who employs trances in practicing the art of a medicine man
ba·li·ba·go \,bälē'bä(,)gō\ *n* -s [Tag & Bisayan] *Philippines* **:** MAJAGUA a
bal·i·bun·tal *or* **bal·li·bun·tl** \,balē'bəntᵊl, -lə'-\ *n* -s [*bali-* (fr. *Balinog,* town on Luzon, Philippines) + Tag *buntál* talipot-palm fiber, hat made of talipot-palm fiber] **1 :** a fine lightweight straw of glossy smooth buntal **2 :** a hat made of balibuntal
ba·li·ja \bə'lējə\ *n* -s *usu cap* **:** a member of a numerous caste of traders of Madras and Madhya Pradesh states, India
ba·lim·bing \bə'lim(,)biŋ\ *n* -s [Tag] *Philippines* **:** CARAMBOLA
¹ba·li·nese \¦bälə¦nēz, ¦ba-, -lē-, -nēs\ *n, pl* **balinese** *usu cap* [D *Balinees,* adj. & n., fr. *Bali,* island of Indonesia + connective *-n-* + D *-ees* -ese] **1 a :** a people of chiefly Hindu-Javanese extraction prob. with Papuan and Polynesian admixture inhabiting the island of Bali **b :** a member of such people **2 :** the Malayo-Javanese language of the Balinese people
²balinese \"\ *adj, usu cap* [D *Balinees*] **:** of or relating to the island of Bali or its inhabitants or their language or culture
baling *pres part of* BALE
bal·in·ger \'balənjə(r)\ *n* -s [ME *balynger,* fr. MF *balengier, baleinier* whale ship, fr. *baleine* whale — more at BALEEN] **:** a small British seagoing ship of the 15th to 17th centuries
baling hook *n* [fr. pres. part. of ⁴*bale*] **:** a longshoreman's implement consisting of a metal hook with short shank and wooden handle at right angles to the shank
ba·lin·ta·wak \bə¦lintə¦wäk\ *n* -s [Tag] **:** a native dress of Filipino women consisting of dress and skirt woven of local fibers with a kerchief and apron to match
ba·li·saur \'bälə,sȯ(ə)r\ *n* -s [Hindi *bālū* sand (fr. Skt *vālukā,* prob. fr. *valate* he turns) + *sūar* pig, fr. Skt *sūkara* — more at VOLUBLE, SOW] **:** HOG-NOSED BADGER
ba·li·sier \bə'lēzē,ā\ *n* -s [F] *in the West Indies* **:** WILD PLANTAIN
balista *var of* BALLISTA
ba·lis·tes \bə'li(,)stēz\ *n, cap* [NL, fr. L *balista, ballista;* fr. the way in which the first spine snaps down when pressure is applied on the second spine — more at BALLISTA] **:** the type genus of Balistidae
¹ba·lis·tid \-stəd\ *adj* [NL *Balistidae*] **:** of or relating to the family Balistidae
²balistid \"\ *n* **:** a fish of the family Balistidae
ba·lis·ti·dae \-stə,dē\ *n pl, cap* [NL, fr. *Balistes,* type genus + *-idae*] **:** a family of long-snouted small-eyed marine fishes having a deep compressed body and rough spinose scales, comprising the triggerfishes and sometimes the filefishes, and with a few related forms constituting a suborder of Plectognathi
bal·is·toi·dea \,balə'stȯidēə\ *n pl, cap* [NL, fr. *Balistes* + *-oidea*] **:** a suborder of marine plectognath fishes including the filefishes, triggerfishes, and related chiefly tropical forms
bal·is·trar·ia \,balə'stra(a)rēə\ *n, pl* **balistrari·ae** \-rē,ē\ [NL, fr. LL, fem. of *balistrarius, ballistrarius* of slinging, fr. L *balista, ballista* sling — more at BALLISTA] **:** a narrow often cruciform opening in a wall (as of a tower or fortress) for discharging arrows (as from a crossbow)
ba·li·tao \¦bälə¦taù\ *n* -s [native name in the Philippines] **:** a Philippine peasant dance in mazurka rhythm and semi-European style depicting work movements
baliti *var of* BALETE
¹balk *or* **baulk** \'bȯk *sometimes* -ȯlk\ *n* -s [ME *balke,* fr. OE *balca* ridge; akin to OHG *balko* beam, ON *bjālki,* L *fulcire* to prop, Gk *phalanx* log, line of battle, Skt *bhurij* arm] **1 a :** a ridge of land left unplowed between furrows or formerly between the acres or fields in common lands **b :** a piece missed in plowing (as by carelessness) **2 :** a rough-squared length of timber **:** BEAM, RAFTER, TIE BEAM **3** *dial Eng* **a :** the beam of a balance **b :** the often unfloored loft above the tie beams of a house — usu. used in pl. **4** *obs* **:** OMISSION **5 :** HINDRANCE, DISAPPOINTMENT, CHECK, DEFEAT **6 a :** the space behind the balkline on a billiard table **b :** any of the eight outside divisions of a billiard table made by the four balklines **7 :** headrope connecting fishing nets **8 a :** a failure of a competitor after making his approach to the starting line to follow through with his jump, vault, or dive **b :** an illegal motion by the pitcher in baseball toward the plate or toward a base when there are men on base esp. without delivering the ball, the baserunners automatically advancing a base **c** *in racket games* **:** interference with an opponent's stroke **9 :** one of the stringers placed from boat to boat on which the flooring is placed in a floating bridge **10 :** an abrupt thinning out of a coal seam
²balk *or* **baulk** \"\ *vb* -ED/-ING/-S [ME *balken* to make balks in plowing, to pass over, fr. *balke,* n.] *vt* **1** *archaic* **:** to pass over **:** let pass by **:** OVERLOOK, IGNORE, AVOID ⟨~ an invitation⟩ ⟨~ a touchy topic of conversation⟩ ⟨~ dessert at a banquet⟩ ⟨~ no expense⟩ ⟨~ an opportunity⟩ ⟨~ a hand offered in friendship⟩ **2 :** to defeat, check, or stop by or as if by an obstacle, block, or barrier **:** block from things wished, contemplated, or planned causing ensuing disappointment and vexation **:** block or halt occurrence, indication, performance, or execution of ⟨the French ambassadors had neither been ~*ed* nor been frightened —Francis Hackett⟩ ⟨snarled in a knot of words which ~*s* the understanding —Edmund Wilson⟩ **3** *cribbage* **:** to give (the dealer's crib) cards that are unlikely to make fifteens or sequences ~ *vi* **1 a :** to stop short and refuse to go ⟨they ~*ed* like seasoned steers at a loading-chute gate —Lewis Nordyke⟩ **:** cease or decline progress, action, or development suddenly, arbitrarily, or unexpectedly ⟨many of the more interesting bacteria distinctly prefer to grow at this higher temperature and . . . are apt to ~ if not provided with their favorite heat —Justina Hill⟩ **b :** to refuse abruptly or decisively (as for reasons of taste, propriety, or temperament) **:** RECOIL — used with *at* ⟨his aggressive nature ~*ed* at the association —*Amer. Guide Series: Oregon*⟩ ⟨I ~*ed* at snails but Bill got them down without a quiver —W.A. White⟩ **c :** to commit a balk in sports **2 :** to engage in foolish or trivial argument **:** QUIBBLE **syn** see DEMUR, FRUSTRATE
bal·kan \'bȯlkən *sometimes* 'bal-\ *also* **bal·kan·ic** \(')=¦kanik\ *adj, usu cap* [fr. the *Balkan* peninsula in southeastern Europe] **:** of or relating to the Balkan peninsula, the Balkan mountain range, or the people of Balkan states
balkan frame *n, usu cap B* [fr. the *Balkan* countries, where it was first used] **:** a frame employed in the treatment of fractured bones of the leg or arm that provides overhead weights and pulleys for suspension, traction, and continuous extension of the splinted fractured limb
balkan grippe *n, usu cap B* **:** Q FEVER
bal·kan·ism \-,nizəm\ *n* -s *usu cap* **1 :** the quality or state of being balkanized ⟨a country fated to endure a century of ~⟩ **2 :** BALKANIZATION
bal·kan·ite \-,nīt\ *n* -s *cap* **:** a native or inhabitant of the Balkan states
bal·kan·i·za·tion \,==nə'zāshən, -,nī'z-\ *n* -s *often cap* **:** the process of balkanizing **:** the state of being balkanized ⟨regretted the ~ of South Africa and were anxious for some form of federation —Leo Marquard⟩ ⟨perpetuate the ~ of the Christian Commonwealth by validating the concept of separate sovereignties —E.A.Walsh⟩
bal·kan·ize \'==,nīz\ *vt* -ED/-ING/-S *often cap* [*Balkan* peninsula + E *-ize;* fr. the way in which this territory has been broken up into many small states] **:** to break up (as a region) into smaller ineffectual and frequently conflicting units ⟨opposed the partition of Germany, and holds that the economic consequences of *Balkanizing* the country would be serious —*Times Lit. Supp.*⟩
balkan pine *n, usu cap B* **:** an ornamental pine (*Pinus peuce*) of the Balkan mountains of dense pyramidal habit and having needles in fascicles of five
bal·kar \'bäl,kär\ *n* -s *cap* [Russ, of Turkic origin; akin to Kara-Kalpak *balqar,* Balkar *bolqar,* OTurk *bulgar* mixed breed — more at BULGAR] **:** one of a mixed Mongoloid people of the Caucasus in the Kabardino-Balkarian Republic, U.S.S.R.
balk·i·ly \'bȯkəlē, -li *sometimes* 'bȯlk-\ *adv* [*balky* + *-ly*] **:** in a balky manner ⟨the horse crossed the river ~ and only with severe coercion from the whip⟩
balk·i·ness \-kēnəs, -ki-\ *n* -ES **:** the quality or state of being balky
balk·ing·ly *adv* **:** in a balking manner
balkline \'=,=\ *n* **1 :** a line across a billiard table near one end behind which the cue balls are placed in lagging for lead and making opening shots (as in English billiards, pool, or bagatelle) **2 a :** one of four lines drawn parallel to and 14 or 18 inches from the cushions of a billiard table dividing it into nine compartments **b :** a carom billiards game that sets restrictions (as in scoring) determined by these lines; *specif* **:** the billiard game in which it is ruled that if the two object balls rest in one of the eight compartments formed by the cushions and these lines at least one of the balls must be driven out at the second shot or sometimes at each shot
balks *pl of* BALK, *pres 3d sing of* BALK
balky \'bȯkē, -i *sometimes* 'bȯlk-\ *adj* -ER/-EST [¹*balk* + *-y*] **:** balking or likely to balk **:** refusing or apt to refuse to proceed in an indicated or expected direction or to act according to direction or suggestion ⟨will appeal directly to the voters for support if Congress gets ~ —*Look*⟩ ⟨order ~ witnesses to appear⟩ ⟨a ~ horse⟩ ⟨acting just like a ~ mule⟩ **syn** see CONTRARY
¹ball \'bȯl\ *n* -s [ME *bal,* fr. ON *bǫllr;* akin to OE *bealluc* testis, OHG *balla* ball, OE *bula* bull — more at BULL] **1 :** a round or roundish body or mass: as **a :** a spherical or ovoid body of any kind for throwing, hitting, or kicking in games or sports ⟨the baseball player knocked the ~ down the third-base line⟩ ⟨kick the ~ over the goalposts⟩ **b :** a celestial body **:** EARTH, GLOBE **c :** any of various spherical, rounded, or conical missiles or projectiles (as for a catapult, cannon, or firearm); *also* **:** projectiles used in firearms **:** BULLETS ⟨powder and ~⟩ **d :** a roundish protuberant part of the body: as (1) **:** the rounded eminence by which the base of the thumb is continuous with the palm of the hand (2) **:** the rounded broad part of the sole of the human foot between toes and arch and on which the main weight of the body first rests in normal walking; *also* **:** the corresponding part of a shoe or of a last (3) **:** the padded rounded underside of a human finger or toe near the tip **e :** EYEBALL **f :** a ball-shaped dabber made usu. of pelt stuffed with wool and fastened to a handle and formerly used by printers for inking a form **g :** a mandrel upon which steel piping is welded by concave rolls **h :** BALL BEARING **i :** TESTIS — usu. considered vulgar **j :** a spherical architectural ornament often hollow and of considerable size crowning a cupola or dome **k :** a small globose fruit or seed pod **:** SEED BALL **l :** the compact mass of earth and roots often tightly bound (as with burlap) and moved with a transplanted tree, shrub, or herbaceous plant **m :** a solidified mass of iron in the manufacture of wrought iron intimately mixed with siliceous slag and being the result of puddling or of pouring molten refined iron into slag **n :** a large pill (as one used in veterinary medicine) **:** BOLUS **o** (1) **:** a ball-shaped mass (as of candy, pastry, vegetable, minced fish, or meat) (2) **:** a small roundish mass ranging in consistency from soft to hard and formed when sugar is boiled to a certain temperature and then quickly chilled **2 :** a game in which a ball is thrown, kicked, or struck; *esp* **:** BASEBALL ⟨play ~ for two hours⟩ **3 a :** the delivery of the ball (as in baseball) ⟨a fast ~⟩ ⟨a curve ~⟩ **b :** a pitched baseball not struck at by the batter that fails to pass through the strike zone ⟨a count of three ~*s* and two strikes⟩ **c** *cricket* **:** a fair delivery of the ball by bowling — opposed to *no ball;* compare WIDE **4** *slang* **:** FELLOW, CHARACTER ⟨this narrator . . . is an odd ~ indeed —Hollis Alpert⟩ **5 balls** *pl* [fr. pl. of *ball* (testis)] **:** NONSENSE — often used interjectionally to express disapproval or annoyance; often considered vulgar **6 :** main authority over or direction of an enterprise or activity **:** RESPONSIBILITY ⟨to take the ~ away from the incompetent director and give it to a new man⟩ — **get the ball rolling** *or* **start the ball rolling :** to initiate an activity usu. to be engaged in by two or more people hesitant to begin ⟨the teacher *started the ball rolling* by posing a large and general question on which all were sure to have an opinion⟩ — **keep the ball rolling :** to give continued impetus or momentum to an activity already in progress ⟨when the conversation began to lag, the host always *kept the ball rolling* by introducing a new topic of common interest without seeming to have done it purposely⟩ — **on the ball** *adv (or adj)* **1** *slang* **:** knowledgeable and competent **:** purposively active **:** ALERT ⟨she was no chicken perhaps, but she was *on the ball* —Theodora Keogh⟩ ⟨when the men know some of the lesson, the instructor really

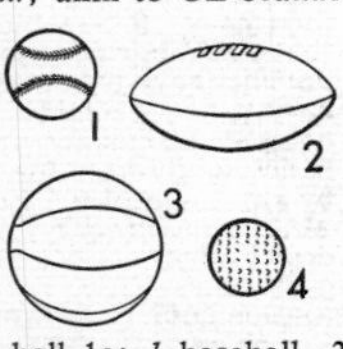

ball 1a: *1* baseball, *2* football, *3* basketball, *4* golf ball

has to stay *on the ball* —*Infantry Jour.*⟩ **2** *slang* **:** of ability **:** of competence ⟨to have a lot *on the ball*⟩ ⟨the average man of 40 had appreciably more *on the ball* than the person of 30 —J.E.Gibson⟩

²**ball** \"\ *vb* -ED/-ING/-S *vt* **1 :** to form into a ball: as **a :** to squeeze into a more or less compact mass ⟨~*ing* each sheet of paper into a wad before throwing it away⟩ — often used with *up* **b :** to wind up (as string) upon itself **c :** to form (as molten iron) into balls in the manufacture of wrought iron **d :** to cluster densely about (the queen bee) — used of bees **2 :** to clog (the hoof of an animal) with balls ⟨the pony's hoofs got badly ~*ed* in the mud⟩ **3 :** to compact a ball of earth about (a tree, shrub, or herbaceous plant or its roots) for storing or transporting **4 :** to give a medicinal ball to (as a horse) ~ *vi* **:** to form, gather, collect, or pack into a ball or balls ⟨the stallion's right forefoot ~*ed* with snow and sand —W.V.T.Clark⟩ ⟨the boiled sugar ~*ed* when dropped into cold water⟩ ⟨smaller shotgun pellets liable to ~ in the barrel⟩ — often used with *up* ⟨danger of the stuff ~*ing* up, i. e. the fibers clot up into small inseparable balls of fiber —F.H.Norris⟩ — **ball the jack** *slang* **:** go fast **:** HURRY ⟨a hot rodder *balling the jack* up highway 102⟩

³**ball** \"\ *n* -S [F *bal*, fr. OF, fr. *baller* to dance, fr. LL *ballare*, fr. Gk *ballizein;* akin to Skt *balbaliti* he whirls] **1 :** a large formal gathering for social dancing **2 :** a good time **:** PICNIC ⟨a fairly monstrous cowboy actor in from the Coast for a ~ —Gilbert Millstein⟩ ⟨it's a ~ for a while, but it's no life to lead —David Hulburd⟩

bal·la·bi·le \bä'läbə,lā\ *n* -S [It, fr. *ballare* to dance (fr. LL) + *-abile* -able — more at BALL] **:** a dance in classic ballet performed by the corps de ballet by itself or with the principal dancers

¹**bal·lad** \'baləd\ *n* -S [ME *balade*, fr. MF, fr. OProv *balada* dancing song, dance, fr. *balar* to dance, fr. LL *ballare* — more at BALL] **1 :** a song sung while dancing or to accompany a dance **2 :** a part-song often in stanzas with a refrain **:** a light madrigal **3 a :** a narrative composition in verse of strongly marked rhythm suited to simple singing or dancing; *specif* **:** a composition handed down by oral transmission from medieval and early modern times and having narrative combined with lyrical and sometimes dramatic elements — see BALLAD METER, BALLAD STANZA **b :** an art song imitating such a composition **c :** BROADSIDE BALLAD **4 :** BALLADE **5 :** a popular song; *esp* **:** a dance song of romantic or sentimental character and slow tempo

²**ballad** \"\ *vt* -ED/-ING/-S [ME *baladen*, fr. *balade*, n.] *obs* **:** to tell or sing of in ballads

bal·lade \bə'läd, ba-, -ād,-ad; bå'läd, bä'läd\ *n* -S [ME *balade*] **1 :** a medieval French verse form or the English verse form derived from it having usu. three stanzas of 7, 8, or 10 lines, maintaining the same three or four rhymes throughout, and concluding with an envoi of half the stanzaic length usu. in the form of an apostrophe addressed to an individual, the last line of each stanza and of the envoi being an identical refrain **2 a :** an elaborate musical setting of a ballad with or without text **b :** a musical composition usu. for piano suggesting the theme or spirit of an epic ballad

bal·lad·eer *also* **bal·lad·ier** \,balə'di(ə)r, -iə\ *n* -S [¹*ballad* + *-eer, -ier*] **:** a singer of ballads ⟨guitar-strumming ~*s*⟩

ballade royal \=,=ˈrȯiəl; bälädrwäyäl\ *n, pl* **ballade royals** \-əlz,-äl\ [ME *balade royal*, fr. MF, royal ballade] **:** a ballade having its stanzas usu. in rhyme royal

ballad horn *n* **:** a circular althorn

bal·lad·ic \bə'ladik, (')ba¦l-\ *adj* **:** of or relating to a ballad

bal·lad·ist \-,dəst\ *n* -S **:** one who writes or sings ballads

ballad meter *n* **:** the meter common in English ballads consisting chiefly of iambic lines of 7 accents each arranged in rhymed pairs and usu. printed as the 4-line ballad stanza

balladmonger \'==,==\ *n* **1 :** a seller or composer of ballads **2 :** a poor or inferior poet

balladmongering \'==,=(=)=\ *n* **1 :** the selling or composing of ballads **2 :** the composing of popular verse having little or no artistic value

ballad opera *n* **:** a theatrical entertainment consisting of folk melodies and popular airs with new texts interspersed with spoken dialogue

bal·lad·ry \'balədrē, -ri\ *n* -ES **1 :** the art or practice of ballad singing **2 :** BALLADS ⟨the ~ of Scotland⟩

ballad stanza *n* **:** a verse stanza common in English ballads that consists of 2 lines in ballad meter usu. printed as a 4-line stanza with lines 1 and 3 of 4 accents each unrhymed and with lines 2 and 4 of 3 accents each rhymed

bal·la·hoo *or* **bal·la·hou** \¦balə¦hü\ *n* -S [Sp *balahú*] **1 :** a schooner of Bermuda and the West Indies having its foremast raking forward and mainmast aft **2 :** a lubberly untrim ship

ball alley *n* [¹*ball*] **:** ¹ALLEY 2a

bal·lam \bə'läm\ *n* -S [Malayalam *vaḷḷam*] **:** a canoe of the Malabar coast

bal·lan *or* **ballan wrasse** *also* **bal·len wrasse** \'balən-\ *n* -S [origin unknown] **:** a European wrasse (*Labrus bergylta*)

ball and chain *n, pl* **balls and chains** [so called fr. the ball and chain stereotypically attached to prisoners' legs to prevent escape] **1 :** something that severely restricts one's activity usu. oppressively ⟨marriage, intended to enslave woman, was also a *ball and chain* for man —H.M.Parshley⟩ ⟨his aristocratic birth proved a *ball and chain* throughout his life⟩ **2** *slang* **:** WIFE ⟨this is a book for females, but if any male can get the *ball and chain* to read it, maybe the skillets won't fly so fast —Burton Rascoe⟩

ball-and-claw foot *n* **:** CLAW-AND-BALL FOOT

ball-and-socket joint *n* **:** a joint in which a ball moves within a socket so as to admit of rotary motion in every direction within certain limits (as the hip joint) — called also *ball joint*

ball-and-socket joint (with part of socket cut away)

bal·lant \'balənt\ *n* -S [by alter.] *chiefly Scot* **:** BALLAD

bal·las \'baləs\ *n* -ES [prob. fr. Pg *balas*, pl. of *bala*, lit., ball bullet, fr. It *palla*, of Gmc origin; akin to OHG *balla* ball — more at BALL] **:** a nearly spherical aggregate of diamond grains having a radial or granular structure and used as an industrial diamond because of a toughness that is due to the lack of through-going cleavage planes

¹**bal·last** \'baləst\ *n* -S [prob. fr. LG, of Scand origin; akin to Dan & Sw *barlast*, lit., mere load, fr. *bar* bare (fr. ODan & OSw) + *last* load, fr. MLG; akin to ON *berr* bare and to OHG *hlast* load — more at BARE, LAST] **1 :** a relatively heavy substance used to maintain a ship at its proper draft or trim or to improve its stability (as rock stowed in holds or water in tanks) **2 :** something that gives stability or weight esp. in character, conduct, ideas, or morals ⟨it is profitable for cultures to carry a considerable degree of ~ in the shape of consistency and continuity —A.L.Kroeber⟩ **3 :** something heavy (as sand or water) put into the car of a balloon to be thrown out if necessary to reduce the load **4 a :** gravel or broken stone laid in a roadbed esp. of a railroad to provide a firm surface for the track, to hold the track in line, and to facilitate drainage **b :** the larger solids (as broken stone or gravel) used in making concrete — compare ³AGGREGATE 3b **5 :** a resistance used to stabilize the current in a circuit (as of an arc lamp, a mercury-vapor lamp, or a fluorescent lamp) **6 :** ROUGHAGE — **in ballast** *of a ship* **:** with only ballast as a load

²**ballast** \"\ *vt* -ED/-ING/-S **1 :** to steady or equip with ballast ⟨~ a canoe with large rocks⟩ **2** *archaic* **:** weight down **:** BURDEN, LOAD **3 a :** to steady or stabilize in mind, morals, or conduct ⟨a little security to ~ your life⟩ **b :** to act as a counterpoise to ⟨some common sense to ~ the general flightiness of the group⟩ **4 :** to fill in (as a railroad bed) with ballast **syn** see STABILIZE

bal·last·age \-ij\ *n* -S [¹*ballast* + *-age*] **:** a toll paid for the privilege of taking up ballast in a port or harbor

ballast car *n* **:** a freight car (as for carrying ballast) that may be unloaded from the side or bottom

ballast engine *n* **:** a steam engine used in excavating and for digging and raising stones and gravel for ballast

ballast fin *n* **:** a fin-shaped metal extension of the keel of a yacht that acts as ballast **:** FIN KEEL

ballasting *n* -S [¹*ballast* + *-ing*] **:** material used for ballast

ballast line *n* **:** the water line of a ship in ballast

ballast master *n* **:** a harbor official who sees that ships take on and discharge ballast according to regulations

ballast port *n* **:** a large port in the side of a ship for taking in or discharging ballast

ballast pump *n* **:** a pump for discharging water ballast

ballast tank *n* **:** a tank in the hold of a ship that can be pumped full of or free from water ballast

bal·lat \'balət\ *archaic var of* BALLAD

bal·la·ta \bə'läd·ə\ *n, pl* **bal·la·te** \-ä,tā\ [It, fr. OIt, fr. OProv *balada* — more at BALLAD] **:** a medieval Italian song accompanied by or alternated with dancing and having stanzas and refrain alternating

ball-bank indicator *n* **:** a bank indicator consisting of a slightly curved tube in which a ball remains centered while the airplane is flying straight and level or while the airplane is making a properly banked turn

ball bat *n* **:** a baseball bat

ball bearing *n* **1 a :** a bearing in which the journal turns upon loose hardened steel balls that roll easily in a race and thus convert sliding friction into rolling friction **b :** any of the balls in such a bearing **2 :** a bearing in which the disk of a watt-hour meter is mounted on a vertical shaft that rotates with minimized friction because of rolling action on a single steel ball between cupped jewels

ball boy *n* [¹*ball*] **:** a tennis court attendant who retrieves balls for the players

ball breaker *n* **:** SKULL CRACKER

ball cactus *n* **:** a low tuberculated cactus (*Neobessya missouriensis*) having short spines and predominantly yellow flowers and resembling a ball

ballcarrier \'=,===\ *n* **:** the football player carrying the ball in an offensive play

ball cartridge *n* **:** a general-purpose cartridge having a ball, a primer, and a full charge of powder

ball change *n* **:** a quick change of weight from the ball of one foot to the other in ballroom and tap dancing

ball-check valve *n* **:** a ball valve in which the ball is pushed against or away from its seat by fluid pressure opposed to the action of a spring

ball clay *n* **:** a sometimes refractory plastic clay that has a tendency to ball, that fires to a light buff color, and that is used as a constituent of many ceramic wares **:** PIPE CLAY

ball clover *n* **:** any of certain clovers with globular flower heads (as cluster clover)

ball club *n* **1 :** a club or professional organization whose main purpose is the support and building up of a baseball team **2 :** a ball team; *esp* **:** a baseball team

ball cock *n* **:** a float valve with a spherical float — called also *ball valve*

ball dahlia *n* **:** any of a class of dahlias having globular flower heads usu. more than three inches in diameter — compare POMPON 2c

balldress \'=,=\ *n* [³*ball* + *dress*] **1** *Brit* **:** a suit or dress worn on official or formal occasions **2** *Brit* **:** formal attire

balled *past of* BALL

ballen wrasse *var of* BALLAN

ball·er \'bȯlə(r)\ *n* -S **1 :** one that makes something into balls: as **a :** a warper who balls the warp **b :** *or* **baller-out** \'==,=\ **:** BATTER 2a (1) **2 :** a laundry worker who irons parts of garments that cannot be ironed on a flat press or with a hand iron by moving them back and forth over heated metal forms — called also *puffer*

bal·le·ri·na \,balə'rēnə\ *n* -S [It, fr. *ballare* to dance, fr. LL — more at BALL] **1 a :** a female ballet dancer **:** DANSEUSE **b :** PRIMA BALLERINA **2 :** a lightweight flexible slipper with a very low heel for street and evening wear by women — compare BALLET SLIPPER

¹**bal·let** \'balət\ *n* -S [alter. of ¹*ballad*] **1** *dial* **:** BALLAD 3 **2** *also* **bal·lett** \"\ **:** BALLAD 2

²**bal·let** \'ba,lā, ba'lā *sometimes* bə'lā *or* 'ba,lā *or* 'balē *or* 'bali\ *n* -S [F, fr. It *balletto*, dim. of *ballo* dance, fr. *ballare* to dance, fr. LL — more at BALL] **1 :** artistic dancing in which conventionalized poses and steps are combined with light and flowing figures and movements (as leaps and turns) ⟨a lesson in ~ usu. includes exercises in balancing⟩ **2 a :** a theatrical art form by which ballet dancing together with music, scenery, costume, and sometimes pantomime or speech conveys a story, theme, or atmosphere to the audience **b :** a theatrical performance of the ballet art form ⟨attend the ~⟩ **c :** a musical score for such a performance **d :** the script for a ballet performance ⟨the microfilm copy of a ~⟩ **e :** a performance resembling a ballet (as by a troupe of ice skaters or trapeze artists) **3 :** a company of persons who perform ballets ⟨the New York City *Ballet*⟩ **4 :** BALLET SLIPPER

ballet blanc \¦=(,)=ˈblän, =¦=ˈ=\ *n, pl* **ballets blancs** \-āz'blän, -ēz',-iz'-; -ā'blän(z), -ē'-,-i'-\ [F, lit., white ballet] **:** a ballet in which the ballerinas wear white skirts

ballet bouffe \-'büf\ *n, pl* **ballets bouffes** \-āz'büf, -ēz'-,-iz'-; -ā'büf(s), -ē'-,-i'-\ [F] **:** a comic ballet usu. with stock characters

bal·let d'ac·tion \bålädåksyōn\ *n, pl* **ballets d'action** \"\ [F] **:** a ballet with a plot

ballet girl *pronunc at* ²BALLET +,-\ *n* **:** a female ballet dancer

bal·let·ic \(')ba¦led·ik\ *adj* [²*ballet* + *-ic*] **:** of, typical of, relating to, resembling, or suitable for ballet — **bal·let·i·cal·ly** \-d·ək(ə)lē\ *adv*

ballet leg *n* **:** a synchronized group-swimming stunt in which from a starting back floating position with legs extended one knee is drawn to the chest, the leg is then extended vertically, the knee then bent, and the leg then returned to the starting position

ballet master *n* [²*ballet*] **:** a man who directs, trains, and sometimes acts as choreographer for a ballet company

ballet mistress *n* [²*ballet*] **:** a woman who directs, trains, and sometimes acts as choreographer for a ballet company

bal·let·o·mane \ba'led·ə,mān, bə-\ *n* -S [*ballet* + *-o-* + *-mane* (fr. *mania*)] **:** one who takes extraordinary delight in ballets

bal·leto·mania \=¦==+\ *n* [²*ballet* + *-o-* + *mania*] **:** extraordinary enthusiasm for ballets

ballet slipper *or* **ballet shoe** *n* [²*ballet*] **1 :** a slipper without a heel made usu. of kid or fabric, often reinforced in the toe, and worn by ballet dancers **2 :** a woman's shoe for street or evening wear resembling a ballet slipper

ball fern *n* **:** a feathery fern (*Davallia bullata*) of tropical Asia and Malaya cultivated chiefly in fern balls that its creeping rhizomes help to form

ball-flower \'=,=\ *n* **:** an ornament characteristic of 13th century English Gothic architecture consisting of a ball placed in the hollow of a circular flower and usu. inserted in a hollow molding

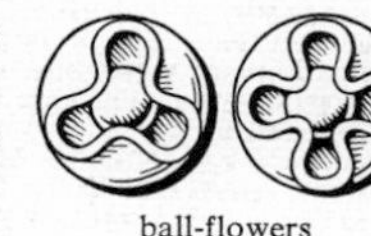
ball-flowers

ball foot *n* **:** a large turned foot often found on 17th-century case furniture — see BUN FOOT, MELON FOOT, TURNIP FOOT; FOOT illustration

ball fringe *n* **:** a decorative fringe (as for upholstery, curtains, or clothing) made with covered balls or yarn balls hanging at even intervals along one edge

ball game *n* **:** a game played with a ball; *esp* **:** a baseball game

ball governor *n* [¹*ball*] **:** a governor that operates by the centrifugal force of revolving balls

ball handler *n* **:** one who controls the ball in a ball game (as basketball or football) — **ball handling** *n*

ball hawk *n* **1 :** one skillful in taking the ball away from opponents (as in basketball or football) **2 :** a fielder in baseball skilled in catching fly balls — **ball hawking** *n*

ballhooter \'=,==\ *n* **:** a logger who rolls logs down slopes too steep for teams — called also *brutter*

ballibuntl *var of* BALIBUNTAL

ballies *pl of* BALLY

¹**bal·ling** \'bȯliŋ, 'bäl-, -lēŋ\ *adj, usu cap* [*Balling* (*scale*)] **1 :** according to a Balling scale ⟨a sugar solution of 19° *Balling*⟩ **2 :** calibrated in accordance with a Balling scale ⟨a *Balling* hydrometer⟩

²**balling** \"\ *n* -S *usu cap* **:** concentration in percent by weight of a soluble solid (as sugar) according to a Balling scale ⟨the *Balling* of a syrup⟩

ball·ing furnace \'bȯl-\ *n* **:** PUDDLING FURNACE

ball·ing iron *or* **balling gun** \"\ *n* **:** a long metal instrument with a cup-shaped depression at one end for placing solid medicine in the form of a ball or cylinder in the posterior part of the mouth of a horse or ox so that it will have to be swallowed whole

bal·ling scale \'bȯl-,'bäl-\ *n, usu cap B* [after Karl J. N. *Balling* †1868 Ger. chemist] **:** a hydrometer scale that registers the percentage by weight of soluble solids in a solution (as sugar in grape juice or wine), one degree on the scale being equal to one percent

bal·lism \'ba,lizəm\ *or* **bal·lis·mus** \ba'lizməs\ *n, pl* **ballisms** *or* **ballismuses** [NL *ballismus*, fr. Gk *ballismos* dance, act of jumping about, fr. *ballizein* to dance, jump about, fr. *ballein* to throw] **:** the abnormal swinging jerking movements sometimes seen in chorea

bal·lis·ta \bə'listə *also* ba-\ *also* **ba·lis·ta** \"\ *n, pl* **ballis·tae** \-,tē, -,tī\ *also* **ballistas** \-,təz\ *or* **balis·tae** \-,tē, -,tī\ *or* **bali·stas** \-,təz\ [L, fr. (assumed) Gk *ballistas* or *ballistēs*, fr. *ballein* to throw — more at DEVIL] **:** an ancient military engine often in the form of a crossbow for hurling large missiles

bal·lis·ter \'baləstə(r)\ *n* -S [by alter.] **:** BALUSTER

bal·lis·tic \bə'listik, -ēk *also* ba-\ *adj* [L *ballista* + E *-ic*] **1 :** of or belonging to the hurling of missiles ⟨the ~ power of a crossbow⟩ **2 :** of or relating to ballistics or to a body in motion when the characteristics of such motion are determined by the laws of ballistics **3 :** belonging to or actuated by a sudden impulse (as that due to an electric discharge) — **bal·lis·ti·cal·ly** \-tək(ə)lē, -tēk-, -li\ *adv*

ballistic cap *n* **:** a hollow metal cap placed over an armor-piercing cap to continue the ogival curve of the head of the projectile and reduce the resistance to the air

ballistic coefficient *n* **:** a constant in ballistics that represents the efficiency of a projectile in overcoming air resistance

ballistic galvanometer *n* **:** a moving-coil galvanometer that indicates the presence of an electric charge by the single impulse imparted to the coil by a sudden brief current, the quantity of electricity that passes being proportionate to the first deflection of the coil

bal·lis·ti·cian \,balə'stishən\ *n* -S [fr. *ballistics*, after such pairs as E *statistics: statistician*] **:** an authority on or one versed in ballistics; *esp* **:** a member of a police force who studies the evidence and determines the facts relating to the use of firearms in criminal cases

ballistic missile *n* **:** a guided missile designed to fly roughly in the high-arch trajectory of a true ballistic object, self-powered for most of its ascent and guided in the ascending part of its flight but becoming a free-falling object in descent

ballistic pendulum *n* **:** a pendulum with a bifilarly suspended bob that retains objects striking it and registers the amplitude of the swing caused by the impact, the velocity of the object (as a rifle bullet) penetrating the bob being computed by application of the principles of conservation of momentum and energy — compare GUN PENDULUM

bal·lis·tics \bə'listiks, -ēks *also* ba-\ *n pl* **1 a** *usu sing in constr* **:** the science of the motion of powder-propelled projectiles in flight — compare EXTERIOR BALLISTICS, INTERIOR BALLISTICS **b** *sometimes sing in constr* **:** the characteristics of flight of a projectile **c** *sometimes sing in constr* **:** the firing characteristics of a firearm or cartridge **2** *usu sing in constr* **:** the cardiac movements involved in the forcing of blood into the arteries and the bodily recoil movements that maintain adjustment within the body

bal·lis·tite \'balə,stīt\ *n* -S [fr. *Ballistite*, a trademark] **:** a smokeless powder consisting essentially of soluble cellulose nitrates and nitroglycerin approximately in equal parts

bal·lis·to·cardiogram \bə¦li(,)stō, ba-+\ *n* -S [*ballistic* + *-o-* + *cardiogram*] **:** the record made by a ballistocardiograph

bal·lis·to·cardiograph \"+\ *n* -S [*ballistic* + *-o-* + *cardiograph*] **:** a device for measuring the amount of blood passing through the heart in a specified time by recording the recoil movements of the body that result from contraction of heart muscle in ejecting blood from the ventricles — **bal·lis·to·cardiographic** \"+\ *adj* — **bal·lis·to·cardiography** \"+\ *n*

bal·lis·to·spore \bə'listə,spō(ə)r\ *n* -S [L *ballista* + E *-o-* + *-spore* — more at BALLISTA] **:** one of the spores borne on sterigmata of certain fungi and forcibly discharged at maturity

bal·li·um \'balēəm\ *n* -S [ML, fr. ME *baile* — more at BAIL (outer wall)] **:** BAILEY

ball·iz·ing \'bȯ,līziŋ\ *n* -S [fr. gerund of *ballize*, fr. ¹*ball* + *-ize*] **:** the process of sizing and surface-finishing a hole by pressing a hardened steel ball through it

ball joint *n* **:** BALL-AND-SOCKET JOINT

ball jointing *n* **:** concentric joints in homogeneous rock

ball lightning *n* **:** an extremely rare form of lightning consisting of highly luminous balls that move with moderate speed and usu. disappear without an explosion

ball mill *n* **:** a pulverizing machine consisting of a hollow drum that contains material to be pulverized along with pebbles or heavy steel balls and sometimes also water or some other liquid and that is revolved or agitated so that the pebbles or balls crush the material as they roll about

ball-mill *vt* **:** to pulverize in a ball mill

ball moss *n* **:** an epiphytic plant (*Tillandsia recurvata*) of the southern U. S. that often grows in compact masses

ball mustard *n* **:** a yellow-flowered European plant (*Neslia paniculata*) of the family Cruciferae having globose seed pods and being adventive in eastern No. America

ball nettle *n* **:** HORSE NETTLE

ball nut *n* **:** a nut having ball bearings that run (as in a ball race) between its threads and those of the screw it engages

bal·lock \'bälik, -ēk,-ək\ *n* -S [ME *ballok*, fr. OE *bealluc* — more at BALL] **:** TESTIS — usu. used in pl. and considered vulgar

ball of fire : a person of unusual energy, vitality, or drive esp. manifest in speed of accomplishment ⟨no mental *ball of fire*, but a few things quickly become clear to her —*Time*⟩

bal·lo·gan \'bäl(ə)gən\ *n* -S [ScGael *bolgan*, dim. of *bolg* bag, swelling, pimple; akin to OE belg bag, skin — more at BELLY] **:** NIPPLEWORT

bal·lon *also* **ba·lon** \ba'lōn\ *n* -S [F *ballon*, lit., balloon] **:** the lightness of movement that allows a ballet dancer to appear to remain in the air unusually long during a jump **:** BUOYANCY

bal·lon d'es·sai \bålōndāsā\ *n, pl* **ballons d'essai** \"\ [F] **:** TRIAL BALLOON

bal·lo·net *or* **bal·lon·net** \¦balə¦nā\ *n* -S [F *ballonnet*, dim. of *ballon*] **:** a gas-tight compartment of variable volume within the interior of a balloon or airship used for controlling its ascent or descent and for maintaining pressure on the outer envelope so as to prevent deformation and kept inflated under the control of valves by a blower or by the action of wind caught in an air scoop

bal·lon·né \¦balə¦nā\ *n* -S [F, fr. *ballon*] **:** a wide circular jump in ballet with a battement

¹**bal·loon** \bə'lün\ *n* -S [It dial. *ballone* (It *pallone*), aug. of It dial. *balla*, of Gmc origin; akin to OHG *balla* ball — more at BALL] **1 a** (1) **:** a large inflated leather ball used in a now obsolete sport that involved striking and kicking the ball back and forth (2) **:** the game formerly played with such a ball **b** (1) **:** a bag of silk or other tough light material shaped usu. like a sphere, made nonporous, and filled with heated air or a gas lighter than air **:** an aerostat without a propelling system — see FREE BALLOON, KITE BALLOON, PILOT BALLOON, SOUNDING BALLOON (2) **:** a small-necked inflatable bag of thin usu. gaily colored rubber used as a toy ⟨held a bright red ~⟩ **2 :** something resembling a balloon in contour, buoyancy, inflation, or insubstantiality: as **a** *obs* **:** a fireworks shell **b :** ¹BALL 1i **c :** a spherical glass vessel usu. with a short neck (as a receiver) or with a stopcock

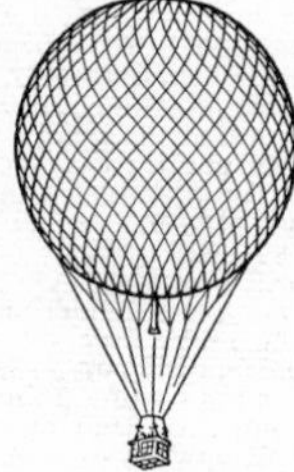
balloon 1b (1)

for use in weighing gases **d :** an area (as of a cartoon) in which presumed spoken words are printed or thoughts represented typically having a rounded outline and being connected with the speaker's or thinker's mouth by a single line **e :** BALLOON TIRE **f** (1) **:** the ball-shaped mass of yarn strands produced in the mechanical spinning, twisting, or winding of thread as the strands pass between a guide and the revolving spool on which they are wound (2) **:** a revolving cylindrical reel used in woolen warp drying **g** *or* **balloon glass :** SNIFTER **3 a :** outward appearance **:** SHOW, DISPLAY ⟨punctured their ~ of confidence —Speed Lamkin⟩ **b :** a poorly substantiated or shallow attitude, belief, or assumption ⟨dogmatists who take delight in shooting ~*s* and asking a man for proofs —Van Wyck Brooks⟩

²**balloon** \"\ *vb* -ED/-ING/-S *vt* **1 :** to cause to assume a smooth rounded form by or as if by inflation **:** DISTEND ⟨a sudden breeze ~*ing* the spinnaker⟩ ⟨he ~*ed* his cheeks in imitation of a fat lady⟩ **2 :** to increase or augment usu. beyond what is average, normal, or expected ⟨a lusty increase in European consumption helped ~ prices —*Wall Street Jour.*⟩ ~ *vi* **1 a :** to ascend or travel in a balloon ⟨in 1935 he had ~*ed* to a world's altitude record —*Time*⟩ **b :** to rise abruptly and become fully airborne in an airplane after the initial landing impact **c** *of a young spider* **:** to travel through the air supported by a strand of silk that catches the wind **2 a :** to swell out into a smoothly rounded surface **:** belly out ⟨the curtains ~*ing* in the morning breeze⟩ **b :** to issue or burst forth in or as if in rounded distended form ⟨the fat mushroom of smoke that ~*ed* out of the mouth of the English chase guns —Frank Yerby⟩ ⟨magniloquent phrases ~ from his lips —Neville Cardus⟩ **3 :** to increase rapidly ⟨clerical costs ~*ed* . . . in every department of business —*Newsweek*⟩ **:** grow suddenly and beyond average proportion or normal expectation ⟨the church's enrollment has ~*ed* 130% —*Time*⟩ — sometimes used with *out* or *up* ⟨houses in fashionable architectural styles ~*ed* up and expired in endless succession —T.H.Robsjohn-Gibbings⟩ ⟨the young republic ~*ed* out to its present proportions in a few decades⟩

³**balloon** \"\ *adj* **1 :** of, relating to, resembling, or suggesting a balloon esp. in contour or silhouette ⟨a ~ sleeve⟩ ⟨a ~ figure⟩ ⟨a ~ sail⟩ **2** *of cargo* **:** consisting of light bulky goods **3 :** having a final installment that is much larger than preceding ones in a term or installment loan ⟨a ~ note⟩ ⟨a ~ payment mortgage⟩

balloon back *n* **:** a chair back of rounded outline

balloon barrage *n* **:** a screen of balloons moored to the ground as a barrage against enemy airplanes

balloonberry \ˈ=ˌ=,==\ *n* **:** STRAWBERRY RASPBERRY

balloon cloth *or* **balloon fabric** *n* **:** a fine strong cloth of plain weave made usu. of cotton and used primarily with special finishes for balloons and airplanes

bal·loon·er \bəˈlünə(r)\ *n* -S **:** BALLOON SAIL

balloon feather *n* **:** an arrow vane with convex outline

balloonfish \ˈ=ˈ=,=\ *n* [so called fr. its ability to distend its body] **:** GLOBEFISH

balloonflower \ˈ=ˈ=,=\ *n* **:** an Asiatic plant (*Platycodon grandiflorum*) with showy corollas like balloons — called also *bellflower, Chinese bellflower*

balloon fly *n* **:** a small fly (family Empididae) in whose courtship ritual the male presents the female with food supported by a silken balloon

balloon foresail *or* **balloon jib** *n* **:** a large sail set usu. between the fore-topmast head and the end of the bowsprit or jib boom with the clew led abaft the foremast — compare BALLOON SAIL

balloon frame *also* **balloon framing** *n* **1 :** a frame for a building constructed of small members nailed together instead of heavy timbers joined by mortises and tenons — compare BRACED FRAME **2 :** construction utilizing the balloon frame

ballooning *pres part of* BALLOON

bal·loon·ist \bəˈlünəst\ *n* -S **:** one that ascends in a balloon (as for exhibition purposes)

balloons *pl of* BALLOON, *pres 3d sing of* BALLOON

balloon sail *n* **:** a large light sail (as a spinnaker) set in addition to or in place of an ordinary light sail esp. by yachts in moderate weather

balloon tire *n* **:** a pneumatic tire with a light flexible carcass and large cross section designed to provide cushioning through a large volume of air at low pressure

balloon trawl *n* **:** a trawl designed to skim over rather than thoroughly drag the bottom

balloon vine *n* **:** a cultivated vine (*Cardiospermum halicacabum*) introduced into northern No. America from tropical America and bearing numerous large ornamental bladdery pods

¹**bal·lot** \ˈbalət, *usu* - əd·+V\ *n* -S [It *ballotta*, fr. It dial., dim. of *balla* ball — more at BALLOON] **1 a :** a small ball dropped into a box or urn in secret voting **b :** a ticket or sheet of paper (as one printed with the candidates' names or the proposition to be voted on) used to cast a secret vote (as during public elections) — see AUSTRALIAN BALLOT **2 a :** the action or system of secret voting by the use of ballots or by any device for casting or recording votes (as a voting machine) **b :** the right to vote in such a way **c :** ¹VOTE 1a **3 :** the whole number of votes cast at an election **4 :** the drawing of lots

²**ballot** \"\ *vb* -ED/-ING/-S [It *ballottare*, fr. *ballotta*] *vi* **:** to vote or decide by ballot ⟨~ for a candidate⟩ ⟨~ against a referendum⟩ ⟨the ~*ing* continued until eight in the evening⟩ ~ *vt* **1 :** to obtain a vote from (a body of voters) ⟨~ the men on the proposal⟩ **2 :** to select by ballot or by the drawing of lots ⟨~ all able-bodied men for service in the army⟩

bal·lo·ta \bəˈlōd·ə\ *n, cap* [NL, alter. of L *ballote* black horehound, fr. Gk *ballōtē*] **:** a genus of plants (family Labiatae) having small bracteate flowers in axillary clusters — see BLACK HOREHOUND

bal·lo·tade \ˌbaləˈtād, -ˈäd\ *n* -S [F *ballottade*, fr. *ballotter* to toss (fr. *ballotte* small ball, fr. It dial. *ballotta*) + *-ade* — more at BALLOT] **:** a forward leap performed by a horse trained in manège in which fore and hind legs are gathered under the body and the hind hoofs are turned outward so that the shoes are visible

bal·lo·tage \ˌbaləˈtäzh\ *n* -S [F *ballottage*, fr. *ballotter* to subject to a second ballot, lit., shake, toss + *-age*] **:** a second ballot taken to decide between the two or three highest candidates when no candidate receives a majority of the votes on the first ballot

ballot box *n* **1 :** a box for receiving ballots **2 :** the system or practice of secret voting **:** ¹BALLOT 2

bal·lot·ta·ble \bəˈläd·əbəl, ba-\ *adj* [*ballottement* + *-able*] **:** identifiable by ballottement

bal·lot·té \ˌbaləˈtā\ *adj* [F, past part. of *ballotter*] *of a leap* **:** made in ballet with a rocking motion and with the free leg cut out to the side

bal·lotte·ment \bəˈlätmənt, ba-, F bálótmäⁿ\ *n* -S [F, lit., act of tossing, shaking, fr. *ballotter* + *-ment*] *med* **:** a method of determining the presence or absence of a floating object by using the sense of touch: as **a :** the act of pushing up the uterus with a finger inserted below in order to detect pregnancy by feeling the return impact when a fetus displaced in the amniotic fluid sinks back **b :** a similar procedure for diagnosing floating kidney

ballow *n* -S [origin unknown] *obs* **:** CUDGEL, STICK

ball park *n* **:** a park in which ball games are played ⟨knocked a home run right out of the *ball park*⟩

ball peen *n* **:** a hemispherical peen

ball peen hammer *n* **:** a machinist's hammer having a head with a cylindrical convex-faced surface at one end and a ball peen at the other

ball pen *n* **:** BALL-POINT PEN

ball planting *n* **:** the transplanting of balled plants

ballplayer \ˈ=ˌ==\ *n* **:** one that plays ball; *specif* **:** a professional baseball player

ball point \ˈ=ˌ=\ *n* **:** a device like a ball for forming a seat for a leg of a divider or the head of a trammel in describing curves around a hole

ball-point pen \ˈ=ˌ=-\ *also* **ball-point** \ˈ=ˌ=\ *n* **:** a pen having as the writing point a small steel ball that rotates in its socket and inks itself by contact with an inner magazine of ink

ball powder *n* **:** a progressive-burning spherical-grained smokeless gunpowder

ball python *n* **1 :** a small burrowing Central African snake (*Calabaria reinhardti*) that twists itself into a tight ball when alarmed **2 :** a small West African python (*Python regius*) — called also *royal python*

ball race *n* **:** one of the races in a ball bearing

ball rest *n* **:** a lathe rest having a circular traverse and a radial feed for turning spherical objects

ballroom \ˈ=ˌ=\ *n* **:** a large room (as in a hotel) set aside or suitable for dances

ballroom dance *also* **ballroom** *n* **:** a social dance adapted to the modern ballroom and including couple dances in embrace position (as the fox trot, tango, two-step, waltz), face-to-face position (as the jazz dances (as the charleston), and certain folk dances (as the czardas, mazurka, polka, schottische) done usu. for recreation and sometimes for exhibition

balls *pl of* BALL, *pres 3d sing of* BALL

ball sage *n* **:** BLACK SAGE 3

ball screw *n* **:** a screw attachable to a ramrod used to extract lead bullets from muzzle-loading guns

ball signal *n* **:** an object like a ball hoisted manually to the top of a track-side pole in early railroading to indicate that the way was clear for an approaching train — compare HIGHBALL

ball smut *n* **:** ²BUNT

ball snake *n* **:** RUBBER BOA

ballstock \ˈ=ˌ=\ *n* [¹*ball* + *stock*] **:** the handle on a printer's ink ball

ball turret *n* **:** a usu. retractable gun turret used on large combat aircraft and capable of being rotated so that a gunner may obtain a full circle of fire

¹**bal·lup** \ˈbaləp\ *n* -S [alter. of earlier *baglap*, fr. ¹*bag* + *lap* (flap of cloth)] *now dial* **:** a flap resembling a codpiece on the front of the trousers

²**ball-up** \ˈbȯ,ləp\ *n* -S [*ball up*] *slang* **:** a balled up state of affairs **:** CONFUSION

ball up *vt* **:** to make a mess of **:** CONFUSE, MUDDLE ⟨a mind that could *ball* anything *up*⟩ ⟨my educational routine was so hopelessly *balled up* that my mother made only one more effort to reform me —Elsa Maxwell⟩ ⟨got his signals crossed and hopelessly *balled up* the program⟩ ~ *vi* **:** to get balled up **:** become badly muddled or confused ⟨so tired he *balled up* on even simple problems⟩

ball valve *n* **1 :** a valve in which a ball fits into a spherical seat and regulates the aperture by its rise and fall due to fluid pressure, to a spring, or to its own weight **2 :** BALL COCK

¹**bal·ly** \ˈbali\ *adv (or adj)* [euphemism for ³*bloody*] *slang Brit* — used as a mild imprecation and intensifier ⟨he was ~ well sure he was right⟩ ⟨ask the whole ~ lot to . . . dinner —John Buchan⟩

²**bal·ly** \ˈbalē, -li\ *n* -ES [by shortening] **:** ¹BALLYHOO 1

³**bally** \"\ *vt* -ED/-ING/-ES [by shortening] **:** ²BALLYHOO 1 ⟨a sideshow barker noisily ~*ing* a group of loiterers⟩

bal·ly gum \ˈbälē-\ *n* [by alter.] **:** BOLLY GUM

bal·ly·hack \ˈbalē,hak\ *n* [origin unknown] *slang* **:** HELL, HADES, PERDITION — used especially in the expression *go to ballyhack*

¹**bal·ly·hoo** \ˈbalē,hü, -li-\ *n* -S [origin unknown] **1 :** an attention-getting demonstration or talk (as by a barker) to arouse interest in an entertainment ⟨a stunt of sticking a trick knife through one arm to attract a crowd and then starting his ~ —F.B.Gipson⟩ **2 a :** publicity characterized by exaggeration, gross flamboyant display, or excessive sensationalism ⟨a good deal of ~ for safer driving⟩ ⟨burlesque . . . election campaign tactics and advertising ~ —W.R.Frye⟩ **b :** empty or false talk **:** NONSENSE ⟨every face powder must claim a "scientific" uniqueness, and by this ~ millions are impressed —Ruth Benedict⟩ ⟨this claim cannot be dismissed as mere . . . ~ —L.G.Pine⟩ **syn** see PUBLICITY

²**ballyhoo** \" *sometimes* ˌ==ˈ=\ *vt* **ballyhooed; ballyhooed; ballyhooing; ballyhoos 1 :** to direct ballyhoo at ⟨~ the crowd with songs and speeches⟩ ⟨~ the public with false advertising⟩ **2 :** to drum up interest in by means of ballyhoo **:** PUBLICIZE ⟨gladiatorial meets were ~*ed* on the walls of ancient Rome —*Dun's Rev.*⟩ ⟨new cars carry on their bodies a shield or some such insigne ~*ing* the dealer from whom they were bought —*New Yorker*⟩

³**bal·ly·hoo** *also* **bal·ly·hu** \ˈbalē,hü, -li-\ *n* -S [by folk etymology fr. AmerSp *balajú*] **:** HALFBEAK; *esp* **:** either of two common tropical American halfbeaks (*Hemiramphus brasiliensis* and *Hyporamphus unifasciatus*) much used for bait

bally platform *n* **:** a platform at a carnival or sideshow on which a barker stands

ballyrag *var of* BULLYRAG

¹**balm** \ˈbä(l)m, ˈbȧ| *also* |lm; *sporadic & archaic* ˈbam\ *n* -S [ME *baume, basme*, fr. OF *basme*, fr. L *balsamum* balsam, fr. Gk *balsamon*, prob. of Sem origin; akin to Heb *bāśām* spice, balsam] **1 :** any of several balsamic resins; *esp* **:** the resinous and aromatic exudation from trees of the genus *Commiphora* **2 :** an aromatic preparation: as **a :** a healing ointment ⟨his hands were covered with blisters . . . doctored with some smelly iodine ~ —Vicki Baum⟩ **b** *obs* **:** an oil or ointment for anointing **3 :** any of various aromatic plants: as **a :** a plant of the genus *Melissa; esp* **:** LEMON BALM **b :** a plant of the genus *Monarda; esp* **:** OSWEGO TEA **4 :** a spicy odor **:** an agreeably pungent or aromatic redolence ⟨the white lilies in the garden, the herb bed near the bees — everything sent out fragrance and ~ into the soft air —Agnes S. Turnbull⟩ **5 :** a soothing restorative agency **:** something that brings comfort and relieves pain ⟨bound up her wound . . . with the ~ of understanding —Josephine Pinckney⟩ ⟨friendship is . . . the finest ~ for the pangs of disappointed love —Jane Austen⟩ **6 :** a sticky resinous substance used by honey bees to varnish the inside of certain cells in the hive before eggs are laid in them — compare PROPOLIS

²**balm** \"\ *vt* -ED/-ING/-S [ME *baumen*, fr. *baume*, n.] **1** *obs* **:** to anoint esp. with balm **2 :** SOOTHE, ALLEVIATE ⟨~ one's injured feelings⟩

bal·ma·caan \ˌbalməˈkan, -aa(ə)n *sometimes* -ˈän *or* -ˈȧn\ *n* -S [fr. *Balmacaan*, estate near Inverness, Scot.] **:** a loose boxy overcoat made orig. of rough woolens and with raglan sleeves, a short turnover collar, and a closing that may be buttoned to the throat ⟨a ~ collar⟩ — called also *bal*

bal mas·qué \ˌbälmȧskā\ *n, pl* **bals masqués** \"\ [F] **:** a masked ball

balm cricket *n* [by folk etymology fr. *baum-cricket*, part trans. of G *baumgrille*, fr. *baum* tree (fr. OHG *boum*) + *grille* cricket — more at BEAM] **:** CICADA

balm·i·ly *pronunc at* ¹BALM + əlē, -li\ *adv* **:** in a balmy manner

balm·i·ness *pronunc at* ¹BALM + -ēnəs, -in-\ *n* -ES [*balmy* + *-ness*] **:** the quality or state of being balmy ⟨the ~ of the warm summer air⟩

balm of gil·ead \-ˈgilēəd, -lyəd, -lē,ad\ *usu cap G* [fr. *Gilead*, region of ancient Palestine known for its "balm" (Jer 8:22)] **1 :** a small evergreen African and Asian tree (*Commiphora meccanensis*) with leaves that yield a strong aromatic odor when bruised **2** *also* **balm in gilead a :** any of several aromatic plant secretions; *esp* **:** a fragrant yellow or greenish oleoresin with a somewhat bitter taste obtained from the balm of Gilead and valued esp. in biblical times as an unguent and cosmetic — called also *Mecca balsam* **b :** an agency that soothes, relieves, or heals **3 :** a fragrant herb (*Dracocephalum canariense*) **4 :** BALSAM FIR 1 **5 :** either of two poplars: **a :** a hybrid northern tree (*Populus gileadensis*) used in cultivation and differing from the balsam poplar in having broadly cordate leaves that are pubescent esp. on the under side **b :** BALSAM POPLAR

bal·mo·ny \ˈba(l)mənē\ *n* -ES [origin unknown] **:** a turtlehead (*Chelone glabra*)

bal·mor·al \balˈmȯrəl, -ˈmär-\ *n* -S [fr. *Balmoral* Castle, Aberdeen, Scot.] **1 :** a boot or shoe that is laced in front; *esp* **:** an oxford shoe with quarters meeting and centered over a separate tongue — called also *bal* **2** *usu cap* **:** a round flat cap with a top projecting all around, somewhat resembling a tam-o'-shanter, and worn esp. in Scotland

balmy *pronunc at* ¹BALM + ē, i\ *adj* -ER/-EST [¹*balm* + *-y*] **1 a :** having the soothing, healing, or aromatic qualities of balm or suggesting those attributed to balm ⟨the first ~ presage of this repose —Laurence Sterne⟩ ⟨~ flowery vegetation —John Muir †1914⟩ ⟨a ~ medicinal syrup⟩ **b :** MILD ⟨the ~ breeze of morning —T.L.Peacock⟩ ⟨a pleasant ~ climate⟩ **2** [alter. of BARMY] **:** FOOLISH, SILLY, INSANE ⟨with weather so cold, one would be ~ to think of going swimming⟩ ⟨the country has gone slightly ~ —G.A.Parks⟩ **syn** see SOFT

balne- *or* **balneo-** *comb form* [L *balne-*, fr. *balneum* bath — more at BAGNIO] **:** bath **:** bathing ⟨*balne*al⟩ ⟨*balneo*therapy⟩

bal·ne·al \ˈbalnēəl\ *or* **bal·ne·ary** \-ē,erē\ *adj* [L *balneum* bath + E *-al, -ary*] **:** of or relating to a bath, bathing, or a bathroom ⟨the *balneal* reek of grim-tiled lavatories —William Sansom⟩ ⟨not . . . the slightest sign of the presence of *balneary* appurtenances in bedrooms; not even of ewers, lavers, and basins, nor of pails and tubs —E.V.Mitchell⟩

bal·ne·a·tion \ˌbalnēˈāshən\ *n* -S [LL *balneatus* (past part. of *balneare* to bathe, fr. L *balneum* bath) + E *-ion*] **:** the act or action of bathing

bal·neo·log·ic \ˌbalnēəˈläjik\ *or* **bal·neo·log·i·cal** \-jəkəl\ *adj* **:** of or relating to balneology

bal·ne·ol·o·gist \ˌbalnēˈäləjəst\ *n* -S **:** an expert in balneology

bal·ne·ol·o·gy \-jē\ *n* -ES [ISV *balne-* + *-logy*] **:** the science of the therapeutic application of baths esp. with natural mineral waters

bal·neo·therapy *also* **bal·neo·therapeutics** \ˈbalnēō +\ *n* [ISV *balne-* + *-therapy, -therapeutics*] **:** the treatment of disease by baths

balochi *or* **baloch** *usu cap, var of* BALUCHI

ba·lo·ghia \bəˈlōgēə\ *n, cap* [NL, fr. Joseph *Balogh*, 19th cent Hung. botanist + NL *-ia*] **:** a small genus of Australasian trees and shrubs (family Euphorbiaceae) with opposite-stalked leaves and small dioecious flowers — see BLOODWOOD a(2)

balon *var of* BALLON

¹**ba·lo·ney** \bəˈlōnē, -ni\ *var of* BOLOGNA

²**baloney** \"\ *n* -S [alter. of ²*bologna*] *slang* **:** pretentious nonsense **:** something false or insincere **:** BUNKUM — often a generalized expression of disagreement ⟨everything he says is just plain ~⟩ ⟨forget this ~ about temperament and concentrate more on the game —Jack Crawford⟩

bal·op \ˈba,läp\ *n* -S [short for *balopticon*] **1 :** a balopticon for projecting images into a television transmitting apparatus **2 :** the slide or card bearing the picture or other visual material for projection by the balop; *also* **:** the visual material for projection

bal·op·ti·con \baˈläptə,kän, bə-\ *n* -S [fr. *Balopticon*, a trademark] **:** a projector that utilizes reflected light for projecting the images of opaque objects

ba·low \baˈlō\ *or* **ba·loo** \-ˈlü\ *n* -S *now chiefly Scot* **:** LULLABY

bals *pl of* BAL

bal·sa \ˈbȯlsə *also* -äl-\ *n* -S [Sp] **1 a :** a tree (*Ochroma lagopus*) of Central America, the West Indies, and northern So. America with wood that is lighter than cork but strong and used esp. for floats **b :** the wood of this tree **2 :** a Central American, So. American, or Philippine raft made of bundles of grass or reeds lashed together **3 :** a life raft made of two cylinders of metal or wood joined by a framework and often used for landing through surf

bal·sam \ˈbȯlsəm\ *n* -S *often attrib* [L *balsamum* — more at BALM] **1 a :** an aromatic substance flowing spontaneously or by incision from a plant and not necessarily remaining liquid **b** (1) **:** any of various oleoresins (as copaiba and Canada balsam) (2) **:** any of several resinous substances (as balm of Gilead and benzoin) that contain benzoic or cinnamic acid in addition to resin and usu. essential oil — called also *true balsam* **c :** any of various pharmaceutical preparations containing resinous substances and having a balsamic odor **2 :** any of several balsam-yielding trees: as **a :** BALSAM FIR **b :** BALSAM POPLAR **c :** the tree that produces balsam of Tolu **3 :** something that heals or soothes ⟨music was ~ to the senses⟩ ⟨the ~ of flattery⟩ **4 :** a plant of the genus *Impatiens; esp* **:** GARDEN BALSAM **5 :** CYPRESS SPURGE **6 :** BALSAMWEED 1

balsam apple *n* **1 :** either of two small East Indian ornamental vines of the gourd family (*Momordica balsamina* and *M. charantia*) with red or orange oblong warty fruits extensively naturalized in the West Indies and used sometimes for poultices and for liniments **2 :** the fruit of the balsam apple plant

balsam bog *n* **1 :** a plant (*Azorella glebaria*) of the Falkland islands and Patagonia that belongs to the carrot family, forms dense woody hillocks often several feet in height, and yields a gum used as a folk remedy **2 :** a usu. sphagnous bog in northeastern America containing the balsam fir

balsam bottle *n* **:** a bottle fitted with a dropper and glass cap to prevent evaporation and exclude dust and used for storing Canada balsam

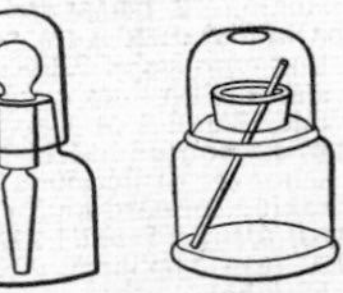
balsam bottles

balsam copaiba *n* **:** COPAIBA

balsam fig *n* **:** PITCH APPLE

balsam fir *n* **1 :** a medium-sized fir (*Abies balsamea*) that is widely distributed in northeastern No. America, has a rather smooth gray or brown bark with many resin-filled blisters, flat dark green needles with rounded tips, upright purplish cones, and soft weak wood resembling but inferior as lumber to that of the eastern spruce, is the source of Canada balsam, and is much used for pulpwood and for Christmas trees — called also *balm of Gilead;* see TREE illustration **2 :** any of certain southern and western firs of the genus *Abies:* as **a :** FRASER FIR **b :** WHITE FIR 1a(1)

balsam-fir sawfly *n* **:** a greenish sawfly (*Neodiprion abietis*) that is widespread in the northern U.S. and Canada and has larvae which feed on and defoliate various spruces and the balsam fir

balsam herb *n* **:** COSTMARY

balsam hickory *n* **:** a No. American tree (*Carya ovalis*) having a small sweet nut and aromatic hard tough wood

bal·sam·ic \(ˈ)bȯlˈsamik\ *adj* **1 :** of, relating to, yielding, or containing balsam ⟨a ~ wood⟩ ⟨leaves which exude a ~ fragrance —David Fairchild⟩ **2 :** having the qualities of balsam **:** SOOTHING, HEALING, RESTORATIVE, BALMY ⟨a ~ medicinal preparation⟩

bal·sam·if·er·ous \ˌbȯlsəˈmif(ə)rəs\ *adj* [*balsam* + *-i-* + *-ferous*] **:** producing balsam

bal·sa·mi·na·ce·ae \ˌbȯlsəməˈnāsē,ē, -ˌsam-\ *n pl, cap* [NL, fr. *Balsamina*, type genus (fr. Gk *balsaminē*) + *-aceae*] **:** a family of plants (order Geraniales) distinguished from members of the Geraniaceae by the irregular flowers — see IMPATIENS — **bal·sa·mi·na·ceous** \ˌ=(ˌ)==ˈnāshəs\ *adj*

bal·sa·mine \ˈbȯlsə,mēn\ *or* **bal·sam·i·na** \bȯlˈsamənə\ *n* -S [F *balsamine*, fr. Gk *balsaminē*, fr. *balsamon* balsam — more at BALM] **:** GARDEN BALSAM

bal·sa·mo \ˈbȯlsə,mō\ *n* -S [AmerSp *bálsamo*, fr. Sp, balsam, fr. L *balsamum* — more at BALM] **:** a tree yielding BALSAM OF TOLU

balsam of copaiba *n* **:** COPAIBA

balsam-of-copaiba tree *n* **:** a tree yielding true copaiba

balsam of fir *n* **:** CANADA BALSAM

balsam of pe·ru \-pəˈrü, -pē-\ *usu cap P* **:** a dark brown syrupy balsam obtained from a tropical American tree (*Myroxylon pereirae*) growing esp. in El Salvador and used chiefly in perfumery and in medicine (as in dressing wounds and in certain skin diseases)

balsam of to·lu \-təˈlü, -tō-\ *usu cap T* [fr. Santiago de *Tolú*, Colombia] **:** a brown or yellowish brown plastic solid balsam obtained from a tropical American tree (*Myroxylon balsamum* or *M. toluiferum*) and used as a stimulating expectorant and a flavoring for cough syrups and in perfumes

bal·sa·mor·rhi·za \ˌbȯlsəməˈrīzə\ *n, cap* [NL, fr. Gk *balsamon* balsam + NL *-rhiza*] **:** a small genus of coarse western American perennial herbs (family Compositae) with large roots containing an aromatic balsam, velvety basal leaves, and large heads of yellow flowers — see BALSAMROOT

balsam pear *n* **:** a balsam apple (*Momordica charantia*)

balsam poplar *n* **:** a No. American poplar (*Populus balsamifera* syn. *P. tacamahaca*) that is often cultivated as a shade tree and has buds thickly coated with an aromatic resin — called also *balm of Gilead, tacamahac*

balsamroot \ˈ==ˌ=\ *n* **:** a plant of the genus *Balsamorrhiza*

balsams *pl of* BALSAM

balsam tree *n* **:** a tree that yields balsam: as **a :** BALSAM FIR **b :** MASTIC TREE **c :** BALSAM POPLAR **d :** a large tropical tree (*Myroxylon balsamum*) with small pinnate dark green leaves that yields balsam of Tolu

balsam-tree family *n* **:** GUTTIFERAE

balsam twig aphid *n* **:** a common aphid (*Mindarus abietinus*) of the northern U.S. and Canada feeding chiefly on spruces and balsam fir and often producing much honeydew
balsamum *n, pl* **balsami** [ME, fr. L — more at BALM] *obs* **:** BALSAM
balsamweed \'⸗⸗,⸗\ *n* **1 :** either of two fragrant American everlastings (*Gnaphalium macounii* and *G. obtusifolium*) **2 :** JEWELWEED
balsam willow *n* **:** a low shrub or small tree (*Salix pyrifolia*) of northern No. America often occurring up to the tree line and having leaves prominently reticulate when mature and balsamic when crushed
balsam woolly aphid *n* **:** an aphid (*Adelges piceae*) native to northern Europe and widespread in No. America that severely damages fir (as balsam fir) causing swollen twigs and abnormal growth and covering the stems with a dirty white flocculent encrustation
bal·samy \'bȯlsəmē, -mi\ *adj* **:** like balsam (as in fragrance)
balshem *var of* BAALSHEM
balt \'bȯlt\ *n* -s *usu cap* [LL *Balti, Balthi, Balthae*, pl., fr. a Gothic word akin to *balthei* boldness — more at BOLD] **1 a :** one of the Lithuanians or Letts identified with the Aestii of Tacitus **b :** a native or inhabitant of the Baltic states of Lithuania, Latvia, and Estonia **2 :** a German born or resident in one of the Baltic states; *esp* **:** a member or descendant of the former German-speaking landed aristocracy of the Baltic states **3** *Austral* **:** a recently arrived immigrant from Central Europe
balter *vi* -ED/-ING/-s [ME *balteren*] *archaic* **:** to dance or tread clumsily
bal·te·us \'baltēəs, 'bȯl-\ *n, pl* **bal·tei** \-ē,ī\ [L] **1 a :** an ancient Roman belt or baldric **b :** one of the passages between the tiers of seats in an auditorium of ancient Rome **2** *also* **bal·the·us** \-lthēəs\ **:** a belt worn by an ecclesiastic; *specif* **:** SUBCINCTORIUM
bal·thaz·ar \bal'thazə(r), bȯl-\ *n* -s *usu cap* [after *Balthazar* (Belshazzar), 6th cent. B.C. king of Babylon mentioned in the Bible (Dan 5)] **:** an oversize wine bottle holding about 16 quarts ⟨a ~ of champagne⟩
bal·ti \'bəltē\ *n, pl* **balti** *or* **baltis** *usu cap* **1 a :** a muslimized Tibetan people in northern Kashmir having some physical resemblances to the Indo-Aryan Dards, having a castelike system of social hierarchy, and possibly being descendants of the Scythian Sacae **b :** a member of such people **2 :** a Tibeto-Himalayan language of the Balti people
¹bal·tic \'bȯltik, -ēk\ *adj, usu cap* [ML *balticus*, fr. LL *Balti*, pl., Balts + L *-icus* -ic] **1 a :** of or relating to the sea enclosed by Sweden, Denmark, Germany, Poland, the Baltic States, and Finland **b :** situated on the Baltic sea **c :** of or relating to the Baltic states of Lithuania, Latvia, and Estonia ⟨two *Baltic* ministers in Washington⟩ **2 :** of or relating to a branch of the Indo-European languages containing Latvian, Lithuanian, and Old Prussian
²baltic \"\ *n* -s **1** *cap* **:** the Baltic languages **2** *often cap* **:** MYRTLE 3b
baltic ivy *n, usu cap B* **:** a small-leaved hardy form (*Hedera helix baltica*) of English ivy
baltic pine *n, usu cap B* **:** SCOTCH PINE
baltic rush *n, usu cap B* **:** a small tufted rush (*Juncus balticus*) of cool regions that grows from extensively creeping and forking rootstocks and has usu. loosely forking flower clusters
¹bal·ti·more \'bȯltə,mō(ə)r, -mȯ(ə)r,-mōə,-mȯ(ə),-,mə(r) *sometimes* -ltēm- *or, locally & in rapid speech,* -lәm-\ *adj, usu cap* [fr. *Baltimore*, Maryland] **:** of or from the city of Baltimore, Md. ⟨*Baltimore* crowds⟩ **:** of the kind or style prevalent in Baltimore
²baltimore \"\ *n* -s *usu cap* [after Lord *Baltimore* (George Calvert) †1632 Eng. proprietor and colonizer of Maryland] **:** an eastern No. American nymphalid butterfly (*Euphydryas phaëton*) that is black above with orange-red, yellow, and white spots, has a larva which is social in nests when young, hibernates before maturity, and feeds on turtlehead and related plants
bal·ti·mor·e·an \,bȯltə'mōrēən, -ȯr-\ *n* -s *cap* [*Baltimore*, Maryland + E *-an*] **:** a native or resident of Baltimore, Md.
baltimore clipper *n, usu cap B* [fr. *Baltimore*, Maryland] **:** a fast sharp-hulled ship of usu. less than 200 tons built chiefly between 1830 and 1850 on Chesapeake Bay and usu. having sharply raked masts and a brig or schooner rig
baltimore oriole *or* **baltimore bird** *n, usu cap B* [after Lord *Baltimore*] **:** a common American oriole (*Icterus galbula*) that builds a finely woven pendent nest of various fibers and grasses and that in the female has prevailingly brown and greenish yellow plumage and in the male has a black head, upper back, and tail base, black and white wings, and a yellow⸗orange outer part of the outer tail feathers and has the remaining plumage a brilliant orange
bal·to–slavic \¦bȯl,tō+\ *n, cap B&S* [*Balto-* (fr. *Baltic*) + *Slavic*] **:** a subfamily of Indo-European languages consisting of the Baltic and the Slavic branches
balts *pl of* BALT
ba·lu·chi \bə'lüchē\ *or* **ba·luch** \-ch\ *also* **ba·lo·chi** \-lōchē\ *or* **ba·loch** \-ōch\ *or* **be·lu·chi** \bə'lüchē\ *n, pl* **baluchi** *or* **baluchis** *or* **baluch** *or* **baluches** *usu cap* [Per *Balūch, Balūchī*] **1 a :** an Indo-Iranian people blended from a mixture of the Veddoid type isolated in the Hadhramaut and of the Irano⸗Afghan type and located in Baluchistan in the southwestern part of Pakistan **b :** a member of such people **2 :** the Iranian language of the Baluchi people
ba·lu·chi·stan *or* **be·lu·chi·stan** \bə¦lüchə¦stan, -än\ *n* -s *usu cap* [fr. *Baluchistan*, country of western Asia, fr. Per *Balūchistān*] **:** a rug in somber colors (as mulberry and deep blue) woven by nomad tribes in Baluchistan and esp. Seistan
ba·lu·chi·there \bə'lüchə,thi(ə)r\ *n* -s [NL *Baluchitherium*] **:** BALUCHITHERIUM 2
ba·lu·chi·the·ri·um \bə,lüchə'thirēəm\ *n* [NL, fr. *Baluchistan* (country) + NL *-therium*] **1** *cap* **:** a genus of very large Oligocene mammals related to the rhinoceros the remains of which are found in central Asia **2** *pl* **baluchithe·ria** \-ēə\ **:** an animal or fossil of the genus *Baluchitherium*
ba·lu·ga \¦bälə¦gä\ *n, pl* **baluga** *or* **balugas** *usu cap* [Tag *baluga*] **:** a person of mixed Negrito and non-Negrito Philippine ancestry in central Luzon
bal·un \'ba,lən\ *n* -s [*bal*anced + *un*balanced] **:** a radio device for converting from a balanced to an unbalanced line and usu. used at high radio frequencies
bal·us·ter \'baləstə(r)\ *n* -s [F *balustre*, fr. It *balaustro*, fr. *balaustra* flower of the wild pomegranate, modif. of L *balaustium*, fr. Gk *balaustion*; fr. the similarity of form] **1 :** a short support like a column often with a circular section and a molded vaselike outline; *esp* **:** one of a series (as in a balustrade or stair rail) **2 :** a vertical member (as the leg of a table, a round in the back of a chair, the stem of a glass, the shaft of a candlestick) having a vaselike or turned outline

balusters 1

¹bal·us·trade \'balə,strād, ,⸗⸗'⸗\ *n* -s [F, fr. It *balaustrata*, fr. *balaustro* baluster] **1 a :** a row of balusters topped by a rail to serve as an open parapet (as along the edge of a balcony, terrace, bridge, staircase, or the eaves of a building) **b :** a stair rail; *esp* **:** a wide rail having massive supports **2 :** a low parapet or barrier
²balustrade \"\ *vt* -ED/-ING/-s **:** to furnish with a balustrade
bal·us·trad·ing \-diŋ\ *n* -s **:** the architectural members that constitute a balustrade
ba·lut \bä'lüt, bə-\ *n* -s [Tag *balót, balút*] **:** a food in the Philippines consisting of duck eggs incubated almost to the point of hatching and then boiled
bal·zacian \(')bal¦zāshən; (')bȯl¦zakēən, (')bal¦zak-\ *adj, usu cap* [Honoré de *Balzac* †1850 French novelist + E *-ian*] **1 :** of, relating to, or befitting Balzac or his voluminous writings **2** *of a literary work* **:** large and comprehensive or minute and faithful in presentation of the realistic details of contemporary life or of lives of odd and undistinguished types
¹bam \'bam\ *vt* **bammed; bammed; bamming; bams** [perh. short for *bamboozle*] *archaic* **:** FOOL, HOAX ⟨now you're *bamming* me — don't attempt to put such stories off on your old granny —Frederick Marryat⟩
²bam \"\ *n* -s [imit.] **:** a dull resounding noise (as one made by a flat surface of a bulky object striking against another flat surface) ⟨the crates fell with ~s and crashes⟩
³bam \"\ *vi* **bammed; bammed; bamming; bams :** to make or emit a bam **:** strike making the noise of a bam ⟨the planes *bammed* against the deck of the carrier⟩
ba·mah \'bä,mä, ⸗'⸗\ *n, pl* **ba·moth** \-mōth, -ōt,-ōs\ [Heb *bāmāh*] **:** a high place; *esp* **:** one that serves as a sanctuary (as one orig. devoted to a non-Israelite religion that later served as a place where Yahweh was worshiped)
ba·ma·ko \'bämə,kō, bä'ma(,)kō\ *adj, usu cap* [fr. *Bamako*, Mali, West Africa] **:** of or relating to Bamako, capital of Mali, West Africa **:** of the kind or style prevalent in Bamako
bam·ba \'bämbə\ *n* -s *often cap* [AmerSp] **:** a foot-tapping couple dance deriving from one of the huapangos of the Mexican Pacific-coast Negro-Indian population and danced in ballrooms of the U.S. — called also *la bamba*
bam·ba·ra \bäm'bärə\ *n, pl* **bambara** *or* **bambaras** *usu cap* **1 a :** a Negroid people of the upper Niger noted for their delicate mask carving **b :** a member of the Bambara people **2 :** a Mande language of the Bambara people widely used as a trade language in French Sudan — compare MANDINGO
bam·bar·ra groundnut *also* **bambarra nut** \"-\ *n, usu cap B* **:** a tropical leguminous African creeping herb (*Voandzeia subterranea*) that ripens its edible fruits underground
bam·bi·no \bam'bē(,)nō, bäm-\ *n, pl* **bambinos** \-(,)nōz\ *or* **bam·bi·ni** \-,nē\ [It, dim. of *bambo* child, simpleton] **1 :** CHILD, BABY **2** *pl usu* **bambini :** a representation of the infant Christ
bam·boche \bäm'bōsh\ *n* -s [AmerF (Haiti), fr. F, spree, back-formation fr. *bambochade* spree, rustic genre painting often depicting drinking scenes, fr. It *bambocciata* rustic genre painting, fr. It *Bamboccio* (lit., the simpleton, fr. *bambo* child, simpleton), nickname of Pieter van Laar (or Laer) †1642 Dutch painter] **:** a social get-together in Haiti characterized by noisy singing and dancing
¹bam·boo \(')bam¦bü, -aam-\ *n* -s [Malay *bambu*, fr. Kannada or Tulu] **1 :** a woody or arborescent grass of *Bambusa, Arundinaria, Dendrocalamus*, and related genera (tribe Bambuseae) widely distributed chiefly in the tropics and subtropics of both hemispheres; *esp* **:** a large woody plant (*B. arundinacea*) having hollow stems that attain a diameter of five or six inches and are so hard and durable as to be used for furniture, cooking utensils, and structural framing, the smaller stalks being also used (as for walking sticks and flutes) and the young shoots utilized as food **2 a :** a variable color averaging a grayish yellow that is greener, lighter, and stronger than chamois, lighter and stronger than old ivory, and redder, lighter, and stronger than crash **b :** a light to moderate yellowish brown that is yellower than lion

A portion of bamboo stem; *B* longitudinal section of *A*

²bamboo \"\ *adj* **1 :** of, relating to, or made of bamboo ⟨a ~ hut⟩ **2 :** belonging or peculiar to or suggestive of a native population esp. of a tropical Pacific area ⟨a ~ train⟩ ⟨a ~ prison⟩; *specif* **:** having dropped Western habits and affiliations — used of an American or European ⟨Mac stayed because he was ~, but you couldn't use that word to his face —R.O.Bowen⟩
bamboo borer *n* **:** an auger beetle (*Dinoderus minutus*) that is blackish with yellow markings on the elytra, green on the thorax, and red on the antenna bases and that bores in bamboo and in the southern U.S. attacks stored grain
bamboo brier *n* **:** BULLBRIER
bamboo cocktail *n* **:** a cocktail consisting of dry sherry, French vermouth, and usu. a dash of bitters
bamboo curtain *n, often cap B&C* **:** a political, military, and ideological barrier in the Orient (as that isolating territory controlled by Communist China) — compare IRON CURTAIN
bamboo dance *n* **:** a popular dance in India and the Philippines that involves skillful hopping over and between bamboo poles as they are manipulated by two or four men
bamboo fern *n* **:** a fast-growing sturdy Japanese fern (*Coniogramme japonica*) having mostly once-pinnate fronds and grown esp. under glass and for ornament
bamboo fish *n* **:** a southern African fish (*Sarpa salpa*) of the family Sparidae often used as bait
bamboo grass *n* **1 :** BAMBOO **2 :** a grass resembling the bamboo (*Bambusa arundinacea*) in structure or appearance **3 :** a cane grass (*Glyceria ramigera*)
bamboo oyster *n* **:** a small oyster of the Chinese coast cultivated on bamboo stakes thrust into the mud
bamboo palm *n* **1 :** ¹BAMBOO **2 :** any of several palms of the genus *Raphia* (esp. *R. vinifera*)
bamboo partridge *n* **:** any of certain east Asian partridges (genus *Bambusicola*) having a spurred tarsus, 14 tail feathers, and the first primary shorter than the tenth
bamboo pipe *n* **:** a simple easily made whistle flute
bamboo powder-post beetle *n* **:** BAMBOO BORER
bamboo rat *n* **1 :** any of several burrowing ratlike rodents of the genus *Rhizomys* found in the Orient **2 :** CANE RAT 1
bamboo reed *n* **:** GIANT REED 1
bamboo seaweed *n* **:** a brown seaweed (*Ecklonia buccinalis*) common on the coasts of southern Africa and resembling the bladder kelps of the No. Pacific ocean
bamboo shoot *n* **:** one of the young expanding buds from the rhizome of bamboo cut as soon as it appears aboveground and used as a vegetable esp. by Chinese and Japanese
bamboo sugar *n* **:** TABASHEER
bamboo telegraph *or* **bamboo wireless** *n* **:** the Oceanian native grapevine telegraph
bamboo vine *n* **:** a bull brier (*Smilax bona-nox*) having 4⸗angled stems with stellate scurfy bases
bamboo ware *n* [so called fr. its color] **:** a ware resembling but darker than caneware introduced by Josiah Wedgwood in 1770
bamboo worm *n* [so called fr. the resemblance of the segmentally striped body to a jointed bamboo stalk] **:** a common slender cylindrical reddish polychaete worm (*Clymenella torquata*) dwelling in tubes in the littoral zone along the New England coast
bam·boo·zle \bam'büzəl, baam-\ *vt* **bamboozled; bamboozled; bamboozling** \-z(ə)liŋ\ **bamboozles** [origin unknown] **:** to conceal one's true motives from esp. by elaborately feigning good intentions so as to gain an end or achieve an advantage **:** MISLEAD, HOODWINK ⟨campaigns to ~ workers into turning out more work for less pay —*Progressive Labor World*⟩ — often used with *into* ⟨she'd *bamboozled* Grandfather into marrying her —Ngaio Marsh⟩ **syn** see DUPE
bam·boo·zle·ment \-zəlmənt\ *n* -s **:** the quality or state of being bamboozled
bam·bou·la \bam'bülə, bäm-\ *n* -s [F, fr. Bantu] **1 :** a primitive drum used by Negroes of western Africa and the West Indies esp. in voodoo ceremonies and incantations **2 :** the dance performed to the beating of the bamboula
bam·bu·co \bam'bü(,)kō\ *n* -s [AmerSp] **:** a Colombian dance song with alternating six-eight and three-quarter meter
bam·buk butter \'bam,bük-\ *n, often cap 1st B* [fr. *Bambuk*, region in western Africa] **:** SHEA BUTTER
bam·bu·sa \bam'byüsə\ *n, cap* [NL, fr. D *bamboes* bamboo, modif. of Malay *bambu*] **:** a genus (tribe Bambuseae) comprising typical bamboos that are woody or arborescent grasses native to the warmer parts of Asia, Africa, and So. America sometimes attaining a height of 120 feet, growing in clumps, and having spikelets bearing several flowers
bam·bu·se·ae \-sē,ē\ *n pl, cap* [NL, fr. *Bambusa* + *-eae* (fem. pl. of *-eus*)] **:** a tribe of the family Gramineae comprising the bamboos and being characterized by perennial usu. rhizomatous rootstocks that send up numerous culms which typically form clumps but are sometimes solitary or climbing
ba·mia \'bämyə\ *n* -s [Turk *bamya*] **:** OKRA
bammed *past of* BAM
bamming *pres part of* BAM
bamoth *pl of* BAMAH
bams *pl of* BAM, *pres 3d sing of* BAM
¹ban \'ban, -aa(ə)n\ *vb* **banned; banned; banning; bans** [ME *bannen* to curse, summon, fr. OE *bannan* to summon; akin to OHG *bannan* to command, ON *banna* to prohibit, L *fari* to speak, Gk *phanai* to say, *phōnē* sound, voice, Skt *bhanati* he speaks] *vt* **1** *archaic* **:** CURSE ⟨he blessed his friend and *banned* his foe⟩ **2 :** to prohibit esp. by legal means or social pressure the performance, activities, dissemination, or use of ⟨~ a political party⟩ ⟨~ a book⟩ ⟨good manners ~ slovenly dress in restaurants⟩ ⟨a bill to ~ birth-control literature⟩ ~ *vi* **:** to utter maledictions ⟨the serious world will scold and ~ —J.R.Drake⟩ **syn** see FORBID
²ban \"\ *n* -s [ME, partly fr. *bannen*, v. & partly fr. OF *ban* summoning of the king's vassals for military service, of Gmc origin; akin to OHG *ban* command, prohibition, jurisdiction, *bannan* to command, ON *bann* prohibition] **1 :** the summoning in feudal times of the king's vassals for military service; *also* **:** the body of feudal vassals so summoned — compare ARRIÈRE-BAN **2 a** *obs* **:** a public proclamation or edict **:** summons by public proclamation **b** *archaic* **:** BANNS 1 **3 :** a solemn curse formally made by ecclesiastical authority **:** ANATHEMA ⟨a person under the pope's ~⟩ ⟨a city placed under ~ of pope and church⟩ **4 a :** a curse that calls down evil or harm upon a person or thing **:** an incantatory malediction ⟨a father's ~ upon his wayward son⟩ **b** *archaic* **:** a maledictory oath **:** a profane exclamation ⟨blasphemous ~s and shouts⟩ **5 :** legal prohibition **:** official interdict ⟨the Senate committee also voted to continue the ~ on price support of potatoes —*Wall Street Jour.*⟩ ⟨lift the ~ on the sale of a product⟩ ⟨the delegates voted against the ~ of Communists from the teaching profession —*Key Reporter*⟩ **6 :** censure or condemnation esp. through public opinion, social pressure, or moral or ethical considerations **:** severe disapproval ⟨a ~ on the use of atomic weapons⟩ ⟨a ~ on high-pressure salesmanship⟩ ⟨he became a lawyer; but the profession was under ~ with the upper classes —*Encyc. Americana*⟩
³ban \'bän\ *n* -s [Serbo-Croatian *bān* lord, ruler; akin to ORuss *bojanŭ* rhapsodist, of Turkic origin; akin to Turk *bay* rich man] **:** a provincial governor of former times in Hungary, Croatia, or Slavonia with military powers in time of war
⁴ban \'bän\ *n, pl* **ba·ni** \'bä(,)nē\ [Romanian] **1 :** a Romanian unit of value equal to $\frac{1}{100}$ leu — see MONEY table **2 :** a coin representing one ban
ba·na·ba \¦bänə¦bä\ *n* -s [Tag & Bisayan] **1 :** an Asiatic timber tree (*Lagerstroemia speciosa*) with large red or rose⸗purple flowers **2 :** the tough durable reddish wood of the banaba much used for ship planking
ba·nak \'bä,näk\ *n* -s [prob. native name in Honduras] **:** any of several Central American timber trees of the genus *Virola* (esp. *V. merendonia*) extensively shipped from British Honduras
¹ba·nal \'bānᵊl; bə'nal, -äl,-ål *also* ba-\ *adj* [F, fr. MF, of compulsory feudal service, possessed in common, commonplace, fr. *ban* summoning of the king's vassals + *-al* — more at BAN] **1 :** wanting originality, freshness, or novelty **:** failing to stimulate, appeal, or arrest attention **:** TRITE, WORN-OUT, COMMONPLACE ⟨the poor working girl of the ~ songs —J.T. Farrell⟩ ⟨little books on great subjects are generally intolerably ~ —*Times Lit. Supp.*⟩ ⟨the food there was ~ —Jean Stafford⟩ ⟨the new Custom House, a towering structure, sound in plan but ~ in decoration —Lewis Mumford⟩ **2** *med* **:** COMMON, ORDINARY ⟨~ inflammation⟩ **syn** see INSIPID
²ban·al \'bänᵊl\ *adj* [³*ban* + *-al*] **:** of or relating to a ban or banat
ba·nal·i·ty \bā'nalәd·ē, bə-, -әtē, -i *also* ba-\ *n* -ES [F *banalité*, fr. *banal* + *-ité* -ity] **1 a :** the quality or state of being banal ⟨their love affairs had a tedious ~ —W.S.Maugham⟩ **b :** something banal **:** COMMONPLACE ⟨the *banalities* of our rhymed radio commercials —C.M.Fuess⟩ **2 :** a lord's right in old French law to require his vassals to use his wine press, oven, or mill
ba·nal·ly \'bānᵊlē; bə'nallē, -ällē,-ållē *also* ba-; -i\ *adv* **:** in a banal manner
ba·nana \bə'nanə, *chiefly Brit* -'nä-\ *n* -s *often attrib* [Sp or Pg; Sp, fr. Pg, of African origin; akin to Wolof *banäna*, Mandingo *banāna, banānda, barānda* plantain, Teoni *bänana*] **1 a :** the elongated often curved and usu. tapering fruit of the banana plant having soft pulpy flesh and a rind that is usu. yellow or orange-colored when ripe and dark brown to black at full maturity — see DWARF BANANA, PLANTAIN **b :** any of several treelike perennial herbs of the genus *Musa* (esp. *M. paradisiaca sapientum*) that are native to tropical Asia but are cultivated or naturalized throughout the tropics, that have a soft herbaceous stalk, very large simple leaves, flowers enveloped in colored bracts and collected into a large pendent bunch each flower of which produces a single usu. seedless fruit, and that usu. reproduce only vegetatively by means of suckers formed at the base of the plant **2 :** a grayish yellow that is paler and slightly greener than chamois, redder, lighter, and stronger than crash, and lighter, stronger, and very slightly redder than old ivory — called also *sunbeam*

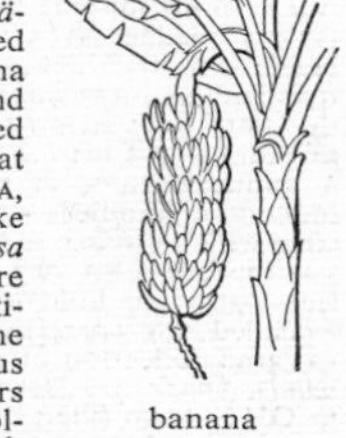
banana

banana bird *n* **1 :** BANANA QUIT **2 :** any of several Australian birds
banana boa *n* **:** a boa frequenting bananas; *specif* **:** a moderate-sized snake (*Boa imperator*) often imported with bunches of bananas
banana family *n* **:** MUSACEAE
banana fish *n* **:** BONEFISH 1
banana freckle *n* **:** a disease of the fruit and leaves of the banana caused by an imperfect fungus (*Macrophoma musae*) producing brown or black spots
banana melon *or* **banana muskmelon** *n* **:** a long slender muskmelon with salmon-colored flesh and a shallow-ribbed rind that is not netted
banana oil *n* **1 a** (1) **:** ISOAMYL ACETATE (2) **:** AMYL ACETATE a **b :** a lacquer containing amyl acetate; *often* **:** a solution of cellulose nitrate usu. in amyl acetate **2** *slang* **:** HOKUM ⟨the pure *banana oil* of the propagandist —Hesketh Pearson⟩
banana-plant \⸗'⸗⸗,⸗\ *n* **:** an aquatic perennial herb (*Nymphoides aquatica*) with cordate leaves and tubers in clusters like bananas
banana plug *n* **:** a single-conductor electrical plug with a banana-shaped tip of spring metal
banana quit *n* **:** any of several typical honeycreepers (genus *Coereba*)
banana republic *n* [so called fr. the fact that some small tropical countries are economically dependent on their fruit exporting trade] **:** a small country usu. in the tropics that is economically dependent on foreign capital and dominated by it
banana root borer *also* **banana root weevil** *n* **:** a stout orange or reddish black-marked weevil (*Cosmopolites sordidus*) whose larvae bore in banana plant roots
banana shrub *n* **:** a Chinese evergreen shrub (*Michelia fuscata*) with flowers having a fragrance like banana
banana spider *n* **1 :** a large tropical crab spider (*Heteropoda venatoria*) often introduced into temperate regions with bunches of bananas **2 :** TARANTULA
banana split *n* **:** a dessert consisting of a banana sliced in half lengthwise, topped with one or more balls of ice cream, and usu. garnished with whipped cream and nuts
banana squash *n* **:** a winter squash having elongated fruits that taper at both ends
banana water lily *n* **:** a yellow-flowered water lily (*Nymphaea mexicana*) having seeds that serve as feed for wild fowl esp. from Florida to Mexico
banana wilt *n* **:** PANAMA DISEASE
ba·na·ras \bə'närəs\ *or* **be·na·res** \", -rēz\ *adj, usu cap* [fr. *Banaras* or *Benares*, India] **:** of or from the city of Banaras, India **:** of the kind or style prevalent in Banaras
ba·na·ro \'bänə,rō\ *n, pl* **banaro** *or* **banaros** *usu cap* **1 :** a Papuan people of the Sepik district, Territory of New Guinea **2 :** a member of the Banaro people
ban·at *also* **ban·ate** *or* **ban·nat** \'bänət\ *n* -s [Serbo-Croatian *bānat*, fr. *bān* lord, ruler — more at BAN] **:** a province under the jurisdiction of a ban

ba·nau·sic \bə'nȯsik, -ȯzik\ *adj* [Gk *banausikos* of artisans, fr. *banausos* artisan + *-ikos* -ic] **1 a :** governed by or suggestive of utilitarian purposes **:** PRACTICAL ⟨my approach to this literature was . . . ~. I wanted advice, instruction, not aids to reflection —John Buchan⟩ **b :** common in taste, thought, or intention **:** dull and menial ⟨this sort of ~ performance is not mitigated by the striking of a few brave attitudes —John Wain⟩ **2 :** MONEYMAKING, BREADWINNING **:** VOCATIONAL ⟨a class freed from ~ pursuits and enjoying its leisure⟩ **:** commercially minded **:** MATERIALISTIC ⟨a ~ civilization⟩

Ban·bury \'ban,berē-, -,bərē\ *trademark* — used for any of various mechanical mixers for processing rubber, plastic, and other compositions

banbury tart *n*, *usu cap B* [fr. *Banbury*, England] **:** an often triangular tart with a fruit filling esp. of raisins

banc \'baŋk, -ai-\ *n* -s [ME *banck*, fr. OF *banc* — more at BANK] **:** the bench on which the judges of a court sit — **in banc** *also* **in ban·co** \-'bæŋ(,)kō, -aiŋ-\ **:** in full court **:** with full judicial authority ⟨sittings *in banc*⟩ — used of a court held by such a number of judges as constitute a quorum; compare NISI PRIUS

ban·ca *also* **bang·ka** *or* **ban·ka** \'bäŋkə\ *n* -s [PhilSp & Tag; PhilSp *banca*, fr. Tag *bangkâ*] **:** a small boat found in Pacific waters esp. around the Philippines; *usu* **:** a dugout canoe often provided with outriggers and a roof of bamboo

ban·cal \bäŋ·'käl\ *n* -s [Sp, fr. Bisayan *bañkal*] *Philippines* **:** a large tree (*Nauclea orientalis*) of the family Rubiaceae that has rather soft straight-grained yellow to orange wood which is used locally for cabinetwork and construction

ban·cha \'bän(,)chä\ *also* **bancha tea** *n* -s [Jap *bancha*, fr. *ban* number + *cha* tea] **:** a coarse Japanese tea that is usu. not exported

¹ban·co \'baŋ(,)kō, -aiŋ-\ *adj* [It, money of account, bank, bench, var. of *banca* bank, bench — more at BANK] *of a coin, note, unit of value* **:** issued or used by a bank at the time of a depreciated government currency ⟨a 19th century Swedish skilling ~⟩

²banco \"\ *n* -s [F, fr. It, total sum offered by the banker in a gambling game, fr. *banco* bank, bench] **:** an announcement by a bettor in certain gambling games (as baccarat or chemin-de-fer) signifying that he elects to accept alone the entire sum offered by the banker to meet the bets of all bettors, his bet taking precedence over any lower bet previously offered — often used interjectionally

³banco \"\ *n* -s [Sp, sandbar, bench, of Gmc origin; akin to OHG *bank* bench — more at BENCH] **:** a portion of the floodplain or channel of a river cut off and left dry by the shifting of its course

ban·croft·i·an filariasis \'ban,krȯftēən-, *also* -aŋ-,k- *or* ='===-\ *or* **ban·croft's filariasis** \'=,krȯf(t)s-\ *n*, *usu cap B* [Joseph *Bancroft* †1894 Eng. physician + E *-ian*] **:** filariasis caused by a slender white filaria (*Wuchereria bancrofti*) that is transmitted in larval form by mosquitoes, lives in lymph vessels and lymphoid tissues periodically shedding larvae into the peripheral blood stream, and often causes elephantiasis by blocking the lymphatic drainage of a part

bancroft's law *n*, *usu cap B* [after Dr. Edith S. W. *Bancroft* *b*1893 Am. botanist] **:** a statement in ecology: a community or an organism tends to attain a state of dynamic equilibrium with its environment

¹band \'band, -aa(ə)-\ *n* -s [ME *band, bond*, fr. ON *band*; akin to OE *bend* fetter, OHG *bant*, Goth *bandi*, Skt *bandha* fetter, OE *bindan* to bind — more at BIND] **1 :** something that confines or constricts while allowing or imparting a limited or necessary degree of movement: **a** (1) *archaic* **:** something used to make fast the body or limbs (as a fetter, manacle, shackle) (2) *obs* **:** a leading string **:** TETHER **b** *obs* **:** a hinge of a gate or door; *esp* **:** STRAP HINGE **2 :** something that binds or restrains by legal, moral, or spiritual authority: as **a :** a restraining obligation or tie affecting one's relations to another, to others, or to a tradition, concept, or condition ⟨two New Jersey sculptors of the same period who helped break the ~s of neoclassic traditions —*Amer. Guide Series: N.J.*⟩ **b** *archaic* (1) **:** a formal promise or guarantee **:** BOND (2) **:** a pledge given **:** SECURITY, SURETY **3** [partly fr. ME *bande* strip, fr. MF *bande, bende*] **:** a strip serving to join, hold together, or integrate two or more things: as **a :** a string or tie (as of hay, straw, rushes) used to bind stalks into a sheaf or bundle **b :** BELT 2 **c :** the endless loop of cotton cord on a spinning frame or twister that is used as a belt to drive individual spindles — called also *spinning band* **d :** a cord or strip which crosses the backbone of a book and to which the sections are sewn **e :** a window came **f :** a metallic hoop or sleeve used to hold the barrel and stock of a gun together — called also *barrel band* **g :** a printed strip used as a label ⟨a large collection of cigar ~s⟩ **4** [ME *bande* strip, fr. MF *bande, bende*, fr. (assumed) VL *binda*, of Gmc origin; akin to OHG *binta* fillet; akin to OHG *bintan* to bind — more at BIND] **:** a thin flat encircling strip, strap, or flat belt of material serving chiefly to bind or contain something: as **a :** a close-fitting strip that confines material at the waist, neck, or cuff of clothing; *specif* **:** HATBAND **b** (1) *obs* **:** a strip of cloth for swathing the body **:** BANDAGE (2) **:** a strip of cloth used to protect a newborn baby's navel — called also *bellyband* **c :** a ring or endless strip of elastic (as for holding or compressing wrapping or keeping small objects together) **d :** a strengthening piece of canvas sewed across a sail (as at the eyelet holes used in reefing) **e :** a container without a bottom and usu. of wood-veneer or treated paper in which plants are grown individually prior to transplanting or benching — called also *plant band* **5** [ME *bande* strip, fr. MF *bande, bende*] **:** an elongated surface or section with parallel or roughly parallel sides: as **a :** a strip separated by some characteristic color or texture or considered apart from what is adjacent ⟨a yellow ~ of light upon the street pours from an open door —Amy Lowell⟩: as (1) **:** a stripe, streak, or other elongated mark on an animal; *esp* **:** one transverse to the long axis of the body ⟨the ~ is an important show feature on a Hampshire hog⟩ (2) **:** a line or streak of differentiated cells; *often* **:** GERM BAND (3) **:** one of the alternating dark and light segments of skeletal muscle fibers (4) **:** STAB CELL (5) **:** a strip of abnormal tissue either congenital or acquired; *esp* **:** a strip of connective tissue that causes obstruction of the bowel (6) **:** a thin seam of ore or other mineral stratified between other kinds of rock **b** (1) **:** a transverse ridge raised by a cord or strip on the backbone of a book and often continued onto the front and back covers — see RAISED BAND (2) **:** a false ridge raised on the binding of a book for decoration or to protect lettering — compare HUB 4 **c :** a long narrow feature or surface running along, across, or around something ⟨along the coast . . . lies a ~ of sand dunes —Samuel Van Valkenburg & Ellsworth Huntington⟩ **d :** a more or less well-defined range of wavelengths, frequencies, or energies of optical, electric, or acoustic radiation ⟨~ spectrum⟩ ⟨radio-frequency ~⟩ **6** [ME *bande* strip, fr. MF *bande, bende*] **:** a narrow circular, curved, or straight strip serving chiefly as decoration: as **a :** a narrow strip of material (as cloth) applied as binding, trimming, or finish to an article of dress **b** (1) **bands** *pl* **:** a pair of strips hanging at the front of the neck as part of a clerical, legal, or academic dress — compare GENEVA BANDS (2) **:** FALL 1d (2) **c :** any of several flat lines stamped or tooled on a book cover in gold or color or blind to simulate bands — compare FILLET 5b **d :** a flat usu. horizontal member (as a continuous tablet, a stripe, or a series of ornaments as of carved foliage, of color, or of brickwork) dividing or ornamenting a wall or part (as the molding or suite of moldings which encircles the pillars and small shafts in Gothic architecture or one of the sections of the banded column used in French Renaissance) **e :** a ring without raised portions ⟨a wedding ~⟩ **7** [ME *bande* strip, fr. MF *bande, bende*] **:** ¹BAND SHELL **8 :** a strip of the grooves of a phonograph record on which a single piece or a section of a long piece is recorded

²band \"\ *vb* -ED/-ING/-S *vt* **1 :** to affix a band to: as **a :** to bind together or tie up with a band ⟨~ asparagus⟩ ⟨automatically ~ed and delivered in 5 packs of 50 cards each —*Theory & Practice of Presswork*⟩ **b :** to encircle (a tree trunk) with a band of cloth, paper, or sticky substance as protection against injurious insects **c :** to mark (a bird) with a band for identification **2 a :** to finish with a band ⟨the jacket was ~ed with black⟩ ⟨the interior walls, ~ed in light and dark gray stone —*Amer. Guide Series: Minn.*⟩ **b :** to create or form a band on ⟨wide gray eyes ~ed her face with intensity and intellect —Elizabeth Pollet⟩ **3 a :** to attach (oneself) to a group ⟨the royalists ~ed themselves against the popular movement⟩ **b :** to gather together or summon esp. for some purpose ⟨he ~ed all his resources together against the coming struggle⟩ **c :** to unite in a troop, company, or confederacy ⟨farmers had long been ~ed against certain government controls⟩ **4 :** to distribute (as grass seed, legume seed, or fertilizer) in strips under the soil surface rather than broadcast ~ *vi* **:** to confederate esp. for some common purpose **:** UNITE ⟨all the first-rate critics are, in some measure, ~ed in one army —C.E. Montague⟩ — often used with *together* ⟨housewives ~ together and serve chicken and turkey —*Amer. Guide Series: Texas*⟩

³band \"\ *n* -s [MF *bande* troop, prob. fr. OProv *banda*, of Gmc origin; akin to Goth *bandwa, bandwo* sign; fr. the use of a standard by a troop of soldiers — more at BANNER] **:** a group of persons, animals, or things: as **a :** a body of armed men **:** GANG ⟨a guerrilla ~⟩ ⟨a ~ of Indians⟩ ⟨a ~ of outlaws⟩ ⟨a ~ of men who wrecked the tobacco crop of those of their neighbors who refused to join a would-be monopolistic association —E.R.Bentley⟩ **b :** a body of persons often brought together by a common purpose or bound together by a common fate or lot ⟨a ~ of refugees⟩ ⟨a ~ of patriotic ladies who made clothing for the soldiers —*Encyc. Americana*⟩ ⟨the small and select ~ of Europeans who have made the overland journey from China to India —*Geog. Jour.*⟩; *specif* **:** a relatively self-sufficient tribal subgroup that is mainly united for social and economic reasons **c :** a group of animals sharing often more or less permanently a common existence either in nature or under domestication: as (1) **:** a herd or flock usu. of domestic mammals ⟨a ~ of well-fattened cattle⟩; *esp* **:** a large flock of range sheep tended by one herder (2) **:** a flock of birds ⟨a ~ of jays⟩ (3) **:** a swarm of insects; *specif* **:** a circumscribed aggregation of migratory grasshoppers functioning as a unit — used often of the immature hoppers as distinguished from swarms of flying adults **d :** a group of musicians organized for playing together **:** ORCHESTRA: as (1) **:** a group composed chiefly of percussion and wind instruments ⟨military ~⟩ or of percussion and brass wind instruments only ⟨brass ~⟩ (2) **:** any group capable of playing while marching (3) **:** a group composed chiefly of one kind of instrument ⟨a harmonica ~⟩ ⟨a pipe ~⟩ (4) **:** a dance orchestra of any composition (5) **:** one of the groups of related instruments in an orchestra **e :** AGGREGATE, COLLECTION, NUMBER ⟨a ~ of ideas⟩ ⟨the small numerable ~ of runaway planets —A.N.Whitehead⟩

⁴band \"\ *vt* -ED/-ING/-S [prob. fr. MF *bander*, lit., to be tight — more at BANDY] **:** BANDY

ban·da \'bandə\ *n* -s [native name in Africa] **:** a thatched house of central Africa

¹ban·dage \'bandij, -aan-, -dēj\ *n* -s [MF, fr. *bande* strip + *-age* — more at BAND] **1 :** a narrow length of fabric used to cover a wound, hold a dressing in place, immobilize an injured part, or apply pressure **2 :** a flexible strip used like a bandage (as one bound over or around something to cover, strengthen, or compress it); *specif* **:** a strip of coarse-mesh fabric (as cheesecloth) used in cheesemaking to line the hoop before the curd is put in for pressing

bandages: *1* spiral bandage of finger, *2* gauntlet bandage, *3* spiral reverse bandage of forearm, *4* figure-of-eight bandage of knee and spiral reverse below knee

²bandage \"\, *esp in pres part* -dəj\ *vb* -ED/-ING/-S *vt* **:** to bind, dress, or cover with a bandage ⟨~ a wound⟩ ⟨~ a sprained ankle⟩ ⟨*bandaging* and whitewashing the apple trees —Miles Franklin⟩ ~ *vi* **:** to apply a bandage ⟨were taught how to ~⟩

ban·dag·er \-jə(r)\ *n* -s **:** one that bandages

Band–Aid \'ban,dād, -aan-\ *trademark* — used for a small adhesive strip with a gauze pad for covering minor wounds

ban·da·ite \'bandə,īt, -n,dīt\ *n* -s [*Bandai*, volcano on Honshu Island, Japan + E *-ite*] **:** a siliceous often quartz-bearing basalt of andesitic texture with labradorite as its feldspar

ban·da·ka *also* **ban·dak·ka** \'bandəkə\ *or* **ban·di·kai** \-də-,kī\ *n* -s [Kanarese *bende-kāyi* or Telugu *benda-kāya*] **:** OKRA

ban·da·lore \'bandə,lō(ə)r\ *n* -s [origin unknown] **:** a toy with an automatically winding cord by which it is brought back to the hand when thrown — called also *quiz*

ban·dan·na *also* **ban·dana** \ban'danə, baan-, *Brit also* -dä-; *attrib* (')=¦==\ *n* -s [Hindi *bādhnū*, a variegated-color dyeing process involving tying the cloth in knots, cloth so dyed, fr. *bādhnā* to tie, fr. Skt *badhnāti* he ties — more at BIND] **1 :** a large cotton or silk handkerchief that usu. has a solid background of red or blue with simple figures or geometrical forms in white or yellow and is printed by tie-and-dye **2 :** any of various large plain or printed handkerchiefs or kerchiefs often made to imitate the tied-and-dyed ones

ban·dan·naed \-nəd\ *adj* **:** covered with a bandanna

ban·dar *also* **bhun·der** *or* **bun·der** \'bəndə(r)\ *n* -s [Hindi *bādar, bādar* monkey, fr. Skt *vānara*, fr. *vanar-, vana* forest; akin to Av *vana* forest] **:** RHESUS

ban·dar-log \'bəndə(r),lȯg, -läg\ *n*, *pl* **bandar-log** *or* **bandar-logs** [Hindi *bādar* monkey + *log* people; fr. the portrayal of the monkey race as chatterers and poseurs in the jungle stories of Rudyard Kipling †1936 Eng. writer — more at LOG] **:** a vacuous chattering person ⟨he's evidently picked up some congenial *bandar-logs* —Booth Tarkington⟩

¹band·box \'ban(d),bäks, -aan-\ *n* [¹*band* + *box*] **1 :** a usu. cylindrical box of pasteboard or thin wood for holding light articles of attire (as ruffs, collars, hats) **2 :** a structure (as a baseball park) resembling a bandbox esp. in having relatively small interior dimensions — **band·box·i·cal** \(')=¦=səkəl\ *adj* — **band·boxy** \'=,=ē\ *adj*

²bandbox \"\ *adj* **1 :** of flimsy unsubstantial nature or construction ⟨a fragile ~ reputation⟩ **2 :** exquisitely neat, clean, or ordered **:** being as though fresh-taken from a bandbox ⟨the quiet ~ scenery of cultivated England —Leslie Stephen⟩

band brake *n* **:** a friction brake used esp. in vehicles, cranes, and hoists that consists of a flexible band around a revolving drum and is operated by tightening the band

band cell *n* **:** STAB CELL

band clutch *n* **:** a clutch in which a friction band resembling a brake band tightens around a shaft or drum

band conveyor *n* **:** CONVEYER 2a (1)

band course *n* **:** BELT COURSE

band creaser *n* **:** a tool used in bookbinding to crease lines on either side of bands

ban·deau \'ban,dō, -aan-, =¦=\ *n*, *pl* **ban·deaux** \-ōz\ [F, dim. of *bande* strip — more at BAND] **1 a :** a fillet or a wide band (as for the hair) **b :** a bandlike hat for women **2 :** BRASSIERE; *esp* **:** a lightweight narrow one for a young figure

banded *adj* **1 a :** having a band or bands; *esp* **:** marked with or showing bands or stripes ⟨a ~ collar⟩ ⟨a ~ rock⟩ **b** *heraldry* **:** having a band of a specified color **2** *of an architectural feature* **:** having the regular profile interrupted by blocks or projections crossing it at right angles ⟨a ~ architrave⟩ ⟨a series of ~ piers⟩

banded anteater *n* **:** a marsupial anteater of the genus *Myrmecobius* of Australia — called also *numbat*

banded drum *n* **1 :** the black drum when immature **2** *or* **banded croaker :** a scianeid fish (*Larimus fasciatus*) of the So. Atlantic and the Gulf coast of the U.S.

banded duiker *n* **:** a small forest antelope (*Cephalophus doriae*) of Liberia with dark cross stripes on a fulvous ground

banded krait *or* **banded adder** *n* **:** a sluggish krait (*Bungarus fasciatus*) banded with black and yellow or buff

banded leaf monkey *n* **:** a Malayan langur of the genus *Presbytis*

banded mackerel *n* **:** BANDED RUDDERFISH

banded olive snake *n* **:** a small harmless snake (*Natrix olivaceus*) of tropical and southern Africa

banded palm civet *n* **:** any of several East Indian civets that constitute the genus *Hemigalus* and usu. have a light coat with dark transverse stripes

banded pickerel *n* **:** CHAIN PICKEREL

banded purple *n* **:** a nymphalid butterfly (*Limenitis arthemis*) of northeastern No. America with blue-black wings crossed by a broad white band — called also *white admiral*

banded rattlesnake *n* **:** TIMBER RATTLESNAKE

banded rudderfish *n* **:** a common amberfish (*Seriola zonata*) of the western Atlantic — called also *banded mackerel*

banded spindle *n* **:** ¹BAND SHELL

banded stilt *n* **:** a web-footed Australian stilt (*Cladorhynchus leucocephalum*) with reddish brown pectoral markings

banded structure *n* **:** a geological structure characterized by an arrangement of different minerals in layers that appear as bands in cross section (as in a fissure vein) or of different colors or textures in layers in a rock consisting of one mineral (as in onyx marble)

banded sunfish *n* **:** BLACK-BANDED SUNFISH

banded veins *n pl* **:** mineral veins that when seen in cross section present a banded structure

banded water snake *n* **:** a common No. American water snake (*Natrix sipedon*) represented in the U.S. by several widely distributed subspecies

banded whelk *n* **:** ¹BAND SHELL

ban·de·let \¦bandə¦let, 'bandlət\ *also* **ban·de·lette** \¦bandə¦let\ *or* **band·let** \'bandlət\ *n* -s [F *bandelette*, dim. of *bande* strip — more at BAND] *archit* **:** a little band or flat molding about a column

bandelier *var of* BANDOLIER

ban·deng \'ban,deŋ\ *n* -s [native name in Indonesia] **:** the milkfish (*Chanos chanos*) used for mosquito control and cultivated in ponds in Indonesia

band·er \'bandə(r), -aan-\ *n* -s **:** one that bands: as **a :** a sewing-machine operator who attaches neckbands, waistbands, and trimming bands to garments **b :** a worker who wraps labels around items (as shoelaces or cigars) or who bands together a specified number of articles (as envelopes, hose, or knitted garments)

ban·de·ri·lla \,bandə'rē(y)ə, ,bän-, -ēlyə\ *n* -s [Sp, dim. of *bandera* banner, of Gmc origin; akin to Goth *bandwa* sign — more at BANNER] **:** a decorated barbed dart that the banderillero thrusts into the neck or shoulder of the bull in a bullfight

ban·de·ri·lle·ro \,bandərē(l)'ye(,)rō, ,bän-\ *n* -s [Sp, fr. *banderilla*] **:** one who thrusts in the banderillas in bullfighting

ban·de·roie *or* **ban·de·rol** \'bandə,rōl\ *or* **ban·drol** \-,drōl\ *n* -s [F *banderole*, fr. It *banderuola*, dim. of *bandiera* banner, of Gmc origin; akin to Goth *bandwa* sign — more at BANNER] **1 :** a long narrow forked flag or streamer **2 :** a ribbonlike scroll bearing an inscription or a device; *specif* **:** a sculptured band often bearing an inscription and used as architectural decoration esp. in the Renaissance period **3 :** a flag about one yard square formerly displayed at funerals of great men

ban·der·snatch \'bandə(r),snach\ *n* -ES [fr. *Bandersnatch*, a fabulous animal in *Through the Looking Glass* (1872) by Lewis Carroll (Charles L. Dodgson) †1898 Eng. mathematician & writer] **:** a wildly grotesque or bizarre individual ⟨like teaching metaphysics to a ~ —F.B.Ebersole⟩

band file *n* **:** a machine tool resembling a band saw but with a cutting edge in the form of a file

bandfish \'=,=\ *n* **:** RIBBONFISH 1b

band form *n* **:** STAB CELL

ban·di·coot \'bandē,küt\ *n* -s [Telugu *pandikokku*, fr. *pandi* pig + *kokku* bandicoot] **1** *or* **bandicoot rat :** any of several very large rats of *Nesokia* and related genera of India and Ceylon that do much injury to rice fields and gardens **2 :** any of certain small active insectivorous and herbivorous marsupial mammals constituting the family Peramelidae and found in Australia, Tasmania, and New Guinea — see RABBIT BANDICOOT

Australian bandicoot

ban·di·do \ban'dē(,)dō\ *n* -s [Sp, fr. It *bandito* — more at BANDIT] *Southwest* **:** an outlaw esp. of Mexican extraction or origin

ban·die \'bandē\ *n* -s [prob. alter. of *banstickle*] *chiefly Scot* **:** STICKLEBACK

bandied *past of* BANDY

bandies *pres 3d sing of* BANDY, *pl of* BANDY

bandikai *var of* BANDAKA

bandileer *var of* BANDOLIER

banding *n* -s [fr. gerund of ²*band*] **1 :** a uniting or confederating ⟨a ~ of man and man⟩ **2 a :** narrow fabric (as tape, braid, or ribbon) that is used for bands **b :** a series or configuration of bands ⟨the ~ on a sectionalized mineral⟩ ⟨veneer ~ on furniture⟩

ban·dit \'bandət, -aan-, *usu* -əd-+V\ *n*, *pl* **bandits** \-əts\ *also* **bandit·ti** \=ˈdid·ē, -it|, |i\ *see sense 1* [It *bandito*, fr. past part. of *bandire* to banish, of Gmc origin; akin to OHG *ban* command, prohibition, prob. influenced in form by a Gmc word akin to Goth *bandwa* sign — more at BAN, BANNER] **1** *pl often* **banditti :** one who is outlawed **:** BRIGAND — often used of a member of one of the marauding bands in the mountainous districts of the Mediterranean lands **2** *pl* **bandits :** one who steals, profiteers, or kills esp. in a shameless, inglorious, or pitiless manner **:** GANGSTER ⟨~ killings⟩ ⟨a theater held up by masked ~s⟩ ⟨the war against the Communist ~s —Amry Vandenbosch⟩ **3** *pl* **bandits**, *slang* **:** one who takes unfair advantage over others usu. to procure inordinate payment or profit ⟨the taxi ~s who tie up traffic —Bennett Cerf⟩ **4** *pl* **bandits :** an enemy plane — used in the armed forces in the identification and recognition of aircraft ⟨a ~ approaching at 15,000 feet⟩

ban·dit·ry \'bandətrē, -aan-, -ri\ *n* -ES **:** the practice of marauding esp. in semiorganized groups ⟨juvenile ~⟩ ⟨civil wars and ~ are still common in Tibet —Christopher Rand⟩

band·ke·ram·ik \¦bäntkə¦rämik, *Ger* -rääm-\ *n* -s *usu cap* [G, fr. *band* band (fr. OHG *bant*) + *keramik* ceramics, fr. F *céramique* — more at BAND, CERAMICS] **:** a European Neolithic pottery with banded decoration

band knife *n* **:** a knife having the form of an endless belt running over a set of pulleys and used for splitting hides into two or more thicknesses and for cutting many thicknesses of cloth

B and L *abbr* building and loan

bandleader \'=,==\ *n* [³*band* + *leader*] **:** the director of a band (as a dance band)

band·less \'bandləs, 'baan-\ *adj* **:** being without a band

bandlet *var of* BANDELET

bandman *var of* BANDSMAN

band·mas·ter \'=,==\ *n* [³*band* + *master*] **:** a conductor of a military or concert band

band mill *n* [*band* (*saw*)] **:** a sawmill whose headsaw is a band saw

band neutrophil *n* **:** STAB CELL

band nippers *n pl but sometimes sing in constr* **:** metal pliers designed for shaping the bands on the backbone of a book

ban·do·bust \'bandə,bəst\ *var of* BUNDOBUST

bandoeng *usu cap, var of* BANDUNG

ban·dog \'ban, -aan +\ *n* -s [ME *bandogge, band-dogge*, fr. *band* + *dogge* dog] **:** a dog (as a mastiff or bloodhound) formerly kept tied or chained as a watchdog or because ferocious

bandoleer fruit \see BANDOLIER\ *n* **:** the fleshy berrylike fruit of an East Indian vine (*Zanonia indica*)

ban·do·le·ris·mo \,bandə(,)le'riz(,)mō, ,bän-\ *n* -ES [Sp, fr. *bandolero* + *-ismo* -ism] *Philippines* **:** HIGHWAY ROBBERY

ban·do·lier *or* **ban·do·leer** *also* **ban·de·lier** *or* **ban·di·leer** \¦bandə¦li(ə)r, -aan-, -liə\ *n* -s [MF *bandouliere*, fr. OSp *bandolera*, fr. *bandolero* highwayman, partisan, fr. Catal *bandoler*, fr. *bàndol* band, fr. Sp *bando*, of Gmc origin; akin to

Goth *bandwo, bandwa* sign — more at BANNER] **:** a belt worn over the shoulder and across the breast often for the suspending of some article or as a part of an official or ceremonial dress: as **a** *obs* **:** one used to carry a wallet **b :** one from which the small tubular cases containing charges for a musket were suspended **c** (1) **:** one having a series of loops for individual cartridges (2) **:** one having a series of pouches, each holding one or more cartridge clips, and now used chiefly for carrying ammunition supplementary to that in the cartridge belt

ban·do·ni·on *or* **ban·do·ne·on** \ban'dōnē,än\ *n* -s [*bandonion* fr. G, fr. Heinrich *Band*, 19th cent. German musician, its inventor + G *-on-* (as in *harmonika* harmonica, accordion, fr. E *harmonica*) + *-ion* (as in *akkordion* accordion); *bandoneon*, fr. Sp *bandoneón*, fr. G *bandonion* — more at HARMONICA, ACCORDION] **:** an accordion popular in So. America having buttons for both treble and bass notes with each bass button representing or sounding a single note not a chord

ban·dore \ban,dō(ə)r\ *or* **ban·do·ra** \ban'dōrə\ *n* -s [Sp *bandurria* or Pg *bandurra*, fr. LL *pandura, pandurium* — three-stringed lute, fr. Gk *pandoura*] **:** a bass stringed instrument that resembles a guitar with scalloped sides and that was popular in the Renaissance — called also *pandora*

band–pass filter \'ˌ=,=-\ *n* **:** FILTER 3a

bandrol *var of* BANDEROLE

bands *pl of* BAND, *pres 3d sing of* BAND

B and S *abbr* brandy and soda

band saw *n* **:** a saw in the form of an endless steel belt running over pulleys; *also* **:** a power sawing machine using this device — compare SCROLL SAW

¹band shell *n* [¹*band*] **:** any of numerous large marine snails that have thick-walled spiral shells with an expanded body whorl, constitute *Fasciolaria* and related genera, and are common in warm shallow seas — called also *banded spindle, banded whelk*

²band shell *n* [³*band*] **:** a bandstand having at the rear a sounding board shaped like a huge concave seashell

bands·man \'ban(d)zmən, 'baan-\ *also* **band·man** \-n(d)mən, -,man, -,maa(ə)n\ *n, pl* **bandsmen** *also* **bandmen :** a member of a band esp. of musicians

band spectrum *n* **:** an optical spectrum consisting of groups of narrowly spaced lines — used of a molecular spectrum

bandstand \'=,=\ *n* [³*band* + *stand*] **1 :** a stand in which a band may play an outdoor concert; *usu* **:** a roofed platform open on all sides — see BAND SHELL **2 :** a raised platform (as in a hall or restaurant) on which a band or orchestra performs

band·stra·tion \(')ban(d)z'trāshən, -n(d)'st-\ *n* -s [³*band* + orche*stration*] **:** the scoring of music for a band

bandstring \'=,=\ *n* [¹*band* (collar) + *string*] **:** one of a pair of strings for fastening a 16th century ruff or a 17th century collar

band-tailed \'=,=\ *adj* **:** marked by a band or bands upon the tail

band-tailed pigeon *also* **band-tail pigeon** \'=,=-\ *or* **bandtail** \'=,=\ *n* **:** a wild pigeon (*Columba fasciata*) of western No. America that is often confused with the now extinct passenger pigeon but is distinguished by a rounded tail with a black transverse band

band tool *n* **:** a machine tool having an endless belt (often of metal) that contains cutting elements (as for sawing, shaping, or finishing materials)

ban·dung *or* **ban·doeng** \'bän,dŭŋ, 'ban,dŭŋ, 'ban,dəŋ *sometimes* 'bän,dəŋ\ *adj, usu cap* [fr. *Bandung* or *Bandoeng*, Indonesia] **:** of or from the city of Bandung, Indonesia **:** of the kind or style prevalent in Bandung

ban·du·ra \ban'dürə\ *n* -s [Russ, fr. Pol, fr. It *pandura, pandora*, fr. LL *pandura, pandurium* three-stringed lute — more at BANDORE] **:** a Russian stringed instrument of the lute class — **ban·du·rist** \-rəst\ *n* -s

ban·dur·ria \ban'dùryə\ *n* -s [Sp — more at BANDORE] **:** a Spanish stringed instrument of the lute family

b and w *abbr, often cap B & W* **1** black and white **2** bread and water

bandwagon \'=,==\ *n* [³*band* + *wagon*] **1 :** a usu. ornate and high wagon for a band of musicians esp. in a circus parade **2 a :** a party, faction, or other element that attracts adherents by its timeliness, showmanship, vigor, or novelty ⟨the Prohibition ~ rolled victoriously through several states⟩; *specif* **:** such a party, faction, or other element held together by or capable of attracting new members through opportunity for personal gain ⟨the ~ mentality⟩ **b :** a social, cultural, or racial movement that amasses power by or as if by sheer size, momentum, or internal unity ⟨fascists certain they were on history's ~⟩ ⟨the reform ~ that swept across the country⟩ **c :** a current or fashionable taste or trend ⟨the sports car ~⟩ ⟨to beat the Mozart ~ as early as 1903 with a penetrating study of the classical concerto —Joseph Kerman⟩

band wheel *n* **1 :** BELT PULLEY **2 :** a wheel on which a band saw runs

bandwidth \'=,=\ *n* **:** the range within a band of wavelengths, frequencies, or energies; *specif* **:** the number of cycles per second expressing the difference between the limiting frequencies of a band ⟨a television channel with a ~ of 6 megacycles⟩

bandworm \'=,=\ *n* **:** TAPEWORM

¹ban·dy \'bandē, -aan-, -di\ *vb* -ED/-ING/-ES [prob. fr. MF *bander* to be tight, to bandy at tennis, fr. *bande* strip — more at BAND] *vt* **1 :** to bat (as a tennis ball) to and fro **2** *obs* **:** to toss aside (as rumors) **:** drive or throw away **:** REJECT ⟨~ a suitor⟩ **3 a :** to toss from side to side or from one to another in a rough or inappropriate manner ⟨a firearm is no toy to be *bandied* about⟩ **:** treat carelessly or highhandedly ⟨so that's the way he *bandies* me about, I'll teach him —Anne Green⟩ **b :** EXCHANGE ⟨~ blows⟩ ⟨~ compliments⟩; *esp* **:** to exchange (words) petulantly, heatedly, or argumentatively ⟨the senator never deigned to ~ words with members of the opposition⟩ **c :** to discuss lightly or banteringly esp. among a number of people ⟨the ~*ing* of statistics⟩ **:** use (as in writing or conversation) in a glib, facile, or offhand manner — often used with *about* ⟨I beg the privilege of ~*ing* generalizations and theories —E.R.Bentley⟩ **4** *archaic* **:** to band together **:** UNITE ~ *vi* **1** *obs* **:** CONTEND, STRIVE — usu. used with *with* **2** *archaic* **:** UNITE

²bandy \"\ *n* -ES [perh. fr. MF *bandé*, past part. of *bander*] **1** *obs* **:** an old game played with a ball and racket; *also* **:** a stroke or return in this game **2 :** a game similar to and reputedly the prototype of hockey; *also* **:** the bent club with which the ball is struck in this game

³bandy \"\ *adj* [prob. fr. ²*bandy* (hockey stick)] **1** *of legs* **:** BOWED **2 :** BOWLEGGED ⟨a case of china . . . stood beyond the ~ table —Dylan Thomas⟩

⁴bandy \", 'bə-\ *n* -ES [Kanarese-Telugu *baṇḍi*] **:** a carriage or cart used in India; *esp* **:** one drawn by bullocks

ban·dy-ban·dy \'bandē,bandē\ *n* [native name in Australia] **:** a common poisonous ringed snake (*Furina annulata*) of Australia with a mouth so small as to be incapable of biting a man

bandy-leg \'==,=\ *n* [³*bandy*] **1 :** BOWLEG **2 :** a cabriole furniture leg

ban·dy-legged \'==,leg(ə)d\ *adj* **:** BOW-LEGGED

ban·dy·lite \'bandē,līt\ *n* -s [after Mark C. *Bandy*, 20th cent. mining engineer who collected it + E *-lite*] **:** a mineral $Cu_2B_2O_4Cl_2.4H_2O$ consisting of a rare hydrous borate and chloride found near Calama, Chile

ban·dy·man \'bandēmən, 'bə-\ *n, pl* **bandymen** [⁴*bandy* + *man*] *India* **:** a driver of a bandy

¹bane \'bān\ *n* -s [ME, fr. OE *bana*; akin to OE *benn* wound, OHG *bano* death, destruction, ON *ben* wound, *bani* slayer, Goth *banja* wound, Av *banta* ill] **1 a** *obs* **:** one that causes death **:** MURDERER, SLAYER **b :** POISON ⟨was there ~ in that tea you did tell Tivvy to give Mother —Mary Webb⟩ — see HENBANE, RATSBANE **c** (1) **:** DEATH, DESTRUCTION ⟨drink will be the ~ of him⟩ ⟨money, thou ~ of bliss, and source of woe —George Herbert⟩ ⟨the cup of deception spiced and tempered to their ~ —John Milton⟩ (2) **:** HARM, WOE ⟨from deepest ~ will he bring her back to highest blessing —George Meredith⟩ **2 a :** any pernicious or fatal element, feature, or flaw **:** CURSE ⟨the aristocratic tradition embedded in British higher education is its ~ —Bertrand Russell⟩ ⟨used cars have been called the ~ of the automobile industry —C.W.Phelps⟩ ⟨this rage for novelty is the ~ of literature —T.L.Peacock⟩ **b :** a person who makes another completely miserable ⟨the ~ of my existence⟩ **:** one that perversely or persistently spoils or thwarts ⟨the pitcher was the ~ of right-handed batters⟩ **syn** see POISON

²bane \"\ *vb* -ED/-ING/-S *vt, obs* **:** to kill esp. with poison ~ *vi, archaic* **:** to do injury **:** HARM

³bane \"\ *n* -s [ME (northern dial.) *ban*, fr. OE *bān* — more at BONE] *chiefly Scot* **:** BONE

baneberry \'=,==\ *n* [*bane* (poison) + *berry*] **1 :** the acrid poisonous berry of any plant of the genus *Actaea* **2 :** a plant of the genus *Actaea*

bane·ful \'bānfəl\ *adj* [¹*bane* + *-ful*] **1** *archaic* **:** having poisonous qualities **:** NOXIOUS **2 :** creating destruction, woe, or ruin **:** RUINOUS, HARMFUL ⟨~ effects⟩ ⟨constantly influencing our foreign policy in a ~ way —S.F.Bemis⟩ **3 :** perversely productive of discomfort or misery ⟨then came an east wind, ~ to me at all times —William Cowper⟩ ⟨her love for him is a possessive and ~ love —J.D.Scott b.1915⟩ ⟨students undergoing three hours of ~ examinations⟩ **4 :** darkly or grimly threatening or foreboding **:** OMINOUS ⟨picturing their country in more lurid and ~ lights —Robert Brennan⟩ ⟨the story, which has been acquiring a ~ intensity —Malcolm Cowley⟩ **syn** see PERNICIOUS

bane·ful·ly \-fəlē, -li\ *adv* **:** in a baneful manner **:** with a baneful effect

banes *obs var of* BANNS

banewort \'=,=\ *n* [¹*bane* + *wort*] **1 :** BELLADONNA 1 **2** *Brit* **:** LESSER SPEARWORT

banff·shire \'bam(p)f,shi(ə)r, -,shər\ *or* **banff** \-f\ *adj, usu cap* [fr. *Banffshire* or *Banff*, Scotland] **:** of or from the county of Banff, Scotland **:** of the kind or style prevalent in Banff

¹bang \'baŋ, -aiŋ\ *vb* -ED/-ING/-S [prob. of Scand origin; akin to Icel *banga* to hammer, OSw *banga*; prob. of imit. origin like ON *bang* hammering, MHG *bungen* to drum] *vt* **1** *archaic* **:** to beat soundly (as with a cudgel) **:** THRASH **2 :** to strike against **:** BUMP ⟨fall and ~ one's knee⟩ **3 :** to knock (an object) a distance with noisy vigor ⟨~*ed* a homer over the center-field bleachers⟩ **4 a :** to thrust, put, push, or force vigorously often with a sharp noise ⟨~ a book down⟩ ⟨~ a receiver up⟩ ⟨the driver ~*ed* in the clutch —G.A.Wagner⟩ **b :** to copulate with — usu. considered vulgar **5 :** to produce a resounding report or series of reports by striking ⟨~ a drum⟩ ⟨don't ~ the door⟩ ⟨~ a gavel⟩ **6 a :** to treat roughly or carelessly ⟨packages badly ~*ed* around by the post office⟩ **:** mistreat so as to leave dents, bruises, or other signs of damage ⟨~ furniture⟩ **b :** to cause extensive damage to **:** RUIN — used with *up* ⟨~*ed* up his car⟩ **7** *chiefly dial* **:** BEAT, SURPASS, OUTDO ⟨don't it just ~ anything you ever heard of —Mark Twain⟩ ~ *vi* **1 a :** to strike with a sharp noise ⟨the falling chair ~*ed* against the wall⟩ ⟨the door ~*ed* shut⟩ **b :** to strike repeatedly ⟨buckles of his helmet straps ~*ing* against his cheeks —K.M. Dodson⟩ **:** beat or thump with a resounding series of blows ⟨~ on a door⟩ **2 :** to produce a sharp often metallic explosive or percussive noise or series of such noises ⟨drums thumped, crackers ~*ed*, horns screamed —John Blofeld⟩ ⟨a brass band ~*ing* away on the village green⟩ **3 a :** to move or proceed rapidly or noisily **:** DASH, RUSH ⟨we grab our coats and ~ down the stairs⟩ ⟨a train ~*ing* along down the valley⟩ **b :** to go from one thing to another **:** frequent a place without definite or sustained purpose — used with *about* or *around* ⟨in 1923, when I was ~*ing* around Madison Avenue —William Benton⟩ **4 :** to shoot esp. in a sporadic or desultory manner — usu. used with *away* ⟨the town got out its shotguns . . . and ~*ed* away at the flock going over —Paul Annixter⟩

²bang \"\ *n* -s [prob. of Scand origin, akin to ON *bang* hammering] **1 :** a resounding blow **:** THUMP, WHACK ⟨gave the ball a terrific ~⟩ ⟨a ~ on the head⟩ **2 a :** a sudden loud noise ⟨closed the door with a ~⟩ ⟨the ~ of a rifle⟩ — often used interjectionally ⟨saw flashes and heard an automatic go ~ ~ —Erle Stanley Gardner⟩ **b :** earsplitting noise often of a metallic quality ⟨the deafening clang and ~ of a . . . boiler factory —*Lamp*⟩ ⟨they played with a virile blare and ~ —S.H. Adams⟩ **3 :** sudden emotional pleasure **:** THRILL ⟨the kind that will try anything once — for the ~ of it —J.P.Marquand⟩ — often used with *get* or *give* ⟨I get a ~ out of all this —W.H. Whyte⟩ ⟨Jean looked very beautiful and it gave him a ~ to be with her —Frederic Wakeman⟩ **4 a :** a sudden or abrupt burst of showiness, brilliancy, or éclat ⟨you've got to have a press campaign. Not a big one, necessarily, after the first big ~ —Dorothy Sayers⟩ **b :** sudden effectiveness or success ⟨went over with a ~⟩ **5 a :** emotional or physical vitality ⟨no ~ left in him⟩ **b :** a quick burst of energy or activity ⟨start off with a ~⟩ **:** sudden fervor ⟨fell for her with a ~⟩

³bang \"\ *vt* -ED/-ING/-S **1 :** to cut (the hair) in a bang **2 :** to cut (the hair of an animal) like a bang ⟨~ a horse's tail⟩

⁴bang \"\ *adv* **:** RIGHT, DIRECTLY, EXACTLY ⟨~ on time⟩ ⟨married ~ in the middle of the war⟩ ⟨ran ~ up against more trouble⟩ ⟨open spaces . . . ~ on top of old colliery workings —Sam Pollock⟩

⁵bang \"\ *n* -s [prob. back-formation fr. *bangtail* short tail — more at BANGTAIL] **:** the front hair or a section of it cut short and worn straight or curled over the forehead — usu. used in pl.

A bang

⁶bang \"\ *n* -s [origin unknown] **1 :** a common sardine (*Sardinella anchovia*) of the western Atlantic esp. abundant in the Caribbean area **2 :** ALEWIFE

⁷bang \"\ *var of* BHANG

⁸bang \"\ *n* -s *usu cap* [Skt *Vaṅga* Bengal] **1 :** an ancient people of Bengal, India, differing racially and culturally from the Aryans whose literature refers to them disdainfully **2 :** a member of the Bang people

ban·ga \'bäŋ'ä\ *n* -s [Tag] **:** a large spherical baked-clay water jar of the Philippines

bang·al·ay \baŋ'alē\ *n* -s [native name in Australia] **:** BASTARD MAHOGANY 1a(1)

ban·ga·lore \'baŋgə,lō(ə)r\ *adj, usu cap* [fr. *Bangalore*, India] **:** of or from the city of Bangalore, India **:** of the kind or style prevalent in Bangalore

bangalore torpedo \"\ *also* **bangalore** \'==,=, ,=='=\ *n* -s [fr. *Bangalore*, city in India] **:** a metal tube containing explosives and a firing mechanism often designed so that it can be joined to other such tubes and used to cut wire entanglements and detonate buried mines by being exploded flat on the ground

ban·ga·low palm *also* **bangalow** \'baŋgə,lō\ *n* -s [native name in Australia] **:** either of two Australian palms (*Auchontophoenix alexandrae* and *A. cunninghamii*) cultivated for their tall erect form and pinnate foliage and having a terminal bud that is sometimes used as food

ban·gash \'ban,gash\ *n, pl* **bangash** *or* **bangashes** *usu cap* **1 :** a Pathan people in the Punjab **2 :** a member of the Bangash people

bang away *vi* **1 :** to work with determined effort ⟨students *banging away* on their homework⟩ **2 :** to attack esp. in an indirect, persistent, hounding way — used with *at* ⟨police are going to keep *banging away* at you —Erle Stanley Gardner⟩

bang–bang \'=,=\ *n* **:** SHOOTING; *broadly* **:** violent action ⟨plenty of *bang-bang* in that movie⟩

bangboard \'=,=\ *n* [¹*bang* + *board*] **1 :** an extra sideboard mounted above the far sideboard of a wagon from which the ears of corn tossed by a husker rebound into the wagon **2 :** a tennis practice board usu. of plywood with a line marked at the height of a net

bange \'banj\ *vi* **banged; banged; bangeing; banges** [origin unknown] *NewEng* **:** to lounge about **:** LOAF

ban·ghy \'baŋgē\ *n* -ES [Hindi *bahaṅgī*] *India* **:** a shoulder yoke for carrying loads; *also* **:** the yoke with its pair of suspended boxes or baskets

bang·i·a·ce·ae \,banjē'āsē,ē\ *n pl, cap* [NL, fr. *Bangia*, type genus (fr. Hoffman *Bang*, 19th cent. Dan. botanist + NL *-ia*) + *-aceae*] **:** a family of chiefly marine red algae (order Bangiales) having a simple unbranched mostly thin or membranaceous thallus with a single stellate axile chromatophore in each cell and no pits in the cell walls — **bang·i·a·ceous** \'==;=shəs\ *adj*

bang·i·a·les \,baŋē'ā(,)lēz\ *n pl, cap* [NL, fr. *Bangia* + *-ales*] **:** an order of red algae usu. considered coextensive with the subclass Bangioideae

bang·ing \'baŋiŋ, ŋēŋ\ *adj* [fr. pres. part. of ¹*bang*] **:** HUGE, WHOPPING ⟨a ~ lie⟩

bang·i·oi·de·ae \,baŋē'óidē,ē\ *n pl, cap* [NL, fr. *Bangia* genus of algae + *-oideae* — more at BANGIACEAE] **:** a subclass of Rhodophyceae comprising red algae that usu. lack a growing point, undergo diffuse growth, and have a filamentous or foliose and often unbranched thallus — compare FLORIDEAE

bangka *var of* BANCA

bang·kal \bäŋ·'käl\ *n* -s [Bisayan *baṅkal*] **:** BANCAL

¹bang·kok \'baŋ,käk, -aiŋ- -, =\'=\ *adj, usu cap* [fr. *Bangkok*, Thailand] **:** of or from Bangkok, the capital of Thailand **:** of the kind or style prevalent in Bangkok

²bangkok \"\ *n* -s **1 :** a fine buntal **2 :** a hat made of bangkok

¹bang·le \'baŋəl\ *vt* -ED/-ING/-S [origin unknown] *now dial Eng* **:** to fritter away **:** WASTE ⟨~ away a fortune⟩

²ban·gle \'baŋgəl, -aiŋ-\ *n* -s [Hindi *baṅgṛī, baṅgrī, baṅglī*] **1 :** a stiff usu. ornamental bracelet or anklet slipped or clasped on **2 :** something that hangs loosely; *esp* **:** an ornamental disk (as on a bracelet, necklace, tambourine)

ban·go \'baŋ(,)gō\ *or* **bango reed** *n* -s [native name in East Africa] **:** an East African grass (*Phragmites mauritianus*) used in thatching buildings

bang off *vi, of a loom* **:** to stop normal operation due to the failure of the shuttle to enter the box

ban·gón \baŋ'gōn\ *n, pl* **bangón** *or* **bangóns** *usu cap* [Tag] **1 :** a pagan people inhabiting central Mindoro, Philippines **2 :** a member of the Bangón people

ban·gor ladder *also* **bangor** \'baŋ,gō(ə)r, -aiŋ-, -,gō(ə),-,gə(r)\ *n, usu cap B* [fr. *Bangor*, Maine, where it was invented] **:** a long extension ladder controlled by means of poles and used in fire fighting

bang·os \'bäŋōs\ *n, pl* **bangos** [Tag] *Philippines* **:** MILKFISH

bang out *vt* **:** to produce in a hurried manner ⟨a typist *banging out* copy⟩ ⟨authors continually are being importuned to *bang out* a brief article, speech, or foreword —Bennett Cerf⟩

bangs *pres 3d sing of* BANG, *pl of* BANG

bang's disease *also* **bang's** \'baŋz-, -aiŋz-\ *n, usu cap B* [after Bernhard L.F. *Bang* †1932 Dan. veterinarian] **:** BRUCELLOSIS; *specif* **:** contagious abortion of cattle

bangsring *var of* BANXRING

bang·ster \'baŋztər, -ŋ(k)st-\ *n* -s [¹*bang* + *-ster*] **1** *Scot* **:** BULLY, ROUGHNECK **2** *Scot* **:** WINNER, VICTOR

bangtail \'=,=\ *n* [fr. *bangtail* short tail, prob. fr. ¹*bang* + *tail*] **1 a :** RACEHORSE **b :** a wild horse; *esp* **:** one with a short stubby tail **2** *Austral* **:** any bovine that has had its tail banged to indicate that it has been counted during a muster and to prevent the possibility of recounting it

bangtail muster *n* [*bangtail* short tail; fr. the practice of cutting the tuft at the end of the tail straight across as the animal is counted] *Austral* **:** a roundup of cattle for counting them

ban·gui \'bäŋ(,)gē\ *adj, usu cap* [fr. *Bangui*, Central African Republic] **:** of or from Bangui, capital of the Central African Republic **:** of the kind or style prevalent in Bangui

¹bang-up \'=,=\ *adj* [¹*bang*] **:** FIRST-RATE, EXCELLENT ⟨a *bang-up* job⟩

²bang-up \"\ *n* -s [origin unknown] **:** a heavy overcoat

ban·gy \'baŋgē\ *var of* BANGHY

bani *pl of* BAN

bania *or* **banian** *var of* BANYAN

ba·nig \bä'nēg\ *n* -s [Tag *banig*] *Philippines* **:** PETATE

baning *pres part of* BANE

ban·ish \'banish, -ēsh, *in pres part* -əsh\ *vt* -ED/-ING/-ES [ME *banishen*, fr. *baniss-*, stem of MF *banir*, of Gmc origin; akin to OHG *ban* command, prohibition — more at BAN] **1 a :** to require (a person) by authority to leave esp. his own country or the country in which he is staying ⟨political foes ~*ed* by the dictator⟩ **b :** to forbid (a person) to frequent a certain area, group, or class ⟨~ from court⟩ ⟨~ newsmen from the captured city⟩ **c :** to send (a person) away often in a summary manner **:** DISMISS ⟨stood confronting her visitor as though to ~ her from the house —Robert Grant †1940⟩ **2 a :** to remove esp. from a significant or dominant position **:** DEPOSE ⟨genetic theories . . . are to be ~*ed* from Russian laboratories —*Collier's Yr. Bk.*⟩ ⟨the . . . towboat is fighting the railroad that ~*ed* the packet boat —Murray Schumach⟩ **b :** to do away with or cast out esp. in a retributive, truculent, or vindictive manner ⟨the club signified its displeasure by ~*ing* his portrait from the library — *Amer. Guide Series: N.Y. City*⟩ ⟨the gray squirrels will entirely ~ the old red ones—Lord Dunsany⟩ **3 :** to clear away **:** DISSIPATE, DISPEL ⟨a smudge to ~ mosquitoes —B.A.Williams⟩ ⟨literacy . . . will ~ the desperation on which communism feeds —Jerome Ellison⟩ ⟨anesthesia has done much to ~ the fear of operations⟩

syn BANISH, EXILE, EXPATRIATE, OSTRACIZE, DEPORT, TRANSPORT, and EXTRADITE mean, in common, to remove by force or authority from a country, state, or sovereignty. To BANISH is usu. to compel, usu. by public edict or sentence, to leave and stay out of a country or section, although not necessarily one's own ⟨the Reverend John Wheelwright, who had been *banished* from the Massachusetts Bay Colony —*Amer. Guide Series: N.H.*⟩ ⟨the Newtonian scheme of the universe does not *banish* God from the universe —*Times Lit. Supp.*⟩ ⟨Plato wished to *banish* poetry utterly from the Republic because it could be intoxicating to its victims —Max Lerner & Edwin Mims⟩ To EXILE is usu. to banish a person from his own country or section or oneself voluntarily from one's own country ⟨criminals sent to Siberia for political offenses⟩ ⟨many American writers *exiled* themselves in Paris⟩ ⟨the fallen champion chose to *exile* himself to his southern ranch —*Time*⟩ To EXPATRIATE implies not only exile but often a loss of citizenship in one's country, often voluntarily imposed by naturalization in another country ⟨a man all too willing to be *expatriated*⟩ ⟨*expatriate* oneself to England for emotional reasons for a number of years⟩ To OSTRACIZE is to exclude by common consent from recognition or acceptance by society ⟨a person *ostracized* for religious reasons⟩ ⟨the dangers inherent in *ostracizing* from public service men of eminence —Kimmis Hendrick⟩ ⟨after the Normans conquered England in 1066, Anglo-Saxon was *ostracized* from the schools⟩ To DEPORT is to banish (a person) from a country of which he is not a citizen, often to the country from which he came ⟨aiding the Chinese government to *deport* to their homeland the remnants of Japanese forces —*Current Biog.*⟩ ⟨an alien *deported* because of illegal entry into the country⟩ To TRANSPORT, in this sense, is to banish a person convicted of crime to a penal colony or a place regarded as like one ⟨English convicts *transported* to Australia⟩ To EXTRADITE is to deliver over (a person, usu. an alleged criminal) to authorities of another jurisdiction ⟨a criminal *extradited* by Texas at the request of Massachusetts for a confessed murder in Massachusetts⟩

ban·ish·ment \-mənt\ *n* -s **1 a :** legal expulsion from a country ⟨in 1940 his sentence was changed to ~ —*Current Biog.*⟩ **b :** exclusion or dismissal, self-imposed or prescribed by some authority, esp. from a particular area, group, or class ⟨his ~ from amateur sports⟩ ⟨~ from good society⟩ **2 :** a casting off **:** DISCARDING ⟨the ~ of the textbook from the classroom —Theodore Collier⟩

ban·is·ter *also* **ban·nis·ter** \'banəstə(r)\ *n* -s [alter. of *baluster*] **1 :** a slender vertical post sometimes having a turned or molded outline; *specif* **:** one of the upright supports of a handrail alongside a staircase — compare BALUSTER **2** *often pl but sing or pl in constr* **a :** a handrail (as of a staircase) and its supporting posts **b :** the handrail esp. of a staircase ⟨Alice went downstairs, walking with one hand on the ~*s* —Audrey Barker⟩ **3 :** one of several upright members, typically split turnings, that support the crest rail of a chair back

ba·ni·va *also* **ba·ni·wa** \bə'nēvə\ *n, pl* **baniva** *or* **banivas** *usu cap* [Sp *baniva*, of AmerInd origin] **1 a :** an Arawakan people of the upper Orinoco and Rio Negro, Venezuela and Colombia **b :** a member of such people **2 :** the language of the Baniva people

baniya *var of* BANYAN

ban·jo \'ban(,)jō, -aan-, *in S often* -jə\ *n, pl* **banjos** *also* **banjoes** [prob. of African origin; akin to Kimbundu *mbanza*, a similar stringed instrument] **1 a :** a musical instrument of the guitar class with a long narrow fretted neck and small drumlike body and usu. five strings plucked or strummed

banjo 1b

with the fingers **b** : a banjo with a larger body and four wire strings played usu. with a pick — called also *tenor banjo* **2** : BANJO SIGNAL **3** : something bearing some resemblance to a banjo in shape: as **a** : a miner's shovel **b** : a working device for the placer mining of tin **c** : a transmission housing of a certain design

banjo clock *n* : a shelf or wall pendulum clock whose shape suggests a banjo; *esp* : such a clock designed by Simon Willard of Roxbury, Mass. and patented by him in 1802

a banjo clock

banjo hit *n* : BLOOPER 3b

ban·jo·ist \-,jōəst, -,jəwə̇-\ *n* -s : a banjo player

ban·jo·rine \,banjə¦rēn\ *n* -s [*banjo* + *-rine* (as in *tambourine*)] : a banjo with a short neck, tuned a fourth higher than the common banjo

banjo signal *n* : a former railroad-signal apparatus having a circular box with a glass window in which a red disk appeared as the danger signal

ban·jo·uku·le·le \¦=(,)= +\ *also* **ban·jo-uke** \"+\ *n* : a ukulele with a drumlike body

[1]**bank** \'baŋk, -aiŋk\ *n* -s [ME *banke*, prob. of Scand origin; akin to ON *bakki* ridge, bank; akin to OE *benc* bench — more at BENCH] **1** : a mound, pile, or ridge raised by natural processes or artificial means above the surrounding level: **a** *now dial Eng* : ELEVATION, HILL **b** *obs* : EARTHWORK **c** : something piled or accumulated in the form of a mound and often having a broad or long base and flat top ⟨a ~ of snow⟩; *specif* : a piled-up mass of cloud, fog, or mist often extending upward from the horizon **d** : an underwater elevation of mud, gravel, or sand; *specif* : an undersea elevation rising esp. from the continental shelf and usu. with a broad flat top ⟨the cod ~s off Norway —Irwin Shaw⟩ — compare REEF, SEAMOUNT, SHOAL **2 a** : the margin of a watercourse : the rising ground bordering a lake, river, or sea or forming the edge of a cut or other hollow **b** *obs* : SEACOAST **3 a** : a steep acclivity (as the side of a hill, pile, or mound) : GRADE, SLOPE **b** : the lateral inward tilt of a vehicle or other moving object when taking a curve ⟨the bomber crossed the target area in a sharp ~⟩ : the lateral inward tip of a surface (as a road or track) along a curve ⟨the engineers hadn't given the road enough ~⟩ **4** : a protective or cushioning rim or piece: as **a** (1) : the slightly elevated ground surrounding a bowling green on the outer side of the ditch (2) : CUSHION 3e **b** : a ramp of earth (as that leading to the upper story of some bank barns) **c** : BANKING PIN **5 a** *Brit* : the place in a bog where peat is dug **b** (1) : the face of coal being worked (2) : a deposit of ore or coal worked by excavations above water level (3) : the ground at the top of a shaft ⟨the cost of an ore on the ~⟩

[2]**bank** \"\ *vb* -ED/-ING/-S *vt* **1** : to raise a bank about : enclose, protect, or fortify with a bank : EMBANK: as **a** : to cover (as a fire) with fresh fuel or other material, usu. adjusting the draft to slow the rate of burning and maintain fire for a prolonged period — often used with *up* **b** : to heap earth along the row of (a growing crop, as of celery) to protect or blanch : HILL, EARTH **c** : to build (a railway curve) with the outer rail elevated above the inner rail or to build (a curve in a road or track) with the roadbed or track inclined laterally upward from the inside edge to the outside edge so as to prevent a fast-moving vehicle or runner from being carried off the track or toppled over by centrifugal force in rounding the curve ⟨it is necessary to ~ the curves very steeply for bobsled racing⟩ **2** *obs* : to pass by the banks of : SKIRT **3** : to heap (as sand) or pile (as logs) in a bank ⟨lumberjacks . . . ~ed the cut timber on rollways to await the spring drives —*Amer. Guide Series: Mich.*⟩ — often used with *up* ⟨there is ~ed up a great mass of purchasing power —Clement Atlee⟩ **4 a** : to drive (the cue ball in billiards) into a cushion before striking an object ball **b** (1) : to drive (an object ball in pool) into a cushion in an attempt to pocket or to place advantageously on the rebound (2) : to drive (a cue ball in pool) into a cushion to hit an object ball on the rebound or to play a safe shot **5** : to form or group in a tier ⟨~ electric lights⟩ ~ *vi* **1** : to rise in or form a bank : lie in banks (as of clouds) — often used with *up* ⟨in the rainy season the clouds would ~ up about midday, and showers fall with true tropical violence —William Beebe⟩ **2** : to swing so far as to strike against a banking pin — used of the lever of a lever escapement in a watch or clock **3** : to fish on the banks of Newfoundland **4 a** (1) : to incline an airplane laterally (2) *of an airplane* : to incline laterally ⟨torpedo planes . . . darting in to attack, then ~ing off —K.M.Dodson⟩ **b** : to execute a movement like that of an airplane banking ⟨comets . . . appear without warning, race in through the planets, ~ sharply around the sun, then head out toward the stars —A.C. Clarke⟩ — used esp. of birds in flight and fishes swimming

[3]**bank** \"\ *n* -s [ME *banck*, fr. OF *banc*, of Gmc origin; akin to OHG *bank* bench — more at BENCH] **1 a** *obs* : the bench or seat on which the judges of a court of law sit **b** : a bench upon which the rowers of a galley sit **2** : a group or series of objects arranged near together in a row or a tier: as **a** : a tier of oars esp. of an ancient galley **b** : a tier of keys belonging to a keyboard **c** : a set of two or more elevators ⟨eighteen passenger elevators, in three ~s of six —*New Yorker*⟩ **3 a** *archaic* : a table for holding unprinted and printed sheets **b** : a slant-topped stand or sometimes a flat-topped table on which type matter in galleys is corrected and prepared for makeup **4** : one of the horizontal divisions of a headline; *esp* : a secondary or lower division — compare [1]DECK 6 **5** : the backboard to which a basketball hoop is attached — **in bank** *adv, law* : in full court — compare BANC

[4]**bank** \"\ *n* -s [ME, fr. MF or OIt; MF *banque*, fr. OIt *banca*, lit., bench, of Gmc origin; akin to OHG *bank* bench] **1 a** (1) *obs* : the table, counter, or place of business of a money-changer (2) : an establishment for the custody, loan, exchange, or issue of money, for the extension of credit, and for facilitating the transmission of funds by drafts or bills of exchange; *also* : an institution incorporated for performing one or more of such functions **b** : GAMBLING HOUSE **2 a** : the stockholders or directors of a bank acting in their corporate capacity **b** : a person or persons conducting a gambling house or game; *specif* : DEALER **3** : a supply of something useful or valuable held in reserve: as **a** (1) *obs* : a sum of money (2) : the sum of money in certain gambling games (as chemin de fer) that is deposited or stated by the dealer as a fund from which to pay his losses **b** (1) : the whole supply of chips available for purchase and use by players in a gambling game (as poker) (2) : a fund of pieces belonging to a game (as dominoes) from which the players are allowed to draw **c** : an excess of logs cut or skidded during a given period and held as a reserve to make up deficiencies in daily quotas **4** : a place where something useful or valuable is held available: as **a** : LANDING 2b **b** : a small container for holding coins to be accumulated as savings or for a special purpose — see PIGGY BANK **c** : a depot for the collection and storage of a biological product of human origin for medical use ⟨a semen ~⟩ ⟨a nerve ~⟩ ⟨bone ~⟩ — **in the bank** *adv (or adj), Brit* : in debt

[5]**bank** \"\ *vb* -ED/-ING/-S *vi* **1 a** : to keep a bank **b** : to carry out the business of banking **2 a** : to deposit money in a bank ⟨a trip into town to shop and ~⟩ **b** : to have an account with a bank or banker ⟨the company ~s at the First National⟩ ~ *vt* **1** : to deposit in a bank ⟨~ your salary⟩ **2** : to deposit (as blood, plasma, bone) for storage in a bank (sense 4c) ⟨whole blood . . . could be ~ed indefinitely —*Time*⟩ **3** : to act as banker for (as a gambling game) **4** : FINANCE ⟨members who help ~ political campaigns —*New Republic*⟩ — **bank on** *or* **bank upon** : to expect with confidence or assurance : depend upon : rely on ⟨*bank on* a person's help⟩ ⟨Hitler . . . *banked on* the moral collapse of the Western Powers —*Times Lit. Supp.*⟩ **syn** see RELY

banka *var of* BANCA

bank·a·ble \'baŋkəbəl, -aiŋ-\ *adj* [[5]*bank* + *-able*] : acceptable to or at a bank ⟨a ~ risk⟩ ⟨~ currency⟩ ⟨the bank did not find . . . the proposed loan . . . and the project was abandoned —*N.Y.Times*⟩

bank acceptance *n* [[4]*bank*] : a draft drawn on and accepted by a bank or banker

bank account *n* [[4]*bank*] : an account with a bank created by the deposit of money or its equivalent and subject to withdrawal of money (as by check or passbook) ⟨thought it wise to put his savings in a *bank account*⟩

bank and turn indicator *n* [[1]*bank*] : TURN AND BANK INDICATOR

bank annuities *n pl* [[4]*bank*] : CONSOLS

bank balance *n* [[4]*bank*] **1** : the amount credited to a depositor of a bank as of a particular time **2** : a balance against or in favor of a bank at a financial clearinghouse ⟨an increasingly substantial *bank balance*⟩

bank barn *n* [[1]*bank*] : a two-story barn, typical of northern and central parts of No. America, built into a slope of earth that provides an outside entrance into the second story on one side, the lower story being enterable from the other side

bank beaver *n* [[1]*bank*] **1** : OTTER **2** : a beaver that inhabits burrows in stream banks instead of making a house and dam

bank bill *n* [[4]*bank*] **1** : an obsolete Bank of England note — called also *sealed bank bill* **2** : BANK NOTE 1

bankbook \'=,=\ *n* [[4]*bank* + *book*] : the depositor's book in which a bank enters his deposits and withdrawals — called also *passbook*

bank call *n* [[4]*bank*] : a periodic demand made usu. quarterly by the Comptroller of Currency of the U.S. upon national banks and by the heads of the banking departments of the several states upon state banks and trust companies for sworn detailed statements showing the condition of the banks as of a definite date

bank check *n* [[4]*bank*] : an order by a depositor on a commercial bank to pay a specified sum on demand to a designated payee or, when the check is endorsed by the payee, to others

bank commissioner *n* [[4]*bank*] : an appointed official in charge of supervising banks; *esp* : a state superintendent of banks

bank craps *n* [[4]*bank*] : the game of craps played in gambling houses where every bet made against the house is under special rules established by the house

bank debit *n* [[4]*bank*] : the charge against a bank-deposit account resulting from the drawing of checks or from cash withdrawals

bank deposit *n* [[4]*bank*] : any funds credited to a depositor's account by a bank

bank deposit insurance *n* : the insurance of deposit accounts up to $10,000 (formerly up to $5000) in banks in the U.S. that belong to the Federal Deposit Insurance Corporation

bank discount *n* [[4]*bank*] : the interest discounted in advance on a note and computed on the face value of the note ⟨the *bank discount* on $1000 for one year at 5% is $50⟩ — compare ARITHMETICAL DISCOUNT

bank draft *n* [[4]*bank*] : a demand draft drawn by one bank upon funds to its account in another bank

banked *adj* [fr. past part. of [2]*bank*] **1** : arranged in tiers ⟨~ microphones⟩ ⟨~ windows⟩ **2** : laterally tipped or made while laterally tipped esp. inward along or while taking a curve ⟨a ~ railroad track⟩ ⟨the ~ glide of an airplane⟩ **3 a** : piled up into or as if into a bank ⟨~ earth⟩ ⟨~ clouds⟩ **b** : protected by a bank ⟨~ cellar windows⟩ ⟨guns ~ in concrete⟩

bank engine *n* [[1]*bank* (slope)] *Brit* : a helper locomotive used to assist heavy trains over steep grades — called also *banker*

[1]**ban·ker** \'baŋkə(r), -aiŋ-\ *n* -s [ME, fr. OF *banquier*, fr. *banc* bench — more at BANK] *archaic* : a covering (as of tapestry) for a bench or chair

[2]**bank·er** \"\ *n* -s [MF *banquier*, fr. *banque* bench, table, bank + *-ier* -er — more at BANK] **1** : one who engages in the business of commercial or investment banking **2 a** : the player who keeps, sells, and redeems the supply of chips used in a game — compare [4]BANK 3b(1) **b** : the person who agrees to cover the bets of all players up to a certain limit established as the bank **c** : a dealer (as in blackjack) or a gambling house or its representative against whom all bets must be placed **d** : BANKER AND BROKER

[3]**bank·er** \"\ *n* -s [[1]*bank* + *-er*] **1** : a man or a vessel employed in the cod fishery on the banks of Newfoundland **2** *Austral* : a river running full to the top of its banks

[4]**bank·er** \"\ *n* -s [[3]*bank* + *-er*] : a bench of stone or wood or a support on which a sculptor, mason, or bricklayer shapes or gauges his material

[5]**bank·er** \"\ *n* -s [[1]*bank* + *-er*] : BANK ENGINE

banker and broker *n* [[2]*banker*] : any of various card games in which two or more opposing players lift off a packet from the deck and show the card at the bottom of the packet, the highest-ranking card so shown determining the winner

banker-mark \'=,=\ *n* [[4]*banker*] : a mark cut by the stonecutter on dressed stones in medieval times to identify the person preparing the stone — called also *mason's mark*

banker mason *n* [[4]*banker*] : a workman who does by hand the final preparation work on stone-masonry blocks

banker's acceptance *n* [[2]*banker*] : BANK ACCEPTANCE

banker's bank *n* [[2]*banker*] : a bank that deals only with other banks; *specif* : a central bank (as a U.S. Federal Reserve bank or the Bank of England)

banker's bill *n* [[2]*banker*] : a bill of exchange drawn by a bank on a foreign bank

bankers' blanket bond *n* [[2]*banker*] : insurance sold to financial institutions covering theft by employees and losses due to burglary, robbery, or forgery — compare FIDELITY BOND

banker's check *n* [[2]*banker*] : TRAVELER'S CHECK

banker's draft *n* [[2]*banker*] : a check or bill drawn by one bank against balances deposited with another

ban·ket \'ban,ket\ *n* -s [Afrik, lit., a kind of confectionery, banquet, fr. MD, banquet, fr. MF *banquet* — more at BANQUET] : the auriferous conglomerate rock of the Transvaal

bank examiner *n* [[4]*bank*] : a federal or state official empowered to examine the records and affairs of a bank

bank fish *n* [[1]*bank*; so called fr. its being caught on the banks of Newfoundland] : COD

bank-full \'=¦=\ *adj* [[1]*bank* + *full*] : full to the top of the banks ⟨a *bank-full* river⟩

bank gravel *n* [[1]*bank*] : gravel or sand as found in natural deposits

bank guarantee *n* [[4]*bank*] : a statement issued by an importer's bank guaranteeing the payment of drafts to the exporter

bank guaranty *n* [[4]*bank*] : insurance to protect depositors in a bank against loss in case of failure — see DEPOSITORY BOND

bank head *n* [[1]*bank* + *head*] : the mouth and immediate environs of a coalmine

bank holiday *n* [[4]*bank*] **1** *Brit* : a holiday on which banks are closed by law : LEGAL HOLIDAY **2** : a period when banks in general are closed often by government fiat (as for the stabilization of currency or for the reform of banking practices)

ban·kia \'baŋkēə\ *n, cap* [NL, fr. Sir Joseph *Banks* †1820 Eng. naturalist + NL *-ia*] : a genus of boring mollusks (family Teredinidae) including the giant northwest shipworm (*B. setacea*) of the Pacific coast of No. America

bank indicator *also* **banking indicator** *n* [[1]*bank*] : RELATIVE INCLINOMETER

[1]**banking** *n* -s [fr. gerund of [5]*bank*] : the business of a bank, orig. restricted to money changing and now devoted to taking money on deposit subject to check or draft, loaning money and credit (as by discounting notes and bills), issuing drafts, and any other associated form of general dealing in money or credit

[2]**banking** *n* -s [fr. gerund of [2]*bank*] **1 a** : the construction of embankments **b** : [1]BANK 2a : EMBANKMENT **2** : fishing on the banks of Newfoundland

banking doctrine *also* **banking principle** *n* : the principle that bank notes represent a form of banker's credit and should not be subject to special regulation and that freedom from regulation is essential to an elastic currency the fluctuation of which will be regulated by business conditions — compare CURRENCY DOCTRINE

banking game *n* : a gambling game in which bets must be placed against a gambling house, banker, or dealer

banking pin *n* [fr. pres. part. of [2]*bank*] **1** : either of two upright pins limiting the angular motion of the pallet fork in a timepiece having a lever escapement **2** : a pin emerging horizontally from the rim of a balance in a cylinder escapement or verge escapement to limit the arc of the balance **3** : REGULATOR PIN

banking screw *n* [fr. pres. part. of [2]*bank*] : an adjustable screw in a chronometer escapement for regulating the depth of escape-tooth locking

bank kiln *n* [[1]*bank*] : an Oriental kiln (as in China) built on a slope of a hill to obtain draft

bank letter *n* [[4]*bank*] : a periodical reviewing economic and financial developments that is issued by a bank

bank line *n* [[1]*bank*] : a fishing line attached to the shore and not tended by a fisherman : SETLINE

bank loan *n* [[4]*bank*] : a loan by a bank to be repaid at a fixed future date with interest — compare DISCOUNT

bank·man \'baŋkmən, -aiŋ-\ *n, pl* **bankmen** [[1]*bank* + *man*] : a compositor or apprentice who works at a stand on which type matter in galleys is corrected and prepared for makeup

bank martin *n* [[1]*bank*] : BANK SWALLOW

bank money *n* [[4]*bank*] : the equivalent of money as a medium of exchange constituted by checks, drafts, or bank credits other than bank notes — compare CURRENCY

bank night *n* [[4]*bank*] : a copyright form of lottery conducted by proprietors of motion-picture theaters with a drawing of prizes for distribution among patrons who have registered and are present at an appointed evening performance

bank note *n* [[4]*bank*] **1** : a promissory note issued by a bank payable to bearer on demand but without interest and circulating as money — compare NATIONAL BANK NOTE **2** : a strong durable pliable bond paper made of cotton and linen rags and used in paper money

bank of deposit [[4]*bank*] : a bank that receives money for safekeeping

bank of issue *also* **bank of circulation** [[4]*bank*] : a bank authorized by law to issue bank notes (as the Bank of England or the U.S. Federal Reserve banks)

bank paper *n* [[4]*bank*] **1 a** : circulating bank notes **b** : bankable commercial paper (as drafts or bills accepted by a bank or notes good enough to be discounted at a bank) **2** : a thin strong paper similar to but lighter than bond paper and commonly used for business letterheads

bank pole *n* [[1]*bank*] : a fishing pole secured to the shore and not tended by a fisherman

bank rate *n* [[4]*bank*] : the discount rate fixed by a central bank (as by the Bank of England) — compare DISCOUNT RATE

[1]**bankroll** \'=,=\ *n* [[4]*bank* + *roll*] : supply of money : FUNDS ⟨rising taxes had made a great dent in the family ~⟩

[2]**bankroll** \"\ *vt* : to supply the capital for or pay the cost of (a business or project) ⟨the project was ~ed by the government⟩

bank·roll·er \"ə(r)\ *n* [*bankroll* + *-er*] : one that bankrolls ⟨was ~ for a television show⟩

bank run *n* [[1]*bank*] : BANK GRAVEL

[1]**bank·rupt** \'baŋk,rəpt, -aiŋ-, -ŋ,krəpt\ *n* -s [modif. (influenced by L *ruptus*) of MF & OIt; MF *banqueroute*, fr. OIt *bancarotta*, fr. *banca* bank + *rotta* broken, fr. L *rupta*, fem. of *ruptus*, past part. of *rumpere* to break — more at BANK, REAVE] **1** *obs* : BANKRUPTCY **2 a** *obs* : a person who to avoid payment of his debts secretes himself, flees the country, or defrauds or simply avoids his creditors and is in consequence legally a criminal **b** : any person who has done any of the acts that the law provides shall entitle his creditors to have his estate administered for their benefit (as by the making of a general assignment) **c** : a person who has on the petition of his creditors or on his own petition been judicially declared subject to having his estate administered under the bankrupt laws for the benefit of his creditors **d** : a person who becomes insolvent — not used technically **3** : one who is destitute of or completely lacking in a particular thing ⟨a moral ~⟩ ⟨a ~ in all that is intellectually valuable⟩

[2]**bankrupt** \"\ *vt* -ED/-ING/-S **1 a** : to bring about the legal bankruptcy of ⟨high taxes and poor sales ~ed the company⟩ **b** : DEPLETE, IMPOVERISH ⟨war had ~ed the nation's natural resources and manpower⟩ **2 a** : to render destitute of : DEPRIVE ⟨a nervous breakdown ~ed him of courage to face society⟩ **b** : to spoil completely : RUIN ⟨his revision made the novel more accurate historically but ~ed it as a work of art⟩ **syn** see DEPLETE

[3]**bankrupt** \"\ *adj* **1 a** : in a state of financial ruin ⟨the nation's finances are ~⟩ : IMPOVERISHED ⟨~ peasantry⟩; *specif* : declared legally insolvent and with assets taken over by judicial process in order that they may be distributed among creditors ⟨a ~ corporation⟩ ⟨the original owner of the company went ~⟩ **b** : having to do with bankrupts or bankruptcy ⟨~ laws⟩ **2 a** : BROKEN, RUINED ⟨a ~ professional career⟩ : come to an end : FINISHED ⟨~ politicians⟩ **b** : DEPLETED, STERILE, EXHAUSTED ⟨the conviction . . . that the world was morally and religiously ~ —G.G.Coulton⟩ ⟨a ~ soil⟩ **c** : DESTITUTE, DEPRIVED — used with *of* or *in* ⟨~ of all merciful feelings⟩ ⟨~ in resources⟩

bank·rupt·cy \-p(t)sē, -si\ *n* -ES [[3]*bankrupt* + *-cy*] **1** : the quality or state of being bankrupt ⟨the company went into ~⟩ **2 a** : utter failure ⟨the ~ of Hitler's soaring ambitions —G.P. Gooch⟩ : RUIN ⟨our policy . . . in ~, the nation in mortal peril —C.B.Marshall⟩ **b** : DEPLETION, EXHAUSTION ⟨physical ~⟩ ⟨quitting is a tacit admission of moral ~ —W.R.Miller⟩ **c** : STERILITY, BARRENNESS ⟨the ~ of his propaganda⟩

bankrupt worm *n* [so called fr. its injurious effect on sheep and cattle] : a roundworm of the genus *Trichostrongylus*

banks *pl of* BANK, *pres 3d sing of* BANK

banks·hall \'baŋks,hȯl\ *n* -s [by folk etymology fr. Malay *bangsal* shed] **1** *India* : WAREHOUSE **2** *India* : the office of a harbor master or port officer

bank shot *n* [[1]*bank*] **1** : a shot in billiards and pool in which a player banks the cue ball or the object ball **2** : a shot in basketball played to rebound from the backboard into the basket

banks·ia \'baŋksēə\ *n* [NL, fr. Sir Joseph *Banks* †1820 Eng. naturalist + NL *-ia*] **1** *cap* : an important genus of Australian evergreen trees or shrubs (family Proteaceae) with alternate coriaceous leaves, apetalous yellowish flowers often in showy heads, and large woody follicles containing winged seeds — see AUSTRALIAN HONEYSUCKLE **2** -s : a plant of the genus *Banksia*

banks·ian pine \-ēən-\ *also* **banks' pine** \-ŋks(əz)-\ *or* **banks' air pine** *n, usu cap B* [after Sir Joseph *Banks*] : JACK PINE 1

banksia rose *also* **banksian rose** *n, sometimes cap B* : a Chinese evergreen climbing rose (*Rosa banksiae*) having yellow or white single flowers and being cultivated in several horticultural varieties in mild climates

bankside \'=,=\ *n* [[1]*bank* + *side*] : the slope of a bank esp. of a stream

bank·sku·ta \'baŋk,skŭd·ə\ *also* **bank·skoi·te** \-kȯid·ə\ *n* -s [*bankskuta* fr. Sw, fr. *bank* + *skuta* sloop, smack; *bankskoite* fr. Norw *bankskøite*, fr. *bank* + *skøite* sloop, smack] : a usu. ketch-rigged Scandinavian fishing craft designed for use in the North Sea bank fisheries and averaging from 30 to 70 tons burden

banks·man \'baŋksmən\ *n, pl* **banksmen** [[1]*bank* + *-s* + *man*] : an overseer at the bank of a mine drift

banksring *var of* BANXRING

bank statement *n* [[4]*bank*] **1** : a statement showing the condition of a bank or banks **2** : a statement by a bank of a customer's account

bank stock *n* [[4]*bank*] : the capital stock of any banking company

bank superintendent *n* [[4]*bank*] : BANK COMMISSIONER

bank swallow *n* [[1]*bank*] : a small swallow (*Riparia riparia*) of the northern hemisphere that nests in a hole it makes in a bank — called also *bank martin*

bank vole *n* [[1]*bank*] : the common red-backed mouse (*Clethrionomys glareolus*) of Europe

bank winding *n* [[1]*bank*] : a type of winding of coils which is used esp. in radios and in which the turns are staggered so as to reduce the capacity of the whole coil

bank-wound \'=,=\ *adj* [[1]*bank*] : of or having to do with bank winding

ban·lieue *also* **ban·lieu** \bäⁿlyœ\ *n, pl* **banlieues** *also* **banlieux** \"\ [F *banlieue*, fr. OF, fr. *ban* summoning of the king's vassals, tribute, ban + *lieue* league, fr. LL *leuca* — more at BAN, LEAGUE] : the outlying residential area of a city : ENVIRONS — often used in pl. ⟨trainload after trainload of young men and women from the ~ was disgorged into the capital —Max Beerbohm⟩ ⟨from the location of all these puppet theaters in the ~s of town it is evident that they were the resorts . . . of common people —Paul McPharlin⟩

bannack *var of* BANNOCK

bannat *var of* BANAT

banned *past of* BAN

1ban·ner \'banə(r)\ *n* -s [ME *baner, banere,* fr. OF *banere, baniere,* fr. *ban-* (modif. — influenced by OF *ban* proclamation, summons — of an assumed word in some Gmc language akin to Goth *bandwa, bandwo* sign) + *-ere, -iere* (fr. L *-aria* -ary); akin to ON *benda* to give a sign and prob. to Gk *phainein* to show — more at FANCY, BAN] **1 a :** a piece of cloth attached by one edge to a staff and used by a monarch, feudal lord, knight, or other commander as his standard which served as a rallying point for his men in battle **b :** FLAG 1 — used esp. in literary context or for emotional effect **c :** a quadrangular piece of cloth bearing armorial ensigns (as of an individual) **d** (1) **:** an ensign displaying some distinctive or symbolic device, motto, or legend; *esp* **:** one used as the emblem of a guild, fraternity, club, or other organization or presented as an award of honor or distinction (2) **:** such an ensign extended on a crosspiece, in a frame, or between poles **2 :** STANDARD 16a **3 a :** any of the primary divisions of the Manchu army, each having its distinctive banner **b :** a military subdivision of Mongolian tribes **4 :** a headline in large type running across an entire newspaper page usu. the first page **5 :** the actuated part of a disk or wigwag signal on a railroad **6 :** a strip of cloth on which a sign is painted ⟨welcoming ~s stretched across the street⟩ ⟨political ~s⟩ ⟨sideshow ~s — the pictorials that describe the freaks and the wonders on the midways —Emmett Kelly⟩ **syn** see FLAG

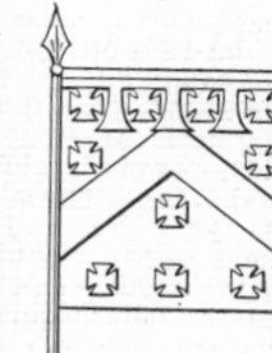
banner 1a

2banner \"\ *vt* -ED/-ING/-S **1 :** to furnish with a banner **2 :** to give extreme prominence to; *esp* **:** to print (a news story) under a banner usu. on the front page

3banner \"\ *adj* **:** distinguished from all others esp. in excellence **:** OUTSTANDING ⟨a ~ year for business⟩ ⟨a ~ student⟩ ⟨a bureau that has done ~ work in drawing up scientific recipes —*Consumers' Guide*⟩

banner cloud *n* **:** a cloud touching and extending out from the lee side of a mountain peak

bannered *adj* **1 :** bearing or furnished with a banner **:** hung with banners **2 :** blazoned or borne on a banner

1ban·ner·et \'banərət, ¦==¦ret\ *n* -s *often cap* [ME *baneret,* fr. OF *baneret, banerez,* fr. *banere* banner — more at BANNER] **1 :** a knight who was entitled to lead his vassals into the field under his own banner and who therefore ranked above a knight bachelor **:** KNIGHT BANNERET **2 :** a civil officer in some of the Swiss cantons and Italian republics

2ban·ner·et *also* **ban·ner·ette** \¦banə¦ret\ *n* -s [ME *banerett,* fr. MF *banerete,* dim. of *banere*] **:** a small banner

banner head *or* **banner headline** *n* **:** BANNER 4

ban·ner·less \'banərləs, -R -nəl- *or* -nᵊl-\ *adj* **:** lacking a banner

1bannerline \'==,=\ *n* [1*banner* + *line*] **:** 1BANNER 4

2bannerline \"\ *vt* **:** 2BANNER 2

ban·ner·man \'banə(r)mən\ *n, pl* **bannermen 1 :** STANDARD-BEARER **2 :** a Manchu belonging to a banner

banner man \-,man\ *n* **:** one who posts bills advertising coming amusements

ban·ne·rol *also* **ban·ner roll** \'banə,rōl\ *n* -s [*bannerol* fr. MF, var. of *banderole; banner roll* by folk etymology fr. *bannerol* — more at BANDEROLE] **:** BANDEROLE; *esp* **:** a banner displayed at a funeral and set over the tomb

banner plant *n* **:** any of several plants constituting the genus *Anthurium* and having a bright-colored reflexed bannerlike spathe

banner pompano *n* [so called fr. its long dorsal and anal fins] **:** LONGFIN POMPANO

banner screen *n* **:** a fire screen consisting of an upright pole usu. mounted on a tripod and carrying a rectangular frame covered with tapestry or needlework

bannerstone \'==,=\ *n* **:** a perforated stone reported only from archaic sites in midwestern and eastern No. America and having usu. two symmetrical wings that are apparently used primarily as a weight attached to a throwing stick but doubtless had considerable ceremonial significance, having been often buried with the dead — compare ATLATL

bannerstone from Rhea county, Tenn.

banning *pres part of* BAN

bannister *var of* BANISTER

ban·nis·ter harness \'banəstə(r)-\ *n, usu cap B* [prob. fr. the name *Bannister*] **:** a harness used for weaving wide patterns in fine reeds from a small jacquard loom

1ban·nock \'banək, -nik\ *n* -s [ME *bannok,* prob. fr. ScGael *bannach, bonnach*] **1 :** an often unleavened bread of oat or barley flour baked in flattish loaves that is common in the British isles esp. in the north **2** *NewEng* **:** CORNBREAD; *esp* **:** a thin cake baked on a griddle

2bannock \"\ *also* **ban·nack** \"\ *n, pl* **bannock** *or* **bannocks** *also* **bannack** *or* **bannacks** *usu cap* [Bannock *Banákwŭt*] **1 a :** a Shoshonean people of southern Utah and neighboring states **b :** a member of such people **2 :** the language of the Bannock people

banns \'banz, -aa(ə)-\ *n pl* [pl. of *bann,* alter. (influenced by 2*ban*) of earlier *bane,* fr. ME, var. of 2*ban* (proclamation)] **1 :** notice of a proposed marriage proclaimed in a church or other place prescribed by law in order that any person may object if he knows any impediment to the marriage **2** *obs* **:** the proclamation or prologue of a play

ban·nut \'banət\ *n* -s [ME *bannenote*] *dial Eng* **:** ENGLISH WALNUT

ba·no·vi·na \'bänə,vēnə\ *n, pl* **banovi·ne** \-,nā\ [Serbo-Croatian *bānovina,* fr. *bān* lord, ruler] **:** a former administrative subdivision of Yugoslavia

1ban·quet \'baŋkwət, 'bank-,'baank- *sometimes* -n,kwet *or* -ŋ,kwet; *usu* -d·+V\ *n* -s [MF, fr. OIt *banchetto* judge's bench, banquet, dim. of *banco* bench — more at BANCO] **1 a :** an elaborate and often ceremonious meal attended by numerous people and often honoring a person or marking some incident (as an anniversary or reunion) **b** *obs* **:** a drinking feast **2** *obs* **a :** DESSERT **b :** a repast between meals

2banquet \"\ *vb* -ED/-ING/-S [MF *banqueter,* fr. *banquet*] *vt* **:** to treat with a banquet **:** FEAST ⟨~*ed* the visiting notables⟩ ~ *vi* **:** to partake of a banquet **:** enjoy good food and drink ⟨didn't just eat; we ~*ed*⟩

ban·que·teer \,baŋkwə¦ti(ə)r, -a(a)nk-\ *n* -s **:** BANQUETER 2

ban·quet·er *pronunc at* 1BANQUET + ə(r)\ *n* -s **1** *obs* **:** a host at a banquet **2 :** a guest at a banquet **:** a person prone to participate in banquets

ban·quette \(')baŋ¦ket, -aiŋ·-, -an¦k-,-aan¦k-, *in sense 2b often* 'baŋkət *or* -aiŋ-\ *n* -s [F, fr. Prov *banqueta,* dim. of *banc* bench, of Gmc origin; akin to OHG *bank* bench — more at BENCH] **1 a :** a raised way or foot bank along the inside of a parapet or trench on which soldiers and guns are posted to fire upon the enemy — see BASTION illustration **b** *South* **:** a raised footway beside a thoroughfare **:** SIDEWALK **2 a :** a benchlike upholstered seat **b :** a narrow window seat **c :** a sofa having one roll-over arm **d :** a built-in upholstered bench along a wall or partition (as in a restaurant) **e :** a raised shelf (as at the back of a buffet) **3 :** an elevated platform or bench along the wall in a cliff dwelling or a kiva **4 :** an embankment constructed at the toe of the land side of a levee to protect the levee from sloughing off when saturated with water

banquette slope *n* **:** the slope of earth connecting the banquette tread of a fortification with the terreplein or parade

banquette tread *n* **:** the standing surface of a banquette (sense 1a) — called also *firing tread*

bans *pl of* BAN, *pres 3d sing of* BAN

ban·sal·a·guin \(,)bän,sälə'gēn\ *also* **ban·sal·a·gue** *or* **ban·sal·a·gui** \bän'sälәgē\ *or* **ban·sal·a·que** \-əkē\ *n* -s [Tag & Bisayan *bansalagin*] **1 :** a large tree (*Mimusops parvifolia*) of the Philippines and southwest Pacific area that produces an edible fruit and a very dense fine-grained wood that is reddish or reddish white in color **2 :** the wood of the bansalaguin

ban·shee *also* **ban·shie** \'ban(,)shē\ *n* -s [ScGael *bean-sìth,* fr. or akin to OIr *ben síde* woman of fairyland, fr. *ben* woman + *síde,* gen. of *síd* fairy abode; akin to Gk *gynē* woman — more at QUEAN, SIDHE] **:** a female spirit in Gaelic folklore that warns a family of the approaching death of a member by her appearance or esp. by wailing unseen under the windows of the house a night or two before the time of the death she foretells

ban·stick·le \'banz,tikəl, -n,st-\ *n* -s [ME *banstickel,* prob. fr. *ban-* (fr. OE *bān* bone) + *stickel* sting, fr. OE *sticel* — more at BONE, STICKLE] **:** THREE-SPINED STICKLEBACK

bant \'bant\ *vi* -ED/-ING/-S [short for *bantingize* to reduce by bantingism, fr. *banting* + *-ize*] **:** to practice banting **:** DIET

1ban·tam \'bantəm, -aan-\ *n* -s [fr. *Bantam,* former residency in Java] **1** *usu cap* **a :** a very small domestic fowl having feathered legs and feet and believed to have come from Java **b :** any of numerous small chiefly ornamental domestic fowls that are often miniatures of members of the standard breeds ⟨a Cochin ~⟩ ⟨a Brahma ~⟩ **2 :** a person of diminutive stature and often combative disposition **3 :** BANTAMWEIGHT **4 :** JEEP

2bantam \"\ *adj* **1 a :** SMALL ⟨~ sized⟩ **b :** easily handled **:** small and manageable ⟨a ~ edition of Shakespeare's complete works⟩ ⟨~ English cars⟩ **2 :** SAUCY **:** pertly combative ⟨her valiant ~ spirit —H.G.Wells⟩ **3 :** of the junior age-group ⟨a ~ baseball team⟩

ban·tam·ize \-,mīz\ *vt* -ED/-ING/-S *see -ize in Explan Notes* **:** to cause (a breed of fowls) to become bantam or to produce a bantam strain

bantamweight \'==,=\ *n* **:** a boxer of the class whose maximum weight is 118 pounds — compare FEATHERWEIGHT

ban·tay \bän·'tī\ *n* -s [Tag *bantáy*] *Philippines* **:** a guard or sentinel

ban·ta·yan \bän·'tä,yän\ *n* -s [Tag, fr. *bantáy*] *Philippines* **:** LOOKOUT, SIGNAL TOWER

ban·teng \'bän·,teŋ\ *also* **ban·tin** \-ntᵊn, -n(·,)tin\ *or* **bant·ing** \-n,tiŋ\ *n* -s [Malay *banteng, banting*] **:** a wild ox (*Bibos banting,* syn. *sondaicus*) of the Malay peninsula and archipelago sometimes used for draft

1ban·ter \'bantə(r), -aan-\ *vb* **bantered; bantered; bantering** \-ntəriŋ *also* -n·triŋ\ **banters** [origin unknown] *vt* **1 :** to speak to or address in a witty and teasing manner ⟨the students enjoyed their teacher's ~*ing* them about mistakes⟩ **:** act playfully and teasingly with ⟨~ the ladies⟩ **2** *archaic* **:** to delude or trick esp. by way of jest **3** *obs* **:** RIDICULE **4** *chiefly South & Midland* **:** DARE, CHALLENGE ⟨I'll ~ you to a game of checkers⟩ ⟨he ~*ed* him for a fight⟩ **5 :** *chiefly South & Midland* **:** to coax into action by argument or haggling **:** WHEEDLE ⟨he'd like to ~ you for a horse swap⟩ ~ *vi* **:** to tease good-naturedly **:** speak or act playfully or wittily ⟨he ~*ed* and romped with his grandchildren —*Time*⟩

2banter \"\ *n* -s **1 a** *obs* **:** absurd or nonsensical language used as ridicule **b :** good-natured and usu. witty and playful teasing ⟨the sprightly ~ of a tea party⟩ **:** animated joking back and forth ⟨~ between husband and wife⟩ **:** PLAYFULNESS ⟨the tragic mood predominates but a considerable infusion of delightful ~ relieves it —Arthur Berger⟩ **2** *archaic* **:** an instance of good-natured teasing

ban·ter·ing·ly *adv* **:** in a bantering manner

Ban·thine \'ban,thēn\ *trademark* — used for methantheline

1ban·ting \'bantiŋ\ *also* **ban·ting·ism** \-,izəm\ *n* -s *often cap* [after William *Banting* †1878 Eng. undertaker and writer] **:** a method of dieting for obesity by avoiding sweets and carbohydrates

2ban·ting \", 'bän-\ *n* -s [Malay] **:** a sailing dugout of Johore, Malaya

ban·ti's disease *or* **banti's syndrome** \'bäntēz-\ *n, usu cap B* [after Guido *Banti* †1925 Ital. physician] **:** a disorder characterized by congestion and great enlargement of the spleen usu. accompanied by anemia, leukopenia, and cirrhosis of the liver

bant·ling \'bantliŋ\ *n* -s [perh. modif. of G *bänkling* bastard, fr. *bank* bench (fr. OHG) + *-ling* — more at BENCH] **:** a very young child **:** INFANT ⟨a woman with a ~ in her arms⟩ ⟨the record of the ~ American language remains incomplete —H.M.Reynolds⟩

ban·toid \'ban,tȯid\ *adj, usu cap* [*Bantu* + *-oid*] **1 :** of, relating to, or characteristic of the Bantu people **2 :** of, relating to, or characteristic of the Bantu language

ban·tu \'ban,tü, -aan- *also* -än- *or* -ān-\ *n, pl* **bantu** *or* **bantus** *usu cap* **1 a :** a family of Negroid peoples (as the Ngoni, Ganda, Kikuyu, Lunda, Zulu, Swahili, and peoples whose names begin with *Aba-, Ama-, Ma-, Wa-,* and other variants of the Bantu plural personal prefix *Aba-*) who occupy equatorial and southern Africa and who apart from language do not show a great degree of racial or cultural uniformity — used chiefly in linguistic classification; see KAFFIR **b :** a member of such people **2 a** *in former classifications* **:** an independent family of African languages **b :** a group of African languages within the Central branch of the Niger-Congo family, comprising over 300 languages, spoken generally south of a line from Cameroons to Kenya, and being generally very similar in structure, characteristically having a highly developed system of noun classes marked by prefixes and determining a system of concord, each dependent word having a prefix of the same class as the noun

ban·tu·ist \-üəst\ *n* -s *usu cap* **:** a specialist in the Bantu languages or the Bantu-speaking peoples

bantu ka·vi·ron·do \-,kävə'rän(,)dō\ *n, usu cap B&K* **:** a group consisting of two distinct but neighboring and related Bantu-speaking peoples, the Logoli and Vugusa of eastern Africa

ban·ty \'bantē, -aan-, -ain-, -ti\ *n or adj* [by alter.] **:** BANTAM

ba·nus \'bänəs\ *n* -ES [ML, fr. Serbo-Croatian *bān* lord, ruler — more at BAN] **:** 3BAN

ba·nu·yo \bə'nü(,)yō\ *n* -s [Tag] **1 :** a Philippine timber tree (*Wallaceodendron celebicum*) of the family Leguminosae **2 :** the fine hard wood of the banuyo, similar to acle, of pale golden-brown or dark coffee color, much used in cabinetwork

banx·ring \'baŋks,riŋ\ *or* **bangs·ring** \-ŋz,r-\ *or* **banks·ring** \-ŋks,r-\ *n* -s [Jav *bangsring*] **:** TREE SHREW

ban·yan *or* **ban·ian** \'banyən *sometimes* -n,yan *or* -nēən *or* -nē,an *or* 'bənyən\ *n* -s [Hindi *baniyā,* fr. Skt *vāṇija* merchant, fr. *vaṇij* merchant] **1** *or* **ba·nia** *or* **ba·niya** \-nyə,-nēə,-nē,(y)ä\ **a :** one of a caste of Hindu merchants and traders **b :** a loose shirt, gown, or jacket that is worn in India **2** [fr. a banyan pagoda erected under a tree of the species grown near Bandar Abbas, southern Iran] *also* **ban·yan tree :** an East Indian tree (*Ficus bengalensis*) the branches of which send out numerous trunks that grow down to the soil and form props so that a single tree thus covers a very large area

banyan 2

banyan day *n* [so called fr. the banyans' abstinence fr. flesh] **1 :** a day on which no meat is served to the crew of a ship **2** *Austral* **:** a day on which the food is of inferior quality (as on the last day of a weekly ration)

ban·zai \(')bän'zī, -ān-\ *n* -s [Jap, hurrah, fr. *ban* ten thousand + *sai* year] **:** a Japanese cheer **:** a cry of enthusiasm or triumph — used interjectionally

ban·zai attack *or* **banzai charge** \'bän,zī, -an-,-aan-,-ān-\ *n* **:** a reckless desperate mass attack originated by Japanese soldiers and accompanied by yells of "banzai" and insulting taunts

bao·bab \'baů,bab, 'bāə,-\ *n* -s [prob. native name in Africa] **:** a tree (*Adansonia digitata*) esp. of Africa, India, and Australia having a trunk that often grows to a diameter of 30 feet, a gourdlike fruit that yields a pleasantly acid edible pulp which also furnishes a beverage, leaves and bark formerly used medicinally, and bark that is used in papermaking and that is also made into cloth and ropes by the natives — see MONKEY BREAD

bap \'bap\ *n* -s [origin unknown] *chiefly Scot* **:** a small loaf or roll of bread

bap *or* **bapt** *abbr* baptized

baph·ia \'bafēə\ *n, cap* [NL, fr. Gk *baphē* dye (fr. *baptein* to dip, dye) + NL *-ia* — more at BAPTIZE] **:** a small genus of trees and shrubs (family Leguminosae) native to tropical Africa and Madagascar having unifoliolate leaves and bracteolate flowers with a sheathing calyx and 10 free stamens — see CAMWOOD

baph·o·met·ic \¦bafə¦med·ik\ *adj, usu cap* [*Baphomet,* idol the Templars were accused of worshiping (fr. F, alter. of *Mahomet* Muhammad †632 Arabian prophet, fr. Ar *Muḥammad*) + E *-ic*] **:** of or relating to the idol Baphomet

bap·tise *chiefly Brit var of* BAPTIZE

bap·ti·sia \bap'tizh(ē)ə, -ēzh-\ *n, cap* [NL, fr. Gk *baptisis* baptism (fr. *baptein* to dip) + NL *-ia* — more at BAPTIZE] **:** a genus of No. American herbs (family Leguminosae) with showy yellow, blue, or white pealike flowers and an inflated pod — see WILD INDIGO

bap·tism \'bap,tizəm, ÷'bab,t-\ *n* -s [ME *bapteme, baptisme,* fr. OF & LL; OF *baptesme,* fr. LL *baptisma,* fr. Gk, fr. *baptizein* to baptize — more at BAPTIZE] **1 a :** the ceremony of proclaiming one a Christian or of admitting one into membership in a Christian church with the use of water by immersion, pouring, or sprinkling and with the recital of a form of words (as "I baptize thee in the name of the Father and of the Son and of the Holy Ghost") **b :** the Christian sacrament (as in the Roman Catholic and many Protestant churches) of purification from sin and of spiritual rebirth as a Christian that is administered before any other sacrament (often in infancy) **c :** a rite resembling Christian baptism usu. in using water for ritual purification **d :** an experience of spiritual purification and renewal **e** *Christian Science* **:** purification by or submergence in Spirit **2 :** an act, experience, or ordeal by which one is purified, sanctified, initiated, or named ⟨the ~ of the gutter —W.B.Yeats⟩ ⟨giving bomber crews their ~ in mock atomic warfare —*N.Y.Times*⟩ ⟨the official ~ of a new battleship⟩

bap·tis·mal \(')=¦tizməl\ *adj* [ML *baptismalis,* fr. LL *baptisma* + L *-alis* -al] **:** of or relating to baptism ⟨~ certificates⟩ ⟨~ vows⟩ ⟨the first ~ shock . . . had worn off —Evelyn Barkins⟩ — **bap·tis·mal·ly** \-məlē, -li\ *adv*

baptismal name *n* **:** CHRISTIAN NAME; *esp* **:** one given at baptism

baptismal regeneration *n* **:** the theological doctrine that regeneration is effected in and through Christian baptism

baptism for the dead : the baptism of a living person as proxy for one who has died unbaptized (as practiced in modern times by Mormons)

baptism of fire [trans. of LGk *baptisma pyros*] **1 :** a spiritual baptism by the gift of the Holy Spirit — often used in allusion to Acts 2:3–4; Mt 3:11 (RSV) **2 :** an introductory or initial experience that is a severe ordeal; *specif* **:** a soldier's first exposure to enemy fire

1bap·tist \'baptəst, ÷'babtə-, ÷'babdə-\ *n* -s [ME *baptiste,* fr. OF, fr. LL *baptista,* fr. Gk *baptistēs,* fr. *baptizein* to baptize — more at BAPTIZE] **1 :** one that baptizes **2** *cap* **:** a member or adherent of a denomination of Trinitarian Protestant Christians that are congregational in polity and for the most part doctrinally Calvinistic and maintain that baptism should be administered by immersion to believers only

2baptist \"\ *adj, usu cap* **:** of or relating to Baptists or their doctrines and practices

bap·tis·tery \'baptəstrē, -ri, ÷'babtə-, ÷'babdə- *also* -stər- *sometimes* bap'tis-tər- *or* ÷ bab't-\ *or* **bap·tis·try** \'==-trē, -ri\ *n* -ES [ME *baptisterie,* fr. MF, fr. LL *baptisterium,* fr. LGk *baptistērion,* fr. Gk, swimming tank, fr. *baptizein* to dip, baptize — more at BAPTIZE] **1 :** a usu. round or polygonal building used in early times for baptismal services **2 a :** a part of a church containing a font and used for baptismal services **b :** a large tank used in modern Baptist and other churches for immersion

baptistery 1

bap·tis·tic \(')bap¦tistik, ÷-ab¦t-\ *adj, usu cap* **:** of or relating to Baptists; *esp* **:** in accord with Baptist doctrines and practices

bap·tize \bap'tīz, ÷bab't-, '=,=\ *vb* -ED/-ING/-S *see -ize in Explan Notes* [ME *baptizen,* fr. OF *baptiser,* fr. LL *baptizare,* fr. Gk *baptizein* to dip, baptize, fr. *baptein* to dip; akin to ON *kafa* to dive, swim under water, *kvefja* to quench] *vt* **1 a :** to dip or immerse in water or to pour or sprinkle water on as a rite of spiritual or moral purification or of initiation into a religious society **:** administer baptism to ⟨~ a child in the Episcopal Church⟩ **b :** to make a member of (a particular sect) by baptism ⟨in San Antonio, he was *baptized* a Catholic —Green Peyton⟩ **2 a :** to initiate or launch ⟨both developments were *baptized* under last season's conditions of scanty snow —*N.Y.Times*⟩ **b :** to purify or cleanse spiritually esp. by a purging experience or ordeal ⟨*baptized* with pain and rapture, tears and fire —Sidney Lanier⟩ **3 :** to give a name to (as at baptism) **:** CHRISTEN ⟨I know you're not always called the name you're *baptized* by —Agatha Christie⟩ ⟨he was *baptized* Samuel⟩ ~ *vi* **:** to administer baptism

bap·tiz·er \-zə(r)\ *n* -s [ME, fr. *baptizen* to immerse + *-er*] **:** one that baptizes **:** BAPTIST

bap·tor·nis \bap'tȯrnəs\ *n, cap* [NL, fr. Gk *baptein* to dip + *-ornis*] **:** a genus of swimming birds from the Cretaceous of Kansas that is imperfectly known but prob. related to *Hesperornis*

ba·pu \'bə,pü, 'bä-\ *n* -s [Hindi, fr. Skt *papu* protector] *India* **:** FATHER

1bar \'bär, 'bå(r\ *n* -s *often attrib* [ME *barre,* fr. OF] **1 a** (1) **:** a straight piece of wood or metal that is longer than it is wide, is used to fasten (as a door), and that can be unlatched or unfastened (2) **:** a similar piece of wood or metal so fixed or placed as to obstruct passage through any opening or over any way and often forming a part of a continuous barrier (as of a fence or grating) ⟨heavy ~s across prison windows⟩ **b :** a rodlike piece of iron or steel often pointed at one or both ends or terminating at one end in a cutting edge and used as a digging, breaking, or prying tool **c :** a solid piece or block of some material usu. rectangular and considerably longer than it is wide ⟨a ~ of gold⟩ **d :** a piece (as of wood or metal) longer than it is wide and usu. having considerable rigidity that is used as a lever, handle, support, or division maker: as (1) **:** a part of a machine usu. designed to activate a certain mechanism or to hold replaceable parts (as cutting teeth or needles)

bars 6a, *B;* double bar, *D*

(2) : a handrail along the walls of a dance studio used as an aid to maintain balance during ballet exercises (3) : a slender strip of wood that divides and supports the glass in a window : SASH — called also *sash bar* **e** (1) : the part of the wall of a horse's hoof that is bent inward toward the frog at the heel on each side and that extends toward the center of the sole (2) : the sidepiece joining the pommel and cantle of a saddle (3) : the mouthpiece of a bridle when solid **2** : BARRIER, IMPEDIMENT : something that obstructs, hinders, or prevents passage, progress, or action: as **a** : the gate or the gatehouse of a castle or fortified town ⟨the four principal entrances along the main highroads were defended by the four ~*s* —Edwin Benson⟩ **b** : the complete and permanent destruction of an action or claim in law ⟨matter in ~⟩ ⟨defense in ~⟩; *also* : a plea or objection that effects such destruction **c** (1) : any intangible or nonphysical impediment or obstacle ⟨agreed that long sentences are a ~ to easy reading —F.L.Mott⟩ ⟨one of the biggest ~*s* standing in the way of developing a vaccine —*Monsanto Mag.*⟩ (2) **bars** *pl* : standards of inclusion or admission : restrictions or precautions against inclusion or admission of undesirable or supposedly inferior elements ⟨let down the ~*s* against this microbial enemy —Justina Hill⟩ ⟨the club will not let down its ~*s*⟩ **d** : a submerged or partly submerged bank of sand, gravel, or other material along a shore or in a river often obstructing navigation esp. at the mouth of the river or approaching a harbor — compare BANK 1d, BARRIER 2b (1), HOOK, REEF, SPIT, TOMBOLO **3 a** (1) : the railing in a courtroom that encloses the place about the judge where prisoners are stationed for arraignment, trial, or sentence or where the business of the court is transacted in civil cases ⟨summoned the prisoner to the ~⟩ (2) : COURT, TRIBUNAL ⟨see that justice is done at the ~⟩ (3) : a particular system of courts ⟨the New York bench and ~ acquitted themselves wisely . . . in defense of liberty and law —Telford Taylor⟩ ⟨practice at the Massachusetts ~⟩ (4) : any authority or tribunal that renders judgment or makes a final evaluation ⟨he must summon to the ~ of a nobler philosophy the current standards of value and conduct —V.L.Parrington⟩ ⟨be judged at the ~ of public opinion⟩ **b** (1) : the barrier or partition in the English Inns of Court that formerly separated the seats of the benchers or readers from the body of the hall occupied by the students who in time were called to take their place within the barrier to enter into the debates of the house — called also *utter bar* (2) : the whole body of barristers or lawyers qualified to practice in any jurisdiction ⟨be admitted to the ~⟩ ⟨a ~ association⟩ (3) : the profession of barrister or lawyer ⟨heighten respect for members of the ~ and judiciary —W.L.Hoyt⟩ **c** : a railing in a room, office, or hall of assembly designed to reserve a space for those having special privileges ⟨the ~ of the House of Commons⟩ **4** : a straight stripe, band, or line much longer than it is wide: as **a** : one of two or more horizontal stripes on a heraldic shield — see FESS **b** : a transverse ridge on the roof of a horse's mouth — usu. used in pl. **c** : the space in front of the molar teeth of a horse in which the bit is placed **d** : a metal or embroidered strip worn on a uniform to indicate rank or service in the armed forces ⟨a second lieutenant's ~⟩ ⟨overseas ~*s*⟩ or as an award for merit or achievement ⟨awarded ~*s* to volunteer Red Cross workers⟩ or to signify that the holder of a medal or distinction has again merited its award ⟨a Distinguished Flying Cross with ~⟩ **e** : RIBBON 1c **f** : a mark or stripe crossing at right angles to the length of a feather **g** : the space between the inner and outer table on a backgammon board **h** *geol* : VEIN, DIKE **i** : a mark long in proportion to its width, used in print or writing (as the superscript mark in ā or the subscript mark in t̲h̲ or the mark |) **5 a** : a counter at which food or esp. alcoholic beverages are served ⟨had a cocktail at the ~⟩ ⟨snack ~⟩ ⟨milk ~⟩ **b** : a room or public establishment containing such a counter : BARROOM **c** : a piece of furniture on wheels to be moved about having a counter on top and storage space for liquor and equipment below **d** : a counter or section of a store where a particular item or items of merchandise are featured ⟨hat ~⟩ ⟨gift ~⟩ ⟨slipper ~⟩ **6 a** *or* **bar line** : a vertical line across the musical staff before the initial measure accent **b** : MEASURE ⟨a passage of eight ~*s*⟩ ⟨two ~*s'* rest⟩ **c** : BASS-BAR **d** : a stanzaic song form in medieval music related to the French ballade but without the refrain; *specif* : this form (a a b) as practiced by minnesingers **7 a** : a lace and embroidery joining for connecting various parts of the pattern that is usu. covered with buttonhole stitch for needlepoint lace and cutwork **b** : the strengthening threads covered with buttonhole stitch placed at one or both ends of a buttonhole **8** : banded ferruginous rock — called also *jasper bar* **9** : a recorded time of performance in horse racing taken on an occasion or at an event not conducted according to the rules of racing that debars a horse from entry in a class of slower record **10** : an area of a crap table in which a bettor may place a bet against the caster, one cast (1-1, 6-6, or 1-2) being barred **11** *or* **bar arm** : HAMMERLOCK; *esp* : one combined with another hold **syn** see OBSTACLE — **at bar 1** : legally before the court : in open court **2** *or* **at the bar** : before the full court ⟨trial *at bar*⟩ ⟨trial *at the bar*⟩ — **go to the bar** : to become a barrister ⟨*went to the Bar* as a very young man —W.S.Gilbert⟩ — **in bar of** : as a sufficient reason against : PREVENTING — **within the bar** : in or to the office of King's or Queen's Counsel — used in the phrase *called within the bar;* in allusion to the fact that King's Counsel plead within the bar of the court

²**bar** \"\ *vt* **barred; barred; barring; bars** [ME *barren,* fr. OF *barrer,* fr. *barre* bar] **1 a** : to fasten with a bar ⟨~ the gate⟩ ⟨~ a door⟩ **b** : to place bars across to prevent ingress or egress **2** : to mark with bars : STRIPE ⟨a feather *barred* with brown⟩ **3 a** : to confine or shut in by or as if by bars ⟨~ a prisoner in his cell⟩ **b** : not to take into consideration : set aside ⟨the picnic will be on Saturday, *barring* the possibility of rain⟩ ⟨if man does not want to change his culture, then, *barring* outside compulsions, it will not be changed —W.D.Wallis⟩ **c** : to shut or keep out : EXCLUDE — often used with *from* ⟨*barred* enlisted men from the club⟩ ⟨*barred* aliens from sensitive positions⟩; *also, archaic* : to exclude from ⟨I will ~ no honest man my house —*Shak.*⟩ **4 a** : to interpose or serve as a sufficient and permanent legal objection to (as an action) or to the claim of (as a person) **b** : PREVENT, HINDER ⟨nothing *barred* them from meeting together⟩ : FORBID, PROHIBIT ⟨a convention *barring* the use of poison gas in war⟩ **c** : to obstruct, block up, or shut off (as an entrance or road) by or as if by a barrier ⟨~ a residential street to heavy traffic⟩ **d** : to obstruct or prevent (as a person's movement) ⟨rushed fresh reserves to ~ the enemy's advance⟩ **5** : to reinforce (as a buttonhole) with a bar **6** : to move or turn (as a flywheel or a locomotive driving wheel) by a bar used as a lever **7** : to divide (a music staff) into measures with bar lines **8** *in veterinary practice* : to dissect free and ligate (a vein in a horse's leg) above and below the site of a projected operative procedure **syn** see HINDER

³**bar** \"\ *prep* : EXCEPT, SAVE, EXCLUDING ⟨all was over ~ the formal recording of the votes —*Sydney (Australia) Bull.*⟩ ⟨language can describe anything ~ the ineffable —Edna Daitz⟩

⁴**bar** \"\ *n* -s [F, fr. OF, fr. MD *baers;* akin to OE *bærs* bass — more at BASS] : ²MAIGRE

⁵**bar** \"\ *n* -s [LaF *boire* mosquito net] : MOSQUITO NETTING ⟨see that you drive all the mosquitoes out of their ~ —Mark Twain⟩

⁶**bar** *n* -s [ScGael *bàir* game, goal] **1** *Scot* : PRACTICAL JOKE **2** *Scot* : an amusing situation

⁷**bar** \"\ *n* -s [G, fr. Gk *baros* weight — more at GRIEVE] **1** : a unit of pressure equal to one million dynes per square centimeter or about 0.98697 standard atmosphere **2** : the absolute cgs unit of pressure equal to one dyne per square centimeter — called also *barye*

BAR \ˌbēˌāˈär, -ˈāˈä(r\ *abbr or n* -s Browning automatic rifle ⟨an infantry squad leader . . . carries a *BAR* —Donald Howard⟩

bar *abbr* **1** bark; barque **2** barometer; barometric **3** barrel

bar- *or* **baro-** *comb form* [Gk *baros* — more at GRIEVE] : weight : pressure ⟨*bar*agnosis⟩ ⟨*baro*graph⟩

ba·ra \ˈbä(ˌ)rä\ *var of* BURRA

ba·ra·ba·ra \ˌbärəˈbärə\ *or* **ba·ra·bo·ra** \ˌ≈≈ˈbōrə\ *n* -s [Russ dial. *barabora*] : a sod or turf hut of northern Siberia or of Alaska; *esp* : a hut of the Aleutian islanders built partly or wholly underground

bar·a·boo \ˈbarəˌbü, ˌ≈≈ˈ≈\ *n* -s [fr. *Baraboo* mts., Wis.] : a disinterred monadnock

bar·ag·no·sis \ˌbaˌragˈnōsə̇s, baˈragˌnō-\ *n, pl* **baragno·ses** \-ōˌsēz\ [NL, fr. *bar-* + ²*a-* + *-gnosis*] : loss of barognosis

ba·ra·gouin \ˌbarəˈgwaⁿ\ *n* -s [F] : outlandish unintelligible speech : JARGON

ba·rai·ta *or* **ba·rai·tha** \bəˈrītə\ *n, pl* **baraitas** *or* **baraithas** *also* **ba·rai·toth** \ˌbärīˈtōt, -tōth, -tōs\ *or* **barai·tot** \-ˈtōt, -ˈtōs\ *or* **barai·thoth** \-t,-th,-s\ *or* **barai·thot** \-t,-s\ *usu cap* [Aram *barrāythā* extraneous matter] : a traditional Jewish interpretation or statement of biblical law dating from the tannaitic period but not included in the Mishnah

ba·ra·ji·llo \ˌbarəˈhē(ˌ)(y)ō\ *n* -s [AmerSp, perh. fr. Sp *barajar* to entangle] : a Central American perennial herb (*Desmodium rensoni*) used as forage

ba·ra·ka \bəˈräkə\ *n* -s [Ar *barakah*] : a blessing that is regarded in various Eastern religions as an indwelling spiritual force and divine gift inhering in saints, charismatic leaders, and natural objects

bar·a·min \ˈbarəmə̇n\ *n* -s [Heb *bara* created + *min* kind] *among some antievolutionists* : a created plant or animal as distinguished from one that has developed through the process of evolution

bar-and-dot \ˈ≈≈ˈ≈\ *adj* [¹*bar*] : of or relating to a system of writing numbers used by the Maya and some other ancient peoples of Middle America in which a bar stood for five and a dot for one (as in the following examples)

1 2 5 6 9 10 18

baranduki *var of* BARONDUKI

¹**ba·ran·gay** \ˌbärənˈgī\ *n* -s [Iloko *baranggáy* hamlet, community] : a unit of administration in primitive Philippine society consisting of from 50 to 100 families under a headman

²**barangay** *var of* BALANGAY

ba·rani \bəˈranē, -ränē\ *or* **ba·roni** \-ˈrānē\ *n* -s [prob. fr. the name *Barani*] : a trampoline and tumbling stunt in which the performer does a front somersault with a half twist

bá·rá·ny chair \bəˈrānē-, *Hung* ˈbäˌränʸ-\ *n, usu cap B* [after Robert *Bárány* †1936 Austrian physician] : a chair for testing the effects of circular motion esp. on airplane pilots

ba·rar·ite \bəˈräˌrīt\ *n* -s *cap* [*Barari,* Bengal, India + E *-ite*] : a mineral $(NH_4)_2SiF_6$ consisting of ammonium fluosilicate occurring in hexagonal crystals and in crusts on the rocks about Vesuvius

bar arm *n* [¹*bar*] : ¹BAR 11

ba·ra·singh \ˈbärəˌsiŋ\ *or* **ba·ra·sin·gha** \ˌbärəˈsiŋgə\ *n* -s *sometimes cap* [Hindi *bārahsiṅghā,* lit., having twelve tines, fr. *bārah* twelve + *sīg* horn (fr. Skt *śṛṅga*) — more at HORN] : SWAMP DEER

¹**ba·rat** \bəˈrät\ *n* -s [native name in Indonesia] : a violent squall from the northwest that occurs in Menando Bay on the coast of Celebes Island and is prevalent from December to February

²**barat** *var of* BERAT

bar·a·thea \ˌbarəˈthēə\ *n* -s [fr. *Barathea,* a trademark] : a closely woven clothing fabric that has a broken twill weave which produces a pebbly-surface effect and is made of silk, rayon, cotton, wool, or combinations of these yarns

bar·a·thrum \ˈbarəthrəm\ *n, pl* **bara·thra** \-rə\ [L & Gk; L *barathrum,* fr. Gk *barathron;* akin to Gk *bibrōskein* to devour — more at VORACIOUS] : a bottomless pit or abyss : HELL

ba·ratte \bəˈrat\ *n* -s [F, churn, fr. MF, fr. *baratter* to shake, fr. *baratte, barate* agitation, confusion] : a churn in which alkali cellulose is converted into cellulose xanthate in the manufacture of viscose

¹**barb** \ˈbärb, ˈbȧb\ *n* -s [ME *barbe* barb, beard, fr. MF, fr. L *barba* — more at BEARD] **1 a** : a sharp projection extending backwards (as from the point of an arrow, spear, or fishhook) preventing easy extraction from a wound; *also* : any sharp projection with its point similarly oblique or crosswise to something else **b** : the point of a weapon or missile **c** : a biting or pointedly critical remark or comment ⟨~*s* of ridicule⟩ ⟨attacks the . . . government and its leaders with personal ~*s* of astonishing virulence —Faubion Bowers⟩ : painful impact or effect ⟨the first violators felt the ~ of Mulrain's enforcement tactics —G.S.Perry⟩ **2** : a part of a medieval linen or cotton headdress that is usu. starched and sometimes pleated, that passes over or under the chin and covers the neck and sometimes the shoulders, and that is now worn only by nuns of certain orders **3** : a fleshy projection under the snout or around the mouth in fishes like sturgeons or cod; *esp* : BARBEL **4** : one of the little projections of the mucous membrane that mark the opening of the submaxillary glands under the tongue in horses and cattle; *esp* : such a projection when inflamed and swollen — usu. used in pl. **5** *heraldry* : one of the projecting leaves of the calyx of a rose **6** : one of the side branches of the shaft of a bird's feather **7** : one of the minute branches on fur fiber **8** *bot* : a hair or bristle ending in a hook, often a double one

barb 1a

²**barb** \"\ *vb* -ED/-ING/-S [ME & MF; ME *barben* to clip wool, fr. MF *barber* to shave, clip, fr. *barbe* beard, barb] *vt* **1 a** *obs* : to shave or trim the beard of **b** : CLIP, MOW **2** [¹*barb*] : to furnish (as an arrow or fishhook) with a barb ⟨~ arrows with points of fish bone⟩ ~ *vi, obs* : to shave or trim the beard

³**barb** \"\ *n* -s [by alter.] *obs* : ²BARD 1

⁴**barb** \"\ *n* -s [F *barbe,* fr. It *barbero,* fr. *barbero* of Barbary, fr. *Barberia* Barbary, coastal region of northern Africa] **1 a** : a horse of the stock native to Barbary **b** *usu cap* : a horse of a breed related to the Arabs that is noted for speed and endurance and was introduced into Spain by the Moors **2** : a pigeon of a domestic breed related to the carriers that has a short broad beak, much bare skin about the eyes, and the skin about the nostrils swollen **3** : a black kelpie

⁵**barb** \"\ *n* -s [prob. fr. ¹*barb*] **1** : any of several whitings of the eastern and southeastern coasts of the U.S. **2** : any of several brightly colored tropical fishes (genus *Barbus*) kept in aquariums

⁶**barb** \"\ *n* -s [by shortening] *slang* : BARBARIAN 2

bar·ba am·a·ril·la \ˌbärbəˌaməˈrilə, -rē(y)ə\ *n, pl* **barba amarillas** [AmerSp, lit., yellow beard] : FER-DE-LANCE

bar·ba·coa \ˌbärbəˈkōə\ *n, pl* **barbacoa** *or* **barbacoas** *usu cap* [Sp, of AmerInd origin] **1 a** : a Chibchan people of northern Ecuador and southern Colombia **b** : a member of such people **2** : a language of the Barbacoa people — **bar·ba·co·an** \ˌ≈≈ˈ≈ən\ *adj, usu cap*

¹**bar·ba·di·an** \(ˈ)bärˈbādēən\ *adj, usu cap* [*Barbados,* island in the West Indies + E *-ian*] **1** : of, relating to, or characteristic of Barbados, West Indies **2** : of, relating to, or characteristic of Barbadians

²**barbadian** \"\ *n* -s *cap* : a native or resident of Barbados

bar·ba·dos \(ˈ)bärˈbādəs, -(ˌ)äs,-(ˌ)ōz\ *adj, usu cap* [fr. *Barbados,* West Indies] : of or from the island of Barbados, West Indies : of the kind or style prevalent in Barbados

bar·ba·dos aloe *n, usu cap B* : a stemless aloe (*Aloe vera*) with grayish green spiny-margined leaves and spikes of yellow flowers that is native to northern Africa but naturalized throughout the tropics and widely grown as a greenhouse ornamental

barbados cherry *n, usu cap B* **1** : any of several West Indian shrubs of the genera *Malpighia* and *Bunchosia* (esp. *M. urens*) **2** : the slightly acid berry of the Barbados cherry somewhat resembling cherries in flavor **3** : SURINAM CHERRY 2

barbados-cherry family *n, usu cap B* : MALPIGHIACEAE

barbados earth *n, usu cap B* : an earthy marl of Miocene age occurring in Barbados and noted for its richness in radiolarians

barbados flower fence *n, usu cap B* : any of several tropical shrubs or small trees used for hedges: as **a** : PRIDE OF BARBADOS **b** : BRASILETTO **c** : JERUSALEM THORN 2

barbados gooseberry *n, usu cap B* **1** : a West Indian cactus (*Peireskia aculeata*) **2** : the smooth edible fruit of the Barbados gooseberry

barbados lily *n, usu cap B* : a bulbous tropical American herb (*Hippeastrum puniceum*) related to the amaryllis

barbados pride *n, usu cap B* **1** : PRIDE OF BARBADOS **2** : RED SANDALWOOD 2

barbados tar *n, usu cap B* : a thick black petroleum from Barbados

barb·al·o·in \bärˈbaləwən\ *n* -s [*Barbados aloe* + *-in*] : a yellow crystalline compound $C_{20}H_{18}O_9$ isolated from aloin that yields aloe-emodin and D-arabinose on hydrolysis

bar·ba·ra's buttons \ˈbärb(ə)rəz-\ *n pl but sing or pl in constr, usu cap 1st B* [fr. the name *Barbara*] : a plant of the genus *Marshallia* (family Compositae); *esp* : a low-growing perennial herb (*M. trinervia*) sometimes cultivated and having purplish flowers in globose heads

bar·ba·rea \ˌbärbəˈrēə\ *n, cap* [NL, fr. St. *Barbara,* 3d cent. martyr + NL *-ea*] : a small genus of yellow-flowered sometimes weedy biennial or perennial herbs (family Cruciferae) of the north temperate zone having lyrate or pinnatifid lower leaves and clasping stem leaves and basal rosettes of leaves that overwinter — see WINTER CRESS

¹**bar·ba·resque** \ˌbärbəˈresk\ *adj* [F, fr. It *barbaresco,* fr. *Barbaria, Barberia* Barbary, coastal region of northern Africa + It *-esco* -esque] **1** *usu cap* : of, relating to, or characteristic of Barbary **2** : barbaric in style ⟨~ architecture⟩

²**barbaresque** \"\ *n* -s *cap* : one of the natives of Barbary formerly noted for their piratical activity ⟨seventy thousand peasants huddled together because it had not been safe to remain out for fear of the ~*s* —Bernhard Berenson⟩

¹**bar·bar·i·an** \(ˈ)bärˈberēən, (ˈ)bȧˈ-, -ˈba(a)r-, -ˈbär-\ *adj* [L *barbarus* + E *-ian* — more at BARBAROUS] **1** : of or relating to a land, culture, or people alien and usu. believed to be inferior to one's own ⟨~ tribes massing on the borders of the Roman Empire⟩ ⟨the Chinese emperor received with civility a mission from the ~ West⟩ **2** : lacking refinement, gentleness, learning, or artistic or literary culture : marked by a tendency toward brutality, violence, or lawlessness but sometimes displaying a rough vigor or vitality ⟨introduced me to his loud, boisterous, ~ mother⟩ ⟨a ~ race which possesses neither virtue nor humanity —R.L.Bruckberger⟩ **3** *among some anthropologists* : of or relating to a people or group in a stage of cultural development about midway between savagery and full civilization; *also* : of or relating to such a stage

syn BARBARIC, BARBAROUS, SAVAGE: BARBARIAN frequently applies to a state about midway between full civilization and tribal savagery ⟨some *barbarian* peoples have brought their mores into true adjustment to their life conditions and have gone on for centuries without change —W.G.Sumner⟩ BARBARIC and BARBAROUS may also be used to express this notion ⟨they had passed the *barbaric* stage when they invaded Chaldea. They knew the use of metals; they were skillful architects and . . . good engineers —Edward Clodd⟩ ⟨Caesar's short sketch of the Germans gives the impression of *barbarous* peoples . . . they had not yet reached the agricultural stage, but were devoted to war and hunting —H.O.Taylor⟩ SAVAGE implies even less advancement ⟨for *savage* or semicivilized men . . . authority is needed to restrain them from injuring themselves —C.W.Eliot⟩ BARBAROUS and SAVAGE are somewhat more common than BARBARIC and BARBARIAN to indicate uncivilized cruelty, but all may be used ⟨he required as a condition of peace that they should sacrifice their children to Baal no longer. But the *barbarous* custom was too inveterate —J.G.Frazer⟩ ⟨the King's greed passed into *savage* menace. He would hang all, he swore — man, woman, the very child at the breast —J.R.Green⟩ ⟨they had further traits and customs which are *barbaric* rather than specifically Teutonic: cruelty and faithlessness toward enemies, feuds, wergeld —H.O.Taylor⟩ ⟨for him those chambers held *barbarian* hordes, hyena foeman, and hot-blooded lords —John Keats⟩ BARBARIC and BARBAROUS are more common in relation to taste and refinement. BARBARIC connotes a wild, profuse lack of restraint ⟨this audacious and *barbaric* profusion of words — chosen always for their color and their vividly expressive quality —Arthur Symons⟩ ⟨the march became rather splendid and *barbaric.* First rode Feisal in white, then Sharraf at his right in red headcloth and henna-dyed tunic and cloak, myself on his left in white and scarlet, behind us three banners of faded crimson silk with gilt spikes —T.E.Lawrence⟩ BARBAROUS implies an utter lack of cultivated taste and refinement ⟨a race of unconscious spiritual helots. We shall become utterly *barbarous* and desolate —Ludwig Lewisohn⟩ ⟨but this deeply *barbarous* book may, in its very vulgarity of expression, be in advance of its time —Dorothy Thompson⟩

²**barbarian** \"\ *n* -s **1** : one that is barbarian ⟨a cultural conceit which divided the world into Greeks and ~*s* —Frederick Bodmer⟩ ⟨he is . . . a ~ in the arts of the table —Sinclair Lewis⟩ ⟨he would be a ~ indeed who failed to appreciate exquisite flowers, rare lace, . . . and feminine charm —H.M.Parshley⟩ **2** *slang* : an undergraduate not a member of a fraternity or sorority

bar·bar·i·an·ism \≈ˈ≈≈≈ˌnizəm\ *n* -s : BARBARISM, BARBARITY

bar·bar·ic \(ˈ)bärˈbarik, (ˈ)bȧˈ-, -rēk *also* -ˈber-\ *adj* [L *barbaricus* foreign, barbaric, fr. Gk *barbarikos,* fr. *barbaros* foreign + *-ikos* -ic — more at BARBAROUS] **1** : of, relating to, or characteristic of barbarians ⟨a war was bloodier and more bestial wars than our ~ ancestors —Edward Glover⟩ ⟨full of the virility of ~ health and vigor —William Baucke⟩ ⟨men may be considered to have risen into the ~ state when they take to agriculture —E.B.Tylor⟩ **2** *of artistic style or expression* : marked by a lack of restraint or by unchecked exuberance ⟨the ~ use of color or ornament⟩ : having a bizarre, primitive, or unsophisticated quality ⟨the ~ splendor of the carving —*Notes and Queries*⟩ ⟨the ~ richness of color of Stravinsky's *Rite of Spring*⟩ ⟨I sound my ~ yawp —Walt Whitman⟩ ⟨wild ~ music —Sir Walter Scott⟩ ⟨the tangled, loose ~ magnificence of the Elizabethan drama —*Think*⟩ **syn** see BARBARIAN

bar·bar·i·cal·ly \-ə̇k(ə)lē, -ēk-, -li\ *adv* : in a barbaric manner

bar·bar·i·ous \(ˈ)≈ˈberēəs, -ˈba(a)r-,-ˈbär-\ *adj* [by alter.] : BARBAROUS

bar·ba·rism \ˈbärbəˌrizəm, ˈbȧb-\ *n* -s [MF *barbarisme,* fr. L *barbarismus,* fr. Gk *barbarismos,* fr. *barbaros* foreign + *-ismos* -ism — more at BARBAROUS] **1 a** : a word or expression which in form or use offends against contemporary standards of correctness or purity in a language esp. in the derivative construction of words **b** : any idea, act, or performance that runs counter to prevailing standards of good taste or of what is intellectually or artistically sound or correct ⟨the ~ seen on some of the Assyrian sculpture, where inscriptions were scrawled right across the work without regard to design —Edward Clodd⟩ ⟨the idea of . . . a unit of international exchange based upon an unchanging value in terms of gold is an economic ~ —E.H.Collins⟩ **2 a** : a barbarian or barbarous social or intellectual condition ⟨that peculiar taint of ~ which makes men prefer occasional disobedience to systematic liberty —H.T.Buckle⟩ : BACKWARDNESS ⟨drew the country out of its economic ~ and illiteracy⟩ **b** (1) : the practice or display of barbarian acts, attitudes, or ideas esp. of barbarous cruelty or brutality ⟨the reversion to ~ in political trials and punishments —Alfred Cobban⟩ ⟨the ~ with which the revolt was suppressed⟩ (2) : a particular trait or characteristic of this condition ⟨I had been taught that war was an outmoded ~ —A.W.Turnbull⟩ **c** *among some anthropologists* : a stage of cultural development between savagery and civilization characterized by a primitive agricultural and pastoral economy but lacking a written language

bar·bar·i·ty \bärˈbarəd·ē, bȧˈb-, -ətē, -i *also* -ˈber-\ *n* -ES [L *barbarus* + E *-ity*] **1** : BARBARISM ⟨liberties . . . which were now threatened by the rising tide of ~ —Walter Lippmann⟩ ⟨many American writers fled to exile . . . in disgust at the ~ of their homeland —Horace Sutton⟩ ⟨a ~ which deserves the ridicule which we bestow upon the rites of savages —Virginia Woolf⟩ **2 a** : barbarous cruelty : INHUMANITY ⟨to mitigate the ~ of the criminal law —W.R.Inge⟩ **b** : an act or instance of barbarous cruelty : ATROCITY ⟨there were few inhuman *barbarities* aside from the custom of scalping —*Amer. Guide Series: Maine*⟩

bar·ba·ri·za·tion \ˌbärbərəˈzāshən, ˌbȧb-, -ˌrīˈz-\ *n* -s **1** : the act of making barbarous : the action of becoming barbarous **2** : the state of being barbarized

bar·ba·rize \ˈ≈≈ˌrīz\ *vb* -ED/-ING/-S [partly fr. Gk *barbarizein* to act or speak like a barbarian, fr. *barbaros* + *-izein* -ize; partly fr. E *barbarous* + *-ize*] *vi* **1** : to use barbarisms in speech or writing **2** : to become barbarous ⟨Christianity began rapidly to ~ —H.H.Milman⟩ ~ *vt* : to make barbarian or barbarous ⟨the Greek world had been cut off and the Roman world *barbarized* —Gilbert Highet⟩ ⟨an aristocratic and ruling class may just as well ~ culture as revive it —William Barrett⟩

⟨with the end of the Roman schools the Latin used was terribly *barbarized* —F.B.Artz⟩

bar·ba·rous \'bärb(ə)rəs, 'bȧb-\ *adj* [L *barbarus*, fr. Gk *barbaros* foreign, rude, ignorant; perh. akin to Skt *barbara* stammering, non-Aryan — more at BABBLE] **1 :** characterized by the use of barbarisms in speech or writing ⟨~ language⟩ **:** constituting a barbarism in speech or writing ⟨a ~ phrase⟩ **2 a :** BARBARIAN, UNCIVILIZED ⟨so ~ are some of these jungle lands that when . . . mapping planes dipped low, savage Indians launched futile spears . . . at them —*Nat'l Geographic*⟩ **b :** lacking culture or refinement **:** PHILISTINE ⟨a large enough advance to permit him to escape . . . from this ~ country to lodgings in Paris or Rome —Harrison Smith⟩ **c :** contrary to good or fashionable standards (as of taste or deportment) ⟨the ~ taste of our time and country, which had loaded . . . the furniture with bric-a-brac —Ambrose Bierce⟩ ⟨wolfing my dinner in order to arrive at the opera house at the ~ hour of seven-fifteen —Winthrop Sargeant⟩ **d :** BARBARIC, INHUMANE ⟨the crimes in this country are more ~ —W.C.Reckless⟩ **syn** see BARBARIAN, FIERCE

barbarously *adv* **:** in a barbarous manner

bar·ba·rous·ness \-nəs\ *n* -ES **:** BARBARISM, BARBARITY ⟨the provincialism and crudity, if not outright ~, of . . . society —R.T.LaPiere⟩

bar·ba·ry ape \'bärb(ə)rē-, 'bȧb-, -ri-\ *n, usu cap B* [fr. *Barbary*, coastal region in northern Africa] **:** a tailless monkey (*Macaca sylvana*) of No. Africa and the Rock of Gibraltar that is the only monkey now native to Europe and is often trained by showmen

barbary coast *n, usu cap B & often cap C* [fr. the *Barbary Coast*, former notorious vice-ridden section of San Francisco, after the *Barbary coast* of northern Africa, former pirate center] **:** a district or section of a city noted as a center of gambling, prostitution, and riotous night life ⟨a *Barbary Coast* in the Colorado desert —Frank Waters⟩

barbary fig *n, usu cap B* **:** a common prickly pear (*Opuntia vulgaris*) of the eastern U.S. introduced into No. Africa

barbary horse *n, usu cap B* **:** ⁴BARB 1

barbary lion *n, usu cap B* **:** the No. African lion

barbary mastic *n, usu cap B* **:** a mastic obtained from a plant (*Pistacia atlantica*) of the Mediterranean region; *also* **:** the plant itself

barbary sheep *n, usu cap B* **:** AOUDAD

bar·bas \'bärbəs, -bəz\ *n, pl* **barbas** \-bəz,-bəs\ [Pg, lit., beards, pl. of *barba* beard, fr. L — more at BEARD] **:** a tropical American timber tree (*Vitex longeracemosa*) with yellowish brown lustrous wood — called also *jocote de mico*

bar·bas·co \bär'ba(,)skō, -r'bä-\ *also* **ba·bas·co** \bä'b-,bə'b-\ *n* -S [AmerSp *barbasco*, perh. alter. of Sp *verbasco, varbasco* mullein, fr. L *verbascum*] **1 :** WILD CINNAMON 1 **2 :** JOEWOOD **3 a :** any of various plants used by the Indians of northern So. America in making fish poison; *esp* **:** ³CUBE 1 **b :** the poison (as rotenone) contained in these plants

bar bass *n* [¹*bar*; fr. its resting on gravel bed bars] **:** CHANNEL BASS

bar·ba·stel *or* **bar·ba·stelle** \ˌbärbəˌstel\ *n* -S [F *barbastelle*, fr. It *barbastello*, fr. It dial. (Ferrara) *barbastel, barbastrel*, fr. L *vespertilio* bat — more at VESPERTILIO] **:** a long-eared European bat (*Barbastellus barbastellus*)

bar·bate \'bär,bāt\ *adj* [L *barbatus*, fr. *barba* beard + *-atus* -ate — more at BEARD] **1 :** BEARDED **2** *bot* **:** bearing long stiff hairs

bar·ba·ti·mao \ˌbärbətē'maůⁿ\ *n* -S [Pg *barbatimão*, fr. Tupi *barbatimão*] **:** a Brazilian tree (*Stryphnodendron barbatimao*) of the family Mimosaceae that yields tanning material

barb bolt *n* [¹*barb*] **:** RAG BOLT

barbe \'bärb, 'bȧb\ *n* -S [ME, fr. MF, lit., beard — more at BARB] **1 :** ¹BARB 2 **2 :** a short scarf or lappet of lace formerly worn at the throat or on the head

bar·beau \'bär,bō, ₌'₌\ *n* -S [F, fr. *barbe* beard] **:** CORNFLOWER 1b

¹bar·be·cue *also* **bar·be·que** \'bärbə,kyü, 'bȧb-, -bē,k-\ *n* -S *often attrib* [AmerSp *barbacoa*, prob. fr. Taino] **1 a :** a metal rack on which meat and fish are roasted **b :** an often portable fireplace with such a rack **2 a :** a hog, steer, or other large animal roasted or broiled, whole or split, over an open fire or barbecue pit **b :** a social gathering of many people esp. in the open air at which whole or sides of large animals (as beef) are roasted over a barbecue pit **c :** pieces of meat, chicken, or fish broiled over or in front of a source of cooking heat outdoors or indoors **d :** meat or chicken cooked in a barbecue sauce **3 :** a place where barbecued meat is sold

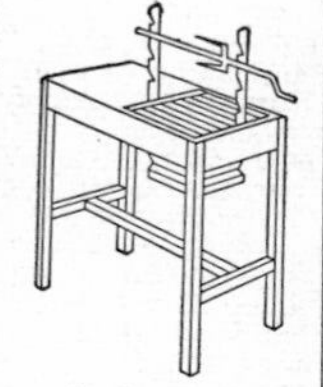

barbecue 1b

²barbecue \"\ *vt* -ED/-ING/-S **1 :** to dry or cure (as meat) by exposure to heat **2 :** to roast or broil (as beef or fish) on a rack over hot coals or on a revolving spit before or over a source of cooking heat **3 :** to cook (as beef or fish) in a highly seasoned vinegar sauce

barbecue pit *n* **:** a trench in which wood is burned to make a bed of hot coals over which meat is barbecued

bar·be·cu·er \-üə(r)\ *n* -S **:** one that barbecues

barbecue sauce *n* **:** a highly seasoned sauce of vinegar, condiments, and spices that may be used in cooking, basting, or serving meat or fish

¹barbed \'bärbd, 'bȧbd\ *adj* [³*barb* + *-ed*] **:** equipped with barbs ⟨under his feet he treads the armed Saracens and ~ steeds —Richard Carew⟩

²barbed \"\ *adj* [obs. E *barb* beard (fr. ME) + *-ed* — more at BARB] **1 a :** emblazoned with a beard ⟨an antelope argent ~ or⟩ **b :** emblazoned with wattles ⟨a cock vert ~ gules⟩ **c :** emblazoned with sepals showing between petals ⟨a rose gules ~ vert⟩ **d :** emblazoned with a pointed head ⟨an arrow argent ~ azure⟩ **2** [fr. past part. of ²*barb*] **a** *of a stream* **:** joined by tributaries at an acute angle pointed upstream ⟨a ~ tributary⟩ **b :** consisting of streams of this nature ⟨~ drainage⟩

barbed wire \'bä(r)b'(d)wī(ə)r; 'bȧb'(d)wīə, 'bäb-; *attrib* ₌'₌\ *n* [fr. past part. of ²*barb*] **:** a wire or a strand of twisted wires armed with barbs or sharp points

bar·bei·ro \bär'bā(,)rü, -rō\ *n* -S [Pg, lit., barber, fr. *barba* beard, fr. L; fr. its blood-sucking apparatus — more at BEARD] **:** a large black red-spotted cone-nose bug (*Triatoma*, or *Conorhinus, megistus*) of the American tropics that transmits the trypanosome causing Chagas' disease

barbed wire

¹bar·bel \'bärbəl, 'bȧb-\ *n* -S [ME, fr. MF, fr. (assumed) VL *barbellus*, dim. of L *barbus* barbel — more at BARBUS] **1 :** a large European freshwater fish (*Barbus fluviatilis*) with four barbels on its upper jaw **2 :** any of various species of the genus *Barbus*

²barbel \"\ *n* -S [obs. F (now *barbeau*), fr. MF, dim. of *barbe* barb, beard, fr. L *barba* — more at BEARD] **1 :** a slender tactile process on the lips of certain fishes (as catfishes and cyprinoids) **2 barbels** *pl* **:** ¹BARB 4 — used esp. when the processes are inflamed and turgid **3 :** a fleshy process on the chin or neck of some turtles

bar·bell \'bär,bel, 'bȧ,b-\ *n* [¹*bar* + *bell*] **:** a bar with adjustable weighted disks attached to each end used for exercise and in weight lifting

bar·bel·late \'bärbə,lāt, (')bär'belət\ *adj* [NL *barbella* short stiff hair (dim. of L *barbula*, dim. of *barba* beard + E *-ate* — more at BEARD] *biol* **:** having short stiff hooked bristles or hairs

bar·bel·lu·la \bär'belyələ\ *n, pl* **barbellu·lae** \-,lē\ [NL, dim. of *barbella* short stiff hair, dim. of L *barbula* little beard — more at BARBULA] *biol* **:** a very small barb or bristle — **barbel·lu·late** \(')₌'₌₌lət, -,lāt\ *adj*

barbeque *var of* BARBECUE

¹bar·ber \'bärbər, 'bȧbə(r\ *n* -S [ME *barbour, barber*, fr. MF *barbeor*, fr. *barbe*, fr. L *barba* beard + *-eor* -or — more at BEARD] **1 :** one whose business is cutting and dressing hair, shaving and trimming beards, and performing related services (as giving facials or scalp treatments or formerly performing dentistry and surgery) **2 a :** a Tasmanian fish (*Caesioperca rasor*) of the family Serranidae **b :** an African catfish (*Clarias capensis*) **3 :** FROST SMOKE

²barber \"\ *vb* **barbered; barbered; barbering** \-b(ə)riŋ\ **barbers** *vt* **1 :** to render the services of a barber to; *esp* **:** to cut, trim, dress, or groom the hair or beard of ⟨~*ed* him and bathed him and sent him to a tailor —T.W.Duncan⟩ **2 :** to cut or trim closely (as a lawn) ⟨green acres of ~*ed* landscape —*Time*⟩ ~ *vi* **:** to perform usu. professionally the actions or services of a barber ⟨he'd been ~*ing* . . . for well over twenty years —G.S.Perry⟩

barber chair *n* **1 :** a specially constructed chair used in barbershops and usu. having a footrest, a backrest that may be lowered to reclining position, and a hydraulic mechanism for adjusting the height of the chair **2 :** a stump on which a slab is left standing when a tree is felled

barberfish \'₌₌,₌\ *n* **:** any of several bright red fishes of the genus *Anthias* (family Berycidae); *esp* **:** a fish (*A. anthias*) of Madeira and the Mediterranean

barbermonger \'₌₌,₌₌\ *n* [¹*barber* + *monger*] *obs* **:** FOP

bar·bero \bär'be(,)rō\ *n* -S [AmerSp, fr. Sp, barber, fr. *barba* beard, fr. L — more at BEARD] **:** SURGEONFISH

barber pole *or* **barber's pole** *n* **:** a usu. rotating pole with diagonal stripes of red and white or of red, white, and blue used as a sign for a barbershop

bar·ber·ry \'bär,berē, 'bȧ,-, -b(ə)rē, -ri\ *also* **ber·ber·ry** *or* **ber·bery** \'bər,-, 'bə,-\ *n* [by folk etymology (influence of ¹*berry*) fr. ME *barbere*, fr. MF *barbarin, berberis, berbere*, fr. Ar *barbārīs*] **1 :** any shrub of the genus *Berberis* — see AMERICAN BARBERRY, COMMON BARBERRY, JAPANESE BARBERRY **2 :** the dried rhizome and roots of various shrubs of the genus *Mahonia* used as a bitter tonic

barberry family *n* **:** BERBERIDACEAE

barberry rust *n* **:** the wheat stem rust in its aecial stage on barberry, formerly thought to be a distinct species (*Aecidium berberidis*)

¹bar·ber·shop \'₌₌,₌\ *n* **:** a barber's place of business

²barbershop \"\ *adj* [fr. *barbershop (quartet)*, male quartet traditionally associated with old-style barbershops] **1** *of singing* **:** in the style of impromptu unaccompanied vocal harmonizing of popular songs esp. by a male quartet or any informal singing group **2 a** *of harmony* **:** marked by avoidance of spread chords and by the favoring of chromatically altered tones — compare CLOSE HARMONY **b :** of, relating to, or marked by such harmony ⟨a ~ quartet⟩ ⟨a ~ chord⟩

³barbershop \"\ *n* **:** barbershop singing **:** barbershop harmony ⟨singing ~ for an hour after supper⟩

barber's itch *n* **:** ringworm of parts of the face and neck caused by any of several parasitic fungi

barber's pole worm *n* **:** a stomach worm (*Haemonchus contortus*)

bar·ber·ton daisy \'bärbərtᵊn-, -tən-, 'bȧbət-, *prob also* 'bärbət- *by r-dissimilation*\ *n, usu cap B* [fr. *Barberton*, town in eastern Transvaal, Union of South Africa] **:** TRANSVAAL DAISY

bar·ber·ton·ite \-tᵊn,īt, -tə,nīt\ *n* -S [*Barberton* + E *-ite*] **:** a mineral $Mg_6Cr_2(OH)_{16}(CO_3)·4H_2O$ consisting of a hydrous basic carbonate of magnesium and chromium

bar·bery \'bärbərē\ *n* -ES [MF *barberie*, fr. *barbier* barber (fr. *barbe* beard, fr. L *barba*) + *-ie* -y — more at BEARD] **:** the craft of a barber ⟨a fashionable dentist . . . who seems to have graduated from ~ to dentistry —Harvey Graham⟩

barbes *pl of* BARBE

bar·bet \'bärbət\ *n* -S [prob. fr. ¹*barb* + *-et*] **1 :** any of numerous loud-voiced tropical birds constituting a family (Capitonidae) of the Piciformes being closely related to the honey guides but having a large stout bill bearing bristles and usu. swollen at the base — see COPPERSMITH **2 :** PUFFBIRD

barbet

bar·bette \(')bär¦bet\ *n* -S [F, dim. of *barbe* nun's barb — more at BARB] **1 :** a nun's barb; *often* **:** one consisting only of a band passing under the chin and pinned on top of the head **2** [so called fr. the resemblance of the earthwork encircling the cannon to a nun's barb] **:** a mound of earth or an often specially protected platform on which guns are mounted to fire over a parapet **3 :** a cylinder of armor on a warship that gives protection to the rotating part of the turret below the gunhouse — **in barbette** *of a gun* **:** in such a position as to fire over a parapet rather than through embrasures

barbette carriage *n* **:** a gun carriage that elevates the gun sufficiently for it to be in barbette

barbette gun *n* **:** a gun mounted in barbette

bar·bi·can \'bärbəkən\ *n* -S [ME, fr. OF *barbacane*, fr. ML *barbacana*] **:** an outer defensive work of a city or castle; *esp* **:** a tower at a gate or bridge

bar·bi·cel \'bärbə,sel\ *n* -S [NL *barbicella*, dim. of L *barba* beard — more at BEARD] **:** one of the small processes on a barbule of the distal side of a barb of a feather that bear the hooks which hold the web of the feather together

bar·bier·ite \bär'bi,rīt\ *n* -S [Philippe *Barbier* fl1908 French chemist + E *-ite*] **:** a hypothetical monoclinic soda feldspar $NaAlSi_3O_8$ believed to be isomorphous with orthoclase

barb·ing \'bärbiŋ, 'bȧb-, -bēŋ\ *n* -S [fr. gerund of ²*barb*] **:** oblique cutting to form sharp points when forming barbed wire

bar bit *n* [¹*bar*] **:** a bit for horses of which the mouthpiece is a solid bar of metal sometimes covered (as with rubber) and having no lever action — see BIT illustration

bar·bi·tal \'bärbə,tȯl, 'bȧb- *sometimes* -bəd·ᵊl *or* -bət·ᵊl *or* bə,tal\ *n* -S [*barbituric* + *-al* (as in *Veronal*)] **:** a white crystalline habit-forming hypnotic $C_8H_{12}N_2O_3$ often administered in the form of its soluble sodium salt; diethyl-barbituric acid

bar·bi·ton \'₌₌,tän\ *n, pl* **barbitons** *or* **barbita** [L *barbitos*, *barbiton*, fr. Gk] **1** *also* **barbitos :** an ancient Greek musical instrument resembling a lyre **2** *obs* **:** LUTE, VIOL

bar·bi·tone \'₌₌,tōn\ *n* -S *sometimes cap* [*barbituric* + *-one*] *Brit* **:** BARBITAL

bar·bi·tu·rate \bär'bichərət, bȧ'b-, -,rāt *sometimes* -chrət; *also* ,bärbə'tů,rāt *or* ,bȧb- *or* -ə'tyů- *or* -t(y)ü- *sometimes* -ə'chü- *or* -ə'chü- *or* '₌₌,₌₌; *substand* 'bichəwət *or* -chə,wāt; *usu* -ād· *or* -ād· + V\ *n* -S [*barbituric* + *-ate*] **1 :** a salt or ester of barbituric acid **2 :** any of a large group of slightly bitter crystalline acids (as barbital, phenobarbital) or their salts derived from barbituric acid that are used as sedatives, hypnotics, and antispasmodics

bar·bi·tu·ric acid \ˌbärbə¦türik-, ¦bȧb-, -ə¦tyů-, -t(y)ü-, -rēk-\ *n* [part trans. of G *barbitursäure*, irreg. fr. the name *Barbara* + G *-ur-* (fr. ISV *uric*) + *säure* acid] **:** a crystalline acid $CH_2(CONH)_2CO$ that is a derivative of pyrimidine and is usu. obtained from malonic acid and urea; malonylurea; *also* **:** any of the acids derived from this acid, many of them being used as hypnotics

bar·bi·zon \'bärbə,zän\ *adj, usu cap* [fr. *Barbizon*, village near Fontainebleau Forest, France] **:** depicting landscape and rural genre subjects from direct observation of nature and with much attention to the expression of light and atmosphere — used esp. of a middle 19th century school of French painting

bar·ble \'bärbəl\ *n* -S [by alter.] **:** ¹BARB 4

barb·less \'bärbləs, 'bȧb-\ *adj* **:** being without a barb ⟨considered it unsporting to use anything other than a ~ hook⟩

bar·blet \'bärblət\ *n* -S [irreg. fr. ²*barbel* + *-let*] **:** a small barbel

bar·bo·la work \bär'bōlə, bȧ'b-\ *also* **barbola** *n* -S [origin unknown] **:** the decoration of small articles (as of wood or glass) with colored models of flowers, fruit, or other ornamental objects made from a plastic paste

bar·bo·ne \bär'bōnē\ *also* **barbone disease** *n* -S [It, lit., long beard, aug. of *barba* beard, fr. L — more at BEARD] **:** pasteurellosis of the domestic buffalo

bar·bo·tine \'bärbə,tēn\ *n* -S [F, fr. *barboter* to splash about + *-ine*] **1 :** ⁷SLIP 1a **2** *or* **barbotine ware :** early European ware decorated with raised slip designs

bar·botte \(')bär¦bät\ *also* **bar·booth** \-¦büt(h)\ *or* **bar·bu·di** \bär'büdē\ *n* -S [CanF & Turk; CanF *barbotte*, fr. Turk *barbut*] **:** a dice game in which a throw of 3-3, 5-5, 6-6, or 6-5 wins, a throw of 1-1, 1-2, 2-2, or 4-4 loses, and other throws do not count

barboy \'₌,₌\ *n* [¹*bar* (counter) + *boy*] **:** a bartender's helper who keeps the bar supplied (as with glasses and ice) and performs related duties (as peeling fruit and carrying off waste)

barbs *pl of* BARB, *pres 3d sing of* BARB

bar·bu·do \bär'bü(,)dō\ *n* -S [AmerSp, fr. Sp, adj., bearded, fr. *barba* beard, fr. L; fr. the barbels — more at BEARD] **1 :** any of several threadfins used as food; *esp* **:** a common species (*Polynemus virginicus*) of the Caribbean and adjacent areas **2 :** any of several berycoid fishes (genus *Polymixia*) widely distributed in the deeper waters of the Atlantic and Pacific oceans

bar·bu·la \'bärbyələ\ *n, cap* [NL, fr. L *barbula* little beard, dim. of *barba* beard — more at BEARD] **:** a large genus of slender tufted mosses (family Pottiaceae) with 16 mostly long spirally twisted peristome teeth

bar·bu·la·tion \ˌbärbyə'lāshən\ *n* S [*barbule* + *-ation*] **:** the occurrence of barbules — used of feathers

bar·bule \'bär(,)byül\ *n* -S [L *barbula* little beard] **:** a minute barb or beard: **a :** ²BARBEL 1 **b :** one of the processes along either side of a barb of a feather, those on the upper side resembling slender scroll-like plates and terminating in a thickened flange with which the hooks of the barbicels that terminate the barbules of the lower margin of an adjacent barb mesh

bar·buled \-ld\ *adj* **:** having barbules

bar burner *n* [¹*bar*] **:** one who secures samples of steel bars from each heat and prepares them for carbon analysis

bar·bus \'bärbəs\ *n, cap* [NL, fr. L, barbel] **:** a very large genus of chiefly small often brilliantly colored Old World fishes related to the carps and including a number that are popular in the tropical aquarium

barb·wire \'bä(r)b'wī(ə)r; 'bȧb'wīə, 'bäb-; *attrib* '₌¦₌\ *n* [¹*barb* + *wire*] **:** BARBED WIRE

bar car *n* [¹*bar*] **:** a parlor car or lounge car with facilities for preparing and serving beverages or other refreshments

bar·ca·role *or* **bar·ca·rolle** \'bärkə,rōl, 'bȧk-\ *n* -S [F *barcarolle*, fr. It *barcarola*, fr. *barcarolo* gondolier, fr. *barca* bark, barge, fr. LL — more at BARK] **1 :** a boat song esp. as sung by Venetian gondoliers and typically characterized by the alternation of a strong and a weak beat in 6/8 time and suggesting a rowing rhythm **2 :** an art song or other piece of music imitating a barcarole

¹bar·ce·lo·na \ˌbärsə¦lōnə, ¦bȧs-\ *adj, usu cap* [fr. *Barcelona*, Spain] **:** of or from the city of Barcelona, Spain **:** of the kind or style prevalent in Barcelona

²barcelona \"\ *n* -S **:** a handkerchief or scarf of twilled silk

barcelona nut *n, usu cap B* **:** a Spanish variety of hazelnut kiln-dried before exportation to preserve its flavor

bar·ce·lo·nese \¦₌₌(,)lō¦nēz, -ēs\ *n, pl* **barcelonese** *usu cap* [*Barcelona*, city & province of Spain + E *-ese*] **:** a native or resident of Barcelona, esp. Barcelona, Spain

bar·chan *or* **bar·chane** *or* **bar·khan** \(')bär¦kän, -¦k-\ *n* -S [Russ *barkhan*, fr. Kirghiz] **:** a moving sand dune shaped like a crescent and found in several very dry regions of the world

bar chart *n* [¹*bar*] **:** a graphic representation for comparing numbers by means of rectangles of uniform widths but of lengths proportional to the numbers being represented — called also *bar graph*

bar clamp *n* [¹*bar*] **:** a frame consisting of a long bar with two adjustable clamping jaws that is used usu. in woodwork or cabinetmaking for holding large work

bar·coo rot \(')bär¦kü-\ *n, often cap B* [fr. *Barcoo*, district of Australia, where the disease was common] **:** DESERT SORE

barcoo spew *or* **barcoo vomit** *n, often cap B* **:** a sickness occurring in Australia that is characterized by painless attacks of vomiting

bar creaser *n* [¹*bar*] **:** an operator of a machine for creasing paper-box blanks along lines where they are to be folded

¹bard \'bärd, 'bȧd\ *n* -S [ME, fr. ScGael & MIr; akin to W *bardd* poet and prob. to Skt *gṛṇāti* he praises — more at GRACE] **1 a :** a tribal poet-singer (as among the ancient Celts) gifted in composing and reciting verses usu. to harp accompaniment in honor of the chief or successive chiefs and their deeds and as a record in verse of tribal history, tradition, genealogy, or religious law **b :** any similar poet-singer of the period before the use of writing; *esp* **:** a composer, singer, or declaimer of epic or heroic verse **2** *obs* **:** one of a class of wandering musicians or minstrels in early Scotland often treated as vagabonds in Scottish law and opinion **3 a :** POET; *esp* **:** a poet who writes impassioned, lyrical, or epic verse ⟨the ~ walks in advance, leader of leaders —Walt Whitman⟩ **b :** a writer of insipid or mediocre verse **:** VERSIFIER ⟨newspaper ~*s*⟩

²bard *or* **barde** \"\ *n* -S [MF *barde*, fr. OSp *barda* horse armor, fr. Ar *barda'ah*] **1 a :** a piece of spiked or bossed armor for a horse's neck, breast, or flank — usu. used in pl. **b :** an ornamental imitation of such armor made of velvet or other rich cloth and often used in tournaments — usu. used in pl. **2 bards** *pl* **:** plate armor formerly worn by a man-at-arms **3 :** a slice of bacon used to cover meat or game for cooking

³bard \"\ *vt* -ED/-ING/-S [MF *barder*, fr. *barde*] **1 :** to equip or accouter with bards **2 :** to cover (meat or game) with slices of bacon for cooking

bar·dane \'bär¦dän\ *n* -S [F] **:** BURDOCK

bar·dash \(')bär¦dash\ *n* -ES [MF *bardache*, fr. OIt dial. *bardascia* youth, homosexual, fr. Ar *bardaj* slave, fr. Per *bardah*] **:** a homosexual male **:** CATAMITE

bar·dé \(')bär¦dā *F* bȧrdā\ *adj* [F, past part. of *barder* to bard (cover with bacon)] **:** covered with salt pork or slices of bacon before cooking

bar·dee *also* **bar·dy** \'bärdē\ *n, pl* **bardees** *also* **bardies** [prob. a native name in Australia] **:** a large Australian roundheaded borer that is the larva of a beetle (*Bardistus cibarius*) and is esteemed as food by the aborigines

bard·ic \'bärdik, 'bȧd-, -ēk\ *adj* [¹*bard* + *-ic*] **:** being, belonging, or relating to a bard or his poetry ⟨a ~ poet⟩ ⟨a ~ lay⟩

bard·ie \'bärdi\ *n* -S [¹*bard* + *-ie*] *Scot* **:** a minor poet

bar·di·glio \bär'dēl(,)yō\ *n* -S [It, fr. It dial. *bardiglio* grayish (It *pardiglio*) fr. Sp *pardillo* grayish, brown, fr. *pardo* gray, brown, prob. fr. L *pardus* panther; fr. the color of the panther — more at PARD] **:** an Italian marble commonly having a dark gray or bluish ground traversed by veins and occurring in its principal varieties in the neighborhood of Carrara and in Corsica

bard·ing \'bärdiŋ\ *n* -S [fr. gerund of ³*bard*] **:** the armorial or armorlike ornamental trappings of a horse — usu. used in pl.

bar ditch \'bär,-\ *n* [alter. of *borrow*] *chiefly West* **:** BORROW DITCH

bard·let \'bärdlət\ *or* **bard·ling** \-liŋ\ *n* -S **:** POETASTER

bar·do \'bär(,)dō\ *n* -S *often cap* [Tibetan, lit., between two] *Lamaism* **:** the intermediate or astral state of the soul after death and before rebirth

bard·ol·a·ter \bär'däləd·ər\ *also* **bard·ol·a·trist** \-lə·trəst\ *n* -S *sometimes cap* [*Bard (of Avon)*, nickname of William Shakespeare †1616 Eng. poet & playwright + *idolater*] **:** one who idolizes Shakespeare ⟨an ardent ~⟩

bard·ol·a·try \-ə·trē\ *n* -ES *sometimes cap* **:** the worship of Shakespeare

bard·ship \'bärd,ship\ *n* [¹*bard* + *-ship*] **:** the office of or condition of a bard

bardy \'bärdi\ *adj* -ER/-EST [prob. fr. ¹*bard* (minstrel) + *-y*] *Scot* **:** BOLD, FORWARD, INSOLENT

¹bare \'ba(a)(ə)r, 'be(ə)r,'ba(a)ə, 'beə\ *adj* -ER/-EST [ME, fr. OE *bær*; akin to OHG *bar* naked, ON *berr*, Lith *basas* barefoot, Arm *bok*] **1 a :** lacking its natural covering (as of hair, flesh, bark, or foliage) ⟨a stroke that left the bone ~⟩ ⟨a ~ hillside⟩ ⟨trees standing gaunt and ~⟩ ⟨a ~ scalp⟩ **b** (1) **:** lacking clothing **:** UNCOVERED ⟨expose a ~ back to the sun⟩ ⟨walk in ~ feet⟩ (2) *obs* **:** BAREHEADED **c** (1) **:** lacking its customary or appropriate covering (as of paint or carpets) ⟨~ aluminum gutters⟩ ⟨a ~ floor⟩ (2) **:** lacking armor or weapons **:** UNARMED — usu. used in the phrase *bare hands* or the word *bare-handed* ⟨fought and killed him with ~ hands⟩ (3) *of cloth* **:** THREADBARE (4) *of a sword* **:** UNSHEATHED ⟨and ~ was the Niblung sword —William Morris⟩ (5) *of a ship's mast* **:** having no sails set ⟨rode out the storm with ~ poles⟩ **d** *obs* **:** laid waste or desolate **2 :** exposed or open to view or comprehension — often used in the phrase *lay bare* ⟨lays ~ with admirable simplicity the essentials of the problem⟩ ⟨laid ~ the innermost secrets of the society⟩ **3 a :** lacking the usual or appropriate furnishings, equipment, or contents **:** EMPTY **:** unfurnished or scantily supplied ⟨tenant farmers who live in ~ shacks —*Amer. Guide Series: Texas*⟩ ⟨a ~ room, dusty and cold⟩ **b :** DESTITUTE, NEEDY, LACKING — usu. used with *of* ⟨a house ~ of all comforts save the devotion of the parents⟩ ⟨deny the right to livelihood of individuals ~ of all legal protection —Robert Lekachman⟩ **4 a :** having nothing left over or added ⟨a ~ living⟩ ⟨the ~ dinner of potatoes —Lewis Mumford⟩ **:** MINIMUM ⟨the ~ necessities of life⟩ **:** MERE ⟨the father drowned . . . when Nathan was a ~ two years old —Mary S. Watts⟩ ⟨rage . . . at the ~ idea that the tenant of a furnished house should interfere with the owner's timber —F.M.Ford⟩ **b :** having no more or little more than essentials **:** devoid of amplification or of adornment, refinement, or polish **:** severely plain **:** AUSTERE ⟨state the ~ truth⟩ ⟨the ~ folk tale, a simple narration of some happening or action —R.A.Hall b. 1911⟩ ⟨a ~ outline of a novelette⟩ **c :** SCANTY, MEAGER ⟨only a ~ portion of the available gold was being secured —Irving Stone⟩ **5** *obs* **:** WORTHLESS, PALTRY, INADEQUATE **6** *bridge* **:** unaccompanied by others of the same suit ⟨a ~ king⟩ ⟨hold the ace ~⟩

syn BARE, NAKED, NUDE, BALD, BARREN all indicate lack of some usual covering, shrouding, or overlaying. In reference to bodily matters, BARE usu. describes bodily parts, indicates simply an unclothed or uncovered condition, and lacks especial connotation ⟨maidens whose *bare* feet make no sound —Lafcadio Hearn⟩ ⟨legs *bare* or swathed from the knee to the ankle —Edna S. V. Millay⟩ NAKED usu. indicates complete lack of clothing; it may suggest a primitive or natural condition, rare and complete beauty, pitiful destitution, or wanton and shameless exhibitionism ⟨a boy and an old man — both islanders, the former nearly *naked* and the latter dressed in an old naval frock coat —Herman Melville⟩ ⟨a radiant spirit arose all beautiful in *naked* purity —P.B.Shelley⟩ ⟨hunt for food and be a *naked* man —S.T.Coleridge⟩ ⟨down with Reticence, down with Reverence — forward — *naked* — let them stare —Alfred Tennyson⟩ Especial connotations are lacking for NUDE, a synonym more sophisticated and less common before the 20th century, except that it is frequently used in relation to artistic productions ⟨standing before a picture of *nude* beauty —P.E.More⟩ In reference to bodily matters BALD also lacks especial connotation. In other contexts BARE stresses a lack of some covering, furniture, addition, or amplification usu. expected ⟨the house seemed *bare* and cold, a bareness scarcely modified by the few old pieces of furniture —Mary Austin⟩ ⟨scorched and blackened by the long summer, the country was as *bare* as a conquered province after the march of an invader —Ellen Glasgow⟩ ⟨the *bare* statement that "art is useless" is so vague as to be really meaningless, if not inaccurate and misleading —Havelock Ellis⟩ NAKED strongly suggests exposure or revelation ⟨it is not asked that poetry should offer *naked* argument and skeleton plans —C.D. Lewis⟩ ⟨numberless *naked*, detached coral formations are seen, just emerging, as it were, from the ocean —Herman Melville⟩ BALD indicates absence of natural covering, particularly on the top of something ⟨Texas, spanning a widely divergent region between the lush green coastal prairies and a semiarid trans-Pecos expanse of *bald* hills —*Amer. Guide Series: Tex.*⟩ It may also imply severe curt plainness and lack of adornment ⟨he invented no fancy phrases to decorate a *bald* fact —Agnes Repplier⟩ ⟨lend verisimilitude to an otherwise *bald* and unconvincing narrative —W.S.Gilbert⟩ BARREN stresses lack of natural covering ⟨the country was *barren* and rocks stuck up through the clay. There was no grass —Ernest Hemingway⟩ Otherwise it suggests impoverishment or fruitlessness ⟨my life is a *barren* and lonely one, and so full of work that I have not had much time for friendships —Bram Stoker⟩

²bare \"\ *vt* -ED/-ING/-S [ME *baren*, fr. OE *barian*; causative fr. the root of E ¹*bare*] **:** to make or lay bare **:** UNCOVER, REVEAL ⟨~ his back to the sun⟩ ⟨~ her teeth in a smile⟩ ⟨~*s* the remote origins of bolshevism —S.T.Possony⟩ ⟨demanding that men ~ their private opinion or else go to jail —Herbert Agar⟩ **syn** see STRIP

³bare \"\ *adv* [ME, fr. *bare*, adj.] *obs* **:** BARELY

⁴bare \"\ *archaic past of* BEAR

⁵ba·ré \bəˈrā, ˈbä(ˌ)rā\ *n, pl* **baré** *or* **barés** *usu cap* [Sp & Pg, of AmerInd origin] **1 a :** an Arawakan people on the Rio Negro and Rio Cassiquiare in northern Brazil and Venezuela **b :** a member of such people **2 :** the language of the Baré people

bare-assed \ˈ=ˌ=\ *adv (or adj)* **:** in the nude **:** UNCLOTHED — sometimes considered vulgar ⟨a boy swimming *bare-assed*⟩ ⟨a small *bare-assed* boy running along the beach⟩

bareback *or* **barebacked** \ˈ=ˌ=\ *adv (or adj)* **:** on the bare back of a horse without using a saddle ⟨a young boy riding ~⟩ ⟨learned ~ riding among the Indians⟩

bareback rider *n* **:** an entertainer (as in a circus) who performs acrobatic feats or feats of balance bareback while the horse is trotting or cantering

bareboat \ˈ=ˌ=\ *adj, of a charter* **:** placing on the charterer of a vessel once it has been outfitted and equipped by the owner full responsibility for operating and manning it and paying operation, repair, and insurance costs as if it were his own

bare bones *n pl* **:** the barest essentials, facts, or elements (as of a situation) ⟨the afternoon paper had reported the *bare bones* of the case —Thomas Thursday⟩ ⟨he finally stripped his proposition to its *bare bones* —A.H.Vandenberg †1951⟩

ba·re'e \bəˈrā,ā\ *n* -S **:** an Austronesian language of central Celebes

bare-eyed cockatoo \ˈ=ˌ=-\ *n* **:** a widely distributed small corella (*Kakatoe sanguinea*) with patches of bare bluish gray skin about the eyes

bareface \ˈ=ˌ=\ *adj, of a fabric* **:** having a clear finish and no nap

barefaced \ˈ=ˌ=\ *adj* **1 :** having the face uncovered: **a :** having no beard or whiskers **:** BEARDLESS **b :** wearing no mask **2 a :** UNCONCEALED, OPEN, OBVIOUS ⟨a ~ mockery of the new . . . trading class —Sam Pollock⟩ ⟨out of this ~ and unashamed formula evolves one of the most entertaining . . . tales of the lightly fantastic —John Nerber⟩ **b :** lacking scruples **:** SHAMELESS, BRAZEN ⟨a policy of ~ imperialism —W.K. Ferguson⟩ ⟨cheat each other in ways that were often ~ and sometimes violent —Havelock Ellis⟩ ⟨a ~ lie⟩ **c :** BLUNT, STRAIGHTFORWARD ⟨never slandered personalities, but he was . . . ~ about facts as he saw them —Peggy Bennett⟩ **syn** see SHAMELESS

bare·fac·ed·ly \(ˈ)=ˈfāsədlē, -stlē, -li\ *adv* **:** in a barefaced manner

barefaced tenon *n* **:** a tenon having a shoulder on one side only

bare fallow *n* **:** land remaining uncropped for a season and kept free from vegetation by cultivation

barefisted \ˈ=ˈ==\ *adv (or adj)* **:** BAREKNUCKLE ⟨fight ~⟩ ⟨a ~ exchange of blows⟩

bare·fit \ˈbär(ˌ)fit, -er-, -är-\ *adj* [by alter.] *Scot* **:** BAREFOOT

barefoot \ˈ=ˌ=\ *or* **barefooted** \ˈ=ˈ==\ *adv (or adj)* [ME *barefot*, fr. OE *bærfōt* (akin to MHG *barvuoz*, OFris *berfōt*, ON *berfættr*), fr. *bær* bare + *fōt* foot — more at BARE, FOOT] **1 a :** with the feet bare **:** without shoes or stockings ⟨a ~ boy⟩ ⟨go ~ in the summertime⟩ **b** *of a horse* **:** UNSHOD **2 :** wearing only sandals on the feet — used esp. of certain religious communities **3 :** set up and fastened without a mortise and tenon (as a post or stud in a balloon frame) **4** *of an oil well* **:** drilled without a casing

B barefaced tenon

barefoot auger *n* **:** SHIP AUGER

ba·rege \bəˈrezh\ *n* -S [F *barège*, fr. *Barèges*, a town in the Pyrenees, France] **:** a sheer fabric of open weave for women's clothing usu. made of wool in combination with silk or cotton

bare-handed \ˈ=ˈ==\ *adv (or adj)* **1 :** without covering on the hands **:** UNGLOVED ⟨box *bare-handed*⟩ **2 :** without tools, implements, or weapons ⟨fight an animal *bare-handed*⟩ ⟨efforts to survive *bare-handed* in a hostile world —Lewis Mumford⟩

bareheaded \ˈ=ˈ==\ *also* **barehead** \ˈ=ˌ=\ *adv (or adj)* [ME *barehed*, fr. *bare* + *hed* head] **:** without a hat or other covering for the head ⟨standing ~ in the rain —*New Republic*⟩ ⟨go ~ in the hot sun⟩ ⟨a ~ boy who had lost his cap⟩ — **bare·head·ed·ness** *n* -ES

ba·reil·ly \bəˈrālē\ *adj, usu cap* [fr. *Bareilly*, India] **:** of or from the city of Bareilly, India **:** of the kind or style prevalent in Bareilly

¹bareknuckle *or* **bareknuckled** \ˈ=ˈ=ˌ=\ *adj* [¹*bare* + *knuckle* or *knuckled*] **1 :** not using boxing gloves — used of fighting or a fighter ⟨champion ~ prizefighter of England —Dennis Craig⟩ **2 :** having an aggressive fierce unrelenting character ⟨led a *bareknuckled* fight against waste of public funds —J.R. Aswell & E.J.Michelson⟩

²bareknuckle *or* **bareknuckled** \ˈ=ˈ==\ *adv* **:** in a bareknuckle way ⟨the early days of pugilism in which men fought ~⟩ ⟨fighting ~ in congress for his beliefs⟩

barely *adv* [ME, fr. ¹*bare* + -*ly*] **1 :** by the narrowest margin ⟨~ escaped injury⟩ **:** lacking any excess **:** with nothing to spare **:** SCARCELY, HARDLY ⟨~ enough food to sustain life⟩ **2 :** SCANTILY, MEAGERLY, PLAINLY ⟨a ~ furnished room⟩

ba·ren \(ˈ)bäˈren\ *n* -S [prob. fr. Jap] **:** a pad of twisted cord covered with paper, cloth, and bamboo leaf with which a printmaker transmits pressure typically by rubbing to paper laid on an inked woodcut

bare·ness *n* -ES [¹*bare* + -*ness*] **:** the quality or state of being bare ⟨a room furnished with a simplicity bordering on ~⟩ ⟨a story with a marked ~ of outline⟩

bare·sark \ˈ=ˌsärk\ *n* -S [intended as trans. of ON *berserkr* — more at BERSERK] **:** BERSERKER

ba·res·ma \ˈbarəsmə, -əzmə\ *n* -S [Av *barəsman-*] **:** BARSOM

bare trust *n* **:** PASSIVE TRUST

ba·ret·ta \bəˈredə\ *n* -S [modif. of MexSp *barreta*, fr. Sp *barreta, barrete* cap, biretta, fr. Catal *barret*, fr. Prov *berret* — more at BERET] **:** a rutaceous evergreen shrub (*Helietta parvifolia*) of Texas with opposite trifoliolate leaves and purple flowers

barff \ˈbärf\ *vt* -ED/-ING/-S [after *F.S.Barff* — more at BOWER-BARFF PROCESS] **:** to protect (iron or steel) with a coating of iron oxide Fe_3O_4 by the Bower-Barff process

barfish \ˈ=ˌ=\ *n* [¹*bar*; fr. the stripes on the back] **1 :** WHITE BASS **2 :** YELLOW BASS

barfly \ˈ=ˌ=\ *n* -ES [¹*bar* (counter) + *fly*] **:** a drinker who frequents bars

¹bar·gain \ˈbärgən, ˈbäg-\ *n* -S *often attrib* [ME *bargayn*, fr. MF *bargaigne*, fr. OF, fr. *bargaignier*] **1** *obs* **:** discussion of terms of agreement **:** HAGGLING **2 a :** an agreement between parties settling what each gives or receives in a transaction between them or what course of action or policy each pursues in respect to the other ⟨struck a ~ to sell only to each other⟩ ⟨the two armed camps made a ~ to cease fire⟩ **b** *dial Eng* **:** a piece of contract work at an agreed rate esp. in mining and quarrying **3 a :** a thing acquired by or as if by bargaining ⟨chaffered for half an hour before acquiring his ~⟩ **b :** an advantageous purchase **:** something whose value to the purchaser considerably exceeds its cost ⟨at that price the house is a ~⟩ **4 :** a transaction, situation, or event regarded in the light of its good or bad consequences or results ⟨make the best of a bad ~⟩ — **in the bargain** *or* **into the bargain :** over and above what is agreed on or might be anticipated **:** BESIDES ⟨singers . . . subdued and colorless, often naturally mediocre and conspicuously untrained *in the bargain* —H.F.Mooney⟩ ⟨destroyed the Popular Front and ruined the Spanish Republic *into the bargain* —*Times Lit. Supp.*⟩

²bargain \"\ *vb* -ED/-ING/-S [ME *bargaynen*, fr. MF *bargaignier*, fr. OF, of Gmc origin; akin to OE *borgian* to borrow — more at BURY] *vi* **1 :** to negotiate over the terms of an agreement or contract **:** haggle esp. over a purchase price ⟨nosegays bought from the urchins who ~*ed* on the carriage roads —Jean Stafford⟩ ⟨~*ed* for the use of the property⟩ ⟨considered the possibility of ~*ing* with the enemy⟩; *specif* **:** to engage in collective bargaining ⟨ask that both management and labor ~ in good faith⟩ **2 :** to agree to certain terms or conditions **:** come to terms ⟨~*ed* on setting me ashore tonight⟩ ~ *vt* **1 a :** to bring (a price) to a desired level by bargaining ⟨~ the price of meat down⟩ **b :** to sell or dispose of by bargaining ⟨~ his services to the highest bidder —*Springfield (Mass.) Daily News*⟩ **:** BARTER, TRADE ⟨~ one horse for another⟩ **c :** to resolve or settle (as differences) by bargaining ⟨~*ed* out the remaining obstacles to an agreement⟩ **d :** to bring (a party) to a specific agreement by bargaining ⟨tried . . . to ~ Britain out of her share of this region —R.W.Van Alstyne⟩ **2 :** to give assurances or make a commitment **:** PLEDGE — usu. used with clause as object ⟨I couldn't ~ that my mind should remain suggestive at that age —O.W.Holmes †1935⟩ ⟨I ~ that he'll be there on time⟩ — **bargain for :** to expect or plan for **:** count on in advance ⟨find mountain climbing harder than one *bargained for*⟩ — often used in negative construction ⟨they had not *bargained for* anything on so large a scale —Jean Stafford⟩ — **bargain on :** to count on **:** EXPECT ⟨*bargain on* making a fortune early in life⟩ ⟨hadn't *bargained on* so cold a reception⟩

bar·gain·a·ble \-nəbəl\ *adj* **:** subject to bargaining; *esp* **:** legitimately subject to collective bargaining ⟨a ~ contract⟩

bargain and sale *n, law* **:** a conveyance by which the vendor contracts for a consideration paid to convey the lands to the vendee and becomes by such contract a trustee for and seized to the use of the vendee — see BARGAINEE, BARGAINOR

bargain basement *n* **:** a section of a store (as the basement) where merchandise is sold at bargain prices

bargain-basement \ˈ==ˈ===\ *adj* [*bargain basement*] **:** markedly cheap or inexpensive ⟨a bill to . . . sell it to them at *bargain-basement* rates — A.J.Liebling⟩

bargain counter *n* **:** a counter where merchandise is sold at bargain prices

bargain-counter \ˈ==ˈ==\ *adj* [*bargain counter*] **:** BARGAIN-BASEMENT ⟨*bargain-counter* divorces —Morris Ploscowe⟩

bar·gain·ee \ˌ=gəˈnē\ *n* -S [²*bargain* + -*ee*] **:** the vendee in a bargain and sale

bar·gain·er \-nə(r)\ *n* -S [ME *bargayner*, fr. *bargaynen* to bargain + -*er*] **:** one that bargains

bargain hunter *n* **:** one that goes shopping for bargains

bargaining power *n* **:** the relative capacity of each of the parties to a negotiation or dispute to compel or secure agreement on its own terms ⟨widespread unemployment is adding to employers' *bargaining power* in their talks with the unions⟩

bargaining unit *n* **:** the group of employees on whose behalf a union seeks to negotiate a collective agreement

bar·gain·or \ˈ=gəˌnȯ(ə)r, -ōə, ˈ=gənə(r)\ *n* -S **:** the vendor in a bargain and sale

bargain plea *n, slang* **:** a plea of guilty to one usu. the least of several charges allowed by the prosecution when the prosecution stands to gain thereby (as where an offer of prosecution under a lesser charge is useful in persuading an offender to turn state's evidence)

¹barge \ˈbärj, ˈbäj\ *n* -S [ME, fr. OF, fr. LL *barca*] **1** *obs* **:** a sailing vessel; *specif* **:** one next larger than the balinger **:** BARK **2 :** any of various boats: as **a :** a roomy usu. flat-bottomed boat used principally in harbors or inland waterways though often sea-going for the transport of goods (as coal, oil, lumber, or grain) and sometimes passengers and usu. propelled by towing **b :** a large boat formerly a double-banked rowboat but now a powerboat supplied to a naval flagship for the use of a flag officer **c :** a roomy pleasure boat; *esp* **:** a boat of state elegantly furnished and decorated **d :** a racing boat somewhat broader and heavier than a shell and often used for practice purposes **e :** a towed or self-propelled boat used to transport freight cars over or across water routes not provided with bridges **3 :** ²KEEL 1b **4 :** a tub or box for bread for the crew's mess on a ship **5** *chiefly NewEng* **:** a large horse-drawn omnibus usu. used for excursions or the transportation of groups (as from a railroad station to a hotel)

²barge \"\ *vb* -ED/-ING/-S *vt* **:** to carry by barge ⟨ore will be *barged* down the Orinoco —*Newsweek*⟩ ⟨have already *barged* out the virgin forests in the form of lumber —*Sat. Eve. Post*⟩ ~ *vi* **1 :** to move or charge in a lumbering, ponderous, or clumsy manner ⟨he was a particularly cheeky saurian and soon came *barging* along to inspect us —Francis Birtles⟩ or in a headlong, impetuous, heedless, or aimless fashion ⟨a bat flew in the front door, *barged* around for 20 minutes until finally knocked down —*Time*⟩ **2 :** to thrust oneself unceremoniously (as into a place where one is unwanted) — used with *in* or *into* ⟨~ in on some friends while they are eating dinner⟩

³barge \ˈbärj, ˈbäj\ *vt* -ED/-ING/-S [E dial. (Ireland), *barge* shrewish woman, fr. IrGael *bairseach*] *dial Brit* **:** SCOLD, REBUKE ⟨she could have *barged* me all night telling me I was a cur and a coward —D'Arcy Niland⟩

bargeboard \ˈ=ˌ=\ *n* [origin unknown] **:** a piece of board often elaborately ornamented that conceals roof timbers projecting over gables

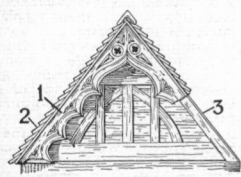

barge couple *n* [origin unknown] **:** one of the two rafters in a gable that project beyond the gable wall and carry the overhanging part of the roof

barge course *n* [origin unknown] **1 :** a part of the tiling on the sloping edges of a gable roof usu. projecting beyond the principal rafters or the bargeboards **2 :** the course of bricks laid on edge to form the coping of a wall

1 bargeboard, cut away at right to show *2* barge course; *3* barge couple

barg·ee \(ˈ)bärˈjē, (ˈ)bäˈj-\ *n* -S [¹*barge* + -*ee*] *Brit* **:** BARGEMAN

barge·man \ˈbärjmən, -äj-\ *n, pl* **bargemen** [ME, fr. ¹*barge* + *man*] **:** the master or a deckhand of a barge

bar gemel *or* **bar gemelle** *n, pl* **bars gemel** *or* **bars gemels** *or* **bars gemelles** *heraldry* **:** a pair of narrow bars borne close together — called also *gemel*

barge pole *n* [¹*barge*] **:** a long pole used on a barge for propelling, for fending off objects, or with an attached hook for holding onto a wharf

barg·er \ˈbärjər, ˈbäjə(r\ *n* -S [¹*barge* + -*er*] **:** BARGEMAN

barge spike *n* [¹*barge*] **:** a long square spike used in heavy timber construction — called also *boat spike*

barge stone *n* [origin unknown] **:** one of the stones that make the sloping edge of a gable

bar·gham \ˈbärfəm, -rkəm\ *n* -S [ME, perh. fr. OE *beorgan* to protect + *hama* covering — more at BURY, HAME] *now dial Eng* **:** a horse collar

bar·ghest *also* **bar·guest** \ˈbärgəst\ *n* -S [perh. fr. E dial. *bar, bargh* ridge (fr. ME *bergh* hill) + E dial. *ghest*, alter. of *ghost* — more at BARROW] *dial Eng* **:** a ghost or goblin believed to portend misfortune and sometimes appearing in the shape of a large dog

bar graph *n* [¹*bar*] **:** BAR CHART

barhal *var of* BHARAL

bar-headed goose \ˈ=ˌ==-\ *or* **barhead goose** \ˈ=ˌ=-\ *n* [¹*bar*] **:** an Asiatic goose (*Anser indicus*) having a white head with two black bars on the occiput

barhop \ˈ=ˌ=\ *vi* **barhopped**; **barhopped**; **barhopping**; **barhops** [¹*bar* (counter) + *hop*] **:** to visit and usu. to drink at a series of bars esp. in one evening staying only a short time in any one bar ⟨to spend a vacation *barhopping* in Paris and London⟩ **:** PUB-CRAWL

¹ba·ri \ˈbärē\ *n, pl* **bari** *or* **baris** *usu cap* **1 a :** a Nilotic Negro people in the Sudan near Gondokoro **b :** a member of the Bari people **2 :** a Nilotic language of the Bari

²bari \"\ *adj, usu cap* [fr. *Bari*, Italy] **:** of or from the city of Bari, Italy **:** of the kind or style prevalent in Bari

ba·ria \bəˈrēə\ *n* -S [AmerSp *baria*] **:** PRINCEWOOD 1

ba·ri·ba \bəˈrēbə, ¦bärēˈbä\ *n, pl* **bariba** *or* **baribas** *usu cap* **1 a :** a Negro people of northern Dahomey, West Africa **b :** a member of such people **2 :** a Gur language of the Bariba people

bar·ic \ˈbarik\ *adj* [NL *barium* + E -*ic*] **:** of or relating to barium

ba·ri·lla \bəˈrēlyə, -ē(y)ə\ *n* -S [modif. of Sp *barrilla*] **1 a :** either of two European saltworts (*Salsola kali* and *S. soda*) **b :** an Algerian plant (*Halogeton souda*) formerly burned as a source of sodium carbonate **2 :** an impure sodium carbonate made from the ashes of barillas formerly used esp. in making soap and glass

bar·ing \ˈba(a)riŋ, ˈber-, -rēŋ\ *n* -S **:** something that is removed in making bare: as **a :** the surface soil removed from ore or rock **b barings** *pl* **:** the small coal made in undercutting coal seams

ba·ri·o·lage \¦barēōˈlāzh\ *n* -S [F, fr. MF, fr. *barioler* to variegate (prob. blend of *barrer* to cross out, streak, bar + *rioler* to cross out, streak, fr. *riole* rule, ruler, fr. L *regula*) + -*age* — more at BAR, RULE] **1 :** MEDLEY **2 a :** a cadenza for a solo musical instrument; *specif* **:** a special effect in violin playing obtained by playing in rapid alternation upon open and stopped strings

bar iron *n* [¹*bar*] **:** wrought iron in the form of bars

ba·ris \ˈbärəs\ *n, pl* **baris** [native name in Bali] **:** a Balinese spear dance or warriors' dance with angular movements depicting a sham battle

bar·i·sal guns \ˈbarəˌsȯl-\ *n pl, cap* B [fr. *Barisal*, town in East Bengal, Pakistan] *meteorol* **:** brontides heard near the town of Barisal on a mouth of the Ganges

bar·ish \ˈba(a)rish, ˈber-\ *adj* [¹*bare* + -*ish*] **:** rather bare **:** scant in furnishings, equipment, or contents **:** thinly covered (as with hair or tree growth)

ba·rit \bəˈrēt\ *n* -S [Tag] **:** a stoloniferous marsh grass (*Leersia hexandra*) of the Philippines that is used as horse fodder

bar·ite *or* **bar·yte** \ˈbaˌrīt *also* ˈbe-\ *or* **ba·ry·tes** \bəˈrīd-ēz, ˈbarəˌtēz\ *n, pl* **barites** *or* **barytes** [Gk *barytēs* weight, fr. *barys* heavy — more at GRIEVE] **:** a white, yellow, or colorless mineral consisting of native barium sulfate $BaSO_4$ occurring in orthorhombic and generally tabular crystals, in granular form, or in compact massive forms resembling marble (sp. gr. 4.3–4.6) — called also *heavy spar*

bar·i·ten·or \ˈbarəˌtenə(r)\ *n* -S [blend of *baritone* and *tenor*] **1 :** a baritone singing voice with virtually a tenor range **2 :** a singer having a baritenor voice

bar·i·tone *or* **bar·y·tone** \ˈbarəˌtōn *also* ˈber-\ *n* -S *often attrib* [F *baryton* or It *baritono*, fr. Gk *barytonos*, adj., deep sounding, fr. *bary-* + *tonos* tone — more at TONE] **1 a :** a male singing voice of medium compass between bass and tenor and partaking somewhat of the quality of both **b :** one having such a voice **2 :** VIOLA BASTARDA **3 :** the saxhorn intermediate in size between althorn and tuba

baritone oboe *n* **:** HECKELPHONE

bar·i·um \ˈba(a)rēəm, ˈber-,ˈbār-\ *n* -S [NL, fr. *bar-* + -*ium*] **:** a silver-white malleable toxic bivalent metallic element of the alkaline-earth group that tarnishes rapidly in air, that occurs only in combination esp. as barite and witherite, that is made by reduction of barium oxide or by electrolysis of a fused salt (as barium chloride), and that is used in the form of alloys chiefly as a getter in electron tubes — symbol *Ba*; see ELEMENT table

barium carbonate *n* **:** a water-insoluble toxic salt $BaCO_3$ occurring in nature as witherite, made artificially by precipitation as a white powder, and used chiefly in making other barium compounds, in removing sulfates from aqueous solutions, in ceramics as a flux, and in optical glass

barium chloride *n* **:** a water-soluble toxic salt obtained usu. as colorless crystals $BaCl_2.2H_2O$ by treating barium sulfide with hydrochloric acid and used chiefly as a raw material (as for blanc fixe) and a reagent in analysis

barium chromate *n* **:** a yellow crystalline toxic salt $BaCrO_4$ used chiefly as a pigment

barium enema *n* **:** a suspension of barium sulfate injected into the lower bowel to render it radiopaque, usu. followed by injection of air to inflate the bowel and increase definition, and used in the roentgenographic diagnosis of intestinal lesions

barium hydroxide *n* **:** a strong toxic base $Ba(OH)_2.8H_2O$ obtained usu. as colorless crystals by dissolving barium oxide in water and used chiefly in making lubricating greases and esp. formerly in recovering sugar from molasses

barium meal *n* **:** a solution of barium sulfate that is swallowed by a patient to facilitate fluoroscopic or roentgenographic diagnosis

barium nitrate *n* **:** a colorless crystalline toxic salt $Ba(NO_3)_2$ used chiefly in pyrotechnics (as in green lights) and in explosives

barium oxide *n* **:** any oxide of barium; *esp* **:** the monoxide BaO obtained usu. as a white to grayish toxic powder by heating barium carbonate or barium sulfate with carbon and used chiefly in making barium hydroxide and barium peroxide, in coating cathodes of electron tubes, and as a drying agent

barium peroxide *also* **barium dioxide** *n* : a compound BaO_2 obtained as a grayish white toxic powder by heating barium monoxide in air or oxygen and used chiefly in making hydrogen peroxide and in pyrotechnics

barium sulfate *n* : a colorless crystalline insoluble salt $BaSO_4$ occurring in nature as barite, obtained artificially by precipitation, and used chiefly as a pigment and extender, as a filler, and as a radiopaque substance — see BLANC FIXE, LITHOPONE

barium sulfide *n* : any sulfide of barium; *esp* : the colorless crystalline toxic monosulfide BaS obtained usu. as a gray to black substance by reducing barite with coal and used chiefly in making other barium compounds, pigments (as lithopone), and luminous paints

barium titanate *n* : a white crystalline compound $BaTiO_3$ characterized by ferroelectric and piezoelectric properties and used in hearing aids, phonograph pickups, and ceramic transducers

barium yellow *n* **1** : barium chromate used as a pigment **2** : a pale to light yellow — called also *colonial buff*

[1]bark \ˈbärk, ˈbȧk\ *vb* -ED/-ING/-S [ME *berken*, fr. OE *beorcan*; akin to ON *berkja* to bark, Lith *burgėti* to growl, quarrel] *vi* **1 a** *of a dog* : to emit or utter its characteristic short loud explosive cry **b** : to make a noise resembling a bark ⟨a fox ~*ed* far away —Ellen Glasgow⟩ ⟨a squirrel ~*ed* at him from a beech tree —Edwin Granberry⟩ ⟨a seal ~*s*⟩ ⟨a solitary cannon ~*ed* —Louis Bromfield⟩ **2** : to speak in a curt loud or explosive and usu. angry tone : SNAP ⟨Mr. Webb . . . alternately ~*ing* at his "son" and accusing his wife of an unforgivable breach of taste —Hollis Alpert⟩ ⟨~*ing* at his crew⟩ ⟨spends his life ~*ing* into phones —J.S.Sandoe⟩ ~ *vt* **1** : to utter in a curt loud usu. angry tone ⟨he would suddenly ~ out harsh, bitter, and coarse sayings —V.S.Pritchett⟩ ⟨~*ed* orders into the telephone for coffee and food —Barnaby Conrad⟩ **2** : to advertise (goods for public sale or use) by loud persistent outcry ⟨newsboys will be found ~*ing* their wares on the . . . steps —*Brit. Books of the Month*⟩

[2]bark \"\ *n* -s **1 a** : the short loud explosive sound made by a dog; *also* : a similar sound made by some other animals **b** : any other similar sound (as a cough or a pistol shot) **2** : a short sharp peremptory tone of speech or utterance ⟨the . . . ~ of the coxswain —W.H.Mansfield⟩

[3]bark \"\ *n* -s [ME *barke*, fr. ON *bark-*, *börkr*; akin to MD & MLG *borke* bark and prob. to ON *björk* birch tree — more at BIRCH] **1 a** : the exterior dead cellular covering of woody roots and stems, often rough when older, that consists at first mainly of cork layers and cortical parenchyma together with epidermis, pericycle, and phloem of which only phloem and cork persist indefinitely, and is considered to include (1) all tissues outside the true cambium or (2) only those tissues external to the innermost cork cambium — compare PERIDERM **b** : the outer layer or covering; *specif* : the human skin ⟨fell, knocking all the ~ off his shins⟩ **2 a** : TANBARK **b** : CINCHONA BARK **3** : a dark olive brown — called also *mocha*

[4]bark \"\ *vt* -ED/-ING/-S [ME *barken*, fr. *barke*, n.] **1** : to treat with an infusion of tanbark : TAN **2** : to strip the bark from; *specif* : [2]GIRDLE 3 **3** : to rub a portion of skin off or break the skin of usu. by banging or rubbing sharply against a rough or sharp object ⟨they kept on colliding with the cabinet in the dark, bruising their elbows and ~*ing* their shins —Hamilton Basso⟩ **4** : to bring down or kill (a squirrel in a tree) by striking the bark of the tree with a bullet

[5]bark *or* **barque** \"\ *n* -s [ME *bark*, fr. MF *barque*, fr. OProv *barca*, fr. LL] **1 a** : any small sailing ship (as a fishing smack or pinnace) **b** : ROWBOAT **2** : a three-masted vessel with her foremast and mainmast square-rigged and her mizzenmast fore-and-aft rigged — compare FOUR-MASTED BARK **3** : a craft of any size or character propelled by sails or oars ⟨some lone ~ buoy'd on the dense marine —Walt Whitman⟩

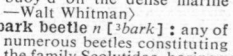

bark 2

bark beetle *n* [[3]*bark*] : any of numerous beetles constituting the family Scolytidae, boring under bark of trees both as larvae and adults, and including certain destructive pests of conifers — see DENDROCTONUS

bark canker *n* [[3]*bark*] any of various cankers of woody plants; *specif* : a canker of rubber trees caused by a fungus (*Phytophthora faberi*)

bark cloth *n* [[3]*bark*] **1** : a papery fabric made by primitive peoples from the bark of certain trees usu. by retting and beating; *specif* : TAPA CLOTH **2** : a loosely woven cotton or rayon cloth resembling linen but with a heavier fiber and used for drapes, slipcovers, or bedspreads

bark cloth tree *n* : any of various trees (as the paper mulberry or members of the genera *Ficus* and *Brachystegia*) having a strong fibrous inner bark from which bark cloth is made

bark disease *n* [[3]*bark*] : CHESTNUT BLIGHT

barked *past of* BARK

bar keel *n* [[1]*bar*] : a solid keel of rectangular section in an iron or steel ship — distinguished from *plate keel* and *trough keel* — see SHIP illustration

barkeeper \ˈ=,==\ *or* **barkeep** \ˈ=,=\ *n* -s : one that keeps or tends a bar for the sale of alcoholic beverages

[1]bark·en \ˈbärkən, ˈbȧk-\ *vb* -ED/-ING/-S [[3]*bark* + *-en*] *dial Brit* : to dry into a crust : ENCRUST

[2]barken \ˈbärkən, ˈbȧk-\ *adj* [[3]*bark* + *-en*] : made of bark

bar·ken·tine *or* **bar·kan·tine** *also* **bar·quen·tine** *or* **bar·quan·tine** \ˈbärkən,tēn\ *n* -s [[5]*bark*, *barque* + *-entine*, *-antine* (as in *brigantine*)] : a three-masted ship having the foremast square-rigged and the mainmast and mizzenmast fore-and-aft rigged

[1]bark·er \ˈbärkər, ˈbȧkə(r\ *n* -s [[1]*bark* + *-er*] : one whose work requires or involves the use of loud voluble glib speech or patter: as **a** : one whose occupation is to attract a crowd (as for a sales talk at a fair booth) or patrons (as for a circus sideshow) **b** : a sightseeing guide — called also *spieler* **c** : a theater employee who stands outside to announce attractions and answer questions about the availability of seats and the time and length of the show

[2]barker \"\ *n* -s [[4]*bark* + *-er*] **1 a** : one that removes bark : ROSSER; *specif* : one that removes bark and dirt from logs and pulpwood by subjecting them to water pressure in a stream barker or to tumbling in a drum barker — called also *power barker* **b** *in tanning* : one that prepares or shovels bark **2 a** : a machine used esp. in pulp mills to remove bark from logs **b** : BARK SPUD

bar·ke·vik·ite \ˈbärkə,vi,kīt, ,==ˈ=,=\ *n* -s [Norw *barkevikit*, fr. *Barkevik*, Norway, its locality + Norw *-it* -ite] : a mineral consisting of a velvet-black amphibole resembling arfvedsonite (sp. gr. 3.43) — **bar·ke·vik·it·ic** \ˌ==(ˌ)vi¦kid·ik\ *adj*

bark graft *n* [[3]*bark*] : a plant graft made by slitting or slipping the bark of the stock and inserting the scion beneath it and used esp. in topworking and frameworking where two or more scions are inserted in the end of each truncated branch of the stock — compare CROWN GRAFT

bark grafting *n* : grafting by bark grafts

barkhan *var of* BARCHAN

bark·hau·sen effect \ˈbär,kau̇zᵊn-, -rk,hau̇-\ *n*, *cap B* [after Heinrich *Barkhausen* †1956 Ger. physicist and electrical engineer] : the series of abrupt changes or jumps in the magnetization of a substance when the magnetizing field is gradually altered

barkhausen-kurz oscillation \-¦ku̇rts-\ *or* **barkhausen oscillation** *n*, *usu cap B&K* [after H.*Barkhausen* & K.*Kurz*, 20th cent. Ger. scientists] : ultrahigh-frequency oscillation produced in a triode oscillator by means of a positively biased grid that causes the cathode electrons passing through it to oscillate at a frequency characteristic of the tube and applied voltages

barking *pres part of* BARK

barking bird *n* [fr. pres. part. of [1]*bark*] : any of several birds with harsh discordant notes likened to the barking of a dog

barking deer *n* : MUNTJAC

barking drum *n* [fr. pres. part. of [4]*bark*] : a revolving drum in which pulp logs are placed for loosening and removing bark by repeated impacts

barking fits *n pl but sing in constr* [fr. pres part. of [1]*bark*] : CANINE HYSTERIA

barking iron *n* [fr. pres. part. of [4]*bark*] : BARK SPUD

barking squirrel *n* [fr. pres. part. of [1]*bark*] : PRAIRIE DOG

bar·kle \ˈbärkəl, ˈbȧk-\ *vb* -ED/-ING/-S [freq. of [4]*bark* "to cover with bark"] *dial Eng* : ENCRUST, CAKE

bark·less \ˈbärkləs, ˈbȧk-\ *adj* : having no bark

bark louse *n* [[3]*bark*] : any of a number of small insects living on the bark of plants (as certain psocids, scales, and aphids)

bark·ly·ite \ˈbärklē,īt\ *n* -s [Sir Henry *Barkly* †1898 Eng. colonial administrator + E *-ite*] : a magenta-colored nearly opaque variety of corundum found in Australia

bark mill *n* [[3]*bark*] **1** : a machine for removing bark from pulpwood usu. by means of rotating knives **2** : a mill in which bark is ground (as for tanning)

bark·om·e·ter \bär¦kämәd·ər\ *n* -s [[3]*bark* + *-o-* + *-meter*] : a hydrometer with a special scale for determining the strength of tanning liquor

barkpeel \ˈ=,=\ *vi* -ED/-ING/-S [[3]*bark* + *peel*] : to peel the bark from a tree — **barkpeeler** \ˈ=,==\ *n* -s

bark pocket *n* [[3]*bark*] : a patch of bark partially or wholly enclosed in the wood of the tree

barks *pres 3d sing of* BARK, *pl of* BARK

bark scorch *n* [[3]*bark*] : sunscald usu. following sudden exposure to sunlight

bark spud *n* [[3]*bark*] : a tool for peeling off bark

bark·stone \ˈ=,=\ *n* [[3]*bark* + *stone*] : [1]CASTOR 2

bark tree *n* [[3]*bark*] **1** : CINCHONA 2 **2** : BARK CLOTH 1

barky \ˈbärkē, ˈbȧk-, -ki\ *adj* -ER/-EST [[3]*bark* + *-y*] : covered with or resembling bark ⟨from one ~ post to another⟩ ⟨a diamondback rattlesnake . . . ruffles his ~ scales —Marjory S. Douglas⟩

bar-le-duc \ˌbärlə¦d(y)ük, -du̇k\ *n* -s *often cap* [F, fr. *Bar-le-Duc*, commune in Meuse dept., northeastern France] **1** : a preserve of whole white currants from which the seeds have been removed **2** : any preserve of whole fruit (as berries)

bar·less \ˈbärləs, ˈbȧl-\ *adj* : being without a bar

[1]bar·ley \ˈbärlē, ˈbȧlē, -li\ *n* -s [ME *barly*, fr. OE *bærlic* of barley, fr. *bær-* (akin to OE *bere* barley) + *-lic* -ly; akin to ON *barr* barley, Goth *barizeins* of barley, L *far* spelt] **1** : any cereal grass of the genus *Hordeum* cultivated since prehistoric times and widely adaptable being grown for forage and as a nurse or a smother crop **2** : the seed or grain of barley and its many varieties (esp. *Hordeum vulgare*) commonly used in the manufacture of malt beverages and also in breakfast foods and as feed for stock — see SIX-ROWED BARLEY

barley head

[2]barley \"\ *n* -s [prob. by folk etymology fr. *parley*] : TRUCE, RESPITE — used in children's games ⟨save oneself from being caught by crying ~⟩

bar·ley·break *also* **bar·ley·brake** \-,brāk\ *n* -s [prob. fr. [2]*barley* + *break*] : an old British group game in which one couple or player stationed in a defined area called "hell" or the "barley field" tries to catch the others as they venture into it

barley-bree *also* **barley-broo** \ˈ==,=\ *n* -s [[1]*barley* + *bree* or *broo* (liquor)] **1** *chiefly Scot* : WHISKEY **2** *chiefly Scot* : BEER, ALE

barley broth *n*, *dial Brit* : BARLEY-BREE

barley candy *n* : BARLEY SUGAR

barley coal *also* **barley** *n* : anthracite coal of a small size : number 3 buckwheat coal — see ANTHRACITE table

barleycorn \ˈ==,=\ *n* -s [ME *barly corn*] **1** : a grain of barley **2** : an old unit of length equal to the average length of a grain of barley : the third part of an inch **3** : a basket weave with an allover design of small geometric figures **4** : a pointed front gunsight common in British military rifles that appears like a triangle with the sharp point at the top when the rifle is aimed

barley feed *n* : by-products from the manufacture of pearl barley used for feed

barley fork *n* : a pitchfork with a guard at the base of the handle used to gather up barley or other short-stemmed grains

barley grass *n* : WALL BARLEY

barley itch *n* : GROCER'S ITCH

barley jointworm *n* : a jointworm (*Harmolita hordei*) attacking the stems of barley and sometimes extremely destructive to crops in eastern Canada

barley pearler *n* : a device containing a revolving abrasive stone that rubs the hull, bran, and germ from the barley kernel to produce pearled barley, small models being used to test the density of the kernels of barley, wheat, and other grains

barley reel *n* : a machine having a rotating reel of corrugated woven-wire screen for separating wild oats from tame oats and barley and pin oats from wheat

barley scald *n* : a disease of barley caused by an imperfect fungus (*Rhynchosporium secalis*) producing bluish green to yellow blotches, often with brown margins, and blighting of the foliage

barley smut *n* : either of two diseases of barley: **a** : a naked or loose smut caused by a fungus (*Ustilago nuda*) **b** : a covered smut caused by a related fungus (*U. hordei*)

barley stripe *n* : a disease of barley caused by a fungus (*Helminthosporium gramineum*) and characterized by green or pale yellow and finally dark brown and frayed-out stripes on the leaves

barley sugar *or* **barley candy** *n* : a transparent brittle confection produced by melting and then cooling cane sugar

barley water *n* : a decoction of barley used esp. in diarrheal disorders of infants

barley wine *n* : an ale of more than average strength

bar lift *n* [[1]*bar*] : J-BAR LIFT, T-BAR LIFT

bar line *n* [[1]*bar*] : BAR 6a

bar lock *n* [[1]*bar*] : a door lock consisting of a lug or lugs on the doorframe and a bar fitting into them

bar·low \ˈbär,lō, ˈbȧ,lō\ *n* -s [after Russell *Barlow*, 18th cent. Englishman, its maker] : a large sturdy 1- or 2-bladed jackknife with a long bolster

barlow's plate *n*, *usu cap B* [after Peter *Barlow* †1862 Eng. mathematician] : an iron plate formerly used on a ship to compensate for the action of part of the ship's magnetism on the compass — compare FLINDERS BAR

barm \ˈbärm, ˈbȧm\ *n* -s [ME *berme*, fr. OE *beorma*; akin to MLG *barm* yeast, L *fermentum* yeast, *fervēre* to boil — more at BURN] : yeast formed during the fermentation of alcoholic beverages

bar magnet *n* [[1]*bar*] : a magnet in the shape of a bar with poles at its ends

barmaid \ˈ=,=\ *n* [[1]*bar* (counter) + *maid*] *chiefly Brit* : a female bartender

barman \ˈbärmən, ˈbȧm-\ *n*, *pl* **barmen** [[1]*bar* (counter) + *man*] **1** : BARTENDER **2** : a metalworker who makes or prepares bars

bar·mas·ter \ˈ=,==\ *n* [alter. of earlier *bargh-master*, prob. part modif., part trans. of G *bergmeister*, fr. *berg-* mining (fr. *berg* mountain, fr. OHG) + *meister* master — more at BARROW] **1** : a local official arbiter or judge among English miners **2** : an officer of the barmote who presides at meetings, collects dues, and acts as manager

barm·brack \ˈbärm,brak\ *n* -s [IrGael *bairghean breac*, lit., speckled cake, fr. *bairghean* cake, loaf (fr. OIr *bairgen* bread) + *breac* speckled, fr. OIr *brecc*; akin to L *perca* perch — more at FARRAGO, PERCH] *Irish* : a rich currant bun or cake

bar·me·cid·al \ˌbärmə¦sīdᵊl\ *or* **bar·me·cide** \ˈ==,sīd\ *adj*, *usu cap* [*Barmecide* a member of a wealthy Persian family *fl* 752–803 (fr. Ar *barmak* chief priest) + E *-al*] : providing only the illusion of plenty or abundance : UNREAL, ILLUSORY ⟨he could persuade his guests that they had eaten well, though the meal had really been a ~ one —Hesketh Pearson⟩ ⟨a *Barmecide* room, that always had a great dining table in it and never had a dinner —Charles Dickens⟩ ⟨it was the first crumb of proof he had obtained after a long *Barmecide* banquet on pure theory —Fletcher Pratt⟩

bar mitz·vah \(ˈ)bär¦mitsvə, -(,)vä\ *n*, *pl* **bar mitzvahs** \-vəz, -(,)väz\ *or* **bar mitz·vot** *or* **bar mitz·voth** \-,vōth, -ōt, -ōs\ *often cap B&M* [Heb *bar miṣwāh*, lit., son of the (divine) law or precept] **1** : a Jewish boy who has reached his 13th birthday and has attained the age of religious duty and responsibility — compare BATH MITZVAH **2** : the initiatory synagogue ceremony recognizing a boy as a bar mitzvah

barmkin *n* -s [ME, perh. alter. of *barbican*] *obs* : BARBICAN

bar money *n* [[1]*bar*] : money in the form of bars of metal; *esp* : the stamped copper bars issued 1796–1818 for use as money in the Dutch East Indies

bar·mote \ˈbär,mōt\ *n* -s [alter. of earlier *barghmoot*, prob. modif. of G *berg-* mining + E *moot* (meeting) — more at BARMASTER] : a court held in Derbyshire, England, for deciding controversies between miners

bar movement *n* [[1]*bar*] : an old type of watch movement in which the upper pivot bearings are in separate bridges instead of in a full top plate — called also *Geneva movement*

barm·skin \ˈbärmz,kin, -m,sk-\ *n* -s [ME *barm-skin*, fr. *barm* bosom, lap (fr. OE *bearm*) + *skin*; akin to OHG *barm* bosom, ON *barmr*, Goth *barms*, OE *beran* to bear — more at BEAR] *dial Brit* : a leather apron

barmy \ˈbärmē, ˈbȧmē, -mi—ˈbāmē *or* -mi *is also -R pronunc for* "balmy" (*see sense 2*)\ *adj* -ER/-EST [*barm* + *-y*] **1** : full of froth or ferment **2** : BALMY 2

[1]barn \ˈbärn, ˈbȧn\ *n* -s [ME *bern*, fr. OE *bereærn*, fr. *bere* barley + *ærn* place — more at BARLEY, REST] **1 a** : a usu. large farm building orig. for the storage of farm products and feed (as grain and hay) but now used as a general storage building (as for hay, drying tobacco, and farm equipment or vehicles) and usu. for the housing of farm animals typically in separated sections **b** : the section of such a building that is used for the housing of farm animals (as horses or cows) and their feed **c** : a building for the housing of cattle or horses and their feed ⟨stabling accommodations for nearly nine hundred horses in ~*s* of the latest type —*New Yorker*⟩ **d** : a large building for the housing of a fleet of vehicles (as trolley cars or trucks) — compare CARBARN **e** : an unusually large and usu. bare building ⟨a great ~ of a hotel with roomy porches —W.A.White⟩ **2** *railroad slang* : ROUNDHOUSE **3** [so called fr. its having been considered "as big as a barn" with respect to nuclear bombardment] : a unit of area that equals 10^{-24} sq. cm. used in nuclear physics for measuring cross section

[2]barn \"\ *vt* -ED/-ING/-S : to store (a crop) in a barn

[3]barn \ˈbȧn\ *var of* BAIRN

bar·na·bite \ˈbärnə,bīt\ *n* -s *usu cap* [It *barnabita*, fr. Santa *Barnaba*, monastery in Milan where the order was founded + It *-ita* -ite (fr. L)] : REGULAR CLERK OF ST. PAUL

bar·na·by bright \-,bē-\ *or* **barnaby day** *n*, *usu cap 1st B* [after St. *Barnabas* (Acts 4:36-37), whose feast day is June 11] : June 11 Old Style, the longest day in the year — called also *St. Barnabas' day*; contrasted with *Lucy light*

bar·na·by's thistle \ˈbärnəbēz-\ *n*, *usu cap B* [fr. *Barnaby* (*day*), the time of its flowering] : any of several weeds of the genus *Centaurea*; *esp* : a European herb (*C. solstitialis*) adventive in the eastern U.S. and having a winged stem and tomentose leaves

[1]barnacle \ˈbärnəkəl, ˈbȧn-, -nēk-\ *n* -s [ME *bernak*, *bernacle*, fr. OF *bernac*] **1 a barnacles** *pl* : an instrument for restraining a horse by pinching his nose **b** : a conventionalized heraldic representation of a pair of barnacles — sometimes used in pl. **2** *obs* : an instrument of torture resembling a pair of barnacles — usu. used in pl. **3 barnacles** *pl*, *dial Eng* : SPECTACLES

[2]barnacle \"\ *n* -s [ME *barnakylle*, alter. of *bernekke*, *bernake*, of Celt origin; akin to W *brenig* limpets, Corn *brennyk*, Bret *bernic* barnacle, MIr *bairnech* limpet; fr. a popular belief in the Middle Ages that the goose grew from the shellfish; prob. akin to MIr *bern* cleft, L *forare* to bore — more at BORE] **1** : BARNACLE GOOSE **2** : any of numerous marine crustaceans constituting the order Cirripedia, being free-swimming in the larval state but permanently fixed as adults and protected by a calcified shell of several pieces, and having usu. six pairs of biramous feathery cirri that are modified limbs and are protruded and drawn back with a grasping motion serving to catch the food that floats within reach — see ACORN BARNACLE, GOOSE BARNACLE **3 a** : a person who clings tenaciously (as to an easy or comfortable job) or who sticks close to another against his will ⟨forced to avoid predatory people and ~ friends —Corra Harris⟩ **b** : anything (as a venerable trait, institution, or vestige from the past) that mars or hinders (as progress of any kind) ⟨the judicial process is clumsy and covered with ~*s* —T.W.Arnold⟩

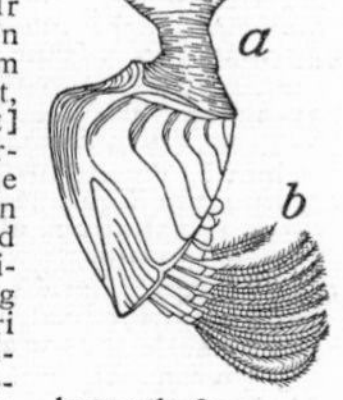

barnacle 2: *a* peduncle, *b* cirri

[3]barnacle *vt* **barnacled**; **barnacled**; **barnacling** \-k(ə)liŋ\ **barnacles** : to fasten or attach (oneself) securely or persistently to ⟨there are the legends, the "scandals" . . . which ~ such a public figure —Trevor Allen⟩ : cover with something so that it clings persistently ⟨the ancient Egyptians . . . *barnacled* their heads with lumps of nard —D.W.Dresden⟩

bar·na·cled \-kəld\ *adj* : covered with barnacles ⟨the ~ hull of a wrecked ship⟩ ⟨foundations have occasionally become so ~ with steady pensioners . . . that they have lost almost all freedom of maneuver —Dwight Macdonald⟩

barnacle goose *n* : a European goose (*Branta leucopsis*) breeding in the far north that is related to but larger than the brant

barnacle scale *n* : a soft scale (*Ceroplastes cirripediformis*) attacking orange and quince trees in Florida and having a scale that resembles a sessile barnacle in form

bar·na·ul \ˌbärnə¦u̇l\ *adj*, *usu cap* [fr. *Barnaul*, U.S.S.R.] : of or from the city of Barnaul, Altai territory, U.S.S.R. : of the kind or style prevalent in Barnaul

barn·brack \ˈbärn,brak\ *var of* BARMBRACK

barn dance *n* **1** : a rollicking American social dance held in a barn with square dances, certain round dances, and traditional music and calls **2** : an American ballroom dance developed in England early in the 20th century that is similar to the schottische but characterized by three running steps and a hop

barn door *n* : a hinged opaque panel mounted usu. in a pair on a motion-picture or TV studio lamp and used to screen light from an area or from the camera

barn-door fowl \ˈ=¦=-\ *n* : BARNYARD FOWL

barn-door skate *n* : a large No. American skate (*Raja laevis*) growing four feet or more long

barn-dry *or* **barn-finish** *vt* : to complete the drying of (partly cured hay stored in a barn) by forced ventilation often with heated air ⟨*barn-dried* hay⟩

barne \ˈbarn, ˈbȧn\ *dial Brit var of* BAIRN

barned *past of* BARN

bar·nett effect \(ˈ)bär¦ned·-, -net-\ *n*, *usu cap B* [after Samuel J. *Barnett* †1956 Am. physicist] : magnetization produced by rotating a body the direction of the magnetization being that of the rotation axis — compare EINSTEIN-DE HAAS EFFECT

bar·ne·veld·er \ˈbärnə,veldər\ *n* -s *usu cap* [D, fr. *Barneveld*, commune of eastern Netherlands + D *-er*] : a Dutch breed of large dual-purpose fowls laying numerous deep-brown eggs

bar·ney \ˈbärnē, ˈbȧn-, -ni\ *n* -s [perh. fr. the name *Barney*] **1** *Brit* **a** : a noisy argument : ALTERCATION, ROW ⟨what's the big ~ about⟩ **b** : a boisterous good time **2** : a small car attached to a cable used to push cars up a slope in a mine

barn·ful \ˈbärn,fu̇l, ˈbȧn-\ *n* -s : the amount or number that fills a barn

barn grass *var of* BARNYARD GRASS

barn gun \ˈbärn,gən\ *n* [E dial. *barn* (alter. of *burn*) + dial. *gun*, *gund* scab, fr. OE *gund-* matter, pus; akin to OHG *gunt* pus, Norw *gund* dandruff, scab, Goth, cancerous tumor, and prob. to Gk *kanthylē* swelling, tumor] *dial Eng* : a skin eruption; *specif* : SHINGLES

barning *pres part of* BARN

barn itch *n* : any contagious irritation of the skin of livestock (as sarcoptic mange or ringworm)

barn lantern *n* : a portable kerosine lantern similar to a standard kerosine lamp but having also a tubular frame with handle and guard encircling the chimney — see LANTERN illustration

barn lot *n*, *chiefly South & Midland* : BARNYARD

barn·man \-mən, -,man\ *n*, *pl* **barnmen** : one who takes care of cows and the barn and usu. does the milking

barn owl *n* : a nearly cosmopolitan owl (*Tyto alba*, syn. *Strix flammea*) having plumage mottled with buff brown and gray above and chiefly white below and frequenting barns and other buildings where it is an important factor in rodent control

barn raising *n* **:** a gathering for the purpose of erecting a barn — compare ¹BEE 3a

barn red *n* **:** a variable color averaging a moderate reddish brown that is stronger and slightly redder and lighter than mahogany, yellower and stronger than roan, and stronger and slightly redder than oxblood

barns *pres 3d sing of* BARN, *pl of* BARN

barns-break·ing \ˈbärnz,brākən\ *n* -s *Scot* **:** MISCHIEF **:** idle play

barn·storm \ˈbärnz,tȯrm, ˈbȧnz,tȯ(ə)m, -n,st-\ *vb* -ED/-ING/-S *vi* **1 :** to tour through rural districts staging theatrical performances in barns or makeshift theaters usu. in one-night stands ⟨traveled with Will Benbon's road show . . . ~*ing* through Mississippi —*Tomorrow*⟩ **2 :** to travel from one town or locality to another making brief stops (as in campaigning or in the course of a concert or exhibition tour) ⟨the candidates ~*ed* through the Eastern states last week⟩ ⟨~*ing* in Boston, Chicago, and Manhattan lecture halls —*Time*⟩; *specif* **:** to pilot one's airplane in sightseeing flights with passengers or in exhibition stunts in an unscheduled itinerant course esp. in rural districts ⟨his ~*ing* plane was forced down in a Minnesota swamp —Grace H. Flandrau⟩ **~** *vt* **:** to travel across while barnstorming ⟨figure-skating troupes that ~ the country —*Amer. Guide Series: Minn.*⟩ — **barn·storm·er** \-mə(r)\ *n* -s

barn swallow *n* **:** the common European swallow (*Hirundo rustica*) or its No. American variety (*H. r. erythrogaster*) both usu. attaching their nests to beams and rafters of barns

barny \ˈbärnē\ *adj* -ER/-EST **:** like or suggesting a barn esp. in size, shape, or characteristic smell

¹**barnyard** \ˈ=,=\ *n* [ME *bernyerde*, fr. *bern* barn + *yerde* yard] **:** a usu. fenced area adjoining a barn — compare FARMYARD

²**barnyard** \"\ *adj* **:** EARTHY, SMUTTY, SCATOLOGICAL ⟨the ~ school of novelists⟩ ⟨~ humor⟩

barnyard fowl *n* **:** the common domestic fowl; *esp* **:** the mongrel fowl allowed to pick up its living casually about the farmstead

barnyard golf *n, slang* **:** the game of horseshoes

barnyard grass *also* **barn grass** *or* **barnyard millet** *n* **:** a coarse annual grass (*Echinochloa crusgalli*) that has terminal panicles of one-sided flower clusters resembling spikes, is near cosmopolitan as a weed in cultivated ground, and is occas. used for hay or grazing — see JAPANESE MILLET

baro- — see BAR-

barocco *var of* BAROQUE

baro·cy·clon·om·e·ter \ˌbarō,sī,klōˈnäməd·ə(r)\ *n* -s [*bar-* + *cyclone* + *-o-* + *-meter*] **:** a form of aneroid barometer used in conjunction with a dial having adjustable arrows to determine the location and movement of a tropical cyclone

ba·ro·da \bəˈrōdə\ *adj, usu cap* [fr. *Baroda*, India] **:** of or from the city of Baroda, India **:** of the kind or style prevalent in Baroda

baro·dynamic \ˌbarō+\ *adj* [*bar-* + *dynamic*] **:** of or relating to barodynamics

bar·o·dynamics \"+\ *n pl but sing in constr* **:** mechanics applied to the behavior of heavy structures (as bridges, dams, and mine shafts) liable to failure because of their own weight

bar off *vi* [²*bar*] **:** to move soil from each side of row plants usu. in a cropped field and usu. with a turn plow or similar implement so as to leave the plant roots in a high narrow bed

bar of mi·chel·an·ge·lo \-,mīkəˈlanjə,lō, -,mik- *also* -,mēk-\ *usu cap M* [so called from its prominence in the statues of Michelangelo] *in sculpture* **:** SUPERCILIARY RIDGE

bar of sa·nio \-ˈsänē,ō\ *usu cap S* [after Carl *Sanio*, 19th cent. botanist] **:** CRASSULA

bar·og·no·sis \,ba,rägˈnōsəs, ,barəg- *n, pl* **barognoses** \-ō,sēz\ [NL, fr. *bar-* + *-gnosis*] *psychol* **:** the perception of weight by the cutaneous and muscle senses

bar·o·gram \ˈbarə,gram\ *n* -s [ISV *bar-* + *-gram*] **:** a tracing showing variations of atmospheric pressure that is usu. made by a barograph

bar·o·graph \-,graf\ *n* -s [ISV *bar-* + *-graph*] **:** an automatic instrument for recording variations of atmospheric pressure **:** a self-registering barometer — **bar·o·graph·ic** \ˌ==ˈgrafik\ *adj*

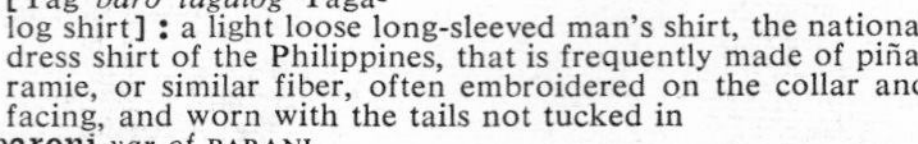

barograph

ba·rom·e·ter \bəˈrämədə(r), -ətə-\ *n* -s [*bar-* + *-meter*] **1 :** an instrument for determining the pressure of the atmosphere and hence for assisting in judgment as to probable weather changes and for determining the height of an ascent — see ANEROID BAROMETER, CUP BAROMETER, SIPHON BAROMETER **2 :** something that serves to register accurately changes in fluctuating activity or state (as in public opinion) ⟨retail sales, perhaps the most sensitive ~ of general prosperity —*Time*⟩

barometer crab *n* **:** a crab (*Carpillius maculatus*) of the Great Barrier reef that is lilac colored with 11 symmetrically placed blood-red spots that are said to change in appearance with the state of the weather

bar·o·met·ric \ˌbarəˈme·trik,-rēk *also* ˌber-\ *also* **bar·o·met·ri·cal** \-rəkəl, -rēk-\ *adj* [*barometer* + *-ic*, *-ical*] **:** relating to the barometer **:** made or indicated by a barometer — **bar·o·met·ri·cal·ly** \-rək(ə)lē, -rēk-, -li\ *adv*

barometric gradient *n, meteorol* **:** the rate of fall in atmospheric pressure between two stations **:** the slope of an isobaric surface

barometric pressure *n* **:** the pressure of the atmosphere usu. expressed in terms of the height of a column of mercury — compare BAROMETER

barometric surface *n* **:** a surface having the same barometric pressure at all points **:** an isobaric surface

barometric tendency *n* **:** the change of atmospheric pressure during the last few (generally three) hours before a regular observation

barometric tide *n* **:** a regular daily fluctuation in barometric pressure

barometric wave *n* **:** a change of atmospheric pressure that occurs progressively over an area

bar·o·met·ro·graph \ˌbarəˈme·trə,graf\ *n* -s [*barometro-* (fr. *barometer*) + *-graph*] **:** a self-recording barometer **:** BAROGRAPH

ba·rom·e·try \bəˈrämə·trē, -i\ *n* -ES **:** the science or process of making barometric measurements

bar·on \ˈbarən *also* ˈber-\ *n* -s [ME *barun, baroun, baron*, fr. OF *baron*, of Gmc origin; akin to OHG *baro* man, freeman, prob. akin to ON *berjask* to fight, OE *borian* to bore — more at BORE] **1 a :** one of a class of tenants in chief of a feudal superior holding his rights and title by military or other honorable service **b :** one of a class of tenants in chief of the king summoned by writ to the central council of the king's tenants in chief **c** *from the time of Henry III* **:** one of the king's tenants in chief personally summoned to Parliament — called also *baron by writ, great baron* **d :** a lord of the realm **:** NOBLE, PEER **2 a :** a member of the fifth and lowest grade of the peerage in Great Britain being entitled to be addressed as "Lord" and to sit in the House of Lords **b :** a nobleman on the continent of Europe whose rank and status vary from country to country **c :** a member of the lowest order of nobility in Japan **3 :** one of the former freemen of London, York, and other places who were bound to attendance upon and service to the king as homagers **4 :** a joint of meat consisting of two loins or sirloins not cut apart at the backbone ⟨a ~ of beef⟩ **5 :** a man of great or overweening power or influence in some field of activity (as business or industry) — usu. used with a specifying noun adjunct ⟨coal ~⟩ ⟨oil ~⟩ ⟨lumber ~⟩ ⟨cattle ~⟩ **6 :** HUSBAND — used in law and heraldry usu. with the correlative term *feme* ⟨an escutcheon per pale ~ and feme⟩

bar·on·age \-nij\ *n* -s [ME *barnage, barunage*, fr. OF *barnage*, fr. *baron* + *-age*] **:** the whole body of barons or peers **:** NOBILITY 2

baron bailie *n* **:** a Scottish magistrate of a barony or burgh

baron court *n* **:** COURT BARON

bar·on·du·ki *also* **bar·an·du·ki** *or* **bar·un·du·ki** \,barən-ˈdükē\ *or* **bu·run·du·ki** \,bür-\ *n* -s [Russ *burunduk*] **1 :** a Siberian ground squirrel (*Eutamias asiaticus* or *E. sibiricus*) with 5 conspicuous dark stripes down its back **2 :** the fur or pelt of the baronduki

bar·on·ess \ˈbarənəs *also* ˈber-\ *n* -ES [ME *barnesse*, fr. MF, fr. *baron* + *-esse* -ess] **1 :** the wife or widow of a baron **2 a :** a woman who holds a baronial title in her own right

¹**bar·on·et** \,barəˈnet (*apparently infrequent in Brit*), ˈbarənət, -,net *also* -ber-; *usu* -d·+V\ *n* -s [ME, fr. *baron* + *-et*] **1** *obs* **a :** a young or a lesser baron **b** *in Ireland* **:** the holder of a small barony **c :** ¹BANNERET 1 **2 :** the holder of a dignity or degree of honor, the lowest that is hereditary, ranking immediately below a baron but having precedence of all orders of knights except those of the garter

²**baronet** \"\ *vt* -ED/-ING/-S **:** to raise to the baronetcy

bar·on·et·age \-d·ij,-tij\ *n* -s [¹*baronet* + *-age*] **1 :** the rank of a baronet **2 a :** the whole body of baronets **b :** a list or record of baronets

bar·on·et·cy \-tsē, -i\ *n* -ES [¹*baronet* + *-cy*] **1 :** the rank or position of a baronet **2 :** the possession of a baronetcy

bar·on·et·i·cal \ˌ==ˈned·əkəl\ *adj* [¹*baronet* + *-ical*] **:** of or belonging to a baronet or baronetcy

ba·rong \bəˈrȯŋ, bä-, -räŋ\ *n* -s [native name in the Philippines] **:** a broad-bladed knife or sword with thick back and thin edge used by the Moros

ba·rong-ba·rong \=ˌ==ˈ=\ *n* -s [Tag] *Philippines* **:** a makeshift dwelling **:** HUT, SHANTY

barong ta·ga·log \-təˈgä-läg\ *n* -s *sometimes cap T* [Tag *barò tagalog* Tagalog shirt] **:** a light loose long-sleeved man's shirt, the national dress shirt of the Philippines, that is frequently made of piña, ramie, or similar fiber, often embroidered on the collar and facing, and worn with the tails not tucked in

barong and sheath

baroni *var of* BARANI

ba·ro·ni·al \bəˈrōnēəl, -nyəl\ *adj* [*barony* + *-al*] **1 :** of or relating to a baron or the baronage **2 :** SPLENDID, STATELY, SPACIOUS, AMPLE ⟨a ~ room⟩ ⟨the logs are of ~ dimensions —George Santayana⟩ **3** *of an envelope* **:** being smaller and squarer than envelopes used for ordinary commercial purposes and designed esp. for short social or personal correspondence or business announcements

ba·ronne \bəˈrän, ba-, -ȯn\ *n* -s [F, fr. OF, fem. of *baron*] **:** BARONESS

bar·on·ry \ˈbarənrē, -ri *also* ˈber-\ *n* -ES [ME *barunrie*, fr. MF *baronerie*, fr. *baron* + *-erie* -ery] **1 :** the domain, rank, or dignity of a baron **2 :** the body of barons

barons *pl of* BARON

bar·ony \ˈbarənē, -ni *also* ˈber-\ *n* -ES [ME *baronie*, fr. OF, fr. *baron* baron + *-ie* -y — more at BARON] **1 a :** the fee or domain of a baron **b :** the rank or dignity of a baron **2 a** *in Ireland* **:** a division of a county roughly corresponding to an English hundred **b** *in colonial So. Carolina* **:** a large tract of land of 12,000 acres granted to a landgrave or cacique **c** *in Scotland* **:** an extensive freehold **3 :** a vast or extensive private landholding ⟨to operate and maintain this ~, the billionaire employed some 350 people —Andrew Tully⟩ ⟨a cotton ~⟩ **4 :** a region or field of activity under the unchecked or predominant control or sway of a single individual or family ⟨the power of . . . the last of the nation's old-fashioned political *baronies* is perceptibly ebbing —Gladwin Hill⟩

bar opal *n* **:** jade-colored opal

baro·phil·ic \ˌbarəˈfilik\ *adj* [*bar-* + *-philic*] **:** thriving under high environmental pressures — used of deep-sea organisms

¹**ba·roque** \bəˈrōk, ba-; bəˈräk, bə-; *also* baˈrȯk *or* bə- *sometimes* ˈba,r-\ *adj* [F, fr. Pg *barrôco* irregularly shaped pearl] *of a pearl* **:** irregular in form

²**baroque** \"\ *n* -s [F] **:** a baroque pearl

³**baroque** \"\ *adj* [F, fr. It *barocco*, perh. after Federigo *Barocci* or *Baroccio* †1612 Ital. painter] **1** *also* **ba·roc·co** \bəˈrä(,)kō, -rō-\ **:** of, relating to, or having the characteristics of a style of artistic expression prevalent esp. in the 17th century: as **a** (1) **:** of, relating to, or being a style of art and architecture prevalent from the latter part of the 16th century to the latter part of the 18th century, marked by dynamic opposition and energy, by the use of curved and plastic figures, and esp. in its later phases by elaborate and sometimes grotesque ornamentation, and represented typically by the sculpture of Bernini and the painting of Rubens (2) **:** ROCOCO ⟨many writers draw no distinction between the words *rococo* and ~, which are far from synonymous —M.S.Briggs⟩ **b** (1) **:** of, relating to, or being a style of musical composition prevalent from about 1600 to 1750, marked by elaborate ornamentation and improvisation, the use of contrasting effects, and the creation of powerful tensions and climaxes, and culminating in the work of J.S.Bach and Handel (2) *of an organ* **:** built according to the specifications of the time of J.S.Bach **c :** of, relating to, or being a style of literary composition prevalent from the late 16th century to the early 18th century and marked typically by complexity and elaborateness of form and by the use of bizarre, calculatedly ingenious, and sometimes intentionally ambiguous imagery — compare EUPHUISM, GONGORISM **2 :** characterized by grotesqueness, extravagance, or flamboyance ⟨a truly ~ act of sabotage —G.N.Shuster⟩ ⟨a *baroque*-style desperado who had brought his western trimmings to New York —John Lardner⟩ **syn** see ORNATE

⁴**baroque** *n* -s **:** baroque work or style

ba·roque·ly *adv* [³*baroque* + *-ly*] **:** in a baroque manner

bar·o·scope \ˈbarə,skōp\ *n* [*bar-* + *-scope*] **:** an apparatus for showing that the loss of weight of an object in air equals the weight of the air displaced by it

ba·ros·ma \bəˈräzmə\ *n, cap* [NL, fr. *bar-* + *-osma*] **:** a genus of southern African strong-scented evergreen shrubs (family Rutaceae) having small pentamerous flowers — see BUCHU

bar·o·stat \ˈbarə,stat\ *n* -s [ISV *bar-* + *-stat*] **:** a usu. automatic device for maintaining a constant pressure (as in an airplane cabin or in a pressure cooker)

bar·o·switch \ˈ==+\ *n* [*bar-* + *switch*] **:** an electrical switching device in the radiosonde that is operated by the atmospheric pressure and used to switch temperature and humidity measuring elements alternately into the circuit

bar·o·tac·tic \ˈbarō,taktik\ *adj* **:** of, relating to, or being a barotaxis

bar·o·tax·is \ˌ==ˈtaksəs\ *n, pl* **barotaxes** [NL, fr. *bar-* + *-taxis*] **:** a taxis in which pressure is the orienting stimulus

bar·o·taxy \ˈ==,sē\ *n* -ES [ISV *barotax-* (fr. NL *barotaxis*) + *-y*] **:** BAROTAXIS

bar·o·thermograph \ˌbarō+\ *n* -s [ISV, blend of *barograph* and *thermograph*] **:** an instrument for recording both pressure and temperature (as of the atmosphere)

bar·o·ther·mo·hygrograph \ˌbarəˌthərmō+\ *n* -s [blend of *barograph, thermograph* and *hygrograph*] **:** an instrument for automatically recording on the same sheet of paper the pressure, temperature, and humidity of the atmosphere

ba·ro·to \bəˈrōd·(,)ō\ *n* -s [PhilSp] *Philippines* **:** a dugout canoe that is larger and heavier than a banca

bar·o·trauma \"+\ *n, pl* **barotraumata** [NL, fr. *bar-* + *trauma*] **:** injury of a part or organ as a result of changes in barometric pressure; *specif* **:** AERO-OTITIS MEDIA

ba·rot·se \bəˈrätsə\ *n, usu cap* **1** *pl* **barotse** *or* **barotses** **:** LOZI **2 :** a breed of large long-horned African cattle

ba·rouche \bəˈrüsh, ba-\ *n* -s [modif. of G *barutsche*, fr. It *baroccio, biroccio*, fr. (assumed) VL *birotium* two-wheeled vehicle, fr. LL *birotus* two-wheeled, fr. L *bi-* ¹bi- + *rota* wheel — more at ROLL] **:** a four-wheeled shallow carriage with a driver's seat high in front, two double seats inside, one facing back and the other front, and a folding top over the back seat, the entire carriage being suspended on C springs

barouche

ba·rou·chet \,ba(,)rü-ˈshā\ *or* **ba·rou·chette** \-shet\ *n* -s **:** a light barouche

bar pilot *n* [¹*bar*] **:** a pilot who navigates a ship from a pilot station over a bar and often into the harbor or to the harbor docks

bar pin *n* [¹*bar*] **:** a long narrow ornamental pin

bar pit \ˈbär,-\ *n* [by alter.] *chiefly West* **:** BARROW PIT

bar plate *n* [¹*bar*] **:** a drawbar follower on a railroad car

bar point *n* [¹*bar*] **:** the backgammon point nearest the bar on each player's outer table **:** the player's seventh point

barque *var of* BARK

bar·quen·tine *also* **bar·quan·tine** *var of* BARKENTINE

bar·qui·si·me·to \ˌbärkəsəˈmād·(,)ō\ *adj, usu cap* [fr. *Barquisimeto*, Venezuela] **:** of or from the city of Barquisimeto, Venezuela **:** of the kind or style prevalent in Barquisimeto

barr *abbr* barrister

bar·ra·ble \ˈbärəbəl, ˈbȧr-\ *adj* [²*bar* + *-able*] **:** capable of being barred esp. by legal process

bar·ra·bo·ra \,barəˈbōrə\ *n* -s [origin unknown] **:** an Eskimo earth lodge below the surface of the ground with a roof of sod or dirt shaped like a dome — compare KEEKWILEE-HOUSE

¹**bar·rack** \ˈbarək *also* ˈber- *or* -rik *or* -rēk\ *n* -s [F *baraque*, fr. MF, fr. OCatal *barraca*] **1 :** a hut used for temporary shelter esp. for soldiers ⟨he lodged in a miserable hut or ~ composed of dry branches and thatched with straw —Edward Gibbon⟩ **2** *or* **barracks** *pl but sing or pl in constr* **a :** an often permanent building or set of buildings used esp. for lodging soldiers in garrison ⟨stepped into the ~ and blew his whistle —L.M.Uris⟩ ⟨the dormitory where I was quartered was like an army ~*s* —John Cheever⟩ **b :** the regular quarters of the Salvationists **3** *or* **barracks** *pl but sing or pl in constr* **a :** a building or a group of buildings often like a shed or barn in structure and appearance that provides temporary housing (as for a group of workmen) ⟨the construction gang occupied a wooden ~ on the site of the job⟩ ⟨accommodated in a barely furnished ~*s* for commercial travelers —William Sansom⟩ **b :** a large building or set of buildings housing a number of people (as a crowded tenement house) that is characterized by extreme plainness or an air of dreary uniformity ⟨the big house on the hill . . . and the factory ~*s* in the valley —W.A.White⟩ ⟨the grim, topfofty ~*s* that we are now building —Lewis Mumford⟩ **4** *Northeast* **:** a structure with a movable roof sliding on four posts used to cover a hay or straw rick

²**barrack** \"\ *vt* -ED/-ING/-S **:** to lodge in barracks ⟨buildings . . . used to ~ George Washington's troops in 1775 —*Official Register of Harvard Univ.*⟩

³**barrack** \"\ *vb* -ED/-ING/-S [origin unknown] *vi, chiefly Austral* **:** to shout usu. derisively or sarcastically at a person or team engaged in a contest ⟨his game would lose a lot of its venom if the crowd were not ~*ing* —Jack Crawford⟩ **~** *vt, chiefly Austral* **:** JEER ⟨the crowd started to ~ me and shout for me to kick the ball clear —*Irish Digest*⟩

bar·rack·er \-kə(r)\ *n* -s *chiefly Austral* **:** one that barracks **:** a noisy partisan

barracks bag *n* **:** a heavy cotton bag in which a soldier carries personal equipment (as uniforms) except in the field

bar·ra·coon \ˌbarəˈkün\ *n* -s [Sp *barracón*, aug. of *barraca* hut, fr. Catal] **:** an enclosure or barrack formerly used for temporary confinement of slaves or convicts

bar·ra·cou·ta \,barəˈküd·ə, -ütə *also* ,ber-\ *also* **bar·ra·cou·da** \-üdə\ *n, pl* **barracouta** *or* **barracoutas** [modif. of AmerSp *barracuda* (*Sphyraena barracuda*)] **:** a large reddish-brown food fish (*Thyrsites atun*) related to the escolar and common on the coasts of Australia, New Zealand, and southern Africa — called also *snoek*

bar·ra·cu·da \,barəˈküdə *also* ,ber-\ *also* **bar·ra·cou·ta** \-üd·ə,-ütə\ *n, pl* **barracuda** *or* **barracudas** [AmerSp *barracuda*] **1 :** any of several voracious pikelike marine mugiloid fishes related to the gray mullets, constituting the genus *Sphyraena* and family Sphyraenidae cosmopolitan in warm seas, and including excellent food fishes as well as forms regarded as toxic — see GREAT BARRACUDA **2 :** a large scombroid food and game fish (*Scomberomorus commersonii*) of the warmer Indo-Pacific seas

¹**bar·rage** \ˈbärij, ˈbȧr-, -rēj\ *n* -s [F, fr. *barrer* to bar + *-age* — more at BAR] **1 :** the act or the result of barring; *specif* **:** an artificial dam placed in a river or watercourse to increase the depth of water or to divert it into a channel for navigation or irrigation **2 :** the application of the forefinger of the left hand across some or all of the strings (as of a guitar) to change their pitch **3 :** a space between two masses of mycelium caused by lack of compatibility between them

²**bar·rage** \bəˈräl(zh, -äl *also* |j *sometimes* ba-, *Brit usu* ˈba,räzh\ *n* -s [F (*tir de*) *barrage* barrier fire] **1 a :** a barrier of fire esp. of artillery and mortar fire laid on a line close to friendly troops to screen and protect them by inflicting losses on the enemy and by impeding or preventing enemy movement and fire — see BOX BARRAGE, EMERGENCY BARRAGE, NORMAL BARRAGE, ROLLING BARRAGE, STANDING BARRAGE **b :** a screen of antiaircraft-artillery fire **c :** a barrier consisting of a series of barrage balloons — called also *aerial barrage* **d :** a barrier of mines preventing the passage of ships **e :** a barrier created by nonexplosive weapons ⟨the bowmen . . . laid down a ~ of arrows from the flanks —G.H.Fathauer⟩ **f :** a massive concentrated and usu. continuous discharge or shower (as of missiles or blows) ⟨killed by a ~ of stones . . . by sardonic townspeople —*Springfield (Mass.) Union*⟩ **2 :** a rapid-fire massive or concentrated delivery or outpour (as of speech or writing) ⟨a ~ of footnotes —Geoffrey Bruun⟩ ⟨speakers kept up an oratorical ~ —*N.Y.Times*⟩

³**barrage** \"\ *vt* -ED/-ING/-S **:** to deliver a barrage against **:** attack with or subject to a barrage ⟨the besiegers immediately *barraged* the enemy stronghold with a torrent of rifle fire —*Sericana Quarterly*⟩ ⟨patrons . . . *barraged* the Post Office Department with letters of complaint —*Newsweek*⟩

barrage balloon *n* [²*barrage*] **:** a small captive balloon used to support wires or nets as protection against air attacks

barrage reception *n* [¹*barrage*] **:** a system of radio reception in which interference from one or more directions is prevented (as by directional properties of antennas)

barragudo *var of* BARRIGUDO

bar·ra·mun·da \,barəˈməndə\ *or* **bar·ra·mun·di** \-dē\ *n, pl* **barramunda** *or* **barramundas** *or* **barramundi** *or* **barramundis** *or* **barramundies** [native name in Australia] **:** any of several Australian fishes: **a :** a large red-fleshed lungfish (*Neoceratodus* or *Ceratodus forsteri*) of Australian rivers that attains a length of 6 feet and is highly esteemed as food — called also *Burnett salmon, salmon* **b :** a river fish (*Scleropages leichhardtii*) esteemed as food **c :** *in northern Australia* **:** BEGTI

bar·ran·ca \bəˈraŋkə\ *or* **bar·ran·co** \-ŋ(,)kō\ *n* -s [Sp, of non-IE origin] **1 :** a deep gulley or arroyo with steep sides **2 :** a steep bank or bluff

bar·ran·dite \bəˈran,dīt, ˈbarən-\ *n* -s [F *barrandite*, fr. Joachim *Barrande* †1883 Fr. geologist + F *-ite*] **:** a mineral $(Fe,Al)PO_4.2H_2O$ consisting of a pale-gray hydrous phosphate of iron and aluminum belonging to the isomorphous series strengite-variscite

bar·ran·qui·lla \ˌbarənˈkē(y)ə\ *adj, usu cap* [fr. *Barranquilla*, Colombia] **:** of or from the city of Barranquilla, Colombia **:** of the kind or style prevalent in Barranquilla

bar·ra·tor *also* **bar·ra·ter** *or* **bar·re·tor** \ˈbarəd·ə(r)\ *n* -s [ME *baratour*, fr. MF *barateor* deceiver, fr. *barater* to deceive, barter + *-eor* -or] **:** one who engages in barratry

bar·ra·trous \-rə·trəs\ *adj* [*barratry* + *-ous*] **:** tainted with or constituting barratry — **bar·ra·trous·ly** *adv*

bar·ra·try \-rə·trē\ *n* -ES [ME *barratrie*, fr. MF *baraterie* deception, fr. *barater* + *-erie* -ery] **1 :** the purchase or sale of office or preferment in church or state **:** SIMONY **2 :** a fraudulent breach of duty or willful act of known illegality on the part of a master of a ship or of the mariners to the injury of the owner of the ship or cargo and without his consent (as running away with the ship, sinking or deserting her, or embezzling the cargo) **3 :** the practice of exciting and encouraging or maintaining lawsuits or quarrels **:** the persistent incitement of litigation

¹**bar·ré** \bäˈrā\ *n* -s *often attrib* [F, fr. past part. of *barrer* to bar — more at BAR] **1 :** a weftwise bar or striped pattern in fabrics **2 :** a defect in the weaving, knitting, or printing process that causes a weftwise streak

²**bar·ré** \(ˈ)bäˈrā\ *adv* (*or adj*) [F, fr. past part. of *barrer*] **:** with all strings stopped by the forefinger laid across them — compare ¹BARRAGE 2

³**barre** \ˈbär, ˈbȧ(r\ *n* -s [F] **:** ¹BAR 1d(2)

¹**barred** \ˈbärd, ˈbȧd\ *adj* [¹*bar* + *-ed*] **:** having, marked by, or divided off by bars; *specif*, *of a bird* **:** having alternate bands of different color crossing the feathers

²barred \"\ *adv (or adj)* [trans. of F *barré*] : BARRÉ

barred owl *n* : a large American owl (*Strix varia* or *Syrnium varium*) with bars of dark brown on the breast

barred perch *n* : a silvery sea perch (*Amphistichus argenteus*) that is barred and spotted with brassy olive along the sides and is a valued game fish along the California coast

barred pickerel *n* : REDFIN PICKEREL

barred rock *n, often cap R* : a barred Plymouth Rock

barred spiral *n* : a spiral galaxy whose arms apparently spring from the extremities of a luminous bar that extends across the nucleus giving the object somewhat the appearance of a letter S

barred stamp *n* : a postage stamp that is a canceled remainder

¹**bar·rel** \'barəl *also* 'ber-\ *n* -s [ME *barell, barel,* fr. MF *baril*] **1** : a round bulging vessel of greater length than breadth that is usu. made of staves bound with hoops and has flat ends of equal diameter **2 a** : a barrel with its contents **b** : the contents of a barrel **c** : the amount contained in a barrel **d** : any of various units of capacity or volume: as (1) : a U.S. unit of liquid measure equal to 31½ gallons; *also* : a unit of measure for fermented beverages equal to 31 gallons (2) : a unit of measure for petroleum equal to 42 gallons (3) : a unit of dry measure (as for fruits or vegetables) equal to 105 dry quarts or about 3.9 bushels; *also* : a measure for cranberries equal to about 87 quarts or about 2.7 bushels — abbr. *bbl.* **e** : a great quantity : LOT ⟨have a ~ of fun⟩ **3** : a drum or cylinder or similar round part: as **a** : the body of a windlass or capstan about which the cable winds **b** : the tube of a gun from which the projectile is discharged **c** : the revolving cylinder of a barrel organ **d** : the flat cylindrical metal box that encloses the mainspring of a timepiece **e** : the upper inside part of a bell **f** : the large cylindrical part of a locomotive boiler containing the tubes **g** : the core of various cylindrical devices (as a spool or bobbin) on which yarn or cloth is wound **h** : the cylindrical part of a clarinet connecting the mouthpiece with the first joint **i** : the part of a fountain pen or of a pencil containing the writing fluid or the lead **j** : a cylindrical or tapering housing containing the optical components of a photographic-lens system and the iris diaphragm usu. equipped with a flange on the outside for mounting on a camera **k** : a revolving hollow cylinder or drum within which metal may be cleaned by tumbling with abrasive material or may be dissolved from ore by mixing with a leaching solution **l** : the cylinder in which a piston travels **m** : the fuel outlet from the carburetor on a gasoline engine **4** : the trunk of a quadruped esp. of a domestic animal — see COW illustration

barrel: *H* hoop, *S* stave, *B* bunghole

²**barrel** \"\ *vb* **barreled** *or* **barrelled; barreled** *or* **barrelled; barreling** *or* **barrelling; barrels** [ME *barellen,* fr. *barell,* n.] *vt* **1** : to put or pack in a barrel **2** : to clean or otherwise treat (metal) in a barrel **3 a** : to transport at a high speed ⟨~*s* heavy loads up steep hills⟩ **b** : to cause (as an automobile) to travel fast ⟨~*ed* the convertible for a distant roadhouse⟩ **4** : to fit (a firearm) with a barrel ~ *vi* : to travel at a high speed ⟨~*ing* along in excess of the speed limit⟩

bar·rel·age \-lij\ *n* -s : amount in barrels

barrel arch *n* : an arch resembling a segment of a barrel in that its length is considerable compared to its span

barrel band *n* : ¹BAND 3f

barrel bolt *n* : a door or sash bolt made to slide into a cylindrical socket

barrel cactus *n* : a cactus of the genus *Ferocactus*

barrel ceiling *n* : a ceiling that is semicircular in cross section and resembles a segment of a barrel

barrel chair *n* : an upholstered easy chair with a high solid rounded back suggestive of a barrel with a section removed

barrel chest *n* : the enlarged rounded thorax with fixed horizontal position of the ribs occurring in chronic pulmonary emphysema

barrel–chested \ˌ⸗⸗ˈ⸗⸗\ *adj* : having a large rounded chest ⟨he was powerful and *barrel-chested* —Alan LeMay⟩

barrel clover *or* **barrel medic** *n* : a clover (*Medicago tribuloides*) native to Australia and used there and elsewhere for pastures esp. on alkaline soil

barrel cuff *n* : a single soft unfolded cuff on a shirt usu. fastened by a button — distinguished from *French cuff*

barrel distortion *n* : distortion (as by an optical instrument or television receiver) in which the image of a straight line appears to be curved convexly away from the axis — compare PINCUSHION DISTORTION

barreled *adj, of an arrow* : tapered toward both ends

bar·rel·ful \'barəlˌfu̇l *also* 'ber-\ *n, pl* **barrel·fuls** \-əlˌfu̇lz\ *or* **barrels·ful** \-əlzˌfu̇l\ [ME *barel ful*] : BARREL 2c

barrelhead \'⸗⸗ˌ⸗\ *n* : the flat end of a barrel — **on the barrelhead** *adv (or adj)* : asking for or granting no credit : in cash ⟨was paid for, cash *on the barrelhead* —*Time*⟩ ⟨prepared to pay *on the barrelhead* for what it needs —*Newsweek*⟩

barrel helm *n* : a cylindrical helmet with flat top worn esp. in the 13th century

¹**barrelhouse** \'⸗⸗ˌ⸗\ *n* [so called fr. the row of barrels sometimes stacked along its walls] **1** : a cheap drinking establishment usu. with facilities for dancing and sometimes for gambling and lodging **2** : a style of jazz characterized by a very strongly accented beat, syncopation, dissonance, free improvisation, and when performed by a group continuous simultaneous improvisation by each member throughout an entire number

²**barrelhouse** \'⸗⸗ˌhau̇s, -au̇z\ *vb* -ED/-ING/-S : BARREL ⟨every crow in hearing distance will come *barrelhousing* in, gang up, and drive this most hated enemy from the neighborhood —Eugene Kinkead⟩

barrel key *n* : PIPE KEY

barrel knot *n* : either of two knots used for tying fishing leaders together: **a** : a knot made by twisting the ends of two standing parts one around the other usu. two or three times and then pushing the ends back through the center twist — called also *blood knot* **b** : a knot made by tying double or triple overhand knots with each end around the opposite standing part — called also *double Englishman's knot, double fisherman's knot, grapevine knot*

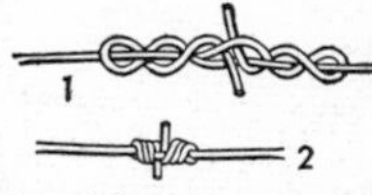

barrel knot a: *1* before, and *2* after ends are pulled tight

barrel organ *n* **1** : an instrument used chiefly by street musicians for producing music by the action of a revolving cylinder studded with pegs upon a series of valves that admit air from a bellows to a set of pipes **2** : a church organ operated like a barrel organ

barrel palm *n* : BOTTLE PALM

barrel plating *n* : the electroplating of objects placed in a revolving perforated barrel

barrel process *n* : a process of extracting gold or silver by treating the ore in a revolving barrel with mercury, chlorine, cyanide solution, or other reagent

barrel pump *n* : a hand pressure pump attached to a barrel containing a liquid spray

barrel quartz *n* : the quartz of certain folded gold-bearing quartz veins (as in Nova Scotia) whose outcrops resemble barrels

barrel roll *n* : an aerial maneuver in which a complete revolution about the longitudinal axis is made while the direction of flight is approximately maintained

barrel roof *n* **1** : a roof like the interior of a barrel vault **2** : BARREL VAULT

barrels *pl of* BARREL, *pres 3d sing of* BARREL

barrel saw *n* : a saw of cylindrical shape used to cut such rounded pieces as barrel staves, chair backs, and brush backs

barrel scale *n* : CYLINDER SCALE

barrel spindle *n* : a thick removable spindle for the turntable of a record player designed esp. for adapting the turntable to play 45 r.p.m. records with large center holes

barrel vault *n* : a semicylindrical vault having parallel abutments and the same section throughout; *also* : a similar vault that is curved in plan or rampant — see VAULT illustration

barrel vaulting *n* : vaulting consisting of barrel vaults

bar·re·mi·an \bəˈrāmēən, -rēm-\ *adj, usu cap* [F *barrémien,* fr. *Barrême,* town in southeast France + F *-ien* -an] : of or relating to a subdivision of the European Cretaceous

¹**bar·ren** \'barən *also* 'ber-\ *adj, often* -ER/-EST [ME *bareyne,* fr. OF *baraine,* fem. of *barain, brehaing,* prob. of non-IE origin; akin to the source of Alb *beronjë* sterile] **1 a** : having produced or borne no young : seemingly incapable of pregnancy or reproduction : STERILE ⟨spinsters and ~ women were not allowed to benefit under wills at all and their loss was the gain of their fruitful sisters —Robert Graves⟩ **b** *of an animal* : not with young : not pregnant at the usual season **c** *of a plant* : not bearing fruit or seed **d** *of land or a region* : deficient in producing vegetation : BARE, DESOLATE ⟨obtain wretchedly poor crops . . . from the ~ soil immediately round their cabins —Anthony Trollope⟩ **e** : producing ore in too small quantities to be commercially profitable ⟨a ~ mine⟩ **2** : DEVOID, LACKING — used with *of* ⟨~ of all love —John Keats⟩ ⟨a sea ~ of seals —Jack London⟩ ⟨~ of troublesome conventions and artificialities —Mark Twain⟩ **3** : providing little or no aesthetic or intellectual stimulation or gratification : lacking interest, information, or charm ⟨nameless millions performing ~ office routines —Edmund Wilson⟩ ⟨religion . . . buried under an even narrower and more ~ scholasticism —J.H.Randall⟩ **4** : unproductive of results or gain : lacking the intended effect or force : FRUITLESS, UNPROFITABLE ⟨a ~ conquest which brought him no special repute —John Buchan⟩ ⟨a high-sounding but ~ title, which gratified the Duke's vanity and signified nothing —J.L.Motley⟩ **5** : lacking inspiration or ideas : DULL, UNRESPONSIVE ⟨a dull suspicion in leaden, opaque, and ~ minds that wit, brilliancy, and imagination are incompatible with great mental power and solidity of judgment —J.J.Ingalls⟩ **syn** see BARE, STERILE

²**barren** \"\ *n* -s **1** : a tract of barren land **2 barrens** *pl* : an extent of usu. level land that lacks trees, has an inferior growth of trees, or has little vegetation of any kind whether due to natural factors (as climate or poor soil) or to accident (as fire) ⟨covered largely with stunted pine woods — the famous pine ~*s* —*Amer. Guide Series: N.J.*⟩

barren brome grass *or* **barren brome** *n* : a feathery Eurasian grass (*Bromus sterilis*) adventive in waste places in No. America

bar·ren·er \-nə(r)\ *n* -s [¹*barren* + *-er*] *Brit* : a barren or a relatively infertile cow

barren–ground \ˈ⸗⸗ˈ⸗\ *adj, usu cap B&G* : of or living in the Barren Grounds of northern Canada

barren ground bear *n, usu cap 1st B&G* : a peculiar bear that inhabits the Barren Grounds of northern Canada and is believed to be a variety of the grizzly bear

barren ground caribou *n, usu cap B&G* : any of several rather small caribou of the Barren Grounds of No. America and Greenland

bar·ren·ly *adv* [¹*barren* + *-ly*] : in a barren manner ⟨a time when technical philosophy seems ~ timid —M.R.Cohen⟩

bar·ren·ness \'barənnəs\ *n* -ES [ME *bareynesse,* fr. *bareyne* barren + *-nesse* -ness — more at BARREN] : the quality or state of being barren

barren oak *or* **barrens oak** *n* **1** : BLACKJACK 5 **2** : BEAR OAK

barren strawberry *n* **1** : a low herb (*Waldsteinia fragarioides*) resembling a strawberry and having yellow flowers and dry fruits **2 a** *Brit* : a cinquefoil (*Potentilla fragariastrum*) with hairy carpels **b** : ROUGH CINQUEFOIL

barrenwort \'⸗⸗ˌ⸗\ *n* -s [so called fr. the belief that it causes sterility] : any of certain plants of the genus *Epimedium* having or believed to have sudorific properties: as **a** : a European herb (*E. alpinum*) often cultivated and having bitter leaves **b** : a Japanese herb (*E. diphyllum*) with small bluish flowers **c** : an herb (*E. hexandra*) of the Pacific coast of No. America having ternate leaves and small nodding flowers on a scapelike stalk

bar·rer \'bärər, bärə(r\ *n* -s [²*bar* + *-er*] : a shoeworker who stitches in parallel rows across parts of shoe uppers that need to be strengthened

bar·rera \bəˈrerə, bäˈ-\ *n* -s [Sp, fr. *barra* bar] **1** : the red wooden fence surrounding a bullring **2** : the first row of seats in the amphitheater of a bullring

bar·ret \ˈbarət, bəˈret\ *also* **bar·rette** \bəˈret\ *n* -s [F *barrette,* fr. It *berretta* — more at BIRETTA] : a small cap; *esp* : BIRETTA

barretor *var of* BARRATOR

bar·rette \bäˈret, bə-\ *n* -s [F, dim. of *barre* bar] : a clip or pin shaped like a bar and used to hold a woman's hair in place

barrettes

bar·ret·ter \bəˈred·ə(r)\ *n* -s [modif. of OF *bareter* to exchange] : an early form of radio detector operating by increased resistance when subjected to the influence of electric waves

¹**bar·ri·cade** \ˈbarəˌkād, ˌ⸗⸗ˈ⸗ *also* -er-\ *vt* -ED/-ING/-S [MF *barricader,* fr. *barricade*] **1** : to block off or stop up (as a street or passage) with a barricade esp. in order to prevent the advance of an enemy : BLOCKADE ⟨angry workers *barricaded* the narrow streets with furniture, carriages, and piles of lumber⟩ **2** : to prevent access to by means of a barricade ⟨*barricaded* myself behind my study door —Bentz Plagemann⟩

²**barricade** \"\ *n* -s [F, fr. MF, fr. *barriquer* to barricade, fr. *barrique* barrel (a typical component of barricades, fr. dial. —Gascon— *barrico*) + *-ade*; akin to OF *barril* barrel] **1 a** : an obstruction or rampart hastily improvised and thrown up across some way or passage (as in revolutionary street fighting) to check the advance of the enemy — usu. used in pl. ⟨men, women, and children manned the ~*s*⟩ **b** : material barrier or obstacle that prevents passage ⟨a man behind a floor-to-ceiling concrete ~ was looking through a glass porthole —Stanley Frank⟩ **2** : a nonmaterial barrier or protective shield ⟨sat stiff as a poker behind his flimsy ~ of silence —Claud Cockburn⟩ ⟨guarded by . . . legal ~*s* —W.P.Webb⟩ **3** : a field of disagreement, dispute, or combat ⟨would die upon the literary ~ of defending the noble proportions of "War and Peace" —Ellen Glasgow⟩

¹**bar·ri·ca·do** \ˌ⸗⸗ˈkā(ˌ)dō\ *vt* **barricadoed; barricadoed; barricadoing; barricadoes** *also* **barricados** [modif. of F *barricade*] *archaic* : BARRICADE

²**barricado** \"\ *n, pl* **barricadoes** *also* **barricados** *archaic* : BARRICADE

bar·ri·co \bəˈrē(ˌ)kō, *Brit often* ˈbrākə\ *n, pl* **barricoes** *also* **barricos** [modif. of Sp *barrica*] : a small cask : KEG

¹**bar·ri·er** \ˈbarēə(r) *also* ˈber-\ *n* -s [ME *barere,* fr. MF *barriere,* fr. *barre* bar] **1** *obs* : BARRICADE; *esp* : an outer defense to impede or stop an enemy **2** : a material object or set of objects that separates, keeps apart, demarcates, or serves as a unit or barricade: as **a** : the palisades that enclosed the lists in medieval tournaments — usu. used in pl. **b** (1) *or* **barrier beach** *also* **barrier bar** : a long narrow sandy island lying parallel to a shore and built up by the action of waves, currents, and wind — called also *offshore bar*; see BARRIER ISLAND (2) *sometimes cap* : an extension of the antarctic continental ice sheet into the sea resting partly on the bottom **c** : the gate where customs duties are collected at the boundaries of some European countries **d** : a railing or other separation between the station building and train platforms in some European countries with openings to permit the passage of arriving and departing passengers **e** (1) : POTENTIAL BARRIER (2) : a movable net or structure serving in an emergency to halt a landing airplane esp. on an aircraft carrier when the tail hook has failed to engage the arresting gear **f** : a porous partition (as a thin sheet of silver-zinc alloy from which the zinc has been dissolved out) used in atmolysis **g** *in packaging* : a flexible material that can be formed into a container preventing or limiting the entrance of moisture, retaining flavors or oils, and otherwise protecting its contents **h** : a solid usu. white or yellow warning line painted between traffic lanes of a highway **3 barriers** *pl, often cap* : a medieval war game in which combatants fought on foot with a fence or railing between them — often used in the phrase *at barriers* **4 a** : the starting point in an ancient racecourse **b** : the movable gate or device at the starting line in a modern racetrack which is opened to signal the start of a race **5** : something intangible or immaterial that acts as a barrier (as by impeding or separating) ⟨psychological and social ~*s* to increased agricultural production —G.P. Wibberley⟩ ⟨the ~ between the craft and scholarly traditions —S.F.Mason⟩ **6** : a factor (as a topographic feature or a physical or physiological quality) that tends to restrict the free movement and mingling of individuals or populations — compare ISOLATING MECHANISM

²**barrier** \"\ *vt* -ED/-ING/-S : to obstruct or confine by a barrier

barrier berg *n* : a usu. large flat-topped iceberg that has broken from the antarctic barrier

barrier cell *n* : a barrier-layer cell

barrier chain *n* : a series of barriers extending along a considerable length of coast

barrier cream *n* : any of several cosmetic creams applied to the skin as a protective measure against dermatitis caused by chemical irritants

barrier ice *n* : floating freshwater ice of the antarctic barrier

barrier island *n* : a barrier so broadened as to be much more than a barrier beach; *also* : a long series of such barriers

barrier layer *n* : the surface of contact between a semiconductor (as cuprous oxide) and a metal (as copper) that acts as an alternating current rectifier or photovoltaic cell when included in a circuit

barrier line *n* : a line painted or otherwise marked on a roadway as a guide to traffic; *esp* : such a line that is not to be crossed by vehicles

barrier reef *n* **1** : a coral reef roughly parallel to a shore and separated from it by a lagoon **2** : limestone produced by the consolidation of materials in a barrier reef

barrier spit *n* : a barrier connected at one end to the mainland

barries *pl of* BARRY

bar·ri·gu·da \ˌbarəˈgüdə\ *n* -s [Pg, fr. fem. of *barrigudo*] : a large Brazilian thatch palm (*Iriartea ventricosa*) having its trunk much swollen between the top and the ground

bar·ri·gu·do *also* **bar·ra·gu·do** \ˌ⸗⸗ˈ⸗(ˌ)dō\ *n* -s [Pg *barrigudo,* fr. *barrigudo* big-bellied, fr. *barriga* belly, barrel] : WOOLLY MONKEY

¹**bar·ring** \ˈbäriŋ, ˈbȧr-, -rēŋ\ *pres part of* BAR

²**barring** \"\ *n* -s [ME, fr. gerund of *barren* to mark with bars, to bar — more at BAR] : BARS; *esp* : the arrangement of bars ⟨the curious ~ on a raccoon's back⟩

³**barring** \"\ *prep* [ME, fr. pres. part. of *barren* to bar] : excluding by exception : EXCEPTING ⟨they knew that, ~ a miracle, they would never be able to save the large cash outlay required —Warner Olivier⟩

barring–out \ˈ⸗⸗ˈ⸗\ *n, pl* **barrings–out** : the shutting out of a schoolmaster from the schoolroom as a prank or to win certain concessions

bar·ring·to·nia \ˌbariŋˈtōnēə, -nyə\ *n, cap* [NL, fr. Daines *Barrington* †1800 Eng. judge and naturalist + NL *-ia*] : a genus of tropical trees (family Lecythidaceae) with alternate leaves often crowded toward the branch ends and large white flowers in spikes or racemes

bar·rio \ˈbärēˌō\ *n* -s [Sp, fr. Ar *barrī* of the open country, fr. *barr* exterior, outside, open country] **1** : a ward, quarter, or district of a city or town in Spanish-speaking countries **2** : a village or rural community unit in Latin America and the Philippines — see POBLACIÓN, SITIO **3** : a Spanish-speaking quarter or neighborhood in a city or town in the U.S. esp. in the Southwest

bar·ris·ter \ˈbarəstə(r)\ *n* -s [¹*bar* + *-i-* + *-ster*] **1** : a counsel admitted to plead at the bar and undertake the public trial of causes in an English superior court : COUNSELOR-AT-LAW — distinguished from *solicitor*; see LAWYER; compare ADVOCATE, ATTORNEY **2** : LAWYER, ATTORNEY

barrister–at–law \ˈ⸗⸗⸗⸗ˈ⸗\ *n, pl* **barristers–at–law** : BARRISTER — used chiefly as a formal title

bar·ris·te·ri·al \ˌbarəˈstirēəl\ *adj* : of or relating to a barrister

bar roller *n* [¹*bar*] : a roller that consists of one or more rotating cylinders whose surfaces are made up of horizontal tubular bars with spaces between and that is used for crushing clods and packing surface soil without leaving a smooth surface

barroom \ˈ⸗ˌ⸗\ *n* [¹*bar* + *room*] : a room or establishment whose main feature is a bar for the sale of liquor : TAPROOM, SALOON

¹**bar·row** \ˈba(ˌ)rō, -ˌrə *also* ¹be- *often* -ˌrəw+V; *dial or sporadic & old-fash* ˈbä-\ *n* -s [ME *berwe, bergh,* fr. OE *beorg;* akin to OHG *berg* mountain, ON *berg* rock, Goth *bairgahei* hill country, Skt *bṛhant* high] **1** : MOUNTAIN, HILL, MOUND — now used only in the names of hills in England ⟨Cadon *Barrow*⟩ **2** : a large mound of earth or stones over the remains of the dead and often enclosing a sepulchral cell or an apartment built of large rocks : TUMULUS — see LONG BARROW, ROUND BARROW

²**barrow** \"\ *n* -s [ME *barow,* fr. OE *bearg;* akin to OHG *barug* barrow, ON *börgr,* Russ *borov* barrow, OE *borian* to bore — more at BORE] : a male hog castrated before it reaches sexual maturity

³**barrow** \"\ *n* -s [ME *barew, barowe,* fr. OE *bearwe* basket, handbarrow; akin to OFris *bare* handbarrow, LG *berwe,* ON *barar* bier, OE *beran* to carry — more at BEAR] **1 a** : HANDBARROW **b** : WHEELBARROW **2** : a cart with a shallow box body, two wheels, and shafts for pushing it : PUSHCART ⟨street vendors pushing their ~*s*⟩

barrow boy *also* **bar·row·man** \-mən, -ˌman\ *n* [³*barrow* + *boy* or *man*] : COSTERMONGER

bar·row·ist \ˈbarəwəst\ *n* -s *usu cap* [Henry *Barrow* or *Barrowe* †1593 Eng. church reformer + E *-ist*] : a follower of Henry Barrow, a founder of Congregationalism in England who was executed for nonconformity

bar·row pit \ˈbarō-, ˈbä- *also* ˈbe-\ *n* [by alter.] *chiefly West* : BORROW PIT; *esp* : a ditch dug along a roadway to furnish fill and provide drainage

bar·row's goldeneye \ˈbarōz-, -rəz *also* ˈbe-\ *n, usu cap B* [after Sir John *Barrow* †1848 Eng. traveler and admiralty official] : a No. American goldeneye (*Bucephala islandica*) distinguished from the American goldeneye by the somewhat more crested head and white patch shaped like a crescent in front of the eye of the male

bar·ru·let \ˈbar(y)ələt\ *n* -s [¹*bar* + *-ule* + *-et*] *heraldry* : a diminutive of the bar usu. half to a fourth as wide

bar·ru·ly \ˈbar(y)əlē\ *also* **bar·ru·lé** *or* **bar·ru·lée** \ˌbar(y)əˈlā\ *adj* [ME *berle,* prob. modif. of MF *burelé,* fr. OF — more at BURELLY] *heraldry* : divided into a large number of horizontal bars

¹**bar·ry** \ˈbärē, ˈba-\ *adj* [ME, fr. AF *barré,* fr. OF *barre* bar — more at BAR] *heraldry* : divided into an even number of horizontal bars of two tinctures arranged alternately

²**bar·ry** \ˈbarē\ *n* -ES [by shortening and alter.] : BARRACUDA

bar·ry–bendy \ˌbärēˈbendē, ˌbar-\ *adj* [¹*barry* + *bendy*] *heraldry* : divided by bars and bends with tinctures alternate — see BENDY

barry–nebuly \ˌ⸗⸗ˈ⸗⸗⸗\ *adj* [¹*barry* + *nebuly*] *heraldry* : composed of bars having nebuly bounding lines — compare BARRY-WAVY

barry–pily \ˌ⸗⸗ˈ⸗⸗\ *adj* [¹*barry* + *pily*] *heraldry* : divided into equal piles arranged horizontally — see PILY

barry–wavy \ˌ⸗⸗ˈ⸗⸗\ *adj* [¹*barry* + *wavy*] *heraldry* : divided into an even number of wavy bars — compare BARRY-NEBULY

bars *pl of* BAR, *pres 3d sing of* BAR

bar·sac \ˈbärˌsak\ *n* -s *usu cap* [fr. *Barsac,* dept. Gironde, France] : a white semisweet Bordeaux wine produced near the Garonne river in the department of Gironde, France

bar screen *n* [¹*bar*] : a screen or sieve with parallel uniformly spaced bars instead of wire mesh — see GRIZZLY

bars gemel *or* **bars gemels** *pl of* BAR GEMEL

bar share *n* [¹*bar*] : a plowshare welded to the landside

bar shoe *n* [¹*bar*] : a horseshoe having a flat piece across the usual opening at the heel to protect a tender frog from injury

bar sight *n* [¹*bar*] : a rear sight on a firearm consisting of a movable bar with an open notch or peep

bar sinister *n* [¹*bar*] **1** : a supposed heraldic charge widely believed to be a mark of bastardy **2** : the fact or condition of being of illegitimate birth ⟨started with the initial handicap of the *bar sinister* —G.D.Brown⟩ **3** : an enduring stigma, stain, or reproach (as of improper conduct or irregular status) ⟨the loyalty determinations presented a special situation involving the imposition of a *bar sinister* —N.L.Nathanson⟩ ⟨a number of the great universities still ignore ecology or accord it the *bar sinister* —*Amer. Naturalist*⟩

bar soap *n* [¹*bar*] : soap sold in the form of solid oblong cakes commonly for laundry purposes

bar·som \'bärsəm\ *n* -s [Per *barsam,* fr. MPer *barsum,* fr. Av *barəsman;* akin to Skt *barhis* sacrificial grass, *brhati* he plucks] **:** a bundle of sacred twigs or metal rods used by priests in Zoroastrian ceremonies

bar spade *n* [¹*bar*] **:** a trenching spade with a cutting blade welded across the ends of three parallel bars for use in spading wet sticky soil

bar·spoon \'=,=\ *n* [¹*bar* (counter) + *spoon*] **:** a spoon equivalent to a teaspoonful that is used in measuring ingredients for mixed drinks

bar·stool \'=,=\ *n* [¹*bar* (counter) + *stool*] **:** a high stool that usu. has a round seat fixed permanently on a central post and that usu. is one of a row of such stools standing in front of a bar

bart \'bärt, 'bȧt\ *n* -s *often cap* [by abbr.] **:** BARONET

bar tack *n* [¹*bar*] **:** a reinforcement for points of strain in clothing consisting of a bar-shaped line of small stitches worked across several threads — **bartacked** \'=,=\ *adj*

bar–tailed godwit \'=,=-\ *n* **:** a godwit (*Limosa lapponica*) that has a slightly curved bill, a closely barred tail, and relatively short legs and that breeds in extreme northern Europe and Asia and winters chiefly in Africa and Australasia

bar·tangi \bär'täŋē\ *n, pl* **bartangi** *or* **bartangis** *usu cap* [fr. the *Bartang* river valley, Tadzhik S.S.R., U.S.S.R.] **1 :** an Iranian people from the Bartang river valley in the western Pamirs **2 :** a member of the Bartangi people

bar·tend \'bär,tend, 'bȧ,-\ *vi* -ED/-ING/-S [back-formation fr. *bartender*] **:** to act as a bartender esp. professionally

bar·tend·er \-ə(r)\ *n* -s [¹*bar* (counter) + *tender*] **:** one that serves liquor at a bar **:** BARKEEPER

¹**bar·ter** \'bär|d·ər, 'bȧ|, |tə(r)\ *vb* **bartered; bartered; bartering** \|d·əriŋ, |təriŋ *also* |·triŋ\ **barters** [ME *bartren,* fr. MF *barater* to cheat, exchange] *vi* **1 :** to trade by exchanging one commodity for another ⟨~*ed* for furs with tobacco and rum⟩ **:** TRUCK ⟨stores ~*ing* with farmers⟩ **2 :** to trade in intangible or nonmaterial values ⟨the Americans refused to ~ for peace unless the British granted independence to the colonies — *Amer. Guide Series: N.Y.City*⟩ ~ *vt* **1 :** to trade or exchange by bartering ⟨~ unlimited surpluses for strategic materials — *New Republic*⟩ ⟨Indians . . . ~*ed* their services for "ironmongery" —C.B.Hitchcock⟩ **2 :** to trade or exchange (as an ideal or intangible value) for a material or unworthy consideration — often used with *away* ⟨would cheerfully ~ away all the social gains of the last century for one first-class new symphony —Hunter Mead⟩

²**barter** \"\ *n* -s **1 :** the act or practice of carrying on trade by bartering **:** an exchange of goods for goods ⟨the former system of ~ has virtually ceased to exist, replaced by money economy —H.S.Tschopik⟩ **2 :** the thing given in exchange in bartering ⟨the trinkets were ~ for food and manual service from the natives⟩

¹**barth·ian** \'bärd·ēən, -rthē-\ *adj* [Karl *Barth* b1886 Swiss theologian + E *-ian*] *usu cap* **:** of or relating to Barth or to his theology which has exercised a formative influence in the development of the neoorthodox school of Protestant theology

²**barthian** \"\ *n* -s *usu cap* **:** a follower or adherent of the theology of Karl Barth

barth·ian·ism \-,nizəm\ *n* -s *usu cap* **:** the Barthian crisis theology or dialectical theology that rejects theological liberalism and its emphasis on empirical methods and stresses instead reliance on supernatural revelation

barth·ite \'bär,thīt, -rd-,īt\ *n* -s [G *barthit,* fr. *Barth,* 20th cent. mining engineer in southwestern Africa + G *-it* -ite] **:** CONICHALCITE

bar·tho·lin·itis \bär,tōlə'nīd·əs\ *n, pl* **bartholin·ites** \-ī,tēz\ *sometimes cap* [NL, fr. ISV (glands of) *Bartholin* + NL *-itis*] **:** inflammation of the glands of Bartholin

bartholin's gland *n, usu cap B* **:** GLAND OF BARTHOLIN

bar·ti·zan \'bärd·əzən, ¦==¦zan\ *n* -s [alter. of ME *bretasynge,* fr. *bretasce* parapet — more at BRATTICE] **:** a small structure (as a turret) overhanging or projecting from a building near an entrance for lookout or defense or for support for a flagpole — **bar·ti·zaned** \-nd\ *adj*

bartizans

bar·ton \'bärtᵊn\ *n* -s [ME *berton,* fr. OE *beretūn* threshing floor, barn, fr. *bere* barley + *tūn* enclosure — more at BARLEY, TOWN] **1** *now dial Eng* **:** a large farm; *esp* **:** a demesne farm or the demesne lands of a manor **2** *now dial Eng* **a :** a farmyard or the outbuildings behind a farmhouse **b :** a poultry yard or hen coop

bar·ton·el·la \,bärtᵊn'elə\ *n* [NL, fr. A.L.*Barton fl*1909 + NL *-ella*] **1** *cap* **:** the type genus of Bartonellaceae including the causative organism of Oroya fever and verruga peruana in man **2** -s *sometimes cap* **:** any member of the genus *Bartonella*

bar·ton·el·la·ce·ae \,bärtᵊn,e'lāsē,ē\ *n pl, cap* [NL, fr. *Bartonella,* type genus + *-aceae*] **:** a family of microorganisms (order Rickettsiales) that invade blood and tissue cells of man and other vertebrates and are often transmitted by blood-sucking arthropods

bar·ton·el·lo·sis \-'lōsəs\ *n, pl* **bartonello·ses** \-ō,sēz\ *sometimes cap* [NL, fr. *Bartonella* + *-osis*] **:** a disease of man and other mammals orig. in the valleys of the Andes of Peru but now in other parts of So. America characterized by severe anemia and high fever followed by an eruption like warts on the skin and caused by an organism (*Bartonella bacilliformis*) like rickettsia that invades the red blood cells and is transmitted by sandflies (genus *Phlebotomus*)

¹**bar·to·nia** \bär'tōnēə\ *n* [NL, fr. Benjamin S. *Barton* †1815 Amer. botanist + NL *-ia*] *syn of* MENTZELIA

²**bartonia** \"\ *n* [NL, fr. B.S.*Barton* + NL *-ia*] **1** -s **:** MENTZELIA 2a **2** *cap* **:** a genus of very small herbs (family Gentianaceae) with scalelike leaves and small yellow flowers

bar tracery *n* [¹*bar*] **:** tracery formed by the curves and intersections of the molded bars of mullions

bar·tra·mia \bär'trāmēə\ *n, cap* [NL, fr. William *Bartram* †1823 Am. naturalist + NL *-ia*] **:** a genus (the type of the family Bartramiaceae) of acrocarpous mosses with globular capsules which dry in ridges and folds

bar·tra·mi·an sandpiper *or* **bartramian plover** \(')bär-¦trāmēən-\ *n, usu cap B* [Wm. *Bartram* + E *-ian*] **:** UPLAND PLOVER

bar·tram oak \'bärtrəm-\ *n, usu cap B* [after John *Bartram* †1777 Am. botanist] **:** an oak (*Quercus heterophylla*) of the eastern U.S. usu. considered a natural hybrid between the northern red oak and the willow oak

bartram's sandpiper *n, usu cap B* [after William *Bartram*] **:** UPLAND PLOVER

bartree \'=,=\ *n* -s [¹*bar* + *tree*] **:** WARPING BOARD

barts *pl of* BART

bart·sia \'bärtsēə\ *n* [NL, irreg. fr. Johann *Bartsch* †1738 Ger. physician in Surinam + NL *-ia*] **1** *cap* **:** a small genus of partly parasitic herbs (family Scrophulariaceae) of the northern hemisphere with opposite leaves and showy irregular flowers in terminal leafy spikes — see ALPINE BARTSIA **2** -s **:** any plant of the genus *Bartsia*

ba·rukh·zy \bə'rüksē\ *also* **barukhzy hound** *n* -ES *often cap B* [Russ, fr. Pashto *Bārakzi* people of Afghanistan] **:** AFGHAN HOUND

barunduki *var of* BARONDUKI

barway \'=,=\ *n* [¹*bar* + *way*] **:** a gateway closed by bars usu. fitting into posts

bar winding *n* [¹*bar*] **:** an armature winding consisting of a series of metallic bars connected at their extremities

bar·wing \'=,=\ *n* [so called fr. the wide white wing stripe] *Austral* **:** WHITE-EYED DUCK

bar·wise \'=,wīz\ *also* **bar·ways** \-,wāz\ *adv* [¹*bar* + *-wise* or *-ways*] **1** *heraldry* **:** in the direction of a bar **:** HORIZONTALLY **2** *heraldry* **:** in a line in the direction of a bar — used of two or more charges esp. when not across the middle of the field; compare *in fess* at FESS

barwood \'=,=\ *n* [¹*bar* + *wood*] **:** a hard red dyewood of tropical Africa from a tree of the genus *Pterocarpus* but supposed by some to be camwood; *also* **:** redwood from any of several other African trees

bar–wound \'=,=\ *adj* **:** made with bar winding ⟨bought a *bar-wound* armature⟩

bary- *comb form* [Gk *bary-,* fr. *barys* — more at GRIEVE] **:** heavy ⟨*bary*lite⟩ ⟨*bary*sphere⟩

bar·y·cen·ter \'barə,sentə(r)\ *n* -s [part trans. of G *baryzentrum,* fr. *bary-* + *zentrum* center] **:** CENTER OF MASS — **bar·y·cen·tric** \,==¦sentrik, -ēk\ *adj*

bar·ye \'barē\ *n* -s [F, fr. Gk *barys* heavy] **:** ⁷BAR 2

bar·y·lambda \,barə'lamdə\ *n, cap* [NL, fr. *bary-* + Gk *lambda,* the letter; fr. the shape of the upper molars] **:** a genus of large powerful herbivorous mammals (order Pantodonta) from the upper Paleocene of Colorado that have tails like kangaroos and small heads

bar·y·lite \'barə,līt\ *n* -s [ISV *bary-* + *-lite;* orig. formed as G *barylit*] **:** a mineral $BaBe_2Si_2O_7$ consisting of rare silicate of barium and beryllium occurring in colorless prismatic crystals (hardness 7, sp. gr. 4.03)

ba·ryp·o·da \bə'ripədə\ [NL, fr. *bary-* + *-poda*] *syn of* EMBRITHOPODA

ba·rys·i·lite \bə'risə,līt, ,barə'si,līt\ *n* -s [Sw *barysil* (fr. *bary-* + *silikon* silicon) + E *-ite*] **:** a rare lead silicate $Pb_3Si_2O_7$ occurring in white cleavable masses

bar·y·sphere \'barə,sfi(ə)r, -iə\ *n* -s [ISV *bary-* + *-sphere*] **:** the heavy interior portion of the earth within the lithosphere

baryt- *or* **baryto-** *comb form* [ISV, fr. *baryta*] **:** baryta — barytic ⟨*baryto*calcite⟩

ba·ry·ta \bə'rīd·ə\ *n* -s [alter. of *barytes* — more at BARITE] **:** any of several compounds of barium; *esp* **:** barium monoxide

baryta paper *n* **:** paper that is coated with a preparation of barium sulfate in gelatin and used after calendering as a support for the light-sensitive emulsion used in photography

baryta water *n* **:** an aqueous solution of barium hydroxide

baryta white *n* **:** barium sulfate used as a pigment or extender

baryta yellow *n* **:** BARIUM YELLOW 2

baryte *or* **barytes** *var of* BARITE

ba·ryt·ic \bə'rid·ik\ *adj* [*baryta* + *-ic*] **:** of or relating to baryta

bar·y·tine \'barə,tēn\ *n* -s [F, fr. *baryte* barite + *-ine*] **:** BARITE

ba·ry·to·cal·cite \bə,rīd·ə+\ *n* -s [*baryt-* + *calcite*] **:** a mineral $BaCa(CO_3)_2$ consisting of white monoclinic barium calcium carbonate (hardness 4, sp. gr. 3.66)

bar·y·ton \'barə,tän\ *n* -s [F — more at BARITONE] **1 :** BARITONE 2, 3 **2** [G, fr. It *baritono* — more at BARITONE] **:** a tenor vox humana organ stop of 16- or 8-foot pitch

¹**bar·y·tone** \'barə,tōn\ *adj* [Gk *barytonos,* lit., deep-sounding — more at BARITONE] **:** having an unaccented final syllable — used esp. in Greek grammar

²**barytone** \"\ *n* -s **:** a barytone word (as Greek *philos* "dear" contrasted with *sophós* "wise") — used esp. in Greek grammar

³**barytone** *var of* BARITONE

¹**bas** *pres 3d sing of* BA, *pl of* BA

²**bas** \'bəs\ *adv* [Hindi *bas,* fr. Per] *India* **:** ENOUGH, STOP — often used interjectionally

bas *abbr* basso

ba·sad \'bā,sad\ *adv* [¹*base* + *-ad*] **:** toward the base ⟨with small bony processes lying ~ to the true fin rays⟩

¹**ba·sal** \'bāsəl *also* -āz-\ *adj* [¹*base* + *-al*] **1 :** relating to, situated at, or forming the base; *specif* **:** ¹RADICAL 1a(2) ⟨~ leaves⟩ **2 a :** of or relating to the foundation, base, or essence **:** FUNDAMENTAL, BASIC, ESSENTIAL ⟨accept the ~ doctrines of Christianity —Frank Thilly⟩ **b :** of, relating to, or essential for maintaining the fundamental vital activities of an organism (as respiration, heartbeat, or excretion) **:** MINIMAL ⟨~ diet⟩ — see BASAL METABOLISM **3 :** serving as or serving to induce an initial comatose or unconscious state that forms a basis for further anesthetization ⟨~ narcosis⟩ ⟨~ anesthetic⟩ — **ba·sal·ly** \-əlē, -əli\ *adv*

²**basal** \"\ *n* -s **:** a basal part or structure; *esp* **:** a basal plate of an echinoderm

basal age *n* **:** the mental age level at which all the items on an intelligence test can be creditably passed

basal area *n* **:** the area of a breast-high cross section of a tree or of all the trees in a stand

basal body *n* **1 :** BASAL GRANULE **2 :** KINETOPLAST

basal cell *n* **:** one of the innermost cells of the Malpighian layer of the skin

basal–cell carcinoma *n* **:** a skin cancer derived from and preserving the form of the basal cells of the skin

basal cleavage *n* **:** cleavage parallel to the base of a crystal or to the plane of the lateral axes

basal complex *n* **:** FUNDAMENTAL COMPLEX

basal conglomerate *n* **:** a conglomerate that resting on a surface of erosion and consequently marking an unconformity forms the bottom member of a sedimentary series

basal disk *n* **:** an expanded basal portion by which certain stalked sessile organisms are attached to the substrate

ba·sa·le \bə'sa(,)lē, -za-, -ā(,)lē, -ä(,)lē\ *n, pl* **ba·sa·lia** \-lēə\ [NL, fr. E *basal*] **:** the proximal one of the two or more cartilaginous or bony portions in the axis of any of the paired fins of a fish — compare BASIPTERYGIUM

basal ganglion *n* **:** any of four deeply placed masses of gray matter within each cerebral hemisphere comprising the caudate nucleus, the lenticular nucleus, the amygdaloid nucleus, and the claustrum — usu. used in pl.

basal granule *n* **:** a minute distinctively staining granule typically found at the base of every flagellum or cilium — called also *blepharoplast*

ba·sa·lis \-ləs\ *n, pl* **basa·les** \-,lēz\ [NL, fr. E *basal*] **:** the basal part of the endometrium that is not shed during menstruation

basal lamina *n* **:** the part of the gray matter of the embryonic neural tube from which the motor nerve roots arise

basal length *n, anthrop* **:** distance from gnathion to basion

basal metabolic rate *n* **:** the rate at which heat is given off by an organism at complete rest usu. determined 12 to 15 hours after ingestion of food and expressed in large calories per square meter of body surface per hour and as a percentage above or below a standard value

basal metabolism *n* **:** the metabolism of an organism in the fasting and resting state when it uses just enough energy to maintain vital cellular activity, respiration, and circulation as measured by the basal metabolic rate

basal–nerved \¦==¦=\ *adj, of a leaf* **:** having the veins radiating from the base

basal plane *n* **1 :** a plane parallel to the lateral or horizontal axis **2 :** a basal pinacoid

basal plate *n* **:** an underlying structure: as **a :** the ventral portion of the neural tube **b :** the part of the decidua of a placental mammal that is intimately fused with the placenta **c :** the part of a coral corallium immediately below the polyp **d :** any of certain chiefly ventral skeletal plates of an echinoderm

basal ration *n* **:** a ration furnishing the necessary energy but lacking in one or more accessory food substances (as vitamins) that may be added in varying proportion for the study of their effects

basal rot *n* **:** a rot affecting the basal parts of a plant; *specif* **:** a rot of narcissus bulbs due to a fungus (*Fusarium bulbigemum*)

ba·salt \bə'sȯlt, 'bā,sȯlt, 'ba,sȯlt *also* 'bā,zȯlt *sometimes* 'basəlt *or* 'bazəlt\ *n* -s [alter. of earlier *basaltes,* fr. L, MS var. of *basanites* touchstone, fr. Gk *basanitēs,* fr. *basanos* touchstone (fr. Egypt *bḫnw*) + *-itēs* -ite] **1 :** a dark-gray to black dense to fine-grained igneous rock that is the extrusive equivalent of gabbro, that consists of basic plagioclase, augite, and usu. magnetite with olivine or basalt glass or both sometimes present, that is often vesicular the cavities sometimes being filled with secondary minerals, and that sometimes has a prismatic parting (as in the basalts of the Giant's Causeway, Northern Ireland) and occas. a pillow or ellipsoidal structure **2** *usu* **ba·sal·tes** \bə'sȯl(,)tēz\ **:** a hard fine-grained black stoneware introduced by Josiah Wedgwood in 1768

basalt dome *n* **:** a broad rounded dome-shaped volcano formed almost exclusively of basaltic lava — compare SHIELD VOLCANO

basalt glass *n* **:** a black glassy form of basalt — called also *hyalobasalt, vitrobasalt*

ba·sal·tic \bə'sȯltik\ *adj* **:** relating to, formed of, containing, or resembling basalt ⟨~ lava⟩

ba·sal·ti·form \bə'sȯltə,fȯrm\ *adj* [*basalt* + *-iform*] **:** like basalt in form **:** COLUMNAR

basalt–porphyry *n* **:** a basalt characterized by prominent phenocrysts of olivine or augite

bas·aluminite \¦bās+\ *n* -s [*basic* + *alumin-* + *-ite*] **:** a mineral $Al_4(SO_4)(OH)_{10}\cdot5H_2O$ consisting of a basic hydrated aluminum sulfate found in veinlets in siderite at Irchester and Brighton Hill, England, and in France

basal wall *n, bot* **:** the primary wall in archegoniates that divides the oospore into an anterior and a posterior half

bas·a·nite \,basə,nīt, -azə-\ *n* -s [L *basanites* — more at BASALT] **1 :** TOUCHSTONE 1 **2 :** an extrusive-igneous rock composed of plagioclase, augite, olivine, and either nephelite or leucite

bas bleu \bäblœ\ *n, pl* **bas bleus** \-œ(z)\ [F *bas-bleu,* fr. *bas* stocking + *bleu* blue] **:** BLUESTOCKING 1

bas·cart \'ba,skärt\ *n* [blend of *basket* and *cart*] **:** a waist-high wire basket or pair of baskets on wheels into which shoppers in supermarkets gather their purchases

bas·cine *or* **bas·sine** \bə'sēn\ *adj* [F *bassine,* lit., pan, fr. *bassin* basin, fr. OF *bacin* — more at BASIN] *of a watchcase* **:** having a flush joint that is barely visible

bascinet *var of* BASINET

bas·col·o·gist \ba'skäləjəst\ *n* -s *usu cap* **:** a specialist in the Basque language or culture

bas·col·o·gy \-əjē\ *n* -ES *usu cap* [*Basco-* (fr. *Basque*) + *-logy*] **:** the study of the Basque language or culture

bas·cule \'ba,skyül\ *n* -s [F, seesaw, fr. MF, alter. (influenced by *bas* low) of earlier *bacule,* fr. *baculer* to punish by beating the buttocks against the ground, fr. *bas* low + *cul* buttocks — more at BASE, CULET] **:** an apparatus or structure in which one end is counterbalanced by the other on the principle of the seesaw or by weights (as in a bascule bridge)

bascule bridge *n* **:** a counterpoised or balanced drawbridge

bascule escapement *n* **:** the detent escapement in which the detent is pivoted, the tension being supplied by a small hair-spring

¹**base** \'bās\ *n, pl* **bas·es** \'bāsəz\ [ME, fr. MF, fr. L *basis,* fr. Gk, step, stepping, base, pedestal, fr. *bainein* to go, step — more at COME] **1 a :** the bottom of something considered as its support **:** that on which something rests or stands **:** FOUNDATION ⟨the ~ of the lamp⟩ ⟨the ~ of the pyramid⟩ ⟨the ~ of the mountain⟩ **b** (1) **:** the lower part of a wall, pier, or column considered as a separate architectural feature (2) **:** the lower part of a complete architectural design (as of a monument) **c :** the line or surface constituting that part of a geometrical figure on which it is supposed to stand ⟨the ~ of a triangle⟩ ⟨the ~ of a cone⟩ **d :** that part of a bodily organ by which it is attached to another more central structure of the organism ⟨the ~ of the thumb⟩ **e** (1) **:** the part on, to, or in which the frame and operating parts of a mechanism are fastened (2) **:** the part (as a panelboard) upon which other parts (as buses, switches, terminal and contact parts) are mounted (3) **:** the insulated part of a lamp bulb or electron tube through which its intervals make electrical connection with the circuit associated with it **f :** ¹BLOCK 4g **2 :** the main ingredient ⟨an exotic drink with a rum ~⟩: as **a** (1) **:** an essential ingredient of an explosive — compare DOUBLE-BASE POWDER, SINGLE-BASE POWDER (2) **:** the predominating substance held in solution in a crude petroleum or left as a residue on refining ⟨mixed-*base* crudes⟩ — see ASPHALT-BASE, NAPHTHENE-BASE, PARAFFIN-BASE **b** (1) **:** an inert supporting or carrying ingredient **:** an absorbent or adsorbent (as kieselguhr in dynamite) **:** CARRIER 9 — compare DOPE 3a (2) **:** an active supporting ingredient (as wood pulp mixed with an oxidizing agent in dynamite) **c** (1) **:** the usu. inactive ingredient of a preparation serving as the vehicle for the active medicinal principle ⟨the fatty ~ of an ointment⟩ (2) **:** the chief active ingredient of a preparation — called also *basis* **d** (1) **:** a transparent support for photographic film (2) **:** the paper support used for photographic paper **3 a :** the fundamental part of something **:** basic principle **:** ESSENCE, FOUNDATION, BASIS, GROUNDWORK ⟨tried to furnish criticism with a psychological ~ —C.I.Glicksberg⟩ ⟨rejuvenating the moral ~ of a society—Herbert Agar⟩ **b** (1) **:** the fundamental unit or pattern of a rhythm or one of its component parts or the norm of this unit (2) **:** the nuclear pattern in a complex rhythmic figure or system (3) **:** BASIS 5 **4** *bases pl, archaic* **:** a skirt often of velvet or brocade and sometimes of mailed armor that reaches from the waist to the knees **5 :** the lower or back part of something without reference to its function as a support: as **a :** the lower part of an heraldic field — usu. used in the phrase *in base;* compare ESCUTCHEON 1 **b :** the lowest part of the hilt of a saber **c :** the pavilion of a cut gem **d :** the underside of a cloud ⟨fly below the cloud ~⟩ **6 a :** the point or line from which a start is made in an action or undertaking ⟨plans to make this city his ~ of operation for six to eight weeks —J.A.Loftus⟩ **b :** a line in a survey which when accurately determined in length and position serves as the origin for computing the distances and relative positions of remote points and objects by triangulation **c** (1) **:** the locality or the installations on which a military force relies for supplies or from which it initiates operations ⟨a large naval ~⟩ ⟨an advanced ~⟩ (2) **:** the element on which a military movement or formation is regulated **d :** the number with reference to which a set of numbers or a mathematical table is constructed ⟨the ~ of a system of logarithms⟩ **e** (1) *historical and comparative linguistics* **:** ROOT, STEM, THEME; *esp* **:** one reconstructed from words or from the relationships among words in several languages (as assumed Indo-European *bher-* "to carry" reconstructed from Greek *pherein,* Latin *ferre,* Old English *beran,* and their cognates) (2) *descriptive linguistics* **:** the word or morpheme, which may be a bound form but not an affix, selected as a convenient point of departure in the analysis of complex words or derivatives (as *play* used in the analysis of *played* and *playful, sing* used in the analysis of *sings, sang, sung,* and *song,* or *acet-* used in the analysis of *acetal* and *acetate*) **f :** the basal pinacoid of a crystal **g :** the quantity equaling 100 from which variations in an index number are measured ⟨the 1946–49 profit ~⟩ **7 a :** the starting place or goal in various games **b** *obs* **:** PRISONER'S BASE **c :** any one of the four stations at the corners of a baseball infield ⟨was thrown out at first ~⟩ **8 a :** a compound (as lime, ammonia, a caustic alkali, or an alkaloid) capable of reacting with an acid to form a salt either with or without the elimination of water, its aqueous solutions if it is water-soluble having an acrid brackish taste and turning litmus blue **b :** a compound (MOH) containing the hydroxide ion (OH^-) or hydroxyl group (OH) that is capable of yielding in aqueous solution a hydroxyl ion together with the cation (M^+), the degree of ionization in dilute solutions of strong bases (as sodium hydroxide, calcium hydroxide, and choline) being virtually complete and that of weak bases (as ammonium hydroxide and many organic bases) being in the neighborhood of one per cent or less **b** *according to the Brønsted-Lowry system* **:** a molecule (as ammonia) or ion (as hydroxyl or nitrate) that can take up a proton from an acid **:** a proton acceptor ⟨the chloride ion is the conjugate ~ of hydrogen chloride⟩ **c** *according to the G.N.Lewis system* **:** a compound (as ammonia, ether, or benzene) or a negative ion (as hydroxyl) capable of giving up to an acid an unshared pair of electrons which then form a covalent chemical bond — called also *Lewis base* **9 :** the least number of natural cards that will form a canasta when a required number of natural or wild cards is added — **off base 1 :** completely or absurdly mistaken ⟨any man who said such a thing is certainly *off base*⟩ **2 :** by surprise **:** UNAWARES ⟨the sudden question caught him *off base*⟩

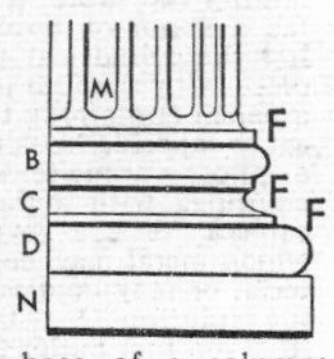

base of a column: *B* upper torus; *C* scotia; *D* lower torus; *F, F, F,* fillets; *M* shaft; *N* plinth

²**base** \"\ *vb* -ED/-ING/-S *vt* **1 a :** to make or form a foundation for ⟨great roots *based* the tree columns —George Macdonald⟩ **b :** to serve as a base for ⟨these carriers can ~ 100 planes⟩ **c :** to establish or maintain a base for ⟨would be necessary to ~ them at specially designated . . . strategic points —Vera M. Dean⟩ **2 :** to use as a base or basis for **:** ESTABLISH, FOUND — used with *on* or *upon* ⟨~s his position on a wide and shrewd scrutiny of man —A.L.Locke⟩ ⟨*basing* her life-sized portrait . . . on contemporary evidence —Harry Levin⟩ ~ *vi* **1 :** to become based — used with *on* or *upon* ⟨the value of diamonds ~s on the gem value —G.S.Brady⟩ **2 :** to establish or main-

tain one's base ⟨would fly on to Luzon after the attack and ~ there overnight —Fletcher Pratt⟩
syn BASE, FOUND, GROUND, BOTTOM, STAY, and REST can mean, in common, to provide with or serve as a basis. BASE now usu. applies to what underlies a belief, a system of thought, a judgment, a hope, and so on ⟨a conviction not *based* on any ascertainable fact⟩ ⟨a tax *based* on prospective earnings⟩ ⟨a religion *based* on faith as much as principle⟩ FOUND is very close to BASE but usu. adds the idea of something consciously advanced as support (of an opinion, a judgment, and so on) ⟨an opinion *founded* on a careful written analysis of facts⟩ ⟨this criticism is *founded* in misconception —B.N.Cardozo⟩ ⟨the terrible old mythic story on which the drama was *founded* —Matthew Arnold⟩ GROUND implies or connotes an implanting (as in the ground) to give solidity and firmness ⟨a love *grounded* in understanding and trust⟩ ⟨*grounded* all his work as a novelist on the faithful study of human nature —M.P.Linehan⟩ ⟨America was *grounded* not in the overthrow of the feudal past but in escape from it —Richard Hofstadter⟩ BOTTOM, rarer in this sense than the other terms, implies a broad and strong base ⟨his report was *bottomed* on sober statistics —*Time*⟩ ⟨*bottomed* on ideas to which everyone subscribes today —C.G.Bowers⟩ STAY implies a support that keeps upright or prevents from falling ⟨*stay* a tipping barn with heavy supporting timbers on one side⟩ ⟨his nature looked coldly upon its early faith and sought to *stay* itself with rational knowledge —H.O.Taylor⟩ REST stresses reliance upon something as a base or fundamental support, usu. figurative ⟨continuing progress based on science and technology . . . the foundation upon which our prosperity and our increasing standard of living *rest* —H.H.Curtice⟩ ⟨their academic reputations *rest*, quite largely, upon their academic power —C.W.Mills⟩ ⟨the cultures of the ancient empires of the Near East, of Greece and Rome, and of medieval Europe, all *rest* on the technical achievements of the Neolithic Age —Benjamin Farrington⟩

³base \"\ *adj* [¹*base*] **1 :** constituting or serving as a base ⟨are now setting up a string of ~ camps —*Time*⟩ **2 :** BASIC ⟨the right to work is a ~ right —Ira Mosher⟩

⁴base \"\ *adj* -ER/-EST [ME *bas*, fr. MF, fr. ML *bassus* fat, short, low] **1** *archaic* **:** of little height **:** not high or tall ⟨the cedar stoops not to the ~ shrub's foot —Shak.⟩ **2** *obs* **:** low in place or position ⟨fall to the ~ earth from the firmament —Shak.⟩ **3** *obs* **:** ³BASS **4** *archaic* **a :** of humble birth or position **:** LOWLY, PLEBEIAN, POOR ⟨~ in kind and born to be a slave —William Cowper⟩ **b :** of illegitimate birth **:** BASTARD ⟨Edmund the ~ shall top the legitimate —Shak.⟩ **5 a :** like a villein **:** SERVILE ⟨a ~ tenant⟩ **b :** held by villenage ⟨~ tenure⟩ **6 :** of inferior quality **:** SHABBY, COARSE, DEBASED: as **a** (1) **:** alloyed with inferior metal ⟨~ gold⟩ (2) **:** made of inferior metal ⟨~ coins of aluminum⟩ **b** *of language* **:** not classical ⟨~ Latin⟩ **7 :** having no dignity of sentiment or trustworthiness **:** LOW-MINDED, MEANSPIRITED, SHAMEFUL, IGNOBLE, UNWORTHY ⟨seemed a ~ betrayal of idealism —L.M.Sears⟩ **8 :** lacking higher values **:** DEGRADING, MENIAL ⟨citizens go on existing with a ~ mechanical kind of life like that of insects —Stephen Spender⟩ **9 :** of comparatively little value **:** not precious — compare BASE METAL
syn LOW, VILE: BASE stresses the ignoble; it may suggest cruelty, treachery, greed, or grossness ⟨all those features which distinguish the errors of magnanimous and intrepid spirits from *base* and malignant crimes —T.B.Macaulay⟩ ⟨*base* self-centered indulgence and selfish ambition —W.R.Inge⟩ LOW may connote crafty cunning, vulgarity, or immorality ⟨a man who by exercising a *low* sort of cunning, has managed to grab three or four millions of money selling bad whiskey —G.B. Shaw⟩ ⟨some sporting events of a *low* type, such as setting on men, women, or animals to fight —G.M.Trevelyan⟩ VILE, the most extreme of these three words, often suggests depravity or filth ⟨a jeering intention in his meanly unctuous tone, something more *vile* than mere cruelty —Joseph Conrad⟩ ⟨*vile* abuse and unbelievable blasphemies poured from her snarling lips —W.H.Wright⟩ ⟨the jail was a *vile* place, in which most kinds of debauchery and villainy were practiced, and where dire diseases were bred —Charles Dickens⟩ or, unlike BASE and LOW, is often used as a strong synonym for *objectionable* or *poor* ⟨curses . . . for the *vile* drinks he had been the means of introducing there —W.M.Thackeray⟩

⁵base [⁴*base*] *obs var of* ²BASS

base angle *n* [³*base*] **:** the horizontal angle between the base line and the orienting line in artillery fire measured from the base line in the same direction as angles are measured by the sight on the gun

base·ball \'≈,≈\ *n, often attrib* [¹*base* (goal) + *ball*] **1 :** a game played with a ball, bat, and gloves between 2 teams of 9 players each on a large field centering upon 4 bases that form the corners of a square 90 feet on each side, each team having a turn at bat and in the field during each of the 9 innings that constitute a normal game, the winner being the team that scores the most runs — see BALL 3a, b, STRIKE, OUT; FAIR BALL, FOUL BALL; INFIELD, OUTFIELD **2 :** a ball having a cork or rubber center wound tightly with twine and covered with two pieces of bleached white horsehide stitched together, officially from 5 to 5¼ ounces in weight and from 9 to 9¼ inches in circumference **3 :** a form of seven-card stud poker in which nines and threes are wild and threes and fours when dealt face up give the recipient certain special privileges

baseball field: *1* pitcher, *2* catcher, *3* first baseman, *4* second baseman, *5* third baseman, *6* shortstop, *7* left fielder, *8* center fielder, *9* right fielder, *a* first base, *b* second base, *c* third base, *d* home plate, *e* batter's box, *f* catcher's line, *g* foul line, *h* coach's box

baseball stitch *n* **:** a stitch for making two edges just meet worked under and over from the inside outward and used esp. in seaming baseball covers and mending tears in sails

baseboard \'≈,≈\ *n* [¹*base* + *board*] **:** a board situated at or forming the base of something ⟨the ~ of a camera⟩; *specif* **:** a protecting or finish molding of board or other material covering the joint of a wall and the adjoining floor

baseboard heating *n* **:** panel heating by means of baseboards

baseborn \'≈¦≈\ *adj* [⁴*base* + *born*] **1 a :** of humble birth **:** LOWLY **b :** of illegitimate birth **:** BASTARD **2 :** MEANSPIRITED, IGNOBLE

base box *n* **:** a unit of area for tin plate and terneplate equal to 31,360 square inches or 217.78 square feet or 20.232 square meters corresponding to the area covered by 112 plates of 14 by 20 inches each

base broom *n* **:** WOODWAXEN

base bullion *n* [⁴*base*] **:** crude lead containing silver or gold and silver

base burner *n* [¹*base*] **:** a stove in which the fuel is fed from a hopper as the lower layer is consumed

base circle *n* [¹*base*] **:** the circle of an involute gear wheel from which the involute forming the outline of the tooth face is generated

base coat *n* [³*base*] **1 :** the plaster underlying the finish coat and consisting of a single coat or of separately applied scratch coat and brown coat **2 :** PRIMING 1b(2)

base course *n* [³*base*] **1 a :** the first or lowest course of a wall (as of a foundation wall or of the wall of a building above the basement) **b :** the bottom layer of material laid down in the construction of a pavement **2** *of a ship* **:** a straight-line course ⟨the destroyer turned back to *base course*⟩

base–court \'≈,≈\ *n* [MF *basse-court*, fr. *basse* (fem. of *bas* low) + *court* — more at *base*] **1 a :** the lower or outer court of a castle or mansion **:** BAILEY **b :** the rear courtyard of a farmhouse **2 :** an English inferior court of law

based \'bāst\ *adj* [¹*base* + *-ed*] **:** having a base or having as a base ⟨firmly ~ ice⟩ ⟨a soundly ~ argument⟩

ba·se·dow's disease \'bäzə,dōz-\ *n, usu cap B* [after Karl von *Basedow* †1854 Ger. physician] **:** EXOPHTHALMIC GOITER

base elbow *n* [¹*base*] **:** a cast-iron pipe bend having a flange or pad cast on it as a seat for a supporting column or bracket

base esquire *n* [⁴*base*] *heraldry* **:** the lower of the halves of a canton divided diagonally

base exchange *n* [¹*base*] **:** CATION EXCHANGE

base fee *or* **base fee simple** *n* [³*base*] **1 :** a determinable fee; *broadly* **:** a defeasible fee-simple estate (as a conditional fee) **2** *obs* **a :** an estate held by a tenant at the will of his lord or superior **b :** the status of an estate conveyed by a tenant in tail out of possession as a fee simple without proper adherence to the relevant rules of law

basehearted \'≈¦≈\ *adj* **:** having a base heart

base hit *n* [¹*base*] **:** a hit in baseball that enables the batter to reach base safely with no error being made and no base runner being forced out on the play

base horehound *n* [⁴*base*] **1 :** WHITE DEAD NETTLE **2 :** a common European woundwort (*Stachys germanica*) with ashy gray foliage and pinkish white flowers

base knob *n* [¹*base*] **:** a knob often made partly of rubber and fastened to a baseboard to prevent a door from striking the wall

ba·sel \'bäzəl, 'bäz-\ *adj, usu cap* [fr. *Basel*, Switzerland] **:** of or from the city of Basel, Switzerland **:** of the kind or style prevalent in Basel

base·less \'bāsləs\ *adj* [¹*base* + *-less*] **:** having no base **:** GROUNDLESS ⟨a ~ fear⟩ — **base·less·ly** *adv* — **base·less·ness** *n* -ES

¹baselevel \'≈¦≈≈\ *n* [¹*base* + *level*] **:** the level below which a land surface cannot be reduced by running water

²baselevel \"\ *vt* **:** to reduce to or toward the condition of a plain at baselevel

baselevel plain \'≈,≈≈-\ *n* **:** a plain produced by the degradation of a region to its baselevel — compare PENEPLAIN

base line *n* [¹*base*] **:** a main line taken as or representing a base: as **a :** BASE 6b; *specif* **:** a line extending east and west from a chosen reference point on a principal meridian and forming with the meridian a pair of coordinate axes for locating township and section corners — used in U.S. public-land surveying **b :** the line joining the base piece and the base point in artillery fire **c :** the lowest horizontal line in a profile drawing of a ship used as a base for vertical measurements **d** *of a perspective drawing* **:** the line formed by the intersection of the ground plane and the picture plane **e :** the area within which a baseball player must keep when running between bases **f :** the back line at each end of a tennis court — see TENNIS illustration **g :** the lower horizontal guideline for aligning capitals in freehand lettering **h :** a known quantity used as a control for further experimentation

base·lin·er \'bā¦slīnə(r)\ *n* -S [*base line* + *-er*] **:** a tennis player who usu. plays near the base line

ba·sel·la \bə'selə, -'ze-\ *n, cap* [NL, prob. fr. a native name in India] **:** a genus of herbaceous annual or biennial vines (the type of the family Basellaceae) having sessile flowers on thickened pedicels and being natives of tropical Asia and Africa where they are used as potherbs — see MALABAR NIGHTSHADE

bas·el·la·ce·ae \,basə'lāsē,ē, -azə-\ *n pl, cap* [NL, fr. *Basella*, type genus + *-aceae*] **:** a small family of usu. climbing herbs (order Caryophyllales) sometimes included in the Chenopodiaceae but distinguished by having the calyx and corolla dissimilar — **bas·el·la·ceous** \¦≈≈¦≈shəs\ *adj*

base·ly *adv* [⁴*base* + *-ly*] **:** in a base manner **:** DISHONORABLY, IGNOBLY, SHAMEFULLY ⟨few . . . have been clearly and ~ faithless to their society —C.W.deKiewiet⟩

base·man \'bāsmən\ *n, pl* **basemen :** a man stationed at a base

base map *n* [³*base*] **:** a map having only essential outlines and used for the plotting or presentation of specialized data of various kinds

base·ment \'bāsmənt\ *n* -S *often attrib* [prob. fr. ¹*base* + *-ment*] **1 :** the architectural member that serves as a pedestal or substructure for the main order; *specif* **:** the ground floor facade in Renaissance architecture **2 a :** the part of a building that is wholly or partly below ground level; *esp* **:** such a room having overlaid or hard-surface flooring and housing a furnace — compare CELLAR **b :** the interior at ground level in a basement house or in a building having a basement facade **3 :** the lowest or fundamental part of anything ⟨the ~ of the fountain —Charles Dickens⟩ **4 a :** BASEMENT COMPLEX **b :** a compact firm rock underlying less firmly consolidated earth materials ⟨atolls can grow on various types of ~s —F.P.Shepard⟩ **5** *chiefly New Eng* **:** an indoor school toilet or washroom ⟨the boy's ~⟩

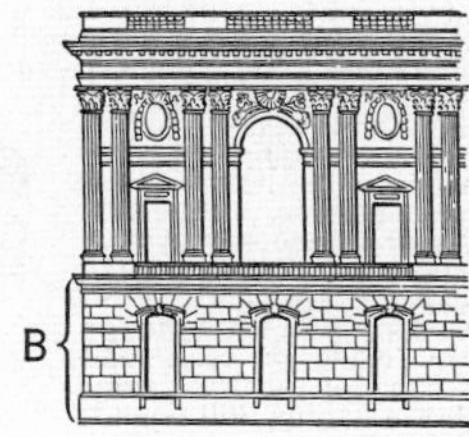

B basement

basement complex *n* **1 :** the assemblage of metamorphic and igneous rocks underlying stratified rocks in a particular region **2 :** the Archean rocks — compare FUNDAMENTAL COMPLEX

basement house *n* **:** a dwelling in which the principal drawing rooms are located at least one story above ground level with the main entrance at ground level or one story above and reached by exterior steps

basement membrane *n* **:** a delicate connective tissue membrane commonly composed of a single layer of flat cells and underlying the epithelial cells of many organs

base metal *n* [⁴*base*] **1 :** a metal or alloy (as zinc, lead, or brass) of comparatively low value and relatively inferior in certain properties (as resistance to corrosion) — opposed to *noble metal* **2 :** the metal to which a coating or plating is applied **:** the metal existing underneath a coating or plating **3 :** the chief constituent of any alloy **4 :** the metal composing parts to be welded

base molding *n* [¹*base*] **:** a molding along the upper margin of a baseboard or other plinth

bas·en·dite \'ba'sen,dīt\ *n* -S [¹*base* + *endite*] **:** either of a pair of lobes attached at the end of each of the specialized paired appendages of a crustacean — compare ENDITE, EXITE

base·ness \'bāsnəs\ *n* -ES [⁴*base* + *-ness*] **1 :** the quality or state of being base ⟨moral ~⟩ **2 :** a base act or trait ⟨perpetrate a ~ so unmixed —Robert Browning⟩

base net *n* [¹*base*] **:** a system of triangles and quadrilaterals including and immediately adjacent to a base line in a triangulation system

ba·sen·ji \bə'senjē\ *n* [of Bantu origin; akin to Lingala & Tshiluba *basenji*, pl. of Lingala *mosenji*, Tshiluba *musenji* native, inhabitant of the hinterland] **1** *usu cap* **:** an African breed of small compact curly-tailed chestnut-brown dogs that rarely bark **2** -S *sometimes cap* **:** any dog of the Basenji breed

base of fire [¹*base*] **:** an element of one or more military units that give supporting fire to an attacking unit

base on balls [¹*base*] **:** an advance to first base given to a baseball player who during his time at bat receives four pitches outside the strike zone ⟨was given an intentional *base on balls* in the seventh inning⟩ — called also *pass, walk*

base paper *or* **base stock** *n* [¹*base*] **:** BODY PAPER

base path *n* [¹*base*] **:** the area between the bases of a baseball field used by a base runner

base pay *or* **base salary** *or* **base wage** *n* [³*base*] **:** BASIC WAGE; *specif* **:** the minimum pay for a given rank or grade of a member of the armed forces ⟨retired for life upon three-quarters of his *base pay* —Nancy B. Shea⟩

base period *n* [³*base*] **:** a period of business or economic activity used as a basis or reference point esp. for indexing, calculating, estimating, or adjudicating prices, taxes, compensation, income, and production

base piece *n* [³*base*] **:** the piece of a gun battery for which the initial firing data are computed

baseplate \'≈,≈\ *n* [³*base* + *plate*] **1 :** a plate that serves as a base or support: as **a :** the foundation plate of heavy machinery (as of a steam engine) **:** BEDPLATE **b :** the steel or cast-iron plate on which a column rests **c :** the metal plate that serves as a base and firing support for the breech end of a mortar **2 a :** the portion of an artificial denture in contact with the jaw **b :** the sheet of plastic material used in the making of trial denture plates

baseplug \'≈,≈\ *n* [¹*base* + *plug*] **:** an electric wall receptacle; *esp* **:** one in or near the baseboard

base price *n* [³*base*] **1 :** a price for a standard commodity from which variations are readily computed (as by a formula) **2 :** a price before discounts and extras

baser *comparative of* BASE

base rate *n* [³*base*] **:** an established and usu. guaranteed rate of pay per unit of time (as per hour or day) or for production at the standard rate

base right *n* [³*base*] **:** the right in Scots law acquired by a disponee taking feudal property to hold as subvassal

base ring *n* [¹*base*] **1 :** a projecting band of metal around the breech of a muzzle-loading cannon — see CANNON illustration **2 :** the circular base of a heavy gun carriage

base rocker *or* **base rocking chair** *n* [¹*base*] **:** a rocking chair fastened upon a base that is usu. mounted on casters

base runner *n* [¹*base*] **:** a baseball player of the team at bat who is on base or is attempting to reach a base — **base·run·ning** \'≈,≈≈\ *n*

bases *pl of* BASE *or of* BASIS, *pres 3d sing of* BASE

base shoe *n* [¹*base*] **:** a narrow molding often of quarter round joining the bottom of a baseboard and the floor

basest *superlative of* BASE

base stock method *n* [³*base*] **:** an accounting method of valuing inventories by carrying on the books a minimum quantity of a commodity at the same low fixed price from year to year and valuing the quantity in excess of the minimum at a separate price which is usu. the lower of cost or market value — compare LAST IN, FIRST OUT

base stone *n* [³*base*] **:** FOOTING STONE

base surge *n* [¹*base*] **:** the cloud of mist, water, and debris that spreads outward from the surface point of an underwater atomic explosion

base time *n* [³*base*] **:** the time calculated as the normal time required by a qualified individual working at normal pace for completion of a given work cycle with no allowance for delay or fatigue and personal needs

¹bash \'bash, -aa(ə)-, -ai-\ *vb* -ED/-ING/-ES [origin unknown] *vt* **:** to strike violently **:** BEAT, KNOCK ⟨~ him on the head with a club⟩ **:** smash by a blow — often used with *in* ⟨the tree ~*ed* in the roof⟩ ~ *vi* **1 :** CRASH ⟨the car ~*ed* into a tree⟩ **2** *Brit* **:** HIT, KNOCK ⟨a branch ~*ing* against the house⟩; *also* **:** to punch with the fist — **bash one's ear** *chiefly Austral* **:** to talk long and insistently to one

²bash \"\ *n* -ES **1** *chiefly Brit* **:** a forceful blow **2** *slang Brit* **:** a good time **:** ENTERTAINMENT

ba·sha \bä'shä, '≈(,)≈\ *n* -S [Assamese] **:** an Assamese hut typically made of bamboo and grass

bash·am's mixture \'bashəmz-\ *n, usu cap B* [after William R. *Basham* †1877 Eng. physician] **:** an aromatic solution of iron and ammonium acetate formerly used as a hematinic

bashaw *often cap, var of* PASHA

bash·er \'bashə(r), -aash-,-aish-\ *n* -S [¹*bash* + *-er*] **:** one that bashes; *esp, chiefly Austral* **:** a criminal who beats and robs his victims

bash·ful \'bashfəl, -aash-, -aish-\ *adj* [obs. *bash* to be abashed (fr. ME *basshen*, short for *abasshen*) + *-ful* — more at ABASH] **1 :** inclined to shrink from public attention **:** socially shy or timid **:** SELF-CONSCIOUS, DIFFIDENT ⟨he hesitated, awkward and ~, shifted his weight from one leg to the other —Jack London⟩ ⟨they considered themselves a tough outfit and weren't ~ about letting anybody know it —F.B. Gipson⟩ **2 :** characterized by, showing, or resulting from extreme sensitiveness, self-consciousness, or shyness ⟨found that ~ words tumbling from his tongue's end really spelled themselves out into sensible talk —Carl Sandburg⟩ **syn** see SHY

bashful billy *n, usu cap 2d B* **:** LORIS 1b

bash·ful·ly \-fəlē, -li\ *adv* **:** in a bashful manner

bash·ful·ness \-fəlnəs\ *n* -ES **:** the quality or state of being bashful

bashi–ba·zouk \,bashēbə'zük\ *n* -S [Turk *başı bozuk* irregular soldier, fr. *baş* head, leader + *bozuk* depraved, corrupt] **1 a :** a member of an irregular ill-disciplined auxiliary of the Ottoman Empire **b :** IRREGULAR **2 :** a turbulent ill-disciplined person

bashing *n* -S [fr. gerund of ¹*bash*] **:** BEATING ⟨they have both had a ~⟩

bash·kir \(')bash¦ki(ə)r\ *n, pl* **bashkir** *or* **bashkirs** *usu cap* [Russ, of Turkic origin; akin to Jagatai *badžkyr* Bashkir, Chuvash *puškərt*] **1 a :** a Turkic-speaking Muslim people between the Volga and the Ural mountains regarded as tatarized Finns **b :** a member of the Bashkir people **2 :** the language of the Bashkirs

bash·lyk *also* **bash·lik** \(')bash¦lik\ *n* -S [Russ *bashlyk*, fr. Turk *başlık* hood, fr. *baş* head] **:** a protective hood with long ends for use as a scarf worn esp. by the Russian military

ba·si \'bäsē\ *n* -S [native name in the Philippines] **:** a fermented beverage prepared by natives of the Philippines

basi- *in pronunciations below* ¦≈≈ = ¦bāsē (*bef vowels or consonants*) *or* -sə (*bef consonants*)\ *also* **baso-** *comb form* [ISV, fr. L *basis*] **1 a :** base **:** lower part ⟨*basipetal*⟩ **b :** at or near the base ⟨*basifixed*⟩ ⟨*basiglandular*⟩ **c :** of or belonging to the base of ⟨*basicranial*⟩ **2 a :** chemical base ⟨*basify*⟩ **b :** subsilicic and ⟨*basiophitic*⟩

ba·si·al \'bāsēəl\ *adj* [*basi-* + *-al*] **:** of or relating to the basion

¹ba·si·branchial \¦≈≈ *at* BASI- + \ *adj* [*basi-* + *branchial*] **:** of, relating to, or being a median bone or cartilage at the ventral point of a branchial arch

²basibranchial \"\ *n* -S **:** a basibranchial bone or cartilage

ba·si–bregmatic height \¦≈≈+ . . . -\ *var of* BASION-BREGMA HEIGHT

¹ba·sic \'bās¦ik, ¦ēk *sometimes* -āz¦\ *adj* [¹*base* + *-ic*] **1 :** of, relating to, or forming the base or essence **:** FUNDAMENTAL, ESSENTIAL, IRREDUCIBLE ⟨a ~ fact⟩ ⟨a ~ argument⟩ ⟨~ truths⟩ **2 :** constituting or serving as the basis or starting point ⟨a ~ house⟩ **3 a :** of, relating to, or characteristic of a base ⟨~ groups⟩ ⟨~ nitrogen⟩ — compare ALKALINE **b :** having an alkaline reaction ⟨~ compounds⟩ ⟨a ~ catalyst⟩ **c** *of salts* **:** derived by partial neutralization ⟨~ lead carbonate⟩ ⟨~ bismuth chloride⟩ **d :** containing or involving the use of alkaline material ⟨a furnace with a ~ lining⟩ — see BASIC PROCESS **e :** base-forming ⟨lime is a ~ oxide⟩ **4** *of rocks* **:** containing relatively little silica **:** SUBSILICIC — opposed to *acid* **5 :** relating to or made by a basic process ⟨~ steel⟩ ⟨~ rails⟩ **6** *of language* **:** having a vocabulary that consists of a very small number of words but that can be used to convey a wide range of ideas or information ⟨~ French⟩ **7 :** assigned for general duties within a military organization ⟨a ~ private⟩ **8 :** prescribed and nominal — used of standards (as of size) that are the basis for the calculation of allowances and tolerances

²basic \"\ *n* -S **1 :** something that is basic **:** FUNDAMENTAL — usu. used in pl. ⟨the ~*s* of honesty⟩ ⟨the ~*s* of sewing⟩ **2 :** BASIC TRAINING ⟨took his ~ at Keesler Field⟩

basic airman *n* **:** an airman undergoing basic training in the U.S. Air Force

ba·si·cal·ly \|ək(ə)lē, |ēk-, -li\ *adv* **:** FUNDAMENTALLY, ESSENTIALLY

basic anxiety *n, psychol* **:** a feeling of helplessness and personal isolation

basic crew *n* **1 :** the group or number of employees considered necessary for continuous operation (as of a business or factory) **2 :** a limited number or prescribed group of employees subject to guaranteed wage provisions in a labor contract

basic crop *or* **basic commodity** *n* **:** an agricultural product deemed of sufficient economic or political importance to be designated by the U.S. Congress for special production controls or price supports

basic dress *n* **:** a simple classic dress usu. of a solid color and adaptable to many occasions by a change of accessories

basic dye *or* **basic color** *n* **:** any of various chiefly synthetic dyes reacting as bases because of the presence of certain nitrogen-containing groups (as amino groups), producing clear

brilliant colors that are not very fast to light, and being used in the form of water-soluble salts in the dyeing of textiles and as histological stains or as water-insoluble free bases as the coloring ingredient of certain products (as inks, plastics, or shoe polishes) — see DYE table I
basic english *also* **basic** *n* -s *cap B&E* **:** a copyrighted system of simplified English consisting of the 850 words considered most essential and of a short list of grammatical rules and designed to serve both as an auxiliary language and as an introduction to English
basic fuchsin *n* **:** a complex red phenyl methane dye important as a biological stain
ba·si·chromatic \¦≠≠ *at* BASI- +\ *adj* [*basi-* + *chromatic*] **1 :** capable of being stained with basic dyes **2** [*basichromatin* + *-ic*] **:** composed of basichromatin **:** BASICHROMATINIC
ba·si·chromatin \"+\ *n* -s [ISV *basi-* + *chromatin;* orig. formed in G] **:** basophilic chromatin — **ba·si·chromatinic** \"+\ *adj*
basic iron *n* **:** pig iron that contains a high percentage of phosphorus and is used for making steel by a basic process that removes the phosphorus
ba·sic·i·ty \bā'sisəd·ē\ *n* -ES [*basic* + *-ity*] **1 :** the quality, state, or degree of being a base ⟨the ~ of a slag⟩ **2 :** the power of an acid to react with one or more equivalents of a base according to the number of replaceable hydrogen atoms contained in the acid
basic lime *n* **:** a superphosphate to which enough lime has been added to change water-soluble phosphate to the citrate-soluble form
basic-lined \¦≠≠¦≠\ *adj, of a metallurgic furnace* **:** lined with basic material (as dolomite, magnesite, or basic slag)
basic nitrogen *n* **:** nitrogen present in the form of a base; *specif* **:** nitrogen or the proportion of the total nitrogen present in protein or its products of hydrolysis in predominantly basic radicals (as in arginine, histidine, and lysine) as distinguished from nitrogen in radicals whose basicity is modified by adjacent acidic radicals
basic pay *n* **:** pay that includes the base pay and longevity of a member of the armed forces
basic pilot training *n* **:** the second stage of flying training in the U.S. Air Force in which students qualify to solo single-engine jet fighter aircraft or multi-engine aircraft and at the conclusion of which they receive pilot ratings and, if cadets, commissions as second lieutenants
basic process *n* **:** a process (as in steelmaking) carried on in a furnace lined with basic material (as magnesite, dolomite, lime, or iron oxide) and under a slag that is dominantly basic — opposed to *acid process;* compare BESSEMER PROCESS
basic proposition *or* **basic statement** *n* **:** PROTOCOL STATEMENT
ba·si·cranial \¦≠≠ *at* BASI- +\ *adj* [*basi-* + *cranial*] **:** of or relating to the base of the skull
basic rate *n* **:** BASE RATE
basic science *n* **:** any one of the sciences (as anatomy, physiology, bacteriology, pathology, or biochemistry) fundamental to the study of medicine
basic size *n* **:** a sheet size used as a standard in the paper industry (as 17 x 22 in. for ledger, bond, and writing papers)
basic slag *n* **:** a slag low in silica and high in base-forming oxides; *specif* **:** a slag that is used to remove phosphorus and other elements from pig iron in the basic process of steelmaking and that contains sufficient phosphorus after such use to be used as a fertilizer
basic stain *n* **:** a basic dye used as a stain
basic steel *n* **:** steel made by a basic process
basic training *n* **:** the initial period of training of a military recruit
basic wage *or* **basic salary** *n* **1 :** a wage or salary based on the cost of living and used as a standard for calculating rates of pay **2 :** a rate of pay for a standard work period exclusive of such additional payments as bonuses and overtime
basic weight *also* **basic substance weight** *n* **:** BASIS WEIGHT
basic yield *n* **:** the rate of return in interest or dividends upon the actual amount of an investment
basidi- *or* **basidio-** *comb form* [NL, fr. *basidium*] **:** basidium **:** basidial ⟨*basidio*spore⟩ ⟨*Basidio*mycetes⟩
basidia *pl of* BASIDIUM
ba·sid·i·al \bə'sidēəl\ *adj* [NL *basidium* + E *-al*] **:** relating to, characterized by, or consisting of a basidium or basidia ⟨a ~ layer⟩
ba·si·dig·i·ta·le \¦≠≠ *at* BASI- + ,dijə'ta(,)lē, -ā(,)lē,-ä(,)lē\ *n, pl* **basidigita·lia** \-lēə\ [NL, fr. *basi-* + L *digitalis* pertaining to the fingers — more at DIGITAL] **:** a cartilage or bone at the base of a digit **:** METACARPAL, METATARSAL
ba·sid·io·carp \bə'sidēō,kärp, -ēə,-\ *n* -s [*basidi-* + *-carp*] **:** the basidium-bearing fruiting body of a basidiomycete
ba·sid·io·lichen \≠¦≠≠≠+\ *n* [NL *Basidiolichenes*] **:** a lichen of the group Basidiolichenes — compare ASCOLICHEN, DISCOLICHEN
ba·sid·io·lichenes \≠,≠≠≠+\ *n pl, cap* [NL, fr. *basidi-* + *Lichenes*] **:** a group of lichens consisting of the few genera in which the component fungus is a basidiomycete — compare ASCOLICHENES
ba·sid·io·my·cete \≠,≠≠≠+'mī,sēt,mī'sēt\ *n* -s [NL *Basidiomycetes*] **:** a fungus of the Basidiomycetes
ba·sid·io·my·ce·tes \"+mī'sēd·,ēz\ *n pl, cap* [NL, fr. *basidi-* + *-mycetes*] **:** a large class of higher fungi distinguished by having septate hyphae and bearing the spores on a basidium produced either directly from the mycelium or as an outgrowth of a spore — see HETEROBASIDIOMYCETES, HOMOBASIDIOMYCETES; compare PROMYCELIUM — **ba·sid·io·my·ce·tous** \≠¦≠≠≠+mī¦sēd·əs\ *adj*
ba·sid·io·phore \≠'≠≠≠+,fō(ə)r\ *n* -s [*basidi-* + *-phore*] **:** a sporophore bearing basidia
ba·sid·io·spore \≠'≠≠≠,spō(ə)r\ *n* -s [*basidi-* + *spore*] **:** a spore produced by a basidium — **ba·sid·io·spo·rous** \≠,≠≠≠'spōrəs, ≠¦≠≠¦äspərəs\ *adj*
ba·sid·i·um \bə'sidēəm\ *n, pl* **basid·ia** \-ēə\ [NL, fr. *basi-* + *-idium*] **:** a structure on a basidiomycete in which nuclear fusion occurs followed by meiosis and on which usu. four basidiospores are borne — compare HEMIBASIDIUM, PROMYCELIUM
ba·si·facial \¦≠≠ *at* BASI- +\ *adj* [*basi-* + *facial*] **:** of or relating to the lower part of the face
ba·si·fi·ca·tion \,bāsəfə'kāshən\ *n* -s **:** the act or process of basifying
ba·si·fixed \¦≠≠ *at* BASI-+\ *adj* [*basi-* + *fixed*] *bot* **:** attached at or near the base ⟨a ~ anther⟩ — compare VERSATILE 3b
ba·sif·u·gal \(')bā¦sif(y)əgəl\ *adj* [*basi-* + *-fugal*] **:** ACROPETAL
ba·si·fy \'bāsə,fī\ *vt* -ED/-ING/-ES [¹*base* + *-ify*] **:** to convert into a base **:** make alkaline
¹**ba·si·hy·al** \¦≠≠ *at* BASI- + ¦hīəl\ *adj* [ISV *basi-* + *hyoid* + *-al*] **1 :** of, relating to, or being a median element or bone at the ventral point of the hyoid arch that in man forms the body of the hyoid bone **2 :** HYPOHYAL
²**basihyal** \"\ *n* -s **:** a basihyal bone
ba·si·hyoid \¦≠≠ *at* BASI- +\ *adj or n* [*basi-* + *hyoid*] **:** BASIHYAL
¹**bas·il** \'bazəl *also* 'bās- *or* 'bas- *or* 'bāz-\ *n* -s [MF *basile*, fr. LL *basilicum*, fr. Gk *basilikon*, fr. neut. of *basilikos* royal — more at BASILICA] **:** any of several aromatic plants: as **a :** any plant of the genus *Ocimum; esp* **:** SWEET BASIL — see BUSH BASIL **b :** MOUNTAIN MINT 1
²**basil** \"\ *n* -s [modif. of F *basane*, fr. Prov *bazana*, fr. Sp *badana*, fr. Ar *biṭānah*, lit., lining] **:** sheepskin tanned with bark — distinguished from *roan*
³**bas·il** \'bazəl\ *n* -s [by alter.] **:** BEZEL 1
bas·i·lar \'basələ(r)\ *also* **bas·i·lary** \-,lerē\ *adj* [irreg. fr. *basis* + *-ar, -ary*] *biol* **:** of, relating to, or situated at the base
basilar artery *n* **:** an unpaired artery formed by the uniting of the two vertebrals, running forward within the skull just under the pons, dividing into the two posterior cerebrals, and supplying the pons, cerebellum, posterior part of the cerebrum, and the internal ear
basilar groove *n* **:** the depression in the upper surface of the basilar process on which the medulla rests
basilar index *n* **:** the ratio of the distance between the basion and the alveolar point to the total length of the skull multiplied by 100
basilar membrane *n* **:** a supporting membrane; *specif* **:** the membrane that extends from the margin of the bony shelf of the cochlea to the outer wall and that supports the organ of Corti
basilar meningitis *n* **:** a usu. tuberculous inflammation of the meninges at the base of the brain
basilar plate *n* **:** a cartilaginous plate formed of the fused parachordals and anterior notochord that gives rise to the ethmoid and certain other bones of the vertebrate skull
basilar process *n* **:** an anterior median projection of the occipital bone in front of the foramen magnum articulating in front with the body of the sphenoid by the basilar suture
basil balm *n* [¹*basil*] **1 :** a perennial herb (*Monarda clinopodia*) of eastern No. America with aromatic foliage and whitish or yellowish pink flowers **2 :** a fragrant European mint (*Satureia acinos*) naturalized esp. in eastern No. America
ba·si·leus \,bäsə'leüs\ *n, pl* **basi·leis** \-'lās\ [Gk] **:** a ruler of the Eastern Roman Empire
¹**ba·sil·ian** \bə'zilēən, -lyən *also* -'si-\ *adj, usu cap* [St. *Basil* †*ab* A.D.379 Cappadocian church father + E *-ian*] **:** of or relating to St. Basil or to the order following his monastic rule
²**basilian** \"\ *n* -s *usu cap* **:** one who follows the Basilian rule
basilian rule *n, usu cap B* **:** a series of ascetic precepts for cenobites of either sex written by St. Basil and forming the basis of the statutes of practically all monasteries in the Eastern churches
¹**ba·sil·ic** \bə'silik, -lēk *also* -'zi-\ *also* **ba·sil·i·cal** \-lәkəl, -ēk-\ *adj* [L *basilicus*, fr. Gk *basilikos*] **:** of great importance **:** KINGLY, ROYAL
²**basilic** \"\ *n* -s [F *basilique*, fr. L *basilica*] **:** BASILICA
³**basilic** \"\ *also* **basilical** \"\ *adj* **:** BASILICAN
ba·sil·i·ca \bə'silәkə, -lēkə *also* -'zi-\ *n, pl* **basilicas** \-kəz\ *also* **basili·cae** \-,kī, -,sē, -,chā\ [L, fr. Gk *basilikē*, fr. fem. of *basilikos* royal, fr. *basileus* king + *-ikos* -ic] **1 :** an oblong building typically with a broad nave flanked by colonnaded aisles or porticoes and ending in a semicircular apse used in ancient Rome esp. for a court of justice and place of public assembly **2** [LL, fr. L] **:** an early Christian church building consisting of nave and aisles with clerestory, sometimes a narthex, and a large high transept from which an apse projects and in its simplest form having a wooden roof, brick walls, and decorations usu. in mosaic or interior painting **3 :** a Roman Catholic church or cathedral having certain liturgical privileges — used as a canonical title ⟨the church was raised to the rank of ~⟩

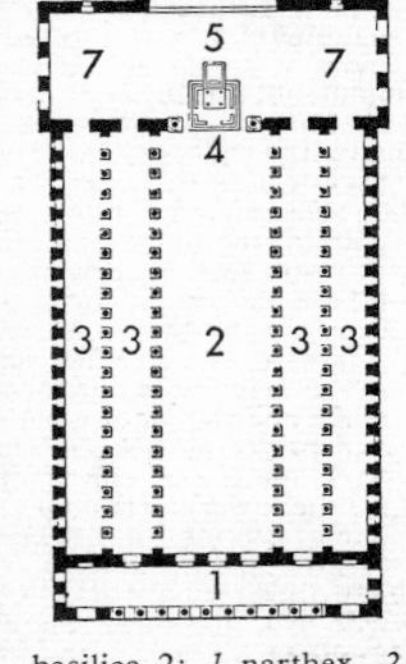

basilica 2: *1* narthex, *2* nave, *3* aisle, *4* altar, *5* bema, *6* apse, *7* transept

ba·sil·i·can \-kən\ *adj* [ML *basilicanus*, fr. LL *basilica* + L *-anus* -an] **:** of, relating to, or resembling a basilica **:** having nave and aisles with clerestory ⟨churches of the ~ form⟩
ba·sil·i·con ointment \-kən-, -lə-,kän-\ *n* [L, fr. Gk *basilikon*, fr. neut. of *basilikos* royal] **1** *obs* **:** an ointment composed of opopanax, galbanum, pitch, resin, and oil **2 :** an ointment composed of rosin, yellow wax, and lard — called also *resin cerate*
basilic vein *n* **:** a vein of the upper arm lying along the inner border of the biceps muscle, draining the whole limb, and opening into the axillary vein
¹**bas·i·lid·i·an** \¦basə¦lidēən, -azə-\ *adj, usu cap* [*Basilides* †*ab* A.D.140 gnostic of Alexandria + E *-ian*] **:** of, relating to, or taught by Basilides, a Gnostic of Alexandria
²**basilidian** \"\ *n* -s *usu cap* **:** a follower of Basilides
bas·i·lis·cus \,basə'liskəs, -azə-\ *n, cap* [NL, fr. L, basilisk] **:** a genus of active carnivorous lizards (family Iguanidae) that have rising above the occiput a membranous pouch which can be inflated with air and along the back a movable crest which can be raised or lowered at will — see BASILISK 3
¹**bas·i·lisk** \'basə,lisk, -azə- *sometimes* -āsə-\ *n* -s [ME, fr. L *basiliscus*, fr. Gk *basiliskos*, lit., little king, dim. of *basileus* king] **1 :** a legendary reptile that is hatched from the egg of a 7-year-old cock and that has a fatal breath and glance — compare COCKATRICE **2 :** a large cannon usu. made of brass and capable of throwing stone shot weighing 200 pounds **3 :** any of several tropical American lizards (genus *Basiliscus*) noted for their activity and ability to run at high speed upon their hind legs

basilisk 3

²**basilisk** \"\ *adj* **:** like a basilisk **:** SPELLBINDING, FATAL ⟨the eyes fell full upon me with all their blaze of ~ horror —Bram Stoker⟩
basil mint *n* [¹*basil*] **:** a mountain mint (*Pycnanthemum virginianum*) of eastern No. America with narrow leaves and inconspicuous greenish white flowers
basil oil *n* [¹*basil*] **:** a yellowish essential oil obtained from the flowering tops of sweet basil and used as a flavoring material and in perfumery — called also *sweet basil oil*
bas·i·lo·sau·rus \,basəlō'sȯrəs\ *n, cap* [NL, fr. Gk *basileus* king + NL *-o-* + *-saurus*] **:** a genus (the type of the family Basilosauridae) of large slender-bodied Eocene whales that are found most abundantly in Alabamian and Floridian rocks and that have serrated posterior teeth with two roots — see ZEUGLODONTIA
basils *pl of* BASIL
basil thyme *n* [¹*basil*] **:** any of several fragrant herbs or shrubs: as **a :** BASIL BALM 2 **b :** FIELD BALM 1
basilweed \'≠≠,≠\ *n* [¹*basil*] **:** WILD BASIL
¹**ba·sin** \'bās°n\ *n* -s [ME *basin*, fr. OF *bacin*, fr. LL *bacchinon*, fr. (assumed) VL *bacca* water vessel, perh. of non-IE origin; akin to the source of L *baca* berry — more at BAY] **1 a :** an open usu. circular vessel or dish with sloping or curving sides and wider than its depth used typically for holding water for washing **b :** a container of similar shape: as (1) **:** the scalepan of a balance (2) **:** a tank or reservoir used for the treatment of liquids **c :** the quantity contained in a basin **2 a** (1) **:** a dock built in a tidal river or harbor and used esp. for ships discharging or loading cargo, floodgates serving to keep the water level constant ⟨constructing ships in ~s resembling drydocks from which they float out on completion —*Time*⟩ (2) **:** a part of a river or canal widened and provided with wharves **b** (1) **:** a water area enclosed or partly enclosed by land and suitable for anchorage of ships **:** a landlocked harbor **:** a little bay ⟨a ~ . . . provides mooring space for eighty yachts —*Amer. Guide Series: Md.*⟩ (2) **:** a water area artificially enclosed or partly enclosed (as by jetties) that is designed to shelter small craft ⟨rates for mooring boats at boat ~s —*N. Y. Herald Tribune*⟩ **3 a** (1) **:** a large or small depression in the surface of the land, the lowest part often being occupied by a lake or pond ⟨the ~ of Lake Michigan⟩ (2) **:** a similar depression in the ocean floor ⟨some 2000 fathoms down, but it still separates broad eastern and western ~s —R.E.Coker⟩ **b :** an area that does not drain to the ocean **c :** an area largely enclosed by higher lands but having an outlet and being drained ⟨the Big Horn ~⟩ **d :** the entire tract of country drained by a river and its tributaries — called also *river basin* ⟨appropriations for flood control in the Missouri ~ —*New Republic*⟩ **e :** a great depression in the surface of the lithosphere occupied by an ocean ⟨the ~ now filled by the Pacific ocean —Waldemar Kaempffert⟩ — called also *ocean basin* **4 a :** a broad area of the earth beneath which the strata dip usu. from the sides toward the center ⟨the Richmond coal ~⟩ — called also *structural basin, synclinal basin* **b :** a depression of the earth in which sedimentary materials accumulate or have accumulated usu. characterized by continuous deposition over a long period of time ⟨a salt ~⟩ **c :** rocks of such composition and having such structural and topographic relations as to facilitate the presence of artesian water ⟨an artesian ~⟩ **5 :** the depression at the apex of an apple or similar fruit **6 a :** an area enclosed so as to be flooded for subsequent cultivation ⟨a ~ for irrigation⟩ **b :** a hollow or enclosure made about the base of a tree to receive water for moistening the roots **c :** a small depression or pocket made (as with a basin lister) in a field to check water runoff

basin 1a

²**basin** \"\ *vb* **basined; basined; basining** \-s(°)niŋ\ **basins** *vt* **:** to bend down (a part of the earth's crust) in the form of a basin ⟨the rocky surface of Greenland is actually ~*ed* as if by the weight of the existing icecap —R.A.Daly⟩ **~** *vi* **:** to form a basin by erosion
ba·sin·al \-s°n°l,-snəl\ *adj* [*basin* + *-al*] **:** of or relating to a basin ⟨thick ~ deposits⟩ ⟨~ facies⟩ — **ba·sin·al·ly** \-°lē,-əlē\ *adv*
ba·sined \'bās°nd\ *adj* [¹*basin* + *-ed*] **:** enclosed in a basin
bas·i·net *or* **bas·ci·net** *also* **bas·si·net** \¦basə¦net\ *n* -s [ME *bacinet*, fr. OF, dim. of *bacin* basin — more at BASIN] **:** a light often pointed steel helmet orig. open and worn under the battle helmet but subsequently made with a visor
basing *pres part of* BASE
basing point *n* [fr. pres. part. of ²*base*] **:** a location agreed upon by sellers from which they compute transportation charges so that all customers in an area pay uniform delivery charges regardless of the exact distance to the sellers
basing point system *n* **:** a pricing system using one or more basing points
basin irrigation *n* **:** irrigation of land by surrounding it with embankments to form a basin and flooding it with water
basin range *n* [fr. the Great *Basin*, region of the western U.S.] **:** a mountain range that owes its present elevation essentially to faulting and tilting **:** a tilted fault block
basin stand *n* **:** a light table usu. made to fit into a corner to hold a basin **:** WASHSTAND
¹**ba·si·occipital** \¦≠≠ *at* BASI- +\ *adj* [*basi-* + *occipital*] **:** relating to or being a bone in the base of the cranium immediately in front of the foramen magnum, represented in man by the basilar process of the occipital
²**basioccipital** \"\ *n* -s **:** the basioccipital bone
ba·si·on \'bāsē,än *also* -zē-\ *n* -s [NL, irreg. fr. L *basis* base — more at BASE] **:** the midpoint of the anterior margin of the foramen magnum
basion-bregma height \'≠≠,≠'≠≠-\ *or* **basi-bregmatic height** \¦≠≠ *at* BASI- + . . . -\ *n* **:** the distance between basion and bregma
basion-prosthion line *n* **:** a line from the basion to the prosthion
ba·si·ophthalmite \¦≠≠ *at* BASI- +\ *n* -s [*basi-* + *ophthalmite*] **:** the lowest joint of the eyestalk of certain crustaceans — **ba·si·oph·thal·mous** \"+¦äf¦thalməs\ *adj*
ba·sip·e·tal \(')bā¦sipəd·°l\ *adj* [ISV *basi-* + *-petal*] **:** from the apex toward the base or from above downward ⟨~ differentiation of an inflorescence or leaf primordium⟩ ⟨~ movement of dissolved materials in a plant body⟩ — compare ACROPETAL — **basipetally** *adv*
ba·sip·o·dite \≠'≠≠,dīt\ *n* -s [ISV *basi-* + *-podite*] **1 :** the proximal joint of the arthropod limb **2 :** the second joint, next succeeding the coxopodite, of certain limbs of crustaceans (as the ambulatory limbs of a decapod). — **ba·sip·o·dit·ic** \≠¦≠≠did·ik\ *adj*
ba·sip·ter·yg·i·al \(¦)bā,siptə¦rij(ē)əl\ *adj* [NL *basipterygium* + E *-al*] **:** of, relating to, or being a basypterygium
ba·sip·ter·yg·i·um \-jēəm\ *n, pl* **basipteryg·ia** \-jēə\ [NL, fr. *basi-* + Gk *pterygion* fin, lit., small wing — more at PTERYGIUM] **:** a basal bone or cartilage forming a support of one of the paired fins of a fish: **a :** a large cartilage supporting the radialia in ganoids and selachians **b :** a large bone supporting the rays of a pelvic fin in teleosts **c :** the posterior member of a group of three such supporting elements in certain fishes — compare MESOPTERYGIUM, METAPTERYGIUM, PROPTERYGIUM
ba·si·rhinal \¦≠≠ *at* BASI- +\ *or* **ba·sir·rhi·nal** \"\ *adj* [ISV *basi-* + *rhinal*] **:** situated at the base of the rhinencephalon
ba·si·rostral \¦≠≠ *at* BASI- +\ *adj* [ISV *basi-* + *rostral*] **:** related to or situated at the base of the bill of a bird
¹**ba·sis** \'bāsəs\ *n, pl* **ba·ses** \-ā,sēz\ [L — more at BASE] **1 a :** the bottom of anything considered as a foundation for the parts above **:** BASE, FOOT **b** *obs* **:** the pedestal of a column, pillar, or statue ⟨if no ~ bear my rising name —Alexander Pope⟩ **c :** any of certain anatomical structures that function as bases: as (1) **:** the membranous or calcareous base by which a barnacle is attached to the substrate (2) **:** BASIPODITE (3) **:** the articulated proximal part of the capitulum of a tick — called also *basis capituli* **2 :** the principal component of anything **:** fundamental ingredient **:** BASE ⟨a combination of fruit or fruit juices and sugar is the fundamental ~ of jelly⟩ **3 :** something that supports or sustains anything immaterial **:** ESSENCE ⟨his argument rested on a ~ of conjecture⟩ **4 a :** something on which anything is constructed or established ⟨Indian trails . . . were the ~ for many of their roads —*Amer. Guide Series: N.C.*⟩ **:** the basic principle **:** GROUNDWORK ⟨the frustrating task of putting international affairs on a permanent ~ of law and order —A.E.Stevenson †1965⟩ **b :** FOOTING 6 ⟨a club where everyone was on a first-name ~ —J.P.Marquand⟩ **5 a :** a rhythmic unit constituted by a given proportion of arsis to thesis without reference to the order or placement of long and short elements ⟨trochaic and iambic feet represent the same ~⟩ **b :** a free first foot in some ancient verse that admits more variation from the norm of the line than appears in subsequent feet **6 :** a glassy or felsitic noncrystalline granular material that is a last product of solidification of a volcanic rock and that forms a cement for earlier minerals **7 a :** the price difference between a specified grade of a commodity and a designated futures delivery **b :** the actual yield on an investment in bonds **c :** the original cost of property used in computing capital gains or losses for income tax purposes
²**basis** \'bä,sēz\ *pl of* BASI
ba·si·scop·ic \¦≠≠ *at* BASI- +\ *adj* [*basi-* + *-scopic*] *bot* **:** facing or on the side toward the base ⟨the sori of most ferns are ~⟩ — compare ACROSCOPIC
¹**ba·si·sphenoid** \¦≠≠ *at* BASI- +\ *also* **ba·si·sphenoidal** \"+\ *adj* [ISV *basi-* + *sphenoid, sphenoidal*] **:** relating to or being the part of the base of the cranium that lies between the basioccipital and the presphenoid and that usu. ossifies separately and becomes a part of the sphenoid only in the adult
²**basisphenoid** \"\ *n* **:** the basisphenoid bone
basis point *n* **:** one hundredth of one percent in the yield of an investment
basis rate *n* **:** the amount of premium per unit of insurance assumed and used as a starting point for computing the specific rates to be charged to policyholders
ba·si·sternum \¦≠≠ *at* BASI- +\ *n* [NL, fr. *basi-* + *sternum*] **:** the anterior of the two sternal skeletal plates of insects
ba·si·style \"+\ *n* [*basi-* + *style*] **:** either of a pair of more or less flexible processes on the hypopygium of certain male two-winged flies
basis weight *n* **1 :** the weight in pounds of a 500-sheet ream of paper cut to a basic size — called also *basic weight, substance, substance number* **2 :** the weight of a sheet of paper expressed in terms of the weight of a ream of that paper
ba·si·tarsus \"+\ *n* [NL, fr. *basi-* + *tarsus*] **:** the basal segment of an arthropod tarsus being often conspicuously enlarged or differentiated from other segments
¹**ba·si·temporal** \"+\ *adj* [ISV *basi-* + *temporal*] **:** of, relating to, or being one of a pair of membrane bones of the skull of birds underlying and uniting with the part of the true cranium formed by the basisphenoid and basioccipital bones
²**basitemporal** \"\ *n* **:** a basitemporal bone
ba·si·vertebral \¦≠≠ *at* BASI- +\ *adj* [ISV *basi-* + *vertebral*] **:** of or relating to the centrum of a vertebra
bask \'bask, -aa(ə)-,-ai-,-á-\ *vb* -ED/-ING/-S [ME *basken*, fr. ON *bathask*, refl. of *batha* to bathe — more at BATHE] *vi* **1 :** to lie in or expose oneself to a pleasant warmth or atmosphere **:** LUXURIATE ⟨pretend that I'm still ~*ing* on the beach —Hamilton Basso⟩ ⟨the house ~*ed* in the moonlight —Agatha Christie⟩ ⟨spent 10 days in the capital, ~*ing* in civilization's comfort—*Nat'l Geographic*⟩ **2 :** to take pleasure or derive en-

joyment — usu. used with *in* ⟨he ~*ed* in the smiles of the girls and was patted and complimented by the old men —Stephen Crane⟩ ~ *vt, obs* **:** to warm by continued exposure to heat ⟨~*s* at the fire his hairy strength —John Milton⟩

¹**bas·ket** \'baskət, -aas-,-ais-,-ȧs-, *usu* -d.+V\ *n* -s [ME, prob. fr. (assumed) ONF *baskot* (akin to F dial. *bâchot* wicker basket), fr. (assumed) ONF *baskou, baskoue* (akin to OF *baschoue* wooden or wicker vessel), fr. L *bascauda* dishpan, of Celt origin; akin to MIr *basc* necklace — more at FASCIA] **1 a :** a receptacle made of interwoven osiers, cane, rushes, splints, or other flexible material **b :** any of various lightweight usu. wood containers in which berries, fruits, or vegetables are packed, shipped, or sold **c :** the quantity contained in a basket ⟨fishing upstream, I have sometimes in my youth had good ~*s* with the red worm —John Buchan⟩ **2** *archaic* **:** CHARITY **3 :** anything that resembles a basket esp. in shape or use: as **a** *Brit* **:** the two back seats facing one another on the outside of a stagecoach **b :** a shallow receptacle sometimes with a bail handle used to serve cake, bread, or rolls **c :** the perforated container for the ground coffee through which heated water seeps in a coffee maker **d :** a metal liner of coarse mesh made to fit into a deep fat fryer and used to hold the food for frying and to lift it from the fryer **e :** the typebars of a typewriter taken as a unit **f :** the perforated metal container in a centrifugal for holding material being processed **4 :** the box, cage, or other vessel suspended from a balloon to carry passengers, ballast, and equipment **5 a :** a net of white cord that is 15 to 18 inches long, open at the bottom, and suspended from a metal ring 18 inches in diameter and that constitutes the goal in basketball **b :** the score made by putting the ball through the basket in basketball; *esp* **:** FIELD GOAL ⟨an occasional game is won with more points scored on fouls than ~*s* —Jimmy Jemail⟩ **6 :** a square-dance pattern formed by the raised interlocking arms of concentric circles of men and women

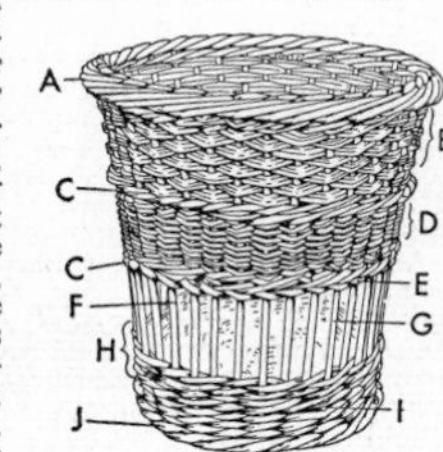

a form of basket: *A* border, *B* slew, *C* wale, *D* rand, *E* fitch, *F* stake, *G* by-stake, *H* upset, *I* end of by-stake, *J* foot

²**basket** \"\ *vt* -ED/-ING/-S **:** to put or throw into a basket ⟨the pigeons were ~*ed* and sent to several race points⟩

³**basket** \"\ *adj* **1 :** made like a basket **:** made of basketwork ⟨a ~ carriage⟩ **2 :** used for baskets or basketmaking ⟨~ osiers⟩ **3 :** with provisions brought in a basket ⟨an old-fashioned ~ picnic⟩

basket ash *n* **:** ¹BLACK ASH 1

basketball \'==,=\ *n, often attrib* **1 :** a game played with a ball between 2 teams of 5 players each, 6 in a women's game, on a rectangular court usu. indoors, each team attempting to throw the ball through its own basket and to prevent the other team from scoring, the winner being the team that scores the most points — see FIELD GOAL, FOUL **2 :** a spherical ball made of an airtight rubber case covered with leather officially from 29 to 30 inches in circumference and from 20 to 22 ounces in weight

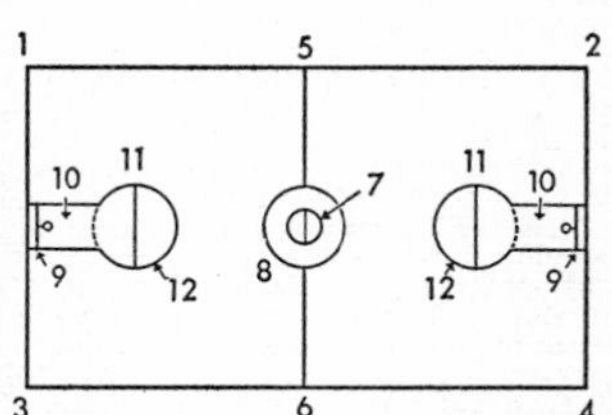

basketball court: *1 2, 3 4* sidelines, *1 3, 2 4* end lines, *5 6* division line, *7* center circle, *8* restraining circle, *9* backboard and basket, *10* free throw lane, *11* free throw line, *12* free throw circle

basket capital *n* **:** a capital of the Byzantine style with interlaced bands like those of a basket

basket case *n* **:** one who has all four limbs amputated ⟨rumors have been heard in this country about the large number of *basket cases* among our war casualties —Bruce Bliven b.1889⟩

basket cell *n* **:** any of the cells in the molecular layer of the cerebellum whose axis-cylinder processes pass inward and end in a basketlike network around the cells of Purkinje

basket chair *n* **:** a deep low wicker armchair with back and arms in one and rounded at the top

basket clam *n* **:** BASKET SHELL 1

basket cloth *n* **1 :** cloth with a basket weave **2 :** book cloth with an embossed wicker pattern

basket dance *n* **:** a women's vegetation dance of certain peoples of medieval Europe and certain Indians of the southwestern U.S., a basket serving as the focal prop

bas·ke·teer \,=ə'ti(ə)r\ *n* -s [*basketball* + *-eer*] **:** a basketball player

basket fern *n* **1 :** MALE FERN **2 :** a tropical American sword fern (*Nephrolepis pectinata*) often cultivated for its finely divided grayish green foliage

basket–fired \'==,=\ *adj, of Japanese longleaf tea* **:** fired in baskets rather than metal pans or other containers

basket flower *n* **1 :** an annual plant (*Centaurea americana*) of the southwestern U.S. often cultivated for its purple-rayed flower heads with involucres like baskets **2 :** a spider lily (*Hymenocallis calathina*) having umbels of two to four flowers, each with linear perianth segments

bas·ket·ful \'==,fu̇l\ *n, pl* **basketfuls** *also* **basketsful** \-t,fu̇lz, -t,sfu̇l\ **1 :** as much or as many as a basket will hold ⟨a ~ of apples⟩ **2 :** a considerable quantity ⟨a whole ~ of allegories —Thomas Wood †1950⟩ ⟨a ~ of ironic commentary on contemporary truths —Henry Hewes⟩

basket grass *n* **:** TURKEY BEARD

basket–handle arch *n* **:** a low-crowned elliptical arch drawn from three or more centers — see ARCH illustration

basket hilt *n* **:** a hilt with a guard wrought like basketwork to protect the hand

basket–hilted \,==¦==\ *adj* **:** having a basket hilt

basketing *pres part of* BASKET

basket maker *n, usu cap B&M* **1 :** any of three stages of an ancient culture of the plateau area of southwestern U.S. that preceded and formed one cultural development with the Pueblo, was characterized by excellent basketry and use of the spear thrower, and was marked by development from an initial nomadic preagricultural state through a cave-dwelling phase with limited agriculture to a village economy with semisubterranean houses, agriculture, the beginnings of pottery, and use of bow and arrow **2 :** a member of the people who produced the Basket Maker culture

basketmaking \'==,==\ *n* **:** the making of baskets

basket mast *n* **:** an obsolete type of mast formerly used on some battleships and composed of a number of straight elements of steel tubing arranged as a hyperboloid of revolution — called also *cage mast*

basket meeting *n* **:** a usu. all-day meeting esp. for religious purposes to which food is brought in baskets

basket oak *n* **:** a rather large oak (*Quercus prinus*) of the southeastern and central U.S. having a durable wood that is used as timber and often split and woven into baskets — called also *cow oak, swamp chestnut oak*

basket–of–gold \,===¦=\ *n* **:** a European perennial herb (*Alyssum saxatile*) widely cultivated esp. in rock gardens and having grayish foliage and yellow flowers in compact clusters that elongate in fruit — called also *golden tuft*

basket osier *n* **:** either of two European osier willows (*Salix purpurea* and *S. viminalis*)

basket phaeton *n* **:** a phaeton carriage with a body of wickerwork

basket plant *n* **:** a trailing plant (as Kenilworth ivy) that can be grown in a hanging basket

basket rummy *n* **:** CANASTA 1

bas·ket·ry \-kətrē, -ri\ *n* -ES **1 :** the art or craft of assembling slender elongated elements (as reeds, osiers, wooden splints, or metal ribbons) into baskets or other objects (as chair seats, mats, or boats) usu. by weaving, braiding, or sewing **2 :** objects or any fabrication produced by basketry ⟨delicate ~ panels⟩

baskets *pl of* BASKET, *pres 3d sing of* BASKET

basket salt *n* **:** salt that has drained from baskets after being drawn from the evaporating pans

basket shell *n* **1 :** a bivalve mollusk of a family (Corbulidae) having unequal valves, the right usu. larger, and a single large hinge tooth on each valve — called also *basket clam* **2** *also* **basket whelk :** any of several marine snails (family Nassariidae) living on muddy bottoms and feeding on other mollusks

basket sponge *n* **:** GLASS SPONGE; *specif* **:** VENUS'S-FLOWER-BASKET

basket star *also* **basket fish** *n* **:** any of numerous ophiuroids (order Euryalida) having slender complexly branched interlacing arms that serve to entrap the fish on which they feed — called also *sea spider*

basket weave *n* **1 :** a textile weave with two or more adjacent warp and weft threads worked as one in plain-weave manner resembling the checkered pattern of a plaited basket **2** *radio* **:** a type of coil winding in which the windings of successive layers are woven in and out of one another

basket willow *n* **:** OSIER 1

basketwork \'==,=\ *n* **:** BASKETRY 2

basking *pres part of* BASK

basking shark *n* **1 :** one of the largest of sharks (*Cetorhinus maximus*) attaining a length of 40 feet, commonly lying at the surface of the water basking in the sun and feeding on plankton which it strains from the water by means of gill rakers, the water straining out through very long gill slits and the minute teeth being nearly functionless, and being of commercial interest because of its immense liver which yields large quantities of oil **2 :** WHALE SHARK

basks *pres 3d sing of* BASK

bas mitzvah *var of* BATH MITZVAH

baso– — see BASI-

ba·so·cellular \,bā̇sō¦===\ *adj* [*baso-* + *cellular*] **:** of, relating to, or derived from basal cells

ba·so·cyte \'==,sīt\ *n* -s [*baso-* + *-cyte*] **:** BASOPHIL

¹**bas·oid** \'bā,sȯid\ *adj* [¹*base* + *-oid*] *of certain soil substances* **:** potentially basic — compare ACIDOID

²**basoid** \"\ *n* -s **:** a basoid substance

ba·som·ma·toph·o·ra \bə,sämə'täf(ə)rə\ *n pl, cap* [NL, fr. *baso-* + ISV *ommatophore*] **:** a suborder of Pulmonata comprising snails that have the eyes at the base of the nonretractile tentacles and including many common pond snails — **ba·som·ma·toph·o·rous** \=¦==¦täf(ə)rəs\ *adj*

bason \'bās°n\ *var of* BASIN — now used chiefly in the Church of England

ba·so·nym \'bāsə,nim, -sō-\ *n* -s [*baso-* + *-nym*] **:** the earliest validly published name of a taxon, being in the case of a binomial or trinomial the source of the valid specific or subspecific epithet when the taxon is transferred to a new combination and in technical usage always accompanied by the name of the original author ⟨*Crataegus spicata* Lamarck is the ~ of *Amelanchier spicata*⟩

ba·so·phil \'==,fil\ *or* **ba·so·phile** \-,fīl\ *n* -s **:** a basophilic substance or structure: as **a :** a white blood cell with basophilic cytoplasmic granules **b :** a secretory cell of the anterior lobe of the pituitary with similar granules

basophile \"\ *also* **ba·soph·i·lous** \(')bā¦säfələs\ *adj* [*baso-* + *-phile, -philous*] **:** attracted to or growing best in alkaline soils ⟨~ plants⟩

ba·so·phil·ia \,bāsō'filēə\ *n* -s [NL, fr. *baso-* + *-philia*] **1 :** tendency to stain with basic dyes ⟨cytoplasmic ~⟩ **2 :** an abnormality of which increased basophilia of some tissue element is a feature: as **a :** leukocytosis in which the number of circulating basophils is elevated **b :** the presence of basophilic granules in red blood cells (as in lead poisoning) — called also *punctate basophilia*

ba·so·phil·ic \,==¦filik\ *also* **ba·soph·i·lous** \(')bā¦säfələs\ *or* **ba·so·phile** \'bāsō,fīl\ *or* **ba·so·phil** \-,fil\ *adj* [ISV *baso-* + *-philic, -philous, -phile, -phil*] *biol* **:** staining readily with basic stains

ba·soph·i·ly \bā'säfəlē\ *n* -ES **:** the condition of being basophilic

¹**basque** \'bask, -aa(ə)-,-ai- *also* -ȧ-\ *n* -s [F, fr. L *Vasco*] **1** *cap* **:** one of a people inhabiting from pre-Roman times the region of the western Pyrenees on the Bay of Biscay in Spain and France, being of obscure origin but believed by some authorities to represent a pre-Aryan people, and constituting a distinct people become distinctive through long isolation **2** *cap* **:** the language of the Basques, of unknown relationship though attempts have been made to connect it with the Caucasic languages, the Berber languages, Etruscan, or Iberian — called also *Euskarian* **3** [F, fr. MF, alter. (influenced by *Basque*, the people) of *baste*, fr. OProv *basta* seam, tuck] **a** (1) **:** a short skirtlike continuation of a man's doublet (2) **:** a similar continuation of a woman's bodice **b :** any of various tight-fitting bodices for women copied from the Basque costume

²**basque** \"\ *adj, usu cap* [F, fr. *basque*, n.] **1 a :** of, relating to, or characteristic of the Basque provinces **b :** of, relating to, or characteristic of the Basque people **2 :** of, relating to, or characteristic of the Basque language

basque shirt *n* **:** a pullover sweaterlike shirt often of knitted cotton and usu. having a round ribbed neck and a design of horizontal stripes

bas·quine \(')ba¦skēn\ *n* -s [F, fr. MF, fr. OSp *basquiña*, fr. OPg *vasquinha*, fr. *vasco* Basque, fr. L *Vasco*] **1 :** a tightly fitting corsetlike underbodice of heavy material worn esp. in the 16th century **2 :** a rich outer petticoat worn by Basque and Spanish women

bas·ra *or* **bas·rah** \'bä|srə, 'bə|, 'ba|, |zrə\ *adj, usu cap* [fr. *Basra*, Iraq] **:** of or from Basra, Iraq **:** of the kind or style prevalent in Basra

bas–relief \,bä, ¦bä+=¦= *sometimes* ¦bas *or* ¦baas *or* ¦bais+\ *n* -s [F (trans. of It *bassorilievo*), fr. *bas* low + *relief* raised work — more at BASE, RELIEF] **1 :** sculptural relief in which the projection from the surrounding surface is slight and no part of the modeled form is undercut ⟨heraldic emblems carved in *bas-relief*⟩ — compare HIGH RELIEF **2 :** sculpture or a sculptural form executed in bas-relief ⟨an early Wedgwood *bas-relief*⟩ **3 :** a photographic print having the appearance of sculpture made from a positive transparency and its negative in contact but with the images not quite coinciding

¹**bass** \'bas, -aa(ə)-,-ai- *sometimes in NE* -ȧ-\ *n, pl* **bass** *or* **basses** [ME *bace, base*, alter. of OE *bærs*; akin to MHG *bars* perch, OE *byrst* bristle — more at BRISTLE] **1 a :** a European perch (*Perca fluviatilis*) **b :** any of numerous edible spiny-finned freshwater and marine fishes esp. of the families Centrarchidae and Serranidae — see SEA BASS, BLACK BASS, CHANNEL BASS, KELP BASS, SAND BASS, STRIPED BASS, WHITE BASS **2 :** the flesh of any bass used as food

²**bass** \'bās\ *n* -ES [alter. (influenced by F *basse* & It *basso*) of ⁵*base*] **1 :** a deep or grave tone **:** low-pitched sound **2 a** (1) **:** the lowest part in polyphonic or harmonic music; *specif* **:** the lowest tone of a chord — distinguished from *root* (2) **:** the lower half of the whole vocal or instrumental tonal range — contrasted with *treble* **b** (1) **:** the lowest male singing voice (2) **:** a person having such a voice **c :** the lowest member in range of a family of instruments: as (1) **:** CONTRABASS (2) **:** a bass tuba

³**bass** \'bās\ *adj* [alter. (influenced by F *basse* & It *basso*) of ⁴*base*] **:** deep or grave in tone **:** of low pitch ⟨a ~ voice⟩ ⟨a ~ lute⟩

⁴**bass** \'bas, -aa(ə)-,-ai- *sometimes* -ȧ-\ *n* -ES [alter. of *bast*] **1 a :** the usu. coarse tough fiber found on the sheathing leaf bases or leafstalks of many palms **b :** any of various articles (as a mat or basket) made of bast or similar material **2 :** BASSWOOD 1

¹**bas·sa** \'bäsə\ *n, pl* **bassa** *or* **bassas** *usu cap* **1 a :** a seafaring people of Liberia **b :** a member of such people **2 :** a Kwa language of the Bassa people

²**bassa** \"\ *adj* [It, fem. of *basso* low — more at BASSO] **:** OTTAVA BASSA

bas·sa·lia \bə'sālēə\ *n, usu cap* [NL, fr. LL *bassus* thick, short, low + NL *-alia* — more at BASE] **:** ABYSSAL ZONE

bas·sa·li·an \bə'sālēən\ *adj, usu cap B* [NL *bassalia* + E *-an*] **:** ABYSSAL

bas·sa·nel·lo \,basə'ne(,)lō, ,bäs-\ *n, pl* **bassanel·li** \-(,)lē\ [It, from Giovanni *Bassani* †1716 Ital. composer] **:** a 17th century double-reed woodwind instrument

bas·sa·nite \bə'sä,nīt\ *n* -s [It, fr. Francesco *Bassani*, 20th cent. Ital. geologist + It *-ite*] **:** a mineral $CaSO_4 \cdot \frac{1}{2}H_2O$ consisting of calcium sulfate found in white opaque crystals in blocks ejected from Vesuvius in 1906 (sp. gr. 2.69-2.76) — compare PLASTER OF PARIS

bas·sa·ris·cus \,basə'riskəs\ *n, cap* [NL, fr. Gk *bassaris* fox + NL *-iscus* (dim. suffix)] **:** a genus of carnivorous mammals that comprises the cacomistles of western No. America, is usu. included with the raccoons in the family Procyonidae, but is sometimes made type of a separate family

bas·sa·risk \'basə,risk\ *n* -s [modif. of NL *Bassariscus*] **1 :** CACOMISTLE **2 :** the fur or pelt of the cacomistle

bass–bar \'bās,=\ *n* [²*bass*] **:** an oblong piece of wood attached lengthwise to the top or belly within the body of instruments of the violin class for withstanding the pressure at the bridge

bass broom *n* [⁴*bass*] **:** a broom made from piassava fiber

bass bug *n* [¹*bass*] **:** an artificial floating lure used usu. with a fly rod in fishing for bass

bass clarinet *n* [³*bass*] **:** a large clarinet that is lower in pitch by an octave than the ordinary B-flat clarinet

bass clef *n* [³*bass*] **1 :** F CLEF **2 :** the bass staff

bass drum *n* [³*bass*] **:** a large drum having a cylindrical body with two heads and giving a booming sound of low indefinite pitch — see DRUM illustration

basse–cour \(')bä¦skü(ə)r\ *n, pl* **basse–cours** \-r(z)\ [F, fr. MF *basse-court* — more at BASE-COURT] **:** BASE-COURT 1

basse danse \(')bäs¦dä^ns\ *n, pl* **basses danses** \-ä^ns(əz)\ [F *basse-danse, danse basse*, lit., low dance] **:** a stately 15th century court dance that was ancestor to the minuet

basse–lisse \(')bä¦slēs\ *adj* [F, fr. *basse* low (fem. of *bas*) + *lisse* warp — more at BASE, LISSE] **:** LOW-WARP

basses *pl of* BASS

¹**bas·set** \'basət, *usu* -əd.+V\ *or* **basset hound** *n* [F *basset*, fr. MF, fr. *basset*, adj., short, low, fr. *bas* low — more at BASE] **1** *often cap B* **:** a long-established French breed of short-legged slow-moving hunting dogs that have very long ears, crooked front legs, and a typical hound coat, are used chiefly on hares and rabbits, and are noted for the depth and quality of their voice when trailing **2** -s **:** any dog of the basset breed

bass clarinet

²**basset** \"\ *n* -s [F *bassette*, fr. It *bassetta*, fr. *basso* low — more at BASSO] **:** a game at cards that resembles faro and was popular in the 18th century

³**basset** \"\ *n* -s [perh. fr. obs. F, low stool, fr. *basset*, adj., short, low] **:** the outcropping edge of a geological stratum

⁴**basset** \"\ *vi* -ED/-ING/-S **:** to appear at the surface **:** crop out ⟨a seam of coal ~*s*⟩

basse–taille \(')bä¦stī\ *adj* [F, lit., a low cutting, fr. *basse* (fem. of *bas* low) + *taille* act of cutting — more at BASE, TAIL (tax)] **:** having a background carved in low relief — used of an enameling technique in which translucent enamels are applied over such a background or of objects enameled by this method ⟨a *baisse-taille* silver brooch⟩

bas·set horn \'basət-\ *n* [prob. fr. G *bassetthorn*, fr. It *bassetto* (dim. of *basso* bass) + G *horn* (fr. OHG) — more at BASSO, HORN] **:** a tenor clarinet in F pitched lower than the normal clarinet

bas·set·ite \'basəd.,īt\ *n* -s [*Basset* mines, Redruth, Cornwall, England + E *-ite*] **:** a mineral that consists of a yellow phosphate of calcium and uranium and that is close to autunite in composition

basset oboe *n* [It *bassetto*] **:** HECKELPHONE

bass fiber *n* [⁴*bass*] **:** any of several strong bast fibers: as **a :** fiber from a West African palm (*Raphia vinifera*) **b :** piassava fiber

bass fiddle *n* [³*bass*] **:** the contrabass esp. as used in jazz orchestras

bass flute *n* [³*bass*] **1 :** ALTO FLUTE **2 :** an organ stop in the pedal division

bass fly *n* [¹*bass*] **:** any of certain large artificial flies used in fishing for bass

bass horn *n* [³*bass*] **1 :** a former wind instrument shaped like the bassoon but having a cup-shaped mouthpiece and a metal bell — compare SERPENT 7a **2 :** TUBA

bassi *pl of* BASSO

¹**bas·sia** \'basēə\ *n, cap* [NL, fr. Ferdinando *Bassi* †1774 Ital. naturalist + NL *-ia*] **:** a small genus of European herbs (family Chenopodiaceae) that have corolla lobes without appendages, sepals usu. in two pairs, and seeds without endosperm and that are naturalized locally in eastern No. America

²**bassia** \"\ [NL, fr. F *Bassi* + NL *-ia*] *syn of* MADHUCA

bas·sie \'basi, 'bä-\ *n* -s [perh. irreg. fr. ¹*basin* + *-ie*] *Scot* **:** a wooden bowl

¹**bas·sine** \(')ba¦sēn\ *n* -s [⁴*bass* + *-ine*] **:** the coarse leaf fiber of the palmyra palm used esp. in the manufacture of brushes and brooms

²**bassine** *var of* BASCINE

¹**bassinet** *var of* BASINET

²**bas·si·net** *also* **bas·si·nette** \,basə,net, *usu* -ed.+V\ *n* -s [prob. modif. (influenced by ¹*bassinet*) of F *barcelonnette*, dim. of *berceau* cradle] **1 :** an infant's bed made of wickerwork, plastic, or other material and often having a hood over one end **2 :** CRIB **3 :** an infant's bed in a hospital usu. as representative of the equipment and services required to care for one infant in an obstetrical service — compare BED 1j **4 :** a perambulator that resembles a bassinet

bassinet 1

bass·ing \'basiŋ, 'baas-,'bais-, -sēŋ *sometimes in NE* 'bȧs-\ *n* -s [²*bass* + *-ing*] **:** fishing for bass (as striped bass) particularly with rod and reel ⟨night ~⟩

bass·ist \'bāsə̇st\ *n* -s [²*bass* + *-ist*] **1 :** a contrabass player **2 :** a bass singer

bass·ly \'bāslē\ *adv* **:** in a bass manner

bass·ness \'bāsnə̇s\ *n* -ES **:** the quality or state of being bass

bas·so \'ba(,)sō, 'baa-,'bai-,'bä'bȧ-\ *n, pl* **bassos** \-ōz\ *or* **bas·si** \-ä(,)sē, -ȧ-\ [It, fr. ML *bassus*, fr. *bassus*, adj., fat, short, low] **1 :** a bass singer; *esp* **:** an operatic bass **2 :** a bass part (as in a chorus or opera)

basso oboe *n* [³*bass*] **:** HECKELPHONE

basso buf·fo \¦=(,)=¦bü(,)fō\ *n, pl* **bassi buf·fi** \-(,)fē\ *or* **basso buffos** \-(,)fōz\ [It, lit., comic bass] **:** a bass singer of comic roles in opera

basso can·tan·te \¦=(,)=kən'tantē; -(,)kän'täntē, -tän-,tā\ *n, pl* **bassi cantan·ti** \-ntē, -n-,tē\ [It, lit., singing bass] **:** a bass voice with a well-developed upper range ⟨a *basso cantante* . . . he combines baritone agility with bass sonority and boom —*Time*⟩ — compare BASSO PROFUNDO

basso continuo *n, pl* **basso continuos** [It, lit., continuous bass] **:** CONTINUO

basso da ca·me·ra \-də'kam(ə)rə, -'kaamrə,-'kämərə\ *n, pl* **bassi da camera** [It, lit., chamber bass] **:** a small contrabass esp. for use in ensemble playing

bas·son russe \bäsō^nrüs\ *n, pl* **bassons russes** \"\ [F, lit., Russian bassoon] **:** BASS HORN 1

bas·soon \bə'sün, ba's- *sometimes* bə'zün\ *n* -s [F *basson*, fr. It *bassone*, fr. *basso* bass — more at BASSO] **1 :** a tenor or bass double-reed woodwind instrument having a long doubled conical wooden body connected to the mouthpiece by a thin metal tube **2 :** a 16-foot pipe organ stop imitating the bassoon in tone

bassoon

bas·soon·ist \-nəst\ *n* -s **:** a bassoon player

basso osti·na·to \-,ästə'näd·(,)ō, ,ōs-, ,ós-\ *n, pl* **basso ostinatos** [It, lit., obstinate bass] **:** GROUND BASS

basso pro·fun·do \-prə'fən(,)dō, -ün-,-ün-\ *n, pl* **bassi profun·di** \-(,)dē\ *or* **basso profundos** \-(,)dōz\ [It *basso profondo*, lit., deep bass] **1 :** a deep heavy bass voice with a compass extending to about C below the bass staff — compare BASSO CANTANTE **2 :** a person having a basso profundo voice

bas·so·ra gum \'bas(ə)rə-, 'bəs-\ *n, often cap B* [fr. *Bassorah* (Basra), Iraq] **:** STERCULIA GUM; *esp* **:** a gum derived from an Asiatic tree (*Cochlospermum gossypium*)

bas·so-re·lie·vo *also* **bas·so-ri·lie·vo** \¦ba(,)sōrē'lē(,)vō, ¦baa-, ¦bai-, ¦bä-, ¦bá-; ¦bä(,)sōrēl'yä-, ¦bá-, -ye-\ *n, pl* **basso-relievos** \-vōz\ *or* **bas·si-ri·lie·vi** \¦bä(,)sērēl'yä(,)vē, ¦bá-, -ye-\ [It *bassorilievo*, fr. *basso* low + *rilievo* relief, fr. *rilevare* to raise, fr. L *relevare* — more at BASSO, RELIEVE] **:** BAS-RELIEF

bas·so·rin \'basərən, 'bəs-\ *n* -s [ISV *bassor-* (fr. *Bassora gum*) + *-in*] **:** a substance obtained from certain gums (as tragacanth) that is insoluble in water but swells to form a gel — compare TRAGACANTHIN

bass player *n* [²*bass*] **:** a performer on a bass musical instrument (as the contrabass) ⟨allows the pianist, the *bass player*, and the drummer to get in a few licks —*New Yorker*⟩

bass·ra locust \'basrə-, 'bəs-\ *n* [origin unknown] **:** ANGELIQUE 1a

bass reflex *n* [²*bass*] **:** a vent arrangement in the front surface of a loudspeaker enclosure designed to improve the reproduction of low-pitched tones

bass trumpet *n* [³*bass*] **:** a valve trumpet sounding usu. an octave lower than the ordinary trumpet and often considered to be a valve trombone

bas·sus \'basəs\ *n, pl* **bassi** [ML — more at BASSO] **:** the bass part in early polyphonic music

bass viol *n* [³*bass*] **1 :** VIOLA DA GAMBA **2 :** CONTRABASS

¹**basswood** \'⸗,⸗\ *n* [⁴*bass* + *wood*] **1 a :** a tree of the genus *Tilia* (esp. *T. americana*) — called also *bass, linden*; see TREE illustration **b :** the wood of any of these trees **2 a :** TULIP TREE **b :** the wood of this tree

²**basswood** \"\ *adj* **:** of or relating to a basswood **:** made of basswood

bast \'bast, -aa(ə)-,-ai-\ *n* -s [ME, fr. OE *bæst*; akin to OHG & ON *bast*] **1 :** PHLOEM **2** *or* **bast fiber :** any of certain strong woody fibers obtained chiefly from the phloem but also sometimes from the pericycle or cortex of various plants and used esp. in the manufacture of ropes, cordage, matting, and fabrics

bas·ta \'bastə, -äs-\ *or* **bas·to** \-stō\ *n* -s [Sp *basto*, fr. *bastón* stick — more at BASTINADO] **:** the third-highest trump in various card games: as **a :** the ace of clubs in omber **b :** the queen of spades in solo

bas·taard \'bastə(r)d, 'baas-,'bais-, -,stärd, -tȧd\ *or* **bas·tard** \-,stə(r)d\ *n* -s *cap* [obs. Afrik *Bastaard* (now *Baster*), lit., bastard, fr. MD *bastaert*, fr. OF *bastard*] **:** GRIQUA 2

¹**bas·tard** \'bastə(r)d, 'baas-,'bais- *also* 'bȧstəd-\ *n* -s [ME, fr. OF *bastart, bastard*, fr. *bast*, perh. meaning "barn" (in *fils de bast* bastard, perh. of Gmc origin; akin to Goth *bansts* barn) + *-art, -ard* -ard — more at BOOSE] **1 :** one born out of wedlock **:** an illegitimate child — compare LEGITIMATE, NULLIUS FILIUS **2 :** a sweet Spanish wine resembling muscatel that was esp. popular in England in Elizabethan times **3 :** something that is spurious, irregular, inferior, or of questionable origin ⟨the . . . residence is a ~ of the architectural era which followed the building of the Imperial Hotel —Hugh Byas⟩ **4 :** HYBRID — now used chiefly to imply inferior quality or to indicate a product of chance interbreeding **5 :** writing paper 16x20 inches in size **6 :** an inferior brown sugar made from the syrups that have already had several boilings **7 a :** an obnoxious or mean overbearing person — used as a generalized term of abuse ⟨they made him an officer and right away he became the biggest ~ you ever saw —T.O. Heggen⟩ **b :** an unfortunate victim ⟨once the sequence of events was set going the poor ~ never had a chance —Samuel Yellen⟩ **c :** FELLOW — used as a generalized term of approval ⟨the nicest thing an Aussie can call you is a bloody fine ~ —*Life*⟩

²**bastard** \"\ *adj* [ME, fr. OF *bastart, bastard*, fr. *bastart, bastard*, n.] **1 :** born out of wedlock **:** ILLEGITIMATE ⟨the ~ son of a rich old noble —J.T.Farrell⟩ **2 :** of inferior breed or stock **:** MONGREL, HYBRID, LOWBRED ⟨~ dogs⟩ ⟨~ oats⟩ **3 a :** of abnormal shape or irregular size **:** of unusual make or proportions ⟨a sash and door catalog with its fifty or more ~ sizes of doors and windows —R.E.Flanders⟩ — usu. used in technical phrases ⟨~ car⟩ ⟨~ connection⟩ ⟨~ bolt⟩ **b** *of printing type* (1) **:** having a face of one size and a body of another size (2) **:** not cast on the point system (3) **:** of a size arbitrarily classed as nonstandard **4 :** having the appearance of **:** resembling to some extent **:** being an inferior kind of ⟨~ sugar⟩ ⟨~ marble⟩ ⟨~ measles⟩ **5 :** lacking genuineness or authority **:** SPURIOUS, DEBASED, FALSE ⟨a ~ poetic form⟩ ⟨houses of ~ design⟩ ⟨the indiscriminate use of Greek letters by ~ groups not connected with the higher learning —C.W. Ferguson⟩

bas·tar·da \ba'stärdə, bä-\ *n* -s [It, fr. OIt, fr. *bastardo* bastard, fr. OF *bastart, bastard*] **:** a Gothic script used in France and Germany in the 14th and 15th centuries having mixed cursive and book hand features and characterized by flourishes and hairlines

bastard alkanet *n* **:** CORN GROMWELL

bastard aloe *n* **1 :** a Mexican century plant (*Agave vivipara*) cultivated for its fiber **2 :** the fiber of bastard aloe

bastard apple *n* **:** a bastard box (*Eucalyptus cambagei*)

bastard asphodel *n* **:** BOG ASPHODEL

bastard bar *n* **:** BATON 3b

bastard box *n* **:** any of several Australian or New Caledonian trees of the genera *Eucalyptus* (esp. *E. goniocalyx* and *E. cambagei*) and *Tristania* (esp. *T. neriifolia*) with strong hard wood that resembles boxwood

bastard bullet tree *n* **:** any of several tropical American timber trees of the genus *Humiria* (esp. *H. floribunda*)

bastard canna *n* **:** SAFFLOWER 1

bastard cedar *n* **:** any of several trees: as **a :** INCENSE CEDAR **b :** SEQUOIA **c :** SPANISH CEDAR **d :** CHINABERRY 2 **e :** a medium-sized West Indian tree (*Guazuma ulmifolia*) that is used for forage and timber and yields a cordage fiber **f :** RIBBONWOOD 3

bastard cherry *n* **1 :** a shrub (*Ehretia tinifolia*) bearing small black edible berries **2 :** GROUND-CHERRY 2

bastard chinaroot *n* **:** a prickly-stemmed No. American vine (*Smilax pseudo-china*) resembling the chinaroot

bastard cress *n* **1 :** FIELD CRESS **2 :** PENNYCRESS

bastard-cut \'⸗⸗,⸗\ *adj* **:** TANGENT-SAWED

bastard dittany *n* **1 :** a European mint (*Ballota pseudodictamnus*) **2 :** FRAXINELLA

bastard dogwood *n* **:** an Australasian shrub or small tree (*Pomaderris apetala*)

bastard eigne *or* **bastard elder** *n* **:** a bastard son of parents who afterward marry each other and have a legitimate son — compare MULIER PUISNE

bastard elm *n* **:** a hackberry (*Celtis occidentalis*)

bastard feverfew *n* **:** a tropical American annual weed (*Parthenium hysterophorus*) with small radiate heads of white flowers that is adventive in the southern U.S.

bastard file *n* **:** a file having teeth of a grade next finer than coarse

bastard gemsbok *n* **:** ROAN ANTELOPE

bastard gentian *n* **1 :** a No. American gentian (*Gentiana acuta*) **2 :** ORANGE GRASS

bastard grain *n* **:** grain appearing when the angle of cut is such that the growth rings of a timber form angles of 30 to 60 degrees with the face of a board cut from the timber

bastard granite *n* **:** GNEISS

bastard halibut *n* **:** CALIFORNIA HALIBUT

bastard hartebeest *n* **:** SASSABY

bastard hellebore *n* **1 :** HELLEBORINE **2 :** ARETHUSA 2 **3 :** GREEN HELLEBORE 2

bastard hemp *n* **1 :** either of two herbs of the genus *Datisca:* **a :** an Asiatic herb (*D. cannabina*) **b :** an American herb (*D. glomerata*) **2 :** HEMP AGRIMONY **3 :** HEMP NETTLE

bastardies *pl of* BASTARDY

bastard indigo *n* **1 :** FALSE INDIGO 1 **2 :** an East Indian shrub (*Tephrosia purpurea*)

bastard ipecac *n* **1 :** FEVERROOT **2 :** an ipecac from the roots of a milkweed (*Asclepias curassavica*)

bastard ironwood *n* **1 :** a small prickly tree (*Zanthoxylum fagara*) of the southern U.S. and tropical America **2 :** a tropical American tree (*Trichilia hirta*) with odd-pinnate leaves and pendulous flower clusters

bas·tard·i·za·tion \,bastə(r)də'zāshən, ,baas-, ,bais- *also* ,bȧstəd-\ *n* -s **:** the act or process of bastardizing ⟨~ of the chief principle of which they had the custody —Philip Wylie⟩

bas·tard·ize \'⸗⸗,dīz\ *vb* -ED/-ING/-S [¹*bastard* + *-ize*] *vt* **1 :** to stigmatize as or prove to be a bastard **:** declare or decide legally to be illegitimate ⟨they can therefore ~ the issue of the second marriage —Morris Ploscowe⟩ **2 :** to reduce from a higher to a lower state or condition **:** DEBASE ⟨decide whether we want to propagate opera or ~ it —Irving Kolodin⟩ ~ *vi* **:** to become debased **:** DEGENERATE, DETERIORATE

bastard jasmine *n* **1 :** MATRIMONY VINE **2 :** a plant of the genus *Cestrum*

bastard jute *n* **:** KENAF

bastard lignum vitae *n* **1 :** a tropical American tree (*Guaiacum sanctum*) yielding a wood similar to the lignum vitae **2 :** a West Indian shrub (*Badiera diversifolia*)

bastard locust *n* **:** ANGELIQUE 1a, 1b

bas·tard·ly \'⸗tə(r)dlē, -li\ *adj* [¹*bastard* + *-ly*] **1 :** of no worth or value **:** CONTEMPTIBLE, MEAN — usu. a generalized term of abuse ⟨quarts of that ~ stuff —Calder Willingham⟩ ⟨I'm not just doing it to be ~ —James Jones⟩ **2** *obs* **:** of no authority **:** SPURIOUS, CORRUPT ⟨apocryphal and ~ canons which they father upon the Apostles —John Donne⟩

bastard mahogany *n* **1 a** *also* **bastard jarrah** (1) **:** an Australian tree (*Eucalyptus botryoides*) — called also *bangalay, woolly butt* (2) **:** the timber of this tree that is hard and durable though inferior to the other so-called mahoganies of the continent **b :** JARRAH 1 **2 :** a West Indian tree (*Ratonia apetala*) of the family Sapindaceae

bastard mar·ga·ret \-'märg(ə)rət\ *n* **:** a ronco (*Haemulon parra*)

bastard marjoram *n* **:** WILD MARJORAM

bastard mouse-ear *n* **:** an Italian hawkweed (*Hieracium tenoreanum*)

bastard myall *n* **:** any of several Australian wattles (esp. *Acacia glaucescens* and *A. acuminata*)

bastard oak *n* **1 :** SCARLET OAK **2 :** a moderate-sized oak (*Quercus durandii*) of the south-central U.S. with rather small ovoid acorns — called also *bastard white oak, pin oak*

bastard parsley *n* **:** BUR PARSLEY

bastard pennyroyal *n* **:** BLUE CURLS 1

bastard pimpernel *n* **:** CHAFFWEED

bastard pine *n* **1 :** LOBLOLLY PINE 1 **2 :** POND PINE **3 :** CARIBBEAN PINE **4 :** WHITE FIR 1a(1)

bastard plantain *n* **1 :** WILD PLANTAIN **2 :** MUDWORT

bastard quartz *n* **:** massive quartz with no accessory minerals and valueless as an ore — called also *bull quartz*

bastard quince *n* **:** a European shrub (*Sorbus chamaemespilus*) with pink flowers and red inedible fruit

bastard rosewood *n* **1 :** an Australian tree (*Synoum glandulosum*) of the family Meliaceae **2 :** the valuable hard timber of bastard rosewood — called also *Australian rosewood*

bastards *pl of* BASTARD

bastard saffron *n* **:** CARTHAMUS RED

bastard sandalwood *n* **1 :** FALSE SANDALWOOD **2 :** any of several trees of the family Myoporaceae: as **a** (1) **:** either of two small shrubby Australian trees (*Myoporum platycarpum* and *M. tenuifolium*) with pleasantly scented wood (2) **:** NAIO c **b :** an aromatic shrub or shrubby tree (*Eremophila mitchelli*) of Australia **3 :** a small tree (*Zelkova abelicea*) of Crete **4** *New Zeal* **:** AKEAKE

bastard-saw \'⸗⸗¦⸗\ *vt* **:** TANGENT-SAW

bastard sensitive plant *n* **:** a tropical American herb (*Aeschynomene americana*) the leaves of which are sensitive like those of mimosas

bastard spikenard *n* **:** a European matgrass (*Nardus strictus*) adventive in Newfoundland and Massachusetts

bastard strangles *n pl but sing or pl in constr* **:** atypical strangles in which abscess formation occurs elsewhere than in the cervical lymph glands

bastard thread *n* **:** BUTTRESS THREAD

bastard title *n* **:** HALF TITLE 1

bastard toadflax *n* **1** *Brit* **:** a plant of the genus *Thesium* **2 :** a plant of the genus *Comandra* (esp. *C. umbellata* and *C. pallida*)

bastard tree *n* **:** REDWOOD 3a

bastard trout *or* **bastard weakfish** *n* **:** SILVER SQUETEAGUE

bastard turtle *n* **:** RIDLEY

bastard white oak *n* **:** BASTARD OAK 2

bastard wing *n* **:** the process of a bird's wing corresponding to the thumb and bearing a few short quills — called also *alula*

bas·tardy \'bastə(r)dē, 'baas-,'bais- *also* 'bȧs-\ *n* -ES [ME *bastardie*, fr. OF, fr. *bastart, bastard* bastard + *-ie* -y] **1 :** the quality or state of being a bastard **:** ILLEGITIMACY ⟨acutely conscious of his ~ —*Time*⟩ **2 :** the begetting of an illegitimate child

bastard yellowlegs *n* **:** STILT SANDPIPER

¹**baste** \'bāst\ *vt* -ED/-ING/-S [ME *basten*, fr. MF *bastir* to build, baste, of Gmc origin; akin to OHG *besten* to patch, mend, fr. *bast* — more at BAST] **:** to sew (as a garment) by hand or machine with long loose stitches in order to hold in place during fittings or for final stitching

²**baste** \"\ *vb* -ED/-ING/-S [origin unknown] *vt* **:** to moisten (foods, esp. meat) at intervals with melted butter, fat, pan drippings, or other liquids esp. during the cooking process to prevent drying and to add flavor ⟨~ a roast every half hour⟩ ~ *vi* **:** to become moistened with fat, drippings, or other liquids during cooking

³**baste** \"\ *n* -s **:** the liquid used in basting food during cooking

⁴**baste** \"\ *vt* -ED/-ING/-S [prob. fr. ON *beysta*; akin to ON *bauta* to beat — more at BEAT] **1 :** to beat severely or soundly **:** CUDGEL, THRASH **2 :** to scold vigorously **:** BERATE, DENOUNCE **syn** see BEAT

bas·tel house *or* **bas·tle house** \'bastᵊl-, -səl-\ *n* [ME *bastel, bastile* tower, fortress, fr. MF *bastile* — more at BASTILLE] **:** a fortified house esp. on the English and Scottish border usu. having its lowest floor vaulted

bast·en \'bastən, -aas-,-ais-\ *adj* [OE *bæsten*, fr. *bæst* bast + *-en* — more at BAST] **:** made of bast

¹**bast·er** \'bāstə(r)\ *n* -s [¹*baste* + *-er*] **:** one that bastes garments, parachutes, or other articles by hand or machine

²**baster** \"\ *n* -s [²*baste* + *-er*] **:** one that bastes foods; *specif* **:** a device that consists of a large glass tube fitted with a rubber bulb at one end and is used in basting meat

bast fiber *n* **:** BAST 2

bas·tide \(')ba¦stēd\ *n* -s [MF, fr. OProv *bastida* — more at BASTILLE] **1 :** a village or town in medieval France built esp. for defense and usu. laid out according to a definite geometric plan **2 :** a small country house in the south of France

¹**bas·tille** *or* **bas·tile** \(')ba¦stēl, -aa¦-, -ai¦-\ *n* -s [F *bastille*, fr. the *Bastille*, tower in Paris used as a prison, fr. MF *bastille* tower, fortress, modif. of OProv *bastida*, fr. *bastir* to build, of Gmc origin; akin to OHG *besten* to patch, mend] **:** a place of detention or imprisonment **:** PRISON, JAIL ⟨found that the ~ harbored as many drunkards and fighting men as before she began her campaign —Herbert Asbury⟩

²**bas·tille** *or* **bas·tile** \"\ *vt* -ED/-ING/-S **:** to confine in or as if in a bastille **:** IMPRISON

bastille day *n, usu cap B&D* [after *Bastille*, the fortress-prison in Paris] **:** July 14, the anniversary of the fall of the Bastille in 1789, observed in France as a national holiday

¹**bas·ti·na·do** \,bastə'nā(,)dō, -nä-\ *or* **bas·ti·nade** \¦bastə¦nād, -äd\ *n, pl* **bastinadoes** *or* **bastinades** [modif. of Sp *bastonada*, fr. *bastón* stick (fr. LL *bastum*) + *-ada* -ade — more at BASTON] **1 :** a blow with a stick or cudgel **2 a :** a beating esp. with a stick **:** CUDGELING **b :** a form of corporal punishment practiced in Asia that consisted of beating the soles of the culprit's feet with a stick **3 :** STICK, CUDGEL

bastinado 2b

²**bastinado** \"\ *vt* -ED/-ING/-S **:** to subject to repeated blows **:** BLUDGEON, BEAT

¹**basting** *n* -s [fr. gerund of ¹*baste*] **1 :** the action of a sewer who bastes **2 a :** the thread used by a baster **b :** the line of stitching made by a baster

²**basting** *n* -s [fr. gerund of ²*baste*] **1 :** the action of one that bastes food **2 :** the liquid used by a baster

bas·tion \'baschən *also* -stēən *sometimes* -styən *or* -schēn\ *n* -s [MF, fr. *bastille* fortress — more at BASTILLE] **1 :** a projecting part of a fortification ⟨the old fort with a ~ at each of its five corners⟩ **2 :** a fortified area or position ⟨planes disrupted surface communications and bombed island ~*s*⟩ **3 :** something that is considered a stronghold **:** BULWARK, SAFEGUARD ⟨one of the main ~*s* of order in a world so badly in need of them —D.W.Brogan⟩ ⟨responsible for weakening the final and greatest ~ of civil liberty —R.K.Carr⟩ **4 :** a pronounced salient of rock projecting from the wall of a glaciated valley and most commonly formed where a tributary joins a trunk glacier

bastion: *1* gorge, *2* ramp, *3* banquette, *4* salient angle, *5* face, *6* flank, *7* curtain

bas·tioned \-nd\ *adj* **:** having or defended by a bastion

bas·tite \'ba,stīt, 'bä-\ *n* -s [G *bastit*, fr. *Baste*, town near Harzburg, Germany + G *-it* -ite] **:** SCHILLER SPAR

bastle house *var of* BASTEL HOUSE

bast·naes·ite *or* **bast·näs·ite** \'bastnə,sīt\ *n* -s [Sw *bastnäsit*, fr. *Bastnäs*, Riddarhyttan dist., Västmanland, Sweden + Sw *-it* -ite] **:** a mineral consisting of a fluocarbonate of the cerium metals that is wax-yellow to reddish brown

basto *var of* **basta**

bas·ton \'bastən\ *n* -s [ME, fr. OF, fr. LL *bastum* stick, staff, prob. fr. (assumed) VL *bastare* to carry, fr. Gk *bastazein* to lift, carry] **1 :** BATON 3 **2 :** a convex round molding **:** TORUS

bast parenchyma *n* **:** PHLOEM PARENCHYMA

bast ray *n* **:** PHLOEM RAY

ba·su·ral \,bä(,)sü'räl\ *n, pl* **basura·les** \-ä,lās\ [AmerSp, rubbish heap, fr. Sp *basura* rubbish, fr. (assumed) VL *versura*, fr. L *verrere* to drag along, sweep — more at WAR] **:** an ancient refuse heap **:** MIDDEN

ba·su·to \bə'süd·(,)ō *sometimes* -'zü-\ *n, pl* **basuto** *or* **basutos** *usu cap* **1 :** one of the Bantu Southern Sotho-speaking people of Lesotho **2 :** a southern African breed of hardy ponies developed by interbreeding Arabs and Barbs

¹**bat** \'bat, *usu* -d.+V\ *n* -s [ME, fr. OE *batt*, prob. of Celt origin; akin to Gaulish *andabata* gladiator that fought while wearing a helmet without eye openings and to the source of L *battuere* to beat; akin to L *fatuus* silly, Russ *bat* cudgel] **1 :** a stout solid stick **:** CLUB, CUDGEL **2 :** a sharp blow **:** STROKE ⟨getting only one halfhearted ~ on his ear and a small scratch on his cheek —A.B.Mayse⟩ **3 a :** a wooden implement used for hitting the ball in various games (as baseball or cricket) **b :** a racket used in various games (as squash or badminton) **c :** the short whip used by a jockey **4 a :** BATSMAN ⟨a handy ~ and a good fast bowler⟩ **b :** the act of batting esp. in baseball **:** a turn at batting — usu. used in the phrase *at bat* ⟨the second baseman was at ~⟩ **5 a :** a part of a brick with one end whole and the other broken off **b :** a sun-dried brick **c** (1) **:** a flat round slab of clay or plaster esp. as representing the first stage in plate or saucer making (2) **:** a flat slab of fired clay serving as a kiln shelf (3) **:** the flat plaster disk supporting clay on the potter's wheel **6 a** *or* **batt** \"\ **:** BATTING 2 — usu. used in pl. **b** *or* **batt :** a continuous sheet of cotton or wool fiber prepared for carding or for layering in felt making **c** *also* **batt :** a layer of felt as used in making hats **7** *Brit* **:** rate of speed **:** CLIP, GAIT ⟨it can travel at a fair ~ —Alan Marshall⟩ **8 :** a drinking bout **:** SPREE, BINGE ⟨went off on a monumental ~ —Robert Wilder⟩ **9 :** a corrugation across the face of a masonry stone having a tooled finish — **go to bat for :** to give active support or assistance to **:** DEFEND, CHAMPION ⟨many friends stepped forward to *go to bat for* him and try to get him reinstated —James Jones⟩ — **off one's own bat :** through one's own efforts **:** on one's own account ⟨able to win the war *off its own bat* —George Orwell⟩ — **off the bat** *adv* **:** without delay **:** at once **:** IMMEDIATELY ⟨lock these people up right *off the bat* without letting them run around —Clare Hoffman⟩

²**bat** \"\ *vb* **batted; batted; batting; bats** [ME *batten*, fr. *bat*, n.] *vt* **1 :** to strike or hit with or as if with a bat **:** BEAT, CUDGEL ⟨~ each of the studio audience over the head —Richard Maney⟩ ⟨easily *batted* down the opposition's arguments⟩ **2** *in baseball* **a :** to advance (a base runner) by batting **:** DRIVE — see BAT IN **b :** to have a batting average of **:** HIT ⟨some players are never able to ~ .300⟩ **c :** to send to bat **d :** to lead to victory by batting ⟨*batted* his team to a 2-1 win last night⟩ **3 :** to compose esp. in a casual, careless, or hurried manner — usu. used with *out* ⟨*batted* out the first draft of the document on the typewriter —Charles Michelson⟩ **4 :** to discuss at length **:** consider in detail — usu. used with *around* or *back and forth* ⟨the plan was *batted* around for weeks⟩ ⟨we *batted* the subject back and forth —C.E. LeMay⟩ ~ *vi* **1 a :** to strike or hit a ball with a bat **:** HIT ⟨he ~*s* unusually well for a pitcher⟩ **b :** to take one's turn at bat (as of a player or a team) ⟨the shortstop was *batting* when the rain began⟩ **2 :** to travel from one place to another esp. in an aimless fashion **:** WANDER ⟨almost convinced myself that I was ready to ~ around the mountains with the snake nooses and cameras and guns —Saul Bellow⟩ **3 :** to strike repeatedly **:** BEAT ⟨the moths *batted* and trembled on the screens —Hamilton Basso⟩

³**bat** \"\ *n* -s [alter. of ME *bakke*, prob. of Scand origin; akin to OSw *nattbakka* bat] **1 :** any one of the numerous flying mammals that constitute the order Chiroptera, the only mammals capable of true flight, having the forelimbs modified to form wings, the metacarpals and finger bones except those of the thumb being greatly elongated and supporting like the ribs of an umbrella a cutaneous membrane that also extends a little in front of the arm and embraces the hind limbs except the feet and sometimes the whole length of the tail;

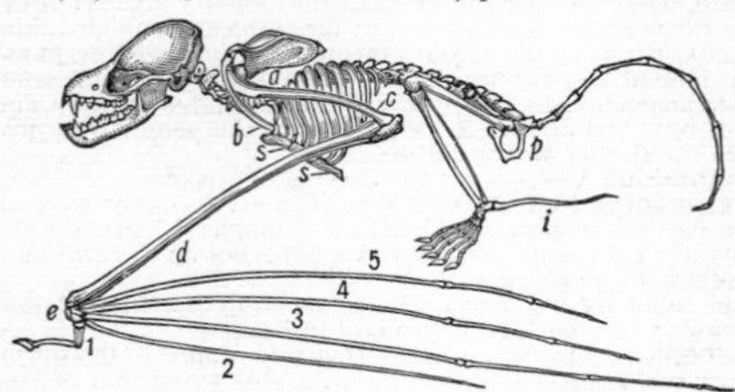

skeleton of a bat: *a* scapula; *b* clavicle; *c* humerus; *d* radius; *e* carpal bones; *1* thumb; *2, 3, 4, 5* second to fifth metacarpals; *ss* sternum; *p* pelvis; *i* calcar

having a thumb and toes with claws by which the animal suspends itself often head downward when at rest; being nocturnal in habit and among the most perfectly aerial of all animals, locomotion other than by flight being comparatively difficult for it; occurring most abundantly and attaining the largest size in warm countries; and being mostly insectivorous though some are frugivorous (as the flying fox) and a few suck the blood of other mammals — see VAMPIRE **2** *in the West Indies* **:** any of certain large moths and butterflies **3 :** IRON GRAY **4** *slang* **a :** PROSTITUTE **b :** an unattractive usu. unpleasant woman — often used as a generalized expression of abuse ⟨we ain't got around to telling the old ~ we're married yet —Maxwell Griffith⟩ — **have bats in the belfry :** to be foolish, eccentric, or insane

4bat \"\ *adj* [ME *batt*, fr. MF *bat, bast*, n., packsaddle, fr. (assumed) VL *bastum*, fr. (assumed) VL *bastare* to carry — more at BASTON] **:** for carrying a packsaddle or baggage ⟨~ mules⟩ ⟨a ~ and forage allowance⟩

5bat \"\ *vt* **batted; batted; batting; bats** [prob. alter. of 2*bate*] **1 a :** WINK ⟨*batting* her eyelids⟩ ⟨the son-in-law had begun to ~ his eyes rapidly —William Faulkner⟩ **b :** FLUTTER ⟨she *batted* mascaraed eyelashes foolishly —Lael Tucker⟩ **2 :** to show surprise or emotion by or as if by blinking (the eyes) **:** blink (the eyes) in or as if in surprise ⟨no one would have *batted* an eye had Bruce admitted to ten years more —Jane Woodfin⟩

6bat \"\ *n* -s [Hindi *bāt* speech, language, news, fr. Skt *vārttā* news, fr. *vartate* it turns, happen — more at WORTH (to become)] **:** the colloquial language of a foreign country **:** LINGO — used esp. in the phrase *sling the bat*

7bat *var of* BAHT

ba·taan \bəˈtan, -ˈän\ *n* -s [fr. *Bataan* province, Luzon, Philippines] **:** a valuable Philippine timber tree (*Shorea polysperma*) that yields a resin

1ba·tak \bəˈtäk, bäˈ-\ *n, pl* **batak** *or* **bataks** *usu cap* [Tagbanuwa *Baták*] **1 :** a small predominantly pagan native group inhabiting northern Palawan Island, Philippines **2 :** a member of the Batak group

2ba·tak \ˈbäˌtäk\ *also* **bat·tak** \"\ *n, pl* **batak** *or* **bataks** *usu cap* [Malay] **1 a :** an Indonesian ethnic group inhabiting the highlands of Sumatra **b :** a member of this group **2 :** an Austronesian language of the Batak people

bataleur *var of* BATELEUR

ba·ta·mote \ˌbädəˈmōt, -mōd·(ˌ)ā\ *n* -s [AmerSp] **:** WATER WALLY

ba·tan \bəˈtän\ *n, pl* **batan** *or* **batans** *usu cap* **:** IVATAN

ba·tan·gan \bəˈtaŋgən, -täŋ-\ *n, pl* **batangan** *or* **batangans** *usu cap* [Tag *Batángan*] **1 :** a small pagan group inhabiting central Mindoro, Philippines **2 :** a member of the Batangan group

bâ·tarde \bəˈtärd\ *n* -s [F, fr. fem. of *bâtard* bastard, fr. OF *bastard, bastart* — more at BASTARD] **:** a French round handwriting developed in the early 17th century and modified by the current English commercial cursive

ba·ta·ta \bəˈtäd·ə\ *n* -s [Sp, fr. Taino] **:** SWEET POTATO

ba·ta·tas \bəˈtäˌtas\ [NL, fr. Sp *batata* sweet potato] *syn of* IPOMOEA

ba·ta·ti·lla \ˌbädəˈtēyə, -tilə\ *n* -s [AmerSp, dim. of Sp *batata*] *in the West Indies* **:** any of numerous plants of the genus *Ipomoea*

ba·ta·via cassia *or* **batavia cinnamon** \bəˈtāvēə-, -vyə-\ *n, usu cap B* [fr. *Batavia*, now Djakarta, Java] **:** FAGOT CINNAMON

ba·ta·vi·an \-vēən,-vyən\ *n* -s *cap* [L *Batavi*, ancient inhabitants of the Low Countries + E *-an*] **1 :** one of an ancient people of the Low Countries **2** [NL *Batavia* Holland + E *-an*] **:** DUTCHMAN

2batavian \"\ *adj, usu cap* **1 :** of, relating to, or characteristic of the ancient Batavians **2 :** of, relating to, or characteristic of the Netherlands

3batavian \"\ *adj, usu cap* [*Batavia*, Java + E *-an*] **1 :** of, relating to, or characteristic of the city of Batavia, now Djakarta, Java **2 :** of, relating to, or characteristic of Batavians

4batavian \"\ *n* -s *cap* **:** a native or resident of the city of Batavia (now Djakarta) Java

bat bolt *n* [3*bat*] **:** a bolt that is barbed or jagged at its butt or tang

bat boy *n* [1*bat*] **:** a boy who looks after the bats and other equipment of a baseball team

bat bug *n* [3*bat*] **:** any of a family (Polyctenidae) of small flattened elongated hairy bugs related to the bedbug that are ectoparasites of bats

1batch \ˈbach\ *n* -ES [ME *bache* process of baking, batch of bread; akin to OE *bacan* to bake — more at BAKE] **1 :** the quantity (as of bread) baked at one time **:** BAKING ⟨the first ~ of cookies⟩ **2 a :** the quantity of material prepared or required for one operation; *specif* **:** a quantity of properly proportioned and mixed raw materials ready for fusion into glass **b :** the quantity (as of beer or concrete) produced at one operation ⟨a detailed record of all ~*es* manufactured⟩ **3 :** a quantity or number of persons or things considered as a group **:** LOT, SET, GROUP ⟨taken out in ~*es* to a firing squad —Green Peyton⟩ ⟨a ~ of childish braggarts who marry nasal bossy women —Claudia Cassidy⟩ ⟨a uniformed official stamped a ~ of yellow passes —Andy Logan⟩ ⟨my report on the latest ~ of office buildings —Lewis Mumford⟩ ⟨a great ~ of rules and regulations —St. Clair McKelway⟩; *specif* **:** a lumber raft made up of a number of units fastened together

2batch \"\ *adj* **1 :** by the batch **:** in a batch or batches ⟨a qualitative and quantitative analysis on a *batch*-sampling basis —*Science*⟩ **2 :** of, relating to, or intended for use in a batch ⟨the ~ materials must be as inexpensive as possible —C.J.Phillips⟩

3batch \"\ *vt* -ED/-ING/-ES **1 a :** to bring together (a quantity or number of things) for processing at one time **b :** to put (a quantity or number of things) through a manufacturing process at one time **2 :** to measure out (the material required for a batch) ⟨concrete was ~*ed* at a conveniently located plant⟩

4batch \"\ *var of* BACHE

5batch \"\ *var of* BACH

batch·er \-chə(r)\ *n* -s [3*batch* + *-er*] **:** one that batches: as **a :** one who operates a batching plant — called also *batching man, batch man* **b :** a machine that weighs the materials for batches of concrete **c :** BAGGER b

batching plant *n* [fr. pres. part. of 3*batch*] **:** an assemblage of bins, conveyers, and weighing equipment arranged for the purpose of weighing the materials entering into a batch of concrete

batch mixer *n* **:** a mixer into which the ingredients for one batch are placed, mixed, and discharged before another batch is introduced — opposed to *continuous mixer*

batchwise \ˈ=,=\ *adv (or adj)* [1*batch* + *-wise*] **:** by the batch **:** in a batch or batches ⟨data were obtained ~⟩ ⟨~ production⟩

1bate \ˈbāt, *usu* -d·+V\ *vb* -ED/-ING/-S [ME *baten*, short for *abaten* to abate (beat down)] *vt* **1 :** to reduce the force or intensity of **:** MODERATE, RESTRAIN ⟨he *bated* his breath⟩ **2 :** to take away **:** DEDUCT, SUBTRACT ⟨that grave and orderly senior was not going to ~ a jot of his dignity —George Eliot⟩ **3** *archaic* **:** to lower esp. in amount or estimation **:** DIMINISH, LESSEN ⟨and I shall have to ~ my price —A.E.Housman⟩ **4** *archaic* **:** to make dull the point or edge of **:** BLUNT ⟨and now I have *bated* your curiosity —J.F.Cooper⟩ **5 :** to leave out of consideration **:** EXCEPT, OMIT ⟨*bating* their jewels . . . I would not give three sous —Laurence Sterne⟩ **6** *archaic* **:** DEPRIVE ⟨when baseness is exalted do not ~ the place its honor for the person's sake —George Herbert⟩ ~ *vi, dial* **:** to fall off **:** DIMINISH, DECREASE ⟨the wind is *bating*⟩

2bate \"\ *vi* -ED/-ING/-S [ME *baten*, fr. MF *batre* to beat, fr. L *battere, battuere* — more at BAT] *of a falcon* **:** to beat the wings suddenly **:** flutter wildly downward from the fist or perch

3bate \"\ *n* -s [prob. of Scand. origin; akin to Sw *beta* to macerate; akin to OHG *beiza* maceration — more at BAIT] **:** a bath used by tanners after liming to remove the lime and soften the hides — compare PUER

4bate \"\ *vt* -ED/-ING/-S **:** to steep (as hides) in bate

5bate *var of* BAIT 5

6bate *var of* BETE

7bate *dial Brit past of* BITE

ba·tea \bəˈtēə, -tāə\ *n* -s [Sp, perh. fr. Ar *bāṭiyah* tub] **1 :** a large shallow pan of wood or iron used for washing sand and gravel to recover gold or valuable minerals **2 :** a painted or lacquered tray made of wood or from gourds

bat ear *n* [3*bat*] **:** an ear (as of certain dogs) that is large, erect, and rounded at the tip and resembles that of a bat

ba·teau *also* **bat·teau** \baˈtō, bə-, ˈba(ˌ)tō\ *n, pl* **ba·teaux** \-tōz,-tō\ [CanF, fr. F, boat, fr. OF *batel*, fr. OE *bāt* boat + OF *-el* (dim. suffix) — more at BOAT] **:** any of various small craft used esp. in the U.S. and Canada; *esp* **:** a flat-bottomed boat with raked bow and stern, flaring sides, strong sheer, and rockered bottom used esp. on rivers by lumbermen

a Canadian bateau

bateau bridge *n* **:** a pontoon bridge supported on bateaux

bateau neck *or* **bateau neckline** *n* **1 :** a wide neckline that follows the line of the collarbone and is high in front and back **2 :** any of various high or low necklines that extend toward the tips of the shoulders

bateless *adj* [1*bate* + *-less*] *obs* **:** that cannot be blunted

ba·te·leur *or* **ba·ta·leur** \ˌbad·əlˈər(·)\ *or* **bateleur eagle** *n* -s [F *bateleur*, fr. OF *bastelleur* juggler, puppet player, fr. *baastel* puppet] **:** a short-tailed African eagle (*Terathopius ecaudatus*) that is basically black with ruddy chestnut back, reddish tail, legs, bill, and cheeks, a silver-gray patch at the bend of each wing, and a white undersurface with a black margin along the hind edge of the wing

bate·ment light \ˈbātmənt-\ *n* [short for *abatement;* fr. the reduced line of the window] **:** a window or one division of a window having vertical sides but with the sill curved or inclined (as where it follows the rake of a staircase)

bat·er \ˈbād·ə(r), -ātə-\ *n* -s [4*bate* + *-er*] **:** one that bates; *specif* **:** a tannery worker who treats hides in bate to remove lime that was used for unhairing

-bates \bəd·ˌēz, bəˌtēz\ *n comb form* [NL, fr. Gk *-batēs* one that goes, fr. *bainein* to go, walk — more at COME] **:** walker — in generic names of animals ⟨*Hydrobates*⟩ ⟨*Pelobates*⟩

bates·i·an mimicry \ˈbātsēən-\ *n, usu cap B* [Henry Walter *Bates* †1892 Eng. naturalist + E *-ian*] *zool* **:** resemblance of an innocuous species to another that is protected from predators by unpalatability or other qualities

ba·te·te \bəˈtäd·(ˌ)ā\ *n* -s [native name in the Philippines] **1 :** a Philippine tree (*Kingiodendron alternifolium*) of the family Leguminosae with an aromatic sap used in making incense **2 :** the reddish brown oily wood of batete used in cabinetwork and furniture

batfish \ˈ=,=\ *n* [3*bat* + *fish*] **:** any of several fishes having more or less winglike processes: as **a :** any of the flattened fishes constituting a family Ogcocephalidae of the Pediculati (as a common West Indian form *Ogcocephalus vespertilio*) **b :** the flying gurnard (*Dactylopterus volitans*) of the Atlantic **c :** a California stingray (*Aetobatus californicus*)

batfish

bat fly *n* [3*bat*] **:** any of numerous small flies constituting the families Streblidae and Nycteribiidae, being ectoparasitic on bats, and having larvae completely developed in the body of the mother

batfowl \ˈ=,=\ *vi* [ME *batfowlyn*, fr. *bat* + *fowlyn, foulen* to fowl — more at FOWL] **:** to catch birds at night by blinding them with a light and knocking them down with a stick or netting them ⟨he taught them to throw flies and bait crawfish nets, to ~, and ferret for rabbits —Thomas Hughes⟩

1bath \ˈbath, -aa(ə)th,-aith,-àth\ *n, pl* **baths** \-thz,-ths\ [ME, fr. OE *bæth;* akin to OHG *bad* bath, ON *bath*, OHG *bāen* to warm — more at BAKE] **1 :** a washing or soaking of all or part of the body (as in water, steam, mud, or sunshine) ⟨a cool ~ refreshed him⟩ ⟨he took sun ~*s* for his health⟩ ⟨a mud ~⟩ **2 a :** water or any other medium used for bathing ⟨told her maid to draw her a ~⟩ ⟨baby played in its ~⟩ **b :** a contained liquid for a special purpose (as for immersion of something to be acted upon in dyeing, metallurgy, or photography) ⟨a mercury ~⟩ ⟨a fixing ~ containing a small amount of silver⟩ **c :** a medium (as water, air, sand or oil) for regulating the temperature of something placed in or on it **3 a :** a room where one may bathe **:** BATHROOM ⟨went into the ~ to take a shower⟩ **b (1) :** a building containing an apartment or a series of rooms designed for bathing ⟨went twice a week to the public ~⟩ **(2) :** one of the elaborate bathing establishments of the ancients — usu. used in pl. ⟨the Roman ~*s* in this quarter were found covered by an old burying ground —Tobias Smollett⟩ **c :** a place resorted to esp. for medical treatment by bathing **:** SPA — usu. used in pl. ⟨spent the summer at the ~*s*⟩ **d :** SWIMMING POOL ⟨the sound of swimmers diving into ~*s* —William Sansom⟩ **4 :** the quality or state of being covered with a liquid ⟨his head all over in a ~ of sweat —Bernard Mandeville⟩ **5 a :** a receptacle for water in which to bathe **:** BATHTUB ⟨cast-iron ~*s* were introduced during the early 19th century —J.E. Gloag⟩ **b :** a receptacle for holding a liquid preparation in which something is immersed (as in dyeing, metallurgy, or photography) **c :** a vessel containing a medium for regulating the temperature of something placed in or on it and used esp. in chemistry

2bath \ˈbàth\ *vb* -ED/-ING/-S *vt, Brit* **:** to give a bath to ⟨you'll have your little girl to ~ and put to bed —Richard Llewellyn⟩ ~ *vi, Brit* **:** to take a bath ⟨he was expected to shave, expected to ~ —H.G.Wells⟩

3bath \ˈbath\ *n* -s [Heb] **:** an ancient Hebrew unit of capacity for liquids equal to $\frac{1}{10}$ homer or about 10 gallons and corresponding to the ephah of dry measure

bath- *or* **batho-** *comb form* [ISV, fr. Gk *bathos*, fr. *bathys* deep — more at BATHY-] **1 :** depth ⟨*bathic*⟩ ⟨*batholith*⟩ ⟨*bathometer*⟩ ⟨*bathophobia*⟩ **2 :** downward **:** lower ⟨*bathochrome*⟩

bath asparagus \ˈbath-, ˈbàth-\ *n* [fr. *Bath*, city and county borough, England] **:** the edible young shoots of a European star-of-Bethlehem (*Ornithogalum pyrenaicum*)

bath brick *n, usu cap 1st B* [fr. *Bath*, England] **:** an unfired brick of siliceous material used as a scourer and polisher of metals

bath bun *n, usu cap 1st B* [fr. *Bath*, England] **:** a round bun made of sweet yeast dough containing eggs, butter, and currants and usu. decorated with sugar, nuts, or pieces of candied fruit

bath chair *n, sometimes cap B* [fr. *Bath*, England] **:** a hooded and sometimes glassed wheeled chair used esp. by invalids that is drawn by a horse or pushed by an attendant; *sometimes* **:** WHEELCHAIR

bath coup *n, usu cap B* [fr. *Bath*, England] **:** the refusal by a bridge or whist player holding the ace, jack, and at least one other card of a suit to take a king led by the opponent on his left

1bathe \ˈbāth\ *vb* -ED/-ING/-S [ME *bathen*, fr. OE *bathian;* akin to OHG *badōn* to bathe, ON *batha*, OE *bæth* bath — more at BATH] *vt* **1 :** to wash in water or another liquid esp. for the purpose of cleanliness, refreshment, or health **:** give a bath to ⟨shall wash his clothes and ~ himself in water —Lev 15:5 (RSV)⟩ ⟨hurried upstairs to ~ the baby⟩ **2 :** to moisten or suffuse with water or another liquid **:** WET ⟨and let us ~ our hands in Caesar's blood —Shak.⟩ **3 :** to apply water or a liquid medicament to ⟨was advised to ~ the eye with warm water⟩ **4 :** to touch in flowing **:** flow along the edge of **:** LAVE ⟨the lake which *bathed* the foot of the Alban mountain —Thomas Arnold⟩ **5 :** to suffuse with or as if with light **:** COVER, OVERSPREAD ⟨the sunlight *bathing* the ragged lawn —Ellen Glasgow⟩ ⟨the refulgent glow which ~*s* this story of an English mansion —John Barkham⟩ ~ *vi* **1 :** to take a bath **:** bathe oneself ⟨after dinner at the New York Café he *bathed* and dressed —Carson McCullers⟩ **2 :** to swim for pleasure **:** go in bathing ⟨he could ~ and lie in the sun for long hours —W.G.MacCallum⟩ **3 :** to become suffused as if with water **:** become immersed or absorbed ⟨our two ladies were privileged to ~ in those luscious strains each Sunday —Osbert Sitwell⟩

2bathe \"\ *n* -s **1** *Brit* **:** 1BATH 1 ⟨a ~ in blood like that can change the world —H.J.Laski⟩ **2** *Brit* **:** SWIM, DIP ⟨you walk right out of the front door on to the sands and into the sea for a ~ —William Aspden⟩

bath·er \ˈbāthə(r)\ *n* -s **1 :** one that bathes **2** *Brit* **:** SWIMMER **3** *Austral* **:** a bathing suit — usu. used in pl.

ba·thet·ic \bəˈthed·ik, -etik, -ēk\ *adj* [*bathos* + *-etic* (as in *pathetic*)] **:** characterized by bathos ⟨neither could his stout rationality lapse into ~ extravagance —Douglas Bush⟩ — **ba·thet·i·cal·ly** \-ək(ə)lē, -ēk-, -li\ *adv*

bath·house \ˈ=,=\ *n* **1 :** a house or building equipped and used for bathing ⟨though it was not Saturday he went early to the ~ with his sons —Hope Muntz⟩ **2 :** a building (as at the seashore) containing dressing rooms for bathers ⟨resembled a ~ under a cliff —Sinclair Lewis⟩

Bath·i·nette \ˌ=thəˈnet\ *trademark* — used for a portable bathtub for babies

bath·ing \ˈbāthiŋ, -ēŋ\ *n* -s [fr. gerund of *bathe*] **1 :** the act or sport of one who bathes ⟨the chief attraction of the resort is ~⟩ **2 :** the conditions (as the temperature of the water and the safeness of the beach) under which one may bathe and swim ⟨the ~ is good on the east coast⟩

bathing beauty *n* **:** an attractive woman in a bathing suit; *esp* **:** one who competes in a beauty contest

bathing box *n, chiefly Brit* **:** a small detached building in which bathers dress and undress ⟨clothes were lying all about as in a *bathing box* —Robert Lynd⟩

bathing dress *n, now chiefly Brit* **:** BATHING SUIT ⟨a middle-aged woman and her husband were sitting in *bathing dresses* in deck chairs —Nevil Shute⟩

bathing machine *n* **:** a small bathhouse on wheels which is capable of being driven into the water and in which bathers dress and undress ⟨*bathing machines* are ranged along the beach —Tobias Smollett⟩

bathing suit *n* **:** a one-piece or two-piece garment worn esp. by swimmers

bath kol \ˌbätˈkōl, ˌbäˈsk-\ *n* -s [Heb *bath qōl*] *in Jewish tradition* **:** a divine revelation given in the postprophetic age to certain Jewish teachers

bath·less \ˈ=ləs\ *adj* **1 :** without a bath **:** not having or not having had a bath ⟨they went ~ for a week⟩ **2 :** without a bathroom ⟨an old ~ farmhouse⟩

bath mat *n* **:** a mat that is usu. made of a washable material and is used in a bathroom

bath·mic \ˈbathmik, -ēk\ *adj* [*bathmism* + *-ic*] **:** of or relating to bathmism

bath·mism \ˈ=,mizəm\ *n* -s [Gk *bathmos* step (fr. *bainein* to go) + *-ism* — more at COME] **:** a hypothetical growth force — compare ÉLAN VITAL

bath mitz·vah \(ˈ)bäthˈmitsvə, -ät'-,-äs'-, -(ˌ)vä\ *or* **bas mitzvah** \-äs-\ *also* **bat mitzvah** \-ät-\ *n, often cap B & M* [Heb *bath miṣwāh* daughter of the (divine) law or precept] **1 :** a Jewish girl who at about 13 years of age assumes religious duties and responsibilities — compare BAR MITZVAH **2 :** the initiatory synagogue ceremony recognizing a girl as a bath mitzvah

bath·mo·trop·ic \ˌbathməˈträpik\ *adj* [Gk *bathmos* step + E *-tropic*] **:** modifying the degree of excitability of the cardiac musculature — used esp. of the action of the cardiac nerves

bath·mot·ro·pism \=ˈmä·trəˌpizəm\ *n* -s **:** the state of being bathmotropic

batho- — see BATH-

bath·o·chrome *also* **bath·y·chrome** \ˈbathəˌkrōm\ *n* -s [G *bathychrom*, fr. *bathy-* + *-chrom* -chrome] **:** an atom or group that when introduced into a compound (as a dye) causes a visible deepening of color (as from yellow toward green) — contrasted with *hypsochrome* — **bath·o·chro·mic** \ˌ=ə=ˈkrōmik\ *adj*

bath·o·lith *also* **bath·o·lyth** *or* **bath·y·lith** \ˈbathəˌlith\ *or* **bath·o·lite** *or* **bath·y·lite** \-ˌlīt\ *n* -s [ISV *bath-* or *bathy-* + *-lith* or *-lite;* orig. formed as G *batholith*] **:** a great mass of intruded igneous rock that for the most part stopped in its rise a considerable distance below the surface and that extends downward to unknown depth ⟨the Sierra Nevada ~⟩ ⟨the Boulder ~ of Montana⟩ — **bath·o·lith·ic** *also* **bath·y·lith·ic** \ˌ=ə=ˈlithik\ *or* **bath·o·lit·ic** *or* **bath·y·lit·ic** \-ˈlid·ik\ *adj*

bath ol·i·ver \-ˈäləvə(r)\ *n, usu cap B&O* [fr. *Bath*, England and William *Oliver* †1764 Eng. physician who invented the biscuit] **:** an unsweetened biscuit

ba·thom·e·ter \bəˈthäməd·ə(r)\ *n* [*bath-* + *-meter*] **:** an instrument for measuring depths in water

bat·horse \ˈbat+ˌ-\ *n* [part trans. of F *cheval de bât* packhorse, fr. *bât* packsaddle, fr. OF *bast* — more at BAT] **:** a horse that carries baggage (as of an officer) during a military campaign

ba·thos \ˈbāˌthäs, -ōs,-ōs *also* ˈba-\ *n* -ES [Gk, depth, fr. *bathys* deep — more at BATHY-] **1 :** the lowest phase **:** BOTTOM, NADIR ⟨the very ~ of stupidity —Frederick Marryat⟩ **2 a :** the sudden or unexpected appearance of the commonplace in writing or speaking otherwise elevated in style or content ⟨this habit of cultivating ~ . . . has become one of modern poetry's most persistent vices —D.J.Enright⟩ **b :** ANTICLIMAX, COMEDOWN ⟨spring was the real apex of the year. Summer was ~ —Jan Struther⟩ **3 :** exceptional commonplaceness **:** TRITENESS, FLATNESS ⟨some have deplored the aridity and attributed to it the ~ and prosing of the less successful ballads —Roger Sharrock⟩ ⟨its relentless conformity . . . filled him at first with a deep feeling of ~ —Fred Majdalany⟩ **4 :** insincere or overdone pathos **:** excessive sentimentality **:** SENTIMENTALISM, MAUDLINISM ⟨the ~ of the "my old mammy" theme —Lillian Smith⟩

bathrobe \ˈ=,=\ *n* **:** a loose ankle-length or knee-length garment usu. of a warm or absorbent material that is worn before and after bathing and sometimes as a dressing-gown

bathroom \ˈ=,=\ *n* **1 :** a room containing a bathtub or shower and usu. a washbowl and toilet **2 :** TOILET

bath salts *n pl* **:** a usu. colored crystalline compound for perfuming and softening bath water

bath sponge *n* **1 :** a sponge used in or for bathing **2 :** any of several fairly large sponges (family Spongidae) lacking spicules and having elastic skeletons of spongin that are gathered commercially in the Mediterranean, the Caribbean, and the Gulf of Mexico

bath stone *n, usu cap B* [fr. *Bath*, England, near which it was quarried] **1 :** an oolitic limestone used for building **2 :** FREESTONE 3

bath towel *n* **:** a towel usu. large and with a rough nap used after a bath

bathtub \ˈ=,=\ *n* **1 :** a tub that is usu. permanently fixed in a bathroom and in which a bath can be taken **2 :** SITZMARK

bathtub gin *n* **:** a usu. strong liquor made often illicitly and under makeshift conditions from spirits flavored with essences and essential oils so as to resemble gin ⟨the speakeasies, the *bathtub gin*, the gangsters —Carl Jonas⟩

bath·urst burr \ˈbathə(r)st-\ *n, usu cap 1st B* [fr. *Bathurst*, New South Wales, Australia] **:** a plant of the genus *Xanthium; esp, Austral* **:** SPINY CLOTBUR

bath·vill·ite \ˈbathvəˌlīt\ *n* -s [*Bathville*, West Lothian, Scotland + E *-ite*] **:** an oxygenated hydrocarbon occurring as brown porous lumps in coal

bath white *n, usu cap B & often cap W* **:** a European pierid butterfly (*Pontia daplidice*) that is largely white but with green marbling the undersurface of the wings

bathy- *comb form* [ISV, fr. Gk, fr. *bathys* deep; akin to W *boddi* to drown, Skt *gāhate* he dives into] **1 :** deep ⟨*bathyseism*⟩ **:** depth ⟨*bathythermograph*⟩ **2 :** deep-sea ⟨*bathypelagic*⟩ ⟨*bathyplankton*⟩ ⟨*bathysphere*⟩ **3 :** inner parts of the body ⟨*bathyesthesia*⟩

bathy·al \ˈbathēəl\ *also* **bathy·al·ic** \ˌ=ēˈalik\ *adj* [*bathy-* + *-al* or *-alic* (fr. *-al* + *-ic*)] **:** of or relating to the deeper parts of the ocean esp. between 100 and 1000 fathoms **:** DEEP-SEA

bathyal zone *or* **bathyal district** *n* **:** the slope from the continental shelf to the abyssal zone at 1000 fathoms to 1000 fathoms
ba·thyb·ic \bə'thibik\ *or* **ba·thyb·i·al** \-bēəl\ *adj* [NL *bathybius* + E *-ic* or *-ial*] **:** of, relating to, or living in the deepest parts of the sea
ba·thyb·i·us \-bēəs\ *n* -ES [NL, fr. *bathy-* + Gk *bios* life — more at QUICK] **:** a gelatinous substance precipitated by alcohol from mud dredged from the Atlantic and orig. regarded as free-living protoplasm but now recognized as a form of calcium sulfate
bathychrome *var of* BATHOCHROME
bathy·clinograph \¦bathə+\ *n* [*bathy-* + *clinograph*] **:** an instrument for measuring vertical currents in the deep sea
bathy·er·gi·dae \,bathə'ərjə,dē\ *n pl, cap* [NL, fr. *Bathyergus*, type genus (fr. Gk *bathyergein* to plow deeply, fr. *bathy-* + *ergein* to plow) + *-idae*] **:** a family of aberrant hystricomorph rodents that includes the mole rats and sand rats of Africa
bathy·gram \'bathə,gram\ *n* -S [*bathy-* + *-gram*] **:** a record obtained from sonic sounding instruments
bath·yl \'bathəl\ *adj* [by alter.] **:** BATHYAL
bathy·limnetic \¦bathə+\ *adj* [*bathy-* + *limnetic*] **:** relating to or inhabiting a bathylimnion
bathy·limnion \¦bathə+\ *n, pl* **bathylimnia** [NL, fr. *bathy-* + *-limnion*] **:** the deeper part of the hypolimnion distinguished by rather constant rates of heat absorption at different depths — compare CLINOLIMNION
bathylith *or* **bathylite** *var of* BATHOLITH
bathy·mas·ter·i·dae \,bathə(,)ma'sterə,dē\ *n pl, cap* [NL, fr. *Bathymaster*, type genus (fr. *bathy-* + Gk *mastēr* seeker, fr. *masteuein* to seek) + *-idae*] **:** a family of percoid fishes comprising the ronquils
ba·thym·e·ter \bə'thimәd·ə(r)\ *n* -S [*bathy-* + *-meter*] **:** a device for the sounding of depths
bathy·metric *or* **bathy·metrical** \¦bathə, -thē+\ *adj* [*bathymetric* ISV *bathy-* + *-metric*; orig. formed as F *bathymétrique*; *bathymetrical* fr. *bathy-* + *metrical*] **1 :** relating to the measurement of depths of water in oceans, seas, and lakes **2 :** relating to the contour of the bottoms of oceans, seas, and lakes ⟨a ~ map⟩ **3 :** relating to the distribution in depth of marine or lacustrine organisms ⟨~ range⟩ — **bathy·metrically** \"+\ *adv*
ba·thym·e·try \bə'thimə·trē\ *n* -ES [ISV *bathy-* + *-metry*; orig. formed as F *bathymétrie*] **:** the measurement of depths of water in oceans, seas, and lakes; *also* **:** the information derived from such measurements
bathy·orographical \¦bathē+\ *adj* [*bathy-* + *orographical*] **:** of or relating to ocean depths and mountain heights ⟨a ~ map⟩
bathy·pelagic \¦bathə+\ *adj* [*bathy-* + *pelagic*] **:** of, relating to, or living in the deeper waters of the ocean, esp. those several hundred feet below the surface — distinguished from *abyssal, pelagic*
bathy·pi·tot·me·ter \¦bathəpē'tō,mēd·ə(r)\ *n* -S [*bathy-* + Henri *Pitot* †1771 Fr. physicist and engineer + E *-meter*] **:** an instrument designed to record the current velocity and water temperature at indicated depths below the surface of a sea or lake — compare BATHYTHERMOGRAPH
bathy·scaphe \'bathə,skaf, -thē- *also* -āf\ *n* -S [ISV *bathy-* + Gk *skaphē* light boat; orig. formed in F] **:** a navigable submersible ship that is used for deep-sea exploration, has a spherical watertight cabin attached to its underside, and uses gasoline and shot for ballast
bathy·seism \'bathə,sīzəm\ *n* [*bathy-* + *-seism*] **:** an earthquake of deep origin recordable at seismographic stations the world over
ba·thys·mal \bə'thizməl\ *adj* [Gk *bathysma* deep place (fr. *bathys* deep) + E *-al*] **:** of or relating to the bottom of the deeper parts of the sea, esp. those parts between 100 and 1000 fathoms deep
bathy·sophical *also* **bathy·sophic** \¦bathə+\ *adj* [*bathy-* + *sophical, sophic*] **:** of or relating to a knowledge of the depths of the sea or of the things found there
bathy·sphere \'bathə, -thē+,-\ *n* [*bathy-* + *sphere*] **:** a strongly built steel diving sphere used for deep-sea observation and study
bathy·thermogram \"+\ *n* [*bathy-* + *thermogram*] **:** a record obtained with a bathythermograph
bathy·thermograph \"+\ *n* [ISV *bathy-* + *thermograph*] **:** an instrument designed to record the temperature of sea or fresh water as a function of depth
bathy·ther·mo·sphere \'bathə'thərmə+,-\ *n* -S [*bathy-* + *therm-* + *sphere*] **:** BATHYTHERMOGRAPH
bathy·vessel \'bathə+,-\ *n* [*bathy-* + *vessel*] **:** a ship (as a submarine or a bathysphere) designed for exploration of or navigation in water far below the surface of a sea or lake
bat·i·a·tor root \'bad·ēād·ə(r)-\ *n* [origin unknown] **:** the root of a tropical African shrub (*Vernonia nigritiana*) that yields vernonin
ba·ti·cu·lin *or* **ba·ti·ku·lin** \,batəkə'lēn\ *or* **ba·ti·cu·ling** *or* **ba·ti·ku·ling** \-'liŋ\ *n* -S [Tag *batikuling*] **:** any of several Philippine timber trees of the family Lauraceae (esp. *Litsia robusta*) that yield a wood much used for carvings and cabinetwork
bat·i·da·ce·ae \,bad·ə'dāsē,ē\ *n pl, cap* [NL, fr. *Batid-, Batis*, type genus + *-aceae*] **:** a family of low straggling dioecious shrubs (order Caryophyllales) having succulent opposite leaves and a conelike inflorescence — see BATIS — **bat·i·da·ceous** \¦=¦dāshəs\ *adj*
ba·tik \bə'tēk; 'bad·ik, -atik, -ēk *also* 'bä-\ *n* -S [Malay, fr. Jav. painted] **1 a :** an Indonesian method of hand-printing textiles by coating parts of the fabric with wax to resist dye, dipping in a cold dye solution, boiling off the wax, and repeating the process for each color used **b :** a design so executed **2 a :** a fabric printed by the batik method **b :** an imitation of such a fabric
bat in *vt* **:** to bring about (a run) by batting
bat·ing \'bād·iŋ, -ātiŋ, -ēŋ\ *prep* [fr. pres. part. of ¹*bate*] **:** with the exception of **:** EXCEPTING
ba·ti·no \bə'tē(,)nō\ *n* -S [Tag] **:** a Philippine tree (*Alstonia macrophylla*) that yields a moderately valuable timber
ba·tis \'bād·əs\ *n, cap* [NL, fr. L, samphire, fr. Gk] **:** a genus of plants constituting the family Batidaceae and characterized by flowers in scaly spikes — see SALTWORT 3
ba·tiste \bə'tēst, ba'-\ *n* -S [F, fr. MF (*toile de*) *baptiste*, prob. after *Baptiste* of Cambrai, 13th cent. Fr. textile maker, its inventor] **:** a fine soft sheer fabric of plain weave made of any of the principal fibers (as cotton, linen, rayon, silk, or wool) and used esp. for clothing
ba·ti·ti·nan \,bäd·ə'tē,nän\ *n* -S [Tag] **:** a Philippine tree (*Lagerstroemia pyriformis*) yielding a grayish or brown wood
bat·lan *or* **bat·lon** \bät'län, -ōn, '=,=\ *n, pl* **bat·la·nim** *or* **bat·lo·nim** \=ˈlänəm, -lōn-, -ēm\ [Heb *batlān*] **:** an unemployed Jewish man who spends most of his time in the synagogue or study hall or who is available for making up the number required for religious services or for singing prayers in memory of the dead
¹**bat·man** \'batmən\ *n* -S [Turk] **:** any of various old Persian or Turkish units of weight: as **a :** a Tabriz unit equal to 6.5 pounds **b :** a Turkish unit equal to 16.96 pounds
²**batman** \'batmən\ *n, pl* **batmen** [⁴*bat* + *man*] **1 :** one in charge of a bathorse and its load **2 :** the personal military servant of an officer in the British forces **:** ORDERLY
bat mitzvah *var of* BATH MITZVAH
batn *abbr* battalion
ba·toc·ri·nus \bə'täkrənəs\ *n, cap* [NL, fr. Gk *batos* skate (fish) + NL *-crinus*] **:** a genus (the type of the family Batocrinidae) of extinct crinoids esp. well represented in Lower Carboniferous rocks
bat·o·den·dron \,bad·ə'dendrən\ *n, cap* [NL, fr. Gk *batos bramble* + *-dendron*] *in some classifications* **:** a genus of recent and fossil shrubs usu. included in *Vaccinium*
ba·toi·dea \bə'tōidēə\ *n pl, cap* [NL, fr. *Batis*, genus of fish (fr. Gk, a flat fish) + *-oidea*] **:** Batoidei when considered a suborder of Hypotremata
ba·toi·dei \bə'tōidē,ī\ *n pl, cap* [NL, fr. *Batis* + *-oidei*] **:** an order or suborder of Hypotremata comprising somewhat dorsoventrally flattened elasmobranch fishes including the skates, rays, guitarfishes, sawfishes, and sometimes torpedoes
ba·to·ko plum \bə'tō(,)kō-\ *n* [origin unknown] **:** INDIAN PLUM

ba·tol·o·gist \bə'täləjəst\ *n* -S [Gk *batos* bramble + E *-logy* + *-ist*] **:** one who specializes in the study of brambles
¹**ba·ton** \bə'tän, ba'-, -'tänⁿ, -tōⁿ *sometimes* -tòn; *also* 'ba,= *or US sometimes and Brit usu* 'batⁿn\ *n* -S [F *bâton*, fr. OF *baston* — more at BASTON] **1 :** a club used as a weapon **:** CUDGEL, TRUNCHEON; *esp* **:** a policeman's billy **2 :** a staff borne as a symbol of office ⟨the ~ of a field marshal⟩ **3** *heraldry* **a :** a narrow bend **b :** a narrow bend with the ends cut off that is borne sinister and used as a mark of illegitimate descent in English heraldry **4 :** a stick or wand with which a leader directs a band or orchestra **5** *also* **baton de com·man·de·ment** \bätōⁿdəkōmäⁿd(ə)mäⁿ, bätōⁿtk-\ **:** an artifact of Aurignacian and later paleolithic times consisting of a reindeer or stag horn having one or more perforations and usu. engraved or carved and possibly used as a shaft straightener — compare ARROW STRAIGHTENER **6 :** a hollow wooden, paper, or plastic cylinder carried by each member of a relay team and passed to the succeeding runner in the exchange zone **7 a :** a long loaf of bread **b :** a thin short stick made of bread or pastry dough and sometimes flavored (as with cheese) **8 :** a smooth staff weighted with a ball at one end for balance and carried by a drum major or baton twirler

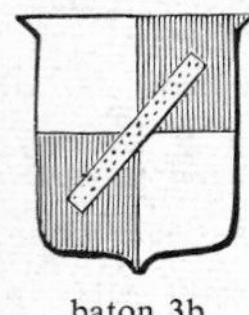
baton 3b

²**bat·on** \'batⁿn\ *vt* **batoned; batoned; batoning** \'bat(ⁿ)niŋ\ **batons :** to beat or strike with a baton **:** CUDGEL ⟨threatened to ~ him to death —Sir Walter Scott⟩
³**ba·ton** \bə'tän, ba'- *sometimes* -'tòn *also* 'ba,=\ *vi* -ED/-ING/-S **:** to lead a band or orchestra **:** CONDUCT
ba·ton·eer \bə,tä'ni(ə)r, ba,-, =ˈ=,=\ *n* -S [¹*baton* + *-eer*] **:** a leader of an orchestra or band
ba·ton·ist \bə'tänəst, ba'-\ *n* -S [¹*baton* + *-ist*] **:** one who uses a baton **:** CONDUCTOR
ba·ton·is·tic \bə(,)tä¦nistik, ¦batⁿn¦is-\ *adj* **:** relating to the use of the conductor's baton and to the art of conducting ⟨~ experience⟩
ba·ton·né paper \¦bätⁿn¦ā-, ba-, -tò¦nā-, -tō-\ *n* [part trans. of F *papier batonné* ruled paper, fr. *papier* paper + *batonné* ruled, crossed out, past part. of *bâtonner* to rule, cross out, fr. *bâton*] **:** a paper watermarked with widely spaced parallel lines and used esp. by philatelists
ba·ton·nier \,bätò'nyā, ,ba-, -tō-\ *n* -S [F *bâtonnier*, fr. MF *bastonnier*, fr. *baston* staff — more at BASTON] **:** the chief of the advocates of a court or bar
bat·on rouge \¦batⁿn¦rüzh\ *adj, usu cap B&R* [fr. *Baton Rouge*, La.] **:** of or from Baton Rouge, the capital of Louisiana ⟨a *Baton Rouge* residence⟩ **:** of the kind or style prevalent in Baton Rouge
bâ·tons rom·pus \bätōⁿrōⁿpue\ *n pl* [F, broken sticks] **:** the short straight billets or portions of molding usu. of rounded section forming the zigzag molding in Romanesque architecture
ba·ton twirler *n* **:** one who twirls a baton — compare DRUM MAJORETTE
batoon *n* -S [modif. of F *bâton*] *archaic* **:** BATON
bat printing *n* [¹*bat*] **:** a mode of printing on glazed ware by transferring the impression from the engraving to the ware on a thin slab of gelatin with the impression being taken in varnish and dusted with color after transfer
batrach- *or* **batracho-** *comb form* [ISV, fr. Gk, frog, fr. *batrachos*; perh. akin to OHG *kreta, krota* toad] **1 :** frog **:** toad ⟨*batracho*phobia⟩ **2 :** ranula ⟨*batracho*plasty⟩
¹**ba·tra·chia** \bə'trākēə\ [NL, fr. *batrach-* + *-ia*] *syn of* SALIENTIA
²**batrachia** \"\ [NL, fr. *batrach-* + *-ia*] *syn of* AMPHIBIA
³**batrachia** \"\ *n pl, sometimes cap* [NL, fr. *batrach-* + *-ia*] **1 :** SALIENTIANS — usu. used collectively **2 :** members of the class Amphibia
¹**ba·tra·chi·an** \bə'trākēən\ *adj* [F *batracien*, fr. *batrac*-batrach- + *-ien* -ian] **1 :** of or relating to the Batrachia **2 :** relating to or having the characteristics of frogs and toads
²**batrachian** \"\ *n* -S **:** one of the Batrachia
ba·tra·chi·ate \-kēət\ *adj* [NL ¹*Batrachia* + E *-ate*] **:** SALIENTIAN
ba·trach·i·dae \bə'trakə,dē\ [NL, fr. *Batrachus*, genus of amphibians (fr. Gk *batrachos* frog) + *-idae*] *syn of* BATRACHOIDIDAE
ba·tra·chi·um \-'trākēəm\ *n, cap* [NL, fr. L *batrachion*, a medicinal plant, fr. Gk, fr. *batrachos* frog + *-ion* (dim. suffix)] **:** a genus of aquatic or marsh herbs (family Ranunculaceae) having finely dissected or lobed leaves, small white flowers, and wrinkled achenes
¹**bat·ra·choid** \'ba·trə,kòid\ *adj* [*batrach-* + *-oid*] **:** like a frog or toad
²**batrachoid** \"\ *adj* [NL *Batrachoididae*] **:** of or relating to the Batrachoididae
bat·ra·choi·di·dae \,==ˈkòidə,dē\ *n pl, cap* [NL, fr. *Batrachoides*, type genus (fr. Gk *batrachos* frog + NL *-oides*) + *-idae*] **:** a family of marine fishes (order Haplodoci) having the head large and depressed and the mouth very wide and including the common toadfishes
bat·ra·choph·a·gous \¦==¦käfəgəs\ *adj* [*batrach-* + *-phagous*] **:** feeding on frogs
bat·ra·cho·sper·mum \¦ba·trə(,)kō¦spərməm\ *n, cap* [NL, fr. *batrach-* + *-spermum*] **:** a genus (the type of the family Batrachospermaceae) of red algae of the order Nemalionales found in slow-moving fresh waters and having a thallus that consists of a conspicuous central axis bearing transverse whorls of short branches at regular intervals
-bat·ra·chus \'batrəkəs\ *n comb form* [NL, fr. Gk *batrachos*] **:** batrachian — in generic names of animals ⟨Mega*lobatrachus*⟩
bat ray *or* **bat stingray** *n* [³*bat*] **:** BATFISH c
¹**bats** *pl of* BAT, *pres 3d sing of* BAT
²**bats** \'bats\ *adj* [by alter.] *slang* **:** BATTY 2 ⟨nothing to do but sweat out the old degree and try not to go ~ —Theodore Morrison⟩
bats·man \'batsmən\ *n, pl* **batsmen 1** [*bats* (gen. of ¹*bat*) + *man*] **:** BATTER — the usual term in cricket; see CRICKET illustration **2** [*bats* (pl. of ¹*bat*) + *man*] **:** a man who guides aircraft with a pair of bats; *esp* **:** one who guides incoming aircraft in this manner from the deck of a carrier
batsman's ground *n* **:** GROUND 5h (2)
bats·man·ship \-,ship\ *n* -S **:** ability at bat esp. in cricket
batt *var of* BAT
batt *abbr* **1** battalion **2** batten **3** battery **4** battle
¹**bat·ta** \'bad·ə, -atə\ *n* -S [Hindi *bhattā* allowance for food, fr. Skt *bhakta* allotted, something distributed or enjoyed, food, fr. *bhajati* he distributes, allots & *bhajate* he receives, enjoys — more at BAKSHEESH] **1** *India* **:** subsistence money (as for a witness or prisoner) **:** maintenance or traveling expenses of an employee **2** *India* **:** extra pay; *esp* **:** an extra allowance on special grounds to British officers, soldiers, and others serving in India
²**batta** \"\ *n* -S [Hindi *baṭṭā*] **1** *India* **:** rate of exchange **:** AGIO **2** *India* **:** discount on uncurrent coins
bat·tail·ous \'bad·ᵊləs\ *adj* [ME *bataillous*, fr. MF *bataillos*, fr. *bataille* battle + *-os* -ous — more at BATTLE] *archaic* **:** ready for battle **:** WARLIKE
battak *usu cap, var of* ²BATAK
bat·ta·lia \bə'tälyə, -tāl-\ *n* -S [It *battaglia* company of soldiers, battle — more at BATTALION] **1** *obs* **:** a large body of men in battle array **2** *archaic* **:** order of battle **:** battle array
bat·tal·ion \bə'talyən\ *n* -S [MF *bataillon*, fr. OIt *battaglione*, aug. of *battaglia* company of soldiers, battle, fr. LL *battalia* combat — more at BATTLE] **1 :** a considerable body of troops organized to act together **:** ARMY **2 :** a tactical military unit composed basically of a headquarters and two or more companies, batteries, or similar units **3 :** a large group of persons or things usu. marked by similarity of characteristics, condition, or purpose ⟨a ~ of instructors teaching elementary composition to freshmen —Douglas Bush⟩ — often used in pl. ⟨summoned new ~s to the service of the liberal ideal —M.W.Straight⟩ **4 :** a fire department unit made up of several fire companies **5 :** the headquarters of a military battalion ⟨someone . . . up from ~ —W.C.Fridley⟩
batteau *var of* BATEAU
batted *past of* BAT
¹**bat·tel** \'bad·ᵊl, -atᵊl\ *n* -S [perh. fr. ⁵*battle*] **:** the account for college expenses at Oxford University; *specif* **:** the account for board and provisions supplied from the college kitchen — usu. used in pl. ⟨Father would have the money put by for my first year's ~s —Thomas Wood †1950⟩
²**battel** \"\ *vi* -ED/-ING/-S **:** to have an account with or to be supplied with provisions from a college kitchen or buttery at Oxford University
bat·tel·er *or* **bat·tler** \-lə(r)\ *n* -S **:** one that battels
bat·te·ment \batmäⁿ, 'batmənt\ *n* -S [F, fr. *battre* to beat + *-ment* — more at BAT] *ballet* **:** an extension of the free foot in any direction followed by a beat against the supporting foot
¹**bat·ten** \'batⁿn\ *vb* **battened; battened; battening** \'bat(ⁿ)niŋ\ **battens** [prob. fr. ON *batna* to improve; akin to ON *betr* better — more at BETTER] *vi* **1 a :** to grow fat **:** thrive by feeding ⟨skepticism ~*ing* at the vitals of belief —C.J.Rolo⟩ **b :** to feed gluttonously **:** glut oneself — usu. used with following *on* or *upon* ⟨foreigners who had been ~*ing* on the carcass of the peninsula —G.C.Sellery⟩ **2 :** to grow prosperous **:** thrive esp. at the expense or to the detriment of another ⟨the pilgrim . . . was expected to serve the state, not ~ on it —Agnes Repplier⟩ ~ *vt* **:** to cause to thrive by feeding **:** FATTEN ⟨we drove afield . . . ~*ing* our flocks with the fresh dews of night —John Milton⟩
²**batten** \"\ *n* -S [F *bâton* stick — more at BATON] **1 a :** a strip of sawed timber that is usu. seven inches wide, less than four inches thick, and more than six feet long and is used esp. for flooring — compare BOARD 3a **b** *dial Eng* **:** a deal less than seven inches wide **2 a :** a strip of wood used for nailing across two other pieces (as to hold them together or to cover a crack) **b** (1) **:** a strip usu. of wood used to strengthen or to help seal a structure (2) **:** a reinforcing strip usu. of wood attached to the end or base of a box, a barrelhead, or a crate (3) **:** a piece of wood used to hold and strengthen loads in freight handling **3 a :** a strip of light wood sewed into a ship's sail at approximately right angles to the leech to make it set flat **b :** an iron bar used to stretch and hold a tarpaulin over the hatch covers or gratings of a ship **c :** a strip of wood nailed or clamped around the edges of the covering of a ship's hatchway to hold it in place **d :** a strip of wood used to keep cargo away from the steel hull of a ship or to prevent it from shifting — see SHIP illustration **4 :** a stripped log less than 11 inches in diameter at the small end **5 a :** a thin strip usu. of wood used in fairing a ship's lines in the mold loft **b :** a thin strip usu. of wood used as an auxiliary for reference or measurement in erecting structures during the building of a ship or in setting up a dry dock to receive a ship **6 a :** a length of wood or pipe suspended from the gridiron and used to support the scenery or lighting instruments in a theater **b :** a strip of lumber usu. 1x3 inches used in the construction of stage scenery **c :** a strip of wood fastened to the top and bottom of a stage drop
³**batten** \"\ *vb* -ED/-ING/-S *vt* **1 :** to furnish with battens ⟨the wall had to be ~*ed*⟩ **2 :** to fasten by or as if by means of battens — often used with *down* ⟨had ~*ed* down his hatches long before the first gale winds began to blow —Bennett Cerf⟩ ~ *vi* **:** to make oneself secure by or as if by battens — often used with *down* ⟨we ~*ed* down at the first hurricane warning⟩
⁴**batten** \"\ *n* -S [origin unknown] *dial Eng* **:** a bundle of straw
⁵**batten** \"\ *n* -S [F *battant*, fr. pres. part. of *battre* to beat — more at BAT] **:** the movable bar carrying the reed of a loom that strikes home each filling thread as it is interlaced with the warp by the passage of the shuttle
⁶**batten** \"\ *dial var of* BATTING
bat·ten·berg lace \'batⁿn,bərg-\ *n, usu cap B* [fr. *Battenberg*, village in Prussia, Germany] **:** RENAISSANCE LACE
batten door *n* [²*batten*] **:** a door made of usu. narrow boards set lengthwise and secured by battens nailed crosswise
bat·ten·er \'bat(ⁿ)nə(r)\ *n* -S [³*batten* + *-er*] **:** one that battens; *specif* **:** a person who attaches cleats to packing cases
batten plate *n* [²*batten*] **:** a short plate used to connect two parallel parts of a built-up structural-steel member of a bridge or building
¹**bat·ter** \'bad·ə(r), -atə-\ *vb* -ED/-ING/-S [ME *bateren*, prob. freq. of *batten* to bat — more at BAT] *vt* **1 a :** to beat with successive blows **:** beat repeatedly and violently so as to bruise, shatter, or demolish ⟨he's got sense enough not to ~ his head against a stone wall for a lost cause —Mary Deasy⟩ ⟨they ~*ed* open the door —E.E.Shipton⟩ **b :** to assail orig. with a battering ram but now esp. with an artillery bombardment so as to break down or demolish **:** BOMBARD ⟨they ~*ed* down with cannon the beautiful apartment houses —Sinclair Lewis⟩ **2 a :** to subject to strong, overwhelming, or repeated attack ⟨the English professional class has been ~*ed* by change —V.S.Pritchett⟩ **b :** to drive by strong, overwhelming, or repeated attack ⟨the constant change of theme soon ~*s* the reader into exhaustion —A.J.P.Taylor⟩ **3 :** to wear or damage by blows or hard usage ⟨the raincoat and the hat were now ~*ed* by weather out of their former glossiness —John Buchan⟩ ⟨seems so much cruder in sensibility and expression as well as rather ~*ed* in appearance —Willa Cather⟩ ~ *vi* **:** to strike heavily and repeatedly **:** BEAT, POUND ⟨flies ~*ed* against and buzzed around the electric-light bulbs —D.B.Chidsey⟩ **syn** see MAIM
²**batter** \"\ *n* -S [ME *bater*, prob. fr. *bateren*] **1 :** a mixture (as for cake or waffles) that consists of flour, liquid, and other ingredients and is thin enough to pour or drop from a spoon — compare DOUGH **2** *Scot* **:** a paste of flour and water **3 :** the act or result of battering: as **a :** a damaged area on a printing surface (as a plate or type) **b** (1) **:** the wear on the surface of a railhead at or near a track joint (2) **:** a deviation from the vertical in the upright members forming a trestle bent
³**batter** \"\ *vb* -ED/-ING/-S [origin unknown] *vi* **:** to have a receding upward slope ~ *vt* **:** to give a receding upward slope to (as a wall)
⁴**batter** \"\ *n* -S **:** a receding upward slope of the outer face of a wall or other structure usu. causing a decrease in thickness as it ascends
⁵**batter** \"\ *n* -S [²*bat* + *-er*] **1 :** one that bats; *esp* **:** the player (as in baseball or cricket) whose turn it is to bat **2 a** *or* **batter–out** \'==,=\ (1) **:** a pottery worker who shapes balls of soft clay and throws them into the hollow molds used in forming wares — called also *baller, cup baller* (2) **:** a pottery worker who spreads bats for plates or similar dishes and throws them upon the center of the mold **b :** a plaster block with a handle used in ceramics in making bats
batter board *n* [⁴*batter*] **:** one of a pair of horizontal boards nailed to posts set near the corners of an excavation for a building and used by the builders to indicate a desired level and also as a fastening for stretched strings to mark outlines
batter brace *n* [⁴*batter*] **:** an inclined brace at the end of a truss used to give added strength and support — called also *batter post*
batter bread *n* [²*batter*] *chiefly Midland* **:** SPOON BREAD
battercake \'==,=\ *n* [²*batter* + *cake*] *chiefly South&Midland* **:** GRIDDLE CAKE
batter head *n* [¹*batter*] **:** the upper head of a snare drum — compare SNARE HEAD
bat·te·rie *like* BATTERY, *or (as F)* bà·trē\ *n* -S [F, fr. *battre* to beat + *-erie* -ery — more at BATTERY] **1 :** a ballet movement consisting of beating together the feet or calves of the legs during a leap **2 :** BATTERY 12
battering ram *n* [fr. pres. part. of ¹*batter*] **1 :** a military siege engine that consisted of a large wooden beam with a head of iron and was used in ancient times to beat down the walls of a besieged place **2 :** a heavy metal bar with handles that is used (as by firemen) to batter down doors and to breach brick walls
batter pile *n* [⁴*batter*] **:** a pile driven at an angle with the vertical to resist a lateral force

battering ram 1

batter post *n* [⁴*batter*] **1 :** BATTER BRACE **2 :** a post set at the corner of a building or at one side of a gateway as protection against damage by vehicles

batter pudding *n* [²*batter*] **:** an unsweetened pudding of flour, eggs, and milk or cream baked or boiled

batter rule *n* [⁴*batter*] **:** an instrument consisting of a rule or frame and a plumb line and bob and used to regulate the batter of a wall in building

batters *pres 3d sing of* BATTER, *pl of* BATTER

batter's box *n* [⁵*batter*] **:** the rectangular area on either side of home plate in which the batter stands while at bat

bat·ter·sea enamel \'bad-ə(r)sē-, -atə-, -si-\ *n, usu cap B* [fr. *Battersea,* metropolitan borough of London, England] **:** 18th century English decorative enamel work with painted or transfer designs on a usu. white background

bat·tery \'bad-ərē, -atərē, -a-trē, -ri\ *n* -ES [MF&F *batterie,* fr. OF, beating, fr. *battre* to beat — more at BAT] **1 :** metal or metal articles esp. of brass or copper wrought by hammering; *specif* **:** metallic kitchen utensils **2 a :** the act of battering or beating **b :** the unlawful beating of another including every willful, angry and violent, or negligent unlawful touching of another's person or clothes or anything attached to his person or held by him — compare ASSAULT 3a **c** *obs* **:** BOMBARDMENT ⟨keep the bulwark fronts from ~ —Christopher Marlowe⟩ **3 a :** a temporary grouping (as of mortars or searchlights) for tactical purposes **b** (1) **:** the entire armament of a warship (2) **:** a group of a warship's guns ⟨the starboard ~⟩ ⟨the main ~⟩ **4 a :** an emplacement where artillery is mounted ⟨a fortress crowned with *batteries* —S.P.B.Mais⟩ **b** (1) **:** SINKBOX (2) **:** a blind usu. of turf used on English and Scottish moors esp. by grouse shooters **5 :** the basic tactical and administrative artillery unit usu. consisting of from two to six pieces with the necessary personnel, transportation, communications, and equipment — compare COMPANY **6 a :** a combination of apparatus for producing a single electrical effect ⟨a ~ of dynamos⟩ **b** (1) **:** a group of two or more cells connected together to furnish electric current (2) **:** a single voltaic cell **7 a :** a number of similar articles, devices, or machines arranged, connected, or used together **:** SET, SERIES, GROUP ⟨a ~ of files⟩ ⟨a ~ of roman candles⟩ ⟨a ~ of coke ovens⟩ ⟨a ~ of exhausted brooms and mops leaned against the rail —Philip Wylie⟩: as (1) **:** a group or series of tests esp. of intelligence or personality given to a subject as an aid in psychological analysis (2) **:** a series of cages or compartments for raising or fattening poultry (3) **:** a closely packed group of nematocysts on the tentacle of a coelenterate **b :** an imposing series or group of similar things **:** ARRAY ⟨has equipped his book with . . . a formidable ~ of prepublication comments —Robert Bierstedt⟩ **c :** an impressive group of persons having similar characteristics, occupations, or interests ⟨a ~ of specialists . . . all testified that the bill was too high —Milton Silverman⟩ **d :** a group of bulls kept for breeding **8 a :** the position of readiness (of a gun) for firing ⟨the breechblock failed to close and the gun would not return to ~ —*Infantry Jour.*⟩ ⟨in ~⟩ ⟨out of ~⟩ **b :** the part of a flintlock the flint strikes against in firing **9 a :** a series of usu. five stamps operated in one box or mortar for crushing ores **b :** the box in which such stamps are operated **10 :** a tank with its electrical and chemical accessories in which an electrotype shell is formed by electrodeposition **11 :** the pitcher and catcher of a baseball team **12 :** the percussion section of an orchestra

battery acid *n* **:** dilute sulfuric acid for use in storage batteries — called also *electrolyte acid*

battery charger *n* **:** CHARGER 1c

battery eliminator *n* **:** a device to supply voltage to electron tubes from electric power supply mains — compare A POWER SUPPLY, B POWER SUPPLY, C POWER SUPPLY

battery indicator *n* **:** a small direct-current ammeter that continuously indicates the net charging or discharging current of an automobile battery

battery jar *n* **:** a glass container that has straight sides and a round, square, or rectangular bottom and is entirely open at the top and that is used esp. in biology and chemistry laboratories

bat·tery·man \-mən\ *n, pl* **batterymen 1 :** one who charges and repairs storage batteries — called also *chargeman, charger* **2 :** an electrotyper who works at the battery **3 :** one who tends the battery cells in which sugar is extracted from beets

battier *comparative of* BATTY

battiest *superlative of* BATTY

bat·ting \'bad-iŋ, -atiŋ, -ēŋ; *in sense 2 sometimes* -tᵊn *by speakers who usu pronounce ng* ŋ *in -ing words*\ *n* -S [fr. gerund of ²*bat*] **1 :** the act of one who bats: as **a :** the use of a bat in beating raw cotton or wool to separate and clean it **b :** the use of or ability with a bat (as in baseball or cricket) **:** HITTING **2 :** layers or sheets usu. of raw cotton or wool used esp. for lining quilts or for stuffing or packaging

batting average *n* **1 a :** the average (as of a baseball batter) determined by dividing the number of official times at bat into the number of base hits ⟨ended the season with a *batting average* of .312⟩ **b :** the ratio of runs scored by a batsman in cricket to innings completed **2 :** a record of achievement or accomplishment ⟨has maintained an almost unbelievably high *batting average* in gaining and holding the friendship of the home folk —G.S.Perry⟩

batting block *n* **:** a solid block of plaster on which the batter beats out the clay in making a bat

batting cage *n* **:** CAGE 9a

batting crease *n* **:** POPPING CREASE

batting eye *n* **:** visual judgment by a baseball batter of balls thrown by a pitcher ⟨the coach's suggestion greatly improved the rookie's *batting eye*⟩

¹**bat·tle** \'bad-ᵊl, -atᵊl\ *n* -S *often attrib* [ME *bataile, batel,* fr. OF *bataille* battle, battalion, fr. LL *battalia* combat, alter. of *battualia* fencing exercises, fr. L *battuere* to beat, of Celt origin; akin to Gaulish anda*bata* gladiator that fought while wearing a helmet without eye openings — more at BAT] **1 :** a general fight or encounter between armies, ships of war, or aircraft **:** a general and prolonged military engagement **:** COMBAT ⟨the 4-month ~ at Anzio⟩ **2 :** a combat between two persons; *specif* **:** the combat by which disputes were legally decided — see TRIAL BY BATTLE **3 :** participation in armed conflict **:** WARFARE ⟨and drunk delight of ~ with my peers —Alfred Tennyson⟩ **4** *archaic* **:** a body of troops composing an army or one of its chief divisions; *esp* **:** BATTALION **5 :** an extended contest, struggle, or controversy (as between athletic teams or political parties) **:** WAR ⟨the advocates of the old classical education have been . . . fighting a losing ~ for over half a century —W.R.Inge⟩ ⟨a ~ for control of the railroad⟩ **6** *obs* **:** the main body of a military force esp. as distinct from the van and rear

²**battle** \"\ *vb* **battled; battled; battling** \-d·ᵊliŋ, -t(ᵊ)l-\ **battles** [ME *batailen,* fr. MF *bataillier,* fr. *bataille*] *vi* **1 :** to engage in battle **:** FIGHT ⟨the king will bid you ~ presently —Shak.⟩ **2 :** to contend with full strength, vigor, craft, or other resources **:** STRUGGLE ⟨*battled* like an avenging angel for the seamen's rights —Van Wyck Brooks⟩ ⟨like one who having *battled* with the waves —L.G.White⟩ **~** *vt* **1 :** to engage in battle with **:** fight against ⟨when the nobles rebelled the king *battled* them⟩ **2 :** to engage in an extended contest, struggle, or controversy with **:** FIGHT ⟨for three years he *battled* factions of both parties —Oscar Handlin⟩ ⟨they are *battling* tremendous odds —Henry Hewes⟩ **3 :** to force, thrust, or drive by contending or resolute battling ⟨a small boy *battled* his way through the crowd —Virginia Woolf⟩ **syn** see CONTEND

³**battle** \"\ *vt* -ED/-ING/-S [ME *batailen,* fr. MF *bataillier* to fortify, fr. OF, fr. *bataille* fortifying tower, battle] *archaic* **:** to fortify with battlements ⟨beneath the *battled* tower —Alfred Tennyson⟩

⁴**bat·tle** \'bā-,'be-\ *var of* BAITTLE

⁵**battle** *vb* -ED/-ING/-S [perh. of Scand origin; akin to ON *beit* pasture land — more at BAIT] *vt, obs* **:** to feed well **:** NOURISH **~** *vi, obs* **:** to feed well **:** THRIVE

⁶**bat·tle** *like* ¹BATTLE\ *vt* -ED/-ING/-S [prob. freq. of ²*bat*] *chiefly South & Midland* **:** to beat (clothes) with a stick or paddle during laundering

¹**battle-ax** *or* **battle-axe** \'ˌˌ,ˌ\ *n* [ME *bataile-axe,* fr. *bataille* battle + *axe*] **1 :** a broadax formerly used as a weapon of war **2** *slang* **:** a quarrelsome, irritable, domineering woman ⟨was a formidable old *battle-ax* —G.W.Johnson⟩

²**battle-ax** *or* **battle-axe** \"\ *adj, usu cap B&A* **:** of or belonging to a Neolithic culture of northern Europe characterized by the decoration of pottery with cord impressions and the depositing of perforated stone battle-axes in graves

battle-axes

battle bill *n* **:** a list of battle assignments on a warship

battle-board tennis *n* **1 :** modified tennis in which opponents play side by side on a half court with the net hung at one end in front of a board from which the ball rebounds **2 :** a practice tennis game for one player in which the rebound from a board simulates a return shot from an opponent

battle chess *n* **:** chess in which each player places his men in a permissible arrangement of his own choosing on the first three ranks of his side of the board, a screen separating the two opponents until play begins

battle clasp *n* **:** CLASP 1c(1)

battlecraft \'ˌˌ,ˌ\ *n* **:** skill in the technics of military combat and in the procedures of living under battle conditions

battle cruiser *n* **:** a warship of battleship size and of the highest speed and heaviest battery but without the heavy armor protection of the battleship and designed for high-speed cruising, scouting, and long-range fighting

battle cry *n* **1 :** a war cry of forces engaged in battle **2 :** a slogan used esp. in a campaign or contest **:** CATCHWORD ⟨the *battle cry* of freedom⟩

battled *adj* [ME *batailed,* fr. past part. of *batailen* to battle] **:** EMBATTLED 2

battle dance *n* **:** WAR DANCE 1

bat·tle·dore \'bad-ᵊl,dō(ə)r, -atᵊl-, -ó(ə)r,-ōə,-ó(ə)\ *n* -S [ME *batyldore,* prob. modif. of OProv *batedor* beating instrument, fr. *batre* to beat, fr. L *battere, battuere* — more at BATTLE] **1 a :** a beetle or bat that is used in washing or smoothing clothes **b :** a tool with a long flat blade with a square end that is used in glassworking to flatten the bottoms of vessels **c :** a long-handled paddle that is used for placing loaves in an oven **2 a :** a light flat bat or racket that is used in striking a shuttlecock **b :** BATTLEDORE AND SHUTTLECOCK **3 :** a child's primer usu. made of two or three pages of stiff cardboard on which were printed or impressed the alphabet, numerals, and other rudimentary material and used esp. in the 17th and 18th centuries

battledore and shuttlecock *n* **:** a game of ancient Oriental origin that evolved into badminton

battle dress *n* **:** military uniform that is designed for field service

battle fatigue *n* **:** COMBAT FATIGUE

battlefield \'ˌˌ,ˌ\ *n* **:** BATTLEGROUND

battlefield flower *n* **:** JOHNNY-JUMP-UP

battlefront \'ˌˌ,ˌ\ *n* **:** the region where armed forces face the enemy

battle game *n* **:** a variety of tenpins in which a score of 12 can be made by knocking down all of the pins except the kingpin 3 balls being rolled to the frame, 4 or 6 frames constituting a game, and strikes and spares not being counted

battleground \'ˌˌ,ˌ\ *n* -S **1 :** the territory on which a battle is waged **2 :** an area of conflict ⟨human nature as a ~ between the forces of evil and the forces of good —F.B.Millett⟩

battle group *n* **:** a military unit that is normally a fifth part of a division and is normally made up of five companies

battle jacket *n* **1 :** a waist-length woolen jacket worn by members of the armed forces **2 :** any jacket cut like a battle jacket

battle lantern *n* **:** one of the lanterns on a naval vessel; *esp* **:** a portable battery-powered electric light for emergency use on such a vessel ⟨he fumbled through the dim glow of the *battle lanterns* —Keith Wheeler⟩

battle light *n* **:** a special low-intensity red light used inside a warship at night

battle line *n* **1 :** a line along which a battle is waged **2 :** battleships, cruisers, and supporting warships organized to function as a fighting unit

bat·tle·ment \'bad-ᵊlmənt, -atᵊl-\ *n* -S [ME *batelment,* fr. MF *bataille* fortifying tower + ME *-ment* — more at BATTLE] **1 :** a parapet that consists of alternate solid parts and open spaces, that surmounts a wall, and that is used in fortified buildings for purposes of defense and in other edifices (as a church) for decoration ⟨pinnacles on the ~s are frequent but not universal —Nikolaus Pevsner⟩ **2 :** an embattled roof or platform

battlements: *A* merlon: *B* crenel, *C* machicolations

bat·tle·ment·ed \-,mentəd, *esp Brit* -mən-\ *adj* **:** furnished with or as if with battlements

battle piece *n* **:** a work (as a painting, musical composition, or poem) concerned with or descriptive of a battle

battleplane \'ˌˌ,ˌ\ *n* **:** WARPLANE

battle police *n pl* **:** military policemen detailed to prevent straggling during battle

battle position *n* **:** a defensive position on which is concentrated the main effort of the defense

¹**bat·tler** \'batlə(r), -ad-ᵊl-,-atᵊl-\ *n* -S [²*battle* + *-er*] **:** one that battles; *esp* **:** a dogged fighter

²**battler** *var of* BATTELER

battle range *n* **:** the range for which the sights of a military weapon are adjusted when in the normal or carrying position — compare BATTLE SIGHT

battle royal *n, pl* **battles royal** *or* **battle royals 1 a :** a fight participated in by more than two combatants ⟨he tells of seeing a *battle royal* among five, each gashing, slashing, and puncturing the nearest to him until only one was left alive —J.W. Lippincott⟩; *esp* **:** such a contest in which the last man in the ring or on his feet is declared the winner **b :** a fight to the finish **:** a violent struggle ⟨after a *battle royal* the cops hauled Jack off to jail —*Sat. Eve. Post*⟩ **2 :** a heated discussion, disagreement, or dispute ⟨these *battles royal* between him and Lady Henry were not uncommon —Mrs. Humphry Ward⟩

battles *pl of* BATTLE, *pres 3d sing of* BATTLE

battleship \'ˌˌ,ˌ\ *n* [short for *line-of-battle ship*] **1 :** a warship of the largest and most heavily armed and armored class usu. having at least 10-inch armor and carrying in the main battery guns of 12-inch or larger caliber **2** *slang* **:** a large railroad locomotive **3 :** BATTLESHIP GRAY **4 battleships** *pl but sing in constr* **:** SALVO 4

battleship

battleship gray *n* **:** a nearly neutral slightly bluish medium gray that is darker than pearl — called also *Denver*

battle sight *n* **:** an arrangement of sights that makes possible the rapid aiming of a firearm at short ranges

bat·tle·some \'bad-ᵊlsəm, -atᵊl-\ *adj* [*battle* + *-some*] **:** inclined to battle **:** QUARRELSOME ⟨the young fellows were tough and the girls ~ —Saul Bellow⟩

battlewagon \'ˌˌ,ˌˌ\ *n* **1 :** BATTLESHIP 1 **2 :** a large heavily armored and heavily armed bombing plane or tracked vehicle

battlewise \'ˌˌ,ˌ\ *adj* **:** having knowledge of or experience in battle ⟨~ troops⟩

battling *pres part of* BATTLE

battling stick *n* [fr. pres. part. of ⁶*battle*] *chiefly South & Midland* **:** a paddle or stick used to battle clothes

bat tree *n* [³*bat*] **:** EVERGREEN MAGNOLIA

¹**batts** \'bats\ *n pl* [origin unknown] *Scot* **:** COLIC

²**batts** *pl of* BATT

bat·tu \bàtü, ba'tü, ba·'tyü\ *adj* [F, past part. of *battre* to beat] *of a ballet movement* **:** BEATEN — see ¹BEAT 1c

bat·tue \ba'tü, ba·'tyü, *Fr* bàtü̅\ *n* -S [F, fr. fem. of *battu,* past part. of *battre* to beat, fr. OF *batre,* fr. L *battere, battuere* — more at BATTLE] **1 a :** the driving or drawing out of game from cover esp. by beating woods and bushes **b :** a hunt in which this procedure is used ⟨I never cared much for a ~ of pheasants or a grouse drive —John Buchan⟩ **2 :** a concerted action by a number of persons performed with bustle ⟨once a year a grand ~ is organized when every nook and cranny of the church is raked from roof to floor —Richard Free⟩ **3 :** indiscriminate slaughter ⟨a huge prison ~ was ordered . . . on the principle that many should pay for one —Bernard Pares⟩

bat·ture \ba'tů(ə)r, ba·'tyů-, *Fr* bàtü̅r\ *n* -S [LaF, fr. F *battre* to strike + *-ure* — more at BATTUE] **:** the alluvial land between a river at low-water stage and a levee — used esp. of such land along the lower Mississippi river

bat·tu·ta \bə'tüd-ə\ *n* -S [It, fr. fem. of *battuto,* past part. of *battere* to beat, fr. L *battere, battuere* — more at BATTLE] **1 :** the beat of a musical composition **2 :** MEASURE 4c(1)

bat·ty \'bad-ē, -atē, -i\ *adj, usu* -ER/-EST [³*bat* + *-y*] **1 :** belonging to or resembling a bat **:** like a bat's ⟨large ~ wings⟩ **2** *slang* **:** mentally unstable **:** CRAZY, INSANE ⟨undoubtedly the *battiest* critical judgment of the year —Wolcott Gibbs⟩

ba·tu \bə'tü\ *n* -S [Malay, lit., stone] **:** a yellow to brown or black hard semifossil dammar resin derived from any of certain trees of the genus *Agathis* (esp. *A. dammara*)

ba·tu·que \bə'tükə\ *n* -S [Pg, prob. fr. a native name in Africa] **:** an impassioned Brazilian Negro courtship dance of African origin

ba·twa \'bä,twä\ *n, pl* **batwa** *or* **batwas** *usu cap* **1 a :** a Bantu-speaking pygmy people of the Kasai region and elsewhere in Africa **b :** a member of such people **2 :** any African pygmy or pygmoid

batwing \'ˌ,ˌ\ *adj* [³*bat* + *wing*] **:** shaped like the wing or wings of a bat ⟨the ~ doors of a saloon⟩ ⟨a ~ collar⟩: as **a** *of a necktie* **:** worn in a bowknot and having ends of equal length ⟨a black ~ tie for evening wear⟩ **b** *of a sleeve* **:** made with a deep armhole ⟨the ~ sleeves of a knitted blouse⟩ **c** *of chaps* **:** having wide flared sides and snap or buckle fastenings ⟨he picked up the scarred ~ chaps —W.V.T.Clark⟩

batyl alcohol \'bad-əl-\ *n* [ISV *bat-* (fr. NL *Batis,* genus of fish) + *-yl* — more at BATOIDEA] **:** a colorless crystalline alcohol $C_{18}H_{37}OCH_2CH(OH)CH_2OH$ obtained esp. from many shark-liver oils and ray-liver oils and from the yellow marrow of cattle bones; glycerol α-octadecyl ether

batz \'bäts\ *n, pl* **batz·en** \-sən\ [G (now usu. *batzen*), fr. *batz, batzen* lump, fr. *batzen* to stick together, freq. of *backen* to stick together, bake, fr. OHG *backan* to bake — more at BAKE] **1 :** an old base silver coin of southern Germany and Switzerland worth four kreuzers **2 :** a unit of value equivalent to one batz ⟨in Switzerland ½*-batz* and 10*-batzen* and 40*-batzen* coins were issued⟩

baubee *var of* BAWBEE

bau·ble \'bóbəl, 'bäb-\ *n* -S [ME *babel,* fr. MF *babel, baubel*] **1 :** something that is bright, showy, sometimes expensive, and usu. of little use **:** TRINKET, GEWGAW, PLAYTHING ⟨he affixed the ~, with a kiss, upon her middle finger —Elinor Wylie⟩ **2 :** a fool's scepter ⟨the licensed jester . . . brandished his ~ —Sir Walter Scott⟩ **3 :** a child's toy ⟨a child asleep with a ~ —R.P.Warren⟩ **4 a :** something that is considered childish, foolish, or worthless **:** TRIFLE ⟨the Right Honorable before my name is a ~ —T.B.Macaulay⟩ **b** *obs* **:** a childish, foolish, or worthless person ⟨thither comes the ~ and falls me thus about my neck —Shak.⟩

bauble 2

bau·bling \-bliŋ\ *adj* [*bauble* + *-ing*] *archaic* **:** INSIGNIFICANT, CONTEMPTIBLE

bauch \'bäk, 'bòk\ *adj* [perh. of Celt origin; akin to ScGael *beag* little, short, disagreeable, trifling, OIr *becc, bec* small, W *bach,* Bret *biban*] *chiefly Scot* **:** INFERIOR, SUBSTANDARD — **bauch·ly** *adv*

bauch·le \'bákəl, 'bòk-\ *n* -S [perh. fr. *bauch* + *-le*] **1** *Scot* **:** an old shoe; *esp* **:** one worn down at the heel **2** *Scot* **:** something useless, worn out, or worthless ⟨a ~ of a creature⟩

bauck·ie \'bäki, 'bò-\ *or* **bauckiebird** \'ˌˌ,ˌ\ *n* -S [alter. of ME *bakke* bat + E *-ie* — more at BAT] *Scot* **:** ³BAT 1

baud \'bòd\ *n* -S [after J.M.E. *Baudot* †1903 Fr. inventor] **:** a unit equal to one dot per second or the equivalent interval per second and used in measuring the speed of signaling in telegraphic code

bau·de·kin \'bòdəkən\ *n* -S [ME, fr. MF *baudequin, baldequin* — more at BALDACHIN] **:** BALDACHIN 1

bau·drons \'bädrənz, -athr-\ *n* -ES [ME] *chiefly Scot* **:** CAT, PUSS, KITTY ⟨and ~ was watching a rathole⟩

bau·era \'baùərə\ *n* [NL, after Ferdinand *Bauer* †1826 and Franz A. *Bauer* †1840 Austrian botanical painters] **1** *cap* **:** a small genus of evergreen shrubs (family Saxifragaceae) native to eastern Australia with pink or purple long-stalked flowers resembling single roses **2** *pl* **bauera :** a plant of the genus *Bauera*

bau·haus \'baù,haùs\ *adj, usu cap* [fr. G *Bauhaus,* lit., architecture house, an academy of the arts founded in Weimar, Germany, in 1919, fr. *bau-* architecture (fr. *bauen* to build) + *haus* house] **:** of, relating to, or influenced by a school of design founded by Walter Gropius at Weimar in 1919 and noted for its association with functional architecture, abstract art, innovation in the use of building materials, and the absence of applied ornament in design and for a program that synthesized technology, craftsmanship, and design esthetics and disregarded the distinction between fine and applied art ⟨*Bauhaus* furniture⟩ ⟨the *Bauhaus* point of view⟩

bau·hin·ia \bō'inēə, -'hin-, bò'-\ *n* [NL, fr. Jean *Bauhin* †1613 and Gaspard *Bauhin* †1624 Swiss botanists + NL *-ia*] **1** *cap* **:** a large genus of tropical trees, shrubs, or lianas (family Leguminosae) with leaves that are usu. bifoliolate and tough fibrous bark — see MOUNTAIN EBONY **2** *pl* **bauhinia** *or* **bauhinias :** a plant of the genus *Bauhinia* ⟨the trees on the street . . . are to be ~s, an Asiatic variety that puts out mauve blooms in the fall —Christopher Rand⟩

bauk \'bák, 'bòk\ *dial var of* BALK

bauld \'bäl(d), 'bòl-\ *chiefly Scot var of* BOLD

¹**baule** \,bäü'lā, 'ˌˌ,ˌ\ *n, pl* **baule** *or* **baules** *usu cap* **1 :** a people of the Ivory Coast region of West Africa linguistically related to Ashanti and other peoples eastward and renowned for their carved statuary in wood **2 :** a member of the Baule people

²**baule** \'bòl, 'bōl\ *n* -S [origin unknown] **:** the theoretical amount of nitrogen or other essential mineral constituent necessary to produce one-half of the maximum possible yield of a crop

baulk *var of* BALK

bau·mé *also* **bau·me** *or* **beau·mé** \bō'mā, 'ˌ(,)ˌ\ *adj, usu cap* [after Antoine *Baumé* †1804 Fr. chemist] **:** according to a Baumé scale ⟨a hydrometer indicating degrees *Baumé*⟩ **:** calibrated in accordance with a Baumé scale ⟨*Baumé* hydrometer⟩

bau·mer \'bòmə(r)\ *adj, usu cap* [fr. the name *Baumer*] **:** of or belonging to an ancient culture of southern Illinois and adjacent areas characterized by fabric-impressed flat-based pottery, stone implements and ornaments, and permanent villages with large square houses

baumé scale *n, usu cap B* [after Antoine *Baumé*] **:** either of two arbitrary hydrometer scales, one for liquids lighter than water and the other for liquids heavier than water, that indicate specific gravity in degrees, the intervals between the degree graduations being of equal length, readings on the scale being approximately reducible to specific gravities by the following formulas given by the U.S. Bureau of Standards (*n* in each case being the reading on the Baumé scale): (a) for liquids heavier than water, sp. gr. = 145÷(145 − *n*) at 60° F; (b) for liquids lighter than water, sp. gr. = 140 ÷ (130 + *n*) at 60° F

baum·hau·er·ite \(')baù'maùə,rīt, (')baùm'haù-\ *n* -S [H.A. *Baumhauer* †1926 Swiss mineralogist + E *-ite*] **:** a mineral $Pb_4As_6S_{13}$ consisting of a lead thioarsenite and occurring in metallic gray monoclinic crystals

bau·mier \bōm'yā\ *n* -S [F, fr. *baume* balm, fr. OF *basme* — more at BALM] **1 :** BALSAM POPLAR **2 :** BALSAM FIR 1 **3 :** any of several plants of the genera *Ocimum, Amyris,* and *Trigonella*

baum marten \'baùm,-\ *n* [part trans. of G *baummarder,* fr. *baum* tree (fr. OHG *boum*) + *marder* marten — more at BEAM] **:** the pelt or fur of the European pine marten

bau·no \bä'ü(,)nō, 'baü-\ *n, pl* **baunoes** *or* **baunos** [Cebuan & Taw-sug] **:** a wild mango (*Mangifera verticillata*) found in the Philippines having a juicy rich subacid fruit

bau·ple nut \'bȯpəl,-\ *n* [origin unknown] **:** MACADAMIA 2

bauré \baü'rā\ *n, pl* **bauré** *or* **baurés** *usu cap* [Sp, of AmerInd origin] **1 a :** an Arawakan people living in the Baures river valley in northeastern Bolivia **b :** a member of such people **2 :** the language of the Bauré people

bau·sching·er effect \'bȯ(,)shiŋə(r)-\ *n, usu cap B* [after Johann *Bauschinger* †1893 Ger. technologist] **:** the phenomenon by which plastic deformation of a metal increases the yield strength in the direction of plastic flow and decreases the yield strength in the opposite direction

bau·son \'bȯsᵊn\ *n* -s [ME *bausen*, fr. MF *baucent*, fr. *baucent*, adj., spotted] *archaic* **:** BADGER

bau·sond \'bäsənd, 'bȯ-\ *adj* [ME *bausand*, fr. MF *baucent*, perh. fr. L *balteus* belt, prob. fr. Etruscan] *dial Brit, of an animal* **:** having a white spot or streak on a dark ground esp. on the forehead or face

bau·ta \'baüdə\ *n* -s [modif. of ON *bautasteinn*, fr. *bauta* (meaning and origin unknown) + *steinn* stone] **:** a prehistoric upright gravestone or memorial stone sometimes 20 feet high that was often placed at the summit of a barrow — compare MENHIR

ba·ut·ta \bä'üdə\ *n* -s [It, fr. It dial. (Venice) *bauta*, prob. fr. *bava* slobber, fr. (assumed) VL] **:** a black cloak with a hood that falls so as to mask the face esp. for masquerades

baux·ite \'bȯk,sīt, 'bäk,s-, -k,z- *sometimes* 'bō,zīt, *usu* -d·+V\ *also* **beaux·ite** \'bō,zīt, *usu* -d·+V\ *n* -s [F *bauxite*, fr. Les *Baux*, near Arles, Dept. Bouches-du-Rhône, France + F *-ite*] **:** an impure mixture of earthy hydrous aluminum oxides and hydroxides that commonly contains similar compounds of iron and occas. of manganese, usu. has a concretionary or oolitic structure, and is the principal source of aluminum used in commerce and industry

baux·it·ic \(')bȯk¦sid·ik, (')bäk¦-, -k¦z- *sometimes* (')bō¦zi-\ *adj* **:** containing or resembling bauxite ⟨~ clay⟩

ba·var·dage \,bavə(r)'däzh, '==,=\ *n* -s [F, fr. *bavarder* to gossip, chatter (fr. MF, fr. *bavard* chatterbox, fr. *bave* slobber, fr. — assumed — VL *bava*) + *-age*] **:** SMALL TALK, CHITCHAT

1ba·var·i·an \bə'verēən, -va(a)r-,-vār-\ *adj, usu cap* [*Bavaria*, region of Germany + E *-an*] **1 :** of, relating to, or characteristic of Bavaria **2 :** of, relating to, or characteristic of Bavarians **3 :** of, relating to, or characteristic of the Bavarian dialect

2bavarian \"\ *n* -s *cap* **1 :** a native or inhabitant of Bavaria **2 :** the High German dialect of Bavaria and Austria

bavarian cream *also* **bavarian** *n* -s *usu cap B* **:** a dessert of a flavored whipped gelatine mixture into which whipped cream is folded

ba·ve·nite \bə'vē,nīt, -vä-\ *n* -s [It, fr. *Baveno*, on Lake Maggiore, Italy + It *-ite*] **:** a mineral $Ca_4BeAl_2Si_9O_{24}(OH)_2$ consisting of a basic calcium beryllium aluminosilicate, belonging to the zeolite group, and occurring in radiated groups of white fibrous crystals (hardness 5.5, sp. gr. 2.7)

ba·vi·an \'bāvēən, -vyən\ *n* -s [obs. G or D; obs. G *bavian* (now *pavian*), fr. D *baviaan*, alter. of *babiaen* — more at BABIANA] **:** CHACMA

bav·in \'bavən\ *n* -s [origin unknown] *Brit* **:** a bundle of brushwood or kindling used for fuel or in fences or drains

baw·bee *or* **bau·bee** \'bä(,)bē, 'bȯ- ='=\ *n* -s [prob. after Alexander Orrok, laird of Sille*bawbe*, appointed mintmaster 1538] **1 :** an old Scottish billon coin issued by James V and Mary, Queen of Scots, at three halfpence **2 :** a Scottish copper coin worth sixpence issued by Charles II and William III **3 :** a unit of value equivalent to a bawbee coin ⟨half-*bawbee* coins were made⟩ **4 :** an English halfpenny **5 :** something of small value **:** TRIFLE ⟨no Scotsman who can write worth a ~ is ever quite happy until he has done a book about his glorious native tipple —Clifton Fadiman⟩

baw·cock \'bȯ,käk\ *n* -s [by folk etymology, fr. F *beau coq*, fr. *beau* fine + *coq* fellow, cock (bird)] **:** a fine fellow ⟨how now, my ~ —Shak.⟩

1bawd \'bȯd\ *n* -s [ME *bawde*, perh. fr. MF *baud* (fem. *baude*) bold, merry, of Gmc origin; akin to OHG *bald* bold — more at BOLD] **1** *obs* **:** GO-BETWEEN, PANDER **2 a :** one who keeps a house of prostitution **:** MADAM **b :** PROSTITUTE ⟨there will be ~s aplenty when we reach Saint-Domingue —Frank Yerby⟩

2bawd \'bäd, 'bȯd\ *n* -s [perh. short for *baudrons*] *chiefly Scot* **:** HARE

bawd·i·ly \'bȯdᵊlē, -dəlē, -li\ *adv* **:** in a bawdy manner

bawd·i·ness \-dēnəs\ *n* -ES **:** the quality or state of being bawdy ⟨his ribaldry and ~⟩

bawd·ry \'bȯdrē, -ri\ *n* -ES [ME *bawderie*, fr. *bawde* + *-erie* -ery] **1** *obs* **:** the practice or business of a bawd **2** *obs* **:** illicit intercourse **:** UNCHASTITY ⟨we must be married or we must live in ~ —Shak.⟩ **3 :** offensively suggestive, coarse, or obscene language **:** BAWDINESS ⟨smoking-room ~⟩

1bawdy \'bȯdē, -di\ *adj, usu* -ER/-EST [1*bawd* + *-y*] **:** of, relating to, or having the characteristics of a bawd **:** OBSCENE, LEWD, INDECENT, SMUTTY ⟨a ~ woman⟩ ⟨a ~ story⟩

2bawdy \"\ *n* -ES [prob. fr. 1*bawdy*] **:** BAWDRY 3 ⟨how can that . . . coachman talk so much ~ to that lean horse —Laurence Sterne⟩

bawdy house \'==,=\ *n* [2*bawdy* + *house*] **:** BROTHEL

1bawl \'bȯl\ *vb* -ED/-ING/-S [ME *baulen*, prob. of Scand origin; akin to Icel *baula* to low, LG *bolen*, and prob. to ON *bylja* to resound — more at BELLOW] *vi* **1 :** to cry out loudly and unrestrainedly **:** YELL, BELLOW ⟨as the circle of sage lessened the steers began to ~ —Zane Grey⟩ ⟨Herr Direktor ~*ed* at them, worked them to weariness, and reduced Tania to nervous exhaustion —Winifred Bambrick⟩ **2 :** to cry loudly or lustily esp. from distress **:** WEEP, WAIL ⟨he collapsed in an armchair in the lobby and ~*ed* . . . uncontrollably —E.J.Kahn⟩ ~ *vt* **1 :** to cry out at the top of one's voice ⟨the sergeant ~*ing* commands⟩ **:** SHOUT, PROCLAIM ⟨a hawker ~*ing* his wares⟩ **2 :** to reprimand loudly or severely **:** REBUKE, REPROVE, SCOLD — used with *out* ⟨he ~*ed* me out for letting such dangerously infectious material get on my fingers —Fredric Wertham⟩ *syn* see ROAR, SCOLD

2bawl \"\ *n* -s **:** a loud prolonged cry **:** OUTCRY ⟨despite all political ~s and bellows about cattle prices —*Time*⟩

baw·ley \'bȯlē, -li\ *or* **bawley boat** *n* -s [origin unknown] **:** a broad-beamed shallow-draft cutter-rigged fishing boat used esp. for shrimping around the Thames and Medway estuaries

bawn \'bȯn\ *n* -s [IrGael *badhūn* enclosure, bulwark, fr. MIr *bōdhūn*, fr. *bō* cow + *dūn* enclosure, fr. OIr, castle, fortified town; akin to OE *cū* cow — more at COW, TOWN] **:** an enclosure usu. of mud or stone walls about a farmhouse or castle in Ireland: as **a :** the fortified court of a castle **b :** a fold for livestock, esp. cattle

baw·neen \'bä,nēn\ *n* -s [IrGael *báinín* flannel, white flannel jacket, fr. *báin-*, *bán* white (fr. OIr *bān*) + *-ín* (dim. suffix); akin to Skt *bhāti* he shines — more at FANCY] **:** a man's work jacket of homemade undyed wool flannel worn esp. in Ireland

bax·ter \'bakstə(r)\ *n* -s [ME *baxestre*, *baxtere*, fr. OE *bæcestre*, fr. *bæcere* baker + *-stre* -ster — more at BAKER] **:** BAKER ⟨the excelling stewards, cunning ~s, excellent cooks —Sir Walter Scott⟩

1bax·te·ri·an \(')bak¦stirēən\ *adj, usu cap* [Richard *Baxter* †1691 Eng. Puritan scholar and writer + E *-ian*] **:** of or relating to Richard Baxter or his doctrines which sought to promote tolerance and restrain fanaticism by emphasizing certain fundamental tenets — **bax·te·ri·an·ism** \-ə,nizəm\ *n* -s

2baxterian \"\ *n* -s *usu cap* **:** an adherent or follower of Richard Baxter

1bay \'bā\ *adj* [ME, fr. MF *bai*, fr. L *badius*; akin to OIr *buide* yellow] **:** reddish brown **:** chestnut-colored — usu. used of a horse ⟨a ~ mare⟩

2bay \"\ *n* -s **1 :** an animal of a bay color; *specif* **:** a horse having a reddish brown body color with mane, tail, and points black ⟨a dashing pair of ~s⟩ — compare CHESTNUT **2 a :** a moderate brown that is deeper and slightly redder than auburn, redder, stronger, and slightly darker than chestnut brown, lighter, stronger, and very slightly redder than tobacco, and darker and slightly yellower and less strong than toast brown — called also *Malabar, mummy brown, Trotteur tan*

3bay \"\ *n* -s [ME, weir, millrace] **:** a bank to keep back water **:** DAM

4bay \"\ *vt* -ED/-ING/-S **:** DAM — usu. used with *up* or *back* ⟨~ water up⟩

5bay \"\ *n* -s [ME *baye*, fr. MF *baie*, fr. L *baca*, prob. of non-IE origin; akin to the source of Gk *Bakchos* Bacchus, a name of Dionysus, god of fruits including esp. the grape] **1** *obs* **:** a berry esp. of the laurel **2 a :** LAUREL 1a **b :** any of several shrubs or trees esp. of the genera *Magnolia, Myrica*, and *Gordonia* resembling the laurel **3 a :** a garland or crown esp. of laurel given as a prize for victory or excellence — often used in pl. **b :** HONOR, FAME, RENOWN — usu. used in pl. ⟨the patriot's honors and the poet's ~s —John Trumbull⟩

6bay \"\ *n* -s [ME, fr. MF *baée* open part, opening, fr. OF *baee*, fr. fem. of *baé*, past part. of *baer* to be open, gape — more at ABEYANCE] **1 :** a principal compartment of the walls, roof, or other part of a building or of the whole building ⟨in a Gothic cathedral the transverse arches and adjacent piers of the arcade divide the building into ~s —Helen Gardner⟩ **2 :** a main division of any structure: as **a :** a compartment in a barn ⟨chaff packed into a whole ~ of the barn —Adrian Bell⟩ **b :** BAY WINDOW **c :** a straight section of trench between two adjacent traverses **d :** the length of bridge between center and center of adjacent pontoons in a pontoon bridge **e :** the forward part of a ship on each side between decks often used as a ship's hospital **f** (1) **:** a longitudinal portion of an elongated structure (as a truss or wing) lying between two adjacent transverse members or walls (as uprights or ribs) of an airship (2) **:** any of several compartments in the fuselage of an aircraft; *esp* **:** BOMB BAY **3 a :** a vertical support or group of such supports on which various pieces of electronic apparatus are mounted — used esp. of radio and telephone equipment **b :** one of the units including a dipole and a reflector that comprise an antenna array

7bay \"\ *vb* -ED/-ING/-S [ME *baien*, alter. of *abaien*, fr. OF *abaiier*, of imit. origin] *vi* **1** *of a dog* **:** to bark (as at a thief or at the game that is pursued) esp. with deep prolonged tones ⟨the wakeful dogs did never cease to ~ —Edmund Spenser⟩ **2 :** to cry out loud and long **:** SHOUT ⟨the prosecutor ~*ed* for a death penalty —*Time*⟩ ~ *vt* **1 :** to bark at **:** set upon with barking ⟨the dogs ran mad and ~*ed* the sky — Clinton Scollard⟩ **2 :** to bring to bay **:** hold at bay ⟨hounds jumping a fox . . . run it down and ~ it —Hart Stilwell⟩ **3 :** to pursue with barking ⟨killed by the aid of dogs ~*ing* and driving him up a tree —C.R.Darwin⟩ **4 :** to utter in deep prolonged tones ⟨a deep voice ~*ed* a question —Anne Green⟩

8bay \"\ *n* -s [ME *baye*, *abay*, fr. OF *abai*, fr. *abaier*, v.] **1 :** the position of one (as an animal) forced to face an antagonist ⟨a handsome young huntsman facing a furious boar at ~ —H.A.Overstreet⟩ **2 :** the position of one checked (as in pursuit, growth, or development) ⟨such infections can be kept at ~ if a wound is kept clean —C.L.Boltz⟩ **3 :** the barking of dogs; *esp* **:** a deep prolonged barking of dogs closing in on their quarry ⟨in full ~ the hounds followed the trail⟩

9bay \"\ *n* -s *often attrib* [ME *baye*, fr. MF *baie*, perh. alter. of *baiée* open part, opening, fr. OF *baiee*, fr. *baee*] **1 a :** an inlet of the sea or other body of water usu. smaller than a gulf but of the same general character **b :** a large tract of water around which the land forms a curve **c :** a recess or inlet between capes or headlands **2 :** a small body of water set off from the main body: as **a :** a compartment containing water for a wheel **b :** the portion of a canal just outside the gates of a lock **3 :** any of various terrestrial formations felt to resemble a bay of the sea: as **a :** a recess of plain within a curve in a range of hills **b :** an opening of prairie in the edge of a forest **c :** CAROLINA BAY **d :** a recess (as in the forepart of a shrubbery) for the display of specimen or accent plants

10bay *n* -s [back-formation fr. earlier *bayse*, fr. MF *baies*, pl. — more at BAIZE] *obs* **:** BAIZE — usu. used in pl.

ba·ya \'bīyə, bī'yä\ *or* **baya weaver** *n* -s [Hindi *bayā*, *baiyā*] **:** an East Indian weaverbird (*Ploceus philippinus*) that feeds on seeds and insects and is sometimes destructive to grain crops

bayacura root *var of* BIACURU

baya·dere \'bī(y)ə,di(ə)r, -de(ə)r\ *n* -s [fr. *bayadere* Hindu dancing girl, fr. F *bayadère*, fr. Pg *bailadeira* female dancer, fr. *bailar* to dance, fr. LL *ballare* — more at BALL] **1 :** a fabric made with a design of horizontal stripes in strongly contrasted colors **2 a :** a design of horizontal stripes in strongly contrasted colors **b :** decoration applied in horizontal stripes (as in a printed pattern on textiles)

ba·ya·mo \bə'yä(,)mō\ *n* -s [fr. *Bayamo*, Cuba] **:** a violent thundersquall that occurs on the south coast of Cuba esp. near Bayamo, the gusts being modified foehn winds

bay antler \'bā-\ *or* **bes antler** \'bes-, 'bās-\ *or* **bez antler** \'bez-, 'bāz-\ *n* [*bay antler* by folk etymology fr. *bes antler*, *bez antler*; *bes antler*, *bez antler* fr. *bes-*, *bez-* secondary (fr. ME *bes-*, fr. MF, fr. L *bis-* twice) + E *antler* — more at BIS-] **:** the second tine from the base of a stag's antler — called also *bay point*; see ANTLER illustration

bay bar *or* **bay barrier** *n* [9*bay*] **:** a bank of sand or of sand and gravel deposited by waves and currents across the mouth of a bay so that the bay is no longer connected or is connected only by a narrow outlet with the main body of water — called also *baymouth bar*

bay-bay \'bī'ē,bī, 'bī,bī\ *n* -s [Island Carib *bai-bai*] **:** a tropical American shrub or small tree (*Byrsonima spicata*) with racemose flowers and fleshy fruits

bay bean *n* **1 :** a tropical vine (*Canavalia lineata*) growing on the seashore **2 :** one of the brown seeds of bay bean

bayberry \'=(,)==, '== — *see* BERRY\ *n* [5*bay* + *berry*] **1 a :** a West Indian tree (*Pimenta acris*) that is closely related to the allspice tree and that is a source of bay oil — called also *bay rum tree, Jamaica bayberry, wild cinnamon*; see BAY RUM **b :** the fruit of the bay tree **2 a :** any of several plants of the genus *Myrica* (esp. the eastern *M. pensylvanica*) common mostly near No. American coasts **b :** the fruit of wax myrtle **3 :** a variable color averaging a grayish green that is bluer, lighter, and stronger than slate green and yellower and lighter than average blue spruce

bayberry bark *n* **:** the bark of the root of either of two trees (*Myrica cerifera* and *M. pensylvanica*) used as a tonic and astringent — called also *candleberry bark*

bayberry family *n* **:** MYRICACEAE

bayberry gray *n* **:** a pale green that is bluer and very slightly duller than celadon gray, bluer and duller than spray green, and bluer and duller than aloes green

bayberry wax *or* **bayberry tallow** *n* **:** a fragrant green waxlike fat obtained from the wax myrtle and used esp. in making candles

bay bird *n* [9*bay*] **:** any of various limicoline birds that frequent the shores of bays and inlets

baybolt \'=,=\ *n* [6*bay* + *bolt*] **:** a bolt with a barbed shank

bay-breasted warbler \'=¦==-\ *n* [1*bay*] **:** an American warbler (*Dendroica castanea*) having the breast and crown of the head of the male a rich chestnut brown

bay bush \'=,=\ *n* [9*bay* + *bush*] **:** SWEET GALE

bay camphor *n* [9*bay*] **:** LAURIN

bay cat *n* [1*bay*] **:** a wildcat (*Felis bodia*) of Borneo and adjacent regions

bay cedar *n* [9*bay*] **1 :** a common Central American timber tree (*Guazuma ulmifolia*) with wood not unlike that of the American elm **2 :** any of several plants of the genus *Suriana* (esp. the tropical *S. maritima*) with alternate entire leaves and yellow flowers — called also *tassel plant*

bay-ce·dar family \'=¦==-\ *n* **:** SURIANACEAE

bay coot *n* [9*bay*] **:** an American scoter: as **a :** SURF SCOTER **b :** an immature or female white-winged scoter

bayed *past of* BAY

bay·er·ite \'bāə,rīt, 'bīə-,-\ *n* -s [fr. the name *Bayer* + E *-ite*] **:** an artificially prepared compound $Al(OH)_3$ that is a polymorph of gibbsite

bay·er process \'bāə(r)-, 'bīə-\ *n, usu cap B* [after Karl J. *Bayer* †1904 Ger. chemist] **:** a process for producing alumina from bauxite by digesting it in hot sodium hydroxide solution

bay·er's acid \'bīə(r)z-\ *n, usu cap B* [after Friedrich *Bayer* †1880 Ger. industrialist] **:** CROCEIN ACID

bay·er 205 \'bīə(r)¦tü,ō'fīv\ *n, usu cap* [after Friedrich *Bayer* and Co., 19th cent. Ger. chemical company] **:** SURAMIN

baye·ta \bī'ād·ə, -'yā-\ *n* -s [Sp, prob. fr. obs. F *baiette*, fr MF, dim. of *baie* baize — more at BAIZE] **1 :** BAIZE 1 **2 :** an imitation of baize woven by the Navahos

bay floe *n* [9*bay*] **:** a floe of bay ice

baygall \'=,=\ *n* [9*bay* + *gall*] **1 :** RED BAY **2 :** a tract of swampy land; *esp* **:** a low-lying tract of boggy or spongy land in the southern U.S. usu. overgrown with the inkberry and with bay trees

bay grass *n* [9*bay*] **:** LOVE GRASS

bayhead \'=,=\ *n* [9*bay* + *head*] **:** the part of a bay that is most remote from the larger body of water with which the bay is confluent

bayhead bar *or* **bay head barrier** *n* **:** a bank of sand or of sand and gravel deposited across a bay near its head often with a narrow breach to serve as outlet of the nearly confined water

bayhead beach *n* **:** a beach at the head of a bay

bay ice *n* [9*bay*] **:** sea ice that is formed in the shelter of a bay in the arctic or antarctic and that is relatively smooth since it is not subjected to wind or pressure

baying *pres part of* BAY

bay laurel *n* [5*bay*] **1 :** BAY TREE **2 :** OLEANDER **3 :** CHERRY LAUREL 1 **4 :** CALIFORNIA LAUREL

bay lavender *n* [9*bay*] **:** a fleshy shrub (*Mallotonia gnaphalodes*) of the family Boraginaceae of Florida, Central America, and the West Indies having silky gray leaves in clusters near the ends of the branches

bayl·don·ite \'bāldə,nīt\ *n* -s [John *Bayldon*, 19th cent. Englishman + E *-ite*] **:** a mineral $(Cu,Pb)_2(AsO_4)(OH)$ consisting of a lead copper arsenate and occurring in mammillary green masses

bay leaf *n* [5*bay*] **:** the dried leaf of the bay tree (*Laurus nobilis*) used as an herb in cooking

bay-leaf willow *or* **bay-leaved willow** \'=,=-\ *n* **:** BAY WILLOW 1

bay·ley·ite \'bālē,īt\ *n* -s [William S. *Bayley* †1943 Am. geologist + E *-ite*] **:** a mineral $Mg_2(UO_2)(CO_3)_3.18H_2O$ consisting of a rare hydrous magnesium uranyl carbonate of yellow color found in Arizona

bay lynx *n* [1*bay*] **:** a wildcat (*Lynx rufus*) that is the common wildcat of the eastern U.S. — see DESERT CAT

bay mackerel *n* [9*bay*] **:** a Spanish mackerel (*Scomberomorus maculatus*)

bay·man \'bāmən\ *n, pl* **baymen** [9*bay* + *man*] **:** one who lives or works on or about a bay

bay·mouth bar \'bā,maüth-\ *n* [9*bay* + *mouth*] **:** BAY BAR

bay myrtle *n* [5*bay*] **:** WAX MYRTLE

bay oak *n* [5*bay*] **:** ENGLISH OAK

bay·o·gou·la \,bī(y)ō'gülə, -(y)ə'-\ *n, pl* **bayogoula** *or* **bayogoulas** *usu cap* [Choctaw *Bāyuk-ókla*, lit., bayou people] **1 :** an extinct Muskogean people of southern Louisiana **2 :** a member of the Bayogoula people

bay oil *n* [5*bay*] **1 :** a yellow aromatic antiseptic essential oil obtained from the leaves of the West Indian bayberry and used in perfumes and esp. in bay rum — called also *myrcia oil* **2 :** a light-yellow essential oil obtained from the leaves of the California laurel — called also *California bay oil*

ba·yok \(')bī¦(y)ōk\ *also* **ba·yog** \-¦(y)ōg\ *n* -s [Tag *bayok*] **:** any of several Philippine timber trees of the genus *Pterospermum* (esp. *P. diversifolium*) the bark of which yields an inferior fiber and a dye

1bay·o·net \'bāənət, -,net, ¦bāə'net, *usu* -d·+V\ *n* -s *often attrib* [F *baïonnette*, fr. *Bayonne*, France, where first made + F *-ette*] **1 :** a steel blade made to be attached to or at the muzzle end of a shoulder arm and used esp. for stabbing and slashing in hand-to-hand combat **2 :** a pin that plays in and out of holes made to receive it and serving to engage or disengage parts (as of machinery) ⟨~ joint⟩ ⟨~ lamp base⟩

2bayonet \"\ *vb* **bayoneted** *also* **bayonetted**; **bayoneted** *also* **bayonetted**; **bayoneting** *also* **bayonetting**; **bayonets** *vt* **1 :** to stab with a bayonet ⟨we found their bodies *bayoneted* right through the blankets —Burtt Evans⟩ **2 :** to compel or drive by or as if by the bayonet ⟨troops to sabre and to ~ us into a submission —Edmund Burke⟩ ~ *vi* **:** to use a bayonet ⟨taught soldiers to ~ and to survive hand-to-hand combat⟩

bayonets 1

bayonet gauge *n* **:** a graduated stick or rod esp. for testing the depth of oil in a crankcase

bayonet grass *n* **:** a pale-green sedge (*Scirpus paludosus*) of alkaline marshes and shores chiefly of western No. America with ovoid to cylindric spikelets in clusters

bayonet mount *n* **:** a mount in which prongs or bayonets on the rim of the lens or lens accessory of a camera fit into slots in the camera to facilitate quick attachment (as in interchanging lenses)

bayonet plant *n* **:** YUCCA; *esp* **:** an Adam's needle (*Yucca filamentosa*)

bayonet stack *n* **:** an exhaust pipe whose open end is cut off diagonally and partly flattened and has the edges curved inward to increase the muffling effect

bay·ong \bī'ȯŋ, -'yȯŋ\ *also* **bay·on** \-'ȯn, -'yōn\ *n* -s [Tag & Bisayan *bayóng*, *bay-óng*] **:** a coarse sack of woven strips of pandanus or palm leaves used esp. in the Philippines

bay·ott \(')bī¦ät, -¦yät\ *n* -s [origin unknown] **:** PALOSAPIS

bay·ou \'bī,(y)ü; *S usu* -,(y)ō, *esp La also* -,(y)ə *or sometimes* bäyü\ *n* -s [LaF, fr. Choctaw *bayuk*] **1 :** a creek, secondary watercourse, or minor river that is tributary to another river or other body of water **2 :** any of various bodies of water: as **a :** a large stream or creek or a small river that is characterized by a slow or imperceptible current; *esp* **:** a sluggish stream that follows a tortuous course through alluvial lowlands, swamps, or plantations **b :** a clear brook or rivulet that rises in the hills esp. of northern Arkansas or southern Missouri **c :** an effluent usu. sluggish or stagnant branch of a main stream: as (1) **:** a natural canal connecting two bodies of water (2) **:** a by-channel of a river enclosing a low island (3) **:** a branch of a river discharging through a delta **d :** an intermittent, partly closed, or disused watercourse that is sluggish or stagnant: as(1) **:** a partly closed channel of a river delta (2) **:** *or* **bayou lake :** a lake or pool in an abandoned channel of a stream (3) **:** a swampy or miry offshoot of a lake or river subject to overflow (4) **:** an outlet for a coastal lake or swamp (5) **:** a slough in a salt marsh (6) **:** a shallow or stagnant inlet opening into a bay, lake, or river **e** (1) **:** an estuarial creek or inlet on the Gulf coast (2) **:** a small bay, open cove, or harbor (3) **:** a lagoon, lake, or bay esp. in a sea marsh or among salt-marsh islands **f** (1) **:** a passage connecting two bodies of open water (as bays) (2) **:** a navigable channel through sandbars or mud flats

bayou bass *n* **:** LARGEMOUTH BLACK BASS

bay plum *n* [9*bay*] **:** GUAVA 1, 2

bay point *n* [*bay* (antler)] **:** BAY ANTLER

bay poplar *n* [5*bay*] **1 :** TUPELO GUM **2 :** the wood of tupelo gum

bay rum *n* [5*bay*] **:** a fragrant liquid used for cosmetic and medicinal purposes, the original from the West Indies being prepared by distilling the leaves of the bayberry (*Pimenta acris*) with rum and that of the National Formulary being prepared from bay oil (sense 1), orange oil (sense a), pimenta oil, alcohol, and water

bay-rum tree \'=¦=-\ *n* **:** BAYBERRY 1a

bays *pl of* BAY, *pres 3d sing of* BAY

bay salt *n* [9*bay*] **:** SOLAR SALT

bay scallop *n* [9*bay*] **:** a small delicate-flavored scallop (*Pecten irradians*) formerly abundant in shallow water from Maine to the Gulf of Mexico but now greatly reduced by excessive commercial fishing

bay shark *n* [9*bay*] **:** a common shark (*Carcharhinus lamiella*) widespread in shallow waters of warm or temperate seas and very destructive to nets and fishes

bay shilling *n, usu cap B* [fr. Massachusetts *Bay* Colony, where it was coined] **:** PINE TREE SHILLING

bay stall *n* [6*bay*] **:** a seat fixed in a window bay

bay stater *n, usu cap B&S* [*Bay State*, nickname for Massachusetts + E *-er*] **:** a native or resident of Massachusetts — used as a nickname

bay stone *n* [perh. alter. of *base stone*] **:** a stone laid on the ground as part of a surface foundation for a structure
bay–top palmetto \'=,=-\ *n* [⁵*bay*] **:** a tropical American thatch palm (*Coccothrinax argentea*) with silvery leaves and black fruit
bay tree *n* [⁵*bay*] **1 :** LAUREL 1a **2 :** CALIFORNIA LAUREL **3 :** BAYBERRY 1a
bay willow *n* [⁵*bay*] **1 :** a European willow (*Salix pentandra*) with shining coriaceous leaves **2 :** FIREWEED b
bay window *n* [ME *baye wyndowe*, fr. *baye*, *bay* bay (compartment)] **1 :** a window or series of windows forming a bay or recess in a room and projecting outward from the wall in a rectangular, polygonal, or curved form — compare BOW WINDOW, ORIEL **2 :** a large protruding stomach esp. of a man **:** PAUNCH, POTBELLY ⟨men with weak hearts and bay windows⟩

bay window

bay–winged bunting \'=¦=-\ *n* [¹*bay*] **:** VESPER SPARROW
bay·wood \'bā+,-\ *n* [*Bay* of Campeche, Mexico + E *wood*] **:** MAHOGANY 1a (2)
ba·zaar *also* **ba·zar** \bə'zär, -'zȧ(r\ *n* -s [Per *bāzār*, alter. of MPer *bāchār*, fr. OPer *abēcharish*] **1 :** an Oriental market place or market that usu. consists of rows of shops or stalls where all kinds of goods are offered for sale ⟨the mock Rajah is reduced to going about the ~ and the villages soliciting alms —J.G.Frazer⟩ **2 a :** a place or establishment (as a large hall) for the sale of goods (as fine fabrics and odd knickknacks) ⟨days were spent in the big ~s where already the Christmas stocks were beginning to fill the counters —Winifred Bambrick⟩ **b :** a departmentalized retail store **:** DEPARTMENT STORE ⟨the great city ~ crushed its country rivals with branch stores —Edward Bellamy⟩ **3 :** a fair for the sale of useful and ornamental articles esp. for charitable or religious ends ⟨one of those nabobs . . . first thought of helping the local church by means of a ~ —Ernest Weekley⟩
ba·ze·ries cylinder \,baz(ə)'rē,-, '=(=),=,-\ *n*, *usu cap B* [after Etienne *Bazeries* †1931 Fr. cryptographer credited with its invention] **:** a cryptographic cylinder assembled of disks that can be rotated on a common shaft, each disk having on its periphery a different mixed alphabet and used for multiple substitution

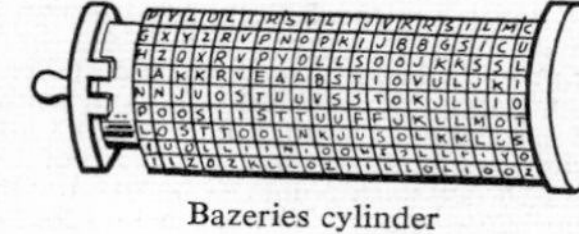
Bazeries cylinder

ba·zi·gar \,bäzə'gär\ *n*, *pl* **bazigar** *or* **bazigars** *usu cap* [Hindi *bāzīgar*, fr. Per, lit., player] **1 :** a gypsylike nomadic Muslim people in India **2 :** a member of the Bazigar people
ba·zoo \bə'zü\ *n* -s [origin unknown] **1 :** KAZOO **2** *slang* **:** MOUTH ⟨she's always blowing off her ~ —J.T.Farrell⟩ **3 :** a sound of disapproval **:** RASPBERRY ⟨the British ~ is higher and clearer than the Madison Square Garden variety —*Newsweek*⟩
ba·zoo·ka \bə'zükə\ *n* -s [fr. *bazooka*, a crude musical instrument made of pipes and a funnel and used by Bob Burns †1956 Am. comedian, prob. fr. *bazoo*] **1 :** a light portable usu. crew-served shoulder weapon consisting of an open-breech smooth-bore firing tube and used esp. to launch armor-piercing rockets **2 :** a rocket launcher placed on the underside of the wing of a warplane

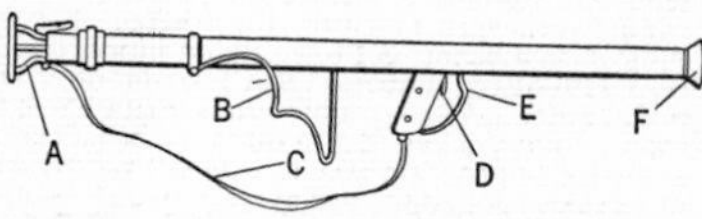

bazooka: *A* breech guard, *B* shoulder rest, *C* strap for carrying, *D* trigger *E* guard, *F* muzzle

ba·zoo·ka·man \-,man,-maa(ə)n\ *n*, *pl* **bazookamen :** a man armed with a bazooka
baz·zite \'ba,zīt, 'bät,sīt\ *n* -s [It, fr. Alessandro E. *Bazzi* †1929 Ital. engineer + It *-ite*] **:** a mineral consisting of a silicate of scandium and other rare-earth metals and occurring in small azure-blue hexagonal prisms
bb \'bēbē\ *or* **beebee** \"\ *n* -s *usu cap both Bs* [prob. fr. the letter *b*] **1 :** a shot pellet 0.18 inch in diameter for use in shotgun cartridges **2 :** a shot pellet 0.175 inch in diameter for use in a BB gun
BB *abbr*, *often not cap* **1** bail bond **2** ball bearing **3** balloon barrage **4** bankbook **5** base on balls **6** bearer bond **7** best of breed **8** bill book **9** blessed **10** blue book **11** break bulk
b battery \'bē,-\ *n*, *usu cap 1st B* **:** an electric battery connected in the plate circuit of an electron tube to cause flow of electron current in the tube — called also *plate battery*; compare A BATTERY, C BATTERY
bbb *abbr* **1** bed, breakfast, and bath **2** *usu cap all 3 Bs* better business bureau
bbc *abbr*, *often cap both Bs&C* **1** baseball club **2** basketball club
bb cap \'bēbē,-\ *n*, *usu cap both Bs* **:** a .22 caliber metallic cartridge about 0.43 inch long overall that consists of a rimfire case and a small (as about 20 grain) round-nose lead bullet and in which orig. the primer served as the propellant
bb gun *n*, *usu cap both Bs* **:** a smooth-bore air gun actuated by a spring-loaded plunger that upon release from the cocked position compresses the air behind the pellet and propels it from the tube — compare AIR RIFLE 1
bbl *abbr* barrel
BBT *abbr* basal body temperature
BC *abbr* **1** [It *basso continuo*] thorough bass **2** battery commander **3** before Christ **4** bicycle club **5** board of control **6** boat club **7** borough council **8** bowling club **9** broadcast
BCD *abbr* bad conduct discharge
BCE *abbr* before the Common Era
BCG *abbr* bacillus Calmette-Guérin
bcg vaccine \¦bē,sē'jē-\ *n*, *usu cap B&C&G* **:** a vaccine prepared from a living attenuated strain of tubercle bacilli and used to vaccinate human beings against tuberculosis
bch *abbr* bunch
BCL \¦bē,sē'el\ *abbr or n* -s **:** a bachelor of civil law
BCL *abbr* broadcast listener
bcn *abbr* beacon
b complex \'bē,-\ *n*, *usu cap B* [by shortening] **:** VITAMIN B COMPLEX
bc soil \(')bē'sē,-\ *n*, *usu cap B&C* **:** a soil with a profile having only B-horizons and C-horizons
bd *abbr* **1** band **2** board **3** bond **4** bound **5** boundary **6** brindled **7** bundle
BD *abbr or n* -s **:** a bachelor of divinity
BD *abbr*, *often not cap* **1** back dividend **2** bank draft **3** barrels per day **4** bills discounted **5** bomb disposal **6** brought down
bde *abbr* brigade
bdell- *or* **bdello-** *comb form* [F & NL, fr. Gk, fr. *bdella*] **:** leech ⟨*Bdelloura*⟩ ⟨*Bdelloida*⟩ ⟨*bdellotomy*⟩
-bdel·la \-b+'delə\ *n comb form* -s [NL, fr. Gk *bdella*] **:** leech — esp. in generic names in helminthology ⟨Malaco*bdella*⟩
bdel·li·dae \'delə,dē\ *n pl*, *cap* [NL, fr. *Bdella*, type genus (fr. Gk *bdella* leech) + *-idae*] **:** a family of mites (order Acarina) comprising the snout mites that feed on insects and on other mites
bdel·li·um \'delēəm, -lyəm\ *n* -s [ME, fr. L, fr. Gk *bdellion*, perh. of Semitic origin; akin to Heb *bĕdhōlah*] **:** a gum resin obtained from various trees of the genus *Commiphora* that is similar to myrrh and used for the same purposes — compare BISABOL
bdel·lod·ri·lus \de'lädrələs\ *n*, *cap* [NL, fr. *bdell-* + Gk *drilos* earthworm] **:** a genus of small leechlike oligochaete worms parasitic on the gills of crayfishes
¹**bdel·loid** \'de,lȯid\ *adj* [*bdell-* + *-oid*] **:** like or relating to a leech
²**bdelloid** \"\ *n* -s **:** LEECH
bdel·loi·da \de'lȯidə\ [NL, fr. *bdell-* + *-oida*] *syn of* BDELLOIDEA
bdel·loi·dea \-'lȯidēə\ *n pl*, *cap* [NL, alter. of *Bdelloida*] **:** an order of Rotifera comprising forms that swim freely by means of the ciliated disk and also creep like leeches
bdel·lo·nemertea \¦delō+\ *n pl*, *cap* [NL, fr. *bdell-* + *Nemertea*] **:** an order of Nemertea (class Enopla) comprising short thick-bodied forms with a large posterior sucker and no eyes or cerebral organ — see MALACOBDELLA
bdel·lo·nys·sus \,delə'nisəs\ *n*, *cap* [NL, fr. *bdell-* + *-nyssus* (fr. Gk *nyssein*, *nyttein* to prick, sting) — more at NUMEN] **:** a genus of mites (family Dermanyssidae) parasitic on vertebrates and including serious pests (as *B. bursa* and *B. sylviarum*) of domestic fowl and the tropical rat mite
bdel·lou·ra \de'lürə, -'laù-\ *n*, *cap* [NL, fr. *bdell-* + Gk *oura* tail; akin to Gk *orrhos* buttocks — more at ASS] **:** a genus (the type of the family Bdellouridae) of triclad flatworms that live in the gills of the horseshoe crab
bdg *abbr* binding
BDI *abbr*, *often not cap* **1** both dates inclusive **2** both days inclusive
bdl *abbr* bundle
bdr *abbr*, *often cap B* **1** bombardier **2** brigadier
bdry *abbr* boundary
BDS *abbr* bomb disposal squad
bdy *abbr* boundary
¹**be** \(¦)bē, ,bi\ *vb*, *past 1st & 3d sing* **was** \(¦)wəz, (¦)wäz *also* (¦)wȯz\ *or dial* **were** *see below*\ *or* **war** \(¦)wär\; *2d sing* **were** \,wə(r); ¦wər, + V ¦wər-, ¦wə, + V " *or* ¦wər- *also* ¦wər; *archaic or Brit* (¦)w\|a(ə)(r *or* \|e(ə)r *or* \|a(ə *or* \|eə\ *or dial & archaic* **was** *or dial* **war** (with *you*) *or archaic* **wast** (with *thou*) \,wəst, (¦)wäst *also* (¦)wȯst\ *or* **wert** (with *thou*) \,wə(r)t, ¦wər\|t, (¦)wə\|t, (¦)wəi\|t, *usu* \|d·+V\ *pl* **were** *or substand & archaic* **was** *or dial* **war**; *past subjunctive* **were** *or substand & archaic* **was** *or archaic 2d sing* **wert** (with *thou*); *past part* **been** \(¦)bin, ,bən; ben (*in standard speech more often unstressed or with secondary stress than with primary stress*); *Brit usu & US sometimes* (¦)bēn\ *or dial* **ben** \(¦)ben\ *pres part* **be·ing** \¦bēiŋ, ¦bēeŋ, *rapid* (¦)bēŋ\ *or dial Brit & archaic* **been** \(¦)bēn, ¦bēən\ *pres 1st sing* **am** \,əm, (¦)am *also* (¦)aa(ə)m; *after "I" often* m\ *or dial* **is** *or* **be**; *2d sing* **are** (with *you*) \,ə(r), (¦)är, (¦)ȧ(r; *after a vowel-final pronoun often* r\ *or archaic* **art** (with *thou*) \,ə(r)\|t, (¦)är\|t, (¦)ȧ\|t, +V *usu* \|d·\ *or dial* **be** *or* **is** (with *you*) *or dial Brit* **beest** (with *thou*) \(¦)bēst, ¦bēəst\ *or* **bist** (with *thou*) \(¦)bist\ *3d sing* **is** \(¦)iz, ,əz; *after vowels & after voiced consonants other than* z, zh, & j: *often* z; *after voiceless consonants other than* s, sh, & ch: *often* s\ *or dial Brit* **be** *or substand* **is** *or dial & archaic* **be** *or archaic* **been** *the last like past part* BEEN\ *pres subjunctive* **be** *or obs 2d sing* **beest** (with *thou*) [ME *been*, fr. OE *bēon*; akin to OHG *bim* am, ON *būa* to live, dwell, Goth *bauan*, L *fui* I have been, *futurus* about to be, *fieri* to become, Gk *phyein* to bring forth, *phynai* to be born, be, Skt *bhavati* he is] *vi* **1 a :** to equal in meaning **:** have the same connotation (sense 3) as ⟨God *is* love⟩ ⟨January *is* the first month⟩ ⟨let *x* ~ 10⟩ **:** represent symbolically ⟨the seven lampstands *are* the seven churches —Rev 1:20 (RSV)⟩ **b :** to constitute the same idea or object as **:** have individual identity with ⟨the first person I met *was* my brother⟩ ⟨the pianist himself *was* the composer of the piece⟩ ⟨$50 *was* all I had⟩ **c :** to constitute the same class as ⟨these three books *are* the authoritative works on the president's life⟩ **d :** to have a meaning that includes or implies the meaning of ⟨fish *are* vertebrates⟩ ⟨red *is* a color⟩ **:** have a (specified) qualification or characterization ⟨the leaves *are* green⟩ ⟨this book *is* heavy⟩ **e :** to belong as an individual to the class of ⟨the fish you caught *was* a trout⟩ **f :** to belong as a class to the larger class of ⟨some animals with horns and divided hoofs *are* graminivorous animals⟩ — used regularly in senses 1a through 1f as the copula of simple predication **g :** SIGNIFY **:** amount to ⟨her death *was* nothing to him⟩ **h :** to show oneself as an outstanding example of — used with main stress in spoken sentences ⟨the doctor pleased the parents by commenting, "That *is* a baby"⟩ **i :** to constitute genuinely **:** actualize well the type of ⟨one of the few great elegies which *are* elegies —Douglas Bush⟩ **j :** to seem to consist of **:** show oneself gripped or dominated by (a feeling) ⟨she *was* all scorn at the proposition⟩ **:** become completely covered with ⟨road *was* all mud⟩ **2 a :** to exist either absolutely or in relations or under conditions specified **:** have an objective existence **:** have reality or actuality **:** LIVE ⟨Thee, which *wert* and *art* and evermore shalt *be* —Reginald Heber⟩ ⟨I think, therefore I *am*⟩ — often used with *there* ⟨once upon a time there *was* a knight⟩ ⟨there *is* a wreck ahead⟩ **b :** to have, maintain, or occupy a place, situation, or position **:** show a certain characteristic — often used with a prepositional phrase ⟨the book *is* on the table⟩ ⟨he *was* at ease⟩ **c :** to remain unmolested, unbothered, or uninterrupted — used only in infinitive form ⟨let him ~ ; stop pestering him⟩ **d :** HAPPEN, OCCUR **:** take place ⟨the concert *was* last night⟩ ⟨where will the meeting ~⟩ **e** *archaic* **:** BELONG, PERTAIN ⟨to thine and Albany's issue ~ this perpetual —Shak.⟩ **f** (1) **:** to come or go **:** JOURNEY ⟨we will ~ on our way shortly⟩ ⟨have you *been* home since Christmas⟩ (2) **:** to make a stay **:** show oneself or be present ⟨they will ~ in town all week⟩ ⟨*was* your sister at the party last night⟩ — not used in the present; use of the past tense followed by *to* ⟨I *was* to town yesterday⟩ often considered nonstandard **g :** to come around in due course often in following a schedule or appointed round — used only in perfect forms ⟨has the postman *been* this morning⟩ **h** *substand* **:** ACT — used only in the perfect; used as an intensive ⟨see what you have *been* and done⟩ **3** *now dial Brit* **:** to stand good for expense (as in a treat) ⟨offering to ~ his friend's dinner⟩ ~ *verbal auxiliary* **1 :** to undergo an action — used with the past participle of transitive verbs as a passive-voice auxiliary ⟨the money *was* found⟩ ⟨German *is* spoken here⟩ ⟨the house is *being* built⟩ **2 :** to perform a continuous action **:** be supposed to perform a future action — used as the auxiliary of the present participle in the so-called progressive tenses, usu. expressing continuous action ⟨he *is* reading⟩ ⟨I have *been* sleeping⟩ ⟨the house *is* being built⟩ but sometimes in present-tense form expressing future noncontinuous action ⟨he *is* leaving tomorrow⟩ **3 :** to have changed place or condition as a result of completing an action — used with the past participle of certain intransitive verbs as an auxiliary forming archaic perfect tenses ⟨Christ *is* risen from the dead —1 Cor 15:20 (DV)⟩ ⟨the minstrel boy to the war *is* gone —Thomas Moore⟩ **4 :** become supposed **:** become destined — used with the infinitive with *to* to express futurity, arrangement in advance, or obligation ⟨I *am* to interview him today⟩ ⟨he *was* to become one of the most famous men of his century⟩ ⟨you *are* to repay the loan in monthly installments⟩ — usu. not used in the form of an infinitive or participle **5 :** to undergo a continuous action **:** be in the process of — used in a passive sense with the present participle or with the gerund preceded by the prefix *a-* or the preposition *a* ⟨while the ark *was* building —1 Pet 3:20 (NCE)⟩ ⟨when the ark *was* a building —1 Pet 3:20 (DV)⟩; now usu. replaced by the passive construction with *being* followed by the past participle, as in 1 and 2 — **be oneself :** to act, talk, or comport oneself in a usual or fitting manner **:** show that one has attained to a suitable self-realization — **to be sure :** GRANTED, ADMITTEDLY
²**be** *var of* BEE
be- *prefix* [ME, fr. OE *be-*, *bi-*; akin to OE *bī* by, near, OHG *bi-* be-, *bī* by, near, Goth *bi-* be-, *bi* by, about, at — more at BY] **1 :** on **:** around **:** over ⟨*be*daub⟩ ⟨*be*smear⟩ **2 :** to a great or greater degree **:** thoroughly — esp. in intensive verbs formed from simple verbs ⟨*be*cudgel⟩ ⟨*be*fuddle⟩ ⟨*be*smite⟩ ⟨*be*spatter⟩ ⟨*be*rate⟩ **3 :** excessively **:** ostentatiously — in intensive verbs formed from simple verbs ⟨*be*deck⟩ ⟨*be*laud⟩ and in adjectives based on adjectives ending in *-ed* ⟨*be*ribboned⟩ ⟨*be*furbelowed⟩ **4 :** about **:** to **:** at **:** upon **:** against **:** across — in transitive verbs formed from intransitive simple verbs ⟨*be*stride⟩ ⟨*be*speak⟩ ⟨*be*croak⟩ **5 :** make **:** cause to be **:** treat as — in verbs formed from adjectives or nouns ⟨*be*little⟩ ⟨*be*numb⟩ ⟨*be*fool⟩ ⟨*be*friend⟩ **6 :** call or dub esp. excessively — in verbs formed from nouns ⟨*be*lady⟩ ⟨*be*rascal⟩ ⟨*be*doctor⟩ **7 :** affect, afflict, treat, provide, or cover with esp. excessively — in verbs formed from nouns ⟨*be*famine⟩ ⟨*be*devil⟩ ⟨*be*glue⟩ ⟨*be*blood⟩ and sometimes only in the form of a past participle or adjective ending in *-ed* ⟨*be*capped⟩ ⟨*be*cobwebbed⟩
Bé *abbr* Baumé
BE *abbr* **1** band elimination **2** bill of entry **3** bill of exchange **4** board of education **5** Buddhist Era
Be *symbol* beryllium
¹**beach** \'bēch\ *n* -ES [origin unknown] **1 :** shore pebbles **:** SHINGLE **2 a :** a gently sloping shore of an ocean, sea, or lake or the bank of a river that is covered by sand, sand and gravel, or larger rock fragments, is usu. orig. water-borne, and is typically devoid of much vegetation **:** STRAND; *also* **:** the deposit of sand, gravel, or rock fragments along a shore **b :** a seashore area ⟨a vacation at the ~⟩ **c** *in New Jersey* **:** a low sand island along the coast **d :** a stretch of sand placed beside a bathing area for the bathers' pleasure and recreation ⟨putting in a ~ by the pool⟩ **e :** naval or mercantile offices or instrumentalities ashore ⟨the ~ handed over the sealed orders to the captain⟩ **f :** an African trading or shopping center not necessarily located near a shoreline **3 :** a light olive gray to light grayish olive that is very slightly redder and paler than sage gray — called also *chip*, *smoke yellow* — **on the beach 1 :** UNEMPLOYED, DOWN-AND-OUT **:** badly needing money or work **:** STRANDED **2 :** assigned to a post ashore ⟨a living allowance for officers *on the beach*⟩
²**beach** \"\ *vt* -ED/-ING/-ES **1 :** to run or haul (a ship) ashore or aground esp. when mooring, anchoring, or docking is unfeasible or when quick landing of supplies and personnel is required ⟨the mutineers ~*ed* the ship on the island⟩ ⟨~*ing* the landing craft in the assault⟩ **2 a :** to force or drive ashore or aground usu. with considerable damage ⟨the storm ~*ed* half the fleet⟩ ⟨sinking one enemy ship and ~*ing* another⟩ **b :** to draw ashore or moor and relegate to desuetude
³**beach** \"\ *adj* **:** on, of, or relating to a beach; *often* **:** designed for wear on a beach ⟨lounging casually in a ~ shirt⟩
beach apple *n* **1 :** a fig marigold (*Carpobrotus chilensis* syn. *Mesembryanthemum chilense*) native to southern Africa — called also *beach strawberry*, *sea fig* **2 :** the fruit of the beach apple plant
beach aster *n* **:** SEASIDE DAISY
beach ball *n* **:** a large inflated ball for use at the beach
beach bird *n* **:** any of various limicoline birds (as the knot) that frequent beaches
beachboy \'=,=\ *n* **:** a male beach attendant; *esp* **:** an entertainer and instructor in surfing and swimming
beach buggy *n* **:** a motor vehicle with oversize tires for use on sand beaches
beach·comb \'=+,kōm\ *vb* [back-formation fr. *beachcomber*] *vi* **:** to live or act as a beachcomber **:** engage in a beachcomber's activities or lack of them ~ *vt* **:** to search (an area) as a beachcomber **:** find by a beachcomber's procedure
beach·comb·er \-mə(r)\ *n* -s **1 :** a casual often in So. Pacific areas who may ship as a short-haul sailor or engage in short-term work or irregular ventures in coastal areas ashore **2 a :** a disreputable unemployed or derelict seaman **:** a drifter or loafer usu. along the seacoast; *esp* **:** a white man (as an American or Britisher) leading a bum's existence in the So. Pacific **b :** a seashore lounger or vacationist **c :** a hanger-on in Bohemian circles **3 :** one who searches along a shore for worthwhile flotsam, refuse, or specimens; *sometimes* **:** WRECKER
beach crab *n* **:** any of various crabs living on seabeaches; *esp* **:** a common tropical American grapsoid (*Sesarma ricordi*)
beach cusp *n* **:** sand and gravel deposits formed by wave action into points that project seaward along a coast
beach flea *n* **:** any of numerous amphipod crustaceans of the family Orchestiidae living on seabeaches and leaping like fleas
beach fly *n* **:** any of certain two-winged flies that frequent beaches; *esp* **:** any biting fly (as a horsefly) encountered in such an area
beach gear *n* **:** rope, winches, and other equipment for handling boats on a beach
beach goldenrod *n* **:** SEASIDE GOLDENROD
beach grass *n* **:** any of several tough strongly rooted grasses that grow on exposed sandy shores; *esp* **:** a perennial European grass (*Ammophila arenaria*) with hard creeping rhizomes that is widely planted to bind sandy blowing slopes — called also *marram grass*, *sand reed*
beach·head \'bēch,hed\ *n* **1 :** an area on a hostile shore seized and defended to secure further landing of troops and supplies **2 :** an initial advance position or foothold to be used as vantage ground for extending to new areas
beach heather *n* **:** a plant of the genus *Hudsonia*; *esp* **:** a small heathlike plant (*H. tomentosa*) growing on beaches in northeastern No. America
beaching gear *n* **:** a wheeled cradle that may be attached to the hull of a seaplane for hauling it ashore and moving it on land
beach–la–mar \¦bēchlə¦mär\ *n* -s *usu cap* [by folk etymology] **:** BÊCHE-DE-MER 2
beach·less \'bēchləs\ *adj* **:** being without a beach
beachline \'=,=\ *n* **:** shoreline esp. if marked by a series of well-developed beaches
beach·man \'=mən, -,man\ *n*, *pl* **beachmen 1 :** a person who works (as at odd jobs) on a beach **2 :** a worker who hauls flying boats from the water by means of special beaching gear
beachmaster \'=,==\ *n* **1 :** an officer in charge of disembarkation of troops and munitions **2 :** a bull fur seal on its breeding ground
beach morning glory *n* **:** a creeping fleshy glabrous herb (*Ipomoea pes-caprae*) occurring on sandy beaches throughout the tropics and subtropics and having rounded leaves notched at the apex and purple flowers
beach mouse *n* **:** a pale buff-colored field mouse (*Peromyscus polionotus*) occurring as distinct subspecies on sandy beaches of the Florida east coast and adjacent islands
beach pea *n* **:** a wild pea (*Lathyrus maritimus*) with long tough roots and purple flowers that is found along seashores of the north temperate zone and that is useful as a sand binder
beach pine *n* **:** LODGEPOLE PINE a
beach plover *n* **:** any of certain plovers or sandpipers that frequent beaches (as the sanderling)
beach plum *n* **1 :** a shrub (*Prunus maritima*) of the seacoast of northeastern No. America with showy white flowers and edible fruit often used for jam **2 :** the dark purple fruit of the beach plum
beach pool *n* **:** a pool of water between two beaches or two beach ridges **:** a more or less transitory pool that adjoins a lake and is often the result of wave action — compare TIDE POOL
beach ridge *n* **:** a ridge of sand and gravel built up along the beach by wave action
beach robin *n* **:** ³KNOT
beach–sap \'bēch,sap\ *n* **:** a sea rocket (*Cakile chapmani*) with pale purple flowers and jointed pods that is found along the Gulf coast
beach seine *n* **:** a long net that is made fast to the shore at one end and then circled about a school of fish and drawn ashore
beach strawberry *n* **1 :** BEACH APPLE **2 :** CHILEAN STRAWBERRY
beach tan *n* **:** SEDGE 3
beach umbrella *n* **:** a large umbrella used to shade part of a beach, patio, or recreation area
beach wagon *n* **:** STATION WAGON
beach wormwood *n* **:** an herb (*Artemisia stelleriana*) with greyish foliage found along the eastern coast of the U.S. and used as an ornamental plant — called also *dusty miller*
beachy \'bēchē\ *adj* -ER/-EST **:** covered with pebbles, shingle, or sand
¹**bea·con** \'bēkən\ *n* -s [ME *beken*, fr. OE *bēacen* sign; akin to OHG *bouhhan* sign and perh. to Gk *phainein* to show — more at FANCY] **1 :** a signal fire commonly on a hill, tower, or pole **2 a :** a lighthouse or other signal mark ashore or in shoal water usu. to guide mariners **b :** an unattended light or other signaling device for the guidance of aviators **c :** a fixed automatic radio transmitter emitting characteristic signals for the guidance of aircraft **d :** a traffic light or other signal serving a similar purpose **3 a** *Brit* **:** a high hill with a conspicuous outlook **b** *Brit* **:** a watchtower or signaling station **c :** a pole that marks **4 :** a very clear or conspicuous signal or indication **:** a monumental indication often serving as a source of

light and inspiration ⟨the ~ to the oppressed of all countries —Adrienne Koch⟩ ⟨a ~ for creative artists the world over —A.R.Katz⟩ **5** *heraldry* **:** a fire basket usu. depicted inflamed set up on a pole against which a ladder leans **:** CRESSET

2**beacon** \"\ *vb* -ED/-ING/-s *vt* **1 a :** to light as a beacon ⟨fires where the hedgers had been at work ~*ed* the darkness —Adrian Bell⟩ **b :** to give light to **:** inspire and guide **:** summon to achievement ⟨one truth would dimly ~ me —Robert Browning⟩ **2 :** to furnish or mark with a beacon ⟨~ the headland⟩ ~*vi* **:** to shine as a beacon ⟨then Adventure ~*ed* from far off, and his heart leapt —Maurice Hewlett⟩

bea·con·age \-(,)nij\ *n* -s **:** charges levied for the maintenance of beacons

bea·con·ite \-,nīt\ *n* -s *usu cap* [A *Beacon* to the Society of Friends, book by Isaac Crewdson †1844 Eng. religious leader + E *-ite*] **:** a member of an English party of Quakers that were led by Isaac Crewdson to secede from other English Quakers in 1836 on the basis that the doctrines of the latter were scripturally unsound

bea·con·less \ˈbēkənləs\ *adj* **:** being without a beacon

bea·con·ry \ˈbēkənrē\ *n* -ES **:** the technique of using radio beacons

1**bead** \ˈbēd\ *n* -s *often attrib* [ME *bede* prayer, prayer bead, fr. OE *bed, gebed* prayer; akin to OHG *beta* request, *gibet* prayer, Goth *bida* prayer, OE *biddan* to entreat, pray — more at BID] **1 a** *obs* **:** PRAYER, SUPPLICATION — usu. used in pl. **b beads** *pl* **:** a series of prayers and devotional meditations made with the use of a rosary ⟨saying his ~*s* in solitude⟩ **2 :** a small often round piece of stone, glass, shell, wood, metal, or other material that is pierced for threading on a string or wire ⟨the ~*s* of the necklace⟩ ⟨~*s* for trade with the natives⟩ ⟨children stringing ~*s*⟩; *specif* **:** a bead of a rosary **3 beads** *pl* **a :** ROSARY ⟨~*s* blessed by the bishop⟩ **b :** a necklace of beads or pearls **4 :** a drop like a bead or a small body shaped like a ball ⟨letting the ~*s* of lead pour as easily as sand —Kay Boyle⟩: **a :** a drop of sweat or blood ⟨~*s* of pain broke out on her forehead —Ellen Glasgow⟩ **b :** a minute bubble formed in or on a beverage; *specif* **:** the bubbles that are formed on the surface of a distilled beverage when it is shaken and that by their number and duration may indicate proof and quality ⟨this whiskey holds a good ~⟩ **c :** a small knob of metal on a firearm near the muzzle used for a front sight in aiming ⟨to draw a ~ on a target⟩ **:** AIM ⟨to take a ~ on a man⟩ **d :** a blob of weld metal or a continuous deposit of weld metal blobs **e :** the globule of precious metal obtained by the cupellation process in assaying **f :** a glassy drop of flux (as borax or microcosmic salt) used as a solvent and color test for several metallic oxides and salts (as of iron, manganese) that is formed by fusion in the loop of a usu. platinum wire **g :** one of a series of tiny bosses or raised dots on a coin, token, medal, or plate **5 :** a projecting rim, band, or molding: **a :** a small salient molding of rounded surface, continuous or broken, the section being usu. an arc of a circle — compare ASTRAGAL 1 **b :** any of various pieces or members (as a parting strip) usu. having a section somewhat like such a molding **c :** a similarly rounded or cordlike projecting band (as the exposed portion of the headband of a book or a projecting band round a metal box) **d :** one of the strips around the inner periphery of a pneumatic tire shaped often with external ridge or rounded fold for engaging the rim of a wheel **e :** a wood or metal strip embedded in the plaster at a salient corner of a wall and serving as a guide and support for the plaster **f :** an extended rounded rim or flange (as on a pot or kettle) **g :** a ledge below the finish on a glass jar or bottle to aid in removal of pry-off closure **h :** a groove or rounded elevation on the surface of a metal can, fiber drum, glass jar, or metal closure to improve appearance and to stiffen **i :** the outer edge of circled heading that fits into the croze of barrel staves **j :** a raised ridge on sheet metal

beads 5a: *A* cock bead; *B, C* quirk beads; *D* double-quirked bead

2**bead** \"\ *vb* -ED/-ING/-s *vt* **1 :** to trim, furnish, or adorn with beads or beading **:** cover with beads **2 :** to string together like beads ⟨row houses ~*ed* together⟩ **3 :** to cause beads to develop on ⟨her face was flushed and rosy, ~*ed* with small particles of rain —Thomas Wolfe⟩ ⟨tears were ~*ing* Dorinda's lashes —Ellen Glasgow⟩ **4 :** to form a bead on (as sheet metal) ~ *vi* **1 :** to form into a bead **:** develop as beads ⟨sweat ~*ed* on his forehead —Hartley Howard⟩ **2 :** to take aim ⟨the major ~*ed* too low⟩

bead and butt *n* **:** framing in which the panels are flush, having beads stuck or run upon the two edges with the grain

bead and flush *n* **:** beadflush work

bead and reel *n* **:** a round convex molding with disks alternating singly or in pairs with oblong beads

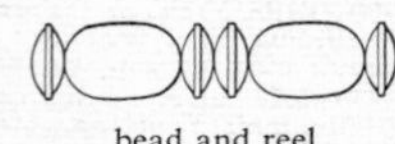
bead and reel

bead chain *n* **:** a chain formed of small hollow metal spheres connected by short dumbbell-shaped metal links that is used esp. in electric pull sockets and switches

bead curtain *n* **:** a curtain formed of vertical strands threaded with beads

bead·ed \ˈbēdəd\ *adj* **:** having the edges skived thin and turned in to present a finished edge — used of shoes

beaded esker *n* **:** an esker with numerous expansions and contractions in width

beaded lightning *also* **bead lightning** *n* **:** a streak of lightning that seems to be broken up into short segments

beaded lizard *n* **:** GILA MONSTER

beaded ribs *n pl* **:** ribs with beading (sense f)

bea·del \ˈbēdᵊl\ *archaic var of* BEADLE

bead·er \ˈbēdə(r)\ *n* -s **1 a :** a tool or machine for making a bead (as about the end of a boiler tube) **b :** BEADING PLANE **2 :** a worker who attaches beads or finishes with beading **3 a :** one that sews together pieces of leather or fabric on a machine which sews with a zigzag stitch **b :** one that machine-sews around collar neckbands to make the seam between collar and neckband flat **c :** one that sews beads by hand onto dresses and other articles of theatrical wardrobes

bead·flush \ˈbēd,fləsh\ *adj, of a panel or paneling work* **:** surrounded by a bead usu. worked in the edges of the frame so that panel, bead, and frame are flush at their front faces

beadier *comparative of* BEADY

beadiest *superlative of* BEADY

bead·i·ly \ˈbēdᵊlē, -dəlē\ *adv* [*beady* + *-ly*] **:** in a beady manner

bead·ing *n* -s [1*bead* + *-ing*] **:** a part or piece consisting of a bead or beads **:** beaded material **:** BEADS **:** the result of beading: **a :** a molding or rounded projecting band **b :** an edging of small loops used on lace or ribbon **c :** an insertion or edging with openings through which ribbon, tape, or elastic may be laced **d :** decorative bead trimming on fabric or leather **e :** a bead design on a coin, token, or medal **f :** the beadlike nodules occurring in rickets at the junction of the ribs with their cartilages — called also *rachitic rosary*

beading plane *n* **:** a carpenter's plane with a cutter having a semicircular concave edge for making beads on molding

bea·dle \ˈbēdᵊl\ *n* -s [ME *bedel, bidel, budel,* fr. OE *bydel;* akin to OHG *butil* bailiff, OE *bēodan* to offer, command — more at BID] **1 :** a herald or messenger esp. in the service of a law court **2 :** a parish officer whose duties include ushering and preserving order at church services **3 :** a synagogue officer who maintains order

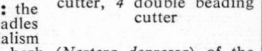

beading plane: *1* cutter, *2* fence, *3* single beading cutter, *4* double beading cutter

bea·dle·dom \-ldəm\ *n* -s **:** the characteristics felt to mark beadles as a class; *usu* **:** stupid officialism

bead plant *n* **:** a creeping herb (*Nertera depressa*) of the southern hemisphere cultivated for its tiny leaves and orange-colored fruit

bead pointing *n* **:** masonry pointing that forms a protruding bead

beadroll \ˈ=,=\ *n* [1*bead* + *roll*] **1** *archaic* **:** a list of persons for whom prayers were to be said **2 :** an often long list or series of names **:** CATALOG ⟨the ~ of substantive and noteworthy poems in English —George Saintsbury⟩ **3 :** ROSARY **4 :** a bookbinder's finishing roll designed to impart a bead pattern

bead-ruby \ˈ=,==\ *n* **:** FALSE LILY OF THE VALLEY

beads *pl of* BEAD, *pres 3d sing of* BEAD

bead saw *n* **:** a short saw with a curved blade and backward-pointing teeth that is used for scoring grooves in window and door frames in preparation for weatherstrips

beads·man *also* **bedes·man** \ˈbēdzmən\ *or* **bede·man** \-dmən\ *n, pl* **beadsmen** [ME *bedeman,* fr. *bade* prayer, prayer bead + *man* — more at BEAD] **1** *archaic* **:** one who prays for the soul of another — used until the 17th century in England in letters as a complimentary close ⟨your grace's ~ and servant⟩ **2 a :** an almshouse inmate usu. charged with praying for the souls of his benefactors **b :** a licensed beggar in Scotland ⟨a king's ~ being given a blue gown on the king's birthday⟩

bead snake *n* [so called fr. its markings resembling beads] **:** the common venomous coral snake (*Micrurus fulvius*) of southeastern No. America

bead tree *n* [so called fr. its bright scarlet seeds, used for necklaces] **1 :** CHINABERRY 2 **2 :** NECKLACE TREE **3 :** RED SANDALWOOD 2

beadwork \ˈ=,=\ *n* **1 :** ornamental work in beads **2 :** joinery beading

beady \ˈbēdē, -di\ *adj* -ER/-EST **1 :** seeming to resemble beads **:** small, round, prominent, and intent esp. with interest or greed ⟨a look of avid interest crept into the ~ eyes of the priest —T.B.Costain⟩ **2 :** marked by bubbles or beads ⟨a ~ liquor⟩

1**bea·gle** \ˈbēgəl\ *n* -s [ME *begle*] **1 :** a small short-legged smooth-coated hound said to have originated as a definite breed in England at least four centuries ago, being about 12 to 15 inches high with pendulous ears and coat of hound colors, the tricolor being common **2 :** CONSTABLE **:** sheriff's officer **:** SPY **:** a zealous aide given to ferreting ⟨the senator's ~*s* probing the deal⟩ **3** *usu cap* **:** VIRGINIAN — used as a nickname

2**beagle** \"\ *vi* **beagled; beagled; beagling** \-g(ə)liŋ\ **beagles :** to hunt game with a beagle or a pack of beagles

bea·gler \-g(ə)lə(r)\ *n* -s **:** one that beagles

bea·gling *n* -s **:** hunting with beagles

1**beak** \ˈbēk\ *n* -s [ME *bec,* fr. OF, fr. L *beccus,* fr. Gaulish] **1 a :** the bill of a bird; *sometimes* **:** the bill of a bird of prey adapted for striking and tearing — often distinguished from *bill* **b :** the long projecting sucking mouth of some insects and other invertebrates (as in the typical bugs) **c :** the bill of some other animals (as the turtle and octopus) **d** (1) **:** the tip of the umbo of a bivalve shell or a brachiopod (2) **:** the prolongation of certain univalve shells containing the canal **e :** the human nose ⟨his face, with small ~ and the pricked skin of smallpox —Saul Bellow⟩ **f :** the projecting bony elements of the jaws of a fish (as in the pike) or of the upper jaw only (as in swordfish or sawfish) or of the lower jaw alone (as in the halfbeak) **2 :** a pointed structure, formation, or construction: **a :** PEAK **b :** a beam shod or armed with a metal head or point projecting from the bow of an ancient galley for piercing the ship of an enemy **c :** PROMONTORY **d** (1) **:** the spout of a vessel (as a teakettle) (2) **:** the tapering tube of a retort **e :** one of the jaws of a forceps or pliers **f :** a continuous slight architectural projection ending in an arris or narrow fillet **:** the part of a drip from which water is thrown off — see MOLDING illustration **g :** a process terminating the fruit or other parts of a plant and somewhat resembling the beak of a bird; *esp* **:** a short awn on the outer chaff of wheat **h :** the mouthpiece of a musical instrument (as the flageolet, clarinet, or flûte à bec) **3 a** *chiefly Brit* **:** MAGISTRATE, JUSTICE OF THE PEACE **b :** a master at certain British public schools

2**beak** \"\ *vt* -ED/-ING/-s [ME *beken,* fr. OF *bequer, bequier,* fr. *bec*] **:** PECK **:** peck at **:** strike or seize with the beak

beaked \ˈbēkt, ˈbēkəd\ *adj* [1*beak* + *-ed*] **1 :** having a beak: **a :** ROSTRATE ⟨a ~ fruit⟩ **b :** having a mouth or proboscis resembling a beak **2 a :** resembling a beak ⟨a gaunt, grizzled man of middle age, with a ~ nose —Ellen Glasgow⟩ **b :** having a beaked nose ⟨a gaunt, ~ lady of eighty-odd —Frances G. Patton⟩

beaked cockle *n* **:** a mollusk of the genus *Nuculana* or family Nuculanidae — called also *elongate nut shell*

beaked hazel *or* **beaked hazelnut** *n* **:** an American hazel (*Corylus cornuta*) with involucral bracts that enclose the nut and form a tubular beak

beaked nightshade *n* **:** BUFFALO BUR

beaked parsley *n* **:** CHERVIL 1

beaked salmon *n, Austral* **:** SANDFISH

beaked whale *n* **:** a toothed whale of the family Ziphiidae

1**beak·er** \ˈbēkə(r)\ *n* -s [ME *biker,* fr. ON *bikarr,* prob. fr. OS *bekari;* akin to OHG *behhari* beaker; both fr. a prehistoric OHG-OS word derived fr. ML *bicarius* goblet, beaker, fr. Gk *bikos* earthen jug, prob. of non-IE origin] **1 :** a large drinking cup without handles that has a wide and often flaring mouth and is sometimes supported on a foot or standard **2 :** a deep openmouthed thin vessel (as of glass, porcelain, or metal) that often has a projecting lip for pouring and is used esp. by chemists and pharmacists **3 :** a breaker or other storage vessel esp. for water on shipboard

beakers 1

2**beaker** \"\ *adj, usu cap* **:** of or relating to the beaker folk

beaker folk *also* **beaker people** \ˈbēkə(r)-\ *or* **beaker·men** \-mən,-,men\ *n pl, often cap B* **:** a prehistoric people living in Europe in the early Bronze Age whose culture was characterized by bell beakers buried with their dead in round barrows

beak flute *n* [trans. of F *flûte à bec*] **:** FIPPLE FLUTE

beakhead \ˈ=,=\ *n* **1 a :** a ship's beak **b :** a space forward of a forecastle containing latrines for crewmen **2 :** an architectural ornament resembling a head with a beak used in some Norman doorways

beak·horn stake *n* [*beak* + *horn*] **:** a stake or small bench anvil having a slender horn on one side — see STAKE illustration

beak·ing joint \ˈbēkiŋ-\ *n* **:** a joint formed by the meeting in a continuous line of several heading joints

beak·iron \ˈbikə(r)n, ˈbē,kīə(r)n\ *n* [by folk etymology (influence of E *beak & iron*) fr. earlier *bickern, bycorne* — more at BICKIRON] **:** BICKIRON

beak molding *n* **:** an architectural molding whose profile resembles a beak — see MOLDING illustration

beak rush *or* **beaked rush** *or* **beak sedge** *n* **:** a sedge of the genus *Rhynchospora* having a tubercle like a beak crowning the fruit

beak wattle *n* **:** one of the fleshy outgrowths at the base of both mandibles of carrier pigeons

beak willow *or* **beaked willow** *n* **:** a No. American shrub or small tree (*Salix bebbiana*) with broad leaves and long conic capsules

beaky \ˈbēkē\ *adj* -ER/-EST **:** having a beak, esp. a noticeable one **:** resembling a beak ⟨his overcivilized, prim, finely drawn, ~ profile —Christopher Isherwood⟩

1**beal** \ˈbē(ə)l\ *vi* -ED/-ING/-s [prob. fr. obs. E *beal* boil, fr. ME *bele,* prob. var. of *bile* — more at BOIL] *now dial* **:** to swell and become infected **:** SUPPURATE, FESTER

2**beal** \"\ *vi* -ED/-ING/-s [perh. alter. of 3*bell*] *dial Eng* **:** BELLOW, ROAR ⟨a bull ~*ing*⟩

bealing *n* -s [fr. gerund of 1*beal*] *now dial* **:** BOIL, SUPPURATION

beal·lach *also* **beal·ach** \ˈbe,läk\ *n* -s [IrGael *bealach* road, path, mountain pass, fr. MIr *belach* gap, pass] *Scot & Irish* **:** a mountain pass

be-all and end-all \ˈbē,ȯl . . . ˈen,dȯl\ *n* **:** prime cause **:** essential element **:** dominant or definitive factor; *sometimes* **:** WHOLE, TOTALITY ⟨the *be-all and end-all* of the detective story is to conceal the identity of the criminal —*Times Lit. Supp.*⟩

bealtine *usu cap, var of* BELTANE

1**beam** \ˈbēm\ *n* -s [ME *beem,* fr. OE *bēam* tree, beam; akin to OHG *boum* tree, ON *bathmr,* Goth *bagms,* and perh. to Gk *phyma* growth, *phyein* to bring forth — more at BE] **1 a** *obs* **:** a sizable metal bar **b :** a long piece of heavy often squared timber suitable for use in house construction **c** (1) **:** a large cylinder of wood or metal on which yarns comprising a warp are wound before weaving or warp knitting or on which woven or knitted cloth is wound as it is made (2) **:** a hand-weaving loom part over which warp yarns travel up and forward during the weaving process **d :** the part of a plow to which handles, standard, and colter are attached and by which the implement is drawn — see PLOW illustration **e :** the crossbar of a balance from the ends of which scales or weights are suspended; *sometimes* **:** the whole balance **f** *obs* **:** the shaft of a chariot **g :** a structural member (as an iron girder) usu. supported at the two ends that is laid horizontally to bear a load and brace a frame **:** a horizontal supporting span (as between opposite foundation walls of a building) **h** (1) **:** a horizontal structural member supporting the deck of a ship and aiding in holding her sides in place — see SHIP illustration (2) **:** the extreme width of the hull of a ship including projecting structures **:** the widest part of a ship; *also* **:** the maximum width of a seaplane float or hull measured between the chines — see SHIP illustration (3) **:** the side of a ship **:** the direction outward from the side **i :** a lever having an oscillating motion on a central axis and connected at one end with an engine piston rod from which it receives motion and at the other with the crank or its equivalent **j :** a sloping board or frame upon which hides are worked in tanning **k :** a long structural member not supported everywhere along its length and subject to the force of flexure (as a rod resting on supports at the ends and bearing a weight at the center) **:** SPAR, BOOM, LEVER **2 a :** a light ray **:** a radiating line (as of light or color) ⟨how far that little candle throws his ~*s* —Shak.⟩ **:** a shaft of light rays from a lamp ⟨the ~*s* from the searchlights⟩ **b :** a collection of nearly parallel rays (as of light or X rays) or of particles (as electrons) **c :** GLANCE **d :** a gleam or other emanation or manifestation **e** (1) **:** a directional radio signal transmitted in quadrants from a radio range station audible as a continuous tone or whine as long as an aircraft proceeds directly on the proper course but audible as dot-dash or dash-dot as it veers to left or right (2) **:** the exact course indicated by a radio beam **f** (1) **:** stream of electrons in a vacuum tube flowing from an emitting electrode to a collecting electrode (2) **:** a directed flow of a radio signal in space **g :** the zone in which a microphone or loudspeaker functions best **3 :** the main stem of a deer's antler **4 :** the width of the buttocks **:** RUMP ⟨a massive woman, much taller than her husband and immensely broad in the ~ —Ann Bridge⟩ — **abaft the beam :** in an arc of the horizon between a line that crosses a ship at right angles to the keel and that point of the compass toward which her stern points — **before the beam :** in an arc of the horizon included between a line that crosses a ship at right angles to the keel and that point of the compass toward which the ship heads — **off the beam :** not following a guiding beam **:** proceeding on a wrong course **:** deviating from the normal or true ⟨truly *off the beam* and wandering in a Stygian darkness —Peggy Bennett⟩ — **on the beam :** following a guiding beam **:** proceeding correctly **:** following the normal or true **:** operating well — **the beam in one's own eye :** a blemish as palpable as a house beam ⟨cast *the beam* out of *thine own eye* —Matt 7:5 (AV)⟩

2**beam** \"\ *vb* -ED/-ING/-s [ME *beemen,* fr. *beem,* n.] *vt* **1 :** to send out, radiate, or project in beams or as a beam **2 a :** to wind (warp yarn or cloth) on a beam **b :** to dress or work (hides) on a beam **3 :** to equip or support with beams ⟨a roof ~*ed* with heavy timbers⟩ **4 a :** to aim (a broadcast) by directional antennas ⟨programs ~*ed* at Britain⟩ **b :** to aim (sound) from a loudspeaker **c :** to direct (a broadcast) to a particular audience ⟨a program ~*ed* to women⟩ **:** address special attention to ⟨a sales campaign ~*ed* at sportsmen⟩ ~ *vi* **1 :** to send out beams of light ⟨the sun ~*ing* overhead⟩ **2 :** to smile broadly or blandly with unreserved satisfaction, pleasure, or joy ⟨~*ing* with good nature —R.L.Stevenson⟩

3**beam** \"\ *adj* [1*beam*] **1 :** moving toward or directed at a ship's beam ⟨a ~ sea⟩ ⟨a ~ wind⟩ **2 :** relating to wave transmission in a fairly well-defined beam as distinguished from substantially uniform transmission in all directions ⟨~ antenna⟩

beam·age \ˈbēmij\ *n* -s [1*beam* + *-age*] **:** a deduction for loss by evaporation of weight in a freshly dressed animal carcass cooling on a beam

beam anchor *n* **:** a building anchor used to tie walls firmly to floors

beam and scales *n* **:** BALANCE

beam antenna *n* **:** ANTENNA ARRAY

beam arm *n* **1 :** a forked timber bolted to a beam next to a deck opening — called also *fork beam* **2 :** a split end of a steel deck beam bent over so as to be bolted to the frame where it forms a knee

beambird \ˈ=,=\ *n* **:** SPOTTED FLYCATCHER

beam board *n* **:** the platform of a steelyard or balance

beam bracket *n* **:** a riveted or welded steel plate connecting a ship's beam to its frame

beam caliper *n* **1 :** CALIPER SQUARE **2** *or* **beam divider :** a trammel fitted with caliper legs

beam ceiling *n* **:** a ceiling with exposed beams

beam compass *n* **:** a compass that consists of a beam with sliding sockets which carry steel or pencil points and that is used for drawing large circles

beamed *past of* BEAM

beam-ends \ˈ=,=\ *n pl* **:** ends of beams usu. on a ship — **on her beam-ends :** inclined so much on one side that beams approach a vertical position with danger of capsizing — **on one's beam-ends 1 :** laid up **2 :** at the end of one's material resources **:** in extremities

beam·er \ˈbēmə(r)\ *n* -s [1*beam* + *-er*] **1 a :** a machine for winding yarn or cloth on a beam **b :** an operator of such a machine — compare WARPER a **2 :** a leather worker who scrapes wet hides with a beaming knife to remove flesh and traces of hair **3 :** a bone implement like a drawknife found in Mississippi sites and in later cultural stages of the southwestern U.S., usu. made from metapodal bones of deer or elk, and having cutting and scraping edges midway between the handles

beam·fill·ing \ˈbēm,filiŋ\ *n* **1 :** masonry placed between the ends of beams in a wall **2 :** cargo that is or can be stowed between beams

beamhouse \ˈ=,=\ *n* **:** a tannery section where hides are prepared for tanning

beam·i·ly \ˈbēməlē\ *adv* **:** in a beamy manner

beaming *adj* **1 :** marked by, emitting, or reflecting strong or clear rays of light ⟨the ~ sun above⟩ **2 :** marked by or expressive of extreme and unreserved joy, happiness, or satisfaction ⟨~ parents watching a baby⟩ ⟨quiet, confident, bright, and smiling eyes, ~ with a consciousness of being associated with a cause far higher —Sir Winston Churchill⟩ **syn** see BRIGHT

beaming knife *or* **beam knife** *n* **:** a tanner's 2-handled knife used to shave hides stretched over a beam

beam·ing·ly *adv* **:** with radiance **:** RADIANTLY

beaming machine *n* **1 :** a machine for working hides to remove hair roots — compare SCUD **2 :** a machine for filling beams with yarn or cloth

beam·ish \ˈbēmish\ *adj* **:** beaming and bright with optimism, promise, or achievement ⟨those ~ young men you encounter on . . . recruiting posters —John McCarten⟩

beam knee *n* **1 :** a knee supporting a ship's beam **2 :** BEAM ARM

beam·less \ˈbēmləs\ *adj* **:** being without a beam or ray

beam light *n* **:** a candle kept burning before the rood in a church

beam pump *n* **:** an oil-well pump actuated by a walking beam

beam-rider \ˈ=,==\ *n* **:** a missile guided along a radio beam

beams *pl of* BEAM, *pres 3d sing of* BEAM

beams·man \ˈbēmzmən\ *n, pl* **beamsmen :** a worker at a tannery beam

beam splitter *n* **:** a mirror that is sometimes built into a prism, that reflects part of a beam of light and transmits part, and that is used for diverting a portion of the beam to one side in color separation cameras, in photomicrography, and for superposition of images in projected pictures or printers

beam·ster \ˈbēmstə(r)\ *n* -s [1*beam* (for tanning) + *-ster*] **:** one that beams hides

beam trawl *n* **:** a trawl net with its mouth spread by a beam — compare OTTER TRAWL

beam-trawl \'=,=\ *vi* [*beam trawl*] **:** to fish with a beam trawl

beam trawler *n* **:** a fishing boat equipped with a beam trawl

beam tree *n* **:** WHITEBEAM

beam tube *n* **:** a power amplifier vacuum tube in which the flow of electrons is channeled by means of beam-forming plates and similarly spaced control and screen grids

beam well *n* **:** an oil well having a beam pump

beamy \'bēmē\ *adj* -ER/-EST [ME *beemy*, fr. *beem* beam + *-y*] **1 a :** marked by, emitting, or reflecting beams of light **:** BRIGHT, RADIANT **b :** radiantly joyful **:** flushed with optimism or marked by happy benignness **2 :** resembling a beam in size and weight **:** MASSIVE, BROAD **3 :** having horns or antlers ⟨~ stags —John Dryden⟩ **4 :** notably broad in the beam ⟨a ~ cargo ship⟩ **syn** see BRIGHT

¹bean \'bēn\ *n* -S *often attrib* [ME *bene*, fr. OE *bēan*; akin to OHG *bōna* bean, ON *baun*, and prob. to L *faba* bean, Gk *phakos* lentil] **1 a :** BROAD BEAN **b :** the seed of any of various other erect or climbing leguminous plants esp. of the genera *Phaseolus, Dolichos*, and *Vigna* — see KIDNEY BEAN, LIMA BEAN, SIEVA BEAN, SNAP BEAN **c :** a plant bearing beans **d :** a bean pod used when immature as a vegetable **2 a :** a valueless item ⟨not worth a ~⟩ **b** *slang Brit* **:** a sovereign or a guinea **c :** a small amount of money ⟨he didn't have a ~ when they were married⟩ ⟨haven't spent a ~ on it in years⟩ **d** *slang* **:** DOLLAR **e beans** *pl* **:** an appreciable amount ⟨he doesn't know *beans* about it⟩ ⟨I haven't heard *beans* about the matter lately⟩ **3 a :** any of various seeds or fruits that resemble beans ⟨a coffee ~⟩ ⟨catalpa ~*s* littering the walk⟩ **b :** any of several plants producing such beans — usu. used in combination ⟨a field of castor ~*s*⟩; see BLACK BEAN, CORAL BEAN **4 a :** a bean used in balloting **b :** a man that becomes leader of Twelfth Night festivities through having drawn a piece of cake containing a bean **5 :** something felt to resemble a bean: as **a :** a protuberance on the upper mandible of waterfowl (as of certain geese) — see GOOSE illustration **b :** a nipple or similar device placed in an oil-well line to restrict the flow of the oil **c :** a hardened mass of fatty secretion in the sheath of a stallion or gelding that if allowed to accumulate may block the urethra causing colicky pain and impeding urination **6** *slang* **a beans** *pl* **:** BEATING, PUNISHMENT, PAIN, CENSURE — usu. used with *give* ⟨giving the enemy ~*s* when they came within range⟩ ⟨giving the opposition ~*s* in a stinging speech⟩ **b :** HEAD, SKULL, BRAIN ⟨every whim and caprice which enters his ~ —Henry Miller⟩

²bean \"\ *vt* -ED/-ING/-S [¹*bean* (head)] **:** to strike typically with a hurled or propelled object and on the head ⟨a caddie ~*ed* by a wild shot⟩; *specif* **:** to hit (a baseball batter) esp. on the head with a pitched ball

bean anthracnose *n* **:** a disease of the bean caused by an imperfect fungus (*Colletotrichum lindemuthianum*) producing pinkish or brown lesions on the pod and seed and rusty to black discolorations on the veins on the lower leaf surface — see BEAN BLIGHT

bean aphid *also* **bean aphis** *n* **:** an aphid attacking bean plants; *specif* **:** a dull black or dark green aphid (*Aphis fabae* or *A. rumicis*) that feeds in great numbers on succulent parts of many cultivated and native plants

beanbag \'=,=\ *n* **1 :** a cloth bag partly filled with dried beans or comparable small firm objects and used (as for tossing or passing) in many games **2 :** a game played with one or more beanbags

beanball *n* **:** a baseball deliberately pitched at a batter's head

bean beetle *n* **:** MEXICAN BEAN BEETLE

bean blight *n* **:** a disease caused by a bacterium (*Xanthomonas phaseoli*) distinguished from bean anthracnose by more irregular diffuse extended and water-soaked lesions on stem, leaf pod, and seed that later become yellowish brown

bean cake *n* **:** oil cake made from soybeans

bean caper *n* **:** any of several perennial plants constituting the genus *Zygophyllum* and having usu. ill-smelling foliage and flower buds that are used as capers; *esp* **:** a small shrub or tree (*Z. fabago*) of the eastern Mediterranean region and southwestern Asia that has yellow 5-petaled flowers brick red at the base

bean-caper family \'=,==-\ *n* **:** ZYGOPHYLLACEAE

bean clam *n* **:** a small wedge-shaped clam (*Donax gouldii*) of southern California and Mexico

bean curd *also* **bean cheese** *n* **:** a soft vegetable cheese extensively eaten in the Orient that is prepared by treating soybean milk with magnesium chloride, dilute acids, or other coagulants and draining and pressing

bean cutworm *n* **:** a pinkish brown larval noctuid moth (*Loxagrotis albicosta*) that feeds on developing bean pods and seeds

bean-eater \'=,==\ *n*, *sometimes cap B&E* **1 :** BOSTONIAN — used as a nickname **2 :** MEXICAN — used as a nickname

bean·ery \'bēnərē\ *n* -ES **:** a restaurant often of the cheaper class

beanfeast \'=,=\ *n* **1** *Brit* **:** an annual dinner given to employees by their employers **2** *chiefly Brit* **:** a festive occasion often including an outing and a meal

bean flour *n* **:** a ground meal made of dried ripe beans

bean fly *n* **:** a small dark fly (*Agromyza phaseoli*) having larvae that are leaf miners esp. in the leaves of beans and are a serious pest of cultivated crops in Australia and adjacent regions

bean goose *n* **:** a common brownish Eurasian wild goose (*Anser fabalis*) having a bean-shaped mark on the bill

bean harvester *n* **:** a machine consisting of a cutting device of two long horizontal knives inclined to the rear for cutting bean plants and a raking device for gathering them into cocks or windrows

bean hole *n* **:** a hole in the ground sometimes lined with stones or bricks that is heated to serve as a slow-baking oven esp. for beans

bean huller *n* **:** BEAN THRESHER

bean·ie *also* **beany** \'bēnē\ *n*, *pl* **beanies** [prob. fr. ¹*bean* (head) + *-ie, -y*] **1 :** a small round tight-fitting skullcap worn esp. by schoolboys and collegians **2 :** a woman's small round hat worn off the face

bean king *n* **:** BEAN 4b

bean leaf beetle *n* **:** a reddish or yellowish beetle (*Cerotoma trifurcata*) that as an adult feeds on the leaves of beans and peas and sometimes other legumes

bean leaf roller *n* **:** a larval skipper butterfly (*Urbanus proteus*) that sometimes injures the foliage of beans, peas, and related plants in the southeastern U.S.

bean mosaic *n* **:** a virus disease of the bean transmitted by plant lice and by the seed and characterized by light green and dark green mottling and puckering of the leaves

¹beano \'bē(,)nō\ *n* -S [alter. of *beanfeast*] **1** *slang chiefly Brit* **:** BEANFEAST **2** *slang chiefly Brit* **:** a noisy good time

²beano \"\ *n* -S [by alter. (influenced by *bean*)] **:** BINGO

bean oil *n* **:** SOYBEAN OIL

bean-pod borer \'=,=-\ *n* **:** a larval pyralid moth (*Etiella zinckenella*) that feeds in the developing seeds of beans and other legumes

bean pole *n* **1 :** a pole up which bean vines may climb **2 :** a tall thin person

bean pot *n* **1 :** a covered pot of heavy crockery made esp. for the slow cooking of beans **2 :** any crockery or metal pot or utensil used in the slow cooking of foods (as beans) ⟨an electric *bean pot*⟩ ⟨individual *bean pots* of brown pottery⟩

beans *pl of* BEAN, *pres 3d sing of* BEAN

bean·shooter \'=,==\ *n* **1 :** PEASHOOTER **2 :** SLINGSHOT

bean sprouts *n pl* **:** the sprouts of bean seeds esp. of the mung bean germinated in humid darkness and used as food

beanstalk \'=,=\ *n* **:** the stem of a bean plant

be·ant \'bēənt\ [by alter. & contr.] *dial* **:** be not

bean thresher *n* **:** a thresher that removes beans from pods by a combination of a low-speed cylinder that threshes out dry pods and two high-speed cylinders that thresh out damp or green pods

bean·town·er \'bēn,tau̇nə(r)\ *n* -S *usu cap* [fr. *Bean Town*, nickname for Boston, Mass. + *-er*; fr. the proverbially famous Boston baked beans] **:** BOSTONIAN — used as a nickname

bean tree *n* **:** any of several trees having fruits that are felt to resemble a bean pod: as **a :** an Australian leguminous tree (*Catanospermum australe*) with bright yellow flowers, large pods containing three or four seeds like chestnuts, and dark strong wood — called also *Moreton Bay chestnut* **b :** CATALPA 2

bean trefoil *n* **1 :** a shrub (*Anagyris foetida*) of southern Europe with trifoliolate leaves and yellow flowers **2 :** BUCKBEAN **3 :** CORAL TREE **4 :** LABURNUM 2

bean-vine \'=,=\ *n* **:** a perennial climbing American herb (*Phaseobus perennis*) with minutely pubescent stem and slender racemes or panicles of purple or whitish flowers

bean weevil *n* **:** any of several small weevils that deposit their eggs in the pods of beans and peas, the larva burrowing in and feeding on the seed; *specif* **:** a mottled olive-brown weevil (*Acanthoscelides obtectus*) native to America but now a cosmopolitan pest of growing and stored beans

¹beany \'bēnē\ *adj* -ER/-EST **1 :** METTLESOME, SPIRITED **2** *of an oil* **:** marked by an off-flavor suggestive of that of beans

²beany *var of* BEANIE

be·aproned \(')bē+\ *adj* [*be-* + *aproned*] **:** wearing an apron

¹bear \'be(ə)r, 'ba(a)(ə)r, 'beə, 'ba(a)ə\ *n* -S *see sense 1, often attrib* [ME *bere*, fr. OE *bera*; akin to OHG *bero* bear, Lith *bėras* brown, OE *brūn* — more at BROWN] **1** *or pl* **bear a :** an animal of the family Ursidae (order Carnivora) of large heavy mammals having long shaggy hair, rudimentary tail, and plantigrade feet, feeding largely on fruit and insects as well as on flesh, and though ordinarily slow and clumsy moving very fast for short distances esp. on rough or steep ground — see GRIZZLY BEAR, POLAR BEAR **b** *Austral* **:** KOALA **c :** the fur or pelt of any bear **2 a :** a person felt to resemble a bear esp. in surly irascibility, coarse uncouthness, or shambling burliness ⟨bad-tempered and demanding, he was a perfect ~ all morning⟩ ⟨a lumbering good-natured ~ of a man⟩ **b :** a person having a special aptitude, excellence, or enthusiasm ⟨a ~ at mathematics⟩ **:** one showing resolution or ruggedness in enduring ⟨a ~ for punishment⟩ **3** [prob. fr. *bear* as used in the proverb about *selling the bearskin before catching the bear*] **a** *obs* **:** a stock or commodity sold short **b :** one that sells short **:** one interested in price decline **:** one who wishes or expects a fall in stock prices — compare BULL **4 :** a mat or matting-covered block esp. for scouring decks; *sometimes* **:** HOLY STONE **5 :** a small invertebrate animal felt to resemble a bear: as **a :** WATER BEAR **b :** ANT BEAR **c :** WOOLLY BEAR **6 :** a nearly neutral slightly brownish dark gray — called also *Chaetura drab* **7 :** a cub scout of the third rank who is at least nine years old

²bear \"\ *vt* -ED/-ING/-S **:** to lower prices in or at **:** DEPRESS ⟨attempts to ~ the stock market⟩

³bear \'bē(ə)r, 'be(ə)r\ *n* -S [ME *bere*, fr. OE — more at BARLEY] *chiefly Scot* **:** BARLEY

⁴bear \'be(ə)r, 'ba(a)(ə)r, 'beə, 'ba(a)ə\ *vb* **bore** \'bō(ə)r, 'bȯ(ə)r, 'bōə, 'bȯ(ə)\ *or archaic* **bare** *pronounced like* BEAR\ **borne** \'bō(ə)rn, 'bȯ(ə)rn, 'bōən, 'bȯ(ə)n\ *also* **born** \'bȯ(ə)rn, 'bȯ(ə)n\ (*see vt 2a,d,e,f*) *or dial* **bore** *pronounced like* BORE *above*\ **bearing; bears** [ME *beren*, fr. OE *beran*; akin to OHG *beran* to carry, ON *bera*, Goth *bairan*, L *ferre*, Gk *pherein*, Skt *bharati* he carries] *vt* **1 a :** to move while holding up or supporting often with effort or special care **:** CARRY ⟨let four captains ~ Hamlet, like a soldier to the stage —Shak.⟩ ⟨~*ing* gifts to the newborn prince⟩ **b :** to be accoutered or fitted out with **:** carry as equipment ⟨the right to ~ a sword in the king's presence⟩ **c :** to harbor or entertain mentally or emotionally; *sometimes* **:** CHERISH ⟨~*ing* malice in his heart⟩ ⟨the love he *bore* his mother⟩ **d :** to carry as a communication and usu. to relate ⟨killing the runner ~*ing* the orders⟩ ⟨constantly ~*ing* tales⟩ **e :** BEHAVE, CONDUCT, DEPORT — used reflexively ⟨~*ing* himself well in battle⟩ **f** *archaic* **:** MANAGE, WIELD, EXERCISE ⟨~ his power wisely⟩ ⟨~*ing* the rule in the land⟩ **g :** to have as an attribute, feature, or characteristic ⟨~*ing* a likeness to the suspect⟩ ⟨~*ing* the scars of old wounds⟩ **:** be capable of (as meaning or significance) ⟨a word ~*ing* many meanings⟩ **h :** to adduce in testifying ⟨~*ing* false witness⟩ ⟨~ testimony⟩ **i :** to have attached to one by way of identification, characterization, or evaluation ⟨~*ing* the name of John Doe⟩ ⟨~*ing* a good local reputation⟩ ⟨~*ing* a high price⟩ **j :** to use as an armorial emblem ⟨~*ing* the family coat of arms⟩ **k :** to have as a bodily part ⟨~*ing* a good pair of eyes⟩ **l** *obs* **:** WIN **:** prevail in — used only with *it* ⟨~ it by speaking a great word —Francis Bacon⟩ **m :** LEAD, ESCORT ⟨~ the officer to his quarters⟩ **n :** RENDER, GIVE, TENDER ⟨~ a hand in helping⟩ **o :** TRANSPORT ⟨goods *borne* in neutral ships⟩ ⟨air*borne* troops⟩ **2 a :** to give birth to (offspring) **:** bring forth (young) — *borne* is the usual past participle form in active uses ⟨she has *borne* several children⟩ and is commonly used in passives seeming to suggest the action of giving birth esp. as used with *by* ⟨several children *borne* by her⟩; *born* is the usual form in passives indicating the fact of birth ⟨a son *born* to her⟩ ⟨he was *born* in the city⟩ and in adjective uses indicating condition or status often with durative aspect ⟨new-*born* kittens⟩ ⟨a suitor lowly *born* —W.S.Gilbert⟩ **b :** PRODUCE **:** send forth as yield esp. as leaf, flower, or fruit ⟨a tree ~*ing* late pears⟩ ⟨a bush ~*ing* red flowers⟩ **c :** AFFORD: (1) **:** to permit growth of often readily ⟨this soil ~*s* good cotton⟩ (2) **:** to contain in quantity and form permitting extraction ⟨oil-*bearing* shale⟩ (3) **:** to yield to the owner ⟨a bond that ~*s* interest⟩ **d :** to call into being — used only in the passive; *born* is the usual past participle form ⟨with this discovery a new age was *born*⟩ **e :** to give birth to or to develop with a special predisposition or bent — used only in the passive; *born* is the usual past participle form ⟨he loved teaching; he had been *born* to it⟩ **f :** EXTRUDE — used mainly in the passive; *born* is the usual past participle form ⟨after the lamb's head was *born*⟩ **3 a :** SUSTAIN **:** support or hold up without moving **b** (1) **:** TOLERATE **:** sustain with opposing or resisting — usu. used in negative constructions ⟨a nuisance not to be *borne* longer⟩ (2) **:** to endure esp. without giving way, collapsing, or succumbing ⟨~*ing* his sorrows as best he could⟩ ⟨pain more than he could ~⟩ (3) **:** to tolerate without discomfort or distaste **:** come to accept the presence of — usu. used in negative constructions ⟨he could not ~ his sister-in-law⟩ **c** (1) **:** ASSUME, ACCEPT ⟨he must ~ the blame⟩ (2) **:** to incur and defray ⟨~ by himself the whole cost of the arrangement⟩ **d :** to hold up **:** keep from falling ⟨columns that ~ the roof⟩ — often used with *up* ⟨a support that ~*s* up the weight⟩ **e :** to hold above, on top, or aloft — usu. used with adverb or prepositional phrase ⟨a banner *borne* aloft⟩ ⟨a table ~*ing* several vases⟩ **f :** to endure with ill will, resentment, or grievance **:** experience with bitterness or other deep unpleasant feeling — usu. used with *hard* or *heavy* ⟨he *bore* it hard to be ignored⟩; obs. with a personal object ⟨Ligarius doth ~ Caesar hard —Shak.⟩ **g** (1) **:** to show as written, inscribed, or otherwise displayed on a surface ⟨a cornerstone ~*ing* a Latin inscription⟩ ⟨a letter ~*ing* the date of 1900⟩ ⟨a shield ~*ing* strange symbols⟩ (2) **:** to enter on a list **:** ENROLL, REGISTER — used passively ⟨inactive personnel still *borne* on the rolls⟩ **h** (1) **:** to allow or admit of **:** be capable of sustaining without violence or wrenching ⟨a style that can ~ adornment⟩ ⟨a work that will not ~ close scrutiny⟩ (2) **:** SUGGEST, PROVOKE, INVITE ⟨his book *bore* heavy praise⟩ ⟨the answer of this witness will ~ examination⟩ **i** *archaic* **:** PURPORT, IMPORT, SIGNIFY ⟨her sentence *bore* that she should stand a certain time upon the platform —Nathaniel Hawthorne⟩ **j :** TAKE, PLAY ⟨~*ing* only a secondary part⟩ **4 :** THRUST, DRIVE, PRESS **:** impel with force ⟨the defenders being *borne* backward⟩ ⟨a canoe *borne* down the rapids⟩ **~** *vi* **1 a :** to force one's way **:** make way against resistance **:** PRESS ⟨*bear* back that the prince may pass⟩ **b :** to be situated, often as to compass direction ⟨the land ~*s* N by E⟩ ⟨the fleet ~*ing* directly off the point⟩ **c :** to extend or continue usu. along a direction indicated or implied ⟨a stream ~*ing* south for several miles⟩ **d :** to show a certain direction, range, or aim **:** to have a position commanding an objective (as an enemy position) — used with *on* or *upon* ⟨to bring guns to ~ upon a target⟩ **e :** GO, PROCEED ⟨nearer and nearer the foe are ~*ing*⟩; *often* **:** to direct or take a course (in an indicated way) esp. with a slight veering or inclination rather than a right-angle turn ⟨the road ~*s* west beyond the lake⟩ ⟨~ right into the outer lane at the next corner but do not turn⟩ **2 a :** to relate or have relevance **:** APPLY, PERTAIN ⟨facts ~*ing* on the question⟩ **b :** to exert influence or force **:** AFFECT, SWAY **:** put into effect ⟨to bring pressure to ~⟩ ⟨how this discovery will ~ on later developments⟩ ⟨legislation brought to ~ directly upon industry —Harriet Martineau⟩ **c :** to exert pressure or repose weight **:** push on or against something ⟨the wall ~*ing* on the floor⟩ ⟨an arch ~*ing* against piers⟩ **3 a :** to become subjected to a strain esp. in a structure **:** withstand a strain ⟨a wall added later that does not ~⟩ ⟨these small joists will not ~⟩ **b** *obs* **:** to hold good **:** be convincing **c :** to support a person's or a vehicle's weight without cracking or breaking ⟨wondering if the thawing ice would still ~⟩ **4 :** to produce as fruit **:** be fruitful **:** YIELD ⟨plants that ~ well⟩

syn PRODUCE, YIELD, TURN OUT: BEAR in the sense here involved usu. implies a giving birth to or a bringing forth naturally ⟨*bearing* children⟩ ⟨a sow may *bear* litters of over a dozen⟩ ⟨these fruit trees *bear* very well⟩ PRODUCE is very wide in its application and is used for any act of bringing forth or making ⟨the tree will *produce* no fruit⟩ ⟨a pair will *produce* over a hundred offspring⟩ ⟨the factory is *producing* more silk than ever⟩ ⟨he *produced* a book on the subject at the publisher's request⟩ ⟨not until the end of the tenth century did the English *produce* a truly notable prose writer —Kemp Malone⟩ ⟨George was dead. This death *produced* no effect of sadness on me at all —Arnold Bennett⟩ YIELD may center attention on the fact of giving forth or out of something within ⟨the farms *yielded* a variety of fruit, vegetables, poultry, and cattle —*Amer. Guide Series: N.J.*⟩ ⟨these areas *yield* about one hundred thousand barrels of oil a day —*Current Biog.*⟩ TURN OUT indicates production or result of previous labor or effort ⟨the factory is now *turning out* more automobiles⟩

syn ENDURE, SUFFER, ABIDE; TOLERATE, STAND: BEAR is likely to indicate the power of sustaining an affliction onerous or difficult without breaking or flinching ⟨*bear* the brunt of the fighting⟩ ⟨*bear* the major part of the loss⟩ ⟨*bear* the pain of the illness⟩ ⟨his decency, which has made him *bear* prolonged and intolerable humiliation with control and courtesy —Marya Mannes⟩ ⟨a hardy crew, these men who *bore* the hardships of the lumbering industry —*Amer. Guide Series: Wash.*⟩ ENDURE indicates the fact of lasting without succumbing, of continuing unbroken or firm through trials and difficulties ⟨he had endured, and was to *endure* again, a life of tragic penury —W.B. Yeats⟩ ⟨an element of the austere which has allowed him to *endure* the miseries of prison life with indifference —*Times Lit. Supp.*⟩ ⟨Chinese culture has *endured* many conquerors but has always managed to absorb them —Stuart Chase⟩ SUFFER indicates the experiencing of affliction, or what is felt to be like affliction, sometimes with voluntary acceptance ⟨identify himself so thoroughly with the cause of the exploited Indian that he denounced his Puritan fellows and *suffered* exile —H.A.Overstreet⟩ ⟨braves *suffered* their hands and noses to be cut off for their defiance of Spanish authority —*Amer. Guide Series: Fla.*⟩ ⟨for a moment the girl *suffered* the caress; almost she seemed to nestle closer to the Dowager's shoulder —Rafael Sabatini⟩ ABIDE may refer notably to looking forward to afflictive circumstances or agencies as well as trying to endure them with patience and stoicism ⟨I had been grossly wrong, and must *abide* the consequences —Jane Austen⟩ ⟨he fled to Sicily, with a tacit confession that he dared not *abide* his trial —J.A.Froude⟩ ⟨she was a professional do-gooder, a professional busybody; Hawthorne could not *abide* her —H.S.Commager⟩ TOLERATE suggests an enduring or countenancing conditioned in part by individual characteristics or inclinations ⟨the Father of all mankind seems always to have *tolerated* a diversity of views among His children —M.R. Cohen⟩ ⟨children have been found quite able to *tolerate* eyeglasses at the age of fifteen months —Morris Fishbein⟩ ⟨Arnold swallowed an injustice which others would not have *tolerated* —R.G.Adams⟩ STAND, which sometimes has informal suggestion, may apply to bearing with steady firmness, without discomposure or flinching ⟨his wife could not have *stood* another winter here —Owen Wister⟩ ⟨this interference, is more than we can *stand* —W.S.Gilbert⟩ **syn** see in addition CARRY, PRESS

— **bear a hand :** to extend help **:** join in and help out **:** PARTICIPATE — **bear arms 1 :** to carry or possess arms ⟨the right of the people to keep and *bear arms* —*U.S. Constitution*⟩ **2 :** to serve as a soldier — **bear arms against :** to fight against **:** wage war on — **bear date :** to have the date of execution (as of a document) written down explicitly ⟨a letter *bearing date* of 1800⟩ — **bear fruit :** to come to satisfying fruition, production, or development repaying expenditure or compensating for quiescence ⟨his conduct in the primary election *bore fruit* in November⟩ — **bear in hand 1 :** MANAGE, CONTROL **2 :** MAINTAIN, ASSERT, CHARGE ⟨*bearing in hand* that he is guilty⟩; *sometimes* **:** PROMISE ⟨*bear in hand* to marry the princess⟩ **3** *obs* **:** to deceive or gull with pretenses or false promises ⟨how you were *borne in hand*, how crossed —Shak.⟩ — **bear in mind :** to think of esp. as a cautionary or reservation **:** REMEMBER ⟨*bear in mind* that your supplies are limited⟩ — **bear in with :** to run or tend toward ⟨a ship *bears in with* the land⟩ — **bear low sail** *archaic* **:** to comport oneself humbly — **bear with :** to be indulgent, patient, or forbearing with **:** ENDURE ⟨*bear with* the old bore for a while longer⟩

bear·a·ble \-rəbəl\ *adj* [⁴*bear* + *-able*] **:** capable of being borne or endured **:** TOLERABLE — **bear·a·bly** \-rablē, -blī\ *adv*

bear animalcule *n* **:** one of the Tardigrada **:** WATER BEAR

bear away *vt* **:** to carry off or attain to in victory ⟨*bear away* the spoils⟩ **~** *vi* **:** to change course so as to sail with the wind farther aft

bear·baiting \'=,==\ *n* -S [ME *berebaiting* fr. *bere* bear + *baiting*, fr. gerund of *baiten* to bait — more at BEAR, BAIT] **:** the former practice of setting dogs on a chained bear

bearberry \'=- — *see* BERRY\ *n* [¹*bear* + *berry*] **1 :** any of several plants of the genus *Arctostaphylos* (esp. *A. uva-ursi*) with astringent foliage and glossy red berries **2 :** AMERICAN CRANBERRY **3 :** a deciduous shrub (*Ilex decidua*) of the southern U.S. with green flowers and red fruit **4 :** CASCARA BUCKTHORN

bearberry willow *n* **:** a dwarf prostrate shrub (*Salix uva-ursi*) of the arctic and alpine regions of northeastern No. America with deep green elliptical leaves that taper toward their base

bear·bine \'=,=\ *n* [¹*bear* + *bine*] **1** *or* **bear·bind** \-,bīnd\ **:** any of various European plants of the genus *Convolvulus* (as *C. arvensis* and *C. soldanella*) **2 :** BLACK BINDWEED 1

bear brush *n* **:** a shrub (*Garrya fremonti*) of the western U.S. with oblong shining leaves and dark purple berries — called also *California feverbush*

bear bush *n* **:** INKBERRY 1

bear cat *n* **1 :** BINTURONG **2 :** PANDA **3 :** a person or thing that is marked by especial power or force ⟨obviously this new skipper was a *bear cat*, at least insofar as getting into action with the enemy was concerned —E.L.Beach⟩ ⟨mosquitoes that are regular *bear cats* in action⟩

bear caterpillar *n* **:** WOOLLY BEAR

bear clover *n* **:** MOUNTAIN MISERY

bear corn *n* **:** AMERICAN HELLEBORE

¹beard \'bi(ə)rd, 'bi(ə)d\ *n* -S [ME *berd*, fr. OE *beard*; akin to OHG *bart* beard, L *barba*, OSlav *brada*] **1 :** the hair on the chin, lips, and adjacent parts of the human face usu. of an adult male ⟨he has a very light ~ and does not shave every day⟩: **a :** such hair esp. on cheek and chin permitted to grow until capable of being shaped or trimmed ⟨wearing a ~ to conceal the scar on his chin⟩ **b :** hair growing over the face except that on the upper lip — compare MOUSTACHE, WHISKER **2 :** any of certain appendages of animals felt to resemble a beard: as **a :** a tuft or fringe of hair about the mouth or chin of certain mammals (as some dogs or the goat) **b :** any of various groups of processes about the mouth (as of barbels on catfish or hairy feathers at the base of the bill of some birds) **c :** any of certain groups, tufts, or clusters of hairs, filaments, or processes located on the bodies of animals elsewhere than about the mouth (as the gills of certain bivalve mollusks or the tuft of coarse hair on the breast of adult male turkeys) **3 a :** bristlelike often barbed hairs on plants; *esp* **:** the awns of a head of grain **b beards** *pl* **:** the bristly hairs on the acorn cup of the valonia oak used in tanning **4 :** a projecting element: **a :** a barb or point projecting backward or outward (as on a crochet hook) **b :** a spring piece on the back of a lock bolt to prevent rattling **c :** a crosspiece fastened below the upper lip of a flue pipe of an organ to aid in promptness of speech **d :** BEVEL 1e; *sometimes* **:** the bevel plus the shoulder — see TYPE illustration **5 :** the tail of a comet often when preceding the nucleus **6 :** a noticeable error in performance in a broadcast **:** a word misread or mispronounced **:** FLUFF **7 :** a person who diverts attention or suspicion from another; *esp* **:** a person employed to place bets for another whose reputation might affect the odds — **to one's beard :** to one's face **:** in open defiance

[2]**beard** \"\ *vt* -ED/-ING/-S [ME *berden*, fr. *berd*, n.] **1 :** to cause to have a beard — usu. used in adjective uses of the past participle ⟨letters that may be ~*ed*⟩; *specif* **:** to cut barbs on (fishhooks) **2 a :** to remove the gills of (a shellfish) **b :** to bevel or round the edges of (timber) to a required angle or curve **3 :** to confront and oppose with boldness and resolution often to the point of affronting or defying a powerful or secure opponent ⟨no . . . subject on which he has not taken a clear and open stand even to the point of ~*ing* selfish groups —John Steinbeck⟩ **syn** see FACE

beard dance *n* **:** a rhythmic animal dance among No. American Indians imitating the bear and primarily propitiatory for aid in hunting or in effecting cures or in connection with totemic worship

bearded *adj* [ME *berded*, fr. *berd* beard + *-ed*] **1 :** having a beard ⟨a ~ meteor⟩ ⟨a ~ man⟩ — often used in names of animals and plants **2 :** awned or having a growth of hairs **3 :** having a jagged point like a fishhook **:** BARBED

bearded argali *n* **:** AOUDAD

bearded darnel *n* **:** a weedy annual grass (*Lolium temulentum*) with very long awns on the glumes and seeds sometimes considered poisonous that often occurs in grainfields and other cultivated land — called also *cheat*

bearded iris *n* **:** any of numerous wild or cultivated irises with bearded falls — compare BEARDLESS IRIS; see GERMAN IRIS

bearded lizard *also* **bearded dragon** *n* **:** JEW LIZARD

bearded needle *n* **:** SPRING NEEDLE

bearded pig *n* **:** a wild swine (*Sus barbatus*) of Borneo and Malaya with short rounded ears, a wartlike outgrowth between the nostril and eye, and curly whitish whiskers covering the cheeks

bearded seal *n* **:** a large grayish or yellowish arctic seal (*Erignathus barbatus*) having a tuft of flattened bristles on each side of the muzzle

bearded tit *also* **bearded titmouse** *n* **:** a small long-tailed European titlike bird (*Panurus biarmicus*) that frequents reedy places, is largely orange-brown, black, and white, and in the male has a tuft of black feathers on each side of the face — called also *reedling*

bearded tongue *var of* BEARD TONGUE

bearded tortoise *n* **:** MATAMATA

bearded vulture *n* **:** LAMMERGEIER

bearded wheatgrass *n* **:** a wheatgrass (*Agropyron subsecundum*) with straight terminal awns on the lemmas

beard·er \-də(r)\ *n* -S **:** one that beards; *also* **:** one that tends a bearding machine

beard grass *n* **1 :** a grass of the genus *Polypogon* (esp. *P. monspeliensis*) with a densely bearded spike **2 :** any of several common grasses of the genus *Andropogon* (as *A. scoparius*) **3 :** NEEDLEGRASS 2 **4 :** any perennial grass of the genus *Gymnopogon* (family Gramineae) with short rigid leaves and numerous slender flower spikes **5 :** PLUME GRASS 1

beard hair *n* **:** coarse medullated hair of many mammals that grows through and partly covers shorter wool or down (as in goats or seals) **:** KEMP, GUARD HAIR

beard·ie \'birdē\ *n* -S [*beard* + *-ie*; fr. its bristly gills] **1 :** an Australian codlike fish (*Lotella callarias*) with a barbel beneath the lower lip **2 :** a small vigorous shaggy collielike sheep dog of Scottish origin

bearding *n* -S [[1]*beard* + *-ing*] **1 :** a beardlike growth **2 a :** the beveling of a timber to fit the angle of a ship's side **b :** the forward edge of a rudder **:** the corresponding edge of a sternpost

bearding line *n* **:** a line on the side of the stem, deadwoods, keel, and sternpost of a ship marking the intersection of the outer face of the frames with these members

bearding machine *n* **:** a machine that barbs fishhooks

beard·less \'⸗+ləs\ *adj* [ME *berdles*, fr. *berd* beard + *-less*] **1 :** lacking a beard ⟨a ~ barley⟩ **2 a :** too young to have a beard **b :** YOUTHFUL, INEXPERIENCED, CALLOW — **beard·less·ness** *n* -ES

beardless iris *n* **:** any of numerous wild or cultivated irises having no beard on the falls — compare BEARDED IRIS; see JAPANESE IRIS

beardless wheat *n* **:** a wheat in which the outer glumes are without prominent awns — see WHEAT illustration

beard lichen *or* **beard moss** *n* **:** a greenish gray pendulous lichen (*Usnea barbata*) growing on trees

bear dog *n* [[1]*bear*] **:** any of several massive carnivorous extinct mammals of *Amphicyon* and related genera (family Canidae) that suggest but were probably not ancestral to the bears

bear down *vt* [[4]*bear*] **1 a :** to subdue in battle or contention **:** OVERWHELM ⟨the castle defenders were *borne down*⟩ **b :** to overcome in argument or discussion ⟨*borne down* by the weight of evidence⟩ **2 :** to weigh down **:** drag down ⟨branches of the tree *borne down* by the large yield⟩ **~** *vi* **1 a :** to sail esp. with the wind **b** *of ships* **:** to sail toward each other **2 :** to be arduous and zealous **:** exert full strength and concentrated attention ⟨to hold his place he had to *bear down*⟩ ⟨the pitcher *bore down* in the pinches and won the game⟩ **3 :** to contract the abdominal muscles and the diaphragm during childbirth — **bear down on** *or* **bear down upon 1 :** to sail toward often in force or with hostile intent ⟨an enemy frigate *bearing down on* the sloop⟩ **:** proceed toward esp. impressively, awesomely, or forcibly **2 :** to give major attention to **:** STRESS ⟨a lecture that *bore down on* economic causes⟩ **3 :** to weigh heavily on **:** AFFLICT, BURDEN **:** treat in a noticeably demanding way ⟨a tax that *bore down on* the poorer groups⟩ ⟨*bear down on* a man whose work has fallen off⟩

beards *pl of* BEARD, *pres 3d sing of* BEARD

beards·lee trout \'birdzlē-\ *n*, *usu cap B* [after Rear Admiral L.A. *Beardslee* †1903 Am. naval officer] **:** BLUEBACK TROUT b

beard·tongue *also* **beards·tongue** \'⸗,⸗\ *or* **bearded tongue** *n* **:** PENTSTEMON

beardy \'birdē\ *adj* -ER/-EST **:** BEARDED

beared *past of* [2]BEAR

[1]**bear·er** \'berə(r), 'ba(a)r-\ *n* -S [ME *berere*, fr. *beren* to carry + *-er* — more at BEAR] **1 a :** one bearing a communication to or involving another ⟨rewarding the ~ before reading the note⟩ **b :** one who holds a check, note, draft, or other order for the payment of money; *specif* **:** the person in possession of a check payable to bearer whether so drawn or having become so by being last endorsed in blank **2 a :** one that bears: as (1) **:** CARRIER, PORTER ⟨the ~*s* stopped at the door⟩ (2) **:** a man carrying baggage and supplies for travelers in a situation in which other means of transport are lacking ⟨native ~*s* serving the safari⟩ **b :** one that aids actually or symbolically in carrying a dead person in a funeral proceeding **:** PALLBEARER **c :** a palanquin bearer **d** *India* **:** a personal or household servant **e :** a military corpsman who carries stretchers and attends the wounded **3 :** one that affords, yields, produces, or supplies ⟨trees that are good ~*s*⟩ **4 a :** one that holds or enjoys an indicated rank, office, or endowment; *specif* **:** INCUMBENT ⟨an office-*bearer*⟩ **b :** one marked by a distinctive cultural tradition ⟨the invasion of Mexico by Spanish culture ~*s*⟩ **5 a :** one that supports or upholds **:** one that bears a weight ⟨posts, walls, and other ~*s*⟩ **:** a small member (as one of a series) used primarily to support another member or structure (as one of the short pieces of quartering supporting the winders of winding stairs) **b :** something that protects a printing surface from excessive pressure (as from an inking or impressing mechanism) or prevents the inking of a blank part: as (1) **:** one of the pieces of type-high material placed near the corners of the bed of a handpress (2) **:** a track on the bed of a press against which cylinder or rollers rotate (3) **:** type-high material placed in the blank parts of a form or left on the face of an engraving or plate to protect it during molding

[2]**bearer** \"\ *adj* **1 :** freely negotiable by the holder ⟨a ~ check⟩ **2 :** not registered with full title being transferred merely by delivery ⟨~ securities⟩

bear family *n* **:** URSIDAE

bear garden *n* **1 :** an establishment for bearbaiting or similar practices or entertainment **2 :** a scene or procedure marked by unruly rowdy disturbance **:** HURLY-BURLY

bear grape *var of* BEAR'S-GRAPE

bear grass *n* **1 :** any of several liliaceous plants chiefly of the southern and western U.S. that have foliage which resembles coarse blades of grass: as **a :** any of several yuccas (esp. *Yucca glauca* and *Y. filamentosa*) **b :** SOUR GRASS 2 **c :** a plant of the genus *Nolina* native to desert regions of the southwestern U.S. and Mexico and sometimes cultivated as greenhouse succulents **2 a :** a needle grass (*Stipa setigera*) **b :** a bur grass (*Cenchrus pauciflorus*)

bear huckleberry *n* **1 :** any of certain low huckleberries of eastern No. America (esp. *Gaylussacia ursina* and *G. baccata*) **2 :** a low blueberry (*Vaccinium hirsutum*) of the southeastern U.S.

bear hug *n* **:** a rough tight embrace; *specif* **:** a wrestling hold in which a contestant facing his opponent locks his arms around the opponent's back and forces him backwards to the mat

[1]**bear·ing** \'beriŋ, 'ba(a)r-, -rēŋ\ *n* -S [ME *bering*, fr. gerund of *beren* to bear — more at BEAR] **1 a :** the manner in which one bears oneself **:** CARRIAGE ⟨a man of erect and soldierly ~⟩ **b :** the manner in which one comports oneself **:** BEHAVIOR, MIEN ⟨a sedate and dignified ~⟩ ⟨a confident and cheerful ~ —Sheridan LeFanu⟩ **c :** pleasing, impressive, or assured carriage or mien ⟨a man of ~⟩ **2 a :** the act of bringing forth young ⟨weakened by this succession of child-*bearings*⟩ ⟨an older woman past ~⟩ **b :** the action or fact of bringing forth fruit, flowers, or other yield **:** CROP ⟨three ~*s* in a year⟩ **3 :** PRESSURE, THRUST **4 a :** an object, surface, or point that supports **:** supporting power **:** point of support **b :** the act or fact of carrying or supporting **c :** a machine part in which a journal, gudgeon, pivot, pin, or other part revolves, oscillates, or slides — see BALL BEARING, NEEDLE BEARING, ROLLER BEARING, THRUST BEARING **5 a :** a single charge in a coat of arms ⟨the lion is a frequent heraldic ~⟩ **b bearings** *pl* **:** COAT OF ARMS ⟨the ~*s* of Scrope are: azure a bend or⟩ **6 bearings** *pl* **a :** the widest part of a ship below plank-sheer **b :** the line of flotation of a ship when properly trimmed **7 a :** relative situation or position **:** the situation of one point with respect to another or its direction from another **b bearings** *pl* **:** relative positions or directions (as in reference to the compass or to landmarks) **c :** the horizontal direction of an object or point from an observer (as on a ship or aircraft) usu. measured clockwise from a reference direction and expressed in degrees from 0° to 360° **:** AZIMUTH 1b — see COMPASS BEARING, MAGNETIC BEARING, RELATIVE BEARING, TRUE BEARING **d :** an examination or determination of one's position or situation ⟨let's take a ~⟩ **e bearings** *pl* **:** comprehension or appreciation of one's position, environment, or situation **:** perception aiding orientation ⟨time for a newcomer to get his ~*s*⟩ ⟨to lose your ~*s*⟩ **f :** RELATION, CONNECTION **:** full consequence ⟨to consider the matter in all its ~*s*⟩ **:** RELATIONSHIP, INFLUENCE ⟨the question had no ~ on the outcome⟩ **g :** PURPORT, SIGNIFICANCE ⟨the ~ of a remark⟩ **8 a :** the part of any member of a building that rests upon its supports ⟨a lintel or beam with 4 inches of ~ upon the wall⟩ **b :** an unsupported span ⟨the beam has 20 feet of ~ between its supports⟩ **9 a** *sometimes pl* **:** the genital tract of a female domestic animal; *often* **:** its uterus **b bearings** *pl* **:** eversion of the vagina at parturition in the ewe; *also* **:** the everted part

[2]**bearing** \"\ *adj* [ME *bering*, fr. pres. part. of *beren* to bear] **1 :** producing or yielding ⟨an interest-*bearing* note⟩ ⟨fruit-*bearing* trees⟩ **:** marked by or fit for producing or yielding ⟨a good ~ year⟩ ⟨a *bearing*-age tree⟩ **2** *of a structural member* **:** SUPPORTING **:** withstanding a weight, thrust, or strain ⟨a ~ partition⟩

bearing arrow *n* [[1]*bearing*] **:** a war arrow

bearing block *n* [[2]*bearing*] **1 :** a block of material acting as a bearing plate **2** *or* **bearing box** [[1]*bearing*] **:** JOURNAL BOX

bearing brass *n* [[1]*bearing*] **:** a brass or bronze step, bushing, or lining for a bearing

bearing cloth *n* [[1]*bearing*] **:** a cloth with which a child is covered when carried to baptism

bearing off spar *n* [fr. pres. part. of [4]*bear*] **:** a spar to keep two boats apart

bearing pile *n* [[2]*bearing*] **:** a pile driven into the ground so as to carry a vertical load

bearing plate *n* [[2]*bearing*] **:** a plate placed under one end of a truss beam, girder, or column to distribute the load

bearing rein *n* [[2]*bearing*] **:** CHECKREIN 1a

bearing robe *n* [[1]*bearing*] **:** a garment used as a bearing cloth formerly given to a child by his sponsors

bearing value *n* [[1]*bearing*] **:** the compression a rivet will stand

bear·ish \'berish, 'ba(a)rish, -rēsh\ *adj* **1 :** felt to resemble a bear in roughness, gruffness, irascibility, or surliness ⟨disappointed and ~ this morning⟩ **2 a :** marked by or tending to a decline in stock prices ⟨present trends are ~⟩ ⟨a decline in stock prices⟩ **:** DECLINING ⟨present trends are ~⟩ ⟨a ~ effect on the market⟩ **b :** expecting a decline **:** investing on the notion that prices will fall **:** dubious or pessimistic about developments ⟨a ~ stock-market operator⟩ ⟨~ about the new issues of the company⟩ — **bear·ish·ly** *adv*

bear leader *n* [[1]*bear*, fr. the way trained bears were led around on a chain by their masters] **:** one that takes charge of a young man on cultural travels **:** a traveling tutor ⟨sent with a *bear leader* to the continent for years to be ripened —P.E.More⟩

bear mat *n* **:** MOUNTAIN MISERY

bear moss *n* **:** a haircap moss (*Polytrichum juniperinum*)

béar·naise \,ber'nāz, ,ba(a)r'-, ,bär'-, -'nez\ *or* **béarnaise sauce** *n* -S *sometimes cap B* [F *béarnaise*, fem. of *béarnais* of Béarn, region of southwestern France] **:** hollandaise sauce seasoned (as with minced shallots, tarragon, and chervil) and served with meat or fish

bear oak *n* [so called fr. its acorns' serving as food for bears and other wildlife] **:** a shrubby evergreen oak (*Quercus ilicifolia*) of the southeastern U.S. usu. forming dense thickets

bear off *vb* [[4]*bear*] *vt* **1 a :** to ward off **b :** to remove to a distance **:** to keep off or clear from rubbing against anything ⟨*bear off* a boat⟩ **2 :** GAIN **:** carry off (as a prize) **~** *vi* **1 :** to steer away **2 :** to remove the backgammon men finally from the board after they are all home

be around *vi* **:** to have experience **:** become sophisticated; *sometimes* **:** to have sexual experience — used only in perfect tenses ⟨he'll know how to act; he's *been around*⟩

bear out *vt* [[4]*bear*] **:** CORROBORATE, CONFIRM, SUBSTANTIATE ⟨recent discoveries that have *borne out* his theory⟩ ⟨history will *bear* his prediction *out*⟩

bear-paw \'⸗,⸗\ *n* [[1]*bear*] **:** a snowshoe typically blunt and tailless that is suitable for use in mountains or on rocky terrain

bear pig *n* [[1]*bear*] **:** HOG-NOSED BADGER

bear raid *n* [[1]*bear*] **:** concerted selling of securities usu. by short sellers to force down prices

bears *pl of* BEAR, *pres 3d sing of* BEAR

bear's-bed \'⸗,⸗\ *n*, *pl* **bear's-beds :** the soft cushionlike tuft or mat of certain mosses (as *Polytrichum commune*)

bear's-breech \'⸗,⸗\ *n*, *pl* **bear's-breeches :** either of two prickly European herbs (*Acanthus mollis* and *A. spinosus*) having rough-pubescent leaves

bear's-bush \'⸗,⸗\ *var of* BEAR BUSH

bear's-ear \'⸗,⸗\ *also* **bear's-ears** \'⸗,⸗\ *n*, *pl* **bear's-ears :** AURICULA 1

bear's-foot \'⸗,⸗\ *n*, *pl* **bear's-foots :** a hellebore (*Helleborus foetidus*) with digitate leaves, an acrid taste, an offensive odor, and irritant qualities when taken internally

bear's-grape \'⸗,⸗\ *also* **bear grape** *n*, *pl* **bear's-grapes** *also* **bear grapes :** BEARBERRY 1

bear's grease *or* **bear's oil** *n* **:** the rendered fat of the bear

bear's-head \'⸗,⸗\ *n*, *pl* **bear's-heads :** an edible fungus (*Hydnum caput-medusae*) growing on trees in irregular masses

bear·skin \'⸗,⸗\ *n* **1 :** an article (as a rug) made of the skin of a bear **2 :** an often large full-dress military hat made of bearskin **3 :** a coarse shaggy woolen cloth used for making overcoats

bear's-paw \'⸗,⸗\ *n*, *pl* **bear's-paws :** the shell of a large East Indian clam (*Hippopus hippopus*)

bear's-weed \'⸗,⸗\ *n*, *pl* **bear's-weeds :** YERBA SANTA

bear-trap dam \'⸗,⸗-\ *n* **:** a movable dam usu. consisting of two leaves that is used to deepen shallow parts in a river

bear up *vb* [[4]*bear*] *vt* **:** SUPPORT, ENCOURAGE **:** check from sinking, flagging, or becoming discouraged ⟨aid that should *bear* them *up*⟩ ⟨*borne up* in adversity by his faith⟩ **~** *vi* **1 :** to summon up courage, resolution, morale, or strength **:** find stamina to cope or resist ⟨*bearing up* under the long strain⟩ ⟨she *bore up* well during her convalescence⟩ **2 :** to check a horse's head with a checkrein **3 :** to put the helm to windward and so change the ship's course to leeward **:** take a leeward course ⟨the ship *bore up*⟩ **4 :** to keep pace ⟨fain he would *bear up* with his neighbors in that —John Milton⟩ — **bear up for :** to sail toward esp. on a leeward course

bearwalker \'⸗,⸗⸗\ *n* [[1]*bear* + *walker*] **:** a person powerful and malevolent and believed able to assume the shape of a bear or other animal — compare WEREWOLF

bear wallow *n* **:** a declivity or sink in the ground made or capable of having been made by bears

bear·ward \'⸗+,wȯrd\ *n* [ME *bereward*, fr. *bere* bear + *ward* keeper] **:** a bear keeper

bearwood \'⸗,⸗\ *n* **:** CASCARA BUCKTHORN

beas·lings \'bēzlənz, -liŋz\ *dial var of* BEASTINGS

beast \'bēst\ *n* -S *often attrib* [ME *beest*, *beste*, fr. OF *beste*, fr. L *bestia*; perh. akin to Lith *dvasas* spirit, breath — more at DUST] **1 a :** a living creature **:** animal as distinguished from plant **b :** any lower animal as distinguished from man **c :** a 4-footed mammal as distinguished on the one hand from man and on the other from birds and lower vertebrates (as fishes and reptiles) and from invertebrates **d** (1) *obs* **:** any domesticated mammal (2) **:** a game mammal (3) **:** a wild mammal fierce by nature; *esp* **:** a carnivorous wild mammal (4) **:** an animal used for riding or draft; *esp* **:** HORSE (5) **:** a domestic bovine; *esp*, *Brit* **:** a fat or fattening butcher's steer **2 a :** a person arousing contempt or loathing for any of a number of traits (as folly, great stupidity, coarseness, vileness, degradation, lust, or insensate brutality) ⟨called me a ~ and a satyr and asked me whether I had gone mad —Robert Graves⟩ **b :** a thing, situation, or condition felt to be hateful or offensive ⟨a ~ of a day, bleak, cold, and rainy⟩ **3** *slang* **:** GIRL **:** young woman; *esp* **:** a coarse or unattractive woman

beast epic *n* **:** a long verse narrative with climactic epic construction comprising stories of animals represented as acting with human feelings and motives

beast fable *n* **:** a prose or verse fable or short story which usu. points a moral and in which animal characters are represented as acting with human feelings and motives

beast god *n* **:** a god represented wholly or partly in animal form

beastial *obs var of* BESTIAL

beast·ie \'bēstē, -ti\ *n* -S [*beast* + *-ie*] **:** ANIMAL ⟨the buffalo were stubborn ~*s* —W.F.Harris⟩; *often* **:** a small creature ⟨rats and other small ~*s* —W.H.Hudson †1922⟩

beast·i·ly \'bēstəlē\ *adv* **:** BESTIALLY

beast·ings *or* **beest·ings** \'bēstiŋz, -stēŋz\ *also* **beast·lings** \-liŋz, -lēŋz\ *n pl but sing or pl in constr* [ME *bestynge*, fr. OE *bȳsting*, fr. *bēost* beestings; akin to OHG *biost* beestings, ON *beysti* ham — more at BOAST] **:** COLOSTRUM; *esp* **:** the colostrum given by a cow after calving

beast·li·ly \'bēstlēlē\ *adv* **:** in a beastly manner

beast·li·ness \'bēstlēnəs\ *n* -ES [ME *beestlynesse*, fr. *beestly* + *-nesse* -ness] **:** the quality or state of being beastly **:** brutal or disgusting behavior

[1]**beast·ly** \-lē, -li\ *adj* -ER/-EST [ME *beestly*, *bestly*, fr. *beest*, *beste* beast + *-ly*] **1 :** like a beast **:** marked by the traits of an animal and by lack of man's dignity or refinement; *often* **:** lustful or brutal ⟨a ~ froth of rage —Robert Browning⟩ ⟨the abstentious and ~ crudeness of the battlefield —Lewis Mumford⟩ **2 :** like, characteristic of, or relating to animals as opposed to man ⟨~ divinities and droves of gods —Matthew Prior⟩ **3 :** ABOMINABLE, DISGUSTING, DISTASTEFUL, UNPLEASANT ⟨~ weather⟩ ⟨the ~ stench almost made him faint —W.S.Maugham⟩ ⟨the ~ dullness of the village⟩ **syn** see BRUTAL

[2]**beastly** \"\ *adv* -ER/-EST/ [ME *beestly*, *bestly*, fr. *beestly*, *bestly*, adj.] **:** to a beastly degree or in a beastly manner **:** ABOMINABLY, EGREGIOUSLY ⟨~ vulgar —Henry James †1916⟩

beast·man \'bēstmən, -,man\ *n*, *pl* **beastmen 1** *Brit* **:** HERDSMAN **2 :** a low or brutal person

beast of burden : an animal employed to carry heavy material or to perform other heavy work (as pulling a cart or a plow)

beast of chase 1 : any of the animals (as fallow deer, roe deer, fox, marten) that might be kept in or hunted under a chase in medieval England — compare *beast of venery*, *beast of warren* **2 :** a game mammal — not used technically

beast of prey : a carnivorous animal

beast of venery : any of the animals (as red deer, boar, wolf, hare) that might be hunted in the forests (sense 1) in medieval England — called also *beast of the forest;* compare BEAST OF CHASE, BEAST OF WARREN

beast of warren : either the hare or the coney when kept and hunted in a warren (sense 1) — compare BEAST OF CHASE, BEAST OF VENERY

beast tale *n* **:** a prose or verse narrative similar to the beast fable but usu. without a moral

[1]**beat** \'bēt, *usu* -d·+V\ *vb* **beat** \"\ **beaten** \'bēt[ə]n\ *also* **beat** \'bēt, *usu* -d·+V\ *or now dial* **bet** \'bet\ **beating; beats** [ME *beten*, fr. OE *bēatan*; akin to OHG *bōzan* to beat, ON *bauta*, L *-futare* to beat, *fustis* club] *vt* **1 :** to strike repeatedly: **a :** to hit repeatedly with hand, fist, weapon, or other instrument so as to inflict pain (as in order to punish or warn) often cruelly or oppressively ⟨arrested for ~*ing* his wife⟩ ⟨~*ing* the dog for barking at night⟩ ⟨*beaten* by thugs⟩ **b :** to walk on **:** TREAD ⟨~*ing* the streets looking for work⟩ **c :** to strike (part of one's own body) repeatedly in the throes of emotion ⟨the wedding guest he ~ his breast —S.T.Coleridge⟩ or in accordance with musical rhythm ⟨the natives watching the dance, ~*ing* their thighs⟩ **d :** to strike directly against forcefully and repeatedly **:** dash against ⟨a house *beaten* by repeated storms⟩ **e** *obs* **:** to assail or importune with repeated sounds ⟨~*ing* our ears with his endless complaints⟩ **f :** to flail, flap, or thrash at futilely ⟨the trapped bird ~*ing* the air⟩ **g** (1) **:** to strike, lash, or poke at (as in order to rouse game animals or birds) ⟨~*ing* the hedgerow for rabbits⟩ **:** range over in quest of game ⟨~ the woods and rouse the bounding prey —Matthew Prior⟩ **:** SEARCH, SCOUR ⟨~*ing* the woods for the lost child⟩ (2) **:** to sweep a net across to dislodge and capture insects ⟨~*ing* the limb for injurious insects⟩ (3) **:** to hit repeatedly in order to knock something off or out ⟨~*ing* the dirty rugs⟩ ⟨~*ing* the olive trees and picking up the fruit⟩ **h :** to mix together or to bring about frothing in by mixing with air by means of repeated strong turning, stirring, whirling, or agitating **:** WHIP ⟨~*ing* eggs⟩ ⟨~*ing* pancake batter⟩ **i :** to strike repeatedly to produce musical, rhythmical, or meaningful sound ⟨~*ing* a drum⟩ ⟨~*ing* a gong⟩ **2 :** to effect by or as if by repeated striking or hitting: **a :** to drive, force, or impel by blows ⟨*beaten* back by the defenders of the castle⟩ ⟨~*ing* off the savage dogs with a club⟩ **b** (1) **:** to pound into a powder, paste, or pulp ⟨pebbles *beaten* to a fine dust⟩ (2) *papermaking* **:** to subject (fibrous materials) to a mechanical process (as in a beater) causing disintegration, cutting, bruising, and fraying out **c :** to force or drive home by repeated strong admonition or injunction ⟨trying to ~ some sense into these dolts⟩ **d :** BATTER **:** bring or make by hard or crushing blows ⟨*beaten* to the ground by a series of blows⟩ ⟨*beaten* black-and-blue⟩ ⟨*beaten* to death by the mob⟩ ⟨a beached ship *beaten* to pieces in the storm⟩ — used in a number of metaphoric phrases such as *to beat the daylights out of, to beat the tar out of, to beat the devil out of, to beat the life out of, to beat the ears off* **e :** to make by repeated treading, walking, or driving over ⟨~ a path through the thicket⟩ ⟨the trail he used was *beaten* into a road by the feet and wagons of the first homesteaders —*Amer. Guide Series: Mich.*⟩ **f** (1) **:** to dislodge by repeated hitting ⟨~*ing* dust from the carpet⟩ (2) **:** to lodge securely by repeated striking ⟨~*ing* the stakes into the ground⟩ **g :** to shape by beating ⟨~ swords into plowshares⟩; *esp* **:** to flatten out by hammer blows sometimes into leaf thinness ⟨gold *beaten* into strips⟩ **:** make ornamental dents in by beating ⟨*beaten* pewter⟩ **h** (1) **:** to sound by drumming ⟨~*ing* a martial tune⟩ ⟨rain ~ a tattoo on the roof⟩ **:** give a signal for or express a wish for by beat of drum or sound of other instrument ⟨~ an alarm⟩ ⟨~*ing* a charge⟩ ⟨~ the reveille⟩ ⟨~*ing* a parley⟩ (2) *of a drum* **:** to express or signify when beaten ⟨the drums ~ a merry tune⟩ ⟨drums ~*ing* a march⟩ **i :** to flatten (book leaves) by hammering **j :** to ink (a printing surface) by dabbing with ink

balls **3** : to cause to beat, strike, or flap repeatedly ⟨a bird ~*ing* its wing⟩ ⟨~ his foot nervously on the ground —Charles Dickens⟩ ⟨~*ing* their hands in time to the music⟩ **4** : OVERCOME, DEFEAT: **a** : to achieve victory over : conquer, vanquish, or subdue in a battle, contest, strife, race, game, or other competition ⟨~*ing* the insurgents in a bloody battle⟩ ⟨Central ~*ing* Suburban in football⟩ ⟨~*ing* his rival in the election⟩ : bring about the defeat of ⟨his own great wealth ~ him in the election⟩ ⟨*beaten* in the game by their own mistakes⟩ **b** : SURPASS, TOP, EXCEL : be or be judged superior to ⟨a meal hard to ~⟩ ⟨for loveliness it would be hard to ~ —Matthew Arnold⟩ ⟨this dog ~ the others for the blue ribbon⟩ : outdo and supersede ⟨his performance ~*s* the record⟩ — used in a number of phrases sometimes adverbially: *to beat hell, to beat the cars, to beat the band, to beat the devil, to beat the Dutch* ⟨I lay down and cried to ~ the band all afternoon —Scott Fitzgerald⟩ **c** *archaic* : to beat down : endeavor to bring down in price or terms ⟨~*ing* the bargain⟩ **d** : to get the better of, win against, or prevail over or despite ⟨~*ing* the bank with his system⟩ ⟨~*ing* the odds against him⟩ **e** (1) : CHECK : defy all efforts of (one) at solving ⟨a problem that ~ the engineers⟩ (2) : MYSTIFY, BEWILDER, PERPLEX, BAFFLE ⟨it ~*s* me how he does it⟩ (3) : to be too canny to outwit or too capricious to outguess **f** : FATIGUE, EXHAUST — used mostly in passives and adjective uses of the past participle ⟨feeling completely ~ after the race⟩ **g** : CHEAT, DEFRAUD ⟨~*ing* him out of his due return⟩ **h** : to check and leave dispirited, irresolute, or hopeless ⟨a failure at fifty, a *beaten* man⟩ **i** : to escape the possible consequences of : defeat or check the effect of : NULLIFY, VITIATE, SURMOUNT : prevail over ⟨~*ing* the sultry weather⟩ ⟨~*ing* the inflationary trend⟩ **j** : to report a news item in advance of or to the exclusion of (competing newsmen or news media) **k** : ELUDE : break through : get past ⟨the batsman was *beaten* and bowled by an inswinger⟩ **5 a** : FORESTALL, ANTICIPATE : get ahead of : take important or decisive action before ⟨he was going to bid at the auction but I ~ him⟩ **b** : to act ahead of usu. so as to forestall or make ineffective the engaging in a like action of (another) ⟨~*ing* his enemy to the draw⟩ ⟨he ~ his opponent to the punch⟩ **c** : to act or to complete an act before (a determined final point in time) ⟨~ the deadline⟩ **d** : to come to, arrive at, or sojourn at before ⟨another man ~ me to the empty chair⟩ : arrive at a goal or destination before ⟨the fielder's throw ~ the baserunner⟩ **e** : to start or to do something before (an official signal to begin) ⟨~ the gun⟩ ⟨leaving early and ~*ing* the whistle⟩ **f** : CIRCUMVENT : surmount or escape from by devious procedure ⟨no system can be devised that cannot be *beaten* by collusion —*Jour. of Accountancy*⟩ **6** : to indicate by one's motions (a musical beat or tempo) ⟨a young conductor will ~ wildly almost any tempo —Warwick Braithwaite⟩ ~ *vi* **1 a** : DASH, STRIKE : become forcefully impelled : fall violently ⟨waves ~ against the shore⟩ ⟨rain ~*ing* on the roof⟩ **b** : to glare with continuing oppressive intensity ⟨burning hot weather, with the sun ~*ing* down —G.W.Talbot⟩ : become projected steadily with unpleasant force or intensity ⟨the heat in the shadeless fields ~*s* down on the steaming black earth —Marjory S. Douglas⟩ **c** : to sustain violent or strident activity with a demanding distracting effect ⟨the turbulence of the Renaissance and the quarrels of England and Spain ~*ing* about his head —Douglas Stewart⟩ **d** : to make a succession of strokes on a drum ⟨the drummers ~ to call soldiers to their quarters⟩ **2 a** : to course or operate with perceptible strokes : PULSATE ⟨my pulse ~ so quickly and hardly that I felt the palpitation of every artery —Mary W. Shelley⟩ **b** : to throb with animation : pulsate strongly; *often* : to demand attention with agitating exigency ⟨her dominant will ~ so strongly within her —Hugh Walpole⟩ ⟨his breathing was hard and . . . the blood ~ in his ears and eyes —Robertson Davies⟩ ⟨a question was ~*ing* unanswered at the back of her brain —Ellen Glasgow⟩ **c** *of a timepiece* : to operate audibly : TICK ⟨the ~*ing* of the clock⟩ **d** (1) : to sound upon being struck ⟨the drums ~⟩ (2) : to become sounded by or as if by drums ⟨before the assembly ~*s* —W.M.Thackeray⟩ **e** : to result in beats (as produced by two simultaneous tones of slightly different frequencies) ⟨the B ~*s* unpleasantly with the C⟩ **3 a** : to strike repeatedly : inflict repeated blows : knock or pound vigorously or loudly ⟨their air attack still ~*ing* upon us —Sir Winston Churchill⟩ ⟨~*ing* on the door of the cabin⟩ **b** *of a hare* : to tap the ground as a mating gesture **c** : to strike the air : FLAP ⟨the wings of the bird ~*ing* feebly⟩ **d** : to strike bushes or other cover to rouse game; *also* : to range or scour for or as if for game **4** : to progress with changes of direction or procedure: **a** : to make progress to windward by sailing in a zigzag line (as by tacking) **b** : to sail with much tacking ⟨~*ing* along the coast⟩ **c** : to make one's way persistently and often arduously usu. by a series of expedient choices ⟨the castaways ~*ing* inland⟩ **5** : WIN ⟨our team will ~⟩

syn POUND, PUMMEL, THRASH, THRESH, BUFFET, BASTE, BELABOR: BEAT is a general word to designate repeated striking ⟨*beat* a carpet⟩ ⟨*beat* a child, hitting him repeatedly⟩ ⟨a savage *beating*⟩ POUND may apply to beating with heavier, more massive, damaging, or crushing blows ⟨a tropical hurricane *pounded* the island with giant waves —Martin Gardner⟩ ⟨the artillery and the dive bombers *pounded* the defense —S.L.A. Marshall⟩ PUMMEL may apply to a continuous shower of blows not massive but fairly heavy and damaging ⟨with Dick fastened on him, *pummeling* away most unmercifully —Samuel Lover⟩ ⟨the piers are *pummelled* by the waves —W.H.Auden⟩ THRASH and THRESH apply to repeated striking as with a flail, stick, or whip ⟨*thrashing* grain⟩ ⟨*thrash* a child or servant⟩ ⟨Indians paddle into the swamp, two men in each canoe; while one rows the other *threshes* the rice heads into the boat with two sticks —*Amer. Guide Series: Minn.*⟩ BUFFET, often used figuratively, implies a repeated striking, heavy slapping, cuffing to and fro ⟨Sung Yung was shoved about and *buffeted* by angry hands —T.B.Costain⟩ ⟨the two hands of Madame Defarge *buffeted* and tore her face —Charles Dickens⟩ ⟨*buffeted* by the bewildering passions and divided loyalties —C.J.Rolo⟩ BASTE may imply a thorough cudgeling, thrashing, or beating ⟨if you will give me the loan of a horsewhip, I'll *baste* the backs of these lazy fellows of yours —J.H. Wheelwright⟩ BELABOR suggests a prolonged beating or drubbing ⟨a group of demonstrating Egyptians being *belabored* by police —R.C.Doty⟩ **syn** see in addition CONQUER, PULSATE

— **beat about the bush** *also* **beat around the bush** : to fail or refuse to come to the point in discourse — **beat a retreat** : to retreat or retire often in haste or with loss of dignity — **beat goose** *or* **beat the booby** : to thrust the hands under the armpits to warm them — **beat hollow** *or* **beat all hollow** : to defeat or surpass utterly ⟨*beat* his opponents *hollow*⟩ ⟨this movie *beats* that one *all hollow*⟩ — **beat it 1** : to hurry away : get out in a rush : SCRAM ⟨the youngsters *beat it* when the police came⟩ **2** : HURRY, RUSH ⟨the reporter *beat it* to a telephone to call in the news⟩ — **beat one's brains out** *or* **beat one's brains** : to cudgel one's brain : try continually and energetically to think out something difficult — **beat one's breast** *or* **beat one's chest** : to declaim often vaingloriously or vauntingly and usu. in vindicating oneself — **beat one's gums** : to talk continually or excessively; to talk with little effect — **beat one's time** : to surpass one's understanding : leave one puzzled or mystified — **beat one's way** : to make one's way usu. against difficulties by a series of resourceful expedients or varied means ⟨*beating his way* across country doing odd jobs —Elmer Davis⟩ ⟨*beating his way* on foot, muleback, raft, and canoe⟩ — **beat the air** : to flail away at nothing — **beat the bounds** : to survey the bounds of an English parish by marching in procession and marking them at various points by switching with boughs — **beat the bushes** : to scour or search through all likely or possible areas ⟨*beating the bushes* for promising talent⟩ — **beat the drum** *also* **beat a drum** : to declaim as meritorious or esp. significant : publicize or argue noisily ⟨publicity men *beating the drum* about the new star⟩ ⟨*beat the drum* for him as a candidate⟩ — **beat the rap** : to escape or evade the penalties connected with an accusation or charge ⟨he was charged with arson but he *beat the rap*⟩ — **beat the time of** : to cut out esp. with a date : court and win the choice of (another suitor) — **beat time** : to measure or mark off musical time by strokes or taps — **beat to leeward** : to sail before the wind with mainsail and headsails trimmed for a broad reach at an angle to the course first on one side of the course and then after jibbing on the other — **beat to windward** : BEAT *vi* 4a

[2]**beat** \"\ *n* -s **1 a** : a single stroke, blow, or pulsation; *also* : the sound so produced **b** : a stroke in a series or a set of strokes as on a drum; *also* : the sound so given **c** : the driving impact of or as if of steady blows ⟨the full force of the surf ~ —Joyce Allan⟩ ⟨the fierce ~ of the eastern sun —T.B.Costain⟩ **d** : the number of strokes per minute rowed by a racing crew or completed by a swimmer ⟨the cox lifted the ~ to 36⟩ **2 a** : one swing of the pendulum or the balance of a timepiece **b** : the tick or other sound made as a tooth of the escape wheel in a timepiece engages a pallet face of the escapement **3** : each of the pulsations of amplitude recurring at regular intervals produced by the union of sound waves, radio waves, or electric currents having different frequencies, the frequency of the beats being the sum or difference between the frequencies of the waves or currents **4 a** : a sharp tap delivered on a fencing opponent's blade esp. to open up a line of attack **b** : an accented stroke in dancing (as of one leg or foot against the other, one prop against another, or the hand against a part of the body) **5 a** : a recurring stroke : THROB, PULSATION ⟨a heart ~⟩; *also* : the sound of such a throb **b** : the sound of a steady sequence of blows or strokes ⟨the ~ of the waves on the rock⟩ : a steady sequence of sounds **c** : an effect of rhythmical repetition ⟨the ~ of a poet's verse⟩ : metrical or rhythmical stress **6 a** : a grace or ornament in early English music probably equivalent to a mordent **b** : the recurring periodic accent that constitutes the basis of meter in all metrical music **c** : the unit of time or tempo measurement indicated to the performer (as by a movement of a conductor's hand or baton or by the tick of a metronome) **d** : the pronounced and swinging rhythm that is characteristically the generating or driving force in jazz music and jazz bands ⟨that band has a fine ~⟩ **e** : a noteworthy rhythmical effect ⟨the irregular ~ of city life⟩ **7 a** : a round, course, or stretch frequently gone over : an habitual range or resort : an area frequently traversed esp. in the course of work or duty ⟨a policeman's ~⟩ **b** : a tract with more or less definite bounds over which sportsmen customarily range for game **c** (1) : a scouring of a tract of land to rouse or drive out game (2) : those engaged in a beat **d** : the area of one's special duty, responsibility, or jurisdiction **e** : a group of news sources that a reporter covers regularly **f** : one's special range of knowledge or interests **8** : the part of a valve surface that contacts the seat when the valve is closed **9 a** : an administrative subdivision of a county in Alabama or Mississippi — called also *supervisor district* **b** : an election precinct in Alabama or Mississippi **10 a** : something that excels or surpasses ⟨I have never seen the ~ of it⟩ **b** : the reporting of an important news story ahead of or to the exclusion of one's competitors; *broadly* : an action defeating or checking a competitor **11 a** : DEADBEAT 2 **b** : one that fails to make returns **c** : a shiftless character : LOAFER **12 a** : an act of beating to windward **b** : one of the reaches in the zigzag course so traversed : TACK — **in beat** : in a condition in which a timepiece pendulum or balance receives its impulses when at equal distances from the dead point — **off one's beat** : out of one's accustomed sphere or scope — **off the beat** *or* **off beat** : out of tempo : showing irregularity : off the beam — **out of beat** : in a condition in which a pendulum or balance receives its impulses at unequal distances from the dead point

[3]**beat** \"\ *adj* [ME *bete*, fr. *bete, beten*, past part. of *beten* to beat] **1** : EXHAUSTED : used up : completely tired ⟨so ~ that I'd flop down and go to sleep fully dressed —Polly Adler⟩ **2** : BEATEN 3 **3** : marked by injury or weakness brought about by the jarring impacts incident to working with a pick ⟨a miner with a ~ hand⟩ **4** : of, relating to, or having the characteristics of beatniks ⟨~ jargon⟩ ⟨~ generation⟩ ⟨~ poet⟩

[4]**beat** \"\ *n* -s : BEATNIK

[5]**beat** \'bēt, 'bāt\ *dial Brit var of* [3]BEET

[6]**beat** \"\ *n* -s [origin unknown] *Brit* : turf pared from fallow land for spreading and burning on cropland as a fertilizer

be·a·ta \bā'ād·ə, -ätə,-äd·(,)ä,-ä(,)tä *sometimes* bē'ād·ə, -ätə\ *n, pl* **bea·tae** \bā'äd·(,)ā, -ä(,)tā *sometimes* bē'äd·(,)ē, -ä(,)tē, -äd·,ī,-ä,tī\ *also* **beatas** \-əz,-äz\ [L, fr. fem. of *beatus* happy — more at BEATIFY] *Roman Catholic Church* : a woman or girl who has been beatified

beat about *vi* **1** : to range about in quest or search **2** : to change course repeatedly : TACK; *esp* : to experiment to find an expedient course

beat back *vt* : REPULSE, REPEL : drive back ⟨*beat back* the enemy⟩

beat board *n* [[2]*beat*] : a short slanted platform used as a take-off in vaulting and broad jumping

beat down *vt* **1** : to harass, subdue, or crush the spirit of ⟨he *beat down* the arrogance of a heretic —H.O.Taylor⟩ : VANQUISH ⟨the enemy was *beaten down*⟩ **2 a** : to haggle for a reduction of : force down by haggling ⟨*beating* the price *down*⟩ : cause lowering of **b** : to force esp. by haggling into accepting a lower price or more advantageous arrangement ⟨we *beat* him *down* to a dollar⟩

beat·em·est *also* **beat·'em·est** \'bētəməst\ *adj* [prob. alter. of *beatingest*, fr. superl. of *beating*, pres. part. of [1]*beat*] *dial* : BEST : most outstanding or powerful

beaten *adj* [ME *beten*, fr. past part. of *beten* to beat] **1** : wrought by hammering : hammered into shape : hammered thin or fine ⟨~ gold⟩; *sometimes* : REPOUSSÉ **2 a** : much trodden and worn smooth or bare; *sometimes* : FAMILIAR, WELL-KNOWN ⟨a ~ path⟩ **b** *archaic* : TRITE **3** : defeated or checked and sapped of strength, resolution, and morale ⟨too ~ to pull himself out of the latest mess —Laurent Le Sage⟩ **4 a** : [3]BEAT 1 **b** : worn out : exhausted of fertility ⟨~ soil⟩ **c** : much worn : BATTERED, TATTERED, DILAPIDATED ⟨one of my most precious volumes is a ~ old volume —Christopher Morley⟩

beaten biscuit *n* : a biscuit made of a dough of flour, water, and shortening lightened by beating and folding

beaten-up \'==,=\ *adj* : WORN, BATTERED, DILAPIDATED ⟨a *beaten-up* old car⟩

beaten zone *n* : the elliptical ground area struck by the fire of automatic weapons or by artillery projectiles

beater \'bēd·ə(r), -ētə\ *n* -s [ME *beter*, fr. *beten* to beat + *-er*] **1** : one that beats: as **a** : a plasterer's staff for beating mortar **b** : a tool for packing tamping on a charge of powder in a blasthole **c** : MAUL **d** : a device like a fan placed at the back of the cylinder in a grain thresher for directing straw to straw racks **e** : DOWN-BEATER **f** : an attachment to the discharge end of a manure spreader for pulverizing the manure as it passes from the spreader **g** : the part of a flail that strikes the grain in threshing **h** : a revolving cylinder bearing chains or flails that chop up standing cornstalks, potato vines, brush, or sugar-beet tops **i** : a tailor's paddle used in pressing **j** : a kitchen utensil used for beating, stirring, or whipping **k** : a device on a cotton picker or opener for separating raw cotton **l** : a knife for breaking flax or hemp **m** : the lay of a loom for driving the weft from the shed into the cloth **n** : a machine consisting essentially of a tank equipped with adjustable cutting elements between which paper stock passes to be cut or beaten and in which coloring, loading, and sizing are sometimes done — compare HOLLANDER **o** : a heavy iron for beating basketwork into compactness **p** : a worker who spreads filler material evenly in quilts or mattresses **2 a** : one that beats up game in hunting ⟨engaged a native ~⟩ **b** : an advance publicity agent **3** *in Newfoundland* : a young harp seal on its first journey northward from the breeding area

beater 1j

beater chest *n* : a reservoir into which paper pulp is discharged from beaters

beat·er·man \'==mən, -,man\ *n, pl* **beatermen** : one in charge of a beater in paper manufacturing

beater roll *n* : a rotating roller in a papermaking beater that is faced with a series of parallel bars or knives that brush against similar bars in the bedplate

beater-size \'==,=\ *vt* : to make (paper) from pulp mixed with a sizing agent in a beater — compare SURFACE-SIZE, TUB-SIZE

beati *pl of* BEATUS

be·a·tif·ic \,bēə'tifik\ *also* **be·a·tif·i·cal** \-fəkəl\ *adj* [L *beatificus*, fr. *beatus* happy (fr. past part. of *beare* to bless, make happy) + *-i-* + *-ficus* -fic; akin to L *bonus* good — more at BOUNTY] **1** : of, possessing, or imparting beatitude **2** : marked by an appearance of complete bliss or utter benignity : SAINTLY, ANGELIC, SERAPHIC — **be·a·tif·i·cal·ly** \-fək(ə)lē, -li\ *adv*

be·a·tif·i·cate \,bēə'tifə,kāt, bē'ad·əfə,-, *usu* -ād· + V\ *vt* -ED/-ING/-S [It *beatificato* (past part. of *beatificare*), fr. LL *beatificatus*, past part. of *beatificare*, fr. L *beatificus*] : BEATIFY

be·at·i·fi·ca·tion \bē,ad·əfə'kāshən, -,atəf-\ *n* -s [LL *beatification-, beatificatio*, fr. *beatificatus* + L *-ion-, -io* -ion] **1** : the act of beatifying **2** : the state of being beatified

beatific vision *n* : the immediate sight of God in the glory of heaven : the direct intuition of God

be·at·i·fy \bē'ad·ə,fī, -'atə,fī\ *vt* -ED/-ING/-ES [MF *beatifier*, fr. LL *beatificare*] **1** : to make supremely happy : endow with beatitude and bliss **2** *Roman Catholicism* : to declare (a deceased person) to have attained the blessedness of heaven and authorize the title "Blessed" and limited public religious honor for — compare CANONIZE

beat·in'·est *or* **beat·in·est** *also* **beat·en·est** \'bēt[ə]nəst\ *adj* [alter. of *beatingest*, fr. superl. of *beating*, pres. part. of [1]*beat*] *chiefly South & Midland* : surpassing all others : most unusual or surprising

beating *n* -s [ME *beting*, fr. gerund of *beten* to beat] : a material or immaterial injury, impairment, or detriment like the bruising of heavy blows ⟨taking a ~ in the stock market⟩

beating engine *n* : BEATER 1n

beating reed *n* : a reed covering an air opening in a musical instrument so as to vibrate against the edge of an air slot (as in a clarinet or organ pipe) — compare FREE REED

be·at·i·tude \bē'ad·ə,tüd, -'atə,-, -ə,tyüd\ *n* -s [L *beatitudo*, fr. *beatus* happy + *-tudo* -tude] **1** : the quality or state of being blessed : consummate bliss **2** : transcendent happiness **3** : a declaration of a specific condition for being blessed or gaining a kind of bliss **4** : BEATIFICATION **5** : a patriarch in either the Eastern or Western Orthodox Church : the head of any of certain autocephalous Eastern churches — used mostly as a title ⟨his ~ the Patriarch⟩ **syn** see HAPPINESS

beat man *n* [[2]*beat*] : a newsman with a regular beat

beat·nik \'bētnik, -nēk\ *n* -s [[3]*beat* + *-nik* (as in *nudnik*)] : a person having a predilection for unconventional behavior and dress and often a preoccupation with exotic philosophizing and self-expression

beat off *vt* : REPEL, REPULSE : drive back

beat·om·est \'bētəməst\ *var of* BEATEMEST

beat out *vt* **1** : to make or perform by or as if by beating ⟨*beating out* pewter ware⟩ : accomplish by beating ⟨*beat out* a path⟩ **2** : to prevail over (a rival or competitor) ⟨*beat out* another firm in bidding⟩ ⟨*beat out* others for a job⟩ **3** : EXHAUST, WEARY **4 a** : to mark or accompany by beating ⟨*beat out* the rhythm strongly⟩ **b** : PLAY ⟨*beat out* jazz⟩ **5** : to turn (a ground ball) into a hit in baseball by fast running to first base

beat-out *adj* [fr. past part. of *beat out*] : WEARY, EXHAUSTED : [3]BEAT 1 ⟨too *beat-out* to think, even about home —L.M.Uris⟩

beats *pres 3d sing of* BEAT, *pl of* BEAT

beat up *vi* **1** : to sail or attempt to sail against adverse winds or currents ⟨*beating up* for hours trying to enter the harbor⟩ **2** : to go about zealously seeking ⟨*beat up* for likely recruits⟩ ~ *vt* **1** : DISTURB, ALARM, AROUSE ⟨urgent messengers *beating up* the general's quarters⟩ **2** : to muster up ⟨*beating up* volunteers for the corps⟩ **3** : to bring to froth or mix thoroughly by repeated beating, stirring, or whipping : [1]BEAT 1h ⟨*beat up* an egg⟩ **4** : to beat soundly with fists or clubs or other weapons : THRASH ⟨thugs and brutes who *beat up* their victims without compunction —J.H.Plumb⟩ ⟨*beat up* a scab⟩ **5** : to remove (a depression or mark) from the face of an engraver's plate by striking the back **6** : to drive (the filling) into its proper position in a fabric being woven **7** : to force (as by haggling) into acceptance of a higher price or offer

[1]**beat-up** \'=;=\ *adj* [fr. past part. of *beat up*] : worn or damaged by hard or long use or by neglect : DILAPIDATED, EXHAUSTED ⟨a *beat-up* car fifteen years old⟩ ⟨a *beat-up* suit⟩

[2]**beat-up** *n* -s [*beat up*] : tufts per inch warpwise in Axminster and chenille carpeting

be·a·tus \bā'äd·əs, -ätəs,-äd·(,)üs,-ä(,)tüs *sometimes* bē'ād·əs, -ātəs\ *n, pl* **bea·ti** \bā'äd·(,)ē, -ä(,)tē *sometimes* bē'äd·,ī, -ä,tī\ [L, blessed, happy — more at BEATIFIC] *Roman Catholicism* : a man or boy who has been beatified

beat your neighbor *n* : a form of poker in which a player must drop unless his exposed cards form a higher-ranking combination than the exposed cards of the player to his right

[1]**beau** \'bō\ *adj* [ME, fr. MF] : FAIR, GOOD, GALLANT

[2]**beau** \"\ *n, pl* **beaux** \'bōz, 'bō\ *or* **beaus** \'bōz\ [F, fr. *beau* fine, beautiful, fr. OF *biau, bel*, fr. L *bellus* pretty — more at BEAUTY] **1** : a man who shows careful, meticulous, or vain addiction to the latest fashions in dress, bearing, and etiquette : DANDY — formerly used as an epithet or sobriquet ⟨the magnificent ~, dancing to the light of chandeliers —T.L.Peacock⟩ **2 a** : a man or boy who goes frequently or steadily with a woman or girl : ESCORT, STEADY **b** : a man or boy in an intimate relationship with a woman or girl : LOVER, SWEETHEART ⟨her ~'s gone and left her —William Faulkner⟩

[3]**beau** \"\ *vt* -ED/-ING/-S : go with : act as beau to : ESCORT ⟨all of us ~*ed* the girls to the little dances —W.A.White⟩

beau brum·mel *also* **beau brummell** \(')bō'brəməl\ *n, pl* **beau brummels** *also* **beau brummells** *usu cap both B's* [after *Beau Brummell*, nickname of George B. Brummell †1840 Eng. dandy] **1** : a typical or extreme dandy **2** : a man's dressing table of 18th century design with an adjustable mirror, side leaves, and many small drawers or compartments

beaufet *archaic var of* [3]BUFFET

beau·fort cipher \'bōfə(r)t-\ *n, usu cap B* [after Sir Francis *Beaufort* †1857 Eng. naval officer and hydrographer] : a system of polyalphabetic substitution equivalent to Vigenère cipher with a reversed normal cipher sequence, the keying formula of which is P+C=K

beaufort scale *n, usu cap B* [after Sir Francis *Beaufort*] : a

BEAUFORT SCALE

BEAUFORT NUMBER	NAME	MILES PER HOUR	DESCRIPTION
0	Calm	Less than 1	Calm; smoke rises vertically
1	Light air	1–3	Direction of wind shown by smoke but not by wind vanes
2	Light breeze	4–7	Wind felt on face; leaves rustle; ordinary vane moved by wind
3	Gentle breeze	8–12	Leaves and small twigs in constant motion; wind extends light flag
4	Moderate breeze	13–18	Raises dust and loose paper; small branches are moved
5	Fresh breeze	19–24	Small trees in leaf begin to sway; crested wavelets form on inland waters
6	Strong breeze	25–31	Large branches in motion; telegraph wires whistle; umbrellas used with difficulty
7	Moderate gale	32–38	Whole trees in motion; inconvenience in walking against wind
8	Fresh gale	39–46	Breaks twigs off trees; generally impedes progress
9	Strong gale	47–54	Slight structural damage occurs; chimney pots and slates removed

(*Continued*)

BEAUFORT SCALE — *continued*

BEAUFORT NUMBER	NAME	MILES PER HOUR	DESCRIPTION
10	Whole gale	55–63	Trees uprooted; considerable structural damage occurs
11	Storm	64–72	Very rarely experienced; accompanied by widespread damage
12	Hurricane	73–82	Devastation occurs
13	Hurricane	83–92	Devastation occurs
14	Hurricane	93–103	Devastation occurs
15	Hurricane	104–114	Devastation occurs
16	Hurricane	115–125	Devastation occurs
17	Hurricane	126–136	Devastation occurs

wind scale in which the force of the wind is indicated by a series of numbers from 0 to 17, orig. from 0 to 12, with corresponding descriptive terms, these terms being commonly used by the U.S. Weather Bureau

beau geste \(ˈ)bōˈzhest\ *n, pl* **beaux gestes** *or* **beau gestes** \"\ [F, lit., beautiful gesture] **1 :** a graceful pleasing fine or magnanimous gesture **2 :** a gracious conciliatory insubstantial or ineffectual gesture

beau greg·o·ry \(ˈ)bōˈgregərē\ *also* **beau gre·goire** \-greˈgwär\ *n, pl* **beau gregories** \-(ˌ)rēz\ *also* **beau gregoires** \-ˈgwärz\ *often cap B&G* [¹*beau* + the name *Gregory*] **:** a small blue-and-gold pomacentrid fish (*Eupomacentrus leucostictus*) found along the coasts of Florida and the West Indies

beau ideal \(ˈ)bō,īˈdēl, *esp bef pause or cons* -ēəl\ *n* [F *beau idéal* ideal beauty] **1** *pl* **beaus ideal** \(ˈ)bōˌzī-\ *or* **beaux ideal** \" *also* (ˈ)bō,ī-\ **:** ideal or perfect beauty **2** *pl* **beau ideals** \(ˈ)bō,īdē(ə)lz\ **:** the perfect type or model **:** a type attaining to highest excellence ⟨the *beau ideal* of all that was romantic, exquisite, and passionate —Harrison Smith⟩ **syn** see MODEL

beau·jo·lais \ˌbōzhəˌlā\ *n, pl* **beaujolaises** \-āz\ *usu cap* [F, fr. *Beaujolais*, region of central France] **:** a red Burgundy table wine from grapes grown between the Loire and Saône around Beaujeu in the department of Rhone, France

beaumé *usu cap, var of* BAUMÉ

beau monde \(ˈ)bōˌmōnd, -mänd\ *n, pl* **beau mondes** *or* **beaux mondes** [F, lit., fine world] **:** the world of high society and fashion

beau·mon·tage \bōˈmäntij\ *n* -s [origin unknown] **:** a composition used by artisans to fill and conceal holes or cracks in wood or metal

beau·mon·tia \bōˈmänsh(ē)ə, -tēə\ *n, cap* [NL, fr. Lady *Beaumont*, 19th cent. Englishwoman + NL *-ia*] **:** a small genus of East Indian woody vines (family Apocynaceae) having very large showy fragrant white flowers and being grown as ornamental climbers in warm regions

beau·mont root \ˈbō(ˌ)mänt-, -ōmənt-\ *n, usu cap B* [prob. fr. the name *Beaumont*] **:** CULVER'S ROOT

beaune \ˈbōn\ *n* -s *usu cap* [F, fr. *Beaune*, France] **:** a usu. red table wine produced in the department of Côte d'Or, France

beaus *pl of* BEAU, *pres 3d sing of* BEAU

beau sa·breur \ˌbōsaˈbrər\ *n, pl* **beau sabreurs** \-rz\ *or* **beaux sabreurs** \ˌbōsa-\ [F, lit., handsome swordsman] **:** a dashing adventurer

¹**beau·sé·ant** \ˌbōsāˈäⁿ\ *n* -s [MF *beaucéant*, fr. OF *baucent* spotted with white — more at BAUSOND] **:** the black-and-white banner of the Knights Templars

²**beauséant** \"\ *interj* — used as a battle cry by the Knights Templars

beaut \ˈbyüt, usu -d.+V\ *n* -s [short for *beauty*] *slang* **:** a beautiful, outstanding, or egregious example **:** BEAUTY

beau·te·ous \ˈbyüd·ēəs, -ütēəs, -ü·tyəs *sometimes* ÷ üchəs\ *adj* [ME, fr. *beaute* + *-ous*] **:** replete with beauty **:** commanding rapt appreciation for sensuous beauty ⟨~ even where beauties most abound —Lord Byron⟩ **syn** see BEAUTIFUL

beau·te·ous·ly *adv* [ME, fr. *beauteous* + *-ly*] **:** in a beauteous manner

beau·te·ous·ness *n* -ES **:** the quality or state of being beauteous

beau·ti·cian \byüˈtishən\ *n* -s [*beauty* + *-ician*] **:** COSMETOLOGIST

beau·ti·fi·ca·tion \ˌbyüd·əfəˈkāshən, -ütəf-\ *n* -s **:** BEAUTIFYING

beau·ti·fi·er \ˈ⸗⸗ˌfī(ə)r\ *n* -s **:** one that beautifies

¹**beau·ti·ful** \ˈbyüd·əfəl, -yütə- *also* -yüd·ēf-, -yütēf-\ *adj, sometimes* -ER/-EST [*beauty* + *-ful*] **1 :** marked by beauty: **a :** keenly delighting the senses as approaching perfection or the ideal in form, proportion, arrangement, grace, color, or sound ⟨seldom have I seen . . . so ~ a face. She was a blonde, golden-haired, blue-eyed —A. Conan Doyle⟩ ⟨the Song of Songs, ~, orientally sensuous, too glowing perhaps for western taste —H.O.Taylor⟩ ⟨a ~ sonorous and flexible language —H.T.Buckle⟩ **b :** delighting with a higher, more exalted appeal **:** calling forth great spiritual, intellectual, and aesthetic appreciation **:** lofty in effect ⟨an Aquinas in his cell before a crucifix or a Narcissus . . . equally ~ —W.H.Mallock⟩ **2 a :** attractive or impressive through expressing or suggesting fitness, order, regularity, rhythm, cogency, or perfection of structure ⟨this most ~ system of the sun, planets, and comets —Isaac Newton⟩ ⟨the deep canyon of Broadway, between those vast structures, ~ but sinister —P.E.More⟩ ⟨his arguments were ~ and deserved to be true —Francis Galton⟩ **b :** perfect, nearly perfect, or extremely attractive through such qualities as honesty, devotion, charity, or self-sacrifice ⟨young children not infrequently have an exquisitely ~ saintliness of character —W.R.Inge⟩ **c :** marked by practically perfect unerring art, skill, finesse, technique, or polish ⟨he made a ~ shot on that leopard —Ernest Hemingway⟩ ⟨its accurate and ~ record of folk dialect —*Amer. Guide Series: Ind.*⟩ ⟨a ~ book so technically perfect that the professional writer stands in awe of it —*Saturday Rev.*⟩ **d :** perfect as an illustration **:** outstanding as a type or model ⟨a case of disease may be so typical in its exhibition of characteristic relations as to be called ~ —John Dewey⟩ **3 :** generally pleasing **:** FINE, EXCELLENT, DELECTABLE **:** superlatively good **:** lacking anything detracting from enjoyment ⟨~ weather⟩ ⟨a ~ friendship⟩ ⟨a ~ roast turkey⟩

syn LOVELY, BEAUTEOUS, PULCHRITUDINOUS, PRETTY, COMELY, BONNY, FAIR, HANDSOME, GOOD-LOOKING: BEAUTIFUL, wide in its application and extreme in praise, describes a close approach to an ideal and indicates a quite keen delight in contemplation ⟨O Cynthia, ten times bright and fair! . . . too divine art thou, too keen in beauty . . . how *beautiful* thou art —John Keats⟩ ⟨after nursery rhymes they should learn equally *beautiful* songs —Bertrand Russell⟩ ⟨the Deanery is now a *beautiful* private residence with herbaceous borders —E.V. Lucas⟩ LOVELY suggests sensuous or emotional delights ⟨Freydis now showed as the most *lovely* of womenkind. She had black plaited hair, and folds of crimson silk were over her white flesh, and over her shoulders was a black coat embroidered with little gold stars —J.B.Cabell⟩ BEAUTEOUS, a rather literary word, and PULCHRITUDINOUS, a relatively new word uncommon outside journalism, stress rich appeal ⟨young maidens came, *beauteous* and calm, like shapes of living stone, clothed in the light of dreams —P.B.Shelley⟩ PRETTY suggests presence of grace, charm, vivacity, daintiness, or petiteness, an absence of perfection, ideality, stateliness, and dignity ⟨she was *pretty* at all times . . . with her light-brown ringlets, her delicately tinged but healthful cheek, her sensitive, intelligent, yet most feminine and kindly face. But every few moments, the *pretty* and girlish face grew beautiful and striking, as some inward thought and feeling brightened, rose to the surface —Nathaniel Hawthorne⟩ ⟨as a *pretty* household toy, Pussy was carried from Africa to Europe —Agnes Repplier⟩ COMELY and BONNY, which has a Scotch suggestion, stress pleasant wholesomeness and fitness ⟨a quick brunette, well molded, falcon-eyed. . . . '*Comely*, too, by all that's fair' —Alfred Tennyson⟩ ⟨your *bonny* face sae mild and sweet his honest heart enamors —Robert Burns⟩ FAIR, less common as a synonym for BEAUTIFUL in today's English, may suggest lightness or freshness ⟨the girl was certainly *fair* to look upon. Many heavens were in her sunny eyes, and the outline of that arm of hers . . . was the very curve of beauty —Herman Melville⟩ The words preceding refer more commonly to women than to men; HANDSOME and GOOD-LOOKING refer about equally to men, women, and things. HANDSOME suggests a pleasing appearance, due proportions, and a measure of dignity and taste ⟨Cleveland was . . . a he-man, *handsome* with a certain bull-like pulchritude, which was the outer symbol of his inner courage —W.A.White⟩ ⟨she was very *handsome;* a bold beauty, with shining black hair, red lips, and eyes not afraid of men —George Meredith⟩ ⟨*handsome* houses rich in mahogany, plate, and pier glasses —Allan Nevins & H.S.Commager⟩ GOOD-LOOKING is less expressive and is not rich in especial connotations ⟨a *good-looking* young fellow of twenty-five. His cheeks were dyed with fine Saxon red . . . his blue eye opened well, and a profusion of fair hair curled over a well-shaped head —Herman Melville⟩

²**beautiful** \"\ *n* -s **:** the abstract or ideal essence or principle of that which appeals to aesthetic tastes and dispositions — used with *the* ⟨studying the ~⟩

beautiful letters *n pl* [trans. of F *belles-lettres*] **:** BELLES LETTRES

beau·ti·ful·ly \-f(ə)lē, -lī\ *also substand* **beautiful** *adv* **:** in a beautiful manner

beau·ti·ful·ness \-fəlnəs\ *n* -ES **:** the quality or state of being beautiful

beau·ti·fy \ˈbyüd·əˌfī, -yütə-,-\ *vb* -ED/-ING/-ES [*beauty* + *-fy*] *vt* **:** to make beautiful: as **a :** adorn in order to mask or transform the plain or unpleasant **:** EMBELLISH ⟨plants and flowers used to ~ all public parks and buildings —*Amer. Guide Series: Minn.*⟩ **b :** to grace with pleasurable, worthy, or ennobling attributes ⟨a scholarly formula for ~*ing* the corporation way of life —Norman MacKenzie⟩ ⟨religious faith . . . not only stabilizes one's life; it *beautifies* and consecrates it —Rufus Jones⟩ ~ *vi* **:** to grow beautiful ⟨her face ~*ing* at the encouraging answer⟩ **syn** see ADORN

¹**beau·ty** \ˈbyüd·ē, -yütē, -ī\ *n* -ES *often attrib* [ME *beaute*, *bealte*, fr. OF *biauté*, *belté*, fr. *biau*, *bel* beautiful (fr. L *bellus* pretty) + *-té* -ty; akin to L *bonus* good — more at BOUNTY] **1 a :** extreme physical attractiveness and loveliness **:** perfect combination of characteristics pleasurable to see ⟨the ~ of the actress⟩ ⟨the ~ of the scenery⟩ **b :** a characteristic or combination of characteristics affording great sensory pleasure ⟨the ~ of the sonata⟩ **c** (1) **:** one notably marked by beauty ⟨the new car was a ~⟩ ⟨fishing for trout and catching several *beauties*⟩; *esp* **:** a person so marked ⟨a bold ~, with shining black hair, red lips, and eyes not afraid —George Meredith⟩ (2) **:** the aggregate of those marked by beauty ⟨the ~ and chivalry of the county were gathered there —Raymond Weeks⟩ **d** (1) **:** a particular grace, adornment, or excellence **:** a single characteristic or attribute marked by beauty ⟨he had two great *beauties*, the pale flat white of his skin, and his great shaggy mass of dark hair —Dorothy C. Fisher⟩ (2) **beauties** *pl* **:** passages of literature strongly marked by beauty ⟨a collection of the poet's *beauties*⟩ **e :** a trait or combination of traits calling forth admiration, praise, or respect ⟨the ~ of his character⟩ ⟨the ~ of this mathematical demonstration⟩ **f :** a brilliant, extreme, or egregious example or instance ⟨the goalie's save was a ~⟩ ⟨his bruise after the fall was a ~⟩ ⟨this mistake in strategy was a ~⟩ **g :** most cogent feature **:** characteristic insuring effectiveness **:** climactic detail ⟨the ~ of it is that everyone can play⟩ ⟨the ~ of the scheme is that the trickster is defrauded⟩ **2 a :** perfection that excites admiration or delight for itself rather than for its uses **:** a quality in a consummate thing that induces immediate and disinterested pleasure **:** something that is beautiful as determined by subjective awareness and by such reactions as delightful sensation, moral exaltation, or reverie ⟨the ~ of a silent eve —John Keats⟩ **b :** the characteristic value of a beautiful thing apart from any effect it produces **:** perfection of form attained through the flawless sensible manifestation of an artist's conception or by an independent self-subsistent product of the creative imagination **c** (1) **:** the absolute perfection of the ideal or idea as suggested by or reflected in the relative sensuous perfection of works of art (2) **:** the ideal itself apprehended through the medium of a beautiful thing

²**beauty** \"\ *vt* -ED/-ING/-ES [ME *beautien*, fr. *beaute*, n.] *archaic* **:** BEAUTIFY

beauty-berry \ˈ⸗⸗-\ — see BERRY\ *n* **:** a plant of the genus *Callicarpa* — see FRENCH MULBERRY, JAPANESE BEAUTY-BERRY

beauty bush *n* **:** a Chinese shrub (*Kolkwitzia amabilis*) with yellow-throated pinkish flowers and a fruit covered with bristles that is often planted as an ornamental

beauty contest *n* **:** an assemblage of girls or women at which judges select the most beautiful

beauty culture *n* **:** COSMETOLOGY

beauty-fruit \ˈ⸗⸗,⸗\ *n* **:** any of several plants of the genus *Callicarpa*; *esp* **:** FRENCH MULBERRY

beauty operator *n* **:** COSMETOLOGIST

beauty shop *or* **beauty parlor** *n* **:** an establishment or a department in an establishment where hairdressing, facials, and manicures are done

beauty sleep *n* **:** sleep before midnight

beauty spot *n* **1 :** ¹PATCH 2 **2 a :** NEVUS **b :** a minor blemish **3 :** a beautiful scenic area

beau·vais \(ˈ)bōˌvā\ *adj, usu cap* [fr. *Beauvais*, commune, Oise dept., France] **:** of or relating to fine tapestry and embroidery originating at Beauvais, France and noted for its delicate floral designs

beau·ve·ria \bōˈvirēə\ *n, cap* [NL] **:** a genus of imperfect fungi (order Moniliales) that is sometimes included in the genus *Botrytis* and that comprises several fungi used in biological control of insects — see CALCINO

beaux *pl of* BEAU

¹**beaux arts** \(ˈ)bōˈzär, -ˈzȧ(r\ *n pl* [F *beaux-arts*] **:** FINE ARTS

²**beaux arts** \"\ *adj* **1** *archit* **:** characterized by formalism, the reapplication of historic forms and details, and a tendency toward monumental conception ⟨a *beaux arts* design⟩ **2 :** relating to a method of architectural education esp. prominent in the 19th century in which hypothetical problems are solved by individual students working in an atelier under a master critic and the solutions are judged by a jury of architects that rates them on a competitive basis

beaux esprits *pl of* BEL ESPRIT

beauxite *var of* BAUXITE

beaux mondes *pl of* BEAU MONDE

beaux sabreurs *pl of* BEAU SABREUR

¹**bea·ver** \ˈbēvə(r)\ *n, pl* **beaver** *or* **beavers** *often attrib* [ME *bever*, fr. OE *beofor*; akin to OHG *bibar* beaver, ON *björr*, L *fiber*, Lith *bebrus* beaver, Skt *babhru* large ichneumon, *babhru* reddish brown — more at BROWN] **1 a :** either of two large semiaquatic rodents having webbed hind feet and a broad flat tail, feeding chiefly on bark and twigs, being remarkable for ingenuity in the construction of lodges and dams, and yielding valuable fur and castor: (1) **:** an Old World rodent (*Castor fiber*) formerly abundant over much of northern Europe and Asia (2) **:** a New World congener (*C. canadensis*) whose skins were a major factor in the exploration and settlement of much of No. America and served in early times as a basic standard of exchange **b :** any of certain other rodents that resemble beavers; *esp* **:** MOUNTAIN BEAVER **2 a :** the fur or pelt of the beaver **b :** the fur or pelt of any of various animals processed to resemble that of the beaver — often used with a qualifying word **3 a :** a hat with a tall approximately cylindrical crown made of beaver fur or a fabric imitation of beaver ⟨tall men wearing ~*s*⟩ **b :** SILK HAT **4** *also* **beaver cloth a :** a thick woolen coating in twill weave made with a deep nap to resemble beaver fur **b :** a cotton cloth for clothing napped on both sides **c :** plush used for millinery **5 a :** MADE-BEAVER **b :** one of the 5-dollar or 10-dollar gold coins with the picture of a beaver on the obverse that were issued by the state of Oregon in 1849 **6** *or* **beaver brown :** a grayish brown that is yellower, less strong, and slightly lighter than chestnut, less strong and slightly yellower and lighter than coconut, and less strong and slightly lighter than new cocoa — called also *mushroom*, *starling* **7** [approximate trans. of Beaver *Tsattine*, lit., dwellers among the beavers] *usu cap* **a :** an Athapaskan people of the Peace river valley in Alberta **b :** a member of such people **8 :** the language of the Beaver people **9 a :** a full beard **b :** a man wearing a full beard **c :** a game in which one shouts "beaver" when he sees a bearded man **10 :** EAGER BEAVER

²**beaver** \"\ *n* -s [ME *baviere*, fr. MF, beaver, bib, fr. *bave* slobber — more at BAVARDAGE] **1 :** a piece of armor protecting the lower part of the face **2 :** a helmet visor ⟨saw you not his face? O, yes, my lord; he wore his ~ up —Shak.⟩

B beaver 1

beaver board *n* [fr. *Beaverboard*, a trademark] **:** a fiberboard used for partitions and ceilings

beaver bundle *n* [¹*beaver*] **:** a Blackfoot Indian medicine bundle

beaver dam *n* [¹*beaver*] **1 :** a dam built by beavers **2 :** the pond formed behind a beaver dam

beaver eater *n* [¹*beaver*] **:** WOLVERINE

bea·ver·ette \ˌbēv(ə)ˈret\ *n* -s [¹*beaver* + *-ette*] **:** rabbit fur dyed and processed to imitate beaver

beaver gray *n* [¹*beaver*] **:** a dark gray to brownish gray that is darker and slightly yellower than hair brown

bea·ver·ite \ˈbēvəˌrīt\ *n* -s [*Beaver* co. Utah + E *-ite*] **:** a mineral $Pb(Cu,Fe,Al)_3(SO_4)_2(OH)_6$ consisting of a hydrous sulfate of copper, lead, and iron occurring in microscopic canary-yellow plates

beaver lily *n* [¹*beaver*] **:** SPATTERDOCK 1

beaverpelt \ˈ⸗⸗,⸗\ *n* [¹*beaver* + *pelt*] **:** NUTRIA 2

beaver poison *n* [¹*beaver*] **:** WATER HEMLOCK

beaver rat *n* [¹*beaver*] **:** a golden Australian water rat (*Hydromys chrysogaster*) with an elongated flattened body, broad flat head, short limbs, large feet, and a short heavy white-tipped tail

beaverroot \ˈ⸗⸗,⸗\ *n* [¹*beaver*] **1 :** SPATTERDOCK 1 **2 :** a water lily (*Nymphaea odorata*) with fragrant flowers

beaver stone *n* [¹*beaver*] **:** either of a pair of glandular pouches in the groin of a beaver that secrete castor

beaver tail *n* [¹*beaver*] **:** a prickly-pear cactus (*Opuntia basilaris*) of southwestern U.S. and adjacent Mexico often cultivated for its showy purple, reddish, or white flowers

beavertail \ˈ⸗⸗,⸗\ *n* [so called fr. its flat, wide shape] **:** a rifle or shotgun fore-end made wider than standard to afford a better grip and improve the balance

bea·ver·teen \ˌbēvə(r)ˈtēn, ˈ⸗⸗,⸗\ *n* -s [¹*beaver* + *-teen* (as in *velveteen*)] **:** a heavy twilled cotton cloth made with an uncut pile and a short nap

beaver trade *n* [¹*beaver*] *obs* **:** trade with the Indians; *specif* **:** trade in beaver skins

beaver tree *n* [¹*beaver*] **:** SWEET BAY 2

beaverwood \ˈ⸗⸗,⸗\ *n* [¹*beaver* + *wood*] **1 :** a hackberry (*Celtis occidentalis*) **2 :** SWEET BAY 2

bea·very \ˈbēv(ə)rē\ *n* -ES [blend of *beaver* and *-ry*] **:** a place in which beavers live or are kept

beb \ˈbeb\ *chiefly Scot var of* ¹BIB

bebb willow \ˈbeb-\ *n, often cap B* [after Michael S. *Bebb* †1895 Amer. botanist] **:** BEAK WILLOW

be·bee·rine \bəˈbiˌrēn, -ˌrən; ˈbeb(ē)əˌrēn\ *also* **bi·bi·rine** \bəˈbiˌrēn, -ˌrən; ˈbibəˌrēn\ *n* -s [G *bebeerin*, fr. *bebeerubaum* bebeeru tree (fr. Sp & Pg *bibirú*) + *-in* -ine] **:** a crystalline alkaloid $C_{36}H_{38}N_2O_6$ known in two optically different forms; *esp* **:** the dextrorotatory form obtained from the bark of the bebeeru and the pareira — see CURINE

be·bee·ru \bəˈbi(ˌ)rü, ˌbebēəˈrü\ also **bi·bi·ru** \bəˈbi(ˌ)rü, ˌbibəˈrü\ *n* -s [Sp & Pg *bibirú*, of Cariban origin; akin to Macusi *bibiru*] **:** a tropical So. American evergreen tree (*Nectandra rodioei*) — called also *greenheart*

be·bi·za·tion \ˌbābəˈzāshən\ *n* -s [G *bebisation*, irreg. fr. *be*, one of the notes of this scale + *-isation* -ization] **:** an obsolete musical solmization using the syllables *la, be, ce, de, me, fe, ge*

be·bop \ˈbēˌbäp\ *n* -s [imit. of a staccato 2-tone phrase distinctive in this music] **:** ³BOP

be·bop·per \-pə(r)\ *n* -s **:** BOPPER

be·bouldered \bə, bē+\ *adj* [*be-* + *bouldered*] **:** strewn with boulders

be·bung \ˈbā(ˌ)bůŋ\ *n, pl* **be·bung·en** \-ŋən\ [G, lit., trembling, fr. *beben* to tremble (fr. OHG *bibēn*) + *-ung* -ing (fr. OHG *-unga*); akin to OE *bifian* to tremble, ON *bifa*, L *foedus* ugly, Gk *pithēkos* ape, Skt *bhayate* he is afraid; basic meaning: fearing] **:** a tremolo effect that is similar in sound to a violin vibrato and is produced on the clavichord by sustaining a varying pressure on the key after striking a note

bec *abbr* because

be·call \bə, bē+\ *vt* -ED/-ING/-S [*be-* + *call*] **:** to call names **:** MISCALL

be·calm \bə, bē+\ *vt* -ED/-ING/-S [*be-* + *calm*, adj. or v.] **1 :** to keep from motion or stop the progress of by lack of wind ⟨the fleet was ~*ed*⟩ **2 :** to make calm: as **a :** SOOTHE, TRANQUILIZE ⟨~ an agitated mind⟩ **b :** to bring about a cessation of the work, progress, or activity of ⟨a committee ~*ed* by analysis of trivia⟩

became *past of* BECOME

be·card \bāˈkärd\ *n* -s [F *bécarde*, fr. *bec* beak — more at BEAK] **:** any of several large-billed tropical American birds of the family Cotingidae

be·casse \bāˈkäs\ *n* -s [F *bécasse*, fr. OF *becaz*, fr. *bec* beak — more at BEAK] **:** WOODCOCK 1a

be·cas·sine \bākäˈsēn\ *n* -s [F *bécassine*, fr. *bécasse* + *-ine*] **:** SNIPE; *esp, in Louisiana* **:** any of several American snipes

be·cause \bəˈkȯz, bē-, -(ˌ)kəz, *chiefly in substand speech* -ōs\ *conj* [ME, fr. *be*, *bi* by + *cause*] **1 :** SINCE **:** for the reason that **:** on account of the cause that — used to introduce dependent clauses ⟨we stopped at the filling station ~ we needed gasoline⟩ **2** *obs* **:** in order that **:** to the end that ⟨"Why laugh you?" "*Because* you should see my teeth" —John Lyly⟩ **3 a :** THAT **:** the fact that — used to introduce a noun clause serving as the subject or the complement of a sentence ⟨one of the reasons why it has seemed to me to be desirable to speak on this subject is ~ it may contribute —E.N.Griswold⟩ ⟨~ men are still incapable of being angels is no good reason why they should be ants —E.A.Mowrer⟩; in reputable use though disapproved by some **b :** on account of being ⟨a rather stuffily written book, but the material is interesting ~ firsthand —A.W.Long⟩

because of *prep* **:** by reason of **:** on account of ⟨the game was postponed *because of* rain⟩ ⟨*because of* losses the unit was not at full strength⟩ — in reputable use though sometimes disapproved in constructions complementary to expressions of the notion of reason or cause ⟨the reason we do not now have such a trained reserve . . . is *because of* lack of foresight and energy —*N.Y.Times*⟩

bec·ca·fi·co \ˌbekəˈfē(ˌ)kō\ *n, pl* **beccaficos** *or* **beccaficoes** [It, fr. *beccare* to peck (fr. *becco* beak, fr. L *beccus*) + *fico* fig, fr. L *ficus* — more at BEAK] **:** any of various European songbirds esteemed as a table delicacy when fat on fruit and grains in autumn; *specif* **:** GARDEN WARBLER

be·cer·ris·ta \ˌbāsəˈrēstə, -āthə-\ *n* -s [Sp, fr. *becerro* yearling bull (fr. OSp *bezerro*, prob. fr. a word cognate to the non-IE source of L *ibex* chamois) + *-ista* -ist] *in bullfighting* **:** one who fights calves

bé·cha·mel \ˌbāshəˈmel\ *or* **béchamel sauce** *n* -s *sometimes cap B* [F *(sauce) béchamelle*, after Louis de *Béchamel* (Béchameil) †1703 Fr. courtier] **:** a white sauce sometimes enriched with cream

²**bé·champ reduction** \(ˈ)bāˌshäⁿ-\ *n, cap B* [after Pierre J. A. *Béchamp* †1908 Fr. physician, surgeon, and chemist] **:** a method of reducing aromatic nitro compounds to amines by means of iron usu. in acid solution

be·chance \bə, bē+\ *vb* -ED/-ING/-S [*be-* + *chance* (v.)] *vi, archaic* **:** HAPPEN, BEFALL ~ *vt, obs* **:** to happen to ⟨my sons — God knows what hath *bechanced* them —Shak.⟩

be·charm \bə, bē+\ *vt* [ME *becharmen*, fr. *be-* + *charmen* to charm] **:** to hold under or as if under a spell

be·chatter \bə, bē+\ *vt* [*be-* + *chatter* (v.)] **:** to oppress with chatter

bêche-de-mer \ˌbāshdəˈme(ə)r\ *n* [F, lit., sea grub] **1** *pl* **bêche-de-mer** \"\ *or* **bêches-de-mer** \-āsh(əz)d-\ **:** TREPANG **2** *usu cap B&M* [so called fr. the trepang's having been an important commercial item in these islands, its designation thus becoming a type-word to designate the pidgin]

: a pidgin based on English and used as a lingua franca in New Guinea, the Bismarck archipelago, the Solomon islands, and other islands nearby

bech·tel crab \'bektᵊl-\ *or* **bech·tel's crab** \-ᵊlz-\ *n, usu cap B* [after Ernst A. *Bechtel*, 19th cent. Am. nurseryman] : a flowering crab derived from the Iowa crab apple and having very large double pink flowers

bech·te·rew's nucleus \'bektə,refs-, -,revz-\ *n, usu cap B* [after V. M. Bekhterev (*Bechterew*) †1927 Russ. neuropathologist] : the upper part of the vestibular nucleus

bech·u·a·na \,bech(ə)'wänə\ *n, pl* **bechuana** *or* **bechuanas** *usu cap* : a member of one of the various Bantu-speaking Negro peoples dwelling between the Orange and Zambezi rivers esp. in Botswana, So. Africa

[1]**beck** \'bek\ *n* -s [ME *bek*, fr. ON *bekkr;* akin to OE *bæc* brook, OHG *bah*, MIr *būal* flowing water] *Brit* : a small stream usu. with a stony bed

[2]**beck** \"\ *vb* -ED/-ING/-S [ME *becken*, alter. of *beknen* — more at BECKON] *vi* **1** *archaic* : GESTURE, SIGNAL **2** *chiefly Scot* : BOW, CURTSY ~ *vt, archaic* : to signal to : BECKON

[3]**beck** \"\ *n* -S [ME, fr. *becken*] **1** *chiefly Scot* : a gesture of salutation or respect : BOW, CURTSY, NOD ⟨coming into the parlor with a low ~⟩ **2 a** (1) : a gesture or signaling motion (2) : a nod, wave, or other signal summoning or commanding **b** (1) : an indication whereby one gives a command or expresses a desire (2) : full and absolute control — **at beck and call** : in obedient readiness to obey any command or fulfill any wish ⟨a thousand servants and a huge palace *at* his *beck and call* —Robert Keable⟩

[4]**beck** \"\ *n* -S [prob. alter. (influenced by [1]*beck*) of [5]*back*] : a large vat : [5]BACK; *esp* : a vat used in dyeing by hand

[5]**beck** \"\ *n* -S [back-formation fr. *beckiron*] : the beak of an anvil

beck·e·lite \'bekə,līt\ *n* -S [Friedrich *Becke* †1931 Austrian mineralogist + E *-lite*] : a mineral $Ca_3(Ce,La,Y)_4(SiZr)_3O_{15}$ consisting of the cerium metals and calcium and occurring in wax-yellow isometric crystals (hardness 5, sp. gr. 4.15)

beck·en \'bekən\ *n pl* [G, lit., basin, fr. OHG *beckīn*, fr. LL *bacchinon* — more at BASIN] : CYMBALS

[1]**beck·et** *also* **beck·ett** \'bekət\ *n* -S [origin unknown] : a simple device for holding something in place: as **a** : a small grommet or a loop of rope with a knot at one end to catch in an eye at the other **b** : a ring of rope or metal **c** : BRACKET **d** : POCKET **e** : HOOK

[2]**becket** \"\ *vt* -ED/-ING/-S : to secure by beckets : provide with beckets

becket bend *n* : SHEET BEND

becke test \'bekə-\ *n, usu cap B* [after Friedrich *Becke* — more at BECKELITE] : a method of determining with a microscope the relative indices of refraction of a transparent particle (as a plant or animal cell or a mineral) immersed in or in contact with a standard medium of known refractive index

beck·iron \'bek·+,-\ *n* -S [by folk etymology fr. earlier *bickern*, fr. *bycorne*, fr. MF *bigorne*, fr. (assumed) VL *bicornia*, fr. L *bicornis* with two horns — more at BICORN] : a horned anvil; *esp* : a cooper's anvil used in clinching nails or rivets

beck·ite \'bek·,īt\ *n* -S [by alter.] : BEEKITE

beck·mann rearrangement \'bekmən-, -,män-\ *n, usu cap B* [after Ernst O. *Beckmann* †1923 Ger. chemist] : a rearrangement by which a ketoxime [as the oxime $(C_6H_5)_2C$:NOH of benzophenone] changes into an amide derivative (as benzanilide) on treatment usu. with phosphorus pentachloride or an acid

beckmann thermometer *n, usu cap B* [after Ernst O. *Beckmann*] : a very sensitive thermometer that has a small range adjustable for any desired values and that is used for determining accurately small differences in temperature (as the change in freezing point or boiling point of a liquid when some substance is dissolved in it)

beck·mes·ser \'bek,mesə(r)\ *n* -S *usu. cap* [G, after Sixtus *Beckmesser*, pedantic musical philistine in the opera *Die Meistersinger von Nürnberg* (1867) by Richard Wagner †1883 Ger. composer] : a critic or teacher of music characterized by timid and excessive reliance upon rules : PEDANT

[1]**beck·on** \'bekən\ *vb* **beckoned; beckoned; beckoning** \-k(ə)niŋ\ **beckons** [ME *beknen*, fr. OE *bīecnan*, fr. *bēacen* sign — more at BEACON] *vi* **1** : to gesture or signal typically with a wave, nod, or other motion in summons or command ⟨he . . . ~*ed* to the other generals to come and stand where he stood —H.E.Scudder⟩ **2** : to appear inviting : offer strong attraction or allure ⟨Australian goldfields ~*ed*, and he sailed —L.R.Hafen⟩ ⟨sending his ships wherever profit ~*ed* —*Time*⟩ ~ *vt* **1** : to signal to typically with a wave in summons or request to approach or follow ⟨my guide ~*ed* me off the narrow path —John Connell⟩ ⟨they ~*ed* us to come⟩ **2** : to seem to invite : extend attraction, interest, allure, or appeal to ⟨it ~*s* men . . . into the calm of the absolute and eternal —John Dewey⟩

[2]**beckon** \"\ *n* -S : a signaling gesture esp. to approach

beck·on·ing *adj* : inviting by or as if by attraction or allure : APPEALING ⟨myth reveals beauty in ~ imagery —J.P. Anton⟩ — **beck·on·ing·ly** *adv*

beckoning crab *n* : FIDDLER CRAB

becks *pres 3d sing of* BECK, *pl of* BECK

be·clad \bə̇, bē+\ *adj*. [*be-* + *clad*] *archaic* : CLOTHED

be·clip \bə̇, bē+\ *vt* [ME *beclippen*, fr. OE *beclyppan*, fr. *be-* + *clyppan* to clasp, embrace — more at CLIP] *archaic* : EMBRACE, CLASP, ENCIRCLE

be·cloud \bə̇, bē+\ *vt* -ED/-ING/-S [*be-* + *cloud*, v, or n.] **1** : to cover over with a cloud : OBSCURE, MASK ⟨the ink of the cuttlefish ~*ing* the water⟩ **2 a** : to confuse and check from incisive thought ⟨scrambling up the issues and ~*ing* the minds and memories of witnesses —R.H.Rovere⟩ **b** : to muddle and prevent clear perception or realization of ⟨disputes . . . threatened to ~ the real issues —M.J.Adler⟩ **syn** see OBSCURE

be·come \bə̇'kəm, bē-\ *vb* **be·came** \-kām\ **become; becoming; becomes** [ME *becomen*, fr. OE *becoman, becuman* to come to, approach, happen, befit (akin to OHG *biqueman* to come to, meet, Goth *biquiman* to come to) fr. *be-* + *coman, cuman* to come — more at COME] *vi* **1 a** *obs* : COME, ARRIVE : GO ⟨where is Warwick then ~ —Shak.⟩ **b** (1) : to come to exist or occur (2) : to emerge as an entity : grow to manifest a certain essence, nature, development, or significance ⟨we do not know our own identity since we are always in a state of *becoming* —J.D.Adams⟩ ⟨what ~*s* has duration —A. N.Whitehead⟩ **c** *archaic* : to come to experience — used with an infinitive **2 a** : to pass from a previous state or condition and come to be : grow or change into being through taking on a new character or characteristic ⟨as the pain ~*s* more intense⟩ ⟨that they might rest and ~ warm —T.B.Costain⟩ **b** : to take on a new role, essence, or nature and come to be ⟨he *became* the nation's first president⟩ ⟨his former foes *becoming* loyal allies⟩ ⟨materials formerly wasted *becoming* profitable by-products⟩ **c** : to come to be — used as an auxiliary in passive constructions ⟨she *became* influenced by these ideas⟩ ⟨men *becoming* hurt in the battle⟩ **3 a** : HAPPEN ⟨it sometimes ~*s* that these accounts are misleading⟩ **b** : to ensue by way of fate, destiny, or disposition — usu. used with *of* ⟨he wondered what had ~ of his boyhood friends⟩ ⟨investigating what *became* of the missing ship⟩ ~ *vt* **1 a** : to accord with : be suitable to : lack jarring contrast to or incongruity with ⟨rough clothes *becoming* their lowly condition⟩ ⟨brash confidence ill *becoming* his record of failures⟩ **b** : to suit with propriety : be quite proper for ⟨dignity *becoming* a lord⟩ ⟨the humility that ~*s* the amateur —B.N.Cardozo⟩ **2** : GRACE: **a** : to adorn or look well on while befitting or according with ⟨a hat that ~*s* her⟩ **b** : to occupy, use, or wear with suitable bearing or pleasing grace ⟨he ~*s* his high office⟩

becomed *adj* [fr. obs. past part. of *become*] *obs* : BECOMING, DECOROUS

[1]**becoming** *adj* [fr. pres. part. of *become*] **1** : marked by fitness or propriety : SUITABLE, SEEMLY ⟨~ modesty⟩ ⟨~ respect and obedience⟩ ⟨monks for whom self-effacement is ~ —H.O. Taylor⟩ **2** : having an attractive effect : tending to grace or adorn ⟨a fashionable ~ dress⟩ ⟨a hairdo ~ to her⟩

[2]**becoming** *n* -S [fr. gerund of *become*] **1** *obs* **a** : the action of befitting **b** : something that befits or becomes **2 a** : a coming into being : emergence into change that leads to a distinct stage or condition ⟨life is a constant ~: all stages lead to the beginning of others —G.B.Shaw⟩ **b** : a process in which the new appears : a passage of events in time : CHANGE ⟨there is a constant ~; there was no beginning, there can be no ending —John Burroughs⟩ — **be·com·ing·ly** *adv*

be·com·ing·ness \-nəs\ *n* -ES **1** : the quality or state of being becoming **2** : the character or fact of becoming ⟨that ultimate ~ which is the creative advance of nature —A.N.Whitehead⟩

be·coom \bə̇'küm, bē-\ *vt* -ED/-ING/-S [*be-* + *coom* soot] *Brit* : to begrime with smut or soot

bec·que·rel effect \(')be¦krel-, ¦bekə¦rel-\ *n, usu cap B* [after Antoine H. *Becquerel* †1908 Fr. physicist] : a photovoltaic electromotive force manifested by certain electrolytic cells with identical but unequally illuminated electrodes

bec·que·rel·ite \be'kre,līt, ,bekə're-\ *n* -S [F *becquerelite*, fr. A. H. *Becquerel* + F *-ite*] : a mineral $UO_2.2H_2O$ consisting of uranium hydroxide and occurring in small yellow crystals and crusts on pitchblende from Katanga, Belgian Congo

becquerel ray *n, usu cap B* [after A. H. *Becquerel*] : a ray emitted by a radioactive substance — used before adoption of the terms *alpha ray, beta ray, gamma ray*

be·crime \bə̇, bē+\ *vt* -ED/-ING/-S [*be-* + *crime*] : to make guilty of crime

be·cross \bə̇, bē+\ *vt* [*be-* + *cross* (n.)] **1** : [2]CROSS *vt* 3a **2** : to decorate with a cross

be·crush \bə̇, bē+\ *vt* [*be-* + *crush*] : to crush utterly or repeatedly

bec-scie *F* beksē\ *n* -S [CanF *bec-scie* (trans. of E *sawbill*), fr. F *bec* beak + *scie* saw, fr. *scier* to saw, fr. L *secare* to cut — more at BEAK, SAW] : MERGANSER

be·cui·ba *or* **bi·cu·hy·ba** \bə̇'kwēbə\ *or* **bi·cu·hy·bao** \-ē,baů\ *or* **bi·cui·ba** \-ēbə\ *n* -S [Pg *becuiba*, fr. Tupi *bicuiba*] : a Brazilian timber tree (*Virola becuhyba*) of the family Myristicaceae with nuts that yield a wax

be·cu·na \bā'künə\ *or* **be·cune** \-ün\ *n* -S [F & Sp; F *bécune*, fr. Sp *becuna*] : GREAT BARRACUDA

be·curl \bə̇, bē+\ *vt* [*be-* + *curl* (n. or v.)] : to furnish or adorn with curls

[1]**bed** \'bed\ *n* -S *often attrib* [ME, fr. OE *bedd;* akin to OHG *betti* bed, ON *bethr*, Goth *badi* bed, L *fodere* to dig, Lith *besti*] **1 a** : a piece of furniture on or in which one may lie down and sleep often including bedstead, legs or supports, spring, mattress, and bedding **b** (1) : a place of marital sex relations (2) : marital relationship ⟨dishonoring her ~ with a lover⟩ **c** : any improvised place or arrangement for sleeping ⟨hikers making their ~*s* under the trees⟩ **d** (1) : a place of procreation (2) : marital union ⟨the eldest son of his second ~ —Edward Hyde⟩ (3) : PROGENY **e** : situation or fact of being in bed : SLEEP, SLEEPING : time for sleeping ⟨taking a walk before ~⟩ **f** : place of repose : REPOSE ⟨the bugle calling them from their ~*s*⟩ **g** : a flat sack or mattress filled with some soft material in distinction from the bedstead on which it is placed ⟨a feather ~⟩; *also* : a mattress and bedclothes **h** : BEDSTEAD **i** : lodging for the night with accommodations for sleeping ⟨getting a ~ at the inn⟩ **j** : a measure of the equipment and services needed in a hospital to care for one hospitalized patient or in a hotel to care for one guest ⟨a new wing of 200 ~*s*⟩ **2** : a flat or level surface: as **a** (1) : a plot in a garden or lawn often a little raised above the adjoining ground : the plants grown in such plot; *also* : HOTBED (2) : an area in a greenhouse or conservatory in which plants are grown (3) : a cluster or concentration of plants ⟨a ~ of ferns⟩ **b** : the bottom of a watercourse or of any other body of water; *esp* : an area of sea bottom supporting a heavy growth of a particular kind of organism ⟨a kelp ~⟩ ⟨an oyster ~⟩ **c** : the surface of a bowling alley along which the ball is bowled **d** : the surface on which the cloth of a billiard table is fastened **e** : the canvas surface of a trampoline upon which a gymnast performs **3** : a grave as a place of last sleep ⟨digging out his narrow ~⟩ **4** : SUPPORT, REST: **a** : the supporting part of a gun carriage **b** (1) : an extended base : MATRIX (2) : a layer of specialized or altered tissue; *often* : such a layer or zone separating dissimilar structures ⟨a ~ of vigorous granulation tissue is essential for a satisfactory skin graft⟩ — see VASCULAR BED **c** : a framework or support on or in which a piece of machining or carpentry work rests **d** : the cradle of a ship on the stocks **e** : a foundation for a machine or apparatus ⟨the ~ of an engine⟩ : the rigid part of a machine serving to support or secure **f** : the superficial earthwork that supports the ballast and track of a railroad **g** : the body, box, or supporting frame of a vehicle (as a wagon, truck, or trailer); *sometimes* : the floor or bottom of a truck or trailer **h** : the inclined piece of a carpenter's plane against which the plane iron bears **i** : the lower die of a punching machine **j** : the surface on which the printing form is locked on a flatbed press **k** *or* **bed ladder** : the lower section of an aerial ladder **l** : a drawer or layer supporting a typewriter in an office desk **m** : the base of a bellows camera usu. including the focusing guide rails **5** : a nest of small animals crowded together ⟨a ~ of snakes⟩ **6** : a layer esp. if placed with something above ⟨salad served on a ~ of lettuce⟩: as **a** : a rock stratum; *esp* : a bedding plane of stratified rock **b** (1) : a horizontal surface of a brick or stone in position ⟨in the upper ~⟩ (2) : a course of stone or brick in a wall (3) : the place or material in which a block or brick is laid (4) : the lower surface of a brick, slate, or tile (5) : BED JOINT **c** : a layer containing a concentration of paleontological or anthropological evidence (as bones) **d** : FILTER BED **e** : FIRE BED **7** : the place where an animal sleeps; *esp* : a place arranged or covered for a domestic or farm animal to sleep **8 a** : a mass or heap felt to resemble a bed ⟨a ~ of ashes⟩ ⟨the judging tent floor was a deep ~ of sawdust —Christopher Rand⟩ **b** : a mass of solid catalyst or solid chemical reactant that may be either in a fixed state or in a moving fluidized state **c** : a stack of raw hides or skins spread flat and salted for curing and preserving **9 a** : a water solution of gum tragacanth used as a couch in the process of marbling book edges **b** : the impression base used by bookbinders in stamping, graining, or embossing covers or materials

[2]**bed** \"\ *vb* **bedded; bedded; bedding; beds** [ME *bedden, beddien*, fr. OE *beddian*, fr. *bedd* bed] *vt* **1 a** : to furnish with a bed : accommodate with sleeping quarters ⟨the innkeeper was unable to ~ all the guests⟩ — sometimes used with *down* ⟨a garrison of about seventy, which the captain *bedded* down in the ground floor —Earle Birney⟩ **b** : to put to bed ⟨getting the children *bedded*⟩ **c** : to put (a couple) to bed — used with the implication that sex relations will ensue **d** : to furnish (an animal) with a bed or bedding : settle (an animal) in sleeping quarters ⟨*bedding* the mare —Ellen Glasgow⟩ — often used with *down* ⟨~ down the cattle —Andy Adams⟩ **e** : to take to bed for sexual intercourse : have sex relations with ⟨when he had *bedded* his wife and . . . had left her bed —B.A.Williams⟩ **f** : to put to bed with an illness — used mostly in the passive ⟨*bedded* for a week with influenza⟩ **2 a** : EMBED : place, sink, bury, or cover over securely in an enclosed place or situation ⟨the tremendous mortar . . . was *bedded* in the great timbers of her foredeck —Frank Yerby⟩ ⟨edges *bedded* in rabbets⟩ **b** : to plant or arrange in beds : set or cover esp. in a bed of soft earth ⟨*bedding* roots in mold⟩ ⟨~ out geraniums⟩ — often used with *up, down*, or *out* **c** : BASE, ESTABLISH **d** : to fit (a rifle barrel) to a fore-end **3 a** : to lay or embed in a layer : lay flat ⟨*bedding* bricks in the mortar⟩ ⟨*bedding* metal plates together to test them⟩ **b** : to dress the bearing surface of a brick or stone block **c** : to form (soil) into a bed or ridge (as for cotton) by plowing two or more furrows together — often used with *up* **d** : to spread or strew in a layer ⟨the floor of the pen being *bedded* with straw⟩ **e** : to prepare the ground about a tree by leveling and other means so as to lessen the chances of its shattering when felled **f** : to lay, place, or set (something) in a plastic bedding material (as masonry units in mortar or glass in putty) **4** : to place (oysters) in beds for setting ~ *vi* **1 a** : to find or make sleeping accommodations — often used with *down* ⟨*bedding* down in a sleeping bag —Hamilton Basso⟩ ⟨halted beside a haystack and told to ~ down —E.J.Kahn⟩ **b** : to go to bed with opportunity for sex relations or in order to have sex relations : to have coition ⟨the couple *bedded* that night at the inn⟩ — used with *with, down with, up with* ⟨man may ~ with slaves, concubines, mistresses —H.M.Parshley⟩ **c** *of an animal* : to make its bed or lair — often used with *down* ⟨the deer *bedded* down on the sope⟩ **d** : to go to bed to sleep : RETIRE ⟨accustomed to ~ early⟩ **e** : to burrow into a mud bottom ⟨the side of the lake where the eels ~⟩ **2** : to form a layer usu. compact — often used with *down* ⟨litter in the hen coop ~*s* down if it is not raked⟩ **3** : to lie or be placed on or as if on a bed in a mechanical operation : lie flat or flush against another part ⟨countersunk rivets ~ well against a flat plate⟩

be·dabble \bə̇, bē+\ *vt* -ED/-ING/-S [*be-* + *dabble*] : to wet or soil by dabbling ⟨clothes *bedabbled* with blood⟩

be·dad \bə̇'dad, bē-\ *interj* [euphemism for *by God*] *Irish* — used as a mild oath

be·damn \bə̇, bē +\ *vt* [*be-* + *damn*] : to swear at : DAMN

bed and board *n* : sleeping quarters and meals esp. in marital cohabitation ⟨his wife has left his *bed and board*⟩

be·dash \bə̇, bē\ *vt* [*be-* + *dash*] **1** : DASH : splash esp. with color or rain **2** : to dash against **3** : RUIN ⟨hopes ~*ed*⟩

be·daub \bə̇, bē+\ *vt* [*be-* + *daub*] **1** : to daub over : besmear or soil with anything thick, dirty, or sticky ⟨~*ed* with clay⟩ **2** : to ornament with vulgar excess : BEDIZEN

be·daux system \bə̇'dō-\ *also* **bedaux plan** *n, usu cap B* [after Charles E. *Bedaux* †1944 Fr. efficiency engineer in U.S.] : POINT SYSTEM

be·da·wi *or* **ba·da·wi** \bə'däwē\ *n, pl* **beda·win** \-,wēn\ *or* **bedawis** \-(,)wēz\ *or* **bada·win** \-,wēn\ *or* **ba·da·wis** \-(,)wēz\ *often cap* [Ar *badāwi* — more at BEDOUIN] : BEDOUIN

be·daze \bə̇'dāz, bē-\ *vt* [*be-* + *daze*] : DAZE : stun and confuse — **be·daze·ment** \-mənt\ *n* -S

be·dazzle \bə̇, bē+\ *vt* [*be-* + *dazzle*] **1** : DAZZLE : confuse by a strong light **2** : to impress awesomely or most forcefully and take away power to think or notice : ENCHANT ⟨*bedazzled* by the mountains and the ranch —Jean Stafford⟩ — **be·dazzle·ment** \"+\ *n* -S

bed board *n* : a stiff thin wide board inserted usu. between bedspring and mattress

bed bolt *n* : a metal bolt with a tapered square head

bed book *n* : a book typically light and interesting for reading in bed

bedbug \'=,=\ *n* **1 a** : a wingless bloodsucking bug (*Cimex lectularius*) sometimes infesting houses and esp. beds and feeding on human blood **b** : any other bloodsucking bug of the genus *Cimex* **2** : CONENOSE

common bedbug

bedbug hunter *n* : a bug (*Reduvius personatus*) of the family Reduviidae that is said to prey esp. on bedbugs

bedchamber \'=,==\ *n* : BEDROOM

bedchamber woman *n* : WOMAN OF THE BEDCHAMBER

bed check *n* : a night inspection to check the presence of persons (as soldiers) required by regulations to be in bed or in quarters

bedclothes \'=,=\ *n pl* [ME, fr. [1]*bed* + *clothes*] : sheets, blankets, or other coverings used on a bed

bedclothing \'=,==\ *n* [*bed* + *clothing*] : BEDCLOTHES

bedcord \'=,=\ *n* [*bed* + *cord*] : a rope drawn from one side of a bedstead to another to support a mattress

bedcover \'=,==\ *n* **1** : BEDSPREAD **2** : [2]COVER 2g

bed-curtain \'=,==\ *n* : a curtain hung from a bed canopy

beddal *Scot var of* BEADLE

bed·da nut \'bedə-\ *n* [Marathi *behḍā*] : NUT OF BAHERA

bed·ded \'bedəd\ *adj* [[1]*bed* + *-ed*] *geol* : deposited in layers : STRATIFIED

bed·der \'bedə(r)\ *n* -S [[1,2]*bed* + *er*] **1** : one that makes up beds esp. in an English university **2** : one that places or fixes something in a bed: as **a** : a pottery worker who arranges greenware in piles with sand and clay between to protect and support the pieces during biscuit firing **b** : a leatherworker who salts hides and piles them in beds to preserve them **3** : a bedding plant : a plant grown in a bed for ornamental purposes (as a rose, begonia, or geranium) **4** *Brit* : BEDROOM **5** : a device for adjusting contact between rifle barrel and fore-end consisting of one or more adjustable contact points mounted in the forearm by means of which compensation may be made for error in initial fit of forearm to barrel, minor stock warpage due to weather conditions, and barrel vibration under given powder loads

[1]**bed·ding** \'bediŋ, -ēŋ\ *n* -S [ME, fr. OE, fr. *bedd* bed + *-ing*] **1** : BEDCLOTHES **2** : a bottom layer : FOUNDATION **3** : litter (as straw or wood chips) for livestock **4** : the arrangement of rock in layers : STRATIFICATION **5** : a layer of soft material (as jute yarn) put on an electric cable underneath its armor **6** : the mortar, putty, or other substance used to bed building units (as bricks or glass)

[2]**bedding** \"\ *n* -S [fr. gerund of [2]*bed*] **1** : the act of putting or taking a bride to bed **2** : the storing of different ores in thin layers or beds for future reclamation as a nearly uniform mixture

[3]**bedding** \"\ *adj* [fr. gerund of [2]*bed*] : appropriate or adapted for culture in beds in the open air; *specif* : adapted to produce a massed effect for decoration, ⟨a ~ plant⟩ ⟨a ~ geranium⟩

bedding course *n* : CUSHION 3 l

bedding fault *n* : a displacement along or parallel to a bedding plane

bedding plane *n* : the surface that separates each successive layer of a stratified rock from its preceding layer : a depositional plane : a plane of stratification

bedding-slip \'==,=\ *n* : a bedding fault with slight displacement

be·deck \bə̇, bē+\ *vt* [*be-* + *deck*] : to deck out : ornament profusely : decorate in a showy manner ⟨~*ed* in fine silks and laces⟩ : GRACE **syn** see ADORN

be·deen \bə̇'dēn\ *adv* [ME *bedene*] *chiefly Scot* : STRAIGHTWAY, FORTHWITH, ANON

bed·e·guar *or* **bed·e·gar** \'bedə̇,gär\ *n* -S [MF *bedegard*, fr. Per *bādāward*] : gall like a moss produced on rosebushes (as the sweetbrier or eglantine) by a gall wasp (*Rhodites rosae* or related species)

be·del *or* **be·dell** \bə̇'del, be-\ *n* -S [ME *bedel* — more at BEADLE] : an English university officer who walks at the head of processions of officers and students — usu. spelled *bedel* at Oxford, *bedell* at Cambridge

bed·er·al \'bed(ə)rəl\ *n* -S [by alter.] *Scot* : BEADLE 2

bedesman *or* **bedeman** *var of* BEADSMAN

be·devil \bə̇, bē+\ *vt* **bedeviled** *or* **bedevilled; bedeviled** *or* **bedevilled; bedeviling** *or* **bedevilling; bedevils** [*be-* + *devil*] **1** : to possess with or as if with a devil : BEWITCH **2** : to change for the worse ⟨a room ~*ed* by a poor decorator⟩ : SPOIL, CORRUPT **3 a** : to treat diabolically : torment and abuse or maltreat **b** : to drive frantic with or as if with care and worry **c** : HARASS, VEX, ANNOY, PESTER ⟨~*ing* city officials in little matters —Green Peyton⟩ ⟨hard to hold the horses on a straight course with the insects ~*ing* them —H.L.Davis⟩ **d** : to make worse often by obscuring or muddling : confuse and aggravate ⟨racial tensions that ~ politics —*Times Lit. Supp.*⟩ ⟨how tendentious maps can ~ an international problem —G.R.Crone⟩

be·dev·il·ler \-lə(r)\ *n* -S : one that bedevils

be·dev·il·ment \-lmənt\ *n* -S **1** : a situation or condition that bedevils : CONFUSION, DISORDER, VEXATION, TROUBLE **2** : possession by a devil ⟨mad conduct and other signs of ~⟩

be·dew \bə̇, bē+\ *vt* -ED/-ING/-S [ME *bedewen*, fr. *be-* + *dewen* to wet with dew — more at DEW] : to moisten with dew or with something felt to resemble dew (as tears or sweat) ⟨sympathetic tears my cheeks ~ —W.S.Gilbert⟩

bedfast \'=,=\ *adj* [[1]*bed* + *fast* (fixed)] : confined to bed because of sickness or weakness : BEDRIDDEN

bedfellow \'=,=(,)=\ *n* [ME *bedfelawe*, fr. *bed* + *felawe* fellow] **1** : a person sharing one's bed **2** : one found in proximity to or cooperation with another ⟨the press, like politics, makes strange ~*s* — *Newsweek*⟩ : ASSOCIATE, ALLY

bed·fel·low·ship \'=,=_=,ship\ *n* : the condition of being bedfellows

bedflower \'=,=\ *n* : YELLOW BEDSTRAW

bed·ford \'bedfə(r)d\ *adj, usu cap* [fr. *Bedford*, England] : of or from the municipal borough of Bedford, England : of the kind or style prevalent in Bedford

bedford cord *n, usu cap B* : a plain or twill-weave clothing fabric with wide or narrow lengthwise ribs made in various weights of cotton, wool, or other fibers singly and in combination

bed·ford·shire \'bedfərd,shi(ə)r, -fəd,shiə(r, -fə(r)dshə(r)\ *or*

bedford \-fə(r)d\ *adj, usu cap* [fr. *Bedfordshire* or *Bedford* county, England] **:** of or from the county of Bedford, England **:** of the kind or style prevalent in Bedford
bed fuel *n* **:** the bottom layer of fuel in a cupola furnace
bedgery *var of* PITURI
bedgown \ˈ=,=\ *n* **1 :** NIGHTGOWN **2** *dial Brit* **:** a woman's short loose jacket formerly worn for general work
bed-ground \ˈ=,=\ *n* **:** an area on which a drove of cattle or sheep sleep for a night
bedhead \ˈ=,=\ *n* [¹*bed* + *head*] **:** the head of a bed
be·dias·ite \bēˈdī,zīt\ *n* -s [fr. *Bedias*, town in Grimes county, Texas + E *-ite*] **:** TEKTITE
be·dight \bə̇ˈdīt, bē-\ *vt* **bedighted** *or* **bedight; bedighted** *or* **bedight; bedighting; bedights** [ME *bedighten*, fr. *be-* + *dighten* to put in order — more at DIGHT] *archaic* **:** EQUIP, ACCOUTER, ARRAY, BEDECK
be·di·kah \bə(,)dēˈkä, =ˈ=(,)=\ *n, pl* **bedikahs** \-äz\ *or* **bedikoth** \=(,)=ˈkōt, -ōth, -ōs\ [Heb *bĕdhīqāh* inspection] **:** the ritual inspection (as of a ceremonial act, person, or object) to ascertain fitness or unfitness according to rabbinical law
be·di·kath ha·metz \bə(,)dēˈkätkə̇ˈmäts, -ˈdē,kät-, -äthk-, -äsk-, -ˈkō,mets\ *or* **be·di·kat hametz** \-kät-, -käs-\ *n* [Heb *bĕdhīqath hāmēṣ* search for leaven] **:** the Jewish ceremony of searching for leaven in the home on the evening before Passover
be·dim \bə̇, bē+\ *vt* **bedimmed; bedimmed; bedimming; bedims** [*be-* + *dim* (v. or adj.)] **:** to make less bright or lustrous by or as if by covering ⟨clouds ~ the sun⟩ ⟨the surface was *bedimmed* by exposure to air⟩ **:** DIM **:** to make indistinct or confused **syn** see OBSCURE
be·dimple \bə̇, bē+\ *vt* [*be-* + *dimple*] **:** to mark with dimples
be·di·zen \bə̇ˈdīzᵊn, bē-, -diz-\ *vt* -ED/-ING/-S [*be-* + *dizen*] **:** to dress or adorn with gaudy and meretricious vulgarity ⟨a bold and shameless creature, *~ed*, painted and overdressed —Kenneth Roberts⟩
be·di·zen·ment \-mənt\ *n* -s **:** vulgar gaudy ornamentation ⟨*~s* of purple, scarlet, and apricot —Osbert Sitwell⟩
bed jacket *n* **:** a short lightweight jacket worn over a nightgown often when sitting up in bed
bed joint *n* **1 :** a horizontal joint in masonry **2 a :** a horizontal crack or fissure in massive rock **b :** one of a set of cracks or fissures parallel with the bedding of a rock
bedkey \ˈ=,=\ *n* [¹*bed* + *key*] **:** a wrench for adjusting the nuts and bolts or the ropes of a bedstead
bed ladder *n* **:** ¹BED 4k
¹**bed·lam** \ˈbedləm\ *n* -s [fr. *Bedlam*, popular name for the Hospital of St. Mary of Bethlehem, London, England, an insane asylum, fr. ME *Bedlem, Bethlem*, alter. of *Bethlehem*, town of Palestine] **1** *obs* **a :** MADMAN, LUNATIC **b** *sometimes cap* **:** a discharged often imperfectly cured patient of an asylum who is licensed to beg **2** *archaic* **:** a hospital for the insane **:** a lunatic asylum **3 a :** a place or scene of wild mad uproar ⟨after the speech the meeting became a ~⟩ **b :** an extremely confused scene **:** a situation making for confusion ⟨the ~ of roads, crescents, drives and avenues that forms the suburbs —*Irish Digest*⟩
²**bedlam** \"\ *adj* **:** MAD, LUNATIC **:** of or appropriate to an insane asylum
bed·lam·er \ˈbedləmə(r)\ *n* -s [origin unknown] **:** an immature harp or hooded seal
¹**bed·lam·ite** \ˈbedlə,mīt\ *n* -s *sometimes cap* [¹*bedlam* + *-ite*] **:** MADMAN, LUNATIC
²**bedlamite** \"\ *adj* **:** MAD, LUNATIC ⟨the ~ yells of carnival in the street —Joseph Conrad⟩
bed lathe *n* **:** a lathe whose bed extends to the floor
bed·less \ˈbedlə̇s\ *adj* **:** being without a bed
bed linen *n* **:** linen or cotton articles for a bed; *esp* **:** sheets and pillowcases
bed·ling·ton terrier \ˈbedliŋtən-\ *n, usu cap B* [fr. *Bedlington*, Eng.] **:** a swift rough-coated terrier of a breed originating in Northumberland, England, being of light build with arched loin, roached back, and tapering neck and tail, and weighing from 22 to 24 pounds
bed load *n* **:** sediment not in suspension rolled or dragged along a stream bottom
bed·man \ˈbedmən\ *n, pl* **bedmen :** one who prepares sand beds in which pig iron is cast
bedmate \ˈ=,=\ *n* **:** one that shares one's bed; *sometimes* **:** MISTRESS, CONCUBINE, WIFE
bed molding *or* **bed mold** *n* **:** the molding of a cornice immediately below the corona and above the frieze; *also* **:** a molding below a deep projection
be·doctor \bə̇, bē+\ *vt* [*be-* + *doctor* (n.)] **1 :** to confer a doctoral degree upon **2 :** to address as doctor
bed of roses : a place or situation of agreeable ease **:** a relaxed carefree luxurious situation
be·dog \bə̇, bē+\ *vt* [*be-* + *dog* (n. & v.)] **1 :** to call (a person) a dog **2 :** ²DOG *vt* 1
¹**bed·ou·in** *also* **bed·u·in** \ˈbedəwə̇n, -dwə̇n, -də,win, -də,wēn\ *or* **bed·oui** \ˈbedə(,)wē\ *n, pl* **bedouin** *or* **bedouins** *also* **beduin** *or* **beduins** *or* **bedouis** *often cap* [F *bédouin*, fr. Ar *badāwī* (colloq. Ar *bidwān*), pl. of *badawi, badwi* desert dweller] **:** a nomadic Arab of the Arabian, Syrian, or No. African deserts
²**bedouin** *also* **beduin** \"\ *adj, often cap* **:** of or relating to the bedouin
bedpan \ˈ=,=\ *n* **1** *obs* **:** WARMING PAN **2 :** a shallow vessel so constructed that it can be used by a person in bed for urination or defecation
bed piece *n* **1 :** a skid piece placed under a pile of lumber **2 :** a bank-note engraving die consisting of a flat hardened hand-engraved steel plate from which the printing plates are made by transference
bed plane *n* **:** BEDDING PLANE
bedplate \ˈ=,=\ *n* **:** a plate or framing used as a bed or support for something: as **a :** the heavy foundation framing or plate giving support and stability to the lighter parts in a machine ⟨an engine ~⟩ **b :** a stationary set of mounted knives or bars in a papermaking beater against which corresponding knives of the beater roll brush as they rotate
bedpost \ˈ=,=\ *n* **1 :** the usu. turned or carved post of a bed **2 :** the 7-10 split in bowling — usu. used in pl.
bedpost clock *n* **:** LANTERN CLOCK
be·drabble \bə̇, bē+\ *vt* -ED/-ING/-S [*be-* + *drabble*] **:** to wet and dirty with rain and mud
be·draggle \bə̇, bē+\ *vt* -ED/-ING/-S [*be-* + *draggle*] **:** to wet thoroughly ⟨little ducklings suffering from being *bedraggled*⟩
be·drag·gled \-gəld\ *adj* **1 :** left wet and limp or dragging by or as if by rain ⟨the ~ flags after the shower⟩ **2 :** soiled and stained by or as if by trailing in mud ⟨the ~ clothes of the beggar⟩ **3 :** lacking all former impressiveness **:** DILAPIDATED, DECREPIT, SOILED, WORN ⟨the ~ buildings of the slums⟩
bed·ral \ˈbedrəl\ *n* -s [by alter.] *Scot* **:** BEADLE 2
be·dress \bə̇, bē+\ *vt* [*be-* + *dress*] **:** to dress up
bed rest *n* **:** continuous confinement of a sick person to bed (as in treatment of tuberculosis or certain nerve disorders)
bed·rid·den \ˈbe,dridᵊn\ *also* **bed·rid** \-id\ *adj* [alter. of ME *bedrede, bedreden*, fr. OE *bedreda, bedrida*, fr. *bedreda, bedrida*, n., one who is confined to bed, fr. *bedd* bed + *-reda, -rida* rider (fr. *rīdan* to ride) — more at RIDE] **1 :** confined to one's bed by illness, injury, or weakness ⟨a ~ invalid⟩ **2 :** DECREPIT, WORN-OUT, ENERVATED ⟨~ notions⟩
¹**bedrock** \ˈ=ˈ=\ *n* [¹*bed* + *rock*] **1 :** the solid rock underlying the soil and other unconsolidated materials or appearing at the surface where these are absent — called also *ledge* **2 a :** lowest point **:** NADIR, MINIMUM **:** least quantity ⟨his resources were at ~⟩ **b :** BASIS, FOUNDATION ⟨a ~ of elementary learning on which an intermediate teacher could build⟩ **:** basic situation or consideration after matters adventitious have been stripped away
²**bedrock** \"\ *adj* **:** stripped of nonessential matter obscuring or adorning **:** BASIC, FUNDAMENTAL **:** SOLID, FACTUAL ⟨the great advantage of reality is its hard, ~, concrete quality —Lionel Trilling⟩
bedrock valley *n* **:** a valley eroded in bedrock
bedroll \ˈ=,=\ *n* [¹*bed* + *roll*] **:** bedding often of blankets only that is rolled up for ready carrying
¹**bedroom** \ˈ=,=\ *n* **1 :** a room furnished with a bed and intended primarily for sleeping **2 :** a private room on a railroad sleeping car larger than a roomette and smaller than a compartment and containing toilet facilities and usu. two berths
²**bedroom** \"\ *adj* **1 :** dealing with, suggestive of, or inviting to sex relations usu. illicit ⟨a ~ farce concerning a wife and her lover⟩ ⟨~ eyes which caressed the female on whom he looked —Ethel Wilson⟩ **2 :** inhabited or used by commuters ⟨a fringe of ~ towns around the city⟩
bedroom slipper *n* **:** a fabric or soft leather slipper often without heel or counter
be·drop \bə̇, bē+\ *vt* **bedropped; bedropped; bedropping; bedrops** [*be-* + *drop* (n.)] **:** to sprinkle with or as if with drops
bed rot *n* **:** DAMPING-OFF
beds *pl of* BED, *pres 3d sing of* BED
bed setter *n* **:** one that arranges blocks of granite on a bed of wooden beams and levels them in preparation for polishing of the tops — called also *setter*
¹**bedside** \ˈ=,=\ *n* [ME *bedside, beddes side*, fr. *bed* or *beddes* (gen. of *bed*) + *side*] **:** the side of a bed **:** a place beside a bed (as a sickbed or a deathbed) ⟨by her ~ when she died⟩
²**bedside** \"\ *adj* **1 :** relating to or conducted at the bedside of a patient ⟨~ teaching⟩ ⟨a ~ diagnosis⟩ **2 :** suitable for reading in bed esp. in short bits; *sometimes* **:** light and entertaining ⟨a ~ book⟩ ⟨~ literature⟩
bedside manner *n* **:** the manner often solicitous and sympathetic that a physician assumes toward his patients
bed-sitter \ˈ=ˈ==\ *n* [by shortening and alter.] **:** BED-SITTING-ROOM
bed-sitting-room \ˈ=ˈ==,=\ *n, Brit* **:** a one-room apartment serving as both bedroom and sitting room
bed slat *n* **:** a board supporting bedsprings usu. extending from side to side of a bedstead
bedsore \ˈ=,=\ *n* **:** an ulceration of tissue deprived of nutrition by prolonged pressure; *specif* **:** ulceration of tissue covering a prominent bony point (as the spine or a hipbone) in patients bedfast or animals recumbent for long periods
bedspread \ˈ=,=\ *n* **:** a large usu. ornamental cloth used as a cover for a bed
bedspring \ˈ=,=\ *n* **:** a spring supporting a mattress
bedstaff \ˈ=,=\ *n* **:** BED SLAT
bed·stead \ˈbed,sted *sometimes* -,stə̇d\ *n* -s [ME *bedstede*, fr. *bed* + *stede* stead, place — more at STEAD] **:** a framework of a bed usu. including a head with legs, a foot with legs, and connecting sides or rails
bed steps *n pl* **:** steps used to climb into a quite high bed
bedstock \ˈ=,=\ *n* [ME *bedstoke*, fr. *bed* + *stoke, stok* stock — more at STOCK] *dial Eng* **:** a structure supporting bed slats that runs either from side to side or from head to foot
bed stone *n* **1 :** a large foundation stone **2 :** the stationary lower stone of a pair of millstones
bedstraw \ˈ=,=\ *n* [ME, fr. *bed* + *straw*] **1 :** straw used in place of a mattress **:** straw used to fill a mattress **2 :** an herb of the genus *Galium*
bed tester *n* **:** fittings about the head of a bed; *sometimes* **:** CANOPY
bedtick \ˈ=,=\ *n* **:** TICK
bedticking \ˈ=,==\ *n* **:** TICKING
bed timber *n* **:** a foundation timber
bedtime \ˈ=,=\ *n* [ME, fr. *bed* + *time*] **:** time to go to bed
bedtime story *n* **:** a simple story for young children often about animals
be·du \ˈbe(,)dü\ *n, pl* **bedu** *sometimes cap* [Ar *badāwi* — more at BEDOUIN] **:** BEDOUIN
beduin *var of* BEDOUIN
bed up *vt* **:** to plow (two or more furrows) together to form a ridge on which a crop (as cotton or sweet potatoes) is grown
bed vein *n* **:** a vein that runs parallel to a bedding plane in a rock formation
bed wagon *n* **:** a wagon carrying bedding and supplies on a cattle roundup
bed·ward \ˈbedwə(r)d\ *or* **bed·wards** \-dz\ *adv* [ME *bedward*, fr. ¹*bed* + *-ward*] **1 :** toward bed **2** *obs* **:** towards bedtime
bed warmer *n* **:** a covered pan containing hot coals used to warm a bed
bedway \ˈ=,=\ *n* **1 :** the bed of a child's slide **2 :** one of the rails or guides on the bed of a lathe
be·dwell \bə̇, bē+\ *vt* [*be-* + *dwell*] **:** to dwell in **:** INHABIT
bed wetter *n* **:** a person that habitually urinates in bed during sleep
bed-wetting \ˈ=,==\ *n* **:** ENURESIS
¹**bee** \ˈbē\ *n* -s *often attrib* [ME, fr. OE *bēo*; akin to OHG *bini, bīa* bee, ON *bȳ*, W *bydaf* beehive, Lith *bitis* bee] **1 a :** a social colonial hymenopterous insect (*Apis mellifera*) often maintained in a state of domestication for the sake of the honey that it produces and for use as a pollinator **:** HONEYBEE; *broadly* **:** any of numerous membranous-winged noncarnivorous insects constituting a superfamily (Apoidea) of the order Hymenoptera that differ from the closely related wasps in possession of a heavier hairier body and sucking as well as chewing mouthparts, feed on pollen and nectar and store both and often also honey, the fertile females and workers usu. having functional stings **2 :** an eccentric, fantastic, or delusive notion **:** WHIM, FANCY ⟨he has a new ~ that he'd like to be an actor⟩ **3** [perh. alter. of E dial. *been, bean* voluntary help given by neighbors toward the accomplishment of a particular task, prob. fr. ME *bene* boon, prayer, fr. OE *bēn* prayer — more at BOON] **a :** a usu. social gathering of people to accomplish cooperatively a specific purpose — often used in combinations ⟨husking ~⟩ ⟨quilting ~⟩ **b :** PARTY 10a ⟨a square-dancing ~⟩ **c :** SPELLING BEE **4 :** a lump of a yeast (*Saccharomyces pyriformis*) intermittently rising and releasing bubbles in brew — usu. used in pl. — **bee in one's bonnet :** ¹BEE 2 ⟨he has the presidential *bee in his bonnet* —O.W.Holmes †1935⟩
²**bee** \"\ *or* **bee block** *n* -s [ME *beghe, beh* ring, bracelet, fr. OE *bēag, bēah*; akin to OHG *boug* ring, bracelet, ON *baugr*, Skt *bhoga* coil (of a snake), OE *būgan* to bend, bow — more at BOW] **:** a piece of hard wood bolted to the side of a bowsprit sometimes with metal sheaves to reeve fore-topmast stays through
³**bee** *also* **be** \"\ *n* -s **:** the letter *b*
be-east \bē+\ *prep* [ME (northern dial.) *be est, be eist*, fr. *be* by (fr. OE *be, bi, bī*) + *est, eist* east — more at BY, EAST] **:** east of
bee-ball \ˈbē+,-\ *n* **:** a game that combines elements of rugby and soccer and is played on a football field between two teams of nine players using a leather ball slightly smaller than a soccer ball
bee balm *n* **1 :** LEMON BALM **2 :** either of two common monardas: **a :** OSWEGO TEA **b :** a wild bergamot (*Monarda fistulosa*)
¹**bee·bee** *var of* BIBI
²**beebee** *var of* BB
bee bird *n* **:** any of several birds reputed to eat bees (as the European flycatchers and the kingbird)
beebread \ˈ=,=\ *n* **:** bitter yellowish brown pollen stored up in honeycomb cells and used mixed with honey by bees as food
bee brush *n* **:** a soft brush for removing bees from the honeycomb
bee-butt \ˈbē,bət\ *n* [¹*bee* + E dial. *butt* straw beehive, fr. OCorn] *dial Eng* **:** BEEHIVE
bee candy *n* **:** sugar with another substance (as honey) incorporated in it for feeding bees
bee cellar *n* **:** a cellar where bees are kept through the winter
¹**beech** \ˈbēch\ *n, pl* **beeches** *or* **beech** [ME *beche*, fr. OE *bēce*; akin to OE *bōc* beech, OHG *buohha*, ON *bōk*, L *fagus* beech, Gk *phēgos* oak, and perh. to Russ *buzina* elder] **1 :** any tree of the genus *Fagus* characterized by smooth gray bark, hard fine-grained wood, deep green foliage, and small sweet-flavored edible triangular nuts enclosed in burs — see AMERICAN BEECH, COPPER BEECH, EUROPEAN BEECH; TREE illustration **2 :** the wood of the beech **3** *Austral* **:** any of numerous trees resembling the true beech esp. in their timber — compare FLINDOSA **4 :** a tree of the genus *Nothofagus*
²**beech** \"\ *adj* [ME *beche*, fr. *beche*, n.] **1 :** of or relating to the beech **2 :** made of beech
beech agaric *n* **:** a white glutinous edible mushroom (*Armillaria mucida*) that is a wound parasite on the beech
beech bark disease *n* **:** a disease of beech esp. destructive in eastern Canada and northern U.S. that is due to the combined activities of the beech scale (*Cryptococcus fagi*) and a fungus (*Nectria coccinea faginata*) and causes destruction of living bark, wilting of foliage, and finally death of the tree
beechdrops \ˈ=,=\ *n pl but sing or pl in constr* **1 :** a low wiry plant (*Epifagus virginiana*) parasitic on the roots of beeches **2 :** SQUAWROOT
beech·en \ˈbēchən\ *adj* [ME *bechen*, fr. OE *bēcen*, fr. *bēce*, n. + *-en*] **:** consisting or made of beech **:** derived from or belonging to the beech
beech family *n* **:** FAGACEAE
beech fern *n* **:** either of the two ferns (*Dryopteris phegopteris* and *D. hexagonoptera*) that grow frequently in beechwoods — see BROAD BEECH FERN
beech fungus *n* **:** a So. American edible fungus — see CYTTARIA
beech leaf snake *n, dial* **:** COPPERHEAD
beech marten *n* **:** STONE MARTEN
beech mast *n* **:** beechnuts esp. as they lie under trees
beech·nut \ˈbēch,nət *sometimes* -,nət\ *n* **:** the nut of the beech
beech scale *n* **:** a destructive European scale (*Cryptococcus fagi*) now established in the northeastern U.S. and adjacent parts of Canada where it is destructive to stands of native beech
beech seal *n, in Vermont* **:** a beech rod **:** a flogging with beech rods
beech-tree \ˈ=,=\ *n* [ME *bech-tre*, fr. *beche* beech + *tre* tree] **:** BEECH 1
beechy \ˈbēchē\ *adj* -ER/-EST **:** of, relating to, or abounding in beeches
bee-eater \ˈ=,==\ *n* **:** any of numerous brightly colored chiefly tropical Old World birds constituting the family Meropidae and distinguished by a strong graceful flight like that of a swallow
bee-escape \ˈ==,=\ *n* **:** a device to permit the escape of bees but prevent their return (as from a compartment of a hive)
¹**beef** \ˈbēf\ *n, pl* **beefs** \-ēfs\ *or* **beeves** \-ēvz\ *also* **beef** *see numbered senses* [ME, fr. OF *buef* ox, beef, fr. L *bov-, bos* head of cattle — more at COW] **1 :** the flesh of a steer, cow, or other adult bovine animal when killed for food **2 a** *pl* **beeves** *also* **beefs** *or* **beef :** an ox, cow, or bull in a full-grown or nearly full-grown state; *esp* **:** a steer or cow fattened for food ⟨*beeves* of quality —P.A. Rollins⟩ ⟨Texan *beefs* were loaded in the Abilene yards —R.A. Billington⟩ ⟨a herd of *beef* —E.C. Abbott & Helena Smith⟩ **b** *pl* **beeves** *also* **beefs :** the dressed carcass of a beef animal ⟨*beeves* hanging in the slaughterhouse⟩ **c :** beef animals ⟨growing ~ on the range⟩ **3 a :** muscular flesh **:** BRAWN, WEIGHT **:** bulky strength ⟨a heavyweight wrestler with a great deal of ~⟩ **b :** strength and power ⟨an engine with added ~⟩ **c :** ARGUMENT, QUARREL, BRAWL, FIGHT **4** *pl* **beefs** [fr. the verb] **a** *slang* **:** PROTEST, OBJECTION **:** grievance or ground for complaint **:** point at issue ⟨*~s* and grumbling by disappointed contestants —Bennett Cerf⟩ **b** *slang* **:** COMPLAINT, ACCUSATION **:** criminal charge ⟨parole officer said he was going straight — no *~s* anywhere —Thurston Scott⟩

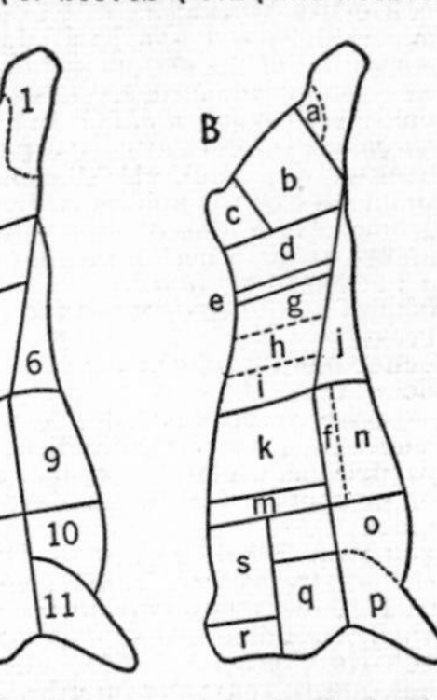

A. wholesale cuts of beef: *1* shank; *2* round (with rump and shank cut off); *3* rump; *4* sirloin; *5* short loin; *6* flank; *7* rib; *8* chuck; *9* plate; *10* brisket; *11* shank B. retail cuts of beef: *a* heel pot roast; *b* round steak; *c* rump roast; *d* sirloin steak; *e* pinbone steak; *f* short ribs; *g* porterhouse steak; *h* T-bone steak; *i* club steak; *j* flank steak; *k* rib roast; *m* blade rib roast; *n* plate; *o* brisket; *p* crosscut shank; *q* arm pot roast; *r* boneless neck; *s* blade roast

²**beef** \"\ *vb* -ED/-ING/-S *vt* **1 :** to add weight, strength, force, or power to — usu. used with *up* ⟨de-emphasize their navy and ~ up their army —*Fortune*⟩ ⟨the inspector general's office would be *~ed* up with additional investigators —*Time*⟩ **2 :** to fatten or kill (a beef animal) for food ~ *vi* **1 :** to complain, object, or protest often angrily or emphatically ⟨seamen can always find something to ~ about —S.E.Morison⟩ **2** *slang* **a :** to make a complaint **b :** to inform or give evidence ⟨if the mark *~s* and goes to the police —D.W.Maurer⟩ **syn** see COMPLAIN
³**beef** \"\ *adj* **1 :** of, from, or relating to the ox kind ⟨~ blood⟩ ⟨a ~ serum⟩ **2 :** raised for or suitable for beef ⟨a ~ animal⟩
beef bacon *n* **:** beef plate or brisket cured in the same way as pork bacon
beef boat *n* **:** a supply ship or boat
beef bread *n* **:** the pancreas of a mature animal (as a beef) used for food
beef breed *n* **:** any breed of cattle developed primarily for the efficient production of meat (as the Angus, Hereford, or Shorthorn) and characterized by capacity for rapid growth, heavy rectangular well-fleshed body, and comparatively short stocky neck and legs — compare DAIRY BREED
beef·burg·er \ˈbēf,bərgə(r)\ *n* -s [¹*beef* + *hamburger*] **:** HAMBURGER
beefcake \ˈ=,=\ *n, slang* **:** display (as in photographs featuring bare chests) of robust or vigorous masculine physique — compare CHEESECAKE
beef cattle *n* **:** cattle suitable for beef; *esp* **:** cattle of one of the beef breeds
beef cow *n* **:** a cow of a beef breed
beef critter *n, dial* **:** a mature beef
beefeater \ˈ=,==\ *n* **1 :** a yeoman of the guard that forms part of an English monarch's train on state occasions **2 :** a warder of the Tower of London uniformed like a beefeater
¹**beef·er** \ˈbēfə(r)\ *n* -s [¹*beef* + *-er*] **:** an animal of the ox kind produced for meat
²**beefer** *n* -s *slang* **:** one that beefs ⟨was a constant ~; nothing ever pleased him⟩
beef extract *n* **:** an extract of the soluble constituents of beef or beef blood used to stimulate gastric secretion — compare BEEF TEA
beefheaded \ˈ=ˈ==\ *adj* **:** STUPID ⟨resented the ~ ward heelers —John Fischer⟩
beef juice *n* **:** the juice of beef extracted by pressure rather than by cooking
beef·less \ˈbēflə̇s\ *adj* **:** being without beef ⟨this hungry, thirsty . . . ~ land —Richard Ford⟩
beeflower \ˈ=,==\ *n* **:** BEE PLANT
bee fly *n* **1 :** any of numerous flies constituting a family (Bombyliidae) having many members resembling bees **2 :** a fly (*Heterostylum robustum*) that parasitizes wild bees by laying its eggs in the nesting cells

beefeater 1

beef measles *n pl but sing or pl in constr* **:** the infestation of beef muscle by cysticerci of the beef tapeworm which make oval white vesicles giving a measly appearance to the beef
beefs *pl of* BEEF
beef's blood *n* **:** OXBLOOD
beefsteak \ˈ=,=\ *n* **:** a steak of beef usu. cut from the hindquarter and suitable for broiling or frying
beefsteak begonia *or* **beefsteak geranium** *n* **:** a rhizomatous begonia (*Begonia feastii*) with round fleshy leaves reddish colored beneath
beefsteak fungus *also* **beefsteak mushroom** *n* **:** a fungus (*Fistulina hepatica*) of the family Polyporaceae growing on dead trees in bright-red shelving masses and esteemed as a table delicacy — called also *beeftongue*

beefsteak plant *n* **:** any of several plants having red or purple foliage: as **a :** an ornamental foliage plant (*Perilla frutescens crispa*) **b :** a wood betony (*Pedicularis canadensis*) **c :** a plant of the genus *Begonia; esp* **:** BEEFSTEAK BEGONIA

beef tapeworm *n* **:** an unarmed tapeworm (*Taenia saginata*) that infests the human intestine as an adult, has a cysticercus larva that develops in cattle, and is contracted by man through ingestion of the larva in raw or rare beef

beef tea *n* **:** a beverage prepared by extracting finely cut lean beef with hot water or by dissolving commercial beef extract in boiling water — compare BEEF EXTRACT, BOUILLON

beeftongue \ˈ=,=\ *n* **:** BEEFSTEAK FUNGUS

beef-witted \ˈ=ˈ==\ *adj* **:** STUPID

beefwood \ˈ=,=\ *n* **1 :** any of several hard heavy reddish chiefly tropical woods including some that are used for cabinetwork **2 :** any tree yielding beefwood: as **a :** any of several casuarinas; *esp* **:** a common Australian tree (*Casuarina equisetifolia*) now widely grown as an ornamental in warm regions — called also *Australian pine* **b :** either of two Australian silk oaks (*Grevillea striata* and *Stenocarpus salignus*) **c :** BLOLLY 1 **d :** a bully tree (*Manilkara bidentata*)

beefwood family *n* **:** CASUARINACEAE — compare CASUARINA

beefy \ˈbēfē, -fi\ *adj* -ER/-EST [¹*beef* + -*y*] **1 :** brawny or fleshy with suggestions of grossness **:** THICKSET, HEAVY ⟨coarsened and ~, with a neck like a bull's and a rapidly spreading girth —Ellen Glasgow⟩ ⟨~ and sturdy, with heavy legs —Joseph Bennett⟩ **2 a :** promising a good yield of beef ⟨~ cattle⟩ **b :** coarsely overfleshed **:** obesely heavy

bee·ger·ite \ˈbēgə,rīt\ *n* -s [Hermann *Beeger*, 19th cent. Amer. metallurgist + E -*ite*] **:** a mineral $Pb_6Bi_2S_9$ consisting of massive gray sulfide of lead and bismuth

bee glue *n* **:** PROPOLIS

bee gum *n* **1** *chiefly South & Midland* **:** a hollow gum tree in which wild bees hive **2** *chiefly South & Midland* **:** a beehive made from sections of a hollow tree; *broadly* **:** BEEHIVE **3** *chiefly South & Midland* **:** a tall silk hat

beeheaded \ˈ=ˈ==\ *adj* **:** ECCENTRIC, CRAZY

beehive \ˈ=,=\ *n* [ME, fr. ¹*bee* + *hive*] **1 :** a hive for bees **2 :** something felt to resemble a hive for bees: as **a :** a rounded conical shape ⟨a ~ hut⟩ **b :** a scene of swarming buzzing activity **3 :** SHAPED CHARGE

beehive coke *n* **:** coke that is made in a beehive oven and is usu. of large size and hard stringy structure

beehive kiln *n* **:** a circular brick kiln with a domed roof

beehive oven *n* **:** a now little used arched coke oven in which heat is supplied by partial combustion of the coal within the oven chamber and no by-products are recovered

old-fashioned beehive

beehive tomb *n* **:** a tomb shaped like a beehive cut in a hillside and usu. approached by a horizontal passage, distinctive of the Mycenaean age in Greece

beehouse \ˈ=,=\ *n* **:** a house for bees **:** APIARY

beek \ˈbēk\ *vb* -ED/-ING/-S [ME *beken*] *chiefly Scot* **:** WARM ⟨~ before a fire⟩ **:** BASK

beekeeper \ˈ=,==\ *n* **:** one that engages in beekeeping esp. as a means of livelihood

beekeeping \ˈ=,==\ *n* **:** the branch of agriculture concerned with the production of and caring for bees and honey **:** APICULTURE

bee killer *n* **:** a large robber fly that feeds on or is supposed to feed on bees

beek·ite \ˈbē,kīt\ *n* -s [Henry *Beeke* †1837 dean of Bristol, who first called attention to it + E -*ite*] **:** a pseudomorph of chalcedony after coral or shell

¹**beeline** \ˈ=ˈ=\ *n* [¹*bee* + *line*; fr. the belief that nectar-laden bees return to their hives in a direct line] **:** a straight line**:** a straight direct course traversed rapidly — usu. used with *make* ⟨make a ~ to safer quarters⟩

²**beeline** \ˈ"\ *vi* -ED/-ING/-S **:** to go fast over the straightest quickest course — sometimes used with *it* ⟨ambulances *beelining* it for the hospital⟩

bee-lin·er \ˈbē¦līnə(r)\ *n* [blend of ¹*beeline* and *liner*] **:** a self-propelled diesel railroad car

bee louse *n* **:** a minute wingless fly (*Braula coeca*) parasitic on honeybees

bee·ze·bub \bēˈelzə,bəb, ˈbēl-,ˈbel-\ *n* -s [after *Beelzebub*, called "prince of the devils" in Mt 12:24, fr. L, fr. Gk *Beelzeboub*, fr. Heb *Ba'al Zĕbhūbh*, lit., lord of flies] **1** *sometimes cap* **:** DEVIL **2 a :** a So. American howler monkey (*Alouatta beelzebul*)

bee·man \ˈbēmən, -,man\ *n, pl* **beemen :** BEEKEEPER

bee-martin \ˈ=,==\ *n* **:** KINGBIRD

beemaster \ˈ=,==\ *n* **:** BEEKEEPER

bee moth *n* **:** a dull brownish or ashen moth (*Galleria mellonella*) whose larva feeds on the wax of the combs of the honeybee fouling the honey and injuring the brood and sometimes destroying weak colonies of bees — called also *wax moth*

been *past part of* BE, *dial Brit & archaic pres pl of* BE

bee·na marriage \ˈbēnə-\ *n* [Ar *bīnah* distinct, separate] **:** a marriage in parts of India and Ceylon in which the husband enters the wife's kinship group and has little authority in the household — compare MUTA

bee nettle *n* **1 :** HEMP NETTLE **2 :** HENBIT

bee orchis *or* **bee orchid** *n* **:** a European orchid (*Listera apifera*) whose flowers bear a resemblance to bees, flies, or other insects

¹**beep** \ˈbēp\ *n* -s [imit.] **1 :** a sound from a horn on a moving vehicle (as an automobile, boat, or locomotive) serving as a signal or warning **2 :** a short high-pitched note as if from a reed instrument sounded esp. as a time signal in radio broadcasting or as an indication that a telephone conversation is being recorded or that a recording has been made by telephone

²**beep** \ˈ"\ *vb* -ED/-ING/-S *vi* **:** to sound a horn ⟨drivers ~*ing* behind us⟩ **:** make a beep ⟨horns ~*ing*⟩ ~ *vt* **1 :** to cause (a horn) to sound **2 :** to make by sounding — sometimes used with *out* ⟨~*ing* out a warning⟩

beep·er \-pə(r)\ *n* -s **1 :** a device emitting beep signals esp. to pilotless aircraft **2 :** one that governs the flight of pilotless aircraft by remote control

bee plant *n* **:** a plant much frequented by bees for nectar: as **a :** a heavy-scented herb (*Cleome serrulata*) with numerous pink flowers **b :** any of various plants of the genus *Scrophularia* **c :** BEE BALM

¹**beer** \ˈbi(ə)r, -iə\ *n* -s *often attrib* [ME *ber*, fr. OE *bēor*; akin to OHG *bior* beer and perh. to OE *bȳsting* beestings — more at BEASTINGS] **1 :** a malted and hopped somewhat bitter alcoholic beverage; *specif* **:** such a beverage brewed by bottom fermentation — compare ALE, BOCK BEER, LAGER, PORTER **2 :** a carbonated nonalcoholic or a fermented slightly alcoholic beverage with flavoring derived from roots and other plant parts — used chiefly in compounds; see BIRCH BEER, GINGER BEER, ROOT BEER, SPRUCE BEER **3 :** fermented mash **:** WASH **4 :** a drink of beer ⟨order a ~⟩

²**beer** \ˈ"\ *also* **bier** \ˈ"\ *n* -s [perh. fr. ¹*bier*] **:** one of the groups in weaving usu. consisting of 40 threads into which the threads of the warp are divided; *also* **:** the corresponding group of dents on the reed consisting usu. of 20

beer·age \ˈbirij\ *n* -s [blend of *beer* and *peerage*] **:** the British peerage — usu. used disparagingly

beer and skittles *n* **:** drink and play **:** easygoing enjoyment

beer barrel *n* **:** a large common tun shell (*Tonus cerevisina*) of the Australian coast

beer cellar *n* **1 :** a cellar for storing beer **2 :** RATHSKELLER

beer gallon *n* **:** ALE GALLON

beer garden *n* **:** a garden where beer and other liquors are served at tables

beer hall *n* **:** an establishment featuring beer and sometimes offering entertainment

beerhouse \ˈ=,=\ *n, Brit* **:** a public house licensed to sell only malt liquors

beer·i·ly \ˈbirəlē\ *adv* **:** in a beery and esp. a muddled or maudlin way ⟨they may sound as ~ nostalgic . . . at 2:00 a.m. —*Saturday Rev.*⟩

beerpull \ˈ=,=\ *n* **:** BEER PUMP; *also* **:** its handle

beer pump *n* **:** a pump for drawing up beer from casks (as from cellar to bar)

beer's law \ˈbāərz-\ *n, usu cap B* [after August *Beer* †1863 Ger. physicist] **:** a law in physics: the absorption of light by different concentrations of the same solute dissolved in the same solvent is an exponential function of the concentration provided the thickness of the absorbing medium remains constant

beer stone *also* **beer scale** *n* **:** a grayish brown scale composed of calcium oxalate and organic substances forming on the inside surfaces of brewing apparatus

beery \ˈbirē, -ri\ *adj* -ER/-EST **1 :** inspired or influenced by beer drinking **:** convivial, mellowed, muddled, or maudlin ⟨~ song⟩ ⟨~ reminiscenses⟩ **:** affected or conditioned by beer ⟨a ~ face⟩ ⟨~ voices⟩ **2 a :** smelling of beer ⟨a ~ tavern⟩ **b :** mixed or flavored with beer

bees *pl of* BEE

bee sage *n* **:** a shrub (*Hyptis emorgi*) of the family Labiatae of southwestern U.S. and Mexico with aromatic white woolly foliage and purple flowers

bee smoker *n* **:** a device for blowing smoke into a hive to quiet bees before working on or about the hive

bee space *n* **:** a space a little less than ¼ inch that provides for the passage of bees in a hive

¹**beest** \ˈbēst\ *n* -s [by shortening] **:** BEASTINGS

²**beest** *dial Brit pres 2d sing of* BE, *obs pres subjunctive 2d sing of* BE

bee-sting \ˈbē,stiŋ\ *n* [¹*bee* + *sting*] **1 :** the burning itching swollen lesion produced by the stinging of a bee **2** *or* **bee's sting :** the modified ovipositor of a bee that is typically associated with a venom gland and that serves as the bee's chief weapon

beest·ings \ˈbē,stiŋz, -,stenz\ *var of* BEASTINGS

¹**bees·wax** \ˈbēz,waks\ *n* [*bee's* (gen. of ¹*bee*) + *wax*] **1 :** WAX 1a **2 a :** a wax obtained as a yellow to brown solid by melting a honeycomb with boiling water, straining, and cooling and used esp. in polishes, modeling, and making patterns — called also *yellow wax* **b :** bleached yellow wax used esp. in cosmetics, ointments, and cerates and in church candles — called also *white wax* **3 :** a moderate yellowish brown that is slightly lighter than Bismarck brown or antique bronze, yellower and slightly lighter and stronger than cinnamon brown, darker than maple sugar, and redder and lighter than bronze — called also *linoleum brown, wax brown*

²**beeswax** \ˈ"\ *vt* -ED/-ING/-ES **:** to rub, coat, or polish with beeswax

beeswax flint *n* **:** a paleolithic flint of the color of beeswax

bees·wing \ˈbēz,wiŋ\ *n* [*bee's* (gen. of ¹*bee*) + *wing*] **1 :** a film of shining scales of tartar formed in port and some other wines after long keeping **2 :** very thin filmy pieces of bran — **bees·winged** \-ŋd\ *adj*

¹**beet** \ˈbēt, *usu* -ēd·+V\ *n* -s *often attrib* [ME *bete*, fr. OE *bēte*, fr. L *beta*] **1 :** any biennial plant of the genus *Beta* (esp. *B. vulgaris*) with large thick leaves used esp. when young as greens and with a bulbous root **2 :** the enlarged root of the beet cultivated as a garden vegetable or as a source of sugar or for forage — usu. used in pl. when referring to a table vegetable; see CHARD, MANGEL, SUGAR BEET

²**beet** \ˈ"\ *vt* -ED/-ING/-S [ME *beten, beeten* to improve, amend, kindle or feed a fire, fr. OE *bētan*; akin to OHG *buozzen* to improve, amend, ON *bæta*, Goth *gabotjan*, all causatives fr. the root of OE *bōt* help, relief — more at BOOT] *dial Brit* **:** to add fuel to (a fire) **:** FEED

³**beet** \ˈ"\ *n* -s [ME *bete, beite*] **:** a tied bundle or sheaf of fiber flax plants

beet armyworm *n* **:** an armyworm (*Spodoptera exigua*) that eats the foliage of beets, alfalfa, and vegetables

bee·tewk \ˈbē·tyük\ *n, usu cap* [Russ *bityug, bityuk*, prob. fr. the *Bityug* river, Russia] **:** a Russian breed of heavy draft horses

bee·tho·ve·nian \ˌbā,tō¦vēnēən, -nyən *also* -äd-,ō¦v- *or* -äd-ə¦v-\ *adj, usu cap* [Ludwig van *Beethoven* †1827 German composer + E -*ian*] **:** of, relating to, or characteristic of Ludwig van Beethoven or his musical style or works ⟨possessed of a *Beethovenian* genius⟩

¹**bee·tle** \ˈbēd·ᵊl, -ētᵊl\ *n* -s [ME *bityl, betylle*, fr. OE *bitula*, fr. *bītan* to bite — more at BITE] **1 :** an insect of the order Coleoptera — sometimes distinguished from *weevil* **2 :** any of various insects (as cockroaches) more or less resembling those of the order Coleoptera esp. in being of large size and dark color — not used technically

beetle

²**beetle** \ˈ"\ *vi* **beetled; beetled; beetling** \-ēd·ᵊliŋ, -ēt(ᵊ)liŋ\ **beetles :** to scuttle like a beetle either with speed or with awkward bumbling ⟨while the heavy buses ~ past —Thomas Wolfe⟩

³**beetle** \ˈ"\ *n* -s [ME *betel*, fr. OE *bietel*, fr. *bēatan* to beat — more at BEAT] **1 :** a heavy wooden hammering or ramming instrument for driving stakes, tamping paving blocks, and performing similar heavy tasks of pounding **2 :** a wooden pestle or bat for such domestic tasks as beating linen and mashing potatoes **3 :** a machine for giving cotton and linen fabrics a compact appearance and a lustrous finish (as by hammering over rollers)

⁴**beetle** \ˈ"; *for pres part see* ²BEETLE\ *vt* -ED/-ING/-S **:** to flatten and compact (a fabric) in a beetle

⁵**beetle** \ˈ"\ *adj* [ME *bitel-* (as in *bitel-browed* beetle-browed)] **:** prominent and overhanging — usu. used of eyebrows with suggestion of lowering sullenness

⁶**beetle** \ˈ"; *for pres part see* ²BEETLE\ *vi* -ED/-ING/-S **:** to project, overhang, jut, or loom often ominously or threateningly ⟨the dark heavy brows *beetling* in a frown —Ellen Glasgow⟩ ⟨spending my strength in vain to scale the *beetling* crags —R.L.Stevenson⟩ **syn** see BULGE

beet leafhopper *n* **:** a destructive homopterous insect (*Circulifer tenellus*) widely distributed in the western U.S. where it serves as a vector of curly top on a large number of crop and ornamental plants

beetled *adj* [fr. past part. of ⁶*beetle*] **:** BEETLE

beetle green *n* **:** an iridescent color that under normal viewing is a deep yellowish green

beetlehead \ˈ==,=\ *n* [³*beetle* + *head*] **1 :** a stupid person **2 :** BLACK-BELLIED PLOVER

beetleheaded \ˈ==ˈ==\ *adj* **:** STUPID

beetle mite *n* [so called fr. their hard, shining bodies] **:** any of numerous free-living mites (superfamily Oribatoidea) that are abundant and widespread in soil and that include several important intermediate hosts of tapeworms of domestic animals

bee·tler \ˈbēd·ᵊlə(r), -ēt(ᵊ)lə(r)\ *n* -s [⁴*beetle* + -*er*] **:** one that beetles cloth

beetleweed \ˈ==,=\ *n* [prob. fr. ¹*beetle* + *weed*] **:** GALAX 2

beet puller *or* **beet lifter** *n* **:** an implement that lifts sugar beets out of soil at harvest time

beet pulp *n* **:** wet or dried slices of sugar beet after the sugar has been extracted used as a stock feed

bee tree *n* **1 :** a hollow tree in which honeybees have a nest **2 :** BASSWOOD 1

beetroot \ˈ=,=\ *n* -s **1** *chiefly Brit* **:** BEET 2 **2 :** a pigweed (*Amaranthus retroflexus*) with stem base of a reddish color

beets *pl of* BEET, *pres 3d sing of* BEET

beet sugar *n* **:** sugar made from sugar beets by extraction of juice from the finely sliced roots, evaporation of excess water, and crystallization of the resulting syrup

beet webworm *n* **:** the green or yellowish larva of a small brownish pyralidid moth (*Loxostege sticticalis*) that feeds on and defoliates garden beets and sugar beets and many other cultivated plants

beeve \ˈbēv\ *n* -s [back-formation fr. *beeves*, pl. of *beef*] **:** ¹BEEF 2a

bee veil *n* **:** a protective device of fine fabric or wire mesh worn about the head by beekeepers when working with bees

beeves *pl of* BEEF *or of* BEEVE

beev·ish \ˈbēvish\ *adj* [*beeve* + -*ish*] **:** resembling or suggesting cattle

beeware \ˈ=,=\ *n* [¹*bee* + *ware*] **:** materials used by beekeepers

beeway \ˈ=,=\ *n* [¹*bee* + *way*] **:** BEE SPACE

beeweed \ˈ=,=\ *n* [¹*bee* + *weed*] **:** any of several bee plants; *esp* **:** an American woodland aster (*Aster cordifolius*)

beeyard \ˈ=,=\ *n* [¹*bee* + *yard*] **:** APIARY

bee·zer \ˈbēzə(r)\ *n* -s [perh. blend of *beak* and *sneezer*] *slang* **:** NOSE

bef *abbr* before

be·fall \bəˈfȯl, bē-\ *vb* **be·fell** \-ˈfel\ **be·fall·en** \-fȯlən, *also in poetry & sometimes* + *V in prose* -fȯln\ **befalling; befalls** [ME *befallen*, fr. OE *befeallan* (akin to OHG *bifallan* to fall), fr. *be-* + *feallan* to fall — more at FALL] *vi* **1** *archaic* **:** to fall due **:** PERTAIN ⟨taking only what *befell* to him⟩ **2 :** to take place esp. as if by the prompting of destiny or fate **:** come to pass ⟨these things *befell* —George Santayana⟩ **3** *obs* **:** BECOME — used with *of* ~ *vt* **:** to happen or occur to esp. in the course of events ⟨the saddest thing that ~*s* a soul is when it loses faith —Alexander Smith⟩ **syn** see HAPPEN

be·fettered \bə, bē+\ *adj* [*be-* + *fettered*] **:** ENSLAVED

be·fezzed \bəˈfezd, bē-\ *adj* [*be-* + *fez* + -*ed*] **:** wearing a fez

be·fit \bəˈfit, bē-, *usu* -id·+V\ *vt* **befitted; befitted; befitting; befits** [ME *befitten*, prob. fr. *be-* + *fit*, adj.] **1 :** to accord with **:** be in harmony with **:** be proper or becoming to **:** SUIT ⟨clothing that ~*s* his position⟩ ⟨as *befitted* his New England background he was a staunch protectionist —Broadus Mitchell⟩ **2** *obs* **:** to fit out

befitting *adj* **1 :** SUITABLE, APPROPRIATE ⟨the matter was written in ~ prose⟩ ⟨the ~ elegance of a royal court⟩ **2 :** in harmony with moral, ethical, or social norms **:** PROPER, DECENT ⟨act in a ~ manner⟩ — **be·fit·ting·ly** *adv* — **be·fit·ting·ness** *n* -ES

be·flagged \bəˈflagd, bē-, -aa(ə)gd, -aigd\ *adj* [*be-* + *flag* + -*ed*] **:** decorated with or as if with flags ⟨the ~ balcony⟩

be·flatter \bə, bē+\ *vt* -ED/-ING/-S [*be-* + *flatter*] **1 :** to dupe by flattery **2 :** to flatter greatly

be·flour \bə, bē+\ *vt* -ED/-ING/-S [*be-* + *flour*, n.] **:** to dust over with or as if with flour ⟨bees ~*ed* with yellow⟩

be·flowered \bə, bē+\ *adj* [*be-* + *flower* + -*ed*] **:** adorned with flowers

be·flum \bəˈfləm, bē-\ *vt* **beflummed; beflummed; beflumming; beflums** [*be-* + *flum*; perh. influenced by Sc *blaflum* to cajole] *chiefly Scot* **:** to deceive esp. by flattery

be·flustered \bə, bē+\ *adj* [*be-* + *flustered*] **:** much flustered

be·fog \bə, bē+\ *vt* **befogged; befogged; befogging; befogs** [*be-* + *fog*, n.] **1 :** to obscure with or as if with fog ⟨*befogged* roads⟩ ⟨cigar smoke *befogged* the room⟩ ⟨television . . . *befogged* with zigging and zagging lines —Philip Hamburger⟩ **2 a :** to make indistinct, vague, or confused ⟨the issue was *befogged* with bias⟩ **b :** to lessen or impair the clarity, perceptivity, or sensitivity of ⟨drink *befogged* his senses⟩ **c :** to throw into a state of uncertainty, indecision, or confusion **:** PUZZLE ⟨questions of rising or not and shaking hands or not ~ many people —Agnes M. Miall⟩ **syn** see OBSCURE

be·fool \bə, bē+\ *vt* -ED/-ING/-S [*be-* + *fool*, n.] **1 a :** to make a fool of **:** cause to appear foolish ⟨~*ing* a pedant with questions⟩ **b :** to lead on or astray esp. into something foolish or stupid **c :** to cause to believe something false **:** DECEIVE ⟨the masses . . . browbeaten and ~*ed* by bureaucrats —A. R.Williams⟩ **2** *obs* **:** to call (a person) a fool **syn** see DUPE

¹**be·fore** \bəˈfō(ə)r, bē-, -ˈfȯ(ə)r, -ōə, -ȯ(ə)\ *adv* [ME *before, beforen*, adv. & prep., fr. OE *beforan*, fr. *be-* + *foran* before, fr. *fore* — more at FORE] **1 :** in advance **:** AHEAD ⟨racing on ~ to give warning⟩ ⟨the army encamped with its tanks covering the rear and some infantry units ~⟩ **2 :** in time past ⟨he had known it ~⟩ **:** PREVIOUSLY ⟨two weeks ~⟩ **:** ALREADY ⟨the names ~ mentioned⟩ — often used with *go* ⟨in terms of the experience that has gone ~ —C.E.Kellogg⟩ **3 :** in the future **:** to come ⟨forgetting the things that are behind, and stretching forth myself to those that are ~ —Phil 3:13 (DV)⟩ **4 :** EARLIER, SOONER **:** until then ⟨you'll get it tomorrow, not ~⟩ ⟨he was surprised at the news and said he hadn't known it ~⟩

²**before** \ˈ"\ *prep* [ME *before, beforen*] **1 a :** preceding (a point, turn, or incident in time) **:** earlier than ⟨20 minutes ~ 12⟩ ⟨returning ~ dark⟩ ⟨making up his mind long ~ the meeting⟩ **b :** preceding (something or someone in a chronological series) ⟨he lived in New York as did his father ~ him⟩ **2 a :** in the presence of ⟨speaking ~ the conference⟩ **:** in sight or notice of **b :** face to face with **:** CONFRONTING ⟨powerless ~ such restrictions⟩ **c :** in defiance of **:** in firm opposition to ⟨~ successful crime he stood unmoved . . . the inflexible judge of its manifest wrong —W.L.Sullivan⟩ **3 a :** in advance of (someone or something moving in the same direction) **:** ahead of ⟨destroyers zigzagging ~ a convoy⟩ ⟨the captain going ~ his troops⟩ **b :** driven in front by ⟨refugees ~ barbarian armies⟩ **:** harassed by ⟨fleeing ~ a storm⟩ **c :** in the same direction as the main force of ⟨a ship running ~ a heavy sea⟩ ⟨sailing ~ the wind⟩ **4 a :** in a position facing, opposing, or close to **:** in front of ⟨stand ~ the fire⟩ **b :** just preceding (as in a spatial series) **:** next to ⟨the road to the left ~ the junction⟩ **:** just in front of **5 a :** at the disposal of **:** available to ⟨the six candidates ~ the people⟩ ⟨great sums of money were placed ~ the scientists⟩ **b :** in store for **:** AWAITING ⟨still thirty years of life ~ him —H.O.Taylor⟩ ⟨a whole glorious summer was ~ the children⟩ **6 a :** in the estimation of ⟨make the Europeans lose face ~ the common people —Peggy Durdin⟩ **b :** according to the precepts, doctrines, or views emanating from or associated with ⟨man and wife ~ God⟩ ⟨a crime ~ the law⟩ **7 a :** to be judged or acted on by ⟨the case went ~ the court⟩ ⟨a bill coming up ~ Congress⟩ **b :** under the official or formal consideration of ⟨in order that there may be a debate, a definite proposal . . . must ordinarily be ~ the House —C.J.Friedrich⟩ **8 :** occupying, inviting, or compelling the attention of ⟨the problems ~ the American public⟩ **9 a :** in greater esteem, significance, or value than ⟨thou shalt have none other gods ~ me —Deut 5:7 (AV)⟩ ⟨put profits ~ conscience⟩ **b :** more important than — used with *else* ⟨he is ~ all else a gentleman⟩ **10 :** in advance of **:** superior to ⟨~ all nations in cheap-car production⟩ **11 :** as a result of **:** in consequence of ⟨forests have dwindled ~ ax and saw —*Amer. Guide Series: Wash.*⟩ ⟨these archaic people . . . disappeared suddenly, evidently ~ the pressure of a new people —R.W. Murray⟩ **12 :** up to but not including or taking into account **:** exclusive of ⟨his yearly income ~ taxes⟩

³**before** \ˈ"\ *conj* [ME *before, beforen*, fr. *before, beforen*, prep.] **1 :** earlier than the time when ⟨~ the year was out⟩ — sometimes used archaically with a postpositive *that* ⟨it is not the custom of the Romans to give up any man, ~ that the accused have the accusers face to face —Acts 25:16 (ASV)⟩ **2 :** sooner than ⟨he will starve ~ he will steal⟩

beforehand \ˈ=ˈ=,=\ *adv* (*or adj*) [ME *before hand, beforen hand*, fr. *before, beforen* before + *hand*] **1 a :** in anticipation **:** so as to be prepared ⟨all equipment must be in the trucks ~⟩ ⟨taken . . . pains to inform himself ~ concerning the subject matter —Vera M. Dean⟩ **b :** in advance ⟨demanding his fee ~⟩ ⟨payment ~⟩ **2 :** BEFORE, PREVIOUSLY ⟨the city had ~ borne a different name⟩; *specif* **:** before the appointed time ⟨he arrived at the meeting place ~⟩ **3 a :** in a sound financial state **:** possessing enough or somewhat more than enough ⟨he was ever a little ~ and never lived precariously⟩ **b** *of money* **:** in reserve or excess ⟨having nothing ~⟩ **4 :** in a position to or being able to forestall or anticipate something — used with *with* ⟨a general ever ~ with his enemy⟩

be·fore·ness \ˈ=ˈnəs\ *n* -ES **:** the condition of having existed previously **:** PREEXISTENCE **:** the quality or state of having been before

beforetime \ˈ=ˈ=,=\ *also* **be·fore·times** \-,tīmz\ *adv* [ME *beforetime*, fr. *before, beforen* + *time*] **:** FORMERLY ⟨neither shall the children of wickedness afflict them any more as ~ —2 Sam 7:10 (AV)⟩

be·fortune \bə, bē +\ *vb* -ED/-ING/-S [*be-* + *fortune*] *archaic* **:** BEFALL ⟨good things *befortuned* him⟩

be·foul \bə, bē +\ *vt* -ED/-ING/-S [ME *befoulen*, alter. (influenced by *foul*) of *befilen* to befoul, fr. OE *befȳlan*, fr. *be-* + *fȳlan* to foul — more at FILE] **1 :** to make foul with or as if with dirt or filth ⟨a building ~*ed* with soot⟩ ⟨mudslinging ~*ed* his speeches⟩ **2 a :** SLANDER, CALUMNIATE ⟨~*ing* his reputation⟩ **b :** DISGRACE, BLACKEN, DENIGRATE ⟨scandals that ~*ed* the administration⟩

be·friend \bə, bē+\ *vt* -ED/-ING/-S [*be-* + *friend*, n.] **:** to act as a friend to **:** show kindness, sympathy, and understanding to ⟨~ a helpless person⟩

be·frilled \bə'frild, bē-\ *adj* [*be-* + *frill* + *-ed*] **:** furnished with frills
be·fringe \bə, bē +\ *vt* -ED/-ING/-S [*be-* + *fringe*, n.] **:** to border with a fringe
be·frogged \bə'frägd, bē-, -ägd\ *adj* [*be-* + *frog* + *-ed*] **:** adorned with frogging
be·fuddle \bə, bē +\ *vt* -ED/-ING/-S [*be-* + *fuddle*] **1 :** to dull, muddle, or stupefy ⟨a mind *befuddled* with fatigue⟩ ⟨the old doctor is *befuddled* with drink all the time —Ellen Glasgow⟩ **2 :** to throw into confusion or perplexity **:** PUZZLE ⟨the problem *befuddled* the experts⟩ — **be·fud·dle·ment** \-mənt\ *n* -S
be·furred \bə'fərd, bē-, -fȯd\ *adj* [*be-* + *fur* + *-ed*] **:** adorned with fur

¹beg \'beg, 'bāg — *some who have* ā *in "leg" and "egg" have* e *in "beg"*\ *vb* **begged; begged; begging; begs** [ME *beggen*, perh. alter. of OE *bedecian*; akin to Goth *bidagwa* beggar, OE *biddan* to entreat — more at BID] *vt* **1 :** to ask for as a charity esp. habitually or from house to house ⟨~ his bread from door to door⟩ **2 :** to ask earnestly for **:** request warmly or humbly **:** ENTREAT ⟨~ forgiveness⟩ — often used in expressions of polite deference ⟨I ~ your pardon⟩ ⟨I ~ leave to disagree⟩ **3 a :** EVADE, SIDESTEP ⟨Maynard ~*s* the difficulties set . . . by designating its principles as "simply Christian" —C.T.Harrison⟩ **b :** to assume the fact of established solution, settlement, or proof of (a question or issue) ⟨grave danger that these questions may be *begged* —Walter Moberly⟩ — compare PETITIO PRINCIPII **4 :** to obtain release of esp. by entreaty — used with *off* ⟨~ a person off from a duty⟩ ~ *vi* **1 :** to ask for alms or charity ⟨*begging* from door to door⟩ **:** live by asking for charity ⟨a license to ~⟩ **2 :** to ask earnestly **:** entreat humbly ⟨~ for mercy⟩ — often used as a term of polite deference ⟨I ~ to state⟩ **3** *of a dog or other pet animal* **:** to make a formalized gesture of request; *esp* **:** to sit erect on the haunches with the forepaws raised **4 :** DECLINE, RENEGE **:** back out — used with *off* ⟨men of stern morality ~ off from all discussions of . . . morality —R.H.Rovere⟩ **5 :** to reject the turned-up trump in the game of all fours thereby giving the dealer certain privileges
syn IMPLORE, ENTREAT, BESEECH, SUPPLICATE, ADJURE, IMPORTUNE: these seven verbs are closely related in all signifying the making of an appeal in some way. BEG is often used in certain forms of politeness ⟨I *beg* leave to return tomorrow⟩ Otherwise it suggests strongly the personal urgency of the appeal, often to the point of a certain self-abasement of the doer ⟨now that you're through, you come *begging* me to marry you —Barnaby Conrad⟩ ⟨turning to Foley he *begged* silently for some help —Morley Callaghan⟩ ⟨we watched the fat, lazy squirrels lollop inquisitively round us *begging* the crumbs —Wilfred Fienburgh⟩ ⟨he, casting himself prostrate on the ground, implored her forgiveness and *begged* to know her will —W.H.Hudson⟩ IMPLORE usu. emphasizes even more strongly than BEG personal urgency and earnestness although usu. implying more dignity in the doer ⟨how she pleaded, and *implored* me to wait —George Meredith⟩ ⟨the last look of my dear mother's eyes, which *implored* me to have mercy —Charles Dickens⟩ ⟨the one thing the doctor *implored* him to avoid was that kind of exertion —J.C.Powys⟩ ENTREAT suggests the earnestness of a persuasive petition, implying generally less personal, emotional involvement than do BEG or IMPLORE ⟨smooth-tongued barkers *entreat* passerby to stop and inspect bargains —*Amer. Guide Series: Tenn.*⟩ ⟨he did not *entreat* or plead; he announced —Margaret Deland⟩ ⟨he earnestly *entreated* her to name the day that was to make him the happiest of men —Jane Austen⟩ BESEECH, not as strong as ENTREAT in the suggestion of personal urgency, sometimes stresses an earnestness arising from anxiety or solicitude ⟨a Cape captain, whose bride *beseeched* him to write while he was away —R.W.Hatch⟩ ⟨the girl *besought* her so earnestly that Lady Drum was driven into warm language to defend herself —William Black⟩ ⟨a beggar *beseeches* him in the name of Allah —Jean & Franc Shor⟩ SUPPLICATE emphasizes the humbleness of the doer, suggesting strongly a respectful or prayerful attitude ⟨invite, entreat, *supplicate* them to accompany you —Earl of Chesterfield⟩ ⟨to visit the governor and *supplicate* for more welfare aid⟩ ADJURE usu. suggests a certain seriousness or solemnity of request, an invocation of duty or responsibility or of something bindingly sacred ⟨the wives and daughters . . . rushed about the camp . . . *adjuring* their countrymen to save them from slavery —J.A.Froude⟩ ⟨the student who seeks a closer acquaintance with the playwrights mentioned . . . is *adjured* to make any contact he can achieve with the living theater —W.Bridges-Adams⟩ ⟨"You must give the people an example of poverty, misery and denial," he sometimes *adjures* his disciples —*Time*⟩ IMPORTUNE implies an insistence, esp. in repetition, of appeal or request, usu. to the point of annoyance or irritation ⟨they are *importuned* to spread the official gospel throughout the community via their patients to the utmost of their ability —J.H.Means⟩ ⟨she knew how to look after him without ever imposing herself on him or *importuning* him —Edmund Wilson⟩
²beg \'beg\ *n* -S [Russ *beg, bek*, of Turkic origin; akin to Jagatai *bäg* beg, Turk *bey*] **:** a central Asian, Turkish, or Mogul Indian chieftain or official — often used as a title; compare BEY
beg *abbr* begin; beginning
be·gad \bə'gad, bē-, -gaa(ə)d\ *interj* [euphemism for *by God*] — a mild oath
be·gam \'bēgəm, 'bā-\ *var of* BEGUM 1
began *past of* BEGIN
be·gar \'bā,gär\ *n* -S [Hindi *begār*, fr. Per] *India* **:** forced labor
be·ga·ri \bā'gä(,)rē\ *n* -S [Hindi *begārī*, fr. Per, fr. *begār*] *India* **:** a forced laborer
begass *or* **begasse** *var of* BAGASSE
begat *archaic past of* BEGET
be·gats \bə'gats, bē-\ *n pl* [*begat* + *-s*; fr. its frequent use in the Bible, esp. Gen 5] **1** *slang* **:** a genealogical list ⟨the Old Testament ~⟩ **2** *slang* **:** OFFSPRING ⟨some ~ . . . died without issue —*Time*⟩
be·gaud \bə, bē+\ *vt* -ED/-ING/-S [*be-* + *gaud*] **:** to make gaudy
be·gem \bə, bē+\ *vt* **begemmed; begemmed; begemming; begems** [*be-* + *gem*, n.] **:** to adorn with or as if with gems ⟨a *begemmed* sword hilt⟩ ⟨morning sun *begemmed* the lake⟩
be·get \bə'get, bē-, *usu* -ed·+V\ *vt* **be·got** \-gät, *usu* -äd·+V\ *or archaic* **be·gat** \-gat, *usu* -ad·+V\ **be·got·ten** \-gät°n\ *or* **begot; begetting; begets** [ME *begeten*, alter. (influenced by *geten* to get) of *beyeten*, fr. OE *begietan* to get, beget, fr. *be-* + *gietan* to get — more at GET] **1** *obs* **:** to acquire esp. through effort **2 a :** to procreate as the father **:** SIRE ⟨and Mehujael *begat* Methusael and Methusael *begat* Lamech —Gen 4:18 (AV)⟩ ⟨no conquering race ever lived . . . among a tributary one without *begetting* children on it —A.T.Quiller-Couch⟩ **b :** to give birth to **:** BREED ⟨excellent cows do not ~ only excellent daughters —V.A.Rice & F.N.Andrews⟩ **3** *obs* **:** to make (a woman) pregnant **4 :** to produce usu. as an effect or as a natural outgrowth ⟨economic dependency ~*s* a moral subserviency —J.M.Morse⟩ ⟨emotionally *begotten* rationalizations —Ernest & Pearl Beaglehole⟩
be·get·tal \-ged·°l, -et°l\ *n* -S **:** the act or fact of being begotten
be·get·ter \-ged·ə(r), -etə(r)\ *n* -S [ME *begetere*, fr. *begeten* + *-ere* -er] **:** one that begets
¹beg·gar \'begə(r), -āg-\ *n* -S [ME *beggare, beggere*, fr. *beggen* to beg + *-are, -ere* -er — more at BEG] **1 a :** one that begs; *esp* **:** one that lives by asking for gifts **b :** one that asks (as for a gift) earnestly or humbly ⟨he must be a good ~ — money raiser the vestries call it —Nelson Rightmyer⟩ **2 :** a poor or impoverished person ⟨this system only created ~*s*, completely dependent on outside help —Darcy Ribeiro⟩ **3 :** FELLOW ⟨the poor little ~*s* in the orphanages⟩ ⟨a good-hearted ~⟩
²beggar \"\ *vt* **beggared; beggared; beggaring** \-g(ə)riŋ\ **beggars 1 :** to reduce to beggary **:** IMPOVERISH ⟨wars that ~ a nation⟩ **:** reduce the value of ⟨~*ing* the very policy he was advocating —*Time*⟩ **2 :** to reduce to inadequacy **:** exceed the resources of ⟨the costumes of the performers almost ~ description —Bess A. Garner⟩
beg·gar·li·ness \-gə(r)lēnəs, -lin-\ *n* -ES **:** the quality or state of being beggarly
¹beg·gar·ly \-gə(r)lē, -li\ *adv* [ME, fr. *beggare* + *-ly*] *archaic* **:** in a mean, servile, or despicable manner ⟨entreated them ~ for alms⟩
²beggarly \"\ *adj* [¹*beggar* + *-ly*] **1 :** befitting or like a beggar **:** marked by low mean unrelieved poverty ⟨~ starved-out paupers —Anthony Trollope⟩ **2 :** meriting or arousing contempt or disdain esp. by being mean, scant, or paltry ⟨the poorest and most ~ things . . . in the whole range of criticism —George Saintsbury⟩ **syn** see CONTEMPTIBLE
beggar-my-neighbor \¦⸗⸗(,)⸗'⸗⸗\ *n* **:** a game of cards in which the object is to gain all the opponent's cards
beggar's-buttons \¦⸗⸗,⸗⸗\ *n pl but sing or pl in constr* **:** BURDOCK; *esp* **:** its flower heads
beggar's dance *or* **begging dance** *n* **1 :** a dance of India and Central Europe performed for the purpose of obtaining gifts **2 :** an American Indian dance consisting largely of a masked procession and performed for the purpose of obtaining gifts
beggar's-lice *or* **beggar-lice** \'⸗⸗,⸗\ *n pl but sing or pl in constr* **1 :** any of several plants esp. of the genera *Lappula, Desmodium,* and *Galium* bearing prickly or adhesive fruits that cling to clothing **2 :** the fruit of beggar's-lice
beggar's needle *n* **:** LADY'S-COMB
beggar-ticks *or* **beggar's-ticks** \'⸗⸗,⸗\ *n pl but sing or pl in constr* **1 :** a plant of the genus *Bidens* **2 :** the fruit of beggar-ticks (sense 1) **3 :** BEGGAR'S-LICE **4 :** a plant of the genus *Agrimonia* **5 :** the fruit of beggar-ticks (sense 4)

beggar-ticks 2

beggarweed \'⸗⸗,⸗\ *n* **1 :** any of various plants that grow in waste ground (as knotweed, spurry, and dodder) **2 :** any of several tick trefoils of the genus *Desmodium; esp* **:** a West Indian forage plant (*D. tortuosum*) cultivated in the southern U.S.
beg·gary \'begərē, 'bāg-, -gəri\ *n* -ES [ME *beggarie*, fr. *beggare* beggar + *-ie* -y] **1 :** the quality or state of being impoverished **:** PENURY ⟨the ~ to which the . . . tribesmen have been reduced —M.J.Herskovits⟩ **2 :** the class or occupation of beggars **3 :** the act of begging esp. as a livelihood **:** MENDICANCY ⟨suffered the bitterest privation, and were even . . . threatened with ~ —H.E. Barnes & H.P.Becker⟩ **4 :** BASENESS, CONTEMPTIBLENESS ⟨the ~ of his lies⟩ **5 :** mean impoverished appearance **:** DISREPUTABLENESS ⟨shabby and unshaven almost to the point of ~ —Edmund Wilson⟩
begged *past of* BEG
beg·giatoa \bə'jad·əwə, ,bejə'tōə\ *n, cap* [NL, fr. F. S. *Beggiato*, 19th cent. Ital. botanist] **:** a genus (the type of the family Beggiatoaceae) of colorless filamentous sulfur bacteria of the order Beggiatoales that in form and motility resemble algae of the family Oscillatoriaceae and that often form thick mats of unsheathed filaments in swamps, sulfur springs, and seawater — **beg·giato·a·ceous** \bə,jad·ə¦wāshəs, ¦bejə,tō¦ā-\ *adj*
beg·giat·o·a·les \bə,jad·ə'wā(,)lēz\ *n pl, cap* [NL, fr. *Beggiatoa* + *-ales*] **:** an order of free-living bacteria having relatively large rigid cells often in filaments, lacking flagella and moving by gliding like some of the blue-green algae, and often containing sulfur granules within or on the surface of the cells — see BEGGIATOA
begging *pres part of* BEG
beg·ging·ly *adv* **:** in a begging manner
beg·hard \'be,gärd, -eg,härd, -egərd\ *n* -S *usu cap* [ML *Beghardus, Begardus*, prob. fr. OF *begard*] **:** a member of one of many semimonastic associations of laymen founded in the 13th century in the Low Countries in imitation of the Beguines and eventually proscribed as heretical by the medieval church and in the 14th century all but extinct
be·gild \bə, bē+\ *vt* [*be-* + *gild*] **:** to gild esp. to excess
be·gin \bə'gin, bē-\ *vb* **be·gan** \-'gan, -aa(ə)n\ *or dial* **be·gun** \-'gən\ **begun; beginning; begins** [ME *beginnen*, fr. OE *beginnan*, fr. *be-* + *-ginnan* to begin; akin to OE *onginnan* to begin, OHG *biginnan*, Goth *duginnan*] *vi* **1 a :** to perform or execute the first part of an action, activity, or procedure **:** START **:** set about or enter on some course or operation ⟨after the introduction, the speaker *began*⟩ ⟨the night shift ~*s* at five o'clock⟩ **b :** COMMENCE **:** show occurrence or performance of first steps or stages ⟨work on the project *began* in May⟩ **2 a :** to come into existence **:** ARISE **:** originate or be called into being ⟨World War I *began* in 1914⟩ ⟨the organization *began* at a discussion meeting⟩ **b :** to have initial or starting point ⟨the alphabet ~*s* with *A*⟩ **3 :** to do or succeed in the least degree **:** make an appreciable approach to doing ⟨can't even ~ to describe the beauty of the scene⟩ ~ *vt* **1 a :** to set about **:** go into activity of ⟨they *began* the attack at dawn⟩ — often used with the infinitive or gerund ⟨*beginning* to study⟩ ⟨he *began* to speak⟩ ⟨the children *began* laughing⟩ ⟨~ doubting his comments⟩ **b :** to perform the first steps or stages of **:** do or perform the first actions or activities of **:** enter on ⟨he *began* his career as a teacher⟩ ⟨he *began* his collection in early summer⟩ **2 a :** to found or call into being **:** bring about a start or establish an origin for ⟨he *began* the movement with a series of magazine articles⟩ ⟨~ a dynasty⟩ **b :** start on a way or course **:** INITIATE ⟨where I *began* poor Nell upon the woman's road to hell —John Masefield⟩ **c :** to come first in or come in an initial position in ⟨the letter *A* ~*s* the alphabet⟩
syn START, COMMENCE, INITIATE, INAUGURATE: BEGIN, START, and COMMENCE are often interchangeable in meaning. BEGIN, opposed to *end*, is general and lacks especial connotation ⟨*begin* a job⟩ ⟨*begin* a journey⟩ ⟨*begin* the day with hope⟩ START, opposed to *stop*, may apply esp. to the first actions, steps, or stages of a course, career, or progression ⟨the conversation stopped, and it refused to *start* again —Arnold Bennett⟩ ⟨the movement recently *started* by such psychoanalysts —H.J.Muller⟩ COMMENCE is sometimes more formal than BEGIN or START, more bookish in suggestion ⟨they sat down and tried to *commence* a conversation —George Meredith⟩ ⟨things never began with Mr. Borthrop Trumbull; they always *commenced* —George Eliot⟩ INITIATE always suggests taking or facilitating first steps or preliminary measures culminating in an actual start, without suggesting any necessary continuation ⟨the art of recording thought, invented ages ago, *initiated* history —A.C.Morrison⟩ ⟨a third section called Ardencroft was *initiated* by Frank Stephens, but was not developed —*Amer. Guide Series: Del.*⟩ INAUGURATE indicates a starting or a bringing into effect or operation with some formality, seriousness, notion of significance, sweep, utility, or service ⟨since it was *inaugurated* in 1894 the May Festival has presented numerous important American and world premieres —*Amer. Guide Series: Mich.*⟩ ⟨the New Light theology *inaugurated* by Jonathan Edwards —T.D.Bacon⟩ ⟨a passionately modern mind who feels that science has *inaugurated* a new era —J.C.Powys⟩ ⟨not until 1786 was a ferry *inaugurated* between the two towns —Green Peyton⟩
be·gin·ner \-'ginə(r)\ *n* -S [ME, fr. *beginnen* + *-er*] **:** one that begins anything; *specif* **:** a young or inexperienced person **:** TYRO
beginner's luck *n* **:** the good fortune felt to attend one's first ventures (as at gambling, hunting, or fishing)
¹be·gin·ning \bə'giniŋ, bē-, -nēŋ\ *n* -S [ME, fr. gerund of *beginnen*] **1 :** the point at which something begins to exist ⟨the ~ of the world⟩ ⟨the ~ of the war fell in May⟩ **2 :** the first part **:** initial section or division ⟨the first few chapters at the ~ of a novel⟩; *specif* **:** the first third ⟨the ~ of the play was good but the middle and end were dull⟩ **3 :** anything that has given rise to something **:** ORIGIN, SOURCE ⟨nobody knows what the ~ of the feud was⟩ **4 a :** rudimentary stage **:** early period ⟨this small ~ political corruption was to grow to tremendous proportions —Carol L. Thompson⟩ — often used in pl. ⟨Canada has had a dramatic and colorful history, particularly in her ~*s* —J.D.Adams⟩ **b :** anything that is undeveloped, only partially realized, or far from completion ⟨the Alaska highway system . . . is still incomplete and still only a ~ —Harold Griffin⟩ **5 :** the act or action of calling or being called into existence ⟨ascribing the blame for the ~ of a war⟩ **6 :** the first principle or basic assumption ⟨the ~ of justice is the capacity to generalize and make objective one's private sense of wrong —Earl Warren⟩
²beginning \"\ *adj* [fr. pres. part. of *begin*] **1 :** just called into existence **:** INCIPIENT ⟨elected president of the ~ organization⟩ **2 a :** of the introductory part or first third ⟨the ~ chapters of a book⟩ **b :** very first **:** INITIAL ⟨the ~ canto of an epic —*New Yorker*⟩ **:** ORIGINAL ⟨he quickly modified his ~ plan⟩ **3 a :** treating the rudiments or basic elements of ⟨a course in ~ chemistry⟩ **b :** just becoming familiar with the rudiments, skills, practice, or routine ⟨a ~ machinist⟩ ⟨the ~ fisherman⟩ ⟨a ~ dentist⟩
beginning rhyme *n* **1 :** rhyme at the beginning of successive lines of verse **2 :** ALLITERATION
be·gird \bə, bē+\ *vt* **begirt** *also* **begirded; begirt; begirding; begirds** [ME *begyrden*, fr. OE *begyrdan*, fr. *be-* + *gyrdan* to gird — more at GIRD] **1 :** to bind about or around ⟨a warrior *begirt* with sword and dagger⟩ **2 :** to surround, envelop, or encompass ⟨*begirt* by wilderness enemies —V.L.Parrington⟩ ⟨we are *begirt* with spiritual laws —R.W.Emerson⟩
be·girdle \bə, bē+\ *vt* -ED/-ING/-S [*be-* + *girdle*] **:** to surround as if with a girdle
be·glamour \bə, bē+\ *vt* -ED/-ING/-S [*be-* + *glamour*, n.] **1 :** to impart glamour to **:** GLAMORIZE **2 :** to impress or deceive with glamour
beg·ler·beg \'beglə(r),beg\ *also* **beg·ler·bey** \-,bā\ *or* **bey·ler·bey** \'bālə(r),bā\ *n* -S [Turk *beylerbeyi*, fr. *beyler-* (pl. of *bey* prince) + *bey* + *-i* (possessive suffix)] **:** a governor of a province of the Ottoman Empire next in dignity to the grand vizier
be·gloom \bə, bē+\ *vt* [*be-* + *gloom*, n. or v.] **:** to make gloomy
be·gnaw \bə, bē+\ *vt, past part* **begnawn** [*be-* + *gnaw*] *obs* **:** to gnaw at ⟨the worm of conscience still ~ thy soul! —Shak.⟩
be·gob \bə'gäb, bē-\ *or* **be·gobs** \-bz\ *interj* [euphemism for *by God*] *Irish* — a mild oath
be·god \bə, bē+\ *interj* [euphemism for *by God*] — a mild oath
be·goggled \bə, bē+\ *adj* [*be-* + *goggle* + *-ed*] **:** wearing goggles
be·gone \bē, bə+\ *vi* [ME, fr. *be* (imper. of *been* to be) + *gone* — more at BE] **:** to go away **:** DEPART — used in the infinitive ⟨she was ordered to ~⟩ and esp. in the imperative ⟨gather up your gold now, and ~ from my sight —J.M.Synge⟩
be·go·nia \bə'gōnyə, -nēə, bē-\ *n* [NL, fr. Michel *Bégon* †1710 Fr. governor of Santo Domingo + NL *-ia*] **1** *cap* **:** a large genus of succulent herbs or rarely subshrubs (family Begoniaceae) native to the tropics but widely cultivated with asymmetrical leaves and monoecious flowers succeeded by 3⸗ winged capsular fruit **2** -S **:** a plant of the genus *Begonia* — see FIBROUS-ROOTED BEGONIA, REX BEGONIA, TUBEROUS BEGONIA **3** -S **:** a deep pink that is bluer, lighter, and stronger than average coral (sense 3b), bluer than fiesta, and bluer and stronger than sweet william — called also *gaiety*
be·go·ni·a·ce·ae \⸗,⸗nē'āsē,ē\ *n pl, cap* [NL, fr. *Begonia*, type genus + *-aceae*] **:** a family of monoecious plants (order Parietales) distinguished by the asymmetrical leaves and consisting of five tropical genera of which *Begonia* is much the largest — **be·go·ni·a·ceous** \⸗¦⸗⸗¦āshəs\ *adj*
begonia rose *n* **:** a moderate red that is bluer and lighter than cerise, claret (sense 3a), or average strawberry (sense 2a)
be·good *or* **be·goud** \bə'güd\ [ME (northern dial.) *begouthe*, alter. (influenced by *couthe* could, past of *can*) of *began*, past of *beginnen*] *chiefly Scot past of* BEGIN
be·gor·ra \bə'gȯrə, -är-, bē-\ *or* **be·gor·ry** \-rē, -ri\ *also* **be·gor** \-ō(ə)r, -är\ *interj* [euphemism for *by God*] *Irish* — a mild oath
begot *past of* BEGET
begotten *past part of* BEGET
be·gowk \bə, bē+\ *vt* [*be-* + Sc *gowk*, n.] *Scot* **:** to make a fool of
be·grime \bə, bē+\ *vt* -ED/-ING/-S [*be-* + *grime*] **1 :** to make dirty with grime ⟨*begrimed* streets⟩ **2 :** SULLY, TARNISH, CORRUPT ⟨graft had *begrimed* the town's politics⟩
be·grudge \bə'grəj, bē-\ *vt* -ED/-ING/-S [ME *begrucchen*, fr. *be-* + *grucchen, gruggen* to murmur, grudge — more at GRUDGE] **1 a :** to give reluctantly ⟨the government did not ~ the millions spent on flood control⟩ **b :** to yield or concede with displeasure ⟨they *begrudged* every minute taken from their work⟩ **2 a :** to look upon or acknowledge with reluctance, hesitation, or disapproval ⟨we shall not ~ this exquisite soul the pleasure of his sensations —C.I.Glicksberg⟩ **b :** to be annoyed by or take little pleasure in ⟨he *begrudged* reading newspapers because it meant taking "time from Tacitus and Horace" —E.W. Parks⟩ **3 :** to envy the pleasure or enjoyment of ⟨no one . . . has ever *begrudged* his recreations —J.E.Sayers⟩
be·grudg·ing·ly *adv* **:** in a begrudging manner **:** GRUDGINGLY
be·grutch \bə'grəch, -rüch\ [ME *begrucchen*] *now dial var of* BEGRUDGE
be·grut·ten \bə'grət°n\ *adj* [*be-* + Sc *grutten*, alter. of ME *graten, greten*, fr. OE *grēten, grǣten*, past part. of *grǣtan, grētan* to weep — more at GREET] *Scot* **:** TEAR-STAINED
begs *pres 3d sing of* BEG, *pl of* BEG
beg·ti \'begtē, -ek-\ *also* **bek·ti** \-ek-\ *n* -S [Bengali] **:** a large percoid fish (*Lates calcifer*) of river mouths and brackish waters of eastern and southern Asia, New Guinea, and northern Australia that is esteemed as food and in India often reared in ponds — called also *cockup, giant perch*
be·guile \bə'gīl, bē, *esp bef pause or cons* -īəl\ *vb* -ED/-ING/-S [ME *begilen*, fr. *be-* + *gilen* to guile, deceive — more at GUILE] *vt* **1 a :** to lead or draw by deception ⟨*beguiled* into ambush⟩ **b :** to lead away **:** DIVERT ⟨*beguiled* from these prejudices only by the president's prestige⟩ **2 a :** DECEIVE, HOODWINK ⟨*beguiled* by vague promises⟩ **b :** to deprive by guile **:** CHEAT — used with *of* or *out of* ⟨worries ~ him of sleep⟩ **3** *obs* **:** to cause to fail **:** DISAPPOINT, SHATTER **4 :** to cause to dwindle or vanish painlessly or without notice ⟨*beguiling* sorrow with music⟩ ⟨the seven poems were written to ~ the tedium of a sea voyage —V.L.Parrington⟩ **5 :** to gain the notice of by the use of wiles **:** CHARM ⟨her ways *beguiled* him⟩ ~ *vi* **:** to deceive by wiles **:** CHARM ⟨all her intent was to ~⟩ **syn** see DECEIVE
be·guil·er \-īlə(r)\ *n* -S [ME *begiler*, fr. *begilen* + *-er*] **:** one that beguiles
beguiling *adj* **:** provoking pleased interest and diverting from concern or vexation **:** ATTRACTIVE, PLEASING, INTRIGUING — **be·guil·ing·ly** *adv*
bé·guin \bāgaⁿ\ *n* -S [F, lit., hood of a beguine (influenced in meaning by *s'embéguiner* to become infatuated, fr. *béguin* hood), fr. MF, fr. *béguine*] **:** INFATUATION ⟨the girl has a ~ for you —W.S.Maugham⟩
¹be·guine \'bā,gēn, 'be-, ⸗'⸗; bə'g-\ *n* -S *usu cap* [MF, fr. OF] **:** a member of one of a number of semimonastic associations for women not bound by the vows of a religious but interested in devotional life and works of charity
²be·guine \bə'gēn, bā-\ *n* -S [AmerF *béguine*, fr. F *béguin* flirtation] **:** a vigorous popular dance of the islands of Saint Lucia and Martinique somewhat like the rumba
be·gum \'bēgəm, 'bā-\ *n* -S [Hindi *begam*, fr. a Turkic word akin to the fem. of Jagatai *bäg* beg — more at BEG] **1** *India* **:** a Muslim queen, princess, or lady of high rank **2** *Brit* **:** an Anglo-Indian heiress
be·gummed \bə, bē+\ *adj* [*be-* + *gum* + *-ed*] **:** smeared or clogged with or as if with gum
begun *dial past of* BEGIN, *past part of* BEGIN
be·gunk \bə'gəŋk\ *n* -S [*be-* + Sc *gunk*] *chiefly Scot* **:** a piece of deception **:** TRICK
be·half \bə'haf, bē-, -aa(ə)f, -aif, -äf, -äf\ *n, pl* **be·halves** \-vz\ [ME, fr. *be* by (fr. OE *be, bi, bī*) + *half* side — more at BY, HALF] **1** *archaic* **:** RESPECT, QUARTER — used as the object of *in* ⟨more can be said in this ~⟩ **2 :** INTEREST, BENEFIT, SUPPORT — used as the object of *in* or *on* and with a possessive noun or pronoun ⟨a good word in a friend's ~⟩ ⟨the senator who is now stumping the state on his own ~⟩ ⟨intervening in her ~ —Warren Beck⟩ — **in behalf of** *or* **on behalf of** *prep* **:** in the interest of **:** as the representative of **:** for the benefit of ⟨this letter is written *in behalf of* my client⟩
behari *usu cap, var of* BIHARI
be·hatted \bə, bē+\ *adj* [*be-* + *hat* + *-ed*] **:** wearing a hat **:** adorned with a hat
be·have \bə'hāv, bē-\ *vb* -ED/-ING/-S [ME *behaven*, fr. *be-* + *haven* to have — more at HAVE] *vt* **1 a :** to bear or comport (oneself) in a particular way ⟨the plaintiff *behaved* himself with great composure⟩ **b :** to conduct (oneself) in a correct, obedient, or proper manner ⟨he *behaved* himself, got good marks, never made a fuss, was always right —G.W.Brace⟩ **2** *obs* **:** RESTRAIN, REGULATE ~ *vi* **1 a :** to act or react in a particular way ⟨he *behaved* to the emperor as an equal —Edith Sitwell⟩ ⟨under fire the troops *behaved* admirably⟩ **b :** to conform to the accepted patterns of society ⟨his conscience that is trying to make him ~ —Weston La Barre⟩ **:** do the right thing or what one is told ⟨children who won't ~⟩ **2 a :** to perform or function in a particular way ⟨all vehicles *behaved* well on their test runs⟩ **b :** to react under stimulus in a par-

ticular way ⟨the alloy *behaved* unpredictably under intense heat⟩
syn CONDUCT, COMPORT, DEMEAN, DEPORT, ACQUIT, QUIT: BEHAVE indicates performing various actions or saying various things in the manner indicated by modifiers ⟨one must keep one's contracts, and *behave* as persons of honor and breeding should behave —Rose Macaulay⟩ ⟨you will bitterly reproach him in your own heart, and seriously think that he has *behaved* very badly to you —Oscar Wilde⟩ Used without modifiers, it indicates action and conduct adjudged proper and seemly; in this use it is common in relation to children and adolescents ⟨the average parent is likely to say that the child *behaves* if the child conforms to what the parent thinks is right —Morris Fishbein⟩ CONDUCT often applies to actions showing direction or control of one's actions or bearing with command, will, knowledge, and resolution ⟨he *conducted* himself with patience and tact, endeavoring to enforce the laws and to check any revolutionary moves —W.E.Stevens⟩ COMPORT, in this sense always reflexive, is somewhat more formal than BEHAVE and CONDUCT but lacks any other special suggestion ⟨the missionaries . . . *comported* themselves in a way that did not rouse general antagonism or they could have been easily ousted —E.H.Spicer⟩ ⟨a man is judged now by how well he *comports* himself in the face of danger —J.W.Aldridge⟩ ⟨after having seen him thus publicly *comport* himself, but one course was open to me — to cut his acquaintance —W.M.Thackeray⟩ In this sense DEMEAN and DEPORT are close synonyms for COMPORT; the former is becoming rare ⟨it shall be my earnest endeavor to *demean* myself with grateful respect towards her —Jane Austen⟩ The latter may suggest deportment according to a code ⟨Dido and Aeneas, in the "Roman d'Eneas", *deport* themselves in accordance with the strictest canons of courtly love —J.L.Lowes⟩ ACQUIT and QUIT, the latter archaic, are always used reflexively in this sense; they are likely to apply to action deserving praise or meeting expectations ⟨I trust we *acquit* ourselves worthily as custodians of this sacred mystery —Elinor Wylie⟩ ⟨he then *acquitted* himself well as a hard-working and level-headed chairman of the judiciary committee of the House —C.C.Pearson⟩ ⟨the endless heroes of life and death who still bravely meet their separate hours . . . and *quit* themselves like men —*Yale Rev.*⟩ **syn** see in addition ACT

be·hav·ior \bə'hāvyə(r), bē-\ *n* -s *see -or in Explan Notes* [alter. (influenced by *havior*) of earlier *behaviour*, fr. ME, fr. *behaven* to behave + *-our* -or] **1 a :** the manner in which a person behaves in reacting to social stimuli ⟨his flustered ~ before women⟩ or to inner need ⟨his ~ under the impress of loneliness⟩ or to a combination thereof ⟨hunger and poverty left their mark on her adult ~⟩ **b :** an activity of a defined organism; *esp* **:** observable activity when measurable in terms of quantifiable effects on the environment whether arising from internal or external stimulus **c** (1) **:** anything that an organism does that involves action and response to stimulation (2) **:** the response of an individual, group, or species to the whole range of factors constituting its environment **2 a :** the treatment shown by a person toward another or others esp. in its conformity with or divergence from the norms of good manners or social decorum ⟨the gracious ~ of the hostess⟩ ⟨loyal ~ toward his brothers⟩ **b** *obs* **:** good manners **3 :** the peculiar reaction of (a thing) under given circumstances ⟨the ~ of a new car⟩ ⟨the ~ of dyes in certain weathers⟩ ⟨the ~ of steel under stress⟩

be·hav·ior·al \-yərəl\ *adj* **:** of or relating to behavior ⟨~ similarities⟩ ⟨~ disturbances⟩ — **be·hav·ior·al·ly** \-yərəlē, -li\ *adv*

be·hav·ior·al·ist \-yərələst\ *n* -s **:** one who studies, accepts, or observes the point of view of behavioristics

behavioral science *n* **:** a science (as psychology, sociology, or anthropology) dealing with human action and aiming at the establishment of generalizations of man's behavior in society —compare SOCIAL SCIENCE

behavior disorder *n* **:** a mental usu. functional disorder

be·hav·ior·ism \-yə,rizəm\ *n* -s **1 :** the doctrine that the data of psychology consist exclusively of the observable evidences of organismic activity esp. when expressible in operational or physicalistic terms — compare BEHAVIOR 1b, INTROSPECTIONISM, MENTALISM **2 :** the application of principles of behavioral science to industry, personality evaluation, the arts, or literary criticism **3 :** the characteristic behavior of a defined organism or group under defined conditions

¹be·hav·ior·ist \-yərəst\ *n* -s **:** one who accepts or assumes the point of view of behaviorism

²behaviorist \"\ *or* **be·hav·ior·is·tic** \=ˌ==ˈristik, -ēk\ *adj* **:** of or belonging to behaviorism ⟨~ psychology⟩ — **be·hav·ior·is·ti·cal·ly** \-tək(ə)lē, -ēk-, -li\ *adv*

be·hav·ior·is·tics \=ˌ=='=tiks, -ēks\ *n pl but sing in constr* **:** a physicalistic science of individual and social behavior wherein an organism's responses to its environment are studied

behavior problem *n* **1 :** symptomatic expression of emotional or interpersonal maladjustment esp. in children (as by nail-biting, enuresis, negativism, or by overt hostile or antisocial acts) **2 :** an individual evidencing maladjustment by indulging in behavior problems; *esp* **:** a child indulging in such problems

behavior psychology *n* **:** BEHAVIORISM

be·head \bə'hed, bē-\ *vt* -ED/-ING/-S [ME *beheden, beheveden*, fr. OE *behēafdian*, fr. *be-* + *hēafdian* to behead, fr. *hēafod* head —more at HEAD] **1 :** to sever the head or crown from **:** DECAPITATE ⟨~ a prisoner⟩ ⟨~ a tree⟩ **2 a :** to divert the headwaters of (a stream) into another drainage system by stream piracy — compare BETRUNK **b :** to remove the upper part of the drainage area of (a stream) by wave erosion

be·head·al \-dᵊl\ *n* -s **:** BEHEADING

beheld *past of* BEHOLD

¹be·he·moth \bə'hēməth, bē'hēməth *also* 'bēə,mōth *sometimes* =ˈ=,mōth *or* =ˈ=,məth *or* '==,məth *or* '==,mōth\ *n* -s [ME *bemoth, behemoth*, fr. L *behemoth*, fr. Heb *bĕhēmōth*, pl. (expressing magnitude) of *bĕhēmāh* beast] **1** *often cap* **:** an animal, prob. the hippopotamus, described in Job 40: 15–24 (RSV) **2 :** something of oppressive or monstrous size ⟨a ~ of a book⟩ or power ⟨a ~ of a tractor⟩ or appearance ⟨he stood there, a dirty and unshaven ~⟩

²behemoth \"\ *adj* **:** very large **:** MONSTROUS ⟨~ football linesmen⟩ — **be·he·moth·i·an** \ˌbēəˈmōthēən, -māth-,-mōth-\ *adj*

behen *var of* BEN

be·hen·ate \bə'he,nāt, bə'hē,n-, 'bāə,n-, 'bēə,n-\ *n* -s [ISV *behenic* + *-ate*] **:** a salt or ester of behenic acid

be·hen·ic acid \bə'henik, -ēn-\ *n* [ISV *behen* (var. of ⁷*ben*) + *-ic*; prob. orig. formed as F *béhénique*] **:** a crystalline fatty acid $CH_3(CH_2)_{20}COOH$ occurring in the form of esters esp. in the fats and oils from seeds (as ben oil, peanut oil) and in some waxes — called also *docosanoic acid*

be·hest \bə'hest, bē-\ *n* -s [ME, fr. OE *behǣs*, fr. *behātan* to promise, fr. *be-* + *hātan* to promise, command, call — more at HIGHT] **1** *obs* **:** PROMISE ⟨the land of ~⟩ **2 a :** COMMAND ⟨at divine ~⟩ ⟨signs of imperfect obedience to military ~s —A.M. Young⟩ **b :** a strong often authoritative request **:** DEMAND ⟨at the ~ of Congress an investigation was made⟩ **c :** urgent prompting **:** insistent desire ⟨at the ~ of friends he would sometimes read his own poems aloud⟩

be·hight *vt, past or past part* **behight** *or* **behighted** *also* **be·hote**; *pres 3d sing* **behighteth** [ME *behighten, beheten*, alter. (influenced by *behight, behet*, past of *beheten*) of *beheten*, fr. OE *behātan*] **1** *obs* **:** PROMISE **2** *obs* **:** COMMAND **3** *obs* **:** CALL, NAME

¹be·hind \bə'hīnd, bē-\ *adv (or adj)* [ME *behinde, behinden*, fr. OE *behindan*, fr. *be-* + *hindan* from behind, behind — more at HIND] **1 :** in the place or situation left (as by someone or something gone or departed) ⟨leaving much unfinished work ~⟩ ⟨only a small group stayed ~⟩ ⟨little residue remained ~ after evaporation⟩ **2** *archaic* **:** to come **:** UNREALIZED ⟨his heritage that is yet ~⟩ **3 a :** in arrears ⟨~ with the rent⟩ ⟨~ in his dues⟩ **b :** in a secondary or inferior position ⟨lag ~ in competition⟩ **:** REMISS ⟨~ in his work⟩ — often used with a negative ⟨the opposition was not ~ in the use of bitter words⟩ **c :** SLOW ⟨the clock was ~⟩ ⟨the train was an hour ~⟩ **4 a :** in back ⟨the car ~⟩ **:** to the rear ⟨the men in poor condition fell ~ early in the march⟩ **b :** toward the back **:** BACKWARD ⟨to look ~⟩ **5 :** in the past **:** gone by ⟨the drab days in a furnished room in Rome seem well ~ —*Time*⟩ **6 :** BEYOND **:** on the other or far side of ⟨the stream, slowing through broad meadows, has the Green mountains ~ —H.E.McDaniel⟩

²behind \"\ *prep* [ME *behinde, behinden*, fr. *behinde, behinden*, adv.] **1 a** *of something having a front and back* **:** at the back of ⟨a garden ~ a house⟩ ⟨taking cover ~ barricades⟩ — sometimes used with a reflexive object ⟨he looked ~ him⟩ **b** — used as a function word to indicate anything that lies or intervenes between or as if between one thing (as an observer) and another ⟨hills hidden ~ clouds⟩ ⟨~ his friendly manners was maliciousness⟩ ⟨drop ~ the horizon⟩ **2 a** — used as a function word to indicate someone who has departed or is at a distance ⟨the staff remained ~ the troops⟩; often used with a reflexive object ⟨they left wives and children ~ them⟩ ⟨left ~ him a great reputation⟩ **b :** as past experience for ⟨believe that . . . we have ~ us, at least in most parts of the country, the crudest of the pioneering period —M.Eucharista⟩ ⟨with several generations of devoted service to the church ~ him —M.H.Thomas⟩ **c :** not in prospect for **:** gone by for ⟨his best jobs are all ~ him⟩ **3 a** (1) **:** FOLLOWING ⟨there was rain ~ the wind —H.D.Skidmore⟩ ⟨~ the band marched the infantry⟩ (2) **:** in pursuit of ⟨a fox with a pack of hounds ~ him⟩ **b** (1) **:** BELOW ⟨way ~ his last year's average⟩ **:** inferior to ⟨sales were only a few percentage points ~ those for the previous year⟩ **:** retarded in relation to ⟨~ the times⟩ ⟨with theory running ~ practice, we will not be surprised to meet some inconsistencies —Hunter Mead⟩ (2) **:** not up to but competing with ⟨the firm was close ~ the leader in the field⟩ (3) *of a pitcher in baseball* **:** in the situation of having thrown more balls than strikes to ⟨the pitcher was ~ the batter⟩ (4) *of a batter in baseball* **:** in the situation of having a count of more strikes than balls **4 a :** later than understood or stipulated ⟨a train ~ schedule⟩ ⟨~ time in his appointments⟩ **b** — used as a function word to indicate anything that belongs in a period later than or subsequent to another ⟨looking back ~ the vast technological superstructure of western civilization to a quieter day —H.J.J.Winter⟩ **5 a :** in the background of **:** as an ever-present quality or feature of ⟨~ United States-Mexican relations lies the constant question of unsettled damage claims —H.E.Davis⟩ **b :** out of the mind or consideration of ⟨he put unpleasant memories ~ him⟩ **c :** BEYOND ⟨an analysis of the story ~ the news⟩ **:** PAST ⟨whenever possible he has gone ~ the printed book to the manuscript —*Times Lit. Supp.*⟩ **6 a :** on the side of **:** SUPPORTING ⟨in a crisis Latin America would probably be ~ the U.S.⟩ **b :** serving as a foundation for or basis of **:** UPHOLDING, BACKING ⟨~ his arguments are years of experience⟩ ⟨a good picture . . . must have intelligent thinking ~ it —F.L.Mott⟩ **7 a :** serving as motivation for **:** PROMPTING, PROVOKING ⟨economic pressure was ~ the thievery⟩ ⟨the real reasons ~ his actions⟩ **b :** in control of **:** GUIDING, REGULATING ⟨the person ~ the wheel of a car⟩ ⟨~ the throttle of a locomotive⟩

³behind \"\ *n* -s [¹*behind*] **1 :** the back side (as of a garment) **2 :** BUTTOCKS — sometimes considered vulgar

behindhand \=ˈ=,=\ *adv (or adj)* [²*behind* + *hand*] **1 :** in arrears **:** in debt ⟨a company that has been run ~ for years⟩ ⟨to live ~⟩ **2 :** REMISS ⟨were ~ in providing aid⟩ ⟨she was ~ in courtesy to Mrs. Andersen —Willa Cather⟩ **:** after the fact ⟨wise only ~⟩ **3 a :** behind the times **:** BACKWARD ⟨a country so ~ in matters of art⟩ **b :** in an inferior position **:** BEHIND ⟨men . . . are not in the least ~ with women in their love of flattery —Earl of Chesterfield⟩ **c :** behind schedule **:** not caught up ⟨~ with what one wants to do⟩ **syn** see TARDY

behind-the-scenes \=ˌ==ˈ=\ *adj* **:** kept or made in secret or private **:** not revealed ⟨a *behind-the-scenes* conference⟩ ⟨the colonel has actually held *behind-the-scenes* power since 1949 —J.S.Roucek⟩

behite *past of* BEHIGHT

behither *prep* [*be-* + *hither*] *obs* **:** on this side of

behmenism *cap, var of* BOEHMENISM

be·hold \bə'hōld, bē-\ *vb* **be·held** \-held\ **beheld** \"\ *or archaic* **be·hold·en** \-hōldən\ **beholding**; **beholds** [ME *beholden* to hold, keep, behold, fr. OE *behaldan, behealdan*, fr. *be-* + *haldan, healdan* to hold — more at HOLD] *vt* **1** *obs* **:** to look at **:** examine closely **:** WATCH **2 :** to receive the impression of through or as if through visual means **:** see intently and fully **:** APPREHEND, EXPERIENCE ⟨the author ~s life on earth as molded by forces that are blindly mechanical⟩ ⟨a truth . . . so central that it shall commend itself to the eye at whatever angle *beholden* —R.W.Emerson⟩ **~** *vi* **1** *obs* **:** LOOK **2** — used in the imperative as an interjection esp. to call attention ⟨~, he cometh with the clouds, and every eye shall see him —Rev 1: 7 (AV)⟩ **syn** see SEE

beholden \bə'hōldən, bē'-\ *adj* [ME, fr. *beholden*, past part. of *beholden*, fr. OE *behealden*, past part. of *behaldan*] **1 :** being under obligation to return a favor or gift ⟨getting support without becoming ~ for it⟩ **2 :** indebted (as for aid or inspiration) ⟨no poet likes to acknowledge that he is ~ to an older — or a contemporary one —O.S.J.Gogarty⟩ **3 :** DEPENDENT — usu. used with *to* ⟨domesticated animals are plainly dominated by and ~ to adult human beings —Weston La Barre⟩ ⟨politically ~ to the industrial strength of the state —R.E. McGill⟩

be·hold·er \-də(r)\ *n* -s [ME, fr. *beholden* + *-er*] **:** one that beholds

be·hold·ing \-dən\ *adj* [alter. of *beholden*] *now dial Brit* **:** OBLIGED, BEHOLDEN

be·hoof \bə'hüf, bē-\ *n, pl* **be·hooves** \-üvz\ [ME *behof*, fr. OE *behōf*; akin to OFris *behōf* advantage, MHG *behuof* something useful, business, purpose, ON *hōf* correct measure, OE *hebban* to raise — more at HEAVE] **:** ADVANTAGE, PROFIT — used in prepositional phrases ⟨spending the money directly for his own ~ —George Eliot⟩ ⟨diversions of public money to their own use and ~ —A.J.Nock⟩

be·hoove \bə'hüv, bē-\ *or* **be·hove** \-hōv\ *vb* -ED/-ING/-S [ME *behoven*, fr. OE *behōfian*, fr. *behōf*] *vt* **1** *obs* **:** to have need of **:** REQUIRE **2 a :** to be morally or ethically necessary for — usu. used impersonally ⟨it ~s the archaeologist as a scientist to work objectively —G.W.Brainerd⟩ **b :** to be fitting or proper for ⟨he played the piano well, as *behooved* the son of a musical father⟩ — usu. used impersonally ⟨it *behooved* Punch to fold up his clothes neatly on going to bed —Rudyard Kipling⟩ **3 :** to be worthwhile, advantageous, or profitable for — chiefly used impersonally ⟨it would ~ us to examine our motives⟩ **~** *vi* **1 :** to be necessary, fit, or proper — used esp. with *it* as the subject ⟨it *behoved* to pass these points swiftly and unobtrusively —John Buchan⟩ **2** *now Scot* **:** to be in duty bound ⟨he ~s to rejoice at it —E.B.Ramsay⟩

be·hoove·ful *or* **be·hove·ful** \-vfəl\ *adj* [ME *behoful, behoveful*, fr. *behof* + *-ful*] *archaic* **:** ADVANTAGEOUS, PROFITABLE, NEEDFUL

be·hoov·ing·ly *adv* **:** in a behooving manner

behote *past of* BEHIGHT

be·howl \bə, bē+\ *vt* -ED/-ING/-S [*be-* + *howl*] **:** to howl at (as in lamentation)

be·hung \bə, bē+\ *adj* [fr. past part. of obs. *behang* to hang around, fr. ME *behangen*, fr. OE *behōn*, fr. *be-* + *hōn* to hang — more at HANG] **:** HUNG, DRAPED — used with *with* ⟨a hall ~ with decorations⟩

bei·del·lite \bī'de,līt\ *n* -s [*Beidell*, locality in Colo. + E *-ite*] **:** a mineral ideally $Ca_{0\text{-}16}Al_3Si_{3\text{-}17}O_{10}(OH)_2$ that is a common constituent of certain clays and consists of basic aluminosilicate with exchangeable calcium, sodium, or other cation

¹beige \'bāzh\ *n* -s [F, perh. fr. It *bambagia* cotton, fr. ML *bambac-, bambax*, fr. MGk *bambak-, bambax*, prob. fr. a Turkish word represented now by Turk *pamuk* cotton, prob. of Per origin; akin to Per *pamba* cotton] **1 :** cloth (as dress goods) made of natural undyed wool **2 a :** a variable color averaging light grayish yellowish brown **b :** a pale to grayish yellow

²beige \"\ *adj* [F, fr. *beige*, n.] **1 :** of the color beige **2 :** having the natural color — used of fabrics made of undyed or unbleached wool

beige brown *n* **:** a grayish yellowish brown to light olive brown — called also *mist brown*

beige gray *n* **:** MOUSE 4a

bei·gnet \(')bān'yā\ *n, pl* **beignets** \-ā(z)\ [F, fr. MF *bignet, buignet*, fr. *buigne* bump, bruise] **:** FRITTER

bein \'bēn\ *var of* BIEN

¹be·ing \'bēiŋ, 'bē-ēŋ, *rap.* 'bēŋ\ *n* -s [ME, fr. gerund of *been, beon* to be — more at BE] **1 a :** the quality or state of existing **:** material or immaterial existence ⟨artistic form comes into ~ only when two elements are successfully fused —Carlos Lynes⟩ **b** (1) **:** something that is more abstract and has less intension than existence, nonexistence, or any other predicate ⟨pure ~ is the empty absolute —W.T.Harris⟩ — used esp. by Hegelians (2) **:** something that is logically conceivable and hence capable of existence **:** something that has or may have reality (3) **:** something that exists as an actuality or entity in time or space or in idea or matter (4) **:** the totality comprising the possible and the actual **:** something that is common to the objects within a class and to the objects not included in the same class **c :** conscious or mortal existence **:** LIFE ⟨the mother who gave him his ~⟩ **2 :** the complex of physical and spiritual qualities that constitute an individual ⟨it thus enlarges our ~ and gives us strength —M.R.Cohen⟩ **:** PERSONALITY ⟨one of history's most enigmatic ~s⟩ **3 a** *now dial Eng* (1) **:** LIVELIHOOD, LIVING (2) **:** dwelling place **:** HOME **b** *archaic* **:** station in life **:** STANDING **4 :** ESSENCE ⟨an analysis that probes the very ~ of religion⟩ **5 a :** HUMAN, PERSON ⟨always a well-dressed ~⟩ **b :** INDIVIDUAL ⟨a human ~⟩ ⟨the incredible ~s you see in the circus⟩

²being \"\ *pres part of* BE

³being \"\ *adj* [ME, fr. pres. part. of *been, beon* to be] **:** PRESENT — used postpositively with *time* ⟨enough for the time ~⟩

⁴being \" *or more often* 'bēən *or* 'bēn; *"being as" is often* 'bēənz *or* 'bēnz\ *conj, now dial* **:** SINCE, BECAUSE ⟨~ I'm late already⟩ — often used with *as* or *that* ⟨~ that he's your cousin⟩ ⟨~ as it's you⟩

be·ing·less *pronunc at* ¹BEING + ləs\ *adj* **:** having no being **:** not existing ⟨to be meaningless is to be ~ —J.H.Muirhead⟩

be·ing·ness *n* **:** the quality of having existence

bei·ra *also* **bai·ra** \'bīrə\ *n* -s [native name in Africa] **:** a small antelope (*Dorcatragus megalotis*) of Somaliland that is purplish black and brightly marked with yellowish fawn

bei·rut \(')bā'rüt, *usu* -üd.+V\ *adj, usu cap* [fr. *Beirut*, Lebanon] **:** of or from Beirut, the capital of Lebanon **:** of the kind or style prevalent in Beirut

bei·sa \'bāzə, -,zä\ *n* -s [Amharic *be'zā*] **:** an antelope (*Oryx beisa*) found in Somaliland and northeastern Africa

be·ja \'bājə\ *n, pl* **beja** *or* **bejas** *usu cap* **1 a :** a nomadic pastoral people living between the Nile and the Red sea — compare BENI AMER, BISHARIN, HADENDOA **b :** a member of such people **2 :** the Cushitic language of the Beja people

be·jab·bers \bə'jabə(r)z\ *also* **be·ja·bers** \-jā-\ *interj* [euphemism for *by Jesus*] — a mild oath; used in noun function virtually without meaning ⟨beat the ~ out of him⟩

bejade *vt* -ED/-ING/-S [*be-* + *jade*] *obs* **:** to tire out **:** JADE

be·jan \'bājən\ *or* **be·jant** \'bējənt\ *also* **ba·jan** \'bājən\ *n* -s [F *béjaune*, fr. MF *becjaune* beak of young birds, fr. *bec* beak + *jaune* yellow — more at BEAK, JAUNDICE] **:** a freshman at certain Scottish universities

bej·el \'bejəl\ *n* -s [Ar *bajlah*] **:** a disease that is chiefly endemic in children in northern Africa and Asia Minor, is marked by bone and skin lesions, and is caused by a spirochete of the genus *Treponema*

be·jesuit \bə, bē+\ *vt* -ED/-ING/-S [*be-* + *jesuit*] **:** to make Jesuitic

be·je·sus \bə'jēzəs, bē- *also* -zəz; *esp by speakers subject to Irish influence* -jā-\ *interj* [alter. of *by Jesus*] — a mild oath; used in noun function virtually without meaning ⟨kick the ~ out of him⟩

be·jewel \bə, bē+\ *vt* [*be-* + *jewel*] **:** to ornament with or as if with jewels

be·ju·co \bə'hü(,)kō\ *n* -s [Sp, fr. Taino] **1 :** a climbing woody vine of the tropics with the habit of a liana **2** *Philippines* **:** RATTAN

be·juggle \bə, bē+\ *vt* [*be-* + *juggle*] **:** to deceive as if by sleight of hand **:** DELUDE, CHEAT

be·kah *or* **be·ka** \'bā(,)kä, -,kə\ *n* -s [Heb *beqaʽ*] **:** an ancient Hebrew unit of weight equal to half a shekel

be·kiss \bə, bē+\ *vt* [*be-* + *kiss*] **:** to kiss intensely or excessively

be·knave \"+\ *vt* -ED/-ING/-S [*be-* + *knave*, n.] **:** to call knave **:** treat as a knave

bek·ra \'bekrə\ *n* -s [prob. native name in India] **:** FOUR-HORNED ANTELOPE

bekti *var of* BEGTI

¹bel \'bel\ *also* **bael** \", 'bāl, 'bīl\ *n* -s [Hindi *bel* fruit of the bel, fr. Skt *bailva*, fr. *bilva* bel tree, of Dravidian origin; akin to Tamil *vilā, vilavu* bel tree] **1 :** a thorny tree (*Aegle marmelos*) of India **2 :** the aromatic edible fruit of the bel tree — called also *Bengal quince, golden apple*

²bel \'bel\ *n* -s [after Alexander Graham *Bell* †1922 Scottish-Am. inventor of the telephone] **:** ten decibels — abbr. *b*

bel *abbr* below

be·labor \bə, bē+\ *vt, see -or in Explan Notes* [*be-* + *labor*] **1 a** *obs* **:** to work diligently on or at **b :** to work on or at to absurd lengths ⟨~ an argument⟩ ⟨~ the obvious⟩ **2 a :** to beat soundly **b :** ASSAIL, ATTACK ⟨she ~s the foibles of grandparents, great-aunts, uncles, and cousins —Virginia Peterson⟩ **syn** see BEAT

be·lah \'bēlə\ *also* **be·lar** \-lə(r)\ *n* -s [native name in Australia] **1 :** a beefwood (*Casuarina glauca*) of Australia **2 :** a tall forest tree (*Acacia excelsa*) of Queensland with oblong phyllodia and globular heads of flowers

belamour *n* -s [MF *bel amour* fair love, fr. *bel* fair, beautiful + *amour* love — more at BEAUTY, AMOUR] *obs* **:** one who is loved

belanda *cap, var of* BLANDA

be·late \bə, bē+\ *vt* -ED/-ING/-S [*be-* + *late*, adj.] *archaic* **:** to retard or make late **:** DELAY

be·lat·ed \bə'lād.əd, bē-, -ātəd\ *adj* **1** *archaic* **:** overtaken by night **:** BENIGHTED **2 a :** delayed beyond the usual time ⟨one of the men was ~ and did not join us at all —B.A.Botkin & A.F.Harlow⟩ **b :** staying, existing, or appearing past the normal time or season ⟨nothing but an occasional rabbit and a ~ heron —John Buchan⟩ **c :** OUT-OF-DATE, PASSÉ ⟨his policies are now quite ~⟩ — **be·lat·ed·ly** *adv* — **be·lat·ed·ness** *n* -ES

be·laud \bə, bē+\ *vt* [*be-* + *laud*] **:** to praise esp. unduly or excessively

¹be·lay \bə'lā, bē-\ *vb* -ED/-ING/-S [ME *beleggen*, fr. OE *belecgan*, fr. *be-* + *lecgan* to lay — more at LAY] *vt* **1** *obs* **:** ORNAMENT, ADORN **2** *obs* **a :** BESIEGE **b :** WAYLAY **c :** to occupy (a place) for the purpose of intercepting or guarding **3 a :** to secure (as a rope or cable) by one or more figure-eight turns around a cleat, pin, or bitt **b :** to make fast **:** fasten down ⟨~*ing* ammunition on deck⟩ **4** *naut* **:** STOP **:** hold back on ⟨~ that last order⟩ **:** CANCEL, DISREGARD **5 a :** to secure (a person) at the end of a rope ⟨our guides ~*ed* us and accepted belays from us —*Appalachia*⟩ ⟨~*ing* each other over the difficult places —*Nat'l Geographic*⟩ **b :** to secure (a rope) to a person or to a firm object **~** *vi* **1** *chiefly naut* **:** to make be fast ⟨knowing where each rope ~s on deck⟩ **2** *naut* **:** STOP, QUIT — used in the imperative ⟨~ there⟩ **3 :** to make fast by belaying ⟨he kept going when he ought to have ~*ed*⟩

²belay \"\ *n* -s **1 :** the obtaining of a hold (as for a rope) during mountain climbing ⟨~s are more difficult to secure on ice and snow than on rock —K.A.Henderson⟩ **2 :** a method of obtaining a hold or anchor (as for a rope) during mountain climbing **3 :** something to which a mountain climber's rope is anchored (as a projection of rock or an embedded pick)

belaying pin *n* **1 :** a pin around which ropes on shipboard are belayed to make them fast **2 a :** a rock projection used by mountain climbers to belay a rope

belaying pin 1

bel can·to \(')bel 'kän,tō, -ån-\ *n* [It, lit., beautiful singing] **:** operatic singing originating in 17th century and 18th century Italy and stressing ease, purity, and evenness of tone production and an agile and precise vocal technique

¹belch \'belch\ *vb* -ED/-ING/-S [ME *belchen*, fr. OE *bealcian*] *vi* **1 :** to expel gas suddenly from the stomach through the mouth **2 :** to erupt, explode, or detonate violently ⟨artillery growled and ~*ed* on the horizon —Earle Birney⟩ **3 :** to issue forth spasmodically **:** GUSH ⟨the wind ~*ing* down the narrow alleys —G.G.Carter⟩ ⟨obscenities ~*ed* out of him —Albert Morgan⟩ **~** *vt* **1 a :** to throw out or cast forth violently **:** EJECT ⟨smokestacks of rumbling smelters ~ forth their fumes —Tom Marvel⟩ **b :** to vent forcibly **:** EMIT, EJACULATE ⟨~*ing* blasphemies⟩ **2 a :** to expel (gas) from the stomach suddenly **:** ERUCT **b :** to burp (a baby)

²belch \"\ *n* -ES **1 :** an act or instance of belching **:** ERUCTATION

2 : a sudden violent gush ⟨a ~ of flame⟩ ⟨a ~ of angry words⟩ **3 :** beer of poor quality

¹**bel·cher** \ˈbelchə(r)\ *n* -s [after James *Belcher* †1811 Eng. pugilist] **1 :** a blue neckerchief having large white spots with dark blue spots at their centers **2 :** a multicolored handkerchief worn about the neck

²**belcher** \ˈ"\ *adj, often cap* [fr. the name *Belcher*] **:** BROAD — used of jewelry (as of rings and the links of chains)

beld \ˈbeld\ *Scot var of* ¹BALD

bel·dam \ˈbeldəm, -ˌdam, -ˌdaa(ə)m\ *or* **bel·dame** \-ˌdəm, -ˌdām\ *n* -s [ME *beldam*, fr. MF *bel* fair, beautiful + ME *dam*, *dame* lady, mother — more at BEAUTY, DAME] **1** *obs* **:** GRANDMOTHER **2 :** a woman of advanced age ⟨old Lady Shropshire and some other old ~ —Edith Sitwell⟩ **3 a :** an old and loathsome woman **:** HAG **b :** a raging woman **:** VIRAGO ⟨performed in an opera house with a posse of fat ~s throwing themselves about the stage —H.L.Mencken⟩

be·lea·guer \bəˈlēgə(r), bē-\ *vt* **beleaguered; beleaguered; beleaguering** \-g(ə)riŋ\ **beleaguers** [D *belegeren*, fr. *be-* + *leger* camp, fr. MD *lēgher*; akin to OHG *legar* couch, lair — more at LAIR] **1 :** to surround with an army so as to prevent escape **:** BESIEGE, BESET ⟨~ a town⟩ **2 :** to hem in **:** bottle up **3 :** to subject to oppressive or grievous forces **:** HARASS ⟨pests that ~ Alberta wheat farmers —*Lamp*⟩ ⟨~*ed* parents⟩

be·lecture \bə, bē+\ *vt* [*be-* + *lecture*] **:** to subject to much lecturing

belee *vt, past part* **beleed** [*be-* + *lee*, n.] *obs* **:** to cut off from or as if from favorable wind ⟨I . . . must be *beleed* and calmed —Shak.⟩

be·lém *or* **be·lem** \bəˈlem\ *adj, usu cap* [fr. *Belém* or *Belem*, Brazil] **:** of or from the city of Belém, Brazil **:** of the kind or style prevalent in Belém

bel·em·nite \ˈbeləmˌnīt, bəˈlem-\ *n* -s [F *bélemnite*, fr. Gk *belemnon* dart + F *-ite*; akin to Gk *belos* arrow, *ballein* to throw — more at DEVIL] **:** a conical calcareous Mesozoic fossil tapering to a point at the lower extremity, having a conical cavity at the other end that is usu. broken but when perfect contains a small chambered phragmocone prolonged on one side into a delicate concave blade, and being the internal shell of any of numerous extinct cephalopods (family Belemnitidae) related to the surviving spirulas — compare THUNDERSTONE — **bel·em·nit·ic** \ˌbeləmˈnid-ik, -ˌlem-\ *adj*

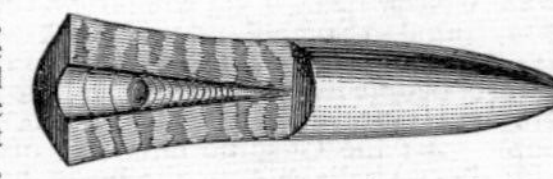
belemnite (partly in section)

bel·em·nit·i·dae \ˌbeləmˈnid-əˌdē\ *n pl, cap* [NL, fr. *Belemnites*, type genus (fr. F *bélemnite* or E *belemnite*) + *-idae*] **:** a family of extinct Mesozoic dibranchiate cephalopods comprising the belemnites

¹**bel·em·noid** \ˈbeləmˌnȯid, bəˈlem-\ *adj* [Gk *belemnon* dart + E *-oid*] **1 :** shaped like a dart **2** [NL *Belemnoidea*] **:** of, relating to, or like the Belemnoidea

²**belemnoid** *n* -s **:** a belemnite or a closely related cephalopod

bel·em·noi·dea \ˌbeləmˈnȯidēə\ *n pl, cap* [NL, fr. *Belemnites* + *-oidea*] **:** an order or other division of Dibranchiata comprising the belemnites and sometimes the genus *Spirula*

belemnoid process *n* **:** STYLOID PROCESS

beleper *vt* [*be-* + *leper*] *obs* **:** to affect with or as if with leprosy

bel es·prit \ˌbe,leˈsprē, ˌbelə'sˈ-\ *n, pl* **beaux es·prits** \ˌbō,zeˈsprē, ˌbōzə'sˈ-\ [F, lit., fine mind] **:** a person with a fine and gifted mind ⟨as a *bel esprit* she despised pedantry whether in a man or in a bluestocking —Robert Halsband⟩

bel étage \ˌbelāˈtäzh\ *n* [F, lit., beautiful story] **:** the chief story of a house

be·letter \bə, bē+\ *vt* [*be-* + *letter* (of the alphabet)] **:** to decorate the name of (a person) by appending abbreviations of official or academic rank ⟨the most academic and ~*ed* conventionalist —Joseph Macleod⟩

bel·fast \ˈbel,fast, ˈbeu̇,f-, -aa(ə)st,-aist,-ȧst; *in Belfast often, in US also* ='=; *in US also* ˈbelfəst\ *adj, usu cap* [fr. *Belfast*, Ireland] **:** of or from Belfast, the capital of Northern Ireland **:** of the kind or style prevalent in Belfast

bel·fry \ˈbelfrē, -ri\ *n* -ES [ME *belfray* tower, bell tower, alter. (influenced by ME *belle* bell or ML *belfredus* tower) of *berefreid*, *berfrey*, fr. OF *berfrei*, fr. MHG *bervrit*, prob. fr. ML *berfredus*, *belfredus*, *balfredus*, perh. fr. an (assumed) L word derived fr. Gk *pyrgos phorētos* movable war tower] **1 a :** BELL TOWER; *esp* **:** one surmounting or attached to another structure — compare CAMPANILE, CARILLON **b** *obs* **:** the bell ringer's floor or room under the bells in a tower **c** (1) **:** a room in which the bell is hung in a tower (2) **:** a cupola, turret, or framework designed to enclose a bell **d :** the framing by which a ship's bell is suspended **2** *slang* **:** HEAD **:** mental capacities ⟨man's cocksureness that he was master of his own ~ —*Newsweek*⟩ — see ³BAT

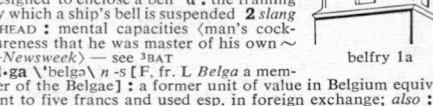

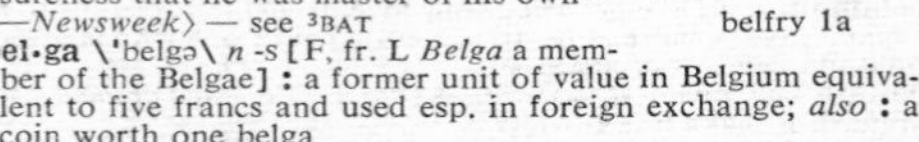
belfry 1a

bel·ga \ˈbelgə\ *n* -s [F, fr. L *Belga* a member of the Belgae] **:** a former unit of value in Belgium equivalent to five francs and used esp. in foreign exchange; *also* **:** a coin worth one belga

bel·gae \ˈbel,jē, -l,gī\ *n pl, usu cap* [L] **:** a people occupying northern France and Belgium in Caesar's time who were prob. of Celtic stock and may have been the ancestors of the modern Belgians

belgard *n* -s [It *bel guardo*] *obs* **:** a loving look

¹**bel·gian** \ˈbeljən *sometimes* -jēən\ *adj, usu cap* [*Belgium*, country of Europe + E *-an*] **1 :** of, relating to, or characteristic of Belgium **2 :** of, relating to, or characteristic of the Belgians

²**belgian** \ˈ"\ *n* **1** -s *cap* **:** a native or inhabitant of Belgium — compare FLEMING, WALLOON **2** *usu cap* **:** a Belgian breed of heavy draft horses that are usu. roan or chestnut in color and have massive compact deep bodies and esp. well-developed hindquarters

belgian block *n, usu cap 1st B* **:** a stone paving block cut as a truncated pyramid with base 5 to 6 inches square, depth 7 to 8 inches, and the face opposite the base not more than 1 inch smaller than the base; *also* **:** any stone paving block

belgian endive *n, usu cap B* **:** ENDIVE 2

belgian fence *n, usu cap B* **:** a trellis with diamond-shaped openings used to support espaliered fruit trees

belgian hare *n, usu cap B* **:** a rabbit of a breed of slender long-legged long-eared domestic rabbits of a dark red or mahogany color

belgian pansy *n, usu cap B* **:** the common pansy with blended, blotched, or streaked petals

belgian sheepdog *or* **belgian shepherd** *n, usu cap B* **:** a dog of a breed of hardy working dogs developed in Belgium esp. for herding sheep, being about 23 inches in height and over 50 pounds in weight, and occurring in two varieties — see GROENENDAEL, MALINOIS

bel·gic \ˈbeljik\ *adj, usu cap* [L *Belgicus*, fr. *Belgae* + *-icus* -ic] **1 :** of, relating to, or characteristic of the Belgae **2 :** BELGIAN

bel·gium \ˈbeljəm *sometimes* -jēəm\ *adj, usu cap* [fr. *Belgium*, country of Europe] **:** of or from Belgium **:** of the kind or style prevalent in Belgium **:** BELGIAN

belgo- *comb form, cap* [*Belgium* + *-o-*] **1 :** Belgium **:** Belgian ⟨*Belgo*phile⟩ **2 :** Belgian and ⟨*Belgo*-Luxembourg⟩ **:** Belgian and ⟨*Belgo*-Dutch⟩

bel·grade \ˈbel,grād *also* -ȧd *or* -ad *or* -ȧd *or* -aa(ə)d *or* ='=\ *adj, usu cap* [fr. *Belgrade*, Yugoslavia] **:** of or from Belgrade, the capital of Yugoslavia **:** of the kind or style prevalent in Belgrade

bel·gra·via \belˈgrāvēə, -vyə\ *n* -s *usu cap* [*Belgrave* Square, London, center of a fashionable residential section in the 19th cent.] **:** a fashionable residential section — **bel·gra·vian** \(ˈ)=ˈ=vēən, -vyən\ *adj, usu cap*

be·lial \ˈbēlēəl, -lyəl\ *n* -s *usu cap* [Heb *bĕlīya'al*, prob. fr. *bĕlī* without + *ya'al* use] **:** worthlessness or wickedness — often personified in the Old Testament ⟨children of *Belial* —Deut 13:13 (DV)⟩

be·libel \bə, bē+\ *vt* [*be-* + *libel*] **:** to attack with libels **:** CALUMNIATE

be·lie *also* **be·ly** \bəˈlī, bē-\ *vt* **belied; belied; belying; belies** [ME *belien*, fr. OE *belēogan*, fr. *be-* + *lēogan* to lie — more at LIE] **1** *archaic* **:** to tell lies about **:** defame by lies ⟨~ a person shamefully⟩ **2** *obs* **:** to deny the authority, presence, or validity of **:** REJECT **3 a :** to give a false impression of ⟨the rasping and combative voice . . . which *belied* him because he was really friendly and good-humored —J.J.Mallon⟩ **b** (1) **:** to stand in contrast to ⟨a hard pair of eyes that *belied* his unmanly, almost effeminate face —Barnaby Conrad⟩ (2) **:** to present an appearance that is not in agreement with ⟨the imperturbable gentlemen . . . nearly all ~ their origins —Bill Wolf⟩ **4 a :** to prove false ⟨the event has *belied* this reasoning —Walter Moberly⟩ **b :** to run counter to **:** CONTRADICT ⟨at first sight Home Term Court . . . appeared to ~ all the rosy things I had heard about it —Katherine T. Kinkead⟩ **5 :** to cover up **:** HIDE, DISGUISE ⟨an air of rural charm . . . ~s the community's industrial activity —*Amer. Guide Series: Pa.*⟩ **syn** see MISREPRESENT

be·lief \bəˈlēf, bē-, *rap.* ˈblēf\ *n* -s [alter. (influenced by such pairs as E *grief*: *grieve*) of ME *beleve*, *beleave*, prob. alter. (influenced by *beleven* to believe) of OE *gelēafa*, fr. *ge-*, collective prefix + *lēafa* belief; akin to *lēfan*, *lȳfan* to allow, believe — more at CO-, BELIEVE] **1 :** a state or habit of mind in which trust, confidence, or reliance is placed in some person or thing **:** FAITH **2 a :** something believed; *specif* **:** a statement or body of statements held by the advocates of any class of views **b :** trust in religion **:** persuasion of the validity of religious ideas ⟨the war of ~ against unbelief —Thomas Carlyle⟩ **:** a statement of religious doctrines believed **:** CREED **3 a :** conviction of the truth of some statement or the reality of some being or phenomenon esp. when based on an examination of the grounds for accepting it as true or real **:** reflective assurance **:** intellectual assent ⟨~ in the validity of logical propositions and scientific statements⟩ **b :** a statement or a state of affairs on the basis of which one is willing to act; *specif* **:** a deliberate habitual readiness to act in a certain manner under appropriate conditions **4 :** immediate assurance or feeling of the reality of something ⟨~ in sensation⟩

syn FAITH, CREDENCE, CREDIT: BELIEF signifies mental acceptance of or assent to something offered as true, with or without certainty ⟨we tend to speak of faith when we are designating the less sure *beliefs*. We believe our eyes, and we believe the proposition that twice two are four —G.W.Allport⟩ ⟨the *belief* that the dead shall rise and live again is purely a matter of faith with which reason has nothing to do directly —Frank Thilly⟩ FAITH applies to full and certain assent, often on grounds other than those afforded by the senses and reason and often with a complete trust or confidence ⟨the *faith* that human science and freedom would advance hand in hand to usher in an era of indefinite human perfectibility —John Dewey⟩ ⟨he's still touchingly full of *faith*, even after all that has happened, in a new heaven and a new earth —Rose Macaulay⟩ CREDENCE suggests the fact of intellectual assent without implying anything about grounds for assent; it may refer to less intimately significant matters than FAITH and BELIEF ⟨we are not now concerned with the finality or extent of truth in this judgment. The point is that it gained a widespread *credence* among the cultured class in Europe —C.D.Lewis⟩ ⟨the colonial office statement is too pitiably thin for *credence* —*New Statesman & Nation*⟩ CREDIT suggests that a notion is held worthy of trusting consideration although it practically never connotes certainty or conviction in acceptance ⟨giving no *credit* to such reports⟩ **syn** see in addition OPINION

be·li·er \bəˈlīə(r), bē-\ *n* -s [*belie* + *-er*] **:** one that belies

be·liev·a·bil·i·ty \bə,lēvəˈbiləd-ē, bē-\ *n* -ES **:** the quality or state of being believable ⟨advertising exists basically on a foundation of ~ —C.B.Larrabee⟩

be·liev·a·ble \=ˈ=vəbəl\ *adj* [ME *belevable*, fr. *beleven* + *-able*] **:** capable of instilling faith, trust, or acceptance ⟨a ~ explanation⟩ ⟨a ~ portrayal of the doctor's character⟩

be·liev·a·bly \-vəblē, -li\ *adv* **:** in a believable manner

be·lieve \bəˈlēv, bē- *rap.* ˈblēv\ *vb* -ED/-ING/-S [ME *bileven*, *beleven*, fr. OE *belēfan*, *belȳfan*, fr. *be-* + *lēfan*, *lȳfan* to allow, believe; akin to OE *gelȳfan* to believe, *alȳfan* to allow, OHG *gilouben* to believe, *irlouben* to allow, ON *leyfa* to allow, Goth *galaubjan* to believe, *uslaubjan* to allow, OE *lēof* dear — more at LOVE] *vi* **1 a :** to have a firm or wholehearted religious conviction or persuasion — usu. used with *in* ⟨~ in the Scriptures⟩ and sometimes with *on* ⟨and many *believed* on him there —Jn 10:42(AV)⟩ **b :** to receive in faith or trust **:** ACCEPT ⟨a story that divided the audience into those who *believed* and those who didn't⟩ — often used with *in* ⟨serfs incapable of *believing* in the sincerity of a master who desired to help them —E.J.Simmons⟩ ⟨because of its sincerity . . . this is the kind of play one would like to ~ in —*Punch*⟩ **2** *obs* **:** to give credence **:** TRUST — used with *to* ⟨~ to your own virtues⟩ **3 :** to have a firm conviction as to the beneficial, genuine, or good quality of something — used with *in* ⟨~ in physical culture⟩ **4 :** THINK, SUPPOSE ⟨inclined to ~ in accordance with her husband⟩ ~ *vt* **1 a :** to take (a statement or person making a statement) as true, valid, or honest **:** give credence to ⟨~ the reports⟩ **b :** to accept or receive as genuine, valid, or good ⟨a bland assumption that all scientists . . . decide and publish what science ~s —R.M.Weaver⟩ **2** *obs* **:** to assume the existence of as true or valid ⟨~ a God⟩ **3 :** to be of the opinion **:** SUPPOSE, SUSPECT. ⟨~ it will rain⟩ ⟨the dye is *believed* to be a complex acid⟩

be·liev·er \-və(r)\ *n* -s [ME *biliver*, fr. *bileven* to believe + *-er*] **1 :** one that believes ⟨a ~ in the power of words⟩ **2 :** one who professes a religious faith; *esp* **:** one who believes in the saving power of the Christian faith

believer's baptism *n* **:** baptism administered (as among Baptists) only to those old enough to make an independent profession of faith

be·like \bə, bē +\ *adv* [ME, fr. *be-* (fr. *bi* by) + *like*, adj.] *archaic* **:** most likely **:** PROBABLY ⟨a tale one told to me — for a jest —Rudyard Kipling⟩

belime *vt* [*be-* + *lime*] *obs* **:** BIRDLIME

bel·i·nu·rus \ˌbelə'n(y)u̇rəs\ *n, cap* [NL, irreg. fr. Gk *belonē* needle + NL *-urus*] **:** a genus (the type of the family Belinuridae) of Devonian and Carboniferous arthropods related to the modern king crab

be·li·sha beacon \bəˈlēshə-\ *n, usu cap 1st B* [after Leslie Hore-*Belisha* †1957 Eng. political leader] **:** an orange traffic signal for the protection of pedestrians at street crossings in English cities

be·lite \ˈbē,līt\ *n* -s [Sw *belit*, fr. *be* (name of the letter *b*) + Sw *-lit* -lite] **:** larnite found as a constituent of portland-cement clinker

be·littered \bə, bē +\ *adj* [*be-* + *littered*] **:** strewn with litter

be·lit·tle \bəˈlid-ᵊl, bē-, -itᵊl\ *vt* **belittled; belittled; belittling** \-itliŋ, -id-ᵊl-, -itᵊl-\ **belittles** [*be-* + *little*] **1 :** to make small or make appear as small ⟨the bulk of the warehouse *belittles* the houses around it⟩ **2 :** to speak of slightingly **:** DISPARAGE, DEPRECIATE ⟨~ a person's efforts⟩ **syn** see DECRY

be·lit·tle·ment \-id-ᵊlmənt. -itᵊl-\ *n* -s **:** the act of belittling

be·lit·tler \-itlə(r), -id-ᵊl-, -itᵊl-\ *n* -s **:** one that belittles

be·live \bəˈlīv, bē-\ *adv* [ME *bilive*, fr. *bi* by + *live*, dat. of *lif* life — more at LIFE] **1** *now Scot* **:** SPEEDILY, QUICKLY **2** *now Scot* **:** in due time **:** by and by

¹**bell** \ˈbel\ *n* -s *often attrib* [ME *belle*, fr. OE; akin to MLG *belle* bell, ON *bjalla* bell, OE *bellan* to roar — more at BELLOW] **1 a :** a cup-shaped, saucer-shaped, or hollow spherical metallic device that vibrates and gives forth a ringing sound when struck by a clapper or hammer or by a loose ball inside — see CHIME, GONG, SLEIGH BELL **b :** DOORBELL ⟨the ~ began to chime more frequently —A.R.Foff⟩ **2 :** the ringing or sound of a bell as a signal ⟨school ~⟩ or summons ⟨dinner ~⟩ or warning ⟨fire ~⟩ **3 a :** a bell (as of a clock) rung to tell the hour **b :** the stroke of such a bell esp. on shipboard — often used in pl. **c :** the time so indicated **d** *naut* **:** a half hour — compare WATCH (see column 3) **e :** a signal to a ship's engine room given orig. by striking a bell **f :** the gong sounded at the beginning and end of a round in boxing **4 :** a mark of superiority or merit **:** AWARD, PRIZE — used in such phrases as *to bear the bell, to carry away the bell* **5 :** something having the form of a bell: as **a :** the cup or corolla of a flower ⟨in a cowslip's ~ I lie —Shak.⟩ **b :** a hollow inverted vessel (as a diving bell or bell jar) **c :** a bell-shaped organ or part (as the umbrella of a jellyfish or the nectocalyx of a siphonophore) **d :** a small pouch of hairy skin that hangs from the neck of a deer **e :** the part of the capital of a column between the abacus and neck molding; *esp* **:** the nearly bell-shaped naked core assumed to exist within the leafage of a Corinthian capital **f :** a flaring mouth (as of a trumpet or other musical wind instrument or of an old firearm) **g :** a bell-shaped cover of metal or glass placed over food in cooking or serving — called also *cloche* **h :** the cone-shaped part in a bell and hopper **i :** the enlarged end of a section of pipe that receives the spigot end of the adjoining section **j :** the cup-shaped endpiece of a stethoscope that is placed against a body area (as the chest) **6 a :** a musical percussion instrument consisting of a number of metal bars or tubes of various graded lengths that when struck with a hammer give out tones resembling those of different-sized bells — usu. used in pl.; called also *chimes* **b :** GLOCKENSPIEL **7 bells** *pl* **:** heel clicks performed in the air in tap dancing — **with bells on** *adv* **:** in full party dress and spirits **:** with readiness and zeal **:** in full force **:** with clear superiority

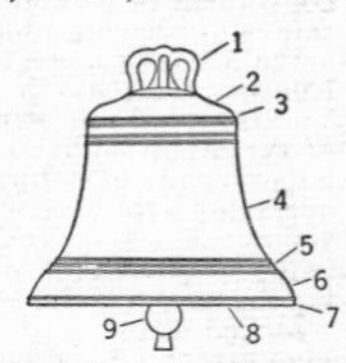

bell 1a: *1* crown, *2* head, *3* shoulder, *4* waist, *5* bead lines, *6* sound bow, *7* lip, *8* mouth, *9* clapper

SHIP'S BELLS

NO. OF BELLS	HOUR (A.M. OR P.M.)		
1	12:30	4:30	8:30
2	1:00	5:00	9:00
3	1:30	5:30	9:30
4	2:00	6:00	10:00
5	2:30	6:30	10:30
6	3:00	7:00	11:00
7	3:30	7:30	11:30
8	4:00	8:00	12:00

²**bell** \ˈ"\ *vb* -ED/-ING/-S *vt* **1 :** to put a bell upon **:** provide with a bell ⟨camels had got away from them in the dark and . . . were not ~*ed* —Myrtle R. White⟩ **2 a :** to ring a bell for ⟨~ the man to come up⟩ **b :** to cause to ring ⟨the ground, so hard it hurt our brittle feet, ~*ed* the iron rakes —Whitney Balliett⟩ **3 :** to make bell-mouthed ⟨~ out the end of a tube⟩ **4 :** to cover by a bell or bell jar ⟨artificial fruit . . . the stuff your grandmother ~*ed* under glass —Walter de la Mare⟩ ~ *vi* **1 :** to ring a bell or bells ⟨trams ~ against motors and drays —William Sansom⟩ **2 :** to make a sound suggestive of a bell ⟨a great ~*ing* chorus of thrushes —H.E.Bates⟩ **:** RING ⟨his head ~*ing* with interrupted sleep —D.C.Peattie⟩ **3 a :** to take the form of a bell **:** swell up or puff out into the shape of a bell ⟨~*ing* sleeves⟩ ⟨~*ed* flowers⟩ ⟨skirts inclined to ~ at the hemline —*Women's Wear Daily*⟩ **b :** to develop bells or corollas **:** BLOSSOM ⟨hops ~*ing* at the end of August⟩ — **bell the cat :** to do a daring or risky deed ⟨everybody made suggestions but no one actually offered to *bell the cat*⟩

³**bell** \ˈ"\ *vi* -ED/-ING/-S [ME *bellen*, fr. OE *bellan* — more at BELLOW] **:** to make a resonant bellowing or baying sound ⟨the bobcat . . . was ahead of the ~*ing* hounds —William Faulkner⟩ **:** BELLOW, ROAR ⟨the distant ~*ing* of the herds of deer —Sacheverell Sitwell⟩

⁴**bell** \ˈ"\ *n* -s **:** the noise of one that bells **:** BELLOW, ROAR ⟨the ~ of a stag⟩

bel·la \ˈbelə\ *n* -s [It, fr. *bella*, adj., fem. of *bello*, fr. L *bellus* — more at BEAUTY] **:** the king and queen of trumps given a special scoring value in European card games

bel·la·bel·la \ˌbeləˈbelə\ *n, pl* **bellabella** *or* **bellabellas** *usu cap* [alter. of *Millbank*, Brit. Columbia, Canada] **1 a :** a Wakashan people or group of peoples of the coast of British Columbia **b :** a member of the Bellabella people or group of peoples **2 :** the language of the Bellabella people

bel·la·coo·la \ˌbeləˈkülə\ *n, pl* **bellacoola** *or* **bellacoolas** *usu cap* [Kwakiutl *Bīlxula*] **1 a :** a Salishan people of the vicinity of Queen Charlotte Sound, British Columbia **b :** a member of such people **2 :** the language of the Bellacoola people

bel·la·don·na \ˌbeləˈdänə\ *n* -s [It, lit., fine lady, fr. *bella*, fem. of *bello* beautiful (fr. L *bellus*) + *donna* lady; fr. its use as a cosmetic — more at BEAUTY, DONNA] **1 :** a European poisonous plant (*Atropa belladonna*) which is extensively grown in the U.S., which has reddish bell-shaped flowers and shining black berries, and from the root and leaves of which atropine is produced — called also *deadly nightshade* **2 :** a medicinal extract from the belladonna plant **3 :** BELLADONNA LILY

belladonna lily *n* **:** a southern African bulbous plant (*Amaryllis belladonna*) often cultivated for its fragrant usu. white or rose-colored flowers which resemble lilies

belladonna ointment *n* **:** an official ointment containing belladonna extract, wool grease, yellow wax, and petrolatum

bell and hopper *n* **:** an apparatus at the top of a blast furnace consisting of a large hopper closed by a cone which is pulled up from below by the apex and through which the charge may be introduced without escape of the gases

bell-and-spigot joint *n* **:** a pipe joint formed by the insertion of the spigot end of one length of pipe into the bell end of the next length

bell animalcule *n* **:** any of many bell-shaped stalked ciliated infusorians of *Vorticella* and related genera

bell apple *n* **:** JAMAICA HONEYSUCKLE

bell arch *n* **:** a round arch on two corbels faced convexly to a wider space below

bel·lar·mine \ˌbelärˈmēn, -ˌlär-; ˈbelərmən\ *n* -s [after Roberto Cardinal *Bellarmine* (Bellarmino) †1621 Ital. prelate whom such jugs orig. caricatured] **:** a narrow-necked large-bellied stoneware drinking jug typically adorned with the figure of a bearded man

bell beaker *n* **:** a bell-shaped pottery vessel of the prehistoric Beaker folk

bell·bind \ˈbel,bīnd\ *or* **bell·bind·er** \-ndə(r)\ *or* **bell·bine** \-n\ *n* -s **1 :** FIELD BINDWEED **2 :** HEDGE BINDWEED

bellbird \ˈ=,=\ *n* [so called fr. its bell-like note] **:** any of several birds whose notes are likened to the sound of a bell: as **a :** a loud-voiced white So. American bird (*Procnias nivea*) having a fleshy caruncle on the head or a related bird **b :** a honey eater (*Manorina melanophrys*) of Australia or a honey eater (*Anthornis melanura*) of New Zealand **c :** a western Australian bird (*Oreoica cristata*) **d :** WOOD THRUSH 1

bellbird a

bell book *n* [so called fr. the shipboard use of bells for signals] **:** a book in which a ship's engineer records speeds, directions, and engine data

bell boot *n* [so called fr. its shape] **:** a rubber covering fitted over the hoof of a horse to protect the hoof surface

bell-bottom \ˈ=ˌ==\ *also* **bell-bottomed** \(ˈ)=ˌ==\ *adj, of trousers* **:** having legs with wide flaring bottoms ⟨sailors wearing *bell-bottom* pants⟩

bell-bottoms \(ˈ)=ˌ==\ *n pl* **:** a pair of bell-bottom trousers

bellboy \ˈ=ˌ=\ *n* **1 :** a hotel or club employee who escorts guests to their rooms, assists them with their luggage, and is available for running errands — called also *bellhop, bellman* **2 :** a logging signalman who uses a bell system

bell buoy *n* **:** a buoy with a bell that rings by the action of the waves and usu. marks a shoal or rocks

bell button *n* **1 :** a push button to ring a bell **2 :** a bell-shaped button used esp. on some dress uniforms

bell cage *n* **:** a timber frame constructed to support a large bell

bell canopy *n* **1 :** BELL GABLE **2 :** an open-roofed structure for protecting a bell

bell captain *n* **:** ¹CAPTAIN 1m(2)

bell center punch *n* **:** a center or prick punch mounted on the axis of a hollow cone that when placed over the end of round stock and struck marks the center of the stock

bell cord *n* **:** a cord that rings a bell when pulled (as in a room for summoning a servant or on a railroad car for giving a signal)

bell cot *or* **bell cote** *n* **:** a small or subsidiary construction frequently corbeled out from the walls of a structure and used to contain and support one or more bells

bell cow *n* **1 :** a cow with a bell attached to its neck; *esp* **:** a lead cow **2** *slang* **:** LEADER ⟨the *bell cow* in county politics —James Street & J.S.Childers⟩
bell crank *n* [so called fr. the bell wires used to transfer motion] **:** a lever having its fulcrum at the apex of the angle formed by its two arms
bell crown *n* **:** a silk hat or a beaver with a crown shaped like an inverted bell
bell deck *n* **:** the floor of a belfry serving as a roof to the rooms below

bell crank

belle \'bel\ *n* -S [F, fr. fem. of *beau* beautiful, handsome — more at BEAU] **:** a girl or woman who is popular and beautiful or attractive **:** a girl or woman whose charm and beauty make her a favorite ⟨the ~ of the ball⟩
bell ear *n* **:** a rabbit's ear with a large lopped tip that is rated as a disqualifying fault in show stock
belled \'beld\ *adj* [¹*bell* + *-ed*] **:** having bell-shaped flowers ⟨the ~ hyacinth⟩
bel·leek \bə'lēk\ *n* -S [*Belleek*] **:** CHAMPAGNE 3
Belleek \"\ *trademark* — used for a thin translucent often ornately decorated porcelain covered with a lustrous often iridescent glaze
belle isle cress \(')be¦lī(ə)l-\ *n, usu cap B&I* [prob. fr. *Belle Isle*, Orange county, Fla.] **:** WINTER CRESS
bel·ler \'belə(r)\ *dial var of* BELLOW
bel·ler·ic \bə'lerik\ *n* -S [F, fr. Ar *balīlaj*, fr. Per *balīlah*] **:** the fruit of the bahera — compare MYROBALAN
bel·ler·o·phon \bə'lerə,fän, -,fən\ *n, cap* [NL, fr. *Bellerophon*, mythological character who slew the Chimera with the help of Pegasus, fr. L, fr. Gk *Bellerophōn*] **:** a genus (the type of the family Bellerophontidae) of extinct Palaeozoic gastropod mollusks having a somewhat loosely coiled plain spiral shell and often placed in the superfamily Bellerophontacea of the Aspidobranchia — **bel·ler·o·phont** \-,fänt\ *adj or n*
belles let·tres \bel(l)et(rᵊ), -le·tr(ə)\ *n pl but sing in constr* [F *belles-lettres*, lit., beautiful letters] **:** literature that is an end in itself (as most poetry, fiction, and drama) and not practical or purely informative ⟨a magazine more concerned with public affairs than *belles lettres*⟩; *specif* **:** light entertaining literature often of a facile or sophisticated nature ⟨the *belles lettres* fragrance that clings to the humanities repelled the social scientists —A.L.Guérard⟩
bell·et·er \'bələd·ə(r)\ *n* -S [¹*bell* + *-eter* (fr. obs. *yeter* metal caster, fr. OE *gēotere*, fr. *gēotan* to cast, pour + *-ere* -er) — more at YET] **:** a bell founder
bel·le·trism *or* **belles–let·trism** \bel'le·,trizəm\ *n* -S [*belles lettres* + *-ism*] **:** an interest in belles lettres to the neglect of more practical or informative literature **:** literary aestheticism ⟨emphasis upon ~ . . . is an educational luxury in this chaotic era —W.L.Moore⟩
bel·le·trist *also* **belle–let·trist** \-le·trəst\ *n* -S [*belles lettres* + *-ist*] **:** a writer of or a person devoted to belles lettres
bel·le·tris·tic *also* **bel·let·tris·tic** \¦belə¦tristik\ *adj* **:** belonging to or suggestive of belles lettres ⟨~ writing⟩ ⟨a ~ trifler⟩ ⟨~ qualities⟩
bellflower \'=,=\ *n* **1 :** any of several plants having bell-shaped flowers: as **a :** a plant of the genus *Campanula* or a closely related genus **b :** CHILEAN BELLFLOWER **c :** BALLOONFLOWER **2 :** MAZARINE BLUE
bellflower family *n* **:** CAMPANULACEAE
bell gable *n* **:** a piece of walling pierced with openings that are usu. arched and arranged for the hanging of large bells and are often upward prolongations above the roof of a gable wall (as of a church or chapel)
bell gamba *n* **:** CONE GAMBA
bell glass *n* **:** BELL JAR
bellhanger \'=,==\ *n* **:** one who hangs, puts up, or repairs bells esp. as a trade
bell harp *n* **:** an 18th century musical instrument consisting of a psaltery mounted in a triangular frame and plucked with plectra attached to the thumbs
bell heather *n* **1 a :** a European heather (*Erica tetralix*) with rose-colored flowers **b :** a European heather (*E. cinerea*) with purple flowers — called also *heather bell* **2 :** an alpine plant (*Cassiope mertensiana*) of western No. America found in wet places and resembling a heath
¹bell·hop \'bel,häp\ *n* -S [short for *bell-hopper*, fr. ¹*bell* + *hopper*] **1 :** BELLBOY **2 :** one who does messenger service within a bank
²bellhop \"\ *vi* **:** to work as a bellhop
bellhouse \'=,=\ *n* [ME *bellhous*, fr. OE *bellhūs*, fr. *belle* bell + *hūs* house] **:** a structure for containing a bell (as a detached building or a belfry)
bel·li·cist \'beləsəst\ *n* -S [L *bellicus* of war + E *-ist*] **:** one who advocates war — opposed to *pacifist*
bel·li·cose \'belə,kōs, -lē-\ *adj* [ME, fr. L *bellicosus*, fr. *bellicus* (fr. *bellum* war — fr. OL *duellum* — + *-icus* -ic) + *-osus* -ose — more at DUEL] **:** WARLIKE ⟨~ young officers⟩ **:** favoring or inclined to favor war or strife **:** inclined to foment contention and quarrels **:** AGGRESSIVE, COMBATIVE **syn** see BELLIGERENT
bellicosely *adv* **:** in a bellicose manner
bel·li·cos·i·ty \,==ˈkäsəd·ē, -ətē, -i\ *n* -ES **:** showy, demonstrative, or arrant truculence or aggressiveness ⟨confuse courage with ~ —*Yale Rev.*⟩
bel·lied \'belēd, -lid\ *adj* [¹*belly* + *-ed*] **1 :** possessed of a belly ⟨a man ~ like a hog⟩ — often used in combination ⟨a great-*bellied* person⟩ ⟨empty-*bellied* children⟩; *specif* **:** possessing a large or pronounced belly ⟨to produce long, fine, not too ~ animals —Poul Vestbirk⟩ **2 :** possessing a convex, rounded, or bulging surface ⟨a ~ sail⟩ ⟨a ~ file⟩
bellies *pl of* BELLY, *pres 3d sing of* BELLY
bel·lig·er·ence \bə'lij(ə)rən(t)s\ *sometimes* bē-\ *n* -S **:** an attitude, atmosphere, or disposition distinguished by aggressiveness or truculence ⟨to circumvent ~ and reduce suspicion of adult control —*Newsweek*⟩
bel·lig·er·en·cy \-rənsē, -si\ *n* -ES **1 :** the state of being at war or in conflict; *specif* **:** the status whereby a recognized military force is granted the protection of the international laws and usages of war (as those laid down by the Hague Convention in 1899) **2 :** BELLIGERENCE ⟨over against this persistent ~ of the German militarists stood the ideology of British pacifism —*Hibbert Jour.*⟩
¹bel·lig·er·ent \-rənt\ *adj* [irreg. fr. L *belligerant-, belligerans*, pres. part. of *belligerare* to be at war, fr. *belliger* waging war, fr. *bellum* war + *gerere* to wage — more at CAST] **1 :** waging war **:** carrying on war ⟨~ factions⟩ ⟨~ powers⟩; *specif* **:** belonging to or recognized as an organized military power protected by and subject to the laws of war ⟨~ embassies in neutral countries⟩ ⟨a ~ nation⟩ — often used of a party in revolt after its establishment of and recognition as a de facto government **2 :** inclined to or exhibiting assertiveness, hostility, truculence, or combativeness ⟨an obnoxious, ~, argumentative adolescent —Hannah Smith⟩ ⟨such ~ verbalizing as makes peaceful action more difficult to achieve —H.A.Overstreet⟩
syn BELLICOSE, PUGNACIOUS, COMBATIVE, CONTENTIOUS, QUARRELSOME: BELLIGERENT may describe a country or group actually at war ⟨a truce of six months between the *belligerent* parties —W.H.Prescott⟩ Less legalistically, it indicates an aggressive, truculent attitude and connotes very hostile feelings ⟨still fighting some of the battles . . . and he is at times unnecessarily *belligerent* —H.S.Commager⟩ ⟨and the most *belligerent* of all . . . she who at tea heroically slaughtered not only German men but all women and viperine children —Sinclair Lewis⟩ BELLICOSE likewise suggests a pronounced inclination to fight ⟨Calhoun joined with Clay in driving through Congress a war policy. In this he seems to have represented his constituents, whose patriotism was always somewhat *bellicose* —V.L. Parrington⟩ ⟨they were a *bellicose* people, wielding axes, spears, and clubs against their enemies —John Murra⟩ PUGNACIOUS indicates ready and pleasurable willingness to fight ⟨their *pugnacious* dispositions are well known, and they not only fight among themselves but are incessantly quarreling with their neighbors —John Burroughs⟩ ⟨a certain *pugnacious* virtue that would inculcate righteousness by means of a broken head — V.L.Parrington⟩ COMBATIVE may indicate either pertaining to combat or, more positively, willingly ready for combat ⟨combat in the field of sports, contests in various forms of games . . . are generally approved. The *combative* impulses in human nature may thus find an expression —M.R.Cohen⟩ ⟨on Mary's face there was . . . something *combative* and alert as well. She was still fighting, but Will was obviously beaten —Dorothy Sayers⟩ PUGNACIOUS and COMBATIVE may lack unpleasant connotation; CONTENTIOUS implies a perverse and irritating fondness for arguments and strife ⟨ideal wives are thought to be like sisters or mothers, cherishing and submissive; others are considered *contentious* —A.L.Kroeber⟩ ⟨his experience with the *contentious* Dominion council led him often abruptly to silence lengthy and unprofitable debates —Viola F. Barnes⟩ QUARRELSOME suggests a fretful ill-natured disposition to quarrel for petty ill-grounded reasons ⟨you also feel very *quarrelsome*, and you swear at each other in hoarse whispers —J.K. Jerome⟩ ⟨she was such a confounded *quarrelsome* high-bred jade —W.M.Thackeray⟩
²belligerent \"\ *n* -S **:** a belligerent nation, state, or person ⟨recognized the Confederacy as a ~ —W.C.Ford⟩
belligerently *adv* **:** in a belligerent manner
¹bell·ing \'beliŋ, -lēŋ\ *n* -S [ME, fr. gerund of *bellen* to roar — more at BELL] **:** the crying or bellowing of animals (as the baying of foxhounds or the sound made by deer in rutting season)
²belling \"\ *n* -S [fr. gerund of ²*bell*] *chiefly Midland* **:** SHIVAREE
bel·linger·ite \'beliŋə,rīt, -lənjə,r-\ *n* -S [Herman C. *Bellinger* †1940 metallurgist + E *-ite*] **:** a mineral $3Cu(IO_3)_2.2H_2O$ consisting of a light-green hydrous copper iodate found at Chuquicamata, Chile
bel·li·ni's duct *also* **bellini's tube** *or* **bellini's tubule** \bə'lēnēz-\ *n, cap B* [after Lorenzo *Bellini* †1704 Ital. anatomist] **:** any of the excretory ducts of the kidney — usu. used in pl.
bel·lip·o·tent \(')be¦lipəd·ənt\ *adj* [L *bellipotent-, bellipotens*, fr. *bellum* war + *potent-, potens* powerful — more at BELLICOSE, POTENT] **:** mighty in war
bel·lis \'beləs\ *n, cap* [L, white daisy, perh. fr. *bellus* pretty — more at BEAUTY] **:** a small genus of scapose herbs (family Compositae) having solitary heads of ray flowers with involucral bracts that are nearly equal — see DAISY 1, WESTERN DAISY
bell jar *n* **:** a bell-shaped usu. glass vessel designed to cover and protect objects, to contain gases, or to enclose a vacuum
bell–less \'belləs\ *adj* **:** being without a bell
bell–lyra \(')=¦==\ *or* **bell lyre** *n* **:** a glockenspiel mounted in a portable lyre-shaped frame and used esp. in marching bands
bell–ma·gen·die law \'bel,mä,zhaⁿ 'dē-\ *n, usu cap B & M* [after Sir Charles *Bell* †1842 Scottish anatomist & François *Magendie* †1855 Fr. physiologist] **:** BELL'S LAW
bell magpie *n* [so called fr. its bell-like call note] **:** CURRAWONG

bell jar

bell·man \'belmən *also* -,man *or* -,maa(ə)n\ *n, pl* **bellmen** [ME, fr. *belle* bell + *man*] **1 :** a man who rings a bell (as a town crier or a night watchman) **2 :** one who assists a diver by checking his equipment and pulling in or letting out the lifeline according to his instructions **3 :** BELLBOY **4 :** a construction-crew signalman who uses a bell
bell mare *n* **:** a female horse, mule, or ass wearing a bell and serving as leader of a packtrain or herd
bellmaster \'=,==\ *n* **:** CARILLONNEUR
bell metal *n* **:** bronze that consists usu. of three to four parts of copper to one of tin and is used for making bells
bell–metal ore *n* **:** STANNITE
bell–mouthed \'=¦=\ *adj* **:** flaring at the mouth
bell olive tree *n* [so called fr. the shape of the flowers] **:** SILVER BELL
bello·ta *also* **bello·te** \bə'lōd·ə, bə'yō-\ *n* -S [MexSp *bellota*, fr. Sp, acorn, fr. Ar *ballūṭa*] **1 :** GAMBEL OAK **2 :** the acorn of the gambel oak
¹bel·low \'be(,)lō, -lə, *often* -lə̇w+V\ *vb* -ED/-ING/-S [ME *belwen*, fr. OE *bylgian*; akin to OE & OHG *bellan* to roar, ON *belja* to bellow, *bylja* to resound, Skt *bhāṣate* he talks] *vi* **1 :** to emit a loud deep hollow prolonged sound (as of a bull) **2 :** to speak or shout in a deep voice and unrestrained manner **:** BAWL ⟨~*ing* with hoarse merriment —Kenneth Roberts⟩ ~ *vt* **:** to utter in a bellowing manner **:** BAWL ⟨the captain ~*ed* out commands⟩ ⟨the cannon ~*ed* forth their salvos⟩ **syn** see ROAR
²bellow \"\ *n* -S **:** a loud deep forceful reverberating outcry; *typically* **:** the roaring of a bull
¹bel·lows \'be(,)lōz, -ləz, *formerly often & still sometimes esp in S* - ləs\ *n pl but sing or pl in constr* [ME *bely, below* belly, bellows — more at BELLY] **1 :** an instrument or machine that by alternate expansion and contraction or by rise and fall of the top draws in air through a valve or orifice and expels it more or less forcibly through a tube; *also* **:** any of various forms of rotary and other blowers — compare BLOWER 5 **2 :** LUNGS ⟨the yell from the deep ~ of the man —Barnaby Conrad⟩ **3 :** the pleated expansible part of leather, cloth, or similar material in a camera making a light-tight passage between the lens and the light-sensitive material at the back of the camera — see CAMERA illustration **4 :** any of various enclosures of variable volume with walls like those of an accordion (as in sealed expansion joints and thermostats)

bellows 1

²bellows *vt* -ED/-ING/-ES *obs* **:** to blow with or as if with bellows
bellows fish *n* **1 :** any of several fishes (family Macrorhamphosidae) having a deep compressed body and long tubular snout — called also *snipefish, trumpet fish* **2 :** ANGLER 2a **3 :** a globefish (*Sphoeroides maculatus*)
bellows pocket *n* **:** a pocket with an expansion pleat applied to the outside of a garment
bellows tongue *n* **:** a wide folding tongue of a shoe or boot (as of a blucher) attached at the sides to the uppers so as to make the shoe watertight
bellows top *n* **:** a folding top of a carriage
bell pepper *n* [so called prob. fr. the shape] **:** SWEET PEPPER
bellpull \'=,=\ *n* **:** a handle or knob attached to a cord or wire by which one rings a bell; *sometimes* **:** the cord itself
bell push *n* **:** a button that is pushed to ring a bell
bell ringer *n* **1 :** one that rings a bell: as **a :** CARILLONNEUR **b :** one that rings a church bell; *esp* **:** one that takes part in change ringing **c :** a performer on musical hand bells **2 :** something that succeeds or makes a hit
bell ringing *n* **:** the art or occupation of playing a chime, carillon, or other set of musical bells
bell rope *n* **:** a rope attached to a bell or to the tongue of a bell
bells *pl of* BELL, *pres 3d sing of* BELL
bell scraper *n* **:** a flattened bell-shaped metal instrument with sharpened edges used for scraping the hair from hog carcasses as they come from the scalding vat
bell shape *n* **:** the shape in full or in outline of vertical section of an inverted cup with flaring rim and convex crown — compare CAMPANIFORM
bell's law \'belz-\ *n, usu cap B* [after Sir Charles *Bell* †1842 Scottish anatomist] **:** a statement in physiology: the roots of the spinal nerves coming from the ventral portion of the spinal cord are motor in function and those coming from the dorsal portion are sensory — called also *Bell-Magendie law*
bells of ireland *usu cap I* [so called fr. the green bell-shaped calyx] **:** MOLUCCA BALM
bell's palsy *n, usu cap B* [after Sir Charles *Bell*] **:** paralysis of the facial nerve producing distortion of one side of the face
bell sparrow *or* **bell's sparrow** *n, often cap B* [after J.G.*Bell* †1889 Am. physician and ornithologist] **:** a California desert sparrow (*Amphispiza belli belli*) that is brownish gray above and white below with a black tail and yellowish wing margins
bell's vireo *n, usu cap B* [after J.G.*Bell*] **:** a vireo (*Vireo bellii bellii*) of the central U.S. with a brownish olive back, white throat, and yellow underparts
belltail \'=,=\ *n* **:** RATTLESNAKE
bell toad *n* **:** a small drab upland toad (*Ascaphus truei*) of the northwestern U.S.
bell tone *n* **1 :** the tone or timbre peculiar to a bell (as a church bell) and composed of a unique series of harmonics beginning 1 : 2 : 2 : 4 : 3 : 4 **2 :** a musical tone (as produced on a trumpet) characterized by a strong initial accent followed by a sharp diminuendo similar in dynamics to a tone struck on a bell
belltopper \'=¦==\ *n* [so called fr. its bell-shaped crown] *chiefly Austral* **:** a tall silk hat
bell tower *n* **:** a tower either freestanding or surmounting a civil or religious building that supports or shelters a bell — compare BELFRY, CAMPANILE, CARILLON
bell trap *n* **:** a bell-shaped trap below the inlet of a floor drain
bell tree *n* **:** SILVER BELL
bell turret *n* **:** a turret (as of a small church or chapel having no bell tower) where a bell is hung
bel·lum \'beləm\ *n* -S [modif. of Per *balam*] **:** a Persian-gulf boat holding about eight persons and propelled by paddles or poles
bell vine *n* [so called fr. the bell-shaped corolla] *New Zeal* **:** HEDGE BINDWEED
bellwaver \'=,==\ *vi* **:** to wander aimlessly **:** FLUCTUATE, RAMBLE ⟨with a ~*ing* air —Muriel Rukeyser⟩
bellwether \'=¦==\ *n* [ME, fr. *belle* bell + *wether*] **1 :** a belled wether or sheep **2 :** one that takes the lead or initiative **:** LEADER ⟨distinguished for his outstanding work as a ~ bomber pilot —R.G.Hubler & J.A.DeChant⟩ ⟨California, traditional ~ of the canning industry —*Wall Street Jour.*⟩
bell wire *n* **:** a small-size wire insulated with paraffin-coated cotton and used esp. for electric bell circuits
bellwood \'=,=\ *n* **:** SILVER BELL
bellwort \'=,=\ *n* **1 :** a plant of the family Campanulaceae **2 :** a plant of the genus *Uvularia* having yellow flowers shaped like bells
¹bel·ly \'belē, -li\ *n* -ES [ME *bely, baly*, fr. OE *belg, bælg* bag, skin; akin to OHG *balg* bag, skin, ON *belgr*, Goth *balgs* wineskin, Skt *upabarhaṇa* cushion, L *flare* to blow — more at BLOW] **1 a** (1) **:** the front part of the human body between the breast and the thighs enclosing the abdominal viscera **:** ABDOMEN (2) **:** the underpart of an animal's body corresponding to the human belly; *also* **:** the hide from the underside of an animal — see HIDE illustration **b :** WOMB, UTERUS **c :** the internal cavity of the body **:** the abdominal cavity **d :** the part of a garment that covers a person's belly **e :** the piece of wool from the sheep's belly — usu. used in pl. **2 :** the internal cavity of something **:** INTERIOR ⟨a boat carrying a half dozen freight cars in its ~⟩ **3 :** APPETITE ⟨thoughts that rose little above his ~⟩ **:** satisfaction of hunger ⟨always intent on his ~⟩ **4 :** a surface or object so curved or rounded as to resemble or suggest the human or animal belly ⟨the ~ of a flask⟩ ⟨the ~ of an airplane⟩ ⟨a cold ~ of fog advancing down the street⟩ **5 a :** the convex inner side of an archer's bow **b :** the part of a sail that swells out when filled with wind **c :** the enlarged fleshy body of a muscle between the usu. slender points of attachment **d :** the side of a piece of printer's type opposite the back and having the nick — see TYPE illustration **e :** the part of a blast furnace at the top of the bosh where the diameter is greatest **f** (1) **:** the front or upper plate of the sound box of instruments of the violin and lute classes — called also *table* (2) **:** the soundboard of a piano
²belly \"\ *vb* -ED/-ING/-ES *vt* **1 :** to round out **:** SWELL, FILL ⟨wind ~*ing* the sails⟩ **2** *Austral* **:** to remove the wool on the belly of (a sheep) before shearing **3 :** to disable the treads of (an army tank) esp. in such a way as to expose the underside to enemy fire ⟨*bellied* by concrete blocks⟩ ~ *vi* **1 :** to swell out **:** bulge out ⟨his blouse *bellied* out round him —F.M. Ford⟩ **2 :** to move along on the belly ⟨the patrol *bellied* across the field under enemy fire⟩ or with the belly foremost ⟨the cowboys *bellied* up to the bar⟩
¹bellyache \'==,=\ *n* [¹*belly* + *ache*] **:** pain in the abdomen and esp. in the bowels **:** COLIC
²bellyache \"\ *vi* **:** to complain and find fault whiningly or with disgruntled peevishness ⟨*bellyached* about small matters —Stanley Walker⟩ **syn** see COMPLAIN
bellyache–bush *or* **bellyache–weed** \'==,=,=\ *n* **:** a shrub (*Jatropha gossipiifolia*) of the southeastern U.S. that is reputedly poisonous and has seeds with purgative properties
bellyband \'=,=,=\ *n* **:** a band that passes around or across the belly: as **a :** a band that goes around or under the belly of a horse and holds the saddle, harness, or shafts in place **:** GIRTH — see HARNESS illustration **b :** a strengthening band of canvas sewed across a sail below the lower reef band **c :** a strip of fabric worn around the abdomen; *esp* **:** BAND 4b(2)
belly brace *n* **:** a vertical steel plate that is used to secure a locomotive boiler to a casting that binds together the frames of a locomotive at a point just in front of the firebox — compare WAIST SHEET
belly bump *also* **belly bumper** *n or adv or vi, chiefly NewEng* **:** BELLY FLOP
belly bunt *n or adv or vi, NewEng* **:** BELLY FLOP
belly bust *or* **belly buster** *n or adv or vi* **:** BELLY FLOP
belly button *n* **:** NAVEL 1
bellycheer *n* **1** *obs* **:** gratification of the belly **:** GLUTTONY **2** *obs* **:** FOOD
belly dance *n* **:** a dance emphasizing movement of the abdominal muscles — called also *danse du ventre*
¹belly flop *also* **belly flopper** *n* **:** a dive (as into water or in coasting prone on a sled) in which the front of the body strikes flat against another surface
²belly flop *adv* **:** with a belly flop **:** on the belly **:** PRONE ⟨slide *belly flop* downhill⟩
³belly flop *vi* **:** to execute a belly flop
belly–footed \¦==¦==\ *adj* **:** of or having to do with a gastropod mollusk
bel·ly·ful \'belē,fu̇l, -li-\ *n* -S **:** an amount over and above what can be stood with comfort ⟨a ~ of advice⟩
belly–god \'==,=\ *n, archaic* **:** GLUTTON
belly–gun \'==,=\ *n* **:** an easily concealed short-barreled revolver used only at very close range
belly gut \'==,=\ *also* **belly gut·ter** \¦==gəd·ə(r)\ *n or adv or vi, dial* **:** BELLY FLOP
belly in *vi* [²*belly*] **:** to crash-land an aircraft with landing gear retracted **:** BELLY-LAND
bellying *pres part of* BELLY
belly–land \¦==¦=\ *vi* [¹*belly* + *land* (v.)] **:** to land an airplane without use of landing gear — **belly landing** *n*
belly laugh *n* **:** a deep hearty laugh
bel·ly·man \'belē,man\ *n, pl* **bellymen :** a worker who assembles and adjusts the soundboard of a piano
belly offal *n* **:** hide from the belly that does not measure up to the standard of that from other parts
belly robber *n, slang* **:** COOK, STEWARD
belly tank *n* **:** an auxiliary jettisonable fuel tank mounted under the belly of an airplane
belly whop *also* **belly whopper** *n or adv or vi* **:** BELLY FLOP
be·lo hor·i·zon·te \¦bā(,)lō,hȯrə'zäntē, ¦be-\ *adj, usu cap B &H* [fr. *Belo Horizonte*, Brazil] **:** of or from the city of Belo Horizonte, Brazil **:** of the kind or style prevalent in Belo Horizonte
be·loid \'bē,lȯid\ *adj* [Gk *belos* dart, arrow + E *-oid*; akin to Gk *ballein* to throw — more at DEVIL] **1 :** having a shape like that of an arrow **2** *of a skull or head* **:** having a contour broad in the occipital and narrow in the frontal regions when viewed from above
bel·o·man·cy \'belə,man(t)sē\ *n* -ES [Gk *belos* dart, arrow + E *-mancy*] **:** divination by drawing arrows at random from a container
bel·o·mys \'belə,mis\ *n, cap* [NL, fr. Gk *belos* dart + NL *-mys*] **:** a genus of Asiatic flying squirrels
bel·o·ne \'belə,nē\ *n, cap* [NL, fr. L, fr. Gk *belonē* needle, a sea fish, fr. *belos* dart; prob. akin to Gk *ballein* to throw — more at DEVIL] **:** a genus (the type of the family Belonidae) of needlefishes — **bel·o·nid** \'belənəd, -,nid\ *n or adj*
be·long \bə'lȯŋ, bē- *also* -äŋ\ *vi* -ED/-ING/-S [ME *belongen*, fr. *be-* + *longen* to belong — more at LONG (to be suitable)] **1 a :** to be suitable, appropriate, or advantageous (for a person or thing) ⟨strong meat *belongeth* to them that are of full age — Heb 5:14 (AV)⟩ ⟨a dictionary ~*s* in every office⟩ **b :** to be in a proper, rightful, or fitting place, situation, or connection ⟨books placed where they don't ~⟩ ⟨a man of his ability ~*s* in business⟩ **2** *archaic* **:** to have relation or reference (to a person or thing) — used with *to* or *unto* **3 a :** to be the property of a person or thing — used with *to* ⟨the money ~*s* to him⟩ ⟨buildings ~ to the government⟩ **b :** to become attached or bound (as to a person, group, or organization) by birth, allegiance, residence, or dependency — used with *to* ⟨soldiers ~*ing* to a famous regiment⟩ **c** (1) **:** to be a member of a club

or similar association — used with *to* ⟨~ to the golf club⟩ (2) **:** to have the social qualifications or ability to be a member of a group, circle, or society ⟨she's smart and jolly and everything, but she just doesn't ~ —Edna Ferber⟩ **4 :** to be an attribute, part, adjunct, or function (of a person or thing) — used with *to* ⟨good humor and wit ~ to his personality⟩ **5** *chiefly South & Midland* **:** to become accustomed **:** OUGHT ⟨he ~*s* to come at 8 o'clock⟩ **6 :** to be properly classified ⟨whales ~ among the mammals⟩

belonging *n* -s **1 belongings** *pl* **:** relative matters, circumstances, or features **:** ADJUNCTS ⟨reality or its ~*s*⟩ **2 :** POSSESSION ⟨favorite ~⟩ — usu. used in pl. ⟨left all his ~*s* to his brother⟩ **3 belongings** *pl* **:** RELATIVES ⟨followed his female ~*s* up the aisle —Dorothy Sayers⟩ **4 :** close or intimate relationship **:** mutual loyalty ⟨each member had a sense of ~⟩

be·long·ing·ness \-nə̇s\ *n* -ES **:** the quality or state of being essential, integral, or important ⟨a feeling of ~ through participation in the discussion —K.H.Recknagel⟩

bel·o·nite \ˈbelə,nīt\ *n* -s [G *belonit*, fr. Gk *belonē* needle + G *-it* -ite — more at BELONE] **:** an elongated crystallite with rounded or pointed ends

bel·o·noid \ˈbelə,nȯid\ *adj* [Gk *belonoeidēs*, fr. *belonē* needle + *-eidēs* -oid] **:** needlelike in shape **:** STYLOID

1belo·russian \ˌbelō+\ *also* **bielo·russian** *or* **byelo·russian** \ˌbēˌelō, ˌbye- +\ *n* -s *cap* [*Belorussia, Bielorussia, Byelorussia*, region of the U.S.S.R. (fr. Russ *Byelorussiya*, fr. *byelo-* white — fr. *byely* — + *Russiya* Russia) + E *-an*; akin to Skt *bhāti* he shines — more at FANCY] **1 :** a native or inhabitant of Belorussia, U.S.S.R. — called also *White Russian* **2 :** the Slavic language of the Belorussians

2belorussian \"\ *also* **bielorussian** *or* **byelorussian** \"\ *adj, usu cap* **1 a :** of, relating to, or characteristic of Belorussia **b :** of, relating to, or characteristic of Belorussians **2 :** of, relating to, or characteristic of the Belorussian language

bel·o·stom·a·tid \ˌbeləˈstäməd·əd\ *n* -s [NL *Belostomatidae*] **:** a bug of the family Belostomatidae

bel·o·sto·mat·i·dae \ˌbeləstōˈmad·ə,dē\ *n pl, cap* [NL, fr. *Belostomat-, Belostoma*, type genus (fr. Gk *belos* dart + NL *-stomat-, -stoma*) + *-idae* — more at BELONE] **:** a family of large predaceous water bugs with piercing and sucking mouthparts that may be very destructive to young fishes

bel·o·stom·i·dae \ˌbeləˈstämə,dē\ [NL, fr. *Belostoma*, type genus + *-idae*] *syn of* BELOSTOMATIDAE

be·lote *or* **be·lotte** \bəˈlät\ *n* -s [F *belote*, after F. *Belot*, 20th cent. Frenchman] **:** a card game played with a 32-card pack similar to klaberjass and very popular in France

belouga *var of* BELUGA 1

1be·loved \bə̇ˈləvd, bē-— *compare* 2BELOVED *and* 3BELOVED\ *past part* [ME, past part. of *beloven* to love, fr. *be-* + *loven* to love — more at LOVE] **:** LOVED — used as a passive transitive with *of* or *by* ⟨I was ~ of the Italian and Chinese —Eve Langley⟩

2be·loved \-v(ə̇)d — *usu* -vd *when modified by an adverb of degree other than "dearly"; after "dearly" and when there is no adverb of degree both pronunciations are frequent, the frequency of* -vəd *after "dearly" prob being due to the analogy of the noun "dearly beloved", for which* -və̇d *is usual*\ *adj* [ME, fr. 1*beloved*] **:** dear to the heart **:** dearly loved ⟨his ~ aunt⟩ ⟨a well-*beloved* novel⟩ ⟨a post ~ to old soldiers⟩

3be·lov·ed *usu* -və̇d\ *n* -s **:** one who is loved; *esp* **:** SWEETHEART

1be·low \bə̇ˈlō, bē-\ *adv (or adj)* [*be-* + *low* (adv.)] **1 a** (1) **:** at a lower level ⟨the pencil rolled off the desk and fell on the floor ~⟩ **:** further down (as along a river, valley, or slope) ⟨several houses ~ on the right bank of the stream⟩ (2) **:** directly under **:** down under ⟨the elevator was let down to pick up the men on the floor ~⟩ — sometimes used interjectionally to express warning ⟨in spite of a shout "*Below!*" an engineer was hit on the shoulder —John May⟩ **b** (1) **:** on earth ⟨if man is born in sin . . . improvements in conditions here ~ can be of only secondary importance —*Times Lit. Supp.*⟩ (2) **:** in Hades or hell ⟨the fiends ~⟩ **2 a :** lower in rank **:** in a lower station ⟨the kindergarten ~⟩ **b :** in or to a court or tribunal of inferior jurisdiction ⟨the learned judge ~ did not distinguish —*Amer. Jour. of International Law*⟩ **3 :** inside or into the superstructure of a boat or down from an upper deck or structure (as a bridge or pilothouse) to a lower deck ⟨set his course, and went ~ to sleep —*Saturday Rev.*⟩ **4 a :** below zero ⟨20 ~⟩ **b :** BELOW-THE-LINE

2below \"\ *prep* **1 a :** downward from ⟨flower boxes ~ the windows⟩ **b :** further down from ⟨a river barge moored a mile ~ town⟩ **:** at a lower level than ⟨lava beds lying ~ the volcanic cone⟩ **c :** at the bottom of **:** directly underneath ⟨the caption ~ a picture⟩ **d :** farther south than ⟨Richmond is ~ Washington⟩ **2 :** BENEATH ⟨he thought manual labor ~ him⟩ **3 :** inferior to **:** lower down the scale than ⟨fairly high in the scale of animal life and only a little ~ the vertebrates —R.E.Coker⟩ **4 :** covered, concealed, or hidden by ⟨the real reason ~ the mass of pretexts⟩ ⟨~ the sod⟩

3below \"\ *n* -s **1 :** matter located lower on the same page or on a following page ⟨the ~ is iambic⟩ **2 a :** a lower class (as of people) ⟨churches have always drawn their recruits from ~ —A.W.Long⟩ **b :** a lower region (as of a building interior, land, or water)

4below \"\ *adj* **:** located lower on the same page or on a following page ⟨the ~ list contains about 500 names⟩

belowdecks \ˈ=ˌ=ˈ=\ *adv* [2*below* + *decks*, pl. of *deck*] **:** 1BELOW 3 ⟨stayed ~ all afternoon⟩

belowground \ˈ=ˌ=ˈ=\ *adj* [2*below* + *ground*] **1 :** under the ground ⟨~ storage⟩ **2 :** dead and buried ⟨most of his friends are now ~⟩

1belowstairs \ˈ=ˌ=ˈ=\ *adv* [2*below* + *stairs*] **:** DOWNSTAIRS ⟨many works . . . kept ~ . . . are accessible only on demand —Denys Sutton⟩

2belowstairs \"\ *adj* **1 :** on a lower floor ⟨the servants' quarters are ~⟩ **2 :** COMMON, UNREFINED ⟨a ~ love affair⟩

below-the-line \ˈ=ˌ=ˈ=\ *adv (or adj)* **1 :** in that part of the score sheet in bridge reserved for the trick score **2 :** classified as an unusual or nonrecurring expense or revenue item rather than as a current expense or asset

Bel Pa·e·se \ˌbelpäˈāzē\ *trademark* — used for a mild soft creamy cheese in a firm rind

bels *pl of* BEL

belsire *n* -s [ME *belsyre*, fr. *bel* fair, beautiful (fr. OF) + *syre* sire — more at BEAUTY] *obs* **:** GRANDFATHER, ANCESTOR

belswagger *n* [origin unknown] **1** *obs* **:** PIMP **2** *obs* **:** BULLY

1belt \ˈbelt\ *n* -s [ME, fr. OE; akin to OHG *balz* belt, ON *belti*; all fr. a prehistoric Gmc word borrowed fr. L *balteus* girdle, belt] **1 a :** a strip of flexible material (as leather, plastic, cloth) used in a circular form with or without a buckle or other closing and for wear generally around the waist (as a support for trousers, a decoration for dresses, or a means of carrying weapons, tools, or ornaments) ⟨sword ~⟩ **b :** a similar article worn as a corset or as a protection for the body (as a medical bandage or support) or for safety (as by airplane passengers or telephone linemen) **c :** a mark or symbol of distinction in the form of a belt ⟨the championship ~ of heavyweight boxing⟩ **2 :** a continuous band of tough flexible material (as leather, rubber, fabric, wire) for transmitting motion and power from one pulley to another or for conveying materials — see CHAIN BELT illustration **3 a :** an area distinctively characterized by its species or forms of life ⟨a pine ~⟩ ⟨a forest ~⟩ **b :** an elongated area characterized by some particular geologic feature or occurrence and generally not so extensive as a zone ⟨mountain ~⟩ ⟨~ of volcanoes⟩ ⟨coal ~⟩ ⟨oil ~⟩ **c :** a region marked by the prevalence of some type of inhabitant or noteworthy condition ⟨the goiter ~⟩ ⟨the vacationland ~⟩ **4 :** a horizontal band of brick or stone running across a face of a masonry wall or pier **5** [Dan *bælt*; akin to MHG *Beltemeer* Baltic sea] **:** a strait leading to the Baltic sea **6 :** one of several roads or routes arranged concentrically **:** BELT HIGHWAY — **below the belt** *adv* **1 :** in the area below the waistline ⟨a boxer disqualified for hitting *below the belt*⟩ **2 :** in an unfair or cowardly manner ⟨most of the criticism hit *below the belt*⟩ — **under one's belt 1 :** in one's stomach ⟨a couple of drinks *under his belt*⟩ **2 :** in one's possession ⟨with four flourishing papers *under their belts* —*Newsweek*⟩ **:** as part of one's past or experience ⟨she now had three great classic roles *under her belt* —Agnes de Mille⟩

A belt 2

2belt \"\ *vb* -ED/-ING/-S [ME *belten*, fr. *belt*, n.] *vt* **1 a :** to encircle, girdle, or fasten with a belt ⟨a cord ~*ing* a gown⟩ ⟨paraphernalia ~*ed* together⟩ **b :** to gird on ⟨~ on a gun and ammunition⟩ **c :** to invest (a person) with a distinction or title ⟨~ a squire with the rank of knight⟩ **2 a :** to beat with or as if with a belt **:** THRASH **b :** to strike vigorously **:** HIT ⟨~ a person in the jaw⟩ — often used with *out* ⟨~*ing* out a triple⟩ **3 :** to mark with or as if with a band ⟨all equipment to be sold was ~*ed* in green⟩ ⟨~*ed* with a shining porch of enormous pillars —Robinson Jeffers⟩; *specif* **:** GIRDLE 3a ⟨~ a tree⟩ **4 :** to sing in a very loud forceful manner or style ⟨the hoydenish numbers are ~*ed* across effectively —Bill Simon⟩ — usu. used with *out* ⟨~ out a high note⟩ **~** *vi* **:** to move, act, or perform in a vigorous or violent manner ⟨~ along in a car⟩ ⟨waves ~*ing* over a ship⟩

3belt \"\ *n* -s **1 :** a jarring blow **:** JOLT, WHACK ⟨gave the ball a terrific ~⟩ ⟨a ~ of lightning⟩ **2** *slang* **:** a strong emotional reaction ⟨get a terrific ~ out of this tale —*New Republic*⟩

belt ammunition *n* **:** ammunition of usu. small caliber loaded in web or metallic link belts for an automatic weapon

bel·tane \ˈbel(,)tān, -ˌtin\ *also* **beal·ti·ne** \ˈbyau̇ltənə\ *n* -s *usu cap* [ME, fr. ScGael *bealltainn*; akin to MIr *beltene*] **1 :** the first day of May in the old Scottish calendar **2 :** the May Day festival once widely celebrated in Celtic lands with bonfires on the hills, dancing, and various rites

belt conveyor *n* **:** CONVEYER 2a(1)

belt course *n* **:** a horizontal band forming part of an interior or exterior architectural composition (as around pillars or engaged columns) — called also *band course*

B belt course

belted *adj* [ME, fr. past part. of *belten*] **1 :** wearing or encircled by a belt; *esp* **:** girded by a king in an investiture ⟨the son of a ~ earl —Sir Walter Scott⟩ **2 :** marked or furnished with a band (as about the body of an animal) ⟨a ~ hog⟩

belted cattle *n* **:** cattle of any breed characterized by a white band about the body

belted coastal plain *n* **:** a coastal plain on which there are two or more roughly parallel cuestas

belted galloway *n, usu cap B&G* **:** a breed of black or dun-colored cattle developed from the Galloway and having a white band about the body

belted kingfisher *n* **:** a No. American kingfisher (*Ceryle*, or *Megaceryle, alcyon*) that is about a foot long and slate-blue above and white below with a chestnut band across the breast and is sometimes a pest about fish hatcheries

bel·ter \ˈbeltə(r)\ *adj, often cap* [after John H. *Belter* †1863 Ger.-Am. cabinetmaker] **:** belonging to or suggestive of a style of richly carved 19th century furniture ⟨a ~ chair⟩

belt-fed \ˈ=ˌ=\ *adj* **:** using belt ammunition ⟨*belt-fed* weapons⟩

belt highway *n* **:** a highway skirting an urban area — called also *beltway, ring road*

belt·ian \ˈbeltēən\ *adj, usu cap* [Big *Belt* & Little *Belt* Mountains, Montana + E *-ian*] **:** of or relating to a division of Proterozoic geologic era in No. America region — see GEOLOGIC TIME table

1belting *n* -s [1*belt* + *-ing*] **1 :** BELTS **2 :** material for belts: as **a :** a firm narrow fabric usu. of cotton made in various weights and thicknesses **b** *or* **belting leather :** heavy cattle-hide leather used for power transmission belts

2belting *n* -s (fr. gerund of 2*belt*] **:** THRASHING, BEATING

bel·tir \ˈbel,ti(ə)r\ *n, pl* **beltir** *or* **beltirs** *usu cap* **1 :** a turkicized Samoyed people of Yeniseisk province, Siberia **2 :** a member of the Beltir people

belt leather *n* **:** leather used to make waist belts — compare 1BELTING 2b

beltline \ˈ=ˌ=\ *n* **1 :** production line ⟨manufacture requiring only simple ~ operations⟩ **2 :** WAISTLINE

belt line *n* **1 a :** a railroad going wholly or partly around a city for the interchange of traffic between trunk lines or for handling traffic to off-trunkline terminals **b :** a transport line that makes a fairly complete circuit (as around a city) **2 :** a line of rope carried at the belt by a fireman for use in emergency

belt loom *n* **:** a primitive loom consisting usu. of two parallel sticks supporting the warp, one being attached to a tree or post and the other to the weaver's belt

belt·man \ˈbeltmən, -ˌman\ *n, pl* **beltmen :** a worker who tends and repairs machine belts

belt of cementation : the portion of the zone of fracture in which mineral matter is commonly deposited in cracks, fissures, intergranular spaces, and other openings of the earth

belt of fire : an area of active volcanoes

bel·ton \ˈbeltᵊn *also* -tən\ *n* -s [fr. *Belton*, Northumberland, Eng.] **1 :** a blended, flecked, or finely mottled combination orig. of gray and yellow but now of any two colors including esp. white — used of the coats of dogs (as of certain setters) ⟨blue ~⟩ ⟨orange ~⟩ **2 :** a dog with a belton coat

belt pulley *n* **:** a pulley designed to drive or be driven by a belt

belt punch *n* **:** a punch for making holes (as in leather)

belt railroad *n* **:** BELT LINE 1a

belts *pl of* BELT, *pres 3d sing of* BELT

belt sander *n* **:** a machine for belt-sanding

belt-sanding \ˈ=ˌ==\ *n* **:** the sanding or smoothing of a flat wood surface by means of a mechanically driven abrasive belt

belt punch

belt shifter *n* **:** a device for placing a belt on a pulley or for shifting a belt from one pulley to another

belts·ville small white \ˈbelts,vil-, *esp S* -ˌvəl-\ *n, usu cap B&S&W* [fr. *Beltsville*, Maryland] **:** a small white domestic turkey of a variety developed by the U.S. Department of Agriculture to meet the demand for a smaller table bird

belt tightening *n* **:** the curbing of unnecessary expenditure

beltway \ˈ=ˌ=\ *n* **:** BELT HIGHWAY

beltwise \ˈ=ˌ=\ *adv* [1*belt* + *-wise*] **:** in the manner of a belt

beltwork \ˈ=ˌ=\ *n* **:** an operation in which power from a stationary tractor is applied to other machines through a pulley and belt

beluchi *var of* BALUCHI

beluchistan *usu cap, var of* BALUCHISTAN

be·lu·ga *also* **be·lou·ga** \bəˈlügə\ *n* -s [Russ *byeluga*, fr. *byely* white; akin to OSlav *bělŭ* white, Skt *bhāti* he shines — more at FANCY] **1 :** a white sturgeon (*Acipenser huso*) of the Black sea, Caspian sea, and their tributaries that reaches a length of 18 feet and has a swim bladder that is used to make isinglass and roe that is made into caviar **2** [Russ *byelukha*, fr. *byely* white] **:** a cetacean (*Delphinapterus leucas*) of the family Delphinidae becoming about 10 feet long and white when adult and occurring chiefly in northern seas and esp. in the lower St. Lawrence river — called also *white whale*

1bel·ve·dere *also* **bel·vi·dere** \ˈbelvə,di(ə)r, ˌ==ˈ=\ *n* -s [It *belvedere*, lit., beautiful view, fr. *bel, bello* beautiful (fr. L *bellus*) + *vedere* view, fr. *vedere* to see, fr. L *vidēre* — more at BEAUTY, WIT] **:** a structure (as a cupola or a summerhouse) designed to command a view

2belvedere *also* **belvidere** \"\ *n* -s [It *belvedere* (alter. of It dial. — Tuscany — *bedduvidiri*), fr. *bel* + *vedere*] **:** SUMMER CYPRESS

bely *var of* BELIE

belying *pres part of* BELIE

be·lyve *var of* BELIVE

bel·ze·buth \ˈbelzə(,)bəth, -ˌbüth\ *n* -s [NL (specific epithet of *Ateles belzebuth*) prob. alter. of *Beelzebub*] **:** a Brazilian spider monkey (*Ateles belzebuth*)

be·ma \ˈbēmə\ *n* -s [LL & LGk; LL, fr. LGk *bēma*, fr. Gk, step, tribune, fr. *bainein* to step, go — more at COME] **1 :** the part of an early Christian and modern Eastern Orthodox church that contains the altar and synthronon and corresponds to the sanctuary of Western churches — see BASILICA illustration **2 :** ALMEMAR

bemad *vt* [*be-* + *mad*] *archaic* **:** to make insane or frantic

be·master \bə̇, bē+\ *vt* [*be-* + *master*] **:** to master thoroughly **:** bring under control

be·maul \bə̇, bē+\ *vt* [*be-* + *maul*] **:** to maul thoroughly

be·mazed \bə̇ˈmāzd, bē-\ *adj* [ME *bemased*, fr. past part. of *bemasen* to stupefy, fr. *be-* + *masen* to stupefy — more at MAZE] *archaic* **:** BEWILDERED, STUPEFIED

bem·ba \ˈbembə\ *n, pl* **bemba** *or* **bembas** *usu cap* **1 a :** a prominent primarily agricultural Bantu-speaking people in northern Rhodesia **b :** a member of the Bemba people **2 :** a Bantu language of the Bemba people

1bem·bex \ˈbem,beks\ [NL, alter. of *Bembix*] *syn of* BEMBIX

2bembex \"\ *n* -ES [NL, fr. 1 *Bembex*] **:** a bembicid wasp

bem·bi·cid \ˈbembəsəd, -ˌsid\ *adj* [NL *Bembicidae*, fr. *Bembic-, Bembix*, type genus + *-idae*] **:** of or relating to the genus *Bembix* or the family Bembicidae

bem·bix \ˈbembiks\ *n, cap* [NL, fr. Gk, buzzing insect, top, whirlpool, cyclone; akin to Gk *bombos* booming or humming sound — more at BOMB] **:** a genus (the type of the family Bembicidae) of wasps comprising the large solitary or gregarious burrowing sand wasps

be·mean \bə̇ˈmēn, bē-\ *vt* -ED/-ING/-S [*be-* + *mean* (adj.)] **:** DEBASE, LOWER

be·med·aled *or* **be·med·alled** \bə̇ˈmedᵊld, bē-\ *adj* [*be-* + *medal* + *-ed*] **:** wearing or decorated with medals esp. in excessive numbers

bemeet *vb* [*be-* + *meet*] *obs* **:** MEET

be·ment·ite \ˈbēmənt-ˌīt\ *n* -s [C. S. *Bement* †1923 Am. manufacturer and mineral collector + E *-ite*] **:** a mineral consisting of a hydrous silicate of manganese occurring in grayish yellow radiated masses

be·mire \bə̇, bē+\ *vt* [*be-* + *mire* (n.)] **1 :** to cover or soil with or as if with mud or dirt ⟨surveyed his extended leggings, his immense *bemired* boots —F.M.Ford⟩ **2 :** to drag through, encumber with, or sink in mire ⟨*bemired* in a ditch⟩

be·mist \bə̇, bē+\ *vt* [*be-* + *mist* (n.)] **:** to envelop, involve, or obscure in or as if in mist ⟨a ~*ed* mind⟩

be·moan \bə̇, bē+\ *vt* [alter. (influenced by *moan*) of ME *bemenen*, fr. OE *bemǣnan*, fr. *be-* + *mǣnan* to moan — more at MOAN] **1 a :** to express grief over **:** LAMENT ⟨she ~*ed* her brother's death⟩ **b** *archaic* **:** to subject (oneself) to lamentations ⟨people grieve and ~ themselves, but it is not half so bad with them as they say —R.W.Emerson⟩ **2** *obs* **:** to express pity or sorrow for ⟨they ~*ed* him and comforted him over all the evil . . . brought upon him —Job 42:11 (AV)⟩ **3 :** to look upon with regret, displeasure, or disapproval ⟨the governmental control which industrialists ~ so consistently —Douglas McGregor⟩ **syn** see DEPLORE

be·moan·ing·ly *adv* **:** in a bemoaning manner

be·mock \bə̇, bē+\ *vt* [*be-* + *mock*] **:** to mock or mock at

bemoil *vt* [*be-* + *moil*] *obs* **:** to soil or encumber with mud and dirt

be·monster \bə̇, bē+\ *vt* -ED/-ING/-S [*be-* + *monster* (n.)] **1** *obs* **:** to make ugly or vicious as a monster **2 :** to address or refer to as a monster

be·mouth \bə̇ˈmau̇th, bē-\ *vt* [*be-* + *mouth*] **:** to talk bombastically about **:** put into a specified condition by bombastic talk

be·mud \bə̇, bē+\ *vt* [*be-* + *mud* (n.)] **1** *archaic* **:** to cover or spatter with mud **2 :** MUDDLE ⟨*bemudded* thought⟩

be·muffled \bə̇, bē+\ *adj* [*be-* + *muffled*] **:** muffled up

be·muse \bə̇ˈmyüz, bē-\ *vt* [*be-* + *muse*] **1 :** to make confused or muddled ⟨he drinketh strong waters which do ~ a man —W.S.Gilbert⟩ **:** BEWILDER ⟨the extraordinary dialect used in this case . . . would have *bemused* the acutest jury —Malcolm Muggeridge⟩ **2 :** to cause to dream or muse **:** induce a state of reverie in ⟨there is another theory that ~*s* the pilots in the islands —Corey Ford⟩ **syn** see DAZE

be·mused \-ˈmyüzd\ *adj* **1 :** marked by confusion or bewilderment **:** DAZED ⟨he was fumbling with the sheets and looking down at them with a slightly ~ expression —R.P.Warren⟩ **2 :** lost in thought or reverie **:** ABSTRACTED ⟨as distant and ~ as a professor emeritus listening to the prattling of his freshman class —M.W.Straight⟩ — **be·mus·ed·ly** \-zədlē, -li\ *adv*

be·muse·ment \-zmənt\ *n* -s **:** the quality or state of being bemused ⟨this ~ by superficial ideas —H.L.Mencken⟩

1ben \ˈben\ *adv* [ME *ben, binne, binnen*, fr. OE *binnan*, fr. *be-* + *innan* within, from within, fr. *in* — more at IN] *Scot* **:** in or into the inner part or parlor of the house **:** INSIDE, WITHIN ⟨with kindly welcome Jenny brings him ~ —Robert Burns⟩ — opposed to *but*

2ben \"\ *prep, Scot* **:** in or into the inner room of **:** WITHIN ⟨~ the house⟩

3ben \"\ *adj, Scot* **:** situated in the inner part of a house **:** INNER, INTERIOR

4ben \"\ *n* -s *Scot* **:** the inner room or parlor of a house (as of a but-and-ben) — compare 6BUT

5ben \"\ *n* -s [ScGael *beann* peak, horn; akin to MIr *benn* peak, horn, W *ban* peak — more at PIN] *Scot* **:** a high hill **:** MOUNTAIN — often used in place names ⟨*Ben* Nevis⟩ ⟨*Ben* Lomond⟩

6ben *dial past part of* BE

7ben \ˈben\ *also* **be·hen** \bəˈhen, ˈbāən, ˈbēən\ *n* -s [Ar *bān*] **:** the seed of any tree of the genus *Moringa* — see BEN OIL

bena \ˈbenə\ *n, pl* **bena** *or* **benas** *usu cap* **1 :** an African Bantu-speaking people north of Lake Nyasa **2 :** a member of the Bena people

be·nab \bəˈnab\ *n* -s [prob. native name in Guiana] **:** a native hut or shelter in Guiana

Ben·a·dryl \ˈbenədrəl, -ˌdril\ *trademark* — used for diphenhydramine

be·na·mi *also* **be·na·mee** \bəˈnämē\ *adj* [Hindi *benāmī*, fr. Per *banām* in the name of + *-ī*] **:** made, held, done, or transacted in the name of (another person) — used in Hindu law to designate a transaction, contract, or property that is made or held under a name that is fictitious or is that of a third party who holds as ostensible owner for the principal or beneficial owner

benares *usu cap, var of* BANARAS

be·nasty \bə̇, bē+\ *vt* [*be-* + *nasty*] *dial* **:** to make nasty **:** SOIL

ben·ben \ˈben,ben\ *n* -s [alternate transliteration of Egypt *bnbn*] **:** an Egyptian stone of pyramidal shape

bence-jones protein \ˈben(t)s,jōnz-\ *n, usu cap B&J* [after Henry *Bence-Jones* †1873 Eng. physician and chemist] **:** a globulin or a group of globulins found in the blood serum and urine in multiple myeloma and occas. in other bone diseases and usu. characterized by coagulation at 50-60°C with partial redissolving at higher temperatures

1bench \ˈbench\ *n* -ES [ME, fr. OE *benc*; akin to OHG *bank* bench, ON *bekkr*] **1 a :** a long usu. wooden seat often for two or more persons and sometimes with a back ⟨a park ~⟩ **b :** a thwart or seat in a boat **c** (1) **:** a seat on which members of an athletic team sit while awaiting a turn or an opportunity to play (2) **:** the reserve players of a team **2 a :** the seat where a judge sits in court **:** the seat of justice **b :** the office or dignity of a judge ⟨a recent appointment to the ~⟩ **c :** the place where justice is administered **:** COURT **d :** the persons who sit as judges — see COURT OF KING'S BENCH **3 a :** a seat or seat and table or desk for an official **b :** the office or dignity of such an official ⟨he aspires to the civic ~⟩ **c :** the officials occupying seats ⟨the bishops' ~ in the House of Lords⟩ **4 a :** a long worktable having a level top ⟨a carpenter's ~⟩ **b :** a usu. metal table forming part of a machine **c :** any of various machines (as for drawing wires or tubes) that are developments of the simple workbench **5 :** TERRACE, SHELF: as **a :** an area of level or gently sloping land with steep slopes above and below formed by differential erosion of rocks of varying resistance or by a change of base-level erosion **b :** a former wave-cut shore of a sea or lake or floodplain of a river **c :** a shelf formed in working an open excavation on more than one level **d :** a shelf or ledge made in a mine tunnel or working when an upper section is cut back **e** (1) **:** a stratum of coal forming part of a seam (2) **:** one of two or more portions of a coal seam often separated (as by slate) **6 a** (1) **:** a platform with wooden sides and back and often a heavy screen top and front on which a dog is placed at a dog show (2) **:** a public exhibition of dogs **b :** a raised platform with sides that is used for supporting potted plants or for holding soil in which plants are grown (as in a greenhouse or conservatory) **7 a :** a group of retorts in an oven or furnace for generating coal gas **b :** the complete oven or furnace containing a set or group of retorts — **on the bench 1 :** sitting as a judge **2 a :** awaiting a turn or opportunity to play **b :** temporarily out of a game

²**bench** \"\ *vb* -ED/-ING/-ES [ME *benchen*, fr. *bench*, n.] *vt* **1 :** to furnish with benches **2 a :** to seat on a bench (as of justice or honor) **b :** to remove (a player) from a game or keep (a player) on the bench ⟨the infielder was ~*ed* for poor fielding⟩ **c :** to set out (plants) in greenhouse benches or beds **3 a :** to exhibit (dogs or other show animals) in a bench show **b :** to arrange the bench for (a dog or other animal show) **4 :** to cut ledges or steps in (as an embankment) ~ *vi* **1** *obs* **:** to sit on a seat of justice **2 :** to form a bench by natural processes ⟨the soil showed a tendency to ~ off levelly between the tree rows —Russell Lord⟩

benchboard \ˈ=,=\ *n* **:** a horizontal or slightly inclined switchboard with or without vertical instrument sections

bench·er \ˈbenchə(r)\ *n* -S [¹*bench* + *-er*] **:** one that sits on, works at, or presides at a bench: as **a :** one that sits on an official bench (as a judge) — see BACK BENCHER, FRONT BENCHER **b :** one of the senior and governing members of an Inn of Court

ben chervil \ˈben+,-\ *n* [origin unknown] **:** HEDGE PARSLEY

¹**bench graft** *n* [¹*bench* + *graft*] **:** a plant propagated by bench grafting

²**bench graft** *vt* **:** to graft indoors (as on a greenhouse bench during the winter) ⟨cherries were *bench grafted* successfully⟩

bench hardening *n* **:** the hardening of wire by drawing after annealing

bench hook *n* **:** any of various hook-shaped stops on a bench against which work may be pushed (as while planing or chiseling)

benching *n* -S [¹*bench* + *-ing*] **1 :** benches esp. around a room **2 :** ¹BENCH 6a(1)

bench jockey *n* **:** a baseball player who heckles the members of the opposing team ⟨all the *bench jockeys* on the circuit were quickly counting ten on every pitch Lefty made —G.S.Cochrane⟩

bench key *or* **bench winder** *n* **:** a watchmaker's adjustable clock or watch key

bench knife *n* **:** an adjustable stop with a projecting knife or hook that holds a piece of work on the bench

benchland \ˈ=,=\ *n* **1 :** a bench esp. along a river **2 :** a land surface composed largely of benches

bench lathe *n* **:** a lathe mounted on a workbench

bench–legged \ˈbench¦leg(ə)d\ *adj* [*bench leg* + *-ed*] **:** having the legs spread wide apart ⟨a *bench-legged* pony⟩

bench–made \ˈ=¦=\ *adj* **:** made on a bench usu. by hand **:** HANDMADE — used esp. of shoes

bench·man \ˈbenchmən\ *n, pl* **benchmen :** one that works at a bench: as **a :** a repairer of shoes **b :** one that cleans, fits, assembles, tests, or repairs component parts of a product **c :** a bakery worker who prepares dough for baking by kneading, shaping, weighing, and placing in pans **d :** a chemist who performs laboratory tests during the processing of sugar

bench mark *n* **1 :** a mark on a fixed and enduring object (as on an outcropping of rock or a concrete post set into the ground) indicating a particular elevation and used as a reference in topographical surveys and tidal observations **2 :** a point of reference from which measurements of any sort may be made

bench plane *n* **:** a plane (as a jack plane or smoothing plane) used by a carpenter or joiner in benchwork

bench press *n* **:** a small punch press mounted on a workbench

benchrest \ˈ=,=\ *n* **:** a sturdy table on which a heavy target rifle is cradled usu. by means of sandbags and a pedestal so as to ensure maximum steadiness when it is aimed and fired

bench saw *n* **:** a circular saw mounted on a bench

bench screw *n* **:** a long wood or iron screw used in operating the jaws of a bench vise or clamp

bench show *n* **:** an exhibition of small animals in competition for prizes on the basis of physical conformation and condition — compare FIELD TRIAL

bench table *n* **:** a projecting course at the base of a wall (as in a church) or round a pillar sufficient to form a seat

bench terrace *n* **:** an artificial land terrace with flat top and often nearly vertical side and used esp. in series to convert mountainous slopes to arable land (as in certain Old World vineyards)

bench warmer *n* **:** one that sits on a bench; *specif* **:** a substitute player on an athletic team

bench warrant *n* **:** a warrant issued by a presiding judge or by a court against a person guilty of some contempt or indicted for some crime — compare JUSTICE'S WARRANT

benchwork \ˈ=,=\ *n* **:** work done at a bench

benchy \ˈbenchē\ *adj* [¹*bench* + *-y*] **:** occurring in benches or tending to split horizontally — used esp. of a bed of coal or stone

¹**bend** \ˈbend\ *n* -S [ME, fr. OE *bend* bend, chain, fetter & MF *bende, bande* band, ring, stripe — more at BAND] **1** *obs* **:** a thin flat strip (as of iron) used for strengthening **2** *heraldry* **:** a diagonal band **3 :** the half of a butt or a hide trimmed of the thinner parts and containing the best quality of sole leather — see HIDE illustration **4 :** a knot by which one rope is fastened to another or to some object — **in bend 1 :** in a line in the direction of a bend — used of two or more heraldic charges **2 :** BENDWISE — **in bend dexter :** in bend — used only in contrast with *in bend sinister*

²**bend** \"\ *vb* **bent** \-nt\ *or archaic* **bended; bent** *or archaic* **bended; bending; bends** [ME *benden*, fr. OE *bendan;* akin to ON *benda* to bend, OE *bend* fetter — more at BAND] *vt* **1 a :** to constrain or strain to tension (as a bow) **b** *archaic* **:** to strain, brace, or bring into a tense condition **2 a :** to turn, press, or force with stress concentrated at specific points from straight, level, or even to curved, angular, uneven, or cambered ⟨~ a pipe⟩ ⟨a *bent* glass tube⟩ **b :** to press or force back to an original straight, level, or even condition ⟨~ a crooked bar straight again⟩ **c :** to force, prize, or crush from a proper, intended, or usable shape ⟨he *bent* the can opener⟩ **3 :** FASTEN ⟨~ one rope to another⟩ ⟨~ a sail to its yard⟩ ⟨~ a cable to the ring of an anchor⟩ **4 :** to make submissive **:** SUBDUE ⟨natives unwilling to be *bent* by colonial power⟩ **5 :** to determine usu. after considerable thought **:** RESOLVE — used in passive and with *on* or *upon* ⟨he seemed *bent* on self-destruction⟩ **6 a :** to cause to turn at an angle or on a curve from a straight line, course, or pattern **:** DEFLECT ⟨*bent* rays emerging from a prism⟩ **b :** to guide or turn toward **:** DIRECT ⟨Tictocq ~*s* his rapid steps in the direction of the headquarters of the Paris gendarmerie —O.Henry⟩ ⟨Santayana ~*s* his genius . . . to deal with the concrete facts of actual political life —*Times Lit. Supp.*⟩ **c :** INCLINE, DISPOSE, PREDISPOSE **:** induce a liking, inclination, or partiality or a distaste or antipathy in ⟨ignoring other peoples and ~*ing* their minds to the Buddhist concept of eternity —Christopher Rand⟩ **d :** to influence or constrain from a usual, expected, or individual course or pattern ⟨how society ~*s* its individual members to function in conformity with its needs —A.N.Whitehead⟩ **7 a** *obs* **:** to direct (as a weapon) with hostile intent **b :** to direct strenuously or with interest ⟨~ their efforts to the task⟩ **:** APPLY ⟨*bent* themselves to the work at hand⟩ **c** *Scot* **:** DRINK, GUZZLE ~ *vi* **1 :** to curve over or away from a vertical line or position; *specif* **:** to incline the body often in token of submission or reverence ⟨*bent* to the queen⟩ **2 a :** to move out of a straight line **:** be or become curving **:** CROOK, BOW ⟨trees ~*ing* under the weight of snow⟩ **b :** to have a direction or inclination away from a straight line **:** CURVE, TREND ⟨beyond the rocks the coastline *bent* west⟩ **3** *archaic* **:** to direct oneself **:** take one's course **:** TURN **4 :** INCLINE, LEAN, TEND ⟨an individual who always ~*s* toward his own tastes⟩ **5 :** to work vigorously ⟨sailors ~*ing* to the oars⟩ **6** *Scot* **:** to drink hard **syn** see CURVE — **bend an ear :** to listen closely ⟨*bend an ear* toward how the man in the street feels about this business —*Frontier*⟩ — **bend one's ear :** to talk to at length esp. to the point of boredom ⟨Humphrey *bent the ear* of . . . Charles Murphy for nearly two hours —*Newsweek*⟩

³**bend** \ˈbend\ *n* -S **1 a :** the act or action of bending ⟨a quick ~ of the body⟩ **b :** the quality or state of being bent or curved ⟨the graceful ~*s* of Gothic windows⟩ **2 :** something that is bent or curved: as **a :** a curved part of a stream, lake, inlet, or coastline **b :** the thickest and strongest planks in the sides of a wooden ship **:** WALES — usu. used in pl. **c :** a curved piece of pipe **d :** the part of a fishhook lying between the shank and the barb **3 bends** *pl but sing or pl in constr* **:** CAISSON DISEASE, AEROEMBOLISM; *specif* **:** the form of aeroembolism that is marked by intense pain in muscles and joints due to formation of gas bubbles in the tissues — usu. used with preceding *the* **4 :** the distance between a bow braced ready for use and its string **5 :** a stylistic effect produced by varying the pitch of a sustained note and commonly employed by brass-wind instruments in jazz bands

bend \ˈbe¦end\ *n, usu cap B* **:** the end of a railway car on which the hand brake is located

bend·a·ble \ˈbendəbəl\ *adj* [²*bend* + *-able*] **:** capable of being bent

¹**ben·day** \(ˈ)ben¦dā\ *vt* -ED/-ING/-S [fr. *Ben Day* process, after *Benjamin Day* †1916 Am. printer] **:** to produce or prepare by the benday process ⟨~ a plate⟩ ⟨a ~*ed* area⟩

²**benday** \"\ *adj, often cap B* [fr. *Ben Day* process] **:** involving or used in a method of adding tints made up of dots, lines, or other patterns to original copy, negatives, or plates for reproduction as line engravings

bended *archaic past of* BEND — **on bended knee :** kneeling or as if kneeling in supplication

bend·er \ˈbendə(r)\ *n* -S [ME, fr. *benden* + *-er*] **1 :** one that bends or folds: as **a :** an instrument or power-driven machine for bending **b :** a factory worker who bends and shapes wooden or metal parts by hand or by machine; *specif* **:** one that shapes wooden parts of furniture that have been made flexible by steaming **c :** a paper-products worker who folds blanks (as for boxes or bags) along scored lines to prepare them for further processing or to collapse them for shipment **d :** a paperboard suitable for folding — called also *bending board* **2 :** SPREE ⟨go out on a ~⟩ **3** *slang Brit* **:** SIXPENCE **4** *dial chiefly Eng* **:** an extraordinary specimen ⟨it's a ~ of a night —Rudyard Kipling⟩ **5 benders** *pl* **:** BENDER COTTON

bend·er cotton \ˈbendə(r)-\ *n* [³*bend* + *-er*] **:** cotton grown on land partly enclosed by the bends of the Mississippi river

ben·der gestalt test \ˈbendə(r)-\ *n, usu cap B&G* [after Lauretta *Bender* *b*1897 Am. psychiatrist] **:** a performance test requiring reproduction of the configuration in line drawings

bending *pres part of* BEND

bending moment *n, physics* **:** the resultant moment about the neutral axis of any cross section of a rod or beam of the system of forces that produce bending

bending shackle *n* **:** a shackle joining a chain cable to an anchor

bending slab *n* **:** a slab consisting of several large cast-iron blocks with holes for pins around which frames and other structural members of ships are bent

bend·let \ˈbendlət\ *n* -S [¹*bend* (in heraldry) + *-let*] *heraldry* **:** a narrow bend

bend over backward *vi* **:** to lean over backward

bends *pl of* BEND, *pres 3d sing of* BEND

bend sinister *n* [¹*bend*] *heraldry* **:** a bend drawn from sinister chief to dexter base — **in bend sinister 1 :** in a line in the direction of a bend sinister — used of two or more heraldic charges **2 :** BENDWISE SINISTER

bend sinister

bend–sin·is·ter·wise \(ˈ)=¦===,wīz\ *also* **bend–sin·is·ter·ways** \-,wāz\ *adv* **:** BENDWISE SINISTER

¹**bend·wise** \ˈben,dwīz\ *also* **bend·ways** \-wāz\ *adv* [¹*bend* + *-wise*] *heraldry* **:** in the direction of a bend **:** DIAGONALLY

²**bendwise** \"\ *adj* **:** having the direction of a bend in a coat of arms **:** DIAGONAL

bendwise sinister *adv* **:** in the direction of a bend sinister

¹**bendy** \ˈbendē\ *adj* [ME, fr. ¹*bend* + *-y*] *heraldry* **:** divided into an even number of bends, usu. six

²**ben·dy** \"\ *n* -S [Hindi *bhindī*] **:** OKRA

ben·dy tree \"-\ *n* [Marathi *bhēḍī*] **:** PORTIA TREE

bendy–wavy \¦==¦==\ *adj* [¹*bendy*] *heraldry* **:** composed of an even number of wavy bends

bene *var of* BENNE

be·neaped \bə, bē+\ *adj* [*be-* + *neaped*] **:** NEAPED

¹**be·neath** \bəˈnēth, bē-\ *adv (or adj)* [ME *benethe, benethen*, adv. & prep., fr. OE *beneothan*, fr. *be-* + *neothan* below; akin to OFris *nitha* below, OHG *nithana*, ON *nithan* — more at NETHER] **1 a :** directly under ⟨look at the illustration and read what is ~⟩ **b :** underneath esp. in relation to something screening, sheltering, surmounting ⟨an awning with chairs and tables ~⟩ ⟨the sky above and the earth ~⟩ **c :** in a low position (as in relation to something else) **:** lower down ⟨the mountains and the little towns ~⟩ **2 :** lower in rank, dignity, or quality ⟨a man intolerant of those above and merciless to those ~⟩ **3 :** on the further side **:** beyond what intervenes ⟨slashes in the glaze to show the beige pottery ~ —*New Yorker*⟩

²**beneath** \"\ *prep* [ME *benethe, benethen*] **1 a :** unworthy of **:** unbecoming or lowering to ⟨an occupation ~ his dignity⟩ **b :** too low, vile, or wretched for **:** far below ⟨his words were ~ contempt⟩ **2 a** (1) **:** at or to a level lower than ⟨the sun sank ~ the horizon⟩ **:** further down from ⟨a town located a mile ~ the crest of a hill⟩ (2) **:** at the foot or base of ⟨a chair ~ a wall⟩ ⟨a camp ~ a hill⟩ (3) **:** immediately under **:** UNDERNEATH ⟨the floor echoed ~ his tread⟩ ⟨a cellar ~ the first floor⟩ **b :** lower than (as in rank, dignity, excellence) **:** BELOW ⟨he in turn became something of a bully to the men ~ him —Sherwood Anderson⟩ **3 :** overhung, shaded, or screened by **:** BELOW ⟨~ an umbrella⟩ **4 :** under esp. in relation to something that exerts pressure, influence, control ⟨trees bent down ~ their weight of fruit⟩ ⟨the Higher Order ~ which men carry on their fantastic mummeries —W.L.Sullivan⟩ **5 a :** concealed by **:** covered by ⟨wearing a vest ~ his coat⟩ **b :** on the other side of **:** below the surface of **:** BEYOND ⟨detected moral truth ~ the veil of antique fable⟩

¹**be·ne·di·ci·te** \,benəˈdisəd·ē, -səd·i,-sə(,)tē, -ˈdikə,tā, -ˈdēchə,tā, ,bānāˈdēchē,tā *Brit usu* ,beniˈdīsiti\ *n* -S [ME, fr. LL, bless ye] **:** an invocation of a blessing ⟨the friar answered his reverend greeting with a paternal ~ —Sir Walter Scott⟩ ⟨a general and excellent custom is to substitute the *Benedicite* for the Te Deum during Advent —Percy Dearmer⟩

²**benedicite** \"\ *interj* [ME, fr. LL, bless ye, imper. pl. of *benedicere* to bless — more at BENEDICTION] *obs* — used to express a wish ⟨grace go with you, ~ —Shak.⟩

¹**benedict** *adj* [LL *benedictus*, past part. of *benedicere* to bless] *obs* **:** BLESSED, BENIGN, MILD

²**ben·e·dict** \ˈbenə,dikt\ *also* **ben·e·dick** \-ik\ *n* -S *sometimes cap* [after *Benedick*, newly married man in Shakespeare's *Much Ado about Nothing*] **:** a married man: *esp* **:** a newly married man who has long been a bachelor ⟨he had married our great-aunt . . . shortly before the death of our parents and so became our guardian while still a ~ —Mary McCarthy⟩

¹**ben·e·dic·tine** \,benəˈdik,tēn, -,tən — *the second is the usu pronunc in the order*\ *n* -S *usu cap* [after St. *Benedict* of Nursia †*ab* 543, who founded it] **:** a member of a monastic order founded in the sixth century and noted esp. for its liturgical worship and its scholarly activities

²**benedictine** \¦==¦=(,)=\ *adj, usu cap* **1 :** of or relating to St. Benedict of Nursia **2 :** of or relating to the Benedictines

ben·e·dic·tin·ism \,==ˈ=,tə,nizəm, -,tē,n-\ *n* -S *usu cap* **:** the state, system, or practices of Benedictines

ben·e·dic·tion \,benəˈdikshən\ *n* -S [ME *benediccioun*, fr LL *benediction-, benedictio*, fr. *benedictus* (past part. of *benedicere* to bless, fr. L *bene dicere* to praise, speak well, fr. *bene* well + *dicere* to say) + L *-ion, -io* -ion — more at BOUNTY, DICTION] **1 :** an expression or utterance of blessing or good wishes ⟨departing with his parents' ~⟩ ⟨yearning for the ~ of the New York critics —*Time*⟩ **2 :** the invocation of a blessing on persons or things being dedicated to God: as **a :** the short blessing pronounced by a clergyman with which public worship is concluded **b :** the blessing before or after meals **c :** the Roman Catholic rite of solemnly blessing and hallowing (as a person or house) or of solemnly blessing and dedicating (as bells or vestments intended for sacred use) **3 :** a Roman Catholic service consisting of the exposition of the eucharistic Host in the monstrance, the incensing of the exposed Host, at least one prescribed hymn, sometimes a prayer, and the blessing of the people by a formal sign of the cross made with the monstrance containing the Host **4 :** something that blesses or promotes goodness, well-being, or betterment ⟨the Mexican sun is no pleasant ~ like our northern sun —Gertrude Diamant⟩ **5 :** a prayer or scripture passage pronounced to dismiss a meeting

¹**ben·e·dic·tion·al** \-shənᵊl,-shnəl\ *n* -S [ML *benedictionale*, fr. neut. of *benedictionalis* of a benediction (in *benedictionalis liber* book of benedictions), fr. LL *benediction-, benedictio* + L *-alis* -al] **:** a book of benedictions

²**benedictional** \¦==¦=(=)=\ *adj* [*benediction* + *-al*] **:** of or relating to benediction ⟨the ~ attitude of the child —Herbert Read⟩

ben·e·dic·tive \¦==¦. iv\ *adj* [LL *benedictus* (past part. of *benedicere* to bless) + E *-ive*] *of a set of verb forms* **:** expressing a wish **:** PRECATIVE — used of an aorist optative in Sanskrit and of moods with similar grammatical meaning in other languages —**ben·e·dic·tive·ly** *adv*

ben·e·dic·to·ry \-t(ə)rē\ *adj* [*benediction* + *-ory*] **:** of or expressing benediction ⟨a ~ prayer⟩

ben·e·dict's test \ˈbenə,dik(t)s-\ *n, usu cap B* [after Stanley R. *Benedict* †1936 Am. physiological chemist] **:** a test for the presence of a reducing sugar in a solution (as urine) made by heating with a complex reagent containing sodium carbonate and citrate and copper sulfate, a colored precipitate being indicative of the presence of a reducing sugar

ben·e·dight \ˈbenə,dīt\ *adj* [ME, fr. LL *benedictus* — more at BENEDICTION] *archaic* **:** BLESSED

ben·e·fact \ˈbenə,fakt\ *vt* -ED/-ING/-S [back-formation fr. *benefactor*] **:** to act as a benefactor of

ben·e·fac·tion \ˈbenə,fakshən, ,==ˈ=\ *n* -S [LL *benefaction-, benefactio*, fr. L *benefactus*, past part. of *benefacere* to do good to (fr. *bene* well + *facere* to make, do) + *-ion-, -io* -ion — more at BOUNTY, DO] **1 :** an act or action of doing good esp. by generous donation ⟨the ~*s* of the American GIs to the . . . children of Korea —*Hartford (Conn.) Times*⟩ **2 :** a charitable donation **:** GRANT, GIFT ⟨this ~ totals almost $5 million —*Americana Annual*⟩

¹**ben·e·fac·tive** \¦==¦=tiv\ *adj* [L *benefactus* + E *-ive*] *of a linguistic form* **:** indicating that someone is benefited — used esp. of affixes and verb forms in various American Indian languages

²**benefactive** \"\ *n* -S **:** a benefactive form or set of forms in a language

ben·e·fac·tor \ˈbenə,faktə(r), ,==ˈ== *sometimes* ,==ˈ=,tȯ(ə)r *or* -,tȯ(ə)\ *n* -S [LL, fr. L *benefactus* + *-or*] **:** one that gives help or confers a benefit ⟨a ~ of mankind⟩; *specif* **:** one that makes a gift or bequest ⟨his endowments . . . placed him high among the ~*s* of the convent —Jane Austen⟩

ben·e·fac·tress \-==,trəs, ,==ˈ==\ *or* **ben·e·fac·trix** \-triks\ *n, pl* **benefactresses** \-trəsəz\ *or* **benefactrixes** \-triksəz\ *or* **benefactri·ces** \,==ˈfaktrə,sēz, -,fakˈtrī(,)sēz\ [*benefactor* + *-ess* or *-trix*] **:** a female benefactor

be·nef·ic \bəˈnefik, be-\ *adj* [L *beneficus*, fr. *bene* well + *-ficus* (fr. *facere* to make, do) — more at BOUNTY, DO] **:** of, having, or exerting a favorable or beneficent influence ⟨a ~ star⟩ ⟨a ~ force⟩

¹**ben·e·fice** \ˈbenəfəs\ *n, pl* **benefic·es** \-fəsəz, -,fis-\ [ME (also, "favor, advantage, benefit"), fr. MF, fr. ML, LL, & L; ML *beneficium* ecclesiastical and feudal benefice, LL, right, benefit, fr. L, kindness, favor, support, promotion, fr. *beneficus* + *-ium*] **1 :** an ecclesiastical post or office to which property or a determined revenue is attached (as a rectory, vicarage, or perpetual curacy) **2 :** a feudal estate in lands **:** FIEF; *specif* **:** an estate granted for life only and held on the mere good pleasure of the donor **3 :** GIFT ⟨a ~ of love —Amy Lowell⟩

²**benefice** \"\ *vt* **beneficed; beneficed; beneficing** \-fəsiŋ, -,fis-\ **benefic·es** [ME *beneficen*, fr. *benefice*, n.] **:** to endow or invest with a benefice ⟨a *beneficed* clergyman⟩

be·nef·i·cence \bəˈnefəsən(t)s\ *n* -S [L *beneficentia*, fr. *beneficus* + *-entia* -ence] **1 :** the quality or state of being beneficent **:** active goodness or kindness ⟨men who might be more profitably employed in works of a wider ~ —Clive Bell⟩ **2 :** a beneficent act or gift **:** BENEFACTION ⟨bestow your ~*s* generously but as though no such thing as gratitude existed —W.L.Sullivan⟩

be·nef·i·cent \-nt\ *adj* [fr. *beneficence*, after such pairs as E *benevolence: benevolent*] **1 :** doing or producing good ⟨a ~ influence⟩; *specif* **:** performing acts of kindness and charity ⟨a ~ king⟩ **2 :** productive of benefit ⟨~ bacteria⟩ — **be·nef·i·cent·ly** *adv*

beneficia *pl of* BENEFICIUM

ben·e·fi·cial \¦benə¦fishəl\ *adj* [*benefice* (in obs. sense "advantage, benefit") + *-ial*] **1 :** conferring benefits **:** contributing to a good end **:** HELPFUL, ADVANTAGEOUS ⟨~ animals⟩ ⟨a ~ organization⟩ ⟨~ effects⟩ — often used with *to* ⟨moist, cool summers, which are not ~ to such crops as maize —P.E. James⟩ **2 :** receiving or entitling one to have or receive in one's own right and for one's own benefit an advantage, use, or benefit that need not be monetary ⟨the ~ owner of securities⟩ ⟨a ~ interest in an estate⟩ — see CESTUI QUE TRUST; compare TRUSTEE

syn ADVANTAGEOUS, PROFITABLE: BENEFICIAL, the most general of the three words, may describe anything conducive to well-being, esp. to personal health and feeling and to social welfare ⟨only his daughter had the power of charming this black brooding from his mind . . . the touch of her hand had a strong *beneficial* influence with him almost always —Charles Dickens⟩ ⟨the relative ability of individuals and public bodies to make a *beneficial* use of the money —J.A.Hobson⟩ ADVANTAGEOUS stresses a choice or preference for the thing referred to over something else or over its lack or absence ⟨primitive rules of moral action . . . are all more or less *advantageous* and helpful on the road of primitive life —Havelock Ellis⟩ ⟨the republican government found it to be very *advantageous* to pay its troops promptly, for thereby a discipline was secured that surprised the Spaniards —J.L.Motley⟩ PROFITABLE suggests a pleasing return or remuneration in matters financial or in matters of education and character development ⟨the war boom demonstrated positively that mass production and distribution in books are both feasible and highly *profitable* —J.T.Farrell⟩ ⟨give . . . yourselves to *profitable* meditation at home —Robert Browning⟩

beneficial improvement *n* **:** an improvement on land that enhances the value of a property but is not necessary to prevent deterioration

ben·e·fi·cial·ly \-shəlē, -li *also* -shl-\ *adv* **:** in a beneficial manner

ben·e·fi·cial·ness \-shəlnəs\ *n* -ES **:** the quality or state of being beneficial

¹**ben·e·fi·ciary** \,benəˈfishē,erē, -shərē, -ri\ *n* -ES [ML *beneficiarius* (influenced in meaning by ML *beneficium*), fr L, privileged soldier, fr. *beneficium* favor + *-arius* -ary — more at BENEFICE] **1 a :** one who holds a feudal benefice **:** FEUDATORY, VASSAL **b :** one who holds an ecclesiastical benefice **2 :** one who receives something: as **a :** the person designated to receive the income of a trust estate **b :** the person named (as in an insurance or annuity policy) as the one who is to receive proceeds or benefits accruing **c :** a person in whose favor a letter of credit is issued entitling him to draw a draft or bill of exchange

²**beneficiary** \¦==¦=-\ *adj* [ML *beneficiarius* (influenced in meaning by ML *beneficium*), fr. L, of a favor, fr. *beneficium* + *-arius* -ary] **:** arising from, held as, or having a benefice ⟨~ services⟩ ⟨a ~ baron⟩

beneficiary heir *n, Scots law* **:** an heir who enters upon the estate of his predecessor with the benefit of an inventory that determines the exact limits of his liability for the predecessor's debts

ben·e·fi·ci·ate \,benəˈfishē,āt\ *vt* -ED/-ING/-S [Sp *beneficiar* to benefit, to derive profit from working land or a mine, to beneficiate (fr. *beneficio* benefit, fr. LL *beneficium*) + E *-ate*] **:** to process (as a raw material) so as to improve the physical and chemical properties: as **a :** REDUCE ⟨~ ores⟩ **b :** to concentrate or otherwise prepare for smelting (as iron ore) esp. by drying, sintering, or magnetic concentration — **ben·e·fi·ci·a·tion** \-,fishēˈāshən\ *n* -S

ben·e·fi·ci·um \,benəˈfikēəm, -kē,ům, -fishēəm\ *n, pl* **benefi·cia** \-ikēə, -kē,ä, -ishēə\ [LL — more at BENEFICE] *Roman & civil law* **:** RIGHT, BENEFIT, PRIVILEGE, BENEFICE

beneficium abs·ti·nen·di \-,äbztəˈnen(,)dē, -,äpst-; -,abztəˈnen(,)dē, -,dī\ *n* [LL, privilege of refusing] **:** POTESTAS ABSTINENDI

beneficium ce·den·da·rum ac·ti·o·num \-,kā,denˈdärəm-,äktēˈōnəm, -ä,rü-, -ō,nüm; -,sē,denˈda(a)rə,makshēˈōnəm\ *n*

[LL, right of yielding the suits] *Roman & civil law* **:** the right of a surety before paying his principal's debt to a creditor to insist that the creditor's cause of action against the debtor or any cosurety first be assigned to the surety making the payment
beneficium cler·i·ca·le \-,klerə'kālē, -ä,lā,-alē,-äle\ *n* [ML] **:** BENEFIT OF CLERGY 1
beneficium com·pe·ten·ti·ae \-,kämpə'tentē,ī, -tenchē,ē\ *n* [ML, right to a competency] **1** *Roman law* **:** the right of a defendant debtor bearing to plaintiff a special relationship (as ascendant, patron, husband, former partner, or one who has promised but not delivered a gift or dowry) to a judgment that will not deprive him of the means of existence **2 a** *civil law* **:** the right of a gratuitous grantor to reserve if indigent a competency to himself out of the subject of his grant **b** *Scots law* **:** this right extended to fathers and grandfathers with respect to provisions granted to their children
beneficium di·vi·si·o·nis \-də,wēsē'ōnəs, -də,vizhē'ō-\ *n* [LL, right of division] *Roman, civil, & Scots law* **:** the right of a surety sued by a creditor to compel the creditor also to sue the cosureties; *also* **:** the right of such surety to be held liable only for his proportionate share, with other solvent sureties, of the debt
beneficium ex·cus·si·o·nis \-(,)ek,skůsē'ōnəs, -,skəs(h)ē'ō-\ *or* **beneficium dis·cus·si·o·nis** \-də,skůsē'ōnəs, -,skəs(h)ē-'ō-\ *or* **beneficium or·di·nis** \-'ȯrdᵊnəs\ *n* [*beneficium excussionis* fr. ML, right of discussion; *beneficium discussionis* fr. LL, right of discussion; *beneficium ordinis* fr. LL, right of rank] *Roman, civil, & Scots law* **:** the right granted to a surety or cautioner to compel a creditor suing him first to sue the principal debtor — called also *benefit of discussion*
beneficium in·ven·ta·rii \-,in,wen'tärē,ē, -,in,ven·'ta(a)rē,ī\ *n* [LL] **:** BENEFIT OF INVENTORY
beneficium se·pa·ra·ti·o·nis \-,sepə,räd·ē'ōnəs, -,rāshē'ō-\ *n* [LL, right of separation] **:** SEPARATIO BONORUM
¹ben·e·fit \'benə,fit, *US sometimes* -,fət, *S sometimes* -ni- *or* -nē-, *Brit usu* -ni,fit; *US sometimes* -d·+V\ *n* -s [ME *benefet, benefit*, alter. (influenced by L *bene*) of *benfet*, fr. AF, fr. L *bene factum*, fr. neut. of *bene factus*, past part. of *bene facere* to do good, benefit, fr. *bene* well (adv. of *bonus* good) + *facere* to do — more at BOUNTY, DO] **1** *archaic* **:** an act of kindness **:** good deed **:** BENEFACTION ⟨bless the Lord, O my soul, and forget not all his ~*s* —Ps 103:2 (RSV)⟩ **2 a :** something that guards, aids, or promotes well-being **:** ADVANTAGE, GOOD ⟨no voice is louder than that of business in affirming the ~*s* of political democracy —W.H.Whyte⟩ **b :** useful aid **:** HELP, MEANS, AGENCY — used esp. in the phrase *without benefit of* ⟨the attack proceeded without ~ of artillery —P.W.Thompson⟩ **3 :** PAYMENT, GIFT: as **a :** financial help in time of sickness, old age, or unemployment — see BENEFIT SOCIETY **b** *obs* **:** a winning ticket or prize in a lottery **c :** a cash payment or service provided for under an annuity, pension plan, or insurance policy **4** *obs* **:** a natural advantage ⟨disable all the ~*s* of your own country —Shak.⟩ **5 :** an entertainment or social event to raise funds for a person, public program, or cause ⟨a ~ luncheon⟩; *specif* **:** a theatrical performance whose proceeds are given to a particular actor or a designated cause
²benefit \"\ *vb* **benefited** *or* **benefitted** \-,fid·əd, -,fitəd, *Brit usu* -fitid\ **benefited** *or* **benefitted** \"\ **benefiting** *or* **benefitting** \-,fid·iŋ, -,fitiŋ, *Brit usu* -,fitiŋ\ **benefits** \-,fits, *US sometimes* -,fəts, *Brit usu* -,fits\ *vt* **:** to be useful or profitable to **:** AID, ADVANCE, IMPROVE ⟨medicines that ~ mankind⟩ ~ *vi* **:** to receive benefit **:** become protected, aided, or advanced ⟨~ from experience⟩ ⟨a novel that would ~ by revision⟩
benefit of clergy [trans. of ML *beneficium clericale*] **1 :** the privilege claimed by the medieval church of demanding a trial and punishment by an ecclesiastical court for a member of the clergy accused of crime before a temporal court **2 :** the ministration or sanction of the church — used chiefly of the marriage rite ⟨a man and a girl living together without *benefit of clergy* —Wolcott Gibbs⟩
benefit of discussion [trans. of LL *beneficium discussionis*] **:** BENEFICIUM EXCUSSIONIS
benefit of inventory [trans. of LL *beneficium inventarii*] *Roman & civil law* **:** the right of an heir to have an inventory of his ancestor's estate made in the presence of a notary and representatives of the creditors of the estate upon the heir's election within 30 days after notice that he was instituted as an heir; *also* **:** the right to be liable for debts and legacies only to the amount of three fourths of the estate, the remaining one fourth being for the use of the heir
benefit of the doubt : the advantage derived from doubt about guilt, a possible error, or the weight of evidence
benefit society *n* **:** an association by which life insurance, sick allowances, the payment of funeral expenses, provision for old age, or other similar benefits are secured by means of regular dues or special assessments paid by its members
benefit theory of taxation : the theory that taxes should be considered as payments for services rendered by the state to the taxpayers and so proportioned
benefit year *n* **:** a one-year period during which workers may collect unemployment insurance benefits
ben·e·lux \'benᵊl,əks\ *adj, usu cap* [*Belgium* + *Netherlands* + *Luxembourg*] **:** of or relating to the countries of Belgium, the Netherlands, and Luxembourg esp. with reference to their customs union formed in 1947
be·net \bə̇, bē+\ *vt* [*be-* + *net*] **:** to ensnare with or as if with a net ⟨a man *benetted* by a woman's charms⟩
ben·e·ven·tan \¦benə¦ventᵊn, -ntən\ *adj, usu cap* [It *beneventano*, fr. ML *Beneventanus*, fr. *Beneventum* Benevento, province of Italy + L *-anus* -an] **:** LOMBARDIC 2
be·nev·o·lence \bə'nevələn(t)s\ *n* -s [ME, fr. L *benevolentia*, fr. *benevolent-, benevolens* + *-ia*] **1 :** benevolent feeling **:** kindly disposition to do good and promote the welfare of others **:** GOODWILL ⟨we shook hands and I again glowed with ~ to my fellow men —Richard Aldington⟩ **2** *archaic* **:** personal regard or affection ⟨his dislike of application and control prevented his acquiring the ~ of his superiors —James Mill⟩ **3 :** an expression of benevolence: **a :** an act of kindness **b :** a generous gift **4 :** a compulsory contribution or tax formerly levied by certain English kings with no other authority than the claim of prerogative
be·nev·o·lent \-lənt\ *adj* [ME, fr. L *benevolent-, benevolens*, fr. *bene* well + *volent-, volens*, pres. part. of *velle* to will, wish — more at WILL] **1 :** marked by a kindly disposition to promote the happiness and prosperity of others or by generosity in and pleasure in doing good works ⟨a ~ donor⟩ **2 :** marked by or suggestive of goodwill or benign feelings **:** lacking any hostility ⟨a ~ judge⟩ ⟨a ~ smile⟩ **3 :** arising from or prompted by motives of charity or a sense of benevolence **:** PHILANTHROPIC ⟨a ~ society⟩ — **be·nev·o·lent·ly** *adv* — **be·nev·o·lent·ness** *n* -ES
¹ben·gal \(')ben¦gȯl, -eŋ¦-, -¦gäl, '≈gəl\ *adj, usu cap* [fr. *Bengal*, region of the Indian subcontinent] **:** of or from the region of Bengal in northeastern India and East Pakistan **:** of the kind or style prevalent in Bengal **:** BENGALESE, BENGALI
²bengal \"\ *n* -s *usu cap* [fr. *Bengal* (region)] **:** any of various fabrics: as **a :** a silk or striped cotton woven in Bengal **b :** an imitation of such a fabric
bengal bean *n, usu cap 1st B* [*Bengal* (region)] **:** an annual plant (*Mucuna aterrima*) with long trailing stems used esp. in Brazil, Australia, and Ceylon for forage
bengal catechu *n, usu cap B* **:** CATECHU 1a
ben·gal·ee *like* BENGALI\ *n* -s *usu cap* [fr. *Bengali, Bengalee* native of Bengal] **:** any of several small tropical songbirds commonly kept as cage birds: as **a :** CORDON BLEU **b** *also* **bengalese :** SOCIETY FINCH
¹ben·gal·ese \¦beŋgə¦lēz, -eŋg-, -ēs; ben'gȯ,l-, beŋ-, -'gä,-l-\ *n, pl* **bengalese** *cap* [*Bengal* (region) + E *-ese*] **:** a native or resident of Bengal, India
²bengalese \"\ *adj, usu cap* **1 :** of, relating to, or characteristic of Bengal **2 :** of, relating to, or characteristic of the Bengalese
bengal gram *n, usu cap B* **:** CHICK-PEA
bengal grass *n, usu cap B* **:** FOXTAIL MILLET
bengal hemp *n, usu cap B* **:** SUNN
¹ben·gali *also* **ben·gal·ee** \(')ben¦gȯlē, (')beŋ-, -¦gä-, -li; 'bengəˌlē, -eŋg-\ *n, pl* **bengali** *or* **bengalis** *also* **bengalee** *or* **bengalees** *cap* [Hindi *baṅgālī*, fr. *baṅgāl* Bengal, fr. Skt *vaṅga*] **1 :** a native or resident of Bengal **2 :** the modern Indic language of Bengal

²bengali *also* **bengalee** *adj, usu cap* **1 a :** of, relating to, or characteristic of Bengal **b :** of, relating to, or characteristic of the Bengali people **2 :** of, relating to, or characteristic of the Bengali language
ben·ga·line \'beŋgə,lēn, -eŋg-, ,≈≈'≈\ *n* -s [F, fr. *Bengal* (region) + *-ine*] **:** a drapery and clothing fabric woven with a pronounced crosswise rib and made from the major textile fibers or a combination of these
bengal isinglass *n, usu cap B* **:** AGAR 1a
bengal kino *n, usu cap B* **:** BUTEA GUM
bengal light *or* **bengal fire** *n, usu cap B* **1 :** a bluish white light composed usu. of a mixture of potassium nitrate, sulfur, and realgar and used formerly in signaling and for illumination (as in theaters) — called also *Indian fire* **2 :** any of various colored lights or flares ⟨red and blue *Bengal lights* flared up —J.G.Frazer⟩
bengal monkey *n, usu cap B* **:** RHESUS MONKEY
bengal quince *n, usu cap B* **:** BEL
bengal rose *n, usu cap B* **:** CHINA ROSE 1a
bengal sage *n, usu cap B* **:** a camphor-scented medicinal mint (*Meriandra bengalensis*) of India
bengal tiger *n, usu cap B* **:** the southern short-haired tiger
ben·ga·si *or* **ben·ga·zi** *or* **ben·gha·zi** \(')ben¦gäzē, -gazē\ *adj, usu cap* [fr. *Bengasi, Bengazi, Benghazi*, Libya] **:** of or from Bengasi, joint capital of Libya **:** of the kind or style prevalent in Bengasi
ben·go·la \ben'gōlə, beŋ\ *or* **bengola light** *n, usu cap B* [irreg. fr. *Bengal*, the region] **:** BENGAL LIGHT
beni *usu cap, var of* BINI
beni amer \,benē'āmər\ *n, pl* **beni amer** *usu cap B&A* **1 :** a pastoral Tigre-speaking Hamitic people belonging to the same racial group as the Bisharin and Hadendoa **2 :** a member of the Beni Amer people
be·night \bə̇, bē+\ *vt* -ED/-ING/-S [*be-* + *night*, n.] **1 :** to overtake by darkness or night esp. before the end of a journey — usu. used in the passive ⟨there was no fear of our being ~*ed*, for in Norway at this season it never gets dark —Frances Pitt⟩ **2 :** to envelop in intellectual, moral, or social darkness ⟨what men . . . call religion now ~*ing* half the earth —John Wilson †1854⟩ — usu. used in the passive **3 :** to make dark esp. by depriving of light **:** OBSCURE ⟨the cliffs were so high that the bay itself was already ~*ed* —Clemence Dane⟩
benighted *adj* **1 :** overtaken by darkness or night ⟨~ travelers . . . have seen his midnight candle glimmering —W.B. Yeats⟩ **2 :** in a state of intellectual, moral, or social darkness **:** UNENLIGHTENED ⟨to some ~ souls even antiquarians seem peculiar —*Antiques*⟩ ⟨how long have you been in this ~ country —Charles Beadle⟩ — **be·night·ed·ness** *n* -ES
be·nign \bə̇'nīn, bē-\ *adj* [ME *benigne*, fr. MF, fr. L *benignus*, fr. *bene* well + *-ignus* (fr. *genere, gignere* to produce, beget) — more at KIN] **1 :** of a kind and gentle disposition **:** GRACIOUS ⟨a ~ teacher⟩ **2 a :** acting or appearing kind, gracious, or gentle ⟨an ominous frown gathered upon Mr. Littlepage's ~ forehead —Ellen Glasgow⟩ **b :** arising from or prompted by generous or gracious kindliness ⟨~ contributions⟩ ⟨~ actions⟩ **3 a :** tending to promote or indicative of happiness, goodness, or favorable outcome **:** SALUTARY, WHOLESOME ⟨a ~ balance between firmness and laxity⟩ ⟨a ~ rather than a malevolent phenomenon —Margaret Halsey⟩ **b :** FAVORABLE, PROPITIOUS ⟨born under a ~ planet⟩ **c :** of a mild type or character **:** not threatening health or life ⟨~ malaria⟩ ⟨a ~ tumor⟩ **:** having a good prognosis ⟨a ~ psychosis⟩ — opposed to *malignant* **4 :** forgivingly or understandingly tolerant ⟨viewed the antagonism shown his eccentricities with ~ complacency —Alvin Redman⟩ **syn** see FAVORABLE, KIND
be·nig·nan·cy \bə̇'nignənsē, bē-, -si\ *n* -ES **:** benignant quality ⟨filled with a special, protective ~ for her —Elizabeth Bowen⟩
be·nig·nant \-gnənt\ *adj* [*benign* + *-ant* (as in *malignant*)] **1 :** KINDLY, MILD, GENTLE ⟨a ~ face⟩ ⟨a ~ counselor⟩ **2 :** FAVORABLE, BENEFICIAL ⟨a ~ power⟩ **syn** see KIND
be·nig·nant·ly *adv* **:** in a benignant manner
be·nig·ni·ty \-nignəd·ē, -ətē, -i\ *n* -ES [ME *benignite*, fr. MF *benignité*, fr. L *benignitat-, benignitas*, fr. *benignus* benign + *-itat-, -itas* -ity] **1 :** the quality or state of being benign ⟨the angelic spinster . . . smiled with soft ~ —Arnold Bennett⟩ ⟨the ~ or malignancy of the tumor —*Biol. Abstracts*⟩ **2** *archaic* **:** a kind or generous deed, gift, or manifestation **:** KINDNESS
be·nign·ly \-nīnlē, -li\ *adv* [ME *benignely*, fr. *benigne* + *-ly*] **:** in a benign manner ⟨~ help a person in distress⟩ ⟨look upon his criticisms ~⟩ ⟨a ~ growing foreign trade⟩
beni–israel \,benē +\ *n, pl* **beni–israel** *usu cap B&I* [Ar *banī Isrā'īl* the children of Israel] **1 :** a people of Jewish descent living in the neighborhood of Bombay, India, and known to history at least as early as the 12th century A.D. **2 :** a member of the Beni-Israel people
ben·in·ca·sa \,benən'käsə\ *n, cap* [NL, after Giuseppe *Benincasa*, 16th cent. Italian who developed the botanical garden at Pisa] **:** a small genus of Asiatic herbaceous vines (family Cucurbitaceae) with large yellow flowers and fleshy fruit that is used for pickles —see WAX GOURD
ben·i·son \'benəsən, -əzən\ *n* -s [ME *beneson, benesoun*, fr. OF *beneïçon, beneïçun*, fr. LL *benediction-, benedictio* benediction — more at BENEDICTION] **1 :** BLESSING ⟨with no help except their hands and the ~ of God —A.E.Stevenson b.1900⟩ **2 :** the pronouncing of a blessing **:** BENEDICTION ⟨the prelate's ~⟩
bé·ni·tier \bānē·tyā\ *n* -s [F, fr. OF *beneoitier*, fr. *beneoit*, past part. of *beneïr* to bless, fr. LL *benedicere* — more at BENEDICTION] **:** a holy-water stoup
be·ni·to·ite \bə'nēd·ə,wīt, -ēd·,ō,īt\ *n* -s [San *Benito* co., Calif. + E *-ite*] **:** a mineral $BaTiSi_3O_9$ consisting of sapphire-blue crystallized barium titanosilicate sometimes used as a gem
¹ben·ja·min \'benjəmən\ *n* -s [by folk etymology fr. MF *benjoin* — more at BENZOIN] **1 :** BENZOIN 1 **2 :** any of several plants of the genus *Trillium* **3 :** BALSAM 4
²benjamin \"\ *n* -s [prob. fr. the name *Benjamin*] *slang* **:** a man's close-fitting overcoat
benjamin bush *n* [*¹benjamin*] **:** SPICEBUSH
ben·ja·min·ite \-mə,nīt\ *n* -s [Marcus *Benjamin* †1932 Am. museum official + E *-ite*] **:** a mineral Pb (Cu, Ag) Bi_2S_4 consisting of sulfobismuthite of lead, silver, and copper occurring in gray masses
benjamin tree *n* [*¹benjamin*] **1 :** BENZOIN 3 **2 :** SPICEBUSH
ben·ja·mite \-,mīt\ *or* **ben·ja·min·ite** \-mə,nīt\ *n* -s *usu cap* [*Benjamin*, youngest of Jacob's 12 sons in the Bible (Gen 35) + E *-ite*] **:** a member of the Hebrew tribe of Benjamin
ben·jy \'benji\ *n* -ES [perh. fr. *Benjy*, dim. of the name *Benjamin*] **1** *slang Brit* **:** ²BENJAMIN **2** *slang Brit* **:** ¹BENNY 1
ben marcato \¦ben+,-\ *adv (or adj)* [It, well-marked] **:** MARCATO — used as a direction in music
ben·ne *also* **ben·ni** *or* **bene** \'benē, -ni\ *n* -s [of African origin; akin to Wolof & Mandingo *bĕne* sesame, Bambara *bene*] **:** SESAME 1, 2
benne cake *n* **:** a candy consisting of a small flat cake of benne seeds boiled with sugar
ben·net \'benət\ *n* -s [short for *herb bennet*] **1 :** HERB BENNET **2 :** either of two American avens (*Geum virginianum* or *G. canadense*) **3** *in the writings of early herbalists* **a :** HEMLOCK **b :** GARDEN HELIOTROPE **4 :** DAISY 1a **5 :** BURNET SAXIFRAGE
ben·net·ti·ta·ce·ae \bə,ned·ə'tāsē,ē\ *n pl, cap* [NL, fr. *Bennettites*, type genus + *-aceae*] **:** a family of fossil gymnospermous plants of the order Bennettitales having strobili usu. bisexual and the female sporophyll more reduced than that of the male — **ben·net·ti·ta·ceous** \≈¦≈≈'tāshəs\ *adj*
ben·net·ti·ta·le·an \≈¦≈≈tə'tālēən\ *adj* **:** of, relating to, or characteristic of the order Bennettitales
ben·net·ti·ta·les \≈,≈≈'tā(,)lēz\ *n pl, cap* [NL, fr. *Bennettites* + *-ales*] **:** an order of fossil gymnospermous plants first known from the Carboniferous and probably becoming extinct during the Cretaceous that appear to have derived from the seed ferns but have megasporophylls aggregated into cones and with little resemblance to foliage leaves, that are in general structurally similar to the cycads from which they differ chiefly in having the reproductive organs on the trunk embedded in a thick external covering of persistent leaf bases, and that have been considered as possible ancestors of the angiosperms — see BENNETTITACEAE
ben·net·ti·tes \,benə'tīd·ēz\ *n, cap* [NL, fr. John Joseph *Bennett* †1876 Eng. botanist + L *-ites* -ite] **:** a genus of fossil gymnospermous plants (family Bennettitaceae) known only from seeds and parts of the fruits and often considered not demonstrably distinct from *Cycadeoidea*

ben·ni·seed *also* **beni·seed** \'benē,sēd, -ni-\ *n* [*benni* + *seed*] **:** SESAME 2
ben nut *n* [*⁷ben*] **:** ⁷BEN
¹ben·ny \'benē, -ni\ *n* -ES [prob. fr. the name *Benny*] **1** *slang* **:** a low-crowned broad-brimmed straw hat **2** *slang* **:** OVERCOAT — compare BENJAMIN
²benny \"\ *n* -ES [by alter. and shortening fr. *benzedrine*] *slang* **:** a tablet of amphetamine taken as a stimulant to the central nervous system
be·no *or* **bi·no** \'bē(,)nō\ *n* -ES [modif. of Sp *vino* wine, fr. L *vinum* — more at WINE] **:** a strongly alcoholic drink of the Philippines distilled from the fermented sap of certain palms — compare ³TUBA
ben oil *also* **behen oil** *n* [*⁷ben, behen*] **:** a fatty oil or semisolid fat that is obtained from ben and used esp. in cosmetics and in cooking
be·no·ni \bə'nōnē\ *adj, usu cap* [fr. *Benoni*, Union of So. Africa] **:** of or from Benoni, Union of So. Africa **:** of the kind or style prevalent in Benoni
be·north \bi'nȯrt(h)\ *prep* [ME *benorth*, fr. OE *be northan*, fr. *be* by (fr. *bī, bī*) + *northan* from the north, fr. *north* — more at BY, NORTH] *Scot* **:** north of
be·note \bə̇, bē+\ *vt* [*be-* + *note*] **:** to annotate excessively or absurdly
ben·rath line \'ben,rät-, -ät-\ *n, usu cap B* [trans. of G *benrather linie*, fr. *Benrath*, Germany, near which the isogloss dividing HG *machen* "to make" from LG *maken* crosses the Rhine] **:** one of a bundle of isoglosses crossing Germany roughly from Aachen and Düsseldorf to Frankfurt an der Oder and dividing High German to the south, with fricatives and affricates for proto-Germanic *p, t, k*, from the rest of the West Germanic speech area to the north and northwest, with proto-Germanic *p, t, k* remaining intact (as in E *pipe*, *that*, *to*, *make*, contrasted with G *pfeife*, *das*, *zu*, *machen*)
¹ben·sel *also* **ben·sil** \'ben(t)səl, -nzəl\ *n* -s [prob. of Scand origin; akin to ON *benzl* bent state of a bow, fr. *benda* to bend — more at BEND] *chiefly Scot* **:** sudden violent motion or action
²bensel *also* **bensil** \"\ *vt* **benseled** *or* **bensellled; benseled** *or* **bensellled; benseling** *or* **benselling; bensels** *chiefly Scot* **:** to strike violently **:** BEAT
bensh \'bench\ *vb* -ED/-ING/-ES [Yiddish *bentshen*, fr. LL *benedicere* to bless — more at BENEDICTION] *vt* **:** BLESS ~ *vi* **:** to say a blessing **:** recite prayers
¹bent \'bent\ *n* -s [ME, grassy place, bent grass, fr. OE *beonot-* (in place names); akin to OHG *binuz* rush] **1 a :** unenclosed pastureland **:** FIELD, MOOR ⟨curlews crying over the snow-patched ~ —John Buchan⟩ **b** *archaic* **:** HILLSIDE, SLOPE **2 a** (1) **:** a reed, rush, or reedlike grass ⟨a coastline grown over with sedge and ~⟩ (2) **:** a stalk of stiff coarse grass ⟨his spear a ~, both stiff and strong —Michael Drayton⟩ **b :** a beach grass (*Ammophila arenaria*) **c :** DOGSTAIL 1 **d** *or* **bent grass :** any grass of the genus *Agrostis*; *esp* **:** any of several important pasture and lawn grasses that are typically perennial, rhizomatous, resistant to adverse conditions, and noted for their fine velvety or wiry herbage — see CREEPING BENT
²bent \"\ *adj* [ME, fr. past part. of *benden* to bend — more at BEND] **1 a :** changed by bending or being bent so as to be no longer in an original straight, level, or even condition ⟨a boy fishing with a ~ pin⟩ ⟨a ~ automobile fender⟩ ⟨a ~ head and sloping shoulders⟩ **b :** braced by being bent ⟨a ~ bow⟩ **c :** CURVED ⟨~ glass⟩ **2 a :** strongly inclined **:** RESOLVED, DETERMINED — used with *on* or *upon* ⟨a country ~ upon world domination⟩ **b :** actively engaged or occupied — used with *on* or *upon* ⟨housewives ~ on spring cleaning⟩
³bent \"\ *n* -s [fr. *bend*, v., after such pairs as E *descend*: *descent*] **1** *obs* **:** something curved or crooked **:** BEND **2 a :** particular inclination or tendency **:** strong interest conducive to bias **:** BIAS ⟨the ~ of his mind . . . was at all times much to metaphysical theology —William Wordsworth⟩ **b :** a special and often inherent inclination, disposition, or capacity; *esp* **:** one facilitating ready and easy learning or mastery ⟨a decided ~ for language⟩ **3** *archaic* **:** a curved state or form **:** CURVATURE **4 :** capacity of endurance ⟨they fool me to the top of my ~ —Shak.⟩ **5 :** a framework transverse to the length of a structure (as a trestle, bridge, or long shed) usu. designed to carry lateral as well as vertical loads **syn** see GIFT
be'nt \(')bēnt\ *var of* BEANT
ben·tang \'ben·,taŋ\ *n* -s [Wolof *benteng, bentengi*] **:** CEIBA 2a
ben–teak \'ben·,tēk\ *n* -s [origin unknown] **:** the wood of an East Indian tree (*Lagerstroemia lanceolata*)
bent grass *n* [*¹bent*] **:** ¹BENT 2d
ben·tham·ic \(')ben¦thamik\ *adj, usu cap* [J. *Bentham* + E *-ic*] **:** of or belonging to Benthamism
ben·tham·ism \'ben(t)thə,mizəm, -ntə,m-\ *n* -s *usu cap* [Jeremy *Bentham* †1832 Eng. jurist and philosopher + E *-ism*] **:** the utilitarian philosophy of Bentham and his followers; *esp* **:** the theory that the morality of actions is estimated and determined by their utility and that pleasure and pain are both the ultimate standard of right and wrong and the fundamental motives influencing human desires and actions
ben·tham·ite \-,mīt\ *n* -s *usu cap* [J. *Bentham* + E *-ite*] **:** one that adheres to Benthamism
ben·thic \'ben(t)thik *or* **ben·thal** \-thəl\ *adj* [*benthos* + *-ic* or *-al*] **1 :** of, relating to, or occurring on the bottom underlying a body of water ⟨mud-dwelling ~ mollusks⟩ **2 :** of, relating to, or occurring in the depths of the ocean or the bottom underlying these depths
ben·tho·graph \'benthə,graf\ *n* -s [*benthos* + *-graph*] **:** an instrument consisting of a hollow steel sphere that contains cameras and lighting equipment and is designed for underwater photographic exploration at great depths
ben·thon \'ben,thän\ *n* -s [*benthos* + *-on* (as in *plankton*)] **:** organisms that live on the bottom — compare PLANKTON
ben·thon·ic \(')ben¦thänik\ *adj* [irreg. fr. Gk *benthos* + E *-ic*] **:** BENTHIC 1
ben·thos \'ben,thäs\ *n* -ES [Gk, depth; akin to *bathys* deep — more at BATHY-] **1 :** the bottom of the sea esp. in the deep parts of the oceans **2** [G, fr. Gk] **:** organisms that live on or in the bottom of bodies of water
ben·tho·scope \'benthə,skōp\ *n* -s [*benthos* + *-scope*] **:** a deep-sea diving instrument consisting of a hollow steel sphere capable of carrying an observer to depths of several thousand feet
ben·tinck \'benti(ŋ)k\ *n* -s *usu cap* [after John A. *Bentinck* †1775 Brit. naval officer, its inventor] **:** a triangular sail superseded by the storm staysail
bentinck boom *n, usu cap 1st B* [after J.A.*Bentinck*, its inventor] **:** a boom used to stretch the foot of the foresail in some small square-rigged ships
bent leg *n* [*²bent*] **:** a bowed condition of the forelegs of lambs suggesting and possibly being a form of rickets
ben·ton·ite \'bentᵊn,īt, -tə,nīt\ *n* -s [Fort *Benton*, Montana + E *-ite*] **1 :** a soft porous moisture-absorbing rock composed essentially of clayey minerals often of volcanic origin **2 :** any of numerous variously colored clay deposits containing montmorillonite as the essential mineral, characterized either by the ability to swell in water or by the ability to be slaked and to be activated by acid, and used chiefly in oil-well drilling muds, as fillers and plasticizers (as in paint and soap), as suspending agents (as in pharmaceutical preparations), and as carriers for agricultural chemicals — **ben·ton·it·ic** \¦bentᵊn¦id·ik, -tə¦ni-\ *adj*
ben tro·va·to \,ben·trō'vä,tō\ *also* **ben tro·va·ta** \-ä(,)tä\ *adj* [It, lit., well found, well thought up] **:** characteristic or appropriate but not true ⟨of Baudelaire, who was a bit overfond of shocking, is told this tale, which is probably *ben trovato* —C.H.Grandgent⟩
bents *pl of* BENT
bentwood \'≈,≈\ *adj* [*²bent* + *wood*] **:** made of wood that is bent and not cut into shape ⟨a ~ chair⟩
benty \'bentē\ *adj* [*¹bent* + *-y*] **1 :** of, relating to, or suggestive of bent ⟨the herb had a ~ stalk⟩ **2 :** abounding in bent ⟨a wide ~ moor —John Buchan⟩
be·numb \bə̇, bē+\ *vt* -ED/-ING/-S [ME *benomen*, fr. *benome*, *benomen* (past part. of *benimen* to take away, deprive), fr. OE *benumen*, past part. of *beniman* to take away, fr. *be-* + *niman* to take — more at NIMBLE] **1 :** to make inactive **:** DEADEN, STUPEFY ⟨a spirit of the blindest imitation . . . ~*ed* the intel-

lectual faculties —Van Wyck Brooks⟩ **2 :** to make numb esp. by cold **:** deprive of sensation ⟨the fearful cold that overtakes and ~s the traveler —John Burroughs⟩ **syn** see DAZE

be·numb·ing·ly *adv* **:** in a benumbing manner

ben·weed \ˈben,wēd\ *n* [origin unknown] *chiefly Scot* **:** TANSY RAGWORT

benz- *or* **benzo-** *comb form* [ISV, fr. *benzoin*; prob. orig. formed in F] **1 :** related to benzene or benzoic acid ⟨*benz*azide⟩ ⟨*benzo*pinacol⟩ **2 :** containing a benzene ring fused on one side to one side of another ring ⟨*benz*acridine⟩ ⟨*benzo*pyrone⟩

ben·zal \ˈben,zal\ *n* -s [ISV *benz-* + *al*dehyde] **:** the bivalent radical $C_6H_5CH=$ derived from benzaldehyde by removal of the oxygen atom — called also *benzylidene*

benzal chloride *n* **:** a colorless highly refractive liquid compound $C_6H_5CHCl_2$ made by chlorinating toluene and used esp. in the synthesis of benzaldehyde; α,α-dichloro-toluene — called also *benzylidene chloride*

benz·al·de·hyde \benz+\ *n* -s [G *benzaldehyd*, fr. *benz-* + *aldehyd* aldehyde] **:** a colorless nontoxic liquid aldehyde C_6H_5CHO that has an odor like that of bitter almond oil, that occurs in many essential oils (as bitter almond oil and peach-kernel oil) and is usu. made from toluene, and that is used chiefly in flavoring and perfumery, in pharmaceutical preparations, and in synthesis (as of dyes) — called also *artificial bitter almond oil;* see AMYGDALIN

benz·ald·ox·ime \,benzal'däk,sēm, -,səm\ *n* -s [ISV *benzaldehyde* + *oxime*] **:** a crystalline oxime $C_6H_5CH{=}NOH$ derived from benzaldehyde and known in two stereoisomeric forms usu. distinguished as *syn-benzaldoxime* and *anti-benzaldoxime* — compare STRUCTURAL FORMULA

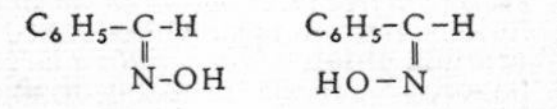

$C_6H_5{-}C{-}H$ / $N{-}OH$ *syn*-benzaldoxime — $C_6H_5{-}C{-}H$ / $HO{-}N$ *anti*-benzaldoxime

ben·zal·ko·ni·um \-ˈkōnēəm\ *n* -s [*benz-* + *alk*yl + *ammonium*] **:** a mixture of alkyl-benzyl-dimethyl-ammonium radicals $C_6H_5CH_2N(CH_3)_2R$ in which the alkyl groups range from C_8H_{17} to $C_{18}H_{37}$

benzalkonium chloride *n* **:** a white or yellowish white salt obtained as a bitter aromatic powder or gelatinous pieces that is used as an antiseptic and germicide

benz·am·ide \benˈza,mīd, -,məd, ˈbenzə,mīd\ *n* -s [G *benzamid*, fr. *benz-* + *amid* amide] **:** a colorless crystalline compound $C_6H_5CONH_2$ obtained usu. by the action of ammonia on benzoyl chloride; the amide of benzoic acid

benzamido- *comb form* [ISV, fr. *benzamide* + *-o-*] **:** containing the univalent radical $C_6H_5CONH{-}$ derived from benzamide ⟨α-*benzamido*cinnamic acid⟩

ben·za·mine brown 3GO \ˈbenzə,mēn . . . ,thrē,gēˈō\ *n, usu cap both Bs* **:** a direct dye — see DYE table I (under *Direct Brown 1*)

benz·anilide \benz+\ *n* [ISV *benz-* + *anilide*] **:** a white crystalline compound $C_6H_5CONHC_6H_5$ made from benzoic acid and aniline and used in the manufacture of pharmaceuticals and dyes

benz·anthracene \"+\ *n* [ISV *benz-* + *anthracene*] **:** a crystalline feebly carcinogenic cyclic hydrocarbon $C_{18}H_{12}$ that is isomeric with naphthacene and is found in small amounts in coal tar — called also *1,2-benzanthracene, benz[a]anthracene*

benz·anthrone \"+\ *n* [ISV *benz-* + *anthrone*] **:** a pale yellow crystalline ketone $C_{17}H_{10}O$ made from anthraquinone and glycerol and used as a dye intermediate

Ben·ze·drine \ˈbenzə,drēn *sometimes* benˈzedrən\ *trademark* — used for amphetamine

ben·zene \ˈben,zēn, ·ˈ·\ *n* -s [ISV *benz-* + *-ene*] **:** a colorless volatile flammable toxic liquid aromatic hydrocarbon C_6H_6 that burns with a luminous flame, that is usu. obtained commercially from the carbonization of coal (as from the light oil from coke-oven gas) or from certain petroleum fractions by catalytic dehydrogenation, and that is used chiefly in organic synthesis (as of styrene, phenol, aniline, and cyclohexane), as a solvent, and as a motor fuel (as for blending with gasoline) — called also *benzol*

ben·zene·di·a·zo·ni·um \,ben,zēn,dīəˈzōnēəm\ *n* -s [*benzene* + *diaz-* + *-onium*] **:** a univalent cation $C_6H_5N_2^+$ known best in the form of crystalline explosive salts (as the chloride $C_6H_5N_2Cl$ made by reaction of aniline hydrochloride and nitrous acid)

benzene hexachloride *n* **:** a compound $C_6H_6Cl_6$ occurring in several stereoisomeric forms, obtained usu. as a white to grayish musty powder containing some of these forms by chlorinating benzene in the presence of actinic light, and used as an insecticide — see LINDANE

benzene ring *or* **benzene nucleus** *n* **:** the structural arrangement of atoms believed to exist in benzene and other aromatic compounds showing six carbon atoms in planar symmetrical hexagonal fashion numbered 1 to 6 for convenience in designating the location of substituting groups and linked by alternate single and double bonds with each carbon attached to hydrogen in benzene itself or to other atoms or groups in substituted benzenes of which there is but one variety for each monosubstituted product (as toluene, phenol) but three for each disubstituted product — see META- 4b, ORTH- 3b, PARA- 2b(1); compare CYCLOHEXANE, PYRIDINE, STRUCTURAL FORMULA

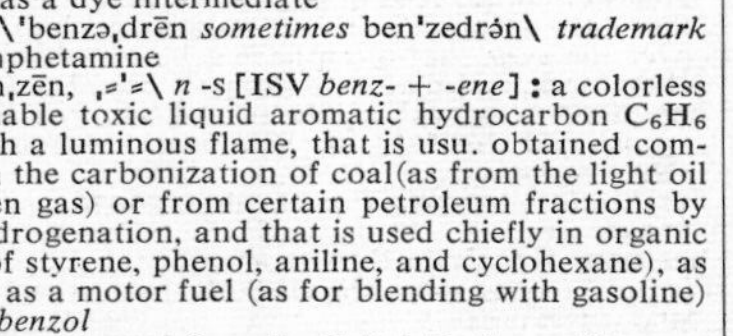

Kekulé formula for benzene (three methods of representation, the plain hexagon without double bonds being acceptable only when it cannot be mistaken for cyclohexane)

benzene series *n* **:** a series of liquid and solid aromatic hydrocarbons containing the benzene ring of which benzene is the simplest member and toluene the next higher member and from which hydrocarbons with condensed rings (as naphthalene) are sometimes excluded

ben·zene·sulfonate \ˈben,zēn+\ *n* [ISV *benzene* + *sulfonate*] **:** a salt or ester of benzenesulfonic acid

ben·zene·sulfonic acid \;··+. . .-\ *n* [ISV *benzene* + *sulfonic*] **:** a colorless crystalline acid $C_6H_5SO_3H$ made by sulfonating benzene and used chiefly in organic synthesis and in the form of derivatives as detergents

ben·ze·noid \ˈbenzə,nȯid\ *adj* [*benzene* + *-oid*] **:** like benzene esp. in structure or linkage **:** of the benzene series — sometimes contrasted with *alicyclic, naphthalenoid, quinonoid*

ben·zes·trol \benˈze,strōl, -,strōl\ *n* -s [*benz-* + *estrogen* + *-ol*] **:** a crystalline estrogenic diphenol $C_{20}H_{26}O_2$ derived from diphenyl-propane

benz·hydrol \benz+\ *also* **ben·zo·hydrol** \,benzō+\ *n* -s [ISV *benz-* + *hydrol*] **:** a colorless crystalline secondary alcohol $(C_6H_5)_2CHOH$ made usu. by reduction of benzophenone and used in organic synthesis

ben·zi·dine \ˈbenzə,dēn, -dən\ *n* -s [prob. fr. G *benzidin*, blend of *benzin* benzine and *-id* -ide] **:** a white or reddish gray crystalline base $NH_2C_6H_4C_6H_4NH_2$ made usu. by a series of reactions from nitrobenzene and used chiefly in making dyes (as Congo red), in chemical analysis, and in the detection of blood; 4,4′-biphenyl-diamine

benzidine yellow *n* **:** any of several azo pigments — see DYE table I (under *Pigment Yellow 12*)

ben·zil \ˈben,zil, -,zəl, ·ˈzil\ *n* -s [F, fr. *benzoin* + *-il*] **:** a yellow crystalline diketone $C_6H_5COCOC_6H_5$ made by oxidizing benzoin

ben·zil·ic acid \(ˈ)ben¦zilik\ *n* [F *benzilique*, fr. *benzil* + *-ique* -ic] **:** a white crystalline acid $(C_6H_5)_2C(OH)COOH$ obtained by warming benzil with alcohol and alkali; diphenyl-glycolic acid

benz·imidazole \,benz+\ *or* **benz·iminazole** \"+\ *n* -s [ISV *benz-* + *imidazole* or *iminazole*] **:** a crystalline base $C_7H_6N_2$ made by reaction of *ortho*-phenylenediamine with formic acid; *also* **:** a derivative of this base

ben·zine \ˈben,zēn, ·ˈ·, ·ˈzən\ *also* **ben·zin** \ˈbenzən\ *n* -s [G *benzin*, fr. *benz-* + *-in*] **1 :** BENZENE — not used scientifically **2 :** any of various volatile flammable petroleum distillates that are lighter than kerosene, consist of mixtures chiefly of aliphatic hydrocarbons, and are used esp. as solvents or as motor fuels: as **a :** LIGROIN **b :** GASOLINE — see PETROLEUM BENZIN

benzine cup *n* **:** a watermark-detector tray used in stamp collecting

ben·zin·er \ˈben,zēnə(r)\ *n* -s [*benzine* + *-er;* fr. the use of *benzine* in dry cleaning] **:** DRY CLEANER

benzo- — see BENZ-

ben·zo·ate \ˈbenzə,wāt, *usu* -ād·+V\ *n* -s [*benz-* + *-ate*] **:** a salt or ester of benzoic acid

benzoate of soda : SODIUM BENZOATE

ben·zo·caine \ˈbenzō,kān\ *n* -s [ISV *benz-* + *-caine*] **:** a white crystalline ester $NH_2C_6H_4COOC_2H_5$ used as a local anesthetic; ethyl *para*-aminobenzoate — called also *ethyl aminobenzoate*

ben·zo·dioxan \¦ben(,)zō+\ *or* **ben·zo·dioxane** \"+\ *n* -s [ISV *benz-* + *dioxan, dioxane*] **:** a compound containing a benzene ring fused to a dioxane ring; *esp* **:** PIPEROXAN

benzo dye \"+\ *n, usu cap B* [*benzo* fr. *benz-*] **:** any of numerous direct dyes — see DYE table I (under *Direct*)

ben·zo·flavine \"+\ *n* -s [ISV *benz-* + *flavine*] **:** a basic acridine dye that dyes leather yellow

ben·zo·furan \"+\ *n* -s [*benz-* + *furan*] **:** COUMARONE

ben·zo·hydrol \"+\ *var of* BENZHYDROL

ben·zo·ic acid \(ˈ)ben¦zōik-\ *n* [ISV *benz-* + *-ic*] **:** a lustrous white crystalline acid C_6H_5COOH occurring in benzoin and other resins, in cranberries, and combined in the urine of herbivorous animals, made chiefly by decarboxylation of phthalic acid and by oxidation of toluene, and used esp. as a preservative of foods, pharmaceuticals, and cosmetics, in medicine for the treatment of ringworm, and in organic synthesis

benzoic aldehyde *n* **:** BENZALDEHYDE

benzoic sulfimide *n* **:** SACCHARIN

ben·zoin \ˈbenzəwən, -,wēn, -,zōin, ·ˈzōən\ *n* [MF *benjoin*, fr. OCatal *benjui*, fr. Ar *lubān jāwī* frankincense of Java (prob. confused with Sumatra)] **1** -s **:** a balsamic resin that is obtained from various trees of the genus *Styrax* growing esp. in Sumatra, Java, and Thailand, that appears in commerce in yellowish to brown hard brittle tears or masses having a fragrant odor, and that is used chiefly in treating irritations of the skin, as a stimulating expectorant, as a fixative in perfumes, and as incense **2** -s **:** a white crystalline hydroxy ketone $C_6H_5COCHOHC_6H_5$ made usu. by condensation of two molecules of benzaldehyde in the presence of potassium cyanide **3** -s **:** a tree yielding benzoin **4 a** *cap, in some classifications* **:** a genus of aromatic shrubs comprising the American spicebush and certain other plants often included in the genus *Lindera* **b** -s **:** a plant of the genus *Benzoin; esp* **:** SPICEBUSH 1

ben·zoi·nat·ed \¦benzəwə¦nād·əd, -¦zōə¦n-, -¦zōi¦n-\ *adj* **:** containing or impregnated with benzoin resin ⟨~ lard⟩

ben·zol \ˈben,zōl, -ōl\ *also* **ben·zole** \-ōl\ *n* -s [G, fr. *benz-* + *-ol*] **:** BENZENE; *also* **:** a mixture containing other aromatic hydrocarbons as well as benzene ⟨motor ~⟩ — usu. used commercially

ben·zo·lize \ˈbenzə,līz\ *vt* -ED/-ING/-S [*benzol* + *-ize*] **:** to treat with benzene

ben·zo·ni·trile \¦ben(,)zō¦nī·trəl\ *n* -s [G *benzonitril*, fr. *benz-* + *nitril* nitrile] **:** a colorless toxic oily compound C_6H_5CN of almond-oil odor made by fusing a mixture of sodium cyanide and sodium benzenesulfonate and in other ways and used chiefly as a solvent for synthetic resins — called also *cyanobenzene, phenyl cyanide*

ben·zo·phe·none \,·(,)··ˈnōn, -ˈfē,nōn\ *n* -s [ISV *benz-* + *-phenone*] **:** a colorless crystalline ketone $C_6H_5COC_6H_5$ with a roselike odor made by the pyrolysis of calcium benzoate or from benzene and carbon tetrachloride by the Friedel-Crafts reaction and used chiefly in perfumery — called also *diphenyl ketone*

ben·zo·purpurine \¦ben(,)zō+\ *also* **ben·zo·purpurin** \"+\ *n* -s *often cap* [ISV *benz-* + *purpurine, purpurin*] **:** any of several closely related direct disazo red dyes: as **a** *or* **benzopurpurine 4B :** a red dye made from *ortho*-tolidine and naphthionic acid and used on cellulosic textiles and as an indicator and plasma stain — see DYE table I (under *Direct Red 2*) **b** *or* **benzopurpurine 10B :** a carmine-red dye made from *ortho*-dianisidine and naphthionic acid — see DYE table I (under *Direct Red 7*)

ben·zo·pyrene \"+\ *or* **benz·pyrene** \benz+\ *n* -s [ISV *benz-* + *pyrene*] **:** a yellow crystalline cancer-producing hydrocarbon $C_{20}H_{12}$ found in coal tar

ben·zo·quinone \¦ben(,)zō+\ *n* -s [ISV *benz-* + *quinone*] **:** QUINONE 1

ben·zo·sul·fi·mide \ˈben(,)zōˈsəlfə,mīd\ *n* -s [*benz-* + *sulf-* + *imide*] **:** SACCHARIN

ben·zo·thiazole \¦ben(,)zō+\ *n* -s [ISV *benz-* + *thiazole*] **:** a liquid compound C_7H_5NS made by cyclization from *ortho*-amino-thiophenol and formaldehyde well known as a parent compound of mercaptobenzothiazole and many dyes

ben·zo·thiophene \"+\ *n* -s [ISV *benz-* + *thiophene*] **:** THIANAPHTHENE

ben·zo·triazole \"+\ *n* -s [ISV *benz-* + *triazole*] **:** a white crystalline compound $C_6H_5N_3$ made by the action of nitrous acid on *ortho*-phenylenediamine and used in photographic developing solutions as an antifoggant

ben·zo·trichloride \"+\ *n* -s [ISV *benz-* + *trichloride*] **:** a colorless highly refractive liquid compound $C_6H_5CCl_3$ made by the action of chlorine on boiling toluene and used chiefly in the manufacture of dyes; α,α,α-trichloro-toluene

benzoxy- *comb form* [ISV *benz-* + *oxy-*] **:** containing the benzoate radical $C_6H_5COO{-}$; benzoyl-oxy ⟨*benzoxy*acetanilide⟩

ben·zo·yl \ˈbenzəwəl, -,wēl\ *n* -s [G — more at -YL] **:** the radical $C_6H_5CO{-}$ of benzoic acid — compare -YL

benzoyl acetyl peroxide *n* **:** ACETYL BENZOYL PEROXIDE

ben·zo·yl·ate \ˈbenzōə,lāt, ,·ˈ··,·\ *vt* -ED/-ING/-S [*benzoyl* + *-ate*] **:** to introduce benzoyl into (a compound) — **ben·zo·yl·a·tion** \,·(,)···ˈlāshən\ *n* -s

benzoyl chloride *n* **:** a colorless very pungent liquid compound C_6H_5COCl made by partial hydrolysis of benzotrichloride and in other ways and used chiefly in organic synthesis (as of dyes)

ben·zo·yl·glycine \¦benzəwəl, -,wēl+\ *n* -s [*benzoyl* + *glycine*] **:** HIPPURIC ACID

benzoyl peroxide *n* **:** a white crystalline flammable compound $(C_6H_5CO)_2O_2$ made usu. by reaction of benzoyl chloride with sodium peroxide and used chiefly in initiating vinyl-type polymerizations and in bleaching (as flour, fats, oils)

benz·pyr·in·i·um \,benzpə̇ˈrinēəm\ *n* -s [*benz-* + *pyridinium*] **:** the substituted pyridinium ion $[C_6H_5CH_2NC_5H_4OOCN(CH_3)_2]^+$ derived by benzylation of dimethyl-carbamoyl-oxy-pyridinium; *also* **:** a salt containing this radical (as the bromide used to relieve postoperative urinary retention)

ben·zyl \ˈben,zēl, -zil\ *n* -s [ISV *benz-* + *-yl*] **:** the univalent radical $C_6H_5CH_2$ derived from toluene by removal of one hydrogen atom from the side chain

benzyl acetate *n* **:** a colorless fragrant liquid ester $CH_3COOCH_2C_6H_5$ occurring in jasmine oil and other essential oils, made synthetically, and used chiefly in perfumery

benzyl alcohol *n* **:** a colorless liquid primary alcohol $C_6H_5CH_2OH$ occurring free and in the form of esters in many essential oils, made usu. by hydrolysis of benzyl chloride, and used chiefly as a solvent and in making esters

ben·zyl·amine \¦ben,zil, -zēl+\ *n* -s [ISV *benzyl* + *amine*] **:** a colorless liquid base $C_6H_5CH_2NH_2$ made synthetically (as by the action of ammonia on benzyl chloride)

ben·zyl·ate \ˈbenzə,lāt\ *vt* -ED/-ING/-S [*benzyl* + *-ate*] **:** to introduce benzyl into (a compound) — **ben·zyl·a·tion** \,··ˈlāshən\ *n* -s

benzyl benzoate *n* **:** a colorless oily ester $C_6H_5COOCH_2C_6H_5$ occurring esp. in balsams (as balsam of Peru), made synthetically, and used chiefly in medicine as an antispasmodic and in the form of a lotion as a scabicide and in perfumery as a fixative and solvent

benzyl cellulose *n* **:** any of various white granular thermoplastic substances made by benzylating alkali cellulose and used similarly to ethyl cellulose

benzyl chloride *n* **:** a colorless pungent lacrimatory liquid compound $C_6H_5CH_2Cl$ made usu. by treating boiling toluene with chlorine and used chiefly in organic synthesis (as of pharmaceuticals and dyes); α-chloro-toluene

benzyl cinnamate *n* **:** an aromatic white crystalline ester $C_{16}H_{14}O_2$ found in balsam of Peru, balsam of Tolu, and storax and used in perfumery — called also *cinnamein*

benzyl cyanide *n* **:** an oily aromatic compound $C_6H_5CH_2CN$ found in some essential oils (as of garden peppergrass) and also made synthetically; phenyl-acetonitrile

ben·zyl·ic \(ˈ)ben¦zilik, -ēk\ *adj* [ISV *benzyl* + *-ic*] **:** relating to benzyl

ben·zyl·i·dene \benˈzilə,dēn\ *n* -s [ISV *benzyl* + *-idene*] **:** BENZAL

benzylidene chloride *n* **:** BENZAL CHLORIDE

ben·zyl·oxy \¦benzə̇¦läksē\ *adj* [*benzyloxy-*] **:** relating to or containing the radical $C_6H_5CH_2O{-}$

benzyloxy- *comb form* [ISV *benzyl* + *oxy-*] **:** containing the univalent radical $C_6H_5CH_2O{-}$ composed of benzyl united with oxygen ⟨*benzyloxy*amine⟩

ben·zyl·penicillin \¦benzəl, -(,)zēl+\ *n* [*benzyl* + *penicillin*] **:** PENICILLIN 2b

benzyl violet *n, often cap B&V* **:** a basic dye — see DYE table I (under *Basic Violet 13*)

be·o·thuk \ˈbāə,thu̇k\ *n, pl* **beothuk** *or* **beothuks** *usu cap* **1 a :** an extinct Indian people of Newfoundland **b :** a member of such people **2 :** a language of the Beothuk people that is of unknown relationship — **be·o·thuk·an** \ˈ··,·kən\ *adj*

be·paint \bə̇, bē+\ *vt* [*be-* + *paint*] **1** *archaic* **:** to paint esp. heavily or gaudily **:** smear with paint ⟨~*ed* Indians⟩ **2** *archaic* **:** to tinge with color ⟨the ~*ed* sky of dawn⟩

be·paper \bə̇, bē+\ *vt* [*be-* + *paper*] **:** to cover with paper **:** encumber with papers

be·patched \bə̇, bē+\ *adj* [*be-* + *patched*] **1 :** covered with patches **:** wearing patched clothing **2 :** wearing an ornamental patch or patches on the face

be·picture \bə̇, bē+\ *vt* [*be-* + *picture*, n.] **1 :** to adorn with or as if with a picture or pictures **2 :** to show in or as if in a picture

be·plaster \bə̇, bē+\ *vt* [*be-* + *plaster*] **:** to plaster over **:** cover profusely ⟨a uniform ~*ed* with medals⟩ **:** smear thickly ⟨~*ing* her cheeks with cosmetics⟩

be·powder \bə̇, bē+\ *vt* [*be-* + *powder*] **:** to cover with powder

be·praise \bə̇, bē+\ *vt* [*be-* + *praise*] **:** to praise greatly, repeatedly, or excessively

be·pranked \bə̇, bē+\ *adj* [*be-* + *pranked*] **:** showily dressed or adorned

be·puffed \bə̇, bē+\ *adj* [*be-* + *puffed*] **1 :** praised unduly **2 :** very puffy or swollen

be·puzzle \bə̇, bē+\ *vt* [*be-* + *puzzle*] **:** to puzzle greatly — **be·puzzlement** \"+\ *n* -s

be·queath \bə̇ˈkwēth, -ēth, bē-\ *vt* -ED/-ING/-S [ME *bequethen* to say, assign, allot, bequeath, fr. OE *becwethan*, fr. *be-* + *cwethan* to say — more at QUOTH] **1 a :** to give or leave by will **:** give by formal declaration so that the thing given passes into the ownership of the recipient after the death of the donor **:** give by testament — used esp. of personalty; compare DEVISE **b :** to hand down (as to successors or posterity) **:** TRANSMIT ⟨politicosocial myths ~*ed* to us by the 19th century —Ignazio Silone⟩ **2** *archaic* **:** to consign trusting that the recipient will accept and take care of that which is consigned **:** ENTRUST, COMMEND **3** *obs* **:** to assign or make over by formal declaration so as to give the recipient immediate possession **:** transfer ownership of **syn** see WILL

be·queath·al \-əl\ *n* -s **:** BEQUEST

be·queath·ment \-mənt\ *n* -s **:** BEQUEST

be·quest \bə̇ˈkwest, bē- *sometimes* ˈbē,k-\ *n* -s [ME *bequeste*, irreg. fr. *bequethen* to bequeath] **1 :** the action of bequeathing **2 :** something (as personal property) bequeathed **:** LEGACY

ber \ˈbe(ə)r\ *n, pl* **ber** *also* **bers** [Hindi, fr. Skt *badara*] **:** JUJUBE 1

be·rai·rou \bəˈrī,rau̇\ *n* -s [prob. native name in New Zealand] **:** RED KAURI

be·ra·kah *or* **be·ra·chah** \bəˈrä(,)kä, ·,·ˈ·\ *n, pl* **bera·koth** *or* **bera·choth** \-kōth, -ōt,-ōs\ *or* **bera·kot** *or* **bera·chot** \-ōt,-ōs\ [Heb *bərākhāh* blessing] *Jewish relig* **:** BENEDICTION, BLESSING ⟨the kiddush is a well-known ~⟩

be·rat *or* **ba·rat** \bəˈrät\ *n* -s [Turk *berat*, fr. Ar *barā'ah*] **:** a formal authorization granting a privilege or conferring a dignity issued by a sovereign in the Near East

be·rate \bə̇ˈrāt, bē-, *usu* -ād·+V\ *vt* -ED/-ING/-S [*be-* + *rate* (to chide)] **:** to heap reproaches on **:** criticize vigorously ⟨hearing Ed Hall ~ a farmer who doubted the practicability of the machine —Sherwood Anderson⟩ **:** scold or chide vehemently ⟨an Italian shrew *berating* her unemployed husband —John McCarten⟩ **syn** see SCOLD

berattle *vt* [*be-* + *rattle*] *obs* **:** to scold at **:** cry down

be·raun·ite \bəˈrau̇,nīt, bāˈr-, ˈbā,r-\ *n* -s [G *beraunit*, fr. *Beraun* (Beroun), Czechoslovakia + G *-it* -ite] **:** a mineral consisting of a hydrous basic iron phosphate commonly in brown or dark red druses or radiated globules

beray *vt* -ED/-ING/-S [*be-* + *ray* (soil)] *obs* **:** to spatter with dirt or filth; *esp* **:** to defile with excrement

ber·ba·mine \ˈbərbə,mēn, -,mən\ *n* -s [ISV *berberine* + *amine;* orig. formed as G *berbamin*] **:** a crystalline alkaloid $C_{37}H_{40}N_2O_6$ found esp. in barberry

ber·ber \ˈbərbər; ˈbəbə(r), ˈbəib-\ *n* -s *cap* [Ar *Barbar*] **1 :** a member of a Caucasoid people of northern Africa west of Tripoli closely related to southern Europeans, Egyptians, and Ethiopians **2 :** a branch of the Afro-Asiatic language family comprising languages spoken by minorities in No. Africa and the Sahara **3 :** any one of the Berber languages or the whole group considered as one language with numerous dialects

ber·beri \ˈbərbərē\ *n, pl* **berberi** *or* **berberis** *usu cap* **1 :** a people of Mongol origin in the Afghan-Iran frontier region **2 :** a member of the Berberi people

ber·ber·i·da·ce·ae \,bərbərəˈdāsē,ē, bər,ber-\ *n pl, cap* [NL, fr. *Berberid-, Berberis*, type genus + *-aceae*] **:** a family of shrubs or herbs (order Ranales) having the sepals and petals imbricated in several series and the fruit either a berry or a capsule

ber·ber·i·da·ceous \¦bərbərə¦dāshəs, bər¦ber-\ *adj* [NL *Berberidaceae* + E *-ous*] **:** of or relating to the Berberidaceae

[1]**ber·ber·ine** \ˈbərbə,rēn, -,rən\ *n* -s [G *berberin*, fr. NL *Berberis* + G *-in* -ine] **:** a bitter crystalline yellow alkaloid $C_{20}H_{19}NO_5$ obtained from the roots of the barberry, goldenseal, and other plants and used as a tonic and antiperiodic

[2]**berberine** \"\ *also* **berberine tree** *n* -s **:** an African tree (*Xylopia polycarpa*) yielding a yellow dye containing berberine

[3]**ber·ber·ine** \ˈbərbə,rēn, -īn\ *adj, usu cap* [*Berber* + *-ine*] **:** of or relating to the Berbers or their languages

ber·ber·is \ˈbərbərəs\ *n* [NL, alter. of ML *barbaris* barberry, fr. Ar *barbāris*] **1** *cap* **:** a large genus of shrubs (family Berberidaceae) natives of the north temperate zone and of the Andes to Tierra del Fuego having prickly stems and yellow flowers succeeded by red berries — see BARBERRY **2** -ES **:** the dried rhizome and roots of certain barberries of the genus *Mahonia* that contain the alkaloids berberine, oxyacanthine, and berbamine — called also *Oregon graperoot*

berberry *or* **berbery** *var of* BARBERRY

ber·ceuse \berˈsə(r)z, -sœz; beəˈsœz\ *n, pl* **berceuses** \-z(əz)\ [F, fr. *bercer* to rock] **1 :** CRADLESONG **2 :** a vocal or instrumental composition of a tranquil or soothing character

ber·che·mia \(,)bərˈkēmēə\ *n, cap* [NL] **:** a genus of widely distributed woody vines (family Rhamnaceae) having bright green foliage — see SUPPLEJACK

ber·cy \(ˈ)ber¦sē\ *also* **bercy sauce** *n* -ES *usu cap B* [fr. *Bercy*, quarter of Paris, France] **:** velouté sauce with minced shallots, parsley, lemon juice, white wine, and butter

ber·dache \bə(r)ˈdash\ *n* -s [F *bardache* homosexual male — more at BARDASH] **:** an American Indian transvestite assuming more or less permanently the dress, social status, and role of a woman

be·re·an \bəˈrēən\ *n* -s *usu cap* [*Berea* or *Beroea*, ancient name for Veroia, town in Macedonia, Greece; Bire, Palestine; and Alep, Syria + E *-an*] **:** a native or inhabitant of the ancient city Beroea

be·reave \bə̇ˈrēv\ *vt* **bereaved** \-vd\ *or* **be·reft** \-reft\ **bereaved** *or* **bereft** *or archaic* **be·reav·en** \-rēvən\ **bereaving; bereaves** [ME *bereven*, fr. OE *berēafian*, fr. *be-* + *rēafian* to rob — more at REAVE] **1 :** to deprive esp. by death **:** STRIP, DISPOSSESS — used with *of* before that which is taken away ⟨the war *bereaved* them of their three sons⟩ ⟨*bereft* of all hope⟩

⟨*bereft* of their senses⟩ **2** *obs* **:** to take away (a cherished or valued possession) esp. by force or violence **syn** see DEPRIVE

be·reave·ment \-ēvmənt\ *n* -s **:** the state or fact of being bereaved **:** DEPRIVATION; *esp* **:** loss of a loved one by death

berendo *var of* BERRENDO

ber·en·gar·i·an \ˌberən'ga(a)rēən\ *n* -s *usu cap* [*Berengarius* (Bérenger de Tours) †1088 Fr. ecclesiastic + E *-an*] **:** one who follows Bérenger de Tours in denying transubstantiation

ber·en·ge·lite \ˌberən'gəˌlīt\ *n* -s [San Juan de *Berengela*, Peru + E *-ite*] **:** a brown resinous substance used in caulking ships

be·res·o·vite \bə'resəˌvīt\ *n* -s [F, fr. *Beresov*, Ural mts., U.S.S.R., its locality + F *-ite*] **:** a mineral perhaps $Pb_6(CrO_4)_3(CO_3)O_2$ consisting of a deep red lead chromate-oxide-carbonate

be·ret \bə'rā, be-\ *n* -s [F *béret*, fr. Prov *berret*, fr. OProv, cap — more at BIRETTA] **1 :** a soft flat visorless cap of woolen material orig. worn by Basque peasants **2 :** a woman's hat the design of which is based on the beret

beret 2

beretta *var of* BIRETTA

berettina *var of* BERRETTINO

berewick *n* -s [OE *berewīc*, lit., barley-village, fr. *bere* barley + *wīc* village — more at BARLEY, WICK] **:** a detached portion of farmland that belonged to a medieval manor and was reserved for the lord's own use

¹berg \'bərg, -ēg, -əig\ *n* -s [by shortening] **:** ICEBERG

²berg \'berk\ *n* -s [Afrik, fr. MD *bergh*, *berch*; akin to OHG *berg* mountain — more at BARROW] *chiefly Africa* **:** MOUNTAIN

berg adder *n* [²*berg*] **:** a small venomous snake (*Bitis atropos*) inhabiting the highlands of the Transvaal and the southern African uplands

ber·ga·ma \'bərgəmə, 'ber-, bər'gämə\ *or* **ber·ga·mo** \ˌbergəˌmō\ *or* **ber·ga·mot** \ˌbergəˌmō\ *n* -s *usu cap* [fr. *Bergama*, town in western Turkey] **:** a rug of long loose pile, strong geometric designs, and rich vivid colors

ber·ga·mo \'bergəˌmō\ *adj, usu cap* [fr. *Bergamo*, Italy] **:** of or from the city of Bergamo, Italy **:** of the kind or style prevalent in Bergamo

ber·ga·mot \'bərgəˌmät, -ˌmət, *usu* -d·+V\ *or* **bergamot orange** *n* -s [F *bergamote*, fr. It *bergamotta*, fr. a Turkic word akin to Turk *bey-armudu*, lit., prince's pear] **1 a :** an orange (*Citrus bergamia*) with a pear-shaped fruit whose rind yields an essential oil much used in perfumery **b :** any of several mints (esp. *Mentha aquatica*, *Mentha citrata*, *Monarda fistulosa*, and *Monarda didyma*) **2 :** the oil or perfume made from bergamot fruit **3 :** a snuff scented with bergamot perfume

bergamot camphor *n* **:** BERGAPTEN

bergamot mint *n* **:** a bergamot (*Mentha citrata*) with thick flower spikes and mostly ovate or elliptic obtuse leaves

bergamot oil *n* **:** a greenish or brownish yellow fragrant essential oil expressed from the rind of the fruit of a tree (*Citrus bergamia*) and used chiefly as a perfume (as in colognes)

ber·gan *or* **ber·gen** \'bərgən\ *n* -s *usu cap* [fr. *Bergen*, Norway] **:** a rucksack supported by a wooden frame and having a belt to fasten around the waist

ber·gan·der \bə(r)'gandə(r)\ *n* -s [origin unknown] *chiefly Brit* **:** the common European sheldrake

ber·gap·ten \bə(r)'gaptən\ *or* **ber·gap·tene** \-ˌtēn\ *n* -s [ISV *bergamot* + *-pten -ptene* (as in *eleoptene*)] **:** a crystalline lactone $C_{12}H_8O_4$ that separates from crude bergamot oil on standing — called also *bergamot camphor*

berg crystal \'bərg-\ *n* [part trans. of G *bergkristall*, fr. *berg* mountain (fr. OHG) + *kristall* crystal — more at BARROW] **:** ROCK CRYSTAL **:** transparent quartz

berg·da·ma \'bergˌdämə\ *or* **berg·dam·a·ra** \-ˌdamərə, -ˌdəˌmärə\ *n, pl* **bergdama** *or* **bergdamas** *or* **bergdamara** *or* **bergdamaras** *usu cap* [Afrik, fr. *berg* mountain + *Dama*, *Damara* — more at BERG] **:** a branch of the Damara

ber·gen \'bərgən, 'ber-\ *adj, usu cap* [fr. *Bergen*, Norway] **:** of or from the city of Bergen, Norway **:** of the kind or style prevalent in Bergen

ber·ge·nia \(ˌ)bər'gēnēə, -nyə\ *n, cap* [NL, fr. Karl A. von *Bergen* †1760 Ger. physician and botanist + NL *-ia*] **:** a genus of perennial spring-blooming herbs (family Saxifragaceae) often included in the genus *Saxifraga* but having large thick rootstocks that produce typical colonies or clumps of plants with very thick heavy leaves

ber·gère \(')ber'zhe(ə)r\ *n* -s [F, lit., shepherdess, fem. of *berger* shepherd, fr. OF *bergier*, fr. (assumed) VL *berbicarius*] **:** an upholstered armchair of a style fashionable in the 18th century

ber·ge·rette \ˌberzhə'ret\ *n* -s [F, dim. of *bergère* shepherdess] **1 :** a 16th century pastoral song or dance **2 :** an 18th century French song or other composition resembling the pastoral form

ber·ger rhythm \'bərgər-, 'ber-\ *n, usu cap B* [after Hans *Berger* †1944 Ger. neurologist] **:** ALPHA RHYTHM

berg·haan \'berkˌhän, -ån\ *n* -s [Afrik, fr. *berg* mountain (fr. MD *berch, bergh*) + *haan* cock, fr. MD *hāne*; akin to OHG *berg* mountain and to OHG *hano* cock — more at BARROW, HEN] **:** any of several southern African eagles; *esp* **:** BATELEUR

berg ice *n* [¹*berg*] **:** the ice of a broken iceberg

ber·gi·ni·za·tion \ˌbergənə'zāshən, -ˌnī'z-\ *n* -s [*Bergius* (*process*) + connective *-n-* + *-ization*] **:** subjection to the Bergius process

ber·gi·us process \'bergēəs-\ *n, usu cap B* [after Friedrich *Bergius* †1949 Ger. chemist] **:** a process of hydrogenating usu. powdered coal mixed with oil and a catalyst under heat and high pressure in order to obtain chiefly liquid products (as fuel oil and gasoline)

berg·mann's rule \'bərgmənz, 'berg-\ *n, usu cap B* [after Carl *Bergmann*, 19th cent. Ger. biologist] **:** a statement of the principle that within a polytypic wide-ranging species of warm-blooded animals the average body size of members of each geographic race varies inversely with the mean environmental temperature

berg·schrund \'berkˌshrünt\ *n* -s [G, fr. *berg* mountain (fr. OHG) + *schrund* crack, fr. OHG *scrunta*; akin to MD *schronde* crack, OFris *schran* sharp, Norw *skrunda* wooden box, OHG *scrintan* to crack open, OPruss *skrundos* shears — more at BARROW] **:** a deep and often broad crevasse or series of such crevasses frequently occurring near the head of a mountain glacier

¹berg·so·nian \(')berg'sōnēən, -nyən\ *adj, usu cap* [Henri Bergson †1941 Fr. philosopher + E *-ian*] **:** of or relating to Bergson or Bergsonism

²bergsonian \"\ *n* -s *usu cap* **:** an adherent of Bergsonism

berg·so·nian·ism \=ˌnēəˌnizəm, -nyə-\ *n* -s *usu cap* **:** BERGSONISM

berg·son·ism \'bergsəˌnizəm\ *n* -s *usu cap* [F *bergsonisme*, fr. H. *Bergson* + F *-isme* -ism] **:** the theories of the philosopher Bergson according to whom the world is a process of creative evolution in which the novelty of successive phenomena rather than the constancy of natural law is the significant fact, reality being regarded as time or duration that is the same as free motion and that is the expression of a vital impetus or creative force while the space world of science and common sense is taken to be an interpretation put upon sense images in the interest of practical activity and social cooperation and as a falsification of free-moving reality so that a true apprehension of reality is to be gained not by the analytic procedures of mathematics and science but by that intuition that can grasp wholes as such

berg·stock \'bərgˌstäk, *Ger* 'berkˌshtōk\ *n* -s [G, fr. *berg* mountain (fr. OHG) + *stock* staff, fr. OHG *stoc* — more at BARROW, STOCK] **:** ALPENSTOCK

berg till \'bərgˌtil\ *n* [¹*berg*] **:** lacustrine clay with boulders and other glacial debris dropped in it by melting icebergs

bergy bit \'bərgē-\ *n* [¹*berg* + *-y*] **:** a great chunk of ice broken free of a large ice body (as an iceberg)

berg·ylt \'bergəlt\ *n* -s [Sw or Norw *berggylta*, fr. *berg* rock (fr. ON *berg*) + *gylta* sow (pig), fr. ON — more at BARROW, GILT] **:** ROSEFISH

be·rhyme *or* **be·rime** \bə̇, bē+\ *vt* [*be-* + *rhyme, rime*] *archaic* **:** to use as the subject of a rhyme; *esp* **:** to lampoon in rhyming verse

be·rib·boned \bə̇'ribənd, bē-\ *adj* [*be-* + *ribbon* + *-ed*] **:** adorned with ribbons ⟨dressed in a child's shorts, blouse, socks, and ~ sailor hat —John Buchan⟩ ⟨colored lapels, ~ and bemedaled chests, and vertical rows of golden buttons —Nicolas Nabokov⟩

beri·beri \ˌberē'berē\ *n* -s [Sinhalese *bæribæri*] **:** a deficiency disease marked by inflammatory or degenerative changes involving the nerves, digestive system, and heart and caused by a lack of or inability to assimilate vitamin B_1

ber·ing·ite \'beriŋˌīt, 'bir-\ *n* -s [G *beringit*, fr. *Bering* island, Kamchatka, U.S.S.R. + G *-it* -ite] **:** a melanocratic alkali-trachyte rock composed of barkevikite, albite, and orthoclase

bering sea *adj, usu cap B&S* [fr. *Bering Sea*, part of the northern Pacific] **:** OLD BERING SEA

be·rith *or* **brith** *or* **be·rit** *also* **briss** *or* **bris** \bə'rith, 'bri-, -it,-is\ *n, pl* **beriths** *also* **brisses** [Heb *bĕrīth* covenant] **1 :** BERITH MILAH **2 :** the Jewish rite or ceremony of circumcision performed on the male child on the eighth day after his birth

berith mi·lah \-'mē(ˌ)lä\ *n* [Heb *bĕrīth mīlāh*] *Jewish relig* **:** the covenant of circumcision

¹berke·le·ian *or* **berke·ley·an** \'bər(ˌ)klēən, ˌbər'k-, *Brit. usu* 'bä(ˌ)k- *or* bä'k-\ *adj, usu cap* [George *Berkeley* †1753 Irish philosopher + E *-ian*] **:** of or relating to Bishop Berkeley or his system of philosophical idealism

²berkeleian *or* **berkeleyan** \'=ˌ==, (ˌ)='==\ *n* -s *usu cap* **:** one who believes in or advocates Berkeleianism

berke·le·ian·ism *or* **berke·ley·an·ism** \'= ==ˌnizəm, (ˌ)='==-\ *n* -s *usu cap* **:** a system of philosophical idealism first taught by George Berkeley maintaining that so-called material things exist only in being perceived and that the material universe is not independent reality but exists as a perception of the divine mind and also partially as perceived by the finite minds of men

berke·ley \'bərklē\ *adj, usu cap* [fr. *Berkeley*, Calif.] **:** of or from the city of Berkeley, Calif. ⟨*Berkeley* stores⟩ **:** of the kind or style prevalent in Berkeley

berke·ley·ism \'bərklēˌizəm, *Brit usu* 'bäk-\ *n* -s *usu cap* [G. *Berkeley* + E *-ism*] **:** BERKELEIANISM

berke·ley·ite \-ˌīt\ *n* -s *usu cap* [G. *Berkeley* + E *-ite*] **:** BERKELEIAN

berke·li·um \'bərklēəm (*the coiners' pronunc*), ˌbər'kēl-\ *n* -s [NL, fr. *Berkeley*, Calif., location of the Univ. of Calif., where it was discovered + NL *-ium*] **:** a radioactive metallic element discovered by bombarding americium 241 with helium ions — symbol *Bk*; see ELEMENT table

ber·ko·vets \'berkəˌvets\ *n, pl* **berkov·tsi** \-kəfˌtsē\ [Russ *berkovets*, fr. ORuss *bĭrkovĭskŭ*, *berkovĭskŭ*, fr. OSw *Biærkö* Björkö (Koivisto), fortress of Vyborg, U.S.S.R.] **:** a Russian unit of weight equal to 361.13 pounds

¹berk·shire \'bərkˌshi(ə)r, -iə, -ˌshə(r), *Brit usu* 'bäk-\ *adj, usu cap* [fr. *Berkshire*, England] **:** of or from Berkshire, England **:** of the kind or style prevalent in Berkshire

²berkshire \"\ *n* -s *usu cap* [fr. *Berkshire*, England, where the breed originated] **1 :** a breed of medium-sized swine black with white markings **2 :** a Berkshire swine

ber·le·se funnel \bə(r)'lāzē-, -äsē-\ *n, cap B* [after Antonio *Berlese*, 20th cent. Ital. entomologist] **:** an apparatus that separates and preserves small insects found in ground litter and consists of a sieve placed over a funnel connected at the bottom to a preserving bottle

ber·ley \'bərlē\ *n* -s [origin unknown] *Austral* **:** GROUND BAIT

¹ber·lin \bə(r)'lin; ˌbər'l-,bə̄'l-,bəi'l-, '=ˌ=\ *adj, usu cap* [fr. *Berlin*, Germany] **:** of or from the city of Berlin, Germany **:** of the kind or style prevalent in Berlin

²ber·lin \bə(r)'lin, ˌbər'l-,bə̄'l-,bəi'l-\ *also* **ber·line** \", -'lēn; bər'lēn, beə'l-\ *n* -s [F *berline*, fr. *Berlin*, Germany, where it was fashionable in the late 17th & 18th cent.] **1 a** *sometimes cap* **:** a 4-wheeled 2-seated covered carriage with a hooded rear seat **b :** an enclosed automobile body having at the rear of the driver's seat a glass partition with usu. one movable window **2** [by shortening] *sometimes cap* **a :** BERLIN WOOL **b :** something (as a glove) made of Berlin wool

berlin black *n, often cap 1st B* [¹*berlin*] **:** a black varnish that dries with an almost dead surface and is used for coating the better kinds of ironwork

berlin blue *n, often cap 1st B* **1 :** any of various iron-blue pigments **2 :** PRUSSIAN BLUE 2

berlin brown *n, often cap 1st B* **:** a grayish red that is yellower and duller than livid brown, bluer and duller than Pompeian red, and duller and slightly yellower than bois de rose — called also *iron minium*

ber·lin·er \bə(r)'linə(r), ˌbər'l-,bə̄'l-,-bəi'l-\ *n* -s *cap* [G *berliner*, fr. *Berlin*, Germany] **:** a native or inhabitant of Berlin, esp. Berlin, Germany

ber·lin·ite \(ˌ)bər'liˌnīt, 'bərlə̇ˌn-\ *n* -s [Sw *berlinit*, fr. N. H. *Berlin*, 19th cent. Swedish pharmacologist + Sw *-it* -ite] **:** a mineral $AlPO_4$ consisting of a hydrous aluminum phosphate occurring in colorless to rose-red masses (sp. gr. 2.6)

berlin porcelain *n, usu cap B* [¹*berlin*] **:** a hard resistant variety of porcelain

berlin red *n, often cap B* **:** ²BOLE 3

berlin ware *n, often cap B* **:** Berlin-porcelain ware

berlin wool *n, usu cap B* **:** a fine worsted yarn for knitting and embroidery

berlin work *n, usu cap B* **:** embroidery (as cross-stitch and needlepoint) usu. done with Berlin wool on canvas

ber·lock dermatitis \bər'läk-, 'bərˌl-\ *n* [F *berloque, breloque*, lit., charm for a watch or bracelet; fr. the pattern of the discoloration] **:** a brownish discoloration of the skin that develops on exposure to sunlight after the use of perfume containing ethereal oils

ber·loque \bər'läk, -lōk\ *n* -s [F *berloque, breloque* (also, charm for a watch or bracelet)] **:** a drumbeat in which one stick beats twice to the other's once and which is used as a signal for certain fatigue duties (as at breaking ranks); *also* **:** a corresponding trumpet call

berm *or* **berme** \'bərm\ *n* -s [F *berme*, fr. D *berm* strip of ground along a dike; akin to ON *barmr* edge, brim — more at BRIM] **:** a narrow shelf, edge, or path typically at the bottom or top of a slope or along a bank: as **a :** a ledge between the foot of the exterior slope and the top of the scarp of a fortification **b :** a narrow shelf near the top of a trench or dugout to prevent dirt slides and to provide supports for beams **c :** the level space between the edge of a ditch and the bank of earth excavated from it **d :** the bank of a canal opposite the towpath ⟨poorly constructed sections of the canal's ~ and towpath . . . were dangerously vulnerable to muskrat burrowings and flood pressure —S.H.Adams⟩ **e :** the shoulder of a road ⟨deer . . . were feeding on the ~ of the highway between the concrete and the guardrails —Norman Erickson⟩ **f :** the nearly horizontal portion of a beach generally bounded on one side or other by a beach ridge or beach scarp ⟨waves wash across the beach to the ~ —W.C.Krumbein & R.L.Miller⟩ **g :** BENCH 5a **h** *North & Midland* **:** TREE BELT

ber·man·ite \'bərməˌnīt\ *n* -s [Harry *Berman* †1944 Am. mineralogist + E *-ite*] **:** a mineral $(Mn,Mg)_5(Mn,Fe)_8(PO_4)_8(OH)_{10}.15H_2O(?)$ consisting of a reddish brown basic hydrous phosphate of manganese, iron, and magnesium

¹ber·mu·da \bə(r)'myüdə, *S also* -mü-; *attrib sometimes* 'bərˌm- *or* 'bə̄ˌm- *or* 'beiˌm-\ *adj, usu cap* [fr. *Bermuda* islands, western No. Atlantic] **:** of or from Bermuda **:** of the kind or style prevalent in Bermuda **:** BERMUDIAN

²bermuda \"\ *n* -s *often cap* [fr. *Bermuda* islands] **1 :** GERANIUM PINK 2 **2 bermudas** *pl* **:** BERMUDA SHORTS ⟨*Bermudas* . . . made from an older pair of trousers —Herbert Barsale⟩

bermuda arrowroot *n, usu cap B* **1 :** arrowroot obtained from a maranta (*Maranta arundinacea*) **2 :** the plant that yields Bermuda arrowroot

bermuda buttercup *n, usu cap 1st B* **:** a southern African bulbous wood sorrel (*Oxalis cernua*) cultivated for its showy yellow flowers

bermuda cedar *n, usu cap B* **:** a juniper (*Juniperus bermudiana*) endemic in Bermuda that has tough hard wood, scalelike leaves, and dark blue fruit

bermuda chub *n, usu cap B* **:** a gray percoid fish (*Kyphosus sectatrix*) striped with blue or yellow that is a common food and game fish of the warmer waters of the western Atlantic esp. about the Florida keys and Bermuda

bermuda cress *n, usu cap B* **:** WINTER CRESS

bermuda grass *n, usu cap B* **:** a grass (*Cynodon dactylon*) of trailing and stoloniferous habit native to southern Europe but now widely distributed in warm countries and used for lawns and pasture esp. in the southern U.S. and in India — called also *Bahama grass, devil grass, doob, scutch grass*

Bermuda grass

bermuda high *n, usu cap B* **:** a semipermanent system of high atmospheric pressure near Bermuda in the Atlantic ocean found particularly well developed in the summer

bermuda lily *n, usu cap B* **:** a lily that is a variety (*Lilium longiflorum eximium*) of the white trumpet lily with flowers green tinged toward the base and with a long narrow tube the upper part of which flares like a trumpet formerly much cultivated in Bermuda and sold as an Easter lily

bermuda lobster *n, usu cap B* **:** a large brightly colored spiny lobster (*Panulirus argus*)

bermuda maidenhair *n, usu cap B* **:** a delicate endemic Bermudian fern (*Adiantum bellum*) with a creeping rootstock

bermuda mulberry *n, usu cap B* **:** FRENCH MULBERRY 1

bermuda olivewood bark *n, usu cap B* **:** an endemic Bermudian evergreen tree (*Elaeodendron laneanum*) with dioecious axillary flowers and roundish white-fleshed fruit

bermuda onion *n, usu cap B* **:** a large flat yellow-skinned mild-flavored onion that probably originated in Italy or the Canary islands and is now widely grown in southern Texas; *broadly* **:** any of several long-season onions that differ from the Bermuda onion chiefly in skin color

bermuda rig *or* **bermudian rig** *n, usu cap B* **:** a fore-and-aft rig marked by a triangular sail and a mast with an extreme rake

bermuda shorts *n pl, usu cap B* **:** knee-length walking shorts worn by men and women

¹ber·mu·di·an \bə(r)'myüdēən, *S also* -mü-; *attrib sometimes* 'bərˌm- *or* 'bə̄ˌm- *or* 'bəiˌm-\ *or* **ber·mu·dan** \-d°n\ *adj, usu cap* [*Bermuda* islands + E *-ian* or *-an*] **1 :** of, relating to, or characteristic of Bermuda **2 :** of, relating to, or characteristic of Bermudians

²bermudian \"\ *n* -s *cap* **:** a native or resident of Bermuda

bern *or* **berne** \'bərn, 'be(ə)rn\ *adj, usu cap* [fr. *Bern* or *Berne*, Switzerland] **:** of or from Bern, the capital of Switzerland **:** of the kind or style prevalent in Bern **:** BERNESE

¹ber·nard·ine *R* 'bərnə(r)ˌdēn, –*R* 'bə̄nə,d- *or* 'bəinə,d-\ *adj, usu cap* [F *bernardin*, fr. St. *Bernard* of Clairvaux †1153 Fr. ecclesiastic + F *-in* -ine] **1 :** of or relating to St. Bernard of Clairvaux **2 :** of or relating to the branch of the Cistercian order instituted by St. Bernard of Clairvaux

²bernardine \"\ *n* -s *usu cap* **:** a nun of one of several non-Cistercian congregations following a rule modeled on the original Cistercian observance

ber·ne \'bernə\ *n* -s [Pg] **:** TORSALO

¹bern·ese \ˌbər'nēz, (')ber-, -ēs\ *adj, usu cap* [*Bern*, city and canton in Switzerland + E *-ese*] **1 :** of, relating to, or characteristic of Bern, a city and canton in Switzerland **2 :** of, relating to, or characteristic of the Bernese

²bernese \"\ *n, pl* **bernese** *cap* **:** a native or resident of Bern

bernese mountain dog *n, usu cap B & sometimes cap M&D* **:** one of a Swiss breed of large powerful long-coated black dogs that have deep tan or russet-brown markings on the legs and over the eyes, that often have a blaze, white feet, and white chest mark, and that were formerly used for draft

ber·ni·cla \'bərnə̇klə, (ˌ)bər'nik-\ [NL, fr. F *bernicle* barnacle (goose and shellfish), fr. Bret *bernic* — more at BARNACLE] *syn of* BRANTA

ber·ni·cle \'bərnə̇kəl\ *or* **bernicle goose** *n* -s [MF] **:** BARNACLE GOOSE

ber·noul·li distribution \bər'nülē-, ¦berˌnü¦yē-\ *n, usu cap B* [after Jacques *Bernoulli* †1705 Swiss mathematician] **:** BINOMIAL DISTRIBUTION

ber·noul·li effect \"-\ *n, usu cap B* [after Daniel *Bernoulli* †1782 Swiss mathematician and scientist] **:** an effect observed in hydrodynamics: the pressure in a stream of fluid is reduced as the speed of flow is increased — compare BERNOULLI'S THEOREM 2

bernoulli's theorem *n, usu cap B* **1** [after Jacques *Bernoulli*] **:** a basic principle of statistics: as the number of independent trials of an event of theoretical probability *p* is indefinitely increased, the observed ratio of actual occurrences of the event to total trials approaches *p* as a limit; — called also *law of averages* **2** [after Daniel *Bernoulli*] **:** a law of hydrodynamics: in a stream of liquid the sum of the elevation head, the pressure head, and the velocity head remains constant along any line of flow provided no work is done by or upon the liquid in the course of its flow and decreases in proportion to the energy lost in viscous flow — see HEAD 14b

ber·oë \'berəˌwē\ *n, cap* [NL, fr. L, a nymph] **:** a widely distributed genus that is coextensive with the class Nuda and comprises delicately iridescent thimble-shaped ctenophores

be·ro·i·da \bə'rōədə\ *n pl, cap* [NL, fr. *Beroë* + *-ida*] **:** an order of ctenophores coextensive with the class Nuda

be·rok \bə'räk\ *n* -s [origin unknown] **:** PIG-TAILED APE

be·rouged \bə̇, bē + \ *adj* [*be-* + *rouged*] **:** obviously or thickly rouged

ber·ren·do *or* **be·ren·do** \bə'ren(ˌ)dō\ *n* -s [Sp, fr. *berrendo*, adj., spotted] *Southwest* **:** PRONGHORN

berretta *var of* BIRETTA

ber·ret·ti·no \ˌberə'tē(ˌ)nō\ *or* **ber·et·ti·na** \-ēnə\ *n* -s [It, dim. of *berretta* biretta — more at BIRETTA] **:** a cardinal's scarlet skullcap

ber·ri·chon \berēshōⁿ\ *n* -s *usu cap* [F, fr. *Berry*, region of central France] **:** a native or inhabitant of the former province of Berry in central France

ber·ried \'berēd, -rid\ *adj* **1 :** furnished with berries **:** BACCATE **2 :** bearing eggs ⟨a ~ lobster⟩

ber·ri·gan \'berə̇gən\ *n* -s [native name in Australia] **:** EMU BUSH

ber·ru·ga·te \ˌberə'gädˌē\ *n* -s [prob. fr. AmerSp *verrugato*, fr. Sp *verruga* wart (fr. L *verruca*) + *-ato* -ate — more at WART] **:** a tripletail fish (*Verrugato pacificus*) found at Panama and used for food

¹ber·ry \'berē, -ri; *in compounds in which a stressed syllable immediately precedes*, ˌb(ə)rē *or* ˌb(ə)ri *is usual in Brit speech and is used by some US speakers esp in compounds that are well known and that are in attrib position (as in "strawberry jam"); in compounds in which an unstressed syllable immediately precedes (as "huckleberry"), this pronunc is less freq in Brit speech and is little heard in US speech*\ *n* -ES [ME *berye*, fr. OE *berie*; akin to OHG *beri* berry, ON *ber*, Goth *weinabasi* grape] **1 a :** a pulpy and usu. edible fruit of small size irrespective of its structure (as the strawberry, raspberry, checkerberry, and hip of the rose) **b** *dial Brit* **:** GOOSEBERRY **c :** any simple fruit that has a pulpy or fleshy pericarp (as the currant, grape, gooseberry, cranberry, tomato, or banana) **d :** the dry seed or kernel of certain grains ⟨a coffee ~⟩ ⟨a wheat ~⟩ **2 :** one of the eggs of a fish or lobster **3 :** the black knob on the bill of the mute swan — **in berry :** carrying ova or spawn — used of lobsters and crabs

²ber·ry \'berē, -ri\ *vi* -ED/-ING/-ES **1 :** to bear or produce berries ⟨a ~*ing* shrub⟩ **2 :** to gather berries **:** pick berries ⟨when the wild strawberries were ripe, they went ~*ing*⟩

berry alder *n* **:** ALDER BUCKTHORN

berry basket *or* **berry box** *or* **berry cup** *n* **:** a small nesting container of wood veneer, paper, or plastic usu. in standard sizes of ½ pint, 1 pint, or 1 quart used for berries or other small fruit

berry cone *n* **:** the ripened berrylike fruit of certain conifers (as the juniper) in which the fleshy cone scales are fused together

ber·ry·less \-lə̇s\ *adj* **:** having no berries

ber·ry·like \'=ˌ=ˌ=\ *adj* **1** *of a fruit* **:** resembling a berry esp. in size or structure **2 :** small and rounded **:** COCCOID

berry pepper *n* **:** BIRD PEPPER

berry spoon *n* **:** a large spoon with a broad deep bowl used in serving berries, salad, and other juicy foods

berry sugar *n* **:** finely granulated sugar **:** CASTOR SUGAR

berry tree *n* **:** GOOSEBERRY 1b

berry wax *n* **:** a wax obtained from the berries of a southern

African shrub (*Myrica cordifolia*) and used in making polishes and soap

bers *pl of* BER

ber·sag horn \'bər,sag-\ *n, usu cap B* [*Bersaglieri*] **:** a bugle with one valve on which a diatonic scale may be played

ber·sa·glie·re \,bersəl'yerē, -ye(,)rā\ *n, pl* **bersaglie·ri** \-e(,)rē\ *often cap* [It, fr. *bersaglio* target, fr. OIt, fr. OF *bersail*, fr. *berser* to shoot, hit] **:** a member of the Italian army infantry corps organized about 1850 as sharpshooters or riflemen

ber·seem \bər'sēm\ *or* **berseem clover** \(')=¦=-\ *or* **ber·sim** \bər'sēm\ *or* **ber·sine** \-'sēn\ *n* -s *sometimes cap B* [Ar *barsīm, birsīm*, fr. Copt *bersim*] **:** a clover (*Trifolium alexandrinum*) generally more succulent than alfalfa or other clovers and extensively cultivated as a forage plant and green-manure crop in the alkaline soils of the Nile valley and to some extent in the southwestern U.S. — called also *Egyptian clover*

ber·serk \R bər'sərk, ,bər-, -'zərk *also* bə'sərk *or* bə'zərk *or* 'bər,sərk *sometimes* 'bər,sə(r)k *or* 'bər,zərk; *-R* bə's|ək, |əik, bə's|ək, bəi's|əik, -'z| *also* 'bə,sək *or* 'bəi,səik *sometimes* 'bə,sək *or* 'bəi,sək *or* 'bə,zək *or* 'bəi,zəik\ *also* **ber·serk·er** \R -kər, *-R* -kə(r\ *adj* **:** marked by a display of violent erratic behavior indicative of extreme excitement or agitation and suggestive of sudden mental unbalance **:** FRENZIED, CRAZED, MAD, WILD ⟨attacked the fish with ~ fury —Claude Dredge⟩ ⟨a machinist's mate went ~ with a knife —F.J.Bell⟩

berserker \"\ *or* **berserk** \"\ *n* -s [ON *berserkr*, from *ber-* (stem of *bjǫrn* bear) + *serkr* shirt — more at BEAR, SARK] **1 :** an ancient Scandinavian warrior reputed to be invulnerable, of enormous strength, and filled with wild frenzy in battle **2 :** one whose actions are marked by a headstrong intractable spirit or by reckless defiance (as of orthodox views or attitudes) ⟨a political ~ whose course was completely unpredictable⟩

ber·tat \bər'tat\ *n, pl* **bertat** *or* **bertats** *usu cap* **1 :** an agricultural Negro people of the Shangalla group dwelling along the tributaries of the Blue Nile **2 :** a member of the Bertat people

ber·te·roa \,bərtē'rōə, (,)bər'terəwə\ *n, cap* [NL, after Carlo G. *Bertero* †1831 Ital. botanist] **:** a small genus of Eurasian herbs (family Cruciferae) with narrow entire leaves, white racemose flowers, and oblong or nearly round pods — see HOARY ALYSSUM

¹berth \'bərth, 'bəth, 'bəith\ *n, pl* **berths** \-ths *sometimes* -thz\ *n* -s [prob. fr. ⁴*bear*, after E *birth*: ⁴*bear*] **1 a :** convenient sea room **:** sufficient or safe distance for maneuvering maintained between a ship and another object ⟨keep a clear ~ of the shoals⟩ ⟨give the lighthouse a wide ~⟩ **b :** distance preserved for the sake of safety — used esp. with *wide* ⟨an orderly place to which outlaws and criminals gave wide ~ —S.H.Holbrook⟩ **2 a :** the place where a ship lies when at anchor or at a wharf ⟨an ocean liner riding quietly at her ~⟩ **b :** the place in a shipyard where a ship is built **:** SHIPWAY **c :** a space designed to accommodate an automotive vehicle (as a truck or train or plane) at rest for a specific purpose (as loading) ⟨plenty of room for 20 parking ~*s*⟩ **3 a** *archaic* **:** a room in which a number of the officers of a ship or the ship's company mess and reside **b :** a place to sit or sleep **:** ACCOMMODATION ⟨vainly looked for a ~ in the crowded bus⟩ ⟨helped him find a ~ during his visit to town⟩ **4 a :** a billet on board ship ⟨waiting for a ~ as a ship's surgeon —Bernard Keelan⟩ **b :** JOB, POSITION, SITUATION, POST ⟨dissatisfied with his prewar truck driving ~ —*Newsweek*⟩ ⟨the sales department is an excellent ~ for a young man —Jo Ranson & R.M.Pack⟩ ⟨high-school seniors having difficulty in locating ~*s* in leading colleges⟩; *specif* **:** a playing position on a team ⟨won a regular first-string ~⟩ ⟨the left-field ~⟩ **5 :** a sleeping accommodation (as on a ship, train, or plane) that consists typically of a shelf or frame fixed to a wall or of unfolded facing seats and is provided with a mattress and bedding **syn** see ROOM, WHARF — **on the berth :** properly moored so as to be ready to load or unload cargo

²berth \"\ *vb* -ED/-ING/-S *vt* **1 a :** to bring to anchorage **:** MOOR **:** maneuver to a suitable place for anchoring or docking ⟨tugs when ~*ing* a ship sometimes work by pushing with their bow against the ship's side —D.W.Pye⟩ **b :** to put or maneuver (as a bus) into a berth ⟨~*ing* the plane in the hangar⟩ ⟨~*ed* the car in the space reserved for it⟩ **2 :** to allot a berth to **:** furnish with a berth ⟨a cabin with 16 bunks in it to ~ the crew⟩ ~ *vi* **1 :** to come into a position suitable for mooring **:** arrive at a berth **:** stop at a berth ⟨the ship glided in and effortlessly ~*ed*⟩ **2 :** to have a berth or a lodging place ⟨~*ed* beside him —Frederick O'Brien⟩

ber·tha \'bərthə, -əthə,-əithə\ *n* -s [in sense 1, fr. F *berthe*, after *Berthe* (Bertha) †783 queen of the Franks, noted for her modesty; in sense 2, fr. G *Bertha*, after Frau *Bertha* Krupp von Bohlen und Halbach †1957 proprietress of the Krupp Works, Essen, Germany — more at BIG BERTHA] **1 a :** a woman's shoulder cape **b :** a wide round collar covering the shoulders (as for a dress or blouse) **2** *usu cap* **:** BIG BERTHA

bertha 1b

bertha armyworm *n* [prob. fr. the name *Bertha*] **:** a destructive climbing cutworm (*Mamestra configurata*) feeding on a variety of cultivated crops in the north-central states and adjacent parts of Canada

berth·age \-thij\ *n* -s **1 :** accommodation for mooring or anchoring; *specif* **:** space (as at a wharf) reserved to take care of shipping **2 :** a toll for anchorage **:** berthing duties **:** DOCKAGE

berth cargo *n* **:** cargo taken by a ship at less than the regular line rates to fill surplus cargo space

berth deck *n* **1 :** the deck on which the hammocks on a warship were formerly swung **2 :** a space containing the crew's sleeping quarters

berthe \'be(ə)rt\ *n* -s [F — more at BERTHA] **:** BERTHA 1

ber·thi·er·ite \'bərthēə,rīt\ *n* -s [F *berthierite*, after Pierre *Berthier* †1861 Fr. chemist + F *-ite*] **:** a mineral $FeSb_2S_4$ consisting of a sulfide of antimony and iron of a dark steel-gray color (sp. gr. 4.0)

¹berth·ing \'bərthiŋ, 'bəth-, 'bəith-, -thēŋ\ *n* -s [fr. gerund of ²*berth*] **:** BERTHAGE 1

²berthing \"\ *n* -s [fr. gerund of obs. *berth* to cover with boards, perh. of Scand origin; akin to ON *byrthi* side of a ship, fr. *borth* border, side of a ship — more at BOARD] **:** the planking outside of a wooden ship above the sheer strake; *also* **:** the upright planking of the sides and partitions

ber·thol·le·tia \,bərthə'lēsh(ē)ə\ *n, cap* [NL, after Comte Claude L. *Berthollet* †1822 Fr. chemist + NL *-ia*] **:** a genus of tall So. American trees (family Lecythidaceae) having flowers with six petals and a 2-parted deciduous calyx succeeded by hard-shelled capsules — see BRAZIL NUT

ber·thol·lide \'bərthə,līd; (,)bər'thä,līd, -,ləd\ *n* -s [C.L. *Berthollet* + E *-ide*] **:** a solid chemical compound (as some metallic hydrides and the tungsten bronzes) that does not conform to the law of definite proportions **:** a nonstoichiometric compound — distinguished from *daltonide*

ber·thon boat \'bər,thän-\ *n, often cap 1st B* [after Edward L. *Berthon* †1899 Eng. ecclesiastic and physician, its inventor] **:** a collapsible lifeboat often carried on small ships

berths *pl of* BERTH, *pres 3d sing of* BERTH

ber·tia \'bərd-ēə, 'ber-\ [NL, fr. Paul *Bert* †1886 Fr. physiologist and politician + NL *-ia*] *syn of* BERTIELLA

ber·ti·el·la \,=d-ē'elə\ *n, cap* [NL, fr. P. *Bert* + NL *-i-* + *-ella*] **:** a genus of medium-sized taenioid tapeworms parasitizing apes, monkeys, and in rare instances man

ber·til·lon·age \;bərd-ᵊl;änäzh, bertēyō'nàzh\ *n* -s [F, fr. Alphonse *Bertillon* + F *-age*] **:** BERTILLON SYSTEM

ber·til·lon system \'bərd-ᵊl,än-, bertēyōⁿ-\ *n, usu cap B* [after Alphonse *Bertillon* †1914 Fr. criminologist] **:** a system for the identification of persons by a physical description based on anthropometric measurements, standardized photographs, notation and classification of markings, color, bodily anomalies, thumb line impressions, and other data that has been largely superseded by fingerprinting

bertin's column *n, usu cap B* **:** COLUMN OF BERTIN

ber·to·lo·nia \,bərd-ᵊl'ōnyə, -nēə\ *n, cap* [NL, fr. Antonio *Bertoloni* †1869 Ital. botanist + NL *-ia*] **:** a small genus of ornamental Brazilian herbs (family Melastomaceae) having showy leaves and white, rose, or purple flowers in one-sided racemes

ber·trand curve \'ber,tränd-, ber·trāⁿ-\ *n, usu cap B* [after Joseph L. F. *Bertrand* †1900 Fr. mathematician] **:** either of two twisted curves having the property that the principal normals to one of them are also principal normals to the other

ber·trand·ite \'bər·trən,dīt\ *n* -s [F, fr. E. *Bertrand*, 19th cent. Frenchman who first described it + F *-ite*] **:** a mineral $Be_4Si_2O_7(OH)_2$ consisting of a beryllium silicate occurring in hard colorless or pale-yellow prismatic crystals (hardness 6–7, sp. gr. 2.59–2.60)

bertrand lens *n, usu cap B* [prob. after Joseph L. F. *Bertrand*] **:** an auxiliary removable lens in the tube of a polarizing microscope used to obtain interference figures

ber·wick·shire \'berik,shi(ə)r, -shər\ *or* **ber·wick** \'berik\ *adj, usu cap* [fr. *Berwickshire*, Scotland] **:** of or from the county of Berwick, Scotland **:** of the kind or style prevalent in Berwick

be·ryc·i·dae \bə'risə,dē\ *n pl, cap* [NL, fr. *Beryc-*, *Beryx*, type genus + *-idae*] **:** a family of fishes that have a narrow compressed body and thoracic ventral fins, are usu. black or bright scarlet, and live chiefly in rather deep water

ber·y·coid \'berə,kȯid\ *n* -s [NL *Berycoidei*] **:** a fish of the group Berycoidei or the order Berycomorphi

ber·y·coi·dei \,==ˈkȯidē,ī\ *n pl, cap* [NL, fr. *Beryc-*, *Beryx*, genus of fishes + *-oidei*] *in some classifications* **:** a suborder or other division of Acanthopterygii comprising a number of marine fishes possessing an orbitosphenoid bone and other primitive features

berycoid

be·ry·co·mor·phi \bə,rīkō'mȯr,fī\ *n pl, cap* [NL, fr. *Beryc-*, *Beryx* + *-o-* + *-morphi*] **:** an order of spiny-rayed fishes that is nearly coextensive with Berycoidei and that includes a number of families of marine chiefly deepwater fishes intermediate in some respects between clupeoid fishes and the Percomorphi, some of which (as the Australian red snapper) are of considerable commercial value

ber·yl \'berəl, -(,)ril\ *n* -s [ME, fr. OF *beril*, fr. L *beryllus*, fr. Gk *bēryllos*, of Indic origin; akin to Skt *vaiḍūrya* cat's-eye gem] **1 :** a mineral $Be_3Al_2Si_6O_{18}$ consisting of a silicate of beryllium and aluminum of great hardness and occurring in green, bluish green, yellow, pink, or white hexagonal prisms **2 :** a light greenish blue that is bluer and deeper than average aqua, greener than average robin's-egg blue (sense 1), bluer and paler than average turquoise blue, and greener and deeper than beryl blue

beryl blue *n* **:** a light greenish blue that is bluer and paler than beryl or average light turquoise blue and bluer and slightly paler than average aqua

beryl green *n* **:** a light bluish green that is greener and deeper than average aqua green (sense 1), greener and slightly lighter than average turquoise green, and bluer and stronger than robin's-egg blue (sense 2)

ber·yl·late \bə'ri,lāt, -lət; 'berə,lāt\ *n* -s [ISV *beryll-* (fr. NL *beryllia*) + *-ate*] **:** a salt formed by the reaction of a strong alkali with beryllium oxide ⟨sodium ~⟩

be·ryl·lia \bə'rilēə\ *n* -s [NL, fr. *beryllium*] **:** BERYLLIUM OXIDE

ber·yl·line \'berə,līn, -lēn\ *adj* [*beryl* + *-ine*] **:** like beryl esp. in color

be·ryl·li·o·sis \bə,rilē'ōsəs\ *also* **ber·yl·lo·sis** \,berə'lō-\ *n, pl* **beryllio·ses** \-ō,sēz\ *or* **beryllo·ses** \-lō-\ [NL, fr. *beryllium* + *-osis*] **:** poisoning resulting from exposure to fumes and dusts of beryllium compounds or alloys and occurring chiefly as an acute pneumonitis or as a granulomatosis involving the lungs or other organs or tissues

be·ryl·li·um \bə'rilēəm\ *n* -s [NL, fr. Gk *bēryllion*, dim. of *bēryllos* beryl — more at BERYL] **:** a steel-gray light strong brittle toxic bivalent metallic element having high electric conductivity and high permeability to X rays that occurs in combination (as in beryl, chrysoberyl, and phenakite), that is produced by reduction of its compounds (as by electrolysis), and that is used chiefly as a hardening agent in alloys (as with copper), as windows in X-ray tubes, and as a moderator and reflector in nuclear reactors — symbol *Be*; called also *glucinium*; see ELEMENT table

beryllium oxide *n* **:** a white amorphous compound BeO having high thermal conductivity and high electrical resistance that is usu. obtained by treatment of beryl ore and is used chiefly as a high-temperature refractory (as in crucibles) and in phosphors (as for television screens, X-ray equipment, and formerly fluorescent lamps)

ber·yl·loid \'berə,lȯid\ *n* -s [ISV *beryll-* (prob. fr. L *beryllus*) + *-oid*; fr. the frequent occurrence of beryl crystals in this form] **:** a form consisting of a double 12-sided pyramid **:** the dihexagonal dipyramid

berylloid

be·ryl·lo·nite \bə'rilə,nīt\ *n* -s [NL *beryllium* + E *-on* + *-ite*] **:** a mineral $NaBePO_4$ consisting of sodium beryllium phosphate occurring in light-colored topazlike orthorhombic crystals (hardness 5.5–6, sp. gr. 2.85)

ber·ze·lian formula \(,)bər'zēlyən-, -lēən-\ *n, usu cap B* [Jöns J. *Berzelius* †1848 Swedish chemist + E *-an*] **:** DUALISTIC FORMULA

ber·ze·lian·ite \(,)bər'zēlyə,nīt, -lēə,-\ *n* -s [Sw *berzelianit*, irreg. fr. Baron J. J. *Berzelius* †1848 Swedish chemist + Sw *-it* -ite] **:** a mineral Cu_2Se consisting of copper selenide having a silver-white color when freshly broken (sp. gr. 6.7)

ber·ze·li·ite \(,)bər'zēlē,īt\ *or* **ber·ze·lite** \(,)bər'zē,līt, 'bərzə,-\ *n* -s [G *berzeliit*, fr. Baron J. J. *Berzelius* + G *-it* -ite] **:** a mineral $(Mg,Mn)_2(Ca,Na)_3(AsO_4)_3$ consisting of a bright yellow arsenate of calcium, magnesium, and manganese (sp. gr. 4.03)

bes *pl of* BE

be·sa \'bāsə\ *n, pl* **be·se** \-(,)sā\ *or* **besas** [It] **1 a :** a bronze coin issued 1909–21 for use in Italian Somaliland where it was worth ¹⁄₁₀₀ of a rupee **b :** a corresponding unit of value ⟨the circulation of 2-*besa* and 4-*besa* coins⟩ **2 a :** a copper coin formerly used in Ethiopia where it was worth ¹⁄₁₀₀ of a talari **b :** a corresponding unit of value ⟨a ½-*besa* coin was struck⟩

besant *var of* BEZANT

bes antler *var of* BAY ANTLER

be·scattered \bə̇, bē+\ *adj* [*be-* + *scattered*] **:** sparsely covered **:** BESPRINKLED, BESTREWED

be·screen \bə̇, bē+\ *vt* [*be-* + *screen*] *archaic* **:** SCREEN

be·scribble \bə̇, bē+\ *vt* [*be-* + *scribble*] **1 :** to scribble very illegibly **2 :** to scribble about **:** scribble upon

besee *vt* **besaw; beseen; beseeing; besees** [ME *beseen*, fr. OE *besēon*, fr. *be-* + *sēon* to see — more at SEE] *obs* **:** to treat well or badly **:** provide or furnish with

¹be·seech \bə̇'sēch, bē-\ *vb* **be·sought** \-'sȯt, *usu* -ȯd·+V\ *or* **beseeched; besought** *also* **beseeched; beseeching; beseeches** [ME *besechen*, fr. *be-* + *sechen* to seek — more at SEEK] *vt* **1 :** to ask earnestly for **:** BEG, SOLICIT ⟨*besought* their collaboration in the work of reform⟩ **2 :** to address oneself earnestly to **:** call upon **:** IMPLORE, ENTREAT, SUPPLICATE ⟨a Cape captain whose bride ~*ed* him to write while he was away —R.W.Hatch⟩ ~ *vi* **:** to make supplication **:** engage in entreaty **syn** see BEG

²beseech *n* -ES *obs* **:** ENTREATY, PETITION

beseeching *adj* **:** marked by earnest entreaty **:** SUPPLICATING ⟨he met her gaze with a look of ~ intensity —J.C.Powys⟩ — **be·seech·ing·ly** *adv* — **be·seech·ing·ness** *n* -ES

be·seem \bə̇'sēm, bē-\ *vb* -ED/-ING/-S [ME *besemen*, fr. *be-* + *semen* to seem — more at SEEM] *vi* **1** *archaic* **:** SEEM **2** *archaic* **:** to be in accordance with what is proper **:** be fitting **:** be becoming ⟨with such embellishment as well ~*s* —William Wordsworth⟩ ~ *vt, archaic* **:** to be suitable to the nature or appearance of **:** BECOME, BEFIT ⟨as might ~ so bright a dame —S.T. Coleridge⟩

beseeming *adj, archaic* **:** SUITABLE, PROPER — **be·seem·ing·ly** *adv, archaic* — **be·seem·ing·ness** *n* -ES *archaic*

be·set \bə̇'set, bē-, *usu* -ed·+V\ *vt* **beset; beset; besetting; besets** [ME *besetten*, fr. OE *besettan*, fr. *be-* + *settan* to set — more at SET] **1 a :** to set at intervals **:** stud esp. with ornaments ⟨leaves whose edges were *beset* with thorns —J.G.Frazer⟩ ⟨a crown *beset* with pearls⟩ **b :** to cover esp. with plant growth ⟨*beset* with tangled vegetation —Xavier Herbert⟩ **:** fill or strew esp. with impediments ⟨the road is *beset* with dragons and evil magicians —T.B.Costain⟩ **2 :** PLAGUE, TROUBLE, HARASS **:** weigh down **:** DOG, BEDEVIL ⟨subject to none of the pressures that ~ American and English papers —F.L.Mott⟩ ⟨distrust of himself had always *beset* and hampered him —S.H. Adams⟩ **3 a :** to set upon **:** attack repeatedly **:** ASSAIL ⟨throughout the long trek the settlers were *beset* by savages⟩ **b :** to lay siege to **:** surround so as to compel surrender **:** BESIEGE ⟨enemy troops *beset* the fortress⟩ **c :** to occupy, take possession of, or overrun in such a way as to prevent free passage **:** choke off **:** BLOCKADE ⟨a screaming mob *beset* every road into the town⟩ **d** (1) **:** to close or hem in **:** ENCOMPASS, SURROUND ⟨a town *beset* with towering mountains⟩ (2) **:** to surround (as a task or problem) with immaterial or nonphysical perils or obstacles ⟨his task was *beset* with many difficulties⟩ (3) **:** to surround (as a ship) on all sides with ice so that free movement is totally checked — used of ice fields ⟨in danger of being *beset* by the worst pack we'd ever seen —Glen Jacobsen⟩

be·set·ment \-tmənt\ *n* -s **1 :** the action of besetting or the condition of being beset ⟨would invite ~ in the frozen sea —Glen Jacobsen⟩ **2 :** something by which one is beset **:** TROUBLE, VEXATION ⟨the small ~*s* and annoyances of life⟩; *esp* **:** a besetting sin, weakness, or failing

besetting *adj* **:** constantly in evidence **:** persistent or deeply rooted **:** PRINCIPAL, DOMINANT ⟨the ~ sin of woman, her passion to discuss her private affairs with anyone who is willing to listen —W.S.Maugham⟩ **:** OBSESSIVE, HAUNTING ⟨a ~ idea⟩ ⟨a strange ~ desire to know what to do when the time came —Charles Dickens⟩

be·shawled \bə̇'shȯld, bē-\ *adj* [*be-* + *shawl* + *-ed*] **:** wearing a shawl ⟨a ~ woman⟩

be·show \bə̇'shō\ *n* -s [Makah *bishowk*] **:** SABLEFISH

be·shrew \bə̇, bē+\ *vt* -ED/-ING/-S [ME *beshrewen*, fr. *be-* + *shrewen* to curse — more at SHREW] *archaic* **:** CURSE — often used in mild imprecations ⟨~ all them that are in love untrue —William Wordsworth⟩

¹be·side \bə̇'sīd, bē-\ *adv* [ME *beside, besiden*, adv. & prep., fr. OE *be sīdan* at or to the side, fr. *be* at, by (fr. *bī*) + *sīdan*, dat. & acc. of *sīde* side — more at BY, SIDE] **1** *archaic* **:** in a nearby position **:** close by **:** ALONGSIDE **2** *archaic* **:** BESIDES ⟨myself and divers gentlemen ~ —Shak.⟩

²beside \"\ *prep* [ME *beside, besiden*] **1 a :** at or by the side of ⟨walk ~ me⟩ **:** along or on one side of ⟨the ditch ~ the road⟩ ⟨the road leads ~ a branch of the White river —Bernard DeVoto⟩ **b :** close to **:** NEAR **:** next to ⟨there's an orchard ~ the house, about a half mile off⟩ **c :** in comparison with ⟨a writer needs to be a Walt Whitman if his faults of technique are to be rated unimportant ~ the vigor of his personality —Douglas Stewart⟩ **d :** on a par with ⟨a musical achievement that can be ranked ~ that of the masters⟩ **2 :** BESIDES 1 ⟨~ being taken into a world of escapist literature a thoughtful reader can go somewhat further —J.P.Marquand⟩ **3 :** BESIDES 2 ⟨many creatures ~ man live in communities —Stuart Chase⟩ **4 a** *obs* **:** outside of **b :** away from (as through irrelevance) **:** wide of ⟨~ the point⟩ **c** *archaic* **:** beyond the range of **:** contrary to — **beside oneself :** carried out of oneself (as through extreme excitement) **:** out of one's wits or senses ⟨*beside* himself with embarrassment —Sherwood Anderson⟩ ⟨filled them with such delirious emotions that they were *beside* themselves —Liam O'Flaherty⟩

¹be·sides \bə̇'sīdz, bē-\ *adv* [ME, alter. of *beside* + *-s*] **1 a :** in addition **:** over and above ⟨possessing a wealth of printed material and many original manuscripts ~⟩ **b :** MOREOVER, FURTHERMORE ⟨the play is excellent, and ~ the tickets cost very little⟩ **2 :** OTHERWISE, ELSE ⟨knows the rules of grammar, but very little ~⟩

²besides \"\ *prep* [ME] **1 :** in addition to ⟨~ being a model of scholarly thoroughness, the biographical chapters are vivid and engrossing —C.J.Rolo⟩ **2 :** other than **:** EXCEPT ⟨there's nothing you can do ~ making the best of the situation⟩

be·siege \bə̇'sēj, bē-\ *vt* -ED/-ING/-S [ME *besegen*, fr. *be-* + *sege* siege — more at SIEGE] **1 a :** to surround (as a city) with armed forces for the purpose of compelling surrender **:** lay siege to **b :** to surround closely **:** hem in **:** crowd upon or around ⟨I was *besieged* by four small Bedouin children —A.J. Liebling⟩ ⟨on Saturday nights the "picture house" in the town is *besieged* by eager young men and women —J.M.Mogey⟩ ⟨the land offices . . . were *besieged* daily by dozens of new settlers —*Amer. Guide Series: Ind.*⟩ **2 a :** to press esp. with requests **:** IMPORTUNE ⟨hungry for jobs and patronage, they *besieged* the president from morning to night —H.F.Wilkins⟩ ⟨*besieging* the royal ministers with petitions —T.B.Costain⟩ ⟨I was constantly *besieged* for an opinion —Henry Miller⟩ **b :** ASSAIL, BESET — used of fears or other troubling ideas or sensations ⟨such doubts and hesitations ~ one now and again —B.N.Cardozo⟩ ⟨a kind of loneliness . . . that ~*s* us —J.A.Pike⟩ — **be·sieg·er** \-jə(r)\ *n* -s

be·sieg·ing·ly *adv* **:** in a besieging manner

be·silver \bə̇, bē+\ *vt* -ED/-ING/-S [*be-* + *silver*] **:** to cover with or as if with silver

be·sing \bə̇, bē+\ *vt* [*be-* + *sing*] **1 :** to sing about **:** celebrate esp. in song or poetry **2 :** to sing to

be·slabber \bə̇, bē+\ *vt* **:** BESLOBBER

beslave \bə̇, bē+\ *vt* -ED/-ING/-S [*be-* + *slave*] **1** *obs* **:** ENSLAVE **2** *obs* **:** to address as a slave **3 :** to fill with slaves

be·slobber \bə̇, bē+\ *vt* [*be-* + *slobber*] **1 :** to slobber upon **:** smear with or as if with slobber **2 :** to praise fulsomely

be·slubber \bə̇, bē+\ *vt* [*be-* + *slubber*] **:** to besmear esp. with something thick or oily

be·smear \bə̇, bē+\ *vt* [ME *bismerwen*, fr. OE *be- smierwan*, fr. *be-* + *smierwan* to smear — more at SMEAR] **1 :** to smear with any thick, sticky, or greasy substance ⟨savages whose faces and bodies were ~*ed* with war paint⟩ **2 :** TARNISH, SULLY ⟨~*ing* the reputation of a distinguished scholar⟩

be·smirch \bə̇, bē+\ *vt* [*be-* + *smirch*] **:** to lessen the purity, luster, or beauty of **:** SULLY, SOIL, TARNISH, STAIN ⟨high ideals were ~*ed* by cruelty and greed —R.A.Newhall⟩ ⟨having his name ~*ed* in a litigation —M.R.Cohen⟩

be·smirch·ment \-mənt\ *n* -s **:** the action or an instance of besmirching **:** the condition of being besmirched ⟨a ~ of all that had gone before —Richard Joseph⟩

be·smoke \bə̇, bē+\ *vt* [ME *besmoken*, fr. *be-* + *smoken* to smoke — more at SMOKE] **1 :** to soil with smoke **2 :** to fill with smoke **3 :** to cure (as bacon) by smoking

be·soil \bə̇, bē+\ *vt* [ME *besoilen*, fr. *be-* + *soilen* to soil — more at SOIL] **:** to make very dirty

be·som \'bēzəm, 'biz-,'bis-,'bəz-\ *n* -s [ME *beseme*, fr. OE *besma*; akin to OHG *besmo, besamo* broom] **1 :** BROOM; *esp* **:** a broom made with a bundle of twigs **2 a :** BROOM 1a **b** *dial Eng* **:** a heath of the genus *Erica* **3** *dial Brit* **:** WOMAN; *esp* **:** a woman of slovenly, shrewish, or morally unacceptable character — usu. a generalized term of disparagement

besom moss *n* **:** HAIRCAP MOSS

¹besort *vt* -ED/-ING/-S [*be-* + *sort*] *obs* **:** to be suitable to

²besort *n* -s *obs* **:** suitable company

be·sot \bə̇'sät, bē-, *usu* -äd·+V\ *vt* **besotted; besotted** *also* **besot; besotting; besots** [*be-* + *sot* (to befool)] **1 :** to make or cause to be besotted ⟨the king . . . was *besotted* by her purely carnal attractions —*Times Lit. Supp.*⟩ ⟨*besot* by rhythm, visual . . . as well as auditory —Agnes de Mille⟩ ⟨*besotted* as we are by names —William Wordsworth⟩ ⟨permitted . . . to ~ themselves in the company of their favorite revelers —T.B.Macaulay⟩

besotted *adj* **1 :** characterized by a condition of blind doting affection **:** utterly fascinated **:** INFATUATED, OBSESSED ⟨~ with a dancing girl —W.E.Allen⟩ ⟨seemed absolutely ~ about the damned woman —Agatha Christie⟩ ⟨only the most ~ classicist would prefer the smell of ancient Athenians to the smell of his compatriots —Katharine F. Gerould⟩ **2 a :** STUPID, DULL-WITTED, DOLTISH, DAZED, MUDDLED ⟨the empress was not so ~ as to take his . . . word for it —A.M.Young⟩ ⟨half-starved and . . . frequently idle, ~ and fever-stricken —Van Wyck Brooks⟩ ⟨his ~ confidence, his sober radiant face . . . made them uncomfortable —Willa Cather⟩ **b :** intoxicated or stupefied esp. with drink ⟨the ~ fool had been drinking steadily for weeks⟩

besought *past of* BESEECH

be·soul \bə̇, bē+\ *vt* -ED/-ING/-S [*be-* + *soul*, n.] **:** to endow with a soul

be·spangle \bə̇, bē+\ *vt* -ED/-ING/-S [*be-* + *spangle*] **:** to adorn with spangles **:** dot or sprinkle with brilliantly sparkling or glittering objects ⟨the grass . . . is all *bespangled* with dewdrops —William Cowper⟩

be·spatter \bə̇, bē+\ *vt* [*be-* + *spatter*] **1 :** to spatter esp. with muck ⟨in his little room with the dingy walls . . . ~*ed* with printer's ink —Van Wyck Brooks⟩ **2 a :** to heap (as abuse or criticism) upon ⟨~*ed* him with all the vitriolic language at her command⟩ **:** cover with abuse **:** SLANDER ⟨no man in public life had ever been so foully ~*ed*⟩ **b :** to render less attractive or valuable **:** MAR, SPOIL ⟨the slick, heartless, elegant phrases of the past still ~ the poetry —J.H.Plumb⟩ ⟨the meaningless abstractions which ~ history books —*Times Lit. Supp.*⟩

bespawl *vt* -ED/-ING/-S [*be-* + *spawl*] *obs* **:** to spatter with or as if with saliva

¹be·speak \bə̇'spēk, bē-\ *vb* **be·spoke** \-pōk\ *or archaic* **be·spake** \-pāk\ **be·spo·ken** \-pōkən\ *or archaic* **bespoke**; **bespeaking; bespeaks** [ME *bespeken*, fr. OE *besprecan* to speak about, accuse of, complain, fr. *be-* + *specan, sprecan* to speak — more at SPEAK] *vi, archaic* **:** SPEAK ⟨and thus *bespake* sweet Christabel —S.T.Coleridge⟩ ~ *vt* **1 :** to arrange for in advance **:** hire or engage beforehand **:** ORDER ⟨if the place is not *bespoken* you will be welcome —O.W.Holmes †1935⟩ ⟨the taxi *bespoken* by cousin Francis to drive him back again to the station —Elizabeth Bowen⟩ **:** lay claim to beforehand ⟨the Rockefellers, the Fricks, the Morgans entered the North Star Country . . . ~*ing* the ore "forever" —Meridel Le Sueur⟩ **2 :** to speak to esp. with some formality **:** ADDRESS ⟨sends one of his friends to ~ the girl to whom he has been betrothed —A.H.J.Prins⟩ ⟨we were *bespoken* through public address megaphones and told what to do —Christopher Morley⟩ **3 a** *obs* **:** to request or engage (a person) to do something **b :** REQUEST **:** ask for ⟨~ a favor⟩ ⟨he *bespoke* me a job with Flood the next time he met him —Andy Adams⟩ ⟨~*ing* Federal assistance in the problem —*N.Y. Times*⟩ **:** request to know **:** ask about ⟨the letter Sir Austin lifted his head from to ~ his son's wishes —George Meredith⟩ **4 a :** to give evidence of **:** testify to **:** INDICATE, SIGNIFY, REVEAL ⟨noise is the loud laugh that ~*s* the empty mind —O.S.J.Gogarty⟩ ⟨shrugged in that faint way which *bespoke* total indifference —Marcia Davenport⟩ ⟨these names ~ the quality and sincerity of this compilation —J.C.Smith⟩ **b :** to speak of or show beforehand **:** FORETELL, PORTEND ⟨murmurings that *bespoke* imminent rebellion⟩ **syn** see INDICATE

²bespeak \"\ *n* -S **1 :** a request (as by an actor's patrons) for the presentation of a particular play to be given usu. as a benefit performance **2** *Brit* **:** a request made to a lending library by a borrower for the loan of a book when it is available

be·speckle \bə̇, bē+\ *vt* [*be-* + *speckle*] **:** SPECKLE, BESPRINKLE

be·spectacled \bə̇, bē+\ *adj* [*be-* + *spectacle* + *-ed*] **:** wearing spectacles

be·spell \bə̇, bē+\ *vt* -ED/-ING/-S [*be-* + *spell*, n.] **:** to cast a spell on **:** ENCHANT

bespete *vt; past* **bespet**; *past part* **bespate** [ME *bespeten*, fr. *be-* + *speten* to spit — more at SPET] *obs* **:** to spit upon **:** spatter with saliva

be·spoke \bə̇'spōk, bē-\ *or* **be·spo·ken** \-kən\ *adj* [fr. past part. of *bespeak*] **1** *Brit* **a :** CUSTOM-MADE **:** made to order — used esp. of wearing apparel ⟨~ suits⟩ **b :** dealing in or producing custom-made articles ⟨~ dressmaking⟩ ⟨a ~ tailor⟩ **2** *dial* **:** ENGAGED; *esp* **:** engaged to be married

be·spot \bə̇, bē+\ *vt* [ME *bespotten*, fr. *be-* + *spotten* to spot — more at SPOT] *archaic* **:** to mark with or as if with spots

be·spread \bə̇, bē+\ *vt* [ME *bespreden*, fr. *be-* + *spreden* to spread — more at SPREAD] *archaic* **:** OVERSPREAD ⟨a region that is *bespread* with lush vegetation⟩

be·sprent \bə̇'sprent, bē-\ *adj* [ME *bespreynt*, fr. *bespreynt*, *besprenged*, past part. of *besprengen* to besprinkle, fr. OE *besprengan*, fr. *be-* + *sprengan* to scatter, sprinkle, burst, causative fr. the root of *springan* to spring — more at SPRING] *archaic* **:** sprinkled over ⟨glistening grass ~ with raindrops⟩

be·sprinkle \bə̇, bē+\ *vt* [ME *besprengeln*, freq. of *besprengen*] **:** to sprinkle over **:** SPRINKLE ⟨white and yellow flowers *besprinkled* the banks —Van Wyck Brooks⟩ ⟨the surnames of authors quoted ~ the text —F.L.M.Dawson⟩

¹bes·sa·ra·bi·an \ˌbesəˈrābēən\ *adj, usu cap* [*Bessarabia*, region of southeastern Europe + E *-an*] **1 :** of, relating to, or characteristic of Bessarabia, **2 :** of, relating to, or characteristic of Bessarabians

²bessarabian \"\ *n* -S *cap* **:** a native or inhabitant of Bessarabia

bess-bug \'bes,bəg\ *or* **bes·sy·bug** \-sē,-\ *also* **bess beetle** *n* [prob. of imit. origin] **:** any of various gregarious flattened dark-colored beetles constituting a family (Passalidae) and living in decaying wood

bes·sel function \'besəl-\ *n, usu cap B* [after Friedrich W. *Bessel* †1846 Prussian astronomer] **:** one of a class of transcendental functions expressible as infinite series and occurring in the solution of the differential equation $x^2\frac{d^2y}{dx^2}+x\frac{dy}{dx}=(n^2-x^2)y$

besselian elements *n, usu cap B* [F.W. *Bessel* + E *-ian*] **:** mathematical-astronomical data employed by Bessel for facilitating precise prediction of a solar eclipse at any place on the earth

bes·sel's day numbers \'besəlz-\ *or* **bessel's star numbers** *n pl, usu cap B* [after F.W. *Bessel*] **:** four numbers, *A, B, C, D,* constant for all stars, whose logarithms are tabulated for different dates and used in calculating the apparent change in right ascension and declination for any date from any date

bes·se·mer \'besəmə(r)\ *or* **bessemer converter** *n* -S *usu cap B* [after Sir Henry *Bessemer* †1898 Eng. engineer and inventor] **:** the type of furnace used in the Bessemer process

bessemer copper *n, often cap B* [after H. *Bessemer*] **:** BLISTER COPPER

bessemer iron *or* **bessemer pig** *n, usu cap B* [after H. *Bessemer*] **:** a cast iron that contains not more than 0.10 percent of phosphorus and is suitable for the manufacture of Bessemer steel by the acid process

bes·se·mer·ize \-mə,rīz\ *vt* -ED/-ING/-S *often cap* [*Bessemer (process)* + *-ize*] **:** to treat with a blast of air (as in the Bessemer process)

bessemer process *n, usu cap B* [after H. *Bessemer*] **1 :** a process of making steel from pig iron by burning out carbon and other impurities through the agency of a blast of air that is forced through the molten metal, the blowing usu. being continued until nearly all the carbon is removed, the desired proportion being restored together with manganese by adding ferromanganese while the blown metal is being poured into a large ladle from which the ingot molds are filled **2 :** a process of refining copper matte by burning out the sulfur in a similar way

bessemer steel *n, usu cap B* **:** steel made by the Bessemer process

bes·sy \'besē, -si\ *n* -ES *usu cap* [fr. the name *Bessy*] **:** a stock character in English folk dances and plays played by a man dressed as a woman

bes·sy cer·ka \ˌbesēˈsərkə, ˌbesi-\ *n, usu cap B* [perh. by folk etymology fr. AmerSp *pejepuerco*] **:** QUEEN TRIGGERFISH

¹best \'best\ *adj, superlative of* GOOD [ME, adj. & adv., fr. OE *betst*; akin to OHG *bezzist* best, ON *beztr*, Goth *batista*; superlative of the root found in OE *bōt* remedy, compensation — more at BETTER] **1** *of a person* **a :** excelling all others (as in moral, intellectual, or physical qualities) ⟨the ~ boxer in his class⟩ ⟨the ~ teacher of the subject I ever knew⟩ ⟨the ~ person in the community — kind, gentle, and understanding⟩ **b :** excelling or leading all others in social and usu. financial standing — used esp. in the phrases *the best families* or *the best people* ⟨the ~ people, alas, were no longer always the people with money —Brian Glanville⟩ ⟨the rich and arrogant, the traditional "~ families" —Bess A. Garner⟩ **2** *of a thing* **:** excelling or surpassing all others of its kind in inherent quality or according to some standard **:** most productive of good **:** providing or offering the greatest advantage, utility, or satisfaction ⟨ready to receive ideas and to devote life's ~ energies to developing . . . their implications —M.R.Cohen⟩ ⟨what is the ~ thing to do⟩ ⟨a luxurious yet practical material, the ~ you can buy⟩ ⟨the ~ road⟩ ⟨the ~ way to make coffee⟩ ⟨the ~ of Shakespeare's plays⟩ **3 :** LARGEST, MOST ⟨they passed the ~ part of the three weeks at the seashore⟩

²best \"\ *adv, superlative of* WELL [ME] **1 :** in the best way **:** to the most advantage **:** with the most success, ease, profit, benefit, or propriety ⟨of his many roles, he appears ~ as Hamlet⟩ ⟨adjusted to the situation as ~ they could⟩ **2 :** to the highest degree **:** to the fullest extent **:** MOST ⟨my *best*-loved friend⟩ ⟨those ~ able to fight⟩

³best \"\ *n* -S [ME, fr. *best*, adj.] **1 :** something that is best: as **a :** the point or circumstance that is best ⟨the ~ of it all is, they are willing to give even more⟩ **b :** best state or condition ⟨a fine actor who is at his very ~ in this play⟩ **c :** best part ⟨always managing to get the ~ out of life⟩ **2** *usu pl in constr* **:** best individuals ⟨even the ~ of us make mistakes⟩ **3 :** all that one can do **:** one's utmost or maximum effort ⟨do your ~ and you'll win⟩ **4 :** best clothes ⟨wearing their ~, for it was Sunday⟩ **5** ADVANTAGE — used in the phrase *the best of it* ⟨in the 3d round the challenger seemed to be having the ~ of it⟩ ⟨when it comes to ridin' pitchin' horses them little bench-legged fellows usually has all the ~ of it —Ross Santee⟩

⁴best \"\ *vt* -ED/-ING/-S [¹*best*] **:** to get the better of **:** OUTDO ⟨in every game they were ~*ed* by their opponents⟩

⁵best \"\ *verbal auxiliary* [by shortening] **:** had best — not often in formal use ⟨you ~ get home in a hurry⟩

be·stain \bə̇, bē +\ *vt* [*be-* + *stain*] **:** to stain thoroughly

be·starred \bə̇, bē +\ *adj* [*be-* + *starred*] **:** decorated with stars

best-ball foursome *n* **:** a golf match of two players against two others, the best score of the two on each side being the one counted on each hole

best-ball match *n* **:** a golf match in which one player competes against the best ball of two or more players

best bet *n* **:** safest or most reliable course of action **:** surest means to a desired end **:** most advantageous approach **:** most satisfactory choice ⟨the pilot's *best bet* was to make an emergency landing⟩ ⟨the *best bet* for stabilizing the national economy⟩

best bib and tucker *n* **:** best clothes — not often in formal use ⟨strutting in their *best bib and tucker* —C.G.Bowers⟩

best bower *n* **:** a ship's spare anchor about the same size as the bowers usu. used and often about 15 percent heavier

¹be·stead *also* **be·sted** \bə̇'sted, bē-\ *adj* [ME *bested*, *bestad*, fr. *be-* + *sted*, *stad*, past part. of *steden* to place, stead — more at STEAD] **1** *archaic* **:** PLACED, VESTED ⟨my faith [is] *bestead* in the love of my own land —W.R.Benét⟩; *esp* **:** placed in a difficult or hazardous situation ⟨thank you for sending your knights . . . when we were really hard *bestead* —Charles Kingsley⟩ **2** *archaic* **:** HARASSED, ENDANGERED

²bestead \"\ *vt* **besteaded; bestead; besteading; besteads** [*be-* + *stead*] **1** *archaic* **:** to be of assistance to **:** HELP ⟨so long as they are behoveful, they may ~ each other —Sir Richard Burton⟩ **2** *archaic* **:** to be useful to **:** AVAIL

best foot *n* **:** one's most prepossessing or favor-winning appearance or traits ⟨there was no reason for him to concentrate on putting his *best foot* forward —Hamilton Basso⟩

best girl *n* **:** a favorite girl sweetheart

best gold *n* **:** the shot nearest the exact center of the bull's-eye in an archery contest

¹bes·tial \'bestyəl\ *n* -S [ME *bestaile*, *bestial*, fr. OF & ML; OF *bestail*, fr. ML *bestialia*, fr. L, adj., neut. pl. of *bestialis*] *Scot* **:** a domestic animal esp. of the bovine kind; *collectively* **:** CATTLE, LIVESTOCK

²bes·tial \'bes(h)chəl, 'bēs-, *Brit usu & US sometimes* -styəl *or* -stiəl\ *adj* [ME, fr. MF, fr. L *bestialis*, fr. *bestia* beast + *-alis* -al — more at BEAST] **1 a :** of or relating to a beast ⟨in their ~ form the dead men extend a benign protection to their living human kinsfolk —J.G.Frazer⟩ **:** like or resembling a beast in form or appearance ⟨things of ~ shape and with hideous voices —Oscar Wilde⟩ **b** *of a sign of the zodiac* **:** represented by the figure of an animal **2 a :** lacking intelligence or reasoning power **:** moved by unthinking prejudice or passion **:** BRUTISH, BARBAROUS ⟨the ~ man has no sense of right and wrong —J.E.Hankins⟩ ⟨some historians, to prove their immunity from ~ prejudice . . . are prone to treat the American Revolution almost apologetically —C.G.Bowers⟩ **b :** marked by, indicating, or gratifying base, inhuman, or immoderate instincts or desires **:** BRUTAL, DEPRAVED ⟨the ~ commander of a notorious concentration camp⟩ ⟨~ lust⟩ ⟨supplied an abundance of wine and brandy, and a scene of ~ intoxication was the natural consequence —Herman Melville⟩ **syn** see BRUTAL

bes·ti·al·i·ty \ˌbes(h)chēˈalədē, bes(h)ˈchal-, -ēs-, -lətē, -i *Brit usu & US sometimes* ˌ==stiˈal-\ *n* -ES [ME *bestialite*, fr. MF *bestialité*, fr. *bestial* + *-ité* -ity — more at BESTIAL] **1 :** the condition of being a beast (sense 1b) ⟨all this which marks the difference between ~ and humanity . . . is because man remembers, preserving and recording his experiences —John Dewey⟩ **2 a :** the display, gratification, or an instance of bestial traits or impulses ⟨the ~ and degradation that war brings —Drew Middleton⟩ ⟨the calculated *bestialities* of sadistic conquerors⟩ **b :** a debased brutalized condition of life ⟨the ~ of existence in a tenement jungle is well portrayed⟩ **3 :** sexual relations between a human being and a lower animal

bes·tial·ize *pronunc at* ²BESTIAL+ˌīz\ *vt* -ED/-ING/-S [²*bestial* + *-ize*] **1 :** to change into a beast (sense 1b) ⟨a man who has been *bestialized* into a gigantic beetle —*Time*⟩ **2 :** to cause to display bestial qualities **:** BRUTALIZE, DEGRADE ⟨such values as those of technics, the state, the race or the class ~ man —J.H.Hallowell⟩

bes·tial·ly *pronunc at* ²BESTIAL+ē *or* i\ *adv* [ME, fr. *bestial* + *-ly*] **:** in a bestial manner

bes·ti·a·rist \-s(h)ch(ē)ərəst, 'bēs-, -stēər-\ *n* -S **:** a writer of bestiaries

bes·ti·ary \'s(h)chē,erē, -stē,-\ *n* -ES [ML *bestiarium*, fr. L, neut. of *bestiarius* of beasts, fr. *bestia* beast + *-arius* -ary — more at BEAST] **1 :** a medieval often illustrated work in verse or prose describing with an allegorical moralizing commentary the appearance and habits of real and fabled animals **2 :** the sculptured or painted representation of a group of real or imaginary animals (as in a medieval cathedral) often vested with a symbolical significance

bes·ti·culture \'bestə, 'bēs- +,-\ *n* [L *bestia* beast + E *culture*] **:** exploitation and utilization of wild animals (as by hunting and fishing)

besting *pres part of* BEST

be·stir \bə̇, bē+\ *vt* [ME *bestiren*, *besteren*, fr. *be-* + *stiren*, *steren* to stir — more at STIR] **:** to stir up **:** rouse into brisk vigorous action ⟨she had grown fat because she no longer *bestirred* herself —Elizabeth Taylor⟩

best man *n* **:** the principal groomsman at a wedding

best·ness \'bes(t)nəs\ *n* -ES **:** the quality or state of being best

be·stow \bə̇'stō, bē-\ *vt* -ED/-ING/-S [ME *bestowen*, fr. *be-* + *-stowen* (fr. *stowe* place) — more at STOW] **1 a :** to put to use **:** APPLY, DEVOTE ⟨hours quite as well ~*ed* as hours spent in golfing —A.C.Benson⟩ **b** *obs* **:** to lay out (money) **:** SPEND **2 a :** to set in a given place, position, or situation **:** PUT, PLACE, LOCATE ⟨they saw her down the path and ~*ed* in her car with tender solicitude by the chauffeur —Frances Towers⟩ **b :** to put away (as in storing) **:** deposit for safekeeping **:** STOW ⟨parcels which she ~*ed* in the corners of the vehicle —Arnold Bennett⟩ ⟨without pausing to take breath till the whole cargo was ~*ed* —R.L.Stevenson⟩ **3** *obs* **:** to give in marriage **:** marry off **4 :** to provide with a lodging place **:** put up **:** QUARTER ⟨~*ed* Clotilde in lodgings of her own —Rayner Heppenstall⟩ **5 :** to present as a gift **:** GIVE, GRANT, CONFER ⟨a favor that the Roman was pleased to ~ —L.C.Douglas⟩ — usu. used with *on* or *upon* ⟨he ~*s* on them more praise than critical judgment —R.A.Cordell⟩ **6** *obs* **:** to conduct or acquit (oneself)

be·stow·al \-ōəl\ *n* -S **1 :** the act of bestowing or conferring **:** PRESENTATION ⟨conditions for ~ of a name —Leslie Spier⟩ **:** an instance of bestowing **:** GIFT ⟨viewed these afflictions as God's ~*s* upon his saints⟩ **2 :** the act or an instance of bestowing in a given place or position **:** the condition of being bestowed **:** STORAGE ⟨an odor of mothballs that told of long ~ —Marguerite Steen⟩

be·stow·er \-ō(ə)r, -ōə\ *n* -S **:** one that bestows

be·stow·ing \-ōiŋ\ *n* -S **:** a casing of burned brick on the upper part of a brickmaking clamp

be·stow·ment \-ōmənt\ *n* -S **:** BESTOWAL

bestraught *adj* [*be-* + *straught*, short for *distraught*] *archaic* **:** DISTRAUGHT

be·streak \bə̇, bē+\ *vt* [*be-* + *streak*] **:** to cover with streaks

be·strew \bə̇, bē+\ *vt* **bestrewed** *or archaic* **bestrewed**; **bestrewed** *also* **bestrewn** *or archaic* **bestrowed** *also* **bestrown**; **bestrewing** *or archaic* **bestrowing; bestrews** *or archaic* **bestrows** [ME *bestrowen*, *bestrewen*, fr. OE *bestrēowian*, fr. *be-* + *strēowian*, *strewian* to strew — more at STREW] **1 :** to cover with objects lying scattered about **:** STREW ⟨with some flowers my grave ~ —Robert Herrick †1674⟩ ⟨a sea of blood ~*ed* with wrecks —S.T.Coleridge⟩ **2 :** to lie or be scattered over (as an area) ⟨the isolated farmhouses of today which so liberally ~ Ordnance Survey maps —J.H.G.Lebon⟩

be·stride \bə̇, bē+\ *vt* **bestrode** *also* **bestrid; bestridden** *also* **bestrid** *or* **bestrode; bestriding; bestrides** [ME *bestriden*, fr. OE *bestrīdan*, fr. *be-* + *strīdan* to stride — more at STRIDE] **1 a :** to ride astride ⟨I saw fair boys *bestriding* steeds —R.W.Emerson⟩ **:** MOUNT ⟨*bestrode* his precious bike, and . . . went roaring out —Elizabeth Goudge⟩ **b :** to sit astride ⟨two small boys *bestriding* a fallen log⟩ **c :** to lie on either side of **:** STRADDLE ⟨one rather formal consultation about a dead balsam that *bestrode* the property line —A.B. Mayse⟩ **:** SPAN ⟨a bridge *bestriding* the torrential river⟩ **2 a :** to stand astride (as a fallen man) **:** stand over **b :** to dominate absolutely **:** have unquestioned control over **:** tower over ⟨~*s* the new Democratic Congress as . . . in the past —W.S.White⟩ **3** *archaic* **:** to stride across

bests *pres 3d sing of* BEST, *pl of* BEST

best seller *n* **1 a :** a book or other publication whose sales are among the highest of its class **b :** an article of merchandise whose sales are among the highest of its class **2 :** the author of a best-selling book or other publication; *also* **:** the maker of a best-selling phonograph record ⟨the band has been a *best seller* in the record shops for weeks⟩

best·sell·er·dom \(')bes(t)'selə(r)dəm\ *n* -S **:** the category of a best seller **:** the condition of being a best seller ⟨wrote obscurely . . . before he came into ~ —*Saturday Rev.*⟩

best-selling \'=;==\ *adj* **:** ranking among best sellers

be·stud \bə̇, bē+\ *vt* [*be-* + *stud*] **:** to set (a surface) with or as if with studs

be·su·go \bə̇'sü(ˌ)gō\ *n* -S [Sp] **:** a European red porgy (*Pagrus pagrus*)

¹bet \'bet, *usu* -ed·+V\ *n* -S [origin unknown] **1 a** (1) **:** something that is laid, staked, or pledged typically between two parties on the outcome of a contest or any contingent issue **:** WAGER ⟨a ~ on the game⟩ ⟨lay a ~ on a racehorse⟩ (2) **:** a sum put into a poker pot requiring other players to stay or drop; *esp* **:** the first such sum put in after a deal or draw — compare ²ANTE, ²CALL 8, ²RAISE **b :** the act of giving or promising such a pledge **2 :** something on which one lays a bet **:** a thing to wager on ⟨the gray horse is the best ~ to win the race⟩ **3 :** a choice decided on with consideration of probabilities ⟨your best ~ is to avoid short cuts if you do not know the route⟩ ⟨he is a poor ~ for the job⟩

²bet \"\ *vb* **bet** *or* **betted; bet** *also* **betted; betting; bets** *vt* **1 :** to stake (money) on the outcome of an issue or the performance of a contestant ⟨*betting* $2 on the race⟩ ⟨*betting* $100 on the election⟩ **2 a :** to maintain with or as if with a bet ⟨I will ~ that he will be elected⟩ **b :** to make a bet with or against (a person) ⟨I ~ him on the game⟩ **c :** to lay a bet on ⟨he ~ the track favorite to place⟩ ~ *vi* **:** to lay a bet

³bet *now dial past of* BEAT

⁴bet *var of* BETH

bet *abbr* between

¹be·ta \'bād·ə, -ātə *also* 'bē-\ *n* -S [Gk *bēta*, of Sem origin; akin to Heb *bēth*- — more at BETH] **1 :** the second letter of the Greek alphabet — symbol B or β; see ALPHABET table **2 :** BETA PARTICLE, BETA RAY

²beta *or* **β-** \"\ *adj* **1 :** of or relating to one of two or more closely related chemical substances ⟨β-yohimbine⟩ — used somewhat arbitrarily to specify ordinal relationship or to specify a particular physical form, esp. an allotropic modification (as in β-iron), or an isomeric or sometimes polymeric or stereoisomeric form (as in β-D-glucose); abbr. sometimes *b-* **2 :** second in position in the structure of an organic molecule from a particular group or atom or having a structure characterized by such a position ⟨the ~ positions of furan⟩ ⟨β-hydroxy acids⟩ ⟨β-naphthol⟩ **3 :** producing a zone of decolorization when grown on blood media — used of certain hemolytic streptococci or of the hemolysis they cause **4 :** second in order of brightness — used of a star in a constellation

³be·ta \'bēd·ə, -ētə\ *n, cap* [NL, fr. L, beet — more at BEET] **:** a small genus of glabrous succulent herbs (family Chenopodiaceae) having greenish flowers and aggregate fruits — see BEET, CHARD, SEA BEET

betabacterium \ˌ==;==+\ *n* [NL, fr. L ³*Beta* + *bacterium*] **1** *cap* **:** a genus or subgenus of heterofermentative lactobacilli **2** *pl* **betabacteria :** a member of the genus *Betabacterium* **:** a heterofermentative lactobacillus

beta brass *n* [²*beta*] **:** a copper-zinc alloy with a copper content of approximately 50 to 55 percent

beta cell *n* [²*beta*] **:** any of certain secretory cells distinguished by their basophilic staining characters: as **a :** a pituitary basophil **b :** an insulin-secreting cell of the islets of Langerhans

beta cellulose *n* [²*beta*] **:** CELLULOSE 2c

be·ta·cism \'bād·ə,sizəm *also* 'bē-\ *n* -S [NL *betacismus*, fr. L *beta* (fr. Gk *bēta*) + LL *-cismus* (as in *iotacismus* iotacism)] **:** loss of distinction between the sounds of *b* and *v* in a language or dialect

¹be·ta·coc·cus \'bēd·ə,käkəs\ [NL, fr. L *beta* beet + NL *coccus*] *syn of* LEUCONOSTOC

²betacoccus \"\ *n, pl* **betacoc·ci** \-ä,kī, -äkē, -äk,sī, -äksē\ [NL, fr. L *beta* beet + NL *coccus*] **:** a heterofermentative streptococcus

bet·a·fite \'bed·ə,fīt\ *n* -S [F, fr. *Betafo*, Madagascar, its locality + F *-ite*] **:** a mineral consisting of an oxide of niobium, titanium, and uranium occurring as greenish black isometric crystals near Betafo, Madagascar

beta gauge *n* [¹*beta*] **:** a device for measuring the thickness of a material by its absorption of beta rays

beta globulin *n* [²*beta*] **:** any of several globulins of human or animal plasma or serum that have electrophoretic mobilities intermediate between those of the alpha globulins and gamma globulins — see LIPOPROTEIN

beta hemolysis *n* [²*beta*] **:** a sharply defined clear colorless zone of hemolysis surrounding colonies of certain streptococci on blood agar plates

beta–hypophamine \ˌ==+\ *n* [²*beta*] **:** a polypeptide hormone that is secreted together with oxytocin by the posterior lobe of the pituitary, that is also obtained synthetically, that increases blood pressure in mammals and exerts an antidiuretic effect, and that is used esp. in treating diabetes insipidus

be·ta·ine \'bēd·ə,ēn\ *n* -S [ISV *beta-* (fr. NL *Beta*) + *-ine*; prob. orig formed as G *betain*] **1 a :** a crystalline sweet-tasting quaternary ammonium salt that occurs in beet juice and other plant substances and in some marine animals and that is regarded as an inner salt or as a dipolar ion $(CH_3)_3N^+CH_2COO^-$ derived from glycine by methylation or from choline by oxidation; *also* **:** the hydrated form $(OH)(CH_3)_3NCH_2COOH$ **b** *or* **betaine hydrochloride :** the chloride $Cl(CH_3)_3NCH_2COOH$ of the hydrated form used as a source of hydrochloric acid esp. in medicine **2 :** any of several quaternary ammonium salts analogous in structure to betaine ⟨alanine trimethyl*betaine* $(CH_3)_3N^+CH(CH_3)COO^-$⟩

beta iron *n* [²*beta*] **:** the nonmagnetic form of iron that exists between 768° and 910°C and that is identical with alpha iron except that alpha is magnetic — compare ALPHA IRON, GAMMA IRON

be·take \bə̇, bē+\ *vb* **betook; betaken; betaking; betakes** [ME *betaken*, fr. *be-* + *taken* to take — more at TAKE] *vt* **1** *obs* **:** to deliver over **:** give for disposal **:** give up **:** GRANT ⟨Phoebe to a nymph her babe *betook* —Edmund Spenser⟩ **2** *archaic* **:** OCCUPY, COMMIT ⟨they *betook* themselves to a short debate —John Bunyan⟩ **3 :** to cause (oneself) to go ⟨he *betook* himself to the steamship offices —C.G.D. Roberts⟩ ~ *vi*, *obs* **:** to take oneself **:** have recourse **:** GO ⟨then to her . . . wagon she ~*s* —Edmund Spenser⟩

beta–naphthol \ˌ≈≈+\ *n* [²*beta*] **:** NAPHTHOL 1b

beta–naphthyl \ˌ≈≈+\ *n* [²*beta*] **:** NAPHTHYL b

be·ta·nin \ˈbēd·ənən\ *n* -s [blend of NL *Beta* and E *cyanin*] **:** a nitrogen-containing anthocyanin constituting the chief coloring matter of garden beets

beta oxy naphthoic acid *n* **:** HYDROXYNAPHTHOIC ACID a

beta particle *n* [¹*beta*] **:** an electron or positron emitted by the nucleus of an atom during radioactive decay

beta ray *n* **1 :** BETA PARTICLE **2** *or* **beta radiation :** a stream of beta particles

beta rhythm *or* **beta wave** *n* [¹*beta*] **:** a brain wave current having a frequency of more than 10 pulsations per second

betas *pl of* BETA

be·tassel \bə̇, bē+\ *vt* [*be-* + *tassel*] **:** to adorn with or as if with tassels

beta test *n* [¹*beta*] **:** a nonverbal group intelligence test used in the U.S. Army during World War I

be·ta·tron \ˈbād·əˌträn, -ātə-— *also* ˈbē-\ *n* -s [ISV ¹*beta* + *-tron*] **:** an accelerator in which electrons are propelled by the inductive action of a rapidly varying magnetic field

betch·er·y·gah \ˈbechərēˌgä, -gä\ *n* -s [native name in Australia] **:** BUDGERIGAR

¹**bete** \ˈbāt\ *adj* [prob. fr. F *bête*, lit., blockhead, beast (in *faire la bête* to pass in a card game), fr. OF *beste* beast — more at BEAST] *in certain card games* **:** subject to a penalty for failure to fulfill one's contract; *also* **:** DOWN, BEATEN

²**bete** \ˈ"\ *n* -s **:** failure by the bidder (as in auction pinochle) to fulfill his contract; *also* **:** the penalty for such failure

beteem *vt* -ED/-ING/-S **1** *obs* **:** VOUCHSAFE, GRANT, ACCORD, CONCEDE **2** *obs* **:** ALLOW, PERMIT

be·tel \ˈbēd·ᵊl, -ētᵊl\ *or* **betel pepper** *n* -s [Pg *betel*, *betle*, fr. Tamil *verrilai*] **:** a climbing pepper (*Piper betle*) whose dried leaves are wrapped around or mixed with a whole betel nut or scrapings from it together with lime made from burnt coral and chewed as a stimulant masticatory esp. by southeastern Asians

betel nut *n* **:** the astringent seed of the betel palm used as a vermifuge and myotic and in the East for chewing — called also *areca nut*

betel palm *n* **:** an Asiatic pinnate-leaved palm (*Areca cathecu*) having a slender ringed trunk and an orange-colored pungent astringent drupe with an outer fibrous husk — see BETEL NUT; compare BETEL

betel phenol *n* **:** CHAVIBETOL

bête noire *also* **bête noir** \ˌbātnəˈwär, bāt'nw-, -et-, -wä(r\ *n*, *pl* **bêtes noires** *also* **bêtes noirs** \-är(z),-äz,-ä(r\ [F *bête noire*, lit., black beast] **:** a person or thing usu. strongly and persistently detested, feared, or avoided **:** BUGBEAR

beth \ˈbāth, -āt,-ās\ *also* **bet** \-āt,-ās\ *n* -s [Heb *bēth-*, construct form of *bayith*, lit., house] **1 :** the second letter of the Hebrew alphabet — symbol ב; see ALPHABET table **2 :** the letter of the Phoenician or of any of various other Semitic alphabets corresponding to Hebrew beth

be·thab·a·ra \beˈthabərə\ *n* -s [origin unknown] **:** any of several British Guiana timber trees of the genus *Tabebuia* yielding dense hard wood

beth din *or* **bet din** \≈ˈdin, -ˈdēn\ *n* [Heb *bēth dīn*, lit., house of judgment] **1 :** a Jewish court in ancient times composed of three or four judges **2 :** a judicial body composed of a rabbi and two or more assistants having jurisdiction in matters of Jewish law

beth·el \ˈbethəl\ *n* -s [Heb *bēthʼēl* house of God] **:** HOUSE OF WORSHIP: as **a :** a chapel for nonconformists **b :** a place of worship for seamen

beth·ell process \ˈbethəl-\ *n*, *usu cap B* [after John *Bethell*, 19th cent. Am. inventor] **:** a method of preserving wood with creosote under pressure

be·thes·da \bəˈthezdə, be-\ *n* -s [fr. *Bethesda*, Biblical pool believed to have curative powers (Jn 5:2–4), fr. Gk *Bēthesda*] **:** a hallowed place **:** CHAPEL; *esp* **:** BETHEL a

beth ha·mi·drash \ˌbāth,hämiˈdräsh, ˌbāth·häˈmi,dräsh, -ät-,-äs-\ *or* **bet hamidrash** \-ät-,-äs-\ *n* [Heb *bēth hammidhrāsh*, lit., house of study] **:** a hall or school where Jews esp. in eastern Europe study the Bible, the Talmud, and later Hebrew literature

beth ha·se·pher *or* **bet ha·se·fer** \ˌ≈ häˈsāfər\ *n* [Heb *bēth hassēpher* house of the book] **:** a Jewish elementary school

beth ha·te·fil·lah *or* **bet ha·te·fil·lah** \ˈ≈,hätəˈfilə, -təfiˈlä\ *n* [Heb *bēth hattĕphillāh* house of prayer] **:** a Jewish house of worship **:** SYNAGOGUE

be·think \bə̇, bē +\ *vb* **bethought; bethought; bethinking; bethinks** [ME *bethinken*, *bethenken*, *bethenchen*, fr. OE *bethencan*, fr. *be-* + *thencan* to think — more at THINK] *vt* **1 a** *archaic* **:** to call to mind **:** REMEMBER ⟨~ how those of old . . . clove to their word —Edwin Arnold⟩ **b :** to cause (oneself) to call something to mind ⟨he *bethought* him of his responsibility as head of the house —Mary Webb⟩ **2** *obs* **a :** to consider with a view to decision or action **:** think over ⟨~ what clemency . . . they would desire —Francis Bland⟩ **b :** to cause (oneself) to consider something with a view to decision or action ⟨may find the grace . . . to ~ themselves and recover —John Milton⟩ **3 :** to give (oneself) up to reflection **:** devote (oneself) to thought ⟨Rip *bethought* himself a moment —Washington Irving⟩ **4** *obs* **:** to contrive as a result of thought **:** DEVISE ⟨we ~ a means to break it off —Shak.⟩ **5 :** to bring (oneself) to a conclusion **:** RESOLVE ⟨has *bethought* himself of joining profit and pleasure together —Richard Steele⟩ ~ *vi* **:** to engage in thought **:** CONSIDER ⟨~ ere thou dismiss us —Lord Byron⟩ **syn** see REMEMBER

beth·le·hem \ˈbethlə,hem, -lē,h-, ˈbethlēəm, -lēhəm, *rapid* ˈbethləm, ÷ -lə,ham *or* ÷ -lē,ham\ *n* -s *usu cap* [fr. the Hospital of St. Mary of *Bethlehem*, London, England] **:** ¹BEDLAM 4

beth·le·hem·ite \-,mīt\ *n* -s *cap* [*Bethlehem*, Palestine + E *-ite*] **:** a native or inhabitant of Bethlehem

bethlehem sage *n*, *usu cap B* **:** a European herb (*Pulmonaria saccharata*) with white or reddish violet flowers shaped like bells

bethlehem's–star \ˌ≈ . . . ˈ≈\ *n*, *pl* **bethlehem's–stars** *usu cap B* **:** STAR-OF-BETHLEHEM 1

beth·root \ˈbeth+,-\ *n* -s [alter. of *birthroot*] **1 :** BIRTHROOT **2 :** TRILLIUM 2

be·thumb \bə̇, bē +\ *vt* [*be-* + *thumb*] **:** to wear or soil with or as if with thumbs

be·thump \bə̇, bē +\ *vt* [*be-* + *thump*] **:** to beat or pelt soundly

be·thwack \bə̇, bē +\ *vt* [*be-* + *thwack*] **:** to beat, thrash, or pelt thoroughly

beth·y·lid \ˈbethələd, -,lid\ *adj* [NL *Bethylidae*] **:** of or relating to the family Bethylidae

be·thyl·i·dae \bəˈthilə,dē\ *n pl*, *cap* [NL, fr. *Bethylus*, type genus (fr. Gk *bēthylos*, a kind of bird) + *-idae*] **:** a family of small wasps the females of which oviposit on other insects that they sting and paralyze

be·tide \bə̇ˈtīd, bē-\ *vb* **betided** \-tīdəd\ *also archaic* **be·tid** \-tid\; **betided** *also archaic* **betid; betiding; betides** [ME *betiden*, fr. *be-* + *tiden* to happen — more at TIDE] *vt* **1 :** to happen to **:** BEFALL — now used chiefly in the expression *woe betide* ⟨woe ~ the man who recognizes no law⟩ ⟨woe ~ our enemies⟩ **2 :** FOREBODE, PRESAGE ⟨such omens ~ no good⟩ ~ *vi* **1 :** BEFALL, HAPPEN ⟨hope . . . must abide with all of us, whate'er ~ —William Wordsworth⟩ **2** *obs* **:** to be the fate or end — used with *of* or *on* ⟨if he were dead, what would ~ on me —Shak.⟩ **3 :** BETOKEN, FOREBODE **syn** see HAPPEN

betime *adv* [ME, fr. *be-* + *time*] *obs* **:** BETIMES

be·times \bə̇ˈtīmz, bē-\ *adv* [ME, fr. *betime* + *-s*] **1 :** in good season or time **:** SEASONABLY, EARLY ⟨that Friday morning Stephen awoke ~ with a sense that something was to happen —Winston Churchill⟩ **2** *archaic* **:** in a short time **:** SOON, SPEEDILY ⟨my father and sister very ~ took their leave —Samuel Pepys⟩ **3** *chiefly dial* **:** at times **:** OCCASIONALLY ⟨to write local items ~ —W.A.White⟩

be·tis \ˈbēd·əs\ *n* -ES [Sp, fr. Tag *bitis*] **:** a Philippine tree (*Payena betis*) of the family Sapotaceae the fruit of which yields an illuminating oil

bê·tise \bāˈtēz\ *n*, *pl* **bê·tises** \-z(əz)\ [F, fr. *bête* foolish, fr. *bête* blockhead, beast — more at BETE] **1 :** FOLLY, STUPIDITY, IGNORANCE ⟨one more exhibition of the ~ of an audience when confronted with something fresh —Arnold Bennett⟩ **2 :** an act of foolishness or stupidity ⟨he had committed as many literary as ideological ~*s* and he was soundly chastised for both —D.U.McDowell⟩

be·title \bə̇, bē +\ *vt* [*be-* + *title*] **1 :** to give a title to ⟨a *betitled* elder statesman⟩ **2 :** to call by a title **:** call by the title of ⟨*betitled* "king of the Anglo-Saxons" in some charters⟩

be·toil \bə̇, bē +\ *vt* [*be-* + *toil*] **:** to oppress or exhaust with toil

be·to·ken \bə̇ˈtōkən, bē-\ *vt* **betokened; betokened; betokening** \-k(ə)niŋ\ **betokens** [ME *betacnien*, *betokenen*, fr. *be-* + *tacnien*, *tokenen* to token — more at TOKEN] **1 a** *obs* **:** to be a symbol of **:** signify visibly **:** REPRESENT ⟨in the cloud a bow ~*ing* peace from God —John Milton⟩ **b :** to show esp. by signs or tokens **:** give evidence of ⟨thin, tall, and of that ash-gray color which ~*s* constant sleeplessness —Osbert Sitwell⟩ ⟨an elderly man, of . . . strong, square features, ~*ing* a steady soul —Nathaniel Hawthorne⟩ **2 :** FORESHOW, PRESAGE ⟨no sighing in the woods to ~ a big weather change — John Muir⟩ **syn** see INDICATE

be·ton·i·ca \bə̇ˈtänəkə\ *n*, *cap* [NL, fr. L *betonica*, *vettonica* betony] *in some esp. former classifications* **:** a small genus of Eurasian herbs (family Labiatae) often included in *Stachys* having the corolla tube greatly exceeding the calyx

bet·o·ny \ˈbetᵊnē\ *n* -ES [ME *betone*, fr. OF *betoine*, fr. L *betonica*, *vettonica*, fr. *Vettones*, an ancient people inhabiting the Iberian peninsula] **1 :** any of several woundworts formerly included in the genus *Betonica*; *esp* **:** PURPLE BETONY **2 :** any of several plants of the genus *Teucrium*; *esp* **:** AMERICAN GERMANDER

betook *past of* BETAKE

be·toss \bə̇, bē +\ *vt* [*be-* + *toss*] **:** to toss violently **:** AGITATE

be·to·yan \bäˈtōyən, -tȯi(y)ən\ *n* -s *usu cap* [*Betoya*, a So. American Indian people, the language of the Betoya (fr. Sp *betoya*, *betoy*, *betoye*, of AmerInd origin) + E *-an*] **1 :** a language family of Chibchan stock in eastern Colombia **2 :** TUCANO 1b

be·trample \bə̇, bē +\ *vt* [*be-* + *trample*] **:** to mark or dirty by trampling

be·tray \bə̇ˈtrā, bē-\ *vb* -ED/-ING/-S [ME *betrayen*, fr. *be-* + *trayen* to betray, fr. OF *traïr*, fr. L *tradere* to betray, deliver — more at TRAITOR] *vt* **1 :** MISLEAD: as **a :** to lead astray (as into error, sin, or danger) ⟨a peaceful man ~*ed* by anger into violence⟩ ⟨their heroes are still victims ~*ed* by circumstances into criminal follies that lead to disasters —Malcolm Cowley⟩ **b :** to lead astray and abandon (a girl or woman) **:** SEDUCE ⟨a girl ~*ed* in her teens by a much older man⟩ **2 :** to deliver into the hands of an enemy by treachery or fraud in violation of trust ⟨~ a citadel by opening its gates in the night to enemy forces⟩ **3 :** to prove faithless or treacherous to **:** fail or desert esp. in time of need ⟨~ his own people by going over to the enemy⟩ ⟨use the poor as a stepping-stone to power, and then to ~ them —*Encounter*⟩ **4 :** REVEAL: as **a :** reveal unintentionally (as something more prudently concealed) **:** DISCLOSE ⟨even his best writings ~ a limited imagination and a sour view of life⟩ ⟨~ an almost morbid sense of guilt —*N.Y.Times*⟩ **b :** to show or indicate (as something not obvious on the surface) ⟨only a tension of mouth muscles ~*ed* his uneasiness⟩ ⟨his best columns ~ . . . the philosophical bent of his mind —John Mason Brown⟩ **c :** to disclose in violation of confidence ⟨~ government secrets⟩ ~ *vi* **:** to prove false ⟨when lovely woman stoops to folly and finds too late that men ~ —Oliver Goldsmith⟩ **syn** see DECEIVE, REVEAL

be·tray·al \-ā(ə)l\ *n* -s **:** the act of betraying or fact of being betrayed ⟨his ~ of that trust by his unthinking egotism —Mark Schorer⟩ ⟨the hesitation was a ~ of his uncertainty⟩

be·trim \bə̇, bē +\ *vt* [*be-* + *trim*] **:** to adorn on both or all sides

be·troth \bə̇ˈträth, bē-, -ōth,-ōt͟h *also* -ōth *or* -ät͟h *or* -ōt͟h\ *vt* -ED/-ING/-S [ME *betreuthen*, *betrouthen*, fr. *be-* + *treuthe*, *trouthe* truth, troth — more at TRUTH] **1** *archaic* **:** to promise to take in marriage **:** plight one's troth to **2 a :** to promise in marriage **:** AFFIANCE ⟨a daughter ~*ed* to a rising young lawyer⟩ ⟨two children of noble blood ~*ed* almost from birth⟩ **b** *obs* **:** PLEDGE ⟨a fool that ~*s* himself to unquietness —Shak.⟩ **3 :** to give or pledge in religious faith and affiliation

be·troth·al \-thəl,-t͟həl\ *n* -s [*betroth* + *-al*] **:** the act of betrothing or fact of being betrothed **:** a mutual promise or contract for a future marriage — called also *espousal*

be·trothed \-tht,-t͟hd *sometimes* -thəd *or* -t͟həd\ *n* -s **:** one betrothed; *esp* **:** the person to whom one is betrothed

be·troth·ment \-thmənt, -t͟h-\ *n* -s **:** BETROTHAL

be·trousered \bə̇, bē +\ *adj* [*be-* + *trousers* + *-ed*] **:** wearing trousers

be·trunk \bə̇ˈtrəŋk, bē-ˈ-\ *vt* -ED/-ING/-S [*be-* + *trunk* (to truncate)] **:** to remove the lower part of the course of (a stream) esp. by submergence of a valley or by recession of the land along a shore — compare BEHEAD

betrust *vt* [*be-* + *trust*] *obs* **:** TRUST

bets *pres 3d sing of* BET, *pl of* BET

bet·sey bug *or* **bet·sy bug** \ˈbetsē-\ *also* **betsy beetle** *n*, *sometimes cap 1st B* [by folk etymology] **:** BESS-BUG

bet·si·mi·sar·a·ka \ˌbetsēməˈsarəkə\ *n*, *pl* **betsimisaraka** *or* **betsimisarakas :** a native of the east coast of Madagascar of predominantly Malay blood and type — compare MALAGASY

bet·ta \ˈbed·ə\ *n* [NL] **1** *cap* **:** a genus of small brilliantly colored long-finned freshwater anabantid fishes of southeastern Asia related to the climbing perch **2** -s *sometimes cap* **:** any fish of the genus *Betta*; *esp* **:** one (*B. splendens*) often kept in the tropical aquarium — called also *Siamese fighting fish*

betted *past of* BET

¹**bet·ter** \ˈbed·ə(r), -etə-\ *adj*, *comparative of* GOOD [ME *bettre*, fr. OE *betera*; akin to OHG *bezziro* better, ON *betri*, Goth *batiza*; comparative (with the suffix represented by OE *-ra*) of the root found in OE *bōt* remedy, compensation, *batian* to get better, OHG *bazzēn*, ON *batna* to get better, Goth *gabatnan* to receive as a benefit, Skt *bhadra* fortunate, good — more at -ER] **1 :** more than half; *esp* **:** much more than half ⟨waiting the ~ part of an hour⟩ **2 :** improved in health ⟨the patient is much ~ after a good night's rest⟩ **3 :** of high quality (as in breeding, style, or workmanship) ⟨a ~ class of people⟩ ⟨a ~ line of yard goods⟩ ⟨a ~ type of car⟩ — **bet·ter·ly** *adv* — **bet·ter·ness** *n* -ES

²**better** \ˈ"\ *adv*, *comparative of* WELL [ME *bettre*, fr. *bettre*, adj.] **1 :** in a superior or more excellent manner ⟨he writes ~ than I do⟩ **2 a :** to a higher or greater degree ⟨he knows the story ~ than you do⟩ **b :** MORE ⟨it is ~ than 10 miles to the lake⟩ ⟨the book was published ~ than 50 years ago⟩

³**better** \ˈ"\ *n* -s [ME *bettre*, fr. *bettre*, adj.] **1 a :** something better ⟨I expected ~⟩ ⟨I never looked for ~ at his hands —Shak.⟩ **b :** one who has a claim to precedence **:** a superior esp. in merit or rank ⟨the common man has been put and kept in his place by his ~*s* —C.G.Benjamin⟩ ⟨I like novels to be about my ~*s*, in body, wit, energy, breeding, or bank balance —W.H. Auden⟩ **2 :** superior position **:** ADVANTAGE, VICTORY — usu. used with *of* ⟨have the ~ of an argument⟩ ⟨get the ~ of a rival⟩ — **for the better :** so as to produce improvement ⟨making alterations *for the better* in the design of a house⟩

⁴**better** \ˈ"\ *vb* -ED/-ING/-S [ME *bettren*, fr. *bettre*, adj.] *vt* **1 :** make better **:** IMPROVE: as **a :** AMELIORATE ⟨strive toward ~*ing* the condition of the slum dwellers⟩ **b :** to advance or make sounder the condition or circumstances of ⟨as time goes by and we ~ our acquaintance —A.T.Quiller-Couch⟩ ⟨closer proofreading would have ~*ed* the book —M.B.Emeneau⟩ ⟨~ his lot⟩ **2 :** to surpass in excellence **:** EXCEED, EXCEL ⟨ran the mile in four minutes flat, ~*ing* his own previous record by several seconds⟩ ⟨industrial production this year considerably ~*ed* that of last year⟩ **3 :** to increase (a previous bet) in certain card games **:** RAISE ~ *vi* **:** become better **:** IMPROVE ⟨the general condition . . . must be ~*ing* instead of worsening —Thomas Carlyle⟩ ⟨the cattle . . . , though they doubled in weight and shortened their horns, but little ~*ed* in temper —P.A.Rollins⟩ **syn** see IMPROVE

⁵**better** \ˈ"\ *verbal auxiliary* **:** had better — not often in formal use ⟨the boy felt he ~ go before the fight started⟩ ⟨you ~ not do it⟩

⁶**better** *var of* BETTOR

Better Business Bureau *trademark* — used for a bureau maintained by businessmen in a town or city for keeping up local standards of honesty in business transactions

better half *n*, *pl* **better halves :** SPOUSE; *esp* **:** WIFE

bettering house *n*, *archaic* **:** ²REFORMATORY

bet·ter·ment \ˈbed·ə(r)mənt, -etə-\ *n* -s **1 :** a making or becoming better **:** IMPROVEMENT: as **a :** an improvement of an estate (as by the addition of new buildings) that makes it better and more valuable than mere repairing would do **b :** an improvement (as of a highway, railroad, or business establishment) that does more than restore to a former good condition **c :** the replacement in accounting of an existing asset with one of greater cost or superior value **2 :** the sum of money assessed, required, or used for a betterment ⟨~*s* for street construction⟩; *specif* **:** an expenditure that adds greater worth (as extended life or increased capacity) to a fixed asset

bet·ter·most \-,mōst\ *adj* **1** *now chiefly dial* **:** BEST ⟨my lady might wear some of her ~ gowns —Emily Eden⟩ **:** SUPERIOR ⟨the ~ person who shows her superiority by wearing kid gloves —Flora Thompson⟩ **2** *now chiefly dial* **:** GREATER ⟨the ~ part of the time⟩

better nature *or* **better self** *n* **:** the more virtuous, amiable, or kindly instincts of a person

better 'ole \ˌbed·ə(r)ˈōl\ *n* [*'ole* alter. of ¹*hole*] **:** the more tolerable of two undesirable things

¹**better–to–do** \ˌ≈≈≈ˈ≈\ *adj* [intended as comparative of *well-to-do*] **:** in prosperous economic circumstances **:** better off ⟨many of the *better-to-do* urban Frenchmen acquire homes in the country —S.K.Padover⟩

²**better–to–do** \ˈ"\ *n*, *pl* **better–to–do :** one who is better-to-do ⟨the *better-to-do* on whom the burden of the expense of the liberal program had fallen —C.L.Jones⟩

betting *pres part of* BET

betting machine *n* **:** PARI-MUTUEL

bet·tong \ˈbe,tȯŋ, -äŋ\ *also* **bet·ton·ga** \-ŋgə\ *n* -s [native name in Australia] **:** any of several kangaroos of the genus *Bettongia*

bet·ton·gia \beˈtäŋgēə\ *n*, *cap* [NL, fr. E *bettong* + NL *-ia*] **:** a common Australian genus of small leaping rat kangaroos

bet·tor *or* **bet·ter** \ˈbed·ə(r), -etə-\ *n* -s **:** one that bets

betts' process \ˈbets(əz)-\ *n*, *usu cap B* [after Anson G. *Betts* b1876 Am. metallurgist] **:** an electrolytic process for refining lead, the electrolyte being a solution of lead fluosilicate $PbSiF_6$ and fluosilicic acid

bet·ty \ˈbedē, ˈbetē, -i\ *n* -ES *usu cap* [back-formation fr. *brown betty*] **:** a dessert made of alternate layers of fruit and buttered crumbs, sugar, and spices baked in a large baking dish or in individual dishes ⟨cranberry ~⟩; *specif* **:** BROWN BETTY

betty lamp \ˈ"-\ *n*, *usu cap B* [prob. fr. the name *Betty*] **:** a lamp consisting of a shallow lidded metal vessel with a small spout for a coarse wick, fueled by tallow, grease, or oil, usu. hung by a hook and chain, and used esp. in the American colonies

Betty lamp

bet·u·la \ˈbechələ\ *n*, *cap* [NL, fr. L *betula*, *betulla* birch, fr. Gaulish *betulla*; akin to MIr *bethe*, *beithe* box (tree), W *bedw* birch, and to the (prob. Celtic) source of L *bitumen* mineral pitch; fr. the use of the birch tree as a source of tar — more at CUD] **:** a genus of north-temperate and arctic trees and shrubs (family Betulaceae) comprising the birches and having hard close-grained wood, alternate toothed leaves, monoecious flowers in catkins, the fruiting bracts 3-lobed or entire, thin, and deciduous, and the fruit a small samara

bet·u·la·ce·ae \ˌbechəˈlāsē,ē\ *n pl*, *cap* [NL, fr. *Betula*, type genus + *-aceae*] **:** a family of trees and shrubs (order Fagales) having simple leaves, monoecious or rarely dioecious flowers, and one-seeded nutlike fruits and comprising the birches and certain related plants (as alders, hornbeams, and hazels) — **bet·u·la·ceous** \ˌ≈≈ˈlāshəs\ *adj*

betula oil *n* **:** BIRCH OIL 2

bet·u·lin \ˈbechələn\ *n* -s [ISV *betul-* (fr. NL *Betula*, genus name of *Betula alba*) + *-in*] **:** BETULINOL

bet·u·lin·ic acid \ˌbechəˈlinik\ *n* [ISV *betulin* + *-ic*] **:** a crystalline triterpenoid acid $C_{29}H_{46}(OH)COOH$ found in various plants (as flowering dogwood) and obtained from betulinol by oxidation

bet·u·lin·ol \-lə,nōl, -ōl\ *n* -s [*betulin* + *-ol*] **:** a crystalline triterpenoid alcohol $C_{30}H_{48}(OH)_2$ occurring esp. as the white pigment of the outer bark of the European birch (*Betula alba*)

bet·u·li·tes \ˌbechəˈlīd·(,)ēz\ *n*, *cap* [NL, fr. *Betula* + L *-ites*] **:** a genus of extinct Cretaceous trees resembling the genus *Betula*

be·turbaned \bə̇, bē+\ *adj* [*be-* + *turban* + *-ed*] **:** wearing a turban

be·twat·tled \bə̇ˈtwäd·ᵊld, bē-\ *adj* [*be-* + *twattled*, past part. of *twattle*] *dial* **:** ADDLED, CONFUSED

¹**be·tween** \bə̇ˈtwēn, bē-\ *prep* [ME *betwene*, prep. & adv., fr. OE *betwēonum*, fr. *be-* + *-twēonum* (dat. pl. of an old distributive numeral akin to Goth *tweihnai* two each); akin to OE *twēgen*, *twā*, *tū* two — more at TWO] **1 a :** involving the reciprocal action of **:** involving as participants **:** jointly engaging ⟨the job was completed ~ the two of them⟩ ⟨two years of quiet talks ~ the three —*Time*⟩ **b :** shared by ⟨there are many interrelationships, and many mutual interests, ~ linguistics, philosophy, and psychology —J.B.Carroll⟩ **c :** by giving a portion of the total to each of ⟨the fortune was divided ~ the four grandchildren⟩ ⟨the food was shared ~ three families⟩ **2 a :** in the time interval that separates ⟨the two days ~ Monday and Thursday⟩ ⟨~ bites of food, they talked to their teacher⟩ **b :** in the space that separates **:** BETWIXT ⟨an alleyway ~ two tall buildings⟩ ⟨a vacuum ~ two electrodes⟩ **:** in the midst of **:** surrounded by ⟨a lion rampant ~ eight crosses⟩ **c :** in intermediate relation to in respect to quantity, quality, or degree ⟨weighing somewhere ~ a pound and a pound and a half⟩ ⟨a grade ~ passing and failing⟩ **3 a :** from one to the other of ⟨air service ~ the two cities⟩ **b :** JOINING, CONNECTING ⟨a passageway ~ two rooms⟩ **c :** in common to **:** in the joint possession, action, or agency of ⟨an agreement ~ states⟩ ⟨there is no continuity of mood ~ the three books —F.A.Swinnerton⟩ ⟨mutual understanding ~ the brothers⟩ **d :** SEPARATING, DISTINGUISHING **:** setting apart ⟨the lines ~ different new media —F.L.Mott⟩ ⟨a distinction must be drawn ~ the . . . three functions of authority —Abram Kardiner⟩ **4 :** after a comparison of **:** in point of comparison of ⟨there is not much to choose ~ the two coats⟩ **5 :** in confidence restricted to ⟨a secret ~ ourselves⟩ ⟨there's nothing private ~ you and me —Walter de la Mare⟩ **6 :** taking together the total effect of (a series of things) ⟨~ making beds, washing dishes, sewing, cleaning, and raising her children, she was kept busy⟩

²**between** \ˈ"\ *adv* [ME *betwene*] **1 a :** in an intermediate position in relation to two other objects ⟨two desks with a wastebasket ~⟩ **b :** filling the space limited by two objects ⟨two buildings with a parking area ~⟩ **2 :** in the interval **:** in intervals ⟨two short movies with a newsreel ~⟩ ⟨dancing all the dances with very little rest ~⟩ **3 :** through a space limited by two objects ⟨since he could not go around the two strolling men, he went ~⟩

³**between** \ˈ"\ *n* -s **:** the time, space, state, or way between

betweenbrain \≈ˈ≈,≈\ *n* -s [²*between*] **:** DIENCEPHALON

¹**between decks** \≈ˈ≈,≈\ *adv* [¹*between*] **:** in the space on a ship between decks **:** BELOWDECKS **:** below the main deck

²**between decks** \≈ˈ≈,≈\ *n pl but sing in constr* **1 :** the space belowdecks **:** the space below the main deck **2 :** a deck below the main deck; *specif* **:** a raised deck in the hold of a cargo ship

betweenmaid \≈ˈ≈,≈\ *n* -s [²*between*] *Brit* **:** a maidservant whose work supplements that of cook and housemaid

be·tween·ness \-ēnnəs\ *n* -ES **:** the quality or state of being between two others in an ordered series

between-the-lens shutter *n* **:** DIAPHRAGM SHUTTER

between the lines *adv* **:** by implication **:** in an indirect way ⟨made it clear, *between the lines,* that he would be in line for J's present job —W.S.Carlson⟩ **:** INFERENTIALLY ⟨read *between the lines*⟩

between the sheets *n* **:** a cocktail consisting of equal parts of rum, an orange-flavored liqueur, and brandy and flavored with lime or lemon juice

be·tween·times \-ˈ-ˌtīmz\ *adv* **:** at or during intervals ⟨spent the bulk of his time writing but ~ worked as a janitor and a car salesman⟩

be·tween·whiles \-ˈ-ˌ(h)wīlz\ *adv* **:** BETWEENTIMES

¹be·twixt \bəˈtwikst, bē·-\ *prep* [ME *betwix, betwixte,* fr. OE *betweoh, betweox, betwyxt,* fr. *be-* + *-tweoh, -tweox, -twyxt* (fr. an old distributive numeral akin to Goth *tweihnai* two each); akin to OE *twēgen, twā, tū* two — more at TWO] *now chiefly dial* **:** BETWEEN ⟨~ the eyes⟩

²betwixt \"\ *adv* [ME *betwix, betwixte,* fr. *betwix, betwixte,* prep.] *now chiefly dial* **:** ²BETWEEN

betwixt and between *adv* **:** in a midway position **:** neither one thing nor the other ⟨wrote . . . in such wise that he seemed more or less *betwixt and between —Amer. Guide Series: Pa.*⟩

betz cell \ˈbet(s),s-\ *n, usu cap B* [after Vladimir A. *Betz* †1894 Russ. anatomist] **:** a very large pyramidal nerve cell of the motor area of the cerebral cortex

beu·dant·ite \ˈbyüdᵊnˌtīt, byüˈdan-\ *n* -S [F *beudantite,* fr. François S. *Beudant* †1852 Fr. mineralogist + F *-ite*] **:** a mineral PbFe$_3$(AsO$_4$)(SO$_4$)(OH)$_6$ consisting of a basic ferric lead arsenate and sulfate occurring in green to black rhombohedral crystals

beuk \ˈbyük\ *chiefly Scot var of* BOOK

beurre \ˈbər\ *n* -S [F, fr. L *butyrum* — more at BUTTER] **:** BUTTER — usu. used with *au* ⟨peas au ~⟩

beurre noir \ˌbərn(ə)ˈwär\ *n, pl* **beurres noirs** \-ˈär(z)\ [F, lit., black butter] **:** butter browned and seasoned with vinegar and parsley

BEV *abbr, often not cap* billion electron volts

¹bev·el \ˈbevəl\ *adj* [fr. (assumed) MF *bevel,* n.] **:** having the slant of a bevel **:** OBLIQUE, BEVELED ⟨a ~ edge⟩

²bev·el \"\ *n* -S [fr. (assumed) MF *bevel* (whence MF *béveau, biveau*), fr. OF *baif* with open mouth, fr. *baer* to gape + *-if* -ive (fr. L *-ivus*) — more at ABEYANCE] **1 a :** the angle that one surface or line makes with another when they are not at right angles **b :** the slant or inclination of such a surface or line **c :** the surface or line at such a slant or inclination **d :** ¹FLEAM 2 **e :** the part of a piece of printer's type extending from the face to the shoulder — compare BEARD 4d; see TYPE illustration **2** *or* **bevel square :** an instrument consisting of two rules or arms jointed together and opening to any angle for drawing angles or adjusting the surfaces to be given a bevel **3 :** BEVEL WHEEL 2 **4 :** the direction in which the bolt of a lock tapers

A

A bevel 1c

³bevel \"\ *vb* **beveled** *or* **bevelled; beveled** *or* **bevelled; beveling** *or* **bevelling** \-v(ə)liŋ\ **bevels** *vt* **1 :** to cut or shape to a bevel **:** slope the edge or surface of **:** put a bevel on ⟨a carpenter must often ~ the bottom edge of a door to fit a slanting sill⟩ ⟨a printer ~*s* a rule in a mitering machine⟩ ⟨an engraving or electrotype is ~*ed* for fastening to patent bases⟩ **2** *geol* **:** to cut across ⟨the waves ~*ed* a volcanic island⟩ ⟨the erosion surface ~*s* an anticlinal structure⟩ ~ *vi* **:** to deviate or incline so as not to be at right angles with a line or surface **:** SLANT

bevel chisel *n* **:** a wood carver's chisel with a cutting edge that makes an oblique angle with the sides

beveled *or* **bevelled** *adj* **1** *mineralogy* **:** replaced by two planes inclining equally upon the adjacent planes ⟨a ~ edge⟩ **2** *mineralogy* **:** having its edges replaced by sloping planes

bev·el·er *or* **bev·el·ler** \-v(ə)lə(r)\ *n* -S **:** one that bevels: as **a :** one that bevels and smooths the edges of optical glass by means of an abrasive wheel **b :** one that files and sands slabs of slate for building purposes

bevel gauge *n* **:** ²BEVEL 2

bevel gear *n* **:** one of a pair of toothed wheels whose working surfaces are inclined to nonparallel axes

bevel pinion *n* **:** the smaller of a pair of bevel gears

bevel protractor *n* **:** a protractor with an arm pivoted so that it serves also as a bevel — see PROTRACTOR illustration

bevel siding *n* **:** siding tapered or beveled so that its upper edge is thinner than its lower and lapped in laying to cover the horizontal joint between adjoining pieces

bevel wheel *n* **: 1 :** a bevel gear **2 :** a wheel having a conical surface that rolls in contact with a disk or another bevel wheel

bevel gear

¹bever *obs var of* BEAVER

²bev·er \ˈbevə(r), ˈbi-, ˈbā-\ *vi* -ED/-ING/-S [freq. of ME *biven* to tremble, fr. OE *beofian* — more at BEBUNG] *dial chiefly Brit* **:** SHIVER, TREMBLE

³bever \"\ *n* -S *dial chiefly Brit* **:** TREMBLING ⟨all of a ~ with cold⟩

⁴be·ver \ˈbēvə(r), ˈbā-\ *n* -S [ME, drinking, potation, fr. MF *beivre,* fr. *beivre* to drink] *chiefly dial* **:** a light lunch eaten between regular meals

bev·er·age \ˈbev(ə)rij, -ēj\ *n* -S [ME, fr. MF *bevrage,* fr. *beivre* to drink, fr. L *bibere* — more at POTABLE] **1 :** liquid for drinking; *esp* **:** such liquid other than water (as tea, milk, fruit juice, beer) usu. prepared (as by flavoring, heating, admixing) before being consumed **2** *archaic* **:** any of several prepared drinks: as **a :** a drink made by passing water through pressed grapes **b :** weak beer **c :** diluted cider **3** *dial Brit* **:** a drink or drink money esp. when exacted from someone wearing manifestly new clothes

beverage room *n, Canad* **:** a hotel barroom that serves only beer

bev·er·en \ˈbev(ə)rən, ˈbāv-\ *n, usu cap* [fr. *Beveren,* commune of Belgium] **1 :** a breed of blue-eyed rabbits of Belgian origin raised for meat, fur, and show **2** -S **:** a rabbit of the Beveren breed

be·vue \bāvˈtē\ *n* -S [F *bévue,* fr. *bé-,* pejorative prefix (fr. L *bis* twice) + *vue* sight, view, fr. OF *veue* — more at BIS, VIEW] **:** an error due to ignorance or inadvertence

bevy \ˈbevē, -vi\ *n* -ES [ME *bevey, bevie*] **1 a :** a usu. large group or collection ⟨amorous involvement with a ~ of young women —Rex Lardner⟩ ⟨a ~ of balloons filling the sky⟩ ⟨a ~ of nature activities —*Ford Times*⟩ **b :** ¹BEE 3a **2 :** a number of animals (as birds) together — used chiefly of quail

be·wail \bə, bē +\ *vb* -ED/-ING/-S [ME *bewailen,* fr. *be-* + *wailen* to wail — more at WAIL] *vt* **1 :** to express deep sorrow for **:** wail over **:** LAMENT ⟨~ your injuries or losses⟩ ⟨a servant ~*ing* her hard luck —W.A.White⟩ **2 :** to express deep regret for **:** DEPLORE ⟨he ~*ed* the breaches of the Constitution —H.D.Jordan⟩ ~ *vi* **:** to express grief **:** LAMENT **syn** see DEPLORE

be·wail·ing·ly *adv* **:** in a bewailing manner

be·wail·ment \-ā(ə)lmənt\ *n* -S **:** the act or the sound of bewailing **:** LAMENTATION

be·ware \bəˈwa(a)(ə)r, bē-, -we(ə)r,-wa(a)ə,-weə\ *vb* -ED/-ING/-S [ME *been war,* fr. *been* to be + *war* careful — more at BE, WARE] *vi* **1 :** to be on one's guard **:** be cautious **:** take care — usu. used with *of* or *lest* and now chiefly in imperative or infinitive ⟨~ of straying into . . . absurdities —*Manchester Guardian Weekly*⟩ **2** *obs* **:** to have a special regard **:** pay heed ⟨~ of him and obey his voice —Exod 23:21 (AV)⟩ ~ *vt* **1 :** to take care of **:** have a care for — now chiefly in imperative or infinitive ⟨~ your pocketbook when he is around⟩ **2 :** to be wary of — used chiefly in imperative or infinitive constructions ⟨~ the exceedingly tenuous generalization —Matthew Lipman⟩

be·weep \bə, bē+\ *vt* **bewept; bewept; beweeping; beweeps** [ME *bewepen,* fr. OE *bewēpan,* fr. *be-* + *wēpan* to weep — more at WEEP] *archaic* **:** to weep over **:** LAMENT

be·west \biˈwest\ *prep* [ME, fr. OE *be westan,* fr. *be* by, at (fr. *bi, bī*) + *westan* from the west, fr. *west* west, westward — more at BY, WEST] *Scot* **:** to the west of

bewet *vt* [ME *beweten,* fr. *be-* + *weten* to wet — more at WET] *obs* **:** WET

be·whisker \bə, bē +\ *vt* -ED/-ING/-S [*be-* + *whisker*] **:** to put whiskers on

bewhiskered *adj* **1 :** wearing whiskers **2 :** staled by repetition **:** OLD ⟨a ~ joke⟩

bewhore *vt* -ED/-ING/-S [*be-* + *whore,* n.] **1** *obs* **:** to call or name (a woman) a whore **2** *obs* **:** to make a whore of

bew·ick's swan \ˈbyüik(s)ˈs-\ *also* **bewick swan** *n, usu cap B* [after Thomas *Bewick* †1828 Eng. wood engraver who illustrated a book about birds] **:** a white swan (*Cygnus bewicki*) of northern Asia and northeastern Europe that occas. appears in western Europe in winter and is smaller than the whooper swan with a smaller and more orange patch of naked skin in front of the eye

bewick's wren \-iksˈr-\ *n, usu cap B* [after T. *Bewick*] **:** a brown wren (*Thyromanes bewickii*) common in the southern half of the U.S.

be·wig \bə, bē +\ *vt* **bewigged; bewigged; bewigging; bewigs** [*be-* + *wig,* n.] **:** to furnish with a wig ⟨hatless but *bewigged* and protected by flowing baronial robes —*Amer. Guide Series: Va.*⟩

bewigged *adj* **:** clothed in or marked by official dignity or importance ⟨the Age of Reason, with its ~ platitudes —L.P. Smith⟩

be·wil·der \bəˈwildə(r), bē-\ *vb* **bewildered; bewildered; bewildering** \-d(ə)riŋ\ **bewilders** [*be-* + *wilder*] *vt* **1 :** to cause to lose one's bearings **:** perplex or confuse by revealing no clear or right path to follow ⟨~*ed* by the maze of streets in the town⟩ **2 :** to perplex, confuse, or lead mentally astray esp. by a complexity, variety, or multitude of objects or considerations ⟨so many questions ~ him⟩ ⟨events which have caused ~*ed* and angry anxiety —Thomas Cadett⟩ ~ *vi* **:** CONFUSE ⟨the ~*ing* expansion of science during the last century —C.H. Grandgent⟩ ⟨a complexity of logic that ~*s* and confuses⟩ **syn** see PUZZLE

be·wil·dered·ly \-ldə(r)dlē, -li\ *adv* **:** in a bewildered manner

be·wil·dered·ness \-də(r)dnəs\ *n* -ES **:** the quality or state of being bewildered

be·wil·der·ing·ly \-ld(ə)riŋlē, -ŋli\ *adv* **:** in a way that bewilders ⟨a ballet which is ~ beautiful —Stephen Graham⟩ ⟨~ rapid conquests —J.P.Baxter b.1893⟩

be·wil·der·ment \-ldə(r)mənt\ *n* -S **1 :** the quality or state of being bewildered ⟨his complete ~ as to what had really taken place —F.W.Crofts⟩ **2 :** a bewildering tangle or confusion ⟨led his now grumbling men . . . into a ~ of headwaters, beaver ponds, mountains, and unfriendly Indians —Ralph Gray⟩

bew·it *or* **bew·et** \ˈbyüət\ *n* -S [ME *bewette,* fr. MF *buie, beue* fetter (fr. L *bojae,* pl., neck-collar, fr. (assumed) Gk *boeiai,* fr. fem. pl. of *boeios* of an ox, fr. *bous* ox, cow) + ME *-ette* -et — more at COW] **:** a slip of leather by which bells are fastened to a hawk's legs in falconry

be·witch \bəˈwich, bē-\ *vb* -ED/-ING/-ES [ME *bewicchen,* fr. *be-* + *wicchen* to witch — more at WITCH] *vt* **1 a :** to influence or control by witchcraft **:** dominate by witchcraft **:** affect (as injuriously) by charms or incantations ⟨look how I am ~*ed;* behold, mine arm is like a blasted sapling withered up —Shak.⟩ ⟨charged with ~*ing* a girl, who had been seized with a sudden illness that the doctor could not diagnose —*Amer. Guide Series: Tenn.*⟩ **b :** to cast a spell over ⟨the spotlight was on them, and the spell, and they stood there ~*ed* and helpless —Dorothy Baker⟩ **2 :** to attract or please to such a degree as to take away all power of resistance or considered reservation **:** ENCHANT, CHARM, FASCINATE ⟨she ~*ed* King James no less than her first lover —*N.Y.Times*⟩ ⟨that time-honored privilege of saying foolish things in the grand manner which seems to have ~*ed* our gallant forefathers —Norman Douglas⟩ ~ *vi* **:** to act in a way that bewitches **:** CHARM, FASCINATE ⟨a book that ~*es* and enchants as it teaches —*Americas*⟩ **syn** see ATTRACT

be·witchedness \-chədnəs, -ch(t)n-\ *n* -ES **:** the quality or state of being bewitched

be·witch·ery \-ch(ə)rē, -ri\ *n* -ES **:** BEWITCHMENT 1 ⟨a great ~ in the idea —Nathaniel Hawthorne⟩

be·witch·ing·ly *adv* **:** in a bewitching manner **:** to a bewitching degree ⟨a ~ beautiful girl⟩

be·witch·ing·ness *n* -ES **:** the quality or state of being bewitching

be·witch·ment \-chmənt\ *n* -S **1 a :** the act or power of bewitching **:** FASCINATION ⟨the ~ of forbidden pleasures⟩ **b :** a spell that bewitches **2 :** the state of being bewitched ⟨the ~ of a young man in love⟩

bewpers *n, pl* **bewpers** [perh. fr. *Beaupréau,* near Cholet, Maine-et-Loire dept., France] *obs* **:** a fabric prob. of linen used for flags

be·wrap \bə, bē +\ *vt* [ME *bewrappen,* fr. *be-* + *wrappen* to wrap — more at WRAP] **:** to wrap up **:** clothe in a wrap

¹be·wray \bəˈrā, bē-\ *vt* -ED/-ING/-S [ME *bewreyen,* fr. *be-* + *wreyen* to accuse, inform on, fr. OE *wrēgan;* akin to OHG *ruogen* to accuse, ON *rægja* to defame, Goth *wrōhjan* to accuse, and prob. to Lith *rėkti* to cry out] **1** *archaic* **:** to make known **:** DIVULGE, DISCLOSE; *esp* **:** to reveal (as a secret) to one's disadvantage often unintentionally **2** *archaic* **:** to reveal the true character of **syn** see REVEAL

²bewray \"\ *vt* -ED/-ING/-S [alter. (influenced by ¹*bewray*) of *beray*] *archaic* **:** BERAY

be·wray·er \-āə(r)\ *n* -S [ME *bewreyer,* fr. *bewreyen* + *-er*] **:** one that bewrays ⟨a ~ of secrets —Joseph Addison⟩

be·wreath \bəˈrēth, bē-, -th\ *vt* -ED/-ING/-S [*be-* + *wreath*] **:** to decorate with wreaths

be·write \bə, bē +\ *vt* **bewrote; bewritten; bewriting; bewrites** [*be-* + *write*] **:** to write about ⟨a public figure who has been much *bewritten* in the newspapers⟩

be·wusst·seins·la·ge \bəˈvu̇st,zīn(t)s,lägə, -zīnz,l-, -lägə\ *n, pl* **bewusstseinslagen** \-gən\ *usu cap* [G, fr. *bewusstsein* consciousness (fr. *bewusst* conscious — past part. of *bewissen* to know, fr. *be-* + *wissen* to know, fr. OHG *wizzan* — + *sein* being, fr. *sein* to be, fr. OHG *sīn*) + *lage* situation, fr. OHG *lāga* act of laying; akin to OHG *ligen* to lie — more at WIT, IS, LIE] *psychol* **:** a state of consciousness or a feeling devoid of sensory components

bey \ˈbā\ *n* -S [Turk, gentleman, chief, prince] **1 a :** the governor of a district or minor province in the Ottoman Empire **b :** the sovereign of the former kingdom of Tunis **c :** the native and often nominal sovereign of the former monarchy of Tunisia **2 :** the bearer of a title of courtesy or honor formerly used in Turkey and Egypt

be·yant \-ˈ(y)än(t), -an-\ *chiefly Irish var of* BEYOND

bey·er·ite \ˈbīəˌrīt\ *n* -S [Adolph *Beyer* †1805 Ger. mining engineer and mineralogist + E *-ite*] **:** a mineral Ca(BiO)$_2$(CO$_3$)$_2$ consisting of a rare calcium bismuth oxide and carbonate occurring in yellow crystals

beylerbey *var of* BEGLERBEG

bey·lic *or* **bey·lik** \ˈbālik\ *n* -S [Turk *beylik,* fr. *bey* + *-lik* (suffix used to form abstract nouns)] **:** the territory ruled by a bey **:** the jurisdiction of a bey — **bey·lic·al** \-kəl\ *adj*

¹be·yond \bēˈänd *also* bēˈyä- *or* bəˈyä- *sometimes* -ˈ(y)ȯ- *or* -ˈ(y)ə-\ *adv* [ME *beyonde,* adv. & prep., fr. OE *begeondan,* fr. *be-* + *geondan* beyond, fr. *geond* yond, yonder — more at YOND] **1 a :** farther away or farther along in space, time, or any developing temporal activity ⟨along the road through the valley and ~ to town⟩ ⟨the class lasts until four o'clock and seldom goes ~⟩ ⟨through the secondary school and ~⟩ **b :** on the farther side ⟨a hayfield with a pond ~⟩ **2 :** in addition **:** FURTHER, BESIDES ⟨to provide the essentials of education but nothing ~⟩

²beyond \"\ *prep* [ME *beyonde*] **1 :** on or to the farther side of **:** in the same direction as but farther on or farther away ⟨a house ~ a field and a small wood⟩ ⟨traveling ~ the larger cities to a village on the same route⟩ ⟨he made his native town his home, never journeying many miles ~ its borders —H.E. Starr⟩ **2 a :** out of the reach or sphere of ⟨then we grew ~ it —H.A.Overstreet⟩ **:** greater than the grasp or power of ⟨a task ~ his strength⟩ ⟨a sick man far ~ medical help⟩ ⟨the job was clearly ~ him —Merle Miller⟩ **b :** in a degree or amount surpassing ⟨angry ~ measure⟩ ⟨beautiful ~ expression⟩ **c :** out of or passing the comprehension of ⟨his reasoning is ~ us⟩ ⟨God's ways are ~ us —M.R.Cohen⟩ **3 :** in addition to **:** OVER AND ABOVE, BESIDES ⟨decided to make traffic control their personal business ~ their regular duties —*Lamp*⟩ ⟨without any treatment ~ sedatives and rest —Stuart Chase⟩

³beyond \"\ *n* -S [¹*beyond*] **1 :** something that lies beyond ⟨a river for small boats for twenty miles back into the ~ —R.W.Hatch⟩ **2** *sometimes cap* **:** something that lies outside the scope of ordinary experience ⟨there's a ~ that the mind can't see, and that's where the answers are —Robert Nathan⟩; *specif* **:** ²HEREAFTER

be·yond·ness \-nəs\ *n* -ES **:** the quality or state of being beyond ⟨their dream of ~ was forgotten in the immediacy of the sky, breeze, and turf of earlier experience —Viola Meynell⟩

be·yont \-n(t)\ *or* **be·yonst** \-nzt,-n(t)st\ *dial var of* BEYOND

bez·ant *also* **bes·ant** \ˈbezᵊnt, bəˈzant\ *or* **byz·ant** \ˈbizᵊnt, bəˈzant\ *n* -S [ME *besand, besant,* fr. OF *besant,* fr. ML *Byzantius* Byzantine, fr. *Byzantium,* ancient city (now Istanbul, Turkey)] **1 :** the Byzantine gold solidus as designated in western Europe where it circulated up to the 16th century **2 :** a flat disk used in architectural ornament sometimes as one of many overlapping circular scales arranged in a single row (as in a molded jamb or archivolt) **3** *heraldry* **:** a roundel or

¹be·zan·tée *or* **be·zan·té** \bəˈzantē, ˌbezᵊnˈtā\ *also* **be·zan·ty** \bəˈzantē\ *adj* [F *besanté,* fr. *besant*] **1 :** set with bezants **2** *heraldry* **:** semé of bezants

²be·zan·tee \bəˈzantē\ *n* -S **:** BEZANT 2

bez antler [OF *bes* twice, fr. L *bis* — more at BIS] *var of* BAY ANTLER

¹bez·el *or* **bez·il** \ˈbezəl\ *n* -S [prob. fr. a dial. form of F *biseau,* perh. fr. L *bis* twice — more at BIS] **1 :** a sloping edge or face esp. on a cutting tool — called also *basil* **2** *also* **biz·el** \ˈbizəl\ **a :** the top part of a ring that may be a flat table or hold a gem, bear an intaglio, or have some other ornamentation **b :** the oblique side or face of a cut gem; *specif* **:** the upper faceted portion of a brilliant projecting from the setting between the table and the girdle **:** CROWN — compare PAVILION; see BRILLIANT illustration **c :** the grooved rim that holds the crystal on a watch **d :** a similar rim that holds a glass or plastic covering (as on a clock dial or headlight)

²bez·el *or* **bez·il** \"\ *vt* **bezeled** *or* **bezelled** *or* **beziled** *or* **bezilled; bezeled** *or* **bezelled** *or* **beziled** *or* **bezilled; bezeling** *or* **bezelling** *or* **beziling** *or* **bezilling** \-z(ə)liŋ\ **bezels** *or* **bezils :** to form the edge of to an angle **:** BEVEL

be·zique \bəˈzēk\ *n* -S [F *bésique*] **1 :** a card game similar to pinochle that is played with a pack of 64 cards and in which the points are made chiefly by winning tricks (as those containing brisques) and thereupon declaring any of certain combinations in the hand (as a marriage, a sequence, or four of a kind) **2 :** a combination of a queen and a jack (as the queen of spades and jack of diamonds) in bezique commonly scored as 40 but counting as 500 when doubled

be·zoar \ˈbēzō(ə)r\ *or* **bezoar stone** *n* -S [MF *bézoard,* fr. Sp *bezoar,* fr. Ar *bāzahr, bādizahr,* fr. Per *bād-zahr, pād-zahr* fr. *pād* protecting (against) + *zahr* poison] **:** any of various concretions found in the alimentary organs (esp. of certain ruminants) formerly believed to possess magical properties and used in the Orient as a medicine or pigment — see GERMAN BEZOAR, ORIENTAL BEZOAR, PHYTOBEZOAR, TRICHOBEZOAR, WESTERN BEZOAR

bezoar antelope *n* **:** BLACK BUCK 1

bezoar goat *n* **:** the wild goat (*Capra aegagrus*) of Iran and adjacent regions

be·zold-brücke phenomenon \ˌbātˌsōltˈbrikə-, -rækə-\ *n, usu cap both Bs* [after Wilhelm von *Bezold* †1907 Ger. meteorologist and Ernst W. von *Brücke* †1892 Ger. physiologist] **:** the shift in the hue of colors that occurs when the intensity of the corresponding energy stimulus is materially increased, except in the case of the stimuli for certain invariable hues approximating the psychologically primary hues

be·zo·ni·an \bəˈzōnēən, bē-, -nyən\ *n* -S *sometimes cap* [modif. (influenced by E *-ian*) of It *bisogno* recruit from Spain, lit., need, fr. ML *bisonium*] **1** *archaic* **:** a military recruit **2** *archaic* **:** a mean dishonest person **:** SCOUNDREL

bez·po·po·vets \ˌbespəˈpȯvəts, ˌbezp-\ *n, pl* **bezpo·pov·tsy** \-ˌȯftsē\ *usu cap* [Russ, fr. *bez* without (fr. ORuss) + *-popovets* (fr. *popov-* — pl. stem of *pop* priest, fr. OHG *pfaffo* fr. Goth *papa,* fr. LGk *papas,* fr. Gk, father — + *-ets,* agent suffix); akin to OSlav & Pol *bez* without, Lith *bė,* Skt *bahis* outside — more at POPE] **:** a member of a Raskolnik priestless sect in Russia — compare POPOVETS

bez tine *n* [OF *bes* twice — more at BAY ANTLER] **:** BAY ANTLER

bez·zle \ˈbezəl\ *vb* -ED/-ING/-S [ME *besilen,* fr. MF *besillier* to destroy, kill] *vt, now dial Brit* **:** WASTE, PLUNDER ~ *vi* **:** to drink or eat to excess

bf *abbr* **1** boldface **2** brief

BF *abbr* **1** beat frequency **2** *often not cap* board foot **3** brought forward

b flat \ˈ-ˈ-\ *n, usu cap B* **1 :** the keynote of B-flat major or B-flat minor **2 :** the tone a half step below B

b-flat major \ˈ-ˌ-ˈ--\ *n, usu cap B* **:** the major musical key having a signature of two flats

b-flat minor \ˈ-ˌ-ˈ--\ *n, usu cap B* **:** the minor musical key having a signature of five flats

BFO *abbr* beat-frequency oscillator

bg *abbr* **1** bag **2** background **3** being

BG *abbr* **1** bonded goods **2** brigadier general

bght *or* **bgt** *abbr* bought

b-girl \ˈbē+ˌ-\ *n, usu cap B* [prob. fr. *bar* + *girl*] **:** a woman employed frequently on a commission basis to entertain and listen to bar patrons and encourage them to spend freely

BH *abbr* **1** base hospital **2** bill of health

bha·bar \ˈbäbə(r)\ *n* -S [Hindi *bhābar*] **1 :** a valuable Indian fiber grass (*Ischaemum angustifolium*) used for making mats, rope, and paper — called also *baib grass* **2 :** a sedge (*Eriophorum comosum*) found with bhabar and used for the same purposes

bha·don \ˈbäˌdōn\ *n* -S *usu cap* [Hindi *bhādõ,* fr. Skt *bhādrapada,* fr. *Bhadrapadā,* either of two lunar asterisms, fr. fem. of *bhadrapada* having fortunate steps or feet, fr. *bhadra* fortunate + *pada* step, foot; akin to Skt *pad* foot — more at BETTER, FOOT] **:** a month of the Hindu year — see MONTH table

bha·gat \ˈbəgət\ *n* -S [Hindi *bhagat*] **:** a Hindu saint or religious devotee

bha·ga·vat \ˈbəgəvət\ *n, usu cap* [Skt, lit., possessing good fortune, fr. *bhaga* good fortune; akin to Skt *bhajati* he grants, allots — more at BAKSHEESH] **:** blessed one **:** LORD — used chiefly as an epithet of deities in Hinduism and Buddhism

bha·ga·va·ta \ˌbägəˈvəd·ə\ *n* -S [Skt *bhāgavata* relating to the blessed one, fr. *bhagavat*] **:** a devotional worshiper of a deity, esp. of Vishnu **:** BHAKTA

bhai \ˈbäē\ *n* -S [Hindi *bhāī* brother, fr. Skt *bhrātṛ* — more at BROTHER] *India* **:** BROTHER, FRIEND — used in address as an expression of friendship

bhak·ta \ˈbəktə\ *n* -S [Skt, one who resorts or is devoted to (a god), belonging to, allotted — more at BATTA] *Hinduism* **:** a religious devotee **:** WORSHIPER — compare BHAKTI

bhak·ti \ˈbəktē\ *n* -S [Skt, lit., portion, share, fr. *bhajati* he grants, allots] *Hinduism* **:** religious devotion **:** love directed toward a personal deity — **bhak·tic** \ˈbaktik, ˈbək-\ *adj*

bhak·ti-mar·ga \ˌbəktēˈmärgə\ *n* [Skt *bhaktimārga,* fr. *bhakti* + *mārga* path, fr. *mṛga* deer, gazelle] *Hinduism* **:** approach to salvation by way of ardent devotion to a deity — compare KARMA-MARGA

bhakti yoga *n* [Skt *bhaktiyoga,* fr. *bhakti* + *yoga*] **:** devotional yoga

bha·lu \ˈbäˌlü, ˈbä-\ *n* -S [Hindi *bhālū,* fr. Skt *bhallūka,* fr. *bhalla* bear; akin to OE *bera* bear — more at BEAR] **:** BEAR; *specif* **:** SLOTH BEAR

bhang *also* **bang** \ˈbaŋ\ *n* -S [Hindi *bhāg,* fr. Skt *bhaṅga;* akin to Per *bang* hemp] **1 a :** HEMP 1 **b :** the leaves and flowering tips of hemp, esp. of the female plant **:** CANNABIS — compare GANJA, HASHISH, MARIHUANA **2 :** any of several narcotic and intoxicant products obtained from bhang: as **a :** an Asian decoction of bhang usu. fermented in milk or water **b :** MAJOON **c :** a resinous extractive rich in narcotic principles

bhan·gi *or* **bhun·gi** \ˈbəŋ(ˌ)gē\ *n* -S [Hindi *bhangī,* lit., one addicted to bhang, fr. *bhāg*] **:** a Hindu sweeper or scavenger being a member of one of the lowest untouchable castes

bhar \ˈbär\ *n, pl* **bhar** *or* **bhars** *usu cap* **1 :** a caste of agricultural laborers in India linguistically of the Kol group inhabiting central India **2 :** a member of the Bhar caste

bhar·al *also* **barh·al** *or* **burrh·el** \ˈbərəl\ *n* -S [Hindi *bharal*] **:** a wild sheep (*Pseudois nahoor*) having down-curved horns and living at high elevations in the Himalayas and Tibet

bhar·a·ta \'bärəd·ə, -rətə\ *n* -s *cap* [Skt *bhārata* inhabiting India, of India, descended from Bharata, of Bharata, fr. *Bharata*, a legendary monarch of India whose descendants are the principal characters in the Mahabharata, one of the two great Sanskrit epics] **:** an inhabitant of India

bhar·a·ta na·tya \¦bərəd·ə'nä·tyə, -rətə'-\ *or* **bharata na·tyam** \-·tyəm\ *n* [Skt *bharatanātya*, lit., Bharata's dancing, fr. *Bharata*, a sage reputed to be the author of the Natyashastra, a manual of dramatic art + *nātya* dramatic art, dancing — more at NATYA] **:** a traditional Indian dance formerly exclusively performed by devadasis — compare KATHAK, KATHAKALI, MANIPURI

bhar·a·ti \'bärəd·ē, -rətē, -i\ *adj, usu cap* [Skt *bhāratī*, fem. of *bhārata*] **:** of or relating to India **:** INDIAN

bhar·ti \'bär|d·ē, 'bȧ|d·ē, |tē, -i\ *n* -s [native name in India] *India* **:** BARNYARD GRASS

bhat \'bät\ *n* -s [Hindi *bhāṭ*, fr. Skt *bhaṭṭa*] **:** a member of an Indian caste of bards or entertainers

bhat·pa·ra \(')bät¦pärə\ *adj, usu cap* [fr. *Bhatpara*, India] **:** of or from the city of Bhatpara, India **:** of the kind or style prevalent in Bhatpara

bhav·na·gar \(')bau̇¦nəgə(r)\ *adj, usu cap* [fr. *Bhavnagar*, India] **:** of or from the city of Bhavnagar, India **:** of the kind or style prevalent in Bhavnagar

BHC *abbr* benzene hexachloride

bhd *abbr* bulkhead

bhees·ty *or* **bhees·tie** *or* **bhis·ti** \'bēstē, -ti\ *n, pl* **bhees·ties** *or* **bhistis** [Hindi *bhīstī*, fr. Per *bihishtī* heavenly one] *India* **:** a water carrier esp. of a household or a regiment

bher tree \'be(ə)r-, 'ba(a)(ə)r-\ *n* [Hindi *ber*, fr. Skt *badara*] **:** CHINESE JUJUBE

bhik·ku \'bi(,)kü, -ikə\ *n* -s [Pali, fr. Skt *bhikṣu*] **:** a Buddhist monk or religious mendicant — compare BONZE

bhik·shu \'bikshə\ *n* -s [Skt *bhikṣu*, fr. *bhikṣate* he desires, begs, desiderative of *bhajati* he grants, allots — more at BAKSHEESH] **:** a Hindu or Buddhist monk or religious mendicant

bhil \'bē(ə)l\ *n, pl* **bhil** *or* **bhils** *usu cap* [Hindi *Bhīl*, fr. Skt *Bhilla*] **1 :** a hill people of west central India having a bow-and-arrow culture **2 :** a member of the Bhil people

bhil·a·wan nut \'bilə,wän-, 'bēl-, -,wən\ *n* [prob. fr. *Bhilawan*, *Bhilwara*, district in central India] **:** MARKING NUT

bhi·li \'bēlē\ *n* -s *cap* [Hindi *Bhīlī*, fr. *Bhīl*] **:** the Indic language of the Bhil people

BHN *abbr* Brinell hardness number

bhoj·pu·ri \'bōjpə,rē\ *n* -s *cap* [Hindi *Bhojpurī*, fr. *Bhojpur*, village in Shahabad district, western Bihar, India] **:** the dialect of Bihari spoken in western Bihar and the eastern United Provinces, India

bho·kra \'bōkrə\ *n* -s [Gujarati] **:** FOUR-HORNED ANTELOPE

bhoo·sa *also* **bhu·sa** \'büsə, -(,)sä\ *n* -s [Hindi *bhus*, *bhūsā*, fr. Prakrit *bhusa*; akin to Skt *busa* chaff] *India* **:** the broken straw and husks from the threshing floor used as fodder **:** CHAFF

bho·ra \'bōrə, -rä\ *or* **bo·ho·ra** \bō'hōr-\ *n, pl* **bhora** *or* **bhoras** *or* **bohora** *or* **bohoras** *usu cap* [Hindi *bohrā*] **:** a modern Shi'ite sect of western India retaining some Hindu elements

b–horizon \'bē·¦==\ *n, usu cap B* **:** the soil layer immediately beneath the A-horizon from which it obtains humic and other organic matter chiefly by illuviation and is usu. distinguished by less weathering — see C-HORIZON

bho·tan pine \(')bō¦tan-, -tän\ *also* **bhu·tan pine** \(')bü¦-\ *n, often cap B* [fr. *Bhotan*, *Bhutan*, country in eastern Himalayas] **:** a very resinous pine (*Pinus excelsa*) that resembles the American white pine and is native to the Himalayas but grown in Australia for timber and turpentine

bho·tia *also* **bho·ti·ya** \'bōd·ē(y)ə, -ōtē-, -ē(,)yä\ *or* **bhu·tia** \'büd·ē-, -ütē-\ *n, pl* **bhotia** *or* **bhotias** *also* **bhotiya** *or* **bhotiyas** *or* **bhutia** *or* **bhutias** *usu cap* [Skt *bhoṭiya* Tibetan (adj.), fr. *Bhoṭa* Tibet] **1 a :** the peoples of southern Tibet and Bhutan **b :** a member of such peoples **2 a :** TIBETAN **b :** any or all of the Sino-Tibetan languages spoken in Tibet or in the Himalayan region

b'hoy \bə'hȯi\ *n* -s *slang* [alter. (representing Irish pronunc.) of *boy*] **:** ROWDY, TOUGH

bhp *abbr* bishop

BHP *abbr* brake horsepower

bhpric *abbr* bishopric

bhui·ya \'büē(y)ə, -(,)(y)ä\ *n, pl* **bhuiya** *or* **bhuiyas** *usu cap* **1 :** a people in the Orissa and Bengal regions of India **2 :** a member of the Bhuiya people

bhu·mi·dar \¦bümē¦där\ *n* -s [Hindi *bhūmidār*, fr. *bhūmi* earth, land (fr. Skt) + *-dār* holder (fr. Per); akin to Skt *bhavati* he is and to Skt *dhārayati* he holds, possesses — more at BE, FIRM] *India* **:** a landholder having full title to his land

bhu·mij \'bümij\ *n, pl* **bhumij** *usu cap* [Hindi *bhūmij*, lit., earth-born, fr. Skt *bhūmija*, fr. *bhūmi* earth + *-ja* born; akin to Skt *janati* he begets — more at KIN] **1 a :** a Munda people of Chota Nagpur, India **b :** a member of this people **2 :** the Munda language of the Bhumij people

bhunder *var of* BANDAR

bhungi *var of* BHANGI

bhut \'büt, *usu* -d·+V\ *n* -s [Hindi *bhūt*, fr. Skt *bhūta*, lit., having come into being, fr. *bhavati* he becomes, is — more at BE] *India* **:** an esp. malevolent spirit **:** GHOST, DEMON, GOBLIN

bhu·tan \(')bü¦tan, -tän\ *adj, usu cap* [fr. *Bhutan*, country in eastern Himalayas] **:** of or from Bhutan **:** of the kind or style prevalent in Bhutan **:** BHUTANESE

bhutan cypress *n, usu cap B* **:** a lofty East Indian cypress (*Cupressus torulosa*) venerated by the natives

¹bhu·ta·nese \¦büt°n¦ēz\ *adj, usu cap* **1 a :** of, relating to, or characteristic of Bhutan **b :** of, relating to, or characteristic of the people of Bhutan **2 :** of, relating to, or characteristic of the Bhutanese language

²bhutanese \"\ *also* **bhu·ta·ni** \bü'tanē, -tä-\ *or* **bho·ta·ni** \bō'-\ *n, pl* **bhutanese** *or* **bhutani** *or* **bhutanis** *or* **bhotani** *or* **bhotanis** *usu cap* **1 a :** a Tibetan Mongolian people of Bhutan **b** (1) **:** a member of the Bhutanese people (2) **:** an inhabitant of Bhutan **2 :** the Tibetan language of Bhutan

bhu·ta·ta·tha·ta \,büd·əd·ə'te,tä\ *n* -s [Skt *bhūtatathatā*] **:** the essence of suchness in Buddhism

¹bhutia *usu cap, var of* BHOTIA

²bhu·tia \'büd·ēə\ *n* -s *usu cap* **:** any of a breed of chiefly gray riding ponies native to Nepal and adjacent regions

¹bi- *prefix* [ME, fr. L; akin to OE *twi-* — more at TWI-] **1 a :** two ‹*bi*muscular› ‹*bi*cycle› ‹*bi*racial› **b :** lasting two **:** coming or occurring every two ‹*bi*ennial› ‹*bi*monthly› ‹*bi*weekly› **c :** into two parts ‹*bi*sect› **2 a :** twice **:** doubly **:** on both sides ‹*bi*conic› ‹*bi*convex› ‹*bi*serrate› **b :** coming or occurring two times ‹*bi*diurnal› ‹*bi*quarterly› ‹*bi*weekly› — often disapproved in this sense because of the likelihood of confusion with sense 1b; compare SEMI- **3** *anat* **:** between, involving, or affecting two (specified) symmetrical parts ‹*bi*gonial› ‹*bi*-iliac› **4** *chem* **a :** containing one (specified) constituent in double the proportion of the other constituent or in double the ordinary proportion — esp. in names of acid salts formed with twice as much acid as is required for a normal salt ‹*bi*urate› **b :** DI- 2 — esp. in names of organic compounds to denote the doubling of a radical or molecule ‹*bi*tolyl› ‹*bi*phenol›

²bi- *or* **bio-** *comb form* [Gk, fr. *bios* mode of life — more at QUICK] **:** life ‹*bio*blast› **:** living organisms or tissue ‹*bio*psy› *bio*dynamics›

Bi *symbol* bismuth

-bia \bēə, *sometimes US and usu Brit* byə\ *n comb form* [NL, fr. fem. sing. and neut. pl. of *-bius* having a (specified) mode of life — more at -BIUS] **:** one or ones having a (specified) mode of life — in generic names as a singular ‹Bryo*bia*› and in descriptive biological group names as a plural ‹aero*bia*› ‹coeno*bia*›

bi·acetyl \¦bī, (')bī+\ *n* [ISV ¹*bi-* + *acetyl*] **:** a greenish yellow liquid diketone $(CH_3CO)_2$, with an odor like that of quinone that is found in some essential oils (as bay oil), that is chiefly responsible for the flavor of butter and also contributes to the aroma of coffee and tobacco, and that is made synthetically and used as a flavoring agent in foods (as margarine); 2,3-butane-dione — called also *diacetyl*

bi·acromial \-¦bī+\ *adj* [ISV ¹*bi-* + *acromial*] **:** of, relating to, or between the two acromion processes ‹~ diameter›

bi·a·cu·ru \,bī(y)əkə'rü, '===,=\ *or* **ba·ya·cu·ra root** \¦bī-(y)ə¦kürə-\ *n* -s [Pg *bayucuru*, fr. Tupi] **:** the powerfully astringent root of a So. American herb (*Limonium brasiliense*); *also* **:** the plant itself

bi·a·jai·ba \,bēə'hībə\ *n* -s [AmerSp] **:** LANE SNAPPER

bi·ak \bē'(y)äk\ *n, pl* **biak** *or* **biaks** *usu cap* **1 a :** a Papuan people of western New Guinea inhabiting the islands of Biak, Numfor, and Japen **b :** a member of such people **2 :** the language of the Biak people

bi·alate \(')bī+\ *adj* [¹*bi-* + *alate*] **:** having two wings **:** DIPTEROUS

bia·ly·stok \byä'wi,stȯk, ,bēə'-, -'li,s-\ *adj, usu cap* [fr. *Białystok*, Poland] **:** of or from the city of Bialystok, Poland **:** of the kind or style prevalent in Bialystok

bian·chi \'byäŋkē, bē'äŋ-\ *n pl, usu cap* [It, lit., whites, pl. of *bianco* white, of Gmc origin; akin to OHG *blanch* shining, white — more at BLANK] **:** a political faction of the Guelphs in Tuscany, Italy, about 1300 opposed to the Neri

bi·an·chite \bē'aŋ,kīt\ *n* -s [It, fr. Angelo *Bianchi* b1892 Ital. mineralogist + It *-ite*] **:** a rare mineral $(Zn,Fe)SO_4.6H_2O$ consisting of hydrous sulfate of zinc and iron occurring as white crystalline crusts

bian·co so·pra bianco \¦byäŋ(,)kō¦sōprə¦-, bē¦äŋ-\ *n* [It, white on white] **:** a technique of porcelain decoration using white glaze in floral or scroll designs on a near-white usu. pale gray or blue ground

bi·anisidine \¦bī+\ *n* -s [¹*bi-* + *anisidine*] **:** any of several isomeric compounds $C_{14}H_{16}N_2O_2$ the molecule of which is a doubled anisidine molecule; *esp* **:** the white crystalline ortho isomer derived from benzidine, made by reducing *ortho*-nitro-anisole, and used as an intermediate for many azo dyes — called also *dianisidine*

bi·annual \(')bī+\ *adj* [¹*bi-* + *annual*] **:** occurring, appearing, or being made, done, or acted upon twice a year; *sometimes* **:** BIENNIAL — compare SEMIANNUAL — **bi·annually** \"+\ *adv*

bi·articular \¦bī+\ *adj* [¹*bi-* + *articular*] *anat* **:** of or relating to two joints

bi·articulate *or* **bi·articulated** \¦bī+\ *adj* [¹*bi-* + *articulate* or *articulated*] *biol* **:** having or consisting of two joints

¹bi·as \'bīəs\ *n, pl* **bi·as·es** \-əsəz\ [MF *biais*, fr. OProv, perh. irreg. fr. Gk *epikarsios* athwart, oblique, fr. *epi* on + *-karsios* (as in *enkarsios* athwart, oblique); akin to Lith *skersas* oblique, Russ *cherez* over, across] **1 :** a line diagonal to the grain of a fabric; *esp* **:** a line at a 45° angle to the selvage producing a cut with some stretchability and often utilized in the cutting of garments for smoother fit **2 a :** an inclination of temperament or outlook ‹a strong liberal ~›; *often* **:** such prepossession with some object or point of view that the mind does not respond impartially to anything related to this object or point of view ‹the most pernicious kind of ~ consists in falsely supposing yourself to have none —Walter Moberly› **:** PREJUDICE **b :** BENT, TENDENCY, TREND ‹a panel of experts of psychiatric ~› ‹the present ~ of trade in our favor›; *sometimes* **:** INCLINATION ‹my brother had a strong ~ toward the scholarly life› **c** *statistics* **:** a tendency of an estimate to deviate in one direction from a true value (as by reason of nonrandom sampling) **3** *now dial Eng* **:** established procedure **:** settled way or course ‹there is no putting him out of his ~. He is a regular piece of clockwork —Samuel Richardson› **4** *archaic* **:** anything tending to influence one in a particular direction **:** a determining influence **5** *lawn bowling* **a :** a peculiarity in the shape of a bowl that causes it to swerve when rolled on the green **b :** a tendency of the bowl to swerve; *also* **:** the impulse causing this tendency **c :** the swerve of the bowl **6 :** an unvarying component of the electric potential difference between a given element of an electron tube and the cathode — see GRID BIAS **syn** see PREDILECTION — **on the bias 1 :** diagonally to the grain — used of cloth **2 :** OBLIQUELY, ASKEW

²bias \"\ *adj* **1 :** DIAGONAL, SLANTING, OBLIQUE ‹a ~ light› ‹trimmed with ~ bands of velvet› — used chiefly of fabrics and their cut; compare ¹BIAS 1 **2** *obs* **:** swelled or weighted on one side **3 :** of, relating to, or exhibiting bias — **bi·as·ness** *n* -ES

³bias \"\ *adv* [²*bias*] **1 :** in a slanting manner **:** OBLIQUELY, DIAGONALLY ‹cut cloth ~› **2** *obs* **:** AWRY, AMISS

⁴bias \"\ *vt* **biased** *or* **biassed**; **biased** *or* **biassed**; **biasing** *or* **biassing**; **biases** *or* **biasses** [¹*bias*] **1 :** to give a bias to **:** incline to one side **:** give a particular direction to **:** INFLUENCE, PREJUDICE, PREPOSSESS ‹he was ~*ed* by his ignorance› **2 :** to apply a slight negative or positive voltage to (as a vacuum-tube grid)

bias binding *or* **bias tape** *n* **:** a narrow strip of cloth cut on the bias, folded once or twice, and used chiefly for finishing and decorating clothing

biased *or* **biassed** *adj* **:** exhibiting or characterized by bias ‹a ~ estimate of the book's worth› — **biasedly** *adv*

bi·as·ter·ic \¦bīə¦sterik, -tir-\ *adj* [¹*bi-* + *asterion* + *-ic*] **:** of, relating to, or between the two asterions

bias·wise \'==+,wīz\ *adv* **:** OBLIQUELY, ASKEW

biaural *var of* BINAURAL

bi·auricular \¦bī +\ *adj* [¹*bi-* + *auricular*] **1 :** BIAURICULATE **2 a :** of or relating to the two auditory openings **b :** joining the two auricular points ‹the ~ diameter of the skull›

bi·auriculate \¦bī +\ *adj* [¹*bi-* + *auriculate*] **:** having two auricles esp. of the heart of mammals, birds, and reptiles

bi·axial *also* **bi·axal** *or* **bi·axiate** \(')bī +\ *adj* [¹*bi-* + *axial* or *axal* or *axiate*] **:** having two axes ‹~ crystals› — **bi·axiality** \¦bī +\ *n* -ES — **bi·axially** \(')bī +\ *adv*

¹bib \'bib\ *vb* **bibbed**; **bibbed**; **bibbing**; **bibs** [ME *bibben*, perh. fr. L *bibere* to drink — more at POTABLE] *archaic* **:** DRINK, SIP, TIPPLE

²bib \"\ *n* -s **1 a :** a piece of cloth worn across the chest and often tied around the neck to protect a child's clothing **b :** a similar part of an adult's dress or costume that is usu. for decoration **c :** the part of a garment (as an apron) rising above the waist **d :** a canvas throat protector attached to a fencing mask **e :** a patch of differently colored feathers or fur immediately below the chin of a bird or mammal **f :** a leather shield fitting behind the lower jaw and attached to the halter of a horse to prevent interference (as with blanket or bandages) while permitting eating and drinking **2 :** a small cod (*Gadus luscus*) of European coasts having on the head a distensible membrane like a bib **3** *or* **bibb** \"\ **a :** BIBCOCK **b :** BIB NOZZLE **4 :** a long projection of land sloping gradually into the sea

bib *abbr* **1** *often cap* Bible **2** biblical

bi·ba·cious \bə'bāshəs, (')bī¦b-\ *adj* [L *bibac-*, *bibax* bibulous (fr. *bibere* to drink) + E *-ious* — more at POTABLE] **:** addicted to drinking **:** BIBULOUS

bi·bac·i·ty \-'basəd·ē\ *n* -ES [L *bibac-*, *bibax* + E *-ity*] *archaic* **:** addiction to drink **:** TIPPLING

bib and tucker *n* **:** an entire outfit of clothing — usu. used in the phrase *best bib and tucker*

bi·ba·tion \bə'bāshən, bī-\ *n* -s [¹*bib* + *-ation*] **:** TIPPLING, IMBIBING

¹bibb \'bib\ *n* -s [alter. of ²*bib*] **:** a side piece of timber bolted to the hounds of a ship's mast to support the trestletrees

²bibb *var of* BIB

bibbed \'bibd\ *adj* [²*bib* + *-ed*] **:** having a bib ‹a ~ apron›

bib·ber \'bibə(r)\ *n* -s [¹*bib* + *-er*] **:** one addicted to drinking **:** TIPPLER — often used in combination ‹winebibber› — **bib·bery** \-b(ə)rē\ *n* -ES

bib·ble \'bibəl\ *vb* [freq. of ¹*bib*] *now dial* **:** TIPPLE

bib·ble-babble \'bibəl+¦-\ *n* [redupl. of ²*babble*] **:** idle talk **:** BABBLE

bib·bler \'bib(ə)lə(r)\ *n* -s *archaic* **:** TIPPLER

bib·by \'bibē\ *n* -ES *often cap* [after the *Bibby* Line, Ltd., on whose ships (between England and India) such rooms were first used] **:** a stateroom on a passageway of a ship

bibcock \'=,=\ *also* **bibb cock** *n* [²*bib* + *cock*] **:** a stopcock or faucet having a bent-down nozzle

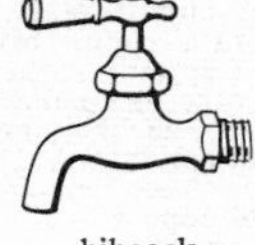
bibcock

bi·be·lot \'bi(,)blō, 'bibə,lō, bēblō\ *n* -s [F] **1 :** a small household ornament or decorative object **:** TRINKET ‹a whatnot cluttered with figurines and other ~s› **2 :** a miniature book esp. of elegant design or format

bi·be·ron \'bibə,rän, -,rən, bebrōⁿ\ *n* -s [F, fr. L *bibere* to drink — more at POTABLE] **:** a drinking vessel with an elongated spout as its only opening formerly used for invalids, travelers, or children

bi·bi \'bē(,)bē\ *n* -s [Hindi *bībī*, fr. Per] *India* **:** a lady usu. of a European country; *sometimes* **:** the Hindu mistress of a house **:** WIFE — used as a term of respect

bib·i·on·id \'bibēənəd\ *adj* [NL *Bibionidae*] **:** of or relating to the family Bibionidae

bib·i·on·i·dae \,bibē'änə,dē\ *n pl, cap* [NL, fr. *Bibion-*, *Bibio*, type genus (fr. L *bibion-*, *bibio* small insect found in wine) + *-idae*; perh. akin to L *bibere* **:** a family of two-winged flies (suborder Nematocera) comprising the March flies and having larvae that feed on the roots of grasses and other plants

bi·bi·ri \bə'birē\ *n* -s [Sp & Pg *bibiri bibirú* — more at BEBEERU] **:** BEBEERU

bibirine *var of* BEBEERINE

bibiru *var of* BEBEERU

bib·i·to·ry \'bibə,tōrē, -tȯrē\ *adj* [ML *bibitorius*, fr. L *bibitus* (past part. of *bibere*) + *-orius* -ory] **1 :** concerned with or relating to drinking ‹a ~ muscle› **2 :** capable of taking up moisture ‹~ papers›

bi·bivalent \¦bī, (')bī +\ *adj* **:** relating to or being an electrolyte that dissociates into two bivalent ions

bibl *abbr* **1** biblical **2** bibliography

¹bi·ble \'bībəl\ *n* -s *often attrib* [ME, Bible, book, fr. OF, Bible, fr. ML *biblia*, fr. Gk, pl. of *biblion* book, dim. of *biblos*, *byblos* book, papyrus, fr. *Byblos* (now Jubayl), Phoenician city from which papyrus was exported] **1** *usu cap* **a :** the book composed of writings generally accepted by Christians as inspired by God and of divine authority **b :** the portion of this book that antedates the Christian era **:** an integrated segment of this earlier work (as the Torah) **c :** a book containing the sacred writings of a religion ‹the Koran is the Muslim *Bible*› **2** *obs* **:** BOOK **3** *obs* **:** a library or collection of books **4** *usu cap* **:** a copy or an edition of the Bible **5 :** a publication likened to the Bible esp. in authoritativeness or in the regularity with which it is consulted: as **a :** an outstanding or definitive reference work in any field ‹Blackstone was the lawyer's ~ in those days› **b :** a publication regularly read and regarded as indispensable ‹the ~ of show business› **c :** a book of rules **6 :** something suggesting a book: as **a :** a small holystone **b :** OMASUM **c :** a piece of whale blubber sliced into leaves like those of a book to facilitate heating in the try-pot

²bible \"\ *vt* -ED/-ING/-S **:** to supply with Bibles ‹~ a hotel›

bible belt *n, usu cap both Bs* **:** an area chiefly in the southern portion of the U.S. supposedly holding uncritical allegiance to the literal accuracy of the Bible; *broadly* **:** any area characterized by an ardent fundamentalism

bible box *n, usu cap 1st B* **:** a miniature chest of the 17th century or earlier with flat top and with or without a till

bible church *n, usu cap B&C* **:** a Christian congregation that lays special emphasis on the Bible as the basis of faith and the inerrant word of God — used frequently in names of churches that hold such doctrines and do not have other denominational affiliations

bible class *n, often cap B* **:** a Sunday-school or church-school class devoted to the study of the Bible

bible clerk *n, usu cap B* **:** one of certain scholars who read the lessons in chapel or say grace in hall at some colleges of Oxford University

bible college *or* **bible institute** *n, usu cap B* **:** a Christian college offering courses in religion and specializing in training students as ministers and religious workers

bible leaf *n* **1 :** COSTMARY **2 :** one of the thin segments making up a bible of whale blubber

bible oath *n, usu cap B* **:** a solemn oath; *esp* **:** one sworn upon the Bible

bible paper *n, cap B* **:** INDIA PAPER

bible school *n, usu cap B* **:** SUNDAY SCHOOL, CHURCH SCHOOL 2

bible society *n, usu cap B* **:** an association for securing the wide distribution of the Christian Bible

bib·less \'bibləs\ *adj* **:** being without a bib

bi·blia a·bi·blia \¦biblēə(')ā¦biblēə\ *n pl* [NL, books that are no books] **:** volumes of no humanist interest or worth

biblia pau·pe·rum \'biblē(,)ä'pau̇pə,rüm, -blēə'p-, -'pȯpərəm\ *n pl, usu cap B* [NL, lit., Bible of the poor] **:** one of a class of biblical picture books that depicted important scriptural events and were used in medieval and somewhat later times as a means of instructing large numbers of people in the Christian faith

biblic- *or* **biblico-** *comb form, often cap* [obs. *biblic* biblical (prob. fr. ML *biblicus*, fr. *biblia* Bible + L *-icus* -ic) + E *-o-*] **:** Bible ‹*biblic*ist› **:** biblical and ‹*biblico*literary›

bib·li·cal \'biblə̇kəl, -blēk-\ *adj, sometimes cap* [obs. *biblic* + E *-al*] **1 :** of, relating to, derived from, or in accord with the Bible **2 :** like that of the Bible ‹a ~ inevitability› ‹~ styles in writing›; *sometimes* **:** like that of the time and region where the Bible was produced ‹~ costume› ‹a beard of ~ proportions› — **biblically** *adv, sometimes cap*

biblical hand *n, usu cap B* **:** a book hand of the Byzantine period (about A.D. 300–650) characterized by squarish uncials of somewhat heavy appearance

biblical hebrew *n, usu cap B&H* **:** the Hebrew language of the Old Testament — see AFRO-ASIATIC LANGUAGES table

bib·li·cal·i·ty \,biblə'kaləd·ē\ *n* -ES **:** biblical quality or something embodying it

biblical theology *n, often cap B* **:** theology based on the Bible; *specif* **:** theology that seeks to derive its categories of thought and the norms for its interpretation from the study of the Bible as a whole

bib·li·cism \'biblə,sizəm\ *n* -s *often cap* [*biblic-* + *-ism*] **:** narrow or exclusive use of the Bible; *specif* **:** adherence to the letter of the Bible

bib·li·cist \-,səst\ *n* -s [*biblic-* + *-ist*] **1** *often cap* **:** one that adheres to or practices biblicism **2 :** a Bible scholar

biblio- *comb form* [MF, fr. L, fr. Gk, fr. *biblion* — more at BIBLE] **:** book ‹*biblio*graphy› ‹*biblio*mania›

bib·li·o·clast \'biblēə,klast, -blēō,-\ *n* -s [*biblio-* + *-clast*] **:** a destroyer or mutilator of books

bib·li·o·film \'===+,=\ *n* [*biblio-* + *film*] **:** a microfilm used esp. for photographing pages of books

bib·li·o·genesis \¦===+\ *n* [*biblio-* + *genesis*] **:** BIBLIOGONY

bib·li·og·nost \'biblēäg,näst\ *n* -s [F *bibliognoste*, fr. *biblio-* + *-gnoste* (fr. Gk *gnōstēs* one who knows, fr. *gignōskein* to know) — more at KNOW] **:** one that has comprehensive knowledge of books and bibliography — **bib·li·og·nos·tic** \¦===¦nästik\ *adj*

bib·li·og·o·ny \,biblē'ägənē\ *n* -ES [*biblio-* + *-gony*] **:** production of books — called also *bibliogenesis*

bib·li·o·graph \'biblēə,graf, -lēō,-\ *vt* -ED/-ING/-S [back-formation fr. *bibliographer*, *bibliographic*, & *bibliography*] **1 :** to enter in a bibliography **2 :** to provide (as a book) with a bibliography **3 :** to compile a bibliography of

bib·li·og·ra·pher \,biblē'ägrəfə(r)\ *n* -s [F *bibliographe* bibliographer (prob. back-formation fr. *bibliographie*) + E *-er*] **1 :** one that writes about or is informed about books, their authorship, format, publication, and similar details **2 :** a compiler of bibliography

bib·li·o·graph·ic \¦biblēə¦grafik, -lēō-, -fēk\ *also* **bib·li·o·graph·i·cal** \-¦grafə̇kəl, -fēk-\ *adj* [*bibliographic* fr. F *bibliographique*, fr. *bibliographie* + *-ique* -ic; *bibliographical* fr. F *bibliographique* + E *-al*] **:** of, relating to, or dealing with bibliography — **bib·li·o·graph·i·cal·ly** \-fə̇k(ə)lē, -fēk-, -li\ *adv*

bib·li·o·graph·i·ca \,===¦grafə̇kə\ *n, pl* **bibliographica** [NL, fr. neut. pl. of *bibliographicus* bibliographic, fr. ISV *bibliographic*] **:** bibliography esp. when bearing on a particular subject, period, or author

bib·li·og·ra·phy \,biblē'ägrəfē, -fi\ *n* -ES [prob. fr. F *bibliographie*, prob. fr. NL *bibliographia*, fr. *biblio-* + L *-graphia* -graphy, fr. Gk] **1 a :** the history, identification, or analytical and systematic description or classification of writings or publications considered as material objects **b :** the investigation or determination of the relationships of varying texts or multiple editions of a single work or a related group of works — called also *analytic bibliography*, *descriptive bibliography* **2 :** a list or catalog, often with descriptive or critical notes, of writings relating to a particular subject, period, or author ‹a ~ of modern poetry› ‹a ~ of the 17th century›; *also* **:** a list of works written by an author or printed by a publishing house ‹the ~ of Walt Whitman› ‹a publisher's ~› **3 :** the works, or a list of them, referred to in a text or consulted by an author in the production of that text — usu. included as an appendix to the work ‹a ~ of 40 books and articles› **4 :** the study of bibliography or bibliographic methods ‹an intensive course in ~›

bib·li·o·klept \'biblēə,klept, -lēō,-\ *n* -s [*biblio-* + *-klept*] **:** one who steals books

bib·li·ol·a·ter \,biblē'älədə(r)\ *also* **bib·li·ol·a·trist** \-'älə·trəst\ *n* -s [*biblio-* + *-later*] **:** one characterized by bibliolatry **:** a book worshiper

bib·li·ol·a·trous \¦==¦älətrəs\ *adj* [*bibliolatry* + *-ous*] **:** given to bibliolatry

bib·li·ol·a·try \,==¦älə·trē\ *n* -ES [*biblio-* + *-latry*] **1 :** extravagant devotion to or concern with books **2 :** excessive veneration of or absolute dependence on a group of sacred writings as infallible; *specif* **:** worship of the Bible

bib·li·ol·o·gy \-'äləjē\ *n* -ES [*biblio-* + *-logy*] **1 :** the history and science of books as physical objects in all aspects **:** bibliography in its widest sense **2** *often cap* **:** the study of the theological doctrine of the Bible

bib·li·o·man·cy \'biblēə,man(t)sē, -lēō,-\ *n* -ES [*biblio-* + *-mancy*] **:** divination by books, esp. the Bible

bib·li·o·mane \-,mān\ *n* -s [F, back-formation fr. *bibliomanie*] **:** BIBLIOMANIAC

bib·li·o·mania \,biblēə, ,biblēō +\ *n* [modif. (influenced by E *mania*) of F *bibliomanie*, fr. *biblio-* + *manie* mania, fr. LL *mania*] **:** extreme preoccupation with books, esp. with their acquisition and possession

¹bib·li·o·maniac \" +\ *n* [fr. *bibliomania*, after E *mania: maniac*] **:** one affected with bibliomania; *esp* **:** an avid book collector

²bib·li·o·maniac *also* **bib·li·o·maniacal** \¦===+\ *adj* **:** characteristic of bibliomania; *also* **:** characterized by or noted for bibliomania

bib·li·o·peg·ic \-¦pejik, -pēj-\ *adj* [*bibliopegist* + *-ic*] **:** relating to bookbinding — **bib·li·o·peg·i·cal·ly** \-jək(ə)lē\ *adv*

bib·li·op·e·gist \,biblē'äpəjəst\ *n* -s [perh. fr. obs. F *bibliopégiste*, fr. F *biblio-* + obs. F *-pégiste* (fr. Gk *pēgnynai* to fasten together + F *-iste* -ist) — more at PACT] **:** BOOKBINDER

bib·li·op·e·gis·tic \¦==¦==¦jistik\ *also* **bib·li·op·e·gis·ti·cal** \-təkəl\ *adj* **:** BIBLIOPEGIC

bib·li·op·e·gy \,biblē'äpəjē\ *n* -ES [*bibliopegist* + *-y*] **:** the art of binding books

bib·li·o·phage \'biblēə,fāj, -lēō,-\ *n* -s [ISV *biblio-* + *-phage*] **:** BOOKWORM — **bib·li·oph·a·gous** \¦biblē¦äfəgəs\ *adj*

bib·li·o·phile \'biblēə,fīl, -lēō,-\ *n* -s [F, fr. *biblio-* + *-phile* (fr. Gk *philos* friend)] **:** a lover of books esp. for beautiful or rare qualities of format; *also* **:** a book collector — **bib·li·o·phil·ic** \¦===¦filik, -lēk\ *adj*

bib·li·oph·i·lism \,biblē'äfə,lizəm\ *n* -s **:** love of books ⟨a center of good music, serious art, ~, the ballet —William Manchester⟩

bib·li·oph·i·list \-,ləst\ *n* -s **:** BIBLIOPHILE — **bib·li·oph·i·lis·tic** \¦==¦==¦listik, -tēk\ *adj*

bib·li·oph·i·ly \-'äfəlē, -li\ *n* -ES [F *bibliophilie*, fr. *bibliophile* + *-ie* -y] **:** the love of books characteristic of the bibliophile

bib·li·o·phobe \'biblēə,fōb, -lēō,-\ *n* -s [ISV *biblio-* + *-phobe*] **:** a person with bibliophobia

bib·li·o·pho·bia \,===¦fōbēə\ *n* -s [*biblio-* + *-phobia*] **:** strong dislike of books

bib·li·o·pole \'===,pōl\ *or* **bib·li·op·o·list** \,biblē'äpələst\ *n* -s [L *bibliopola* bookseller, fr. Gk *bibliopōlēs*, fr. *biblio-* + *-pōlēs* (fr. *pōlein* to sell) — more at MONOPOLY] **:** a dealer in books (as secondhand, rare, or curious books) — **bib·li·o·pol·ic** \¦biblēə¦pälik, -lēō¦-, -¦pä-\ *adj*

bib·li·o·taph *also* **bib·li·o·taphe** \'biblēə,taf, -lēō,-\ *n* -s [F *bibliotaphe*, fr. *biblio-* + *-taphe* (fr. Gk *taphos* tomb) — more at EPITAPH] **:** one that hides away or hoards books — **bib·li·o·taph·ic** \¦===¦tafik\ *adj*

bib·li·o·the·ca \,===¦thēkə\ *n*, *pl* **bibliothecas** \-kəz\ *or* **bibliothe·cae** \-ē(,)kē,-ē(,)sē,-ē,kī,-ē,sī\ [L *bibliotheca* collection of books, fr. Gk *bibliothēkē*, fr. *biblio-* + *thēkē* case, chest; akin to Gk *tithenai* to put, place — more at DO] **1** *archaic* **:** BIBLE 1a **2 :** a library or collection of books **3 :** a list or catalog of books — **bib·li·o·the·cal** \¦===¦thēkəl\ *adj*

bib·li·o·the·car·i·al \¦===thə'ka(a)rēəl, ¦biblē,ath-\ *adj* [L *bibliothecarius* librarian (fr. *bibliotheca* + *-arius* -ary) + E *-al*] **:** of or related to a library

bib·li·o·therapeutic \¦biblēə, ¦biblēō +\ *adj* [*biblio-* + *therapeutic*] **:** of, relating to, or involving bibliotherapy

bib·li·o·therapist \" +\ *n* -s [*bibliotherapy* + *-ist*] **:** one skilled in bibliotherapy

bib·li·o·therapy \" +\ *n* [ISV *biblio-* + *therapy*] **:** the use of selected reading materials as therapeutic adjuvants in medicine and in psychiatry; *also* **:** guidance in the solution of personal problems through directed reading

bib·li·ot·ic \¦biblē¦äd·ik\ *adj* [fr. *bibliotics*, after such pairs as E *aesthetics* **:** *aesthetic*] **:** of or relating to bibliotics

bib·li·ot·ics \-ks\ *n pl but sing or pl in constr* [*biblio-* + connective *-t-* + *-ics*] **:** the scientific study of handwriting, documents, and writing materials esp. for determining genuineness or authorship — **bib·li·o·tist** \'biblēəd·əst, -lēō-, -təst\ *n* -s

bi·blism \'bībə,lizəm *also* 'bī,bli- *sometimes* 'bi,bli-\ *n* -s *often cap* [*bible* + *-ism*] **:** adherence to the Bible as the sole rule of faith

bib·list *in sense 1* 'bibləst *also and in sense 2 usu* 'bībələst, 'bībləst\ *n* -s *often cap* [*bible* + *-ist*] **1 :** a biblical scholar **2 :** one who practices or advocates biblism

bib·lus \'bibləs\ *also* **bib·los** \", -,läs\ *n* -ES [Gk & L; L *biblus*, fr. Gk *biblos*, *byblos* — more at BIBLE] **:** PAPYRUS 2

bib nozzle *n* [²*bib*] **:** a bent-down nozzle of a cock or faucet often threaded for attachment of a hose

bi·borate \(')bī +\ *n* [¹*bi-* + *borate*] **:** TETRABORATE

biborate of soda : BORAX — not used scientifically

bi·bos \'bī,bäs, -,bōs\ *n*, *cap* [NL, prob. fr. *Bison* + *Bos*] **:** a genus of Asiatic wild oxen (family Bovidae) comprising the gaur and related animals — **bi·bo·vine** \'bībə,vēn, -,vīn, -vən\ *adj*

bib pout *n* **:** ²BIB 2

bibs *pl of* BIB, *pres 3d sing of* BIB

bib·u·los·i·ty \,bibyə'läsəd·ē\ *n* -ES [*bibulous* + *-osity*] **:** state of being bibulous

bib·u·lous \'bibyələs\ *adj* [L *bibulus*, fr. *bibere* to drink — more at POTABLE] **1 :** readily taking up fluids or moisture ⟨the ~ paper with which the dentist keeps his working area dry⟩ **2 a :** inclined to drink **:** addicted to tippling **b :** of, relating to, or affected by tippling ⟨a ~ farewell⟩ **c :** of or relating to drink ⟨the ~ history of wine country⟩ — **bib·u·lous·ly** *adv*

bi·cameral \(')bī+\ *adj* [¹*bi-* + *camera* + *-al*] **1 a :** consisting of two chambers ⟨the ~ heart of a fish⟩ **b :** having or made up of two distinct legislative bodies ⟨the Congress is ~, consisting of the Senate and the House of Representatives⟩ **2 :** based on or involving legislative bicameralism ⟨the evident advantages of the ~ system⟩ — **bi·camerally** \"+\ *adv*

bi·cameralism \(')bī+\ *n* -s **:** bicameral organization of a legislative body

bi·cameralist \(')bī+\ *or* **bi·cam·er·ist** \(')bī¦kamərəst\ *n* -s **:** an advocate of bicameralism

bi·canine \(')bī+\ *adj* [¹*bi-* + *canine*] **:** between the outer borders of the canine teeth of a jaw ⟨the ~ width of the chimpanzee⟩

bi·capsular \(')bī+\ *adj* [prob. fr. F *bicapsulaire*, fr. *bi-* ¹bi- + *capsulaire* capsular] **1** *biol* **:** having two capsules **2** *biol* **:** having a bilocular capsule

bi·carb \(')bī¦kärb, -kab\ *n* -s [short for *bicarbonate*] **:** SODIUM BICARBONATE

bi·carbonate \(')bī+\ *n* [ISV ¹*bi-* + *carbonate*] **:** an acid carbonate **:** a hydrogen carbonate — see ¹BI- 4

bicarbonate of soda : SODIUM BICARBONATE — not used scientifically

bi·carinate \(')bī+\ *adj* [fr. (assumed) NL *bicarinatus*, fr. NL ¹*bi-* + L *carinatus* carinate] **:** having two projections like keels ⟨the strongly ~ shell of certain marine snails⟩

bi·caudal *also* **bi·caudate** \(')bī+\ *adj* [NL *bicaudalis* & (assumed) NL *bicaudatus*, fr. NL ¹*bi-* + *caudalis* caudal & *caudatus* caudate] **:** having or terminating in two tails

bice blue \'bīs\ *n* [ME *bis*, fr. *bis* (adj.) dark gray, fr. MF; akin to OProv *bis* dark gray, It *bigio*] **:** AZURITE BLUE

bice green *n* **:** MALACHITE GREEN 2

bi·cellular \(')bī+\ *adj* [¹*bi-* + *cellular*] **:** having or composed of two cells

bi·centenary \¦bī, (')bī+\ *adj or n* [¹*bi-* + *centenary*] **:** BICENTENNIAL

¹bi·centennial \¦bī+\ *n* -s [¹*bi-* + *centennial*] **:** a 200th anniversary or its celebration

²bi·centennial \"+\ *adj* **:** relating to a 200th anniversary

bi·centric \(')bī+\ *adj* [¹*bi-* + *centric*] **1 a** *of a taxon* **:** having two centers of origin ⟨it is doubtful that *Zea* is ~⟩ ⟨*Limulus* is an outstanding example of a ~ genus⟩ **b :** having or involving two centers ⟨the ~ distribution of certain Scandinavian plants⟩ ⟨a lichen of ~ origin⟩ **2 :** having two centromeres — **bi·centricity** \¦bī+\ *n* -ES

bi·cep \'bī,sep\ *n* -s [back-formation fr. *biceps*, taken as a plural] **:** BICEPS

bi·cephalous \(')bī+\ *or* **bi·cephalic** \¦bī+\ *adj* [¹*bi-* + *-cephalous* or *-cephalic*] **:** having two heads

bi·ceps \'bī,seps\ *n*, *pl* **bi·ceps·es** \-,sepsəz\ [NL *bicipit-*, *biceps*, fr. L, two-headed, fr. *bi-* ¹bi- + *-cipit-*, *-ceps* (fr. *capit-*, *caput* head) — more at HEAD] **:** a muscle having two heads or origins: as **a :** the large flexor muscle of the front of the upper arm arising by its short head from the coracoid process and by its long head from the upper margin of the glenoid cavity and being inserted into the tuberosity of the radius — called also *biceps brachii*, *biceps humeri*, *biceps flexor cubiti* **b :** a muscle that arises by its long head from the ischial tuberosity and by its short head from the shaft of the femur, that is inserted into the head of the fibula, its tendon forming the outer hamstring, and that flexes the leg on the thigh and extends the thigh on the trunk — called also *biceps femoris*, *biceps flexor cruris*

bich·ir \'bichə(r)\ *n* -s [F] **:** a large primitive fish (*Polypterus bichir*) of the order Cladistia found in the upper Nile and certain neighboring waters and esteemed as food

bichir

bi·chloride \(')bī +\ *n* [ISV ¹*bi-* + *chloride*] **1 :** DICHLORIDE **2** *or* **bichloride of mercury :** MERCURY CHLORIDE b

bi·chord \'bī +,-\ *adj* [¹*bi-* + *chord*] *of musical instruments* **:** having two strings in unison for each note ⟨the mandolin is a ~ instrument⟩

bi·chromate \(')bī +\ *n* [ISV ¹*bi-* + *chromate*] **:** DICHROMATE — used chiefly commercially and esp. of the dichromates of sodium and potassium

bichromate cell *n* **:** a zinc-carbon cell having an acid bichromate solution as electrolyte and developing an electromotive force of about two volts

bi·chromated \(')bī +\ *adj* **:** treated or combined with a bichromate ⟨~ gelatin⟩

bi·chromatic \¦bī +\ *adj* [¹*bi-* + *chromatic*] **:** DICHROMATIC

bi·chromatized \(')bī +\ *adj* [fr. past part. of (assumed) *bichromatize* to treat or combine with a bichromate, fr. *bichromate* + *-ize*] **:** BICHROMATED

bi·chrome \'bī + ,-\ *adj* [¹*bi-* + *-chrome*] **:** two-colored **:** having two colors

bi·ciliate *or* **bi·ciliated** \(')bī +\ *adj* [¹*bi-* + *ciliate* or *ciliated*] **:** having two cilia

bi·cip·i·tal \(')bī¦sipəd·əl\ *adj* [NL *bicipit-*, *biceps* + E *-al*] **1 a** *of certain muscles* **:** having two heads or origins **b :** of or relating to a biceps muscle **2** *bot* **:** dividing into two parts at one extremity

bicipital fascia *n* **:** an aponeurosis given off from the tendon of the biceps of the arm and continuous with the deep fascia of the forearm

bicipital groove *n* **:** a furrow on the upper part of the humerus occupied by the long head of the biceps

bicipital tuberosity *n* **:** the rough eminence which is on the anterior inner aspect of the neck of the radius and into which the tendon of the biceps is inserted

bi·circular \(')bī +\ *adj* [ISV ¹*bi-* + *circular*] **:** consisting of or like two circles

bick \'bik\ *n* -s [ON *bikkja* — more at BITCH] *Scot* **:** BITCH

¹bick·er \'bikə(r)\ *n* -s [ME *biker*] **1 a :** an act of bickering **:** CONTENTION, ALTERCATION **:** petulant quarreling **b :** a sound of or as if of bickering ⟨the ~ and plash of the fountain⟩ **2** *Scot* **:** TUSSLE, BRAWL, FRACAS

²bick·er \"\ *vb* **bickered**; **bickered**; **bickering** \-k(ə)riŋ\ **bickers** [ME *bikeren*; akin to ME *biker*] *vi* **1** *archaic* **:** to skirmish esp. with missiles **:** FIGHT **2 :** to contend in petulant or petty altercation **:** WRANGLE ⟨America . . . ~s with the Asian countries about the price of rubber —Mochtar Lubis⟩ ⟨they had ~*ed* so long as to quite forget the original quarrel⟩ **3 :** to move quickly and unsteadily often with a rapidly repeated noise ⟨water ~*ing* over stones⟩ **:** QUIVER, FLICKER ⟨a wistful smile ~*ed* across her face⟩ **4** *Scot* **:** to make a quick short run **:** SPRINT ~ *vt*, *archaic* **:** to attack or assail with (as missiles) ⟨if we're going to ~ adverbs —Christopher Morley⟩

³bicker \"\ *n* -s [ME *biker* beaker — more at BEAKER] **1** *chiefly Scot* **:** a drinking vessel esp. of wood **2** *chiefly Scot* **:** a porridge dish often made of wooden staves

bickering *n* -s [ME *bikeringe* skirmishing, fr. *bikeren* + *-inge* -ing] **:** petty and petulant quarreling esp. when prolonged or habitual ⟨the factional ~ that has wrecked many a well-meaning organization⟩; *sometimes* **:** an instance of this ⟨those childish ~s that are part of growing up⟩ **syn** see QUARREL

bick·er·ment \-mənt\ *n* -s [²*bicker* + *-ment*] *now dial Eng* **:** BICKERING

bick·er·ton·ite \'bikə(r)tə,nīt\ *n* -s *usu cap* [William Bickerton 19th cent. Am. religious leader, who founded the denomination + *-ite*] **:** a member of the Church of Jesus Christ founded 1862 in Pennsylvania

bick·ford fuse \'bikfə(r)d-\ *n*, *usu cap B* [after William *Bickford* †1834 Eng. leather merchant, its inventor] **:** SAFETY FUSE 1

bick·iron \'bikə(r)n, -,kīə(r)n\ *n* [by folk etymology (influence of E *iron*) fr. earlier *bickern*, *bycorne* taper end of an anvil, anvil with two taper ends, modif. of MF *bigorne* anvil with two taper ends, fr. L *bicornia*, neut. pl. of *bicornis*] **:** the taper end of an anvil

bick·nell's thrush \'biknəlz-, -,nelz-\ *also* **bicknell thrush** \-nəl-, -,nel-\ *n*, *usu cap B* [prob. after Eugene P. *Bicknell* †1925 Am. botanist and ornithologist] **:** a small slender-billed thrush (*Hylocichla minima bicknelli*) of upland areas of northeastern No. America that is olive-brown above and buffy-white below

bi·clin·i·um \bī'klinēəm\ *n*, *pl* **biclin·ia** \-nēə\ [L, fr. *bi-* ¹bi- + *-clinium* (fr. Gk *-klinion* — as in *triklinion* triclinium)] **:** an ancient Roman dining couch for the use of two persons

bicol *usu cap*, *var of* BIKOL

bi·collateral \¦bī +\ *adj* [ISV ¹*bi-* + *collateral*] *of a vascular bundle* **:** having the phloem both external and internal to the xylem — compare COLLATERAL — **bi·collaterality** \" + \ *n* -ES

bi·colligate \(')bī +\ *adj* [fr. (assumed) NL *bicolligatus*, fr. NL ¹*bi-* + L *colligatus* bound together, past part. of *colligare* to bind together — more at COLLIGATE] *of certain birds* **:** having the three anterior toes connected by webs

¹bi·color *also* **bi·colored** \(')bī +\ *adj* [*bicolor* fr. L *bicolor*, fr. *bi-* ¹bi- + *color*; *bicolored* fr. ¹*bi-* + *colored*] **:** having or marked with two colors ⟨a ~ jonquil⟩ **:** printed in two colors (as of a postage stamp)

²bicolor \"\ *n* -s **:** a bicolor individual (as a postage stamp or a flower)

bicolor lespedeza *n* **:** an Asiatic shrub (*Lespedeza bicolor*) that has conspicuous purple flowers in axillary racemes and is now widely used as an ornamental, as a source of wild-bird food, and in erosion control

bi·col·or·ous \(')bī¦kələrəs\ *adj* [L *bicolor* + E *-ous*] **:** BICOLOR

bi·concave \(')bī, +\ *adj* [ISV ¹*bi-* + *concave*] **:** concave on both sides **:** CONCAVO-CONCAVE ⟨~ vertebrae⟩ ⟨a ~ lens⟩ —see LENS illustration — **bi·concavity** \¦bī + \ *n* -ES

bi·conditional \¦bī + \ *n* [¹*bi-* + *conditional*] **1 :** a statement of a relation between a pair of propositions such that one is true only if the other is simultaneously true, or false if the other is simultaneously false **2 :** the symbolic representation of a biconditional — called also *sentential connective*

bi·condylar \(')bī +\ *adj* [¹*bi-* + *condylar*] **:** of, relating to, or between two condyles ⟨the ~ breadth of the jaw⟩

bi·cone \'bī,kōn\ *n* [prob. back-formation fr. *biconical*] **:** an object in the form of two cones with their bases placed together; *specif* **:** a bead having this form found among Sumerian and early Egyptian jewelry

bi·conical \(')bī +\ *adj* [ISV ¹*bi-* + *conical*] **:** having the form of a bicone

bi·conjugate \(')bī +\ *adj* [fr. (assumed) NL *biconjugatus*, fr. NL ¹*bi-* + L *conjugatus* joined together — more at CONJUGATE] **:** twice paired (as when each branch of a forking petiole bears a pair of leaflets)

bi·consonantal *also* **bi·consonantic** \(¦)bī +\ *adj* [¹*bi-* + *consonantal* or *consonantic*] **:** of or containing two consonants

bi·convex \(¦)bī +\ *adj* [ISV ¹*bi-* + *convex*] **:** convex on both sides **:** CONVEXO-CONVEX ⟨a ~ lens⟩ — see LENS illustration

bi·corn \'bī,kȯrn\ *or* **bicorned** \-nd\ *also* **bicornous** \(')bī¦kȯrnəs\ *adj* [*bicorn* fr. L *bicornis*, fr. *bi-* ¹bi- + *-cornis* (fr. *cornu* horn); *bicorned* fr. L *bicornis* + E *-ed*; *bicornous* fr. L *bicornis* + E *-ous* — more at HORN] **:** two-horned **:** like a crescent

bi·corne *also* **bi·corn** \'bī,kȯrn\ *n* -s [F *bicorne*, fr. L *bicornis* two-horned] **:** COCKED HAT 1b

bi·cor·nu·ate \(')bī¦kȯrnyü,āt, -yüət\ *also* **bi·cor·nate** \-,nāt, -,nət\ *or* **bi·cor·nu·ous** \-nyüəs\ *adj* [*bicornuate* fr. ¹*bi-* + L *cornu* horn + E *-ate*; *bicornate* fr. L *bicornis* two-horned + E *-ate*; *bicornuous* fr. ¹*bi-* + L *cornu* + E *-ous*] **:** having two horns or horn-shaped processes ⟨a ~ uterus⟩

bi·corporal \(')bī +\ *adj* [¹*bi-* + *corporal*] *of a sign of the zodiac* **:** represented by two figures

bi·costate \(')bī +\ *adj* [¹*bi-* + *costate*] *of a leaf* **:** having two principal ribs running longitudinally

bi·cris·tal \(')bī¦kristəl\ *adj* [¹*bi-* + L *crista* crest + E *-al* — more at CREST] **:** of, relating to, or between the iliac crests

bi·crural \(')bī +\ *adj* [¹*bi-* + *crural*] **:** having two legs

bicuhyba *or* **bicuhybao** *or* **bicuiba** *var of* BECUIBA

bi·cultural \(')bī +\ *adj* [¹*bi-* + *cultural*] **:** combining two distinct cultures ⟨a recognition of . . . Canada's ~ character —*Dict. of Canadian Biog.*⟩

bi·cur·sal \(')bī¦kərsəl\ *adj* [¹*bi-* + L *cursus* course + E *-al* — more at COURSE] **:** having two paths, one for each of two moving points — used of a curve (as a hyperbola); opposed to *unicursal*

¹bi·cuspid *also* **bi·cuspidate** \(')bī +\ *adj* [*bicuspid* fr. NL *bicuspid-*, *bicuspis*, fr. ¹*bi-* + L *cuspid-*, *cuspis* point; *bicuspidate* fr. (assumed) NL *bicuspidatus*, fr. NL ¹*bi-* + L *cuspidatus* pointed, past part. of *cuspidare* to make pointed, fr. *cuspid-*, *cuspis*] **:** having two points or prominences **:** ending in two points ⟨~ teeth⟩ ⟨~ leaves⟩

²bicuspid \bī +\ *n* -s [NL *bicuspid-*, *bicuspis*, fr. ¹*bi-* + L *cuspid-*, *cuspis* point] **:** either of the two double-pointed teeth that intervene in man between the canines and the molars on each side of each jaw **:** PREMOLAR — see DENTITION illustration

bicuspid valve *n* **:** the mitral valve of the heart

¹bi·cy·cle \'bī,sikəl, -,sək-,-,sek *sometimes* -,sīk-\ *n* -s [F, fr. *bi-* ¹bi- + *-cycle* (as in *tricycle*)] **1 :** a vehicle that has two wheels one behind the other, a steering handle, and a saddle seat or seats and is usu. propelled by the action of the rider's feet upon pedals **2 :** a traveling block used on a cable in skidding logs **3** [so called fr. the picture of the ace, two, three, four, and five of hearts formerly printed on the container of a pack of Bicycle brand playing cards] **:** the best possible hand in lowball comprising ace, two, three, four, and five of mixed suits **4 :** a literal translation **:** PONY

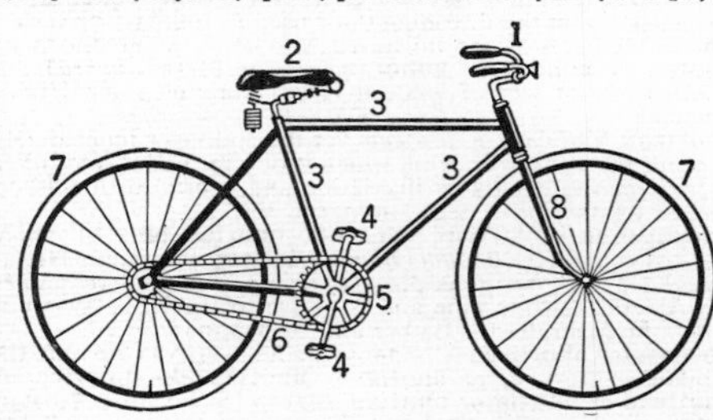

bicycle: *1* handlebar, *2* saddle, *3* frame, *4* pedal, *5* sprocket wheel, *6* chain, *7* tire, *8* fork

²bicycle \"\ *vb* **bicycled**; **bicycled**; **bicycling** \-k(ə)liŋ\ **bicycles** *vi* **1 :** to ride a bicycle **2** *West* **:** to spur a bucking horse repeatedly, alternately on the right and on the left side ~ *vt* **:** to send (a recorded radio, television, or motion-picture program) directly from one broadcasting or exhibition point to another to facilitate distribution or to avoid payment of fees — **bi·cy·cler** \-k(ə)lə(r)\ *n* -s

bicycle gear *n* **:** a landing gear configuration in airplanes in which the main wheels or sets of wheels are placed under the center of the fuselage to take the main weight of the airplanes and are supplemented by small outrigger wheels under the wings

bi·cy·clic \(')bī¦sīklik, -¦sik-\ *also* **bi·cy·cli·cal** \-klәkәl\ *adj* [ISV ¹*bi-* + *cyclic* or *cyclical*] **1 :** consisting of or arranged in two cycles or circles ⟨a ~ flower with the petals in two whorls⟩ **2 :** containing two usu. fused rings in the structure of the molecule (as in naphthalene) ⟨a ~ terpene⟩

bi·cy·clist \'bī,sikləst, -sək-,-sek- *sometimes* -,sīk-\ *n* -s **:** one that rides a bicycle; *specif* **:** a bicycle racer

bicyclo- *comb form* [ISV, fr. *bicyclic*] *chem* **:** bicyclic ⟨*bicycloalkane*⟩

bi·cylindrical \¦bī +\ *adj* [¹*bi-* + *cylindrical*] **:** having two cylindrical surfaces usu. with their axes parallel ⟨certain lenses are ~⟩

¹bid \'bid\ *vb* **bade** \'bad, 'baa(ə)d\ *or* **bid** *or archaic* **bad** \'bad\ **bidden** \'bidᵊn\ *or* **bid** *also* **bade**; **bidding**; **bids** [partly fr. ME *bidden* to entreat, pray, invite, command, fr. OE *biddan* to entreat, pray, command; akin to OHG *bitten* to entreat, ON *bithja*, Goth *bidjan* to entreat, ask for, Skt *bādhate* he presses, harasses; partly fr. earlier *bede* to invite, command, fr. ME *beden* to offer, proclaim, invite, command, fr. OE *bēodan* to offer, proclaim, command; akin to OHG *biotan* to offer, ON *bjōtha* to offer, command, Goth *anabiudan* to command, Gk *pynthanesthai* to learn by inquiry, Skt *bodhati*, *bodhate* he wakes, is awake, observes] *vt* **1 a** *archaic* **:** to ask for insistently **:** BESEECH, ENTREAT, PRAY **b :** to issue an order to either mildly and without especial emphasis or authoritatively or peremptorily ⟨the servant did as he was *bidden*⟩ ⟨they *bade* him enter⟩ **c :** to request to come **:** INVITE ⟨as many as ye shall find, ~ to the marriage —Mt 22:9 (AV)⟩ **2 a** *obs* **:** to make known **:** DECLARE, REVEAL, PROCLAIM **b :** to give expression to (as a greeting, a farewell, or a wish) to someone ⟨she *bade* me a tearful farewell⟩ **3 a :** OFFER — obs except in the phrase *to bid defiance* **b** (1) **:** to offer (a price) whether for payment or acceptance ⟨~ $10,000 less than his nearest competitor⟩ ⟨surely you can afford to ~ one dollar⟩ (2) **:** to obtain (goods) by offering a price or premium ⟨*bidding* scarce goods away from the open market⟩ (3) **:** to make (a bid) to someone ⟨I'll ~ you 50 cents and not one penny more⟩ **c** *past or past part bid* **:** to make a bid of or in ⟨~ hearts⟩ ⟨he *bid* one spade⟩ **d :** to enter a claim for (a vacant job) on the basis of seniority ~ *vi* **1 :** to make a bid: as **a :** to state what one will pay or take **b :** to try to obtain or attain something — usu. used with *for* ⟨*bidding* for the support of special-interest groups⟩ **c :** to enter a claim for a vacant job on the basis of seniority — usu. used with *in* or *for* ⟨he *bid* in the operation of the big crane⟩ **2 :** SEEM, APPEAR — usu. used with *fair* (sense 8a(1)) and now with a complementary infinitive ⟨his effort ~s fair to succeed⟩ though formerly also with *for* **syn** see COMMAND

²bid \"\ *n* -s **1 a :** the act of one who bids **:** an offer of a price (as at an auction) **:** a statement of what one will give or do for something to be received or will take for something to be done or furnished **b :** something offered as a bid **2 :** an opportunity to bid ⟨the ~ is with you, sir⟩ **:** one's turn at bidding ⟨it's your ~⟩ **3 :** INVITATION ⟨a ~ to join a sorority⟩ **4** *card games* **a :** an announcement of willingness to attempt to accomplish a certain result under specified conditions (as to take a stated number of tricks in bridge if a stipulated suit is trumps) **b** : the amount of such a bid ⟨a 3-heart ~⟩ ⟨a 350 bid⟩ **c** : a bridge hand on which one may reasonably bid ⟨I haven't had a ~ in the last three hands⟩ **5** : an attempt or effort to win, achieve, or attract ⟨he made a strong ~ for the championship⟩; *sometimes* : an appeal or plea esp. for sympathy

³bid *archaic past part of* BIDE

BID *abbr* [L *bis in die*] twice a day

bi·dac·tyl \(ˈ)bī¦daktəl\ *or* **bi·dac·tyle** \ˈ", -ˌtīl\ *also* **bi·dac·ty·lous** \-ˈdaktələs\ *adj* [*bidactyl* & *bidactyle* fr. F *bidactyle*, fr. *bi-* ¹bi- + *-dactyle* -dactylous (fr. Gk *-daktylos*); *bidactylous* fr. *bidactyl* + *-ous*] : DIDACTYL

bi·dai \ˈbēˌdī\ *n, pl* **bidai** *or* **bidais** *usu cap* [prob. fr. Caddo *bidai* brushwood] **1** : an Atakapan people of the Trinity river valley, Texas **2** : a member of the Bidai people

bid ale *n* [ME *bede ale*, fr. *bede, beden*, past part. of *bidden* to invite + *ale* — more at BID] *obs* : a feast commonly held in past centuries in England for the benefit of a destitute person

bid–and–asked \ˌ==ˈ=\ *adj* **1** *of market quotations* : showing both the least price acceptable to a seller and the highest acceptable to a buyer **2** *of a market or exchange* : functioning on the basis of bid-and-asked quotations

bi·dar *also* **bai·dar** \bīˈdär\ *n* -s [Russ *baidara;* akin to Russ *baidak* boat, Ukrainian *bajdak* boat, canoe] : a large skin-covered boat used chiefly by the Aleuts

bi·dar·ka *also* **bai·dar·ka** \bīˈdärkə\ *or* **bi·dar·kee** \-kē\ *n* -s [Russ *baidarka*, dim. of *baidara*] : a portable boat made of skins stretched over wood frames and widely used by Alaskan coastal natives and Aleuts

bid bond *n* : a surety bond often required of contractors bidding on construction work to provide that the bidder, if successful, shall furnish a satisfactory bond ensuring completion of the work — called also *proposal bond*

bid·da·bil·i·ty \ˌbidəˈbiləd·ē, -i\ *n* : the state or quality of being biddable : DOCILITY

bid·da·ble \ˈbidəbəl\ *adj* **1** : OBEDIENT, DOCILE **2** *of a hand or suit at cards* : capable of being bid : strong enough to warrant a bid **syn** see OBEDIENT

bid·da·bly \ˈbidəblē, -bli\ *adv* : OBEDIENTLY, DOCILELY

bid·dance \ˈbidᵊn(t)s\ *n* -s : the act of bidding : INVITATION, COMMAND

bidden *past part of* BID, *archaic past part of* BIDE

bid·der \ˈbidə(r)\ *n* -s [ME *biddere*, fr. OE, *petitioner*, fr. *biddan* to entreat + *-ere* -er — more at BID] : a person who bids: as **a** : one that commands or orders **b** : the giver of an invitation **c** : the maker of a bid (as at an auction or in a card game)

bid·der's ganglion \ˈbidə(r)z-\ *n, usu cap B* [after Friedrich H. *Bidder* †1894 Ger. physician] : a nerve-cell ganglion in the vicinity of the atrioventricular groove in frogs

bidder's organ *n, usu cap B* : a rudimentary ovary present near the fat body in both sexes of some toads sometimes becoming functional in old males

bid·dery \ˈbid(ə)rē\ *var of* BIDRI

bid·ding \ˈbidiŋ, -dēŋ\ *n* -s [ME *biddinge, bidding*, fr. *bidden* to entreat, pray, command + *-inge, -ing* -ing] **1** *archaic* : ENTREATY, PRAYER **2 a** : the act of making bids; *also* : the period during which bids are made (as in a card game or at an auction) **b** : an offer of a price **3** : COMMAND, INJUNCTION, ORDER, BEHEST, DIRECTION, SUMMONS ⟨shall I give up all the joys of life at your ~⟩ ⟨writing only at the ~ of a deep love of nature⟩; *sometimes* : INVITATION ⟨we gathered at his ~⟩

bidding prayer *n* **1** : a prayer said in English churches down to the Reformation for those living and dead whose names were on the list of persons to be prayed for **2** : a prayer taking the form of a series of petitions for specified objects or classes of persons said esp. in Anglican churches before the sermon

bid·dul·phia \bəˈdəlfēə\ *n, cap* [NL, prob. fr. G. *Biddulph*, 19th cent. Eng. botanist + NL *-ia*] : a large genus (the type of the family Biddulphiaceae) of rectangular diatoms having winglike or hornlike projections at the corners of the valves and being locally abundant in the marine plankton

¹bid·dy \ˈbidē, -di\ *n* -ES [perh. of imit. origin] **1 a** : an adult female domestic fowl — often used as a call **b** : a young chicken ⟨a hen and her *biddies*⟩ **2** : any of various wild fowls in some respect suggesting a domestic hen

²biddy \ˈ"\ *also* **biddie** *n* -s [dim. of *Bridget* (the name)] **1** : a hired girl or maidservant; *esp* : an elderly housemaid or cleaning woman in a dormitory **2** : WOMAN: **a** : an elderly and often gossipy or dissolute woman — used disparagingly **b** : a young woman — often used disparagingly **c** *slang* : a female school teacher **3** : a toothless old ewe : GUMMER

biddy–bid \ˈbidēˌbid\ *also* **biddy–biddy** \ˈ==ˌ==\ *or* **bid·a–bid** \ˈbidəˌbid\ *n* -s [modif. of Maori *piripiri*] **1** *NewZeal* : PIRIPIRI **2** *NewZeal* : the bur of piripiri

bide \ˈbīd\ *vb* **bode** \ˈbōd\ *or* **bided** \ˈbīdəd\ *also* **bade** \ˈbad, ˈbaa(ə)d\ *or archaic* **bad**; **bided** *or archaic* **bid** *or* **biden** *or* **bidden**; **biding**; **bides** [ME *biden*, fr. OE *bīdan;* akin to OHG *bītan* to wait, ON *bītha*, Goth *beidan* to wait, L *fidere* to trust, Gk *peithesthai* to believe, be persuaded, obey, Russ *beda* misfortune] *vi* **1** : to continue in some state or condition ⟨~ still until you feel better⟩ **2 a** : WAIT, TARRY — used esp. with an expression of time ⟨~ yet a little⟩ **b** *of things* : to await one's pleasure : be left unchanged ⟨let the matter ~⟩ **3** : ABIDE, SOJOURN, DWELL ⟨the old man still ~*s* in the shanty though the mill has fallen to ruin⟩ ~ *vt* **1** *past usu* **bided** : to wait for ⟨their ready answer suggested that they had long *bided* that demand⟩ — now used chiefly in the phrase *bide one's time* **2** *archaic* : to encounter and resist : WITHSTAND, FACE ⟨the ships that ~ the storm⟩ **3** *now chiefly dial* : to put up with : TOLERATE, ENDURE ⟨couldn't ~ children on his place —J.W.Riley⟩ ⟨aggregated power does not readily ~ legal restraints —M.O.Hudson⟩ — **bide by** *archaic* : abide by

bi·dens \ˈbīˌdenz\ *n, cap* [NL, fr. L, having two teeth, 2-pronged, fr. *bi-* ¹bi- + *dent-, dens* tooth — more at TOOTH] : a large genus of herbs (family Compositae) native to the warmer parts of both hemispheres that have divided or compound leaves and yellow flowers and the usu. flattened achenes armed with barbed awns — see BEGGAR-TICKS, BUR MARIGOLD, SPANISH NEEDLE

bi·dent \ˈbīdᵊnt\ *n* -s [L *bident-, bidens*, fr. *bident-, bidens* 2-pronged] : a 2-pronged instrument

bi·dentate \(ˈ)bī+\ *adj* [fr. (assumed) NL *bidentatus*, fr. NL ¹*bi-* + *-dentatus* -dentate] : having two teeth or two processes suggestive of teeth

bi·denticulate \(ˌ)bī+\ *adj* [¹*bi-* + *denticulate*] *biol* : having two small teeth

bid·er \ˈbīdə(r)\ *n* -s : one that bides

bi·det \bəˈdet, bēˈ-, ˈ-dā\ *n* -s [F, fr. MF, fr. *bider* to trot] **1** : a small horse esp. in pack or courier service in an army **2** : a vessel about the height of the seat of a chair that often has fixtures for running water and is used esp. for bathing the external genitals and the posterior parts of the body

bi·di \ˈbē(ˌ)dē\ *var of* BIRI

bi·di–bi·di \ˈbēdēˌbēdē\ *n* -s [modif. of Maori *piripiri*] : PIRIPIRI

bi·digitate \(ˈ)bī+\ *adj* [fr. (assumed) NL *bidigitatus*, fr. NL ¹*bi-* + L *digitatus* digitate] : having two fingers or digitate projections or parts

bi·dimensional \(ˌ)bī+\ *adj* [¹*bi-* + *dimensional*] : having or perceived in terms of two dimensions — **bi·dimensionality** \(ˌ)bī+\ *n* -ES

bid in *vt* : to retain (property offered at auction) by overbidding the highest bid of a bona fide customer

bid·ing \ˈbīdiŋ\ *n* -s [ME *bidinge, biding*, fr. OE *bīding*, fr. *bīdan* to bide + *-ung, -ing* -ing] **1** *archaic* : an awaiting or remaining : STAY, RESIDENCE **2** *obs* : a lodging place : ABODE

biding place *n, archaic* : a place of abode : lodging place

bi·directional \(ˌ)bī+\ *adj* [¹*bi-* + *directional*] : reactive or functioning in two usu. opposite directions; *esp of a microphone* : having two sensitive areas

bid off *vt* : to receive (property offered at auction) immediately upon one's bid

bid price *n* : the price that a buyer offers to pay

bi·dri \ˈbidrē\ *n* -s [Hindi *bidrī*, fr. *Bidar*, town in India] : a pewter formerly used in India for making ware inlaid with gold or silver; *also* : BIDRI WARE

bidri ware *n* : the ware made by inlaying bidri

bids *pl of* BID, *pres 3d sing of* BID

bid up *vt* : to raise the price of (as property at auction) by a succession of offers ⟨the dealer clique *bid up* everything worth having to shut out the amateurs⟩; *also* : to raise (the price of something) by such means ⟨they *bid* the prices *up* sky-high to maintain their monopoly⟩

bid whist *n* : whist in which the players bid for the privilege of naming the trump suit

bie·ber·ite \ˈbēbəˌrīt\ *n* -s [G *bieberit*, fr. *Bieber*, town in Hesse, Germany + G *-it* -ite] : a mineral $CoSO_4.7H_2O$ consisting of hydrous cobalt sulfate occurring esp. in pale red crusts and stalactites

bie·brich scarlet \ˈbēˌbrik-\ *n, usu cap B & often cap S* [prob. trans. of G *biebricher scharlach*, fr. *Biebrich*, former city (now part of Wiesbaden), Prussia, Germany] : PONCEAU 3RB

¹bie·der·mei·er \ˈbēdə(r)ˌmīə(r)\ *adj, usu cap* [after Gottlieb *Biedermeier* ("Papa *Biedermeier*"), satirical name for a simple, fussy, uninspired Ger. bourgeois, the imaginary author of poems by Adolf Kussmaul †1902, Ludwig Eichrodt †1892, and others] **1** *of furniture* : of a type developed in Germany between 1815 and 1848, derived from French Empire styles but at once simpler in detail and weaker and heavier in design **2** : artistically, intellectually, or socially staid, conventional, humdrum, limited; *also* : bourgeois or Philistine ⟨*Biedermeier* writers⟩ ⟨a comfortable *Biedermeier* pastor⟩

²biedermeier \ˈ"\ *n* -s *usu cap* : one that is Biedermeier ⟨the story was a nice piece of *Biedermeier*⟩

bielby *var of* BILBY

¹bield \ˈbē(ə)l(d)\ *vt* [ME *belden* to assist, encourage, protect, fr. OE *beldan, byldan* to encourage, denominative fr. the stem of OE *bald, beald* bold — more at BOLD] *now chiefly Scot* : SHELTER, PROTECT

²bield \ˈ"\ *n* -s [ME *belde* shelter, confidence, boldness, fr. OE *beldo, byldo* boldness; akin to OHG *beldī* boldness, Goth *balthei;* derivative fr. the stem of OE *bald, beald* bold] **1** *chiefly Scot* : SHELTER, PROTECTION **2** *chiefly Scot* **a** : a place affording shelter : REFUGE **b** : a habitation for man or beast

bieldy \-ldē\ *adj* [²*bield* + *-y*] *chiefly Scot* : SHELTERING

bie·le·feld \ˈbēləˌfelt\ *adj, usu cap* [fr. *Bielefeld*, Germany] : of or from the city of Bielefeld, Germany : of the kind or style prevalent in Bielefeld

bielorussian *usu cap, var of* BELORUSSIAN

bien \ˈbēn\ *adj* [ME *bene* pleasant, comfortable, in good condition] **1** *Scot* **a** : COMFORTABLE, COZY, SNUG **b** : PROSPEROUS, WELL-TO-DO **2** *obs slang* : GOOD, FINE

¹bi·en·ni·al \(ˈ)bī¦enēəl, -nyəl\ *adj* [L *biennium* period of two years (fr. *bi-* + *-ennium*, fr. *annus* year) + E *-al* — more at ANNUAL] **1** : occurring, appearing, or being made, done, or acted upon every two years — compare BIANNUAL **2** : continuing or lasting for two years — used specif. of plants (as the parsnip) that require two growing seasons in which to go from seed to seed; compare ANNUAL

²biennial \ˈ"\ *n* -s : something that is biennial (as an exhibition or examination); *esp* : a biennial plant

biennial bearing *n* : the production of a heavy crop one year followed by a light or no crop the next (as in certain varieties of apple trees) — called also *alternate bearing*

bi·en·ni·al·ly \-əlē, -li\ *adv* : every two years

bi·en·ni·um \(ˈ)bī¦enēəm\ *n, pl* **bienniums** \-mz\ *or* **bien·nia** \-nēə\ [L] : a period of two years

bien·ve·nue *also* **bienvenu** \byaⁿv(ə)nüe\ *n* -s [ME *bienvenue*, fr. MF, fr. OF, fr. *bienvenu* welcome (adj.), fr. *bien* well (fr. L *bene*, adv. of *bonus* good) + *venu*, past part. of *venir* to come, fr. L *venire* — more at BOUNTY, COME] **1** : WELCOME — formerly common in English but now usu. a conscious borrowing from the French **2** *obs* : a fee demanded of a new workman by his fellows

¹bier \ˈbi(ə)r, ˈbiə\ *n* -s [ME *bere*, fr. OE *bǣr, bēr;* akin to OS & OHG *bāra* bier; derivative fr. the stem of OE *beran* to carry — more at BEAR] **1** *archaic* : a framework (as a litter or stretcher) for carrying; *also* : HANDBARROW **2** : a stand on which a corpse or coffin is placed or carried to the grave; *sometimes* : a coffin and the stand on which it is placed **3** *archaic* : the place where someone is buried : GRAVE, SEPULCHER

²bier *var of* BEER

bier·mer's anemia \ˈbirmərz-\ *also* **biermer's disease** *n, usu cap B* [after Anton *Biermer* †1892 Ger. physician] : PERNICIOUS ANEMIA

bier right *n* : an ordeal formerly used to test the guilt of one accused of murder by requiring him to vindicate himself in the presence of the corpse, the victim's wounds being believed to bleed afresh if the body were touched by the murderer

bier·stu·be \ˈbirˌs(h)tübə\ *n, pl* **bierstubes** \-bəz\ *or* **bier·stu·ben** \-bən\ [G, fr. *bier* beer (fr. OHG *bior*) + *stube* room (fr. OHG *stuba* heated room) — more at BEER, STOVE] : a room or other place (as in a German or German-style tavern) used primarily for the serving of beer

biestings *var of* BEASTINGS

bi·face *also* **bi·facial** \ˈbī+,-\ *n* [*biface* prob. back-formation fr. *bifacial*, adj.; *bifacial*, n. fr. *bifacial*, adj.] *archaeol* : a stone tool usu. of flint made from a core flattened on both sides : HAND AX

bi·facial \(ˈ)bī+\ *adj* [¹*bi-* + *facial*] : having opposite surfaces alike (as of certain chipped flint tools or some leaves); *sometimes* : having two fronts ⟨a representation of the Roman Janus is ~⟩

bi·facially \(ˈ)bī+\ *adv* : on two sides

bi·fanged \(ˈ)bī+\ *adj* [¹*bi-* + *fanged*] *of a tooth* : having two roots

bif·a·ra \ˈbifərə\ *n* -s [perh. fr. It *bifara, bifra*] : an organ stop of 8-foot or 4-foot pitch in which each pipe has two mouths of which one is cut a little higher than the other, causing a gentle vibrato effect; *also* : a similar stop with two ranks of pipes one of which is slightly sharped to produce a comparable vibrato effect

bi·far·i·ous \(ˈ)bī¦fa(a)rēəs\ *adj* [L *bifarius*, fr. *bifariam* in two ways, fr. *bi-* ¹bi- + *-fariam* (akin to Skt root *dhā* in *dvidhā* in two ways, *dadhāti* he places, sets) — more at DO] *archaic* : TWOFOLD, AMBIGUOUS ⟨some strange, mysterious verity in old ~ prophesy —Ned Ward⟩ — **bi·far·i·ous·ly** *adv*

¹biff \ˈbif\ *n* -s [prob. imit.] *slang* : WHACK, BLOW

²biff \ˈ"\ *vt* -ED/-ING/-s **1** *slang* : to deal a blow to : WHACK, SOCK **2** *chiefly Austral* : THROW

bif·fin \ˈbifən\ *n* -s [earlier *beefen*, fr. obs. *beefin* ox for slaughter, fr. ME, fr. (assumed) ME *beefing*, fr. ME *beef* + *-ing* one of a (specified) kind; fr. its deep-red color — more at -ING] **1** : an English apple of a variety often sold after being dried in the oven **2** *Brit* : an apple that has been baked and flattened into a cake

bif·fy \ˈbifē\ *n* -ES [origin unknown] *slang* : TOILET; *often* : OUTHOUSE, PRIVY

bi·fid \ˈbīˌfid, -ˌfəd\ *adj* [L *bifidus*, fr. *bi-* ¹bi- + *-fidus* (fr. the stem of L *findere* to split) — more at BITE] **1** : divided into two equal lobes or parts by a median cleft ⟨a ~ leaf⟩ ⟨claws ~⟩ **2** *of a cipher alphabet* : constructed by matching the letters of the alphabet with 2-unit equivalents of such a nature that exactly as many of them can be constructed as there are letters of the alphabet (as by using the 25 possible pairs made up of combinations of one or more of the numerals 1,2,3,4, and 5 for a 25-letter alphabet) — compare FRACTIONAL SUBSTITUTION — **bi·fid·i·ty** \bīˈfidəd·ē\ *n* -ES — **bi·fid·ly** *adv*

bi·filar \(ˈ)bī+\ *adj* [ISV ¹*bi-* + *fil-* (fr. L *filum* thread) + *-ar* — more at FILE] **1** : composed of or employing two threads or wires ⟨a ~ suspension of a waving part of an instrument⟩ **2** : composed of or employing a single thread or wire doubled back upon itself ⟨~ winding of a resistance coil⟩ — **bi·filarly** *adv*

bi·flabellate \ˌbī+\ *adj* [fr. (assumed) NL *biflabellatus*, fr. NL ¹*bi-* + (assumed) NL *flabellatus* flabellate] *of an insect antenna* : having short joints with long flattened processes on opposite sides

bi·flagellate \(ˈ)bī+\ *adj* [¹*bi-* + *flagellate*] : having two flagella ⟨a ~ zoospore⟩

bi·fluoride \(ˈ)bī+\ *n* -s [ISV ¹*bi-* + *fluoride*] : an acid fluoride of the formula MHF_2 (as lithium bifluoride $LiHF_2$)

¹bi·focal \(ˈ)bī+\ *adj* [ISV ¹*bi-* + *focal*] **1 a** : having two focal lengths **b** *of an eyeglass lens* : having one part that corrects for near vision and one for distant vision **2** : marked by two distinct often seemingly incompatible approaches or points of view ⟨the ~ nature of medieval historiography with its mixture of myth and history —Keith Spalding⟩ ⟨an Indian, educated in England and America, and hence able to give a sort of ~ view of the people and problems of Asia —*Nation*⟩

²bifocal \ˈ"\ *n* -s **1** : a bifocal glass or lens **2 bifocals** *pl* : eyeglasses with bifocal lenses

bi·fold \(ˈ)bī+\ *adj* [¹*bi-* + *-fold*] : TWOFOLD, DOUBLE

bi·foliate \(ˈ)bī+\ *adj* [fr. (assumed) NL *bifoliatus*, fr. NL ¹*bi-* + L *foliatus* leaved — more at FOLIATE] **1** : two-leaved **2** : BIFOLIOLATE

bi·foliolate \(ˈ)bī+\ *adj* [fr. (assumed) NL *bifoliolatus*, fr. NL ¹*bi-* + LL *foliolum* foliole + L *-atus* -ate — more at FOLIOLE] *of compound leaves* : having two leaflets

bi·follicular \ˌbī+\ *adj* [¹*bi-* + *follicular*] : having two follicles or twin pods esp. of milkweed

bi·fo·rate \ˌbīˌfōˌrāt, ˈbīfə,-, ˈbifə,-, (ˈ)bī¦fōrət\ *adj* [fr. (assumed) NL *biforatus*, fr. NL ¹*bi-* + L *foratus* pierced, bored, past part. of *forare* to bore — more at BORE] *biol* : having two perforations

bi·forked \(ˈ)bī+\ *adj* [¹*bi-* + *forked*] : so forked as to have two branches or peaks

bi·form \ˈbī,+\ *adj* [*biform* fr. L *biformis*, fr. *bi-* ¹bi- + *-formis* (fr. *forma* form); *biformed* fr. L *biformis* + E *-ed* — more at FORM] **1** : combining the qualities or forms of two distinct kinds of individuals ⟨a ~ crystal⟩ ⟨the ~ body of a satyr⟩ **2** : having or appearing in two dissimilar guises — used of characters in classical mythology that appeared to mortals in other than their customary bodily form ⟨whence Europa fled with ~ Jove⟩

biformed *obs var of* BIFORM

bi·fo·rous \ˈbīfərəs, ˈbif-\ *adj* [L *biforus* having two doors, fr. *bi-* ¹bi- + *-forus* (fr. *fores* door) — more at DOOR] : BIFORATE

bi·front \ˈbī+,-\ *or* **bi·fronted** \(ˈ)bī+\ *adj* [*bifront* fr. L *bifront-, bifrons*, fr. *bi-* ¹bi- + *front-, frons* forehead; *bifronted* fr. L *bifront-, bifrons* + E *-ed* — more at BRINK] *archaic* : having two faces or fronts

bi·furcal \(ˈ)bī+\ *adj* [L *bifurcus* 2-pronged (fr. *bi-* ¹bi- + *-furcus*, fr. *furca* fork) + E *-al* — more at FORK] : BIFURCATE

¹bi·fur·cate \ˈbīfə(r)ˌkāt, (ˈ)bī¦fər,kāt, -ˌfə,-, *usu* -d·+V\ *vb* -ED/-ING/-s [ML *bifurcatus*, past part. of *bifurcare* to bifurcate, fr. L *bifurcus*] *vi* : to branch or separate into two parts — often used with *into* ⟨the stream *bifurcated* into two narrow winding channels⟩ ~ *vt* : to cause to branch or separate into two parts ⟨it might be possible to ~ the beam of light⟩ **syn** see BRANCH

²bifurcate \ˈbīfə(r)ˌkāt, -kət; (ˈ)bī¦fərkət, -ˌfək-, -ˌkāt, *usu* -d·+V\ *adj* [ML *bifurcatus*, past part. of *bifurcare*] : divided into two branches : DICHOTOMOUS — used chiefly of physical objects — **bi·furcately** *adv*

bifurcate collateral *adj, of kinship name classes* : distinguishing collateral relatives both from lineal relatives of the same generation and from one another on the basis of the sex of connecting relatives

bifurcated *adj* [fr. past part. of ¹*bifurcate*] **1** : BIFURCATE **2** : combining or made up of two aspects, factors, or parts ⟨a ~ E layer in the ionosphere⟩ ⟨socially ~ populations⟩; *sometimes* : BIFOCAL 2 ⟨Freneau's peculiarly ~ view of the Indian, his agrarianism and primitivism, his warm humanitarianism —J.T.Flanagan⟩

bifurcate merging *adj, of kinship name classes* : identifying collateral relatives with lineal relatives of the same sex and generation when the connecting relative is of the same sex but distinguishing them when the connecting relative is of the opposite sex ⟨in a *bifurcate merging* terminology a father's brother would be identified as father but a mother's brother as uncle⟩

bi·furcation \ˌbī+\ *n* -s [F *bifurcation*, prob. fr. NL *bifurcation-, bifurcatio*, fr. ML *bifurcatus* + L *-ion-, -io* -ion] **1** : separation or branching into two parts, areas, aspects, or connected segments ⟨the Cartesian ~ of reality into mind and matter⟩ **2** : the point at which bifurcation occurs — used almost wholly of physical objects ⟨inflammation may occlude the ~ of the trachea⟩ **3** : either member of a pair produced by bifurcation : BRANCH ⟨the left ~ of the common iliac artery⟩ ⟨a ~ of the Japan current that carries warmth and moisture to the Alaska coastline⟩

¹big \ˈbig\ *adj* **bigger**; **biggest** [ME, prob. of Scand origin; akin to Norw dial. *bugge* important man — more at BOAST] **1 a** *obs* : of great physical strength : powerful in body ⟨Sir Launcelot was ~ and strong again —Thomas Malory⟩ **b** : of great force or vehemence : VIOLENT ⟨farewell the ~ wars that make ambition virtue —Shak.⟩ — now used only of natural phenomena ⟨the night of the ~ blow⟩ **2** : LARGE 4a: **a** : large in physical dimensions, bulk, or mass ⟨a ~ bag of potatoes⟩ ⟨the ~ white house on the hill⟩ **b** : of great extent ⟨a ~ tract of open country⟩ **c** : large in magnitude ⟨a ~ change from our simple country life⟩; *also* : large in quantity, number, or amount ⟨a ~ fleet⟩ **d** : formed or conducted on a large scale ⟨~ government⟩ ⟨a ~ merchandising combine⟩ **e** : having the largeness of — used chiefly in the comparative ⟨a little fish scarcely *bigger* than a mosquito larva⟩ **3** : FULL: **a** : PREGNANT; *esp* : nearly ready to give birth — usu. used with *with* ⟨a white heifer ~ with calf⟩ **b** : full to bursting : FILLED, BRIMMING, SWELLING, TEEMING — usu. used with *with* ⟨eyes ~ with tears⟩ ⟨~ with rage⟩ ⟨no period *bigger* with opportunity for the daring man⟩ **c** *of the voice* : full and resonant **4** : conspicuous or noteworthy in some respect: **a** : CHIEF, LEADING, PREEMINENT ⟨the ~ issue of this campaign⟩ ⟨the ~ shopping center is on 10th Avenue⟩ **b** : NOTORIOUS, BAD — used esp. in the superlative ⟨the *biggest* rascal on two feet⟩ **c** : OUTSTANDING, PROMINENT ⟨a ~ banker⟩; *esp* : outstandingly worthy or able ⟨a truly ~ man⟩ ⟨the *bigger* they are the harder they fall⟩ **d** : of importance, moment, or significance : IMPRESSIVE ⟨the ~ moment of his life⟩ ⟨a ~ piece of news⟩ **e** : IMPOSING, HIGH-SOUNDING, PRETENTIOUS ⟨such ~ words to put abroad such petty thoughts⟩; *often* : BOASTFUL, POMPOUS, THREATENING ⟨his ~ words were never backed by deeds⟩ **f** : having or showing greatness of spirit : MAGNANIMOUS, GENEROUS ⟨a heart ~ enough to hold no grudges⟩ ⟨he can be trusted to do the ~ thing⟩ — **too big for one's breeches** *also* **too big for one's pants** *or* **too big for one's boots** : exhibiting self-approval not justified by circumstances : above oneself

²big \ˈ"\ *adv* **1** : to a large amount or extent : LARGELY ⟨pay ~ for a privilege⟩ ⟨I eat ~ in the mornings⟩ **2** : in a big manner : to a marked degree: **a** *slang* : so as to bring notable success or advantage ⟨if the new line goes ~ he should clean up a fortune⟩ : with pronounced effect ⟨the only one to score ~ was George S. Kaufman —*Time*⟩ **b** : POMPOUSLY, PRETENTIOUSLY ⟨to talk ~⟩ **c** : BRAVELY, COURAGEOUSLY ⟨taking his losses ~⟩ **3** *dial* : VERY, EXTREMELY ⟨~ rich⟩ ⟨~ lazy⟩

³big \ˈ"\ *vt* **bigged**; **bigged**; **bigging**; **bigs** *chiefly Midland* : IMPREGNATE : make pregnant

⁴big \ˈ"\ *n* -s : an individual or organization of outstanding importance or power ⟨competition with the ~*s* of the aviation industry⟩

⁵big \ˈ"\ *vt* **bigged**; **bigged**; **bigging**; **bigs** [ME *biggen* to build, dwell, inhabit, fr. ON *byggja;* akin to OE *bēon* to be — more at BE] *dial Brit* : BUILD, CONSTRUCT, ERECT ⟨~ a new house⟩

BIG *abbr* best in group

bi·ga \ˈbēgə, ˈbīgə, -gə\ *n, pl* **bi·gae** \ˈbēˌgī, -(ˌ)gē, -(ˌ)jē; ˈbī(ˌ)jē\ [L, fr. *bi-* ¹bi- + *-ga* (fr. *jugum* yoke) — more at YOKE] : a two-horse chariot of ancient Mediterranean countries

big·a·mist \ˈbigəməst\ *n* -s [*bigamy* + *-ist*] : one that practices bigamy; *esp* : one that has two wives or mates at the same time — **big·a·mis·tic** \ˌ==ˈmistik, -tēk\ *adj*

big·a·mize \ˈ==ˌmīz\ *vi* -ED/-ING/-s [*bigamy* + *-ize*] : to commit bigamy

big·a·mous \ˈbigəməs\ *adj* [*bigamy* + *-ous*] **1** : guilty of bigamy ⟨a ~ man⟩ **2** : involving bigamy ⟨a ~ marriage⟩ — **big·a·mous·ly** *adv*

big·a·my \-mē, -mi\ *n* -ES [ME *bigamie*, fr. ML *bigamia*, fr. L *bi-* ¹bi- + LL *-gamia* -gamy, fr. Gk, fr. *gamos* marriage + *-ia* -y; akin to L *gener* son-in-law, Skt *jāmi* being a brother or sister, *jāmi* daughter-in-law] **1** *criminal law* **a** : unlawful polygamy **b** : the statutory offense of entering into a ceremonial marriage with one person while still legally married to another **2** *canon law* : any of several offenses that disqualify one from holding ecclesiastical office or entering holy orders: **a** : the offense of marrying two persons successively whether the first spouse be dead or divorced or of marrying a widow — called also *real bigamy* **b** : the offense of marrying one already carnally known by another — called also *interpretative bigamy* **c :** the offense of one in holy orders or under a vow of continence in marrying anyone

big apple *n, often cap B&A* **:** a jazz dance combining circular group formations with improvised solos and duets

big·a·rade \'bigə,räd\ *n* -s [F, fr. Prov *bigarrado*, fr. past part. of *bigarra* to variegate, fr. (assumed) OProv *bigarrar*, prob. fr. MF *bigarrer*] **:** SOUR ORANGE ⟨roast duck with a sauce ~⟩

big·ar·reau cherry \,bigə'rō-\ *also* **bigarreau** *n* -s *usu cap B* [F *bigarreau*, fr. MF, fr. *bigarrer* to variegate, fr. *bi-* ¹bi- + *-garrer* (fr. *garre* variegated)] **:** any of several cultivated sweet cherries with rather firm, often light-colored globular fruits — compare DUKE 5, HEART CHERRY

big bedbug *n* **:** CONENOSE

big bertha *n, usu cap both Bs* [approximate trans. of G *dicke Bertha*, lit., fat Bertha, after Frau *Bertha* Krupp von Bohlen und Halbach †1957 proprietress of the Krupp Works, Essen, Germany, where during the First World War a particularly celebrated and effective 42-centimeter mortar was made] **1 :** a German gun of large bore or of long range used in World War I **2 a :** something large or cumbersome of its kind — used esp. of machines or tools **b :** something effective at long range — used esp. of cameras and photographic lenses

bigbloom \'=,=\ *n* **:** LARGE-LEAVED MAGNOLIA

big bluegrass *n* **:** a grass (*Poa ampla*) used in the Pacific Northwest for forage and pasture having flat leaf blades, glabrous sheaths, and spikelets that are little compressed and have the lemma obscurely keeled

big bluestem *n* **:** BLUESTEM 1a

big board *n, often cap both Bs, often attrib* **:** a quotation board for securities listed on the New York Stock Exchange; *also* **:** the exchange

big-boned \'=¦=\ *adj* **:** having the skeletal structure large and rugged in comparison to the fleshy parts **:** somewhat rawboned

big-bore \'=¦=\ *adj* **1** *of firearms* **:** having a large or relatively large caliber — distinguished from *small-bore* **2 :** of, relating to, or involving the use of big-bore firearms ⟨*big-bore* shooting⟩

big boss *n* **:** the person ultimately in charge of an enterprise (as the active head of a business enterprise or the officer in charge of a military organization)

big boy *n* **:** a man of prominence in some field of endeavor (as a sport, a racket, or the ladies' garment trade) — often used ironically as a term of address ⟨come on, *big boy*, head for home before I run you in for loitering⟩

big brother *n* **1 :** an older brother **2 :** one that is like or likened to an older brother: **a :** a man who befriends a delinquent or friendless boy **b** *often cap both Bs* (1) **:** the leader of an authoritarian state or movement (2) **:** such a state or movement — called also *Big Brotherism*

big brown bat *n* **:** a rather large widely distributed No. American bat (*Eptesicus fuscus*) having soft loose brown fur, naked flight membranes, and moderately short rounded ears

big bud *n* **1 :** any of several diseases of plants characterized by abnormal swelling of the buds: as **a :** such a condition in currants caused by a gall mite (*Eriophyes ribis*) **b :** a virus disease of the tomato **2** *also* **big-bud hickory :** MOCKERNUT

big bug *n, slang* **:** a person of consequence **:** BIGWIG

big business *n* **1 :** large aggregations of capital and business organizations; *esp* **:** monopolies or trusts regarded collectively — often used derogatorily **2 :** any business having a large turnover and income **3 :** an institution of prominence or importance; *sometimes* **:** a nonbusiness organization unpleasantly suggestive in its methods or acts of big business (sense 1)

big casino *n, in casino* **:** the ten of diamonds for winning which a score of two is earned

big cat *n* **:** a hand recognized in some poker games that consists of king, queen, jack, ten, and eight, contains no pairs, includes cards from two or more suits, and ranks next below a flush — compare LITTLE CAT

big cheese *n, slang* **:** a person of consequence **:** BIGWIG

big chief *n, slang* **:** an important or influential person

big-city \'=¦==\ *adj* **:** typical of or restricted to large urban areas ⟨*big-city* delinquency problems⟩

big-cone pine \'=,=-\ *n* **:** COULTER PINE

big-cone spruce *n* **:** an evergreen tree (*Pseudotsuga macrocarpa*) of the western U.S. having cones 4 to 7½ inches long with their bracts protruding little beyond the scales — compare DOUGLAS FIR

big crab *n* **:** DUNGENESS CRAB

big dick *n, usu cap B&D, in craps, slang* **:** a throw of 10

big ditch *n* **:** a large artificial water channel (as the Erie Canal or the main channel of an irrigation system) — usu. cap. when designating a particular channel ⟨when the *Big Ditch* finally joined the Atlantic and Pacific oceans⟩

big drum *n* **:** BLACK DRUM

big-eared bat \'=¦=-\ *n* **:** any of numerous bats having exceptionally large ears (as members of a No. American genus *Corynorhimes* or of an Old World tropical family Megadermatidae)

big-eared fox *n* **:** LONG-EARED FOX

big·e·lowia \,bigə'lōēə\ *n* [NL, fr. Jacob *Bigelow* †1879 Am. physician and botanist + NL *-ia*] **1** *cap* **:** a genus of herbaceous or shrubby plants (family Compositae) with alternate linear or lanceolate leaves and flower heads arranged in corymbs **2** -s **:** a plant of the genus *Bigelowia*

big·em·i·nal \(')bī¦jemənəl\ *adj* [LL *bigeminus* doubled (fr. L *bi-* ¹bi- + *geminus* twofold, twin) + E *-al* — more at GEMINI] **:** DOUBLE, PAIRED ⟨the ~ optic parts of the brain in fishes⟩

bigeminal pulse *n, med* **:** a pulse characterized by two beats close together with a pause following each pair of beats

bi·geminate *also* **bi·geminated** \(')bī+\ *adj* [*bigeminate* fr. (assumed) NL *bigeminatus*, fr. NL ¹*bi-* + L *geminatus* geminate; *bigeminated* fr. (assumed) NL *bigeminatus* + E *-ed*] **:** twice geminate **:** having two pairs: **a :** BICONJUGATE **b** *mineralogy* **:** having two pairs of crystal forms

bi·gem·i·ny \bī'jemənē\ *n* -ES [ISV *bigemin-* (fr. LL *bigeminus* doubled) + *-y*] **:** the state of being bigeminal; *specif* **:** that of having a bigeminal pulse

big end *n* **:** the crankpin end of an engine connecting rod

bi·ge·ner \'bījənə(r)\ *n* -s [L, hybrid (adj.), fr. *bi-* ¹bi- + *gener-, genus* kind, race — more at KIN] **:** a bigeneric hybrid

bi·generic \¦bī+\ *adj* [*bi-* + *-ic*] **:** of, relating to, or involving two genera ⟨a ~ hybrid is produced by interbreeding members of species belonging to different genera and is rare in nature⟩

big·eye \'bi,gī\ *n* **:** either of two small widely distributed catalufas (*Priacanthus cruentatus* and *P. arenatus*) that are reddish to silvery and esteemed as food in areas where they are abundant

bigeye bass *or* **big-eyed bass** *n* **:** a small percoid fish (*Xenistius californiensis*) of the coast of California sometimes used as bait or for food

big-eyed \'=¦=\ *adj* **:** having big eyes; *also* **:** ASTONISHED **:** deeply impressed **:** WONDERING ⟨*big-eyed* with delight⟩

big-eyed bug *n* **:** a lygaeid bug; *esp* **:** any of certain bugs of the genus *Geocoris* that suck the juices from and destroy large numbers of leafhoppers

big-eyed herring *n* **1 :** TENPOUNDER **2 :** an alewife (*Pomolobus pseudoharengus*)

big-eyed mackerel *n* **:** CHUB MACKEREL

big-eyed scad *or* **bigeye scad** *n* **:** a small carangid fish (*Trachurops crumenophthalmus*) with large prominent eyes that is widely distributed in tropical seas and in some areas is an important food fish — called also *akule, goggler*

big four yellow *n, often cap B&F* **:** a strong to vivid orange that is slightly yellower and lighter than Navaho and redder than orpiment orange

¹**bigg** \'big\ *var of* ⁵BIG

²**bigg** \"\ *n* -s [ME *byge*, fr. ON *bygg* barley; akin to OE *bēow* barley and perh. to Gk *phyein* to bring forth — more at BE] *dial Brit* **:** FOUR-ROWED BARLEY

biggah *var of* BIGHA

big-gait·ed \'=¦==\ *adj, of a horse* **:** having a long easy stride

big game *n* **1 :** the large animals sought or taken by hunting or fishing for pleasure rather than profit ⟨*big game* angling is not without its risks⟩ **2 :** an important object of quest; *esp* **:** one involving risk

bigged *past of* BIG

big·gen \'bigən\ *vi* -ED/-ING/-S [¹*big* + *-en*] *now dial Brit* **:** to become big **:** increase in size

bigger *comparative of* BIG

biggest *superlative of* BIG

big·gety *or* **big·gity** \'bigəd·ē, -ətē, -i\ *adj* [prob. irreg. fr. ¹*big* + *-y*] **1** *South & Midland* **:** CONCEITED, VAIN **2** *South & Midland* **:** rudely self-important **:** assertively independent **:** IMPUDENT ⟨all that ~ talk of his⟩ ⟨a little authority and some folks act mighty ~⟩

big·gie *also* **big·gy** \'bigē\ *n* -s [¹*big* + *-ie* or *-y*] *slang* **1 :** one that is big **2 :** a person of consequence **:** BIG SHOT, BIGWIG

¹**big·gin** *or* **big·ging** \'bigən\ *n* -s [ME *bigginge, bigging*, fr. *biggen* to build, dwell, inhabit + *-inge, -ing* -ing — more at ⁵BIG] *dial Brit* **:** any of certain buildings: as **a :** HOUSE **b :** OUTBUILDING

²**biggin** \"\ *n* -s [MF *beguin*, fr. *beguine* Beguine, fr. OF] *now dial Brit* **:** CAP, HOOD: **a :** a child's cap **b :** NIGHTCAP

³**biggin** \"\ *n* -s [after Mr. *Biggin fl*1800 its inventor] **:** a coffee percolator used in the early 19th century; *also* **:** a pot with stand and lamp used in the same period for keeping coffee warm

bigging *pres part of* BIG

big·gish \'bigish, -gēsh\ *adj* [¹*big* + *-ish*] **:** somewhat big **:** comparatively big

big goldenrod *n* **:** a stout coarse goldenrod (*Solidago squarrosa*) of eastern No. America with the tips of its involucral bracts squarrose

big·go·net \'bigə,net\ *n* -s [irreg. fr. ²*biggin* + *-et*] *chiefly Scot* **:** a woman's cap or coif of linen

big gun *n* **:** a person or factor of outstanding importance esp. in some particular relation ⟨a *big gun* in the diplomatic corps⟩ ⟨ecology may be the *big gun* in the battle to keep the world's wild animals alive —W.A.Bridges⟩

bi·gha *or* **big·gah** \'bēgə\ *n, pl* **bigha** *or* **bighas** *or* **biggah** *or* **biggahs** [Hindi *bighā*, fr. Skt *vigraha* division, fr. *vigrhnāti* he separates, divides, fr. *vi* apart + *grhnāti* he seizes — more at WITH, GRAB] **:** any of various Indian units of land area varying between ⅓ acre and 1 acre

bighead \'=,=\ *n* -s **1 :** any of several diseases of animals: as **a :** equine osteoporosis **b :** an acute photosensitization of sheep and goats that follows the ingestion of certain plants and is characterized by subcutaneous edema of the head, ears, and neck, by impairment of vision, and by fever **c** *Austral* **:** a malignant edema of rams due to infection of head wounds with a bacterium (*Clostridium novyi*) causing gelatinous infiltration of the head and neck usu. followed by death **2 :** an exaggerated opinion of one's worth or importance **:** CONCEIT, POMPOSITY — **big·head·ed** \'=¦==\ *adj*

big-headed gurnard *n* **:** a sea robin (*Prionotus tribulus*) of the So. Atlantic and Gulf coasts of the U.S.

bighearted \'=¦==\ *adj* **:** generous and kindly **:** OPENHANDED, LIBERAL — **bigheartedly** *adv*

big hole *n, railroading, slang* **:** emergency application of brakes

big hook *n, railroading, slang* **:** a wrecking crane

bighorn \'=,=\ *also* **bighorn sheep** *n, pl* **bighorn** *or* **bighorns :** a usu. grayish brown wild sheep (*Ovis canadensis*) of mountainous western No. America resembling the Asiatic argali but smaller and with less massive horns — compare DALL SHEEP

bighorn

big house *n, often cap B&H* **1 :** the outstanding residence of a locality; *esp* **:** the seat of the local magnate ⟨mother worked for years in the kitchen of the *big house*⟩ **2** *slang* **:** PENITENTIARY **3** *South & Midland* **:** the social or living area of a house; *specif* **:** LIVING ROOM, PARLOR

¹**bight** \'bīt, *usu* -d·+V\ *n* -s [ME, fr. OE *byht*; akin to MLG *bocht* bend, ON *ölbogabōt* elbow joint; derivative fr. the stem of OE *būgan* to bend, bow — more at BOW] **1** *obs* **:** a corner, bend, or angle esp. of a body part **2 a :** the middle part of a slack rope — distinguished from *end* **b :** a curve or loop esp. in a rope, hose, or chain **3 a :** a bend or curve esp. in a river or a mountain chain; *specif* **:** a bend in a coast forming an open bay **b :** a bay formed by such a bend ⟨the *Bight* of Benin⟩ ⟨the Great Australian ~⟩ **4 :** the length of a sewing-machine stitch

²**bight** \"\ *vt* -ED/-ING/-S **1 :** to arrange, lay, or fasten (a rope) in bights **2 :** to fasten with a bight of rope ⟨~*ing* the canvas of a sail⟩

big idea *n, slang* **:** PURPOSE, INTENT

big if *n, slang* **:** something that is both important and uncertain **:** a fundamental question

big inch *n* **:** a very long oil or gas pipeline 24 inches in diameter

big jaw *n* **:** actinomycosis of the jaw of cattle **:** LUMPY JAW

big joker *n* **:** JOKER 2b(1) — used in certain card games (as canasta) in which other wild cards of lower scoring value also take the name of *joker;* compare LITTLE JOKER

big knife *n, usu cap B&K* **:** an American colonist esp. of Virginia — used orig. by the Indians to distinguish established settlers from the English; called also *Long Knife*

big laurel *n* **1 :** EVERGREEN MAGNOLIA **2 :** a large large-leaved evergreen rhododendron (*Rhododendron maxima*) of eastern No. America having the leaves hairy below and rosy bell-shaped flowers more or less speckled with green — called also *great laurel, rosebay*

big-leaf maple \'=,=-\ *n* **:** OREGON MAPLE

big league *n* **1** *often cap B&L* **a :** MAJOR LEAGUE **b :** any comparable sports association **2 :** something or some group that is outstanding of its kind (as in stature, quality, or worth) ⟨there is only one commercially sponsored dramatic program in the *big league* —*New Republic*⟩ ⟨*big league* politics⟩

big-leagu·er \'bi'glēgə(r)\ *n* **:** one that belongs to or plays in a big league

big leg *n* **:** an acute lymphangitis of equines usu. affecting the hind legs, accompanied by severe pain and high fever, and commonly the result of overfeeding though sometimes due to local infection

big lie *n, sometimes cap B&L* [trans. of G *grosse lüge*] **:** untruth on a large scale consciously used as a propaganda technique on the assumption that it is more likely to compel belief than untruth on a modest scale

big-lip sucker \'=,=-\ *n* **:** COLUMBIA RIVER SUCKER

big liver disease *n* **:** that form of avian leukosis in which the liver is greatly enlarged and infiltrated with white blood cells; *broadly* **:** AVIAN LEUKOSIS COMPLEX

big·ly \'biglē, -li\ *adv* [ME, fr. ¹*big* + *-ly, -liche* -ly] **:** in a big manner: as **a :** with great scope **:** LARGELY, COMPREHENSIVELY ⟨few things done, but those done ~⟩ **b** *archaic* **:** in a swelling blustering manner **:** HAUGHTILY, POMPOUSLY

big man *n, slang* **:** LEADER; *esp* **:** an unlawful wholesale dealer in narcotics

big meeting *n* **:** a series of revival meetings held successively in one locality

bigmitt \'=,=\ *n* [¹*big* + *mitt;* fr. the use of sleight of hand] **:** a confidence game involving dishonest card play

¹**bigmouth** \'=,=\ *n* **1 :** any of various fishes having noticeably large mouths: as **a :** LARGEMOUTH BLACK BASS **b :** WARMOUTH **c :** SQUAWFISH **d :** the common buffalo fish **2 :** a loudmouthed, talkative, and often maliciously gossipy person

²**bigmouth** \"\ *adj* **:** BIGMOUTHED

bigmouth buffalo *or* **bigmouth buffalo fish** *n* **:** the largest of the suckers (*Megastomatobus cyprinella*) that inhabits large rivers, bayous, and oxbows in central No. America and sometimes exceeds 3 feet in length and 50 pounds in weight

bigmouthed \'=,=\ *adj* **1 :** having a large mouth **2 :** LOUDMOUTHED, LOUD, BOISTEROUS; *often* **:** indiscreetly talkative

big name \'=¦=\ *n* **:** a big-name performer or personage ⟨the *big name* is the one you read about on page one —N.M. Loomis⟩ ⟨get some *big names* for the show⟩

big-name \'=¦=\ *adj* **1 :** of top rank in popular recognition **:** NOTABLE ⟨a *big-name* industrialist⟩ ⟨a *big-name* university⟩ ⟨*big-name* guests at a hotel⟩ **2 :** of or involving a big-name person, organization, or product ⟨a *big-name* committee⟩ ⟨a *big-name* novel⟩

big neck *n* **:** goiter of livestock

big-neck clam \'=,=-\ *n* **:** a large gaper (*Schizothaerus nuttallii*) of the Pacific coast of No. America

big·ness \'bignəs\ *n* -ES **1 :** quality or state of being big **2 :** size, whether great or small ⟨a painful lump having the ~ of a pea⟩ **3 :** broadness of outlook or scope; *sometimes* **:** POMPOSITY **:** self-assertive quality ⟨the ~ of their bandied words⟩

big noise *n, slang* **:** a person of consequence **:** BIGWIG

big·no·nia \big'nōnēə\ *n, cap* [NL, fr. J.P.*Bignon* †1743 French royal librarian + NL *-ia*] **:** a small genus of American and Japanese woody vines (family Bignoniaceae) climbing by small disks at the ends of tendrils and having compound leaves and showy somewhat irregular tubular flowers in axillary cymes — see CROSS VINE

big·no·ni·a·ce·ae \-nē'āsē,ē\ *n pl, cap* [NL, fr. *Bignonia*, type genus + *-aceae*] **:** a family of trees, shrubs, woody vines, or occas. herbs (order Polemoniales) growing widely in the tropics, a few in temperate regions, and having opposite or occas. alternate leaves and irregular showy flowers with 2 or 4 stamens — **big·no·ni·a·ceous** \=¦==¦āshəs\ *adj*

big·no·ni·ad \big'nōnē,ad\ *n* -s [NL *Bignonia* + E *-ad*] **:** a plant of the family Bignoniaceae or the genus *Bignonia*

big one *n* **:** WHOPPER

bi·go·net \'bigə,net\ *var of* BIGGONET

bi·go·ni·al \(')bī¦gōnēəl\ *also* **bi·go·ni·ac** \-nē,ak\ *adj* [¹*bi-* + *gonial* or *goniac*] **:** of, relating to, or joining the two gonia

bigonial diameter *also* **bigonial** *n* -s *anthrop* **:** the distance between the gonia

¹**big·ot** \'bigət, *usu* -d·+V\ *n* -s [MF, bigot, hypocrite, fr. OF *bigot* Norman, perh. fr. (assumed) OE *bī God* by God, fr. OE *bī* by + *God* — more at BY, GOD] **1** *obs* **:** HYPOCRITE; *esp* **:** a superstitious religious hypocrite **2 :** one obstinately and irrationally, often intolerantly, devoted to his own church, party, belief, or opinion **syn** see ENTHUSIAST

²**bigot** \"\ *adj* **:** BIGOTED

big·ot·ed \'bigəd·əd, -ətəd\ *adj* **:** obstinately and blindly attached to some creed, opinion, or practice **:** unreasonably devoted to a system or party and illiberal, often intolerant, toward others' opinions — **big·ot·ed·ly** *adv*

big·ot·ry \'bigətrē, -ri\ *n* -ES [F *bigoterie*, fr. MF, fr. *bigot* + *-erie* -ery] **:** state of mind of a bigot **:** obstinate and unreasoning attachment to one's own belief and opinions with intolerance of beliefs opposed to them; *also* **:** behavior or beliefs ensuing from such a condition

big·ot·ty \'bigəd·ē, -ətē, -i\ *var of* BIGGETY

big pine *n* **1 :** PONDEROSA PINE **2 :** SUGAR PINE

bi·gram \'bī,gram\ *n* [¹*bi-* + *-gram*] *cryptography* **:** DIGRAPH

big·root \'=,=\ *n* **:** an herbaceous California vine (*Echinocystis fabacea*) with an enormous tuberous root

bigs *pl of* BIG, *pres 3d sing of* BIG

big sagebrush *n* **:** SAGEBRUSH

big shellbark *or* **big shellbark hickory** *also* **big shagbark** *n* **:** a hickory (*Carya laciniosa*) of the eastern U.S., resembling the shagbark but having a much larger nut — called also *king nut*

big shot *n* **:** a person of consequence or prominence ⟨a *big shot* in gambling circles⟩ ⟨what's your problem, *big shot*⟩

big sister *n* **1 :** an older sister **2 :** one that is like an older sister: as **a :** a woman who befriends a delinquent or friendless girl **b :** a girl in an upper class at college who acts as adviser to a girl in the freshman class

big skunk *n* **:** a skunk of the genus *Mephitis*

big stick *n* **1 :** coercive power, esp. military or political ⟨we must speak softly but carry a *big stick* —Theodore Roosevelt⟩ **2** *slang* **:** a long ladder; *esp* **:** AERIAL LADDER

big talk *n* **:** boastful talk **:** BLUSTER

big thing *n* **:** something that is prominent, important, or in wide use ⟨tweed is the *big thing* this fall⟩

big-ticket \'=¦==\ *adj* **:** high-priced **:** having a large initial cost ⟨credit buying of *big-ticket* items such as refrigerators is on the increase⟩

big-time \'=¦=\ *adj* **1 :** of or relating to the big time **2 :** OUTSTANDING, PROMINENT, TOP-NOTCH, FIRST-CLASS ⟨her presentation was definitely *big-time*⟩

big time *n* **1 :** any high-paying vaudeville circuit requiring only two performances a day **2 :** the top rank of professional performance or of large-scale enterprise esp. as indicated by high income or great popular prestige ⟨a prize fighter may have a long wait before breaking into the *big time*⟩

big-tim·er \'big,tīmə(r), =¦==\ *n* **:** one who has reached the big time ⟨a television *big-timer*⟩

big toe *n* **:** the innermost and largest digit of the foot

bigtooth aspen *or* **bigtoothed aspen** \'=,=\ *n* **:** LARGE-TOOTHED ASPEN

bigtooth maple *n* **:** WESTERN SUGAR MAPLE

big top *n* **1 :** the main tent of a circus ⟨the glamour of the *big top*⟩ **2 :** CIRCUS 1c

big tree *n* **1 :** a California evergreen (*Sequoiadendron giganteum*) that often exceeds 300 feet in height and 30 feet in girth — called also *giant sequoia* **2 :** NOBLE FIR

big-tree plum \'=¦=-\ *n* **:** a small tree (*Prunus mexicana*) of the southeastern U.S. that is sometimes cultivated for ornament, that has glandless, abruptly acuminate, coarsely serrate leaves broadly rounded at the base and softly pubescent beneath, and that produces a purplish red fruit

big trefoil *n* **:** a European perennial legume (*Lotus uliginosus*) used in the U.S., chiefly in the Northwest, as a forage crop esp. on acid and wet soil

bi·gua·nide \(')bī¦gwä,nīd, -nəd\ *n* -s [ISV ¹*bi-* + *guan-* (fr. *guanidine*) + *-ide*] **:** a strong amorphous base $NH[C(=NH)NH_2]_2$ some of whose derivatives (as aryl derivatives) find use as antimalarial drugs or as precipitants for dyes in color photography

bi·guttate \(')bī+\ *adj* [¹*bi-* + *guttate*] **:** having a pair of droplike spots

big vein *or* **big vein disease** *n* **:** a soil-borne virus disease of lettuce characterized by strikingly enlarged light-yellow leaf veins and more or less stunting of the plants

big wheel *n, slang* **:** a person of consequence or authority **:** BOSS, BIGWIG

big·wig \'big,wig\ *n* **:** a person of consequence or self-importance; *esp* **:** one of high official position ⟨a couple of senators and some other political ~*s*⟩

bi·ha·ri *or* **be·ha·ri** \bē'här(,)ē\ *n, pl* **bihari** *or* **biharis** *or* **behari** *or* **beharis** *usu cap* [Hindi *bihārī*, fr. *Bihār* Bihar, state in northeastern India] **1 :** a native or inhabitant of Bihar, India **2 :** a group of Indic dialects spoken by the inhabitants of Bihar

bi·har tree \bē'här-\ *n* [prob. fr. *Bihar*, state in northeastern India] **:** LACQUER TREE

bi-iliac \(')bī+\ *adj* [¹*bi-* + *iliac*] **:** of, relating to, or between the two most prominent points of the crests of the iliac bones ⟨a large *bi-iliac* diameter⟩

bi·ischial \(')bī+\ *also* **bi·ischiadic** *or* **bi·ischiatic** \(¦)bī+\ *adj* [¹*bi-* + *ischial* or *ischiadic* or *ischiatic*] **:** of, relating to, or between both ischia

bi·ja \'bējə\ *n* -s [short for *bijasal*] *India* **:** KINO 2

bi·jar \bə'jär\ *n* -s [fr. *Bijar*, town in northwest Iran] **:** a thick-piled Persian rug of very close weave and variable design produced in Bijar

bi·ja·sal \'bējə,säl\ *n* -s [prob. fr. an Indic word akin to Skt *bīja* seed and *sāla* sal tree] **:** BIJA

¹**bi·jou** \'bē,zhü, =¦=\ *n, pl* **bi·joux** \-üz, -ü\ [F, fr. Bret *bizou* ring, fr. *biz* finger; akin to W *bys* finger, OCorn *bis, bes*] **:** TRINKET, JEWEL **:** a small dainty usu. ornamental piece of delicate workmanship and fine material

²**bijou** \"\ *adj* **:** small of its kind and usu. marked by fine detail and workmanship ⟨can Americans be persuaded to pay out dollars for ~ cars⟩ — used esp. of buildings ⟨a ~ theater with delicate rococo decorations⟩

bi·jou·te·rie \bē'zhütə,rē, *F* bēzhü·trē\ *n* -s [F, fr. *bijou*] **1 a :** a collection of trinkets or ornaments ⟨proud of his Gothic ~⟩; *collectively* **:** TRINKETS, JEWELS **b :** jewelry in which delicate or intricate metalwork contributes more to the value than do the constituent materials **2 :** an apt turn of phrase **:** BON MOT

bi·ju·gate \'bījə,gāt; (')bī¦jügət, -,gāt\ *also* **bi·ju·gous** \-gəs\ *adj* [*bijugate* fr. ¹*bi-* + *jugate; bijugous* fr. ¹*bi-* + L *jugum* yoke + E *-ous* — more at YOKE] *of a pinnate leaf* **:** having two pairs of leaflets

bi·ka·ner \,bikə'ne(ə)r, ,bē-, -¦ni(ə)r\ *adj, usu cap* [fr. *Bikaner*, India] **:** of or from the city of Bikaner, India **:** of the kind or style prevalent in Bikaner

bik·a·neri \,bikə'nerē, ,bē-, -nirē\ *also* **bik·a·ner** \-'ne(ə)r,

-ni(ə)r\ *n* -s *usu cap* **:** a sheep of an Indian breed of wool-type sheep having the body white and the face usu. colored

[1]**bike** \'bīk\ *n* -s [ME] **1** *chiefly Scot* **:** a nest of wild bees, wasps, or hornets **2** *chiefly Scot* **:** a crowd or swarm of people ⟨the busy ~ of the city —R.L. Stevenson⟩

[2]**bike** \"\ *n or vb* [by shortening and alter.] **:** BICYCLE — **bik·er** \-kə(r)\ *n* -s

bikh \'bik\ *n* -s [Hindi, fr. Skt *viṣa* poison — more at VIRUS] *India* **:** a poison extracted from certain plants of the genus *Aconitum*

bikh·a·con·i·tine \,bikə'känə,tēn, -,tən\ *n* -s [ISV *bikh* + *aconite* + *-ine*] **:** a toxic crystalline alkaloid $C_{36}H_{51}NO_{11}$ obtained from the root of certain plants of the genus *Aconitum*

bi·ki·ni \bə'kēnē\ *n* -s [F, fr. *Bikini*, atoll of the Marshall islands in the northern Pacific, site of atomic bomb tests of 1946; fr. the comparison of the effects wrought by a scantily clad woman to the effects of an atomic bomb] **:** a woman's abbreviated two-piece bathing suit

bi·ki·ni·an \-nēən,-nyən\ *n* -s *usu cap* [*Bikini* + E *-an*] **:** a native of the Marshallese island Bikini

bik·ku·rim \bi,kü'rēm, -'kürim\ *n pl* [Heb *bikkūrīm* first fruits] **1 :** the first ripe fruits offered in thanks to God on the altar of the Temple in ancient Palestine **2** *in modern Israel* **:** the products of the orchards and fields gathered and sold to further the Jewish National Fund

bi·kol *also* **bi·col** \bē'kōl\ *n, pl* **bikol** *or* **bikols** *also* **bicol** *or* **bicols** *usu cap* [Bikol & Tag] **1 a :** a Christianized people in southeastern Luzon and adjacent islands of the Philippines **b :** a member of such people **2 :** the Austronesian language of the Bikol people

bi·la·an \bē'lä,än, -'län\ *n, pl* **bilaan** *or* **bilaans** *usu cap* [Bisayan *Bilaan*, fr. Bilaan *Blaan*] **1 a :** a predominantly pagan people inhabiting southern Mindanao and the Sarangani islands, Philippines **b :** a member of such people **2 :** the Austronesian language of the Bilaan people

[1]**bi·labial** \(')bī+\ *adj* [ISV [1]*bi-* + *labial*] **1** *of a consonant* **:** produced with both lips ⟨\p\ and \b\ and \m\ are ~ consonants⟩ — compare LABIAL **2 a :** of, relating to, or between the lips **b** *anthrop* **:** between the highest point on the upper lip and the lowest point on the lower lip

[2]**bilabial** \"\ *n* -s **:** a bilabial consonant

bi·labiate \(')bī+\ *adj* [[1]*bi-* + *labiate*] **:** having two lips ⟨a ~ corolla of a flower⟩

bi·laminate *or* **bi·laminated** *also* **bi·laminar** \(')bī+\ *adj* [[1]*bi-* + *laminate* or *laminated* or *laminar*] **:** formed of or having two laminae

bil·an·der \'biləndə(r), 'bī-\ *n* -s [obs. D *billander* (now *bijlander*), alter. of (assumed) obs. D *binlander*, fr. obs. D *bin* inside (fr. MD, alter. of *binnen*, fr. *be-* + *innen* inside) + D *land* + *-er*; akin to OE, OHG & ON *innan* from the inside, Goth *innana*, OE *in*, and to OHG *lant* land — more at IN, LAND] **:** a small 2-masted merchant ship

bi·lat·er·al \(')bī¦lad·ərəl, -lat(ə)rəl\ *adj* [[1]*bi-* + *lateral*] **1 :** having two sides ⟨a problem that poses a ~ difficulty⟩ **2 :** affecting reciprocally two sides or two parties ⟨a ~ contract⟩ ⟨a ~ treaty⟩; *specif* **:** of or relating to bilateralism in trade ⟨~ trade policies⟩ **3** *biol* **a :** of or relating to the right and left sides of a central area, organ, or plane **b :** possessing bilateral symmetry **4 :** related or tracing descent through both maternal and paternal ancestors — contrasted with *unilateral* **5 :** of or relating to a system of tolerance specification that allows variation both above and below the basic size — **bi·lat·er·al·ly** \-lad·ərəlē, -lat(ə)rəlē, -li\ *adv*

bi·lat·er·al·ism \-ə,lizəm\ *n* -s **1 :** the state of being bilateral; *esp* **:** BILATERAL SYMMETRY **2 :** the practice of advancing trade between two countries by concluding agreements governing such factors as the volume and composition of trade, the price of commodities, and the settling of accounts — contrasted with *multilateralism*

bi·lat·er·al·is·tic \-ə¦listik\ *adj* **:** BILATERAL 2

bi·lat·er·al·i·ty \¦bī,lad·ə¦raləd·ē, -latə¦-, -ralətē, -i\ *n* -ES **:** BILATERALISM

bilateral monopoly *n* **:** a market condition in which only one buyer or one group of associated buyers confronts only one seller or one group of associated sellers

bilateral symmetry *n* **:** the condition of having the right and left sides (as of the body) counterparts one of the other — compare RADIAL SYMMETRY

[1]**bi·la·te·ria** \,bīlə'tirēə\ [NL, fr. [1]*bi-* + L *later-, latus* side + NL *-ia* — more at LATERAL] *syn of* EXOCYCLOIDA

[2]**bilateria** \"\ *also* **bi·lat·er·a·lia** \,bī,lad·ə'rālēə\ *n pl, cap* [*bilateria*, NL, fr. [1]*bi-* + L *later-, latus* side + NL *-ia*; *bilateralia*, NL, fr. [1]*bi-* + L *lateralia*, neut. pl. of *lateralis* lateral — more at LATERAL] **:** bilaterally symmetrical animals

bil·bao \(')bil¦bä(,)ō, -¦bau̇ *also* -¦bā(,)ō\ *adj, usu cap* [fr. *Bilbao*, Spain] **:** of or from the city of Bilbao, Spain **:** of the kind or style prevalent in Bilbao

bil·bao glass \"-\ *also* **bilboa** \'bil(,)bō(ə)\ *n* -s **:** a mirror with a marble or marble and mahogany frame frequently ornamented in filigree

bil·ber·ry \'bil- — *see* BERRY\ *n* [*bil-* (prob. of Scand origin; akin to Dan *bølle* whortleberry) + *berry*; akin to ON *beyla* hump — more at BILE] **1 :** any of certain plants of the genus *Vaccinium* that differ from the typical blueberries in having their flowers solitary or in very small clusters and arising from axillary buds: **a :** WHORTLEBERRY 1 **b :** any of several chiefly alpine or boreal No. American plants (as *V. membranaceum, V. caespitosum*, or *V. uliginosum*) **2 :** the sweet edible blue or bluish black fruit of a bilberry **3 a :** a bearberry (*Arctostaphylos uva-ursi*) **b :** a withe rod (*Viburnum nudum*)

[1]**bil·bo** \'bil(,)bō\ *or* **bil·boa** \-(,)bō(ə)\ *n, pl* **bilboes** *or* **bilbos** *or* **bilboas** [fr. *Bilboa*, earlier form of *Bilbao*, Spain] **:** a finely tempered sword

[2]**bilbo** \"\ *n* -ES [earlier *bilbowe*, perh. fr. *Bilboa*, Spain] **:** a long bar of iron with sliding shackles and a lock at the end that is used to confine the feet of prisoners esp. on shipboard

bil·bo·quet \,bilbə'ket\ *n* -s [F, fr. MF *billeboquet*, fr. *bille* ball (of Gmc origin; akin to MHG *bickel* die, ankle) + *bouquer* to thrust, fr. *bouc* male goat, of Celt origin; akin to OIr *bocc* male goat — more at BUCK] **:** a device having a cup or spike at the top of a stick to which is attached a ball on a string; *also* **:** the game of maneuvering the device so as to catch the ball in the cup or on the spike — compare CUP AND BALL

bil·by *also* **bil·bi** \'bilbē, -bi\ *or* **biel·by** \'bēl-\ *n, pl* **bilbies** *also* **bilbis** *or* **bielbies** [native name in Australia] **:** the rabbit bandicoot of Australia

bil·cock \'bil,käk\ *n* -s [origin unknown] *Brit* **:** WATER RAIL

bil·dar \bil'där\ *n* -s [Hindi *beldār*, fr. Per *beldār*, fr. *bel* spade + *-dar* holder] *India* **:** DIGGER, EXCAVATOR

bil·dungs·ro·man \'bil,du̇ŋ(k)srō,män, -u̇ŋzr-\ *n, pl* **bildungsromane** \-nə\ *or* **bildungsromans** *usu cap* [G, fr. *bildung* education, culture + *roman* novel] **:** a novel about the usu. early development or spiritual education of the main character ⟨a long, detailed *Bildungsroman*⟩

[1]**bile** \'bī(ə)l\ *n* -s [ME, fr. OE *bȳl*; akin to OHG *būlla* boil, ON *beyla* hump, growth, Goth *ufbauliths* swollen with pride, Serb *buljiti* to stare with goggle eyes — more at BOAST] *dial* **:** [1]BOIL

[2]**bile** \'bīl, *esp bef pause or cons* -ī\ə\l\ *n* -s [F, fr. L *bilis*; akin to W *bustl* bile] **1 a :** a yellow or greenish viscid alkaline fluid secreted by the liver from which it passes into the duodenum where it mixes with the duodenal and pancreatic secretions, aids in the digestive processes by emulsifying fats and otherwise assisting in their digestion and absorption, and may also aid in neutralizing the acid chyme from the stomach, in promoting peristalsis, and in reducing putrefactive action **b :** HUMOR 1b(1) **:** (1) **:** YELLOW BILE (2) **:** BLACK BILE **2 :** proneness to anger **:** ILL HUMOR, IRASCIBILITY, SPLEEN ⟨the villain in every novel gives you somebody "to shoot at", rather than firing your stored-up ~ at yourself —T.V.Smith⟩

[3]**bile** \'bī(ə)l\ *vb* -ED/-ING/-S [by alter.] *dial* **:** [2]BOIL

[4]**bile** \"\ *n* -s [by alter.] *dial* **:** [3]BOIL

bile acid *n* **:** any of several acids (as cholic acid) that occur in bile usu. in the form of sodium salts of the acids conjugated with glycine or taurine (as in glycocholic acid or taurocholic acid), that are formed in the body from cholesterol and belong to the class of steroids, that promote the digestion of fats and other lipides by their emulsifying and solubilizing actions, and that aid in the absorption of many water-insoluble organic substances by forming soluble complexes with them; *also* **:** any conjugated bile acid

bilection *var of* BOLECTION

bile cyst *n* **:** GALLBLADDER

bile duct *n* **:** an excretory duct of the liver — see COMMON BILE DUCT

bile fluke *n* **:** CHINESE LIVER FLUKE

bile pigment *n* **:** any of several coloring matters (as bilirubin or biliverdin) in the bile that pass on oxidation through a succession of colors useful as tests for the pigments

bile salt *n* **1 :** a salt of a bile acid; *esp* **:** a naturally occurring sodium salt of a conjugated bile acid **2 bile salts** *pl* **:** a dry mixture of the principal salts of ox gall consisting of sodium glycocholate and sodium taurocholate in varying proportions used as a liver stimulant and laxative

bile vessel *n* **:** any of numerous fine channels within the liver that conduct bile

[1]**bilge** \'bilj\ *n* -s [origin unknown] **1 a :** the point of largest circumference of a cask or barrel usu. located at the middle **b :** the difference in width between the midsection of a barrel stave and the end **2 a :** the part of the underwater body of a ship lying between the flat of the ship's bottom and the straight vertical topsides; *specif* **:** the point of greatest curvature **b :** the lowest point of a ship's inner hull adjacent to the keelson **3 a :** BILGE WATER **b :** stale, offensive, or worthless remarks or ideas ⟨all his sanctimonious ~ —John Buchan⟩

[2]**bilge** \"\ *vb* -ED/-ING/-S *vt* **1 :** to fracture or otherwise damage the bilge of (a ship) **:** stave in the bottom of ⟨the boat was *bilged* by a snag —W.S.Campbell⟩ **2** *slang* **:** to require to resign (as from a naval academy) because of failure in studies ⟨a couple of midshipmen got *bilged*⟩ ~ *vi* **1 a :** to undergo a fracture or other damage in the bilge **:** spring a leak through damage to the bilge ⟨the ship *bilged* when it struck the reef⟩ **b :** to rest on the bilge (as after running aground) ⟨for three hours the ship lay *bilging* on the sand bar⟩ **2** *slang* **:** to fail in one's studies and resign under compulsion ⟨he *bilged* out⟩

bilge block *n* **:** one of the blocks supporting the bilge of a ship at the turn of the bilge while in a dry dock or under construction

bilge·board \'=,=\ *n* **1 :** a plane of wood or metal sliding in a case like a centerboard but built into each bilge of a ship **2 :** LIMBER BOARD

bilge keel *also* **bilge piece** *n* **:** a steel plate or other longitudinal projection like a fin secured for a distance along a ship near the turn of the bilge on either side to check rolling — called also *rolling chock*; see SHIP illustration

bilge keelson *n* **:** a keelson located near the turn of the bilge

bilge log *n* **:** one of the logs of the bilge ways

bilge saw *n* **:** a saw similar to a barrel saw but having the diameter at the middle greater than at the ends

bilge strake *n* **:** one of the strakes at the turn of the bilge

bilge water *n* **1 :** water that collects by seepage or leakage in the bilge of a ship or other vessel **2 :** BILGE 3b

bilge ways *n pl but sometimes sing in constr* **1 :** heavy timbers that rest on the ground ways and carry the weight of a vessel in launching — compare DOGSHORE **2 :** transverse timbers or supports on which the bilge blocks travel

bilgy \'biljē, -i\ *adj, usu* -ER/-EST **:** suggestive of or like bilge water; *esp* **:** highly offensive in odor

[1]**bil·har·zia** \bil'härzēə\ [NL, fr. Theodor *Bilharz* †1862 Ger. helminthologist + NL *-ia*] *syn of* SCHISTOSOMA

[2]**bilharzia** *n* -s [NL, fr. T. *Bilharz* + NL *-ia*] **1 :** SCHISTOSOME **2 :** SCHISTOSOMIASIS — **bil·har·zi·al** \(¦)=¦=zēəl\ *or* **bil·har·zic** \-zik\ *adj* — **bil·har·zi·al·ly** \-zēəlē\ *adv*

bil·har·zi·a·sis \,bilhär'zīəsəs\ *or* **bil·har·zi·o·sis** \(,)bil-,härzē'ōsəs\ *n, pl* **bilharzia·ses** \-ə,sēz\ *or* **bilharzio·ses** \-'ō,sēz\ [NL, fr. [1]*Bilharzia* + *iasis* or *-osis*] **:** SCHISTOSOMIASIS

bili- *comb form* [MF, fr. L, fr. *bilis* — more at BILE] **1 :** bile ⟨*bilification*⟩ **2 :** derived from bile ⟨*bilirubin*⟩

bil·i·ary \'bilē,erē, -lyər-, -i\ *adj* [F *biliaire*, fr. *bili-* + *-aire* -ary] **1 a :** of or relating to bile, the bile ducts, or the gallbladder ⟨~ acids⟩ **b :** conveying bile ⟨~ ducts⟩ **2** *archaic* **:** BILIOUS

biliary calculus *n* **:** GALLSTONE

biliary canal *n* **:** a passage for the bile **:** HEPATIC DUCT

biliary dyskinesia *n* **:** pain or discomfort in the epigastric region resulting from spasm esp. of the sphincter of Oddi following cholecystectomy

biliary fever *n* **:** piroplasmosis esp. of dogs and horses

biliary tract *n* **:** the bile ducts and gallbladder

bil·ic \'bilik\ *adj* [[2]*bile* + *-ic*] **:** of, relating to, or derived from bile

bil·i·cy·a·nin \¦bilə¦sīənən\ *n* -s [ISV *bili-* + *cyan-* (fr. Gk *kyanos* dark blue) + *-in*] **:** a blue pigment found in gallstones and formed by oxidation of biliverdin or bilirubin

bil·i·fi·ca·tion \,biləfə'kāshən, ,bī-\ *n* -s [*bili-* + *-fication*] **:** formation and excretion of bile

bil·i·fus·cin \,==='fəsən\ *n* -s [*bili-* + *fusc-* (fr. L *fuscus* dark) + *-in* — more at DUSK] **:** a brown pigment found in human gallstones and in old bile and formed by oxidation of biliverdin

bi·lim·bi \bə'limbē\ *or* **bi·lim·bing** \-'lim(,)biŋ\ *n* -s [Konkani & Malay; Konkani *bilimbi*, fr. Malay *bĕlimbing*] **1 :** an East Indian evergreen tree (*Averrhoa bilimbi*) resembling the carambola **2 :** the very acid fruit of the bilimbi that is used for preserves or pickles — compare CARAMBOLA

biliment *n* -s [short for *habiliment*] *obs* **:** an ornamental part of women's dress (as a jeweled headdress or special lace) esp. in the 16th century

bi·lin \bə'lēn\ *n* -s *usu cap* **:** the Cushitic language of the Bogos — compare HAMITIC LANGUAGES

bi·linear \(')bī + \ *adj* [[1]*bi-* + *linear*] **1 :** of or relating to two lines ⟨~ coordinates⟩ **2 :** of or relating to an algebraic form each term of which involves one variable to the first degree from each of two sets of variables

biling *pres part of* BILE

[1]**bi·lin·gual** \(')bī¦liŋgwəl\ *adj* [L *bilinguis* (fr. *bi-* [1]*bi-* + *lingua* tongue) + E *-al* — more at TONGUE] **1 :** containing or expressed in two written languages ⟨a ~ inscription⟩ ⟨a ~ street sign⟩ **:** involving the use of two languages ⟨books printed in ~ form⟩ **:** having reference to two languages written, spoken, or manual ⟨~ study⟩ ⟨the ~ deaf⟩ **2 :** having or using two languages esp. as spoken with the fluency characteristic of a native speaker ⟨a practically ~ control of French and English⟩ ⟨a ~ speaker⟩ — **bi·lin·gual·ly** \-gwəlē, -li\ *adv*

[2]**bilingual** \"\ *n* -s **1 :** an inscription in two languages **2 :** a person using two languages esp. habitually and with a control like that of a native speaker

bi·lin·gual·ism \bī'liŋgwə,lizəm\ *also* **bi·lin·gual·i·ty** \,==gwaləd·ē\ *n, pl* **bilingualisms** *also* **bilingualities** **:** the quality or state of being a bilingual; *also* **:** the use (as by a community) of two languages

bil·i·nite \'bilə,nīt\ *n* -s [Czech *bilinit*, fr. *Bilina*, Czechoslovakia + Czech *-it* -ite] **:** a mineral $FeSO_4.Fe_2(SO_4)_3.22H_2O$ consisting of a hydrous iron sulfate occurring in yellowish radiating fibers

bil·ious \'bilyəs *sometimes* -lēəs\ *adj* [MF *bilieux*, fr. L *biliosus*, fr. *bilis* bile + *-osus* -ose — more at BILE] **1 a :** of or relating to bile **b :** marked or accompanied by disordered liver function ⟨a ~ attack⟩; *broadly* **:** due to or associated with excessive secretion of bile ⟨suffered three years with a ~ ague⟩ **c :** affected by a bilious disorder ⟨a ~ patient⟩ **d :** appearing as though affected by a bilious disorder ⟨a sickly ~ face⟩ — compare JAUNDICE **2 :** of a peevish ill-natured disposition **:** marked by a glum and morosely sour attitude **:** fretfully irascible **:** CHOLERIC ⟨a ~ disagreeable old skinflint⟩ ⟨looking at life with a ~ eye⟩ **3 :** sickeningly unpleasant **:** of a kind that makes one queasy **:** NAUSEATING, REVOLTING ⟨utterly ~ weather⟩ ⟨with clapboards painted red and ~ yellow —Sinclair Lewis⟩ — **bil·ious·ly** *adv* — **bil·ious·ness** *n* -ES

bil·i·ru·bin \¦bilə¦rübən, ,bī-\ *n* -s [ISV *bili-* + L *ruber* red + ISV *-in* — more at RED] **:** a reddish yellow crystalline pigment $C_{33}H_{36}N_4O_6$ occurring in bile, blood, urine, and gallstones sometimes in combination with protein and formed by reduction of biliverdin

bil·i·ru·bi·ne·mia *or* **bil·i·ru·bi·nae·mia** \,====='nēmēə\ *n* -s [NL, fr. ISV *bilirubin* + NL *-emia, -aemia*] **:** the presence of bilirubin in the blood in excess of the normal slight quantity

bil·i·ru·bi·nu·ria \-'n(y)u̇rēə\ *n* -s [NL, fr. ISV *bilirubin* + NL *-uria*] **:** excretion of bilirubin in the urine

bi·literal \(')bī+\ *adj* [[1]*bi-* + *literal*] **1 :** consisting of or employing two letters or types of letters: as **a :** having two root consonants ⟨Semitic ~ nouns⟩ **b :** written in two different alphabets **2** *cryptography* **a :** composed of or employing a cover text in which two letter forms or type faces are used in significant combinations — see BACON BILITERAL CIPHER **b :** representing one letter by two

bi·lith \'bī,lith\ *or* **bi·lith·on** \bī'li,thän\ *n* -s [[1]*bi-* + *-lith, -lithon* (fr. Gk *lithos* stone)] **:** a prehistoric monument composed of two stones usu. constituting a pillar capped by a slab

bil·i·ver·din \,bilə'vərdən, ,bī-\ *n* -s [Sw, fr. *bili-* + obs. F *verd* green (now *vert*) + Sw *-in* — more at VERDANT] **:** a green crystalline pigment $C_{33}H_{34}N_4O_6$ occurring as the chief bile pigment of amphibians and birds and chiefly as a precursor of bilirubin in man and carnivorous mammals and formed at least in part by the breakdown of hemoglobin

[1]**bilk** \'bilk\ *vt* -ED/-ING/-S [perh. alter. of [2]*balk*] **1 :** to block the free development, functioning, or fulfillment of **:** BALK, CHECK ⟨whatever measures one suggests are bound to be resisted if not ~*ed* —*Saturday Rev.*⟩ **2 a :** to cheat out of what is due **:** DEFRAUD ⟨~*ed* insurance companies of more than $1,000,000 —Henry La Cossitt⟩ **b** *archaic* **:** to evade payment of or for ⟨don't intend to ~ my lodgings —Henry Fielding⟩ **3 a** *archaic* **:** to slip away from **b :** AVOID, SHUN ⟨~*ed* the problem of slavery by making Heaven democratic —Waldo Frank⟩

[2]**bilk** \"\ *n* -s **:** an untrustworthy tricky individual **:** CHEAT

[1]**bill** \'bil\ *n* -s [ME *bile*, fr. OE; akin to OE *bill* sword]

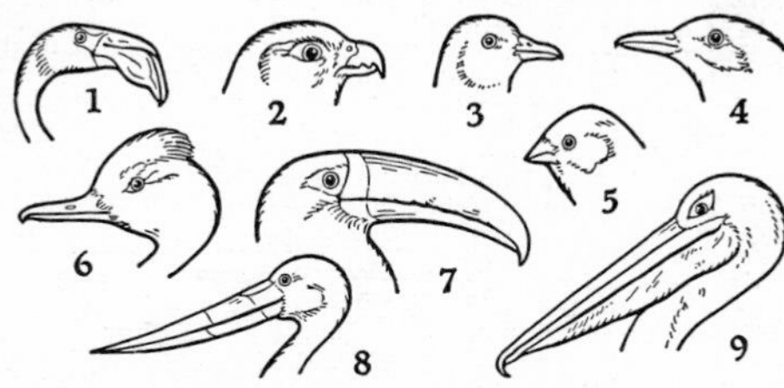

bills: *1* flamingo, *2* hawk, *3* pigeon, *4* thrush, *5* finch, *6* duck (merganser), *7* toucan, *8* saddle-bill, *9* pelican

1 : the jaws of a bird together with their horny covering, the whole varying greatly in form according to the food and habits of the various kinds **:** BEAK, NIB **2 a :** any mouthpart similar to or likened to a bill (as the horny jaws of a turtle, the elongated snout of a marlin, or the sensitive skin-covered beak of a platypus) **b :** a thin flattened part of the shell margin of the broad end of an oyster **3 :** a projection of land like a beak **:** PROMONTORY, HEADLAND **4 :** the point of the end of an anchor fluke or of a yard — see ANCHOR illustration **5 :** the prong of the metal hook of a pompier ladder **6 :** one of the blades of a pair of scissors **7 :** the visor of a cap

[2]**bill** \"\ *vb* -ED/-ING/-S [ME *bilen*, fr. *bile*, n.] *vi* **1** *obs* **:** PECK **2 :** to touch and rub bill to bill ⟨a pair of doves gently ~*ing*⟩ **3 :** to show affection through fondling and kissing ⟨lovers ~*ing* and cooing⟩ ~ *vt* **:** to catch or pick up with the bill ⟨swift birds ~*ing* insects on the wing⟩

[3]**bill** \"\ *n* -s [ME *bil*, fr. OE *bill*; akin to OHG *bill* pickax, ON *bildr* instrument for letting blood, Gk *phitros* log, OSlav *biti* to strike] **1 :** a weapon used up to the 17th century mainly by infantry and up to the 18th by civic guards that consisted of a long staff terminating in a hook-shaped blade usu. with pikes at the back and top — compare HALBERD **2 :** BILLHOOK

head of a bill

[4]**bill** \"\ *n* -s [ME *bille*, fr. ML *billa*, alter. of *bulla* document, seal, fr. L *bulla* bubble, boss, stud, amulet — more at POLL (head)] **1 :** a written or printed statement: as **a :** a written document **b :** MEMORANDUM **c :** LETTER **2** *obs* **:** a formal and usu. written petition **:** SUPPLICATION **3 :** a draft of a law presented to a legislature for enactment **:** a proposed or projected law ⟨a new ~ was set before Congress⟩ — compare [1]ACT 3, [1]STATUTE **4 :** a declaration in writing stating some wrong a complainant has suffered from a defendant or stating a breach of law by some person — used chiefly in various phrases (as *bill of complaint*) **5 a :** a written list **:** a paper carrying a statement of particulars ⟨a ~ of quantities containing specifications of building materials⟩ **b** *obs* **:** a list of drugs **:** medical prescription **c :** a list of men and their duties esp. as part of a ship's crew **:** a chart or organization sheet listing functions or assignments ⟨watch quarter and station ~⟩ **d :** a list of a complete correctly proportioned assortment of printer's type of one size and style; *also* **:** the assortment itself **:** FONT ⟨a ~ of pica⟩ **6 a :** an itemized account that states the separate costs of goods sold, services rendered, or work done **:** INVOICE ⟨the ~ accompanying a large consignment of furniture⟩ **b :** a statement in gross of a creditor's claim **:** statement of account **:** total amount indicated as due **:** total charge ⟨last month we had a huge grocery ~⟩ **c :** a statement of charges for food or drink consumed (as in a restaurant) **:** CHECK ⟨ask the waiter to bring the ~⟩ **7** *obs* **:** LABEL **8 a :** a written or printed advertisement that is posted or otherwise distributed to announce an event (as an exhibition or an auction) of interest to the public **:** PLACARD, POSTER, HANDBILL; *esp* **:** a written or printed announcement of a theatrical entertainment **:** PLAYBILL ⟨~*s* about the new play were in nearly every store window⟩ **b :** a programmed presentation (as a motion picture, play, lecture, concert) **:** the entertainment or other event of interest presented on a given program ⟨the newly built theater was offering a wonderful ~ that evening⟩ **9 a :** a piece of paper money ⟨a 10-dollar ~⟩ **b :** an individual or commercial note ⟨~*s* receivable⟩ ⟨a discounted ~⟩

[5]**bill** \"\ *vt* -ED/-ING/-S [ME *billen*, fr. *bille*, n.] **1 a :** to enter in a book of accounts **:** prepare a bill of (charges to customers or clients) ⟨~*ing* each month's purchases⟩ **b :** to submit a bill of charges to ⟨the company ~*s* its customers every other month⟩ **c :** to enter (as passengers or freight) in a waybill **:** consign to a destination **:** BOOK **d :** to issue a bill of lading to or for **2 a :** to advertise esp. by posters or placards ⟨the circus was ~*ed* well in advance of its arrival in town⟩ **b :** to present or arrange for the presentation of (an event or attraction of interest to the public, as a motion picture, lecture, or concert) ⟨the theater is ~*ing* the play for three weeks⟩ **c :** to present or arrange for the presentation of (as an entertainer or group of entertainers) **:** bring before the public **:** offer on a program ⟨an astute producer who ~*ed* the country's leading actress in the new play⟩ ⟨was ~*ed* as a brilliant dance team⟩; *esp* **:** to allot a specific part (as a role in a play) to **:** CAST ⟨for three consecutive seasons he was ~*ed* in leading roles⟩

[6]**bill** \"\ *n* -s [by alter.] *Scot* **:** [1]BULL 1

[7]**bill** \"\ *n* -s [alter. of *bell*] **:** the cry of the bittern ⟨the bittern's hollow ~ was heard —William Wordsworth⟩

bil·la·bong \'bilə,bȯŋ, -äŋ\ *n* -s [native name in Australia] *Austral* **1 a :** a blind channel leading out from a river **b :** a stream bed usu. dry but filled seasonally **2 :** a backwater caused by overflow from a river and forming a stagnant pool

billback \'=,=\ *n* [[4]*bill* + *back*] **:** a charge to members of a marketing group when the commodity sells for less than the sum advanced to members

billbeetle \'=,==\ *n* [[1]*bill* + *beetle*] **:** BILLBUG

billbergia \bil'bərjēə\ *n* [NL, fr. J.G.*Billberg* †1844 Swedish botanist + NL *-ia*] **1** *cap* **:** a genus of tropical American epiphytes (family Bromeliaceae) with stiff spiny-edged leaves and showy flowers **2** -s **:** a plant of the genus *Billbergia*

[1]**billboard** \'=,=\ *n* [[1]*bill* (point of an anchor fluke) + *board*] **:** a projection or ledge fixed on the bow of a vessel for the anchor to rest on

[2]**billboard** \"\ *n* [[4]*bill* + *board*] **1 :** a flat surface (as of a panel, wall, or fence) on which notices are posted; *specif* **:** a large panel designed to carry outdoor advertising and mounted on a building or framework near a road **2 :** an announcement at the beginning of a television or radio program that lists starring performers or other features

bill broker *n* [4*bill* + *broker*] *chiefly Brit* **:** one who negotiates the discount of bills of exchange either as agent or usu. by buying and selling them or buying them and carrying them with money borrowed upon them as security — compare NOTE BROKER — **bill·brok·ing** \'bil,brōkiŋ, -ēŋ\ *n* -s

billbug \'ˌ=ˌ=\ *n* [1*bill* + *bug*] **:** any of numerous weevils (as members of the genus *Calendra*) having larvae that are destructive to the roots of grasses and cereal crops

billed \'bild\ *adj* [ME *biled*, fr. *bile* + *-ed*] **:** having a bill ⟨a thick-*billed* bird⟩ ⟨a long-*billed* cap⟩

bill·er \'bilə(r)\ *n* -s [5*bill* + *-er*] **:** one that bills: as **a :** a clerk who makes out bills; *esp* **:** a billing-machine operator **b :** BILLING MACHINE **c :** a worker in a planing mill who having calculated from blueprints or shop drawings designates on shop orders the wood to be used in making such units as sashes and doors

1**bil·let** \'bilət, *usu* -d·+V\ *n* -s [ME *bylet*, fr. MF *billette*, *bullette*, dim. of *bulle* document, fr. ML *bulla* — more at BILL] **1** *archaic* **:** a brief usu. informal letter **:** NOTE **2 a :** an official order directing that a member of a military force be provided with board and lodging (as in a private home) ⟨the townspeople received ~s ordering them to lodge the regiment overnight⟩ **b :** quarters assigned (as by a billet) **:** a lodging place ⟨the old mansion served as the soldiers' ~ for nearly a week⟩ **3 a :** POSITION, JOB, POST, APPOINTMENT ⟨he landed a lucrative ~ with a New York publishing house⟩ **b :** a place allotted **:** DESTINATION ⟨every bullet has its ~⟩

2**billet** \"\ *vb* -ED/-ING/-s *vt* **1** *obs* **:** to enter in a list **2 :** to assign quarters to (as soldiers) by a note or other directive **:** assign a place to **:** LOCATE ⟨the troops were ~*ed* with the friendly inhabitants of the village⟩ ⟨~*ing* visitors in private homes —Harry Gordon⟩ **3 :** to serve with a billet requiring lodgings ⟨the farmer had already been ~*ed* when a fresh group of soldiers arrived⟩ ~ *vi* **:** to have quarters **:** LODGE ⟨for a time they ~*ed* in a ramshackle house⟩

3**billet** \"\ *n* -s [ME *bylet*, fr. MF *billete*, dim. of *bille* log, of Celt origin; akin to OIr *bile* sacred tree; prob. akin to L *florēre* to bloom — more at BLOW] **1 a :** a chunky piece of wood (as one for firewood) **:** a short round log **:** a section obtained by halving, quartering, or otherwise splitting or sawing logs lengthwise **b** *obs* **:** a thick usu. knobbed stick **:** CUDGEL **2 a :** a strap that enters a buckle (as the ends of harness reins or of the cheek pieces that buckle on the bit) **b :** a loop that receives the end of a buckled strap **3 :** a heraldic bearing in the form of an upright rectangle **4 a :** a bar of metal (as of gold or iron) **b :** a piece of semifinished iron or steel nearly square in section made by rolling an ingot or bloom until it has been reduced in size to 1½ to 6 in. square **c :** a section of nonferrous metal ingot hot-worked by forging, rolling, or extrusion **d :** a nonferrous metal casting suitable for rolling or extrusion **5 :** an ornament in Norman moldings that resembles a billet of wood of rounded or sometimes polygonal cross section

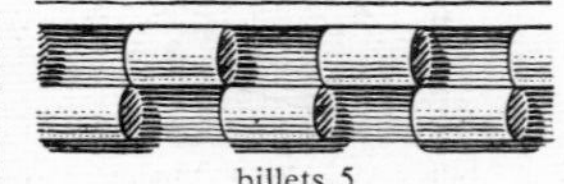
billets 5

4**billet** \"\ *n* -s [prob. alter. of earlier *billard* coalfish] *chiefly Brit* **:** a young pollack or coalfish

bil·let-doux \'bilā'dü, -lē-, *F* bēyādü\ *n, pl* **billets-doux** \-'düz, *F* bēyādü\ [F *billet doux*, lit., sweet letter] **:** a love letter

billethead \'ˌ=ˌ=\ *n* [3*billet* + *head*] **1 :** a round piece of timber at the bow or stern of a whaleboat around which a harpoon line may be run out **2 :** a scroll or ornamental carving used in place of a figurehead on a ship

billet rolls *n pl* [3*billet*] **:** ROUGHING ROLLS

billets *pl of* BILLET, *pres 3d sing of* BILLET

billetwood \'ˌ=ˌ=\ *n* [3*billet* + *wood*] **:** a tropical African timber tree (*Diospyros dendo*) with wood similar to ebony

bil·lety *also* **bil·let·ty** \'biləd-ē, -ətē, -i\ *or* **bil·let·té** \ˌbilə'tā, *F* bēyətā\ *adj* [F *billeté*, fr. *billette* billet — more at BILLET (log)] **:** charged or studded with heraldic billets

billfish \'ˌ=ˌ=\ *n* [1*bill* + *fish*] **:** any of numerous fishes having long slender jaws like a bird's bill (as the saury, the marine and freshwater gars, the spearfish, the sailfish)

billfold \'ˌ=ˌ=\ *n* -s [short for earlier *billfolder*] **1 :** a folding pocketbook for paper money about the size of bills that will fit into it without previous folding and usu. carried in a pocket or larger pocketbook **2 :** WALLET 2b

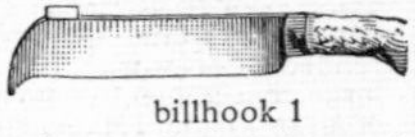
billfold

billhead \'ˌ=ˌ=\ *n* [4*bill* + *head*] **:** a printed form commonly headed with the seller's name and address on which accounts of money owed are rendered

billholder \'ˌ=ˌ==\ *n* [4*bill* + *holder*] **1 :** one that holds a bill or acceptance **2 :** a device by means of which bills are held

billhook \'ˌ=ˌ=\ *n* [3*bill* + *hook*] **1 :** a cutting tool consisting of a blade with a hooked point fitted with a handle and used in pruning and similar work **2 :** KNOTTING BILL

billhook 1

bil·li·an \'bilēən, -lyən\ *n* -s [Malay (*pokok*) *bĕlian*, lit., sorcerer's tree, fr. *pokok* tree + *bĕlian* sorcerer] **:** a valuable timber tree (*Eusideroxylon zwageri*) of the family Lauraceae of Borneo having heavy hard antproof wood

bil·liard \'bilyə(r)d\ *n* -s [back-formation fr. *billiards*] **1 :** CAROM 1 **2 :** a tobacco pipe with slightly rounded sides

billiard ball *n* [*billiards*] **:** one of the balls used in playing billiards

billiard cloth *n* **:** the smooth green woolen cloth thoroughly shrunk and felted that is used to cover billiard and pool tables

billiard green *n* **:** a deep yellowish green

bil·liard·ist \-dəst\ *n* -s **:** one who plays billiards esp. professionally

billiard room *or* **billiard hall** *or* **billiard parlor** *or* **billiard saloon** *n* **:** a room in which billiards is played **:** POOLROOM

bil·liards \'bilyə(r)dz\ *n pl but usu sing in constr* [MF *billard* curved stick used in certain games, billiard cue, billiards, fr. *bille* log — more at BILLET] **:** any of several games played on an oblong table in which small balls are driven against one another or into pockets by means of a cue; *specif* **:** a game in which one scores by causing a cue ball to hit in succession two object balls — see CAROM BILLIARDS, POOL 2b

billiard table *n* **:** a table having a slate bed covered with billiard cloth and surrounded by cushioned rails on which billiards is played; *also* **:** any similar table provided with six pockets for the playing of pool or English billiards

bil·lie *also* **bil·ly** \'bilē\ *n, pl* **billies** [prob. fr. the name *Billie, Billy*] **1** *chiefly Scot* **:** COMRADE, COMPANION ⟨my old school ~⟩ **2** *chiefly Scot* **:** BROTHER **3** *chiefly Scot* **:** LAD, FELLOW, BOY ⟨when chapman *billies* leave the street —Robert Burns⟩

billies *pl of* BILLIE *or of* BILLY

bil·lie·tite \'bil(ē)ə,tīt, bə'lē,t-\ *n* -s [F, fr. Valère Louis *Billiet* †1945 Belg. mineralogist] **:** a mineral consisting of a hydrous barium uranium oxide closely related to becquerelite

bil·li·ken \'biləkən\ *n* -s *often cap* [prob. fr. the name *Billy* + *-ken* (alter. of *-kin*)] **:** a squat smiling comic figure used as a mascot

bill in aid of an execution : a creditor's bill filed to reach assets subject to execution but fraudulently transferred

bill in equity : the process instituting an action or proceeding in a suit in equity setting forth the plaintiff's cause of action

bill·ing \'biliŋ, -ēŋ\ *n* -s [fr. gerund of 5*bill*] **1 :** the making out or forwarding of customer invoices and bills ⟨a battery of clerks to take care of the firm's monthly ~⟩ **2 a :** advertising (as by posters or placards) ⟨a widely publicized product that lived up to its advance ~⟩ **b :** presentation (as of an actor or play) to the public ⟨he spent much time arranging for the ~ of the controversial production⟩ **3 :** total amount of business or investments (as of an advertising agency) within a given period ⟨~s of leading agencies for a one-year period hit a record high⟩ **4 :** the relative prominence given a name (as of an actor) in publicizing, advertising, or other promotional programs ⟨the marquee of every theater gave him top ~⟩

billing machine *n* **:** a machine designed specif. for some or all of the mechanical operations (as typing, adding or computations, and sometimes duplicating) usu. involved in filling out and providing a record of customer invoices or bills

bil·lings·gate \'biliŋz,gāt, -ˌgit\ *n* -s *sometimes cap* [fr. *Billingsgate*, old gate and fish market, London, England, noted for the abusive language used there] **:** condemnatory language marked by the coarse or offensive and scornfully abusive or contentious ⟨the ~ common to the lower political quarreling —H.R.Warfel⟩ ⟨a kind of ~ Falstaff at his worst never approached —Edith Hamilton⟩ **syn** see ABUSE

bil·lion \'bilyən\ *n* -s *often attrib* [F, fr. *bi-* 1bi- + *-illion* (as in *million*) — more at MILLION] **1** — see NUMBER table **2 :** a very large number

bil·lion·aire \ˌbilyə'na(a)(ə)r, -ne(ə)r, -na(a)ə,-neə, 'ˌ=ˌ=\ *n* -s [*billion* + *-aire* (as in *millionaire*)] **:** one whose wealth is about a billion dollars, pounds, or other monetary units

bil·lion-dol·lar grass \'ˌ=ˌ=ˌ=-\ *n* **:** JAPANESE MILLET

1**bil·lionth** \'bilyən(t)th\ *adj* [*billion* + *-th*] **1 :** being number one billion in a countable series — see NUMBER table **2 :** being one of a billion equal parts into which anything is divisible

2**billionth** \"\ *n, pl* **billionths** \-yən(t)s,-yən(t)ths\ **1 :** number one billion in a countable series **2 :** the quotient of a unit divided by one billion **:** one of a billion equal parts of anything

1**bill·man** \'bilmən\ *n, pl* **billmen** [3*bill* + *man*] **:** one using or armed with a bill — see 3BILL

2**billman** \"\ *n, pl* **billmen** [4*bill* + *man*] **:** one that posts advertising bills **:** BILLPOSTER

bill of attainder : a bill or statute attainting a person

bill of complaint : COMPLAINT 1c

bill of costs : COST 4b

bill of credit 1 : LETTER OF CREDIT **2 :** a bill issued by a state (as in the American colonial period) involving the faith and credit of the state and designed to circulate as money on the credit of the state

bill of divorce *or* **bill of divorcement** *Jewish law* **:** a written document prepared according to prescribed form and given by the husband to his wife by which the marriage relation is dissolved — called also *get*

bill of entry : a written account of goods entered at the customhouse whether imported or intended for exportation

bill of exceptions : a statement of exceptions to the rulings or decision of a judge in the trial of a cause made for the purpose of a writ of error or an appeal to a superior court

bill of exchange : an unconditional written order addressed by one person to another and signed by the person giving it that requires the person to whom it is addressed to pay on demand or at a fixed or determinable future time a certain sum of money to or to the order of a specified person or to bearer, the drawee not being liable on it until he has accepted it — usu. used of foreign transactions; see ACCEPTANCE 4; compare DRAFT 14a(1); ACCEPTOR, DRAWER, PAYEE; NEGOTIABLE

bill of fare 1 : a printed or written list of the dishes that may be ordered (as in a restaurant) or of specially prepared dishes that are to be served (as at a banquet) **:** MENU **2 :** a listing of something offered to customers, clientele, or audience ⟨two sonatas on the musical *bill of fare*⟩

bill of goods : a consignment of merchandise

bill of health : a duly authenticated certificate of the state of health of a ship's company and of a port with regard to infectious diseases, the bill being given to the ship's master at the time of leaving the port; *broadly* **:** a usu. satisfactory report about a condition or situation ⟨getting a clean *bill of health* in the loyalty investigation⟩

bill of indictment : an indictment before it is found or ignored by the grand jury

bill of interpleader : INTERPLEADER

bill of lading 1 : a written account of goods shipped by any person signed by the agent of the owner of the ship or by its master and acknowledging the receipt of the goods and promising to deliver them safe at the place directed, dangers of the sea excepted **2 :** a written document issued by a common carrier acknowledging the receipt of the goods and setting forth the terms of the contract of carriage

bill of mortality : a periodical official statement of the number of deaths (later also of births) within a given time formerly issued in districts of London and vicinity

bill of pains and penalties : a legislative act imposing upon those who have previously committed a certain designated act or acts punishment or disability by which the act was not punishable at the time of its commission — compare EX POST FACTO LAW

bill of parcels : an account given by the seller to the buyer of the several articles purchased with their prices

bill of particulars : a detailed statement of the items of a plaintiff's demand in an action or of the defendant's setoff or counterclaim

bill of peace : a bill in equity to secure relief from repeated vexatious litigation

bill of rights *often cap B&R* **:** a summary of certain fundamental rights and privileges guaranteed to a people against violation by the state — used esp. of the first 10 amendments to the U.S. Constitution

bill of sale : a formal instrument for the conveyance or transfer of title to goods and chattels

bill of sight : a form of entry at the customhouse by which goods respecting which the importer is not possessed of full information may be provisionally landed for examination

bill of store 1 : a license formerly granted at the customhouse to merchants to carry stores and provisions necessary for a voyage custom free **2 :** a license permitting the reimportation of exported dutiable goods

bill of sufferance : a license to load and discharge cargo at specified ports without paying duty

bil·lon \'bilən\ *n* -s [F, fr. MF, fr. *bille* log — more at BILLET] **1 :** an alloy of silver with more than its weight of copper, tin, or other metal **2 :** gold or silver alloyed with a considerable amount of some less valuable metal

1**bil·low** \'bi(,)lō, -lə, *often* -ləw+V\ *n* -s [prob. fr. ON *bylgja*; akin to MHG *bulge* billow, MLG *bülge*, ON *belgr* bag — more at BELLY] **1 a :** a large swelling wave of water esp. in the open sea ⟨the ~s rose and fell, flashing in the sunlight⟩ **b :** a marked undulation of water ⟨the small boat cut swiftly through the lake's quiet ~s⟩ **2 :** a rolling or swirling surge ⟨~s of flame swept through the forest⟩ **:** an undulating or swelling mass ⟨~s of marching regiments wound through the valley⟩

2**billow** \"\ *vb* -ED/-ING/-s *vi* **1 :** to rise or roll in waves or surges **:** SURGE, UNDULATE ⟨the restless ~*ing* sea⟩ ⟨the smoke from the houses thickened and spread, bellied out, ~*ed* up —Kenneth Roberts⟩ **2 :** to bulge or swell out in billows (as through the action of the wind) ⟨~*ing* clouds⟩ ⟨the flags in front of the Supreme Court building ~*ed* out in pride —G.B. Oxnam⟩ ⟨the girl flashed on, her pretty skirt ~*ing* —Irwin Shaw⟩ ~ *vt* **:** to cause to billow ⟨a high wind was blowing from the west, ~*ing* the sleeves and skirts of women's dresses —Ellen Glasgow⟩ ⟨a field of burning grass ~*ing* thick black clouds of smoke into the sky —Donald Windham⟩

billow cloud *n* **:** a long narrow cloud or usu. a series of such clouds roughly parallel to each other caused by the flow of one layer of air over another producing waves at their interface the relatively cold crests of which are cloud-capped and their relatively warm troughs clear when the humidity is just right

bil·low·i·ness \'biləwēnəs, -win-\ *n* -ES **:** the quality or state of being billowy

bil·lowy \'biləwē, -wi\ *adj, sometimes* -ER/-EST **1 :** characterized by billows ⟨the ~ sea⟩ **2 :** suggestive of billows ⟨the ~ prairie⟩

billposter \'ˌ=ˌ==\ *n* [4*bill* + *poster*] **1 :** one that posts advertising bills **2 :** an advertising bill **:** POSTER

billposting \'ˌ=ˌ==\ *n* [4*bill* + *posting* (gerund of *post*)] **:** the action or occupation of posting advertising bills

bill quia timet \-ˌ'kwēə'tē(,)met, -kwīə'tī-\ *n* [L *quia timet* because he fears] **:** a bill by which a petitioner asks aid to prevent a wrong that he fears he may suffer from an act or an omission of another

bill rate *n* [4*bill*] **:** the rate of return on bills: **a :** the interest rate at which treasury bills are allotted in the weekly auction **b :** the rates at which outstanding bill issues are traded in the bill market

bills *pres 3d sing of* BILL, *pl of* BILL

billsticker \'ˌ=ˌ==\ *n* [4*bill* + *sticker*] **:** BILLPOSTER 1

billsticking \'ˌ=ˌ==\ *n* [4*bill* + *sticking*] **:** BILLPOSTING

1**billy** *var of* BILLIE

2**bil·ly** \'bilē, -li\ *n, pl* **billies** *also* **billys** \-(ˌ)lēz, -liz\ [prob. fr. the name *Billy*] **1 :** a slubbing frame **2 :** a heavy usu. wooden weapon for delivering blows **:** CLUB; *esp* **:** a policeman's club **3** [by shortening] **:** BILLY GOAT

3**billy** \"\ *n* -ES [prob. back-formation fr. *billycan*] *chiefly Austral* **:** a cylindrical container usu. made of metal or enamelware, having a set-in lid and a wire bail and often used for outdoor cooking or for carrying food or liquid ⟨tea fresh from the ~⟩

billyboy \'ˌ=ˌ=\ *n* [prob. fr. the name *Billy* + *boy*] *Brit* **:** a flat-bottomed bluff-bowed river or coasting boat usu. rigged as a ketch or sloop and carrying leeboards

billycan \'ˌ=ˌ=\ *n* [by folk etymology fr. *billa* water (a native name in Australia) + E *can*] **:** 3BILLY

billy club *n* [2*billy*] **:** 2BILLY 2

billycock \'ˌ=,käk\ *also* **billycock hat** *n* [origin unknown] *Brit* **:** DERBY 2a

billy gar *n* [1*bill* + *-y*] **:** LONG-NOSED GAR

billy gate *n* [2*billy*] **:** the moving carriage in a slubbing machine

billy goat *n* [fr. the name *Billy*] **:** a male goat

billy-goat weed \'ˌ=ˌ=-\ *n* **:** a tropical American annual low herb (*Ageratum conyzoides*) widely cultivated as a border and bedding plant for its bluish or white flowers

billy owl *n, often cap B* [prob. fr. the name *Billy*] **:** BURROWING OWL

billy webb \-ˌ'web\ *n, usu cap B&W* [origin unknown] **:** a tropical American timber tree (*Sweetia panamensis*) of the family Leguminosae having brown hard wood

bil·ly·wix \'ˌ=ˌ,wiks\ *n* -ES [origin unknown] *dial Eng* **:** TAWNY OWL

bi·lo \'bē(,)lō\ *n* -s [Serbo-Croatian] **:** an area of wide and roughly parallel ridges in the Karst topography of the Dinaric region of the Balkan peninsula

bi·lobate *also* **bi·lobated** \(')bī+\ *adj* [1*bi-* + *lobate*] **:** divided into two lobes

bi·lobed \'bī+\ *adj* [*bi-* + *lobe* + *-ed*] **:** BILOBATE

bi·lobular \(')bī+\ *adj* [1*bi-* + *lobular*] **:** having or divided into two lobules

bi·location \ˌbī+\ *n* [1*bi-* + *location*] **:** the state or power of being in two places at the same time

bi·loc·u·lar \(')bī¦läkyələ(r)\ *adj* [1*bi-* + NL *loculus* + E *-ar*] **:** divided into two cells or compartments

bi·loc·u·late \(')bī¦läkyələt, -ˌlāt\ *adj* [1*bi-* + *loculate*] **:** BILOCULAR

bi·loc·u·li·na \bī¦läkyə'līnə\ *n, cap* [NL, fr. 1*bi-* + *loculus* + *-ina*] **:** a genus of calcareous imperforate foraminiferans extraordinarily abundant in the North sea where their remains form much of the ooze covering the bottom

bi·loc·u·line \(')bī¦läkyə,līn, -lən\ *adj* [1*bi-* + NL *loculus* + E *-ine*] **1 :** having two chambers **2** [NL *Biloculina*] **:** relating to the genus *Biloculina*

bi·loph·o·dont \(')bī¦läfə,dänt, -lōf-\ *adj* [1*bi-* + *lophodont*] *zool* **:** having two transverse ridges or crests ⟨the molar teeth of the tapirs are ~⟩ — **bi·loph·o·dont·ism** \(')=¦=ˌ=¦dän,tizəm\ *n* -s

bilos *pl of* BILO

bi·loxi \bə'läksē\ *n, pl* **biloxi** *or* **biloxis** *usu cap* **1 a :** a Siouan people in the lower Pascagoula river valley, Mississippi **b :** a member of the Biloxi people **2 :** the language of the Biloxi people

bil·sted \'bil,sted\ *n* -s [origin unknown] **:** SWEET GUM

bil·ston \'bilstən\ *n* -s *usu cap* [fr. *Bilston*, urban district, Staffordshire, England] **:** a type of English enameled ware often characterized by rich ground colors and gilding

bilt·more ash \'bilt,mō(ə)r-, -ō(ə)r-,-ōə-,-ō(ə)-\ *n, usu cap B* [from the *Biltmore* estate, Asheville, N.C.] **:** a medium-sized tree (*Fraxinus biltmoreana*) of the southeastern U.S. resembling and closely related to the white ash

biltmore stick *n, usu cap B* **:** a graduated rule used by timber estimators in determining tree diameters

bil·tong \'bil,tȯŋ, -äŋ\ *n* -s [Afrik, fr. *bil* buttock (fr. MD *bille*) + *tong* tongue, fr. MD *tonghe*; fr. its source & its tongue-like appearance; akin to OHG *arspelli* buttock, G dial. *bille* penis, OE *bealloc* testicle, and to OHG *zunga* tongue — more at BULL TONGUE] *Africa* **:** jerked meat; *esp* **:** jerked beef, venison, or ostrich

bim *n* -s [origin unknown] *slang* **:** WOMAN; *esp* **:** a woman of loose morals

BIM *abbr* best in match

bi·maculate *also* **bi·maculated** \(')bī+\ *adj* [1*bi-* + *maculate*] **:** marked with two maculae

bi·mah *also* **bi·ma** \'bēmə\ *n* -s [Yiddish *bime*, fr. Russ *bima* bema, fr. LGk *bēma* — more at BEMA] **:** ALMEMAR

bima·na \'bimənə, bī'mānə\ *also* **bima·nes** \-,nēz\ *or* **bima·nus** \-,nəs\ *n pl* [NL, fr. F *bimane* two-handed, fr. *bi-* 1bi- + *-mane* (fr. L *manus* hand) — more at MANUAL] *zool* **:** man considered as sole representative of a group distinguished by having hands unlike the feet — compare QUADRUMANA — **bi·mane** \'bī,mān\ *adj or n*

bima·nal \'bimən°l, (')bī¦mān-\ *or* **bima·nous** \-nəs\ *adj* [F *bimane* + E *-al* or *-ous*] **:** having two hands **:** TWO-HANDED

bi·manual \(')bī+\ *adj* [1*bi-* + *manual*] **:** done with two hands **:** requiring the use of both hands ⟨a machine designed for ~ operation⟩ — **bi·manually** \(')bī+\ *adv*

bi·mas·tic \(')bī¦mastik\ *adj* [1*bi-* + *mast-* + *-ic*] **:** having two mammae — **bi·mas·tism** \bī'ma,stizəm\ *n* -s — **bi·mas·ty** \'bī,mastē\ *n* -ES

bi·mastoid \(')bī+\ *adj* [1*bi-* + *mastoid*] **:** of, relating to, or joining the two mastoid processes

bi·maxillary \(')bī, ¦bī+\ *adj* [1*bi-* + *maxillary*] **1 :** of or relating to the two halves of the maxilla **2** *anthrop* **:** of or relating to the distance between the lower margins of the sutures of the maxilla and malar bones

bim·bo \'bim(,)bō\ *n, pl* **bimbos** *or* **bimboes** [origin unknown] **1** *slang* **:** MAN, FELLOW — often a generalized expression of disparagement ⟨a couple of ~s slouching down the street⟩ **2** *slang* **:** WOMAN; *esp* **:** a woman of loose morals

bime·by \(')bīm¦bī, ¦bīm¦bī, ˌbəm'bī\ *adv* [by alter.] *chiefly dial* **:** by and by

bime·ler·ite \'bīmlə,rīt\ *n* -s *usu cap* [Joseph M. *Bimeler* (Bäumler) †1853 German-American founder of Separatist Society of Zoar, Ohio + E *-ite*] **:** ZOARITE

bi·mes·ter \(')bī¦mestə(r)\ *n* -s [1*bi-* + *-mester* (as in semester)] **:** a period of two months

bi·mes·tri·al \-trēəl\ *adj* [L *bimestris* (fr. *bi-* 1bi- + *-mestris*, fr. *mensis* month) + E *-al* — more at MOON] **:** continuing two months **:** BIMONTHLY

1**bi·metal** \(')bī+\ *adj* [by shortening] **:** BIMETALLIC

2**bimetal** \"\ *n* -s **:** a bimetallic material or device

1**bi·metallic** \ˌbī+\ *adj* [F *bimétallique*, fr. *bi-* 1bi- + *métallique* metallic — more at METALLIC] **1 :** relating to, based on, or using bimetallism **2** [1*bi-* + *metallic*] **:** composed of two different metals: as **a :** formed of two different metals or alloys (as in sheets, layers, or strips) bonded together (as by fusing, welding, plating, or riveting) — often used of devices in which a change in temperature causes bending of a part composed of two metals that expand differently **b** *of offset printing plates* **:** surfaced with two metals, one grease-repellent and one grease-receptive — compare LITHOGRAPHY

2**bimetallic** \"\ *n* -s **:** BIMETAL

bi·met·al·lism \(')bī¦med-°l,izəm, -et°l-\ *n* -s [F *bimétallisme*, fr. *bi-* 1bi- + *métal* metal + *-isme* -ism — more at METAL] **:** the policy or practice of using two metals (as gold and silver) jointly as a monetary standard by specifying that both constitute legal tender at a predetermined ratio

bi·met·al·list \-°ləst\ *n* -s [prob. fr. F *bimétalliste*, fr. *bi-* 1bi- + *métal* + *-iste* -ist] **:** an advocate of bimetallism — **bi·met·al·lis·tic** \(ˌ)=¦=°l¦istik\ *adj*

1**bi·millenary** \(')bī, ¦bī+\ *or* **bi·millenial** \ˌbī+\ *n, pl* **bimillenaries** *or* **bimillenials** [1*bi-* + *millenary* or *millenial*] **1 :** a period of 2000 years **2 :** a 2000th anniversary or its celebration

2**bimillenary** \"\ *adj* **:** of or relating to a bimillenary

bi·millennium \ˌbī+\ *n, pl* **bimillenniums** *also* **bimillennia** [NL, fr. *bi-* + *millennium*] **:** BIMILLENARY

bim·li·pa·tam hemp \ˌbimlē'päˌtam-, -ˌtām-\ *or* **bim·li hemp** \'bimlē-\ *or* **bimlipatam jute** *or* **bimli jute** *n, usu cap B* [fr.

Bimlipatam, Bimlipatnam, city in northeastern Madras, India] : KENAF

bim·me·ler \'bim(ə)lə(r)\ *n* -s *usu cap* [after J.M. *Bimeler* — more at BIMELERITE] : ZOARITE

bi·modal \(')bī+\ *adj* [¹*bi-* + *modal*] : possessing two statistical modes — **bi·modality** \ˌbī+\ *n* -ES

bi·molecular \ˌbī+\ *adj* [ISV ¹*bi-* + *molecular*] : relating to or formed from two molecules ⟨~ reaction⟩ : being two molecules thick ⟨~ layers⟩ — **bi·mo·lec·u·lar·ly** *adv*

¹**bi·monthly** \(')bī+\ *adj* [¹*bi-* + *monthly*] : occurring, appearing, or done every two months; *sometimes* : occurring, appearing, or done twice a month ⟨a ~ magazine⟩ — compare SEMIMONTHLY

²**bimonthly** \"\ *n* -ES : a bimonthly publication

³**bimonthly** \"\ *adv* : once every two months; *sometimes* : twice a month

bi·morph \'bī,mȯrf\ *n* -s [¹*bi-* + *-morph*] : a device consisting of two layers of a crystal (as Rochelle salt) cemented together and often used in a phonograph pickup because of the ability to convert the vibration of the needle into electrical voltage

bi·morphemic \ˌbī+,-\ *adj* [¹*bi-* + *morphemic*] : consisting of two morphemes (sense 2) ⟨the ~ word *tied*⟩ : involving two morphemes

bi·motored \(')bī+\ *adj* [¹*bi-* + *motored*] : equipped with two separate motors — used esp. of airplanes

bims *pl of* BIM

bi·muscular \(')bī+\ *adj* [¹*bi-* + *muscular*] : having two adductor muscles ⟨most bivalves are ~⟩

¹**bin** \'bin\ *n* -s [ME *binne,* fr. OE *binn, binne* manger, basket, prob. of Celt origin; akin to Gaulish *benna* two-wheeled cart with a wicker body; akin to Gk *phatnē* manger, OE *bindan* to bind — more at BIND] : a box, frame, crib, or enclosed place used for storage ⟨coal ~⟩ ⟨apple ~⟩ ⟨grain ~⟩

²**bin** \"\ *vt* **binned; binned; binning; bins** : to put into a bin; *esp* : to stow and age (bottled wine) in a bin

³**bin** \'bēn\ *n* -s [Hindi *bīn,* fr. Skt *vīṇā*] : VINA

⁴**bin** \"\ *n* -s [modif. (influenced by ³*bin*) of Hindi *ben,* fr. Skt *veṇu* bamboo, flute] : PUNGI

bin- *comb form* [ME, fr. LL, fr. L *bini* two by two; akin to OE *twin* twine — more at TWINE] **1** : two : two by two : two at a time ⟨*binary*⟩ ⟨*binate*⟩ ⟨*binaural*⟩ **2** *chem* : BI- 4 ⟨*binoxalate*⟩ ⟨*binoxide*⟩ — in some words of which the last constituent begins with a vowel; compare BI-

bina *var of* VINA

¹**bi·na·ry** \'bīnərē, -ri *sometimes* -,ner-\ *adj* [LL *binarius,* fr. L *bini* two by two + *-arius* -ary] **1** : compounded or consisting of two things or parts : characterized by two : DUAL, DOUBLE **2** : composed of two chemical elements, of an element and a radical that acts as an element, or of two such radicals ⟨a ~ compound⟩ ⟨~ salts⟩ **3 a** : of, relating to, or being a system of numbers having two as its base **b** : involving two variables ⟨a ~ form⟩ **4** *logic* : relating two arguments or terms (of functions and propositions) ⟨a ~ relation⟩ **5 a** : having two musical subjects or two divisions or sections one complementary to the other ⟨a song in ~ form⟩ **b** : DUPLE — used of measure or rhythm

²**binary** \"\ *n* -ES [ME *binarie,* fr. ML *binarius,* fr. LL, consisting of two] : something that is constituted of two figures, things, or parts; *specif* : BINARY STAR

binary color *n* : a color made by mixing two primary colors : SECONDARY COLOR

binary combination *or* **binary name** *n* : ³BINOMIAL

binary digit *n* **1** : either of the two digits, conventionally 0 and 1, used in a binary system of numeration **2** : ⁷BIT 1

binary fission *n* : reproduction of a cell by division into two approximately equal parts ⟨the *binary fission* of protozoans⟩

binary granite *n* : a granite composed only of quartz and feldspar or one containing two kinds of mica

binary nomenclature *n* : a system of nomenclature in which the designation of a species consists of two parts that may or may not be single names — compare BINOMIAL NOMENCLATURE

binary opposition *n, phonetics* : one of a number of pairs of diametrically opposed characteristics (as voicedness or voicelessness) taken as a basis for the classification of speech sounds

binary star *also* **binary system** *n* : a system of two stars that revolve around each other under their mutual gravitation and falling into one or more of three classes — compare ECLIPSING VARIABLE, SPECTROSCOPIC BINARY, VISUAL BINARY

binary system *n* : a system having two components

binary theory *n* : DUALISM 4

¹**bi·nate** \'bī,nāt, *usu* -ād.+V\ *adj* [*bin-* + *-ate*] *bot* : growing in pairs or couples : DOUBLE — **bi·nate·ly** *adv*

²**binate** \"\ *vi* -ED/-ING/-S [NL *binatus,* past part. of *binare,* prob. fr. L *bini* two by two — more at BIN-] : to celebrate two masses on the same day

bi·na·tion \bī'nāshən\ *n* -s [NL *bination-, binatio,* prob. fr. *binatus* + *-ion-, -io* -ion] : celebration of mass twice on the same day by the same priest

bi·national \(')bī+\ *adj* [¹*bi-* + *national*] : composed of, belonging to, or connected with two nations or nationalities

bin·aural \(')bī,n+,-\ *adj* [ISV *bin-* + *aural*] **1** *also* **bi·aural** \(')bī+\ : of or relating to two ears ⟨~ perception of sound⟩ : involving the use or function of both ears ⟨a ~ stethoscope⟩ **2** : of, relating to, or characterized by directional techniques and systems that utilize the actual placement of sound sources (as in sound transmission and recording) to achieve in sound reproduction an effect on the listener of hearing the sound sources in their original positions, so creating the illusion of added dimension and fuller fidelity ⟨~ broadcasting⟩ ⟨a ~ tape recorder⟩ — usu. limited to techniques and systems using two separate transmission or recording paths and sometimes limited in sound reproduction to the use of earphones; compare STEREOPHONIC — **binaurally** *adv*

bin·auricular \ˌbī,n, ˌbi,n+\ *adj* [*bin-* + *auricular*] : BIAURICULAR

bin-burn \'=,=\ *vi* [¹*bin*] *of cereal grains* : to become discolored and poor in quality through heat generated and moisture accumulated in bin storage

binche lace \'bansh-, -anch-\ *n, usu cap B* [fr. *Binche,* Belgium, where it was originally made] : a bobbin lace of Flemish origin having flat designs of floral scrolls on a coarse mesh ground with a scattered snowflake pattern

¹**bind** \'bīnd\ *vb* **bound** \'baund\ **bound** *or archaic* **bounded; binding; binds** \'bīn(d)z\ [ME *binden,* fr. OE *bindan*; akin to OHG *bintan* to bind, ON *binda,* Goth *bindan,* Gk *peisma* cable, Skt *badhnāti* he binds] *vt* **1 a** : to make secure by tying (as with a cord) ⟨they *bound* his hands⟩ **b** : to confine with or as if with chains or other bonds so as to deprive of liberty : make captive ⟨he was *bound* and thrown into prison⟩ ⟨she was not wholly *bound* in mind by her middle-class existence —Delmore Schwartz⟩ **c** : to hold in check : keep in place : RESTRAIN ⟨a sense of fair play ~s them and preserves their open-mindedness⟩ **d** : to hamper the free movement of : exert an uncomfortably restrictive and chafing force upon ⟨tight-fitting clothes that ~ the hiker⟩ **e** : to put under an obligation (as by making, accepting, or exacting a solemn promise) ⟨the knight *bound* himself with an oath to serve faithfully⟩ **f** : to constrain with legal authority : ⟨the court's decision ~s them to pay the fine⟩ **2 a** : to wrap around so as to cover (as with cloth) : SWATHE ⟨a broad sash *bound* her waist⟩ **b** : to wrap up (an injury) with a cloth : BANDAGE ⟨~*ing* up the gash with clean gauze⟩ **3** : to fasten round about : ENCIRCLE, GIRD, WREATHE ⟨a statue of a poet, laurel *bound* about the head⟩ **4** : to tie together (as stalks of wheat) ⟨~*ing* the reaped grain into sheaves⟩ **5 a** : to cause (particles) to stick together in a usu. hard mass ⟨wet sand that had been baked and *bound* by the sun⟩ **b** : to cause to cohere : unite into a cohesive whole ⟨~ the chopped celery and apples with mayonnaise⟩ : give a moist or thickened consistency to ⟨~ poultry dressing with beaten eggs⟩ **c** : to take up and hold usu. by chemical forces : combine with ⟨cellulose ~s water⟩ **6** : to make costive : CONSTIPATE **7** : to make firm or sure : SETTLE ⟨~*ing* our agreement with a friendly handshake⟩ **8** : to protect, strengthen, or decorate by a band or binding ⟨a carpet *bound* with a yellow edging⟩ **9 a** : to apply the parts of the cover to (a book) in successive stages (as in hand binding) **b** : CASE *vt* 1d **10** : INDENTURE, APPRENTICE ⟨he was *bound* out to the tailor for one year⟩ **11** : to cause to be attached (as by gratitude or affection) ⟨some gracious instinct ~s her to her home —Agnes Repplier⟩ **12** : to fasten together : CONNECT, UNITE ⟨a jeweled pin *bound* the ends of the scarf⟩ **13** : to move (a fencing opponent's blade) from one line to another by exerting pressure against **14** : to effect (an insurance policy) by means of an oral commitment or by a binder **15** *logic* : to convert (a free variable in a statement or formula) into a bound variable by prefixing a quantifier or other operator — compare QUANTIFICATION ~ *vi* **1 a** : to form a usu. hard lump or mass ⟨heat causes clay to ~⟩ **b** : to form a cohesive mass ⟨a little milk added to the ingredients will quickly make the mixture ~⟩ **2** : to hamper free movement : exert an uncomfortably restrictive and chafing force ⟨shorts that are guaranteed not to ~⟩ **3** : to become hindered from free operation : become blocked or jammed ⟨rust caused the door to ~ in its frame⟩ **4** : to exert a restraining, compelling, or uniting influence ⟨a promise that ~s⟩ **5** *falconry* : to close with or grapple quarry in the air **6** *printing* : to lock up improperly ⟨oversize cuts caused the form to ~⟩

²**bind** \" *but* 'bin(d) *in sense* 2\ *n* -s [ME *binde,* fr. *binden,* v.] **1** : something that binds or ties : the act of binding : a place where binding occurs : the state or an instance of being bound **2** : BINE **3** *Scot* : capacity esp. for drink : LIMIT **4 a** : TIE **b** : SLUR **5** : the action of forcing a fencing opponent's blade from one line to another by means of pressure against his blade **6** : a position that restricts an opponent's freedom of action (as in chess) ⟨White gets a ~ on Black's position⟩ — **in a bind** *slang* : in distress : in trouble

bind·er \'bīndə(r)\ *n* -s [ME, fr. *binden* + *-er*] **1** : one that binds: as **a** : BOOKBINDER **b** : BUNCHER **c** : a worker who stitches decorative or reinforcing bindings to wearing apparel, household furnishings, or upholstery **2 a** : something that is used in binding (as a fillet, band, or cord) **b** : a broad bandage applied (as about the chest or abdomen) for support ⟨breast ~⟩ ⟨obstetrical ~⟩ **c** : a detachable cover or other device for holding together sheets of paper or similar material (as sheet music or magazines) in loose-leaf form — see POST BINDER, RING BINDER, SPRING BINDER **d** : the sheet of tobacco that binds the filler in a cigar next to the wrapper **e** : a band (as of straw) used for binding sheaves of grain; *also* : a band (as of wire) used for binding bales **f** : a series of extra warp or weft threads that hold together the face and back of a cloth (as a double cloth) by interweaving without disturbing the surface patterns **g** *North* : RUBBER BAND **3 a** : something (as tar or cement) that produces or promotes cohesion in loosely assembled substances **b** : the nonvolatile portion of a paint vehicle **c** : a substance (as flour or cornstarch) used in cooking as a thickening agent or as an agent to improve consistency (as of a sauce) **d** : a fibrous material used in plaster and stucco to increase their cohesiveness while in the plastic state **e** : an adhesive used in a coated paper or a material used in the paper stock to make the paper firmer and less fuzzy **f** : a substance (as cereal, oil, clay, resin, or pitch) that causes cohesion of the grains of sand in foundry molds or cores **g** : a substance added to metal powder to assist in cohesion of the metal particles during sintering **h** : a substance (as glucose or acacia) used in pharmacy to hold together the ingredients of a compressed tablet **4** : a mechanical device used in binding: as **a** : a sewing-machine attachment for putting on bindings **b** : a harvesting machine that cuts grain and binds it into bundles **c** : a single machine designed to perform several operations in the construction of a book **5 a** : a beam, girder, or frame used to bind together the parts of a structure **b** : a springy pole used for tightening a chain binding together a load of logs **c** *weaving* : a lever in a shuttle box that prevents the rebound of the shuttle **d** : BONDSTONE, HEADER **e** : one of the fibers connecting the staples so as to form a piece or fleece of wool **6 a** : a written instrument used when an insurance policy cannot be immediately issued to evidence that the insurance coverage attaches at a specified time and continues subject to a maximum limitation until the policy is issued or the risk is declined and notice thereof given **b** : BINDING RECEIPT **7** : a receipt for money paid to the owner or his agent to secure the right to purchase a piece of real estate upon agreed terms; *also* : the money itself **8** : BINDER LINE

binder course *n* : a coarse aggregate bound with bitumen between the foundation and the wearing course of an asphalt pavement

binder line *n* : a large-type identifying line that heads an esp. long newspaper story or group of related stories carried on an inside page

binder's board *also* **binder board** *n* : a smooth hard tough pulpboard much used in covers by bookbinders

binder's cloth *n* : cotton fabric with a finish suitable for book covers — compare BOOK CLOTH

binder's title *n* : the title printed or stamped by the binder on the outside of the cover of a book

binder twine *n* : a coarse slack-twisted twine or thin rope (as of sisal or henequen) used in binding esp. of grain after cutting

bind·ery \'bīnd(ə)rē, -ri\ *n* -ES [¹*bind* + *-ery*] : a place where books are bound

bind·heim·ite \'bint,hī,mīt\ *n* -s [G *bindheimit,* fr. Johann J. *Bindheim* †1825 Ger. chemist + G *-it* -ite] : a mineral $Pb_2Sb_2O_6(O,OH)$ consisting of hydrous lead antimony oxide produced from the alteration of other ores

bin·di-eye \'bindē,ī\ *n* [origin unknown] : a grayish perennial Australian herb (*Calotis cuneifolia*) of the family Compositae with globular fruiting heads resembling burs

¹**bind·ing** \'bīndiŋ, -dēŋ\ *n* -s [ME, fr. gerund of *binden*] **1** : the action of one that binds **2** : a material or device used to bind: as **a** : the fastening of the sections of a book; *esp* : this fastening and the cover **b** : a narrow fabric (as tape) or a narrow piece of fabric (as bias fabric) used to finish, strengthen, or decorate raw edges (as of a garment, carpet, or blanket) **c** : a band of masonry so laid as to fasten together or strengthen adjoining parts **d** : an ingredient (as flour, eggs, or starch) used in cooking to give cohesion or a richer or thicker consistency (as to a sauce) **e** : the set of ski fastenings for holding the toe of the boot firm on the ski

²**binding** \"\ *adj* [ME, fr. pres. part. of *binden*] **1** : that binds or causes to bind : tending to bind **2** : imposing an obligation, duty, or responsibility ⟨a solemnly ~ promise⟩ **3** : requiring submission, conformity, or obedience ⟨the ~ force of wise laws⟩ — **bind·ing·ly** *adv* — **bind·ing·ness** *n* -ES

binding course *n* : a row (as of bricks) set across an inner and an outer course to bind them together

binding edge *n* : the edge (as of an insert or leaf) that is bound into a book, pamphlet, or magazine

binding energy *n* : the energy required to break up a molecule, an atom, or an atomic nucleus completely into its constituent particles; *also* : the portion of the energy acquired by one part when separated from the rest, being in the case of nuclear disintegration large enough to give a measurable change in mass — compare MASS DEFECT

binding joist *n* : a joist framed into the girders of a double-framed floor to support the bridging joists

binding post *n* **1** : a metallic post attached to electrical apparatus for convenience in making connections **2** : any of the posts holding the sheets in place in a loose-leaf binder

binding rafter *n* : a longitudinal timber (as a purlin) between the plate and the ridge of a roof for the support of rafters

binding receipt *n* : a receipt given to an applicant for life insurance when he signs the application and pays his first premium stipulating that the insurance shall go into effect immediately if the risk proves to be acceptable irrespective of the date of delivery of the policy and providing for return of the money if risk is declined — called also *binder, conditional receipt*

binding screw *n* : a setscrew used to hold parts together (as for making a firm electrical connection or for clamping a glass lampshade in place)

binding strake *n* : a heavy strake of planking next to and under the sheer strake

binding tape *n* : FRICTION TAPE

bin·dle \'bindᵊl\ *n* -s [prob. alter of *bundle*] **1** *slang* **a** : a bundle usu. containing clothing and cooking utensils **b** : BLANKET ROLL 1, BEDROLL **2** *slang* : a small package, envelope, or paper containing a narcotic (as morphine, heroin, or cocaine); *also* : a usu. small quantity of a narcotic : a narcotic dose

bindle stiff *n, slang* : a transient usu. carrying a bundle (as of clothing or bedding): as **a** : a migratory worker **b** : TRAMP, HOBO

bind off *vt* : to decrease (stitches) in knitting in order to form an edge by slipping the first of two stitches over the second and repeating across

bind over *vt* : to put under bonds to do something (as to appear at court) ⟨he was *bound over* to the grand jury⟩

binds *pres 3d sing of* BIND, *pl of* BIND

bindweed \'=,=\ *n* [¹*bind* + *weed*; fr. their twining habit] : any of numerous plants of more or less twining habit and dense or prickly form that tend to mat together or interlace with plants among which they grow: as **a** : any of several plants of the genus *Convolvulus* — see FIELD BINDWEED, HEDGE BINDWEED, ROUGH BINDWEED **b** : knotgrass or a closely related plant (as black bindweed)

bindweed nightshade *n* : ENCHANTER'S NIGHTSHADE

bine \'bīn\ *n* -s [alter. of ²*bind*] : a twining stem or flexible shoot: as **a** : the stem of common hop varieties **b** : BINDWEED **c** : WOODBINE 1

bi·negation \ˌbī+\ *n* -s [¹*bi-* + *negation*] : JOINT DENIAL

bi·nervate \(')bī+\ *adj* [¹*bi-* + *nervate*] : TWO-NERVED

bi·net age \bə'nā-, bi-\ *n, usu cap B* [after A. *Binet*] : mental age as determined by the Binet-Simon test

binet-si·mon test \-sē'mōⁿ-\ *n, usu cap B & S* [after Alfred *Binet* †1911 and Théodore *Simon* †1961, Fr. psychologists] : an intelligence test consisting orig. of tasks graded in difficulty from the level of the average 3-year-old to that of the average 12-year-old but later revised and extended in range — called also *Binet test*; see STANFORD-BINET TEST

¹**bing** \'biŋ\ *n* -s [ME, of Scand origin; akin to ON *bingr* divided space, bin, OSw *binge* storage room, Icel *bingur* heap; akin to OHG *bungo* tuber — more at BUNCH] **1** *dial Brit* **a** : a heap or pile for storage ⟨a ~ of potatoes⟩ **b** : a storage bin **2** *slang* : a solitary-confinement prison cell

²**bing** \"\ *vi* [origin unknown] *archaic* : GO

³**bing** \"\ *interj* [imit.] — used to suggest a sharp ringing sound

¹**binge** \'binj\ *vb* -ED/-ING/-S [origin unknown] *vt, dial Brit* : to soak (a wooden vessel) so as to swell the wood and prevent leakage ~ *vi, dial Brit* : to stand soaking so as to swell and prevent leakage ⟨putting vats to ~⟩

²**binge** \"\ *n* -s [E dial. *binge* to drink heavily, fr. ¹*binge*] **1 a** : uninhibited and usu. excessive indulgence esp. in alcoholic beverages : CAROUSAL ⟨bleary-eyed from a week-end ~⟩ **b** : unreserved and often riotous indulgence in or abandonment to any form of activity : a riotous display : ORGY, RAMPAGE, SPLURGE ⟨a buying ~⟩ ⟨an emotional ~⟩ **2** : a social gathering : PARTY ⟨fancy-dress ~s have always been my dish —P.G.Wodehouse⟩ ⟨the intimate ~ or book tea —R.G.G. Price⟩

bin·gee *also* **bin·gy** \'binjē\ *n, pl* **bingees** *also* **bingies** [native name in Australia] *Austral* : STOMACH, BELLY

bing·hi \'biŋ,ī\ *n* -s *often cap* [native name in Australia] *slang Austral* : ABORIGINE

¹**bin·gle** \'biŋgəl\ *n* -s [prob. alter. (influenced by ³*bing*) of *single*] : BASE HIT

²**bingle** \"\ *n* -s [*bob* + *shingle*] : a woman's short bob partly shingled at the back

bing·ley terrier \'biŋlē-\ *n, usu cap B* [fr. *Bingley,* Yorkshire, England] : AIREDALE TERRIER

¹**bin·go** \'biŋ(,)gō\ *interj* [alter. of ³*bing*] **1** — used to point up the occurrence of a sudden or unexpected event **2** — used in the game of bingo to indicate that one has completed a 5-number row

²**bingo** \"\ *n* -s *sometimes cap* [¹*bingo,* the winner's exclamation] **1 a** : a game resembling lotto or keno, the card used being a grid on which five numbers that are covered in a row in any direction constitute a win, the center square being counted as an already drawn number — called also *beano* **b** : a social gathering at which bingo is played **2** : a dice game with usu. petty merchandise as stakes

binh dinh \'bin,din\ *adj, usu cap B&D* [fr. *Binh Dinh,* So. Vietnam] : of or from the city of Binh Dinh, So. Vietnam : of the kind or style prevalent in Binh Dinh

bi·ni *also* **be·ni** \bə'nē\ *n, pl* **bini** *or* **binis** *usu cap* : EDO

bin·io·dide \(')bī,n, (')bi,n+,-\ *n* [*bin-* + *iodide*] : DIIODIDE ⟨mercury ~⟩

biniou \bē'nyü, bi'-\ *n* -s [F, fr. Bret] : the Breton bagpipe consisting of one drone and a chanter with seven finger holes

bi·nit \'bīnət\ *n* -s [*binary digit*] : BINARY DIGIT

bink \'biŋk\ *n* -s [ME (northern dial.) *bink, benk,* fr. OE *benc* — more at BENCH] **1** *chiefly Scot* : a bench to sit on **2** *chiefly Scot* : an open rack of shelves for dishes **3** *chiefly Scot* : a bank of earth

bin·man \'binmən\ *n, pl* **binmen** [¹*bin* + *man*] : a worker who fills hoppers or tends the flow of material through bins connected by conveyors

bin·na \'binə\ *conj* [*be,* pres. subjunctive of *be,* v.i. + *na* (adv.)] *Scot* : UNLESS

¹**bin·na·cle** \'binəkəl, -nēk-\ *n* -s [alter. (perh. influenced by *bin*) of earlier *bittacle,* fr. ME *bitakle,* fr. OPg *bitácola,* or OSp *bitácula,* fr. L *habitaculum* dwelling place, fr. *habitare* to dwell — more at HABIT] : a case, box, or stand containing a ship's compass and a lamp

²**binnacle** \"\ *also* **bin·ne·kill** \"\ *n* -s [D *binnenkil,* fr. *binnen* within + *kil* channel — more at BILANDER, KILL] *in New York & Pennsylvania* : a secondary channel of a stream

binnacle list *n* : a sick list posted at or near the binnacle for the use of the officer of the deck

binned *past of* BIN

binning *n* -s [fr. gerund of ²*bin*] : the action of putting into a bin; *esp* : the stowing and aging of bottled wine in a bin

bin·ny \'binē\ *n* -ES [NL *bynni,* specific epithet of *Barbus bynni*] : a very large cyprinid fish (*Barbus bynni*) common in the Nile river and sometimes used as food

bino *var of* BENO

¹**bin·oc·u·lar** \(')bī,näkyələ(r) *also* bə'n-\ *adj* [*bin-* + *ocular*] **1** : of or relating to both eyes ⟨~ infection⟩ **2** : employing both eyes at once; *specif* : producing an appearance of solidity or depth because of the slight difference in the two retinal images due to the angle from which each eye views an object ⟨~ vision⟩ **3** : adapted to the use of both eyes ⟨a ~ microscope⟩ — **bin·oc·u·lar·i·ty** \(,)bī,näkyə'larəd.ē *also* bə,n-\ *n* -ES — **bin·oc·u·lar·ly** \(')bī,näkyələ(r)lē, bə'n-\ *adv*

²**binocular** \bə'näkyələ(r) *also* bī-\ *n, pl* **binoculars** *but sometimes sing in constr* : an optical instrument composed of two refracting telescopes mounted on a single frame and containing erecting systems usu. with both focusing tubes simultaneously adjustable by means of a single screw ⟨a 6-power ~⟩ ⟨the ~s are in that leather case⟩ — usu. used in pl. and often with *pair* ⟨a pair of ~s⟩

binocular

binocular rivalry *n* : RETINAL RIVALRY

bin·oculate \(')bī,n, bə'n+,-\ *adj* [*bin-* + *oculate*] : having two eyes

bin·oc·u·lus \bī'näkyələs, bə'-\ *n* -ES [NL, fr. *bin-* + L *oculus* eye — more at EYE] : the two eyes and their central nervous connections regarded as a functional whole

bi·nodal \(')bī+\ *adj* [¹*bi-* + *nodal*] : consisting of or having two nodes ⟨a ~ stem of a plant⟩ ⟨a ~ quartic curve⟩

bi·no·kid \'binəkəd, ,=='kid\ *n* -s *usu cap* [of Philippine origin; akin to Bisayan *bukidnon* — more at BUKIDNON] : BUKIDNON 2

bi·no·men \(')bī'nōmən\ *n, pl* **binom·i·na** \-'nämənə\ [NL, fr. ¹*bi-* + L *nomen* name — more at NAME] : a binomial naming a species ⟨*Canis latrans* is the ~ of the coyote⟩

bi·no·men·cla·ture \bī'nōmən,klāchə(r)\ *n* -s : BINOMIAL NOMENCLATURE

¹**bi·no·mi·al** \bī'nōmēəl\ *n* -s [NL *binomium* (fr. neut. of ML *binomius*) + E *-al*] : a mathematical expression consisting of two terms connected by a plus sign or minus sign (as $a+b$ or $7-3$)

²**binomial** \(')=¦===\ *adj* [ML *binomius* having two names (alter. of L *binominis,* fr. *bi-* ¹*bi-* + *-nominis,* fr. *nomin-, nomen* name) + E *-al* — more at NAME] **1** [¹*binomial*] : relating to binomials **2** : consisting of two terms or names — **bi·no·mi·al·ly** \-ēəlē, -li\ *adv*

³**binomial** \=¦===\ *n* -s : a species name consisting of two terms — see BINOMIAL NOMENCLATURE

binomial coefficient *n* **:** the coefficient of any term resulting from the expansion of the binomial $(x+y)^n$

binomial distribution *n* **:** a frequency distribution of the probability that an attribute that occurs with a given probability among the members of a population will occur a certain number of times in a succession of samples of the population — called also *Bernoulli distribution*

binomial expansion *n* **:** the expansion of a binomial

bi·no·mi·al·ism \bī'nōmēə,lizəm\ *n* -s **:** the theory or use of binomial nomenclature

binomial law *n* **:** a theorem in mathematics: the probability of an event whose probability on each trial is *p* occurring *r* times in *n* trials is given by the term containing p^r in the binomial expansion of $(p + q)^n$ in which $q=1-p$

binomial nomenclature *n* **:** a system of nomenclature in which each species of plant or animal receives a name of two terms of which the first identifies the genus to which it belongs and the second the species itself and which was first standardized by Linnaeus about the middle of the 18th century — compare LINNAEAN

binomial theorem *n* **:** a theorem in mathematics: a binomial may be raised to any power according to $(x+y)^n = x^n+nx^{n-1}y+\frac{n(n-1)}{1\cdot 2}x^{n-2}y^2+\frac{n(n-1)(n-2)}{1\cdot 2\cdot 3}x^{n-3}y^3+\ldots$

bi·nominal \(')bī+\ *adj* [L *binominis* having two names + E *-al* — more at BINOMIAL] **:** using a combination of two names **:** BINOMIAL

bi·normal \bī+\ *n* -s [¹*bi-* + *normal*] **:** the normal to a twisted curve at a point of the curve that is perpendicular to the osculating plane of the curve at that point

bin·ovular \¦bī¦n+-\ *adj* [*bin-* + *ovular*] **:** BIOVULAR

bin·oxalate \(')bī¦n, (')bī¦n+-\ *n* -s [*bin-* + *oxalate*] **:** an acid oxalate (as sodium binoxalate $NaHC_2O_4$) formed from oxalic acid by the replacement of half the acid hydrogen

bin·oxide \"+-\ *n* -s [*bin-* + *oxide*] **:** DIOXIDE

bins *plural of* BIN, *pres 3d sing of* BIN

bint \'bint\ *n* -s [Ar, girl, daughter] *slang Austral* **:** GIRL, WOMAN, DAME

bin·tang·or \bin'taŋə(r)\ *n* -s [Malay *bĕntangor*] **:** POON

bin·tu·rong \bin·'tü,rȯŋ\ *n* -s [Malay *bĕnturong, binturong, binturon*] **:** an Asiatic prehensile-tailed civet (*Arctictis binturong*)

bi·nuclear *or* **bi·nucleate** *or* **bi·nucleated** \(')bī+\ *adj* [¹*bi-* + *nuclear* or *nucleate* or *nucleated*] **:** having two nuclei

bi·nucleolate \¦bī, (')bī+\ *adj* [¹*bi-* + *nucleolate*] **:** having two nucleoli

bio \'bī(,)ō\ *n* -s [by shortening] **:** BIOGRAPHY

bio- — see ²BI-

bio·acoustic \¦bī(,)ō +\ *adj* [²*bi-* + *acoustic*] **:** of or relating to the relation between living beings and sound

bio·acoustician \"+\ *n* [*bioacoustics* + *-ian*] **:** a specialist in bioacoustics

bio·acoustics \"+\ *n pl but sing in constr* [fr. *bioacoustic*, after such pairs as E *acoustic: acoustics*] **:** a branch of science that deals with the relation between living beings and sound

bio-aer·a·tion \¦bī(,)ō+\ *n* [²*bi-* + *aeration*] **:** the activation of sewage by mechanical means

¹**bio·assay** \¦bī(,)ō+\ *n* [*biological assay*] **:** determination of the relative effective strength of a substance (as a vitamin, hormone, or drug) by comparing its effect on a test organism with that of a standard preparation; *also* **:** a particular test of this kind ⟨do a ~ on the sample⟩

²**bio·assay** \¦bī(,)ō+\ *vt* **:** to perform a bioassay on

bio·bibliographical \¦bī(,)ō+\ *adj* **:** of, relating to, or being a biobibliography

bio·bibliography \¦bī(,)ō+\ *n* [²*bi-* + *bibliography*] **:** a bibliography with biographical notes about the author or authors listed; *also* **:** a usu. short biography esp. concerned with the bibliography of the biographee

bi·o·blast \'bīō,blast\ *n* -s [ISV ²*bi-* + *-blast*; orig. formed in G] **:** ALTMANN'S GRANULE — **bioblastic** \¦==¦=stik\ *adj*

bio·catalyst \,bīō+\ *n* [²*bi-* + *catalyst*] **:** a substance (as an enzyme or a trace element) that plays a fundamental role in living organisms by activating or accelerating biological processes (as metabolic processes) — **bi·o·catalytic** \¦bīō+\ *adj*

bi·ocel·late \¦bī, (')bī+\ *adj* [¹*bi-* + *ocellate*] **:** having two ocelli

bi·o·ce·nol·o·gy *also* **bi·o·coe·nol·o·gy** \,bī(,)ōsə'nälə̇jē\ *n* -ES [²*bi-* + *coen-* + *-logy*] **:** a branch of biology concerned with the study of natural communities and the interaction of the members of such a community — compare ECOLOGY

bi·o·ce·no·sis *or* **bi·o·coe·no·sis** \,bīōsə'nōsə̇s\ *or* **bi·o·ce·nose** *also* **bi·o·coe·nose** \-'sēnōs\ *n, pl* **bio·ceno·ses** *or* **biocoeno·ses** \-sə'nō,sēz\ [NL *biocenosis, biocoenosis*, fr. ²*bi-* + Gk *koinōsis* sharing (fr. *koinoun* to make common, fr. *koinos* common) — more at COEN-] **:** an assemblage of diverse organisms inhabiting a common biotope **:** a biotic community — **bi·o·ce·not·ic** *or* **bi·o·coe·not·ic** \¦==sə¦näd·ik\ *adj*

bio·centric *also* **bio·central** \¦bīō+\ *adj* [²*bi-* + *centric* or *central*] **:** centering in life **:** taking life as a central fact — **bio·cen·trist** \"+¦sen·trəst\ *n*

¹**bio·chemical** *also* **bio·chemic** \¦bīō, ¦bīə+\ *adj* [ISV ²*bi-* + *chemical* or *chemic*; orig. formed as G *biochemisch*] **:** of or relating to biochemistry **:** characterized by, produced by, or involving chemical reactions in living organisms ⟨~ mutants⟩ — **bio·chemically** \"+\ *adv*

²**biochemical** \"\ *n* **:** a biochemical product

biochemical oxygen demand *n* **:** the oxygen used in meeting the metabolic needs of aerobic microorganisms in water rich in organic matter (as water polluted with sewage) — called also *biological oxygen demand*

bio·chemist \¦bīō, ¦bīə+\ *n* [²*bi-* + *chemist*] **:** one trained in or engaged in biochemistry

bio·chemistry \"+\ *n* [ISV ²*bi-* + *chemistry*; orig. formed as G *biochemie*] **1 :** the chemistry of plant and animal life **:** biological chemistry or physiological chemistry **2 :** chemistry in relation to life processes ⟨~ of chlorophyll⟩ ⟨~ of microorganisms⟩

bio·chemor·phol·o·gy \¦bīō¦ke(,)mȯr'fälə̇jē\ *n* [²*bi-* + blend of *chem-* and *morphology*] **:** the study of the relationship between the chemical structure of a compound and its biological action

bi·o·chore \'bīō,kō(ə)r\ *n* -s [ISV ²*bi-* + *-chore*] **:** a group of similar biotopes (as temperate forests)

bi·o·chrome \-,krōm\ *n* -s [²*bi-* + *-chrome*] **:** a coloring matter that can be extracted from a plant or animal **:** a natural pigment

bi·o·chron \-,krän\ *n* -s [²*bi-* + *-chron* (fr. Gk *chronos* time)] **:** a fossil fauna or flora of relatively short time range

bi·o·cide \'bīə,sīd\ *n* -s [²*bi-* + *-cide*] **:** PESTICIDE

bi·o·clas·tic \¦bīō¦klastik\ *adj* [²*bi-* + *-clastic*] *of rock or similar material* **:** attaining its present form through the action of living organisms ⟨concrete, like the consolidated muds of certain coral reefs, may be considered a ~ substance⟩

bio·climatic \¦bī(,)ō+\ *adj* [²*bi-* + *climatic*] **:** of, relating to, or concerned with the relations of climate and living matter ⟨~ research⟩ ⟨~ peculiarities of desert regions⟩

bioclimatic law *n* **:** a statement in ecology: phenological events in temperate No. America are generally altered about 4 days for each change of 5° of latitude northward, 5° of longitude eastward, or 400 feet of altitude upward, the vernal alteration being retardation (as of flowering), the autumnal being acceleration (as of leaf fall)

bio·cli·mat·ics \¦bī(,)ō,klī'mad·iks\ *n pl but sing or pl in constr* **:** BIOCLIMATOLOGY

bio·cli·mat·o·graph \¦bī(,)ō,klī¦mad·ə,graf\ *n* -s [²*bi-* + *climatograph* climograph (fr. *climate* + *-o-* + *-graph*)] **:** a climograph constructed to show the relation between climatic conditions and some living organism and used esp. to determine the points most susceptible to attack in the life cycle of various pests and parasites

bio·climatological \¦bī(,)ō+\ *adj* [²*bi-* + *climatological*] **:** of, relating to, or involving the methods of bioclimatology ⟨~ research⟩

bio·climatologist \"+\ *also* **bio·cli·ma·ti·cian** \¦bī(,)ō-,klīmə'tishən\ *n* [*bioclimatologist* fr. *bioclimatology* + *-ist*; *bioclimatician* fr. *bioclimatics* + *-ian*] **:** a specialist in bioclimatology

bio·climatology \¦bī(,)ō+\ *n* [²*bi-* + *climatology*] **1 :** a branch of knowledge concerned with the direct and indirect impact of climate or sometimes other geophysical factors on living matter **2 :** the interrelation of an organism and climate

biocoenology *var of* BIOCENOLOGY

biocoenosis *also* **biocoenose** *var of* BIOCENOSIS

bio·colloid \¦bīō+\ *n* -s [²*bi-* + *colloid*] **:** a colloid or colloidal mixture of plant or animal origin — **bio·colloidal** \¦bī(,)ō+\ *adj*

bio·cycle \'bīō+,-\ *n* [²*bi-* + *cycle*] **:** a group of related biochores constituting a major division of the biosphere ⟨the ~s usu. recognized are saltwater, freshwater, and terrestrial⟩

bi·o·cy·tin \,bīō'sītᵊn\ *n* -s [blend of *biotin* and *cyt-*] **:** a colorless crystalline peptide $C_{16}H_{28}N_4O_4S$ occurring naturally (as in yeast) and yielding biotin and lysine on hydrolysis

bio·dynamic \¦bī(,)ō+\ *adj* [ISV ²*bi-* + *dynamic*] **1 :** of, relating to, or concerned with the dynamic relation between organisms and their environment ⟨~ concepts in psychology⟩ **2 :** of, relating to, or being a system of farming that depends wholly on organic materials for fertilizing and soil conditioning ⟨~ agriculture⟩

bio·dynamics \"+\ *n pl but sing or pl in constr* [ISV ²*bi-* + *dynamics*] **:** biodynamic state, factors, or condition ⟨the ~ of a watercourse⟩ ⟨the ~ of sewage purification⟩

bio·ecological *also* **bio·ecologic** \¦bīō+\ *adj* **:** of or relating to bioecology

bio·ecologist \"+\ *n* **:** a specialist in bioecology

bio·ecology \"+\ *n* [²*bi-* + *ecology*] **:** general ecology **:** ecology dealing with the interrelation of plants and animals with their common environment — sometimes opposed to *biocenology*

bio·electric *also* **bio·electrical** \¦bī(,)ō+\ *adj* [²*bi-* + *electric, electrical*] **:** of or relating to electrical phenomena in plants or animals — **bio·electricity** \¦bīō+\ *n*

bio·energetic \¦bīō+\ *adj* [²*bi-* + *energetic*] **:** of or relating to bioenergetics or bioenergy

bio·energetics \"+\ *n pl but sing or pl in constr* [²*bi-* + *energetics*] **:** the branch of biology that deals with the energy relations in or the energy changes produced by living organisms

bio·energy \"+,-\ *n* [²*bi-* + *energy*] **:** energy available for the bodily work of the living organism

bio·engineering \"+\ *n* [²*bi-* + *engineering*] **:** engineering relating to the biosynthesis or processing of animal or plant products; *specif* **:** engineering relating to fermentation processes

bio·facies \"+,-\ *n* [NL, fr. ²*bi-* + *facies*] *geol* **:** a part of a stratigraphic unit in which the fossil fauna or flora differs significantly from that found elsewhere in the same unit

bio·filter \"+,-\ *n* [²*bi-* + *filter*] **:** a filter bed in which sewage is subjected to the action of microorganisms that assist in decomposing it

bio·filtration \¦bī(,)ō+\ *n* [²*bi-* + *filtration*] **:** the process of treating sewage by passing it through a biofilter

bio·flavonoid \¦bīō+\ *n* [²*bi-* + *flavonoid*] **:** a flavonoid compound (as rutin) having in mammals biological activity related to its reducing and chelating properties and its effect on the functioning of minute blood vessels but in many cases (as some such compounds obtained commercially from citrus fruits) not having nutritional functions — called also *vitamin P*

bi·o·gen \'bīəjən\ *n* -s [ISV ²*bi-* + *-gen*; orig formed in G] **:** a hypothetical ultimate living unit of which cells are built up **:** BIOPHORE

bio·genesis \¦bīō+\ *n* [NL, fr. ²*bi-* + L *genesis*] **1 :** the development of life from preexisting life — opposed to *abiogenesis* **2 :** the supposed tendency for stages in the evolutionary history of a race to briefly recur during the development and differentiation of an individual of that race — compare RECAPITULATION THEORY

bio·gen·e·sist \"+¦jenəsə̇st\ *n* -s [irreg. fr. NL *biogenesis* + E *-ist*] **:** a student or protagonist of biogenesis

bio·ge·net·ic *also* **bio·ge·net·i·cal** \¦bī(,)ō+\ *adj* [F *biogénétique*, fr. *bio-* ²*bi-* + *génétique* genetic, genetical] **1 :** of, relating to, or produced by biogenesis **2 :** BIOGENOUS — **bio·genetically** \"+\ *adv*

biogenetic law *n* **:** RECAPITULATION THEORY

bi·o·gen·ic \¦bīō¦jenik\ *adj* [²*bi-* + *-genic*] **1 :** produced by the action of living organisms ⟨~ rocks⟩ **2 :** essential to life and its maintenance ⟨sleep, food, and water are among the ~ needs of the organism⟩

bi·og·e·nous \(')bī¦äjənəs\ *adj* [²*bi-* + *-genous*] **1 :** produced from living organisms (as by growing on them) **2 :** BIOGENIC

bi·og·e·ny \-jənē\ *n* -ES [²*bi-* + *-geny*] **:** BIOGENESIS

bio·geo·chemical \,bīō,jēō+\ *adj* [²*bi-* + *ge-* + *chemical*; trans. of Russ *biogeokhimicheskiǐ*] **:** of or relating to biogeochemistry ⟨~ prospecting⟩

bio·geo·chemistry \"+\ *n* -ES [²*bi-* + *ge-* + *chemistry*; trans. of Russ *biogeokhimiya*] **:** the science that deals with the relation of earth chemicals to plant and animal life in an area **:** chemistry in relation to geology and plant and animal life ⟨~ of iron⟩

bio·geographic *or* **bio·geographical** \¦bīō+\ *adj* [²*bi-* + *geographic, geographical*] **:** of, relating to, or involved with biogeography — **bio·geographically** \"+\ *adv*

bio·geography \"+\ *n* -ES [ISV ²*bi-* + *geography*] **:** a branch of biology that deals with the geographical distribution of animals and plants and includes both zoogeography and phytogeography — compare ECOLOGY, GEOGRAPHY

bi·og·no·sis \,bī,äg'nōsə̇s\ *n, pl* **biogno·ses** \-ō,sēz\ [NL, fr. ²*bi-* + *-gnosis*] **:** the scientific investigation of life

bi·o·graph \'bīə,graf, -raa(ə)f,-raif,-räf\ *vt* -ED/-ING/-S [back-formation fr. *biographer, biography*] **:** to write a life or biographical sketch of ⟨after ~ing the painter⟩

bi·og·ra·phee \(,)bī¦ägrə¦fē *also* bē¦äɡrə- *sometimes* ¦bīə,gra¦fē\ *n* -s [*biography* + *-ee*] **:** the person about whom a biography is written

bi·og·ra·pher \bī'ägrəfə(r) *also* bē'ä-\ *n* -s [*biography* + *-er*] **:** a writer of a biography or of biography

bi·o·graph·i·cal \¦bīə¦grafə̇kəl, -fēk- *sometimes* ¦bēə-\ *or* **bi·o·graph·ic** \-fik,-fēk\ *adj* [*biography* + *-ical, -ic*] **1 :** of, relating to, or being biography ⟨~ material⟩ ⟨a ~ interest⟩ ⟨a ~ work⟩ **2 :** consisting of biographies or biographical matter ⟨a ~ dictionary⟩ ⟨a ~ novel⟩ — **bi·o·graph·i·cal·ly** \-fə̇k(ə)lē, -fēk-, -lī\ *adv*

bi·og·ra·phize \bī'ägrə,fīz *also* bē'ä-\ *vt* -ED/-ING/-S [*biography* + *-ize*] **:** ²BIOGRAPHY

¹**bi·og·ra·phy** \bī'ägrəfē, -fi *also* bē'ä-\ *n* -ES [LGk *biographia*, fr. Gk *bio-* ²*bi-* + *-graphia* -graphy] **1 :** a usu. written history of a person's life **2 :** biographical writings in general; *esp* **:** such writings considered as a genre ⟨the field of ~⟩ **3 :** an account in biographical form of the life of something (as an animal, a coin, or a building) ⟨the ~ of the commonwealth⟩

²**biography** \"\ *vt* -ED/-ING/-ES **:** to write a biography of

bi·o·herm \'bīō,hərm\ *n* -s [²*bi-* + Gk *herma* sunken rock, reef — more at WART] **:** a body of rock built up by or composed mainly of sedentary organisms (as corals, algae, or mollusks) and enclosed or surrounded by rock of different origin — compare BIOSTROME — **bi·o·her·mal** \¦==¦hərməl\ *adj*

bioi *pl of* BIOS

bi·o·lith \'bīō,lith\ *also* **bi·o·lite** \-,līt\ *n* -s [ISV ²*bi-* + *-lith* or *-lite*; orig formed as G *biolith*] **:** a rock of organic origin **:** a rock produced directly by the activities of organisms

¹**bi·o·log·ic** \¦bīə¦läjik, -jēk\ *or* **bi·o·log·i·cal** \-jə̇kəl, -jēk-\ *adj* [ISV *biology* + *-ic, -ical*] **1 :** of or relating to biology or to life and living things **:** belonging to or characteristic of the processes of life — compare PHYSIOLOGICAL **2 :** used in or produced by practical application of biology ⟨*biological* methods⟩ ⟨*biologic* supplies⟩ — **bi·o·log·i·cal·ly** \-jə̇k(ə)lē, -jēk-, -lī\ *adv*

²**biologic** \"\ *or* **biological** \"\ *n* -s **:** a biological product (as a globulin, serum, vaccine, antitoxin, or antigen) used in the prevention or treatment of disease

biological assay *n* **:** BIOASSAY

biological balance *n* **:** a dynamic equilibrium existing between members of any relatively stable natural community and being the resultant of all the effects (as in food chains, parasitism, or pollinization) of the constituent organisms on one another

biological control *n* **:** attack upon noxious organisms (as insects) by interference with their ecological adjustment (as by the introduction of parasites not previously present)

biological dye *or* **biological stain** *n* **:** STAIN 4b

biological efficiency *n* **:** the relative ability of a protein or protein foodstuff to meet adequately the metabolic needs of an animal — compare BIOLOGICAL VALUE

biological environment *n* **:** the natural biological factors (as wild animals and plants or bacteria) that affect human life (as in a particular place or period)

biological geography *n* **:** BIOGEOGRAPHY

biological half-life *n* **:** the time that a living body requires to eliminate one half the quantity of an administered substance (as a radioisotope) through its normal channels of elimination

biological method *or* **biological test** *n* **:** a method or test involving experiment on organisms — compare BIOASSAY

biological oceanography *n* **:** a science that deals with the animal and plant inhabitants of ocean waters

biological oxygen demand *n* **:** BIOCHEMICAL OXYGEN DEMAND

biological product *n* **:** a complex pharmaceutical substance, preparation, or agent of organic origin depending for its action on the processes effecting immunity and used esp. in diagnosis and treatment of disease (as a vaccine or pollen extract); *also* **:** any such complex product of organic or synthetic origin obtained or standardized by biological methods or assay (as arsphenamine, pituitary extract, or insulin) **:** BIOLOGICAL

biological race *n* **:** PHYSIOLOGIC RACE — used esp. of insects

biological species *n* **:** PHYSIOLOGIC RACE

biological value *n* **:** a measure of the efficiency of the protein in a foodstuff for the maintenance and growth of the bodily tissues of an individual usu. computed as the percentage of protein intake actually utilized in the body but sometimes as the percentage of digestible protein assimilated from a foodstuff

biological warfare *n* **:** warfare involving the use of living organisms (as disease germs and toxic substances produced by them) against men, animals, or plants; *also* **:** warfare involving the use of synthetic chemicals harmful to plants

biological zone *n* **:** ZONE 3b

biologic false-positive *n* **:** a positive serological reaction for syphilis given by blood of a nonsyphilitic person

bi·ol·o·gism \bī'äləjizəm\ *n* -s [*biology* + *-ism*] **1 a :** a doctrine or system formulated from the biological point of view or based on biological modes of explanation **b :** adherence to such a doctrine, system, or point of view; *esp* **:** preoccupation with biological explanations in the analysis of social situations **2 :** the use of scientific phraseology peculiar to biologists; *also* **:** an expression peculiar to biologists

bi·ol·o·gist \-jə̇st\ *n* -s [*biology* + *-ist*] **:** a specialist in biology

bi·ol·o·gis·tic \¦bī¦älə¦jistik, bī¦ä-\ *adj* **:** of or relating to biologism — **bi·ol·o·gis·ti·cal·ly** \-tə̇k(ə)lē\ *adv*

bi·ol·o·gize \bī'älə,jīz\ *vb* -ED/-ING/-S [*biology* + *-ize*] *vi* **:** to engage in biological investigations esp. superficially or amateurishly ~ *vt* **:** to treat (as a problem) biologically

bi·ol·o·gy \bī'äləjē, -ji\ *n* -ES *often attrib* [G *biologie*, fr. *bi-* ²*bi-* + *-logie* -logy] **1 a :** the science of life **:** a branch of knowledge that deals with living organisms and vital processes broadly including zoology, botany, morphology, genetics, embryology, and allied sciences but commonly being restricted to consideration of principles of wide application to the origin, development, structure, functions, and distribution of living matter as represented by plants and animals and to the generally recurrent phenomena of life, growth, and reproduction **b :** ECOLOGY **2 a :** the plant and animal life of a particular region or environment considered as a unit ⟨the ~ of the plains⟩ **b :** the laws and phenomena relating to an organism or group ⟨the ~ of the honeybee⟩ ⟨the ~ of parasitic worms⟩ **3 :** a treatise on biology

bio·luminescence \,bī(,)ō+\ *n* [ISV ²*bi-* + *luminescence*] **:** the emission of light from living organisms as the result of internal oxidative changes; *also* **:** the light so produced — compare PHOSPHORESCENCE — **bio·luminescent** \¦bī(,)ō+\ *adj*

bi·ol·y·sis \bī'äləsə̇s\ *n, pl* **bioly·ses** \-ə,sēz\ [NL, fr. ²*bi-* + *-lysis*] **1 :** death and the bodily disintegration that follows **2 :** decomposition by living organisms of sewage and other complex materials — **bi·o·lyt·ic** \¦bīō¦lid·ik\ *adj*

biolytic tank *n* **:** a chamber having a hopper bottom in which the oxidation of organic matter is hastened by agitating the sludge with raw sewage

bio·mass \'bīō+,-\ *n* [²*bi-* + *mass*] **:** the amount of living matter in the form of one or more kinds of organisms present in a particular habitat usu. expressed as weight of organisms per unit area of habitat or as volume or weight of organisms per unit volume of habitat — used esp. of plankters

bio·mathematical \¦bīō +\ *adj* [²*bi-* + *mathematical*] **:** of or relating to biomathematics

bio·mathematics \" +\ *n pl but usu sing in constr* [²*bi-* + *mathematics*] **:** the principles of mathematics that are of special use in biology and medicine

bi·ome \'bī,ōm\ *n* -s [²*bi-* + *-ome*] **:** an ecological formation considered in terms of both plants and animals of the area concerned and usu. identified in terms of characteristic vegetation forms

bio·mechanical \¦bī(,)ō +\ *adj* [²*bi-* + *mechanical*] **:** of, relating to, or involving biomechanics

bio·mechanics \" +\ *n pl but sing or pl in constr* [²*bi-* + *mechanics*] **:** the mechanical bases of biological, esp. muscular, activity; *also* **:** the study of the principles and relations involved

bio·meteorological \" +\ *adj* **:** of or relating to biometeorology

bio·meteorology \" +\ *n* -ES [²*bi-* + *meteorology*] **:** a science that deals with the relationship between living beings and atmospheric phenomena

bi·om·e·ter \bī'ämə̇d·ə(r)\ *n* -s [ISV ²*bi-* + *-meter*] **:** a device for measuring carbon dioxide given off by living matter

bi·o·met·ric \,bīō'me·trik\ *also* **bi·o·met·ri·cal** \-rə̇kəl\ *adj* [back-formation fr. *biometrics*] **:** of, relating to, or concerned with biometrics — **bi·o·met·ri·cal·ly** \-rə̇k(ə)lē\ *adv*

bi·o·me·tri·cian \,bīōmə'trishən, ,bī,ämə-\ *also* **bi·o·met·ri·cist** \,bīō'me·trəsə̇st\ *n* -s [*biometrics* + *-ian* or *-ist*] **:** a specialist in biometrics

bi·o·met·rics \,bīō'me·triks\ *n pl but sing or pl in constr* [ISV *biometry* + *-ics*; prob. orig. formed as F *biométrique*] **:** the statistical study of biological observations and phenomena

bi·om·e·try \bī'ämə·trē\ *n* -ES [ISV ²*bi-* + *-metry*] **:** BIOMETRICS

bio·microscope \,bīō +\ *n* [²*bi-* + *microscope*] **:** a low-power binocular microscope placed horizontally and used with a slit lamp for detailed examination of the anterior part of the eye

bio·microscopic \¦bīō +\ *adj* **:** of, relating to, or by means of biomicroscopy or the biomicroscope — **bio·microscopically** \" +\ *adv*

bio·microscopy \" +\ *n* [²*bi-* + *microscopy*] **:** the microscopic examination and study of living cells and tissues; *specif* **:** examination of the living eye with the biomicroscope

bio·molecule \" +\ *n* [²*bi-* + *molecule*] **:** a hypothetical living molecule — compare BIOGEN, BIOPHORE

bi·o·mor·phic \¦bīō¦mȯrfik\ *adj* [²*bi-* + *morphic*] **:** related to, derived from, or incorporating the forms of living beings — used esp. of primitive and abstract art

bio·negative \¦bīō +\ *adj* [²*bi-* + *negative*] **:** DISRUPTIVE, RETROGRESSIVE; *specif* **:** relating to the phase of radiation damage to living tissue in which organization is disrupted

bi·o·nom·ic \¦bīō¦nämik\ *or* **bi·o·nom·i·cal** \-mə̇kəl\ *adj* [prob. fr. F *bionomique*, fr. *bionomie* bionomy + *-ique* -ic, -ical] **:** of or relating to ecology — **bi·o·nom·i·cal·ly** \-mə̇k(ə)lē\ *adv*

bi·o·nom·ics \-miks\ *n pl but sing or pl in constr* **:** ECOLOGY

bi·on·o·mist \bī'änəmə̇st\ *n* -s **:** ECOLOGIST

bi·on·o·my \-mē\ *n* -ES [²*bi-* + *-nomy*] **1 :** PHYSIOLOGY **2 :** ECOLOGY

bi·ont \'bī,änt\ *n* -s [²*bi-* + *-ont*] **:** a discrete unit of living matter **:** ORGANISM

-bi·ont \¦bī,änt, ,bē,änt\ *n comb form* -s [prob. fr. G, modif. of Gk *biount-, biōn* living, pres. part. of *bioun* to live, fr. *bios* mode of life — more at QUICK] **:** one having a (specified) mode of life ⟨aero*biont*⟩

bi·on·tic \(')bī¦äntik\ *adj, biol* **:** INDIVIDUAL — opposed to *phyletic* — **bi·on·ti·cal·ly** \-tə̇k(ə)lē\ *adv*

bi·operculate \¦bī+\ *adj* [¹*bi-* + *operculate*] **:** having two opercula

bi·oph·a·gous \(')bī¦äfəgəs\ *adj* [²*bi-* + *-phagous*] **:** using living organisms as food ⟨a ~ plant⟩ — **bi·oph·a·gy** \bī'äfəjē\ *n* -ES

bi·oph·i·lous \(ˈ)bī¦äfələs\ *adj* [²*bi-* + *-philous*] : PARASITIC 2a
bi·o·phore \ˈbīə,fō(ə)r, -ȯ(ə)r\ *also* **bi·o·phor** \-fō(ə)r\ *n* -s [G *biophor*, fr. *bio-* ²*bi-* + *-phor* -phore] : the ultimate supramolecular vital unit in Weismann's theory of life processes, being conceived as the basic building block of living structures — see DETERMINANT 5a, ID
bio·photogenesis \¸bī(¸)ō +\ *n* [NL, fr. ²*bi-* + *photogenesis*] : production of bioluminescence
bio·photometer \" +\ *n* [²*bi-* + *photometer*] : an instrument for measuring the rate and efficiency of dark adaptation of the eye used esp. in detecting vitamin A deficiency
bio·physical \¦bīō +\ *adj* [²*bi-* + *physical*] **1** : of or relating to biophysics **2** : involving biological and physical factors or considerations
bio·physicist \" +\ *n* [²*bi-* + *physicist*] : a specialist in biophysics
bio·physics \" +\ *n pl but sing or pl in constr* [ISV ²*bi-* + *physics*] : the physics of living organisms : the application of physical principles and methods to biological problems
bio·physiography \" +\ *n* [²*bi-* + *physiography*] : descriptive zoology and botany
bio·physiologist \" +\ *n* [²*bi-* + *physiologist*] : a specialist in general physiology
bio·physiology \" +\ *n* [²*bi-* + *physiology*] : GENERAL PHYSIOLOGY
bi·o·pic \ˈbīō,pik\ *n* -s [*bio*graphical *pic*ture] : a biographical motion picture
bi·o·plasm \ˈbīō,plazəm\ *n* -s [²*bi-* + *-plasm*] : living protoplasm as distinguished from ergastic substances — **bi·o·plas·mic** \¦bīō¦plazmik\ *adj*
bi·o·plast \ˈbīō,plast\ *n* -s [²*bi-* + *-plast*] **1** : ALTMANN'S GRANULES **2** : a functional unit of living protoplasm : CELL
bio·positive \¦bīō +\ *adj* [²*bi-* + *positive*] : REGENERATIVE; *specif* : relating to the phase of radiation damage to living tissue in which repair of previously disrupted tissue takes place (as in the replacing of X-ray-destroyed tumor cells by connective tissue)
bio·potency \" +\ *n* [²*bi-* + *potency*] : capacity to function in a biological system ⟨the ~ of a synthetic hormone⟩
bio·potential \" +\ *n* [*bio*electric *potential*] : a bioelectric potential
bio·precipitation \" +\ *n* [²*bi-* + *precipitation*] : precipitation brought about by biological agents (as in the activated-sludge process for sewage treatment)
bi·op·sy \ˈbī¸äpsē, ˈbīəp-, -si\ *n* -ES [ISV ²*bi-* + *-opsy*; orig. formed as F *biopsie*] : the removal of tissue, cells, or fluids from the living body for examination or study; *also* : the examination of such material esp. for diagnostic purposes
bio·psychic *also* **bio·psychical** \¦bīō +\ *adj* [²*bi-* + *psychic*, *psychical*] : of, relating to, or involving both psychic and biological phenomena : relating to the place of mind in life
bio·psychological \" +\ *adj* : of, relating to, or involving biology and psychology ⟨the human ~ makeup⟩
bio·psychology \" +\ *n* [²*bi-* + *psychology*] : psychology as related to biology or as a part of the vital processes
bi·o·pyr·i·bole \¸bīōˈpirə,bōl\ *adj* [*bio*tite + *pyr*oxene + amphi*bole*] *of igneous rocks* : composed of biotite, pyroxene, or amphibole
bi·orbital \(ˈ)bī +\ *adj* [¹*bi-* + *orbital*] : of or relating to the two orbits; *specif* : relating to a measure taken between the outer borders of the bony orbits on the skull or between the outer corners of the eyes on the living
¹**bi·os** \ˈbī,äs\ *n, pl* **bi·oi** \ˈbī,ȯi\ *or* **bioses** \ˈbī,äsəz\ [NL, fr. Gk, mode of life — more at QUICK] **1 a** : living beings **b** : organic nature **2** [F, fr. Gk] : a mixture of vitamins of the B complex including biotin, *meso*-inositol, and pantothenic acid extracted from various yeasts and essential for the optimum growth of these yeasts
²**bios** *pl of* BIO
bi·o·scope \ˈbīə,skōp\ *n* -s [²*bi-* + *-scope*] **1** : a motion-picture projector **2** *chiefly Brit* : a motion-picture theater
bi·ose \ˈbī,ōs\ *n* -s [ISV ¹*bi-* + *-ose*] **1** : DISACCHARIDE **2** : DIOSE
bio·seston \ˈbīō+,-\ *n* [²*bi-* + *seston*] : the living constituents of seston
-bi·o·sis \¸bīˈōsəs\ *n comb form, pl* **-bioses** [NL, fr. Gk *biōsis*, fr. *bioun* to live (fr. *bios* mode of life) + *-ōsis* -osis] : mode of life ⟨aero*biosis*⟩ ⟨necro*biosis*⟩
bio·social *or* **bio·sociological** \¦bīō+\ *adj* [²*bi-* + *social* or *sociological*] : of, relating to, or involving the interaction of the biological and the social : of or relating to animal or human aspects of social life as affected by biological principles or processes ⟨speech is a ~ activity⟩ : viewing the organism and environment as a complex unity
biosocial environment *n* : domesticated plants and animals as a factor affecting human life
bio·sociology \"+\ *n* [²*bi-* + *sociology*] : the study of social interaction in terms of analogy with the vital processes of the living organism
bi·o·some \ˈbīə,sōm\ *n* -s [²*bi-* + *-some*] : a self-perpetuating organized unit within protoplasm (as a chromonema)
bio·sphere \ˈbīō+,-\ *n* -s [²*bi-* + *sphere*] **1** : the part of the world in which life can exist including parts of the lithosphere, hydrosphere, and atmosphere **2** : living beings together with their environment
bio·statistical \¦bī(¸)ō+\ *adj* : relating to or according with biostatistics
bio·statistician \¸bī(¸)ō+\ *n* -s : a specialist in biostatistics
bio·statistics \"+\ *n pl but sing in constr* [²*bi-* + *statistics*] : statistical processes and methods applied to the analysis of biological phenomena
bio·stratigraphic *also* **bio·stratigraphical** \¦bīō+\ *adj* : of or relating to biostratigraphy : by the methods of biostratigraphy
biostratigraphic unit *n* : a group of geologic strata characterized by a particular fossil fauna or flora rather than by lithologic features
bio·stratigraphy \¦bī(¸)ō+\ *n* [²*bi-* + *stratigraphy*] : the part of paleontology that is directly related to the conditions and order of deposition of the sedimentary rocks : stratigraphic paleontology
bi·o·stromal \¦bīə¦strōməl\ *adj* : of or relating to a biostrome
bi·o·strome \ˈbīə,strōm\ *n* -s [²*bi-* + LL *stroma* coverlet, fr. Gk *strōma* bed, mattress] : a distinctly bedded or broadly lenticular body of rock composed mainly of the remains of sedentary organisms (as shell beds, crinoid beds, or coral beds) — compare BIOHERM
bio·synthesis \¸bīō+\ *n* [NL, fr. ²*bi-* + *synthesis*] : the production of a chemical compound by a living organism by either synthesis or degradation (as of adrenaline by vertebrates or of alcohol by yeasts) — **bio·synthetic** \¦bī(¸)ō+\ *adj* — **bio·synthetically** \"+\ *adv*
bio·systematic \¦bīō+\ *adj* : of or relating to biosystematy
bio·systematics \"+\ *n pl but sing or pl in constr* : BIOSYSTEMATY
bio·systematist \"+\ *n* -s : a specialist in biosystematy
bi·o·sys·tem·a·ty \¦bīōsəˈstemədē\ *n* -ES [²*bi-* + Gk *systēmat-*, *systēma* system + E *-y* — more at SYSTEM] : experimental taxonomy esp. as based on cytogenetics
¹**bi·o·ta** \bīˈōdə, ˈbīədə\ *n* -s [NL, fr. Gk *biotē* way of life, sustenance, fr. *bios* life — more at BIOTIC] : the animal and plant life of a region : living things : flora and fauna
²**biota** \"\ *n, cap* [NL, fr. Gk *biotē*] *in some classifications* : a genus of evergreen shrubs or small trees having branchlets in vertical planes and that is often included in *Thuja*
bio·technic *also* **bio·technical** \¦bīō+\ *adj* [²*bi-* + *technic*, *technical*] : of or relating to biotechnics; *also* : concerned with the adaptation of technology to the betterment of human life
bio·technics \"+\ *n pl but sing or pl in constr* [²*bi-* + *technics*] **1** : the control and adaptation of living organisms to the needs and ends of man **2** : the application of natural forms to problems of design and engineering
bio·technological \"+\ *adj* : of or relating to biotechnology
bio·technology \¦bī(¸)ō+\ *n* [²*b-* + *technology*] : the aspect of technology concerned with the application of biological and engineering data to problems relating to the mutual adjustment of man and the machine
bio·test \ˈbīō+,-\ *n* [²*bi-* + *test*] : BIOASSAY
bio·therapy \¦bīō+\ *n* [²*bi-* + *therapy*] : treatment of disease with products produced by living organisms (as vaccines, antisera, toxoids, or antigens)

¹**bi·ot·ic** \(ˈ)bī¦äd·ik, -ät|, |ēk *also* bēˈä-\ *also* **bi·ot·i·cal** \|əkəl, |ēk-\ *adj* [*biotic* fr. Gk *biōtikos* of life, fr. *biōtos* livable, worth living (fr. *bioun* to live, fr. *bios* life) + *-ikos* -ic; *biotical* fr. Gk *biōtikos* + E *-al*] : of or relating to life : BIOLOGIC ⟨a ~ community⟩ : induced or caused by the action of living beings ⟨~ alteration of a habitat⟩
²**biotic** \"\ *n* -s [by shortening] : ANTIBIOTIC
-biotic \(¸)ō¦=+\ *adj comb form* [prob. fr. NL *-bioticus*, fr. Gk *biōtikos*] **1** : relating to life : life ⟨anti*biotic*⟩ **2** : having a (specified) mode of life ⟨aero*biotic*⟩ ⟨necro*biotic*⟩
biotic climax *n* : an ecological climax primarily due to the action of living organisms
biotic formation *n* : BIOME
biotic potential *n* **1** : the inherent capacity of an organism or species to reproduce and survive, being usu. expressed in terms of numbers that could be produced under optimum conditions and in the absence of environmental resistance **2** : CARRYING CAPACITY
biotic province *n* : a geographic region characterized by the presence of one or more ecological associations that differ at least quantitatively from those of adjoining provinces and marked by a tendency to act as a center of ecological dispersion
bi·o·tin \ˈbīətən\ *n* -s [ISV *biot-* (fr. Gk *biotos* life, sustenance, fr. *bios* life, way of life) + *-in*; orig. formed in G] : a colorless crystalline growth vitamin $C_{10}H_{16}N_2O_3S$ of the vitamin B complex that occurs widely (as in yeast, liver, and egg yolk) usu. in combined form, that is inactivated by combination with avidin in the case of egg-white injury, and that is involved in the fixation of carbon dioxide (as by pyruvate to form oxalacetate) in mammals and bacteria
bi·o·tite \ˈbīə,tīt\ *n* -s [G *biotit*, fr. Jean B. *Biot* †1862 Fr. mathematician + G *-it* -ite] : a generally black or dark green form of mica $K_2(Mg,Fe,Al)_6(Si,Al)_8O_{20}(OH)_4$ forming a constituent of crystalline rocks and being a silicate of iron, magnesium, potassium, and aluminum (hardness 2.5-3) — **bi·o·tit·ic** \¦bīə¦tid·ik\ *adj*
bi·o·tit·ize \ˈbīə,tīd·,īz, -ətə,tīz\ *also* **bi·o·tize** \ˈbīə,tīz\ *vt* -ED/-ING/-S : to transform (a metamorphic rock) into biotite by replacement of other components
bi·o·tope \ˈbīə,tōp\ *n* -s [²*bi-* + Gk *topos* place — more at TOPIC] : a region uniform in environmental conditions and in its populations of animals and plants for which it is the habitat
biot-sa·vart law \¦bē,ōsə¦vär-, ¦byōsə-\ *n, usu cap B&S* [after Jean B. *Biot* †1862 Fr. mathematician and Félix *Savart* †1841 Fr. physician & physicist] : a statement in electromagnetism: the magnetic intensity at any point due to a steady current in an infinitely long straight wire is directly proportional to the current and inversely proportional to the distance from point to wire — compare AMPERE'S LAW
bi·o·type \ˈbīə,tīp\ *n* -s [ISV ²*bi-* + *type*; orig. formed as G *biotypus*] **1** : all the organisms sharing a specified genotype; *also* : the genotype so shared or the peculiarity distinguishing such a genotype ⟨the silver ~ in red foxes⟩ ⟨the species may be considered a complex assemblage of ~s⟩ **2** : a group of individuals sharing many psychological traits — **bi·o·typ·ic** \¦=¦tipik\ *adj*
bi·o·ty·po·gram \¦bīə¦tīpə,gram\ *n* [*biotype* + *-o-* + *-gram*] : a set of diagrams or test scores reflecting the basic physical and psychological characteristics of an individual
bi·o·ty·pol·o·gy \¸bīə,tīˈpäləjē\ *n* -ES [*biotype* + *-o-* + *-logy*] : the study of biotypes
bi·ovular \(ˈ)bī+\ *adj* [¹*bi-* + *ovular*] : derived from two ova — used of fraternal twins or their characteristic state; compare MONOVULAR
bi·oxalate \(ˈ)bī+\ *n* [¹*bi* + *oxalate*] : BINOXALATE
bio·zone \ˈbīō+,-\ *n* [²*bi-* + *zone*] : the temporal and stratigraphic range of a kind of organism (as of a species) as reflected by its occurrence in fossiliferous rocks
bi·pack \ˈbī+,-\ *n* -s [¹*bi-* + *pack*] : a pair of films each sensitive to a different color that are used in color photography by simultaneous exposure one through the other usu. with the emulsion surfaces in contact — compare TRIPACK
bi·pa·li·um \bīˈpālēəm\ *n, cap* [NL, fr. L, double mattock, fr. *bi-* ¹*bi-* + *pala* shovel, spade + *-ium*] : a genus (the type of the family Bipaliidae) of terrestrial mostly large triclad flatworms occurring in tropical countries and having the head end expanded into a semicircular plate
bi·palmate \(ˈ)bī+\ *adj* [¹*bi-* + *palmate*] : palmate with the segments again palmate ⟨some compound leaves are ~⟩
bi·parasitic \¦bī+\ *adj* [¹*bi-* + *parasitic*] : parasitic upon or in a parasite
bi·parental \"+\ *adj* [¹*bi-* + *parental*] : of, relating to, or derived from two parents — **bi·parentally** \"+\ *adv*
bi·parietal \"+\ *adj* [ISV ¹*bi-* + *parietal*] *anthrop* : of or relating to the parietal bones; *specif* : being a measurement between the most distant opposite points of the two parietal bones
bip·a·rous \ˈbipərəs\ *adj* [¹*bi-* + *-parous*] **1** : bringing forth two young at a birth **2** *of a plant part* : having branches or axes dichotomous ⟨a ~ cyme⟩
bi·par·ti·ent \(ˈ)bī¦pärd·ēənt\ *adj* [L *bipartient-*, *bipartiens*, pres. part. of *bipartire* to divide into two parts, fr. *bi-* ¹*bi-* + *partire*, *partiri* to divide — more at PART] : dividing into two parts : dividing twice
bi·parting \ˈbī+,-\ *adj* [¹*bi-* + *parting*] *of a door or gate* : composed of two sections that open away from each other
bi·partisan *also* **bi·partizan** \(ˈ)bī+\ *adj* [¹*bi-* + *partisan*, *partizan*] : representing or composed of members of two parties; *specif* : marked by accord and cooperation between two major political parties ⟨a ~ foreign policy⟩
bi·partisanism \"+\ *n* -s : the quality or state of being bipartisan
bi·partisanship \"+\ *n* -s : a bipartisan relation; *esp* : formulation of governmental policy by compromise and agreement between two major political parties esp. in respect to foreign affairs
bi·par·tite \(ˈ)bīˈpär,tīt, -pä| *also* |d·,īt, *usu* īd· +V\ *adj* [L *bipartitus*, past part. of *bipartire* to divide into two parts] **1** : being in two parts : having two correspondent parts one for each party ⟨a ~ contract⟩ ⟨~ writing⟩ : shared by two ⟨a ~ treaty⟩ **2** : divided into two parts almost to the base ⟨~ leaf⟩ : consisting of two subdivisions — **bi·par·tite·ly** *adv*
bi·par·ti·tion \¦bī(¸)pärˈtishən, ¸bīpər-\ *n* [L *bipartitus* + E *-ion*] : the act of dividing or state of being divided into two parts, esp. two corresponding parts
bi·party \(ˈ)bī+\ *adj* [¹*bi-* + *party*] : TWO-PARTY
bi·paschal \"+\ *adj* [¹*bi-* + *paschal*] : including two Passover feasts — used of a theory that regards Christ's public ministry as of only about one year's duration
bi·pectinate \"+\ *adj* [¹*bi-* + *pectinate*] **1** *also* **bi·pectinated** \"+\ : having two margins toothed like a comb — used esp. of the antennae of certain moths **2** : branched like a feather on both sides of a main shaft ⟨the organ of smell in certain snails is ~⟩
¹**bi·ped** \ˈbī,ped *sometimes* -,pəd\ *adj* [L *biped-*, *bipes*, fr. *bi-* ¹*bi-* + *ped-*, *pes* foot — more at FOOT] : two-footed
²**biped** \-,ped\ *n* -s **1** : a two-footed animal (as man) **2** : any two of the legs of a horse or other quadruped — called also according to the legs involved *anterior biped*, *diagonal biped*, *lateral biped*, *posterior biped*
bi·ped·al \(ˈ)bī¦pedᵊl *also* -¦pē- *sometimes* ˈbipədᵊl\ *adj* [¹*bi-* + *pedal*] **1** : having two feet : BIPED **2** : of or relating to a biped
bi·ped·al·ism \(ˈ)bī¦pedᵊl,izəm *also* -¦pēd- *sometimes* ˈbipəd-\ *or* **bi·pe·dal·i·ty** \¦bīpəˈdaləd·ē *sometimes* ¸bip-\ *n, pl* **bipedalisms** *or* **bipedalities** : the condition of having but two feet or of using only two for locomotion if more are present ⟨the ~ of some desert lizards⟩
bi·peltate \(ˈ)bī+\ *adj* [¹*bi-* + *peltate*] **1** *zool* : having a shell or covering like a double shield **2** *bot* : having two shield-shaped parts
bi·penniform \"+\ *adj* [¹*bi-* + *penniform*] : resembling a feather barbed on both sides — used of certain muscles from the arrangement of their fibers
bi·phasic \"+\ *adj* [¹*bi-* + *phasic*] : having two phases; *specif* : having both a sporophytic and a gametophytic phase in the life cycle
bi·phenyl \(ˈ)bī+\ *n* [ISV ¹*bi-* + *phenyl*] : a white crystalline hydrocarbon $C_6H_5C_6H_5$ obtained usu. by heating vapors of benzene to about 800°C and used chiefly in a mixture with phenyl ether as an industrial heat-transfer medium — called also *diphenyl*
bi·phonemic \¦bī+\ *adj* [¹*bi-* + *phonemic*] : constituting, consisting of, or standing for two phonemes
bi·phosphate \(ˈ)bī+\ *n* [¹*bi-* + *phosphate*] : an acid phosphate (as sodium acid phosphate) : a monobasic phosphate
bi·phyletic \¦bī+\ *adj* [¹*bi-* + *phyletic*] : descended or evolved in two branches from common ancestry — **bi·phyletically** \"+\ *adv*
bi·pin \ˈbī,pin\ *adj* [¹*bi-* + *pin*] : having two terminal pins that fit into corresponding sockets — used of certain lamp or vacuum-tube bases and cable terminals
bi·pin·nar·ia \¸bīpəˈna(a)rēə\ *n* -s [NL, fr. ¹*bi-* + L *pinna* feather + NL *-aria* — more at FIN] : a bilaterally symmetrical free-swimming larva of certain starfishes that swims by means of ciliated bands
bi·pinnate \(ˈ)bī+\ *adj* [¹*bi-* + *pinnate*] : twice pinnate — **bi·pinnately** \"+\ *adv*
bi·pinnatifid \¦bī+\ *adj* [¹*bi-* + *pinnatifid*] : pinnatifid with the segments or divisions also pinnatifid
bi·place \ˈ=,=\ *adj* [¹*bi-* + *place*] *of an airplane* : having space for two occupants
bi·planar \(ˈ)bī+\ *adj* [¹*bi-* + *planar*] : lying in two planes
¹**bi·plane** \ˈbī+,-\ *n* [¹*bi-* + *plane*] : an airplane with two main supporting surfaces usu. placed one above the other
²**biplane** \"\ *adj* [¹*bi-* + *plane*] : acting in or taking place from two planes ⟨a ~ examination of the hip joint⟩ ⟨~ fluoroscopy⟩ : having parts arranged in two planes esp. at right angles to one another ⟨a ~ filament lamp⟩
biplane fluoroscope *n* : an X-ray machine by means of which examinations and roentgenograms can be made in the horizontal and the vertical planes

biplane

bipli·cate \(ˈ)bīˈplī,kāt, ˈbipləkət\ *adj* [¹*bi-* + *plicate*] : twice folded
bi·pod \ˈbī,päd\ *n* -s [¹*bi-* + *-pod* (as in *tripod*)] : a two-legged mount (as for an automatic rifle) or support (as for a mast)
bi·polar \(ˈ)bī+\ *adj* [¹*bi-* + *polar*] **1 a** : having or involving the use of two poles ⟨a ~ dynamo⟩ ⟨~ encephalograph leads⟩ **b** *of a neuron* : having an afferent and an efferent process **2** : relating to or associated with the polar regions ⟨certain marine organisms have a ~ distribution and are found only north and south of an equatorial or median zone⟩ **3** : having or marked by two mutually repellent forces or two diametrically opposed natures, qualities, or views
bi·polarity \¦bī+\ *n* -ES [ISV *bipolar* + *-ity*] : the quality or state of being bipolar: as **a** : identity or similarity between fauna of northern regions and that of southern, the fauna of the intervening regions being different **b** : AMBIVALENCE
bi·po·lar·ize \(ˈ)bī+ˈ-\ *vt* : to bring into a bipolar state
bi·post \ˈbī,pōst\ *adj* [¹*bi-* + *post*] : BIPIN — used esp. of a high-power lamp base having heavy pins
bi·potential \¦bī+\ *adj* [¹*bi-* + *potential*] *biol* : having potentiality for development in either of two mutually exclusive directions ⟨the larva of *Bonellia* is ~ for sex⟩
bi·potentiality \"+\ *n* : capacity to function as male or female : HERMAPHRODITISM
bi·prism \ˈbī+,-\ *n* [¹*bi-* + *prism*] : a triangular prism with vertex angle of nearly 180° used to obtain images of a single source in observing the interference of light — called also *Fresnel biprism*
¹**bi·propellant** \¦bī+\ *n* [¹*bi-* + *propellant*] : a rocket propellant consisting of separate fuel and oxidizer that come together only in a combustion chamber; *also* : either of these substances — compare MONOPROPELLANT
²**bipropellant** \"\ *adj* : of, relating to, or employing a bipropellant
bi·punctal *or* **bi·punctual** \(ˈ)bī+\ *adj* [¹*bi-* + *punctal* or *punctual*] : having or relating to two points
bi·punctate \"+\ *adj* [¹*bi-* + *punctate*] *bot* : marked with two spots
bi·pyramid \(ˈ)bī+\ *n* [¹*bi-* + *pyramid*] : DIPYRAMID
bi·pyramidal \¦bī+\ *adj* [¹*bi-* + *pyramidal*] : DIPYRAMIDAL
¹**bi·quadratic** \"+\ *adj* [¹*bi-* + *quadratic*] : of or relating to the fourth power in mathematics
²**biquadratic** \"\ *n* **1** : a fourth power in mathematics **2** : a biquadratic equation
biquadratic equation *n* : an algebraic equation of the fourth degree — called also *quartic equation*
bi·quarterly \(ˈ)bī+\ *adj* [¹*bi-* + *quarterly*] : occurring twice every three months
bi·quartz \ˈbī+,-\ *n* [¹*bi-* + *quartz*] : a quartz plate made up of a dextrorotatory and a levorotatory half and used in detecting polarization
bi·quintile \(ˈ)bī+\ *n* [¹*bi-* + *quintile*] : an aspect of the planets when their positions are twice the fifth part of a great circle apart or at an angle of 144 degrees
bi·racial \(ˈ)bī+\ *adj* [¹*bi-* + *racial*] : of, relating to, or involving members of two races ⟨~ strife⟩ ⟨~ organizations⟩; *esp* : concerned with the separate coexistence of white and Negro populations ⟨a ~ school system⟩ — **bi·racialism** \"+\ *n* -s
bi·radial \(ˈ)bī+\ *adj* [¹*bi-* + *radial*] : having both bilateral and radial symmetry ⟨a ~ ctenophore⟩ — see CTENOPHORA
bi·radiate *also* **bi·radiated** \(ˈ)bī+\ *adj* [¹*bi-* + *radiate*] : having two rays
bi·radical \(ˈ)bī+\ *n* [¹*bi-* + *radical*] : a free radical or compound (as sulfur monoxide ·SO·) with two unpaired electrons
bi·ramous *also* **bi·ramose** \(ˈ)bī+\ *adj* [¹*bi-* + *ramous*, *ramose*] : having or consisting of two branches ⟨a ~ antenna⟩
¹**birch** \ˈbərch, ˈbəch, ˈbəich\ *n* -ES *often attrib* [ME *birche*, *birk*, fr. OE *birce*, *beorc*; akin to OHG *birka* birch, ON *björk* birch, L *fraxinus* ash tree, Skt *bhūrja* birch, OE *beorht* bright — more at BRIGHT] **1 a** : a tree of the genus *Betula* — see PAPER BIRCH, RIVER BIRCH, SWEET BIRCH, WHITE BIRCH, YELLOW BIRCH **b** *Austral* : PIRIPIRI **c** *NewZeal* : any of various trees resembling those of the genus *Betula* (as the kamahi or the native beeches) **d** : GUMBO-LIMBO **2** : the wood or timber of the birch **3** : a birch rod or a bundle of twigs for whipping an offender : SWITCH **4** : BIRCHBARK
²**birch** \"\ *vt* -ED/-ING/-ES : to beat with or as if with a birch : CANE, WHIP : punish (as a schoolboy) by caning or whipping
birchbark \ˈ=,=\ *n* : a canoe made of birch bark
birch beer *n* : a sweetened effervescent beverage including oil of birch or oil of wintergreen among its flavoring ingredients and prepared by carbonating or fermenting
birch borer *n* : an insect larva that bores in the wood of birch trees; *esp* : the bronze birch borer (*Agrilus anxius*) that burrows just beneath the bark
birch·en \-chən\ *adj* [ME *birchen*, *birken*, fr. *birche*, *birk* + *-en*] : of or relating to birch
birch family *n* : BETULACEAE
birching *n* -s : a beating with a birch : CANING, WHIPPING
birch-leaf mahogany \ˈ=,=-\ *n* : a hardtack (*Cercocarpus betuloides*)
birch leaf miner *n* : a small black sawfly (*Fenusa pusilla*) native to Europe but now established in much of eastern No. America with a larva that mines in the leaves of various birches often causing serious defoliation
birch oil *n* **1** : BIRCH-TAR OIL **2** : an essential oil obtained from the bark or twigs of the sweet birch that resembles wintergreen oil in consisting chiefly of methyl salicylate and is used similarly to methyl salicylate — called also *sweet-birch oil*
birch partridge *n* : RUFFED GROUSE
birch rod *n* : BIRCH 3
birch skeletonizer *n* : a small tineoid moth (*Bucculatrix canadensisella*) whose larva attacks birch leaves
birch-tar oil \ˈ=,=-\ *n* : a brown toxic phenolic oil obtained by destructive distillation of the bark and wood of the European white birch and used in finishing Russia leather to which it gives the characteristic odor and sometimes in ointments for skin diseases (as eczema) — called also *birch oil*
birchwood \ˈ=,=\ *n* **1** : BIRCH 2 **2** : a wood or grove of birch trees

¹bird \'bərd, 'bə̄d, 'bəid\ *n* -s [ME *brid, bird* young bird, bird, fr. OE *bridd* young bird] **1 a** *archaic* **:** the young of a feathered vertebrate (as a chick, eaglet, or duckling) **:** NESTLING **b :** any young animal as: (1) *obs* **:** CHILD, YOUNGSTER (2) **:** a girl or young woman — now usu. used somewhat facetiously or as a term of endearment **2 a :** a member of the class Aves all differing from the ancestral reptiles in possession of a covering of feathers instead of scales, a completely four-chambered heart served by a single (the right) aortic arch, fully separate systemic and pulmonary circulations, a warm-blooded metabolism, and large eggs with hard calcareous shells, and all recent forms having the forelimbs modified into wings, the jaws without teeth and enclosed in horny sheathes, and usu. the breastbone enlarged by a ventral keel for the attachment of the pectoral muscles that control the action of the wings **b :** an adult of any variety of domestic poultry ⟨a table ~⟩ ⟨a show ~⟩ ⟨housing for 3000 ~s and 1000 poults⟩ **3 :** GAME BIRD; *esp* **:** PARTRIDGE **4 :** a saucer (as of pottery) made to be thrown from a spring trap and used in skeet and as a substitute for a live bird in trapshooting **:** CLAY PIGEON **5** *slang* **a :** FELLOW, CHAP **:** a peculiar or inconsequential person — usu. used somewhat patronizingly ⟨a queer ~⟩ ⟨a gay old ~⟩ **b** (1) **:** a notably clever or accomplished person — often used ironically ⟨her grandfather really is a ~⟩ (2) **:** something admirable of its kind ⟨a ~ of a filly⟩ ⟨a ~ of a scheme⟩ **6 :** SHUTTLECOCK 1a **7 :** a hissing or jeering expressive of disapproval ⟨the crowd gave him the ~⟩; *also* **:** dismissal from employment ⟨I've got to get busy if I don't want to get the ~⟩ **8 :** a small thin piece of meat rolled up with stuffing and skewered, browned, and braised — see VEAL BIRD **9 :** GUIDED MISSILE — **bird in the hand** [from the proverb "a bird in the hand is worth two in the bush"] **:** something assured or definite rather than the merely possible — **for the birds :** WORTHLESS, RIDICULOUS, NONSENSICAL ⟨that's *for the birds*⟩

bird (waxwing): *1* bill, *2* forehead, *3* crown, *4* crest, *5* auricular region, *6* throat, *7* breast, *8* abdomen, *9* under tail coverts, *10* tail, *11* primaries, *12* secondaries, *13* upper wing coverts, *14* scapulars

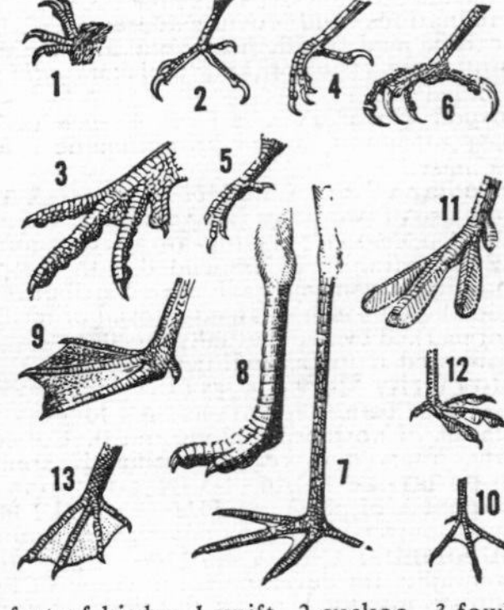

feet of birds: *1* swift, *2* cuckoo, *3* fowl, *4* finch, *5* kingfisher, *6* hawk, *7* stork, *8* ostrich, *9* duck, *10* sandpiper, *11* grebe, *12* coot, *13* pelican

²bird \"\ *vi* -ED/-ING/-S **:** to observe or identify wild birds in their natural environment

bird-alane \ˌbərdəˈlān\ *var of* BURD-ALANE

birdbander \'ₑ,ₑₑ\ *n* **:** one that bands birds — **birdbanding** \'ₑ,ₑₑ\ *n*

birdbath \'ₑ,ₑ\ *n* **1 :** a usu. ornamental vessel provided esp. in gardens for birds to bathe in **2** *also* **birdbath dish :** a small usu. oval saucedish used esp. formerly for the serving of individual portions of vegetables

bird-batting \'ₑ,ₑₑ\ *n, now dial* **:** BATFOWLING

bird bell *n* **:** RATTLESNAKE ROOT a

birdberry \'ₑ- — *see* BERRY\ *n* **:** PEPPER VINE 2

bird bills *n pl* [so called fr. the shape of the flowers] **:** SHOOTING STAR 2

bird-bolt \'ₑ,ₑ\ *n* **:** a short blunt missile (as a blunt arrow) formerly used for killing birds without piercing them

bird box *n* **:** a box for wild birds to nest in **:** BIRDHOUSE

birdbrain \'ₑ,ₑ\ *n* **:** a flighty thoughtless person **:** SCATTERBRAIN **:** a stupid person — **bird-brained** \'ₑ¦ₑ\ *adj*

birdcage \'ₑ,ₑ\ *n* [ME, fr. *bird* + *cage*] **1 :** a cage for confining birds **2 :** something resembling a birdcage (as a wire cage for dice) **3 :** CHUCK-A-LUCK **4** *Brit* **:** a paddock in which horses are saddled at a racecourse **5 :** a double-block construction to allow the top of a tilt-top table to revolve as well as to tip up when not in use

birdcage clock *n* **:** LANTERN CLOCK

birdcall \'ₑ,ₑ\ *n* **1 :** the note or cry of a bird or a sound made in imitation of it **2 :** an instrument (as a whistle) used in imitating a birdcall

bird cherry *n* **1 :** any of several small-fruited cherry trees frequented or fed on by birds: as **a :** EUROPEAN BIRD CHERRY **b :** PIN CHERRY 1 **2 :** the fruit of a bird cherry

bird-claw \'ₑ¦ₑ\ *adj* **:** like the claw of a bird esp. in gauntness and lack of flesh ⟨trembling *bird-claw* hands⟩

bird colonel *n* [so called fr. the eagle of the insignia] *slang* **:** a colonel as distinguished from a lieutenant colonel

bird dog *n* **1 :** a gun dog trained to locate or to retrieve birds for the hunter **2 :** one that seeks out or locates: as **a :** CANVASSER; *esp* **:** one who locates prospects for a salesman **b :** a talent scout esp. in sports **c :** one (as a detective) who pries after information **d :** one who steals another's date

bird-dog \'ₑ,ₑ\ *vb* [*bird dog*] *vi* **:** to play the part of a bird dog **:** watch closely **~** *vt* **:** to seek out **:** follow and detect **:** FERRET, DOG

birded *past of* BIRD

bird·er \-də(r)\ *n* -s [ME, fr. *bird* + *-er*] **1 :** a catcher or hunter of birds; *esp* **:** a person who kills birds in quantity for market **2 :** an observer or identifier of wild birds in their natural surroundings

birdeye \'ₑ,ₑ\ *n* [so called fr. the spot resembling an eye in the flower's center] **:** a partially woody herb (*Caperonia castaneaefolia*) of the spurge family occurring in wet soils of the southeastern U.S. and having alternate toothed leaves and flowers in elongate interrupted spikelike clusters — called also *Mexican weed*

bird-eyed \'ₑ¦ₑ\ *adj* **1 :** having eyes like a bird **:** having something (as spots) suggesting the eyes of a bird ⟨a *bird-eyed* tissue⟩ **2 :** easily frightened **:** SKITTISH — used chiefly of horses

bird flower *n* **1 :** BIRD-OF-PARADISE **2 :** any of several flowers the pollination of which is accomplished by birds (usu. hummingbirds): as **a :** OSWEGO TEA **b :** CARDINAL FLOWER **3 :** BIRD PLANT

bird font *n* **:** BIRDBATH

bird-foot *var of* BIRD'S-FOOT

bird-foot delta *n* **:** a delta (as that of the Mississippi river) having many levee-bordered channels extending seaward like outstretched claws

bird grape *n* **:** a wild grape (*Vitis munsoniana*) of Florida, Georgia, and the Bahamas closely related to the muscadine

bird grass *n* **1 :** KNOTGRASS 1 **2 :** ROUGH BLUEGRASS

birdhouse \'ₑ,ₑ\ *n* **1 :** an artificial nesting site (as a box or other container) for birds **2 :** an enclosure or building where birds are confined and exhibited **:** AVIARY

¹bird·ie \-dē,-di\ *n* -s [¹*bird* + *-ie*] **1 :** a little bird — often used as a pet name **2 :** a golf score of one stroke less than par on a hole **3 :** any of various sounds suggesting the chirp or trill of a bird

²birdie \"\ *vt* -ED/-ING/-S **:** to shoot (a hole in golf) in one stroke under par ⟨*birdied* the 18th hole to win the match⟩

birdie in the cage *or* **bird in the cage** *n* **:** a square-dance figure in which three members of a two-couple team encircle the fourth dancer

birdier *comparative of* BIRDY

birdiest *superlative of* BIRDY

birding *pres part of* BIRD

bird-in-the-bush \ˈ¦ₑₑₑˈₑ\ *n* **:** PRICKLY POPPY

bird knotgrass *n* **:** KNOTGRASS 1

bird·less \-dləs\ *adj* **:** being without a bird

birdlife \'ₑ,ₑ\ *n* **:** AVIFAUNA; *also* **:** the activities and habits of the constituent birds ⟨~ of this state⟩

bird·like \'ₑ,ₑ\ *adj* **:** like a bird esp. in dainty alertness or in voice

¹birdlime \'ₑ,ₑ\ *n* [ME *birdlim, bridlim*, fr. *bird, brid* bird + *lim* lime — more at BIRD, LIME] **1 :** an extremely adhesive sticky substance usu. made from the bark of the holly (*Ilex aquifolium*) but also from other plants (as the European mistletoe or the breadfruit) and used esp. formerly to entrap small birds by smearing twigs where they are accustomed to perch **2 :** something that entraps or ensnares ⟨a ~ of words⟩ **3 :** CLEAVERS

²birdlime \"\ *vt* **:** to smear with or as if with birdlime **:** catch with birdlime **:** ENSNARE

bird·ling \'ₑ + (,)liŋ, (,)lēŋ\ *n* -s [¹*bird* + *-ling*] **:** a little bird **:** NESTLING, FLEDGLING

bird louse *n* **:** any of numerous wingless insects of the order Mallophaga mostly parasitic on birds, a few on mammals, all having mouths adapted to biting, not sucking, and feeding on the feathers, hair, or skin of the host often causing injury — called also *biting louse*

bird malaria *n* **:** a febrile disease of wild birds and poultry that is physiologically comparable to human malaria and caused by related protozoan parasites of *Plasmodium* and related genera

bird·man \'ₑ + mən, -,man, ,ma(ə)n; *in sense 2 usu* + mən\ *n, pl* **birdmen 1 :** one that deals with birds (as a fowler or an ornithologist) **2 :** AVIATOR, AIRMAN; *sometimes* **:** an airplane passenger

bird mite *n* **:** any of numerous small mites parasitic upon birds; *esp* **:** CHICKEN MITE

bird of freedom : BALD EAGLE; *also* **:** a representation of it (as on the coat of arms and coins of the U.S.)

bird of jove *usu cap J* [after *Jove* (Jupiter), ancient Roman divinity — more at JOVE] **:** EAGLE

bird of ju·no \-'jü(,)nō\ *usu cap J* [after *Juno*, ancient Roman goddess, consort of Jupiter, fr. L] **:** PEACOCK

bird of minerva *usu cap M* [after *Minerva*, ancient Roman goddess] **:** OWL

bird of night : OWL

bird of paradise 1 : any of a number of birds of the family Paradisaeidae inhabiting New Guinea and the adjacent islands notable for the brilliant colors, graceful plumes, and often remarkably developed tail feathers of the adult males, the females and young being without plumes and plainly colored **2 :** *in New South Wales* **:** LYREBIRD

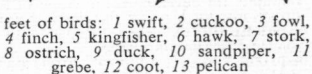

bird of paradise

bird-of-paradise \ˈ¦ₑₑˈₑₑ(,)ₑ\ *or* **bird-of-paradise flower** *n* [*bird of paradise*] **1 :** an ornamental bananalike plant (*Strelitzia reginae*) having scapes of orange and purple flowers suggestive of a bird **2 :** a poinciana (*Poinciana gilliesii*) with colorful red and yellow flowers

bird of passage 1 : a migratory bird **2 :** a person who moves freely from one place to another and usu. has no permanently fixed abode **:** ROLLING STONE; *sometimes* **:** an immigrant laborer temporarily in a country

bird of prey : any of various carnivorous birds that feed wholly or chiefly on meat taken by hunting as opposed to carrion and including most members of the orders Falconiformes and Strigiformes (as hawks, eagles, and owls)

bird of wonder : PHOENIX

bird-on-the-wing \ˈ¦ₑₑₑˈₑ\ *n* [so called fr. the shape of the flower] **:** GAYWINGS

bird peck *n* **:** a small spot of distorted grain or a hole in wood attributed to damage by birds

bird pepper *n* **:** a pepper having very small oblong red fruits that are among the most pungent of all peppers, commonly occurring wild or spontaneously in warm countries, and being considered to constitute the type of a species (*Capsicum frutescens*) or to be a variety (*C. frutescens baccatum*) of this species

bird pest *or* **bird plague** *n* **:** FOWL PLAGUE

bird plant *n* **:** a Mexican herb (*Heterotoma lobelioides*) having yellow-and-purple flowers that suggest the form of a bird — called also *bird flower, canarybird flower*

bird pox *n* **:** FOWL POX

bird rattle *n* **:** a device for scaring birds away from fields or gardens by making a rattling noise

bird-ringer \'ₑ,ₑₑ\ *n, Brit* **:** BIRDBANDER — **bird-ringing** \'ₑ,ₑₑ\ *n* -S

birds *pl of* BIRD, *pres 3d sing of* BIRD

bird's-beak \'ₑ,ₑ\ *n, pl* **bird's-beaks 1 :** an architectural molding with a section resembling a beak **2** [so called fr. the shape of the flower] **:** a California herb of the genus *Cordylanthus* (family Scrophulariaceae)

bird's-bread \'ₑ,ₑ\ *n, pl* **bird's-breads :** a stonecrop (*Sedum acre*)

birdseed \'ₑ,ₑ\ *n* **1 :** a mixture of small seeds (as those of hemp, millet, and certain grasses) used chiefly for feeding cage birds **2 :** the common groundsel (*Senecio vulgaris*)

birdseed grass *n* **:** CANARY GRASS 1

bird's-egg green \'ₑ,ₑ-\ *n* **:** ROBIN'S-EGG BLUE

¹bird's-eye \'ₑ,ₑ\ *n, pl* **bird's-eyes 1 :** any of numerous plants with bright-colored flowers: as **a :** a primrose (*Primula farinosa*) having a pale lilac flower with a yellow eye **b** *Brit* (1) **:** GERMANDER SPEEDWELL (2) **:** PHEASANT'S-EYE (3) **:** BIRD'S-FOOT TREFOIL (4) **:** HERB ROBERT **2 a :** an allover geometric pattern for textiles consisting of a small diamond with a center dot resembling a bird's eye **b :** a fabric esp. of cotton, linen, or worsted woven with this pattern **3 :** a small spot with the wood fibers arranged around it in the form of an ellipse in some lumber **4 :** a spot on coated paper caused by a particle of grease in the coating mixture

²bird's-eye \"\ *adj* **1 a :** seen from above as if by a flying bird **:** PANORAMIC ⟨a *bird's-eye* view⟩ **b :** GENERAL, CURSORY, SUPERFICIAL ⟨a *bird's-eye* survey of American politics⟩ **2 :** marked with spots resembling birds' eyes ⟨*bird's-eye* diaper⟩ ⟨a *bird's-eye* scarf⟩ **3** [*bird's-eye (maple)*] **:** made of bird's-eye maple ⟨a *bird's-eye* chest⟩ ⟨*bird's-eye* veneer⟩

bird's-eye maple *n* **:** wood of the sugar maple in which a wavy grain causes eyelike markings

bird's-eye primrose *n* **:** any of several bright-flowered primroses; *esp* **:** BIRD'S-EYE 1a

bird's-eye rot *n* **:** anthracnose of the grape caused by a fungus (*Elsinoe ampelina*) and manifested by small sunken dark fruit spots with light centers

bird's-eyes \'ₑ,ₑ\ *n pl but sing or pl in constr* **:** an erect annual garden herb (*Gilia tricolor*) with dissected leaves and corolla having a yellowish tube, a purple-marked throat, and violet or lilac lobes

bird's-eye spot *n* **:** a disease of plants characterized by round dark spots with lighter surrounding tissue suggesting the appearance of a bird's eye: as **a :** a disease of tea leaves caused by a fungus (*Orcospora theae*) **b :** a leaf spot of the Hevea rubber tree caused by a fungus (*Helminthosporium heveae*)

bird's-foot *also* **bird-foot** \'ₑ,ₑ\ *n, pl* **bird's-foots** *also* **bird-foots :** any of numerous plants having leaves or flowers resembling the foot of a bird; *specif* **:** a plant of the genus *Ornithopus* having bent and jointed pods or of the related genera *Lotus* and *Trigonella*

bird's-foot clover *n* **:** BIRD'S-FOOT TREFOIL

bird's-foot fern *n* **:** a rock brake (*Pellaea ornithopus*) of the Pacific coast of No. America having some of the lower pinnules replaced by secondary pinnae each consisting of three sessile pinnules arranged so as to suggest a bird's foot

bird's-foot trefoil *n* **1 :** a plant of the genus *Lotus*: as **a :** a European plant (*L. corniculatus*) having claw-shaped pods and now widely used esp. in the U. S. as a forage and fodder plant — called also *babies'-slippers* **b :** PRAIRIE BIRD'S-FOOT TREFOIL **2 :** a glabrous annual or perennial prostrate Old World herb (*Trigonella ornithopodioides*) related to fenugreek

bird's-foot violet *also* **bird-foot violet** *n* **:** a common violet (*Viola pedata*) of the eastern U.S. with pedate leaves and large pale blue or purple flowers that resemble pansies — see PANSY VIOLET

bird shot *n* **:** shot of small size for shooting birds

birds-in-the-bush \ˈ¦ₑₑₑˈₑ\ *n* **:** PRICKLY POPPY

bird skin *n* **:** the skin of a bird; *specif* **:** the external part of a bird prepared for study or display by removing most parts internal to the skin and replacing them with cotton or tow

bird's knotgrass *n* **:** KNOTGRASS 1

bird's-mouth \'ₑ,ₑ\ *n, pl* **bird's-mouths :** an interior angle of notch cut across the end of a piece of timber to receive the edge of another piece

bird snake *n* **:** a back-fanged tree snake (*Thelotornis kirtlandii*) of tropical and southern Africa having a slender body and a green head that allow it to be mistaken for a liana by the birds and lizards on which it preys

bird's nest *n* **1 :** the nest in which a bird lays eggs and hatches young **2 a :** EDIBLE BIRD'S NEST; *also* **:** a substitute used in the preparation of soup **b :** any of several dishes commonly containing nuts or fruit (as an apple dumpling or a cobbler) **3 :** any of several plants having a real or fancied resemblance to a bird's nest; *esp* **:** WILD CARROT **4 :** CROW'S NEST 1a **5 :** a snarl of fishing line at the reel **:** BACKLASH

bird's-nest \'ₑ,ₑ\ *vi* [*bird's nest*] **:** to hunt for or take birds' nests or their contents — **bird's-nester** \'ₑ,ₑₑ\ *n*

bird's-nest cactus *n* **:** BALL CACTUS

bird's-nest fern *n* **1 :** an Australian epiphytic fern (*Asplenium nidus*) frequently forming tufts in tree crotches **2 :** a fern (*Pycnodoria vittata*) of the southern U.S. having prostrate rosettes

bird's-nest fungus *n* **:** a fungus of the family Nidulariaceae

bird's-nest moss *n* **:** a Mexican club moss (*Selaginella lepidophylla*)

bird's-nest orchid *or* **bird's-nest orchis** *n* **:** a European orchid (*Neottia nidusavis*) having closely matted roots

bird's-nest plant *n* **1 :** INDIAN PIPE **2 :** BIRD'S NEST 3

birdsong \'ₑ,ₑ\ *n* **:** the song of a bird; *also* **:** sound suggesting the singing of birds

bird's-pep·per \'ₑ,ₑₑ\ *n, pl* **bird's-peppers :** a wild peppergrass (*Lepidium virginicum*) with nearly orbicular seed pods

bird spider *n* **:** any of a number of large hairy spiders (family Theraphosidae) chiefly of tropical America that are reputed to capture small birds in their strong webs

bird·stone \'ₑ,ₑ\ *n* **:** a stone artifact known only from archaic sites in midwestern and eastern No. America that resembles a bird and is thought to have been an atlatl weight — compare BANNERSTONE, BOATSTONE

bird's-tongue \'ₑ,ₑ\ *n, pl* **bird's-tongues** [so called fr. the shape of the leaves] **1 :** JOINT GRASS 1 **2 :** SCARLET PIMPERNEL **3 :** a common European maple (*Acer campestre*) used as an ornamental **4 :** a stitchwort (*Alsine holostea*)

birds·ville disease \'bərdz,vil-, 'bə̄dz-, -,vəl\ *n, usu cap B* [fr. *Birdsville*, village and cattle region in Queensland, Australia] **:** a disease of Australian horses marked by drowsiness, emaciation, incoordination, and labored breathing, frequently ending fatally in 7 to 10 days, and being of uncertain etiology, both poisonous forage and heavy worm burdens having been suggested as possible causes

bird tick *n* **1 :** a fly of the family Hippoboscidae parasitic on birds **2 :** any of several ticks (family Argasidae) attacking birds

bird vetch *n* **:** TUFTED VETCH

birdvine \'ₑ,ₑ\ *n* **:** a plant of the genus *Loranthus*

bird walk *n* **:** a walk usu. by a group of people and often under the guidance of a skilled leader for the purpose of observing and identifying wild birds in their natural surroundings

bird-watch \'ₑ,ₑ\ *vi* [back-formation fr. *bird watcher*] **:** ²BIRD

bird watcher *n* **:** BIRDER 2

birdweed \'ₑ,ₑ\ *n* **:** KNOTGRASS 1

bird wheat *n* **:** PIGEON-WHEAT

bird-wing butterfly \'ₑ,ₑ-\ *also* **bird wing** *n* **:** any of various very large often brilliantly colored butterflies (family Papilionidae) of southeast Asia, the East Indies, and tropical Australia

bird-wit·ted \'ₑ¦ₑₑ\ *adj* **:** FLIGHTY **:** lacking capacity for prolonged attention

birdy \-dē\ *adj, often* -ER/-EST [¹*bird* + *-y*] **1 :** like or like that of a bird ⟨~ curiosity⟩ **2 a :** abounding in birds, esp. game birds ⟨quartering an upland slope that should have been very ~⟩ **b** *of a gun dog* **:** skilled at finding game birds

bi·rectangular \(ˈ)bī + *adj* [¹*bi-* + *rectangular*] **:** having two right angles ⟨a ~ spherical triangle⟩

bi·refracting \ˌbī +\ *adj* [¹*bi-* + *refracting*] **:** BIREFRINGENT

bi·refraction \ˌbī +\ *n* -s [¹*bi-* + *refraction*] **:** DOUBLE REFRACTION

bi·refractive \ˌbī +\ *adj* [¹*bi-* + *refractive*] **:** BIREFRINGENT

bi·refringence \ˌbī +\ *n* -s [ISV ¹*bi-* + *refringence*] **:** DOUBLE REFRACTION

bi·refringent \ˌbī +\ *adj* [¹*bi-* + *refringent*] **:** having or characterized by double refraction

bi·reme \'bī,rēm\ *n* -s [L *biremis*, fr. *bi-* ¹bi- + *-remis* (fr. *remus* oar) — more at REMI-] **:** a galley with two banks of oars common in the early classical period — compare TRIREME

bi·ret·ta *also* **ber·ret·ta** *or* **be·ret·ta** \bə'red·ə, -etə\ *n* -s [It *berretta, berretto*, fr. OProv *berret* cap, irreg. fr. LL *birrus* cloak with a hood, of Celt origin; akin to MIr *berr* short, W *byr*] **:** a square head covering worn by ecclesiastics that has three or four projections above the crown, often with a tassel at the top, and is red, purple, or black to correspond to the rank of cardinal, bishop, or priest

biretta

bir·gus \'bərgəs\ *n, cap* [NL] **:** the genus containing the purse crab

birh·or \'bi,rȯr\ *n, pl* **birhor** *or* **birhors** *usu cap* **1 :** a Dravidian people in the plateau jungles in east-central India **2 :** a member of the Birhor people

bi·ri \'bē(,)rē\ *n* -s [Hindi *bīṛī, bīrī* betel quid, cigar, fr. Skt *vīṭikā* betel quid] *India* **:** a cheap locally made cigarette

bi·ri·ba \ˌbirē'bä\ *n* -s [Pg *biribá*, fr. Tupi] **:** a Brazilian tree (*Rollinia deliciosa*) whose fruit resembles the custard apple

bi·rimose \(ˈ)bī +\ *adj* [¹*bi-* + *rimose*] *bot* **:** opening by two slits (as of an anther)

birk \'bi(ə)rk, 'bərk\ *n* -s [ME — more at BIRCH] *chiefly Scot* **:** BIRCH

birk·en \-kən\ *adj* [ME — more at BIRCHEN] *chiefly Scot* **:** BIRCH, BIRCHEN

bir·ken·head \ˈbərkənˌhed\ *adj, usu cap* [fr. *Birkenhead*, England] **:** of or from the county borough of Birkenhead, England **:** of the kind or style prevalent in Birkenhead

bir·ke·nia \bər'kēnēə\ *n, cap* [NL, fr. *Birkenhead* Burn, Lanark county, Scotland + NL *-ia*] **:** a genus (the type of the family Birkeniidae of the order Anaspida) of Upper Silurian ostracoderms having no cephalic armor and having the body covered with small scales

birk·ie \'birki, 'bər-\ *n* -s [origin unknown] **1** *Scot* **:** a lively smart assertive person ⟨a gay stout ~⟩ **2** *Scot* **:** FELLOW, BOY

birl \'bərl, 'bərəl; *in sense 1 usu* 'bir(ə)l\ *vb* -ED/-ING/-S [ME *birlen*, fr. OE *byrelian*; akin to OE *byrele* cup-bearer, OS *biril* basket, and perh. to OE *beran* to bear — more at BEAR] *vt* **1** *also* **birle** \'bir(ə)l\, 'bər(ə)l\ *chiefly Scot* **a :** POUR ⟨come ~ the ale, lass⟩ **b :** to ply with drink ⟨she ~*ed* him with strong beer⟩ **2 :** to revolve or cause to revolve: **a :** to cause (a floating log) to rotate by treading (as in log driving or in a logrolling contest) **b :** SPIN ⟨~ a coin on the table⟩ **~** *vi* **1** *chiefly Scot* **:** to drink in company **:** CAROUSE **2 :** to progress with a curved or rotary motion **:** SPIN, WHIRL **3 :** to birl a log esp. in competition — **birl the bawbee** *Scot* **:** to spend freely esp. for drink

bir·ler \-lə(r)\ *n* -s **:** one that birls; *esp* **:** a person who birls logs

bir·lie·man \'birlēmən\ *var of* BYRLAWMAN

¹bir·ling \'birliŋ\ *or* **birlinn** \-lən\ *n* -s [ScGael *birlinn*, prob. (like MIr *birling*), fr. ON *byrthingr* merchant ship, fr. *byrth-* (akin to *borth* board) + *-ingr* -ing — more at BOARD] **:** a chieftain's galley or barge used about the Hebrides

²birl·ing \'bərliŋ\ *n* -s [fr. gerund of *birl*] **:** the sport of logrolling

bir·ma \'bərmə\ *n* -s [origin unknown] **:** SANTA MARIA TREE

birman *usu cap, var of* BURMAN

bir·ming·ham *see separate senses*\ *adj, usu cap* [fr. *Birmingham*, England] **1** \'bərmiŋəm *sometimes* -ŋ,ham\ **:** of or from the city of Birmingham, England **:** of the kind or style prevalent in Birmingham — compare BRUMMAGEM **2** \'bərmiŋ,ham *sometimes* -ŋəm\ [fr. *Birmingham*, Alabama] **:** of or from the city of Birmingham, Ala. ⟨a *Birmingham* industry⟩ **:** of the kind or style prevalent in Birmingham

birn \'bərn\ *n* -s [G (now usu. *birne*), lit., pear, fr. MHG *bir*, fr. OHG *bira*, fr. ML *pira* — more at PEAR] **:** the pear-shaped socket of an instrument of the clarinet class into which the mouthpiece is fitted

bir·ne \'birnə\ *n* -s [G, lit., pear] **:** ⁴BOULE

bir·nirk \(')bir¦ni(ə)rk\ *adj, usu cap* [fr. *Birnirk*, locality near Point Barrow, Alaska] **:** of or belonging to an Eskimo culture centered around Point Barrow in northeastern Alaska, intermediate between Old Bering Sea and Thule, dated about A.D. 600–1000, and characterized by toggle harpoon heads and elements suggesting Asiatic derivation

bi·rotation \¦bī + \ *n* [ISV ¹*bi-* + *rotation*] **:** MUTAROTATION

bi·rot·u·lar \(')bī¦räǀchələ(r), -rōl, ǀ·tyə-\ *or* **bi·rot·u·late** \-lət, -,lāt\ *adj* [*birotular* fr. ¹*bi-* + *rotular*; *birotulate* fr. ¹*bi-* + L *rotula* little wheel + E *-ate* — more at ROLL] **:** being or resembling a birotulate

bi·rot·u·late *like adj*\ *or* **bi·ro·tule** \'bīrə,tyül, -rō,-\ *n* -s [*birotulate* fr. *birotulate*, adj.; *birotule* prob. back-formation fr. *birotulate*, adj.] **:** a sponge spicule having two wheel-shaped ends

¹birr \'bər, 'bə̄\ *n* -s [ME *bir*, *birr* strong wind, force, attack, fr. OE *byre* strong wind and ON *byrr* favoring wind; both akin to OE *beran* to bear — more at BEAR] **1 a :** force esp. of the wind or of an onslaught in battle **:** onward rush **:** IMPETUS; *also* **:** ENERGY, VIGOR ⟨full of ~ and go⟩ **b :** BLOW, THRUST, PUSH **2 :** a whirring sound (as of a spinning wheel) **:** BURR

²birr \'bi(ə)r, 'bər\ *vi* -ED/-ING/-S *chiefly Scot* **:** to make a whirring sound

bir·rus *or* **byr·rus** \'birəs\ *n, pl* **bir·ri** *or* **byr·ri** \-(,)rē, -,rī\ [LL — more at BIRETTA] **:** a woolen cape or cloak usu. with a hood worn by the Romans and by members of the poorer classes in the middle ages

birse \'bi(ə)rs, 'bərs\ *n* -s [fr. (assumed) ME *birst*, fr. OE *byrst* — more at BRISTLE] **1** *chiefly Scot* **:** a bristle or tuft of bristles **2** *chiefly Scot* **:** ANGER, IRRITATION

bir·sle \'birsəl, 'bər-\ *vb* -ED/-ING/-S [origin unknown] *Scot* **:** BROIL, TOAST, DRY ⟨*birsled* peas⟩ ⟨~ yourselves at the fire⟩

birsy \'birsi\ *adj* [*birse* + *-y*] *Scot* **:** BRISTLY, IRRITABLE

¹birth \'bərth, 'bə̄th, 'bəith\ *n, pl* **births** \-ths *sometimes* -thz\ *often attrib* [ME *birthe*, *burthe*, fr. ON *byrth*; akin to OE *gebyrd* birth, OHG *giburt*, Goth *gabaurths*, ON *bera* to bear — more at BEAR] **1 a :** the act of coming forth from the womb **:** the condition of being born **:** the emergence of a new individual from the body of its parent; *specif* **:** the period during which and processes by which the mammalian fetus becomes established as an individual physically independent of its mother's body ⟨several years after the ~ of the princess⟩ ⟨the ~ of the head was delayed⟩ ⟨a child sickly from ~⟩ **b :** the act or process of bringing forth young from the womb ⟨she had a very hard ~ after a prolonged labor⟩ **2 :** state resulting from being born esp. at a particular time or place or into a particular kinship ⟨a Frenchman by ~⟩**: a :** LINEAGE, EXTRACTION, DESCENT ⟨marriage between those unequal in ~ and ability is risky⟩; *often* **:** high or noble birth ⟨a lady of ~ descended from the kings of Ireland⟩ **b** *obs* **:** NATIVITY 4 **3** *obs* **:** FETUS **4 a** *archaic* **:** one that is born **:** CHILD, OFFSPRING, YOUNG **b :** a coming into existence **:** BEGINNING, START ⟨the ~ of an idea⟩

²birth \"\ *vb* -ED/-ING/-S *vt* **1** *now chiefly dial* **:** to bring forth (as a child) **2 :** to give rise to **:** ORIGINATE, PRODUCE ⟨provided the weapons that won the war and . . . ~*ed* the Atomic Age —Philip Wylie⟩ ~ *vi, dial* **:** to bring forth a child or young ⟨two women due to ~ 'bout the same time —Ralph Ellison⟩

birth canal *n* **:** the channel formed by the cervix, vagina, and vulva through which the mammalian fetus is expelled during parturition

birth certificate *n* **:** a certificate embodying a copy of an official record of the date and place of birth and parentage of a person

birthcoat \'=,=\ *n* **:** the dense coat of wool of a newborn lamb

birth control *n* **:** control or limitation of the number of children born esp. by preventing or lessening the frequency of impregnation (as by the use of contraceptives or by avoiding coitus when ovulation is likely) **:** CONTRACEPTION — compare PLANNED PARENTHOOD

birth controller *n* **:** an advocate of birth control

birth·day \'=(,)dā, -,dē, -di\ *n* [ME *birthe day*, fr. *birthe* birth + *day*] **1 a :** the day on which a person is born **b :** a day of origin or commencement **2 a :** an anniversary of one's birth; *also* **:** a celebration of an anniversary of it **b :** YEAR — chiefly in figurative or poetic use

birthday cake *n* **:** a cake for a birthday celebration

birthday honor *n* **:** recognition (as a title) bestowed by the British sovereign at the celebration of the ruler's official birthday — usu. used in pl.

birthday suit *n* **:** unclothed skin — used chiefly in the phrase *in one's birthday suit*

birth·dom \'=dəm\ *n* -s [*birth* + *-dom*] *obs* **:** domain by birthright **:** native land

birth flower *n* **:** a flower considered as appropriate to or symbolic of the month of one's birth

birthing *n* -s [fr. gerund of ²*birth*] **1** *chiefly dial* **:** the act of giving birth **:** BEARING ⟨on tenterhooks like she was the one that had to go through ~ —Conrad Richter⟩ **2 :** BIRTH

birth·land \'=,land, -,lənd\ *n* **:** the land where someone or something is born

birth·less \'=ləs\ *adj* **1 :** ABORTIVE, FRUITLESS **2 :** having unknown or unimportant parents or ancestors

¹birthmark \'=,=\ *n* [¹*birth* + *mark*] **1 :** an unusual mark or blemish on the skin at birth **:** NEVUS **2 :** a distinguishing characteristic or quality ⟨words sang for him, and that is the ~ of a poet —Dylan Thomas⟩

²birthmark \"\ *vt* **:** to fix a birthmark on — usu. used passively

birthnight \'=,=\ *n* **:** the night in which a person is born **:** the anniversary of that night in any succeeding year; *specif* **:** the celebration formerly held on the evening of a royal birthday

birth pang *n* **1 :** one of the regularly recurrent pains that are characteristic of childbirth — usu. used in pl. **2 birth pangs** *pl* **:** disorder and distress incident to a major organizational or social change ⟨the *birth pangs* of civilization⟩

birth phantasy *n, psychoanalysis* **:** a primitive or childish notion of the process of childbirth

birthplace \'=,=\ *n* **1 :** the place (as a house or town) where a person is born **2 :** the place of origin of something ⟨the ~ of freedom⟩

birthrank \'=,=\ *n* **:** order of birth among siblings

birthrate \'=,=\ *n* **:** the ratio between number of births and number of individuals in a specified population and period of time often expressed as number of live births per hundred or per thousand population

birthright \'=,=\ *n* **:** a right, privilege, or possession to which a person is entitled by birth (as an estate or as civil liberty guaranteed under a constitution); *esp* **:** the inheritance of the firstborn ⟨to sell his ~ for a mess of pottage⟩ **syn** see RIGHT

birthroot \'=,=\ *n* [so called fr. its use to ease childbirth] **:** any of several trilliums having astringent roots that were formerly used in folk medicine; *esp* **:** PURPLE TRILLIUM

births *pl of* BIRTH, *pres 3d sing of* BIRTH

birth sin *n* **:** ORIGINAL SIN

birthstone \'=,=\ *n* **:** a precious stone considered as appropriate to or symbolizing the influences due to the month of one's birth

birth·stool \'=,=\ *n* **:** a seat formerly used by women in childbirth

birth trauma *n* **:** the physical injury or emotional shock sustained by an infant in the process of birth

birthwort \'=,=\ *n* -s **1 :** any of several plants of the genus *Aristolochia* (as *A. longa*, *A. pistolochia*, *A. clematitis*, or *A. serpentaria*) the aromatic roots of which are reputed to aid in parturition **2 :** either of two European herbs (*Corydalis fabacea* and *C. tuberosa*) whose roots are reputed to aid in parturition **3 :** BIRTHROOT

birthwort family *n* **:** ARISTOLOCHIACEAE

bis \'bis\ *adv* [F, fr. L, twice, fr. OL *dvis*; akin to MHG *zwis* twice, OHG *zwiro*, ON *tvisvar* twice, Goth *twis-* apart, Gk *dis* twice, Skt *dvis* twice, L *duo* two — more at TWO] **1 :** AGAIN — used to direct repetition of a passage of music or to request an encore **2** [L] **:** TWICE — used to call attention to the occurrence of an item twice (as in an account or an address)

bis- *comb form* [L, fr. *bis*] **1 a :** both **:** of or belonging to both — chiefly in anatomical or medical words of which the second constituent begins with a vowel ⟨*bis*ischiatic⟩ **b :** two ⟨*bis*marine⟩ **2 :** twice **:** doubled — esp. in complex chemical expressions ⟨*bis*dimethylamino-⟩

bis *abbr* bissextile

BIS *abbr* best in show

bis·a·bol \'bisə,bōl, -bōl\ *or* **bisabol myrrh** *also* **bis·sa·bol** *like first form*\ *n* -s [of African origin; akin to Wolof *bisap u ala*, a Senegambian tree] **:** a gum resin that resembles true myrrh and is obtained from two African trees (*Commiphora kataf* and *C. erythraea*) — called also *opoponax*

bis·a·bol·ene \,bisəbə'lēn, '=≈=,=\ *n* -s [ISV *bisabol* + *-ene*] **:** a colorless oily sesquiterpene $C_{15}H_{24}$ derived from cyclohexene and found in many essential oils (as oil of bisabol and lime oil)

bi·sag·re \bə'sä(,)grē, bi'sä(,)grā\ *n* -s [MexSp] **:** a small spiny cactus (*Echinocactus horizonthalonius*) of Mexico and southwestern U.S. that is sometimes cut into slices and candied

bi·sal·tae \bə'sal(,)tē\ *n pl, usu cap* [L, fr. Gk *Bisaltai*] **:** a people of ancient Thrace

bi·sa·yan \bə'sī(y)ən\ *also* **bi·sa·ya** \-(y)ə\ *n, pl* **bisayan** *or* **bisayans** *also* **bisaya** *or* **bisayas** *usu cap* [*Bisayan* fr. Bisayan *Bisayâ* + E *-an*; *Bisaya* fr. Bisayan *Bisayâ*] **1 a :** any of several Christianized peoples in the Visayan islands, Philippines **b :** a member of any of such peoples **2 :** the Austronesian language of the Bisayan peoples; *collectively* **:** the Bisayan languages — see AKLAN, CEBUAN, HANTIK, HILIGAYNON, SAMAR-LEYTE

bis·azo \(')bis+\ *adj* [*bisazo-*, fr. *bis-* + *-az-*] **:** DISAZO

bis·bi·glian·do \'bisbēl¦yän(,)dō\ *or* **bis·bi·glia·to** \-¦yäd-, (,)ō, -ä(,)tō\ *adj* [*bisbigliando* fr. It, verbal of *bisbigliare* to whisper, of imit. origin; *bisbigliato* fr. It, past part. of *bisbigliare*] **:** very light and murmuring — used as a direction in music for a fingered tremolo on the harp

biscacha *var of* VIZCACHA

¹bis·cay·an \(')bis¦kā(y)ən\ *n* -s *cap* [*Biscay* or *Biscaya*, province of Spain (fr. Sp *Vizcaya*) + E *-an*] **1 :** a native or resident of Biscay province, Spain **:** BASQUE **2 a :** the Basque language **b :** the westernmost dialect of Basque spoken in the Spanish province of Biscay

²biscayan \"\ *adj, usu cap* **:** BASQUE

bis·cay green \'bi(,)skā-\ *n, often cap B* [fr. *Biscay*, *Biscaya*, province of Spain] **:** a moderate yellow green that is greener and lighter than average moss green, yellower and less strong than average pea green, and yellower and duller than apple green (sense 1)

bis·cay·ner \'bi(,)skānər\ *also* **bis·cay·neer** \,=≈'ni(ə)r\ *n* -s *usu cap* [obs. *Biskaine*, *Biscayne* Biscayan (fr. *Biscay*, province of Spain) + *-er* or *-eer*] **:** a seaman or ship from Biscay

bisch·of·ite \'bishə,fīt, -,vīt\ *n* -s [G *bischofit*, fr. Gustav *Bischof* †1870 Ger. geologist + G *-it* -ite] **:** a mineral $MgCl_2.6H_2O$ composed of hydrous magnesium chloride

bis·cuit \'biskət, *usu* -d·+V\ *n, pl* **biscuits** *also* **biscuit** [ME *bisquite*, *besquite*, fr. MF *bescuit*, fr. (*pain*) *bescuit* twice-cooked bread, fr. *pain* bread + *bescuit*, past part. of *bescuire* to cook twice, fr. *bes-* bis- (fr. L *bis-*) + *cuire* to cook, fr. L *coquere* — more at COOK] **1 :** any of certain hard or crisp dry baked products: **a** *Brit* (1) **:** CRACKER 4 (2) **:** COOKIE 1 **b :** PILOT BISCUIT **c :** DOG BISCUIT **2 :** earthenware or porcelain that has undergone the first firing before it is subjected to the glazing **:** BISQUE **3 a :** a quick bread made in a small shape from dough that has been rolled and cut or dropped and that is raised in the baking by a leavening agent other than yeast ⟨baking-powder ~s⟩ **b :** ROLL 2d(1) **4 a :** ALMOND BROWN **b :** a grayish yellow **5 :** a flat rounded cake of crude rubber (as Para rubber) or of synthetic rubber **6 a :** a small piece of plastic suitable for the pressing of a single disc record; *also* **:** plastic stock from which such pieces are prepared **b** *slang* **:** a phonograph record

biscuit beetle *n* **:** DRUGSTORE BEETLE

biscuit cutter *n* **:** a circular device for cutting out biscuits from rolled dough

biscuit fire *n* **:** the first fire that changes ceramic clay to biscuit — called also *bisque fire*

bis·cuit·ing \'biskəd·iŋ, -ətiŋ\ *n* -s **:** the first firing of earthen or similar ware by which biscuit is formed

biscuit leaves *n pl but sing or pl in constr* [so called fr. the edible leaves] **:** a greenbrier (*Smilax rotundifolia*)

biscuit plant *n* **:** a greenbrier (*Smilax rotundifolia*)

biscuit-root \'=≈,=\ *n* [so called fr. their being used for meal by the Indians] **1 :** CAMAS 1 **2** *West* **:** a plant of the genus *Lomatium*

biscuit shooter *n, slang* **:** a cook or waiter esp. in a camp or on a ranch

biscuit tortoni \bēskwē- *also* 'biskət-\ *n* **:** tortoni frozen and served in a paper cup

biscuit ware *n* **:** unglazed porcelain or pottery

bis·diapason \¦bis+\ *n* -s [*bis-* + *diapason*] **:** a musical interval of two octaves

bise \'bēz\ *n* -s [ME, fr. OF, of Gmc origin; akin to OHG *bīsa* north wind, OS *bīsa* whirlwind, D dial. *bijs* gust of wind, OHG *bisōn* to run around in confusion, OSw *bisa* to run, and perh. to OHG *bibēn* to tremble — more at BEBUNG] **1 :** a cold wind; *esp* **:** a cold dry north wind of southern France, Switzerland, and Italy

¹bi·sect \(')bī¦sekt\ *vb* -ED/-ING/-S [¹*bi-* + *-sect*] *vt* **1 :** to divide into two usu. equal parts **2 :** to cut (a postage stamp) into two or occas. more pieces each representing a corresponding fraction of the postage value of the whole — used chiefly as a participial adjective ⟨~*ed* copies of some stamps are very valuable⟩ ~ *vi* **:** SEPARATE; *also* **:** CROSS, INTERSECT — used chiefly of roads and ways

²bisect \'=,=\ *n* -s **1 :** one of the pieces of a bisected stamp **2 a :** examination of the lateral and vertical dimensions of the above-ground and below-ground parts of plants by means of a cross-section through soil exposing the profile of underground parts (as roots, tubers, rhizomes) **b :** a graphic representation of the findings of such an examination

bi·sec·tion \(')bī¦sekshən\ *n* -s **:** division into two usu. equal parts

bi·sec·tion·al \-nəl\ *adj* **:** of or relating to bisection **:** that bisects — **bi·sec·tion·al·ly** \-nəlē\ *adv*

bi·sec·tor \(')bī¦sektə(r)\ *n* -s **:** one that bisects; *esp* **:** a straight line that bisects an angle or a line segment

bi·sec·trix \-,triks\ *n, pl* **bisectri·ces** \,=≈'trī(,)sēz\ [*bisec*- (fr. *bisector*) + *-trix*] **:** BISECTOR; *specif* **:** a line bisecting the angle between the optic axes of a biaxial crystal

bi·segmentation \¦bī+\ *n* [¹*bi-* + *segmentation*] **:** complete or partial division into two parts

bi·sel·li·um \bī'selēəm\ *n, pl* **bisel·lia** \-lēə\ [L, fr. *bi-* ¹bi- + *-sellium* (fr. *sella* seat, chair, saddle) — more at SELLATE] **:** an ancient Roman seat of honor for occupancy by two persons

bi·serial \(')bī+\ *adj* [¹*bi-* + *serial*] **:** arranged or characterized by an arrangement in two rows or series — **bi·serially** *adv*

bi·seriate \(')bī+\ *adj* [¹*bi-* + *seriate*] **:** BISERIAL — **bi·seriately** *adv*

bi·serrate \(')bī+\ *adj* [¹*bi-* + *serrate*] **1 :** doubly serrate **:** having the serrations serrate ⟨~ leaves⟩ **2 :** serrate on both sides ⟨~ antennae⟩

bi·setose *also* **bi·setous** \(')bī+\ *adj* [¹*bi-* + *setose*, *setous*] *biol* **:** having two bristles

bi·sexed \'bī,sekst\ *adj* [¹*bi-* + *sex* + *-ed*] **:** BISEXUAL 1a

¹bi·sexual \(')bī+\ *adj* [¹*bi-* + *sexual*] **1 a :** HERMAPHRODITIC **:** possessing characters (as mental and behavioral qualities) typical of both sexes **b :** having sexual desire commonly on an unconscious level for members of both sexes **2 :** relating to, consisting of, or involving two sexes ⟨a ~ hormone⟩ ⟨~ progeny⟩ ⟨~ reproduction⟩ — **bi·sexuality** \¦bī+\ *n* -ES — **bi·sexually** \(')bī+\ *adv*

²bisexual \"\ *n* -s **:** a bisexual person, animal, or plant

bish·a·rin *also* **bish·a·reen** \,bishə'rēn\ *n pl, usu cap* **:** one of the three main divisions of the Beja

¹bish·op \'bishəp\ *n* -s [ME *bisshop*, fr. OE *bisceop*, *biscop*; akin to OS *biskop* bishop, OHG *biscof* MD *bisskop*; all fr. a prehistoric WGmc word borrowed fr. (assumed) VL *biscopus*, *episcopus*, fr. LL *episcopus* bishop, overseer, fr. Gk *episkopos*, fr. *epi* on, over + *skopos* watcher; akin to Gk *skeptesthai* to view — more at EPI-, SPY] **1 :** a chief priest of a non-Christian religion **2 :** a clergyman of the highest order in Christian churches usu. charged with an administrative function such as the supervision of a diocese and in certain communions held to be ordained in direct succession from the apostles **3 :** OVERSEER; *esp* **:** a spiritual guide and overseer **4 :** one of two pieces in a set of chessmen that move diagonally across any number of unoccupied squares **5 :** a mulled beverage with a base of port wine flavored with roasted orange and cloves **6 :** a bustle worn in 18th and 19th century America **7** *or* **bishop bird :** any of various African weaverbirds the males of which are scarlet and black or orange and black **8 :** a Mormon high priest ordained and set apart as the administrative and executive officer of a ward and head of the Aaronic priesthood

²bishop \"\ *vt* -ED/-ING/-S [ME *bisshopen*, fr. OE *bisceopian*, fr. *bisceop*, n.] **1** *archaic* **a :** to administer the sacrament of confirmation to **:** CONFIRM **b :** to approve formally **:** SANCTION **2 :** to appoint as bishop **:** to make a bishop of **3** *dial Eng* **:** to burn or scorch while cooking ⟨the milk is ~*ed*⟩

³bishop \"\ *vt* -ED/-ING/-S [fr. the name *Bishop*] **:** to make (a horse) seem younger by operating on the teeth

bishop coadjutor *n* **1 :** a Roman Catholic bishop assisting a diocesan and usu. having the right of succession **2 a :** a Church of England bishop appointed or consecrated to assist an infirm diocesan in matters of jurisdiction as well as in the performance of purely episcopal duties **b :** a Protestant Episcopal bishop elected as assistant to a diocesan with right of succession upon the latter's death or resignation

bish·op·dom \-dəm\ *n* -s **:** the episcopal body of bishops

bish·oped \'bishəpt\ *adj* [origin unknown] *of pigeons* **:** having white shoulder patches or wing margins

bish·op·ess \-pəs\ *n* -ES [¹*bishop* + *-ess*] **:** the wife of a bishop

bishop in par·ti·bus in·fi·de·li·um \-,in'pärd·əbə,sinfə'dālēəm\ [part trans. of ML *episcopus in partibus infidelium* bishop in infidel parts] **:** TITULAR BISHOP

bish·op·less \-pləs\ *adj* **:** being without a bishop

bishop pine *or* **bishop's pine** *n* [so called fr. its discovery near the mission of San Luis Obispo de Tolosa, Calif., lit., "Saint Louis, bishop of Toulouse"] **:** a California pine (*Pinus muricata*) having a spreading flattened crown and small prickly cones that remain attached to the tree for many years

bish·op·ric \'bishə(,)prik\ *n* -s [ME *bisshopriche*, *bisshoprike*, fr. OE *bisceoprice*, fr. *bisceop* bishop + *rīce* realm; akin to OE *rīce* rich, powerful — more at RICH] **1 :** the administrative area under the jurisdiction of a bishop; *specif* **:** DIOCESE **2 :** the office of a bishop **3 :** a bishop's seat or residence **4 :** a Mormon administrative body of a ward consisting of a bishop and two high priests as counselors

bishops *pl of* BISHOP, *pres 3d sing of* BISHOP

bishop's apron *n* **:** a shortened cassock formerly worn by Anglican clergy out of doors but now used by bishops, deans, and archdeacons only

bish·op's-cap \'=≈,=\ *n, pl* **bishops'-caps** [so called fr. the shape of the seedpod] **1 :** MITERWORT **2 :** STAR CACTUS

bishop's-leaves \'=≈,=\ *n pl but sing or pl in constr* **:** WATER BETONY

bishop sleeve *n* **:** a long full sleeve usu. gathered on a wristband and adapted from a bishop's robe

bishop's length *n* **:** an artist's canvas measuring 58 by 94 inches

bishop's-miter \'=≈,=\ *n, pl* **bishops'-miters :** a miter shell — compare MITRA

bishop's purple *n* **1 :** a violet glaze occurring in Oriental porcelain — called also *aubergine purple* **2 :** BISHOP'S VIOLET

¹bishop's ring \'bishəps-\ *n* **:** a ring worn by bishops on the third finger of the right hand signifying that the bishop is wedded to his diocese

²bishop's ring \'==-\ *n, usu cap B* [after Sereno E. *Bishop* †1909 Am. missionary in Hawaii, who first explained it] **:** a faint reddish brown corona due to the sun's shining through fine dust in the atmosphere

bishop's staff *n* **:** CROSIER

bishop's stone *n* **:** AMETHYST

bishop·stool \'=≈,=\ *n* [ME *bisshopstol*, fr. OE *bisceopstōl*, fr. *bisceop* bishop + *stōl* stool, throne, see — more at BISHOP, STOOL] *archaic* **:** a bishop's seat or see

bishop suffragan *n* **:** a Church of England bishop consecrated with the title of some town or see usu. within the diocese where he assists the diocesan in duties purely episcopal — compare SUFFRAGAN 1a

bishop's violet *n* **:** a moderate reddish purple that is bluer, stronger, and slightly lighter than heliotrope (sense 4b) and bluer and duller than eupatorium purple — called also *bishop's purple*

bishop's-weed *also* **bishop-weed** \'=≈,=\ *n, pl* **bishops'-weeds** *also* **bishop-weeds 1 :** a plant of the genus *Ammi* **2 :** GOUTWEED **3 :** WATER MINT

bis·hy·droxy·coumarin \,bis·,hī,dräksē+\ *n* -s [*bis-* + *hydroxy-* + *coumarin*] **:** DICOUMAROL — not used systematically

bi·silicate \(')bī+\ *n* [¹*bi-* + *silicate*] **:** METASILICATE

bi·sinuate \(')bī+\ *adj* [¹*bi-* + *sinuate*] **:** having two sinuate edges — **bi·sinuation** \¦bī+\ *n* -s

bisk *var of* BISQUE

bisk·op \'biskəp\ *n* -s [Afrik, lit., bishop, fr. MD *bisscop*; fr. the supposed grave appearance of the head — more at BISHOP] **:** either of two large sparid marine food and sport fishes of southern Africa — called also *musselcracker*, *steenbras*; see BLACK BISKOP, WHITE BISKOP

¹bis·marck \'biz,märk, 'bi,sm-\ *n* -s [prob. after Prince Otto Edward Leopold von *Bismarck*-Schönhausen †1898 Ger. chancellor] **1** [short for *Bismarck brown*] *often cap* **:** a moderate reddish brown that is yellower, stronger, and slightly lighter than roan and lighter and stronger than mahogany **2** *sometimes cap* **:** a raised doughnut shaped like a ball with filling usu. of jelly

²bis·marck \'biz,-\ *adj, usu cap* [fr. *Bismarck*, North Dakota] **:** of or from Bismarck, the capital of North Dakota **:** of the kind or style prevalent in Bismarck

bismarck brown \'biz,-, 'bi,sm-\ *n* [trans. of G *bismarckbraun*, after Prince Otto von *Bismarck*-Schönhausen] **1** *often cap 1st B* **:** a moderate yellowish brown that is yellower and very slightly stronger than cinnamon brown, darker and very slightly yellower than maple sugar, redder and lighter than bronze, and very slightly less strong than antique bronze — called also *bunny*, *Havana* **2** *often cap both Bs* **:** either of two basic diazo dyes: **a :** a dye made from *meta*-phenylenediamine that dyes wool, silk, and leather brown — called also *Bismarck Brown G*; see DYE table I (under *Basic Brown 1*) **b :** a dye made from *meta*-tolylenediamine that dyes wool, jute, and leather reddish brown — called also *Bismarck Brown R*; see DYE table I (under *Basic Brown 4*, *Pigment Brown 3*, and *Solvent Brown 3*)

bismarck herring *n, usu cap B* [trans. of G *bismarckhering*, after Prince Otto von *Bismarck*-Schönhausen] **:** filleted salt herring marinated in wine, vinegar, and spices and served cold with raw onion and lemon

bis·marck·i·an \(')biz¦märkēən, (')bi¦sm-\ *adj, usu cap* [Prince Otto von *Bismarck*-Schönhausen + E *-ian*] **:** of, relating to, or characteristic of Bismarck who was noted for his aggressiveness, executive capacity, relentlessness, and far-sighted diplomacy — **bis·marck·i·an·ism** \-kēə,nizəm\ *n* -s *usu cap*

bis·mil·lah \bi'smilə\ *interj* [Ar *bismi 'llāh* in the name of Allah] — a Muslim invocation

bis·mite \'biz,mīt, 'bi,sm-\ *n* -s [*bismuth* + *-ite*] **:** bismuth trioxide Bi_2O_3 occurring as a straw-yellow earth

bis·mo·clite \'bizmō,klīt, 'bism-\ *n* -s [*bismuth* + *O* (symbol for oxygen) + *Cl* (symbol for chlorine) + *-ite*] **:** a bismuth oxychloride BiOCl isomorphous with daubreelite

bismut- *or* **bismuto-** *comb form* [G *bismut-, bismuto-*, fr. *bismut* (now *wismut*)] **:** bismuth ⟨*bismut*ite⟩ ⟨*bismuto*plagionite⟩

bis·muth \'bizməth, 'bism-\ *n* -s [obs. G *bisemutum, bismut* (now *wismut*), modif. of *wismut*, fr. *wise* meadow (fr. OHG *wisa*) + *mut* claim to a mine, fr. *muten* to claim, fr. OHG *muotōn*, fr. *muot* mind; akin to OE *wāse* mire, marsh — more at OOZE, MOOD] **:** a heavy brittle highly diamagnetic chiefly trivalent metallic element resembling arsenic and antimony chemically, crystallizing usu. in grayish white rhombohedrons with a pinkish tinge and high luster, characterized by low melting point, expansion on solidification, low thermal conductivity and electric conductivity, occurring widely but sparingly both native in veins (as in arborescent, foliated, or granular forms) and in combination (as in bismuthinite, bismite, and bismutite), but being usu. recovered as a by-product from ores of other metals (as lead, copper, or tin), and used chiefly in making fusible alloys, casting alloys, and bismuth compounds for chemical and pharmaceutical use — symbol *Bi;* see ACTINIUM SERIES, THORIUM SERIES, URANIUM SERIES; ELEMENT table

bis·muth·al \'bizməthəl, 'bism-, -mathəl; (')biz¦mə-, -¦myü-\ *adj* **:** of or relating to bismuth

bis·muth·ate \'bizmə,thāt, 'bism-, -,that, -,thət,-thət\ *n* -s [*bismuth* + *-ate*] **:** a salt (as sodium bismuthate $NaBiO_3$) containing pentavalent bismuth in the anion

bismuth blende *n* **:** EULYTITE

bismuth glance *n* **:** BISMUTHINITE

bis·muth·ic \(')bizmə,thik, (')bism-; (')biz¦məth-, (')bi¦sm-, -myü-; -thik, -ēk\ *adj* **:** of, relating to, or containing bismuth ⟨~ oxide Bi_2O_5⟩ — used esp. of compounds in which this element is pentavalent

bis·muth·ine \'bizmə,thēn, 'bism-, -mə,thēn,-məthən,-məthən\ *n* -s [F, fr. *bismuth* + *-ine*] **1 :** BISMUTHINITE **2 :** an unstable gaseous hydride of bismuth BiH_3 of which stable organic derivatives [as trimethyl-*bismuthine* $Bi(CH_3)_3$] are known; *also* **:** any of such derivatives ⟨the aliphatic ~*s*⟩

bis·muth·in·ite *n* -s \'bizməthə,nīt, 'bism-, -məthə,-; (')biz¦mə-, -myü-\ [*bismuthine* + *-ite*] **:** a mineral Bi_2S_3 consisting of native bismuth sulfide usu. in foliated or fibrous masses of lead-gray color and metallic luster

bis·muth·ite \'bizmə,thīt, 'bism-, -,thīt\ *n* -s [G *bismutit*, *bismut* bismuth + *-it* -ite] **:** a nitrate of bismuth: as **a :** the normal nitrate $Bi(NO_3)_3.5H_2O$ obtained as colorless lustrous hygroscopic crystals by the action of nitric acid on bismuth and used chiefly in making other bismuth compounds **b :** BISMUTH SUBNITRATE

bismuth ocher *n* **:** BISMITE

bismuth oxide *n* **:** an oxide of bismuth; *esp* **:** the trioxide Bi_2O_3 occurring naturally as bismite, obtained synthetically as a yellow powder, and used chiefly in painting porcelain

bismuth oxychloride *n* **:** a white crystalline basic salt approximately BiOCl made usu. by reaction of an acid solution of bismuth nitrate with a solution of sodium chloride and used chiefly as a pigment and a cosmetic

bismuth spar *n* **:** BISMUTITE

bismuth subcarbonate *n* **:** a basic salt obtained as a white powder of varying composition by reaction of a carbonate with a bismuth salt (as bismuth subnitrate) and used chiefly in treating gastrointestinal disorders and in cosmetics

bismuth subchloride *n* **:** BISMUTH OXYCHLORIDE

bismuth subgallate *n* **:** a basic salt obtained as a bright yellow powder usu. by reaction of hydrated bismuth oxide with gallic acid and used chiefly as a dusting powder in treating skin diseases (as eczema)

bismuth subnitrate *n* **:** a basic salt or usu. a mixture of basic salts obtained as a white powder from normal bismuth nitrate (as by reaction with sodium bicarbonate) and used similarly to bismuth subcarbonate and also in ceramics

bismuth subsalicylate *or* **bismuth salicylate** *n* **:** a basic salt obtained as a white or nearly white powder of varying composition and sometimes used as an adjuvant to penicillin in the treatment of syphilis

bismuth white *n* **1 :** bismuth oxychloride used as a pigment **2 :** BISMUTH SUBNITRATE

bismuth yellow *n* **1 :** bismuth chromate used as a pigment **2 :** bismuth trioxide used as a pigment

bis·muth·yl \'bizmə,th¦il, 'bis-, -,th¦ēl; -məth|əl, -məth|\ *n* -s [ISV *bismuth* + *-yl*] **:** a univalent radical BiO regarded as existing in some basic salts of bismuth

bismuthyl chloride *n* **:** BISMUTH OXYCHLORIDE

bis·mut·ite \'bizməd·,īt, 'bism-, -mə,tīt\ *n* -s [G *bismutit*, fr. *bismut-* + *-it* -ite] **:** a mineral $(BiO)_2CO_3$ consisting of an earthy and amorphous basic bismuth carbonate usu. dull white or yellowish

bismuto- — see BISMUT-

bis·mut·o·tantalite \,bizməd·ə, ,bizmətə, ,bis-+\ *n* -s [*bismut-* + *tantalite*] **:** a mineral $Bi(Ta,Cb)O_4$ consisting of an oxide of bismuth and tantalum commonly with some columbium

bis·na·ga *also* **biz·na·ga** \bi'snägə\ *n* -s [Sp *biznaga*, prob. by folk etymology (influence of *biznaga* parsnip, fr. Ar *bastināj, bashnāqah*, fr. L *pastinaca*) fr. earlier *vitznauac*, fr. Nahuatl *huitz-nahuac*, lit., surrounded by thorns, fr. *huitztli* thorn + *nahuac* around — more at PARSNIP] **:** any of several thorny cacti of the genera *Ferocactus* and *Echinocactus* (esp. *F. peninsulae* of Lower California and adjacent regions)

bi·sociation \,bī+\ *n* -s [¹*bi-* + *association*] **:** the simultaneous mental association of an idea or object with two fields ordinarily not regarded as related ⟨the pun is perhaps the simplest form of ~⟩

bi·sociative \(')bī+\ *adj* **:** of, or relating to bisociation

bi·son \'bīsᵊn, 'bīzᵊn\ *n* [L *bisont-, bison*, of Gmc origin; akin to OE *wesend* aurochs, OHG *wisant, wisunt*, ON *visundr;* akin to OPruss *wissambrs* aurochs and perh. to L *virus* slimy liquid, poison, stench; fr. its musky odor — more at VIRUS] **1** *pl* **bison** *also* **bisons a :** any of several large shaggy-maned usu. gregarious recent or extinct bovine mammals constituting the genus *Bison* and having a large head with short horns and heavy forequarters surmounted by a large fleshy hump formed by the withers and supported by prolonged spinous processes of the ribs **b :** a recent member of this group: (1) **:** WISENT (2) **:** BUFFALO 1c **2** *cap* **:** the genus of Bovidae comprising bison and sometimes being regarded as a subgenus of *Bos* **3** *pl* **bison :** any of certain Asiatic wild oxen; *specif* **:** GAUR **4** -s **:** a dark grayish yellowish brown that is stronger and slightly yellower and lighter than seal, slightly redder and lighter than sepia brown, and very slightly yellower and paler than lama

bi·son·tine \-ᵊn,tīn, -,tən\ *adj* [L *bisont-, bison* + E *-ine*] **:** of, relating to, or characteristic of bison

bi·sphenoid \(')bī+\ *n* -s [¹*bi-* + *sphenoid*] **:** DISPHENOID

bi·spi·nous *or* **bi·spi·nose** \(')bī+\ *adj* [¹*bi-* + *spinous, spinose*] **:** having two spines

bi·spo·ran·gi·ate \¦bīspə¦ranjēət, -jē,āt\ *adj* [¹*bi-* + NL *sporangium* + E *-ate*] **:** having two different kinds of sporangia — compare MONOCLINOUS

bi·spore \'bī+,-\ *n* -s [¹*bi-* + *spore*] **:** an asexual spore produced in pairs by certain red algae — compare TETRASPORE — **bi·sporous** \(')bī+\ *adj*

1bisque *also* **bisk** \'bisk\ *n* -s [F *bisque*] **:** odds allowed an inferior player in certain games: **a :** a point to be taken when desired in a set of tennis **b :** an extra turn in croquet **c :** one or more strokes to be deducted from the whole or part score in golf

2bisque *also* **bisk** \"\ *n* -s [F *bisque*] **1 :** a thick cream soup made of crayfish or other shellfish or of the flesh of birds or rabbits; *also* **:** a cream soup of pureed vegetables ⟨tomato ~⟩ **2 :** ice cream containing powdered nuts or macaroons

3bisque \"\ *n* -s **1 :** a variable color that is brownish pink, light grayish yellowish brown, and pale orange yellow to yellowish gray **2 :** a light grayish brown esp. used in textiles

4bisque \"\ *n* -s [by shortening & alter.] **:** BISCUIT 2; *esp* **:** unglazed ceramic ware that is not to be glazed but is hard-fired and vitreous ⟨Sèvres ~⟩

bisque fire *n* [⁴*bisque*] **:** BISCUIT FIRE

bissabol *var of* BISABOL

bis·sex·tile day \(')bī, bə+\ *n* [ML *bissextilis, bisextilis* of a bissextus, fr. LL *bissextus, bisextus*, an intercalary day in the Julian calendar, fr. *bi-* ¹bi or *bis-* + *sextus* sixth; fr. its following Feb. 24, the 6th day before the calends of March — more at SIXTH] **:** LEAP DAY

bissextile year *n* **:** leap year in the Julian or Gregorian calendar

bisson *adj* [ME *bisen*, fr. OE *bisene*] *obs* **:** BLIND, PURBLIND; *also* **:** BLINDING

bist *dial Brit pres 2d sing of* BE

bi·state \'¦=¦=\ *adj* [¹*bi-* + *state*] **:** of two states **:** established and maintained by two states acting as a unit ⟨a ~ water commission⟩

bis·ter *or* **bis·tre** \'bistə(r)\ *n* -s [F *bistre*] **1 a :** an artist's medium for use with brush or pen made with a brown extract obtained from the soot of wood after the soot has been soaked or boiled in water and ranging in color from yellowish brown to dark brown **b :** a watercolor medium having the general color characteristics of bister **2 :** MANGANESE BROWN **3 :** SOOT BROWN

bis·tered *also* **bis·tred** \-tə(r)d\ *adj* **:** colored with or as if with bister; *esp, of skin* **:** SWARTHY

bister green *n* **:** a dark grayish to dark yellow that is slightly darker than pyrite yellow and very slightly duller than sulphine yellow

bis·tort \'bi,stȯrt\ *n* -s [MF *bistorte*, fr. (assumed) ML *bistorta*, fr. L *bis-* + *torta*, fem. of *tortus*, past part. of *torquere* to twist — more at TORTURE] **:** any of several plants of the genus *Polygonum; esp* **:** either a European herbaceous plant (*P. bistorta*) or a related American form (*P. bistortoides*) the twisted roots of which are used as astringents

bis·tour·nage \'bistə(r),nij\ *n* -s [F, fr. *bistourner* to twist (fr. MF, fr. OF *bestourner*, fr. *bes-* — fr. L *bis-* — + *tourner* to turn) + *-age* — more at TURN] **:** castration by torsion of the spermatic cord

bis·tou·ry \'bistərē\ *n* -ES [F *bistouri*, fr. MF *bistorie, bistorit* dagger] **:** a small slender straight or curved surgical knife sharp-pointed or probe-pointed

bi·stratal \(')bī+\ *adj* [¹*bi-* + *stratal*] **:** having or belonging to two layers

bi·striate \(')bī+\ *adj* [¹*bi-* + *striate*] **:** marked with two parallel striae

bi·stro *also* **bi·strot** \'bi(,)strō, 'bē(,)-\ *n* -s [F] **1 :** a small or unpretentious European wineshop or restaurant **2 a :** a usu. small and often out-of-the-way bar, tavern, or other place selling drinks and often food to patrons and marked by an atmosphere of extreme casualness **b :** NIGHTCLUB — **bi·stro·ic** \(')¦strōik\ *adj*

bi·sulcate \(')bī+\ *adj* [¹*bi-* + *sulcate*] *of a hoof or foot* **:** CLOVEN

bi·sulfate \(')bī+\ *n* [ISV ¹*bi-* + *sulfate*] **:** an acid sulfate (as potassium bisulfate $KHSO_4$) **:** a hydrogen sulfate — see ¹BI-4

bi·sulfide \(')bī+\ *n* [ISV ¹*bi-* + *sulfide*] **:** DISULFIDE 1 — used chiefly commercially in the term *carbon bisulfide*

bi·sulfite \(')bī+\ *n* [F, fr. *bi-* ¹bi + *sulfite*] **:** an acid sulfite (as potassium bisulfite $KHSO_3$) **:** a hydrogen sulfite — see ¹BI-4

bisulfite of lime : CALCIUM BISULFITE

bi·syllabic \¦bī+\ *adj* [¹*bi-* + *-syllabic*] **:** DISYLLABIC

1bit \'bit, *usu* -d.+V\ *n* -s [ME *bitt*, fr. OE *bite;* akin to OE *bītan* to bite — more at BITE] **1** *obs* **:** the action of biting; *also* **:** GRAZING, EATING **2 :** something that is bitten or held with the teeth: **a** *obs* **:** ²BITE 5 **b :** the part of a usu. steel bridle that is inserted in the mouth of a horse together with its appendages (as the rings to which the reins are fastened) — see BAR 1e (3), BRIDOON, CURB, SNAFFLE, BRIDLE illustration **c :** the rimmed mouth end on the stem of a pipe or a cigar or cigarette holder ⟨a fishtail ~⟩ **3 a :** the biting or cutting edge or part of a tool (as of an ax, adz, or rock drill); *also* **:** a replaceable part of a compound tool that actually performs the function (usu. some form of cutting) for which the whole tool is designed (as a screwdriver blade or boring tool for use with a brace, an inserted saw tooth, a plane iron, or the copper head of a soldering iron) **b bits** *pl* **:** the jaws or nippers of tongs or pincers **4 :** something that curbs or imposes a restraint on something or someone ⟨folly curbed by honor's ~⟩ **5 :** the part of a key which enters the lock and in which are cut the wards that act upon the bolt and tumblers **6 :** a triangular earmark (as for identifying cattle) — see EARMARK illustration **7 :** a piece of wire or brass fixed to a dandy roll to make a watermark in paper — **bit in one's teeth :** control of affairs esp. on a headlong or willful course — used chiefly with *get* or *take* ⟨he took the *bit in his teeth* and soon dissipated his fortune⟩

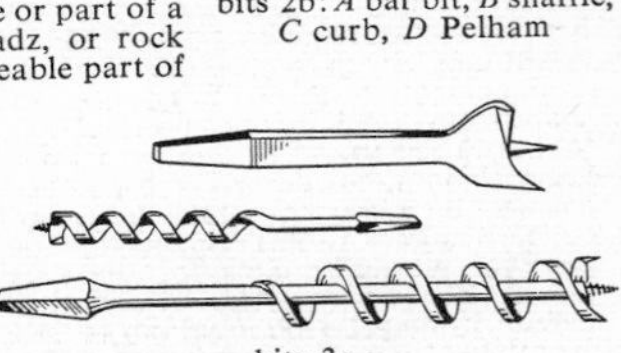

bits 2b: *A* bar bit, *B* snaffle, *C* curb, *D* Pelham

bits 3a

2bit \"\ *vt* **bitted; bitted; bitting; bits; 1 a :** to put a bit in the mouth of (a horse) **b :** to accustom (a horse) to the bit **c :** to control with or as if with a bit **:** CURB, CHECK **2 :** to form a bit on (a key)

3bit \"\ *n* -s [ME, fr. OE *bita;* akin to OE *bītan* to bite — more at BITE] **1 :** a small quantity of food: **a** *obs* **:** a piece of food such as may be bitten off at once **:** BITE **b :** MORSEL; *esp* **:** a small delicacy **c :** fragment of food **:** SCRAP, LEAVING — usu. used in pl. ⟨we can make supper from the ~*s*⟩ **2 :** a small piece, portion, or quantity of some material thing: as **a** (1) *chiefly Scot* **:** PLACE, SPOT ⟨may I never stir from the ~ —Sir Walter Scott⟩ (2) *of land or lands* **:** a small or relatively small amount ⟨planting the level ~*s* to grain and terracing the hills for their vineyards⟩ ⟨a ~ of the old country set down in the midst of this American state⟩ **b** (1) **:** an old one-real piece worth ⅛ of a Spanish peso (2) **:** a unit of value equivalent to ⅛ of a Spanish peso — used esp. in designating the value of a piece of cut money ⟨each piece of a peso cut into four parts was worth two ~*s*⟩ (3) **:** a unit of value equal to ⅛ of a dollar (12½ cents) — used only of even multiples ⟨two ~*s*⟩ ⟨four ~*s*⟩ (4) **:** a unit of value equal to ¹⁄₁₀₀ of a daler ⟨2½-, 5-, 10-, 25-, and 50-*bit* coins were issued⟩ — used in the Virgin islands of the U.S. when they were the Danish West Indies (5) *in British Guiana* **:** FOURPENCE; *also* **:** a corresponding unit of value equal to ⅙ of a florin (6) *Brit* **:** any particular small coin ⟨a threepenny ~⟩ ⟨a sixpenny ~⟩ **c :** a small piece of hot glass gathered on an iron rod ready to be attached to a glass vessel (as to form a foot or handle) **d** *ceramics* **:** a loose material (as flint fragments) sprinkled over the bottom of a sagger to prevent glazed pieces (as cups) from adhering to it — called also *bitstone* **e :** a section of rootstock or rhizome (as of bananas) used in propagation **3** *chiefly of immaterial objects* **:** something small or unimportant of its kind: as **a** *of time* (1) **:** a brief period **:** WHILE ⟨rest a ~ longer⟩ (2) *chiefly Scot* **:** the exact or critical moment ⟨he came just at the ~⟩ (3) *slang* **:** a term of imprisonment **b :** SOMEWHAT **:** some degree or extent — used chiefly in the phrase *a bit of* ⟨there is a ~ of the cad in all men⟩ ⟨a ~ of a mystery⟩ **c :** the smallest or an insignificant amount or degree **:** WHIT, MITE — often used adverbially with *a* ⟨the sauce is a ~ too sweet⟩ ⟨she felt a ~ better after her nap⟩ **d :** one's contribution however small to a cause — used chiefly in the phrase *do one's bit* **e :** a sketch or incident in a literary work or in a theatrical performance ⟨leafing the pages seeking the ~*s* that had brightened his childhood⟩ ⟨one of the best ~*s* was the bawdy exchange between the two brothers in the second act⟩; *often* **:** a sketch forming a unit in a burlesque or nightclub show **f :** a small part usu. with some spoken lines in a theatrical performance — compare WALK-ON **4** *slang* **:** a young woman **:** GIRL — sometimes used disparagingly — **a bit of all right** *chiefly Brit* **:** something or someone regarded with full and hearty approval

4bit \"\ *adj, chiefly Scot* **:** SMALL ⟨a ~ lassie⟩ ⟨~ portraits of worthies like Rob Roy —*New Yorker*⟩

5bit \"\ *past or substand past part of* BITE

6bit \"\ *Scot var of* BUT

7bit \"\ *n* -s [*binary digit*] **1 :** a unit of information equivalent to the result of a choice between two equally probable alternatives — used esp. in communication and information theory **2 :** a unit of memory corresponding to the ability to store the result of a choice between two alternatives — used esp. in connection with digital computing devices

bit·a·ble *also* **bite·a·ble** \'bīd·əbəl, 'bītə-\ *adj* [*bite* + *-able*] **:** that may be bitten

bi·tan·hol \,bē,tän'hōl\ *n* -s [Tag *bitanhól*] **:** a tropical tree (*Calophyllum blancoi*) common in the Philippines with bark and seeds that yield an aromatic resin and a bitter oil

bi·tartrate \(')bī+\ *n* -s [ISV ¹*bi-* + *tartrate;* prob. orig. formed in F] **:** an acid tartrate (as sodium bitartrate $NaHC_4H_4O_6$) **:** a hydrogen tartrate — see ¹BI- 4

bitbrace \'=,=\ *n* [¹*bit* + *brace*] **:** ¹BRACE 4

bit by bit *adv* **:** PIECEMEAL **:** little by little **:** by degrees

1bitch \'bich\ *n* -ES [ME *bicche*, fr. OE *bicce;* akin to ON *bikkja* female dog, OE *bæc* back — more at BACK] **1 a :** the female of the dog or of a closely related animal (as the wolf or fox) **b :** the female of certain other carnivorous mammals (as the ferret or otter) **2 a :** a lewd or immoral woman **:** TROLLOP, SLUT — a generalized term of abuse **b :** a malicious, spiteful, and domineering woman **3 :** any of several mechanical devices designed to grasp and hold something in position **4 :** a makeshift lamp consisting of a can or cup of grease with a wick of twisted rag much used in pioneer western and northwestern No. America **5** *slang* **:** something regarded as outstanding of its kind esp. in unpleasantness ⟨we'll have a ~ of a time getting home at this hour⟩ **6** *slang* **:** COMPLAINT, GRUMBLING

2bitch \"\ *vb* -ED/-ING/-ES *vt* **1** *slang* **:** SPOIL, BOTCH — often used with *up* ⟨someone had really ~*ed* things up for fair —R.H.Newman⟩ **2** *slang* **:** to complain of (someone or something) **:** gripe about **3** *slang* **:** CHEAT, DO, DOUBLECROSS ~ *vi, slang* **:** COMPLAIN, GROUSE

bitch chain *n* **:** a short logging chain with hook and ring used for fastening the lower end of a gin pole to a sled or car when loading logs

bitch·ery \'bich(ə)rē, -ri\ *n* -ES **:** behavior of or like that of a bitch

bitch goddess *n* **:** SUCCESS; *esp* **:** material or worldly success

bitch·i·ly \'bichəlē, -li\ *adv* **:** in a bitchy manner

bitch·i·ness \'bichēnəs, -chin-\ *n* -ES **:** the quality of being bitchy or of acting like a bitch

bitchy \'bichē, -chi\ *adj* -ER/-EST **1 :** suggestive of a bitch esp. in malice or arrogance **2** *of a male dog* **:** EFFEMINATE

1bite \'bīt, *usu* -d.+V\ *vb* **bit** \'bit, *usu* -d.+V\ *or dial Brit* **bate** \'bāt\ *or* **bote** \'bōt\ **bitten** \'bitᵊn\ *or substand* **bit; biting; bites** [ME *biten*, fr. OE *bītan;* akin to OHG *bīzan* to bite, ON *bīta*, Goth *beitan* to bite, L *findere* to split, Skt *bhedati* he splits] *vt* **1 a** (1) **:** to seize with the teeth so that they enter, grip, or wound ⟨the dogs *bit* the child savagely⟩ (2) **:** to remove (a part of something) with the teeth ⟨a piece was *bitten* from the apple⟩ **:** sever by biting ⟨she *bit* the thread in two⟩ **b :** to seize, pinch, or sever with the jaws (as of a snapping turtle) or with a jawlike organ (as the claw of a lobster) **c :** STING: (1) **:** to pierce with any of certain sharp-pointed buccal organs (as the proboscis of a mosquito or the fangs of a snake) (2) **:** to pierce with any of certain other pointed organs not associated with the mouth (as the stinger of a bee) — not used technically **2 :** CUT, PIERCE — used of edged weapons or their wielders ⟨the sword cleft his armor and *bit* him to the bone⟩ **3** *obs* **:** EAT, NIBBLE, CHEW **:** GRAZE **4 :** to cause sharp pain or stinging discomfort to ⟨the wind howling, the sleet *biting* our necks⟩ **5 a :** to take hold of **:** hold fast ⟨the scored jaws of a vise help it ~ the work⟩ **b :** to act like teeth or jaws in removing (part of something) ⟨the giant shovels *bit* 5-yard chunks from the hill⟩ **c :** affect profoundly **:** IMPRESS **6 :** to eat into **:** CORRODE ⟨acid ~*s* an etcher's plate⟩; *sometimes* **:** to etch with acid ⟨he *bit* and printed his lithographs —Margery Allingham⟩ **7 a :** to cheat, trick, or take in; *esp* **:** to borrow with little intention of repaying ⟨he *bit* me for a fiver⟩ **b :** to catch as with teeth by a sudden turn of events — usu. used in passive ⟨he was badly *bitten* on the market⟩ **8** *slang* **:** PERTURB, WORRY, DISTRESS ⟨well, what's *biting* him today⟩ **~** *vi* **1 a :** to seize something with the teeth or jaws **:** wound with the teeth **:** pierce or sting esp. with proboscis or fang ⟨the mosquitoes *bit* fiercely all evening long⟩ **b :** to have the habit of so doing ⟨does that dog ~⟩ **2** *of a weapon or tool* **:** to cut, pierce, or take hold — used esp. with reference to power or quality ⟨this saw ~*s* well⟩ **3 :** to cause an irritation or smarting ⟨his words *bit* deeply into our spirit⟩ **:** be pungent ⟨the sauce is a bit too sharp, it really ~*s*⟩ **4 :** SNAP, SNARL, CARP — usu. used with *at* ⟨why are you always *biting* and bickering at one another⟩ **5** *of a chemical* **:** PENETRATE ⟨few dyes will ~ until the wool has been boiled with some mordant —Karis E. Legge⟩; *specif* **:** CORRODE, EAT ⟨if the acid fails to ~ well, the fault may be with the metal of the etcher's plate⟩ **6 :** to produce an impression **:** have an effect ⟨such thoughts ~⟩ **7 a** *of fish* **:** to take a bait **b** *chiefly slang* **:** to respond so as to be caught by something (as a trick or deceit) used as bait **8 :** to take or maintain a firm hold ⟨be sure the anchor ~*s* well⟩ **9** *printing* **:** to cause a bite **10 :** to grip the surface of the ground momentarily esp. so as to rebound in a manner influenced by a previously imparted spin — used of a bowled ball in cricket — **bite one's lip** *or* **bite one's tongue :** to hold back a remark one would like to make — **bite the dust** *also* **bite the ground 1 :** to fall dead esp. in a battle ⟨many a redskin *bit the dust* that day⟩ **2 a :** to fall from a horse **b :** to come a cropper **:** suffer humiliation or defeat — **bite the hand that feeds one :** to injure a benefactor maliciously — **bite the thumb at :** to insult provocatively **:** JEER

2bite \"\ *n* -s [ME, fr. *biten*, v.] **1 a :** the act of seizing with the teeth or mouth or of bringing the teeth together as in seizing **b :** the act of wounding or separating with the teeth or mouth **c :** a seizure (as of a bait) with the teeth or mouth **d :** the act (as of some insects) of puncturing or abrading with the mouth parts **2 :** FOOD, VICTUALS: **a :** the amount of food taken at a bite **:** MORSEL ⟨I couldn't eat another ~⟩ **b :** a small amount of food **:** SNACK ⟨we had just a ~ at tea⟩ **c :** a meal esp. if impromptu ⟨why not have a ~ of dinner now and finish the work later⟩ **d :** herbage for grazing **3 :** an unintended blank area on a printed sheet caused by the accidental covering (as by foreign matter) of part of the inked surface during printing **4** *archaic* **:** CHEAT, TRICK; *also* **:** SHARPER, CHEATER **5 :** a wound made by biting ⟨the ~ became infected⟩ **6 :** the hold or grip by which friction is created or purchase obtained (as the hold of the short end of a lever upon the thing to be lifted or of one part of a machine upon another) **7 :** a surface that creates friction or is brought into contact with another for the purpose of obtaining a hold; *specif* **:** the holding surfaces of the jaws of a chuck **8 :** the keen incisive quality or the smart, tang, or penetrating effect of a sharply impinging sensation ⟨the ~ of raw whiskey⟩ ⟨the ~ of his words was sharp⟩ ⟨the ~ of wind on our cheeks⟩ **9 :** the corroding of an etcher's plate by acid; *also* **:** a period during which the plate is exposed to the action of the acid **10 :** the distance between the point and the bottom of the bend of a fishhook **11 :** an amount (as of money) taken usu. in one operation for one purpose **:** CUT, SLICE, SHAVE ⟨the tax ~⟩ ⟨a 10 percent ~ for his manager⟩

biteable *var of* BITABLE

bite block *n* **:** a device used chiefly in dentistry for recording the spatial relation of the jaws esp. in respect to the occlusion of the teeth

bi·teg·mic \(')bī¦tegmik\ *also* **bi·teg·mi·nous** \-'tegmənəs\ *adj* [¹*bi-* + NL *tegmin-, tegmen* + E *-ic* or *-ous*] *bot* **:** having two integuments ⟨~ ovules⟩

bite in *vt* **:** to corrode or eat (lines or figures) into an etcher's plate by means of an acid

bi·temporal \(ˈ)bī+\ *adj* [¹*bi-* + *temporal*] **:** relating to, involving, or joining the two temporal bones or the areas that they occupy

bite off *vt* **1 :** to remove by or as if by biting ⟨great chunks of the countryside *bitten off* for cheap housing⟩ **2 a :** to eliminate (as music or dialogue) from a radio program while it is being broadcast **b :** to cut short (a program) — **bite off more than one can chew :** to undertake more than one can perform

bit·er \ˈbīd·ə(r), ˈbītə-\ *n* -s [ME, fr. *biten* + *-er*] **1 :** one that bites; *esp* **:** one that is inclined to bite or bites habitually ⟨a dog that is a known ~⟩ **2** *obs* **:** one that cheats **:** SHARPER

bi·ternate \(ˈ)bī+\ *adj* [¹*bi-* + *ternate*] **:** doubly ternate — used esp. of a ternate leaf in which each division is also ternate — **bi·ternately** *adv*

bites *pres 3d sing of* BITE, *pl of* BITE

bite-wing \ˈ⸗,⸗\ *n* **:** a dental X-ray film designed to show the crowns of the upper and lower teeth simultaneously and having a fin for the teeth to bite upon and hold the film in place during exposure

bit extension *n* [¹*bit*] **:** a metal rod with a tang at one end and a socket at the other and used for increasing the effective length of an auger bit

bit-gatherer \ˈ⸗,⸗⸗⸗\ *n* [³*bit*] **:** a glassworker who gathers bits

bit gauge *n* [¹*bit*] **:** a device attached to the shank of a drilling or boring bit to control the depth of the hole

bi·theism \ˈbī(,)thē,izəm, ˈbīˈth-\ *n* -s [¹*bi-* + *-theism*] **:** belief in the existence of two gods (as one good and one evil)

bi·thyn·ia \bəˈthinēə\ [NL, fr. *Bithynia*, Asia Minor] *syn of* BULIMUS

¹bi·thyn·i·an \-nēən\ *adj, usu cap* [*Bithynia*, ancient country of northwestern Asia Minor (fr. L, fr. Gk) + E *-an*] **1 :** of, relating to, or characteristic of Bithynia in Asia Minor **2 :** of, relating to, or characteristic of Bithynians

²bithynian \"\ *n* -s *usu cap* **:** a native or inhabitant of ancient Bithynia

biting *adj* [ME, fr. pres. part. of *biten*] **:** that bites or tends to bite esp. with the production of mental or physical discomfort **:** SHARP, CUTTING, CAUSTIC ⟨a ~ acid odor⟩ ⟨~ sarcastic words⟩ ⟨chill ~ winds⟩ **syn** see INCISIVE

biting crowfoot *n* **:** BULBOUS BUTTERCUP

biting fly *n* **:** a fly (as the mosquito, midge, or horsefly) having mouthparts adapted for piercing and biting man and other vertebrates

biting housefly *n* **:** STABLE FLY

biting knotweed *n* **:** WATER PEPPER

biting louse *n* **:** BIRD LOUSE

bit·ing·ly *adv* [ME, fr. *biting* + *-ly*] **:** in a biting manner

biting midge *n* **:** a midge of the family Ceratopogonidae

bit·ing·ness *n* -ES **:** the quality or state of being biting

biting stonecrop *n* **:** a stonecrop (*Sedum acre*)

bi·tis \ˈbīd·əs\ *n, cap* [NL] **:** a genus of African vipers including the Old World puff adder, the Gaboon viper, and a few other heavy-bodied rather sluggish venomous snakes

bit key *n* [¹*bit*] **:** a key having a wing bit (as for lever tumbler locks)

bi·to \ˈbēd·(,)ō\ *or* **bito tree** *n* -s [origin unknown] **:** a small scrubby tree (*Balanites aegyptiaca*) that grows in dry regions of tropical Africa and Asia and has bark that yields a fish poison and seeds that yield a medicinal oil — called also *desert date;* see BALANITES

bi·tonal \(ˈ)bī +\ *adj* [¹*bi-* + *tonal*] **:** using two musical tonalities simultaneously — **bi·tonality** \ˌbī + \ *n* -ES

bi·tot's spots \(ˈ)bēˈtōz,-\ *n pl, usu cap B* [after Pierre A. *Bitot* †1888 Fr. physician] **:** shiny pearly spots of triangular shape occurring on the scleras in severe vitamin A deficiency esp. in children

bit part *n* [³*bit*] **:** ³BIT 3f

bit pincers *n pl* [¹*bit*] **:** pincers having curved jaws

bi·trochanteric \(ˈ)bī +\ *adj* [¹*bi-* + *trochanteric*] **:** of, relating to, or between the two trochanters or trochanterions

bits *pl of* BIT, *pres 3d sing of* BIT

bit·stock *also* **bit·stalk** \ˈ⸗,⸗\ *n* [¹*bit* + *stock* or *stalk*] **:** a handle or other device for holding and turning a bit by hand; *specif* **:** a carpenter's brace

bit·stone \ˈ⸗,⸗\ *n* [³*bit* + *stone*] **:** ³BIT 2d

bit·sy \ˈbitsē\ *adj* [prob. alter. of *bitty*] *dial* **:** TINY

¹bitt \ˈbit, *usu* -d· + V\ *n* -s [perh. fr. ON *biti* beam, thwart — more at BOAT] **1 :** a single or double post of metal or wood fixed on the deck of a ship and around which mooring lines or other lines are made fast **2 :** BOLLARD 1a

²bitt \"\ *vt* -ED/-ING/-S **:** to make (a cable) fast about the bitt of a ship (as in mooring)

bit·ta·ci·dae \bəˈtasə,dē\ *n pl, cap* [NL, fr. *Bittacus*, type genus (fr. Gk *bittakos, psittakos* parrot) + *-idae*] **:** a family of chiefly tropical predacious red-and-black flies (order Mecoptera) comprising the scorpion flies

bit·ta·cle \ˈbid·əkəl\ *archaic var of* BINNACLE

bitted *past of* BIT *or of* BITT

bitten *past part of* BITE

bitten-leaf disease \ˈ⸗⸗,⸗-\ *n* **:** LEAF BITE

¹bit·ter \ˈbid·ə(r), ˈbitə-\ *adj, usu* -ER/-EST [ME, fr. OE *biter;* akin to OHG *bittar* bitter, ON *bitr* sharp, biting, Goth *baitis* bitter, OE *bītan* to bite — more at BITE] **1 a :** indicating or inducing the one of the four basic taste sensations that is mediated by end organs in the circumvallate papillae, is produced chiefly by organic compounds (as alkaloids and certain glucosides), and when strongly developed is markedly unpleasant and lingering ⟨the medicine left a ~ taste in her mouth⟩ — compare SALT, SOUR, SWEET **b :** distasteful to the mind **:** distressing to contemplate **:** UNPALATABLE, GALLING ⟨~ truths⟩ ⟨a ~ sense of shame⟩ **2 :** marked by intensity or severity **:** RIGOROUS: **a :** accompanied by severe pain or suffering of mind or body **:** difficult to bear ⟨a ~ death⟩ ⟨there was a ~ moment when they parted for the last time⟩ **b :** VEHEMENT, RELENTLESS, DETERMINED ⟨a ~ partisan⟩ ⟨the ~ struggle for economic freedom⟩; *often* **:** exhibiting intense animosity ⟨~ enemies⟩ **c** *obs* **:** cruel and oppressive **d** (1) *of modes of expression* **:** harshly reproachful **:** sharp and resentful **:** BITING ⟨~ complaints⟩ (2) *of a person or attitude* **:** marked by cynicism and rancor **:** intensely unfriendly ⟨~ contempt⟩ ⟨a ~ answer⟩ **e** *of weather or its manifestations* **:** intensely unpleasant esp. in coldness or rawness **:** PIERCING, RAW ⟨a ~ wind whistled about our ears⟩ **3** *obs* **:** causing or designed to cause pain or anguish **4 :** caused by or expressive of severe pain, grief, or regret ⟨~ tears shed too late⟩

syn ACRID stresses astringent effects accompanying strong, pungent, unpleasant tastes or penetrating or suffocating odors ⟨in its green state, it is exceedingly *acrid*, but boiled or baked, had the sweetness of the sugarcane —Herman Melville⟩ ⟨there was an *acrid* musty smell; the raw air was close with breathing —Rose Macaulay⟩ BITTER, a more general and often less extreme word, indicates a marked pungent taste, usu. unpleasant, and an absence of sweetness or mildness ⟨*bitter* as aloes, it parched my tongue —Elinor Wylie⟩ ⟨McCoy had made some beer, once, with ti roots . . . It was *bitter* stuff and fair gagged ye to get it down —C.B.Nordhoff & J.N.Hall⟩ Sometimes, as with BITTER chocolate, BITTER winter cress and tonics, and flavors called bitters, the unpleasant suggestion is lacking. Both words refer to acid, misanthropic temperaments. ACRID suggests malevolent, caustic sarcasm ⟨the thin, angular woman, with her haughty eye and her *acrid* mouth —Lytton Strachey⟩ BITTER may add to this the suggestion of cynicism ⟨the good-humoured, affectionate-hearted Godfrey Cass was fast becoming a *bitter* man, visited by cruel wishes —George Eliot⟩

syn SORE, GRIEVOUS: BITTER applies to that which may hurt by or as if by stinging or biting and to that which is unpleasant or unpalatable in the extreme because galling, chagrining, inducing sharpest regret ⟨a *bitter* winter⟩ ⟨a *bitter* period of frustration⟩ ⟨no act of Caesar's showed more sagacity than the introduction of Gallic nobles into the Senate; none was more *bitter* to the Scipios and Metelli, who were compelled to share their august privileges with these despised barbarians —J.A.Froude⟩ ⟨one had a *bitter* sense of waste when one read how tuberculosis had taken him at last up in Switzerland —Rebecca West⟩ In descriptions of persons and their moods, utterances, and activities, BITTER indicates deep, virulent, implacable resentment and hate ⟨an ugly story of low passion, delusion, and waking from delusion, which needs not to be dragged from the privacy of Godfrey's *bitter* memory —George Eliot⟩ SORE applies to what occasions severe trial, tribulation, or painful affliction ⟨Baltimore's tribulations were indeed *sore;* there was no peace for him day nor night —Herman Melville⟩ ⟨an exceptionally long history of struggle and suffering has left many *sore* and sensitive spots in the body of Israel —M.R.Cohen⟩ Applied to persons SORE may indicate either painful sensitivity or smarting resentment ⟨the worst of suffering such as hers was that it left one *sore* to the gentlest touch —Edith Wharton⟩ ⟨many of the delegates were *sore* and angry about places in the Constitution that they didn't like and had worked hard to cut out —Dorothy C. Fisher⟩ GRIEVOUS, rather archaic in effect, applies to the painfully onerous or sorely lamentable ⟨though his hurts were many and *grievous*, and his lifeblood ebbing fast —William Morris⟩ ⟨Europe had suffered *grievous* losses of men and materials —Vera M. Dean⟩

²bitter \"\ *adv* [ME, fr. OE *bitere*, fr. *biter*, adj.] **1 :** BITTERLY — used esp. in the phrase *bitter cold* **2** *dial Eng* **:** EXTREMELY, VERY ⟨this drug is wanted ~ bad, sir —R.L.Stevenson⟩

³bitter \"\ *n* -s [ME, fr. *bitter*, adj.] **1 a :** something bitter; *also* **:** bitter quality ⟨take the ~ with the sweet⟩ **b :** a bitter taste sensation ⟨the medicine has a ~ all its own⟩ **2 a bitters** *pl* **:** a usu. alcoholic liquor prepared by maceration or distillation of a bitter herb, leaf, fruit, seed, or root and used as a mild tonic or stimulant to increase the appetite and improve digestion and as a flavoring agent esp. in cocktails and sauces **b** *Brit* **:** a very dry heavily hopped ale usu. sold on draft

⁴bitter \"\ *vt* -ED/-ING/-S [ME *bitteren*, fr. OE *biterian*, fr. *biter*, adj.] **:** to make bitter ⟨~*ed* ale⟩ **:** EMBITTER

⁵bitt·er \"\ *n* -s [¹*bitt* + *-er*] **:** a turn of cable round the bitts

bitter almond *n* **:** an almond that has a very bitter seed and forms a variety (*Amygdalus communis amara*) of the common almond; *also* **:** the seed of this plant

bitter almond oil *n* **1 :** ALMOND OIL 1b, 2 **2 :** BENZALDEHYDE

bitter aloes *n pl* **:** ALOE 4

bitter apple *n* **:** COLOCYNTH

bitter ash *n* **1 :** BITTERWOOD 1a **2 :** ²WAHOO a

bitterbark \ˈ⸗⸗,⸗\ *n* **1 :** any of several woody plants having bitter bark: as **a** *Austral* (1) **:** a woody shrub (*Alstonia constricta*) with a bark sometimes used as a febrifuge (2) **:** NATIVE QUINCE (3) **:** a shrub or small tree (*Tabernaemontana orientalis*) having evergreen leaves, sweet-scented flowers with slender tubes, and orange-colored fruit **b :** FEVER TREE b **c :** CASCARA BUCKTHORN **2 :** the bark from a bitterbark esp. when used medicinally

bitterbloom \ˈ⸗⸗,⸗\ *n* **:** an American centaury (*Sabbatia angularis*)

bitterbrush \ˈ⸗⸗,⸗\ *n* **:** a much-branched silvery shrub (*Purshia tridentata*) with 3-toothed leaves and yellow flowers that is common in arid regions of western No. America and valuable for winter forage — called also *antelope bitterbrush, antelope brush*

bitter bugle *n* **:** either of two mints of the genus *Lycopus* (*L. americanus* and *L. europaeus*) with bitter foliage

bitterbush \ˈ⸗⸗,⸗\ *n* **1 :** BEAR OAK **2 :** a tropical American shrub or small tree (*Picramnia pentandra*) with red berries

bitter buttons *n pl but sing or pl in constr* **:** a tansy (*Tanacetum vulgare*)

bitter cassava *n* **:** a cassava (*Manihot utilissima*) commonly used to make cassiri and other intoxicating drinks

bitter cherry *n* **:** a wild cherry (*Prunus emarginata*) of the western U.S. with bitter fruit

bitter chocolate *n* **:** CHOCOLATE 1

bitter clover *n* **:** a yellow-flowered Eurasian annual sweet clover (*Melilotus indica*) used as a cover crop in the western U.S. and now naturalized there and eastward

bitter cress *n* **1 :** a plant of the genus *Cardamine* (as the European *C. amara* and the American *C. hirsuta*) **2 :** WINTER CRESS

bitter cucumber *n* **:** COLOCYNTH

bitter damson *n* **:** MARUPA

bitter dock *n* **:** a European dock (*Rumex obtusifolius*) having broad obtuse leaves and bitter rootstocks that is very common as a weed in the U.S. — called also *broad-leaved dock, yellow dock*

bitter dogbane *n* **:** a No. American dogbane (*Apocynum androsaemifolium*) with pink flowers

¹bitt·er end *n* [⁵*bitter*] **:** the inboard end of a ship's anchoring cable or line

²bit·ter end *n* [prob. fr. ¹*bitter*] **:** the last extremity however painful, distasteful, or calamitous ⟨to the *bitter end*⟩

bitter-ender \ˈ⸗ˈ⸗⸗\ *n* -s [²*bitter end* + *-er*] **:** one who inflexibly rejects opportune compromising or yielding on any part of an effort or policy **:** EXTREMIST, DIEHARD

bitterer *comparative of* BITTER

bitterest *superlative of* BITTER

bitter gourd *n* **1 :** COLOCYNTH **2 :** an edible gourd of Australia and Asia that is prob. identical with a snake gourd (*Trichosanthes anguina*)

bitterhead \ˈ⸗⸗,⸗\ *n* **1 :** BLACK CRAPPIE **2 :** GOLDEN SHINER

bitter herb *n* **1 :** an annual centaury (*Centaurium umbellatum*) with purplish rose flowers in dense clusters **2 :** TURTLEHEAD **3 :** a salad usu. of horseradish and sometimes supplemented by cos lettuce eaten during the seder of Passover as maror ⟨with *bitter herbs* they shall eat it —Exod 12:8 (AV)⟩

bit·ter·ish \ˈbid·ərish, ˈbitə-, -rēsh\ *adj* [¹*bitter* + *-ish*] **:** somewhat bitter

bitter lake *n* **:** a lake the water of which contains in solution large quantities of sodium sulfate as well as lesser amounts of the carbonates and chlorides ordinarily found in salt lakes

bit·ter·less \-ləs\ *adj* [¹*bitter* + *-less*] **:** without a bitter taste — used of pharmaceutical preparations in which the bitter principle is masked or eliminated ⟨~ syrup of quinidine⟩

bit·ter·ling \ˈbid·ə(r)liŋ\ *n* -s [G, fr. *bitter* (fr. OHG *bittar*) + *-ling* — more at BITTER] **:** a small European cyprinid fish (*Rhodeus amarus*) introduced and locally common about New York that is much used in bioassay of mammalian hormones — see BITTERLING TEST, JAPANESE BITTERLING

bitterling test *n* **:** a test for human pregnancy based on response of the female Japanese bitterling to substances excreted in pregnant urine and made by adding test urine to the water containing the fish, a positive test being reported if the ovipositor enlarges markedly

bit·ter·ly *adv* [ME, fr. OE *biterlice*, fr. *biter* + *-lice* -ly] **:** in a bitter manner ⟨spoke ~⟩ **:** to a bitter degree ⟨~ exhausted⟩

¹bit·tern \ˈbid·ə(r)n, ˈbitə-\ *n* -s [ME *bitoure, botor*, fr. MF *butor*, perh. fr. (assumed) VL *butitaurus*, fr. L *butio* bittern (prob. of imit. origin) + *taurus* ox, bull — more at STEER] **:** any of various small or medium-sized herons of *Botaurus* and related genera that frequent reedy bogs and swamps, nest on the ground, are nocturnal in habit, and have soft streaked and speckled plumage and a characteristic booming cry — see LEAST BITTERN, STAKE DRIVER

European bittern

²bittern \"\ *n* -s [irreg. fr. ¹*bitter*] **1 :** the bitter mother liquor that remains in saltworks after the salt has crystallized out and that contains other salts (as magnesium chloride, magnesium sulfate, bromides, and iodides) **2 :** a very bitter mixture of quassia and other drugs formerly used in adulterating beer

bit·ter·ness \ˈbid·ə(r)nəs, ˈbitə-\ *n* -ES [ME *bitternesse*, fr. OE *biternes*, fr. *biter* bitter + *-nes* -ness — more at BITTER] **1 :** the quality or state of being bitter **2 :** something bitter

bitter nightshade *n* **:** BITTERSWEET 2a

bit·ter·nut \ˈ⸗⸗,⸗\ *or* **bitternut hickory** *n* **:** a hickory (*Carya cordiformis*) of the eastern U.S. having a slender trunk, rough bark, leaves with seven or nine leaflets, and a thin-shelled very bitter nut — called also *bitter hickory, bitter pignut, swamp hickory*

bitter orange *n* **:** SOUR ORANGE

bitter orange oil *n* **:** ORANGE OIL b

bitter osier *n* **:** PURPLE WILLOW

bitter pecan *n* **:** WATER HICKORY

bitter pepper *n* **:** an Asiatic tree (*Evodia daniellii*) with compound deciduous leaves, white flowers, and black fruit

bitter pill *n* **:** an extreme vexation or humiliation; *esp* **:** one constituting a punishment, retribution, or unavoidable expedient ⟨having to seek his foe's aid was a *bitter pill* to take⟩

bitter pit *n* **:** a nonparasitic disease of the apple, pear, and quince of uncertain etiology but suspected of being caused by upset in the water balance between leaves and fruit and producing spots of dead brown tissue in the flesh of the fruit and discolored depressions on its surface — called also *Baldwin spot, stippen*

bitter principle *n* **:** any of various neutral substances of strong bitter taste (as aloin) extracted from plants

bitterroot \ˈ⸗⸗,⸗\ *n* **1 :** a succulent plant (*Lewisia rediviva*) of the Rocky mountains with fleshy farinaceous roots and pink flowers **2 :** DOGBANE 1

bitter rot *n* **1 :** a very destructive disease of apples, grapes, and other fruit caused by a fungus (*Glomerella cingulata*) and producing cankers on the twigs, limbs, and fruit spurs and a spotting or blistering and decay of the fruit characterized by bitterness of the pulp — called also *anthracnose, ripe rot* **2 :** a rot of ripening grapes caused by an imperfect fungus (*Melanconium fuligineum*)

bitter rubberweed *n* **:** an erect herb (*Actinea odorata*) of the family Compositae of the southwestern U.S. having alternate leaves often sprinkled with resinous globules and chiefly yellow terminal flower heads and causing poisoning of livestock

bitters *pl of* BITTER

bitter salt *n* **:** EPSOM SALTS

bitter spar *n* **:** DOLOMITE

¹bittersweet \ˈ⸗⸗,⸗\ *n* [ME *biterswete*, fr. *biter* bitter + *swete* sweetness — more at SWEET] **1 :** something that is bittersweet **:** pleasure alloyed with pain ⟨all the ~ of their long separation —Christopher Morley⟩ **2 a :** a sprawling Old World poisonous plant (*Solanum dulcamara*) that is common as a weed in America and has purple flowers and oval coral-red berries and a taste at first sweetish and then bitter **b :** a No. American ornamental woody vine (*Celastrus scandens*) having clusters of small greenish flowers succeeded by yellow capsules that burst open when ripe disclosing the scarlet aril — called also *climbing bittersweet, false bittersweet;* see EVERGREEN BITTERSWEET, JAPANESE BITTERSWEET **3 a :** a deep orange that is deeper than bittersweet orange **b :** a dark to deep reddish orange — called also *lobster*

²bittersweet \"\ *adj* **1 :** at once bitter and sweet ⟨a ~ apple⟩; *esp* **:** pleasant but attended by elements or twinges of suffering or regret ⟨~ hunger of desire —Hamlin Garland⟩ **2 :** of or relating to a prepared chocolate containing little sugar; *also* **:** of or relating to syrups and candy coatings made of this chocolate or confections covered with such coatings

bittersweet orange *n* **:** a deep orange that is paler than bittersweet — called also *neutral orange*

bittersweet pink *n* **:** a strong yellowish pink that is yellower and darker than salmon pink, yellower than peach red, and yellower and slightly lighter than average salmon — called also *Du Barry*

bitter thistle *n* **:** BLESSED THISTLE 1

bitter vetch *n* **:** any of several reputedly bitter or toxic vetches: as **a :** ERS **b :** CHICKLING **c :** an erect glabrous European vetch (*Lathyrus montanus*) with creeping and tuberous rhizomes **d :** a western No. American vetch (*Lathyrus lanszwertii*) with narrow coriaceous leaflets and pale lavender to pinkish violet flowers

bitter waternut *n* **:** NUTMEG HICKORY

bitterweed \ˈ⸗⸗,⸗\ *n* **1 :** any of several American plants containing a bitter principle: as **a :** RAGWEED 2 **b :** HORSEWEED **c :** SNEEZEWEED 1a **d :** any of several trees of the genus *Xylopia; esp* **:** a West Indian tree (*X. glabra*) **:** BITTER RUBBERWEED **2 :** the wood of a bitterweed tree

bitter willow *n* **:** PURPLE WILLOW

bitterwood \ˈ⸗⸗,⸗\ *n* -s **1 a :** a West Indian tree (*Picrasma excelsum*) of the family Simaroubaceae that yields Jamaica quassia **b :** PARADISE TREE 1 **2 :** QUASSIA 2

bitterworm \ˈ⸗⸗,⸗\ *n* [so called fr. the creeping scaly root and the bitter principle contained in the plant] **:** BUCKBEAN

bitthead \ˈ⸗,⸗\ *n* [¹*bitt* + *head*] **:** the upper end of a bitt

¹bit·tie *var of* BITTY

²bittie \"\ *n* [³*bit* + Sc *-ie* (dim. suffix)] *Scot* **:** ³BIT

³bittie \"\ *adj, Scot* **:** LITTLE

¹bitting *pres part of* BIT *or of* BITT

²bit·ting \ˈbid·iŋ, ˈbitiŋ\ *n* -s [¹*bit* + *-ing*] **:** the shape of the bit of a key that causes it to fit or actuate the lock

bit·ti·um \ˈbid·ēəm\ *n, cap* [NL] **:** a genus of rather small marine snails (family Arithiidae) having elongated spiral shells with a granulated sculpture

bit·tock \ˈbitək\ *n* -s [³*bit* + *-ock*] *chiefly Scot* **:** a little bit

bitt pin *n* **:** a pin thrust through the bitthead to keep the cable from slipping off

bitts *pl of* BITT, *pres 3d sing of* BITT

¹bit·ty *or* **bit·tie** \ˈbid·ē, ˈbitē\ *adj, often* -ER/-EST [³*bit* + *-y*, *-ie*] **:** made up of bits **:** SCRAPPY; *also* **:** containing particulate matter

²bitty *or* **bittie** \"\ *adj* [(*little*) *bitty*, prob. fr. *little bit* + *-y*, *-ie*] *dial* **:** SMALL, TINY — used esp. in the phrase *little bitty*

bitty cream *n* [¹*bitty*] **:** sweet cream curdled by bacteria that survive pasteurization — compare ¹BROKEN 2j

bi·tubercular \ˌbī +\ *adj* [¹*bi-* + *tubercular*] *of a tooth* **:** having two cusps

bi·tu·mas·tic \ˌbī·tyüˈmastik\ *n* -s [fr. *Bitumastic*, a trademark] **:** a composition of asphalt and filler (as asbestos shorts) used chiefly as a protective coating on structural metals exposed to weathering or corrosion

bi·tu·men \bīˈt(y)ümən, bəˈ-, -(,)men; *US sometimes and Brit usu* ˈbityü-\ *n* -s [ME *bithumen* mineral pitch, fr. L *bitumen*, prob. of Celt origin; akin to MIr *bethe, beithe* box (tree), W *bedw* birch; fr. the use of the birch tree as a source of tar — more at CUD] **1 a :** an asphalt of Asia Minor used in ancient times as a cement and mortar **b :** any of various mixtures of hydrocarbons (as asphalt, crude petroleum, or tar) often together with their nonmetallic derivatives that are usu. dark brown or black and occur naturally or are obtained as residues from naturally occurring substances by heat refining; *specif* **:** such a mixture soluble in carbon disulfide — see ASPHALTENE **c :** a roadbed or other surface faced with bitumen **2 :** CONGO 4

bitumen process *n* **:** a photographic process in which advantage is taken of the fact that prepared bitumen is rendered insoluble in benzene or other organic solvents by exposure to light (as in photolithography)

bi·tu·mi·ni·za·tion \bī,t(y)ümənəˈzāshən, bə,-\ *n* -s **1 :** treatment with bitumen **2 :** the natural development of oil shale from ordinary shales

bi·tu·mi·nize *also* **bi·tu·men·ize** \-ˈ⸗⸗,nīz\ *vt* -ED/-ING/-S [L *bitumin-, bitumen* + E *-ize*] **:** to prepare or treat with bitumen

bi·tu·mi·noid *also* **bi·tu·men·oid** \-,nȯid\ *adj* [L *bitumin-, bitumen* + E *-oid*] **:** like bitumen

bi·tu·mi·nous \(ˈ)bīˈt(y)ümənəs, bəˈt-\ *adj* [F or L; F *bitumineux*, fr. MF, fr. L *bituminosus*, fr. *bitumin-, bitumen* + *-osus* -ous] **1 a :** resembling, containing, or impregnated with bitumen **b** *of a mineral* **:** having an odor of bitumen **2 :** impregnated with, infiltrated by, or containing bitumen ⟨~ shale⟩ ⟨~ paint⟩ ⟨a stretch of ~ road⟩ **3 :** of or relating to bituminous coal ⟨the ~ production of the U.S.⟩

bituminous coal *n* **:** a coal that yields when heated considerable volatile bituminous matter — called also *soft coal*

bituminous grout *n* **:** a grout that has bituminous material as a binder and sandy mineral matter as an aggregate and that can be poured when heated

bituminous macadam *n* **:** a pavement constructed by spreading two or more layers of crushed stone on a suitable base and pouring a bituminous binder on each

bit-wise \ˈ⸗,⸗\ *adj* [¹*bit* + *-wise*] *of a saddle horse* **:** responsive to pressure on the bit

bi·typic \(ˈ)bī+\ *adj* [¹*bi-* + *typic*] *of a genus* **:** consisting of two species

-bi·um \bēəm\ *n comb form, pl* **-bia** [NL, fr. neut. of *-bius*] **:** organism or group having a (specified) mode of life — in taxonomic names ⟨*Anobium*⟩ and group names ⟨*coenobium*⟩ in biology

bi·unguiculate \ˈbī+\ *adj* [¹*bi-* + *unguiculate*] **:** of or having a double claw ⟨the ~ leg of a crustacean⟩

bi·u·ni·al \(ˈ)bī¦yünēəl\ *also* **bi·une** \ˈbī,yün\ *adj* [*biunial* fr. ¹*bi-* + L *unus* one + E *-ial*; *biune* fr. ¹*bi-* + L *unus* — more at ONE] **:** combining two in one

bi·u·ret \,bīyəˈret, ˈ≈≈,≈\ *n* -S [ISV ¹*bi-* + *-uret*] **:** a white crystalline compound $NH_2CONHCONH_2$ formed by heating urea — called also *allophanamide*

biuret reaction *n* **:** a reaction shown by biuret, proteins, and most peptides on treatment in alkaline solution with copper sulfate, resulting in a violet color, and used esp. in testing for proteins

-bi·us \bēəs\ *n comb form* [NL, fr. -*bius* having a (specified) mode of life, fr. Gk -*bios*, fr. *bios* mode of life — more at QUICK] **:** one that has a (specified) mode of life — chiefly in generic names in zoology ⟨Entero*bius*⟩

bi·valence *or* **bi·valency** \(ˈ)bī+\ *n, pl* **bivalences** *or* **bivalencies** [¹*bi-* + *valence*; trans. of G *zweiwertigkeit*] **:** the quality or state of being bivalent

¹**bi·valent** \(ˈ)bī+\ *adj* [¹*bi-* + *valent*; trans. of G *zweiwertig*] **1 :** having a valence of two **2 :** DOUBLE — used of homologous chromosomes associated in pairs in synapsis **3 a** *of an antigen, hapten, or antibody* **:** having two sites for combination with antibody or antigen **b** *of an antibody* **:** capable of producing agglutination or precipitation under ordinary experimental conditions

²**bivalent** \"\ *n* -S **:** a pair of synaptic chromosomes

¹**bi·valve** *also* **bi·valved** \(ˈ)bī+\ *adj* [¹*bi-* + *valve* or *valved*] **1 :** having a shell composed of two usu. movable valves that open and shut ⟨~ oysters⟩ ⟨~ clams⟩ **2** *of a shell or capsule* **:** having two valves ⟨the ~ wall of a diatom⟩ **3 :** consisting of two corresponding movable pieces suggesting the shells of mollusks ⟨a ~ speculum⟩

²**bivalve** \"\ *n* -S **:** an animal with a 2-valved shell; *esp* **:** a mollusk of the class Lamellibranchia (as a clam, mussel, or oyster) — compare UNIVALVE

³**bivalve** \"\ *vt* [¹*bi-* + *valve*] **:** to split (a cast) along one or two sides (as to renew surgical dressings or to restore circulation)

bi·val·via \bīˈvalvēə\ *n pl, cap* [NL, fr. E ²*bivalve* + NL *-ia*] *in former classifications* **:** the Lamellibranchia and Brachiopoda considered as a natural group; *sometimes* **:** LAMELLIBRANCHIA

bi·variant \(ˈ)bī+\ *adj* [¹*bi-* + *variant*] **:** capable of twofold variation **:** having two degrees of freedom — used of a system in which the number of components equals the number of phases — compare PHASE RULE

bi·variate \(ˈ)bī+\ *adj* [¹*bi-* + *variate*] **:** of, relating to, or involving two variables ⟨a ~ frequency distribution⟩

bi·vascular \(ˈ)bī+\ *adj* [¹*bi-* + *vascular*] **:** having two blood or other body vessels

bi·venter \(ˈ)bī+\ *n* [NL, fr. ¹*bi-* + *venter*] **:** a muscle with two fleshy bellies

bi·ventral \(ˈ)bī+\ *adj* [¹*bi-* + *ventral*] **:** having two bellies **:** DIGASTRIC

bi·verbal \(ˈ)bī+\ *adj* [¹*bi-* + *verbal*] **:** relating to or involving two words or expressions; *also* **:** PUNNING

bi·vinyl \(ˈ)bī+\ *n* -S [ISV ¹*bi-* + *vinyl*] **:** BUTADIENE

bi·visible \(ˈ)bī+\ *n* [¹*bi-* + *visible*] **:** a dry fly tied from hackles of contrasting colors so that it may be seen readily by both fish and angler

bi·vittate \(ˈ)bī+\ *adj* [¹*bi-* + *vittate*] *zool* **:** having two longitudinal stripes

biv·i·um \ˈbivēəm, ˈbīv-\ *n, pl* **bivia** [NL, fr. L, crossroads, fr. neut. of *bivius* having two roads, fr. *bi-* ¹*bi-* + *-vius* (fr. *via* road, way) — more at VIA] **:** the two rays of a starfish between which is the madreporite — opposed to *trivium*

bi·vol·tine \bīˈvōl,tēn, (ˈ)≈¦≈,tᵊn\ *also* **bi·vol·tin** \-,tᵊn\ *adj* [F *bivoltin*, fr. *bi-* ¹*bi-* + It *volta* time, instance (fr. — assumed — VL *volvita*, fr. L *volvere* to turn) + F *-in* -ine — more at VOLUBLE] **1 :** producing two broods in a season — used esp. of silkworms **2** *of insects* **:** having two generations a year, a summer generation without diapause and a winter generation with diapause — **bi·vol·tin·ism** \-,tᵊn,izəm\ *n* -S

bi·vol·tin·ize \≈ˈ≈tə,nīz\ *vt* -ED/-ING/-S **:** to treat (silkworm eggs) so as to produce bivoltine progeny

¹**biv·ouac** \ˈbiv,wak *also* -və,w-\ *n* -S [F, fr. LG *biwake*, fr. *bi* at, by (fr. MLG *bī*) + *wake* guard; akin to OHG *bī* by, at and to OHG *wahha* guard, *wahhēn*, *wahhōn* to wake — more at WAKE] **1 a** *obs* **:** the watch of a whole army by night when in danger of surprise or attack **b :** an encampment under little or no shelter usu. for a short time; *also* **:** the site of such encampment **2 :** a camping out for a night; *also* **:** a temporary or casual shelter or settlement

²**bivouac** \"\ *vi* **bivouacked**; **bivouacked**; **bivouacking**; **bivouacks** *also* **bivouacs 1 :** to encamp with little or no shelter ⟨the troops *bivouacked* there for a week⟩ **2 a :** to spend the night in the open **b :** to put up temporarily **:** make a casual or temporary settlement ⟨the troupe . . . *bivouacked* at a three-story house —Milton Esterow⟩

bivouac sheet *n* **:** ZDARSKY TENT

biv·er \ˈbivə(r)\ *dial chiefly Brit var of* ²BEVER

bivvy *also* **bivy** \ˈbivē\ *n or vb* [by shortening & alter.] *slang* **:** BIVOUAC

bi·wa \ˈbē(,)wä\ *n* -S [Jap] **:** a 4-stringed Japanese lute

¹**bi·weekly** \(ˈ)bī+\ *adj* [¹*bi-* + *weekly*] **1 :** occurring or appearing every two weeks **:** having a 2-week interval between recurrences **:** FORTNIGHTLY — now usu. used with this meaning in respect to publication dates; compare SEMIWEEKLY **2 :** occurring or appearing twice a week **:** SEMIWEEKLY — used esp. of transportation schedules

²**biweekly** \"\ *adv* **1 :** every two weeks **2 :** twice a week

³**biweekly** \"\ *n* -ES **1 :** a publication issued every two weeks **2 :** SEMIWEEKLY

bixa \ˈbiksə\ *n, cap* [NL, fr. AmerSp *bija*, *bixa* achiote, fr. Taino *bixa*] **:** an American genus (the type of the family Bixaceae) of trees with cordate leaves and large pink or rose flowers — see ANNATTO TREE

bix·a·ce·ae \bikˈsāsē,ē\ *n pl, cap* [NL, fr. *Bixa*, type genus + *-aceae*] **:** a family of tropical shrubs or trees (order Parietales) having alternate leaves, perfect flowers, a superior ovary, and valvate capsules — **bix·a·ceous** \-ˈsāshəs\ *adj*

bix·by·ite \ˈbiksbē,īt\ *n* -S [Maynard *Bixby*, 19th cent. American who discovered it + E *-ite*] **:** a mineral $FeO.MnO_2$ consisting of an iron manganese oxide occurring in black isometric crystals

bix·in \ˈbiksən\ *n* -S [ISV *bix-* (fr. NL *Bixa*, genus name of *Bixa orellana*) + *-in*] **:** a red-brown carotenoid acid ester $HOOCC_{22}H_{26}COOCH_3$ constituting the chief coloring matter of annatto and used similarly

bi·yearly \(ˈ)bī+\ *adj* [¹*bi-* + *yearly*] **1 :** BIENNIAL **2 :** BIANNUAL

biz \ˈbiz\ *n* [by shortening & alter.] *slang* **:** BUSINESS

¹**bizarre** \bəˈzär, bēˈz-, -zȧ(r\ *adj* [F, fr. It *bizzarro*] **:** being strikingly out of the ordinary or at variance with some standard real or implied: as **a :** not suited to the situation; *esp* **:** being at variance with good taste or accepted standards (as of fashion, design, or color) ⟨a ~ little house, fit home for a troll⟩ ⟨her ~ hanging sleeves⟩ **b :** odd, extravagant, or eccentric in style or mode ⟨~ art forms of the early 20th century⟩ ⟨he became increasingly ~ in speech⟩ **c :** involving sensational contrasts or marked incongruities **:** FANTASTIC ⟨the ~ assurance of this mousy little man⟩ **d :** not falling within the bounds of what is recognized as normal **:** ATYPICAL ⟨~ bone formation⟩ ⟨the ~ test scores indicated a schizophrenic tendency⟩ **syn** see FANTASTIC

²**bizarre** \"\ *n* -S **:** any of certain flowers with atypical striped markings: **a :** a carnation with white or yellowish flowers striped and flecked with two or more other colors **b :** a yellow tulip with stripes and blotches of usu. scarlet or brown

bi·zarre·ly *adv* **:** in a bizarre manner

bi·zarre·ness *n* -ES **:** the quality or state of being bizarre

bi·zar·re·rie \bəˈzärə,rē, bēˈzä-\ *n* -S [F, fr. *bizarre* + *-erie* -ery] **1 :** bizarre quality **2 :** something bizarre

bizel *var of* BEZEL

bizen *var of* BYZEN

bi·zet \bəˈzet\ *n* -S [prob. by alter.] **:** BEZEL 2b

biznaga *var of* BISNAGA

bi·zonal \(ˈ)bī+\ *adj* [¹*bi-* + *zonal*] **:** of, relating to, or concerned with the combined affairs of two administrative areas — often cap. when referring to the British and American occupied zones in Germany after World War II ⟨*Bizonal* currency⟩

bi·zone \ˈbī+,-\ *n* -S [prob. back-formation fr. *bizonal*] **:** a bizonal area; *specif* **:** a zone governed or administered by two powers acting together

¹**bi·zygomatic** \(ˈ)bī+\ *adj* [¹*bi-* + *zygomatic*] **:** of or relating to the two cheekbones; *specif* **:** relating to a measure of facial width taken between the most lateral points on the external surfaces of the zygomatic arches

²**bizygomatic** \"\ *n* -S **:** the bizygomatic width of the face

bizz \ˈbiz\ *dial var of* BUZZ

biz·zar·ro \bətˈsä(,)rō\ *adj* [It] **:** BIZARRE — used as a direction in music

bk *abbr* **1** backwardation **2** balk **3** bank **4** bark **5** black **6** block **7** book **8** brake **9** brook

Bk *symbol* berkelium

bkcy *abbr* bankruptcy

bkg *abbr* **1** banking **2** bookkeeping **3** breakage

bkgd *abbr* background

bkp *abbr* bookplate

bkpg *abbr* bookkeeping

bkpr *abbr* bookkeeper

bkpt *abbr* bankrupt

bkry *abbr* bakery

bks *abbr* **1** backstrip **2** barracks

bkt *abbr* **1** basket **2** bracket

bl *abbr* **1** bale **2** barrel **3** black **4** blessed **5** block **6** blue

BL *abbr or n* -S **1 :** a bachelor of laws **2 :** a bachelor of letters

BL *abbr* **1** base line **2** bill of lading **3** black letter **4** breadth-length **5** breech-loading **6** building line

blaa *or* **blaa–blaa** *var of* BLAH

blaas·op \ˈblä,säp\ *n* -S [Afrik, fr. *blaas* (imper. of *blaas* to blow, fr. MD *blāsen*) + *op* up, fr. MD; akin to OHG *blāsan* to blow and to OHG *ūf* up — more at BLAST, UP] *Africa* **:** GLOBEFISH

blaauwbok *var of* BLAUBOK

blaauw wildebeest \ˈblō-\ *n* [obs. Afrik (now *blouwildebees*), lit., blue wildebeest] *Africa* **:** BRINDLED GNU

¹**blab** \ˈblab, -aa(ə)b\ *n* -S [ME *blabbe*; akin to ME *blaberen* to blabber] **1 :** one that blabs ⟨who will open himself to a ~ or a babbler —Francis Bacon⟩ **2 :** idle or excessive talk **:** the telling of secrets **:** CHATTER **3 :** a word or series of usu. high sounding or pretentious words, that is empty of meaning or too vague in meaning to serve as a basis of discussion ⟨"that's just ~", came the rude interruption⟩ — **blab·by** \-ē, -i\ *adj*

²**blab** \"\ *vb* **blabbed**; **blabbed**; **blabbing**; **blabs** *vt* **:** to reveal (as a secret) esp. by talking without reserve or discretion ⟨confessions made to him are rarely . . . *blabbed* —Christopher Morley⟩ — often used with *out* ⟨expect me to ~ out my private feelings —Robertson Davies⟩ **~** *vi* **1 :** to reveal a secret esp. by talking without reserve or discretion ⟨he will be sure to ~, and it will be all over the town in no time —Joseph Conrad⟩ **2 :** to talk idly or thoughtlessly **:** CHATTER, GAB

³**blab** \"\ *n* -S [origin unknown] *West* **:** a thin piece of board attached to a calf's nose to prevent suckling

⁴**blab** \"\ *vt* **blabbed**; **blabbed**; **blabbing**; **blabs** *West* **:** to attach a blab to **:** wean with a blab

¹**blab·ber** \ˈblabə(r)\ *vb* **blabbered**; **blabbered**; **blabbering** \-ab(ə)riŋ\ **blabbers** [ME *blaberen*, prob. of imit. origin like OHG *blabbizōn* to babble, ON *blabbra*] *vi* **:** to talk indiscreetly, excessively, or nonsensically **:** BABBLE **~** *vt* **:** to say or utter indiscreetly or foolishly — often used with *out* ⟨he ~*ed* out some kind of reply⟩

²**blabber** \"\ *n* -S **:** indiscreet, excessive, or nonsensical talk

³**blabber** \"\ *archaic var of* ³BLUBBER

⁴**blabber** \ˈblabə(r), -laab-\ *n* -S [²*blab* + *-er*] **:** one that blabs

⁵**blabber** \"\ *n* -S [by alter.] **:** BLUBBERER 2

blabbermouth \ˈ≈≈,≈\ *n* -S [²*blabber* + *mouth*] **:** one that talks too much **:** BLABBER

blabmouth \ˈ≈,≈\ *n* -S [¹*blab* + *mouth*] **:** BLABBERMOUTH

blab school *n* [²*blab*] **:** a school common in the U.S. during pioneer days in which pupils study their lessons by repeating them aloud separately or in chorus until one is called forward to recite

¹**black** \ˈblak\ *adj* -ER/-EST [ME *blak*, fr. OE *blæc*; akin to OHG *blah* black, ON *blakra* to blink, L *flagrare* to burn, Gk *phlegein*, Skt *bharga* radiance, OE *bǣl* fire, pyre — more at BALD] **1 a :** of the color black **:** having the color of soot or coal ⟨~ cloth⟩ ⟨~ as ebony⟩ **b :** very dark in color ⟨his face ~ with rage —T.B.Costain⟩ **c** *of written or printed letters* **:** characterized by thickness of form and consequent intense contrast with the white of a page ⟨a heavy ~ type⟩ **d :** covered or darkened with numerous dark objects close together ⟨the . . . ceiling was . . . ~ with flies —Ann Bridge⟩ ⟨the boxcars going north would be ~ with harvesters sitting on the top —Meridel Le Sueur⟩ **2 a** *of human beings* (1) **:** having darkly pigmented skin, hair, and eyes **:** dark-complexioned **:** BRUNET ⟨whether the writer . . . be a ~ or a fair man —Joseph Addison⟩ (2) **:** dark in comparison to the average complexion of a group or race **:** SWARTHY ⟨a ~ Irishman⟩ (3) **:** being a member of a group or race characterized by dark pigmentation ⟨organized Negro regiments commanded by ~ officers⟩; *esp* **:** NEGROID — compare BROWN 2a, COLORED, WHITE, YELLOW **b :** of, belonging to, consisting of, or connected with black, esp. negroid, people ⟨~ Africa⟩ ⟨~ races⟩; *esp* **:** having a large Negro population ⟨a ~ belt⟩ **c :** advocating more rights for Negroes — used esp. in reference to the slavery controversy of the 19th century in the U.S. ⟨~ abolitionist⟩ ⟨~ Republican⟩ **3 a :** characterized by wearing black clothes or black armor ⟨the ~ knight⟩ **b :** of, belonging to, or being a member of a group characterized or formerly characterized by wearing black: as (1) **:** clerical in politics (2) **:** FASCIST ⟨the red and ~ totalitarians —Mark Starr⟩ — see BLACKSHIRT **4 :** soiled with dirt **:** DIRTY ⟨how ~ your hands are⟩ ⟨the pot calls the kettle ~⟩ **5 a :** characterized by the absence of light or the presence of very little light ⟨a ~ night⟩ **:** reflecting or transmitting little or no light ⟨~ water⟩ ⟨~ glass⟩ **b** *of coffee* **:** served without cream or milk and sometimes also without sugar **6 a :** outrageously wicked **:** deserving unmitigated condemnation ⟨a ~ deed⟩ ⟨a ~ heart⟩ ⟨a ~ villain⟩ ⟨a moralist to whom everything is either ~ or white⟩; *sometimes* **:** DISHONORABLE, DISCREDITABLE **b :** expressing or indicating disgrace, dishonor, discredit, or guilt sometimes through symbolic use of an object that is black in color ⟨a ~ mark for tardiness⟩ ⟨with evidence so ~ against him —Charlotte Armstrong⟩ **7 :** connected with some baneful aspect of the supernatural, esp. the devil ⟨a ~ curse⟩ ⟨~ magic⟩ ⟨the ~ art⟩ **8 a :** unrelievedly sad, gloomy, or calamitous ⟨~ despair⟩ ⟨things are looking ~⟩ ⟨the autumn of 1776 was a ~ season for the Continental Army —J.D.Hart⟩ **b** *sometimes cap, of a day* **:** marked by the occurrence of a disaster ⟨on September 24, 1869, when Jay Gould, James Fisk, Jr., and their associates effected the partial corner in gold that ended so disastrously in the panic of ~ Friday —S.A.Nelson⟩ **9 :** expressing or characterized by menace or angry discontent **:** SULLEN, HOSTILE ⟨he gave me a ~ look⟩ ⟨~ resentment filled his heart —Miriam James⟩ **10 :** being such to the greatest possible extent **:** EXTREME, UNQUALIFIED, UTTER ⟨it was a ~ born fool I had for a son —J.M.Synge⟩ ⟨they were all ~ strangers to me —Mary Deasy⟩ **11 :** constituting, committing, or connected with a violation of an official quota, price ceiling, rationing restriction, or other public regulation **:** ILLICIT, ILLEGAL ⟨the ~ market⟩ ⟨~ gasoline⟩ **12** [short for ¹*blackleg*] *chiefly Brit* **:** subject to boycott by trade-union members as employing or favoring nonunion workmen or as operated, conducted, or made under conditions considered unfair by trade-union members ⟨a ~ ship⟩ ⟨declare a pub ~⟩ **13 :** marked by or as if by a black section on a map or chart as being affected by some undesirable condition (as infection or a high rate of unemployment) ⟨the polio situation is improving but there are still some ~ areas⟩ **14 :** covered with a dark scale of oxide **:** not galvanized ⟨~ iron pipe⟩ **15 a** *of propaganda* **:** conducted so as to appear to originate within an enemy country and designed to weaken enemy morale — opposed to *white* **b :** characterized by or connected with the use of black propaganda ⟨~ psychological warfare⟩ ⟨~ radio⟩

²**black** \"\ *n* -S [ME *blak* black color, black particle, black material, fr. OE *blæc* ink, fr. *blæc*, adj.] **1 :** any of various substances (as bone black, carbon black, lampblack) containing elemental carbon usu. as the chief constituent **2 a :** the neutral or achromatic object color of least lightness **:** the darkest gray **:** the achromatic color bearing the least resemblance to white **b :** the one of the six psychologically primary colors that is characteristically perceived to belong to objects that neither reflect nor transmit an appreciable fraction of the incident light **c :** any object color of very low lightness and saturation ⟨the painter's ~*s* and browns⟩ **3 :** a black part or area **:** a black speck or stain **4 :** a black material or substance: **a :** black clothing ⟨~ is becoming to her⟩ esp. as worn as a sign of mourning ⟨wear ~ for her father⟩ **b :** a black garment esp. as worn as a sign of mourning or by men on formal occasions ⟨the lawyer . . . in his ~*s* and his silk hat —G.K.Chesterton⟩ ⟨uncomfortable in his wedding ~*s* —Edna Ferber⟩ — usu. used in pl. **5 :** a Negro, Negrito, or Australian aborigine **:** a person belonging to a darkly pigmented race **:** a person whose appearance shows that some of his ancestors belonged to a darkly pigmented race **6 :** a poacher in 18th century England who operated as a member of a band disguised by blackened faces **7 :** the dark-colored pieces in a two-handed board game; *also* **:** the player by or the side of the board from which these pieces are played **8 a :** a black animal: as (1) **:** a black horse (2) **:** an Aberdeen Angus (3) **:** a Norfolk turkey **b :** an individual of a black or melanistic variety of certain common mammals (as squirrel or skunk) **9** *usu cap* **:** one of the Neri **10 :** the black circle of a target; *also* **:** a shot that hits it **11** *usu cap* **:** a member or adherent of a group characterized or formerly characterized by wearing black: as **a :** a member or adherent of a clerical political party **b :** FASCIST **12 :** something deserving unmitigated condemnation ⟨pure whites and seamy ~*s* of character, inviting sighs and hisses —Leslie Rees⟩ ⟨the tendency to think only in terms of ~ or white —D.K.Berninghausen⟩ **13** *print* **:** BOLDFACE 2 **14 :** total or nearly total absence of light **:** DARKNESS ⟨the ~ of night⟩ **15** [fr. the bookkeeping practice of entering credit items in black ink] **:** the condition of making a profit — usu. used with *the* ⟨the company is now operating in the ~⟩; opposed to *red*

³**black** \"\ *vb* -ED/-ING/-S [ME *blaken*, fr. *blak*, n.] *vi* **1 :** BLACKEN — often used with *over* ⟨the sky ~*ed* over⟩ **2 :** to put black coloring matter on one's face in preparation for playing the role of a Negro — used with *up* ⟨~ up for the minstrel show⟩ **~** *vt* **1 a :** BLACKEN 1 **b :** to bruise and discolor (an eye) by a blow ⟨say that again and I'll ~ your eye⟩ **2 :** BLACKEN 2 **3 :** to apply black coloring matter to: as **a :** to make black and shiny by applying blacking to ⟨who will ~ these shoes⟩ ⟨they ~*ed* the stove⟩ **b :** to put black coloring matter on in preparation for playing the role of a Negro ⟨the makeup man ~*ed* the actor's face⟩ — often used with *up* ⟨he ~*ed* himself up for the next performance⟩ **c :** to obliterate with or as if with black ink **:** BLOT **:** delete or suppress through censorship — used with *out* ⟨ordered the passage ~*ed* out from all copies in the school libraries —Upton Sinclair⟩ **d :** to treat (a ship's rigging) with tar or with a mixture containing a black oil or grease — used with *down*

⁴**black** \"\ *adv* [¹*black*] *dial Brit* **:** EXTREMELY ⟨~ afraid⟩ **:** UTTERLY, COMPLETELY ⟨the fire was ~ out⟩

black abalone *n* **:** a comparatively small dark-shelled abalone (*Haliotis cracherodii*) feeding on plankton along the coast from Oregon to Lower California

black acacia *n* **:** LOCUST 3a(2)

blackacre \ˈ≈,≈≈\ *n, law* **:** a particular piece of land esp. in distinction from whiteacre — used esp. as an arbitrary name

black alder *n* **1 :** a shrub (*Ilex verticillata*) with clusters of axillary flowers — called also *winterberry* **2 :** an alder (*Alnus glutinosa*) with broadly oval leaves and with very glutinous young parts

black alkali *n* **:** alkali containing carbonates that dissolve organic matter and blacken soil or crusts **:** soil blackened by such alkali

black·a·moor \ˈblakə,mu̇(ə)r *also* -mō(ə)r *or* -mȯ(ə)r\ *n* -S [alter. of earlier *black More*, fr. *black* + *More*, earlier form of *Moor*] **:** a dark-skinned person **:** a person belonging to a darkly pigmented race; *esp* **:** NEGRO

black-and-blue \¦≈≈¦≈\ *adj* **:** darkly discolored **:** livid or bluish black from a bruise causing rupture of blood vessels and effusion of blood in the tissues

black-and-tan \¦≈≈¦≈\ *adj* **1** *of a dog's coat* **:** having a dominant color pattern that occurs typically in the dachshund, doberman, bloodhound, Manchester terrier, and several other breeds, the body being black with deep tan or rusty red on feet, breeching, and cheek patches, above eyes, and inside ears **2** *often cap B & T* **:** favoring or practicing proportional representation of whites and Negroes in politics ⟨in the campaign of 1912 the Roosevelt supporters in the southern states broke away from the *black-and-tan* regulars and excluded Negroes from the bolting conventions —D.D.McKean⟩ — opposed to *lily-white* **3 :** frequented by both Negroes and whites ⟨a *black-and-tan* bar⟩

black and tan \"\ *n* [*black-and-tan*] **1** *often cap B & T* **:** a black-and-tan dog; *specif* **:** a black-and-tan hound **2** *usu* **black-and-tan :** a nightclub frequented by both Negroes and whites **3** *often cap B & T* **:** a member of the black-and-tan faction of the Republican party in the southern U.S. — opposed to *lily-white* **4** *cap B & T* **:** a recruit enlisted in England in 1920–21 for service in the Royal Irish Constabulary against the armed movement for Irish independence

black-and-tan coonhound *n* **:** a strong vigorous American coonhound having a black-and-tan coat and commonly regarded as constituting a distinct breed

black and white *n* **1 :** WRITING, PRINT ⟨the facts have been set down in *black and white*⟩ **2 :** a drawing or print executed in black or a dark pigment on a white or light ground or in a light pigment on a dark ground **:** the mode or practice of executing such drawings or prints **3 :** a monochrome printed reproduction of a work of art; *also* the mode or practice of executing such reproductions **4 :** monochrome reproduction of visual images (as by photography or television)

black-and-white \¦≈≈¦≈\ *adj* [*black and white*] **1 :** being in writing or print ⟨a *black-and-white* statement of the true situation⟩ **2 :** partly black and partly white in color ⟨a *black-and-white* desert hawk —Zane Grey⟩ **3 a :** executed in black or a dark pigment on a white or light ground or in a light pigment on a dark ground ⟨a *black-and-white* sketch⟩ ⟨*black-and-white* work⟩ **b :** working with such pigment on such a ground ⟨a *black-and-white* artist⟩ **4 a :** printed in ink of one color only ⟨a *black-and-white* map⟩ **b :** characterized by the reproduction or transmission of visual images in tones of gray rather than in colors ⟨*black-and-white* photography⟩ ⟨*black-and-white* television⟩ **5 :** sharply divided into good and evil groups, camps, or sides ⟨a *black-and-white* world where a guy is either your pal or probably a bum —Hal Boyle⟩ **:** evaluating things as altogether bad or good ⟨*black-and-white* morality⟩ ⟨a *black-and-white* judgment⟩

black-and-white warbler *also* **black-and-white creeper** *n* **:** an eastern No. American warbler (*Mniotilta varia*) that is streaked with black and white and that creeps about on trunks and stems

black-and-white work *n* **:** timber framework the interstices of which are filled in with rough masonry or coarse plastering

black-and-yellow warbler \¦≈≈¦≈-\ *n* **:** MAGNOLIA WARBLER

black angelfish *n* **:** a large dark-colored angelfish (*Pomacanthus arcuatus*) of the warm western Atlantic sometimes used as a food fish

black angelica *n* **:** BLACK HOREHOUND

black ape *n* **:** a sooty black monkey (*Cynopithecus niger*) of Celebes having an extremely short tail and a long muzzle and being intermediate in several characteristics between the macaques and the baboons

black apple *n* **1 :** an Australian tree (*Sideroxylon australe*) — called also *brush apple, native plum, wild plum* **2 :** the large plumlike fruit of the black apple

black apricot *n* **:** PURPLE APRICOT

black archangel *n* **:** BLACK HOREHOUND

blackarm \ˈ≈,≈\ *also* **blackarm disease** \(ˈ)≈¦≈-\ *n* **:** a form of angular leaf spot producing dark lesions on the stem and petioles of cotton

¹**black ash** *n* [*ash* (tree)] **1 :** a No. American ash (*Fraxinus nigra*) having dark brown heavy wood — called also *basket ash, brown ash, hoop ash* **2 :** an Australian eucalyptus (*Eucalyptus stellulata*) **3 :** BOX ELDER

²**black ash** *n* [*ash* (combustion product)] **1 :** any of various

dark-colored crude products obtained in industrial processes: as **a :** crude sodium carbonate obtained in the Leblanc process **b :** crude barium sulfide **2 :** a black mass containing chiefly soda in the form of sodium carbonate and usu. also sodium sulfide with some carbon and produced esp. for recovery of its soda content by concentrating and burning black liquor (sense 2) in rotary furnaces

black-a-vised \'blakə,vīst, -,vīzd,-,vēst\ *also* **black-a-viced** \-st\ *adj* [¹*black* + F *à vis* as to face + E *-ed*] : DARK-COMPLEXIONED

blackback \'=,=\ *n* **1 :** any of certain black-backed fishes: as **a :** MENOMINEE WHITEFISH **b :** WINTER FLOUNDER **2 :** any of certain black-backed birds (as the black-backed gull)

black-backed gull \'=,=-\ *n* **:** any of several gulls having the back and upper surface of the wings of a very dark slate or black color as adults — see GREAT BLACK-BACKED GULL, LESSER BLACK-BACKED GULL

black-backed jackal *n* **:** a common So. African jackal (*Canis mesomelas*) with a dark dorsal saddle mark — called also *saddle-backed jackal*

black bag *n* **:** BLUE BAG 2

¹**blackball** \'=,=\ *vt* -ED/-ING/-S [¹*black* + *ball*] **1 a :** to prevent from becoming a member of an organization by casting an adverse vote esp. by putting a black ball into a ballot box or urn ⟨if he applies for membership, I'll ~ him⟩ **b :** to vote against **:** make impossible by casting an adverse vote **:** VETO ⟨~*ed* the membership applications of some candidates of unsavory character⟩ **2 :** to exclude socially **:** OSTRACIZE ⟨he was ~*ed* by all his former friends⟩ **:** exclude from normal professional or economic relations **:** BLACKLIST, BOYCOTT ⟨an advertisement inviting the population at large to ~ me —Victor Ross⟩ **syn** see EXCLUDE

²**blackball** \'=,=\ *n* [¹*black* + *ball*] **1 :** a small black ball that may be put into a ballot box or urn to constitute a vote against admitting someone to membership in an organization **2 :** an adverse vote esp. as excluding an applicant from membership in an organization

black bamboo *n* **:** a small Asiatic bamboo (*Phyllostachys nigra*) having black branches

blackband \'=,=\ *n* **:** the mineral siderite when occurring mixed with clay, sand, and considerable carbonaceous matter and frequently being associated with coal

black-banded snake \'=,==-\ *n* **:** a small brownish back-fanged snake (*Coniophanes imperialis*) with three black bands extending along its back and sides that is native to Mexico and southern Texas

black-banded sunfish *n* **:** a small yellowish gray sunfish (*Mesogonistius chaetodon*) with vertical black bars that is sometimes kept in the aquarium

black bass *n* **1 :** any of several widely distributed and highly prized freshwater game fishes (genus *Micropterus*) of the family Centrarchidae that is native to eastern and central No. America and has been introduced into several western states — see LARGEMOUTH BLACK BASS, SMALLMOUTH BLACK BASS, SPOTTED BLACK BASS **2 :** any of several dark-colored fishes: as **a :** BLACK SEA BASS 1 **b :** PRIESTFISH **c :** BLACK CROAKER a

black-bead \'=,=\ *n* **:** CAT'S-CLAW 1b

black bean *n* **1 :** the seed or wood of Moreton Bay chestnut **2 :** HYACINTH BEAN **3 :** any of several black-seeded beans of the genus *Phaseolus* used esp. in So. America for food

black bear *n* **1 :** the common American bear (*Ursus americanus* or *Euarctos americanus*) known in a number of color phases from typical black through various shades of brown or gray to white **2 :** an Asiatic bear (*Selenarctos thibetanus* or *Ursus thibetanus*) that is usu. black and larger than the American black bear

black bearberry *n* **:** a depressed arctic-alpine shrub (*Arctostaphylos alpinus*) with evergreen leaves and black fruit

black beast *n* [trans. of F *bête noire*] **:** BÊTE NOIRE

black bee *n* **:** a dark-colored ill-tempered honeybee of a race supposedly of German origin — called also *German bee*

black beech *n* **1 :** AMERICAN HORNBEAM **2** *NewZeal* **:** a forest tree (*Nothofagus solanderi*) having entire leaves

black beetle \'=,=\ *n* **:** either of two glossy black burrowing beetles that are very destructive to turf and certain cultivated plants in Australia: **a :** a beetle (*Heteronychus sanctae-helenae*) that was accidentally introduced from Africa **b :** a native beetle (*Metanastes vulgivagus*)

blackbeetle \'=,==\ *n, chiefly Brit* **:** ORIENTAL COCKROACH

black-bellied plover \'=,==-\ *n* **:** a large plover (*Squatarola squatarola* or *Charadrius squatarola*) highly esteemed as a game bird that breeds in the arctic regions of both continents but winters in Africa and So. America and differs from related birds in its jet-black throat and underparts when in breeding plumage

black-bellied sandpiper *n* **:** RED-BACKED SANDPIPER

black-bellied snake *n* **:** a common slightly venomous snake (*Denisonia signata*) widely distributed in eastern Australia that is olive or brownish above with the underparts very dark gray or black

black-berried elder \'=,==-\ *n* **:** ELDERBERRY 1b

¹**blackberry** \'=(,)==, '== — *see* BERRY\ *n* [ME *blakberie*, fr. OE *blæcberie*, fr. *blæc* black + *berie* berry — more at BLACK, BERRY] **1 a :** any of various usu. black or dark purple juicy but seedy and sweet to somewhat bitter edible berries that technically are aggregate fruits consisting of numerous small drupes crowded upon a fleshy receptacle to which, unlike those of the closely related raspberries, they usu. adhere even when fully ripe **b :** any of various trailing or erect usu. prickly brambles of the genus *Rubus* that bear blackberries, are usu. considered to constitute a distinct subgenus, readily form complex hybrids, and include numerous forms cultivated for their fruits **2 :** any of various plants or their black or dark berrylike fruits: as **a :** WHORTLEBERRY 1 **b :** BLACK CURRANT **c :** CROWBERRY 1a

²**blackberry** \"\ *vi* -ED/-ING/-ES **:** to pick blackberries — usu. used in the form *blackberrying* ⟨they went ~*ing*⟩

blackberry bark *n* **:** the dried bark of the rhizome and roots of any species of blackberry (genus *Rubus*) used as an astringent in diarrhea

blackberry lily *n* **:** a garden plant (*Belamcanda chinensis*) of the family Liliaceae with lilylike leaves and flower clusters whose capsule discloses when ripe a mass of seeds resembling a blackberry

blackberry liqueur *n* **:** a dark red liqueur made from blackberry juice often with the addition of red wine and alcohol

blackberry mite *n* **:** a minute mite (*Aceria essigi*) infesting the fruit of blackberries and interfering with their ripening

blackberry wine *n* **:** a variable color averaging a dark purplish red that is bluer and duller than pansy purple, redgrape, raisin, or Bokhara and bluer and less strong than dahlia purple (sense 1)

blackberry winter *n, South & Midland* **:** a period of cold weather in late spring when the blackberries are in bloom

black bile *n* [trans. of L *atra bilis*, prob. trans. of Gk *melaina cholē*] *in medieval physiology and natural philosophy* **:** a humor (sense 1b(1)) believed to be secreted by the kidneys or spleen and to cause gloominess

black-billed cuckoo \'=,=-\ *n* **:** a common No. American cuckoo (*Coccyzus erythropthalmus*) that constructs a nest and hatches its own eggs and is grayish brown above with a circle of bare red skin about the eye and a solid-black bill

black bindweed *n* **1 :** a twining herb (*Polygonum convolvulus*) naturalized in America from Europe and frequently troublesome as a weed **2 :** BLACK BRYONY

blackbine \'=,=\ *n* **:** BLACK BINDWEED 1

black birch *n* **1 :** SWEET BIRCH **2 :** any of several western birches; *esp* **:** RIVER BIRCH **3 :** BEECH 4

¹**blackbird** \'=,=\ *n* [ME *blakbrid*, fr. *blak* black + *brid, bird* bird] **1 :** any of various birds of which the males are largely or entirely black: as **a** *Brit* **:** a common and familiar thrush (*Turdus merula*) that is black with orange bill and eye rim — called also *merl* **b :** any of several American birds of the family Icteridae: as (1) **:** REDWING BLACKBIRD (2) **:** PURPLE GRACKLE (3) **:** RUSTY BLACKBIRD **2 :** a Kanaka kidnaped for use as a plantation laborer esp. in Australia

²**blackbird** \"\ *vb* -ED/-ING/-S *vi* **:** to kidnap Kanakas for use or sale as laborers esp. in Australia — usu. used in the form *blackbirding* ⟨that . . . man who became the terror of the Pacific in the lawless days of ~*ing* and piracy —*Times Lit. Supp.*⟩ ~ *vt* **:** to kidnap (Kanakas) for use or sale as laborers

black·bird·er \-də(r)\ *n* **1 :** a person that blackbirds **2 :** a ship used in blackbirding

black biskop *n* **:** a large biskop (*Cymatoceps nasutus*) sometimes exceeding 100 pounds in weight that is dark mottled gray above and white below with blackish fins and a bulbous snout that overhangs the lower lip

black blight *n* **:** any of several tropical plant diseases caused by superficial sooty molds

black blister beetle *n* **:** an all-black blister beetle (*Epicauta pennsylvanica*) widespread in eastern No. America that feeds destructively on the foliage of potatoes and certain other cultivated plants as an adult

black blizzard *n* **:** a dust storm esp. in the dust-bowl area of the U.S.

black blowfly *n* **:** a rather large dark greenish black typically cold-weather blowfly (*Phormia regina*) breeding chiefly in carrion but also in open wounds of sheep and other animals including man

black blueberry *n* **1 :** a shrub (*Vaccinium atrococcum*) of the eastern U.S. having nearly black fruit without a bloom **2 :** the fruit of the black blueberry

blackboard \'=,=\ *n, often attrib* **:** a thin broad piece of a hard material with a smooth surface formerly always black but now often white or tinted and used esp. in a classroom for chalk writings and drawings that are to be made visible to a group — called also *chalkboard*

blackbody \'=¦==\ *n* **:** an ideal body or surface that completely absorbs all radiant energy of any wavelength falling upon it with no reflection of energy, the temperature on the absolute scale being determined by measuring the intensity and spectral distribution of the radiated energy

blackbody radiation *n* **:** the characteristic thermal radiation emitted by a blackbody when heated — called also *Planckian radiation;* compare PLANCK RADIATION LAW 2

black bone *n, often cap both Bs* **1 :** a member of the Nosu ruling class — distinguished from *white bone* **2 :** a Kazak commoner — distinguished from *white bone*

black bonito *n* **:** COBIA

black bonnet *n, Scot* **:** REED BUNTING 1

black book *n* **:** a book listing persons that have committed offenses against morality, law, or any set of regulations or giving an account of the offenses of a person or group ⟨six of the exile governments, which have indicted thousands of quisling and Axis culprits in detailed, documented *black books* —*Newsweek*⟩ — **in one's black books :** out of one's favor **:** in disgrace with one

black-bordered oyster \'=,==-\ *n* **:** a large edible oyster (*Saxostrea gradiva*) of northern Australia with a bluish black shell

black bottle *n* **:** a bottle from which according to folklore a dose of poison is administered to unwanted patients in hospitals

black bottom *n* **1** *sometimes cap both Bs* **:** a tract of low-lying land with black soil **2** *often cap both Bs* [prob. fr. *black bottom* "low-lying Negro section of a southern town"] **:** an American dance popular from 1926 to 1928 with sinuous movements of the hips and rocking steps

black-bottom \'=¦==\ *vi* -ED/-ING/-S [*black bottom*] **:** to dance the black bottom

black box *n* **:** any of several Australian eucalypts with dark foliage (as *Eucalyptus bicolor, E. baueriana, E. boormani*)

blackboy \'=,=\ *n* **1** *Austral* **:** BLACKFELLOW **2** *Austral* **:** GRASS TREE 1

blackboy gum *n* **:** ACAROID RESIN

black brant *n* **:** a small brownish black goose (*Branta nigricans*) having a white bar across the front of the neck and white on belly, flanks, and tail coverts, breeding along the north coast of No. America, and wintering along the west coast from Puget Sound to Lower California

black bread *n* **:** dark-colored bread; *esp* **:** a close-grained sour rye bread of central and northern Europe

black bream *n* **1** *Austral* **:** any of several dark-colored edible fishes: as **a :** an important percoid food and game fish (*Chrysophrys australis*) **b :** LUDERICK **2** *Africa* **:** GALJOEN

blackbreast \'=,=\ *n* **1 :** RED-BACKED SANDPIPER **2 :** PLOVER; *esp* **:** BLACK-BELLIED PLOVER

black-browed \'=¦=\ *adj* **:** SCOWLING, GLOOMY, FORBIDDING

black-browed albatross *n* **:** a large albatross (*Diomedea melanophrys*) with a dark mark above the eye

blackbrush \'=,=\ *n* **1 :** TARBUSH 3 **2 :** a desert shrub (*Coleogyne ramosissima*) of the family Rosaceae of the southwestern U.S. with spiny twigs and solitary apetalous flowers

black bryony *n* **:** a common European twining vine (*Tamus communis*) with tuberous roots and cordate leaves

black buck *n* **1 :** the common medium-sized antelope (*Antilope cervicapra*) of India having in the male long spirally twisted closely ringed horns **2 :** SABLE ANTELOPE

black buffalo *n* **1 :** a buffalo fish (*Ictiobus niger*) chiefly of the southern part of the Mississippi valley **2 :** CAPE BUFFALO

black bullhead *n* **:** a small dusky greenish brown to black bullhead (*Ameiurus melas*) having a flattened head and plump body and being widely distributed chiefly in sluggish waters in much of temperate No. America — called also *horned pout*

black bunch grass *n* **:** GALLETA GRASS

black·burn \'blak(,)bərn, -,bə̄n,-,bən\ *adj, usu cap* [fr. *Blackburn*, England] **:** of or from the county borough of Blackburn, England **:** of the kind or style prevalent in Blackburn

black·burn·ian \blak'bərnēən\ *or* **blackburnian warbler** \(')=¦===-\ *n* -S *often cap B* [Mrs. Hugh *Blackburn*, 18th cent. Englishwoman + E *-ian*] **:** a No. American warbler (*Dendroica fusca* syn. *blackburniae*) strongly marked in the male with orange, yellow, and black on the head and neck and with an orange-yellow breast

blackbush \'=,=\ *n* **:** BLACKBRUSH 2

blackbutt \'=,=\ *n* **:** any of several Australian timber trees of the genus *Eucalyptus* (esp. *E. pilularis*) in which the bark of the lower part of the trunk resembles charred wood

black cabbage tree *n* **:** a tree (*Melanodendron integrifolium*) of the family Compositae of the island of St. Helena having dark alternate oblong or lanceolate leaves and a campanulate involucre about the flower head

black caiman *n* **:** a very large So. American reptile (*Caiman niger*) that is related to the typical crocodiles but has the snout rounded like that of the alligator and is abundant in parts of the Amazon drainage

black calabash *n* **:** a tree (*Crescentia ovata*) of tropical America having a thin-shelled gourdlike fruit

black calla *n* **:** an ornamental aroid (*Arum palaestinum*) cultivated in greenhouses for its dark purple or almost black spathe somewhat resembling that of the calla

black cancer *n* **:** MELANOMA

black canker *n* **1** *archaic* **:** severe diphtheria **2 :** any of several plant diseases characterized by dark-colored cankers: as **a :** INK DISEASE **b :** a disease of willows caused by a fungus (*Physalospora miyabeana*) — called also *willow blight*

blackcap \'=,=\ *n* **1** *also* **blackcap raspberry :** a black-fruited raspberry (*Rubus occidentalis*) native to eastern No. America that is the source of several cultivated varieties — called also *black raspberry* **2 :** any of several birds with black heads or crowns: as **a :** a small European warbler (*Sylvia atricapilla*) with a black crown **b :** CHICKADEE **c :** WILSON'S WARBLER **3 :** the common cattail (*Typha latifolia*)

black cap *n* **:** the black cap worn by a British judge when passing sentence of death

black-capped \'=¦=\ *adj, of a bird* **:** having the top of the head black

black-capped chickadee *n* **:** CHICKADEE; *esp* **:** the common chickadee (*Parus atricapillus* or *Penthestes atricapillus*) of northern and eastern No. America having the throat and crown of the head jet black — called also *willow tit*

black-capped petrel *n* **:** a heavy-bodied petrel (*Pterodroma hasitata*) with a dark crown and whitish nape, neck, forehead, and tail coverts that is now rare and that has unknown breeding grounds

black-capped vireo *n* **:** a vireo (*Vireo atricapillus*) of western No. America having the top and sides of the head black

black caraway *n* **:** an herb (*Nigella sativa*) of the Mediterranean region having pungent seeds that are used like those of caraway — called also *black cumin*

black carib *n, usu cap B&C* **:** a member of an ethnic group of mixed Negro and Carib ancestry, Arawakan speech, and Caribbean-Arawakan culture that originated on St. Vincent Island but was deported in the late 18th century to Roatán Island and now lives chiefly along the Caribbean coast of Honduras, Guatemala, and British Honduras

black carpet beetle *n* **:** CARPET BEETLE b

black cat *n* **:** FISHER 2

black catechu *n* **:** CATECHU 1a

black cattle *n, archaic* **:** beef cattle of any color

black cayuga *n, usu cap B&C* [fr. *Cayuga*, lake and county, N.Y.] **:** CAYUGA DUCK

black chaff *n* **:** a disease of wheat caused by a bacterium (*Xanthomonas translucens undulosa*) and producing dark stripes running lengthwise of the chaff

black chalk *n* **:** a dark carbonaceous clay, shale, or slate used as a pigment or crayon

black chamber *n, usu cap B&C* [trans. of F *chambre noire*] **:** a government office or department engaged in cryptographic work, esp. cryptanalysis

black chaser *n* **:** BLACK SNAKE 1a

black check *n* **:** a defect common in western hemlock characterized by pockets in the bark containing resin

black cherry *n* **1 :** SWEET CHERRY **2 a :** a large American wild cherry (*Prunus serotina*) with dark bark, thick oval leaves, white flowers in racemes, and black astringent fruits — called also *rum cherry* **b :** the strong reddish brown wood of this tree used esp. for cabinetwork **3 :** any cultivated cherry having black fruit

black cherry aphid *n* **:** a large black shiny aphid (*Myzus cerasi*) feeding on and causing curling and distortion of the terminal growth of various cherries

black cherry fruit fly *n* **:** a small black fruit fly (*Rhagoletis fausta*) having a larva that burrows in and feeds on the fruit of native and cultivated cherries in western No. America — compare APPLE MAGGOT

black-chinned hummingbird \'=,=-\ *n* **:** a hummingbird (*Archilochus alexandri*) of western No. America, the male being greenish above with the upper part of the throat velvety black, the lower a brilliantly iridescent violet, and the under parts of the body dull white

black chokeberry *n* **:** a shrub (*Pyrus melanocarpa*) of eastern No. America with white flowers like those of the pear and nearly black fruit

black choler *n* **:** BLACK BILE

black cinnamon *n* **:** BAYBERRY 1

black citrus aphid *n* **:** a black aphid (*Toxoptera aurantii*) widely distributed in warm regions that feeds on a number of cultivated plants and is considered to be a vector of tristeza disease of citrus in Brazil

black-clawed crab \'=,=-\ *n* **:** a small active crab (*Lophopanopeus bellus*) having claws with black tips that is common along rocky shores of Puget Sound and adjacent areas

black clergy *n* **:** monks of the Russian Orthodox Church — distinguished from *white clergy*

black coal *n* **:** BITUMINOUS COAL

blackcoat \'=,=\ *n* **1 :** CLERGYMAN — usu. used disparagingly **2** *Brit* **:** a member of the black-coated class

black-coated \'=¦==\ *adj, Brit* **:** WHITE-COLLAR

blackcock \'=,=\ *n* [ME *blakcok*, fr. *blak* black + *cok* cock] **:** BLACK GROUSE; *specif* **:** the male black grouse

black cockatoo *n* **:** any of several Australian cockatoos (genus *Calyptorhynchus*) that are chiefly rusty black but distinguished by different bright colors of their tail feathers

black cod *n* **:** SABLEFISH

black code *n, often cap B&C* [fr. *Black Code*, a code of laws promulgated in Louisiana in the 18th cent. to define the status of the Negro, trans. of F *Code Noir*] **:** a code of laws esp. as adopted by some southern states of the U.S. shortly after the Civil War limiting the rights of Negroes

black cohosh *n* **:** a bugbane (*Cimicifuga racemosa*)

black comb *n* **:** a disease of Australian pullets resembling and perhaps identical with blue comb

black copper *n* **1 :** MELACONITE **2 :** a product containing usu. 70 to 99 percent of copper formed in smelting copper ores direct to metal without first forming matte or by re-melting old or scrap copper and copper alloys

black coral *n* **:** an antipatharian coral having a black horny axis

black core *n* **:** a flaw in ceramic ware attributed to the decomposition of iron pyrites

black cosmos *n* **:** a Mexican perennial herb (*Cosmos atrosanguineus*) grown for its dark purplish red flowers

black cotton *or* **black cotton soil** *n* [so called fr. its suitability for growing cotton] **:** a soil formed in the Deccan region of India by the disintegration of a black lava

black cottonwood *n* **1 :** a tree (*Populus trichocarpa*) of the Pacific coast of No. America with dark green leaves shining above and rusty or silvery beneath **2 :** SWAMP COTTONWOOD

black cow *n* **:** a dark carbonated drink (as root beer) with ice cream in it

black crab *n* **:** a brilliantly marked edible land crab (*Gecarcinus ruricola*) of southern Florida and the West Indies that is noted for its annual mass migrations to the sea for the hatching of the eggs and is considered a great delicacy

black crappie *n* **:** a common sunfish (*Pomoxis nigro-maculatus*) that is black-mottled on a silvery ground, widely distributed throughout the Mississippi drainage and much of the eastern U.S., and regarded as both a food and game fish through most of its range — called also *calico bass*

black-crested monkey \'=¦==-\ *n* **:** SIMPAI

black-crested titmouse *n* **:** a titmouse (*Parus atricristatus*) of the southwestern U.S. and Mexico

black croaker *n* **:** any of several marine fishes of the Pacific coast of America: **a :** a croaker (*Sciaena saturna*) that is dusky blue or blackish above and silvery below **b :** SPOTFIN CROAKER **c :** SARGO 2

black crowberry *n* **:** CROWBERRY 1a

black-crowned night heron \'=,=-\ *n* **:** a No. American night heron (*Nycticorax nycticorax hoactli*)

black cumin *n* **:** BLACK CARAWAY

black curlew *n* **:** the Old World glossy ibis (*Plegadis falcinellus*)

black currant *n* **1 :** a European currant (*Ribes nigrum*) with loosely flowered drooping racemes of yellow flowers and black aromatic fruit **2 :** WILD BLACK CURRANT **3 :** NORTHERN BLACK CURRANT

black-currant rust *n* **:** the white pine blister rust in its uredinial and telial stages

black cutworm *n* **:** an abundant almost cosmopolitan cutworm (*Agrotis ypsilon*) of dark color and waxen appearance — called also *greasy cutworm*

black cyanide *n* **:** CALCIUM CYANIDE

black cypress *n* **:** a bald cypress (*Taxodium distichum*)

black cypress pine *n* **:** an Australian evergreen coniferous tree (*Callitris calcarata*) having small flattened scales as leaves and being valued for its timber and resin

black dammar *also* **black damar** *n* **:** a resin obtained mostly from an East Indian tree (*Canarium strictum*)

blackdamp \'=¦=\ *n* [¹*black* + *damp* (gas)] **:** a nonexplosive mine gas that is heavier than air, that consists of a mixture of carbon dioxide and other gases, and that will not support life or flame — called also *chokedamp;* compare FIREDAMP

black death *n, sometimes cap B&D* **:** the form of plague that was epidemic in Asia and Europe in the 14th century and was marked by hemorrhages into the skin forming large dark patches

black diamond *n* **1 black diamonds** *pl* **:** ¹COAL 3a **2 :** ³CARBONADO **3 :** dense black hematite that takes a polish like metal and is sometimes used for intaglios

black disease *n* **:** a rapidly fatal toxemia of sheep characterized by liver necrosis and subcutaneous hemorrhage resulting from growth of an anaerobic toxin-producing bacterium (*Clostridium novyi* or *Clostridium oedematiens*) in liver tissue damaged by the common liver fluke — compare BLACKLEG, BRAXY, LIVER ROT, MALIGNANT EDEMA

black dog *n* **1 :** a coin made of base silver or pewter **2 :** depression of spirits **:** BLUES, DEJECTION, MELANCHOLY, DESPONDENCY ⟨shake the *black dog* from your back —J.B.Cabell⟩

black dogwood *n* **:** ALDER BUCKTHORN

black dot *n* **:** DARTROSE

black draft *n* **1 :** an infusion of senna with magnesium sulfate used as a purgative **2 :** BLACK DRINK
black drink *n* **:** a drink prepared from the leaves of the yaupon by the Indians of the southeastern U.S. as a medicine and ceremonial beverage
black drongo *n* **:** a small-billed purplish black drongo (*Dicrurus macrocercus*) having a long deeply forked tail and being common in India and southeastern Asia
black drop *n* **1 :** VINEGAR OF OPIUM **2 :** an optical phenomenon observed in transits of Mercury and Venus near the instant of internal contact when the planet seems for the moment attached to the sun's limb by a dark ligament that is probably due to irradiation and the imperfections of the telescope — called also *black ligament*
black drum *n* **:** a large sluggish gray or coppery croaker (*Pogonias cromis*) of the eastern coast of No. America that is usu. considered inferior as a food or sport fish
black duck *n* **:** any of various ducks that are predominantly black or dusky in color: as **a :** a common duck (*Anas rubripes*) of the northeastern U.S. and Canada related to the mallard but having in both sexes plumage that is chiefly dusky brown with lighter edging to the feathers **b :** SCOTER; *esp* **:** BLACK SCOTER **c :** RING-NECKED DUCK **d :** a brownish duck (*Anas superciliosa*) of Australia, New Zealand, and Polynesia highly regarded as a game and table bird
black eagle *n* **1 :** a young golden eagle — used esp. when the bird is supposed to be a representative of a separate species **2 :** a large powerful eagle (*Aquila verreauxii*) of mountainous parts of southern and eastern Africa that is chiefly black but has white tail coverts and a V-shaped band across the shoulders
black-eared bushtit \'≠,≠-\ *n* **:** a bushtit that has conspicuously black cheek patches (as members of several races of the southwestern U.S., Mexico, and Central America)
black-ears \'≠,≠\ *n pl but sing or pl in constr* **:** LONGEAR SUNFISH
black earth *n* **:** CHERNOZEM
black east indian *n, usu cap B&E&I* **:** a small domestic duck of a breed having black plumage with greenish reflections and an olive-green bill
black ebony *n* **:** the black or nearly black wood of any of several ebony trees (genus *Diospyros*); *usu* **:** the heartwood of such a tree
blacked *past of* BLACK
black elderberry *n* **1 :** BLUE ELDERBERRY **2 :** a common elder (*Sambucus canadensis*) of central and eastern No. America
black·en \'blakən\ *vb* **blackened; blackened; blackening** \-k(ə)niŋ\ **blackens** [ME *blaknen*, fr. *blak* black + *-enen* -en — more at BLACK] *vi* **1 :** to become black **2** *of paper* **:** to become darker in color than intended because of improper calendering ~ *vt* **1 :** to make black ⟨the house burned down, leaving only a ~*ed* chimney⟩ ⟨mosquitoes capable of ~*ing* a man with their bodies within a minute —E.T.Gilliard⟩ ⟨the shadow of the possibility of famine ~*ed* everybody's life —G.E.Fussell⟩ **2 :** to speak evil of ⟨~ the past rather than to report it faithfully —Ernest Beaglehole⟩ **:** make infamous ⟨he ~*s* opponents by giving them . . . names such as Barbarian and Philistine —*Times Lit. Supp.*⟩ **3 :** ³BLACK 3a, 3b, 3d
black end *n* **1 :** a nonparasitic disease of the pear characterized by a blackening of the epidermis and flesh of the calyx end and believed to be caused by a disturbed water relation aggravated by uncongenial stocks **2 :** a disease of the banana caused by fungi (esp. *Gloeosporium musarum*) and characterized by a discoloration or rot of the fruit stem
black·en·er \-k(ə)nə(r)\ *n* -s **:** a leather worker that brushes blackening compound onto the grain side of tanned hides — called also *blacker*
blackening *n* -s [ME *blakning*, fr. gerund of *blaknen* to blacken] **1 :** BLACKING **2 :** DENSITY 5b
¹black·er \'blakə(r)\ *comparative of* BLACK
²blacker \"\ *n* -s [³*black* + *-er*] **:** any of several workers that apply blacking to articles: as **a :** BOOTBLACK **b :** BLACKENER
blackest *superlative of* BLACK
blackey *var of* BLACKIE
black eye *n* **1 a :** a darkening of the skin about the eye resulting from a bruise **b** (1) **:** a severe defeat **:** SETBACK, REBUFF ⟨voters gave the administration a *black eye*⟩ (2) **:** a discrediting **:** a bad reputation ⟨pleasant views may greet visitors instead of sore spots which might give the community a *black eye* —*N.Y. Times*⟩ ⟨the word "aristocracy" in this country has a *black eye* —A.N.Whitehead⟩ **2 :** an eye with a very dark iris
blackeye \'≠,≠\ *or* **blackeye bean** *or* **black-eyed bean** \'≠,≠-\ *n* [so called fr. its black hilum] **:** COWPEA 1
black-eyed pea *also* **blackeye pea** *n* **1 :** COWPEA 1 **2** *black-eyed pea* **:** a tropical vine (*Dolichos sphaerospermus*) having a seed that is used in the West Indies for food
black-eyed su·san \-'süzᵊn\ *n, usu cap S* [*black-eyed* (fr. ¹*black* + *eyed*) + *Susan* (the name)] **1 :** either of two coneflowers, one (*Rudbeckia hirta*) of central and eastern No. America and one (*R. serotina*) of the southeastern U.S., having flower heads with deep yellow to orange rays and dark conical disks **2 :** FLOWER-OF-AN-HOUR **3** *also* **black-eyed susan vine :** a tropical African vinelike herb (*Thunbergia alata*) with yellow flowers having a dark purple center
blackface \'≠,≠\ *n, often attrib* **1 :** a sheep with a black face; *esp* **:** one of the Scottish Blackface breed **2 a :** makeup for Negro roles, esp. comic ones ⟨he appeared in ~⟩ ⟨a ~ comedian⟩ **b :** an actor that plays a comic Negro role esp. in a minstrel show **3 :** BOLDFACE 2
black-faced \'≠¦≠\ *adj* **:** BOLD-FACED 3
black-faced highland *n, usu cap B&H* **:** SCOTTISH BLACKFACE
black-fast \'≠¦≠\ *vi* **:** to undergo a black fast
black fast *n* **:** a fast of the most severe kind
blackfeet *pl of* BLACKFOOT
blackfellow \'≠,≠(,)≠\ *n* **:** an Australian aborigine
blackfellows' bread *n* **:** the usu. large sclerotia of an Australian pore fungus (*Polyporus mylittae*) used as food by the aborigines
black fever *n* **:** any of various febrile diseases characterized by a hemorrhagic rash: as **a :** KALA AZAR **b :** ROCKY MOUNTAIN SPOTTED FEVER **c :** TYPHUS 1a
black fiber *n* **:** KITTUL
black fig *n* **1 :** a West Indian tree (*Ficus laurifolia*) with thick leathery leaves and inedible fruit **2 :** MORETON BAY FIG
¹black-figure \'≠,≠\ *or* **black-figured** \'≠¦≠\ *adj* **:** of, belonging to, or constituting a style of ceramic painting practiced by or in imitation of Greeks of the 6th century B.C. in which the decoration is in black with occasional added details in white slip on the red body clay of the vessel and in which the subjects are usu. drawn from mythology, athletic events, or the hunt in an archaic and stiff style ⟨a *black-figure* vase⟩ ⟨*black-figure* ware⟩ — compare POLYCHROME, RED-FIGURE
²black-figure \'≠¦≠\ *n* [¹*black-figure*] **:** black-figure ware
blackfin \'≠,≠\ *also* **blackfin cisco** *n* **:** a whitefish (*Leucichthys nigripinnis*) of the Great Lakes valued as a food fish
blackfin shark *n* **:** BLACKTIP SHARK
blackfin snapper *n* **:** a common West Indian market fish (*Lutjanus buccanella*)
blackfire \'≠,≠\ *n* **:** a disease of tobacco caused by a bacterium (*Pseudomonas angulata*) and characterized by angular leaf spots without a surrounding halo that are at first dark green but become zonate and turn grayish, tan, or dark brown and may drop out leaving ragged holes — compare WILDFIRE
blackfish \'≠,≠\ *n* **1 :** any of several dark-colored fishes: as **a :** the female salmon just after spawning **b :** a deep-sea stromateoid fish (*Centrolophus niger*) of the Atlantic, esp. of the European coast **c :** TAUTOG **d :** RIVER BLACKFISH **e :** BLACK SEA BASS 1 **f :** a small but important food fish (*Dallia pectoralis*) common in shallow freshwaters (as sphagnum swamps) of Alaska and Siberia and noted for its resistance to cold **g :** a California cyprinid fish (*Orthodon microlepidotus*) **h :** any of several marine Australian bass-type food fishes of the genus *Girella*; *esp* **:** LUDERICK **i** *Austral* **:** a food and game fish of Australia that is either identical with or closely related to the Bermuda chub **j :** any of several small serranid fishes (genus *Dinoperca*) of the Indian ocean that are highly esteemed as food **k :** GALJOEN **l :** BOWFIN **2 :** any of several small toothed whales (genus *Globicephala*) related to the dolphins and found in all the warmer seas
blackfisher \'≠,≠≠\ *n* [*blackfish* + *-er*] *Scot* **:** one that engages in blackfishing
blackfishing \'≠,≠≠\ *n* [*blackfish* + *-ing*] *Scot* **:** the illegal catching of blackfish (sense 1a)
black flag *n* **:** a flag black in color or having a device on a black field (as a pirate flag) — see JOLLY ROGER
black flower *n* **:** a bunchflower (*Melanthium virginicum*) of the eastern and southern U.S.
black flux *n, metallurgy* **:** a reducing flux composed of powdered carbon and alkali-metal carbonate
blackfly \'≠,≠\ *n* **:** any of several black or dark-colored insects: as **a :** a small two-winged biting fly of *Simulium* and related genera whose larvae live in flowing usu. clear streams — called also *buffalo gnat* **b :** BEAN APHID **c :** CITRUS BLACKFLY **d :** GREENHOUSE THRIPS
¹blackfoot \'≠,≠\ *n, pl* **blackfeet** *sometimes sing in constr, or* **blackfoot** *usu cap* [trans. of Blackfoot *Siksika*] **1 a :** an Indian confederacy comprising the Siksika (sense 1a), the Bloods, and the Piegan ⟨the *Blackfeet* were the toughest — Chad Oliver⟩ ⟨gave the *Blackfoot* their present home — Edward Sapir⟩ — called also *Siksika* **b :** a member of a people belonging to the Blackfoot confederacy ⟨the heart of a *Blackfoot* —Washington Irving⟩ ⟨the official . . . calls himself a *Blackfeet* —Marcus Rosenblum⟩ **c :** the Algonquian language of the Blackfeet **2 :** SIKSIKA 1 **3 :** SIHASAPA 2
²blackfoot \"\ *n* [¹*black* + *foot*] *Scot* **:** a lovers' go-between
black-footed albatross \'≠,≠≠-\ *n* **:** an albatross (*Diomedea nigripes*) of the Pacific that is chiefly blackish with dusky bill and black feet and legs — called also *gooney*
black-footed cat *n* **:** a southwestern African desert wildcat (*Felis nigripes*) that resembles a dwarf serval, that is colored cream or grayish faun and mottled and striped with black or dark brown, and that is the smallest of the true cats and readily hybridizes with domesticated cats
black-footed ferret *n* **:** an American weasel (*Mustela nigripes*) related to the European polecat and resembling a yellow mink with dark feet, tail, and mask
black fox *n* **1 a :** a melanistic red fox **b :** the fur or pelt of a melanistic red fox at one time much prized because of its rarity and the beauty of its pure-black fur **2 :** SILVER FOX 1a
black friar *n, often cap B&F* [so called fr. the black mantle worn by Dominicans] **:** a Dominican friar
black frost *n* **:** frost or cold so intense as to blacken vegetation and usu. unaccompanied by hoarfrost
black fungus *n* [so called fr. the production of dark excrescences that look like charred spots] **:** FIRE FUNGUS 1
black game *n* **1 :** BLACK GROUSE **2 :** one of a black variety of the old English Game fowl
black gang *n* [so called fr. the grime traditionally associated with them] **:** the stokers or the engineer's crew on a ship
black garget *n* [so called fr. the dark color of the udder in the late stages of the disease] **:** BLUE BAG 2
black ginger *n* **:** the rootstock of ginger dried and unscraped — called also *coated ginger, unpeeled ginger, unscraped ginger;* distinguished from *white ginger*
black gold *n* **:** a dark-colored product containing gold or resembling gold in value: as **a :** MALDONITE **b :** PETROLEUM
black gown *n* **:** a Jesuit missionary to the Indians of the western U.S. esp. in the 19th century
black gram *n* **1 :** HORSE GRAM **2 :** URD
black grama *n* **1 a :** HAIRY GRAMA **b :** a grama (*Bouteloua eriopoda*) important as a forage grass esp. of the plains and western coastal region of No. America — compare BLUE GRAMA **2 :** GALLETA GRASS
black granite *n* **:** a dark-colored intrusive rock (as diorite or gabbro) — not used technically
black grass *n* **1 :** a grasslike rush (*Juncus gerardi*) of salt marshes that is good for hay **2 :** SLENDER FOXTAIL **3 :** SPINY ROLLING GRASS **4 :** BLACK MEDIC
black greasewood *n* **:** GREASEWOOD 1
black grouper *n* **1 :** BLACK JEWFISH **2 :** a large dark grouper (*Mycteroperca bonaci*) having a protruding jaw and widely distributed in the warmer waters of the Atlantic **3 :** SPOTTED JEWFISH
black grouse *n* **:** a large grouse (*Lyrurus tetrix*) widely distributed in western Asia and Europe including most of the heath districts of England and Scotland of which the male is chiefly black with white wing patches and outwardly curved tail feathers and the female has barred and mottled plumage — see BLACKCOCK, GRAY HEN
black growth *n* **:** a forest or woods consisting largely of conifers (as hemlock, pine, and spruce)
black grub *n* **:** a larval fluke (family Strigeidae) encysted in the flesh of fish (as black bass)
black grunt *n* **1 :** TRIPLETAIL 1a **2 :** any of several grunts with dark coloration; *esp* **:** a grunt (*Haemulon bonariense*) widely distributed in the western Atlantic from Florida to Argentina
¹black·guard \'blagə(r)d, -aigə-, -a,gärd, -ai,gärd, -ak,gärd, -,gäd\ *n* [¹*black* + *guard*] **1** *obs* **a :** the kitchen servants of a noble or royal household **b :** the servants and hangers-on of an army **c :** a black, black-clothed, or villainous retinue **d :** street urchins esp. as employed in blacking shoes, carrying torches, or running errands **e :** the criminal element of a community **2** *obs* **:** a vagabond child **:** a street urchin esp. as employed in blacking shoes, carrying torches, or running errands **3 a :** one whose conduct or character is disgraceful **:** a contemptible scoundrel — a generalized term of abuse **b :** a foulmouthed person **4 :** ⁵SNUFF 1a **syn** see VILLAIN
²blackguard \"\ *adj* **1** *obs* **:** of or relating to a shoeblack or street urchin **2 :** BLACKGUARDLY ⟨my schoolfellows were a very ~ set —George Borrow⟩ ⟨~ talk⟩
³blackguard \"\ *vb* -ED/-ING/-S *vi* **1 :** to act in a ruffianly or scoundrelly manner **:** engage in disorderly behavior **:** run riot ⟨~*ing* about the streets till he got his head cut and his clothes torn —Charles Lever⟩ **2 :** to talk obscenely ~ *vt* **:** to talk about or address in abusive or obscene terms ⟨he ~*ed* the war, and the people that started it —Mark Twain⟩
black·guard·ery \-d(ə)rē, -ri\ *or* **black·guard·ry** \-dr-\ *n* -ES **:** behavior characteristic of a blackguard (sense 3a)
black·guard·ism \-,dizəm\ *n* -s **:** behavior characteristic of a blackguard (sense 3a); *esp* **:** use of abusive language
black·guard·ly \-,dlē, -li\ *adj* **:** being, belonging to, or characteristic of a ruffian or scoundrel ⟨~ street rows —Rudyard Kipling⟩ ⟨a ~ fellow⟩; *esp* **:** SCURRILOUS ⟨~ language⟩
black guava *n* **:** a tree (*Guettarda argentea*) of Jamaica and Guiana with black edible fruit
black guillemot *n* **:** a small red-footed guillemot (*Cepphus grylle*) that is black with white wing patches in summer and largely mottled with white in winter — called also *white guillemot*
black gum *n* **1 :** either of two trees of the genus *Nyssa:* **a :** a tree (*Nyssa sylvatica*) of the eastern, central, and southern U.S. having close-grained wood, entire obovate or ovate leaves, and small blue-black drupaceous fruits with nearly ribless stones — called also *pepperidge, sour gum, tupelo* **b :** a tree (*N. biflora*) of the southern U.S. with spatulate leaves and ribbed stones **2 :** WHITE FIR 1a(1) **3 :** BLACK SALLY
black gyrfalcon *n* **:** a very dark slaty gyrfalcon (*Falco rusticolus obsoletus*) of northern No. America
black hand *n, often cap B&H* [fr. *Black Hand*, a lawless Sicilian and Italian-American secret society of the late 19th and 20th centuries, an imitation of an Andalusian anarchist society of the 19th century, trans. of It *Mano Nera*, trans. of Sp *Mano Negra;* fr. the black hand on their emblem] **:** a lawless secret society practicing terrorism, extortion, or other crimes
black-hand·er \'≠,≠də(r)\ *n* **1 :** a member of a black hand society **2 :** EXTORTIONER
black harry *n, often cap H* **:** BLACK SEA BASS 1
black haw *n* **1 :** a shrub (*Viburnum prunifolium*) bearing cymes of white flowers and bluish black drupes **2 a :** SOUTHERN BUCKTHORN **b :** FALSE BUCKTHORN **3 :** either of two trees (*Bumelia tenax* and *B. lanuginosa*) of the southern U.S. **4** *also* **black hawthorn :** a hawthorn (*Crataegus douglasii*) of the western U.S.
black hazel *n* **:** HOP HORNBEAM
¹blackhead \'≠,≠\ *n* **1 :** any of various birds with more or less black about the head; *esp* **:** SCAUP DUCK **2 :** COMEDO **3 :** a destructive disease of turkeys and in a milder form of chickens and other related birds caused by a protozoan (*Histomonas meleagridis*) that invades the intestinal ceca and liver causing tissue destruction and necrosis and intense systemic reaction and that is commonly transmitted from bird to bird by fecal contamination but maintained in nature by intermediate stages developed in the cecal worm (*Heterakis gallinae*) from which it may pass directly to the bird — called also *enterohepatitis, infectious hepatitis* **4 :** a glochidium larva of a freshwater clam or mussel attached to the skin or gills of any of several freshwater fishes and with the cells of its host growing around it in a blackish mass
²blackhead \"\ *adj* **:** having a black head
blackhead disease *n* **1 :** a disease of the banana caused by eelworms of the family Tylenchidae **2 :** a rot of the banana rootstock caused by a fungus (*Thielaviopsis paradoxa*)
black-headed budworm \'≠¦≠≠-\ *n* **:** the bright green brownish headed (black when young) larva of a small variably marked grayish moth (*Acleris variana*) that is a serious pest of hemlock, spruce, and fir throughout much of the northern U.S. and Canada feeding on the new foliage and webbing it into mats
black-headed grosbeak *n* **:** a grosbeak (*Pheucticus melanocephalus*) of western No. America that in the adult male has the head black, the neck, rump, and underparts orange-brown, and the belly and under-wing parts yellow, the female being chiefly brown
black-headed gull *n* **:** any of certain small gulls with a black head
blackhead minnow *n* **:** FATHEAD MINNOW
blackhead persian *n, often cap B & usu cap P* **:** a sheep of an African breed having the head and neck black and the body white that is much used in crossing to introduce superior mutton quality or hardiness into other breeds
blackheart \'≠,≠\ *n* **1 :** a heart cherry having a dark flesh and skin **2 :** WHORTLEBERRY 1 **3 :** any of several plants of the genus *Polygonum* having black seeds **4 :** RED-BACKED SANDPIPER **5 :** a plant disease in which the central tissues blacken; *specif* **:** a disease of potato tubers caused by high temperature or poor ventilation **6 :** a dark coloration of undetermined cause in the wood of certain hardwoods (as maple and ash)
blackhearted \'≠¦≠≠\ *adj* **:** having a wicked disposition **:** MALIGNANT
black heat *n* **:** a heat just below a dull-red heat at which iron or steel turns black
black heath *n* **:** a European heath (*Erica cinerea*)
black hellebore *n* **1 :** either of two hellebores: **a :** an herb (*Helleborus orientalis*) with greenish to dark purple flowers **b :** CHRISTMAS ROSE **2 :** the root of black hellebore **3 :** BLACK SANICLE 1
black hemlock *n* **:** MOUNTAIN HEMLOCK
black henbane *n* **:** HENBANE 1a
black hickory *n* **1 :** any of several hickories: as **a :** MOCKERNUT **b :** any of several pignut trees (esp. *Carya glabra*) **2 :** BLACK WALNUT 1
black hills beetle *n, usu cap B&H* [fr. *Black Hills*, mountains in So. Dak. and Wyo.] **:** a bark beetle (*Dendroctonus ponderosae*) of the Rocky mountain area that feeds chiefly on mature ponderosa pine destroying the cambium and causing the death of great numbers of valuable timber trees
black hills spruce *n, usu cap B&H* **:** a compact tree (*Picea glauca densata*) of central No. America that is used for ornament and hedges and has bright green or bluish green leaves
black hole *n, sometimes cap B&H* [fr. *Black Hole (of Calcutta)*, a military lockup in Calcutta, India, where 146 Europeans were disastrously incarcerated in 1756] **:** a place of confinement for punishment; *specif* **:** a military lockup
black hollander *n, usu cap H* **:** ALMOND WILLOW 1
black horehound *n* **:** an ill-smelling European herb (*Ballota nigra*) with ovate rugose leaves and whorls of dark purple flowers — called also *black archangel, fetid horehound, stinking horehound*
black horse *n* **:** HOG SUCKER
black house *n, Scot* **:** a low windowless cottage
black huckleberry *n* **1 :** a rather low shrub (*Gaylussacia baccata*) of eastern No. America that produces a shining black somewhat acid drupe and that is the best known of the huckleberries **2 :** the fruit of the black huckleberry; *broadly* **:** any huckleberry black in color — compare DANGLEBERRY
black hu·ron *n* **:** LARGEMOUTH BLACK BASS
black hurts *n pl* [*hurts*, pl. of *hurt* (hurtleberry)] **:** the fruit of any plant of the genus *Gaylussacia*
black ice *n* **:** dark-colored glacial ice formed by freezing of silt-laden water — compare BLUE ICE, WHITE ICE
black·ie *also* **black·ey** *or* **blacky** \'blakē, -ki\ *n, pl* **blackies** *also* **blackeys** *or* **blackies :** one that is black: as **a :** a person belonging to a darkly pigmented race; *esp* **:** NEGRO **b :** any of several largely black or dark-colored birds: as (1) *Brit* **:** BLACKBIRD 1a (2) **:** RING-NECKED DUCK (3) **:** CANADA GOOSE (4) **:** BLACK DUCK a
black indian hemp *n, usu cap I* **:** INDIAN HEMP 1
blacking *n* -s [fr. gerund of ³*black*] **:** a substance that is applied to objects and makes them black: as **a :** a paste or liquid used in shining black shoes **b :** a carbon facing for foundry molds or cores usu. consisting of charred wood, coal, coke, or graphite ground to a powder
black ipecac *n* **1 :** a tropical American shrub (*Psychotria emetica*) **2 :** the powerfully emetic root of the black ipecac
black ironwood *n* **1 :** a shrub or small tree (*Krugiodendron ferreum*) of the family Rhamnaceae of southern Florida and the West Indies having hard dark very heavy wood **2 :** a southern African timber tree (*Olea laurifolia*) with dark wood
black·ish \'blakish, -kēsh\ *adj* [ME *blakish*, fr. *blak* black + *-ish*] **:** somewhat black
black italian poplar *n, usu cap I* **:** a rapid-growing hybrid poplar produced by crossing an Old World black poplar (*Populus nigra*) with the cottonwood of eastern No. America and widely used in screen plantings, often being treated by the nursery trade as a separate species (*P. serotina*)
black ivory *n* **:** Negroes subject to economic exploitation esp. in plantation industry; *specif* **:** Negro slaves ⟨the old rich traffic in *black ivory* is no more —Lawrence & Sylvia Martin⟩
¹black·jack \'blak,jak\ *n* -s [¹*black* + *jack* (jacket)] *archaic Scot* **:** a black leather jerkin
²blackjack \"\ *n* -s **1** [¹*black* + *jack* (vessel)] **:** a capacious vessel for beer or ale usu. of tar-coated leather **2** *or* **black jack** [¹*black* + *jack* (man); fr. its presence in lead ore, considered by the miners an impish intrusion of a worthless substance] **:** SPHALERITE **3** [¹*black* + *jack* (bird)] **:** any of several dark-colored No. American ducks: as **a :** SCAUP DUCK **b :** BLACK DUCK a **c :** RUDDY DUCK **4** [¹*black* + *jack* (instrument)] **:** a small striking weapon typically consisting at the striking end of a leather-enclosed piece of lead or other heavy metal and at the handle end of a strap or springy shaft that increases the force of impact **5** *or* **blackjack oak** [so called fr. the club-shaped leaves] **:** a common often somewhat scrubby oak (*Quercus marilandica*) of the southeastern and southern U.S. that has a black bark, broad-ovate leaves, and a rather large ovoid-oblong acorn and that tends to form dense thickets — called also *scrub oak* **6** [¹*black* + *jack* (knave of cards)] **a :** TWENTY-ONE **b :** a card game identical with twenty-one except that additional rules make it possible for any player to become the dealer **c :** an ace and a face card or ten received by a player as his first two cards in the game of blackjack (sense 6a or 6b) — called also *natural*
³blackjack \"\ *vt* -ED/-ING/-S **1 :** to strike with a blackjack **2 :** to coerce by threats or pressure
blackjack pine *n* [¹*black* + *jack (pine)*] **:** JACK PINE 1
black jew *n, often cap B&J* **1 :** a member of a community of persons professing Judaism as their religion but belonging to the same darkly pigmented biological type as their neighbors who do not profess Judaism; *esp* **:** FALASHA **2 a :** one of a Negro Christian sect called the Church of God and Saints of Christ that holds the Negro race to be descended from the ten lost tribes of Israel, observes the Jewish Sabbath, and practices immersion and foot washing **b :** COMMANDMENT KEEPER
black jewfish *n* **:** a very large grouper (*Garrupa negrita*) sometimes weighing several hundred pounds and widely distributed in the warmer parts of the western Atlantic
black kernel *or* **black kernel disease** *n* **:** a disease of rice caused by a fungus (*Curvularia lunata*) and characterized by a dark discoloration of the kernels

black kingfish *n* : COBIA
black kirghiz *n, usu cap B&K* : KARA KIRGHIZ
black kite *n* [so called fr. its dark color] : a large brown hawk (*Milvus migrans*) that feeds chiefly on carrion and is an important scavenger over much of the Old World
black knot *n* **1** : a destructive disease of plum and cherry trees characterized by black excrescences on the branches and caused by a fungus (*Dibotryon morbosa*) **2** : a destructive disease of the gooseberry characterized by black excrescences on the branches and caused by a fungus (*Dibotryon ribesia*) **3** : a disease of the filbert and hazel characterized by black warty excrescences on the bark and caused by a fungus (*Cryptosporella anomala*) **4** : a cane infection of the grape caused by the crown-gall bacterium
black lady *n* **1** : the queen of spades **2** : a variety of hearts in which the queen of spades counts as 13 hearts
blackland \'⸗,land\ *n* : a heavy sticky black soil such as that covering extensive areas in Texas
black land crab *n* : a large active burrowing land crab (*Gecarcinus lateralis*) that is widely distributed on the Caribbean islands and the northern coast of So. America
blackland plow *n* : a plow built with a low front and a moldboard and share so shaped that the plow penetrates and sheds sticky heavy soil
black larch *n* : a tamarack (*Larix laricina*)
black latten *n* : LATTEN 1
black laurel *n* **1** : LOBLOLLY BAY 1 **2** : an evergreen fetterbush (*Leucothoe davisiae*) of springy wet places in the western U.S. that in some areas causes stock poisoning
black lead \'⸗'led\ *n* : [1]GRAPHITE 1
blacklead \"\ *vt* [*black lead*] : to apply graphite to; *esp* : to cover the face of (matter to be molded for electrotyping) with graphite to prevent adhesion of wax or the face of (a wax mold) with graphite to induce electrodeposition
[1]**blackleg** \'⸗,⸗\ *n* [[1]*black* + *leg*] **1** : an enzootic usu. fatal toxemia of young cattle and less commonly of sheep, goats, and swine characterized by high fever and crackling discolored swellings under the skin and caused by toxins produced by an anaerobic soil bacterium (*Clostridium feseri* syn. *C. chauvoei*) usu. entering the tissues through minor wounds or abrasions — called also *black quarter, symptomatic anthrax;* compare MALIGNANT EDEMA **2** : a professional gambler : SHARPER, SWINDLER **3** *chiefly Brit* : a worker hostile to trade unionism or acting in opposition to union policies : STRIKEBREAKER, SCAB **4 a** : a destructive disease of cabbage and other plants esp. of the family Cruciferae caused by certain fungi (as *Phoma lingam*) and characterized by lesions in the stem near the soil surface that become sunken and dark and may girdle the stem **b** : a disease of potato plants caused by a bacterium (*Erwinia atroseptica*) that rots the bases of the stems with subsequent yellowing, wilting, and sometimes rotting of the tubers
[2]**blackleg** \"\ *vb* **blacklegged; blacklegged; blacklegging; blacklegs** *chiefly Brit, vt* : to act as a blackleg (sense 3) against ~ *vi* : to act as a blackleg (sense 3)
black·leg·gery \'⸗,⸗ərē\ *n* -ES : behavior characteristic of a blackleg (sense 2)
black·leg·ism \-,gizəm\ *n* -S : BLACKLEGGERY
black lemur *n* : a large dark lemur (*Lemur macaco*)
black leopard *n* : a melanistic variety of the common leopard
black letter *n* : a style of type or lettering characterized by a heavy face and angular outlines and used chiefly by the earliest European printers or sometimes for the printing of German — called also *Gothic, Old English*
black level *n* : the instantaneous amplitude of a television signal that corresponds to a black area in the transmitted image
black ligament *n* : BLACK DROP 2
black light *n* : invisible ultraviolet or infrared light
black lignite *n* : low-grade coal that is intermediate between ordinary lignite and bituminous coal
black lily *n* : either of two bulbous plants (*Fritillaria biflora* and *F. camschatcensis*) of the Pacific coast of No. America that have a dark purple perianth
black line *n* : a nonparasitic disease of walnuts esp. of English varieties grafted onto black walnuts that appears to be associated with incompatibility between certain stocks and is characterized by a black line of dead tissue at the graft union, later dying of the bark below, and subsequent decline and death of the tree
black linn \-'lin\ *n* : CUCUMBER TREE 1
black lip *n* : a pearl oyster (*Pinctada margaritifera*) that has valves with a black margin
black liquor *n* **1** : IRON LIQUOR **2** : the dark-colored alkaline waste liquor which comes from the sulfate and soda processes of making cellulosic pulp and from which tall oil and lignin are recovered — compare [2]BLACK ASH 2
[1]**blacklist** \'⸗,⸗\ *n* [[1]*black* + *list*] : a list of persons that are disapproved of or are to be punished or discriminated against: as **a** : an employers' privately circulated list of workers that are to be refused employment because they are reputed to hold opinions or engage in actions contrary to the employers' interests **b** : a union list of employers that are to be boycotted because they are reputedly unfair to workers **c** : a list of firms and individuals with whom the nationals of a belligerent country are forbidden to trade because of their reputed contribution to the economic strength of the enemy **d** : a public or privately circulated list often used to screen for employment applicants suspected of or charged with holding views or engaging in activities subversive of the national interest
[2]**blacklist** \"\ *vt* -ED/-ING/-S : to put on a blacklist
black locust *n* **1** : LOCUST 3a(2) **2** : HONEY LOCUST 1a(1)
black lotion *n* : BLACK WASH 1
black·ly *adv* : in a black manner
black lye *n* : BLACK LIQUOR 2
black mahogany *n* : a Mexican mahogany (*Swietenia humilis*) that has harder, heavier, and darker wood than the common mahogany
black maidenhair *n* **1** : VENUSHAIR **2** : BLACK SPLEENWORT
[1]**black·mail** \'blak,māl\ *n* -S [[1]*black* + *mail* (tribute)] **1** : a tribute of money or commodities exacted in the 16th and early 17th centuries in the north of England and south of Scotland by freebooting chiefs for protection or immunity from pillage **2** : extortion of money or anything of value by threats esp. of subjecting someone to criminal prosecution or revealing something injurious to his reputation : something of value extorted by such threats
[2]**blackmail** \"\ *vt* -ED/-ING/-S : to extort money or anything of value from by threats esp. of subjecting someone to criminal prosecution or revealing something injurious to his reputation ⟨his former mistress tried to ~ him⟩ : to compel to act in a particular way by threats ⟨~ a government employee into giving military information to the enemy⟩
black maire *n* **1** : a New Zealand tree (*Olea cunninghamii*) with coriaceous leaves and stout flower clusters **2** : the dense hard light brown wood of the black maire
black mallard *n* : BLACK DUCK a
black mamba *n* : a mamba in its black phase
black man *n* **1** : BLACK 5 **2** : an evil spirit : BOOGEYMAN, DEVIL
black manganese *n* : PYROLUSITE
black mangrove *n* **1** : a mangrove (*Avicennia marina*) of the West Indies and the southern Florida coast that usu. occurs in dense thickets and that has numerous short roots that bend up or away from the ground **2** : an Australian plant (*Aegiceras majus*) of the family Verbenaceae that resembles the black mangrove of the West Indies and Florida
blackman reaction *n, cap B* [after Frederick F. Blackman †1947 Eng. botanist] : the secondary part of the process of photosynthesis involving only chemosynthesis
black maple *n* **1** : a sugar maple (*Acer nigrum*) having black bark and dark soft leaves **2** : the wood of the black maple
black margate *n* : [2]POMPON
black ma·ria \-mə'rīə\ *n, usu cap B&M* [prob. fr. the name *Maria*] **1** : PATROL WAGON **2** : BLACK LADY
black market *n* : trading activity in violation of public regulations (as price ceilings, rates of exchange, tax laws, or rationing); *also* : a place where such activity is carried on
black-market \'⸗'⸗⸗\ *vb* [*black market,* n.] *vi* : to buy or sell goods in the black market ~ *vt* : to sell in the black market
black mar·ke·teer \,⸗,⸗⸗'⸗\ *n* [*black market* + *-eer*] : one that sells goods in the black market
black-marketeer \"\ *vi* -ED/-ING/-S [*black marketeer*] : to sell goods in the black market
black mar·ket·er \⸗'⸗⸗⸗\ *n* [*black market* + *-er*] : BLACK MARKETEER
black marlin *n* : either of two Pacific ocean game fishes (*Makaira mazara* and *M. marlina*) that may attain a weight of 1000 pounds and a length of 14 feet
black mass *n* **1** *usu cap B&M* : a travesty of the Christian mass ascribed to the reputed worshipers of Satan — compare SATANISM **2** : a mass for the dead in which the priest's vestments are black : a requiem mass
black measles *n* **1 a** : hemorrhagic measles **b** : ROCKY MOUNTAIN SPOTTED FEVER **2** : a disease of grapevines in California of obscure and undetermined cause characterized by black spotting of the skin of the berries and browning and drying up of the leaf tissue between the veins and often developing suddenly and severely, the leaves dropping and the canes dying back from the tips in a few days — called also *apoplexy*
black medic *n* : a prostrate herb (*Medicago lupulina*) with heads of small yellow flowers and curved black pods — called also *yellow trefoil*
black mercury *n* : POISON IVY 1
black miao *n, pl* **black miao** *or* **black miaos** *usu cap B&M* [part trans. of Chin *hei*[1] *miao*[2]] : HEI-MIAO
black mica *n* : BIOTITE
black mint *n* : a peppermint with dark green stems and foliage that is widely cultivated for its oil — compare WHITE MINT
black mold *n* **1** : a mold or fungus like a mold with dark mycelium or spores: as **a** : a fungus of the order Mucorales; *esp* : the common bread mold (*Rhizopus stolonifer*) — compare [5]MOLD **b** : a sooty mold of the families Perisporiaceae and Capnodiaceae **c** : an imperfect fungus of the family Dematiaceae **2** : a diseased and blackened condition produced by a black mold; *esp* : a disease of roses that is caused by a fungus (*Chalaropsis thielavioides*) and that causes serious losses in rose grafts esp. on Manetti stock by growing over the cut surface of the scion and thus preventing proper union
black mollie *or* **black mollienisia** *n* -S [*black mollie* by shortening fr. *black mollienisia*] : a small jet-black poeciliid fish (*Mollienisia sphenops*) from Yucatan that is often kept in the tropical aquarium
black monday *n, usu cap B&M* [ME *blak Monunday*] *obs* : EASTER MONDAY
black money *n* : base coin; *esp* : the coins issued as silver but containing a high alloy of base metal that were current in England esp. in the 14th century
black monk *n, often cap B&M* [ME *blak monek;* fr. the color of the habit] : a Benedictine monk
black moss *n* : SPANISH MOSS
blackmouth \'⸗,⸗\ *also* **blackmouth salmon** *n* : a king salmon esp. when immature
black mulberry *n* **1** : a European mulberry (*Morus nigra*) with dark foliage and fruit **2** : the purplish to black fruit of the black mulberry **3** : RED MULBERRY
black muskrat *n* : a melanistic muskrat fur or pelt
black mustard *n* [so called fr. the dark-colored testae] : a much-branched annual Eurasian herb (*Brassica nigra*) now widespread as a weed that is the principal source of table mustard and that has small bright yellow flowers and a thin-beaked seed pod which is closely appressed to the stem — compare WHITE MUSTARD
black muzzle *n* : HEAD SCAB
black myrobalan *n* : CHEBULE
blackneb \'⸗,⸗\ *n* **1** *Brit* : a black-billed bird; *esp* : CARRION CROW **2** *Scot* : a sympathizer with the French Revolution **3** *Brit* : [1]BLACKLEG 3
black·neck \'⸗,⸗\ *n* : SCAUP DUCK
black-necked cobra \'⸗,⸗-\ *n* : a venomous and aggressive elapid snake (*Naja nigricollis*) common and widely distributed in Africa that rarely bites but discharges by spitting a venom that is harmless to the intact skin but may cause blindness if it enters the eyes — called also *spitting cobra*
black-necked grebe *n* : EARED GREBE
black-necked stilt *n* : a stilt (*Himantopus mexicanus*) that ranges from the western and southern U.S. to northern So. America and that has the characteristic black mantle extended forward along the back of the neck to the crown of the head and about the eyes
black·ness *n* -ES [ME *blaknes,* fr. *blak* black + *-nes* -ness] : the quality or state of being black
black nightshade *n* : a cosmopolitan weed (*Solanum nigrum*) with hairy poisonous foliage, white flowers, and edible black berries
black·nob \'blak,näb\ *n* [[1]*black* + *knob*stick] *Brit* : [1]BLACKLEG 3
black nonesuch *n* : BLACK MEDIC
black norway pine *n, usu cap N* : a pitch pine (*Pinus rigida*) with slightly curved and twisted needles in threes
blacknose \'⸗,⸗\ *n* : a physiological disease of the date that is characterized by darkening, cracking, and shriveling of the distal end of the fruit
blacknose dace *also* **black-nosed dace** \'⸗,⸗-\ *n* : a common No. American dace (*Rhinichthys atronasus* or *Atratulus atronasus*) with a black stripe along either side passing from the base of the tail to the tip of the nose — called also *striped dace*
black oak *n* **1** : any of several American oaks having dark bark or foliage (as blackjack or scarlet oak); *esp* : a large timber tree (*Quercus velutina*) of the eastern and central U.S. that has foliage resembling that of the red oak and a yellow inner bark that is used for tanning — called also *quercitron* **2** *Austral* : SHE-OAK 1
black oat *n* : an annual European oat (*Avena strigosa*) with a lemma having two long apical bristles
black oat grass *n* : an oat grass (*Stipa avenacea*) of the eastern U.S. that has a spikelet with a black third scale
black ocher *n* : [5]WAD 2
black oil *n* : any of various dark-colored oils obtained esp. from petroleum (as heavy crude lubricating oils)
black oldwife *n* : a plectognath fish of the genus *Melichthys; esp* : GALAFATE
black olive *n* **1** : a tropical American tree (*Bucida buceras*) of the family Combretaceae with dark-colored very durable wood and a fruit that is a one-seeded drupe **2** : a dark grayish olive to olive-green color
black onyx *n* : chalcedony that is artificially colored black
black opal *n* : a dark-colored opal showing usu. red or green internal reflections
black out *vi* **1 a** : to turn off the stage lighting in order to indicate the end of a theatrical performance or of a scene in a play **b** : to become enveloped in darkness ⟨as the heroine speaks this line the scene *blacks out*⟩ ⟨astronomers have observed that stars sometimes *black out*⟩ **2 a** : to undergo a transient dulling or loss of vision or consciousness as a result of temporary impairment of cerebral circulation ⟨an airplane pilot may *black out* while pulling out of a dive⟩ or retinal anoxia, traumatic emotional blows, or an alcoholic bout **b** : to have a lapse of memory **c** : to lose consciousness ⟨became ill and *blacked out* behind the wheel —*Springfield (Mass.) Union*⟩ **3 a** : to make an object or area invisible or less conspicuous by extinguishing or screening all lights for protection esp. against air attack ⟨my orders are to *black out* at sunset⟩ **b** : to become invisible or less conspicuous by the extinguishing or screening of all lights for protection esp. against air attack : become blacked out ⟨I have a truck to sleep in . . . It can . . . *black out,* and has a huge map board so one can work at night —G.S.Patton⟩ **4** : to become inoperative or ineffectual : cease to exist or act ⟨shortwave radio transmission *blacked out* because of a sunspot⟩ ⟨telephones *blacked out* over a wide area⟩ ~ *vt* **1 a** : to envelop in darkness ⟨a dust storm *blacked out* the city⟩; *esp* : to make (an object or area) invisible or less conspicuous by extinguishing or screening all lights for protection against air attack ⟨the city was *blacked out*⟩ **b** : to extinguish or screen esp. in order to make an object or area invisible or less conspicuous for protection against air attack ⟨the lights were *blacked out*⟩ ⟨we had to *black out* all our windows⟩ **c** : to debar from transmitting or receiving information and ideas ⟨a nation that had been *blacked out* from the rest of the world — Sigrid Arne⟩ **2** : to silence or jam (radio transmission) effectively **3** : to make inoperative, ineffectual, or temporarily nonexistent ⟨falling trees *blacked out* several electric power lines⟩ ⟨some intercollegiate sports were *blacked out* by the war⟩ : DESTROY ⟨the newspaper was *blacked out* by insolvency⟩ : cause the forgetting or ignoring of ⟨relief emergencies . . . must not *black out* the longer task of recovery —*Air Transport*⟩ **4** : to cause (a person) to undergo transient dulling or loss of vision or consciousness ⟨the first drag at the cigarette had nearly *blacked* him *out* —J.A.Phillips⟩ **5** : to restrict or forbid the telecasting of (a program to which admission is charged) esp. in the area of origination in order to protect gate receipts ⟨a program *blacked out* in the city⟩ : prohibit such telecasting in ⟨the city is *blacked out* for this game⟩
blackout \'⸗,⸗\ *n* -S *often attrib* [*black out*] **1 a** : a turning off of the stage lighting for the purpose of separating scenes in a play or of closing a skit in a revue, burlesque show, or musical comedy **b** : a skit that ends with a blackout **2 a** : transient dulling or loss of vision or consciousness resulting from temporary impairment of cerebral circulation **b** : a lapse of memory **c** : a loss of consciousness **3** : an action of blacking out an object or area : a condition or period of being blacked out **4** : a blotting out, suppression, obscuring, or cessation esp. when temporary ⟨a ~ of waterfront commerce over the whole North Atlantic coast —A.H.Raskin⟩ ⟨unless a ~ on science be decreed in every land —A.J.Carlson⟩ **5** : a condition of severe loss of radio signal during intense phases of magnetic storms **6** : a restriction or prohibition of the telecasting of a program to which admission is charged esp. in the area of origination for the purpose of protecting gate receipts
black ox *n* **1** : bad luck **2** : old age ⟨the *black ox* has trod on his foot⟩
black oyster catcher *n* : a blackish brown oyster catcher (*Haematopus bachmani*) of the Pacific coast of No. America
black palm *n* **1** : an Australian palm tree (*Areca normanbyi*) **2** : any palm tree of the genus *Astrocaryum*
black partridge *n* : a francolin (*Francolinus francolinus*) that is now restricted to southern Asia though formerly extending into southern Europe and that is distinguished by the black plumage of the male
black patch *n* : a disease of red clover caused by an unidentified sterile fungus and characterized by groups of blackened plants resulting from the spread of the disease
black pea *n* : a European bitter vetch (*Lathyrus niger*) with foliage that turns black in drying
black peach aphid *n* : an aphid (*Brachycaudus persicaecola*) having the adult shiny black and the young reddish brown, wintering on the roots of peach trees, and feeding during the growing season on the leaves and young fruit
black pear *n* : BLACK CHOKEBERRY
black pepper *n* **1** : a pungent condiment consisting of the fruit of an East Indian plant (*Piper nigrum*) ground with the black husk still on **2** : the black pepper plant
black peppermint *n* : BLACK MINT
black perch *n* : any of various dark-colored saltwater or freshwater fishes: as **a** *chiefly Midland* : SMALLMOUTH BLACK BASS **b** : BLACK SEA BASS 1 **c** : TRIPLETAIL 1a **d** : a common surf fish (*Embiotoca jacksoni*) of the Pacific coast
black petrel *n* : a rather large common sooty to brownish black petrel (*Oceanodroma melania*) of the coast of southern California and Mexico
black phoebe *n* : a phoebe (*Sayornis nigricans*) of the southwestern U.S. and Mexico that is chiefly dull or slaty black with a pure-white abdomen
black pigment *n* : coal-tar lampblack used chiefly in printer's ink
black pilot *n* **1** : BEAU GREGORY **2** : BLACK RUDDER FISH
black pine *n* **1** : any of several American pines having dark-colored bark: as **a** : LOBLOLLY 3 **b** : LODGEPOLE PINE **b c** : JEFFREY PINE **d** : POND PINE **e** : JACK PINE 1 **2 a** : AUSTRIAN PINE **b** : CORSICAN PINE **3** *Austral* : any of several coniferous trees: as **a** : either of two podocarps of New Zealand (*Podocarpus ferruginea* and *P. spicata*) **b** : BLACK CYPRESS PINE **c** : CAMPHORWOOD 2 **4** : JAPANESE BLACK PINE
black pit *n* **1** : a spot disease of lemons and less frequently of other citrus fruits that is caused by a bacterium (*Erwinia citrimaculans*) — compare CITRUS BLAST **2** : a disease of peas that is prevalent in the Netherlands and that produces black spots in the seeds
black plantain *n* : a common ribgrass (*Plantago lanceolata*)
black plate *n* : sheet steel or sheet iron that has not yet been made into tin plate by being coated with tin or that is used uncoated where the protection afforded by tin is unnecessary (as in certain cans)
black plum *n* **1** : an Australian date plum (*Diospyros microcarpa*) **2** : JAVA PLUM **3** : a purplish black that is redder and less strong than mulberry (sense 2b)
black pod *n* : a pod rot of cacao caused by a fungus (*Phytophthora faberi*)
black point *n* : a worldwide disease of wheat and other cereal grains that is caused by various bacteria and fungi esp. of the genera *Alternaria* and *Helminthosporium* and that blackens the embryo ends of the grains, sometimes impairs germination, and lowers the market value of the grain
black poison *or* **black poisonwood** *n* : a West Indian poisonous tree (*Metopium brownei*) of the family Anacardiaceae that has alternate pinnate leaves and small greenish flowers
black-poll warbler \'⸗,⸗-\ *also* **blackpoll** \'⸗,⸗\ *n* : a No. American warbler (*Dendroica striata*) having the top of the head of the male bird black when in full plumage
black·pool \'blak,pül\ *adj, usu cap* [fr. *Blackpool,* England] : of or from the county borough of Blackpool, England : of the kind or style prevalent in Blackpool
black pope *n, usu cap B&P* [so called fr. the habit of the order and the great power its leader had during the papacy of Pius IX] : the head of the Jesuits
black poplar *n* **1** : a European poplar (*Populus nigra*) of which the Lombardy poplar is a variety **2 a** : SWAMP COTTONWOOD **b** : the wood of the swamp cottonwood **3** : BALSAM POPLAR **4** : a European aspen (*Populus tremula*) with petioles strongly compressed laterally
blackpot \'⸗,⸗\ *n* **1** *archaic* : a beer or ale mug **2** *dial Eng* : BLOOD SAUSAGE
black pottery *n* : a fine thin black Chinese pottery burnished and made on a wheel that is characteristic of the ancient Ch'eng-tzu-yai culture
black powder *n* : an explosive consisting of black gunpowder now used chiefly as an ignition charge and primer, as a propellant in older guns fired as a hobby, and in pyrotechnics; *also* : a similar explosive consisting of a mixture of sodium nitrate instead of potassium nitrate and charcoal and sulfur used chiefly in blasting — see BLASTING POWDER
black prairie *n* : prairie land having rich black soil
black pudding *n* : BLOOD SAUSAGE
black purslane *n* : SPOTTED SPURGE
black quahog *n* : [1]QUAHOG 2
black quarter *n* : [1]BLACKLEG 1
black racer *n* : an American black snake of a typical subspecies (*Coluber constrictor constrictor*) common in the eastern U.S.
black rail *n* : a small dark No. American rail (*Laterallus,* or *Creciscus, jamaicensis*) with a short bill and tail and a chestnut-brown patch on the back
black rain *n* : rain blackened by gathering in its fall particles of smoke, black fungus spores, or atmospheric dust
black raspberry *n* : BLACKCAP 1
black rat *n* : a rat (*Rattus rattus*) of a species that infests houses
black rattlesnake *n* : MASSASAUGA a
black rent *n, Eng law* : rent paid in grain, meat, or the lowest coin — opposed to *white rent*
black rhinoceros *n* : a rhinoceros (*Diceros bicornis*) of the species that is most common in Africa
black ring *also* **black ring spot** *n* **1** : a virus disease of cabbage and other members of the cabbage family (Cruciferae) that is characterized by necrotic, dark, and often sunken rings on the leaf surface **2** : a virus disease of the tomato that is characterized in its initial stage by numerous small black rings on young leaves
black robe *n* : a Roman Catholic priest; *esp* : a Roman Catholic missionary to the American Indians
black rock cod *n* **1** : a large Australian grouper (*Epinephelus*

damelii) **2 :** either of two common rockfishes: **a :** BLACK ROCKFISH 1b **b :** PRIESTFISH

black rockfish *n* **1 :** either of two common rockfishes: **a :** PRIESTFISH **b :** a common dark-colored scorpaenid food fish (*Sebastodes melanops*) of the Pacific coast of No. America **2 :** BLACK GROUPER 2

black rod *n* [so called fr. his staff of office] **1 :** an officer of the Order of the Garter that is also usher to the British House of Lords and that has as one of his duties the occasional summoning of the Commons and their speaker to the House of Lords to hear a speech from the throne **2 :** an usher in the legislature of some of the British dominions or colonies

black root *n* **1 :** any of several plants or their dark-colored roots: as **a :** a perennial plant (*Pterocaulon undulatus*) of the southern U.S. that has large black rootstocks **b :** CULVER'S ROOT **c :** COLICROOT 1 **d :** a common comfrey (*Symphytum officinale*) with the upper part of the stem and inflorescence densely hispid **2 :** any of several plant diseases characterized by dark discoloration of roots: as **a :** COTTON WILT 1 **b :** a disease of radishes, beets, and sugar beets caused by fungi (genus *Aphanomyces*) and producing brown or black lesions on the roots, deformation of the roots, and a damping off of seedlings

black root rot *n* **:** any of several diseases of plants marked by dark often confluent lesions of the root and sometimes the crown often involving the whole cortex: as **a :** a disease of apples caused by a fungus (*Xylaria mali*) **b :** a disease of tobacco and various other plants caused by a fungus (*Thielaviopsis basicola*)

black rot *n* **:** any of various diseases of cultivated plants caused by fungi or bacteria and producing dark brown discoloration and decay: as **a :** a disease of the apple, pear, and quince caused by a fungus (*Physalospora cydoniae*) **b :** a disease of the grape caused by a fungus (*Guignardia bidwellii*) — see GRAPE ROT **c :** a disease of cabbage and related plants caused by a bacterium (*Xanthomonas campestris*) **d :** a disease of the sweet potato caused by a fungus (*Ceratostomella fimbriata*) **e :** a disease of the potato caused by a bacterium (*Erwinia atroseptica*)

black rouge *n* **:** chemically precipitated magnetite used as a polishing agent and pigment

black rudder fish *n* **:** a blackish stromateoid fish (*Palinurichthys perciformis*) that is common off the New England coast

black ruff *n* **1 :** BLACKFISH 1b **2 :** a stromateoid fish closely related to the blackfish (sense 1b)

black runner *n* **:** BLACK SNAKE 1a

black rush *n* **1 :** GREAT BULRUSH **2 :** PIASSAVA 1

black rust *n* **1 :** a plant rust producing black discoloration; *esp* **:** BLACK STEM RUST **2 :** STEM RUST 2; *esp* **:** the uredostage of this fungus

blacks *pres 3d sing of* BLACK, *pl of* BLACK

black sage *n* **1 :** a woolly-leaved plant (*Trichostema lanatum*) native to southern California and Mexico **2 :** any of several plants of the genus *Cordia; esp* **:** an introduced weed (*C. macrostachya*) that is a serious pest in sugar plantations on Mauritius **3 :** a common highly inflammable California sage (*Salvia mellifera*) that is the chief source of sage honey **4 :** either of two sagebrushes (*Artemisia arbuscula* and *A. tridentata*) of the western U.S. **5 :** a California herb (*Audibertia stachyoides*)

black salamander *n* **:** ALPINE SALAMANDER

black sally \-'salē\ *n* **:** an Australian tree (*Eucalyptus stellulata*) having rough dark-colored bark near the butt and yielding a red kino

black salmon *n* **:** any of several dark-colored salmons or similar fishes: as **a :** COBIA **b :** KING SALMON

black salsify *n* **:** a European herb (*Scorzonera hispanica*) cultivated for the edible root and for winter greens

black salt *also* **black salts** *n* **:** crude potassium carbonate obtained from wood ashes or in the Leblanc process

black saltwort *n* **:** SEA MILKWORT

black samp·son \-'sam(p)sən\ *n* **:** PURPLE CONEFLOWER

black sanctus *n, archaic* **:** confused singing or speaking by several persons at one time without regard to each other **:** a burlesque of a hymn

black sand *adj, usu cap B&S* [so called fr. the glacial sand of the Illinois river flood plain near Liverpool, Ill., where remains were found] **:** of or relating to a component of Woodland culture and a physical type first found in central Illinois

black sanicle *n* **1 :** a sanicle (*Sanicula marylandica*) of the eastern U.S. with thickish leaves and a thick rhizome **2 :** MASTERWORT b

black sapote *n* **:** a Mexican persimmon (*Diospyros ebenaster*) with an almost seedless dark-fleshed fruit

black sassafras *n* **:** OLIVER'S BARK

black scab *n* **:** POTATO WART

black scale *n* **:** a large dark brown or black unarmored scale (*Saissetia oleae*) destructive to olive, citrus, and other cultivated plants **2 :** a serious disease of Easter lilies caused by a fungus (*Colletotrichum lilii*) that produces black lesions on the bulb scales

black scoter *n* **:** a common European scoter (*Oidemia nigra*) having the adult male completely black and the female and young birds largely dark brown above and mottled brown and white below

black scour *n, pl* **black scours** *sing or pl in constr* **:** a hemorrhagic enteritis of sheep, swine, and cattle that affects esp. young animals and is usu. associated with a heavy worm burden but sometimes results from bacterial infection or improper feeding

black scour worm *n* **:** a small nematode worm (genus *Trichostrongylus*) parasitizing the small intestine and fourth stomach of sheep

black scrub oak *n* **:** BEAR OAK

black scurf *n* **:** RHIZOCTONIA DISEASE 2

black sea bass *n* **1 :** an abundant and important food fish (*Centropristes striatus*) of the Atlantic coast of the U.S. that is dark bluish with black bands and more or less varied with small white spots and blotches — called also *sea bass* **2 :** GIANT BASS

black sea devil *n* **:** a fish of the family Ceratiidae

blackseed \'⸗,⸗\ *n* **1 :** SMUT GRASS **2 :** BLACK MEDIC

black shank *n* **:** a disease of tobacco caused by a fungus (*Phytophthora parasitica nicotianae*) and producing a black rot of the stem, brown blotches on the leaves, and damping off of seedlings

black shark *n* **1 :** BLACKTIP SHARK **2 :** a small dark-colored shark (*Scymnorhinus licha*) widely distributed in warm seas

black sheep *n* **1 :** a recessive black-fleeced individual in a flock of normally white-fleeced sheep — compare MELANISM 1a **2 :** a member of a group that stands in conspicuous and unfavorable contrast to the other members esp. by reason of socially undesirable characteristics or behavior ⟨he's the *black sheep* of his family⟩

blackshirt \'⸗,⸗\ *n, usu cap* **:** a member of a fascist organization having a black shirt as a distinctive part of its dress or uniform; *esp* **:** a member of the Italian Fascist party

black·shop \'⸗,⸗\ *n* **:** the part of an electrotyping plant where blackleading is done

black-shouldered kite \'⸗,⸗⸗-\ *n* **:** a common Asiatic and African hawk (*Elanus caeruleus*) that is chiefly bluish gray above and white below with a black patch on each shoulder

black·side darter *n* **:** a small darter (*Hadropterus maculatus*) of the upper Mississippi drainage that is greenish yellow with dark blotches along the sides

black silver *n* **:** STEPHANITE

black skimmer *n* **:** a black-and-white skimmer (*Rhynchops nigra*) that has a bright red bill tipped with black and is widely distributed along the east coast of No. America

black slash pine *n* **:** LOBLOLLY PINE 1

black sloe *n* **:** a wild plum (*Prunus umbellata*) of the southern U.S. that has small sour fruits

black smallpox *n* **:** a highly fatal form of smallpox characterized by cutaneous hemorrhages

blacksmith \'⸗,⸗\ *n* [ME *blaksmith*, fr. *blak* black + *smith*; fr. his working with iron, known as black metal] **1 a :** a smith who works in iron with a forge — sometimes distinguished from *whitesmith* **b :** a blacksmith who shoes horses — called also *farrier, horseshoer* **c :** one who makes metal into tools, machine parts, and other objects by heating it in a forge and hammering it into shape on an anvil — called also *smith, striker* **2 :** an edible blackish pomacentrid fish (*Chromis punctipinnis*) of the Pacific coast **3** *or* **blacksmith plover :** a spur-winged plover (*Hoplopterus armatus*) of Africa

black·smith·ery \-(ə)rē\ *n* **:** BLACKSMITHING

black·smith·ing \-iŋ\ *n* **:** the craft or job of a blacksmith

blacksmith shop *or* **blacksmith's shop** *n* **:** the workshop of a blacksmith

blacksmith welding *n* **:** forge welding by manual hammering

black snake \'⸗,⸗\ *n* **1 :** any of several snakes predominantly dark or black in color: as **a :** a widely distributed colubrid snake (*Coluber constrictor*) of No. America that may reach a length of six feet **b :** PILOT BLACK SNAKE **c :** a colubrid snake (*Ocyophis ater*) of Jamaica **d :** any of several venomous elapid snakes of Australia: as (1) **:** a venomous elapid snake (*Pseudechis porphyriacus*) that is black above with a cherry-red belly (2) **:** TIGER SNAKE 1 **2** *usu* **blacksnake** *or* **blacksnake whip :** a long tapering braided whip of rawhide or leather ending in a leaf-shaped piece that serves as a snapper

blacksnake \"\ *vb* -ED/-ING/-S [*blacksnake*, n. (whip)] **:** to whip with a blacksnake

black snakeroot *n* **1 :** a bugbane (*Cimicifuga racemosa*) **2 :** SANICLE a **3** *or* **black snakeweed :** WILD GINGER 2a

black snapper *n* **:** any of several dark-colored marine fishes: as **a :** SCHOOLMASTER 3 **b :** PRIESTFISH

black snowbird *n* **:** SLATE-COLORED JUNCO

black southern beech *n* **:** BLACK BEECH 2

black spanish *n, usu cap B&S* **:** an old Mediterranean breed of glossy black domestic fowls with blue legs and white faces

black speck *n* **1 :** RHIZOCTONIA DISEASE 2 **2 :** DARTROSE

black spleenwort *n* **:** a European spleenwort (*Asplenium adiantum-nigrum*) having foliage that resembles that of the maidenhair and yielding an astringent

black sponge *n* **:** a commercial sponge that has not been cleaned or trimmed

black spot *n* **1 :** any of several plant diseases characterized by black spots or blotches: as **a :** APPLE SCAB **b :** APPLE ANTHRACNOSE **c :** a common destructive disease of roses caused by a fungus (*Diplocarpon rosae*) and characterized by black spots or blotches on the leaves, yellowing of the remaining portions, and premature falling of the leaves **d :** a disease of citrus fruits caused by an imperfect fungus (*Phoma citricarpa*) **e :** a disease of peaches and plums caused by a bacterium (*Xanthomonas pruni*) **f :** a disease of beets caused by boron deficiency in the soil **2 :** a spotting of frozen meat caused by an imperfect fungus (*Cladosporium herbarum*) **3 :** BLACK GRUB

black-spotted trout \'⸗,⸗⸗-\ *n* **:** CUTTHROAT TROUT

black spruce *n* **1 :** a spruce (*Picea mariana*) of northeastern No. America that grows chiefly in wet boggy areas and has inferior wood, spreading branches, deep green and very dense foliage, and oval persistent cones — see TREE illustration **2 :** DOUGLAS FIR

black squall *n* **:** a squall accompanied by dark clouds — compare WHITE SQUALL

black squirrel *n* **:** a squirrel that is black or exceptionally dark in color; *esp* **:** a fox squirrel with such coloring typically found in the southern and western parts of its range

black stem *n* **:** any of various diseases of plants characterized by darkening of the stem: as **a :** a disease of alfalfa caused by a fungus (*Ascochyta imperfecta*) **b :** a disease of cabbage and cauliflower caused by a fungus (*Phoma lingam*)

black stem rust *n* **:** stem rust in the teliospore stage

blackstick \'⸗,⸗\ *n* **:** quinoidine molded into sticks

black stinkwood *n* **:** a stinkwood (*Ocotea bullata*)

black stock *n* **:** the dark-colored material that in papermaking is discharged from a digester at the end of an alkaline cook of wood chips and contains the fiber, the alkali, and about half the weight of the wood in solution

black stork *n* **:** an Old World stork (*Ciconia nigra*) that is glossy black above and white below

blackstrap \'⸗,⸗\ *n* [¹*black* + *strap*] **1 :** a common red wine of the Mediterranean **2 :** a drink consisting of a mixture of rum and molasses **3** *or* **blackstrap molasses a :** the final molasses that is obtained in the last of successive processes of raw sugar manufacture and used as a constituent of many mixed cattle feeds and as a raw material for the production of industrial alcohol **b :** any thick and very dark molasses **4 :** a dark heavy oil used esp. for lubricating mine-car wheels

black streak *n* **:** BLACK CHECK

black stripe *n* **1 :** BLACK STRAP 2 **2** *or* **black stripe canker :** BLACK THREAD

black sucker *n* **:** any of several suckers; *esp* **:** HOG SUCKER

black sugar *n* **:** Spanish licorice or its juice

black sugar maple *n* **:** BLACK MAPLE

black sumac *n* **:** DWARF SUMAC

black swallower *n* **:** a small dark deep-sea percoid fish (*Chiasmodon niger*) that is remarkable for the distensibility of its stomach and body

black swallowtail *n* **:** a common butterfly (*Papilio polyxenes*) of eastern No. America that is black with yellow spots and has a larva that often feeds on the foliage of carrots, parsley, and related plants

black swallow-wort *n* **:** a European perennial twining herb (*Cynanchum nigrum*) that is occas. cultivated and sometimes escaped in No. America and has purple-brown or dark purple flowers with triangular ovate petals

black swan *n* **:** an Australian swan (*Cygnus atratus*) that is black with white wing tips and red bill

black sweetwood *n* **:** a tropical American evergreen tree (*Ocotea floribunda*) with dioecious greenish flowers

blacktail \'⸗,⸗\ *n* **1** *also* **blacktail deer :** BLACK-TAILED DEER **2 a :** a young salmon trout **b :** DASSIE 2 **3 :** BLACK-TAILED GODWIT

black-tailed deer \'⸗,⸗-\ *n* **1 :** a deer (*Odocoileus columbianus*) of British Columbia, Oregon, and Washington that is in many respects intermediate between the mule deer and the Virginia deer **2 :** MULE DEER

black-tailed gnatcatcher *n* **:** a gnatcatcher (*Polioptila melanura californica*) of southern California and Lower California

black-tailed godwit *n* **:** a long-legged European godwit (*Limosa limosa*) with a long straight bill and a broad black band on the white tail

black-tailed jackrabbit *n* **:** a jackrabbit (*Lepus californicus*) of the southwestern U.S. and Mexico that has a tail with a black upper surface

black-tailed native cat *n* **:** a native cat (*Dasyurus geoffroyi*) distinguished from the common native cat by possession of a distinct hallux

black-tailed rattlesnake *n* **:** a medium-sized black-tailed heavy-bodied rattlesnake (*Crotalus molossus*) of Texas, Arizona, and northern Mexico

black-tailed shrimp *n* **:** a dark-colored edible shrimp (*Crago nigricauda*) common from California to Alaska in relatively shallow water

black tamarind *n* **1 :** VELVET TAMARIND **2 :** a tropical American timber tree (*Pithecolobium arboreum*)

black tang *n* **:** BLADDER WRACK 1

black tea *n* **:** tea that is dark in color due to the leaf's being fully fermented before firing

black tellurium *n* **:** NAGYAGITE

black tern *n* **:** any of several very small short-tailed terns with largely dark gray or black plumage that breed in marshes and constitute a genus (*Chlidonias*) of nearly cosmopolitan distribution

blackthorn \'⸗,⸗\ *n* [ME *blakthorn*, fr. *blak* black + *thorn*] **1 a :** a European spiny tree or shrub (*Prunus spinosa*) that has hard wood and bears small white flowers before the leaves and small purplish or blue black astringent fruits — see SLOE **b :** a cane made of the wood of this tree or shrub **c** *or* **blackthorn cocktail :** a cocktail variously made from sloe gin or rye whiskey and French or Italian vermouth flavored with bitters and occas. anisette **2 :** PEAR HAW

blackthorn winter *n, chiefly Brit* **:** cold weather in spring when the blackthorn is in bloom

black thread *n* **:** a disease of the tapped area of the Para rubber tree that is caused by a fungus (*Phytophthora meadii*) and that is characterized by black lines extending through the exposed bast into the cambium or wood — called also *black stripe, stripe canker*

black thrips *n, Austral* **:** GREENHOUSE THRIPS

black-throated blue warbler \'⸗;⸗⸗-\ *n* **:** a common warbler (*Dendroica caerulescens*) of eastern No. America the male of which has a conspicuously black throat and breast and bluish upper parts

black-throated bunting *n* **:** DICKCISSEL

black-throated gray warbler *n* **:** a grayish warbler (*Dendroica nigrescens*) of western No. America that has black markings on head, throat, and sides

black-throated green warbler *n* **:** a common warbler (*Dendroica virens*) of eastern No. America the male of which has a black throat, yellow sides of the head, and olive-green upperparts

black tie *n* **1 :** the black bow tie worn with men's semiformal evening dress — compare WHITE TIE **2 :** semiformal evening dress for men ⟨a *black-tie* dinner⟩

black tip *n* **1 :** any of several plant diseases characterized by dark-colored necrotic areas at the end of the fruit or seed: as **a :** a nonparasitic disease of the mango that is of undetermined cause and is characterized by a dark area at the distal end of the fruit **b :** BLACK POINT **2 :** BLACKTIP SHARK

blacktip shark *or* **black-tipped shark** \'⸗,⸗-\ *n* **:** a small grayish shark (*Carcharias limbatus*) with black-tipped fins that is widely distributed in warm seas

black titi *n* **:** ¹TITI 1a

blacktongue \'⸗,⸗\ *n* **1 :** a dark discoloration of the tongue that is sometimes associated with a fungous growth **2 a :** STUTTGART DISEASE **b :** a disease of dogs that is characterized by ulcers in the mouth, inflammation of the alimentary canal, erythema, and severe nervous symptoms and that results from certain deficiencies in the diet and has been found to be identical with pellagra in man

black tooth *n* **1 :** NEEDLE TOOTH **2 :** a mottled condition of the teeth caused by excess fluorides in the drinking water of growing children

¹**blacktop** \'⸗,⸗\ *n, often attrib* [¹*black* + *top*] **1** *also* **blacktopping** \'⸗,⸗⸗\ **:** a blackish bituminous material used esp. for surfacing roads, playgrounds, and airport runways and spread while in a plastic state over a base course of crushed rock, concrete, or an existing surface in need of resurfacing **2 :** an area (as a road) surfaced with blacktop

²**blacktop** \"\ *vt* **:** to surface (a road) with a blacktop coating

blacktracker \'⸗,⸗⸗\ *n, Austral* **:** an aborigine employed to help police in the backcountry find fugitives and lost people

blacktree \'⸗,⸗\ *n* **:** BLACK MANGROVE 1

black tree fern *n* **:** SILVER TREE FERN

black trevally *n* **:** a small spiny-finned fish (*Siganus nebulosus*) occurring on the coast of New South Wales

black tupelo *n* **:** BLACK GUM 1

black turkey *n* **:** NORFOLK TURKEY

black turnstone *n* **:** a common turnstone (*Arenaria melanocephala*) of the Pacific coast of No. America that has a black back with a bronzy-green sheen and white underparts

black turpentine beetle *n* **:** a bark beetle (*Dendroctonus terebrans*) that is extremely destructive to pines esp. of the southeastern U.S.

black twinberry *n* **:** a fly honeysuckle (*Lonicera involucrata*) of western No. America with bitter black fruit

black udder *n* **:** BLUE BAG 2

black-varnish tree *n* **:** a Burmese tree (*Melanorrhoea usitata*) that yields a black varnish — called also *theetsee*

black velvet *n* **1** *Austral* **:** an aboriginal girl or woman; *collectively* **:** aboriginal girls or women **2 :** a drink that is half champagne and half stout — compare VELVET

black vetchling *n* **:** BLACK PEA

black vine weevil *n* **:** a small elongated dull-black flightless weevil (*Brachyrhinus sulcatus*) of which the adult feeds on foliage and the larva on the roots of many crop and ornamental plants

black vomit *n* **1 a :** vomitus consisting of dark-colored matter (as broken-down blood) seen in yellow fever and cancer of the stomach — called also *coffee-ground vomit* **b :** a condition characterized by such vomitus; *esp* **:** YELLOW FEVER **2 :** HEMATEMESIS

black vulture *n* **:** an American vulture (*Coragyps atratus*) that is smaller than the turkey buzzard and heavier in flight

black·wall hitch \'blak-,wȯl-\ *n, usu cap B* [fr. *Blackwall*, shipyard in Poplar district, London, England] **:** a hitch used for temporarily securing a line to a hook and made by passing the end of the line round the shank of the hook and crossing it under the standing part in the mouth of the hook

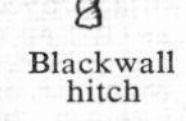

Blackwall hitch

black walnut *n* **1 a :** a tall timber tree (*Juglans nigra*) of eastern No. America that has hard strong heavy dark brown wood much used for furniture and implements and that bears oily edible roughly spherical nuts — see TREE illustration **b :** the wood of this tree **c :** one of the nuts of this tree **2 :** an aromatic timber tree (*Cryptocarya palmerstonii*) of Australia **3 :** CALIFORNIA BLACK WALNUT

black wart *n* **:** POTATO WART

blackwash \'⸗,⸗\ *vt* **1 :** to color with blackwash **2 :** ¹DEFAME 2 — contrasted with *whitewash*

black wash \"\ *n* **1 :** a lotion of calomel and lime water used on syphilitic sores — called also *black lotion* **2** *usu* **blackwash a :** a wash that colors a surface black — compare WHITEWASH **b :** DEFAMATION 2 **3 :** a wash of blacking and other ingredients used for coating foundry molds and cores to prevent their being burned by the molten metal

blackwater \'⸗,⸗⸗\ *n* **:** any of several diseases of animals or man that are characterized by dark-colored urine: as **a :** RED WATER 1b **b :** BLACKWATER FEVER **c :** TEXAS FEVER **d :** azoturia of horses

blackwater fever *n* [so called fr. the blackish or dark red urine passed during the disease] **:** a febrile condition occurring after repeated attacks of malaria (as falciparum malaria) and marked by destruction of blood cells with hemoglobinuria and extensive kidney damage

black wattle *n* **:** any of several Australian acacias (esp. *Acacia mollissima*) that yield tanning materials

black waxy *also* **black wax** *n, West* **:** a black soil that is sticky when moist

blackweed \'⸗,⸗\ *n* **:** RAGWEED 2a

black weevil *n* **:** RICE WEEVIL

black whale *n* **1 :** SOUTHERN RIGHT WHALE **2 :** SPERM WHALE

black wheatear *n* **:** a large European wheatear (*Oenanthe leucura*) having the plumage black with the rump, under tail coverts, and sides of the tail white

black-whiskered vireo \'⸗,⸗⸗ \ *n* **:** a vireo (*Vireo altiloquus barbatulus*) of Florida and the West Indies that has black markings on the sides of the head

black widow *n* **1 :** a venomous New World spider (*Latrodectus mactans*) that is black with an hourglass-shaped red mark on the underside of the abdomen; *broadly* **:** any other spider of the genus *Latrodectus* **2 :** BLACK LADY

black wildebeest *n* **:** WHITE-TAILED GNU

black will \-'wil\ *n* **:** BLACK SEA BASS 1

black willow *n* **1 :** any of several willows with dark bark; *esp* **:** an American tree (*Salix nigra*) with linear leaves that grows close to streams and lakes **2 :** MULE FAT

black-winged stilt \-,wiŋd-\ *n* **:** a stilt (*Himantopus himantopus*) of southern Europe, Africa, and Asia that is distinguished by very long pinkish red legs and plumage largely white but with black wings and upper parts

black witch *n* **:** a very large noctuid moth (*Erebus odora*) having dark mottled-brown wings with an eyespot in each and being native to tropical America but migrating as far north as Canada in summer

black wolf *n* **1 :** a melanistic color phase of the European wolf once common in the Pyrenees **2 :** a melanistic color phase of the American gray wolf **3 :** KARAKURT

blackwood \'⸗,⸗\ *n* **:** any of several hardwood trees or their dark-colored wood: as **a :** BLACK MANGROVE 1 **b :** an East Indian tree (*Dalbergia latifolia*) having a useful dark purple wood — called also *East Indian rosewood* **c :** LOGWOOD 1 **d :** LIGHTWOOD 2a

black·wood convention \'blak-,wu̇d-\ *n, usu cap B* [after Easley F. *Blackwood*, 20th cent. American who devised it] **:** a bidding method used in reaching slam contracts in contract bridge and consisting of the use of four no-trump as an asking bid to which the bidder's partner is supposed to respond five clubs if he holds no ace, five diamonds if he holds one ace, five hearts if he holds two aces, five spades if he holds three aces, or five no-trump if he holds four aces and the use of five no-trump as an asking bid to which the bidder's partner is supposed to respond six clubs with no king, six diamonds with one king, six hearts with two, six spades with three, or six no-trump with four

blackwork \ˈ=,=\ *n* **1 :** metal products (as forgings or rolled work) that have not undergone a process (as pickling or machining) that gives a bright finish **2 :** embroidery worked in black thread on white material

black wrack *n* **:** a rockweed (*Fucus serratus*) common in the No. Atlantic

¹blacky \ˈblakē, -ki\ *adj* [¹*black* + *-y*] **:** somewhat black **:** BLACKISH

²blacky *var of* BLACKIE

black yeast *n* **:** any of various yeasts or similar organisms (as of the genera *Torula* and *Monilia*) that form colonies of a characteristic black color

blacky-white \ˈ=,=ˈ=\ *n* **:** ²ANGLO-INDIAN 2 — usu. used disparagingly

¹blad \ˈblad, -ȧd\ *vt* **bladded; bladded; bladding; blads** [origin unknown] **1** *chiefly Scot* **:** slap hard **:** STRIKE **2** *chiefly Scot* **:** to beat against **:** BUFFET ⟨the wind *bladding* the young trees⟩

²blad \"\ *n* -s **1** *Scot* **:** SLAP, BLOW **2** *Scot* **a :** PORTION **b :** SELECTION, FRAGMENT

¹blad·der \ˈbladə(r)\ *n* -s [ME *bladdre*, fr. OE *blǣdre* bladder, blister; akin to OHG *blātara* bladder, ON *blathra* blister, OE *blāwan* to blow — more at BLOW] **1 a :** a membranous sac in animals that serves as the receptacle of a fluid or contains gas ⟨urinary ~⟩ ⟨gall ~⟩ — usu. used of the urinary bladder when unqualified; see AIR BLADDER **b :** a vesicle or pouch forming part of an animal body ⟨the ~ of a larval tapeworm⟩ **c :** VESICLE c **2 a :** a urinary bladder dressed and used for some purpose, esp. as a container ⟨a ~ of lard⟩ **b :** a man-made flexible and elastic container (as a toy balloon or the rubber lining of an inflatable ball) suggesting such a bladder **3 :** something resembling a bladder esp. in being inflated, empty, or unsound; *specif* **:** a pretentious self-important person

²bladder \"\ *vb* -ED/-ING/-S *archaic* **:** to puff up **:** swell out **:** INFLATE

bladder-and-string \ˈ===ˈ=\ *n* **:** an ancient burlesque bass fiddle consisting of a string stretched on a pole and over a bladder and bowed with a notched stick — called also *bumbass*

bladder campion *n* **1 :** any of several plants of the genus *Silene* having a much-inflated calyx; *esp* **:** a bluish green herb (*S. latifolia*) **2 :** an alpine plant (*Wahlbergella apetala*) of the Rocky mountain region having a calyx in shape suggestive of a Chinese lantern

bladder catchfly *n* **:** a bladder campion (*Silene latifolia*)

bladder cell *n* **:** any of numerous large vacuolated cells conspicuous in the outer layers of the tunic of certain tunicates

blad·der·et \ˌbladəˈret\ *n* -s [¹*bladder* + *-et*] *archaic* **:** a little bladder

bladder fern *n* **:** a fern of a genus (*Cystopteris*) characterized by a hooded or bladderlike indusium; *esp* **:** a common No. American fern (*C. fragilis*) with finely dissected fronds

bladder fucus *n* **:** BLADDER WRACK 1

bladder green *n* **:** SAP GREEN 2b

bladder kelp *n* **:** any of various brown algae with prominent floats: as **a :** BLADDER WRACK 1 **b :** SEA-OTTER'S-CABBAGE

bladder ket·mia \-ˈketmēə\ *n* **:** FLOWER-OF-AN-HOUR

bladderlike \ˈ==,=\ *adj* **1 :** similar to a bladder esp. in form or distensibility ⟨the ~ float of a Portuguese man-of-war⟩ **2 :** inflated like a bladder **:** BLADDERY 1

bladdernose \ˈ==,=\ *n* [so called fr. the inflatable sac on the head] **:** HOODED SEAL

bladdernut \ˈ==,=\ *n* **1 :** a shrub or small tree of the genus *Staphylea* **2 :** the bladderlike seed pod of any bladdernut shrub or tree

bladdernut family *n* **:** STAPHYLEACEAE

bladderpipe \ˈ==,=\ *n* **:** a primitive bagpipe with an animal's bladder used for the bag

bladder plum *n* **:** PLUM POCKET

bladderpod \ˈ==,=\ *n* **:** any of certain plants having inflated pods: as **a :** an American herb of the genera *Physaria* and *Lesquerella* **b :** INDIAN TOBACCO **c :** a European plant of the genus *Vesicaria* **d :** a California shrub (*Isomeris arborea*) of the family Capparidaceae **e :** BAGPOD

bladderseed \ˈ==,=\ *n* **:** a plant of a European genus (*Physospermum*) of the family Umbelliferae with seeds that are somewhat inflated and have large oil tubes

bladder senna *n* **1 :** any of several leguminous shrubs of the genus *Colutea; esp* **:** a yellow-flowered European shrub (*C. arborescens*) cultivated for its flowers and bladdery pod and as a source of wildlife food **2 :** a southern African shrub (*Sutherlandia frutescens*) with a much-inflated pod

bladder snout *n* **:** BLADDERWORT

bladder tree *n* **:** BLADDERNUT 1

bladderweed \ˈ==,=\ *n* **:** a seaweed (as the bladder wrack) with air bladders in the fronds

bladder worm *n* **1 :** a saclike or bladderlike tapeworm larva (as a cysticercus, a coenurus, or a hydatid) **2 :** a parasitic worm infesting the urinary bladder; *esp* **:** a nematode (*Capillaria plica*) of the bladder of many carnivores

bladderwort \ˈ==,=\ *n* -s **:** any of several aquatic plants of the genus *Utricularia* having bladderlike floats; *broadly* **:** any of numerous members of the family (Lentibulariaceae) to which *Utricularia* belongs

bladderwort family *n* **:** LENTIBULARIACEAE

bladder wrack *n* **1 :** a common black rockweed (*Fucus vesiculosus*) used in preparing kelp and as a manure **2 :** a seaweed (*Ascophyllum nodosum*) closely related to bladder wrack and often found intermingled with it

blad·dery \ˈbladərē, -ri\ *adj* **1 a :** resembling a bladder esp. in being swollen but empty **b :** PUFFY, INFLATED ⟨a fruit with ~ pulp⟩ **2 :** having or characterized by bladders ⟨certain ~ kelps⟩

¹blade \ˈblād\ *n* -s [ME, fr. OE *blæd;* akin to OHG *blat* leaf, ON *blath*, L *folium*, Gk *phyllon* leaf, OE *blōwan* to blossom — more at BLOW] **1 a :** a leaf of a plant; *esp* **:** a leaf of an herb or more narrowly of a grass ⟨~*s* of stunted grass⟩ **b** *chiefly Scot* **:** a leaf that is broad and flat ⟨a ~ of rhubarb⟩ **c** (1) **:** the expanded portion of a leaf or a plant organ resembling a leaf **:** LAMINA 2b(1) — distinguished from *petiole* (2) **:** the broad terminal part of certain petals — distinguished from *claw* **2 :** an object or part of an object resembling the blade of a leaf esp. in broadness and flatness: as **a :** the broad flattened part of an oar or paddle that exerts force against the water to propel a boat **b :** something with an action basically similar to that of the blade of an oar: as (1) **:** a fluke of a whale (2) **:** a float of a paddle wheel (3) **:** an arm of a screw propeller, centrifugal fan, or steam turbine (4) **:** an airfoil used as a propeller to produce thrust or as a part of the lift-producing system of a rotary-wing aircraft **c :** a broad flat bone (as one of the rami of a mandible); *specif* **:** SCAPULA — now used chiefly in naming cuts of meat ⟨a ~ chop⟩; see BEEF illustration **d :** a piece of mace **e :** the part of the arm of an anchor behind the palm **f :** the expanded rear portion of the comb of a single-comb fowl — see COCK illustration **g :** the striking surface of a golf club or a hockey stick **h** *phonetics* (1) **:** the portion of the tongue immediately behind the tip and lying approximately opposite the teethridge when the tongue is at rest (2) **:** this portion of the tongue together with the tip **i :** the light-obstructing portion of the shutter of a camera **j :** an inclined metal slab that functions as an ink reservoir in the fountain mechanism of a printing press **k :** the broad, flat, or concave part of a road grader, bulldozer, or snowplow that comes into direct contact with the material to be moved **3 :** an object or part of an object resembling a blade of grass: as **a :** the cutting part of an instrument ⟨the ~ of a sword⟩ ⟨well-set saw ~*s*⟩ **b :** an edged instrument: as (1) **:** SWORD (2) **:** a stone tool similar to a knife and having one or more sharp cutting edges **c :** the runner of an ice skate **d :** the long arm of a T square or carpenter's square **e :** a single plate of baleen from a right whale **f :** one of the movable conducting bars of an electrical switch **g :** a slat esp. in a venetian blind, louver, or shutter **4 :** a human being: **a :** SWORDSMAN **b :** a sharp-witted, dashing, wild, or reckless fellow ⟨such a gay ~ of a fellow⟩ **c :** WOMAN ⟨the old ~ shouldn't last much longer⟩ **5 :** one of the principal rafters of a roof

²blade \"\ *vb* -ED/-ING/-S [ME *bladen*, fr. *blade*, n.] *vt* **1 :** to furnish with a blade **2** *chiefly Scot* **:** to pluck leaves from (a plant) ⟨*blading* cabbages for market⟩ **3 :** to remove (as gravel or dirt) with machinery having a blade (as a grader or bulldozer) ~ *vi* **1 :** to leaf out **:** put forth leaves **2 :** to remove typically gravel, dirt, or muck with machinery having a blade

³blade \"\ *adj* [¹*blade*] *of speech sounds* **:** articulated with or involving the participation of the blade of the tongue ⟨\s\ and \z\ are ~ consonants⟩

blade angle *n* **:** the angle between the chord of a propeller or rotor blade and a plane normal to the axis of rotation, its value varying along the span and decreasing from root to tip because of blade twist

blade apple *n* **:** BARBADOS GOOSEBERRY

blade back *n* **:** the surface of a propeller or rotor blade that corresponds to the upper surface of a lifting airfoil

bladebone \ˈ=,=\ *n* -s **1 :** SCAPULA **2 :** a cut of meat containing part of the bladebone

blad·ed \ˈblādəd\ *adj* [¹*blade* + *-ed*] *of a mineral* **:** composed of plates shaped like knife blades

blade face *n* **:** the surface of a propeller or rotor blade that corresponds to the lower surface of a lifting airfoil — called also *driving face, thrust face*

blade harrow *n* **:** ACME HARROW

blade loading *n* **:** the gross weight of a rotary-wing aircraft divided by the total area of the rotor blades

blade plate *n* **:** a metal plate consisting of a shank terminated by a blade at an angle used in correcting and holding fractures in the upper end of the femur

blade-point \ˈ=ˈ=\ *adj, of a speech sound* **:** articulated with or involving the participation of the blade and raised tip of the tongue ⟨\sh\ is a *blade-point* sound with many speakers⟩

blad·er \ˈblādə(r)\ *n* -s [¹*blade* + *-er*] **1 :** a bladed implement or vehicle **2 :** a worker who fits blades on turbines

blades *pl of* BLADE, *pres 3d sing of* BLADE

blade section *n* **:** a cross section of a propeller blade in a plane parallel to that containing the axis of rotation

bladesmith \ˈ=,=\ *n* **:** a cutler who makes blades

blad·ing \ˈblādiŋ\ *n* -s [¹*blade* + *-ing*] **:** a set of blades (as of a cutter bar or in a turbine)

blads *pres 3d sing of* BLAD, *pl of* BLAD

blady \ˈblādē\ *adj* -ER/-EST [¹*blade* + *-y*] **1 :** having or made up of blades ⟨coarse ~ fodder⟩ **2 :** like a blade ⟨~ elbows⟩

bladygrass \ˈ==,=\ *n, Austral* **:** COGON

blae \ˈblā\ *adj* [ME *bla* (northern dial.), *blo* (southern dial.), fr. ON *blār* — more at BLUE] *chiefly Scot* **:** dark blue or bluish gray **:** BLUISH: **a** *of the skin* **:** livid or lead-colored (as from a bruise) **b** *of weather* **:** DARK, BLEAK, CHEERLESS ⟨the ~ east wind⟩

blae·ber·ry \ˈblā- — *see* BERRY\ *n* [ME (northern dial.) *blaberie*, fr. *bla* blae + *berie* berry] *chiefly Scot* **:** BILBERRY

blae·wort \ˈblāwərt\ *var of* BLAWORT

blaf·fert \ˈbläfə(r)t\ *n* -s [MHG] **:** a base silver coin of Switzerland and Germany in the 15th century — called also *plappert*

blaf·lum \ˈblaf(l)əm, bləˈf(l)əm\ *n* -s [origin unknown] *chiefly Scot* **:** empty talk **:** HOAX

blag·gard *n* -s [by alter.] **:** BLACKGUARD

¹blague \ˈbläg, -ȧg\ *n* -s [F] **:** HUMBUG, CLAPTRAP, RAILLERY

²blague \"\ *vi* -ED/-ING/-S **:** to talk pretentiously and usu. inaccurately **:** lie boastfully

¹blah \ˈblä, -ȧ\ *also* **blah-blah** \ˈ=ˈ=\ *or* **blaa** \ˈblä, -ȧ\ *or* **blaa-blaa** \ˈ=ˈ=\ *n* -s [prob. fr. *blah-blah*, interj. used as a derogatory comment on meaningless chatter, of imit. origin] **:** silly or pretentious nonsense **:** BUNKUM, HOKUM ⟨this week a record is being made in the output of ~, bunkum, and hypocrisy —Raymond Moley⟩

²blah \"\ *adj* **:** dull and unattractive ⟨when the dormitory fare gets too ~ to bear —*Mademoiselle*⟩ **:** without verve or originality ⟨she was just ~ but her friend wasn't so bad⟩

blah-blah \ˈblä,blä, ˈblȧ,blȧ\ *also* **blah** *vb* -ED/-ING/-S [prob. fr. *blah-blah*, interj.] *vi* **:** to utter blah ~ *vt* **:** REPEAT, MOUTH ⟨*blah-blahing* their outworn slogans⟩

blain \ˈblān\ *n* -s [ME *blein*, fr. OE *blegen;* akin to MLG *bleine* blain, OSw *blena* blain, OE *blāwan* to blow — more at BLOW] **:** an inflammatory swelling or sore **:** BULLA, PUSTULE, BLISTER — now used chiefly of animals

blake \ˈblāk\ *adj* [ME, pale, fr. OE *blāc* — more at BLEACH] *dial Eng* **:** YELLOW — often used of foodstuffs ⟨fine ~ butter⟩

blake·ite \ˈblā,kīt\ *n* -s [William P. *Blake* †1910 Am. geologist & mineralogist + E *-ite*] **:** a mineral consisting of an iron tellurite found sparingly in the mines at Goldfield, Nev.

bla·lock-taus·sig operation \ˈblā,läkˈtausig-\ *n, usu cap B&T* [after Alfred *Blalock* b1899 & Helen B. Taussig b1898 Am. physicians who devised it] **:** surgical correction of the congenital malformation of the heart known as tetralogy of Fallot — called also *blue-baby operation*

blam·a·ble *also* **blame·a·ble** \ˈblāməbəl\ *adj* [ME *blamable*, fr. *blamen* + *-able*] **:** deserving reproach, blame, or censure **:** REPREHENSIBLE ⟨the most ~ act of his life⟩ **syn** see BLAMEWORTHY

blam·a·bly *also* **blame·ably** \-məblē, -li\ *adv* **:** in a blamable manner

¹blame \ˈblām\ *vt* -ED/-ING/-S [ME *blamen*, fr. OF *blamer*, *blasmer*, fr. (assumed) VL *blastemare*, alter. of LL *blasphemare* to revile, blaspheme, fr. Gk *blasphēmein* to speak ill of, blaspheme, fr. *blasphēmos* evil-speaking, fr. *blas-* (perh. akin to Gk *meleos* futile, unhappy) + *-phēmos* (fr. *phanai* to say); akin to MIr *mell* error, Lith *melas* lie, Av *mairya* deceitful — more at BAN] **1 :** to express disapproval of **:** find fault with **:** REPROACH ⟨Aristotle, while *blaming* the man who is unduly passionate, ~*s* equally the man who is insensitive —G.L.Dickinson⟩ **2 a :** to attribute responsibility to **:** make answerable — usu. used with *for* ⟨he *blamed* himself for the failure on the agricultural front —T.P.Whitney⟩ **b :** to ascribe responsibility for **:** account for by placing culpability — usu. used with *on* ⟨dimly conscious that something was wrong, he *blamed* it on his father —E.L.Acken⟩ **3** *obs* **:** to bring reproach upon **:** LOWER, ABASE **4 :** BLAST, DAMN — used in the imperative as a mild imprecation ⟨~ this rainy weather⟩ **syn** see CRITICIZE — **to blame :** deserving blame **:** at fault **:** RESPONSIBLE ⟨the conductor was *to blame* for the accident⟩ ⟨I know the cucumbers were *to blame* for his upset⟩

²blame \"\ *n* -s [ME, fr. MF, fr. OF, *blamer*] **1 :** expression of disapproval or reproach **:** REPROOF, CENSURE ⟨saying nothing . . . either in the way of ~ or praise —R.L.Stevenson⟩ **2 a :** CULPABILITY, FAULT ⟨acknowledge the world as a world of common ~ —Muriel Rukeyser⟩ **b** *archaic* **:** GUILT, CRIME, SIN ⟨that we should be holy and without ~ before him —Eph 1:4 (AV)⟩ **3 :** responsibility for something that deserves or is felt to deserve censure ⟨the low-tax lobby at home must share the ~ for starving local and state governments —K.F.Zeisler⟩ **4** *obs* **:** HURT, INJURY

¹blamed \ˈblām(d)\ *also* **blame** \-m\ *adj* **:** DARNED, BLASTED, CONFOUNDED — used as a mild imprecation ⟨it's a ~ shame⟩

²blamed \"\ *or* **blame** \"\ *adv, dial* **:** EXCEEDINGLY, DEUCEDLY, VERY ⟨a ~ cold winter⟩

blame·ful \-mfəl\ *adj* [ME, fr. ²*blame* + *-ful*] **:** deserving disapproval, blame, or punishment **:** GUILTY ⟨by our peculiar double standard the taker of the bribe is considered more ~ than the giver —Estes Kefauver⟩ — **blame·ful·ly** \-fəlē, -li\ *adv*

blame·less \-mləs\ *adj* [ME, fr. ²*blame* + *-less*] **:** free from blame or fault **:** IRREPROACHABLE ⟨has lived a ~ life and . . . has prospered —Green Peyton⟩ — **blame·less·ly** *adv* — **blame·less·ness** *n* -ES

blam·er \-mə(r)\ *n* -s [ME, fr. *blamen* + *-er*] **:** one that blames

blameworthiness \ˈ=,===\ *n* -ES **:** the quality or state of being blameworthy

blameworthy \ˈ=,==\ *adj* [ME, fr. ²*blame* + *worthy*] **:** deserving blame **:** at fault **:** CENSURABLE

syn BLAMABLE, GUILTY, CULPABLE: BLAMEWORTHY and BLAMABLE, wide in application and lacking specific suggestions, are used when GUILTY and CULPABLE are too severe ⟨anyone in any party who falls below the level of the high spirit of national unity which alone can give national salvation is *blameworthy* —Sir Winston Churchill⟩ ⟨a *blamable* or at least questionable, lack of such doings —G.G.Coulton⟩ GUILTY usually refers to serious offenses ⟨in old German law infanticide was treated as the murder of a relative. The *guilty* mother was buried alive in a sack —W.G.Sumner⟩ It may indicate legal proof or conviction of guilt ⟨tried, all five, found *guilty*, and put to death —Robert Browning⟩ It may indicate a state of mind or the expression of it ⟨the woman's face was *guilty* —Arnold Bennett⟩ CULPABLE suggests less stringent blame than GUILTY and connotes malfeasance or errors of omission, negligence, or ignorance ⟨a most urgent telegram was dispatched to you from London by Godfrey Staunton at six-fifteen yesterday evening — a telegram which is undoubtedly associated with his disappearance — and yet you have not had it. It is most *culpable* —A. Conan Doyle⟩ ⟨the prevailing abuses, *culpable* stupidity, common dishonesty and empty political buncombe, which too often passes for statesmanship —J.H.Robinson †1936⟩

blam·ing·ly *adv* **:** in a blaming manner

blanc \ˈblaŋk, -ai-, ˈbläⁿ\ *also* **blank** \ˈblaŋk, -ai-\ *n* -s [F *blanc*, fr. OF, fr. *blanc*, adj., white — more at BLANK] **:** a French coin of the 14th to 18th centuries orig. of silver but later debased

blanc de chine \ˌbläⁿdəˈshēn\ *n* [F, lit., white of China] **:** a white Chinese porcelain made at Te-hua and often decorated with embossed ornament but without color

blanc fixe \ˈbläⁿ ˈfēks\ *n* [F, lit., fixed white] **:** barium sulfate obtained as a fine heavy white precipitate from aqueous solutions of a soluble barium compound (as barium sulfide) and sodium sulfate

¹blanch \ˈblanch, -aa(ə)n-,-ain-,-ȧn-\ *adj* [ME *blaunche*, *blanche*, fr. MF *blanche*, fem. of *blanc* white — more at BLANK] **1** *Eng law* **:** of or relating to a white rent **2** *or* **blench** \-len-\ *Scots law* **:** of or relating to a nominal duty paid as a quitrent or the tenure held by payment of such rent

²blanch \"\ *vb* -ED/-ING/-ES [ME *blaunchen*, fr. MF *blanchir*, fr. OF, fr. *blanche*] *vt* **1 :** to take the color out of and make white **:** BLEACH ⟨~*ing* linen on the grass⟩ ⟨age has ~*ed* his hair⟩: **a :** to bleach by excluding light; *esp* **:** to bleach (the leaves or stalks of plants) by earthing, boarding, or wrapping **b :** to scald or parboil (foods) in boiling water or steam in order to remove the skin from (as almonds), whiten (as kidney), or stop enzymatic action in (as fruits or vegetables for canning or freezing) **c :** to clean (a coin blank) in an acid solution **d :** to cover (sheet iron or steel) with a coating of tin **2 :** to make ashen or pale ⟨fear ~*es* the cheek and stills the heart⟩ **3 :** to give a favorable appearance to **:** WHITEWASH, GLOSS — often used with *over* ~ *vi* **:** to become pale **:** WHITEN **:** grow pallid or ashen ⟨his face ~*ed* with horror⟩ ⟨some red roses ~ in the direct sun⟩

³blanch \"\ *vb* -ED/-ING/-ES [alter. of ¹*blench*] *vt* **:** to cause to turn aside or back **:** HEAD 5b ⟨crashed through the brush and ~*ed* a deer⟩ ~ *vi* **:** to flinch or shrink back

¹blanch·er \-nchə(r)\ *n* -s [²*blanch* + *-er*] **:** one that blanches something (as foods, metals, linens)

²blancher *n* -s [³*blanch* + *-er*] *obs* **:** a person or object stationed for turning driven game in the desired direction

blanching *adj* [fr. pres. part. of ²*blanch*] **:** destructive of color — **blanch·ing·ly** *adv*

blanc·mange \bləˈmänj, -äⁿzh\ *n* -s [alter. of ME *blancmanger*, fr. MF *blanc manger*, fr. *blanc* white (fr. OF) + *manger* food, fr. OF *mangier*, fr. *mangier* to eat, fr. L *manducare* to chew, eat — more at BLANK, MANGER] **:** a dessert made from gelatinous or starchy substances and milk usu. sweetened, flavored, and shaped in a mold

blancmanger *n* -s [ME] *archaic* **:** BLANCMANGE

blan·co \ˈblaŋ(,)kō\ *vt* -ED/-ING/-ES [*Blanco*] **:** to whiten with Blanco whitening

Blanco \"\ *trademark* — used for a substance used to whiten belts or other equipment esp. in the British army

¹bland \ˈbland, -aa(ə)nd\ *adj, usu* -ER/-EST [L *blandus*] **1 a :** smooth and soothing in manner **:** GENTLE, SUAVE, INGRATIATING ⟨~ approval⟩ ⟨a ~ smile⟩ **b :** exhibiting no personal concern or embarrassment **:** UNCONCERNED, UNPERTURBED ⟨the criminal made a ~ confession⟩ **2 a :** having soft and soothing qualities **:** not drastic or irritating **:** not stimulating or vigorous ⟨a ~ oil⟩ ⟨a simple ~ diet⟩ ⟨the ~ climate of the southern coast⟩ **b :** FLAT, DULL, INSIPID, WISHY-WASHY ⟨a ~ pudding⟩ ⟨he submits and becomes ~ and tasteless —Norman Kelman⟩ **3 :** not infected ⟨a ~ infarct⟩ **syn** see SOFT, SUAVE

²bland \"\ *n* -s [ON *blanda*, fr. *blanda* to mix — more at BLEND] **:** a drink of the Orkney and Shetland islands consisting of buttermilk and water

blan·da \ˈbländə\ *or* **be·lan·da** \bəˈländə, ˈbl-\ *n* -s *cap* [Malay *bĕlanda*, fr. a Dravidian word derived fr. Pg *Holanda* Holland] **:** DUTCHMAN — used esp. in the Malay peninsula

bland dollar \ˈbland-, -aa(ə)nd-\ *n, usu cap B* [after Richard P. *Bland* †1899 U.S. congressman] **:** the U.S. silver dollar of 412½ grains troy coined under the Bland-Allison Act of 1878 that provided for the free coinage of silver

bland·for·dia \blanˈfȯrdēə\ *n, cap* [NL, fr. George, Marquis of *Blandford*, 19th cent. Englishman + NL *-ia*] **:** a genus of Australian tuberous-rooted plants (family Liliaceae) having large orange or crimson flowers

blan·ding's turtle \ˈblandiŋz-\ *n, usu cap B* [after William *Blanding*, 19th cent. Am. herpetologist] **:** a freshwater turtle (*Emys blandingii*) of the northeastern U.S. and Canada having a black or dark olive shell with small yellow spots

blan·din's gland \bläⁿdaⁿz-, ˈblandənz-\ *n, usu cap B* [after Philippe F. *Blandin* †1849 Fr. surgeon] **:** ANTERIOR LINGUAL GLAND

blan·dish \ˈblandish, -aan-, -dēsh, *esp in pres part* -dəsh\ *vb* -ED/-ING/-ES [ME *blandishen*, fr. MF *blandiss-*, stem of *blandir*, fr. L *blandiri*, fr. *blandus* mild, flattering] *vt* **:** to flatter with soft words or affectionate actions **:** COAX, CAJOLE ⟨found herself being ~*ed* by millionaires —Lee Rogow⟩ ~ *vi* **:** to act or speak in a flattering manner

blan·dish·er \-shə(r)\ *n* -s **:** one that blandishes **:** FLATTERER, CAJOLER

blandishing *adj* [ME, fr. pres. part. of *blandishen*] **:** FLATTERING, CAJOLING — **blan·dish·ing·ly** *adv*

blan·dish·ment \-shmənt\ *n* -s [*blandish* + *-ment*] **:** speech, action, or device that flatters and tends to coax or cajole **:** ALLUREMENT — often used in pl. ⟨he refuses to yield to their ~*s* —Irving Babbitt⟩

bland·ly *adv* [¹*bland* + *-ly*] **:** in a bland manner

¹blank \ˈblaŋk, -aiŋk\ *adj, usu* -ER/-EST [ME, fr. MF *blanc*, of Gmc origin; akin to OHG *blanch* shining, bright, white, OE *blanca* white horse, ON *blakkr;* akin to L *flagrare* to burn — more at BLACK] **1** *archaic* **:** of a white or pale color **:** lacking color **2 a** *archaic* **:** lacking resource or answer **:** DISCONCERTED **:** taken aback **:** ABASHED ⟨the Damsel of Burgundy at sight of her own letter was soon ~ —John Milton⟩ **b** *of emotions* **:** OVERMASTERING, INTENSE, SHEER **:** lacking relief or break ⟨watched with ~ awe⟩ ⟨~ terror gripped them⟩ **c** *of expressions* **:** lacking animation as though dazed, confounded, or nonplused ⟨her face ~ with wonder⟩ **3 a :** devoid of interest or event, of variety or change, or of affections or hopes ⟨a ~ prospect⟩ ⟨if it is a bad day, he can occupy his ~ hours looking at the scenery —Michael Warr⟩ **b :** devoid of covering or content **:** UNOCCUPIED, UNFILLED ⟨a ~ space⟩ **c :** free from writing or marks — used of paper or other substances normally written on ⟨give me a ~ sheet to do my sums⟩ **d :** having an empty space or spaces to be filled in with some special writing ⟨a ~ application form⟩ ⟨a ~ check⟩ **e :** BLIND 6d **f** (1) **:** lacking some critical ingredient ⟨a ~ solution used as a control⟩ (2) **:** involving the use of such a blank substance (as in analysis or pharmacological experimentation) ⟨a ~ test⟩ ⟨a ~ run⟩ **g** (1) **:** lacking any card **:** VOID ⟨a ~ suit⟩ ⟨he was ~ in spades⟩ (2) **:** containing no valuable cards **:** WORTHLESS ⟨a ~ hand⟩ **4 :** ABSOLUTE, DOWNRIGHT, UNMIXED, ⟨the ~ impossibilities of Lilliput —Thomas De Quincey⟩ **5 :** having a plain or unbroken surface where an opening, finish, or other interruption of continuity is usual: as **a** *of a key* **:** not yet having had the slots made **b** *of an architectural feature* **:** lacking the opening that is characteristic of such a feature ⟨a ~ arch⟩ ⟨~ window over a stair well⟩ **6 :** of a kind denoted euphemistically or for the occasion by a blank (sense) 4 — often used as a substitute for an abusive or imprecatory epithet ⟨you ~ idiot⟩ or for something (as a date or address) that one cannot or is unwilling to supply ⟨when the ~ regiment was transferred to Ireland⟩ **syn** see EMPTY

[2]**blank** \"\ *n* -s **1 a :** an empty space on a paper or in any written or printed instrument ⟨leave a ~ for his signature⟩ **b :** a paper with spaces left to be filled with desired or appropriate data (as names, dates, descriptions); *esp* **:** a paper containing the substance of a document or legal instrument (as a deed, release, or charter) with spaces to be filled in before execution ⟨a deed made out in ~⟩ **c :** a sheet, card, leaf, or other object without printing, writing, or other impression on it ⟨this machine turns out few ~*s*⟩ **2 a :** an empty form without substance or significance ⟨he is a mere ~ of what he once was⟩ **b :** an empty place or space ⟨my mind became a ~ when I heard the question⟩ **c :** an empty interval; *esp* **:** a period devoid of consciousness, interest, action, or result ⟨a long ~ in American history between the decline of the Mayans and the Aztec civilization⟩ ⟨they say I talked rationally enough but for me the time after the accident was a total ~⟩ **d :** something useless, valueless, or undesirable; *specif* **:** a lottery ticket that does not win a prize — usu. used as object of *draw* **3 :** something aimed at; *specif* **:** the bull's-eye of a target **4 :** a dash written or printed as a substitute for an omitted word — see [1]BLANK 6 **5** *archaic* **:** BLANK VERSE ⟨and rhyme and ~ maintain an equal race —Lord Byron⟩ **6 :** something in an unfinished or incomplete state that is designed for further working or manipulation: as **a :** a piece of flint or shell roughly blocked out for later shaping into a prehistoric tool **b :** a wooden gunstock before it is cut to receive the metal parts **c :** a piece of material prepared to be made into something (as a coin, key, screw, tile, or container) by a further operation; *esp* **:** a small segment (as one produced by punching, sawing, or cleaving a large sheet, block, or billet) suitable for the production of a single finished piece (as a dowel, key, or button) **d :** an unrecorded lacquer disc **7 :** BLANK DETERMINATION **8 :** any of certain cardboards made in standard thicknesses with a white or colored liner and combining stiffness and printability **9 :** an old moneyers' unit of weight equal to $\frac{1}{24}$ perit or $\frac{1}{230400}$ grain **10 a :** something lacking a critical element and used (as in experimental medicine or chemical analysis) to provide a control for comparison with the complete material; *esp* **:** a solution for use in a blank determination **b :** BLANK CARTRIDGE **11 :** a domino without any spots on one of its halves **12 a :** an instance of having no cards in a specified suit **:** VOID ⟨a ~ in spades⟩ **b :** CARTE BLANCHE

[3]**blank** \"\ *vb* -ED/-ING/-S *vt* **1** *archaic* **a :** NONPLUS, FOIL, DISCONCERT **b :** to make void or ineffective **:** FRUSTRATE **2 a :** OBSTRUCT, OBSCURE, BLOT — usu. used with *out* ⟨an announcement apparently timed to ~ out their opponents' claims of progress⟩ **b :** to seal (as an oil sand, a tunnel, or part of a pipeline) against the unwanted flow of oil or water — used with *off* **c :** to make (a radio or television signal) undetectable at the output for short periods of time in order to avoid undesirable effects (as return traces in a television receiver) **3 a :** to indicate by a written or printed dash — compare [2]BLANK 4 **b :** DAMN ⟨~ him! that is just like him —Charles Reade⟩ **4 :** to keep (an opposing team) from scoring **5 :** to cut with a die from a sheet or flat piece of stock **:** form into blanks — often used with *out* ⟨levers ~*ed* out of strip steel⟩ **6 :** to fill out with space (as a short line of type, a column, a page, or the nonprinting areas of a form) — often used with *out* **7 :** [2]BLIND 4 ~ *vi* **1 :** to become obscure or tenuous **:** FADE — usu. used with *out* ⟨laughter and music that ~*ed* out as he passed on his way⟩ **2 :** to become confused or distrait **:** black out ⟨her mind seemed to have ~*ed* out —Peggy Bennett⟩

[4]**blank** *var of* BLANC

blank bar *n* **:** COMMON BAR

blankbook \'=,=\ *n* -s [[1]*blank* + *book*] **:** a book of mostly blank pages or of printed forms; *esp* **:** one in a strong flat easily opened style of binding

blank cartridge *n* **:** a cartridge having instead of a projectile a wadding (as of paper) sealed in the mouth of the case

blank charter *n* **: 1** *obs* **:** a charter given to a crown agent in Richard II's time with liberty to fill it out as he pleased **2 :** liberty to do as one pleases ⟨our substitutes at home shall have *blank charters* —Shak.⟩

blank check *n* **1 :** a check signed by the maker but with the amount left to the discretion of the recipient **2 :** complete control or freedom of action **:** CARTE BLANCHE

blank determination *n* **:** a determination in analytical chemistry made as nearly as possible under the same conditions as a true determination but with the omission of the substance to be tested for the purpose of ascertaining the effect due to associated factors (as impurities in the reagents) — compare CONTROL EXPERIMENT

blank endorsement *n* **:** an endorsement of commercial paper that omits the name of a person in whose favor the endorsement is made and makes the paper payable to the bearer and that is usu. made by simply writing the name of the endorser on the back of the paper

blank·er \-kə(r)\ *n* -s [[3]*blank* + *-er*] **:** one that blanks; *specif* **:** a worker who cuts or punches blanks from sheet metal or other stock

[1]**blan·ket** \'blaŋkət, -aiŋ-, *usu* -əd·+V\ *n* -s [ME, fr. OF *blanqete*, fr. *blanc* white + *-et* (dim. suffix) — more at BLANK] **1 a** *archaic* **:** a white or undyed woolen cloth **b :** a cloth woven with samples of various designs usu. used as a display sample or for experimental purposes **c** *or* **blanket cloth** (1) **:** a heavy reversible cotton fabric often with jacquard figures and usu. with a dense nap used for blankets and clothing (as bathrobes) (2) **:** a similar woolen cloth in solid colors used for coats **2 :** a sheet of fabric adapted to a particular purpose: as **a :** a piece of warm fabric for use as a bed covering being of wool, cotton, or synthetic yarns and usu. oblong and napped on both sides — compare QUILT, ROBE, SHEET **b :** a similar piece of fabric used as a body covering (as for a horse or dog) or among certain primitive peoples as a cloak **c :** a band of fabric running beneath the cloth in a cloth-printing machine and forming the covering of a slasher cylinder **d** (1) **:** a heavy cloth used to catch fine gold or valuable minerals (as in blanket sluices or on concentrating tables (2) **:** the permeable cloth sheet or membrane used in flotation cells in ore dressing **e** (1) **:** a sheet of wool, felt, or rubber in the packing of an impression cylinder to soften the impression or reduce makeready in printing (2) **:** a rubber sheet in an offset press that receives the inked impression from the plate and transfers it to the surface being printed **3 :** a covering layer or sheet ⟨a ~ of clouds⟩ ⟨the still-white snow ~⟩: as **a :** a covering (as of sauce, chopped vegetable, bacon) on a service of food (as of meat or fish) ⟨a thick ~ of glutinous cream sauce⟩ **b :** a thin surface formed by one or more coats of bituminous material on a roadway **c :** a thin widespread geologic deposit ⟨a ~ ore deposit⟩ ⟨an alluvial ~⟩ — compare TABULAR **d :** a streak or layer of blubber in whales **e :** a floral display for a funeral designed to be spread over the coffin like a bed blanket **f :** a layer of a fire-extinguishing agent (as foam or gas) spread over a burning surface in order to smother the fire **g :** a layer of less active material surrounding the highly reactive core of an atomic reactor **h :** insulating or shock-absorbing material formed into batts or sheets for ease of application **4 :** a large pelt; *esp* **:** a beaver pelt of the largest market size **5 :** something that covers and encloses ⟨a ~ of gloom descended on us⟩ or serves to guard, isolate, and protect ⟨the airfield was under security ~*s*⟩ ⟨the vast Civil Service ~*s* which Presidents Roosevelt and Truman threw over Federal personnel —Arthur Krock⟩

[2]**blanket** \"\ *vt* -ED/-ING/-S **1 :** to cover with or as if with a blanket ⟨new green grass ~*ing* the slopes⟩ ⟨designed to ~ the Iron Curtain countries and other critical areas with powerful standard broadcasts —*N.Y.Times*⟩ **2** *archaic* **:** to toss in a blanket (as by way of punishment) **3 :** to cover so as to obscure, interrupt, suppress, or extinguish: as **a :** to cover (food) with a blanket **b :** to interfere with or stop (the fire of friendly forces) by coming into the line of fire or interposing friendly forces in the line of fire **c :** to make (radio receiving sets) ineffective by powerful signals or interference **d :** to take the wind out of the sails of by sailing to windward of (another ship) **e :** to control or extinguish (a fire) by means of a foam or gas blanket **f :** EXCLUDE, ELIMINATE — usu. used with *out* ⟨using an inert gas to ~ out corrosive fumes⟩ **4 a :** to cover or apply to uniformly despite wide separation or diversity among the elements included ⟨legislation ~*ing* subversive acts⟩ ⟨freight rates that ~ a region⟩ **b :** to cause to belong **:** cause to be included — often used with *into* or *in* ⟨every area . . . had automatically been ~*ed* into the San Jose Unified School District —*Fortnight*⟩ ⟨will result in ~*ing* additional millions into the old-age pension system⟩

[3]**blanket** \"\ *adj* **1 a :** including or covering a group or class without any individual apportionment ⟨~ insurance coverage⟩ ⟨a ~ wage increase⟩ **b :** effective or applicable in all instances or contingencies ⟨a ~ price⟩ ⟨~ rules⟩ ⟨a ~ complaint⟩ **2 a :** of, relating to, or suggestive of a blanket **b :** having contestants extremely close together — used of the finish of a race **3 :** consisting of one or more large sheets of newsprint folded once to make four pages each — often used in distinguishing the modern large newspaper from the tabloid

blanket ballot *n* **:** a single ballot listing all the offices to be filled and candidates to be voted upon and sometimes containing legislative proposals — called also JUNGLE BALLOT, LONG BALLOT; compare SHORT BALLOT

blanket bond *n* **1 :** an insurance policy covering a wide variety of risks (as loss from dishonesty of employees, burglary, misplacement, damage, or destruction of property) **2 :** a fidelity bond covering all or all of a category of the employees of the insured

blanket chest *n* **:** a piece of case furniture with hinged lid, a deep well, and one or two drawers underneath

blanket-coat \'==,=\ *n* **:** a heavy short coat of blanket material **:** MACKINAW

blanket cylinder *n* **1** *archaic* **:** IMPRESSION CYLINDER **2 :** the cylinder of an offset press that carries the rubber blanket

blanket deposit *n* **:** MANTO 2a

blanket fish *also* **blanket ray** *n* **:** MANTA 3

blanketflower \'==,=\ *n* **:** a flower or plant of the genus *Gaillardia* — compare INDIAN BLANKET

blanket indian *n, usu cap I* **:** an Indian who retains or returns to tribal costume and custom

blanketing *n* -s [[1]*blanket* + *-ing*] **1 :** cloth for blankets **2 :** supply of blankets

blanket leaf *or* **blanket plant** *n* **:** MULLEIN

blanket mortgage *n* **:** a mortgage that covers a group or class of things or properties instead of one or more things mentioned individually (as a mortgage that secures various debts as a group or subjects a group or class of different pieces of property to one general lien)

blanket moss *n* **:** a felted scum of dead algae (as members of the genera *Spirogyra* or *Cladophora*) often found stranded after high water; *also* **:** an alga that is a constituent of such scum

blanket piece *n* **:** one of the large strips into which blubber is cut in removing it from a whale

blanket policy *n* **:** an insurance policy in which various items or classes of property (as buildings and contents) are covered

blanket rate *n* **1 :** GROUP RATE **2 a :** an insurance rate applying to two or more risks of a similar character but at different locations **b :** the insurance rate applying under a blanket policy

blanket roll *n* **1 :** a cylindrical pack made up of kit or accessories rolled in bedding and often in an outer water-resistant cover (as a shelter half or poncho) and used esp. by hikers and the military **2 :** a method of cheating at craps involving the throwing of the dice so that they will rotate only on their horizontal axes

blanket shawl *n* **:** a shawl made of blanketing or heavy woolen cloth

blanket sheet *n* **1 :** a newspaper of blanket size **2 :** a bed sheet or thin blanket of cotton having a nap on both sides

blanket stiff *n* **:** an itinerant usu. unskilled workman who travels with a blanket roll

blanket stitch *n* **:** a buttonhole stitch with spaces of variable width between the stitches

blanket-stitch \'==,=\ *vt* [*blanket stitch*] **:** to sew or finish with blanket stitches

blanketweed \'==,=\ *n* -s **:** a green alga of the genus *Cladophora* that often forms felted sheets along the shoreline

[1]**blank·ety-blank** \ˌblaŋkəd·|ē¦blaŋk, -aiŋkəd·|d¦blaiŋk, -kət|, |i¦-\ *also* **blankety** \'===\ *adj* (*or adv*) [redupl. of [1]*blank*] **:** DAMNED — used as a generalized expression of disapproval ⟨the interruptions for those *blankety-blank* . . . commercials —Jack Gould⟩ ⟨do what he *blankety-blank* well pleases —Gerard Smith⟩

[2]**blankety-blank** \"\ *n* **:** WRETCH, FOOL — used as a generalized expression of disapproval ⟨that *blankety-blank* can't make up his mind whether he's for us or against us —*Newsweek*⟩

blanking *pres part of* BLANK

blanking die *n* **:** a cutting die that in conjunction with a blanking punch cuts out flat pieces of stock

blanking punch *n* **:** a punch used in conjunction with a blanking die

blank·ly *adv* [[1]*blank* + *-ly*] **1 :** in a blank manner **:** without expression **:** VACUOUSLY ⟨gaze ~ at one⟩ **2 :** UTTERLY, COMPLETELY ⟨contains little that is not ~ medieval —H.O.Taylor⟩

blank·ness *n* -ES **:** the quality or state of being blank

blanks *pl of* BLANK, *pres 3d sing of* BLANK

blank signature *n* **:** a signature appended to a document (as a blank bill or note) that still has essential parts to be added and usu. authorizing any person to whom the document is delivered to fill it up as a bill for any amount subject to any limits stated in or on the instrument

blank tooling *n* **:** BLIND TOOLING

blank verse *n* **:** unrhymed verse; *specif* **:** the unrhymed iambic pentameter verse used esp. in English dramatic and narrative poetry

blank wall *n* **:** an impenetrable obstacle or barrier ⟨they suddenly saw a *blank wall* raised between government and a man —Vannevar Bush⟩

blanky \'blaŋki\ *adj* [[1]*blank* + *-y*] *Brit* **:** BLANKETY-BLANK

blanquette \blä^nket\ *n* -s [F, prob. fr. Prov *blanqueto*, fr. *blanc* white, of Gmc origin; akin to OHG *blanch* white — more at BLANK] **:** a light meat (as veal or breast of chicken) in a white sauce

blan·qui·llo \bläŋ·'kē(ˌ)(y)ō\ *n* -s [Sp, fr. *blanco* white (fr. OSp, fr. OF *blanc*) + *-illo*, dim. suffix — more at BLANK] **:** a marine fish of the percoid family Branchiostegidae including several important food fishes (as the ocean whitefish and the tilefish)

blan·quism \'bläŋˌkizəm\ *n* -s *usu cap* [Louis-Auguste *Blanqui* †1881 Fr. socialist + E *-ism*] **:** the revolutionary doctrine that a socialist state could be established only by an immediate seizure of power by the workers themselves

blan·quist \-ˌkəst\ *n* -s *usu cap* [Louis-Auguste *Blanqui* + E *-ist*] **:** an advocate of Blanquism

[1]**blare** \'bla(a)(ə)r, -le(ə)r,-la(a)ə,-leə\ *vb* -ED/-ING/-S [ME *bleren, bloren;* akin to MHG *blēren*, *blerren* to bleat, *brüelen* to bellow, moo, OE *blætan* to bleat — more at BLEAT] *vi* **1** *now dial* **:** to utter a prolonged cry ⟨the calf *blared* for its mother⟩ **2 :** to sound with or as if with the loud and somewhat harsh tone characteristic of a trumpet ⟨radios *blaring* in the night⟩ **3** *of lights* **:** to shine forth brilliantly and often garishly **:** GLARE ~ *vt* **1 a :** to sound loudly and usu. harshly or vehemently ⟨sat *blaring* the car horn⟩ **b :** to proclaim loudly or announce sensationally or flamboyantly ⟨headlines *blared* his disgrace⟩ **2 :** to give off (light) brilliantly or garishly **:** GLARE ⟨the chandelier . . . *blared* light like a trumpet —Eleanor Clark⟩

[2]**blare** \"\ *n* -s **1 :** the loud and somewhat harsh sound of a trumpet **2 a :** a sound felt to resemble the blast of a trumpet ⟨an automobile passed before the house, its horn giving off a ~ —Hamilton Basso⟩ **b :** sound that is loud and often harsh ⟨the jukebox filled the room with ~⟩ **3 :** dazzling and often garish brilliance ⟨tunnels with their sudden ~ of daylight —Osbert Sitwell⟩ **4 :** sensationalism or flamboyance that often exceeds good taste ⟨for general ~ and blarney and pandemonium —C.L.Becker⟩; *also* **:** an instance of this ⟨a ~ of publicity⟩ **5 :** tar mixture used in caulking

bla·ri·na \bla(a)'rīnə, -rēnə\ *n* [NL, perh. irreg. fr. *Blair*, Nebr. + NL *-ina*] **1** *cap* **:** a genus of short-tailed shrews widely distributed in No. America **2** -s *also* **blarina shrew** **:** any shrew of the genus *Blarina*

[1]**blar·ney** \'blärnē, -ån-, -ni\ *vb* **blarneyed**; **blarneyed**; **blarneying**; **blarneys** *vt* **:** to influence or gain by smooth talk **:** WHEEDLE ⟨demagogues who pleasingly ~ the electorate —B.I.Bell⟩ ~ *vi* **:** to use flattering speech ⟨then would she wheedle and laugh and ~ —Nathaniel Hawthorne⟩

[2]**blarney** \"\ *n* -s [fr. *Blarney stone*, a stone in Blarney castle, near Cork, Ireland, reputed to bestow talent for eloquent cajolery upon those who kiss it] **:** smooth wheedling talk **:** FLATTERY ⟨made fun of his gift for ~, his adroitness in playing up to whatever an audience or a situation demanded of him —Eleanor Dark⟩

blart \'blåt\ *n or vb* [prob. of imit. origin] *dial Eng* **:** CRY, BLEAT, BLARE

blas \'blas, -äs\ *n* -ES [D, fr. *blazen* to blow, fr. MD *blāsen;* akin to OHG *blāsan* to blow — more at BLAST] **:** a supposed emanation from the stars

bla·sé \(')blä¦zā, -lå- *also* -la-\ *adj* [F] **:** apathetic to pleasure or life esp. as a result of excessive indulgence or enjoyment **:** SOPHISTICATED ⟨the ~ traveler likes to refer to the ocean he has crossed as "the pond" —R.E.Coker⟩ **:** WORLD-WEARY ⟨the ~ indifference of . . . the people —Jack Belden⟩

[1]**blash** \'blash\ *n* -ES [prob. of imit. origin] **1** *dial Brit* **:** a splash of liquid or mud **2** *dial Brit* **:** a shower of rain or sleet

[2]**blash** \"\ *vb* -ED/-ING/-ES *dial Brit* **:** SPLASH, SPLATTER

blashy \-shi\ *adj* [[1]*blash* + *-y*] **1** *dial Brit* **:** RAINY, GUSTY, SPLASHY **2** *dial Brit, of food* **:** THIN, WATERY

blas·pheme \(')bla¦sfēm, -laa-,-lai-\ *vb* -ED/-ING/-S [ME *blasfemen*, fr. LL *blasphemare* — more at BLAME] *vt* **1 :** to speak of or address with irreverence **:** revile impiously ⟨and when he reproved them they *blasphemed* all the saints in the calendar —W.H.Hudson †1922⟩ **2 :** to speak evil of **:** REVILE, ABUSE ⟨he has been *blasphemed* more than he deserves —*Wildlife Rev.*⟩ ~ *vi* **:** to utter blasphemy

blas·phem·er \-mə(r) *sometimes* '=ˌsfəmə(r)\ *n* -s [ME *blasfemer*, fr. *blasfemen* + *-er*] **:** one that blasphemes

blaspheme-vine \'=,=,=\ *n* **:** a greenbrier (*Smilax laurifolia*) of the southeastern U.S. with thick coriaceous leaves

blas·phe·mous \'blasfəməs, -laa-,-lai-, *now chiefly in substand speech* (')=¦sfēməs\ *adj* [LL *blasphemus*, fr. Gk *blasphēmos* evil-speaking — more at BLAME] **1 :** speaking or writing blasphemy **:** impiously irreverent ⟨the ~ Swinburne is a very good though hardly a great poet —H.N.Fairchild⟩ **2 :** constituting blasphemy ⟨observing stiffly that such audacious claims were ~ —M.L.Bach⟩ **:** PROFANE ⟨a ~ epithet⟩ **syn** see IMPIOUS

blas·phe·mous·ly *adv* **:** in a blasphemous manner

blas·phe·my \'blasfəmē, -laa-,-lai-, -mi\ *n* -ES [ME *blasphemie*, fr. LL *blasphemia*, fr. Gk *blasphēmia*, fr. *blasphēmos* evil-speaking + *-ia* -y] **1 :** irreverence toward God ⟨the crime of ~ in 17th century England was the crime of dissenting from whatever was the current religious dogma —T.C.Clark⟩: **a** *Jewish law* (1) **:** the cursing or reviling of God or the king (2) **:** the pronouncing of the forbidden name of God — compare TETRAGRAMMATON **b** (1) **:** indignity offered to God in speaking, writing, or signs ⟨~ . . . is now an offense against the common law —R.C.Mortimer⟩ (2) **:** the act of claiming the attributes or prerogatives of deity ⟨for a mere man to suggest that he was both messiah and divine could only be viewed . . . as ~ —John Bright †1889⟩ **2 :** irreverence toward something considered sacred or held in high regard ⟨an outraged House of Commons officer sourly viewing the breach of precedent, muttered: "This is ~" —*Time*⟩ **syn** see PROFANATION

[1]**blast** \'blast, -aa(ə)st, -aist,-åst\ *n* -s [ME, fr. OE *blæst;* akin to OHG *blāst* blast, *blāsan* to blow, ON *blāstr* blast, *blāsa* to blow, Goth uf*blesan* to inflate with self-importance, OE *blāwan* to blow — more at BLOW] **1 a :** a violent gust of wind ⟨heavy ~*s* whistling about our ears⟩ **b :** a blowing or battering of winds ⟨this prosperous handsome town has withstood the ~ of hurricanes —G.S.Perry⟩ **c :** something borne by a gust of wind ⟨a ~ of sleet⟩ ⟨the drizzle became a ~ and then a deluge —John Buchan⟩ **2 a :** the sound produced from a horn or whistle at one breath **b :** the sound produced by a steam whistle or any comparable mechanical instrument ⟨the ~ of an auto horn⟩ **c :** a signal made by a ship's whistle **d :** an inadvertent loud sound so intense as to overload a sound-recording or sound-transmission system and produce a discordant effect **3 :** something resembling a gust of wind: as **a :** BREATH; *esp* **:** air exhaled in breathing or coughing **b :** a violent or vigorous outburst or onslaught ⟨let out a great ~ of mirth —Marcia Davenport⟩ ⟨the senator's angry ~ against special privilege⟩ **c :** the continuous blowing to which one charge of ore or metal is subjected in a furnace ⟨melt so many tons of iron at a ~⟩ **d** (1) **:** the exhaust steam from a steam engine that drives a column of air up the smokestack and thus creates an intense draft through the fire (2) **:** the draft thus created **e :** the exhaust from an internal-combustion engine or a rocket or jet engine **f** *chiefly Scot* **:** a smoke of tobacco **:** PIPE ⟨a quiet cup and a peaceful ~ by the fire⟩ **4 a :** a sudden pernicious influence or effect ⟨virtue preserved from fell destruction's ~ —Shak.⟩ ⟨the ~ of a great pestilence⟩ **b :** any of certain diseases (as erysipelas) that suggest the effect of a noxious wind or that spread as though distributed by wind; *esp* **:** a disease of plants that causes the foliage or flowers to appear as though dried by a hot wind, that is sometimes marked by spotting and cracking and in some crops (as rice) by rotting of the neck or (as in oats) by failure of the buds or flowers to open, and that is caused by infection (as with bacteria or fungi) or by environmental conditions (as drought) **5 a :** an explosion or violent detonation: as (1) **:** the discharge of a shot or series of shots of an explosive (as dynamite) used to break rock and other solid material; *also* **:** the charge used for this purpose (2) **:** an explosion of gas or dust in a mine (3) **:** muzzle blast **b :** the violent effect produced in the vicinity of an explosion that consists of a wave of increased atmospheric pressure followed by a wave of decreased atmospheric pressure **6 :** a season's run from a particular furnace in glass manufacturing **7 :** ACTIVITY, OPERATION, CAPACITY, SPEED — usu. used in phrases to indicate relative degree or level of activity ⟨the new educational system going full ~⟩ ⟨the plant had run at half ~ for several months⟩ **syn** see WIND

[2]**blast** \"\ *vb* -ED/-ING/-S [ME *blasten*, fr. *blast*, n.] *vi* **1 :** to give out blasts; *specif* **:** to produce sounds of undesired loudness ⟨a good voice marred by a tendency to ~ when before a microphone⟩ **2** *dial Eng, of an animal* **:** BLOAT **3 a :** to employ an explosive to shatter or open something **b :** to employ the most vigorous means to attain an end ⟨you'll have to ~ to make her change her mind⟩ **4 a :** to fire a gun **:** SHOOT ⟨as we walked in they started ~*ing*⟩ **b :** to attack with vigor — often used with *away* ⟨he ~*ed* away at the false idealism of his opponents⟩ **5 :** to hit a golf ball out of a sand trap with an explosion shot — usu. used with *out* ⟨it was a poor lie but he ~*ed* out successfully⟩ **6** *slang* **:** to smoke marijuana ~ *vt* **1 :** to injure by or as if by the action of wind ⟨seedlings ~*ed* by the hot dry wind⟩ **:** stop or check from growth or fruit bearing ⟨we'll have no peaches; frost ~*ed* the blossoms this year⟩ **:** WITHER, STUNT, BLIGHT, SHRIVEL **2 :** to affect with some violence, plague, calamity, or blighting influence that thwarts or destroys **:** WRECK, RUIN ⟨time has ~*ed* his ambition⟩ **3** *obs* **:** to confound by a blast of or as if of trumpets **4 :** to denounce vigorously ⟨his own lack of hesitation in . . . ~*ing* any and all dignitaries —J.T.Farrell⟩ **:** CURSE, DAMN ⟨I am not making this up, ~ you; it is all in the book —Samuel Grafton⟩ **5 a :** to shatter (as rock) by an explosive agent **b :** to remove (as an obstruction) or open (as a ditch) by blasting — often used with *away* or *out* ⟨set himself to ~ away these barriers to progress —Elmer Davis⟩ ⟨they ~*ed* out a new course for the stream⟩ **c :** to kill by shooting or bombing — often used with *down* ⟨when the senator rose to speak the conspirators ~*ed* him down⟩ **6 a :** to apply a forced draft to (as a fuel bed) **b :** to blow particles of abrasive against (a metal object) for the purpose of cleaning the surface **7 a :** to defeat (as an opposing team) decisively ⟨they ~*ed* the home team by a score of 12 to 2⟩ **b :** to hit vigorously and effectively (as in baseball) ⟨~*ed* a homer over the right-field wall⟩

blast- *or* **blasto-** *comb form* [G *blast-*, *blasto-*, fr. Gk, fr. *blastos*] **1 :** bud **:** budding **:** germ **:** embryo in its early stages ⟨*blasto*derm⟩ **2 :** metamorphic and ⟨*blasto*granitic⟩

-blast \ˌblast, -aa(ə)st,-aist\ *n comb form* -s [NL *-blastus*, fr. Gk *blastos*; akin to OE *molda* top of the head, Gk *blōthros* tall, *melathron* roof, Skt *mūrdhan* head, Toch A *malto* first] **1** *biol* **a** : germ : shoot : sprout **b** : embryonic or formative cell — in names of formative cells corresponding to names of fully developed cells ending in *-cyte* ⟨erythro*blast*⟩ **c** : germ layer : formative layer of cells ⟨splanchno*blast*⟩ **d** : formative constituent unit of living matter ⟨idio*blast*⟩ **2** *geol* : crystal formed during metamorphism ⟨porphyro*blast*⟩

blas·taea \blaˈstēə\ *n* -s [NL, irreg. fr. Gk *blastos*] : a hypothetical metazoan ancestral form corresponding in organization to the blastula — **blas·tae·al** \(ˈ)ˌstēəl\ *adj*

blast burner *n* : a gas burner in which combustion is intensified by means of a controlled blast of air or oxygen — called also *blast lamp*

blast cleaning *n* : the removal of sand or scale from metal objects by the impinging action of a current of abrasive material (as sand, shot, or grit)

blasted *adj* [fr. past part. of ²*blast*] **1** : BLIGHTED, WITHERED ⟨upon this ~ heath —Shak.⟩ **2** : CONFOUNDED, ACCURSED, DETESTABLE — often used as a mild imprecation ⟨if I ever get out of this ~ mess⟩ **3** : cleft, torn, or injured by or as if by an explosive, lightning, or the wind ⟨an old ~ apple tree⟩

blas·te·ma \blaˈstēmə\ *n, pl* **blastemas** \-məz\ *or* **blastema·ta** \-məd·ə\ [NL, fr. Gk *blastēma* offspring, offshoot, fr. *blast-* + *-ēma* -eme] : a mass of living substance capable of growth and differentiation: **a** : the protoplasmic portion of a fertilized egg **b** : a mass of indifferentiated embryonic cells from which an organ or definitive structure will develop : ANLAGE **c** : undifferentiated tissue that is capable in an emergency (as loss of a body part) of renewed growth and differentiation sometimes (as in salamanders) to the extent of restoring a missing part — **blas·te·mal** \(ˈ)blaˈstēməl\ *or* **blas·te·mat·ic** \ˌ==ˈmad·ik, -stē-\ *or* **blas·tem·ic** \(ˈ)=ˈstēmik, -ste-\ *adj*

blast·er \ˈblastə(r), -aas-,-ais-,-ȧs-\ *n* -s : one that blasts: as **a** : one whose work is blasting with an explosive — called also *chargeman, firer, shooter* **b** : a golf club with a broad face and rounded base

blast-freeze \ˈ=,=\ *vt* : to quick-freeze by rapidly circulating cold air

blast furnace *n* : a furnace in which combustion is forced by a current of air under pressure; *specif* : such a furnace for obtaining iron by the reduction of the ore with suitable fuel and fluxes at a high temperature

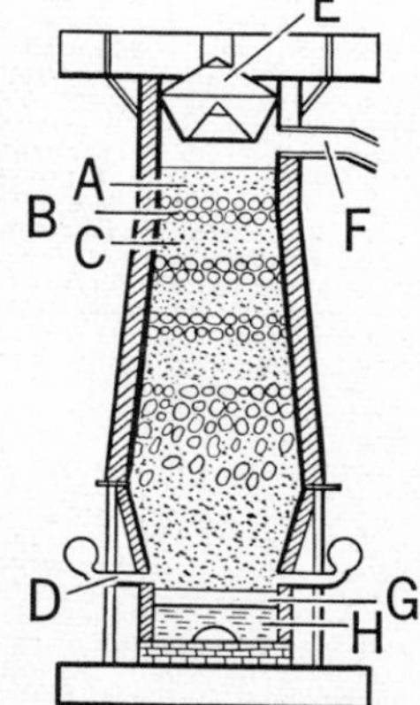

cross section of a typical blast furnace: *A* coke, *B* ore, *C* limestone, *D* hot blast, *E* charging hopper, *F* downcomer, *G* slag, *H* molten iron

blast gate *n* : a damper (as of the butterfly-valve type) used for controlling the volume of a blast of air or exhaust gases

blast heater *n* : a heating unit (as a coil of steam pipes) through or over which air is driven by a fan and then circulated through the rooms to be heated

blasthole \ˈ=,=\ *n* -s **1** : a hole in the bottom of a pump stock through which water enters **2** : the hole into which a blasting charge is inserted

blas·tic \ˈblastik, -laa-,-lai-, -tēk\ *adj* [Gk *blastikos* budding, fr. *blast-* + *-ikos* -ic] : involving growth of new constituents in metamorphic rocks

-blastic \ˈ==\ *adj comb form* [ISV, fr. *-blast* + *-ic*] : sprouting or germinating (in a specified way) ⟨hetero*blastic*⟩ : having (such or so many) sprouts, buds, or germ layers ⟨calypto*blastic*⟩ ⟨mono*blastic*⟩

blas·tid \ˈ=təd\ *n* -s [*blast-* + *id*] : an echinoderm or fossil of the class Blastoidea

blast·ie \ˈblastē\ *n* -s [Sc *blast* to curse, wither (fr. ²*blast*) + *-ie*] *Scot* : an ill-favored little being (as a dwarf or elf)

blastier *comparative of* BLASTY

-blasties *pl of* -BLASTY

blastiest *superlative of* BLASTY

blasting *n* -s [fr. gerund of ²*blast*] **1** : BLIGHT **2** : the practice or occupation of breaking up heavy masses (as of rock) by means of explosives **3** : abrasion or attrition effected by the impact of fine particles moved against or past a stationary body — often used in combination ⟨sand*blasting* by the wind⟩

blasting cap *n* : a small usu. metal or plastic tube closed at one or both ends, containing a detonating agent together with other charges (as a priming composition), and used in detonating high explosives

blasting gelatin *n* : a translucent tough rubbery very powerful explosive consisting chiefly of nitroglycerin and lower-nitrated cellulose nitrate and used esp. in submarine work — compare GELATIN DYNAMITE

blasting machine *n* : a hand-operated magneto or dynamo for firing explosives by electricity

blasting powder *n* : black powder usu. containing sodium nitrate manufactured in grains or pellets and used esp. for blasting soft materials (as in coal mines) — called also *black blasting powder*

blast injury *n* : the harmful effects on the body of sudden changes in pressure produced by explosion

blast lamp *n* **1** : BLAST BURNER **2** : BLOWTORCH

blast main *n* : BLAST PIPE

blast·man \-stmən, -ˌman\ *n, pl* **blastmen** : SANDBLASTER c

blast·ment \-stmənt\ *n* -s : a blasting process or influence : BLIGHTING

blas·to- — see BLAST-

blas·to·car·pous \ˌblastōˈkärpəs, -təˈ-\ *adj* [*blast-* + *-carpous*] : germinating in the pericarp

blas·to·chyle \ˈ==+ˌkīl\ *n* -s [*blast-* + *chyle*] : the fluid that fills the blastocoel

blas·to·cla·dia \ˌ==·ˈklādēə\ *n, cap* [NL, fr. *blast-* + *clad-* + *-ia*] : a genus of fungi (family Blastocladiaceae) lacking false septa and having cylindrical sporangia with one collar

blas·to·cla·di·a·ce·ae \ˌ===ˌdēˈāsē,ē\ *n pl, cap* [NL, fr. *Blastocladia*, type genus + *-aceae*] : a family of saprobic fungi (order Blastocladiales) having resistant sporangia with walls that are often conspicuously pitted

blas·to·cla·di·a·les \-ˈā(ˌ)lēz\ *n pl, cap* [NL, fr. *Blastocladia* + *-ales*] : an order of fungi (subclass Oomycetes) having a eucarpic thallus and carrying out asexual reproduction by thick-walled often punctate resting spores that produce zoospores upon germination

blas·to·coel *or* **blas·to·coele** *also* **blas·to·cele** \ˈ==,sēl\ *n* -s [ISV *blast-* + *-coel, -coele, -cele*] : the cavity of a blastula — called also *segmentation cavity*; see BLASTULA illustration — **blas·to·coel·ic** \ˌ==ˈsēlik\ *adj*

blas·to·col·la \ˌ==ˈkälə\ *n* -s [NL, fr. *blast-* + Gk *kolla* glue] : the gummy or balsamic varnish on certain buds (as of the horse chestnut)

blas·to·cone \ˈ==+ˌ-\ *n* -s [*blast-* + *cone*] : an incomplete blastomere; *esp* : one at the periphery of an egg undergoing discoidal cleavage

blas·to·cyst \"+ˌ-\ *n* [*blast-* + *-cyst*] **1** : the modified blastula characteristic of placental mammals **2** [NL *Blastocystis*] : a yeast of the genus *Blastocystis*

blas·to·cys·tis \ˌ==+\ *n, cap* [NL, fr. *blast-* + *cystis*] : a cosmopolitan genus of commensal yeasts common in human feces and a frequent source of confusion in fecal examinations for the detection of pathogenic protozoans

blas·to·cyte \ˈ==ˌsīt\ *n* -s [*blast-* + *-cyte*] **1** : an undifferentiated embryonic cell **2** : a residual undifferentiated cell capable of replacing lost or damaged tissues esp. in certain lower animals — compare BLASTEMA

blas·to·derm \ˈ==ˌdərm\ *n* -s [G, fr. *blast-* + *-derm*] **1** : a blastodisc after completion of cleavage and formation of the blastocoel **2** : the part of insect and certain other invertebrate embryos corresponding to the vertebrate blastoderm — **blas·to·der·mat·ic** *or* **blas·to·der·mic** \ˌ==+\ *adj*

blastodermic vesicle *n* : BLASTOCYST 1

blas·to·disc *also* **blas·to·disk** \ˈ==+ˌ-\ *n* [*blast-* + *disc, disk*] : the embryo-forming portion of a megalecithal egg with discoidal cleavage, usu. appearing as a small disc on the upper surface of the yolk mass — called also *germinal disc;* see EGG illustration

blast off *vi* : to take off : begin to travel — used esp. of rocket-propelled missiles and vehicles

blast-off \ˈ=,=\ *n* -s [*blast off*] : the action of blasting off — used esp. of rocket-propelled missiles and vehicles

blas·to·genesis \ˌ==+\ *n* [NL, fr. *blast-* + L *genesis*] **1** : reproduction by budding **2** : the transmission of inherited characters through the germ plasm — opposed to *pangenesis*

blas·to·genetic \ˌ==+\ *adj* [*blast-* + *genetic*] **1** : of or relating to blastogenesis **2** : BLASTOGENIC 1a

blas·to·genic \"+\ *adj* [*blast-* + *-genic*] **1 a** *of somatic characters* : originating in the germ plasm — compare SOMATOGENIC **b** *of castes of social insects* : determined genetically — opposed to *trophogenic* **2** : promoting or initiating tissue proliferation

blas·tog·e·ny \blaˈstäjənē\ *n* -ES [*blast-* + *-geny*] : BLASTOGENESIS

¹blas·toid \ˈblaˌstȯid\ *n* -s [NL *Blastoidea*, fr. *blast-* + *-oidea*] : an echinoderm or fossil of the class Blastoidea

²blastoid \"\ *adj* : of, relating to, or like the Blastoidea

blas·toi·dea \blaˈstȯidēə\ *n pl, cap* [NL, fr. *blast-* + *-oidea*] : a class, formerly considered a division of Crinoidea, of extinct Paleozoic short-stemmed or stemless pelmatozoan echinoderms shaped somewhat like a flower bud and having five ambulacral areas with slender appendages along their margins and flattened tubes along their internal surface — **blas·toi·de·an** \(ˈ)=ˈ=dēən\ *adj or n*

blas·to·kinesis \ˌblastō, ˌblastə+\ *n* [NL, fr. *blast-* + *kinesis*] : movement of the developing embryo in some insect eggs into the yolk mass usu. involving partial revolution of the body — **blas·to·kinetic** \ˌ==+\ *adj*

blas·to·mere \ˈ==ˌmi(ə)r\ *n* -s [ISV *blast-* + *-mere*] : a cell produced during cleavage : a blastula cell — **blas·to·mer·ic** \ˌ==ˈmerik\ *adj*

blas·to·my·ces \ˌ==ˈmīˌsēz\ *n, cap* [NL, fr. *blast-* + *-myces*] *in some classifications* : a genus of yeastlike fungi coextensive with the group Blastomycetes

blas·to·my·cete \ˌ==ˈmīˌsēt, -ˌmīˈsēt\ *n* -s [NL *Blastomycetes*] : a fungus of the group Blastomycetes

blas·to·my·ce·tes \ˌ==ˌmīˈsēd·ēz\ *n pl, cap* [NL, fr. *blast-* + *-mycetes*] *in some classifications* : a group of pathogenic fungi growing typically like yeasts by budding but sometimes forming mycelium and conidia on artificial media and being usu. classed among the Moniliales or formerly sometimes made synonymous with Saccharomycetaceae

blas·to·my·ce·tic \ˌ==,=ˈsēd·ik\ *adj* [NL *Blastomycetes* + E *-ic*] **1** *also* **blas·to·my·ce·tous** \-ˈsēd·əs\ : of or relating to the group Blastomycetes ⟨~ fungi⟩ **2** : of, relating to, or caused by blastomycetes ⟨~ dermatitis⟩

blas·to·my·co·sis \ˌ==,=ˈkōsəs\ *n, pl* **blastomyco·ses** \-ō-ˌsēz\ [NL, fr. *Blastomycetes* + *-osis*] : a disease of man and less often of other animals caused by infection with any of several blastomycetes and involving invasion of the skin, mucous membrane, lymph nodes, or internal organs — see NORTH AMERICAN BLASTOMYCOSIS, SOUTH AMERICAN BLASTOMYCOSIS — **blas·to·my·cot·ic** \ˌ==,=ˈkäd·ik\ *adj*

blas·to·neuropore \ˌ==+\ *n* -s [*blast-* + *neuropore*] : a temporary opening formed by the union of the blastopore and neuropore in some embryos

blas·toph·a·ga \blaˈstäfəgə\ *n* [NL, fr. *blast-* + *-phaga*] **1** *cap* : a common genus of fig wasps essential to the pollination of Smyrna figs **2** *pl* **blastophaga** *or* **blastophagas** : a wasp of the genus *Blastophaga*

blas·to·phore \ˈ==ˌfō(ə)r\ *n* -s [*blast-* + *-phore*] **1** : the residual cytoplasm detached during transformation of a spermatid to a spermatozoon **2** : an amorphous cytoplasmic core that holds together the cells of the male morula of developing oligochaete germ cells and is produced by segregation of part of the cytoplasm of each spermatoblast of the morula — **blas·to·phor·ic** \ˌ==ˈfȯrik\ *adj*

blas·toph·tho·ria \ˌblastäfˈthōrēə\ *also* **blas·toph·tho·ry** \blaˈstäfthərē\ *n, pl* **blastophthorias** *also* **blastophthories** [NL *blastophoria*, fr. *blast-* + Gk *phthoria* decay, fr. *phtheirein* to destroy — more at PHTHIRIASIS] : degeneration of the germ cells believed to be due to chronic poisoning (as by alcohol) or to disease — **blas·toph·thor·ic** \ˌblastäfˈthȯrik\ *adj*

blas·to·po·ral \ˌblastō, ˌblastə+ˈpōrəl\ *or* **blas·to·por·ic** \"+ˈpōrik\ *adj* : of, relating to, or involving a blastopore

blas·to·pore \ˈ==+ˌ-\ *n* -s [*blast-* + *-pore*] : the mouth or opening of the archenteron — see GASTRULA

blas·to·porphyritic \ˌ==+\ *adj* [ISV *blast-* + *porphyritic;* orig. formed as G *blastoporphyritisch*] *of rocks* : having a palimpsest texture showing traces of the original porphyritic texture

blas·to·sphere \ˈ==+ˌ-\ *n* -s [*blast-* + *sphere*] : BLASTULA; *esp* : BLASTOCYST — **blas·to·spheric** \ˌ==+\ *adj*

blas·to·spore \"+ˌ-\ *n* -s [*blast-* + *spore*] : a fungous spore that is produced by budding and that acts as a resting spore or (as in yeasts) gives rise to another spore or a hypha while still attached to the parent cell and without an intervening dormant period

blas·to·style \"+ˌstīl\ *n* -s [*blast-* + *-style*] : a process in certain hydroids that may be regarded as a zooid without mouth or tentacles whose function is to produce medusoid buds

blas·tot·o·my \blaˈstäd·əmē\ *n* -ES [*blast-* + *-tomy*] : separation of cleavage cells during early stages of embryonic development ⟨both polyembryony and identical twinning may be explained in terms of ~⟩

blas·to·zooid \ˌblastə+\ *n* -s [*blast-* + *zooid*] : a zooid or individual produced by budding — distinguished from *oozooid*

blast pipe *n* : a pipe delivering steam or air so as to cause a blast — called also *blast main*

blast roasting *n* : the process of roasting finely divided ores by means of a blast maintaining internal combustion in the charge (as in desulfurizing ores of lead or copper) — called also *roast sintering*

blasts *pl of* BLAST, *pres 3d sing of* BLAST

-blasts *pl of* -BLAST

blas·tu·la \ˈblaschələ\ *n, pl* **blastulas** \-ləz\ *or* **blastu·lae** \-ˌlē\ [NL, fr. *blast-* + *-ula*] : an early metazoan embryo typically having the form of a hollow fluid-filled rounded cavity bounded by a single layer of cells — compare GASTRULA, MORULA — **blas·tu·lar** \-lə(r)\ *adj*

blas·tu·la·tion \ˌ==ˈlāshən\ *n* -s [NL *blastula* + E *-ation*] : formation of a blastula

a
mi
c
ma
v

section of blastula: *c* blastocoel, *ma* macromere, *mi* micromere, *a* animal pole, *v* vegetal pole

blast wall *n* : a protective work designed to minimize blast damage to buildings or other structures exposed to bombing or other types of explosions

blasty \ˈblastē, -laa-,-lai-,-lȧ-, -ti\ *adj, usu* -ER/-EST [¹*blast* + *-y*] **1** : subject to or marked by blasts esp. of wind : GUSTY ⟨this bleak and ~ shore —Nathaniel Hawthorne⟩ **2** : causing or impaired by blast ⟨a good recording but a bit ~ at times⟩

-blas·ty \ˌblastē, -laa-,-lai-, -ti\ *n comb form* -ES [ISV, fr. *-blastic* + *-y*] : manner or condition of germinating ⟨hetero*blasty*⟩

¹blat \ˈblat, *usu* -d·+V\ *vb* **blatted; blatted; blatting; blats** [imit.] *vi* **1** : to cry esp. like a calf or sheep : BELLOW, BLEAT ⟨the calf *blatted* in fear as it was borne to the ground —F.D. Davison⟩ **2 a** : to make a senseless or raucous noise ⟨like an oboe *blatting* . . . inside a barrel of feathers —R.P.Warren⟩ **b** : to talk loudly and often foolishly ⟨someone has to be constantly *blatting* around the house —Wilder Hobson⟩ ~ *vt* : to utter (as an opinion) loudly and often foolishly or unthinkingly : BLURT ⟨you don't want to go *blatting* this all over town —Mary S. Watts⟩

²blat \"\ *n* -s **1** : a bleat or bleatlike cry ⟨the thin ~ of a sheep beneath the barn —Mary E. Waller⟩ **2** : a senseless or raucous noise ⟨the never-ending ~ of airhorns piercing the dusk —E.L.DeGolyer⟩

bla·tan·cy \ˈblātᵊnsē, -si\ *n* -ES **1** : the quality or state of being blatant ⟨human-interest stories . . . may be ruined by ~ —F.L. Mott⟩ **2** : something blatant ⟨attacks the *blatancies* of our culture in a series of oracular essays —*New Yorker*⟩

bla·tant \ˈblātᵊnt\ *adj* [perh. fr. L *blatire* to chatter, gossip + E *-ant;* perh. of imit. origin like MLG *pladderen* to chat, gossip, Sw *pladder* loose gossip, Dan *bladre* to gossip, L *blaterare* to chatter, bleat, croak] **1** : noisy esp. in a vulgar or offensive manner : loud and clamorous ⟨an enormous ~ jukebox —Dan Wickenden⟩ **2** : obtrusive in an offensive manner: **a** : conspicuous or enforcing attention in a vulgar manner (as by gaudy pretense) ⟨the predominant tendency toward a coarse and ~ westernization —Harold Strauss⟩ **b** : completely or crassly obvious : PROMINENT ⟨loathed the squalor and ~ poverty —Willard Robertson⟩; *esp* : BRAZEN ⟨found this ~ form of intellectual seduction irresistible —Anthony West⟩

syn see VOCIFEROUS

bla·tant·ly *adv* : in a blatant manner

¹blate \ˈblāt\ *adj* [ME, prob. fr. OE *blāt* pale; akin to OHG *bleizza* pallor, OSlav *blēdŭ* pale, Gk *phalos* white — more at BALD] **1** *chiefly Scot* : BASHFUL, TIMID, SHY ⟨you are not ~ — you will never lose fair lady for faint heart —Sir Walter Scott⟩ **2** *chiefly Scot* : DULL, SLOW

²blate \"\ *vb* -ED/-ING/-S [by alter] : BLEAT

¹blath·er \ˈblathə(r)\ *also* **bleth·er** \ˈbleth-\ *vi* **blathered; blathered; blathering** \-th(ə)riŋ\ **blathers** [ON *blathra* to talk unintelligibly; akin to MHG *blōdern* to chatter, gurgle, prob. of imit. origin] : to talk foolishly or nonsensically ⟨he ~s about goodness and beauty and his own genius —Herman Wouk⟩

²blather \"\ *n* -s [ON *blathr* nonsense, fr. *blathra* to talk unintelligibly] **1 a** : voluble, foolish, or nonsensical talk ⟨sensible people can get up . . . and talk such ~ —Francis Neilson⟩ **b** : bubbling sound ⟨the ~ that the water made —Wallace Stevens⟩ **2** : ADO, STIR, COMMOTION ⟨out of all this ~ will come a demand . . . to rewrite the . . . law —*New Republic*⟩

³blather \ˈblāthər\ *Scot var of* BLADDER

blath·er·er \ˈblath(ə)rə(r)\ *n* -s [¹*blather* + *-er*] : one that blathers

blath·er·skite \ˈblathə(r),skīt\ *n* -s [alter. of earlier *blether-skate*, fr. ¹*blether* + *skate* (fish)] **1** : a blustering, talkative, and often incompetent person ⟨elect fewer cowards . . . and fewer ~s who will do anything for publicity —Elmer Davis⟩ **2** : NONSENSE, BLATHER ⟨your literary fakers . . . talk ~ about Celtic poetry —Thomas Beer⟩ **3** : RUDDY DUCK

blat·ta \ˈblad·ə\ *n, cap* [NL, fr. L, cockroach, chafer, moth; perh. akin to Lith *blakts* bedbug, Latvian *blãkê*] : a genus (the type of the family Blattidae) of cockroaches including the common Oriental cockroach that infests buildings in America and most other parts of the world

blat·tar·ia \bləˈta(a)rēə, -ter-\ *n pl, cap* [NL, fr. *Blatta* + *-aria*] : an order of medium to large-sized broadly oval flattened cursorial insects consisting of the roaches and having the head concealed from above beneath the pronotum, strong chewing mouthparts, long many-jointed antennae, two pairs of wings when present with the forewings membranous and veined, prominent jointed cerci at the end of the abdomen, incomplete metamorphosis, and eggs produced in an ootheca

blat·tar·i·ae \-rē(ˌ)ē\ *syn of* BLATTARIA

blatted *past of* BLAT

blat·tel·la \bləˈtelə\ *n, cap* [NL, fr. L *blatta* + NL *-ella*] : a genus of cockroaches including the abundant small domestic croton bug

¹blat·ter \ˈblad·ə(r), -atə-\ *vi* -ED/-ING/-S [perh. fr. L *blaterare* to chatter — more at BLATANT] **1** *dial* : to talk noisily and fast : PRATTLE ⟨he ~*ed* along and managed to inquire about pretty much everybody —Mark Twain⟩ **2** *chiefly Scot* : PATTER, BEAT ⟨the rain that ~*ed* in my face⟩

²blatter \"\ *n* -s *chiefly Scot* : a clatter of repetitive sounds : a prattle of words or sounds ⟨listening to the ~ of snow and wind —*Nat'l Geographic*⟩

¹blat·tid \ˈblad·əd, -atəd\ *adj* [NL Blattidae] : of or relating to the family Blattidae

²blattid \"\ *n* -s [NL *Blattidae*] : an insect of the family Blattidae; *broadly* : ROACH

blat·ti·dae \ˈblad·ə,dē\ *n pl, cap* [NL, fr. *Blatta*, type genus + *-idae*] : a family of Blattaria including domestic pest roaches

blat·ti family \ˈblad·ē-\ *n* [Malayalam *plātti*] : SONNERATIACEAE

blatting *pres part of* BLAT

blat·to·dea \bləˈtōdēə\ [NL, fr. *Blatta* + *-odea*] *syn of* BLATTARIA

blau·bok *or* **blaauw·bok** \ˈblau̇ˌbäk\ *n, pl* **blaubok** *or* **blauboks** [obs. Afrik *blauwbok* (now *bloubok*), fr. *blauw* blue (fr. MD *blā, blau*) + *bok* male antelope, male goat, fr. MD *boc;* akin to OHG *blāo* blue and to OHG *boc* male goat — more at BLUE, BUCK] **1** : a southern African antelope (*Hippotragus leucophaeus*) closely related to the sable antelope but now exterminated **2** : BLUE DUIKER

blaud \ˈblad, ˈblȯd\ *var of* BLAD

blaud's pill \ˈblȯdz-, ˈblō(d)z-\ *n, usu cap B* [after Paul *Blaud* †1858 Fr. physician] : a pill consisting essentially of ferrous carbonate used in the treatment of anemia

blaue rei·ter \ˌblau̇əˈrītə(r)\ *adj, usu cap B & R* [G, n. pl., blue riders] : of, relating to, or characteristic of a short-lived group of German artists concerned esp. with the emotional use of color in primarily nonrepresentational art

blau gas \ˈblau̇-\ *n* [fr. *Blaugas*, a trademark] : an oil gas consisting chiefly of a mixture of lower saturated and unsaturated hydrocarbons supplied in liquid form under pressure and used esp. formerly for heating and lighting and as a motor fuel — distinguished from *blue gas*

bla·ver \ˈblāvə(r)\ *n* -s [origin unknown] **1** : CORN POPPY **2** : CORNFLOWER 1b

blaw \ˈblȯ, ˈblō\ *vb* **blawed; blawn; blawing; blaws** [ME (northern dial.) *blawen*, fr. OE *blāwan* — more at BLOW] *chiefly Scot* : BLOW

bla·wort *or* **blae·wort** \ˈblawərt, -lāw-\ *n* [Sc *bla* + E *wort* — more at BLAE] **1** *chiefly Scot* : CORNFLOWER 1b **2** *chiefly Scot* : HAREBELL 1

¹blay \ˈblā\ *n* -s [fr. (assumed) ME, fr. OE *blǣge;* akin to MD *blei* bleak, MLG *blei, bleig*] : ²BLEAK

²blay \"\ *adj* [alter. of *blae*] *Irish* : UNBLEACHED ⟨~ linen⟩

¹blaze \ˈblāz\ *n* -s [ME *blase*, fr. OE *blæse* torch, firebrand; akin to MHG *blas* bald, Icel *blesa* blaze on a horse's face, OE *bǣl* fire, pyre — more at BALD] **1 a** : a bright and lambent flame ⟨with what a ~ the lamp shines forth⟩ **b** : intense direct light often accompanied by heat ⟨the ~ of noon⟩ **2 a** : FIRE: (1) : a freely burning flaming fire ⟨we'll have a good ~ in a minute⟩ (2) : a fire that flares up suddenly and spreads rapidly ⟨fires would appear in the most distant places from the main ~ —Mary H. Vorse⟩ **b** : an instance of blazing : a burning with brightness and flame ⟨the crackle and ~ of dry oak logs⟩ — compare SMOLDER **3** : something suggesting or resembling a flame or fire: as **a** : a display of or as if of light ⟨the Christmas ~ of shops —Saul Bellow⟩; *esp* : a striking or brilliant display ⟨hills covered with a ~ of flowers⟩ ⟨a ~ of love, and extinction, was better than a lantern glimmer of the same —Thomas Hardy⟩ **b** : a bursting forth or active display of some quality ⟨a great ~ of patriotism⟩ : OUTBURST ⟨her words came in a ~ of fury⟩ **c** : BRILLIANCE, BRIGHTNESS ⟨the ~ of his auburn hair⟩ **d** : HELL — usu. used in pl. ⟨go to ~s⟩ often as an intensive with *in* ⟨where in ~s have you been⟩ **4 a** : a hand or combination of cards in certain old card games containing only face cards **b** : such a hand in some poker games where it ranks between two pairs and three of a kind

²blaze \"\ *vb* -ED/-ING/-S [ME *blasen*, fr. *blase*, n.] *vi* **1 a** : to burn with bright flame ⟨he stirred the fire and the logs *blazed* up⟩ **b** : to burn with fervor or passion ⟨his eyes *blazed* with anger⟩ **c** : to flare up like a fire ⟨must this old conflict ~ up again⟩ **2 a** : to send forth or reflect glowing or brilliant light ⟨the sun *blazing* overhead⟩ **b** : to be or become conspicuous or resplendent ⟨an intellect that *blazed* above his fellows like a meteor⟩ ⟨the air was frosty, the ridges *blazing* with color⟩ **3 a** : to shoot esp. rapidly and repeatedly — usu. used with *away* ⟨any but the best would have lost their nerve and *blazed* away —Fred Majdalany⟩ **b :** to do or continue to do something vigorously; *esp* **:** to utter arguments or reproaches with great intensity ⟨they keep *blazing* away about ideals and principles —John Buchan⟩ ⟨she *blazed* out in anger and disgust⟩ **~ *vt* 1 a :** to cause to blaze **:** BURN ⟨the forests were *blazed* by the contemptuous use of wood fuel —Bernard Pares⟩ **b :** to cause the surface of (a food) to flame ⟨a pudding *blazed* with brandy⟩ **2 a :** to shine with **:** be resplendent with ⟨the sugar maples ~ their orange glory —L.S.Gannett⟩ **b :** to show forth **:** call attention to ⟨he *blazed* his wrath to all who would listen⟩ ⟨the stalls and stores *blazing* their bargains⟩

syn FLAME, FLARE, GLARE, GLOW: BLAZE implies great activity in burning, with suggestions of leaping flame or of radiation of intense heat. Figuratively, it applies to what commands notice by fervency, marked activity, or intensity ⟨the pine branches were soon *blazing*⟩ ⟨the sun *blazing* down on the prairie⟩ ⟨Cobbett, the tough, bluff Englishman . . . lived in the United States from 1792 to 1800 and made the country too hot to hold him by *blazing* antirevolutionary propaganda —Gilbert Highet⟩ ⟨Conkling, eyes *blazing*, rose to reply and lashed out with all the oratorical fury and savage invective at his command —Sidney Warren⟩ ⟨after the heavy rains which come at infrequent intervals, the desert *blazes* with colorful flowers —*Amer. Guide Series: Calif.*⟩ FLAME calls attention to leaping or darting tongues of fire, perhaps with less steadiness, intensity, and effectiveness than BLAZE ⟨the paper fire *flamed* up⟩ ⟨discontent with harsh treatment and long hours without pay *flamed* into open protest —*Amer. Guide Series: Ark.*⟩ ⟨she *flamed* forth in public life as an embodiment of democracy, as the hope and cheer of common men —Marvin Lowenthal⟩ ⟨the windowpanes, which *flamed* with a reflected glow —Ellen Glasgow⟩ FLARE may suggest single flames or fires darting up with sudden light or similar lighting effects or sudden bursts of activity or feeling ⟨torches *flared* in the darkness —F.V.W. Mason⟩ ⟨the shore shut off the bottom of the tower. You could only see the top, the white tapering over the brown sand until it *flared* into the red crown that held the light which mariners on a tall bridge could see for more than thirty miles in the night —Wirt Williams⟩ ⟨national guardsmen stand ready to move in if violence should *flare* between the trigger-tempered factions —H.H.Martin⟩ ⟨on the Republican side of the aisle tempers *flared* and fighting words were hurled —*N.Y.Times*⟩ GLARE suggests a quite bright or dazzling steady light that compels notice and often becomes unpleasant; in figurative uses it may apply to the egregious or flagrant or may connote antipathy or malevolence ⟨the sun *glaring* on the snow⟩ ⟨an unshielded light bulb *glaring* in his eyes⟩ ⟨this injustice was peculiarly *glaring* —T.B.Macaulay⟩ ⟨watch a pair of cats, crouching on the brink of a fight. Balefully the eyes *glare* —Aldous Huxley⟩ GLOW stresses emission of light without flame and may suggest steadiness, luminousness, and duration; in extensions it may indicate showing strong bright color or diffused strong feeling ⟨the sun was low in the west, and the sky was *glowing* —Charles Dickens⟩ ⟨the beauty of hills *glowing* purple with heather —O.S.Nock⟩ ⟨what mattered . . . was the fire that burned within him, that *glowed* with so strange and marvelous a radiance in almost all he wrote —Aldous Huxley⟩

[3]**blaze** \"\ *vt* -ED/-ING/-S [ME *blasen* to blow (an instrument), to proclaim, fr. MD *blāsen* to blow; akin to OHG *blāsan* to blow — more at BLAST] **1 :** to make public or conspicuous **:** PROCLAIM, DISSEMINATE ⟨~ those virtues which the good would hide —Alexander Pope⟩ — often used with *abroad* ⟨people who ~ abroad each new bit of scandal⟩ **2** *obs* **:** BLAZON 2

[4]**blaze** \"\ *n* -S [G *blas*, fr. OHG *plas;* akin to MD & MLG *bles* blaze, Sw *bläs* blaze, horse with a blaze, ON *blesóttr* with a blaze, MLG *blare* blaze, OE *blæse* torch — more at BLAZE (fire)] **1 a :** a white mark on the face of a horse, cow, or other animal; *esp* **:** a white stripe running down the face to the lips **b :** a facial pattern in certain cats in which two colors (as red and black) meet along a line down the nose **c :** a white or gray streak in the hair of the head; *esp* **:** one clearly demarked and extending back from the forehead **2 a :** a mark made on a tree usu. by chipping off a piece of the bark **b :** a trail or road marked out by blazes **c :** something serving as a clew to or identification of a course or way to be followed ⟨she must try to find her way by the ~*s* of former emotion —Kathleen Sproul⟩ **3 :** [1]PATCH 5

[5]**blaze** \"\ *vt* -ED/-ING/-S **1 :** to mark (a tree) usu. by chipping off a piece of bark ⟨go through the lot and ~ the trees to be cut this winter⟩ **2 a :** to mark out (as a path) by making blazes on trees ⟨*blazed* a trail through the mountains⟩ **b :** to lead or pioneer in some direction or activity ⟨the new Russia promised, for a time, to follow the liberal democratic path the United States had *blazed* —Oscar Handlin⟩ ⟨we ~ open a vast new territory of enjoyment —John Gassner⟩

[1]**blaz·er** \'blāzə(r)\ *n* -S [ME *blasour*, fr. *blasen* to proclaim + *-our* -or] *obs* **:** one who spreads reports ⟨babblers of folly and ~*s* of crime —Edmund Spenser⟩

[2]**blazer** \"\ *n* -S [[2]*blaze* + *-er*] **1 :** a single-breasted sports jacket of flannel or other fabric in bright stripes or solid color made usu. with a notched collar, patch pockets, and sometimes decorated edges **2** *slang* **:** an overheated railroad-car journal with its packing afire

[3]**blazer** \"\ *n* -S [[5]*blaze* + *-er*] **:** one that blazes trees to mark them for cutting or to mark a path

blazer

blaze–up \'=,=\ *n* -S [fr. *blaze up*, v.] **:** FLARE-UP

blaz·ing·ly *adv* **:** in a blazing manner

blazing star *n* **1** *archaic* **:** COMET 1 **2** *archaic* **:** one that is a center of attraction **:** CYNOSURE **3 :** any of several plants with showy inflorescence: as **a :** a plant of the genus *Liatris* **b :** a plant of the genus *Chamaelirium* **c :** a colicroot (*Aletris farinosa*) **d :** TRITONIA 2 **e :** a plant of the genus *Mentzelia; esp* **:** a yellow-flowered biennial herb (*M. laevicaulis*) of California

[1]**bla·zon** \'blāzᵊn\ *n* -S [ME *blason*, fr. MF] **1 a :** COAT OF ARMS **:** ARMORIAL BEARINGS **b :** the proper description or representation of heraldic or armorial bearings **2 :** DESCRIPTION, REPRESENTATION ⟨let me set forth a ~ of her charms⟩; *esp* **:** ostentatious display ⟨obtruding the ~ of their accomplishments on all present⟩

[2]**blazon** \"\ *vt* -ED/-ING/-S **1** [prob. influenced in meaning by [3]*blaze*] **:** to make public **:** publish far and wide **:** PROCLAIM ⟨I'll ~ it to high heaven from every street corner in this town —Kenneth Roberts⟩; *esp* **:** to boast of ⟨the entertainment world daily ~*s* a new play or film as "the epic to end all epics" —*English Digest*⟩ **2 a :** to describe (heraldic or armorial bearings) in proper technical language **b :** to represent (armorial bearings) in drawing or engraving **:** EMBLAZON **3 a :** to depict or inscribe in colors **b :** to exhibit conspicuously **:** DISPLAY ⟨carry photographs of their girls ~*ed* on their planes —Dixon Wecter⟩ **4 :** to cover as if with blazons **:** DECK, EMBELLISH ⟨permitted the Communist Party to ~ Indonesia with hammer and sickle posters —*Time*⟩

bla·zon·er \'blāz(ᵊ)nə(r)\ *n* -S **:** one that blazons; *esp* **:** one that blazons coats of arms

bla·zon·ing \'blāz(ᵊ)niŋ\ *n* -S **1 :** the act or process of blazoning **2 :** heraldic or armorial bearings

bla·zon·ry \'blāzᵊnrē\ *n* -ES **1 :** BLAZON 1b **2 :** BLAZON 1a **3 a :** artistic or brilliant representation or display **b :** a superficial finish or ornamental covering ⟨for she did look remarkably young, despite her ~ of makeup —Mary McCarthy⟩

blazy \'blāzē\ *adj, often* -ER/-EST [[1]*blaze* + *-y*] **:** that blazes

blc *abbr* balance

bldg *abbr* building

bldr *abbr* builder

[1]**bleach** \'blēch\ *vb* -ED/-ING/-ES [ME *blechen*, fr. OE *blǣcean*, causative-denominative fr. the root of OE *blāc* pale; akin to MHG *bleichen* to make pale, OHG *bleih* pale, ON *bleikja* to bleach, *bleikr* pale, Lith *blizgėti* to glitter, shine, OE *bǣl* fire, pyre — more at BALD] *vt* **1 a :** to remove the color or stains from (as natural fibers, cellulosic pulp, or fats) esp. by chemical means (as by oxidizing agents or less often by reducing agents) — compare BLANCH, DECOLORIZE **b :** PURIFY **c :** to whiten esp. by an oxidizing agent ⟨~*ing* flour⟩ **d :** to lighten the shade of (hair) by use of a chemical (as hydrogen peroxide) that removes color **2 a** *archaic* **:** to cause to whiten **:** make pale as from fear ⟨liberty . . . ~*ed* the tyrant's cheek —Tobias Smollett⟩ **b :** to make pure and decent ⟨~*ing* the barroom stories for polite use⟩ **c :** to make pallid and dull **:** remove the emotional intensity from ⟨~*ing* the affect⟩ **3 :** to remove the original silver image from (a photographic negative or positive) **~ *vi* 1** *of a material object* **:** to grow white **:** lose color **2** *of the countenance* **:** to become pale **:** BLANCH

[2]**bleach** \"\ *n* -ES **1 :** the act or process of whitening or lightening the color of something ⟨this cloth is still stained; you'll have to give it another ~⟩ **2 :** a chemical or preparation used in bleaching ⟨peroxide is a common ~ for the hair⟩ **3 :** the result of bleaching **:** the color or degree of whiteness obtained by bleaching ⟨a perfect ~ is seldom attained in one treatment⟩

bleach·a·ble \-chəbəl\ *adj* **:** capable of being bleached

bleached ginger *n* **:** LIMED GINGER

bleached rattler *or* **bleached rattlesnake** *n* **:** a moderate-sized pale-colored rattlesnake (*Crotalus mitchellii*) of desert areas of the southwestern U.S.

bleach·er \-chə(r)\ *n* -S **1 a :** one that bleaches or is used in bleaching; *specif* **:** a worker who works at the bleaching of materials (as flour, cloth, or certain leathers) **b :** one that carries out bleaching and often also preliminary and subsequent treatments **c :** a vessel (as a tank or bin) used in bleaching **2 a** *usu* **bleachers** *pl but sometimes sing in constr* **:** a stand of tiered planks providing relatively inexpensive and usu. unreserved undivided seating space for spectators (as in a ball park) usu. in a section without protection from sun or weather and affording a less advantageous view than that afforded by a grandstand ⟨*bleacher* seats available⟩; *also* **:** a similarly constructed stand erected elsewhere (as in a gymnasium) ⟨in front of a ~*s* filled with VIPs —K.M.Dodson⟩ **b bleachers** *pl* **:** all these seats of a particular place (as of a stadium) **c bleachers** *pl* **:** the occupants of the bleachers ⟨the ~*s* booed the umpire⟩

bleach·er·ite \'blēchə,rīt\ *n* -S [*bleacher* + *-ite*] **:** one seated in the bleachers

bleach·ery \-ch(ə)rē\ *n* -ES [[1]*bleach* + *-ery*] **:** a place or an establishment where bleaching is done

bleachfield \'=,=\ *n* [[2]*bleach* + *field*] *Brit* **:** an area where textiles are exposed to the sun for bleaching

bleaching *n* -S **:** the act or process of bleaching; *esp* **:** the process of improving the whiteness of a textile material by other means than scouring only

bleaching clay *or* **bleaching earth** *n* **:** an adsorbent clay or earth (as activated clay) used for removing the coloring matter from liquids (as oils)

bleaching powder *n* **:** a nearly white powder made by passing chlorine gas over hydrated lime, believed to consist chiefly of compounds or mixtures of calcium hydroxide, calcium chloride, and calcium hypochlorite with varying contents of available chlorine and of water, and used as a bleaching agent, disinfectant, and deodorant — called also *chloride of lime, chlorinated lime;* compare TROPICAL BLEACH

bleach liquor *n* **:** a liquid for bleaching; *usu* **:** a solution of calcium hypochlorite or of bleaching powder used esp. for bleaching paper pulp and textile materials — compare LIQUID BLEACH

bleach–out process \'=,=-\ *n* **:** any of several processes of color photography in which light-sensitive dyes are bleached directly by the action of light — distinguished from *dye-bleach process*

[1]**bleak** \'blēk\ *adj* -ER/-EST [ME *bleke* pale, prob. alter. (influenced by ME *blok* pale, fr. OE *blāc*) of *bleche*, fr. OE *blǣc;* akin to OE *blāc* pale — more at BLEACH] **1** *dial Eng* **:** lacking color **:** PALE **2 :** lacking vegetation **:** exposed and barren and often windswept ⟨~ alkali soils⟩ ⟨watching the sunset from the ~ crest of the ridge⟩ **3 :** COLD, RAW **:** bitter and chilling ⟨the snow was deep, the wind ~⟩ ⟨on a ~ November evening⟩ **4 a :** lacking in warmth or kindliness **:** DRAB, FRIGID, CHEERLESS, GRIM ⟨the ~*est* woman I ever knew⟩ ⟨with the ~ dogmas of election and reprobation put away, with the God of wrath dethroned —V.L.Parrington⟩ **b :** lacking likelihood of favorable termination or solution **:** wholly distressing **:** DEPRESSING ⟨these desires . . . stand in ~ contradiction to our central proposals —J.R.Oppenheimer⟩ ⟨a ~ outlook⟩ ⟨~ facts⟩ **c :** lacking petty or softening detail **:** severely simple **:** AUSTERE ⟨some who have been repelled by the ~ isolation of the mystic's final climb —W.R.Inge⟩ ⟨I like ~ thinking, as I like austerity in religion —H.L.Stuart⟩ ⟨the brittle, ~ photography . . . is a lesson in realism —J.P.Lyford⟩ **syn** see DISMAL

[2]**bleak** \"\ *n, pl* **bleak** *or* **bleaks** [ME *bleke*, prob. alter. (influenced by *bleke* pale) of OE *blǣge* — more at BLAY] **:** a small European cyprinid river fish (*Alburnus lucidus*) having silvery pigment lining its scales that is used in making artificial pearls — see PEARL ESSENCE

bleak·ly *adv* **:** in a bleak manner

bleak·ness *n* -ES **:** the quality or state of being bleak

bleaky \'blēkē\ *adj* **:** somewhat bleak

[1]**blear** \'bli(ə)r, 'bliə\ *vb* -ED/-ING/-S [ME *bleren;* perh. akin to LG *bleer-oged*, blear-eyed] *vi* **:** to look or observe dully with or as if with watery eyes ⟨young men ~*ing* at suffering with no understanding in their eyes —Bruce Marshall⟩ **~ *vt* 1 a :** to make (the eyes) sore or watery ⟨wind gluing coats to bodies, ~*ing* eyes, ripping at corners —Stanford Whitmore⟩ **b :** DIM, BLUR ⟨~*ed* sight⟩ **2** *archaic* **:** DECEIVE, HOODWINK, TRICK — usu. used in the phrase *to blear the eyes of* ⟨the king was crafty and cautious; he sought to ~ the eyes of the world before he struck⟩

[2]**blear** \"\ *adj* [ME *blere;* akin to *bleren* to blear] **1 :** dim with water or tears — used of the eyes **2 :** DULL, DIM, CLOUDY

[3]**blear** \"\ *n* -S **1 a :** a bleared state or appearance **2 a :** a film or other impediment that causes the eyes to be bleared

bleared \'bli(ə)rd, -iəd\ *adj* [ME *blered*, fr. past part. of *bleren*] **1** *of the eyes* **:** dimmed esp. by a watery secretion or a covering film **2 :** BLURRED **:** indistinct as though seen through bleared eyes ⟨a dull ~ old voice⟩

blear–eyed \'=;=\ *adj* [ME *bleereyed*] **1 :** having blear eyes **2 :** STUPID, DULL-WITTED; *sometimes* **:** SHORT-SIGHTED

blear–eyed herring *n* **:** ALEWIFE 1a

blear·i·ly \'blirəlē, -li\ *adv* **:** in a bleary manner

blear·i·ness \-rēnəs\ *n* -ES **:** the state of being bleary

blear–witted \'=;==\ *adj* **:** dull of mind

bleary \'blirē, 'blērē, -ri\ *adj, often* -ER/-EST [[2]*blear* + *-y*] **1** *of the eyes or vision* **:** partially or temporarily blear **:** dull or dimmed esp. from fatigue or sleep **2 :** poorly outlined or defined **:** DIM ⟨the world had had the ~ white look of a country seen through a train window —Josephine Pinckney⟩ **3 :** tired to the point of exhaustion **:** WORN-OUT ⟨after 12 hours of conferences the ~ aide staggered home to bed⟩

bleary–eyed \'==;=\ *adj* [by alter.] **:** BLEAR-EYED

[1]**bleat** \'blēt, *usu* -d.+V\ *vb* -ED/-ING/-S [ME *bleten*, fr. OE *blǣtan;* akin to OHG *blāzan* to bleat, L *flēre* to weep, Russ *bleyat'* to bleat, OE *bellan* to roar — more at BELLOW] *vi* **1 a** *of a sheep or goat or sometimes a calf* **:** to utter its natural cry **b :** *of various animals or man* **:** to make a sound suggestive of the call of a sheep; *sometimes* **:** WHIMPER, WHINE ⟨a dog cringing and ~*ing* in the cold⟩ **2 a :** to talk complainingly or with a whine **b :** to talk without due consideration **:** BLATHER ⟨we ~ once a year about peace on earth and goodwill to men —G.B.Shaw⟩ **~ *vt* :** to utter as though a bleat ⟨~*ing* their good-nights at the door⟩; *often* **:** to utter in a bleating manner ⟨the bigwigs in the Capitol are ~*ing* their fears —*Wall Street Jour.*⟩

[2]**bleat** \"\ *n* -S **1 a :** the cry of a sheep, goat, or calf **b :** any sound similar to or imitative of this cry **2 :** whining or foolish talk **:** BLATHER

bleat·er \'blēd·ə(r), -ētə-\ *n* -S **1 :** one that bleats; *specif* **:** SHEEP **2 :** SNIPE 1a

bleating *n* -S [ME *bleting*, fr. gerund of *bleten*] **:** BLEAT; *also* **:** the uttering of bleats

bleat·ing·ly *adv* **:** in a bleating manner

bleaty \'blēd·ē\ *adj* [[2]*bleat* + *-y*] **:** like a bleat

ble·aunt \'blēənt\ *n* -S [ME *bleaunt, blihand*, fr. MF *bliaud, bliaut*, fr. OF *bliaut, blialt*] **:** BLIAUT

bleb \'bleb\ *n* -S [perh. alter. of *blob*] **1 :** a small circumscribed elevation of the cuticle usu. containing serum **:** a small blister — compare BULLA **2 :** a bubble esp. in water or glass; *also* **:** a small bit or particle of distinctive material (as of mercury ore in quartzite) — **bleb·by** \'blebē\ *adj*

blebbed \'blebd\ *adj* **:** covered with or full of blebs

[1]**blech·noid** \'blek,nȯid\ *adj* [NL *Blechnum* + E *-oid*] **:** of or resembling the genus *Blechnum*

[2]**blechnoid** \"\ *n* -S **:** a fern of the genus *Blechnum*

blech·num \-nəm\ *n, cap* [NL, fr. L *blachnon, blechnon*, a fern, fr. Gk *blēchnon*] **:** a genus of chiefly tropical ferns (family Polypodiaceae) having rather stiff pinnate leaves with the sori linear and parallel to the midvein of the pinnae

[1]**bleck** \'blek\ *n* -S [ME *blek* ink, fr. *blæc*, fr. OE *blæc* black — more at BLACK] **1** *now chiefly Scot* **:** a black substance as: **a :** shoe blacking **b :** black grease **c :** SOOT, SMUT **2** *Scot* **:** NEGRO **3** *Scot* **:** BLACKGUARD, SCOUNDREL

[2]**bleck** \"\ *vt* [ME *blecken*, fr. *blek*, n.] *dial Brit* **:** BLACKEN

bled \'bled\ *n* -S [Ar *bilād* land] **:** a prairie or treeless plain in northern Africa; *also* **:** open country **:** COUNTRYSIDE, HINTERLAND

bled ingot \'bled-\ *n* **:** an ingot or casting from the interior of which, while cooling, liquid steel has escaped through a rupture

blee \'blē\ *n* -S [ME *ble, bleo*, fr. OE *blēo;* akin to OS & OFris *blī* color, OE *blīthe* happy — more at BLITHE] **1** *archaic* **:** COLOR, HUE, COLORATION ⟨under a banner of mingled ~⟩ **2** *archaic* **:** COMPLEXION, COLORING — used chiefly in the phrase *bright of blee* ⟨three fair sisters bright of ~⟩

[1]**bleed** \'blēd\ *vb* **bled** \'bled\ *obs* **bleeded; bled** *obs* **bleeded; bleeding; bleeds** [ME *bleden*, fr. OE *blēdan*, fr. *blōd* blood — more at BLOOD] *vi* **1 a :** to emit blood ⟨the wound *bled* freely⟩ **:** to lose blood ⟨hemophiliacs often ~ severely from the slightest scratch⟩ **b :** to lose blood from wounds **:** to sacrifice one's blood (as in battle) ⟨men who fought and *bled* along this rocky coast⟩ **2 a :** to feel anguish, pain, or sympathy ⟨his heart ~*s* for the distress of his fellows⟩ **b :** to be in grave distress or seriously disordered circumstances ⟨the human race . . . ~*ing* in its uneasy sleep —Irwin Shaw⟩ **c :** to become upset or bothered ⟨only steak and four eggs for breakfast? I ~ for you⟩ **3 a :** to ooze, drop, or flow from or as though from a wound ⟨grease ~*ing* through a wrapper⟩; *also* **:** to escape by such a process ⟨pitch ~*s* freely from any little break in the bark⟩ **b** *of life or its phenomena* **:** to terminate as a result of bleeding — usu. used with *away* ⟨retaining but a quantity of life, which ~*s* away —Shak.⟩ **c :** to give up some constituent or content by bleeding ⟨fruits sulfured at high temperatures . . . ~ more readily than when sulfured at lower temperatures —*Experiment Station Record*⟩ **4 :** to exude something **:** DISCHARGE: as **a :** to exude water or sap from a wounded surface (as of a tree) **b :** to diffuse or run when wetted — used chiefly of textile dyes or dyed fabrics **c :** to diffuse into and show through a covering layer — used of various pigments or of the paints, enamels, or varnishes into which they are incorporated **5** *dial Brit, of grain crops* **:** to yield well **6 a :** to pay out or give money ⟨willing to ~ freely for the cause⟩ **b :** to have money drawn or extorted ⟨hang those city fellows, they must ~ —W.M.Thackeray⟩ **7 :** to be printed so as to run off one or more edges of a printed page or sheet after trimming — often used with *off* ⟨the halftones ~ off all round the edges of the 4-page spread⟩ **8 :** to separate from a mixture — used esp. of oils (as from grease) **9 :** to exude bituminous material — used of pavements or creosoted timber bound or impregnated with such material **~ *vt* 1 :** to remove or draw blood from ⟨at one time the surgeon *bled* the patient for any or every ill⟩ ⟨the meat will keep better if the carcass is *bled* immediately and thoroughly⟩ **2 a :** to obtain money from esp. by improper or unlawful methods ⟨the company . . . had *bled* consumers in western Mississippi of $2 to $3 million a year in excessive rates —*New Republic*⟩ **b :** to take away **:** EXTRACT ⟨mobilization plans call for ~*ing* just as much metals out of the durable-goods industries as they can stand —*Newsweek*⟩ **3 :** to draw the sap from (a tree) **4 :** to drain or empty of liquid, gas, or other contents esp. slowly: as **a :** to empty of accumulated water (as a steam cylinder, air reservoir, or a leaking buoy in which water has accumulated) **b :** to let out the air from (a reservoir or other container) so as to diminish pressure **c :** to let out grain from (a sack) by slitting (as in stowing a cargo) **d :** to draw off or extract (low-pressure steam) from any of the stages of the expansions of a steam turbine for heating buildings, for boiler feed water, for process work, or for other purposes **5 :** to cause (as a printed illustration) to bleed; *also* **:** to trim (as a page) so that some of the printing bleeds **6** *of a dyed article* **:** to give up (dye or color) when wetted — **bleed white :** to drain or be drained of blood or resources

[2]**bleed** \"\ *n* -S **1** *print* **:** something that bleeds or is bled (as an illustration or a page); *also* **:** the part trimmed off in bleeding or the corresponding area of the printing plate **2 :** a stain discoloration showing on a surface resulting from diffusion of coloring matter from a substance **3 a :** BLEEDER 4a **b :** a narrow opening in the surface of an air inlet through which low-energy boundary-layer air is bled off from the main stream

bleed·er \'blēdə(r)\ *n* -S **1 :** one that draws blood: **a :** a person (as a barber-surgeon) who draws blood for medical reasons **:** BLOODLETTER **b :** STICKER **2 :** one that gives up blood: **a :** HEMOPHILIAC **b :** a large blood vessel divided during surgery **c :** a prizefighter who cuts and bleeds easily in the ring **d :** a horse or other animal immunized against some pathogen and regularly bled for the production of serums **3 a :** one that bleeds another of money or resources **:** SPONGE, PARASITE **b** *slang* **:** ROGUE, RASCAL — often used as a deprecatory or affectionate term of address ⟨you old ~, you⟩ **4 a :** a device or arrangement that permits bleeding (as an escape valve or the device controlling the extraction of steam from a turbine) **b :** an electrical resistor connected across a power supply in parallel with the load and of such value that normal variations in load resistance have little effect on the terminal voltage

bleeder turbine *n* **:** a steam turbine from the casing of which steam is drawn at one or more points to be used for heating of feedwater or industrial fluids or for district steam heating

[1]**bleeding** *adj* [ME *bleding* fr. pres. part. of *bleden*] **1 :** that bleeds or appears to bleed ⟨a ~ wound⟩ **2 :** feeling anguish or compassion **3** — used as a generalized intensive ⟨a ~ idiot⟩; compare BLOODY 6

[2]**bleeding** \"\ *n* -S [ME *bleding*, fr. gerund of *bleden*] **:** an act, instance, or result of being bled or the process by which something is bled: as **a :** the escape of blood from vessels **:** HEMORRHAGE; *also* **:** the operation or an instance of performing the operation of bleeding a person medically **:** BLOODLETTING **b :** the diffusion of pigment or other materials to alter an overlying surface (as in leather) **c :** the exudation of bituminous material (as from pavements or creosoted lumber) **d :** extraction of steam from a turbine for use in heating or low pressure pump operation **e :** the autogenous flow of mixing water within freshly mixed concrete or mortar or its emergence therefrom

bleeding bread *n* **:** bread containing reddish patches produced by a bacterium (*Serratia marcescens*)

bleeding canker *n* **:** a disease of hardwoods (as of maples) caused by a fungus (*Phytophthora cactorum*), characterized by the exudation of a reddish ooze from small cracks in cankers on the trunk and branches, and leading to wilting and branch dieback

bleeding disease *n* **:** a disease of the coconut palm caused by a fungus (*Ceratostomella paradoxa*) and characterized by a reddish brown or rusty liquid exudation from cracks in the stem

bleeding heart *n* **1 :** any of several plants of the genus *Dicentra; esp* **:** a garden plant (*D. spectabilis*) with racemes of deep-pink drooping heart-shaped flowers **2** *dial Eng* **:** a wallflower (*Cheiranthes cheiri*) **3** *Austral* **:** CORAL PEA **4** *South* **:** [2]WAHOO a **5** *West Indies* **a :** TARO **b :** CALADIUM 2 **6 :** a person who makes a show of great concern for any oppressed individual that can be made to appear persecuted

bleeding–heart pigeon \'==;=-\ *n* **:** a Philippine pigeon (*Gallicolumba luzonica*) with a greenish blue back, a white throat, and a patch of stiff crimson feathers on the breast

bleeding time *n* **:** a period of time of usu. about 2½ minutes during which a small wound (as a pinprick) continues to shed blood

bleeding tooth *n* **:** a marine gastropod mollusk (*Nerita peloronta*) of the Caribbean area having projections resembling teeth reddish about the base on the inner wall of the aperture; *also* **:** any of several related mollusks some of which lack the colored projections

blees *pl of* BLEE

[1]**bleeze** \'blēz, ,blāz\ *Scot var of* [1]BLAZE, [2]BLAZE

[2]**bleeze** \"\ *vi* -ED/-ING/-S [alter. of [3]*blaze*] *chiefly Scot* **:** BRAG **:** talk officiously

blel·lum \'blelәm\ *n* -S [perh. blend of Sc *bleber* to babble (alter. of *blabber*) and *skellum* rascal] *Scot* **:** a lazy talkative person

STATE BIRDS

CAROLINA WREN
(SOUTH CAROLINA)
PURPLE FINCH
(NEW HAMPSHIRE)
GOLDFINCH
(IOWA, NEW JERSEY, WASHINGTON)
LARK BUNTING
(COLORADO)
HERMIT THRUSH
(VERMONT)
BLACK-CAPPED CHICKADEE
(MAINE, MASSACHUSETTS)
MOUNTAIN BLUEBIRD
(IDAHO, NEVADA)
CARDINAL
(ILLINOIS, INDIANA, KENTUCKY, NORTH CAROLINA, OHIO, VIRGINIA, WEST VIRGINIA)
YELLOW-SHAFTED FLICKER
(ALABAMA)
BROWN THRASHER
(GEORGIA)
ROADRUNNER
(NEW MEXICO)
BALTIMORE ORIOLE
(MARYLAND)
EASTERN BLUEBIRD
(MISSOURI, NEW YORK)
SCISSOR-TAILED FLYCATCHER
(OKLAHOMA)
WESTERN MEADOWLARK
(KANSAS, MONTANA, NEBRASKA, NORTH DAKOTA, OREGON, WYOMING)
CACTUS WREN
(ARIZONA)
MOCKINGBIRD
(ARKANSAS, FLORIDA, MISSISSIPPI, TENNESSEE, TEXAS)
BLUE HEN CHICKEN
(DELAWARE)
RING-NECKED PHEASANT
(SOUTH DAKOTA)
CALIFORNIA QUAIL
(CALIFORNIA)
AMERICAN ROBIN
(CONNECTICUT, MICHIGAN, WISCONSIN)
RHODE ISLAND RED
(RHODE ISLAND)
CALIFORNIA GULL
(UTAH)
WILLOW PTARMIGAN
(ALASKA)
NENE
(HAWAII)
RUFFED GROUSE
(PENNSYLVANIA)
BROWN PELICAN
(LOUISIANA)
COMMON LOON
(MINNESOTA)

¹blem·ish \ˈblemish, -mēsh\ *vt* -ED/-ING/-ES [ME *blemisshen*, fr. MF *blemiss-*, *blesmiss-*, stem of *blemir*, *blesmir* to make pale, wound, of Gmc origin; akin to G *blass* pale, MHG *blas* bald — more at BLAZE] : to produce flaws in ⟨too much heat will ~ the glass⟩ : **a** : to spoil by a flaw (as something well formed or excellent) : IMPAIR ⟨these little singularities . . . rather set off than ~ his good qualities —Joseph Addison⟩ **b** : SULLY, STAIN, TAINT **c** *archaic* : DISCREDIT, DEFAME ⟨whether a man should be permitted to ~ himself, by pleading his own insanity —William Blackstone⟩

²blemish \"\ *n* -ES **1** : a flaw of character or spirit : a moral defect : TAINT, STAIN ⟨I suppose that human character will never free itself entirely from the ~ of prejudice —A.E. Stevenson b. 1900⟩ **2** : a mark of physical deformity or injury ⟨a calf and a lamb, both a year old without ~, for a burnt offering —Lev 9:3 (RSV)⟩: **as a** : any small mark on the skin (as a pimple or birthmark) ⟨~*es* on the adolescent skin may be a symptom of acne —*Today's Health*⟩ **b** : a defect of an animal (as a horse) that detracts from its appearance but does not interfere with its usefulness — compare UNSOUND **c** : any flaw in wood that mars its appearance without necessarily impairing its strength or durability — compare DEFECT **3** : a fault or imperfection esp. of workmanship or art ⟨he played his minor role without ~ if without distinction —C.L.Becker⟩

syn DEFECT, FLAW: BLEMISH applies to a marring external or superficial spot or to something likened thereto ⟨he studiously perfected nature by correcting all the little *blemishes* of manner and little weaknesses of character in order to produce an immaculate effect —V.L.Parrington⟩ ⟨they assure you that complete, 99 percent waterproof, governmentally organized thought control in China is just a temporary pimple, a passing *blemish* —Peggy Durdin⟩ DEFECT applies to an imperfection or incompleteness, superficial or not, impairing value or operation ⟨a *defect* in the machine⟩ ⟨a *defect* in his hearing⟩ ⟨the moral *defects* of the thinker are such as make him unfaithful to his work, e.g. laziness or prejudice —Samuel Alexander⟩ ⟨the Spartan state, in fact, by virtue of that excellence which was also its *defect* —the specializing of the individual on the side of discipline and rule — carried within it the seeds of its own destruction —G.L.Dickinson⟩ FLAW may refer to defect in continuity or cohesion (as a crack, fissure, or break) or to something compared to a break or weak spot ⟨we have already seen *flaws* in the great structure, which were to widen into breaches —John Buchan⟩ ⟨we most enjoy, as a spectacle, the downfall of a good man, when the fall is justified by some *flaw* in his being —A.L.Guérard⟩ ⟨while Milton's work is immaculate, Wordsworth's is full of *flaws* —Richard Garnett †1906⟩

blem·ish·er \ˈblemə̇shə(r), -mēsh-\ *n* -S [ME *blemissher*, fr. *blemisshen* + *-er*] : one that blemishes

blem·my·es \ˈblemē,ēz\ *n pl, usu cap* [L, fr. Gk] : an ancient Ethiopian Hamitic people dwelling between the Nile and the Red Sea

¹blench \ˈblench\ *vb* -ED/-ING/-ES [ME *blenchen* to deceive, blench, fr. OE *blencan* to deceive; akin to ON *blekkja* to impose on; prob. causative fr. the root of E *blink*] *vi* : to draw back or turn aside from lack of courage or resolution : FLINCH, QUAIL, SHRINK ⟨though sometimes you do ~ from this to that —Shak.⟩ ~ *vt* **1** *obs* : BAFFLE, DISCONCERT, FOIL **2** *archaic* : to draw back from : AVOID, EVADE **syn** see RECOIL

²blench \"\ *vb* -ED/-ING/-ES [alter. (influenced by ¹*blench*) of ²*blanch*] : PALE, BLEACH, WHITEN

³blench *var of* BLANCH

blenching *adj* [fr. pres. part. of ²*blench*] : PALING, BLEACHING, WHITENING — **blench·ing·ly** *adv*

¹blend \ˈblend\ *vt* **blend** \"\ *or* **blent** \ˈblent\ **blend·ed**; **blending**; **blends** [ME *blenden*, lit., to blind, fr. OE *blendan*; akin to OHG *blenten* to blind, OFris *blenda*, causatives fr. the root of E *blind*] *archaic* : BEDAZZLE, BLIND, DECEIVE ⟨a villainous affair . . . and will one day so ~ and confound us —Laurence Sterne⟩

²blend \"\ *vb* **blended** \ˈblendə̇d\ *also* **blent** \ˈblent\ **blended** *also* **blent**; **blending**; **blends** [ME *blenden*, modif. of ON *blanda*; akin to OE *blandan* to mix, OHG *blantan* to mix, Goth *blandan* to associate, Lith *blandus* thick (of soup), Skt *bradhna* pale red, ruddy; basic meaning: obscure, indistinct] *vt* **1** : MIX, MINGLE; *esp* : to mingle, combine, or associate so that the separate constituents or the line of demarcation cannot be distinguished ⟨the new North Africa, in order to endure, must successfully ~ the cultures of East and West —*Lamp*⟩ ⟨~*ing* flour with broth to thicken a gravy⟩ **2** : to prepare (as whiskey, flour, tobacco, or tea) by mixing and thoroughly intermingling different varieties or grades whether for purposes of adulteration or of standardization and improvement of qualities : make by mixing or blending **3** : to darken the hairs, (as the tips of the hairs) of (a fur) with dye **4** : to cause (paints or pigments) to mingle and shade into each other **5** : to reduce the bulk of (a turned seam) by trimming one edge ~ *vi* **1 a** : to mingle intimately : pass or shade insensibly into one another ⟨that vein of contempt for the crowd, which runs across Leonardo's writings, ~*ed* . . . with his vein of human sweetness —Havelock Ellis⟩ **b** : to combine into an integrated whole : UNITE ⟨various traditional dishes ~ into a distinctive and tasty meal⟩ **2** : to produce a harmonious effect : agree with or balance one another : HARMONIZE — used esp. of color, design, or objects in which these are of prime importance ⟨how well the new curtains ~ with the rug⟩ ⟨pick a color that will ~ with your skin⟩ **3** *biol* : to exhibit or possess a character that does not directly show the result of mendelian dominance or segregation but is intermediate between contrasting characters of the parents — compare BLENDING INHERITANCE **syn** see MIX

³blend \"\ *n* -S : something produced by blending: as **a** : a product (as a whiskey, a flour, or a tobacco) prepared by blending **b** : a congruous mixture of articles, qualities, or characteristics ⟨the little sketch . . . is a wonderful ~ of charm and gentle sadness —Bergen Evans⟩; *often* : the harmonious product of such a mixture ⟨associated with a racial ~ that was henceforth to be distinctively English —Herbert Read⟩ **c** : a merging of one color or musical timbre into another ⟨a little more concern for tonal quality and ~ would have been welcome —Irving Kolodin⟩ **d** : a word composed of parts of two words (as *chortle* from *chuckle* and *snort*), all of one word and part of another (as *bookmobile* from *book* and *automobile*), or two entire words and characterized invariably in the latter case and frequently in the two former cases by single occurrence of one or more sounds or letters that appear in both the component words (as *motel* from *motor hotel*, *camporee* from *camp* and *jamboree*, *aniseed* from *anise seed*) — compare CONTAMINATION 3

☞ In this dict. the term *blend* is used in etymologies only when the entry word is characterized by single occurrence of one or more sounds or letters that appear in both the component words or by infixation of all or part of one component word within all or part of the other

e *biol* : a blending character; *also* : an individual exhibiting such a character — compare BLENDING INHERITANCE **f** : a compound of two or more elementary sensations that is experienced as a homogeneous unit ⟨the color orange is a ~ of red and yellow⟩ **g** : MIXTURE 2d

blende \ˈblend\ *n* -S [G, fr. *blenden* to blind, fr. OHG *blenten* — more at BLEND] **1** : SPHALERITE **2** : any of several minerals, chiefly metallic sulfides, with somewhat bright but nonmetallic luster

blended whiskey *n* : whiskey consisting of either a blend of two or more straight whiskeys or a blend of whiskey and neutral spirits with the proof adjusted by addition of distilled water

blend·er \-də(r)\ *n* -S [²*blend* + *-er*] : one that blends: as **a** : an instrument (as a blunt brush) used in blending colors **b** : a worker who blends various materials or grades of material to produce a finished product (as a whiskey, a flour, a tobacco, or a gasoline) of a desired quality or flavor **c** : a machine or device by which materials are blended ⟨a pastry ~⟩; *sometimes* : BLENDOR

blending *n* -S [fr. gerund of ²*blend*] : a product resulting from blending : BLEND

blending inheritance *n* : inheritance by the progeny of characters intermediate between those of the parents that is now usu. explained on a mendelian basis by use of the multiple factor hypothesis — compare BLOOD 2, MULTIPLE FACTORS, PARTICULATE INHERITANCE, QUANTITATIVE INHERITANCE

blen·dor \-də(r)\ *n* -S [²*blend* + *-or*] : a mechanical device for producing a fine uniform suspension or blend

blend-word \ˈ⸗,⸗\ *n* : ³BLEND d

blen·heim spaniel \ˈblenəm-\ *n, usu cap B* [fr. *Blenheim* Palace, seat of the Duke of Marlborough, in England] : a spaniel of a red and white variety of the English toy spaniel

blen·ni·idae \bleˈnīə,dē\ *n pl, cap* [NL, fr. *Blennius*, type genus (fr. L, a sea fish) + *-idae* — more at BLENNY] : a large family of small carnivorous marine fishes comprising the typical blennies and with related forms constituting a suborder of the Percomorphi — see BLENNIOIDEA

¹blen·ni·oid \ˈblenē,ȯid\ *adj* [NL *Blennioidea*] : of or relating to the suborder Blennioidea

²blennioid \"\ *n* -S [NL *Blennioidea*] : a blennioid fish

blen·ni·oi·dea \,blenēˈȯidēə\ *n pl, cap* [NL, fr. *Blennius* + *-oidea*] : a suborder of Percomorphi that includes the Blenniidae and other families of blennies and comprises marine fishes with the pectoral fins large but the pelvic fins reduced or absent, scales partially or wholly lacking, and a usu. elongated body often specialized for tide pool existence

blen·ni·oi·dei \-dē,ī\ [NL, fr. *Blennius* + *-oidei*] *syn of* BLENNIOIDEA

blen·noid \ˈble,nȯid\ *adj* [Gk *blennos* mucus + E *-oid*] : resembling mucus : MUCOID

blen·nor·rhea *also* **blen·nor·rhoea** \,blenəˈrēə\ *n* -S [NL, fr. Gk *blennos* mucus + NL *-o-* + *-rrhea*, *-rrhoea*] : an excessive secretion and discharge of mucus — **blen·nor·rheal** *also* **blen·nor·rhoeal** \¦⸗⸗¦rēəl\ *adj*

blen·ny \ˈblenē\ *n* -ES [L *blennius*, a sea fish, fr. Gk *blennos*] : any of numerous usu. small fishes belonging to Blenniidae and related families having a usu. elongate, often scaleless body tapering to a more or less rounded tail with the ventral fins jugular or wanting and the dorsal and anal fins long, living about rocky shores of all regions and occas. in fresh water, and often having protective coloration

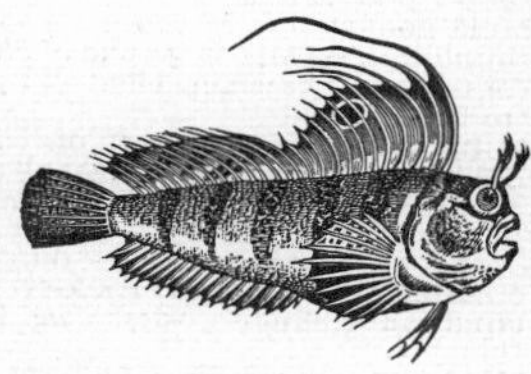

European blenny

blent *past of* BLEND

blephar- *or* **blepharo-** *comb form* [NL, fr. Gk, fr. *blepharon*] **1** : eyelid ⟨*blephar*itis⟩ ⟨*blepharo*spasm⟩ : of the eyelid and ⟨*blepharo*conjunctivitis⟩ **2** : cilium : flagellum ⟨*blepharo*plast⟩

bleph·a·ra \ˈblefərə\ *n, pl* **blepharae** \-,rē,-rī\ [NL, fr. Gk *blepharon* eyelid] : one of the peristome teeth of a moss

bleph·a·ral \-rəl\ *adj* [*blephar-* + *-al*] : of or relating to the eyelids

bleph·a·ri·glottis \,blefərə + \ [NL, fr. Gk *blepharis* eyelash + *glōttis* tongue — more at GLOTTIS] *syn of* HABENARIA

bleph·a·rism \ˈblefə,rizəm\ *n* -S [ISV *blephar-* + *-ism*] : spasm of the eyelids

bleph·a·risma \,⸗⸗ˈrizmə\ *n, cap* [NL, fr. *blephar-* + *-isma* (fr. L *-ismus* -ism)] : a genus of large ovoid or pyriform frequently rose-colored free-living ciliates (order Spirotricha) having the peristome highly developed

bleph·a·ri·tis \-ˈrīd·ə̇s\ *n, pl* **blepharit·i·des** \-ˈrid·ə,dēz\ [NL, fr. *blephar-* + *-itis*] : inflammation of the eyelids, esp. of the margins

bleph·a·ro·conjunctivitis \¦blefə(,)rō, ¦blefərə + \ *n* [NL, fr. *blephar-* + *conjunctivitis*] : inflammation of the eyelid and conjunctiva

bleph·a·ro·plast \" + ,plast\ *n* -S [*blephar-* + *-plast*] : a basal granule or kinetoplast — usu. used in botany or by cytologists when the nature of the body is uncertain — **bleph·a·ro·plastic** \" + ¦plastik\ *adj*

bleph·a·rop·to·sis \,blefəräpˈtōsə̇s\ *n* [NL, fr. *blephar-* + *-ptosis*] : a drooping or abnormal relaxation of the upper eyelid

bleph·a·ro·spasm \ˈblefə(,)rō, -,rə + ,-\ *n* [NL *blepharospasmus*, fr. Gk *blephar-* + L *spasmus* spasm] : spasmodic winking from involuntary contraction of the orbicular muscle of the eyelids

ble·phil·ia \bləˈfilēə\ *n, cap* [NL, irreg. fr. Gk *blepharis* eyelash] : a small genus of No. American herbs (family Labiatae) with opposite hairy leaves and purplish or bluish flowers in dense clusters

bles·bok \ˈbles,bäk\ *also* **bles·buck** \-,bək\ *n, pl* **blesbok** *or* **blesboks** [Afrik *blesbok*, fr. *bles* blaze (fr. MD) + *bok* male antelope, male goat, fr. MD *boc*; akin to OHG *boc* male goat — more at BLAZE, BUCK] : a So. African antelope (*Damaliscus albifrons*) resembling the bontebok and having a large white spot on a face divided by a dark crossbar between the eyes

bles·mol \ˈbles,mōl, -mōl\ *or* **bles mole** \ˈbles,mōl\ *n* -S [Afrik *blesmol*, fr. *bles* blaze + *mol* mole, fr. MD — more at MOLE] : any of several grayish burrowing southern African rodents of *Bathyergus* and related genera that are very destructive to root crops

¹bless \ˈbles\ *vb* **blessed** \ˈblest\ *also* **blest** \"\ **blessed** \"\ *also* **blest** \"\ **blessing**; **blesses** [ME *blessen*, fr. OE *bletsian*, *blētsian*, *blēdsian*, fr. *blōd* blood; fr. the use of blood in consecration or sacrifice — more at BLOOD] *vt* **1** : to consecrate or hallow by religious rite or word : make or pronounce holy ⟨and God ~*ed* the seventh day, and sanctified it —Gen 2:3 (AV)⟩ ⟨this little touch of ceremony . . . seemed to ~ the union —Margaret A. Barnes⟩ **2** : to make the sign of the cross upon or over — often used reflexively ⟨they shivered and ~*ed* themselves as they passed the gloomy opening⟩ **3** : to invoke divine care for ⟨then the bishop shall ~ them —*Bk. of Com. Prayer*⟩ : pray for ⟨we may as well ~ our enemies; they are too many to fight⟩ **4 a** : PRAISE, GLORIFY : to extol for excellences ⟨~ the Lord, O my soul —Ps 103:1 (RSV)⟩ **b** : to regard with great favor : approve highly ⟨your cameraman may ~ you because he can go all out for atmosphere —Richard Harrison⟩ **5** : to make happy : give good fortune or satisfaction to : confer prosperity upon ⟨a child soon ~*ed* the union⟩ ⟨the whole region is ~*ed* with good soil and abundant water⟩ **6** : GUARD, PROTECT, KEEP, PRESERVE — formerly usu. used with *from* and often reflexively ⟨~ me from marrying a usurer —Shak.⟩ ⟨he ~*ed* himself from such customers —Tobias Smollett⟩; now used almost wholly in exclamations ⟨God ~ me, what's happened now⟩ **7** : FAVOR, ENDOW ⟨few persons have been ~*ed* as he has in his every endeavor⟩ — usu. used with *with* ⟨a man ~*ed* with a happy nature and a healthy appetite⟩ : to give approval to ⟨the president would ~ the reopening of this issue⟩ **8** *archaic* : to account happy : FELICITATE — used reflexively ⟨the nations shall ~ themselves in him —Jer 4:2 (AV)⟩ **9** : CURSE, DAMN, CONDEMN — usu. used in the first person present ⟨I'm ~*ed* if I know what went wrong⟩ or future ⟨I'll be ~*ed* if I do⟩ or absolutely ⟨~*ed* if I care⟩ ~ *vi* : to offer thanksgivings or ask for blessings ⟨if you ~ with the spirit —1 Cor 14:16 (RSV)⟩ ⟨his historic sense would have *blest* and feasted —*Atlantic*⟩

²bless *vt* [origin unknown] *obs* : WAVE, BRANDISH

¹blessed \ˈblesə̇d *sometimes esp for meter's sake or when imperative "be" follows* -est\ *or* **blest** \-est\ *adj, sometimes* **blesseder** *sometimes* **blessedest** [ME, fr. past part. of *blessen*] **1** : HALLOWED, CONSECRATED, HOLY ⟨the ~ death of the martyr⟩; *also* : worthy of blessing or adoration : held in adoration ⟨the ~ Trinity⟩ **2** : highly favored (as with blessings or divine care) : existing in or enjoying happiness ⟨the ~ saints⟩ **3** : bringing pleasure or contentment : PLEASING, ENJOYABLE, DELIGHTFUL ⟨that extra ~ quarter hour in bed —A.C.Spectorsky⟩; *sometimes* : FORTUNATE ⟨a ~ state of unquestioning trust⟩ ⟨traveled about Amazonia with greater ease than most who have been so ~ —*Geog. Jour.*⟩ **4** : enjoying or relating to spiritual contentment ⟨cast out from God and ~ vision —John Milton⟩ **5** *Roman Catholicism* : BEATIFIED **6** : CURSED, DAMNED, DARNED, DOGGONE, DRATTED — used as an intensive ⟨not a ~ drop of rain⟩ ⟨will those ~ boys never stop ringing⟩

²bless·ed \ˈblesə̇d\ *n, pl* **blessed** *also* **blesseds** : a person beatified by the Roman Catholic Church

blessed bread \ˈblest-\ *n, Eastern Church* : ANTIDORON

bless·ed event \-sə̇d-\ *n* : the birth of a baby

bless·ed·ly \-esə̇dlē, -li\ *adv* : in a blessed manner

bless·ed·ness \ˈblesə̇dnə̇s\ *n* -ES [ME, fr. *blessed* + *-ness*] : the quality or state of being blessed **syn** see HAPPINESS

bless·ed sacrament \-sə̇d-\ *n, usu cap B&S* : the consecrated Host

bless·ed thistle \-sə̇d-\ *n* **1** : an annual pubescent herb (*Cnicus benedictus*) with large heads of yellow flowers **2** : MILK THISTLE 1

bless·ed word \-sə̇d-\ *n* : CATCHWORD, SHIBBOLETH

blessing *n* -S [ME, fr. OE *blētsung*, fr. *blētsian* to bless — more at BLESS] **1 a** : act of one that blesses **b** : words used in such an act **c** : BENEDICTION 1 **d** : APPROVAL, ENCOURAGEMENT ⟨presumably had the ~ . . . of the British government —*Time*⟩ ⟨tried to obtain the president's ~ for higher steel prices⟩ **2 a** : a thing conducive to happiness or welfare ⟨able to appreciate the ~ of peace⟩ **b** : a present or gift accorded as a token of esp. divine favor **3** : PRAISE, WORSHIP; *esp* : grace said at a meal ⟨father will ask the ~⟩ **4** *chiefly Midland* : CURSING, SCOLDING; *esp* : a severe or wordy rebuke — often with *out* ⟨I'll give her a real ~ out when she gets home⟩

bless·ing·ly *adv* : in a blessing manner

blessing way *n, usu cap B&W* : a Navaho rite intended to attract good fortune by establishing harmony with good spirits

bless out *vt, chiefly Midland* : to rebuke sternly : SCOLD

¹blest *past of* BLESS

²blest *var of* BLESSED

blether *var of* BLATHER

²bleth·er \ˈblethə(r)\ *dial Brit var of* BLADDER

bleth·er·a·tion \,blethəˈrāshən\ *n* -S [¹*blether* + *-ation*] *chiefly Scot* : NONSENSE

blethernose \ˈ⸗⸗,⸗\ *n* [²*blether* + *nose*] : HOODED SEAL

bleth·ers \ˈblethərz\ *n pl* [¹*blether*] *Scot* : foolish talk

ble·tia \ˈblēsh(ē)ə, -ēd·ēə\ *n, cap* [NL, fr. Luis *Blet*, 18th cent. Span. pharmacist and botanist + NL *-ia*] : a genus of terrestrial cormose orchids of tropical America with linear plicate leaves and a slender scape of large purple or pink flowers — see BLETILLA

ble·til·la \bləˈtilə\ *n, cap* [NL, alter. of *Bletia*] : a small genus of chiefly Asiatic terrestrial orchids that resemble those of the genus *Bletia* and include one (*B. striata*) that is cultivated in several horticultural forms in the open in mild climates or in the cool greenhouse

blet·ting \ˈbled·iŋ\ *n* -S [fr. gerund of *blet* to become overripe, fr. F *blettir*, fr. *blet* overripe, fr. OF] : the ripening and softening of certain fruits in storage

bleu cheese \ˈblü-\ *n* [part trans. of F *fromage bleu*, fr. *fromage* cheese + *bleu* blue, of Gmc origin; akin to OHG *blāo* blue — more at BLUE] : BLUE CHEESE

bleu de ly·on \blœ̄dlēōⁿ\ *n, pl* **bleus de lyon** \"\ *often cap L* [F, lit., Lyons blue, fr. *Lyons* (Lyon), France] : NATIONAL BLUE

bleu de roi \blœ̄d(ə)·rwä\ *n, pl* **bleus de roi** \"\ [F, lit., king's blue] : SÈVRES BLUE 2b (2)

bleu lou·ise \blœ̄lü(w)ēz\ *n, pl* **bleus louise** \"\ *often cap L* [F, lit., Louise blue] : EMAIL 2

bleu pas·sé \blœ̄päsā\ *n, pl* **bleus passés** \"\ [F, lit., faded blue] : OLD BLUE

¹blew *obs var of* BLUE

²blew *past of* BLOW

blew·its \ˈblüə̇ts\ *n* -ES [prob. irreg. fr. *blue*] : an edible agaric (*Tricholoma personatum*) that is pale lilac when young

bli·aut *or* **bli·aud** \ˈblē(,)ō\ *n* -S [F, fr. OF *bliaut*, *blialt*] : a close-fitting often laced medieval tunic with long skirts and sleeves

blickey *or* **blickie** *also* **blicky** \ˈblikē\ *n, pl* **blickeys** *or* **blickies** [D *blikje*, dim. of *blik* pail, tin, fr. MD *blic*, *blec*; akin to OHG *bleh* tin, ON *blik* gleam, OE *blice* act of becoming visible, OHG *bleih* pale — more at BLEACH] *North* : a small pail; *esp* : a covered metal lunch pail

¹blight \ˈblīt, *usu* -d·+V\ *n* -S [origin unknown] **1 a** : any disease, symptom of disease, or injury of plants characterized by or resulting in withering, cessation of growth, and a more or less general death of parts (as leaves, flowers, and stems) without rotting and caused by fungi or bacteria, viruses, unfavorable climatic conditions, or insect attack — often used with a qualifying word that describes the disorder ⟨black ~*s* of various plants⟩ or that names the plant or part affected **b** : any organism causing blight; *esp* : an insect (as the woolly apple aphid) that causes such a condition **2** : something that frustrates one's plans or withers one's hopes ⟨suffering the pervading ~ of poverty⟩ **3 a** : something that impairs or destroys ⟨the censorship . . . has brought under its ~ Ireland's greatest poets, dramatists, and scholars —Paul Blanshard⟩ **b** : a condition or influence that lowers the value of real estate ⟨industrial expansion may create urban ~⟩; *often* : the state resulting from such a condition ⟨congested slums and decaying areas of ~ which are the outstanding disgrace of American city life —*Pencil Points*⟩ **4** *chiefly Brit* : APHID; *esp* : WOOLLY APPLE APHID **5** *Austral* : an inflammation of the eye in which the eyelids discharge a thick mucous substance that often seals them up for days and minute granular pustules develop inside the lid — called also *sandy blight*

²blight \"\ *vb* -ED/-ING/-S *vt* **1** : to affect (as a plant) with blight : BLAST ⟨last night's hard frost ~*ed* the late flush of growth⟩ **2** : to cause to deteriorate : RUIN, FRUSTRATE ⟨some human beings ruin and ~ themselves by old-fashioned sex suppression while others ruin and ~ themselves by new-fashioned sex excess —J.C.Powys⟩ ~ *vi* : to suffer from or become affected with blight : become blasted ⟨our potatoes ~*ed*⟩

blightbird \ˈ⸗,⸗\ *n* : any of several silvereyes of Australia and New Zealand that feed freely on various insect pests

blight canker *n* : a phase of fire blight characterized by cankers

blight·ed \ˈblīd·ə̇d, -ītə̇d\ *adj* **1** *slang* : BLASTED 2 **2** : affected by blight ⟨a ~ rose⟩; *esp, of real estate* : marked by termination of healthy growth and development accompanied by deterioration and decline of property values ⟨the ~ areas that are the shame of every metropolis⟩

blight·er \ˈblīd·ə(r), -ītə-\ *n* -S **1** : one that blights **2** *slang Brit* **a** : a worthless or contemptible person **b** : FELLOW, GUY ⟨we're for you against the other ~*s* —John Buchan⟩

blight·ing \ˈblīd·iŋ, -ītiŋ\ *adj* : causing blight — **blight·ing·ly** *adv*

blighty \ˈblīti\ *n* -ES [by folk etymology fr. Hindi *bilāyatī*, *wilāyatī* foreign country, England, fr. Ar *wilāyat* province, country] **1** *often cap, slang Brit* : one's native land (as England) **2** *slang Brit* **a** : a wound whereby a member of the armed forces is invalided home **b** : FURLOUGH

blij·ver \ˈblīvə(r)\ *n* -S [D, one that remains, fr. *blijven* to remain (fr. MD *bliven*) + *-er*; akin to OE *belīfan* to remain — more at LEAVE] : a European typically of mixed blood who is a permanent resident of the Netherlands Indies

blim·bing \ˈblimbiŋ\ *n* -S [Tag *balimbing*, *bilimbing* + Malay *bělimbing*] : CARAMBOLA

bli·mey *also* **bli·my** \ˈblīmi\ *interj* [by shortening] *chiefly Brit* : GORBLIMEY

blimp \ˈblimp\ *n* -S [perh. fr. (*type*) *B* + *limp*] **1 a** : a nonrigid airship **b** : a fat person **2** : a soundproof housing for a motion-picture camera used in taking pictures with sound **3** [after Col. *Blimp*, character created by David Low *b*1891 British cartoonist] *often cap* : a diehard of ultraconservative nationalistic outlook and complacent stupidity

blimp·ish \-pish,-pēsh\ *adj, often cap* : in the manner of or resembling a blimp ⟨the pig-headed ~ obstinacy with which Britain clung to the imperial defense plan —*Sydney (Australia) Daily Telegraph*⟩ — **blimp·ish·ly** *adv*

blin \ˈblin\ *n, pl* **blini** *or* **bliny** \ˈblinē\ *or* **blinis** [Russ — more at BLINTZE] : BLINTZE

¹blind \ˈblīnd\ *adj, usu* -ER/-EST [ME, fr. OE; akin to OHG *blint* blind, ON *blindr*, Goth *blinds* blind, OE *blandan* to mix — more at BLEND] **1 a** : lacking the sense of sight by natural defect or by deprivation **b** : not having an eye or having an eye that does not see ⟨that horse will shy if you come up on his ~ side⟩ **c** : deficient in or lacking a physical sense other than sight — usu. with a qualifying term ⟨taste-*blind*⟩ **d** : for sightless persons ⟨~ care⟩ ⟨~ home⟩ **2 a** : not having the faculty of discernment : lacking in intellectual light : unable or unwilling to judge rationally ⟨~ to his own defects⟩ **b** : unsupported by evidence or plausibility : not substantially based ⟨~ faith⟩ **3 a** : without regard to rational discrimination, guidance, or restriction ⟨if they persist in such a ~ choice they must suffer for it⟩ **b** *of an impersonal force* **:** lacking any directing or controlling consciousness ⟨our fate is in the hands of ~ chance⟩ **c :** marked by complete insensibility ⟨lying helpless in a ~ stupor⟩; *esp* **:** drunken to the point of insensibility **:** DEAD-DRUNK **4 :** made or done without sight of objects or knowledge of facts comprising the chief or usual means of guidance or judgment ⟨a ~ purchase⟩: as **a :** performed solely by the aid of data given by instruments within an airplane and without direct sight of landmarks ⟨a ~ landing⟩ ⟨~ flying⟩ **b** *in card games* **:** made without seeing some relevant factor (as one's own hand or the dummy) ⟨a ~ lead⟩ **c :** made or done from psychological test data without reference to other case material ⟨~ analysis⟩ ⟨~ interpretation⟩ **5 :** DEFECTIVE, INCOMPLETE, ABORTIVE: **a** *of plants or plant parts* (1) **:** SUPPRESSED (2) **:** lacking a growing point (3) **:** failing to produce flowers or seeds — used esp. of buds and bulbs **b** *music* **:** having alternate tones in different registers ⟨a ~ trill⟩ ⟨a ~ octave series⟩ **c :** incapable of producing a print — used of a lithographic surface ⟨the plate went ~ after 10,000 impressions⟩ **6 a** *archaic* **:** lacking in light or brightness **:** DARK ⟨the little ~ bedchamber —Samuel Pepys⟩ **b** *obs* **:** UNLIGHTED ⟨a ~ candle⟩; *also* **:** having its light concealed ⟨a ~ lantern⟩ **c :** DULL **:** lacking in brightness or luster; *esp* **:** not polished or brought to a high gloss **:** finished dull ⟨a mellow ~ finish to the paneling⟩ **d :** impressed or tooled without gilding, inking, or coloring ⟨~ lettering⟩ ⟨~ scoring⟩ **7 :** difficult to discern, make out, or discover **:** hard to locate or identify **:** OBSCURE, HIDDEN: as **a** *archaic* **:** out of the way; *also* **:** SECRET ⟨a ~ meeting place⟩ **b** *archaic, of a track or way* **:** dim and ill-defined; *also* **:** not easily followed or traced **:** INVOLVED, INTRICATE ⟨the ~ mazes of this tangled wood —John Milton⟩ **c** (1) *of writing* **:** ILLEGIBLE; *esp, of mail* **:** lacking a complete or legible address (2) **:** concerned with the handling of blind mail **d** *of the sense of a passage* **:** unintelligible or uncertainly determinable **e** *of material objects* **:** constructed or arranged so as to be hidden from sight **:** COVERED ⟨a ~ veneer⟩ ⟨~ seams in a shoe⟩: as (1) *of a ditch or other water channel* **:** consisting of a cut in the soil filled loosely with stones between which water can trickle or percolate (2) *of minerals and lodes and strata* **:** not appearing in an outcrop at the surface ⟨a ~ vein⟩ (3) *of roads, driveways, and crossings* **:** screened from the view of oncoming drivers or engineers ⟨a ~ crossroad⟩ **8 a :** having but one opening or outlet **:** closed at one end **:** not permitting passage or flow all the way through ⟨a ~ alley⟩ ⟨~ sockets⟩ ⟨the ~ gut⟩ **b** *of a rivet or other fastener* **:** designed to be inserted and made fast from one side **c** *geol* **:** terminating abruptly where it might be expected to continue ⟨a ~ joint in rocks⟩ ⟨a ~ valley that ends downstream where drainage disappears underground⟩ **9 :** having no opening for light or passage **:** BLANK ⟨a ~ wall⟩: as **a** *of a hedge* **:** too thick to see through or pass through **b** *of a structural member* **:** made without an opening but like a member that normally has an opening ⟨a ~ arch⟩ ⟨a ~ window over the stairs⟩ **10** *railroading* **:** turned edgewise — used of a target or of its position

²blind \"\ *vt* -ED/-ING/-S [ME *blinden*, fr. *blind*, adj.] **1 :** to make blind: **a :** to deprive of the sense of sight ⟨his right eye was ~*ed* when he was a child⟩ **b :** to deprive of insight or understanding ⟨prejudice usually ~*s* judgment⟩ **c :** DECEIVE, FOOL, BEDAZZLE **d :** to deprive temporarily or partially of vision **:** make seeing difficult for or painful to **:** DAZZLE ⟨the hot glare ~*ed* her as she stepped into the street⟩ **2 a :** to withhold light from **:** DARKEN ⟨shrubbery ~*ing* all their windows⟩ **b :** HIDE, CONCEAL **c :** to make dim by comparison **:** OUTSHINE, ECLIPSE ⟨torches that ~ the candles⟩ **d :** to render nonlustrous **:** DULL ⟨a synthetic fabric may need to be ~*ed* in the finishing process⟩ **3 :** to fill the interstices of **:** CLOG: as **a :** to cover (a newly paved road) with a coating of sand and gravel in order that joints may be filled **b :** to cover (drain tiles) with earth while the trench is being filled **4 :** to stamp (as a book cover) without gilding or coloring — often used with *in* **5 :** to protect with blindages or with blinds

³blind \"\ *n* -S **1 :** something to hinder sight or keep out light: as **a :** a screen used to deflect or redirect light or to restrict observation from without: as (1) **:** WINDOW SHUTTER (2) **:** a roller window shade (3) **:** VENETIAN BLIND (4) *chiefly Brit* **:** AWNING (5) **:** BRISE-SOLEIL (6) **:** a shutter for a porthole **b :** BLINDER **c :** a cloth covering for the eyes used esp. in games **2 :** a place or means of concealment **:** AMBUSH 1; *esp* **:** a concealing enclosure from which a person may shoot game or observe wildlife **3 a :** something put forward to screen or cover another object or design **:** SUBTERFUGE, DECEPTION ⟨the holding company was a ~ for out-of-state interests⟩ ⟨his helpful offer is no more than a ~⟩ **b** (1) **:** a person serving as an agent for another who keeps under cover (2) **:** one who acts as a decoy or distraction **4 :** hand tooling without gilding or coloring ⟨bindings decorated in ~⟩ **5 a :** BLINDAGE **b :** a strong frame of uprights and crosspieces used to support a blindage **6** *card games* **a :** an obligatory opening bet in some forms of draw poker made by the player at the dealer's left before the cards are dealt and often constituting a raise of the ante **b :** the player who makes this bet **c :** WIDOW 3 **7** *railroading* **a :** BLIND BAGGAGE **b :** the platform of a blind baggage immediately behind the tender — usu. used in pl. **8** *slang Brit* **:** a noisy usu. drunken party **:** BRAWL

⁴blind \"\ *adv* [¹*blind*] **:** BLINDLY: as **a :** to the point of insensibility ⟨~ drunk⟩ **b :** without the aid of visual or other indicators that are usu. a source of guidance or judgment ⟨learning to fly ~⟩ **c :** RECKLESSLY, HEEDLESSLY ⟨I'd rather go it ~ than not get home at all⟩

blind advertisement *n* **:** an advertisement that does not disclose the name of the advertiser

blind·age \'blīndij\ *n* -S [F, fr. *blinder* to screen, protect (fr. *blinde* blind to screen military operations, fr. G *blende*, fr. *blenden* to blind, fr. OHG *blenten*) + *-age* — more at BLIND] **:** an overhead protection: as **a :** an earth-covered screen supported by a blind for an advanced trench or approach **b :** a large deep dugout often with bunks and other fittings

blind alley *n* **:** something that offers no opportunity for progress or advancement

blind area *n* **:** a wholly or partly covered area outside the wall of a building to keep moisture from the wall

blind attic *n* **:** a closed unfinished dead space immediately beneath the roof of a building

blind baggage *n* **:** a railway baggage, express, or postal car that has no door or opening at one end; *esp* **:** one immediately behind a tender

blind blocking *n* **:** BLIND 4

blind bond *n* **:** a masonry bond in which the headers extend only halfway through the tier of face brick all of which are stretchers and some of which are split lengthwise to accommodate the ends of the headers

blind bridle *n* **:** a bridle provided with blinders

blind catch *n* **:** BLINDFAST

blind date *n* **1 :** a date arranged by a third person between two persons of opposite sex who have not previously met **2 :** either participant in a blind date

blinded *adj* **1 :** made blind **:** DAZZLED, OBSCURED, DARKENED **2 :** furnished with a blind or blinds ⟨green-*blinded* windows⟩ **3 :** having the window blinds closed

blind eel *n* **1 :** CONGO SNAKE **2 :** seaweed accidentally hauled up in a net — used esp. by fishermen

¹blinder *comparative of* BLIND

²blind·er \'blīndə(r)\ *n* -S **1 :** either of two flaps on a horse's bridle to prevent sight of objects at his sides **2 blinders** *pl* **:** an obstruction to sight or discernment **:** an impediment to clear thinking

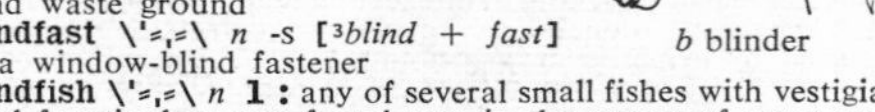

b blinder

blindest *superlative of* BLIND

blind·eyes \'⸗,⸗\ *n pl but sing or pl in constr* **1 :** CORN POPPY **2 :** a scarlet-flowered poppy (*Papaver dubium*) often occurring as a weed in cultivated fields and waste ground

blindfast \'⸗,⸗\ *n* -S [³*blind* + *fast*] **:** a window-blind fastener

blindfish \'⸗,⸗\ *n* **1 :** any of several small fishes with vestigial and functionless eyes found usu. in the waters of caves and subterranean streams in No. and So. America and Africa (as certain catfishes or members of the genus *Amblyopsis*) **2 :** any of certain eyeless deep-sea fishes

blind flange *n* **:** a cover plate bolted or otherwise fastened across a pipe flange to seal the pipe

¹blind·fold \'blīn(d),fōld\ *vt* -ED/-ING/-S [by folk etymology fr. ME *blindfelden*, alter. of *blindfellen* to strike blind, to blindfold, fr. *blind* + *fellen* to fell, strike down — more at FELL] **1 :** to cover the eyes of with or as if with a bandage **2 :** to hinder from seeing; *esp* **:** to keep from comprehension

²blindfold \"\ *adj* [by folk etymology fr. ME *blindfeld*, *blindfelled*, fr. past part. of *blindfellen*] **1 :** having the eyes covered **2 a :** lacking mental vision or understanding **b :** lacking consideration **:** HEEDLESS, RECKLESS ⟨a ~ fury⟩

³blindfold \"\ *n* **1 :** a bandage for covering the eyes and shutting out light or vision **2 :** something that acts as a blindfold esp. in obscuring mental or physical vision ⟨do not let the wool grow down into a ~ that interferes with grazing⟩ ⟨his arrogance was a ~ shutting him away from his fellows⟩

blindfold chess *n* **:** chess played without sight of the board

blind·fold·ed·ness *n* -ES **:** the quality or state of being blindfolded

blind gentian *n* **:** CLOSED GENTIAN

blind goby *n* **:** PINKFISH

blind gut *n* [so called fr. its having only one opening] **:** CECUM

blind head *n, obs* **:** a cover without outlet for a retort or other distilling vessel; *also* **:** the whole apparatus of which the cover is a part

blind header *n* **:** a masonry header in the interior of a wall; *also* **:** SNAP HEADER

blind hookey *n, card games* **:** a variety of banker and broker

¹blinding *n* -S [ME, fr. gerund of *blinden*] **1 :** the act of making or the fact of becoming blind **2 :** the sand and fine gravel used to blind a road

²blinding *adj* [fr. pres. part. of ²*blind*] **1 :** making blind or as if blind: **a :** depriving of sight **b :** depriving of understanding **:** CONFUSING **c :** brilliant with light or color **:** DAZZLING **d :** OBSCURING ⟨~ tears⟩ **2** *slang* **:** DARNED, BLAMED, BLASTED ⟨what are you in such a ~ hurry over⟩ — **blind·ing·ly** *adv*

blinding tree *n* **:** BLIND-YOUR-EYES

blind·ish \'blīndish, -dēsh\ *adj* [¹*blind* + *-ish*] **:** somewhat blind

blind·ism \-,dizəm\ *n* -S **:** a form of behavior characteristic of blind persons

blind·less \-dləs\ *adj* [³*blind* + *-less*] **:** having no blind

blind lift *n* **:** a catch for raising or lowering a window blind

blind-loaded \'⸗,⸗⸗\ *adj* **1 :** containing no bursting charge but loaded with sand so as to come up to service weight — used of a shell **2 :** not having a fuse, the bursting charge being exploded by the heat of impact — used of a shell

blind·ly *adv* [ME, fr. ¹*blind* + *-ly*] **:** in a blind way ⟨groping ~ in the dark passage⟩: **a :** without reason or understanding **:** without comprehension or consideration ⟨let no one follow me ~⟩ **b :** without conscious purpose **:** MECHANICALLY ⟨toying ~ with the ringlet on her neck⟩ **c :** without an opening or outlet ⟨the path ended ~ at a high brick wall⟩

blind·man \-dmən\ *n, pl* **blindmen** [*blind* (*mail*) illegible or insufficiently addressed mail + *man*] *chiefly Brit* **:** BLIND-READER

blind·man's buff \'blīn(d),manz-, -,maa(ə)nz-\ *n* [*blind man* + *buff* (buffet)] **1 :** a group game in which a blindfolded player tries to catch and identify any other member of the group **2 :** something concerted with trickery and bedazzlement or carried out without awareness of the facts and issues involved

blindman's holiday \"-\ *n* [*blind man*] *archaic* **:** TWILIGHT

blind mortise *n* **:** a mortise that does not extend entirely through the material in which it is cut

blind-nail \'⸗,⸗\ *vt* **:** to nail in such a way that nailheads are not visible on the face of the work

blind·ness \'blīnnəs\ *n* -ES [ME, fr. ¹*blind* + *-ness*] **1 :** want of discernment esp. with reference to some particular object or matter **:** failure to exercise understanding, judgment, or discrimination **2 a :** the quality or state of being blind; *specif* **:** that of having less than $\frac{1}{10}$ of normal vision in the more efficient eye when refractive defects are fully corrected by suitable lenses — compare COLOR BLINDNESS **b :** psychic inability to perceive visual images although the visual receptors are functional — called also *mental blindness, mind blindness, psychic blindness* **c :** lack of sensory perception involving all or part of some sense other than sight ⟨taste ~⟩ ⟨smell ~⟩ **3 a** *obs* **:** CONCEALMENT **b :** OBSCURITY **4** *of plants* **:** failure to produce a growing tip or flowers or to develop vegetative parts — compare ¹*blind* 5a

blind nettle *n* [ME *blind netyll*, fr. OE *blindnetle*, fr. *blind* + *netle* nettle — more at NETTLE; fr. its lack of sting] **1 :** WHITE DEAD NETTLE **2 :** HENBIT

blind officer *n* [*blind* (*mail*) illegible or insufficiently addressed mail] *chiefly Brit* **:** BLIND-READER

blind P \-'pē\ *n* [so called fr. the fact that the loop is inked in] **:** the paragraph mark ⟨¶ is one form of *blind P*⟩

blind pig *n, slang* **:** BLIND TIGER

blind pit *n, bot* **:** a pit lacking a complementary pit and commonly found opposite an intercellular space — see PIT-PAIR

blind pocket *also* **blind pocket psorosis** *n* **:** a phase of psorosis of citrus trees characterized by a creasing of the trunk of the tree that results in a fluted effect

blind pool *n* **:** a pool of funds placed at the discretion of the manager

blind pull *n* **:** BLIND LIFT

blind pulley *n* **:** DEADEYE

blind-punch \'⸗,⸗\ *vt* **:** to punch (as metal) only a part of the way through

blind rat *n* **:** MOLE RAT

blind-reader \'⸗,⸗⸗\ *n* [*blind* (*mail*) illegible or insufficiently addressed mail] *chiefly Brit* **:** a post-office clerk whose duty is the deciphering of illegible or insufficient addresses

blind robin *n* **:** a smoked herring

blinds *pl of* BLIND, *pres 3d sing of* BLIND

blind-seed disease \'⸗,⸗-\ *also* **blind seed** *n* **:** a disease of forage grasses (as rye grass and fescue) caused by an ascomycetous fungus (*Phialea temulenta*) and resulting in abortion of the seed

blind set *n* **:** an unbaited trap hidden in the runway or burrow of an animal — compare BAIT SET

blind shaft *n* **:** WINZE

blind shell *n* **1 a :** a blind-loaded shell **b :** ¹DUD 5 **2** [so called fr. the closing of the apex at maturity] **:** a mollusk of the family Caecidae

blind side *n* **1 :** the side on which one that is blind in one eye cannot see **2 :** an aspect of a matter in which one can see no fault **3 :** the ground on the side of a rugby scrum opposite to the side the referee stands on

blind siding *n* **:** a railroad siding located at a point where there is no agent or means of communication

blind snake *n* **1 :** a snake of the family Typhlopidae or of the related Leptotyphlopidae — called also *worm snake* **2 :** any of various limbless burrowing lizards

blind snipe *n* **:** WOODCOCK 1a(2)

blind spot *n* **1 a :** the point in the retina not sensitive to light where the optic nerve passes through the inner coat of the eyeball — see EYE illustration **b :** a portion of a field not seeable or inspectable with available equipment ⟨one limitation of radar is the existence of *blind spots* at low levels⟩ **2 :** an area in which one fails to exercise understanding, judgment, or discrimination **3 :** a locality in which radio reception is markedly poorer than in the surrounding area

blind staggers *n pl but sing or pl in constr* **1 a :** ²STAGGER 1a **b :** SELENOSIS; *esp* **:** a severe acute form of this condition **2 a :** dizziness accompanied by staggers **b :** extreme drunkenness

blind stamp *n* **:** an impression made by blind stamping

blind-stamp \'⸗,⸗\ *vt* [*blind stamp*] **:** to stamp (as the cover of a book) without gilding or coloring

blind stitch *n* **:** a sewing stitch so made as to be invisible on the right side and often nearly invisible on the wrong side

blind-stitch \'⸗,⸗\ *vt* [*blind stitch*] **:** to sew with blind stitches

blind·story \'⸗,⸗⸗\ *n* **:** a story without windows; *specif* **:** the triforium of a Gothic church without windows in the outer wall

blind teat *n* **:** a teat that does not permit passage of milk (as an occluded or inverted teat)

blind tiger *n* [prob. so called fr. the evasion of prohibition laws by selling liquor in establishments disguised as halls for exhibiting natural curiosities] *slang* **:** a place that sells intoxicants illegally **:** SPEAKEASY

blind tire *n* **:** BALD TIRE

blind-tool \'⸗,⸗\ *vt* **:** to hand-tool (as the cover of a book) without gilding or coloring — compare BLIND-STAMP

blindworm \'⸗,⸗\ *n* [¹*blind* + *worm*] **1 :** a small burrowing limbless lizard with minute eyes; *esp* **:** a small-scaled European lizard (*Anguis fragilis*) that feeds on grubs and worms and is popularly believed to be blind — called also *slowworm* **2** *archaic* **:** ADDER

blind-your-eyes \'⸗⸗,⸗\ *n, pl* **blind-your-eyes** [so called fr. its volatile juice] **:** an Australian tree (*Excoecaria agallocha*) — called also *milky mangrove, poison tree*

bling·er \'bliŋə(r)\ *n* -S [origin unknown] *slang* **:** a superlative example of its kind ⟨his cold was a real ~⟩

blini *or* **blinis** *pl of* BLIN

¹blink \'bliŋk\ *vb* -ED/-ING/-S [ME *blinken* to open one's eyes; prob. akin to MD & G *blinken* to glitter, shine, OHG *blanch* shining, bright, white — more at BLANK] *vi* **1 a** *obs* **:** to look glancingly **:** PEEP, GLANCE **b :** to look with half-shut winking eyes (as when roused from sleep or dazzled by strong light) ⟨seated in her obscure corner ~*ing* at the fire⟩ ⟨the glare on the snow made us ~⟩ **c :** to open and shut the eye repeatedly or rapidly **:** wink involuntarily ⟨one eye ~*ing* and twitching⟩ **2** *of light or a source of light* **a :** to shine intermittently **:** FLICKER, TWINKLE **b :** to shine dimly or uncertainly ⟨sun ~*ing* through the strands of fog⟩ **3 a :** to look evasively **:** look with ignoring or condoning — usu. used with *at* ⟨modern popular philosophy ~*s* at these facts —M.R.Cohen⟩ **b :** to look with surprise **:** become startled, amazed, or dismayed — used with *at* ⟨a professional statistician might ~ at the methods though the results seem reasonable⟩ **~** *vt* **1** *obs* **:** to cause to sour **:** make sour (as milk or beer) **2** *of a sporting dog* **:** to refuse to see and point (game) ⟨his dog *blinked* the first bevy of the day⟩ **3 a :** to close and open (the eye) involuntarily **:** WINK ⟨he ~*ed* his tired eyes⟩ **b :** to remove (as tears) from the eye by blinking **4** *chiefly Scot* **:** to put the evil eye on **:** BEWITCH **5 a :** to deny recognition to **:** deliberately evade **:** IGNORE — often used in negative constructions ⟨there was no ~*ing* the fact that she had been worried —Helen Howe⟩ or with *away* ⟨truths that at the turn of the century were firmly ~*ed* away —*Saturday Rev.*⟩ **b :** to be aware of **:** RECOGNIZE ⟨if we ~ the truth we must admit our share of responsibility⟩ **6 a :** to cause to emit flashes or twinkles of light ⟨he ~*ed* his flashlight to show us the way⟩ **b :** to signal by a blinker

²blink \"\ *n* -S **1** *chiefly Scot* **:** GLIMPSE, GLANCE ⟨a view on a bit of empty road, houses, and a ~ of sea —R.L.Stevenson⟩ **2 a :** a brief show of light **:** GLEAM, GLIMMER, SPARKLE ⟨a ~ of bright flame⟩ **b :** a brief period of time **:** INSTANT, MOMENT, TRICE **3 :** an involuntary shutting and opening of the eye **:** WINKING **4** *dial* **:** milk that is slightly sour **5 a :** a whitish or mottled appearance of the sky about the horizon caused by the reflection of light from an ice field or from scattered ice — compare ICEBLINK **b :** a dark appearance of the sky about the horizon caused by the absence of reflected light due to open water — compare WATER SKY — **on the blink** *adv* (*or adj*) **:** in or into a disabled or useless condition **:** INDISPOSED **:** out of order

³blink \"\ *adj* **:** BLINK-EYED

⁴blink \"\ *n* -S [by shortening] **:** BLINKER 3

blink·ard \'bliŋkə(r)d\ *n* -S [¹*blink* + *-ard*] **1** *archaic* **:** one that blinks with or as if with weak eyes **2 :** a stupid, slow-witted, or obtuse person

blink comparator *n* **:** an optical instrument by means of which two pictures identical in all but a few details may be registered in a single visual field and viewed alternately in rapid succession

blinked *adj* [fr. past part. of ¹*blink*] **:** affected with blinking

¹blink·er \'bliŋkə(r)\ *n* -S [¹*blink* + *-er*] **1 :** one that blinks: as **a** *archaic* **:** COQUETTE **b :** a sporting dog that refuses to see and point game or to hold to a point and flush his game **c** (1) **:** a device consisting essentially of a light that can be flashed on and off regularly as a warning (as at a railway crossing) (2) **:** a traffic light arranged to blink rather than show a color for a sustained period **d** (1) **:** a device consisting essentially of a light that can be flashed on and off in a sequence of coded intervals for signaling a message (as from ship to ship) (2) **:** a message sent by means of a blinker **2 a** (1) **:** BLINDER 1 (2) **:** a cloth hood with shades projecting at the sides of the eye openings used on skittish racehorses — usu. used in pl. **b :** something that impairs mental or moral perception **3** *also* **blink :** a young or undersized mackerel smaller than a tinker

²blinker \"\ *vt* **blinkered; blinkered; blinkering** \'bliŋk(ə)riŋ\ **blinkers 1 :** to put blinders or blinkers on ⟨they ~*ed* themselves against the facts⟩; *specif* **:** HOODWINK ⟨a person ill-equipped for his task, ~*ed* as he is by long association with partisan groups⟩ **2 :** to send (a message) by means of a blinker ⟨~*ed* a breakfast invitation from shore —*Newsweek*⟩

blinkered *adj* **:** NARROW, OBTUSE, LIMITED

blinker tube *n* **:** a tube for confining signals by blinker to a single direction

blink-eyed \'⸗,⸗\ *adj* **:** habitually winking

blinking *adj* [fr. pres. part. of ¹*blink*] *slang Brit* **1 :** DAMNED, BLASTED ⟨a ~ nuisance⟩ **2 :** COMPLETE, UTTER ⟨a ~ fool⟩

blink·ing·ly *adv* **:** with blinking eyes **:** EVASIVELY

blink microscope *n* **:** a blink comparator in which the compared images are magnified

¹blinks *pres 3d sing of* BLINK

²blinks *n, pl* **blinks** [fr. pl. of ²*blink*; fr. the fact that the flowers do not open fully] **:** a small herb (*Montia lamprosperma*) of northern regions — called also *blinking chickweed, water chickweed*

blinky \'bliŋkē, -ki\ *adj, usu* -ER/-EST [¹*blink* + *-y*] **1 :** BLINKING, BLINK-EYED **2** *dial* **:** slightly sour — used esp. of milk or beer

blin·ter \'blintə(r)\ *vi* -ED/-ING/-S [prob. freq. of obs. Sc *blent* to gleam, glance, fr. ME (northern dial.) *blenten*, fr. *blent, blenked* past part. of *blenken* to deceive, swerve, gleam, glance, fr. OE *blencan* to deceive — more at BLENCH] **1** *Scot* **:** FLICKER, GLIMMER ⟨the firelight ~*ed* on her face⟩ **2** *Scot* **:** BLINK

blin·tze \ blintsə\ *or* **blintz** \'blints\ *n, pl* **blintzes** [Yiddish *blintse*, fr. Russ *blinets*, dim. of *blin* pancake, fr. ORuss *mlinŭ*; akin to Russ *molot'* to grind, OHG *malan* — more at MEAL] **:** a thin rolled pancake with a filling usu. of cream cheese

bliny *pl of* BLIN

¹blip \'blip\ *n* -S [imit.] **1 :** a short crisp sound ⟨the ~ of a switch button⟩ **2 :** an image on a radar screen

²blip \"\ *vb* **blipped; blipped; blipping; blips** *vt* **:** to strike or slap **~** *vi* **:** to make or cause a blip

blirt \'bli(ə)rt, 'blərt\ *Scot var of* BLURT

bliss \'blis\ *n* -ES [ME *blis, blisse*, fr. OE *bliss, blīths*; akin to OS *blīdsea* bliss; derivative fr. the root of E *blithe*] **1 :** a state of complete or ecstatic happiness ⟨they lived in perfect loving ~⟩ ⟨the ~ of complete understanding can only come to the equally endowed⟩ **2 a :** the perfect and exalted joy of saved souls **:** BEATITUDE 1 **b :** the place where such joy is experienced **:** PARADISE, HEAVEN **c :** the state of enjoying such joy **3** *archaic* **:** a cause of happiness **syn** see HAPPINESS

bliss·ful \'-fəl\ *adj* [ME *blisful*, fr. *blis* + *-ful*] **1 :** full of, marked by, or causing bliss **:** very happy ⟨a ~ couple of young lovers⟩ **2 :** content with things as they are **:** oblivious of existing incongruities, improprieties, or inequities ⟨Meddling's ~ lack of sensitivity to other people's feelings —Gordon Merrick⟩ ⟨new regulations issued in ~ ignorance of the real situation⟩ — **bliss·ful·ly** \-fəlē, -li\ *adv* — **bliss·ful·ness** \fəlnəs\ *n* -ES

bliss·less \-ləs\ *adj* **:** being without bliss

blissom *vb* [ME *blissomen*, of Scand origin; akin to ON *blæsma* in heat (said of goats); akin to ON *blāsa* to blow — more at BLAST] *vt, obs, of a ram* **:** TUP **~** *vi, obs, of a ewe* **:** to be in heat

¹blis·ter \'blistə(r)\ *n* -S [ME *blester, blister*, modif. of OF or MD; OF *blostre* boil, pustule, fr. MD *bluyster* blister; akin to OE *blǣst* blast — more at BLAST] **1 :** an elevation of the epidermis containing watery liquid or serum : BLEB, BULLA **2** : an enclosed raised spot on the surface of an organism caused by the separation of skin or other covering (as one resulting from a bruise on a plant) **3** : an agent that causes a blister (as a blistering plaster) **4** : a flaw on a surface caused by nonadherence or by separation of an applied substance: as **a** : a nodule on a painted surface filled with air, solvent, or water **b** : an elevated layer of rock resulting from the flow of molten rock into low wet areas and the generation of steam pockets **c** : BLISTER PEARL **d** : a fault in plywood or veneer resulting from failure to obtain uniform binding of the surface layer **e** : a large bubble in glass **f** : a spot of emulsion in a photographic film or plate loosened from its base in processing **g** : a rounded elevation on the surface of metal caused by expansion of gas within or through the subsurface metal while it is hot or plastic **5** : an oyster smaller than a quarter dollar **6** : BLISTER COPPER **7 a** : a disease of plants caused by ascomycetous fungi (genus *Taphrina*) that produce large swollen patches on the leaves (as that of the pear caused by *T. bullata*) **b** : any of various similar diseases (as a nonparasitic disorder of the apple) — see BLISTER BLIGHT, BLISTER CANKER, BLISTER SPOT **8** : any of various structures that bulge out from the main mass of which they are part: as **a** : a watertight compartmented structure applied to the hull of certain vessels esp. below the waterline to offer added protection (as against torpedoes or mines) **b** : a gunner's or observer's compartment protruding from the fuselage of an airplane and often covered by a transparent dome **c** : a glass observation dome built into and protruding above the roof of a railroad car **d** : a housing for a radar antenna — see RADOME **9** *slang* : PERSON; *esp* : [1]BAG 5 — usu. used disparagingly

[2]**blister** \"\ *vb* **blistered**; **blistered**; **blistering** \'blist(ə)riŋ\ **blisters** [ME *blisteren*, fr. *blister*, n.] *vi* **1 a** : to become affected with blisters ⟨lips will ~ and chap in the wind⟩ **b** : to raise a blister ⟨that sauce is hot; it positively ~*s*⟩ **2** : to have or take on the form of a blister ⟨the trumpeter's cheeks were ~*ing* like a child's balloon⟩ ~ *vt* **1 a** : to raise a blister on ⟨she ~*ed* her hand with hot grease⟩ : cause a blister to form on ⟨the hot sun will ~ the paint⟩ **b** : to treat by blistering or by means of blisters — now usu. restricted to veterinary usage ⟨the doctor physicked him, and bled him, and ~*ed* him, but he lived all the same⟩ **2** : to affect as if to the point of raising blisters: **a** : to administer severe physical punishment to esp. by whipping or beating ⟨get in here this minute or I'll ~ your bottom when you do⟩ **b** : to scorch with words (as in anger or contempt) : censure harshly : EXCORIATE ⟨the sergeant ~*ed* the men and set them to drilling again⟩

blister beetle *n* : any of certain beetles (as the Spanish fly) that when dried and powdered are used to raise blisters on the skin (as in the relief of certain forms of neuritis); *broadly* : any of numerous soft-bodied beetles that constitute the family Meloidae, have a complex metamorphosis, and include the blister beetles and some that as adults are destructive pests of economic plants

blister blight *n* **1** : a blister disease affecting the leaves of the tea plant caused by a fungus (*Exobasidium vexans*) **2** : a disease of Scotch pine caused by a rust (*Cronartium asclepiadeum*) that causes lesions like blisters on the twigs and gradually kills them

blister canker *n* : a disease of the apple tree caused by an ascomycetous fungus (*Nummularia discreta*) producing roughened and blackened cankers on the trunk and larger limbs — called also *apple pox*

blister cone *n* : a small cone produced by the expansion and escape of gas or vapor from liquid lava

blister copper *n* : metallic copper of a black blistered surface, being the product of converting copper matte and being about 98.5 to 99.5 per cent pure — called also *Bessemer copper*

blister cress *n* : any of certain pungent cresses (esp. of the genera *Erysimum* and *Cheiranthus*)

blister disease *var of* BLISTER

blistered *adj* **1** : affected with blisters : having the surface irregular and often pebbled, nodular, or covered with blisters ⟨certain fabrics are ~⟩ **2** : having slashes or openings through which cloth of another material or color shows or is drawn in puffs — used of a 16th century decoration esp. of doublets, breeches, and sleeves

blister figure *n* : an uneven appearance in some woods caused by irregular depressed and elevated rounded areas in the annual rings

blister fly *or* **blistering fly** *n* : BLISTER BEETLE

blister gas *n* : VESICANT

blistering *adj* **1** : extremely hot : hot enough to blister ⟨a ~ sun⟩ **2** *slang* : BLAMED, DARNED, DAMNED **3** : ACRIMONIOUS, WITHERING, SCATHING ⟨a ~ letter⟩ **4** : SEVERE, INTENSE ⟨the troops fell back under a ~ assault from the enemy⟩ ⟨invest human existence with something more . . . than a ~ misery —Norman Cousins⟩ **5** : very rapid : such as might be expected to cause blistering from frictional heat : SCORCHING, GRUELING ⟨the leader set a ~ pace⟩ **6** : of pressing and immediate importance ⟨a ~ local issue⟩ — **blis·ter·ing·ly** *adv*

blistering cerate *n* : a cerate composed of cantharides, glacial acetic acid, oil of turpentine, yellow wax, rosin, and benzoinated lard — called also *cantharides cerate*

blister mite *n* : any of several mites esp. of the genus *Eriophyes* producing a gall on leaves (as the pear-leaf blister mite)

blister pearl *n* : a pearly excrescence on the inside of the shell of a mollusk (as the oyster) commonly enclosing a foreign body (as a bit of mud or a parasite)

blister plant *or* **blister flower** *n* : a crowfoot (*Ranunculus acris*)

blister rust *n* : any of several diseases of pines caused by rust fungi (genus *Cronartium*) in the aecial stage, affecting the sapwood and inner bark and producing blisters externally; *often* : WHITE-PINE BLISTER RUST

blisters *pl of* BLISTER, *pres 3d sing of* BLISTER

blister spot *n* : a disease of the apple caused by a bacterium (*Pseudomonas papulans*) and characterized by dark brown blisters on the fruit and rough bark cankers on the limbs

blister steel *n* : crude steel formerly formed from wrought iron by cementation

blis·tery \'blist(ə)rē, -ri\ *adj* [[1]*blister* + *-y*] : having, full of, or marred by blisters

blite \'blīt\ *n* -S [ME, fr. L *blitum* orach, fr. Gk *bliton*] : any of several herbs of the family Chenopodiaceae: **a** : STRAWBERRY BLITE **b** : SEA BLITE **c** : GOOD-KING-HENRY

[1]**blithe** \'blīth, 'blīth\ *adj* -ER/-EST [ME, fr. OE *blīthe;* akin to OHG *blīdi* kind, joyous, ON *blīthr* gentle, Goth *bleiths* merciful, Lith *blyvas* violet-blue, OE *bǣl* fire, pyre — more at BALD] **1** : of a happy contented character or disposition : JOYFUL, GLAD, CHEERFUL; *also* : exhibiting light-hearted gaiety **2** : without due thought, consideration, or knowledge : LIGHT-MINDED : CASUAL, HEEDLESS ⟨a ~ disregard of the rights of others⟩ ⟨acting in ~ ignorance of historic precedent⟩ **syn** see MERRY

[2]**blithe** \"\ *adv* [ME, fr. OE *blīthe*, fr. *blīthe*, adj.] : BLITHELY

blithe·ful \-fəl\ *adj* [ME *blithful*, fr. *blithe* + *-ful*] : GAY, JOYOUS — **blithe·ful·ly** *adv*

blithe·ly *adv* [ME *blithely, blitheliche*, fr. OE *blīthelīce*, fr. *blīthe* + *-līce* -ly] : in a blithe manner

blithe·meat \'blīth+,-\ *n* [*blithe* + *meat*] *chiefly Scot* : food prepared for a feast to celebrate the birth of a child

blith·en \'blīthən, -īth-\ *vt* -ED/-ING/-S [[1]*blithe* + *-en*] : to make blithe

blithe·ness \-thnəs, -th-\ *n* -ES [ME *blitheness*, fr. OE *blīthnes*, fr, *blīthe* + *-nes* -ness] : the quality or state of being blithe

[1]**blith·er** \'blithə(r)\ *vi* -ED/-ING/-S [by alter.] : BLATHER — used chiefly in the present participle form ⟨a ~*ing* idiot⟩

[2]**blither** \"\ *n* -S [by alter.] : BLATHER

blith·ered \'blithə(r)d\ *adj, Austral* : DRUNK

blithe·some \'blīthsəm, -īth-\ *adj* [[1]*blithe* + *-some*] : CHEERY, GAY, MERRY — **blithe·some·ly** *adv*

blit·ter \'blitər\ *n* -S [perh. alter. of *bleater*] *Scot* : the common Old World snipe (*Capella gallinago*)

[1]**blitz** \'blits\ *n* -ES [short for *blitzkrieg*] **1 a** : BLITZKRIEG 1 **b** : an intensive all-out aerial attack or campaign; *also* : AIR RAID ⟨Hitler's ~*es* in 1941 —*Time*⟩ **2** : a fast intensive nonmilitary campaign ⟨the top GOP strategists . . . can hold the Senate by a last-minute ~ —*Newsweek*⟩ ⟨a ~ of spot announcements introduced the new models⟩

[2]**blitz** \"\ *vt* -ED/-ING/-ES **1 a** : to subject to a blitz ⟨the district was ~*ed* regularly —*Reader's Digest*⟩ **b** : to make a vigorous attack on ⟨an army of doctors ~*ed* the disease⟩ **2** : to damage by or as if by blitz ⟨Congress ~*ed* them last month by cutting their budgets —*Newsweek*⟩ — used chiefly as a past participle ⟨not one English city, no matter how badly ~*ed* —Elmer Davis⟩ **3** : HUSTLE, PUSH, MOVE ⟨I was ~*ed* off my lunch-counter seat —*Collier's*⟩; *also* : to cause to act without due consideration : STAMPEDE ⟨a drive to ~ the Chicago convention into an early ballot —*Christian Science Monitor*⟩

[3]**blitz** \"\ *adj* **1** : of, resulting from, typical of, or used in a blitz ⟨~ tactics⟩ ⟨~ ground units⟩ **2** : like a blitz esp. in speed and effectiveness ⟨making a ~ tour of Europe⟩ **3** : involving the offer of unusual discounts or other advantages to stimulate immediate volume sales — used chiefly in the retail automobile trade ⟨clearing last year's models in a ~ sale⟩

blitz can *n* : the standard U. S. government issue 5-gallon container used esp. to transport water or gasoline

blitzed *adj* : subjected to blitz

[1]**blitz·krieg** \'=,krēg\ *n* -S [G, lit., lightning war, fr. *blitz lightning* + *krieg* war] **1** : war conducted with great speed and force; *specif* : a violent surprise offensive by massed air forces and mechanized ground forces in close coordination, and with objectives (isolation of bodies of troops, disruption of communications, and capture of matériel) such that mobility may be exploited to the fullest **2** : any sudden overpowering bombardment (as with propaganda)

[2]**blitzkrieg** \"\ *vt* -ED/-ING/-S : to subject to or overpower with a blitzkrieg

blitzweed \'=,=\ *n* [[1]*blitz* + *weed;* fr. its use in England during World War II to cover areas devastated by bombing] *Brit* : FIREWEED b

bliz·zard \'blizə(r)d\ *n* -S [origin unknown] **1** *archaic* : a shot or volley of shots **2 a** : a severe and prolonged snowstorm **b** : an intensely strong cold wind filled with fine snow **3** : something likened to a blizzard of snow ⟨a ~ of volcanic ash⟩; *esp* : a sudden outbreak : unexpected occurrence : RASH ⟨a ~ of damage suits⟩ ⟨the ~ of bureaus that swirls around our nation's capital —T.W.Arnold⟩

blizzard head *n* : a woman television performer having hair so blond as to require special lighting to prevent a flare or halo from appearing

bliz·zar·dy \-dē,-di\ *also* **bliz·zard·ly** \-lē,-li\ *adj* : marked by blizzard ⟨a ~ day⟩ : tending to become or produce a blizzard ⟨the wind picked up, the storm became ~⟩

blk *abbr* **1** black **2** blank **3** block **4** bulk

blkd *abbr* bulkhead

blo \'blō\ *adj* [ME — more at BLAE] *dial Eng* : BLUE-BLACK

bloak *var of* BLOKE

[1]**bloat** \'blōt, *usu* -d·+V\ *adj* [alter. (prob. influenced by obs. *bloat* cured in such a way as to be comparatively soft and moist) of earlier *blowt*, fr. ME *blout*, prob. fr. ON *blautr* soft, weak, soaked; akin to OE *blēat* miserable, *blēath* timid, OHG *blōz* proud, MHG *blōz* naked, OHG *blōdi* timid, ON *blauthr* timid, Goth *blauthjan* to annul, Gk *phlydan* to be too moist, become soft, OE *blāwan* to blow — more at BLOW] : BLOATED, PUFFY, STUFFED

[2]**bloat** \"\ *vb* -ED/-ING/-S *vt* **1** : to make turgid (as with water or air): **a** : to cause swelling of the cellular tissue of by accumulation of serous fluid : produce edema in **b** : to cause or result in accumulation of gas in the digestive tract of ⟨cucumbers sometimes ~ me⟩ **2 a** : to fill to capacity or overflowing : INFLATE, STUFF **b** : to puff up : make vain ⟨encourage him and ~ him up with praise —John Dryden⟩ ~ *vi* : to become turgid : puff out : SWELL

[3]**bloat** \"\ *n* -S [[2]*bloat*] **1 a** : one that bloats or is bloated **b** *slang* : DRUNKARD **2 a** : distention of the rumen of ruminant mammals with gases from fermenting foodstuffs that is usu. associated with feeding on wet legumes but sometimes involves anaphylactic reactions and is esp. common in domestic cattle but sometimes also affects sheep and goats **b** : any flatulent digestive disturbance of domestic animals

bloat colic *n* : BLOAT — used esp. of a horse

[1]**bloat·ed** \'blōd·əd, -ōtəd\ *adj* [fr. past part. of obs. *bloat* to cure (a herring) by a process that leaves it comparatively soft and moist, fr. obs. *bloat*, adj., cured in such a way as to be comparatively soft and moist, fr. ME *blote* soft and moist, prob. of Scand origin; akin to ON *blotna* to become soft, lose courage, *blautr* soft, weak, soaked] *of a fish* : cured by a process involving salting and smoking that leaves it comparatively soft and moist

[2]**bloated** \"\ *adj* [fr. past part. of [2]*bloat*] **1** *of living things* : distended beyond the natural size by fluid (as serum or gas) : EDEMATOUS; *also* : excessively or unhealthily fat : GROSS, PAUNCHY, STUFFED **2 a** : enlarged beyond usual or expected bounds : SWOLLEN ⟨a river ~ by bursting dams and heavy rains⟩ ⟨increases in the already ~ defense budget⟩ **b** : giving an effect of swollen clumsiness ⟨the ~ side-wheelers that he had seen all his life —Marcia Davenport **3** : puffed up with pride : POMPOUS

bloated clay *n* [[2]*bloated*] : clay caused to swell naturally or by gas-forming additives and used esp. as insulation in concrete because of its porosity and lightness

bloat·ed·ness *n* -ES : the quality or state of being bloated

[1]**bloat·er** \'blōd·ə(r), -ōtə-\ *n* -S [obs. *bloat* to cure + *-er*] : one that is bloated: as **a** : a large fat herring lightly salted and smoked for a short time so that it remains plump and moist **b** : a large fat mackerel similarly cured or suitable for such curing

[2]**bloater** \"\ *vt* -ED/-ING/-S : to process (as herrings) into bloaters

[3]**bloater** \"\ *n* -S [[2]*bloat* + *-er*] **1** : a fruit or vegetable containing hollow spaces as a result of gaseous fermentation during processing **2** : a small but common cisco (*Leucichthys hoyi*) of the Great lakes formerly of no importance but now often marketed with related larger forms

[1]**blob** \'bläb\ *n* -S [ME] **1** *now dial Brit* : BLISTER, BUBBLE **2 a** : a small drop, globule, or lump of something viscid or thick ⟨a ~ of melting butter⟩ **b** : a spot of color ⟨candles burned in a golden ~ —Bruce Marshall⟩; *also* : DAUB 4 ⟨to the uninitiated his paintings were mere ~*s*, rich in color but meaningless⟩ **c** : something ill-defined or amorphous ⟨small ~*s* and faint glimmers of satire —*Time*⟩ ⟨a ~ of land looming up in the dusk⟩ — sometimes used of persons when considered only as shapes viewed ⟨a big sluggish ~⟩ **3** : an imperfect or harsh note on a wind instrument **4** : MILLER'S-THUMB 1 **5** : a score of zero in cricket : GOOSE EGG **6** *NewEng* : BLOSSOM

[2]**blob** \"\ *vt* **blobbed**; **blobbed**; **blobbing**; **blobs** [ME (northern dial.) *bloben*, fr. *blob*, n.] : to mark with blobs : SPLOTCH, BLOT

blobbed \'bläbd\ *adj* : SPOTTED, SPECKLED

blob·ber \'bläbə(r)\ *dial or archaic var of* BLUBBER

blob·by \'bläbē, -bi\ *adj* -ER/-EST **1** : covered or filled with blobs **2** : made up of blobs; *also* : like a blob

bloc \'bläk\ *n* -S *often attrib* [F, lit., block, fr. MF — more at BLOCK] **1 a** : a temporary combination of parties in a legislative assembly; *esp* : one organized to support the government in power in a country having a multiparty system **b** : a group of legislators in a U.S. legislative assembly who act together for some common purpose irrespective of party lines ⟨the farm ~⟩ **2 a** : a combination of persons, groups, or nations forming a unit with a common interest or purpose : UNION **b** : a group of nations united by treaty or agreement for mutual support or joint action ⟨the Western ~⟩ ⟨a middle course between the two power ~*s*⟩; *esp* : a group of nations whose currencies are so linked as to be convertible into each other at fixed rates and usu. freely transferable within the group ⟨the sterling ~⟩ ⟨the dollar ~⟩

blo·cage \blō'käzh, -äj\ *n* -S [F, fr. *bloc* block + *-age*] : rough cheap masonry usu. with a facing built up of irregular usu. small stones laid in mortar

bloch wall \'bläk-, 'blȯk-\ *n, usu cap B* [after Felix *Bloch* *b*1905 Swiss-Amer. physicist] : the boundary between two domains in a magnetic material marked by a layer wherein the direction of magnetization is assumed to change gradually from one domain to the other

[1]**block** \'bläk\ *n* -S [ME *blok*, fr. MF *bloc*, fr. MD *blok;* akin to OHG *bloh* block, MIr *blog* fragment, and perh. to OHG *bliuwan* to beat — more at BLOW (stroke)] **1** : a compact usu. solid piece of substantial material (as wood, stone, or metal) ⟨a fine ~ of marble⟩; *esp* : one worked or altered from its natural or rough state to serve a particular purpose: as **a** : a bulky piece of strong hard wood usu. having the upper surface dressed and serving as a base on which some operation (as the cutting of firewood) is performed: as (1) : such a block on which a butcher cuts meat (2) : the piece of wood on which a person condemned to be beheaded lays his neck for execution **b** : a mold or form upon which articles or materials are shaped or displayed: as (1) : a wooden form upon which hats are shaped; *also* : the pattern or style of a hat (2) : a hollow wooden or metal device in which a gather of glass is shaped (3) : a cast or turned plaster form around which plaster is cast to make a potter's mold **c** : HORSE BLOCK **d** : a piece of stone or other natural or artificial composition dressed or formed usu. to uniform size for use as a structural unit ⟨paving ~*s*⟩; *esp* : a hollow rectangular building unit of terracotta, concrete, glass, burned clay, or gypsum — compare BRICK, TILE **e** : BLOCK COAL **f** : a piece of solid material used to strengthen, support, or retain in position: as (1) : CHOCK 1 ⟨put a ~ behind the rear wheel⟩ (2) : a piece of wood or other material glued into an interior angle to strengthen a joint (3) : a support placed behind a wainscot to hold it out from the wall (4) : BREECHBLOCK (5) : SPRING BLOCK (6) : BRAKE BLOCK (7) : one of the supports on which the keel of a ship is laid (8) : a rectangular prism of wood placed to support a vessel in dry dock (as under its keel or under any stiffened part between keel and turn of the bilge) **g** : a percussion musical instrument consisting of a hollow slotted block of wood played usu. with a drumstick — called also *wood block* **h** : a cylinder that revolves drawing an attached wire through a die and coiling it **i** : a lightweight usu. cubical and solid wooden or plastic toy that is typically decorated on each face with a letter or picture and is usu. provided in sets permitting varied arrangement and building activities — called also *building block* **j** : the casting that contains the cylinders of an internal-combustion engine — called also *cylinder block* **2** : something (as a person or a body part) suggesting or likened to a piece of wood: **a** : a stupid doltish person **b** : a harsh inconsiderate hard-hearted person **c** *now slang* : HEAD 1 ⟨knock his ~ off⟩ **d** : a dressed and trimmed carcass (as of beef) **3** : an obstruction or cause of obstruction : STUMBLING BLOCK, HINDRANCE, OBSTACLE, STOP, CHECK, IMPEDIMENT: as **a** : something interfering with free passage (as a military roadblock or a traffic jam) **b** : any of several kinds of or procedures for interference (as with other contestants or players) in sports: (1) : the obstruction with the hand or arm of a punch in boxing (2) : BLOCK BALL (3) : the checking of a player in football by use of one's body esp. to keep him out of the path of the ball carrier ⟨a rolling ~⟩ ⟨a shoulder ~⟩ (4) : GUARD 5b (5) : BLOCKHOLE **c** : a situation in various card and other games (as checkers or dominoes) in which no player can make a further legal move and which in most games results in a draw but in checkers wins the game for the player making the last move **d** : interruption of normal physiological function of a tissue or organ (as by fatigue or the presence of a chemically abnormal environment) ⟨respiratory ~ due to carbon monoxide⟩ ⟨mucosal ~ may accompany certain gastrointestinal disorders⟩; *esp* : HEART BLOCK **e** (1) : BLOCK ANESTHESIA (2) : NERVE BLOCK **f** : an instance or the result of psychological blockage or blocking **g** : DIAPAUSE **4** : a base, platform, or supporting frame: **a** : a wooden or metal case enclosing one or more pulleys, provided with a hook, eye, or strap by which it may be attached to an object, and used to change the direction of motion of the object or, when two or more pulleys are compounded, to change the rate of motion or exert increased force **b** : a platform from which slaves or other property are displayed for sale at auction; *broadly* : sale at auction — used chiefly with *on* **c** : a permanent base for mounting a device or machine (as for exhibition, testing, or support) **d** : PEDESTAL, PLINTH 2 **e** : a frame for supporting a log while sawing it **f** : a base commonly of wood or metal on which a relief printing plate is mounted — compare PATENT BASE **g** : a bookbinder's stamp too large for handwork **h** : GAGE BLOCK **5** : a whole made up of like or unlike elements esp. when itself a part of some greater whole : AGGREGATE: **a** : a quantity, number, or section of things dealt with as a unit ⟨a large ~ of shares⟩ ⟨the experimental ~ of trees was far more productive than the control⟩ **b** : [1]PAD 7 **c** [prob. trans. of D *blok*] (1) : a large building divided into separate functional units (as shops or offices) (2) : a line of row houses (3) : a group of neighboring buildings (as houses built by a single agency) (4) : a part of a building or integrated group of buildings distinctive in some respect (as in function, origin, or styling); *sometimes* : WING — used almost entirely of large complex structures ⟨a ~ of classrooms⟩ ⟨the laboratory ~ is nearing completion⟩ ⟨a magnificent refectory was then designed in one ~ of the palace⟩ (5) : CELLBLOCK **d** : something of a convenient or appropriate size (as for handling, working, using, or considering) ⟨a ~ of questions⟩ ⟨a design for a quilt ~⟩ **e** [prob. trans. of D *blok*] : a portion of land: as (1) : a usu. rectangular space (as in a city) enclosed usu. by streets but sometimes by other bounds (as rivers or railroads) and occupied by or intended for buildings ⟨a factory covering an entire ~⟩ (2) : the distance along one of the sides of such a block ⟨living only two ~*s* from the bus⟩ ⟨walked 10 ~*s*⟩ : the side of a block abutting on a street (3) : an area of land ⟨four ~*s* of woodland⟩; *esp* : a tract of land leased for drilling a wildcat oil well (4) : a part of the earth's crust bounded by faults and behaving as a unit in earth movements due to faulting (5) *chiefly Austral* : one of the large lots of public land divided by the government and opened to settlers (6) *often cap, Austral* : a street or quarter of a city; *often* : a section popular as a promenade — usu. used with *the* **f** [F *bloc*] : BLOC **g** : a group of four or more attached stamps in square or rectangular arrangement — contrasted with *strip* **h** : a length of railroad track of defined limits the use of which is governed by block signals **i** : a group of points considered together in determining transportation rates **j** : two or more lines of type set flush left and right **6 a** : CUT 3k(1); *esp* : WOODCUT **b** : material (as linoleum or rubber) mounted (as on wood or plywood) and having on its surface a hand-cut design from which impressions are to be printed — see BLOCK PRINT *vt* 1a

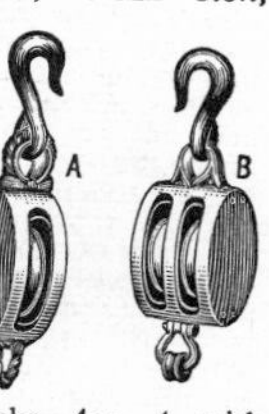

blocks 4a: *A* with single sheave; *B* with double sheave

[2]**block** \"\ *vb* -ED/-ING/-S *vt* **1 a** : to render (as a way) unsuitable for passage or progress by obstruction ⟨they ~*ed* the road with a barricade⟩ — sometimes used with *up* ⟨if grease ~*s* up the pipe⟩ ⟨my nose is all ~*ed* up⟩ **b** *archaic* : BLOCKADE, INVEST ⟨a city . . . besieged and ~*ed* about —John Milton⟩ **c** : to obstruct the passage, progress, or accomplishment of (someone or something) esp. by a positive obstacle ⟨they made every effort to ~ his election⟩ ⟨the ambulance was ~*ed* by traffic⟩ ⟨his brother ~*ed* him at every turn⟩ **d** : to interfere usu. legitimately with (an opponent's action or equipment) in various games or sports (as by use of a block): as (1) : to end (as a game of dominoes) with a block (2) : to check the play of (as a piece in checkers by suitable arrangement of pieces or a suit in bridge by withholding a high card of the suit from play) (3) : to halt or impede the progress of (a ball) usu. in a particular manner (as in cricket, volleyball, or football) (4) : to obstruct or interfere with (an opponent, his play, or his movement) by bodily contact; *specif* : to so impede the progress of (a basketball player who does not have the ball) **e** : to prevent normal functioning of (a bodily element) ⟨~ the reticuloendothelial system with trypan blue⟩ ⟨~ a nerve with novocaine⟩ **f** : to stop the output of alternating current from (an electron tube) by overloading the input **g** *chem* : to obstruct the effect of : render inactive : HINDER, MASK ⟨a carboxyl group ~*ed* by esterification⟩ **h** : to pro-

hibit conversion of (foreign-held funds) into foreign exchange; *also* : to limit the use to be made of (such funds) within the country — compare FREEZE **2** : to mark or indicate the outline or chief lines of — usu. used with *out*, sometimes with *in* ⟨let's ~ out our plan of action⟩ ⟨it's a good idea to ~ in the main masses of light and shade before touching any details of the drawing⟩ **3** : to shape on, with, or as if with a block: as **a** : to shape or restore (as a garment) to original dimensions by applying steam and adjusting sometimes over a form ⟨~ a sweater to a person's measurements⟩ **b** (1) : to emboss (book covers) with a frame or block containing the entire device (2) : 1STAMP 3e **4** : to form or divide into blocks ⟨~ coal⟩: as **a** : to remove (as sugar-beet seedlings) from drills with a hoe or other tool so as to leave small bunches for thinning later to single plants **b** : to set (two or more lines of type) flush left and right **c** : to separate (hair) into squared-off sections for waving **d** : to divide (beef) into wholesale cuts **5 a** : to secure, support, provide, or raise with a block ⟨~*ing* a plate for printing⟩ — often used with *up* ⟨~ up one rear wheel⟩ **b** : to secure (as two boards at their angles of intersection) by pieces of wood glued to each **c** : to raise the walls of (a log cabin) — used with *up* **6** : to run (trains) by the block system **~** *vi* **1** : to make or commit a block (as in football, boxing, basketball) : block an opponent **2** *of paper* : to stick together under the influence of heat and pressure **3** : to experience or exhibit psychological blocking or blockage **4** *of a photographic print or negative* : to lack halftones or gradations in highlights or shadows — usu. used with *up* **syn** see HINDER

3block \"\ *adj* **1 a** : made or taken in the block ⟨a ~ sum⟩ **b** : formed (as by pressing) into a block ⟨~ rubber⟩ **c** : of or forming block or a block : formed of blocks **2** *of an address, heading, or paragraph* : forming a block without an indentation at the left **3** : resembling a block : BLOCK-UNIVERSE

1block·ade \(ˈ)blä¦kād\ *n* -S *often attrib* [2*block* + *-ade*] **1 a** : a measure of war involving the isolation by a belligerent of a particular area vital to the interests of an enemy through deployment of any part of its armed forces so as to effectively hamper ingress and egress and harass the enemy by cutting off trade, communications, and supplies, being commonly agreed as legal against neutral nations only after due notice has been given and when carried on with such force as required to make passage through the area a real hazard but when so established and maintained permitting the seizure, detention, or sometimes destruction of neutral property found in the area; *broadly* : any restrictive measure or measures designed to obstruct the commerce and communications of an unfriendly nation whether or not a formal state of war exists **b** : something that acts in the manner of a blockade to prevent free and normal exchange (as of ideas) ⟨only clear thinking can free us from our emotional ~ and dissipate our prejudices⟩ **2 a** : something that constitutes an obstacle to passage; *esp* : a blocking of a pass or way (as by snow) **b** 1BLOCK 3b, 3c **c** : the filling of the receptive cells of the reticulo-endothelial system with material that is expected to prevent their taking up any new antigenic material — compare BLOCKING ANTIBODY **3** *chiefly Midland* : MOONSHINE 3

2blockade \"\ *vt* -ED/-ING/-S **1** : to effect a blockade of (as a port, coast, or fleet) : subject (as a nation) to a blockade : INVEST **2** : to close with obstructions : BLOCK, OBSTRUCT

block·ad·er \-də(r)\ *n* -S **1** : one that blockades; *specif* : a ship employed in blockading a port **2** *South & Midland* : MOONSHINER

blockade-runner \(ˈ)ˌ=ˌ=ˌ==\ *n* : a ship or person that runs or attempts to run through a blockade — **blockade-running** \(ˈ)ˌ=ˌ=ˌ==\ *n*

block·ad·ing \(ˈ)=¦diŋ\ *n* -S *South & Midland* : the distilling of moonshine

block·age \ˈbläkij, -ēj\ *n* -S [2*block* + *-age*] : an act or instance of obstructing : the state of being blocked: as **a** : BLOCKADE 1a, 2c **b** : 1BLOCKING 4 **c** : internal resistance of an individual to understanding a communicated idea, to learning new material, or to adopting a new mode of response because of existing habitual ways of thinking, perceiving, and acting — compare BLOCKING 3

block and block *adj* : CHOCKABLOCK

block and tackle *also* **block and fall** *or* **block and falls** *n* : pulley blocks with associated rope or cable for hoisting or hauling : TACKLE

block anesthesia *n* : anesthesia of an area produced by interruption of the flow of impulses along a nerve trunk (as by the injection of an anesthetic near it) — compare REGIONAL ANESTHESIA

block ball *n* : a batted or thrown baseball interfered with when in play by a person not a player

blockboard \ˈ=ˌ=\ *n* : a plywood board in which veneer layers used in the core are replaced by blocks of wood, the direction of grain of the blocks running at right angles to that of the adjacent veneer

block bond *n* **1** : FLEMISH BOND **2** : ENGLISH BOND

block book *n* : a book in which the entire text and illustrations are block printed

block booking *n* : the licensing for exhibition of motion-picture films in a block or group, the licensee being compelled to take an entire group of films or none

block brake *n* : a friction brake consisting of one or more shoes (as wooden blocks) to be pressed against a wheel or other moving part

blockbuster \ˈ=ˌ==\ *n* [1*block* (space in a city) + *buster*, fr. *bust*, v. + *-er*] **1** : a huge high-explosive demolition bomb usu. several tons in weight designed to be dropped from an airplane **2** : something or someone notably outstanding, effective, or violent ⟨they predict the new show will be a ~⟩ ⟨his speech was a real ~⟩

block-busting \ˈ=ˌ==\ *adj* : suggesting the action of a blockbuster esp. in vigor or effectiveness

block capital *n* : a square bold capital letter without serifs — compare BLOCK LETTER

block-caving \ˈ=ˌ==\ *n* -S : a mining in which sections of a large ore body are undercut by working places and then permitted to cave in, the ore so crushed being recovered through drifts

block chain *n* : a drive chain (as on a bicycle) made up of alternate transverse blocks or cylinders and side links held together by pins, the blocks engaging the driving-wheel teeth and the pins and side links giving flexibility

block chain

block chords *n pl* : a succession of musical chords produced by the component voices or parts moving in the same rhythm

block coal *n* : very coarse lump coal

block coefficient *n* : the ratio of the volume of the displacement of a ship to that of a rectangular block having the same length, breadth, and draft

block dance *n* : a public dance commonly featuring folk and other specialty dancing that is held outdoors (as in a street temporarily closed to traffic) — compare BLOCK PARTY

block diagram *n* **1** : a perspective diagram of a three-dimensional object used orig. for physiographic illustration of parts of the earth's surface but later adapted to other uses (as demonstration of the relation of cells in tissue) **2** : a drawing in which labeled squares, rectangles, and other arbitrary figures represent the relative position and function of the parts of an apparatus ⟨a *block diagram* of a radio receiving set⟩

block dissection *n* : the operation of dissecting out and removing all the lymph nodes that provide lymphatic drainage for a cancerous area in an effort to prevent lymphatic spread of cancer cells

block down *vt* : to force (sheet metal) into a die esp. by covering with a thick blanket of lead and then hammering

blocked *adj* **1** : OUTLINED; *also* : shaped, supported, or stamped with or as if with a block ⟨finely ~ linens⟩ **2** : closed by or as if by a block or blocks : OBSTRUCTED, OCCLUDED **3** *of money or other assets* **a** : not available for international circulation esp. by reason of the action of a monetary bloc ⟨~ accounts limit the free exchange of goods between nations⟩ **b** : not available to the owner by reason of government action ⟨the ~ assets of enemy nationals are administered by a special office⟩

blocked ball *n* : BLOCK BALL

block·er \ˈbläkə(r)\ *n* -S : one that blocks: as **a** : a tool or device used in blocking or blocking out something; *esp* : a forging die used for giving a forging approximately its final shape — compare BREAKDOWN 5, FULLER **b** : a worker who blocks something or whose work is done on or with blocks: as (1) : one that blocks clothing (as hats or knitted garments) (2) : one that operates the blocks in wiredrawing (3) : 2BRACER 1c **c** : a football player who engages in or is esp. proficient in blocking **d** : BLOCKING ANTIBODY **e** : CASER 2 **f** : one who blocks out with water colors the imperfections or unwanted parts of negatives to be used in photoengraving

block faulting *n* : geological faulting that produces blocks

block figure *n* : a sculpture in which natural form is expressed as a composition of geometric solids

block·flö·te \ˈbläk,flœd·ə, -flərd·ə\ *n, pl* **blockflö·tes** \-d·əz\ *or* **blockflö·ten** \-d·ən\ *usu cap* [G, fr. *block* block of wood (fr. LG, fr. MLG) + *flöte* flute, fr. MHG *vloite, flöute*, fr. MD *flūte, fleute, floite*, fr. OF *flaüte, fleute*; akin to OHG *bloh* block — more at BLOCK, FLUTE] **1** : RECORDER 3a **2** : a flute organ stop of 16-, 8-, 4-, or 2-ft. pitch tonally similar to the recorder

block foot *n* : a furniture foot in the shape of a cube generally used with a square untapered leg — see FOOT illustration

blockfront \ˈ=ˌ=\ *n* **1** : a front (as of a chest of drawers or a desk) characterized by a sunken center panel flanked on either side by a raised panel **2** : the frontage of a block : one side (as the main side) of a block with a portion of land abutting esp. when considered as the site of a single building ⟨the structure is going on the north ~ of the street⟩

block grant *n* : a fixed grant of money made by the British parliament to local governing authorities

blockhead \ˈ=ˌ=\ *n* **1** *obs* **a** : a wooden head serving as a block for hats or wigs **b** : a head dull and wanting in intelligence **2** : a dull and stupid person : one deficient in understanding or intellect

blockhead board *n* : a device that consists of a pair of conspicuously numbered boards one of which rises while the other falls and that is used as a detector on a jacquard loom to show if the cards are working correctly

blockheaded \ˈ=¦==\ *adj* : STUPID, DULL, UNINTELLIGENT — **block·head·ed·ly** *adv* — **block·head·ed·ness** *n* -ES

block·head·ism \ˈ=ˌ=ˌizəm\ *n* -S : the stupidity of or that might be expected of a blockhead

1blockhole \ˈ=ˌ=\ *n* : a light indentation in the ground just behind the popping crease and in front of the wicket made by a batsman in cricket with the end of his bat to mark the position of his guard

2blockhole \"\ *vt* : to shatter (a boulder) by drilling a hole and exploding dynamite in it — **block·hol·er** \ˈ=ˌ=ə(r)\ *n*

blockhouse \ˈ=ˌ=\ *n* [1*block* (impediment) + *house*] **1** *obs* : a detached fort blocking or covering access (as to a landing, bridge, or pass) **2 a** : a structure of heavy timbers or logs formerly used for military defense having its sides loopholed and pierced for gunfire and often an upper story projecting over the lower or so placed upon it as to have its sides make an angle with the sides of the lower story, thus enabling the defenders to fire downward and in all directions **b** : a small defensible wood, iron, or concrete building usu. partially dug in that gives protection from enemy fire and provides a firing base for defense **3** : a house of squared logs **4** : a building usu. more or less hemispherical and formed of reinforced concrete as a shelter against and observation point of certain dangerous operations likely to be accompanied by heat, blast, or radiation hazard

blockhouse 2a

blockier *comparative of* BLOCKY

blockiest *superlative of* BLOCKY

block·i·ly \-kəlē\ *adv* [*blocky* + *-ly*] : in a blocky manner

block-in-course \ˈ=ˌ=ˌ=\ *n* : squared stone masonry with good close joints to give great strength and soundness

block-in-course bond *n* : a bond used in brick arches in which the arch is divided into sections similar in shape to the voussoirs of stone arches with the brick in each section laid with any desired bond but with the radial joints between sections continuous from intrados to extrados

blocking *n* -S **1** : the act of one that blocks: as **a** : the act of obstructing, supporting, shaping, or stamping with or as if with a block or blocks **b** : the act or process of signaling by the block system **2 a** : blocks in quantity ⟨stack the ~ to one side⟩ **b** : a wooden block, jack, or other device used as a temporary support esp. in structural and machine erecting operations and in shipping; *broadly* : material used to secure or brace something (as freight in a car) **3** *psychol* : interruption of a trend of associative thought by the arousal of a countertrend or through the welling up into consciousness of a complex of unpleasant ideas — compare BLOCKAGE c **4** : adhesion between sheets of paper in a pile or in a roll in storage or use that can result in damage or loss — compare 2BLOCK *vi* 2 **5** : an atmospheric process that is often produced by a deep well-developed anticyclone and that deflects strong westerlies and eastward-moving storms from their usual paths

blocking antibody *n* : an antibody that combines with an antigen without producing visible reaction but preventing another antibody from later combining with or producing its usual effect on that antigen — called also *incomplete antibody, univalent antibody*

blocking course *n* : the finishing course of a wall showing above a cornice usu. serving as a solid parapet and forming a small architectural attic

blocking layer *n* : BARRIER LAYER

blocking patent *n* : FENCING PATENT

blocking press *n Brit* : a press for stamping titles and designs on book covers

block interlocking system *n* : BLOCK SYSTEM 2

block·ish \-kish, -kēsh\ *adj* [1*block* + *-ish*] : like a block : lacking in intellect and understanding : STUPID, DOLTISH — **block·ish·ly** *adv*

block lava *n* : AA

block letter *n* : a letter of the alphabet written or printed in sans serif; *also* : sans-serif type or lettering

blocklike \ˈ=ˌ=\ *adj* : like a block

block·man \ˈ=mən, -ˌman, -ˌmaa(ə)n\ *n, pl* **blockmen 1** : a workman who makes blocks (as of stone) or works with or at a block **2** : a manufacturer's representative acting as a district agent and intermediary between the company and its local agents in an assigned block of territory — used esp. in the field of agricultural supplies and equipment

block mold *n* **1** : the original mold for a pottery form made directly from the model and used only for making working molds **2** : a one-piece unjointed mold for pressed glassware (as tumblers, saucers, or bowls)

block mountain *n* : a mountain caused by faulting and uplifting or tilting — compare BASIN RANGE

block operator *n* : a railroad worker who operates block signals manually

block out *vt* **1** : to shut from view : SCREEN ⟨that vine on the porch *blocks out* all the sunlight⟩: **a** : to prevent (a part of a photographic negative) from printing by painting over with opaque or a comparable substance **b** : to cancel (printed matter) by overprinting with a solid patch of ink **2 a** : to excavate (as ore and gravel) by making a drive in the wall and taking out the material in blocks or strips along the sides of the drive **b** : to subdivide (a lode) into blocks in advance of the working stopes by shafts, winzes, and intersecting drives or levels so as to be ready for stoping and to keep a known amount of reserve ore in sight

blockout \ˈ=ˌ=\ *n* -S [*block out*] : a reproduction (as a photographic negative or a halftone) of which a part has been blocked out

block paper *n* : paper printed with a pattern usu. in color from blocks (as of wood or linoleum) and used esp. as wallpaper or for endpapers or box covers

block paragraph *n* : a paragraph (as in a news story) written as an independent unit to allow its deletion or rearrangement in the order of paragraphs without loss of coherence

block party *n* : a public party held in the open air (as in a stretch of street temporarily barred to traffic) commonly under the auspices of a public figure or organization — compare BLOCK DANCE

block plan *n* : an outline sketch : a plan in which only broad general features are indicated

block plane *n* : a small plane having the iron set at a lower pitch than other planes and used chiefly on end grains of wood — see PLANE illustration

1block print *vt* **1 a** : to print (as books) from hand-cut wooden blocks — used chiefly of printers' practice before the general adoption of movable types **b** : to print from blocks ⟨a linen scarf *block printed* in black⟩ **2** : to write in block letters ⟨it may be easier to *block print* the lessons at first⟩

2block print *n* **1** : a large founding core print the impression of which receives a core that also replaces a part of the mold **2** : a print produced by block printing

blockprinter \ˈ=ˌ==\ *n* : one that block prints; *esp* : a designer and user of blocks for decorative printing (as of textiles)

block programming *n* : the arrangement of programs on radio or television so that several items of one general class (as soap operas or popular music) occur in sequence

block rate *n* **1** : a certain price charged for the first definite number of units (as of electricity) used : a successively lower price for each additional block used **2** : GROUP RATE

blocks *pl of* BLOCK, *pres 3d sing of* BLOCK

block salt *n* : salt often with accompanying trace elements or medicaments that is pressed into blocks for salting livestock

block-saw \ˈ=ˌ=\ *vt* : to slab (a log) on four sides so as to form a block

block·ship \ˈ=ˌ=\ *n* [1*block* (impediment) + *ship*] : a ship intended to be sunk in a channel or fairway to block its use

block shot *n* : HALF VOLLEY

block signal *also* **block signal system** *n* : a fixed signal at the entrance of a block to govern railroad trains entering and using that block — compare BLOCK SYSTEM 2

blocks·man \ˈbläksmən\ *n, pl* **blocksmen** : a worker who shapes highway curbs or lays paving blocks

block station *n* : a place at which railroad manual block signals are displayed

block sugar *n* : CUBE SUGAR

block system *n* **1** : a system of mountain ranges composed of tilted or uplifted fault blocks — compare BASIN RANGE **2** : a system by which a railroad track is divided into short sections (as of three or four miles) and trains are so run by the guidance of electric or combined electric and pneumatic signals that (1) no train enters a section or block until the preceding train has left it or that (2) a train may be allowed to follow another into a block as long as it proceeds with extreme caution — called also respectively (1) *absolute blocking*, (2) *permissive blocking* **3** : a method of betting in draw poker comprising a 19-chip ante by the dealer, a 2-chip blind, and a 4-chip straddle

block teeth *n pl* : two or more artificial teeth in one piece

block test *n* : a test of an internal-combustion engine in which it is mounted on a block and checked as to workmanship and performance

block tin *n* : commercial tin cast into blocks and partly refined but containing small quantities of various impurities (as copper, lead, iron, or arsenic) : solid tin as distinguished from tin plate

block-universe \ˈ=¦=ˌ==\ *n* : the universe conceived as resembling a block in being a closed system, monistic and without any real novelty, plurality, and individuality

block vote *n* : a method of voting (as at a convention) by which each delegate's vote has a value proportional to his representation; *also* : such a vote

blockwood \ˈ=ˌ=\ *n* : LOGWOOD 1a

block worker *n* : a person who actively campaigns on the most local level (as a city block) as one of the organized workers of a political party or pressure group

blocky \-kē, -ki\ *adj* -ER/-EST **1 a** : like a block in form or massiveness ⟨the hood lines of these car models are high and ~⟩ **b** *of a body or its parts* : heavily or sturdily built : somewhat square or boxy : CHUNKY ⟨a fine ~ steer⟩ ⟨a ~ tireless man⟩ ⟨a terrier with a ~ head⟩ **2** : filled with or made up of blocks or blocklike parts ⟨a ~ soil aggregate⟩; *often* : full of or marked with patches esp. of light and shadow : DAPPLED

bloe·dite \ˈblō,dīt\ *also* **blö·dite** \", ˈblər,d-, ˈblœ,d-\ *or* **blo·dite** \ˈblō,d-\ *n* -S [G *blödit*, fr. Carl A. *Bloede* †1820 Ger. chemist + G *-it* -ite] : a mineral $Na_2Mg(SO_4)_2.4H_2O$ consisting of a hydrous sodium magnesium sulfate that is colorless or white when pure and occurs in monoclinic crystals or massive

bloed·pens \ˈblüt,pen(t)s\ *n pl but sing or pl in constr* [Afrik, fr. *bloed* blood (fr. MD *bloet*) + *pens* belly, paunch, fr. MD *pense, panse*, fr. OF *pance*; akin to OE *blōd* blood — more at BLOOD, PAUNCH] *Africa* : enterotoxemia of lambs

bloem·fon·tein \¦blümfȯn¦tān\ *adj, usu cap* [fr. *Bloemfontein*, Union of So. Africa] : of or from the city of Bloemfontein, Union of So. Africa : of the kind or style prevalent in Bloemfontein

bloke *or* **bloak** \ˈblōk\ *n* -S [origin unknown] *chiefly Brit* : MAN, CHAP, FELLOW — used informally and commonly implying mild disrespect when applied to a superior and slight or affected deprecation when used of oneself ⟨the admiral was a jolly old ~ but no administrator⟩ ⟨I'm a peaceful sort of a ~ if folks let me alone⟩

blol·ly \ˈblälē\ *n* -ES [short for *loblolly*] **1** : a shrub or small tree (*Torrubia longifolia*) of southern Florida and the West Indies with smooth oval leaves and bright red fruit **2** : a low shrub (*Chiococca alba*) of southern Florida and the West Indies with yellow flowers and white fruit

blom·strand·ine \ˈblämstrən,dēn, -ˌdən\ *n* -S [C.W.*Blomstrand* †1897 Swedish chemist + E *-ine*] : PRIORITE

1blond *also* **blonde** \ˈbländ\ *adj, sometimes* -ER/-EST [F *blond* (masc.), *blonde* (fem.), prob. of Gmc origin; akin to OE *blondenfeax, blandenfeax* gray-haired, old, fr. *blondan, blandan* to mix — more at BLEND] **1 a** *of human hair* : flaxen, golden, light auburn, or pale yellowish brown **b** *of human skin* : pale white or rosy white **c** *of persons* : having blond hair and skin and usu. blue or gray eyes **d** *of peoples* : consisting of blond individuals ⟨a ~ tribe from the northern hills⟩ **2 a** : light-colored ⟨~ long-furred pelts will be preferred this year⟩ **b** : of the color blond **c** *of wood and wood products* : rendered light-colored by bleaching ⟨a table of ~ oak⟩ — **blond·ness** *also* **blonde·ness** \-n(d)nəs\ *n* -ES

2blond *or* **blonde** \"\ *n* -S **1** [F *blonde*, fr. *blonde*, adj.] *usu* **blonde lace** *also* **blond lace** : a silk bobbin lace orig. unbleached and now bleached white or dyed black made with a mesh ground of fine thread and floral patterns of a soft heavy thread **2** : a blond person : a person with fair complexion and light hair and eyes; *sometimes* : a person of noticeably lighter coloring than that typical of the population to which he belongs **3** : a light yellowish brown to dark grayish yellow

blond beast *n, sometimes cap both Bs* : the blond type of primitive man of northern Europe often regarded (as by Nietzsche) as a splendid animal, a superior or ideal physical type, or a predatory creature; *broadly* : anyone who acts in a predatory manner

blonde *or* **blonde ray** *n* -S : a large sluggish ray (*Raja blanda*) of the French and English coasts that is sometimes used as food

1blondine \(ˈ)blän¦dēn\ *n* -S [F, fr. *blond* + *-ine*] **1** : a bleach for the hair; *also* : a person with bleached hair **2 a** : BLOND 3 **b** : WOODBARK

2blondine \"\ *vt* -ED/-ING/-S : to bleach (hair) to a blond color

blondined *adj* **1** *of hair* : BLEACHED **2** *of a person* : having bleached hair

blond·i·nette \¦bländə¦net\ *n* [F, young blond girl, dim. of *blondine*] **1** *usu cap* : a breed of small plump show pigeons that are bred in several colors usu. with the plumage more or less laced with white and with the feathers somewhat frilled **2** -S *sometimes cap* : a bird of the Blondinette breed

blond·ish \ˈbländish, -dēsh\ *adj* : somewhat blond : nearer blond than brunet; *esp* : rather light in color ⟨a . . . chemical can turn ~ pine to the flaming red of cherry —*Geog. School Bull.*⟩

blond·ism \-,dizəm\ *n* -S : the state of being blond; *specif* : the occurrence of blond traits in a predominantly dark or colored population

1blood \ˈbləd\ *n* -S *see sense 9, often attrib* [ME, fr. OE *blōd*; akin to OHG *bluot* blood, ON *blōth*, Goth *blōth*, and prob. to OE *blōwan* to bloom — more at BLOW] **1 a** : the fluid that circulates in the principal vascular system of vertebrate animals carrying nourishment and oxygen to all parts of the body and bringing away waste products for excretion and that consists of a liquid plasma containing dissolved nutrients, waste products, and other substances and suspended red blood cells, leukocytes, and blood platelets — see CIRCULATION, RESPIRATION; COAGULATION **b :** any fluid of similar function and comparable composition in an invertebrate animal usu. containing a respiratory pigment dissolved in the plasma and one or more kinds of cells often amoeboid **c :** any fluid suggestive of or likened to vertebrate blood esp. in color or in vital quality (as the juice of the grape or the sap of a plant) **2 a :** blood regarded as a vital principle **:** LIFEBLOOD; *broadly* **:** LIFE **b :** human blood regarded as a hereditary differentiating factor typical of and specific to a given family, stock, lineage, or race ⟨English ~⟩; *esp* **:** the national blood royal — used with *the* ⟨a prince of the ~⟩ **c :** the whole body of physical traits passed from parent to offspring whether in man, animals, or plants **d :** relationship by descent from a common ancestor ⟨the Delaware grape shows a strong strain of vinifera ~⟩ **:** KINSHIP, CONSANGUINITY ⟨~ is thicker than water⟩ **e :** persons related through a common familial or racial descent **:** KINDRED, LINEAGE, STOCK, RACE; *also, obs* **:** KINSMAN, RELATIVE **f :** honorable birth or descent; *often* **:** aristocratic or high birth or lineage ⟨a gentleman of ~ and breeding —Shak.⟩ **g** *of animals or plants* **:** descent from parents of recognized breed or pedigree; *specif, of horses* **:** descent from Thoroughbred ancestors — see HALF BLOOD **3 a :** blood shed in the taking of life esp. in sacrifice; *specif* **:** the blood shed in the atonement offered by Christ ⟨the ~ of the Lamb⟩ **b** *cap* **:** the wine or its equivalent in the sacrament of the Lord's Supper, held by some to be and by others to represent the blood of Jesus Christ **4 a :** the shedding of blood; *also* **:** the taking of life **:** MURDER, MANSLAUGHTER ⟨~ ever demands revenge⟩ **b :** murderous habit or deed ⟨a man of ~⟩ **c** *archaic* **:** BLOODGUILT ⟨His ~ be on us and on our children —Mt 27:25 (RSV)⟩ **5 a :** blood regarded as the seat of the emotions **:** TEMPER, PASSION ⟨when you perceive his ~ inclined to mirth —Shak.⟩ ⟨he was no mean adversary when his ~ was up⟩ — compare HUMOR, SANGUINE; see BAD BLOOD, COLD BLOOD **b** *obs* **:** bodily passion **:** animal appetite **:** LUST **c :** a gay showy foppish man **:** one unduly preoccupied with the trivia of fashionable life and lacking restraint or regard for proprieties **:** BUCK, DANDY, RAKE **6 :** PERSONNEL — used regularly with a qualifying term implying new and additional ⟨we need young ~ in this office⟩ ⟨give me enough new ~ and we'll get everything straightened out⟩ **7 :** a measure of the fineness of wool fiber based on Merino wool as full blood with others in decreasing order of fineness (as three-quarter blood, half blood, quarter blood) — now used without any implication as to the breeding of the sheep producing the wool **8** *Brit* **:** a lurid work of fiction: *esp* **:** a cheap and ill-written book of adventure or crime **9** *or pl* **blood** *usu cap* **a :** a people that comprise a division of the Blackfeet **b :** a member of such people — **in blood** *obs, of an animal* **:** full of life **:** abounding in vigor — **in one's blood :** acting as a fundamental factor or guiding principle in one's life — used esp. of something that may be construed as having such influence because of family or ancestral association ⟨religion is *in his blood;* both his father and his uncles are ministers⟩ — **out of blood** *obs, of an animal* **:** lacking in vigor **:** spiritless and sluggish

²blood \ˈ"\ *vt* -ED/-ING/-S **1** *archaic* **:** to let the blood of **:** BLEED **2 :** to stain, smear, or wet with blood **:** BLOODY; *esp* **:** to mark the face of (an inexperienced fox hunter) with blood of the prey when a hunt is successful **3 a :** to familiarize (a hunting dog) with its intended prey by exposing it to sight, scent, or taste of the blood of this prey **b :** to give (soldiers) experience in battle; *broadly* **:** to give (a novice) experience in any field **c :** to use (a new weapon) in conflict **4 :** to heat the blood of **:** EXASPERATE

blood albumin *n* **1 :** SERUM ALBUMIN **2 :** soluble dried blood
blood-al·bu·min glue \ˈ⸗⸗¦⸗⸗-\ *n* **:** BLOOD GLUE
blood alley *n* **:** an alley used in the game of marbles that is spotted or streaked with red
bloodalp \ˈ⸗,⸗\ *n* -S [*blood* + *alp* (bullfinch)] *dial Eng* **:** a male bullfinch
blood-and-feather-dressed \¦⸗⸗¦⸗⸗,⸗\ *adj* **:** NEW YORK DRESSED
blood-and-guts \¦⸗⸗¦⸗\ *adj* **:** marked by vigor and attention to fundamentals **:** INTENSIVE ⟨few people ever get down to real *blood-and-guts* self-criticism⟩
blood and iron *n* [trans. of G *blut und eisen*] **:** reliance on and use of force; *esp* **:** the use of military power rather than normal diplomatic means
blood and thunder *n* **:** violence and uproar such as characterizes melodrama ⟨novels full of *blood and thunder*⟩
blood bank *n* **:** a place for storage of or an institution storing blood or plasma; *also* **:** blood so stored
bloodbath \ˈ⸗,⸗\ *n* **:** a great slaughter **:** MASSACRE — compare PURGE
blood bay *n* **:** a dark reddish bay color; *often* **:** a horse of this color
bloodberry \ˈ⸗- — *see* BERRY\ *n* **:** a tropical American herb (*Rivina humilis*) with racemes of red berries resembling those of pokeweed
bloodbird \ˈ⸗,⸗\ *n* **:** an Australian honey eater (*Myzomela sanguinolenta*) having the head, neck, breast, and back bright scarlet, the wings and tail black, and the under parts buff
blood blister *n* **:** a blister containing blood or bloody serum usu. caused by an injury
blood bond *n* **:** the familial bond of common descent or of a similarly close relationship established by adoption or other ceremony
blood brother *n* **1 :** a brother by birth **2 :** one that is bound by a blood bond by virtue of a ceremony (as of the mingling of blood) **3 :** something viewed as basically related to some other often apparently incongruous item ⟨the social idealist is declared to be *blood brother* to the snake-oil practitioner —M.B.Smith⟩ ⟨soldiering and drinking have always been *blood brothers* —James Jones⟩
blood brotherhood *n* **:** a solemn friendship established between usu. unrelated men by a ceremonial use of each other's blood
blood cancer *n* **:** LEUKEMIA
blood cell *n* **:** any cell present in blood (as a leukocyte) **:** HEMOCYTE
blood clam *n* **:** a clam of a genus (*Arca*) of widely distributed red-blooded clams with a thick equivalve shell, pointed foot, and numerous marginal compound eyes on the mantle
blood corpuscle *n* **:** BLOOD CELL
blood count *n* **1 :** the determination of the blood cells in a definite volume of blood by partial enumeration and extrapolation — compare RED COUNT, WHITE COUNT; DIFFERENTIAL BLOOD COUNT **2 :** the number of blood cells in a definite volume of the blood of an individual as determined by a blood count, a figure that varies with sex, physiologic state, and health but in normal man approximates 5,000,000 red cells and 7000 white cells per cubic millimeter, the latter divided among 55 percent or more neutrophils, about 30 percent lymphocytes, and small percentages of eosinophils, monocytes, and basophils
blood crisis *n* **:** a sudden appearance of large numbers of nucleated red blood cells in the circulation presumably due to stimulation of the erythropoietic tissues
blood crystal *n* **:** one of the crystals obtained by heating a hemoglobin solution with acetic acid containing a little common salt, the form of the crystal differing according to the animal from which the hemoglobin was obtained
blood cup *n* **1 :** a cup-shaped ascomycetous fungus of a widely distributed genus (*Peziza*); *esp* **:** a scarlet European fungus (*P. coccinea*) **2 :** a heavy elongated metal vessel attached to the jaw of a table bird to catch the blood during dressing
bloodcurdler \ ⸗,⸗(⸗)⸗\ *n* -S **:** one that is bloodcurdling; *specif* **:** a lurid melodramatic theatrical or literary production
bloodcurdling \ˈ⸗,⸗(⸗)⸗\ *adj* **:** such as might be expected to congeal the blood through fear or horror ⟨a ~ scream⟩ ⟨recovering slowly from the shock of that ~ experience⟩
blood disease *n* **:** an important vascular disease of the banana in the Celebes probably caused by a bacterium (*Xanthomonas celebensis*) and characterized by blighting of the leaves and reddish brown rot of the fruits
blood disk *n* **:** a mammalian red blood cell
blood donor *n* **:** a person who gives blood for use in transfusion
blooddrop \ˈ⸗,⸗\ *n* **:** a terebellid bloodworm
blooddrops \ˈ⸗,⸗\ *n pl but sing or pl in constr* [so called fr. its bright red flowers] **:** WIND POPPY
blood dust *n* **:** HEMOCONIA
blood dyscrasia *n* **:** an abnormal condition or disease of the blood
blooded *adj* [ME *bloded*, fr. ¹*blood* + *-ed*] **1 :** entirely or largely of pure blood ⟨~Jerseys⟩ **:** of the best stock ⟨good ~ animals⟩ **2 :** having blood of a specified kind — used in combination ⟨low-*blooded*⟩ ⟨warm-*blooded*⟩
blood feud *n* **:** a feud between the members of different clans or families arising out of a crime of violence (as a killing) committed by a member of one upon a member of the other and requiring a continuing series of alternative retaliations in kind — called also *vendetta;* compare BLOOD MONEY, WERGILD
bloodfin \ˈ⸗,⸗\ *n* **:** a small So. American characin (*Aphyocharax rubripinnis*) with silvery body and deep-red fins often kept in the tropical aquarium
blood fine *n* **:** a fine for shedding blood **:** BLOODWITE, WERGILD
blood flour *n* **:** finely ground blood meal
bloodflower \ˈ⸗,⸗⸗\ *n* **1 :** a tropical herb (*Asclepias curassavica*) with orange-red flowers **2 :** BLOOD LILY
blood fluke *n* **:** SCHISTOSOME
blood gill *n* **:** one of the thin-walled fimbriated blood-filled evaginations more or less completely free from tracheae that are characteristic of certain chiefly aquatic insects and may be concerned with respiratory or osmotic activity
blood gland *n* **:** ENDOCRINE GLAND
blood glue *n* **:** an adhesive made chiefly from blood, esp. soluble dried blood, and used because of its water resistance in making plywood
blood groove *n* **:** a longitudinal groove on the shaft of an arrow or spear or on the blade of a bayonet or knife said to have been introduced to cause increased bleeding of a wound produced and possibly actually facilitating withdrawal of bayonet or knife by preventing suction
blood group *n* **1 :** a group of persons related by a blood bond **2 :** one of the classes into which human beings can be separated on the basis of their possession or nonpossession of certain antigens, the classical ABO antigens subdividing human blood into four groups: O, A, B, and AB — compare ISOANTIBODY, RH FACTOR
blood grouping *n* **:** the act of determining to what blood group a sample of blood belongs
bloodguilt \ˈ⸗,⸗\ *also* **bloodguiltiness** \ˈ⸗,⸗⸗⸗\ *n* **:** guilt resulting from the shedding of blood; *esp, anthrop* **:** a formal state of guilt produced by killing human beings (as in war) and subject to removal by suitable ritual acts
bloodguilty \ˈ⸗,⸗⸗\ *adj* **:** guilty of murder or bloodshed; *esp* **:** affected with bloodguilt
blood heat *n* **:** a temperature approximating that of the human body and being usu. taken as about 98° Fahrenheit — used esp. of fluids the temperature of which is estimated by dropping a portion on the skin and noting the sensation of relative warmth or chill ⟨heat the baby's bottle to *blood heat*⟩
blood horse *n* **1 :** THOROUGHBRED **2 :** any purebred horse
¹bloodhound \ˈ⸗,⸗\ *n* [ME *bloodhound, bloodhund,* fr. *blood* + *hound, hund* hound] **1 a :** a large powerful hound of a breed (Bloodhound) originated in European monasteries but largely developed in England, distinguished by long smooth pendulous ears, long head, and wrinkled face and by remarkable acuteness of smell, and used formerly in tracking game but now almost entirely in tracking criminals or lost persons **b :** any hound hunting by scent and used for tracking humans **2 :** a person keen or relentless in pursuit

bloodhound

²bloodhound \ˈ"\ *vt* **:** to pursue (as an aim) relentlessly or keenly
bloodied *past of* BLOODY
bloodier *comparative of* BLOODY
bloodies *pres 3d sing of* BLOODY
bloodiest *superlative of* BLOODY
blood·i·ly \ˈblədᵊlē, -dəlē, -li\ *adv* **:** in a bloody manner
blood·i·ness \-dēnəs, -din-\ *n* -ES **:** the quality or state of being bloody
blooding *pres part of* BLOOD
blood island *also* **blood islet** *n* **:** any of the reddish areas in the extraembryonic mesoblast of developing vertebrate eggs where blood cells and vessels are forming
blood kin *n* **:** RELATIVES **:** those that are kin by reason of common ancestry; *also* **:** a group united by blood bond
blood knot *n* **1 :** a multiple overhand knot esp. when tied in a cat-o'-nine-tails **2** *Brit* **:** BARREL KNOT a
bloodleaf \ˈ⸗,⸗\ *n* **:** any of several plants of the family Amaranthaceae having colored foliage; *esp* **:** a member of either of two genera (*Iresine* and *Aerva*) including several that are used as ornamental and bedding plants
blood·less \ˈbləd·ləs\ *adj* [ME *blodles,* fr. OE *blōdlēas,* fr. *blōd* blood + *-lēas* -less — more at BLOOD] **1 a :** lacking or apparently lacking blood **:** free from blood ⟨the meat must be made completely ~⟩ ⟨a ~ surgical field⟩; *often* **:** PALE, PALLID, BLANCHED ⟨a wan and ~ countenance⟩ **b :** LIFELESS ⟨the ~ carcass of my Hector sold —John Dryden⟩ **2 :** not accompanied by bloodshed or slaughter ⟨a ~ victory⟩ ⟨a ~ revolution⟩ **3 :** lacking in spirit or vitality ⟨a ~ descendant of a noble race⟩; *also* **:** lacking in originality or vigor ⟨the ~ art of the mid-19th century⟩ ⟨make his novels and dramas rather ~ exercises in abstract morality —F.B.Millett⟩ **4 :** lacking in human feeling **:** COLD-HEARTED, UNEMOTIONAL, UNFEELING ⟨a batch of ~ statistics —F.L.Allen⟩ ⟨a curious ~ attempt to examine and pry into the lives of his fellows⟩ — **blood·less·ly** *adv* — **blood·less·ness** *n* -ES
bloodless surgery *n* **1 :** manipulative procedures for the correction of deformities or reduction of fractures or dislocations **2 :** surgery performed with a minimum effusion of blood (as by electrocoagulation or with the patient in a state of hypothermia)
bloodletter \ˈ⸗,⸗⸗\ *n* -S [ME *bloodletere,* fr. OE *blodlǣtere,* fr. *blōd* blood + *-lǣtere* -letter (fr. *lǣtan* to let + *-ere* -er) — more at BLOOD, LET] **:** one that engages in bloodletting: **a :** a practitioner of venesection **b :** a warlike or bloodthirsty person
bloodletting \ˈ⸗,⸗⸗\ *n* -S [ME *bloodleting,* fr. *blood* + *leting,* gerund of *leten* to let — more at LET] **1 a :** VENESECTION **b :** a draining away (as of strength or character) ⟨the intellectual ~ Germany has suffered, owing to the emigration of many of her greatest writers —H.F.Garten⟩ **2 :** BLOODSHED
bloodlike \ˈ⸗,⸗\ *adj* **:** like or like that of a Thoroughbred ⟨a trim horse with small ~ head and well-set ears⟩
blood lily *n* **:** any of various southern African plants (genus *Haemanthus*) of the family Amaryllidaceae; *esp* **:** one of a species (*H. coccineus*) having brilliant red flowers and often cultivated
bloodline \ˈ⸗,⸗\ *n* **1 :** a sequence of direct ancestors esp. in a pedigree regarded as transmitting the distinctive traits or characters of the sequence ⟨there's a sound young bull of proven performance and with the best of ~s behind him⟩ **2 :** a group of individuals linked by ancestry and usu. by distinctive qualities ⟨a ~ outstanding in productivity and finish through several generations⟩ **:** FAMILY, STRAIN
bloodlust \ˈ⸗,⸗\ *n* [*blood* + *lust*] **:** desire for bloodshed
bloodlusting *adj* **:** desiring bloodshed
blood meal *n* **:** the ground dried blood of animals characterized by a high protein content and used for feeding livestock and as a nitrogenous fertilizer
blood·mo·bile \ˈ⸗mō,bēl, -mə,-, -,bil\ *n* -S [*blood* + *-mobile*] **:** an automobile staffed and equipped for the purpose of collecting blood from donors
blood money *n* **1 :** money or other benefit obtained as the price or at the cost of another's life or sometimes of his happiness, good name, or welfare — used esp. of a reward for supporting a capital charge, of money received for betraying a fugitive or for committing murder, or of the price obtained by sale of something that will destroy the purchaser **2 :** money paid by a manslayer or members of his family, clan, or tribe to the next of kin of a person killed by him — compare WERGILD
blood·noun \ˈbləd,naün\ *n* -S [imit.] *South & Midland* **:** BULLFROG
blood orange *n* **:** any of several varieties of the sweet orange with deep-red pulp
blood pheasant *n* **:** any of several pheasants (genus *Ithaginis*) of the mountains of India and China remarkable for the bright red colors of their throat and breast
blood picture *n* **:** the condition and quality of the blood as indicated by a blood count, hemoglobin determination, and various other chemical and physical tests
blood pink *n* **:** a perennial pink (*Dianthus cruentus*) of southern Europe with dense clusters of bloodred flowers
blood plasma *n* **:** the fluid portion of whole blood — compare BLOOD SERUM
blood platelet *n* **:** one of the minute protoplasmic disks occurring in vertebrate blood, playing a role in blood clotting, and believed to originate as bits of cytoplasm pinched off the megakaryocytes
blood poisoning *also* **blood poison** *n* **:** SEPTICEMIA
blood poor *adj* **:** very poor **:** POVERTY-STRICKEN
blood pressure *n* **:** pressure exerted by the blood upon the walls of the blood vessels varying with the muscular efficiency of the heart, the blood volume and viscosity, the age of the individual, and the state of the vascular wall, being usu. measured on the radial artery by means of a sphygmomanometer and expressed in millimeters of mercury either as a fraction having as numerator the maximum pressure that follows systole of the left ventricle of the heart and as denominator the minimum pressure that accompanies cardiac diastole ⟨a *blood pressure* of $\frac{120}{80}$⟩ or as a whole number representing the first value only ⟨a *blood pressure* of 120⟩, tending to increase normally with age and excessively with certain vascular kidney and endocrine disorders and decreasing in hemorrhage, hypothyroidism, and various debilitating diseases — compare DIASTOLIC PRESSURE, PULSE PRESSURE, SYSTOLIC PRESSURE; HYPERTENSION, HYPOTENSION; ARTERIOSCLEROSIS
blood price *n* **:** BLOOD MONEY 2
bloodproof paper \ˈ⸗,⸗-\ *n* **:** BUTCHER PAPER
blood pudding *n* **:** BLOOD SAUSAGE
blood purge *n* **:** the elimination en masse by massacre or execution of individuals considered to constitute an untrustworthy or undesirable element within a party or movement
blood rain *n* **:** rain colored red by blood dust from the air
bloodred \ˈ⸗¦⸗\ *adj* [ME, fr. OE *blōdrēad,* fr. *blōd* blood + *rēad* red — more at BLOOD, RED] **:** having the color of blood **:** bright red ⟨~ tomatoes⟩
blood red *n* **:** a moderate to strong red that is yellower and darker than camellia — called also *cadmium vermilion, para red, Parma red, perma red, permanent red, scarlet lake*
blood-relationship \ˈ⸗⸗¦⸗⸗,⸗\ *n* **:** CONSANGUINITY
blood revenge *n* **:** BLOOD VENGEANCE
bloodroot \ˈ⸗,⸗\ *n* **1 :** a scapose woods plant (*Sanguinaria canadensis*) having a red root and red sap, bearing a solitary lobed leaf and white flower in early spring, and having acrid emetic properties and a rootstock that is used as a stimulant expectorant — called also *bloodwort, Indian paint, puccoon, redroot, tetterwort, turmeric* **2** *Brit* **:** TORMENTIL
blood royal *n* **:** royal family; *specif* **:** those members of the royal family by birth ⟨a prince of the *blood royal*⟩
bloods *pl of* BLOOD, *pres 3d sing of* BLOOD
blood sacrifice *n* **:** a religious rite involving bloodshed
blood sausage *n* **:** sausage containing a large proportion of blood so that it is very dark in color
blood scours *n pl but sing or pl in constr, Austral & New Zeal* **:** a bloody diarrhea of calves prob. due to intestinal infection following malnutrition and lowered resistance
blood serum *n* **:** blood plasma from which the fibrin has been removed (as by clotting or defibrinating)
bloodshed \ˈ⸗,⸗\ *n* -S [ME, fr. *blood* + *-shed* (fr. *sheden* to shed) — more at SHED] **1 :** the shedding or spilling of blood **:** act of shedding human blood **2 :** the taking of life (as in war or murder) **:** SLAUGHTER, CARNAGE
bloodshedder \ˈ⸗,⸗⸗\ *n* **:** one that sheds blood **:** MURDERER
bloodshedding \ˈ⸗,⸗⸗\ *n* [ME *bloodsheding,* fr. *blood* + *sheding,* gerund of *sheden* to shed] **:** BLOODSHED
blood-shot \ˈ⸗,⸗\ *adj* [alter. of earlier *bloodshotten*] **1** *of an eye* **:** red and inflamed **:** suffused with blood or having the vessels turgid with blood (as when the conjunctiva is inflamed or irritated) **2 :** INFLAMING, CHALLENGING, TENSE ⟨another thought came in mad ~ pursuit —Liam O'Flaherty⟩
blood·shot·ten \ˈbləd¦shätᵊn\ *adj* [*blood* + *shotten,* obs. past part. of *shoot*] *now dial* **:** BLOODSHOT
blood spavin *n* **:** distention of the saphenous vein of a horse in the vicinity of the hock causing a soft swelling
bloodspilling \ˈ⸗,⸗⸗\ *n* [*blood* + *spilling*] **:** BLOODSHED
blood sport *n* **:** a sport (as hunting) involving bloodshed
blood spot *n* **:** a clot of blood in a hen's egg due to hemorrhage within the ovarian follicle during the growth of the egg
bloodspotting \ˈ⸗,⸗⸗\ *n* -S **:** the occurrence of blood spots **:** the tendency to produce blood spots, which appears to be inherited in certain strains of fowls
bloodstain \ˈ⸗,⸗\ *n* [*blood* + *stain*] **:** a discoloration caused by blood
bloodstained \ˈ⸗,⸗\ *adj* **:** stained or soiled with blood **:** BLOODY; *esp* **:** BLOODGUILTY
blood-stanch \ˈ⸗,⸗\ *n* -ES **:** HORSEWEED 1
blood star *also* **blood starfish** *n* **:** a small bright red starfish (*Henricia sanguinolenta*) lacking pedicellaria and widely distributed in shallow seas
blood·stock \ˈ⸗,⸗\ *n* **:** horses of Thoroughbred breeding; *esp* **:** such horses when used for or considered in relation to racing
blood·stone \ˈ⸗,⸗\ *n* **1 :** a stone consisting of green chalcedony sprinkled with red spots resembling blood and resulting from oxidizing of the green — called also *heliotrope* **2 :** HEMATITE
bloodstream \ˈ⸗,⸗\ *n* [ME *bloodstrem,* fr. *blood* + *strem* stream — more at STREAM] **1 :** the flowing blood in a circulatory system **2 :** something regarded as comparable to the living bloodstream esp. in pervasive or vital quality ⟨the influence of communism had entered the ~ of national politics in southeast Asia —*N.Y. Times*⟩ ⟨Lancashire might be in thriving health if its ~ of labor had not been so ruthlessly tapped during the war —*Economist*⟩
bloodsucker \ˈ⸗,⸗⸗\ *n* [ME *blood soukere,* fr. *blood* + *soukere* sucker — more at SUCKER] **1 :** an animal that sucks blood; *esp* **:** LEECH **2 :** a person who bleeds another preying upon his money, ideas, or other resources **:** SPONGER, EXTORTIONER; *sometimes* **:** a rapacious and exacting master, landlord, or moneylender **3 a :** any of several Indian lizards (genus *Calotes*) having the throat blotched with red **b :** any of several Australian lizards
bloodsucking \ˈ⸗,⸗⸗\ *adj* **:** that draws blood from the body of another by or as if by sucking ⟨the plague of ~ insects⟩; *broadly* **:** that behaves as a bloodsucker
bloodsucking bat *n* **:** VAMPIRE 3
blood sugar *n* **1 :** the glucose in the blood; *also* **:** the amount or proportion of such sugar, normally from 0.08 to 0.11 percent but much increased in certain diseases, esp. diabetes mellitus **2 :** a determination of the amount of glucose in the blood ⟨some days we may do a dozen *blood sugars,* others not one⟩
blood test *n* **:** a test of the blood (as to determine parentage or ascertain the nature of an infection); *specif* **:** a serologic test for syphilis
blood-test \ˈ⸗,⸗\ *vt* [*blood test*] **:** to make a blood test on ⟨chicks from *blood-tested* stock⟩
bloodthirst \ˈ⸗,⸗\ *n* [*blood* + *thirst*] **:** desire for bloodshed
bloodthirstily \ˈ⸗,⸗⸗⸗\ *adv* **:** in a bloodthirsty manner
bloodthirstiness \ˈ⸗,⸗⸗⸗\ *n* -ES **:** the quality or state of being bloodthirsty
bloodthirsty \ˈ⸗,⸗⸗\ *adj* **1 :** eager for the shedding of blood **:** SANGUINARY; *also* **:** MURDEROUS **2 :** vehement in partisan-

ship or antagonism as though seeking the shedding of blood ⟨the ~ yells of the fans⟩
blood transfusion *n* : TRANSFUSION
blood tree *n* **1** : a small West Indian tree (*Croton draco*) yielding a red kino **2** : an Australian bloodwood (*Eucalyptus corymbosa*)
blood type *n* : BLOOD GROUP
blood–type \'=,=\ *vt* [*blood type*] : to determine the blood group of (an individual)
blood–vascular \'=¦===\ *adj* : of, relating to, or involving blood vessels ⟨the *blood-vascular* system⟩ ⟨a serious *blood-vascular* lesion⟩
blood vengeance *n* : vengeance for bloodshed requiring bloodshed in return — compare BLOOD FEUD
blood vessel *n* : a vessel or canal in an animal in which blood circulates : ARTERY, VEIN, CAPILLARY
blood–warm \'=¦=\ *adj* : as warm as blood in the living body; *specif* : warmed to blood heat
bloodwealth \'=,=\ *n* [*blood* + *wealth*] : an indemnity for murder paid in some African tribes to the family of the victim
bloodweed \'=,=\ *n* **1** : BLOOD LILY **2** : BLOODFLOWER 1 **3** : GREAT RAGWEED
bloodwite *also* **bloodwit** \'=,=\ *n* [ME, fr. OE *blōdwīte*, fr. *blōd* blood + *wīte* punishment — more at WITE] **1** *early English law* **a** (1) : a fine or amercement for the shedding of blood payable to the king, lord, or other superior in compensation for the breach of his peace — compare WERGILD (2) : a penalty for murder **b** (1) : the right to levy such a fine (2) : exemption from payment of such a fine **2** *Scots law* : a broil or riot in which blood is spilled
bloodwood \'=,=\ *n* : any of numerous trees having a red juice or red wood: as **a** *Austral* (1) : any of several eucalypts (as *Eucalyptus corymbosa*) (2) : a tree (*Baloghia lucida*) the sap of which is used as a paint **b** *in tropical America* (1) : LOGWOOD (2) : FALSE LOGWOOD (3) : any of several plants of the genus *Pterocarpus* (4) : a tree of the genus *Vismia* **c** *in the East Indies* : QUEEN'S CRAPE MYRTLE
bloodworm \'=,=\ *n* **1** : any of certain annelid worms that are more or less red in color: **a** : any of several small reddish earthworms used as bait **b** : any of several red-blooded polychaete worms: (1) : a soft-bodied terebellid worm of the genus *Polycirrus* (2) : a common intertidal worm (*Glycera dibranchiata*) common on the east coast of Canada and used for bait **2** : the red aquatic larva of certain midges of the family Tendipedidae **3** : PALISADE WORM
bloodwort \'=,=\ *n* [ME *bloodwurt*, fr. *blood* + *wurt*, *wort* wort — more at WORT] **1** : a plant of the family Haemodoraceae the members of which contain a deep red coloring matter in the roots **2 a** : a European dock (*Rumex sanguineus*) with red-veined leaves **b** : WATER DOCK **3 a** : European elder (*Sambucus ebulus*) **4** : a centaury (*Centaurium umbellatum*) **5** : SALAD BURNET **6** : YARROW **7** : BLOODROOT **8** : HERB ROBERT
bloodwort family *n* : HAEMODORACEAE
[1]**bloody** \'blədē, -di\ *adj* -ER/-EST [ME, fr. OE *blōdig*, fr. *blōd* blood + *-ig*, -y — more at BLOOD] **1 a** : containing or made up of blood ⟨a ~ boil⟩ ⟨a ~ sweat⟩ **b** : of or in the blood ⟨lust is but a ~ fire —Shak.⟩ **2 a** : smeared or stained with blood ⟨your scarf is all ~⟩ **b** : dripping blood : BLEEDING ⟨too many minor arguments were ending in ~ noses⟩ **3 a** : portending or calling for bloodshed ⟨a ~ augury⟩ ⟨I do begin to have ~ thoughts —Shak.⟩ **b** : accompanied by or involving bloodshed, often cruel or needless bloodshed : SANGUINARY ⟨a bitter ~ quarrel⟩; *esp* : marked by great slaughter ⟨a ~ battle was once fought here⟩ **4 a** : given or tending to the shedding of blood : MURDEROUS ⟨there was no escape from this ~ rule⟩ **b** : having a cruel savage disposition : MERCILESS, CRUEL ⟨a foul ~ villain⟩ **5** : suggesting or like blood in color : BLOODRED ⟨maples ~ at the touch of Jack Frost⟩ **6** *Brit* — used as a generalized expression of intensification ⟨a ~ rascal⟩ often losing all force ⟨pass the ~ salt⟩; often considered vulgar
[2]**bloody** \"\ *vt* -ED/-ING/-ES : to make bloody ⟨let me alone or I'll ~ your nose⟩; *esp* : to stain or redden with or as if with blood ⟨autumn already ~*ing* the dwarf shrubs of the plain —Farley Mowat⟩ ⟨the battles that have *bloodied* this sacred soil⟩
[3]**bloody** \"\ *adv*, *Brit* — used as an intensive ⟨a ~ good lot⟩ ⟨he can ~ well get his own dinner⟩; often considered vulgar
bloody–back \'==,=\ *n*, *archaic* : a British soldier : REDCOAT
bloody bark *n* : a showy Australian woody vine (*Lonchocarpus blackii*) with rusty red twigs and foliage and purple flowers in drooping racemes
bloodybone *n* -S *obs* : BLOODYBONES
bloody·bones \'==,=\ *n pl but sing or pl in constr*, *archaic* [alter. of earlier *bloodybone*] : HOBGOBLIN, SPECTER — used esp. in the phrase *rawhead and bloodybones*
bloody bread *n* : BLEEDING BREAD
bloody clam *n* : BLOOD CLAM
bloody dock *n* : BLOODWORT 2
bloody fingers *n pl but sing or pl in constr* **1** : FOXGLOVE 1 **2** : MALE ORCHIS
bloody flux *n* **1** : a diarrhea in which blood is mixed with the intestinal discharge — now archaic when used of man **2** : SWINE DYSENTERY
bloody hand *n* **1** : a hand stained with deer's blood being sufficient evidence in old English forest laws of a man's trespass in the forest against venison **2** *heraldry* : a red hand (as in the arms of Ulster) that is now the distinguishing mark of a baronet of the United Kingdom or of Ireland
bloody man's fingers *n pl but sing or pl in constr* : FOXGLOVE 1
bloody mary \-'merē, -ma(a)rē, -mārē, -ri\ *n*, *often cap B&M* [prob. after *Bloody Mary*, nickname for Mary I †1558 queen of England, notorious for her persecution of Protestants; fr. the red color] : a beverage consisting of vodka and tomato juice to which is usu. added seasoning and sometimes lemon juice
bloody murder *adv* : as though face to face with a gory murder ⟨he thought of screaming *bloody murder* so that they would let him get out of the car —Jean Stafford⟩
bloody murrain *n* : TEXAS FEVER
bloody–nosed beetle \'==¦=-\ *n*, *Brit* : a dull blue Old World chrysomelid beetle (*Timarcha tenebricosa*) that exudes a drop of reddish fluid from its head when disturbed
bloody·noun \'blədē,naun, -di,-\ *var of* BLOODNOUN
bloody scours *n pl but sing or pl in constr* : a bloody diarrhea of domestic animals; *also* : a disease characterized by such a diarrhea (as swine dysentery or coccidiosis of calves)
bloody shirt *n* : the blood-stained shirt of a slain man used to incite vengeance for his death; *broadly* : a symbol used to inflame to anger or to retaliative action — used specif. in the U.S. after the Civil War of any means employed to stir up or revive party or sectional animosity esp. in the phrase *wave the bloody shirt*
bloo·ey *also* **bloo·ie** \'blüē\ *adj* [origin unknown] *slang* : out of order : AWRY : incomprehensibly wrong — used chiefly with *go* ⟨the ladder slipped, then everything went ~⟩
[1]**bloom** \'blüm\ *n* -S [OE *blōma* mass, lump of metal] **1** : a mass of wrought iron from the Catalan forge or from the puddling furnace deprived of its dross and shaped in the form of an oblong block by shingling **2** : a semifinished mass of steel usu. nearly square in section and not smaller than 6 by 6 inches formed directly from an ingot by hot rolling — compare BILLET, SLAB **3** : a mass of iron or steel formed by consolidating scrap at a high temperature by hammering or rolling
[2]**bloom** \"\ *n* -S [ME *blome*, fr. ON *blōm*, *blōmi*; akin to OHG *bluomo* flower, blossom, Goth *blōma* lily, OE *blōma* mass, lump of metal, *blōwan* to bloom — more at BLOW] **1 a** : the flower of a seed plant : an individual flower : BLOSSOM 1a; *collectively* : flowers or amount of flowers esp. of a plant or a season ⟨look at the ~ on that bush⟩ ⟨the apples had a very light ~ this spring⟩ **b** : the flowering state ⟨the roses are all in ~⟩ **c** : a period or instance of flowering ⟨there are usually two ~*s*, a heavy one in May and another in late September⟩ ⟨the spring ~ in the park⟩ **2 a** : one (as a girl) that is estimable, outstanding, or lovely ⟨it is hard to accept the frailty of so fair a ~⟩ **b** : a state or time of beauty, freshness, and vigor ⟨the ~ of youth⟩; *also* : highest development : PERFECTION, PEAK, CULMINATION ⟨if automation comes into fuller ~ —J.I.Snyder⟩ ⟨a world that has become sufficiently relaxed to allow its tendencies toward a diversification of manners to reach their ~ —Irving Howe & Eliezer Greenberg⟩ **c** : a period of development or improvement (as in quality or standing) ⟨the clavichord had . . . a second ~ almost unique in history —Curt Sachs⟩ **3** : a surface coating or appearance: as **a** : the delicate powdery coating on certain fresh fruits (as grapes or plums) and leaves (as of cabbage or carnation); *also* : the waxy material that forms such a coating **b** : a rosy appearance of the cheeks : FLUSH ⟨recovered all her health and ~⟩; *broadly* : an outward evidence of freshness or healthy vigor : GLOW ⟨a new, fresh world, with all the ~ upon it —W.M.Thackeray⟩ **c** : a deposit or coating of ellagic acids that appears on leather **d** : the grainy or powdery surface of a newly minted coin **e** : the fluorescence of petroleum or its products or of rosin oil **f** : the cloudy appearance often observed on a film of varnish or lacquer **g** : a milky appearance on the surface of glass produced by slight decomposition **h** : luster or brightness of textile fibers or materials esp. when dyed ⟨wool with a fine ~⟩ ⟨the soft ~ of silk velvets⟩ **i** : WATER BLOOM **j** : the surface appearance characteristic of freshness and quality in dressed meat and poultry **k** : the protective cuticle of an eggshell **l** : a healthy well-kept appearance of the coat and skin of a domestic animal; *also* : FATNESS, FINISH **m** : a grayish discoloration on chocolates resulting from the deposit of microscopic crystals of fat or sugar on the surface of the coating **n** : glare caused by an object reflecting too much light into a television camera **o** : an appearance of brightness on dyed material ⟨a red ~ on indigo navy⟩ **4** : a mineral that is frequently found as an efflorescence ⟨cobalt ~⟩ ⟨antimony ~⟩ **5** : the characteristic aroma of a wine : BOUQUET 4a
[3]**bloom** \"\ *vb* -ED/-ING/-S [ME *blomen*, fr. *blome*, n.] *vi* **1** : to produce or yield blossoms : flower or be in flower : BLOSSOM ⟨bulbs that ~ in the spring⟩ ⟨that bush will ~ soon⟩ **2 a** : to attain, undergo, or acquire bloom; *esp* : to flourish esp. in youthful beauty, freshness, or excellence ⟨the arts ~*ed* in this heady environment⟩ ⟨we could not believe that scrawny child had ~*ed* into such a lovely lass⟩ **b** : to become affected or marred with bloom ⟨a beautiful finish but it ~*s* so easily⟩ **c** : to exhibit bloom : shine out : GLOW ⟨the stove ~*ed* warm and bright in the dark room⟩ **d** : to cause bloom ⟨this polish does not ~ or become sticky⟩ **3** : to come out like a bloom on a plant; *esp* : to appear or occur unexpectedly or in surprising quantity or degree ⟨subscription selling ~*ed* splendidly —Bernard Kalb⟩ ⟨the senator ~*ed* as an enthusiastic liberal⟩ **4** : to become colored usu. brown or red — used of the sea or of bodies of fresh water that show a seasonal increase in the numbers of planktonic microorganisms ~ *vt* **1** *obs* : to cause to bloom; *esp* : to make flourishing **2** : to give bloom or a bloom to: as **a** : to make glowing or radiant : BRIGHTEN ⟨while barred clouds ~ the soft-dying day —John Keats⟩ **b** : to cloud or mar with a bloom ⟨dampness can ~ the best of varnishes⟩ **c** *Brit* : to coat (a photographic lens) with a thin layer of low-refracting material to reduce surface reflection
[1]**bloom·er** \-mə(r)\ *n* -S [[3]*bloom* + *-er*] **1** : a plant that blooms; *sometimes* : a person that reaches full competence, skill, or maturity ⟨some youngsters are late ~*s*⟩ **2** : a workman who removes bloom (as a leather scourer) **3** : a workman or a rolling mill that shapes blooms **4** *slang chiefly Brit* : a gross error : a stupid blunder : BONER, BLOOPER
[2]**bloomer** \"\ *n* -S [after Mrs. Amelia *Bloomer* †1894 Am. pioneer in social reform who advocated such clothing] **1** : a costume for women introduced about 1850 consisting of a short skirt and long loose trousers gathered closely about the ankles and usu. with a coat and broad-brimmed hat **2 a bloomers** *pl* : the trousers of a bloomer costume **b** : full loose trousers gathered at the knee formerly worn by women for athletics — usu. used in pl. **c** : underpants of similar design but less bulk worn chiefly by girls — usu. used in pl. **3** : a woman wearing a bloomer (sense 1); *esp* : one adopting such a costume as an indication of adherence to the fight for the rights and freedom of women during the 19th century
bloo·me·ria \blü'mirēə\ *n*, *cap* [NL, fr. H. G. *Bloomer*, 19th cent. Amer. botanist + NL *-ia*] : a genus of bulbous California plants (family Liliaceae) with grasslike leaves and showy orange flowers — see GOLDEN STAR 3
bloomer pit *n* [[1]*bloomer*] : TAN VAT
bloom·ery *also* **bloom·a·ry** \'blüm(ə)rē\ *n* -ES [[1]*bloom* + *-ery* or *-ary*] : a furnace and forge in which wrought-iron blooms were formerly made directly from the ore or more rarely from cast iron
bloom·field·ian \(')blüm¦fēldēən\ *n* -S *usu cap* [Leonard *Bloomfield* †1949 Am. linguist + E *-ian*] : a follower of the principles of linguistic analysis taught by Leonard Bloomfield
bloom·i·ness \'blümēnəs\ *n* -ES : the state of having the surface covered with bloom
[1]**blooming** *adj* [fr. pres. part. of [3]*bloom*] **1** : having blooms unfolding : FLOWERING ⟨a ~ violet⟩; *also* : attaining full development or improved status **2** : thriving in health, beauty, and vigor : exhibiting the freshness and beauties of youth or health **3** [prob. euphemism for *bloody*] *slang* — used as a generalized intensive ⟨a ~ fool⟩; compare BLOODY 6 — **bloom·ing·ly** *adv* — **bloom·ing·ness** *n* -ES
[2]**blooming** \"\ *n* -S [fr. gerund of [3]*bloom*] **1** : BLOOM **2** : the process of coating the surface of glass (as of a lens) with a film designed to increase transmission of light through the glass by reducing loss due to reflection
[3]**blooming** \"\ *n* -S [[1]*bloom* + *-ing*] *metallurgy* : the process of making blooms
blooming mill *n* [[3]*blooming*] : a rolling mill in which blooms are produced from ingots in steel manufacture : ROUGHING MILL, COGGING MILL
blooming sal·ly \-'salē\ *also* **blooming willow** *n* [[1]*blooming*] : GREAT WILLOW HERB
bloom·less \'blümləs\ *adj* : lacking bloom; *sometimes* : incapable of flowering ⟨a ~ apple tree⟩
bloom poison *n* : either of two poisonous Australian shrubs (*Gastrolobium ovalifolium* and *Oxylobium retusum*) of the family Leguminosae — compare POISON BUSH
blooms *pl of* BLOOM, *pres 3d sing of* BLOOM
blooms·bury \'blümz,berē, -zb(ə)rē, -ri\ *adj*, *usu cap* [fr. *Bloomsbury*, district of London, England] : cultivating or displaying literary and artistic interests flourishing among an informal group of intellectuals associated with the residential district of Bloomsbury ⟨the *Bloomsbury* group⟩ ⟨he is more *Bloomsbury* than the British Museum —Harvey Breit⟩
bloom side *n* : the hair side of a skin or hide
bloom spray *n* : a pesticidal orchard spray applied when 90 percent or more of the flowers are in full bloom
bloomy \'blümē\ *adj*, *often* -ER/-EST **1** : full of or characterized by flowers : FLOWERY ⟨a ~ sunlit slope⟩ **2** : covered with bloom (sense 3) **3** *archaic* : FLOURISHING; *esp* : exhibiting youthful beauty and vigor ⟨but all the ~ flush of life is fled —Oliver Goldsmith⟩
[1]**bloop** \'blüp\ *vb* -ED/-ING/-S [imit.] *vi* : to make a howling noise : operate a radio receiving set that makes such a noise — see BLOOPER 1 ~ *vt* : to silence bloops in by the application of a mask or by electrical cutoff of the sound output
[2]**bloop** \"\ *n* -S **1** : an unpleasing sound; *specif* : the noise made when the beam of light in a sound reproducer is interrupted in its passage through the film by a splice or other unwanted abrupt change in the density of the film **2** : a special mask applied over a splice in a film to prevent a bloop
bloop·er \'blüpə(r)\ *n* -S **1** : a radio receiving set that generates current of radio frequency thus causing radiation from the receiving antenna and under certain circumstances causing nearby sets to bloop **2** : an embarrassing public blunder ⟨his prize ~ was introducing the speaker by the wrong name⟩ **3** *baseball* **a** : a high pitch lobbed to the batter with backspin **b** : a lofting fly ball hit barely beyond the infield
blooth \'blüth\ *var of* BLOWTH
[1]**blore** \'blü(ə)r, -üə\ *vi* [ME *bloren* — more at BLARE] *dial Eng* : BELLOW, LOW — used of cattle or those (as children) that cry out loudly
[2]**blore** \'blō(ə)r\ *n* -S [ME; perh. akin to ME *blowen* to blow — more at BLOW] *archaic* : a roaring wind : BLAST, BLUSTER
blos·my \'bläs(ə)mē\ *adj* [ME — more at BLOSSOMY] *archaic* : BLOSSOMY
[1]**blos·som** \'bläsəm\ *n* -S [ME *blosme*, fr. OE *blōstm*, *blōstma*; akin to MHG *bluost* blossom, OE *blōwan* to bloom — more at BLOW] **1 a** : the flower of a seed plant : [2]BLOOM 1a — used esp. of flowers having a colored or conspicuous perianth, rarely of apetalous flowers, and often preferred to *flower* or *bloom* when the reference is to plants producing edible fruits ⟨the scent of apple ~*s* mingled with that of woodland flowers⟩ **b** : the mass of bloom on a single plant ⟨this tree had an excellent ~ this year⟩; *also* : the state of bearing flowers ⟨those plums are in full ~ now⟩ **2** : a period or stage of development analogous to the unfolding of a flower ⟨in the ~ of one's youth⟩ **3** : something resembling a blossom esp. in freshness, loveliness, or rich promise ⟨a ~ of literature⟩ ⟨my babe, my ~, ah, my child —Alfred Tennyson⟩ **4** : the weathered outcrop of a coal or ore deposit **5** : a moderate pink that is yellower and duller than arbutus pink, yellower and less strong than blossom pink, stronger than chalk pink, and deeper than hydrangea pink — called also *Venetian pink*
[2]**blossom** \"\ *vi* -ED/-ING/-S [ME *blosmen*, fr. OE *blōstmian*, fr. *blōstm*, *blōstma*] **1 a** *of plants* : to put forth flowers : come into bloom : FLOWER ⟨this lily ~*s* very early⟩ **b** *of places* : to be or become full of flowers ⟨during its short season the desert ~*s* gloriously⟩ **2** : to unfold like a blossom ⟨smoke ~*ed* out from the cracks⟩: as **a** : to flourish and prosper ⟨the romance . . . ~*ed* for six or seven months and then wilted —Saxe Commins⟩ **b** : DEVELOP, EVOLVE, EXPAND — often used with *into*, sometimes with *out* ⟨the town ~*ed* into a metropolis⟩ ⟨genuine culture often ~*s* tardily⟩ ⟨he started small and ~*ed* out as he gained experience⟩ **c** : to come into being : put in an appearance : APPEAR ⟨under rental control trickery and connivance ~*ed*⟩ ⟨new industries can ~ overnight if we find an outlet for their products⟩ **d** *of a parachute* : to open and expand **3** : to be or become changed by or notable for the appearance or addition of something — usu. used with *with* or *out* ⟨the ward had ~*ed* out in shiny plaster casts —Earle Birney⟩ ⟨Apple Valley ~*s* with dude ranches —Ralph Friedman⟩
blossombill \'==,=\ *n* [so called fr. the colored spot on the bill] : SURF SCOTER
blossom bud *n* : FLOWER BUD; *esp* : a flower bud of a fruit tree that is formed during one growing season but develops during the next
blossomed *adj* [ME *blossumed*, fr. *blossum*, *blosme* blossom + *-ed*] : bearing blossoms : FLOWERING ⟨a fully ~ rose⟩; *often* : having blossoms of a specified kind — used in combination ⟨scarlet-*blossomed*⟩ ⟨double-*blossomed*⟩
blossom–end rot \'==,=-\ *n* **1** : any fruit rot originating at the blossom end **2** : a common physiological disease of the tomato attributed to great fluctuation in available moisture and characterized by slightly sunken leathery areas around the tip end of the fruit that appear water-soaked or colored lead to brown
blossomhead \'==,=\ *n* : SURF SCOTER
blossom–headed parakeet \'==¦==-\ *n* : a common parakeet (*Psittacula cyanocephala*) of India and southeast Asia, having a green back, a greenish yellow breast, and a red head with bluish iridescence
blos·som·less \'bläsəmləs\ *adj* : being without a blossom
blossom pink *n* : a moderate pink that is yellower and deeper than arbutus pink, bluer and stronger than chalk pink, and bluer and deeper than hydrangea pink — called also *cherry pink*
blos·som·ry \'bläsəmrē\ *n* -ES : BLOSSOMS
blos·somy \'bläsəmē, -mi\ *adj* [alter. of earlier *blosmy*, fr. ME, fr. *blosme* blossom + *-y*] : full of blossoms : like a blossom : FLOWERY
[1]**blot** \'blät, — *usu* -d·+V\ *n* -S [ME *blot*, *blotte*, perh. fr. MF *blotte*, *bloste*, *blostre* clod, perh. of Gmc origin; akin to MD *bluyster* blister — more at BLISTER] **1 a** : a soiling or disfiguring mark, spot, or stain (as of ink or earth) ⟨a letter full of ~*s*⟩ **b** : something resembling such a spot or mark esp. in detracting from the excellence or beauty of the whole of which it is a part ⟨these filthy streets are a ~ on our city⟩ **2** : a spot on a reputation : a moral flaw : DISGRACE, REPROACH, BLEMISH **3** *archaic* : a deliberate obliteration of something written or printed; *specif* : a mark covering something unwanted in a piece of writing
[2]**blot** \"\ *vb* **blotted**; **blotted**; **blotting**; **blots** [ME *bloten*, *blotten*, fr. *blot*, *blotte*, n.] *vt* **1** : to spot, stain, or bespatter with some discoloring substance ⟨her tears *blotted* the page as she wrote⟩ **2** *obs* : to spoil (as paper) with bad writing : write ineptly or clumsily **3** : to make obscure or indistinct : blot out : ECLIPSE **4** *obs* **a** : to cause flawing of : MAR, SOIL, IMPAIR ⟨it ~*s* thy beauty, as frosts do bite the meads —Shak.⟩; *esp* : to stain with infamy : DISGRACE ⟨to do me honor in that very thing, wherein these men thought to have *blotted* me —John Milton⟩ **b** : CALUMNIATE, STIGMATIZE ⟨there's a good mother, boy, that ~*s* thy father —Shak.⟩ **5 a** : to dry (as writing) with blotting paper or other absorbing agent ⟨she hastily *blotted* her letter⟩ **b** : to remove (an unwanted deposit) by blotting the surface on which it occurs — often used with *up* ⟨get a towel and ~ up the gravy you spilled before it soaks into the cloth⟩ ~ *vi* **1** : to make a blot or blots ⟨this pen ~*s* badly⟩; *sometimes* : to make an erasure **2** : to become marked with a blot : take a blot ⟨this paper ~*s* easily⟩ — **blot one's copybook** : to do something that spoils one's record (as for probity or good sense)
[3]**blot** \"\ *n* -S [origin unknown] **1** : a backgammon man exposed to capture by being placed or left alone on a point **2** *archaic* : a weak point : FAILING; *also* : an exposed point or mark ⟨he is too great a master of his art to make a ~ which may be so easily hit —John Dryden⟩
[1]**blotch** \'bläch\ *n* -ES [prob. alter. (influenced by *blister* or *blain*) of *botch* swelling] **1 a** : IMPERFECTION, BLEMISH ⟨face covered with ~*es*⟩; *sometimes* : a moral flaw : FAULT **b** : a spot or mark (as of color or ink) esp. when large or irregular **2** : a disease of plants characterized by dark, irregular, and often diffusely margined spots on the leaves or fruit: **a** : a disease of apples caused by an imperfect fungus (*Phyllosticta solitaria*) producing small dark spots on the leaves and fruit and cankers on the tree **b** : BLACK SPOT 1c — see NET BLOTCH, SPOT BLOTCH
[2]**blotch** \"\ *vb* -ED/-ING/-ES **1** : to mark or mar with blotches — used almost wholly as a past participle and often adjectivally **2** : to make or cause a blotch — used almost wholly as a past participle and often adjectivally
[3]**blotch** \"\ *adj*, *of textile printing* : involving production of a black or colored ground
blotchy \'bläche, -chi\ *adj* -ER/-EST **1** : having or marked with blotches **2** : like a blotch
blot·less \'blätləs\ *adj* : free from blots or spots : IMMACULATE
blot on the escutcheon : a disgrace in a family record : a stain in reputation
blot out *vt* **1 a** : to alter (as writing) by covering with a blot : correct or cancel (something written) by blotting ⟨my name be *blotted out* from the book of life —Shak.⟩ **b** : to render insignificant or inconsequential : withdraw from awareness or need for consideration ⟨time will *blot out* these bitter memories⟩ ⟨one act like this *blots out* a thousand crimes —John Dryden⟩ **2** : to make obscure or invisible ⟨mist slowly *blotted out* the hills⟩ **2** : to make obscure or invisible : HIDE, CONCEAL, DARKEN ⟨acquired prejudices . . . can spread a fog over verbal messages, *blotting out* common meanings, distorting common experiences —Stuart Chase⟩ **3** : DESTROY, ANNIHILATE, KILL ⟨*blot out* the nations of men —Lewis Mumford⟩ **syn** see ERASE
blot·ter \'bläd·ə(r), -ätə-\ *n* -S **1** : one that blots; *esp* : a piece of blotting paper **2** : a book in which entries (as of transactions or occurrences) are made temporarily pending their transfer to permanent record books ⟨a police ~⟩ **3** *slang* : a person who blots up liquor : DRUNK, SOT **4** [so called fr. its having been made of blotting paper] : a disk of compressible material (as a cloth or felt gasket in the mounting of a grinding wheel) for avoidance of excessive pressure by clamping nuts **5** : a coat of gravel, crushed rock, or crushed slag spread over a layer of bituminous material with which it consolidates to form a bonded road surface **6** *West* : a cattle thief who attempts to conceal his depredations by altering the brands of stolen cattle
blot·tesque \(')blä¦tesk\ *adj* [[1]*blot* + *-esque* (as in *grotesque*)] : painted with heavy touches or blotlike brushwork
blotting *n* -S [by shortening] : BLOTTING PAPER
blotting book *n* : a book of blotting paper

blot·ting·ly *adv* **:** with blots **:** in a blotting style or manner

blotting pad *n* **:** a pad of blotting paper

blotting paper *n* **:** a soft spongy unsized paper used to absorb ink from freshly written manuscript

blot·to \'bläd·(,)ō, -ä(,)tō\ *adj* [prob. irreg. fr. ²*blot*] **1** *slang* **:** completely drunk **:** made unconscious by drink **2** *slang* **:** CONFUSED, DISORDERED, UNCONSCIOUS

blot·ty \'bläd·ē, -ätē\ *adj, often* -ER/-EST [¹*blot* + -*y*] **:** covered or disfigured with blots **:** DAUBY

blou·bis·kop \'blaů,biskəp\ *n* -s [Afrik, fr. *blou* blue (fr. MD *blā, blau*) + *biskop;* akin to OHG *blāo* blue — more at BLUE] *Africa* **:** BLACK BISKOP

¹blouse \'blaůz\ *var of* BLOWZE

²blouse \'blaůs, 'blaůz\ *n, pl* **blouses** \'blaůsəz, -aůzəz\ [F] **1 :** a loose overgarment like a shirt or smock, hiplength to calf-length, belted or unbelted, and worn esp. by workmen, artists, and peasants **2 :** the dress and undress uniform coat of the U.S. Army; *also* **:** the upper outer garment of any uniform ⟨a postman's gray ~⟩ **3 :** a usu. loose-fitting garment covering the body from the neck to the waist or just below, made with or without a collar, sleeves, or belt, and worn over or tucked inside a waistband (as of a skirt) **4 :** a bloused draping of cloth (as in a coat or dress)

Russian blouse

³blouse \"\ *vi* -ED/-ING/-S **1 :** to fall in folds like those of a loose blouse when closely belted — used of textiles and garments ⟨the new coats ~ gracefully above the hipline⟩ **2 :** DROOP, BAG ⟨sails bellying and *blousing* in a fitful breeze⟩

bloused \'blaůst, -aůzd\ *adj* **1 :** wearing a blouse **2 :** made with fullness like that of a blouse **3 :** having a bulge or droop similar to the effect of a blouse belted at the waist

blous·ette \blaů'set, -'zet\ *n* -s [²*blouse* + -*ette*] **:** a woman's sleeveless blouse

¹blousy *var of* BLOWSY

²blousy *also* **blous·ey** \'blaůsē, -aůzē, -i\ *adj* **blousier; blousiest** [¹*blouse* + -*y*] **:** like a blouse **:** BLOUSED

blou·wil·de·bees·oog \'blaů,vildə,bā,sōk\ *n* -s [Afrik, fr. *blouwildebees* brindled gnu + *oog* eye, fr. MD *ōghe;* akin to OE *ēage* eye — more at BLUE WILDEBEEST, EYE] *Africa* **:** a disease marked by exophthalmos, blindness, and frequently rupture of the eyeball occurring in sheep that come in contact with the gnu and prob. due to an unidentified infective agent

blo·vi·ate \'blōvē,āt\ *vi* -ED/-ING/-S [prob. irreg. fr. *blow* + -*i*- + -*ate*] **:** to orate verbosely and windily

¹blow \'blō\ *vb* **blew** \'blü\ *or dial* **blowed** \'blōd\ **blown** \'blōn\ *or dial* **blowed; blowing; blows** [ME *blowen,* fr. OE *blāwan;* akin to OHG *blāen* to blow, inflate, L *flare* to blow, *follis* bellows, Gk *phallos* penis, Skt *bhāṇḍa* pot; basic meaning: to swell] *vi* **1** *of air or air currents* **:** to move with speed or force ⟨the wind *blew* in gusts⟩ — often used with *it* as an impersonal nominative ⟨let it ~, we're snug and warm⟩ **2 a :** to produce a current of air (as by expelling it forcibly from the lungs through the mouth) ⟨never ~ on your soup to cool it⟩ **b :** to drive air or other gas ⟨the fan is ~*ing* on my neck⟩ **c :** to escape (as of natural gas or oil) from a region of high pressure **3 a :** to make a sound by or as if by blowing **:** HISS, WHISTLE, TOOT ⟨the train *blew* for the crossing⟩ **b :** to play a wind instrument; *also, slang* **:** to play jazz on any instrument **c** *of a wind instrument* **:** SOUND ⟨there let the pealing organ ~ —John Milton⟩ **d** *of an animal* **:** SNORT ⟨the horse stood stamping and ~*ing* restlessly in the cold⟩ **4 a :** to talk emptily **:** BOAST ⟨he kept us awake half the night ~*ing* about his family⟩ **b :** STORM, BLUSTER, FULMINATE; *also* **:** to be or become enraged **:** blow up ⟨when he heard what they had done he really *blew*⟩ **5 a :** to breathe hard or rapidly **:** PANT, PUFF, GASP ⟨my, those stairs make me ~⟩ **b** *of whales and other cetaceans* **:** to eject moisture-laden air from the lungs through the blowhole **6** *obs, of flies* **:** to lay eggs **7 a :** to move or be carried by or as if by wind ⟨the echo of a lost world ~*s* through her sparkling prose —Beatrice Washburn⟩ ⟨the soil is ~*ing* badly all along the hedge⟩ **b :** to flutter, billow, or flap in a current of air ⟨curtains ~*ing* out the open window⟩ **:** be carried by the wind ⟨the kite *blew* away⟩ **8 :** to be damaged in a manner involving swelling or expansion: **a :** to become destroyed by explosion **:** EXPLODE ⟨if this old blunderbuss doesn't ~ we may have duck for dinner⟩ **b** *of cement* **:** to swell and crack due to imperfect preparation and curing **c** *of foods* **:** to become swollen by the products of abnormal fermentation ⟨certain bacteria cause cheeses to ~⟩ **d** *of an electrical fuse* **:** to melt when overloaded ⟨an overloaded outlet often causes fuses to ~⟩ **e** *of a pneumatic tire* **:** to release its air through a spontaneous rupture **:** blow out **f** *of pottery* **:** to blow apart from too rapid heating in the kiln **g** *of paper* **:** to blister esp. from air entrapped between the wet sheet and the felt or from too sudden drying on the cylinder; *also, of paperboard* **:** to blister from air entrapped between two plies **9** *slang* **:** to move off **:** clear out **:** DEPART ⟨~ now, nobody wants the likes of you around here⟩ **10** *of a horse or mule* **:** to pause for breath ⟨let the mare ~ at the end of the furrow⟩ **~** *vt* **1 a :** to drive (gas or vapor) from a region of greater to a region of lower pressure ⟨use the bellows to ~ air on the forge⟩; *specif* **:** to eject (breathed air) from the lungs during normal or forced exhalation ⟨don't ~ your breath in my face⟩ **b :** to set (gas or vapor) in motion (as by the action of a fan) ⟨the fan *blew* the hot air about our heads⟩ **c :** to force a current of gas or vapor upon, through, or into, usu. to produce a particular effect (as of warming, cooling, drying) ⟨come on out, let the breeze ~ your hair dry⟩ ⟨~ the fire into a good blaze⟩ ⟨oil being *blown* with air and oxygen⟩ **d** (1) **:** to force air through (molten metal) to refine (as in a Bessemer or other converter) (2) **:** to force air into (a blast furnace) to support the combustion of coke **2 a :** to play on (a wind instrument); *also, slang* **:** to play jazz on (any instrument) **b :** to sound a signal for (as an assault or retreat) on a wind instrument **c :** to sound (as a note or blast) on or with a wind instrument **d** *of a wind instrument* **:** SOUND **e :** to direct (hunting dogs) with the sound of a horn **f :** to play (jazz) on an instrument **3 a :** to spread by report **:** noise abroad **:** make public **:** DISCLOSE ⟨through the court his courtesy was *blown* —John Dryden⟩ — now usu. used with *about* or *abroad* ⟨they have *blown* all sorts of silly rumors about⟩ **b** *obs* **:** to give utterance to **:** UTTER — used esp. of emotional expression **c** *archaic* **:** to inform against (a person) or inform a person of (as an act or secret) **:** BETRAY — formerly used with *up;* now only in the phrase *blow the gaff* **d :** DARN, DAMN, BLAST ⟨~ it, my watch has stopped⟩; *often* **:** pay no attention to **:** put aside from consideration **:** IGNORE, DISREGARD ⟨~ the expense⟩ ⟨risk be *blowed*⟩ **4 a :** to drive, activate, or act upon with a current of gas or vapor ⟨the storm *blew* the boat aground⟩ **b :** to clear of contents by the passage of such a current: (1) **:** to free (the nose) of mucus and debris by forcible exhalation (2) **:** to empty (an egg) by forcing out the contents through one small hole with a current of air introduced through another small hole (3) **:** to expel (the contents of a wood-pulp digester) by relief of pressure at the completion of a cook **5 a :** to distend with or as if with gas **:** blow up **:** BLOAT ⟨his face *blown* out like a bladder⟩ ⟨small boys ~*ing* their balloons⟩ **b** *obs* **:** to puff up with pride ⟨look how imagination ~*s* him —Shak.⟩ **c :** to expand and shape (glass) by the action of injected air **d :** to produce or shape (as a glass vessel) by the action of blown or injected air ⟨~*ing* iridescent soap bubbles⟩ ⟨the wind *blew* a hollow on the edge of the dune⟩ **6** *of insects* **:** to deposit eggs or larvae on or in — now used only of blowflies and flesh flies ⟨wounds *blown* by flies often healed faster than supposedly clean wounds⟩ **7 :** to shatter, burst, or destroy by explosion — used commonly with *out, in, up* ⟨be ready to charge when we ~ in the gate⟩ or with phrases expressing degree of damage ⟨they were *blown* to bits⟩ **8 a :** to put out of breath **:** cause to pant with fatigue ⟨take it easy on the hills or you'll ~ your horse⟩ **b :** to let (as a horse) pause to catch the breath — often used with *out* **c** *of a saddle horse* **:** to keep the chest of expanded by holding the breath while being girthed — used with *out* ⟨the stud frequently *blew* himself out⟩ **9 a :** to spend (money) recklessly or extravagantly **:** SQUANDER ⟨he *blew* his pay at the gambling tables⟩ **b :** to treat with unusual or lavish expenditure — used with *to* ⟨come on, I'll ~ you to a steak⟩ ⟨I may live on beans for a month, but I'm going to ~ myself to a really good handbag now⟩ **10 :** to cause (a fuse) to blow **11 :** to rupture (as a seal or cover) by too much pressure ⟨the engine *blew* a head gasket⟩ **12** *slang* **:** to lose control of (a winning position) **:** toss away **:** MISPLAY, MUFF ⟨two chances to win and he *blew* them both⟩ ⟨~ an easy putt⟩ **13 :** to leave esp. hurriedly ⟨he *blew* town after running up huge bills⟩ — **blow a fuse** *or* **blow a gasket** *slang* **:** to exhibit anger **:** become enraged **:** make a big fuss ⟨when he saw what they had done he like to *blew a fuse*⟩ — **blow great guns** *of wind* **:** to blow furiously and with roaring gusts — **blow hot and cold :** to be favorable at one moment and adverse the next **:** react or respond both favorably and unfavorably **:** SHILLY-SHALLY — **blow into** *slang* **:** to appear or arrive at casually or unexpectedly ⟨he *blew into* town last night⟩ — **blow one's horn** *or* **blow one's own horn :** to praise oneself **:** boast of one's achievements — **blow one's lines 1** *theater* **:** to forget one's lines or make an error in speaking them **2 :** to deviate from an announced or prescribed course **:** fall into inconsistency **:** FALTER ⟨before the week was out he had *blown his lines* as president and perhaps blown the Democratic party out of office —*Time*⟩ — **blow one's top** *or* **blow one's lid** *or* **blow one's stack** *slang* **:** to lose control of oneself: **a :** to become furiously angry **:** be incoherent with rage **b :** to go crazy **:** become insane — **blow the lid :** to expose something to view — usu. used with *off* ⟨this book *blew the lid* off the secret corruption and gangsterism in these unions⟩ — **blow the whistle** *slang* **:** BETRAY, INFORM — **blow upon :** to bring into disrepute or discredit **:** render unsavory or worthless **:** BLEMISH, TAINT, DEFAME ⟨the reputation of her house, which was never *blown upon* before, was utterly destroyed —Henry Fielding⟩

²blow \"\ *n* -s **1 :** a blowing of wind esp. when strong or violent **:** WINDSTORM, GALE ⟨recurrent ~*s* sweep the coastal islands bare⟩ **2 :** the act of certain insects of depositing eggs or larvae; *sometimes* **:** a larva so deposited (as in a wound) — used chiefly of blowflies and flesh flies **3 a :** BOASTING, BRAG **b** *slang* **:** BOASTER **4 a :** an act or instance of forcing air through or from some instrument ⟨give the fire a ~ with the bellows⟩ ⟨a single loud ~ of his horn⟩ **b :** forcible ejection of air from the body (as in freeing the nose of mucus and debris) ⟨Junior, give your nose a good ~ before we start⟩ **5 :** the spouting of a whale **6 a :** a short rest **:** BREATHING SPELL, BREATHER **b :** a brief stop (of a horse) for rest **7 a :** PARISON **b :** the vacuity in the stem of certain blown-glass vessels **8 :** HUFF 5 **9** *slang* **:** a social affair; *esp* **:** BLOWOUT, BINGE, SPREE **10 :** BLOAT 2 — usu. pl. but sing. or pl. in constr. **11 a :** a leak in the packing of a valve or cylinder (as of a steam locomotive) **b :** the failure of a cofferdam or dike causing a sudden inrush of water through or under the structure **12 :** BLOWHOLE **13 a :** the period in the manufacture of water gas in which a blast of air is admitted to the ignited fuel bed for heating the bed by combustion before the run **b :** the blowing of gas from an open well **c** (1) **:** the blast of air forced through molten metal to refine it (as in a Bessemer or other converter) (2) **:** the time during which air is being forced through molten metal to refine it (3) **:** the quantity of metal refined during that time

³blow \"\ *vb* **blew; blown** *or obs* **blowe; blowing; blows** [ME *blowen,* fr. OE *blōwan;* akin to OHG *bluoen* to bloom, L *florēre* to bloom, *flos* flower, *folium* leaf, Gk *phyllon*] *vi* **:** FLOWER, BLOSSOM, BLOOM ⟨I know a bank where the wild thyme ~*s* —Shak.⟩ **~** *vt* **1** *archaic* **:** to cause to blossom **2** *obs* **:** to put forth (blossoms or flowers) ⟨banks that ~ flowers —John Milton⟩

⁴blow \"\ *n* -s **1 a :** a display of flowers ⟨the south border made a fine ~ this spring⟩ **b :** ²BLOOM 1b — used chiefly in the phrases *in blow, in full blow* ⟨the old lilac by the fence is in full ~⟩ **c** *archaic* **:** an individual flower **2 :** full and perfect development **:** ²BLOOM 2b **3 a :** BLOSSOM 4 **b :** BLOWOUT 8

⁵blow \"\ *n* -s [ME (northern dial.) *blaw;* perh. akin to OHG *bliuwan* to beat, ON *blegthi* wedge, Goth *bliggwan* to beat, OE *bealu* evil — more at BALE] **1 a :** a forcible stroke delivered with a part of the body (as the fist or head) or with an instrument (as a hammer) **:** BUFFET, PUNCH, SLAP **b** *Austral* **:** a single stroke in shearing sheep **c** *slang* **:** BASE HIT **2 :** a hostile act or state **:** COMBAT, FIGHTING — usu. used in pl. and used esp. in the phrase *come to blows* ⟨nations like small boys have come to ~*s* over the most trivial issues⟩ **3 :** a forcible, determined, or sudden and unexpected act or effort **:** IMPACT, ASSAULT ⟨such a language . . . would solve many of his . . . difficulties at a single ~ —Edward Sapir⟩ ⟨shall we not support the downtrodden in their ~ for freedom⟩ **4 :** a severe and usu. sudden misfortune or calamity ⟨hail at this season was like a ~ from heaven⟩ **:** something that suddenly or unexpectedly produces mental, physical, or financial suffering or loss ⟨the loss of her husband was a ~ from which she never recovered⟩ **5** *sports* **:** MISPLAY; *specif* **:** failure to bowl a spare when no split exists — **at a blow :** SUDDENLY **:** at one effort **:** by a single vigorous act

blow accordion *n* **:** an accordion in which the air is furnished by the player's lungs

blow away *vt* **:** to dissipate or remove (something) as if with a current of air ⟨the whole well-ordered system has been *blown away* —Roger Fry⟩ ⟨even this caution . . . might well be *blown away* by the rush of buying . . . before the holiday —*Newsweek*⟩

blowback \'⸗,⸗\ *n* -s *often attrib* [*blow back,* v.] **1 :** an act of blowing back; *esp* **:** escape backward of imperfectly burned gunpowder after a shot **2 :** the action of a recoil-operated automatic or semiautomatic weapon that uses in its operation no locking or inertia mechanism to delay the rearward motion of the slide or breechblock; *also* **:** a weapon using such an action

blowball \'⸗,⸗\ *n* **:** a fluffy seed ball (as of the dandelion); *also* **:** a plant bearing such a ball

blow-by \'⸗,⸗\ *n* -s [*blow by,* v.] **:** leakage of gas or liquid between a piston and its cylinder during operation

blow-by-blow \¦⸗⸗¦⸗\ *adj* **:** minutely detailed ⟨a *blow-by-blow* account of the campaign⟩

blowcase \'⸗,⸗\ *n* **:** ACID EGG

blow down *vt* **:** to blow off

blowdown \'⸗,⸗\ *n* -s [*blow down*] **1 a :** the action of blowing down something **b :** a severe wind storm that blows over trees or structures **c :** WINDFALL **:** an area in which trees have been blown down **2 a :** the act or process of blowing off **b :** an apparatus for blowing off steam or gas

blowdown tunnel *n* **:** an intermittent wind tunnel in which the air flow is produced by the rapid discharge of a high-pressure storage tank or by suction from an evacuated reservoir

blowdown turbine *n* **:** a turbine driven by the escaping exhaust gases of a reciprocating internal-combustion engine

blowed *dial past of* BLOW

blow·en \'blōən, 'blaůən\ *n* -s [origin unknown] **:** WENCH, STRUMPET

blow·er \'blō(ə)r, 'blōə\ *n* -s [ME, fr. OE *blāwere,* fr. *blāwan* to blow + -*ere* -er — more at BLOW] **1 :** one that blows; *specif* **:** a worker who blows something (as furs), produces something (as glassware) by blowing, or operates a blowing machine or blowing equipment (as a blast furnace) **2 :** PUFFER 4a **3 :** a boastful person **:** BRAGGART **4** *slang* **:** a communication system; *esp* **:** a closed or private system (as between police headquarters and cruisers on duty or between bookmakers and their representatives at a track) **b :** the receiving device of such a system **5 :** a device for producing a current of air or gas (as to increase the draft of a furnace, ventilate a building or shaft, cool electronic equipment, or move or raise hay, silage, grain, or sawdust pneumatically)

blowfish \'⸗,⸗\ *n* **1 :** PUFFER 4a **2** *South* **:** WALLEYED PIKE

blowfly \'⸗,⸗\ *n* **:** any of various two-winged flies (family Calliphoridae) that deposit their eggs or maggots on meat and other foodstuffs or in wounds on living creatures; *esp* **:** the widely distributed bluebottle (*Calliphora vicina*) that is larger than the housefly and has a dark steel-blue abdomen and hairy thorax — compare STRIKE

blow gas *n* **:** gas leaving the generator during a blow period in the manufacture of water gas

blowgun \'⸗,⸗\ *n* **1 :** a tube (as of cane or reed) generally about 10 feet long through which a projectile (as a poisoned dart) may be impelled by the force of the breath **2 :** a device used for cleaning or spraying with a blast (as of air or liquid)

blowhard \'⸗,⸗\ *n* -s [¹*blow* + *hard* (adv.)] **:** BRAGGART

blowhole \'⸗,⸗\ *n* -s **1 :** a hole in a metal ingot or casting caused by a bubble of gas captured in the solidifying metal and constituting a flaw or defect **2 :** a nostril in the top of the head of a whale or other cetacean, there being two in the whalebone whales and only one in the toothed whales and related forms **3 :** a hole or fissure in rocks along a shore through which incoming waves force air to rush upward or water to spout intermittently **4 :** a hole in the ice to which aquatic mammals (as whales or seals) come to breathe

blowier *comparative of* BLOWY

blowiest *superlative of* BLOWY

blow in *vi* **1** *slang* **:** to appear or arrive casually or unexpectedly ⟨he *blew in* last night about eight⟩ **2** *of an oil well* **:** to come into production **:** start discharging oil and gas **~** *vt* **:** to start (a blast furnace) in operation — opposed to *blow out*

blow·ing \'blōiŋ, -ēŋ\ *n* -s [ME, fr. OE *blāwung,* fr. *blāwan* to blow + -*ung* -ing — more at BLOW] **1 :** a noise caused by the forcible ejection of air, steam, or gas **2 :** a sound that is habitually produced by the vibration of the nostrils in some horses during breathing and is not considered an unsoundness or associated with roaring **3 :** a step in the processing of textile fibers, fabrics, or furs in which air or steam is forced through the material **4 :** a process of forming hollow wares (as of plastic) by use of internal pressure (as of compressed air) to press the material against the inside of a mold — called also *blow molding*

blowing adder *or* **blowing viper** *n* [so called fr. its habit of distending the surface of its head before striking] **:** HOGNOSE SNAKE

blowing agent *n* **:** a substance (as sodium bicarbonate) that produces gas used in making expanded cellular or spongy products (as of rubber)

blowing cave *or* **blowing cavern** *n* **:** a cave into or from which a strong current of air passes

blowing charge *n* **:** a small charge of powder or of a mixture of powder and coal dust having just sufficient strength to blow out the fuse plug of a shell without rupturing the shell

blowing cone *n* **:** a small volcanic cone built up of congealed drops of lava from which steam or other vapors escape — compare DRIBLET CONE

blowing iron *n* **:** BLOWPIPE 4

blowing machine *n* **:** a machine for blowing bottles and other hollow glassware

blowing pipe *or* **blowing tube** *n* **:** BLOWPIPE 4

blowing-up \¦⸗⸗¦⸗\ *n, pl* **blowings-up** [fr. gerund of *blow up*] **:** a violent scolding

blow·iron \'blō+,-\ *n* **:** BLOWPIPE 4

blowlamp \'⸗,⸗\ *n* **:** BLOWTORCH

blow land *n* **:** land subject to wind erosion

blowline \'⸗,⸗\ *n* **:** a fishing line so light that the wind will carry it with the lure out over the stream

blow·mo·bile \'blōmō,bēl, -mə,-, -,bil\ *n* [blend of ¹*blow* and *snowmobile*] **:** a sledge driven by an airplane propeller

blow mold *n* **:** a usu. hinged mold in which a glass article may be shaped as it is blown

blow molding *n* **:** BLOWING 4

¹blown *adj* [ME *blowen,* fr. OE *geblōwen,* fr. past part. of *blōwan* to blossom — more at BLOW] **1** *of a flower* **:** OPEN **2** *of a place or plant* **:** covered with flowers **:** FLOWERY

²blown *adj* [ME *blowen,* fr. past part. of *blowen* to blow — more at BLOW] **1 :** SWOLLEN, INFLATED, DISTENDED: **a** *of animals* **:** having the stomach distended (as with food that develops gas) **:** afflicted with bloat **b** *of a sealed food container* **:** swollen or misshapen by pressure resulting from spoilage of the contents **2 :** moved or acted upon by moving air or vapor ⟨~ clouds⟩ ⟨~ soil mounded on window sills⟩ **3 a :** SPOILED, TAINTED — used esp. of food **b :** infested with fly larvae **:** FLYBLOWN ⟨caring for ~ sheep⟩ **4 :** out of breath **:** TIRED, EXHAUSTED ⟨their horses much ~ —Sir Walter Scott⟩ **5 :** destroyed or broken to pieces by explosion ⟨troops delayed by a ~ bridge⟩

³blown *n* -s **:** BLOAT 2

blown glass *n* **:** glassware shaped by forcing air into a ball of molten glass

blown–in–the–bottle \¦⸗⸗¦⸗⸗\ *adj* **:** GENUINE, INDUBITABLE

blown joint *n* **:** a plumbing joint formed in soft metal (as lead) by means of a blowtorch

blown–molded \'⸗¦⸗⸗\ *also* **blown–mold** \'⸗¦⸗\ *adj, of glassware* **:** produced by blow molding

blown oil *n* **1 :** a thickened oil obtained by blowing a fatty oil (as linseed oil or a fish oil) and used in paints and varnishes as a drying oil and in lubricants — called also *oxidized oil;* compare BODIED OIL **2 :** a semisolid or solid substance (as an asphalt) obtained by blowing fluid bitumens or residual oils from the distillation of petroleum and used in paints and protective coatings

blown–out shot \'⸗,⸗-\ *n* **:** a blast in which the explosive action breaks little or no coal or rock

blown pattern *n* **:** the unevenly distributed pattern of shotgun pellets that results from the charge of shot overtaking the front wadding of the shell and being disrupted in flight

blown three–mold \'⸗'⸗,⸗\ *adj, of glassware* **:** produced by blow molding in a mold of two or more pieces and designed to simulate hand-cut glass

blown–up \'⸗¦⸗\ *adj* **:** ENLARGED ⟨a *blown-up* photograph⟩ **:** BLOATED ⟨a *blown-up* person⟩ **:** pointlessly or artificially elaborated ⟨a *blown-up* part in a play⟩

blow off *vi* **1 :** to let steam escape through a passage provided for the purpose ⟨the engine is *blowing off*⟩ **2** *slang* **a :** COMPLAIN, GRIPE ⟨always *blowing off* about his superiors⟩ **b :** to speak earnestly and forthrightly **~** *vt* **1 a :** to empty (a boiler) of water through the blowoff pipe while under steam pressure **b :** to eject (steam, water, or sediment) from a boiler **2 :** to relieve (as emotional tension) by vigorous speech or action ⟨all the repressed eagerness of his young years must now be *blown off* —Donn Byrne⟩ ⟨having *blown off* his indigestion⟩ **3 :** to clean (a dusty place) with an air blast ⟨all looms are *blown off* three times each week — *Textiles Industries*⟩ — **blow off steam :** to relieve physical or emotional tension, ill temper, or resentment by vigorous activity or talk; *specif* **:** to talk freely on the topic of one's grievance

blowoff \'⸗,⸗\ *n* -s [*blow off*] **1 a :** a blowing off of or as if of steam, water, or other fluid (as from a boiler); *sometimes* **:** something that is blown off ⟨the drought has made the soil ~ very bad this year⟩ **b :** SPREE, BINGE **2 :** a device for blowing off steam or gas or for discharging water or accumulated matter from pipe lines and sewers **3 :** a climax esp. when marked by a shift from relative passivity to vigorous action ⟨the ~ had come when he had lodged his thousandth complaint about the food —Don Tracy⟩ **:** a strong reaction to an existent condition ⟨upset the military balance of the area, and made some kind of ~ inevitable —*Time*⟩ **4** *slang* **:** a main or featured attraction **:** DRAWING CARD; *esp* **:** a special usu. vulgar performance that follows the main performance in some carnivals and side shows

blow out *vi* **1** *of a flame* **:** to be extinguished by a gust (as of wind) **2 :** to be driven out by the expansive force of a gas or vapor ⟨a spark plug may *blow out*⟩ **3 a** *of a pneumatic tire* **:** to rupture spontaneously in service usu. at a point previously weakened or damaged **b** *of an oil or gas well* **:** to erupt out of control **4** *of a storm* **:** to dissipate by blowing **5** *of an electric fuse* **:** to melt under an excess of current **6 :** to explode without doing any useful work (as of a shot in a drill hole in mining) **~** *vt* **1 :** to extinguish (a flame) by a gust or puff (as of air) ⟨with one puff *blew out* the candle she was wishing on⟩ **2 a :** to clear of contents by blowing **:** clean (as a pipeline) by a current of air **b :** to remove (as dirt or an occlusion) by the action of a current of gas or vapor ⟨keep the pressure up until you have *blown* all the oil *out* of the line⟩ **3 :** to put (a blast furnace) out of operation — opposed to *blow in* **4 :** to walk or exercise (a horse) either to loosen his muscles for further exertion or to prevent chilling and stiffening after a hard workout **5 :** to dissipate (itself) by blowing — used of storms of which wind is a marked feature ⟨many hurricanes *blow* themselves *out* over the sea⟩ ⟨you'll have to stay here until the blizzard *blows* itself *out*⟩ **6 :** to cause (a pneumatic tire or other container) to burst because of internal pressure ⟨*blew out* a tire⟩ **7 :** to cause (an electric fuse) to blow out **8 :** to deflect and extinguish (an arc or spark) ⟨the magnetic field *blows out* an arc⟩

blowout \ˈ=,=\ *n* -s [*blow out*] **1** *slang* **:** a big social affair **:** a convivial party or celebration typically featuring abundant food and drink **2 :** an outburst of temper or disorder **:** ROW **3 a :** a bursting of a container caused by the weight or pressure of the contained material (as of a cofferdam by the weight of water, of a tube pipe by the expansive force of contained gas, or of a pneumatic tire by pressure of the contained air on a weak spot) **b :** the hole made in the container by such bursting **c :** the sudden escape of air from the working chamber of a pneumatic caisson **d :** SAND BOIL **e :** an uncontrolled eruption of an oil or gas well due to excessive natural pressure **4 :** a valley or depression blown out by the wind in areas of shifting sand or of light cultivated soil **5 a** *of an electric fuse* **:** the action of blowing out or the condition of being blown out **b :** MAGNETIC BLOWOUT **6 :** a toy or novelty device consisting essentially of a flexible rolled tube that straightens and extends suddenly when the breath is blown into its open end **7 :** eversion or prolapse of the oviduct of domestic poultry through the vent, being a frequent disorder of heavy-laying hens **8 :** the irregular surface outcrop of certain mineral deposits **9 :** FLAMEOUT **10 :** the lateral thrust of an explosion, being of the extent of its horizontal range of effectiveness

blowout grass \ˈ"-\ *n* **:** any of several grasses growing on interior sand dunes in the western U.S. (esp. *Redfieldia flexuosa* and *Muhlenbergia pungens*)

blow over *vi* **:** to pass away without effect **:** DISSIPATE, SCATTER ⟨it looked like rain but the clouds have all *blown over* now⟩ ⟨be patient, your troubles will soon *blow over*⟩

blowpipe \ˈ=,=\ *n* **1 :** a small tubular instrument for directing a jet of air or other gas into a flame so as to concentrate and increase the heat, used esp. in analysis in which the nature of a substance is studied by means of its characteristic behavior (as with respect to fusibility, flame coloration, or formation of volatile coatings) when exposed to the flame **2 a :** a small simple tubular instrument tapered to a straight or slightly curved tip used in anatomy and zoology for revealing or cleaning a cavity **b :** a blowgun for ejecting compressed air **3 :** BLOWGUN 1 **4** *or* **blowing pipe :** a long metal tube on the end of which a glassmaker gathers a quantity of molten glass and through which he blows to expand and shape it **5 :** BLOWTORCH; *esp* **:** one using acetylene and oxygen (as for cutting metal or welding)

blowpit \ˈ=,=\ *n* **:** a pit or tank into which the contents of a digester are blown at the completion of a cook in papermaking

blowpoint \ˈ=,=\ *n* **:** an old game prob. of blowing arrows at a mark

blow-proof \ˈ=ˈ=\ *adj* **:** proof against failure by blowing out ⟨a ~ gasket⟩

blow run *n* **:** an operation sometimes performed in the making of water gas in which part or all of the blow gas is recovered

blows *pl of* BLOW, *pres 3d sing of* BLOW

blowse \ˈblau̇z\ *var of* BLOWZE

blowsed *var of* BLOWZED

blows·i·ly *or* **blowz·i·ly** \ˈblau̇zəlē, -li\ *adv* **:** in a blowsy manner

blow snake *n* [so called fr. its habit of distending the surface of its head before striking] **:** HOGNOSE SNAKE

blow steam *n* **:** the steam escaping from a digester charge when it is blown in papermaking

blowsy *also* **blowzy** *or* **blousy** \ˈblau̇zē, -zi\ *adj* -ER/-EST [*blowse* or *blowze* or *blouse* + -*y*] **1** *of a person* **:** coarse and ruddy-faced **:** fat and ruddy **:** high-colored and well-fed **2 :** DISHEVELED, FROWZY ⟨a careless ~ wench⟩ ⟨lived in a series of ~ rooms⟩; *often* **:** giving an effect of dishevelment (as by reason of imperfect planning, inattention to detail, or omission of needed polish and finish) ⟨~ novels⟩ ⟨~ metaphysical abstractions —Brendan Gill⟩ **syn** see SLATTERNLY

blow tank *n* **:** BLOWPIT

blowth \ˈblōth\ *n* -s [fr. ³*blow*, after E *grow: growth*] *now dial* **:** the stage of blossoming **:** BLOOM ⟨the bushes were in the ~⟩

blowtorch \ˈ=,=\ *n* **:** a small portable blast burner either supplied with gaseous fuel and air or oxygen through tubes or including a fuel tank (as for kerosene or gasoline) that is pressurized by a hand pump, used esp. in plumbing — called also *blast lamp, blowlamp*

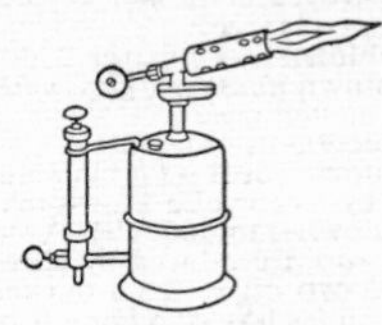

blowtorch

blowtube \ˈ=,=\ *n* **1 :** BLOWGUN 1 **2 :** BLOWPIPE 4

blow up *vt* **1 :** to rend apart, shatter, or destroy by explosion — compare BLOW *vt* 7 **2 a :** to destroy or damage as if by explosion ⟨many biographies have cruelly *blown up* the reputations of some of the great men in history⟩; *esp* **:** to impair the validity, credibility, or significance of ⟨these facts completely *blew up* the case against him⟩ **b :** to reprimand sharply or harshly **3 a :** to fill with or as if with air ⟨*blowing up* a balloon⟩ **b :** to inflate esp. with pride or self-conceit ⟨they *blew* him *up* to ridiculous proportions with their childish adulation⟩ **c :** to expand (as a relatively minor issue) to unreasonable proportions ⟨it is easy to *blow up* the medical school out of all proportion to its place in the university structure —Morley Callaghan⟩ **4 a :** to bring into existence (bad weather) — usu. used with *it* as an impersonal nominative ⟨it looks as though it may *blow up* a storm by nightfall⟩ **b** *archaic* **:** to stir up (as animosity, discord, anger) **:** EXCITE, AROUSE **5 a :** to make an enlargement of (as a photograph) **b :** to enlarge an image of a motion-picture film by optical printing from (a smaller one) ⟨he *blew up* an 8 mm to a 16 mm film⟩ **c :** to enlarge (as original copy or cuts) photographically ~ *vi* **1 a** *of explosives* **:** EXPLODE ⟨all the charges *blew up* at once⟩ **b :** to be disrupted by explosion ⟨it looked as though half the town had *blown up*⟩ **2 a :** to be destroyed as if by explosion ⟨saw his academic career *blow up* in a tabloid scandal —*Time*⟩ **b :** FAIL, COLLAPSE; *esp* **:** to fail to stand up under careful scrutiny ⟨on further investigation the case *blew up*⟩ or stress ⟨many an experienced player *blows up* in his lines on opening night⟩ **c :** to lose self-control; *esp* **:** to become violently angry or abusive ⟨he finally *blew up* and fairly screamed with rage⟩ **3 a :** to become filled with or as if with air **:** SWELL ⟨this tire won't *blow up*, the valve must be blocked⟩ **b :** to become expanded esp. to unreasonable proportions ⟨this matter could *blow up* out of sight if someone doesn't set it straight⟩ **4 a** *of bad weather* **:** to come in on or as if on a blowing of wind — often used with *it* as an impersonal nominative ⟨it's going to *blow up* cold⟩ **b :** to come to the fore **:** appear suddenly or unexpectedly **:** arise without warning ⟨where will the next international crisis *blow up*⟩ ⟨a foolish argument *blew up*⟩ — **blow up in one's face :** to fail completely and publicly esp. in such a way as to embarrass ⟨his whole scheme *blew up in his face*⟩

blowup \ˈ=,=\ *n* -s [*blow up*] **1 :** a blowing up **:** as **a :** EXPLOSION **b :** an outburst of temper **c :** a photographic enlargement (as of original art work, engravings, or type proofs); *sometimes* **:** the production of such blowups **2 :** failure (of a pavement) involving heaving due to excessive expansion **3 :** a tank where crude sugar is dissolved; *also* **:** one in which a solution of crude sugar is clarified

blowy \ˈblōē, -i\ *adj* -ER/-EST [²*blow* + -*y*] **1 :** WINDY ⟨a chill ~ day⟩ **2 :** subject to the action of wind ⟨~ sloping land⟩; *esp* **:** readily blown about ⟨soft full ~ skirts⟩

blowze \ˈblau̇z\ *n* -s [origin unknown] **1** *now dial Eng* **:** WENCH; *esp* **:** a beggar wench **2** *now dial Eng* **:** a coarse or untidy woman **3** *now dial Eng* **:** a wild girl **:** HOYDEN

blowzed *also* **blowsed** \ˈblau̇zd\ *adj* [*blowze* or *blowse* + -*ed*] **:** BLOWSY

blowzily *var of* BLOWSILY

blowzy *var of* BLOWSY

blr *abbr* boiler

BLR *abbr* breech-loading rifle

BLs *pl of* BL

blst *abbr* ballast

blt *abbr* built

blub \ˈbləb\ *vi* **blubbed; blubbed; blubbing; blubs** [by shortening] **:** BLUBBER 2

¹blub·ber \ˈbləbə(r)\ *n* -s [ME *bluber, blober* bubble, foam, prob. of imit. origin] **1 :** a large sea nettle or medusa **2 :** fat which lies between the skin and muscular flesh of whales and other large marine mammals, which serves as an insulating layer, and from which oil is obtained **3 :** superfluous fat on a person or animal **4** [²*blubber*] **:** the act or sound of blubbering

²blubber \"\ *vb* **blubbered; blubbered; blubbering** \-b(ə)riŋ\ **blubbers** [ME *blubren, blobren,* fr. *bluber, blober,* n.] *vi* **1 :** to make a bubbling sound **:** issue with a bubbling sound — often used with *up* or *out* **2 :** to weep noisily and excessively **:** SOB ⟨she wept, she ~*ed*, and she tore her hair —Jonathan Swift⟩ ~ *vt* **1 :** to swell or distort with weeping **:** wet with tears ⟨her face all ~*ed* from weeping⟩ **2 :** to utter haltingly while weeping **:** pour out (words) in tearful broken phrases ⟨he ~*s* all his troubles to the world⟩

³blubber \"\ *adj* [ME *blaber-* (in *blaber-lipped* blubber-lipped), prob. of imit. origin like ME *bluber, blober* bubble] **:** puffed out **:** THICK ⟨full ~ lips⟩ ⟨*blubber*-cheeked⟩

⁴blubber \ˈbləbə(r)\ *adj* [¹*blubber*] **1 :** used for removing blubber esp. in whaling ⟨~ hook⟩ ⟨~ spade⟩ **2 :** using blubber as a fuel ⟨~ lamp⟩ ⟨~ stove⟩

blub·ber·er \ˈbləbərə(r)\ *n* -s **1 :** one that blubbers **2 :** one that scrapes blubber from sealskins

blubber finger *n* [¹*blubber*] **:** SEAL FINGER

blubbering *n* -s [fr. pres. part. of *blubber*] **:** noisy weeping

blub·ber·ing·ly *adv* **:** in a blubbering manner

blubber oil *n* [⁴*blubber*] **:** oil obtained from blubber; *esp* **:** WHALE OIL

¹blub·bery \ˈbləb(ə)rē, -ri\ *adj* [³*blubber* + -*y*] **:** ³BLUBBER ⟨her lips grew broader and more ~ —David Garnett⟩

²blubbery \"\ *adj* [¹*blubber* + -*y*] **:** having or characterized by large or excessive amounts of blubber or fat ⟨a coarse ~ individual for whom he formed an instant dislike⟩

blu·cher \ˈblükə(r), -üchə(r)\ *n* -s [after G.L.von *Blücher* †1819 Prussian field marshal] **1 :** a shoe having the tongue and vamp cut in one piece and the quarters lapped over the vamp and laced together for closing **2 :** the highest bid in the game of napoleon

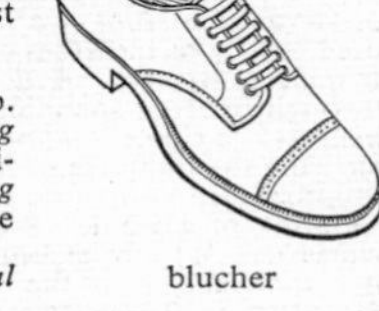

blucher

blude \blæd\ *Scot var of* BLOOD

¹bludge \ˈbləj\ *vb* -ED/-ING/-S [prob. back-formation fr. *bludger*] *vi, slang chiefly Austral* **:** to avoid responsibilities or hard work ~ *vt, slang chiefly Austral* **:** to take advantage of **:** impose on

²bludge \"\ *n* -s *slang chiefly Austral* **:** an easy job **:** SNAP

¹bludg·eon \ˈbləjən\ *n* -s [origin unknown] **1 a :** a short stick used as a weapon usu. having one thick, heavy, or loaded end **:** BILLY **b :** any similar weapon; *esp* **:** BLACKJACK **2 :** a verbal or intellectual attack or criticism ⟨the Victorians, . . . under the ~ of Lytton Strachey and his followers toppled from their high estate —*Saturday Rev.*⟩; *also* **:** the means or instrument of such attack or criticism ⟨substituting . . . for Guillaume's delicacy the ~ of satire —R.A.Hall b. 1911⟩

²bludgeon \"\ *vt* **bludgeoned; bludgeoned; bludgeoning** \-j(ə)niŋ\ **bludgeons 1 :** to hit with a bludgeon **:** BEAT ⟨~*ed* to death⟩ **2 :** to overcome by aggressive argument **:** OVERBEAR, BULLY ⟨we do not talk — we ~ one another with facts and theories —Henry Miller⟩ ⟨conversationally ~*s* his way through the world —Wyndham Lewis⟩ **3 :** COERCE ⟨~*ed* into learning grammatical rules⟩

bludg·er \ˈbləjə(r)\ *n* -s [fr. earlier *bludger* pimp, prob. contr. of *bludgeoner* pimp, bully, fr. ²*bludgeon* + -*er*] *chiefly Austral* **:** LOAFER, SHIRKER

¹blue \ˈblü\ *adj, usu* -ER/-EST [ME *bleu, blew,* fr. OF *blo, blou,* of Gmc origin; akin to OHG *blāo* blue, ON *blār* dark blue, livid; akin to L *flavus* yellow, OE *bǣl* fire, pyre — more at BALD] **1 a :** of the color blue ⟨~ violets⟩ ⟨as ~ as a sapphire⟩ **b :** having the color of the clear sky or the deep sea ⟨the ~ firmament⟩ ⟨the ~ ocean⟩ **2 a :** tinged with blue **:** BLUISH ⟨the ~ haze of tobacco smoke⟩ ⟨~ as a vein⟩ ⟨the ~ mountains⟩ ⟨the milk was ~⟩ ⟨the candle burned ~⟩ ⟨~ lightning⟩ **b** *of the skin* **:** livid esp. with cold or from a blow ⟨a face ~ from the damp —T.B.Costain⟩ **c** *of the coat of an animal* **:** bluish gray ⟨a short-haired ~ cat⟩ **3 a :** low in spirits **:** MELANCHOLY, DEPRESSED ⟨she was ~ and lonesome and half sick —J.B.Benefield⟩ **b :** productive of low spirits **:** UNPROMISING, DEPRESSING ⟨things looked ~ for them⟩ **4 a :** wearing blue ⟨the painting is called "The *Blue* Boy"⟩ **b :** having blue as a distinguishing color ⟨the ~ team defeated the red team⟩ **c :** of or relating to a blue lodge of Freemasons ⟨~ Masonry⟩ **5** *of a woman* **:** really or affectedly learned **:** INTELLECTUAL ⟨the ladies were very ~ and well-informed —W.M. Thackeray⟩ **6 :** characterized by or derived from rigid morals **:** PURITANICAL ⟨a ~ Sunday city by local option —James Street⟩ **7 a :** characterized by indecency or obscenity **:** OFF-COLOR, RISQUÉ ⟨the same joke each time — and a bit *bluer* than anything Charlie had ever heard before in mixed company —J.B.Priestley⟩ **b :** characterized by or filled with cursing and swearing **:** PROFANE ⟨~ language⟩ ⟨shop owners turned the air ~ at a mass meeting —*Time*⟩ **8 :** EXTREME, COMPLETE — used as an intensive ⟨the very name . . . put her in a ~ fear —R.L.Stevenson⟩ **9 :** relating to, suggesting, or suited to blues singing or playing ⟨*blue*-voiced⟩ ⟨a ~ song⟩ — **blue in the face :** in a state of extreme anger or exasperation ⟨argued until he was *blue in the face*⟩

²blue \"\ *n* -s [ME *bleu, blew,* fr. *bleu, blew,* adj.] **1 a :** a color whose hue is that of the clear sky or that of the portion of the color spectrum lying between green and violet **b :** the one of the four psychologically primary hues that is evoked in the average normal observer under normal conditions by radiant energy of the wavelength 475 millimicrons **c :** one of the six psychologically primary object colors **2 a :** any of certain varieties of gray having a bluish appearance — used esp. of pelage or plumage colors in dogs, cats, and poultry **b :** an animal having a coat of such a blue **3 a :** a pigment or dye that colors blue **b :** BLUING 2 **4 a :** blue clothing or cloth ⟨the boys in ~⟩ **b :** one wearing blue or belonging to an organization or party whose uniform or badge is blue ⟨next time you see the ~ ashore —Rudyard Kipling⟩ **5 a** (1) **:** SKY ⟨boomerangs that were once hurled into the ~ —A.J.Toynbee⟩ (2) **:** the far distance **:** SPACE ⟨chuck up Seville and go off somewhere into the ~ —William Sansom⟩ **b :** SEA, OCEAN ⟨the Marianas were right out in the ~ —Fletcher Pratt⟩ **6 :** an object that is blue in color or that belongs to a group whose characteristic color is blue ⟨pieces of Nanking ~⟩ ⟨the poker player bought a stack of ~*s*⟩ **7** [by shortening] **:** BLUESTOCKING **8 a :** a student who represents Oxford or Cambridge University in athletic contests and is awarded the right to wear the university color ⟨was an Oxford ~ in cricket⟩ **b :** the right to wear such a university color ⟨won his ~ in tennis at Cambridge⟩ **9 :** any of numerous small chiefly blue butterflies of the family Lycaenidae **10 a :** the blue third circle of an archery target **b :** a shot that hits such a circle **11 :** first place or first prize **:** BLUE RIBBON ⟨won the ~ at the horse show⟩ **12 :** BLUE CHEESE **13** *Austral* **:** an argument or fight ⟨he got mixed up in a ~⟩ — **out of the blue :** without preliminary warning **:** UNEXPECTEDLY ⟨the job was offered to me *out of the blue* —F.A.Swinnerton⟩

³blue \"\ *vb* **blued; blued; blueing** *or* **bluing; blues** [¹*blue*] *vt* **1 :** to make blue in color: as **a :** to dye or paint blue **b :** to apply bluing to **c :** to make blue (as steel, rifle barrels, or razor blades) by heating in air, steam, or appropriate chemicals — see BLUE HEAT **2** *slang Brit* **:** to spend lavishly or wastefully **:** SQUANDER ⟨while they've got money they ~ it —Ngaio Marsh⟩ ~ *vi* **:** to turn blue

blue acara *n* **:** a small brightly marked acara (*Aequidens latifrons*) of northern So. America having each scale blotched with bright blue and being a popular tropical aquarium fish

blue alert *n* **:** the second stage of alert (as for a threatened air attack or an approaching storm) during which emergency preparations are carried out according to plan; *also* **:** the signal for this — compare RED ALERT, WHITE ALERT, YELLOW ALERT

blue andalusian *n, usu cap A&B* **:** a blue-gray domestic fowl produced by interbreeding black and white Andalusians

blue-and-yel·low macaw \ˌ=ˈ=ˌ=-\ *n* **:** a So. American macaw (*Ara ararauna*) predominantly blue and yellow

blue anemone *n* **:** SQUIRREL CUP

blue angel *or* **blue angelfish** *n* **:** a common chaetodont angelfish of Florida and the West Indies

blue ant *n* **:** a large solitary metallic blue or purple Australian wasp (*Diamma bicolor*) with red legs and antennae, the female being without wings but having a powerful sting

blue asbestos *n* **:** CROCIDOLITE

blue ash *n* **:** an ash (*Fraxinus quadrangulata*) of the central and southern U.S. having bluish green foliage and hard brown wood

blue ashes *n pl but usu sing in constr* **:** AZURITE BLUE

blue baby *n* **:** an infant with a bluish or dusky tint from birth; *specif* **:** one with a congenital defect of the heart in which the flow of venous blood to the lungs is impeded, resulting in the mingling of venous and arterial blood and deficient oxygenation of the hemoglobin

blue-baby operation \ˈ=,==-\ *n* **:** BLALOCK-TAUSSIG OPERATION

blueback \ˈ=,=\ *n* **1 :** any of various fishes (as lake herring or glut herring) having a blue or bluish color on the back **2** [so called fr. the contrast of the blue ink used on its back to the green ink used on the back of the Northern greenback] *archaic* **:** a paper note of Confederate money **3 :** a bluish discoloration of the backs of turkeys resulting from dissemination of feather pigment through the skin when immature feathers are broken **4** [so called fr. the color of the coat] **:** a young hooded seal

blueback mullet *n* **:** LEBRANCHO

blueback salmon *n* **:** a salmon of a species (*Oncorhynchus nerka*) that includes the landlocked kokanee and the sockeye

blueback trout *n* **:** a trout somewhat bluish above: as **a :** OQUASSA **b :** a rainbow trout of a variety restricted to Crescent Lake, Wash.

blue bag *n* **1 :** a barrister's brief bag made of blue material **2 :** gangrenous mastitis of sheep — called also *black bag, black garget, black udder*

blue ball *n* **:** BLUE SCABIOUS

blue basic lead sulfate *n* **:** BLUE LEAD 2

blue bass \-ˈbas\ *n* **:** any of various somewhat blue marine or freshwater fishes (as the black sea bass, the sargo, or the green sunfish)

bluebead \ˈ=,=\ *also* **bluebead lily** *n* [so called fr. the beadlike blue fruit] **:** YELLOW CLINTONIA

blue bear *n* **:** GLACIER BEAR

¹bluebeard \ˈ=,=\ *n* [after *Bluebeard*, a fairy-tale character who murdered six wives, trans. of F *Barbe-Bleue*, the best-known literary version being by Charles Perrault †1703 Fr. writer] **:** a man who marries and kills one wife after another

²bluebeard \"\ *adj* [after *Bluebeard*, the fairy-tale character; fr. his having hidden the bodies of his murdered wives in a room which his seventh wife was forbidden to enter] **:** not to be entered or explored **:** FORBIDDEN ⟨the ~ room of the house —Thomas De Quincey⟩

³bluebeard \"\ *n* -s [¹*blue* + *beard*; fr. the appearance of the flower] **:** a shrub of the genus *Caryopteris*; *esp* **:** an autumn-blooming Asiatic ornamental (*C. incana*) with blue flowers suggesting those of a spirea — called also *blue spirea*

blue beardtongue *n* **:** a Rocky Mountain pentstemon (*Pentstemon virens*) having bluish foliage and deep-blue flowers with conspicuous yellow-bearded sterile stamens

blue beech *n* **:** AMERICAN HORNBEAM

bluebell \ˈ=,=\ *n* **1 :** a plant of the genus *Campanula*, many species of which bear flowers shaped like bells; *esp* **:** HAREBELL 1 **2 :** either of two European plants having racemes of drooping blue flowers shaped like bells: **a :** WOOD HYACINTH **b :** GRAPE HYACINTH **3 :** any of a number of American plants having blue flowers shaped somewhat like bells (as *Viorna crispa, Mertensia virginica, Polemonium reptans, Veronica americana*) **4 :** GARDEN COLUMBINE **5** *NewZeal* **:** any of several plants of the genus *Wahlenbergia* of the bellflower family; *esp* **:** a low tufted plant (*W. gracilis*) that has blue flowers that are shaped like bells

bluebells-of-scotland \ˈ=,==ˈskätlənd\ *n pl, cap S* **:** HAREBELL 1

blue·ber·ry \ˈblü,berē, -b(ə)rē, -ri — *see* BERRY\ *n* **1 a :** the sweet edible blue or blackish berry of any of several plants of the genus *Vaccinium* — see HUCKLEBERRY **b :** any plant that bears this fruit **2 a** (1) **:** the edible berry of an Australian tree (*Myoporum serratum*) — called also *native currant, palberry* (2) **:** the tree that bears this fruit — called also *cockatoo bush, native juniper, native myrtle* **b :** the fruit of the blueberry ash

blueberry ash *or* **blueberry tree** *n* **:** any of several Australian trees of the genus *Elaeocarpus* (as *E. obovatus* and *E. reticulatus*) that yield a strong white wood and bear an edible drupe

blue·ber·ry·ing \ˈblü,bereiŋ\ *n* **:** the act of gathering or looking for blueberries

blueberry maggot *n* **:** the larva of a trypetid fly (*Rhagoletis mendax*) that is similar in habits to the apple maggot but usu. attacks blueberries

blueberry root *n* **:** BLUE COHOSH

blueberry thrips *n* **:** a thrips insect (*Frankliniella vacinii*) prevalent in commercial blueberry areas of eastern Canada feeding on and causing twisting and curling of the leaves and sometimes loss of fruit

blue bice *n* **:** AZURITE BLUE

bluebill \ˈ=,=\ *n* **:** any of various American ducks: as **a :** SCAUP DUCK **b :** WIDGEON **c :** RUDDY DUCK

blue billy *n* [prob. fr. the name *Billy*] **:** a petrel (*Pachyptila desolata*) of the southern oceans with a bluish back and white underparts

blue bindweed *n* **:** BITTERSWEET 2a

blue birch *n* **:** a small tree (*Betula caeruleo-grandis*) growing in dry soils of northeastern No. America and having ovate to deltoid sharply serrate leaves and catkin scales with widely divergent lateral lobes

bluebird \ˈ=,=\ *n* **1 :** any of several small No. American songbirds (genus *Sialia*) that are related to the robin but more or less blue above, the male of the common species (*S. sialis*) of the eastern and central U.S. having a blue back and reddish breast and being among the first of the spring migrants to arrive in the North — see MOUNTAIN BLUEBIRD, WESTERN BLUEBIRD **2 :** FAIRY BLUEBIRD **3 :** a moderate blue that is greener and duller than average copen and redder and deeper than azurite blue, Dresden blue, or pompadour

blue bird *n* **:** a member of the Blue Birds, the junior program of Camp Fire Girls for girls aged 7, 8 and 9

blue biskop *n* **:** BLACK BISKOP

blue-black \ˈ=ˈ=\ *adj* **:** extremely dark; *esp* **:** black with a tinge of blue

blue black *n* **1 :** a pigment of a blue-black color (as a vegetable black or a carbon black) **2 :** a dye producing a blue-black color

blue blazer *n, often cap both Bs* [so called fr. the blue flame of the ignited whiskey] **:** a cocktail made of ignited Scotch whiskey and boiling water with sweetening and lemon peel added

blue blazing star *n* **:** a blazing star (*Liatris squarrosa*) with purplish blue flowers

blue blindness *n* **:** TRITANOPIA

blue blood *n* [trans. of Sp *sangre azul*] **1 :** the blood of noble, aristocratic, or socially prominent families **2 a :** a member of a noble, aristocratic, or socially prominent family ⟨a *blue blood* . . . related to half the noble families in the British isles —*Time*⟩ **b :** the nobility or aristocracy **:** the upper classes ⟨one of high rank and birth, of the *blue blood* —Maria Edgeworth⟩ — **blue-blood·ed** \ˈ=ˈ==\ *adj*

blueblossom \ˈ=,==\ *n* **:** a blue-flowered California shrub (*Ceanothus thyrsiflorus*) — called also *blue myrtle, California lilac*

blue boneset *n* **:** MISTFLOWER

bluebonnet \ˈ=,==\ *n* **1 a :** a wide flat round cap of blue wool formerly worn in Scotland **b :** one that wears such a cap; *specif* **:** SCOT **2 a :** BLUE TIT **b :** an Australian parrot (*Psephotus haematogaster*) with bright blue on its forehead, face, and shoulders **3 a :** CORNFLOWER 1b **b :** a low-growing annual lupine of Texas with silky foliage and blue flowers that is now usu. considered to constitute a single somewhat variable species (*Lupinus subcarnosus*) but is sometimes felt to be divisible into two closely related species (*L. subcarnosus* and *L. texensis*) that differ chiefly in habitat and distribution — called also *buffalo clover* **c :** BLUE SCABIOUS

blue book *n* **1** *often cap both Bs* **:** a government publication providing information on any topic (as a manual or register of officials); *esp* **:** a usu. detailed government report (as the report of a department or commission) ⟨the U.S. Department of State issued . . . a heavily documented 40,000-word *Blue Book* —F.A.Magruder⟩ **2 :** a nongovernmental directory or register esp. of persons of social prominence ⟨the renowned cast that read like the *Blue Book* of the London theatre —Brooks Atkinson⟩ **3 a :** a blank blue-covered booklet used in colleges for writing examinations **b :** a college examination

bluebottle \ˈ⸗,⸗⸗\ *n* **1a :** CORNFLOWER 1b; *broadly* **:** any plant of the genus *Centaurea* **b :** GRAPE HYACINTH **2** *Brit* **:** a person wearing a blue uniform; *esp* **:** POLICEMAN ⟨turns out to be the village ~ —P.G.Wodehouse⟩ **3 :** any of several blowflies that are larger than the houseflies, have the abdomen or the whole body iridescent blue in color, and make a loud buzzing noise in flight **4** *chiefly Austral* **:** PORTUGUESE MAN-OF-WAR

blue brant *n* **:** BLUE GOOSE

blue bream *n* **:** BLUEGILL

bluebreast darter \ˈ⸗,⸗-\ *or* **blue-breasted darter** \ˈ⸗,⸗⸗-\ *n* **:** a brilliantly colored darter (*Poecilichthys camurus*) of clear swift streams from Lake Erie to Tennessee

blue-breasted quail *n* **:** PAINTED QUAIL 1b

blue brick *n* **:** SEWER BRICK

blue brush *n* **:** BLUEBLOSSOM

bluebuck \ˈ⸗,⸗\ *n* [trans. of Afrik *bloubok*] **:** BLAUBOK

blue bug *n* **:** CHICKEN TICK

blue bull *n* **:** NILGAI

blue bunch grass *also* **bluebunch fescue** \ˈ⸗,⸗-\ *n* **:** a fescue grass (*Festuca idahoensis*) of the western U.S. used as forage

bluebunch wheatgrass *n* **:** a tufted grass (*Agropyron spicatum*) of western No. America used for forage and pasture and having stiff pale leaves and strongly compressed spikelets

blue bur *n* [so called fr. the pale blue flowers] **:** STICKSEED

bluebush \ˈ⸗,⸗\ *n* **1 :** a Mexican shrub (*Ceanothus coeruleus*) bearing a profusion of blue flowers **2** *Austral* **:** any of various plants: as **a :** a tomentose saltbush (*Kochia pyramidata*) with short linear leaves **b :** a wattle (*Acacia brachybotrya*) with rather broad phyllodia and linear to narrowly elliptic pods

bluecap \ˈ⸗,⸗\ *n* **1 :** BLUEBONNET 1b **2 a :** BLUE TIT **b :** an Australian fairy wren (*Malurus cyaneus*), the male being largely bright blue and black in summer plumage **3 a :** FIELD SCABIOUS **b :** CORNFLOWER 1b

blue cardinal flower *n* **:** GREAT LOBELIA

blue cat *or* **blue catfish** *or* **blue channel cat** *or* **blue channel catfish** *n* **:** a large bluish catfish (*Ictalurus furcatus*) of the Mississippi valley that may exceed 100 pounds in weight and is an important food fish

blue cheese *n* [trans. of F *fromage bleu*] **:** a cheese usu. made of cow's milk and marked with veins of greenish blue mold

blue chip *n* **1 a :** a blue-colored poker chip usu. of high value **b :** a valuable asset; *esp* **:** one that can be readily used when needed (as in negotiations) ⟨we've got the *blue chips* in the form of our airplanes and ships and fighting men —*Saturday Rev.*⟩ **2 a :** a stock issue esp. of a well-established corporation with substantial assets that usu. commands a high price in relation to its earnings and to the prices of other stocks as a result of public acceptance and confidence in its stability **:** a quality common stock **b :** a venture, investment, or enterprise that is considered to be among the most secure or consistently profitable or successful in its class ⟨the council's drive is supported by the *blue chips* in the advertising field —*N.Y. Times*⟩

blue-chip \ˈ⸗ˈ⸗\ *adj* [*blue chip*] **1 :** of or relating to a blue chip ⟨with the *blue-chip* stocks at record levels, many companies were paying dividends amounting to only 3 percent of their stock purchase price —*Time*⟩ **2 :** being among the leaders in some class **:** being among the most consistently profitable or successful in some field of activity ⟨the *blue-chip* organizations of the electrical world —*Iron Age*⟩ ⟨*blue-chip* farm lands —*Wall Street Jour.*⟩

bluecoat \ˈ⸗,⸗\ *n* **:** one that wears a blue coat: as **a :** a soldier esp. of the U.S. during the Civil War **b :** POLICEMAN

bluecoat boy *n* **:** a student at a bluecoat school

bluecoat school *n* **:** any of certain English charity schools whose students wear long blue coats or gowns

blue cod *n* **1 :** any of several marine fishes of the Pacific coast of No. America: as **a :** LINGCOD **b :** CABEZON 1a **c :** SABLEFISH **2 :** a common marine spiny-finned fish (*Parapercis colias*) of New Zealand

blue cohosh *n* **:** a tall herb (*Caulophyllum thalictroides*) of eastern No. America and Asia having triternate leaves, small greenish yellow or purplish flowers, large blue fruits like berries, and a thick knotty rootstock that was formerly used as an antispasmodic and emmenagogue — called also *blueberry root, papooseroot, squawroot*

blue-collar \ˈ⸗ˈ⸗⸗\ *adj* [so called fr. the contrast of the typically blue collars of work shirts to the typically white collars of dress shirts] **:** belonging or relating to a broad class of wage earners whose duties call for the wearing of work clothes or protective clothing ⟨warehousemen, longshoremen, farmers, miners, mechanics, construction workers, and other *blue-collar* workers —W.J.Hudson⟩ — compare WHITE-COLLAR

blue comb *also* **blue comb disease** *n* [so called fr. its discoloring effect on the combs of fowls] **:** a severe disease of domestic fowl and certain other birds that resembles Bright's disease of man and is due to unknown causes, although both a virus and excessive consumption of common salt have been implicated and hereditary factors may play a part

blue copperas *n* **:** COPPER SULFATE

blue copper ore *n* **:** AZURITE 1

blue coral *n* **:** a massive coral (*Heliopora coerulea*) with a lamellated calcareous skeleton colored blue by iron salts that is widely distributed in the Indian and southwest Pacific oceans and is the sole recent form of a once abundant order (Coenothecalia)

blue crab *n* **1 :** any of several largely blue swimming crabs of

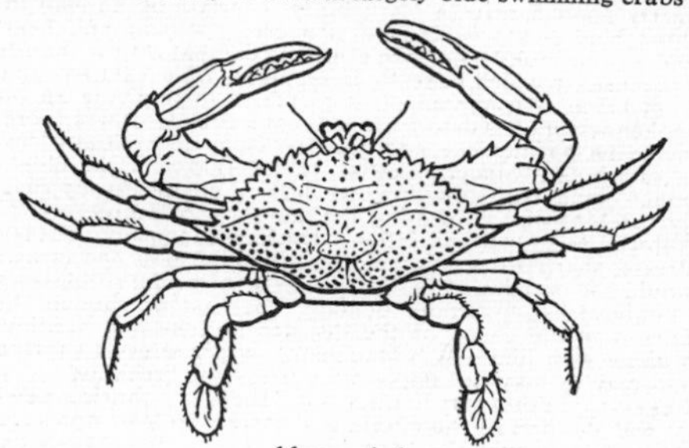

blue crab 1

the genus *Callinectes* of the Atlantic and Gulf coasts of the U.S.; *esp* **:** a crab (*C. sapidus*) that is particularly common from Texas to Delaware and is used extensively as food, providing the soft-shelled crabs of the markets **2** *Austral* **:** an important edible crab (*Portunus pelagicus*)

blue crane *n* **:** GREAT BLUE HERON

blue creeper *n* **:** an Australian vine (*Bredemeyera volubilis*) with showy blue flowers

blue crevally *also* **blue crevalle** *n* **:** a large black-spotted cavalla (*Caranx stellatus*) widely distributed in warmer parts of the Pacific ocean

bluecup \ˈ⸗,⸗\ *n* **:** CORNFLOWER 1b

blue curls *n pl but sing or pl in constr* **1 :** a plant of the genus *Trichostema*: as **a :** a plant (*T. dichotomum*) of the eastern U.S. — called also *bastard pennyroyal* **b :** a plant (*T. lanceolatum*) of California **2 :** SELF-HEAL

blued *past of* BLUE

blue daisy *n* **1 :** an Australian herb (*Felicia amelloides*) with blue-rayed flowers resembling the marguerite **2** *Brit* **:** MICHAELMAS DAISY **3 :** CHICORY

blue dandelion *n* **:** CHICORY

blue darner *n* **:** any of certain large strong-flying often chiefly blue dragonflies of the genus *Aeschna*

blue darter *n* **:** any of several hawks having darting erratic flight rather than soaring (as the sharp-shinned hawk or the Cooper's hawk)

blue devil *n* **1 blue devils** *pl* **:** low spirits **:** DESPONDENCY, MELANCHOLY **2 a :** a common blue-rayed aster (*Aster lowrieanus*) of the eastern U.S. **b blue devils** *pl* **:** BLUEWEED 1 **3 a :** either of two Australian percoid fishes (*Paraplesiops gigas* and *P. meleagris*) brightly marked with light blue dots **b :** a small brilliantly marked blue fish (*Pomacentrus fuscus*) of the West Indies

blue dicks \-ˈdiks\ *n pl but sing or pl in constr* **:** a wild hyacinth (*Brodiaea capitata*) of the western U.S.

blue discharge *n* **:** a discharge on blue paper formerly issued by the U.S. Army or Air Force to one considered undesirable (as through inefficiency or incompatibility)

blue disease *n* **1 :** CYANOSIS **2 :** ROCKY MOUNTAIN SPOTTED FEVER

blue doe *n* [so called fr. its bluish pelt] **:** a female red kangaroo — called also *blue flier*

blue dog *n* **1 :** SMOOTH DOGFISH **2 :** SAND SHARK a

blue dogwood *n* **:** a shrub or small tree (*Cornus alternifolia*) of eastern No. America with small white flowers and blue fruit — see TREE illustration

blue duck *n* **:** a New Zealand duck (*Hymenolaimus malacorhynchos*) with mostly lead-blue plumage

blue duiker *n* **:** any of several small bluish gray antelopes (genus *Cephalophus*) of southern and equatorial Africa of about the same size and weight as a large hare

blue earth *n* **:** KIMBERLITE

blue elder *or* **blue elderberry** *n* **:** a shrub or small tree (*Sambucus caerulea*) of the western U.S. with white flowers and blue berries covered with a whitish bloom

blue ensign *n* **:** a nautical ensign with a blue field borne by various classes of vessels in British government service other than the Royal Navy, under certain conditions by merchantmen commanded by retired officers of the Royal Navy or by officers of the Royal Naval Reserve, and by many British yacht clubs and yachts — see ENSIGN 1

blue-eye \ˈ⸗,⸗\ *n* **1 :** an Australian honey eater (*Entomyzon cyanotis*) **2 :** a small Australian silverside (*Pseudomugil signifer*) used locally in mosquito control and widely known as an aquarium fish **3 :** a faulty or defective eye of a horse; *esp* **:** WALLEYE **4 :** a disease of Indian corn caused by fungi of the genus *Penicillium* and characterized by a rotting and darkening of the germ often after harvesting

blue-eyed \ˈ⸗ˈ⸗\ *adj* **1 :** having blue eyes ⟨*blue-eyed* children⟩ **2 :** FAVORED, PREFERRED ⟨the *blue-eyed* boy can do no wrong⟩

blue-eyed babies *n pl* **:** BLUETS

blue-eyed grass *n* **:** a plant of the genus *Sisyrinchium* having grasslike foliage and delicate blue flowers

blue-eyed mary \-ˈmerē, -ma(a)rē, -marē, -ri\ *n, usu cap M* [fr. the name *Mary*] **1 :** a European navelwort (*Omphalodes verna*) with small blue flowers **2 :** INNOCENCE 3b(1) **3 :** BLUE-EYED GRASS **4 :** a common erect spiderwort (*Tradescantia virginiana*) with blue flowers

blue-faced booby \ˈ⸗,⸗-\ *n* **:** a booby (*Sula dactylatra*) of tropical seas that is white with blackish brown tail and wing tips

blue false indigo *n* **:** a wild indigo (*Baptisia australis*) of the eastern U.S. with racemes of blue flowers

blue fescue *n* **:** a variety (*Festuca ovina glauca*) of sheep's fescue with silvery blue foliage

blue field madder *n* **:** FIELD MADDER

blue fig *n* **:** BRISBANE QUANDONG

bluefin \ˈ⸗,⸗\ *n* **1 :** a deep-water cisco (*Leucichthys cyanopterus*) of Lake Superior **2** *also* **bluefin tuna :** a very large tuna (*Thunnus thynnus*) widely distributed in temperate seas

bluefish \ˈ⸗,⸗\ *n* **1 :** a very active and voracious fish (*Pomatomus saltatrix*) related to the Carangidae but usu. regarded as constituting a separate family (Pomatomidae), that is distributed in many seas and that is an important food fish on the Atlantic coast of the U.S. **2 :** any of various somewhat dark or bluish fishes: as **a :** ARCTIC GRAYLING **b :** POLLACK **c :** BLACK SEA BASS

blue flag *n* **:** a blue-flowered iris; *esp* **:** a common herb (*Iris versicolor*) the dried rhizome of which has been used as a cathartic and emetic

blue flax *n* **1 :** FLAX 1a **2 :** a perennial flax (*Linum lewisii*) of the desert and mountain regions of No. America, esp. California, with blue flowers in loose corymbose clusters

blue flier *n* **:** BLUE DOE

¹blue flower *n, sometimes cap B&F* [trans. of G *blaue blume,* symbol of poetry in *Heinrich von Ofterdingen* (1802), fragmentary novel by Baron Friedrich von Hardenberg (Novalis) †1801 German poet] **:** the mystic vague object of romanticist longing esp. in the 19th century — usu. used with preceding *the* ⟨always in search of the *blue flower* —Willi Apel⟩

²blue flower *n* [¹*blue* + *flower*] **:** a pale blue that is redder, lighter, and stronger than average powder blue or Sistine and greener, lighter, and stronger than average cadet gray

blue-footed booby \ˈ⸗ˈ⸗⸗-\ *n* **:** a Pacific coast booby (*Sula nebouxi*) that is brownish flecked with white above and white below and has bright blue feet and legs

blue fox *n* **1 a :** a color phase of the arctic fox in which the coat remains blue gray in winter **b :** the typical arctic fox in summer pelage **c :** the pelt or fur of one of these foxes often imitated by dyeing white fox pelts **2 :** a dark reddish gray that is lighter and very slightly yellower than average mauve taupe and less strong and slightly bluer and darker than average rose taupe

blue-fronted jay \ˈ⸗ˈ⸗⸗-\ *n* **:** a variety (*Cyanocitta stellere frontalis*) of Steller's jay occurring in the mountains of California

blue gall *n* **:** a small high quality green gall

blue gas *n* **:** uncarbureted water gas burning with a blue nonluminous flame that is used chiefly as a synthesis gas and as a source of hydrogen — distinguished from *blau gas*

blue gentian *n* **1 :** any of several blue-flowered gentians: as **a :** FRINGED GENTIAN **b :** SOAPWORT GENTIAN **c :** CLOSED GENTIAN **2 :** FALSE PENNYROYAL **3 :** an herb (*Eustoma russellianum*) of central No. America with opposite leaves and large purplish flowers

bluegill \ˈ⸗,⸗\ *also* **bluegill bream** *or* **bluegill sunfish** *n* **:** a common sunfish (*Lepomis machrochirus*) of the Mississippi drainage, the Great Lakes region, and much of the southeastern U.S. that is an excellent panfish and often stocked in artificial ponds to provide both food and sport

blue ginseng *n* **:** BLUE COHOSH

blue glede *n* **:** HEN HARRIER

blue goose *n* **:** a No. American wild goose (*Chen caerulescens*) with a grayish plumage resembling that of the young snow goose

bluegown \ˈ⸗,⸗\ *n* [so called fr. the blue gown worn as the badge of office] **:** BEADSMAN 2b

blue grama *n* **:** a grama (*Bouteloua gracilis*) that is an important forage grass in the plains area of No. America and that has the rachis not extended as a point beyond the spikelet — compare BLACK GRAMA

blue grape *n* **:** a native grape (*Vitis aestivalis argentifolia*) of the eastern U.S. with bluish glaucous stems, 3-lobed leaves, and sour bluish black berries

bluegrass \ˈ⸗,⸗\ *n, often attrib* [so called fr. the bluish green color of the culms] **1 :** any of several grasses of the genus *Poa* having bluish green culms: as **a :** KENTUCKY BLUEGRASS **b :** WIRE GRASS a **2** *NewZeal* **:** a grass (*Agropyron scabrum*) having leaves usu. scabrous on both sides **3** *Austral* **:** any of several grasses of the genus *Andropogon* **4 :** DUCK GREEN

blue-gray \ˈ⸗ˈ⸗\ *n* **:** the offspring of a mating of a white Shorthorn bull with an Aberdeen Angus cow or a Galloway cow, having a mixture of black and white hairs that gives it a bluish appearance and being highly esteemed as a beef animal

blue-gray gnatcatcher *n* **:** a common gnatcatcher (*Polioptila caerulea caerulea*) of the eastern U.S., the male being bluish gray above

blue-green alga \ˈ⸗ˈ⸗-\ *n* **:** an alga of the division Cyanophyta

blue grosbeak *n* **:** a grosbeak (*Guiraca caerulea*) that is represented by several subspecies in the U.S. and that has the male very dark blue with two chestnut bars on the wing

blue ground *n* [trans. of Afrik *blougrond*] **:** KIMBERLITE

blue grouse *n* **:** any of several obscurely mottled predominantly slaty gray grouses (genus *Dendragapus*) of western No. America; *esp* **:** DUSKY GROUSE

blue gularis *n* **:** GULARIS

blue gum *n* **1 :** any of several Australian timber trees of the genus *Eucalyptus*; *specif* **:** a tree (*E. globulus*) now much cultivated esp. in California **2 :** a bluish gum held in American Negro folklore to be characteristic of a Negro whose bite is fatally poisonous

blue hawk *n* **:** HEN HARRIER

blue-headed vireo \ˈ⸗ˈ⸗⸗-\ *n* **:** a common vireo (*Vireo solitarius solitarius*) of northeastern No. America with the top and sides of the head a bluish slaty gray

bluehearts \ˈ⸗,⸗\ *n pl but sing or pl in constr* **:** an American herb (*Buchnera americana*) with rough hairy foliage and blue flowers

blue heat *n* **:** a temperature (as 550° to 600° F) at which iron or steel becomes bluish — compare TEMPER COLOR

blue heeler *n* **:** AUSTRALIAN CATTLE DOG

blue hen's chickens *n pl, usu cap B&H&C* [prob. fr. a nickname for a Delaware regiment in the Revolutionary War, known earlier as *Caldwell's gamecocks,* fr. *blue hen,* a kind of hen reputed to breed good gamecocks] **:** DELAWAREANS — used as a nickname

blue heron *n* **:** any of certain herons with somewhat bluish or slaty plumage — see GREAT BLUE HERON, LITTLE BLUE HERON

blue huckleberry *n* **:** DANGLEBERRY

blue ice *n* **1 :** clean compact ice formed in glaciers by recrystallization of snow, often in bands presumably along shear zones **2 :** coarsely crystallized ice on the surface of some seas and lakes — compare BLACK ICE, WHITE ICE

blue indigo *n* **:** BLUE FALSE INDIGO

blueing *var of* BLUING

blueish *var of* BLUISH

blue·jack \ˈblü,jak\ *also* **bluejack oak** *n* [¹*blue* + *-jack* (as in *blackjack oak*); fr. the ashy appearance of the foliage] **:** an oak (*Quercus cinerea*) of the southern U.S. with entire cuneate leaves and numerous small acorns

bluejacket \ˈ⸗,⸗⸗\ *n* **:** an enlisted man in the navy **:** SAILOR

blue jasmine *or* **blue jessamine** *n* **:** a clematis (*Clematis crispa*) of the southern U.S. with bluish purple flowers

blue jay *n* **1 a :** the common jay (*Cyanocitta cristata*) of eastern No. America with a handsome crest and the plumage of the upper parts chiefly bright blue **b :** any of several related largely blue birds of the western U.S. with crests (genus *Cyanocitta*) or without crests (genus *Aphelocoma*) **2 :** ROAD MONKEY

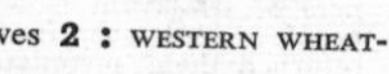

blue jay 1a

blue jeans *n pl* **:** work pants or overalls usu. made of jean or denim and blue in color **:** DENIMS

blue john \ˈ⸗,⸗\ *n* [fr. the name *John*] **1 :** a fibrous or columnar variety of fluorite found in Derbyshire, England and used esp. for vases **2** *sometimes cap J, dial* **:** SKIM MILK; *esp* **:** milk that is just beginning to sour

bluejoint \ˈ⸗,⸗\ *n* **1 :** an American forage grass (*Calamagrostis canadensis*) growing in tussocks and having soft flat often involute leaves **2 :** WESTERN WHEATGRASS 1

bluejoint turkeyfoot *n* **:** LITTLE BLUESTEM

blue kite *n* **:** HEN HARRIER

blue krait *n* **:** a black or blue-black Indian krait (*Bungarus caeruleus*) more or less banded with white

blue lace flower *also* **blue lace** *n* **:** a delicate Australian annual herb (*Trachymene coerulea*) of the family Umbelliferae having flat umbels of tiny blue flowers and used as an ornamental

blue land crab *n* **:** BLACK CRAB

blue lavender *n* **:** ONTARIO VIOLET

blue law *n* [¹*blue* (puritanical)] **1 :** one of numerous extremely rigorous laws designed to regulate morals and conduct in colonial New England **2 :** a statute regulating work, commerce, and amusements on Sundays

¹blue lead \-ˈlēd\ *n* [*lead* (gravel deposit)] **:** tertiary gold-bearing gravel deposits of the Sierra Nevada

²blue lead \-ˈled\ *n* [*lead* (metal)] **1 :** GALENA **2 :** a slate-gray pigment produced by subliming lead ore with coal or coke and used esp. in rust-resistant paints — called also *blue basic lead sulfate, sublimed blue lead*

blue lettuce *n* **:** a plant of the genus *Lactuca* (as *L. pulchella*) with blue-rayed flower heads

blue light *n* [so called fr. the allegation of Commodore Stephen Decatur †1820 American naval officer that on the night of Dec. 12, 1813 American Federalists traitorously signaled to the British by means of blue lights on either end of the mouth of the harbor at New London, Conn.] **:** a member of that wing of the American Federalist party that bitterly opposed the War of 1812 — usu. used disparagingly

blue lily *n* **:** BLUE FLAG

blue line *n* **1 :** ¹LEAD LINE 1 **2 :** either of two lines colored blue and showing through the ice that divide the defensive zones from the center ice area of an ice-hockey rink

blue lips *n pl but sing or pl in constr* **:** any of several blue-flowered herbs of the genus *Collinsia* of the western U.S.

blue lobelia *n* **:** GREAT LOBELIA

blue lodge *n, usu cap B&L* [so called from the color of the decorations of these degrees] **:** a masonic lodge in which the first three degrees are conferred — compare ENTERED APPRENTICE, FELLOWCRAFT, MASTER MASON

blue lotus *n* **:** either of two blue-flowered cultivated water lilies: **a :** a lotus (*Nymphaea stellata*) of India **b :** a lotus (*N. caerulea*) of Egypt

blue louse *n* **:** any of several sucking lice that infest cattle and sheep

blue lucy *n, often cap L* [fr. the name *Lucy*] **:** SELF-HEAL

blue lupine *or* **blue lupin** *n* **:** a blue-flowered plant of the genus *Lupinus* (as *L. perennis* and *L. augustifolius*) of eastern No. America, useful for forage and for soil-building purposes

blue·ly *adv* **:** with a blue or bluish color or tinge **:** in a blue manner

blue magnolia *n* **:** CUCUMBER TREE

blue mahoe *or* **blue mahogany** *n* **:** MAJAGUA b

blue mallow *n* **:** DWARF MALLOW

blue marguerite *n* **:** BLUE DAISY 1

blue marlin *n* **:** a very large marlin (*Makaira nigricans*) widely distributed in warm seas

blue mass *n, pharmacy* **:** a pilular preparation containing finely divided mercury — called also *blue pill, mass of mercury*

blue melilot *n* **:** an erect branching annual (*Trigonella coerulea*) grown for its blue and white flowers borne in long-stalked heads — see SAPSAGO

blue metal *n* **:** broken bluestone or basalt used in macadamizing

blue mold *n* **1 :** a fungus of the genus *Penicillium*; *esp* **:** a mold that produces blue or blue-green surface growths on bread and other foods — compare GREEN MOLD **2** *also* **blue mold rot :** a plant disease caused by a blue-mold fungus **3 :** a serious fungous disease of tobacco seedlings caused by a fungus (*Peronospora tabacina*) and characterized by yellowish spots and a bluish gray mildew on the underside of the leaves — called also *downy mildew*

blue monday *n, often cap B & usu cap M* **:** a Monday that is depressing or trying esp. because of the return to work and routine after a weekend

blue moon *n* **1 :** a very long period of time — usu. used in the phrase *once in a blue moon* ⟨such people happen along only once in a *blue moon* —*Saturday Rev.*⟩ **2 :** the rare blue appearance of the moon that is due to dust particles in the high atmosphere

blue mountain tea *n, usu cap B&M* [fr. the *Blue mountains,* range in Pennsylvania] **:** a goldenrod (*Solidago odora*) of the eastern U.S. from whose aromatic dried leaves a medicinal tea is sometimes made

bluemouth sunfish \ˈ⸗,⸗-\ *or* **blue-mouthed sunfish** \ˈ⸗,⸗-\ *n* **:** BLUEGILL

blue mud *n* **:** a marine sediment that owes its color to organic matter and iron sulfide

blue myrtle *n* **1 :** BLUEBLOSSOM **2 :** PERIWINKLE
blue·ness \ˈblünəs\ *n* -ES **:** the quality or state of being blue
blue nevus *also* **blue naevus** *n* **:** a small blue or bluish black spot on the skin, sharply circumscribed, rounded, and flat or slightly raised that is usu. benign but often mistaken for a melanoma
blue nightshade *n* **:** BITTERSWEET 2a
blue norther *n* [so called fr. the color of the accompanying cloud bank] **:** a cold wind from the north that brings rapidly falling temperatures to the Kansas, Oklahoma, Texas region
bluenose \ˈ⸗ˌ⸗\ *n* **1** [¹*blue* (puritanical) + *nose*] **:** one who advocates a rigorous moral code esp. in matters of individual conscience or personal conduct **:** PURITAN ⟨once the ~*s* were in power they put down all strong language with a brutal hand —H.L.Mencken⟩ **2** *often cap* [perh. so called fr. the extreme cold of the winters in the Maritime Provinces] **:** a native or resident of the Canadian Maritime Provinces; *esp* **:** a native or resident of Nova Scotia — used as a nickname
bluenosed \ˈ⸗ˈ⸗\ *adj* **:** having the characteristics of a bluenose **:** STRAITLACED
blue note *n* [¹*blue* (of blues singing)] **1 :** a minor interval (as at the third and seventh degree) occurring in a melody or harmony where a major would be expected **2 :** a wrong, off-pitch, or badly sounded note
blue nurse *or* **blue nurse shark** *n* **:** a large viviparous gray or bluish shark (*Carcharias tricuspidatus*) of the Indian and western Pacific oceans often taken for its fins and oily liver
blue oak *n* **:** any of several American oaks with somewhat bluish foliage; *esp* **:** an oak (*Quercus douglasii*) of the dry uplands of the California coastal range with thin stiff deciduous leaves that are pale bluish above and yellowish green below — called also *California blue oak, iron oak, post oak, rock oak*
blue ointment *n* **:** mercurial ointment containing 10 percent of mercury
blue oxalis *n* **:** SHAMROCK PEA
blue palm *n* **1 :** a dwarf fan palm (*Sabal adansonii*) of the southern U.S. having a subterranean stem, spineless petioles, and glaucous leaves **2 :** a fan palm (*Erythea armata*) of Lower California with very glaucous leaves and the leaf segments clothed with white filaments
blue palmetto *n* **:** a dwarf fan palm (*Rhapidophyllum hystrix*) of the southern U.S. having a creeping stem that is clothed with fibrous leaf sheaths and occasional spines and leaves that are long-stalked and somewhat glaucous
blue panic *n* **:** a robust glabrous leafy perennial grass (*Panicum antidotale*) of southeastern U.S. with spikelets that are black at maturity
blue parrot fish *n* **1 :** either of two large chiefly West Indian parrot fishes (*Scarus caeruleus* and *Sparisoma chrysopterum*) **2 :** either of two Australian labrid food fishes (*Choerodon ommopterus* and *C. cyanodus*)
blue pea *n* **:** a tropical vine (*Clitoria ternatea*) with pinnate leaves and bright-blue yellow-centered flowers
blue pelt *n* [so called fr. the bluish tinge of the leather side] **:** a pelt taken before priming is complete
blue pencil *n* **:** any instrument (as a blue pencil) with which an editor makes deletions; *also* **:** the act or an instance of deleting ⟨the book is a good one; vigorous use of a *blue pencil* would have made it better —Keith Hutchison⟩
blue-pencil \ˈ⸗ˈ⸗⸗\ *vt* [*blue pencil*] **:** to edit, delete, or revise with or as if with a blue pencil (as in order to eliminate wordiness or irrelevant material or with the aim of censorship) ⟨used to look over Hemingway's early manuscripts . . . and returned them, mercilessly *blue-penciled*, the adjectives gone —*Time*⟩ ⟨bludgeoned by high-ranking officers into *blue-penciling* everything except vague generalities —*Infantry Jour.*⟩
blue perch *n* **:** any of various bluish fishes: as **a :** CUNNER **b :** PRIESTFISH **c :** HALF-MOON
blue peter *n* [fr. the name *Peter*] **1 :** a blue signal flag with a white square in the center used to indicate that a merchant vessel is ready to sail **2 a :** PURPLE GALLINULE **b** *Midland* **:** AMERICAN COOT
blue phlox *n* **:** WILD BLUE PHLOX
blue pigeon *n* **:** a dove-gray Australian cuckoo shrike (*Coracina novae-hollandiae*) with black markings on head, throat, wings, and tail
blue pike *n* **1 :** WALLEYE; *also* **:** any other pike perch (genus *Stizostedion*) **2 :** MUSKELLUNGE
blue pill *n* **1 :** a pill of prepared mercury used esp. as an aperient **2 :** BLUE MASS
blue pimpernel *n* **:** MAD-DOG SKULLCAP
blue pine *n* **1 :** BHOTAN PINE **2 :** CANARY PINE
blue plantain-lily *n* **:** a day lily (*Hosta ventricosa*) having blue flowers with a corolla tube that widens suddenly into a bell
blue plate *n* **1 :** a restaurant dinner plate divided into compartments for serving several kinds of food as a single order **2 :** a main course (as of meat and vegetable) served as a single menu item
blue plum *n* **1 :** an Australian tree (*Notelaea quadristaminea*) having an edible fruit like a plum **2 :** a variable color averaging a dark violet that is stronger and slightly lighter than plum purple (sense 2) and redder and less strong than Derby blue
bluepoint \ˈ⸗ˌ⸗\ *n* [fr. *Blue Point*, Long Island] **:** a small oyster typically from the south shore of Long Island and often served on the half shell — compare LYNNHAVEN
blue point *n* [¹*blue* + *point*] **:** a Siamese cat having a bluish cream body and dark gray points
blue pointer *n* **1** *Austral* **:** BONITO SHARK **2 :** GREAT WHITE SHARK
blue pop *n* **1 :** BLUE GROSBEAK **2 :** INDIGO BUNTING
blue poplar *n* **:** TULIP TREE
blue poppy *n* **:** any of several species of the genus *Meconopsis* (family Papaveraceae) of the north temperate zone
blue powder *n* **:** a mixture of finely divided and partly oxidized metallic zinc formed by the condensation of zinc vapor into droplets; *also* **:** any similar zinc by-product (as dross, skimmings, or sweepings)
¹**blueprint** \ˈ⸗ˌ⸗\ *n* [¹*blue* + *print*] **1 a :** a photographic print in white on a bright blue ground made usu. on paper or cloth sensitized with potassium ferricyanide and a ferric salt, developed after exposure by washing in plain water, and used esp. for copying maps, mechanical drawings, and architects' plans — called also *cyanotype* **b :** a photographic print (as of a map, mechanical drawing, or architect's plans) in white and black or other color (as a vandyke) **2 :** a detailed, thoroughly coordinated plan or program of action for effecting some policy or achieving some goal or solution ⟨had drawn up ~*s* for educating the boys in winter quarters —Dixon Wecter⟩ **3 :** any pattern of action or statement of views, principles, or rules regarded as a guiding program for the achievement of some large objective or objectives ⟨the political leaders of the two countries are guided by the same political ~*s* —Aneurin Bevan⟩ ⟨books on the American Constitution . . . have guided . . . legislatures in drafting their own national ~*s* —D.M.Lacy & Paul Hill⟩ **4 :** a body of experience or a completed project or experiment regarded as a model ⟨a workable ~ . . . is afforded by the reclamation projects . . . which have regenerated Palestine —C.J.Rolo⟩
²**blueprint** \"\ *vt* **1 :** to make a blueprint of **2 :** to work out (as a program or plan) **:** outline in detail **:** DEVISE, ORGANIZE, FORMULATE ⟨the purpose was to ~ a concrete program for bolstering world prosperity —*Newsweek*⟩
blueprinter \ˈ⸗ˌ⸗⸗\ *n* **:** one that makes blueprints
blueprint paper *n* **:** sensitized paper used in making blueprints
blue quail *n* **1 :** SCALED QUAIL **2 :** a small African quail (*Coturnix adansonii*) or an Asiatic or Australian congener
¹**bluer** *comparative of* BLUE
²**blu·er** \ˈblüə(r)\ *n* -S [³*blue* + *-er*] **:** one that works at or supervises bluing: as **a :** a worker who colors the metal parts of guns by immersing them in bluing chemicals or by heat-treating **b :** an auto worker who tests the seating of valves by rotating them after smearing them with a blue compound that will show up high spots
blue racer *n* **:** an American blacksnake of a bluish green subspecies (*Coluber constrictor flaviventris*) occurring in the U.S. from Ohio to Texas
blue rail *n*, *in Louisiana* **:** GALLINULE
blue ribbon *n* **1 a :** a blue ribbon usu. with appropriate words or markings awarded the first-place winner in a competition **b :** an honor, distinction, or award gained for preeminence in some field ⟨this prize was the *blue ribbon* in mathematical research —*Atlantic*⟩ **2 :** a blue ribbon worn by members of certain temperance organizations
blue-ribbon \ˈ⸗ˈ⸗⸗\ *adj* [*blue ribbon*] **:** of the highest quality **:** carefully selected **:** FIRST-RATE ⟨a *blue-ribbon* investigating commission⟩ ⟨*blue-ribbon* beef⟩ **:** OUTSTANDING ⟨the *blue-ribbon* event of the social season⟩
blue-ribbon jury *n* **:** SPECIAL JURY 2
blue rider *adj*, *usu cap B&R* [trans. of G *blauer Reiter*, noun phrase] **:** BLAUE REITER
¹**blue-roan** \ˈ⸗ˈ⸗\ *adj* [¹*blue* + *roan*] **:** of a roan color produced by mingling of black and white hairs
²**blue-roan** \"\ *n* **:** a blue-roan individual (as a horse or dog)
blue rock *n* **:** any of certain somewhat bluish wild or domestic pigeons: as **a** *or* **blue rock pigeon :** ROCK PIGEON **b :** RED-BILLED PIGEON **c :** a blue-barred homing pigeon
blue rot *n* **:** a disease of conifers caused by certain fungi (genus *Ceratostomella*) and producing a blue coloration of the wood — called also *bluing*
blue runner *n* **:** an excellent carangid food fish (*Caranx crysos*) of the warmer parts of the western Atlantic that is bluish green above and golden yellow or silvery below
¹**blues** *pl of* BLUE, *pres 3d sing of* BLUE
²**blues** \ˈblüz\ *n pl but sometimes sing in constr* **1 :** low spirits **:** mental depression **:** DESPONDENCY, MELANCHOLY — usu. used with *the* ⟨staying in this dull place was enough to give anyone the ~ —Joseph Conrad⟩ **2 :** a song sung or composed in a style originating among the American Negroes, characterized typically by the use of three-line stanzas in which the words of the second line repeat the first, expressing a mood of longing or melancholy, and marked by the continual occurrence of blue notes in melody and harmony **3 :** the blue uniform of the U.S. Navy ⟨put on his ~ and went ashore⟩ **4 :** unreserved seats at the two far ends of a circus tent usu. painted blue **syn** see SADNESS
blue sage *n* **1 :** any of several blue-flowered sages of the genus *Salvia*: as **a :** a plant (*S. farinacea*) of Texas **b :** a plant (*S. lancifolia*) of the western U.S. **c :** a plant (*S. azurea*) esp. of dry prairies in the eastern U.S. **2 :** SAGEBRUSH
blue-sail·ors \ˈ⸗ˌ⸗⸗\ *n pl but sing or pl in constr* **:** CHICORY
blue scabious *n* **:** a European herb (*Succisa pratensis*) with opposite leaves and blue flowers
blue sclera *or* **blue sclerotic** *n* **:** FRAGILITAS OSSIUM; *also* **:** the bluish whites of the eyes characteristic of this condition
blue shark *n* **1 :** a voracious and very active pelagic shark (*Prionace glauca*) that may become 20 to 25 feet long and is reputed to be a man-eater **2 :** any of various other sharks; *esp* **:** REQUIN
blue sheep *n* **:** BHARAL
blue shirt *n* **:** one who wears a blue shirt; *esp* **:** a professional fire fighter
bluesides \ˈ⸗ˌ⸗\ *n* **:** a young harp seal
blue skullcap *n* **:** MAD-DOG SKULLCAP
¹**blue-sky** \ˈ⸗ˈ⸗\ *adj* [so called fr. the emptiness of the sky] **1 :** having little or no value **:** UNSOUND, UNSECURED ⟨*blue-sky* stock⟩ **2 :** ill-defined, grandiose, or excessive in scope or object **:** UNREALISTIC, VISIONARY ⟨mass movements, especially of the *blue-sky* variety —Robert Shaplen⟩
²**blue-sky** \"\ *vt* [*blue-sky* (*law*)] **:** to qualify a security issue for sale in a state under its blue-sky law
blue-sky law \ˈ⸗ˈ⸗-\ *n* [¹*blue-sky*] **:** a law providing for the regulation and supervision of the sale of stocks, bonds, or other securities
blue slate *n* **:** SLATE BLUE
blue smelt *n* **:** JACKSMELT
blue spirea *n* **:** ³BLUEBEARD
blue spot *n* **:** a bluish pigmented area near the base of the spine present at birth esp. in infants of Mongoloid ancestry — called also *Mongolian spot*
blue sprat *n* **:** a small clupeoid fish (*Stolephorus robustus*) important as a major food source for the larger sport and food fishes of Australian seas
blue spruce *n* **1 a :** COLORADO SPRUCE; *often* **:** a spruce belonging to a horticultural variety derived from the Colorado spruce **b :** BLACK SPRUCE 1 **2 a :** a variable color averaging a grayish green that is bluer and darker than average bayberry and bluer, lighter, and stronger than slate green **b :** a moderate green that is bluer and paler than average myrtle (sense 3 a) or average laurel green (sense 1) and less strong than sea green (sense 1 a)
blues scale *n* **:** a musical scale having intervals that mutate between major and minor and used esp. in jazz
bluest *superlative of* BLUE
blue stain *also* **blue sap stain** *n* **:** an important bluish stain of sapwood caused in many trees by any of various fungi (as of the genera *Ceratostomella, Penicillium*, or *Fusarium*) — compare BLUE ROT
blue star *n* **:** a star of spectral type *O* or *B* having a high surface temperature and a bluish white color (as Rigel)
bluesteel \ˈ⸗ˈ⸗\ *n* **:** a grayish blue that is redder and duller than electric, greener and duller than copenhagen or old china, and redder and darker than Gobelin
blue·stem \ˈ⸗ˌ⸗\ *n* **1 a :** a tall grass (*Andropogon furcatus*) with smooth bluish leaf sheaths and slender spikes borne in pairs or clusters used in the western U.S. for hay **b** *or* **bluestem wheatgrass :** WESTERN WHEATGRASS 1 **2 a :** a disease of raspberries and blackberries in the Pacific coast region of northwestern No. America caused by a fungus (*Verticillium alboatrum*) and characterized by bluish black discoloration of the stem, stunting, reduction of vigor, and curling of the leaflets **b :** a similar disease of raspberries in the eastern U.S. believed to be caused by a virus — called also *eastern bluestem*
bluestock·ing \ˈ⸗ˌ⸗⸗\ *n* **1** [after *Bluestocking* society, 18th cent. literary clubs, some of whose members wore informal attire often including blue worsted stockings] **:** a woman having or pretending to have intellectual interests or literary tastes **:** a female scholar ⟨she was sensitive, percipient, but in no sense a ~ —George Mallaby⟩ **2** [so called from the color of its legs] **:** the avocet (*Recurvirostra americana*) of No. America
¹**bluestone** \ˈ⸗ˌ⸗\ *n* [¹*blue* + *stone*] **1 :** the hydrated copper sulfate $CuSO_4.5H_2O$ **2 :** a building or paving stone of bluish gray color; *specif* **:** a sandstone quarried near the Hudson river
²**bluestone** \"\ *vt* **:** to treat (as a net or a stream) with copper sulfate
blue·ston·er \ˈblü,stōnə(r)\ *n* **:** one that stains with bluestone
blue·ston·ing \ˈblü,stōniŋ\ *n* **:** a color effect in clay wares caused by reduction of iron oxide
blue streak *n* **1 :** something that moves very fast ⟨ran like a *blue streak*⟩ **2 :** a constant stream of words **:** a seemingly endless flow ⟨talked a *blue streak*⟩
blue-striped grunt \ˈ⸗ˈ⸗-\ *n* **:** YELLOW GRUNT
blue stuff *n* **:** KIMBERLITE
blue succory *n* **:** a So. European plant (*Catananche coerulea*) having heads of flowers with flat blue rays
blue sunfish *n* **:** BLUEGILL
blue swedish *n* **1** *usu cap B&S* **:** a breed of ducks resembling the Pekins but typically smaller and of a blue-gray color **2** *often cap B&S* **:** a duck of the Blue Swedish breed
blue swimming crab *n* **:** BLUE CRAB
blu·et \ˈblüət\ *n* [prob. fr. ¹*blue* + *-et*] **1 a** *dial Eng* **:** CORNFLOWER 1b **b :** FARKLEBERRY **c** (1) **:** a delicate plant (*Houstonia caerulea*) of the U.S. with 4-parted bluish flowers and tufted stems — often used in pl; called also *innocence, quaker-ladies* (2) **:** a Texas plant (*Houstonia patens*) often only 1 to 2 inches high with a single blue flower **2 :** a light to moderate blue that is redder and stronger than king's blue (sense 1)
blue-tailed skink *or* **blue-tailed lizard** \ˈ⸗ˈ⸗-\ *n* **:** a harmless widely ranging No. American scincoid lizard (*Eumeces fasciatus* syn. *quinquelineatus*) having the under surface of the tail bright azure — called also *five-lined lizard, redheaded lizard, scorpion*
blue tangle *n* **:** DANGLEBERRY
blue thistle *n* **1 :** BLUEWEED **2** *Austral* **:** PRICKLY POPPY
bluethroat \ˈ⸗ˌ⸗\ *n* **:** a singing bird (*Erithacus svecicus*) of northern Europe and Asia
blue·tick \ˈ⸗ˌ⸗\ *n*, *sometimes cap* **:** a very speedy American hound having a white coat blotched and flecked with bluish gray and sometimes considered a distinct breed
blue tick *n* **:** a southern African tick (*Boophilus decoloratus*) that feeds on cattle, horses, and other domestic animals and transmits several important diseases (as red-water and anaplasmosis)
blue tit *n* **:** a widely distributed European titmouse (*Parus caeruleus*) having the crown of the head, wings, and tail bright cobalt blue
blue toadflax *n* **:** a weed (*Linaria canadensis*) of sandy soil on coastal plains esp. in southeastern U.S. with violet or purple flowers
bluetongue \ˈ⸗ˌ⸗\ *n* [trans. of Afrik *bloutong*] **1 :** an African horse sickness in which the lesions are most marked about the head — called also *thickhead* **2 :** a serious virus disease of African sheep that is marked by hyperemia, cyanosis, and punctate hemorrhages and by swelling and sloughing of the epithelium esp. about the mouth and tongue, that sometimes affects goats and in a milder form often simulating foot-and-mouth disease occurs in cattle, that is localized in low-lying or marshy areas, and that is thought to be transmitted by biting midges
blue-tongue *or* **blue-tongued lizard** *n* **1 :** BLUE-TONGUED SKINK **2 :** a lizard (*Tiliqua nigrolutea*) of Tasmania
blue-tongued skink *n* **:** a large and stoutly built Australian scincoid lizard (*Tiliqua scincoides*) often kept as a pet
bluetop \ˈ⸗ˌ⸗\ *n* **1 :** HORSE NETTLE **2 bluetops** *pl* **:** KNAPWEED **3 :** BLUEJOINT 1
blue turquoise *n* **:** a light greenish blue that is bluer, lighter, and stronger than average turquoise blue, bluer and paler than average turquoise (sense 2a), and bluer and deeper than average aqua
blue tussock *n* **:** a valuable grazing grass (*Poa colensoi*) native to New Zealand
blue ultramarine ash *n* **:** a strong to vivid greenish blue
blue verditer *n* **1 :** AZURITE BLUE **2 :** a highly basic copper carbonate used as a blue pigment — compare BREMEN BLUE, MINERAL BLUE 1a
blue vervain *n* **:** a tall weed (*Verbena hastata*) of the eastern U.S. with hastate leaves and slender spikes of blue flowers
blue vetch *n* **:** TUFTED VETCH
blue vi·en·na \-vēˈenə\ *n* **1** *usu cap B&V* **:** a breed of blue-coated rabbits resembling and largely derived from New Zealands **2** *often cap B&V* **:** a rabbit of the Blue Vienna breed
blue vine *n* **:** SAND VINE
blue vinny *n*, *often cap B&V* **:** a white cheese made of cow's milk and characterized by blue veining — called also *Dorset*
blue vitriol *n* **:** the hydrated copper sulfate $CuSO_4.5H_2O$
blue water *n* **:** the open sea ⟨talk to the swart men just in from *blue water* —D.C.Peattie⟩
blue water gas *n* **:** BLUE GAS
blue water lily *n* **1 :** BLUE LOTUS **2 :** a blue-flowered African water lily (*Nymphaea capensis zanzibariensis*)
blue-wattled crow \ˈ⸗ˌ⸗⸗-\ *n* **:** a passerine bird (*Callaeas wilsoni*) of New Zealand that resembles a starling
blue wavey *n* **:** BLUE GOOSE
blue waxweed *n* **:** WAXWEED
blueweed \ˈ⸗ˌ⸗\ *n* **1 :** a coarse prickly weed (*Echium vulgare*) of Europe that has been naturalized in the U.S. and that has blue flowers in scorpioid spikes — called also *blue thistle, viper's bugloss* **2 :** CHICORY **3** *in Texas* **:** a Mexican weed (*Larrea densiflora*) introduced as a range plant for alkali soils **4 :** a small perennial (*Helianthus ciliaris*) that is native in southwestern U.S. and often troublesome as a weed and that has blue-green or gray-green foliage
blue whale *n* **:** a rorqual (*Sibbaldus musculus*) common in the northern and southern oceans and sometimes exceeding 80 feet in length
blue wheat grass *n* **:** BLUEGRASS 2
blue-white \ˈ⸗ˈ⸗\ *adj*, *of a diamond* **:** colorless and of the highest quality
blue wildebeest *n* [trans. of Afrik *blouwildebees*, fr. *blou* blue + *wildebees* wildebeest — more at WILDEBEEST] **:** BRINDLED GNU
blue wild rye *n* **:** a tufted perennial No. American grass (*Elymus glaucus*) having very long awns on the lemmas and often cultivated for ornament and in northwest U.S. as a forage crop
bluewing \ˈ⸗ˌ⸗\ *n* **:** BLUE-WINGED TEAL
blue-winged goose \ˈblü,wiŋd-\ *n* **:** an African sheldrake (*Cyanochen cyanopterus*) that superficially resembles a goose
blue-winged teal *n* **:** an American teal (*Anas discors*) resembling the green-winged teal but having blue wing coverts and a large white crescent on each cheek
blue-winged warbler *n* **:** a warbler (*Vermivora pinus*) greenish above, bright yellow below, and with a narrow black line through the eye, found esp. in the east-central U.S.
bluewood \ˈ⸗ˌ⸗\ *n* **1 :** a chaparral shrub (*Condalia obovata*) of western Texas and northern Mexico **2 :** LOGWOOD 2
blue wood aster *n* **:** a common perennial No. American herb (*Aster cordifolius*) with basal cordate leaves and numerous heads of bluish purple flowers
blue wren *n* **:** BLUECAP
¹**bluey** \ˈblüē\ *adj* [¹*blue* + *-y*] **:** BLUISH
²**bluey** \"\ *n* -S **1** [so called fr. the blue blanket that was commonly used to wrap the bundle] *Austral* **:** a swagman's bundle **2 :** BLUE CRAB 2 **3 :** any of several Australian lizards
blue-yellow blindness \ˈ⸗ˈ⸗⸗-\ *n* **:** TRITANOPIA
¹**bluff** \ˈbləf\ *adj* -ER/-EST [obs. D *blaf* flat, broad; akin to MLG *blaff* smooth, even] **1 a :** having a broad flattened front ⟨the ~ bows of a ship⟩ **b :** rising steeply with a broad front either flat or rounded ⟨the ~ banks of the river⟩ **2** *dial Eng* **:** SURLY, ROUGH **3 :** having a good-naturedly abrupt, frank, and outspoken manner **:** heartily blunt ⟨a ~ and rugged natural leader with impulsive determination and an explosive personality —John Warner⟩ ⟨a ~ aggressive manner⟩
syn BLUNT, BRUSQUE, CURT, CRUSTY, GRUFF: BLUFF, the only completely complimentary one of these terms, implies a rough, hearty good nature ⟨a *bluff*, burly, hearty-looking man in a short blue jacket —Kenneth Roberts⟩ ⟨a *bluff* and hearty fellow who looks more like a marine combat officer than the fine musician which he really is —*Current Biog.*⟩ BLUNT ranges from being a near equivalent to BLUFF to implying an outspokenness inconsiderate of or discourteous to others ⟨permit me to be businesslike and perhaps *blunt*, as my train leaves in one hour —Sinclair Lewis⟩ ⟨the Herald said the chief of police could best show his own lack of complicity by speedily catching and convicting the murderer or murderers. The editorial was *blunt* and bitter —Dashiell Hammett⟩ BRUSQUE stresses sharp quickness and unceremoniousness ⟨never again would she exclaim, in her *brusque* tone of genial ruthlessness: "Fiddlesticks" —Arnold Bennett⟩ ⟨at first he thought that Dirk was the cause of the disaster, and he was needlessly *brusque* with him —W.S.Maugham⟩ CURT stresses shortness and may or may not imply discourtesy ⟨at breakfast . . . she was *curt*. "I don't care to discuss it," she said —Sinclair Lewis⟩ ⟨it was the first of the month and there were *curt* notes from the water company —John Steinbeck⟩ CRUSTY suggests a harsh, uncivil, irascible manner, sometimes concealing an inner kindliness ⟨the lashing tongue of a *crusty* disciplinarian —F.V.W.Mason⟩ ⟨this *crusty* old lawyer, who had made no bones about his contempt for the tetrarch —L.C.Douglas⟩ GRUFF also implies a harsh surly manner and curt, perhaps guttural, utterance ⟨a man's voice, ill-tempered and *gruff*, rose through the shadowy room —Louis Bromfield⟩ ⟨"Fool" said the sophist, in an undertone *gruff* with contempt —John Keats⟩
²**bluff** \"\ *n* -S **1 :** a high steep bank (as by a river or the sea or beside a ravine or plain) **:** a cliff with a broad face ⟨a fort on the ~ overlooking the junction of the rivers⟩ **2** *North* **:** a clump of trees on the open plain **:** GROVE
³**bluff** \"\ *vb* -ED/-ING/-S [prob. fr. D *bluffen* to boast, play a kind of card game, fr. MD, to strike, beat, to swell up, alter. of *buffen, boffen*, fr. *buf, bof* blow, swollen face; prob. of imit. origin] *vt* **1** *obs* **:** BLINDFOLD **2 :** to deceive (an opponent in cards) by a bold bet on an inferior hand with the result that the opponent drops a winning hand — often used with *out* **3 a :** to deter, dissuade, or frighten by pretense or a mere show of strength **:** frighten off ⟨with the power of England behind him had ~*ed* the Hamburg merchants out of participating —W.P.Webb⟩ **b :** to cause to believe what is not true **:** MISLEAD, DECEIVE ⟨wanted to ~ them into thinking that the route of

the railroad had been changed⟩ **c :** to make a pretense of **:** FEIGN ⟨the catcher ~*ed* a throw to first base⟩ **~** *vi* **1 a :** to bet boldly on a poor hand in poker in the hope that an opponent will drop **b :** to make any show of strength not justified by the hand held in a card game with the intention of deceiving an opponent **2 :** to make use of pretense, a mere show of strength, or deception **:** SHAM ⟨it is destructive of public goodwill to ~ or fake when you cannot give the information requested —Lou Smyth⟩

4**bluff** \"\ *n* -s **1 :** a blinder or blinker esp. for a horse **2 :** STRAIGHT POKER **3 a :** an act or instance of bluffing ⟨having . . . nothing to support his pretensions he decided to put up a ~ —Sherwood Anderson⟩ ⟨he put on a good ~⟩ ⟨it was all a ~⟩ **b :** the practice of bluffing ⟨the agreement had been reached after weeks of ~ and haggle —*Time*⟩ **4 :** one that bluffs ⟨he was pretty much of a ~⟩

bluff–bowed \'=¦baud\ *adj* [1*bluff*] *of a ship* **:** having a broad flat bow

bluff·er \'bləfə(r)\ *n* -s [3*bluff* + *-er*] **:** one that bluffs

bluff formation *n* [1*bluff*] **:** LOESS

bluff–headed \'=¦==\ *adj* [1*bluff*] **:** BLUFF-BOWED

bluff·ly *adv* [1*bluff* + *-ly*] **:** in a bluff manner

bluff·ness *n* -ES **:** the quality or state of being bluff

bluffy \'bləfē\ *adj, often* -ER/-EST [2*bluff* + *-y*] **:** having or resembling bluffs **:** STEEP

bluft \'bləft\ *vt* -ED/-ING/-S [alter. of 3*bluff*] *dial Eng* **:** BLINDFOLD

blug·gy \'bləgē\ *adj* [euphemism for 1*bloody*] **:** BLOODY

bluid \'blœd\ *Scot var of* BLOOD

blu·ing *or* **blue·ing** \'blüiŋ\ *n* -s [fr. gerund of 3*blue*] **1 :** the act of making blue ⟨the ~ of steel⟩ **2 :** something that gives a bluish tint: as **a :** a rinse for gray or white hair **b :** a preparation of blue or violet dyes used in laundering to counteract the yellowish tinge of white linen or cotton **3 :** BLUE ROT

blu·ish *or* **blue·ish** \'blüish, -üēsh\ *adj* [ME *blewish*, fr. *bleu, blew* blue + *-ish* — more at BLUE] **:** somewhat blue **:** having a tinge of blue ⟨a ~ green⟩ ⟨~ air⟩ — **blu·ish·ness** *or* **blue·ish·ness** *n* -ES

blume \'blœm\ *Scot var of* BLOOM

blu·mea \'blümēə\ *n, cap* [NL, fr. Karl L. *Blume* †1862 Ger. botanist] **:** a genus of tropical Australasian and African herbs or shrubs (family Compositae) with simple alternate leaves and discoid purple or yellow flower heads

1**blun·der** \'bləndə(r)\ *vb* -ED/-ING/-S [ME *blundren, blondren*] *vi* **1 :** to move unsteadily, confusedly, or blindly **:** FLOUNDER, STUMBLE ⟨the cabman ~*ed* up and downstairs with trunks —Arnold Bennett⟩ ⟨in their exhaustion they often ~*ed* against each other —Norman Mailer⟩ **2 :** to come or happen by or as if by accident **:** STUMBLE — usu. used with *on* or *upon* ⟨evidence which I ~*ed* upon in a manuscript —Charlton Laird⟩ **3 :** to make a mistake or commit an error usu. as a result of stupidity, ignorance, mental confusion, or carelessness ⟨while he often ~*ed* he usually won his case by sheer energy and persistence —Edward Preble⟩ **~** *vt* **1** *now dial Eng* **:** to mix up **:** MUDDLE, ROIL **2 :** to utter stupidly, confusedly, or thoughtlessly **:** BLURT — usu. used with *out* ⟨he ~*ed* out an apology⟩ **3 :** to lose usu. by stupidity, carelessness, or thoughtlessness **:** THROW — usu. used with *away* ⟨it maddens me to see people ~*ing* away thousands of pounds —G.B.Shaw⟩ **4 :** to make a stupid, careless, or thoughtless mistake in **:** BOTCH, BUNGLE, MISMANAGE ⟨the risk we run of ~*ing* matters through ignorance —Rafael Sabatini⟩

2**blunder** \"\ *n* -s [ME *blunder, blonder*] **:** an error or mistake resulting usu. from stupidity, ignorance, mental confusion, or carelessness ⟨the building of light-draft monitors was a costly ~ —H.K.Beale⟩ ⟨his chief ~ is his misconception of Aristotle —H.O.Taylor⟩ **syn** see ERROR

blun·der·bush \'bləndər,bush\ *dial var of* BLUNDERBUSS

blun·der·buss \'bləndə(r),bəs\ *n* -ES [by folk etymology fr. obs. D *donderbus*, fr. *donder* thunder (fr. MD *donder, donre*) + obs. D *bus* gun, fr. MD *busse, bosse* box, tube, gun, fr. LL *buxis* box; akin to OHG *thonar* thunder — more at THUNDER, BOX] **1 :** an obsolete short gun or firearm that had a large bore and usu. a bell muzzle, was capable of holding a number of balls, and was intended for shooting at close quarters without exact aim **2 :** a blundering person

blunderbuss

blun·der·er \'blənd(ə)rə(r)\ *n* -s [ME, fr. *blundren* to blunder + *-er*] **:** one that blunders; *esp* **:** one that makes a stupid, careless, or thoughtless mistake

blunderhead \'==,=\ *n* [prob. alter. (influenced by 1*blunder*) of *dunderhead*] **:** a blundering person — **blun·der·head·ed** \¦==¦==\ *adj*

blundering *adj* **:** characterized by or given to making blunders **:** BUNGLING ⟨a ~ attempt to capture the fort⟩ ⟨a ~ lawyer⟩ — **blun·der·ing·ly** *adv*

blunge \'blənj\ *vt* -ED/-ING/-S [prob. blend of *blend* and *plunge*] **:** to amalgamate and blend **:** beat up or mix in water (as clay to form slip)

blung·er \'blənjə(r)\ *n* -s **:** one that blunges; *specif* **:** a vat with mechanical stirrers for mixing clay and water into slip

1**blunt** \'blənt\ *adj* -ER/-EST [ME; perh. akin to ON *blunda* to doze, OE *blind* — more at BLIND] **1 a :** dull or deficient in feeling or perception **:** INSENSITIVE ⟨served his time by showing how ~ the eyes and ears of writers generally are —Norman Foerster⟩ **b :** slow or obtuse in understanding or discernment **:** DULL ⟨this consideration will make it evident to a ~*er* discernment than yours —Edmund Burke⟩ **2 :** having a thick edge or point **:** not sharp or keen ⟨the murderous knife was dull and ~ —Shak.⟩ **3** *archaic* **:** lacking refinement or polish **:** RUDE, ROUGH ⟨though ~ my tale —Alexander Pope⟩ **4 :** abrupt in speech or manner **:** outspokenly frank **:** not suave **:** PLAIN ⟨you are entirely too ~ in your human relations —W.J.Reilly⟩ ⟨the petition was rejected in a ~ one-sentence letter of refusal —Paul Blanshard⟩ **syn** see BLUFF, DULL

2**blunt** \"\ *vb* -ED/-ING/-S [ME *blonten* fr. *blunt, blont*, adj.] *vt* **1 a :** to make (as an edge or point) less sharp **:** DULL ⟨~*ed* the swords⟩ **b :** to make (as an acid or corrosive) less sharp **:** DILUTE ⟨~*s* the acidity of vinegar⟩ **2 :** to make (as the senses or mental faculties) dull or sluggish **:** DEADEN ⟨diminished men's sense of wonder and ~*ed* their sensitiveness to the great mystery —Aldous Huxley⟩ **3 :** to lessen or destroy the force or effectiveness of **:** WEAKEN ⟨their zeal was quickly ~*ed* by the yawn of habit around them —Bruce Marshall⟩ ⟨the attack was ~*ed*⟩ **~** *vi* **:** to become dull or less sharp ⟨its edges will never ~ —John Bunyan⟩

3**blunt** \"\ *n* -s [1*blunt*] **1 :** something blunt; *specif* **:** BLUNT ARROW **2** *slang* **:** ready cash **:** MONEY

blunt arrow *n* **:** an arrow with a blunt head used to kill birds and small game without mangling

blunt dissection *n* **:** surgical separation of tissue layers by means of an instrument without a cutting edge or by the fingers

blunt file *n* **:** a file having parallel edges

blunt·head \'=,=\ *n* **:** a snake of the family Amblycephalidae

blunt·ie \'bləntē\ *n* -s [1*blunt* + *-ie*] *Scot* **:** a stupid person

blunt·ly *adv* **:** in a blunt manner ⟨he is ready to say ~ what every one else is afraid to say —T.S.Eliot⟩

blunt·ness *n* -ES [ME *bluntnes*, fr. *blunt* + *-nes* -ness] **:** the quality or state or being blunt

blunt–nosed crab \'=¦=-\ *n* **:** a large pinkish spider crab (*Hyas lyratus*) of the northwest coast of No. America

1**blur** \'blər + V -ər·; 'blə̄, + V -ər· *also* -ə̄r\ *n* -s [perh. akin to ME *bleren* to blear] **1 :** a moral stain or blot **:** BLEMISH ⟨these ~*s* are too apparent in his life —John Milton⟩ **2 :** a smear or stain that obscures but does not efface (as one made with ink on paper) **:** BLOT ⟨the letter was full of ~*s*⟩ **3 a :** a vague, dim, or confused appearance **:** INDISTINCTNESS ⟨the ~ of spring foliage in the southeast —Ellen Glasgow⟩ **b :** something seen or perceived as vague or lacking definite outline ⟨picked up his book and pretended to read, turning the pages and staring at a dim ~ of words —Josephine Johnson⟩ **4 :** an indistinct somewhat confused sound **:** HUM ⟨his voice came clearly through the ~ of engines —Vincent McHugh⟩

2**blur** \"\ *vb* **blurred**; **blurred**; **blurring**; **blurs** *vt* **1 :** to obscure, soil, or blemish by smearing (as with ink) **:** SMEAR ⟨his damp fingers *blurred* the manuscript⟩ **2 :** SULLY, STAIN, BLOT ⟨his reputation was *blurred*⟩ **:** BLEMISH ⟨an act that ~*s* the grace and blush of modesty —Shak.⟩ **3 :** to make dim, indistinct, or vague in outline or character ⟨the needs of association *blurred* the peculiarities among Dane and Swede and Norwegian —Oscar Handlin⟩ ⟨with memory *blurring* out all but the high light —Ernest Beaglehole⟩ **4 :** to make dim, imperfect, or confused (as the senses or mental faculties) **:** DIM, DARKEN ⟨in her nineties time had begun to ~ her senses —W.A.White⟩ **~** *vi* **1 :** to make blurs ⟨the moths tapped and *blurred* at the window screen —R.P.Warren⟩ **2 :** to become vague, indistinct, or indefinite **:** DIM ⟨the distinctions of politics in both countries tend to ~ —Frank Gorrell⟩

1**blurb** \'blərb, 'blə̄b, 'bləib\ *n* -s [coined 1907 by Gelett Burgess †1951 Am. humorist & illustrator] **:** a short highly commendatory and often extravagant publicity notice; *esp* **:** such a notice printed on the dust jacket of a book ⟨this book fails to give what the ~ describes —O.G.S.Crawford⟩

2**blurb** \"\ *vt* -ED/-ING/-S **1 :** to publicize in or by means of a blurb ⟨whom they now ~ as "the Canadian Mark Twain" —*Time*⟩ **2 :** to advertise in the extravagant manner often characteristic of a blurb ⟨was ~*ed* as a great novel⟩

blurb·ist \-bəst\ *n* -s **:** a writer of blurbs ⟨I have no doubt that the ~ was Walt himself —H.S.Canby⟩

blur circle *n* **:** CIRCLE OF CONFUSION

blurred \'blərd, 'blə̄d, 'bləid\ *adj* [fr. past part. of 2*blur*] **1 :** smeared with or as if with ink ⟨~ sheets of paper⟩ **2 :** characterized by dimness, indistinctness, or obscurity ⟨the ~ names on the gravestones⟩ ⟨a ~ photograph⟩ **:** VAGUE, CONFUSED ⟨the ~ aims of the group⟩ ⟨people of ~ and divided minds⟩ — **blur·red·ly** \'blərədlē *also* 'blə̄r-\ *adv*

blur·ry \'blərē, -ri *also* 'blə̄r-\ *adj, sometimes* -ER/-EST [1*blur* + *-y*] **:** BLURRED ⟨a ~ snapshot⟩

1**blurt** \'blərt, 'blə̄t, 'bləit, *usu* d·+V\ *vb* -ED/-ING/-S [prob. of imit. origin] *vt* **:** to utter abruptly and impulsively **:** divulge unadvisedly **:** EJACULATE — usu. used with *out* ⟨you don't leave me any alternative to ~*ing* it out like this —Lester Atwell⟩ **~** *vi* **1** *obs* **:** to make a contemptuous puffing grimace with the lips **2 :** to speak impulsively ⟨while Henry was ~*ing* and Wolsey thundering —Francis Hackett⟩ **syn** see EXCLAIM

2**blurt** \"\ *n* -s **:** an abrupt impulsive utterance ⟨loudly and lengthily denied his undiplomatic ~ —*Time*⟩

1**blush** \'bləsh\ *vb* -ED/-ING/-ES [ME *blusshen, blisshen*, fr. OE *blyscan* to redden, fr. *blȳsa* flame, torch; akin to MLG *blūs* torch, ON *blys* light, flame, OHG *bluhhen* to burn brightly] *vi* **1 :** to become red in the face esp. from shame, modesty, or confusion **:** FLUSH, COLOR ⟨Clara looked at her aunt and ~*ed* —Sherwood Anderson⟩ ⟨~*ing* more scarlet than ever, slunk off . . . deeply humiliated —Samuel Butler †1902⟩ **2 :** to feel shame **:** be embarrassed ⟨the grossly injurious suspicions which she must ever ~ to have entertained —Jane Austen⟩ ⟨no man ought ever to be called upon to ~ for his wife —W.M.Thackeray⟩ **3 a :** to become red **:** have a red or rosy color ⟨the skies yet ~*ing* with departing light —Alexander Pope⟩ **b :** to have a fresh color **:** BLOOM ⟨full many a flower is born to ~ unseen —Thomas Gray⟩ **4 :** to assume a cloudy appearance — used of varnish or lacquer films; compare 3BLOOM 2b **~** *vt* **1 :** to make red **:** REDDEN ⟨a shielded scutcheon ~*ed* with blood of queens and kings —John Keats⟩ **2** *archaic* **:** to make known by blushing

2**blush** \"\ *n* -ES [ME, prob. fr. *blusshen*, v.] **1 :** appearance, view, or consideration — used esp. in the phrase *at first blush* ⟨at first ~ the answer seems simple enough —Margaret Mead⟩ **2 :** a reddening of the face esp. from shame, modesty, or confusion **:** FLUSH ⟨a ~ revealed his embarrassment⟩ **3 a :** a red or reddish color ⟨light's last ~*es* tinged the distant hills —George Lyttelton⟩ **b :** a rosy glow **:** BLOOM ⟨are meant to amuse while the ~ is on them —Charlton Laird⟩ **4 a :** a light brown that is stronger and slightly redder and darker than alesan, lighter and slightly redder than French beige, and redder and lighter than cork — called also *Josephine, rose blush* **b :** an undesirable whitish or milky appearance of films (as of varnish or lacquer), resins, or plastics — compare 2BLOOM 3f

blushed \'bləsht\ *adj* **:** suffused with a tone of red ⟨the ~ and green sides of apples⟩

blush·er \-shə(r)\ *n* -s **1 :** one that blushes **2** *or* **blushing mushroom :** a yellowish edible agaric (*Amanita rubescens*) that usu. turns red when touched

blush·ful \-fəl\ *adj* **1 :** full of, given to, or provoking blushes ⟨a ~ flirtation⟩ **2 :** blush-colored **:** RUDDY, ROSY ⟨~ mists⟩ — **blush·ful·ly** \-fəlē\ *adv*

1**blushing** *n* -s **1 :** the act or process of blushing **2 :** BLUSH 4b

2**blushing** *adj* **:** marked by blushes — **blush·ing·ly** *adv*

blush rose *n* **:** a grayish red that is bluer and duller than bois de rose or Pompeian red, yellower and duller than appleblossom, and bluer and deeper than livid brown

blushy \'bləshē\ *adj, often* -ER/-EST **:** BLUSHFUL

1**blus·ter** \'bləstə(r)\ *vb* **blustered**; **blustered**; **blustering** \-st(ə)riŋ\ **blusters** [ME *blustren*, prob. fr. MLG *blüsteren* to storm; prob. akin to OHG *blāsan* to blow — more at BLAST] *vi* **1 :** to blow in stormy noisy gusts ⟨with clouds spitting snow and wind ~*ing* off the lake —T.W.Duncan⟩ **:** be windy and boisterous ⟨when autumn ~*s* and the orchard rocks —Robert Browning⟩ **2 :** to talk and act with noisy, swaggering, and often empty threats **:** play the bully **:** STORM, RAGE ⟨it pleased a people who bragged and ~*ed* but felt themselves outsiders in the world of nations —J.D.Hart⟩ **~** *vt* **1 :** to utter with noisy swaggering self-assertiveness ⟨~*ing* I know not what of insolence and love —Alfred Tennyson⟩ **2 :** to drive or force by blustering **:** BULLY, HECTOR ⟨a hurricane ~*ing* its wild way across quiet country —W.S.Maugham⟩ ⟨trying to ~ us into the belief that they are much better than they look —F.A. Swinnerton⟩ **syn** see ROAR

2**bluster** \"\ *n* -s **1 :** a violent boisterous blowing **:** STORM, BLAST ⟨the strong breeze driving them was setting up a ~ on the water —Rose Thurburn⟩ **2 :** boisterous noise or violent commotion ⟨they do their work without ~ or ostentation —Stanley Walker⟩ **3 :** noisy, violent, or threatening talk **:** boastful empty speech ⟨I don't count his ~ worth a cent —Winston Churchill⟩

blus·ter·er \'bləst(ə)rə(r)\ *n* -s **:** one that blusters

blustering *adj* **1 :** blowing boisterously **:** STORMY, TUMULTUOUS ⟨less violent and ~ than the wind of Patagonia —P.E.James⟩ **2 :** uttering noisy often empty threats **:** SWAGGERING, BULLYING ⟨the ~ army officer appeared with an unruly following —R.A.Billington⟩ — **blus·ter·ing·ly** *adv*

blus·ter·ous \'bləst(ə)rəs\ *adj* [2*bluster* + *-ous*] **:** BLUSTERING — **blus·ter·ous·ly** *adv*

blus·tery \'bləst(ə)rē, -ri\ *adj* [2*bluster* + *-y*] **1 :** blowing boisterously **:** STORMY ⟨a cold ~ day⟩ **2 :** noisily self-assertive **:** SWAGGERING ⟨a brusque ~ man⟩

blut·wurst \'blüt,vurst\ *n* -s [G, fr. *blut* blood (fr. OHG *bluot*) + *wurst* sausage, fr. OHG; akin to OHG *werran* to confuse — more at BLOOD, WAR] **:** BLOOD SAUSAGE

blvd *abbr* boulevard

blype \'blīp\ *n* -s [origin unknown] *Scot* **:** a piece or shred of skin

blythe process \'blīth-\ *n, usu cap B* [fr. the name *Blythe*] **:** a wood-preservative process by which carbolic acid or tar is injected into dried timber

bm *abbr* beam

BM \'bē'em\ *abbr or n* -s **:** a bowel movement

BM *abbr* **1** basal metabolism **2** [L *beatae memoriae*] of blessed memory **3** bench mark **4** bill of material **5** bishop and martyr **6** board measure **7** brigade major **8** bronze medal **9** burgomaster

b major \(')bē-\ *n, usu cap B* **:** the major musical key having a signature of five sharps

BMEP *abbr* brake mean effective pressure

b minor \(')bē-\ *n, usu cap B* **:** the minor musical key having a signature of two sharps

BMOC *abbr* big man on campus

BMR *abbr* basal metabolic rate

BMV *abbr* [LL *Beata Maria Virgo*] Blessed Mary the Virgin

bn *abbr* **1** baron **2** battalion **3** beacon **4** been

BN *abbr* bank note

bnd *abbr* **1** band **2** bound

bnss *abbr* baroness

1**bo** *var of* BOO

2**bo** *also* **boe** \'bō\ *n, pl* **boes** [by shortening] *slang* **:** HOBO

3**bo** \"\ *n* -s [prob. short for *bozo* or *hobo*] *slang* **:** FELLOW, BUDDY — used chiefly in informal address ⟨the truth is, ~, that the man's got a good name —Geoffrey Household⟩

4**bo** \"\ *n* -s [Singhalese *bō* — more at BO TREE] **:** PIPAL

BO *abbr* **1** back order **2** blackout **3** body odor **4** box office **5** branch office **6** broker's order **7** brought over **8** buyer's option

boa \'bōə\ *n* [NL, fr. L, a water snake] **1** *cap* **:** a genus (the type of the family Boidae) of nonvenomous snakes of tropical America **2** -s **:** a large snake that crushes its prey (as the boa constrictor, anaconda, or python) **3** -s **:** a long fluffy scarf of fur, feathers, or delicate fabric **4** -s **:** NILE GREEN

bo·a·bab \'bōə,bab\ *n* -s [by alter.] **:** BAOBAB

boa constrictor *n* **1 :** a tropical American boid snake (*Constrictor constrictor*) that is light brown in color and barred or mottled with darker brown, reaches a length of 10 feet or more, is at home on land or in the water, and climbs freely in search of its prey (as small animals) which it kills by constriction and swallows whole **2 :** a large constrictor (as the anaconda or python)

boal \'bōl\ *dial var of* 3BOLE 1

boar \'bō(ə)r, -ȯ(ə)r,-ōə,-ȯ(ə)\ *n* -s [ME *bor*, fr. OE *bār*; akin to OHG & OS *bēr* boar] **1 a :** the uncastrated male of swine **b :** a wild hog (*Sus scrofa*) — see WILD BOAR **2 :** the male of any of various mammals (as the guinea pig) ⟨the first coon, a big old ~, came trundling into camp —Hugh Fosburgh⟩

1**board** \'bō(ə)rd, -ȯ(ə)rd,-ōəd,-ȯ(ə)d\ *n* -s [ME *bord* piece of sawed lumber, table, shield, ship's side, border, fr. OE; akin to OHG *bort* ship's side, ON *borth* piece of sawed lumber, table, ship's side, Goth fotu*baurd* footstool, Skt *bardhaka, vardhaka*, adj., cutting off, *bardhaka, vardhaka*, n., carpenter, and perh. to Gk *perthein* to destroy] **1** *obs* **:** BORDER, SIDE, EDGE **2 a :** the side of a ship **b :** the stretch that a ship makes on one tack in beating to windward **:** TACK 3e **3 a :** a piece of sawed lumber of little thickness but considerable surface area usu. being rectangular and of a length greatly exceeding its width, in technical specifications of a thickness not exceeding 2½ inches and a width of from 6 to 12 inches, and designated according to thickness ⟨a half-inch ~⟩ ⟨a 2-inch ~⟩ — compare BATTEN; see 4DEAL, PLANK **b boards** *pl* (1) **:** STAGE 2b(1) ⟨as good an actor as ever trod the ~*s*⟩ (2) **:** STAGE 15c ⟨if intellectual ideas were to vanish from the ~*s* I am not sure that my heart would break —Max Beerbohm⟩ **c boards** *pl, slang* **:** SKIS **4 a** *archaic* **:** TABLE 3a (1) **b :** a table on which food is customarily served esp. when spread with a meal ⟨bade the fellow call help to clear the ~, where still was set their interrupted noontide meal —Rafael Sabatini⟩ ⟨a feast spread upon the ~⟩ **c :** food in the form of daily meals often provided as payment for services ⟨room and ~⟩ ⟨~ was the most expensive item in his budget⟩ ⟨the job gave him bed, ~, and 10 dollars a week to spend⟩ **d :** a table at which a council or the magistrates of a court sit ⟨sit as a guest at the council ~⟩ **e :** a number of persons appointed or elected to sit in council for the management or investigation of a public or private business, trust, or other organization or institution ⟨a ~ of advisers to the mayor⟩ ⟨~ of directors⟩ ⟨a university examining ~⟩ **f :** LEAGUE, ASSOCIATION ⟨the local ~ of underwriters⟩ **g :** an examination given by an examining board — often used in pl. ⟨passed his ~*s*⟩ **h** (1) **:** the exposed hands of all the players in a stud poker game (2)**:** an exposed dummy hand in bridge **5 a :** a flat usu. rectangular piece of material (as wood) often marked off or provided with pegs and used for some special purpose (as the playing of certain games or the providing of a flat or hard surface on which to cut food or set dishes) ⟨a gaming ~⟩ ⟨a molding ~⟩ — see BACKBOARD, SIDEBOARD, SPRINGBOARD, WARPING BOARD **b :** a wall or a specially constructed flat usu. rectangular device attached to a wall or free standing used for varied purposes (as the posting of notices, the listing of stock-market quotations, or the display of theater advertisements esp. where they may be seen by groups or by the general public) ⟨quotations on the ~ of a brokerage house⟩ ⟨~*s* with playbills in front of a theater⟩ **c :** a panel (as of wood) in which electrical circuit components (as jacks) may be inserted **d :** PARI-MUTUEL MACHINE **e :** any of various forms used in finishing fabrics and knitted garments (as hosiery) — see 2BOARD 8 **f** (1) **:** a device that is used in bridge for holding the four hands of a deal in their original form so that they may be played more than once (as in duplicate bridge) and that consists usu. of a flat oblong container with four pockets for the hands dealt and is marked on its face to show which player is dealer and who is vulnerable — called also *tray* (2) **:** the particular distribution of cards in duplicate bridge constituting any one deal as contained in such a board **:** a deal in duplicate whist or bridge (3) **:** the entire process of bidding and playing such a deal (4) **:** the score accruing to the winning side when such a deal is played; *esp* **:** one match point (5) **:** the greatest number of match points that can be scored on any deal in duplicate bridge **6 a :** any of various wood pulps or composition materials formed or pressed into somewhat stiff or rigid flat usu. rectangular sheets; *specif* **:** material of the same general composition as paper but stiffer and usu. thicker, being in one classification at least 12/1000 inch thick — compare PAPER **b :** the stiff foundation piece for the side of a book cover ⟨bound in ~*s*⟩ ⟨~ binding⟩ **c :** PRESSING BOARD **7** *chiefly Austral* **a :** the part of a woolshed where sheep are sheared **b :** the sheep about to be sheared **c :** the crew of shearers **8 :** an organized exchange providing facilities for buying and selling securities or commodities **9 :** a fixed signal governing the movement of trains ⟨a slow ~⟩ ⟨a clear ~⟩ — **board on board** *or* **board and board** *or* **board by board** *archaic, of ships* **:** side by side **:** close beside each other — **go by the board 1 :** to go or be carried by force over the side of a ship ⟨in the storm the masts *went by the board*⟩ **2 :** to go or be thrown into discard **:** be passed by and beyond recall — **on board :** ABOARD

2**board** \"\ *vb* -ED/-ING -S [ME *borden*, fr. *bord* piece of sawed lumber, table, shield, ship's side, border] *vt* **1** *archaic* **:** to come up against or alongside of (a ship) usu. for the purpose of attacking **2 :** ACCOST, ADDRESS ⟨he ~*ed* me with some light remark —W.A.White⟩ **3 a :** to go on board of or enter (a ship) **b :** ENTER ⟨~ a train⟩ ⟨~ an airplane⟩ **:** MOUNT ⟨~ a motorcycle⟩ **4 :** to cover with boards or boarding ⟨store owners taped and ~*ed* their windows —*Springfield (Mass.) Daily News*⟩ — usu. used with *up* ⟨~*ing* up the windows of the empty house⟩ **5 a :** to provide with regular meals or with regular meals and lodging usu. for a compensation ⟨the question is, will she ~ as well as lodge her guest —Clara Morris⟩ ⟨~*ing* students⟩ **b :** to place where board or board and shelter or other accommodations are provided usu. for a compensation ⟨~ a horse at a livery stable⟩ **6 :** to haul (the tack of a course on a sailing vessel) down to the deck or to the bumpkin **7 :** to work or rub with a board (as in graining leather) **8 :** to shape (knitted garments) by processing on special forms **~** *vi* **1 :** TACK *vi* 1 **2 :** to have one's regular meals or regular meals and lodging provided usu. for a compensation ⟨having ~*ed* for a time at the Rutledge Tavern —Ruth P. Randall⟩

3**board** *var of* BORD

board·a·ble \-d(ə)bəl\ *adj* **:** capable of being boarded ⟨the ship was not ~ in such a rough sea⟩

board–a–match \¦=ə¦=\ *adj* **:** being or relating to a method of scoring used in duplicate bridge whereby each board played between two teams of four counts one point for the team making the higher score on the board and ½ point for each team if they make the same score

board–and–batten \¦==¦==\ *also* **board–and–batt** \¦==¦=\ *n* **:** wall construction that gives the appearance of wide vertical strips with intervening recesses or projections by means of (1) wide boards rabbeted on transverse edges and lapped not to the entire width of the rabbet on one side or (2) wide boards alternating with narrow and thin battens usu. fitting into grooves in the wide boards or (3) wide boards covered at the seams by narrow usu. 2-inch battens

board around *vi* **:** to board at a succession of houses in a community as part of one's compensation ⟨in the early U.S. country teachers and ministers used to *board around*⟩

board boy *n* **:** one who marks up-to-date information on a stock quotations board

board check *n* **:** a body check of an opponent in ice hockey against the rink sideboards

board cloth *n, dial Eng* **:** TABLECLOTH

board company *n* **:** a company having membership in an insurance trade association (as one which makes rates and recommends forms and underwriting rules for the guidance of its members)

board drop hammer *n* **:** a drop hammer in which the ram is raised by means of one or more boards that pass between two friction rollers at the top of the hammer

boarded *adj* **1 :** covered with boards or boarding ⟨a ~ window⟩⟨a pine-*boarded* cellar⟩ **2 :** made of boards ⟨a ~ walk across the lawn⟩

board·er \'bōrdər, 'bȯr-, 'bōədə, 'bȯ(ə)də\ *n* -s **1 :** one that boards: **a :** one (as a man) that is provided with regular meals or regular meals and lodging **:** one (as a horse) that is provided with food and shelter **b :** one that boards or is sent to board a ship (as an enemy ship) **c :** GRAINER 1d **2 :** one that boards knitted garments (as hosiery) **3 :** a cow or chicken that does not produce enough to pay for its keep; *also* **:** an animal (as a dog) that is not worth its keep

board foot *n* **:** a unit of quantity for lumber equal to the volume of a board 12 x 12 x 1 inches — abbr. *bd ft*

board game *n* **:** a game of strategy (as checkers, chess, or backgammon) played by moving pieces on a board; *broadly* **:** a game played on a board

board hole *n* **:** a notch cut in a tree by lumbermen to hold the springboard on which the faller works

boardier *comparative of* BOARDY

boardiest *superlative of* BOARDY

boarding *n* -s [in sense 1, fr. [1]*board* + *-ing*, in sense 2, fr. gerund of [2]*board*] **1 a :** a quantity of boards **b :** a covering made of boards **2 :** the act or an instance of boarding a ship ⟨hundreds of ~*s* by guardsmen all along the coast to enforce the use of safety equipment —John Bunker⟩

boarding home *n* [fr. gerund of [2]*board* (to have regular meals)] **:** a home for foster children

boardinghouse \'⸗⸗,⸗\ *n* [fr. gerund of *board* (to have meals) + *house*] **:** a house that provides board and sometimes rooms

boarding nettings *n pl* **:** a strong network of cords or ropes formerly erected at the side of a ship to prevent an enemy from boarding it

boarding officer *n* **:** a naval officer detailed to board an incoming ship to provide local information (as to the ceremonies or honors expected, uniforms required, or facilities available)

boarding pike *n* **:** a pike formerly used by sailors in boarding a ship or in repelling boarders

boarding school *n* [fr. gerund of [2]*board* (to have meals)] **:** a school in which pupils are boarded and lodged as well as taught

board lot *n* [[1]*board* (wall)] **:** the usual stock-exchange trading unit determined by the rules of the particular exchange (as, in New York, 100 shares of stock) — called also *full lot*

board·man \'⸗mən, ,man,-maa(ə)n\ *n, pl* **boardmen 1 :** one who works at a board: as **a :** one who sorts glazed tile on a large inclined board and marks it according to shade **b :** a motion-picture studio electrician who arranges the lighting and operates control boards during the shooting of scenes **2 :** SANDWICH MAN **3 :** a member of a stock-exchange firm who does the trading on the exchange floor

board measure *n* **:** lumber measurement by the board foot — abbr. *bm*

board mill *n* **:** a sawmill specializing in the cutting of 1-inch and 2-inch lumber — compare TIMBER MILL

board of commissioners : a county administrative board in many states of the U.S. consisting usu. of three, five, or seven elected county commissioners

board of education : a board controlling an educational system or a unit of it; *esp* **:** a board of citizens controlling esp. the elementary and secondary public-school education in a state, county, city, or town — compare SCHOOL BOARD

board of elections : a local bipartisan board in each of the counties of New York state appointed to supervise political elections

board of estimate : a board that is responsible for the direction of fiscal affairs of a city (as New York) and usu. consists of the mayor, the president of the council, and the chief fiscal officer

board of supervisors : a county governing board in many states of the U.S. often having as many as 50 members elected proportionally from the county's cities, towns, townships, or wards — compare BOARD OF COMMISSIONERS

board of trade 1 : a board or an organization that regulates, promotes, supervises, or protects commercial or business enterprises or interests: as **a :** a committee of the English privy council formerly appointed to consider matters relating to trade and the colonies **b :** an English administrative department concerned with the government's commercial and industrial policies **c :** an organization or league of businessmen for the protection and promotion of business interests — compare CHAMBER OF COMMERCE **2 :** a commodities exchange ⟨the Chicago *Board of Trade*⟩

board out *vt, chiefly Brit* **:** to discharge from the service on medical grounds

boardroom \'⸗,⸗\ *n* **1 :** a room that is designated for meetings of a board and usu. contains a large conference table ⟨the board of directors convened once a month in the ~⟩ **2 a :** a room (as in a broker's office or stock exchange) containing a board for the listing of transactions or prices

board rule *n* **:** a measuring stick bearing various scales for computing board feet

boards *pl of* BOARD, *pres 3d sing of* BOARD

board school *n* **:** one of various former elementary schools established in Great Britain during the late 19th century that were maintained out of local taxes and controlled by a locally elected school board

board tree *n* **:** a tree suitable for cutting up into boards; *esp* **:** a pine tree

board wages *n pl* **1 :** wages (as of a domestic servant) paid in the form of board and lodging **2 :** an allowance for food or for food and lodging provided to an employee esp. as part of wages

boardwalk \'⸗,⸗\ *n* **1 :** a low wooden platform providing a walk (as over sand or a worn or slippery area of floor) ⟨bungalows approached by a ~ over the long marsh of the yard —Saul Bellow⟩ ⟨the slatted ~ on the floor behind the bar —Harry Sylvester⟩ **2 :** a promenade along a beach usu. wholly, partly, or orig. consisting of a boardwalk ⟨the ~ . . . of steel and concrete construction overlaid with pine planking —*Amer. Guide Series: N.J.*⟩ ⟨a 1000-foot concrete ~ along its ocean front —C.E.Wright⟩

boardy \-dē\ *adj, often* -ER/-EST [[1]*board* + *-y*] *of fabrics* **:** not pliable **:** HARD, STIFF

boarfish \'⸗,⸗\ *n* **:** any of several fishes that have a projecting snout like that of a hog: as **a :** a deep-bodied zeomorph fish (*Capros aper*) of the Mediterranean and sometimes related forms **b :** any of a number of chiefly tropical percoid fishes (family Histiopteridae)

boar grunt *n* [so called fr. the shape of the snout] **1 :** WHITE GRUNT **2 :** YELLOW GRUNT

boarhound \'⸗,⸗\ *n* **:** a large dog used in hunting wild boars

boar·ish \'bō(ə)rish, -ō(ə)r-, -rēsh\ *adj* **:** of or relating to a boar **:** resembling a boar **:** CRUEL, LECHEROUS

boar's nest *n, slang* **:** living quarters esp. in a camp in which there are only men

boart *var of* BORT

boarwood \'⸗,⸗\ *n* **1 :** a tropical American timber tree (*Symphonia globulifera*) of the family Guttiferae **2 :** the hard greenish brown lustrous wood of boarwood

boas *pl of* BOA

bo·as·i·an \'bō,asēən\ *adj, usu cap* [Franz *Boas* †1942 Ger.-Am. anthropologist + E *-ian*] **:** of or relating to the anthropologist Boas or his anthropological theories

[1]**boast** \'bōst\ *n* -s [ME *boost, bost;* prob. akin to OE *bȳl* boil, OHG *būsi* bad, MHG *būsch* cudgel, ON *beysti* ham, Norw dial. *bugge* important man, Gk *phōides* blisters (pl.), Skt *bhūri* abundant; basic meaning: to swell, inflate] **1 :** the act of boasting or an instance of boasting **:** VAUNT, BRAG ⟨the man's constant ~ was that he had an infallible memory for names⟩ **2 :** a cause of boasting **:** a reason for pride ⟨the university's ~ was its high standard of scholarship⟩

[2]**boast** \"\ *vb* -ED/-ING/-S [ME *bosten*, prob. fr. *boost, bost*, n.] *vi* **1 :** to say or tell something intended to give others a high opinion of one **:** BRAG **:** puff oneself up in speech **:** vaunt oneself ⟨~ of her accomplishments or family line⟩ **2** *archaic* **:** GLORY, EXULT ⟨in God we have ~*ed* continually —Ps 44:8 (RSV)⟩ ~ *vt* **1 a :** to speak of or assert boastfully or in an excessively prideful manner ⟨~ that you have been in every state of the union⟩ ⟨~ their skill at tennis⟩ **b :** to proclaim (oneself) boastfully ⟨~ myself a patriot⟩ ⟨~ himself to be a better man than his neighbor⟩ **2** *now Scot* **:** THREATEN **3** *obs* **:** to display pridefully or vaingloriously **4 a :** to possess usu. conspicuously something one is proud of ⟨the city ~*s* a campanile and a new city hall⟩ **b :** HAVE, POSSESS ⟨the office ~*s* only one desk⟩

syn BOAST, BRAG, VAUNT, CROW, GASCONADE signify, in common, to give oral expression to one's pride in oneself or in something produced by, belonging to, or related to oneself, as one's family, connections, race, or accomplishments. Although BOAST means commonly to claim with a certain pride ⟨the town *boasts* an excellent school system⟩ it can also point to a self-pride often to the point of conceit, ostentation, or exaggeration ⟨childishly anxious to *boast* that he had walked the whole of the six or seven miles —Compton Mackenzie⟩ ⟨*boast* of past triumphs long forgotten⟩ ⟨annoy the company with an incessant *boasting* of one's wealth and position⟩ BRAG, more common in speech than BOAST, suggests a crude self-glorification ⟨a *bragging* politician⟩ ⟨*brag* of one's importance to the community⟩ VAUNT, more literary than BRAG or BOAST, implies more pomp and bombast than BOAST and less crudity than BRAG ⟨a poem . . . in which a peasant sings octaves *vaunting* the beauty of the beloved —R.A.Hall b. 1911⟩ ⟨pamphlets *vaunting* the region's unique opportunities —*Amer. Guide Series: Minn.*⟩ ⟨ashamed of *vaunting* ourselves to claim credit where credit is due —Robert Moses⟩ CROW, most common in speech, is more contemptuous than the others, suggesting an exultant but petty and unbecoming boasting or blatant bragging esp. over an opponent regarded as defeated in some way ⟨the barrister *crowed* with triumph but the professor was in no way put out —Cyril Kersh⟩ ⟨boasted, gloated, and *crowed* —W.E.Buckler⟩ ⟨advocates of the plane against the capital ship *crowed*, "I told you so" —J.P.Baxter b.1893⟩ GASCONADE, a rare term, implies an habitual and extravagant self-glorification ⟨an enlightened statesman, and not a *gasconading* militarist —C.G.Bowers⟩ ⟨the horn, intended for who knows what sonorous *gasconading*, uttering instead a few piteous bleats —*New Yorker*⟩

[3]**boast** \"\ *vt* -ED/-ING/-S [origin unknown] **1 :** to shape (stone) roughly with a broad chisel in sculpture and stonecutting in preparation for finer work to follow **2 :** to finish (the face of a building stone) by making or cutting several cross rows of parallel corrugations

[4]**boast** \"\ *vt* -ED/-ING/-S [prob. modif. of F *bosse* protuberance, place where the ball hits the wall when boasted, fr. OF *boce* — more at BOSS] **1** *court tennis or squash* **:** to return in play by striking (the ball) against either of the side walls or against the end wall on the striker's side **2 :** to make (a stroke) in boasting

[5]**boast** \"\ *n* -s **:** the stroke made in boasting in court tennis or squash

[1]**boast·er** \'bōstə(r)\ *n* -s [ME *boster*, fr. *bosten* to boast + *-er*] **:** one who boasts **:** BRAGGART

[2]**boaster** *n* -s [[3]*boast* + *-er*] **:** DROVE 4a

boast·ful \-fəl\ *adj* [ME *boostful, bostful*, fr. *boost, bost* boast + *-ful*] **:** given to or marked by boasting ⟨silly young officers, who talked in bellicose and ~ terms —*Times Lit. Supp.*⟩ — **boast·ful·ly** \-fəlē, -li\ *adv* — **boast·ful·ness** \-lnəs\ *n* -ES

boast·ing·ly *adv* **:** in a boasting manner

boast·less \-stləs\ *adj* **:** having no boast

[1]**boat** \'bōt, *usu* -d·+V\ *n* -s [ME *boot*, fr. OE *bāt*; akin to ON *beit* boat, *biti* beam, and prob. to OE *bītan* to bite, L *findere* to split; prob. fr. the practice of making a boat by hollowing out a tree trunk — more at BITE] **1 :** a small vessel with or without a deck propelled by oars or paddles or by sail or power — see CANOE, CRUISER, DINGHY, SLOOP **2 a :** SHIP ⟨packet ~⟩ ⟨came from England in the last ~⟩ **b :** SUBMARINE **3 :** a utensil or device shaped like a boat: as **a :** GRAVY BOAT **b :** an ecclesiastical vessel for incense **c :** an open long narrow usu. small receptacle (as of porcelain or nickel) for holding a substance to be heated or burned esp. in chemical analysis by combustion **4 :** a wooden device used in weaving to obtain a strong selvage — **in the same boat :** in the same situation or predicament

boat 3a

[2]**boat** \"\ *vb* -ED/-ING/-S *vt* **1 a :** to place in a boat or ship ⟨the oarsmen ~*ed* their oars when we touched shore⟩ **b :** to bring (a hooked fish) toward and into a boat ⟨I've almost worn out my wrists ~*ing* a 30-pound halibut —Fred Beck⟩ **2 :** to transport by boat ⟨a company of soldiers ~*ed* across a river⟩ ~ *vi* **:** to go by boat **:** ride in a boat often as a pastime ⟨the company ~*ed* to the island⟩ ⟨was ~*ing* on the river last Sunday afternoon⟩

boat·a·ble \'bōd·əbəl, -ōtə-\ *adj* **:** navigable for boats, esp. small river craft ⟨the canal will be ~ for your ark while the others are still mudfast —S.H.Adams⟩

boat·age \'bōd·ij\ *n* -s **1 :** transportation (as of merchandise) by boat **2 :** a charge for boatage

boatbill \'⸗,⸗\ *n* **1** *or* **boat-billed heron** \'⸗¦⸗-\ **:** a wading bird (*Cochlearius cochlearius*) of tropical America related to the night herons and distinguished by a broadly convex bill suggesting an overturned boat **2 :** BROADBILL 2

boatbill 1

boat boom *n* **:** a spar at right angles to the side of a vessel at anchor to which small boats can be attached

boat bug *n* **1 :** any of numerous aquatic hemipterous insects (family Corixidae) having one pair of legs that resemble long oarlike paddles **2 :** BACK SWIMMER

boatbuilder \'⸗,⸗⸗\ *n* **:** one that builds boats

boatbuilding *n* **:** the occupation of building boats

boat cloak *n* **:** a long black naval uniform cloak now optional and worn infrequently with evening dress uniforms

boat deck *n* **:** a ship's upper deck on which lifeboats are stored — see DECK illustration

boat drill *n* **:** drill aboard ship in the launching and manning of lifeboats

boat·er \'bōd·ə(r), -ōtə-\ *n* -s **1 :** one that rows a boat for a livelihood or as a pastime ⟨~*s* on the river⟩ **2** [so called fr. its having been worn typically by boaters] *chiefly Brit* **:** a man's stiff straw hat with a flat crown, ribbon band, and straight brim **3 :** a woman's hat adapted from the man's boater

boat fall *n* **:** a tackle used to hoist or lower a ship's boat from or to the davits — usu. used in pl.

boat form *n* **:** one of the stereochemical conformations of a strainless 6-membered ring (as a cyclohexane ring) in which two atoms directly opposite each other in the ring are above the plane containing the other four atoms — compare CHAIR FORM

boatheader \'⸗,⸗⸗\ *n* **:** one that is in charge of a whaleboat or a small boat putting off from a larger boat in the cod or halibut fisheries; *esp* **:** an officer who stands in the stern sheets of a whaleboat and manipulates the steering oar and lances the harpooned whale

boathook \'⸗,⸗\ *n* **:** a hook with a point or knob on the back fixed on a pole handle and usu. used to pull or push a boat, raft, or log into place

boathook

boathouse \'⸗,⸗\ *n* **1 :** a building usu. built partly over water for the housing or storing of boats and often provided with accommodations for gear or general storage and often with rooms for social activity (as of a sailing club) **2 :** a building near water for the social or club activities of a group owning boats or interested in boats

boathouse rum *n* **:** a variety of rummy in which a player if he takes the top card of the discard pile may then draw another card

boating *n* -s **:** the act or sport of one who boats ⟨an afternoon of ~⟩

boat knot *n* **:** MARLINESPIKE HITCH

boat·less \'bōtləs\ *adj* **:** having no boat

boat line *n* **:** GUEST ROPE

boat livery *n* **:** a boathouse or dock where boats are let out for hire

boatload \'⸗¦⸗\ *n* **1 :** a boat's full load or an amount or number equivalent to such a load ⟨a ~ of passengers arrived on the dock⟩ ⟨a ~ of grain⟩ **2 :** an indefinitely large number ⟨brought in a ~ of books for my entertainment⟩ ⟨dumped a whole ~ of gifts in the boy's lap⟩

boat·man \'⸗mən, -,man,-maa(ə)n\ *n, pl* **boatmen 1 :** one who earns his livelihood by the management or use of a boat or raft: as **a :** DECKHAND **b :** one who operates a tender to carry passengers and supplies between shore and anchored terminals of transoceanic airplanes **c :** a sawmill worker who works from a flatboat or raft and uses a pike pole to shift and sort logs in the pond — called also *poler* **2 :** BOAT BUG

boat·man·ship \'bōtmən,ship\ *n* -s **:** the ability to handle or skill in handling a boat, esp. a small one

boat nail *n* **:** a nail usu. 3 to 10 inches long made with a large oval or round head or often a rosehead and of soft galvanized iron or of copper usu. with a rectangular shaft tapering to a blunt or chisel point and capable of being effectively clinched

boat neck *or* **boat neckline** *n* **:** BATEAU NECK

boat plant *n* **:** OYSTER PLANT 3

boat plug *n* **:** a wood or metal plug stopping up the drainage hole near the keel of a boat and removable when the boat is dry-docked to drain out bilge water

boat rod *n* **:** a fishing rod of rugged construction usu. jointed and used in saltwater trolling

boat rope *n* **:** a rope by which a smaller boat may make fast to a larger boat or which a crew can grasp when leaving or getting aboard

boats *pl of* BOAT, *pres 3d sing of* BOAT

boat-shaped \'⸗¦⸗\ *adj* **:** resembling the hull of a boat

boat shell *n* **1 :** SLIPPER LIMPET **2 :** MELON SHELL

boats·man \'bōtsmən\ *n, pl* **boatsmen :** one who manages, uses, or works at boats

boat spike *n* **:** BARGE SPIKE

boat·steerer \'⸗,⸗⸗\ *n* **:** a crewman in a whaling boat who pulls the harpoon oar, harpoons the whale, and then steers while his superior officer lances the whale

boat·stone \'⸗,⸗\ *n* **:** a stone artifact known only from archaic sites in midwestern and eastern No. America that is shaped like a dugout canoe and is thought to have been an atlatl weight — compare BANNERSTONE, BIRDSTONE

boat·swain \'bōsᵊn *sometimes* 'bōt,swān\ *also* **bo·s'n** *or* **bo's'n** *or* **bo·sun** *or* **bo'·sun** \'bōsᵊn\ *n* [ME *bootswein*, fr. *boot* boat + *swein* young man, servant — more at BOAT, SWAIN] **1 a :** a petty officer on a merchant ship having immediate supervision of the deck force, of boat crews, and of work parties engaged in maintenance of the hull, anchors, boats, and related equipment **b :** a warrant officer in the U.S. Navy who under the first lieutenant is in charge of the hull and all related equipment (as anchors and boats) **2 a :** JAEGER 3 **b :** TROPIC BIRD

boatswain's chair *n* **:** a wooden board slung by a rope and used to sit on while at work aloft or over the side of a ship

boatswain's locker *n* **:** a ship's locker for the small equipment (as tackle) used by the deck force

boatswain's mate *n* **1 :** an assistant to the boatswain **2 :** a petty officer in the U.S. Navy whose specialty is seamanship and who has supervisory duties in the operation of the deck force and the maintenance of equipment

boatswain's pipe *or* **boatswain's whistle** *also* **boatswain's call** *n* **1 :** a silver whistle used by a boatswain's mate (as in relaying orders to the crew or giving orders to winch and crane operators) **2 :** the note or notes sounded on the boatswain's pipe

boatswain's pipe

[1]**boattail** \'bō(t),tāl\ *n* **1 :** BOAT-TAILED GRACKLE **2 :** the part of an artillery projectile in the rear of the rotating band when shaped like the inverted frustum of a cone

[2]**boattail** \"\ *also* **boat-tailed** \'⸗¦⸗\ *adj* **1 :** tapered at the back end like the stern of a boat ⟨a ~ bullet⟩ ⟨a ~ ski⟩ **2** [[1]*boattail*] **:** of, relating to, or having a boattail ⟨bullets of the ~ type⟩

boat-tailed grackle *n* **:** a large grackle (*Cassidix mexicanus*) of the southern U.S. and Mexico having a tail that is keel-shaped when spread or when the bird is in flight

boat train *n* **:** a train scheduled to connect with a boat

boat truck *n* **:** a low platform with casters for moving a heavy, clumsy, or large piece of stage scenery that must be changed quickly during a play

boat-truck \'⸗,⸗\ *n* **:** [5]DUCK

boat·yard \'bōt+,\ *n* **:** a yard near the water with facilities (as docks and rails) for the building, repair, and storage of small boats and yachts

[1]**bob** \'bäb\ *vb* **bobbed; bobbed; bobbing; bobs** [ME *bobben*, perh. of imit. origin] *vt* **1 a** *obs* **:** STRIKE, POMMEL, BUFFET **b :** to strike with a quick light blow **:** TAP, RAP **2 a :** to move with a bob **:** cause to move down and up or up and down in a short quick movement ⟨~ the head⟩ **b :** to move with any sudden quick movement (as back and forth or in and out) ⟨~ your head in and out of the window⟩ **3 :** to polish with a bob **:** BUFF ~ *vi* **1 a** (1) **:** to move down and up or up and down suddenly and briefly and often repeatedly ⟨a cork *bobbing* in the water⟩ ⟨a child *bobbing* along on a pogo stick⟩ (2) **:** to emerge, arise, or appear suddenly or unexpectedly ⟨a few minutes later it *bobbed* free of the boiling water —*Time*⟩ — usu. used with *up* ⟨the same question ~*s* up at each town meeting⟩ ⟨after months in hiding he *bobbed* up in Paris⟩ **b :** to nod the head or curtsy briefly ⟨a little girl *bobbing* before a visitor⟩ **c :** to try to seize with the teeth (as an apple floating in a tub of water or hanging on a string) — used with *for* ⟨~ for apples at a Halloween party⟩ **d :** to move with any sudden quick movement ⟨he *bobbed* to the telephone like a puppet —Carolyn Hannay⟩ **e :** to move or go from place to place fitfully — often used with *around* ⟨*bobbing* around town for a day or two⟩ ⟨small birds *bobbing* all over the yard⟩ **2** *Scot* **:** to dance a bob

[2]**bob** \"\ *n* -s **1 a :** a short quick down-and-up motion ⟨a ~ of the head⟩ ⟨her curtsy was a mere ~⟩ **b** *Scot* **:** any of several dances **2** *obs* **:** a blow, jog, tap, or rap esp. with the fist **3** *obs* **:** TAUNT, GIBE **4 a :** a modification of the coursing order in change ringing **b :** a method of change ringing using a bob ⟨~ major⟩ **5 :** a small polishing wheel of solid felt or leather with rounded edges

[3]**bob** \"\ *vt* **bobbed; bobbed; bobbing; bobs** [ME *bobben*, fr. MF *bober* to deceive, fr. *bobe* deceit] **1** *obs* **:** DECEIVE, FOOL, CHEAT **2** *obs* **:** to take by fraud **:** FILCH

[4]**bob** \"\ *n* -s [ME *bobbe*, perh. of Celt origin; akin to IrGael *baban* tassel, tuft, ScGael, bobbin] **1 a :** a bunch or cluster: as (1) *Scot* **:** a small bouquet of flowers **:** NOSEGAY (2) *now chiefly dial* **:** a bunch of leaves, flowers, or fruit ⟨red clover ~*s*⟩ ⟨a ~ of grapes⟩ (3) **:** a wad of rags, bait, feathers, or hooks used in angling **b :** a knob, knot, twist, or curl esp. of ribbons, yarn, or hair **c :** a wig with tight horizontal or loose vertical curls **d :** a horse's docked tail **:** BOBTAIL **e :** a

very short to shoulder-length haircut on a woman or child **2** *archaic* **:** a grub, worm, or beetle esp. as used for bait in angling **3 :** a ball or weight esp. at the end of something: as **a** *archaic* **:** a pendant worn as an ornament (as in an earring or attached to a necklace) **b :** the weight at the bottom end of a pendulum **c :** the weight on a plumb line **d :** [1]FLOAT 4 **e :** any weighting matter attached to the tail of a kite to steady it **4 a** *archaic* **:** the refrain of a song; *specif* **:** a short and abrupt refrain often of two syllables **b :** a single very short line usu. of two or three syllables occurring in a series of longer lines in English verse **5 :** CLIPPING **:** a small usu. insignificant piece **:** TRIFLE ⟨the ~s and trinkets of criticism —Laurence Sterne⟩ ⟨the animal would be earmarked; that is, assorted crops, bits, and ~s would have been carved out of his long ears —W.F.Harris⟩

[5]**bob** \"\ *vi* **bobbed; bobbed; bobbing; bobs** [[4]*bob* (grub)] **:** to angle with a bob esp. through the ice

[6]**bob** \"\ *vt* **bobbed; bobbed; bobbing; bobs** [[4]*bob* (knob of hair, bobtail)] **1 :** to cut shorter **:** DOCK, CROP — sometimes used with *off* ⟨a show horse with a beribboned mane and *bobbed* tail⟩ ⟨~ off a dog's tail⟩ ⟨prune and ~ shrubbery⟩ **2 :** to cut (hair) in the style of a bob

[7]**bob** \"\ *n, pl* **bob** [perh. fr. *Bob,* nickname for the name *Robert*] *slang Brit* **:** SHILLING

[8]**bob** \"\ *n* -s [back-formation fr. *bobsled*] **1 :** a single pair of sled runners on which the forward ends of logs may be loaded in logging **2** [by shortening] **:** BOBSLED

[9]**bob** \"\ *vb* **bobbed; bobbed; bobbing; bobs** *vi* **1 :** to ride on a bobsled as a recreation **2 :** to transport logs on a bob ~ *vt* **:** to transport (as logs) on a bob

[10]**bob** \"\ *n* -s [by shortening] **:** BOBWHITE

bo·bac *also* **bo·back** \ˈbō,bak\ *n* -s [Pol *bobak*] **:** a marmot (*Marmota bobak*) of eastern Europe and Asia

bobache *var of* BOBECHE

bob·a·chee \ˈbäbə,chē\ *n* -s [Hindi *babarcī,* fr. Per *bāwarchī*] *India* **:** a male cook

bob·a·dil \ˈbäbə,dil\ *n, usu cap* [after Captain *Bobadil,* a character in *Every Man in His Humor* by Ben Jonson †1637 Eng. dramatist] **:** BRAGGART; *esp* **:** a cowardly braggart — **bob·a·dil·ian** \ˌ==ˈdilēən\ *adj* — **bob·a·dil·ish** \-lish\ *adj*

bob and wheel *or* **bob wheel** *n* [[4]*bob*] **:** a bob refrain to a stanza or a bob followed by rhyming lines

bobbed *past of* BOB

bob·be·jaan \ˈbäbə,yän\ *n* -s [Afrik, baboon, fr. obs. D *babiaen* — more at BABIANA] **:** CHACMA

[1]**bob·ber** \ˈbäbə(r)\ *n* -s [[1]*bob* + *-er*] **:** one that bobs: as **a** *angling* (1) **:** FLOAT (2) **:** BOBFLY (3) **:** DROPPER **b :** RUDDY DUCK **c** *logging* **:** DEADHEAD

[2]**bobber** \"\ *n* -s [[9]*bob* + *-er*] **:** one that rides on a bobsled; *esp* **:** a member of a bobsled team

[1]**bob·bery** \ˈbäb(ə)rē, -ri\ *n* -ES [Hindi *bāp re,* lit., oh father, an exclamation] **:** a noisy disturbance **:** ROW, BRAWL

[2]**bobbery** \"\ *adj* [prob. fr. [1]*bobbery*] *of hounds* **:** of miscellaneous or uncertain breed and of mediocre quality

bob·bie \ˈbäbē, -bi\ *var of* BOBBY

bobbies *pl of* BOBBY

bob·bin \ˈbäbən\ *n* -s [origin unknown] **1 a :** any of various small, round, or cylindrical devices usu. of bone, wood, or metal on which threads are wound for working bobbin lace **b :** a cylinder or spindle with a flange at one or both ends and a hole through the center of its length on which slubbing, roving, yarn, or thread is wound in machinery for roving, spinning, twisting, weaving, or sewing or for making lace — called also *cop, pirn, quill, reel, spool* **c :** the little rounded piece of wood at the end of a latchstring **d :** a coil of insulated wire or the reel round which it is wound **e :** an assembly of the carbon electrode with the depolarizer molded around it in dry-cell construction **2 :** a narrow cotton cord formerly used by dressmakers for piping

bobbin and fly frame *n* **1 :** a machine in cotton spinning that draws and twists the sliver and winds the roving on a bobbin **2 :** a cotton-spinning machine that converts the roving into yarn

bob·bi·net *also* **bob·i·net** \ˌbäbəˈnet — *usu* -ed·+V\ *n* -s [blend of *bobbin* and *net*] **:** a machine-made net usu. with a hexagonal mesh made of cotton, silk, or nylon and used plain or appliquéd (as for dresses, curtains, veils)

bobbinet (enlarged)

bobbing *pres part of* BOB

bob·bing joan \ˈbäbiŋˈjōn\ *n, usu cap J* [fr. the pres. part. of [1]*bob* + the name *Joan*] *dial Eng* **:** a lively rustic dance

bobbin lace *n* **:** a handmade lace made by intertwisting threads wound on bobbins and worked over a pillow on which the pattern is marked out by pins

bobbin line *n* **:** a line of rope carried in a pouch by a fire fighter and used in various emergencies

bob·bish \ˈbäbish\ *adj* [perh. fr. [1]*bob* + *-ish*] *slang Brit* **:** HEARTY **:** in good spirits

[1]**bob·ble** \ˈbäbəl\ *vb* **bobbled; bobbling** \-b(ə)liŋ\ **bobbles** [freq. of [1]*bob*] *vi* **1 :** [1]BOB *vi* 1 a (1) ⟨a basketball *bobbling* on the rim of the basket for a moment before dropping in⟩ ⟨laughed . . . so that her black wig *bobbled* —M.F.K.Fisher⟩ **2 :** to make an error or mistake (as in baseball or football) **:** FUMBLE ⟨the catcher *bobbled* at a crucial point⟩ ~ *vt* **:** MUFF, FUMBLE ⟨~ an easy infield grounder⟩

[2]**bobble** \"\ *n* -s **1 :** a repeated bobbing movement ⟨the ~ of the cork in the rough water⟩ **2 :** a small ball; *esp* **:** one in a series of tiny yarn balls used on an edging **3 :** ERROR, MISTAKE ⟨a man who can laugh at his own ~s and stick to his job —*Time*⟩; *esp* **:** an error consisting of momentarily juggling the ball in baseball or fumbling it in football ⟨lost the game because of two ~s by a single ball carrier⟩

bob·by \ˈbäbē, -bi\ *n* -ES [fr. *Bobby,* nickname fr. *Robert,* after Sir *Robert* Peel †1850 Eng. statesman who organized the London police force] *Brit* **:** POLICEMAN

bobby calf *also* **bobby** *n* -ES [E dial. *bob* young calf (prob. fr. the name *Bob*) + *-y*] *Austral & Africa* **:** a young calf; *specif* **:** one of less than 100 pounds live weight

bob·by pin \ˈbäbē-, -bi-\ *n* [[4]*bob* + *-y*] **:** a flat wire hairpin with prongs that press close together used esp. for bobbed hair — see HAIRPIN illustration

bob·by sock \ˈbäbē-, -bi-\ *n, pl* **bobby socks** *or* **bobby sox** \-ˌsäks\ [fr. the name *Bobby* (influenced by *bobby pin*)] **:** a sock reaching above the ankle and usu. worn by teen-age girls and children

bobby-sock *or* **bobby-socks** *or* **bobby-sox** \ˈ==,=\ *adj* **:** consisting of or relating to bobby-soxers ⟨the *bobby-sox* audience —Ruth Inglis⟩ ⟨the *bobby-sock* brigade⟩ ⟨young wives, only a few years away from their *bobby-socks* days —Lois & Don Thorburn⟩

bob·by-sox·er \ˈ==,säksə(r)\ *or* **bob·by-sock·er** \-,säkə(r)\ *n* -s **:** an adolescent girl

bob·cat \ˈbäb,kat\ *n, pl* **bobcats** *also* **bobcat** [[4]*bob* + *cat;* fr. the stubby tail] **1 :** BAY LYNX **2** *pl* **bobcats :** a beginning cub scout who has not advanced to the rank of wolf

bo·beche \bōˈbesh, -ˈbash\ *or* **bo·bache** \-ˈbash\ *n* -s [F *bobèche*] **1 :** a slightly cupped collar (as of glass or plastic) that is placed above a candle socket to catch candle drippings **2 :** an ornamental collar that is fitted to a candlestick, lamp, or chandelier and from which glass prisms are often suspended

bobfly \ˈ=,=\ *n* [[2]*bob* + *fly*] **:** a fishing fly attached to the leader some distance above the tail fly

bob-haired \ˈ=,=\ *adj* [[4]*bob*] **:** having bobbed hair ⟨a *bob-haired* teen-ager⟩

bob-house \ˈ=,=\ *n* [[5]*bob*] **:** a small shack usu. on runners and used for fishing through the ice (as for smelt or lake trout)

bo·bi·er·rite \ˈbōbēə,rīt\ *n* -s [F fr. Pierre A. *Bobierre* †1881 Fr. chemist + F *-ite*] **:** a mineral $Mg_3(PO_4)_2.8H_2O$ consisting of hydrous magnesium phosphate occurring massive or in crystals in guano

bo·bi·za·tion \ˌbōbəˈzāshən\ *n* -s [G *bobisation,* irreg. fr. *bo,* one of the notes of this scale + *-isation* -ization] **:** an obsolete Flemish system of musical solmization using the syllables *bo, ce, di, ga, lo, ma, ni*

bob·let \ˈbäblət\ *n* -s [[8]*bob* + *-let*] **:** a 2-man bobsled

bob·o·link \ˈbäbə,liŋk\ *n* -s [fr. earlier *Bob-o-Lincoln, bob-lincon,* of imit. origin] **1 :** a common American songbird (*Dolichonyx oryzivorus*) of the family Icteridae with the breeding plumage of the male chiefly black and white and the plumage of the female and eclipse male streaky brown above and yellowish brown below that migrates over a wide range, breeds in No. America well north into Canada where it is noted for its rollicking musical song, passes southward in the fall in great flocks toward its winter range south of the Amazon river, and constitutes a serious pest in rice-growing areas through which it passes though formerly regarded as a table delicacy — called also *reedbird, ricebird* **2 :** DEER 4

bo·bo·tie *or* **bo·bo·tee** \bəˈbōd·ē, ¦bōbəd·¦ē\ *n* -s [Afrik *bobotie*] **:** a dish of minced meat with curry and condiments esp. popular in southern Africa

bobs *pl of* BOB, *pres 3d sing of* BOB

[1]**bobsled** \ˈ=,=\ *also* **bobsleigh** \ˈ=,=\ *n* -s [[4]*bob* + *sled* or *sleigh*] **1 :** a short sled usu. used as one of a pair joined by a coupling **2 :** a compound sled formed of two bobsleds and a coupling or a common seat — called also *double-ripper*

bobsled

[2]**bobsled** \"\ *also* **bobsleigh** \"\ *vi* **:** to ride or coast on a bobsled

bob·sled·der \ˈ=,sledə(r)\ *n* **:** one that rides or coasts on a bobsled esp. as a winter sport

bobsledding *n* **:** the act, skill, or sport of riding or racing on a bobsled

bob·stay \ˈ=,=\ *n* [[2]*bob* + *stay*] **:** a rope, chain, or bar extending from the stem of a ship to the end of the bowsprit — see SHIP illustration

[1]**bobtail** \ˈ=,=\ *n* [[4]*bob* + *tail*] **1 :** a bobbed tail **2 :** something with a short or shortened tail: as **a :** OLD ENGLISH SHEEPDOG **b** *also* **bobtail coat** *obs* **:** a man's coat with short skirts as contrasted to one with tails **c :** a switching locomotive **3 :** a bobtailed arrow **4 :** something curtailed, shortened, or abbreviated **5** *slang* **:** a dishonorable discharge from one of the armed services **6 :** a bobtail straight or flush in poker **7 a :** a motortruck with a short wheelbase **b :** the tractor of a trailer truck

[2]**bobtail** \"\ *adj* **1 :** having a bobtail **2 a :** SHORTENED, CURTAILED, ABBREVIATED **:** DEFICIENT **b :** short, esp. shorter than usual or common **3 a** *poker* **:** requiring either of two ranks of cards to make into a straight **:** open at both ends — used of four cards in a sequence **b :** requiring one more card of the same suit to become a flush — used of four cards of the same suit

[3]**bobtail** \"\ *vt* -ED/-ING/-S **1 :** to dock the tail of **2 :** to cut short **:** CURTAIL, ABBREVIATE

bobtail drawbridge *n* **:** a drawbridge that rotates about a pivot near one end

bobtailed \ˈ=,=\ *adj* **1 :** BOBTAIL **2** *of an arrow* **:** decreasing in thickness from the tip to the nock

bobtailed disease *n* [so called fr. the loss of caudal hair accompanying this disease] **:** ALKALI DISEASE 3

bob veal *n* [E dial. *bob* young calf — more at BOBBY] **:** the veal of a very young or unborn calf

bob wheel *var of* BOB AND WHEEL

bob·white \(ˈ)bäb¦(h)wīt, *usu* -d·+V\ *also* **bobwhite quail** *n* -s [imit.] **:** any quail of the genus *Colinis* of which the best-known species (*C. virginianus*) includes a favorite game bird of the eastern and central U.S. that is replaced in Cuba, Texas, and Mexico by members of related varieties and species, all being about 10 inches long and mottled above with gray, rufous, and whitish, the male having the head striped with black and white and a white throat patch — called also *quail, partridge*

bob wig *n* [[4]*bob*] **:** a short wig with bobs worn in British courts

bob wire *n* [by folk etymology fr. *barbed wire*] **:** BARBED WIRE

bobwood \ˈ=,=\ *n* [[1]*bob* + *wood*] **:** BALSA 1

bo·ca \ˈbōkə\ *n* -s [Sp, lit., mouth, fr. L *bucca* cheek, mouth — more at POCK] **:** a river mouth **:** a harbor entrance (as of a So. American seaport)

bo·cac·cio \bōˈkä,chō, bəˈ-\ *n* -s [perh. by folk etymology (influence of Giovanni *Boccaccio* †1375 Ital. writer) fr. an AmerSp word derived fr. Sp *bocacha* big mouth, aug. of *boca* mouth] **:** a large olive to brown red-flushed rockfish (*Sebastodes paucispinis*) of the Pacific coast from British Columbia to southern California being an important market fish in the southern part of its range

bo·ca·chi·ca \ˌbōkəˈchēkə\ *n* -s [modif. of AmerSp *bocachico,* prob. alter. of Sp *boca de chico* boy's mouth, fr. *boca* mouth + *de* of + *chico* boy, fr. *chico* small — more at CHICO] **:** any of several small So. American freshwater fishes (family Characidae)

bo·cage \bōˈkäzh\ *n* -s *often attrib* [F, fr. OF *boscage* — more at BOSCAGE] **:** countryside or landscape (as of western France) marked by intermingling patches of woodland and heath, small fields, tall hedgerows, and orchards

bo·cal \ˈbōkəl, bōˈkal\ *n* -s [F, a kind of vase, mouthpiece, fr. It *boccale,* a kind of vase, fr. LL *baucalis,* fr. Gk *baukalis*] **:** the mouthpiece of a brass-wind instrument

boc·ca \ˈbōkə, ˈbäkə\ *n* -s [It, mouth, fr. L *bucca* cheek, mouth — more at POCK] **1 :** the mouth of a glass furnace **2 :** a vent on the side or near the base of an active volcano from which lava issues

boc·ca·ro \ˈbükə,rō, ˈbäk-\ *n* -s [prob. modif. of Pg *búcaro* clay vase, fr. OPg *púcaro,* fr. Ar dial., fr. L *poculum* cup; akin to L *potare* to drink — more at POTABLE] **:** reddish yellow pottery made at Ihing in Kiangsu, China, and introduced into Europe by the Portuguese

boc·cie *or* **boc·ci** *or* **boc·ce** *also* **boc·cia** \ˈbächē\ *n pl but usu sing in constr* [It *bocce,* pl. of *boccia* ball, fr. (assumed) VL *bottia* — more at BOSS] **:** Italian lawn bowls played in a long narrow court

[1]**boc·co·nia** \bəˈkōnēə\ *n* [NL, fr. Paolo *Boccone* †1704 Sicilian botanist + NL *-ia*] *syn of* MACLEAYA

[2]**bocconia** \"\ *n* -s [NL, fr. P. *Boccone* + NL *-ia*] **:** a garden plant of the genus *Macleaya; esp* **:** PLUME POPPY

boce \ˈbōs\ *n* -s [L *boc-, box,* a sea fish, fr. Gk *bōk-, bōx*] **:** a brightly colored European fish (*Box vulgaris*) of the family Sparidae having a compressed body

[1]**boche** *or* **bosche** \ˈbäsh, ˈbósh, ˈbōsh\ *n, pl* **boches** *or* **boche** *or* **bosches** *or* **bosche** *usu cap* [F *boche,* prob. short for *alboche,* fr. *allemand* German + *-boche* (as in *caboche* cabbage, squarehead) — more at CABBAGE] *slang* **:** GERMAN — usu. used disparagingly ⟨the place is still thick with *Boche* —Fred Majdalany⟩

[2]**boche** *or* **bosche** \"\ *adj, usu cap, slang* **:** GERMAN — usu. used disparagingly ⟨the *Boche* air force⟩ ⟨his hotel here filled . . . with the *Boche* military on leave —Kay Boyle⟩

bocht \ˈbökt\ *Scot var of* BOUGHT

bo·chum \ˈbōkəm\ *adj, usu cap* [fr. *Bochum,* Germany] **:** of or from the city of Bochum, Germany **:** of the kind or style prevalent in Bochum

bochur *also* **bocher** *var of* BAHUR

[1]**bock** \ˈbäk\ *var of* BOKE

[2]**bock** \"\ *n* -s [Hindi *bok* he-goat] **:** leather made from sheepskin and sometimes substituted for morocco in bookbinding

bock beer \ˈbäk-\ *also* **bock** *n* [*bock beer* part trans. of G *bockbier,* by folk etymology (influence of *bock* he-goat) & Bavarian *bockbier,* fr. *Einbecker bier,* lit., beer from Einbeck, fr. *Einbeck,* town in Hannover, Germany; *bock* fr. G, short for *bockbier*] **:** a heavy dark rich beer usu. sold in the early spring

bock·ing \ˈbäkiŋ\ *n* -s [fr. *Bocking,* village in Essex, England] **:** a coarse woolen fabric used esp. as a floor covering

bocks·beu·tel \ˈbäks,bȯid·ᵊl\ *n* -s [G, fr. *bock* he-goat (fr. OHG *boc*) + *beutel* bag, purse, scrotum, fr. OHG *būtil;* fr. the similarity of its shape to the testes of a goat — more at BUCK, BUD] **:** a short-necked bulbous bottle for white table wine produced along the Main river in Germany or for similar wine produced elsewhere

bocland *n* [OE *bōcland* — more at BOOKLAND] *archaic* **:** BOOKLAND

bo·co \ˈbō(,)kō\ *n* -s [F, fr. a native name in the Guianas] **:** a large brightly colored deepwater crab (*Cancer porteri*) from the west coast of Central and So. America

bo·con \bōˈkōn\ *n* -s [Sp *bocón,* fr. *bocón* big-mouthed, fr. *boca* mouth — more at BOCA] **:** any of several Caribbean anchovies; *esp* **:** an anchovy (*Cetengraulis edentulis*) common about the West Indies

bo·cor *also* **bo·kor** \bōˈkō(ə)r\ *n* -s [Haitian Creole] **:** a Haitian witch doctor and magician

[1]**bod** *var of* BOTT

[2]**bod** \ˈbäd\ *n* -s [prob. short for *body*] *Brit* **:** FELLOW, GUY

BOD *abbr* biochemical oxygen demand; biological oxygen demand

bo·dach \ˈbōdək, ˈbäd-\ *n* -s [IrGael & ScGael] **1** *Scot & Irish* **:** a boorish old man **2** *Scot & Irish* **:** GOBLIN, BUGABOO

bo·da·cious \(ˈ)bōˈdāshəs\ *adj* [prob. back-formation fr. *bodaciously*] **1** *South & Midland* **:** complete and unmitigated **:** UNMISTAKABLE **2** *South & Midland* **:** REMARKABLE, NOTEWORTHY

bo·da·cious·ly *adv* [fr. earlier *bodyaciously,* perh. fr. *body* + *-aciously* (as in *graciously*)] *South & Midland* **:** in a bodacious manner **:** THOROUGHLY, UNQUESTIONABLY **:** EXTREMELY

bo·dan·sky unit \bəˈdan(t)skē-, bōˈ-, -dän-\ *n, usu cap B* [after Oscar *Bodansky* b1901 Russ.-Am. physician and biochemist] **:** a unit based on the activity of phosphatase toward sodium beta-glycerophosphate and used as a measure of phosphatase concentration (as in the blood) esp. in the diagnosis of various pathological conditions, the normal value for the blood averaging about 7 for children and about 4 for adults

bodark \ˈbō,därk -dək, -däk\ *var of* BODOCK

boddhisattva *var of* BODHISATTVA

boddice *var of* BODICE

[1]**bode** \ˈbōd\ *n* -s [ME, fr. OE *boda;* akin to OHG *boto* messenger, ON *bothi,* OE *bēodan* to command, proclaim — more at BID] *archaic* **:** MESSENGER, HERALD

[2]**bode** \"\ *vt* -ED/-ING/-S [ME *boden,* fr. OE *bodian;* akin to ON *botha* to proclaim, presage; derivative fr. the root of OE *boda* messenger; akin to OE *bēodan* to proclaim, command — more at BID] **1 a** *archaic* **:** to announce beforehand **:** FORETELL **b :** to indicate by signs (as a future event) **:** be the omen of **:** PORTEND, PRESAGE ⟨her little face puckered up into an expression that *boded* tears —W.H.Hudson †1922⟩ ⟨watched the weather very anxiously, for it *boded* snow —Mary Webb⟩ **2 :** to give promise of ⟨this controversy . . . will ~ ill for both of us —A.H.Lowe⟩ **syn** see FORETELL

[3]**bode** \"\ *n* -s [ME, fr. OE *bod, gebod;* akin to OHG *gabot* command, ON *both,* OE *bēodan* to command — more at BID] **1** *archaic* **:** OMEN, FORESHADOWING **2** *chiefly Scot* **:** BID, OFFER

[4]**bode** *past of* BIDE

bode·ful \ˈbōdfəl\ *adj* [[3]*bode* + *-ful*] **:** PORTENTOUS, OMINOUS

bo·de·ga \bōˈdāgə, -ˈdēgə\ *n* -s [Sp, fr. L *apotheca* storehouse — more at APOTHECARY] **1 a :** a storehouse for wine esp. above ground **b :** WINE CELLAR **c :** WAREHOUSE **2 a :** WINESHOP **b :** a combined wineshop and grocery store **c :** [1]BAR 5 a, 5 b

bo·de·gon \ˌbōdāˈgōn\ *n* -ES **:** a Spanish genre or still-life painting

bode·ment \ˈbōdmənt\ *n* -s [[3]*bode* + *-ment*] **1 :** OMEN, FOREBODING, PRESENTIMENT **2 :** PREDICTION, PROPHECY

bo·den \ˈbōdᵊn\ *adj* [ME *bodin,* prob. fr. ON *bothinn* ready, past part. of *bjōtha* to bid — more at BID] *chiefly Scot* **:** EQUIPPED, PROVIDED

bo·de's law \ˈbōdəz-\ *n, usu cap B* [after Johann E. Bode †1826 Ger. astronomer] **:** an empirical rule of astronomy: the approximate relative distances of most of the planets (excluding Mercury and Neptune but including the asteroid Ceres) from the sun are given in terms of the astronomical unit by means of the formula $D=0.3(2)^{(n-1)}+0.4$ where D is the distance and n is the number of the planet in order outward from the sun (as Venus=1)

bode·wash \ˈbōd,wȯsh, -wäsh\ *n* -ES [by folk etymology fr. AmerF *bois de vache* — more at BOIS DE VACHE] *North & West* **:** BUFFALO CHIPS

[1]**bodge** \ˈbäj\ *n* -s [origin unknown] **:** an English unit of capacity equal to about ½ peck and out of use since the 17th century

[2]**bodge** \"\ *vt* -ED/-ING/-S [by alter.] **:** [2]BOTCH

[3]**bodge** \"\ *n* -s *chiefly dial* **:** [3]BOTCH

bodg·er \ˈbäjə(r)\ *n* -s [origin unknown] *Brit* **:** a wood carver or woodturner; *specif* **:** a turner who makes chairs of beech wood

bo·dhi \ˈbōdē\ *n* -s [Skt, fr. *bodhati* he wakes, is awake — more at BID] **:** the state of enlightenment attained by a Buddhist who has practiced the Eightfold Path and achieved salvation

bo·dhi·satt·va *or* **bod·dhi·satt·va** \ˌbōdēˈsətwə\ *also* **bo·dhi·satta** \-tə\ *n* -s [Skt *bodhisattva* one whose essence is enlightenment, fr. *bodhi* enlightenment + *sattva* being, essence — more at SATTVA] *Buddhism* **:** a being that compassionately refrains from entering nirvana in order to save others **:** a future Buddha; *specif* **:** one worshiped as a deity in Mahayana Buddhism

bodhi tree *n* [Skt *bodhi,* lit., enlightenment] **:** PIPAL

bo·di·a·nus \ˌbōdēˈānəs, -anəs\ *n, cap* [NL] **:** a genus of stout-bodied chiefly tropical percoid fishes (family Labridae) that is sometimes made the type of a separate family (Bodianidae)

bod·ice \ˈbädəs\ *n* -s [fr. earlier *bodies,* pl. of [1]*body* (part of a garment)] **1 :** an undergarment stiffened with whalebone and resembling a corset **:** STAYS **2 a :** the attached or separate waist of a woman's dress **b :** a tight-fitting sleeveless waist or a very wide girdle often laced and worn over or forming part of a dress

[1]**bod·ied** \ˈbädēd, -did\ *adj* [[1]*body* + *-ed*] **1 :** having a body **:** having such a body ⟨full-*bodied*⟩ **2 :** invested with a body **:** INCARNATE

[2]**bodied** \"\ *adj* [fr. past part. of [2]*body*] **:** thickened or made viscous usu. by heating ⟨~ paint⟩

bodied oil *n* **:** an oil thickened by bodying; *esp* **:** a drying oil whose drying properties have been improved in the process — compare BLOWN OIL, BOILED OIL

bo·di·e·ron \bōˈdēˈirən\ *n* -s [origin unknown] **:** the California sea trout or a related greenling

[1]**bodies** *pl of* BODY, *pres 3d sing of* BODY

[2]**bodies** *obs var of* BODICE

bod·i·less *or* **body·less** \ˈbädēləs, -dᵊ-\ *adj* [ME, fr. [1]*body* + *-less*] **:** having no body: as **a :** having no trunk or main part ⟨a ~ head⟩ **b :** lacking substance **:** INCORPOREAL ⟨~ ghosts⟩

[1]**bod·i·ly** \ˈbädᵊlē, -dəlē, -li\ *adj* [ME, fr. *body* + *-ly*] **1 :** having a body or a material form **:** PHYSICAL, CORPOREAL ⟨a ghostlike figure with ~ form⟩ **2 a :** of or relating to the body ⟨~ comfort⟩ **b :** concerning the body ⟨~ fear⟩ **3** *obs* **:** ACTUAL, REALIZED

syn PHYSICAL, CORPOREAL, CORPORAL, SOMATIC: these words agree in referring to the human body and differ so little that they are often interchangeable. BODILY contrasts with *mental* or *spiritual* ⟨*bodily* illness is more easy to bear than mental —Charles Dickens⟩ ⟨if from any *bodily* or mental defect the eldest son is disqualified for ruling —J.G.Frazer⟩ PHYSICAL, in this sense, may be somewhat milder and less explicit than BODILY ⟨even if he dreads no *physical* betrayal, he suffers from terror and morbid sensitiveness at every hint of mental estrangement —George Santayana⟩ ⟨her emotional breakdown had probably more to do with *physical* exhaustion than with any eloquence of his —A.T.Quiller-Couch⟩ CORPOREAL stresses substance and may contrast either with *spiritual* or with *immaterial* ⟨the spiritual life commences where the *corporeal* existence terminates —J.G.Frazer⟩ ⟨we saw . . . the woman, with a *corporeal* body as real at that moment as our own, pass in through the interstice —Bram Stoker⟩ CORPORAL, now less common in these uses than the others, is likely to refer to things which affect the body unpleasantly ⟨*corporal* punishment⟩ In some contexts as "*corporal* works of mercy" it contrasts with *spiritual.* SOMATIC, meaning of or relating to the body, is almost entirely scientific in suggestion ⟨language is produced through the action of definite body parts and is thus a *somatic* function —*Psychoanalytic Rev.*⟩

[2]**bodily** \"\ *adv* [ME, fr. *bodily,* adj.] **1 :** in the body **:** in the flesh **:** in person ⟨the Savior walking ~ among men⟩ **2 :** as a body **:** as a whole **:** ALTOGETHER, ENTIRELY ⟨the first of 160 homes to be moved ~ from this village —*N.Y.Times*⟩

bodily injury liability insurance *or* **bodily injury insurance** *n* **:** insurance against loss from legal liability of the insured for bodily injury to others esp. when caused by accident

bodily oath *n* **:** CORPORAL OATH

bod·i·ment \ˈbädēmənt, -dəm-\ *n* -s [[1]*body* + *-ment*] **:** EMBODIMENT

boding *n* -s [ME, fr. gerund of *boden* to bode, announce — more at BODE] **1 :** OMEN, FOREBODING ⟨laughed at signs and ~s —Mary Webb⟩ **2 :** a prediction usu. of evil

bod·ing·ly *adv* [*boding* (fr. pres. part. of [2]*bode*) + *-ly*] **:** OMINOUSLY, FOREBODINGLY

[1]**bod·kin** \ˈbädkən\ *n* -s [ME *bodekin, boidekin*] **1 a :** DAGGER, PONIARD, STILETTO **b :** a small slender instrument with a sharp point for making holes in cloth and leather and for picking out bastings **c :** an ornamental hairpin shaped like a stiletto **2 :** a blunt needle with a large eye for drawing tape or ribbon through a casing, beading, or hem **3 :** a compositor's sharp-pointed tool used chiefly to push out a character from set type when making corrections **4** *chiefly Brit* **:** a person closely wedged between two others ⟨a ~ squeezed and sweating on a bus⟩

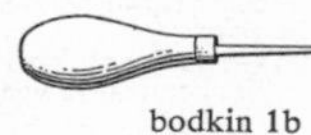

bodkin 1b

[2]**bodkin** \"\ *adv, chiefly Brit* **:** in the position of a bodkin (sense 4) ⟨sitting ~ on the crowded train⟩ ⟨too fat to ride ~ between two friends⟩

bod·le \ˈbädᵊl, ˈbȯd-\ *n* -s [origin unknown] **:** a small copper coin that was issued in Scotland in the 17th century and was worth two Scotch pence

bod·lei·an \(ˈ)bädˈlēən\ *adj, usu cap* [Sir Thomas *Bodley* †1613 Eng. scholar (who restored the Oxford library) + E *-ian*] **:** belonging to the Bodleian Library of Oxford University

[1]**bo·do** \ˈbō,dō\ *n, pl* **bodo** *or* **bodos** *usu cap* **1 a :** a group of peoples living in Assam chiefly along the north bank of the Brahmaputra river as far eastward as the Darrang district and working typically in clannish groups as laborers in tea plantations — called also *Cachari* **b :** a member of such people **2 :** the language of the Bodo people

[2]**bodo** \"\ *n, cap* [NL] **:** a genus (the type of the family Bodonidae) of minute ovoid but plastic biflagellate protozoans (order Protomonodina) common in stagnant water or coprozoic and comprising numerous intestinal commensals of vertebrates as well as water and sewage organisms

bo·dock \ˈbō,däk\ *n* -s [by folk etymology fr. AmerF *bois d'arc* — more at BOIS D'ARC] *chiefly South & Midland* **:** OSAGE ORANGE

bo·do·ni \bəˈdōnē, -dänē\ *n* -s *cap* [after Giambattista *Bodoni* †1813 Ital. printer] **1 :** a book printed by the printer Bodoni **2 :** a text type based on original designs by Bodoni — see MODERN

bo·do·nid \ˈbōdᵊnəd, bōˈdän-\ *n* -s [NL *Bodonidae*, family of protozoans, fr. *Bodon-, Bodo*, type genus + *-idae*] **:** any protozoan of the genus *Bodo* or family Bodonidae

bod-pa \ˈbōdˈpä, bəˈpä\ *n pl* [Tibetan *Bod* Tibet + *-pa* (suffix used in individual and family names)] **:** the Tibetans of southern central Tibet

bods *pl of* BOD

bod-skad \ˈbōdˈskäd, bəˈkäd\ *n* -s *cap B* [Tibetan, fr. *Bod* Tibet + *skad* speech] **:** the Tibetan language

bod stick *var of* BOTT STICK

[1]**body** \ˈbädē, -di\ *n* -ES [ME, fr. OE *bodig*; akin to OHG *botah* body] **1 a :** the total organized physical substance of an animal or plant **:** the aggregate of tissues **:** the physical organism: as (1) **:** the material part or nature of man (2) **:** the dead organism **:** CORPSE (3) **:** the person of a human being **b :** PERSON **:** human being ⟨a feckless ~ who hasn't the faintest idea how to run a house —C.F.Brockington⟩ **2** *relig* **a :** the bread in the sacrament of the Lord's Supper held by some to be and by others to represent Christ's body **b :** the Christian church conceived as a mystical living being of which Christ is the head **c :** the form assumed by man after the resurrection of the dead **3 :** the trunk (as of a person, animal, plant) without appendages **:** the main, central, or principal part of something: as **a :** the nave of a church **b** (1) **:** the bed or box of a vehicle on or in which the load is placed (2) **:** the enclosed or partly enclosed part of an automobile usu. not including the hood and fenders **c :** the part of a garment covering the body or trunk **d** (1) **:** the main part of a document, speech, or literary composition as distinguished from the title, preamble, preface, conclusion, or appendixes (2) **:** the text of a book as distinguished from the front matter, footnotes, and back matter (3) **:** the main part of a social or business letter as distinguished from the heading, salutation, and close **e :** the hull of a ship **f :** the sound box or pipe of a musical instrument **g :** the dominant part of a fortification **h :** TUBE 3a **i :** the statement of a plaintiff's case in a legal action **j :** the main or the larger part of a tool ⟨the ~ of a square is its larger arm⟩ **k :** the fuselage of an aircraft **l** *in printing* (1) **:** text or ordinary reading matter esp. as distinguished from headlines, display lines, footnotes, or tables ⟨a good ~ type⟩ ⟨~ matter⟩ (2) **:** the main matter of a table exclusive of the headings **m :** the largest part of a container; *esp* **:** the part forming the side walls in a metal can body **n :** the main casing of a projectile; *specif* **:** the part of a projectile between the bourrelet and the rotating band **4 a :** a mass or portion of matter esp. distinct in its totality from other masses ⟨a ~ of cold air⟩ ⟨a ~ of water⟩ ⟨no definite proof that the *bodies* found were nitrogen bubbles —H.G.Armstrong⟩ **b** *obs* **:** the real as opposed to the symbolical **:** the substance as opposed to the shadow **c :** one of the seven planets of the old astronomy — called also *celestial body, heavenly body* **d :** one of the seven metals corresponding to the seven planets of the old astronomy — called also *terrestrial body* **e :** a solid figure in geometry **f :** a kind or form of matter **:** a material substance ⟨combining chemical elements to form compound *bodies*⟩ **g :** AMOUNT, QUANTITY **:** BULK, EXTENT **h :** something that embodies, realizes, or gives concrete reality to a thing ⟨see how his theory works in the solid ~ of a novel —C.C.Walcutt⟩ ⟨his intuitions of the future may still give ~ to a better world —*N.Y. Times*⟩; *specif* **:** something that is perceptible or realizable as exhibited in space, that has sensible qualities, or that is the cause of sensation **i** *obs* **:** ENTITY, SUBJECT **j :** ORE BODY **5** *archaic* **:** a vessel for distilling **:** CUCURBIT **6 a :** a group or number of persons or things: as **a :** a fighting unit **:** FORCE ⟨a ~ of cavalry⟩ **b :** a group of individuals united by a common tie or organized for some purpose **:** a collective whole or totality **:** CORPORATION ⟨a legislative ~⟩ ⟨a clerical ~⟩ ⟨the student ~ of the university⟩ ⟨a solid ~ of educated readers —V.S.Pritchett⟩ **c :** a number of particulars regarded as forming a system or embodied in a comprehensive and systematic presentation ⟨a ~ of facts⟩ ⟨a ~ of law⟩ ⟨a ~ of learning⟩ ⟨a ~ of precedents⟩ **7 a :** VISCOSITY, CONSISTENCY — used esp. of oils and grease ⟨a paint with considerable ~ is needed to hide the light undercoating⟩ ⟨oil used in machinery that heats up must have a good deal of ~⟩ **b :** compactness or firmness of texture in cloth **c :** fullness or resonance of a musical tone ⟨his baritone has ~ and richness⟩ **d :** fullness or richness of flavor — used of a beverage **e :** IMPORT, SIGNIFICANCE, MEANINGFULNESS — usu. used of a literary or dramatic work ⟨a play with very little ~ but quite amusing⟩ **f :** strength in intermediate cards (as tens, nines, and eights) in a bridge hand additional to strength in higher cards **8 a :** a clay or a mixture (as of clay and frit or ground rock) from which clayware is made **b :** a piece of ceramic ware distinct from its glaze **9 a :** the part of an attachment plug that screws into a lamp holder **b** (1) **:** the part of a lamp holder or receptacle that contains the contacts (2) **:** a lamp holder and its outer shell **c :** the part of a flexible cord connector that receives the attachment plug cap **10** *of printer's type* **a :** the part extending from foot to shoulder **:** all that underlies the bevel ⟨a kerned letter extends beyond the edge of the ~⟩ — called also *shank*; see TYPE illustration **b :** the distance from belly to back — used as a dimension ⟨a 10-point face on a 12-point ~⟩

[2]**body** \"\ *vt* -ED/-ING/-ES [ME *bodien*, fr. [1]*body*] **1 :** to furnish with a body **:** give material form or shape to **:** EMBODY ⟨believed the sovereign state *bodied* a divine idea⟩ **2 :** to give form or shape to in imagination or art **:** REPRESENT, SYMBOLIZE, INDICATE — often used with *forth* ⟨never been a poet who enjoyed the sensuous world with more gusto . . . or who more solidly *bodied* it forth —Edmund Wilson⟩ ⟨an allegorical figure *~ing* forth the plight of modern man⟩ **3 :** to give strength, substance, or body to; *specif* **:** to increase the viscosity of (an oil) usu. by heating with resulting polymerization — see BODIED OIL

body blow *n* **1 :** a usu. hard blow in boxing that lands between the neck and the waistline **2 :** a serious setback or defeat ⟨the committee has already delivered a *body blow* to wage stabilization —*New Republic*⟩

body brush *n* **:** a stiff bristle brush used in grooming an animal esp. to remove loose scurf and dander from the coat

body brussels *n, usu cap 2d B* [fr. *Brussels*, Belgium] **:** BRUSSELS CARPET 1

body-build \ˈ==,=\ *n* **:** the distinctive physical makeup of a human being **:** CONSTITUTION 3a

body cavity *n* **:** a cavity within an animal body; *specif* **:** the more or less complete space intervening in all higher animals between the body wall and the digestive tract and in mammals and birds divided by the diaphragm into an anterior thoracic cavity that contains heart, lungs, and esophagus and a peritoneal cavity that contains the remainder of the digestive system, the internal parts of the reproductive system, and certain other organs — see COELOM

body cell *n* **1 :** SOMATIC CELL — opposed to *germ cell* **2 :** the one of two cells produced by division of the generative cell in the pollen grain of certain gymnosperms that in turn divides to produce two male nuclei or cells

body-centered \ˈ==¦==\ *adj, of a space lattice* **:** having like points at both ends of every vector parallel and equal to that between the corner and the center of the unit cell **:** having identical atoms or atomic groupings at and about the corners and the center of the unit cell

[1]**body check** *n* **:** a blocking of an opponent with the body in ice hockey and lacrosse

[2]**body check** *vb* [[1]*body check*] **:** to block with a body check

body clothes *n pl* **:** clothing for the body; *esp* **:** UNDERCLOTHES

body coat *n* **:** a coat of opaque paint laid on before translucent coats (as in automobile painting)

body color *n* **1 :** the color of the body of absorbing substances (as gems) due to transmitted light — opposed to *surface color* **2 a :** a pigment that imparts opacity or hiding power to a paint **b :** an opaque coat of paint **c :** the predominant color of a house or other object as contrasted with the color of the trim

body corporate *n, pl* **bodies corporate :** CORPORATION

body english *n, usu cap E* **:** the instinctive attempt of a player to control the movement of a ball or puck after it has been thrown, batted, stroked, or bowled by contorting his body in the desired direction

body fluid *n* **:** a fluid or fluid secretion (as lymph) of the body

bodyguard \ˈ==,=\ *n* [*body* + *guard*] **:** a usu. armed attendant who travels with an individual to protect him from bodily harm

body harness *n* **:** the part of a horse's harness worn on or hanging down from the trunk and hindquarters and including saddle, bellybands, crupper, and breeching

body heat *n* **:** ANIMAL HEAT

body image *n* **:** a subjective picture of one's own physical appearance established both by self-observation and by noting the reactions of others

bodying agent *n* **:** an agent that gives body to a material (as a paint, a plastic, or a cosmetic) with which it is mixed or with which it coalesces

body·kins \ˈbädəkənz, -dēk-\ *interj* [*body* + *-kin* + *-s*] *obs* — a mild oath used esp. in the phrase *God's bodykins*

bodyless *var of* BODILESS

body-line \ˈ==,=\ *or* **body-line bowling** *n* **:** bowling in cricket aimed generally at the leg stump esp. when fast, pitched short, and made to rise sharply — compare LEG THEORY

body louse *n* **:** a louse primarily feeding on the body as distinguished from the extremities or head or from the plumage, pelage, or other modified part of the body; *esp* **:** the sucking louse (*Pediculus humanus humanus*) feeding on the body and breeding in the clothing of man

body mark *or* **body stroke** *or* **body line** *n* **:** the downstroke of a letter

body odor *n* **1 :** the characteristic odor of a living animal body **2 :** an unpleasant odor from a perspiring or unclean person

body out *vt* **:** to make more ample **:** fill out ⟨*body out* the sketchy account of the campaign⟩

body paper *or* **body stock** *n* **:** paper that is to be further processed (as by coating, gumming, impregnating, or vulcanizing) — called also *base paper, raw stock*

body pew *n* **:** a quadrangular enclosed area in the body of a church for a group of worshipers (as a family)

body pigment *n* **:** the chief pigment constituent of a paint

body plan *n* **:** an end elevation in shipbuilding showing the contour of the sides or the transverse vertical cross sections of a ship at certain points of her length

body plasm *n* **:** SOMATOPLASM

body politic *n, pl* **bodies politic 1** *archaic* **:** CORPORATION 2 **2 :** the whole people organized and united under a single political authority **:** a politically organized society **:** STATE

body post *n* **:** STERNPOST

body press *n* **:** a wrestling hold in which one contestant attempts to pin the other on his back by lying on top of him

body rappel *n* **:** a technique of rappelling in which a doubled rope running from the rappel point is passed between the climber's legs, beneath the left buttock, up and around the left hip, across the chest, over the right shoulder, and across the back to the left hand, the right hand grasping the rope above at about shoulder height — called also *Dülfer rappel*

body release *or* **body shutter release** *n* **:** a lever on the body of a camera connected mechanically to the shutter and permitting the shutter to be released easily when the camera is held at eye level

body servant *n* **:** a valet or personal maid

body shop *n* **:** a shop at which automotive bodies are made or repaired

body slam *n* **:** a wrestling throw in which the opponent's body is lifted and brought down hard to the mat

body snatcher *n* **:** one who without authority takes corpses from graves usu. for purposes of dissection or for sale for such purposes **:** RESURRECTIONIST

body stalk *n* **:** the mesodermal cord that connects a fetus with its chorion and through which course the umbilical vessels

body track *n* **:** each of the parallel tracks in a railroad yard upon which cars are switched or stored

body type *n* **:** the type commonly used for the text of a piece of printed matter (as an article, newspaper, or book) as distinguished from the varying type used for such items as headlines, appendixes, footnotes, or advertisements

body varnish *n* **:** RUBBING VARNISH

body wall *n* **:** the external surface of the body in all animals consisting of original ectoderm and mesoderm and enclosing the body cavity

body wave *n* **:** an earthquake vibration transmitted through the earth's interior — contrasted with *surface wave*

body whorl *n* **:** the last and outer whorl of a univalve shell

body·wood \ˈ==,=\ *n* **:** cordwood cut from the bole of a tree

bodywork \ˈ==,=\ *n* **1 :** a vehicle body **2 a :** the act or process of making vehicle bodies **b :** the act or process of repairing vehicle bodies

boe *var of* BO

boea \ˈbüə\ *n* -s [native name in the East Indies] **:** a hard alcohol-soluble Manila copal obtained in the East Indies usu. as a fossil resin

boe·bera \ˈbōbərə\ [NL, after J. von *Boeber* †1820 Ger. botanist] *syn of* DYSSODIA

boeck's sarcoid \ˈbeks-\ *also* **boeck's disease** *n, usu cap B* [after Caesar P. M. *Boeck* †1917 Norw. dermatologist] **:** SARCOIDOSIS

boe·del·hou·der \ˈbüdᵊl,haůdə(r)\ *n* -s [D, fr. *boedel* property (fr. MD) + *houder* holder, fr. *houden* to hold (fr. MD) + *-er*; akin to ON *bōl* farm, abode and to OHG *holtan* to hold — more at BUILD, HOLD] **:** an administrator or a trustee of a boedelhouding

boe·del·hou·ding \-diŋ\ *n* -s [D, fr. *boedel* property + *houding* holding, fr. *houden* to hold + *-ing*] *Roman Dutch law* **:** the holding by an administrator or trustee of the community property of husband and wife as still subject to the community rights after the decease of either

boe·del·schei·ding \ˈbüdᵊl,skādiŋ\ *n* -s [D, fr. *boedel* property + *scheiding* separation, fr. *scheiden* to separate (fr. MD *sceiden, scēden*) + *-ing*; akin to OHG *sceidan* to separate — more at SHED] *Roman Dutch law* **:** partition of an estate

boeh·men·ism *or* **beh·men·ism** \ˈbāmə,nizəm\ *n* -s *usu cap* [after Jakob Böhme (*Boehme* or in England *Behmen*) †1624 Ger. theosophist & mystic] **:** the mystical teaching of Böhme which exerted an influence on George Fox and Quakerism

boeh·men·ist \-nəst\ *also* **boeh·men·ite** \-,nīt\ *or* **boeh·mist** \ˈbāməst\ *n* -s *usu cap* [after J. Böhme (*Boehme*)] **:** an adherent of Boehmenism

boeh·me·ria \bāˈmirēə, bōˈm-\ *n, cap* [NL, fr. G.R.*Boehmer* (Böhmer) †1803 Ger. botanist + NL *-ia*] **:** a large and widely distributed genus of trees, shrubs, and herbs (family Urticaceae) with glomerate flowers in spikes — see RAMIE

boehm·i·an \ˈbāmēən\ *adj, usu cap* [fr. J.Böhme (*Boehme*) †1624 + E *-ian*] **:** of or relating to Boehmenism

boehmite *also* **böhmite** \ˈbā,mīt, ˈbō,m-\ *n* -s *sometimes cap* [G *böhmit*, fr. J.*Böhm* (Boehm), 20th cent. Ger. scientist + G *-it* -ite] **:** a mineral consisting of an orthorhombic form of aluminum oxide and hydroxide AlO(OH) found in bauxite

boehm system \ˈbām-, ˈbōm-\ *n usu cap B* [after Theobald Böhm (*Boehm*) †1881 Ger. musician, its inventor] **:** an improved system of keys and fingering invented for the flute and later adapted to other woodwind instruments

boe·ken·hout \ˈbükən,haůt\ *n* -s [Afrik, fr. *boeken-* beech (fr. MD *boeke, bouke*) + *hout* wood, fr. MD; akin to OHG *buohha* beech and to OHG *holz* wood — more at BEECH, HOLT] **:** a small tree (*Faurea saligna*) of the family Proteaceae of the savanna forests of West Africa with durable wood that is yellowish brown to reddish in color

boe·o·tarch \ˈbēə,tärk, bēˈō,t-\ *n* -s *sometimes cap* [Gk *Boiōtarchēs*, fr. *Boiōtia* Boeotia + *-archēs* -arch] **:** one of the body of chief magistrates elected in ancient times by the cities of central Greece comprising the Boeotian Confederacy

[1]**boe·o·tian** \(ˈ)bēˈōshən\ *adj* [*Boeotia*, district in ancient Greece (fr. L, fr. Gk *Boiōtia*) + E *-an*] **1** *usu cap* **a :** of, relating to, or characteristic of the ancient district of Boeotia in east central Greece **b :** of, relating to, or characteristic of Boeotians **2** *often cap* **:** marked by stupidity and philistinism **:** crudely obtuse **:** DULL, LOUTISH ⟨a ~ distaste for art⟩

[2]**boeotian** \"\ *n* -s **1** *cap* **a :** a native or inhabitant of Boeotia **b :** an Aeolic dialect of ancient Greek used by the Boeotians **2 :** *often cap* **:** a dull obtuse individual **:** a boorish opponent of art and letters **:** PHILISTINE, BOOR

boer \ˈbō(ə)r, ˈbȯ(ə)r, -ōə, -ȯ(ə) *also* bů(ə)r, bůə\ *n* -s *usu cap, often attrib* [D, lit., farmer — more at BOOR] **:** a South African of Dutch or Huguenot descent; *esp* **:** a rural descendant of the early Dutch settlers

boer·haa·via \bůrˈhävēə\ [NL, fr. Hermann *Boerhaave* †1738 Dutch physician + NL *-ia*] *syn of* BOERHAVIA

boer·ha·via \bůrˈhävēə, -ˈhäv-\ *n, cap* [NL, alter. of *Boerhaavia*] **:** a genus of widely distributed pubescent or glandular tropical herbs (family Nyctaginaceae) having small apetalous flowers and club-shaped ribbed fruit

boes *pl of* BO

bo·e·thu·si·an \,bōəˈthüzh(ē)ən\ *n* -s *usu cap* [*Boethus*, 1st cent. B.C. Jewish high priest, founder of the sect + E *-ian*] **:** a member of a Jewish sect associated in Jewish tradition with the Sadducees

boet·i·nese \,bütᵊnˈēz, -ēs\ *n, pl* **boetinese** *or* **boetineses** *usu cap* [irreg. fr. *Boeton, Boetong, Buton*, island of Indonesia + E *-ese*] **1 :** a Papuan people of Netherlands New Guinea **2 :** a member of the Boetinese people

B of E \¦bēə'vē\ *abbr* board of education

boff \ˈbäf\ *n* -s [perh. fr. *box office*] *slang* **1 :** BELLY LAUGH **2 :** a gag or line designed to produce a belly laugh **3 :** HIT 2b **4 :** [2]PUNCH 3

bof·fin \ˈbäfin\ *n* -s [origin unknown] *slang Brit* **:** a scientific expert

boff·o·la \bäˈfōlə, bəˈf-\ *n* -s [irreg. fr. *boff*] **1** *slang* **:** BOFF 1, 2 **2** *slang* **:** HIT 2b

B of H \¦bēə'vāch\ *abbr* board of health

bo·fors gun \ˈbō,fȯrz-, -rs-\ *n, usu cap B* [fr. *Bofors*, munition works in Sweden where it was first made] **:** a double-barreled 40 mm. automatic antiaircraft gun firing an explosive projectile 120 times per minute

B of T \¦bēəv'tē\ *abbr* board of trade

[1]**bog** \ˈbäg, ˈbȯg\ *n* -s *often attrib* [of Celt origin; akin to IrGael & ScGael *bog* soft (respectively fr. & akin to OIr *bocc*), ScGael *boglach* swamp, IrGael *bogach*; akin to OE *būgan* to bend — more at BOW] **1 a :** wet spongy ground where a heavy body is likely to sink **:** QUAGMIRE, MORASS; *esp* **:** an inadequately drained area rich in plant residues, usu. acid in reaction, frequently surrounding a body of open water, and having a characteristic flora (as of sedges, heaths, and sphagnum) — compare MARSH, MEADOW, SWAMP **b :** low-lying land having a thick layer of peat **2 :** land making up a bog

[2]**bog** \"\ *vb* **bogged; bogged; bogging; bogs** *vt* **:** to cause to sink into or as if into a bog **:** submerge in a bog **:** MIRE, IMPEDE **:** slow up ⟨treacherous ground in which you can easily get *bogged*⟩ ⟨too much pedantry *~s* what might otherwise have some interest⟩ — often used with *down* ⟨the book is the result of much careful research, but it is not *bogged* down by it —John Gould⟩ **~** *vi* **:** to become sunk in or as if in a bog **:** become impeded and slowed up — usu. used with *down* ⟨work on the new highway *bogged* down for lack of cement⟩ ⟨the attack would ~ down sooner or later —Norman Mailer⟩

bo·gach *also* **bo·gash** \(ˈ)bōˈgash\ *n* -ES [Ar] **1 :** a subsidiary unit of value in Yemen **2 :** a coin representing one bogach

bo·gan \ˈbōgən\ *n* -s [of Algonquian origin; akin to Malecite *pecelaygan* stopping place] *dial* **:** POKELOGAN

bog asphodel *n* **:** either of two bog herbs (*Narthecium ossifragum*) of Europe and (*N. americanum*) of the U.S.

bo·ga·tyr \,bōgəˈti(ə)r, ˈ==,=\ *n, pl* **bogatyrs** \-rz\ *or* **bogaty·ri** \-irē\ [Russ *bogatyr'* hero, athlete, warrior, fr. ORuss *bogatyrĭ*, of Turkic origin; akin to Turk *batur* brave] **:** one of the legendary medieval heroes of Russia

bogbean \ˈ=,=\ *n* **:** BUCKBEAN

bog bilberry *n* **:** an evergreen shrub (*Vaccinium uliginosum alpinum*) with coriaceous leaves and one to three nearly sessile 4-parted flowers from a scaly bud

bog birch *n* **1 :** YELLOW BUCKTHORN **2 :** SCRUB BIRCH

bog blitter *n, chiefly Scot* **:** the European bittern

bog borer *n* **1 :** WOODCOCK 1a(2) **2 :** an instrument for sampling vegetation below the surface of a bog

bogbuttons \ˈ=,==\ *n* **:** HAIRY PIPEWORT

bog cotton *n* **:** any of several bog sedges of the genus *Eriophorum* with plumose cottony heads

bog cress *n* **:** BITTER CRESS 1

bog crook *n, Irish* **:** chronic aphosphorosis of cattle

bog deal *n* **:** BOG PINE

bog earth *n* **:** a soil composed mostly of fine siliceous matter and partly decomposed vegetable fiber

[1]**bo·gey** *or* **bo·gy** *or* **bo·gie** \ˈbōgē, -gi; *in senses 2&3 often and in the other senses sometimes* ˈbůg- *or* ˈbüg-\ *n, pl* **bogeys** *or* **bogies** [prob. alter. of *bogle*] **1** *usu cap, archaic* **:** DEVIL 1 **2 a :** GOBLIN **b :** SPECTER, PHANTOM **3 a :** an object of dread, fear, or loathing ⟨the ~ of war⟩ **b :** a source of annoyance, perplexity, or harassment ⟨the necessity of grueling study was a ~ he could not escape⟩ **4 :** an unidentified aircraft detected visually or by radar **5** *golf* **a** *chiefly Brit* **:** the number of strokes for each hole set as normally required by an average player **b :** one stroke over par on a hole **6 :** a numerical standard of performance set up as a mark to be attained (as in a contest) **7 a :** a quota, budget, or other estimated figure set up by management in preplanning **b :** a quota restricting output maintained by informal agreement among employees

[2]**bo·gey** \-gē *sometimes* ˈbůg- *or* ˈbüg-\ *vt* **bogeyed; bogeyed; bogeying; bogeys :** to shoot (a hole in golf) in one over par ⟨*~ed* the 17th hole⟩

[3]**bo·gey** \"\ *n* -s [prob. fr. Sc, outhouse, cooking galley on a fishing boat] **:** a small stove

[4]**bogey** *var of* BOGIE

bo·gey·man \ˈbōgē,man, ˈbůg-,ˈbüg-, -gə,-, -,maa(ə)n\ *n, pl* **bogey·men** \-,men\ [*bogey* + *man*] **:** a monstrous imaginary figure used in threatening children; *broadly* **:** a terrifying person or thing **:** MENACE

bogfern \ˈ=,=\ *n* **1 :** a chain fern (*Woodwardia virginica*) **2 :** MASSACHUSETTS FERN

bog garden *n* **:** an ornamental garden in an artificially created or natural bog

bog·gart \ˈbägə(r)t\ *n* -s [earlier *boggard, buggard*, fr.[1]*bug* + *-ard*] **1** *dial chiefly Brit* **a :** GOBLIN **b :** a specter or ghost; *esp* **:** one that is believed to be malicious **2** *dial chiefly Brit* **:** SCARECROW

bog gentian *n* **:** a New Zealand herb (*Gentiana townsoni*) with wiry stems, mostly basal leaves, and white flowers

[1]**bog·gle** \ˈbägəl\ *vb* **boggled; boggled; boggling** \ˈbäg(ə)liŋ\ **boggles** [perh. fr. [3]*boggle*] *vi* **1 a :** to make a sudden jerky movement (as of alarm) **:** start with fright **:** SHY ⟨the prisoner *boggled* at the sight of the gallows⟩ **b :** to be startled (as with

amazement or surprise) : be overwhelmed : be set reeling ⟨the reporters *boggled* over the president's sensational press statement⟩ ⟨the imagination ~*s* at the thought of interstellar distances⟩ **2 a :** to move hesitatingly or evasively : hold back from decisive action (as through doubt, fear, or scruples) : show indecision : SHILLY-SHALLY ⟨his responsibilities coupled with his marked ineptitude caused him to be perpetually *boggling*⟩ **b :** to raise objections usu. minor or petty : hang back from full acceptance or agreement : DEMUR, STICKLE, HAGGLE ⟨no matter how good the argument, he would always pick out something to ~ about⟩ **3 :** to perform an action awkwardly : work unskillfully : make clumsy efforts ⟨uses only one epithet, but it is the right one, and never ~*s* and patches —Leslie Stephen⟩ : BUNGLE, BLUNDER ⟨*boggling* along through the job⟩ ~ *vt* **1 a :** STARTLE **b** *dial Brit* : EMBARRASS, PERPLEX ⟨*boggled* by his father's unexpected return⟩ **2 :** to attend to in an awkward clumsy manner : BUNGLE ⟨*boggling* the little affairs of his own life —Paul de Kruif⟩ **syn** see DEMUR

[2]**boggle** \"\ *n* -s **1 :** the action of boggling **2** *archaic* : a difficult, unpleasant, or bungled situation

[3]**boggle** \"\ *var of* BOGLE

bog grass *n* : any grass or sedge that grows in a bog; *specif* : a sedge of the genus *Carex*

bog·gy \'bägē, 'bȯgē, -gi\ *adj* -ER/-EST [[1]*bog* + *-y*] **1 :** consisting of, containing, or being a bog : SWAMPY **2** *med* : marked by sponginess and turgidity ⟨~ edema of the mucous membrane of the nose in hay fever⟩

bog harrow *n* : a disc harrow with extra-large notched discs for breaking up rank vegetation or hard soil

bog·head coal \'bäg,hed-\ *also* **boghead** *n, often cap B* [fr. *Boghead*, West Lothian, Scotland] : a cannel coal in which algal remains predominate and which is valuable as a source of paraffin oils and gas

boghole \'=,=\ *n* : a hole or depression in a land surface having a miry or spongy bottom

[1]**bo·gie** *also* **bo·gey** *or* **bo·gy** \'bōgē, -gi *sometimes* 'bu̇g-, 'bəg-\ *n, pl* **bogies** *also* **bogeys** [origin unknown] **1 :** a low strongly built truck or cart **2 a** *chiefly Brit* (1) : a swiveling axle or truck on which the leading wheels of a locomotive are fixed (2) : a four-wheel swiveling truck supporting a railroad car **b** *chiefly Brit* : a locomotive or car equipped with a bogie **c :** a swiveling truck including two or more pairs of wheels and used at the end of a vehicle (as a gun carriage) **d :** the drive-wheel assembly and undercarriage of a 6-wheel truck comprising the rear four wheels so mounted as to adjust themselves to sharp curves and road irregularities **3 :** one of the weight-carrying wheels on the inside perimeter of the tread of a tank serving to keep the treads in line

[2]**bogie** \"\ *n* -s [fr. *Bogie* river, Aberdeenshire, Scotland] : tobacco in small twisted ropes

[3]**bogie** *var of* BOGEY

bogie engine *n* [[1]*bogie*] *chiefly Brit* : a locomotive with one or both ends mounted on a bogie

bo·gie·man \'bōgē,man, 'bu̇g-,'bəg-, -gə,-, -,maa(ə)n\ *var of* BOOGEYMAN

bogie roll *n* [[2]*bogie*] : [2]BOGIE

bogie wagon *n* [[1]*bogie*] *chiefly Brit* : a railroad car with one or both ends mounted on a bogie

bo·gi·ji·ab \,bōgē'zhē,ab, -gē'jē,-\ *n, pl* **bogijiab** *or* **bogijiabs** *usu cap* **1 :** an Andaman people of So. Andaman Island **2 a :** member of the Bogijiab people

bog iron ore *or* **bog iron** *n* : a porous variety of limonite

bog kalmia *or* **bog laurel** *n* : SWAMP LAUREL

bog lake *n* : a lake with bogs around its margins

bog·land \'bäg, 'bȯg + ,land\ *n* : BOG 2

bo·gle \'bōgəl, 'bäg-\ *n* -s [E dial. (Sc & northern) *bogill, boggle, bogle* terrifying apparition, goblin; akin to ME *bugge* scarecrow — more at BUG] **1** *also* **bog·gle** \'bäg-\ *dial Brit* : a goblin or specter : any object of dread, fear, or loathing : BOGEY **2** *also* **boggle** *dial Brit* : SCARECROW **3** *chiefly Scot* : HIDE-AND-GO-SEEK

bog lemming *n* : a lemming mouse (*Synaptomys cooperi*) that ranges as far south as the U.S.

bog·let \'bäglət\ *n* -s [[1]*bog* + *-let*] : a little bog

bog lime *n* : earthy impure calcium carbonate deposited in lakes and ponds largely through the chemical action of aquatic plants

bog manganese *n* : a mineral of variable composition being chiefly hydrous manganese oxide : WAD

bog mine *or* **bog–mine ore** \'=,=-\ *n* : BOG ORE

bog moss *n* **1 :** a moss of the genus *Sphagnum* **2 :** a plant of the genus *Mayaca*

bog myrtle *n* **1 :** SWEET GALE **2 :** BUCKBEAN

bo·go \'bō(,)gō\ *n* -s [Hiligaynon, Sugbuhanon, & Magindanao] : a Philippine tree (*Garuga abilo*) of the family Burseraceae with pinnate leaves and fleshy fruits

bog oak *n* : oak that has become dark from long burial in a peat bog

bo·go·do lama \bə'gō(,)dō-\ *n, pl* **bogodo lamas** *usu cap B&L* [Tibetan] : TESHU LAMA

bog·o·mil \'bägə,mil\ *also* **bog·o·mile** \-,mīl\ *n* -s *usu cap* [Russ *bogomil*, after *Bogomilŭ*, 10th cent. Bulgarian priest, founder of the sect] : one of a Bulgarian sect about 1000–1400 which held that the Creator had two sons, Satanaël or Satan, and Christ or Logos

bog·o·mil·ism \'bägəmə,lizəm\ *n* -s *usu cap* : the distinctive doctrines of the Bogomils

bo·gong moth \'bō,gȯŋ-, -gäŋ-\ *or* **bu·gong moth** \'bü,-\ *n* [fr. Mount *Bogong*, highest peak of Victoria, Australia] : an Australian noctuid moth (*Agrotis infusa*) that is made into a paste and eaten by the aborigines when the moths aestivate in huge clusters in rocky mountains to which they migrate from the breeding grounds many miles away

bog onion *n* **1 :** JACK-IN-THE-PULPIT 1 **2** [so called fr. its onion-shaped corm] : ROYAL FERN **3** [so called fr. the onion odor sometimes present in the timber] : an Australian tree (*Owenia venosa*) having foliage with an odor like garlic

bog orchid *n* : any of several orchids growing in bogs; *esp* : a small European orchid (*Malaxis paludosa*) with inconspicuous green flowers

bog ore *n* **1 :** BOG IRON ORE **2 :** BOG MANGANESE

bo·go·tá *or* **bo·go·ta** \,bōgə'tä, -'tō\ *adj, usu cap* [fr. *Bogotá*, Colombia] : of or from Bogotá, the capital of Colombia : of the kind or style prevalent in Bogotá

bog owl *n* : SHORT-EARED OWL

bog pimpernel *n* : a small creeping European herb (*Anagallis tenella*) with delicate pink flowers

bog pine *n* : the wood of pine preserved in peat bogs

bog rose *n* : WILD PINK 2

bog rosemary *n* : a shrub of the genus *Andromeda* — called also *moorwort*

bog rush *n* **1 :** any rush of the genus *Juncus*, growing in bogs **2 :** any of several sedges of the genus *Schoenus* (esp. *S. nigricans*)

bogs *pl of* BOG, *pres 3d sing of* BOG

bog·sha \'bägshə\ *or* **buk·sha** \'bəkshə\ *n* -s [Ar] : BOGACH

bog soil *n* : an intrazonal group of poorly drained dark peat or muck soils underlain by peat and developed under swamp or marsh types of vegetation

bog spavin *n* : a soft swelling usu. on the inner surface of the hock of horses resulting from chronic inflammation of the hock joint with accumulation of fluid in the synovial capsule

bog spruce *n* : BLACK SPRUCE 1

bog star *n* : GRASS-OF-PARNASSUS; *esp* : an herb (*Parnassia palustris*) found in wet places in mountainous or northern regions in the northern hemisphere

bog stitchwort *n* : a bog or marsh chickweed (*Stellaria uliginosa*) with weak stems and tiny white flowers

bog strawberry *n* : MARSH CINQUEFOIL

bog·sucker \'bäg+,-\ *n* : WOODCOCK 1a(2)

bog timber *n* : BOGWOOD

bog torch *n* **1 :** GOLDEN CLUB **2 :** SNOWY ORCHID

bog·trotter \'bäg+,-\ *n* **1 :** a native or resident of Ireland — usu. used disparagingly **2 :** SHORT-EARED OWL **b :** AMERICAN BITTERN

[1]**bogue** \'bōg\ *vi* -ED/-ING/-S [origin unknown] *dial* : to move aimlessly or slowly ⟨just *boguing* around⟩

[2]**bogue** \"\ *also* **bogue bream** *n* -s [F, fr. MF, fr. OProv *boga*, fr. L *boca*, fr. Gk *boak-*, *boax*, a sea fish] : BOCE

[3]**bogue** \"\ *n* -s [LaF, fr. Choctaw *bok, bouk* stream, creek] *chiefly South & Midland* : a passage of water : STREAM

[1]**bo·gus** \'bōgəs\ *adj* [fr. *bogus*, a machine for making counterfeit money, perh. irreg. fr. *bogle*] **1 a :** not genuine : COUNTERFEIT, FORGED ⟨~ currency⟩ ⟨~ documents⟩ : being a spurious imitation of or substitute for the genuine ⟨imitation rosewood or oak panels, false parquetry, ersatz beams, ~ gilt dadoes —Janet Flanner⟩ : SHAM, PRETENDED ⟨a ~ gypsy orchestra⟩ ⟨a ~ king⟩ **b :** pretending to the possession of qualities or character not actually possessed ⟨wrote with ~ elegance —Malcolm Cowley⟩ : false and artificial in tone ⟨a ~ literary flavor⟩ **2** *of a postage stamp, coin, or note* : made privately for fraudulent purposes to appear to be a genuine issue but not in exact imitation of any particular official issue — often distinguished from *counterfeit* **3 :** having qualities like those of a specified paper or board but made partially or wholly of substitute or inferior materials ⟨~ bristol⟩ ⟨~ manila⟩ ⟨~ drawing paper⟩ **syn** see COUNTERFEIT

[2]**bogus** \"\ *n* -ES [fr. *bogus*, a machine for making counterfeit money] **1** *archaic* : counterfeit money **2 a** *slang* : FILLER 1d(1) **b :** printing type or copy set usu. by union requirement in duplication of something that is already typeset and that may have been molded for stereotyping

[3]**bogus** \"\ *n* -ES [short for *calibogus*] : a liquor made of rum and molasses

bog violet *n* : a butterwort (*Pinguicula vulgaris*) with violet-colored flowers

bog whortleberry *n* : BOG BILBERRY

bog willow *n* : a pussy willow (esp. *Salix discolor* and *S. pedicellaris*)

bogwood \'=,=\ *n* : the wood of trees preserved in peat bogs and used chiefly for ornamental purposes

[1]**bogy** *var of* BOGEY

[2]**bogy** *var of* BOGIE

bo·gy·man \'bōgē,man, 'bu̇g-,'bəg-, -gə-, -,maa(ə)n\ *var of* BOOGEYMAN

[1]**boh** \'bō\ *n* -s [Burmese *bō*] *India* : a leader of dacoits

[2]**boh** *var of* BOO

bo·hai \'bō'hī\ *n, pl* **bohai** *or* **bohais** *usu cap* **1 :** an ancient people of northeast Asia once occupying the Sea of Japan coast of the present Soviet Far East **2 :** a member of the Bohai people

[1]**bo·hai·ric** \bō'hīrik\ *n* -s *usu cap* [fr. *Bohairah* Lower Egypt (fr. Ar *buḥairah* lake) + E *-ic*] : a Coptic dialect formerly spoken in the northwestern Nile delta region including Alexandria and surviving in Coptic Christian liturgical use and as the language of the official Bible version of the Coptic Church

[2]**bohairic** \(')=¦==\ *adj, usu cap* : of, relating to, being, or composed in Bohairic

bo·hea \bō'hē\ *n* -s *often cap* [Chin (Pek) wu^3-i^2, hills in China where it was grown] : BLACK TEA — used in the 18th century of the best China black tea and now usu. of inferior grades of black tea

bo·he·mia \bō'hēmēə\ *n* -s *often cap* [fr. *Bohemia*, formerly a kingdom, now a province of western Czechoslovakia, thought of as the home of the gypsies; trans. of F *bohème*] : a community of bohemians : the world of bohemians

[1]**bo·he·mi·an** \bō'hēmēən, -myən\ *n* -s [*Bohemia* + E *-an*] **1** *cap* **a :** a native or inhabitant of Bohemia in central Europe **b :** CZECH **2** *often cap* [trans. of F *bohème*] **a :** one who wanders about not having a definite home : VAGABOND; *esp* : GYPSY **b :** a follower of art, literature, or similar pursuits who adopts an individualistic, easygoing, and sometimes eccentric way of living that reflects protest against or indifference to social conventions

[2]**bohemian** \(')=¦=(=)=\ *adj* **1** *usu cap* **a :** of, relating to, or characteristic of the province of Bohemia **b :** of, relating to, or characteristic of the natives or inhabitants of the province of Bohemia **2** *usu cap* : of, relating to, or characteristic of the Bohemian language **3** *often cap* [trans. of F *bohème*] : of, relating to, or characteristic of bohemians : UNCONVENTIONAL

bohemian bole *n, usu cap 1st B* [*bole* (clay)] : a clay that is a yellow variety of bole

bohemian brethren *n pl, usu cap both Bs* : a Christian body organized in 1467 at Kunwald in Bohemia by followers of Peter of Cheltshic, reformist writer — see MORAVIAN

bohemian earth *n, often cap B* [prob. trans. of G *böhmische erde*] : TERRE VERTE 2

bohemian glass *n, usu cap B* **1 :** ornamental glass noted for its rich colors and incised or engraved patterns **2 :** a hard resistant potash-lime glass much used as a material for chemical ware

bo·he·mi·an·ism \-ə,nizəm\ *n* -s *often cap* : the outlook and way of living typical of bohemians

bohemian ruby *n, usu cap B* [prob. trans. of G *böhmischer rubin*] : a red variety of rock crystal

bohemian waxwing *n, usu cap B* [*bohemian* (gypsy); fr. its extensive and irregular wanderings] : a large waxwing (*Bombycilla garrula pallidiceps*) of northern No. America that closely resembles the smaller cedar waxwing

bohe·reen *or* **bohi·reen** \bō'rēn, ,bōə'r-\ *var of* BOREEN

böhmite *sometimes cap, var of* BOEHMITE

bo·hor \'bō,hȯr\ *n* -s [Amharic *beḥōr*] : a small fawn-colored eastern African reedbuck (*Redunca bohor*)

bohora *usu cap, var of* BHORA

bohr atom \'bō(ə)r-, 'bȯ(ə)r-\ *n, usu cap B* [after Niels H. D. *Bohr* b1885 Dan. physicist] : the atom as described by the Bohr theory

bohr magneton *n, usu cap B* : a magneton based on quantum theory equal to about 9.273×10^{-21} centimeter dyne per gauss per particle

bohr orbit *n, usu cap B* : the hypothetical path of the electron about the nucleus of a Bohr atom

bohr radius *n, usu cap B* : the radius of the smallest or ground-state electron orbit in the hydrogen atom, equal to about 5.29×10^{-9} centimeter — compare BOHR THEORY

bohr theory *n, usu cap B* : a theory of the structure of the hydrogen atom that was later elaborated to apply to atoms of other elements: the hydrogen atom is conceived as a positively charged nucleus with an electron revolving around it in one of many possible circular orbits, each corresponding to a distinct energy state

bo·hunk \'bō,həŋk\ *n* -s [*Bohemian* + *Hunk* central European of the working class, prob. fr. *Hungarian*] **1 a** *often cap* : an eastern or southeastern European (as a Bohemian, Hungarian, or Czech) esp. of the working class — often taken to be offensive **b** *sometimes cap* : a usu. unskilled laborer esp. of foreign origin and usu. of eastern European or southeastern European parentage — often taken to be offensive **2** *slang* **a :** a rough-looking often illiterate or semiliterate individual : LOUT **b :** FELLOW, CHAP

boiar *var of* BOYAR

bo·id \'bōəd\ *n* -s [NL *Boidae*] : one of the Boidae

bo·i·dae \'bōə,dē\ *n pl, cap* [NL, fr. *Boa*, type genus + *-idae*] : a family of sometimes very large nonvenomous snakes having teeth in both jaws and rudiments of hind limbs in the form of hooks or spurs and preying chiefly on warm-blooded animals which they kill by crushing, the family being usu. regarded as including the boas, anacondas, and related snakes of the New World tropics in addition to the Old World pythons — see PYTHONIDAE

bo·i·ga \'bōigə\ *n, cap* [NL] : the type genus of Boigidae

[1]**bo·ig·id** \bō'ijəd\ *adj* [NL *Boigidae*] : of or relating to the family Boigidae

[2]**boigid** \"\ *n* -s : any snake of the family Boigidae

bo·i·gi·dae \bō'ijə,dē\ *n pl, cap* [NL, fr. *Boiga*, type genus + *-idae*] : a widely distributed family (type genus *Boiga*) consisting of somewhat venomous opisthoglyph snakes of which a few (as the African boomslang) are dangerous to man and being sometimes considered a subfamily of Colubridae — see CAT SNAKE

boii \'bȯi,ī, 'bōē,ī\ *n pl, usu cap* [L *Boi, Boii*] : a Celtic people from transalpine Gaul settled partly in northern Italy and partly on the Danube in the region called after them Bohemia

[1]**boil** \'bȯil, *esp bef pause or cons* 'bȯiəl\ *n* -s [alter. (prob. influenced by [2]*boil*) of ME *bile* — more at BILE] **1 :** FURUNCLE **2 :** SEED 4a

[2]**boil** \"\ *vb* -ED/-ING/-S [ME *boilen, boillen*, fr. OF *boillir*, fr. L *bullire* to bubble, boil, fr. *bulla* bubble — more at POLL (head)] *vi* **1 a :** to generate through the action of heat bubbles of vapor that rise and agitate the mass : be agitated by ebullition — used of a liquid **b :** to come to the boiling point ⟨a watched kettle never ~*s*⟩ ⟨the coffee ~*ed* up quickly⟩ **2 a :** to be agitated and tossed about in a manner suggestive of boiling water : bubble or foam violently : SEETHE, CHURN ⟨the sound of the river ~*ing* along the banks —C.S.Forester⟩ **b :** to move in a swirling eddying mass ⟨dust motes ~*ed* in a ray of light —Archie Binns⟩ ⟨a great cloud of dust ~*ed* up past the windows —Hamilton Basso⟩ ⟨black smoke ~*ed* up from the burning warehouse⟩ **3 :** to be moved or excited (as with indignation or anger) : be intensely stirred up ⟨his blood ~*s* at the mention of it⟩ **4 a :** to rush tumultuously or headlong ⟨they ~*ed* through the door in pursuit of the fleeing bandit⟩ ⟨the insects would come ~*ing* out of the swamps —R.P.Warren⟩ **b :** to break forth : gush up or out : ERUPT ⟨the sensational news ~*ed* into headlines and bulletins⟩ **c** *of a fish* : to rise swiftly (as in striking) **5 :** to undergo the action of a boiling liquid ⟨the beans must ~ for some time⟩ ~ *vt* **1 :** to subject to the action of a boiling liquid (as in cooking or cleaning) ⟨the potatoes will need to be ~*ed* longer⟩ ⟨she always ~*ed* the clothes with special care⟩ **2 :** to heat to the boiling point : cause (a liquid) to bubble with heat ⟨the water must be ~*ed* before use⟩ **3 :** to form or separate (as sugar or salt) by boiling or by evaporation involving ebullition ⟨they carefully ~*ed* the salt out of the water⟩ — **boil the pot** **1 :** to provide the means of living ⟨he works 10 hours a day to *boil the pot* for his family⟩ **2 :** to turn out hackwork : produce potboilers ⟨a once-gifted writer who now simply *boils the pot*⟩

[3]**boil** \"\ *n* -s **1 :** the act or state of boiling : AGITATION **2 a :** a swirling upheaval of water; *esp* : one at the surface of a river, a large spring, a pool below a dam, or the sea **b :** the swirl made by a fish moving at or near the surface esp. when feeding **3 :** a disturbance in the surface soil caused by the escape of water under a water-excluding structure (as a levee or cofferdam) **4 :** a stage during which the metal bath in a steelmaking furnace seems to boil as a result of the escape of gas

boil disease *n* [[1]*boil*] : a disease of freshwater fish caused by a myxosporidian protozoan (*Myxobolus pfeifferi*) that invades connective tissue and muscles forming large tumorous masses and commonly causing the death of the host

boil down *vt* **1 :** to reduce in bulk by boiling ⟨*boil down* syrup⟩ **2 :** CONDENSE ⟨*boil down* a narrative⟩; *also* : SIMPLIFY ⟨*boil down* the facts to a short statement⟩ ~ *vi* **1 :** to be reduced in bulk by boiling ⟨the syrup *boils down* in a very short time⟩ **2 :** to be adaptable to condensation ⟨the story *boils down* easily⟩ **3 :** to be equivalent : AMOUNT ⟨the facts *boil down* to very little significance⟩

boildown \'=,=\ *n* -s [*boil down*] : CONDENSATION, ABRIDGMENT

boiled *adj* [ME, fr. past part. of *boilen*] **1 :** subjected to boiling : cooked, cleaned, or otherwise acted upon by boiling ⟨~ beef⟩ ⟨~ clothes⟩ **2** *slang* : very drunk : INTOXICATED ⟨he was ~ as usual⟩

boiled dinner *n* : a dinner of boiled meat (as corned beef or ham) prepared and served with boiled vegetables (as potatoes, cabbage, and turnips)

boiled–off silk \'=,=-\ *n* : silk with the gum removed by boiling in a soap solution

boiled oil *n* : any fatty oil (as linseed oil) whose drying properties have been improved by heating usu. with driers (as lead soaps); *also* : any drying oil made by treating a raw oil with driers in the cold — compare BODIED OIL

boiled shirt *n* : a man's dress shirt with a starched front

boiled sweets *n pl, Brit* : HARD CANDY

boil·er \'bȯilə(r)\ *n* -s [[2]*boil* + *-er*] **1 :** one that boils: as **a :** one that boils ingredients (as of candy, paint, soap) as part of a manufacturing process **b :** a worker who boils fabric **2 a :** a vessel (as a kettle or evaporator) used for boiling **b :** the part of a steam generator in which water is converted into steam and which consists usu. of metal shells, headers, and tubes that form the container for the steam and water under pressure **c :** a tank in which water is heated or hot water is stored (as for domestic use) **3 :** something that is capable of boiling or that is esp. suitable for boiling ⟨milk is a quick ~⟩ ⟨these chickens are good ~*s*⟩ **4 :** a submerged reef; *esp* : a coral reef where the sea breaks

boiler compound *n* : any chemical added to feed water for boilers (as for preventing corrosion, foaming, or the formation of scale)

boiler deck *n* : the deck directly above the boilers of a steamer

boiler horsepower *n* : a unit for measuring the power of a steam boiler, being the equivalent of 34.5 pounds of steam evaporated from and at 212°F per hour

boil·er·less \-ləs\ *adj* : being without a boiler

boilermaker \'==,==\ *n* **1 :** one that performs any or all of the operations in the making, assembling, or repairing of boilers and other objects made of heavy metal plates **2 :** whiskey with a beer chaser — **boilermaking** \'==,==\ *n* -s

boiler plate *n* **1** *or* **boiler iron** : flat-rolled steel usu. about a quarter to a half inch thick used esp. for making boilers and tanks and for covering ships **2 a :** syndicated material supplied esp. to weekly newspapers in matrix or plate form **b :** hackneyed or unoriginal writing **3 a :** a relatively smooth surface (as of flush or overlapping slabs of rock) on a cliff affording little or no foothold **b :** a frozen crusty surface of snow

boiler room *n* **1 :** a room in which one or more steam boilers are located **2** *slang* : a room equipped with many telephones and used for high-pressure selling of stock securities that are often without real value

boiler scale *n* : scale formed on the walls and tubes of a steam boiler

boiler shop *n* : a shop for the manufacture or repair of boilers

boiler suit *n* : COVERALL

boil·ery \'bȯil(ə)rē\ *n* -ES [[2]*boil* + *-ery*] : a place where boiling is carried on ⟨salt *boileries*⟩

[1]**boiling** *adj* [ME, fr. pres. part. of *boilen*] **1 a :** heated to the boiling point : bubbling from the action of heat **b :** intensely hot : TORRID ⟨under a ~ sun⟩ **2 a :** violently agitated : marked by swirling and eddying : SEETHING ⟨winds whipped the ~ sea⟩ ⟨bursting fireworks made the night sky a ~ riot of color⟩ **b :** intensely moved or stirred up ⟨~ with anger⟩ — **boil·ing·ly** *adv*

[2]**boiling** *adv* **1 :** to a boiling degree ⟨some ~ hot coffee⟩ **2 :** EXTREMELY, VERY ⟨~ mad⟩ ⟨they got ~ drunk⟩

[3]**boiling** *n* -s [ME, fr. gerund of *boilen*] **1 :** the action of boiling : subjection to boiling **2** *archaic* : GROUP, BATCH, LOT ⟨the handsomest woman of her day, and the cleverest, the nicest, the best of the whole ~ —George Meredith⟩

boiling flask *n* : FLORENCE FLASK

boiling–house \'==,=\ *n* : a building specially equipped for boiling; *esp* : a building in which sap is reduced to syrup

boiling point *n* : the temperature at which a liquid boils; *specif* : the temperature at which the vapor pressure of a liquid is equal to the external pressure, the boiling point thus decreasing with a decrease in pressure (as 100°C for water at a pressure of 760 mm. of mercury and 51°C at 100 mm.)

boiling spring *n* **1 :** a natural pool of hot water through which bubbles of steam or volcanic gas rise to the surface often with much force **2 :** a spring in which water rises swiftly developing strong vertical eddies

boiling stone *n* : a small object (as a stone or piece of porcelain) used in a boiling liquid to prevent bumping

boil off \'=,=\ *vt* **1 :** to degum (silk) by boiling **2 :** to remove (gum, sizing, wax, dye) from fabric by boiling in a solution

boil–off *n* -s [*boil off*] : the process of removing impurities (as size or gum) by boiling fabrics in a scouring solution

boil out *vt* : to boil off

boil over *vi* **1 :** to overflow while boiling ⟨the milk was on the fire too long and *boiled over*⟩ ⟨use a deep saucepan that won't easily *boil over*⟩ **2 :** to be so excited (as with anger or indignation) as to lose self-control ⟨if you're the least bit late the boss *boils over*⟩

boilover \'=,=\ *n* -s [*boil over*] : the action or process of boiling over : overflow of boiling liquid

boils *pres 3d sing of* BOIL, *pl of* BOIL

boil smut *n* [[1]*boil*] : the common smut of Indian corn caused by a fungus (*Ustilago maydis*) and characterized by grayish white swellings that rupture to expose a black spore mass

bois blanc \bwä'blä"\ *n, pl* **bois blancs** \"\ [CanF, lit., white wood] : AMERICAN BASSWOOD

bois brû·lé \,bwäbrü'lā\ *n, pl* **bois brûlés** \-'lā(z)\ *often cap both Bs* [CanF, lit., burnt wood] **1 :** a Canadian half-breed; *esp* : one of French and Indian blood **2 :** BRÛLÉ

bois co·te·let \-,kōd·ᵊl'ā\ *or* **bois co·te·lette** \-'et\ *n, pl* **bois cotelets** \-ā(z)\ *or* **bois cotelettes** \-et(s)\ [F *bois côtelet*, lit., fiddlewood] *West Indies* : FIDDLEWOOD 1

bois d'arc \'bō,därk, -dak,-däk\ *n, pl* **bois d'arcs** \-ks\ *or* **bois d'arc** *like sing.*\ [LaF, lit., bow wood] : OSAGE ORANGE

bois de fer \,bwädə'fa(ə)(ə)r, bwät'f-, -fe(ə)r\ *n, pl* **bois de fers** \-rz\ *or* **bois de fer** *like sing.*\ [CanF, lit., iron wood] : HOP HORNBEAM

bois de rose \,bwäd(ə)'rōz\ *n, pl* **bois de roses** \-ōzəz\ *or* **bois de rose** *like sing.*\ [F, lit., rose wood] **1 a :** an important tropical American yellow timber derived chiefly from a tree (*Aniba panurensis*) of French Guiana **b :** any tree yielding bois de rose **2 :** a grayish red that is yellower, lighter, and stronger than blush rose, yellower and deeper than appleblossom, bluer and deeper than Pompeian red, and yellower and stronger than livid brown

bois de rose oil *n* **:** a colorless to yellow essential oil obtained from bois de rose and used in perfumery and as a source of linalool — called also *Brazilian bois de rose oil, Cayenne linaloe oil, rosewood oil*

bois de vache \,bwäd(ə)'vash\ *n* [AmerF, lit., cow's wood] : BUFFALO CHIPS

boi·se \'bȯisē, -zē\ *adj, usu cap* [fr. *Boise*, Idaho] **:** of or from Boise, the capital of Idaho ⟨*Boise* shops⟩ **:** of the kind or style prevalent in Boise

boi·se·an \-ēən\ *n* -s *cap* [*Boise*, Idaho + E *-an*] **:** a native or resident of Boise, Idaho

boi·se·rie \,bwäzə¦rē, (')bwäz¦rē\ *n* -s [F, fr. *boiser* to adorn with wood (fr. *bois* wood, fr. OF, forest, wood, of Gmc origin; akin to OHG *busc* bush) + *-erie* -ery — more at BUSH] **:** carved wood paneling

bois im·mor·tel \,bwä,zimȯr'tel, -zēm-\ *n, pl* **bois immortels** \-tel(z)\ [AmerF, lit., immortal wood] *West Indies* **:** a tropical American shrub or tree (*Erythrina umbrosa*) used to shade young cacao plantations

bois in·con·nu \-,zaⁿkə'nü, -'nüē\ *n, pl* **bois inconnus** \-nü(z), -nüē\ [LaF, lit., unknown wood] : HACKBERRY 1

bois pu·ant \,bwäpü'ānt, -püē'äⁿ\ *n, pl* **bois puants** \-pü'änts, -püē'äⁿ\ [LaF, lit., stinking wood] **1 :** HARDY CATALPA **2 :** SYCAMORE 3a

boist \'bȯist\ *n* -s [prob. fr. ME, box, fr. OF *boiste*, fr. ML *buxida*, fr. Gk *pyxida*, acc. of *pyxis* box — more at BOX] *dial* **:** a rough shelter

bois·ter·ous \'bȯist(ə)rəs\ *adj* [ME *boistrous* rough, coarse, alter. of *boistous*, perh. fr. OF *boisteos* lame, rough (said of a road), fr. *boister* to limp (fr. *boiste* knee joint, box) + *-eos* -ous] **1** *obs* **a :** of a strong durable quality ⟨the leathern outside, ~ as it was, gave way —John Dryden⟩ **b :** painfully rough ⟨love . . . is too rough, too rude, too ~ —Shak.⟩ **c :** MASSIVE, CUMBROUS ⟨his ~ club —Edmund Spenser⟩ **2 a :** noisily turbulent **:** loudmouthed and rough in behavior **:** ROWDY, BRAWLING, CLAMOROUS ⟨a ~ mob⟩ ⟨the ~ shantytowns of gold-rush days —*Amer. Guide Series: Calif.*⟩ **b :** full of exuberant uninhibited and often excessive animal spirits **:** completely unrestrained ⟨~ laughter⟩ ⟨children enjoying a ~ play period⟩ **3 a :** rough, stormy and agitated **:** marked by tumultuous violence and fury **:** not calm ⟨~ winds and waves⟩ **b** *obs* **:** savagely fierce **:** TRUCULENT ⟨your indecent and ~ treatment of this man —Alexander Pope⟩ **syn** see VOCIFEROUS

bois·ter·ous·ly *adv* **:** in a boisterous manner

bois·ter·ous·ness *n* -ES **:** the quality or state of being boisterous

boîte \'bwät, 'bwȧt\ *or* **boîte de nuit** \¦=dənü'ē, -nüē'wē\ *n, pl* **boîtes** \'bwät(s), 'bwȧt\ *or* **boîtes de nuit** [*boîte* fr. F, lit., box, fr. OF *boiste*; *boîte de nuit* fr. F, lit., night box] : NIGHTCLUB

bo·ka·dam \'bōkədəm\ *n* -s [prob. native name in the East Indies] **:** an East Indian aquatic venomous snake (*Hurria*, syn. *Cerberus, rhynchops*)

¹boke \'bōk\ *vb* -ED/-ING/-S [ME *bolken*; prob. akin to OE *bealcian* to belch — more at BELCH] **1** *chiefly Scot* **:** VOMIT, RETCH **2** *chiefly Scot* **:** BELCH, BURP

²boke \"\ *n* -s [ME *bolke*, fr. *bolken* v.] **1** *chiefly Scot* **:** RETCHING, VOMITING **2** *chiefly Scot* **:** BELCH, BURP

bo·kha·ra \bō'kärə, -karə\ *also* **bu·kha·ra** \bü'-\ *n* -s [fr. *Bokhara, Bukhara*, region in Uzbek S.S.R., U.S.S.R.] **1** *often cap* **:** astrakhan from Bukhara in central Asia **2** *usu cap* **:** a Turkoman rug in small and large sizes coming from the region of Bukhara, distinguished generally by very fine knotting, geometric allover designs (as octagons, diamonds, angular shrubs, and flowers), and by its prevailing colors of mulberry red with touches of dark blue, vermilion, and ivory white **3** *often cap* **:** a dark purplish red that is redder and duller than red-grape or pansy purple, redder and deeper than raisin, and redder, stronger, and slightly lighter than dahlia purple

bokhara clover *n, usu cap* [fr. *Bokhara*, the region] **:** WHITE SWEET CLOVER

bokharan *usu cap, var of* BUKHARAN

bo·kie \'bōkē\ *Scot var of* BOGEY

bok·ma·kier·ie \,bäkmə'kirē\ *n* -s [Afrik, of imit. origin] **:** a short-winged shrike (*Telophorus zeylonus*) of southern Africa

bo·ko \'bō(,)kō\ *n* -s [origin unknown] *slang Brit* **:** NOSE

bokor *var of* BOCOR

¹bo·la \'bōlə\ *or* **bo·las** \-ləs, -,läs\ *n, pl* **bolas** \-ləz\ *also* **bolases** \-ləsəz\ [AmerSp *bolas*, pl. of Sp *bola* ball, fr. OSp, fr. OProv, fr. L *bulla* bubble, ball — more at POLL (head)] **:** a weapon that consists of two or more usu. stone or iron balls attached to the ends of a cord and that is used for hurling at and entangling an animal

bola

²bola \'bō(,)lä\ *n* -s [Bengali *bolā*, perh. of Dravidian origin; akin to Malayalam & Kanarese *pollu* hollow] *India* **:** MAJAGUA a

bo·lar \'bōlə(r)\ *adj* [²*bole* + *-ar*] **:** of or relating to bole **:** CLAYEY

bol·bo·phyl·lum \¦bälbə¦filəm, ¦bōl-\ *n* [NL, fr. Gk *bolbos* bulb + NL *-phyllum* — more at BULB] **1** *cap* **:** a large genus of epiphytic orchids having small pseudobulbs, stiff leaves, and racemose or solitary showy flowers with a jointed lip, being native chiefly to the Old World tropics, and including a few forms in cultivation **2** -s **:** a plant or flower of the genus *Bolbophyllum*

¹bold \'bōld\ *adj, usu* -ER/-EST [ME, fr. OE *bald, beald*; akin to OHG *bald* bold, ON *ballr* frightful, Goth *balthaba* boldly, and prob. to OE *blāwan* to blow — more at BLOW] **1 a :** fearless in meeting danger or difficulty **:** aggressively daring **:** not shrinking from risk **:** INTREPID, VENTURESOME ⟨~ settlers on some foreign shore —William Wordsworth⟩ **b :** showing or reflecting a courageous daring spirit and contempt of danger ⟨a ~ speech⟩ ⟨a ~ plan⟩ **2 :** presumptuously confident and self-reliant **:** taking undue liberties **:** lacking modesty and restraint **:** FORWARD, RUDE, IMPUDENT ⟨~ triflers with the unknown⟩ ⟨a ~ little urchin⟩ **3** *obs* **:** wholly assured **:** CONFIDENT **4 a :** of great strength or intensity **:** FIERCE ⟨the howling of ~ winds⟩ ⟨~ flames leaping to the sky⟩ **b :** full-flavored **:** HEADY ⟨~ brandy⟩ **:** piquant, pungent, or nippy ⟨~ aromatic peppers⟩ **c :** fully developed **:** MATURE, RIPE ⟨~ fields of grain⟩ **d :** well filled out **:** PLUMP ⟨a laughing girl with a ~ lithe figure⟩ **5 :** rising, sloping, or dropping abruptly **:** SHEER, STEEP ⟨where some of the ~*est* chalk cliffs of England rise from the waters of the Atlantic —Richard Joseph⟩ **6 :** marked by departure from convention or tradition **:** FREE, DARING ⟨a ~ thinker⟩ ⟨a ~ art design⟩ ⟨this ~ modern trend toward loose behavior in love —Ellen Glasgow⟩ **7 :** standing out prominently **:** markedly conspicuous **:** EYE-CATCHING, ARRESTING **:** fully delineated ⟨~ letters scrawled across the wall⟩ ⟨~ newspaper headlines⟩ ⟨a figure carved in ~ relief⟩ **8 :** being or composed of large pieces (as of fossil resin in commerce) **9 :** BOLD-FACED 3 **syn** see BRAVE

²bold \"\ *vb* -ED/-ING/-S [ME *bolden*, fr. OE *bealdian*, fr. *beald* bold] *vi, obs* **:** to be or become bold ~ *vt, obs* **:** EMBOLDEN

³bold \"\ *n* -s [by shortening] **:** BOLDFACE

bol·da·cious \(')bōl¦dāshəs\ *adj* [prob. blend of *bold* and *audacious*] *dial Brit* **:** BRAZEN, IMPUDENT

bold·en \'bōldən\ *vb* -ED/-ING/-S [¹*bold* + *-en*] *vt, now dial Brit* **:** EMBOLDEN ~ *vi, now dial Brit* **:** to take courage

bold·face \'=,=\ *n* **1** *archaic* **:** a forward and usu. impudent individual **2 :** a typeface with downstrokes or all strokes wide producing a relatively heavy impression; *also* **:** boldface print ⟨a paragraph set in ~⟩ ⟨~ letters⟩ — compare LIGHTFACE

bold-faced \'=¦=\ *adj* **1 :** having a bold face **2 :** bold in manner or expression **:** FORWARD, IMPUDENT ⟨*bold-faced* ruffians⟩ **3 :** having the character of boldface **:** set in boldface

boldhearted \'=¦==\ *adj* **:** having a bold heart

bol·dine \'bäl,dēn, -dən\ *n* -s [ISV *boldo* + *-ine*] **:** a poisonous bitter crystalline alkaloid $C_{19}H_{21}NO_4$ found in leaves of the boldo

bold·ly \'bōl(d)lē, -lī\ *adv* [ME, fr. OE *baldlīce, bealdlīce*, fr. *bald, beald* bold + *-līce* -ly — more at BOLD] **:** in a bold manner **:** with assurance **:** DARINGLY

bold·ness \-l(d)nəs\ *n* -ES [ME *boldnesse*, fr. *bold* + *-nesse* -ness] **:** the quality or state of being bold

bol·do \'bäl(,)dō\ *n* -s [AmerSp, fr. Araucan *boldu*] **:** a Chilean evergreen shrub (*Peumus boldus*) with sweet edible fruit

boldo family *n* **:** MONIMIACEAE

bol·du \'bäl,dü\ [NL, fr. AmerSp *boldú* boldo, fr. Araucan *boldu*] *syn of* PEUMUS

¹bole \'bōl\ *n* -s [ME, fr. ON *bolr*; akin to MLG *bole* plank, OE *bula* bull — more at BULL] **1 :** the trunk of a tree; *esp* **:** the lower merchantable portion of such a trunk **2 :** any cylindrically shaped object or mass ⟨massive ~*s* of stone⟩

²bole \"\ *n* -s [ME, fr. MF, fr. LL *bolus* clod, large pill, fr. Gk *bōlos* lump, clod; perh. akin to L *bulla* bubble — more at POLL (head)] **1 :** any of several varieties of friable earthy clay usu. colored red by iron oxide and consisting essentially of hydrous silicates of aluminum or less often of magnesium **2** *archaic* **:** BOLUS 1 **3 :** a moderate reddish brown that is yellower, lighter, and stronger than roan, mahogany, or oxblood, redder, lighter, and stronger than rustic brown, and redder and stronger than russet tan — called also *Antwerp red, Armenian bole, bole Armoniac, oriental bole, red bole, red chalk, red ocher, ruddle, terra Lemnia, terra pozzuoli, terra rosa, terra sigillata, Venice red*

³bole \"\ *n* -s [origin unknown] **1** *chiefly Scot* **:** a small recess or cupboard in a wall **2** *chiefly Scot* **:** an opening in a wall for light and air usu. closed with a wooden shutter

⁴bole \"\ *n* -s [prob. var. of *bowl*] **:** a site of an ancient smelter in Derbyshire, England

bole armoniac *n, often cap A* [ME *bol armoniak*, fr. (assumed) ML *bolus Armeniacus*, lit., Armenian bole, fr. LL *bolus* + L *Armeniacus* Armenian, fr. *Armenia*, ancient country in Asia Minor] **:** ARMENIAN BOLE 1

bo·lec·tion \bō'lekshən\ *or* **bi·lec·tion** \bī'-\ *n* -s [origin unknown] **:** a molding or group of moldings separating two planes (as a stile from a panel) and projecting beyond the surface of both — **bo·lec·tioned** \-shənd\ *adj*

PANEL STILE

typical bolection molding

boled \'bōld\ *adj* [¹*bole* + *-ed*] **:** characterized by or having a bole ⟨a forest of straight-*boled* trees⟩ ⟨a cottage with two ~ walls⟩

bo·le·ite \bō'lā,īt, -'lē,-\ *n* -s [F *boléite*, fr. *Boleo*, village near Santa Rosalía, Lower California, Mexico + F *-ite*] **:** a mineral $Pb_9Cu_8Ag_3Cl_{21}(OH)_{16}.2H_2O$ consisting of a basic and hydrous lead copper silver chloride

bo·le·ro \bō'la(a)(,)rō, bō'-, -le(,)-, -lā(,)-\ *n* -s [Sp, perh. fr. *bola* ball — more at BOLA] **1 a :** a Spanish dance to music in ¾ time and characterized by sharp turns and revolutions of the body and stamping of the feet in syncopated rhythm **b :** a West Indian derivative of the Spanish bolero in ²⁄₄ time **2 :** music for or suited to the bolero **3 :** a jacket of Spanish origin characteristically of waist-length or shorter made with or without sleeves, lapels, and collar and usu. worn open

bo·le·ta·ce·ae \bō¦lə'tāsē,ē\ *n pl, cap* [NL, fr. *Boletus*, type genus + *-aceae*] **:** a family of pore-bearing fleshy fungi (order Agaricales) usu. having the pores easily separating from the pileus and often from each other

bo·le·ta·ceous \¦==¦tāshəs\ *adj* [NL *Boletaceae* + E *-ous*] **:** of or relating to the family Boletaceae

bo·lete \bō'lēt, bə'-\ *n* -s [NL *Boletus*] **:** any fungus of the family Boletaceae

bo·le·tus \bō'lēd·əs, bə'-, -ētəs\ *n, cap* [NL, fr. L, a fungus, fr. Gk *bōlitēs*] **:** a genus (the type and principal representative of the family Boletaceae) of soft early-decaying pore fungi some of which are poisonous and others edible

bo·lide \'bō,līd, -ləd\ *n* -s [F, fr. L *bolid-, bolis* arrow-shaped meteor, fr. Gk, lit., missile, javelin, fr. *ballein* to throw — more at DEVIL] **:** an exploding or exploded meteor or meteorite

bo·li·ta \bə'lēd·ə, bō'-\ *also* **bo·li·to** \-ēd·(,)ō\ *n* -s [AmerSp (Cuba) *bolita*, fr. Sp, little ball, dim. of *bola* ball — more at BOLA] **1 :** a game of chance having the character of a lottery in which a bag of small numbered balls is tossed about until only one remains or until one is grasped at random, the ball so selected being considered as bearing the winning number **2 :** a numbers game in which one attempts to guess a variously determined 2-digit number

bol·i·var \'bälə̇vər, bō'lē,vär\ *n, pl* **bolivars** \-rz\ *or* **bo·li·va·res** \bō'lēvə,rās, -vä,-\ [AmerSp *bolívar*, after Simón *Bolívar* †1830 So. Amer. liberator] **1 :** the basic monetary unit of Venezuela — see MONEY table **2 :** a silver coin representing one bolivar

bo·li·var·i·an \¦bōlə¦verēən, ¦bäl-, -va(a)r-\ *adj, usu cap* [Sp *bolivariano*, fr. S. *Bolívar*, who helped liberate these countries from the rule of Spain + Sp *-iano* -ian] **:** of or relating to the So. American republics of Colombia, Venezuela, Peru, Ecuador, and Bolivia

¹bo·liv·ia \bō'livēə, bə-\ *adj, usu cap* [fr. *Bolivia*, country in So. America] **:** of or from Bolivia **:** of the kind or style prevalent in Bolivia **:** BOLIVIAN

²bolivia \"\ *n* -s **1** [prob. so called fr. the use of Bolivian alpaca in its composition] **:** a twilled woolen fabric for outwear with a surface like plush in diagonal or vertical lines **2** *often cap* [fr. *Bolivia*, the country] **a :** a form of canasta in which sequences and wild cards may be melded **b :** a 7-card meld of wild cards in the game of bolivia

¹bo·liv·i·an \-vēən\ *adj, usu cap* [Sp *boliviano*, adj. & n., fr. *Bolivia* + *-ano* -an] **1 :** of, relating to, or characteristic of Bolivia **2 :** of, relating to, or characteristic of Bolivians

²bolivian \"\ *n* -s *cap* [Sp *boliviano*] **:** a native or resident of Bolivia

bolivian coca *n, usu cap B* **:** COCA 2a

bo·liv·i·a·no \bō,livē'ä(,)nō, bə-\ *n* -s [Sp, fr. *boliviano*, adj.] **1 :** a former basic monetary unit of Bolivia **2 :** a coin or note representing one boliviano

¹boll \'bōl\ *n* -s [ME, prob. var. of *bolle* bowl — more at BOWL] **1 :** any of various old units of capacity used in Scotland and northern England varying from two to six Winchester bushels; *also* **:** a Scottish unit of weight equal to 140 pounds **2 :** the pod or capsule of a plant esp. of flax or cotton **:** a pericarp of a globular form

²boll \"\ *vt* -ED/-ING/-S **:** to strip bolls from (cotton)

bol·land·ist \'bäləndə̇st\ *n* -s *usu cap* [Jean de *Bolland* †1665 Flem. Jesuit hagiologist who began the work + E *-ist*] **:** any of the Jesuit editors of the *Acta Sanctorum*, a collection of biographies of Christian saints and martyrs based on critical evaluation of the sources

bol·lard \'bälə(r)d\ *n* -s [perh. irreg. fr. ¹*bole* + *-ard*] **1 a :** a single or double post of metal or wood fixed on a pier or wharf and around which mooring lines are thrown **:** DOLPHIN **b :** ¹BITT 1 **2** *Brit* **:** any of a series of short posts set at intervals to exclude motor vehicles from an area

bollard timber *n* **:** KNIGHTHEAD 1

bolled \'bōld\ *adj* [¹*boll* + *-ed*] *archaic* **:** producing bolls **:** having bolls ⟨the barley was in the ear, and the flax was ~ —Exod 9:31 (AV)⟩

bol·ley's green \'bälēz-\ *n, usu cap B* [fr. the name *Bolley*] **:** a green copper borate used as a pigment

boll hull *n* [¹*boll*] **:** the bur of cotton

bol·ling·er body \'bälinə(r)-\ *n, usu cap 1st B* [after Otto von *Bollinger* †1909 Ger. physician] **:** one of the inclusion bodies that occur in epithelial cells of birds affected with fowl pox

¹bol·lix *also* **bol·ix** \'bäliks, -lēks, -ləks\ *vt* -ED/-ING/-ES [fr. *bollocks, ballocks*, pl. of *bollock, ballock* testicle, fr. ME *ballock*, fr. OE *beallu*c; akin to ON *böllr* ball — more at BALL] **1 :** to throw into disorder **:** involve in bewildering entanglements — usu. used with *up* ⟨~*ing* up the life of everyone he met⟩ **2 :** to perform or carry out badly **:** BOTCH, BUNGLE ⟨the pilot ~*ed* his takeoff⟩ — often used with *up* ⟨he ~*ed* up his final exams⟩

²bollix *also* **bolix** \"\ *n* -ES **:** a confused jumble **:** HODGEPODGE, MESS ⟨a hybrid art form that at least is earnestly ambitious, at worst is a humorless ~ —*Time*⟩

bol·lo \'bä(,)lō, 'bōl(,)yō\ *n* -s [AmerSp, fr. Sp, bun, muffin, fr. L *bulla* bubble, ball — more at POLL (head)] **:** a fritter made of black-eyed-pea flour and seasonings

bol·lock \'bälək\ *n* -s [by shortening & alter.] **:** BULLOCK BLOCK

boll rot *n* **:** a common rot of cotton bolls caused by various fungi (as *Glomerella gossypii* or *Diplodia gossypii*)

boll weevil *n* **:** a grayish weevil (*Anthonomus grandis*) about ¼ inch long that infests the cotton plant puncturing and laying its eggs in the squares and bolls, the larvae living in and feeding on the interior substance of the buds and bolls and doing great damage to developing cotton

bollworm \'=,=\ *n* **1 :** CORN EARWORM — used chiefly when the larva is feeding on cotton bolls **2 :** any of several noctuid moth larvae other than the corn earworm — usu. used in combination ⟨red ~⟩

bolly \'bōlē\ *n* -ES [¹*boll* + *-y*] **1 :** a cotton boll that has remained unopened or partly opened usu. as a result of frost injury; *also* **:** a quantity of such bolls usu. cracked and ginned **2 :** cotton ginned from undeveloped bolls

bol·ly gum \'bälē-\ *also* **bol·ly·wood** \'bälē,wu̇d\ *n* [origin unknown] **1 :** an Australian tree (*Litsea reticulata*) of the family Lauraceae with scaly bark, alternate oval leaves, and racemose flowers **2 :** the wood of bolly gum

¹bo·lo \'bō(,)lō\ *n* -s [Sp, prob. fr. a native name in the Philippines] **:** a long and usu. rather heavy Philippine single-edged knife resembling a machete

²bolo \"\ *vt* -ED/-ING/-S **:** to cut, hack, or kill with a bolo

³bolo \"\ *n* -s **:** BOLO PUNCH

⁴bolo \"\ *n* -s [perh. fr. Malay *bulu* hairy or feathery covering] **:** a parasitic Malayan plant (*Rafflesia schadenbergii*) with enormous flowers

⁵bolo \"\ *n* -s [fr. *Bolo* Pascha †1918, assumed name of a German agent in France who was convicted of treason] **1** *usu cap* **:** DEFEATIST; *esp* **:** one acting traitorously **2** *usu cap, slang* **:** BOLSHEVIST **3** *slang* **a :** a soldier who fails to qualify on the rifle range **b :** an incompetent or unreliable soldier **:** SAD SACK

⁶bolo \"\ *vi* -ED/-ING/-S **:** to fail to qualify on the rifle range

bo·lo–bo·lo \¦bōlō¦bōlō\ *n* -s [of African origin; akin to Bini *bo'lo³* to peel or strip (as bark from a tree)] **1 :** a West African fiber somewhat resembling jute and derived from the bast of a tree (*Honckenya ficifolia*) of the family Tiliaceae **2 :** the tree that yields bolo-bolo

bolo

¹bo·lo·gna \bə'lōnyə *also* -nə\ *adj, usu cap* [fr. *Bologna*, Italy] **:** of or from the city of Bologna, Italy **:** of the kind or style prevalent in Bologna

²bo·lo·gna \bə'lōnē, -ni *sometimes* -nə *or* -nyə\ *n* -s [short for *Bologna sausage*, trans. of It *mortadella di Bologna*] **1** *or* **bologna sausage** \"-\ *also* **bo·lo·ney** *or* **ba·lo·ney** \bə'lōnē, -ni\ *sometimes* **Bologna :** a large moist sausage usu. made of beef, veal, and pork that is chopped fine, seasoned, enclosed in a casing, boiled, and smoked red **2** *slang* **:** BALONEY

bologna bull *also* **bologna** *n, sometimes cap 1st B* [²*bologna*] **:** a low-grade bull supplying beef of inferior quality

bologna flask *or* **bologna phial** *or* **bologna vial** *n, usu cap B* [¹*Bologna*] **:** a bottle of unannealed glass that will fly into pieces when scratched — compare RUPERT'S DROP

¹bo·lo·gnan \bə'lōnyən *also* -ōnən\ *or* **bo·lo·gnian** \-ōnyən\ *adj, usu cap* [*Bologna*, Italy + E *-an, -ian*] **:** BOLOGNESE

²bolognan \"\ *or* **bolognian** \"\ *n* -s *cap* **:** BOLOGNESE

bologna phosphorus *or* **bolognian phosphorus** *n, usu cap B* [*Bologna* (*stone*)] **:** a phosphorescent sulfide of barium made by reducing Bologna stone or other barium sulfate

bologna stone *or* **bolognan stone** *n, usu cap B* [¹*Bologna* or ¹*Bolognan*; fr. its discovery near Bologna, Italy] **:** the mineral barite when found in roundish masses composed of radiating fibers, being phosphorescent when calcined with charcoal

¹bo·lo·gnese \¦bōlən¦yēz, -ēs, bə'lōn,y- *also* ¦bōlə¦nē-\ *adj, usu cap* [It, adj. & n., fr. *Bologna* + *-ese*] **1 :** of, relating to, or characteristic of Bologna, Italy **2 :** of, relating to, or characteristic of the Bolognese **3 :** having to do with painting in Bologna during the 15th and 16th centuries or with the eclectic late 16th century painters of the Bolognese school

²bolognese \"\ *n, pl* **bolognese** *cap* **:** a native or resident of Bologna

bo·lo·gram \'bōlə,gram\ *n* -s [Gk *bolē* stroke, cast, beam of light (fr. *ballein* to throw) + E *-o-* + *-gram* — more at DEVIL] **:** BOLOGRAPH

bo·lo·graph \-,graf\ *n* -s [Gk *bolē* + E *-o-* + *-graph*] **:** the record made by a bolometer — **bo·lo·graph·ic** \¦==¦fik\ *adj*

bo·lo·ism \'bōlō,izəm, -lə,wi-\ *n* -s *usu cap* [*Bolo* Pascha + E *-ism* — more at BOLO] **:** defeatist activities and propaganda favoring an enemy country

bololo *var of* PALOLO

bo·lo·man \'bōlō,man\ *n, pl* **bolomen** [¹*bolo* + *man*] **:** a man armed with a bolo

bo·lom·e·ter \bō'läməd·ə(r), bə'-\ *n* -s [Gk *bolē* beam of light, stroke, cast (fr. *ballein* to throw) + E *-o-* + *-meter* — more at DEVIL] **:** a very sensitive resistance thermometer used in the detection and measurement of feeble thermal radiation and esp. adapted to the study of infrared spectra — **bo·lo·met·ric** \¦bōlō¦me·trik, -lə¦-\ *adj* — **bo·lo·met·ri·cal·ly** \-trə̇k(ə)lē\ *adv*

bolometric magnitude *n* **:** the magnitude of a star based upon its total radiation in all wavelengths — compare BOLOMETER

¹boloney *var of* BOLOGNA

²boloney *var of* ²BALONEY

bolo punch *n* [³*bolo*] **:** a usu. long uppercut that is started with a downward swing

bolos *pl of* BOLO

¹bol·she·vik \'bōlshə̇,vik, 'bäl-, -,vēk *also* 'bȯl- *sporadically* 'bəl-\ *n, pl* **bolsheviks** \-ks\ *also* **bol·she·viki** \-,vikē, -,vēkē\ [Russ *bol'shevik*, fr. *bol'she* larger (comp. of *bol'shoi* large, great) + *-vik* (nominal suffix); fr. their forming the majority group of the Russian Social Democratic party in 1903; akin to Gk *belteros* better — more at DEBILITY] **1** *usu cap* **a :** a member of the wing of the Russian Social Democratic party that favored revolutionary tactics to achieve full socialization and seized supreme power in Russia during the Revolution (1917–20) for the purpose of setting up a workers' state **b :** a member of the Russian Communist party **2** *often cap* **:** an extreme radical opposed to an existing social, political, and economic order **:** REVOLUTIONARY ⟨began as a literary ~ but ended as a conservative⟩ **3** *usu cap* **:** COMMUNIST

²bolshevik \"\ *adj, usu cap* **:** of, relating to, favoring, or characteristic of bolshevism or Bolsheviks

bol·she·vism \-,vizəm\ *n* -s [¹*Bolshevik* + *-ism*] **1** *often cap* **:** the doctrine or program of the Bolsheviks advocating violent overthrow of the political and economic institutions of capitalism and the establishment of a socialist state controlled by the workers **2 :** communism esp. as developed and practiced by Russian Bolsheviks

¹bol·she·vist \-shə̇,vist, -,vəst\ *n* -s *usu cap* [*Bolshevik* + *-ist*] **:** a supporter or adherent of bolshevism **:** BOLSHEVIK

²bolshevist \"\ *adj, usu cap* **:** BOLSHEVIK

bol·she·vi·za·tion \-,shəvə̇'zāshən, -,vī'z-\ *n* -s *sometimes cap* **:** the process of bolshevizing or the fact of being bolshevized

bol·she·vize \'==,vīz\ *vt* -ED/-ING/-S *see -ize in Explan Notes, sometimes cap* [¹*Bolshevik* + *-ize*] **:** to make Bolshevist in character or principle **:** convert (a country) to a Bolshevist form of government **:** bring under the domination of Bolsheviks

¹bol·shie *or* **bol·shy** \'=shē\ *n, pl* **bolshies** *usu cap* [by shortening & alter.] *slang* **:** BOLSHEVIK

²bolshie *or* **bolshy** \"\ *adj, sometimes cap, slang* **:** BOLSHEVIK

bol·son \bōl,sōn\ *n* -s [AmerSp *bolsón*, aug. of Sp *bolsa* purse, pouch, fr. ML *bursa* — more at PURSE] **:** a flat-floored desert valley that drains to a playa

¹bol·ster \'bōlstə(r)\ *n* -s [ME, fr. OE; akin to OHG *bolstar* bolster, ON *bolstr* bolster, OE *belg* bag — more at BELLY] **1 a :** a long pillow or cushion that is used to support the head of a person lying on a bed and that usu. extends across the bed and is placed under the pillows and often under the sheets **b :** any soft pad, padding, cushion, or support resembling a bolster **2 a :** a structural part of a mechanism designed to eliminate friction between moving parts, reduce pressure, deaden noise, or accomplish similar cushioning effects **b :** any structural part designed to afford support or give a bearing: as (1) **:** a transverse bar above the axle of a wagon on which the bed of the wagon rests (2) **:** a plate often with a hole in the center or T slots on its surface bolted to the top of a punch-press bed (3) **:** the spindle bearing in the rail of a support or spinning frame and the support for the drafting rolls (4) **:** the crossbeam forming the bearing piece of the body of a railroad car **:** the central and principal crossbeam of a railroad-car truck (5) **:** a short timber or block set horizontally upon a post so as to secure a structural advantage (as attaining a greater bearing surface for girders, shortening their span, or allowing erection of an upper post between their ends) (6) **:** the horizontal connection between the volutes of an Ionic capital (7) **:** one of the small pieces of scantling nailed across the outer curve of the centering for an arch and taking the weight of the arch masonry (8) **:** a crosspiece connecting the ribs of the centering that supports the voussoirs of an arch **3 :** any contrivance that prevents chafing; *specif* **:** a block of wood or a stuffed canvas used on shipboard to reduce or eliminate chafing between ropes or other rigging **4 a :** the part of a knife blade that abuts upon the handle **b :** the metallic end of a pocketknife handle **5 :** ²BUNK 2a **6 a :** the slight excrescence at the junction of branch and stem or of the leafstalk and its axis **b :** the cupule of the hazelnut **c :** the husk of the English walnut

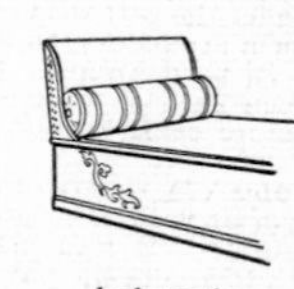
bolster 1a

²bolster \"\ *vb* **bolstered; bolstered; bolstering** \-st(ə)riŋ\ **bolsters** *vt* **1 :** to support with or as if with a bolster — often used with *up* ⟨the sick man lay ~*ed* up in his bed⟩ **2 a :** to give a strong support or foundation to **:** give additional strength to **:** give a boost to **:** REINFORCE, UPHOLD ⟨a convincing argument that was ~*ed* still more by the speaker's respected position⟩ ⟨extra men will ~ already augmented dock details —Stanley Levey⟩ ⟨~*ed* his faltering courage⟩ ⟨~*ing* superstition and prejudice⟩ **b :** to supply for the deficiencies of **:** SUPPLEMENT ⟨a diet that needs to be ~*ed* with more vitamin-rich foods⟩ **3 :** to cause to be increased (as in size, bulk, or intensity) through the addition or presence of something **:** to fill out **:** EXPAND, PAD ⟨a mattress that was ~*ed* to the bursting point⟩ **:** HEIGHTEN, INTENSIFY ⟨a moonless night that ~*ed* the gloom of the forest⟩ **~** *vi, obs* **:** to lie on the same bolster
syn see SUPPORT

bolster plate *n* **:** a circular metal plate bolted to the front axle of a wagon on which the front bolster is pivoted so that the front wheels can be turned

¹bolt \'bōlt\ *n* -s [ME, fr. OE; akin to OHG *bolz* crossbow bolt, Lith *beldéti* to knock, beat] **1 a :** a shaft or missile designed to be shot from a crossbow or catapult; *esp* **:** a short stout usu. blunt-headed arrow **b :** a concentrated flow of usu. atmospheric electricity **:** a lightning stroke **:** THUNDERBOLT **2 a :** a bar or other usu. cylindrically shaped length of metal, wood, or other strong material that moves through guides (as iron staples) attached to a door or other movable frame the end being received into an adjoining fixed socket (as one attached to the jamb or lintel) **b :** the part of a lock that is shot or withdrawn by the key **3 a :** a roll of cloth of specified length **b :** a bundle (as of osiers or straw) **c :** a roll of wallpaper of specified length usu. including two or three separate sections **4** *obs* **:** SHACKLE, FETTER **5 a :** any of several herbs of the genus *Ranunculus; esp* **:** BULBOUS BUTTERCUP **b :** a globeflower (*Trollius europaens*) having lemon-yellow flowers with incurving sepals **6 :** a rod or heavy pin (as one made of steel) designed to fasten two or more objects (as metal plates) together or to hold one or more objects in place often having a head at one end and a screw thread cut upon the other end and being usu. secured by a nut or by riveting **7 a :** a block of timber to be sawed or cut (as into shingles or staves) **b :** a short round section of a log **c :** a bundle of boards joined by an end not sawed through **8 :** a usu. large quantity of matter often like a jet in form or movement ⟨~*s* of water gushing over the dam⟩ ⟨flaming ~*s* erupting from the surface of the sun⟩ **9 :** the breech closure of breech-loading rifles that is designed like a door bolt, has a back-and-forth movement that opens and closes the bore, and is locked in position usu. through rotation; *also* **:** a small-arm breech closure however designed **10 :** the uncut folded paper at the head, fore edge, and foot of a signature (as of a book)

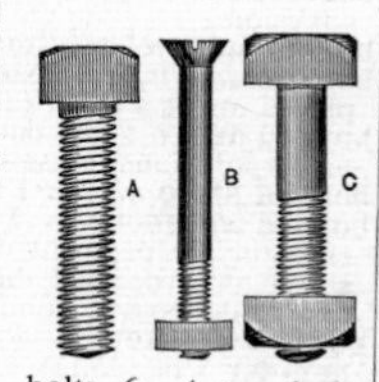

bolts 6: *A* tap bolt, *B* stove bolt, *C* machine bolt

²bolt \"\ *vb* -ED/-ING/-S [ME *bolten, bulten,* fr. *bolt,* n.] *vi* **1 :** to move suddenly or nervously (as from surprise or fright) often involuntarily **:** move with a sudden jerk from one position to another **:** START, SPRING — usu. used with *up* or *upright,* ⟨anger energized me and I ~*ed* upright in bed —Robert Hazel⟩ ⟨the Judge had ~*ed* upright from the pillows —Sir Winston Churchill⟩ **2 :** to move rapidly **:** dart forward **:** DASH ⟨he completely lost his head, ~*ed* out of the yard into the road, and ran up the street —J.C.Powys⟩ **3 a :** to dart off or away (as when fleeing) **:** suddenly make off **:** rush away **:** run off **:** ESCAPE ⟨two sullen-faced aides ~*ed* from the farmhouse and ran —Kenneth Roberts⟩ ⟨a young woman ~*ing* from too much domesticity —E.A.Weeks⟩ **b :** to emerge (as from a lair) and flee ⟨the fox ~*ed*⟩ **c :** to break away from control **:** dash violently aside or off a set course ⟨the horse shied and ~*ed*⟩ ⟨the well-trained bird dog rarely ~*s*⟩ **4** *obs* **:** to fall suddenly like a stroke of lightning ⟨his cloudless thunder ~*ed* on their heads —John Milton⟩ **5 :** to loose an arrow too soon after the draw **6 a :** to produce seed prematurely ⟨the cultivated carrot is a biennial but it may sometimes ~ —J.M. Hector⟩ **b :** to produce a flowering stalk ⟨the lettuce will ~⟩ **7 :** to break away from a political party and go over to the opposition **:** refuse to support the party platform or candidate ⟨many party members were indignant and promptly ~*ed*⟩ ~ *vt* **1** *obs* **:** to put into irons **:** FETTER **2 a** *archaic* **:** to let fly (as a missile) **:** SHOOT, DISCHARGE ⟨~*ing* the arrows straight at the target⟩ **b** *archaic* **:** to drive out by force **:** EXPEL ⟨to have been ~*ed* forth, thrust out abruptly into Fortune's way —William Wordsworth⟩ **c :** to cause to emerge into the open (as from a lair) **:** DISLODGE ⟨they used ferrets to ~ the rabbits⟩ **3 :** to utter explosively or impulsively **:** give voice to or express hastily and usu. with little or no reflection **:** BLURT ⟨~*ing* the word out as if he had restrained it with difficulty until this moment —Virginia Woolf⟩ **4 a :** to secure (as a door) with a bolt **b :** to cause to be shut up or excluded (as by bolting a door) ⟨~*ing* the prisoners in their cells⟩ ⟨keeping prowlers ~*ed* out⟩ **5 a :** to attach or fasten together with bolts ⟨steel plates ~*ed* together⟩ **b :** to furnish or stud with bolts ⟨the newly ~*ed* hull of the ship⟩ **6 :** to consume (as food or drink) hastily or greedily **:** gobble or gulp down **:** eat with little or no chewing **:** swallow whole **:** swallow with spasmodic gulps ⟨tearing the food from one another and ~*ing* what they could keep with convulsive haste —T.B.Costain⟩ ⟨I struggled out of bed, pried open my eyes, shaved and showered, and ~*ed* down some breakfast —H.A.Smith⟩ ⟨~*ing* a cup of coffee⟩ **7 a :** to cut (timber) into bolts ⟨logs that were ~*ed* into 18-inch blocks⟩ **b :** to make up (as lengths of cloth) into bolts **8 :** to break away from or refuse to support (as a political party or candidate) ⟨~*ed* the national ticket⟩

³bolt \"\ *adv* [ME, fr. *bolt,* n.] **1 :** in a rigidly erect or straight-backed position **:** PERPENDICULARLY — usu. used with *upright* ⟨she, sitting ~ upright, paused —Elizabeth Bowen⟩ **2** *archaic* **:** DIRECTLY, STRAIGHT ⟨Mrs. Berry . . . ran ~ out of the house —George Meredith⟩

⁴bolt \"\ *n* -s [*²bolt*] **:** an act or instance of bolting: as **a :** a quick dash or flight ⟨a ~ for shelter⟩ **b :** refusal to support or repudiation of a political party, candidate, or platform ⟨fear of a widespread ~ by party members⟩

⁵bolt \"\ *vt* -ED/-ING/-S [ME *bulten,* fr. OF *buleter,* of Gmc origin; akin to MHG *biuteln* to sift, fr. *biutel* bag, fr. OHG *būtil* — more at BUD] **1 :** to sift (as meal or flour) usu. through fine-meshed cloth; *also* **:** to refine or purify (as meal or flour) through any process **2** *archaic* **:** to examine and separate as though by sifting ⟨time and nature will ~ out the truth of things —Roger L'Estrange⟩

⁶bolt \"\ *n* -s [ME *bult,* fr. *bulten,* v.] **:** ¹BOLTER a

bolt action *n* [*¹bolt*] **:** a rifle action in which the breechblock takes the form of a manually operated sliding rod

bolted *past of* BOLT

bol·tel \'bōltəl\ *also* **bow·tel** *or* **bow·tell** *or* **bou·tell** \'bōd·ᵊl\ *n* -s [ME, perh. fr. *¹bolt* + *-el*] **1 :** a torus or ovolo; *esp* **:** one just below the abacus in the Tuscan and Roman Doric capital **2 :** one of the shafts of a clustered pier

bol·ten·ia \bōl'tēnēə, -tēn-\ *n, cap* [NL, fr. Johannes *Bolten* †1796 Ger. naturalist and physician + NL *-ia*] **:** a genus of simple ascidians related to *Tethyum* but distinguished by a 4-lobed branchial aperture — compare SEA PEAR

¹bolt·er \'bōltə(r)\ *n* -s [ME *bulter,* fr. *bulten* to bolt (sift) + *-er*] **:** one that bolts: as **a :** a machine for bolting (as flour or meal) **b :** an operator of a machine for bolting

²bolter \"\ *n* -s [*²bolt* + *-er*] **:** one that bolts: as **a :** a horse or bird dog given to suddenly breaking away from control **b :** a voter who bolts his party **c :** a plant (as a sugar beet) producing seed prematurely **d :** a machine consisting of one or more circular ripsaws for cutting dimension lumber **e** *also* **bolterman :** a sawmill worker who bolts slabs and short logs into sizes suitable for fuel or by-product conversion — called also *splitterman*

bolt eye *n* [*¹bolt*] **:** a device like a clevis used to terminate a suspension rod or bolt

bolt face *n* [*¹bolt*] **:** the surface of the rifle-bolt end that makes contact with the base of the cartridge case

bolt from the blue [*¹bolt*] **1 :** lightning from a clear sky **2 :** a complete and stunning surprise

bolt handle *n* [*¹bolt*] **:** the projecting lever or knob by which a rifle bolt is manually operated

bolt head *n* [ME *bolthed,* fr. *¹bolt* + *hed* head] **1 :** the head of a bolt **2 :** MATRASS **3 :** the end of a rifle bolt that seats the cartridge in the chamber

bolt–hole \'ˌ,ˌ\ *n* [*⁴bolt*] **:** a place or way of escape; *specif* **:** a hole through which an animal may flee when pursued into its den

bolt hook *n* [*¹bolt*] **:** a hook having a screw and nut so that it can be used like a bolt

bol·ti *also* **bol·ty** \'bōltē\ *or* **bul·ti** \'bu̇l-\ *n, pl* **boltis** *also* **bolties** [Ar *bulṭī*] **:** a cichlid food fish (*Tilapia nilotica*) of the Nile and other rivers of Africa and Asia Minor

bolt·in \'bōltin\ *n* -s [*¹bolt* (bundle) + *-in* (alter. of *-ing*)] *dial Eng* **:** a bundle of straw

¹bolting *n* -s [ME *bulting,* fr. gerund of *bulten* to bolt (sift) — more at BOLT] **1 :** the action or process of bolting (as flour or meal) **2 boltings** *pl* **:** the coarser portion (as of flour or meal) separated from the rest by bolting

²bolting *adj* [fr. pres. part. of *²bolt*] *of an eye* **:** prominent (as in certain pigeons)

bolting cloth *n* [*¹bolting*] **:** a firm fabric now usu. of silk woven in various mesh sizes for bolting (as flour) or for use in screen printing, needlework, or photographic enlargements

bolt·less \'bōltləs\ *adj* **:** having no bolt

bol·ton \'bōltən\ *adj, usu cap* [fr. *Bolton,* England] **:** of or from the county borough of Bolton, Lancashire, England **:** of the kind or style prevalent in Bolton

bol·to·nia \bōl'tōnēə\ *n, cap* [NL, fr. James *Bolton,* 18th cent. Eng. botanist + NL *-ia*] **:** a genus of tall leafy perennial eastern American and eastern Asiatic herbs (family Compositae) with white ray flowers like asters

bol·ton·ite \'bōltə,nīt\ *n* -s [*Bolton,* Mass., its locality + E *-ite*] **:** a greenish granular variety of forsterite

bol·ton thumb \'bōltən-\ *n, often cap B* [alter. of *Boulton,* a glove-manufacturing firm] **:** a thumb whose gusset is formed in the main part of a glove

boltrope \'ˌ,ˌ\ *n* [*¹bolt* + *rope*] **1 :** a strong usu. hemp rope stitched to the edges of a sail to strengthen it **2 :** any rope of superior quality (as of strength)

bolts *pres 3d sing of* BOLT, *pl of* BOLT

boltz·mann's constant \'bōltsmənz-, -,mänz-\ *n, usu cap B* [after Ludwig *Boltzmann* †1906 Austrian physicist] **:** the ideal gas constant per molecule being the ratio of the molar gas constant to the number of molecules of a substance in a gram molecule and having a value of about 1.3803×10^{-16} ergs per degree C

bol·us \'bōləs\ *n* -ES [LL — more at BOLE] **1 :** a rounded mass: as **a :** a large pill (as one used in veterinary practice) **b :** a soft mass of chewed food **2 :** ²BOLE 1 **3 :** ²BOLE 3

bolus al·ba \-'albə\ *n* [NL, white clay] **:** KAOLIN

bom \'bōm\ *or* **bo·ma** \-mə\ *var of* ABOMA

bom *abbr* bombardier

bo·ma \'bōmə\ *n* -s [Swahili] **1 a :** an enclosure (as a barrier of thorn brush or a palisade) erected about a village, camp, or animal pen in central Africa and designed chiefly as a protection against wild beasts **b :** a place of concealment usu. protected (as with thorn brush) and camouflaged (as with foliage) and used by hunters or by animal photographers in central Africa **:** a hunter's blind **2 a :** a police post in central Africa **b :** the office of a district commissioner in central Africa

bo·mar·ea \bō'ma(a)rēə, -mer-\ *n, cap* [NL, after J.C.Valmont de *Bomare* †1807 Fr. naturalist] **:** a large genus of tropical American herbaceous vines (family Amaryllidaceae) with showy and often spotted umbellate flowers — see SALSILLA

¹bomb \'bäm; *sometimes esp South and chiefly archaic* 'bəm\ *n* -s [F *bombe,* fr. It *bomba,* prob. fr. L *bombus* deep hollow sound, fr. Gk *bombos;* of imit. origin like ON *bumba* drum, Lith *bambėti* to hum, buzz, Alb *bumbulit* it is thundering] **1 :** a projectile or other device carrying an explosive charge fused to detonate under certain conditions (as upon impact or through a timing contrivance) and that is hurled (as by a mortar), dropped (as from an aircraft), or merely set into position at a given point (as dynamite) with varying effects (as concussion, or fire-flinging, or the release of gases) depending upon the type used ⟨spangle ~*s* for fireworks displays⟩; *also* **:** any container (as of propaganda leaflets or food) designed to be dropped from aircraft in the manner of an aerial bomb **2 :** a vessel (as a steel cylinder) for compressed gases: as **a :** a pressure vessel for conducting chemical experiments at high temperature and high pressure **b :** a small manually operated dispenser that releases a substance stored under pressure (as an insecticide, a fire-extinguishing liquid, or paint) in the form of a vapor, spray, or gas **3 :** the combustion chamber of a bomb calorimeter **4 :** a mass of lava exploded from a volcanic vent and shaped while viscous by passage through the air into a rounded form ranging from a few inches to many feet in diameter **5 :** an explosive head on a harpoon **6 :** BOMBE **7 :** a lead-lined container for radioactive material used esp. in the radiation treatment of cancer ⟨a cobalt ~⟩ **8 :** BOMBSHELL 2

²bomb \"\ *vt* -ED/-ING/-S **:** to attack with or as if with bombs **:** drop bombs upon **:** hurl bombs at **:** blow up with bombs **:** BOMBARD

bom·ba·ca·ce·ae \,bämbə'kāsē,ē\ *n pl, cap* [NL, fr. *Bombac-,* *Bombax,* type genus + *-aceae*] **:** a widely distributed family of tropical trees (order Malvales) with palmate leaves and large dry or fleshy fruit containing usu. woolly seeds

bom·ba·chas \bəm'bächəz, bōm'-\ *n pl* [AmerSp, pl. of *bombacha,* fr. fem. of Sp *bombacho,* adj.; bomb-shaped, fr. *bomba* bomb, fr. It] **:** loose baggy trousers gathered tightly at the ankle and worn esp. in Argentina and Uruguay for riding and outdoor work

bom·ba·cop·sis \,bämbə'käpsəs\ *n* [NL, fr. ML *bombac-,* *bombax* cotton + NL *-opsis* — more at BOMBAST] **1** *cap* **:** a genus of large trees (family Bombacaceae) with capsular fruits that burst when dry or release a soft brown wool surrounding the small brown seeds **2** *pl* **bombacopses :** any tree of the genus *Bombacopsis*

bom·ba·je palm \bōm'bäzhə-\ *n* [Pg *bombaje*] **:** JIPIJAPA

¹bom·bard \'bäm,bärd, -bäd\ *n* -s [ME *bumbard, bombarde* fr. MF *bombarde,* prob. fr. L *bombus* deep hollow sound — more at BOMB] **1 :** a late medieval cannon that hurled large stone balls **2** *obs* **:** a leather jug or bottle **3 :** a large shawm

²bombard \(')bäm'bärd, -bäd *also* (')bəm-\ *vt* -ED/-ING/-S [MF *bombarder,* fr. *bombarde*] **1 :** to attack with explosive projectiles or other explosive weapons **:** assault with cannon and other heavy ordnance; *esp* **:** BOMB **2 :** to assail vigorously or persistently (as with questions or petitions) ⟨~*ing* the governor with pleas for leniency⟩ **3 :** to subject (a body or substance) to the impact of rapidly moving particles (as electrons or alpha rays) **syn** see ATTACK

bom·barde \(')bōm¦bärd, (')bäm-\ *n* -s [F, prob. fr. It *bombarda,* lit., bombard, fr. OIt, fr. MF *bombarde*] **:** a powerful reed stop of 32-foot or 16-foot pitch in a pipe organ; *also* **:** the manual containing such a stop

bom·bar·dier \¦bämbər¦di(ə)r, -*R & R often* -bə¦d-, -*R* -diə; *sometimes* ¦bəm\ *n* -s [MF, one in charge of a bombard, fr. *bombarde* bombard] **1 a** *archaic* **:** ARTILLERYMAN **b :** a noncommissioned officer in the British artillery **2 :** a bomber-crew member whose duty it is to guide the airplane in the run over the target by means of the bombsight and to release the bombs

bombardier beetle *n* **:** any of numerous carabid beetles of *Brachinus* or related genera that when disturbed discharge audibly a pungent and corrosive vapor from the anal glands

bom·bard·ment \(')bäm¦bärdmənt, -bäd- *also* (')bəm-\ *n* -s **1 :** the act or an instance of bombarding or the state of being bombarded **2 :** a sustained attack (as with guided missiles, aircraft bombs, or artillery)

bom·bar·do \bōm'bär(,)dō\ *n, pl* **bombar·di** \-(,)dē\ *or* **bombardoes** \-,dōz\ [It, alter. of *bombarda* bombarde] **:** BOMBARDON 1

bom·bar·don \bäm'bärdən, 'bämbər-\ *n* -s [F, fr. It *bombardone,* aug. of *bombardo*] **1 :** the bass member of the shawm family **2 :** a bass tuba; *esp* **:** HELICON

bombasine *var of* BOMBAZINE

¹bom·bast \'bäm,bast, -baa(ə)st\ *n* -s [modif. of MF *bombace,* fr. ML *bombac-, bombax* cotton, alter. of L *bombyc-, bombyx* silkworm, silk, fr. Gk *bombyk-, bombyx* silkworm, silk garment, prob. of Per origin; akin to Per *pamba* cotton] **1** *obs* **:** cotton or any soft fibrous material used as padding or stuffing **2 :** a pretentious inflated style of speech or writing ⟨adolescent ~ about Destiny and Youth⟩

syn RHAPSODY, RANT, FUSTIAN, RODOMONTADE: BOMBAST indicates a verbose grandiosity or pretentious inflation of language and style disproportionate to thought ⟨the rant and *bombast* and sentimental cant of politics —Florence Converse⟩ ⟨in the days when a more decorated style was fashionable in many quarters, *bombast* and extravagance were common in the press —F.L.Mott⟩ RHAPSODY may suggest ecstatic effusiveness, extravagant and often incoherent ⟨a *rhapsody* of enchanting images which "led to nothing" —*Times Lit. Supp.*⟩ ⟨his characters, because of the intensity of his feeling about them, are excellently drawn, but he writes as though he had uncovered a new religion and thought it deserved a *rhapsody,* at least —*New Yorker*⟩ RANT is likely to suggest sustained violence of expression ⟨Williams, in a characteristic prose *rant,* writes as if free verse were one of the inalienable rights for which the American Revolution was fought —Irving Howe⟩ ⟨the hoarse *rant* of that demagogue fills the air and distracts the people's minds —Max Ascoli⟩ FUSTIAN suggests or may suggest a filling or padding with the sonorous or grandiloquent but inane ⟨lines of Jonson, detached from their context, look like inflated or empty *fustian* — T.S.Eliot⟩ ⟨condemned as literary because its characters speak the *fustian* of pretentious books —C.E.Montague⟩ RODOMONTADE may suggest the bluster or swaggering rant of the mountebank, braggart, or demagogue ⟨the brothers set about abusing each other in good round terms and with each intemperate sally their phrases became more deeply colored with the tincture of Victorian *rodomontade* —Ngaio Marsh⟩

²bombast \(')ˌ¦ˌ *sometimes* bəm'ˌ\ *vt* -ED/-ING/-S **1** *archaic* **:** PAD, STUFF **2 :** to make speciously impressive **:** INFLATE **:** make bombastic ⟨a book ~*ed* with attempts at wit⟩

³bombast \'bäm,ˌ\ *adj, archaic* **:** PRETENTIOUS, INFLATED

bom·bast·er \(')ˌ¦ˌstə(r) *sometimes* bəm'ˌˌ\ *n* -s **:** one given to bombast ⟨a town that had no use for long-winded orators and other ~*s*⟩

bom·bas·tic \(')ˌ¦ˌstik, -ēk *sometimes* bəm'ˌˌ\ *adj* **:** marked by or given to bombast ⟨a wearisome speech, theatrical and ~⟩ ⟨a ~ writer⟩ — **bom·bas·ti·cal·ly** \-stək(ə)lē, -li\ *adv*

bombastry *n* -ES *obs* **:** BOMBAST

bom·bax \'bäm,baks\ *n* [NL, fr. ML, cotton — more at BOMBAST] **1** *cap* **:** a large genus of trees (family Bombacaceae) chiefly of So. America, a few of India, and one of Africa having digitate leaves and showy white or scarlet flowers — compare CEIBA **2** -ES **:** any tree of the genus *Bombax*

bombax cotton *or* **bombax floss** *n* **:** a fiber obtained from the bombax

bom·bay \(')bäm¦bā\ *adj, usu cap* [fr. *Bombay,* India] **:** of or from the city of Bombay, India **:** of the kind or style prevalent in Bombay

bombay aloe *n, usu cap B* **:** BASTARD ALOE

bombay duck *n, usu cap B* **1 :** a small marine Asiatic lizard fish (*Harpodon nehereus*) the flesh of which is dried and used in India as a relish **2** *India* **:** dried fish eaten with curry

bombay hemp *n, usu cap B* **1 :** SUNN **2 :** KENAF

bombay lamb *n, usu cap B* **:** the gray-dyed pelt of an Indian lamb

bombay senna *n, usu cap B* **:** the leaves of the Indian senna

bombay sumbul *n, usu cap B, pharmacy* **:** the root of an Asiatic perennial herb (*Dorema ammoniacum*) of the family Umbelliferae that is used as a substitute for true sumbul

bom·ba·zet *or* **bom·ba·zette** \¦bämbə¦zet\ *n* -s [*bombazine* + *-et, -ette*] **:** a thin plain or twill-woven worsted cloth with smooth finish used for dresses and coats

bom·ba·zine \¦bämbə¦zēn\ *also* **bom·ba·sine** \", -¦sēn\ *or* **bom·ba·zeen** \-¦zēn\ *n* -s *often attrib* [MF *bombasin,* fr. ML *bombacinum,* alter. of *bombycinum* silken, fr. L, neut. of *bombycinus* silken, fr. *bombyc-, bombyx* silk + *-inus* -ine — more at BOMBAST] **1 :** a silk fabric in twill weave dyed black for mourning wear **2 :** a twilled fabric with silk warp and worsted filling that is dyed various colors

bomb bay *n* **:** a bomb-carrying compartment on the underside of a combat airplane fuselage usu. with down-swinging doors through which bombs are dropped

¹bombe \'bäm(b), 'bōⁿb\ *n* -s [F, lit., bomb — more at BOMB] **:** a frozen dessert consisting of two or more mixtures packed into a round or melon-shaped mold

²bom·bé \(')bäm¦bā, (')bōⁿ¦-\ *adj* [F, fr. *bombe*] **:** having an outward swelling curve (as at front, sides or base) — used chiefly of furniture ⟨a ~ chest of drawers⟩

bombed *past of* BOMB

bomb·er \'bämə(r)\ *n* -s **:** one that bombs; *specif* **:** an airplane specially designed for use in bombing

bomb fly *n* **:** the adult of the northern cattle grub

bom·bic·cite \bäm'bē,chīt\ *n* -s [It, fr. L. *Bombicci* 19th cent. Ital. geologist + It *-ite*] **:** a colorless hydrocarbon mineral found in Tuscan lignite

bom·bi·dae \'bämbə,dē\ *n pl, cap* [NL, fr. *Bombus,* type genus + *-idae*] *in some classifications* **:** a family of medium to very large robust usu. black and yellow hairy bees comprising the bumblebees now often included with honeybees and related bees in the family Apidae

bom·bi·la·tion \,ˌˌ'lāshən\ *n* -s [L *bombilatus* (past part. of *bombilare* to buzz, hum, fr. *bombus* deep hollow sound) + E *-ion* — more at BOMB] **:** a buzzing droning sound

bom·bil·la \bōm'bē(l)yə\ *n* -s [AmerSp (Argentina), dim. of Sp *bomba* pump, perh. fr. L *bombus* deep hollow sound — more at BOMB] **:** a small tube with a strainer at one end used in drinking maté

bom·bi·nate \'bämbə,nāt, *usu* -d·+V\ *vi* -ED/-ING/-S [NL *bombinatus,* past part. of *bombinare,* alter. of L *bombilare* — more at BOMBILATION] **:** BUZZ, DRONE — **bom·bi·na·tion** \,ˌˌ'nāshən\ *n* -s

bombing *pres part of* BOMB

bombing run *n* : BOMB RUN

bomb ketch *n* **:** a small strongly built ketch having mortars mounted for use in naval bombardments

bomb lance *n* **:** a harpoon with an explosive head

bomb·line \ˈ=,=\ *n* -S **:** a demarcation line established in a combat area beyond which aircraft can attack (as by bombing) without danger to their own ground troops

bomb·load \ˈ=,=\ *n* **:** the quantity of bombs carried by an aircraft and measured by weight, by number, or (as for nuclear bombs) by kilotons or megatons of equivalent TNT

bombo *var of* BUMBO

bom·bonne \ˈbäm,bän\ *n* -S [F, fr. Prov *boumbouno*, fr. *boumbo* large ball, fr. L *bombus* deep hollow sound — more at BOMB] **:** a large globular bottle; *specif* **:** an earthenware Woulff bottle

bomb out *vt* **1 :** to subject (as an industrial center) to bombing so that continued operation or inhabitation of the bombed objective is impossible ⟨a munitions factory which was *bombed out* early in the war⟩ ⟨a once beautiful city that was now *bombed out*⟩ **2 :** to force out of a dwelling or place of business by bombing **:** make homeless by bombing ⟨millions of people were *bombed out*⟩

bomb pilot *n* **:** a map or drawing of a bombed target annotated with the location of each bomb hit

1bombproof \ˈ=ˈ=\ *adj* **:** so constructed or placed as to be relatively secure against the explosive force of bombs or shells ⟨a ~ cellar⟩

2bombproof \ˈ=ˈ=\ *n* **:** a bombproof shelter

bomb release line *n* **:** the point on the ground ahead of the target over which an aircraft must release its bombs to get a hit on the target

bomb run *n* **:** the portion of a bomber's attack during which the actual sighting for and release of bombs occurs and which is flown usu. straight and level so that the bombardier's computations may be accurate

bombs *pl of* BOMB, *pres 3d sing of* BOMB

bomb·shell \ˈ=,=\ *n* **1 :** BOMB 1 **2 a :** something that stuns, amazes, or is shatteringly upsetting: as (1) **:** a devastating surprise **:** a totally unexpected occurrence ⟨her arrival was a ~ in the previously tranquil town⟩ (2) **:** an unprecedented and often revolutionary idea or action ⟨a new theory that was a ~ to conservative thinkers⟩ **b :** one who is the cause and object of sensational and usu. widespread attention, excitement, or attraction ⟨a writer who is a literary ~⟩ ⟨a film featuring an actress who can best be described as a blond ~⟩

bombsight \ˈ=,=\ *n* **:** a sighting device for aiming bombs; *specif* **:** a combined optical aiming and calculating mechanism and gyroscopic control for dropping aerial bombs from high altitudes

bomb up *vt* **:** to load (an aircraft) with bombs ⟨can be *bombed up* more or less like loading a clip of cartridges —*Science News Letter*⟩ ~ *vi* **:** to take on a load of bombs

bom·bus \ˈbämbəs\ *n, cap* [NL, fr. L, deep hollow sound, buzzing — more at BOMB] **:** a genus of bees comprising the typical bumblebees — compare BOMBYLIIDAE

1bom·by·cid \ˈbämbəsəd, -,sid\ *adj* [NL *Bombycidae*] **:** of or relating to the family Bombycidae or to silkworms

2bombycid \"\ *n* -S **:** one of the Bombycidae **:** a silkworm or silkworm moth

bom·byc·i·dae \bämˈbisə,dē\ *n pl, cap* [NL, fr. *Bombyc-, Bombyx*, type genus + *-idae*] **:** a family of chiefly Asiatic moderate-sized moths having larvae that feed on leaves and spin cocoons of commercially usable silk and including the domesticated silkworms (genus *Bombyx*) and a few related forms but formerly including many other moths

bom·by·cil·la \,bämbəˈsilə\ *n, cap* [NL, blend of L *bombyc-, bombyx* silkworm, silk and NL *Motacilla* — more at BOMBAST] **:** a genus (the type of the family Bombycillidae) of passerine birds comprising the waxwings

bom·by·cine \ˈbämbə,sīn, -,sən\ *adj* [L *bombyc-, bombyx* silkworm + E *-ine*] **:** of or relating to silkworms

bom·by·li·i·dae \,bämbəˈlīə,dē\ *n pl, cap* [NL, fr. *Bombylius*, type genus (fr. Gk *bombylios* buzzing insect, bumblebee, fr. *bombos* deep hollow sound) + *-idae* — more at BOMB] **:** a family of hairy-bodied often brightly colored two-winged flies many of which resemble bees and are called bee flies

bom·byx \ˈbäm(,)biks\ *n, cap* [NL, fr. L, silkworm — more at BOMBAST] **:** the type genus of Bombycidae including the domestic silkworm moth (*Bombyx mori*) — see SILKWORM

1bon \ˈbän\ *n* -S [perh. fr. D *boon* bean, fr. MD *bōne*; akin to OHG *bōna* bean — more at BEAN] **1 :** BROAD BEAN **2** [perh. another word] **:** KIDNEY BEAN

2bon \ˈbōn\ *n* -S *usu cap* [Jap] **:** a great popular festival of Japan held July 13 to 16 when the spirits of ancestors are supposed to revisit the household altars — called also *Feast of Lanterns*

3bon \"\ *n* -S *cap* [Tibetan *bön*] **:** the pre-Buddhist animistic religion of Tibet

4bon \ˈbän\ *n* -S [origin unknown] **:** CHINA GRASS

bo·na \ˈbōnə\ *n pl* [L, fr. neut. pl. of *bonus* good] **:** PROPERTY — used in Roman and civil law of real and personal property of any kind but chiefly of real property in Roman law and usu. only of movables in common law

bona ad·ven·ti·tia *or* **bona ad·ven·ti·cia** \-,advənˈtish(ē)ə\ *n pl* [L *bona adventicia*] *Roman law* **:** all the property that is acquired by a person by his own labor or from persons other than his father and which he is permitted to keep as his own subject to the right of his father to enjoy its usufruct — called also, in post-Roman times, *peculium adventicium;* compare BONA MATERNA

bo·na·ci \,bōnəˈsē\ *n* -S [Sp *bonasí*] **:** the black grouper (*Mycteroperca bonaci*) or a related marine food fish (as the gag)

bona con·fis·ca·ta \-,känfəˈskädə\ *n pl* [L, confiscated goods] **:** property (as that forfeited for felony) appropriated to the fiscus under Roman law

bona fide \÷ˈbōnə,fīd, ÷ˈbänə,fīd, ˈ==ˈfīdē, ˈ==ˈfīdə\ *adj* [L, in good faith] **1 :** made in good faith without fraud or deceit ⟨a *bona fide* contract⟩ **:** legally valid ⟨return of such persons to place of *bona fide* residence —*U.S. Code*⟩ **2 :** SINCERE ⟨*bona fide* friends of democracy —Sinclair Lewis⟩ **:** made with earnest or wholehearted intent ⟨a *bona fide* proposal⟩ **3 :** GENUINE ⟨just what a *bona fide* United States flag looked like —E.J.Kahn⟩ **:** not specious or counterfeit ⟨*bona fide* dinosaur eggs⟩ ⟨*bona fide* pockets below the waistline —*Women's Wear Daily*⟩ **syn** see AUTHENTIC

bona fide holder *n* **:** a holder of negotiable paper who before it reached maturity acquired title in the ordinary course of business and without actual or constructive notice of any defect in title or of lack of consideration

bona fide purchaser *n* **:** a purchaser who buys in good faith without notice of any defect and for a valuable consideration

bona fi·des \-ˈfī,dēz, -fē,dās\ *n* [L] **:** good faith ⟨a claimant whose *bona fides* is unquestionable⟩ **:** lack of deceit or fraud ⟨the *bona fides* of a transaction⟩ **:** SINCERITY ⟨lays himself open to suspicion as to his *bona fides* and as to his knowledge by his remarks —F.W.Rolfe⟩

bon·aght \ˈbänəkt\ *n* -S [IrGael *buannacht*, fr. *buanna* soldier] **:** a tax formerly imposed by Irish chieftains upon their people for the quartering of soldiers

bon·ail·ie \bäˈnāli\ *n* -S [ME (Scottish dialect), alter. (influenced by MF *bon* good) of MF *bien alee* parting felicitation, gift, or repast, fr. *bien* (fr. L *bene*, adv. of *bonus* good) + *alee*, fr. fem. of *alé*, past part. of *aler* to go — more at BOUNTY, ALLEY] *Scot* **:** a parting drink **:** STIRRUP CUP

bona ma·ter·na \,bōnəməˈtərnə\ *n pl* [L, maternal property] *Roman law* **:** all the property a son subject to paternal power acquires from his mother — compare BONA ADVENTITIA

bo·nang \bōˈnaŋ\ *n* -S [Jav] **:** a Javanese musical instrument consisting of a series of tuned gongs

bo·na no·ta·bi·lia \,bōnə,nōdəˈbilēə\ *n pl* [L, notable goods] *obs* **:** the goods of a deceased person held in a diocese other than his own at the time of his death that according to older English probate law required consideration by the courts if of or exceeding the value of five pounds

bo·nan·za \bəˈnanzə, bō-\ *n* -S *often attrib* [Sp, lit., calm, fair weather, prosperity, rich mine, fr. ML *bonacia*, alter. (influenced by L *bonus* good) of L *malacia* calm at sea, fr. Gk *malakia*, lit., softness — more at BOUNTY, MALACIA] **1 a :** an exceptionally large and rich ore shoot or pocket in veins carrying gold and silver **b :** a mine having such an ore shoot or pocket; *also* **:** the yield of such a mine ⟨a ~ worth millions⟩ **2 a :** something that yields an often unexpectedly large profit ⟨a ~ enterprise⟩ ⟨put the full resources of his studio behind the picture . . . and achieved a box-office ~ —Al Hine⟩ **b :** an extremely large amount ⟨the ~ paid to foreign countries to help them keep out of debt⟩ ⟨a ~ of Socialist sympathy —*Time*⟩ **c :** something excessively rich, lush, or rewarding ⟨the ~ farms of the middle west —Lewis Mumford⟩ ⟨a ~ era⟩ — **in bonanza** *of a mine* **:** producing heavily and profitably

bo·na·parte's gull \ˈbōnə,pärts-\ *or* **bo·na·parte gull** \-rt-\ *n, usu cap B* [after C.L.J.L.*Bonaparte* †1857 Fr. naturalist in U.S.] **:** a No. American black-headed gull (*Larus philadelphia*) about the size of a pigeon

bonaparte's sandpiper *n, usu cap B* [after C.L.J.L.*Bonaparte*] **:** WHITE-RUMPED SANDPIPER

bonaparte's weasel *n, usu cap B* [after C.L.J.L.*Bonaparte*] **:** a small weasel (*Mustela cicognanii*) of northern No. America, slightly larger than a chipmunk, short-tailed, and chocolate-brown turning white in winter

bo·na·part·ism \ˈbōnə,pärd·,izəm, -pȧd·,-, -är,tiz-, -ȧ,tiz-, ˈ===,==\ *n* -S *usu cap* [prob. fr. F *bonapartisme*, fr. Charles Louis Napoléon *Bonaparte* (Napoleon III) †1873 Fr. emperor + F *-isme* -ism] **1 :** the policy of Bonaparte **2 :** a policy advocating or supporting dictatorial rule by a popular leader who has ostensibly received a mandate from the people ⟨it has been a socialist and Communist tradition to be wary of *Bonapartism* —Aneurin Bevan⟩

1bo·na·part·ist \ˈ==,=əst\ *n* -S *usu cap* [prob. fr. F *bonapartiste*, fr. *Bonaparte* + F *-iste* -ist] **:** one attached to the policy or family of Bonaparte

2bonapartist \"\ *adj, usu cap* **:** of, relating to, or supporting Bonaparte or Bonapartism

bo·na per·i·tura \,bōnə,perəˈtu̇rə\ *n pl* [L] *law* **:** perishable property

bo·na·ro·ba \,bōnəˈrōbə, ˈbän-\ *n* -S [It *bona roba* good material, good property, fr. *bona* (var. of *buona*, fem. of *buono* good, fr. L *bonus*) + *roba* property, material, of Gmc origin; akin to OHG *roub* booty, something stolen — more at BOUNTY, ROBE] **:** COURTESAN, PROSTITUTE

bo·na·sa \bōˈnāzə, -āsə\ *n, cap* [NL, prob. alter. of L *bonasus*, aurochs; fr. the similarity of its characteristic drumming sound to the bellowing of a bull] **:** a genus of birds (family Tetraonidae) containing only the ruffed grouse

bo·na·sus \bōˈnāsəs\ *n, pl* **bonasi** \-,sī\ [L, fr. Gk *bonasos, bonassos*] *archaic* **:** WISENT

bona va·can·tia \,bōnəvəˈkansh(ē)ə\ *n pl* [L, ownerless goods] *law* **:** goods without an apparent owner (as shipwrecks or the property of an intestate with no next of kin)

bon·a·ven·ture \,bänəˈvenchə(r), ˈ==,==\ *also* **bonaventure mizzen** *n* -S [prob. fr. It *buonaventura* good luck, fr. *buona* good + *ventura* luck, fortune, short for *avventura*, fr. L *adventura* — more at BONA-ROBA, ADVENTURE] **:** a sail hoisted on the fourth mast of a medieval boat; *also* **:** the mast itself

bon·a·vist \ˈbänəvəst, -,vist\ *also* **bonavist bean** *n* -S [prob. fr. It *buona vista* fine sight, fr. *buona* good + *vista* sight — more at VISTA] **:** HYACINTH BEAN

bona wa·vi·a·ta \,bōnə,wāvēˈäd·ə\ *n pl* [ML] **:** WAIFS

bon·bon \ˈbän,bän\ *n* -S [F, (baby talk), redupl. of *bon* good, fr. L *bonus*] **1 :** a piece of candy; *specif* **:** a small chocolate-coated or fondant-covered candy with a center of sugar fondant to which fruits and nuts are sometimes added **2 :** something cloying and insubstantial ⟨newsstands . . . plastered with gory thrillers, romantic ~*s*, and pornography —Michael Scully⟩

bon·bon·nière \,bänbəˈni(ə)r, ,bōⁿbənˈya(a)(ə)r\ *n* -S [F, fr. *bonbon*] **:** a small fancy box or dish for bonbons

bonbon spoon *n* **:** a spoon with a flat perforated bowl for bonbons and nuts

bonce \ˈbän(t)s\ *n* -S [origin unknown] *dial Eng* **:** a boys' game played with marbles; *also* **:** a large marble

1bond *n* -S [ME *bonde* peasant, serf, fr. OE *bonda, bunda* householder, husband, fr. ON *bōndi*, alter. of *būandi*, fr. pres. part. of *būa* to live, dwell, have a household — more at BOWER] *obs* **:** BONDMAN

2bond *adj* [ME *bonde*, fr. *bonde*, n.] **1** *obs* **:** in serfdom, servitude, or slavery **:** BOUND **2** *obs* **:** of or relating to a slave **:** SERVILE

3bond \ˈbänd\ *n* -S [ME *band, bond* — more at BAND] **1 a :** something that confines or restrains (as a fetter or chain) **:** SHACKLE — usu. used in pl. ⟨you may chain the law down with all manner of clamps and ~*s* —B.N.Cardozo⟩ **b** *archaic* **:** IMPRISONMENT, CONFINEMENT — usu. used in pl. **2 :** an agreement binding one or more parties ⟨a ~ between two governments to aid each other in war⟩ **:** COVENANT, CHARTER ⟨the principles of friendship and ethics as espoused in the ~ of Phi Delta Theta —P.F.Connolly⟩ **3 a :** a hoop, band, or cord used to hold something down or together (as wheat, fagots, thatch) ⟨master the trick of tying the sheaf with its ~ —H.E.Bates⟩ **b :** a piece of building material (as a timber, brick, stone) that serves to bind or unite **c :** a device for bonding the armor or lead sheaths of two or more adjacent cables or for anchoring a cable to the earth **d :** a conductor that provides a continuous path for electric current between adjacent metal parts of a structure: as (1) **:** a conductor between the abutting rails of a track (2) **:** the connection between water mains and gas mains (3) **:** the grounded return of an electric railway system **e :** a mechanism by means of which atoms, ions, or groups of atoms are held together in a molecule or crystal, being usu. represented in chemical formulas by a line, a dot, or a pair of dots or lines denoting paired electrons — called also *link, linkage;* see COVALENT BOND, DOUBLE BOND, ELECTROSTATIC BOND, ELECTROVALENT BOND, HYDROGEN BOND, METALLIC BOND, TRIPLE BOND, VALENCE **f :** an adhesive that binds different ingredients together: as (1) **:** a cementing material that holds abrasive grains together (as in grinding wheels) or that binds the grains to the backing in coated abrasives (as sandpaper) (2) **:** the lime in silica brick (3) **:** a fusible ingredient that imparts strength to fired ceramic ware **4 a :** a uniting or binding element or force **:** TIE ⟨the ~ of fellowship⟩ — often used in pl. ⟨his wish to strengthen the ~*s* between Colombia and the U. S. —*Current Biog.*⟩; *specif* **:** a linkage between a stimulus and a reaction or between one idea and an associated idea ⟨the ~ theory of learning⟩ **b :** the state, result, or an instance of being bonded (as by an adhesive) **:** COHESION ⟨it is impossible to secure the proper ~ of coating to metal when the slightest particle of rust is present —*advt*⟩ **c :** resistance to slipping (as between the major components of a structure) provided by adhesion or friction ⟨precautions were taken to prevent ~ between the concrete roadway and the structural steel beneath it so that the concrete could shorten under the compression —N.J. Sollenberger⟩ **5 a** (1) **:** a writing under seal by which a person binds himself to pay a certain sum on or before an appointed day and usu. containing a condition that if the obligator shall do or abstain from doing a certain act on or before a time specified the obligation shall be void but otherwise shall remain in full force; *also* **:** the amount of money so guaranteed — often used with *give* ⟨each must give ~ for his appearance before the court⟩; compare BAIL, PENAL SUM (2) **:** one who acts as bail or surety **b :** an interest-bearing document giving evidence of a long-term debt and issued by a government body or corporation sometimes secured by a lien on property and often designed to take care of a particular financial need — see CALLABLE, COLLATERAL TRUST BOND, COUPON BOND, DEBENTURE, EQUIPMENT BOND, HIGHWAY BOND, REGISTERED BOND, SAVINGS BOND, SERIAL BOND, SINKING-FUND BOND, TAP BOND **c :** an insurance agreement under which one (as a corporation) becomes surety to pay within stated limits for the financial loss caused to another by the act or default (as breach of trust, negligence, error of judgment, failure to perform a contract) of a third person or from some contingency over which the third person may have no control (as reappearance of a lost instrument or failure to win a lawsuit) **6 :** a connection or system of connections in which adjacent parts of a structure are made to overlap so as to be tied or bound together; *specif* **:** the systematic lapping of brick in a wall ⟨the brickwork is unusually fine and the ~ used on the south front of the house is different from that on the other sides —*Amer. Guide Series: La.*⟩ — see AMERICAN BOND, BLIND BOND, BLOCK-IN-COURSE BOND, CHAIN BOND, CROSS-AND-ENGLISH BOND, CROSS BOND, DIAGONAL BOND, DOG'S-TOOTH BOND, ENGLISH BOND, ENGLISH CROSS BOND, FLEMISH BOND, FLYING BOND, HERRINGBONE BOND, IN-AND-OUT BOND, PLUMB BOND, RANGING BOND, RUNNING BOND, SPLIT BOND **7 :** the state of goods being manufactured, stored, or transported under the care of bonded agencies until the duties or taxes on them are paid ⟨you may leave . . . tobacco in ~ with customs —Richard Joseph⟩ **8 :** a 100-proof straight whiskey that has been aged at least four years under government supervision before being bottled — called also *bonded whiskey* **9 :** BOND PAPER

4bond \"\ *vb* -ED/-ING/-S *vt* **1 :** to bind or tie (a wall, a building, or various masonry units) usu. by lapping one unit over another **2 :** to place under the conditions of a bond: as **a :** to secure the payment of the duties and taxes on (goods or merchandise being manufactured, warehoused, or transported) by giving a bond **b :** to mortgage or issue bonds secured by mortgage upon (property) **c :** to convert into a debt secured by bonds **d :** to give or secure an option upon (as a mine or other property) by a bond tying up the property till the option has expired **e :** to provide a bond (sense 5c) for or cause to provide such a bond ⟨~ a trustee⟩ ⟨~ an employee⟩ ⟨~ an official⟩ **3 :** to bind together or connect by or as if by bonds: as **a :** to cause to adhere firmly (as metal to glass or plastic) **b :** to make secure and adequate electrical connection between (two or more conductors) either to ensure free passage of current ⟨a railroad track with ~*ed* joints⟩ or to maintain uniformity of electric potential (as of water and gas piping or the sheaths of electric cables) — compare 3BOND 3d **c :** to embed in a matrix ⟨abrasive material ~*ed* in a resinous binder to form a grinding wheel⟩ — compare 3BOND 3f **d :** to hold together in a molecule or crystal by means of chemical bonds ~ *vi* **:** to hold together or solidify by or as if by means of a bond or a binder ⟨a cement failing to make materials ~⟩; *specif* **:** to cohere (as the fibers in paper, the coating of the surface of paper, the elements in laminated board) ⟨the coatings ~ tightly to many surfaces —*Graphic Arts Monthly*⟩ — **bond·a·ble** \-dəbəl\ *adj*

bond·age \ˈbändij, -dēj\ *n* -S [ME, fr. ML *bondagium*, fr. ME *bonde* peasant, serf + L *-agium* -age] **1 a :** the tenure or service of a villein, serf, or slave **b** *chiefly Scot* **:** services due from a tenant farmer to his proprietor or from a cottager to the farmer **2 :** the quality or state of being bound: **a :** restraint of personal liberty by compulsion **:** SERFDOM, CAPTIVITY ⟨the ~ of the Hebrews in Egypt⟩ **b :** voluntary subjugation (as to some service or duty) ⟨she had gone into ~ among the aristocracy as a governess —Virginia Woolf⟩ **c :** servitude or subjugation (as to someone superior or dominating or to some power, motive, or appetite) ⟨with the House of Representatives in ~ to its leaders —Lindsay Rogers⟩ ⟨the ~ of specialization⟩ ⟨the obvious and painful ~ of shyness —Helen Howe⟩ **d** *linguistics* **:** the state of being a bound form

bond·ag·er \-jə(r)\ *n* -S **1 :** one that performs bondage service **2** *chiefly Scot* **:** one obligated to perform certain services on a farm; *specif* **:** a woman engaged by a tenant farmer or cotter under his agreement with the proprietor to do field work on the farm

bon·dar \ˈbän,där\ *n* -S [prob. fr. Bengali or Hindi *bā̃da* monkey — more at BANDAR] **:** a palm civet (*Paradoxurus hermaphrodytus*) of India

bond clay *n* [3*bond*] **:** a plastic ceramic clay that gives strength to dry but unfired ware

bond coat *n* [3*bond*] **:** a coat (as of plaster or paint) to ensure adhesion

bond course *n* [*bondstone*] **:** a course of masonry bondstones

bonded *adj* [fr. past part. of 4*bond*] **:** in, operating under, or placed under a bond ⟨a ~ carrier⟩ ⟨~ goods⟩

bonded debt *n* **:** that part of the indebtedness of a government or corporation represented by bonds — called also *funded debt*

bonded store *n, Brit* **:** BONDED WAREHOUSE

bonded warehouse *n* **1 :** a warehouse under bond to the government for payment of customs duties and taxes on goods stored or processed there **2 :** a warehouse insured against loss or damage to goods stored therein

bonded whiskey *n* **:** 3BOND 8

1bond·er \ˈbändə(r)\ *n* -S [4*bond* + *-er*] **1 :** one that bonds: as **a :** an assembler of electromagnet laminations **b :** a worker who welds copper bonds between the joints of rails **2 :** BONDSTONE 1

2bond·er \"\ *n* -S [modif. of Norw *bonde* and Icel *bōndi* householder, fr. ON *bōndi* — more at BOND] **:** a Norwegian or Icelandic farmer or peasant landowner

bond·er·ize \ˈbändə,rīz\ *vt* -ED/-ING/-S [back-formation fr. *Bonderized*, a trademark] **:** to coat (steel) with a patented phosphate solution for protection against corrosion

bondholder \ˈ=,==\ *n* [3*bond* + *holder*] **:** a person who holds a bond (as of a government or corporation)

bon·dieu·se·rie \bōn,dyüzəˈrē\ *n* -S [F, fr. *bon Dieu* dear Lord (fr. *bon* good + *dieu* god, fr. L *deus*) + connective *-s-* + *-erie* -ery — more at BONNY, DEITY] **:** banal and often shoddy religious art; *also* **:** a piece of bondieuserie (as a statue or picture)

bonding *n* -S [fr. gerund of 4*bond*] **:** electrical interconnection between parts (as of an airplane) to minimize differences of voltage

bonding company *n* [fr. pres. part. of 4*bond*] **:** a company issuing fidelity and surety bonds **:** SURETY COMPANY

bonding course *n* **:** BOND COURSE

bonding plaster *n* **:** BOND PLASTER

bond·less \ˈbändləs, *rapid* -nl-\ *adj* **:** being without a bond

1bond·man \ˈbän(d)mən\ *n, pl* **bondmen** [ME *bondeman* peasant, serf, fr. *bonde* peasant, serf + *man* — more at BOND] **:** one who is bound **:** SLAVE, SERF, VILLEIN

2bondman \"\ *n, pl* **bondmen** [Norw *bonde* and Icel *bōndi* householder + E *man* — more at BONDER] **:** 1BONDER 1b

bond miner *n* [3*bond*] **:** a contractor hewer

bon·do \ˈbän(,)dō\ *n, pl* **bondo** *or* **bondos** *usu cap* **1 :** a people of the hill country of the Koraput district in India **2 :** a member of the Bondo people

bond of indemnity [3*bond*] **:** an indemnification agreement filed with a carrier relieving it from liability for something that it would otherwise be liable for

bon·don \(ˈ)bōⁿˈdōⁿ\ *also* **bondon cheese** *n* -S [F *bondon*, lit., bung, fr. *bonde* bung, fr. (assumed) Gaulish *bunda;* akin to MIr *bond, bonn* sole of the foot, L *fundus* bottom — more at BOTTOM] **:** a cheese resembling a bung in form and made in Neufchâtel, France

bond paper *n* [3*bond*] **:** a strong durable paper of a type orig. made for documents (as government bonds) and now commonly used for letterheads and other stationery

bond plaster *n* [3*bond*] **:** a plaster with high adhesive properties made esp. for use as a first coat on interior concrete surfaces

bonds *pl of* BOND, *pres 3d sing of* BOND

bondslave \ˈ=,=\ *n* [2*bond* + *slave*] **:** a person in slavery **:** BONDMAN, SLAVE

1bonds·man \ˈbän(d)zmən\ *n, pl* **bondsmen** [by alter.] **:** 1BONDMAN

2bonds·man \"\ *n, pl* **bondsmen** [3*bond* + *-s* + *man*] **:** one who assumes the responsibility of a bond **:** SURETY

3bondsman \"\ *n, pl* **bondsmen** *usu cap* [Afrik, fr. *Bond* (short for *Afrikanerbond*, lit., alliance of Afrikaners, fr. *Afrikaner* + *bond* alliance, fr. MD, bundle, alliance) + *man*, fr. MD; akin to OE *bundel* bundle and to OE *man, mon* man — more at BUNDLE, MAN] **:** a member of the Afrikanerbond, an organization founded in 1880 to achieve unification and independence of the states and colonies of So. Africa

bondstone \ˈbän,stōn\ *n* [3*bond* + *stone*] **1 :** a stone running through a masonry wall to bind it together **2 :** a stone that joins the coping above a gable to the upper surface of a wall

bond timber *n* [3*bond*] **:** a timber built horizontally into a masonry wall to which battens and laths are fastened — compare CHAIN BOND

bon·duc \ˈbän,dək\ *n* -S [F, fr. Ar *bunduq* hazelnut, filbert] **1 :** NICKER NUT **2** *also* **bonduc tree :** any of several trees of the genus *Caesalpinia* (as *C. bonduc*) with large prickly pods enclosing beanlike seeds **3 :** KENTUCKY COFFEE TREE

bond·wom·an \ˈbän,dwu̇mən\ *also* **bonds·wom·an** \-n(d)z-,w-\ *n, pl* **bondwom·en** *also* **bondswom·en** \-,wimən\ [ME *bondewoman*, fr. *bonde* bond (adj.) + *woman* — more at BOND] **:** a female slave

bone \'bōn\ *n* -s *often attrib* [ME *boon, bon,* fr. OE *bān;* akin to OHG & ON *bein* bone] **1 a :** one of the hard parts of the skeleton of a vertebrate ⟨shoulder ~⟩ ⟨the ~s of the arm⟩ — compare CARTILAGE **b :** any of various hard animal substances or structures akin to or resembling bone (as baleen, ivory, the internal calcareous shell of the cuttlefish) **c :** the hard tissue of which the adult skeleton of most vertebrates is largely composed, being a dense form of connective tissue, hard and rigid from its inorganic matter of chiefly calcium phosphate, and being externally of compact tissue covered except on the articular surfaces with a fibrous coat of vascular connective tissue and internally porous and containing cavities of various sizes — see BONE CELL, CANALICULUS, HAVERSIAN CANAL, LAMELLA, OSSIFICATION, PERIOSTEUM **2 :** ESSENCE, CORE ⟨chilled to the ~⟩ ⟨lying was in his very ~s⟩ ⟨cut expenses to the ~⟩ **3 bones** *pl* **a** (1) **:** the skeleton ⟨reduced to skin and ~s by hunger⟩ or other framework resembling a skeleton ⟨vessels lost on the lakes, many of whose ~s are still ... along the shores —*Amer. Guide Series: Mich.*⟩ (2) **:** BODY ⟨running as fast as his old ~s would carry him⟩ (3) **:** the more enduring parts of a dead body **:** mortal remains ⟨inter a person's ~s⟩ **b :** the essential design or framework (as of a story, novel, picture, or other work of art) **4 :** MATTER, SUBJECT ⟨a ~ of contention⟩ **5 :** something orig. or usu. made of bone: as **a bones** *pl* **:** thin bars of bone, ivory, or wood held in pairs between the fingers and used to produce musical rhythms **:** CLAPPERS, KNACKERS **b :** a strip of whalebone, steel, featherbone, or plastic inserted into a casing to stiffen a garment (as a corset or dress) **c bones** *pl* **:** DICE **d :** DOMINO **6 :** the bow wave of a ship when under way or esp. when traveling at good speed — usu. used with the phrase *in her teeth* ⟨the ship all sails set, was roaring along with a ~ in her teeth⟩ **7 bones** *pl but sing in constr, often cap* **:** an end man in a minstrel show who often performs on the bones — compare TAMBO **8 a :** a layer or fragments of shale, slate, or other rock in a coal seam or in coal **b** *or* **bone coal :** slaty coal often of such a high ash content that it cannot be used in the ordinary ways **:** carboniferous shale — called also *bony, slate* **9** *slang* **:** DOLLAR — **bone to pick :** a point of contention **:** a cause for complaint **:** a matter to argue or complain about ⟨a *bone to pick* with the sales manager over defective merchandise⟩ ⟨a *bone to pick* with the legislature about the raising of taxes⟩

²**bone** \"\ *vb* -ED/-ING/-S [ME *bonen,* fr. *bon, boon,* n.] *vt* **1 :** to remove the bones from ⟨~ a fish⟩ ⟨~ a turkey⟩ ⟨the ribs can be *boned* out and the meat rolled for roasting⟩ **2 :** to provide (a garment) with stays ⟨~ a corset⟩ ⟨a *boned* camisole⟩ **3 :** to rub (as a boot) with a piece of bone in order to remove scratches and smooth the surface **4 :** to sight along (an object or set of objects, as rods or sticks) to arrive at a straight line or ascertain a level **~** *vi* **1 :** to study hard or ploddingly **:** GRIND ⟨~ away at premedical courses⟩ ⟨*boning* through law school⟩ **2 :** to attempt to master necessary or required information in a short time (as in preparation for an examination) **:** CRAM — usu. used with *up* ⟨~ up on a problem⟩ ⟨~ up on Latin⟩; compare SWOT

³**bone** \"\ *adv* [¹*bone* (as in *bone-dry, bone-tired*)] **:** EXTREMELY ⟨a ~ lazy fellow⟩ **:** ABSOLUTELY ⟨a novel ~ clean of sentimentality⟩ **:** UTTERLY ⟨he gets ~ tired and edgy —S.E.Fletcher⟩ **:** DESPERATELY ⟨~ poor⟩ ⟨the poor are ~ hungry —Margaret Shedd⟩

⁴**bône** \"\ *or* **bone** *adj, usu cap* [fr. *Bône* or *Bone,* Algeria] **:** of or from the city of Bône, Algeria **:** of the kind or style prevalent in Bône

bone–ace *n, obs* **:** a card game in which the highest third card took half the stake; *also* **:** the ace of diamonds which was the highest card

bone age *n, usu cap B&A* **:** a prehistoric period characterized by the use of bone and antler implements **:** the period of Magdalenian culture

bone ash *n* **:** the white porous residue containing chiefly tribasic calcium phosphate from bones calcined in air and used esp. in making cupels, pottery, and glass and in cleaning jewelry; *also* **:** synthetic tribasic calcium phosphate used similarly

bone bed *n* **:** any terrestrial or marine stratum in which bones or bone fragments are abundant

bone black *or* **bone char** *n* **:** the black substance containing chiefly tribasic calcium phosphate and carbon into which crushed defatted bones are converted by carbonization in closed vessels and which is used esp. as a black pigment and as a decolorizing adsorbent — called also *animal black, animal charcoal;* compare ACTIVATED CARBON, CARBON BLACK, DROP BLACK, IVORY BLACK

bonebreaker \'ˌ=ˌ==\ *n* **:** any of several large birds (as the giant petrel, the lammergeier, or the osprey)

bone breccia *n* **:** a deposit (as in limestone caves) of fragments of bones of vertebrates often mixed with earth, sand, and calcium carbonate

bone brown *n* **1 :** a pigment similar to bone black made by partially carbonizing bones **2 :** a moderate to dark olive brown — called also *bracken, ivory brown*

bone cell *n* **1** *or* **bone corpuscle :** any of the cells occupying the lacunae of bone **:** OSTEOBLAST **2 :** OSTEOSCLEREID

bone china *n* **:** china made with an admixture of bone ash or calcium phosphate (as developed in England about 1800) and characterized by translucency and whiteness

bone coal *n* **:** ¹BONE 8b

bone conduction *n* **:** the transmission of sound waves to the inner ear through the bones of the skull

boned \'bōnd\ *adj* [ME, fr. *boon, bon* bone (n.) + *-ed* — more at BONE] **1 :** having bones of a specified type ⟨she is slender, erect, and exquisitely ~ —Joseph Mitchell⟩ **2 :** with bones removed ⟨a ~ fish⟩ ⟨a ~ rib roast⟩ **3 :** manured with bone ⟨~ land⟩ **4 :** provided or strengthened with stays ⟨her long neck wrapped in its high ~ collar —Marcia Davenport⟩

bone–dry \'ˌ=ˌ=\ *adj* **1 a :** dry as a weathered bone **:** very dry **:** absolutely dry ⟨fire hazards present in *bone-dry* leaves⟩ **b** *of clay* **:** completely dried but not fired **2 :** without or opposed to intoxicating beverages ⟨a *bone-dry* luncheon⟩ ⟨the county remained *bone-dry* after election⟩

bone dust *n* **:** BONE MEAL

bone earth *n* **:** BONE ASH

bone–eater \'ˌ=ˌ==\ *n* [by folk etymology fr. *bonito*] **:** ATLANTIC BONITO

bo·neen \bä'nēn, bə'-\ *n* -s [IrGael *banabhin,* dim. of *banbh,* fr. OIr *banb;* akin to obs. W *banw* young pig, Breton *bano* sow with a litter, OCorn *baneu* sow] *Irish* **:** a young pig

bone fat *n* **:** the fatty matter in bones obtained by boiling, steaming, or extracting with solvents and used chiefly in candles, cheap soap, and lubricating greases

bone felon *n, dial* **:** ³FELON 2

bonefish \'ˌ=ˌ=\ *n* [so called fr. its many small bones] **1 :** any of several slender silvery small-scaled fishes of the family Albulidae; *esp* **:** an outstanding game and food fish (*Albula vulpes*) of warmer seas that sometimes exceeds 10 pounds in weight — called also *banana fish* **2 :** TENPOUNDER

bone glass *n* **:** a glass of a milky white color due to the presence of bone ash or other form of calcium phosphate

bonehead \'ˌ=ˌ=\ *n* **:** a stupid or slow-thinking person **:** NUMSKULL, BLOCKHEAD ⟨you got ~s running business nowadays —Ira Wolfert⟩ ⟨a ~ play by the shortstop⟩ — **bone·headed** \'ˌ=ˌ==\ *adj*

bone lace *n* [so called fr. the fact that it was made by bone bobbins] **:** BOBBIN LACE

bone·less \'bōnlə̇s\ *adj* [ME *banles,* fr. OE *bānlēas,* fr. *bān* bone + *-lēas* -less — more at BONE] **1 :** being without a bone ⟨jellyfish are ~⟩ **:** having the bone or bones removed ⟨~ roasts of beef⟩ **2 :** lacking character, strength, or vigor ⟨the sentences are occasionally ~ —J.N.Hall⟩

bone·let \-lə̇t\ *n* -s **:** a small bone **:** OSSICLE

bo·nel·lia \bō'nelēə, bə-\ *n, cap* [NL, fr. Francesco A. *Bonelli* †1830 Ital. naturalist + NL *-ia*] **:** a genus of marine worms (group Echiuroidea) that exhibit marked dimorphism and size disparity between the sexes, the male living parasitically in the nephridium of the female and that have what appears to be a unique mechanism of sex determination, the indifferent larva becoming a male if it settles on the proboscis of a mature female and becoming a female if it develops independently on the sea bottom

bone marrow *n* **:** MARROW 1

bone meal *n* **:** bone crushed or ground usu. after extraction of fat and gelatin and used chiefly as a fertilizer but also in the feed of farm animals

bone oil *n* **1 :** a dark-colored ill-smelling oil obtained by carbonizing bones (as in making bone black) that contains hydrocarbons and many nitrogen compounds (as pyrrole and pyridine bases) and is used esp. in sheep dips and in denaturing alcohol — called also *animal oil, Dippel's oil* **2 :** the liquid portion of bone fat used as a lubricant and in leather manufacture

bone phosphate *n* **:** tribasic calcium phosphate from bones

bone picker *n* **:** an American Indian who follows a burial custom of cleaning the flesh from the bones of corpses prior to burial

bone–pointing \'ˌ=ˌ==\ *n* **:** the practice (as among Australian aboriginals) of pointing a sharpened bone at an enemy and uttering incantations conjuring his illness, disability, or death

bone porcelain *n* **:** BONE CHINA

bon·er \'bōnə(r)\ *n* -s [²*bone* + *-er*] **1 :** one that puts bones into garments (as corsets) — called also *stayer, steeler* **2 :** a low-grade beef animal suitable only for boning out (as for the preparation of canned meats or sausage) **3** [¹*bone* + *-er*] **a :** a ridiculous and usu. embarrassing or painful mistake or slip often arising from a sudden and fortuitous lapse of understanding, tact, or decorum — often used with *pull* **b :** a grammatical, logical, or factual blunder in a piece of writing often producing a humorous effect ⟨a few historical ~s ... such as dinosaurs surviving until medieval times —Coulton Waugh⟩ ⟨~s in student themes⟩ **syn** see ERROR

bones *pl of* BONE, *pres 3d sing of* BONE

bone·set \'bōn,set, *usu* -d.+V\ *n* **1 :** any of several American herbs of the genus *Eupatorium* (esp. *E. perfoliatum*) distinguished by opposite perfoliate leaves and white-rayed flower heads and formerly used as a household remedy — called also *agueweed, thoroughwort* **2 :** CLIMBING HEMPWEED **3 :** COMMON COMFREY

bonesetter \'ˌ=ˌ==\ *n* [ME *boone setter,* fr. *boone, boon* bone + *setter*] **:** a person usu. not a licensed physician who sets broken or dislocated bones — **bonesetting** \'ˌ=ˌ==\ *n*

bone·shaker \'bōn,shākə(r)\ *n, slang* **:** a dilapidated, uncomfortable, or outmoded vehicle (as a bicycle of an early model without rubber tires)

bone shark *n* [so called fr. its gill rakers resembling whalebones] **:** BASKING SHARK

bone·shave \'bōn,shāv\ *also* **bone·shaw** \-,shȯ\ *n* [ME *boneschawe*] *archaic* **:** SCIATICA

bone skin *n* **:** PERIOSTEUM

bone spavin *n* **:** a new growth of bone on the hock of the horse that is the result of inflammation and hereditary predisposition and that causes somewhat severe lameness

bone spirit *n* **:** an ammoniacal liquid obtained along with bone oil in the carbonization of bones

bone·tail \'ˌ=ˌ=\ *n* **:** FER-DE-LANCE

bone tankage *n* **:** DIGESTER TANKAGE

bone–throwing \'ˌ=ˌ==\ *n* **:** the throwing of pieces of bone or wood practiced by some primitive peoples for purposes of divination or diagnosis

bone turquoise *n* **:** ODONTOLITE

bone whale *n* **:** a whalebone whale; *esp* **:** RIGHT WHALE

bonewood \'ˌ=ˌ=\ *n* [so called fr. its ivory color and hardness] **:** CHEESEWOOD

boney *var of* BONY

bone·yard \'ˌ=ˌ=\ *n* **1 a** *slang* **:** CEMETERY **b :** a place where domestic animals are disposed of or their bones collected **c :** a restricted area where the bones of wild animals have accumulated ⟨a caribou ~⟩ **2 :** a place where worn-out, obsolete, or irreparably damaged ships, airplanes, or automobiles are collected to await ultimate disposal **3 :** the dominoes remaining after each player has drawn a hand — called also *stock*

bon·fire \'bän + ,-\ *n* [ME *bonefyre,* fr. *bone, bon* bone + *fyre* fire — more at BONE, FIRE] **1 a** *obs* **:** a large public fire in which bones or bones and wood were traditionally burned **b** *obs* **:** a funeral pyre **c** *archaic* **:** a fire in which heretics or officially proscribed articles (as books or religious objects) were publicly burned **2 :** a great open-air fire kindled to mark a religious anniversary (as the eves of St. Peter and St. John) or to highlight some public event (as a political rally, a community outing, a victory celebration, the birthday of a famous person) **3 :** an open-air fire in which waste paper, leaves, brush, or other rubbish is burned

¹**bong** \'bȯŋ, 'bäŋ\ *n* -s [imit.] **:** the deep resonant sound of a bell or one resembling that of a bell ⟨a spittoon slid against the bar with a dull ~ —W.D.Overholser⟩

²**bong** \"\ *vb* -ED/-ING/-S **:** RING ⟨the clock ~*ed* out the hour⟩ ⟨the clerk ... ~*ed* the call bell —John Selby⟩

bonga \'bȯŋə, 'bōŋə\ *also* **bunga** \'bu̇ŋə\ *n* -s [Tag & Bisayan *bunga*] **1** *Philippines* **:** BETEL PALM **2** *Philippines* **:** BETEL NUT

bon·gar \'bäŋ(,)gär\ *n* -s [native name in India] **:** a poisonous snake of India of the genus *Bungarus*

¹**bon·go** \'bäŋ(,)gō, 'bȯŋ-\ *n, pl* **bongo** *or* **bongos** *usu cap* **1 :** a Negro people of eastern Sudan who are agriculturists and efficient metalworkers and are distinguished by their reddish skin — called also *Dor* **2 :** a member of the Bongo people

²**bongo** \"\ *n, pl* **bongo** *or* **bongos** [of African origin; akin to Bobangi *mbangani,* an antelope] **:** any of three large forest antelopes (*Tragelaphus eurycerus* or *T. angasi* of western Africa or *T. isaaci* of eastern Africa) of a reddish or chestnut-brown color with narrow white stripes

³**bongo** *var of* BUNGO

⁴**bon·go** \'bäŋ(,)gō, 'bȯŋ-\ *n* -s [AmerSp] **:** a tropical American timber tree (*Cavanillesia platanifolia*) of the family Bombacaceae that yields a light soft wood resembling balsa

⁵**bongo** \", ='=\ *or* **bongo drum** *n, pl* **bongos** *also* **bongoes** [AmerSp *bongó*] **:** one of a pair of small tuned drums played with the fingers and used esp. in Cuban bands

⁶**bongo** \"\ *n* -s [AmerSp] **:** a sensuous Trinidad Negro dance secularized from an original funeral ritual

bon·grace \'bän,grās\ *n* -s [obs. E, projecting brim for a bonnet, fr. (assumed) MF *bonne-grace* (whence F *bonne-grâce,* a cloth), fr. *bonne* (fem. of *bon* good) + *grâce* grace, favor — more at BONNY, GRACE] *archaic* **:** a hat or bonnet with a brim projecting in front

bon·ham \'bänəm\ *n* -s [modif. of IrGael *banbh* — more at BONEEN] *chiefly Irish* **:** a young pig

bon·heur du jour \bə,nərdə'jü(ə)r, -də'-\ *n, pl* **bonheurs du jour** *like sing.*\ [F, lit., happiness of the day; fr. its tremendous popularity in 18th cent. France] **:** a small desk or writing table with a cabinet top

bon·ho·mie *also* **bon·hom·mie** \'bänə,mē, ,==ˈ=\ *n* -s [F *bonhomie* (formerly *bonhommie*), fr. *bonhomme* good-natured man (fr. *bon* good + *homme* man, fr. L *homo*) + *-ie* -y — more at BONNY, HOMAGE] **:** good-natured easy friendliness **:** warm open geniality **:** atmosphere of good cheer ⟨Christmas ~⟩ ⟨the ~ of a fraternity reunion⟩ ⟨an amazing ~ radiated from her —Jean Stafford⟩

bon·ho·mous \'bänəməs\ *adj* **:** full of bonhomie **:** warmly genial ⟨a ~ master of ceremonies⟩ ⟨stories that can be told only in ~ moments⟩

bo·ni \'bō(,)nē\ *n, pl* **boni** *or* **bonis** *usu cap* [F, of Amer-Ind origin] **1 :** a Bush Negro people of the interior of French Guiana **2 :** a member of the Boni people

bon·ie \'bänī\ *archaic Scot var of* BONNY

bonier *comparative of* BONY

bonies *pl of* BONY

boniest *superlative of* BONY

bon·i·face \'bänəfə̇s, -,fās\ *n* -s *sometimes cap* [fr. *Boniface,* jovial innkeeper in *The Beaux' Stratagem* (1707) by George Farquhar †1707 Irish dramatist] **:** the proprietor of a hotel, nightclub, or restaurant ⟨local ~s preparing to accommodate a political convention⟩

bon·i·fi·ca·tion \,bänəfə'kāshən\ *n* -s [F, fr. ML *bonificatus* (past part. of *bonificare* to ameliorate, fr. L *boni-* — fr. *bonus* good — + *-ficare,* fr. *facere* to do, make) + F *-ion* — more at BOUNTY, DO] **:** betterment of housing conditions and farming practices in a particular area (as a malarial area)

bon·i·form \'bänə,fȯrm\ *adj* [NL *boniformis* (trans. of Gk *agathoeidēs*), fr. L *bonus* good + *-iformis* -iform] *archaic* **:** promoting, perceiving, or akin to good ⟨the ~ powers of knowledge⟩ ⟨man's ~ faculty⟩

bon·ing \'bōniŋ, -nēŋ\ *n* -s [¹*bone* + *-ing*] **:** bones used to stiffen garments

boning knife *n* **:** a short knife with narrow blade and sharp point for boning meat

bon·i·tar·i·an \,bänə'terēən, -ta(a)r-\ *or* **bon·i·tary** \'==,==\ *adj* [L *bonitas* goodness (fr. *bonus* good + *-itas* -ity) + E *-arian* or *-ary* — more at BOUNTY] **1** *Roman law* **:** beneficial or equitable rather than statutory, civil, or quiritarian **2** *Roman law* **:** of or relating to ownership or possession protected not by the jus civile but by praetorian edict

bo·ni·to \bə'nēd·ō, bō'-, -ētō, -ə\ *also* **bo·ni·ta** \-ə\ *n, pl* **bonitos** *or* **bonito** *also* **bonitas** *or* **bonita** [Sp *bonito,* fr. *bonito,* adj., pretty, nice, fr. L *bonus* good + Sp *-ito* (dim. suffix)] **1 :** any of various medium-sized scombroid fishes intermediate in size and in other characteristics between the smaller mackerels and the larger tunas — compare CHILE BONITO, FRIGATE MACKEREL, SKIPJACK **2 :** any of various other fishes somewhat resembling bonitos

bonito shark *n* **:** a common blue or blue-gray mackerel shark (*Isurus glaucus*) of the Pacific ocean notable as a sport fish in the southwest Pacific and sometimes used for food — called also *blue pointer, mako*

bon·jean curves \'bän,jēn-\ *n pl, usu cap B* [origin unknown] **:** curves of areas of transverse sections and their moments about the base line of a ship used in making calculations (as to determine the force of buoyancy during launching)

bonk \'bäŋk\ *n* -s [D, lit., bone, mass (as of flesh), fr. MD *bonc, bonke* bone, jawbone — more at BUNCH] **:** a piece of the old copper bar money of the Dutch East Indies of which pieces worth ½, 1, 2, and 8 stivers were issued

bon mot \bōⁿmō\ *n, pl* **bons mots** *or* **bon mots** \bōⁿmō(z)\ [F, lit., good word] **:** a clever usu. witty remark **:** WITTICISM ⟨his *bons mots* were being repeated ... from coast to coast —W.J.Fisher⟩

bonn \'bän, 'bȯn\ *adj, usu cap* [fr. *Bonn,* Germany] **:** of or from Bonn, the capital of the West German Federal Republic **:** of the kind or style prevalent in Bonn

bon·naz \bə'naz\ *n* -s *usu cap* [after J.Bonnaz, 19th cent. Fr. inventor] **:** embroidery (as chain stitch or appliqué) made with a sewing machine

bonne \'bȯn, 'bən\ *n* -s [F, fr. fem. of *bon* good — more at BONNY] **:** a French maidservant

bonne bouche \bȯn'büsh, bən'-\ *n, pl* **bonnes bouches** *or* **bonne bouches** *like sing.*\ [F, lit., good mouth] **1 :** something supremely delicious or appetizing **:** a choice morsel **:** DELICACY ⟨there was no profusion of unmeaning dishes; each was a *bonne bouche* — Charles Reade⟩ **2 :** a final, unexpected, or supreme delight **:** TREAT ⟨reprints as a *bonne bouche* ... a delightful and characteristic essay —*Saturday Rev.*⟩

bonne femme \(')bȯn¦fam, (')bən-, -fäm\ *adj* [F (*à la*) *bonne femme* in the manner of a good housewife] **:** prepared as in home cooking — often used postpositively ⟨filet of sole *bonne femme*⟩

bonne projection \'bȯn-, 'bən-\ *n, usu cap B* [after Rigobert *Bonne* †1795 Fr. cartographer] **:** a modified conical equal-area map projection having one standard parallel and all meridians curved except the central meridian which is a straight line

¹**bon·net** \'bänə̇t, *usu* -d· + V\ *n* -s [ME *bonet,* fr. MF *bonet, bonnet,* fr. ML *abonnis*] **1 a** (1) *chiefly Scot* **:** a man's or boy's cap (2) **:** a brimless Scotch cap of seamless woolen fabric having usu. an ample soft crown and a snug headband — compare BALMORAL, TAM-O'-SHANTER **b :** a woman's head covering of cloth or straw usu. tied under the chin with ribbons or strings and made with or without a brim, formerly fashionable but now worn chiefly by children or as part of a uniform or habit — see POKE BONNET, SUNBONNET **c :** any bizarre, out-of-the-ordinary, or out-of-fashion headgear ⟨the 19th century ~ of a German infantryman⟩ ⟨the steeple-shaped ~ worn by women in medieval times⟩ **d :** WARBONNET **2 :** something shaped like or suggestive of the shape of a bonnet and used to cover, protect, or enclose: as **a :** an additional piece of canvas laced to the foot of a jib or foresail **b** (1) **:** the second stomach of a ruminant — compare RETICULUM (2) **:** a horny excrescence on the head of the southern right whale **c** *chiefly Midland* (1) **:** SPATTERDOCK — usu. used in pl. (2) **:** the infolded cornucopia-shaped leaf of the southern spatterdock **d** (1) **:** the cover or roof of a mine cage (2) **:** a projecting hood over the platform of a railroad car (3) *Brit* **:** HOOD 3h(2) (4) **:** the parasol-shaped appliance that protects the valve of an airship or balloon against rain **e** (1) **:** a spark arrester for a locomotive funnel (2) **:** the metal shield or cover for the gauze of a miner's safety lamp (3) **:** a cover for an open fireplace or a cowl or hood to increase the draft of a chimney (4) **:** the usu. slightly tapered upper part of the casing of a hot-air furnace from which the hot-air ducts project — called also *hood* **f** (1) **:** a metal covering for valve chambers, hydrants, or ventilators (2) **:** a cap placed over wooden piles to prevent their brooming esp. when being driven **3** *Brit* **:** SHILL

bonnet 1b

²**bonnet** \"\ *vb* -ED/-ING/-S *vi* **:** to remove the bonnet in token of respect **~** *vt* **1 :** to provide with or dress in a bonnet ⟨a mother ~*ing* her children⟩ ⟨~*ed* highlanders⟩ **:** to furnish with or as if with a bonnet ⟨all residences ... are white, ~*ed* with red tile —Aubrey Drury⟩ **2 :** to crush (a person's) hat down around the head ⟨getting drunk and ~*ing* a policeman on Boat Race night —*Atlantic*⟩

bonnet gourd *n* **:** DISHCLOTH GOURD

bonnet grass *n* **1 :** a redtop (*Agrostis alba*) **2 :** POVERTY GRASS 1b

bonnet·head \'==,=\ *or* **bonnethead shark** *n* **:** a shark (*Sphyrna tiburo*) of warm seas related to the hammerhead shark but smaller and having the lobes of the head less developed — called also *bonnet shark, shovelhead*

bonnet laird *n* **:** a petty Scottish landowner wearing a bonnet like the humbler folk

bon·net·less \-lə̇s\ *adj* **:** having no bonnet

bonnet limpet *or* **bonnet shell** *n* [so called fr. the shape of its shell] **:** a snail of *Calyptraea* or a related genus

bonnet monkey *or* **bonnet macaque** *n* [so called fr. the bonnetlike tuft of hair on its head] **:** a monkey (*Macaca radiata*) of the southern part of the Indian subcontinent related to but larger and darker than the toque macaque — called also *capped macaque, crown monkey*

bonnet pepper *n* **:** PIMIENTO; *sometimes* **:** SWEET PEPPER

bonnet piece *n* **:** a Scottish gold coin issued 1539–40 by James V that represented him wearing a bonnet

bon·net rouge \bȯnārüzh\ *n, pl* **bonnet rouges** *or* **bonnets rouges** *like sing.*\ [F, lit., red cap] **:** the red cap adopted by extremists in the French Revolution — compare LIBERTY CAP

bonnets *pl of* BONNET, *pres 3d sing of* BONNET

bonnet shark *n* **:** BONNETHEAD

bonnet skate *n* **1 :** LITTLE SKATE **2 :** a large stingray (*Aetobatus narinari*) common and widespread in tropic seas and an important food fish

bonnet top *n* **:** a broken-arch top in cabinet furniture and doorheads common between 1730 and 1780 with the break extending the entire depth of the top and the center often ornamented with a bust or urn and the corners with urns

bon·ni·ly \'bänᵊlē, -nə̇lē\ *adv* [*bonny* + *-ly*] **:** in a bonny manner

bon·ni·ness \-ānē̇nə̇s, -ānin-\ *n* -ES **:** the quality or state of being bonny

bon·ny *also* **bon·nie** \'bänē, -ni\ *adj* -ER/-EST [ME *bonie,* fr. OF *bon* good (fr. L *bonus*) + ME *-ie* -y — more at BOUNTY] **1** *chiefly Brit* **:** having a pleasing appearance: **a** *of a person* **:** attractive esp. as suggesting health, charm, sweetness, and liveliness ⟨as fair art thou, my ~ lass, so deep in love am I —Robert Burns⟩ **b** *of a place* **:** pleasant esp. through the appeal of the mild, placid, and rural **2 a** *chiefly Brit* **:** of considerable degree, size, or quantity ⟨a ~ fighter, who ... never fought better than when he

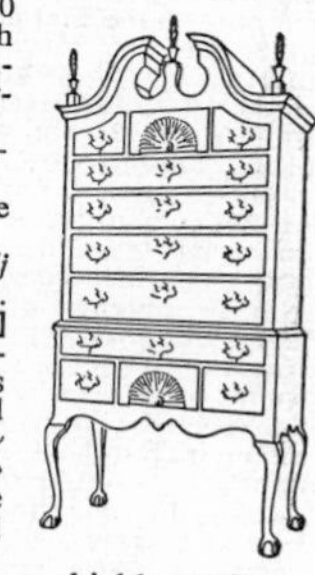
highboy with bonnet top

championed a losing side —Thomas Wood †1950⟩ **b** *Brit* (1) **:** in good health ⟨at the end of three weeks he was . . . ~ . . . and the mother too was . . . recovering —Ruth Mitchell⟩ (2) **:** PLUMP **3** *archaic* **:** HAPPY, GAY **4** *Brit* **:** very pleasant **:** FINE, EXCELLENT — a generalized term of approbation sometimes used ironically ⟨well, my ~ lad, they found you out⟩ **syn** see BEAUTIFUL

bon·ny·clab·ber \ˈbänē,klabə(r)\ *also* **bon·ny·clap·per** \-apə(r)\ *n* [IrGael *bainne clabair*, fr. *bainne* milk (fr. MIr, drop, milk) + *clabair*, gen. of *clabar* sour thick milk; MIr *bainne* akin to Skt *bindu* drop] *North & Midland* **:** 1CLABBER

bo·no·rum pos·ses·sio \bəˈnōrəmpəˈzesē(,)ō, bōˈ-, -ˈses-\ *n* [L, possession of goods] *Roman law* **:** the right of possession of the property of a deceased person; *specif* **:** the effective right to succeed, which changed the order of succession of the older jus civile, given by the praetor to emancipated children along with descendants in power, to cognatic after agnatic relatives, and last to the surviving spouse

bon·pa \bōnˈpä, -ˈpō\ *n* -S *usu cap* [Tibetan] **:** an adherent of the Bon religion

bons *pl of* BON

bon·sai \(ˈ)bän¦sī, (ˈ)bōn-\ *n, pl* **bonsai** [Jap] **:** a potted plant (as a tree) dwarfed by special methods of culture (as by limiting the space for and pruning of roots and by training of shoots by pruning and esp. by coiling wire around the branches); *also* **:** the art of growing such a plant — compare MINIASCAPE

bon-seki \(ˈ)bän¦sākē, ˈbōn-\ *n* -S [Jap, tray-landscape] **:** a landscape constructed of sand and stones on a tray; *also* **:** the art of constructing such a landscape

bon·spiel \ˈbän,spēl\ *n* -S [perh. fr. D *bond* league (fr. MD *bont*) + *spel* game, fr. MD — more at BUND, SPIEL] **:** a match or tournament between curling clubs

bon·te·bok \ˈbäntə,bäk\ *also* **bon·te·buck** \-,bək\ *n, pl* **bontebok** *or* **bonteboks** [Afrik *bontebok*, *bontbok*, fr. *bont* spotted (fr. MD, prob. fr. ML *punctus* dotted) + *bok* male antelope, male goat, fr. MD *boc*; akin to OHG *boc* male goat — more at POINT, BUCK] **:** a southern African antelope (*Damaliscus pygargus*) that is now extinct except in semidomestication and is of a purplish red color with a white face and rump

bon·te quagga \ˈbäntə-, -tē-\ *n* [obs. Afrik (now *bontkwagga*), fr. *bont* spotted + *quagga* — more at QUAGGA] **:** BURCHELL'S ZEBRA

bon·tok *also* **bon·toc** \bänˈtäk\ *n, pl* **bontok** *or* **bontoks** *also* **bontoc** *or* **bontocs** *usu cap* [native name in northern Luzon] **1 a :** a predominantly pagan people inhabiting northern Luzon, Philippines — compare IGOROT **b :** a member of such people **2 :** the Austronesian language of the Bontok people

bon ton \bōⁿˈtōⁿ, (ˈ)bänˈtän\ *n, pl* **bon tons** [F, lit., good tone] **1 :** STYLISHNESS, FASHIONABLENESS ⟨the worldliness and *bon ton* of the characters . . . held me spellbound —S.J.Perelman⟩ **2 :** the fashionable or proper thing ⟨the *bon ton* here is to be grave and learned —Horace Walpole⟩

bont tick \ˈbänt-\ *n* [Afrik *bont* spotted + E *tick* — more at BONTEBOK] **:** a southern African tick (*Amblyomma hebraeum*) attacking livestock, birds, and sometimes man and transmitting heartwater disease of sheep, goats, and cattle; *broadly* **:** any African tick of the genus *Amblyomma*

1bo·nus \ˈbōnəs\ *n* -ES [L, good — more at BOUNTY] **1 :** something given or received that is over and above what is expected ⟨as a ~ she got the day off from school⟩ ⟨a ~ of five days of beautiful weather⟩; *specif* **:** a gift given (as to a person) for complying with the donor's wishes **2 a** *Brit* **:** DIVIDEND 1c **b** (1) **:** money or an equivalent given in addition to the usual compensation ⟨surplus profits distributed among the workers as a ~⟩ (2) **:** the payment made by the employer under a bonus system **c :** a premium (as of stock) given by a corporation to a purchaser of its securities, to a promoter, or to an employee in recognition of his services **d** (1) **:** a government subsidy to an industry ⟨the mills closed down because the city did not provide a $100,000 ~ to keep them operating —*Amer. Guide Series : Mich.*⟩ (2) **:** a government payment to all ex-service men of a war often viewed as compensation for decreased earnings during time spent in the service **e :** a sum in excess of salary given a baseball player for signing with a team ⟨a ~ pitcher⟩ **3 :** a sum of money in addition to interest or royalties charged for the granting of a loan, for the granting of a charter or other privilege to a company, or for the lease or transfer of property (as oil lands) **4 a :** a score in a card game that does not count toward winning: as (1) **:** the score in bridge for honors, for making a doubled or redoubled contract, for a slam, or for winning the rubber — called also *premium* (2) **:** the score in gin rummy for each hand won or game won **b :** an extra amount received in poker for holding an unusually good hand (as a straight flush) — called also *premium*, *royalty*

2bonus \"\ *vt* -ED/-ING/-ES **:** to give a bonus to ⟨~*ing* each family having more than three children⟩ **:** SUBSIDIZE ⟨the enterprise . . . was heavily ~*ed* with land and a certain amount of cash —B.K.Sandwell⟩

bonus system *also* **bonus plan** *n* **:** wage payment whereby a worker is paid an additional amount for accomplishing more than a specified measure of work

bon vi·vant \¦bänvēˈvänt, bōⁿvēvāⁿ\ *n, pl* **bons vivants** *or* **bon vivants** \-vän(t)s, bōⁿvēvāⁿ\ [F, lit., good liver] **:** a person having cultivated or refined tastes esp. in food and drink **:** HIGH LIVER, GOURMET ⟨he was a prodigious worker, a hard and frequent *bon vivant* —Arthur Krock⟩ **syn** see EPICURE

bon vi·veur \¦bänvēˈvər, bōⁿvēvœr\ *n, pl* **bons viveurs** *or* **bon viveurs** \-vər, bōⁿvēvœr\ [F, lit., good liver] **:** a person who lives high and well **:** MAN-ABOUT-TOWN ⟨a *bon viveur* and local Don Juan⟩

bon vo·yage \,bänvwīˈäzh, ,bōn-, bōⁿvwäyäzh\ *n* [F] **:** a good trip ⟨delegates came to wish the explorers *bon voyage*⟩ **:** FAREWELL ⟨*bon voyage* baskets of fruit and flowers —I.V.Morris⟩ — often used as a parting phrase ⟨"*bon voyage* and a happy return," she said formally —Joseph Conrad⟩

bonx·ie \ˈbäŋksē\ *n* -S [perh. of Scand origin; akin to Norw *bunke* heap, corpulent woman, dumpy body, ON *bunki* heap, pile — more at BUNCH] *Scot* **:** GREAT SKUA

1bony *or* **bon·ey** \ˈbōnē, -ni\ *adj* **bonier; boniest** [1*bone* + -*y*] **1 a :** consisting of bone ⟨a ~ substance⟩ **:** made up of bones ⟨the ~ framework of the body⟩ **b :** resembling bone ⟨a ~ tumor⟩ **2 a :** full of bone ⟨a ~ roast⟩ or bones ⟨bass aren't so ~ as pickerel⟩ **b :** having prominent bones ⟨a ~ face⟩ ⟨a ~ horse⟩ **3 a :** SKINNY, SCRAWNY ⟨poor underfed ~ children⟩ **b :** BARREN, LEAN, SPARE ⟨brown and ~ mountains —Norman Cousins⟩ ⟨~, close-mouthed prose —John Woodburn⟩

2bony \"\ *or* **bony coal** *n* -ES **:** BONE 8b

bony bream *n* **:** any of several bony Australian freshwater fishes (genus *Nematalosa*) of the herring family (Clupeidae)

bony·fish \ˈ==,=\ *n* **1 :** MENHADEN **2 :** TENPOUNDER **3 :** BONEFISH

bony fish *n* **:** any of the higher fishes having usu. a well ossified skeleton **:** one of the Teleostomi — compare CARTILAGINOUS FISH

bony labyrinth *n* **:** the cavity in the petrous portion of the temporal bone that contains the membranous labyrinth of the inner ear

bonytail \ˈ==,=\ *or* **bonytail chub** *n* **:** a minnow (*Gila robusta*) of the Colorado river system that is now rarely seen

bonze \ˈbän(d)z\ *n* -S [F, fr. Pg *bonzo*, fr. Jap *bonsō*, Jap pron. of the characters used to designate Chin *fan-seng*] **:** a Buddhist monk of the Far East

bon·zer \ˈbän(d)zə(r)\ *also* **bonza** \-zə\ *adj* [perh. alter. of *bonanza*] *slang Austral* **:** FIRST-RATE, EXCELLENT

1boo \ˈbü\ *also* **bo** *or* **boh** \", ˈbō\ *interj* [ME *bo*] — used to express contempt or disapproval or to startle or frighten

2boo \ˈbü\ *n* -S **1 :** a shout of disapproval **:** a cry of contempt ⟨the unpopular speaker was greeted by ~*s* and hisses⟩ **2 :** any sound at all esp. when uttered in protest or when silence is unexpected ⟨the baby was good as gold and didn't say ~ all through church⟩

3boo \"\ *vb* -ED/-ING/-S *vi* **:** to deride and jeer esp. by uttering or shouting *boo* ⟨the crowd ~*ed* for five minutes⟩ ~ *vt* **:** to boo at **:** express disapproval of or dissatisfaction with (as a person, a performance, an idea) by booing ⟨the play was ~*ed* unmercifully by the gallery —Celia Johnson⟩

1boob \ˈbüb\ *n* -S [short for 1*booby*] **1 :** a stupid awkward person **:** SIMPLETON, DOPE ⟨the big ~ doesn't know enough to come in out of the rain⟩ **2 :** an ignorant insensitive person who is gullible to the point of disgust **:** PHILISTINE ⟨compared to the civilized and educated European, the American seemed a ~ —J.T.Farrell⟩

2boob \"\ *vb* -ED/-ING/-S *vi, slang* **:** to make a mistake **:** GOOF ~ *vt, slang* **:** to make a fool of **:** DUPE

3boob \"\ *n* -S [short for *booby* jail, short for *booby hutch*, prob. alter. of *booby hatch*] *chiefly Austral* **:** JAIL

boob·i·ly \ˈbübəlē, -li\ *adv* **:** in the manner of a booby

boo·boi·sie \,bübwäˈzē, -bwə'-\ *n* -S [1*boob* + -*oisie* (as in *bourgeoisie*)] **:** the class composed of all who are considered boobs ⟨Mencken began his linguistic crusade as part of his attack on middle-class stupidity and the ~ —W.C.Greet⟩

boo-boo \ˈbü,bü\ *n* -S [prob. baby-talk alter. of *boohoo*] **1** *dial* **:** a bruise or sore spot on the body ⟨he fell down and he's got a *boo-boo* on his forehead⟩ **2** *slang* **:** a foolish or embarrassing error **:** a stupid or careless mistake **:** BLUNDER, BONER ⟨committed a *boo-boo* at his press conference⟩

boobook owl \ˈbü(,)bu̇k-, -(,)bük-\ *also* **boobook** *n* -S [imit.] **:** a small Australian owl (*Ninox novae-seelandiae boobook*) or a related species of the Pacific islands

1boo·by \ˈbübē, -bi\ *n* -ES [modif. of Sp *bobo*, fr. L *balbus* stammering; akin to L *babulus* babbler — more at BABBLE] **1 :** an awkward foolish person **:** DOPE **2 :** any of several gannets (genus *Sula*) of tropical seas resembling the common gannet but smaller — see BLUE-FOOTED BOOBY, RED-FOOTED BOOBY **3 :** any of several American ducks; *esp* **:** RUDDY DUCK **4 :** the poorest of a group of performers or contestants **:** the player with the lowest score (as in a card game)

2booby \ˈbu̇bē, -bi\ *n* -ES [alter. of *bubby*] **:** BREAST — often considered vulgar

boo·by·al·la *or* **boo·bi·al·la** \,bübēˈalə\ *n* -S [native name in Australia] **1 :** an Australian wattle (*Acacia longifolia*) — called also *native willow* **2 :** any of several Australian trees of the genus *Myoporum* having alternate leaves and flowers in clusters (esp. *M. acuminatum*)

booby hatch \ˈbübē-\ *n* [perh. fr. *booby* (bird) + *hatch*; fr. its being a favorite resting place of these birds aboard ship] **1 :** a raised framework with a sliding cover over a small hatch; *specif* **:** a hatch in the stern leading to quarters below the deck **2** [influenced in meaning by *booby* (dunce)] **a :** an insane asylum **b :** a place felt to resemble an insane asylum (as in frantic or purposeless activity or in zany characters)

booby hutch *n* [1*booby*] **:** a covered horse-drawn vehicle used esp. in the 18th century

booby prize *n* [1*booby*] **1 :** an award for the poorest score or performance in a game or competition **2 :** an acknowledgement or recognition of notable inferiority ⟨he takes the *booby prize* for bad manners⟩

booby trap *n* [1*booby*] **1 :** a trap for the unwary or unsuspecting: **a :** a trap laid to play a trick on an unwary person ⟨*booby traps* with buckets of water suspended over doors —Robert Graves⟩ **b :** a concealed explosive device usu. attached to some harmless-looking object ⟨the *booby trap* exploded when he touched the doorknob⟩ **c :** an object wired to set off an explosion when touched ⟨the car, which they suspected might be a *booby trap* —*Combined Operations*⟩ **2 :** a critical or potentially dangerous aspect (as of a problem or situation) **:** PITFALL ⟨words and expressions which are *booby traps* when used in the other language —Richard Joseph⟩

booby-trap *vt* **:** to provide with a booby trap ⟨drivers should be trained thoroughly in careful driving through mined and *booby-trapped* roads —*Infantry Jour.*⟩ ⟨Congress . . . *booby=trapped* the bill with unworkable provisions —*Time*⟩

boo·die \ˈbüdē\ *n* -S [modif. of ScGael *bodach* old man, churl, miser, ghost, fr. *bod* penis; akin to OIr *bot* penis, Corn & W *both* nave of a wheel, boss of a shield, OSlav *gvozdĭ* nail] *Scot* **:** HOBGOBLIN

1boo·dle \ˈbüdᵊl\ *n* -S [D *boedel* estate, property, stock, lot (now usu. *boel* in sense "lot"), fr. MD; akin to OS *bōdlos* entire estate, OFris *bōdel* inheritance, ON *būth* booth — more at BOOTH] **1 :** a collection or lot of persons ⟨a big ~ of kids⟩ **:** PACK, CABOODLE **2 a** *slang* **:** counterfeit money **b :** money paid or taken for votes or political favors **:** bribe money ⟨the lobbyist can pocket the money earmarked for bribing and tell his client he passed on the ~ —Jack Lait & Lee Mortimer⟩ **c :** a large amount esp. of money ⟨he's got a ~ hidden away somewhere⟩ **d :** plunder or swag of any sort ⟨the ~ picked up by beachcombers after the storm⟩ **3 :** the game of Michigan

2boodle \"\ *vb* **boodled; boodled; boodling** \ˈbüd(ᵊ)liŋ\ **boodles** *vi* **:** to obtain money through bribery or swindling ~ *vt* **:** SWINDLE, DEFRAUD

boodle card *n* [1*boodle*] **:** a playing card displayed in a layout in various card games (as Michigan) and on which an extra stake is placed to be won by the player who holds or plays that card

boo·dler \ˈbüd(ᵊ)lə(r)\ *n* -S **:** a political grafter

boo·dling \ˈbüd(ᵊ)liŋ\ *n* -S **:** graft and fraud esp. in politics

booed *past of* BOO

boof \ˈbu̇f, ˈbüf\ *n* -S [imit.] **:** the sound made by a dog **:** BARK

1booger *var of* BUGGER

2boog·er \ˈbu̇gə(r)\ *or* **bug·ger** \" *also in sense 1* ˈbəg-\ *n* -S [alter. (prob. influenced by *booger* bugger) of *boggart*] **1 :** BOOGEYMAN **2** *dial* **:** a piece of dried nasal mucus

3booger \"\ *vb* **boogered; boogered; boogering;** \ˈbu̇g(ə)riŋ\ **boogers** *vi, of an animal* **:** to take fright **:** SHY ⟨this horse ~*s* a little at gunfire⟩ ~ *vt, West* **:** to frighten or startle (an animal) into shying or running wild ⟨the cattle were already through the pasture gate when something ~*ed* them —Ross Santee⟩

4booger \"\ *n* -S [prob. alter. (influenced by *booger* boogeyman) of *bug*] *chiefly Midland* **:** HEAD LOUSE

booger dance *n* [2*booger*] **:** a grotesque masked dance included in a satirical mimetic episode of Cherokee Indian winter festivals

boo·gey·man \ˈbu̇gē,man, ˈbüg-, ˈbōg-, ˈgə-, -ma(a)(ə)n *also* ,man\ *or* **boo·ger·man** \-gə(r)-,\ *also* **boo·gie·man** \-gē-, -gə-,\ *n, pl* **boogeymen** *or* **boogermen** *also* **boogiemen** [*boogey*, *boogie* (alter. of 2*booger*) *or* 1*booger* + *man*] *dial* **:** a monstrous imaginary figure used in threatening children ⟨be good or the ~ will get you⟩

boog·ie *also* **boogy** \ˈbu̇gē, ˈbügē, -gi\ *n, pl* **boogies** [prob. alter. of *booger* (boogeyman)] *slang* **:** NEGRO — usu. used disparagingly

1boog·ie-woog·ie \¦bu̇gēˌwu̇gē, ¦bügēˌwü-\ *also* **boogie** *n* -S [origin unknown] **1 a :** a percussive style of playing blues on the piano characterized by a persistent rhythmic ground bass and florid figurations of a simple melody **b :** a piece so played **2 :** a jitterbug dance danced to boogie-woogie music in a sway-backed posture with motions throughout the body, the basic step being a double side step with toe-heel accent

2boogie-woogie \"\ *vi* -ED/-ING/-S **:** to dance the boogie-woogie

boo·gum \ˈbügəm\ *or* **boo·jum** \-üjəm\ *n* -S [perh. fr. *boojum*, an imaginary creature in *The Hunting of the Snark* by Lewis Carroll (C.S.Dodgson) †1898 Eng. mathematician & writer; fr. its grotesque appearance] **:** a spiny tree (*Idria columnaris*) of the family Fouquieriaceae chiefly of Lower California sometimes arching over and rooting at its tips

boo·hoo \bü'hü, ˈ=,=\ *vi* -ED/-ING/-S [imit.] **:** to weep loudly and with sobs ⟨he ~*ed* when he skinned his knee⟩

bo·oi·dea \bōˈōidēə\ [NL, alter. of *Boidea*] *syn of* BOVOIDEA

booing *pres part of* BOO

1book \ˈbu̇k\ *n* -S [ME, fr. OE *bōc*; akin to OHG *buoh* book, ON *bōk*, Goth *bōka* letter, OE *bōc* beech; prob. fr. the early Germanic use of beech wood as a medium for the carving of runic characters — more at BEECH] **1 a** *obs* **:** a formal written document; *esp* **:** a deed of conveyance of land — see BOOKLAND **b** (1) **:** a collection of written sheets of skin or tablets of wood or ivory (2) **:** a continuous roll of parchment or a strip of parchment creased between columns and folded like an accordion **c :** a collection of written, printed, or blank sheets fastened together along one edge and usu. trimmed at the other edges to form a single series of uniform leaves; *specif* **:** a collection of folded sheets bearing printing or writing that have been cut, sewn, and usu. bound between covers into a volume **d** (1) **:** a stack of sheets of paper interleaved alternately with the material whose finish the paper acquires after it passes through the plater — called also *form* (2) **:** the printed but unfolded and uncut sheets for a book **e :** a long systematic literary composition **f :** a major division of a treatise or literary work ⟨an epic in 12 ~*s*⟩ **g :** any of the records (as the daybook, cashbook, salesbook, journal, ledger) in which a systematic record of business transactions may be kept — often used in pl. ⟨their ~*s* show a profit⟩ **h** *in U.S. copyright law* **:** any of various written or printed materials: as (1) **:** a bound volume (2) **:** a private letter (3) **:** a telephone or trade directory (4) **:** an article in an encyclopedia **1 :** a magazine or publication in magazine format **2** *cap* **:** BIBLE ⟨he swore on the *Book* that it was so⟩ **3 a** *obs* **:** LEARNING, STUDY, SCHOLARSHIP **b books** *pl, chiefly Midland* **:** school or the time spent in school ⟨~*s* took up at 8 o'clock —H.E.Giles⟩ **4 a :** something felt to be a source of enlightenment or instruction ⟨drew his knowledge from the great ~ of nature⟩ ⟨her face was an open ~⟩ **b** (1) **:** a particular set of facts, circumstances, or ideas ⟨his past is an open ~⟩ (2) **:** an area of experience or knowledge ⟨calculus was a closed ~ to him⟩ **c :** the total available knowledge and experience that can be brought to bear on a task or problem ⟨tried every trick in the ~ to win the election⟩ **5 a :** an official or personal set of standards, rules, or policies ⟨mules did not, according to the ~, scratch their heads with their hind feet —Herbert Hoover⟩ ⟨the sergeant ran his squad by the ~⟩ **b :** JUDGMENT, OPINION ⟨in my ~ he is a magician with the flute⟩ ⟨in his ~ every man was a neighbor —Alison Blake⟩ **6 a :** the aggregate charges that can be made or pressed against an accused person — usu. used with *throw* ⟨he thought he'd get off with just a reprimand, but they threw the ~ at him⟩ **b :** a position from which one must answer for certain acts **:** ACCOUNT — usu. used with *bring* or *call* ⟨our system of bringing the guilty to ~ —Felix Frankfurter⟩ **7 a :** a libretto esp. of an opera or musical comedy **b :** the script of a play **c :** the repertory of an orchestra or a musician **8 :** a packet of commodities bound together for convenient dispensing and usu. removed and used one at a time ⟨a ~ of 3¢ stamps⟩ ⟨a ~ of matches⟩; *specif* **:** a bundle of skeins of raw silk often 30 in number **9 a** (1) **:** BOOKMAKER (2) **:** a bookmaker's business or base of operations **b :** an event or

BOOK SIZES

The names of book sizes are based on the old system still widely used of considering the size of a page as a fraction of the large sheet of paper on which it was printed. This system is illustrated in Table I below. In printing books an even number (as 4, 8, 16, 24, 32, 48, 64) of pages is printed on each side of a single large sheet which is then folded so that the pages are in proper sequence and the outside edges are cut so that the book will open. Except for the largest size, the folio, the name of the size indicates the fractional part of the sheet one page occupies (as octavo "eighth"). In this system, since the fractional name alone cannot denote an exact size, the name of the sheet size precedes the fractional name. Thus, *royal octavo* is understood to designate a page one-eighth the size of a royal sheet, *medium octavo* a page one-eighth the size of a medium sheet, and *crown octavo* one-eighth the size of a crown sheet. But paper is cut into many sheet sizes and even the terms *crown*, *medium*, and *royal* do not always designate sheets of the same dimensions. Three of the more common sheet sizes have been selected: royal 20 x 25 inches, medium 18 x 23 inches, and crown 15 x 19 inches. Actual page sizes run a little smaller than calculations since the sheets, when folded to page size, are trimmed at top, outside, and bottom, the inside edge becoming part of the binding. British sheet size sometimes differs slightly from American.

Table II illustrates the size names as they are used by the American Library Association, with only the octavo sizes including the name of a sheet size. The dimensional limits given in the table remain standard for this system.

Table III gives equivalent terms and symbols for the size names.

TABLE I

SIZE NAME	TIMES SHEET FOLDED	LEAVES TO SHEET	PAGES TO SHEET	SIZE OF PAGE IN INCHES
royal folio	1	2	4	20 x 12½
royal quarto	2	4	8	12½ x 10
royal octavo	3	8	16	10 x 6¼
royal sixteenmo	4	16	32	6¼ x 5
royal thirty-twomo	5	32	64	5 x 3⅛
royal sixty-fourmo	6	64	128	3⅛ x 2½
medium folio	1	2	4	18 x 11½
medium quarto	2	4	8	11½ x 9
medium octavo	3	8	16	9 x 5¾
medium sixteenmo	4	16	32	5¾ x 4½
medium thirty-twomo	5	32	64	4½ x 2⅞
medium sixty-fourmo	6	64	128	2⅞ x 2¼
crown folio	1	2	4	15 x 10
crown quarto	2	4	8	10 x 7½
crown octavo	3	8	16	7½ x 5
crown sixteenmo	4	16	32	5 x 3¾
crown thirty-twomo	5	32	64	3¾ x 2½
crown sixty-fourmo	6	64	128	2½ x 1⅞

TABLE II
SCALE OF THE AMERICAN LIBRARY ASSOCIATION

SIZE NAME	SYMBOL	OUTSIDE HEIGHT[1]	APPROX. SIZE[2] IN INCHES
folio	F	over 30 cm	12 x 19
quarto	Q	25–30 cm	9½ x 12
octavo	O	20–25 cm	6 x 9
imperial octavo	O		8¼ x 11½
super octavo	O		7 x 11
royal octavo	O		6½ x 10
medium octavo	O		6⅛ x 9¼
crown octavo	O		5⅜ x 8
duodecimo	D	17.5–20 cm	5 x 7⅜
duodecimo (large)	D	17.5–20 cm	5½ x 7½
sextodecimo	S	15–17.5 cm	4 x 6¾
octodecimo	T	12.5–15 cm	4 x 6½
trigesimo-secundo	Tt	10–12.5 cm	3½ x 5½
quadragesimo-octavo	Fe	7.5–10 cm	2½ x 4
sexagesimo-quarto	Sf	less than 7.5 cm	2 x 3

[1]Outside height refers to the head-to-foot dimension of the book's cover.
[2]Approximate size refers to the front cover's rectangular dimensions.

TABLE III
SIZE NAMES AND THEIR EQUIVALENTS

OLD	MODERN—PREFERRED BY PRINTERS	ABBR	SYMBOL[1]
folio	folio	fo *or* f	
quarto	quarto	4to	4°
sexto	sixmo	6to *or* 6mo	6°
octavo	octavo	8vo	8°
duodecimo[2]	twelvemo	12mo	12°
sextodecimo	sixteenmo	16mo	16°
octodecimo	eighteenmo	18mo	18°
vincesimo-quarto } vigesimo-quarto }	twenty-fourmo	24mo	24°
trigesimo-secundo	thirty-twomo	32mo	32°
quadragesimo-octavo	forty-eightmo	48mo	48°
sexagesimo-quarto	sixty-fourmo	64mo	64°

[1]Note also in Table II the symbols used by the American Library Association.
[2]For the terms duodecimo, sextodecimo, etc., printers often use "twelve" or "twelves," "sixteen" or "sixteens," etc. (as in "an ordinary *sixteen*"; "a sheet of *sixteens*")

contingency on which a bookmaker will accept bets together with the odds offered **c :** the record kept by a bookmaker of bets placed with him ⟨he makes ~ on dog races⟩ **d :** a participant or onlooker in a game (as craps) who accepts bets on its contingencies **e :** BANKER 2c **f :** [3]POOL 1b **10 a :** the number of tricks a card player or side must win before any trick can have scoring value: (1) *whist* **:** six tricks (2) *bridge* **:** six tricks for declarer and for his opponents the greatest number declarer can lose without being defeated **b :** a set of cards having scoring value (as all four cards of one kind in authors) **c** *archaic* **:** a deck of cards **11 :** the omasum of a ruminant **12 :** a thick aggregate of mica usu. consisting of a single crystal of considerable dimension in the direction perpendicular to the cleavage **13 :** a stack of half leaves of tobacco from which the stems have been cut **14 :** flat sections of stage scenery joined by hinges ⟨a ~ ceiling⟩ **15 :** a record of membership esp. in a union — **in one's bad books :** in disfavor with one — **in one's book :** in one's own opinion ⟨a trainer of the old school — and *in my book*, there's no better school —G.F.T.Ryall⟩ — **in one's good books :** in favor with one — **one for the book :** an act or occurrence worth recording **:** a notable performance **:** RECORD ⟨that play is *one for the book*⟩ — **on the books :** on the records **:** ENROLLED — **without book 1 :** without authority **2 :** from memory or by rote

[2]book \"\ *vb* -ED/-ING/-S [ME *boken*, fr. OE *bōcian*, fr. *bōc* book] *vt* **1** *obs* **:** to convey or grant (land or property) by charter **2 :** to enter, write, or register (as a name, an act, or an intention) in a record, book, or list: **a :** to engage transportation or conveyance for ⟨a load of eggs ~*ed* for Chicago⟩ ⟨he is ~*ed* to sail Monday⟩ **b :** to schedule a program of engagements for ⟨the orchestra was ~*ed* for a week at the hotel⟩ **c :** to set aside time for **:** SCHEDULE ⟨the president ~*ed* a strategy meeting⟩ **d :** to reserve in advance — chiefly Brit. in all but past participial use and often used with *up* ⟨he paid the dinner bill and stopped to ~ cinema seats⟩ ⟨sorry, but we're all ~*ed* up⟩ **3 :** to enter the name of and tentative charges against (a person) usu. in a police register ⟨they ~*ed* him on suspicion⟩ **4 :** to accept (bets) as a bookmaker ~ *vi* **1 :** to express in advance a desire for something in order to reserve it ⟨we should have ~*ed*⟩ **2 :** *chiefly Brit* **:** to register in a hotel — usu. used with *in* ⟨we went to a hotel and ~*ed* in⟩

[3]book \"\ *adj* **1 a :** put down in writing **:** FORMAL **b :** BOOKISH **2 a :** derived from or based on the matter in a book ⟨an ounce of mother-wit . . . is worth a stone of *book*-knowledge — F.T.Palgrave⟩; *specif* **:** theoretical as opposed to practical ⟨~ farming⟩ **b :** correct or advisable according to a book accepted as authoritative ⟨a ~ bid in bridge⟩ **3 :** shown by a system of accounting ⟨~ value⟩ ⟨the ~ strength of the enemy⟩

book·a·ble \-kəbəl\ *adj, chiefly Brit* **:** that may be booked or reserved in advance ⟨all seats ~ for matinee⟩

book account *n* **:** CURRENT ACCOUNT 1a

book agent *n* **:** a book salesman

bookbinder \'ˌˌ=\ *n* [ME, fr. *book* + *binder*] **:** one that binds or repairs books — called also *binder*

bookbindery \'ˌˌ(=)=\ *n* -ES **:** a place where bookbinding is done

bookbinding \'ˌˌ=\ *n* -S **1 :** the binding of a book **2 :** the trade or art of a bookbinder

book boat *n* **:** a boat fitted with bookshelves and used as a mobile branch library

book burning *n* **:** destruction of writings or pictures regarded as politically or socially harmful or subversive or produced by persons whose ideas or acts are so regarded

book card *n* **:** a record card retained by the library when a book is lent

bookcase \'ˌ=\ *n* **1 :** a case for books; *esp* **:** one having several shelves often with doors **2 :** [2]CASE 2e

book clamp *n* **:** a clamp to hold or press books (as for binding or marbling)

book cloth *n* **:** any of several specially woven fabrics (as cotton) prepared for use in covering books

book club *n* **1 a :** a group of people who buy books for circulation among the group **b :** a club of booklovers or of people with literary interests **2 :** a commercial organization that sends and sells to its members at regular intervals selected new books sometimes of a particular kind and often at discount

book code *n* **:** a code based on an ordinary book or dictionary, the plaintext words being identified by page and line

book corner *n* **:** a protective cap for the corner of a book

bookdealer \'ˌˌ=\ *n* **:** one who deals in books

book debt *n* **:** the amount owed on a current account

booked *adj* **1 :** entered, registered, or otherwise placed in a book **2 a :** engaged or contracted for **b** *Brit, of tickets* **:** SOLD, RESERVED

bookend \'ˌ=\ *n* **:** a supporting device placed at the end of a row of books

book·er \-kə(r)\ *n* -S **:** one that books: as **a :** one that schedules or secures reservations for a traveler or engagements for a performer **b :** BOOKMAKER **c :** one that removes the stems from tobacco leaves by machine and arranges the half leaves into books **d :** a worker in a rubber-goods factory who puts strips of rubber or rubberized material between layers of cloth to facilitate handling

bookends

book·ery \'bu̇k(ə)rē\ *n* -ES **1** *archaic* **:** LIBRARY **2 :** BOOKSTORE

book·e·te·ria *also* **book·a·te·ria** \ˌbu̇kə'tirēə\ *n* -S [*booketeria* fr. [1]*book* + *-eteria* (as in *cafeteria*); *bookateria*, alter. of *booketeria*] **1 :** a self-service bookstore **2 :** a self-service free lending library carrying books owned by a public library but housed elsewhere (as at a grocery store or branch post office)

bookfair \'ˌ=\ *n* **1 :** a display or exhibit of books typically by a group of publishers or bookdealers for promoting sales and stimulating interest **2 :** a fair or bazaar at which books are sold or auctioned to raise money for some worthy cause

book fell *n* [ME, fr. OE *bōcfell*, fr. *bōc* book + *fell* skin — more at BOOK, FELL] **:** a sheet or manuscript of vellum or parchment

book–fold \'ˌ=\ *n* **:** a method of folding cloth so that it can be opened like the pages of a book

book gill *n* **:** a gill found in the king crabs that consists of membranous folds arranged like the leaves of a book

book hand *n* **:** the handwriting designed primarily for legibility and beauty and ordinarily used in officially transcribing manuscripts intended for preservation before printing became common — compare MINUSCULE, RUSTIC CAPITAL, UNCIAL

bookholder \'ˌˌ=\ *n* **:** a device that supports a book — compare BOOKRACK, BOOKREST

bookhunter \'ˌˌ=\ *n* **:** one that looks for books to be bought

book·ie \'bu̇kē, -ki\ *n* -S [by shortening & alter.] **:** BOOKMAKER 2

bookier *comparative of* BOOKY

bookiest *superlative of* BOOKY

booking *n* -S **1 :** the act of one that books **2 :** an engagement or scheduled performance ⟨she has ~*s* to sing several concerts next fall⟩ **3 :** RESERVATION; *esp* **:** one for transportation, entertainment, or lodging ⟨the porter will help with ticket and theatre ~*s*⟩ **4 :** ORDER 3b(2) — usu. used in pl.

booking clerk *n* **1 :** one who registers passengers, baggage, or freight for conveyance **2 :** a ticket seller

booking hall *n, Brit* **:** a room or hall in a railway station that contains the ticket office

booking office *n, chiefly Brit* **:** a ticket office; *esp* **:** one in a railroad station

book inventory *n* **:** an inventory (as of stock or goods) shown on the books of account—distinguished from *physical inventory;* compare PERPETUAL INVENTORY

book·ish \'bu̇kish, -kēsh\ *adj* **1 a :** of or relating to books ⟨a ~ pastime⟩ ⟨a ~ career⟩ ⟨a ~ life⟩ **b :** fond of books and reading ⟨a ~ farmer who carried favorite volumes in his saddle bags —Will Irwin⟩ **2 a :** inclined to rely on knowledge obtained from books as opposed to that gained from practical experience ⟨a ~ approach to life⟩ ⟨a ~ cast of mind⟩ **b** (1) **:** literary and formal as opposed to colloquial and informal ⟨a ~ way of speaking⟩ (2) **:** affectedly learned or pedantic ⟨a ~ writer overly bent on giving his sources and authority to the detriment of both interest and communication⟩ — **book·ish·ly** *adv*

bookit *var of* BOUKIT

book jacket *n* **:** JACKET 3f(1)

bookkeeper \'ˌˌ=\ *n* **:** one who keeps accounts **:** one whose business or vocation is bookkeeping — distinguished from *accountant*

bookkeeping \'ˌˌ=\ *n* **1 :** a branch of accounting that deals with the systematic classification, recording, and summarizing of business and financial transactions in books of account **2 :** the act or practice of keeping books of account

bookkeeping machine *n* **:** a key-operated business machine designed esp. for the keeping of office records and usu. equipped for posting such information as date, description of item, folio number, debits, credits, or extended balances and for such relevant operations as addition, subtraction, or cross computation

book label *n* **:** a book owner's identification label that is usu. small and of distinctive design and is affixed inside the front cover of a book — compare BOOKPLATE

bookland \'bu̇ˌkland\ *n* [trans. of OE *bōcland*] **:** land granted by a book or charter in Anglo-Saxon England

book·lear \'bu̇ˌkler\ *n* [[1]*book* + Sc *lear* learning — more at LEAR] *Scot* **:** BOOK LEARNING

book–learned *in sense 1* 'ˌlərnəd, -lən-; *in sense 2* 'ˌlərnd, -lənd\ *adj* **1 a :** marked by book learning **b :** BOOKISH **2 :** learned through books rather than from practical experience or application

book learning *n* **1 :** learning acquired from books as distinguished from practical knowledge **2 :** formal education **:** SCHOOLING

book·less \'bu̇kləs\ *adj, archaic* **:** UNLEARNED, UNSCHOLARLY

book·let \-lət\ *n* -S **1 :** a usu. paper-covered publication in book format ranging in size from a few pages to a small-scale edition of a book **2 :** STAMP BOOKLET

booklet pane *or* **booklet leaf** *n* **:** PANE 3b

booklift \'ˌ=\ *n* **:** a small usu. electric and automatic lift for moving books from tier to tier in a library

book list *n* **:** a reading list of books having some unifying feature

book·lore \'ˌ=\ *n* [alter. (influenced by *lore*) of Sc *booklear*] **:** BOOK LEARNING

book louse *n* **:** any of several minute wingless insects of the order Corrodentia; *usu* **:** an insect of the family Atropidae (esp. *Liposcelis divinatorius*) that is injurious to books and papers — called also *deathwatch*

booklover \'ˌˌ=\ *n* **:** one fond of books — compare BIBLIOPHILE

book lung *n* **:** a saccular breathing organ occurring in many arachnids that contains numerous thin folds of membrane arranged like the leaves of a book through which gaseous exchange takes place

bookmaker \'ˌˌ=\ *n* **1 :** one that makes books: as **a :** a printer, binder, or designer of books **b :** one that compiles books from the writings of others **2 :** one that determines odds and receives and pays off bets ⟨he placed $2 with the ~ on a horse that never ran⟩

bookmaking \'ˌˌ=\ *n* [ME, fr. *book* + *making*] **1 :** the making of books — used to include design, illustration, typography, materials, and production **2 :** the business of a bookmaker

book·man \'bu̇kmən, -ˌman\ *n, pl* **bookmen 1 :** one having to do with books: as **a :** a man of letters **:** SCHOLAR ⟨the ~ . . . appreciates, enjoys, he communicates pleasure —Van Wyck Brooks⟩ **b :** a bookdealer or book salesman **2 :** the clerk of a tobacco auction

bookmark \'ˌ=\ *or* **bookmarker** \'ˌˌ=\ *n* **:** a narrow strip of material (as an attached ribbon, an insertable card, or a leather slip) to mark a place in a book

book–match \'ˌ=\ *vt* [so called fr. the resemblance of two book-matched pieces of veneer to two opposing pages of a book] **:** to match the grains of (a pair of sheets of veneer or plywood) for symmetrical effect in such a way that one sheet seems to be the mirrored image of the other

book match *n* **:** one of the matches in a matchbook

book·mo·bile \'bu̇kmōˌbēl\ *n* -S [[1]*book* + *automobile*] **:** an autotruck with shelves of books that serves as an itinerant library or bookstore

book mold *n* **:** a split foundry mold hinged at the side

book muslin *n* **1 :** muslin used to strengthen the backbone construction of books **2 :** a thin muslin formerly used for women's dresses

book number *n* **:** a combination of letters and figures used to distinguish an individual book from all others having the same library classification number

book of account 1 : LEDGER **2 :** BOOK OF ORIGINAL ENTRY **3 :** a book or record essential to a system of accounts

book of hours *sometimes cap B&H* **:** a book containing prayers or offices appointed to be said at the canonical hours

book of original entry 1 : JOURNAL **2 :** any one of the books of account in which a transaction is first recorded

book palm *n* **:** an East Indian palm (*Corypha taliera*) whose leaves furnish a substitute for paper — called also *taliera*

book paper *n* **:** a paper suitable for printing books, magazines, and advertising matter including many grades of plain and coated papers but excluding newsprint

bookplate \'ˌ=\ *n* **1 :** a book owner's identification label that is usu. engraved or printed, has a distinctive design, and is pasted to the inside front cover of a book — called also *ex libris;* compare BOOK LABEL **2 :** the plate from which a bookplate is printed

book post *n, chiefly Brit* **:** a postal service providing special low rates for books

book profit *n* **:** profit as shown in or according to books of account

bookrack \'ˌ=\ *n* **:** a rack for holding books

book rate *n* **:** the reduced rate at which books may be sent through the mails

bookrest \'ˌ=\ *n* **:** a support that holds a book while it is being read

book review *n* **1 :** a descriptive and critical or evaluative account of a book **2 :** a newspaper supplement or magazine devoted chiefly to book reviews ⟨a typical book campaign in eight important *book reviews* —*Publishers' Weekly*⟩

book reviewer *n* **:** one who reviews books esp. for a magazine or newspaper

books *pl of* BOOK, *pres 3d sing of* BOOK

book scorpion *n* **:** any of various minute arachnids of the order Pseudoscorpiones that feed on small insects, mites, or other minute animals

bookseller \'ˌˌ=\ *n* **:** one whose business is dealing in books; *esp* **:** the proprietor of a bookstore

book sewer \'ˌˌ=\ *n* **:** one that sews sections together to form books

book–sewing \'ˌˌ=\ *adj* **:** of or relating to the sewing of books

bookshelf \'ˌ=\ *n, pl* **bookshelves :** an open shelf for holding books; *esp* **:** a series of such shelves

book square *n* **:** SQUARE 13

bookstack \'ˌ=\ *n* **:** STACK 7

bookstall \'ˌ=\ *n* **1 :** a stall where books are sold **2** *chiefly Brit* **:** NEWSSTAND ⟨bought a copy of *Punch* at the ~ in the station⟩

book stamp *n* **1 :** a metal plate or die for stamping book covers **2 :** a postage stamp printed for or included in a stamp booklet

bookstore *also* **bookshop** \'ˌ=\ *n* **:** a place of business where books are the main item offered for sale

book support *n* **:** BOOKEND

booksy \'bu̇ksē\ *adj* **:** affectedly or pretentiously intellectual ⟨a ~ crowd⟩

book table *n* **:** a table with shelves beneath for books

book tile *n* **:** a flat clay building tile that has hollow sections, that is usu. 2 to 3 inches thick, 12 inches wide, and from 16 to 24 inches long, and that is shaped roughly like a closed book so that adjoining pieces fit into each other

book truck *n* **1 :** a small wheeled vehicle typically with two or three shelves used esp. in libraries for moving books **2 :** BOOKMOBILE

book value *n* **:** the value of something as shown in or according to the books of account of a business; *specif* **:** the value of capital stock as indicated by the excess of assets over liabilities — distinguished from *market value*

book van *n, Brit* **:** BOOKMOBILE

book wagon *n* **:** BOOKMOBILE

book word *n* **:** a word learned solely or principally from reading and often understood without knowledge of its customary pronunciation ⟨*eleemosynary* is a *book word*⟩ ⟨fine *book words* and long sentences —Charles Kingsley⟩

bookwork \'ˌ=\ *n* **1 :** the manufacture of books as distinct from newspaper or magazine printing or from job work **2 :** work that involves the use of books: as **a :** SCHOOLWORK **b :** PAPER WORK ⟨tax ~ is to be made a little easier for businessmen —*U.S. News & World Report*⟩

bookworm \'ˌ=\ *n* **1 :** the larva of any of various moths or beetles (as the drugstore beetle) that injures books by feeding on the binding and paste and often piercing the leaves **2 :** one unusually devoted to reading or studying books

book wrapper *n* **:** JACKET

booky \'bu̇kē\ *adj, often* -ER/-EST **:** BOOKISH

[1]bool \'bü(ə)l\ *dial var of* BOWL

[2]bool \"\ *n* -S [ME (Scottish dial.) *bowl*, prob. fr. MD *boghel* bow, hoop; akin to MLG *bogel* hoop, OE *būgan* to bend — more at BOW] **1** *dial Brit* **:** any of various objects with a curve or bend (as a semicircular handle, the bow of a key or scissors) **2** *dial Brit* **:** a wooden hoop forming part of the framework of a basket **3 :** a hoop for rolling

[3]bool \"\ *n* -S [ME *boule* ball — more at BOWL] *Scot* **:** a child's marble

bool·e·an *also* **bool·i·an** \'bülēən\ *adj, usu cap* [George *Boole* †1860 Eng. mathematician and logician + E *-an, -ian*] **:** relating to the mathematical or logical systems of Boole

boolean algebra *n, usu cap B* **:** an uninterpreted logical calculus arranged as a deductive system of theorems derived from a set of undefined primitive symbols together with axioms concerning these symbols; *esp* **:** an uninterpreted algebra of classes

bool·ie \'bülē, -li\ *var of* BOWLY

boo·ly \'bülē, -li\ *n* -ES [IrGael *buaile* cattle pen, fr. OIr *būale*, prob. fr. L *bovile, bubile* cattle stall, fr. *bov-, bos* head of cattle — more at COW] **1 :** a temporary enclosure once common in Ireland for the shelter of cattle or their keepers **2 :** a company of herdsmen wandering with their cattle

[1]boom \'büm\ *vt* -ED/-ING/-S [D *bomen*, fr. *boom* tree, pole, beam] **1 :** to extend, move, or manipulate with a boom — usu. used with *off* or *out* ⟨~ out a sail⟩ **2 a :** to confine (logs) by means of a boom **b :** to supply (a body of water) with a boom or booms **3 :** to lift and position (a load attached to a derrick) by raising and swinging the boom

[2]boom \"\ *n* -S *often attrib* [D, tree, pole, beam, fr. MD; akin to OHG *boum* tree — more at BEAM] **1 :** a long spar projecting from a ship used variously to extend the foot of a sail or facilitate handling of cargo or mooring — see SHIP illustration **2 :** any of various devices resembling a ship's boom in appearance or function used usu. to maneuver a piece of equipment into a desired position: as **a :** a long beam projecting from the mast of a derrick to support or guide the body to be lifted or swung **b :** a long movable arm used to manipulate a microphone in a radio, motion-picture, or television studio **3 :** a 2-masted sailing ship used for coastal trade and pearling in the eastern Mediterranean and Indian ocean **4 a :** a line of connected floating timbers across a river or enclosing an area of water to keep saw logs together; *also* **:** the enclosed logs **b :** an obstruction formed of floating logs that retards the flow of a stream **c :** a similar construction arranged to guide floating logs in a certain direction **5 :** a long wooden bar of more or less elliptical cross section supported horizontally and adjustable as to height and used as a support in executing gymnastic stunts and exercises **6 :** a chain cable or line of spars extended across a river or the mouth of a harbor to defend it by obstructing navigation **7 :** a spar or outrigger connecting the tail surfaces and the main supporting structure of an airplane — called also *tail boom*

[3]boom \"\ *vb* -ED/-ING/-S [imit.] *vi* **1 a :** to make a deep hollow sound ⟨the cannon ~*ed* from the deck⟩ ⟨surf ~*ing* on the distant shore⟩ **b :** to utter a deep resonant cry with a hollow note (as of a bird) ⟨in some deep canyon a night owl started ~*ing* —F.B.Gipson⟩ **c :** to make a sonorous humming or croaking sound (as of an insect or animal) ⟨two frogs ~*ed* again, close at hand —William Beebe⟩ **2 a :** to move swiftly and with a booming sound (as of a ship under full sail) **b** *of a person* **:** to move about from place to place idly **:** BUM, TRAMP **3 a** *of a river* **:** to rise suddenly (as during a spring freshet); *specif* **:** to reach a height sufficient to float logs **b** *of logs* **:** to float down a river that is booming **4 a :** to have a sudden increase in popular esteem or importance often occasioned by a compelling exhortation or appeal ⟨the movement to elect him president began to ~ early in the convention⟩ **b :** to experience a sudden rapid growth and expansion usu. including or implying an increase in market value ⟨business was ~*ing*⟩ ⟨stocks began to ~⟩ **c :** to develop rapidly in population and importance often as a result of location or connection with a feature that draws people to the region ⟨California began to ~ when gold was discovered there⟩ ~ *vt* **1 :** to sound forth or give out with a resonant or booming sound — often used with *out* ⟨a 21-gun salute ~*ed* out by the artillery⟩ **2 a :** to cause a rapid growth or increase of (as in price, sales, commercial development, influence, prestige) ⟨skyrocketing rates and unregulated bookings are ~*ing* the market —Eliot Janeway⟩ **b :** to work for and encourage such growth or increase in ⟨real estate operators hopefully tried to ~ the area —*Amer. Guide Series: Conn.*⟩ **:** PUSH, BOOST ⟨enthusiasts ~*ed* the old soldier —E.T.Folliard⟩

[4]boom \"\ *n* -S **1 :** a booming sound: as **a :** a roar esp. of waves **b :** the cry of a bird or animal that booms ⟨the ~ of a bittern⟩ **2 :** a strong rapid expansion movement: as **a :** advocacy and progression into favor of a candidate for office **b :** rapid and often forced settlement and development of a town or district ⟨the Klondike ~ came with the gold rush⟩ **c :** an expansion of economic activity that is characterized by optimistic expectations, increased employment, rising prices and production, and credit expansion ⟨the manufacturing ~ of the reconstruction period following the Civil War —*Amer. Guide Series: Conn.*⟩ ⟨in the midst of an $8,500,000 building ~ —*N.Y.Times*⟩ **d :** the period during which such expansion occurs ⟨during the ~, tremendous tasks of production and administration are performed —Philip Klein⟩

[5]boom \"\ *adj* **:** participating in, arising from, or maintained by an economic boom ⟨the ~ days of lumbering⟩ ⟨~ towns appeared overnight⟩ ⟨~ prices⟩

boom·age \-mij\ *n* -S [[2]*boom* + *-age*] **:** a tax or toll formerly paid for the use of a log boom

boom–and–bust \ˌ=ˌ=\ *n* [[4]*boom*] **:** an alternation of prosperity and depression; *specif* **:** alternate periods of high and low levels of economic activity in the business cycle ⟨we're in for the biggest *boom-and-bust* . . . that we've ever seen —Hal Borland⟩

boom cat *n* [[2]*boom*] **1 :** a derrick mounted on a caterpillar tractor **2 :** one who operates a power shovel at a strip mine to remove overlying ground and load coal into cars

boom crutch *n* [[2]*boom*] **:** a movable prop to support the free end of a ship's boom when it is not in use

boom·das·sie \'bümˌdasē\ *n* -S [Afrik *boomdas*, fr. *boom* tree (fr. MD) + *dassie*, dim. of *das* badger, fr. MD; akin to OHG *boum* tree and to OHG *dahs* badger — more at BEAM, TECHNICAL] **:** any of several African arboreal coneys (genus *Dendrohyrax*) **:** TREE HYRAX

boomed *past of* BOOM

[1]boom·er \'bümə(r)\ *n* -S *often attrib* [[3]*boom* + *-er*] **1 :** one that booms **2 :** one that joins a rush of settlers to a boom area **3 :** a person who moves around the country and works at his trade wherever he happens to be usu. keeping a job for a relatively short period ⟨~*s* who have drifted in from such places as Greenland or Morocco run dredges, build railroads, drive piles —*Time*⟩ **4 a :** MOUNTAIN BEAVER **b :** a large male kangaroo; *specif* **:** GIANT KANGAROO **c** *South & Midland* **:** RED SQUIRREL 1 **5 :** a seller of Salvation Army literature

[2]boomer *n* -S [[2]*boom* + *-er*] **:** a lever-operated device for tightening chains that hold a load (as of logs or pipe) on a truck — called also *load binder*

[1]boo·mer·ang \'bümə,raŋ\ *n* -s *often attrib* [native name in Australia] **1 :** a bent or angular throwing club usu. somewhat flat which can be thrown so as to return near the starting point **2 :** a statement or action that backfires on its originator ⟨such crude methods of conquest would serve as a ~ —Paul Blanshard⟩ **3** [influenced in meaning by [2]*boom*] **a :** a movable platform for supporting painters of theater scenery at various convenient heights **b :** a movable stand or arm for supporting stage lights at various levels

boomerangs

[2]**boomerang** \"\ *vi* -ED/-ING/-S **1 :** to return in the manner of a boomerang **2 :** to produce by word or deed a result directly opposed to that intended; *esp* **:** to injure the originator (as of a policy) instead of the intended target **:** BACKFIRE ⟨his . . . policy had ~*ed* disastrously —*U.N. World*⟩

boom hoist *n* [[2]*boom*] **:** a hoist having a spar projecting from the mast to support and guide the load **:** DERRICK

boom·i·ness \'bümēnəs\ *n* -ES [*boomy* + *-ness*] **:** an excessive amount of bass in the sound reproduced by a loudspeaker

[1]**booming** *adj* -ER/-EST [fr. pres. part. of [3]*boom*] **1 :** making or performing an action with a booming sound ⟨his ~ voice⟩ ⟨the ~ river⟩ **2 :** increasing or growing rapidly ⟨a ~ railroad center⟩ ⟨~ wheat prices⟩ — **boom·ing·ly** *adv*

[2]**booming** *n* -s [fr. gerund of [3]*boom*] **1 :** the sound or act of one that booms **2 :** the process of discharging water behind a dam down a hillside or gorge to wash out deposits of gold

booming ground *n* **:** an area in which the male of certain grouse (as the prairie chicken) takes his stand during the breeding season and performs his characteristic nuptial display accompanied by booming or drumming sounds produced by vibrating the wings in air

boomkin *var of* BUMPKIN

boom·less \'bümləs\ *adj* **:** being without a boom

boom·let \'bümlət\ *n* -s [[4]*boom* + *-let*] **:** a small boom; *specif* **:** a short-term increase in economic activity

boom man *n* [[2]*boom*] **1 :** one who operates the controls of a loading boom or crane **2 :** POLEMAN 2 **3 :** RAFTER

boom pole *n* [[2]*boom*] **:** [2]BOOM 2a

booms *pl of* BOOM, *pres 3d sing of* BOOM

boom shot *n* [[2]*boom*] **:** a motion-picture or television shot; *esp* **:** a traveling shot taken with a camera mounted on a boom

boom·slang \'büm,slaŋ, -laŋ\ *n, pl* **boom·slange** \-äŋə\ *or* **boomslangs** [Afrik, fr. *boom* tree + *slang* snake, fr. MD *slanghe;* akin to OS & OHG *slango* snake, OHG *slingan* to wind — more at BOOMDASSIE, SLING] **:** a large boigid tree snake (*Dispholidus typus*) of southern Africa variously colored green or brownish black and having retiring ways and a back-fanged mouth that render it practically harmless to man despite its powerful venom

boom·ster \'bümstə(r)\ *n* -s [[4]*boom* + *-ster*] **:** BOOMER

boom stick *n* [[2]*boom*] **:** any of the timbers chained end to end to form a boom in logging

boom table *n* [[2]*boom*] **:** a structure around the lower part of a ship's mast to which booms are attached

boom tackle *n* [[2]*boom*] **:** a tackle used on or with a boom

boomtown \'=,=\ *n* -s [[4]*boom* + *town*] **:** a town that has experienced sudden growth as the result of a boom

boomy \'bümē\ *adj, often* -ER/-EST [[4]*boom* + *-y*] **:** having the quality of a boom; *specif, of reproduced sound* **:** having an excessive accentuation on the tones of lower pitch

[1]**boon** \'bün\ *n* -s [ME *boone, bone,* fr. ON *bōn* petition; akin to OE *bēn* prayer, *bannan* to summon — more at BAN] **1** *obs* **:** an order or command in the form of a request **2 :** BENEFIT, FAVOR; *esp* **:** one that is specif. asked for or is given as the result of a request ⟨told he would be granted any ~ he asked⟩ **3 :** an often timely and gratuitous benefit received and enjoyed **:** BLESSING ⟨the rain was a ~ to parched crops⟩

[2]**boon** \"\ *adj* [ME *bon, bone,* fr. MF *bon* good — more at BONNY] **1** *obs* **:** GOODLY, FAVORABLE, PROSPEROUS **2 :** BOUNTEOUS, BENIGN ⟨~ nature⟩ **3 :** MERRY, JOVIAL, CONVIVIAL, INTIMATE ⟨a ~ companion, loving his bottle —John Arbuthnot⟩

[3]**boon** \"\ *n* -s [ME *bone, bunne,* prob. fr. OE *bune* reed — more at BUN] **:** the woody portion of the stem of flax or hemp after the removal of the fiber by retting, braking, and scutching

boon·dock·ers \'bün,däkə(r)z\ *n pl, slang* **:** field shoes

boon·docks \'bün,däks\ *also* **bundocks** \", 'bün-, 'bən-\ *n pl* [Tag *bundok* mountain] **1** *also* **boon·dock** \k\ -s *slang* **:** rough country **:** dense brush **:** JUNGLE — usu. used with *the* **2** *slang* **:** rural backcountry **:** STICKS

[1]**boon·dog·gle** \'bün,dägəl\ *n* -s [coined 1925 by Robert H. Link *b*1897 Am. scoutmaster] **1 :** a handicraft article esp. of leather or wicker fashioned for utility **2 :** an impracticable or useless project wasteful of time and money

[2]**boondoggle** *vi* **boondoggled; boondoggled; boondoggling** \-g(ə)liŋ\ **boondoggles 1 :** to engage in making boondoggles **2 :** to engage in useless or frivolous occupations — **boon·dog·gler** \-g(ə)lə(r)\ *n* -s

boong \'büŋ, 'bō,äŋ\ *n* -s [native name in Australia] *slang Austral* **1 :** ABORIGINE **2 :** a native of New Guinea

boon·ga·ry \'büŋgərē\ *n* -ES [native name in Australia] **:** a small tree wallaby (*Dendrolagus lumholtzi*) native to Queensland

boon·less \'bünləs\ *adj* **:** being without a boon

bo·oph·i·lus \bō'äfələs\ *n, cap* [NL, fr. Gk *boo-* (fr. *bous* head of cattle) + NL *-philus* — more at COW] **:** a genus of ticks some of which are pests of cattle and other ruminants and vectors of disease — see CATTLE TICK

[1]**boor** \'bù(ə)r, 'bùə\ *n* -s [D *boer* peasant, farmer, short for MD *gheboer, ghebuur,* fr. *ghe-* co- + *-boer, buur* dweller; akin to OHG *gi-* co- and to OE *gebūr* dweller, farmer, OHG *gibūro* peasant, fellow countryman, OE & OHG *būan* to dwell — more at BOWER (dwelling)] **1 :** a small farmer **:** PEASANT, HUSBANDMAN **2 :** BOER **3 a :** a rustic or peasant typically rough, crude, insensitive, uncommunicative, or dull **:** YOKEL ⟨a kind of heroic ~ devoid of civilized graces and refinements —F.R.Leavis⟩ **b :** a rude, clumsy, insensitive, or boring individual ⟨an ill-mannered ~⟩

syn CHURL, LOUT, CLOWN, BUMPKIN, CLODHOPPER, HICK, YOKEL, RUBE: BOOR, orig. applicable to any small farmer, now strongly implies rudeness, insensitivity, or dullness; it is an antonym to *gentleman* ⟨he that is rude to a pretty girl when she offers him wine is too great a *boor* to understand —Charles Kingsley⟩ ⟨love makes gentlemen even of *boors* —Henry Adams⟩ CHURL, orig. a rustic or villein, is now more likely to suggest ill-bred surly meanness in general than that associated with rural backgrounds ⟨magic . . . that this divine sweet creature could be allied with that old *churl* —George Meredith⟩ LOUT is applicable to any crude and hulking oaf, rural or urban ⟨a stupid *lout,* seemingly a farmer's boy —Sir Walter Scott⟩ CLOWN, orig. a field worker, now suggests ill-bred clumsiness or gaucheness, perhaps laughable ⟨any *clown,* ignorant of the usages of the house —T.B.Macaulay⟩ BUMPKIN suggests an awkward, gauche, and naive rustic ⟨awkward lads with shy, red faces . . . poor *bumpkins* —James Hilton⟩ CLODHOPPER suggests a shambling heaviness and a cloddish lack of information or urbanity ⟨*clodhoppers* gaping at the stores on Saturday night⟩ HICK is a less forceful term for an unsophisticated simple rustic ⟨*hicks* in the hinterlands disliking city candidates⟩ YOKEL and RUBE may suggest either rustic lack of polish or gullible obtuseness ⟨like a listener in a country store to wondrous tales . . . his mouth was agape in *yokel* fashion —Stephen Crane⟩ Many of these terms are interchangeable ⟨not worthy to be a knight — a *churl,* a *clown* —Alfred Tennyson⟩ ⟨he got off with scorn — he was a *hick,* a *rube* . . . , a rustic, a *boor* or a hillbilly —Bergen Evans⟩

[2]**boor** \"\ *Scot var of* BOWER

boo·rach \'bürək\ *var of* BOUROCK

boord·ly \'bùrdlē\ *var of* BUIRDLY

boor·ish \'bùrish, -rēsh\ *adj* **:** characteristic of or relating to a boor **:** unrefined and insensitive **:** RUDE ⟨~ remarks⟩ — **boor·ish·ly** *adv* — **boor·ish·ness** *n* -ES

boors *pl of* BOOR

boort *var of* BORT

boor·tree \'bùr,trē\ *var of* BOURTREE

boos *pl of* BOO, *pres 3d sing of* BOO

[1]**boose** \'büs\ *n* -s [ME *boos;* akin to OE *bōsig* cow stall, ON *bās,* Goth *bansts* barn, OE *bindan* to bind — more at BIND] *dial Brit* **:** a stall for a horse or a cow

[2]**boose** *var of* BOOZE

[1]**boost** \'büst\ *vt* -ED/-ING/-S [origin unknown] **1 :** to push or shove from below to or towards a higher level ⟨they ~*ed* him up so he could climb the oak tree⟩ **2 a :** to increase (as a price) by a numerically expressible amount **:** RAISE ⟨plans to ~ production by 30 percent next year⟩ **b :** to aid or assist esp. towards progress or increase ⟨an extra holiday to ~ morale⟩ **3 :** to promote the cause or interests of (as a person, city, idea) with enthusiasm and determination **:** recommend vigorously **:** PLUG ⟨they began to ~ him for the presidency early⟩ ⟨an advertising program to ~ local products abroad⟩ **4 a** (1) **:** to raise the voltage of or across (an electric circuit) (2) **:** to charge (a storage battery) at a high rate for a short time **b :** to augment (as by a supercharger) the natural supply of air to (an internal-combustion engine) **c :** to increase the pressure of (as a fluid) **d :** to control or regulate by increase of pressure **5** *slang* **:** STEAL; *esp* **:** SHOPLIFT **syn** see LIFT

[2]**boost** \"\ *n* -s **1 :** an act of boosting **:** a push upwards ⟨give him a ~ so he can climb over the fence⟩ **2 :** an increase esp. of prices, wages, production ⟨a ~ in potato acreage⟩ ⟨a bass ~ on an amplifier⟩ **3 :** assistance or commendation that betters position or enhances reputation ⟨music criticism . . . was given a ~ as an academic subject —*Saturday Rev.*⟩ **4 :** an uplift or encouragement ⟨gave the free world a tonic ~ —*New Yorker*⟩

boost·er \-tə(r)\ *n* -s *often attrib* **1 :** one that boosts **2 :** an enthusiastic supporter or backer ⟨a great ~ for his home town⟩ **3 :** an auxiliary device for increasing force, power, or pressure esp. for the purpose of moving an object: as **a :** an additional locomotive on a train **b :** a hydraulic brake servomechanism **4** *also* **booster pump :** a pump used to increase the pressure of fluids **5 :** a transformer for regulating or modifying a fluctuating or sagging voltage in an electric circuit **6 :** a high explosive charge usu. in the form of one or more pressed pellets in a cup or tube sensitive enough to be set off by a detonator and powerful enough to set off the main charge in a shell, mine, bomb, or other explosive device; *also* **:** a device (as a tube) containing this charge **7 :** a radio-frequency amplifier for intensifying signals picked up by a radio or television antenna before passing them on to the regular receiving set used esp. where reception would otherwise be weak **8 :** an auxiliary part of the propulsive system of a pilotless airplane or missile used to supply a part or all of the thrust during the launching and initial stage of flight **:** the first stage of a multistage rocket **9 :** a pressure blower that draws in air or gas and expels it through an outlet pipe at a higher pressure **10 :** a substance or dose used to renew or increase the effect of a drug or immunizing agent: as **a :** an injection of antigen given after completion of a primary course of immunization ⟨the child was given a ~⟩ ⟨a ~ shot of diphtheria toxoid⟩ — called also *recall dose* **b :** SYNERGIST 2 ⟨a chemical acting as a ~ to sulfa drugs⟩ **11** *slang* **a :** THIEF; *esp* **:** SHOPLIFTER **b :** SHILL

booster battery *n* **:** a battery used to maintain a certain voltage across a crystal detector to increase the sensitivity of the detector by adjusting conditions for increased response for a given input

boost·er·ism \-tə,rizəm\ *n* -s **:** the activities and attitudes typical of boosters (sense 2) ⟨natives deeply in love with their environment with more sincerity than ~ —Al Hine⟩

booster rocket *n* **:** RATO

boost pressure *n* **:** the pressure in the induction system of an aircraft engine in excess of the standard sea-level atmospheric pressure

boosy \'büzē\ *n* -ES [fr. (assumed) ME, fr. OE *bōsig* — more at BOOSE] **:** BOOSE

[1]**boot** \'büt, *usu* -üd·+V\ *n* -s [ME *boote, bote,* fr. OE *bōt* remedy, compensation; akin to OHG *buoza* change for the better, ON *bōt* remedy, compensation, Goth *bōta* advantage, gain, OE *betera* better — more at BETTER] **1** *archaic* **a :** help or relief esp. in time of peril or great want **:** DELIVERANCE **b :** a person or thing that brings such help **2** *now chiefly dial* **:** something to equalize an exchange ⟨give me your sow and $10 ~ or the trade is off for the heifer —Frank Neefe⟩ **3** *obs* **:** profit or advantage towards the accomplishment of an end **:** AVAIL, USE ⟨then talk no more of flight, it is no ~ —Shak.⟩ — **to boot** *adv* **:** in addition **:** over and above **:** BESIDES **:** as a compensation for the difference of value between things bartered ⟨he traded and gave $10 *to boot*⟩

[2]**boot** \"\ *vb* -ED/-ING/-S [ME *booten, boten,* fr. *boote, bote*] *vi, archaic* **:** to be of help, profit, or advantage **:** AVAIL ⟨it ~s not to look backwards —Thomas Arnold⟩ ~ *vt, obs* **:** BENEFIT, ENRICH

[3]**boot** \"\ *n* -s [ME, fr. MF *bote*] **1 a :** a covering for the foot and leg that is usu. made of leather or rubber and is of varying height between the ankle and hip **b** *Brit* **:** a shoe reaching to the ankle **c :** a rubber overshoe **2 :** an instrument of torture applied to the leg and tightened so as to crush the leg and foot **3 :** a sheath or casing resembling a boot that provides a protective covering for the leg: as **a** *obs* **:** a piece of leg armor **b :** a partial covering for the hoof and leg of a horse designed to prevent injury from interference **c :** the feathers on the shank and toes of certain domestic fowls **d :** the part of a stocking between the top and the foot **e :** a canvas or skin mitten used to protect the feet of working dogs from snow or ice **4 :** a protective sheath or casing typically of an object or part resembling a leg: as **a :** the sheath near the uppermost leaves on the stems of grains and many palms that encloses the inflorescence which swells within it **b :** the metal casing and flange fitted about a pipe where it passes through a roof **c :** the box or compartment that contains the reed of a reed pipe of an organ **d :** a large thick patch for the inside of a tire casing **5 a** *obs* **:** a built-in compartment on a horse-drawn coach used orig. as a seat for the coachman and later for storage **b** *Brit* **:** the storage compartment at the rear of an automobile **:** TRUNK **6 :** a usu. leather article that resembles a boot: as **a :** a leather drinking vessel **b :** a leather carrying case for a rifle ⟨with the adoption of the bolt-action Krag . . . a long ~ came into use, covering the entire carbine, up to the stock —W.F. Harris⟩ **c** *aeronautics* **:** a pneumatic rubber cell or tube used for deicing a wing or tail surface **7 a :** the box in which the lower pulley of a grain elevator runs **b :** the chamber and housing at the base of a bucket elevator **8 a :** a blow delivered by or as if by a booted foot **:** KICK **b :** a usu. unexpected and often rude discharge or dismissal — often used with *the* ⟨she gave him the ~ and married another man⟩ ⟨he got the ~ after 14 years and had to find a new job⟩ **c :** pleasure or enjoyment esp. of a momentary sort **:** BANG, KICK ⟨I get a big ~ out of his jokes⟩ **9 :** a fumble in baseball **10 a :** a recruit undergoing basic training in the U. S. Navy or Marines **b :** NOVICE, TRAINEE, APPRENTICE **11** *in glass manuf* **:** a clay receptacle suspended in the nose of a tank furnace to exclude scum and to allow working of the glass without direct contact with heat and gases **12 :** a drain cock in the bottom of a tank car or oil tank

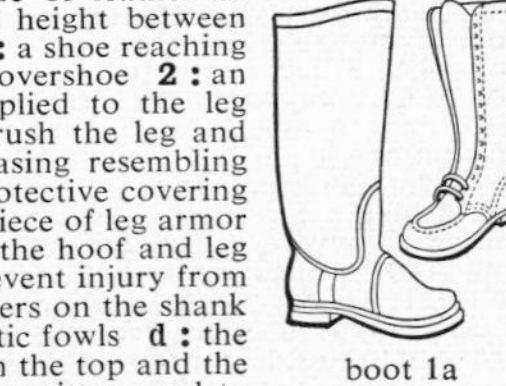

boot 1a

[4]**boot** \"\ *vb* -ED/-ING/-S [ME *booten,* fr. *boot* — more at [3]BOOT] *vt* **1 a :** to put boots on (oneself or another) **b :** to supply with boots ⟨this firm . . . has ~*ed* and spurred every British monarch from George II on —*New Yorker*⟩ **2 a :** to send off or propel with force **:** KICK **b :** to eject or discharge summarily — used often with *out* ⟨he has been quietly ~*ed* out as chief —*Newsweek*⟩ **3 :** to make an error on (a baseball batted on the ground) **:** FUMBLE ⟨he ~*ed* an easy grounder and another run scored⟩ **4** *slang* **:** to ride (a horse) in a race ⟨after a 24-year career in which he ~*ed* home nearly 150 stakes winners⟩ ~ *vi* **:** to put on one's boots

[5]**boot** \"\ *n* -s [[1]*boot* (influenced in meaning by *booty*)] *archaic* **:** BOOTY, PLUNDER

bootblack \'=,=\ *n* **:** one who shines shoes and boots

bootboy \'=,=\ *n* **:** BOOTS

boot camp *n* **:** a station for the basic training of newly enlisted seamen or marines

bootcatcher *n, obs* **:** BOOTS

booted *adj* [fr. past part. of [4]*boot*] **1 :** wearing boots; *specif* **:** equipped for riding ⟨~ and spurred⟩ **2 :** having a continuous horny covering somewhat resembling a boot — used of the tarsus of some birds in distinction from those covered with plates, scales, or soft skin **3 :** having the shanks and toes feathered — used of certain domestic fowls and pigeons

booted eagle *n* **:** a rather small slender Old World eagle (*Hieraetus pennatus*) that breeds in Europe and western Asia and winters in Africa and southern Asia

boo·tee *or* **boo·tie** \(')bü¦tē; *in sense 2 usu* 'büd·ē *or* 'büte *or* -i\ *n* -s [[3]*boot* + *-ee* or *-ie*] **1 :** a boot with a short leg: as **a :** a boot with a front extending from the throat of the vamp over the instep to the ankle **b :** a slipper with the upper extending to or nearly to the ankle **2 :** an infant's sock of knitted or crocheted wool usu. of half-leg length with a tie at the ankle

bootee 2

boot·er \'büd·|ə(r), -üt|\ *n* -s [[4]*boot* + *-er*] **:** one that boots; *specif* **:** a soccer player

boot·ery \|ərē\ *n* -ES [[3]*boot* + *-ery*] **:** a shoe store

booth \'büth, *Brit usu* -th\ *n, pl* **booths** \-ü*th*z, -üths *sometimes* -üz\ [ME *bothe,* of Scand origin; akin to ON *būth* booth; akin to MHG *buode* booth, OE & OHG *būan* to dwell, inhabit — more at BOWER] **1 :** a simple roofed structure often built of any material at hand and used as a temporary shelter for livestock or field workers ⟨in harvest time ~s in fields and vineyards were occupied even at night by some member of the family —Madeleine S. Miller & J.L.Miller⟩ **2 a :** a temporary structure (as at a fair) where articles may be placed for sale or display or where exhibits may be shown ⟨the 4-H ~ at the county fair was a soil conservation exhibit⟩ **b :** a totally or partially enclosed structure often inside a building; *esp* **:** a small enclosure designed to hold one person at a time usu. to afford privacy or to separate its occupant from patrons or customers ⟨a telephone ~⟩ ⟨a voting ~⟩ ⟨the information ~ in the bus station⟩ **c :** a seating and eating accommodation much used in restaurants and bars that consists of a table placed between two backed benches ⟨they sat in the ~ and talked for an hour⟩ **3 :** an enclosure of varying size and construction designed to isolate an area and to prevent the functions carried on within it from being interfered with by the surrounding area ⟨a broadcasting ~ in the ball park⟩

boothale *vb* [[5]*boot* + *hale*] *vi, obs* **:** to forage for booty **:** PLUNDER ~ *vt, obs* **:** PILLAGE, PLUNDER

boot·heel \'=,=\ *n* **1 :** the heel of a boot **2 :** something resembling a bootheel in shape; *esp* **:** a land formation in the shape of a bootheel ⟨the ~ of Missouri⟩

boot hill *n, sometimes cap B&H* [so called fr. the supposition that most persons buried there died with their boots on] *West* **:** a burial-ground esp. for men killed in gunfights ⟨as a wild town in early days, it had its *boot hill* and knew . . . notorious gunfighters —*Amer. Guide Series: Texas*⟩

booth·ite \'bü,thīt, *Brit usu* -th-\ *n* -s [Edwin *Booth* †1917 Am. chemist + E *-ite*] **:** a mineral $CuSO_4.7H_2O$ consisting of a hydrous copper sulfate occurring in indistinct monoclinic blue crystals

boot hook *n* **:** a long cross-handled hook for pulling on riding boots by the straps

boot·hose \'=,=\ *n pl* **:** stockings or protective overstockings worn with or in place of boots

bootjack \'=,=\ *n* [[3]*boot* + *jack*] **1 :** a metal or wood device shaped like the letter V and used in pulling off boots **2 bootjacks** *pl* [so called fr. the flat two-awned achenes] **:** BEGGAR-TICKS 1, 2 **3** *mining engin* **:** a fishing tool consisting of two wings and a latch used in well boring for grabbing bailers

bootlace \'=,=\ *n* **1 :** a lace for a boot **2** *Brit* **:** SHOELACE

[1]**bootleg** \'=,=\ *n* [[3]*boot* + *leg*] **1 a :** the upper part of a boot **b :** an object shaped or used like a bootleg; *specif* **:** a protective cover for railroad track wires where the wires leave the conduit or ground **2 :** a large locking lever in a spinning mule **3 :** something bootlegged; *specif* **:** MOONSHINE

[2]**bootleg** \"\ *vb* **bootlegged; bootlegged; bootlegging; bootlegs** *vt* **1 a :** to carry (alcoholic liquor) on one's person illegally **b :** to manufacture, sell, or transport for sale (alcoholic liquor) contrary to law ⟨*bootlegged* corn whiskey during Prohibition⟩ **2 a :** to produce or obtain for sale or distribution or to sell or distribute illicitly without such inspection, permission, or approval as may be required by law or by existing private agreements ⟨register the number . . so that any watch can be traced should it be *bootlegged* through unscrupulous outlets —*Jewelers' Circular-Keystone*⟩ **b :** SMUGGLE ~ *vi* **1 :** to engage in bootlegging **2 :** to separate and slip — used of the plies of a machine belt

[3]**bootleg** \"\ *adj* **1 :** sold or distributed illicitly or surreptitiously **:** produced, procured, or transported for illicit sale or distribution ⟨~ coal taken from abandoned mines and trucked to the city for sale⟩ ⟨the hills were full of ~ whiskey⟩ **2 :** clandestine or surreptitious esp. in order to avoid laws or regulations ⟨a ~ radio station⟩ ⟨~ wage increases that violated contracts⟩ **3 :** characterized by the presence of, participation in, or dealing with bootlegging ⟨a ~ town⟩

boot·leg·ger \'=,=ə(r)\ *n* -s **:** one that bootlegs esp. alcoholic liquor

bootlegging *n* **:** the act or practice of a bootlegger

bootleg play *n* **:** a football play in which the quarterback fakes giving the ball to a teammate, conceals it on his hip, and runs with it behind interference

boot·less \'bütləs\ *adj* [ME *bootelees,* fr. OE *bōtlēas* inexpiable, fr. *bōt* remedy, compensation + *-lēas* -less — more at [1]BOOT] **1** *archaic* **:** without remedy **:** INCURABLE **2 :** to no advantage or avail **:** fruitless and frustrating ⟨no guides were to be found, and in the next summer the young man returned from his ~ errand —Francis Parkman⟩ — **boot·less·ly** *adv* — **boot·less·ness** *n* -ES

[1]**boot·lick** \'=,=\ *vb* -ED/-ING/-S [[3]*boot* + *lick*] *vt* **:** to fawn on **:** cultivate the favor of through obsequious speech or actions ⟨always beholden to the favor of kings and princes, ~*ing* bishops for a pittance, courting fair ladies for a few crowns —Corra Harris⟩ ~ *vi* **:** to act as a bootlicker **:** play the sycophant

[2]**bootlick** \"\ *n* -s **:** BOOTLICKER **syn** see PARASITE

boot·lick·er \-ə(r)\ *n* -s **:** SYCOPHANT, TOADY **syn** see PARASITE

boot·man \'bütmən, -,man\ *n, pl* **bootmen 1 :** a worker who shapes the sheet-metal fairing for aircraft **2 :** a road worker who applies oil to roads from a specially equipped truck

[1]**boots** *pres 3d sing of* BOOT

[2]**boots** \'büts\ *n pl but sing in constr* [fr. pl. of [3]*boot*] *Brit* **:** SERVANT; *esp* **:** a hotel employee whose main duty is to shine boots and shoes

boots and saddles *n pl but sing in constr* **:** the bugle call preceding assembly for mounted formations

[1]**boot·strap** \'=,=\ *n* **1 :** a looped strap sewed at the side or the rear top of a boot to help in pulling it on **2 bootstraps** *pl* **:** unaided efforts — often used in the phrase *by one's bootstraps* ⟨"well, George, . . . pull yourself up by your own ~s and start in to be a man" —Helen Eustis⟩

[2]**bootstrap** \"\ *adj* **:** based on or carried out with minimum resources or advantages **:** relying on its own efforts ⟨the city recovered from the flood by the ~ method⟩ ⟨a ~ operation⟩

boot top *n* **1 :** the upper part or top of a boot **2 :** a lace ruffle formerly worn so as to conceal the top of the boot

boot topping *n* **1 :** the part of a ship's hull between the light line and the load water line **2** *also* **boot top :** a paint used on the boot topping to prevent corrosion and fouling

boot tree *n* **1 :** SHOE TREE **2 :** BOOTJACK 1

boo·ty \'büd·ē, -ütē, -i\ *n* -ES [modif. (influenced by *boot* profit) of MF *butin,* fr. MLG *būte* exchange, distribution] **1 a :** PLUNDER, SPOILS; *esp* **:** loot taken in war **b :** *international law* **:** spoils taken on land as distinguished from that captured on the high seas — compare PRIZE **2 :** REWARD, PRIZE, GAIN ⟨I made ~ of a great bunch of . . . flowers and scarlet raspberries —Rachel Henning⟩

boo·ty·less *adj* **:** being without booty **:** yielding no booty

booza *var of* BOZA

[1]**booze** *also* **boose** \'büz\ *vi* -ED/-ING/-S [alter. (perh. influenced by Flem *boezen* to tipple) of earlier *bouse,* fr. ME *bousen,* fr. MD *or* MFlem *būsen;* akin to MLG *būsen* to tipple, MHG *būs* swelling, fullness and prob. to OHG *buosam* bosom — more at BOSOM] **:** to drink intoxicating liquor esp. habitually or to

excess ⟨he still *boozed* till daylight and dozed into the afternoon —G.O.Trevelyan⟩

²booze *also* **boose** \"\ *n* -s *often attrib* [alter. (perh. influenced by Flem *boezen* to tipple) of earlier *bouse*, fr. ME *bous*, fr. *bousen*] **1 :** intoxicating drink; *esp* **:** hard liquor ⟨a bottle of ~⟩ **2 :** a drinking bout or spree **:** DRUNK ⟨went on a ~⟩

booze fighter *n* **:** BOOZEHOUND

booze·hound \ˈ=,=\ *n* **:** a heavy or habitual drinker ⟨a violent and lecherous ~ —Joseph Cannata⟩

booz·er \ˈbüzə(r)\ *n* -s **1 :** one that boozes **2** *slang Brit* **:** a drinking place **:** PUB

booz·i·ly \ˈbüzəlē, -li\ *adv* **:** in a boozy manner

boozy \-zē,-zi\ *adj, usu* -ER/-EST **1 :** affected by or showing the influence of liquor **:** slightly drunk **2 :** DRUNK

¹bop \ˈbäp\ *vt* **bopped; bopped; bopping; bops** [imit.] **:** to strike esp. with the fist or a club **:** SOCK, HIT ⟨he reached out and *bopped* me over the head with a rolled-up newspaper —Leslie Ford⟩

²bop \"\ *n* -s **:** a blow esp. with the fist or a club **:** SOCK, HIT ⟨I gave him a ~ that laid him out⟩

³bop \"\ *n* -s *often attrib* [short for *bebop*] **:** jazz characterized by rhythmic harmonic complexity and innovation, lengthened melodic line, usu. loud bravura execution, and the singing of nonsense syllables

bo·peep \bōˈpēp\ *n* -s [¹*boo* + *peep*] **:** PEEKABOO

bop·per \ˈbäpə(r)\ *also* **bop·pist** \-pəst\ *or* **bop·ster** \-pstə(r)\ *n* -s **1 a :** one that plays bop **:** a musician skilled at playing bop **b :** a vocalist that sings with bop accompaniment **2 :** a devotee of bop

bo·pyr·id \bōˈpirəd\ *n* -s [NL *Bopyridae*] **:** an isopod of the family Bopyridae

bo·pyr·i·dae \-rə,dē\ *n pl, cap* [NL, fr. *Bopyrus*, type genus (prob. fr. a proper name *Bopyrus*) + *-idae*] **:** a large family of isopod crustaceans that live as parasites on shrimps and other decapods, the large females attaching themselves to their host by hooked legs, often causing parasitic castration of the host, and themselves becoming extremely degenerated while the minute males live on or near the females and in large measure retain their isopod characters

BOQ *abbr or n* -s bachelor officers' quarters

bor \ˈbō(r)\ *n* -s [prob. alter. of ¹*boor*] *dial Brit* **:** NEIGHBOR, FRIEND — used in address

bor- *or* **boro-** *comb form* [ISV, fr. *boron*] **:** boron ⟨*borism*⟩ ⟨*boryl*⟩ ⟨*boroarsenate*⟩

bor *abbr* borough

¹bo·ra \ˈbōrə, ˈbȯrə\ *n* -s [It dial. (Venetian), fr. L *boreas* — more at BOREAS] **:** an occasional violent cold north to northeast wind that blows over the northern Adriatic from the interior highlands

²bora \"\ *n* -s [Australian, fr. *bōr*, *būr* girdle, circle] **:** a rite in which Australian aborigine boys are initiated into manhood

³bora *usu cap, var of* BORO

borachio *n* -s [modif. of Sp *borracho* drunkard, intoxicated, irreg. fr. L *burrus* red, flushed with food or drink, fr. Gk *pyrrhos* red, tawny — more at PYRRH-] *obs* **:** DRUNKARD

bo·rac·ic \bəˈrasik, bō-, -raas-\ *adj* [ISV *borac-* (fr. ML *borac-, borax*) + *-ic*] **:** BORIC

boracic acid *n* **:** BORIC ACID **a** — not used scientifically

bo·ra·cite \ˈbōrə,sīt, ˈbȯr-\ *n* -s [G *borazit*, fr. ML *borac-, borax* + G *-it* -ite] **:** a mineral $Mg_3B_7O_{13}Cl$ consisting of a borate and chloride of magnesium that is strongly pyroelectric and occurs in hard glassy crystals and in softer white masses (hardness 7, sp. gr. 2.9)

bor·age \ˈbȯrij, ˈbär-, ˈbərij\ *n* -s [ME, fr. MF *bourache*, *bourage*, prob. fr. (assumed) VL *burrago*, fr. LL *burra* shaggy cloth; fr. the hairy leaves — more at BUREAU] **:** a rough-hairy blue-flowered European herb (*Borago officinalis*) used esp. in France as a demulcent and diaphoretic and also as a salad herb and widely naturalized as a weed

borage family *n* **:** BORAGINACEAE

bo·rag·i·na·ce·ae \bə,rajəˈnāsē,ē\ *n pl, cap* [NL, fr. *Boragin-, Borago*, type genus + *-aceae*] **:** a family of herbs, shrubs, or trees (order Polemoniales) of wide distribution distinguished mainly by circinate inflorescence and nutlike fruit

bo·rag·i·na·ceous \bə,rajəˈnāshəs\ *adj* [NL *Boraginaceae* + E *-ous*] **:** of, relating to, or like the Boraginaceae

bo·ra·go \bəˈrā(,)gō, -rä-\ *n, cap* [NL, fr. ML *borago, borrago* borage, prob. fr. (assumed) VL *burrago*] **:** a small genus of perennial herbs (family Boraginaceae) that are natives of the Mediterranean region and distinguished by a rotate corolla and large scar at the base of the nutlet

bor·ak \ˈbȯrək, ˈbär-\ *n* [native name in New South Wales, Australia] *Austral* **:** FUN, RIDICULE — used esp. in the phrase *poke borak at*

bor·al \ˈbōr,al, ˈbȯ,ral, -rəl\ *n* -s [ISV *bor-* (fr. *borate*) + *-al* (fr. *aluminum*)] **:** a fine white astringent powder consisting of a borate and tartrate of aluminum

bo·ran \bəˈran, -rän\ *n, usu cap* [prob. fr. *Borana, Boran*] **:** an East African breed of cattle of the zebu type

bo·rana \bəˈranə, -ränə\ *also* **bo·ran** \-n\ *n, pl* **borana** \-nə\ *or* **boranas** \-nəz\ *also* **boran** \-n\ *or* **bo·rani** \-nē\ *usu cap* [native name in East Africa] **1 :** a widely distributed Hamitic people of southern Ethiopia and northeast Uganda **2 :** a member of the Borana people

bo·rane \ˈbōr,ān, ˈbȯ,rān\ *n* -s [ISV *bor-* + *-ane*] **1 :** a compound of boron and hydrogen; *specif* **:** BORINE 1 — compare DIBORANE **2 :** a derivative (as methyl-diborane) of a borane

boras *pl of* BORA

bo·ras·ca *also* **bor·ras·ca** \bəˈraskə\ *or* **bo·ras·co** \-(,)skō\ *or* **bo·rasque** \-rask\ *n* -s [Sp *borrasca*, fr. LL *borras* north wind, fr. Gk *borras, boreas* — more at BOREAS] **1 :** a squall often attended with a thunderstorm occurring esp. in the Mediterranean **2** [MexSp *borrasca* unproductiveness (of a mine), fr. Sp, squall] **a :** a mine section or an entire mine that is largely oreless **:** an unproductive mine **b :** unproductiveness esp. of a mine; *also* **:** PENURY, WANT

bo·ras·sus \bəˈrasəs\ *n, cap* [NL, fr. Gk *borassos* date palm spadix with immature fruit] **:** a monotypic genus of sugar palms native to tropical Africa and naturalized throughout the tropics and having fan-shaped leaves and very hard wood — see PALMYRA

bo·rate \ˈbōr,āt, ˈbȯ,rāt *also* -rət; *usu* -d·+V\ *n* -s [ISV *bor-* + *-ate* (n. suffix)] **:** a salt or ester of a boric acid

bo·rat·ed \-ād·əd\ *adj* [*bor-* + *-ate* (vb. suffix) + *-ed*] **:** mixed or impregnated with borax or boric acid ⟨~ cream of tartar⟩

¹bo·rax \ˈbōr,aks, ˈbȯ,ra-, -,rəks\ *n* -ES [alter. (influenced by ML *borax*) of earlier *boras*, fr. ME, fr. MF, fr. ML *borac-, borax*, fr. Ar *bawraq*, *būraq*, fr. Per *būrah*] **:** the best-known sodium borate $Na_2B_4O_7.10H_2O$ crystallizing usu. in large monoclinic prisms that occurs naturally in this form as a mineral, that is also obtained from other minerals (as kernite or tincalconite) or from the boric acid of fumaroles by reaction with soda, and that is used chiefly in glass and ceramics, in agricultural chemicals, as a flux, as a cleansing agent and water softener, and as a preservative and fire retardant (as for wood) — called also *sodium tetraborate*

²borax \"\ *n* -ES [so called fr. the reputed custom of a producer of borax soap of giving cheap furniture as a coupon premium] **:** cheap shoddy flashy merchandise; *esp* **:** cheap poorly constructed ostentatious furniture of a nondescript or hybrid style

³borax \"\ *adj* **1 :** characterized by cheapness, shoddy construction, flashiness, and nondescript or hybrid design ⟨~ furniture⟩ ⟨buying ~ goods on the installment plan⟩ **2 :** of, relating to, or dealing in cheap shoddy flashy merchandise, esp. furniture ⟨a ~ credit store⟩; *also* **:** marked by the ballyhoo and high-pressure salesmanship usu. associated with the promotion and sale of such merchandise ⟨~ advertising⟩

borax bead *n* **:** a bead (sense 4f) having borax as the flux

borax carmine *n* **:** an alkaline staining fluid composed of borax, carmine, and water and used with dilute hydrochloric acid in microscopy to produce a permanent red nuclear stain

borax glass *n* **:** a transparent anhydrous glassy solid formed by fusing borax

borax honey *n* **:** a medicinal mixture of borax, glycerin, and purified honey

borax lake *n* **1 :** a lake whose shores are encrusted with borax-rich deposits **2 :** a dry lake bed rich in borax

bor·azole \ˈbōrə,zōl, ˈbȯr-; bəˈra,zōl\ *or* **bor·azine** \-zēn\ *n* -s [*bor-* + *azole* or *azine*] **:** a colorless volatile liquid compound $B_3N_3H_6$ that is formed by heating diborane and ammonia and has a structure like that of benzene with alternating boron and nitrogen atoms in a ring — called also *triborine triamine*

bor·a·zon \ˈbōrə,zän, ˈbȯ-\ *n* -s [*bor-* + *az-* + *-on*] **:** a crystalline boron nitride as hard as a diamond but more resistant to oxidation at high temperatures

bor·bo·ryg·mic \ˌbȯrbəˈrigmik\ *also* **bor·bo·ryg·mat·ic** \-(,)rig,mad·ik\ *adj* [*borborygmic* fr. *borborygmus* + *-ic*; *borborygmatic* fr. NL *borborygmat-*, *borborygma* borborygmus (alter. of *borborygmus*) + E *-ic*] **:** of, relating to, resembling, or caused by borborygmus

bor·bo·ryg·mus \ˌbȯrbəˈrigməs\ *also* **bor·bo·ryg·my** \ˈbȯrbə,rigmē\ *n, pl* **borboryg·mi** \-ˈrig,mī\ *also* **borboryg·mies** \-,rigmēz\ [*borborygmus*, NL, fr. Gk *borborygmos*, fr. *borboryzein* to rumble, of imit. origin; *borborygmy* fr. Gk *borborygmos* + E *-y*] **:** a rumbling sound made by the movement of gas in the intestine

bord \ˈbō(ə)rd\ *also* **board** \ˈbō(ə)rd, ˈbȯ-\ *n* -s [¹*board*; prob. fr. the former practice of laying boards in mine passageways to form a relatively smooth surface along which the coal was dragged in sledges] **:** a straight road or passageway driven at right angles to the main cleavage of the coal in a coal mine

bor·dage \ˈbȯrdij\ *n* -s [OF & MF, fr. OF *borde* hut, cabin + *-age*] **:** the tenure or services of a bordar

bord alexander \ˌbȯrd, -ō(ə)d+\ *n, usu cap A* [alter. (influenced by the name *Alexander*) of ME *borde alisaundre*, perh. fr. MF *bourde*, a cloth + ME *Alisaundre* Alexander or *Alisaundre* Alexandria] **:** ²ALEXANDER

bord-and-pillar \ˌ=ˈ=\ *adj* **:** of or relating to a system of coal mining in which tunnels are driven in a checkerboard pattern having massive square pillars between them which are gradually cut away as the work proceeds

bor·dar \ˈbȯrdər\ *n* -s [ML *bordarius*, fr. *borda* hut, cabin (fr. OF *borde*) + L *-arius* -ary] **:** a feudal tenant holding a cottage and usu. a few acres of land at the will of his lord and bound to menial service

¹bor·deaux \(ˈ)bȯrˈdō, -ō(ə)ˈdō\ *n, pl* **bordeaux** \-ō(z)\ *usu cap* [fr. *Bordeaux*, capital of Gironde dept., France] **1 :** any of the table wines from vineyards near the Dordogne and Garonne rivers and along their estuary, the Gironde, in the Gironde department of France, the majority being fully fermented dry red or occas. white wines averaging from 8 to 11 percent alcohol by volume **2** *or* **bordeaux red** *usu cap B* **:** any of several red acid and direct azo dyes; *esp* **:** FAST RED **b** — see DYE table I (under *Acid Red 17*, *Direct Red 44*) **3** *or* **bordeaux red** *usu cap B* **:** CLARET 3a **4 :** BORDEAUX MIXTURE

²bordeaux \"\ *adj, usu cap* **:** of or from the city of Bordeaux, France **:** of the kind or style prevalent in Bordeaux

bordeaux mixture *n, often cap B* [trans. of F *bouillie bordelaise*] **:** a fungicide made by reaction of copper sulfate, lime, and water

bordeaux turpentine *n, usu cap B* [trans. of F *térébenthine de Bordeaux*] **:** GALIPOT

bor·del \ˈbȯrdᵊl\ *n* -s [ME, fr. MF, brothel, hut, fr. OF, fr. *borde* hut, cabin, of Gmc origin; akin to OE *bord* board — more at ¹BOARD] *archaic* **:** BROTHEL

bor·de·laise \ˌbȯrdᵊlˈāz\ *also* **bordelaise sauce** *n* -s *usu cap B* [F *bordelaise*, fem. of *bordelais* of Bordeaux, fr. *Bordeaux*] **:** a brown sauce flavored with Bordeaux wine

bor·del·lo \bȯrˈde(,)lō\ *n* -s [It, fr. OF *bordel*] **:** BROTHEL

¹bor·der \ˈbȯrdər, ˈbȯ(ə)də(r\ *n* -s *often attrib* [ME *bordure*, fr. MF, fr. OF, fr. *border* to border, fr. *bort* border, ship's side, of Gmc origin; akin to OHG *bort* ship's side — more at BOARD] **1 a :** an outer part or edge **:** the part that parallels the boundary or outline of something **:** MARGIN ⟨at the ~s of the forest is a lake⟩ **b :** a surrounding arrangement (as of material or objects) ⟨a grass plot with a cement ~ running about it⟩ ⟨a roast with a ~ of browned potatoes⟩ **2 a :** a region lying along the edge of a country or territory **:** frontier country ⟨the ~s of the republic are notable for the vast forests there⟩ **b :** a boundary line ⟨travelers crossing the ~ suddenly find themselves in a totally new world⟩ **3 :** a long and usu. narrow bed used for continuous planting; *also* **:** a strip of planted ground or of plants along or around the edge of a garden, bed, or walk ⟨shrub ~s⟩ ⟨a ~ of perennials⟩ **4 a :** an ornamental stripe, print, or other design on or paralleling an edge (as of a fabric, garment, or rug) **b :** a distinctive or functional edging **5 a :** a narrow strip of painted cloth hung above a stage set to conceal the lights and flies **b :** BORDERLIGHT **6 :** a plain or decorative band around or at an edge of printed matter; *also* **:** the type or other material used to produce such a band **7 :** BORDURE 1

syn MARGIN, VERGE, EDGE, RIM, BRIM, BRINK: BORDER indicates either a boundary line or the thin strip just within a boundary line; it may indicate a strip superimposed over an ending or dividing line to emphasize it ⟨the *border* of a flower bed⟩ ⟨the *borders* of the forest⟩ ⟨crossing the *border* between the U.S. and Mexico⟩ ⟨the *border* of a handkerchief⟩ MARGIN may denote a border having definite width and definitely differing in some way from the interior surface ⟨the *margin* of the page⟩ ⟨the nether *margin* of the heath, where it became marshy —Thomas Hardy⟩ VERGE may indicate a very narrow margin area or a boundary line marking an extreme limit; it is more often used figuratively than literally ⟨tethered the horse for half an hour on the *verge* of the road —H.E. Bates⟩ ⟨like two nations which reluctantly accept the fact that a seemingly trivial border incident has brought them to the *verge* of war —Louis Auchincloss⟩ ⟨the entire expedition was on the *verge* of being surrounded and exterminated —John Mason Brown⟩ EDGE indicates a sharply defined terminating line, sometimes between two levels or planes ⟨the *edge* of the precipice⟩ ⟨the *edge* of the shelf⟩ ⟨flat-topped or rolling upland with a steep high *edge* to the west and a long gentle slope to the east —L.D. Stamp⟩ RIM usu. designates a curving or round edge ⟨the *rim* of a wheel⟩ ⟨new *rims* for his glasses⟩ ⟨the *rim* of the canyon⟩ ⟨a *rim* of mountains around the town⟩ BRIM may apply to the upper rim of a vessel or container or whatever else retains a liquid ⟨the *brim* of a goblet⟩ ⟨filling the tub up to the *brim*⟩ ⟨their host predicted that a rain would follow on the heels of the calm and fill the cisterns to the *brim* —Jean Stafford⟩ BRINK may indicate a steep or abrupt edge or brim; it is often figurative ⟨the *brink* of the cliff⟩ ⟨the *brink* of the canyon⟩ ⟨the *brink* of disaster⟩ ⟨the lineaments of that girl on the *brink* of death were those of the woman already dead —Edith Sitwell⟩ ⟨on the *brink* of a horrible danger —Oscar Wilde⟩

²border \"\ *vb* **bordered; bordered; bordering** \-d(ə)riŋ\ **borders** [ME *borduren*, fr. *bordure*, n.] *vt* **1 :** to make a border for **:** furnish with a border **:** put a border on ⟨~*ing* the cloth with lace⟩ **2 a :** to form a border or boundary to **:** BOUND ⟨shade trees ~*ing* the streets of the town⟩ **b** *obs* **:** to confine within bounds **:** LIMIT ⟨that nature which contemns its origin cannot be ~*ed* —Shak.⟩ **3 :** to touch upon the border or boundary of **:** be contiguous or adjacent to **:** ADJOIN ⟨an airport ~*s* the city on the south⟩ ~ *vi* **1 :** to lie on the border **:** be in an adjacent position to ⟨Iowa ~*s* on Missouri⟩ **2 :** to come to be closely similar to a specified thing **:** approach closely the nature or character of a specified thing **:** VERGE — usu. used with *on* ⟨a self-esteem that ~*s* on the ridiculous⟩

border collie *n* **:** a medium-sized black or gray farm dog with white and tan markings that is usu. not recognized as a definable breed though the majority of sheep and herd dogs of the English-Scottish borderlands conform to the type

bor·de·reau \ˌbȯrdəˈrō\ *n, pl* **bordereaux** \-ō(z)\ [F, fr. MF, fr. *bord* border, fr. OF *bort* — more at BORDER] **1 :** a detailed note or memorandum of account; *esp* **:** one containing an enumeration of documents **2 :** a paper setting forth a description of reinsured risks that is prepared by an original underwriter for the information of the reinsuring company

bordered *adj* **:** having a border: as **a :** having a margin differentiated by its structure or marking — used esp. of a leaf **b :** having a border of a specified tincture — used in heraldry

bordered pit *n* [*bordered*, past part. of ²*border*] **:** a wood-cell pit (as of gymnosperm tracheids) having the secondary cell wall arched over the pit cavity

border effect *n, photog* **:** an adjacency effect characterized by a faint dark line just within the high-density side of the margin lying between a lightly exposed and a heavily exposed area

bor·der·er \ˈbȯ(r)dərə(r)\ *n* -s [ME, fr. *border*, *bordure* border + *-er*, *-ere* -er] **1 :** an inhabitant of a border ⟨valiant ~*s* who built their log huts in the woods —Van Wyck Brooks⟩; *specif* **:** an inhabitant of the border between England and Scotland **2** *archaic* **a :** one that is located nearby **:** NEIGHBOR **b :** one that verges ⟨~*s* on the savage state —William Hazlitt⟩ **3** [²*border* + *-er*] **:** one that makes or applies a border

bordering *n* -s [fr. gerund of ²*border*] **:** something that serves as a border **:** EDGING

border irrigation *n* **:** irrigation controlled or directed by short dikes around areas treated

¹bor·der·land \ˈbȯ(r)də(r),land, -laa(ə)nd\ *n* **1 a :** territory at or near a border **:** FRONTIER ⟨rugged folk of the ~⟩ **b :** an outlying region; *esp* **:** fringe area ⟨living from hand to mouth on the ~ of society⟩ **c :** the farthest point proper to or within the scope of a given state, condition, or field of activity **:** BOUNDARY, LIMITS ⟨going beyond the ~ of science⟩ **2 :** a vague region or condition that lacks precise demarcation **:** TWILIGHT ZONE ⟨the ~ between the area of undisputed rights and that of undisputed wrongs —F.L.Mott⟩

²borderland \"\ *adj* **:** BORDERLINE

border leicester *n, usu cap B&L* **:** a strain or variety of the Leicester breed of sheep used in England and Scotland chiefly in the production of superior mutton through crossbreeding esp. with the Cheviot

bor·der·less *adj* **:** being without a border

borderlight \ˈ=,=,=\ *n* **:** a long striplight hung above a theater stage for general illumination

border line *n* **:** a line of demarcation **:** a boundary line

borderline \ˈ=,=,=\ *adj* **1 :** situated at or near a border line ⟨a ~ town⟩ **2 a :** situated between two points or states **:** INTERMEDIATE ⟨mental ~ states between dream and wakefulness —Józef Wittlin⟩ **b :** verging on one or the other place or state without being definitely assignable to either one **:** MARGINAL ⟨a ~ district that was neither opulent nor impoverished⟩; *esp* **:** not quite average, standard, or normal ⟨a person of ~ intelligence⟩ **c :** not quite meeting or conforming to accepted patterns (as of good taste or morality); *esp* **:** verging on the indecent or obscene ⟨a ~ joke⟩ ⟨a ~ book⟩ **d :** not clearly fixed or convincing **:** subject to challenge or debate **:** DUBIOUS, QUESTIONABLE ⟨in their opinion the new theory is of ~ validity⟩ **e :** manifesting typical but not altogether conclusive characteristics **:** apparently existent but lacking definitive development ⟨a patient with ~ diabetes⟩ ⟨attempting some sort of ~ economy⟩

border pen *n* **:** a drawing pen designed for the drawing of ornamental borders

border ruffian *n, often cap B&R* **:** one of a group of proslavery Missourians during the period from 1854 until the beginning of the Civil War who used to cross the border into Kansas to vote illegally, make raids, and intimidate the antislavery settlers

borders *pl of* BORDER, *pres 3d sing of* BORDER

border state *n* **1** *sometimes cap B&S* **a :** a state (as Delaware, Maryland, Virginia, Kentucky, or Missouri) bordering on an antislavery state and favoring slavery before the Civil War **b :** a state (as Maryland, West Virginia, Kentucky, Missouri, Oklahoma, or Tennessee) just north of the Solid South and traditionally voting Democratic **c :** a state (as Montana or No. Dakota) bordering on Canada **2 :** a small country (as Poland) bordering on a larger more powerful country; *esp* **:** such a country lying between two larger more powerful countries **:** BUFFER STATE

border stone *n* **:** a boundary stone **:** CURBSTONE

border terrier *n, usu cap B & often cap T* **:** a small terrier of a breed originating in the border area between England and Scotland with a harsh and dense coat and close undercoat and colored variously red, grizzle and tan, blue and tan, or wheaten

border warrant *n, usu cap B* **:** a writ of arrest issued on one side of the Scottish border for execution on the other side

bor·det-gen·gou \ˌbȯrˈdāˈzhäⁿˈgü\ *adj, usu cap B&G* [Jules J.B.V. *Bordet* b1870 Belgian bacteriologist and Octave *Gengou* †1957 Belgian bacteriologist] **:** of, relating to, or for use in connection with the Bordet-Gengou bacillus ⟨*Bordet-Gengou* media⟩

bordet-gengou bacillus *n, usu cap 1st B&G* **:** a small ovoid bacillus (*Hemophilus pertussis*) held to cause whooping cough

bordet-gengou test *n, usu cap B&G* **:** COMPLEMENT FIXATION TEST; *specif* **:** WASSERMANN TEST

bordroom \ˈ=,=\ *n* **:** a space off a bord from which the coal is being or has been mined — compare BORD-AND-PILLAR

bords *pl of* BORD

bordun *var of* BOURDON

bor·dure \ˈbȯrjər, ˈbȯrdyər, bȯrˈdü(ə)r, *or as F*\ *n* -s [ME, fr. MF — more at BORDER] **1 :** a border about the field often used esp. in Scottish heraldry to difference the arms of a cadet from those of the chief of the family **2 :** BORDER 1; *specif* **:** a border used as a garnish (as around meat, fish, or desserts) ⟨chicken giblets with a ~ of rice⟩

bordure

¹bore \ˈbō(ə)r, ˈbȯ(ə)r,ˈbōə,ˈbȯ(ə)\ *vb* -ED/-ING/-S [ME *boren*, fr. OE *borian*; akin to OHG *borōn* to bore, ON *bora*, L *forare* to bore, *ferire* to strike, Gk *pharos* plow, Russ *borona* harrow] *vt* **1 :** to pierce esp. by or as if by means of a rotatory tool (as a drill, auger, or gimlet) ⟨*boring* a plank at 5-inch intervals⟩ **:** make a cylindrical opening in or through by removal of material ⟨a tree with its center *bored* out⟩ **:** make a hole in or through **:** PENETRATE **2 a :** to form or construct by boring ⟨a tunnel was *bored* through the mountain⟩ **:** sink (as a mine shaft or a well) by boring **b :** to hollow out evenly **:** enlarge (a roughly formed hole) and finish true to size and center by internal turning against a boring tool **3** *of a horse* **:** to push or thrust aside ⟨the leading racehorse *bored* the closest competitor off course⟩ ~ *vi* **1 a :** to make a hole by boring ⟨insects that ~ into trees⟩ **:** sink a mine shaft, well, or other cylindrical opening by boring ⟨~ for oil⟩ **b :** to become pierced or penetrated by an instrument that cuts as it turns ⟨this timber does not ~ well⟩ **2 a :** to make one's way laboriously ⟨we *bored* through the jostling crowds⟩ **b :** to move ahead steadily **:** push forward with constant irresistible force ⟨in spite of furious antiaircraft fire, waves of planes *bored* in over the city⟩ **3** *of a horse* **:** to thrust the head forward and downward putting weight on the bit **4 :** to stare with a fixed penetrating gaze ⟨his eyes were still *boring* into vacancy —William DuBois⟩ **syn** see PERFORATE

²bore \"\ *n* -s [ME, fr. *boren*, v., and ON *bora* hole made by boring (akin to ON *bora* to bore)] **1 :** a hole made by or as if by boring: as **a** *Scot* **:** CREVICE, CHINK **b** (1) **:** a deep vertical hole (as a mine shaft or well) (2) *Austral* **:** a water hole for cattle **c :** a surface opening or outlet (as of a geyser) **d :** TUNNEL **2 a :** an interior cylindrical opening usu. running the entire or nearly the entire length of an object ⟨the ~ of a thermometer⟩ ⟨the ~ of an artery⟩ **b :** the interior tube of a gun: (1) **:** the interior tube of old muzzle-loading ordnance including cylinder and, if present, chamber and the part connecting cylinder and chamber — see CANNON illustration (2) **:** the interior tube of modern breech-loading ordnance; *esp* **:** that between the muzzle and the forward end of the chamber **3 a :** the size of a hole **b :** the interior diameter of a tube (as of a hypodermic needle or a gun barrel) **:** CALIBER, GAUGE **c :** the diameter of an engine cylinder **4 :** a tool (as an auger) for boring

³bore \"\ *past or dial past part of* BEAR

⁴bore \"\ *n* -s [fr. (assumed) ME *bore* wave, fr. ON *bāra*; prob. akin to OE *beran* to carry — more at BEAR] **:** a tidal flood that regularly or occas. rushes with a roaring noise into certain rivers (as the Amazon in So. America) or narrow bays (as the Bay of Fundy) of peculiar configuration or location and proceeds in one or more waves that often present a very abrupt front of considerable height dangerous to shipping

⁵bore *vt* -ED/-ING/-S [perh. alter. of obs. *bourd* to make a fool of, jest with, jest, fr. ME *bourden* to jest, fr. MF *bourder*, *border*, fr. OF, fr. *bourde*, *borde* jest] *obs* **:** to make a fool of **:** TRICK

⁶bore *like* ¹BORE\ *n* -s [origin unknown] **1 :** a cause of ennui: **a :** a dull tiresome annoying person ⟨a loquacious self-centered ~⟩ **b :** something that is monotonous, wearisome, and tediously devoid of interest ⟨an evening that turned out to be one long ~⟩

7bore \"\ *vt* -ED/-ING/-S **:** to afflict with ennui **:** depress, weary, and annoy by dullness **:** crush with irksome tediousness ⟨*bored* by the same old facts —Marston Bates⟩

bo·re·al \ˈbōrēəl, ˈbȯr-\ *adj* [ME *boriall*, fr. LL *borealis*, fr. L *boreas* north wind, *Boreas*, Greek god of the north wind + *-alis* -al] **1 :** of, relating to, or located in northern regions **2 :** NORTHERN: as **a** *usu cap* **:** of, relating to, or constituting a terrestrial biogeographic division comprising the northern and mountainous parts of the northern hemisphere in which mean temperature during the six hottest weeks does not exceed 64.4°F and being equivalent to the Holarctic region exclusive of the Sonoran and Transition zones and corresponding Old World areas; *esp* **:** NEARCTIC **b** *usu cap* **:** of or relating to a terrestrial biogeographic zone between the Arctic and the Transitional zone and made up of Hudsonian and Canadian zones **c :** of or relating to the northern biotic area characterized by dominance of coniferous forests and tundra **3 :** of, relating to, or marked by qualities associated with Boreas **:** COLD, ICY, FROSTY, WINTRY ⟨~ snows and never-thawing ice —J.A.Hillhouse⟩ **4 :** relating to or constituting a period in postglacial times when Europe and No. America had a cooler climate like that of the present Boreal region

bo·re·al·i·za·tion \ˌ≈≈ələˈzāshən\ *n* -S **:** adaptation (as of plants) to life in more northerly regions

boreal sign *n* **:** one of the signs of the zodiac from Aries to Virgo that lie wholly or in part north of the celestial equator

bo·re·as \ˈbōrēəs, ˈbȯr- *also* -ē,as *or* -,aa(ə)s\ *n* -ES [ME, fr. L *boreas* north wind, *Boreas*, Greek god of the north wind, fr. Gk; perh. akin to OSlav *gora* mountain, Skt *giri*] **:** the north wind or wind from north by east

bore bit *n* **:** a bit for drilling rock

bore·cole \ˈbōr,kōl, ˈbȯr-\ *n* -S [modif. of D *boerenkool*, fr. *boeren-* (fr. *boer* peasant) + *kool* cabbage; akin to OE *cāl* cabbage — more at BOOR, COLE] **:** KALE

bored *adj* [fr. past part. of *7bore*] **:** filled with boredom

bore·dom \ˈbōrdəm, ˈbȯrd-,ˈbōd-,ˈbȯ(ə)d-\ *n* -S [*6bore* + *-dom*] **1 :** the state of being bored **:** ENNUI ⟨jaundiced actors suffering from total ~⟩ **2 :** a cause or instance of boredom **:** BORE ⟨every meal with the family was an unmitigated ~⟩

1boree *n* -S [modif. of F *bourrée* — more at BOURRÉE] *obs* **:** BOURRÉE

2bor·ee \ˈbȯrē\ *n* -S [Australian (Queensland) *booreah*, lit., fire] *Austral* **:** any of several wattle trees (as *Acacia pendula* and *A. glaucescens*) — see MYALL

bo·reen \bōˈrēn\ *n* -S [IrGael *bóithrín*, dim. of *bóthar* road, fr. OIr, prob. fr. *bó* ox, cow; akin to L *bos* cow — more at COW] *Irish* **:** a narrow country road or lane esp. in hilly country

bore from within *vi* [*1bore*] **:** to move with caution and secrecy esp. by insinuating oneself into the confidence of others so as to gain an objective otherwise impossible of achievement; *esp* **:** to undermine something insidiously and treacherously ⟨agents infiltrating the government and *boring from within*⟩

bor·e·gat \ˈbȯrə,gat\ *n* -S [origin unknown] **:** CALIFORNIA SEA TROUT

borehole \ˈ≈,≈\ *n* **:** a hole made by boring; *esp* **:** WELL

bor·e·le \ˈbȯrə,lā\ *n* -S [Tswana *bodile*] **:** BLACK RHINOCEROS

bore·mat·ic \bōrˈmad·ik\ *n* -S [*2bore* + *-matic* (as in *automatic*)] **:** an automatic drill press

bore meal \ˈ≈,≈\ *n* **:** the crushed debris brought up by boring (as through rock)

bor·er \ˈbōrə(r), ˈbȯr-\ *n* -S [ME, fr. *boren* to bore + *-er*, *-ere* -er, fr. OE *-ere* — more at 1BORE, -ER] **1 :** one that bores: as **a :** a worker who bores holes **b :** a tool (as a drill) used for boring **2 :** any of various animals that burrow in wood or other substances: as **a :** SHIPWORM **b :** any of various bivalve mollusks (as those of the genera *Saxicava* and *Lithophaga*) that bore in limestone rock — compare PIDDOCK **c :** 5DRILL 4a **d :** any of numerous insects of different orders (as Lepidoptera and Coleoptera) that as larva or adult bore in the woody parts (as bark, stem or roots) of plants **3 :** HAGFISH **4 :** ACCRETION BORER

bores *pres 3d sing of* BORE, *pl of* BORE

bore·scope \ˈbōr,skōp\ *n* -S [*2bore* + *-scope*] **:** a device usu. consisting of either a prism or a tube with a small mirror at one end and used to inspect a cylindrical cavity (as the bore of a gun or the inside of a hydraulic cylinder)

boresight \ˈ≈,≈\ *vt* **1 :** to bring into proper parallel alignment (the bore and sights of a gun) by sighting on a distant point through the bore and adjusting the sights on that same point **2 a :** to aim at (a target) by sighting through the bore **b :** to aim at (a target) very accurately

bore·some \ˈbō(ə)rsəm, ˈbȯ(ə)rs-,ˈbōəs-,ˈbȯ(ə)s-\ *adj* **:** causing or tending to cause boredom **:** TEDIOUS, MONOTONOUS, TIRESOME — **bore·some·ly** *adv*

bore·tree \ˈbōr,trē\ *var of* BOURTREE

bo·ric \ˈbōrik, ˈbȯr-, -rēk\ *adj* [F *borique*, fr. *bore* boron (fr. *borax*, fr. ML) + *-ique* -ic] **:** of, relating to, or derived from boron — used esp. of compounds in which this element is combined with oxygen

boric acid *n* **:** any acid derived from boric oxide: as **a :** a white crystalline toxic weak acid H_3BO_3 that occurs naturally in solution in the fumaroles of Tuscany, that is easily obtained from its salts, and that is used for many of the same purposes as borax and also in electroplating and formerly as a weak antiseptic (as in eyewashes) — called also *boracic acid*, *orthoboric acid* **b :** METABORIC ACID **c :** TETRABORIC ACID

bor·ick·ite \ˈbȯrə,kīt *sometimes* ˈbȯrzhət,sk-\ *n* -S [Emanuel *Bořický* †1881 Czech petrographer + E *-ite*] **:** a mineral consisting of a reddish brown compact hydrous basic phosphate of iron and calcium of uncertain composition

boric oxide *also* **boric anhydride** *n* **:** the trioxide B_2O_3 of boron obtained usu. as a transparent glassy solid by fusing boric acid

bo·ride \ˈbōr,īd, ˈbȯ,rīd, -,rəd\ *n* -S [ISV *bor-* + *-ide*] **:** a binary compound of boron usu. with a more electropositive element or radical

bo·rine \ˈbōr,ēn, ˈbȯ,rēn, -,rən\ *n* -S [*bor-* + *-ine*] **1 :** a borane BH_3 known only in the form of derivatives **2 :** a derivative [as trimethyl-borine $(CH_3)_3B$] of borine

1boring *n* -S [ME *boringe*, fr. *boren* to bore + *-inge*, *-ing* -ing, fr. OE *-ung*, *-ing* — more at BORE, -ING] **1 :** the action or process of one that bores ⟨a successful ~ for oil⟩ ⟨the ~ of wood by insects⟩ **2 a :** an inner cavity (as of a tube) **:** BORE ⟨the ~ of a shotgun⟩ **b :** BOREHOLE **3 :** the residue (as shavings or chips) left after the process of boring — usu. used in pl.

2boring *adj* [fr. pres. part. of *1bore*] **:** that bores **:** PIERCING ⟨a ~ tool⟩

3boring *adj* [fr. pres. part. of *7bore*] **:** causing boredom **:** TIRESOME, TEDIOUS — **bor·ing·ly** *adv* — **bor·ing·ness** *n* -ES

boring bar *n* **:** a cylindrical cutter bar to which a boring tool or cutter is securely attached

boring bit *n* **:** a steel cutter bit to be supported by a boring bar inside a hole (as the bore of a large gun) in process of enlargement

boring block *n* **1 :** a slotted block for holding work to be bored **2 :** the cutter holder on a boring rod

boring clam *n* **:** any of several marine clams that bore into or dissolve away rock, cement, clay, or mud, making chambers in which they live

boring head *n* **:** the cutting end of a boring tool: as **a :** the cutterhead of a diamond drill **b :** the cutter holder on a boring rod

boring machine *n* **:** a machine essentially like a drill press but designed primarily for boring holes in wood with an auger bit

boring mill *n* [*1boring*] **:** a large machine tool essentially a lathe but commonly with rotating work table, fixed cutting tools, and a vertical axis

boring mussel *n* [*2boring*] **:** DATE MUSSEL

boring rod *n* **:** a rod made up of segments carrying at its lower end a tool for earth boring or rock drilling — compare AUGER STEM

boring sponge *n* **:** any sponge of *Cliona* or related genera that penetrates the substance of shells, some species (as *C. celata*) of the Atlantic coast being injurious to oysters

boring tool *n* **:** a boring bit with its supporting boring bar and arbor, used to enlarge and accurately finish a large bore previously formed by casting or otherwise

boring tube *n* [*1boring*] **:** WELL CASING

bo·rin·que·ño \ˌbōriŋˈkān(ˌ)yō\ *n* -S *cap* [Sp, fr. *Borinquén*, *Boriquen*, old name for Puerto Rico, fr. Taino *Boriquen*] **1 :** a native or resident of Puerto Rico **2 :** one of the extinct aboriginal Indians of Puerto Rico — compare ARAWAK

bor·i·ty \ˈbōrəd·ē\ *n* -ES [Swahili *boriti*] *East Africa* **:** a mangrove pole

1born \ˈbȯ(ə)rn, -ō(ə)n\ *adj* [ME *born*, *yborn*, fr. OE *boren*, *geboren*; akin to OHG *giboran* born, carried, ON *borinn*, Goth *baurans*, *gabaurans*; past part. of the verb represented by OE *beran* to bear, carry — more at BEAR] **1 a :** brought into existence by or as if by birth ⟨a newly ~ baby⟩ ⟨a recently ~ idea⟩ **b :** by birth **:** NATIVE ⟨American-*born*⟩ **:** having as place of birth ⟨Maine-*born*⟩ **c :** having origin in or from ⟨sea-*born* breezes⟩ ⟨a country-*born* boor⟩ **:** deriving or resulting from ⟨poverty-*born* crime⟩ **2 a :** having from or as if from birth specified or implied qualities ⟨a ~ leader⟩ or status or character or makeup ⟨a ~ criminal⟩ ⟨a ~ aristocrat⟩ — sometimes used postpositively ⟨though a fisherman ~, he did not want to fish now —Frank Gallagher⟩ **b :** being in specified circumstances from or as if from birth ⟨~ to riches⟩ ⟨nobly ~⟩ **3 :** not acquired **:** NATURAL, INNATE ⟨her ~ dignity⟩ ⟨a ~ respect for old age⟩ **4 :** destined from or as if from birth ⟨~ to succeed⟩ **5** *chiefly dial* **:** existing or elapsed from the time of one's birth — used chiefly in the phrase *born days* ⟨I never saw anything like it in all my ~ days⟩

2born \"\ *vt* **borned** *or* **born**; **borned** *or* **born**; **borning**; **borns 1** *dial* **:** to give birth to **:** BEAR ⟨she ~*ed* four children⟩ **2** *dial* **:** to assist at the birth of **:** DELIVER ⟨I seen him ~ twin calves from a cow —Helen Eustis⟩

bor·na disease \ˈbȯrnə-\ *n*, *usu cap B* [trans. of G *bornasche krankheit*, fr. *Borna*, Saxony, Germany, where the disease was esp. prevalent in the 1890s] **:** a virus disease of equines related to sleeping sickness that occurs as an acute infectious inflammation of the brain and spinal cord usu. giving rise to violent trembling, unsteady gait, inability to swallow, great excitement and signs of pain, or to stupor

bor·nane \ˈbȯr,nān\ *n* -S [ISV *born-* (fr. *borneol*) + *-ane*] **:** a crystalline saturated terpene $C_{10}H_{18}$ that may be regarded as the parent compound of borneol, camphor, and related compounds; 1,7,7-trimethyl-norbornane — called also *camphane*

1borne *past part of* BEAR

2bor·né \(ˈ)bȯrˈnā\ *adj* [F, past part. of *borner* to limit, fr. OF *borner*, *bonner* to delimit, fr. *borne*, *bonne* limit, boundary — more at BOUND] **:** LIMITED **:** lacking scope, depth, or variety esp. in breadth of vision or variety of interests **:** NARROW-MINDED, HIDEBOUND, PROVINCIAL ⟨his slow methodical ~ mind —Walter Bagehot⟩

1bor·ne·an \ˈbȯ(r)nēən\ *adj*, *usu cap* [*Borneo*, island in the Malay archipelago + E *-an*] **1 :** of, relating to, or characteristic of the island of Borneo **2 :** of, relating to, or characteristic of the people of Borneo

2bornean \"\ *n* -S *cap* **:** a native or inhabitant of Borneo

bor·née \(ˈ)bȯrˈnā\ *adj* [F, fem. of *borné*] *of a woman* **:** BORNÉ ⟨a rather ordinary girl, ~, perhaps stupid —E.R.Bentley⟩

bor·neo camphor \ˈbȯ(r)nē,ō-\ *n*, *usu cap B* **:** a camphor that occurs in masses in a tree (*Dryobalanops aromatica*) of the family Dipterocarpaceae and is used as an incense and in embalming; dextrorotatory borneol — called also *Malay camphor*, *Sumatra camphor*

bor·ne·ol \-ē,ȯl, -ōl\ *n* -S [*Borneo* + ISV *-ol*] **:** a crystalline cyclic terpenoid alcohol $C_{10}H_{17}OH$ known in three optically different forms distinguished as dextrorotatory borneol, levorotatory borneol, and racemic borneol, found in many essential oils (as pine oils), formed by reduction of camphor, and used chiefly in the form of esters (as the acetate) in perfumery — called also *bornyl alcohol*; see ISOBORNEOL

borneo tallow *n*, *usu cap B* **:** a hard brittle greenish fat obtained esp. from nuts of trees of the genus *Shorea* growing in the Malay archipelago and used as a substitute for cocoa butter

born·holm disease \ˈbȯrn,hō(l)m-\ *n*, *usu cap B* [*Bornholm*, Danish island in the Baltic sea, where it has been observed] **:** EPIDEMIC PLEURODYNIA

borning *n* -S [fr. gerund of *2born*] *dial* **:** BIRTH 1

born·ite \ˈbȯr,nīt, *usu* -īd.+V\ *n* -S [G *bornit*, fr. Ignaz von *Born* †1791 Austrian mineralogist + G *-it* -ite] **:** a valuable brittle metallic-looking sulfide of copper and iron Cu_5FeS_4 usu. brownish on fresh fracture (hardness 3, sp. gr. 4.9-5.4) — called also *erubescite*, *horseflesh ore*, *purple copper ore* — **born·it·ic** \(ˈ)bȯrˈnid·ik\ *adj*

bor·nyl \ˈbȯrnᵊl, -,nil, -,nēl\ *n* -S [ISV *born-* (fr. *borneol*) + *-yl*] **:** a univalent radical $C_{10}H_{17}$ derived from borneol by removal of hydroxyl — called in full *2-bornyl*

bornyl alcohol *n* **:** BORNEOL

boro- — see BOR-

1bo·ro \ˈbō(ˌ)rō\ *n* -S [Hindi, fr. Skt *vorava*] *India* **:** rice harvested in spring

2boro \" *or* **bo·ra** \ˈbōrə\ *n*, *pl* **boro** *or* **boros** *or* **bora** *or* **boras** *usu cap* [Sp, of AmerInd origin] **1 a :** a Witotoan people of southeastern Colombia, northeastern Peru, and adjacent areas in Brazil **b :** a member of such people **2 :** the language of the Boro people

bo·ro·fluoric acid \ˌbōrō, ˌbȯ-+...-\ *n* [ISV *bor-* + *fluoric*] **:** FLUOBORIC ACID

bo·ro·fluoride \"+\ *n* [ISV *bor-* + *fluoride*] **:** FLUOBORATE

bo·ro·glyceride \"+\ *n* [*bor-* + *glyceride*] **:** a compound of boric acid and glycerol formerly used as an antiseptic

bo·ro·hydride \"+\ *n* [*bor-* + *hydride*] **:** any of a class of compounds containing the anion BH_4^- (as sodium borohydride $NaBH_4$) that are useful reducing agents — called also *hydroborate*, *tetrahydroborate*

bo·ron \ˈbōr,än, ˈbȯ,rän\ *n* -S [*borax* + *-on* (as in *carbon*)] **:** a high-melting trivalent metalloid element that is known both in an extremely hard shiny black crystalline form and in the form of a greenish yellow or brown amorphous powder, that occurs in nature only in combination (as in borax and boric acid and as a trace element in plants and animals), that is usu. obtained by electrolysis of fused potassium fluoborate and potassium chloride or by thermal reduction of other compounds (as boric oxide), and that is used chiefly in metallurgy (as for increasing the hardenability of steel) and in nucleonics because of its high absorption of neutrons — symbol *B*; see ELEMENT table

bo·ro·na·tro·cal·cite \ˌbōrō,nā·trō'kal,sīt\ *n* -S [G *boronatrokalzit*, fr. *bor-* + *natro-* natr- + *kalz-* calc- + *-it* -ite] **:** ULEXITE

boron carbide *n* **:** any binary compound of boron and carbon; *esp* **:** a refractory shiny black crystalline solid B_4C ranking next to the diamond in hardness made usu. by heating boric oxide and coke in an electric furnace and used chiefly as powdered and molded abrasives

bo·ro·nia \bəˈrōnēə\ *n* [NL, fr. Francesco *Borone* 18th cent. Ital. servant + NL *-ia*] **1** *cap* **:** a large genus of Australian aromatic shrubs (family Rutaceae) with highly scented red, purple, or white flowers **2** -S **:** a plant of the genus *Boronia*

bo·ron·ic \(ˈ)bōrˈänik, (ˈ)bȯˈrä-, bəˈrä-\ *adj* **:** of or relating to boron

boron nitride *n* **:** any binary compound of boron and nitrogen; *esp* **:** a fluffy white crystalline powder BN made in various ways (as by the reaction of ammonia and fused boric oxide) and used chiefly as a lubricant and electric insulator

boron trifluoride *n* **:** a colorless pungent gas BF_3 that fumes in moist air, that is made usu. by reaction of a boron compound (as borax) with a fluoride (as hydrogen fluoride) and then sulfuric acid, and that is used chiefly as an acidic catalyst in organic reactions (as alkylations and polymerizations)

bo·ro·ro \bōˈrärō\ *n*, *pl* **bororo** *or* **bororos** *usu cap* [Pg *Bororó*, of AmerInd origin] **1 a :** a people of southern Brazil **b :** a member of such people **2 :** the language of the Bororo people constituting the Bororoan language family of the Borotuke stock — called also *Coroado* — **bo·ro·ro·an** \-ən\ *adj*, *usu cap*

bo·ro·silicate \ˌbōrō, ˌbȯ-+\ *n* [ISV *bor-* + *silicate*] **:** a silicate (as datolite) containing boron in the anion

borosilicate glass *n* **:** a silicate glass having at least 5 percent of boric oxide and used esp. in heat-resistant glassware

bo·ro·tu·ke \ˌbōr,ōd·əˈkā\ *n*, *usu cap* [blend of *Bororo* and *Otuke*] **:** a language stock of Brazil and Paraguay comprising the Bororo and Otuke

bo·ro·tungstic acid \ˌbōrō, ˌbȯ-+...-\ *n* [ISV *bor* + *tungstic*] **:** any of several complex acids of boron and tungsten (as a colorless crystalline acid $H_5BW_{12}O_{40}.xH_2O$) — called also *tungstoboric acid*

bor·ough \ˈbər·(ˌ)ō, ˈbərə, ˈbə·(ˌ)rō, ˈbərə, *often* -r·əw *or* -·rəw+V\ *n* -S [ME *burgh*, *burwe*, *borugh*, fr. OE *burg*, *burh* fortified town, fortress; akin to OHG *burg* fortified place, ON *borg* wall, fortification, Goth *baurgs* city, MIr *brí* hill, Av *bərəz-* high, OE *beorg* mountain, hill, mound — more at BARROW] **1 a :** a medieval fortified group of houses (as in Great Britain) forming a town with special duties and privileges, having in its later form its own courts, the right of burgherhood inheritable, representatives in the national council or parliament, and holding a charter from the king **b :** a town or urban constituency in Great Britain that sends a member or members to Parliament; *also* **:** an organized part of such a constituency sharing in the election of a member **c :** an urban area in Great Britain incorporated for purposes of self-government — see 1COUNTY 3c, METROPOLITAN BOROUGH, MUNICIPAL BOROUGH **d :** an incorporated town in Scotland **:** BURGH; *specif* **:** one returning or contributing to return a member to Parliament **2 a :** a municipal corporation proper in some states (as Connecticut, Pennsylvania, New Jersey, and Minnesota) corresponding in general to the incorporated town or village of the other states **b :** one of the five constituent political divisions of New York City **3 :** a village, township, or town in New Zealand having a special governing body **4 a :** a town area in New So. Wales in Australia as incorporated by an act of Parliament of 1857 or holding a special charter from the crown — compare MUNICIPALITY, SHIRE **b :** a municipal area in Australia of a minimum size and population

borough-english \ˌ≈ˈ≈≈\ *n*, *usu cap E* [earlier *burghenglish*, part trans. of AF *burgh engloys*, fr. *burgh* borough (fr. ME) + *engloys* English] **:** a former custom in some cities and boroughs in Great Britain by which estates descended to the youngest son or sometimes to the youngest daughter or collateral heir

borough-holder \ˈ≈≈,≈≈\ *n* **1 :** one holding property by burgage in certain Yorkshire boroughs in England **2 :** BORSHOLDER

boroughmonger \ˈ≈≈,≈≈\ *n*, *archaic* **:** one who buys or sells the parliamentary seats of boroughs in England

boroughreeve \ˈ≈≈,≈\ *n* **:** the chief municipal officer in certain unincorporated English municipalities before 1835

bor·ra·cha \bəˈräshə\ *n* -S [Pg, lit., leather wine bottle, prob. fr. Sp, fr. *borracho* intoxicated — more at BORACHIO] **1 :** any of several grades of crude Para rubber **2 :** any of several Brazilian latex-producing trees; *also* **:** their coagulated gum (as balata, Ceará rubber, mangabeira rubber, sorva)

borrasca *var of* BORASCA

borrel *adj* [ME *borel*, *burel*, fr. *borel*, *burel* coarse woolen cloth, fr. OF *burel* — more at BUREAU] **1** *obs* **:** belonging to the laity ⟨~ folk —Geoffrey Chaucer⟩ **2** *archaic* **:** UNLETTERED, UNPOLISHED ⟨a coarse, ignorant, ~ man —Sir Walter Scott⟩

bor·rel body \bəˈrel-, bȯˈ-\ *n*, *usu cap 1st B* [after Amédée *Borrel* †1936 Fr. bacteriologist] **:** one of the particles included in a Bollinger body, believed to be actual units of the virus of fowl pox

bor·rel·ia \bəˈrelēə, -rēl-, -lyə\ *n* [NL, fr. Amédée Borrel + NL *-ia*] **1** *cap* **:** a genus of small flexible spirochetes (family Treponemataceae) parasitic upon man and warm-blooded animals, having three to five large wavy spirals and a terminal filament, and including several important pathogens (as *B. anserina*, the cause of septicemia in chickens, *B. recurrentis*, the cause of European relapsing fever, and *B. duttoni*, the cause of the relapsing fever of Africa) **2** -S **:** a spirochete of the genus *Borrelia*

bor·rel·o·my·ce·ta·ce·ae \bəˌrelō,mīsōˈtāsē,ē, -ˌrēl-\ *n pl*, *cap* [NL, fr. Amédée *Borrel* + NL *-o-* + *mycet-* + *-aceae*] *in some classifications* **:** a group of microorganisms coextensive with Mycoplasmataceae

bor·rel's blue \bəˈrelz-, bȯˈ-\ *n*, *usu cap 1st B* [after Amédée *Borrel*] **:** a stain made by adding methylene blue to silver oxide and used in parasitology

bor·re·ria \bəˈrirēə\ *n*, *cap* [NL, fr. William *Borrer* †1862 Eng. botanist + NL *-ia*] **:** a genus of herbs or shrubs (family Rubiaceae) found in warm or tropical regions with opposite entire leaves and small funnel-shaped flowers

bor·rich·ia \bəˈrikēə\ *n*, *cap* [NL, fr. Olaus *Borrichius* †1690 Dan. medical writer + NL *-ia*] **:** a small genus of low shrubby American herbs (family Compositae) having coriaceous or fleshy opposite leaves and solitary heads of yellow flowers with blackish anthers

1bor·row \ˈbä(ˌ)rō, -ˌrə *also* ˈbȯ-; *often* -ˌrəw+V; *chiefly in substand speech* -ˌrē *or* -ˌri\ *vb* -ED/-ING/-S [ME *borwen*, fr. OE *borgian*; akin to OHG *borgēn* to take heed, give security, ON *borga* to go bail, OE *beorgan* to preserve, defend — more at BURY] *vt* **1 :** to receive temporarily from another, implying or expressing the intention either of returning the thing received or of giving its equivalent to the lender **:** obtain the temporary use of ⟨he returned the pen that he had ~*ed* from her⟩; *specif* **:** to receive (a book, magazine, or other circulating material) from a lending library for temporary use outside the library premises ⟨these books may be ~*ed* for two weeks⟩ **2 a :** to appropriate (something not capable of being returned) for one's own esp. immediate or temporary use ⟨the speaker ~*ed* a metaphor from Shakespeare⟩ ⟨the books from which he has ~*ed* his opinions —G.B.Shaw⟩ **b :** to derive (as authority) from another **:** have by a right that is not inherent ⟨~*ing* prestige from the ability of his predecessor⟩ **c :** to derive from an alien source, somewhat radically adapting and modifying the thing so obtained ⟨voodoo practices are frequently blended with rituals ~*ed* from established Christian denominations —*Amer. Guide Series: La.*⟩ **3** *obs* **:** to be surety for **:** set free by or as if by ransom ⟨if thou be taken prisoner . . . I will not ~ thee —John Palsgrave⟩ **4 :** to take (one) from a figure of the minuend in arithmetical subtraction in order to add as 10 to the next lower denomination when the latter figure is less than the corresponding one of the subtrahend ⟨~ 1 from 4 in the number 42 to add as 10 to the 2 in order to carry out the subtraction 42 minus 25 equals 17⟩ **5 :** to introduce (as a word) into one language from another ⟨English *kindergarten* was ~*ed* from German⟩ — see LOANWORD **6 :** to dig (as from a borrow pit) ⟨~*ing* earth to make a fill⟩ **7** *dial* **:** LEND ⟨~ me your pencil⟩ **8 :** to bring in (organ pipes) from a stop in another division **~** *vi* **1 :** to receive, appropriate, or derive something (as by way of a loan) from another ⟨a mixed people freely ~*ing* from others in religion, language, laws, and manners —M.R.Cohen⟩ **2 :** to make a stop or part of a stop in one division of a pipe organ available in another division **3 :** to putt to the left or right of the cup in golf so as to allow for the slant or roll of the green — **borrow trouble :** to take upon oneself needless trouble or anxiety ⟨if you just stick to your own job you won't be *borrowing trouble*⟩

2borrow *n* -S [ME *borwe*, fr. OE *borg*, *borh*, prob. back-formation fr. *borgian*] **1** *obs* **:** something deposited as security **:** PLEDGE **2** *obs* **a :** SURETY **b :** HOSTAGE

3borrow *like* 1BORROW\ *n* -S [*1borrow*] **1** *archaic* **a :** the act of borrowing **b :** something borrowed **2 :** material (as earth or gravel) taken from one location (as a borrow pit) to be used for fill at another location

borrow ditch *n* **:** a ditch dug along a roadway to furnish fill and provide drainage

borrowed light *n* **:** reflected light; *specif* **:** light entering an interior and otherwise dark room or passage from an adjoining space having windows or skylights

borrowed time *n* **:** an unexpected or artifically contrived extension of time usu. of uncertain and limited duration ⟨an old, old man who was merely living on *borrowed time*⟩

bor·row·er \-ˌrəwə(r)\ *n* -S [ME *borwere*, fr. *borwen* to borrow + *-ere* -er] **:** one that borrows

borrowing *n* -S [fr. gerund of *1borrow*] **1 a :** the act of one that borrows **b :** something borrowed; *esp* **:** a word or phrase adopted from one language into another ⟨English is full of foreign-language ~*s*⟩ **2 a :** adoption (as of a custom) from a neighboring people ⟨extensive Indian ~ of material culture —E.H.Spicer⟩ **b :** something (as a custom) adopted from a neighboring people ⟨cultural ~*s* from Italy —R.W.Murray⟩

borrowing days *n pl*, *Scot* **:** the last three days of March, Old Style

borrow pit *n* **:** an excavated area where material (as earth) has been borrowed to be used as fill at another location

bors *pl of* BOR

borsch *or* **borscht** *or* **borsht** *or* **bortsch** *or* **borshch** \'bȯ(ə)rsh(t) *sometimes* -rshch *or* -rch\ *n, pl* **borsches** *or* **borschts** *or* **borshts** *or* **bortsches** *or* **borshches** [Russ *borshch* cow parsnip (*Heracleum sphondylium*), borsch; fr. the soup's being originally made of cow parsnips; akin to Pol *barszcz* cow parsnip, borsch, Latvian *burkšis* cow parsnip, Skt *bhṛṣṭi* spike, point, OHG *burst* bristle — more at BRISTLE] **:** a soup having fermented or fresh red beet juice as the foundation, sour cream or sour milk often being added when the soup is served

borsch circuit *or* **borscht circuit** *n* **:** the summer theaters and nightclubs associated with the Jewish summer camps and resort hotels of the Catskills

bors·hold·er \'bȯ(r)s,hōldə(r), 'bȯ(r),sō-\ *n* -s [by folk etymology (influence of *holder*) fr. earlier *borsolder*, fr. (assumed) ME *borwes alder, borghes alder* (whence AF *borghesaldre*), fr. (assumed) ME *borwes, borghes* of a tithing (fr. ME *borwes, borghes* of a pledge, gen. of *borwe, borgh* pledge) + ME *alder* leader, chief, fr. OE *aldor, ealdor* chief, parent, head of a family — more at BORROW, ALDERMAN] **1 :** the head person of a tithing **2 :** a parish officer in Great Britain corresponding to the petty constable

¹bor·stal *or* **bor·stall** \'bȯrstᵊl, 'bȯr-\ *n* -s [fr. (assumed) ME *borstall*, fr. OE *borgsteall, borhsteall*, fr. (assumed) OE *borg, borh* protection, refuge (fr. OE *borg, borh* pledge, surety) + OE *steall* place; prob. fr. the use of steep hills as places of refuge in war — more at BORROW, STALL] *dial Eng* **:** a pathway up a steep hill

²borstal \'bȯrstᵊl, 'bȯ(ə)s-\ *or* **borstal institution** *n* -s *often cap B* [fr. *Borstal*, village in Kent, England] **:** one of a group of British reform schools for delinquents between the ages of 16 and 23 that follows a system stressing occupational training, special attention to the individual, and highly organized supervision after dismissal

bort \'bȯ(ə)rt\ *n* -s [prob. fr. D *boort*, perh. fr. MF *bourt* bastard, fr. L *burdus* hinny] **1** *also* **boart** *or* **boort** \'bō(ə)rt, 'bȯ(-\ **:** a diamond of inferior quality **:** a diamond not of gem quality; *collectively* **:** material consisting of imperfectly crystallized diamonds or of fragments produced in cutting diamonds used for dressing and truing grinding wheels and in making abrasive diamond powder — called also *bortz* **2 :** ³CARBONADO

bortz \'bȯ(ə)rts\ *n* -ES [alter. of *borts*, pl. of *bort*] **:** BORT 1

bo·ru·ca \bə'rükə\ *n, pl* **boruca** *or* **borucas** *usu cap* [Sp, of AmerInd origin] **1 :** a Chibchan people on the Pacific coast in southeastern Costa Rica in Central America **2 :** a member of the Boruca people

bo·run \bō'rün\ *n* -s *usu cap* [native name] **:** BOTOCUDO

bo·run·duk \¦bȯrən¦dük\ *n* -s [Russ *burunduk*] **:** BARONDUKI

bo·rus·sian \bō'rəsēən, -rəshən\ *n or adj, usu cap* [NL *Borussia* Prussia, historical region at the eastern end of the south shore of the Baltic sea + E *-an*] **:** PRUSSIAN

bor·zi·cactus \¦bȯrzə+\ *n, cap* [NL, fr. Antonio *Borzi* Ital. botanist + NL *Cactus*] **:** a small genus of cylindrical cacti found in the Andes with well-marked ribs, stout spines, and orange or scarlet flowers

bor·zoi \'bȯr,zȯi *also* ='=\ *n* [Russ *borzoĭ*, fr. *borzoĭ* swift; akin to OSlav. *brŭzŭ* swift, Pol *bardzo* very, Lith *burzdùs* agile, L *festinare* to make haste] **1** *usu cap* **:** a breed of tall slender long-haired dogs of greyhound type developed in Russia esp. for pursuing wolves **2** -s *often cap* **:** a dog of the Borzoi breed — called also *Russian wolfhound*

¹bos \'bäs, 'bōs,\ *n, cap* [NL, fr. L, ox, cow — more at COW] **:** a genus of ruminant mammals including the wild and domestic cattle and sometimes the water buffaloes and related forms, distinguished by a stout body and by hollow curved horns standing out laterally from the skull

²bos *pl of* BO

bo·sa *also* **bo·za** \'bōzə\ *or* **boo·za** *or* **bou·za** \'büzə\ *n* -s [Turk *boza*] **:** a drink of the Egyptians and Arabs resembling beer; *esp* **:** an acidulated fermented drink made from millet

bo·sal \bō'sal\ *n* -s [MexSp, fr. Sp, muzzle, bells on a halter, fr. *bozo* mouth, nose of a horse, halter, fr. L *bucca* mouth, cheek — more at POCK] *Southwest* **:** NOSEBAND

bos·cage *also* **bos·kage** \'bäskij\ *n* -s [ME *boskage*, fr. MF *boscage*, fr. OF, fr. *bosc, bois* forest (perh. of Gmc origin; akin to OHG *busc* forest) + *-age* — more at BUSH] **:** a growth of trees or shrubs **:** GROVE, THICKET, UNDERWOOD

bosch·bok *also* **bosh·bok** \'bäs(h),bäk\ *n* -s [obs. Afrik *boschbok* (now *bosbok*), fr. *bosch* (now *bos*) forest (fr. MD *bosch, busch* — akin to OHG *busc*) + *bok* male antelope, he-goat, fr. MD *boc;* akin to OHG *boc* he-goat — more at BUCK] **:** BUSHBUCK

bosche *usu cap, var of* BOCHE

bosch·vark *or* **bosh·vark** \'bäs(h),värk\ *n* -s [obs. Afrik *boschvark* (now *bosvark*), fr. *bosch* (now *bos*) + *vark* pig, fr. MD *varken;* akin to OHG *farh* little pig — more at FARROW] **:** a southern African bushpig

bosch·veld \'bäs(h),felt\ *n* -s [obs. Afrik (now *bosveld*), fr. *bosch* (now *bos*) + *veld* field, fr. MD *velt;* akin to OHG *feld* field — more at FIELD] **:** BUSHVELD

bose \'bōs\ *vt* -ED/-ING/-S [prob. fr. E dial. *boss* to bang] *archeol* **:** to test (ground) by noting the sound of percussion from the blow of a heavy rammer

bose-ein·stein statistics \'bō'sīnz,¦tīn-, -īn,s¦ *sometimes* -īn,sh¦\ *also* **bose statistics** \'bōs-\ *n pl but sing or pl in constr, usu cap B&E* [after Satyendra Nath *Bose* b1894 Indian physicist and Albert *Einstein* †1955 Am. physicist born in Germany] **:** quantum-mechanical statistics according to which subatomic particles of a given class (as photons and pi-mesons) have a quantum-mechanical symmetry that in cases of thermal equilibrium tends to cause an accumulation of many particles of the same kind in each of the possible low-energy quantum-mechanical states — called also *Einstein-Bose statistics;* compare FERMI-DIRAC STATISTICS

bo·sel·a·phus \bō'zeləfəs\ *n, cap* [NL, fr. L *bos* ox, cow + Gk *elaphos* deer — more at ELK] **:** a genus of Asiatic antelopes including only the nilgai

bo·sey \'bōzē, -zi\ *n* -s [irreg. fr. B. J. T. *Bosanquet* †1936 Eng. cricketer + E *-y*] *chiefly Austral* **:** GOOGLY

¹bosh \'bäsh\ *n* -ES [prob. fr. G dial. *bosch* grass-covered slope; akin to OHG *busc*] **1 :** the lower sloping part of a blast furnace where the diameter increases to a maximum above the tuyeres **2 :** a trough used in forging and smelting in which tools and ingots are cooled **3 :** a tank of boiling soda water in which metal parts are washed

²bosh \"\ *n* -ES [Turk *boş* empty, useless] **1 :** absurd or empty talk, actions, ideas, or opinions **:** pretentious nonsense **:** SILLINESS ⟨all the trappings and ~ which goes to make up the autarchic state —*Times Lit. Supp.*⟩ — often used interjectionally to express disapproval or disbelief **2 :** something worthless or trifling ⟨~ consisting of corny short stories, on the gangster or Western pattern —J.B.Priestley⟩

bo·shas \bō'shäs\ *n, pl* **boshas** \-äz\ *usu cap* **1 :** a Gypsy people of the Caucasus living among the Armenians **2 :** a member of the Boshas

bosh·er \'bäshə(r)\ *n* -s **:** a worker who transfers metal sheets to a bosh

bos·jes·man \'bäshəsmən, 'bȯsh-, -shəzm-\ *n, pl* **bosjes·men** \-mən\ *usu cap* [obs. Afrik *Bossiesman* (now *Boesman*), fr. Afrik *bossies-* (fr. *bossie* bush, shrub, dim. of *bos* bush, forest, fr. MD *bosch, busch*) + *man*, fr. MD; akin to OHG *man* — more at MAN] **:** BUSHMAN 1

bosk *or* **bosque** \'bäsk\ *n* -s [prob. back-formation fr. *bosky* (wooded)] *archaic* **:** a small woods **:** wooded area

bos·ker \'bäskə(r)\ *or* **bosh·ter** \'bäshtə(r)\ *adj* [origin unknown] *slang Austral* **:** FIRST-RATE, EXCELLENT

bos·ket *or* **bos·quet** \'bäskət\ *n* -s [F *bosquet*, fr. It *boschetto*, dim. of *bosco* forest, perh. of Gmc origin; akin to OHG *busc* forest — more at BUSH] *archaic* **:** THICKET

bos·kop man *or* **boskop race** \'bä,skäp-\ *n, usu cap B* [fr. *Boskop*, locality in the Transvaal, Union of So. Africa, where remains were found] **:** a late Pleistocene southern African man of moderate stature with a dolichocephalic skull, vertical forehead, orthognathous face, and large brain, this form being orig. described as a separate species (*Homo capensis*) but now commonly regarded as an early strain of *Homo sapiens*, prob. ancestral to modern Bushmen and Hottentots

bos·kop·oid \'bä,skä,pȯid, -¸skə,-\ *adj, usu cap* **1 :** belonging or related to Boskop man **2 :** resembling Boskop man; *esp* **:** showing skull features similar to those of the skull of Boskop man

¹bosky \'bäskē, -ki\ *adj, usu* -ER/-EST [E dial. *bosk* bush (fr. ME) + E *-y* — more at BUSH] **1 :** marked by an abundant growth of woods, bushes, or thickets ⟨the thousand red roofs of a ~ suburb —V.S.Pritchett⟩ **:** richly verdant **:** WOODED ⟨the still, ~ side of the mountain —Joseph Hergesheimer⟩ **2 :** typical or suggestive of a woods **:** like a forest ⟨cool, ~ shade⟩

²bosky \"\ *adj, usu* -ER/-EST *chiefly Brit* **:** TIPSY, DRUNK

bos·mi·na \bäz'mīnə, -mēnə\ *n, cap* [NL] **:** a genus of water fleas resembling in profile microscopic elephants

bos'n *or* **bo's'n** *var of* BOATSWAIN

bos·ni·ac *or* **bos·ni·ak** \'bäznē,ak\ *adj or n, usu cap* [prob. modif. (influenced by *Bosnia*) of Serbo-Croatian *bošnjak*, fr. *Bosna* Bosnia, region of central Yugoslavia] **:** BOSNIAN

¹bos·ni·an \'bäznēən\ *adj, usu cap* [*Bosnia* + E *-an*] **1 a :** of, relating to, or characteristic of Bosnia, central Yugoslavia **b :** of, relating to, or characteristic of Bosnians **2 :** of, relating to, or characteristic of the Bosnian language

²bosnian \"\ *n* -s *cap* **1 :** a native or inhabitant of Bosnia in central Yugoslavia, a region predominantly Serbian in language and ethnic affiliation **2 :** the Serbo-Croatian language of the Bosnians

¹bos·om \'bu̇zəm *also* 'büz-\ *n* -s *often attrib* [ME, fr. OE *bōsm;* akin to OHG *buosam* bosom, Skt *bhūri* abundant — more at BOAST] **1 a :** the fore part of the chest of a human being **:** BREAST **b :** either or both of the breasts; *usu* **:** the female breasts ⟨slipping a quilted housecoat over her broad erect shoulders, pinning it across her ample ~ —Viola G. Liddell⟩ **2 a** *archaic* **:** the breast considered as the center of cherished and secret thoughts **b :** the breast considered as the center of emotions **:** HEART ⟨she has the ability to melt and chill your ~ —Stanley Kauffmann⟩ **c** *obs* **:** DESIRE, WISH ⟨you shall have your ~ on this wretch —Shak.⟩ **d :** a close or intimate relationship usu. marked by affection and protectiveness **:** EMBRACE ⟨for years she lived in the ~ of her family⟩ **:** inner circle ⟨he was accepted into the ~ of the organization⟩ **3 a :** a broad expansive surface ⟨the heaving ~ of the sea —Tom Marvel⟩ **b :** any supporting surface ⟨resting on the ~ of the earth⟩ **c :** an inmost recess **:** intimate center **:** INTERIOR ⟨hiding in the very ~ of the cave⟩ **4 a :** the part of a garment covering the breast; *esp* **:** a distinctive or decorative part of a garment ⟨the pleated ~ of a man's dress shirt⟩ **b :** the space between the breast and the undersurface of whatever garment covers the breast ⟨she seized the letter and thrust it into her ~⟩ **5 a :** the inside of an angle bar **b :** a depression round the eye of a millstone — **in abraham's bosom** *usu cap A* **:** DEAD; *specif* **:** in the realm of the blessed dead

²bosom \"\ *vb* -ED/-ING/-S [ME *bosomen*, fr. *bosom*, n.] *vi* **:** to swell out **:** BELLY ⟨her profuse skirt ~*ed* out with the gusts —Adrian Bell⟩ ~ *vt* **1 :** to put into the bosom ⟨she ~*ed* her letter —E.P.O'Donnell⟩ **2** *archaic* **a :** to take to the bosom **:** EMBRACE **b :** to keep (as a secret) to oneself **c :** to take to heart **:** mull over **3 :** to enclose in or as if in an embrace **:** EMBOSOM ⟨a Gothic, moss-grown structure, half ~*ed* in trees —T.L.Peacock⟩

³bosom \"\ *adj* [¹*bosom*] **:** very intimate or dear ⟨a ~ friend⟩

bos·omed \-md\ *adj* **1 :** kept in the bosom **:** HIDDEN **2 :** having (such) a bosom ⟨full-*bosomed*⟩

bosom-pin \'==,=\ *n* **:** BREASTPIN

bos·omy \-zəmē, -mi\ *adj* **1 :** swelling upward or outward **:** expanding in a curved outline **:** BALLOONING ⟨~ hills⟩ ⟨old ~ trees —Frances G. Patton⟩ **2 a :** having a prominent bosom ⟨a ~ dowager in gray satin —Lewis Mumford⟩; *esp* **:** having prominent and well-developed breasts ⟨a brawny hero and a ~ heroine —P.S.Nathan⟩ **b :** featuring bosomy women ⟨~ photographs⟩ ⟨~ book jackets⟩

bos·on \'bō,sän\ *n* -s [S. N. *Bose* + E *-on* — more at BOSE-EINSTEIN STATISTICS] **:** a particle (as a photon, meson, or alpha particle) having zero spin or an integral number of quantum units of spin and conforming to the Bose-Einstein statistics

bos·po·ran \'bäsp(ə)rən\ *adj, usu cap* [L *bosporanus* of the Bosporus, fr. *Bosporus, Bosphorus* Bosphorus, strait connecting the Sea of Marmara with the Black sea, strait connecting the Sea of Azov with the Black sea (fr. Gk *Bosporos*) + *-anus* -an] **1 :** of or relating to the Bosporus **2 :** of or relating to Kerch strait

bos·po·ran·ic \¦bäspə¦ranik\ *or* **bos·po·ri·an** \(')bä¦spōrēən, -pȯr-\ *adj, usu cap* [*bosporanic* fr. L *bosporanus* + E *-ic; bosporian* fr. Gk *bosporios* of the Bosporus + E *-an*] **:** BOSPORAN

bos·po·rus \'bäsp(ə)rəs\ *or* **bos·pho·rus** \-sf(-\ *n, pl* **bosporuses** *or* **bosphoruses** \-səz\ *also* **bospo·ri** \-pə,rī\ *or* **bospho·ri** \-fə,rī\ [L *Bosporus, Bosphorus*] **:** a strait or a narrow sea connecting two seas or connecting a lake and a sea

¹bos·que \'bä(,)skā\ *n* -s [Sp, woods, perh. of Gmc origin; akin to OHG *busc* forest — more at BUSH] *chiefly Southwest* **:** a dense growth of trees and underbrush **:** a clump of trees

²bosque *var of* BOSK

bosquet *var of* BOSKET

¹boss \'bäs, 'bȯs\ *n* -ES [ME *boce*, fr. OF, fr. (assumed) VL *bottia* (whence also It *bozza* boss, swelling, *boccia* bubble, Romanian *boț* lump)] **1 a :** a protuberant part **:** a round swelling part or body **:** a knoblike process **:** HUMP ⟨~*es* on the horns of an animal⟩ **b :** a raised ornamentation shaped (as by hammering or carving) from the material of the object it ornaments ⟨a metal plaque with ~*es* along its edges⟩ or made of other material ⟨glittering ~*es* on a leather bridle⟩ **:** an ornamental stud or knob ⟨a beautifully wrought ~ on a shield⟩ **c :** an ornamental projecting block or mass used in architecture (as at the intersection of ribs in Gothic vaulting or at the centers of ceiling panels); *also* **:** a block left in the rough to be carved in position **2 a :** a protuberant and often dome-shaped mass of igneous rock congealed beneath the surface of the earth and laid bare by erosion **b :** a smooth mound or hillock of bedrock usu. bare of soil or vegetation **3 :** a soft pad (as of soft leather, corduroy, or silk) used in ceramics and glassmaking for smoothing or making uniform the oil upon which color is to be dusted (as in decorating porcelain) or for cleaning surfaces (as of gilded work) **4 a :** the enlarged part of a shaft on which a wheel is keyed **b :** a flange at the end of a shaft where it is coupled to another shaft **:** a small projection above the general surface of a part to form a seating or reinforcement for another part **c :** a raised rim around a hole (as about the axle hole in a wheel) **:** a hub esp. of a propeller **d :** a projecting part of a screw-steamer sternpost, enclosing the propeller shaft **e :** the part of a ship's propeller to which the blades are attached **f :** a projection on a forging or casting to facilitate handling or to provide extra metal for a test

boss 1c

²boss \"\ *vt* -ED/-ING/-ES [ME *bocen*, fr. MF *bocer*, fr. OF *bocier*, fr. *boce*, n.] **1 :** to ornament with bosses **:** furnish with bosses **:** EMBOSS ⟨a ~*ed* book cover⟩ **2 :** to treat (the surface of porcelain) with a boss

³boss \'bäs\ *adj* [origin unknown] *dial Brit* **:** HOLLOW, EMPTY

⁴boss \'bȯs, 'bäs\ *n* -ES [perh. fr. obs. D *bosse* box (now *bus*), fr. LL *buxis* — more at BOX] **:** a wooden vessel for the mortar used in tiling or masonry that is hung by a hook from the laths or from the rounds of a ladder

⁵boss \'bȯs *also* 'bäs\ *n* -ES [D *baas* master, fr. MD *baes;* akin to Fris *baes* master] **1 :** a chief workman or superintendent (as a foreman, director, or manager) **2 :** someone who exercises control or authority; *esp* **:** a top executive **3 a :** a professional politician who controls a large number of votes in a party organization or who unofficially dictates appointments or legislative measures **b :** a top official regarded as having dictatorial authority over an organization that has wide public contacts ⟨a labor ~⟩

⁶boss \"\ *adj* **1 :** being in charge **:** having authority **:** PRINCIPAL, MASTER ⟨a ~ printer⟩ **2** *slang* **:** marked by superiority **:** EXCELLENT, CHAMPION, FIRST-RATE ⟨she's really a ~ cook⟩

⁷boss \"\ *vt* -ED/-ING/-ES **:** to act as chief workman or superintendent of ⟨we need a good man to ~ that job⟩ **:** exercise control or authority over ⟨wasn't going to have her ~*ing* this show —D.H.Lawrence⟩

⁸boss \'bäs\ *n* -ES [perh. fr. D *bos* bundle (as of straw), bush, forest, fr. MD *bosch, busch* bush, forest — more at BUSH] **1** *now dial Brit* **:** a low seat or hassock; *esp* **:** one made of straw **2 :** the straw back of an archery target made by coiling and sewing straw into a compact round mat

⁹boss \'bȯs, 'bäs *sometimes* 'bəs\ *n* -ES [E dial. *buss, boss* young calf] **:** a cow or other bovine animal — used chiefly in calling

boss·age \'bäsij, 'bȯs-\ *n* -s [F, fr. *bosse* boss (fr. OF *boce*) + *-age* — more at ¹BOSS] **:** the bosses in a piece of architecture considered as a feature of the architecture; *also* **:** such bosses left in the rough for carving in position

boss·dom \'bȯsdəm, -stəm *also* 'bäs-\ *n* -s **1 :** the state of being a political boss **2 :** the power or influence of a political boss **:** control of politics by a boss

bosse \(')bä¦sā, 'bäs,'bōs\ *n* -s [F *bossé*] **1 :** an African tree (*Guarea cedrata*) having glabrous oblong pointed leaflets and small blue flowers **2 :** the pinkish to reddish brown wood of the bosse tree used esp. for plywood

bossed *adj* [fr. past part. of ²*boss*] **:** having bosses **:** EMBOSSED

bos·se·lat·ed \'bäsə,lād·əd, 'bȯs-\ *adj* [modif. of F *bosselé* (after such pairs as F *élevé* elevated: E *elevated*), fr. OF *bocelé* covered with protuberances, fr. past part. of *boceler* to ornament with bosses, fr. *boce* boss] **:** marked or covered with small bosses ⟨a ~ tumor⟩

bosses *pl of* BOSS, *pres 3d sing of* BOSS

bos·set \'bäsət, 'bȯs-\ *n* -s [F *bossette*, fr. OF *bocete, bocette* small protuberance, fr. *boce* boss + *-ete, -ette* -ette] **:** the rudimentary antler of a young male red deer

boss-eyed \'bȯ¦sīd, 'bä¦-\ *adj* [perh. fr. ¹*boss*] **:** CROSS-EYED

boss·i·ness \'bȯsēnəs *also* 'bäs-\ *n* -ES **:** the quality or state of being bossy

boss·ing \'bäsiŋ, 'bȯs-\ *n* -s [ME *bocinge*, fr. *bocen* to boss + *-inge, -ing* -ing — more at ²BOSS] **:** a boss or a swelling resembling a boss

boss·ism \'bȯ,sizəm *also* 'bä,-\ *n* -s **:** the rule, practices, or system of bosses esp. in politics

bos·si work \'bōsē-, 'bäsē-\ *n, usu cap B* [prob. after *Bossi*, 18th cent. Irish artisan] **:** marble inlay

boss plate \'bäs-, 'bȯs-\ *n* **:** one of the after plates on each side of a single-screw ship, covering the boss for the stern tube

boss-ship \'bȯs(h),ship *also* 'bäs(h)-\ *n* -s **:** rule by a political boss

¹bossy \'bäsē, 'bȯsē, -si\ *adj, usu* -ER/-EST [¹*boss* + *-y*] **1 a :** marked by a swelling or roundness resembling a boss **b** *of a dog* **:** having the shoulder muscles overdeveloped **2 :** marked by bosses **:** STUDDED

²bossy \'bȯsē, 'bäsē, -si *sometimes* 'bəs-\ *n* -ES [E dial. *buss, boss* young calf + E *-y*] **:** a cow or calf

³bossy \'bȯsē, -si *also* 'bäs-\ *adj, usu* -ER/-EST [⁵*boss* + *-y*] **:** inclined to domineer **:** DICTATORIAL ⟨childish braggarts who marry nasal, ~ women —Claudia Cassidy⟩

bos·tan·ji *or* **bos·tan·gi** \bō'stanjē\ *n* -s [Turk *bostancı*, lit., gardener, fr. *bostan* garden, fr. Per *bustān* flower or herb garden, fr. *bū* fragrance + *-stān* place, fr. OPer *stāna;* akin to L *stare* to stand — more at STAND] **:** one of the imperial guards of Turkey whose duties include protecting the palace and its grounds, rowing the sultan's barge, and acting as imperial gardeners

bos·thoon \bäs'thün\ *n* -s [IrGael *bastūn*, lit., switch of green rushes, fr. AF *bastun* stick, staff, fr. LL *bastum* — more at BASTON] *Irish* **:** BOOR, DOLT

¹bos·ton \'bȯstən *sometimes* 'bäs-, *rap. sometimes* -sᵊn\ *adj, usu cap* [fr. *Boston*, capital of Massachusetts] **:** of or from Boston, the capital of Massachusetts **:** of the kind or style prevalent in Boston **:** BOSTONIAN

²boston \"\ *n* -s [F, fr. *Boston*, capital of Massachusetts] **1** *usu cap* **:** a variant of whist popular in the late 18th and early 19th centuries in which the players bid for the right to name trumps **2** *often cap* **:** a bid in the game of Boston to win five tricks

³boston \"\ *n* -s *usu cap* [fr. *Boston*, capital of Massachusetts] **1 :** a waltz characterized by a hold of two beats on one foot and an occasional dipping turn **2 :** BOSTON TERRIER

boston bag *n, usu cap 1st B* **:** a traveling bag or general-utility bag that is oblong at the bottom and is tapered or folded in at either end toward a top opening held together by two handles

boston baked beans *n, usu cap 1st B* **:** beans (as navy beans) seasoned with molasses and salt pork and baked for a long time at a low temperature

boston bluefish *n, usu cap 1st B* **:** POLLACK

boston brown bread *n, usu cap 1st B* **:** BROWN BREAD 1c

boston bull *also* **boston bulldog** *or* **boston bull terrier** *n, usu cap 1st B* **:** BOSTON TERRIER

boston butt *n, usu cap 1st B* **:** the upper portion of a pork shoulder containing a small piece of the shoulder blade and characterized by leanness

boston crab *n, usu cap B* **:** a professional wrestling hold in which the aggressor sits on the buttocks of a prone opponent and pulls upward on the opponent's legs

boston cracker *n, usu cap B* **:** a round thick unsalted cracker usu. served split

boston cream pie *n, usu cap B* **:** a round cake that is split and then filled with a custard or cream filling

bos·ton·er \-nə(r)\ *n* -s *cap* **:** BOSTONIAN

¹bos·ton·ese \¦bȯstə¦nēz, -ēs *sometimes* ¦bäs-; *rap. sometimes* -sᵊn¦ē-\ *n, pl* **bostonese** *cap* **1 :** BOSTONIAN **2 :** the speech of Boston and the immediately surrounding region marked by certain features (as the use of \á\ for the *a* in *ask*) that set it off sharply from most other speech patterns of the U.S.

²bostonese \"\ *adj, usu cap* **:** BOSTONIAN

boston fern *n, usu cap B* **:** a luxuriant fern (*Nephrolepis exaltata bostoniensis*) often with drooping foliage and much-divided and delicate or crested fronds of which scores of varieties have been produced since it was first cultivated in 1895

¹bos·to·nian \(')bȯ¦stōnēən, -nyən *sometimes* (')bä¦-\ *adj, usu cap* **1 :** of, relating to, or characteristic of Boston, the capital of Massachusetts **2 :** of, relating to, or characteristic of the people of Boston

²bostonian \"\ *n* -s *cap* **:** a native or resident of Boston

boston ivy *n, usu cap B* **:** a woody Chinese and Japanese vine (*Parthenocissus tricuspidata*) with 3-lobed leaves that is commonly used as a wall cover and climber — called also *Japanese ivy*

boston ledger *n, usu cap B* **:** a columnar ledger in which the account names and money columns are vertically arranged to facilitate the horizontal calculation of daily or periodic balances

boston lettuce *n, usu cap B* **:** any of several butterhead lettuces

boston pink *n, usu cap B* **:** SOAPWORT

boston rocker *n, usu cap B* **:** a rocking chair that is a modification of the Windsor chair, having a wooden seat curved up to meet the spindles of the notably high back, the spindles being held at the top by a usu. flat stenciled headrail

boston rod *n, usu cap B* **:** a light leveling rod

boston round *n, usu cap B* **:** a cylindrical narrow-necked glass bottle of various sizes, its height being about 2¼ times its diameter

boston terrier *n, usu cap B* **:** a dog of a breed of small smooth-coated terriers originating in Massachusetts about 1890 from a crossing of the bulldog and the bullterrier and being brindle or black in color with white markings

Boston rocker

boston two-step *n, usu cap B* **:** a slow two-step incorporating a low jump

¹bos·try·chid \'bästrəkəd, -,kid\ *adj* [NL *Bostrychidae*] **:** of or relating to the family Bostrychidae

²bostrychid \"\ *n* -s **:** a beetle of the family Bostrychidae

bos·trych·i·dae \bä'strikə,dē\ *n pl, cap* [NL, fr. *Bostrychus*, type genus (fr. Gk *bostrychos* curl — or, a winged insect) + *-idae*] **:** a family of small cylindrical beetles having a hoodlike thorax and boring both as larvae and adults in wood, stored products, and lead cables

bos·tryx \'bästriks\ *n, pl* **bostry·ces** \-rə,sēz\ *or* **bostryxes** \-riksəz\ [NL, irreg. fr. Gk *bostrychos* curl; akin to OHG *questa* apron of leaves, OSw *kvaster, koster* tuft, brush, Norw *kvas* small branches when cut off, L *vespices* thick shrubbery, Alb (Gheg) *ghethi* leaf, Skt *guṣpita* accumulation] **:** a cyme with all the flowers on one side of the rachis usu. causing it to curl — called also *helicoid cyme*

bosun *or* **bo'sun** *var of* BOATSWAIN

bo·sun bird \'bōsᵊn-\ *n* [perh. so called fr. its whistle] **:** TROPIC BIRD

bos·well \'bäz,wel, -,wəl\ *n* -s *usu cap* [after James *Boswell* †1795 Scottish lawyer and biographer; fr. the wealth of first-hand detail in Boswell's life (1791) of Samuel Johnson †1784 Eng. lexicographer, critic, and conversationalist] **1 a :** one who out of admiration or hero worship records in detail and usu. contemporaneously the life, conversation, intimate moods, and personal relationships esp. of a famous or otherwise significant contemporary ⟨a *Boswell* to a man of letters⟩ **b :** one who writes with love for and intimate knowledge of any subject ⟨a *Boswell* of the sea⟩ ⟨nature's *Boswell*⟩ **2 :** one who stays in almost constant attendance upon another out of great admiration or hero worship, often in a voluntarily servile position ⟨a faithful and mistreated *Boswell*⟩

bos·well·ia \bäz'welēə\ *n, cap* [NL, perh. fr. James *Boswell* †1795 + NL *-ia*] **:** an important genus of incense-yielding trees (family Burseraceae) of northern Africa and India having triangular 3-celled fruit with winged seeds — see FRANKINCENSE, SALAI

bos·well·ian \(')bäz'welēən\ *adj, usu cap* [James *Boswell* †1795 + E *-ian*] **1 :** relating to or characteristic of Boswell **2 :** characteristic of a Boswell or the writings of a Boswell ⟨a *Boswellian* biography⟩

bos·well·ize \'bäzwə,līz\ *vb* -ED/-ING/-s *often cap, vi* **:** to write a biographical account or other study with the method or manner of a Boswell ⟨*boswellizing* for several pages⟩ ~ *vt* **:** to write of in the manner of a Boswell ⟨an author who *boswellized* the American foot soldier⟩

¹bot *also* **bott** \'bät\ *n* -s [perh. modif. of ScGael *boiteag* maggot] **:** the larva of the botfly, esp. of the species infesting the horse

²bot \"\ *n* -s *Austral* **:** a constant borrower **:** CADGER, SPONGER

³bot \"\ *vi* **botted; botted; botting; bots** [²*bot*] *Austral* **:** to borrow with little or no intention of repaying **:** CADGE, SPONGE

⁴bot *n* -s [OE *bōt* — more at ¹BOOT] *obs* **:** COMPENSATION

bot *abbr* **1** botany **2** bottle **3** bottom **4** bought

BOT *abbr* board of trade

bo·tal·lack·ite \bō'talə,kīt\ *n* -s [*Botallack* mine, Saint Just, Cornwall, England + E *-ite*] **:** a rare bluish green basic chloride of copper prob. $Cu_2(OH)_3Cl.H_2O$

¹bo·tan·i·cal \bə'tanəkəl, -nēk- *also* bō'- *or* bä'-\ *also* **bo·tan·ic** \-nik,-nēk\ *adj* [*botanical* fr. *botanic* + *-al; botanic* fr. F *botanique*, fr. Gk *botanikos* of herbs, fr. *botanē* pasture, herb, fr. *boskein* to feed; akin to Lith *gauja* herd and prob. to L *bos* cow — more at COW] **1 a :** of or relating to plants **b :** relating to botany **2 :** composed of, derived from, or employing vegetable remedial substances **3 :** occurring naturally or in cultivation more or less unchanged from the original wild form ⟨a ~ tulip⟩ — compare HORTICULTURAL — **bo·tan·i·cal·ly** \-nək(ə)lē, -nēk-, -li\ *adv*

²botanical \"\ *also* **botanic** \"\ *n* -s **:** a crude vegetable drug consisting of roots, herbs, leaves, bark, or other plant material as distinguished from a refined or prepared vegetable product **:** a botanical drug as opposed to an animal drug or mineral drug

botanical garden *n* **:** a garden often with greenhouses that is used for the culture and study of plants collected and grown for scientific and display purposes

bot·a·nist \'bät(ᵊ)nəst\ *n* -s [fr. *botanical*, after such pairs as E *chemical: chemist*] **:** a specialist in botany or in a branch of botany **:** a professional student of plants

bot·a·nize \-tᵊn,īz\ *vb* -ED/-ING/-s [*botany* + *-ize*] *vi* **:** to collect plants for botanical investigation **:** study plants esp. on a field trip ~ *vt* **:** to explore for botanical purposes

¹bot·a·ny \'bät(ᵊ)nē, -ni\ *n* -ES [fr. *botanical*, after such pairs as E *astronomical: astronomy*] **1 :** the science of plants **:** the branch of biology dealing with plant life **2 a :** plant life (as of a given region) ⟨the ~ of this section⟩ **b :** the properties and life phenomena exhibited by a plant, plant type, or plant group ⟨the ~ of the orchid⟩ **3 :** a botanical treatise or study; *esp* **:** a particular system of botany ⟨carefully analyzing the earliest *botanies*⟩

²botany \"\ *or* **botany wool** *n* -ES [*Botany* Bay, New South Wales, Australia] **:** a fine grade of usu. merino wool for yarns and fabrics and obtained chiefly from Australia

botany bay greens *n pl but sing or pl in constr, usu cap both Bs* [*Botany Bay*, New South Wales, Australia] **:** an Australasian seashore plant (*Atriplex cinerea*) with an almost woody stem and scurfy foliage

botany bay gum *n, usu cap both Bs* **:** yellow acaroid resin

botany bay kino *n, usu cap both Bs* **:** EUCALYPTUS GUM

botany bay oak *n, usu cap both Bs, chiefly Brit* **:** the wood or timber of the she-oak

botany bay olive *n, usu cap both Bs* **:** an Australasian shrub or small tree (*Olea apetala*) with evergreen leaves and red fruits

bo·tau·rus \bō'tȯrəs\ *n, cap* [NL, modif. (influenced by L *bos* cow and L *taurus* bull) of ME *botor* bittern & OF *butor* bittern; ME *botor* fr. MF *butor*, fr. OF — more at BITTERN, COW, STEER] **:** a genus of birds (family Ardeidae) comprising the typical bitterns

¹botch \'bäch\ *n* -ES [ME *boche*, fr. ONF, fr. (assumed) VL *bottia* protuberance, hump — more at BOSS] **1** *obs* **:** a noninflammatory swelling (as a tumor) **2 a :** an inflammatory sore spot (as a boil or ulcer) **b :** a condition marked by a profusion of boils, ulcers, or other sore spots ⟨the Lord will smite thee with the ~ of Egypt —Deut 28: 27 (AV)⟩

²botch \"\ *vt* -ED/-ING/-ES [ME *bocchen*] **1 :** to repair, mend, or patch usu. in a bungling clumsy inept way ⟨a pair of old trousers that had been ~*ed up* with blue patches⟩ **:** make over, redo, adjust, or alter usu. unskillfully ⟨my best suit had been ~*ed*, and I could no longer wear it⟩ **2 :** to make a mess of through clumsiness, stupidity, or lack of ability **:** foul up hopelessly **:** BUNGLE, SPOIL, RUIN ⟨one of those natural incompetents who ~*es* whatever he puts his hand to —Farley Mowat⟩ **3 :** to assemble, construct, or compose in a makeshift or bungling way ⟨the rest of the report was a patchwork of data ~*ed* together —Dwight Macdonald⟩ ⟨~*ing up* jingles to produce what he fondly thought was a poem⟩

³botch \"\ *n* -ES **1 :** a botched place or part **:** DEFECT, FLAW, BLEMISH ⟨the ~*es* of a poorly constructed building⟩ **2 a :** something that is botched **:** MESS ⟨they made a real ~ of that job⟩ **b :** a bungled piece of work **:** clumsy or careless work ⟨that kind of ~ is worse than no work at all⟩ **c :** a jumbled mixture **:** PATCHWORK, HODGEPODGE, MISHMASH ⟨the script was as often as not a ~ of stolen scenes —Arthur Miller⟩ ⟨a miserable ~ of falsehoods —A.M.Schlesinger b. 1917⟩ **3** *archaic* **:** something used for patching or filling out **:** patching material

botched \'bächt\ *adj* [¹*botch* + *-ed*] **:** afflicted with or as if with boils, ulcers, or other sore spots ⟨the ~ and unfit —H.L. Mencken⟩

¹botch·er \'bächə(r)\ *n* -s [ME *bocchere*, fr. *bocchen* to botch + *-ere, -er* -er] **:** one that does bungling makeshift work; *esp* **:** an incompetent writer ⟨the unconscionable compromises of the artist with the ~ —F.R.Leavis⟩

²botcher \"\ *n* -s [origin unknown] **:** a young salmon **:** GRILSE

botch·ery \'bäch(ə)rē\ *n* -ES **:** ³BOTCH 2

botchwork \'⸗,⸗\ *n* **:** clumsy or careless work ⟨a clumsy craftsman surrounded by his ~ —Samuel Yellen⟩

¹botchy *adj, usu* -ER/-EST [ME *bochy*, fr. *boche* botch + *-y* — more at ¹BOTCH] *obs* **:** having the character of a boil, ulcer, or similar sore spot

²botchy \'bächē, -chi\ *adj, usu* -ER/-EST [³*botch* + *-y*] **:** full of defects **:** poorly done ⟨a ~ piece of work⟩

bote *dial Brit past of* BITE

bo·te·te \bō'tād·ē\ *n* -s [AmerSp] **:** GLOBEFISH

bot·fly \'bät,flī\ *n* **:** any of various medium to large-sized stout two-winged flies with small mouth opening and vestigial mouthparts usu. constituting a group (Oestroidea) of muscoid flies with segmented larvae that are parasitic in cavities or tissues of various mammals including man — see HORSE BOTFLY, HUMAN BOTFLY, SHEEP BOTFLY

¹both \'bōth\ *adj* [ME *bothe, bathe*, fr. ON *bāthir*, adj. & pron.; akin to OHG *beide, bēde* both; both fr. a prehistoric NGmc-WGmc compound whose first constituent is akin to OE *bēgen, bā, bū* both, Goth *bai, ba*, L *ambo*, Gk *amphō*, Skt *ubhau* both, Gk *amphi* around, and whose second constituent is a demonstrative pronoun or definite article (whence E *the*) — more at BY, THE] **:** being the two **:** involving the one and the other — used prepositively with an unmodified noun ⟨~ planes⟩ or with a noun modified by a demonstrative pronoun ⟨~ these armies⟩ or a possessive ⟨~ his eyes⟩ or other attributive word

²both \"\ *pron* [ME *bothe, bathe*, fr. ON *bāthir*, adj. & pron.] **:** the one and the other **:** the two without excepting either **:** the one as well as the other — used (1) alone ⟨I want ~⟩ or (2) with *of* and a pronoun ⟨~ of us⟩ or noun ⟨~ of the books⟩ though with a noun many prefer instead the adjectival form for formal use ⟨~ books⟩ or (3) appositionally with a pronoun ⟨we were ~ happy⟩ or noun ⟨English and French are ~ widely used⟩

³both \"\ *conj* [ME *bothe, bathe*, fr. *bothe, bathe*, adj.] — used as a function word to indicate and stress the inclusion of each of two or more things specified by coordinated words, phrases, or clauses, its position being usu. before the first element while the last element is usu. preceded by *and* ⟨~ New York and London⟩ ⟨speaking ~ with kindness and with understanding⟩ ⟨they were happy ~ when you arrived and when you left⟩ ⟨~ a musician, an archaeologist, and an anti-Fascist —Cyril Connolly⟩

¹both·er \'bäthə(r)\ *vb* **bothered; bothered; bothering** \'bäth(ə)riŋ\ **bothers** [perh. fr. IrGael *bodhar* deaf, bothered, annoyed, fr. OIr *bodar;* akin to W *byddar* deaf and prob. to Skt *badhira*] *vt* **1 a :** to put into a state of agitation **:** put into a flutter **:** cause to be nervous **:** FLUSTER, EXCITE ⟨just the sight of him ~*ed* her and set her heart beating⟩ **b :** to cause to be undecided, uneasy, or perplexed **:** PUZZLE, MYSTIFY ⟨the complexities of life ~*ed* him⟩ **2 a :** to annoy, anger, or upset esp. by petty provocations **:** VEX, IRRITATE, IRK ⟨he would be . . . excessively ~*ed* with details and complaints —Brian Crozier⟩ **b :** to intrude upon **:** force unwelcome attention or company on **:** PESTER, DISTURB ⟨don't ~ me while I'm taking my nap⟩ ⟨they could hardly walk down the street without being ~*ed*⟩ **c :** to cause to be mildly anxious or concerned **:** WORRY, TROUBLE ⟨rest and recovery from what's been ~*ing* you —Richard Joseph⟩ ⟨without ~*ing* their heads about a lot of newfangled nonsense —Green Peyton⟩ ⟨she didn't ~ herself to lower her voice⟩ **d :** to cause to suffer mild discomfort ⟨the sun did not ~ him —Richard Sale⟩ **:** give trouble to ⟨his stomach's been ~*ing* him⟩ — sometimes used as a mild imprecation or interjection expressing annoyance, disagreement, or impatience ~ *vi* **1 :** to feel mild concern or anxiety ⟨she needed help, but they didn't ~ about that⟩ **:** become concerned or interested ⟨I haven't time to ~ with such things⟩ **:** devote time, energy, or attention **2 :** to take pains **:** take the trouble ⟨don't ~ to lock the door⟩ ⟨he did not even ~ to be polite —Fitzroy Maclean⟩ **3 :** to stir up petty trouble **:** make a fuss **syn** see ANNOY, WORRY

²bother \"\ *n* -s **1 a :** a state of petty discomfort, annoyance, or worry ⟨when scenery gets mixed up with our personal ~*s* all the virtue goes out of it —Edith Wharton⟩ **b :** something that causes petty discomfort, annoyance, or worry **:** TROUBLESOMENESS, VEXATION ⟨she valued his gifts by the ~ they cost him —H.G.Wells⟩ **2 :** unnecessary and vexatious fussing ⟨all the ~ of trying to follow this rule —Evelyn Barkins⟩

both·er·ate \'bäthə,rāt\ *vt* -ED/-ING/-s [fr. *botheration*, after such pairs as E *creation: create*] *chiefly Midland* **:** BOTHER

both·er·a·tion \,bäthə'rāshən\ *n* -s **1 :** the act of bothering or the state of being bothered **2 :** something that bothers ⟨I fear that I have been too much of a ~ already —Hamilton Basso⟩ — often used as a mild imprecation

botherheaded \'⸗⸗,⸗⸗\ *adj* **:** MUDDLEHEADED

both·er·ment \'bäthə(r)mənt\ *n* -s **:** BOTHER, BOTHERATION ⟨beefing about the ~*s* which pester those in my spot —James Cagney⟩ — not often in formal use

both·er·some \-(r)səm\ *adj* **:** causing trouble or annoyance

both·i·dae \'bäthə,dē\ *n pl, cap* [NL, fr. *Bothus*, type genus + *-idae*] **:** a widely distributed family of flatfishes (order Heterosomata) having large scales and the eyes on the left side of the body

both·ie \'bäthi, 'bōthi\ *var of* BOTHY

¹both·ni·an \'bäthnēən\ *adj, usu cap* [*Bothnia*, region about the Gulf of Bothnia, northern arm of the Baltic sea + E *-an*] **1 :** of, relating to, or characteristic of Bothnia, a onetime province of Sweden **2 :** of, relating to, or characteristic of the people of Bothnia

²bothnian \"\ *n* -s *cap* **:** a native or inhabitant of Bothnia

both·nic \-nik\ *adj, usu cap* [*Bothnia* + *-ic*] **:** BOTHNIAN

bothr- *or* **bothro-** *comb form* [NL, fr. Gk, fr. *bothros*] **:** trough **:** pit ⟨*bothrenchyma*⟩ — chiefly in generic names ⟨*Bothrodendron*⟩ ⟨*Bothrops*⟩

bothri- *or* **bothrio-** *comb form* [NL, fr. *bothrium*] **:** bothrium ⟨*bothriocidaris*⟩ ⟨*Bothriolepis*⟩

bo·thrid·i·um \bō'thridēəm\ *n, pl* **bothrid·ia** \-ēə\ *or* **bothridiums** [NL, fr. *bothr-* + *-idium*] **:** one of the outgrowths from the head of tapeworms of the order Tetraphyllidea that act as holdfasts

both·rio·ceph·a·lus \,bäthrēō'sefələs\ *n, cap* [NL, fr. *bothri-* + *-cephalus*] **:** a genus of pseudophyllidean tapeworms with two bothria that is sometimes considered to include the common fish tapeworm of man — see DIPHYLLOBOTHRIUM

both·rio·cid·a·ris \-'sidərəs\ *n, cap* [NL, fr. *bothri-* + *Cidaris*] **:** a genus (coextensive with the family Bothriocidaridae and order Bothriocidaroida) of extinct primitive simple sea urchins that somewhat resemble Cystoidea and are known from the Ordovician of the Russo-Baltic area

both·ri·ol·e·pis \,bäthrē'äləpəs\ *n, cap* [NL, fr. *bothri-* + *-lepis*] **:** a genus of Devonian ostracoderms (family Asterolepidae)

both·ri·um \'bäthrēəm\ *n, pl* **both·ria** \-ēə\ *or* **bothriums** [NL, fr. Gk *bothrion* small pit, dim. of *bothros* pit] **:** a slit, groove, or depression esp. on the holdfast of a pseudophyllidean tapeworm

both·ro·den·dron \,bäthrō'dendrən\ *n, cap* [NL, fr. *bothr-* + *-dendron*] **:** a genus (the type of the family Bothrodendraceae) of Paleozoic plants somewhat resembling present-day club mosses of the genus *Lycopodium* and having characters intermediate between those of the fossil genera *Lepidodendron* and *Sigillaria*

bo·throp·ic \bō'thräpik\ *adj* [NL *Bothrop-, Bothrops* + E *-ic*] **:** of, relating to, or produced by the genus *Bothrops*

bo·throps \'bō'thräps\ *n, cap* [NL, fr. *bothr-* + *-ops*] **:** a genus of venomous pit vipers (family Crotalidae) including the fer-de-lance (*B. atrox*) and palm viper (*B. nigroventris*) of Central and So. America, their hemolytic venom causing the breakdown of blood cells and small blood vessels with consequent interstitial hemorrhage

both·ros \'bäthrəs\ *n, pl* **both·roi** \-,thrȯi\ *also* **bothroses** [Gk; perh. akin to L *fodere* to dig — more at BED] *archeol* **:** a hole or pit into which drink offerings to the nether gods were poured by the ancient Greeks

bothy \'bäthi, 'bōthi\ *n* -ES [Sc, prob. fr. obs. Sc *both* booth (fr. ME *bothe*) + E *-y* — more at BOOTH] *chiefly Scot* **:** a rude dwelling **:** HUT: as **a :** a shepherd's or hunter's shelter **b :** quarters for unmarried farm laborers

bo·to·cu·do \,bōd·ə'kü(,)dō\ *n, pl* **botocudo** *or* **botocudos** *usu cap* [Pg, fr. *botoque* wooden plug, alter. of *batoque* plug, bunghole, prob. fr. MF *bartoc* plug, bung; fr. the large cylindrical wooden plugs they wear in their ear lobes and lower lips] **1 :** a So. American labret-wearing people (as the Tupian Indians of eastern Brazil) **2 :** a member of a Botocudo people **3 :** the language of the Botocudo people

bo·tog·e·nin \bō'täjənən, ,bäd·ə'jenən\ *n* -s [*boto-* (perh. irreg. fr. Sp *batata* sweet potato) + *-genin* — more at POTATO] **:** a crystalline steroidal sapogenin $C_{27}H_{40}O_4$ obtained from a yam (*Dioscorea mexicana*)

bot·o·née *or* **bot·on·née** \'bät'ᵊn,ā\ *or* **bot·on·ny** *or* **bot·to·ny** \'bätᵊnē\ *adj* [MF *botonné*, fr. OF *botoné*, past part. of *botoner* to bud, furnish with buttons, fr. *boton* bud, button — more at BUTTON] *of a cross* **:** having a cluster of three balls or knobs at the end of each arm — see CROSS illustration

bo tree \'bō-\ *n* [Singhalese *bō*, fr. Skt *bodhi* — more at BODHI] **:** PIPAL

botry- *or* **botryo-** *comb form* [Gk, fr. *botrys*] **1 :** bunch of grapes ⟨*botryose*⟩ **2 :** botryoid ⟨*botryolite*⟩

bo·trych·i·um \bō'trikēəm\ *n, cap* [NL, fr. Gk *botrychos* stalk of a bunch of grapes (fr. *botrys* bunch of grapes) + NL *-ium;* fr. the grapelike cluster of sporangia] **:** a small widely distributed genus of low fleshy ferns (family Ophioglossaceae) comprising the grape ferns and having a lobed or compound sterile leaf and sporophyll bearing distinct sporangia in spikes or panicles

bo·tryd·i·um \-idēəm\ *n, cap* [NL, fr. Gk *botrydion* small cluster, dim. of *botrys* bunch of grapes] **:** a genus (the type of the family Botrydiaceae of the order Heterosiphonales) of coenocytic yellow-green algae that occur on moist earth as round or pear-shaped vesicles — see PROTOSIPHON

¹bo·tryl·lid \bō'triləd\ *adj* [NL *Botryllidae*, fr. *Botryllus*, type genus + *-idae*] **:** of or relating to the genus *Botryllus* or the family Botryllidae

²botryllid \"\ *n* -s **:** a tunicate of the genus *Botryllus* or the family Botryllidae

bo·tryl·lus \-ləs\ *n, cap* [NL, irreg. fr. Gk *botrys*] **:** a genus (the type of the family Botryllidae) of colonial incrusting tunicates with zooids resembling rays arranged about a common excurrent atrium — see GOLDEN STAR

bot·ry·o·gen \'bä·trēə,jen\ *n* -s [G, fr. *botry-* + *-gen*, fr. Gk *-genēs* born — more at -GEN] **:** a mineral $MgFe(SO_4)_2(OH)\cdot 7H_2O$ consisting of a hydrous sulfate of iron and magnesium that is deep red or deep yellow and usu. botryoid

bot·ry·oid \'bä·trē,ȯid\ *n* -s [*botryoid*, adj.] **:** a formation (as of calcium carbonate on the walls of caves) resembling a bunch of grapes

bot·ry·oi·dal \¦⸗⸗'ȯidᵊl\ *also* **bot·ry·oid** \'⸗⸗,ȯid\ *adj* [*botryoidal* fr. *botryoid*, adj. + *-al; botryoid* fr. Gk *botryoeidēs*, fr. *botry-* + *-oeidēs* -oid] **:** having the form of a bunch of grapes ⟨a ~ mineral structure⟩ ⟨~ growths⟩

bot·ry·o·my·co·ma \,⸗⸗(,)ō,mī'kōmə\ *n, pl* **botryomycomas** \-ōməz\ *or* **botryomycoma·ta** \-ōməd·ə\ [NL, fr. *Botryomyces* + *-oma*] **:** one of the vascular granulomatous masses occurring in botryomycosis

bot·ry·o·my·co·sis \-ōsəs\ *n, pl* **botryomyco·ses** \-ō,sēz\ [NL, fr. *Botryomyces*, former genus name of an organism believed to cause the infection (fr. *botry-* + *-myces*) + *-osis*] **:** a bacterial and prob. always micrococcal infection of domestic animals and man marked by the formation of usu. superficial vascular granulomatous masses, associated esp. with castration or other wounds, and sometimes followed by metastatic visceral tumors — **bot·ry·o·my·cot·ic** \¦⸗⸗(,)⸗,mī¦käd·ik\ *adj*

bot·ry·op·ter·i·da·ce·ae \,bä·trē,äp,terə'dāsē,ē\ *n pl, cap* [NL, fr. *Botryopterid-, Botryopteris*, type genus (fr. *botry-* + *-pterid-, -pteris*) + *-aceae*] **:** a family of three or four genera of primitive ferns found in Devonian and Carboniferous rocks of Europe and having the stem strand of xylem surrounded by phloem and the petioles with characteristic single W-shaped vascular bundle

bot·ry·ose \'bä·trē,ōs\ *adj* [prob. modif. (influenced by *racemose* or *cymose*) of G *botrytisch*, irreg. fr. *botry-* (fr. Gk) + *-isch* -ish, fr. OHG *-isc*] **1 :** RACEMOSE **2 :** BOTRYOIDAL

bo·try·tis \bō'trīd·əs\ *n, cap* [NL, irreg. fr. Gk *botrys*] **:** a form genus of imperfect fungi (family Moniliaceae) having the conidia in bunches like grapes on branched conidiophores and several of them causing serious plant diseases

botrytis disease *n, usu cap B* **:** any of several plant diseases caused by fungi of the genus *Botrytis* and typically characterized by a soft rotting

bots *pl of* BOT, *pres 3d sing of* BOT

bot·swa·na \bät'swänə, bət-\ *adj, usu cap* [fr. *Botswana*, country in southern Africa] **:** of or from the country of Botswana **:** of the kind or style prevalent in Botswana

¹bott *var of* BOT

²bott \'bät\ *or* **bod** \'bäd\ *n* -s [perh. alter. of ¹*bat*] **:** a plug of clay for closing the taphole of a cupola in founding

botted *past of* BOT

bot·te·ga \bō'tāgə, bə'-\ *n, pl* **bottegas** \-gəz\ *also* **botte·ghe** \-gē, -(,)gā\ [It, artist's studio, shop, fr. L *apotheca* warehouse — more at APOTHECARY] **:** the studio or workshop of a major artist in which other artists may participate in the execution of the projects or commissions of the major artist

bot·tery tree \'bäd·ərē-\ *n* [*bottery* alter. of *bourtree*] **:** BOURTREE

bött·ger ware \'betgə(r)-\ *n, usu cap B* [after Johann F. *Böttger* †1719 Ger. maker of porcelains who originated it] **:** a fine reddish brown stoneware

bot·tine \bə'tēn, bä'-\ *n* -s [F, fr. MF *botine*, dim. of *bote* boot] **:** a woman's light boot

botting *pres part of* BOT

¹bot·tle \'bäd·ᵊl, 'bätᵊl\ *n* -s *often attrib* [ME *botel*, fr. MF *boteille, bouteille*, fr. ML *butticula*, dim. of LL *buttis* cask — more at BUTT (cask)] **1 a :** a rigid or semirigid container made typically of glass or plastic, having a round and comparatively narrow neck or mouth that is usu. closed with a plug, screw top, or cap, and having no handle — contrasted with *jar, jug* **b :** a nonrigid container resembling a bag, made of skin, and usu. closed by tying at one end ⟨nomads storing wine in goatskin ~*s*⟩ **c :** the quantity held by a bottle ⟨drank a ~ of wine⟩ **2 a :** intoxicating drinks **:** LIQUOR ⟨fond of the ~⟩ **b :** liquid food usu. consisting of milk and supplements that is fed from a bottle (as to an infant) in place of mother's milk **3 :** a metal container for holding gas

chemical bottles: *1* reagent, *2* weighing, *3* dropping, *4* and *5* washing: *4* for precipitates, *5* for gases

²bottle \"\ *vt* **bottled; bottled; bottling** \-d·ᵊliŋ, -t(ᵊ)liŋ\ **bottles 1 a :** to put into a bottle ⟨*bottling* the wine⟩ **b** *Brit* **:** to preserve (as fruit) by canning in glass jars **:** CAN ⟨she helped to ~ raspberries⟩ **2 a :** to confine as if in a bottle **:** CHECK, RESTRAIN — usu. used with *up* ⟨*bottling* up the anger they felt⟩ **b :** to put or keep in a position or situation that makes escape or free activity impossible **:** CORNER — usu. used with *up* ⟨they successfully *bottled* up the enemy troops in the mountains⟩

³bottle \"\ *n* -s [ME *botel*, fr. MF, dim. of *bote* bundle, fr. MD *bōte* bundle of flax; akin to MD *bōten* to beat, OHG *bōzan* — more at BEAT] *dial Brit* **:** a bundle usu. of straw or hay

bottle baby *n* **:** a baby fed chiefly or wholly on the bottle as contrasted with a baby that is chiefly or wholly breast-fed

bottlebird \'⸗⸗,⸗\ *n* **:** any of various weaverbirds that build nests shaped like a bottle

bottlebrush \'⸗⸗,⸗\ *n* [so called fr. the shape of the flower] **1 a :** any of certain Australian shrubs or trees of the family Myrtaceae that are widely cultivated in warm regions esp. for their spikes of brightly colored flowers: (1) **:** any plant of the genus *Callistemon* (2) *or* **bottlebrush tea tree :** HONEYMYRTLE **b :** AUSTRALIAN HONEYSUCKLE **2** *or* **bottlebrush grass :** a grass of the genus *Hystrix; esp* **:** a No. American grass (*H. patula*)

bottlebrush buckeye *n* **:** a spreading shrub (*Aesculus parviflora*) of the southeastern U.S. that has pinkish flowers

bottlebrush squirreltail *n* **:** SQUIRRELTAIL 1

bot·tle-butt·ed \¦⸗⸗¦bəd·əd\ *adj* **:** SWELL-BUTTED

bottle club *n* **:** an establishment (as a private club) at which patrons are served intoxicating drinks after legal closing hours from the supplies that they have previously purchased or reserved

bot·tled \'bäd·ᵊld, 'bätᵊld\ *adj* [¹*bottle* + *-ed*] **1** *archaic* **:** shaped like a bottle **2 :** kept in or as if in a bottle

bottled gas *n* [*bottled* fr. past part. of ²*bottle*] **:** gas under pressure in portable cylinders; *esp* **:** LIQUEFIED PETROLEUM GAS

bottled in bond *adj, of whiskey* **:** bottled unblended at 100 proof under U. S. government warehouse supervision after aging at least four years and being free of taxation until removal from the bonded warehouse

bottle fern *n* **:** FRAGILE FERN

bottle fly *n* **:** BLUEBOTTLE 3

bot·tle·ful \ˈ==,fu̇l\ *n* -s : BOTTLE 1c

bottle gentian *n* [so called fr. the shape of its flower] : CLOSED GENTIAN

bottle glass *n* : glass from which containers (as bottles or jars) are made: as **a** : GREEN GLASS **b** : soda-lime glass that is clear, white, or colored

bottle gourd *n* : a common cultivated gourd (*Lagenaria siceraria*) whose shell is used as a bottle — called also *calabash*

bottle graft *n* : an approach graft in which the scion is a detached branch protected from wilting by keeping its base in a bottle of water until union is achieved

bottle grass *n* **1** : a foxtail of the genus *Setaria* **2** : RABBIT-FOOT CLOVER

bottle green *n* : a variable color averaging a dark green that is bluer and less strong than forest green (sense 1) and yellower than evergreen

bottlehead \ˈ==,=\ *n, pl* **bottleheads** *or* **bottlehead** **1** : any of several small whales (as the beaked whale or blackfish) **2** : BLACK-BELLIED PLOVER

bottleholder \ˈ==,==\ *n* **1** : a rack or other device for holding bottles **2** [so called fr. the custom of having water held in readiness for boxers by their seconds] : one that assists or supports another : SECOND

bottle jack *n* : a jackscrew somewhat resembling a bottle or jug in shape

bottle jaw *n* : a pendulous edematous condition of the tissues under the lower jaw in sheep and cattle resulting from infestation with bloodsucking parasites esp. stomach worms

bottle kiln *n* : a circular ceramic or lime kiln in which the walls of the hovel are drawn up into a bottle shape

¹bottleneck \ˈ==,=\ *n* **1 a** : a narrow entrance or passageway ⟨entering the harbor through the ~ formed by the reefs⟩ **b** : a narrow stretch of road : narrow route ⟨widened streets are gradually taking the place of the city's ~*s*⟩ **c** : a point of traffic obstruction or congestion ⟨at five o'clock in the afternoon the downtown streets are a series of ~*s*⟩ **2 a** : a condition or situation that obstructs, slows down, or halts free movement and progress ⟨breaking the twin ~*s* of ignorance and prejudice⟩ **b** : the state of blocked activity resulting from a bottleneck : state of checked, frustrated, or paralyzed action : IMPASSE ⟨lack of outside sympathy and understanding leaves the group in an apparently inescapable ~⟩

²bottleneck \"\ *vb* -ED/-ING/-S *vt* : to obstruct, slow down, or halt by or as if by causing or being a bottleneck : produce a bottleneck in : THROTTLE, CHECK, FRUSTRATE, PARALYZE ⟨their stupidity ~*ed* all freedom of expression⟩ ~ *vi* **1** : to be or cause a bottleneck ⟨obstructing progress by constant ~*ing*⟩ **2** : to become obstructed or checked by or as if by a bottleneck ⟨production of material has ~*ed*⟩ **3** : to become narrow or confined like a bottleneck ⟨supply routes run along the rivers, ~*ing* in some spots —*Newsweek*⟩

³bottleneck *or* **bottlenecked** \ˈ==,=\ *adj* **1 a** : shaped like or suggesting the neck and shoulders of a bottle ⟨~ gun cartridges⟩ **b** : narrow or confined like a bottleneck ⟨~ streets⟩ **2** : obstructed or checked by or as if by a bottleneck ⟨progress has unfortunately entered a ~ phase⟩

bottle nose *n* : a swollen or protuberant and sometimes ruddy nose

bottle-nosed \ˈ==ˈ=\ *adj* : having a bottle nose ⟨a large, shapeless man, *bottle-nosed* and evidently no ascetic at table —G.B. Shaw⟩

bottle-nosed diver *n* : SURF SCOTER

bottle-nosed dolphin *or* **bottle-nose dolphin** *also* **bottle-nosed porpoise** *or* **bottle-nose porpoise** \ˈ==ˈ=-\ *or* **bottle-nose** \ˈ==,=\ *n* : any of certain moderately large stout-bodied toothed whales that are usu. all included in the genus *Tursiops*, have a prominent beak and falcate dorsal fin, and are most common in warm seas; *esp* : a nearly cosmopolitan dolphin (*T. truncatus*)

bottle-nosed whale *n* : BOTTLEHEAD 1

bottle palm *n* : any of several palms (as *Colpothrinax wrightii* of Cuba and *Hyophorbe amaricaulis* of the Mascarene islands in the Indian ocean) that have trunks marked by a swelling shaped like a bottle — called also *barrel palm*

bottle party *n* **1** : a private party to which the guests bring their own liquor **2** : BOTTLE CLUB

bottle pool *n* : pool played with a cue ball, two object balls, and a leather bottle placed upside down, points being scored for caroming, pocketing an object ball, or overturning the bottle after hitting an object ball; *broadly* : any pool game in which a leather bottle is used on the table

bot·tler \ˈbäd-ᵊlə(r), ˈbät(ᵊ)l-\ *n* -s : one that bottles: as **a** : a worker or machine that puts up goods in bottles **b** : a concern that makes and bottles beverages, esp. carbonated beverages

bottles *pl of* BOTTLE, *pres 3d sing of* BOTTLE

bottle spring *n* [so called fr. the fact that fresh water may be secured by submerging a stopped bottle directly over the spring and then removing the stopper] : a freshwater spring issuing through the floor of a saline lake or pool

bottle swallow *n* [so called fr. the shape of its nest] : FAIRY MARTIN

bottle tit *n* [so called fr. the shape of its nest] : LONG-TAILED TIT

bottle tree *n* [so called fr. the swollen trunk] : an Australian tree of the genera *Brachychiton* and *Sterculia* (esp. *S. rupestris*) — see KURRAJONG

bottling *n* -s [fr. gerund of ²bottle] : the act or process of putting goods (as beverages) into bottles

¹bot·tom \ˈbäd-əm, -ätəm\ *n* -s [ME *botme*, fr. OE *botm*; akin to OHG *bodam* bottom, ON *botn*, L *fundus*, Gk *pythmēn*, Skt *budhna*] **1 a** : the under surface as opposed to the top surface : the side lying underneath : UNDERSIDE ⟨the ~ of a box⟩ ⟨the ~ of a plank⟩; *specif* : the underside on which a thing normally stands or rests ⟨the ~ of a vase⟩ **b** : a surface facing upwards (as the seat of a chair or the floor of a room) and designed to support something resting on it or to serve as a functional termination of the thing of which it forms a part **c** : the posterior end of the trunk : BUTTOCKS, RUMP **2** : the continuous and gently curved or somewhat flat surface (as of earth, sand, or rock) on which a body of water (as a river, lake, or sea) lies : BED ⟨the ship sank to the ~ of the ocean⟩ **3** *obs* : a very deep place : ABYSS **4 a** : the hull of a boat; *esp* : the part of the hull that lies below the water **b** : BOAT, SHIP — used chiefly of cargo ships ⟨cargo . . . carried by foreign ~*s* —Virginia A. Oakes⟩ **5 a** (1) : the lower or lowest part as opposed to the upper or topmost part ⟨at the ~ of the mountain⟩ (2) : the lower or lowest section, point, region, or level ⟨the ~ of the page⟩ ⟨the ~ of the graph⟩ ⟨traveling to the ~ of the world⟩ ⟨starting out on his career from the ~⟩ (3) : the worst possible level (as of misery, destitution, or degradation) ⟨falling to the ~ of disillusionment⟩ **b** : the farthest removed or inmost point of a recess ⟨sailing to the ~ of the bay⟩ **c** : a position marked by the least dignity or honor ⟨demoted to the ~ of the ranks⟩ : the lowest or last place in point of precedence ⟨marching at the ~ of a procession⟩ **d** (1) : the undermost part of the sole of a shoe; *esp* : the part of the sole extending from the breast of the heel to the toe (2) : the lower part of a garment or a garment worn on the lower part of the body; *esp* : the trousers of pajamas — usu. used in pl. **e** : the card at the bottom of a deck of cards ⟨he cheated by dealing ~*s*⟩ **f** : the last half of an inning of baseball **6** : low-lying land; *esp* : low-lying grassland and fields along a watercourse — usu. used in pl. ⟨the Mississippi river ~*s*⟩ **7** *obs* : CLEW 1 **8 a** : something used underneath or as if underneath another thing to support and strengthen it or to give it an advantageous point from which to develop : FOUNDATION, BASIS ⟨the ~ of a hypothesis⟩ **b** : a solid underlying structure (as of a work of literature) marked by unity and a convincing acceptance and interpretation of reality : SUBSTANCE ⟨their writing lost all grip and ~ —Van Wyck Brooks⟩ **9** : intrinsic nature : ESSENCE : basic character : HEART, CENTER, SOURCE ⟨the ~ of the trouble lay deeper —G.M.Trevelyan⟩ ⟨the tackles problems, tries to get to the ~ of them —H.A.Overstreet⟩ **10 a** : a heavy residuum of impure metal (as in copper smelting) **b** : a residue left in a still (as in refining petroleum) **11** : vigorous physical qualities combined with stamina : capacity to endure strain : SPIRIT — used esp. of horses and dogs ⟨a breed of dogs outstanding for ~⟩ **12** : the main plowing mechanism of a plow comprising the moldboard, share, frame, and landside **13** *Austral* : a gutter in mining **14** : a color applied as a foundation before the dyeing of textile fibers — **at bottom** *also* **at the bottom** : BASICALLY, REALLY, ESSENTIALLY : in reality ⟨he was *at bottom* modest and cautious —H.J.Muller⟩ ⟨a world familiar and close but *at bottom* unknown —Carlo Levi⟩ — **at the bottom of** : being the cause, source, or originator of : BEHIND ⟨they are *at the bottom of* every such scheme⟩ — **at the bottom of one's heart** : within one's own mind : in one's heart ⟨*at the bottom of his heart* he welcomed the news⟩ — **from the bottom of one's heart** : with unreserved sincerity ⟨he speaks *from the bottom of his heart* of something that has impressed and moved him —Stewart Cockburn⟩ — **from the bottom up** : from the very beginning : COMPLETELY ⟨the job will have to be done all over again *from the bottom up*⟩

²bottom \"\ *vb* -ED/-ING/-S *vt* **1** : to furnish (as a chair or shoe) with a bottom **2** *obs* : to wind up (as a ball of thread) **3** : to provide a foundation for : BASE, FOUND, ESTABLISH — usu. used with *on* or *upon* ⟨men who wanted to ~ the dreams of the Romantics on a solid basis —Bonamy Dobrée⟩ **4** : to bring to the bottom ⟨they ~*ed* the submarine on the ocean floor⟩ **5** : to get to the bottom of : figure out : PLUMB, FATHOM ⟨a mystery they hadn't ~*ed*⟩ **6** : to treat with a foundation hue or a mordant preparatory to dyeing ⟨cloth may be ~*ed* with a pale shade of indigo⟩ **7 a** : to underrun (as a gold deposit that is to be worked by the hydraulic method) with a level for drainage **b** : FINISH ⟨~ a borehole or shaft⟩ **c** : EXHAUST ⟨~*ed* the ore in the mine⟩ ~ *vi* **1** : to rest as an ultimate support : become based or grounded — usu. used with *on* or *upon* ⟨find on what foundation any proposition ~*s* —John Locke⟩ **2** : to reach the bottom : strike against the bottom ⟨~*ing* on the bed of the sea⟩; *specif* : to touch bottom so as to impede free action (as when the point of a gear tooth strikes the bottom of a space between two other teeth, a piston strikes the end of a cylinder, or a die forces material solidly into a matrix in coining) **3** : to develop a turf — used of a grass **4** *bot* : to develop a bulb or similar enlargement **syn** see BASE

³bottom \"\ *adj* **1 a** : of, relating to, or situated at the bottom ⟨~ rock⟩ **b** : lower or lowest ⟨the ~ part of the building⟩ ⟨~ prices⟩ **c** : frequenting the bottom ⟨~ fish⟩ **2** : FUNDAMENTAL, BASIC ⟨the ~ reason⟩ ⟨~ ideas⟩

bottom board *n* **1** : the base or floor of a beehive **2 bottom boards** *pl* : removable boards inside a boat at the bottom to protect the outer planking

bottom bracket *n* : BRACKET 2b

bottom break *n* : a branch or shoot arising from the base of a plant without being developed from an axillary bud on a branch and occurring either on grafted or on own-root plants — used esp. of roses

¹bottom-chrome \ˈ==,=\ *adj* [¹*bottom* + *chrome*, n. (in attrib. use)] : CHROME-MORDANT

²bottom-chrome \ˈ==ˈ=\ *vt* : to dye by the chrome-mordant method

bottom dealer *n* : one that deals illegally from the bottom of a deck of cards

bottom disease *n* : any poisoning of stock (as crotalism or Winton disease) caused by the eating of bottomland plants

bottom dog *n* : UNDERDOG

bottom dollar *n* : last dollar ⟨you can bet your *bottom dollar*⟩

bottom drawer *n, chiefly Brit* : a drawer (as in a dresser) used as a hope chest

bottomed *past of* BOTTOM

bot·tom·er \ˈbäd-əmə(r), -ätəm-\ *n* -s : one that bottoms: as **a** : a worker who finishes the bottom part of shoes preparatory to stitching or cementing on the outsoles **b** : a worker who nails bottoms to wooden box frames or makes the bottoms of other containers **c** : a worker stationed at the bottom of a mine shaft or haulage slope to direct the raising of loaded cars to the surface — called also *footman, foot tender*

bottom fermentation *n* : a slow alcoholic fermentation during which the yeast cells collect at the bottom of the fermenting liquid, which takes place at a temperature of 4 to 10° C and which occurs in the production of lager beer and of wines of low alcohol content — compare TOP FERMENTATION

bottom fishing *n* : fishing designed to catch bottom fish in which natural bait is usu. used and the sinker or hook rests on or near the bottom

bottom gear *n, Brit* : LOW SPEED : first gear ⟨he put the car in *bottom gear*⟩

bottom grass *n* **1** : grass growing on bottomlands **2** : any grass of low stature grown in mixtures for turf or sod **3** : TEXAS MILLET

bottom heat *n*: supplemental heat applied beneath greenhouse benches or plant frames to induce rooting of cuttings or to benefit heat-loving plants

bottom-hole \ˈ==,=\ *adj* : at or relating to the bottom of a drilled well ⟨*bottom-hole* temperature⟩

bottom ice *n* : ANCHOR ICE

¹bottoming *n* -s [fr. gerund of ²*bottom*] : the process of attaching the outsole of a shoe to the insole and upper and performing subsequent finishing work on the outsole

²bottoming *n* -s [¹*bottom* + *-ing*] : material (as broken stone) suitable for the bottom coat of a paved road

bottoming drill *n* : a drill designed to form a flat base at the bottom of a drilled hole

bottoming hole *n* : the furnace opening at which a globe of crown glass is exposed in glass manufacture to soften it — called also *glory hole*

bottoming tap *n* : a hand tap cutting a full thread to the bottom of a hole — see TAP illustration

bot·tom·land \ˈ==,land, -laa(ə)nd\ *n* : BOTTOM 6

bot·tom·less \-ləs\ *adj* [ME *botmelees*, fr. *botme* bottom + *-lees* -less] **1 a** : having no bottom ⟨a ~ chair⟩ **b** : lacking a foundation : BASELESS ⟨~ arguments⟩ **2 a** : extremely deep ⟨the ~ sea⟩ **b** : incapable of being plumbed to the depths : UNFATHOMABLE ⟨a ~ mystery⟩ : PROFOUND ⟨~ gloom⟩ **c** : BOUNDLESS, UNLIMITED, INEXHAUSTIBLE ⟨a man whose charity seemed ~⟩ — **bot·tom·less·ly** *adv* — **bot·tom·less·ness** *n* -ES

bot·tom·most \-m,mōst, *esp Brit also* -mməst\ *adj* **1 a** (1) : that is at the very bottom ⟨a village at the ~ part of the mountain⟩ : farthest down : LOWEST ⟨sitting on the ~ step⟩ (2) : that is closest to the end ⟨the ~ part of the day —Alfred Kazin⟩ **b** (1) : DEEPEST ⟨the ~ depths of the sea⟩ (2) : most profound ⟨pangs of ~ grief⟩ **2** : most fundamental : most basic ⟨the ~ problems facing the world⟩

bottom plate *n* **1** : the horizontal beam on which the studs of a partition rest **2** : a plate supporting a foundry mold

bottom rake *n* : CLEARANCE 2e

bottom-road bridge *n* : a bridge having its roadway carried on a floor system at the level of the lower chord in a truss bridge or at the bottom in a tubular bridge — called also *through bridge*

bottom-rooted \ˈ==ˈ==\ *adj* : having roots in the soil of a pool or pond ⟨*bottom-rooted* water lilies⟩

bottom rot *n* **1** : a disease of lettuce caused by a fungus (*Corticium solani*) that first rots the lower leaves and then spreads upward **2** : a decay of the basal portion of a tree trunk by any of various pore fungi (as *Polyporus schweinitzii*)

bottom round *n* : the part of a round steak situated on the outside of the round — compare TOP ROUND

¹bot·tom·ry \ˈbäd-əmrē, -ätəm-, -ri\ *n* -ES [alter. (influenced by *-ry*) of earlier *bottomary*, modif. (influenced by ¹*bottom*) of D *bodemerij*, fr. *bodem* bottom, ship + *-erij* -ery, fr. OF *-erie*; akin to OHG *bodam* bottom — more at BOTTOM] : a contract in the nature of a mortgage by which either the owner of a ship or the master as his agent hypothecates and binds the ship and sometimes the accruing freight as security for the repayment of money advanced or lent for the use of the ship with the lender losing his money if the ship is lost by the perils of the sea but receiving with his loan the interest or premium stipulated if the ship arrives safe — compare RESPONDENTIA

²bottomry \"\ *vt* -ED/-ING/-S : to pledge by a bottomry bond

bottoms *pl of* BOTTOM, *pres 3d sing of* BOTTOM

bottom sawyer *n* : a worker at a saw pit who stands below the timber — called also *pit sawyer*; compare TOP SAWYER

bottomset beds \ˈ==,=-\ *n pl* : layers of sedimentary material lying along the bottom of a body of water near the point of entry of a stream, the material having been carried to the area by the entering stream and being subsequently covered by foreset beds and topset beds in the formation of a delta

bottom shellbark *or* **bottom shellbark hickory** *n* : BIG SHELLBARK

bottom stope *n* : a stope for ore lying on the floor

bottom tool *n* **1** : a tool held under a piece of work and used in conjunction with another tool working on top (as the lowermost of a pair of dies or fullers) **2** : a tool for machining the bottom of a hole

bottom water *n* : the water immediately underlying oil or gas in productive formations — compare TOP WATER

bottom yeast *n* : a yeast that is present in the manufacture of wine and lager beer and that separates after fermentation on the bottom of the fermenting vessel

bottony *var of* BOTONÉE

bot·trop \ˈbä,träp\ *adj, usu cap* [fr. *Bottrop*, city in Germany] : of or from the city of Bottrop, Germany : of the kind or style prevalent in Bottrop

bott stick *also* **bod stick** *n* [²*bott*] : a rod about 10 feet long on the end of which a bott is placed when closing a taphole

bot·tu \ˈbä(,)tü\ *n* -s [Kanarese-Telugu *boṭṭu*] *India* : an ornamental or sectarian mark (as a dot on the forehead)

bot·u·li·form \ˈbächələ,fȯrm; bəˈtül-,bə-ˈtyül-\ *adj* [*botuli-* (fr. L *botulus* sausage) + *-form* — more at BOWEL] : shaped like a sausage

bot·u·lin \ˈbächələn\ *n* -s [prob. fr. NL *botulinus*] : a toxin that is formed by a bacterium (*Clostridium botulinum*) and that is the direct cause of botulism — called also *botulinus toxin, botulismus toxin*

bot·u·li·nal \ˌbächəˈlīnᵊl\ *adj* [NL *botulinus* + E *-al*] : of, relating to, or produced by the botulinus

bot·u·lin·ic \-ˈlinik\ *adj* [ISV *botulin-* (fr. NL *botulinus*) + *-ic*] : BOTULINAL

bot·u·li·nus \ˌbächəˈlīnəs, *attrib* ˈ==ˈ==\ *also* **bot·u·li·num** \-nəm\ *n, pl* **botulinuses** *also* **botulinums** *often attrib* [*botulinus* fr. NL, fr. L *botulus* + *-inus* -ine; *botulinum* fr. NL, neut. of *botulinus*] : a bacterium (*Clostridium botulinum*) that causes botulism — compare BOTULIN

bot·u·lism \ˈbächə,lizəm\ *n* -s [ISV *botul-* (fr. L *botulus*) + *-ism*; orig. formed as G *botulismus*] : acute food poisoning in man, various mammals, and birds caused by ingestion of food containing the toxin secreted by a spore-forming bacterium (*Clostridium botulinum*), characterized by muscle weakness and paralysis, disturbances of vision, swallowing, and speech, and marked by a high mortality rate — see DUCK SICKNESS, LIMBERNECK

bot·u·lis·mus toxin \ˌbächəˈlizməs-\ *n* [G *botulismus* + E *toxin*] : BOTULIN

bou·bou \ˈbü(,)bü\ *also* **boubou shrike** *n* -s [origin unknown] : any of several African shrikes (genus *Laniarius*)

boucan *var of* BUCCAN

bou·chal \ˈbüəkəl\ *n* -s [Ir *buachaill*, fr. MIr, cowherd; akin to W *bugail* shepherd, Bret *bugel*; all fr. a prehistoric Celt compound whose first and second constituents respectively are akin to Gk *bous* cow and to L *colere* to cultivate — more at COW, WHEEL] *chiefly Irish* : young man : BOY; *specif* : HERDBOY

bou·charde \büˈshärd\ *n* -s [F] : a tool for roughening or furrowing the surface of marble

¹bouche \ˈbüsh\ *n* -s [ME, fr. MF, lit., mouth, fr. L *bucca* cheek, mouth — more at POCK] **1** *obs* : an allowance of food and drink for retinue in a royal or noble household **2** : a slit in the edge of a medieval shield for a sword blade or a rounded opening for the shaft of a lance

²bouche \"\ *n* -s [prob. alter. (influenced by F *boucher* to stop up) of *bush* (bushing)] : BUSHING

³bou·ché \(ˈ)büˈshā\ *adj* [F, fr. past part. of *boucher* to stop up, fr. OF, fr. (assumed) OF *bouche* bunch, sheaf (whence MF *bouche*), perh. of Gmc origin; akin to OHG *busc* bush, forest — more at BUSH] : stopped with the hand — used as a direction in music in horn playing

bou·chée \büˈshā\ *n* -s [F, lit., mouthful, fr. (assumed) VL *buccata*, fr. L *bucca* + LL *-ata*, fr. L, fem. of *-atus* -ate)] : a very small patty or cream-puff shell filled with creamed meat or fish

bouche fer·mée \ˌbüsh,ferˈmā\ *adv* (*or adj*) [F, lit., mouth closed] : with the mouth closed — used as a direction in music

bou·che·rie process \ˌbüshəˈrē-, (ˈ)büˈshrē-, ˈbüsh(ə)rē-\ *n, cap B* [after Auguste *Boucherie* †1871 Fr. chemist] : a method of preserving wood involving impregnation with copper sulfate under pressure

bou·chon \(ˈ)büˈshäⁿ, -shōⁿ\ *n* -s [F, bouchon, cork, sheaf, fr. MF, cork, sheaf, fr. *bouche* bunch, sheaf] **1** : a bushing pressed into a bridge or plate of a timepiece **2** : the plug and fuze assembly of a grenade

bou·clé *or* **bou·cle** \(ˈ)büˈklā\ *n* -s [F *bouclé* curly, having a curly appearance (as fabrics), fr. past part. of *boucler* to curl, fr. *boucle* curl, buckle — more at BUCKLE] **1** *also* **bouclé yarn** : an uneven yarn of three plies one of which forms loops at intervals that is made in various weights of the principal clothing fibers **2** : a textile fabric that is used for clothing or decorating, has a rough looped surface, and is knitted or woven of bouclé yarns

bou·din \(ˈ)büˈdan, -aⁿ\ *n* -s [F] **1** : BLOOD SAUSAGE **2** : forcemeat shaped like a sausage and served as an entree **3** : an individual unit in a boudinage

bou·di·nage \ˌbüdᵊnˈäzh, -ˈdij\ *n* -s [F, fr. *boudin* + *-age*] : a structure which is sometimes present in metamorphic rocks apparently as a result of tension and in which a competent bed is thinned and thickened so that it resembles in cross section a string of sausages

bou·doir *R* ˈbü,dwä(r), ˈbu̇,-, =ˈ= *also* -wȯ(ə)r; *–R* -wȧ(r *also* -wȯ(ə)(r\ *n* -s *often attrib* [F, fr. *bouder* to pout, be sulky, prob. of imit. origin] : a woman's dressing room, bedroom, or private sitting room

boudoir chair *n* : a small fully upholstered chair

boudoir lamp *n* : a small ornamental table lamp for a woman's dressing table

bou·et \ˈbüət\ *n* -s [ME *bowett, bowat*, perh. fr. MF *boete* box, fr. OF *boete, boite, boiste*, fr. (assumed) VL *buxita*, irreg. fr. LL *buxis* — more at BOX] *Scot* : a small hand lantern

bouf·fan·cy \ˈbüfənsē\ *n* -ES : an effect of fullness in women's clothing usu. achieved by voluminous skirts

bouf·fant \(ˈ)büˈfänt, -äⁿ\ *adj* [F, fr. MF, fr. pres. part. of *bouffer* to swell, puff, of imit. origin] : puffed out : VOLUMINOUS, FLARING ⟨~ hairdos⟩ — used esp. of very full skirts with tight waistbands

bouffe \ˈbüf\ *n* [by shortening] : OPÉRA BOUFFE

bou·fon \(ˈ)büˈfän, -fōⁿ\ *n* -s [F, buffoon — more at BUFFOON] **1** : MATACHIN **2** : a dancing buffoon in modern Spanish and Mexican fiestas

bou·gain·vil·laea \ˌbügənˈvilyə, ˌbōg-, -vē(y)ə,-vēlyə,-vilēə, -vilēyə\ *n* [NL, fr. Louis Antoine de *Bougainville* †1811 Fr. navigator] **1** *cap* : a small genus of ornamental tropical American woody vines (family Nyctaginaceae) with brilliant red or purple floral bracts **2** -s : ²BOUGAINVILLEA

¹bou·gain·vil·lea \"\ [NL, alter. of *Bougainvillaea*] *syn of* BOUGAINVILLAEA

²bougainvillea \"\ *n* -s : a vine of the genus *Bougainvillaea*

bou·gain·vil·lia \"\ *n* [NL, fr. Louis Antoine de *Bougainville* + NL *-ia*] **1** *cap* : a widely distributed genus of marine hydrozoans forming arborescent colonies and having polyps with a single whorl of tentacles **2** -s : ²BOUGAINVILLEA

bou·gar \ˈbü,gär, -gər\ *n* -s [origin unknown] *chiefly Scot* : a rafter or cross spar of a roof esp. of a cottage — usu. used in pl.

bouge \ˈbüj\ *now dial var of* BULGE

bougee *var of* BURGEE

bou·get \ˈbüjət\ *n* -s [MF *bougette* leather pouch or wallet — more at BUDGET] : WATER BOUGET 2

bough \ˈbau̇\ *n* -s [ME *bow, bough* bough, shoulder, fr. OE *bōg, bōh*; akin to OHG *buog* shoulder, ON *bōgr* shoulder, bow of a ship, Gk *pēchys* forearm, Skt *bāhu* forearm, front foot, Toch A *poke* arm] **1** : a branch of a tree; *esp* : a main branch **2** *archaic* : GALLOWS

boughed \ˈbau̇d\ *adj* [ME *bowed*, fr. *bow, bough* + *-ed*] : having boughs : covered with boughs : having such boughs ⟨heavy-*boughed* oaks⟩

bough·less *adj* : being without a bough

bough·pot *also* **bow·pot** \'bau̇,pät\ *n* [*bough* + *pot*] **1** : a vase for cut flowers or boughs; *also* : BOUQUET **2** : an ornamental design representing a conventionalized vase of flowers — compare ANTHEMION

¹bought [ME *boughte* (past), *bought, ybought* (past part.), fr. OE *bohte* (past), *boht, geboht* (past part.); akin to Goth *bauhta* bought (past), *bauhts* bought (past part.) — more at BUY] *past of* BUY

²bought *adj* [fr. past part. of *buy*] : not homemade : PURCHASED, READY-MADE ⟨unable to let a ~ sauce go by undoctored —*New Yorker*⟩ ⟨~ Christmas cards⟩

³bought \'bȯkt, 'bəkt\ *n* -S [ME (Sc) *bowcht*, prob. fr. MD *bocht, bucht* pen for animals; akin to OE *byht* bend — more at BIGHT] *chiefly Scot* : a shelter of any kind; *esp* : one for animals

⁴bought *n* -S [ME, perh. fr. MLG *bucht, bocht;* akin to OE *byht*] **1** \'bükt, 'bȯkt\ *chiefly Scot* : BEND, CURVE ⟨the ~ of his elbow⟩ **2** *archaic* : TWIST, TURN, COIL

bought-and-sold note *n* : SALE NOTE

bought·en \'bȯtᵊn\ *adj* [*bought* (past part. of *buy*) + *-en* (as in *forgotten*)] *now dial* : ²BOUGHT ⟨my red sled, and my ~ wagon —W.A.White⟩

bou·gie \'bü,zhē, -üjē *sometimes* bü'zhē\ *n* -S [F, fr. *Bougie*, seaport in Algeria from which these candles were first imported into Europe] **1** : a wax candle **2** : a candle-shaped filter **3 a** : a tapering cylindrical medical instrument (as of rubber, waxed silk, or metal) for introduction into tubular passages (as the urethra or anus) to facilitate dilation or exploration or to serve as guide for the passage of other instruments **b** : SUPPOSITORY

bou·gi·nage *or* **bou·gie·nage** \,büzhē¦näzh\ *n* -S [*bougie* + connective *-n-* + *-age*] : the dilation of a tubular cavity (as a constricted esophagus) with a bougie

bou·guer's halo \(')bü¦ge(ə)rz-\ *n, usu cap B* [after Pierre *Bouguer* †1758 Fr. mathematician] : a faint white halo of about 32 degrees minimum radius around the antisolar point

bouguer's law *n, usu cap B* : LAMBERT'S LAW b

bouil·la·baisse \¦büyə¦bās *sometimes* ¦bül(y)ə-\ *n* -S [F, fr. Prov *boui-abaisso*, fr. *boui* (sing. imper. of *boule* to boil, fr. L *bullire*) + *abaisso* (sing. imper. of *abeissa* to lower, fr. — assumed — VL *abbassiare*) — more at BOIL, ABASE] : a fish stew made of at least two and usu. five or six kinds of fish, seasoned with onions and herbs and flavored and colored with saffron

bouil·li \(')bü¦yē\ *n* -S [F, fr. MF, fr. past part. of *bouillir* to boil, fr. OF *boillir*] : boiled meat, esp. beef

bouil·lon \'bü,yän *also* 'bü- *or* ='=; 'bül,yän *also* 'bü- *or* ='=; 'bülyən; bü'yōⁿ, '=,=\ *n* -S [F, fr. OF *boillon*, fr. *boillir* to boil — more at BOIL] : a broth made by slow boiling of beef or other meat in water; *specif* : clarified and seasoned stock served as a soup and made from lean beef unless otherwise stated ⟨clam ~⟩ — compare BEEF TEA, MEDIUM

bouil·lon blanc \büyōⁿblãⁿ\ *n* [F, fr. MF, fr. (assumed) MF *bouillon* mullein (modif. — influenced by MF *bouillon* broth — of LL *bugillon-, bugillo*, a plant, prob. of Celt origin and akin to OIr *buge*, a plant with a blue flower) + MF *blanc* white — more at BLANK] : MULLEIN

bouillon cube *n* : a cube of evaporated seasoned meat extract

bouillon cup *n* : a small cup with two handles for serving bouillon

bouillon spoon *n* : a round-bowled spoon somewhat smaller than a soup spoon

bouil·lotte \bü'yät\ *n* -S [F, fr. *bouillir;* prob. fr. the rapidity of the game] : BRELAN 1

bou·in's fluid *or* **bouin's solution** \(')bü¦anz-, -aⁿz-; 'bwaⁿz-\ *also* **bouin** \-an,-aⁿ\ *n, usu cap B* [after Paul *Bouin*, 20th cent. Fr. histologist] *biol* : a fixing and preserving solution consisting of picric acid, formaldehyde, and glacial acetic acid

¹bouk *in sense 1* 'bük, *in sense 2* 'bu̇k\ *n* -S [ME, belly, body, fr. OE *būc* belly — more at BUCKET] **1** *chiefly Scot* **a** : the body of a person **b** : an animal carcass ⟨a mutton ~⟩ **2** : OMASUM

²bouk \'bük\ *dial Brit var of* BULK

³bouk \"\ *Scot var of* ⁷BUCK

bouk·it \'bükət\ *adj* [²*bouk* + Sc *-it* -ed] *chiefly Scot* : FORMED, BUILT — usu. used with a qualifier ⟨a lad who was wee ~⟩

boul \'bül\ *chiefly Scot var of* BOOL

boul *abbr* boulevard

bou·lan·gère \¦bü,läⁿzhe(ə)r\ *adj* [F, female baker, baker's wife, fr. OF *boulengiere*, fem. of *boulengier* baker, fr. ONF *boulenc* baker (fr. MD *bolle* round loaf of bread + OF *-enc*, n. suffix, of Gmc origin and akin to OHG *-ing* one belonging to) + OF *-ier* -er; prob. akin to OE *bolla* bowl — more at BOWL, -ING] : cooked with sliced onions in a casserole

bou·lan·ger·ite \bü'lanjə,rīt\ *n* -S [G *boulangerit*, fr. C.L. *Boulanger* †1849 Fr. mining engineer + G *-it* -ite] : a bluish gray metallic-looking mineral $Pb_5Sb_4S_{11}$ consisting of antimony lead sulfide occurring usu. in plumose masses (hardness 2.5–3, sp. gr. 5.75–6.0)

¹boul·der *also* **bowl·der** \'bōldə(r)\ *n* -S [short for *boulder stone*, fr. ME *bulder ston*, part trans. of a word of Scand origin; akin to Sw dial. *bullersten* large stone in a stream, fr. *buller* noise (fr. OSw *bulder*) + *sten* stone; akin to MLG *balderen* to make a noise, Dan *buldre*, Lith *bildėti*, OE *bellan* to bellow — more at BELLOW] : a detached and rounded or much-worn mass of rock from 8 or 10 inches to 10 or more feet in diameter typically carried some distance from the parent rock by natural forces and worn by a stream, ocean waves, or glacier or by weathering in situ — see ³COBBLE 1

²boulder *also* **bowlder** \"\ *vt* **bouldered; bouldered; boulder·ing** \'bōld(ə)riŋ\ **boulders 1** : to make into boulders — used chiefly in past participial form **2** : to smooth (a revolving polishing wheel) by crushing against a quartz stone or boulder

boulder beach *n* : a beach deposit consisting largely of boulders

boulder belt *n* : a line or zone of glacial boulders

boulder clay *n* : an unassorted glacial deposit containing much clay in the matrix surrounding pebbles, boulders, and other rock fragments : TILL

boulder fern *n* : HAY-SCENTED FERN 1

boulderhead *also* **bowlderhead** \'==,=\ *n* : a row of piles before a dike to protect it from wave erosion

boul·der·ing *also* **bowl·der·ing** \'bōld(ə)riŋ\ *n* -S : pavement of or paving with small boulders

bouldering stone *n* : pebbles of smooth flint used in abrading or crushing the faces of emery wheels and glazers

boulder pavement *n* : a concentration of boulders as a result of removal of finer particles of a glacial deposit by water

boulder raspberry *n* : a shrub (*Rubus deliciosus*) native to the Rocky mountains and having dark purple fruit

boulder train *n* : a line or fan-shaped spread of glacial boulders that extends from the original rock outcrop often for many miles in the direction of glacial movement

boul·dery *also* **bowl·dery** \'bōld(ə)rē\ *adj* : characterized by boulders

¹bou·le \'bü(,)lē, bü'lā\ *n* -S [Gk *boulē*, lit., will, fr. *boulesthai* to wish, be willing; perh. akin to Gk *ballein* to throw — more at DEVIL] : a legislative council of ancient Greece consisting in Homeric times of an aristocratic body of princes and leaders merely advisory to the king and in Athens in Solon's time of an elective senate acting as a check on the popular assembly and later extending its functions to include certain matters of administration and supervision

²boule *var of* BOULLE

³boule \'bül\ *n* -S [F, ball — more at BOWL (ball)] : a game similar to roulette in which a ball is put in motion in a bowl and players bet on the numbered compartment it will come to rest in

⁴boule \"\ *n* -S [F, ball] : a pear-shaped mass of some substance (as sapphire, spinel, rutile) formed synthetically in the Verneuil furnace with the atomic structure of a single crystal but with crystallographic axes generally in a random position with respect to its length

⁵boule \"\ *n* -S [F, ball] : a log sawed into slabs that are reassembled with spacer strips to form an oval stack resembling the original log

bou·leu·te·ri·on \,bü,lü'tirē,än, ,bül,yü-\ *n, pl* **bouleute·ria** \-ēə\ [Gk *bouleutērion*, fr. *bouleuein* to advise, take counsel, fr. *boulē* counsel, council, will] : an ancient Greek council chamber

¹bou·le·vard \'bu̇lə,värd, -vȧd *also* 'bül-\ *n* -S [F, modif. of MD *bolwerc* — more at BULWARK] **1 a** : a broad thoroughfare; *esp* : one more pretentious than an ordinary street or avenue often having grassplots with trees along the center or between curbings and sidewalks **b** : a grassed or landscaped strip in the center or between the curbings and sidewalks of a boulevard **2** : MOUSE GRAY

²boulevard \"\ *vt* -ED/-ING/-S : to make into a boulevard : provide with boulevards

bou·le·var·dier \¦bül,värd¦yā; ¦bu̇lə,vär¦di(ə)r, ¦bül-\ *n, pl* **boulevardiers** \-yā(z), -i(ə)rz\ [F, fr. *boulevard* + *-ier* -er] : a frequenter of the Parisian boulevards : a sophisticated man of fashion; *also* : BON VIVANT, FLANEUR, TRIFLER

boulevard light *n* : a tall ornamental streetlight with a luminaire like a lantern at the top used chiefly on parkways and principal thoroughfares

boulevard stop *n* : a traffic stop required of vehicles before entering or crossing a through street

boule·verse·ment \bülversəmäⁿ\ *n* -S [F, fr. MF, fr. *bouleverser* to overturn (fr. *boule* ball + *verser* to overturn, fr. L *versare* to turn, overturn + *-ment* — more at VERSATILE] : OVERTURNING, REVERSAL; *also* : CONVULSION, DISORDER

-boulia — see -BULIA

-boulic — see -BULIC

boulimia *var of* BULIMIA

boulle *or* **buhl** *also* **boule** \'b(y)ül\ *n* -S [after André Charles *Boulle* †1732 Fr. cabinetmaker] : inlaid decoration developed under Louis XIV by André Charles Boulle in which tortoiseshell, yellow metal, and white metal are inlaid in cabinetwork, forming scrolls or cartouches

bou·lon·nais \¦bülə¦nā\ *n* [F, fr. *boulonnais* of Boulogne, fr. *Boulogne*, seaport city in northern France] **1** *usu cap* : a French breed of very large quick-maturing draft horses **2** *p* **boulon·naises** \-ā(z)\ *often cap* : a horse of the Boulonnais breed

boult *obs var of* BOLT

boul·ter \'bōltə(r)\ *n* -S [origin unknown] : a long stout fishing line to which many hooks are attached and which is used for bottom fishing esp. in deep water

boul·ter·er \-tərə(r)\ *n* -S : one who fishes with a boulter

¹boun \'bün, 'bau̇n\ *chiefly dial var of* ¹BOUND

²boun \"\ *var of* BOWN

¹bounce \'bau̇n(t)s\ *vb* -ED/-ING/-S [ME *bounsen*, prob. of imit. origin] *vt* **1** *obs* : BEAT, BELABOR **2 a** : to cause to rebound ⟨~ a ball off a wall⟩ : cause to be reflected ⟨~ a light ray off a reflector⟩ **b** : to throw about : handle violently **3** *chiefly Brit* **a** : to bluff or bully with big talk **b** : SCOLD, BROWBEAT **4 a** : to discharge from a post or employ esp. peremptorily and unceremoniously ⟨the old mess sergeant had been *bounced* on recommendation of the mess officer —H.H.Arnold & I.C.Eaker⟩ **b** : to expel or eject esp. precipitately from a room or place or from membership or participation ⟨if the college would only ~ him for something that wasn't too much his fault —Theodore Morrison⟩ ~ *vi* **1** *obs* : to make a loud sudden noise : bang or knock loudly **2** : to strike and rebound ⟨*bouncing* from rock to rock⟩ ⟨the ball will hardly ~ at all⟩ ⟨the car *bounced* all over the road⟩ **3** : to recover from a blow or a defeat quickly or vigorously — usu. used with *back* **4 a** *of a check* : to be returned by a bank as no good (as because of lack of funds) **b** : RECOIL, BOOMERANG ⟨a tendency, which could ~ uncomfortably back on them, to come out and boldly blame the press for everything —Mollie Panter-Downes⟩ **5 a** : to leap or spring suddenly, violently, or noisily : BOUND ⟨*bounced* into the room⟩ ⟨*bouncing* on his seat with ecstasy⟩ **b** : to walk with springing steps **6** *chiefly Brit* : to talk big : BLUSTER, SWAGGER, BOAST **syn** see DISMISS

²bounce \"\ *n* -S **1** *obs* : a heavy sudden often noisy blow or thump; *also* : the sound of an explosion : BANG **2 a** : a sudden leap or bound : a rebound esp. of a ball **3** : BLUSTER, BRAG, SWAGGER : an impudent lie or boast **4** : LIVELINESS, RESILIENCE, VERVE ⟨full of ~ and enthusiasm⟩ **5** *slang* : a peremptory discharge or expulsion ⟨he got the ~⟩ **6** : a pronounced beat characterizing a style of playing jazz usu. in a medium or moderate tempo

bounce·able \-səbəl\ *adj, now dial chiefly Eng* : BUMPTIOUS, PUGNACIOUS — **bounce·ably** \-səblē\ *adv*

bounce back *n* [*bounce back*, v.] **1** : ECHO, REFLECTION ⟨locating submarines by the sonar *bounce back*⟩ **2** : COMEBACK

bounce pass *n* : a basketball pass in which the ball is caromed off the floor

bounc·er \'bau̇n(t)sə(r)\ *n* -S **1** *Brit* **a** : BOASTER, BULLY, LIAR **b** : LIE, WHOPPER **2** : something big : a good stout example of the kind ⟨that baby is a ~⟩ **3** : one that ejects disorderly persons (as at a dance hall, gambling house, or barroom) or keeps gate-crashers out (as at a party or ceremony) **4** *slang* : CABOOSE

bounc·i·ly \-sələ, -li\ *adv* [*bouncy* + *-ly*] : with verve : JAUNTILY, SPRINGILY

bouncing *adj* [fr. pres. part. of ¹*bounce*] **1** : LUSTY, HUSKY ⟨a ~ baby boy⟩ : HEALTHY, VIGOROUS ⟨a ~ young woman⟩ **2** : LIVELY, ANIMATED ⟨a ~ disposition⟩ — **bounc·ing·ly** *adv*

bouncing bet \-'bet\ *or* **bouncing bess** \-'bes\ *n, often cap 2d B* [*bouncing* + *Bet* or *Bess*, nickname for *Elizabeth*] : SOAPWORT 1

bouncing-pin indicator *n* : an instrument that indicates knocking in a gasoline engine by the electrically recorded jumps made by a steel pin resting on a steel plate

bouncing putty *n* : any of various soft elastic silicone polymers that usu. increase in elasticity with rate of application of force and that are used esp. as centers of golf balls, as muscle exercisers in occupational therapy, and as shock-absorbent padding around instruments in high-speed aircraft and rockets

bouncy \'bau̇n(t)sē, -si\ *adj* -ER/-EST [²*bounce* + *-y*] **1** : BOUNCING, BUOYANT, EXUBERANT, LIVELY **2** : RESILIENT ⟨~ chair cushions⟩

¹bound \'bau̇nd\ *adj* [alter. of *boun*, fr. ME, fr. ON *būinn*, past part. of *būa* to live, dwell, make ready — more at BOWER] **1** *archaic* : PREPARED, READY, DRESSED **2** : intending to go : on the way toward : GOING — used with *to* or *for* or with an adverb of motion ⟨a ship ~ for Gibraltar⟩ ⟨homeward ~⟩

²bound \"\ *n* -S [ME *bounde, bunne*, fr. OF *bodne, bonne, borne*, fr. ML *bodina*] **1 a** : the external or limiting line of an object, space, or area ⟨the ~s of a forest reserve⟩ ⟨set ~s on a property⟩ — usu. used in pl. **b** : something that limits or restrains : LIMIT ⟨beyond the ~s of reason⟩ ⟨set a lower ~ to a temperature range⟩; *specif* : limits beyond which military personnel are forbidden to go ⟨out of ~s⟩ **2** *usu pl* **a** : BORDERLAND **b** : the land within certain bounds : DOMAIN ⟨woodland ~s —William Wordsworth⟩ **3** : a number that neither exceeds nor is exceeded by any number associated with a point of a given set or that is a value of a given function

³bound \"\ *vb* -ED/-ING/-S [ME *bounden*, fr. *bounde*] *vt* **1** : to set limits to : establish the bounds of : confine within limits ⟨fields ~*ed* by tall hedges⟩ ⟨art . . . is always greater than the rules with which we may attempt to ~ it —C.S.Kilby⟩ **2** : to form the limits of or lie along the borders of ⟨the sea ~s it on three sides⟩ : CIRCUMSCRIBE, ENCLOSE ⟨the stream that ~s this land⟩ **3** : to name the boundaries of ⟨the class was asked to ~ their country⟩ ~ *vi, archaic* : to form a common boundary — often used with *with*

⁴bound \"\ *adj* [ME *bounden*, fr. past part. of *binden* to bind — more at BIND] **1 a** : fastened by or as if by a band : CONFINED ⟨desk-*bound*⟩ **b** : compelled or constrained esp. by logical necessity : CERTAIN, SURE — used postpositively ⟨such a plan is ~ to fail⟩ ⟨we are ~ to have a frost soon⟩ **2** : under legal or moral restraint or obligation : OBLIGED — usu. used postpositively ⟨~ to pay his wife's debts⟩ ⟨~ by sacred vows⟩ ⟨honor-*bound*⟩ ⟨duty-*bound*⟩; *specif* : APPRENTICED ⟨a ~ girl⟩ **3** : CONSTIPATED, COSTIVE — used postpositively **4** *of a book* **a** : secured to its covers by cords or tapes ⟨a ~ volume⟩ **b** : cased in **5 a** : RESOLVED ⟨~ and determined to have his way⟩ **b** : ASSURED — often used as if spoken under oath ⟨you're a . . . first-rate seaman, I'll be ~ —W.S.Gilbert⟩ **6** : held in chemical or physical combination : COMBINED ⟨some vitamins occur in ~ forms⟩ — opposed to *free* **7** *of a linguistic form* : always occurring in combination with another linguistic form (as *splend-* in *splendor* and *splendid*, *un-* in *unknown*, *-s* in *hats*, *-er* in *speaker*) ⟨a ~ form⟩ ⟨a ~ allomorph⟩ — opposed to *free*

⁵bound \"\ *vt, South & Midland* : BET, WAGER — used chiefly in assertions and affirmations ⟨I ~ you he'll like it⟩

⁶bound \"\ *n* -S [MF *bond*, fr. *bondir*] **1** : a leap or spring usu. made easily and lightly ⟨cleared the hedge at a ~⟩ : one of a continuous series of such springs **2** : BOUNCE, REBOUND **3** : one of a series of relatively short movements by a military unit or by elements of it alternately from one preselected point on the ground to the next **syn** see JUMP

⁷bound \"\ *vi* -ED/-ING/-S [MF *bondir* to leap, bound, resound, fr. (assumed) VL *bombitire* to hum, irreg. fr. L *bombus* deep hollow sound — more at BOMB] **1** : to move with a spring or leap or with a succession of springs or leaps **2** : REBOUND ⟨an elastic ball ~s⟩ : BOUNCE **syn** see JUMP

bound·a·ry \'bau̇nd(ə)rē, ri\ *n* -ES [²*bound* + *-ary*] **1** : something that indicates or fixes a limit or extent : something that marks a bound (as of a territory or a playing field) : a bounding or separating line **2** *cricket* : a hit that sends the ball to or across the boundary **3** *Midland* : a tract of land esp. with timber on it

boundary condition *n, physics* : a condition which a quantity that varies throughout a given space or enclosure must fulfill at every point on the boundary of that space esp. when the velocity of a fluid at any point on the wall of a rigid conduit is necessarily parallel to the wall

boundary layer *n* : the region of retarded flow in a fluid (as air) close to the surface of a body (as an airplane) past which the fluid flows, the retardation being greatest close to the surface of the body and being due to viscosity of the fluid and its adhesion to the surface

boundary light *n* : any light used to indicate the limits of the landing area of an airport

boundary marker *n* : a usu. cone-shaped orange marker that indicates the boundary of an area available for the landing of an airplane

boundary rider *n, Austral* : one that rides around the boundaries of a station and keeps the fences in order

bound bailiff *n* [alter. (influenced by ⁴*bound*) of *bumbailiff*] : a bonded sheriff's officer who serves writs and makes arrests

bound charge *n* [⁴*bound*] : the portion of the electrical charge on a conductor that because of the inductive action of a neighboring charge will not escape to the earth when the conductor is grounded

bounded *past of* BOUND, *archaic past part of* BIND

bound·ed·ness *n* -ES : the quality or state of being bounded

bounded noun *n* [*bounded* fr. past part. of ³*bound*] : a noun (as *book, letter, window*) that in the singular is always accompanied by a determiner

bound·en \'bau̇ndən\ *adj* [ME — more at ⁴BOUND] **1** *archaic* : BOUND : fastened by bonds : in bondage **2** *archaic* : under obligation (as for a favor) : OBLIGED, BEHOLDEN ⟨~ to political supporters⟩ **3** : made obligatory : imposed as a duty : BINDING ⟨our ~ duty⟩

¹bound·er \-də(r)\ *n* -S [³*bound* + *-er*] *archaic* : BOUNDARY

²bounder \"\ *n* -S [⁷*bound* + *-er*] **1** *slang Brit* **a** : DOGCART **b** : a 4-wheeled cab **2** *chiefly Brit* : a man of objectionable manners, taste, or other form of social behavior : OUTSIDER, CAD ⟨a big, jolly fellow, with a touch of the ~ about him —D.H.Lawrence⟩ — often used in general disparagement ⟨almost offensive, the old ~ had been —Norman Douglas⟩ **3** : a batted ball that bounces along the ground : GROUNDER

bound·er·ish \'bau̇ndərish\ *adj* : resembling or typical of a bounder

bounding *pres part of* BOUND

bound·ing·ly *adv* : in a bounding manner

bound·less \'bau̇n(d)ləs\ *adj* [²*bound* + *-less*] : having no boundaries or limits ⟨~ ocean⟩ ⟨the ~ prairie⟩ : IMMEASURABLE, VAST ⟨~ heavens⟩ : without restraining limits ⟨~ joy⟩ ⟨~ optimism⟩ — sometimes distinguished from *infinite* ⟨a spherical surface is ~ but not infinite in extent⟩ — **bound·less·ly** *adv* — **bound·less·ness** *n* -ES

bound·ness *n* -ES : the quality or state of being bound

bounds *pl of* BOUND, *pres 3d sing of* BOUND

bound up *adj* : entirely devoted ⟨he is *bound up* in his family⟩ : inseparable from : dependent on ⟨his career is *bound up* with the fortunes of the enterprise⟩

bound variable *n* [⁴*bound*] *logic* : a variable occurring within the scope of a quantifier and so no longer available for substitution by a constant : an apparent variable

bound water *n* [⁴*bound*] : water that is an essential component of various materials (as animal and plant cells or soils) from which it cannot be removed without changing their structure or composition and distinguishable from free water in such ways as by its inability to dissolve sugar or to form ice crystals

boun·te·ous \'bau̇ntēəs *esp Brit sometimes* -nchəs\ *adj* [ME, alter. (influenced by *bounte* bounty) of *bountevous*, fr. MF *bontif* kind, benevolent (fr. OF, fr. *bonté* goodness, kindness + *-if* -ive) + ME *-ous*] **1** : characterized by bounty : giving or disposed to give freely : GENEROUS, LIBERAL **2** *obs* : abounding in goodness **3** : liberally bestowed : AMPLE, BOUNTIFUL, PLENTIFUL ⟨a ~ yield of corn⟩ ⟨his ~ good looks —J.D.Salinger⟩ **syn** see LIBERAL

boun·te·ous·ly *adv* : in a bounteous manner

boun·te·ous·ness *n* -ES [ME *bounteousnesse*, fr. *bounteous* + *-nesse* -ness] : the quality or state of being bounteous

boun·tied \'bau̇ntēd, -tid\ *adj* **1** : having the benefit of a bounty ⟨a ~ export⟩ **2** : rewarded or rewardable by a bounty ⟨a ~ animal pelt⟩

boun·ti·ful \'bau̇ntəfəl, -tēf-\ *adj* **1** : full of bounty : free in giving : liberal in bestowing gifts and favors : GRACIOUS **2** : ABUNDANT, PLENTIFUL ⟨a ~ supply of food⟩ **syn** see LIBERAL

boun·ti·ful·ly \-f(ə)lē, -li\ *adv* : in a bountiful degree : GENEROUSLY, PLENTIFULLY

boun·ti·ful·ness *n* -ES : the quality or state of being bountiful

boun·tith \'büntəth\ *n* -S [ME, fr. MF *bontet, bonté* goodness, kindness] *Scot* : a supplement to regular wages : BONUS

boun·ty \'bau̇ntē, -ti\ *n* -ES [ME *bounte*, fr. OF *bonté, bunté*, fr. L *bonitat-, bonitas*, fr. *bonus* good (fr. OL *dvenos*) + *-itat-, -itas* -ity; akin to OE *langtwīdig* granted for a long time, MHG *zwīden* to grant, OIr *den* strong, Skt *duvas* gift, reverence] **1** *obs* : GOODNESS, KINDNESS, VIRTUE **2** : liberality in bestowing gifts or favors : gracious or liberal giving : GENEROSITY, MUNIFICENCE **3** : something that is given generously or liberally **4** : yield esp. of a crop **5** : a reward, premium, or subsidy esp. when offered or given by a government: as **a** : an extra allowance to induce entry into the armed services **b** : a grant to encourage an industry **c** : a grant of land to encourage settlement **d** : a payment to encourage the destruction of noxious animals ⟨a ~ on wildcats⟩

bounty hunter *n* **1** : one that hunts predatory animals for the reward offered **2** : one that tracks down and captures outlaws for whom a reward is offered

bounty jumper *n* : one who during the Civil War enlisted in the U.S. service to get a bounty and then deserted

boun·ty·less *adj* : being without a bounty

bou·quet \(')bō¦kā, (')bü¦k- *sometimes* bü'k- *or* bə'k-; (')bō- *is less freq for sense 4 than for the other senses*\ *n* -S [F, fr. MF, *bouquet* thicket, fr. ONF *bosquet* thicket, fr. OF *bosc, bois* forest (perh. of Gmc origin and akin to OHG *busc* forest) + *-et* — more at BUSH] **1 a** : flowers picked and fastened together in a bunch : NOSEGAY **b** : a large flight of fireworks (as rockets) **2** : COMPLIMENT ⟨~s and brickbats⟩ **3** : BOUQUET GARNI **4 a** : the distinctive fragrance (as of a wine or brandy) derived from the processes of fermentation and aging — compare AROMA 2 **b** : a distinctive subtle quality (as of an artistic performance or a piece of writing) **syn** see FRAGRANCE

bouquet gar·ni \-,gär'nē\ *n, pl* **bouquets garnis** \-kā(z). . .nē\ [F, lit., garnished bouquet] : a tied bunch of herbs (as parsley, bay leaf, and thyme) used in soups and other savory dishes

bouquet larkspur *n* : any of several cultivated larkspurs derived from a species (*Delphinium grandiflorum*) having finely cut leaves and flowers with spurs straight or nearly so

bou·qui·niste \bükēnēst\ *n, pl* **bouquinistes** \"\ [F, fr. *bouquin* old book (fr. obs. D *boeckin* little book, dim. of D *boek* book) + *-iste* -ist; akin to OHG *buoh* book — more at BOOK] : a dealer in secondhand books

bour \'bu̇r\ *Scot var of* BOWER

bou·rach \'bürək\ *var of* BOUROCK

bour·bon \'bu̇r\|bən, 'bȯr\|, 'bōr\|, 'bu̇ə\|, 'bōə\|, 'bō(ə)\|; 'bər\| *or* 'bə̄\| *is usual for sense 4 and sometimes occurs for the other senses*\ *n* -S [*Bourbon*, seigniory in central France] **1** *cap* : a member of a French family founded in 1272 by Robert, Count of Clermont, to which belonged the rulers of France from 1589 (Henry IV) to 1793 and from 1814 to 1830, of Spain from 1700 (Philip V) to 1808, from 1814 to 1868, and from 1875 to 1931, of Naples from 1735 (Charles III) to 1805, and of the Two Sicilies from 1815 (Ferdinand I) to 1860 **2** *usu cap* [after *Bourbon,* French royal family, fr. *Bourbon,* seigniory in central France] **:** a person who clings obstinately to the social and political ideas of the old order of things **:** REACTIONARY, CONSERVATIVE; *specif* **:** an extremely conservative member of the Democratic party of the U.S. ⟨the *Bourbons* refused to consider the proposal⟩ **3** *or* **bourbon rose** [*Bourbon* (now Réunion), French island in the Indian ocean, after *Bourbon,* French royal family] **a :** a rose (*Rosa borboniana*) that is generally considered an accidental hybrid between the China rose and the French rose and is of compact upright growth with shining leaves, prickly branches, and clustered flowers **b :** any of various cultivated roses derived from the bourbon rose and typically being hardy and recurrent-blooming **4** *or* **bourbon whiskey** [*Bourbon* county, Kentucky] **:** a whiskey distilled from corn mash; *specif* **:** a whiskey distilled from a mash containing at least 51 percent corn, the rest being malt and rye, and aged in new charred oak containers — compare CORN WHISKEY **5** [perh. fr. *Bourbon* (now Réunion)] **:** a Santos coffee of a superior grade

bour·bon·al \|bə,nal\ *n* -s [perh. fr. *Bourbon,* French royal family + *-al* (aldehyde)] **:** ETHYL VANILLIN

bourbon cotton *n, usu cap B* [*Bourbon* (now Réunion), French island in the Indian ocean] **:** a cotton derived from a West Indian cotton plant (*Gossypium purpurascens*)

bour·bon·ism \|bə,nizəm\ *n* -s *often cap* **1 :** support of the Bourbons (sense 1) **:** LEGITIMISM **2 :** adherence to the Bourbons (sense 2)

bourbon red *n, usu cap B&R* [prob. fr. *Bourbon* county, Kentucky] **:** a variety of domestic turkey of medium size and reddish brown color

bourbon tea *n, usu cap B* [*Bourbon* (now Réunion)] **:** FAHAM

bour·don \'bu̇rdᵊn, -ȯr-,-ər-\ *also* **bor·dun** \'bȯr-\ *n* -s [ME *burdoun,* fr. MF *bourdon* bass horn, of imit. origin] **1 :** ³BURDEN 1 **2 a :** a drone bass (as in a bagpipe or a hurdy-gurdy) **b :** a pipe-organ stop of a droning or buzzing quality usu. of 16-foot pitch **c :** the lowest bell (as in a carillon) in a ring of bells

bour·don gauge \'bu̇r,dōⁿ-\ *n, usu cap B* [after Eugène *Bourdon* †1884 Fr. engineer and inventor] **:** a pressure gauge having a Bourdon tube as its sensitive element

bour·don lace \"-\ *n* [F *bourdon* cord edging on lace, staff of a fish net, pilgrim's staff, fr. LL *burdon-, burdo* hinny, fr. L *burdus*] **:** a net lace with edge and pattern outlined by cording

bour·don·née \¦bu̇rdᵊn¦ā\ *adj* [F *bourdonné,* fr. *bourdon* pilgrim's staff; fr. the knob-shaped handle characteristic of a pilgrim's staff] **:** POMMÉE

bour·don spring \'bu̇r,dōⁿ-\ *n, usu cap B* [after Eugene *Bourdon*] **:** a Bourdon tube coiled into a flat spiral spring

bourdon tube *n, usu cap B* **:** a thin-walled flattened tube of elastic metal bent into a circular arc whose application to certain pressure gauges and thermometers depends upon the fact that increase of pressure inside the tube tends to straighten it — see BOURDON GAUGE, BOURDON SPRING

bou·rette *also* **bour·rette** \bü'ret, bə'\ *n* -s [F *bourrette* coarse silk on the outside of a cocoon, fr. MF, fr. *bourre* (silk) waste, padding (fr. LL *burra* shaggy cloth) + *-ette* — more at BUREAU] **1 :** an irregular slubbed yarn made usu. of silk waste **2 :** a plain-woven fabric that has a rough uneven appearance and is made from bourette yarn

bourg \'bu̇(ə)r(g)\ *n* -s [ME, fr. MF, fr. OF *borc,* fr. L *burgus* fortified place, of Gmc origin; akin to OHG *burg* fortified place — more at BOROUGH] **:** TOWN, VILLAGE: as **a :** one neighboring a castle **b :** MARKET TOWN

bour·gade \bu̇r'gäd\ *n* -s [F, prob. fr. OProv *borgada* village, suburb, fr. *borc* fortified place, fr. L *burgus*] **:** a village of scattered dwellings **:** an unfortified town

¹**bour·geois** \'bu̇rzh,wä, 'bu̇əzh,wä, 'bu̇zh,wä *sometimes* 'büzh-; *sometimes* ≐'≐; *in sense 4* (,)bər'jȯis *or* bə'j- *or* bȯ'j-\ *n, pl* **bourgeois** [MF, fr. OF *borjois,* fr. *borc*] **1 a :** BURGHER **b :** a middle-class person **:** one of the social class whose income derives from the profits of commercial and industrial enterprise esp. as distinguished from the landed gentry, the wage earners and farmers, and sometimes the professions **:** SHOPKEEPER, BUSINESSMAN **2 :** one whose social behavior and political views are determined or influenced by private-property interest **:** CAPITALIST **3 bourgeois** *pl* **:** BOURGEOISIE ⟨the reading public, the ~, who will read the book, go round saying —Madeleine Chapsal⟩ **4 :** an old size of type (approximately 9 point) between brevier and long primer — compare POINT SYSTEM **5 :** one formerly in charge of a trading post in the fur trade of the American Northwest

²**bourgeois** \"\ *adj* [F, fr. OF *borjois,* fr. *borjois,* n.] **1 :** of, belonging to, or characteristic of the townsman or of the social middle class ⟨a solid ~ family⟩ ⟨the ~ virtues of thriftiness, forethought and a serious attitude toward life —Gilbert Cadoffre⟩ ⟨~ culture⟩ **2 :** characterized by selfish concern for material comfort and well-being, by preoccupation with moneymaking or property accumulation, by anxiety about social respectability, and by a tendency toward safe mediocrity in matters of thought, feeling, and artistic taste **:** PHILISTINE — usu. used in disparagement **3** *of a nation* **:** dominated by commercial and industrial interest **:** CAPITALISTIC

bour·geoise \-äz,-äz\ *n* -s [F, fem. of *bourgeois*] **1 :** a wife or daughter of a bourgeois **:** a woman of the middle class **2 :** BOURGEOIS

bour·geoi·sie \¦≐,wä¦zē, -,wȧ-\ *n, pl* **bourgeoisie** [F, fr. *bourgeois*] **1 :** BOURGEOIS **2 :** a social order dominated by bourgeois ⟨civilized society is one huge ~; no nobleman dares now shock his greengrocer —G.B.Shaw⟩

bourgeon *var of* BURGEON

bour·gui·gnon \¦bu̇r(,)gēn¦yōⁿ\ *n* -s *cap* [F, fr. *Bourgogne* (Burgundy), region in east central France] **:** ¹BURGUNDIAN 2

bourkha *var of* BURKA

¹**bourn** *or* **bourne** \'bō(ə)rn, -ȯ(ə)rn, -u̇(ə)rn\ *n* -s [ME *bourne,* fr. OE *burn, burna, burne;* akin to OHG *brunno* spring of water, ON *brunnr,* Goth *brunna,* Gk *phrear* well, L *fervēre* to boil — more at BURN] **:** STREAM, BROOK, RIVULET; *specif* **:** an intermittent stream on chalk downs

²**bourn** *or* **bourne** \"\ *n* -s [MF *bourne, borne,* fr. OF *bodne, bonne, borne* — more at BOUND] **1** *archaic* **:** BOUND, BOUNDARY, LIMIT **2** *archaic* **:** a terminal point aimed at **:** GOAL, DESTINATION ⟨sole ~, sole wish, sole object of my song —William Wordsworth⟩

bourne·mouth \-nməth\ *adj, usu cap* [fr. *Bournemouth,* England] **:** of or from the county borough of Bournemouth, England **:** of the kind or style prevalent in Bournemouth

bour·non·ite \'bu̇rnə,nīt, 'bȯr-, 'bu̇r-\ *n* -s [Count J.L.de *Bournon* †1825 Fr. mineralogist + E *-ite*] **:** a mineral $PbCuSbS_3$ consisting of a steel-gray or black metallic-looking sulfide of antimony, lead, and copper occurring in orthorhombic crystals, and also massive — see WHEEL ORE

bou·rock \'bürək\ *n* -s [prob. fr. *bour* + *-ock*] **1** *Scot* **:** a rude hut; *esp* **:** one used by shepherds **2** *Scot* **a :** MOUND, KNOLL **b :** HEAP, MASS; *specif* **:** a stone heap **3** *Scot* **:** CROWD, GROUP ⟨a ~ of blackguards⟩

bourout *usu cap, var of* BURUT

bour·rée \(')bü¦rā\ *n* -s [F, perh. fr. fem. of *bourré,* past part. of *bourrer* to stuff, beat, fr. MF, fr. *bourre* (silk) waste, padding, fr. LL *burra* shaggy cloth — more at BUREAU] **1 :** a lively old French dance tune usu. in duple time and beginning with an upbeat; *also* **:** a musical composition with the rhythm of such a dance **2 a :** a clogging peasant dance of Auvergne and Berry **b :** a 16th century French court dance with crossing steps **3 :** a ballet combination that consists of small crossing steps

bour·re·let \¦bu̇rə¦lā\ *n* -s [F — more at BURLET] **1 :** BURLET **2 :** a cloth wreath or turban worn on a helmet **3 :** the raised portion of an artillery projectile between the ogive and the body

bourrette *var of* BOURETTE

bour·sault rose \'bu̇r,sō-\ *n, usu cap B* [prob. fr. the name *Boursault*] **:** a climbing hybrid rose (*Rosa lheritierana*) with purplish double flowers

bourse \'bu̇(ə)rs, -u̇əs\ *n* -s [F, lit., purse, fr. ML *bursa* — more at PURSE] **1 :** a place where merchants, bankers, and brokers meet for business at certain hours **:** MARKET, EXCHANGE **2 a :** a sale of numismatic or philatelic items carried on by a number of dealers displaying their wares on tables (as at a convention)

bour·tree \'bu̇r,(,)trē, 'bü·(,)-\ *n* [ME *burtre, bourtre,* perh. fr. *bour* bower + *tre, tree* tree] *Brit* **:** the common large black-fruited elder (*Sambucus nigra*) of Europe and Asia formerly esteemed as a source of dyestuffs and of several folk remedies

¹**bouse** \'büz, 'bau̇z\ *archaic var of* BOOZE

²**bouse** *or* **bowse** \'bau̇z\ *vb* -ED/-ING/-S [origin unknown] *vt, naut* **:** to pull or haul by means of a tackle; *also* **:** to haul well taut and belay (as a purchase) — usu. used with *taut* ~ *vi, naut* **:** to bouse something — usu. used with *taut*

bouser \'büzə(r), 'bau̇z-\ *archaic var of* BOOZER

bous·sin·gaul·tia \,büsᵊn'gōltēə\ *n, cap* [NL, fr. J.B.J.D. *Boussingault* †1887 Fr. chemist + NL *-ia*] **:** a small genus of graceful succulent perennial vines (family Basellaceae) found in tropical America with pedicellate flowers in axillary and terminal spikelike racemes — see MADEIRA VINE

bous·sin·gaul·tite \-l,tīt\ *n* -s [F, fr. J.B.J.D.*Boussingault* + F *-ite*] **:** a mineral $(NH_4)_2Mg(SO_4)_2.6H_2O$ consisting of a crystallized magnesium ammonium sulfate first found in boric-acid fumaroles of Tuscany, Italy

bou·stro·phe·don *also* **bou·stro·phei·don** *or* **bu·stro·phe·don** *or* **bu·stro·phei·don** \,büstrə'fē,dän, -ēdᵊn, ¦≐≐_fē¦dän; bü-¦sträfə¦dän\ *n* -s [Gk *boustrophēdon,* adv., turning like oxen in plowing, fr. *bou-* (fr. *bous* ox, cow) + *-strophēdon* (fr. *strephein* to turn) — more at COW, STROPHE] **:** the writing of alternate lines in opposite directions, one line from left to right and the next from right to left — **bou·stro·phe·don·ic** \¦büstrəfē-¦dänik, (')bü¦sträfə¦-\ *adj*

¹**bout** \'bau̇t, ¦bət\ *prep* [ME, fr. OE *būtan* without, except — more at BUT] *dial Eng* **:** WITHOUT ⟨he came ~ a hat⟩

²**bout** \'bau̇t, *usu* -au̇d·+V\ *n* -s [alter. of *bought* (bend)] **1 a** *dial Brit* **:** a trip going and returning in plowing or mowing **:** TURN **b :** a course or round of knitting **c** *dial chiefly Eng* **:** TIME, OCCASION ⟨won't be caught napping this ~⟩ **2 :** a spell of activity or a period of action having a definite beginning and end: as **a :** a contest or match esp. of boxing, wrestling, fencing **:** TURN ⟨a ~ at cudgels⟩ **b :** OUTBURST, ATTACK, SIEGE ⟨~s of bad temper⟩ ⟨drinking ~⟩ ⟨a ~ of fever⟩ **c :** SESSION ⟨long ~s of stubborn argument⟩ **3 :** one of the six sections or ribs comprising the side walls of the body of a stringed instrument (as a violin); *sometimes* **:** the waist section only

³**bout** \"\ *vt* -ED/-ING/-S **:** to plow (a field) by bouts

bou·tade \bü'täd\ *n* -s [F, fr. MF, fr. *bouter* to thrust + *-ade* — more at BUTT] **1 a :** an outbreak or burst esp. of temper **b :** CAPRICE, WHIM ⟨no need to take his little ~s seriously⟩ **2 a :** an 18th century French dance of impromptu character **b :** an instrumental musical composition similar to the Italian capriccio in an impromptu fanciful style

boutefeu *n* -s [MF, lit., linstock, fr. *bouter* to thrust, put, set + *feu* fire, fr. L *focus* hearth — more at FOCUS] *obs* **:** one who causes contention **:** FIREBRAND

boutell *var of* BOLTEL

bou·te·loua \,büd·ᵊl'üə, ,bōd·ᵊl'ōə\ *n, cap* [NL, irreg. fr. Claudio *Boutelou* †1848 Span. botanist] **:** a large genus of No. American forage grasses distinguished by the one-sided spikes of the inflorescence — see GRAMA

bou·tique \bü'tēk\ *n* -s [F, prob. fr. OProv *botica,* fr. Gk *apothēkē* warehouse — more at APOTHECARY] **1 :** a small retail store; *esp* **:** a specialty shop dealing in ladies' fashionable ready-to-wear clothes and accessories **2 :** a utilitarian or luxury item lavishly decorated (as with gilt, sequins, jewels) ⟨a counter display of ~s⟩ ⟨~ sugar tongs⟩

bou·to \'bō,tü\ *n* -s [Pg *boto,* lit., wineskin, fr. LL *buttis* cask; fr. its shape — more at BUTT (cask)] **:** a river dolphin (*Inia geoffroyensis*) that is peculiar to the Amazon and has a long snout

bou·ton \(')bü¦tōⁿ\ *or* **bouton ter·mi·nal** \-,termə'nal\ *n, pl* **boutons** \-ōⁿ\ *or* **boutons termi·naux** \-'nō\ [F *bouton terminal,* lit., terminal button] **:** a terminal club-shaped enlargement of a nerve fiber lying in contact with the body or dendrites of another neuron — called also *end bulb, end foot*

bou·ton·neuse fever \'bütᵊn,üz-, -,ə(r)z-, -,əz-\ *n* [part trans. of F *fièvre boutonneuse,* fr. *fièvre* fever + *boutonneuse,* fem. of *boutonneux* pimply, fr. *bouton* pimple, button, bud] **:** a disease prevalent in the Mediterranean area that is characterized by headache, pain in muscles and joints, and an eruption over the body including palms and soles and is caused by a rickettsia (*Rickettsia conorii*) which is transmitted by the bite of a tick

bou·ton·niere \¦bütᵊn¦i(ə)r, -iə *also* -tᵊn¦e(ə)r *or* -tən'ye(ə)r *or* -eə\ *n* -s [F *boutonnière* buttonhole, fr. MF *boutonniere,* fr. *bouton* button] **:** a flower or bouquet worn in a buttonhole; *also* **:** BOUQUET

bou·ton pearl \(')bü¦tōⁿ-\ *or* **but·ton pearl** \'bətᵊn-\ *n* [F *bouton* button — more at BUTTON] **:** a pearl flat on one side

bou·tre \'bütr(ᵊ), -t(rə)\ *n* -s [F] **:** a small Arabian coasting boat of the eastern African coast

bouts-ri·més \¦bü(,)rē¦mā(z)\ *n pl* [F, lit., rhymed ends] **:** rhyming words or syllables to which verses are to be written; *also* **:** verses so composed

bou·var·dia \bü'värdēə\ *n* [NL, fr. Charles *Bouvard* †1658 Fr. physician + NL *-ia*] **1** *cap* **:** a genus of tropical American herbs and shrubs (family Rubiaceae) with corymbs of showy tubular red, scarlet, yellow, and white flowers **2** -s **:** a plant or flower of the genus *Bouvardia*

bou·veault-blanc reduction \¦bü,vō¦blaⁿ-\ *n, cap both Bs* [after Louis *Bouveault* †1909 and Gustave *Blanc* fl1903 French chemists] **:** a method for the preparation of alcohols from esters and of amines from oximes or nitriles by reduction with metallic sodium in solution in an alcohol (as ethyl alcohol)

bou·vier des flan·dres \büvyādäflaⁿdr(ᵊ), -d(rə)\ *n, usu cap B&F* [F, lit., cowherd of Flanders] **1 :** a breed of large powerfully built rough-coated dogs originating in Belgium and used esp. for herding and in guard and police work, having a slightly tousled appearance, with definite eyebrows, a mustache, and a beard, and ranging in color from fawn to black, through pepper-and-salt, and gray and brindle **2** *pl* **bouviers des flandres** \"\ **:** a dog of this breed

bouw \'bau̇, 'bōu̇\ *n* -s [D, lit., tillage; akin to OE *bū* dwelling, OHG *bū* tillage, dwelling, ON *bū* household, OE *būan* to dwell — more at BOWER] **:** an Indonesian unit of land area equal to 1.75 acres

bouza *var of* BOSA

bouze \'büz\ *archaic var of* BOOZE

bo·va·rism *or* **bo·va·rysm** \'bōvə,rizəm\ *n* -s [F *bovarysme,* fr. Madame *Bovary* (principal character in the novel *Madame Bovary* by Gustave Flaubert †1880 Fr. novelist) + *-isme* -ism] **:** a conception of oneself as other than one is to the extent that one's general behavior is conditioned or dominated by the conception; *esp* **:** domination by such an idealized, glamorized, glorified, or otherwise unreal conception of oneself that it results in dramatic personal conflict (as in tragedy), in markedly unusual behavior (as in paranoia), or in great achievement

bo·va·rist \-,rəst\ *n* -s [fr. *bovarism,* after such pairs as E *romanticism: romanticist*] **:** a person subject to bovarism ⟨a religious ~⟩ — **bo·va·ris·tic** \¦bōvə¦ristik\ *adj*

bo·vate \'bō,vāt\ *n* -s [ML *bovata,* fr. L *bov-, bos* cow, ox] **:** an old English unit of land area equal to ⅛ carucate

bov·ey coal \'bəvē-\ *n, usu cap B* [*Bovey,* parish in Devonshire, England, its locality] **:** a lignite of the Miocene period found esp. at Bovey, England

bovi- *comb form* [LL *bovi-,* fr. L *bov-, bos*] **:** cattle ⟨*bovi*culture⟩

bo·vic·o·la \bō'vikələ\ *n, cap* [NL, fr. *bovi-* + *-cola*] **:** a genus of biting lice (order Mallophaga) including the red louse of cattle and several other lice infesting the hair of domestic mammals

¹**bo·vid** \'bōvəd\ *adj* [NL *Bovidae*] **:** belonging to the family Bovidae

²**bovid** \"\ *n* -s **:** an animal of the family Bovidae

bo·vi·dae \'bōvə,dē\ *n pl, cap* [NL, fr. *Bov-, Bos,* type genus + *-idae*] **:** a large family of ruminants containing the true antelopes, oxen, sheep, and goats, distinguished from the deer family by the polycotyledonary placenta, the hollow nondeciduous unbranched horns, and by the nearly universal presence of a gall bladder

¹**bo·vine** \'bō,vīn, -ēn *also* ≐'≐\ *adj* [LL *bovinus,* fr. L *bov-, bos* cow, ox + *-inus* -ine — more at COW] **1 :** of or belonging to the genus *Bos* **:** relating to or resembling the ox or cow **2 :** having qualities characteristic of oxen or cows **:** sluggish and patient **:** DULL ⟨a ~ temperament⟩ — **bo·vine·ly** *adv* — **bo·vin·i·ty** \bō'vinəd·ē\ *n* -ES

²**bovine** \"\ *n* -s **:** an animal of *Bos* or of a closely related genus of the family Bovidae

bovine farcy *n* **:** FARCY 2

bovine malaria *n* **:** TEXAS FEVER

bovine mastitis *n* **:** inflammation of the cow's udder resulting from injury or bruising or more commonly from bacterial infection and being a major source of loss to the dairy industry both through direct damage to the animals and through loss of milk — see STREPTOCOCCAL MASTITIS, SUMMER MASTITIS

bovine staggers *n pl but sing in constr* **:** a disease of cattle in southern Africa characterized by staggering, inflammation, emaciation, and finally paralysis and caused by eating a poisonous herb (*Matricaria nigellaefolia*)

bo·vis·ta \bō'vistə\ *n, cap* [NL, fr. G *bofist, bovist* puffball, alter. of MHG *vohenvist,* fr. *vohe* she-fox (fr. OHG *foha*) + *vist, vist* emission of gas from the colon — more at FOX, FEIST] **:** a genus of basidiomycetes (family Lycoperdaceae) including various puffballs having a thin peridium at maturity

bo·vo \'bō(,)vō\ *n* -s [It] **:** a lateen-rigged masted fishing boat of Genoa

bo·void \'bō,vȯid\ *adj* [L *bov-, bos* + E *-oid*] **:** like or belonging to the genus *Bos* or family Bovidae **:** BOVINE

bo·voi·dea \bō'vȯidēə\ *n pl, cap* [NL, fr. *Bov-, Bos* genus of ruminant mammals including the wild and domestic cattle + *-oidea*] **:** a superfamily or other division of horned ruminant mammals (order Artiodactyla) comprising the families Antilocapridae and Bovidae and distinguished by possession of hollow horns that are deciduous in the former family but permanent in the latter

¹**bow** \'bau̇\ *vb* -ED/-ING/-S [ME *bowen,* fr. OE *būgan;* akin to OHG *biogan* to bend, ON *boginn* bent, *beygja* to bend, Goth *biugan* to bend, Skt *bhujati* he bends] *vi* **1** *archaic* **a :** BEND, CURVE **b :** to bend down **:** STOOP **c :** TURN, SWERVE, WEND **2 :** to give in **:** cease from independent resolution, competition, or resistance through courtesy, cooperation, subjugation, admission of defeat, or inferior position **:** DEFER, YIELD ⟨a man who good-humoredly ~*ed* to the inevitable —Willa Cather⟩; *specif* **:** to suffer defeat in a contest ⟨~*ed* to the champion in a close match⟩ **3 :** to bend the head or the body or the knee as an expression of reverence, submission, or shame ⟨~ and scrape⟩ — often used with *down* ⟨~*ing* down before false gods⟩ **4 :** to incline the head or body in salutation ⟨~*ing* to acquaintances⟩ or as a sign of assent (as to a request or order) or to acknowledge applause ~ *vt* **1 :** to cause to incline **:** BEND ⟨the wind ~s the treetops⟩ **2** *obs* **:** TURN, INCLINE ⟨may God ~ their hearts to our cause⟩ **3 :** to bend or incline (the head, neck, body, or knee) esp. as a sign or token of respect, submission, surrender, or self-abasement ⟨the whole nation ~*ed* their necks to tyranny —W.H.Prescott⟩ **4 :** to crush with or as if with a heavy burden ⟨whose heavy hand hath ~*ed* you to the grave —Shak.⟩ **5 a :** to express or signal by bowing ⟨he ~*ed* his thanks⟩ **b :** to usher in or out with a bow ⟨~*ed* in by a footman⟩ **syn** see YIELD

²**bow** \"\ *n* -s **:** a bending of the head or body as an expression of reverence, respect, submission, or assent or as a salutation **:** OBEISANCE — **make one's bow :** to make a first public appearance or, formerly, a final appearance

³**bow** \'bō\ *n* -s [ME *bowe,* fr. OE *boga;* akin to OHG *bogo* bow, ON *bogi,* OE *būgan* to bend] **1 a :** something bent into a simple curve **:** BEND, ARCH ⟨perfect ~s above her eyes⟩ ⟨*bow*-backed⟩ **b :** RAINBOW ⟨I do set my ~ in the cloud —Gen 9:13 (AV)⟩ **c :** a curved or polygonal part projecting from a straight wall of a building **2 :** a weapon made of a strip of wood, metal, or other flexible material with a cord that connects the two ends so as to hold the strip bent in an arc under tension and used to propel an arrow by nocking the arrow on the string and drawing it back against the tension so that upon release it is propelled through the air **3 :** BOWMAN, ARCHER ⟨he was high ~ in the meet⟩ **4 :** SADDLEBOW **5 a** *dial* **:** a U-shaped piece embracing the neck of an ox and fastening it to the yoke; *also* **:** an ox yoke **b** *now dial Brit* **:** an arch esp. of a bridge or gateway ⟨four-and-twenty ~s on the old bridge of Callander⟩ **c :** a bentwood support used in furniture **d :** an early nautical quadrant for measuring arcs, chiefly the sun's altitude **e :** a metal ring or loop forming a handle (as of a key or a pair of scissors) or encircling the winding crown of a pocket watch for attaching a chain **f :** the guard of a sword hilt or trigger **g :** a bent piece of wood or metal supporting the top or cover of a vehicle **:** BAIL **h :** a knot (as an ornamental slipknot) formed by doubling a ribbon or string into two or more loops which usu. can be readily drawn through the knot in untying; *also* **:** BOW TIE **i :** a frame for the lenses of eyeglasses; *also* **:** the curved sidepiece passing over the ear to support eyeglasses **j :** the frame of a snowshoe **6 a :** a resilient wooden rod orig. having a convex curve but from the late 18th century on being slightly concave with a number of horsehairs stretched from end to end and used in playing on a musical instrument of the viol or violin family **b :** a stroke of the bow in playing a stringed instrument ⟨the up ~⟩ **7 :** a contrivance that consists of a bent elastic rod with ends connected by a string and is employed for various purposes (as for giving reciprocating motion to a drill, for wood turning, and for preparing and arranging the hair and fur used by hatters) **8 :** a bent rod or piece in basketmaking; *esp* **:** a rod bent twice at right angles so as to form three sides of a rectangle **9 :** a warping along the length of a piece of lumber — compare CROOK

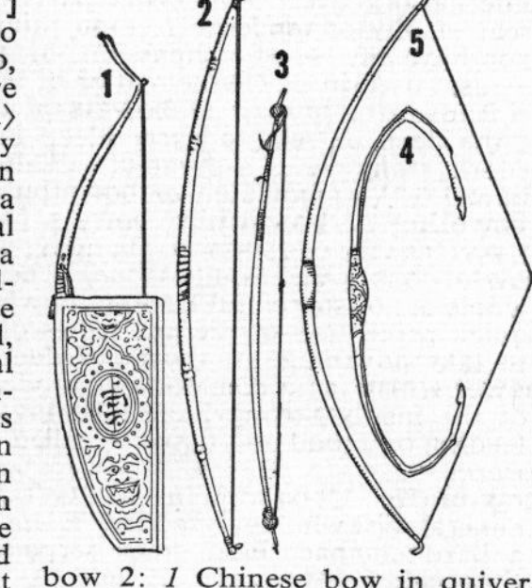

bow 2: *1* Chinese bow in quiver, *2* African cane bow, *3* Brazilian Indian bow, *4* Hindu bow, *5* modern bow; see also CUPID'S BOW illustration

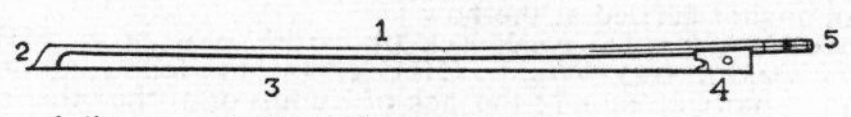

violin bow: *1* stick, *2* head, *3* hair, *4* frog, *5* screw

⁴**bow** \"\ *vb* -ED/-ING/-S *vi* **1 :** to bend into a curve **:** bend out of line ⟨the wall ~s inward⟩ **2 :** to play a stringed musical instrument with a bow; *also* **:** to perform with or manage the bow ~ *vt* **1 :** to make or bend into a curve ⟨a desk with a ~*ed* front⟩ **2 :** to separate and distribute (cotton fibers for felting) by a bow **3 :** to play (a stringed instrument) with a bow

⁵**bow** \'bau̇\ *n* -s [prob. fr. Dan *bov* bow, shoulder, fr. ON *bōgr* — more at BOUGH] **1 :** the forward part of a ship **:** the part where the sides curve inward to terminate in the stem ⟨the ~ lights⟩ — often used in pl. ⟨abeam rather than her ~s⟩ ⟨~s under⟩ — see SHIP illustration **2 :** one that rows in the forward end of a boat **:** BOW OAR — **on the bow** *adv (or adj)* **:** on that part of the horizon bearing within 4 points of 45 degrees on either side of the line ahead

⁶**bow** \'bō, 'bü\ *n* -s [by alter.] **:** ¹BOLL 1

bow–arm \'≐,≐\ *n* **:** the arm that holds the bow in archery or in playing a musical instrument of the violin family

bow–back \'≐,≐\ *adj* [³*bow*] **:** HOOP-BACK

bow bearer *n* [³*bow*] **:** an underofficer of the forest in old England who looked after trespasses affecting vert and venison

bow cap *n* [⁵*bow*] **1 :** a cap of metal or fabric used to reinforce the extreme forward ends of the bow stiffeners of an airship **2 :** the conical or cap-shaped structure at the bow of a rigid airship to which the longitudinal girders are attached and which supports the bow mooring spindle

bow chaser *n* [⁵*bow*] **:** a gun so placed as to be able to fire ahead (as at a ship being chased)

bow china \'bō-\ *n, usu cap B* [Stratford-le-*Bow,* town near London, England, where it was made] **:** china made at Stratford-le-Bow, near London, in the 18th century

bow compass *n* [³*bow*] **:** a small pair of compasses one leg of which carries a pencil, pen, or point, its legs being connected by a bow-shaped spring instead of by a joint

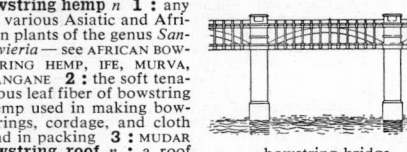

bow compass

bow·darc *or* **bow·dark** \ˈbō,dä(r)k, -dȧk\ *var of* BODOCK

bow·den \ˈbōdᵊn\ *vi* -ED/-ING/-S [earlier Sc *boldin*, fr. ME (Sc) *boldnen*, alter. of ME *bolnen*, modif. of ON *bolgna;* akin to OE & OHG *belgan* to be angry, ON *bolginn* swollen, *belgja* to cause to swell, OE *belg, bælg* bag, skin — more at BELLY] *Scot* **:** SWELL; *specif* **:** BLOAT

bow·den cable *or* **bowden wire** \ˈbōdᵊn, ˈbau̇d-\ *n, usu cap B* [after E.M.*Bowden*, 19th cent. Eng. inventor] **:** spring steel wire enclosed in a spiral wire casing for transmitting longitudinal motion at a distance esp. (as in a hand brake) around a corner

bow·dich·ia \bau̇ˈdichēə\ *n, cap* [NL, fr. Thomas E. *Bowdich* †1824 Eng. traveler + NL -*ia*] **:** a genus of large tropical So. American trees (family Leguminosae) with odd-pinnate leaves, blue or white flowers, and very hard wood

bow·ditch \ˈbau̇(,)dich\ *n* -ES *usu cap* [after Nathaniel *Bowditch* †1838 Am. mathematician and astronomer] **:** a navigation manual

bow divider *n* **:** a bow compass with two divider points

bowd·ler·ism \ˈbōdlə,rizəm, ˈbau̇d-\ *n* -S [T. *Bowdler* + E -*ism*] **:** BOWDLERIZATION, EXPURGATION

bowd·ler·i·za·tion \,bōdlərəˈzāshən, ,bau̇d-, -lə,rīˈz-\ *n* -S **:** the act or result of bowdlerizing

bowd·ler·ize \ˈbōdlə,rīz, ˈbau̇d-\ *vt* -ED/-ING/-S *see -ize in Explan Notes, sometimes cap* [Thomas *Bowdler* †1825 Eng. editor of an expurgated Shakespeare + E -*ize*] **1 :** to remove matter considered indelicate or otherwise objectionable from by expurgation or alteration ⟨~ a text⟩ ⟨a *bowdlerized* version of the scene⟩ ⟨*bowdlerized* the manuscript⟩ **2 :** to alter (something) by removing forceful elements **:** EMASCULATE ⟨~ a philosophy⟩

bow·dock \ˈbō,dȧk\ *var of* BODOCK

bow drill *n* **:** a drill worked by a bow and string to bore holes or make fire

¹**bowed** \ˈbau̇d\ *adj* [ME, fr. past part. of *bowen* to bow — more at ¹BOW] **:** bent down **:** with the head inclined — **bowed·ness** *n* -ES

²**bowed** \ˈbōd\ *adj* [ME, fr. *bowe* bow + -*ed* — more at ³BOW] **:** furnished with a bow **:** shaped like a bow — **bowed·ness** *n* -ES

bowed cotton *n* [*bowed*, past part. of ⁴*bow;* fr. the practice of separating the fiber from the seeds by blows of a bowstring] **:** UPLAND COTTON

bowed tendon *n* [*bowed*, past part. of ⁴*bow*] **:** a suspensory ligament of a horse that has ruptured and shortened in healing, assuming a bowed appearance; *also* **:** the resulting condition of lameness

¹**bow·el** \ˈbau̇(ə)l, *esp S* -au̇wəl\ *n* -S [ME, fr. OF *boel, boiel*, fr. ML *botellus*, fr. L, small sausage, dim. of L *botulus* sausage; prob. akin to OE *cwith* belly, womb, OHG *quiti* vulva, ON *kvithr* belly, womb, Goth *qithus* stomach, womb] **1 :** the intestine or one of its divisions **:** GUT — usu. used in pl. except in medical use ⟨the large ~⟩ ⟨move your ~*s*⟩ **2 a** *obs* (1) **:** an internal organ (2) **:** the inside parts together **b** *archaic* **:** the seat of pity or tenderness ⟨thou thing of no ~*s* —Shak.⟩ ⟨if you have any ~*s* of compassion⟩ or of courage **:** GUTS, HEART — usu. used in pl. ⟨in the matter of backbone, brains, and ~*s* —Rudyard Kipling⟩ **3 bowels** *pl* **:** the interior parts; *esp* **:** the deep or remote parts ⟨deep in the ~*s* of the earth⟩ ⟨dark, stony ~*s* of a pyramid —Walter de la Mare⟩

²**bowel** \"\ *vt* **boweled** *or* **bowelled; boweled** *or* **bowelled; boweling** *or* **bowelling; bowels** [ME *bowelen*, fr. ¹*bowel*] **:** EVISCERATE, DISEMBOWEL ⟨hanging and ~*ing* their enemies⟩

bow·el·less \-əl(l)əs, -ùlləs\ *adj* **:** being without bowels ⟨the whole art of successful trading, in whatsoever degree, lies in a quick perception of the necessities of others and ~ readiness to take advantage of them —Rafael Sabatini⟩

bowel worm *n* **:** a common nematode worm (*Chabertia ovina*) of the family Strongylidae infesting the colon of sheep and feeding on blood and tissue — called also *large-mouthed bowel worm*

bow·en·ite \ˈbōə,nīt\ *n* -S [G.T.*Bowen*, 19th cent. Am. mineralogist who analyzed it + E -*ite*] **:** a mineral consisting of a hard compact light green serpentine resembling nephrite (hardness 5.5–6)

bow·en's disease \ˈbōənz-\ *n, usu cap B* [after John T. *Bowen* †1940 Am. dermatologist] **:** a precancerous lesion of the skin or mucous membranes characterized by small solid elevations covered by thickened horny tissue

¹**bow·er** \ˈbau̇(ə)r, -au̇ə, *esp S* -au̇wə(r\ *n* -S [ME *bour* bedroom, dwelling, fr. OE *būr;* akin to OE & OHG *būan* to dwell, inhabit, cultivate, OHG *būr* dwelling, ON *būa* to prepare, live, dwell, *būr* pantry, Goth *bauan* to live, dwell, OE *bēon* to be — more at BE] **1 :** a rustic cottage **:** an attractive dwelling or retreat **2 :** a lady's private apartment in a medieval hall or castle **3** *also* **bow·ery** \ˈbau̇(ə)rē, -ri\ -ES [*bowery* alter. (prob. influenced by *bough* & -*ery*) of *bower*] **:** a shelter or covered place in a garden made with boughs of trees or vines twined together **:** ARBOR

²**bower** \"\ *vb* -ED/-ING/-S *vt* **:** EMBOWER, ENCLOSE ~ *vi* **1** *obs* **:** LODGE, DWELL **2** *of branches* **:** to form bowers

³**bow·er** \ˈbōər, ˈbüər\ *n* -S [Sc *bow* herd of cattle on a farm (fr. ME, fr. ON *bū* livestock, household) + E -*er* — more at BOUW] *Scot* **:** one that rents or manages for a share of the profits the dairy stock of a farm

⁴**bow·er** \ˈbau̇(ə)r, -au̇ə\ *or* **bower anchor** *n* -S [⁵*bow* + -*er*] **:** an anchor carried at the bow

⁵**bower** \"\ *n* -S [G *bauer* jack (in cards), peasant, fr. MHG *būre* peasant, fr. *gebūre*, fr. OHG *gibūro*, lit., fellow-countryman — more at BOOR] **:** the jack of trumps or of the other suit of the same color in euchre and five hundred — compare LEFT BOWER, RIGHT BOWER

bower actinidia *n* [¹*bower*] **:** a high-climbing Asiatic vine (*Actinidia arguta*) that is sometimes cultivated for its ornamental long-petioled finely serrate leaves, white flowers, and globose greenish yellow edible fruits — called also *tara vine*

bow·er–barff process \ˈbau̇(ə)rˈbärf-\ *n, usu cap both Bs* [after George and A.S.*Bower* and F.S.*Barff*, 19th cent. Am. engineers] **:** a process for producing upon iron or steel an adhering coating of iron oxides to resist atmospheric corrosion

bowerbird \ˈ=,=\ *n* **:** any of a group of large usu. brightly colored passerine birds (family Paradiseidae) of the Australian region that build chambers or passages which are arched over with twigs and grasses and often adorned with bright-colored objects (as shells or feathers) and are used as playhouses or to attract the females rather than as nests — compare BIRD OF PARADISE; see GREAT BOWERBIRD, SATIN BOWERBIRD

bow·er·ly \ˈbȯə(r)lē\ *adj* [prob. alter. of *burly*] *dial Eng* **:** STOUT, BURLY

bowermaiden \ˈ=,==\ *n* [ME *bourmaiden*, fr. *bour* bedroom + *maiden*] *archaic* **:** a lady's maid **:** MAID-IN-WAITING

bower plant *n* **:** an Australian woody vine (*Pandorea jasminoides*) cultivated for its large pink-and-white flowers

bowerwoman \ˈ=,==\ *n, pl* **bowerwomen** [ME *bourwoman*, fr. *bour* bedroom + *woman*] *archaic* **:** CHAMBERMAID

¹**bow·ery** \ˈbau̇(ə)rē, -ri\ *adj* [¹*bower* + -*y*] **:** like a bower **:** full of bowers

²**bowery** \"\ *var of* ¹BOWER 3

³**bowery** \"\ *n* -ES [D *bouwerij*, fr. *bouwer* farmer (fr. *bouwen* to till — fr. MD *bouwen, būwen* — + -*er* — akin to OE -*ere* -er) + -*ij* -y, fr. MD -*ie*, fr. OF -*ie;* akin to OHG *būan* to dwell, cultivate] **1 :** a colonial Dutch plantation or farm (as in early New York or in So. Africa) **2** [The *Bowery*, street in New York City] **:** a city street or district notorious for cheap saloons and homeless derelicts

bow·et \ˈbau̇ət\ *var of* BOUET

bow fast *n* **:** a mooring line at the bow of a ship

bowfin \ˈ=,=\ *n* -S [³*bow*] **:** a voracious dull-green iridescent ganoid fish (*Amia calva*) of little value as food that is found in the fresh waters of the Great lakes, Mississippi valley, and adjacent areas and is the sole surviving representative of a genus known from the Paleocene and formerly widespread in both New and Old Worlds — called also *mudfish*

bowfront \ˈ=,=\ *adj* [³*bow*] **1** *of a case piece of furniture* **:** having an outward curving front **2** *of a house* **:** having a bow window in front

bow·grace \ˈbau̇,grās\ *n* -S [perh. by folk etymology (influence of ⁵*bow*) fr. obs. *bongrace* bowgrace, lit., projecting brim for a bonnet — more at BONGRACE] **:** a fender of rope or waste for protecting a ship from injury by floating ice

bow hair *n* **:** the horsehairs of a bow used in playing a stringed musical instrument — see BOW illustration

bow hand *n* **1 :** the left hand **:** left direction — used esp. in archery in the phrase *on the bow hand* **2 :** the hand that draws the bow of a stringed musical instrument ⟨a light *bow hand*⟩

bowhead \ˈ=,=\ *n* [³*bow*] **:** GREENLAND WHALE

bow–hough'd \ˈbō,häkt\ *adj* [³*bow* + *hough* + -'*d*] *Scot* **:** BOWLEGGED

¹**bow·ie** \ˈbōē\ *n* -S [prob. fr. Sc *bow* bowl (fr. ME *bolle*) + -*ie*] **1** *Scot* **:** a wooden barrel; *esp* **:** one for water or ale **2** *Scot* **:** any of various shallow wooden bowls or dishes **3** *Scot* **:** a bucket or pail made of wood

²**bow·ie** \ˈbüē, ˈbōē\ *or* **bowie knife** *n* -S [after James *Bowie* †1836 Am. soldier, who first used such a knife, probably invented by his brother Rezin P. Bowie †1841 Am. pioneer] **:** a large hunting knife adapted esp. for knife-fighting and common in western frontier regions and having a guarded handle and a strong single-edge blade typically 10 to 15 inches long with its back straight for most of its length and then curving concavely and sometimes in a sharpened edge to the point

bowie knife

bowing *n* -S [fr. gerund of ⁴*bow*] **:** the act or art of managing the bow in playing a stringed musical instrument; *specif* **:** the manner of articulating or grouping the notes of a given phrase or passage with the bow

bowing acquaintance *n* **:** acquaintance limited to bowing in recognition; *also* **:** a person with whom one has such acquaintance

bow·ing·ly *adv* **:** in a bowing manner

bowk \ˈbük, ˈbōk\ *vt* -ED/-ING/-S [ME *bouken* — more at BUCK (to soak)] **:** to steep (textile materials) often with boiling in a bath usu. containing lime, soda, or soap in order to cleanse before bleaching

bow·kail \ˈbō,kāl\ *n* -S [prob. fr. ³*bow* + *kale;* fr. its rounded shape] *Scot* **:** CABBAGE

bowknot \ˈ=,=\ *n* [³*bow*] **:** a knot with decorative loops; *esp* **:** a square knot or granny knot in which the second half-knot is tied with loops instead of ends

¹**bowl** \ˈbōl\ *n* -S [ME *bolle*, fr. OE *bolla;* akin to OHG *bolla* blister, ON *bolli* bowl, OE *blāwan* to blow — more at BLOW] **1 :** a rounded hollow vessel usu. nearly hemispherical in form and generally deeper than a basin and larger or heavier than a cup; *specif* **:** a drinking vessel of this shape ⟨come and fill the flowing ~⟩ **2 :** the contents of a bowl **3 :** a bowl-shaped or concave part: as **a :** the hollow of a spoon, oar, tobacco pipe, flagon, candlestick **b :** the part or parts of such letters as O, b, d, p, q, g, B that are closed curves; *also* **:** the space enclosed by the closed curves **c :** the receptacle of a toilet **4 a :** a natural formation (as a valley) or geographical region shaped like a bowl ⟨the Western dust ~⟩ **b :** a bowl-shaped structure (as an amphitheater) often formed by excavation; *esp* **:** an athletic stadium **c :** a postseasonal football game between specially invited teams ⟨a ~ invitation⟩ ⟨~ squad⟩ **d :** a floor surface sloping toward a center (as in a theater)

²**bowl** \"\ *n* -S [ME *boule, bowle*, fr. MF *boule*, fr. L *bulla* bubble — more at POLL (head)] **1 a** *obs* **:** SPHERE, GLOBE **b :** a usu. lignum vitae ball that is weighted or shaped so as to give it a bias when rolled in lawn bowling **c bowls** *pl but sing in const* **:** LAWN BOWLING **d bowls** *pl but sing in constr, Scot* **:** MARBLES **2 :** a cast or delivery of the ball down the green or alley (as in bowling); *also* **:** a turn in the game of bowling **3 :** a cylindrical roller or drum variously used (as for an antifriction wheel or bearing or in pairs as a means of drawing or pressing fabrics in manufacture)

³**bowl** \"\ *vb* -ED/-ING/-S [ME *bowlen*, fr. *boule, bowle*] *vi* **1 :** to participate in the game of bowls or any of various bowling games (as tenpins) **2 :** to roll a ball down the alley (as in tenpins) or along the green (as in lawn bowling) **3 :** to move on or as if on wheels esp. smoothly and rapidly — usu. with *along* ⟨~*ing* along the highway in a bus⟩ **4 :** to deliver a cricket ball from behind the bowling crease to the batsman with a smooth movement of the arm ~ *vt* **1 a :** to send rolling along the ground or down a green or an alley **b :** to complete by bowling ⟨~ a string⟩ **:** achieve by bowling ⟨~ a 300 game⟩ **:** score by bowling ⟨~*s* a steady 150⟩ **2 :** to deliver (a cricket ball) to the batsman **3 a :** to strike with or as if with a swiftly rolling object esp. so as to displace ⟨~*ed* over by a runaway horse⟩ ⟨~*ed* aside by a man dashing blindly for the exit⟩ **b :** to overwhelm or stun esp. with surprise **:** dismay suddenly **:** DISCONCERT — usu. used with *over* ⟨he was completely ~*ed* over by the news⟩ **4 a :** to put out (a cricket batsman) with a bowled ball that breaks the wicket — often used with *out* **b** *chiefly Brit* **:** to put out of action **:** defeat finally or utterly — often used with *out* or *down* ⟨~*ed* out only by death itself⟩ ⟨~ down an opponent in a debate⟩ — **bowl over the wicket** *cricket* **:** to deliver a ball with the stumps on the same side as one's bowling arm and usu. while standing quite close to the stumps — **bowl round the wicket** *cricket* **:** to deliver a ball from the side of the bowling crease corresponding to the bowling arm (as right for a right-hand bowler) usu. while standing somewhat away from the stumps

bowlder *var of* BOULDER

bowled *past of* BOWL

bowleg \ˈ=,=\ *n* [³*bow*] **:** a leg bowed outward at or below the knee usu. from disease

bow·legged \ˈesp US ˈbō;legəd, *esp Brit* -gd\ *adj* **:** having legs bowed outward

¹**bowl·er** \ˈbōlə(r)\ *n* -S [³*bowl* + -*er*] **:** one that bowls; *specif* **:** the player who delivers the ball to the batsman in cricket

²**bow·ler** \"\ *or* **bowler hat** *n* -S [after *Bowler fl*1861 Eng. hatmaker] **:** DERBY 2a

bow·less \ˈbōləs\ *adj* [³*bow* + -*less*] **:** being without a bow

bow light *n* [⁵*bow*] **:** the white light displayed forward by a ship at anchor or by a power ship under way

bow·line \ˈbōlən, -,līn\ *n* [ME *bouline, bowelyne*, perh. fr. *bowe* bow + *line* — more at ³BOW, LINE] **1 :** a rope fastened near the middle of the perpendicular edge of a square sail and used to keep the weather edge of the sail taut forward when the ship is close-hauled **2** *or* **bowline knot :** a loop knot that neither slips nor jams used esp. for mooring and hoisting — see PORTUGUESE BOWLINE, RUNNING BOWLINE, SPANISH BOWLINE

bowline knot

bow line \ˈbau̇,līn\ *n* [⁵*bow*] **:** the line of intersection of a fore-and-aft vertical plane with the fore-body of a ship

bowline bridle *n* **:** a rope by which the bowline is connected to the leech of the sail — see BOWLINE CRINGLE; SAIL illustration

bowline cringle *n* **:** a loop or eye in the leech of a sail for attaching the bowline bridle

bowline on a bight : a bowline knot with a double loop tied in the bight of a rope

bowling *n* -S [fr. gerund of ³*bowl*] **:** any of several games in which balls are rolled on a green outdoors or down an alley indoors at an object or group of objects; *esp* **:** a game in which pins are set up in a usu. triangular pattern at one end of an alley and balls rolled at them from the other end, the object being to knock down as many pins as possible with each ball — see CANDLEPINS, DUCKPINS, LAWN BOWLING, NINEPINS, TENPINS; compare BOCCIE, SKITTLES

bowling analysis *n* **:** a tabulation of the work of the bowlers in a cricket match or innings showing balls bowled, wickets taken, and runs scored

bowling average *n* **:** the ratio in cricket obtained by dividing the number of runs scored by the number of wickets taken by a bowler

bowling crease *n* **:** one of two lines with wickets pitched in the center of each from or behind which the cricket ball must be bowled

bowling green *n* **:** a level piece of ground for lawn bowling

bowling on the green : LAWN BOWLING

bowling stump *n* **:** a stump marking the cricket bowler's position when a single wicket is used

bowls *pl of* BOWL, *pres 3d sing of* BOWL

¹**bow·ly** \ˈbōlē, ˈbülē\ *adj* [perh. fr. *bool* + -*y*] *Scot* **:** CROOKED, BENT ⟨~ legs⟩

²**bow·ly** \ˈbōlē\ *n* -ES [Hindi *bāwlī*, fr. Skt *vāpī* pond] **:** a large usu. rectangular sunken pool or well in India that serves as a public water supply and a resting place and is usu. provided with terraces and shaded recesses

¹**bow·man** \ˈbōmən\ *n, pl* **bowmen** [ME *boweman*, fr. *bowe* bow + *man* — more at ³BOW] **:** ARCHER

²**bow·man** \ˈbau̇mən\ *n, pl* **bowmen** [⁵*bow*] **:** a boatman, oarsman, or paddler stationed in the front of a boat: as **a :** BOW OAR **b :** a logger who sits in the front of the boat to guide floating logs with a pike pole or peavey

bow·man's capsule \ˈbōmənz-\ *n, usu cap B* [after Sir William *Bowman* †1892 Eng. surgeon] **:** a thin membranous double-walled capsule surrounding the glomerulus of a vertebrate nephron

bowman's glands *n pl, usu cap B* **:** branching tubular glands in the olfactory mucous membrane

bowman's membrane *n, usu cap B* **:** the thin condensed outer layer of the substantia propria of the cornea immediately underlying the epithelium

bow·man's root \ˈbōmənz-\ *also* **bowman root** *or* **bowman** *n, sometimes cap B* [by folk etymology fr. *beaumont root*] **1 :** CULVER'S ROOT **2 :** FLOWERING SPURGE **3 :** INDIAN PHYSIC 1

bown \ˈbau̇n, ˈbün\ *vb* -ED/-ING/-S [ME *bounen*, fr. *boun* ready — more at ¹BOUND] **1** *chiefly Scot* **:** to make ready **2** *chiefly Scot* **:** GO

bow net *n* [³*bow*] **1 :** a trap for lobsters consisting of a wickerwork cylinder with a funnel-shaped entrance at one end **2 :** a net attached to a wooden bow for catching birds

bow oar *n* [⁵*bow*] **1 :** the oar used by the rower nearest the bow; *sometimes* **:** the foremost oar but one in a whaleboat **2 :** one who pulls the bow oar

bow on *adv* **:** head on

bow out *vi* [¹*bow*] **:** to retire or withdraw esp. from a contest ⟨*bowed out* after tiring in the 6th inning⟩ ⟨*bowed out* of the race for governor⟩ **:** work at one's job for the last time **:** make a final appearance at one's post **:** step down ⟨*bowed out* with a great performance⟩ ⟨*bowed out* after 40 years of railroading⟩

bow pen *n* **:** a bow compass for drawing small circles in ink

bow pencil *n* **:** a bow compass provided with a pencil point

bowpin \ˈ=,=\ *n* [³*bow*] **:** a cotter for the bows of an ox yoke

bowpot *var of* BOUGHPOT

bow priest *n* [³*bow* + *priest;* fr. the fact that he is also a leader in war] **:** a Zuñi ceremonial group leader and high-ranking member of the religious hierarchy

bow pulpit *n* [⁵*bow*] **:** PULPIT 4

bow rudder *n* [⁵*bow*] **1 :** one of the forward diving rudders of a submarine — usu. used in pl. **2 :** a steering stroke that is used by a bow paddler to turn a canoe sharply and is executed by bracing the shaft of the paddle against the gunwale while pointing the blade diagonally forward at slight depth

bows *pl of* BOW, *pres 3d sing of* BOW

bow saw *n* [³*bow*] **:** a saw that has a narrow blade held under tension by a light bow-shaped frame and is used for pruning and sawing medium-sized logs

¹**bowse** \ˈbau̇z, ˈbüz\ *archaic var of* BOOZE

²**bowse** *var of* BOUSE

bow·ser \ˈbau̇zə(r)\ *n* -S [fr. *Bowser*, a trademark] *chiefly Austral* **:** a pump usu. at a service station for dispensing liquid fuels, esp. gasoline

bow saw

bowshot \ˈ=,=\ *n* [ME *boweshot*, fr. *bowe* bow + *shot* — more at ³BOW] **:** the distance traversed by an arrow shot from a bow **:** the effective range of a bow ⟨waiting for the foe to come within ~⟩

bow shot *n* [³*bow*] **:** a shot in squash racquets that is hit into a sidewall from rear court, rebounds to the opposite sidewall, and then rebounds to the front wall

bow sight *n* [³*bow*] **:** a device usu. of pins set in a calibrated frame attachable to a shooting bow for aid in aiming for distance

bows·man \ˈbau̇zmən\ *n, pl* **bowsmen** [by folk etymology (influence of ⁵*bow*) fr. F *bosseman*, prob. fr. obs. LG *bossman*, alter. of (assumed) LG *bootsman*, fr. *boots* (gen. of *boot* boat, fr. MLG, fr. ME) + *man*, fr. OS; akin to OHG *man* — more at BOAT, MAN] **:** a crew member of a small boat who is usu. stationed in the bow, not assigned to an oar, and usu. has some supervisory status

bow's notation \ˈbōz-\ *n, usu cap B* [after R.H.*Bow*, 19th cent. Eng. engineer] **:** a method of lettering the cells and outside spaces formed by the directions of the stresses in and loads on a framed structure so that these stresses and loads can be traced by similar letters in the reciprocal diagram

bow·sprit \ˈbau̇,sprit, ˈbō,-\ *n* -S [ME *bouspret*, prob. fr. MLG *bōchsprēt*, fr. *bōch* bow (akin to OE *bōg* shoulder, bough) + *sprēt* pole; akin to OE *sprēot* pole, MHG *spriez* twig, OE *sprūtan* to sprout — more at BOUGH, SPROUT] **:** a large spar projecting forward from the stem of a ship to carry sail forward and to support the masts by stays — see SHIP illustration

bowsprit bed *n* **:** that part of the stem on which the bowsprit rests

bowsprit cap *n* **:** an iron band fitted to the outer end of the bowsprit with a ring on top for the jibboom to run through — compare CRANCE; see SHIP illustration

bowsprit shrouds *n pl* **:** ropes, chains, or rods from the head of the bowsprit to the ship's bows — see SHIP illustration

bows·sen \ˈbau̇sᵊn\ *vt* -ED/-ING/-S [modif. of Corn *beuzi, bedhy, büdhy* to drown, submerge; akin to OIr *bāidim* I drown (transitive), W *boddi* to drown — more at BATHY-] *in Cornwall* **:** to duck in water as a treatment for insanity

bow·stave \ˈbō,stāv\ *n* [back-formation fr. *bowstaves*, pl. of obs. *bowstaff* bowstave, fr. ME *bowestaf*, fr. *bowe* bow + *staf* staff — more at BOW, STAFF] **:** a trimmed rod of wood to be made into a shooting bow

bow·ster \ˈbōstər\ *chiefly Scot var of* BOLSTER

bow stiffener *n* [⁵*bow*] **:** one of the rigid members attached to the bow of a nonrigid or semirigid envelope of an airship to reinforce it against pressure caused by the motion of the ship — called also *nose stiffener*

bow street runner *also* **bow street officer** \ˈbō-\ *n, usu cap B & S* [fr. *Bow Street*, London, England] **:** a London policeman attached to the Bow Street police court; *specif* **:** one of the officers appointed about 1805 to act as detectives in London and elsewhere in England

¹**bowstring** \ˈ=,=\ *n* [ME *bowestring*, fr. *bowe* bow + *string*, *streng* string — more at ³BOW, STRING] **:** a waxed or sized cord usu. of hemp or linen threads joining the ends of a shooting bow ⟨nerves taut as a ~⟩

²**bowstring** \"\ *vt* **bowstringed** *or* **bowstrung; bowstringed** *or* **bowstrung; bowstringing; bowstrings :** to strangle with a bowstring

bowstring beam *or* **bowstring girder** *or* **bowstring truss** *n* **:** a beam or girder consisting of an arched beam strengthened by a tie connecting its two ends

bowstring bridge *n* **:** a bridge with bowstring girders

bowstring hemp *n* **1 :** any of various Asiatic and African plants of the genus *Sansevieria* — see AFRICAN BOWSTRING HEMP, IFE, MURVA, PANGANE **2 :** the soft tenacious leaf fiber of bowstring hemp used in making bowstrings, cordage, and cloth and in packing **3 :** MUDAR

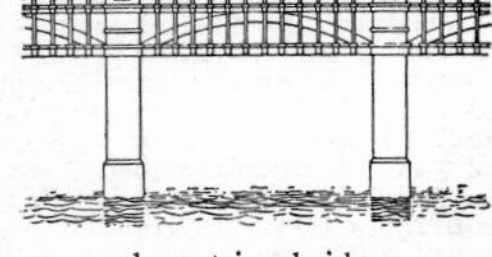
bowstring bridge

bowstring roof *n* **:** a roof with bowstring beams

bowtel *or* **bowtell** *var of* BOLTEL

bow tie \ˈbō\ *n* **:** a short necktie tied in a bowknot

bow trolley *n* [³*bow* + *trolley;* fr. its shape] **:** a bow-shaped member for collecting current by sliding contact with an overhead trolley wire

bow up *vi* [⁴*bow*] *dial* **:** to reach the limit of one's patience and rebel **:** BALK ⟨the chore of it fell to me until I finally *bowed up* —Ross Santee⟩

bow wave \ˈbau̇\ *n* **1 :** the wave on either side of the bow of a ship under way **2 :** SHOCK WAVE

bow weight *n* **:** the force expressed in pounds that is required to draw a bow the length of its arrow

bow window *n* [³*bow*] **:** BAY WINDOW; *esp* **:** one with a curved ground plan

bowwood \ˈ=,=\ *n* **1 :** any of several woods suitable for making archery bows **2 :** OSAGE ORANGE

bow·wow \ˈbau̇,wau̇; ("*bark*") ˈ=¦= *or* =ˈ=\ *n* -S [imit.] **1 :** the bark of a dog; *also* **:** DOG **2 :** noisy clamor or protest **3 :** arrogance or dogmatism of manner ⟨remarks delivered in the big ~ style⟩ **4 bowwows** *pl* **:** RUIN, PERDITION **:** the dogs ⟨headed for the ~*s*⟩ ⟨gone to the ~*s*⟩

bowwow theory *n* **:** a theory that language originated in imitations of natural sounds (as those of birds, dogs, or thunder) — compare DINGDONG THEORY, POOH-POOH THEORY

bow·yang \ˈbō,yaŋ\ *n* -S [alter. of E dial. *bowy-yanks* (pl.) leather leggings] *Austral* **:** a cord or strap tied around a workman's trousers just below the knee — usu. used in pl.

bow·yer \ˈbōyə(r)\ *n* -S [ME *bowyere*, fr. *bowe* bow + *-ere* -er — more at ³BOW] **:** one that makes shooting bows

bowyer's knot *n* **:** TIMBER HITCH

¹**box** \ˈbäks\ *n, pl* **box** *or* **boxes** [ME *box*, fr. OE, fr. L *buxus*, fr. Gk *pyxos*] **1 :** an evergreen shrub or small tree of the genus *Buxus; esp* **:** a widely cultivated typically large shrub (*B. sempervirens*) that is extensively used for hedges, borders, and topiary figures because of its slow growth and compact habit — see BOXWOOD **2** *Austral* **a :** any of several trees of the genera *Alyxia, Eucalyptus, Tristania,* and *Murraya* which have timber resembling boxwood **b :** NATIVE BOX

²**box** \ˈ"\ *n* -ES [ME, fr. OE, fr. LL *buxis*, fr. Gk *pyxis*, fr. *pyxos* boxtree] **1 a :** a rigid typically rectangular receptacle often with a lid or cover in which something nonliquid is kept or carried ⟨shoe ~⟩ ⟨money ~⟩ ⟨take along a ~ lunch⟩ **b :** something constructed of a flat bottom and four upright solid sides (as the carrying part of a wagon) ⟨a ~ of growing seedlings⟩ ⟨playing in the sand ~⟩ ⟨the ~ of a pickup truck⟩ **:** FRAME, FLASK 2 **c :** the contents of a box as a measure of quantity ⟨5 cents a ~⟩ **d :** a closed receptacle to hold contributions (as of money, letters, ballots) **e** *Brit* **:** the money contained in a box **:** FUND **f :** the driver's seat on a carriage or coach **g** *slang* **:** GUITAR, BANJO, FIDDLE **2** *Brit* **:** a gift (as at Christmas) in a box ⟨have you given the postman his ~⟩ — see BOXING DAY **3 a** *in a theater* **:** a space with chairs enclosed by partitions except toward the stage ⟨the royal ~⟩; *also* **:** the occupants of such a space ⟨a favorite of the ~*es*⟩ **b :** a group of spectator seats in a grandstand enclosed by railings **c :** a railed or partitioned enclosure provided for the jury or for witnesses in a courtroom **d :** a space partitioned off in a tavern or public eating house **:** BOOTH **e :** BOX STALL; *also* **:** HORSE BOX **4 a :** a closed case or container for storing or shipping merchandise or belongings **b** *Brit* **:** TRUNK **5 a :** a boxlike protective covering, housing, or mechanical part (as for a bearing or bushing) ⟨gear ~⟩ ⟨journal ~⟩ **b :** an apparatus (as for sending a signal or fire alarm) with its enclosing case ⟨police ~⟩ **c :** the receptacle for a shuttle at the end of a loom lay **6 :** a square or oblong division or compartment: as **a :** any of the compartments in a type case **b :** a cell or pigeonhole in a wall or rack for holding mail **:** POST-OFFICE BOX **7 :** a square or oblong hollow space or recess: as **a :** a recess cut into a tree to collect sap or resin **b :** the part of a window frame for sash windows in which the weight to counterpoise the sash moves up and down **c :** a recess in a window trim into which the shutters may fold **d :** a socket on a doorjamb for the bolt **e :** the portion of a gemstone setting that surrounds the precious stone; *also* **:** a style of such setting **8 a :** a small simple sheltering or enclosing structure (as for a sentry or a watchman) **b** *chiefly Brit* **:** a simple cabin or cottage ⟨a shooting ~⟩ **c :** SINKBOX **d** *Brit* **:** TELEPHONE BOOTH **9 a :** printed matter set off by being enclosed or partly enclosed by rules or white space; *also* **:** the rules or white space enclosing such matter **b :** a hollow rectangle in which a check mark is to be made ⟨please check the ~ that applies to you⟩ **c :** a single unit of a comic strip **d :** LINE 12b **e** *or* **box step :** a combination of ballroom dance steps describing a rectangle on the floor **10 a** *baseball* (1) **:** the space where the pitcher stands formerly outlined with rectangular lines but now marked only by the pitcher's plate (2) **:** a space on either side of the home plate within which the batter must stand while batting (3) **:** either of the rectangular spaces 15 feet from the diamond and opposite first base and third base respectively within which the coaches are required to stand (4) **:** a triangular space behind the home plate in which the catcher must take his stand before every pitch — see BASEBALL illustration **b :** GULLY 4 **11 a :** boarded leather **b :** BOX CALF **12 :** a difficult situation **:** tight corner **:** FIX, PICKLE ⟨I must take some blame on myself for getting into this ~ —Walter H. Page⟩ **13 :** a case that holds a pack of cards so that they may be dealt one by one in the game of faro — called also *dealing box* **14 :** VULVA — usu. considered vulgar — **in the box :** accepting the bets of all the other players on the result of a game with the captain — used of a chouette player

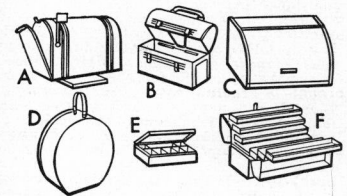

various boxes: *A* rural mailbox; *B* lunch box; *C* bread box; *D* hatbox; *E* cashbox; *F* toolbox

³**box** \ˈ"\ *vt* -ED/-ING/-ES **1 a** *obs* **:** CUP 1 **b :** to cut a hole into (a tree) to collect sap or resin **2 a :** to furnish (as a wheel hub) with a box **b** *Brit* **:** to give a Christmas box to **3 :** to enclose in or as if in a box ⟨~*ed* cigars⟩ ⟨a ~*ed* newspaper story⟩ **:** STOW — often with *up* ⟨~*ed* up and put away⟩ **4 :** BOXHAUL **5 :** to enclose with boarding or lathing so as to bring to a required form — usu. used with *out* or *up* **6** *English & Scots law* **:** to file (a document) with a court of law **7** *Austral* **:** to mix up **:** CONFUSE, BEFUDDLE — orig. used of sheep; often used with *up* **8 :** to mix (paint, varnish) by pouring back and forth between two containers **9 :** to hem in (an opponent or a competitor) — usu. used with *in, out,* or *up* ⟨~*ed* out the opposing tackle⟩ ⟨~*ed* in by a horse to his right⟩ **10 :** to stack (ceramic ware) in a kiln **11 :** to bet on (a specified number to win) in certain games and lotteries; *specif* **:** to bet on each of the 6 permutations of (a 3-digit number) in the numbers game — **box the compass 1 :** to name the 32 points of the compass in their order **2 :** to make a complete turn or reversal (as in policy, opinion) — **box the heart :** to cut slabs or boards in sawmilling from the outside of a log leaving a timber containing the heartwood

⁴**box** \ˈ"\ *n* -ES [ME] **:** a blow with the fist **:** BUFFET; *specif* **:** a cuff on the ear

⁵**box** \ˈ"\ *vb* -ED/-ING/-ES *vt* **1 a** *obs* **:** to hit with the hand or fist **b :** to slap smartly in the region of (the ears) ⟨~*ed* his ears⟩ **2 :** to engage in boxing with (a person) ~ *vi* **:** to fight with the fists **:** engage in boxing **syn** see STRIKE

box and cox \¦bäksən¦käks\ *adv (or adj), usu cap B&C* [*Box and Cox*, farce (1847) by John M. Morton †1891 Eng. playwright, and *Cox and Box*, comic opera (1867) with text by Sir Francis C. Burnand †1917 Eng. playwright and music by Sir Arthur S. Sullivan †1900 Eng. composer, adapted from Morton's farce; fr. the arrangement in the farce and opera whereby the same room is rented to two men named Box and Cox, one occupying it by day and one by night without either's knowing about the other] *Brit* **:** in turn **:** ALTERNATING

box barberry *n* [¹*box*] **:** a dwarf Japanese barberry (*Berberis thunbergii minor*) used for low hedges

box barrage *n* [²*box*] **1 :** a barrage on three sides of a given area to prevent escape or reinforcement of the enemy or to cover the front and flanks of a friendly force **2 :** a barrage of antiaircraft fire intended to block off invaders from a given objective

box beam *n* **:** BOX GIRDER

box bed *n* **1 :** a bed built into an alcove or enclosed with panels **2 :** a bed that folds up into the form of a box

boxberry \ˈ=- — *see* BERRY\ *n* [¹*box*] **1 :** WINTERGREEN 2a **2 :** PARTRIDGEBERRY 1

box bill *n* [²*box*] **:** a fishing tool used in well drilling to recover tools lost in the hole

boxboard \ˈ=,=\ *n* **:** a board from which cardboard boxes are made

box bolt *n* **:** a barrel bolt square or rectangular in cross section

box brier *n* **:** a tropical American spiny shrub (*Randia mitis*) with black fruits and leaves like those of the box — called also *inkberry, wild box*

boxbush \ˈ=,=\ *n* [¹*box*] **:** BURBARK 2

box caisson *n* **:** a heavy-timber watertight box open at the top, floated over a position prepared by dredging, and sunk by building a masonry pier within it

box calf *n* [²*box* + *calf*; fr. the square markings] **:** chrome-tanned calfskin having square markings on the grain because of being rolled lengthwise and then crosswise — compare BOARD *vt* 7

box camera *n* **:** a camera of simple box shape with a simple lens and rotary shutter

box canyon *n* [²*box*] **:** a canyon with approximately vertical walls and typically closed upstream with a similar wall

¹**boxcar** \ˈ=,=\ *n* **1 :** a roofed freight car with enclosed sides and usu. with sliding doors in the sides for the conveyance of lading that must be protected from the weather or pilferage **2 boxcars** *pl but sometimes sing in constr* **:** a throw of 12 in the game of craps **3 :** a truck trailer resembling a railway boxcar in size and shape

²**boxcar** \ˈ"\ *adj* **:** very large ⟨billboards with ~ letters⟩

box chisel *n* **:** a chisel with a notched edge used for prying open nailed wooden boxes — see CHISEL illustration

box cloth *n* [²*box* + *cloth*; prob. fr. its use in making box coats] **:** a heavy feltlike woolen coating made dense and almost waterproof by considerable fulling and shrinking and given a hard smooth face

box coat *n* [²*box* + *coat*; fr. its use by coachmen riding on the box exposed to all kinds of weather] **1 :** a heavy overcoat with or without shoulder capes formerly worn esp. by coachmen and coach passengers **2** *also* **box jacket** [prob. so called fr. its shape] **:** a loose straight-lined single-breasted or double-breasted coat or jacket usu. fitted at the shoulders

box couch *n* **:** a couch with a built-in storage box

box coupling *n* [²*box*] **1 :** a metal collar and tapered key for uniting the ends of shafts or other parts in machinery **2 :** a pipe coupling with threads on the inside

box crab *n* [so called fr. the way the legs fold against the carapace, resembling a box] **1 :** a crab of the tropical oxystomatous family Calappidae **2 :** a large rough anomuran crab (*Lopholithodes foraminatus*) of the Pacific coast of No. America — called also *shamefaced crab*

box culvert *n* **:** a reinforced concrete culvert of rectangular cross section

box day *n* [²*box*] *Scots law* **:** one of the days in vacation appointed for depositing papers with the Court of Sessions

box defense *n* **:** a defensive formation in football in which the players behind the line are arranged in a rectangle

box ditch *n* [²*box*] **:** a wooden irrigation flume resting on the ground and used to replace an earthen head ditch

box dolly *n* **:** a lumber-carrying truck with a single wide-tired wheel in the center of the box frame

box drain *n* **:** a drain that is rectangular in cross section

box drawer *n* **:** a desk drawer divided into compartments resembling boxes

boxed *past of* BOX

boxed heart *n* [*boxed*, past part. of ³*box*] **:** a sawn timber enclosing within its faces the heart of a log

boxed seam *n* **:** a decorative seam having the welt on the outside and made similar to a French seam

box elder *n* [¹*box*] **:** a maple (*Acer negundo*) widely distributed in the central and eastern U. S. and represented to the westward by distinct varieties that has compound leaves and is used as a shade tree because of its rapid growth — called also *ash-leaved maple;* see CALIFORNIA BOX ELDER

box-elder aphid *n* **:** a pale green hairy aphid (*Periphyllus negundinis*) that infests box elder and certain other maple trees

box-elder bug *n* [so called fr. its preference for the box elder] **:** a red-and-black sap-sucking bug (*Leptocoris trivittatus*) of the family Coreidae that sometimes feeds on fruit and hibernates in a partially dormant state often in buildings

box·en \ˈbäksən\ *adj, archaic* **:** of, like, or relating to boxwood or the box

¹**box·er** \ˈbäksə(r)\ *n* -S [⁵*box* + *-er*] **:** one that engages in the sport of boxing **:** one with ability to box rather than merely punch ⟨more of a ~ than a fighter⟩

²**boxer** \ˈ"\ *n* -S [³*box* + *-er*] **1 :** a worker who boxes trees to collect sap or resin **2 :** one that makes boxes or one that packs things in boxes by hand or by machine

³**boxer** \ˈ"\ *n* -S *usu cap* [approx. trans. of Chin *i⁴ hê² ch'üan²*, lit., righteous harmonious fist, alter. of *i⁴ hê² t'uan²* righteous harmonious band (the original name of the society)] **:** a member of a secret society that in 1900 attempted by violence to drive foreigners out of China and to force native converts to renounce Christianity — **box·er·ism** \-ə,rizəm\ *n* -S *usu cap*

⁴**boxer** \ˈ"\ *n* -S [prob. fr. ²*box* + *-er*] *Austral* **:** DERBY HAT

⁵**boxer** \ˈ"\ *n* -S *often cap* [G, fr. E ¹*boxer*; fr. its fighting habits] **:** a medium-sized square-built short-haired dog of a breed originating in Germany with fawn, brindle, or an intermediate coloring, a black mask, and often some white on face, chest, and feet

boxer shorts *n pl* [¹*boxer*] **:** men's underwear shorts characterized by loose fit, a continuous elastic waistband, and an overlapping fly that does not fasten

boxer-up \ˈ==ˈ=\ *n* -S [³*box* + *-er*] **:** a hooper that assembles cylinders and heads of kegs and drums

boxes *pl of* BOX, *pres 3d sing of* BOX

box family *n* [¹*box*] **:** BUXACEAE

boxfish \ˈ=,=\ *n* **:** any of a number of small bright-colored fishes (family Ostraciontidae) of tropical seas that are related to the triggerfishes but have the body and head enclosed in a hard carapace of hexagonal bony plates — called also *trunkfish*

box frame *n* [²*box*] **:** a frame with boxlike members; *specif* **:** a window frame having hollow spaces for sash weights

box girder *n* [²*box*] **:** a girder or beam of rectangular cross section with two or more webs

box green *n* [¹*box*] **:** a moderate yellow green that is greener and deeper than average moss green, yellower and darker than average pea green, and yellower and duller than apple green (sense 1)

box groove *n* [²*box*] **:** a closed groove formed in metalworking by a collar on one roll fitting between collars on another

boxhaul \ˈ=,=\ *vt* [³*box* + *haul*] **:** to put (a square-rigger) on the other tack by luffing and then veering under sternway by bracing the head yards aback

boxhead \ˈ=,=\ *or* **box heading** *or* **boxed head** *n* **:** a printed head or subhead set within a box (as in display composition or at the head of a column in an account book or of figures in a table)

boxholder \ˈ=,==\ *n* **1 :** one having title to a box (as in a theater, opera house, or racetrack) **2 a :** a renter of a post-office box **b :** a holder of a mailbox ⟨folders were sent to ~*s*⟩

box hook *n* **:** a hook with a transverse handle used in handling heavy boxes or crates

box huckleberry *n* [¹*box*] **:** a rare prostrate evergreen shrub (*Gaylussacia brachycera*) of the southeastern U.S. with shiny leaves like those of the box

boxier *comparative of* BOXY

boxiest *superlative of* BOXY

box·i·ness \ˈbäksēnə̇s, -sin-\ *n* -ES [*boxy* + *-ness*] **:** the quality of having unadorned or unrelieved square corners and edges ⟨avoids the barren ~ . . . so often encountered in modern designs —L.G.White⟩

¹**boxing** *n* -S [partly fr. gerund of ³*box*, partly fr. ²*box* + *-ing*] **1 :** a square or oblong enclosure or recess **:** CASING: as **a** *archit* **:** the external case of thin material used to bring a structural member to a required form **b :** a form for poured concrete **2 :** material for making boxes **3 :** the scarf joint uniting the stem and keel of a ship **4 boxings** *pl* **:** coarse flour separated in bolting **5 :** a stiffening material (as leather, wire, shellacked canvas) used in toes of shoes — compare TOE BOX, TOE CAP, TOE PUFF **6 :** a straight strip for joining two sections of a slipcover, bedspread, or upholstery at an angle; *esp* **:** an allowance for the thickness of a cushion or chairback **7 :** FORM 6d

²**boxing** *n* -S [fr. gerund of ⁵*box*] **:** the art of attack and defense with the fists practiced as a sport

boxing day *n, usu cap B&D* [*boxing*, gerund of ³*box*] **:** the first weekday after Christmas observed as a legal holiday in England, Wales, northern Ireland, Australia, New Zealand, and the Union of So. Africa and celebrated by the giving of Christmas boxes to postmen and other service workers

boxing glove *n* [²*boxing*] **:** one of a pair of leather mittens heavily padded on the back and worn in boxing

boxing night *n, usu cap B&N* **:** the night of Boxing Day

boxing shutter *n* **:** one of a set of shutters made to fold back into an oblong recess

box iron *n* [²*box*] **:** a hollow flatiron that is heated by inserting a hot iron core

box jacket *n* **:** BOX COAT

box jig *n* **:** a jig in which work is rigidly held so that it can be drilled or machined from different angles at a single setting depending on which face of the jig is turned toward the tool

boxkeeper \ˈ=,==\ *n* **:** an attendant in charge of the boxes in a theater

box key *n* **:** a T-shaped wrench with a socket in the end of the shank to fit over a nut or bolt head

boxing gloves

box kite *n* **:** a kite without a tail much used formerly in meteorology and consisting of two or more open-ended connected boxes — called also *cellular kite, Hargrave kite, tetrahedral kite*

box-length \ˈ=¦=\ *n* **:** the approximately 12-foot length of a placer gold-mining sluice box

box level *n* **:** a spirit level in which a glass-covered box is used instead of a tube — called also *circular level*

boxlike \ˈ=,=\ *adj* **:** resembling a box esp. in shape **:** rectangular and hollow

box kite

box lock *n* [²*box*] **:** an encased lock for surface mounting

box-loom \ˈ=¦=\ *n* **:** a loom with more than one shuttle box on one or both sides for weaving with two or more shuttles

box magazine *n* **:** a magazine for a repeating firearm which consists of a detachable metal box that fits into the receiver and from which the cartridges are fed into the chamber by the action of the piece

box maker's certificate *n* **:** a statement printed on a shipping container giving test values, rule compliance, the box maker, and other information

box·man \ˈbäksmən\ *n, pl* **boxmen 1 a :** one who takes care of the boxes in which different sizes of coal are washed **b :** a weigher of blast-furnace charges **2 :** CEMENT MIXER 2 **3** *slang* **:** SAFECRACKER

box myrtle *n* [¹*box*] **:** an Asiatic shrub (*Myrica nagi*) whose leaves yield a yellow crystalline dye — see MYRICETIN

box nail *n* **:** a slender wire nail used in making boxes

box nut *n* [²*box*] **:** a nut with a blind hole — called also *cap nut*

box oak *n* **:** BOX WHITE OAK

box off *vt* [³*box*] **:** to turn the bow of (a ship) by bracing the head yards aback

box office *n* [²*box*] **1 :** the office in a theater, auditorium, or stadium where tickets of admission are sold **2 :** success (as of a show, program, or performer) in attracting ticket buyers often in distinction from critical praise **:** popular appeal **:** DRAWING POWER; *also* **:** something that enhances drawing power ⟨almost any sort of publicity may be good *box office*⟩

box oyster *n* [²*box* + *oyster*; fr. being shipped in boxes rather than in barrels] **:** a choice large oyster

box pew *n* **:** an old-fashioned church pew walled in like a box

box pleat *n* [²*box* + *pleat*; fr. its rectilinear form] **1 :** a pleat made by forming two folded edges one facing right and the other left on the front side so that an inverted pleat is formed on the reverse side **2 :** INVERTED PLEAT

box press *n* **:** a device for drawing the covers of boxes into place for nailing

boxroom \ˈ=,=\ *n, Brit* **:** a storeroom (as for trunks) in a house

box score *n* [²*box* + *score*; fr. the compact arrangement of the summaries in a newspaper box] **:** the complete score of a game (as baseball) giving the names and positions of the players and a record of the play arranged in tabular form; *broadly* **:** total count **:** SUMMARY

box seat *n* **1 :** a built-in chest whose top forms a seat; *specif* **:** the driver's seat on a coach **2 a :** a seat in a theater or grandstand box **b :** a position esp. favorable for viewing something

box set *n* **:** a stage set realistically representing three walls and the ceiling of a room

box settle *n* **:** a settle with an enclosed foundation the cover of which forms the seat

box shell *n* **:** ARK SHELL

box shutter *n* **:** BOXING SHUTTER

box sill *n* **:** a sill that is constructed of brick or concrete enclosed in planks and that is used in frame house construction

box social *or* **box sociable** *or* **box party** *or* **box supper** *n* **:** a fund-raising affair at which box lunches or suppers prepared individually by the women are auctioned so that the highest bidder on each box may then share it with its donor

box spanner *n* **:** BOX WRENCH

box spring *n* **:** a bedspring that consists of spiral springs attached to a foundation and enclosed in a cloth-covered frame

box stall *n* **:** an individual enclosure within a barn or stable in which an animal may move about freely without tethering or other restraining device — called also *loose-box*

box staple *n* **:** the box for the bolt of a lock

box step *n* **:** ²BOX 9e

box stirrup *n* **:** a wide stirrup closed at the forward end

box stool *n* **:** a stool with hinged seat that acts as cover to a compartment beneath

box strike *n* **:** a door strike with the socket enclosed to prevent access from the other side of the door

box string *n* [²*box*] **:** CLOSE STRING

box taler *n* **:** a hollow taler the obverse and reverse of which fit or screw together to form a thin box

box tenon *n* [²*box*] **:** an angle tenon (as in a corner post)

boxthorn \ˈ=,=\ *n* [¹*box*] **1 :** MATRIMONY VINE **2** *Austral* **:** NATIVE BOX

box toe *n* **:** a toe of a shoe made with a rigid or a flexible reinforcement

box tool *n* **:** a tool holder that partially surrounds the work piece in an automatic lathe or screw machine and supports it against the pressure of the cutting tool

box tortoise *or* **box turtle** *n* **:** any of three No. American land tortoises (genus *Terrapene* syn. *Cistudo*) that can withdraw entirely within the shell and close it by hinged joints in the lower shell

box trap *n* **:** a trap made of a wooden box supported by an often baited trigger so that the box will drop over an animal seeking the bait

boxtree \ˈ=,=\ *n* [ME, fr. OE *boxtrēow*, fr. *box* + *trēow* tree — more at ¹BOX, TREE] **:** ¹BOX

box truck *n* **1 :** a low flat truck for boxes or bales **2 :** a large light box or crate mounted on casters and used in transferring materials or merchandise in factories or stores

box wagon *n* **1 :** an open wagon with an oblong body with or without seats **2** *Brit* **:** BOXCAR

box·wal·lah \ˈbäk,swälə\ *n* -S [Hindi *bakswālā*, fr. E ²*box* + Hindi *-wālā* man — more at WALLAH] *India* **:** PEDDLER

box white oak *n* [¹*box*] **:** a post oak (*Quercus stellata*) — called also *box oak*

boxwood \ˈ=,=\ *n* [¹*box*] **1 a :** the very hard tough close-grained heavy white to yellow wood of the box that is used in wood-engraving and in the making of musical instruments, rules, inlays, and other fine delicate woodwork — see TURKISH BOXWOOD **b :** any of several other woods having properties and uses similar to those of boxwood — often with a qualifying term ⟨West Indian ~⟩ **2 :** a plant producing boxwood: as **a :** ¹BOX 1 **b :** FLORIDA BOXWOOD **c :** ZAPATERO 2 **d :** FLOWERING DOGWOOD **e :** SHITTIMWOOD 3

boxwood leaf miner *n* **:** a minute orange two-winged fly (*Monarthropalpus buxi*) having a larva that mines in and causes blistering and browning of the foliage of boxwood

boxwork \ˈ=,=\ *n* **:** a mineral-aggregate structure having plates or septa that are often coated with crystals and that intersect at various angles and enclose angular spaces

box wrench *n* [²*box*] **:** a wrench with a socket or a closed ring that fits over the bolt head or nut

box wrench

boxy \ˈbäksē, -si\ *adj* -ER/-EST [²*box* + *-y*] **1 :** like a box **:** SQUARISH — usu. used in disparagement ⟨a ~ automobile design⟩ ⟨a ~ church⟩ **2** *of a horse's hoof* **:** excessively small and contracted **3 :** having an unfitted square straightlined appearance ⟨a jacket of ~ cut⟩

boy \ˈbȯi\ *n* -s *often attrib* [ME; akin to Fris *boi* boy and prob. to OE *Bōia, Bōfa* (masculine proper names), OHG *Buobo* (masculine proper name), MHG *buobe* boy; all perh. fr. prehistoric WGmc words derived by baby talk fr. the WGmc word corresponding to OE *brōthor* brother — more at BROTHER] **1 a :** a male child from birth to puberty ⟨~ baby⟩ **b :** SON **:** male offspring ⟨this is my little ~⟩ **c :** a male person not fully matured or not felt to be mature **:** LAD, YOUTH ⟨a job that separates the men from the ~s⟩ ⟨~ scientist⟩ ⟨~ wonder⟩ **d :** SWEETHEART, BEAU **:** young social partner ⟨she is never seen with a ~⟩ **:** FAVORITE ⟨the fair-haired ~ of the department⟩ **e :** PUPIL, STUDENT ⟨college ~s⟩ ⟨day ~⟩ **2 a :** one native to or orig. belonging to a given place ⟨a country ~ at heart⟩ ⟨a local ~ who made good in the big city⟩ **b :** a member of a group, gang, or any kind of association of equals ⟨wait till the ~s back home hear this⟩ ⟨the ~s at the office⟩ **:** CONFORMIST — usu. used in pl. ⟨trying to be just one of the ~s⟩ **c** *slang* **:** one classed or identified with a particular profession or specialty ⟨what the science ~s have discovered⟩ ⟨the ~s in the drafting room⟩ or doctrine ⟨the hard-money ~s⟩ ⟨the happiness ~s⟩ or faction ⟨controlled by the big-business ~s⟩ — usu. used with some degree of ridicule, hostility, or contempt; usu. used in pl. **3** *obs* **:** RASCAL, KNAVE, VARLET **4 a :** a male servant ⟨house ~⟩ ⟨stable ~⟩ **b :** one who does light work esp. in the service fields ⟨I'll send a ~ over with it⟩ — usu. used in combinations ⟨delivery ~⟩ **c :** a male member of a race felt to be inferior ⟨hiring ~s for a safari⟩ **5 :** MAN, FELLOW — used in affection or admiration or familiarity ⟨a nice old ~⟩ ⟨the boss is quite a ~⟩ ⟨cheer up, old ~⟩

bo·yar *also* **bo·yard** *or* **bo·iar** \bōˈyär, -yȧ\ *n* -s [Russ *boyarin*, fr. ORuss, fr. OSlav *boljarinŭ*, prob. fr. OTurk *boila*] **1 :** a member of a Russian aristocratic order that was next in rank to the ruling princes and was possessed of many exclusive privileges until its abolition by Peter the Great **2 :** a member of a privileged landholding class in Romania

¹**boy·cott** \ˈbȯi,kät, *usu* -äd·+V; *esp Brit* -kət\ *vt* -ED/-ING/-S [Charles C. *Boycott* †1897 Eng. land agent in County Mayo, Ireland, who was ostracized in 1880 for refusing to reduce rents] **1 :** to combine against (a person, employer, a group of persons, or a nation) in a policy of nonintercourse for economic or political reasons **:** withhold wholly or partly social or business intercourse from as an expression of disapproval or means of coercion ⟨a threat to ~ the Security Council⟩ **2 :** to engage in a concerted refusal to have anything to do with the products or services of (an employer) in order to force acceptance of certain conditions desired by a union ⟨agreed to ~ all uncooperative manufacturers⟩

²**boycott** \"\ *n* -s **:** the process or an instance of boycotting — see SECONDARY BOYCOTT

boy·er \ˈbȯiə(r)\ *n* -s [D *boeier*, fr. MD *boeyer, boyer*, fr. *boeyen, boyen* to plank up the side of a ship (perh. fr. *boeye, boye* fetter, chain, fr. OF *buie, boie*, fr. L *boia* shackle for the neck) + *-er* *-er* (akin to OE *-ere* -er)] **:** a small Flemish sailing boat

boyfriend \ˈ=,=\ *n* **1 :** a male friend **2 :** a frequent, regular, or favorite escort or male companion of a girl or woman **3 :** the male partner in an intimate or esp. an illicit relationship **:** LOVER, PARAMOUR

boyg \ˈbȯig\ *n* -s *usu cap* [Norw *bøig* bugbear, ogre, bend, curve; akin to ON *beygja* to bend — more at ¹BOW] **:** a formless or pervasive obstacle, problem, or enemy (as despair or public apathy or popular ignorance) ⟨battling against the great amorphous *Boyg* —Graham Greene⟩

boy·hood \ˈbȯi,hu̇d\ *n* -s **1 :** the state or period of being a boy **2 :** boyish nature **:** BOYISHNESS **3 :** BOYS ⟨outstanding service to ~⟩

boy·ish \ˈbȯi·ish, ˈbȯiēsh\ *adj* **:** like or belonging to a boy **:** IMMATURE **syn** see YOUTHFUL

boy·ish·ly *adv* **:** in a boyish manner

boy·ish·ness *n* -ES **:** the quality or state of being boyish

boy·ism \ˈbȯi,izəm\ *n* -s **1 :** boy nature **:** a boyish trait or feature **2 :** a puerile notion or expression

boy·la \ˈbȯilə\ *n* -s [native name in Australia] *Austral* **:** a native sorcerer

boyle's law \ˈbȯi(ə)lz-\ *n, usu cap B* [after Robert *Boyle* †1691 Brit. physicist, its formulator] **:** a statement in physics: the product of the pressure and the specific volume of a gas at constant temperature is constant — called also *Mariotte's law*

boyo \ˈbȯi(,)ō\ *n* -s [*boy* + *-o*] *Irish* **:** BOY, LAD ⟨"keep out of this, ~," he said grimly —John Fountain⟩

boys *pl of* BOY

boys-and-girls \ˈ=;=;=\ *n pl but sing or pl in constr* **1 :** DUTCHMAN'S-BREECHES **2 :** a slender annual American weed (*Mercurialis annua*) with branching stems

boy scout *n* **1 :** a boy member of the Boy Scouts, a movement founded in Great Britain in 1908 and in the U.S. in 1910 for carrying out among boys a program of outdoor and educational activities aimed at developing good citizenship and healthy useful living — compare GIRL GUIDE, GIRL SCOUT **2 :** a member of the Boy Scouts who is 11, 12, or 13 years old as distinguished from a cub scout or an explorer

boy·sen·ber·ry \ˈbȯizᵊn-, ˈbȯisᵊn- —*see* BERRY\ *n* [after Rudolph *Boysen* fl1923 Am. horticulturist, its originator] **1 :** a very large bramble fruit with a flavor like a raspberry esp. valued for canning and preserving **2 :** the trailing hybrid bramble that bears boysenberries that was developed in California by hybridization from several blackberries and raspberries

boy's-love \ˈ=,=\ *n, pl* **boy's-loves** [so called fr. its use to promote the growth of beard] **1** *dial Eng* **:** SOUTHERNWOOD **2 :** WORMWOOD

boza *var of* BOSA

bo·zal \bōˈsal, -ˈzal\ *var of* BOSAL

bozine *var of* BUSINE

bo·zo \ˈbō(,)zō\ *n* -s [origin unknown] *slang* **:** FELLOW, GUY

boz·zet·to \bətˈsed·(,)ō, bəˈze-\ *n, pl* **bozzet·ti** \-ed·(,)ē\ [It, dim. of *bozzo* sketch, rough stone, alter. of *bozza*, lit., swelling — more at ¹BOSS] **:** a small rough clay study for a larger sculpture — used esp. of baroque sculpture

bp *abbr* **1** baptized **2** birthplace **3** *often cap* bishop **4** boiling point

BP *abbr* **1** band pass **2** before present **3** below proof **4** bill of parcels **5** bills payable **6** blood pressure

BPB *abbr* bank post bill

BPD *abbr* barrels per day

BPH *abbr* barrels per hour

B Phil *abbr or n* -s **:** a bachelor of philosophy

bpl *abbr* birthplace

b power supply *n, usu cap B* **:** a battery or transformer and rectifier supplying electric power in the plate circuit of an electron tube to maintain the electron current in the tube — compare A POWER SUPPLY, C POWER SUPPLY; B BATTERY

bq *or* **bque** *abbr* barque

br *abbr* **1** branch **2** brand **3** brass **4** bridge **5** brief **6** brig **7** brigade **8** broché **9** bronze **10** brother **11** brown **12** brush

BR *abbr* **1** bank rate **2** bedroom **3** bill of rights **4** bills receivable **5** builder's risk

Br *symbol* bromine

bra \ˈbrä, -ȧ *sometimes* -ȯ\ *n* -s [by shortening] **:** BRASSIERE

brab·an·çon \ˈbrabən,sän, brəˈban(t)sən\ *n* -s *usu cap* [F, lit., Brabantine, fr. *Brabant*] **1 :** a Belgian breed of heavy powerful draft horses noted for their quiet temperament **2 :** a horse of the Brabançon breed

bra·bant rose \brəˈbant-\ *n, usu cap B* [fr. *Brabant*, province of central Belgium] **:** a cut (as of a diamond) similar to a Dutch rose but having 12 facets or less — see ROSE illustration

¹**brab·ble** \ˈbrabəl\ *vi* **brabbled; brabbled; brabbling** \-b(ə)liŋ\ **brabbles** [MD *brabbelen* to quarrel, stammer, jabber, of imit. origin] **:** to talk noisily or captiously **:** SQUABBLE ⟨the desultory *brabbling* between the Western Powers and the Russians —*Time*⟩

²**brabble** \"\ *n* -s **1 a :** ALTERCATION, QUARREL ⟨the ~s of the law courts⟩ **b** *obs* **:** a noisy fight **:** BRAWL ⟨in private ~ did we apprehend him —Shak.⟩ **2 a :** BABBLE ⟨a ~ of voices⟩ **:** CHATTER ⟨I'm not to be mollified by any woman's ~ —P.L.Ford⟩ **b :** a discordant sustained murmuring ⟨a fresh nor'-westerly breeze had sprung up . . . and there was a heavy ~ alongshore —G.G.Carter⟩

brab·bler \ˈbrab(ə)lə(r)\ *n* -s **:** one that brabbles

brac·cae \ˈbrä,kī, ˈbra,kē, -ak,sē\ *also* **bra·cae** \ˈbrä,kī, ˈbrā,sē\ *n pl* [L *bracae*, pl. of *braca*, fr. Gaulish *brāca*, of Gmc origin; akin to OHG *bruoh* pair of breeches — more at BREECHES] **:** shapeless trousers of wool or skin tied at the waist and ankles by cords worn chiefly by the ancient Gauls

brac·cio \ˈbrä(,)chō, -chē,ō\ *n, pl* **brac·cia** \-(,)chä, -chē,ä\ [It, lit., arm, fr. L *brachium*] **:** an Italian unit of length varying between 15 and 39 inches

¹**brace** \ˈbrās\ *n, pl* **braces** *also* **brace** *see sense 2* [ME, fr. MF, two arms, fr. L *bracchia, brachia*, pl. of *bracchium, brachium* arm, modif. of Gk *brachīōn*, fr. *brachys* short — more at BRIEF] **1** *obs* **a :** armor esp. for the arm **b :** an arm of water **:** INLET **2** *pl* **brace** *or* **braces :** two of a kind ⟨a ~ of hounds⟩ ⟨several ~ of quail⟩ **:** a pair esp. of things usu. kept together ⟨a ~ of dueling pistols⟩ **3** [ME, prob. influenced in meaning by ME *bracen* to embrace, clasp] *archaic* **:** a clasp, a buckle, or a similar binding or encompassing device **4 :** a crank-shaped instrument with handles and a chuck for holding and turning auger bits **5 :** something that transmits, directs, resists, or supports weight or pressure: as **a :** a piece of material that divides a frame or truss into triangular parts and serves as a tie or strut to bear transverse strains and prevent distortion **b :** one of the slides on the cords of a drum used to tighten the drumhead **c** [perh. influenced in meaning by F *bras*, lit., arm, fr. L *brachium*] **:** a rope rove through a block at the end of a yard of a square-rigged ship and used to swing and trim the yard horizontally — see SHIP illustration **d :** one of the leather straps used to suspend the body of a horse-drawn carriage from the springs **e** *braces pl* **:** SUSPENDERS **f :** an appliance that gives support to movable parts (as a joint or a fractured bone), to weak muscles (as in paralysis), or to strained ligaments (as of the lower back) **g :** an endpiece by which the outer end of the mainspring of a timepiece is attached to the barrel **h :** something (as a chock) used to secure goods and containers during shipment **i :** a device (as a bar or an angle bracket) used to produce stiffness or rigidity **:** REINFORCEMENT **6 a :** a mark { or } or ⏟ used to connect words or items to be considered together, equal, or in pairs or to enclose items of which only one is to be chosen **b :** this mark connecting two or more musical staffs and indicating that the parts on these staffs are to be performed simultaneously; *also* **:** the group of staffs so connected ⟨the upper ~⟩ **c :** one of the pair of such marks used as signs of aggregation in mathematics **d :** BRACKET 4a **7 :** an exaggerated position of attention or of rigidly erect bearing (as while drilling or on parade) ⟨on review, his uniform and ~ were technically correct —*Time*⟩ **8 :** something that arouses energy, increases power of exertion, or strengthens or helps in recovering morale

brace 4

²**brace** \"\ *vb* -ED/-ING/-S [ME *bracen*, fr. MF *bracier* to embrace, fr. *brace*] *vt* **1** *archaic* **:** to fasten tightly **:** BIND, TIE **2 a** *obs* **:** EMBRACE **b** *archaic* **:** ENCIRCLE, SURROUND **3 a :** to prepare for use by making taut ⟨~ a drum⟩; *esp* **:** to place the string of (a bow) in the nocks **b :** to prepare esp. for a struggle, enterprise, shock **:** STEEL ⟨~ his will⟩ ⟨no other country was so . . . *braced* for empire and for glory —Mary S. Douglas⟩ ⟨the class *braced* itself for the examination⟩ — sometimes used with *up* ⟨hearing the words "bad news", the family *braced* itself up⟩ **c :** INVIGORATE, FRESHEN, ENLIVEN ⟨wind ~*ing* the air⟩ — often used with *up* ⟨I took the shower and it *braced* me up a bit —Raymond Chandler⟩ **4** [¹*brace* (rope at the end of a yard)] **:** to turn (a sail yard) by means of a brace **5** [¹*brace*] **a :** to prop up or support with braces ⟨a ~ sagging floor⟩ ⟨a well-*braced* trestle⟩ ⟨the 29-year-old . . . woman, heavily *braced* because of polio —*Springfield (Mass.) Union*⟩ **b :** STRENGTHEN, REINFORCE ⟨the sides were *braced* by tar paper, chicken wire, and timber —S.W.Matthews⟩ ⟨nerves . . . *braced* by long familiarity with danger —T.B.Macaulay⟩ **6 a :** to make rigid **:** STIFFEN ⟨Constance was *braced* into a moveless anguish —Arnold Bennett⟩ **b :** to put or plant firmly ⟨he . . . *braced* his hand on the stone . . . and . . . sprang lightly up —Kay Boyle⟩ **7 a :** to waylay esp. with demands or questions **:** CONFRONT ⟨when *braced*, Willie had naturally denied his identity —*Time*⟩ ⟨he *braced* the owners for a raise —N.M.Clark⟩ **b :** to harry with repeated and abusive questions or criticism **:** dress down **:** BADGER, GRILL, HOUND ⟨the police *braced* him on the charge⟩ ~ *vi* **1 :** to take heart **:** buck up — used with *up* ⟨if you don't ~ up and do something —Upton Sinclair⟩ **2 :** to get ready **:** prepare quickly (as for an attack) **3 :** to assume a brace (sense 7) ⟨today, the plebe need never ~ in public and physical hazing is forbidden —*Newsweek*⟩ **syn** see SUPPORT

³**brace** \"\ *archaic var of* ³BRASS

brace about *or* **brace around** *vt* **:** to turn (a yard of a square-rigged ship) about for the opposite tack

brace bit *n* **:** a bit for use in a brace

brace bumpkin *n* **:** ²BUMPKIN b

brace comb *n* **:** honeycomb built in small pieces by bees to bridge spaces

braced *adj* [fr. past part. of ²*brace* (to embrace, clasp)] *of two or more heraldic bearings* **:** INTERLACED ⟨three chevrons ~⟩

braced arch *n* **:** a truss (as of steel or concrete) in the form of an arch

braced frame *n* **:** a building frame in which the timbers are heavy enough to be mortised and in which diagonal bracing is used — compare BALLOON FRAME

braced framing *n* **:** the method of building that employs the braced frame

brace drill *n* **:** a drill provided with a tang at the end of the shank to fit the chuck of a brace

brace game *n* [¹*brace* (pair); fr. its original application to collusion between the dealer and casekeeper in faro] **:** a gambling game organized for the purpose of swindling

brace head *or* **brace key** *n* **:** an attachment (as a long-handled wrench) for turning a boring rod

brace in *vt* **:** to turn (a ship's yard) more thwartwise by hauling in the weather brace

brace·let \ˈbrāslət\ *n* -s [ME, fr. MF, dim. of *bras* arm, fr. OF *braz*, fr. L *brachium* — more at BRACE] **1 :** an ornamental band, ring, or chain worn around the wrist **2 :** something that in position or appearance suggests a bracelet: as **a :** HANDCUFF — usu. used in pl. **b :** a chain for securing an identification tag to the wrist **c :** one of the dark bands of fur ringing the forelegs of a well-marked tabby cat — compare NECKLACE **d :** ANKLE STRAP ⟨a ~ sandal⟩ **e :** RASCETTE **3 :** a piece of armor (as the vambrace) for the wrist or arm

bracelet watch *n* **:** a small wristwatch; *esp* **:** one for a woman

bracelet wood *n* **:** a small West Indian tree (*Jacquinia armillaris*) of the family Myrsinaceae with hard seeds that are used to make bracelets

bracemate \ˈ=,=\ *n* [¹*brace* (pair) + *mate*] **:** one of two hunting dogs that are shown or worked as a pair

brace molding *n* **:** a molding composed of two ogees connected so as to resemble in outline a printer's brace

brace pendant *n* **:** a rope or chain by which a brace block is attached to a yard

¹**bra·cer** \ˈbrāsə(r)\ *n* -s [ME, fr. MF *braciere*, fr. OF, fr. *braz* arm — more at BRACELET] **:** an arm or wrist protector (as one used by a fencer or a ballplayer); *esp* **:** a guard usu. of leather worn by an archer to shield the left wrist from the snap of the bowstring

²**brac·er** \"\ *n* -s [²*brace* + *-er*] **:** one that braces, binds, or makes firm: as **a** (1) **:** a drink taken as a tonic or stimulant; *esp* **:** a drink of liquor (2) **:** something that acts as a freshener, revitalizer, or reviver ⟨the news was a ~ for us all⟩ **b :** SHORER; *specif* **:** TIMBERMAN **c :** a worker who puts blocks, bracing, and strapping into freight cars and trucks to prevent shifting of load in transit — called also *blocker* **d :** a worker who attaches uppers to the soles of shoes

bra·ce·ro \brəˈse(,)rō\ *n* -s [Sp, laborer, fr. *brazo* arm, fr. L *brachium* — more at BRACE] **:** a Mexican laborer admitted to the U.S. under immigration treaties for chiefly seasonal contract labor in agriculture or industry — compare WETBACK

brace root *n* **:** PROP ROOT

braces *pl of* BRACE, *pres 3d sing of* BRACE

brace to *vt* **:** to brace in

brace up *vt* **:** to turn (a yard) nearer to the fore-and-aft position by hauling in the lee brace ⟨*braced* sharp *up*⟩

brace wrench *n* **:** a wrench with a crank-shaped handle and socket head

brach \ˈbrach\ *n* -ES [ME *brache*, a kind of hound, back-formation fr. *braches, brachez*, pl., fr. MF, fr. OF, pl. of *brachet* — more at BRACHET] *archaic* **:** a bitch hound

brach·el·y·trous \(ˈ)braˈkelə·trəs\ *adj* [Gk *brachys* short + *elytron* covering, shard of a beetle's wing (fr. *eilyein* to enwrap) + E *-ous* — more at BRIEF, VOLUBLE] *of a beetle* **:** having short wing covers

brach·en \ˈbrakən\ *archaic Scot var of* BRACKEN

brach·et \ˈbrachət\ *n* -s [ME, fr. MF, fr. OF, of Gmc origin; akin to OHG *braccho* hunting dog (that uses scent), MLG & MD *bracke*; prob. akin to MHG *bræhen* to smell — more at FRAGRANT] *archaic* **:** BRACH

brachi- *or* **brachio-** *comb form* [L *brachi-* & NL *brachio-*, fr. L *brachium* — more at BRACE] **1 :** arm ⟨*brachi*ferous⟩ ⟨*brachi*otomy⟩ **2 :** brachial and ⟨*brachio*facial⟩

¹**brach·ia** \ˈbrakēə, -rāk-\ *pl of* BRACHIUM

²**brachia** \"\ *n pl* [NL, fr. L, pl. of *brachium* arm] **:** LOPHOPHORE

¹**brach·i·al** \-ēəl\ *adj* [L *bracchialis, brachialis*, fr. *bracchium, brachium* arm + *-alis* -al — more at BRACE] **:** of or relating to the arm or a process like an arm

²**brachial** \"\ *n* -s **:** a brachial part (as a scale or plate)

brachial artery *n* **:** the chief artery of the upper arm, being a direct continuation of the axillary artery and dividing into the radial and ulnar arteries just below the elbow

brachial cavity *n* **:** the anterior space inside the valves of brachiopods into which the brachia are withdrawn

brach·i·al·is \,brakēˈaləs, -āl-,-äl-\ *or* **brachialis an·ti·cus** \-lə,sanˈtēkəs, -tīk-\ *n* -ES [*brachialis*, NL, fr. L, adj., brachial; *brachialis anticus*, NL, front brachialis] **:** a flexor muscle lying in front of the lower part of the humerus whence it arises and being inserted into the ulna

brachial ossicle *n* **:** a small bone of the pectoral fin of a fish

brachial plexus *n* **:** a complex network of nerves that is formed chiefly by the lower four cervical and first thoracic nerves, lies partly within the axilla, and supplies nerves to the chest shoulder, and arm

brachial vein *n* **:** one of a pair of veins accompanying the course of the brachial artery and uniting with each other and with the basilic vein to form the axillary vein

¹**brach·i·ate** \ˈbrakē,āt, -rāk-, -ēət\ *adj* [L *bracchiatus, brachiatus*, fr. *bracchium, brachium* arm + *-atus* -ate] **1 :** having widely spreading branches arranged in alternating pairs ⟨the maple is ~⟩ — compare DECUSSATE **2** *zool* **:** having arms

²**brachiate** \-ē,āt\ *vi* -ED/-ING/-S [*brachi-* + *-ate*] **:** to progress by swinging from one hold to another by the arms (as of the gibbon)

brach·i·a·tion \,==ˈāshən\ *n* -s **:** the act or practice of brachiating

brach·i·a·tor \ˈ==,ād·ə(r)\ *n* -s **:** a brachiating animal

bra·chid·i·um \braˈkidēəm, brəˈ-\ *n, pl* **brachid·ia** \-ēə\ [NL, fr. *brachi-* + *-idium*] **:** the calcareous support of the lophophore of certain brachiopods

brach·i·o·ganoidei \ˌbrakē(,)ō+\ [NL, fr. *brachi-* + *Ganoidei*] *syn of* CROSSOPTERYGII 1

bra·chi·o·la \braˈkēələ, brəˈ-, -kīə-, ,brakēˈōlə\ *n* -s [NL, fr. *brachi-* + L *-ola* (fem. dim. suffix)] **:** one of the three processes of the brachiolaria

brach·i·o·lar·ia \,brakēōˈla(a)rēə\ *n, pl* **brachiolar·i·ae** \-rē,ē\ [NL, fr. *brachiola* + *-aria*] **:** a transitional larva of certain starfishes that develops from the bipinnaria and is distinguished by possession of three anterior processes homologous with those of the adult starfish —**brach·i·o·lar·i·an** \ˈ==;=ˈrēən\ *adj*

brach·ion·ich·thy·i·dae \,brakēə,nikˈthīə,dē\ *n pl, cap* [NL, fr. *Brachionichthys*, type genus (fr. Gk *brachion-, brachiōn* arm + *ichthys* fish) + *-idae* — more at BRACE, ICHTHUS] **:** a family of pediculate fishes comprising the handfishes and distinguished by highly modified pectoral fins that resemble hands

¹**brach·i·o·pod** \ˈbrakēə,päd\ *adj* [NL *Brachiopoda*] **:** BRACHIOPODOUS

²**brachiopod** \"\ *n* -s **:** an animal of the phylum Brachiopoda

brach·i·op·o·da \,brakēˈäpədə\ *n pl, cap* [NL, fr. *brachi-* + *-poda*] **:** a phylum of invertebrates that has persisted with reduced numbers from the Lower Cambrian to the present and that consists of sedentary unsegmented marine animals with well-developed coelom and hemocoel, a lophophore, and often a fleshy stalk extending into the substrate, the body being enclosed in a bivalve chitinophosphatic or calcareous shell the valves of which are unequal, bilaterally symmetrical, and usu. regarded as dorsal and ventral

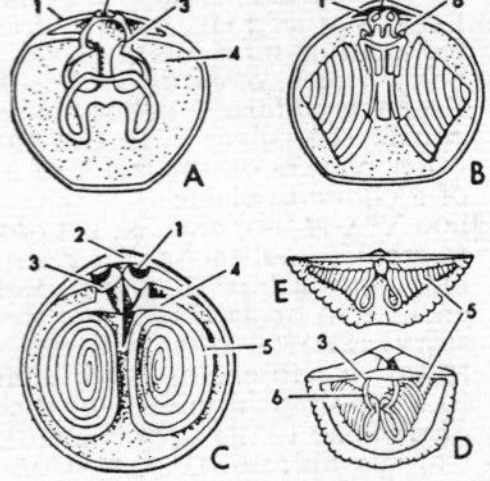

brachiopod shells: looped brachidia, *A;* athyroid, *B;* atrypoid, *C;* spiriferoid, *D* and *E; 1* dental socket, *2* cardinal process, *3* crura, *4* jugal process, *5* spiralium, *6* primary lamella

brach·i·op·o·dist \-dəst\ *n* -s [NL *Brachiopoda* + E *-ist*] **:** one who specializes in the study of Brachiopoda

brach·i·op·o·dous \ˌbrakēˈäpədəs\ *adj* [NL *Brachiopoda* + E *-ous*] **:** of or belonging to the Brachiopoda

brach·i·o·ra·di·al·is \ˌbrakē(,)ō,rādēˈaləs, -āl-,-äl-\ *n, pl* **brachioradial·es** \-,lēz\ [NL, fr. *brachi-* + ML *radialis* radial, fr. L *radius* + *-alis* -al — more at RADIUS] **:** a flexor of the radial side of the forearm arising from the lateral epicondylic ridge of the humerus and inserted into the styloid process of the radius

brach·i·o·saur \ˈbrakēō,sȯ(ə)r\ *n* -s [NL *Brachiosaurus*] **:** a dinosaur of the genus *Brachiosaurus*

brach·i·o·sau·rus \ˌbrakēōˈsȯrəs\ *n, cap* [NL, fr. *brachi-* + *-saurus*] **:** a genus of huge dinosaurs (suborder Sauropoda) of the Upper Jurassic having longer forelegs than hind legs

bra·chis·to·cephalic *also* **brachistocephalous** \braˈkistō, brəˈ-+\ *adj* [Gk *brachistos* (superlative of *brachys* short) + E *-cephalic, -cephalous* — more at BRIEF] **:** brachycephalic with a cephalic index of 85 or more — compare EURYCEPHALIC — **bra·chis·to·ceph·a·ly** \"+ˈsefəlē\ *n* -ES

bra·chis·to·chrone \braˈkistə,krōn, brəˈ-\ *n* -s [F, fr. Gk *brachistos* shortest + *chronos* time] **:** a curve in which a body starting from a point and acted on by an external force will reach another point in a shorter time than by any other path — **bra·chis·to·chron·ic** \ˈ=;=;=ˈkränik\ *adj*

brach·i·um \ˈbrākēəm, -rāk-\ *n, pl* **brach·ia** \-ēə\ [L *bracchium, brachium* arm, forearm — more at BRACE] **1 :** the upper segment of the arm or forelimb from the shoulder to the elbow **2 :** any of certain processes similar to an arm: as **a :** a ray of a crinoid **b :** a tentacle of a cephalopod **c :** a tentaculiferous process **d :** any of certain bands of white matter in the brain in certain jellyfishes **e :** either of the coiled muscular paired appendages that together constitute the lophophore of a brachiopod

brachy- *comb form* [Gk, fr. *brachys* — more at BRIEF] **1 :** short ⟨*brachy*cephalic⟩ **2 :** brachydiagonal — in terms in crystallography ⟨*brachy*dome⟩

brachy·axis \ˈbrakē+\ *n* [*brachy-* + *-axis*] **:** the shorter lateral axis of an orthorhombic or triclinic crystal

brach·y·blast \ˈbrakə̇,blast, -kē-\ *n* -S [ISV *brachy-* + *-blast*] **:** a short shoot often bearing leaves in clusters (as in the pines)

brachy·catalectic \ˈbrakē+\ *adj* [Gk *brachykatalēktos* (fr. *brachy-* + — assumed — *katalēktos*, verbal of *katalēgein* to leave off, stop, fr. *kata-* cata- + *lēgein* to stop, cease, leave off) + E *-ic;* akin to Gk *lagaros* slack, thin — more at SLACK] *prosody* **:** characterized by or due to brachycatalexis

brachy·catalexis \"+\ *n* [LL, modif. of Gk *brachykatalēxia*, fr. *brachykatalēktos* + *-ia* -y] *Greek & Latin prosody* **:** omission of two syllables at the end of a verse composed of the larger metrical units (as dipodies or feet of more than three syllables)

brachy·ceph·al \,brakə̇ˈsefəl, -kēˈ-\ *n* -S [NL *brachycephalus*, fr. *brachy-* + *-cephalus*] **:** a brachycephalic person

brachy·cephalic \ˈbrakə̇, -kē+\ *adj* [NL *brachycephalus* + E *-ic*] **:** short-headed or broad-headed with a cephalic index of over 80 — see CEPHALIC INDEX illustration

brachy·ceph·a·lid \,brakə̇ˈsefələd, -kēˈ-\ *n* -S [NL *Brachycephalidae*] **:** a toad of the family Brachycephalidae

brachy·ce·phal·i·dae \-,səˈfalə,dē\ *n pl, cap* [NL, fr. *Brachycephalus*, type genus (fr. *brachy-* + *-cephalus*) + *-idae*] **:** a large family of small Neotropical toads (suborder Procoela) having partial or complete median fusion of the shoulder girdle

brachy·ceph·a·lism \-ˈsefə,lizəm\ *n* -S [*brachycephalic* + *-ism*] **:** BRACHYCEPHALY

brachy·ceph·a·li·za·tion \-,sefələˈzāshən, -,līˈz-\ *n* -S [*brachycephalic* + *-ization*] **:** transition toward a more brachycephalic condition ⟨the increasing ~ of Europe⟩

brachy·ceph·a·ly \-ˈlē\ *n* -ES [ISV *brachycephalic* + *-y*] **:** the quality or state of being brachycephalic

bra·chyc·era \brəˈkisərə, brə'-\ *n pl, cap* [NL, fr. *brachy-* + *-cera*] **:** a suborder of Diptera including the more highly specialized flies which have palpi with one or two joints and usu. short antennae with one or never more than six joints (as the horsefly, robber fly, and housefly) — compare NEMATOCERA

brachy·cerebral \ˈbrakē+\ *adj* [*brachy-* + *cerebral*] **:** possessing a round or rather short brain

bra·chyc·er·ous \brəˈkisərəs, brə'-\ *adj* [NL *Brachycera* + E *-ous*] **:** having short antennae; *specif* **:** of or relating to Brachycera

brachy·chi·ton \,brakəˈkītᵊn, -akēˈ-\ *n, cap* [NL, fr. *brachy-* + Gk *chitōn* covering, case, tunic — more at CHITON] **:** a genus of Australian trees (family Sterculiaceae) that are grown in warm regions for ornament and have flowers with numerous stamens and woody fruits — see BOTTLE TREE

bra·chyc·o·me \brəˈkikə(,)mē, brə'-\ *n, cap* [NL, fr. *brachy-* + Gk *komē* hair] **:** a genus of mostly Australian herbs (family Compositae) with basal or alternate leaves and solitary or loosely corymbose flower heads

brachy·cranial \ˈbrakē+\ *adj* [*brachy-* + *cranial*] **:** short-skulled or broad-skulled with a cranial index of 80 and above — **brachy·cranic** \"+\ *adj* — **brachy·cra·ny** \ˈbrakē,krānē\ *n* -ES

brachy·cranium \ˈbrakē+\ *n* [NL, fr. *brachy-* + *cranium*] **:** a brachycranial skull

brachy·dac·ty·lism \,brakēˈdaktə,lizəm\ *n* -S [*brachydactylous* + *-ism*] **:** a brachydactylous condition or a tendency toward brachydactyly

brachy·dac·ty·lous \¦==¦==ləs\ *adj* [*brachy-* + *-dactylous*] **:** of or relating to brachydactyly

brachy·dac·ty·ly \-ˈlē\ *also* **brachy·dac·tyl·ia** \,==,=ˈtilyə, -lēə\ *n, pl* **brachydactylies** *also* **brachydactylias** [NL *brachydactylia*, fr. *brachy-* + *dactyl-* + *-ia*] **:** abnormal shortness of the digits (as when the fingers have but two joints)

¹brachy·diagonal \ˈbrakē+\ *adj* [*brachy-* + *diagonal*] **:** of or relating to the brachyaxis

²brachydiagonal \"\ *n* -S **:** BRACHYAXIS

brach·y·dod·ro·mous \ˈbrakə̇ˈdädrəməs\ *adj* [by alter.] **:** BROCHIDODROMOUS

brach·y·dome \ˈbrakə̇,dōm\ *n* [*brachy-* + *dome*] **:** the dome of a crystal having planes parallel to the shorter lateral axis — compare CLINODOME, MACRODOME, ORTHODOME

brachy·dont \-,dänt\ *also* **brachy·odont** \ˈbrakēō,d-\ *adj* [*brachy-* + *-odont*] **1** *of teeth* **:** having short crowns, well-developed roots, and only narrow canals in the roots (as in man) — compare HYPSODONT **2 :** having brachydont teeth

brachy·facial \ˈbrakē+\ *adj* [*brachy-* + *facial*] **:** having a short or broad face

brachy–form \ˈbrakē+,-\ *n* [*brachy-* + *-form*] **:** a rust that does not produce aecia — compare EU-FORM

bra·chyg·na·tha \brəˈkignəthə, brə'-\ *n pl, cap* [NL, fr. *brachy-* + *-gnatha*] **:** a division of the tribe Brachyura comprising the Brachyrhyncha and Oxyrhyncha and including the majority of the true crabs with the mouth field more or less square, sternal female openings, and the last pair of legs usu. normal in size and position

¹bra·chyg·na·than \-thən\ *adj* [NL *Brachygnatha* + E *-an*] **:** of or relating to the Brachygnatha

²brachygnathan \"\ *n* -S **:** a crab of the division Brachygnatha

bra·chyg·ra·phy \-grəfē\ *n* -ES [Gk *brachy-* + E *-graphy*] **:** SHORTHAND

brach·y·lae·mus \,brakə̇ˈlēməs\ [NL, alter. of *Brachylaima*] *syn of* BRACHYLAIMA

brach·y·lai·ma \-ˈlīmə\ *n, cap* [NL, fr. *brachy-* + *-laima* (fr. Gk *laimos* throat, gullet)] **:** a genus (the type of the family Brachylaimidae) of elongated digenetic trematodes including parasites of gallinaceous birds and of swine

¹brach·y·lai·mid \ˈbrakə̇¦līməd\ *also* **brach·y·lae·mid** \-lēm-\ *adj* [NL *Brachylaima* or *Brachylaemus* + E *-id*] **:** of or relating to the genus *Brachylaima*

²brachylaimid \"\ *also* **brachylaemid** \"\ *n* -S **:** a trematode of the genus *Brachylaima*

bra·chyl·o·gy \brəˈkiləjē, brə'-\ *n* -ES [Gk *brachylogia*, fr. *brachy-* + *-logia* -logy] **:** conciseness of expression; *also* **:** a condensed expression

brachy·meiosis \ˈbrakē+\ *n* [NL, fr. *brachy-* + *meiosis*] **:** a second reduction division following the usual two meiotic divisions reputed to occur in the ascus of certain fungi; *also* **:** the entire meiotic process when involving double reduction that has been suggested as an explanation of the restoration of the haploid condition in fungi in which double fertilization has produced a tetraploid primary ascus nucleus

brachy·meiotic \"+\ *adj* [fr. NL *brachymeiosis*, after such pairs as NL *hypnosis:* E *hypnotic*] **:** marked by or relating to brachymeiosis

brachy·mor·phic \ˈbrakə̇ˈmȯrfik\ *adj* [*brachy-* + *-morphic*] **:** ENDOMORPHIC, PYKNIC — opposed to *dolichomorphic* — **brachy·mor·phy** \ˈ==,=fē\ *n* -ES

brachyodont *var of* BRACHYDONT

brachy·oura \,brakēˈ(y)ürə\ [NL] *syn of* BRACHYURA

brachyoural *or* **brachyouran** *or* **brachyourous** *var of* BRACHYURAL

brachyouran *var of* BRACHYURAN

brachy·pha·lan·gy \,brakēfəˈlanjē, -fāˈ-\ *also* **brachy·pha·lan·gia** \-j(ē)ə\ *n, pl* **brachyphalangies** *also* **brachyphalangias** [NL *brachyphalangia*, fr. *brachy-* + *-phalangia*] **:** BRACHYDACTYLY

brach·y·phyl·lum \,brakə̇ˈfiləm\ *n, cap* [NL, fr. *brachy-* + *-phyllum*] **:** a genus of fossil coniferous plants found in rocks ranging from Jurassic to Middle Cretaceous and having appressed, scalelike, relatively short and broad leaves

bra·chyp·ter·ism \brəˈkiptə,rizəm, brə'-\ *n* -S **:** shortness of wings **:** the state of having short wings

bra·chyp·ter·ous \(ˈ)braˈkiptərəs, brəˈk-\ *adj* [Gk *brachypteros*, fr. *brachy-* + *-pteros* (fr. *pteron* wing) — more at FEATHER] **:** SHORT-WINGED **:** having the wings rudimentary or abnormally small — used chiefly of small-winged forms of certain insects

brachy·rhi·nus \,brakə̇ˈrīnəs\ *n, cap* [NL, fr. *brachy-* + *-rhinus*] **:** a very large genus of small short-snouted commonly dark-colored parthenogenetic weevils including a number of destructive pests of economic plants — see BLACK VINE WEEVIL, STRAWBERRY ROOT WEEVIL

brachy·rhyn·cha \,brakə̇ˈriŋkə\ *n pl, cap* [NL, fr. *brachy-* + *rhyncha* (fr. *rhynchos* snout) — more at RHYNCH-] **:** a superfamily of crabs including most of the Brachygnatha and all having the rostrum reduced or absent

brachy·sclereid \ˈbrakē+\ *n* -S [*brachy-* + *sclereid*] **:** a more or less isodiametric sclereid typically occurring in pith, cortex, and bark of many stems and in certain fruits (as pear and quince) — called also *stone cell*

brachy·skelic \ˈbrakə̇¦skelik\ *also* **brachys·ke·lous** \braˈkiskələs, brə'-\ *adj* [*brachy-* + Gk *skelos* leg + E *-ic* or *-ous* — more at SCEL-] **:** having legs short in proportion to the trunk **:** having a skelic index of 75 to 80

brach·ysm \ˈbra,kizəm\ *n* -S [blend of *brachy-* and *-ism*] **:** a dwarfing in plants that is characterized by a shortening of the internodes only — **bra·chyt·ic** \braˈkid·ik, brə'-\ *adj*

brach·y·ste·gia \,brakə̇ˈstēj(ē)ə\ *n, cap* [NL, fr. *brachy-* + Gk *stegos* roof + NL *-ia* — more at THATCH] **:** a small genus of tropical African trees (family Leguminosae) having compound leaves and small flowers with no calyx and small petals

brachy·syllabic \ˈbrakə̇, -kē+\ *adj* [*brachy-* + *syllabic*] **:** of or relating to a short syllable **:** having a short syllable **:** composed of short syllables

bra·chyt·ic \braˈkid·ik, brə'-\ *adj* [irreg. fr. *brachysm* + *-itic*] **:** marked by or relating to brachysm

brachy·ura \,brakēˈyürə\ *n pl, cap* [NL, fr. *brachy-* + *-ura*] **:** a tribe of the suborder Reptantia or in some classifications a suborder of Decapoda comprising crustaceans with the abdomen greatly reduced and more or less folded against the ventral surface of the thorax and including the typical crabs — compare ANOMURA, MACRURA

brachy·ural \ˈbrakē¦yürəl\ *or* **brachy·uran** \-rən\ *or* **brachy·urous** \-rəs\ *also* **brachy·oural** *or* **brachy·ouran** *or* **brachy·ourous** \-ə¦(y)ü-\ *adj* [NL *Brachyura, Brachyoura* + E *-al* or *-an* or *-ous*] **:** of or relating to the Brachyura

brachy·uran \,brakēˈyürən\ *also* **brachy·ouran** \-ˈ(y)ü-\ *n* -S **:** a crustacean of the tribe Brachyura

brachy·uran·ic \ˈbrakēyü¦ranik\ *adj* [*brachy-* + *uran-* + *-ic*] **:** having a short or narrow alveolar arch **:** having a palatomaxillary index of 115 or over — **brachy·ura·ny** \-ē¦yüranē\ *n* -ES

brachy·urus \,brakēˈyürəs\ [NL, fr. *brachy-* + *-urus*] *syn of* CACAJAO

¹bracing *n* -S [fr. gerund of ²*brace*] **:** the act or action of binding, strengthening, or making rigid ⟨the ~ of flood-damaged bridges⟩; *also* **:** material used for such an act or action ⟨beams, logs, and other ~⟩

²bracing *adj* [fr. pres. part. of ²*brace*] **:** imparting strength, vigor, or freshness ⟨~ mountain air⟩ — **brac·ing·ly** *adv* — **brac·ing·ness** *n* -ES

¹brack *chiefly Scot past of* BREAK

²brack \ˈbrak\ *adj* [D *brak* salty fr. MD *brac;* akin to MLG, salty, & perh. to MD *broec* swampy ground, OE *brōc* brook — more at BROOK] **1** *dial* **:** BRACKISH, BRINY ⟨~ water⟩ **2** *or* **brak** \"\ *Africa* **:** ALKALI ⟨~ soil⟩

³brack \"\ *n* -S **1** *dial* **:** salt water **:** BRINE **2** *or* **brak** \"\ *Africa* **:** alkali esp. in soil

⁴brack \"\ *n* -S [alter. of ²*break*] **1** *archaic* **:** a crack or fissure in a solid body **:** BREAK, BREACH **2** *dial* **:** a flaw esp. in cloth

brack·e·busch·ite \ˈbrakə̇,bü,shīt, ,==ˈ=,=\ *n* -S [G *brackebuschit*, fr. Ludwig *Brackebusch* †1906 Ger. mineralogist + G *-it* -ite] **:** a mineral $Pb_4MnFe(VO_4)_4.2H_2O$ consisting of a hydrous vanadate of lead, iron, and manganese

¹brack·en \ˈbrakən\ *n, pl* **bracken** *or* **brackens** [ME *braken*, prob. of Scand origin; akin to OSw *brækne* fern, Norw *brakne*, Icel *burkni;* perh. akin to OE *brecan* to break — more at BREAK] **1 a :** a large coarse fern **b :** the common brake (*Pteridium aquilinum*) and related species of the same genus and of *Pteris* with which it is merged in some classifications **c :** ROYAL FERN **2 :** a growth of brakes (as *Pteridium aquilinum*); *also* **:** an area dominated by such a growth **3 :** BONE BROWN 2

²bracken *var of* BRECHAN

bracken poisoning *or* **bracken staggers** *n* [¹*bracken*] **:** a disease of livestock caused by eating mature bracken and resulting in loss of appetite, diarrhea, weakness, and knuckling of fetlocks and appearing to be a true avitaminosis in that some unknown factor in the bracken renders certain B-complex vitamins unavailable to the animal

¹brack·et \ˈbrakə̇t, *usu* -ə̇d·+V\ *n* -S [earlier *bragget*, fr. MF *braguette* codpiece, dim. of *brague* breeches, fr. OProv *braga*, fr. L *braca* — more at BRACCAE] **1 :** a simple or composite often carved or sculptured overhanging member that projects from a wall, pier, or other structure and is usu. designed to support a vertical load or to strengthen an angle although it sometimes serves merely as a decorative feature only seeming to give support — compare BRACE, CANTILEVER, CONSOLE, CORBEL, CUL-DE-LAMPE, MODILLION, STRUT **2 a** (1) **:** a short crooked ship's timber resembling a knee and used as a support (2) **:** a flat or flanged triangular ship's plate used esp. for connecting frames and deck beams **b :** a piece of formed sheet steel to which the parts of a bicycle frame are fastened and in which the crank axle turns — called also *bottom bracket, crank hanger, main bracket* **3 a :** a short wall shelf (as one with a single support) **b :** a fixture projecting from a wall or column (as for holding a lamp or candle) **c :** the fruiting body of a bracket fungus — called also *conk;* compare POLYPORACEAE **d :** the curved juncture between serif and vertical stem of a type character **4 a :** one of a pair of marks [] used (1) in writing and printing to enclose matter inserted in a direct quotation, matter extraneous or incidental to context, or phonetic symbols or (2) in logic to indicate operands to be grouped and treated as a unit or (3) in mathematics to serve as signs of aggregation — called also *square bracket;* see VINCULUM **b :** one of the pair of marks ⟨⟩ used to enclose a mutilated passage or the expansion of an abbreviation in a text or to enclose quotations or verbal illustrations in a reference work such as a dictionary — called also *angle bracket, broken bracket, pointed bracket* **c :** one of a pair of curves () — called also *parenthesis, round bracket* **d :** BRACE 6b **5 a :** a pair of shots fired to determine the exact distance from gun to target: (1) **:** a pair that falls short of and beyond the target — called also *range bracket* (2) **:** a pair that falls to the right and left of the target — called also *deflection bracket* **b :** the distance often ascertained by instrument between the landings of two shots fired at a distant target and used to correct the aim of the gun **6 :** a section of a continuously numbered or graded series (in the 24 to 55 age ~⟩ ⟨temperatures beyond the 65° to 85° ~⟩; *esp* **:** one of a graded series of income groups ⟨millions of families have risen out of the under $2000 class . . . and climbed a ~ or two —F.L.Allen⟩ **7 a :** a pairing of opponents in an elimination tournament **b :** either half of the draw of an elimination tournament ⟨the upper or lower ~⟩ **8 :** a skating figure in which the skater executes from a simple curve a half turn, a cusp, and then another half turn back to the original curve

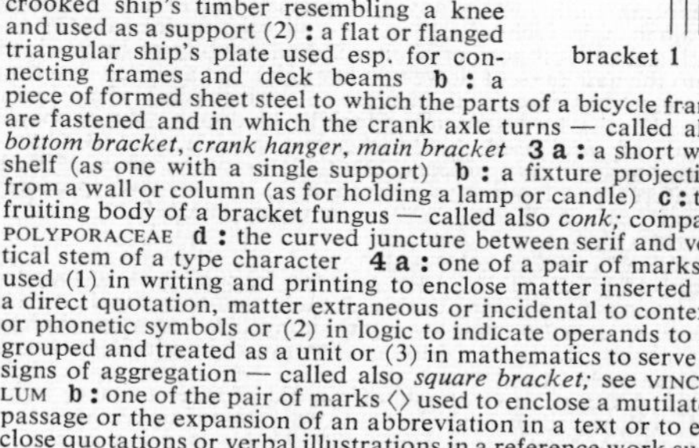

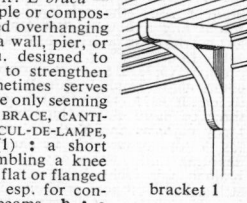

bracket 1

²bracket \"\ *vt* -ED/-ING/-S **1 a :** to place within or as if within brackets ⟨~ a word⟩ ⟨~ the translation of a quotation in a foreign language⟩ ⟨a face ~*ed* with tousled hair⟩ **b :** to set aside **:** separate out **:** eliminate from consideration ⟨the transcendental view requires nature to be ~*ed* on principle —Marvin Farber⟩ — often used with *off* ⟨the danger of a positivistic approach to . . . history that ~*s* off moral questions —*Times Lit. Supp.*⟩ **2 :** to furnish, fasten, or decorate with brackets ⟨an army trunk ~*ed* to its left running board —E.B.White⟩ ⟨its highly stilted and ~*ed* arcading has distinct Moorish effects —*Amer. Guide Series: Tenn.*⟩ **3 a :** to put into the same class with **:** ASSOCIATE ⟨another historical tablet often ~*ed* with the Rosetta stone —Edward Clodd⟩ **b :** CLASSIFY, GROUP ⟨~ together cities of around the same population as if they were alike in all other respects —W.J. Reilly⟩ **4 a :** to treat as a pair **:** deal with simultaneously ⟨Hawaii and Alaska have been ~*ed* together in recent statehood legislation —Ernest Gruening⟩ **b :** to place beside for purposes of comparison **:** COMPARE ⟨teachers at West Point have ~*ed* this retreat with . . . the withdrawal by Napoleon from Moscow —R.L.Neuberger⟩ **5 a :** to obtain a bracket on (as a target) ⟨~ an enemy convoy⟩ **b :** to establish the limits of (as a range of variation or a time interval) ⟨if the guy was murdered in the time you ~ —H.V.Haddock⟩

³bracket \"\ *adj* [modif. of IrGael *breac*, fr. OIr *brec*] *dial* **:** SPOTTED, SPECKLED

⁴bracket \"\ *n* -S [origin unknown] **:** AMERICAN MERGANSER

bracket capital *n* **:** a capital with one or more projecting brackets or corbels to help carry a beam or girder (as in Indian and Syrian architecture and in primitive styles)

bracket clock *n* **:** a clock designed to stand on a shelf or bracket; *esp* **:** a small rectangular clock sometimes with arched top — orig. used of a clock needing space below for weights and pendulum

bracket crab *or* **bracket crane** *n* **:** a hoisting crab placed like a bracket against a wall or post

bracketed *adj, of a serif* **:** curved where it joins the vertical stroke of a letter (as in an old-style *p*)

bracket foot *n* **:** a foot like a bracket found on cabinet furniture mitered at the corner and usu. scrolled on the free sides — see FOOT illustration

bracket fungus *n* **:** a basidiomycete that forms shelflike sporophores (as on tree trunks)

bracketing *n* -S **:** a series or group of brackets; *specif* **:** a framework of wooden ribs (as for supporting a cornice or cove)

brack·et·man \-,man\ *n, pl* **bracketmen :** HANGERMAN

brackets *pl of* BRACKET, *pres 3d sing of* BRACKET

brack·ish \ˈbrakish, -kēsh\ *adj* [²*brack* + *-ish*] **1 :** somewhat salt **:** less salt than sea water but undrinkable ⟨the ~ water in the tidal reaches of a river⟩ ⟨a ~ pond⟩ **2 :** UNPALATABLE ⟨coffee was still a harsh ~ draught —Jack Alexander⟩ **:** DISTASTEFUL ⟨a ~ personality⟩

brackish–water crab *n* **:** a crab (*Sesarina roberti*) living in holes along the banks of tidal streams in the West Indies and Central America

brack·mard \ˈbrak,mär(d)\ *n* -S [F *braquemart*, fr. MF, alter. of *bragamas*, prob. fr. MD *breecmes*, fr. *brēken* to break + *mes, mets* knife; akin to OE *brecan* to break and to OE *metseax* food knife, OHG *mezzisahs, mezzirahs* knife, MLG *metset, mest*, OS *mezas*, all fr. a WGmc compound whose components are akin respectively to OE *mete* food, meat, and to OE *seax* knife — more at BREAK, MEAT, SAX] **:** a short straight broadsword

bracks *pl of* BRACK

¹brac·o·nid \ˈbrakənə̇d\ *adj* [NL *Braconidae*] **:** of or relating to the family Braconidae

²braconid \"\ *n* -S **:** an insect of the family BRACONIDAE

bra·con·i·dae \brəˈkänə,dē\ *n pl, cap* [NL, fr. *Bracon*, type genus (irreg. fr. Gk *brachys* short) + *-idae* — more at BRIEF] **:** a large family of ichneumon flies some of which are parasitic as larvae on living caterpillars and other insect larvae, others on aphids

bra·con·nière \ˈbrakənˈye(ə)r\ *n* -S [F, fr. MF *braconniere, bragonniere*, prob. fr. OIt *braconi*, pl., wide breeches worn by halberdiers, aug. of *braca* breeches, fr. L *braca* — more at BRACCAE] **:** a 16th century piece of armor for the thighs consisting of a short skirt of narrow hoop-shaped plates of steel overlapping one another and moving freely

bract \ˈbrakt\ *n* -S [NL *bractea*, fr. L *brattea, bractea* thin metal plate, gold leaf] **1 :** a somewhat modified leaf associated with the reproductive structures of a plant: as **a :** a leaf from the axil of which a flower or floral axis arises **b :** a leaf borne on the floral axis itself (as one subtending the flower or flower cluster) ordinarily smaller than a foliage leaf but occas. large and showy and simulating petals (as in the fever tree and flowering dogwood) — called also *bracteole, bractlet;* see GLUME, INVOLUCRE, SPATHE; compare SCALE **c :** one of the specialized leaves associated with the sexual organs in mosses **d :** a scalelike structure associated with the ovule in the ovulate cone of certain conifers **2 a :** modified medusae of siphonophores having a protective function **:** HYDROPHYLLIUM **b :** a flattened leaflike part of certain crustacean appendages; *specif* **:** the distal exite of the limb of a phyllopod

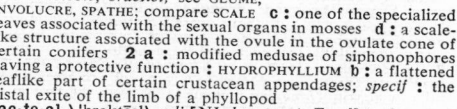

flower showing *1* bracteole, *2* bract

brac·te·al \ˈbraktēəl\ *adj* [NL *bractea* + E *-al*] **:** of, resembling, relating to, or functioning as a bract

¹brac·te·ate \-ēə̇t, -ē,āt\ *n* -S [ML (*nummus*) *bracteatus*, fr. L *nummus* coin + LL *bracteatus* gold-plated, fr. L *bractea, brattea* gold plate + *-atus* -ate] **1 :** a thin metal plate usu. of gold or silver chased on one side and often inscribed with runes and found in early Germanic graves and known to have been used for clothing decoration in the Near East about 2000 B.C. **2 :** a very thin coin usu. of silver having a design stamped on one side only and showing through on the reverse and common esp. in Germany in the 12th to 13th centuries

²bracteate \"\ *adj* [NL *bracteatus*, fr. *bractea* + L *-atus* -ate] **:** furnished with bracts

bract·ed \ˈbraktə̇d\ *adj* [*bract* + *-ed*] **:** BRACTEATE

bracted bindweed *n* **:** a sprawling herbaceous vine (*Convolvulus spithamaeus*) of eastern No. America with large white flowers subtended by two bracts

bracted plantain *n* **:** a troublesome weed (*Plantago aristata*) of the western U.S. with a prominently bracted spike of flowers

brac·te·o·late \brakˈtēələt, -,lāt; ˈbraktēə,lāt\ *adj* [NL *bracteolatus*, fr. *bracteola* + L *-atus* -ate] **:** furnished with bracteoles

brac·te·ole \ˈbraktē,ōl\ *n* -S [NL *bracteola*, fr. L, thin gold leaf, dim. of *bractea, brattea* gold leaf] **:** a small bract; *esp* **:** one on a floral axis — called also *bractlet;* see BRACT illustration

brac·te·ose \-ē,ōs\ *adj* [NL *bractea* + E *-ose*] **:** having numerous or conspicuous bracts

bract·let \ˈbraktlə̇t\ *n* -S [*bract* + *-let*] **:** BRACTEOLE

bract–scale \ˈ=,=\ *n* **:** an annual erect succulent herb (*Atriplex serenana*) of saline soils in the southeastern U.S. with numerous grayish green sparsely scurfy leaves

¹brad \ˈbrad, ˈbraa(ə)d\ *n* -S [ME, alter. of *brod* — more at BROD] **1 :** a thin usu. small nail of the same thickness throughout but tapering in width and with a slight projection at the top on one side instead of a head; *sometimes* **:** a small tapering square-bodied finishing nail with a countersunk head **2 :** a slender wire nail with a small deep round head

²brad \"\ *vt* **bradded; bradded; bradding; brads :** to fasten with brads

bradawl \ˈ=,=\ *n* **:** an awl with chisel edge used to make holes for brads or screws

brad·bury \ˈbrad,berē, *Brit usu* -db(ə)ri\ *n* -S *usu cap* [after Sir John Swanwick *Bradbury* †1950 English treasury official] **:** a British pound note

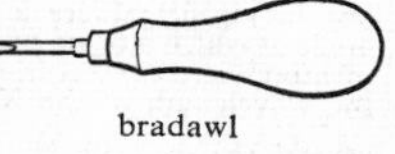

bradawl

brad·dish·er \ˈbradishə(r)\ *n* -S [by alter.] **:** BRATTICER

bra·den·head \ˈbrādᵊn,hed\ *n* [Glenn T. *Braden* †1923 Am. oilman and inventor + E *head*] **:** a casing head in an oil well having a stuffing box packed (as with rubber) to make a gastight connection

brad·ford \ˈbradfə(r)d\ *adj, usu cap* [fr. *Bradford*, England] **:** of or from the city of Bradford, England **:** of the kind or style prevalent in Bradford

bradford frame \"-\ *n, usu cap B* [after Edward H. *Bradford* †1926 Am. surgeon] **:** a rectangular metal frame fitted with adjustable straps of canvas or webbing and used to support a patient with certain diseases or fractures of the spine, hip, or pelvis

bradford system *n, usu cap B* [fr. *Bradford*, England] **:** a method of preparing and spinning long-staple wool into worsted yarn

brad·le·ian *also* **brad·ley·an** \'bradlēən, ⸗'⸗⸗\ *adj, usu cap* [Francis H. *Bradley* †1924 Brit. philosopher + E *-an*] **:** of or relating to Bradley or his objective idealism

brad·ley·ite \'bradlē,īt\ *n* -s [Wilmot H. *Bradley* *b*1899 Am. geologist + E *-ite*] **:** a mineral $Na_3Mg(PO_4)(CO_3)$ consisting of a rare phosphate and carbonate of sodium and magnesium

bradoon *var of* BRIDOON

brad punch *n* **:** a small nail set

brad pusher *n* **:** a tool for grasping and inserting brads by pressure in hard-to-reach places

brad·shaw \'brad(,)shȯ\ *n* -s *usu cap* [short for *Bradshaw's Railway Guide*, a timetable published periodically containing information about all the trains running in the British isles, after George *Bradshaw* †1853 Eng. printer who first issued it in 1839] **:** a comprehensive timetable of British railroad trains

brad·sot \'bradsət\ *n* -s [prob. fr. Icel *brāthasōt*, fr. ON, plague, murrain, fr. *brāthr* sudden, hasty, heated + *sōtt* sickness, disease; akin to ON *brāth* tar and to ON *sjūkr* sick — more at BREATH, SICK] **:** BRAXY 1

brady- *comb form* [MF & NL, fr. Gk *bradys*] **1 :** slow ⟨*brady*cardia⟩ **:** dull ⟨*brady*acusia⟩ **2 :** BRACHY- ⟨*brady*dactylia⟩

brady·auxesis \;bradē+\ *n, pl* **bradyauxeses** [NL, fr. *brady-* + *auxesis*] **:** allometric growth characterized by lagging of a part behind the body as a whole in development — compare TACHYAUXESIS — **brady·auxetic** \"+\ *adj* — **brady·auxetically** \"+\ *adv*

brady·car·dia \;bradə;kärdēə\ *n* -s [NL, fr. *brady-* + *-cardia*] **:** a slow heart rate; *esp* **:** an abnormally slow one (as of 50 beats per minute) in man — compare ARRHYTHMIA

brady·genesis \;bradə+\ *n* [NL, fr. *brady-* + *-genesis*] *biol* **:** retardation of development by prolonging certain ancestral stages — compare LIPOGENESIS, TACHYGENESIS

brad·y·pod \'bradə,päd\ *also* **brad·y·pode** \-pōd\ *n* -s [NL *Bradypodidae*] **:** an edentate of the family Bradypodidae — **bra·dyp·o·doid** \brə'dipə,dȯid, bra'-\ *adj*

brad·y·pod·i·dae \,bradə'pädə,dē\ *n pl, cap* [NL, fr. *Bradypod-, Bradypus*, type genus + *-idae*] **:** a family of edentates comprising the true sloths

brad·y·pus \'bradəpəs, -də,pu̇s\ *n, cap* [NL, fr. Gk *bradypous* slow of foot, fr. *brady-* + *pous* foot — more at FOOT] **:** the genus comprising the three-toed sloths

brady·seism \'bradē,sīzəm\ *n* -s [*brady-* + *-seism*] **:** a slow quiet upward or downward movement of the earth's crust — **brady·seismal** \;bradē+\ *adj* — **brady·seismic** \"+\ *or* **brady·seismical** \"+\ *adj*

brady·tel·ic \;bradə;telik\ *adj* **:** of or relating to bradytely

brady·tely \'bradə,telē\ *n* -ES [*brady-* + *-tely* (irreg. fr. Gk *telos* end, consummation, degree of completion, state of maturity) — more at WHEEL] **:** arrested evolution or evolution at very slow rates outside the rate distribution usual for a given group of plants or animals — compare HOROTELY, TACHYTELY

¹**brae** \'brā\ *n* -s [ME *bra*, fr. ON *brā* eyelash; akin to OE *brǣw* eyebrow, eyelid, OHG *brāwa* eyelid, eyebrow, OE *bregdan* to move quickly — more at BRAID] **1** *chiefly Scot* **:** HILL; *esp* **:** a hillside along a river **2** *chiefly Scot* **:** the brow of a hill **3** *chiefly Scot* **:** a steep road **4** *chiefly Scot* **:** a mountain or hill district **:** UPLANDS — often used in pl.

²**brae** \'bra, -raa,-rā\ *n, pl* **braees** [Norw *bræ*] **:** GLACIER, ICE CAP — used chiefly in toponyms in Scandinavian areas

bra·ford \'brāfərd, 'bräf-\ *n* -s *usu cap* [*Brahman* + *Hereford*] **:** a type of beef cattle developed by crossing Brahman and Hereford; *also* **:** one of these cattle

¹**brag** \'brag, -aa(ə),-aig\ *adj* **bragger**; **braggest** [ME] **1** *archaic* **a :** full of spirits **:** LIVELY, LUSTY **b :** BOASTFUL, PRETENTIOUS ⟨the *braggest* of all soldiers⟩ **2 :** superlatively good **:** FIRST-RATE ⟨a ~ dog⟩ — often used of something displayed with pride or self-congratulation ⟨he showed me his ~ cornfield, which was going to fill his crib —H.C.Nixon⟩

²**brag** \"\ *n* -s [ME] **1 :** a pompous, cocky, or boastful statement, comment, or story **2 a** *obs* **:** ostentatious display **:** POMP ⟨the ~ and show of a royal court⟩ **b :** arrogant or swaggering talk or manner **:** TRUCULENCE, COCKINESS ⟨all his adolescent ~ —A.M.Schlesinger b.1917⟩ ⟨all the ~ and bluster —*Kiplinger Washington Letter*⟩ **3 :** an old card game resembling poker **4 :** BRAGGART

³**brag** \"\ *vb* **bragged**; **bragged**; **bragging**; **brags** [ME *braggen*] *vi* **1 :** to talk about oneself or things pertaining to oneself in a boastful manner **:** BOAST ⟨mechanics *bragging* about their skill⟩ ⟨his luck had been nothing to ~ about⟩ **2** *obs* **:** SWAGGER, STRUT ~ *vt* **1** *now chiefly Scot* **:** THREATEN, DEFY, CHALLENGE ⟨~ a person to a race⟩ **2 :** to assert boastfully or cockily ⟨*bragging* that his crops were the best in the county⟩ **3** *archaic* **:** boast of **syn** see BOAST

brag·ga·do·cian \;bragə;dōsh(ē)ən, ;braig-, -ōsēən,-ōch(ē)ən\ *adj* **:** given to or of the nature of a braggadocio

brag·ga·do·cio \,⸗⸗'⸗shē,ō *also* -(,)shō *or* -,sē,ō *sometimes* -,chē,ō *or* -(,)chō *or* -,shə\ *n* -s [after *Braggadochio*, personification of boasting in *Faerie Queene* by Edmund Spenser †1599 Eng. poet] **1 :** BRAGGART, BOASTER **2 a :** empty boasting **:** BRAGGING ⟨the ~ of dictators⟩ **b :** arrogant pretension **:** COCKINESS ⟨the air of swaggering ~ that all important men are expected to show in fighting —C.W.M.Hart⟩

bragg angle \'brag-\ *n, usu cap B* [after Sir William Henry *Bragg* †1942 and Sir William Lawrence Bragg *b*1890 Eng. physicists] **:** the small angle between an incident X-ray beam and the diffracting planes of a crystal — compare BRAGG'S LAW

¹**brag·gart** \'bragə(r)t, -raag-,-raig- *sometimes* -,gärt *or* -,gat; *usu* -d·+V\ *n* -s [³*brag* + *-art*] **:** a loud or arrogant boaster

²**braggart** \"\ *adj* **1 :** excessively boastful **:** arrogantly pretentious ⟨~ politicians⟩ ⟨he had been loose of tongue and ~ of claims —S.H.Adams⟩ **2 :** of, befitting, or suggestive of an arrant boaster ⟨a large man with a ~ voice⟩ ⟨~ actions⟩ — **brag·gart·ly** *adv*

brag·gart·ism \-d·,izəm, -,tiz-\ *n* -s **:** BOASTFULNESS, SWAGGER

brag·ger \'bragə(r), -raag-,-raig-\ *n* -s [ME *braggere*, fr. *braggen* to brag + *-ere* -er] **1 :** one that brags **:** BOASTER **2 :** CORBEL 2b **3 :** the jack of clubs or nine of diamonds which in the game of brag were wild cards in forming pairs; *also* **:** the player who made the first bet in the game of brag

brag·get \'bragət\ *n* -s [ME *braket, bragot*, fr. MW *bragod*, fr. *brag* malt; akin to MIr *mraich, braich* malt, Gaulish *bracis* grain for making malt, L *marcēre* to wither, droop — more at MARCESCENT] **:** a drink made from ale and fermented honey or from ale sweetened and spiced

brag·ging·ly *adv* **:** in a bragging manner

bragg·ite \'bra,gīt\ *n* -s [Sir W.H. & Sir W.L. *Bragg* + E *-ite*] **:** a mineral PtS consisting of platinum sulfide, usu. containing other metals (as palladium and nickel), and occurring in granitic rocks

bragg reflection \'brag-, -aa-,-ai-\ *n, usu cap B* [after Sir William H. *Bragg* †1942 and Sir William L. *Bragg* *b*1890 English physicists] **:** the action of a crystal in reflecting X rays or particle waves (as electrons or neutrons) in a manner analogous to that of a reflection grating upon light incident at a suitable angle — compare BRAGG'S LAW

bragg's law \-gz-\ *n, usu cap B* [after W.H. & W.L. *Bragg*] **:** a law in physics: there is a definite relationship between the angle at which a beam of X rays must fall on the parallel planes of atoms in a crystal in order that there be strong reflection, the wavelength of the X rays, and the distance between the crystal planes **:** $\sin\Theta = \frac{n\lambda}{2d}$ where Θ is the angle between the incident or the reflected beam and the crystal plane, λ is the X-ray wavelength, d is the crystal plane separation, and n is any integer

brag·gy \'bragē, -aag-,-aig-, gi\ *adj* -ER/-EST [²*brag* + *-y*] **:** BOASTFUL, PRETENTIOUS

brag·less *adj* **:** being without a brag

bra·goz·zo \-brə'gōt(,)sō\ *n, pl* **bragoz·zi** \-t(,)sē\ [It, fr. It dial. (Venice) *bragozo, bargozo*, fr. *braga* trousers, fr. L *braca*; fr. the trouserlike appearance of the nets carried by these boats — more at BRACCAE] **:** a 2-masted trawler common near Venice

brags *pl of* BRAG, *pres 3d sing of* BRAG

¹**brah·ma** *also* **bra·mah** \'brāmə, -ämə,-āmə *also* -amə\ *n* [fr. *Brahma*putra river, India] **1** *usu cap* **:** an Asian breed of very large domestic fowls having pea combs and feathered legs and occurring in light, dark, and buff-color varieties **2** -s **:** a bird of the Brahma breed

²**brahma** \"\ *n* -s *usu cap* [by alter.] **:** BRAHMAN 2

brah·ma·cha·ri \,brämə'chärē\ *n* -s [Skt *brahmacārin*, fr. *brahman* prayer + *cārin* one who practices, fr. *carati* he moves, goes, practices — more at WHEEL] *India* **:** CELIBATE; *specif* **:** one in the stage of brahmacharya

brah·ma·char·ya \-ryə\ *n* -s [Skt *brahmacarya*, fr. *brahman* prayer + *carya* conduct, fr. *carati*] *India* **:** the state of celibate student life **:** the initial stage of the Brahmanic ashramas

brah·man *or* **brah·min** \'brämən, -rȧm-, *in sense 2 often or usu* -ram- *also* -ram-\ *n* -s *usu cap* [Skt *brāhmaṇa*, lit., having to do with prayer, fr. *brahman* prayer] **1** *also* **brahmana** *pl* **brahmana** *or* **brahmanas :** a member of the highest or sacerdotal caste among the Hindus having as chief duty the study and teaching of the Vedas and the performance of religious ceremonies — compare KSHATRIYA, SUDRA, VAISYA **2 a :** any of several breeds of Indian cattle; *specif* **:** a variety or breed of large vigorous heat-resistant and tick-resistant usu. silvery gray cattle evolved in the southern U.S. by interbreeding Indian cattle and now used chiefly for crossbreeding with beef cattle to increase their hardiness and resistance to disease and pests while retaining their beef quality **b :** an animal of this variety or breed — compare ZEBU

brah·ma·na \'brämənə, -rȧm-\ *n* -s *usu cap* [Skt *brāhmaṇa*] **:** one of a class of Hindu sacred writings composed around the 9th to 6th centuries B.C. and devoted chiefly to the instruction of Brahmins in the performance of Vedic ritual — see VEDA

brah·ma·ni *or* **brah·ma·nee** \-nē,-ni\ *n* -s *usu cap* [Skt *brāhmaṇī*, fr. *brāhmaṇa* — more at BRAHMAN] **:** a woman of the Brahma caste

brah·man·ic \(')brä¦manik, -rȧ¦-\ *also* **brah·man·i·cal** \-nəkəl\ *adj, usu cap* **:** of or relating to the Brahmans or their doctrines or worship

brah·man·ism \'brämə,nizəm, -rȧm-\ *n* -s *cap* **:** the religion of the Brahmans and orthodox Hindus; *specif* **:** the later development of the early Vedic religion up to the 12th century A.D.

brah·ma·ny *or* **brah·ma·nee** \-,nē,-ni\ *adj, usu cap* **:** of or relating to the Brahmans

brahmany bull *n, usu cap B* **:** the white male zebu sacred to the Hindus

brah·ma·poo·tra \,brämə'pü·trə, -rȧm- *also* -pyü-\ *n* -s *usu cap* [fr. *Brahmaputra* or *Brahmapootra* river, India] **:** BRAHMA

brah·mi \'brämē, -rȧmē\ *n* -s *usu cap* [Skt] **:** an ancient alphabet of India of Semitic descent which is found in several varieties and from which descend the later Indian alphabets

brah·min \'brämən, -rȧm-\ *n* -s *usu cap* **:** an intellectually and socially cultivated and exclusive person ⟨an old Boston ~ ... has come to mean the lowering of the ~ —C.H.Grandgent⟩; *esp* **:** such a person from one of the older New England families — sometimes used disparagingly ⟨a Boston ~⟩ — **brah·min·ic** \(')brä¦minik, -rȧ¦-\ *or* **brah·min·i·cal** \-nəkəl\ *adj, usu cap*

brah·min·ism \'brämə,nizəm, -rȧm-\ *n* -s *usu cap* **:** the system or practices of or imputed to Brahmins ⟨an ardent devotee of *Brahminism*⟩

brah·mi·ny kite *or* **brah·ma·ny kite** \'brämənē, -rȧm-\ *n, usu cap B* **:** a common kite (*Haliastur indus*) that is largely chestnut red with white breast and head striped with black, is widely distributed from India to the Solomon islands and the Philippines, and is held sacred by the Hindus

brah·mo \'brä(,)mō\ *n* -s *usu cap* [Bengali *Brahmo* (*Samāj*) assembly or church of Brahma, the first member of the Hindu trinity] **:** a member of an eclectic Hindu theistic society noted for its pronounced monotheism and vigorous policy of social and political reform

brah·mo·ism \-,izəm\ *n* -s *usu cap* **:** the doctrines or practices of the Brahmos

brahms·ian \'brämzēən, -rȧm-\ *adj, usu cap* [Johannes *Brahms* †1897 Ger. composer + E *-ian*] **:** of or relating to Brahms or his musical compositions

bra·hui \brä'hüē\ *n, pl* **brahui** *or* **brahuis** *usu cap* **1 a :** a pastoral people dominant in eastern Baluchistan **b :** a member of such people **2 :** the Dravidian language of the Brahui people

¹**braid** \'brād\ *vb* -ED/-ING/-S [ME *breyden* to move suddenly, snatch, weave together, fr. OE *bregdan*; akin to OHG *brettan* to draw (a sword), ON *bregtha* to move suddenly, weave together, Gk *phorkon* something white or gray or wrinkled, Skt *bhrāśate* it glitters; basic meaning: to shine] *vt* **1 a :** to form (three or more strands) into a cord or ribbon by repeatedly crossing a left and then a right strand over a central strand and under an opposite strand **b :** to make by braiding ⟨~ a rug⟩ ⟨~ a lanyard⟩ **2 :** to do up (the hair) by interweaving three or more strands together into one or more lengths **3 a :** to place or arrange in a diagonally woven or crisscross pattern ⟨~*ing* bunting around lampposts⟩ ⟨a secondary plot is ~*ed* through the novel⟩ **b :** INTERMINGLE, MIX ⟨~ fact with fiction⟩ **4 :** to ornament esp. with ribbon or braid **:** TRIM ⟨the girls ~*ed* their hair with flowers⟩ ~ *vi* **1** *dial Eng* **:** to take after **:** RESEMBLE — usu. used with *of* **2 :** to move in a crisscross pattern ⟨streams ~*ing* down a valley floor⟩

²**braid** \"\ *n* -s **1 :** a cord or ribbon having usu. three or more component strands forming a regular diagonal pattern down its length: as **a** (1) **:** a flat or round length of narrow fabric of three or more closely intertwined threads made in various fancy patterns and used for trimming, binding, or outlining (as clothing or lace) (2) **:** a band or cord (as of gold or silver) denoting rank (as on naval uniforms) **b** (1) **:** a length of braided hair ⟨schoolgirls in ~*s* and blue uniforms⟩ (2) **:** a string, band, ribbon, or similar strand binding or intertwined into the hair ⟨a ~ of flowers in her hair⟩ **c :** a woven covering for a central core (as in insulated electrical wire) **d :** a fancy bread made by intertwining lengths of dough **2 :** a coarse grade of wool used chiefly in carpet manufacture **3 :** commissioned military officers; *esp* **:** high-ranking naval officers ⟨differences of opinion between brass and ~ over procurement —Bruce Bliven b.1889⟩ — compare BRASS 5a

³**braid** \"\ *Scot var of* BROAD

⁴**braid** \"\ *dial var of* BREAD

braid·ed \'brādəd\ *adj* [ME *breyded*, fr. past. part. of *breyden* to braid] **1 a :** having braids **b :** adorned with braid **c :** ENTWINED; *specif* **:** made by intertwining three or more threads or fabrics **2 :** divided into or following an interlacing network of channels ⟨a ~ river⟩

braided rug *n* **:** a rug made of a braid of three or more strips of cloth sewed or laced into an oval, round, or rectangle

braid·er \-də(r)\ *n* -s **:** one that braids; *specif* **:** a sewing machine attachment for stitching braid in place

braid·ing \-diŋ,-dēŋ\ *n* -s [ME *breyding*, fr. gerund of *breyden* to braid] **:** something made of braided material: as **a :** trimming or braids esp. for clothes or lace **b :** the woven covering for an electric cable or wire

braid wool *n* **:** LUSTER WOOL

braies \'brā\ *n pl* [F, fr. OF, pl. of *braie*, fr. L *braca* — more at BRACCAE] **1 :** BRACCAE **2 :** breeches or trousers worn in medieval times

¹**brail** \'brāl, *esp bef pause or cons* -āəl\ *n* -s [ME *brayle*, fr. AF *braiel*, fr. OF, girdle, belt, strap, fr. *braies* breeches] **1 :** a rope that is fastened to the leech of a sail and run through a block and by which the sail can be hauled up or hauled in preparatory to furling or in place of furling **2 a :** the feathers at a hawk's rump — usu. used in pl. **b :** a thong of soft leather to restrain a hawk's wing **3 a :** a pipe or rod with many hooks attached that is drawn over a clam bed in harvesting clams **b :** a dip net resembling a small purse seine with which fish are hauled aboard a boat after being gathered in a purse seine or trap; *also* **:** such a dip net full of fish ⟨a ~ of salmon⟩

²**brail** \"\ *vt* -ED/-ING/-S **1 :** to take in (a sail) by the brails ⟨vessels coming into the wind and ~*ing* up their square sails —Kenneth Roberts⟩ ⟨the spanker was of little use and we ... ~*ed* it in —C.V.Reilly⟩ **2 :** to restrain (the wings of a hawk) with a brail **3 :** to hoist (fish) by means of a dip net (as from a trap into a ship's hold) ⟨~ sardines aboard⟩

brail·er \-ālə(r)\ *n* -s **:** BRAIL 3b

¹**braille** \'brāl, *esp bef pause or cons* -āəl\ *n* -s *often cap* [after Louis *Braille* †1852 Fr. teacher of the blind, who invented it] **:** a system of writing for the blind that uses characters made up of raised dots in a 6-dot cell arranged in two vertical columns and that has been adapted for writing various languages and

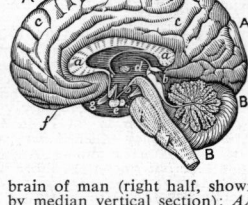

a	b	c	d	e	f	g	h	i	j
1	2	3	4	5	6	7	8	9	0
k	l	m	n	o	p	q	r	s	t
u	v	x	y	z	w	Capital Sign	Numeral Sign		

braille alphabet: the first ten letters serve also as numerals and each letter serves also, when standing alone, as a common word

for transcribing music, mathematics, and scientific symbols — see EMBOSS, GRADE, INTERPOINT, SIGN, STEREOTYPER, TRANSCRIBER, WORD-SIGN

²**braille** \"\ *vt* -ED/-ING/-S *sometimes cap* **:** to transcribe or write in braille characters

braill·er \-ālə(r)\ *n* -s **:** a mechanical device for writing braille; *esp* **:** BRAILLEWRITER

braille slate *or* **braille tablet** *n* **:** SLATE 3d

braillewriter \'⸗,⸗⸗\ *n, often cap* **:** a machine for writing braille that resembles a typewriter in size and action and that has a space bar and six keys, one for each of the six dots of a cell

braill·ist \-āləst\ *n* -s **1 :** an expert in the writing of braille **2 :** one whose work is writing braille

¹**brain** \'brān\ *n* -s [ME, fr. OE *brægen*; akin to OFris *brein* brain, MLG *bregen* brain, Gk *brechmos* front part of the head] **1 a :** the portion of the vertebrate central nervous system that constitutes the organ of thought and neural coordination, including all the higher nervous centers, receiving stimuli from the sense organs, and interpreting and correlating these with stored impressions to formulate the motor impulses that ultimately control all vital activities, that is made up of neurons and their processes organized into layers and nuclei of gray matter and tracts, decussations, and fasciculi of white matter together with various supporting and nutritive structures, and that is enclosed within the skull, being continuous with the spinal cord through the foramen magnum and with the cranial nerves through various other openings — see FOREBRAIN, HINDBRAIN, MIDBRAIN; compare CORTEX, VENTRICLE **b :** a nervous center in invertebrates (as the supraesophageal ganglia of arthropods) corresponding in position and function more or less to the brain of vertebrate animals — compare CEREBRAL GANGLION **2 a** (1) **:** INTELLECT, MIND ⟨it took a queer ~ to think up such a scheme⟩ ⟨successful in reading a man's ~ —Lou Richter⟩ (2) **:** sheer intellect — often used in pl. ⟨he's got ~*s* but no common sense⟩ (3) **:** intellectual endowment **:** INTELLIGENCE — often used in pl. ⟨there's plenty of ~*s* in that family⟩ **b** (1) **:** a supremely bright or intelligent person ⟨he'd been known as a ~ throughout college⟩ (2) **:** the guiding genius or intellectual leader **:** supreme planner — usu. used in pl. ⟨the ~*s* of the Nazi party⟩ ⟨he was the ~*s* of the enterprise⟩ **syn** see MIND — **on the brain :** constantly in mind (as if obsessed) — usu. used with *have* ⟨he had tax reform *on the brain*⟩

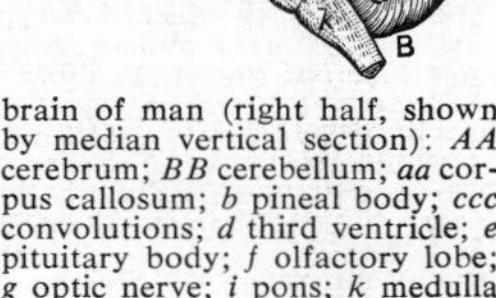

brain of man (right half, shown by median vertical section): *AA* cerebrum; *BB* cerebellum; *aa* corpus callosum; *b* pineal body; *ccc* convolutions; *d* third ventricle; *e* pituitary body; *f* olfactory lobe; *g* optic nerve; *i* pons; *k* medulla oblongata

²**brain** \"\ *adj* [ME, fr. ¹*brain*] *archaic Scot* **:** MAD, FURIOUS

³**brain** \"\ *vt* -ED/-ING/-S [ME *brainen*, fr. ¹*brain*] **1 :** to kill by smashing in the skull ⟨a small flail loaded with lead to ~ the ... assassins —T.B.Macaulay⟩ **2 :** to bang on the head ⟨~ a person with a book⟩

braincap \'⸗,⸗\ *n* **:** the upper part of the skull

braincase \'⸗,⸗\ *n* **:** the bony or cartilaginous case enclosing the brain — compare CRANIUM

brainchild \'⸗,⸗\ *n* **:** a product of one's creative imagination (as an idea or a work of art) ⟨the festival is the ~ of ... a Boston magazine publisher —C.M.Barss⟩

brain coral *n* **:** a massive reef-building coral having the surface covered by ridges and furrows — compare MAEANDRA

brained \;brānd\ *adj* [ME *branyd* having a brain, fr. *bran*, *brain* brain + *-yd*, *-ed* -ed] **:** having a brain of a specified character ⟨bigger ~ than other animal species —Weston La Barre⟩ — usu. used in combination ⟨muddle*brained*⟩

brain fag *n* **:** mental fatigue

brain fever *n* **:** an inflammation of the brain or its coverings; *specif* **:** EQUINE ENCEPHALOMYELITIS

brain–fever bird *n* [fr. the resemblance of its cry to the words *brain fever*] **:** an Indian hawk cuckoo (*Cuculus varius*) having a loud, shrill, repetitive cry; *also* **:** any of several related birds with monotonous cries

brainge \'brānj\ *var of* BREENGE

brainier *comparative of* BRAINY

brainiest *superlative of* BRAINY

brain·i·ness \'brānēnəs, -nin-\ *n* -ES **:** the quality or state of being brainy

brain·ish \-ānish\ *adj* [¹*brain* + *-ish*] **1** *chiefly Scot* **:** HOTHEADED **:** IMPETUOUS **2** *chiefly Scot* **:** mentally unstable **:** DELIRIOUS

brain·less \-nləs\ *adj* [ME, fr. ¹*brain* + *-less*] **1 :** devoid of intellect or intelligence **:** FOOLISH, STUPID ⟨men acting like ~ animals⟩ ⟨the ~ drivers on the highways⟩ **2 :** not demanding understanding or intelligence **:** DULL, STUPEFYING ⟨a ~ task⟩

brainpan \'⸗,⸗\ *n* [ME, fr. ¹*brain* + *pan*] **:** BRAINCASE

brainpower \'⸗,⸗\ *n* **1 a :** intellectual or mental capability ⟨although he was not efficient there were few in his group that had comparable ~⟩ **b :** superior or marked mental ability **:** superior intelligence ⟨~ is no good locked tight behind a handsome brow —*Think*⟩ **2 :** people with developed intellectual or mental ability ⟨mobilizing its ~ for technological warfare⟩

brains *pl of* BRAIN, *pres 3d sing of* BRAIN

brain sand *n* **:** small grains of calcareous matter in the brain (as in the pineal gland and pacchionian bodies) esp. associated with aging

brainsick \'⸗,⸗\ *adj* **1 :** mentally disordered **:** MAD ⟨a ~ criminal⟩ **2 :** arising from mental disorder ⟨~ frenzy⟩ — **brain·sick·ly** *adv*

brainstem \'⸗,⸗\ *n* **:** the axial part of the brain consisting of all except the cerebellum and cerebral cortex and the white matter immediately connected with them and including the motor and sensory tracts and the nuclei of the cranial nerves **:** SEGMENTAL APPARATUS

brainstone \'⸗,⸗\ *or* **brainstone coral** *n* **:** BRAIN CORAL

¹**brainstorm** \'⸗,⸗\ *n* [*brain* + *storm*] **1 :** a violent transient mental derangement **2 :** a sudden inspiration or bright idea **3 :** a harebrained idea **:** a wild or impractical flash of inspiration

²**brainstorm** \"\ *vi* **:** to practice a conference technique by which a group attempts to find a solution for a specific problem by amassing all the ideas spontaneously contributed by its members

brains trust *n, Brit* **:** BRAIN TRUST; *esp* **:** a panel of experts on a radio program

brainteaser \'⸗,⸗⸗\ *n* **:** something demanding mental effort and acuity for its solution **:** PUZZLE

brain trust *n* **:** expert advisers esp. concerned with planning and strategy and often without official or acknowledged status ⟨a Communist *brain trust* convened ... to map plans for keeping the strikes from petering out —*Springfield (Mass.) Union*⟩

brain truster *n* **:** a member of a brain trust **:** an unofficial adviser

brain twister *n* **:** BRAINTEASER

brain vesicle *n* **:** CEREBRAL VESICLE

1brainwash \ˈ⸗,⸗\ *vt* [back-formation fr. *brainwashing*] **1 :** to subject (a person) to brainwashing ⟨denied a previous confession . . . saying that he had been ~*ed* —*Front Page Detective*⟩ ⟨told how he had been *brainwashed* for 527 days in jail —Ed Sullivan⟩ **2 :** to persuade by propaganda ⟨~ the voters⟩

2brainwash \ˈ"\ *n* **1 :** the act of brainwashing ⟨the moral savagery of the ~ —D.H.Gillis⟩ **2 :** an instance of brainwashing ⟨his ~ in prison⟩

brainwashing *n* -s [trans. of Chin *hsi³ nao³*, fr. *hsi³* wash + *nao³* brain] **:** the forcible application of prolonged and intensive indoctrination sometimes including mental torture in an attempt to induce someone to give up basic political, social, or religious beliefs and attitudes and to accept contrasting regimented ideas ⟨life in a highly evolved bureaucratic state where thought control and ~ have dissolved all individual freedom —Laurent LeSage⟩ ⟨~ — the conquest not of a man's body but of his mind and spirit —Gladwin Hill⟩ — compare MENTICIDE

brainwater \ˈ⸗,⸗⸗\ *n* **:** HEARTWATER

brain wave *n* **1 :** rhythmic fluctuations of voltage between parts of the brain resulting in the flow of an electric current; *also* **:** the current produced usu. having a pulsation frequency of 10 or more per second **2 :** a flash of inspiration

brainwood \ˈ⸗,⸗\ *adj* [ME *brainwode*, fr. ¹*brain* + *wode* mad — more at WOOD] *Scot* **:** FRENZIED

brainwork \ˈ⸗,⸗\ *n* **:** deliberate, purposeful, or disciplined mental activity **:** THOUGHT ⟨that fundamental ~ without which no philosopher can get very far —*Times Lit. Supp.*⟩ — **brainworker** *n*

brainy \ˈbrānē, -ni\ *adj* -ER/-EST **1 :** having brains **:** endowed with mental cleverness **:** intellectually active and well developed **:** INTELLIGENT ⟨many men dislike ~ women⟩ **2 :** arising from or showing an alert mentality **:** INGENIOUS ⟨a really ~ suggestion⟩

1braird \ˈbra(a)(ə)rd, -a(a)əd\ *n* -s [ME *breirde*, prob. fr. OE *brerd* edge, rim; akin to OE *brord* point, OHG *brort* point, margin, ON *broddr* point, MIr *brot* goad, OSlav *brŭzda* bridle] *Brit* **:** the first shoots or sprouts (of grass or grain) to appear above the ground

2braird \ˈ"\ *vi* -ED/-ING/-S [ME *breirden*, fr. *breirde*, n.] *Brit* **:** to sprout or spring up from the ground **:** GERMINATE

brai·reau *or* **brai·ro** \ˈbre(,)rō\ *n* -s [modif. of CanF *blaireau*, fr. F, European badger, fr. MF *blarel, blareau*, fr. *bler* spotted, of Celt origin; akin to MW *blawr* gray, ScGael *blar* having a white spot; akin to OHG *blāo* blue — more at BLUE] **:** the badger of No. America

1braise *also* **braize** \ˈbrāz\ *vt* -ED/-ING/-S [F *braiser*, fr. *braise* live coals, fr. OF *brese* — more at BRAZE] **:** to cook (meat or vegetables) slowly in fat and little moisture in a tightly closed pot

2braise *also* **braize** \ˈ"\ *n* -s **:** an item of braised food ⟨squab ~⟩

3braise *or* **braize** \ˈ"\ *n* -s [prob. fr. MLG *brassen, bressem* bream — more at BREAM] **:** a European sea bream (*Pagrus pagrus*)

braj bha·sha \bräjˈbäshə\ *n, usu cap both Bs* [Hindi *braj-bhāṣā*, fr. *Braj*, region round Agra + Skt *bhāṣā* language, fr. *bhāṣate* he takes — more at BELLOW] **:** a dialect of Western Hindi noted for its poetic literature

1brak *Scot past of* BREAK

2brak *var of* BRACK

1brake *archaic past of* BREAK

2brake \ˈbrāk\ *or* **brake fern** *n* -s [ME, fern, prob. of Scand origin; akin to OSw *brækne* fern — more at BRACKEN] **1 :** a fern of the genus *Pteridium* (as *P. aquilinum*) having ternately compound fronds and roots, often growing several feet high, and used for making a beverage, for thatching, and for tanning **2 :** a fern of the genus *Pteris*

3brake \ˈ"\ *vt* -ED/-ING/-S [ME *braken*, fr. MD or MLG, to break flax, to break on the wheel; akin to MD *breken* to break, OE *brecan* — more at BREAK] **:** to break (flax or hemp) with a brake

4brake \ˈ"\ *n* -s [ME, fr. MLG; akin to OE *brecan* to break] **1 :** a toothed instrument or machine for separating out the fiber of flax or hemp by breaking up the woody parts **2 :** a tool resembling scissors used by basket makers to peel the bark from willow stems **3** *dial* **:** a large heavy harrow **:** DRAG **4 :** a baker's kneading machine **5 :** a machine for bending, flanging, folding, and forming sheet metal — called also *cornice brake*

5brake \ˈ"\ *n* -s [ME] **1** *obs* **:** a bridle with a powerful bit **2 :** the handle of a pump; *esp* **:** one long enough so that a number of men can unite in working the pump **3 a** *also* **break** \ˈ"\ (1) **:** a device (as a block or band applied to the rim of a wheel) to arrest the motion of a vehicle, a machine, or other mechanism and usu. employing some form of friction — often used in pl. ⟨to apply the ~s⟩; see AIR BRAKE, EMERGENCY BRAKE, FRICTION BRAKE, HYDRAULIC BRAKE, MAGNETIC BRAKE, SERVICE BRAKE, VACUUM BRAKE (2) **:** something designed or used to slow down or stop movement, momentum, or activity ⟨the interest rate acting as a ~ on expenditures⟩ ⟨the government has applied the ~s on . . . horse players and other gamblers —Harry Levine⟩ **b :** the end man of a bobsled team who operates the brake

6brake \ˈ"\ *vb* -ED/-ING/-S *vt* **:** to retard or stop by or as if by a brake ⟨~ a car⟩ ⟨impulses being *braked* by inhibition —Fredric Wertham⟩ ~ *vi* **1 :** to operate or manage a brake or brakes: as **a :** to act as a brakeman ⟨retired after 40 years of *braking*⟩ **b :** to manage a winding or hoisting engine for a mine **2 a :** to become checked by a brake ⟨the car *braked* to a stop⟩ **b :** to apply a brake **:** slow up by applying the brake ⟨the driver *braked* around curves⟩

7brake \ˈ"\ *n* -s [ME *-brake*, prob. fr. MLG *brake;* akin to MLG *breken* to break, OE *brecan* — more at BREAK] **:** rough, broken, or marshy land thickly overgrown usu. with one kind of plant ⟨cedar ~s⟩ ⟨the thick coastal ~s of the Olympia peninsula⟩ — see CANEBRAKE

8brake \ˈ"\ *n* -s [origin unknown] **1** *obs* **:** CAGE, TRAP, SNARE **2 :** an ancient instrument of torture **:** RACK

9brake *var of* ³BREAK

brake band *n* **:** the flexible band of a band brake

brake beam *also* **brake bar** *n* **:** a horizontal beam or rod on a wagon or railroad car that operates the brake shoes

brake block *n* **1 :** a device for checking by friction the speed of a rope (as in a hoist) **2 :** the part of a brake that holds the shoe

brake club *n* **:** a stout stick used to increase leverage in setting hand brakes on a railroad car

brake cylinder *n* **:** the cylinder in which the piston of an air or hydraulic brake operates

brake drum *n* **:** a revolving cylinder on the wheel of a vehicle or the revolving part of an engine or machine upon which the brake shoe or brake band presses — see HYDRAULIC BRAKE illustration

brake fluid *n* **:** the liquid used in a hydraulic brake cylinder

brake hanger *n* **:** one of the bars or links suspending a brake beam

brake horsepower *n* **:** the power of an engine or other motor as calculated from the force exerted on a friction brake or absorption dynamometer applied to the flywheel or the shaft

brake hose *n* **:** a flexible tube connecting the brake pipes of adjoining vehicles (as railroad cars)

brake·less *adj* **:** being without a brake

brake lining *n* **:** the facing of brake bands esp. on automobiles; *also* **:** the fabric used for such lining

brakeload \ˈ⸗,⸗\ *n* **:** the test load imposed on a prime mover by the brake

brake·man \ˈbrākmən\ *n, pl* **brakemen 1 a** (1) **:** a member of a train crew whose duties include operating hand brakes and track switches, inspecting the train for mechanical deficiencies, watching for signals from the engineer and fireman, and on passenger trains assisting the conductor (2) **:** a worker who rides on trains of mine cars to assist in their operation by motor or cable haulage system — called also *dukey rider, nipper* **b :** ⁵BRAKE 3b **c :** one that inspects, adjusts, and repairs air brakes or hydraulic brakes **2 :** an operator of a power brake for making bends in sheet metal

brake meter *n* **:** a device to measure the decelerating effect of vehicle brakes

brak·en \ˈbrakən\ *dial Brit var of* BRACKEN

brake parachute *n* **:** a deceleration parachute

brake pipe *n* **:** the main pipe of a pressure brake system extending the entire length of the train and connecting the manual and the automatic actuating devices on individual vehicles — called also *train line;* see AIR BRAKE

brak·er \ˈbrākə(r)\ *n* -s [⁴*brake* (kneading machine) + *-er*] **:** a worker who rolls dough for baked goods or macaroni products in a brake — called also *rollerman*

brakes *pl of* BRAKE, *pres 3d sing of* BRAKE

brakes·man \ˈbräksmən\ *n, pl* **brakesmen** *chiefly Brit* **:** BRAKEMAN

brake van *n, Brit* **:** a railway car or compartment containing means for operating the brakes

brak·ie *or* **brak·ey** \ˈbrākē, -ki\ *n* -s [by shortening & alter.] *slang* **:** BRAKEMAN 1

braking *pres part of* BRAKE

braky \ˈbrākē, -ki\ *adj* -ER/-EST [⁷*brake* + *-y*] **:** full of brakes **:** abounding with brambles, shrubs, or ferns ⟨in the woods and ~ glens —William Browne⟩

bramah *var of* BRAHMA

bram·ah lock \ˈbramə-, -ämə-,-āmə-\ *n, usu cap B* [after Joseph *Bramah* †1814 Eng. engineer, its inventor] **:** a lock in which the tumblers are thin flat notched bars receiving endwise movement from the key instead of the swinging movement of the tumblers of an ordinary lock

bramah press *n, usu cap B* [after J.*Bramah*] **:** HYDRAULIC PRESS

bra·man·tesque \ˌbrä,mänˈtesk, -ˌmən-; brəˌmän-\ *adj, usu cap* [It *bramantesco*, fr. Donato d'Agnolo *Bramante* †1514 Ital. architect + It *-esco* -esque] **:** of or relating to a Renaissance style of architecture marked by classical forms

bra·ma·pi·the·cus \ˌbrämәpəˈthēkəs, -ˈpithəkəs\ *n, cap* [NL, irreg. fr. *Brahma*, first member of the Hindu trinity + NL *-pithecus*] **:** a genus of Lower Pliocene dryopithecine apes from the Siwalik hills of India — compare DRYOPITHECINAE

1bram·ble \ˈbrambəl, -raam-\ *n* -s [ME *brembel*, fr. OE *brēmel, brǣmel, brēmbel;* akin to OE *brōm* broom — more at BROOM] **1 :** a plant of the genus *Rubus* or its fruit; *esp, Brit* **:** the blackberry bush or its fruit **2 :** a rough prickly shrub or vine

2bramble \ˈ"\ *n* -s **:** TURNOVER

bram·ble·ber·ry \ˈ⸗—*see* BERRY\ *n, chiefly Brit* **:** BRAMBLE 1

bramblebush \ˈ⸗,⸗\ *n* **1 :** BRAMBLE 1 **2 :** a thicket of brambles

bramble finch *n* **:** BRAMBLING

bramble leafhopper *n* **:** a European leafhopper (*Ribautiana tenerrima*) now established on the Pacific coast of No. America where it is very destructive to loganberries and raspberries

bramble rose *n* **:** DOG ROSE

bramble shark *n* **:** a brownish or purplish shark (*Echinorhinus brucus*) that has hard spiny tubercles scattered on the skin and is nearly cosmopolitan in warm seas though rarely numerous

bramble worm *n* [by folk etymology fr. *brandling worm*] **:** BRANDLING

bram·bling \ˈbram(b)liŋ, -lən\ *n* -s [prob. fr. *bramble* + *-ing*] **:** a brightly colored finch (*Fringilla montifringilla*) that breeds in the northern parts of Europe and Asia and migrates southward in winter and is often kept as a cage bird — called also *bramble finch*

bram·bly \ˈbramblē, -raam-, -li\ *adj* -ER/-EST **:** like or full of brambles

brame *n* -s [It *brama*, fr. *bramare* to desire ardently, prob. fr. a Gmc word meaning "to roar, bellow" (whence It dial. *bramè* to bellow); akin to OHG *bremen* to buzz, rumble, roar — more at FREMITUS] *obs* **:** PASSION, DESIRE, LONGING

bram·i·dae \ˈbramə,dē\ *n pl, cap* [NL, fr. *Brama*, type genus + *-idae*] **:** a widely distributed family of deep-bodied percoid fishes frequenting open seas — compare POMFRET

bramp·ton stock \ˈbra|m(p)tən-\ *or* **bromp·ton stock** \ˈbrä|\ *n, usu cap B* [fr. *Brompton*, suburb of London, England] **:** any of various biennial garden stocks derived from the common stock (*Matthiola incana*) and grown chiefly for early spring bloom — compare TEN-WEEK STOCK

1bran \ˈbran, -aa(ə)n\ *n* -s [ME *bran, bren*, fr. OF] **1 a :** the broken coat of the seed of wheat, rye, or other cereal grain separated from the kernel and used esp. for animal feed **b :** a coarsely ground stock feed obtained as a by-product in food canning ⟨pineapple ~⟩ ⟨shrimp ~⟩ **2** *obs* **:** SORT, CLASS **3 :** a light brown to yellowish brown that is lighter than aloma and less strong than pablo

2bran \ˈ"\ *vt* **branned; branned; branning; brans 1 :** to boil in bran drench **2 :** to cleanse (tinned plate) of oil esp. with bran

bran bug *n* **:** CONFUSED FLOUR BEETLE

bran·car·dier \brä"kärdyā\ *n, pl* **brancardiers** \ˈ"\ [F, fr. *brancard* stretcher, fr. MF, fr. MF dial. (Normandy), large branch, aug. of *branque* branch, fr. LL *branca*] **:** STRETCHER BEARER

1branch \ˈbranch, -aa(ə)-,-ai-,-ȧ-\ *n* -ES *often attrib* [ME

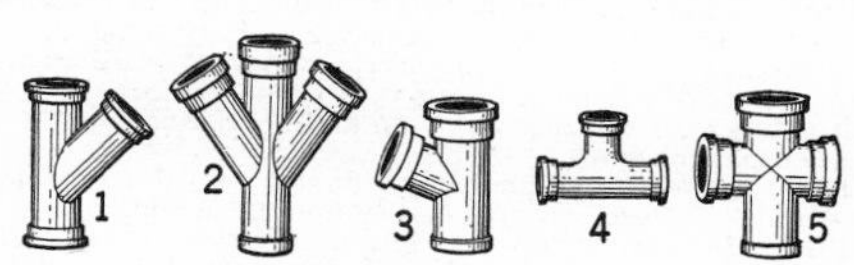

branch 2c(4): *1* Y branch, *2* double Y branch, *3* Y branch, *4* tee, *5* double tee

braunche, fr. OF *branche*, fr. LL *branca* paw] **1 :** a stem growing from the trunk or from a limb of a tree; *specif* **:** a shoot or secondary stem growing from the main stem **2 :** something that extends from, enters into, or is an offshoot of a main body or source: as **a** (1) **:** a stream that flows into another usu. larger stream **:** AFFLUENT, TRIBUTARY (2) *South and Midland* **:** CREEK 2 (3) **:** an effluent stream ⟨a delta ~⟩ (4) **:** a reentrant stream **:** BY-CHANNEL, ANABRANCH (5) **:** a fork of a tidal river (as of the Severn river in Maryland) **b :** a side road or way ⟨a logging railroad whose ~es spread through thousands of square miles —*Amer. Guide Series: Minn.*⟩ **c** (1) **:** a slender projection (as the tine of an antler or arm of a candelabrum) (2) **:** a rib in Gothic vaulting; *esp* **:** one of the smaller ribs in a complicated vault (3) **:** either side of a horseshoe (4) **:** a pipe joined to and diverging from the barrel of another pipe; *also* **:** a forked pipe connection **d** *archaic* **:** SCION, DESCENDANT **e** (1) *math* **:** one of the portions of a curve (as a hyperbola) (2) **:** either of the two partial series of lines in a spectral band that proceed in opposite directions from the zero line of the band **3 :** a part of a complex body: as **a :** a division of a family descending from a particular ancestor as distinguished from those descending from his relations ⟨the Connecticut ~ of an old Boston family⟩ **b :** an area of knowledge that may be considered or studied apart from related areas ⟨pathology is a ~ of medicine⟩ **c** (1) **:** a section, department, or division of an organization ⟨a ~ of the armed service⟩ ⟨the two ~*es* of Congress⟩ (2) **:** a subordinate or dependent part of a central system or organization ⟨a neighborhood ~ of a city library⟩ ⟨a ~ bank in a suburb⟩ **d** (1) **:** a primary division of the animal kingdom — see PHYLUM (2) *in the classification of languages of the eastern hemisphere* **:** a number of related languages forming a category less inclusive than a family or subfamily ⟨the Germanic ~ of the Indo-European language family⟩ **4 :** a warrant or commission given to a pilot authorizing him to pilot ships in certain waters ⟨a ~ pilot⟩

2branch \ˈ"\ *vb* -ED/-ING/-ES [ME *braunchen*, fr. *braunche*, n.] *vi* **1 :** to put or hold forth branches **:** RAMIFY ⟨a great elm ~*ing* over the roof⟩ **2 :** to spring off or out (as from a main stem or root) **:** DIVERGE ⟨streets ~*ing* from either side of the highway⟩ — often used with *off* ⟨his mind kept ~*ing off* into the contemplation of silly things —Liam O'Flaherty⟩ **3 :** to become derived **:** be an outgrowth — used with *from* ⟨poetry that ~*ed* from Baudelaire —Douglas Stewart⟩ **4 :** to extend activities **:** enlarge or develop by taking up something different or by adding on something new — usu. used with *out* ⟨car manufacturers ~*ed out* into tank and cannon manufacture⟩ ~ *vt* **1 :** to ornament with designs of branches or foliage ⟨~ velvet⟩ **2 :** to divide up **:** ARRANGE, SECTION ⟨~*ing* his treatment of the problem into three equal parts⟩

syn RAMIFY, DIVARICATE, FORK, FURCATE, BIFURCATE: BRANCH (often used with *off, from, out*) is applicable to any developing or projecting comparable to the sending out of a branch by a tree or to a split growth comparable to the main fork of a tree trunk ⟨roads *branching* off the main highways⟩ ⟨little streams *branching* from the river⟩ ⟨*branching* out from building houses to selling real estate⟩ ⟨the river *branches* to form the various delta channels⟩ RAMIFY may suggest an intricate dividing or subdividing, sometimes to the extent of interconnecting, permeating, or affecting a whole area ⟨the system of arteries and veins *ramifying* over the whole body⟩ ⟨an inquiry into the nature of the genres and the boundaries of the arts *ramifies* out in every direction —Irving Babbitt⟩ ⟨a *ramifying* network of social relations, with every chance that its force may be multiplied or deflected in the devious process of transmission —Max Lerner & Edwin Mims⟩ DIVARICATE is a technical term indicating splitting into two main branches ⟨elm tree trunks often *divaricate*⟩ FORK indicates a splitting or development at a specific point into what may be likened to tines or branches ⟨the river *forks* forming an island⟩ ⟨the main road *forks* into two smaller roads⟩ FURCATE, now uncommon, and BIFURCATE, explicitly indicating a division into two, are more learned synonyms for FORK ⟨though Islam *bifurcated* into the sects of the Sunnis and the Shi'is as the Christian Church *bifurcated* into the Catholic and Orthodox Churches —A.J. Toynbee⟩ ⟨the inevitable moment when the channel *bifurcated* and a choice had to be made —C.S.Forester⟩

-branch \ˌbraŋk, -aŋ\ *n comb form* -s [NL *-branchia* ones having (such or so many) gills & *-branchus* one having (such or so many) gills, fr. Gk *branchos* gill, irreg. fr. Gk *branchia* gills] **1 :** one having (such or so many) gills ⟨cryptobranch⟩ ⟨dibranch⟩ **2 :** gill ⟨arthrobranch⟩ **:** organ like a gill ⟨actinobranch⟩

branch bar *n* **:** a copper strap that connects a main bus bar with a branch circuit in a wiring system

branch bud *n* **:** LEAF BUD

branch circuit *n* **:** the part of an electric wiring system that extends from any set of outlets as far back as the fuse box, supplying and protecting them

branch-climber \ˈ⸗,⸗⸗\ *n* **:** a tropical or subtropical woody vine supported in climbing by curling branches rather than tendrils

branched chain *n* **:** an open chain of atoms having one or more side chains (as in isobutane $\frac{CH_3}{CH_3}\!>\!CH-CH_3$) — opposed to *straight chain*

bran·chel·lion \braŋˈkelyən\ *n, cap* [NL, alter. of *Branchiobdellion*, fr. *branchi-* + Gk *bdella* leech + *-ion* (dim. suffix)] **:** a genus of leeches with external gills along the sides of the body that are parasitic on fishes

1branch·er \ˈbranchə(r), -aa-,-ai-,-ȧ-\ *n* -s [ME *brauncher*, fr. *braunche* branch + *-er*] **:** a young bird (as a fledgling hawk) that has left the nest and taken to the branches

2brancher \ˈ"\ *n* -s [²*branch* + *-er*] **:** one that makes artificial flowers or feather designs

branches *pl of* BRANCH, *pres 3d sing of* BRANCH

branch gap *n* **:** a gap that surrounds a branch trace

branch grass *n* **:** CREEK SEDGE

branch herring *n* **:** ALEWIFE 1a

branchi- *or* **branchio-** *comb form* [NL *branchio-*, fr. Gk, fr. *branchia*] **1 :** gills ⟨*branchi*ferous⟩ ⟨*branchio*genous⟩ **2 :** branchial and ⟨*branchio*cardiac⟩

bran·chia \ˈbraŋkēə, -aiŋ-\ *n, pl* **branchi·ae** \-ē,ē\ [L *branchia* (sing.) gill, fr. Gk *branchia* gills, pl. of *branchion* gill; akin to Gk *bronchos* trachea — more at CRAW] **:** ³GILL

1-branchia \ˈ"\ *n pl comb form* [NL, fr. L *branchia*] **:** ones having (such or so many) gills — in taxonomic names in zoology ⟨Crypto*branchia*⟩ ⟨Tetra*branchia*⟩

2-branchia \ˈ"\ *n comb form, pl* **-branchi·ae** \-ē,ē\ [NL, fr. L *branchia*] **:** gill ⟨podo*branchia*⟩ **:** organ like a gill ⟨pulmo*branchia*⟩

bran·chi·al \ˈbraŋkēəl, -aiŋ-\ *adj* [*branchi-* + *-al*] **:** of or relating to the gills or to parts of the body derived from the embryonic branchial arches and clefts

branchial arch *n* **:** one of the bony or cartilaginous arches or curved bars extending dorsoventrally and placed one behind the other posterior to the hyoid arch on each side of the pharynx and supporting the gills of fishes and amphibians; *also* **:** a corresponding rudimentary ridge in the embryo of all higher vertebrates

branchial basket *n* **:** the cartilaginous structure supporting the gills in protochordates and lower vertebrates (as ascidians, amphioxi, and cyclostomes)

branchial cleft *n* **:** one of the openings or clefts between the branchial arches in vertebrates that breathe by gills through which water taken in at the mouth passes to the exterior bathing the gills; *also* **:** a rudimentary groove in the neck region of the embryos of air-breathing vertebrates

branchial heart *n* **:** a muscular enlargement of a vein of a cephalopod that contracts and drives the blood into the gills

branchial plume *n* **:** an accessory respiratory organ extending out under the mantle in some gastropods

branchial pouch *n* **:** one of the respiratory cavities in the branchial clefts of cyclostomes and some sharks

branchial sac *n* **:** the dilated pharyngeal part of the alimentary canal in tunicates that has vascular walls pierced with clefts and functions as a gill

bran·chi·a·ta \ˌbraŋkēˈādə, -ädə\ *n pl, cap* [NL, fr. *branchi-* + *-ata*] **:** any of several groups of animals having gills: as **a :** the Crustacea as distinguished from the tracheate arthropods **b :** amphibians and fishes as distinguished from the higher vertebrates

bran·chi·ate \ˈbraŋkēə, -ē,āt\ *adj* [*branchi-* + *-ate*] **:** furnished with gills

bran·chic·o·lous \(ˈ)braŋˈkikələs\ *adj* [*branchi-* + *-colous*] **:** parasitic on gills — used of certain trematode worms

1branchier *comparative of* BRANCHY

2bran·chier \brä"shyā\ *n, pl* **branchiers** \-ā(z)\ [LaF, fr. F *branche* branch, fr. OF — more at BRANCH] **:** WOOD DUCK 1

branchiest *superlative of* BRANCHY

bran·chif·er·ous \(ˈ)braŋˈkif(ə)rəs\ *adj* [ISV *branchi-* + *-ferous*] **:** BRANCHIATE

1bran·chi·hy·al \ˌbraŋkēˈhīəl\ *adj* [*branchi-* + *-hyoid* + *-al*] **:** of or relating to the elements or segments composing the branchial arches

2branchihyal \ˈ"\ *n* -s **:** an element or segment of a branchial arch

branching *n* -s [ME *braunching*, fr. gerund of *braunchen* to branch — more at BRANCH] **:** the process of forming a branch — see FALSE BRANCHING, TRUE BRANCHING

branching foxtail *n* **:** WINDMILL GRASS

bran·chi·ob·del·la \ˌbraŋkē,äbˈdelə, -ēəb-\ *n, cap* [NL, fr. *branchi-* + Gk *bdella* leech] **:** a genus (the type of the family Branchiobdellidae) of small annelid worms that live on the gills and surface of crayfishes, have the posterior end modified into an adhesive sucker, and are now usu. considered to form with a few related forms a superfamily of Oligochaeta though formerly regarded as modified leeches

1bran·chi·ob·del·lid \ˌ⸗⸗(,)⸗ˈ⸗ləd\ *adj* [NL *Branchiobdellidae* family of worms, fr. *Branchiobdella*, type genus + *-idae*] **:** of or relating to the genus *Branchiobdella* or family Branchiobdellidae

2branchiobdellid \ˈ"\ *n* -s **:** a worm of the genus *Branchiobdella*

bran·chio·cardiac \ˌbraŋkē(,)ō+\ *adj* [*branchi-* + *cardiac*] **:** of or relating to the gills and heart

bran·chio·cranium \ˈ"+\ *n* [NL, fr. *branchi-* + *cranium*] **:** one of two main divisions of the fish skull constituting the mandibular and hyal regions and the branchial arches — compare NEUROCRANIUM

bran·chi·og·e·nous \ˌbraŋkēˈäjənəs\ *adj* [*branchi-* + *-genous*] **:** arising from or formed by the branchial clefts or arches

bran·chi·o·mere \ˈbraŋkēə,mi(ə)r\ *n* -s [*branchi-* + *-mere*] **:** a branchial segment; *esp* **:** one of the metameres indicated by the visceral arches and clefts of the embryo of airbreathing vertebrates — **bran·chi·o·mer·ic** \ˌbraŋkēəˈmerik\ *adj* — **bran·chi·om·er·ism** \ˌbraŋkēˈämə,rizəm\ *n* -s

bran·chio·pallial \ˌbraŋkē(,)ō+\ *adj* [*branchi-* + *pallial*] **:** of or relating to the gill and mantle of mollusks

bran·chi·op·neus·tic \ˌbraŋkēˌäp¦n(y)üstik,-ēəp-\ *adj* [*branchi-* + Gk *pneustos* having (such) breath + E *-ic* — more at -PNEUSTA] **:** having the spiracles replaced by gills — used of certain immature aquatic insects

¹bran·chi·o·pod \ˈbraŋkēəˌpäd\ *or* **bran·chi·op·o·dan** \ˌbraŋkēˈäpədən\ *or* **bran·chi·op·o·dous** \¦==¦==dəs\ *adj* [*branchiopod* fr. NL *Branchiopoda; branchiopodan, branchiopodous* fr. NL *Branchiopoda* + E *-an* or *-ous*] **:** of or relating to the Branchiopoda

²branchiopod \"\ *or* **branchiopodan** \"\ *n* -s **:** a crustacean of the subclass Branchiopoda or order Branchiopoda

bran·chi·op·o·da \ˌbraŋkēˈäpədə\ *n pl, cap* [NL, fr. *branchi-* + *-poda*] **1 :** a subclass of crustacea comprising primitive aquatic forms typically having an elongated body, a carapace, and many pairs of foliaceous appendages and including the orders Anostraca, Notostraca, Conchostraca, and Cladocera **2** *in some esp former classifications* **a :** an order of Entomostraca including the Cladocera **b :** an order of Phyllopoda excluding the Cladocera **c :** PHYLLOPODA b

bran·chi·o·saur \ˈbraŋkēəˌsȯ(ə)r\ *n* -s [NL *Branchiosaurus*] **:** an amphibian or fossil of Branchiosaurus

bran·chi·o·sau·rus \ˌbraŋkēəˈsȯrəs\ *n, cap* [NL, fr. *branchi-* + *-saurus*] **:** a group of small fossil amphibians like salamanders from the Permian of Europe formerly regarded as constituting a separate order or suborder but now usu. held to be larvae of typical rhachitomous labyrinthodont amphibians — used orig. as a generic name and still commonly as though it were a generic name

¹bran·chi·os·te·gal \ˌbraŋkē¦ästəgəl\ *adj* [ISV *branchi-* + *steg-* + *-al*] **:** of or relating to the branchiostegals ⟨the ~ membrane⟩

²branchiostegal \"\ *or* **branchiostegal ray** *n* -s **:** one of the bony radiating processes of the hyoid arch that support the membranes enclosing the gill chamber in most fishes

bran·chi·o·steg·i·dae \ˌbraŋkēōˈstejəˌdē\ *n pl, cap* [NL, fr. *Branchiostegus*, type genus (fr. *branchi-* + *-stegus*, fr. Gk *stegē* roof, cover) + *-idae* — more at THATCH] **:** a small family of marine percoid fishes (as the branquillos) having an elongate body, long dorsal and anal fins, and thoracic or subjugular ventral fins

bran·chi·os·te·gite \ˌbraŋkēˈästəˌjīt\ *n* -s [*branchi-* + *steg-* + *-ite*] **:** the extended pleural part of the carapace forming one wall of the gill chamber in crustaceans

bran·chi·os·te·gous \ˌbraŋkē¦ästəgəs\ *adj* [prob. fr. F *branchiostège* + E *-ous*] **1 :** BRANCHIOSTEGAL **2 :** having the gills covered

bran·chi·os·to·ma \ˌbraŋkēˈästəmə\ *n, cap* [NL, fr. *branchi-* + *-stoma*] **:** the type genus of Branchiostomidae comprising lancelets with paired gonads and symmetrical metapleura — see AMPHIOXUS

¹bran·chi·os·to·mid \ˌbraŋkē¦ästəməd\ *adj* [NL *Branchiostomidae*] **:** of or relating to the family Branchiostomidae

²branchiostomid \"\ *n* -s **:** a typical lancelet **:** a member of the family Branchiostomidae

bran·chi·o·stom·i·dae \ˌbraŋkēōˈstäməˌdē\ *n pl, cap* [NL, fr. *Branchiostoma*, type genus + *-idae*] **:** the chief and typical family of Cephalochorda containing most of the known recent lancelets

bran·chi·pus \ˈbraŋkəpəs\ *n, cap* [NL, fr. *branchi-* + *-pus*] **:** a genus of European freshwater branchiopod crustaceans (order Anostraca) that resemble the brine shrimp — see EUBRANCHIPUS

bran·chi·reme \-əˌrēm\ *n* -s [*branchi-* + L *remus* oar — more at ROW] **:** a limb of a branchiopod used both for respiration and locomotion

bran·chi·ura \ˌbraŋkēˈ(y)u̇rə\ *n pl, cap* [NL, fr. *branchi-* + *-ura*] **:** an order of Copepoda comprising copepods that have suctorial mouthparts and are parasitic on fish — compare EUCOPEPODA — **bran·chi·uran** \¦==¦==rən\ *adj or n* — **bran·chi·urous** \-rəs\ *adj*

branch·less *adj* **:** being without a branch

branch·let \ˈbranchlət, -aan-,-ain-,-ȧn-\ *n* -s **:** a small branch or subdivision of a branch; *esp* **:** a terminal one

-branchs *pl of* -BRANCH

branch trace *n* **:** a trace supplying a branch — compare LEAF TRACE

branch water *n* **1 :** water from a small stream **2 :** plain water ⟨bourbon and *branch water*⟩

branchy \-chē,-chi\ *adj* -ER/-EST [ME *braunchy*, fr. *braunche* branch + *-y* — more at BRANCH] **:** covered or overgrown with branches ⟨a ~ tree trunk⟩

¹brand \ˈbrand, -aa(ə)-\ *n* -s [ME *brand, brond* brand, sword, fr. OE; akin to OHG *brant* brand, ON *brandr* brand, blade of a sword, OE *byrnan, bærnan* to burn — more at BURN] **1 a :** a piece of wood that has been or is burning (as one from a hearth or a burning building) **:** FIREBRAND **b :** something that resembles a burning piece of wood ⟨blinding ~*s* of lightning —P.B.Shelley⟩ **2 a :** a sword blade **b :** SWORD **3 a** (1) **:** a mark of a simple easily recognized pattern made by burning with a hot iron to attest manufacture or quality or to designate ownership (2) **:** a mark made with a stamp or stencil for similar purposes **:** TRADEMARK **b** (1) **:** a mark put on criminals with a hot iron (2) **:** a mark of disgrace **:** STIGMA ⟨a reputation bearing the ~ of criminal negligence⟩ **4 a** (1) **:** a class of goods identified as being the product of a single firm or manufacturer **:** MAKE ⟨stores selling well-known ~*s* of canned foods⟩ (2) **:** PRODUCER, MANUFACTURER ⟨a dozen ~*s* of textile goods competing on the open market⟩ **b :** a characteristic or distinctive kind **:** VARIETY ⟨their ~ of love was a tortured and fretful affection —Evelyn Eaton⟩ **5 :** a tool used to produce a brand (as on cattle, manufactured wares, wine casks) **:** BRANDING IRON **6 :** any rust fungus giving a burnt appearance typically to leaves

brands for cattle: *1* diamond X, *2* box X, *3* circle X, *4* bar X, *5* rocking X, *6* swinging X, *7* tumbling X, *8* walking X, *9* flying X, *10* crazy P, *11* lazy P, *12* reverse P

²brand \"\ *vt* -ED/-ING/-S [ME *branden, bronden* fr. *brand, brond*, n.] **1 :** to mark with a brand ⟨~ a criminal⟩ ⟨~ wine casks with the vineyard's name⟩; *esp* **:** to place the brand of ownership on (horses or cattle) **2 :** to mark, signal, or expose as being disgraceful or dishonest **:** STIGMATIZE ⟨refusal of such a demand ~*s* one as stingy —Margaret Mead⟩ **3 :** to impress indelibly ⟨history has once again ~*ed* this lesson on the minds of those who choose to see —T.O.Beachcroft⟩

brand·ed \ˈbrandəd, -n(d)ət\ *adj* [ME *brandit, brended* — more at BRINDED] *dial Brit* **:** BRINDLED

branded drum *n* [fr. past part. of ²*brand*] **:** CHANNEL BASS

bran·den·burg \ˈbrandənˌbərg\ *n* -s *usu cap* [modif. (influenced by *Brandenburg*) of F *brandebourg*, fr. *Brandenburg*, region of Prussia, Germany, 17th cent. soldiers of which wore such ornaments on their uniforms] **:** an ornamental braid trimming — usu. used in pl.

¹bran·der \ˈbran(d)ər\ *n* -s [ME *brandire, brandirne*, fr. *branden* to brand + *ire, irne* iron — more at BRAND, IRON] *chiefly Scot* **:** a ribbed open griddle **:** GRIDIRON

²bran·der \ˈbrandə(r), -raan-, *Scot* -an(d)ər\ *vb* **brandered; brandered; brandering** \-n(d)(ə)riŋ\ **branders** *vt* **1** *chiefly Scot* **:** to broil on a brander **2 :** to apply brandering to ~ *vi* **1** *chiefly Scot* **:** to broil meat **2 :** to apply brandering

³brand·er \ˈbrandə(r), -aan-\ *n* -s [²*brand* + *-er*] **:** one that brands; *esp* **:** one that affixes or stamps an identification on a product

bran·der·ing \ˈbrand(ə)riŋ, -aan-\ *n* -s [¹*brander* + *-ing*; fr. the gridironlike appearance of a wall of brandering] **:** furring strips or small blocks used to set plastering lath out from a beam or other solid surface

bran·died \ˈbrandēd, -aan-, -did\ *adj* **:** preserved in brandy ⟨~ peaches⟩

branding chute *n* **:** a narrow enclosed path down which cattle are driven for branding, spraying, or dehorning

branding iron *n* **:** an iron rod with a brand at one end

brand iron *n* [ME *brandire, brandirne* — more at BRANDER] **1** *now chiefly Scot* **:** ¹BRANDER 1 **2** *now chiefly Scot* **:** TRIVET

bran·dise \ˈbrandəs\ *n* -s [OE *brandīsen*, fr. *brand* burning + *īsen* iron — more at BRAND, IRON] *dial Eng* **:** TRIVET

bran disease *n* **:** a condition resembling rickets occurring in young horses fed excessively on bran and prob. resulting from an unbalanced calcium-phosphorus ratio — called also *bran poisoning*

¹bran·dish \ˈbrandish, -raan-, -dēsh\ *vb* -ED/-ING/-ES [ME *braundisshen*, fr. MF *brandiss-*, stem of *brandir*, fr. OF, fr. *brand* sword, of Gmc origin; akin to OHG *brant* brand — more at BRAND] *vt* **1 :** to shake or wave (a weapon) menacingly ⟨cursed him eloquently . . . and ~*ed* a pistol at him —H.H. Martin⟩ **2 :** to exhibit or expose in an ostentatious, shameless, or aggressive manner ⟨my cherry tree ~*ed* its sparkling blossoms —Adrian Bell⟩ ⟨has . . . not only demonstrated her intellect but ~*ed* it —James Hilton⟩ ~ *vi* **:** FLOURISH, WAVE ⟨swords ~*ed* and banners waved⟩ **syn** see SWING

²brandish \"\ *n* -ES **:** a flourish esp. with a weapon or whip

brand·less *adj* **:** being without a brand

brand·ling \ˈbran(d)liŋ, -lən\ *n* -s [¹*brand* + *-ling*] **1 :** a small yellowish earthworm (*Eisenia foetida*) with brownish purple rings found in dunghills and used as bait by anglers **2 :** a young salmon **:** PARR

brand-new *also* **bran-new** \ˈbran¦n(y)ü, -raan- *sometimes* -nd¦n-\ *adj* [*brand-new* fr. ¹*brand* + *new*; *bran-new*, alter. of *brand-new*] **:** fresh from the manufacturer **:** conspicuously new and unused ⟨thrust a hand into the . . . pocket and fetched out a *brand-new* pigskin wallet —Frances Crane⟩ ⟨an inventive fellow somewhere who would devise a *brand-new* approach —*New Yorker*⟩

bran·dreth *also* **bran·drith** \ˈbrandrəth\ *n* -s [ME, fr. ON *brandreith* grate, fr. *brandr* fire + *reith* wagon — more at BRAND, ROAD] **:** a wooden framework for support (as a stand for a hayrick)

brands *pl of* BRAND, *pres 3d sing of* BRAND

brand spore *n* **1 :** UREDIOSPORE **2 :** a smut chlamydospore

brandt·ite \ˈbrantˌīt\ *n* -s [Sw or G *brandtit*, fr. Georg *Brandt* †1768 Sw. chemist + Sw or G *-it* -ite] **:** a mineral $Ca_2Mn(AsO_4)_2.2H_2O$ consisting of a hydrous arsenate of calcium and manganese

brandt's cormorant \ˈbran(t)s-\ *n, usu cap B* [after J.F. Von *Brandt* †1879 Ger. zoologist] **:** a large chiefly greenish black cormorant (*Phalacrocorax penicillatus*) of the Pacific coast of No. America

bran duster *n* **:** a machine for separating grain or flour from bran

¹bran·dy \ˈbrandē, -raan-, -di\ *n* -ES [short for *brandywine*] **:** an alcoholic liquor distilled from wine or from the fermented juice of peaches, cherries, apples, or other fruit — compare ARMAGNAC, COGNAC, KIRSCH, QUETSCH, SLIVOVITZ

²brandy \"\ *vt* -ED/-ING/-ES **1 :** to flavor, blend, or treat with brandy **2 :** to provide or refresh with brandy

³brandy \"\ *n* -ES [by folk etymology] **:** BARANI

brandy-and-soda \¦===¦==\ *n* **:** a drink of brandy diluted with soda water

brandyball \'==,=\ *n, Brit* **:** a candy flavored with brandy

brandy-bottle \'==,==\ *n* [so called fr. the shape of the seed vessel] *dial Eng* **:** CANDOCK a

brandy mint *n* **:** PEPPERMINT 1a

brandy snap *n* **:** a gingersnap flavored with brandy

bran·dy·wine \'==ˌwīn\ *n* [earlier *brandwine*, fr. D *brandewijn* fr. MD *brantwijn*, fr. *brant* (past part. of *bernen* to burn, distill) + *wijn* wine; akin to OE *biernan* to burn and OE *win* wine — more at BURN, WINE] *obs* **:** BRANDY

brang *substand past of* BRING

bran·gle \ˈbraŋ(g)əl\ *vi* -ED/-ING/-S [blend of ¹*brawl* and *wrangle*] *now dial Brit* **:** SQUABBLE, WRANGLE

²brangle \"\ *n* -s *dial Brit* **:** SQUABBLE, SET-TO

¹brank \ˈbraŋk\ *vi* -ED/-ING/-S [ME *branken*] *dial Brit* **:** PRANCE, CAPER

²brank \"\ *n* -s [origin unknown] **1 a :** an instrument consisting of an iron frame surrounding the head and a sharp metal bit or gag entering the mouth formerly used to punish scolds — called also *scold's bridle*; usu. used in pl. **b branks** *pl, now chiefly Scot* **:** a bridle or halter for horses or cows **2 branks** *pl, Scot* **:** MUMPS

brank·ie *or* **branky** \-kē\ *adj* [¹*brank* + *-ie, -y*] *Scot* **:** GAUDY

brank·ur·sine \braŋˈkərsᵊn\ *n* -s [MF *branque-ursine*, fr. ML *branca ursina*, fr. LL *branca* claw + L *ursina*, fem. of *ursinus* of a bear; fr. the resemblance of the leaves to the claws of a bear — more at URSINE] **:** BEAR'S-BREECH

branle *also* **bransle** \ˈbrä(ä)ᵊl, ˈbrōᵊl\ *or* **brawl** \ˈbrȯl\ *n* -s [MF *branle, bransle*, lit., act of shaking, fr. *branler* to shake, swing, brandish, fr. OF, alter. of *brandir* to brandish — more at BRANDISH] **1 :** one of several couple dances of French origin that were popular in the 16th and 17th centuries, usu. in duple measure, mimetic, accompanied by singing, and danced in groups typically in a circle **2 :** a sideward balance step in a clockwise direction used in branle dances

bran mash *n* **:** a wet mash of bran and hot water

branned *past of* BRAN

bran·ner \ˈbranə(r), -raan-\ *n* -s [²*bran* + *-er*] **1 :** a machine that brans **2 :** the operator of a branning machine

bran·ner·ite \ˈbranəˌrīt\ *n* -s [John C. *Branner* †1922 Am. geologist + E *-ite*] **:** a mineral consisting of a complex uranium titanate with small amounts of rare earths and occurring in black grains and rough prisms

bran-new *var of* BRAND-NEW

bran·ni·gan \ˈbranəgən\ *n* -s [prob. fr. the name *Brannigan*] **1 :** a drinking spree **:** BENDER ⟨go on a ~⟩ **2 :** a difference of opinion **:** CONTROVERSY, SQUABBLE ⟨~ . . . over the location of the schoolhouse —Harry De Lasaux⟩

branning *pres part of* BRAN

bran·ny \ˈbranē, -aan-, -ni\ *adj* -ER/-EST [¹*bran* + *-y*] **:** of, like, or containing bran ⟨the ~ portions of cereal grains⟩

bran poisoning *n* **:** BRAN DISEASE

brans *pl of* BRAN, *pres 3d sing of* BRAN

¹brant \ˈbrant\ *var of* ¹BRENT

²brant \ˈbrant, -aa(ə)-\ *also* **brant goose** \"-\ *or* **brent** \ˈbrent\ *or* **brent goose** *n, pl* **brant** *or* **brants** [origin unknown] **:** any of several wild geese; *esp* **:** any of several small dark geese of the genus *Branta* that breed in the arctic regions and migrate southward chiefly along the coasts — see WHITE BRANT

bran·ta \ˈbrantə\ *n, cap* [NL, fr. E ²*brant*] **:** a genus of birds (family Anatidae) comprising wild geese with rather elaborately patterned commonly dark plumage, long slender neck, and small weakly serrated bill — see BRANT, CANADA GOOSE; compare ANSER

brant bird *n* [²*brant*] **:** TURNSTONE

brant snipe *n* [²*brant*] **:** RED-BACKED SANDPIPER

bran tub *n, Brit* **:** a tub filled with bran in which presents are concealed

bras *pl of* BRA

bra·sen \ˈbrāzᵊn\ *archaic var of* BRAZEN

bra·se·nia \brəˈsēnēə\ *n, cap* [NL] **:** a monotypic genus of widely distributed aquatic plants (family Nymphaeaceae) with floating oval leaves and small dull-purple flowers — see WATER SHIELD

bra·se·ro \brəˈse(ˌ)rō\ *n* -s [Sp, fr. *brasa* live coals — more at BRAZE] **:** a brick stove built into many Mexican kitchens

¹brash \ˈbrash, -aa(ə)-,-ai-\ *n* -ES [obs. E *brash* to breach a wall, prob. fr. MF *breche* breach — more at BREACH] **1** *dial Brit* **a :** ATTACK, BOUT **b :** a burst of activity **2 a** *chiefly Scot* **:** an attack of illness; *esp* **:** a short severe illness **b :** WATER BRASH **3** *chiefly Scot* **:** a sudden shower **4 :** a mass of fragments or debris: as **a** *or* **brash ice :** small floating fragments of ice esp. near an ice pack or floe **b :** clippings of hedges or prunings of trees

²brash \"\ *vt* -ED/-ING/-ES **:** to remove the lower branches of (a tree)

³brash \"\ *adj* -ER/-EST [origin unknown] **1** *of wood* **:** characterized by unusual brittleness and low resistance to shock **:** BRITTLE **2 a :** prone to act in headlong fashion **:** IMPETUOUS ⟨a ~ young cavalry commander⟩ **:** FOOLHARDY ⟨no one was ~ enough to pick a fight with him⟩ **b :** made or done in haste and with little thought or regard for consequences **:** RASH ⟨~ tactics⟩ ⟨meantime you better avoid doing anything ~ —Sinclair Lewis⟩ **3 a :** full of fresh raw vitality **:** EBULLIENT ⟨a ~ and teeming frontier town⟩ **b :** inclined to be uninhibitedly showy or demonstrative **:** BUMPTIOUS ⟨a delightfully ~ comedian⟩ **4 a :** lacking restraint and discernment **:** TACTLESS ⟨he made a ~ speech . . . and told some thunderingly tasteless anecdotes about his wife —*Time*⟩ **b :** shamelessly self-assertive **:** IMPUDENT ⟨an adolescent ~ to the point of arrogance⟩ **c :** lacking refinement, polish, or finesse **:** COARSE ⟨speaking in ~ and raucous accents⟩ **5 a :** piercingly sharp **:** BLATANT ⟨a ~ squeal of brakes⟩ **b :** loudly assertive **:** BLUSTERING ⟨the ~ prophets of political utopias⟩ **6 :** marked by vivid contrast or distinctness of outline **:** BOLD ⟨~ color⟩ **syn** see SHAMELESS

brash·er doubloon \ˈbrashə(r)-\ *n, usu cap B* [after Ephraim *Brasher* or *Brashear*, 18th cent. Am. goldsmith who struck it] **:** a gold coin of the weight of a doubloon struck in New York City in 1787

brash·i·ness \ˈbrashēnəs, -raash-,-raish-, -shin-\ *n* -ES **:** the quality or state of being brashy

brash·ly \-shlē, -li\ *adv* **:** in a brash manner

brash·ness \-shnəs\ *n* -ES **:** the quality or state of being brash

brash oak *n* [³*brash*] **:** a post oak (*Quercus stellata*)

¹brashy \-shē\ *adj* -ER/-EST [³*brash* + *-y*] **:** BRASH ⟨~ timber⟩

²brashy \"\ *adj* [¹*brash* + *-y*] *Scot* **:** SHOWERY

brasier *var of* BRAZIER

bra·sil \brəˈzil\ *n* -s [MexSp, fr. Sp, brazilwood — more at BRAZIL] **:** LOGWOOD 1b

brasilein *var of* BRAZILEIN

bra·si·let·to *or* **bra·zi·let·to** \ˌbrazəˈled·(ˌ)ō\ *n* -s [prob. modif. of Sp *brasilete*, fr. *brasil* brazilwood — more at BRAZIL] **:** a tree that yields brazilwood

bra·si·lia *or* **bra·sí·lia** \brəˈzēlyə, -zil-\ *adj, usu cap* [fr. *Brasília*, capital of Brazil] **:** of or from Brasília, the capital of Brazil **:** of the kind or style prevalent in Brasília

brasilin *var of* BRAZILIN

¹brass \ˈbras, -aa(ə)-,-ai-,-ȧ-\ *n* -ES [ME *bras*, fr. OE *bræs*; akin to OFris *bress* copper, MLG *bras* metal; all fr. a prehistoric WGmc word perh. borrowed fr. a southwest Asiatic language; akin to the source of Heb & Phoenician *barzel* iron — more at FARRIER] **1 a :** a usu. yellow alloy of copper with zinc or formerly tin and sometimes small amounts of other metals that is malleable and ductile and harder and stronger than copper; *esp* **:** one consisting essentially of 50 to 95 percent copper and 5 to 50 percent zinc — compare BRONZE, COMPOSITION METAL, LATTEN, TOMBAC, WHITE BRASS **b :** an article of brass ⟨finely designed ~*es*⟩ **2 a** *or* **brasses** *pl* **:** the brass musical instruments ⟨the strings and ~ never really got together during the performance⟩ **b** *slang Brit* **:** MONEY; *esp* **:** CASH **c :** a memorial tablet (as of copper and zinc) usu. bearing an inscription and a design or picture and fastened to the floor or against the wall of a church or to a gravestone ⟨a student of late Elizabethan ~*es*⟩ **d :** bright metal fittings and equipment (as on a ship) or metal utensils and ornaments (as in a house) ⟨sailors vigorously polishing the ~⟩ **e :** a lining or step for a bearing (as on a railroad-car axle) usu. in pairs and of brass, bronze, or gunmetal **f :** empty fired cartridge shells **3 :** brazen importunity **:** impudent assurance **:** SHAMELESSNESS ⟨the ~ to borrow large sums of money⟩ **4 :** a moderate yellow that is redder and duller than colonial yellow or quince yellow and redder and deeper than mustard yellow — called also *brazen yellow* **5 a :** commissioned military officers; *esp* **:** high-ranking officers of the army or air force — compare ²BRAID 3, BRASS HAT **b :** the higher levels of civil administration or business management ⟨the top ~ of the industry⟩

²brass \"\ *adj* [ME *bras*, fr. *bras*, n.] **1 :** consisting or made of brass ⟨a ~ cannon⟩ **2 :** of the color of brass ⟨a ~ sky⟩ **3 a :** loud and resounding **:** RESONANT ⟨rich boozy ~ voices —Mollie Panter-Downes⟩ **b :** made up of or composed for brass instruments ⟨a ~ choir⟩ ⟨a ~ section⟩

³brass \"\ *n, pl* **brasses** *also* **brass** [F *brasse* length of the arms, fathom, fr. MF *brace* two arms, length of two arms — more at BRACE] **:** a unit of length equal to a fathom

bras·sage \ˈbrasij, brəˈsäzh\ *n* -s [F, act of stirring (as beer mash or fused metal), coining of money, brassage, fr. *brasser* to stir (fr. OF *bracier* to brew, fr. — assumed — VL *braciare*, fr. L *braces*, a kind of spelt, of Celt origin; akin to W *brag* malt) + *-age*] **:** a charge made to an individual under a system of free coinage for the minting of any gold or silver he may bring to the mint and usu. calculated to cover various costs — compare SEIGNIORAGE

brass ankle *n* **1** *usu cap B&A* **:** one of a group of people of mixed white, Indian, and Negro ancestry in So. Carolina — often used disparagingly **2 :** a person sometimes passing as white who is partially Negro — often used disparagingly

bras·sard \brəˈsärd, ˈbraˌs-\ *also* **bras·sart** \-r(t)\ *n* -s [F *brassard*, fr. MF, alter. of *brassal*, fr. OIt *bracciale*, fr. *braccio* arm — more at BRACCIO] **1 :** armor to protect the arm from shoulder to elbow or during the 15th and 16th centuries to protect the entire arm — compare REREBRACE, VAMBRACE **2 :** a cloth band worn around the upper arm usu. to designate its wearer as a member of a special group or service and often bearing some identifying mark

bras·sa·vo·la \ˌbrasəˈvōlə, brəˈsavələ\ *n, cap* [NL, after A.M. *Brassavola* †1570 Ital. botanist] **:** a genus of tropical American epiphytic orchids (family Orchidaceae) with thick solitary leaves

brass band *n* **:** a band consisting solely or chiefly of brass and percussion instruments — compare MILITARY BAND

brassbound \'=¦=\ *adj* **1 :** having trim made of brass or a metal resembling brass or fitted with parts made of brass or a metal resembling brass ⟨a ~ highboy⟩ ⟨a ~ horse pistol⟩ **2 a** (1) **:** tradition-bound and obstinately opinionated ⟨~ naval strategists⟩ (2) **:** UNCOMPROMISING, INFLEXIBLE ⟨a ~ idealist⟩ ⟨~ honesty⟩ **b :** BRAZEN, PRESUMPTUOUS ⟨~ nerve⟩

brass·bound·er \ˈbrȧsˈbau̇ndə(r)\ *n* [so called fr. the gold binding on the uniform] **:** a boy bound as a cadet or apprentice on a British merchant ship who is given for a premium paid by the parents certain privileges not allowed to the common sailors

brass buttons *n* **:** the golden-yellow flower heads of a So. African composite plant (*Cotula coronopifolia*) naturalized along the coast of California and used as an ornamental

brass check *n* **:** money given somewhat secretly to a journalist for services rendered to or expected by a financial interest

brassed off \ˈbrȧst-\ *adj, slang Brit* **:** fed up **:** DISGRUNTLED

bras·se·rie \ˌbrasˈrē\ *n* -s [F, fr. MF, fr. *brasser* to brew + *-erie* -ery — more at BRASSAGE] **:** a restaurant that sells beer and food ⟨breakfast at a little ~ —Frances Alda⟩

brasses *pl of* BRASS

bras·set \ˈbrasət\ *archaic var of* BRASSARD

brass-eye \'=,=\ *n* **:** AMERICAN GOLDENEYE

brass hat *n* [so called fr. the gold braid worn on the cap] **1 :** a high-ranking officer in the armed forces **2 :** a person in a high position in civil life

bras·sia \ˈbrasēə\ *n, cap* [NL, fr. William *Brass*, 18th cent. Eng. botanical collector + NL *-ia*] **:** a genus of tropical American epiphytic orchids (family Orchidaceae) with one or two leaves to each pseudobulb and striking axillary racemes of flowers with narrow long-tailed sepals and warty lips — see SPIDER ORCHID

bras·si·ca \ˈbrasəkə\ *n* [NL, fr. L, cabbage] **1** *cap* **:** a large genus of perennial, biennial, or annual herbs (family Cruciferae) that are native to temperate parts of the Old World but now cosmopolitan in cultivation, include the cabbages, cauliflowers, turnips, mustards, and related plants, and are distinguished by the cylindrical pod tipped with a conical beak and containing a single row of seeds **2** -s **:** a plant of the genus *Brassica*

bras·si·ca·ce·ae \ˌbrasəˈkāsēˌē\ *n pl, cap* [NL, fr. *Brassica*, type genus + *-aceae*] *in some classifications* **:** a family coextensive with the Cruciferae

bras·si·ca·ceous \ˌbrasə¦kāshəs\ *adj* [NL *Brassicaceae* + E *-ous*] **:** of or relating to the family Brassicaceae

bras·si·cas·ter·ol \ˌbrasəˈkastəˌrōl, -ōl\ *n* [NL *Brassica* (genus name of *Brassica napus*) + E *sterol*] **:** a crystalline sterol $C_{28}H_{45}OH$ obtained esp. from rapeseed oil; 7,8-dihydro-ergosterol

bras·sid·ic acid \(ˈ)bra¦sidik-\ *n* [ISV *brass-* (fr. L *brassica* cabbage) + *-id* + *-ic*] **:** a white crystalline acid $C_8H_{17}CH=CH(CH_2)_{11}COOH$ stereoisomeric with erucic acid and formed from it (as by treatment with nitrous acid)

brass·ie *also* **brassy** *or* **brass·ey** \ˈbrasē, -aas-,-ais-,-ȧs-, -si\ *n, pl* **brass·ies** *also* **brass·eys** [¹*brass* + *-ie, -y, -ey*] **:** a wooden golf club soled with brass or other metal and used esp. for long low shots from a favorable lie on the fairway — see WOOD illustration

bras·siere \brəˈzi(ə)r, -iə *sometimes* ¦brasē¦e(ə)r *or* (ˈ)bras¦ye(ə)r *or* -raas- *or* -eə *or* -azē¦e- *or* -az¦ye-\ *n* -s [fr. obs. E, bodice, fr. obs. F *brassière* (now meaning "a kind of infant's undergarment"), fr. OF *braciere* arm protector — more at BRACER] **:** a woman's close-fitting undergarment having cups for bust support, varying in width from a band to a waist-length bodice, made with or without straps, and often boned or wired for additional support or separation; *also* **:** an adaptation of this garment for sportswear

brass·i·ly \ˈbrasəlē, -aas-,-ais-,-ȧs- -li\ *adv* [¹*brassy* + *-ly*] **:** in a brassy manner

brass·i·ness \-sēnəs, -sin-\ *n* -ES **:** the quality or state of being brassy

brass knuckles *also* **brass knucks** *n pl but sing or pl in constr* **:** a set of four metal finger rings or guards attached to a transverse piece and worn over the front of the doubled fist for use as a weapon

brass pounder *n, slang* **:** a telegraph operator

brass ring *n, slang* **:** a prize or rich opportunity ⟨missed the *brass ring* at the Philadelphia convention —Cabell Phillips⟩

brass tacks *n pl* **:** details of immediate practical importance ⟨this monograph has little to reward the tough-minded reader, in the habit of searching for *brass tacks* —Stanley Newman⟩ —usu. used in the phrase *get down to brass tacks*

brassy \ˈbrasē, -aas-,-ais-,-ȧs-, -si\ *adj* -ER/-EST [¹*brass* + *-y*] **1 a :** BRAZEN **:** coarse and impudent **:** unabashedly loud **:** BOLD ⟨~ confidence⟩ ⟨a big ~ blonde who'd already seen her best years⟩ **b :** piercingly loud **:** SHRILL, STRIDENT ⟨~ advertising⟩ ⟨~ nightclub entertainment⟩ **2** *archaic* **:** of or adorned with brass **3 :** resembling brass in hardness, ductility, or other physical property ⟨a metal with a ~ texture⟩; *esp* **:** of the color of brass **4 a :** resembling the sound of a brass instrument ⟨a ~ cough⟩ ⟨a ~ blare⟩ **b :** OVERBLOWN — used of brass musical instruments

brassy bass *n* **:** YELLOW BASS

brast *archaic past of* BURST

¹**brat** \ˈbrat, ˈbrät, -ȧth\ *n* -S [ME, coarse cloak, fr. OE *bratt*, fr. OIr *brat*; akin to W *brethyn* cloth, Bret *broz* skirt and perh. to Gk *pharos* cloth, Lith *burva*, an article of clothing] **1** *dial Brit* **a :** CLOTHING ⟨dressed in their Sunday ~*s*⟩ **b :** a coarse outer garment **:** CLOAK **2** *dial Brit* **:** a work garment (as an apron or smock) **3** *chiefly Scot* **:** SCUM ⟨~ on the porridge⟩

²**brat** \ˈbrat, *usu* -ad·+V\ *n* -S [perh. fr. ¹*brat*] **1 :** CHILD, OFFSPRING ⟨an army ~ whose father was a colonel⟩ **2 a :** an ill-mannered annoying child ⟨like all little girls her age, she could be a ~ —Hamilton Basso⟩

bra·ti·sla·va \¦brad·ə¦slävə, -rä-\ *adj, usu cap* [fr. *Bratislava*, Czechoslovakia] **:** of or from the city of Bratislava, Czechoslovakia **:** of the kind or style prevalent in Bratislava

brat·ling \ˈbratliŋ\ *n* -S [²*brat* + *-ling*] **:** a little brat

brat·tach *n* -S [ScGael *bratach*, fr. or akin to MIr, fr. *brat* cloak] *archaic Scot* **:** BANNER, FLAG

¹**brat·tice** \ˈbrad·əs, -d·ish\ *n* -S [ME *bretais, bretise, bretasce* parapet, fr. OF *bretesche* wooden tower, parapet, fr. ML *breteschia, britaschia*, prob. fr. (assumed) VL *Brittus* Breton, fr. L *Brito, Britto* Briton, Breton — more at BRITON] **:** an often temporary partition consisting of planks or cloth and used esp. in a mine to control ventilation

²**brattice** \"\ *vt* -ED/-ING/-S **:** to provide with a brattice — often used with *up*

brat·tic·er \-s(h)ə(r)\ *n* -S **:** one that erects brattices — called also *airman, braddisher, brattice man*

brat·tish \ˈbrad·|ish, -at|, |ēsh\ *adj* [²*brat* + *-ish*] **:** of, relating to, or suggestive of a brat **:** SPOILED ⟨a ~ kid brother⟩

brat·tish·ing \ˈbrad·əshiŋ\ *n* -S [*brattish* (var. of ¹*brattice*) + *-ing*] **:** a form of openwork cresting of a screen or paneling usu. in a stylized floral form

¹**brat·tle** \ˈbratᵊl\ *n* -S [prob. of imit. origin] **1** *chiefly Scot* **:** a loud clattering noise **2** *chiefly Scot* **:** a sudden forward rush

²**brattle** \"\ *vi* **brattled; brattled; brattling** \-t(ᵊ)liŋ, -lən\ **brattles** *chiefly Scot* **:** to make a rushing, clattering, or rattling sound ⟨the stream well *brattling* over the rocks⟩

brat·ty \ˈbrad·ē, -atē, -i\ *adj* -ER/-EST [²*brat* + *-y*] **:** BRATTISH ⟨~ behavior⟩

brat·wurst \ˈbrat,wərst, -wu̇rst; brät,vu̇rst, -vu̇(r)sht\ *n* -S [G, fr. OHG *brātwurst*, fr. *brāt*, *brāto* meat without waste + *wurst* sausage; akin to OE *brǣd* flesh and to OHG *werran* to confuse — more at BRAWN, WAR] **:** fresh pork sausage for frying

braul \ˈbrau̇(ə)l\ *n* -S [Romanian, fr. F *branle* — more at BRANLE] **:** a lively Romanian round dance related to the French branle

brau·la \ˈbrōlə, -rau̇lə\ *n* -S [NL *Braula*, genus including the bee louse] **:** BEE LOUSE

bra·una \brä'ünə\ *n* -S [Pg *braúna*] **:** a Brazilian tree (*Melanoxylon brauna*) of the family Leguminosae having fine-grained wood

brau·ne·ria \brōiˈnirēə, brau̇ˈ-,brōˈ-\ [NL, fr. J.J.*Bräuner*, 18th cent. Ger. botanist + NL *-ia*] *syn of* ECHINACEA

braun·ite \ˈbrau̇,nīt\ *n* -S [Councilor *Braun*, 19th cent. Ger. treasury official + E *-ite*] **:** a brittle brownish black or steel-gray mineral that consists of manganese silicate and occurs massive and as tetragonal crystals (hardness 6–6.5, sp. gr. 4.75–4.82)

braun·schwei·ger \ˈbrau̇n,shwīgə(r), -shvī, -swī-\ *n* -S *often cap* [G *Braunschweiger (wurst)*, lit., Brunswick sausage, fr. *Braunschweiger* of Brunswick (fr. *Braunschweig* Brunswick, region and city in Germany) + *wurst* sausage] **:** smoked liver sausage

braun's holly fern \ˈbrau̇nz-\ *n, usu cap B* [after Alexander *Braun* †1877 Ger. botanist] **:** PRICKLY SHIELD FERN

braun tube \ˈbrau̇n-\ *n, usu cap B* [after Karl F. *Braun* †1918 Ger. physicist] **:** a cathode-ray tube with a diaphragm through which a beam of cathode rays can pass and a fluorescent screen on which the beam is received

¹**bra·va** \ˈbrävə, -ävə *also* -avə\ *n* -S *usu cap* [fr. *Brava*, one of the Cape Verde islands] **:** a descendant of immigrants from the Cape Verde islands chiefly of Negro and Portuguese stock resident in Massachusetts esp. on Cape Cod and around New Bedford

²**bra·va** \ˈbrä(,)vä, ˈbrȧ(,)vȧ, ⸗ˈ⸗\ *n* -S [It, fem. of *bravo* excellent, courageous — more at BRAVE] **:** BRAVO — used interjectionally in applauding a woman

bra·vade \brəˈväd, -ȧd\ *n* -S [MF] *archaic* **:** BRAVADO

¹**bra·va·do** \brəˈvä(,)dō, -vȧ-\ *n* -ES [MF, OSp & OIt; MF *bravade* & OSp *bravata*, fr. OIt *bravata*, fr. fem. of *bravato*, past part. of *bravare* to threaten, challenge, provoke, show off, fr. *bravo* courageous, wild — more at BRAVE] **1 a :** showy or demonstrative conduct or action often characterized by bluster and swagger ⟨morale is not based on ~ but on deadly competence —*Coast Artillery Jour.*⟩; *also* **:** an instance of such conduct or action ⟨retreating with face-saving ~*es*⟩ **b :** the psychological quality or state conducive to or responsible for perversely capricious, ostentatiously overbearing, or noisy bluffing behavior ⟨to perform idiotic tricks out of sheer ~⟩ **2** *obs* **:** SWAGGERER

²**bravado** \"\ *vi* -ED/-ING/-ES **:** SWAGGER, BLUSTER ⟨~*ing* ward bosses⟩ **:** put on a show of bravado ⟨the mob ~*ed* a while but never got really violent⟩

bra·vais lattice \brəˈva,-vä-; brəˈvā-, brə'-\ *n, usu cap B* [after Auguste *Bravais* †1863 Fr. physicist] **:** one of the 14 possible arrays of points used esp. in crystallography and repeated periodically in 3-dimensional space so that the arrangement of points about any one of the points is identical in every respect (as in dimension and orientation) to that about any other point of the array — compare SPACE LATTICE

¹**brave** \ˈbrāv\ *adj* -ER/-EST [MF, fr. OIt & OSp *bravo* courageous, wild; OIt *bravo* prob. fr. OProv *brau* wild, fr. L *barbarus* barbarous; OSp *bravo* fr. L *barbarus* — more at BARBAROUS] **1 a :** resolute in facing odds **:** able to meet danger or endure pain or hardship without giving in to fear ⟨a ~ and respected man⟩ **b :** of, arising from, or suggestive of mastery of fear and intelligent use of faculties esp. under duress ⟨a ~ defense⟩ ⟨a ~ gesture⟩ **2 :** making a fine show or display **:** BRIGHT, COLORFUL ⟨girls decked out in ~ new dresses⟩ ⟨~ banners flying over the circus grounds⟩ **3 :** EXCELLENT, SPLENDID ⟨the business folded up despite its ~ start⟩

syn COURAGEOUS, UNAFRAID, FEARLESS, INTREPID, VALIANT, VALOROUS, DAUNTLESS, UNDAUNTED, DOUGHTY, BOLD, AUDACIOUS: BRAVE often indicates lack of fear in alarming or difficult circumstances ⟨the *brave* soldier goes to meet Death, and meets him without a shudder —Anthony Trollope⟩ ⟨he would send an explosion ship into the harbor . . . a *brave* crew would take her in at night, right up against the city, would light the fuses, and try to escape —C.S.Forester⟩ COURAGEOUS implies stout-hearted resolution in contemplating or facing danger ⟨I am afraid . . . because I do not wish to die. But my spirit masters the trembling flesh and the qualms of the mind. I am more than brave. I am *courageous* —Jack London⟩ ⟨a man is *courageous* when he does things which others might fail to do owing to fear —Bertrand Russell⟩ UNAFRAID simply indicates lack of fright or fear ⟨enjoy their homes *unafraid* of violent intrusion —Douglas MacArthur⟩ ⟨a young, daring, and creative people —a people *unafraid* of change —Archibald MacLeish⟩ FEARLESS may indicate lack of fear, or it may be more positive and suggest undismayed resolution ⟨joyous we too launch out on trackless seas *fearless* for unknown shores —Walt Whitman⟩ ⟨he gives always the impression of *fearless* sincerity . . . one always feels that he is ready to say bluntly what every one else is afraid to say —T.S.Eliot⟩ INTREPID suggests either daring in meeting danger or fortitude in enduring it ⟨with the *intrepid* woman who was his wife, and a few natives, he landed there, and set about building a house and clearing the scrub —W.S. Maugham⟩ ⟨the *intrepid* guardians of the place, hourly exposed to death, with famine worn, and suffering under many a perilous wound —William Wordsworth⟩ VALIANT suggests resolute courage and fortitude ⟨this *valiant*, steadfast people [of Yugoslavia], whose history for centuries has been a struggle for life —Sir Winston Churchill⟩ VALOROUS suggests illustrious bravery and sometimes has an archaic or romantic ring ⟨the regiment itself is a proud one, with a *valorous* record —*Infantry Jour.*⟩ DAUNTLESS emphasizes determination, resolution, and fearlessness despite danger or difficulty ⟨the *dauntless* English infantry were receiving and repelling the furious charges — W.M.Thackeray⟩ ⟨nothing appalled her *dauntless* soul — William Beckford⟩ UNDAUNTED indicates continued courage and resolution after danger, hardship, or defeat ⟨he watched them at the points of greatest danger falling under the shots from the scorpions, and others stepping *undaunted* into their places to fall in the same way —J.A.Froude⟩ DOUGHTY combines the implications of *formidable, sturdy*, and BRAVE, but may have an archaic or humorous suggestion ⟨when Fisk reached the head of the stairs leading to the board room, the *doughty* president of the endangered railway knocked him down to the ground floor —C.A. & Mary Beard⟩ ⟨so *doughty* a warrior must break a lance —V.L.Parrington⟩ BOLD may indicate a forward or defiant tendency to thrust oneself into difficult or dangerous situations ⟨it was a *bold* man who dared to walk alone through hundreds of miles of lion-infested country with nothing but a spear in his hand to seek work and adventure —Stuart Cloete⟩ ⟨these fellows who attacked the inn tonight—*bold*, desperate blades, for sure —R.L.Stevenson⟩ ⟨he knew a fool and a tyrant in high places, and was *bold* to call them by their true names —V.L.Parrington⟩ AUDACIOUS implies spirited and sometimes reckless daring ⟨the place where the fiery Ethan Allen first sketched his *audacious* move against Ticonderoga —Budd Schulberg⟩ ⟨hitherto no liberal statesman has been so *audacious* as to . . . lay profane hands on the divine right of nations to seek their own advantage at the cost of the rest —Thorstein Veblen⟩

²**brave** \"\ *vb* -ED/-ING/-S [prob. fr. MF *braver*, fr. OIt *bravare* — more at BRAVADO] *vt* **1 a** *archaic* **:** CHALLENGE, DEFY **b :** to face (something involving possible unfortunate or disastrous consequences) or endure (as hardship) usu. with self-control and mastery of fear and often with a particular objective in view ⟨men of the merchant marine who *braved* enemy torpedoes —H.S.Truman⟩ ⟨women who . . . for his sake had *braved* all social censure —Oscar Wilde⟩ **2** *obs* **:** to make showy **:** ADORN ~ *vi, archaic* **:** to make a brave show **:** SWAGGER, BLUFF, BOAST **syn** see FACE

³**brave** \"\ *n* -S [¹*brave*] **1** *archaic* **:** BRAVADO, DEFIANCE, CHALLENGE **2 :** one who is brave **:** WARRIOR ⟨none but the ~ deserves the fair —John Dryden⟩; *specif* **:** a No. American Indian warrior **3** *archaic* **:** BULLY, ASSASSIN

bravehearted \ˈ⸗;⸗⸗\ *adj* **:** having a brave heart

brave·ly *adv* **:** in a brave manner: as **a :** COURAGEOUSLY, VALIANTLY ⟨to fight ~ on the side of justice⟩ **b :** FINELY, SHOWILY, GAILY ⟨~ decked houses⟩ **c :** THRIVINGLY, PROSPEROUSLY, WELL ⟨for three years matters went ~ on —O.S. Nock⟩

brave·ness *n* -ES **:** BRAVERY 4

¹**braver** *comparative of* BRAVE

²**brav·er** \ˈbrāvə(r)\ *n* -S [²*brave* + *-er*] **:** one that braves or defies (as danger, hardship, prodigious tasks) ⟨a ~ of rules⟩

brav·ery \ˈbrāv(ə)rē, -ri\ *n* -ES [prob. fr. MF *braverie*, fr. *braver* + *-erie* -ery] **1** *archaic* **:** an act of defiance or bravado **2 a :** clothes of handsome or striking appearance **:** FINERY ⟨crowds wearing their Sunday ~⟩ **b :** something fine, showy, or of good quality **:** a thing to exhibit ⟨tourists visiting all the *braveries* of the city⟩ **3 :** fine or gaudy show **:** DISPLAY ⟨the streets strewed with flowers and full of pageantry, banners, and ~ —John Evelyn⟩ **4 :** the quality or state of being brave ⟨the ~ of troops under fire⟩ **5** *obs, pl also* **bravery :** a fine gentleman **:** BEAU

bravest *superlative of* BRAVE

brave west winds *n pl* **:** the strong westerly to northwesterly winds between the latitudes 40 degrees and 50 degrees in the oceans of the southern hemisphere

brav·ing·ly *adv* **:** in a braving manner

¹**bra·vo** \ˈbrä(,)vō, -rȧ- *sometimes* -ra-\ *n, pl* **bravos** *or* **bravoes** \-vōz\ *also* **bra·vi** \-(,)vē\ [It, fr. *bravo*, adj., wild, courageous — more at BRAVE] **:** VILLAIN, DESPERADO, CUTTHROAT ⟨the Renaissance ~ turned religious fanatic —H.J.Laski⟩; *esp* **:** a hired assassin

²**bravo** \", ⸗ˈ⸗\ *n, pl* **bravos** \-vōz\ *also* **bra·vi** \ˈ⸗(,)vē\ [It, fr. *bravo*, adj., excellent, courageous, wild] **:** a shout of approval or approbation ⟨frenzied ~*s* for the tenor⟩ — often used interjectionally in applauding a performance (as of an artist or speaker); sometimes restricted in use to a man; compare BRAVA

³**bravo** *like* ²BRAVO\ *vt* -ED/-ING/-ES **:** to show approbation or admiration of esp. by shouts of *bravo* ⟨a wildly ~*ing* audience⟩

⁴**bravo** *like* ¹BRAVO\ *usu cap* — a communications code word for the letter *b*

bra·vo·ite \ˈbrä,vō,īt\ *n* -S [José J. *Bravo* †1928 Peruvian mineralogist + E *-ite*] **:** a mineral $(Ni,Fe)S_2$ consisting of a nickel sulfide containing iron related to pyrite

bra·vu·ra \brəˈv(y)u̇rə, -ürə *also* brä'- *or* brȧ'-\ *n* -S *often attrib* [It, lit., bravado, bravery, fr. *bravare* to show off + *-ura* -ure — more at BRAVADO] **1 a :** a florid brilliant virtuoso musical composition ⟨the stunning ~*s* of Verdi⟩ **b :** the virtuosic execution of a musical composition or passage by a performer **2 :** a show of daring or brilliancy ⟨he organized all sorts of ~ stunts, the more senseless or dangerous the better —Charles Ingle⟩ **3 :** an aggressively confident and commanding air ⟨the sinister smiling figure . . . making a ~ exit before the vote —*New Republic*⟩

¹**braw** \ˈbrō, ˈbrȧ\ *adj* -ER/-EST [alter. of earlier *brawf* brave, fr. ME *brave* — more at BRAVE] **1** *chiefly Scot* **a** (1) **:** FINE, SPLENDID ⟨a ~ house⟩ ⟨a ~ new gown⟩ (2) **:** PLEASANT, FINE — used esp. of the weather ⟨a ~ night⟩ **b** *of a person* (1) **:** GOOD, NICE ⟨my ~ lad⟩ (2) **:** HANDSOME, ATTRACTIVE ⟨a ~ gallant⟩ (3) **:** well dressed **2** *chiefly Scot* **:** PRETTY ⟨it costs a ~ penny⟩ ⟨a ~ fight⟩

²**braw** \"\ *adv, Scot* **:** VERY, QUITE ⟨not feeling ~ well⟩

¹**brawl** \ˈbrōl\ *vb* -ED/-ING/-S [ME *brawlen*; perh. akin to D & LG *brallen* to brag] *vi* **1 :** to quarrel noisily **:** wrangle violently ⟨when statesmen ~*ed* with each other outrageously —*Amer. Guide Series: Texas*⟩ **2 :** to complain loudly **:** raise a clamor ⟨mobs ~*ing* about unfair rationing of food⟩ **3 :** to make a loud confused noise (as of water of a rapid stream running over stones) ⟨the Miami river . . . ~*ed* over 25 feet of rapids in the North Fork —Marjory S. Douglas⟩ ~ *vt* **1** *obs* **:** to call down violently **:** REVILE **2 :** to shout (as orders) in a loud often hoarse voice ⟨sergeants ~*ing* out commands⟩ **3** *archaic* **:** to force or drive by shouting or reviling

²**brawl** \"\ *n* -S [ME, fr. *brawlen*, v.] **1 a :** a loud, angry, or disorderly quarrel ⟨a ~ between husband and wife that kept the whole neighborhood awake⟩ **b** (1) **:** a rough noisy and often prolonged hand-to-hand fight ⟨a barroom ~⟩ (2) *slang* **:** a social affair **:** DANCE, PARTY; *esp* **:** a drinking party ⟨she always tosses a perfectly savage ~ for all the . . . students —A.O.Myrer⟩ **2 :** a loud tumultuous noise ⟨the spring run became quite a trout brook and its tiny murmur a loud ~ —John Burroughs⟩

syn BROIL, RIOT, FRACAS, MELEE, ROW, RUMPUS, SCRAP: BRAWL indicates a noisy fight or quarrel with racket, recrimination, hurly-burly, and angry blows ⟨a howling *brawl* amongst vicious hoodlums —Jean Stafford⟩ ⟨the settlers in the river towns shivered excitedly at the uproar of the loggers' drunken *brawls*, the shattering of the tavern's glassware —*Amer. Guide Series: Minn.*⟩ BROIL indicates a disordered, confused turmoil, conflict, or fight without clear issues or demarcation between contestants ⟨but village mirth breeds contests, *broils*, and blows —P.B.Shelley⟩ ⟨plunging us in all the *broils* of the European nations —Thomas Jefferson⟩ RIOT may indicate a turbulent tumultuous uproar participated in by a number of persons with violent action breaking civil peace ⟨the draft *riots* in Civil War days⟩ ⟨angered supporters of both teams swarmed out of the stands and the game turned into a *riot*⟩ FRACAS may apply to an excited disturbance or noisy quarrel, with or without blows ⟨cowboys hurt in a gambling *fracas* —Laura Krey⟩ MELEE suggests a swirling unclear series of hand-to-hand conflicts or something similar ⟨in such a *melee*, of course, no chronicler could be very clear, and the more active of the knights are much confused —E.V. Lucas⟩ ⟨in 1934, 8000 lettuce pickers struck; when the police attempted to break up picket lines, the resultant *melee* in which blood was shed made headlines —*Amer. Guide Series: Calif.*⟩ ROW applies to any noisy demonstration or fight; RUMPUS may intensify suggestions of disturbance and commotion; SCRAP indicates a fight, often inconsequential, or a noisy sharp quarrel ⟨a crockery-smashing family *row* —Edward Sackville-West & Desmond Shawe-Taylor⟩ ⟨but the *row* went a good deal deeper than a mere squabble in the children's schoolroom —Alan Moorehead⟩ ⟨such a *rumpus* that everybody in the neighborhood took sides —L.C.Douglas⟩ ⟨a bare-knuckled political *scrap* —*New Republic*⟩

³**brawl** *var of* BRANLE

brawl·er \ˈbrōlə(r)\ *n* -S [ME, fr. *brawlen* to brawl + *-er*] **:** one that brawls

brawling *adj* **1 :** noisily quarrelsome ⟨~ neighbors⟩ **2 :** extremely noisy and tumultuous ⟨a ~ hurricane⟩ ⟨a ~ torrent⟩ **3 :** violently active **:** vibrant and teeming ⟨a ~ young democracy⟩ — **brawl·ing·ly** *adv*

brawl·some \ˈbrōlsəm\ *adj* [²*brawl* + *-some*] **:** QUARRELSOME

¹**braw·ly** *also* **braw·lie** \ˈbrōli, ˈbrȧli\ *adv* [*braw* + *-ly, -lie*] *Scot* **:** very well **:** EXCELLENTLY ⟨he knew the way ~⟩

²**brawly** \ˈbrōlē, -li\ *adj* -ER/-EST [²*brawl* + *-y*] **1 :** BRAWLING ⟨the soldiers would . . . get drunk and ~ —Meyer Berger⟩ **2 :** characterized by brawls or brawling ⟨hitherto politically ~ Brazil —F.H.Gervasi⟩

¹**brawn** \ˈbrōn\ *n* -S [ME, fr. MF *braon* fleshy part, muscle, of Gmc origin; akin to OE *brǣd* flesh, OS *brādo* ham, calf of the leg, OHG *brāto* meat without waste, ON *brāth* meat] **1 a :** full strong muscles esp. of the arm or leg **b :** a protuberant muscular part (as on the arm, buttock, or calf) **c** (1) **:** well-developed or powerful-appearing muscles ⟨a youngster with a good build and fine ~⟩ (2) **:** muscular strength ⟨their job — loading and unloading cargo — calls for ~ —*N.Y. Times*⟩ ⟨brains against ~⟩ **d** *obs* **:** thickened or calloused skin **2** *dial Brit* **:** BOAR **3 a** *obs* **:** animal flesh used as food **b** *Brit* **:** flesh of a boar **:** PORK **c :** a product made from chopped, cooked, and molded edible parts of pig's head, feet, legs, and sometimes tongue **4 :** MANPOWER ⟨the West Indian Negro contributed about 60 percent of the ~ required to build the Panama canal —F.J.Haskin⟩

²**brawn** \"\ *vt* -ED/-ING/-S **1** *obs* **:** to make brawny **2** *Brit* **:** to fatten (a pig) for slaughter

brawned \ˈbrōnd\ *adj* [¹*brawn* + *-ed*] **:** BRAWNY — **brawned·ness** \-nəs *also* -ndnəs\ *n* -ES

brawn·i·ness \ˈbrōnēnəs, -nin-\ *n* -ES **:** the quality or state of being brawny

brawny \ˈbrōnē, -ni\ *adj* -ER/-EST **1 :** having large strong muscles **:** MUSCULAR, STRONG ⟨~ arms and legs⟩ ⟨~ stevedores⟩ ⟨~ girls, wide as they were tall —Truman Capote⟩ **2 :** swollen and hard ⟨a ~ and purple infected foot⟩

braws \ˈbrōz, ˈbrȧz\ *n pl* [*braw* + *-s*] *chiefly Scot* **:** best clothes

braxy \ˈbraksē\ *n* -ES [origin unknown] **1 :** a malignant edema of sheep that involves gastrointestinal invasion by a spore-forming bacterium (*Clostridium septicum*), produces an enterotoxemia characterized by staggering, convulsions, coma, and death, and is common in Iceland, Scotland, and Norway — compare BLACK DISEASE **2 :** a sheep dead from natural causes, esp. from disease; *also* **:** mutton from such a carcass

¹**bray** \ˈbrā\ *vb* -ED/-ING/-S [ME *brayen*, fr. OF *braire* to cry, make a noise, fr. (assumed) VL *bragere*, of Celt origin; akin to MIr *braigid* he breaks wind, t-air-*brech* crashing noise; akin to L *fragor* crashing noise, *frangere* to break — more at BREAK] *vi* **1** *obs* **:** to cry out (as in pain) **2 a** *of a donkey* **:** to utter a characteristic loud harsh cry **b :** to utter a loud harsh sound resembling or suggesting that made by a donkey ⟨the sea lions ~*ing* and moving in the green sapphire waters —Josephine Johnson⟩ ⟨cannon roared, trumpets ~*ed* —S.E. Morison⟩ ⟨the politicians wept, ranted, and ~*ed*⟩ ~ *vt* **:** to utter, play, or send forth loudly, harshly, or discordantly ⟨a brass band ~*ing* the national anthem⟩ ⟨she ~*ed* out her grievances before the judge⟩

²**bray** \"\ *n* -S [ME, fr. OF *brait*, fr. *braire*] **1 :** a donkey's characteristic cry **2 :** a loud or discordant noise resembling a donkey's bray ⟨the ~ and roar of traffic⟩

³**bray** \"\ *vt* -ED/-ING/-S [ME *brayen*, fr. MF *broiier*, fr. OF, of Gmc origin; akin to OHG *brehhan* to break — more at BREAK] **1 a :** to pound, crush, or grind small and fine ⟨~ seeds in a mortar⟩ **b :** to wear down as if by this process ⟨sorrow . . . had ~*ed* her —B.A.Williams⟩ **2 :** to spread thin ⟨~ printing ink⟩

⁴**bray** \"\ *or* **brey** \"\ *n* -S **:** a heraldic representation of a brake for braying flax — called also *brake, hemp-brake*

⁵**bray** *var of* ¹BRAE

bray·er \ˈbrāə(r)\ *n* -S [³*bray* + *-er*] **:** one that brays or grinds: as **a** *archaic* **:** a pestle with which ink was brayed before it was dabbed on the printing surface **b :** a printer's hand inking roller

brayer b

bra·yera \brəˈyerə, ˈbrāərə\ *n* -S [fr. NL *Brayera* (genus of trees in some classifications containing *Hagenia abyssinica*) after *Brayer fl*1823 Fr. physician] **:** the dried pistillate flowers of an ornamental Abyssinian tree (*Hagenia abyssinica*) sometimes used as an anthelmintic

bra·yer·in \brəˈyerən, ˈbrāər-\ *n* -S [NL *Brayera* + E *-in*] **:** KOSIN

bray·ton cycle \ˈbrātᵊn-\ *n, usu cap B* [after *Brayton fl*1873 Am. inventor] **:** a thermodynamic cycle composed of two adiabatic and two isobaric changes in alternate order — called also *Joule's cycle*

¹**braze** *vb* -ED/-ING/-S [ME, fr. *brass*, after such pairs as E *glass*: *glaze*] *obs* **:** to make brazen **:** HARDEN

²**braze** \ˈbrāz\ *vb* -ED/-ING/-S [prob. fr. F *braser*, fr. OF, to burn, fr. *brese* live coals, prob. of non-IE origin; akin to the source of OSp *brasa* live coal, OIt *bragia*] **:** to solder with an alloy (as hard solder or brass) that is relatively infusible as compared with common solder

³**braze** \"\ *n* -S **:** a brazed joint

¹**bra·zen** \ˈbrāzᵊn\ *adj* [ME *brasen*, fr. OE *bræsen*, fr. *bræs* brass + *-en* — more at BRASS] **1 :** made of brass ⟨priests drinking from ~ cups⟩ **2 :** sounding harsh and loud like resounding brass **:** BRASSY, CLANGOROUS ⟨the horrible ~ voice of the fire bell —Elmer Davis⟩ **3 a** (1) **:** lacking or insensitive to moral principle **:** UNSCRUPULOUS ⟨a ~ criminal⟩ (2) **:** done in the open or in plain sight with or as if with

complete scorn of public opinion, the common good, or ethical principle ⟨~ aggression⟩ ⟨a ~ violation of the rules⟩ **b :** lacking modesty : SHAMELESS ⟨a ~ hussy⟩ **4 a :** unabashedly frank : lacking delicacy or qualifications ⟨a ~ tongue⟩ ⟨~ announcements⟩ **b :** loud and showy : GAUDY ⟨brand new ~ store fronts⟩ **5 a :** of the color of polished brass : as bright or shiny as polished brass ⟨a ~ sky at sunset⟩ **b :** EXTREME, INTENSE ⟨~ heat⟩ **syn** see SHAMELESS

²brazen \"\ *vt* **brazened; brazened; brazening** \-z(ᵊ)niŋ\ **brazens :** to face (an accusation or an accuser) with resolution or defiance or impudence : carry off (a situation) boldly and imperturbably — used usu. with *out* or *through* and commonly in the phrase *brazen it out* ⟨would the prisoner ~ it out or break down and confess⟩

brazenface \'ˌ\ *n* **:** an impudent or shameless person

bra·zen·faced \'ˌˈfāst\ *adj* **:** IMPUDENT, SHAMELESS — **bra·zen·fac·ed·ly** \ˌˈfāsədlē, -āstlē, -līˌ\ *adv*

brazen law of wages : IRON LAW OF WAGES

bra·zen·ly *adv* **:** in a brazen manner

bra·zen·ness \'brāzᵊn(n)əs\ *n* -ES **:** the quality or state of being brazen

brazen yellow *n* **:** BRASS 4

braz·er \'brāzə(r)\ *n* -S [²*braze* + *-er*] **:** one that brazes metal parts

¹bra·zier *or* **bra·sier** \'brāzhə(r) *also* -zēə- *sometimes* 'brazē-\ *n* -S [ME *brasier*, fr. *bras* brass + *-ier* — more at BRASS] **:** one that works in brass

²brazier *or* **brasier** \"\ *n* -S [F *brasier*, fr. OF, fire of hot coals, fr. *brese* live coals — more at BRAZE] **1 :** a pan for holding burning coals **2 :** a cooking utensil in which the food to be cooked is exposed to the source of heat (as live coals or electricity) through a wire grill

brazier

brazier-head rivet *n* [²*brazier*] **:** a light buttonhead rivet with a wide shallow head used esp. on aircraft

bra·ziery \-zh(ə)rē,-zērē\ *n* -ES [¹*brazier* + *-y*] **:** work done by a brazier

¹bra·zil \brə'zil\ *n* -S [ME *brasile*, fr. OSp or OPg *brasil*, fr. *brasa* live coals; fr. the color of the wood — more at BRAZE] **1 :** BRAZILWOOD **2** *or* **brazil red :** a dark reddish orange that is yellower, stronger, and slightly darker than average lacquer red and redder and stronger than ocher red or burnt sienna — called also *roset*

²brazil \"\ *adj, usu cap* [fr. *Brazil*, country in So. America] **:** of or from Brazil : of the kind or style prevalent in Brazil

³braz·il \'brazəl\ *n* -S [prob. alter. of *brass*; fr. its yellow color] *dial Eng* **:** iron pyrites; *also* **:** coal containing much pyrites

bra·zil·ein *also* **bra·sil·ein** \brə'zilēən\ *n* -S [ISV *brazilin*, *brasilin* + *-ein*; prob. orig. formed as G *brasilein*] **:** a red crystalline dye $C_{16}H_{12}O_5$ — see BRAZILIN

braz·i·lette \ˌbrazəˈlet, ˌbrazəˈled·ē\ *n* -S [prob. fr. Sp *brasilete* brazilwood — more at BRASILETTO] **:** the heartwood of a tropical American brazilwood that yields brazilin

brazilletto *var of* BRASILETTO

¹bra·zil·ian \brə'zilyən\ *adj, usu cap* [*Brazil*, the country + E *-ian*] **1 :** of, relating to, or characteristic of Brazil **2 :** of, relating to, or characteristic of the people of Brazil **3 :** of, relating to, or constituting the subdivision of the Neotropical biogeographic region that includes tropical So. America

²brazilian \"\ *n* -S *cap* **1 :** a native or inhabitant of Brazil **2 :** BRAZILIAN PORTUGUESE

brazilian arrowroot *n, usu cap B* **:** a starch obtained from the bitter cassava and used as a food or industrially as a size, glaze, or laundry starch — compare TAPIOCA

brazilian boxwood *n, usu cap B* **:** a Brazilian tree (*Euxylophora paraensis*) with a lustrous yellowish white wood

brazilian copal *n, usu cap B* **:** copal from the courbaril tree

brazilian cotton *n, usu cap B* **:** KIDNEY COTTON

brazilian duck *n, usu cap B* **:** MUSCOVY DUCK

brazilian emerald *n, usu cap B* **:** a transparent green variety of tourmaline

brazilian guava *n, usu cap B* **:** a So. American tree (*Psidium guineense*) yielding a fruit similar to the true guava

brazilian ipecac *n, usu cap B* **:** IPECAC 2a

bra·zil·ian·ite \brə'zilyəˌnīt\ *n* -S [¹*brazilian* + E *-ite*; fr. its discovery in Brazil] **:** a mineral $NaAl_3(PO_4)_2(OH)_4$ consisting of a basic phosphate of sodium and aluminum

brazilian jalap *n, usu cap B* **:** PIPTOSTEGIA ROOT

brazilian mahogany *n, usu cap B* **1 :** either of two Brazilian timber trees (*Plathymenia foliolosa* and *P. reticulata*) of the family Leguminosae with yellowish brown wood **2 :** JEQUITIBA

brazilian morning glory *n, usu cap B* **:** an ornamental Brazilian pink-flowered vine (*Ipomoea setosa*) densely covered with bristly purplish hairs

brazilian pepper tree *n, usu cap B* **:** a Brazilian evergreen resinous tree (*Schinus terebinthifolius*) with dark green leaflets and a bright red fruit

brazilian pine *n, usu cap B* **:** PARANÁ PINE

brazilian portuguese *n, usu cap B&P* **:** the Portuguese language as spoken or written in Brazil

brazilian rhatany *n, usu cap B* **:** PARÁ RHATANY

brazilian rosewood *n, usu cap B* **:** an important Brazilian timber tree (*Dalbergia nigra*) yielding a heavy hard dark-colored wood streaked with black — called also *caviuna wood, jacaranda*

brazilian sapphire *n, usu cap B* **:** a transparent blue variety of tourmaline

brazilian sassafras *n, usu cap B* **:** a So. American tree (*Nectandra puchury*) whose seed is the pichurim bean

brazilian shrimp *n, usu cap B* **:** a large reddish brown shrimp (*Penaeus aztecus*) common in the Gulf of Mexico that is a leading economic species along the gulf coast — called also *brown shrimp, red shrimp*

brazilian spiderflower *or* **brazilian spiderwort** *n, usu cap B* **:** any of certain Brazilian shrubs of the genus *Tibouchina* (as *T. semidecandra*) used in cultivation and having dark green leaves with conspicuous veins and clusters of large purple flowers

brazilian tea *also* **brazil tea** *n, usu cap B* **:** any of several substitutes for tea: as **a :** the dried leaves of a tropical shrub (*Lantana pseudothea*) **b :** the dried leaves of either of two tropical plants (*Stachytarpheta indica* and *S. jamaicensis*) **c :** MATÉ 2,3

brazilian teal *n, usu cap B* **:** a small brightly colored wild duck (*Amazonetta braziliensis* or *Anas brasiliensis*) of So. American tropical forests highly esteemed as a table bird

brazilian walnut *n, usu cap B* **1 :** IMBUIA **2 :** a Brazilian tree (*Cordia goeldiana*) yielding a wood similar to black walnut

brazilian yellowwood *n, usu cap B* **:** BRAZILIAN MAHOGANY 1

braz·i·lin *also* **bras·i·lin** \'brazələn, brə'zil-\ *n* -S [F *brésiline*, fr. *brésil* brazilwood (fr. OF *bresil*, prob. fr. OSp *brasil*) + *-ine* — more at BRAZIL] **:** a white or pale yellow phenolic compound $C_{16}H_{14}O_5$ obtained from brazilwoods of the genus *Caesalpinia* and used esp. formerly in dyeing because of its ready oxidation to brazilein

brazil nut *n, usu cap B* [²*brazil*] **1** *also* **brazil-nut tree :** a tall So. American tree (*Bertholletia excelsa*) that bears large globular capsules each containing several closely packed roughly triangular nuts **2 :** any of the brown-shelled white-fleshed nuts borne in the fruit of a brazil nut — called also *cream nut, niggertoe, para nut*

brazil red *n* [¹*brazil*] **:** BRAZIL 2

brazils *pl of* BRAZIL

brazil wax *n, usu cap B* [²*brazil*] **:** CARNAUBA WAX

bra·zil·wood \brə'zilˌwu̇d\ *n* [¹*brazil* + *wood*] **1 :** the heavy wood of any of various tropical trees of the genus *Caesalpinia* (as *C. sappan, C. braziliensis,* and *C. crista*) used as red and purple dyewoods and in cabinetwork — see DYE table I (under *Natural Red 24*) **2 :** the wood of a So. American tree (*Haematoxylon brasiletto*) used in the American dye trade

brazing metal *n* [fr. gerund of ²*braze*] **:** the cementing metal used in brazing — compare ²BRAZE, HARD SOLDER, SILVER SOLDER

braz·za·ville \'brazəˌvil, -vēl\ *adj, usu cap* [fr. *Brazzaville*, Congo Republic] **:** of or from Brazzaville, Congo Republic **:** of the kind or style prevalent in Brazzaville

brd *abbr* **1** board **2** braid

brea \'brāə\ *n* -S [AmerSp, fr. Sp, tar, fr. OSp, fr. *brear* to tar, fr. OF *brayer*, fr. ON *brætha*, fr. *brāth* tar — more at BREATH] **1 a** (1) **:** a tree of the genus *Canarium* (2) **:** the soft resin obtained from it — compare ELEMI a **b :** a resinous thorny tree (*Caesalpinia praecox*) of Chile and Argentina that yields a pale brown gum **2 :** MALTHA

breac·an \'brakən\ [ScGael — more at BRECHAN] *Scot var of* BRECHAN

¹breach \'brēch\ *n* -ES [ME *breche*, alter. (influenced by OF *breche* breach, opening made by breaking, fr. OHG *brecha*) of OE *bryce* breach, fracture, breaking; akin to OE *brecan* to break — more at BREAK] **1 a** (1) **:** infraction or violation of a law, obligation, tie, code, or standard ⟨by this ~ of trust they forfeit the power the people had put into their hands —John Locke⟩ (2) **:** unfulfillment or nonfeasance constituting infraction ⟨a ~ of duty⟩ ⟨a ~ of church observances⟩ **b** *archaic* **:** INFRINGEMENT, ENCROACHMENT **c :** the state of being ignored **:** NONOBSERVANCE, DESUETUDE — used only in the phrase *honored more in the breach than in the observance* **d :** BREACH OF PROMISE **e :** the act of breaking or of aiding another to break into or out of ⟨prison ~⟩ **2 a :** a broken, ruptured, or torn condition **:** a place showing rupture, split, or fissure ⟨causing a ~ of the skin or bloodshed —G.G.Coulton⟩ ⟨turning over the picture of the ark with too much haste, I unhappily made a ~ in its ingenious fabric —Charles Lamb⟩ **b :** an opening or gap (as in a wall, rampart, or other fortification) made by or as if by battering ⟨once more unto the ~, dear friends, . . . or close the wall up with our English dead —Shak.⟩ ⟨the fatal ~ in the scholastic wholeness —H.O.Taylor⟩ **c :** a position entailing heavy fighting or strenuous exertion **:** a necessitous situation calling for urgent action ⟨although a thousand fall, there are always some to go into the ~ —R.L. Stevenson⟩ ⟨stepping into the ~ when his leader died⟩ **d :** a way made through a minefield by removing or exploding mines **3 a :** an open break in accustomed friendly or amiable relations **:** a notable division over an issue **:** an estranging difference **:** DISAGREEMENT, QUARREL ⟨a trivial misunderstanding causing a ~ between friends⟩ ⟨a gesture which healed a ~ between the two branches of the family —*Current Biog.*⟩ **b :** an interruption or suspension of something expected to continue **:** HIATUS ⟨imperil that success by any ~ in the continuity of worship —Compton Mackenzie⟩ ⟨the ~*es* of agrarian routine —F.M.Stenton⟩ **c :** a marked difference **:** a difference or lack of accord that prevents unity or integration ⟨the traditional ~ between the artist and the Puritan —S.P.Sherman⟩ **4 a :** the action of the breaking of waves or of the sweeping or pounding of breakers **b** *obs* **:** SURF, BREAKERS **c** *obs* **:** CREEK **5 :** the leap of a whale out of water

syn INFRACTION, VIOLATION, TRANSGRESSION, TRESPASS, INFRINGEMENT, CONTRAVENTION: BREACH usually occurs with modifying phrases specifying the thing offended against ⟨a *breach* of faith⟩ ⟨a *breach* of discipline⟩ ⟨a *breach* of the peace⟩ INFRACTION is more often used than BREACH for the breaking of a law or for an action contravening an obligation ⟨an *infraction* of a traffic regulation⟩ ⟨an *infraction* of school rules⟩ ⟨an *infraction* of a citizen's guaranteed rights⟩ VIOLATION adds the notion of overt disregard of law or the rights of others and often suggests the exercise of force ⟨a *violation* of traffic rules⟩ ⟨a *violation* of fundamental principles of good government⟩ ⟨renewed hostilities constitute an unequivocal *violation* of a peace treaty⟩ TRANSGRESSION applies to any act that goes beyond the limits of a law, rule, or order, usu. a moral law or commandment ⟨mistakes of this sort are resisted as any aesthetic *transgression* might be resisted — as being somehow incongruous —Edward Sapir⟩ ⟨what my father made clear to us as the very crux of our *transgressions* was that we had discredited our bringing up—Mary Austin⟩ ⟨a penalty pronounced upon Eve for her *transgression* in the garden of Eden —J.C. Krantz⟩ TRESPASS also implies an overstepping of prescribed ground but suggests encroachment upon another's rights, comfort, or property ⟨visitors had best avoid *trespass* on the lowlands lying west of the Roosevelt mansion —Morris Kaplan⟩ ⟨*trespass* across tribal frontiers is dangerous unless previous relations are friendly and the arrival is frankly announced —C.D.Forde⟩ ⟨the nature and degree of any *trespass* upon academic integrity—W.A.Dorrance⟩ INFRINGEMENT is sometimes interchangeable with INFRACTION ⟨an *infringement* of the law⟩ Often it implies trespass rather than violation and is the usual term in reference to encroachment upon a legally protected right or privilege ⟨an *infringement* of a patent⟩ ⟨an *infringement* upon a citizen's civil rights⟩ CONTRAVENTION implies a going contrary to the law or an act in defiance of what is regarded as right, lawful, or obligatory ⟨acts in direct *contravention* of the provisions of a treaty⟩ ⟨in flagrant *contravention* of commonly accepted academic principles and practices —*Key Reporter*⟩ ⟨so many judgments of common sense in *contravention* to the prevailing theories of our age —Reinhold Niebuhr⟩

syn BREAK, SPLIT, SCHISM, RENT, RUPTURE, RIFT: of these terms BREACH is the most general, carrying no implication of the cause or seriousness of the separation ⟨the widening *breach* between himself and his mother —Thomas Hardy⟩ ⟨flaws in the great structure, which were to widen into *breaches* —John Buchan⟩ BREAK signifies a breach but carries the idea of strain as a cause ⟨a *break* between the formerly friendly countries over the disposition of foreign aid⟩ SPLIT may imply a complete and usually irreparable breach ⟨he became involved in the *split* of the Socialist party into the "broad" and "narrow" factions —*Current Biog.*⟩ ⟨too wide a *split* in the party's ranks to agree on an acceptable candidate⟩ SCHISM implies a clear-cut division of one group, often religious, into two groups, usually opposed, and a consequent discord and dissension between them ⟨their families were on opposite sides of a *schism* that had occurred within the Society of Friends —*Current Biog.*⟩ ⟨to confirm its divisions, and to render apparently irreparable the *schism* in our culture —Hilaire Belloc⟩ ⟨when the *schism* between craft and industrial unionism resulted in the formation of the CIO —*Amer. Guide Series: Tenn.*⟩ RENT implies the literal sense of an opening, as in a fabric, made by tearing, even in its extended meaning suggesting the violence of the action and the jagged result ⟨the violent squabble over the chairmanship caused a very visible *rent* in the generally amicable relations of the club members⟩ ⟨a *rent* in the social fabric —Gilbert Millstein⟩ RUPTURE is like BREACH but carries more clearly the sense of a break in relations between people or groups, sometimes suggesting an actual break not clearly apparent ⟨the *rupture* of diplomatic relations —*N.Y.Times*⟩ ⟨a disagreement between father and son led to a nine-year *rupture* of their relations —*Current Biog.*⟩ ⟨there was no violent *rupture* of relations; the physicians and surgeons must simply have drifted apart again —Harvey Graham⟩ RIFT, carrying the idea of a breach by some natural process as the cracking of the earth, often suggests a small breach likely to get larger ⟨this little *rift* it was that had widened to a now considerable breach —H.G.Wells⟩ ⟨relations between the two groups were harmonious until politics caused a *rift* —*Amer. Guide Series: Texas*⟩

²breach \"\ *vb* -ED/-ING/-ES *vt* **1 a :** to make a breach in **:** smash a gap through **:** make a hole in by attrition ⟨siege artillery would have been needed to ~ the walls of the city —C.S.Forester⟩ ⟨~*ing* a dam⟩ **b :** to effect an opening in **:** serve successfully as an entering wedge in ⟨~ the wall of racial segregation⟩ ⟨~*ing* his distant reserve⟩ **c :** to wear or cut an opening in by erosion ⟨where the chalk of the South Downs is ~*ed* by the inlet —L.D.Stamp⟩ **d :** to make a gap through (an enemy minefield) **2 :** BREAK, VIOLATE ⟨the Supreme Court . . . held that our contract had not been impaired but ~*ed* —Hodding Carter⟩ ⟨~*ing* disastrously the whole structure of ideas by which . . . they live and govern —Walter Millis⟩ ~ *vi* **:** to break the water by leaping out ⟨they saw a whale spouting and ~*ing* —Charles Kingsley⟩

breach·er \'brēchə(r)\ *n* -S **:** one that makes or commits a breach

breaches *pl of* BREACH, *pres 3d sing of* BREACH

breach of arrest : the military offense committed by one in arrest of leaving without authority the limits within which he is ordered to remain

breach of contract : failure without legal reason to comply with the terms of a contract

breach of faith : a betrayal of confidence or trust

breach of prison : PRISON BREACH

breach of privilege : a violation of the rights of a privileged assembly

breach of promise : violation of one's plighted word, esp. of a promise to marry

breach of the peace : disorderly conduct that disturbs the public peace

breach of trust : violation by a trustee of the terms of a trust (as by fraudulent appropriation or careless handling of funds)

breachway \'ˌ\ *n* **:** a connecting channel

breachy \'brēchē\ *adj* -ER/-EST [²*breach* + *-y*] **1** *now dial* **:** apt to break fences or be wild — used of domestic animals **2** *dial Eng* **:** BRACKISH

¹bread \'bred\ *n* -S *often attrib* [ME *breed*, fr. OE *brēad* crumb, bread; akin to OHG *brōt* bread, ON *brauth* bread, OE *brēowan* to brew — more at BREW] **1 a :** a food made of a dough of flour or meal from grain with added liquid, shortening, and a leavening agent, the dough being kneaded, shaped, allowed to rise, and baked **b :** bread made from flours other than those of cereals ⟨potato ~⟩ **c :** a loaf, biscuit, or cake of sweetened bread dough enriched with eggs and fruit ⟨holiday ~⟩ ⟨Easter ~⟩ **2 :** a loaf, roll, or portion of bread ⟨an altar ~⟩ ⟨the ~*s* for the communicants⟩ **3 a :** FOOD ⟨give us this day our daily ~ —Mt 6:11 (AV)⟩ **b :** LIVELIHOOD; *esp* **:** simple necessities without extras ⟨earning his ~ as a laborer⟩ **c** (1) **:** a sustaining element ⟨the price of the ~ of health —Mary B. Spahr⟩ (2) **:** something that is received or accepted in a way felt to resemble accepting or eating food **d** *slang* **:** MONEY **syn** see LIVING — **bread upon the waters :** resources chanced or charitable deeds performed without expectation of return

²bread \"\ *vt* -ED/-ING/-S **1 :** to cover with bread crumbs before cooking ⟨a ~*ed* pork chop⟩ **2 :** to provide with a supply of bread

³bread \'brēd\ *var of* BREDE

bread and butter *n* **1 :** sliced bread spread with butter **2 a :** ¹BREAD 3b **b :** a sustaining unit or element **:** source of sustaining income ⟨plainer products being the *bread and butter* of the industry⟩ **3 a :** a toadflax (*Linaria vulgaris*) **b :** a greenbrier (*Smilax rotundifolia*) **syn** see LIVING

bread-and-butter \ˌˈˌ\ *adj* [*bread and butter*] **1** *now chiefly Brit* **:** ADOLESCENT **:** marked by the weakness, naïveté, or forcelessness of a juvenile **:** SCHOOLGIRLISH **2 a :** associated or connected with earning a livelihood, making money, or other mundane practical purposes ⟨a practical *bread-and-butter* education⟩ ⟨too busy with the *bread-and-butter* side of life to attend many social functions —A.T.Weaver⟩ **b :** STAPLE, SUSTAINING **:** dependable as a source of income often through being in steady demand ⟨concentrating on *bread-and-butter* products rather than fads⟩ ⟨don't overlook a *bread-and-butter* item that could be boosting your dollar volume —*Circle & Monogram*⟩ **3 :** sent or given by way of thanks for hospitality ⟨a *bread-and-butter* letter to his hostess⟩

bread-and-butter pickle *n* **:** a pickle relish of sliced cucumbers and onions

bread-and-butter plate *n* **:** a plate five to six inches in diameter for individual servings of bread and butter — called also *butter plate*

bread and circuses *n pl* [trans. of L *panis et circenses*] **:** food and entertainment offered by a government (as a dictatorship) to soothe discontent

breadbasket \'ˌ\ *n* **1** *slang* **:** STOMACH **2 :** a typically grain-producing agricultural area that provides much of the food needed by other areas ⟨these wide plains are the ~ of the nation⟩

breadboard \'ˌ\ *n* **1 :** a board on which dough is kneaded or rolled or bread cut **2 :** a board on which electric or electronic circuit diagrams may be laid out and experimental circuits constructed

bread crumb sponge *n* **:** CRUMB-OF-BREAD SPONGE

bread-crust bomb *n* **:** a volcanic bomb whose surface is disrupted by cracks

bread dance *n* **:** a ritual Amerindian dance performed in supplication for food

bread·en \'bredᵊn\ *adj* [¹*bread* + *-en*] *archaic* **:** made of bread

bread flour *n* **:** a flour from which bread dough with a good quality of gluten can be made

breadfruit \'ˌ\ *n* **1 :** a round usu. seedless tropical fruit that varies from 4 to 7 inches in diameter, has a greenish yellow rind and light yellow flesh when ripe, and resembles bread in color and texture when baked **2** *or* **breadfruit tree :** a tall tree (*Artocarpus altilis*) that is prob. native to Malaya but now widespread in the tropics both under cultivation and as an escape, produces breadfruit, has a bark that contains a strong fiber used locally to make cloth, and yields a usable timber and a glutinous material employed in caulking and as a glue or birdlime **3 :** an African tree (*Treculia africana*) that yields numerous seeds used for making meal **4** *Austral* **:** SCREW PINE

breadfruit: branch with fruit and staminate flowers

breadgrain \'ˌ\ *n* **:** cereals (as wheat and rye) that yield flour from which bread is made

breading *pres part of* BREAD

bread knife *n* **:** a knife with a long blade that has a serrated or scalloped edge

bread·less \-ləs\ *adj* [ME *bredlees*, fr. *bred, breed* bread + *-lees* -less] **:** being without bread

breadline \'ˌ\ *n* **:** a line formed by people waiting to receive food given in charity or issued in relief; *also* **:** the people in such a line

bread mold *n* **:** a mold of the family Mucoraceae (esp. *Rhizopus stolonifer*)

breadnut \'ˌ\ *n* **1 :** the nut of a tree (*Brosimum alicastrum*) of Jamaica and Mexico that is roasted and ground into a flour from which bread is made **2 :** a tree (*Brosimum terrabanum*) of British Honduras whose leaves furnish fodder **3 :** a seeded breadfruit

bread riot *n* **:** a riot for food

breadroot \'ˌ\ *n* **1 :** the root of a densely hairy plant (*Psoralea esculenta*) of the western U.S. used for food **2 :** the plant that yields breadroot **3 :** CINNAMON FERN

breads *pl of* BREAD, *pres 3d sing of* BREAD

bread sauce *n* **:** a milk-and-butter sauce thickened with bread crumbs

breadstick \'ˌ\ *n* **:** a crisp stick-shaped roll often served with soup

breadstuff \'ˌ\ *n* **1 :** grain, flour, or other cereal products **2 :** bread of any kind or shape

breadth \'bredth, -etth, *chiefly in substand speech* -eth\ *n* -S [obs. E *brede* breadth (fr. ME, fr. OE *brǣdu*, fr. *brād* broad) + *-th* — more at BROAD] **1 :** distance from side to side **:** measure taken at right angles to length **:** WIDTH **2 a** (1) **:** a piece of fabric of full width as manufactured ⟨a ~ of silk⟩ (2) **:** the width in which a fabric is manufactured ⟨lace in 18-inch ~*s*⟩ **b :** a wide expanse ⟨green ~*s* of undulating park —George Eliot⟩ **3 a :** spacious extent **:** embracing comprehensiveness **:** WIDENESS, SWEEP, SCOPE ⟨~ of culture, an ease with humanism and Renaissance learning —T.S.Eliot⟩ **b :** freedom from narrow concentration or parochial constraint **:** LARGENESS, LIBERALITY, GENEROSITY ⟨viewed with dispassionateness and ~ —Ruth Suckow⟩ **4 :** the quality in works of art brought about by elimination of unnecessary detail to produce an impression of largeness and unity ⟨associating colors in large groups to obtain ~⟩ **5 :** DENOTATION 4

breadth·en \'bredthən, -etthən\ *vi* -ED/-ING/-S [*breadth* + *-en*] **:** BROADEN

breadth extreme *n* **:** the width of a ship over the outside of all planking or plating at the widest frame

breadth-height index *n, anthrop* **:** the ratio of the maximum breadth of the head or skull to its maximum height multiplied by 100

breadth·less \-ləs\ *adj* **:** being without breadth

breadth molded *n, pl* **breadths molded :** MOLDED BREADTH

breadth·rid·er \'ˌ\ *n* **:** a strengthening timber near the broadest part of a wooden ship

breadth·ways \-,wāz\ *or* **breadth·wise** \-,wīz\ *adv (or adj)* **:** in the direction of the breadth **:** not lengthwise

bread tree *n* **1 :** BREADFRUIT 2 **2 :** WILD MANGO **3 :** BAOBAB

bread wheat *n* **:** any wheat (as club wheat) suitable for making into bread flour

breadwinner \'=,==\ *n* **1 :** a means (as a tool or a craft) of obtaining a livelihood **:** VOCATION **2 :** a member of a family or household whose wages solely or largely defray its living expenses

breadwinning \'=,==\ *n* **:** the gaining of a livelihood

[1]**break** \'brāk\ *vb* **broke** \'brōk\ *or archaic* **brake** \'brāk\ *or chiefly Scot* **brack** \'brak\ *or Scot* **brak** \"\ **bro·ken** \'brōkən *sometimes* -kᵊŋ\ *or substand* **broke**; **breaking**; **breaks** [ME *breken,* fr. OE *brecan;* akin to OHG *brehhan* to break, Goth *brikan,* L *frangere* to break, Skt *giribhraj* breaking forth from mountains] *vt* **1 a :** to split into pieces or smash into parts or fragments typically by a blow or stress and with suddenness or violence **b :** to pull, rend, tear, thrust, or shear apart typically forcefully or roughly and often by accident **c** *now dial Eng* **:** TEAR, RIP ⟨~ cloth⟩ ⟨~ paper⟩ ⟨don't ~ your jacket on the fence⟩ **d :** to snap into pieces **:** FRACTURE ⟨~ a bone⟩ **:** fracture the bone of (a bodily part) ⟨the blow *broke* his arm⟩ **:** suffer fracture of a bone in ⟨he *broke* his leg in the wreck⟩ **:** DISLOCATE ⟨~*ing* his neck⟩ **e :** to fracture the limbs of in torture ⟨a captive *broken* on the wheel⟩; *broadly* **:** MAIM, MUTILATE ⟨the *broken* bodies of the dead soldiers⟩ **f** (1) **:** CUT, RUPTURE ⟨~ the skin⟩ (2) **:** to cut or bruise the skin of (the head) ⟨blacked eyes and *broken* heads were common in such fights⟩ **g :** to cut up **:** tear to pieces **:** CARVE, REND — usu. used with *up* ⟨hunters ~*ing* up the deer⟩ ⟨hounds ~*ing* up a fox⟩ **h :** to cut into and turn over the surface of **:** PLOW ⟨~ the soil⟩ ⟨grasslands have been *broken* and planted to wheat —*Amer. Guide Series: Wash.*⟩ **i :** to rupture the surface of and permit flowing out or effusing ⟨~ an artery⟩ **:** undergo such a rupture of ⟨he *broke* several veins during his seizure⟩ **j** (1) **:** to smash or tear open (2) **:** to lay open and distribute or sort the contents of **:** OPEN (3) **:** to uncover for easy collecting ⟨~*ing* ore⟩ (4) **:** to remove and pry apart caked tobacco from (a hogshead) for inspection as to merchantable quality **2 a :** to violate or transgress by failure to follow, observe, or act in accordance with **:** fail to keep ⟨~*ing* the law⟩ ⟨~*ing* a contract⟩ ⟨~*ing* his promise⟩ ⟨every great novel has *broken* many conventions —Ellen Glasgow⟩ **b :** to invalidate (a will) by action at law **3 a :** to force entry into **:** enter by force or violence **:** open for illegal entry — archaic except in law ⟨accused of attempting to ~ a house⟩ **b :** to burst and usu. to force a way through ⟨~*ing* the barriers in his way⟩ **c :** to make one's escape by force from **:** escape by or as if by severing or bursting barriers that confine ⟨~*ing* jail⟩ **d :** to make or effect by or as if by piercing, cutting, forcing, or pressing through ⟨~*ing* a trail⟩ ⟨~*ing* out a ski area⟩ ⟨~*ing* a hole in the ice⟩ ⟨~*ing* open the snow-clogged roads⟩ ⟨~*ing* the packet open⟩ **e :** PENETRATE, PIERCE **4 a :** to separate or shear by or as if by tearing or rending — often used with *off* ⟨a branch *broken* off the tree⟩ **b :** to make ineffective as a binding force **:** LOOSEN, SUNDER ⟨~*ing* his chains⟩ **:** effect release or escape from ⟨~ a wrestling hold⟩ **c** *cricket* **:** to strike (a wicket) and dislodge one or both bails **d :** to subject to breaking ⟨certain consonant combinations may ~ a preceding vowel⟩ **e :** PICK ⟨~ pineapples⟩ ⟨~ oranges⟩ **f :** to soften the fibers of (a skin) by scraping or pounding **5 a :** to disrupt or split with ensuing dispersal ⟨a quarrel that *broke* the party apart⟩ **:** disrupt the order or compactness of ⟨~*ing* ranks⟩ **b :** to end, close, or destroy by or as if by dispersing — often used with *up* ⟨~ up the counterfeiting ring⟩ ⟨~ up our partnership⟩ **c** *archaic* **:** DISSOLVE, DISBAND **d :** to disrupt by death, divorce, or conflict ⟨children from *broken* homes⟩ — often used with *up* ⟨infidelities that *broke* up their marriage⟩ **e :** to prevent effective operation or performance of by disruptive action ⟨~*ing* up bootlegging operations⟩ ⟨~*ing* up a forward pass play⟩ **f :** to give or receive money units of smaller denomination in exchange for ⟨~*ing* a 10-dollar bill⟩ **6 a :** to defeat utterly and end as an effective force **:** overcome the resistance or strength of **:** SMASH, DEMOLISH, DESTROY ⟨he *broke* the enemy by . . . starvation, attrition, and a slow, deadly scientific envelopment —John Buchan⟩ — sometimes used with *down* **b :** to crush the spirit of **:** sap (one's) will to resist, withstand, or persevere **:** afflict with so much distress that hope, resistance, morale, or self-control is weakened **:** cause (one) to yield — often used with *down* ⟨the brutal method finally *broke* the prisoner so that he confessed⟩ ⟨~ down a prisoner by cross-examination⟩; *sometimes* **:** to agitate and depress — often used with *up* ⟨quite *broken* up by his friend's death⟩ **c :** to make tractable or submissive: as (1) **:** to train (an animal) to adjust to the service or convenience of man ⟨bought a number of horses and *broke* them to saddle⟩ (2) **:** INURE, ACCUSTOM **d :** to exhaust in health, strength, energy, or capacity **:** reduce to weakness or ineptness **:** wear out **:** WEARY — often used with *down* ⟨completely *broken* by his struggle for power⟩ ⟨his heavy duties eventually *broke* him down⟩ **e :** to ruin financially **:** BANKRUPT **:** leave virtually without assets **:** exhaust the funds of ⟨~*ing* his competitors by unfair practices⟩ ⟨~*ing* the bank in the gambling house⟩ **f :** to reduce in rank **:** strip of office or privilege **:** CASHIER, DISMISS ⟨*broken* from sergeant to private⟩ **g :** to shatter (something that is advancing or thrusting) by firm resistance **:** turn aside the force or intensity of ⟨the jetty ~*ing* the waves⟩ ⟨a stand of trees ~*ing* the wind⟩ **h :** to separate the fibers from the woody core of (flax or hemp) after retting esp. by means of fluted rollers preparatory to scutching **i :** to cause failure and discontinuance of (a strike) by measures outside bargaining processes **j :** to better (a score, standard, or record) ⟨golfers trying to ~ 90⟩ ⟨~*ing* the mark for innings pitched⟩ **k :** to win against (an opponent's service) in a racket game **l :** to deprive of all chance or hope of success **:** ruin the standing or prospects of ⟨she could make or ~ the ambitious climber —*Amer. Guide Series: R.I.*⟩ **m :** to demonstrate the falsity or lack of credibility of **:** DISPROVE — often used with *down* ⟨~*ing* an alibi⟩ ⟨~*ing* down a witness⟩ **n :** to cause a sharp reduction of **:** reduce the price of sharply ⟨news that will ~ many oil stocks⟩ **7 a :** to stop, cut short, or bring to an end often suddenly **:** disturb the continuance of **:** HALT, STOP — often used with *off,* sometimes with *up* ⟨the home run that ~*s* the tie⟩ ⟨~*ing* the deadlock by decisive action⟩ ⟨~*ing* off what he was saying⟩ ⟨~*ing* off relations with a hostile country⟩ **b :** to cease the regular continuity of **:** INTERRUPT, SUSPEND ⟨~*ing* their journey⟩ ⟨showers ~*ing* the heat wave⟩ ⟨~*ing* the beam of light⟩ — sometimes used with *up* **c :** to open and thus bring about suspension of operation ⟨~*ing* an electric circuit⟩ **d :** to destroy unity or completeness of ⟨this dinner set is *broken;* two cups are missing⟩ ⟨to have a drink and ~ the quart⟩ **e** (1) **:** to change the appearance of uniformity of **:** bring variety or change into **:** serve to change the impression of regular continuity in ⟨plateau lands *broken* by gullies and ravines⟩ ⟨a level roof *broken* by a dormer⟩ (2) **:** to cause lack of regular continuity in ⟨~*ing* joints in Flemish bond⟩ **f :** to split the surface of ⟨flying fish ~*ing* the water⟩ **g** (1) **:** to cause to discontinue indulgence in a habit — used with *of* ⟨his wife tried to ~ him of swearing⟩ (2) **:** DISCONTINUE — often used with *off* ⟨~*ing* a habit⟩ ⟨~*ing* off smoking⟩ **h :** to stop (a telegraph operator) in order to verify matter sent **i** (1) **:** to continue (a story) on a page later than and usu. not consecutive with the starting page (2) **:** to interrupt the continuity of (type or print or matter in type or print) at the end of a line for continuation in the next line **8 a** *archaic* **:** to reveal or impart a confidence harbored in or at **b :** to make known sometimes with caution and after hesitation **:** TELL, IMPART, REVEAL ⟨~ the news of his death to her⟩ **c :** to utter or crack (a jest) ⟨~ no jests that are sharp and biting —George Washington⟩ **d :** to make public or available for publication; *often* **:** to publicize widely or permit wide publicity of sometimes after a period of withholding ⟨the admiralty office *broke* the news of the loss⟩ **e :** to initiate (a campaign or course of action) often with fanfare and publicity ⟨big companies ~*ing* a sales campaign⟩ **f :** to find an explanation or solution for **:** SOLVE, UNRAVEL ⟨the detective who *broke* the case⟩ **g** (1) **:** to discover the essentials of (a code or cipher system) — often used with *down* (2) **:** to solve (an encrypted message) without full knowledge of the keys (3) **:** DECRYPT ⟨~ a message⟩ **9 a :** to split into smaller units, parts, or processes **:** DIVIDE — usu. used with *up* or *down* ⟨*broken* into countless small bands —R.A.Billington⟩ ⟨the primary colors are *broken* up into thousands of colored bands and lines —Waldemar Kaempffert⟩ **b :** to divide (a musical chord) by sounding the component tones separately (as in an arpeggio) **c :** to separate (a color) in painting into component parts and to lay these side by side on the canvas instead of mixing them on the palette so that the observer's eye recomposes the color — compare DIVISIONISM, POINTILLISM **d :** to bunch (cured tobacco leaves) in the center and tear a string away from a lath preparatory to tying into a hand **e :** to separate (an emulsion) permanently into components ⟨cream is *broken* by churning⟩ **f :** to split (grain) into flour and bran in milling **10 :** to alter the direction or course of **:** bring about such alteration in: as **a :** to impart break to (a cricket ball) in bowling **b :** to make (a pitched or thrown baseball) curve, drop, or rise sharply **11 a :** to open or unfold at a seam, bend, groove, or joint; *sometimes* **:** to fold or bend at a seam or joint **b :** to open the action of (certain firearms) ⟨*broke* the shotgun and loaded both barrels⟩ **c :** to make with joints for folding ⟨an airplane with *broken* wings⟩ **12 :** to alter the tone of (a color) by an admixture of another color or shade ~ *vi* **1 a :** to depart or escape usu. with sudden forceful effort and from restraint or constraint **:** burst free from ties or barriers ⟨~*ing* away from home ties⟩ ⟨~*ing* out of jail⟩ **b :** to come forth or move out or forward usu. forcefully or abruptly as if bursting through restraints or barriers ⟨~ through the crowd⟩ ⟨dogs *broke* out of the trees into the open⟩ **c :** to develop or be formed or uttered with or as if with suddenness and force — often used with *out* or *forth* ⟨a wail *broke* from the child's lips⟩ ⟨laughter *broke* out in the audience⟩ ⟨spots *broke* out on the child's face⟩ ⟨the sunlight *broke* forth in splendor⟩ **d :** to come into being by or as if by bursting forth — often used with *forth* or *out* ⟨as day was ~*ing*⟩ ⟨the buds *broke* forth in red⟩ ⟨trouble *broke* out between the two countries⟩ ⟨fire *broke* out in the old warehouse⟩ ⟨yellow fever *broke* out in the city⟩ **e :** to start an action, assume a role, take on a condition, or give vent to expression with abruptness — usu. used with *out* or *into* ⟨~*ing* into a roar of laughter⟩ ⟨~*ing* out in tears⟩ ⟨~*ing* into revolt⟩ **f :** to emerge from the surface of the water **:** leap up from the water ⟨the fish were ~*ing*⟩ **g** (1) **:** to start usu. abruptly as if overcoming restraint — usu. used with *out* ⟨rioting *broke* out⟩ ⟨rifle fire *broke* out at dawn⟩ ⟨when the war finally *broke*⟩ (2) **:** to come to pass **:** OCCUR **h** (1) **:** to become public or available for publication ⟨the disaster story *broke* at 10 o'clock⟩ (2) **:** to attain to wide publicity **:** become publicly known ⟨when the scandal *broke*⟩ **i :** to become detached or disengaged and usu. displaced by or as if by the rending or severing of bonds ⟨the boat *broke* from its mooring⟩ ⟨deck cargo *broke* loose in the storm⟩; *also* **:** to dissociate (from a group) ⟨splinter factions ~*ing* from the political party⟩ **:** take a different course **:** DEPART — often used with *away* ⟨~*ing* away from his former leader⟩ ⟨~*ing* away from old tradition⟩ **j :** to leave cover **:** dash from cover ⟨when the stag *broke*⟩ **k** (1) **:** to make a sudden dash ⟨infantrymen ~*ing* for cover⟩ ⟨a base runner ~*ing* for home⟩ **:** pick up speed quickly ⟨when a basketball player ~*s* for the basket⟩ (2) **:** to leave a starting mark, gate, or barrier ⟨a horse slow at ~*ing*⟩; *also* **:** to start before the proper signal has been given in a sports event (3) *of a hunting dog* **:** to leave a point and move quickly to retrieve ⟨trained to ~ at gunshot⟩ **l** (1) **:** to separate after a clinch in boxing or a hold in wrestling esp. when so ordered by the referee — often used with *away* (2) **:** to separate as if from such a clinch or hold — often used with *away* **m** *chiefly Midland* **:** to let out **:** come to an end **:** DISMISS ⟨what time does church ~⟩ **2 a :** to come apart or split into pieces typically with sudden violence and with damage or ruin **:** BURST, SHATTER ⟨the cup *broke* when it fell on the floor⟩ **b :** to open with or as if with tearing, splitting, or rupturing ⟨the bag *broke* and the sugar spilled⟩ **c :** to open spontaneously or by pressure from within (as of a boil or a bubble) **d** *of a wave* **:** to curl over and fall apart in surf or foam **:** be shattered and lose driving force **e :** to crack without complete separation into parts ⟨the windshield *broke* but did not shatter⟩ **f** (1) **:** to diminish markedly in force or intensity **:** abate and fade away ⟨when the frost ~*s*⟩ ⟨after an hour of heavy rain the storm *broke*⟩ (2) *dial* **:** to become fair **:** CLEAR ⟨when the weather ~*s*⟩ **g :** to be driven back in retreat **:** be dispersed in disorder **:** give way in disorderly retreat ⟨the volunteer units *broke* when the enemy charged⟩ **h** (1) **:** to fail in health or strength **:** suffer loss of strength, vitality, keenness, or control — often used with *down* ⟨he *broke* down under the strain of his position⟩ (2) **:** to suffer complete or marked loss of resistance, composure, resolution, morale, or command of a situation ⟨the prisoner *broke* under cross-examination and told the whole story⟩ — often used with *down* (3) **:** to become severely affected or crushed by grief, disappointment, or anguish — used of the heart conceived as the seat of emotions or affections ⟨his heart *broke* when his wife died⟩ **i :** to become inoperative or ineffectual because of damage, wear, or strain ⟨the toy *broke*⟩ — often used with *down* ⟨the bus *broke* down on the hill⟩ **j :** to go bankrupt **:** fail in business ⟨the bank *broke* as a result of the run⟩ **k :** to undergo a sudden marked decrease in price or value ⟨rail stocks *broke* sharply yesterday⟩ **l :** to undergo breaking **3** *obs* **:** to speak (with a person concerning some subject) ⟨~ with thee of some affairs —Shak.⟩ **4 a :** to end a relationship, connection, accord, or agreement ⟨*broke* with his leader on this issue⟩ ⟨~ with tradition⟩ — often used with *off* or *up* ⟨her parents *broke* up and got a divorce⟩ ⟨*broke* off with his wife completely⟩ **b :** to effect a departure, termination, interruption, or change from the accustomed — often used with *away* ⟨~*ing* away and living a life of her own⟩ **c :** to release a dancing partner's hands **:** loose hands in dancing **:** separate so that another may cut in **d :** to become unfurled **:** stream out at full length ⟨the royal standard *broke* from the mainmast⟩ **5 a :** to make a sharp change in course **:** deviate from a straight line **b** (1) *of a bowled cricket ball* **:** to change direction on touching the ground ⟨a ball that turns from off to leg ~*s* back; one that turns toward the wicket from either side ~*s* in; one that turns away from the wicket to either side ~*s* away⟩ (2) *of a pitched baseball* **:** to curve, drop, or rise sharply ⟨a fast ball that ~*s* away from a batter⟩ **c :** to change sharply in purport, mood, or attitude ⟨~*ing* to the ridiculous⟩ **d** (1) *of the voice* **:** to alter sharply in tone, pitch, or intensity either momentarily (as under stress of emotion) or permanently ⟨his voice *broke* with excitement⟩ **:** shift from one register to another (as when the voice is changing in adolescence) ⟨the boy's voice *broke* momentarily from its deep new bass to its original high soprano⟩ (2) *of a tone on a wind instrument* **:** to shift abruptly from one register to another **:** fail abruptly in musical quality (as by a sudden uncontrolled harshness or shift in register); *also* **:** to die out **:** FAIL ⟨screamed until his voice *broke* completely⟩ **e** *of a horse* **:** to fail to keep a prescribed gait **f** (1) **:** to be interrupted for continuation in another column or on another page usu. not consecutive ⟨the story ~*s* to page five⟩ — compare JUMP (2) **:** to come to a break ⟨the first two columns ~ nicely⟩ ⟨paragraph three *broke* badly at the ends of the lines⟩ **g :** to move a camera to a new location **h** (1) **:** to announce in a game of rummy that play will end after each player has had one more turn (2) **:** to be first to meld in rummy **i :** to interrupt one's activity or occupation usu. for a brief period ⟨at noon we ~ for lunch⟩ **6 a :** to vary from even continuity or regularity **:** develop notable variation or change **b :** to change abruptly in line or set often with suggestion of opening ⟨her face *broke* into a smile⟩ **c :** to become broken or discontinuous ⟨an electric circuit may ~⟩ **d** (1) *of a fish or whale* **:** to leap wholly or partly out of the water (2) **:** to emerge from the surface of the water ⟨shoals that ~ at low tide⟩ **e :** to make the opening shot of a game or frame of pool or billiards **f :** to exhibit variation (as the flowers from hybrid seedlings or those from plants infected with a virus) **:** SPORT **7 a :** to divide into classes, categories, or types **:** ANALYZE, CLASSIFY — usu. used with *down* or *up* ⟨our cases ~ up into three types⟩ **b :** to fold, bend, lift, or come apart at a seam, groove, or joint ⟨a hospital bed that ~*s*⟩ ⟨a pistol that ~*s*⟩ **c** *of cream* **:** to separate during churning into liquid and fat **d :** to fix a round number for the payoff in pari-mutuel betting and disregard uneven winnings (as pennies) ⟨in some states race tracks ~ to the nearest nickel⟩ **e :** to form branches ⟨a tree bough that ~*s*⟩ **f** (1) **:** to thicken and become cloudy **:** produce a precipitate or suspension of gelatinous matter — used esp. of vegetable oils on being heated (2) *of an emulsion* **:** to separate permanently, usu. into oily and aqueous layers — often distinguished from *cream* **8 :** HAPPEN, DEVELOP ⟨everything *broke* right for him⟩

syn CRACK, BURST, BUST, SNAP, SHATTER, SHIVER: BREAK usu. implies a stress or strain strong enough to cause rupture or fracture in one or many places, or a general disruption, but extends commonly to any depriving (of an object, as a machine) of capacity to work ⟨the dam *broke* and flooded neighboring fields⟩ ⟨*break* a rock with a hammer⟩ ⟨*break* a silence⟩ ⟨the clock is *broken* and does not run⟩ CRACK implies a breaking of something hard, brittle, or hollow, usu. without complete separation of parts ⟨*crack* a plate⟩ ⟨*crack* a mirror⟩ ⟨a *cracked* baseball bat⟩ BURST implies a breaking into pieces, usu. with the scattering of parts or contents, often by the force of internal pressure ⟨the glittering bubble *burst* —G.H.Reed b.1887⟩ ⟨a shell *burst* 50 feet in front and showered the area with shrapnel⟩ BUST is interchangeable with BREAK or BURST in extremely informal conversational English ⟨a *busted* alarm clock —Eric Hodgins⟩ ⟨three *busted* ribs —*Time*⟩ ⟨the doors unhinged, the globes *busted* —Henry Miller⟩ SNAP suggests a quick clean complete break, esp. of something brittle or fragile ⟨the branch *snapped* with the weight of the ice and the force of the wind⟩ ⟨to *snap* a stick in two⟩ SHATTER carries the idea of a totally destructive breaking into pieces esp. forcibly and with a wide scattering of fragments ⟨the force of the explosion *shattered* the windows for ½ mile around⟩ ⟨the burst of fire *shattered* all enemy resistance⟩ SHIVER implies a shattering by forceful sudden clashing or smashing and lays even stronger stress than *shatter* on the scattering of small fragments ⟨one of the men tore the paper plaster off the full-length mirror, . . . hurled his soup bowl at it, *shivering* the glass —R.M.Lovett⟩ ⟨the sound of an explosion *shivered* the quiet —Irwin Shaw⟩ — **break a lance :** to engage in spirited controversy often with quixotic ardor ⟨always ready to *break a lance* in defense of his ideas⟩ — **break and enter :** to gain a passage by force or otherwise and enter into another's dwelling, outbuilding, store, or other building — used with varying legal applications in different jurisdictions; see HOUSEBREAKING; compare BURGLARY — **break bread 1 :** to eat in the company of ⟨refusing to *break bread* with his old enemy⟩ **2 :** to give out bread (as in a Communion service) — **break bulk 1 :** to remove, transfer, or displace part of a load or cargo **:** start to unload **:** unload and distribute all or part of a carload, boatload, or truckload **2** *of a bailee* **:** to treat that which is held by bailment in such a manner as to destroy its entirety in the eyes of the law (as by opening a package and removing part of the contents) — **break camp :** to pack up gear and leave a camp or campsite ⟨the troops *broke camp* early in the morning⟩ — **break cover** *or* **break covert :** to start from a covert or lair ⟨the hunted fox *broke cover*⟩ — **break for color** *or* **break up for color :** to separate (imposed letterpress matter) into parts so that each part may be printed in a different color — **break ground 1 :** to dig open the earth often in excavating for new construction ⟨*breaking ground* for the new arsenal⟩ **2 :** to make new discoveries or introduce new procedures or material **:** PIONEER ⟨this report *breaks* new *ground* in the study of human relations⟩ — **break joints :** to arrange bricks or stone in a wall in such a way that the upright joints of two successive courses are nowhere in line with each other — **break no squares** *obs* **:** to make no difference **:** do no harm — **break one's duck** *of a cricket batsman* **:** to score at least one run — **break one's heart :** to afflict with bitter sorrow, hopeless grief, or despair — **break one's neck :** to strive to the utmost — **break one's wrists :** to turn the wrists as part of the swing of a club or bat (as in baseball) — **break service** *of a mare* **:** to fail to conceive — **break sheer** *of a boat* **:** to turn while at anchor so as to lie obliquely to the anchor and in danger of fouling the cable — **break ship :** to fail to rejoin one's ship after leave ⟨facing court-martial for *breaking ship*⟩ — **break step :** to fail to keep step **:** walk or march out of step — **break the back 1 :** to check, subdue, or overcome the main force **:** leave existent but powerless ⟨to *break the back* of enemy resistance⟩ **2** *of a ship* **:** to break the keel and keelson — **break the ice 1 :** to make a beginning **2 :** to get through the first difficulties in starting a conversation or discussion — **break wind :** to expel gas from the intestine

[2]**break** \"\ *n* -s [ME *breke,* fr. *breken,* v.] **1 a :** an act or action of breaking **:** SHATTERING **:** FRACTURE **b :** a grinding of grain or meal **:** any of the grindings in which flour is separated or extracted from bran **c :** a breaking of flax or hemp; *also* **:** BREAKER 2c(1) **d :** the action of breaking open hogsheads; *also* **:** a sale of tobacco from opened hogsheads **e** (1) **:** a pool shot that touches a ball in the arranged triangle at the beginning of a frame (2) **:** the opening shot in a game of billiards **f :** the act of opening a gap in an electrical circuit **2 a :** a condition produced by breaking or appearing as if so produced **:** GAP, OPENING, APERTURE, BREACH, RENT ⟨through a ~ in the hedge⟩ ⟨a ~ in the pipe⟩ ⟨a ~ in the clouds⟩ **b :** a gap in an otherwise continuous electric circuit **3 :** the action or act of breaking in, out, or forth: as **a :** emergence from darkness **:** LIGHTENING ⟨at ~ of day⟩ **b :** a sometimes forcefully effected escape from confinement ⟨the convicts planned a jail ~⟩ **c :** illegal entry accomplished forcefully ⟨a ~ at the store was thwarted by the police⟩ **d :** an abrupt run (as to reach safety) **:** DASH, RUSH ⟨captives making a ~ for freedom⟩ ⟨the startled deer made a ~ for the thicket⟩ ⟨a base runner making a ~ for home⟩; *esp* **:** a quick offensive thrust toward one's own basket in basketball **e :** the start of a race; *esp* **:** the start of a horse race **f :** the act of separating after a boxing or wrestling clinch often by the referee **g :** the occurrence of a disease in a person or esp. in a domestic animal supposed to be immune to or to have been completely isolated from exposure to that disease **4 :** an interruption in continuity ⟨waiting for a ~ in the bad weather⟩: as **a :** discontinuity in the flow or tone of a composition **:** a notable change of subject matter, attitude, or treatment ⟨a sonnet is often marked by a ~ after the eighth line⟩ **b** (1) **:** an abrupt, significant, or noteworthy change or interruption in a continuous process, trend, course of action, or series of events ⟨a ~ in production for retooling⟩ ⟨army service made a ~ in his career⟩ (2) **:** an interruption from work or duty for rest, relaxation, or recreation ⟨taking a ~ for a cigarette⟩ (3) **:** a planned interruption in a radio or television program ⟨a ~ for the commercial⟩ **c :** a noticeable interruption or change in any continuous surface, level, line, or course: as (1) **:** a marked topographical variation ⟨a plain extending 1000 miles without a ~⟩ **:** a portion of land distinct or divided off from adjacent land **:** a plowed area **:** a strip of land in crop or pasture **:** an irregular rough piece of ground **:** a deep valley, ravine, or gorge; *esp* **:** one that cuts through a ridge or mountain (2) **breaks** *pl* **:** a line of cliffs and associated spurs and small ravines (as at the edge of a mesa or canyon) (3) *chiefly Brit* **:** a portion of pasture or grazing crop to be grazed for a limited period of time ⟨grazing rape in ~*s*⟩ (4) **:** a feature breaking the continuity of a structural line **:** a projection from a surface **:** a change in direction ⟨gates, niches, and other ~*s* in the wall⟩ (5) **:** a part in a ship or deck where a partial deck ends leaving a drop to a deck on a lower level (6) **:** change of direction of flight of a bowled cricket ball after bouncing esp. when caused by spin imparted by the bowler — see LEG-BREAK, OFFBREAK (7) **:** deviation of a pitched baseball from a straight line or from a gravitational curve **d** (1) *mining* **:** DISLOCATION, FAULT (2) **:** an abrupt change of fossil content or lithology at a definite horizon in a chronologic sequence of sedimentary rocks indicative of a disconformity or hiatus ⟨a faunal ~⟩ ⟨a stratigraphic ~⟩; *also* **:** any marked change in lithology in a sedimentary sequence **e :** a disturbing or rippling of the surface of water (as by a fish rising) **f :** an abrupt halt, change of direction, or pivoting separation of partners dancing together **g** (1) **:** interruption of a line (as a crease, fold, or seam) in clothing ⟨trousers with a ~ just above the shoe⟩ **:** change in a line at a seam ⟨the ~ where brim and crown of a hat meet⟩ (2) **:** a wrinkle or series of wrinkles formed in leather at a fold **h :** failure of a horse to maintain the prescribed gait in a harness race **:** change from one pace to another **i** (1) **:** an abrupt change in the quality or pitch of musical tone (2) **:** the shift of a rank to a lower octave in organ mixture stops to avoid impractically small pipes (3) **:** any notable variation in pitch,

intensity, or tone in the voice ⟨speaking passionately, with a ~ in her voice⟩ **j :** a switch of a block of votes (as in a political convention) to create a definite trend — compare STAMPEDE **k :** a noticeable change in quality, character, or nature **:** a departure from a previously followed pattern ⟨a ~ from his customary procedure⟩: (1) **:** any striking departure from the normal color of a flower (as in tulips affected by virus) in which the blooms become variously striped and variegated (2) **:** an interruption of the fibers of a fleece by a zone of inferior quality coinciding with the growth of wool during a period of illness or deficiency of food or water **l** *printing* **:** separation of composed matter at an indicated point **5 :** a rupture in previously friendly relations or firm accord **:** disagreement causing separation **:** an abrupt split or difference with or as if with something previously adhered to or followed ⟨a ~ between the president and the secretary on the matter⟩ ⟨a ~ between the two countries⟩ ⟨a ~ with a tradition previously followed⟩ ⟨a clean ~ with his old associates⟩ **6 a :** a number of chests of tea making up a consignment or shipment **b :** the quantity of hemp prepared in a year **c :** a sequence of successful shots in billiards **:** RUN ⟨a ~ of 20⟩ ⟨a 60 ~⟩ **d :** gelatinous matter that separates in some vegetable oils (as raw linseed oil) on being heated; *also* **:** similar matter that separates on aging — compare FOOT 15 **7 :** a device used in breaking, bending, checking, or changing: as **a :** a tool for bending sheet metal to a required angle ⟨a cornice ~⟩ — compare ⁴BRAKE 5 **b :** a bench on which dough is kneaded **:** a machine used in kneading dough **c :** FLAX BREAKER **d :** the roller or stone mill that grinds the original wheat **e :** FIREBREAK **f :** a commutator in telegraphy **8 :** a place or situation at which a break occurs: **a** (1) **:** the point where one musical register changes to another (as of a voice or of wind instruments) (2) *in compound organ stops* **:** a point where the relative pitch of the pipes changes (3) *in blues or jazz* **:** a short ornamental or rhythmically emphatic passage interpolated between phrases by a performer and filling out the form of a short phrase to periodic length **b :** BRANCH; *esp* **:** one formed after pinching or disbudding — see BOTTOM BREAK **c** (1) **:** BREAK LINE (2) **:** the place where calculation shows that a column or page will end and the continuity of composed matter should be broken (3) **:** the place in a form at which matter that is to be printed in another color is separated from neighboring matter (4) **:** the place at which a word is divided (as at the end of a line) (5) **:** the point in a printed story at which it is continued on another page or column (6) **:** the terminal point of a printed line ⟨headline verbs are seldom split by a line ~⟩ (7) **:** the time at which a news story becomes available for publication **d :** a pause or interruption (as a caesura or diaeresis) within or at the end of a verse or other unit of utterance or composition **e :** a failure to make a strike or a spare on a frame in bowling **f :** a forest fire that escapes immediate control **9 :** a sudden and abrupt decline of prices or values; *broadly* **:** any price decline ⟨the news caused a ~ in rails⟩ **10 :** a rough jet of metal on the shank of a newly cast and unfinished foundry type **11 :** an awkward social blunder; *specif* **:** a gauche, naive, or imprudent comment causing embarrassment **12 :** a stroke of fortune ⟨ascribe his fortune to luck, to getting the ~s —J.G.Cozzens⟩; *specif* **:** a favorable or opportune situation or turn arising either through chance or through equitable or kindly consideration or treatment ⟨dwarfs got their best ~ . . . in aircraft factories, inspecting bomber wings from the inside —W.L.Gresham⟩ ⟨a judge often gives a first offender a ~⟩

syn GAP, INTERRUPTION, INTERVAL, INTERIM, HIATUS, LACUNA: BREAK applies to any lapse in continuity of material, course of action, or time ⟨a *break* in the fence⟩ ⟨a *break* in the ice⟩ ⟨the book was written with no *breaks*⟩ ⟨the holiday made a pleasant *break* in the routine⟩ GAP, orig. indicating an opening in a wall, was extended to indicate any means of passage and now may indicate a void, a space unfilled or unfillable ⟨a water *gap*⟩ ⟨a wind *gap*⟩ ⟨a *gap* in the mountain chain⟩ ⟨the *gap* which separates Roman Britain from Anglo-Saxon England has fascinated a long succession of scholars —*Times Lit. Supp.*⟩ INTERRUPTION may apply to breaking of continuity, sometimes disturbing; it may call attention to the action of breaking rather than the result ⟨the time schedule we set up must be tentative, of course, until we find out the *interruptions* — telephone calls, appointments — that are bound to occur —*Better Homes & Gardens*⟩ ⟨the *Newport Mercury*, a publication that has, with one brief *interruption* during the Revolution, come down to the present day —*Amer. Guide Series: R.I.*⟩ INTERVAL may refer to distance in space or period in time between two similar things ⟨along this fertile plain, at *intervals* averaging about seven miles, are thoroughly modern towns —*Amer. Guide Series: Tex.*⟩ ⟨you snatched gladly at such diversions Sunday, for the rest of the day until 2 o'clock was a solemn *interval*, during which all the usual books and plays were interdicted —Mary Austin⟩ INTERIM refers to an interval between specified dates or events ⟨the *interim* between the two wars⟩ ⟨the *interim* between the king's death and the prince's accession⟩ ⟨in a healthy mind there is an *interim* between one duty and another. This prevents them from wearing each other out. These intervals of soothing carelessness, if not unduly prolonged, are very restorative —S.M.Crothers⟩ HIATUS indicates a gap or break, often in regard to something said, composed, or considered ⟨it was believed that a distinct cultural *hiatus* separated the end of the Paleolithic and the beginning of the Neolithic period —R.W. Murray⟩ ⟨it is doubtful if contemporary criticism of fiction, after the critical *hiatus* of the 19th century, has quite found itself again in the classic Aristotelian tradition —R.G. Davis⟩ LACUNA may refer to a blank or gap in or as if in a manuscript ⟨*lacunae* in *Beowulf*⟩ ⟨a difficult man to write a biography of, because there are so many *lacunae* in our factual knowledge of his life —*New Yorker*⟩ **syn** see in addition BREACH, OPPORTUNITY

³break \"\ *also* **brake** \"\ *n* -s [¹*break*] **1 :** a bodiless carriage frame used for breaking in horses **2 :** a four-wheeled straight-bodied horse-drawn pleasure vehicle usu. having a capacity of six or more persons in addition to the driver and footman

⁴break \"\ *var of* BRAKE

¹break·able \'brākəbəl\ *adj* [¹*break* + *-able*] **:** capable of being broken

²breakable \"\ *n* -s **:** an object readily broken ⟨wrap ~s well before mailing⟩

break·age \-kij,-kēj\ *n* -s **1 a :** the act or action of breaking **b :** amount or quantity of items broken ⟨~ in the laboratory was excessive⟩ **:** loss caused by breaking **c :** an interruption caused by breakage **:** BREAK **d :** allowance or compensation for things broken **2 :** space left unfilled in stowing the hold of a ship **3 :** odd cents not paid to winning pari-mutuel bettors because exceeding a payoff figure that is calculated at a multiple of 5 or 10

break and entry *var of* BREAKING AND ENTERING

break away *vt* **:** to break and knock or smash down or away ⟨*breaking away* the bars in the windows⟩

¹breakaway \'≈,≈\ *n, pl* **breakaways** \-āz\ *also* **breaks·away** \-ksə,wā\ [*break away*] **1 :** an act or instance of breaking away (as from a group, affiliation, standard, or tradition) ⟨a ~ from this discontented faction⟩ ⟨a ~ from classical tradition⟩ **2** *Austral* **a :** a stampede esp. of cattle or sheep **b :** an animal that breaks away from the herd **3 a :** a premature start of one or more contestants in a race; *sometimes* **:** the start of a race or speed trial **b :** the moment when hunting dogs are cast off by the handler **c :** a sudden offensive rush toward an opponent's goal **4 :** a theatrical prop (as a chair) made to shatter harmlessly on slight pressure or impact ⟨belaboring each other with ~s in fight scenes⟩ **5** *Austral* **:** an escarpment overlooking a plain or at the edge of a plateau **6 :** a scrummager who does not usu. push but waits in readiness to break away from the scrum immediately after the ball comes out

²breakaway \"\ *adj* **1** *Brit* **:** given to breaking away **:** favoring disaffiliation from a group **:** operating as independent of an original affiliation ⟨a ~ union⟩ ⟨a ~ movement⟩ **2 a :** made as a breakaway **:** constructed to break, shatter, or bend with slight pressure ⟨to slug it out with fists and ~ chairs right up in front of the camera —Gary Cooper⟩ **b :** constructed for very fast dismounting or changing ⟨~ sets cutting time spent between scenes of the play⟩

breakax *or* **breakaxe** \'≈,≈\ *n* **:** any of various hardwoods difficult to chop: as **a :** the wood of a West Indian tree (*Sloanea jamaicensis*) **b :** a quebracho (*Pithecolobium arboreum*)

break back *vi* **1 :** to return usu. abruptly to a former position or state **2** *archit* **:** to return inward from a projection

¹breakback \'≈,≈\ *adj* [*break* + *back*, n.] **:** BACKBREAKING, CRUSHING

²breakback \"\ *n* -s [*break back*] **1 :** a return or setting back **2 :** a bowled cricket ball that breaks back toward the wicket from the off

breakbone fever \'≈,≈-\ *n* **:** DENGUE

break-bulk point \'≈,≈-\ *n* **:** a station or point at which all or portions of a truckload, boatload, or carload are unloaded and distributed

break down *vt* **1 a :** to cause to fall or collapse by breaking or shattering **:** batter down **:** DESTROY ⟨*breaking down* the door⟩ **b :** to wear down into a defective or useless condition by attrition **c :** to bring about loss of force or effectiveness of **:** make ineffective **:** IMPAIR, DISPEL ⟨*breaking down* the old legal codes⟩ **2 a :** to separate (as a chemical compound) into simpler substances **:** DECOMPOSE **b :** to take apart esp. for storage or shipment and for later reassembling ⟨a machine that can be *broken down* quickly and transported by plane⟩ **c** (1) **:** to reduce (a log) to a convenient size for sawing in the mill (2) **:** to saw (a log) into cants **3 a :** to tone down **:** QUALIFY ⟨*break down* a color⟩ **b :** to make (rubber) plastic: SOFTEN, MASTICATE **4 :** to stop (a sawmill or machine) because of an accident ~ *vi* **1 a :** to become inoperative through breakage or wear **:** lose ability to operate or function ⟨the old truck *broke down* on the hill⟩ **b :** to become inapplicable or ineffective ⟨the governor fled, royal authority *broke down* —*Amer. Guide Series: N.C.*⟩ ⟨under critical analysis almost all distinctions previously made tended to *break down*⟩ **2 a :** to be susceptible to analysis or subdivision **:** to be readily analyzed ⟨the chronicle *breaks down* into three large parts —Mark Schorer⟩ **b :** to undergo decomposition ⟨the old highly folded rocks have been *breaking down* gradually into soil —L.D. Stamp⟩ **syn** see ANALYZE

¹breakdown \'≈,≈\ *n* -s [*break down*] **1 :** the action or result of breaking down; *esp* **:** a situation in which machinery becomes inoperative through breakage or wear **:** an ending of effective operation ⟨flooding of the mine caused by a ~ of the pumps⟩ **2 a :** a physical, mental, or nervous collapse **:** a sometimes sudden marked loss of health, strength, faculties, or ability to cope ⟨suffering a ~ after years of overwork⟩ **b :** ²BREAK 3g **c :** surrender to agitation or emotion **:** loss of self-control **3 a :** failure of operation **:** disruption checking progress or effectiveness **:** a condition marked by futile ineffectiveness **:** COLLAPSE, DISINTEGRATION ⟨the ~ of the negotiations between the countries⟩ ⟨a ~ of communications with the territories⟩ ⟨a ~ of tribal customs⟩ **b :** failure of insulation; *esp* **:** failure of an insulating material (as air, oil, porcelain, or rubber) to prevent passage of an electric discharge **4 a :** a noisy rapid shuffling dance; *esp* **:** a dance engaged in competitively by groups or pairs in succession **b :** a tune suitable for such a dance **5 :** the part of a drop-forging die that distributes the metal of the work after it leaves the fuller by bending and shaping it in preparation for forging in the roughing die — called also *edger, side cut* **6 a :** DECOMPOSITION; *esp* **:** chemical decomposition (as of a complex compound) **b :** softening or plasticization of rubber esp. by mastication **c :** a disorganization of cellular tissue (as of stored apples) resulting in internal discoloration **7 a :** division into categories ⟨a statistical ~ of data⟩ **:** ANALYSIS, CLASSIFICATION; *specif* **:** division (of a job or operation) into several distinct processes or operations **b :** an explanation or account with specific headings or categories ⟨a ~ of the casualties according to various service branches⟩ **:** an itemized account ⟨a budget ~⟩ ⟨a ~ as to sources of revenue⟩ **c :** analysis of a movie script in the interest of economy and convenience in filming **8 :** any amateur wrestling maneuver by which a contestant in advantage position forces his opponent to the mat from a position on his hands and knees or from a bridge position

²breakdown \"\ *adj* **1** *Brit* **:** used or employed to make repairs after a breakdown or wreck ⟨a ~ train speeding to the scene of the accident⟩ **2 :** calculated to lower school-attendance requirements or to impair restrictions on child labor ⟨a ~ bill⟩ **3 :** obtained or resulting from disintegration or decomposition of a substance ⟨salvaging ~ products⟩

breakdown block *n* **:** one of a set of forms or chucks over which a sheet-metal object may be successively spun and at each operation brought nearer the final shape

breakdown voltage *n* **:** the potential difference in volts that when applied across a layer of electrically insulating substance is just sufficient to initiate a disruptive discharge

¹break·er \'brākə(r)\ *n* -s [ME *breker*, fr. *breken* to break + *-er* — more at BREAK] **1 :** one that breaks ⟨a ~ of idols⟩ ⟨a ~ of oaths⟩ ⟨a veteran ~ of horses⟩ **2 :** a device or instrument that breaks: **a :** a machine for breaking up the woody part of flax, hemp, or jute **b :** a plow with a moldboard arrangement facilitating turning over virgin land — see PRAIRIE BREAKER, ROD BREAKER **c** (1) **:** a machine that tears apart clumps of textile fiber as a step toward carding and spinning (2) **:** a papermaking machine similar to a beater but used to break up rags and brush out their threads and to disintegrate old papers for reuse (3) **:** one of a series of perforated projections used in a revolving tumbler or drum for treating skins (4) **:** a machine or plant for breaking rocks or for crushing, sorting, and cleaning anthracite **d** (1) **:** FLESHING KNIFE (2) **:** an implement that breaks curd into pieces in cheese making (3) **:** an implement with long teeth replacing a blade for breaking cake into pieces **e** (1) **:** CIRCUIT BREAKER (2) **:** a mechanically operated commutator (3) **:** a spark-coil interrupter **f :** a strip of open-weave fabric placed above the dome of a tire carcass to provide additional protection at the point of its closest approach to contact with the road **3 a :** a wave breaking into foam against the shore, against a sandbank, or against a rock or reef near the surface **b :** a slight furrow across a road for drainage **4 :** a person whose work consists of breaking: as **a** *Brit* **:** one that breaks up ships or autos into salvage and scrap **b :** the operator of a textile breaker **c :** an operator of a machine that softens hides or skins by pounding them with hammers **d :** SCRAPPER **e :** a quarry worker who splits off blocks of stone by driving wedges into previously made holes or channels — called also *ledgeman* **f :** a power-shear operator who cuts formed angle-iron stock to length

²breaker \"\ *n* -s [by folk etymology fr. Sp *barrica*, fr. F dial. (Gascony) *barrique*] **:** a small water cask esp. for use in a lifeboat

breaker boy *n* [¹*breaker*] **:** a boy employed in a coal breaker usu. to pick slate from coal

breaker card *n* [¹*breaker*] **1 :** the first and coarsest of three cards used in producing wool sliver — compare FINISHER CARD, INTERMEDIATE 5a **2 :** BREAKER 2a

break·er·man \'brākə(r)mən\ *n, pl* **breakermen** [¹*breaker* + *man*] **:** one that standardizes the density of cornstarch suspensions that are to be converted into sugar or glucose and pumps the liquid to refinery storage tanks

break even *vi* **:** to emerge from a contest or transaction with balancing gains and losses or other favorable and unfavorable considerations; *esp* **:** to operate a business or enterprise without either loss or profit ⟨the store expects to *break even* next month⟩

break-even \(')≈¦≈≈\ *adj* [*break even*] **:** having equal outgo and return or loss and profit ⟨a *break-even* situation⟩

break-even point *n* **:** the point at which volume of sales or production enables an enterprise to cover related costs and expenses without profit and without loss **:** that volume of trade or degree of activity at which total income equals total expenditures

break facet *n* **:** one of the paired facets on a brilliant-cut gemstone lying next to the girdle

breakfall \'≈,≈\ *n* [*break* + *fall*] **:** a potentially injurious fall (as in judo or tumbling) in which the impact is broken by beating an arm or leg against the mat or floor

¹break·fast \'brekfəst\ *n* -s *often attrib* [ME *brekfast*, fr. *breken* to break + *fast* — more at BREAK] **1 :** the first meal of the day **2 :** a meal eaten early in the day in connection with a ceremonial occasion ⟨a wedding ~⟩ ⟨a Communion ~⟩

²breakfast \"\ *vb* -ED/-ING/-S *vi* **:** to eat breakfast ~ *vt* **:** to supply or entertain with breakfast

breakfast bird *n* [so called fr. its typical early-morning call] *Austral* **:** KOOKABURRA

breakfast food *n* **:** a breakfast cereal

break·fast·less \-fəs(t)ləs\ *adj* **:** being without breakfast

breakfast nook *n* **:** a nook often with built-in table and seats for light meals

breakfast plate *n* **:** a plate of china or earthenware from seven to eight inches in diameter

break flour *n* **:** flour obtained from a break in milling; *also* **:** flour made by mingling that obtained from different breaks

breakfront \'≈,≈\ *n* **:** a large cabinet or bookcase in which a center section projects beyond the flanking end sections

breakfront

breakhead \'≈,≈\ *n* **:** the reinforcement of the bow of a ship for breaking through ice

break in *vi* **1 :** to break and enter ⟨thieves *broke in* and stole the money⟩ **2 :** to interrupt in a conversation **:** say something abruptly and forcefully ⟨impatient, he *broke in* with an oath⟩ **3 :** to start in an activity or enterprise ⟨he *broke in* with a minor-league team⟩ ⟨*breaking in* with the company as an office boy⟩ **:** gain entrée; *also* **:** to gain experience or skill in a new role or function ⟨the new men are *breaking in* well⟩ ~ *vt* **1 a :** to accustom to a certain activity or occurrence ⟨a skiing instructor *breaking in* novices⟩; *esp* **:** to initiate (as into a job, office, or sport) by instruction, demonstration, and correction **b :** BREAK, TRAIN ⟨*break in* a green horse⟩ **c :** to overcome the stiffness of (a new article) ⟨*breaking in* the shoes⟩ **:** operate or use to overcome the uncertainties of the new and unfamiliar **:** operate sufficiently to test all parts thoroughly ⟨*breaking in* a new car⟩ **2 :** to break so as to cause to fall inward ⟨the mob *broke in* the door⟩ **3 :** to place (a pictorial illustration) in a space provided in the text

¹break-in \'≈,≈\ *n* -s [*break in*] **1 :** the act or action of breaking in **2 :** a hole in brickwork to receive the end of a timber, a plug, or other member **3 :** a preliminary performance or series of performances serving as a trial run **4 :** ²BREAK 3c

²break-in \"\ *adj* **:** of or relating to a system or arrangement in which an automatic device permits the transmitting radio operator to receive incoming signals in intervals between his own transmitted signals

break·ing \'brākiŋ, -kēŋ\ *n* -s [ME *breking* act of demolishing, fr. gerund of *breken* to break — more at BREAK] **1** [trans. of G *brechung*] **:** change of a simple vowel sound into a diphthong whether through the influence of a nearby sound (as in Old English *weorc* "work" with *eo* from earlier *e* before *r* plus consonant) or regardless of phonetic environment (as in Italian *nuovo* "new" from Latin *novus*) **2 :** ²BREAK 4k(1) **3 :** plowed virgin sod land

breaking and entering *or* **break and entry** *n* **:** the act of forcing a passage into and entering another's dwelling or other building **:** HOUSEBREAKING

breaking cart *n* **:** a long-shafted 2-wheeled cart for breaking horses to single harness

breaking engine *n* **:** BREAKER 2c(2)

breaking joint *n* **:** a place of weakness between the fused second and third segments of the leg in many decapod crustaceans (as lobsters and crabs) where the appendage may be cut off by reflex muscular action — compare AUTOTOMY

breaking length *n* **:** that length of material hung vertically at which it will break through its own weight

breaking load *n* **:** stress or tension steadily applied and just sufficient to break or rupture

breaking piece *n* **:** a short shaft made narrow and relatively weak in order to break if the machine with which it is connected is subjected to excessive strain

breaking plow *n* **:** BREAKER 2b

breaking point *n* **1 :** the degree of tension or stress at which a material breaks **2 :** the point at which a person gives way under difficulty or at which a situation becomes crucial

breaking strength *or* **breaking stress** *n* **:** the greatest stress esp. in tension that a material is capable of withstanding without rupture

break in on *or* **break in upon** *vt* **:** to thrust in on **:** intrude upon with force or exigence **:** INTERRUPT ⟨minor details *breaking in on* his work⟩

break into *vt* **1 :** to proceed or pass into or turn to with or as if with a sudden throwing off of restraint ⟨he *broke into* swearing⟩ ⟨his opponents *broke into* bitter criticism⟩ ⟨the horses *broke into* a gallop⟩ **2 :** to make entry or entrance into **:** overcome resistance or exclusiveness in order to become a part, member, or contributor of ⟨romantic girls trying to *break into* the movies⟩ ⟨*breaking into* elite social circles⟩ **3 :** INTERRUPT ⟨*breaking into* the radio play with an important news bulletin⟩ **4 :** to force (a code or cipher) to yield the first of its secrets after which success in breaking must follow

break iron *n* **1 :** an iron that holds a plane bit in place and directs shavings upward and out of the throat of the plane **2 :** an iron fitting with two insulator pins for dead-ending wires from opposite directions on the same cross arm

break jaw *n* **:** one of the last contacts broken when an electrical switch is opened — called also *arcing contact*

break joint *n* **1 :** a masonry shift joint **2 :** a cartilaginous part of the shank just above the ankle in lambs that ossifies as the animal matures

break·less \-ləs\ *adj* **:** being without a break

break line *n* **:** the last line of a paragraph esp. when not of full length when printed

breakneck \'≈,≈\ *adj* [¹*break* + *neck*] **:** inviting danger esp. of a broken neck: as **a :** very rapid **:** HEADLONG ⟨traveling at ~ speed⟩ **b :** very steep ⟨~ stairs to the attic⟩

break-of-bulk \¦≈≈¦≈\ *n* **:** the act of unloading, transferring, or distributing part or all of a shipment

break off *vi* **1 :** to stop abruptly **:** leave off **:** interrupt what one is doing or saying ⟨he *broke off* in the middle of a sentence⟩ **2 :** to veer from the course when sailing by the wind because of the wind's drawing ahead

break of forecastle : the extreme end of the forecastle toward the waist

break of poop : the end of the poop toward the waist

break-open \'≈,≈≈\ *adj* [fr. *break open*, v.] **:** characterized by breaking for loading ⟨a *break-open* revolver⟩

break out *vi* **1 a** *of a person or his body* **:** to be affected with a skin eruption ⟨*break out* in spots⟩ esp. with one indicative of the presence of a particular disease ⟨*breaking out* with measles⟩ **b** *of a disease* **:** to manifest itself by skin eruptions **c :** to become covered with ⟨*break out* in a sweat⟩ **2 a :** to break from check or inhibition into displaying or flaunting ⟨to *break out* with a scarlet suit⟩ **:** cast off restraint and express a pent-up emotion or satisfy a desire previously checked **b :** to give vent to sudden forceful or loud utterance or expression ⟨they *broke out* laughing in the middle of the speech⟩ **c :** to become unfurled on being raised ⟨when the flags *break out*⟩ **3 :** to project (as a chimney breast from a wall) ~ *vt* **1 a :** to take from shipboard stowage preparatory to using ⟨a galley helper *breaking out* meat from the locker⟩ ⟨*breaking out* charts in the wheelhouse⟩ **b :** to put into readiness for action or use ⟨the guards *broke out* the machine guns⟩ ⟨time to *break out* life rafts⟩ ⟨*breaking out* tents and preparing to make camp⟩ ⟨*breaking out* a 5-man relief detail⟩ **c :** to unpack, unwrap, or open for consumption **:** to bring out from concealment for eating, drinking, or smoking ⟨*breaking out* champagne to celebrate⟩ **2 a :** to dislodge from the bottom and start pulling up (an anchor) in preparation to sail **b :** to haul up (as a flag) furled and cause to unfurl after reaching the proper height or position ⟨the ensign should never be made up and *broken out;* it should always be hoisted flying⟩; *broadly* **:** FLY **:** display flying and unfurled ⟨patriots *breaking out* the national flags⟩ **c :** DISLODGE; *esp* **:** to start in motion after overcoming inertia or freeing from check or hindrance ⟨*breaking out* the sled from the ice around its runners⟩ **3 :** to draw or paint part of the

surface (as of a mechanism) as if broken away in order to reveal normally hidden detail ⟨a *broken-out* section⟩
breakout \'=,=\ *n* -s [*break out*] **1 :** a violent or forceful breaking from what checks, restrains, circumscribes, or imprisons; *esp* **:** a military attack launched to break through enemy lines **2 :** the process of removing and disconnecting pipes, rods, or casings in well drilling
breakover \'=,==\ *n* -s [*break over*, v.] **:** the portion of a newspaper or magazine story continued on another page
break pin *n* **:** SHEAR PIN
breakpoint \'=,=\ *n* **1 :** the point in one method of chlorinating drinking water at which the amount of available chlorine in the water falls to a minimum and after which it increases proportionately with the amount of chlorine being added indicating that most of the undesirable tastes and odors have been removed **2 :** a point at which mechanical operation (as of a computer) is halted by a manually set switch to permit check and inspection
break roll *n* **:** one of several corrugated rollers between which grain is ground into flour
breaks *pl of* BREAK, *pres 3d sing of* BREAK
breaksaway *pl of* BREAKAWAY
breakstone \'=,=\ *n* [[1]*break* + *stone*] **1 :** SAXIFRAGE **2 :** any plant growing in stony places (as the parsley piert, the burnet saxifrage, or the pearlwort)
breakthrough \'=,=\ *n* -s [*break through*, v.] **1 a :** an act or action of breaking through an obstruction, check, or restriction ⟨a ~ to a radically higher and broader conception —Walter Lippmann⟩ **b :** a place at which such an act or action takes place **2 :** a short passage or narrow opening connecting adjacent or parallel mine workings **3 :** the action by water of breaking or wearing a passage **:** the channel made by water in so doing **4 :** an offensive thrust that penetrates and carries beyond a defensive or reinforcing line in warfare **5 :** a sudden marked increase in prices or values above previous levels ⟨the news caused a ~ in steel prices⟩ **6 :** a sensational advance in scientific knowledge in which some baffling major problem is solved ⟨a ~ like atomic fission⟩
break up *vt* **1** *archaic* **:** to enter forcefully **:** break into **:** break and enter **2 :** to disrupt the continuity or flow of ⟨quotations are apt to *break up* a book by making it less easy to read —J.E.Gloag⟩ **3 a :** to bring about the decomposition or destruction of **b :** DISSIPATE, CURE ⟨*break up* a cold⟩ **c :** to bring to an end by settling or disrupting ⟨a home run in the tenth that *broke up* the game⟩ ⟨a fight that *broke up* the meeting⟩ **4 :** to break into pieces in scrapping or salvaging **:** SCRAP ⟨*breaking up* the obsolete warships⟩ **5 :** to check broodiness in (a hen) usu. by isolation or change of diet — compare BROODY COOP **~** *vi* **1 a :** to cease to exist as a unit **:** split into separate components **:** DISBAND, DISPERSE ⟨the party *broke up* at midnight⟩ ⟨his family had *broken up* and scattered⟩ ⟨when school *breaks up* in the spring⟩ **b :** become separated into parts or fragments **:** DISSOLVE ⟨when the ice *breaks up* on the river⟩ **2 a :** to fail physically **b :** to lose morale, composure, or resolution ⟨likely to *break up* under enemy attack⟩
breakup \'=,=\ *n* -s [*break up*] **1 :** a disruption or dissolution into component parts **:** an ending as an effective entity ⟨the ~ of the empire⟩ ⟨the ~ of a political party⟩ ⟨the ~ of a marriage⟩ **2 :** division into smaller units ⟨the ~ of the large estates⟩ **3 :** the breaking, melting, and loosening of ice in streams and harbors in the spring **4 :** DECOMPOSITION, DISINTEGRATION **5 :** an excavation upward to the arch level made in tunneling from bottom drifts to provide a new face
breakup value *n* **:** the value in liquidation esp. of shares of stock of a financial corporation
breakwater \'=,==\ *n* [[1]*break* + *water*] **1 :** an offshore structure for breaking the force of waves (as to protect a harbor or beach) **2 :** a steel plate or wood V-shaped structure built on the forward weather deck of a ship or boat to keep the sea off the deck
breakwind \'=,=\ *n* [[1]*break* + *wind*] *Brit* **:** SCREEN, WINDBREAK
[1]**bream** \'brim (*usual US pronunc*), 'brēm *sometimes* 'brem\ *n, pl* **bream** *or* **breams** [ME *brem, breme*, fr. MF *breme, bresme, brasme*, fr. OF *braisme, bresme*, of Gmc origin; akin to OHG *brahsima, brahsema* bream, OS *bressemo*, MD & MLG *bressem, brassem* bream, OHG *brettan* to draw a sword — more at BRAID] **1 :** a European freshwater cyprinid fish (*Abramis brama*) of little value as food with a narrow deep body and arched back; *broadly* **:** any of certain related fishes (as the golden shiner of No. America) **2 :** any of various fishes somewhat resembling the European bream in form: as **a :** any fish of the family Sparidae — compare PORGY **b :** any of various freshwater sunfishes of *Lepomis* and related genera; *esp* **:** BLUEGILL **c :** ROSEFISH — compare BLACK BREAM, SEA BREAM
[2]**bream** \'brēm\ *vt* -ED/-ING/-S [prob. fr. D *brem* furze, fr. MD *bremme, brimme;* akin to OE *brōm* broom; fr. the use of burning furze in the cleaning — more at BROOM] **:** to clean (a ship's bottom) by means of fire and scraping
breard \'brērd\ *Scot var of* BRAIRD
breas *pl of* BREA
[1]**breast** \'brest\ *n* -s *often attrib* [ME *brest, breest*, fr. OE *brēost;* akin to OHG *brust* breast, ON *brjōst*, Goth *brusts* (pl.) breast, OIr *brū* belly, Russ *bryukho*] **1 a :** either of two protuberant milk-producing glandular organs situated on the front of the chest or thorax in the human female and some other mammals and normally functional only during the period of lactation following pregnancy **b :** any discrete mammary gland — compare UDDER **c :** a breast in lactation ⟨giving the infant son the ~⟩; *broadly* **:** a source of nourishment ⟨the university serving as the ~ for this intellectual movement⟩ **d :** either of the paired and normally nonfunctional mammary glands of the human male esp. when excessively enlarged and protuberant (as by reason of accumulated fatty tissue) **2 a :** the fore or ventral part of the body between the neck and the abdomen **:** the front of the chest ⟨a soldier shot in the ~⟩ ⟨a bird with an orange ~⟩; *also* **:** either side of the front of the chest ⟨a wound in the right ~⟩ **b** *obs* **:** the whole upper part of the body **:** THORAX **c :** the breastbone with its attached muscles (as of a calf, lamb, or fowl dressed as meat) **d** *obs* **:** the bodily area containing the lungs; *also* **:** singing voice **3 :** the breast regarded as the seat of emotion, affection, sentiment, thought, or intent **:** BOSOM, HEART ⟨opposing the enemy with dauntless ~⟩ ⟨causing little concern in official ~*s*⟩ **4 :** something resembling a breast **:** a front, forward, swelling, bulging, or curving part ⟨the ~ of the lake⟩: **a** (1) **:** the portion of a wall between a window and the floor (2) **:** CHIMNEY BREAST 2 (3) **:** the underside of a member (as a handrail, beam, or rafter) (4) **:** a portion of a wall projecting outward (as at a chimney) **b :** the front part of a plow moldboard **c** (1) **:** the face of a tunnel or mine working (2) **:** a room or stall in a coal mine **d** (1) **:** the fore part of the heel of a shoe next to the shank (2) **:** the front face of a shoe heel **e :** the side of the hearth containing the metal notch in a shaft furnace **f :** the first roller of a carding machine **g :** BREAST FAST **h :** the end of a can having a central raised section containing an opening **5** *archaic* **:** the broad even front of a group or body in motion **6 a :** the part of an article of clothing covering the breast ⟨with pockets at the ~⟩ ⟨their ~*s* were laden with decorations and medals —F.J.Mather⟩ **b :** BREASTPLATE **7 :** the portion of an arrow that touches the bow when in position for shooting
[2]**breast** \"\ *vb* -ED/-ING/-S *vt* **1 :** to oppose the breast to **:** FACE, CONFRONT **:** oppose or contend against manfully ⟨~*ing* the waves⟩ ⟨~*ing* the storm of traffic —Adrian Bell⟩ ⟨to dare to ~ an entrenched political machine⟩ **2** *Brit* **:** to climb resolutely **:** ASCEND ⟨the train had ~*ed* the heavy ascent —O.S.Nock⟩ ⟨the ponies ~*ed* the steep shale slopes —Douglas Carruthers⟩ **3 :** to draw abreast of or alongside of **4 :** to haul or bring broadside on ⟨~*ing* the ship against the dock with the winches⟩ **5 :** to thrust the chest against ⟨the sprinter ~*ed* the tape⟩ **~** *vi* **1 :** to press forward with or as if with the breast ⟨ships ~*ing* through the waves⟩ **2 :** to approach esp. in order to accost ⟨a stranger came ~*ing* up to him⟩
breast auger *n* **:** an auger for soft rock or coal that is advanced under pressure from the miner's chest or breast — compare BREAST DRILL
breast backstay *n* **:** a forward backstay set up to sustain an upper mast when the wind is before the beam
breastband \'=,=\ *n* **1 :** BREAST COLLAR **2 :** a band or rope fastened at both ends to the rigging to support the man who heaves the lead in sounding
breastbeam \'=,=\ *n* **1 :** a beam where the quarterdeck or forecastle breaks **2 :** the beam or rail over which newly woven cloth passes in a loom on its way to the take-up and cloth roll
breast-beater \'=,==\ *n* **:** one that engages in breast-beating
breast-beating \'=,==\ *n* **:** noisy demonstrative protestation (as of grief, anger, or self-recrimination)
breast board *n* **1 :** MOLDBOARD **2 :** a retaining board used at the breast of a mine working to hold back soft ground **3 :** a board at a ship's breastbeam
breastbone \'=;=\ *n* [ME *brestbon*, fr. OE *brēostbān*, fr. *brēost* breast + *bān* bone — more at BREAST, BONE] **:** the sternum esp. when the parts are largely ossified and fused (as in adult mammals and birds)
breast collar *n* **:** a harness strap extending across the chest in place of a collar—called also *breastband;* see HARNESS illustration
breast cylinder *n* **:** the first large roller serving for initial opening of the stock in carding
breast drill *n* **:** a portable drill with a plate that is pressed by the breast in forcing the drill against the work
breast·ed \'brestəd\ *adj* [ME *brested*, fr. *brest* breast + *-ed*] **:** having a breast **:** having (such) a breast — used chiefly in compounds ⟨broad-*breasted*⟩ ⟨red-*breasted*⟩
breasted arrow *n* **:** an arrow having its greatest diameter at the breast
breast·er \'brestə(r)\ *n* -s [[1]*breast* + *-er*] **:** one that cuts breasts on shoe heels
breast fast *also* **breast line** *n* **:** a large rope for fastening the midship part of a ship (as to a wharf)
breast-fed \'=;=\ *adj* **:** fed from a mother's breast ⟨differences between *breast-fed* and bottle-fed babies⟩
breast-feed \'=;=\ *vt* **:** to feed (a baby) from a mother's breast rather than from a bottle **:** SUCKLE

breast drill

breast harness *n* **:** the part of a horse's harness worn on or depending from the fore part of the body and including breast collar and hames with straps, traces, or tugs
breast·height \'=;=\ *n* **:** the height of 4½ feet above ground at which the diameters of standing trees are usu. measured
breast-high scent *n* **:** a scent so strong that dogs course heads up
breast hole *n* **:** a hole in a smelting cupola for raking out cinders
breast·hook \'=,=\ *n* **:** a V-shaped timber or plate connecting ship timbers or stringers of opposite sides where they run into the stem; *also* **:** a similar connecting piece at the stern — called also *crutch*
[1]**breasting** *pres part of* BREAST
[2]**breast·ing** \'brestiŋ, -tēŋ\ *n* -s [[1]*breast* + *-ing*] **1 :** the cutting of a shoe breast to even curve and pitch **2 :** the material covering the breast of a shoe heel — see SHOE illustration **3 :** BREAST STOPING
breasting knife *n* **:** a knife for cutting a clean face on the breast of a heel
breast knee *n* **:** BREASTHOOK
breast·less \-ləs\ *adj* **:** being without a breast
breastmark \'=,=\ *n* [*abreast* + *mark*] **:** a mark placed abreast of some prominent landmark in surveying
breast milk *n* **:** milk from the human breast
breast molding *n* **:** a molding on the breast of a wall or on a window sill
breast off *vi* **1 :** to moor parallel to but at a distance from a dock **:** install spars between a moored ship and wharf to leave space for lighters in between **2 :** to move back from a dock ⟨a boat *breasting off* to make space⟩
breastpin \'=,=\ *n* **1 :** a woman's brooch **2 :** TIEPIN
breastplate \'=,=\ *n* [ME *brestplate*, fr. *brest* breast + *plate*] **1 a :** a metal plate protecting the breast as defensive armor — see ARMOR illustration **b :** SHIELD, DEFENSE **2 :** a vestment worn in ancient times by a Jewish high priest, made of a double piece of rich woven fabric, embroidered, and set with 12 gems bearing the names of the tribes of Israel — see EPHOD illustration **3 :** BREASTSUMMER **4 :** a piece against which the workman presses his breast in operating a breast drill or similar tool **5 :** BREAST STRAP 2 **6 :** a small ornamental metal plate to hold a soldier's shoulder belts at their point of crossing on the breast **7 :** a hard or bony covering of the breast of an animal (as the plastron of a turtle) **8 :** a metal plate for inscriptions on a casket
breastplow \'=,=\ *n* **:** a plow for cutting turf that is driven by the breast of the workman
breast pump *n* **:** a suction apparatus for milking the breast
breast·rail \'=,=\ *n* **1 :** the upper rail of a parapet or a balcony **2 :** the railing of a quarterdeck of a ship
breast roll *n* **:** BREASTBEAM 2
breast·rope \'=,=\ *n* **:** a rope used as a breastband (as around a man making soundings from a ship)
breasts *pl of* BREAST, *pres 3d sing of* BREAST
breast stoping *n* **:** mining in which the ore is broken from a nearly vertical face
breast strap *n* **1 :** a strap attached to the collar and supporting the yoke in team harness **2 :** a band passing around the front of the chest and joining the trace at the saddle and in light and single harness replacing the collar as the point against which the effort of the horse is primarily exerted
breaststroke \'=,=\ *n* **:** a swimming stroke executed prone and with shoulders parallel to the water's surface by extending the arms in front of the head and sweeping them back simultaneously, palms out, while making a frog kick — compare BUTTERFLY
breaststroke kick *n* **:** the leg action used in swimming the breaststroke in which the feet, moving in a horizontal plane, are drawn toward the hips and then thrust sideward and backward — called also *whip kick*
breast·sum·mer \'bres(t),səmə(r), 'bresəm-\ *n* [[1]*breast* + *summer* (beam)] **:** a beam, girder, or lintel placed horizontally over an opening (as a window) to support the superstructure
breast tea *n* [so called fr. its use as a pectoral] **:** a tea prepared from cut and bruised althaea, coltsfoot, licorice root, anise, mullein flowers, and orrisroot and formerly used as a household remedy for respiratory disorders
breast wall *n* **:** a wall built to sustain the face of a natural bank of earth — compare RETAINING WALL
breast·weed \'=,=\ *n* [so called fr. its use in treating mammary inflammation] **:** LIZARD'S-TAIL
breast wheel *n* **:** a waterwheel onto which the water is led at about axle height and which acts partly by impulse and partly by the weight of the descending water in the buckets — compare OVERSHOT WHEEL, UNDERSHOT WHEEL
breastwise \'=,=\ *adv* [[1]*breast* + *-wise*] **:** ABREAST
breastwork \'=,=\ *n* **1 :** an improvised or temporary fortification **2 :** a railing on the quarterdeck and forecastle **3 :** brickwork or masonry making a fireplace breast

section of breast wheel

breastwork log *n* **:** FENDER SKID
breath \'breth\ *n* -s [ME *breeth, breth*, fr. OE *brǣth;* akin to OHG *brādam* breath, heat, ON *brāth* tar, OE *beorma* yeast — more at BARM] **1 a :** steam, smoke, vapor, or other emanation ⟨the ~ of the fire⟩ ⟨the ~ from the river⟩ **b :** air charged with a certain fragrance, odor, or other suggestion ⟨the ~ of roses in the parlor⟩ ⟨carrying with him the ~ of the grave⟩ **:** EMANATION, SUGGESTION ⟨a ~ of mystery about the proceedings⟩ **2 a :** the faculty or power of breathing freely and naturally ⟨he is near death; his ~ is failing⟩ ⟨recovering his ~ after his mad dash⟩ **b :** the act of breathing **:** a single inhalation or exhalation ⟨fighting to his last ~⟩ ⟨speaking also of his brother in the same ~⟩ **c :** opportunity to breathe **:** time to breathe or recover one's breath **:** time for rest or recovery **:** RESPITE **:** ⟨granting some pause, some ~⟩ **3 a :** slight breeze **:** air in gentle motion ⟨not a breeze — no ~ of air —William Wordsworth⟩ **4 a :** air exhaled from the lungs esp. as made apparent by odor or vapor ⟨his ~ smells bad⟩ ⟨a strong smell of whiskey on his ~⟩ ⟨to see one's ~ on a cold day⟩ **b :** air inhaled and exhaled ⟨to draw ~⟩ ⟨after the ~ has left one's body⟩ **c :** INHALATION **:** amount of gas inhaled ⟨a ~ of nitrous oxide⟩ **5 a :** breath used in speech **:** spoken sound or sounds **:** WHISPER, UTTERANCE ⟨no ~ of objection was heard⟩; *sometimes* **:** a slight utterance, gesture or similar act **b :** moisture condensed from one's breath ⟨to see one's ~ on a pane of glass⟩; *sometimes* **:** a slight stain or tarnish ⟨there had never been a ~ on her reputation —Edith Wharton⟩ **c :** air blown through a musical instrument; *also* **:** the resulting sound ⟨the ~ of the trumpet⟩ **6 :** SPIRIT, ANIMATION, VITALITY, LIFE ⟨many a bard's untimely death lends unto his verses ~ —Edna S.V.Millay⟩ **7 :** expiration of air with the glottis wide open so that there is no audible vibration of the vocal cords (as in the formation of \f\ and \s\ sounds) — compare BREATHED, VOICELESS — **below one's breath** *or* **under one's breath :** in a whisper **:** in an inaudible or barely audible voice — **in one breath** *or* **in the same breath :** practically at once **:** almost simultaneously — **out of breath :** gasping for breath (as after strenuous activity) **:** breathing very rapidly
breath·able *also* **breathe·able** \'brēthəbəl\ *adj* **:** fit for being breathed **:** suitable for normal breathing
breathe \'brēth\ *vb* -ED/-ING/-S [ME *brethen*, fr. *breth, breeth* breath] *vi* **1 a** *obs* **:** to emanate into the air as or as if vapor or steam **b** *obs* **:** to send out an odor or fragrance **:** SMELL **c :** to become perceptible **:** be emanated or suggested **:** be expressed ⟨the spirit of the age as it ~*s* from our novelists —*Times Lit. Supp.*⟩ ⟨a fond complacency *breathed* from both girls —Anne D. Sedgwick⟩ **2 a** (1) **:** to draw air into and expel it out of the lungs **:** inhale and exhale **:** RESPIRE (2) **:** to take in oxygen and give out carbon dioxide through natural processes that resemble or are analogous to breathing ⟨plants *breathing* at night⟩ ⟨a fish cannot ~ out of water⟩ **b :** to inhale and exhale freely without sense or feeling of constriction ⟨an atmosphere of intellectual freedom in which he could ~ —Francis Biddle⟩ **c :** to inhale and exhale audibly ⟨the doctor listened to his *breathing*⟩ **3 a :** to continue in existence **:** LIVE **b :** to continue to have vital force or effect **4 :** to pause and rest (as after strenuous activity) **5 :** to make utterance ⟨in making that plea he will ~ in vain⟩ **:** to be uttered ⟨a whisper *breathing* low⟩ **6 :** to blow softly ⟨a light wind *breathing*⟩ **7 :** to draw in and give out air, gas, or vapor (as of a fuel tank) **:** pass air in and out (as of a cushion) or through (as of leather or other membrane) **8** *of an internal-combustion engine* **:** to use air to support combustion **~** *vt* **1 a :** EXHALE **:** send out by exhaling **:** emit as if in breathing out — often used with *out* ⟨*breathing* out his soul⟩ **b :** to instill by breathing in **:** infuse as if by breathing **:** communicate by breath — often used with *in* or *into* ⟨*breathing* new life into the movement⟩ **2 :** UTTER, EXPRESS: as **a :** to utter vehemently **:** cry out ⟨*breathing* threats about revenge⟩ **b :** to utter softly, quietly, or confidentially **:** WHISPER ⟨*breathing* his advice softly⟩ ⟨don't ~ a word of what he said⟩ **c :** to make manifest **:** EVINCE, SHOW ⟨*breathing* the true spirit of his religion⟩ **3 :** to let breathe **:** give a period of rest from exertion or security from danger to ⟨*breathing* their horses after the hard ride⟩ ⟨a chance for the messenger to ~ himself⟩ **4 a :** to exercise briskly ⟨a chase across the fields to ~ the dogs⟩ **b :** to exercise vigorously and deprive of breath **:** WIND, EXHAUST **5 a :** to draw into and usu. press out of the lungs **:** inhale and exhale ⟨*breathing* fresh air⟩ ⟨*breathing* noxious gases⟩ **b :** to pull in and consume (oxygen) in operation — used esp. of an engine — **breathe a vein :** to open a vein to let blood — **breathe down one's neck :** to threaten or loom impending in or as if in pursuit or attack — **breathe easily** *or* **breathe freely :** to enjoy relief from pressure, strain, anxiety, or danger — **breathe one's last :** DIE
breathed \'bretht, *in sense 2 sometimes* 'brēthd\ *adj* [ME *brethed*, fr. *breth* breath + *-ed*] **1 :** having breath **:** having (such) a breath — used esp. in compounds ⟨a long-*breathed* speaker⟩ **2 :** uttered without voice **:** VOICELESS — by some phoneticians not regarded as applicable to voiceless stops
breathe on *or* **breathe upon** *vt* **:** to taint with scandal **:** TARNISH ⟨when her name was *breathed upon*⟩
breath·er \'brēthə(r)\ *n* -s [*breathe* + *-er*] **1 :** one that utters, speaks, or proclaims ⟨scandal that hurt its ~ more than its subject⟩ **2 :** one that breathes usu. in an indicated way ⟨in his sleep the child was a mouth ~⟩ **3 :** a spell of usu. violent exercise **:** something that occasions violent exercise ⟨climbing the mountain was a real ~⟩ **4 a :** a rest period **:** a break in one's activity for rest and relaxation **:** a brief relaxation of effort ⟨taking a ~ after the heavy work⟩ **b :** a game or match against a weak opponent ⟨opened the season with a ~⟩ **5 :** a small vent in an otherwise airtight enclosure for maintaining equality of pressure within and without (as in oil tanks, transformers, crankcases, instrument cases) **6 :** a device to facilitate breathing esp. under unusual circumstances ⟨a new ~ in the diver's equipment⟩
breathes *pres 3d sing of* BREATHE
breathe to *or* **breathe after** *vt, obs* **:** to long for **:** aspire to
breath group *n* **:** a stretch of utterance between two pauses of sufficient length for an intake of breath to be made at each
breath·i·ness \'brethēnəs, -thin-\ *n* -ES **:** the quality of being breathy ⟨singing with a noticeable ~⟩
breath·ing \'brēthiŋ, -thēŋ\ *n* -s [ME *brething* act of respiration, fr. gerund of *brethen* to breathe] **1 a :** a very brief time ⟨it all happened in a ~⟩ **b :** a pause for taking breath **:** DELAY **2 :** either of the marks ʽ and ʼ used in writing Greek, the former to indicate aspiration, the latter to indicate absence of aspiration — see ROUGH BREATHING, SMOOTH BREATHING **3 :** BREATHER 3 **4 :** the passage of air into or out of an aerostat due to changing volume
breathing capacity *n* **:** VITAL CAPACITY
breath·ing·ly *adv* **:** in a breathing manner
breathing mark *n* **:** a comma or other small mark placed over a score to show a singer or wind-instrument player where to take a breath
breathing space *n* **1 :** an unoccupied space **:** an area set aside for or conducive to rest **2** *or* **breathing spell :** a period of inactivity esp. for rest, recreation, and mustering up strength for subsequent efforts ⟨attacking all along the line and giving the enemy no *breathing space*⟩
breathing valve *n* **:** one of certain folds of membrane that control the direction of the flow of water through the mouth, past the gills, and to the exterior in many fishes
breath·less \'brethləs\ *adj* [ME *brethles*, fr. *breth* breath + *-les* -less] **1 a :** not breathing **:** showing suspension of breath **b :** DEAD **2 a :** out of breath **:** panting or gasping for breath after strenuous activity **b :** leaving one breathless **:** STRENUOUS ⟨the pace was rather ~ —A.H.Vandenberg †1951⟩ **c :** out of breath or holding one's breath because of fear, suspense, intense interest, awe, or other strong emotion ⟨~ at the thought of what I had done —Katherine Mansfield⟩ ⟨~ with a strange, painful, yielding ardor —Morley Callaghan⟩ **d :** bringing about or marked by a being out of breath or a holding of one's breath **:** INTENSE, GRIPPING, DOMINATING ⟨the air was so charged with the ~ tension —Hugh Walpole⟩ ⟨caught up into ~ crisis —John Buchan⟩ **e :** suffering from dyspnea **3 :** marked by complete stillness of the air **:** oppressive and close because of absence of breezes ⟨the summer came, ~ and sultry —W.S.Maugham⟩ ⟨sticky with sirocco moisture under the ~ awning —Norman Douglas⟩ — **breath·less·ly** *adv*
breath·less·ness \-nəs\ *n* -ES **1 :** the state of being out of breath **:** a quality making for a breathless condition **2 :** DYSPNEA
breath of heaven 1 : a small southern African shrub (*Adenandra fragrans*) with small leathery leaves and white or pink flowers that is cultivated in California **2 :** an evergreen shrub (*Diosma ericoides*) with perfumed needlelike foliage
breaths *pl of* BREATH
breathtaker \'=,==\ *n* **:** one (as an exciting game, a near accident) that is breathtaking

breath·tak·ing \ˈ=,==\ *adj* **1 :** making one out of breath **:** having shock effects that check breathing ⟨a ~ pain in his side⟩ ⟨a ~ plunge into the icy water⟩ **2 :** commanding intense interest **:** striking with awe and wonder **:** EXCITING, THRILLING ⟨the ~ grandeur of the mountain scenery⟩ ⟨~ in the rapidity and completeness of change —Amy Loveman⟩ ⟨~ beauty⟩ — **breath·tak·ing·ly** *adv*

breathy \ˈbrethē, -thi\ *adj* -ER/-EST [*breath* + *-y*] **1** *of a vocal sound* **:** characterized by or accompanied with the audible passage of unvocalized breath **2** *of a performance on a wind instrument* **:** impaired in purity of tone by the presence of excessive or poorly controlled breath

bre·ba \ˈbrābə, -āvə\ *n* -S [Sp *breva*, alter. of OSp *bebra*, fr. L (*ficus*) *bifera* twice-bearing fig, fr. *ficus* fig + *bifera*, fem. of *bifer* twice-bearing, fr. *bi-* ¹bi- + *-fer* ferous] **:** a fig of the first crop ripening on the old wood

brec·cia \ˈbrech(ē)ə, -esh-\ *n* -S [It] **1 :** a rock consisting of sharp fragments embedded in a fine-grained matrix (as sand or clay) **2 :** an agglomerate deposit of debris in a cave or other site occupied by prehistoric man

brec·cial \-ech(ē)əl, -esh-\ *adj* **:** of or relating to breccia

brec·ciate \ˈbrechē,āt, -e,chāt, -esh-, -e,sh-\ *vt* -ED/-ING/-S **:** to break (a rock or rock formation) into angular fragments **:** form (rock) into a breccia

brecciated *adj* [It *brecciato*, fr. *breccia* + *-ato* -ate] **:** converted into, resembling, or marked by a breccia

brec·ci·a·tion \,brechēˈāshən, -esh-\ *n* -S **:** formation of a breccia

brec·cio·la \breˈchōlə, ,brechēˈō-, -eˈsh-, -esh-\ *n* -S [It, fr. *breccia* + *-ola* -ole] **:** a limestone breccia that is deposited by turbid water and is intraformational in character

brech·am \ˈbrekəm\ *n* -S [ME *berhom, bargham* — more at BARGHAM] *chiefly Scot & Irish* **:** a horse collar

brech·an \ˈbrekən\ *also* **brack·en** \ˈbrakən\ *n* -S [ScGael *breacan*, fr. *breac* spotted, variegated; akin to OIr *brec* spotted, variegated] **:** a plaid of the Scottish Highlands

bre·chi·tes \breˈkīd·ēz, -ī,tēz\ *n, cap* [NL, fr. Gk *brechein* to wet, get wet, to rain + L *-ites* -ite; akin to Russ *morgota* fog, heavy air, Latvian *merguot* to drizzle] **:** a genus of marine bivalve mollusks (suborder Anatinacea) — see WATERING-POT SHELL

¹**breck** \ˈbrek\ *n* -S [ME *brek*, fr. *breken* to break — more at BREAK] *dial Eng* **:** BREACH, GAP

²**breck** \"\ *n* -S [perh. fr. ON *brekka* slope of a hill — more at BRINK] *Brit* **:** a stretch of rough or sandy often undulating ground ⟨scattered trees or the pine hedges which are a feature of the Norfolk ~s —Bruce Campbell⟩; *also* **:** an enclosed portion of such land

breck·an \ˈbrekən\ *chiefly Scot var of* ¹BRACKEN

breck·nock·shire \ˈbrek,näk,shi(ə)r, -,nək-, -kshər\ *or* **breck·nock** \-äk,-ək\ *adj, usu cap* [fr. *Brecknockshire* or *Brecknock* county, Wales] **:** of or from the county of Brecknock, Wales **:** of the kind or style prevalent in Brecknock

¹**bred** *past of* ¹BREED

²**bred** \ˈbred\ *adj* [fr. past part. of *breed*] **1 :** reared or born and reared in (such) a way **:** inculcated with the (specified) traditions — often in compounds ⟨a farm-*bred* youth⟩ ⟨city-*bred* people⟩ **2 :** of (specified) breed — usu. used in compounds ⟨pure*bred*⟩ **3** *of a female animal* **:** IMPREGNATED

bred·berg·ite \ˈbred(,)bər,gīt\ *n* -S [B. G. *Bredberg* 19th cent. American who first described it + E *-ite*] **:** an andradite garnet containing magnesium

brede \ˈbrēd\ *n* -S [alter. of ²*braid*] **1** *archaic* **:** EMBROIDERY **2** *archaic* **:** BRAIDING; *esp* **:** interweaving of colors

bre·di \ˈbrādē\ *n* -ES [Afrik *bredie* (formerly, also a plant of the sorrel family), fr. a native name in Madagascar] *Africa* **:** meat stew containing a vegetable

bred-in-the-bone \ˈ===ˈ=\ *adj* **1 :** very deeply inculcated **:** made an essential of an overall character ⟨his *bred-in-the-bone* honesty⟩ ⟨the *bred-in-the-bone* frugality of the peasantry⟩ **2 :** marked by a quality, trait, or belief that is inveterate, deep, lasting, and genuine ⟨a *bred-in-the-bone* believer in the old religion⟩ ⟨a *bred-in-the-bone* gambler⟩

bred out *adj* **1 :** DEGENERATED **2** *zool* **:** degenerated due to becoming homozygous for latent defective genes by inbreeding

¹**bree** \ˈbrē\ *n* -S [ME *breye, bree* eyelid, eyebrow, fr. OE *brǣw* — more at BRAE] *Scot* **:** EYEBROW, BROW

²**bree** \"\ *n* -S [ME *bre*, prob. alter. of *bri*, fr. OE *brīw, brīg*; akin to OHG *brīo* soup, mush, MD *brī*, OE *brīwan* to cook, MIr *breo* flame, OE *byrnan* to burn — more at BURN] *now chiefly Scot* **:** liquid in which a substance has been boiled or steeped **:** BROTH, SOUP, GRAVY

¹**breech** *in senses 2-4* ˈbrēch *also esp in rural areas* ˈbrich; "**breeches**" (*garment*) *is* ˈbrichəz *sometimes esp in urban areas* -rēch-, *but* -rēch- *is usual for "breeches buoy"*\ *n* -ES [ME *breech* pair of breeches, fr. OE *brēc* breeches, pl. of *brōc* leg covering; akin to OHG *bruoh* pair of breeches, ON *brōk* leg covering, OE *brecan* to break — more at BREAK] **1 breeches** *pl* **a :** short trousers for covering the hips and thighs that fit snugly around the waist at the top and at the lower edges at or just below the knee — called also *knee breeches*; see RIDING BREECHES **b :** PANTS **2 a :** the hind end of the body **:** BUTTOCKS **b :** BREECHING 3 **3 a :** the part of a cannon or other firearm at the rear of the bore — see CANNON illustration **b :** the bottom of a pulley block **:** the end of a block opposite the swallow **c :** the external angle of a timber knee — compare THROAT **4 a** *or* **breech presentation :** a presentation of the fetus in which the breech is the first part to appear at the uterine cervix **b :** a fetus that is presented breech first

²**breech** *in sense 1* ˈbrich *also* ˈbrēch, *in sense 2* ˈbrēch *also* ˈbrich\ *vt* -ED/-ING/-ES **1** *archaic & dial* **:** to put breeches on **2** *archaic* **:** to whip on the buttocks

breechblock \ˈ=,=\ *n* **:** the block in breech-loading firearms that closes the rear of the bore against the force of the charge

breechclout *or* **breechcloth** \ˈ=,=\ *n* [¹*breech* + *clout* or *cloth*] **:** LOINCLOTH

breech delivery *n* **:** delivery of a fetus with the breech appearing first

breeched \ˈbricht, ˈbrēcht — *see* ¹BREECH\ *adj* [¹*breech* + *-ed*] **:** wearing breeches

breeches buoy *see* ¹BREECH\ *n* **:** a canvas seat shaped like a pair of short-legged breeches which is dependent from a circular life buoy suspended from and running upon a hawser and in which a person being rescued is hauled from one ship to another or from ship to shore

1 breeches buoy; *2, 3, 4* tackle for hauling back and forth; *5* supporting block running on the hawser, *6*

breechesflower \ˈ==,=\ *n* **:** DUTCHMAN'S-BREECHES

breeches part *n* **:** a theatrical role that is regularly or frequently played by an actress in male costume

breeches pipe *n* **:** a forked pipe

breech·ing \ˈbrēchiŋ, -chēŋ *also esp in rural areas* ˈbrich- *or* -chən\ *n* -S [¹*breech* + *-ing*] **1 :** the part of a harness that passes around the breech of a draft animal and enables him to hold back a vehicle — see HARNESS illustration **2** *obs* **:** a whipping on the buttocks **3 :** the short coarse wool on the breech and hind legs of a sheep or goat; *also* **:** the hair on the corresponding parts of a dog **4 :** a rope formerly rove through the cascabel of a cannon used for securing the cannon to the side of a ship **5 :** the breech or breech action of a gun **6 :** a sheet-iron or sheet-steel casing at the end of boilers for conveying the smoke from the flues to the smokestack **7 :** a metal fitting, often containing a valve, that serves to connect two lines of hose or to divide a hose into two legs

breech·less \ˈbrichləs, ˈbrēch-\ *adj* **:** being without breeches

breechloader \ˈ=ˈ==\ *n* **:** a breech-loading firearm

breech-loading \ˈ=ˈ==\ *adj, of a firearm* **:** receiving the cartridge or projectile at the breech

breech mechanism *n* **:** the mechanism for opening and closing the breech of a breech-loading firearm, esp. of a heavy-caliber gun

breech pin *n* **:** BREECH PLUG

breech plug *n* **1 :** a plug for closing the breech of a gun **:** BREECHBLOCK **2 :** a cascabel plug screwed through the breech to support the inner tube

breech presentation *n* **:** BREECH 4a

¹**breed** \ˈbrēd\ *vb* **bred** \ˈbred\ **bred; breeding; breeds** [ME *breden*, fr. OE *brēdan*; akin to OHG *bruoten* to brood; denominative fr. the root of OE *brōd* brood — more at BROOD] *vt* **1 :** to produce (offspring) by hatching or gestation **:** give birth to ⟨yet every mother ~s not sons alike —Shak.⟩ **2 a :** BEGET 2 **b :** to cause to come into being **:** PRODUCE, ENGENDER ⟨every scholarly discipline ~s its own jargon —*Times Lit. Supp.*⟩ ⟨extended wars always ~ depression —F.A.Bradford⟩ **3 :** to be the native place of ⟨a pond ~s fish⟩ ⟨a northern country ~s stout men⟩ **:** provide conditions conducive to development of ⟨liberty in all its wildness *bred* iron conscience —Van Wyck Brooks⟩ **4 :** to propagate sexually: **a :** to propagate (plants) by artificial pollination **b :** to improve (a stock) by controlled propagation — compare BREEDING 5 **c :** to develop (desired qualities or characteristics) by breeding ⟨chicks with high production *bred* into them —L.E.Card⟩ **5 a :** to develop by tradition or education **:** bring up **:** NURTURE, TRAIN ⟨no care was taken to ~ him a Protestant —Gilbert Burnet⟩ — often used with *in* or *to* ⟨he was *bred* in the tradition of liberalism —Max Whatman⟩ ⟨ships commanded by men who had not been *bred* to the sea⟩ **b :** to inculcate (a quality) by training ⟨good manners were *bred* into them⟩ **6 a :** to mate or mate with **:** INSEMINATE ⟨this cow was *bred* on the 7th, 27th, and 17th, but failed to settle⟩ ⟨a good mature ram may ~ 60 ewes in a season⟩ **b :** IMPREGNATE ⟨cats normally have their kittens 63 days after being *bred*⟩ **7 :** to produce a fissionable element (as plutonium) from a nonfissionable element (as uranium 238) by bombardment with neutrons from a radioactive element so that more fissionable material is produced than is used up ~ *vi* **1 :** to produce offspring by sexual union **:** reproduce its kind ⟨that they may ~ abundantly on the earth —Gen 8:17 (RSV)⟩ ⟨~ true⟩ **:** MULTIPLY **2 :** to be pregnant **3 :** to propagate animals or plants

²**breed** \"\ *n* -S **1 :** a group of animals or plants presumably related by descent from common ancestors and visibly similar in most characters: **a :** a distinctive group of domestic animals differentiated from the wild type under the influence of man and usu. incapable of maintaining its distinctive qualities in nature, being usu. the sum of the progeny of a known and designated foundation stock without admixture of other blood **b :** a similarly distinctive group of plants — compare HORTICULTURAL VARIETY **2 :** a number of persons of the same line of descent or of the same racial stock ⟨twice fifteen thousand hearts of England's ~ —Shak.⟩ **3 :** a group of persons or things distinguished by similar characteristics, interests, or qualities **:** CLASS, KIND, SORT ⟨the undergraduate ~ —J.C.Ransom⟩ ⟨the new ~ of scientific salesmen —*Time*⟩ ⟨horse lovers, a ~ of folk not yet extinct —H.I.Brock⟩ ⟨a new ~ of ship —Carter Henderson⟩ **4** *dial Brit* **:** a litter of young **:** BROOD **5** *chiefly West* **:** the offspring of a white parent and an Indian parent **:** HALF-BREED **6 :** a distinctively delicate taste discernible in some wines **syn** see VARIETY

breed·er \-də(r)\ *n* -S **1 :** one that produces offspring; *specif* **:** an animal or plant kept primarily for propagation **2 a :** one whose work is to breed a specified organism ⟨plant ~⟩ ⟨poultry ~⟩ ⟨rabbit ~⟩ **b :** the owner of a breeding female animal at the time of conception or at the birth of offspring

breeder reactor *also* **breeder** *n* -S **:** a reactor in which the breeding of fissionable material takes place

breeder tulip *also* **breeder** *n* -S **:** any of certain self-colored late-flowering tulips that resemble Darwin tulips but lack the rectangular flower base and are commonly somewhat more somber in coloring

breed·i·ness \-dēnəs\ *n* -ES **:** the distinctive characters or qualities of a breed as evident in an individual animal

breeding *n* -S [ME *breding*, fr. gerund of *breden*] **1 a :** the action or process of bearing or generating **b :** GESTATION, HATCHING, ORIGINATION, DEVELOPMENT **2 :** ANCESTRY **3 :** TRAINING, EDUCATION, BRINGING-UP ⟨she had her ~ at my father's charge —Shak.⟩ **4 a :** training in the proprieties **:** MANNERS ⟨he sometimes seems like a superior interviewer and goes a little beyond good ~ —O.W.Holmes †1935⟩ ⟨his displays of temper show him to be a person of ill ~⟩ **b :** good manners **:** meticulous or habitual observance of the proprieties **5 :** the propagation of plants or animals; *esp* **:** such propagation for the purpose of improving the plants or animals (as by selection after controlled mating or, esp. in plants, hybridization) **6 a :** an instance of mating **:** SERVICE **b :** condition suitable for mating

breeding crate *n* **:** a stall or narrow open-ended enclosure arranged to restrain a cow or sow and to take the weight of a heavy sire during service

breeding ground *n* **1 :** a place to which animals resort for breeding **2 :** a place or set of circumstances considered favorable to the propagation of certain things, ideas, conditions ⟨the district was a *breeding ground* for gangs —Alfred Prowitt⟩

breeding paralysis *n* **:** DOURINE

breeding plumage *n* **:** NUPTIAL PLUMAGE

breeding population *n* **:** a population within which free interbreeding takes place and evolutionary change may appear and be preserved

breeding potential *n* **:** BIOTIC POTENTIAL 1

breeding range *n* **:** the geographic area over which breeding is carried on by individual pairs or breeding populations of a particular kind of animal

breeding territory *n* **:** a part of an animal's home range which is occupied by a family and defended against intruders

breed of cat *or* **breed of cats :** KIND, SORT — often used with *different* ⟨whether controlled inflation is a different *breed of cat* from runaway inflation —Edgar Scott⟩

breed out *vt* **:** to eliminate (a characteristic) in the course of controlled breeding

breeds *pres 3d sing of* BREED, *pl of* BREED

breed smear *or* **breed method** \ˈbrēd-\ *n, usu cap B* [after Robert S. *Breed* †1956 Amer. bacteriologist] **:** a test of the bacteriological purity of milk by direct examination of a film of fat-free milk stained with methylene blue, often used to detect the organism of bovine mastitis

¹**breedy** \-dē\ *adj* -ER/-EST [¹*breed* + *-y*] **:** PROLIFIC

²**breedy** \"\ *adj* -ER/-EST [²*breed* + *-y*] **:** exhibiting esp. in high degree the characteristics or qualities that distinguish a breed

breef *obs var of* BRIEF

breeks \ˈbrēks\ *n pl* [ME (northern dial.) *breke* pair of breeches, fr. OE *brēc* breeches — more at BREECH] *chiefly Scot* **:** BREECHES ⟨a lot of young lads in short ~ and green sarks —John Buchan⟩

bree·kums \ˈbrēkəmz\ *n pl* [dim. of *breeks*] *Scot* **:** short breeches

¹**breenge** \ˈbrēnj, -rānj\ *vi* -ED/-ING/-S [origin unknown] *Scot* **:** to plunge ahead recklessly or impetuously

²**breenge** \"\ *n* -S *Scot* **:** a clumsy plunge or dash

¹**breer** \ˈbrē(ə)r\ *chiefly Scot var of* BRIER

²**breer** \ˈbrēr\ *n or vi* [by alter.] **:** BRAIRD

brees *pl of* BREE

breest \ˈbrēst\ *dial Brit var of* BREAST

breet \ˈbrēt\ *Scot var of* BRUTE

¹**breeze** *or* **breeze fly** \ˈbrēz\ *n* -S [ME *breese, brese*, fr. OE *brēosa, brīosa*] *dial Eng* **:** GADFLY

²**breeze** \ˈbrēz\ *n* -S [MF *brise*, perh. alter. of *bise* — more at BISE] **1 :** a steady light or moderate air current; *esp* **:** one moving either toward or off a seacoast — see LAND BREEZE, SEA BREEZE **2 a :** a light gentle soft-blowing wind ⟨the languid spring ~ rocked the little green bombshells of maple sprays —T.R.Ybarra⟩ ⟨waved in the ~ of an electric fan⟩ **b :** a wind of from 4 to 31 miles an hour — see FRESH BREEZE, GENTLE BREEZE, LIGHT BREEZE, MODERATE BREEZE, STRONG BREEZE; BEAUFORT SCALE table **3 :** DISTURBANCE, QUARREL **4 a :** something easily managed or accomplished **:** CINCH ⟨that test was a ~⟩ **b :** an easy victory **5 :** something likened to a breeze (as in freshness, transience, lightness) ⟨temper the hot winds of romance with the more sensible ~ of historical fact —*Saturday Rev.*⟩ ⟨high-sounding phrases flutter in the ~ of heroic feeling —R.S.Ellery⟩ ⟨a little ~ of applause broke out —Willa Cather⟩ **syn** see WIND — **shoot the breeze** *or* **bat the breeze :** to engage in small talk **:** GOSSIP ⟨we lounged around, drinking and *shooting the breeze*, when all of a sudden the conversation took a serious turn —Frederic Wakeman⟩

³**breeze** \"\ *vb* -ED/-ING/-S *vi* **1** *of the wind* **a :** to blow gently **b :** FRESHEN ⟨it now began *breezing* strongly from seaward —Herman Melville⟩ — often used with *up* ⟨it had been smooth then, but now it was *breezing* up from the southwest —Archie Binns⟩ **2 a :** to move swiftly and airily ⟨the Senator *breezed* in, wearing a light summer suit and a jaunty straw hat —A.M. Schlesinger b. 1917⟩ **b :** to proceed quickly and easily ⟨the pitcher *breezed* to his third victory⟩ — usu. used with *through* ⟨he *breezed* through the report rapidly, remembering little⟩ ⟨so much of the beauty . . . is lost if you just ~ through —Richard Joseph⟩ **c :** to depart in haste ~ *vt* **:** to exercise (a horse) at a brisk gait without urging to great speed

⁴**breeze** \"\ *n* -S [prob. modif. of F *braise* cinders, live coals, fr. OF *brese* — more at BRAZE] **1 a :** residue from the making of coke or charcoal **b :** dust or fine bits of coke or charcoal **c :** coal or coke dust **2 :** furnace ashes **3 :** a construction material (as brick or concrete) made partly of breeze

breeze in *vi* **:** to win easily ⟨he ran for lieutenant governor and *breezed in*⟩

breeze·less \-ləs\ *adj* **:** being without a breeze

breezeway \ˈ=,=\ *n* [²*breeze* + *way*] **:** a roofed open-air passage or porch connecting two buildings (as a house and garage) or forming a corridor between two halves of a building (as of a cabin) — compare DOGTROT 2

breez·i·ly \ˈbrēzəlē, -li\ *adv* **:** in a breezy manner

breez·i·ness \-zēnəs, -zin-\ *n* -ES **:** a breezy quality or manner

breezy \ˈbrēzē, -zi\ *adj* -ER/-EST [²*breeze* + *-y*] **1 :** swept by breezes ⟨the ~ summit of the tower —Nathaniel Hawthorne⟩ **2 a :** BRISK, ZESTFUL, INFORMAL ⟨a rough and ready, ~, democratic individual —William Land⟩ ⟨delightfully ~ in the telling but serious in its basic intent —Florence Bullock⟩ ⟨a ~ if not chatty descriptive account of his career —Carlos Baker⟩ **b :** AIRY, OFFHAND, BLAND ⟨he talked with a ~ unconcern for her feelings⟩

breg·ma \ˈbregmə\ *n, pl* **bregma·ta** \-məd·ə\ [NL, fr. LL, front part of the head, fr. Gk; akin to Gk *brechma, brechmos* front part of the head — more at BRAIN] **:** the point of junction of the coronal and sagittal sutures of the skull — see CRANIOMETRY illustration — **breg·mat·ic** \(ˈ)bregˈmad·ik\ *adj*

bre·guet hairspring \brəˈgā-\ *n, usu cap B* [after Abraham L. *Bréguet* †1823 Fr. horologist] **:** a flat spiral hairspring whose last outer coil is raised and curved back to a point near the center

bre·hon \ˈbrē,hän, biˈrehüv\ *n* -S [IrGael *breitheamh* judge, fr. OIr *brithem*, fr. *breth* act of bearing, judgment; akin to OIr *biru* I bear, OE *beran* to bear — more at BEAR] **:** one of a class of lawyers in ancient Ireland with power to serve as jurist and referee but without power to enforce decisions

brei \ˈbrī\ *n* -S [G, lit., pap, pulp, fr. OHG *brīo* — more at BREE] *physiol* **:** a finely and uniformly divided tissue suspension used esp. in metabolic experimentation

¹**breid** \ˈbrād, -rēd\ *now dial Brit var of* BRAID

²**breid** \ˈbrēd, -red,-rād\ *chiefly Scot var of* BREAD

breist \ˈbrēst\ *chiefly Scot var of* BREAST

breit·haupt·ite \ˈbrīt,hau̇p,tīt\ *n* -S [G *breithauptit*, fr. J.A.*Breithaupt* †1873 Ger. mineralogist + G *-it* -ite] **:** a copper-colored usu. arborescent mineral NiSb consisting of nickel antimonide

breit·schwantz \ˈbrīt,shfän(t)s, -shvä-\ *n* -ES [G *breitschwanz*, fr. *breit* broad (fr. OHG) + *schwanz* tail, fr. MHG *swanz*, fr. *swanzen* to swing, move back and forth, freq. of *swanken* to move to and fro, fr. *swank* supple, movable, swaying — more at BROAD, SWANK] **:** BROADTAIL 2

bre·lan \brəlä^n\ *n, pl* **brelans** \-ä^n(z)\ [F, fr. OF *brelenc, berlenc* gaming table, gambling house, of Gmc origin; akin to OHG *bretling* small board, fr. *bret* board + *-ling*; akin to OE & OS *bred* board, OE *bord* — more at BOARD] **1 :** an old French gambling game somewhat like poker **2 :** THREE OF A KIND

brelan car·ré \-lä^nkärā\ *n, pl* **brelans carré** *or* **brelan carrés** [F, lit., square brelan] **:** FOUR OF A KIND

bre·loque \brəˈlōk\ *n* -S [F — more at BERLOQUE] **:** a seal or charm for a watch chain

breme \ˈbrēm, ˈbrim\ *adj* [ME *breme, brim* fierce, angry, stormy, perh. fr. OE *brēme* famous, glorious, perh. fr. *bi-* + a word akin to OS *hrōm* honor, glory, praise, OHG *hruom*; akin to OE *hrēth* glory — more at CADUCEUS] **1** *archaic, of weather* **:** SEVERE, FIERCE **2** *archaic, of a person* **:** KEEN, ALERT, SHARP — **breme·ly** *adv*

bre·men \ˈbremən, -rām-\ *adj, usu cap* [fr. *Bremen*, Germany] **:** of or from the city of Bremen, Germany **:** of the kind or style prevalent in Bremen

bremen blue *n, often cap 1st B* [prob. trans. of G *bremerblau*] **1 :** a moderate bluish green that is bluer, lighter, and stronger than porcelain green and bluer and paler than sea blue — called also *chemic green, Neuwied blue, Peligot's blue, water blue* **2 :** any of various greenish blue or bluish green pigments consisting essentially of copper hydroxide containing copper carbonate or of basic copper carbonate — compare BLUE VERDITER

bremen green *n, often cap B* [prob. trans. of G *bremergrün*] **1 :** MALACHITE GREEN 3 **2 :** any of various green pigments similar in composition to Bremen blue — compare GREEN VERDITER

bre·mer·ha·ven \ˈbremə(r),hävən, ˈbrāmərˈhäfən\ *adj, usu cap* [fr. *Bremerhaven*, Germany] **:** of or from the city of Bremerhaven, Germany **:** of the kind or style prevalent in Bremerhaven

bre·mia \ˈbrēmēə, -rām-\ *n, cap* [NL, fr. J. *Bremi*-Wolf †1857 Swiss naturalist + NL *-ia*] **:** a genus of downy mildew fungi (family Peronosporaceae) including a fungus (*B. lactucae*) that attacks lettuce and related plants

brems·strah·lung \ˈbrem,shträlŋ, -m(p)s(h),sht-\ *n* -S [G, lit., decelerated radiation, fr. *bremse* brake (fr. MHG, clamp, muzzle, fr. MLG *premese*, fr. *pramen* to press) + *strahlung* radiation, fr. *strahlen* to radiate (fr. *strahl* ray, beam, fr. OHG *strāla* arrow, lightning bolt) + *-ung* (fr. OHG *-unga* -ing); akin to MHG *pfrengen* to press and to OE *strǣl* arrow, *strēam* stream — more at PRONG, STREAM] **:** the electromagnetic radiation produced by the sudden retardation of an electrical particle (as an electron or positron) in an intense electric field (as in the atomic nucleus)

brem·sung \ˈbrem,zu̇ŋ\ *n* -S [G, lit., deceleration, fr. *bremsen* to decelerate (fr. *bremse* brake) + *-ung*] **:** the sudden slowing down of a moving charged particle on entering an opposing electric field (as that within or surrounding an atomic nucleus) — compare BREMSSTRAHLUNG

¹**bren** *also* **brenn** \ˈbren\ *dial Brit var of* BURN

²**bren** \ˈbren\ *or* **bren gun** *n* -S *usu cap B* [*Brno*, city in Czechoslovakia + *Enfield*, town in England] **:** a light gas-operated air-cooled machine gun that uses .303 caliber ammunition and is fired from the shoulder

¹**brent** \ˈbrent\ *adj* [ME *brent, brant*, fr. OE *brant*; akin to ON *brattr* steep, and prob. to OHG *bor* height, *beran* to bear — more at BEAR] **1** *dial Brit* **:** STEEP, PRECIPITOUS **2** *chiefly Scot* **:** SMOOTH, UNWRINKLED ⟨your bonny brow was ~ —Robert Burns⟩

²**brent** \"\ *or* **brent goose** *var of* BRANT

³**brent** *archaic past of* BURN

bren·ti·dae \ˈbrentə,dē\ *n pl, cap* [NL, fr. *Brentus*, type genus + *-idae*] **:** a family (type genus *Brentus*) of chiefly tropical wood-boring weevils having slender bodies, antennae that are not elbowed, and females with the beak very long and continuing the long axis of the body

brent-new \ˈbren(t)ˈ=\ *adj* [by alter.] *chiefly Scot* **:** BRAND-NEW

brer \,brər(·), ,brə(r, ,brer, ,breə, ,brə\ *n* -S [by contr.] *chiefly South* **:** BROTHER

brere \ˈbri(ə)r\ *archaic var of* BRIER

bre·scia \ˈbreshə, -räshə\ *adj, usu cap* [fr. *Brescia*, Italy] **:** of or from the city of Brescia, Italy **:** of the kind or style prevalent in Brescia

bre·scian \-shən\ *adj, usu cap* [*Brescia*, Italy + E *-an*] **:** of

or relating to Brescia, Italy, or its 16th century school of painters ⟨*Brescian* painting⟩
bresh \'bresh\ *dial var of* BRUSH
bres·lau \'bre,slaů\ *adj, usu cap* [fr. *Breslau*, Germany (now called *Wrocław*, Poland)] : WROCLAW
bres·sum·mer \'bresəmə(r)\ *n* -s [by alter.] : BREASTSUMMER
brest \'brest\ *adj, usu cap* [fr. *Brest*, France] : of or from the city of Brest, France : of the kind or style prevalent in Brest
bre·telle \brə'tel\ *n* -s [F, fr. OF *bretele*, carrying strap, of Gmc origin; akin to OHG *brittil* rein — more at BRIDLE] : one of a pair of ornamental straps that go from the belt on the front of a dress over the shoulders to the belt in back
bretelles
bre·tes·sé *also* **bret·tes·sé** \'bred·ə¦sā, brə·'te,sā\ *adj* [MF *bretessé, breteschié*, past part. of *breteschier* to furnish with parapets, fr. *bretesche* parapet — more at BRATTICE] *heraldry* : embattled on each side with the projections opposite each other
bre·ther \'bre<u>th</u>ər\ *Scot pl of* BROTHER
brethren *pl of* BROTHER — now used chiefly in formal or solemn address, in referring to the members of a profession, society, or sect, or in the names of certain sects ⟨our scientific ~ have been more blamed for this than we of the humanities—F.N.Robinson⟩ ⟨the obligation to instruct them . . . was shared by his clerical ~—G.C.Sellery⟩ ⟨a member of the Church of the *Brethren*⟩
¹bret·on \'bret°n\ *adj, usu cap* [F, fr. ML *Briton-, Brito*, fr. L, Briton — more at BRITON] **1** : of, relating to, or characteristic of Brittany, a region of France **2** : of, relating to, or characteristic of the people of Brittany
²breton \"\ *n* -s **1** *cap* : a native or inhabitant of Brittany in France — called also *Armorican* **2** *cap* **a** : the Celtic language of the Breton people — see INDO-EUROPEAN LANGUAGES table **b** : the Brythonic division of Celtic **3** *sometimes cap* : a woman's hat made on a basic pattern of round crown and wide even brim that is curved upward all around
breton lay *n, usu cap B* : a short medieval French narrative poem usu. based upon Celtic legends
bre·tonne sauce \brə'tän-\ *n, often cap B* [F *sauce bretonne*, lit., Breton sauce] : a brown sauce containing delicately browned fried red onions
brett \'bret\ *n* -s [by shortening & alter.] : BRITSKA
bret·ta·no·my·ces \,bret°nō'mī,sēz\ *n, cap* [NL, fr. Gk *Brettanos, Bretanos* Briton (of Celt origin; akin to W *Brython* Briton) + NL *-myces* — more at BRITON] : a genus of molds (family Moniliaceae) that are sometimes included in the genus *Candida*, are active in the secondary fermentation of beers, and are responsible for some cases of beer spoilage
bret·wal·da \'bret,wōldə, ⸗'⸗⸗\ *n* -s *usu cap* [OE *bretwalda, brytenwealda*, prob. fr. *Bryten* Britain + *-walda, -wealda* (fr. *wealdan* to rule) — more at WIELD] : the chief king in Anglo-Saxon England — used as a title in the Old English Chronicle for several kings said to have held supremacy over kingdoms beyond their own
breun·ner·ite \'brȯinə,rīt, 'brůn-\ *n* -s [G *breunnerit, breunerit*, fr. Count *Breunner* or *Breuner*, 19th cent. Austrian nobleman + G *-it* -ite] **1** : a ferruginous dolomite or magnesite **2** : a mineral consisting of the isomorphous system of magnesium, iron, and manganese carbonate (Mg,Fe,Mn)CO_3
brev *abbr* **1** brevet **2** brevier
breve \'brēv, 'brev\ *n* -s [ME — more at BRIEF] **1** *archaic* : an authorizing letter: as **a** : a royal mandate **b** : a papal brief **2 a** : a mark ˘ placed over a vowel to indicate that the vowel is short **b** : this mark placed over a syllable or used alone to indicate an unstressed or a short syllable in a metric foot **3** : an original writ : any writ or precept under seal that is issued out of any court **4 a** : a note in mensural notation equivalent in duration to either one half or one third of a long **b** : a note in modern notation equivalent to four half notes
breves: *a* obsolete forms; *b* modern form
breve rest *n* : a sign indicating a silence equal in duration to a breve
¹bre·vet \brə'vet, *esp Brit* 'brevət\ *n* -s [ME *brevet, brevette*, fr. MF *brevet*, fr. OF, dim. of *bref, brief* letter — more at BRIEF] **1** *obs* : a written official or authoritative message **2** : an official document from a government granting a privilege, title, or dignity **3** : a commission giving a military officer higher nominal rank than that for which he receives pay; *specif* : such a commission, carrying no right of command, that may be conferred by the president of the U.S. by and with the consent of the Senate upon officers of the Army and Marine Corps for distinguished conduct and public service in presence of the enemy ⟨discharged with the ~ rank of lieutenant colonel⟩ ⟨*Brevet* Major John Doe⟩
²brevet \"\ *vt* **brevetted** *or* **breveted**; **brevetted** *or* **breveted**; **brevetting** *or* **breveting**; **brevets** : to confer rank upon by or as if by brevet
brevi- *comb form* [L, fr. *brevis* — more at BRIEF] : short ⟨*brevi*conic⟩ ⟨*brevi*lingual⟩
bre·via·ry \'brēv(y)ərē, -vē,erē, -ri\ *n* -ES [L *breviarium*, fr. *brevi-* + *-arium* -ary] **1 a** : a brief account or summary : ABRIDGMENT **b** *obs* : EPITOME **2** [ML *breviarium*, fr. L] **a** : an ecclesiastical book containing the daily public or canonical prayers for the canonical hours **b** : the canonical prayers for each day
¹breviate *vt* -ED/-ING/-S [L *breviatus*, past part. of *breviare* to shorten, fr. *brevis* short — more at BRIEF] *obs* : ABBREVIATE, ABRIDGE
²bre·vi·ate \'brēvēət\ *n* -s **1** : COMPENDIUM, SUMMARY, ABSTRACT **2** *obs* : a brief note or dispatch; *also* : a lawyer's brief
brevi·caudate \¦brevə+\ *adj* [*brevi-* + *caudate*] : having a short tail
brevi·cip·i·tid \,brevə'sipəd·əd\ *n* -s [NL *Brevicipitidae*] : a frog or toad of the family Brevicipitidae
brevi·ci·pit·i·dae \-,sə'pid·ə,dē\ *n pl, cap* [NL, fr. *Brevicipit-, Breviceps*, type genus (fr. *brevi-* + L *-cipit-, -ceps*, fr. *caput* head) + *-idae* — more at HEAD] : a large family of tropical frogs or toads (suborder Diplasiocoela) comprising the narrow-mouthed toads feeding chiefly on termites and usu. lacking maxillary teeth and having ridged palates, large vomers, and the mouth usu. small
brevi·cone \'brevə,kōn\ *n* [*brevi-* + *cone*] : a short blunt curved shell characteristic of certain Paleozoic cephalopods; *also* : a fossil animal having such a shell — **brevi·con·ic** \¦brevə¦känik\ *adj*
bre·vier \brə'vi(ə)r, -iə\ *n* -s [prob. fr. D, lit., breviary, fr. ML *breviarium*; fr. the use of this size of type in the printing of breviaries in 16th cent. Holland & Belgium — more at BREVIARY] : a size of type between minion and bourgeois, approximately 8 point — compare POINT SYSTEM
brev·i·ger \'brevəjə(r)\ *n* -s [ML, fr. *breve* + L *-ger* -gerous] : a friar carrying a license for begging
bre·vil·o·quence \bre'viləkwən(t)s, brə'-\ *n* -s [L *breviloquentia*, fr. *breviloquent-, breviloquens* speaking briefly (fr. *brevi-* + *loquent-, loquens*, pres. part. of *loqui* to speak) + *-ia*] : brevity of speaking
bre·vil·o·quent \-nt\ *adj* [L *breviloquent-, breviloquens*] : marked by brevity of speech
brev·i·ped \'brevə,ped\ *adj* [*brevi-* + *-ped*] : having short legs
¹brevi·ros·trine \¦brevə¦rästrən, -ä,strīn\ *adj* [*brevi-* + L *rostrum* beak + E *-ine* — more at ROSTRUM] : of, relatng to, or being any of several extinct Old World Pliocene and Pleistocene mastodons with much-shortened jaws and complex grinding teeth
²brevirostrine \"\ *n* -s : a brevirostrine animal
¹brev·it \'brevət\ *vi* -ED/-ING/-S [origin unknown] **1** *dial Eng* : FORAGE, HUNT ⟨the dog is always ~*ing* about⟩ **2** *dial Eng* : to pry and prowl around : SNOOP ⟨who's ~*ed* through this drawer⟩
²brevit \"\ *n* -s *dial Eng* : a snoopy meddlesome person
brev·i·ty \'brevəd·ē, -ətē, -i\ *n* -ES [L *brevitas*, fr. *brevi-* + *-tas* -ty] **1** : shortness of duration : briefness of time ⟨the ~ of human life⟩ **2** : expression in few words : TERSENESS, CONCISENESS ⟨~ is the soul of wit—Shak.⟩ **3** : a short piece (as of writing, music) ⟨Kipling's work . . . consisted not of a few big books but of an infinite number of significant *brevities*—Katharine F. Gerould⟩

bre·voor·tia \brə'vōrsh(ē)ə\ *n, cap* [NL, prob. fr. J.Carson *Brevoort* †1887 Am. naturalist and ichthyologist + NL *-ia*] : a genus of small marine fishes (family Clupeidae) comprising the menhadens
¹brew \'brü\ *vb* -ED/-ING/-S [ME *brewen*, fr. OE *brēowan*; akin to OHG *briuwan* to brew, ON *brugginn* brewed, L *defrutum* new wine boiled down, *fervēre* to boil — more at BURN] *vt* **1** : to prepare (as beer or ale from malt and hops) by steeping, boiling, and fermentation or by infusion and fermentation : convert into a fermented liquor **2 a** : to bring about (something troublesome or woeful) as if by brewing magical potions or spells ⟨~*ing* mischief⟩ **b** : to produce or bring about as if by mixing ingredients : CONTRIVE, CONCOCT ⟨aggression that the dictator was ~*ing*⟩ ⟨this air is ~*ed* of hot sun and warm sea water—Wolfgang Langewiesche⟩ **3** *obs* : to dilute (liquor) : mix (as liquors) **4** : to prepare (as a drink or other liquid) by infusion esp. in hot water ⟨she is ~*ing* the tea⟩; *broadly* : to prepare any drink ~ *vi* **1** : to brew beer or ale esp. as a business **2** : to be in a state of preparation ⟨revolutionary . . . ways of getting around are ~*ing*—James Cerruti⟩ : be forming ⟨the notion of essence . . . ~*ed* early in Santayana —Justus Buchler⟩ : GATHER ⟨a storm ~*s* in the west⟩ : IMPEND ⟨trouble is ~*ing*⟩
²brew \"\ *n* -s **1 a** : a beverage formed by brewing **b** : a drink of such beverage (as coffee or tea); *also* : a glass of beer ⟨I'll buy you a ~⟩ **2** : a product of brewing : MIXTURE, CONCOCTION, BATCH ⟨a devil's ~ of cynicism, intrigue, and despair —*Time*⟩ ⟨like the ~ of an alchemist —Jean Stafford⟩ — see WITCHES' BREW **3** : the process of brewing or being brewed ⟨it was a loury evening with rain in ~ —A.N.Whitehead⟩
³brew \"\ *n* -s [ME *brewe*, lit., eyebrow, fr. OE *brū* — more at BROW] *dial Brit* : a steep hill or overhanging bank
brew·age \'brüij, -üēj\ *n* -s : something brewed or concocted : BREW
brew·er \'brüə(r); -ü(ə)r, -üə\ *n* -s [ME, fr. *brewen* + *-er*] **1** : one that brews; *esp* : one that manufactures brewed beverages (as ale or beer) **2** : a utensil or appliance used in brewing beverages ⟨a coffee ~⟩
brew·er blackbird *or* **brew·er's blackbird** \-r(z)-,-ə(z)-\ *n, usu cap 1st B* [after Thomas M. *Brewer* †1880 Am. ornithologist] : a blackbird (*Euphagus cyanocephalus*) widely distributed and common in inhabited areas of western No. America, the male being shining greenish black with a purplish black head, the female largely dark brownish gray
brewers' grains *n pl* : the insoluble residue from brewed malt often used as fodder
brewers' grits *n pl* : hulled and coarsely crushed grain that has to be treated in a converter before mashing
brewer's mole *n, usu cap B* [after Thomas M. *Brewer*] : a hairy-tailed mole (*Parascalops breweri*) of eastern No. America
brewer sparrow *or* **brewer's sparrow** *n, usu cap B* [after Thomas M. *Brewer*] : a small sparrow (*Spizella breweri*) of western No. America that is closely related to the chipping sparrow but somewhat smaller and rather more grayish
brewer's pitch *n* : a resinous preparation used esp. for coating the inside of beer casks
brewers' rice *n* : fragments of broken rice from the milling process that may be used as brewers' grits
brewer's spruce *n, usu cap B* [after William H. *Brewer* †1910 Am. scientist] : WEEPING SPRUCE
brewers' yeast *or* **brewer's yeast** *n* : a yeast used or suitable for use in brewing; *specif* : the dried pulverized cells of a top yeast (*Saccharomyces cerevisiae*) used in medicine and as a dietary supplement as a source of B-complex vitamins and of high-grade protein
brew·ery \'brüərē, -ü(ə)rē, -ri *also* -ür-\ *n* -ES [¹*brew* + *-ery*] : a building or plant where beer is manufactured
brewhouse \'⸗,⸗\ *n* [ME *brewhous*, fr. *brewen* to brew + *hous* house] : BREWERY
brewing *n* -s [ME, fr. gerund of *brewen*] **1** : the process of making malt beverages (as beer or ale) by grinding malt into grist, mashing the grist in hot water, boiling the mash, often with the addition of corn or rice, to produce wort, flavoring the wort with hops, fermenting the hopped wort with yeast, and drawing off the fermented wort for storage, packaging, and marketing — compare BOTTOM FERMENTATION, TOP FERMENTATION **2** : a process of preparation : CONCOCTION **3** : a quantity brewed : BATCH ⟨a new ~ of ale⟩
brewis \'brüz, 'brüəs\ *n* -ES [ME *brewes, browes*, fr. OF *broez*, nom. sing. & accus. pl. of *broet* broth, dim. of *breu* broth, of Gmc origin; akin to OHG *brod* broth — more at BROTH] **1** *dial* : broth or pottage; *esp* : broth in which beef has been boiled **2** *dial* : bread soaked in broth, drippings of roast meat, milk, or water and butter
brewmaster \'⸗,⸗⸗\ *n* : one who supervises the brewing processes in a brewery
brews *pres 3d sing of* BREW, *pl of* BREW
brew·ster \'brüstə(r)\ *n* -s [ME, female brewer, brewer, fr. *brewen* + *-ster*] *dial Brit* : BREWER 1
brew·ster angle \"-\ *or* **brew·ster's angle** \"z-\ *n, usu cap B* [after Sir David *Brewster* †1868 Scot. physicist] : POLARIZING ANGLE — compare BREWSTER'S LAW
brewster chair *n, usu cap B* [after William *Brewster* †1644 Am. pioneer] : a heavy turned chair with vertical spindles in two tiers in the back and in one or more tiers below the seat in front
brewster green *n, often cap B* [after Sir David *Brewster*] : a moderate olive green that is yellower, darker, and slightly stronger than cypress green, greener and duller than holly green (sense 2), and greener and darker than Lincoln green
Brewster chair
brew·ster·ite \-ə,rīt\ *n* -s [Sir David *Brewster* + E *-ite*] : a mineral consisting of a zeolite containing barium and strontium (Sr,Ba,Ca)$Al_2Si_6O_{16}$.$5H_2O$ (hardness 5, sp. gr. 2.45)
brewster's booby *n, usu cap 1st B* [after William *Brewster* †1919 Am. ornithologist] : a chiefly grayish brown booby (*Sula leucogaster brewsteri*) occurring from the Gulf of California to the Galápagos islands
brewster's law *n, usu cap B* [after Sir David *Brewster*] : a statement in optics: when unpolarized light of given wavelength is incident upon the surface of a transparent substance it experiences maximum plane polarization at the angle of incidence whose tangent is the refractive index of the substance for that wave length — compare POLARIZING ANGLE
¹brey \'brā\ *n* -s [modif. of F *broie*, fr. MF, prob. alter. of *braie* breeches, fr. L *braca* — more at BRACCAE] : ¹BARNACLE 1b
²brey \"\ *var of* ⁴BRAY
³brey \"\ *vt* -ED/-ING/-S [Afrik *brei*, fr. MD *bereiden* to prepare, fr. *bereit* ready, fr. *be-* + a word akin to OHG *reiti* ready — more at READY] *Africa* : to soften (skins or leather) by working with the hands
brf *abbr* brief
brg *abbr* **1** bearing **2** bridge
¹briar *var of* BRIER
²bri·ar \'brī(ə)r, -īə\ *or* **briar pipe** *n* -s [²*brier, briar* (heath)] **1** : a tobacco pipe made from the root of any of several brier plants; *esp* : a tobacco pipe made from the burl of a brier of southern Europe (*Erica arborea*) **2** : OAK 3
³briar \"\ *n* -s [perh. fr. ¹*brier, briar;* fr. a comparison of the teeth of a saw to the thorns of a brier] : CROSSCUT SAW
briarberry *var of* BRIERBERRY
bri·ard \brē'är(d)\ *n* [F, fr. *Brie*, district in northeastern France + F *-ard*] **1** *usu cap* : an old French breed of large strong usu. black dogs that have a long tail and a stiff slightly wavy long coat and that are esp. useful as sheep dogs **2** -s *sometimes cap* : a dog of the Briard breed
briarroot *var of* BRIERROOT
briarwood *var of* BRIERWOOD
briary *var of* BRIERY
brib·able *or* **bribe·able** \'brībəbəl\ *adj* : capable of being bribed
¹bribe \'brīb\ *vb* -ED/-ING/-S [ME *briben*, fr. MF *briber*, *brimber* to beg, fr. *bribe, brimbe*, n.] *vt* **1** *obs* : ROB, STEAL, PURLOIN, EXTORT **2 a** : to give or promise a bribe to : suborn by bribery ⟨*bribed* to vote against a certain candidate⟩ **b** : to induce or influence as if by bribery ⟨~ a cat with a saucer of milk to come indoors⟩ ~ *vi* : to give a bribe to a person : practice bribery ⟨a man not above *bribing* to gain his end⟩

²bribe \"\ *n* -s [ME, something stolen, fr. MF *bribe, brimbe*, piece of bread given to a beggar, scrap] **1** : a price, reward, gift, or favor bestowed or promised with a view to pervert the judgment or corrupt the conduct esp. of a person in a position of trust (as a public official) **2** : something that serves to induce or influence to a given line of conduct ⟨using ~*s* of candy to get a small child to go to bed⟩ ⟨~*s* offered to new readers ranged from cameras to flannel trousers —E.S.Turner⟩
brib·ee \(')brī¦bē\ *n* -s : one that is bribed ⟨a certain superiority of briber to ~ —Lane Kauffmann⟩
brib·er \'brībə(r)\ *n* -s [ME *bribour* vagrant, scoundrel, thief, fr. MF *bribeur, brimbeur* beggar, scoundrel, fr. *briber, brimber* + *-eur* -or] **1** *obs* **a** : a robber, blackmailer, or extortioner **b** : one that extorts a bribe **c** : something that bribes : BRIBE **2** : one that gives or offers a bribe or that practices bribery
brib·ery \-īb(ə)rē, -ri\ *n* -ES [ME *briberie*, fr. MF *briberie, brimberie* act of begging, fr. *briber, brimber* + *-erie* -ery] **1** *obs* : robbery or theft : EXTORTION **2** : the act or practice of giving or taking a bribe : the act of influencing the action of another by a bribe ⟨~ and legislative favors were in his opinion legitimate party instruments —Helen C. Boatfield⟩
bri·bri \'brē,brē\ *n, pl* **bribri** *or* **bribris** *usu cap* [Sp, of Amer-Ind origin] **1 a** : a Chibchan people of Panama and Costa Rica **b** : a member of such people **2** : the language of the Bribri people
bric-a-brac \'brikə,brak *also* -kər- *sometimes* -,bak\ *n* -s [F *bric-à-brac*] **1** : a miscellaneous collection of often antique articles of virtu : miscellaneous objects regarded as decorative or of a sentimental value and usu. collected in one place : CURIOS ⟨small china figurines, seashells, ornamental ashtrays, and other such *bric-a-brac* around the parlor⟩ ⟨a baby book—a scrapbook . . . filled with pictures, and sentimental *bric-a-brac* like dried flowers and crayon drawings, and other relics and records of my childhood —Richard Lemon⟩ **2** : something resembling or suggesting bric-a-brac esp. in extraneous decorative quality ⟨its plot bristles with . . . curses, poisonings, long-lost daughters, and all the other *bric-a-brac* of old-fashioned Italian dramaturgy —Winthrop Sargeant⟩ ⟨sensational journalistic *bric-a-brac* highlighting the seamy side of the nation's greatest industry —*Utilization*⟩
bricht \'brik̲t\ *Scot var of* BRIGHT
bricht·en \-k̲(t)ən\ *Scot var of* BRIGHTEN
¹brick \'brik\ *n* -s *see sense 2, often attrib* [ME *bryke*, fr. MF *brique*, fr. MD *bricke;* akin to OE *brecan* to break — more at BREAK] **1** : a building or paving material that is made by molding clay into blocks while moist and hardening it sometimes in the sun (as was done extensively in ancient times) but usu. today by baking or burning by fire either in a kiln or in clamps and that is ordinarily red in color due to the presence of iron compounds converted by heat into red oxide, a brown or yellow color being obtained by the addition of lime or magnesia to the clay — see SEWER BRICK **2** *pl* **bricks** *or* **brick a** : an individual molded usu. rectangular block of brick with average dimensions in America usu. of 2¼x3¾x8 inches **b** : a block of other material (as concrete, sand and lime, or glass) of similar size and shape **c** : BRICKBAT ⟨a small boy throwing ~*s* at the side of the house⟩ **3** : a rectangular usu. oblong often compressed mass ⟨a ~ of ice cream⟩ ⟨a ~ of figs⟩ **4** *slang* : a good fellow : one who is esp. good-hearted or selfless ⟨the women behaved like ~*s* and gave up their usual holiday at this time —O.W.Holmes †1935⟩ **5** *or* **brick red a** : a variable color averaging a moderate reddish brown that is redder, lighter, and stronger than mahogany, oxblood, or rustic brown, paler than Tuscan red, redder and deeper than russet tan, and yellower, lighter, and stronger than roan **b** : a moderate brown that is redder, lighter, and stronger than chestnut brown, bay, coffee, or auburn and deeper and slightly redder than toast brown **6** : BRICK CHEESE
²brick \"\ *vt* -ED/-ING/-S **1 a** : to fill up or close with brick — used with *up* or *in* ⟨~ up a doorway⟩ ⟨~ in a hole in the sidewalk⟩ **b** : to face, pave, or line with brick ⟨a shed ~*ed* only on the front⟩ — often used with *over* ⟨~ over the front of the house⟩ ⟨~ over the inside of the well⟩ **c** : to make of brick ⟨~*ed* the front of the house —Angus Mowat⟩ **d** : to enclose, buttress, or make firm with brickwork ⟨~ the shaky trunk of the tree⟩ **2** : to give the appearance of brickwork to (as to plaster by marking it off in brick-shaped areas) ⟨after . . . paint has been applied, guidelines are snapped on regularly over the entire area to be ~*ed* —Herbert Philippi⟩
¹brickbat \'⸗,⸗\ *n* -s [¹*brick* + *bat*] **1 a** : a fragment of a brick **b** : something resembling such a fragment esp. when used as a missile **2** : an uncomplimentary remark; *esp* : an insult or condemnation ⟨it is my purpose in this article to begin with the ~*s* and to end with the bouquets —Angus Wilson⟩ ⟨the religious weeklies and monthlies . . . began to throw ~*s* at him —Van Wyck Brooks⟩
²brickbat \"\ *vt* **brickbatted**; **brickbatted**; **brickbatting**; **brickbats** : to throw a brickbat at ⟨a . . . politician whom he had *brickbatted* —*Time*⟩ ⟨*brickbatting* certain Congressional patriots —*New Yorker*⟩
brick beam *n* : a lintel of bricks with iron straps
brick cheese *n* : a sweet-curd quick-ripened semisoft mellow and smooth cheese about the size and shape of a brick
brick chisel *n* **1** : a cold chisel for cutting brick masonry **2** : a broad-edged chisel used by bricklayers for trimming brick to suitable lengths
brick earth *n* : clay used for making bricks
bric·kel·lia \bri'kelēə\ *n, cap* [NL, fr. John *Brickell* *fl*1730 IrAm. physician and naturalist + NL *-ia*] : a genus of herbs (family Compositae) of the warmer regions of America having greenish or yellowish white flowers with a pappus of slender bristles
brickfield \'⸗,⸗\ *n, Brit* : BRICKYARD
brick·field·er \"+ə(r)\ *n* -s [*brickfield* + *-er;* fr. its having been first applied to dust storms blown up from brickfields near Sydney, Australia] *Austral* : DUST STORM
brick hammer *n* : BRICKLAYER'S HAMMER
brick·ie \'briki\ *n* -s [by shortening + alter.] *Brit* : BRICKLAYER
¹bricking *pres part of* BRICK
²bricking *n* -s [¹*brick* + *-ing*] : brickwork or imitation of brickwork
brickkiln \'⸗,⸗\ *n* **1** : a kiln in which bricks are baked or burned **2** : a pile of green bricks arched to receive underneath the fuel for burning them
bricklayer \'⸗,⸗(⸗)\ *n* -s [ME *brykeleyer*, fr. *bryke* brick + *leyer* layer — more at BRICK, LAYER] : one that constructs buildings, chimneys, or other structures out of brick or building blocks and mortar or that lays brick, blocks, or tile for pavement or sewers or that repairs kilns and fireboxes — called also *brickmason*
bricklayer's hammer *n* : a hammer that has a flat face and sharp peen and is used in dressing or breaking brick
brick·le \'brikəl\ *or* **brick·ly** \-k(ə)lē\ *adj* [ME *brekyl, brickyll, brukyl* fragile, weak, brittle, prob. fr. OE *-brucol* (as in *æbrucol* sacrilegious, *onbrucol* rugged, *scipbrucol* causing shipwreck), fr. *brecan* to break — more at BREAK] *dial* : BRITTLE
brick·low \'bri(,)klō\ *var of* BRIGALOW
brickmaker \'⸗,⸗⸗\ *n* [ME *brykemaker* one who makes bricks, fr. *bryke* brick + *maker*] **1** : one that conducts research in processing clays and sets up improved methods of manufacturing and using brick **2** : a worker who tends a brick-molding machine
brickmaking \'⸗,⸗⸗\ *n* : the act or process of making bricks
brickmason \'⸗,⸗⸗\ *n* : BRICKLAYER
brick nog *or* **brick nogging** *n* : brickwork filled in between the timbers of a wood-framed wall or partition — **brick-nogged** \'⸗,nägd\ *adj*
brick red *n* : BRICK 5
bricks *pl of* BRICK, *pres 3d sing of* BRICK
brick set *n* : BRICK CHISEL
brick stitch *n* : any of several embroidery stitches so spaced and staggered as to resemble laid bricks
brick sugar *n* : CUBE SUGAR
brick tea *n* : a small brick of tea leaves, stalks, and sometimes dust made in China esp. for export to Tibet, Mongolia, and Siberia — compare TABLET TEA
bricktimber \'⸗,⸗⸗\ *n* : MOUNTAIN HOLLY 1
brick trimmer *n* : a trimmer arch of brick
brick trowel *n* : a flat triangular trowel used in bricklaying for cutting brick and spreading mortar or cement

brick veneer *n* **:** a facing of brick on a wall constructed of a material other than brick

brickwork \'=,=\ *n* **:** construction or a particular piece of construction of bricks and mortar

1bricky \'brikē, -ki\ *adj, often* -ER/-EST [1*brick* + *-y*] **1 :** made of bricks **2 :** resembling or suggesting bricks esp. in color

2bricky \-ki\ *var of* BRICKIE

brickyard \'=,=\ *n* **:** a place where bricks are made

bri·cole \bri'kōl\ *n* -s [MF, lit., catapult, fr. ML *bricola*, perh. of Gmc origin; akin to MHG *brechel* breaker, OHG *brehhan* to break — more at BREAK] **1 a :** the rebound of a ball from a wall in court tennis **b :** the side stroke or play by which the ball is driven against the wall in court tennis **2 :** a billiard shot in which the cue ball strikes one of the cushions after contact with the object ball and before hitting the carom ball

brid \'brid\ *now dial var of* BIRD

1brid·al \'brīdᵊl\ *n* -s [ME *bridale*, fr. OE *brȳdealu*, fr. *brȳd* bride + *ealu* ale — more at BRIDE, ALE] **:** a nuptial festival or ceremony **:** MARRIAGE

2bridal \"\ *adj* [ME *bridale*, fr. *bridale*, n.] **:** of or relating to a bride or a wedding **:** NUPTIAL ⟨a ~ veil⟩ ⟨a ~ procession⟩ ⟨~ preparations⟩ ⟨changed the ~ white for the nun's black habit and white coif —*Springfield* (*Mass.*) *Daily News*⟩ — **brid·al·ly** \ᵊl(l)ē\ *adv*

bridal box *or* **bridal chest** *n* **:** HOPE CHEST

brid·ale \'brī,dāl\ *n* -s [ME — more at BRIDAL] **:** a usu. rustic wedding feast **:** BRIDAL

bridal rose *n* **:** CORN MAYWEED 2

brid·al·ty \'brīdᵊltē\ *n* -ES [1*bridal* + *-ty*] *archaic* **:** BRIDAL

bridal veil *n* **:** a northern African shrub (*Genista monosperma pendula*) of the family Saxifragaceae with showy sprays of pealike flowers

bridal wreath *n* **1 :** a spirea (*Spiraea prunifolia*) having copious umbels of small white flowers appearing in spring — called also *St.-Peter's-wreath* **2 :** a Chilean shrub (*Francoa ramosa*) of the family Saxifragaceae that resembles a spirea

1bride \'brīd\ *n* -s [ME, fr. OE *brȳd;* akin to OHG *brūt* bride, ON *brūthr* bride, Goth *brūths* daughter-in-law] **1 :** a woman newly married or about to be married **2 :** a woman taking vows as a member of a Christian religious order ⟨~ of Christ⟩ ⟨the ~*s* then recited together their pledges of chastity —*Springfield* (*Mass.*) *Daily News*⟩

2bride *vi, obs* **:** to appear or act as a bride

3bride \'brīd, 'brēd\ *n* -s [F, lit., reins, bridle, fr. OF, rein, prob. fr. MHG *brīdel, britel* rein, fr. OHG *brittil* — more at BRIDLE] **:** a small joining that resembles a bar, consists of one or more threads with or without ornamentation, and is used to connect the various parts of a lace pattern

bridebed \'=,=\ *n* **:** MARRIAGE BED

bridebox \'=,=\ *n* **:** HOPE CHEST

bridecake \'=,=\ *n* **:** WEDDING CAKE

bridechamber \'=,==\ *n, archaic* **:** the room containing the marriage bed

bridecup \'=,=\ *n* **1** *archaic* **:** a spiced drink served a bridal couple on the wedding night **2 :** the specially prepared cup or bowl from which guests drink at a wedding

bride·groom \'brīd,grüm, -rům\ *n* -s [by folk etymology fr. ME *bridegome*, fr. OE *brȳdguma;* akin to OHG *brūtigomo* bridegroom, ON *brūthgumi;* all fr. a prehistoric NGmc-WGmc compound whose first constituent is the word represented by OE *brȳd* bride and whose second constituent is the word represented by OE *guma* man — more at BRIDE, HOMAGE] **:** a man just married or about to be married

bridelace *n, obs* **:** a ribbon of lace for binding sprigs of rosemary used as favors at weddings

bride·less \-lə̇s\ *adj* **:** being without a bride

bridemaid \'=,=\ *or* **bridemaiden** \'=,==\ *n, archaic* **:** BRIDESMAID

bride·man \'brīdmən\ *n, pl* **bridemen** *archaic* **:** BEST MAN

bride–price \'=,=\ *n* **:** money, property, or services given by or in behalf of a prospective husband to the bride's family esp. among primitive peoples

bride's cake *n* **:** WEDDING CAKE

bride's chest *or* **bride's box** *n* **:** HOPE CHEST

bride service *n* **:** service rendered to the bride's family by the bridegroom as a bride-price or part of a bride-price

brides·maid \'brīdz,mād\ *n* [alter. of earlier *bridemaid*] **:** a usu. young woman who attends the bride during the wedding ceremony often as one of several such attendants — compare MAID OF HONOR, MATRON OF HONOR

brides·man \-,mən\ *n, pl* **bridesmen** [alter. of earlier *brideman*] **:** BEST MAN

bridewealth \'=,=\ *n* -s **:** BRIDE-PRICE

brideweed \'=,=\ *n* **:** TOADFLAX

bride·well \'brī,dwel, -dwəl\ *n* -s *sometimes cap* [fr. *Bridewell*, London house of correction established in the 16th cent.] **:** HOUSE OF CORRECTION, JAIL, PRISON

1bridge \'brij\ *n* -s [ME *brigge*, fr. OE *brycg;* akin to OHG

bridges: *1* simple truss; *2* continuous truss; *3* steel arch; *4* cantilever, *a* suspended span; *5* suspension

brucka bridge, ON *bryggja* gangplank, *brū* bridge, OSlav *brŭvŭno* beam] **1 a :** a structure erected over a depression or an obstacle to travel (as a river, chasm, roadway, or railroad) carrying a continuous pathway or roadway (as for pedestrians, automobiles, or trains) — see ARCH BRIDGE, BAILEY BRIDGE, CANTILEVER BRIDGE, GIRDER BRIDGE, SLAB BRIDGE, SUSPENSION BRIDGE, TRUSS BRIDGE; FOOTBRIDGE, RAILROAD BRIDGE; BOTTOM-ROAD BRIDGE, DECK BRIDGE, THROUGH BRIDGE; BASCULE BRIDGE, LIFT BRIDGE, SWING BRIDGE, TRANSPORTER BRIDGE, TRAVERSING BRIDGE, VERTICAL LIFT BRIDGE; compare OVERPASS, VIADUCT **b :** a time, place, or means of abstract connection (as in transition or reconciliation) **:** a figurative means of crossing ⟨the soldier as he recrosses the ~ from war to peace —Dixon Wecter⟩ ⟨a gulf too wide to be spanned by the one ~ Australians . . . set any store by — the newspaper —Thomas Wood †1950⟩ **2 a** *obs* **:** PIER, JETTY **b :** a movable landing stage for boats **3 :** something resembling a bridge (as in serving as a support for or a way over something else): as **a :** the upper bony part of the nose; *also* **:** the curved part of a pair of glasses that rests upon this part of the nose **b :** an arch or ridge at right angles to the strings of a musical instrument (as a violin or piano) serving to raise them and transmit their vibrations to the body of the instrument — see VIOLIN illustration **c :** BRIDGING JOIST **d :** a platform elevated above the rail and extending across and over the deck of a ship — compare FORE-AND-AFT BRIDGE **e :** the hand used as a rest for a billiard or pool cue in striking the ball; *also* **:** a notched or crossed piece at the end of a thin wooden rod for use as a cue rest **f :** a plank way or elevator used in ironworking to convey fuel or ore to the mouth of a furnace **g :** the position of a wrestler on his back with his body arched so that he is supported by his head and feet and sometimes elbows **h :** BRIDGE BRACKET **i :** one of the lateral bony plates connecting the carapace and plastron of a turtle shell **j :** the metal separating the ports in a machine valve seat **k :** a timber supported on blocks that rest on another timber and have a narrow space between them through which piles may be driven (as in forepoling a mining excavation) **l :** a framework that spans railroad tracks and supports signals **m** (1) **:** a backstage walk equipped with guardrails, mounting battens, and stanchions for lighting instruments that is adjustable as to height and is generally hung directly behind and parallel to the act drop in a theater — called also *light bridge* (2) **:** the portable or fixed scaffold used in a theater in connection with the paint frame for high scenery — called also *paint bridge* **n :** a plate which is attached to the pillar or baseplate of a watch and in which is mounted the bearing for an arbor, wheel pivot, or balance pivot **o :** a bright band across a sunspot **p :** the platform from which a warship is conned **q** (1) **:** the arch formed by a dancer's body in an extreme backbend (2) **:** the arch formed by the joined raised hands of a couple or a series of couples in a folk dance **4 :** something suggesting a bridge in serving the function of connecting: as **a :** LAND BRIDGE **b** (1) *or* **bridge passage :** the transition from the first subject to the second subject in a sonata or other musical form (2) **:** a color or area of color serving as a transition between two other more dominant or significant colors (3) **:** a passage, section, or scene in a literary or dramatic work serving as a transition between two other more significant passages, sections, or scenes **c :** PONS **d :** a strand of protoplasm extending between two cells **e :** a partial denture held in place by anchorage to adjacent teeth **f :** an atom or group of atoms or a valence bond connecting two different parts of a molecule (as opposite sides of a ring) ⟨the valence ~ in naphthalene⟩ ⟨the carbon ~ in camphor⟩ **g :** an area of physical continuity between two chromatids persisting during the later phases of mitosis and constituting a possible source of somatic genetic change **h :** a conductor extending across from one junction of an electric network to another **i :** a short transitional passage (as of music or sound effects) connecting two parts of a radio or TV program or two programs **5 :** a sliding cover usu. on wheels for the top of a mine shaft **6** *or* **bridge circuit :** an electrical instrument or network for measuring or comparing resistances, inductances, capacitances, or impedances by balancing two opposing voltages through a sensitive current detector whose nil reading indicates the equality of the unknown to a known ratio — see WHEATSTONE BRIDGE **7 :** one of the floor elevators running parallel to the proscenium that are raised and lowered to provide various levels for the stage floor **8 :** two men left on the king row in checkers to prevent the opponent from acquiring kings **9 :** an obstruction lodged part way down a drilled hole (as an oil well)

2bridge \"\ *vb* -ED/-ING/-S [ME *briggen*, fr. OE *brycgian*, fr. *brycg*, n.] *vt* **1 a :** to make a bridge over **:** span or make a way across with or as if with a bridge ⟨a model railroad . . . I was going to ~ a little creek for it —John Steinbeck⟩ ⟨*bridging* the gaps between the university and the high schools —J.S. Reeves⟩ ⟨a kinship in spirit that could ~ four centuries —Robert Monteith⟩ ⟨ways to ~ the time from supper to bed —John Gould⟩ ⟨a distance greater than the human shout could ~ —Waldemar Kaempffert⟩ ⟨*bridging* the distance in less than two days of actual walking —Farley Mowat⟩ **b :** to provide with a bridge ⟨small *bridged* streams along the route⟩ ⟨the *bridged* human nose —Weston La Barre⟩ **2 :** to make an electrical connection between ⟨~ the two parts of a circuit⟩ **:** SHUNT **~** *vi, of a wrestler* **:** to assume the position called a bridge

3bridge \"\ *vi* -ED/-ING/-S [prob. by folk etymology (the dealer's passing the declaration of trumps to his partner being regarded as a bridging of the table) fr. earlier *biritch*, v. & n., of unknown origin] *of the dealer in bridge-whist* **:** to delegate to one's partner the duty of selecting a suit to be trump or no-trump — used with *it*

4bridge \"\ *n* -s [prob. by folk etymology (influence of 3*bridge*) fr. earlier *biritch*] **:** any of various widely differing card games for four players in two partnerships, developed from dummy whist and cayenne, having in common that the hand of the declarer's partner is exposed and played by the declarer who also determines the trump suit or the fact of no-trump play, his adversaries being allowed to double the scoring values and the declarer to redouble them; *esp* **:** CONTRACT BRIDGE — see AUCTION BRIDGE, BRIDGE-WHIST; compare WHIST — **at the bridge :** within one point of winning the game in bridge

bridge·able \'brijəbəl\ *adj* **:** capable of being bridged

bridge bar *n* [1*bridge*] **:** TIMBER BAR

bridge bird *n* **:** PHOEBE

bridgeboard \'=,=\ *n* **:** a notched board to support the treads and risers of wooden stairs **:** STRING 14a

A, A bridgeboards

bridge bracket *n* **:** a small slotted bracket bridging a gap in the end frame of a reeling machine in cotton spinning to facilitate doffing the hanks

bridge circuit *n* **:** BRIDGE 6

bridge coat *n* **:** a long coat of very heavy wool worn by officers on a ship's bridge during cold weather

bridge coupler *n* **:** a device for engaging and disengaging the interlocking connection between the shore and a movable bridge span

bridge crane *n* **:** a crane in which a beam or bridge carries the hoisting apparatus — see GANTRY CRANE, ROTARY BRIDGE CRANE

bridge deck *n* **:** a partial deck above a superstructure, usu. amidships — see DECK illustration

bridged–T \'brij(d)¦tē\ *n* **:** a T network with a fourth branch bridging the two series arms of the T from input to output terminal, used to control the ratio of the magnitude of the output to input voltage, their relative phase, or both, such magnitudes or phase relations trips in many cases depending on signal frequency

bridge graft *n* **:** a plant graft made by inserting one or more scions with one end below and the other end above an interruption of the cambium or other weak point in the stock and used esp. to bridge wounds (as from gnawing) or to reinforce weak or defective grafts

bridge guard *n* **:** a guard on a railroad track placed at bridges or gantlet tracks and consisting of two rails gradually drawn in to meet in the center of the track

bridgehead \'=,=\ *n* [trans. of F *tête de pont*] **1 a :** a defensive work covering or commanding the extremity of a bridge nearest the enemy **b :** a locality held by the enemy and garrisoned or fortified to protect a bridge site, ford, or defile on the enemy's side **c :** a position or area around or commanding the end of a bridge ⟨railroad shops were built near the ~ on the north side —*Amer. Guide Series: Ark.*⟩ **2 a :** an advanced position or salient seized in hostile territory and defended as a foothold for further advance **b :** any advanced or initial commanding position (as in politics or commerce) ⟨many ~*s* have been established along the coast and far up the Amazon to exploit commodities in world demand —Allan Murray⟩ ⟨hold a permanent ~ in No. American markets —Dennis May⟩ ⟨the winning of labor's first international ~ —Carol Riegelman⟩

bridge house *n* **:** a structure amidships above the main deck of a ship the top of which forms a bridge deck

bridge islet *n* **:** an island that becomes a peninsula at low water

bridge lamp *n* [4*bridge*] **:** a small floor lamp usu. with an adjustable arm

bridge·less \-lə̇s\ *adj* **:** being without a bridge

bridge line *n* **:** an intermediate railroad connecting two other railroads to form a through route for traffic

bridge lock *n* **:** a mechanical device to ensure that the rails on a movable bridge are in proper position for trains

bridge·man \'brijmən\ *n, pl* **bridgemen 1 :** one who works on a bridge: as **a :** one who tends the landing bridge where a ferryboat docks and supervises the loading and unloading of the ferry **b :** one who operates the machinery for opening and closing drawbridges or who operates the bridge over which railroad cars are run from wharf to scow **c :** a member of a construction crew that builds bridges with structural steel or iron **2 :** one who works on the loading platform of an icehouse selling ice to wholesale and retail customers

bridgemaster \'=,==\ *n* **1** *Brit* **:** an officer (as of a town corporation) in control of a bridge or a pier **2 :** a man stationed on a ship's bridge to transmit directions to the man at the ship's wheel

bridge of boats : a passageway resting on boats moored abreast across a stretch of water

bridge of sighs *often cap B & S* [fr. *Bridge of Sighs*, a covered bridge in Venice, Italy, that leads from the palace of the Doge to a prison, trans. of It *Ponte dei Sospiri*] **:** BRIDGEWAY 2

bridge passage *n* **:** BRIDGE 4b(1)

bridge pewee *n* [so called fr. its nesting under bridges] **:** PHOEBE

bridge piece *n* **:** a plate, shape, or casting arching over the rudder opening between the sternpost and rudderpost of a ship

bridge plate *n* **:** a gangplank usu. of reinforced steel plate used between a railroad car or truck and a landing platform

bridge·port \'brij,pōrt, -ȯrt,-ōət,-ȯ(ə)t, *usu* -d·+V\ *adj, usu cap* [fr. *Bridgeport*, Conn.] **:** of or from the city of Bridgeport, Conn. ⟨*Bridgeport* industries⟩ **:** of the kind or style prevalent in Bridgeport

bridge rail *n* **:** a railroad-track rail in the form of an inverted trough

cross section of bridge rail

bridge rectifier *n* **:** a full wave rectifier consisting of four rectifiers connected in the form of a bridge, in which two pairs of rectifying elements are used, each pair being in series and connected to the input in opposite polarity to the other pair, the output being derived from the center points of the two pairs

bridges *pl of* BRIDGE, *pres 3d sing of* BRIDGE

bridge seat *n* **:** the shelf on the face of a bridge abutment that supports the end of the span

bridge stone *n* **1 :** a stone spanning a gutter or sunken area **2 :** stone for building bridges

bridge table *n* [4*bridge*] **:** CARD TABLE

bridgetender \'=,==\ *n* **:** one that has charge of a bridge; *esp* **:** one that opens and closes a movable bridge to accommodate both waterway and roadway traffic — called also *bridgeman*

bridge tie *n* **:** a timber resting transversely on railroad bridge stringers for support of the rails

bridge tower *n* **:** a tower on a bridge (as for the support of cables or for defense); *also* **:** a tower serving as a bridgehead

bridge train *n* **:** the personnel and equipment of an army train carrying bridge and pontoon materials

bridgettine *usu cap, var of* BRIGITTINE

bridge wall *n* **:** a low separating wall usu. of firebrick in a furnace; *esp* **:** such a wall in a reverberatory furnace

bridge·ward \'brij,wȯrd\ *n* -s **:** the principal ward of a key

bridgeway \'=,=\ *n* **1 :** a road or walk across a bridge **2 :** an enclosed passageway that is suspended above the level of the first floor and connects two otherwise separate buildings

bridge–whist \'=,=\ *n* [4*bridge*] **:** the earliest form of bridge, in which the dealer could name a suit as trump or choose no-trump or require his partner to do so

bridgewing \'=,=\ *n* **:** the end of the bridge of a ship

bridgework \'=,=\ *n* **1 :** the process or trade of bridge building; *also* **:** the structural detail of a bridge **2 :** a dental bridge or dental bridges

bridging *n* -s **1 :** the forming of or causing to assume the form or position of a bridge **2 :** the braces or system of bracing used between floor or other timbers to stiffen them and to distribute the weight — compare CROSS BRIDGING, HERRINGBONE STRUTTING **3 :** the ability of a coating of paint to form a continuous film over a small void or crack

bridging joist *n* **:** a joist resting on the binding joists and supporting the flooring

bridging species *n* **:** a plant species considered to be able to so modify the pathogenicity of a fungus infecting it that the fungus can subsequently infect a plant normally resistant to its attack

1bri·dle \'brīdᵊl\ *n* -s [ME *bridel*, fr. OE *brīdel, brigdils;* akin to OHG *brittil* rein, OE *bregdan* to move quickly — more at BRAID] **1 a :** the headgear with which a horse is governed and restrained, consisting of a headstall, a bit, and reins, often with other appurtenances **b :** a strip of metal joining two parts of a machine esp. for limiting or restraining motion **c :** BRANK 1a **2 :** something resembling or suggesting a bridle esp. in shape or in serving as a restraint: as **a :** a length of rope or cable with the ends secured to different parts or sides of an object (as a ship) and with a second rope or cable attached to the bight to which the force for hauling, lifting, or securing is applied **b :** CURB, CHECK, RESTRAINT ⟨how a soldier behaved . . . depended less upon the ~ of the army than upon self-discipline —Dixon Wecter⟩ **c :** FRENUM **d :** a cord tightening or strengthening the sides of a net **e :** a clevis on a plow **f :** the cord or system of cords by which a kite is attached to its string **g :** a device for controlling the speed of logs on a skid road or the speed of logging sleds **h :** a sling of cordage that has its ends attached to the envelope of a captive balloon or airship or to a preceding bridle and to an intermediate point of which a rope or cable is attached **i :** a cloth stay used in tailoring for the neckline of coats and jackets **3** *Brit* **:** TRIMMER 2

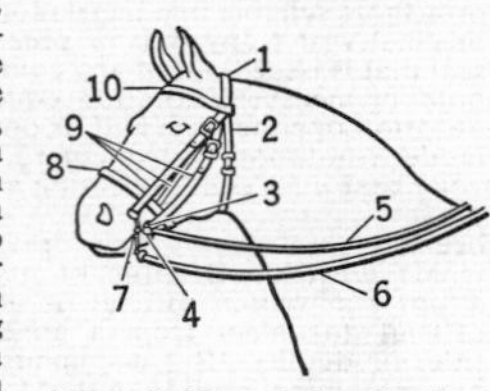

riding bridle: *1* headstall, *2* throatlatch, *3* snaffle ring, *4* snaffle bit, *5* snaffle rein, *6* curb rein, *7* curb bit, *8* noseband, *9* cheek straps, *10* front

2bridle \"\ *vb* **bridled; bridled; bridling** \-d(ᵊ)liŋ\ **bridles** [ME *bridlen*, fr. OE *brīdlian*, fr. *brīdel*, n.] *vt* **1 :** to put a bridle upon **:** equip with a bridle ⟨~ a horse⟩ **2 :** to restrain, arrest, govern, or control with or as if with a bridle; *esp* **:** to moderate steadily or guide away from excess or eccentricity ⟨strong in censuring and *bridling* the wicked —H.O.Taylor⟩ **3 :** to carry or move (as the head) like one that bridles **~** *vi* **:** to give evidence of hostility in one's attitude or behavior out of protest, offended pride, scorn, or resentment esp. by holding up the head and drawing in the chin ⟨we ~ when any one of our institutions sets itself up above another —W.L. Sperry⟩ ⟨military commanders who had *bridled* against . . . interference —*Time*⟩ **syn** see RESTRAIN

3bridle \"\ *n* -s **:** the action of one that bridles

bridle cable *n* **:** a cable secured to a bridle (sense 2a)

bridle chain *n* **1 :** one of the safety chains attaching a cage to the hoisting rope in mining **2 :** ROUGH LOCK

bridled minnow *or* **bridled shiner** *n* **:** a small American cyprinid fish (*Notropis bifrenata*) sometimes kept in aquariums

bridled tern *n* **:** a tern (*Sterna anaethetus*) of tropical seas that resembles the sooty tern but is smaller, grayer of body and whiter on the head

bridled titmouse *n* **:** a titmouse (*Parus wollweberi annexus*) having a black crest and black markings resembling a bridle on the throat and ranging from Arizona to Mexico

bridle hand *n* **:** the hand that usu. holds the bridle in riding; *usu* **:** the left hand

bridle head *n* **:** a horse bridle without a bit

bridle joint *n* **:** a joint in carpentry in which the end of one timber deeply recessed fits over another timber with recessed sides

bri·dle·less \-dᵊl(l)ə̇s\ *adj* [ME *brydiless*, fr. *brydil, bridel* + *-less*] **:** being without a bridle

bridle path *or* **bridle trail** *also* **bridle road** *or* **bridle way** *n* **:** a trail passable to or designed primarily for saddle horses or packhorses as distinguished from one for vehicles

bridle port *n* **:** a port formerly in the bow of a ship through which hawsers, bridle cables, and often gun muzzles were passed

bridle rein *n* [ME *bridel reyne*, fr. *bridel* bridle + *reyne* rein] **:** REIN 1

bridle ring *n* **:** a screw hook having the appearance of a pig's tail used for guiding and retaining telephone and signaling wires on buildings or posts

bridle rod *or* **bridle bar** *n* **:** a steel tie bar used to join the ends of two point rails to hold them to gage in the proper position

bridle sling *n* **:** a contrivance of rings, hooks, and chains or ropes serving to attach heavy loads to a crane

bridlewise \'==,=\ *adj* [1*bridle* + *wise*] *of a horse* **:** responsive to the bridle

bri·doon \brə̇'dün\ *or* **bra·doon** \brə'-\ *n* -s [F *bridon*, fr. *bride* bridle — more at BRIDE] **1 :** a bit resembling a snaffle

but without cheekpieces used chiefly with a separate curb **2 :** a headstall fitted with a bridoon
brids *pl of* BRID
brie \ˈbrē\ *also* **brie cheese** *n* -s *usu cap B* [F *brie,* fr. *Brie,* district in northeastern France, where it is made] **:** a soft perishable cheese ripened by mold
1brief \ˈbrēf\ *adj* -ER/-EST [ME *bref, breve,* fr. MF *brief, bref,* fr. L *brevis;* akin to OHG *murg* short, Gk *brachys,* Sogdian *murzak*] **1 a :** not enduring long **:** markedly limited in duration ⟨a ~ interruption⟩ ⟨a ~ speech⟩ ⟨one of the ~*est* republics in human record —Julian Dana⟩ **b :** of limited extent ⟨down across a ~ meadow —E.W.Smith⟩; *esp* **:** SHORT ⟨a ~ paragraph expressing a firm conviction —Margaret E. Hall⟩ ⟨a jacket . . . waist-length in back and ~*er* in front —Lois Long⟩ ⟨consisting of one ~ street⟩ **2 a :** CONCISE, SUCCINCT ⟨a ~ summary of the day's news⟩ ⟨some ~ remarks on the subject⟩ **b :** CURT, ABRUPT ⟨a cold and ~ welcome⟩ **3** *dial, of a communicable illness* **:** extremely common **:** PREVALENT ⟨measles are very ~ here just now⟩
syn BRIEF and SHORT contrast with *long.* BRIEF usu. applies to duration ⟨it was a fleeting visit, all too *brief;* in three short minutes he had seen them all —W.H.Davies⟩ ⟨a mock episode, as *brief* as a dream —L.P.Smith⟩ ⟨fair but mortal youths who paid with their lives for the *brief* rapture of the love of an immortal goddess —J.G.Frazer⟩ It may suggest conciseness or even curtness ⟨their greetings were *brief.* "Hi, kid", Donald said. "Hi, boy", said Will —Wallace Stegner⟩ SHORT, applying to both duration and extent, may be a close synonym for BRIEF ⟨*short* and narrow bound from morn to eventide —W.E. Gladstone⟩ It may imply a sudden abrupt shortening or conclusion ⟨a *short* but exhilarating experience of the power to control lives for good or evil⟩
2brief \ˈbrēf\ *n* -s [ME *bref, breve,* fr. MF *bref, brief,* fr. ML *brevis, breve,* fr. LL, letter, summary, fr. L *brevis* (masc. & fem.), *breve* (neut.), adj., short] **1 :** a formal or official letter or mandate: as **a :** BREVE 3; *esp* **:** BRIEVE **b** *dial Eng* **:** a statement of the causes of a person's poverty used as a petition **:** a begging letter **c :** a papal letter that is less formal than a bull and is signed by the secretary of briefs and sealed with the pope's ring **d** *obs* **:** DISPATCH 2 **e :** a letter patent formerly issued by the English sovereign as head of the established church authorizing a collection to be made in the churches for some specified purpose **2 :** a brief written item or document: as **a :** a short usu. concise article (as in a newspaper) ⟨local ~*s*⟩ **b :** a short version **:** SYNOPSIS, SUMMARY ⟨a ~ of a large scholarly tome⟩ **c** *obs* **:** CATALOG, LIST **d :** an abridgment or concise statement of a client's case made out for the instruction of counsel in a trial at law — called also *trial brief* **e** *obs* **:** MEMORANDUM, INVOICE **f :** ABSTRACT OF TITLE **3 a :** a plan or outline of an argument; *esp* **:** a formal outline with logically related headings that sets forth the main contentions with supporting statements or evidence **b** *or* **brief of argument :** such a plan in behalf of a client that often has considerable detail dealing with the facts or the law and is presented to a trial or appellate court, an administrative or international tribunal, or to a legislative body **c :** a case at law **4** *Scot* **:** SPELL, CHARM **5 :** short snug-fitting pants or underpants that usu. have elastic at the waist and elastic or ribbing at the slant-cut leg openings and are made in a variety of styles for both men and women — usu. used in pl. **syn** see ABRIDGMENT — **hold a brief for :** ADVOCATE, DEFEND ⟨although a workman, he *holds no brief for* an increase in workman's pay⟩ — **in brief** *adv* **:** in a few words **:** CONCISELY, BRIEFLY ⟨he gave the details of the accident *in brief* before discussing its legal aspects⟩ — **make brief of :** to do or perform very quickly ⟨the host *made brief of* the introductions in order to speed the group into the dining room⟩
3brief \"\ *vt* -ED/-ING/-S [1*brief*] **1 a :** to present in brief or in the form of a brief **:** make a brief, abstract, or abridgment of ⟨entered a solid, old law firm . . . received a salary for ~*ing* up cases —T.W.Duncan⟩ ⟨~ a report⟩ ⟨Miss Sandoz ~*ed* what Cook had said —C.C.Rister⟩ ⟨summarized northeastern Siberian archaeology and has ~*ed* many normally unavailable sources —Wendell Oswalt⟩ **b :** to compose (a written work) in the form of a brief or abstract ⟨a report ~*ed* from the original notes⟩ **2** *Brit* **:** to retain as legal counsel ⟨~ a lawyer⟩ **3 a :** to give final precise and informative instructions to (participants before a mission or action) **b :** to indoctrinate (members of the armed forces) in service standards — compare DEBRIEF **c :** to coach thoroughly in advance, imparting condensed up-to-the-minute information and explicit directions ⟨instructed him in what to say, in other words, ~*ed* him in the current line of propaganda —Evelyn G. Cruickshanks⟩ ⟨thousands of marriages . . . could be kept intact if young couples were properly ~*ed* beforehand on the chief booby traps in married life —*Irish Digest*⟩ **d :** to give usu. essential information to usu. concisely ⟨a visitor can hardly set foot inside the border before someone is ~*ing* him on the general sequence of events —Faubion Bowers⟩
4brief *adv* [1*brief*] *obs* **:** BRIEFLY
brief bag \ˈ≈,≈\ *n* [2*brief*] **1** *Brit* **:** the traditional blue or red bag used by barristers to carry their briefs to and from court **2 :** BRIEFCASE; *esp* **:** a briefcase with expanding sides and bottom designed to carry both documents and clothing for an overnight trip
briefcase \ˈ≈,≈\ *n* [2*brief* + *case*] **:** a flat flexible case usu. with a handle that is designed to carry legal briefs or other papers

briefcase

briefing *n* -s [fr. gerund of 3*brief*] **1 :** the action or an instance of briefing **:** the process of being briefed ⟨at the end of each day authorized spokesmen . . . held ~*s* attended by hundreds of newspaper and radio reporters —Clifton Daniel⟩ ⟨at a ~ session, pilots and navigators . . . get data —*N.Y. Times*⟩ **2 :** the instructions or information imparted at a briefing ⟨do what the ~ calls for⟩
brief·less \ˈbrēfləs\ *adj* [2*brief* + *-less*] *of a lawyer* **:** without clients
brief·ly *adv* [ME *brefly,* fr. *bref* + *-ly*] **1 a :** in a brief way ⟨an attempt has been made to survey ~ the main aspects of this vast . . . subject —W.H.Dowdeswell⟩ **b :** in brief ⟨the procedure adopted consisted ~ of selecting . . . parent trees based on reliability of cropping, yield records, and fruit quality —*Farmer's Weekly (So. Africa)*⟩ **2 :** for a short time ⟨she was ~ associated with the Civil Service Commission —*Current Biog.*⟩
brief·ness *n* -ES [ME *breffnes,* fr. *breff, bref* brief + *nes* -ness — more at BRIEF] **:** the quality or state of being brief
brief of title [2*brief*] **:** ABSTRACT OF TITLE
1bri·er *or* **bri·ar** \ˈbrī(ə)r\ *n* -s [ME *brere,* fr. OE *brǣr, brēr*] **1 a :** a plant (as members of the genera *Rosa, Rubus,* and *Smilax*) with a woody stem bearing thorns or prickles **b** *Brit* **:** WILD ROSE **2 :** a group or mass of brier bushes **3 :** a thorn or twig of a brier **:** a branch of brier
2brier *or* **briar** \"\ *n* -s [F *bruyère* heath, heather, fr. (assumed) VL *brucaria* heath, fr. LL *brucus* heather, of Celt origin; akin to OIr *froech* heather, W *grug;* akin to Gk *ereikē* heather, Lith *viržis*] **:** a heath (*Erica arborea*) of southern Europe the root of which is used for making pipes — see BRIAR, FRENCH BRIER
bri·er·ber·ry *or* **bri·ar·ber·ry** \ˈbrīə(r)- —*see* BERRY\ *n* [1*brier, briar* + *berry*] **1 :** the brownish black fruit of a prickly bush (*Rubus cuneifolius*) of the eastern U.S. **2 :** the plant that bears the brierberry
brierroot *or* **briarroot** \ˈ≈,≈\ *n* [2*brier, briar* + *root*] **:** the root of various plants (as *Erica arborea* of southern Europe or members of the genera *Rhododendron* and *Smilax* of the U.S.) used in the manufacture of tobacco pipes; *esp* **:** the burl of the brier used in the manufacture of briars
brier rose *n* [1*brier*] **:** DOG ROSE
brierwood *or* **briarwood** \ˈ≈,≈\ *n* [2*brier, briar* + *wood*] **:** the wood of the brierroot
bri·ery *or* **bri·ary** \ˈbrīərē, -ri\ *adj* [1*brier, briar* + *-y*] **:** full of briers ⟨they were excessively wet vines and ~ —D.L. Sharp⟩
brieve \ˈbrēv\ *n* -s [alter. of 2*brief*] *Scots law* **:** a chancery writ directing trial usu. by jury to be made of certain specified matters

1brig \ˈbrig\ *n* -s [short for *brigantine*] **1 :** BRIGANTINE **2 :** a 2-masted square-rigged vessel — see HERMAPHRODITE BRIG

brig

2brig \"\ *n* -s [prob. fr. 1*brig*] **:** a temporary place (as on a ship) for confinement of offenders in the U.S. navy **:** GUARDHOUSE
3brig \"\ *now chiefly Scot var of* BRIDGE
1bri·gade \brəˈgād\ *n* -s [F, fr. MF, fr. OIt *brigata,* fem. of *brigato,* past part. of *brigare* to fight — more at BRIGAND] **1 a :** a large body of troops **b :** a tactical and administrative unit composed basically of a headquarters and two or more regiments or groups **2 :** a group of people organized for special activity: as **a :** a supply party in the early American fur trade **b :** BUCKET BRIGADE **c :** FIRE BRIGADE **3** *obs* **:** a train of railroad cars
2brigade \"\ *vt* -ED/-ING/-S **:** to form into a brigade **:** unite to form a brigade ⟨this small body of 500 infantry . . . was *brigaded* with the guards —E.H.Collis⟩
brigade major *n* **:** a brigade staff officer in the British army whose duties are similar to those of a regimental executive in the U.S. Army
brig·a·dier \ˌbrigəˈdi(ə)r, -iə\ *n* -s [F, fr. *brigade* + *-ier*] **1 a :** BRIGADIER GENERAL **b :** an officer in the British army assigned to command a brigade **c :** a noncommissioned officer in the French army **2 :** a Salvation Army officer ranking above a senior major and below a lieutenant colonel
brigadier general *n* **:** an army, marine, or air force officer ranking just below a major general and above a colonel
brig·a·dier·ship \ˌ≈≈ˈ≈,ship\ *n* -s **:** the office or the rank of a brigadier
brig·a·low \ˈbrigə,lō\ *n* -s [native name in Australia] *Austral* **:** any of several plants of the genus *Acacia* with hard heavy elastic wood (esp. *A. harpophylla* and *A. doratoxylon*)
brig·and \ˈbrigənd *sometimes* brəˈgand *or* -ˈgaa(ə)nd\ *n* -s [ME *brigaunt,* fr. MF *brigand,* fr. OIt *brigante,* fr. *brigare* to fight, fr. *briga* strife, of Celt origin; akin to OIr *brīg* strength, virtue, W *bri* fame, honor] **:** one who lives by plunder usu. as a member of a band **:** BANDIT
brig·and·age \-dij\ *n* -s [F, fr. MF, fr. *brigand* + *-age*] **:** depredation as practiced by brigands **:** PILLAGE
brig·an·dine \ˈbrigən,dēn *sometimes* |īn\ *also* **brig·an·tine** \-ən,t|\ *n* -s [ME *brigandyne, brigantyn,* fr. MF *brigandine,* fr. *brigand* + *-ine*] **:** a late medieval coat of body armor consisting typically of overlapping metal scales or plates sewed within canvas, linen, or leather
brig·and·ish \ˈbrigəndish *sometimes* brəˈgan- *or* -ˈgaan-\ *adj* **:** suggesting or resembling a brigand ⟨two ~ men —Dan Wickenden⟩ ⟨~ tendencies⟩
brig·and·ism \-n,dizəm\ *n* -s **:** BRIGANDAGE
brig·an·tine \ˈbrigən,tēn *sometimes* -tīn\ *n* -s [MF *brigantin,* fr. OIt *brigantino,* fr. *brigante* brigand + *-ino* -ine — more at BRIGAND] **1 a :** a former light swift seagoing vessel esp. of the Mediterranean equipped for both rowing and sailing **b** *obs* **:** any of various light European sailing or rowing vessels **2 a :** a 2-masted square-rigged vessel differing from a brig in not carrying a square mainsail **b :** HERMAPHRODITE BRIG
brig·et·ty \ˈbrigəd·ē, -ətē, -i\ *adj* [by alter.] **:** BIGGETY
brigg \ˈbrig\ *now chiefly Scot var of* BRIDGE
briggs logarithm \ˈbrigz-\ *or* **briggs·ian logarithm** \-zēən-\ *n, usu cap B* [after Henry *Briggs* †1631 Eng. mathematician] **:** COMMON LOGARITHM
brig·ham·ite \ˈbrigə,mīt\ *n* -s *usu cap* [*Brigham* Young †1877 Amer. Mormon leader + E *-ite*] **:** a polygamous Mormon
brig·ham tea \ˈbrigəm-\ *n, usu cap B* [after *Brigham* Young; fr. its use in the treatment of gonorrhea, alluding to Mormon polygamy] **:** MORMON TEA
1bright \ˈbrīt, *usu* -īd·+V\ *adj* -ER/-EST [ME, fr. OE *beorht, byrht, bryht;* akin to OHG *beraht* bright, ON *bjartr,* Goth *bairhts* clear, evident, Skt *bhrājate* it shines] **1 a :** marked by shining or radiating light **:** pervaded by, shedding, or reflecting a relatively great amount of light **:** SHINING, LUMINOUS ⟨a ~ sun⟩ ⟨~ flames⟩ ⟨~ eyes⟩ ⟨some diamonds, very ~ and sparkling —Charles Dickens⟩ **b :** marked by qualities that make conspicuous in a way similar to that of a radiating light: as (1) **:** ringing and clear **:** SHARP — used of sounds or musical tones having a predominance of high overtones ⟨a sharp ~ quality of voice⟩ (2) **:** of high or very high saturation or lightness — used of a color ⟨~ red⟩ **c :** having qualities that make markedly, esp. radiantly, attractive **:** illustrious for qualities that charm or affect the mind pleasurably ⟨~ hours with friends⟩ ⟨~ beauty⟩ ⟨a landscape ~ with flowers⟩ **d :** marked by lightness, cheer, happiness, or qualities inspiring optimism **:** PROMISING, AUSPICIOUS ⟨those ~ mornings when you whistle with a light heart —W.H.Auden⟩ ⟨~ prospects of victory⟩ ⟨his voice sounded so ~ and cheerful, and had such a warm infectious gladness running through it —O.E. Rölvaag⟩ **2** *archaic* **:** ILLUSTRIOUS, GLORIOUS ⟨Troy . . . ~ with fame —Shak.⟩ **3 a :** showing mental quickness, ready understanding or learning, prompt responses, or originality ⟨~ young fellows with a charming literary swagger, they aspired to be wits —V.L.Parrington⟩ **b :** showing lively animation, vivacity, or activity ⟨~ and busy and crowded with tourists —*Amer. Guide Series: Mich.*⟩ ⟨she paused for a ~ wave of her hand —Agnes S. Turnbull⟩ **c :** showing glib quickness or facile resourcefulness without deep intellectuality ⟨~ ideas, some of them showing a superb neglect of practical feasibility —*Countryman*⟩ **4 :** CLEAR, TRANSPARENT ⟨a ~ wine⟩ ⟨~ beer⟩ **5 :** light in color or smooth, clean, or lustrous in any of several ways: as **a** *of lumber* **:** newly sawed or planed and smooth or free from discoloration **b** *of woodwork* **:** scraped and cleaned usu. with sand or canvas but not painted **c** *of coal* **:** shining and banded **:** containing high moisture and sulfur content — compare CLARAIN, VITRAIN **d :** having a high sparkling or glazed finish ⟨~ jewelry⟩ ⟨a ~ leather⟩ **e :** free from dirt and having an attractive luster ⟨~ onions ready for market⟩ **f :** having a natural unbleached color (as in certain market grades of hay or grain) **g** *of yarn* **:** LUSTROUS **h** *of silk* **:** DEGUMMED **i** *of wool or cotton* **:** light colored **:** WHITE **j** *of a Negro* **:** light in complexion ⟨a ~ mulatto⟩ **k** *of wire rope* **:** not galvanized, tinned, or otherwise coated **6 :** FLUE-CURED
syn BRILLIANT, RADIANT, LUMINOUS, LUSTROUS, EFFULGENT, REFULGENT, BEAMING, BEAMY, LAMBENT, LUCENT, INCANDESCENT: BRIGHT indicates emission of or pervasion by a high degree of light ⟨like the *bright* spots that move about the sun —John Keats⟩ ⟨the moon was so *bright* that Smith watered and raked and weeded as if it had been day —C.B.Nordhoff & J.N.Hall⟩ BRILLIANT implies intense, often sparkling brightness ⟨midnight streets are more *brilliant* than noon —*Amer. Guide Series: N.Y. City*⟩ ⟨a luscious prairie . . . *brilliant* with bulb flowers in the springtime —H.J.Mackinder⟩ RADIANT may stress emission of light rays but often it is only a colorful equivalent for *bright* ⟨the sun and moon, then at the prime of their *radiant* power and glory —J.G.Frazer⟩ ⟨the *radiant* mist of the afterglow —Ellen Glasgow⟩ ⟨its beautifully terraced garden *radiant* with bloom —V.G.Heiser⟩ LUMINOUS usu. implies emission of a steady, suffused, glowing light ⟨the château began to make itself strangely visible by some light of its own, as though it were growing *luminous* —Charles Dickens⟩ ⟨the inner surface of the glass is *luminous* of itself, shining with a soft and clear green light —K.K.Darrow⟩ LUSTROUS stresses a tendency to reflect light, esp. in a rich and even way ⟨the *lustrous* salvers in the moonlight gleam —John Keats⟩ ⟨*lustrous* as some huge precious pearl —Henry James †1916⟩ EFFULGENT and REFULGENT indicate resplendent or gleaming brilliance, the latter implying reflectivity ⟨the fiery light of the sinking sun . . . mottled the mountains with *effulgent* spaces —John Tyndall⟩ ⟨the glorious sovereign of day, clothed in light *refulgent,* rolling on his gilded chariot, hastened to revisit the western realms —William Bartram⟩ BEAMING and the poetical BEAMY stress emission of light beams or rays ⟨the rising moon fair *beaming* —Robert Burns⟩ ⟨west and away the wheels of darkness roll, day's *beamy* banner up the east is borne —A.E.Housman⟩ LAMBENT often indicates soft luminosity ⟨another moon new risen . . . of *lambent* flame serene —William Cowper⟩ ⟨kind, quiet, nearsighted eyes, which his round spectacles magnified into *lambent* moons —Margaret Deland⟩ LUCENT, various in its uses and romantic in suggestion, may imply a transfiguring light ⟨she walked below the *lucent* sun —Elinor Wylie⟩ ⟨till every particle glowed clean and new and slowly seemed to turn to *lucent* amber in a world of blue —W.W.Gibson⟩ INCANDESCENT suggests intense, glowing brightness ⟨here gush the sparkles *incandescent* like scattered showers of golden sand —Bayard Taylor⟩ ⟨the air rendered *incandescent* by the vehemence of the impacts of the electrons against its molecules —K.K.Darrow⟩ **syn** see in addition INTELLIGENT
2bright \"\ *adv* -ER/-EST [ME *brighte,* fr. OE *beorhte, byrhte, bryhte,* fr. *beorht, byrht, bryht,* adj.] **:** BRIGHTLY ⟨I say it is the moon that shines so ~ —Shak.⟩ ⟨asked which of the two lamps shone ~*er*⟩
3bright \"\ *n* -s [ME, fr. *bright,* adj.] **1** *obs* **:** BRIGHTNESS, SPLENDOR **2 :** tobacco of a light shade; *specif* **:** flue-cured tobacco **3 :** an artist's brush with short flat square-edged bristles — compare FLAT, ROUND **4 brights** *pl* **:** HIGH BEAM
bright and early *adv* **:** early and with time to spare ⟨starting out *bright and early* on a picnic⟩
bright aqua *n* **:** a variable color averaging light bluish green to greenish blue
bright aqua blue *n* **:** a light greenish blue that is greener and deeper than average aqua blue, bluer and deeper than average aqua, and bluer, lighter, and stronger than average turquoise blue
bright aqua green *n* **:** a variable color averaging a light bluish green that is bluer, lighter, and stronger than robin's-egg blue (sense 2) and stronger and slightly lighter than turquoise (sense 2b)
bright cerulean blue *n* **:** a strong greenish blue that is greener, lighter, and stronger than average cerulean blue (sense 1a), bluer and deeper than grotto, and paler than cobalt blue
bright chartreuse *n* **:** a variable color averaging a brilliant yellow that is yellower, stronger, and slightly darker than average chartreuse (sense 2a)
bright chartreuse yellow *n* **:** a variable color averaging a strong greenish yellow that is lighter and stronger than chartreuse yellow — compare BRIGHT CHARTREUSE
bright cherry red *n* **:** a strong to vivid red that is yellower and darker than poinsettia
bright coal *n* **:** a bituminous coal distinguished by its fine banding, higher moisture, nitrogen and sulfur content, and its smaller percentage of ash — compare SPLINT COAL
bright copen blue *n* **:** a variable color averaging a strong blue that is redder and paler than cerulean blue (sense 1b) and redder and lighter than Sèvres
bright coral red *n* **:** a variable color averaging a vivid reddish orange that is redder and lighter than international orange and redder and darker than chrome orange
bright coral rose *n* **:** a moderate reddish orange that is lighter, stronger, and slightly redder than flamingo and redder and slightly paler than crab apple
bright–cut \ˈ≈ˈ≈\ *adj* [2*bright*] *of engraving* **:** executed with short sharp strokes of the graver
bright dip *n* **:** an acid bath for cleaning metal before enameling
bright dutch blue *n, often cap D* **:** a variable color averaging strong blue to purplish blue
bright emerald green *n* **:** a variable color averaging a brilliant bluish green that is greener, lighter, and stronger than average bright turquoise green
bright·en \ˈbrītᵊn\ *vb* **brightened; brightened; brightening** \-t(ᵊ)niŋ\ **brightens** [ME *brightnen,* fr. *bright,* adj.] *vt* **:** to make bright or brighter: as **a :** to cause to shine ⟨~ a tarnished silver mug by polishing⟩ **b :** to make illustrious or more illustrious ⟨~ an already famous name⟩ **c :** to give a brighter hue or luster to ⟨the process of cleaning the oil painting ~*ed* the colors considerably⟩ **d :** to make more cheerful **:** ENLIVEN ⟨his presence ~*ed* up the party⟩ ~ *vi* **:** to become bright or brighter: as **a :** to increase in luminousness ⟨as soon as the moon came out the grove ~*ed* so that one could stroll around without a flashlight⟩ **b :** to become more lively or cheerful ⟨the party began to ~ after the drinks were passed around⟩ **c :** to become more auspicious ⟨business prospects ~*ed* with every year of peace⟩
bright·en·er \-t(ᵊ)nə(r)\ *n* -s **1 :** FLUORESCENT BRIGHTENER **2 :** a chemical or mixture of chemicals added to an electroplating bath to increase the brightness of the plate (as nickel plate)
brighter *comparative of* BRIGHT
brightest *superlative of* BRIGHT
bright–eyed \ˈ≈ˈ≈\ *adj* **:** having or giving the impression of open and youthful innocence ⟨a *bright-eyed* young lady eating an ice-cream cone⟩
brighteyes \ˈ≈,≈\ *n pl but sing in constr* **:** BLUET
bright–field \ˈ≈,≈\ *adj* **:** producing or using a strongly lighted background ⟨*bright-field* microscopy⟩ — compare DARK-FIELD
bright fuchsia purple *n* **:** a strong reddish purple that is redder, stronger, and slightly lighter than average fuchsia purple and redder and paler than purple orchid
bright gold *n* **:** a variable color averaging a strong yellow that is deeper than yolk yellow, goldenrod (sense 2b), or light chrome yellow and greener and deeper than gamboge
bright jade green *n* **:** a variable color averaging a strong green that is bluer, lighter, and stronger than mintleaf (sense 1) and bluer, lighter, and less strong than primitive green
bright kelly green *n, often cap K* **:** a variable color averaging a strong yellowish green that is greener and deeper than Cyprus green and greener, lighter, and stronger than emerald (sense 2b)
bright lavender *n* **:** a variable color averaging a moderate purple that is bluer and stronger than average lilac (sense 3a), bluer and paler than heliotrope (sense 4a), and bluer, lighter, and stronger than average amethyst
bright leaf *n* **:** a type of flue-cured burley or Maryland tobacco
bright lemon yellow *n* **:** a variable color averaging a vivid greenish yellow
bright–light district *n* **:** an urban district devoted chiefly to establishments providing entertainment (as cabarets or theaters) usu. advertised by brightly lighted entrances esp. with marquees
bright lime green *n* **:** a vivid yellow green
bright–line spectrum *n* **:** an emission spectrum consisting of bright lines against a dark background
bright·ly *adv* [ME *brightly, brightliche,* fr. OE *beorhtlīce, byrhtlīce, bryhtlīce,* fr. *beorht, byrht, bryht* bright + *-līce* -ly] **1 :** in a bright manner ⟨~ written handbooks —Milton Wilson⟩ ⟨a ~ shining sun⟩ **2 :** to the point of brightness ⟨a ~ polished metal⟩
bright maize *n* **:** a strong orange yellow that is slightly lighter and stronger than Spanish yellow
bright marigold *n* **:** a vivid orange yellow that is yellower and duller than average national school-bus chrome
bright melon yellow *n* **:** a moderate orange yellow that is redder, lighter, and stronger than yellow ocher or deep chrome yellow
bright mint green *n* **:** a brilliant green that is bluer, lighter, and stronger than emerald (sense 2a) and yellower and paler than scarab green
bright navy *n* **:** a variable color averaging a dark blue that is redder and deeper than Peking blue or Flemish blue and redder, stronger, and slightly lighter than Japan blue
bright·ness *n* -ES [ME *brightnesse,* fr. OE *beorhtnes, byrhtnes, bryhtnes,* fr. *beorht, byrht, bryht* bright + *-nes* -ness] **1 a :** the quality or state of being bright: as (1) **:** BRILLIANCE, LUSTER (2) **:** SPLENDOR, FAME (3) **:** sharpness of wit **:** ACUTENESS **b :** an instance of such a quality or state **2 a :** the attribute of light-source colors by which the light source appears to emit light varying from a minimum for very dim to a maximum for very bright **b :** LUMINANCE
bright nile green *n, often cap N* **:** a brilliant yellowish green that is greener and paler than average Paris green
bright olive green *n* **:** a variable color averaging a moderate

yellow green that is yellower and deeper than average moss green, average pea green, or apple green (sense 1)
brigh·ton \'brīt°n\ *adj, usu cap* [fr. *Brighton*, England] **:** of or from the county borough of Brighton, England **:** of the kind or style prevalent in Brighton
bright orange *n* **:** a variable color averaging a strong and vivid orange
bright peach *n* **:** a strong yellowish pink that is yellower and deeper than salmon pink, melon, or peach red
bright peacock blue *n* **:** a brilliant greenish blue
bright periwinkle blue *n* **:** a variable color averaging a light violet that is bluer, stronger, and slightly lighter than wistaria
bright rose *n* **:** a variable color averaging a strong purplish red that is bluer and deeper than madder rose
[1]**brights** *pl of* BRIGHT
[2]**brights** \'brīts\ *n pl* **:** BRIGHT COAL
bright's disease \'brīts-\ *n, usu cap B* [after Richard *Bright* †1858 Eng. physician who described kidney diseases in 1827] **:** any of several forms of disease of the kidney attended with albuminuria and edema and destructive changes in the kidney **:** GLOMERULONEPHRITIS
bright shell pink *n* **:** a moderate yellowish pink that is redder, lighter, and stronger than dusty pink, redder than peach pink, and redder and lighter than coral pink
brightsmith \'=,=\ *n* [¹*bright* + *smith*] **:** WHITESMITH
bright stock *n* **:** any of various clear oils (as a heavy lubricating oil) obtained usu. from residues of petroleum distillation by refining (as by removal of wax)
bright teal *n* **:** a moderate bluish green that is bluer and deeper than porcelain green and deeper and very slightly bluer than sea blue
bright teal blue *n* **:** a variable color averaging a moderate greenish blue that is greener than average peacock and greener and deeper than Brittany
bright teal green *n* **:** a moderate bluish green that is bluer and deeper than porcelain green and greener and deeper than sea blue
bright turquoise *n* **:** a variable color averaging a strong bluish green that is bluer and paler than Guinea green and bluer and stronger than average emerald (sense 2c)
bright turquoise blue *n* **:** a variable color averaging a strong greenish blue that is greener and very slightly paler than grotto, greener and paler than cobalt blue, and greener, lighter, and stronger than average cerulean blue (sense 1a)
bright turquoise green *n* **:** a variable color averaging a brilliant bluish green that is bluer and duller than average bright emerald green
brightwork \'=,=\ *n* [¹*bright* + *work*] **1 :** polished or plated metalwork (as on a ship, automobile, or appliance) **2 :** woodwork (as rails and coamings on a ship) that is sanded and varnished but not painted
brig·it·tine *or* **brid·get·tine** \'brijə,tēn\ *n* -s *usu cap* [after St. *Brigit* or *Bridget* †1373 Swedish nun and mystic, its founder] **:** a member of a religious order founded in Sweden about 1344
brigs *pl of* BRIG
[1]**brigue** \'brēg\ *vb* -ED/-ING/-S [MF *briguer*, fr. *brigue*, n.] *archaic* **:** PLOT, SCHEME, INTRIGUE
[2]**brigue** \"\ *n* -s [F, fr. MF, fr. OIt *briga* strife — more at BRIGAND] *archaic* **:** CABAL, INTRIGUE
brill \'bril\ *n, pl* **brill** *or* **brills** [perh. fr. Corn *brȳel, brȳthel* mackerel — more at BRIT] **1 :** a European flatfish (*Bothus rhombus*, syn. *Rhombus laevis*) that is related to the turbot and is valued as food **2 :** any of various flatfishes esp. of the family Bothidae **:** TURBOT — see PETRALE SOLE
bril·lan·te \brə'läntē\ *adj* [It, verbal of *brillare* to shine, sparkle — more at BRILLIANT] **:** showy and sparkling in style — used as a direction in music
bril·liance \'brilyən(t)s\ *n* -s **1 :** the state or quality of being brilliant **2 :** performance (as of a musical passage) displaying extraordinary precision and dexterity esp. in achieving speed and clarity; *also* **:** a passage of music calling for such precision and dexterity
bril·lian·cy \-nsē, -si\ *n* -ES **1 :** BRILLIANCE ⟨the ~ of the speech⟩ **2 :** an instance of brilliance ⟨the . . . civilized *brilliancies* of Mendelssohn's Capriccio in B minor —Thomas Heinitz⟩
bril·lian·deer \¦brilyən¦di(ə)r\ *n* -s [D *briljanteren* to cut facets on diamonds — more at BRILLIANTEER] **:** one who cuts small facets on diamonds
[1]**bril·liant** \'brilyənt\ *adj* [F *brillant*, pres. part. of *briller* to shine, sparkle, fr. It *brillare*, fr. *brillo* beryl, fr. L *beryllus* beryl — more at BERYL] **1 a :** sparkling with luster **:** very bright **:** GLITTERING ⟨a ~ star⟩ ⟨a ~ light⟩ ⟨his eyes were ~ with pain —Elinor Wylie⟩ ⟨a hot, cloudless, ~ morning —Kenneth Roberts⟩ **b :** markedly rich or conspicuous in quality: as (1) *of color* **:** strong and light ⟨a ~ red⟩ (2) *of a musical tone* **:** bright, clear, and ringing **:** rich in high harmonics **2 a :** STRIKING, ILLUSTRIOUS, DISTINGUISHED ⟨a ~ career⟩ ⟨a series of ~ exploits⟩ ⟨a ~ victory⟩ **b :** distinguished by unusual mental keenness, alertness, originality, or resourcefulness ⟨clever, witty, ~ and sparkling beyond most of her kind —Rudyard Kipling⟩ ⟨a ~ scholar who has made himself a gifted educator —Ordway Tead⟩ ⟨the prosecutor's ~ argument and summation⟩ **3** [by shortening] **:** BRILLIANT-CUT
syn see BRIGHT, INTELLIGENT
[2]**brilliant** \"\ *n* -s [F *brillant*, fr. *brillant*, adj.] **1 :** a diamond

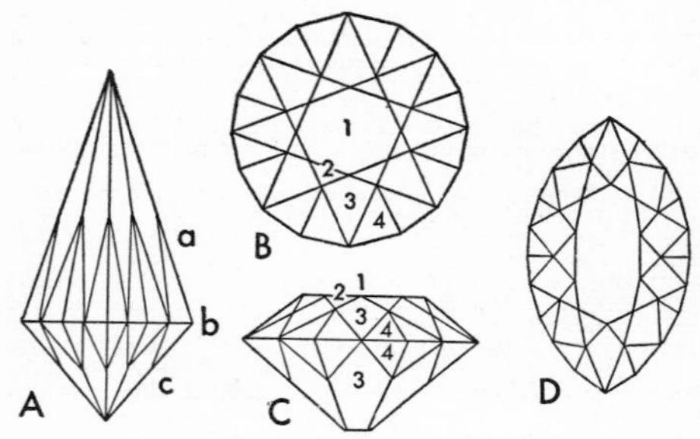

brilliant: *A* briolette; *B*, *C* top and side view of American cut; *D* marquise; *a* bezel, *b* girdle, *c* pavilion; *1* table, *2* star facet, *3* main facet, *4* corner facet, *5* culet

or other gem cut in a particular form with numerous facets so as to have especial brilliancy, ordinarily today cut in two pyramids placed base to base, the upper, usu. with 56 facets, truncated comparatively near its base by the table, the lower, usu. with 24 facets, having only the apex cut off to form the culet around which eight extra facets are sometimes added — compare BEZEL, CROWN, DOUBLE BRILLIANT, GIRDLE, PAVILION, SINGLE BRILLIANT, TABLE, TWENTIETH-CENTURY CUT **2 :** an old size of type (approximately 3½ point) smaller than diamond — compare POINT SYSTEM
brilliant crocein *or* **brilliant croceine** *n, often cap B&C* **:** a bright scarlet acid disazo dye obtained by coupling diazotized *p*-aminoazobenzene with G acid — called also *Croceine Scarlet MOO*; see DYE table I (under *Acid Red 73*)
brilliant-cut \'==¦=\ *adj* [²*brilliant*] *of a gem* **:** cut in the form of a brilliant
brilliant cutting *n* [²*brilliant*] **:** a form of decoration made on glass by means of a wheel with which various types of cuts may be made that are subsequently smoothed and polished
brilliant dye *n* **:** any of numerous acid, basic, direct, mordant, or vat dyes or organic pigments — see DYE table I
bril·lian·teer \¦brilyən·ti(ə)r\ *vi* -ED/-ING/-S [D *briljanteren*, fr. F *brillanter*, fr. *brillant* brilliant (gem) — more at BRILLIANT] **:** to cut and polish the small usu. triangular facets about the girdle of a brilliant — **bril·lian·teer·er** \-irə(r)\ *n* -s

brilliant green *n, often cap B&G* **:** a basic triphenylmethane dye that is prepared similarly to malachite green from benzaldehyde and diethyl-aniline and that gives yellower shades than malachite green — see DYE table I (under *Basic Green 1*)
bril·lian·tine \'brilyən,tēn, ,==¦=\ *n* -s [F *brillantine*, fr. *brillant* brilliant + *-ine* — more at BRILLIANT] **1 :** a usu. colored and perfumed dressing for making hair glossy **2 :** a lightweight lustrous clothing fabric that is similar to alpaca and is woven in plain or fancy weaves usu. with a cotton warp and a mohair or worsted filling
bril·lian·tined \-ēnd\ *adj, of hair* **:** dressed with brilliantine
bril·liant·ly *adv* **:** in a brilliant manner
bril·liant·ness *n* -ES **:** the quality or state of being brilliant
brilliant yellow *n, often cap B&Y* **:** a direct disazo dye derived from stilbene that dyes paper yellow and turns red in alkaline solution — see DYE table I (under *Direct Yellow 4*)
brilliolette *or* **brillolette** *var of* BRIOLETTE
bril·louin zone \¦brēyə¦wa°-\ *n, usu cap B* [after Louis M. *Brillouin* †1948 Fr. physicist] *in solid state theory* **:** one of the limited ranges within which the energy and momentum of an electron in a metallic crystal may vary continuously without any quantum jumps
brills *pl of* BRILL
brill's disease \'brilz-\ *n, usu cap B* [after Nathan E. *Brill* †1925 Am. physician] **:** an acute febrile disease now usu. considered to be a mild recurrence of typhus in an individual who had that disease years before
[1]**brim** \'brim\ *n* -s [ME *brimme*; akin to MHG *brem* edge, trimming, ON *barmr* brim, and perh. to L *frond-, frons* leafy branch, foliage] **1 a** *archaic* **:** the edge or margin of a body of water **b :** the edge or rim esp. of a cup, bowl, or depression resembling a bowl ⟨the ~ of the saucer⟩ ⟨the ~ of the crater⟩ **c :** BRINK, BORDER ⟨on the ~ of unconsciousness⟩ **2 :** the projecting rim of a hat or bonnet **syn** see BORDER

A, brim 2

[2]**brim** \"\ *vb* **brimmed; brimmed; brimming; brims** *vt* **:** to fill to the brim ⟨~ a bowl to good fellowship⟩ **~** *vi* **1 :** to be or become full often to overflowing ⟨a cup *brimming* over onto the table⟩ ⟨children . . . *brimming* over with life and health —F.J.Haskin⟩ ⟨boats . . . ~ with peasants in their folk costumes —Frederic Morton⟩ **2 :** to increase to the point of reaching or overflowing a brim ⟨tears *brimmed* in his eyes⟩ ⟨the sea . . . *brimmed* up to the very lip of the shingle beach —David Garnett⟩
[3]**brim** \"\ *adj* [ME — more at BREME] *archaic* **:** BREME — **brimly** *adv, archaic*
[4]**brim** \"\ *vi* **brimmed; brimmed; brimming; brims** [ME *brimmen*; akin to MHG *brimmen* to roar, OE *bremman* — more at FREMITUS] *now dial Eng, of swine* **:** to be in heat; *also* **:** COPULATE
[5]**brim** \"\ *n* -s [perh. fr. ⁴*brim*] *dial Eng* **:** STRUMPET
[6]**brim** \"\ *dial var of* ¹BREAM
brim·ful *also* **brim·full** \'brim¦fu̇l\ *adj* [¹*brim* + *-ful, -full*] **:** full to the brim **:** ready to overflow ⟨a child, ~ of curiosity about life and people —Caroline Sherman⟩ ⟨letters ~ of reproach —J.D.Adams⟩ ⟨a mind ~ of information —Elmer Davis⟩ ⟨tasks that filled each day ~ —Bruno Frank⟩ — **brim·ful·ly** \-,falē, -,fu̇lē\ *adv* — **brim·ful·ness** \-¦fu̇lnəs\ *n* -ES
bri·ming \'brēmiŋ, -rim-, -miŋ\ *n* -s [origin unknown] *dial Eng* **:** phosphorescence of the sea
brim·less \'brimləs\ *adj* **:** being without a brim
brimmed \'brimd\ *adj* [¹*brim* + *-ed*] **:** having a brim ⟨a woman's small ~ hat⟩ — often used in combination ⟨a broad-*brimmed* sombrero⟩
[1]**brim·mer** \-mə(r)\ *n* -s [²*brim* + *-er*] **:** a cup or glass brimful ⟨feed the flame of their loyalty with copious ~*s* —Sir Walter Scott⟩
[2]**brimmer** \"\ *n* -s [¹*brim* + *-er*] **1 :** a brimmed hat esp. of straw **2 :** a worker who makes brims for hats or provides hats with brims
brim·ming·ly *adv* [fr. pres. part. of ²*brim* + *-ly*] **:** with a fullness that threatens to overflow ⟨feel ~ happy⟩ ⟨filled the cup ~⟩
brim·my \'brimē\ *adj* -ER/-EST [¹*brim* + *-y*] **:** having a broad brim
brim of the pelvis : the upper boundary of the true pelvis formed by the iliopectineal line, the crests of the pubic bones, and the front margin of the base of the sacrum
[1]**brim·stone** \'brimz,tōn, -m,st-, *Brit usu & US sometimes* -,tən\ *n* [ME *brinston, brimston*, prob. fr. *brinnen, birnen* to burn + *ston* stone — more at BURN, STONE] **1 :** SULFUR; *sometimes* **:** native sulfur — used chiefly commercially **2** *or* **brimstone yellow :** SULPHUR YELLOW 2 **3** *archaic* **:** SHREW, VIRAGO **4 :** FIRE AND BRIMSTONE
[2]**brimstone** \"\ *adj* **:** FIRE-AND-BRIMSTONE ⟨preaching a ~ sermon⟩ ⟨an old-fashioned ~ preacher⟩
[3]**brimstone** \"\ *also* **brimstone butterfly** *n* **:** a sulphur butterfly; *esp* **:** a rather large yellow and orange European sulphur (*Gonepteryx rhamni*)
brimstone acid *n* **:** sulfuric acid made from brimstone
brim·stony \-nē\ *adj* [ME, fr. *brimston* + *-y*] **:** SULFUROUS 1, 2
brind·ed \'brindəd\ *adj* [ME *brende, brended*; prob. akin to OE *brand* brand, fire — more at BRAND] *archaic* **:** BRINDLED
brin·di·si \'brində(,)zē, -rēn-\ *n* -s [It, drinking toast, fr. G (*ich*) *bring dirs*, a toasting formula, lit., I bring it (a glass) to you] **:** a drinking or toasting song
brin·dle \'brind°l\ *n* -s [fr. *brindle, brindled*, adj.] **1 :** a brindled color ⟨not white at all . . . but a sort of ~; streaked yellow and gray —Edna Ferber⟩ **2 :** a brindled animal **3 a :** mosaic disease of tobacco **b :** a plant affected with this disease
brin·dled \-d°ld\ *or* **brin·dle** \-d°l\ *adj* [alter. of *brinded*] **:** having dark streaks or spots on a gray or tawny ground esp. with the markings blurred and without sharp margins ⟨eyes that were neither brown nor gray, but a dark ~ mixture of the two —Hamilton Basso⟩ ⟨a ~ dane with black stripes on a brown body⟩
brindled gnu *n* **:** a slaty-blue gnu (*Connochaetes taurinus*) with faint dark transverse bands on neck and withers and dusky blackish mane and tail that is now found in numbers only north of the southern African plains — called also *blue wildebeest*
brindle iron *n* [origin unknown] **:** STIRRUP 2a, 2b
brin·dling \-d(°)liŋ\ *n* -s [*brindle* + *-ing*] **:** the mingling of hairs of more than one color in a single marking **:** a brindled condition or marking
[1]**brine** \'brīn\ *n* -s [ME, fr. OE *brȳne*; akin to MD *brīne* brine, L *fricare* to rub — more at FRICTION] **1 a :** water saturated or strongly impregnated with common salt **b :** a strong saline solution (as of calcium chloride used in refrigeration) **c :** the water of an ocean, sea, or salt lake **d :** SEA, OCEAN **2** *obs* **:** TEARS
[2]**brine** \"\ *vt* -ED/-ING/-S **:** to treat (as by steeping or saturating) with brine ⟨*brined* pork⟩ ⟨*brined* hides⟩ — **brin·er** \-nə(r)\ *n* -s
brine fly *n* **:** any of various acalyptrate flies (family Ephydridae) whose larvae live in brine
brine·less \-ləs\ *adj* **:** being without brine
bri·nell hardness \brə'nel-, 'bri,n-\ *n, usu cap B* [after Johann A. *Brinell* †1925 Swedish engineer] **:** the hardness of a metal or alloy measured by a manually operated vertical hydraulic press in which a hard steel or carbide ball of standard size (as 10 millimeters in diameter) is pressed with a standard load (as 3000 kilograms) into the specimen of metal or alloy under test, the resistance to penetration being expressed by a number denoting the applied load in kilograms divided by the spherical area of indentation in square millimeters
brinell number *n, usu cap B* [after J.A.*Brinell*] **:** a number expressing Brinell hardness
brinell test *n, usu cap B* [after J.A.*Brinell*] **:** the test to determine Brinell hardness
brine·man \'brīnmən\ *n, pl* **brinemen 1 :** one that makes brine for preserving foods **2 :** a worker who prepares briny solution for use in electrolytic cells — called also *saltman*
brine pan *n* **:** a pan in which brine is evaporated to form salt

brine pump *n* **:** a ship's pump for circulating the brine in a refrigerating system or for removing the brine from an evaporator shell
brine shrimp *n* **:** any branchiopod crustacean of the genus *Artemia*
bring \'briŋ\ *vb* **brought** \'brȯt, *usu* -ȯd·+V\ *or substand* **brung** \'brəŋ\ *also* **brang** \'braŋ, -aiŋ\ *or* **brought·en** \'brȯt°n\ **brought** *or substand* **brung** *also* **brang** *or* **brought·en; bringing; brings** [ME *bringen* (past *broughte*, past part. *brought, ybrought*), fr. OE *bringan* (past *brōhte*, past part. *brōht, gebrōht*); akin to OHG *bringan* to bring (past *brāhta*, past part. *brāht*), Goth *bringan* (past *brāhta*), W *hebrwng* to accompany, Toch A *präṅk-* to remove] *vt* **1 a :** to convey, lead, carry, or cause to come along from one place to another, the direction of movement being toward the place from which the action is being regarded ⟨*brought* home a pretty young wife⟩ ⟨*brought* two ponderous lawbooks to the trial⟩ **b :** to cause to be, act, or move in a special way: as (1) **:** ATTRACT ⟨the trial *brought* a crowd to the courtroom⟩ ⟨the turmoil in the street *brought* householders to their windows⟩ (2) **:** PERSUADE, INDUCE ⟨an argument that *brought* many men to his way of thinking⟩ ⟨he may be *brought* to forgive⟩ ⟨we hope to ~ a speaker before you at the next meeting⟩ (3) **:** FORCE, COMPEL ⟨was *brought* sharply to consider his relations to the political state —V.L.Parrington⟩; *esp* **:** to force to go, be, or appear ⟨the new administration *brought* all agencies under a unified control⟩ ⟨the criminal was *brought* before the judge⟩ (4) **:** to handle, act upon, or treat so that the object is in a particular state or condition or acts in a particular way ⟨the helmsman *brought* the boat around and headed for shore⟩ ⟨~ a pot to boil⟩ ⟨the hunter *brought* to bay a lion⟩ ⟨the medicine *brought* the patient around⟩ ⟨the threat *brought* the man to his knees⟩ ⟨the statistics *brought* home the plight of the flood victims⟩ (5) **:** to submit (oneself) ⟨he could not *bring* himself to public confession⟩ **:** overcome the objections in (oneself) ⟨was unable to *bring* himself to do the deed⟩ **c** *now dial* **:** ESCORT, ACCOMPANY ⟨may I ~ you home?⟩ **d** *obs* **:** to carry word or news to **e :** to take or carry along with one ⟨asked for things he needed to ~ to school⟩ ⟨the airplane ~*ing* me from Paris to London⟩ **f :** to carry or bear as an attribute or characteristic ⟨he *brought* to his new life the habits of his old⟩ ⟨the teacher *brought* to his task a fine understanding of children⟩ ⟨~*ing* to the presidency a rich and varied experience⟩ **g :** DELIVER ⟨~ information⟩ ⟨in the absence of the regular minister a visiting preacher *brought* the message⟩ **2 :** to cause to exist or occur in any of a number of ways: as **a :** to cause to appear esp. as a concomitant **:** PRODUCE ⟨winter will ~ snow and ice⟩ ⟨the war *brought* great changes to these grassy shires —L.D. Stamp⟩ ⟨the photograph *brought* the scene clearly before his eyes⟩ ⟨he always *brought* trouble wherever he went⟩ **b :** to cause to follow as a result **:** result in ⟨doing good generally ~*s* honor⟩ ⟨the drug *brought* immediate relief from pain⟩ ⟨the sudden death *brought* great grief to the community⟩ ⟨his actions are sure to ~ trouble⟩ ⟨the sergeant's bravery under fire *brought* him a medal⟩ **c :** INSTITUTE ⟨~ legal action⟩ ⟨~ a complaint⟩ **d :** ADVANCE, ADDUCE ⟨~ an argument⟩ **3 :** PREFER ⟨~ a charge⟩ **4 :** to lead or cause (something) to be **:** arrive at **:** have experience of (something) — usu. used with *to, into, up to*, or *out of* ⟨the action *brought* the men into great difficulties⟩ ⟨the pilot *brought* them safely out of danger⟩ ⟨a few steps *brought* us to the front door⟩ ⟨the medicine seemed to ~ the man back to life⟩ ⟨the popularity of the book *brought* it to a fourth printing⟩ ⟨the donation *brought* the fund to over a million dollars⟩ ⟨this history book ~*s* us up to the present day⟩ ⟨his logic ~*s* me to a completely different conclusion than yours⟩ **5 a :** to cause to be apprehended or experienced esp. by the mind or the emotions ⟨~ certain facts to a man's attention⟩ **b :** RECALL ⟨an incident that ~*s* to mind an old friend⟩ ⟨a single verse may ~ a whole poem back⟩ **6** *obs* **:** DERIVE, DEDUCE, TRACE **7 :** to procure in exchange **:** sell for ⟨how much does coal ~ per ton on the open market⟩ **~** *vi, chiefly Midland* **:** YIELD, PRODUCE — **bring abed** *or* **bring to bed :** to be delivered of (a child) ⟨is *brought to bed* of yet another baby —Virginia Woolf⟩ — **bring by the lee :** to turn (a ship) so rapidly to leeward when sailing large as to bring the lee side suddenly to windward and by laying the sails back incur the danger of capsizing — compare ³BROACH — **bring down the house :** to evoke a furor of laughter or applause — **bring home** *of a jockey* **:** to ride (a horse) to victory — **bring home the bacon 1 :** to earn the living for the family **2 :** to win the prize sought **:** secure the desired results — **bring to account 1 :** to bring to book **2 :** to reprimand esp. for negligence or misconduct — **bring to book :** to compel to give an account or make an accounting ⟨after years of dishonest activity the man was finally *brought to book* and jailed⟩ — **bring to light :** to make clear **:** DISCLOSE, REVEAL — **bring to terms :** to compel to agree, assent, or submit **:** force to come to terms — **bring up the rear :** to come last or behind
bring about *vt* **:** to cause to take place **:** EFFECT, ACCOMPLISH ⟨so revolutionary was the change *brought about* by the abolition of slave labor —*Amer. Guide Series: La.*⟩ ⟨*brought about* a settlement of the fight⟩
brin·gal \'briŋ,gȯl, -gäl, =¦=; 'briŋ(g)əl\ *var of* BRINJAL
bring down *vt* **1 :** to cause to fall esp. by shooting ⟨*brought down* a deer⟩ **2 :** to carry forward (as a balance in bookkeeping)
bring forth *vt* **:** to bear (as fruit or offspring) **:** give birth to **:** PRODUCE ⟨*bring forth* children in pain⟩ ⟨a million and a half . . . acres were *bringing forth* wheat —*Amer. Guide Series: Minn.*⟩ ⟨the Empire style was *brought forth* to glorify . . . Napoleon —*Amer. Fabrics*⟩ **~** *vi* **:** to give birth ⟨the . . . women are not allowed to *bring forth* in the village —J.G.Frazer⟩
bring forward *vt* **1 :** to produce to view **:** INTRODUCE, ADDUCE ⟨*bring forward* some good arguments in one's defense⟩ **2 :** to carry forward
bring in *vt* **1 :** to produce by way of profit or return ⟨each sale *brought in* about five dollars⟩ **2** *obs* **:** to gain an introduction (as to a club) or a place of favor for **3 :** to enable (a man on base) to reach home plate (as by a hit) ⟨his two-bagger *brought in* three men and tied the score⟩ **4 :** to introduce (as a bill in a legislature or a point into a discussion) ⟨members appointed to prepare and *bring in* the bill —T.E.May⟩ **5 :** to report to or lay before a court or other legal body ⟨the jury *brought in* a verdict⟩ ⟨*bring in* a writ of habeas corpus⟩ **6 a :** to cause to produce or be productive (as an oil well) **b :** to win tricks with the long cards of (a suit) in whist or bridge **7 a :** EARN ⟨he *brings in* a good salary each week⟩ **b :** to finish with (as a score) ⟨the golfer *brought in* a 268 for 72 holes of play⟩
bringing *pres part of* BRING
bringing-up \¦==¦=\ *n* **:** training in childhood **:** REARING ⟨people so unlike her in temperament and *bringing-up* —William Black⟩
bring off *vt* **1 :** to cause to escape **:** RESCUE, SAVE **2 :** to achieve or carry to a successful issue esp. somewhat against expectations ⟨the author has *brought off* a tricky tour de force⟩ ⟨*bring off* a significant success in his field⟩ **3 :** HATCH ⟨*brought off* a brood of young⟩
bring on *vt* **:** to cause to come into action or existence ⟨too much activity by the patient *brings on* a fever⟩ ⟨the small border incidents ultimately *brought on* a full-scale war⟩
bring out *vt* **1 a :** to make apparent or more apparent **:** make markedly noticeable ⟨the incident *brought out* the true graciousness of the lady⟩ ⟨the lecturer *brought out* the significant aspects of the problem⟩ **b :** to develop (as a talent) to the point of effectiveness ⟨the teacher *brought out* whatever writing ability the students had⟩ **2 a :** to present (as a book, play, or invention) to the public (as for patronage or purchase) **:** PUBLISH, PRODUCE, MARKET ⟨*brought out* a practical four-wheeled auto —*Amer. Guide Series: Mich.*⟩ ⟨the author has *brought out* three novels to date⟩ **b :** to introduce socially ⟨just the sort of people who have their uses when one is *bringing out* a girl —Victoria Sackville-West⟩ **3 :** UTTER ⟨I know what I will say, or rather *bring out* nonchalantly, in the course of conversation —O.S.J.Gogarty⟩ ⟨so bored . . . that he can hardly *bring out* a good morning —*Punch*⟩
brings *pres 3d sing of* BRING
bring·sel \'briŋzəl, -ŋsəl\ *or* **brin·sell** \-inzəl,-in(t)səl\ *also* **bring·sal** \-iŋzəl,-iŋsəl\ *n* -s [G *bringsel*, fr. *bringen* to bring, fr. OHG *bringan* — more at BRING] **:** a short stick or other

device that is suspended from the collar of a trained dog and that the dog takes in his mouth as a signal to the handler that he has located an objective (as a wounded man)

bring to *vt* **1 :** to check the course of (a boat) : cause (a boat) to lie to or come to a standstill ⟨*brought* the ship *to* by dropping the anchor⟩ ⟨*brought* the enemy craft *to* by firing across her bows⟩ **2 a :** BEND ⟨*bring to* a sail⟩ **b :** to take (a cable) around a capstan **3 :** to restore to consciousness ⟨fainted dead away, but was *brought to* by sympathetic bystanders⟩

bring up *vt* **1 :** REAR, EDUCATE ⟨*bring up* one's children in good surroundings⟩ **2 :** to cause to stop suddenly ⟨*brought up* the car with a screeching of brakes⟩ ⟨a new thought *brought* her *up* sharply —Margaret Mitchell⟩ ⟨the remark *brought* me *up* short⟩ **3 :** to bring to attention **:** INTRODUCE ⟨*brought up* the weather⟩ ⟨his remark *brought up* the subject of the last election⟩ **4 :** VOMIT ⟨promptly *brought up* all the water he had drunk, but he felt better, all the same —C.S.Forester⟩ **5 :** to make ready (a letterpress form) ~ *vi* **:** to stop suddenly **:** come to a standstill ⟨the runaway bus careened down the hill and *brought up* against a building⟩

brin·i·ness \ˈbrīnēnə̇s, -nin-\ *n* -ES **:** the quality or state of being briny

brin·jal *or* **brin·jaul** \ˈbrin,jȯl, -jäl, ⸗ˈ⸗; ˈbrinjəl\ *n* -S [Pg *bringella, beringela,* fr. Ar *bādhinjān,* fr. Per *bādingān,* prob. fr. Skt *vātiṅgaṇa*] *India & Africa* **:** EGGPLANT

brin·jar·ry \brinˈjärē\ *n* -ES [modif. of Hindi *bājārā,* fr. Skt *vaṇijyā* trade (fr. *vaṇij* merchant) + *-kāraka* one who does; akin to Skt *karoti* he does — more at KARMA] **:** a traveling dealer in grain and salt in India

brink \ˈbriŋk\ *n* -S [ME *brinke,* prob. of Scand origin; akin to ON *brekka* slope, Dan *brink* edge of a precipice; akin to MLG & MD *brink* edge of a field, L *front-, frons* forehead, MIr *braine* front, leader, prow] **1 a :** EDGE, MARGIN, BORDER; *esp* **:** the very edge at the top of a steep place ⟨the ~ of a precipice⟩ **b :** a bank or edge esp. of a river **:** BORDER, BORDER LINE ⟨the ~ of the pond⟩ **:** VERGE **c :** the point of onset ⟨at the ~ of tears⟩ ⟨the ~ of war⟩ ⟨on the ~ of starvation⟩ **2** *now dial Eng* **:** the brim of a hat **syn** see BORDER

brink·man·ship \-mən,ship\ *n* [*brink* + *-manship* (as in *horsemanship*)] **:** the practice of pushing a dangerous situation to the limit of safety before stopping

brin·ser \ˈbrinzə(r), -n(t)sə-\ *n* -S *usu cap* [after Matthias *Brinser* *fl*1855 Am. theologist, founder of the sect] **:** a member of a religious body called United Zion's Children that in 1853 separated from the River Brethren

¹briny \ˈbrīnē, -ni\ *adj* -ER/-EST [¹*brine* + *-y*] **:** of, relating to, or like brine or the sea **:** SALTY ⟨a ~ taste⟩

²briny \ˈ"\ *n* -ES *slang* **:** SEA ⟨the pilot descended so fast he disappeared beneath the ~ —Henry La Cossitt⟩

brio \ˈbrē(,)ō\ *n* -S [It, of Celt origin; akin to OIr *brīg* strength, virtue, W *bri* repute, Corn *bry* worth, MBret *bri* regard] **:** VIVACITY, SPIRIT, FIRE ⟨the rector sang with such ~ —Christopher Morley⟩ ⟨driving with the ~ of a Paris taxi-driver —J.M.O'Brien⟩ — see CON BRIO

bri·oche \(ˈ)brēˌōsh, -ˌȯ-\ *n* -S [F, fr. MF dial. (Normandy), fr. dial. *brier* to brake flax, to knead, of Gmc origin; akin to OHG *brehhan* to break — more at BREAK] **:** a fancy roll of very light yeast dough rich with eggs and butter baked in muffin tins or cups

bri·o·lette \ˌbrēəˈlet\ *also* **bril·lio·lette** *or* **bril·lo·lette** \-ē(y)ə-\ *n* -S [F *briolette, brillolette,* prob. irreg. dim. of *brillant,* n., brilliant — more at BRILLIANT] **:** a diamond or other gem in the shape of an oval or pear and having its entire surface cut in triangular facets — see BRILLIANT illustration

briony *var of* BRYONY

¹bri·quette *also* **bri·quet** \(ˈ)briˈket, *usu* -ed.+V\ *n* -S [F *briquette,* dim. of *brique* brick — more at BRICK] **:** a compact mass often in the shape of a brick formed of usu. finely divided material (as coal dust or sawdust for fuel or metal powders for smelting) by mixing with a binder, by pressure, or both

²briquette \ˈ"\ *vt* -ED/-ING/-S **:** to form (as coal dust or metal powders) into briquettes

bris *var of* BERITH

bri·sance \brəˈzän(t)s, brēˈzäⁿs\ *n* -S [F, fr. *brisant,* pres. part. of *briser* to break, fr. OF *brisier,* of Celt origin; akin to OIr *brissim* I break — more at FRICTION] **:** the shattering or crushing effect of an explosive measurable by the crushing of sand or the compression of a metal cylinder and dependent upon the rate of detonation and other factors

bris·bane \ˈbrizbən (*usual Australian pronunc*), -ˌbān\ *adj, usu cap* [fr. *Brisbane,* Queensland, Australia] **:** of or from Brisbane, the capital of Queensland, Australia **:** of the kind or style prevalent in Brisbane

brisbane box *n, usu cap 1st B* **:** BRUSH BOX

brisbane lily *n, usu cap B* **:** a bulbous plant (*Eurycles sylvestris*) of the family Amaryllidaceae that is native to Australia, Malaysia, and the Philippines and has umbels of white flowers resembling lilies

brisbane quandong *n, usu cap B* **:** an Australian tree (*Elaeocarpus grandis*) with hard white timber and edible fruit — called also *blue fig*

bri·sco·la \ˈbrēskō(,)lä\ *n* -S [It] **:** an Italian card game for four players in two partnerships

bri·sé \(ˈ)brēˈzā\ *n* -S [F, fr. *brisé,* past part. of *briser* to break — more at BRISANCE] **:** a movement in ballet in which the feet or legs are clicked together in the air

brise–bise \ˈbrēz,bēz\ *n* [F, lit., windbreaker, fr. *briser* to break + *bise* north wind — more at BISE] **:** a half curtain for the lower part of a window ⟨*brise-bise* curtains in the kitchen⟩

brise–so·leil \ˌbrēzsōˈlā\ *n* -S [F, fr. *brise* (as in *brise-bise*) + *soleil* sun, fr. (assumed) VL *soliculus,* dim. of L *sol* sun — more at SOLAR] **:** an architectural device (as a projection, louvers, or a screen) to block off unwanted sunlight

bri·sé vo·lé \(,)brē,zāvōˈlā\ *n, pl* **brisés volés** \-zāvōˈlā(z)\ [F, lit., flown brisé] **:** a brisé performed with each leg alternately and finished on one foot

¹brisk \ˈbrisk\ *adj* -ER/-EST [prob. modif. of MF *brusque* — more at BRUSQUE] **1 a :** keenly alive and alert **:** LIVELY, VIVACIOUS, SPRIGHTLY ⟨a ~ old lady with no nonsense about her —Jean Stafford⟩ ⟨that ~, managing, lively, imperious woman —W.M.Thackeray⟩ **b** *obs* **:** SPRUCE, SMART **2 :** sharp or keen to the senses: as **a** *of a drink* (1) **:** agreeably lively **:** EFFERVESCENT **:** not flat ⟨a ~ cider⟩ (2) **:** having good flavor **:** pleasingly pungent **:** TANGY ⟨a ~ tea⟩ **b** *of weather conditions* **:** STIMULATING, INVIGORATING, FRESH ⟨~ air⟩ ⟨~ weather⟩ **3 :** sharp in tone or manner ⟨a somewhat ~er sort, with more bite and acid in what he says —R.H.Rovere⟩ **4 :** ANIMATED, QUICK, ENERGETIC **:** not slow or sluggish ⟨a ~ walk⟩ ⟨~ trading on a stock exchange⟩ **syn** see AGILE

²brisk \ˈ"\ *vb* -ED/-ING/-S *vt* **1** *obs* **:** to make spruce or smart in appearance — often used with *up* **2 a :** to make brisk **:** ENLIVEN, ANIMATE, SHARPEN — now used with *up* ⟨a *brisked*-up voice —Rose Thurburn⟩ ⟨~*ed* up with epigrams —*Time*⟩ **b :** to cause to move in a brisk manner ⟨~*ing* a soft cloth over the silver coffeepot —Russell Thacher⟩ ~ *vi* **:** to become brisk esp. in movement or activity — usu. used with *up* ⟨till the market ~*ed up* —H.L.Davis⟩

brisk·en \ˈbriskən\ *vb* -ED/-ING/-S [¹*brisk* + *-en*] **:** BRISK

bris·ket \ˈbriskə̇t, *usu* -ə̇d.+V\ *n* -S [ME *brusket;* akin to ON *brjōsk* gristle, MHG *brūsche* bruise, OE *brēost* breast — more at BREAST] **1 a :** the breast of a quadruped animal; *specif* **:** the part of the lower chest of such an animal that includes portions of five ribs and the breastbone — see COW illustration **b :** a cut of meat (as of beef) consisting of the breast muscles and other tissue with bones removed — see BEEF illustration **2** *dial Brit* **:** BREAST, CHEST

brisket disease *n* **:** dropsy of the brisket of cattle in high altitudes caused by dilatation and consequent weakness of the heart

brisk·ly *adv* **:** in a brisk manner ⟨a popular edition that is now selling ~ —Joseph Wechsberg⟩ ⟨walk ~ along⟩ ⟨she got up ~ and tossed down her pen —William DuBois⟩

brisk·ness *n* -ES **:** the quality or state of being brisk

brisky \ˈbriskē\ *adj* -ER/-EST **:** BRISK, LIVELY, ANIMATED

bris·ling \ˈbrizliŋ, -isl-, -lēŋ\ *or* **bris·tling** \-isl-\ *n* -S [Norw *brisling,* modif. (influenced by *brisa* to flash, burn) of LG *bretling,* fr. *bret* broad + *-ling;* akin to ON *bregtha* to move rapidly and to OE *brād* broad — more at BRAID, BROAD] **:** a small herring (*Clupea sprattus*) that resembles a sardine and that is cured and tinned esp. in Norway for food

brisque \ˈbrisk, ˈbrēsk\ *n* -S [F] **:** an ace or a ten in certain card games (as bezique) in which the ten ranks between the ace and the king

briss *var of* BERITH

¹bris·tle \ˈbrisəl\ *n* -S [ME *bristil, brustel,* fr. *brust* bristle, fr. OE *byrst;* akin to OHG *burst, borst* bristle, ON *burst* bristle, L *fastigium* top, extremity, Skt *bhṛṣṭi* spike, point] **1 :** a short stiff coarse hair **2 :** something resembling a bristle: as **a :** any of various animal structures similar to hair (as a small fine feather) **b :** the stiff short hair of a plant **c :** the manufactured material used in the face of a hairbrush

²bristle \ˈ"\ *vb* **bristled; bristled; bristling** \-s(ə)liŋ, -lēŋ\ **bristles** *vi* **1 :** to rise or stand stiff or erect like bristles ⟨a dragon with fierce eyes and scales *bristling* in defiance —T.B. Costain⟩ ⟨the points of his silvery mustache *bristled* aggressively —D.G.Geraghty⟩ **2 a** *of an animal* **:** to raise the bristles (as in anger) ⟨the dog *bristled* as the stranger approached⟩ **b** *of a person* **:** to assume an aggressive appearance or attitude ⟨I was a little annoyed and *bristled* slightly —A.W. Long⟩ ⟨that sort of antagonism which makes men ~ —Francis Hackett⟩ **3 a :** to become covered with many closely assembled objects thrusting as if aggressively straight upward ⟨the riverbank ~s with factories —*Amer. Guide Series: Pa.*⟩ ⟨a hundred-room house . . . its roof *bristling* with chimneys —*New Yorker*⟩ **b :** to be very noticeably full of a particular kind of thing — usu. used with *with* ⟨his rucksack *bristling* with test tubes —E.E.Shipton⟩ ⟨articles which *bristled* with dark insinuations —Ruth P. Randall⟩ ⟨*bristled* with . . . enthusiasm —J.C.Trewin⟩ ⟨speeches . . . *bristling* with quotations and citations —Van Wyck Brooks⟩ ~ *vt* **1 :** to erect like bristles — sometimes used with *up* ⟨a cock *bristling* up his crest⟩ **2 :** to furnish with bristles **:** attach bristles to **3 :** to make bristly **:** RUFFLE

³bristle \ˈ"\ *vb* -ED/-ING/-S [ME *brystyllen*] *dial Brit* **:** to scorch or parch esp. in cooking

bristle–bird \ˈ⸗⸗,⸗\ *n* **:** any of three Australian birds (genus *Dasyornis*) that resemble wrens and have two or three pairs of strong recurved bristles at the angles of the mouth

bristle cell *n* **:** HAIR CELL

bristlecone fir \ˈ⸗⸗,⸗-\ *n* **:** SANTA LUCIA FIR

bristlecone pine *n* **:** an upland pine (*Pinus aristata*) of the western U.S. that includes the oldest living things ⟨some *bristlecone pines* are demonstrably over 4500 years old⟩

bris·tled \-səld\ *adj* [ME, fr. *bristil, bristle* + *-ed*] **:** emblazoned with bristles on the ridge of the back ⟨a boar rampant argent, tusked, and ~ or⟩

bristle fern *n* **1 :** any fern of the genus *Trichomanes* with coarse pinnatifid fronds — called also *filmy fern* **2 :** HOLLY FERN b

bristle grass *n* [so called fr. the long bristle beneath each spikelet] **:** a grass of the genus *Setaria*

bris·tle·less \-səl(l)ə̇s\ *adj* **:** being without bristles

bristle rat *n* **:** SPINY RAT 1

bristletail \ˈ⸗⸗,⸗\ *n* **1 :** a wingless insect of the orders Thysanura and Entotrophi bearing two or three segmented filaments at the end of the body — compare LEPISMA **2 :** RUDDY DUCK

bristle–thighed curlew \ˈ⸗⸗,⸗-\ *n* **:** a curlew (*Numenius tahitiensis*) with points like bristles on its thigh feathers that breeds in western Alaska and winters chiefly in Polynesia

bristle worm *n* **:** a segmented worm of the class Chaetopoda

bristlewort \ˈ⸗⸗,⸗\ *n* -S **:** a plant of the family Centrolepidaceae

bris·tli·ness \ˈbris(ə)lēnə̇s, -lin-\ *n* -ES **:** the quality or state of being bristly

¹bristling *pres part of* BRISTLE

²bristling *var of* BRISLING

bris·tly \ˈbris(ə)lē, -li\ *adj* -ER/-EST **1 a :** consisting of or like bristles ⟨a horse with a short ~ mane⟩ ⟨a ~ brown mustache —S.H.Adams⟩ ⟨frowning ~ brows — Lucy M. Montgomery⟩ **b :** thickly set with bristles ⟨a ~ skin⟩ ⟨a ~ shrub⟩ **2 :** tending to bristle easily **:** BELLIGERENT ⟨a man with a ~ temperament⟩ ⟨this aura of ~ independence —*Time*⟩

bristly carrot *n* **:** RATTLESNAKE WEED 2

bristly crowfoot *or* **bristly buttercup** *n* **:** a hairy American buttercup (*Ranunculus pennsylvanicus*) with sharp-beaked fruits

bristly foxtail *n* **:** YELLOW FOXTAIL

bristly greenbrier *n* **:** a greenbrier (*Smilax hispida*) with pliant bristly prickles

bristly ground squirrel *n* **:** an African ground squirrel (*Xerus setosus*) with coarse bristly hair

bristly locust *n* **:** a shrub (*Robinia hispida*) of eastern No. America with bristly stems and large clusters of showy pink flowers — called also *moss locust, rose acacia*

bristly oxtongue *n* **:** a European weed (*Picris echioides*) adventive in eastern No. America with bristly foliage and yellow flowers

bristly sarsaparilla *n* **:** a bristly American herb (*Aralia hispida*) with black fruit and medicinal bark having properties like those of sarsaparilla

¹bris·tol \ˈbristᵊl\ *adj, usu cap* [fr. *Bristol,* England] **:** of or from the city of Bristol, England **:** of the kind or style prevalent in Bristol

²bristol \ˈ"\ *n* -S **1** *or* **bristol ware** *usu cap B* **:** ceramic ware produced in or about Bristol, England: as **a** *or* **bristol delft** *usu cap B* **:** 17th and 18th century tin-enameled usu. blue and white earthenware **b** *or* **bristol porcelain** *usu cap B* **:** an 18th century soft paste porcelain containing soapstone and indistinguishable from early Worcester porcelain **c** *or* **bristol porcelain** *usu cap B* **:** hard paste porcelain forming a direct continuation of Plymouth porcelain and produced about 1770–1780 **2** *or* **bristol board :** cardboard with a smooth surface suitable for writing or printing, generally of 6/1000-inch thickness or more

bristol fashion *adj, usu cap B* **:** in good order **:** SHIPSHAPE ⟨spick-and-span, shipshape and *Bristol fashion* —Jack Lusby⟩

bristol glass *n, usu cap B* **:** a semiopaque glass of various color tones, notably deep blue, used for decorative glassware and commonly painted with floral designs

bristol glaze *n, usu cap B* **:** a lead-free and usu. zinc-containing ceramic glaze used on faïence and stoneware

bri·sure *also* **bri·zure** \brəˈzhù(ə)r\ *n* -S [F *brisure,* lit., break, crack, fr. OF, fr. *brisier* to break — more at BRISANCE] **:** CADENCY MARK **:** DIFFERENCE

brit *or* **britt** \ˈbrit\ *n* -S [modif. of Corn *brȳthel* mackerel, lit., speckled, fr. *brȳth* speckled + *-el* (dim. suffix); akin to W *brith* speckled] **1 a :** the young of the common herring **b :** any of certain small herrings **2 :** the minute marine animals, largely crustaceans (Entomostraca) and pteropods, upon which the right whales feed **3 :** any of the silversides

brit·ain \ˈbritᵊn *also* -itən *or* -id·ən\ *n* -S *usu cap* [alter. (influenced by *Britain* Great Britain) of *Briton*] *obs* **:** BRITON

bri·tan·nia \brəˈtanyə, -nēə\ *n* -S *usu cap* [fr. *Britannia,* poetic name for Great Britain, fr. L] **:** a representation of a female figure usu. seated and with helmet and trident that is symbolic of Great Britain or Great Britain and the dominions

britannia metal *or* **britannia** *n* [fr. *Britannia* Great Britain] **:** a silver-white alloy of tin, antimony, copper, and often also zinc and bismuth that is similar to pewter and was formerly much used for domestic utensils

bri·tan·nian \-yən,-ēən\ *adj, usu cap* [*Britannia* Great Britain + E *-an*] **:** BRITISH

¹bri·tan·nic \-nik,-nēk\ *adj, usu cap* [L *Britannicus,* fr. *Britannia* + L *-icus* -ic] **:** BRITISH ⟨her *Britannic* majesty, Queen Victoria⟩ — **bri·tan·ni·cal·ly** \-nə̇k(ə)lē\ *adv, usu cap*

²britannic \ˈ"\ *n* -S **:** AMPHIBRACH

bri·tan·ni·cize \-nə,sīz\ *vt* -ED/-ING/-S *often cap* **:** to make British in quality, customs, or behavior

¹britch \ˈbrich\ *n* -ES [by alter.] *dial* **:** ¹BREECH

²britch \ˈ"\ *vt* -ED/-ING/-ES [by alter.] *dial* **:** ²BREECH

britch·el \ˈbrichəl\ *adj* [ME *bruchel,* fr. OE *-brycel* (as in *hūsbrycel* burglarious); akin to OE *brecan* to break — more at BREAK] *dial Eng* **:** BRITTLE

britch·en *also* **britch·in** \ˈbrichə̇n\ *n* [by alter.] *dial* **:** BREECHING

britch·es \ˈbrichə̇z\ *n pl* [alter. of *breeches*] **:** BREECHES, PANTS — **too big for one's britches :** SWELLHEADED, ARROGANT

brith *var of* BERITH

brith·er \ˈbrit͟hə(r), -ret͟h-\ *n* -S [prob. back-formation fr. dial. *brither,* pl., fr. ME *brether, breither, brither,* pl. of *brother*] *dial* **:** BROTHER

brit·i·cism \ˈbrid·ə,sizəm, -itə-\ *n* -S *usu cap* [*Brit*ish + *-icism* (as in *Gallicism*)] **:** a characteristic feature of British English esp. as contrasted with American English (as *waistcoat* contrasted with *vest, navvy* with *day laborer, to register luggage* with *to check baggage, to engage a servant* with *to hire a servant, tyre* with *tire, kerb* with *curb*)

¹brit·ish \ˈbrid·ish, -it|, |ēsh\ *adj, usu cap* [ME *Bruttische, Brytysshe,* fr. OE *Brettisc, Bryttisc, Brittisc,* of Celt origin; akin to W *Brython* Briton] **1 :** of, relating to, or characteristic of the original inhabitants of Britain **2 a :** of, relating to, or characteristic of Great Britain or its inhabitants **b :** of, relating to, or characteristic of the British Commonwealth **c :** of, relating to, or characteristic of England — **brit·ish·ness** *n* -ES *usu cap*

²british \ˈ"\ *n* -ES *cap* **1 a :** the Celtic language of the ancient Britons **b :** BRITISH ENGLISH **2** *pl in constr* **a :** the people native to or naturalized in Great Britain **b :** the primarily British people of the British Commonwealth **c :** the people of the British Commonwealth

british alpine *n, usu cap B & sometimes cap A* **:** a goat of a strain that is sometimes considered a separate breed developed in England by interbreeding Swiss Alpine goats with native stock

british an·ti–lew·is·ite \-ˈlüə,sīt\ *n, usu cap B* [¹*anti-* + *lewisite*] **:** DIMERCAPROL

british association thread *n, usu cap B&A* **:** a screw thread with an angle of 47½° and rounded crests and roots that is used chiefly in Great Britain and other European countries for very small screws

british co·lum·bi·a \ˌ⸗⸗kəˈləmbēə\ *adj, usu cap B&C* [fr. *British Columbia,* province of Canada] **:** of or from the province of British Columbia **:** of the kind or style prevalent in British Columbia **:** BRITISH COLUMBIAN

¹british co·lum·bi·an \-ən\ *adj, usu cap B&C* **1 :** of, relating to, or characteristic of the province of British Columbia **2 :** of, relating to, or characteristic of the people of British Columbia

²british columbian \ˈ"\ *n, cap B&C* **:** a native or inhabitant of British Columbia

british dollar *n, usu cap B* **:** DOLLAR 2d

british english *n, cap B&E* **:** the native language of most inhabitants of England; *esp* **:** a variety of English characteristic of England and clearly distinguishable from those varieties used in the U.S., Australia, and elsewhere — compare AMERICAN ENGLISH, AUSTRAL ENGLISH, AUSTRALIAN ENGLISH

brit·ish·er \ˈbrid·ishə(r), -it|, |ēsh-\ *n* -S *cap B* **:** BRITON 2

¹british guianese *also* **british guianan** *see* GUIANESE, GUIANAN\ *adj, usu cap B&G* [*British Guiana,* former name of Guyana + E *-ese* or *-an*] **:** GUYANESE

²british guianese *also* **british guianan** \ˈ"\ *n, cap B&G* **:** GUYANESE

british gum *n, usu cap B* **:** DEXTRIN; *esp* **:** dextrin produced by heating starch sometimes with small amounts of acid or alkali and used as size for paper and textiles and as an adhesive

¹british honduran *see* HONDURAN\ *adj, usu cap B&H* [*British Honduras,* country in Central America + E *-an*] **1 :** of, relating to, or characteristic of British Honduras **2 :** of, relating to, or characteristic of the people of British Honduras

²british honduran \ˈ"\ *n, cap B&H* **:** a native or inhabitant of British Honduras

brit·ish·ism \|ē,shizəm, |ə,-\ *n* -S *usu cap* **1 :** BRITICISM **2 a :** the distinctive qualities of the people of the British Commonwealth **b :** one of these qualities

brit·ish·ly *adv, usu cap* **:** in a British way ⟨a ~ calm bystander⟩

british mold *n, usu cap B* **:** a mold of the genus *Brettanomyces*

british oak *n, usu cap B* **:** ENGLISH OAK

british thermal unit *n, usu cap B* **:** the quantity of heat required to raise the temperature of one avoirdupois pound of water one degree Fahrenheit at or near 39.2°F, its temperature of maximum density, being equal to about 0.252 kilogram calorie — abbr. *Btu*

british warm *n, usu cap B* **:** a short double-breasted overcoat worn esp. by British army officers

brito– \ˈbrid·(,)ō, -i,tō\ *n comb form, cap* [prob. fr. L *Brito*] **1 :** of or belonging to the Britons and ⟨*Brito*-Roman⟩ **2 :** British and ⟨*Brito*-Japanese⟩ **3 :** Britain ⟨*Brito*centric⟩

brit·on \ˈbritᵊn *also* -itən *or* -id·ən\ *n* -S *cap* [ME *Breton, Bryton,* fr. MF & L; MF *breton,* fr. L *Briton-, Brito, Britton-, Britto,* of Celt origin; akin to W *Brython* Briton] **1 :** a member of one of the peoples inhabiting Britain previous to the Anglo-Saxon invasions, the majority being presumably Cymric Celts intermixed with earlier non-Indo-European-speaking peoples **2 :** a native or subject of Great Britain; *esp* **:** ENGLISHMAN

brits *pl of* BRIT

brits·ka *or* **britz·ska** \ˈbrichkə, -itskə\ *n* -S [G *britschka, britzka,* fr. Pol *bryczka,* perh. modif. of G *barutsche, birutsche* barouche — more at BAROUCHE] **:** a long open horse-drawn carriage with a folding top over the rear seat and a front seat facing the rear

britt *var of* BRIT

brit·ta·ny \ˈbritᵊnē, -ni\ *or* **brittany blue** *n* -ES *often cap* [*Brittany,* fr. *Brittany,* region of northwestern France] **:** a moderate greenish blue that is bluer and paler than average peacock and bluer and slightly paler than larkspur

brittany spaniel *n, usu cap B* **:** a rather tall active short-tailed spaniel of a French breed having a smooth or slightly wavy coat of orange and white or liver and white somewhat fringed on chest, forelegs, and thighs that was developed by interbreeding pointers with spaniels of Brittany to produce a competent bird dog with an action suggestive of a setter

¹brit·tle \ˈbrid·ᵊl, -itᵊl\ *adj* [ME *britil;* akin to OE *brēotan* to break, OHG *brōdi* frail, ON *brjōta* to break, Skt *bhrūṇa* embryo] **1 a** (1) **:** easily broken, cracked, or snapped **:** apt to break or snap easily esp. under very slight bending or deformation ⟨~ clay⟩ ⟨~ glass⟩ ⟨as ~ as an eggshell⟩ (2) *of a metal or alloy* **:** having very low malleability or ductility **b :** easily disrupted, overthrown, damaged, or disintegrated **:** FRAIL ⟨a ~ promise⟩ ⟨~ honor —Shak.⟩ ⟨a ~ marriage⟩ **c :** requiring careful handling **:** DIFFICULT ⟨a ~ personality⟩ **d :** SHARP, BRILLIANT, TENSE ⟨the light, ~ tones of an orchestra of xylophones —*Asia & the Americas*⟩ ⟨the ~ staccato of the drums —H.A.Sinclair⟩ ⟨could hardly understand what was said to him, so ~ and sharp was the sound —Pearl Buck⟩ **2 a :** PERISHABLE, MORTAL **b :** TRANSITORY, EVANESCENT **3 :** lacking warmth, depth, or generosity of spirit **:** COLD, CALCULATING ⟨she was harder, more ~, than Effie ever was —Rex Ingamells⟩ ⟨a ~ and selfish woman who calculates her ends coldly and by sheer poise and self-possession usually gets her way —Chad Walsh⟩ ⟨the ~, cynical, beautiful legends of Ovid —Gilbert Highet⟩ — **brit·tle·ly** *or* **brit·tly** \-d·ᵊl(l)ē, -tᵊl-, -i); -tlē,-tli\ *adv* — **brit·tle·ness** \-id·ᵊlnə̇s, -itᵊl-\ *n* -ES

²brittle \ˈ"\ *n* -S **:** candy made by boiling sugar to the point of caramelization, adding nuts, and cooling in thin sheets

brittle bones *n pl but sing or pl in constr* **:** FRAGILITAS OSSIUM

brittlebush \ˈ⸗⸗,⸗\ *n* **:** a desert plant of the genus *Encelia* (family Compositae) of the southwestern U.S. and adjacent Mexico having brittle stems, small crowded leaves, and yellow flowers and containing a principle toxic to other plants

brittle fern *n* **:** FRAGILE FERN

brittle maidenhair *n* **:** a tropical American fern (*Adiantum tenerum*) with broad pinnae — see FARLEY MAIDENHAIR

brittle mica *n* **:** a mineral of the clintonite group

brittle snake *n* **:** GLASS SNAKE

brittle star *n* **:** OPHIUROID; *esp* **:** a simple-armed ophiuroid (order Ophiurida)

brittle willow *n* **:** CRACK WILLOW

brittlewood \ˈ⸗⸗,⸗\ *n* **:** YELLOW BUCKTHORN

brit·ton·ic \(ˈ)briˈtänik\ *adj, usu cap* [L *Britton-, Britto* Briton + E *-ic* — more at BRITON] **:** BRYTHONIC 2

britzska *var of* BRITSKA

¹brix \ˈbriks\ *adj, usu cap* [*Brix* (*scale*)] **:** according to a Brix scale ⟨addition of sugar to the juice to about 50° *Brix*⟩ **:** calibrated in accordance with a Brix scale

²brix \ˈ"\ *n* -ES *usu cap* **:** concentration in percent of sugar by weight according to the Brix scale ⟨the *Brix* of a syrup⟩

brix scale *n, usu cap B* [after Adolf F. *Brix* †1870, Ger. scientist, its inventor] **:** a hydrometer scale for sugar solutions so graduated that its readings in degrees Brix at a specified temperature represent percentages by weight of sugar in the solution

bri·za \ˈbrīzə\ *n, cap* [NL, fr. Gk, rye] **:** a genus of grasses (family Gramineae) native to the Old World and So. America and distinguished by broad spikelets and cordate lemmas — see QUAKING GRASS

brizure *var of* BRISURE

brizz \ˈbriz\ *vt* -ED/-ING/-ES [ME *brisen, brusen* — more at BRUISE] *chiefly Scot* **:** CRUSH, BRUISE

brl *abbr* barrel

brlp *abbr* burlap

brm *abbr* barometer

brmc *abbr* barometric

brn *abbr* brown

brno \ˈbər(ˌ)nō, -nō\ *adj, usu cap* [fr. *Brno*, Czechoslovakia] **:** of or from the city of Brno, Czechoslovakia **:** of the kind or style prevalent in Brno

bro *abbr* **1** bronze **2** brother

[1]**broach** \ˈbrōch\ *n* -ES [ME *broche*, fr. MF, fr. OF, fr. (assumed) VL *brocca*, fr. fem. of L *broccus* projecting (of teeth)] **1** *archaic* **:** a pointed rod usu. of wood or iron used as an awl, bodkin, lance, spear **2 :** any of various pointed or spikelike tools, implements, or parts: as **a :** a spit for roasting meat **b :** the stick from which candlewicks are suspended for dipping **c** *now chiefly Scot* **:** a spindle on which newly spun yarn is wound **d :** a wooden rod sharpened at both ends used by thatchers **e** (1) **:** the pin in a lock that enters the barrel of the key (2) **:** the part of the stem of a key beyond the web or bit made to enter a socket **f :** the steel tooth of the doffer comb of a carding machine **3 :** one of the four semipyramidal slopes marking the transition at the corners of a square tower to the sides of an octagonal spire above — compare BROACH SPIRE **4 :** a point of a young stag's horn resembling a spit **5 :** a cutting tool for removing material from a metal or plastic to shape an outside surface or a hole that has been previously formed (as by casting or drilling) consisting of a bar of suitable length provided on its surface with a series of cutting edges or teeth that increase in size from the entering or starting end, the tool being fed through or past the work by a translational movement along its axis and, because the cutting edges are progressively higher, each succeeding tooth removing additional material **6 :** a fine tapered flexible instrument used in dentistry in removing the dental pulp and in dressing a root canal **7 :** BROOCH

[2]**broach** \ˈ"\ *vb* -ED/-ING/-ES [ME *brochen*, fr. MF *brocher*, fr. OF *brochier*, fr. *broche*] *vt* **1** *obs* **:** STAB, PIERCE, PRICK **2** *obs* **:** SPIT **:** fix on a spit **3 a** (1) **:** to pierce (as a cask) in order to draw the contents **:** TAP (2) **:** to open (a vein) to draw blood **b :** to open up or break into (as a mine or stores) **4 :** to shape (a block of stone) roughly by chiseling with a coarse tool **5 :** to shape or enlarge (a hole) with a broach or boring tool **6 :** PRESENT, ANNOUNCE, INTRODUCE ⟨~*ed* a hot lunch program⟩ **:** make known for the first time **:** begin to disclose **:** open up (a subject) for discussion or debate ⟨a suggestion first ~*ed* two years ago⟩ ⟨this is a good time to ~ the subject⟩ **7 :** to drill or cut out (material left between adjacent holes in a row of closely spaced drill holes) in mining and quarrying **~** *vi* **:** to break to the surface from below (as of a whale or a torpedo in the course of a run) **syn** see EXPRESS

[3]**broach** \ˈ"\ *vb* -ED/-ING/-ES [perh. fr. [2]*broach*] *vi* **:** to veer or yaw esp. in a following sea so as to lie beam on to the waves with danger of capsizing or swamping — used chiefly with *to* ⟨strove to keep the tiny boat from ~*ing* to in the heavy seas — G.G.Carter⟩ **~** *vt* **:** to cause (a boat) to swing beam on to the waves

[4]**broach** \ˈ"\ *n* -ES [*Broach, Bharoch*, city in Bombay state, India] **:** a short-staple cotton grown esp. in Bombay state, India

broached work *n* [*broached* fr. past part. of [2]*broach*] **:** the finish on a stone that shows a margin around the edge and has the center broached with continuous grooves

broach·er \ˈbrōchə(r)\ *n* -S **:** one that broaches or works with a broach: as **a :** a broaching machine **b :** the operator of a broaching machine **c :** a worker who finishes holes in jewel bearings by use of a broach with diamond dust

broaching machine *n* [*broaching* fr. gerund of [2]*broach*] **:** a machine tool whose cutting element is a broach

broach post *n* **:** KING POST

broach spire *n* [[1]*broach*] **:** an octagonal spire rising from a square tower without an intervening parapet, the four angles of the tower being covered by corner segments of a pyramid seeming to penetrate the spire

broach turner *n* **:** TURNSPIT

[1]**broad** \ˈbrȯd\ *adj* -ER/-EST [ME *brood*, fr. OE *brād*; akin to OHG *breit* broad, ON *breithr*, Goth *braiths*] **1 a :** marked by ample extent from side to side or by relatively large distance between sides or limits **:** not narrow ⟨~ pen strokes⟩ ⟨~ shoulders⟩ ⟨~ streets⟩ ⟨~ fields⟩ **b :** having extension from side to side of a specified dimension ⟨10 feet ~⟩ **2 :** extending far and wide **:** SPACIOUS ⟨the ~ sea⟩ ⟨the ~ western plains⟩ **3 a :** CLEAR, OPEN, FULL ⟨a crime committed in ~ daylight⟩ **b :** PATENT, UNMISTAKABLE, PLAIN ⟨a ~ hint⟩ **4 :** marked by lack of restraint, delicacy, or subtlety: **a** *obs* **:** OUTSPOKEN ⟨from ~ words ... Macduff lives in disgrace —Shak.⟩ **b :** COARSE ⟨a term thought a little too ~ for a radio program⟩ ⟨merry tales and ~ jests⟩ **:** INDELICATE, RISQUÉ ⟨~ burlesque humor⟩ **5 a :** marked by a generous wide-ranging breadth or tolerance **:** not parochial ⟨a man of ~ views and interests⟩ ⟨~ sympathies that knew no barrier of race or creed⟩ **b :** widely applicable **:** not limited or restricted **:** GENERAL ⟨a ~ rule, not to be narrowly construed⟩ ⟨used the word in its ~ sense⟩ **6 a :** relating to or having to do with the main, essential, or general aspects (as of a problem) ⟨scientific knowledge in its ~ outlines —Bertrand Russell⟩ ⟨achieved ~ agreement on the issue, leaving details to be settled by subordinates⟩ **b** *of a library classification* **:** having relatively large subdivisions — compare CLOSE **7** *often cap* **:** marked by Broad Church attitudes or practices **:** LIBERAL **:** not meticulous about niceties of ritual and dogma **8** *of a coin* **:** having a large diameter and small thickness **9** *of a sailing course* **:** with the wind nearly abeam **10 :** of markedly dialectal nature esp. in pronunciation ⟨a ~ North Country accent⟩ **11** *of textiles* **:** woven wide; *esp* **:** woven in widths (as greater than 30 inches) suitable for clothing and decorating uses — compare NARROW **12** *phonetics* **a** *of a vowel* **:** OPEN — used specif. of *a* (alone or as a member of a digraph) pronounced with a vowel sound that has or approaches the quality of the *a* in *father, calm, par* and esp. in a class of words (as *ask, laugh*) in which the pronunciation is \a\ or \aa(ə)\ in most U.S. speech outside of eastern New England **b** *in certain Celtic languages* (1) *of a vowel* **:** BACK (2) *of a consonant* **:** having the allophone that characterizes it when it is pronounced with a back vowel **13 :** characterized by demand and supply for large blocks of securities or by participation by many customers — used of the market for a security or the market as a whole **14 a** *of wool* **:** straight-fibered and nonelastic **:** coarser than usual for the type in question **b** *of bran* **:** consisting of flakes or nearly whole husks **15** *of pronunciation transcription* **a :** PHONEMIC **b :** representing by distinct nondiacritical symbols all qualitatively and phonemically distinct sounds — compare NARROW **16** *of a radio circuit* **:** having a slowly varying response to different frequencies — opposed to *sharp* **17** *of insurance coverage* **:** covering two or more related risks

syn BROAD, DEEP, and WIDE may all refer to horizontal expansion or dimension. BROAD and WIDE are often interchangeable ⟨*broad* and *wide fields*⟩ ⟨to the *broad* ocean and the azure heavens —William Wordsworth⟩ ⟨view the ocean *wide* and bright —William Wordsworth⟩ WIDE is more common than BROAD when units of measurement are mentioned ⟨rugs eight feet *wide*⟩ and when unfilled space between limits is being considered ⟨a *wide* doorway⟩ When no vertical measurement or measurement from a surface downward is likely to be involved, all three words may be used to indicate extent away from the observer ⟨a *wide, broad*, or *deep* flower garden⟩ DEEP is likely to apply to distance extending straight back from a point considered at the front; BROAD and WIDE to lateral distances ⟨that called on Hertha in *deep* forest glades —S.T. Coleridge⟩ ⟨high on a *broad* unfertile tract of forest-skirted down —William Wordsworth⟩ ⟨that we might look into a forest *wide* —John Keats⟩

[2]**broad** \ˈ"\ *adv* [ME *broode*, fr. OE *brāde*, fr. *brād* broad — more at [1]BROAD] **:** BROADLY, WIDELY — now used chiefly in phrases ⟨~ awake⟩ ⟨~ off⟩

[3]**broad** \ˈ"\ *n* -S [ME *brood*, fr. *brood*, adj. — more at [1]BROAD] **1 :** the broad or flat part of something (as the hand) **2** *Brit* **:** an expansion of a river — often used in pl. ⟨the Norfolk ~*s*⟩ **3 :** BROADPIECE **4 broads** *pl, slang* **:** PLAYING CARDS **5** *slang* **a :** WOMAN **b :** PROSTITUTE **6** [fr. [1]*abroad*, taken as containing the indefinite article *a*] *dial* **:** JOURNEY, TRIP ⟨must give up your ~ ... for I want to have rails right away — *Southern Lit. Messenger*⟩ **7 :** BROADSIDE 6

broad aisle *or* **broad alley** *n* **:** the central aisle of a church

broad arrow *n* [ME *brood arwe*, fr. *brood* broad + *arwe* arrow] **1 :** an arrow with a flat barbed head **2** *heraldry* **:** a pheon that is not engrailed on the inner edge **3** *Brit* **:** an identification mark put on government property including convicts' clothing

broad arrow 3

broadax *or* **broadaxe** \ˈ⸗ˌ⸗\ *n* [ME *broodax*, fr. *brood* broad + *ax*] **:** a large ax with a broad blade (as any of various battle-axes or an ax used for hewing timber) — see AX illustration

broad-base terrace *n* **:** a low wide terrace that permits farm machines to pass over it

broad bean *n* **1 :** a large smooth flattened edible seed that is a staple article of food in parts of southern Europe — called also *fava bean, horsebean*; see FAVISM **2 :** a sturdy upright vetch (*Vicia faba*) that is widely cultivated chiefly in the Old World both for the broad beans which it bears in long pods and as fodder

broad-bean weevil *n* **:** a destructive weevil (*Bruchus rufimanus*) that feeds on broad beans and other vetch seeds

broad beech fern *n* **:** a No. American woodland fern (*Dryopteris hexagonoptera*) with finely dissected leaves and straw-colored stipes

broadbill \ˈ⸗ˌ⸗\ *n* **1 :** any of several ducks with rather wide flat bills: as **a :** SCAUP DUCK **b :** SHOVELER **2 :** any of certain Old World birds (suborder Eurylaimidae) with a wide short bill, often bright plumage, and sluggish habits **3 :** any of several flycatchers (genus *Myiagra*) of the southwest Pacific **4** *or* **broadbill swordfish :** SWORDFISH 1a

broadbill dipper *n* **:** RUDDY DUCK

broad-billed sandpiper \ˈ⸗ˌ⸗-\ *n* **:** a sandpiper (*Limicola falcinellus*) resembling a snipe and breeding in northern parts of the Old World

broad-breasted bronze \ˈ⸗ˌ⸗⸗-\ *n, usu cap all 3Bs* **:** a strain of the Bronze turkey notable for the relatively great amount of breast meat and distinguished by vigor, rapid growth, and exceptionally large size

broadbrim \ˈ⸗ˌ⸗\ *n* **1 :** a hat with a very wide brim (as that worn by Quakers) **2 :** FRIEND 6

[1]**broadcast** \ˈ⸗ˌ⸗\ *adj* [[2]*broad* + *cast*, fr. past part. of *cast* (to throw)] **1 :** cast or scattered in all directions ⟨seed ~ from the hand in sowing⟩ **:** widely diffused **2 :** made public by means of radio or television ⟨the use of ~ appeals to motorists to keep off the roads⟩

[2]**broadcast** \ˈ⸗ˌ⸗\ *n* **1 :** a casting or scattering in all directions (as of seed from the hand in sowing) **2 :** the act of making widely known **:** the act of spreading abroad ⟨in this time of ... excessive ~ of moralities —*Amer. Scholar*⟩; *specif* **:** the act of sending out sound or images by radio or television transmission esp. for general reception ⟨the ~ of court proceedings⟩ **3 :** a single radio or television program ⟨a weekly ~ of world news⟩ ⟨his first appearance in a ~⟩

[3]**broadcast** \ˈ"\ *vb* **broadcast** *also* **broadcasted; broadcast** *also* **broadcasted; broadcasting; broadcasts** *vt* **1 :** to scatter or sow (seed) broadcast **2 :** to make widely known **:** disseminate or distribute widely or at random ⟨it's not really a secret but I wouldn't want it ~⟩ **3 :** to send out from a transmitting station (a radio or television program) for an unlimited number of receivers **~** *vi* **:** to send out radio or television signals ⟨~*ing* on a frequency of 600 kilocycles⟩ **:** speak or perform on a broadcast program ⟨he has lectured and ~ on many subjects⟩ **syn** see DECLARE, STREW

[4]**broadcast** \ˈ"\ *adv* **:** so as to scatter or be scattered in all directions (as of seed) **:** so as to spread widely; *specif* **:** so as to reach by radio or television transmission the greatest possible number of receiving sets

broad·cast·er \-tə(r)\ *n* -S **:** one that broadcasts: **a :** a mechanical device for sowing seed (as of grass or clover) by scattering it broadcast over the ground usu. by centrifugal force **:** a broadcast seeder **b :** an organization or apparatus for broadcasting radio or television programs **c :** a person broadcasting

broadcast spectrum *n* **:** the part of the range of frequencies of electromagnetic waves assigned to broadcasting stations ranging in the U.S. from 550 to 1600 kilocycles per second for AM radio stations

broad church *n, cap B&C* **:** a party or school of theological thought in the Anglican Communion holding liberal views as to doctrine and fellowship and emphasizing a policy of broad inclusiveness, active esp. during the second half of the 19th century under the guidance of such early leaders as Thomas Arnold, Charles Kingsley, A.P.Stanley, and F.W.Robertson

broad churchman *n, usu cap B&C* [*broad church* + *man*] **:** an adherent of the Anglican Broad Church party

broadcloth \ˈ⸗ˌ⸗\ *n* [ME *broodcloth*, fr. *brood* broad + *cloth* — more at [1]BROAD] **1 :** any cloth woven on a wide loom as distinguished from a narrow fabric **2 :** a twilled and napped clothing fabric of woolen or worsted with a smooth lustrous face and a close dense texture **3 :** a clothing and decorating fabric usu. of cotton, silk, or rayon made in plain and rib weaves with a soft semigloss finish

broad command pennant *n* **:** a command pennant that is identical with or similar in shape to a broad pennant and is flown by an officer in the U.S. Navy below flag rank who is temporarily in command of a force, squadron, flotilla, or battleship or cruiser division or of a major unit of aircraft — compare BURGEE COMMAND PENNANT

broad·en \ˈbrȯdᵊn\ *vb* **broadened; broadened; broadening** \-d(ᵊ)niŋ\ **broadens** *vi* **:** to grow or become broad or broader ⟨the street ~*s* into an avenue⟩ — sometimes used with *out* ⟨"textile" has ~*ed* out to include many processes besides weaving —Thomas Munro⟩ **~** *vt* **:** to make broader ⟨a mind ~*ed* by travel and education⟩ **:** extend the limits of ⟨~ the basis on which candidates may be accepted⟩

broader *comparative of* BROAD

broadest *superlative of* BROAD

broadfall \ˈ⸗ˌ⸗\ *adj, of trousers* **:** having a large flap in front that buttons at the sides and top

broad fold *adj, of paper and paperboard* **:** having the machine direction running the short way of the sheet — compare LONG GRAIN

broad-footed pouched mouse \ˈ⸗ˌ⸗-\ *n* **:** any of several Australian pouched mice (genus *Phascogale*) somewhat resembling shrews or tree shrews

broad form *adj, of insurance* **:** covering more property or hazards than the standard form by naming additional specific perils or having fewer restrictions — compare ALL RISK

broad gage *n* **:** any railroad gage that is wider than standard gage

broad-gage *or* **broad-gaged** \ˈ⸗ˈ⸗\ *adj* **1 :** having a broad gage **2** *usu* **broad-gauge** *or* **broad-gauged :** of wide scope

broad glass *n* **:** CYLINDER GLASS

broad goods *n pl but sing or pl in constr* **:** cloth woven in standard or wider widths esp. in distinction from ribbons, bands, or trimmings

broad hatchet *n* **:** a hatchet having a short handle and a broad cutting blade with a rectangular hammering face opposite the blade — see HATCHET illustration

broadhead \ˈ⸗ˌ⸗\ *n* **1 :** a person with a relatively wide head **:** one who is brachycephalic **2 :** a flat pointed steel arrowhead having sharp edges; *also* **:** an arrow having such a head

broad-headed snake \ˈ⸗ˌ⸗⸗-\ *n* **:** an Australian venomous snake (*Hoplocephalus bungaroides*) that is blackish above and marked with a lattice of yellow spots and is related to the tiger snake

broadhorn \ˈ⸗ˌ⸗\ *n* [so called fr. the large oar projecting from the roof on each side near the bow] **:** ARK 2b

broad irrigation *n* **:** irrigation with liquid sewage

broad·ish \ˈbrȯdish\ *adj* **:** rather broad ⟨a ~ face⟩ **:** tending toward broadness ⟨~ jokes⟩

broad jump *n* **:** a jump for distance from a standing position or from a running start in track-and-field athletics — **broad jumper** *n*

broad knife *n* **:** a tool like a putty knife but with a larger and broader blade

[1]**broadleaf** \ˈ⸗ˌ⸗\ *n* -S **1 a :** a tree (*Terminalia latifolia*) of Jamaica whose wood is used for boards, scantlings, shingles, and staves **b :** PUKA 2 **2** *sometimes cap* **:** any of certain tobaccos having broad drooping leaves (as Connecticut valley cigar tobacco and Maryland cigarette tobacco)

[2]**broadleaf** \ˈ"\ *adj* **:** BROAD-LEAVED

broadleaf tree *n* **:** any deciduous tree (as the maple or oak) or any of certain evergreen trees distinguished from trees bearing needlelike leaves (as most conifers) by having relatively broad flat leaves

broadleaf weed *n* **:** any dicotyledonous weedy plant

broad-leaved *or* **broad-leafed** \ˈ⸗ˈ⸗\ *adj* **:** having broad or relatively broad leaves ⟨*broad-leaved* weeds⟩

broad-leaved apple *n* **:** either of two Australian trees: **a :** a medium-sized tree (*Angophora subvelutina*) with large leaves that are used as stock feed **b :** a tree (*Careya australis*) of the family Lecythidaceae that has edible fruits and seeds

broad-leaved asarabacca *n* **:** WILD GINGER 2a

broad-leaved dock *n* **:** BITTER DOCK

broad-leaved maple *n* **:** OREGON MAPLE

broad-leaved plantain *n* **1 :** a European plantain (*Plantago major*) naturalized in No. America that has slender flower spikes and broadly oval leaves with leafstalks which are green to the base **2 :** RUGEL'S PLANTAIN

broad ligament *n* **:** either of the two bilaminate lateral ligaments of the uterus passing from the sides of the uterus to the side walls of the pelvis, giving passage between the two layers of each ligament to the uterine tubes, blood vessels, and the epoophoron and paroophoron, and bearing the ovary suspended from the dorsal surface

[1]**broadloom** \ˈ⸗ˌ⸗\ *adj, of a rug or carpet* **:** woven on a wide loom; *also* **:** so woven in solid color

[2]**broadloom** \ˈ"\ *n* **:** any carpet woven wider than 54 inches, commonly 9 feet or more

broad·ly *adv* **:** in a broad manner: as **a :** WIDELY, EXTENDEDLY **b :** OPENLY, PLAINLY **c** *obs* **:** OUTSPOKENLY **d :** COARSELY, RAUCOUSLY **e :** LIBERALLY, INCLUSIVELY **f :** MAINLY, GENERALLY

broad-minded \ˈ⸗ˈ⸗⸗\ *adj* **1 :** receptive to or tolerant of liberal views esp. in religion or politics **2 :** inclined to tolerate, overlook, or condone minor departures from orthodox social or moral behavior — **broad-mind·ed·ly** *adv* — **broad-mind·ed·ness** *n* -ES

broad mite *n* **:** a widely distributed mite (*Hemitarsonemus latus*) that feeds on a number of crop plants causing mottling and stunting of foliage and russeting of fruits

broad·moor patient \ˈbrȯdˌmu̇ə-, -mōə-,-mȯ(ə)-\ *n, usu cap B* [*Broadmoor*, asylum for criminal lunatics in Berkshire, England] *Brit* **:** one legally detained as a criminal lunatic

broad·ness *n* -ES [ME *broodnesse*, fr. *brood* broad + *-nesse* -ness — more at [1]BROAD] **:** the quality of being broad ⟨~ of viewpoint⟩ ⟨notorious for the ~ of his humor⟩

broad off *or* **broad on** *prep* **:** on a bearing about 45 degrees from a fore-and-aft line at (the bow or stern) ⟨*broad off* the port bow⟩ ⟨*broad on* the starboard quarter⟩

broad pennant *n* **:** a flag with a gradual taper ending in a broad swallowtail with the ratio of breadth in the hoist to length in the fly conspicuously greater than in the long pennant; *esp* **:** such a flag flown by a commodore in a navy — compare BROAD COMMAND PENNANT, BURGEE COMMAND PENNANT, COMMAND PENNANT

broadpiece \ˈ⸗ˌ⸗\ *n* **:** the English 20-shilling piece of hammered gold issued by James I, Charles I, and the Commonwealth — called also UNITE

broads *pl of* BROAD

broad scotch *n, cap S* **:** the dialects of English spoken in the Lowlands of Scotland

broad seal *n* **:** the public seal of a country or state

broad shad *n* **:** a silvery mojarra (*Gerres cinereus*) of Florida and the West Indies

broadshare \ˈ⸗ˌ⸗\ *n* **:** a broad flat plowshare used esp. for surface cultivation

broadsheet \ˈ⸗ˌ⸗\ *n* **1 :** BROADSIDE **2** *Brit* **:** a small wire-stitched pamphlet

[1]**broadside** \ˈ⸗ˌ⸗\ *n* **1 :** the side of a ship above the waterline **2 :** a broad or nearly unbroken surface of an object ⟨couldn't hit the ~ of a barn⟩ **3 a** *archaic* **:** a sizable sheet of paper printed on one side only; *esp* **:** one publicizing a controversy or official proclamation **b :** a sheet printed on one or both sides and folded as for mailing — by some limited in use to a sheet on which the printed text runs from side to side across the folds **c :** printed matter placed broadside **4 :** something printed on a broadside usu. for general sale or distribution; *esp* **:** BROADSIDE BALLAD **5 a :** the whole array of guns on one side of a ship; *also* **:** their simultaneous discharge **b :** a volley esp. of abuse or denunciation **6 :** a large floodlight used to illuminate a film set or television set

[2]**broadside** \ˈ"\ *adj* **1 :** directed broadside ⟨a ~ attack⟩ **2 :** placed broadside ⟨a ~ table of figures⟩

[3]**broadside** \ˈ"\ *adv* **1 a :** with the broadside turned toward a given object or point **b** *of printed matter* **:** set at right angles to the ordinary text direction ⟨a table printed ~ on two facing pages⟩ **2 :** in one volley **:** all together **3 :** at large **:** at random **:** without selection of a specific target ⟨a sales letter sent out ~ to a number of prospects⟩

[4]**broadside** \ˈ"\ *vi* -ED/-ING/-S **1 :** to proceed or go broadside **2 :** to discharge broadsides

broadside ballad *n* **:** a descriptive or narrative verse or song mainly of the 16th and 17th centuries, commonly in a simple ballad form, on a popular theme (as the celebration of an event or in praise of or attack upon a public figure), and sung or recited in public places or printed on broadsides for sale in the streets; *also* **:** a song in imitation of this

broadside on \ˈ⸗ˌ⸗ˈ⸗\ *adv* **:** SIDEWAYS ⟨drifting *broadside on*⟩ **:** with the side or longer dimension foremost

broad sole *n* **:** any of several closely related mostly American flatfishes (family Soleidae)

broad-spectrum \ˈ⸗ˈ⸗⸗\ *adj* **:** effective against a large variety of microorganisms ⟨a *broad-spectrum* antibiotic⟩ ⟨*broad-spectrum* insecticides⟩

broad-spoken \ˈ⸗ˈ⸗⸗\ *adj* **:** PLAINSPOKEN, OUTSPOKEN

broad stone *n* **:** ASHLAR 1

broadsword \ˈ⸗ˌ⸗\ *n* **:** a sword with a broad blade for cutting rather than thrusting — compare BACKSWORD, CLAYMORE

broadtail \ˈ⸗ˌ⸗\ *n* **1** *also* **broadtail sheep a :** KARAKUL 1b **b :** FAT-TAILED SHEEP **2 :** the fur or skin of a very young often prematurely born karakul lamb having a flat and wavy appearance resembling moiré silk — compare CARACUL, PERSIAN LAMB **3** *or* **broad-tailed parrot** \ˈ⸗ˌ⸗-\ **:** any of several parrots (genus *Platycercus*) chiefly of Australia with full brightly colored tails that they frequently spread and display **:** ROSELLA

broad-tailed hummingbird \ˈ⸗ˌ⸗-\ *n* **:** a rather large hummingbird (*Selasphorus platycercus*) of western No. America the male of which resembles the ruby-throated hummingbird but has a metallic reddish purple throat

broad tapeworm *n* **:** the fish tapeworm of man

broad-toothed rat \ˈ⸗ˌ⸗-\ *n* **:** a large dark-colored short-tailed rat (genus *Mastacomys*) of southern Australia and Tasmania

broad tuning *n* **:** FLAT TUNING

[1]**broadway** *or* **broadways** \ˈ⸗ˌ⸗\ *adv* [[1]*broad* + *-way* or *-ways*] **:** BROADWISE

[2]**broadway** \ˈ⸗ˌ⸗\ *n* [[1]*broad* + *way*] **:** a wide road or street **:** HIGHWAY

[3]**broadway** \ˈ⸗ˌ⸗\ *n* [fr. *Broadway*, street in New York City on or near which are located most of New York's legitimate theaters] **:** the New York commercial theater and amusement world

broad·way·ite \ˈ⸗ˌ⸗ˌīt\ *n* -S *usu cap* [*Broadway*, street in New York City + E *-ite*] **:** an habitué of Broadway **:** one that works in or frequents New York professional theaters

broadwife \ˈ⸗ˌ⸗\ *n, pl* **broadwives** [*broad* (fr. *abroad*, prob. after E *alive: live*) + *wife*] **:** a female slave whose husband belonged to another master in the slaveholding states of the U.S.

broad-winged hawk *also* **broad-wing hawk** \ˈ=,=-\ *n* **:** a common American hawk (*Buteo platypterus*) that is dark brown above with lower parts white streaked with brown

broadwise \ˈ=,=\ *adv* (*or adj*) **:** in the direction of the breadth **:** with broad side foremost

brob \ˈbräb\ *n* -s [perh. alter. of *brod*] **:** a brad-shaped spike to be driven alongside the end of an abutting timber to prevent its slipping

brob·ding·nag·ian *also* **brob·dig·nag·ian** \ˌbräbdiŋ¦nagēən, -dig¦n-, -naig- *also* -nāg- *sometimes* -dəŋ¦n-\ *adj, usu cap* [*Brobdingnag*, imaginary country inhabited by giants in *Gulliver's Travels*, by Jonathan Swift †1745 Eng. satirist + E *-ian*] **:** characteristic or suggestive of Brobdingnag or its people **:** marked by tremendous size ⟨the shape of Italy suggests a *Brobdingnagian* boot⟩ **syn** see HUGE

¹bro·cade \brōˈkād *sometimes attributively* ˈ=,=\ *n* -s [Sp *brocado*, fr. Catal *brocat*, fr. It *broccato*, fr. past part. of *broccare* to brocade, spur, fr. *brocco* small nail, projecting tooth, fr. L *broccus* projecting (of teeth)] **1 :** a rich oriental silk fabric with raised patterns embroidered in gold and silver threads **2 :** a clothing and decorating fabric usu. of silk, rayon, or cotton woven in jacquard construction and characterized by allover formal patterns of slightly raised floral and figure designs that are introduced by additional weft threads

²brocade \(ˈ)=¦=\ *vt* -ED/-ING/-S **:** to weave patterns into (as a fabric) or to work in (a design) in the manner of a brocade

bro·cad·ed \(ˈ)brō¦kādəd\ *adj* **1 :** having the weave of a brocade **:** embellished or embroidered with a raised pattern (as in brocade) **2 :** dressed in brocade **:** richly dressed

bro·card \(ˈ)brō¦kärd, ˈbräkərd, ˈbrōkərd\ *n* -s [F, fr. ML *brocardum*, irreg. fr. *Burchardus* Burchard †1025 Ger. bishop who compiled a book of ecclesiastical canons] **:** an elementary principle or maxim **:** a short proverbial rule (as in law, ethics, or metaphysics)

bro·ca's aphasia \(ˈ)brō¦käz-, ˈbrōkəz-\ *n, usu cap B* [after Paul *Broca* †1880 Fr. surgeon] **:** MOTOR APHASIA

broca scale *n, usu cap B* **:** a color chart for rating skin color

broca's convolution *or* **broca's gyrus** *or* **broca's area** *n, usu cap B* [prob. trans. of F *circonvolution de Broca*, fr. Paul *Broca*] **:** CONVOLUTION OF BROCA

broca's point *n, usu cap B* **:** the mid-point of the external auditory meatus

broc·a·telle *also* **broc·a·tel** \ˌbräkə¦tel, -rōk-\ *n* -s [F *brocatelle*, fr. It *broccatello*, dim. of *broccato* brocade] **:** a stiff formal decorating fabric of brocade construction and design distinguished from brocade by patterns in high relief

broc·co·li *or* **broc·o·li** \ˈbräkəlē, -li *also* -kl-\ *n* -s [It *broccoli*, pl. of *broccolo* flowering top of a cabbage or turnip, dim. of *brocco* sprout, small nail, projecting tooth — more at BROCADE] **1 :** a cauliflower that is larger, hardier, and a better keeper than the common cauliflower — called also *heading broccoli* **2 :** a branching cauliflower sometimes considered a separate variety (*Brassica oleracea italica*) that produces a head of functional florets at the end of each main branch which is cut for food while the florets are tight green or purplish buds and is usu. succeeded by smaller heads on secondary branches — called also *sprouting broccoli*

broccoli brown *n* **:** a brownish gray that is yellower, lighter, and stronger than taupe, yellower and lighter than chocolate, and lighter and stronger than castor — called also *goat, loam, plover, rabbit*

broccoli rab \-ˌrab\ *n, pl* **broccoli rabs** [prob. modif. of It *broccoli di rapa* flowering tops of the turnip] **:** ITALIAN TURNIP

¹broch *obs var of* BROOCH

²broch \ˈbräk, ˈbrək\ *n* -s [Sc *broch, bruch*, lit., borough, fr. ME (Sc) *brugh* borough, alter. of ME *burgh* — more at BOROUGH] **1** *Scot* **:** a luminous ring around the moon popularly regarded as an omen of bad weather **2 :** one of the prehistoric circular stone towers found on the Orkney and Shetland islands and the Scottish mainland and usu. consisting of double walls enclosing small apartments about a central court

broch·an \ˈbräkən\ *n* -s [ScGael *brochan* & IrGael *brachān*, *brochān*] *Scot & Irish* **:** porridge or gruel usu. made with oatmeal

bro·chant·ite \brōˈshän,tīt\ *n* -s [A. J. F. M. *Brochant* de Villiers †1840 Fr. geologist + E *-ite*] **:** a mineral $Cu_4SO_4(OH)_6$ consisting of a basic copper sulfate occurring in emerald-green orthorhombic crystals or massive (hardness 3.5–4, sp.gr. 3.91)

¹broche *archaic var of* BROACH

²broche \ˈbrōsh\ *n* -s [F, pointed tool — more at ¹BROACH] **1 :** BROCHETTE 1 **2 :** a bobbin or shuttle used in handweaving of tapestry

³bro·ché \(ˈ)brō¦shā\ *adj* [F, fr. past part. of *brocher* to brocade, sew, fr. MF, to prick — more at ²BROACH] **:** woven with a raised figure

⁴broché \"\ *n* -s [F, fr. *broché*, adj.] **1 :** BROCADE 1 **2 :** a fabric (as a shirting or suiting) with a pinstripe or hairline in the warp **3 :** a silk or rayon fabric of the brocade type with small designs woven in by swivel shuttles and often combining a plain-woven ground with pile-weave designs

bro·chet de mer \brō¦shādəˈme(ə)r\ *n, pl* **brochets de mer** \-shā(z)d-\ [F, lit., sea pike] **:** a snook (*Centropomus undecimalis*)

bro·chette \brōˈshet\ *n* -s [F, fr. OF *brochete*, fr. *broche* spit, pointed tool + *-ete* -ette — more at ¹BROACH] **1 :** a small spit **:** SKEWER; *also* **:** meat broiled on a skewer **2 :** a bar pin for medals, ribbons, decorations

broch·i·dod·ro·mous \ˌbräkə¦dädrəməs\ *also* **bro·chid·o·drome** \brōˈkidə,drōm\ *adj* [NL *brochidodromus*, fr. Gk *brochid-, brochis* small noose (dim. of *brochos* noose) + NL *-o-* + *-dromus* -dromous — more at MERMIS] *of a leaf nerve* **:** forming loops (as in members of the genera *Aristolochia, Olea, Sapindus*)

bro·cho \ˈbrō(,)kō, -kə\ *n* -s [Yiddish, *brokhe, brokho*, fr. Heb *bĕrākhāh* blessing] **:** BERAKAH

brocht *Scot var of* BROUGHT

bro·chure \(ˈ)brō¦shů(ə)r, -ůə *sometimes* ˈbrōshə(r)\ *n* -s [F, fr. *brocher* to stitch, sew + *-ure*] **:** PAMPHLET, BOOKLET; *also* **:** a treatise or article published in such form

bro·chym·e·na \brōˈkimənə\ *n, cap* [NL, perh. irreg. fr. Gk (Aeol) *brochys* short (akin to Gk *brachys* short) + Gk *hymen-, hymēn* membrane, insect wing — more at ¹BRIEF, HYMEN] **:** a widely distributed genus of pentatomid bugs that are predators on phytophagous insects

brock \ˈbräk\ *n* -s [ME, fr. OE *broc*, of Celt origin; akin to W *broch* badger, OIr *brocc*] **1 :** BADGER **2** *now dial chiefly Brit* **:** FELLOW — used as a generalized term of abuse

brock·age \ˈbräkij\ *n* -s [E dial. *brock* rubbish, refuse, scrap of food, broken piece (fr. ME *broc* break in the skin) + E *-age* — more at BROKE] **:** an imperfectly minted coin

brock·ed \ˈbräkit\ *adj* [earlier Sc *brokit*, prob. alter. of *brukit* streaked with black, fr. ME (Sc) *brukit, brukyd* — more at BROOKED] **1** *chiefly Scot, of an animal* **:** striped or spotted with black and white **2** *Scot, of a person* **:** streaked with dirt

brock·en specter *or* **brocken bow** \ˈbräkən-\ *n, usu cap B* [fr. *Brocken*, peak in the Harz mountains, Germany; *Brocken specter*, trans. of G *brockengespenst*] **:** an optical phenomenon sometimes seen from the summit of mountains or from an aircraft when the observer is between the sun and a mass of cloud, the figures of the observer and surrounding objects being seen projected on the cloud much enlarged and often encircled by rainbow colors — compare GLORY 6a (3)

brock·et \ˈbräkət\ *n* -s [ME *broket*, prob. modif. of ONF *brocard, brocart* fallow deer a year old, fr. (assumed) ONF *broque* tine of an antler (akin to OF *broche* tine of an antler, pointed tool) + MF *-ard, -art* — more at ¹BROACH] **1 :** a male red deer two years old — compare PRICKET 2a **2 :** any of several small So. American deer that have unbranched horns and are generally regarded as constituting the genus *Mazama*

brock-faced \ˈ=¦=\ *adj* **:** marked by a white streak on the face like a badger

brock·le-face \ˈbräkəl,fās\ *n* [obs E dial. *brockle* (alter. of E dial. *brocked*) + E *face*] **:** an animal having blotches of colored hair on an otherwise white face

brocoli *var of* BROCCOLI

bro·cot suspension \brəˈkō-, ˈbrōˌkō-\ *n, usu cap B* [after Achille *Brocot* †1878 Fr. horologist] **:** a clock-pendulum suspension in which the clock can be regulated from the front of the dial

¹brod \ˈbräd\ *n* -s [ME, brad, goad, fr. ON *broddr* spike, sting; akin to OE *brord* point, OHG *brort* edge, W *brathu* to sting, stab, Russ *brozda* bridle, bit, OE *byrst* bristle — more at BRISTLE] *now dial Brit* **:** any of various objects having a pointed end (as a goad, prod, thorn, awl)

²brod \"\ *vt* **brodded; brodded; brodding; brods** [ME *brodden*, fr. *brod*, n.] *now dial Brit* **:** GOAD, PROD

brode·glass \ˈbrōd+,-\ *n* [alter. of BROAD GLASS] **:** CYLINDER GLASS

bro·de·quin \ˈbrōdəkən, -räd-\ *n* -s [alter. (influenced by F *brodequin*) of earlier *brodekin, brodkin*, fr. ME *brodkyn*, fr. MF *brodequin*, alter. (influenced by *broder* to embroider) of *brosequin*, of non-IE origin; prob. akin to the source of MF *broissequin*, a sometimes fawn-colored cloth — more at BUSKIN, BROIDER] **:** BUSKIN; *specif* **:** a high shoe once worn by women

bro·der·er \ˈbrōdərə(r)\ *n* -s *usu cap* [ME *broderere, brouderere*, fr. *broderen, brouderen* to embroider (modif. of MF *broder, brouder*) + *-ere* -er] **:** a member of the London City company that represents the guild of embroiderers

bro·de·rie \brōˈdrē\ *n* -s [F — more at BROIDERY] **:** EMBROIDERY; *specif* **:** a style of pottery decoration originating at Rouen, France

bro·de·rie an·glaise \-,äⁿˈglāz\ *n* [F, lit., English embroidery] **:** an embroidery with eyelet and cutwork designs now usu. machine-made and worked in white on white

bro·di·aea \ˌbrōdēˈēə\ *n* [NL, irreg. fr. J. *Brodie* †1824 Scot. botanist] **1** *cap* **:** a genus of western No. American bulbous plants (family Liliaceae) with basal leaves like grass and variously colored flowers **2** -s **:** a plant of the genus *Brodiaea*

bro·die \ˈbrōdē\ *n* -s *sometimes cap* [after Steve *Brodie* *fl*1886 Am. newsboy who claimed to have jumped off the Brooklyn Bridge] **1** *slang* **:** DIVE **:** suicidal leap ⟨do a ~⟩ **2** *slang* **:** FALL, FAILURE **:** BONER ⟨pull a ~⟩ **:** FLOP

brod·mann area \ˈbrädmən-\ *or* **brod·mann's area** \-nz-\ *n, usu cap B* [after Korbinian *Brodmann* †1918 Ger. anatomist] **:** one of the several structurally distinguishable and presumably functionally distinct regions into which the cortex of each cerebral hemisphere can be divided

broenner's acid *usu cap B, var of* BRÖNNER'S ACID

¹brog \ˈbräg\ *n* -s [ME, perh. alter. of *brod*] *now chiefly Scot* **:** a pointed instrument: **a :** AWL **b :** GOAD

²brog \"\ *vt* **brogged; brogged; brogging; brogs** *now chiefly Scot* **:** PROD, GOAD

bro·gan \ˈbrōgən *also* brōˈgan *or* ˈbrō,gan *or* -aa(ə)n\ *also* **brogan shoe** *n* -s [IrGael *brōgan*, dim. of *brōg* shoe — more at BROGUE] **:** a heavy shoe; *esp* **:** a coarse leather work shoe reaching to the ankle — compare BROGUE 1

brög·ger·ite \ˈbrəgə,rīt\ *n* -s [Sw *bröggerit*, fr. W. C. *Brögger* †1940 Norw. mineralogist + Sw *-it* -ite] **:** a thorium-bearing variety of uraninite $(U,Th)O_2$ occurring in octahedral crystals (sp. gr. 9.03)

brogh \ˈbräk, ˈbrək\ *var of* BROCH

¹brogue \ˈbrōg\ *n* -s [origin unknown] *Scot* **:** TRICK, PRANK

²brogue \"\ *n* -s [IrGael & ScGael *brōg*, fr. MIr *brōc*, fr. ON *brōk* leg covering — more at BREECH] **1** *or* **brogue shoe a :** a stout coarse shoe made orig. of half-dressed or untanned leather fastened with thongs and worn formerly in parts of Ireland and in the Scottish Highlands **b :** a heavy shoe often having a hobnailed sole **:** BROGAN **c :** a stout oxford shoe with ornamental foxing and perforations; *esp* **:** one having a wing tip **2 brogues** *pl, obs* **:** TROUSERS, LEGGINGS

brogue 1c

³brogue \"\ *vi* **brogued; brogued; broguing; brogues 1 :** to walk in brogues **2** *chiefly Midland* **:** to go about idly **:** LOAF — used often with *around* ⟨just broguing around⟩

⁴brogue \"\ *n* -s [perh. fr. IrGael *barrōg* grip, wrestling hold; fr. the idea that features of pronunciation noticeably different from one's own must be the result of a physical impediment to the freedom of motion of the speaker's tongue] **:** a dialectal or regional pronunciation; *esp* **:** an Irish accent

⁵brogue \"\ *vt* -ED/-ING/-S **:** to utter with a brogue

brogued vamp \ˈbrōgd-\ *n* [²*brogue* + *-ed*] **:** a vamp having a long usu. perforated tip extension along each side of the shoe

brogue hole \ˈbrōg-\ *n* [*brogue* (prob. alter. of ¹*brog*) + *hole*] **:** a vent in a tin can for the escape of steam and air while in an autoclave

brogu·er \ˈbrōgə(r)\ *n* -s [*brogue* (fr. *brogue hole*) + *-er*] **:** a solderer of brogue holes

brogu·ery \ˈbrōg(ə)rē\ *n* -ES [⁴*brogue* + *-ery*] **:** the use of a dialectal or regional pronunciation; *esp* **:** the use of an Irish accent

brogu·ing \ˈbrōgiŋ\ *n* -s [²*brogue* + *-ing*] **:** an ornamentation of shoes employing heavy perforations and pinkings

broh *var of* BRUH

broid *obs var of* BRAID

broi·der \ˈbrȯidə(r)\ *vt* -ED/-ING/-S [ME *broideren*, modif. (prob. influenced by ME *broiden, broyden*, past part. of *breyden* to weave together) of MF *broder, brouder*, fr. OF *brosder*, of Gmc origin; akin to OE *brord* point, OHG *brort* edge — more at BROD, BRAID] **:** EMBROIDER ⟨they shall make . . . ~*ed* coat —Exod 28:4 (AV)⟩

broi·der·er \-dərə(r)\ *n* -s [ME *broiderere* embroiderer, fr. *broideren* + *-ere* -er] *archaic* **:** EMBROIDERER

broi·dery \-d(ə)rē\ *n* -ES [ME *broiderie*, modif. (prob. influenced by ME *broiden, broyden*) of MF *broderie, brouderie*, fr. *broder, brouder* + *-erie* -ery] **:** EMBROIDERY

broigne \ˈbrȯin\ *n* -s [OF, of Gmc origin; akin to OHG *brunia, brunna* coat of mail — more at BYRNIE] **:** a medieval defensive garment consisting of leather or woven fabric on which were sewed metal rings or plates

¹broil \ˈbrȯil, *esp bef pause or cons* -ȯiəl\ *vb* -ED/-ING/-S [ME *broilen*, fr. MF *bruler* to burn, modif. (perh. resulting from incorrect division of L *amb-ustulare* to roast as *am-bustulare*) of L *ustulare* to scorch, singe, fr. *ustus*, past part. of *urere* to burn — more at EMBER, AMBI-] *vt* **1** *obs* **:** BURN, CHAR **2 :** to cook by direct exposure to radiant heat (as on a grill over live coals or beneath a gas flame or electric coil) **3 :** to subject to great heat ~ *vi* **:** to become subject to the action of heat (as of meat over a fire) **:** to become greatly heated or made uncomfortable with heat (as of a person in hot sunlight)

²broil \"\ *n* -s **1 :** the act or state of broiling **:** an excessive heat **2 :** something broiled (as a broiled steak) **:** GRILL

³broil \"\ *vb* -ED/-ING/-S [ME *broilen*, fr. MF *brouiller* to mix, confuse, fr. OF *broillier*, fr. *breu* broth — more at BREWIS] *vt* **1** *obs* **:** to mix confusedly **:** involve in confusion **:** AGITATE ⟨~*ed* with melancholy —Thomas More⟩ **2 :** to entangle in a quarrel or brawl **:** EMBROIL ~ *vi* **:** to engage in a broil **:** BRAWL, QUARREL

⁴broil \"\ *n* -s **:** a confused or noisy disturbance **:** TUMULT; *esp* **:** QUARREL **syn** see BRAWL

broil·er \-ȯilə(r)\ *n* -s [¹*broil* + *-er*] **1 :** one that broils: as **a :** a utensil (as a grill) or an appliance used in broiling **b :** a compartment in a gas or electric stove with heat supplied overhead and a drip pan beneath **c :** a cook who specializes in the broiling of foods **2 :** a chicken or other bird fit for broiling; *esp* **:** a young chicken weighing up to 2½ pounds dressed **3 :** a very hot day **4 :** a partly developed mushroom with the cap not fully expanded — compare BUTTON

broil·er·man \-mən\ *n, pl* **broilermen :** one engaged in raising broilers on a commercial scale

broil·ing·ly *adv* **:** in a broiling manner

bro·kage \ˈbrōkij\ *n* -s [prob. fr. AF *brocage*, fr. (assumed) AF *brocour* broker, after such pairs as MF *pillour, pilleur* pillager: *pillage* — more at BROKER] *archaic* **:** BROKERAGE

¹broke \ˈbrōk\ *n* -s [ME *broc* break in the skin, fr. OE *broc* trouble, fragment, fr. *brecan* to break — more at BREAK] **1** *archaic* **:** something broken off **:** a fragment (as of kitchen leavings) **2** *obs* **:** a break (as in the skin) **:** WOUND **3 :** paper that becomes unfit for use during any part of its manufacture ⟨wet ~ is from the presses of the paper machine; dry ~ may come from calenders, winders, sorting tables⟩ **4 brokes** *pl* **:** SKIRTINGS **5 :** a grade of tobacco having damaged leaves

²broke \"\ *adj* [ME, alter. of *broken*] **1** *chiefly dial* **:** BROKEN **2 :** without money or resources **:** PENNILESS, BANKRUPT **3 a** *of an animal* **:** tamed and trained to a particular function or activity ⟨a halter-*broke* horse⟩ **b** *of a person* **:** forced to conform or adapt ⟨the old woman's ~ to my ways now⟩

³broke *past and substand past part of* BREAK

⁴broke *vi* -ED/-ING/-S [prob. back-formation fr. *broker*] *obs* **:** NEGOTIATE, TRAFFIC, DEAL

¹bro·ken \ˈbrōkən *sometimes* -kᵊŋ\ *adj* [ME, fr. OE *brocen*, fr. past part. of *brecan* to break] **1 :** violently separated into parts **:** in a state resulting from breaking **:** in fragments **:** SHATTERED ⟨a vase ~ by a fall⟩ ⟨~ bits of glass⟩ **2 :** damaged or altered by or as if by breaking: as **a** *of body parts* **:** FRACTURED, RUPTURED ⟨a ~ leg⟩; *often* **:** having the surface interrupted or flawed (as by a cut or blow) ⟨there'll be more than one ~ head before morning⟩ **b** *obs* **:** TORN, RENT — used chiefly of fabrics **c** *of land or land surfaces* **:** rough and irregular, interrupted (as by cliffs and ravines), or full of obstacles to passage (as rocks, ledges, or gullies) ⟨a ~ country full of springs and streams⟩ ⟨a long ~ ridge⟩ **d :** violated by transgression **:** with integrity destroyed ⟨a ~ promise⟩ **e :** made discontinuous or altered in direction (as by bending or refraction) ⟨the ~ antennae of most weevils⟩ ⟨light rays ~ by a prism⟩; *sometimes* **:** ZIGZAG ⟨following a ~ course⟩ **f :** INTERRUPTED, DISCONTINUOUS ⟨a ~ sleep⟩ ⟨the ~ pattern of his thoughts⟩ **g** *of weather* **:** UNSETTLED; *also, of clouds* **:** overspreading much but not all of the sky **h :** disrupted by change ⟨a home ~ by sickness⟩ **i** *of a plant or flower* **:** affected with break ⟨a ~ tulip⟩ **j** *of cream* **:** separating into large aggregates when shaken due to the action of certain bacteria **k** *of an animal's coat* **:** MOLTING **3 :** reduced in condition: as **a :** made weak or infirm (as by disease, age, or hardships) **b :** SUBDUED, CRUSHED ⟨a ~ spirit⟩ **c :** ruined financially **:** BANKRUPT **d :** made submissive **:** trained for use ⟨a well-*broken* horse⟩ **e :** cashiered or reduced in rank ⟨he was ~ from sergeant to private⟩ **:** ruined officially or professionally ⟨his career was ~ by the scandal⟩ **f** *Scot* **:** declared an outlaw ⟨apprehend all such freebooters and ~ men⟩ **4 :** DISCONNECTED **:** not continuous: as **a :** uttered hesitantly and disjointedly on account of emotion ⟨a few ~ words at parting⟩ **b :** imperfectly spoken or written esp. by a foreigner ⟨~ English⟩ **5 a** *archaic* **:** forming or consisting of remnants or leavings esp. when fragmentary ⟨~ beer⟩ ⟨~ meats⟩ **b :** not complete ⟨a ~ line of goods⟩ or completely full ⟨a ~ bale of wool⟩; *often* **:** containing fewer than the standard number of sheets or boards but not necessarily of poor quality ⟨as ~ ream⟩ ⟨a ~ bundle⟩ ⟨a ~ carton⟩ **6** *of paper* **:** of uneven quality (as when soiled or spotted more than retree) **7 a** *of a color* **:** dulled by an admixture of gray **:** SADDENED; *also* **:** produced by blending of primary colors **b** *of color effects in painting* **:** produced by laying component color elements side by side on canvas or other surface so that at a distance they appear to blend **c :** consisting of two usu. discrete colors — used chiefly of animal eyes and coats ⟨a ~ red and black coat⟩ **8** *of a vowel sound* **:** diphthongized by breaking **9** *of a twill weave* **:** having the diagonal lines reversed at regular intervals to produce a zigzag effect — compare HERRINGBONE **10** *of a noun plural in Arabic* **:** distinguished from the singular by a difference in vowel sounds

²broken \"\ *n* -s **:** BROKE 3 — used chiefly in paper mills

broken arch *n* **:** a decorative arch (as over a door or in the top of a piece of furniture) with a gap at the apex of the curve that is usu. occupied by some decorative feature

broken ashlar *n* **:** ashlar in which the stones are rectangular but of different sizes and shapes

broken-backed \ˈ=¦=\ *adj* [ME, fr. *broken* + *backed*] **:** having a broken back: as **a** *of a ship* **:** HOGGED, SAGGED **:** so weakened as to droop at each end **b** *of a horse* **:** having bones of the back or loins ankylosed or united by a bony growth

broken-backed line *n* **:** a line truncated in the middle — used esp. of many lines in the verse of John Lydgate that have usu. nine syllables and appear to lack an unstressed syllable at the medial break or caesura

broken bank note *n* **:** a note issued by a bank, business firm, or other legal body before the issue of an authorized U.S. paper currency in 1861

broken-bone fever \ˈ=,=-\ *n* **:** DENGUE

broken coal *n* **:** a size of anthracite coal; *also* **:** coal of this size — see ANTHRACITE table

broken consort *n* **:** a group of musical instruments of different families ⟨a *broken consort* of viols and flutes⟩

broken-down \ˈ==¦=\ *adj* **:** infirm or worn to the point of breaking (as in strength, force, power, health, morals, or structure)

broken field *n, football* **:** the area beyond the line of scrimmage where defensive players are rather widely scattered ⟨a good *broken field* runner⟩

broken heart *n* **1 :** a state of extreme grief and depression **2 :** rupture of the heart muscle (as after myocardial infarction)

brokenhearted \ˈ==¦==\ *adj* **:** having the spirits depressed **:** crushed by grief or despair — **bro·ken·heart·ed·ly** *adv* — **bro·ken·heart·ed·ness** *n* -ES

broken-kneed \ˈ==¦=\ *adj* **:** characterized by or suffering from broken knees

broken knees *n pl* **:** the injured or abnormal knees of a horse that falls frequently while in action

broken line *n* **1 :** a line composed of a series of dashes; *often* **:** a guide line painted in dashes on a highway to indicate a stretch on which a driver may lawfully cross the midline of the way (as in passing another vehicle) **2 :** a line made up of straight lines that join a number of given points taken in some specified order

broken lot *n* **:** a lot of less than 100 shares of stock **:** ODD LOT

bro·ken·ly *adv* **:** in a broken manner; *esp* **:** with the voice unsteady from emotion or shock

broken-mouth \ˈ==,=, *in "dentition" sense* ˈ==¦=\ *n* **:** an old sheep that has become broken-mouthed; *also* **:** the faulty dentition of such a sheep

broken-mouthed \ˈ==¦=\ *adj* **:** having lost some of the teeth — used chiefly of old sheep

broken music *n* **1 :** music in parts **2 :** music by different families of instruments sounding together

bro·ken·ness \ˈbrōkən(n)əs\ *n* -ES **:** the quality or state of being broken

broken octave *n* **:** SHORT OCTAVE

broken pediment *n* **:** a pediment frequent in the baroque style having a gap at the apex (as for a statue or vase)

broken reed *n* **:** something or someone that fails when relied on for support or help

broken rhyme *n* **1 :** rhyme in which one of the rhyming elements is divided by the break or by a pause between two words (as in Lord Byron's rhyming ". . . Attic; all . . ." with "mathematical") **2 :** rhyme involving division of a word by the break between two lines in order to end a line with a rhyme provided by the first part of the word (as in G. M. Hopkins's dividing *king-/dom* to rhyme *king/* with *wing*)

broken stowage *n* **:** stowage of cargo with vacant spaces left in it

broken stripe *n* **:** a figure in wood (as veneer) produced when interwoven grain is quarter-cut breaking the strips at irregular intervals — compare RIBBON FIGURE

broken transit *n* **:** a transit whose axis forms part of the right-angled telescope tube, the eyepiece remaining stationary at one end of the horizontal axis

broken-up \ˈ==¦=\ *adj, of a dog's face* **:** having a projecting jaw, the nose short and set well back, a deep stop, and wrinkles

broken wind *n* **:** HEAVES — **broken-winded** \ˈ==¦==\ *adj*

¹bro·ker \ˈbrōkə(r)\ *n* -s [ME *brokour, broker*, fr. (assumed) AF *brocour* (akin to ONF *brokieres* one that sells wine from the tap, AF *brogour* untrustworthy dealer), fr. (assumed) ONF *broquier* to tap (a cask) (akin to OF *brochier* to tap), fr. *broque* tap of a cask (akin to OF *broche* tap of a cask, pointed tool) — more at BROACH] **1 :** NEGOTIATOR, INTERMEDIARY ⟨Sir Winston's offers of his good services as ~ between East and West —Max Ascoli⟩: as **a :** a go-between in affairs of love or sex; *esp* **:** an agent professionally engaged in the arrangement of marriages — called also *marriage broker* **b :** an agent middleman who for a fee or commission negotiates contracts of purchase and sale (as of real estate, commodities, or securities) between buyers and sellers without himself taking title to that which is the subject of negotiation and usu. without having physical possession of it — often used with a qualifying attributive ⟨dealings with a produce ~⟩ ⟨wool ~s⟩ ⟨busy stock*brokers*⟩; compare DEALER, STOCKJOBBER **c** *archaic* **:** a person entrusted with the transmission of information **:** MESSENGER, INTERPRETER **2 :** DEALER: as **a** *Brit* **:** a dealer in secondhand goods; *sometimes* **:** one that buys and sells the loot of thieves **b :** a dealer who for his own profit negotiates purchases and sales (as of negotiable instruments or commodities) himself taking or holding title to and often physical possession of that which is the subject of negotiation but usu. not altering or processing it — not used technically in fields in which a broker is primarily an agent; compare STOCKJOBBER, PROCESSOR **3** *Brit* **:** a person licensed to appraise or sell household distrained goods

²**broker** \"\ *vt* **brokered; brokered; brokering** \-k(ə)riŋ\ **brokers :** to function as a broker in respect to ⟨~*ed* a number of shady deals⟩

bro·ker·age \'brōk(ə)rij, -krēj\ *n* -s [ME, fr. *brokour, broker* broker + *-age*] **1 :** the business of a broker **2 :** the fee or commission for transacting business as a broker

bro·ker·ly \-kə(r)lē\ *adv* **:** in the manner of a broker

brokers' board *n* **:** a stock exchange open only to member brokers of that exchange

broker's loan *n* **1 :** a loan by a bank to a stock-exchange broker secured by negotiable securities **2 brokers' loans** *pl* **:** the aggregate amount of money loaned to brokers (as in the New York market) at any given time

brokery *n* -ES [¹*broker* + *-y*] **1** *obs* **:** BROKERAGE 1, AGENCY 3; *sometimes* **:** shrewd, rascally, or dishonest dealing **2** *obs* **:** secondhand goods

brokes *pl of* BROKE

¹**brok·ing** \'brōkiŋ, -kēŋ\ *n* -s [fr. gerund of ⁴*broke*] **1 :** BROKERAGE 1 **2** *obs* **:** PAWNBROKING; *sometimes* **:** tricky or dishonest dealing

²**broking** \"\ *adj* [fr. pres. part. of ⁴*broke*] **1** *obs* **:** base-dealing **:** CONTEMPTIBLE, GRASPING **2 :** of or relating to brokerage ⟨a ~ business⟩

brol·ga \'brälgə\ *n* -s [native name in Australia] **:** a pale gray crestless Australian crane (*Grus rubicunda*) that is generally seen in pairs and has a habit of gathering in groups and moving about as if dancing — called also *native companion*

brol·ly \'bräli\ *n* -ES [by shortening & alter. fr. *umbrella*] *Brit* **:** UMBRELLA; *also, slang* **:** PARACHUTE

brom- *or* **bromo-** *comb form* [ISV, prob. fr. F *brome* bromine, fr. Gk *brōmos* bad smell] **1 :** bromine ⟨*brom*hydrate⟩ ⟨*bromo*prene⟩ **2** *now usu* **bromo-** **:** containing bromine in place of hydrogen — in names of organic compounds ⟨*bromo*acetic acid⟩ **3** *now usu* **bromo-** **:** containing bromine regarded as replacing hydroxyl or oxygen or as coordinated to a central atom — in names of inorganic acids and salts ⟨*bromo*auric acid⟩ **4 :** containing bromine as bromide and sometimes replacing another element or group — in names of minerals and salts occurring as minerals

bromacetone *var of* BROMOACETONE

brom·ar·gy·rite \brō'märjə,rīt\ *n* -s [F, fr. *brom-* + *argyr-* (fr. NL) + *-ite*] **:** BROMYRITE

¹**bro·mate** \'brō,māt, *usu* -ād+V\ *n* -s [prob. fr. G *bromat,* fr. *brom-* + *-at* -ate] **:** a salt of bromic acid

²**bromate** \"\ *vt* -ED/-ING/-S **1 :** to treat with a bromate, usu. potassium bromate ⟨*bromated* flour⟩ **2 :** BROMINATE —**bro·ma·tion** \brō'māshən\ *n* -s

bro·ma·tium \brō'māsh(ē)əm\ *n, pl* **broma·tia** \-(ē)ə\ [NL, fr. Gk *brōmation* morsel, dim. of *brōmat-, brōma* food, fr. *bibrōskein* to eat, devour — more at VORACIOUS] **:** one of the swollen globular hyphal tips that develop on certain fungi when grown in their nests by ants and that are used as food by the ants

brombenzyl cyanide *var of* BROMOBENZYL CYANIDE

bromcresol green *var of* BROMOCRESOL GREEN

bromcresol purple *var of* BROMOCRESOL PURPLE

brome-grass \'brōm,=\ *or* **brome** *n, pl* **bromegrasses** *or* **bromes** [NL *Bromus*] **:** any grass of the genus *Bromus* — see AWNLESS BROMEGRASS

bro·me·lia \brō'mēlyə, -lēə\ *n* [NL, fr. Olaf *Bromelius* †1705 Swed. botanist + NL *-ia*] **1** *cap* **:** the type genus of Bromeliaceae comprising tropical American plants with deeply cleft calyx that are often placed in the genus *Ananas* **2** -s **:** any plant of the genus *Bromelia; broadly* **:** BROMELIAD

bro·me·li·a·ce·ae \brō,mēlē'āsē,ē\ *n pl, cap* [NL, fr.*Bromelia,* type genus + *-aceae*] **:** a family of tropical American epiphytic or terrestrial herbs or subshrubs (order Xyridales) that have basal often spiny leaves and flowers in dense spikes, panicles, or heads with large often colored bracts and that include several plants (as the pineapple) of economic importance — **bro·me·li·a·ceous** \brō¦mēlē¦āshəs\ *adj*

bro·me·li·ad \brō'mēlē,ad\ *also* **bro·mel** \'brōməl\ *n* -s [*bromeliad* fr. NL *Bromelia* + E *-ad; bromel* short for *bromeliad*] **:** a plant of the family Bromeliaceae

bro·me·lin \'brōmələn\ *n* -s [ISV *bromel-* (fr. NL *Bromelia*) + *-in*] *biochem* **:** a proteinase obtained from the juice of the pineapple

bro·mell·ite \brō'me,līt, 'brämə,l-\ *n* -s [G *bromellit,* fr. Magnus von *Bromell* †1731 Swed. mineralogist + G *-it* -ite] **:** a mineral consisting of beryllium oxide occurring in white hexagonal crystals

bro·mic \'brōmik\ *adj* [F *bromique,* fr. *brom-* + *-ique* -ic] **:** of, relating to, or containing bromine — used esp. of compounds in which this element is pentavalent

bromic acid *n* [ISV *bromic* + *acid*] **:** an unstable strongly oxidizing acid $HBrO_3$ analogous to chloric acid and known only in solution esp. in the form of its salts

¹**bro·mide** \'brō,mīd, *in sense 1 sometimes* -,məd\ *n* -s [ISV *brom-* + *-ide*] **1 a :** a binary compound of bromine and usu. a more electropositive element or a radical, some of these compounds (as potassium bromide) being used as sedatives **:** a salt or ester of hydrobromic acid **b :** a dose of bromide taken usu. as a sedative **2 a :** a conventional and commonplace or tiresome person **:** BORE, DULLARD **b :** a commonplace or hackneyed expression, generalization, or notion ⟨greeting card ~*s*⟩; *also* **:** a trite artistic or dramatic theme or device

²**bromide** \"\ *vt* -ED/-ING/-S **:** to treat with a bromide

bromide paper *n* **:** a sensitized paper coated with an emulsion layer composed chiefly of silver bromide suspended in gelatin — used in photography for enlargements or contact prints

bro·mid·ic \brō'midik\ *adj* **1 :** characterized by bromides **:** TRITE, COMMONPLACE ⟨~ sermons⟩ ⟨a ~ remark⟩ **2 :** given to uttering bromides **:** TIRESOME, UNORIGINAL ⟨a ~ versifier⟩ ⟨~ luncheon speakers⟩—**bro·mid·i·cal·ly** \-dək(ə)lē\ *adv*

bro·mid·i·om \brō'midēəm\ *n* -s [blend of ¹*bromide* and *idiom*] **:** BROMIDE 2b

bro·mid·ism \'brōmə,dizəm, -ō,mī,d-\ *n* -s [¹*bromide* + *-ism*] **:** BROMISM

bro·mi·dro·sis \,brōmə'drōsəs\ *also* **brom·hi·dro·sis** \" *sometimes* -mhi'd-\ *n, pl* **bromidro·ses** *or* **bromhidro·ses** \-ō,sēz\ [NL, fr. Gk *brōmos* bad smell + LGk *hidrōsis* perspiration, sweating, fr. Gk *hidroun* to sweat (fr. *hidrōs* sweat) + *-sis* — more at SWEAT] **:** foul-smelling sweat

bro·mi·nate \'brōmə,nāt\ *vt* -ED/-ING/-S [*bromine* + *-ate*] **:** to treat or cause to combine with bromine or a compound of bromine **:** introduce bromine into (as an organic compound) — **bro·mi·na·tion** \,brōmə'nāshən\ *n* -s

bro·mine \'brō,mēn, -,mən\ *n* -s [F *brome* bromine + E *-ine* — more at BROM-] **:** a nonmetallic chiefly univalent and pentavalent element belonging to the halogens that is normally a deep red corrosive toxic liquid giving off an irritating reddish brown vapor of disagreeable odor, that occurs naturally only in combination in minute quantities in sea water and in many salt lakes, brines, and salt deposits from all of which it can be recovered (as by oxidation with chlorine and driving out of the bromine vapor by steam or air), and that is used chiefly in the manufacture of bromine compounds (as ethylene dibromide for antiknock gasoline), dyes, and pharmaceuticals — symbol *Br;* see ELEMENT table

bromine water *n* **:** a solution of bromine in water; *esp* **:** the red saturated solution

bro·min·ism \'brōmə,nizəm\ *n* -s [*bromine* + *-ism*] **:** BROMISM

bro·min·ize \-,nīz\ *vt* -ED/-ING/-S **:** BROMATE

bro·mism \'brō,mizəm\ *n* -s [ISV *brom-* + *-ism;* prob. orig. formed as F *bromisme*] **:** the abnormal state produced by overdosage with or prolonged use of bromides

brom·lite \'bräm,līt\ *n* -s [*Bromley* Hill (error for *Brownley Hill,* near Alston, Cumberland, England) + E *-ite*] **:** a mineral $BaCa(CO_3)_2$ midway between witherite and strontianite — called also *alstonite*

¹**bro·mo** \'brō(,)mō\ *n* -s [*brom-*] **:** any of certain proprietary effervescent mixtures used as headache remedies, sedatives, and alkalinizing agents; *often* **:** a dose of such a mixture

²**bromo** \"\ *adj* [*brom-*] **:** containing bromine — used esp. of organic compounds; compare BROM-

bro·mo- *in pronunciations below,* ¦== = ¦brō(,)mō *or* -,mə\ — see BROM-

bro·mo·acetone \¦== +\ *also* **brom·acetone** \(')brō¦m+-\ *n* [ISV *brom-* + *acetone*] **:** a colorless lacrimatory not very stable liquid compound CH_3COCH_2Br made by the action of bromine on acetone

bromo acid *n* [²*bromo* + *acid*] **:** EOSIN 1a

bro·mo·benzene \¦== *at* BROMO- +\ *n* [ISV *brom-* + *benzene*] **:** a colorless oily liquid compound C_6H_5Br obtained usu. by bromination of benzene and used chiefly as a solvent and in organic synthesis

bro·mo·benzyl cyanide \¦==+ ... -\ *also* **brom·benzyl cyanide** \(')brōm+¦ . . . -\ *n* [*brom-* + *benzyl cyanide*] **:** a light-yellow oily lacrimatory compound $C_6H_5CHBrCN$ having an odor of sour fruit that is made by brominating benzyl cyanide; α-bromo-phenyl-aceto-nitrile

bro·mo·cresol green \¦== *at* BROMO- + . . . -\ *also* **bromcresol green** *n* [ISV *brom-* + *cresol*] **:** a brominated acid dye of the sulfonephthalein series derived from *meta*-cresol that is obtained as a yellowish crystalline powder and is used as an acid-base indicator

bromocresol purple *also* **bromcresol purple** *n* **:** a brominated acid dye of the sulfonephthalein series derived from *ortho*-cresol that is obtained as a pinkish crystalline powder and is used as an acid-base indicator

bro·mo·form \¦==+,fȯrm\ *n* -s [ISV *brom-* + *-form* (as in *chloroform*)] **:** a colorless heavy liquid compound $CHBr_3$ that is similar to chloroform in properties and methods of preparation and is used chiefly in separating minerals (as in assaying) and in organic synthesis; tribromo-methane

bro·mo·hy·drin \,==+'hīdrən\ *n* -s [ISV *brom-* + *-hydrin*] **:** any of various organic compounds that are analogous to the chlorohydrins but that contain bromine in place of chlorine

bro·moil \'brō,mȯi(ə)l\ *n* -s [*brom-* + *oil*] **:** a print made by the bromoil process

bromoil process *n* **:** a process of making an oil-pigmented photographic print by bleaching the silver image from a bromide print and applying an oil pigment to it with a special brush or roller, the pigment sticking only on those parts where the silver has been

bromoil transfer *n* **:** a photographic print made by transferring under pressure the pigmented image of a bromoil print while still soft to another support

bro·mo·iodide \¦== *at* BROMO- +\ *n* [*brom-* + *-iodide*] **:** a compound or mixture containing anionic bromine and iodine ⟨silver ~ photographic emulsions⟩

bro·mo·met·ric \¦==+¦me·trik\ *adj* [ISV *bromometry* + *-ic*] **:** of or relating to bromometry — **bro·mo·met·ri·cal·ly** \-rək(ə)lē\ *adv*

bro·mom·e·try \brō'mäm·ə·trē\ *n* -ES [ISV *brom-* + *-metry*] **:** quantitative analysis by the use of bromine — compare IODOMETRY

bro·mo·phenol blue \¦== *at* BROMO- + . . . -\ *also* **brom·phenol blue** \(')brōm + . . . -\ *n* [ISV *brom-* + *phenol*] **:** a dye $C_{19}H_{10}Br_4O_5S$ obtained as pinkish crystals and used as an acid-base indicator; tetrabromo-phenolsulfonephthalein

bromos *pl of* BROMO

bro·mo·thymol blue \¦==+...-\ *or* **brom·thymol blue** \(')brōm+...-\ *n* [ISV *brom-* + *thymol*] **:** a brominated dye $C_{27}H_{28}Br_2O_5S$ of the sulfonephthalein series derived from thymol that is obtained as a cream to rose colored powder and is used as an acid-base indicator

bromp·ton stock *usu cap B, var of* BRAMPTON STOCK

Brom·sul·phal·ein \¦brōm,səl'falēən, -fāl-\ *trademark* — used for a dye derived from phenolphthalein that is used in the form of its bitter white crystalline disodium salt in a liver function test

bro·mus \'brōməs\ *n, cap* [NL, fr. L *bromos* oats, fr. Gk] **:** a large genus of grasses (family Gramineae) that are native to temperate regions, comprise the bromegrasses, and have large often drooping spikelets and lemmas usu. awned near the 2-toothed apex

brom·vo·el \'bräm,fül\ *or* **brom·vo·gel** \-ügəl\ *n* -s [obs. Afrik *bromvogel* (now *bromvoël*), fr. *brom* to grumble + *vogel* bird, fr. MD *vōghel;* akin to MD *brimmen, bremmen* to grumble, growl, OHG *brummen* and to OE *fugol* bird — more at FREMITUS, FOWL] **:** a southern African hornbill (*Bucorvus leadbeateri*) of large size and more or less terrestrial habits — called also *turkey buzzard*

bro·my·rite \'brōmə,rīt\ *n* -s [*brom-* + Gk argyros silver + E *-ite* — more at ARGENT] **:** a mineral consisting of native silver bromide AgBr yellow in color — called also *bromargyrite*

bronc \'bräŋk\ *n* -s [by shortening] **:** BRONCO

bronch- *or* **broncho-** *comb form* [prob. fr. F *bronch-, broncho-* trachea, throat, fr. LL *broncho-,* fr. Gk *bronch-, broncho-,* fr. *bronchos* — more at CRAW] **1 :** throat ⟨*broncho*cele⟩ **2 :** bronchial ⟨*bronch*itis⟩ ⟨*broncho*phony⟩ **3 :** bronchial and ⟨*broncho*pulmonary⟩

bronchi *pl of* BRONCHUS

bronchi- *or* **bronchio-** *comb form* [prob. fr. NL *bronchi-,* fr. LL *bronchium*] **:** bronchia ⟨*bronchi*ectasis⟩ ⟨*bronchio*crisis⟩

bronchia *pl of* BRONCHIUM

bron·chi·al \'bräŋkēəl, *esp Brit* -ŋkyəl, *substand* -änəkəl *or* -nkəl *or* -ŋkəl\ *adj* [prob. fr. NL *bronchialis,* fr. LL *bronchium* + L *-alis* -al] **:** of, relating to, or associated with the bronchi or their ramifications in the lungs — **bron·chi·al·ly** \-ŋkēəlē, -li\ *adv*

bronchial artery *n* **:** any branch of the descending aorta or first intercostal artery that accompanies the bronchi

bronchial asthma *n* **:** asthma resulting from spasmodic contraction of bronchial muscles with constriction of the lumen of the bronchi and accumulation of mucus in the respiratory passages due to psychosomatic, allergic, or other causes

bronchial gland *n* **:** any of the lymphatic glands situated at the bifurcation of the trachea and along the bronchi

bronchial pneumonia *n* **:** BRONCHOPNEUMONIA

bronchial tree *n* **:** the bronchi together with their branches

bronchial tube *n* **:** a bronchus or any of its branches

bronchial vein *n* **:** any vein accompanying the bronchi and their branches and emptying into the azygos and superior intercostal veins

bron·chi·ectasis \¦bräŋkē, -äŋkē+\ *also* **bron·chi·ectasia** \"+\ *n, pl* **bronchiectases** *also* **bronchiectasias** [NL, fr. *bronchi-* + *ectasis*] **:** a chronic inflammatory or degenerative condition of one or more bronchi or bronchioles marked by dilatation and loss of elasticity of the walls — **bron·chi·ec·tat·ic** \+,ek¦tad·ik\ *adj*

bron·chio·gen·ic \¦bräŋkēō¦jenik, -äŋk-\ *adj* [*bronchi-* + *-genic*] **:** BRONCHOGENIC

bron·chi·o·lar \¦bräŋkē¦ōlə(r), -äŋk-; (')brän¦kīəl-, -äŋ¦-\ *adj* [*bronchiole* + *-ar*] **:** of, relating to, or affecting a bronchiole

bron·chi·ole \'bräŋkē,ōl, -äŋk-\ *n* -s [NL *bronchiolum,* dim. of LL *bronchium*] **:** a minute thin-walled branch of a bronchus; *esp* **:** one that terminates in one or more pulmonary alveoli

bron·chi·ol·itis \,bräŋkē(,)ō'līd·əs, -äŋk-\ *n* -ES [NL, fr. *bronchiolum* + *-itis*] **:** inflammation of the bronchioles

bron·chi·o·lus \brän'kīələs, -äŋ'-\ *n, pl* **bronchio·li** \-,lī\ [NL, prob. alter. of *bronchiolum*] **:** BRONCHIOLE

¹**bron·chit·ic** \(')brän¦kid·¦ik, -äŋ¦-, it|, ¦ēk\ *adj* [ISV *bronchit-* (fr. NL *bronchitis*) + *-ic*] **:** of, relating to, or affected with bronchitis

²**bronchitic** \"\ *n* -s **:** a bronchitic person

bron·chi·tis \brän'kīd·əs, -äŋ'-, -ītəs\ *n, pl* **bron·chit·i·des** \-kid·ə,dēz, -itə-\ [NL, fr. *bronch-* + *-itis*] **:** acute or chronic inflammation of the bronchial tubes or any part of them; *also* **:** any of several diseases of man or animals of which such inflammation is a characteristic feature — see INFECTIOUS BRONCHITIS

bron·chi·um \'bräŋkēəm\ *n, pl* **bron·chia** \-ēə\ [LL, fr. Gk *bronchion,* dim. of *bronchos*] **:** a branch of a bronchus; *esp* **:** one joining a primary bronchus to its bronchioles

¹**broncho** *var of* BRONCO

²**bron·cho** \'bräŋ(,)kō\ *n* -s [prob. fr. ¹*broncho*] **:** OLD ENGLISH BROWN

broncho- *in pronunciations below,* ¦== = ¦bräŋ(,)kō *or* -äŋ(- *or* -,kə\ — see BRONCH-

bron·cho·dilator \¦== *at* BRONCHO- + \ *n* -s [*bronch-* + *dilator*] **:** any drug that causes relaxation of bronchial muscle resulting in expansion of the air passages of the bronchi — **bron·cho·di·la·to·ry** \"+¦dī¦lād·ərē, -,dəˈl-\ *adj*

bron·cho·gen·ic \¦==+¦jenik\ *adj* [ISV *bronch-* + *-genic*] **:** relating to or arising in or by way of the air passages of the lungs ⟨~ spread of infection⟩ ⟨~ carcinoma⟩

bron·cho·gram \'==+,gram\ *n* -s [ISV *bronch-* + *-gram*] **:** a roentgenogram of the bronchial tree after injection of a radiopaque substance

bron·cho·graph·ic \¦==+¦grafik\ *adj* [ISV *bronchography* + *-ic*] **:** of, relating to, or produced by bronchography — **bron·cho·graph·i·cal·ly** \-fək(ə)lē\ *adv*

bron·chog·ra·phy \brän'kägrəfē, -äŋ'-\ *n* -ES [ISV *bronch-* + *-graphy*] **:** the roentgenographic visualization of the bronchial tree after injection of a radiopaque substance

bron·choph·o·ny \-äfənē\ *n* -ES [ISV *bronch-* + *-phony;* prob. orig. formed as F *bronchophonie*] **:** the sound of the voice heard through the stethoscope over a healthy bronchus and over other portions of the chest in cases of consolidation of the lung tissue — compare PECTORILOQUY

bron·cho·pneumonia \¦== *at* BRONCHO- +\ *n* [NL, fr. *bronch-* + *pneumonia*] **:** pneumonia involving many relatively small areas of the lung adjacent to the smaller bronchi — **bron·cho·pneumonic** \"+\ *adj*

bron·chor·rhea \,==+'rēə\ *n* -s [NL, fr. *bronch-* + *-rrhea*] **:** the excessive discharge of mucus from the air passages of the lung

¹**bron·cho·scope** \'==+,skōp\ *n* -s [ISV *bronch-* + *-scope*] **:** a tubular instrument equipped with a small electric lamp which may be passed through the trachea into the large bronchi and through which the bronchi may be inspected or instruments may be passed for the removal of foreign bodies or other purposes — **broncho·scop·ic** \¦== *at* BRONCHO-+¦skäpik\ *adj* — **bron·cho·scop·i·cal·ly** \-pək(ə)lē\ *adv* — **bron·chos·co·pist** \brän'käskəpəst, -äŋ'-\ *n* -s — **bron·chos·co·py** \-pē\ *n* -ES

²**bronchoscope** \"\ *vt* -ED/-ING/-S **:** to use a bronchoscope on (a patient)

bron·cho·spasm \'== *at* BRONCHO-+,-\ *n* -s [ISV *bronch-* + *spasm*] **:** constriction of the air passages of the lung by spasmodic contraction of the bronchial muscles (as in asthma) — **bron·cho·spastic** \¦==+¦-\ *adj*

bron·cho·spirometry \¦==+\ *n* -ES [ISV *bronch-* + *spirometry*] **:** independent measurement of the vital capacity of each lung by means of a spirometer in direct continuity with one of the primary bronchi

bron·cho·stenosis \¦==+\ *n* [NL, fr. *bronch-* + *stenosis*] **:** stenosis of a bronchus

bron·chus \'bräŋkəs\ *n, pl* **bron·chi** \-än,kī, -äŋ-, -,kē\ [NL, fr. Gk *bronchos* trachea, throat — more at CRAW] **:** either of the two primary divisions of the trachea that lead respectively into the right and the left lung and that are structurally similar to the trachea; *broadly* **:** any of the branches of each bronchus that ramify in the substance of the lung, exhibit increasing reduction and ultimate disappearance of cartilage in passing from the largest to the finest branches, and serve to connect the bronchioles with the primary bronchi and form a channel for the distribution of air in the lung

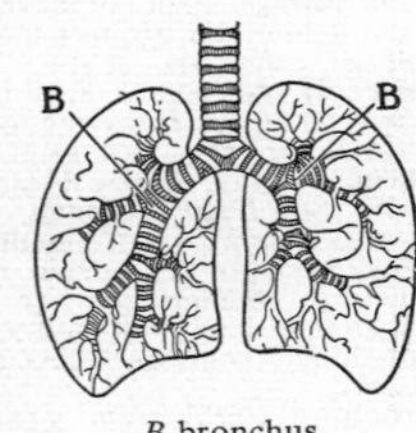

B bronchus

bron·co *also* **bron·cho** \'bräŋ(,)kō, -äŋ(-\ *n* -s [MexSp *bronco,* fr. Sp, rough, wild, fr. (assumed) VL *bruncus* knot in wood (whence It *bronco* stub of a branch, OProv *bronc* projection, roughness)] **1 :** an unbroken or imperfectly broken range horse of western No. America; *sometimes* **:** a vicious or unbreakable horse or one trained to buck — compare CAYUSE **2 :** any range horse **:** MUSTANG

broncobuster \'=(,)=,==\ *n* -s **:** one that breaks wild horses to the saddle

bronco grass *or* **broncho grass** *n* **1 :** a European bromegrass (*Bromus rigidus gussoni*) adventive in Australia and southern Africa **2** *West* **:** CHEAT 3a

bronc peeler *n, West* **:** BRONCOBUSTER

broncs *pl of* BRONC

bron·i·cal *or* **bron·i·chal** *or* **bron·i·kal** *dial var of* BRONCHIAL

bronk \'bräŋk\ *n* -s [by shortening & alter.] **:** BRONCO

brön·ner's acid *or* **broen·ner's acid** \'brenə(r)z-, -rən-,-rön-\ *n, usu cap B* [prob. fr. the name *Brönner*] **:** a colorless crystalline naphthylaminesulfonic acid $NH_2C_{10}H_6SO_3H$ used as a dye intermediate; 6-amino-2-naphthalenesulfonic acid

bront- *or* **bronto-** *comb form* [Gk, fr. *brontē;* akin to Gk *bremein* to roar, *bromos* loud noise] **:** thunder ⟨*bront*ide⟩ ⟨*bronto*meter⟩ — often in generic names esp. of large animals ⟨*Bront*ops⟩ ⟨*Bronto*therium⟩

bron·te·um \brän·'tēəm\ *also* **bron·te·on** \-ēən, -ē,än\ *n* -s [Gk *bronteion,* fr. *brontē* thunder] **:** a device used in the ancient Greek and Roman theater for making a sound of thunder orig. by means of bronze jars or skins filled with stones

bron·tide \'brän·,tīd\ *n* -s [irreg. fr. *bront-*] **:** a low muffled sound like distant thunder heard in certain seismic regions esp. along seacoasts and over lakes and thought to be caused by feeble earth tremors

bron·to·gram \'bräntə,gram\ *n* -s [*bront-* + *-gram*] **:** the record made by a brontometer

bron·to·graph \-af\ *n* -s [*bront-* + *-graph*] **1 :** BRONTOMETER **2 :** BRONTOGRAM

bron·to·lite \-nt°l,īt\ *or* **bron·to·lith** \-°l,ith\ *n* -s [ISV *bront-* + *-lite* or *-lith*] **:** AEROLITE

bron·tom·e·ter \brän-'tämәd·ә(r)\ *n* [ISV *bront-* + *-meter;* prob. orig. formed as F *brontomètre*] **:** an instrument for recording the phenomena of thunderstorms (as times of occurrence, frequency, and intensity of the lightning discharges)

bron·to·pho·bia \,bräntə'fōbēə\ *n* [NL, fr. *bront-* + *-phobia*] **:** abnormal fear of thunder

bron·tops \'brän-,täps\ *n, cap* [NL, fr. *bront-* + *-ops*] **:** a genus of large extinct perissodactyl Oligocene mammals

bron·to·saur \'bräntə,sȯ(ə)r\ *also* **bron·to·sau·rus** \'bräntə¦sȯrəs\ *n* -s [NL *Brontosaurus* (former genus name), fr. *bront-* + *-saurus*] **:** any dinosaur of the genus *Apatosaurus,* being large quadrupedal and probably herbivorous reptiles — called also *thunder lizard* — **bron·to·sau·ri·an** \¦bräntə¦sȯrēən\ *adj*

bron·to·there \'bräntə,thi(ə)r\ *n* -s [NL *Brontotherium*] **:** any mammal or fossil of the genus *Brontotherium*

bron·to·the·ri·idae \,bräntōthə'rīə,dē\ *n pl, cap* [NL, fr. *Brontotherium,* type genus + *-idae*] **:** a large family of extinct Eocene and Oligocene mammals (order Perissodactyla) that were widely distributed in the northern hemisphere and included the titanotheres and a number of related animals

bron·to·the·ri·um \-ntə'thirēəm\ *n, cap* [NL, fr. *bront-* + *-therium*] **:** the type genus of Brontotheriidae comprising large Oligocene ungulate mammals often with horns

bron·to·zo·um \-ntə'zōəm\ *n, cap* [NL, fr. *bront-* + *-zoum* (fr. Gk *zōion* animal) — more at ZOON] **:** a genus of gigantic dinosaurs known from their 3-toed footprints (some 18 inches long) in the Triassic sandstone of the Connecticut valley

¹**bronx** \'bräŋks\ *adj, usu cap* [fr. *the Bronx,* borough of New York City] **:** of or from the borough of the Bronx, New York, N.Y. **:** of the kind or style prevalent in the Bronx

²**bronx** \"\ *or* **bronx cocktail** *n* -ES *usu cap B* **:** a cocktail made from French and Italian vermouth, gin, and orange juice, well shaken, and served with cracked ice

bronx cheer *n, usu cap B* **:** RASPBERRY 3

¹**bronze** \'bränz\ *vb* -ED/-ING/-S [F *bronzer,* fr. MF, fr. *bronze,* n.] *vt* **1 :** to give the appearance of bronze to (as by coating with bronze powder or exposure to the sun) **:** give a bronze

color or luster to ⟨casts carefully *bronzed* and polished⟩ ⟨lounging in the sun *bronzing* their backs⟩ **2** *archaic* **:** to make hard or unfeeling **3 :** to form a colored film of one metal or metal compound on the surface of another metal by chemical treatment **~** *vi* **:** to become like bronze esp. in color ⟨children *bronzing* on the beach⟩

²bronze \"\ *n* -s [F, fr. MF, fr. OIt *bronzo*, perh. fr. L *Brundisium* Brindisi, seaport in southeast Italy famed in ancient times for its bronze] **1 a :** an alloy of copper and tin and sometimes small proportions of other elements (as zinc and phosphorus) that is harder and stronger than brass, is used for a variety of industrial items (as wear plates, bushings, springs, clips, fasteners, and chemical hardware) as well as for objects of art and bells, and is prepared from various proportions of the constituent elements according to the purpose for which it is intended **b :** any of certain copper-base alloys containing considerably less tin than other alloying elements or no tin at all **2 a :** a sculpture or artifact cast or wrought in bronze **b :** a bronze coin; *esp* **:** one of the bronze coins of the Roman Empire (as the sestertius, the dupondius, or the as) **3 a :** a moderate yellowish brown that is yellower and darker than antique bronze, Bismarck brown, or cinnamon brown and yellower, darker, and slightly less strong than maple sugar **b :** a substance (as a pigment, powder, or wash) for imparting a bronze or other brilliant metallic surface (as in printing or decorative stenciling) ⟨fire ~⟩ **4** *usu cap* **:** a domestic turkey of a variety distinguished by large size and coppery brown plumage on a background of black and brown

³bronze \"\ *adj* **1 :** made of bronze ⟨a ~ statue⟩ **2 a :** resembling bronze esp. in color **b :** having a rich resonant tone like that of a bronze bell or casting

bronze age *n, usu cap B&A* **:** the period of human culture characterized by the use of bronze tools beginning in Europe about 3500 B.C. and in western Asia and Egypt somewhat earlier — compare IRON AGE, STONE AGE

bronzeback \'=,=\ *also* **bronzeback bass** *n* **:** SMALLMOUTH BLACK BASS

bronze·back·er \"+ə(r)\ *n* -s [*bronze* + *back* + *-er*] **:** LARGEMOUTH BLACK BASS

bronze bells *n pl but sing or pl in constr* **:** a Rocky mountain bulbous herb (*Stenanthium occidentalis*) of the family Liliaceae with narrow leaves and racemose bell-shaped flowers of bronze color

bronze birch borer *n* **:** a slender elongated olive-bronze beetle (*Agrilus anxius*) widely distributed in No. America and having a slender white larva that mines beneath the bark of various birches

bronze blue *n* **1 :** PRUSSIAN BLUE 2 **2 :** an iron-blue pigment; *esp* **:** one having a bronze tone

bronze bream *n* **:** a sparid food and game fish (*Pachymetopon grande*) of southern Africa that is bronzy above and silvery below with faint longitudinal stripes and dark dorsal and pelvic fins; *also* **:** a rare related fish (*P. aeneum*)

bronze brown *n* **:** a brownish gray that is yellower and stronger than taupe, yellower and lighter than chocolate, and slightly yellower and deeper than castor — called also *Asiatic bronze*

bronze copper *n* **:** a large No. American copper butterfly (*Lycaena thoë*)

bronze cross *n* **:** the highest possible award in the Girl Scouts for gallantry given only when the girl candidate has saved a human life at the risk of her own life

bronzed *adj* [fr. past part. of ¹*bronze*] **:** of a bronze appearance or color; *esp* **:** tanned by or as if by exposure to the sun

bronzed grackle *n* **:** a grackle of a widely distributed variety (*Quiscalus quiscula versicolor*) of the purple grackle, that is distinguished from the typical variety by the bronzy iridescence of the plumage

bronze diabetes *also* **bronzed diabetes** *n* [so called fr. the characteristic skin color that is one of its symptoms] **:** HEMOCHROMATOSIS

bronze-do·ré \¦bränzdə¦rā, -,dȯ¦-\ *n, pl* **bronzes-do·rés** \-nz(,)d..¦ā(z)\ [F *bronze doré*] **:** GILT BRONZE

bronze green *n* **:** a grayish olive green that is greener and slightly paler than average ivy green and greener, stronger, and slightly lighter than privet

bronz·en \'bränzən\ *adj* [²*bronze* + *-en*] **:** BRONZE

bronze nude *n* **:** OLIVE BROWN

bronze pigeon *n* **:** BRONZEWING

bronze powder *n* **:** any metal (as a copper alloy or aluminum) in fine flake form used as a pigment to give the appearance of a metallic surface

bronz·er \'bränzə(r)\ *n* -s **:** one that bronzes, tends a bronzing machine, or applies bronze dust

bronze red *n* **:** PEPPER RED

bronzes *pres 3d sing of* BRONZE, *pl of* BRONZE

bronze·sheen \'bränz(h)¦shēn, -än¦sh-\ *n* -s [³*bronze* + *sheen*] **:** a grayish olive that is greener and duller than average olive drab and greener and darker than average covert brown

bronzesmith \'=,=\ *n* **:** an artisan who works bronze into useful artifacts

bronze turkey *n, usu cap B* **:** BRONZE 4

bronzewing \'=,=\ *also* **bronze-winged pigeon** \'=,=-\ *or* **bronzewing pigeon** *n* **:** any of numerous pigeons of the Australian region that are conspicuous for the metallic spots or areas on the wings

bronze-winged duck \'=,=-\ *n* **:** a So. American duck (*Anas specularis*) having a bronzy speculum

bronze yellow *n* **:** a moderate orange to dark orange yellow — called also *nugget, yellow bronze*

bronzing *n* -s [fr. gerund of ¹*bronze*] **1 a :** the process of imparting a metallic luster (as to a plaster cast) esp. by coating with a powdered metal **b :** a finely ground metal used in bronzing **2 a :** a bronze coloring or discoloration (as of the skin) **b :** a reddish brown discoloration of plant leaves caused by excessive exposure to sun, deficiency of certain nutrients, or the attack of mites or nematodes **c :** PLUMMING

bronzing fluid *or* **bronzing liquid** *n* **:** a liquid for mixing with metallic powders to make a paint or coating

bronz·ite \'brän,zīt\ *n* -s [G *bronzit*, fr. *bronze* (fr. F) + *-it* -ite — more at BRONZE] **:** a mineral consisting of a ferriferous variety of enstatite often having a luster like that of bronze

bronz·itite \-nzə,tīt\ *n* -s [*bronzite* + *-ite*] **:** a hypabyssal rock composed essentially of bronzite

bronzy \-nzē\ *adj* -ER/-EST [²*bronze* + *-y*] **:** like or suggestive of bronze esp. in color or metallic luster ⟨a ~ iridescent surface⟩

¹broo \'brü\ *n* -s [ME *bro*, prob. fr. MF *breu* — more at BREWIS] *chiefly Scot* **:** the liquid in which food has been cooked **:** BROTH, JUICE

²broo \"\ *n* -s [origin unknown] *chiefly Scot* **:** favorable opinion — usu. used with a negative ⟨I have no ~ of him⟩

³broo \"\ *chiefly Scot var of* BROW

¹brooch \'brōch, 'brüch\ *n* -ES [ME *broche* brooch, pointed tool — more at BROACH] **1 :** a fastening device often of precious metal and decked with gems and usu. with a clasp or tongue for making it fast (as to a garment) that is now used chiefly for ornament on women's apparel **2** *obs* **:** a jewel or jeweled ornament

²brooch \"\ *vt* -ED/-ING/-ES **:** to adorn or fasten with or as if with a brooch

¹brood \'brüd\ *n* -s [ME, fr. OE *brōd*; akin to MHG *bruot* incubation, brood, OE *beorma* yeast — more at BARM] **1 :** the young of animals: as **a :** the young of birds hatched or cared for at one time ⟨as a hen doth gather her ~ under her wings —Lk 13:34 (AV)⟩ **b :** the young from the same dam or the offspring of the same mother esp. if nearly of the same age **:** PROGENY **c :** the eggs and young of various bees **d :** progeny produced at a hatch or as a result of a single breeding period ⟨some insects produce a dozen ~s a year⟩ ⟨the first ~ of black flies always seems to bite hardest⟩ **2** *archaic* **:** a brooding or hatching group **3 :** a group likened to a brood of young esp. in respect to similarity of form or nature ⟨a ~ of meteors⟩, community of origin ⟨the entire ~ of chronicle plays —T.S.Eliot⟩, or shared relation to some other item ⟨the ship that some day will mother her own ~ of modern planes —*N.Y. Times*⟩ ⟨a ~ of crystal cups about the bowl⟩ **4 :** a brood bitch — compare STUD

²brood \"\ *vb* -ED/-ING/-S [ME *broden*, fr. *brod*, brood, n.] *vt* **1 a :** to sit on or incubate (eggs) for the purpose of hatching **b :** to produce as if by incubation **:** HATCH **2 a** *of a bird* **:** to cover (young) with the wings **:** warm and protect with the body **b** *obs* **:** to cherish with care **:** hover over protectingly **3 :** to turn over in the mind **:** think anxiously or moodily upon **:** PONDER ⟨I used to ~ these things on my walk —Christopher Morley⟩ **~** *vi* **1 a** *of a bird* **:** to sit on eggs or cover young with the wings **b :** to sit quietly as if brooding eggs or young ⟨birds of calm sit ~*ing* on the charmed wave —John Milton⟩ **2 :** to hover as if enveloping with wings ⟨the old fort ~*ing* above the valley⟩ **3 a :** to dwell continuously or moodily on a subject — usu. used with *over* or *on* ⟨he ~*ed* over their neglect⟩ **b :** to be in a state of mental gloom and depression **:** to indulge in depressing meditation ⟨nothing relieved his distress, he just sat and ~*ed*⟩

³brood \"\ *adj* [¹*brood*] **1** *of a hen* **:** BROODING **:** sitting on eggs **2 a :** kept for breeding ⟨a ~ female⟩ ⟨~ flock⟩ **b :** having or producing young ⟨a ~ sow⟩ **3** *of a plant* **:** infested with insects to an unusual degree ⟨elimination of an occasional ~ tree may cut down insect losses considerably⟩

brood body *n* **:** a gemma (as of a moss or liverwort)

brood bud *n* **1 :** BULBIL **2 :** SOREDIUM

brood capsule *n* **:** one of the secondary scolex-containing cysts that are proliferated from the lining of a hydatid and constitute the infective agent when eaten by a suitable host (as a dog)

brood cell *n* **1 :** GONIDIUM **2 :** a cell in bee comb used for the rearing of a larva

brood chamber *n* **1 :** BROOD POUCH **2** *or* **brood nest** *in a beehive* **:** the part of the comb set aside for brood rearing

brood·er \'brüdə(r)\ *n* -s **1 :** a person or animal that broods **2 a** *also* **brooder house :** a building or enclosed place capable of artificial heating and used for raising chicks and other young fowl without a hen **b :** a heated area or enclosure for keeping young pigs or other animals warm without necessarily separating them from the dam

brooder 2a with section of hover cut away to show oil burner

brooder pneumonia *n* **:** aspergillosis of young birds

brood·i·ness \-dēnəs\ *n* -ES [*broody* + *-ness*] **:** the state of a hen ready to brood eggs that is characterized by cessation of laying and by marked changes in behavior and physiology

brooding *adj* [fr. pres. part. of ²*brood*] **1 :** that broods: as **a :** sitting on eggs **b :** given to meditating moodily or sullenly **2** [fr. gerund of ²*brood*] **:** used for breeding or brooding ⟨a ~ pouch⟩ — **brood·ing·ly** *adv*

brood·less \-dləs\ *adj* **:** being without a brood

broodmare \'=,=\ *n* **:** a mare kept for breeding

brood matron *n* **:** a female domestic animal kept for breeding

brood parasitism *n* **:** social parasitism among birds characterized by a bird of one species laying its eggs in the nest of a bird of another species and giving no parental care to the eggs

brood pouch *n* **:** a sac or cavity of the body of an animal where the eggs or embryos are received and undergo a part of their development

broods *pl of* BROOD, *pres 3d sing of* BROOD

broodsac \'=,=\ *n* **:** BROOD POUCH; *sometimes* **:** GEMMULE 3

brood stock *n* **:** a small population of any animal maintained as a source of population replacement or for the establishment of new populations (as of game birds) in suitable habitats

¹broody \'brüdē, -di\ *adj* -ER/-EST [¹*brood* + *-y*] **1 a** *archaic* **:** tending or seeking to reproduce **:** PROLIFIC **b** *of a hen bird* **:** ready to brood **:** physiologically fit for setting **c** *of a female mammal* **:** suitable for the production of offspring (as by reason of good conformation, vigor, and heredity) ⟨a ~ gilt⟩ **2 :** CONTEMPLATIVE, DEPRESSED, MOODY

²broody \"\ *or* **broody hen** *n* -ES **:** a hen ready to brood — called also *setting hen*

broody coop *n* **:** a small coop designed to break up broodiness of hens by preventing any comfortable settling down

¹brook \'bru̇k\ *vt* -ED/-ING/-S [ME *brouken* to use, enjoy, digest, fr. OE *brūcan*; akin to OHG *brūhhan* to use, Goth *brūkjan* to use, partake of, L *frui* to enjoy] **1 a** *archaic* **:** to possess and enjoy **b** *obs* **:** to merit (a name or epithet); *also* **:** to bear (a name) with credit **2** *obs* **:** to make use of as food **3 :** to put up with **:** ENDURE, BEAR, STOMACH, TOLERATE — now usu. used in negative constructions ⟨they would ~ no interference⟩ ⟨they never would ~ interference⟩

²brook \"\ *n* -s [ME *brook, broke*, fr. OE *brōc*; akin to OHG *bruoh* marshy ground and prob. to OE *brecan* to break — more at BREAK] **1 :** CREEK 2 — in general literary use but used as a common generic term chiefly in England and New England and also in the names of streams in a few northern esp. northeastern states **2 :** BROOK TROUT

³brook \'brük\ *n* -s [Sc *brook, bruik*, fr. *brook, bruik* to soil with soot, make dirty, fr. ME (Sc) *broiken* to make dirty, prob. fr. *brukit, brukyd* streaked with black (taken as a past participle)] *Scot* **:** SOOT

broo·ked \'brükit\ *adj* [ME (Sc) *brukit, brukyd* streaked with black, prob. of Scand origin; akin to Dan *broget* variegated, OSw *brōkoter*] *Scot* **:** streaked with dirt **:** DIRTY

brook feather *n* **:** a Chinese shrub (*Xanthoceras sorbifolia*) of the family Sapindaceae that has showy white racemose flowers that bloom before the leaves expand

brook grass *n* **:** an aquatic perennial grass (*Catabrosa aquatica*) that is widely distributed in the northern hemisphere and sometimes used for pasture, that roots at the lower nodes, and that has overlapping leaf sheaths, soft flat leaves, and a pyramidal inflorescence

¹broo·kie \'brükē\ *n* -s [prob. fr. *brooked* + *-ie*] *Scot* **:** a dirty-faced person; *specif* **:** BLACKSMITH

²brookie \"\ *adj, Scot* **:** DIRTY, SOOTY

³brook·ie \'bru̇kē\ *n* -s [²*brook* + *-ie*] **:** BROOK TROUT

brook·ite \'bru̇,kīt\ *n* -s [Henry J. *Brooke* †1857 Eng. mineralogist + E *-ite*] **:** a mineral consisting of titanium dioxide TiO_2 and identical in composition with rutile and octahedrite but occurring in orthorhombic crystals commonly brown and translucent or brown to black and opaque (hardness 5.5–6, sp.gr. 3.87–4.08)

brook lamprey *n* **:** any of numerous usu. small lampreys that live mostly in brooks

brook·less \'bru̇kləs\ *adj* **:** being without a brook

brook·let \'bru̇klət\ *n* -s **:** a small brook **:** RIVULET, RILL

brook·lime \'bru̇,klīm\ *n* -s [by folk etymology fr. earlier *brooklem*, fr. ME *brokelemke*, fr. *broke* brook + *lemke, lemeke* speedwell, fr. OE *hleomoce*; akin to MLG *lōmeke* speedwell — more at ²BROOK] **1 :** any of certain aquatic or semiaquatic plants of the genus *Veronica* (as *V. beccabunga* and *V. americana*) — see WALL INK **2 :** WATERCRESS **3** *Austral* **:** a plant of the genus *Gratiola*

brook lobelia *n* **:** a delicate waterside plant (*Lobelia kalmii*) of eastern No. America with pale blue irregular evanescent flowers

¹brook·lyn \'bru̇klən\ *adj, usu cap* [fr. *Brooklyn*, borough of New York City] **:** of or from the borough of Brooklyn, New York, N.Y. ⟨*Brooklyn* streets⟩ **:** of the kind or style prevalent in Brooklyn

²brooklyn \"\ *n* -s *usu cap, bowling* **:** a hit in which the ball strikes the headpin to the left of center

brook·lyn·ese \'bru̇klə,nēz, -ēs, ,==ˈ=\ *n, usu cap* **:** the uncultivated speech of greater New York City (including the borough of Brooklyn) and environs among the characteristics of which are the use of \ȯi\ as the vocalic of words like *bird*, the use of the glottal stop for *tt* in words like *bottle*, and the substitution of \t\ or \d(·)\ for \th\ or \t͟h\ of words like *think, these, brother*

brook·lyn·ite \'bru̇klə,nīt\ *n* -s *cap* **:** a native or resident of Brooklyn, N.Y.

brook pimpernel *n* **:** WATER SPEEDWELL

brooks *pl of* BROOK, *pres 3d sing of* BROOK

brookside \'=,=\ *n* [ME *brokeside*, fr. *broke* brook + *side*] **:** the land bordering on a brook

brook tongue *n* **:** either of two water hemlocks: **a :** a European water hemlock (*Cicuta virosa*) **b :** a related American plant (*C. maculata*)

brook trout *n* **:** the common speckled char (*Salvelinus fontinalis*) of eastern No. America highly esteemed as a sport and food fish, widely distributed in cold flowing waters, and introduced in many places outside its natural range — called also *speckled trout, squaretail*

brookweed \'=,=\ *n* **:** either of two small white-flowered herbs (*Samolus valerandi* of Europe and *S. floribundus* of the U.S.) that grow in wet places

brooky \'bru̇kē\ *adj* -ER/-EST [²*brook* + *-y*] **:** full of brooks

brool \'brül\ *n* -s [prob. fr. G *brüllen* to roar, bellow, fr. MHG *brüelen*; akin to MD *brullen* to roar, bellow, MHG *bral* shout; all from a D-G root of imit. origin] **:** a low roar **:** a deep murmur or humming ⟨list to the ~ of that royal forest voice —Thomas Carlyle⟩

¹broom \'brüm, -u̇m\ *n* -s [ME, fr. OE *brōm*; akin to OHG *brāmo* bramble, MHG *brem* edge — more at BRIM] **1 a :** any of various leguminous shrubs chiefly of the genera *Cytisus* and *Genista* with long slender branches, upright growth, small leaves, and usu. showy yellow flowers **b :** BROOM TREE 1 **c :** HEATHER 1a **2 :** a bundle of firm stiff plant shoots or twigs (as of the tops of broomcorn or of birch spray) or of natural or artificial fibers bound tightly together usu. on a long handle and used for sweeping and brushing — compare ¹BRUSH **3 :** the tops of a common broom (*Cytisus scoparius*) formerly used in medicine as a diuretic **4 :** WITCHES'-BROOM **5 :** WOODWAXEN

household brooms

²broom \"\ *vt* -ED/-ING/-S **1 :** to sweep with or as if with a broom; **a :** to cleanse by sweeping ⟨~ off the hearth⟩ **b :** to gather by sweeping ⟨she ~*ed* up the pieces of the broken jar⟩ **c :** to finish (as a surface) by means of a broom ⟨~*ing* the fresh concrete surface gives a pleasing finish⟩ **d :** to apply (as roofing cement or filler in a brick or block pavement) with a broom ⟨carefully ~ the asphalt into the felt⟩ **2 :** to fray or splinter (as a log) at the end by mechanical means ⟨a ~*ed* stick makes a handy stirrer⟩

broom birch *n* **1 :** YELLOW BIRCH **2 :** POPLAR BIRCH

broom brush *n* [so called fr. its use in broommaking] **:** a shrubby American St.-John's-wort (*Hypericum prolificum*) with showy yellow flowers

broom clover *n* **:** INDIGO BROOM

broomcorn \'=,=\ *n* **:** any of several tall cultivated grasses that are derived from a variety of sorghum (*Sorghum vulgare technicum*) and are grown for the stiff-branched elongated panicle which is used for making brooms and brushes

broomcorn millet *n* **:** MILLET 1a

broom crowberry *n* [so called fr. its broomlike appearance] **:** a prostrate shrub (*Corema conradii*) of northeastern No. America resembling the common crowberry but with flowers in terminal heads

broom grass *n* **1 :** BROOM SEDGE 1 **2 :** BROMEGRASS

broom hickory *n* [so called fr. its former use in broommaking] **:** a pignut (*Carya glabra*)

broom·ie *or* **broomy** \'brümē, -u̇-\ *n, pl* **broomies** [*broomtail* + *-ie* or *-y*] **:** BROOMTAIL

broom·ing \-miŋ\ *or* **brooming disease** *n* -s [¹*broom* + *-ing*] **:** abnormal clustering of branches (as in witches'-broom); *also* **:** an abnormal condition of a plant (as of certain walnuts) leading to such brooming

broom man *n* **:** BRUSHMAN 1c

broom millet *n* **:** BROOMCORN MILLET

broom moss *n* **:** a common moss (*Dicranum scoparium*) with tufts that resemble miniature brushes

broom palm *n* **:** COHUNE PALM

broom pine *n* [so called fr. the broomlike appearance of its leaf cluster] **:** LONGLEAF PINE

broom·rape \-m,rāp\ *n* [trans. of NL *rapum genistae*; fr. the parasitic growth of one species like a tuber on the roots of broom] **1 :** any of various root-parasitic plants of the family Orobanchaceae (as of the genus *Orobanche*) **2 :** INDIAN PIPE

broomrape family *n* **:** OROBANCHACEAE

broomroot \'=,=\ *n* [so called fr. its former use in brushmaking] **:** a Mexican grass (*Epicampes macroura*) used for forage and papermaking

brooms *pl of* BROOM, *pres 3d sing of* BROOM

broom sage *n* [so called fr. its use in broommaking] **:** RABBIT BRUSH

broom sedge *n* [so called fr. its use in broommaking] **1 :** any of several grasses of the genus *Andropogon* (esp. *A. scoparius*, *A. virginicus*, and *A. argyraeus*) — called also *broom grass* **2 :** ARROW GRASS 1, 2

broom snakeroot *or* **broom snakeweed** *n* **:** a glabrous and often glutinous low-growing composite shrub (*Gutierrezia sarothrae*) of the southwestern U.S. with narrowly linear leaves and small heads of yellow flowers

broom·stick \'=,=\ *n* -s **:** the long thin handle of a broom

broomstraw \'=,=\ *n* -s **:** BROOM SEDGE 1

broomtail \'=,=\ *n* [¹*broom* + *tail*] **:** a small usu. wild and untrained western range horse of inferior quality — sometimes used specif. of the mare and then contrasted with *fuzztail*

broom top *n* **:** the almost leafless branches of the broom (*Cytisus scoparius*) that contain the alkaloid sparteine; *esp* **:** these tops prepared for pharmaceutical use — used usu. in pl.

broom tree *n* [so called fr. its broomlike appearance] **1 :** a shrub (*Baccharis scoparia*) of Jamaica **2 :** a yellow-flowered prickly shrub (*Genista anglica*) found on the moors of northern Europe and England

broom wattle *n* **:** an Australian shrub or small tree (*Acacia calamifolia*) with showy yellow flowers

broomweed \'=,=\ *n* [so called fr. its use in broommaking] **1 :** an herb (*Scoparia dulcis*) of the family Scrophulariaceae with small whitish flowers that grows in waste places in tropical and subtropical regions — called also *sweet broomweed* **2 :** a tropical American herb (*Corchorus siliquosus*) used for making brooms **3 :** any of several tropical plants of the genera *Sida* and *Triumfetta* used for broommaking **4 :** a shrubby annual plant (*Gutierrezia texana*) of the prairies of the southwestern U.S. with rigid woody branches, glutinous foliage, and yellow flowers

broomwood \'=,=\ *n* **:** a tropical American shrub (*Moluchia tomentosa*) of the family Sterculiaceae that is common in the Bahamas and has papery leaves and bluish purple flowers

broomwort \'=,=\ *n* [so called fr. the parasitic growth of one species on the roots of broom] **1 :** any plant of the family Orobanchaceae **2 :** WATER BETONY

broomy \'brümē, -u̇-\ *adj* -ER/-EST [¹*broom* + *-y*] **:** abounding in broom

broon \'brün\ *Scot var of* BROWN

broon geor·die \-'jȯrdē\ *n, usu cap G* [Sc *broon* + *Geordie*, irreg. dim. of *George* (the name)] *Scot* **:** BROWN GEORGE 1

broos *pl of* BROO

broose \'brüz\ *n* -s [perh. alter. of Sc *brous* violent rush, impact, alter. of ME *brusche* rush — more at BRUSH (encounter)] *chiefly Scot* **:** a race to the bridegroom's house after a country wedding

broo·zled \'brüzəld\ *adj* [*brooz-* (alter. of *bruise*) + *-le* + *-ed*] *Scot* **:** BRUISED, SMASHED

brose \'brōz\ *n* -s [perh. alter. of Sc *bruis* broth, fr. ME *brewes, browes* — more at BREWIS] **:** a chiefly Scottish dish made by pouring some boiling liquid on meal (as oatmeal) and stirring it — usu. used in combination with an attributive indicating the nature of the liquid ⟨water ~⟩ ⟨beef ~⟩

bro·si·mum \'brōsəməm, -räl, ¦zə-\ *n, cap* [NL, fr. Gk *brōsimon*, neut. of *brōsimos* eatable, fr. Gk *bibrōskein* to devour — more at VORACIOUS] **:** a small genus of tropical American trees (family Moraceae) having a milky juice and monoecious flowers and including several of economic importance — see BREADNUT, COW TREE 1, LETTERWOOD

bros·na \'brəsnə\ *n* -s [IrGael, fr. MIr; akin to OE *brȳsan* to bruise — more at BRUISE] *Irish* **:** a bundle of sticks **:** FAGGOT

brosy \'brōzi\ *adj* [*brose* + *-y*] **1** *Scot* **:** fed or smeared with brose **2** *Scot* **:** stout and somewhat bloated in appearance **:** SLUGGISH, TORPID

brotch \'brōch, -räch\ *dial Eng var of* ¹BROACH 2d

bröt·chen \'brœtkən\ *n* -s [G, fr. *bröt-* (fr. *brot* bread, fr. OHG *brōt*) + *-chen*, dim. suffix, fr. MHG *-chīn*; akin to MD *-kijn*, dim. suffix — more at BREAD, -KIN] **:** ROLL 2d(1)

broth \ˈbrȯ|th *also* -rä| \ *n, pl* **broths** \|ths,|(th)z\ [ME, fr. OE; akin to OHG *brod* broth, ON *broth*, L *defrutum* new wine boiled down, OIr *bruth* heat, wrath, L *fervēre* to boil — more at BURN] **1 :** liquid in which meat, fish, cereal grains, or vegetables have been cooked **:** STOCK — compare BOUILLON, CONSOMMÉ **2 :** a fluid culture medium **3 a :** something outstanding of its kind as though produced by boiling down to a savory broth — used chiefly in the phrase *a broth of a boy* **b :** something turbulent, disordered, and ebullient like the surface of a boiling stockpot ⟨matters had reached a ~ of discussion —Agnes de Mille⟩

broth·el \ˈbräthəl, -rȯth-\ *n* -s [ME, fr. *brothen* ruined (past part. of *brethen* to waste away, go to ruin), fr. OE, past part. of *brēothan* to waste away; akin to OHG *brōdi* frail — more at BRITTLE] **1** *obs* **:** a worthless fellow **:** a lewd man or woman **:** PROSTITUTE **2** [influenced in meaning by *bordel*] **:** an establishment (as a house or apartment) in which prostitutes are domiciled and ply their trade usu. as employees or on a commission basis, the keeping of such an establishment being at common law and usu. by statute a misdemeanor

¹broth·er \ˈbrət͟hə(r)\ *n, pl* **brothers** \-ə(r)z\ *also* **breth·ren** \ˈbret͟h(ə)rən *also* -tharn\ [ME, fr. OE *brōthor;* akin to OHG *bruoder* brother, ON *brōthir*, Goth *brothar*, L *frater* brother, Gk *phratēr* member of the same clan, Skt *bhrātṛ* brother] **1 a :** a male human being considered in his relation to another person having the same parents or having one parent in common — see BROTHER-GERMAN, HALF BROTHER; compare UTERINE **b :** a male of any lower animal similarly considered **2 a** (1) **:** a kinsman by blood (2) **:** a male member of the same family, clan, or line, in primitive societies being often charged with the same responsibilities as a brother of common parentage **b :** a person regarded as sharing a common national or racial origin with the user of the word — often used without specific consideration of sex ⟨we must help our ~*s* in the Old Country⟩ **c :** FELLOWMAN ⟨are not all men ~*s*⟩ **3** *pl often* *brethren* **a :** CORELIGIONIST; *esp* **:** a fellow member of a Christian church — often used with a proper noun ⟨*Brother* Jones will pass the collection plate⟩ **b :** a Protestant minister esp. in some evangelical denominations — often used with a proper noun ⟨*Brother* Smith, the Baptist preacher⟩ **4** *pl often brethren* **:** one related or linked to another by some common tie or interest (as of shared rank, profession, membership in a society, suffering, or labor) **5 :** someone or something that closely resembles another in qualities or traits ⟨the ~ qualities of greed and miserliness⟩ **6** *slang* **:** FELLOW, CHAP, MATE — often used as an informal term of address esp. to a person whose name is unknown ⟨hey, ~, what time is it⟩ **7** *Roman Catholicism* **a** *usu cap* **:** a member of a congregation of men usu. not in holy orders but commonly engaged in hospital or school work ⟨a Xaverian *Brother*⟩ **b :** a member of a men's religious order who is not preparing for or ready for holy orders ⟨a lay ~⟩

²brother \"\ *vt* **brothered; brothered; brothering** \-t͟h(ə)riŋ\ **brothers :** to make a brother of **:** address or treat as a brother; *esp* **:** to admit to a brotherhood

³brother \"; ¦brəˈthər, -ˈthə\ *interj* — used typically to indicate intensity of feeling about the topic in hand ⟨~ was I ever sick⟩

brother-german \ˈ⸗⸗⸗⸗\ *n, pl* **brothers-german** [ME *brother germain*, part trans. of MF *frere germain*, fr. *frere* brother + *germain* having the same parents — more at GERMAN] *civil law* **:** a brother through both father and mother **:** a full brother — compare HALF BROTHER

broth·er·hood \ˈbrət͟hə(r),hu̇d\ *n* -s [ME *brotherhod*, alter. (influenced by *-hod* -hood) of *brotherhede*, alter. (influenced by *-hede* as in *godhede* godhead) of *brotherrede*, fr. OE *brōthorrǣden*, fr. *brōthor* brother + *rǣden* condition — more at KINDRED] **1 :** the quality or state of being brothers or a brother **:** the relation between brothers **2 :** brotherly comradeship **:** FELLOWSHIP, COMPANIONSHIP, ALLIANCE ⟨dwelling with the natives in perfect peace and ~⟩ **3 :** an association (as a guild, fraternity, or monastic society) for a particular purpose **4 :** any one of several trade unions; *esp* **:** one among railroad employees **5 a :** the whole body of persons engaged in a business or profession ⟨the medical ~⟩ **b :** a group sharing a common interest or quality ⟨the ~ of wind-swept pines⟩ ⟨the ~ of the handicapped⟩

brother hospitaler of st. john of god \-ˈjän-\ *usu cap B&H, cap S&J&G* [after *St. John of God* †1550 Span. religious, who founded the institute] **:** a member of a Roman Catholic religious institute founded in 1540 at Granada, Spain, and devoted esp. to the care of the sick

brother-in-arms \ˈ⸗⸗⸗ˈ⸗\ *n, pl* **brothers-in-arms :** a close associate; *esp* **:** a fellow member of a military service

brother-in-law \ˈbrət͟hə(r)ən,lȯ, -thrən-,-t͟hə(r)n-\ *n, pl* **brothers-in-law** \-t͟hə(r)zən-\ [ME *brother in lawe;* prob. fr. the fact that the canon law forbids marriage with one's spouse's sister or brother] **1 :** the brother of one's spouse — compare AFFINITY **2 :** the husband of one's sister; *broadly* **:** the husband of one's spouse's sister

brother jon·a·than \,brət͟hə(r)ˈjänəthən\ *n, usu cap B&J* [¹*brother* + *Jonathan* (the name); prob. fr. the frequent use of Old Testament given names among the English colonists in America] *chiefly Brit* **:** a male native or resident of the U.S. — used as a nickname

broth·er·less \ˈ⸗⸗ləs\ *adj* [ME, fr. *brother* + *less*] **:** having no brother

broth·er·li·ness \ˈbrət͟hə(r)lēnəs, -lin-\ *n* -ES **:** the quality or state of being brotherly

¹broth·er·ly \-lē,-li\ *adj* **1 :** of or relating to brothers **2 :** such as is natural for or becoming to brothers; *broadly* **:** AFFECTIONATE, KIND, CHERISHING ⟨~ love⟩

²brotherly \"\ *adv, archaic* **:** as a brother **:** AFFECTIONATELY, KINDLY

brother of the christian schools *usu cap B&C&S* **1 :** a member of a Roman Catholic religious organization founded by St. Jean Baptiste de la Salle in Reims in 1684 and devoted to teaching — called also *Christian Brother* **2 :** a member of a Roman Catholic religious organization founded in Ireland in 1802 and devoted to teaching — called also *Irish Christian Brother*

brothers *pl of* BROTHER, *pres 3d sing of* BROTHER

broths *pl of* BROTH

bro·to·crystal \ˈbrōd·ō+,-\ *n* [*broto-* (fr. Gk *brōtos* eatable, verbal fr. *bibrōskein* to devour + *crystal* — more at VORACIOUS] **:** a crystal occurring in rock and having corroded outlines due to the consolidation of the magma before the crystal was entirely assimilated

¹brot·u·lid \ˈbrächələd\ *n* -s [NL *Brotulidae*] **:** a fish of the family Brotulidae

²brotulid \"\ *adj* **:** of or relating to the family Brotulidae

bro·tu·li·dae \brōˈtülə,dē, -ōˈtyü-\ *n pl, cap* [NL, fr. *Brotula*, type genus (perh. fr. AmerSp *brótula* brotulid fish) + *-idae*] **:** a family of chiefly deep-sea ophidioid fishes superficially resembling the cods but more nearly related to the blennies

brou·ette \(ˈ)brüˈet\ *n* -s [F, fr. OF *brouete, broete* 2-wheeled carriage, fr. (assumed) OF *broue, broe* 2-wheeled carriage (fr. LL *birota*, fr. fem. of *birotus* 2-wheeled, fr. L *bi-* + LL *-rotus*, fr. L *rota* wheel) + *-ete* -ette — more at ROLL] **:** a small 2-wheeled vehicle pulled by a man by means of a pair of shafts in front and used for personal transportation in parts of Europe during the 17th and 18th centuries

brough \ˈbräk, ˈbrəḵ\ *var of* ²BROCH

brougham \ˈbrü(-ə)m, ˈbrō(-ə)m\ *n* -s [after Henry Peter *Brougham*, Baron Brougham and Vaux †1868 Scot. jurist] **1 :** a light closed carriage with seats inside for two or four and with the forewheels capable of turning sharply **2 a :** a 2-door sedan; *esp* **:** one electrically driven **b :** a vehicle similar to a limousine but with the driver's seat outside

brougham 1

brougham-landaulet \ˈ⸗(⸗),⸗⸗ˈ⸗, (ˈ)⸗(⸗)ˈ⸗⸗,⸗ˈ⸗\ *n* **:** a brougham in which the top from the rear doors backward is collapsible

brought [ME *broughte* (past), *brought, ybrought* (past part.), fr. OE *brōhte* (past), *brōht, gebrōht* (past part.); akin to OHG *brāhta* brought (past), *brāht* brought (past part.), Goth *brāhta* (past) — more at BRING] *past of* BRING

broughten [*brought* (past part. of *bring*) + *-en* (as in *forgotten*)] *substand past of* BRING

brou·ha·ha \brüˈhä(,)hä; ¦brüh䦈hä, -ˈühə¦-\ *n* -s [F, perh. modif. of Heb *bārūkh habbā'* blessed be he who enters; fr. the frequent use in the synagogue of a passage containing these words, Ps 118:26 (RSV)] **1 :** a confused medley of sounds esp. of voices **:** HUBBUB **2 :** publicity, attention, or excitement far beyond the merits or importance of its cause **:** HULLABALOO, UPROAR, FURORE

brouil·lon \brüyōⁿ\ *n, pl* **brouillons** \-ōⁿ(z)\ [F, fr. MF, fr. *brouiller* to scrawl, fr. OF *brooillier* to mix, confuse — more at BROIL] **:** a rough draft

brous·so·ne·tia \,brüsəˈnēsh(ē)ə\ *n, cap* [NL, fr. P.M.A. *Broussonet* †1807 Fr. naturalist + NL *-ia*] **:** a genus of Asiatic trees or large shrubs (family Moraceae) with milky juice, sterile flowers in spikes or racemes, and fertile flowers in dense globular heads — see PAPER MULBERRY

¹brow \ˈbrau̇\ *n* -s [ME, fr. OE *brū;* akin to ON *brūn* eyebrow, Gk *ophrys*, Skt *bhrū*] **1 a :** the hair on the ridge over the eye **:** EYEBROW **b :** the superciliary ridge on which the eyebrow grows **c :** either of the lateral prominences of the forehead **d :** FOREHEAD **2 a :** the projecting upper part or margin of a steep place **:** the highest margin of a height as viewed in profile ⟨the wind died down after we crossed the ~ of the slope⟩ **b** *dial Eng* **:** a steep hill or slope **3 a :** the upper face regarded as the seat of expression **:** the general air of the countenance **:** MIEN ⟨a proud contemptuous ~⟩ ⟨the grim ~ of tyranny⟩ **b** *obs* **:** EFFRONTERY, BOLDNESS **4 :** intellectual quality or capacity **5 :** a curved watershed surmounting a porthole or other opening on a ship

²brow \"\ *vt* -ED/-ING/-S **:** to be at or form the edge of **:** BOUND

³brow \ˈbrau̇, -rü\ *var of* ²BROO

⁴brow \ˈbrau̇\ *n* -s [prob. of Scand origin; akin to Dan & Sw *bro* bridge; akin to OE *brycg* bridge — more at BRIDGE] **:** a gangplank usu. fitted with rollers at the end resting on the wharf to allow for the movement of a ship with the tide

bro·wal·lia \brəˈwälēə\ *n* [NL, fr. J. *Browallius* †1755 Swed. theologian and naturalist + NL *-ia*] **1** *cap* **:** a small genus of tropical American annual plants (family Solanaceae) cultivated for their blue, violet, or white flowers **2** -s **:** a plant of the genus *Browallia*

brow antler *n* **:** the first branch of a stag's antler — see ANTLER illustration

browband \ˈ⸗,⸗\ *n* **:** any band designed to cross or cover the forehead; *esp* **:** the part of a bridle, headstall, or halter that passes from one cheekpiece to the other above the eyes and below the ears

browbeat \ˈ⸗,⸗\ *vb* [¹*brow* + *beat*] *vt* **:** to depress or bear down with haughty stern looks or with arrogant speech **:** abash or disconcert by impudence or abuse **:** BULLY ⟨~ witnesses⟩ ~ *vi* **:** to act in an overbearing manner **:** BULLY ⟨they fought, bribed, and ~ in order to achieve their goal⟩ **syn** see INTIMIDATE

brow·beat·er \ˈbrau̇,bēd·ə(r), -ētə-\ *n* **:** one that browbeats

browbound \ˈ⸗,⸗\ *adj* [¹*brow* + *bound* (past part of *bind*)] **:** CROWNED

brow·den \ˈbrau̇dᵊn\ *adj* [ME, fr. OE *brogden*, past part. of *bregdan* to move suddenly, weave together — more at ¹BRAID] *chiefly Scot* **:** fond of **:** intently set upon ⟨less ~ still on cash than verse —Allan Ramsay †1758⟩

browed \ˈbrau̇d\ *adj* [ME, fr. ¹*brow* + *-ed*] **:** having brows of an indicated character or quality ⟨black-*browed* maidens⟩ ⟨smooth-*browed* and carefree⟩

browis \ˈbrōz, ˈbrōəs\ *var of* BREWIS

brow·less \ˈbrau̇ləs\ *adj* [¹*brow* + *-less*] **1 :** UNABASHED **2 :** LACKING EYEBROWS

brow·man \-mən\ *n, pl* **browmen** *mining engin* **:** one who attaches or detaches tubs from the cable at the brow of an incline

¹brown \ˈbrau̇n\ *adj* -ER/-EST [ME *broun*, fr. OE *brūn;* akin to OHG *brūn* brown, shining, ON *brūnn* brown, Gk *phrynē* toad, Skt *babhru* reddish-brown] **1 a :** DARK, DUSKY **b :** GLOOMY ⟨~ years in boarding houses —Sinclair Lewis⟩ **2 :** of the color brown ⟨~ as the oak leaves⟩: as **a** *of a person or a race of men* (1) **:** having skin of the color brown ⟨little ~ men⟩ (2) **:** of dark complexion **:** TANNED **b** *of a kind of animal* **:** distinguished from related kinds by brown coloration ⟨~ bears⟩ ⟨the gamy ~ trout⟩ **3 :** UNBLEACHED — used of linen, cotton cloth, or paper **4** *usu cap* [so called fr. the color of the Storm Troopers' uniform] **:** NAZI ⟨the madness of *Brown* Bolshevism —*Forum*⟩

²brown \"\ *n* -s [ME *broun*, fr. *broun*, adj.] **1 :** one that is brown in color or distinguished by brown coloration: as **a :** a brown-skinned person; *esp* **:** a comparatively light-skinned black **b** *slang chiefly Brit* **:** a copper coin **c :** a flock of game birds in flight ⟨aim at one bird; don't blaze into the ~⟩ **d** (1) **:** BROWN BEAR (2) **:** BROWN TROUT (3) **:** BROWN ALGA **2 :** any pigment or dye that colors brown **3 :** any of a group of colors between red and yellow in hue, of medium to low lightness, and of moderate to low saturation **4 :** a coat color in horses not always distinct from dark bay or from black but identifiable by the presence of light brown or tan hair on the muzzle, legs, and usu. the underline

³brown \"\ *vb* -ED/-ING/-S [ME *brounen*, fr. *broun*, adj.] *vi* **:** to become brown ⟨the roast was ~*ing* in the oven⟩ ~ *vt* **1 :** to make brown or dusky: as **a :** to make brown by scorching slightly (as meat or flour) **b :** to give a bright brown color to (as gun barrels) by forming a thin coat of oxide on the surface **2 :** to apply the brown coat to (a wall) in plastering **3 :** to shoot indiscriminately at (a flock of game birds)

brown alga *n* **:** an alga of the division Phaeophyta

brown ash *n* **1 :** RED ASH 1a **2 :** BLACK ASH 1

brownback \ˈ⸗,⸗\ *n* **:** the dowitcher when in brown-backed summer plumage

brown-banded cockroach *or* **brown-banded roach** \ˈ⸗,⸗⸗-\ *n* **:** a small light brown cockroach (*Supella supellectilium*) with two pale crossbands on the wings

brown-banded snake *n* **:** TIGER SNAKE 1

brown bark spot *n* **:** a nonparasitic disease of apple and pear trees that produces circular brown spots on the bark

brown bast *n* **:** a physiological disease of the Para rubber tree characterized by a grayish brown or greenish brown discoloration of the inner bark near the tapping cut and a stoppage in the flow of latex

brown bat *n* **:** any of various bats somewhat brown in color — see BIG BROWN BAT, LITTLE BROWN BAT

brown bay *n* **:** CHESTNUT 2b

brown bear *n* **:** any of several bears predominantly brown in color; *esp* **:** the common bear (*Ursus arctos*) of Europe

brown bee *n* **:** BLACK BEE

brown beech *n* **:** any of several Australian trees; *esp* **:** NATIVE LAUREL 1

brown bells *n pl but sing or pl in constr* **:** a fritillary (*Fritillaria parviflora*) of California with brownish purple or greenish flowers

brown bent *or* **brown bent grass** *n* [so called fr. its dark panicles] **:** DOG BENT

brown-berried cedar *or* **brown-berried juniper** \ˈ⸗,⸗⸗-\ *n* **:** CADE

brown berry \ˈ⸗,⸗⸗\ *n* **:** a virus disease of the black raspberry characterized by browning, seediness, and drying up of the fruit and by streaking of the foliage — called also *mild streak*

¹brown bess \ˈ⸗ˈbes\ *n, usu cap 2d B* [¹*brown* + *Bess* (nickname of *Elizabeth*); fr. the color of the stock] **:** the flintlock smoothbore musket with bronzed barrel that was formerly used in the British army

²brown bess *n, usu cap 2d B* [prob. alter. of *brown Beth*] **:** PRAIRIE WAKE ROBIN

brown beth \ˈ⸗ˈbeth\ *n, usu cap 2d B* [prob. fr. ¹*brown* + *beth* (short for *beth root*)] **:** a trillium with a dusky purplish flower

brown betty *n, usu cap 2d B* [¹*brown* + *Betty* (nickname of *Elizabeth*)] **:** a betty of sliced or chopped apples, bread crumbs, and spices usu. sweetened with molasses or brown sugar

brown blight *n* **:** a virus disease of lettuce characterized by spotting and streaking of the leaves, reduction in leaf size, and gradual browning of the leaves from the bases upwards

brown blotch *n* **1 :** a disease of the pear possibly caused by the fungus of sooty blotch and characterized by superficial brown spots with indefinite margins on the fruits **2 :** a disease of mushrooms caused by a bacterium (*Pseudomonas tolaasi*) and characterized by brown blocthy discoloration

brown body *n* **1 :** a body formed in many bryozoans by the degenerating internal organs and believed to have an excretory function **2 :** one of numerous flattened or ovoid dark masses in the posterior segments of earthworms resulting from the breakdown of amebocytes and their included debris

brown bread *n* [ME *broun breed*, fr. *broun* brown + *breed* bread] **1 :** any leavened bread darker in color than ordinary wheaten bread: **a :** bread formerly made of native grains (as rye or barley) or maslin often with an admixture of pulses **b :** bread made of whole wheat flour **c :** a dark brown steamed bread made usu. of corn meal, white or whole wheat flours, molasses, soda, and milk or water — called also *Boston brown bread* **2 :** SUDAN BROWN

brown brush *n* **:** BROOM BRUSH

brown bullhead *n* **:** a dark brown or blackish bullhead (*Ameiurus nebulosus*) that is native to eastern No. America and is an excellent panfish affording considerable sport to anglers

brown canker *n* **:** a disease of roses caused by a fungus (*Cryptosporella umbrina*) and characterized by lesions that are initially purple, turn white, and finally become buff

brown catechu *n* **:** CATECHU 1a

brown citrus aphid *n* **:** a brownish aphid (*Toxoptera citricida*) present in many citrus-growing areas and believed to transmit the tristeza disease of citrus trees

brown coal *n* **:** LIGNITE; *esp* **:** loosely consolidated lignite of brownish color and low fuel value

brown coat *n* **:** the usu. brown coat of plaster that precedes the finishing coat and is often preceded by a scratch coat

brown coati *n* **:** a largely brown coati (*Nasua narica*) of Mexico and Central America

brown creeper *n* **:** TREE CREEPER 1a; *esp* **:** a small No. American tree creeper (*Certhia familiaris americana*) that climbs up the trunks of trees supporting itself by the stiff pointed tail feathers as well as by its feet

brown crowberry *n* **:** BROOM CROWBERRY

brown dog tick *n* **:** a widely distributed reddish brown tick (*Rhipicephalus sanguineus*) of the family Ixodidae that occurs on dogs and other mammals and on some birds and that transmits canine babesiasis and possibly other diseases

brown dragon *n* **:** a jack-in-the-pulpit (*Arisaema atrorubens*)

brown duck *n* **1 :** BLACK DUCK d **2 :** a rather rare New Zealand duck (*Anas chlorotis* or *Elasmonetta chlorotis*) grayish brown above with rufous markings and breast

brown earth *n* **:** any of a group of intrazonal soils developed in temperate humid regions under deciduous forests from parent material relatively rich in bases and characterized by a dark brown mull horizon that grades through lighter colored soil into parent material — called also *brown forest soil*

brown ebony *n* **1 :** WAMARA **2 :** GRANADILLA WOOD 4

browned *past of* BROWN

browned-off \ˈ⸗ˈ⸗\ *adj* [*browned* fr. past part. of ³*brown*] *slang* **:** DISGRUNTLED, DISGUSTED **:** fed up

browner *comparative of* BROWN

brownest *superlative of* BROWN

brown·ette \(ˈ)brau̇ˈnet\ *n* -s [²*brown* + *-ette*] **:** a person of intermediate coloring usu. with rather light brown hair, skin fairer than olive, and eyes of blue, gray, or green

brown-eyed su·san \ˈ⸗,⸗ˈsüzᵊn\ *n, usu cap S* [*brown-eyed* (fr. ¹*brown* + *eyed*) + *Susan* (as in *black-eyed Susan*)] **1 :** any of certain dark-centered coneflowers of the genus *Rudbeckia:* as **a :** a black-eyed Susan (*R. hirta*) **b :** a related Texas herb (*R. bicolor*) **c :** an herb (*R. triloba*) of eastern No. America distinguished by tripartite lower leaves **2 :** a blanketflower (*Gaillardia aristata*) of the Rocky mountain area having disk flowers of brownish purple

brown felt blight *n* **:** a foliage disease of conifers caused by any of several ascomycetous fungi (esp. *Herpotrichia nigra* and *Neopeckia coulteri*) and characterized by a dense cobwebby or felty growth of dark brown to black mycelium on the branches that kills the leaves chiefly by excluding air and light

brown george \-ˈjȯ(ə)rj\ *n, usu cap G* [¹*brown* + *George* (the name)] **1** *dial Brit* **:** coarse dark brown bread **2 :** a large brown earthenware water vessel

brown hair worm *n* **:** a small brownish nematode of the genus *Ostertagia* (family Trichostrongylidae) infesting the fourth stomach of sheep

brown hay *n* **:** hay stacked when partly wilted, turned brown as a result of fermentation, and closely approaching green hay in feeding value

brown-headed nuthatch \ˈ⸗,⸗⸗-\ *n* **:** a nuthatch (*Sitta pusilla*) of the southeastern U.S. that is bluish gray above with the top and back of the head grayish brown

brown heart *n* **1 :** ACAPU **2 a :** a physiological disease of stored apples and pears caused by too great a concentration of carbon dioxide and characterized by internal browning **b :** a disease of turnips and related plants caused by a deficiency of boron and characterized by gray or brownish mottling of the outer xylem region of the root

brown hematite *n* **:** LIMONITE

brown hemp *also* **brown indian hemp** *n* **:** SUNN

brown hen *n* **:** GRAY HEN

brown hickory *n* **:** a pignut (*Carya glabra*)

brown horseshoe bat *n* **:** an Australian leaf-nosed bat (*Hipposideros bicolor*)

brown hyena *n* **:** a solitary southern African hyena (*Hyaena brunnea*) often scavenging along the seashore — called also *strand wolf*

brown·ian movement *or* **brownian motion** \ˈbrau̇nēən-\ *n, usu cap B* [after Robert *Brown* †1858 Scot. botanist who discovered it] **:** the peculiar random movement exhibited by microscopic particles of both organic and inorganic substances when suspended in liquids or gases that is caused by the impact of the molecules of fluid surrounding the particles

brown·ie \ˈbrau̇nē, -ni\ *n* -s [¹*brown* + *-ie*] **1 :** a good-natured goblin believed to perform helpful services (as threshing, churning, and sweeping) during the night **2 a :** a member of a group of girls between 7½ and 11 years old who are preparing to be Girl Guides **b :** a member of the Girl Scouts in the age group ranging approximately from 7 through 9 years **3 a** *Austral* **:** a sweet bread made with brown sugar and currants **b :** a small square or rectangle of rich usu. chocolate cake containing nuts **4 :** any of various animals somewhat brown in color: as **a :** PECTORAL SANDPIPER **b :** KODIAK BEAR **c :** BROWN TROUT **d :** SMALLMOUTH BLACK BASS **e :** BRAZILIAN SHRIMP **5** *dial* **:** PENNY, CENT **6** *slang* **:** a demerit given railroad employees for the infraction of certain rules

brownier *comparative of* BROWNY

browniest *superlative of* BROWNY

¹brown·ing \ˈbrau̇niŋ, -nēŋ\ *n* -s [fr. gerund of ³*brown*] **1 :** BROWN COAT **2 :** caramelized sugar or browned flour used for coloring and flavoring **3 :** any of several abnormalities of plants marked by brownish discoloration of the affected parts: as **a :** a disease of flax caused by a fungus (*Polyspora lini*) and characterized by brownish lesions on and breaking of the stem — called also *stem break* **b :** a boron deficiency disease of cauliflower involving brownish patches in the head **c :** discoloration of cut or injured tissue often resulting from disturbances of respiratory mechanisms (as in cut apples or potatoes) and constituting a serious problem in processing certain fruits and vegetables

²brow·ning \"\ *n* -s *usu cap* [after John M. *Browning* †1926 Am. designer of firearms] **:** any of several automatic firearms

browning automatic machine rifle *n, usu cap B* **:** a machine gun identical with the Browning automatic rifle except that the barrel is of the radiator type to facilitate cooling and is provided with a tripod rest

browning automatic rifle *n, usu cap B* **:** a gas-operated air-cooled portable automatic machine rifle fed from a magazine and mechanically capable of firing 200 to 350 rounds a minute — see RIFLE illustration

browning machine gun *n, usu cap B* **:** a water-cooled automatic machine gun fed from a web belt, operated by recoil action, and capable of firing more than 500 shots a minute

brown iron ore *n* [trans. of G *brauneisenstein*] : LIMONITE

brown·ish \'braünish, -nēsh\ *adj* : somewhat brown

brown·ism \'brau̇,nizəm\ *n* -s *usu cap* [Robert *Browne* †1633? Eng. clergyman + E *-ism*] : the views or teachings of Robert Browne who first formulated the principles of Congregationalism and taught that the church is a body of professed believers in Christ united to him and to one another by a covenant, independent of the state, and self-governing by congregations that elect only those officers mentioned in the New Testament

brown·ist \-nəst\ *n* -s *usu cap* : an adherent of Brownism — **brown·is·tic** \(ˈ)brau̇ˈnistik\ *adj, usu cap*

brown king snake *n* : a harmless colubrid snake (*Lampropeltis rhombomaculata*) of the southeastern U.S. that preys upon moles

brown knapweed *n* : a perennial knapweed (*Centaurea jacea*) with purplish flowers and involucral bracts entire or irregularly margined but not regularly toothed

brown kurrajong *n* : an Australasian shrub or small tree (*Commersonia platyphylla*) of the family Sterculiaceae with small white flowers in cymes and a capsular bristly fruit

brown leaf rust *n* : a disease of rye caused by a fungus (*Puccinia dispersa*) — compare STEM RUST

brown lemming *n* : a common arctic lemming (*Lemmus trimucronatus*) lacking seasonal variation in pelage

brown·ly *adv* [¹*brown* + *-ly*] : with brown ⟨~ shadowed⟩ : in a browned condition or manner ⟨a ~ handsome boy⟩

brown madder *n* : CASTILIAN BROWN

brown mahogany *n* : a variable color averaging a dark grayish reddish brown that is lighter, stronger, and slightly yellower than carbuncle and yellower, lighter, and stronger than average Burgundy (sense 2a)

brown mallet *also* **brown mallee** *n, Austral* : any of certain shrubs of the genus *Eucalyptus* (esp. *E. astringens*) that are a rich source of tannin

brown malt *n* : malt for brewing kilned at high temperature over a wood fire

brown mica *n* : PHLOGOPITE

brown·mil·ler·ite \'brau̇n,milə,rīt\ *n* -s [G *brownmillerit*, fr. L. T. *Brownmiller* *b*1902 Am. chemist + G *-it* -ite] : a mineral Ca_2AlFeO_5 consisting of an oxide of calcium, iron, and aluminum

brown mite *n* : CLOVER MITE

brown mixture *n* : a dark brown liquid preparation made of fluid extract of licorice root, tartar emetic, camphorated tincture of opium, spirit of ethyl nitrite, glycerol, and water and used as an expectorant

brown mouth *n* : a virus disease of dogs related to and perhaps a phase of distemper

brown mustard *n* **1** : BLACK MUSTARD **2** : INDIAN MUSTARD

brown·ness \-nnəs\ *n* -ES : the quality or state of being brown

brownnose \'ˌ=\ *vb* [¹*brown* + *nose*; fr. the implication that servility is tantamount to having one's nose in the anus of the person from whom advancement is sought] *slang* : APPLE-POLISH, TOADY

brown oak *n* : an exceptionally dark reddish brown heartwood occurring in certain English oak trees and highly prized for cabinet and finish work

brown ocher *n* **1** : a limonite that is used as a pigment **2** : OCHER BROWN

brown ore *n* : LIMONITE

brownout \'ˌ=\ *n* -s [fr. *blackout*, after E *black*: *brown*] : a curtailment of the use of electric power involving esp. restrictions on the use of lights for advertising or display purposes

brown out *vt* [fr. *black out*, after E *black*: *brown*] : to be responsible for a brownout in ⟨power shortages *browned out* much of the nation that winter⟩

brown owl *n* : an adult leader of a pack of brownies in the Girl Guide movement

brown oxide *n* : OXIDE BROWN

brown patch *n* : a disease of grasses in golf greens and lawns caused by soil-inhabiting fungi (as *Rhizoctonia solani*) that produce circular brown areas each of which is typically surrounded by a band of grayish black mycelium resembling a smoke ring

brown pelican *n* : an American pelican (*Pelicanus occidentalis*) that is dusky brown above with gray wing coverts and tail, head largely white, neck chestnut brown, and grayish brown underparts, that breeds along the Atlantic coast from So. Carolina to Brazil, and that is represented in the Pacific by several varieties

brown pine *n* **1** : LONGLEAF PINE **2** : a large Australian tree (*Podocarpus elatus*) with straight-grained yellowish wood that turns brown on exposure

brown pod *n* : POD ROT

brown podzolic soil *n* : any of a group of acid zonal soils developed in temperate or cool-temperate humid regions under deciduous or mixed deciduous and coniferous forest and characterized by dark brown humus-mineral soil covered with a thin mat of partly decayed leaves and overlying a brown or yellowish brown B-horizon

brown powder *n* : a gunpowder made by the use of an underburned brown charcoal instead of black charcoal — called also *cocoa powder*

brownprint \'ˌ=\ *n* : a photographic print like a blackprint but with white lines on brown ground or vice versa

brown rat *n* : the common domestic rat (*Rattus norvegicus*)

brown red *n* : BOLE 3

brown rice *n* : rice removed from the hulls but not polished and retaining most of the bran layers, endosperm, and germ

brown ring *n* : bundle browning in potato tubers caused by freezing or bacterial or fungous infection

brown root disease *n* : a disease of numerous plants (as cacao, coconut, tea, or rubber) throughout the eastern tropics caused by a fungus (*Hymenochaete noxia*) and characterized by defoliation and incrustation of the roots with masses of earth and stones held together by brownish fungal threads

brown root rot *n* **1** : a disease that most frequently affects plants of the pea, potato, and cucumber families, is caused by a fungus (*Thielavia basicola*), and is characterized by brown to blackish discoloration of the roots and stem base accompanied by decay of these parts **2** : a disease of tobacco and other plants comparable to brown root rot of fungus origin and believed to be caused by attack of meadow nematodes

brown rot *n* **1** : any of certain diseases of plants characterized by browning and decay of tissues: as **a** : a disease of stone and pome fruits caused by fungi of the genus *Sclerotinia* and marked by blighting of twigs, blossoms, and leaves and canker of the stems as well as browning **b** *or* **brown rot gummosis** : a destructive disease of citrus fruits caused by a fungus (*Phytophthora citrophthora*) and marked by gummosis of the trunk as well as browning and decay — called also *foot rot* **c** : a destructive disease of potatoes, tomatoes, tobacco, and related plants caused by a bacterium (*Pseudomonas solanacearum*) and marked by browning of the vascular bundles and wilting — called also *ring disease, ring rot, tobacco wilt* **d** : a decay of timber caused by a fungus (*Polyporus sulphureus*) **2** : any organism causing brown rot

brown rust *n* **1** : ORANGE LEAF RUST **2** : BROWN LEAF RUST

browns *pl of* BROWN, *pres 3d sing of* BROWN

brown sauce *n* : a foundation sauce made of stock thickened with flour browned in fat with added seasonings to taste — called also *espagnole*

brown shark *n* **1** : a small brown cat shark (*Apristurus brunneus*) of the Pacific coast of No. America **2** : a common grayish or brownish shark (*Carcharhinus milberti*) widely distributed in the Atlantic ocean **3** : a large gray, brown, or yellowish shark (*Carcharias taurus*) of tropical seas that is chiefly a bottom scavenger alongshore though regarded in southern Africa as the leading man-eater of the area

brownshirt \'ˌ=\ *n, often cap* [trans. of G *braunhemd*] : a member of the German Sturmabteilung; *broadly* : NAZI

brown shrimp *n* : BRAZILIAN SHRIMP

brownskin \'ˌ=\ *n* : a Negro with rather light skin coloring

brown snail *n* : a common and now nearly cosmopolitan snail (*Helix aspersa*) having a brown shell with paler zigzag markings and being a serious garden pest in some areas

brown snake *n* **1** : any of several Australian venomous elapid snakes esp. of the genus *Demansia*; *specif* : a widely distributed brownish or blackish snake (*D. textilis*) **2** : any of a number of small brownish inoffensive colubrid snakes of No. America

brown soft scale *n* : a soft scale (*Coccus hesperidum*) that is a pest esp. on citrus trees

brown soil *n* : any of a zonal group of soils developed in a temperate to cool semiarid climate under short grass, bunch grass, and shrubs and having a brown surface horizon that grades into a layer of carbonate accumulation by way of a layer of lighter-colored soil

brown spot *n* : any of various diseases of plants producing brown discolorations on the leaves; *specif* : a destructive disease of Indian corn caused by a fungus (*Physoderma zeae-maydis*) affecting the leaves and stalks — called also *Physoderma disease*

brown stain *n* : a discoloration of timber caused by oxidation or by accumulation of certain substances during the seasoning process

brown stem rot *n* : a disease of soybeans caused by a fungus (*Cephalosporium gregatum*) and characterized by a marked yellowing followed by browning and withering of the leaves that is due to a brownish internal rot of the stem

brown stock *n* **1** : stock made from beef (as from beef seared to give color) or from a mixture of meats including beef **2** : the unbleached fibers produced by cooking wood by the alkaline processes of papermaking

brownstone \'ˌ=\ *n* **1 a** : a reddish brown sandstone used for building **b** *also* **brownstone front** : a dwelling faced with brownstone **2** : CHESTNUT 2b — compare BROWN STONE

brown stone \'ˈ=\ *n* : COCONUT 4 — compare BROWNSTONE 2

brown stringy rot *n* : a disease of conifers caused by the Indian paint fungus and characterized by rusty-red or brown fibrous stringy streaks in the heartwood

brown study *n* : a mood of serious perplexed absorption or a state of mental abstraction

brown sugar *n* **1** : soft sugar whose crystals are covered by a film of refined dark syrup that imparts color, flavor, and moisture **2** : a moderate yellowish brown that is duller than cinnamon brown and duller and slightly redder than maple sugar or Bismarck brown — called also *Prout's brown*

brown swiss *n, cap B&S* : a breed of large hardy brown dairy cattle originating in Switzerland

brown-tail moth \'ˌ=-\ *also* **browntail** \'ˌ=\ *or* **brown-tailed moth** \'ˌ=-\ *n* : a white-winged moth (*Nygmia phaeorrhoea*) of the family Lymantriidae native to Europe but found in America and chiefly notable for its larva which is covered with long hairs that are irritating or poisonous to the human skin, its nests of silk and leaves, and its feeding on the foliage of various trees

brown thrasher *n* : the common thrasher (*Toxostoma rufum*) of the eastern U.S. that is reddish brown above and streaked below and like the mockingbird to which it is related is a fine singer

brown tick *n* : an African tick (*Rhipicephalus appendiculatus*) that is a common transmitter of East Coast fever of cattle

brown tiger *n* : COUGAR

browntop \'ˌ=\ *n* : any of several grasses of the genus *Agrostis* (esp. *A. tenuis*)

brown towhee *n* : a towhee (*Pipilio fuscus*) that is chiefly dull grayish brown above and is represented by several subspecies in western No. America

brown trout *n* **1** : a common trout (*Salmo trutta*) native to European streams but found in many parts of the world that is dark olive to purplish black above with yellow or brown sides speckled with various colors and pale white, gray, yellow, or pinkish below and that attains a weight in excess of 10 pounds **2** : SMALLMOUTH BLACK BASS

brownweed \'ˌ=\ *n* : a slender yellow-flowered composite herb (*Bigelowia nudata*) of the southeastern U.S. having disk flowers and resembling a goldenrod in general appearance; *also* : any of several related herbs of the genus *Gutierrezia* of the southwestern U.S.

brown wheat mite *n* : a common mite (*Petrobia latens*) that feeds on growing wheat and other small grains in much of western No. America

browny \'brau̇nē\ *adj* -ER/-EST [¹*brown* + *-y*] : verging on brown : somewhat brown or browned

browpiece \'ˌ=\ *n* [¹*brow* + *piece*] : a heavy upright timber used for underpinning in opening a station for a level in a mine

brow point *n* : BROW ANTLER

browridge \'ˌ=\ *n* [¹*brow* + *ridge*] : SUPERCILIARY RIDGE

brows *pl of* BROW, *pres 3d sing of* BROW

¹**browse** *or* **browze** \'brau̇z, *esp dial* -au̇s\ *n* -s [prob. modif. of MF *brouts*, pl. of *brout* sprout, shoot, fr. OF *brost*, of Gmc origin; akin to OS *brustian* to bud, sprout, OE *brēost* breast — more at BREAST] **1 a** : the tender shoots, twigs, and leaves of trees and shrubs often used as food for cattle and other animals ⟨a good bed of spruce ~⟩ ⟨deer have outmultiplied the available ~⟩ **b** : any plant valued for the production of browse ⟨sagebrush is an important ~⟩ **2** [*browse*, v.] : an act or instance of browsing ⟨cattle out for an evening ~⟩ ⟨at first ~ the book is not impressive⟩

²**browse** *or* **browze** \"\ *vb* -ED/-ING/-s [perh. fr. (assumed) MF *brouser* (whence obs. F *brouser*), prob. fr. *brouts*, pl. of *brout* sprout, shoot] *vt* **1 a** : to consume as browse ⟨a donkey *browsing* thistles⟩ **b** : to feed on the browse of ⟨deer *browsed* the hillside⟩ **c** : GRAZE — not used technically **2** : to feed (as cattle) on browse ⟨farmers forced to ~ their stock when hay ran low⟩ **3 a** : to look over casually (as a book) : SKIM ⟨he lazily *browsed* the headlines⟩ **b** : to make (one's way) by browsing ⟨I *browsed* my way through the agony column⟩ ~ *vi* **1 a** : to feed on or as if on browse ⟨fishes that ~ on algae⟩ **b** : GRAZE — not used technically **2 a** : to skim through a book reading at random passages that catch the eye **b** : to look over books (as in a store or library) esp. in order to decide what one wants to buy, borrow, or read **c** : to casually inspect goods offered for sale usu. without prior or serious intention of buying **d** : to make an examination without real knowledge or purpose

browse line *n* : the boundary between upper normal plant growth and lower stripped and eaten-back growth that indicates the height reached in feeding by the larger browsers

brows·er \-zə(r)\ *n* -s : one that browses; *esp* : an animal that habitually feeds by browsing — compare GRAZER

browsing *n* -s [fr. gerund of ²*browse*] **1** *obs* **a** : BROWSE **b** : a place where there is an abundance of browse **2** : the act of one that browses (as among books or on vegetation) **3** : WHIPPING

browsing room *n* : a room or section in a library designed to allow patrons an opportunity to freely examine and browse in a collection of books

browst \'brau̇st, 'brüst\ *n* -s [prob. back-formation fr. *browster*] **1** *chiefly Scot* : BREWING, BREW **2** *chiefly Scot* : OUTCOME, CONSEQUENCE

brow·ster \-tər\ *chiefly Scot var of* BREWSTER

brow tine *n* : BROW ANTLER

brs *abbr* brass

brt *abbr* brought

bru·ang \'brü,aŋ, =ˈ=\ *n* -s [Malay *bĕruang*] : SUN BEAR

bru·bru \'brü,brü\ *or* **brubru shrike** *n* -s [native name in Africa] : any of several African shrikes (genus *Nilaus*) widely distributed in dry uplands

bru·cel·la \brüˈselə\ *n* [NL, fr. Sir David *Bruce* †1931 Brit. physician and bacteriologist + NL *-ella*] **1** *cap* : the type genus of Brucellaceae comprising nonmotile capsulated bacteria that lack bipolar staining and are pathogenic for man and domestic animals — see BRUCELLOSIS **2** *pl* **brucel·lae** \-e(,)lē\ *or* **brucellas** : a bacterium of the genus *Brucella*

bru·cel·la·ce·ae \,brüsəˈlāsē,ē\ *n pl, cap* [NL, fr. *Brucella*, type genus + *-aceae*] : a family of small gram-negative coccoid to rod-shaped eubacteria that are obligate parasites chiefly of warm-blooded vertebrates and that include a number of serious pathogens — see BRUCELLA; compare HEMOPHILUS, PASTEURELLA

bru·cel·lar \brüˈselə(r)\ *adj* [NL *Brucella* + E *-ar*] : of, with, or resulting from brucellae : of or relating to the genus *Brucella*

bru·cel·ler·gen *or* **bru·cel·ler·gin** \brüˈselə(r)jən\ *n* -s [fr. *Brucellergen*, a trademark] : a nucleoprotein fraction of brucellae used in skin tests to detect the presence of brucella infections

bru·cel·lin \brüˈselən\ *n* -s [fr. *Brucellin*, a trademark] : a cell-free polysaccharide-containing culture filtrate of brucellae used in skin tests to detect the presence of brucellosis

bru·cel·lo·sis \,brüsəˈlōsəs\ *n, pl* **brucello·ses** \-ō,sēz\ [NL, fr. *Brucella* + *-osis*] : a disease caused by bacteria of the genus *Brucella*: **a** : a disease of man of sudden or insidious onset and long duration characterized by great weakness, extreme exhaustion on slight effort, night sweats, chilliness, remittent fever, and generalized aches and pains and acquired through direct contact with infected animals or animal products or from the consumption of milk, dairy products, or meat from infected animals — called also *Malta fever, undulant fever* **b** : CONTAGIOUS ABORTION

bruce spanworm \'brüs-\ *also* **bruce's spanworm** \'brüsəz-\ *n, usu cap B* [prob. after William S. *Bruce* †1921 Brit. explorer and naturalist] : a spanworm (*Operophtera bruceata*) that feeds in early spring on the foliage of deciduous trees in the northeastern U. S. and southern Canada

¹**bru·chid** \'brükəd\ *adj* [NL *Bruchidae*] : of or relating to the family Bruchidae

²**bruchid** \"\ *n* -s : a beetle of the family Bruchidae

bru·chi·dae \'brükə,dē\ *n pl, cap* [NL, fr. *Bruchus*, type genus + *-idae*] : a family (type genus *Bruchus*) of small beetles most of whose larvae infest the seeds of peas and other legumes

bruch's membrane \'brü|ks-, -ü|, |ks-\ *n, usu cap B* [after Carl W. L. *Bruch* †1884 Ger. anatomist] : the inner limiting membrane of the retina separating the pigmented layer of the retina from the choroid coat of the eye

bru·chus \'brükəs\ *n* [NL, fr. L, wingless larva of the locust, fr. Gk *broukos, brouchos* locust, wingless larva of the locust] **1** *cap* : the type genus of the family Bruchidae **2** *pl* **bruchus** *or* **bruchuses** : any of the small seed-eating weevils that constitute the genus *Bruchus*

bru·cia \'brüsēə, -üsh(ē)ə\ *n* -s [NL, alter. of *Brucea*] : BRUCINE

bruc·ine \'brü,sēn, -sən\ *n* -s [prob. fr. F, fr. NL *Brucea* (genus name of *Brucea antidysenterica*, a shrub in which it was erroneously considered to be present, after James Bruce †1794 Scot. explorer of Africa) + F *-ine*] : a bitter poisonous crystalline alkaloid $C_{23}H_{26}N_2O_4$ found with strychnine esp. in nux vomica and ignatia and used chiefly in denaturing alcohol; dimethoxy-strychnine

bruc·ite \-,sīt, *usu* -īd.+V\ *n* -s [Archibald *Bruce* †1818 Am. mineralogist + E *-ite*] : a mineral $Mg(OH)_2$ consisting of native magnesium hydroxide occurring in thin pearly folia and in fibrous form (hardness 2.5, sp. gr. 2.38–2.40)

¹**bruck·le** \'brəkəl, -rük-\ *adj* [ME *brukel* frail, fr. OE *-brucol* — more at BRICKLE] *chiefly Scot* : easily broken or crumbled : BRITTLE

²**bruckle** *vt* -ED/-ING/-s [prob. freq. of Sc *brook, bruik* to soil, begrime] *obs* : DIRTY, BEGRIME

brück·ner cycle \'brüknə(r)-, -rik-, -rœk-\ *n, usu cap B* [after Eduard *Brückner* †1927 Ger. meteorologist] : a climatic cycle marked by the recurrence of warm and dry years and cool and rainy years and averaging about 35 years

¹**brugh** \'brək\ *n* -s [alter. of *borough*] *Scot* : a town or borough

²**brugh** \"\ *var of* ²BROCH

bru·gna·tel·lite \,brünyəˈte,līt\ *n* -s [It *brugnatellite*, fr. Luigi *Brugnatelli* †1928 Ital. mineralogist + It *-ite*] : a mineral $Mg_6Fe(OH)_{13}(CO_3).4H_2O$ consisting of a hydrous ultrabasic carbonate of iron and magnesium occurring in flesh-red lamellar masses

bruh \'brü\ *also* **broh** \'brō\ *n* -s [Malay *bĕrok*] **1** : the pig-tailed macaque (*Macaca nemestrina*) of the East Indies **2** : any of various macaques

bruik \'brük, -rœk\ *Scot var of* BROOK

bru·in \'brüən\ *n* -s [D *Bruin* (name of the bear in the beast epic *Reynard the Fox*), fr. MD *Bruun*, fr. *bruun* brown; akin to OE *brūn* brown — more at BROWN] : BEAR — a conventional epithet esp. in tales and familiar use

¹**bruise** \'brüz\ *vb* -ED/-ING/-s [ME *brusen, brisen*, fr. MF *bruisier* to break, shatter & OE *brȳsan* to bruise, crush; MF *bruisier* of Celt origin; akin to OIr *brūu* I shatter, MW *breu* brittle; OE *brȳsan* akin to OIr *brūu*, MW *breu*, L *frustum* piece, Alb *breshën* hail] *vt* **1 a** *archaic* : to crush or mangle (as by a heavy blow) : DISABLE **b** : BATTER, INDENT ⟨~ armor⟩ **2** : to inflict a bruise on : CONTUSE **3** : to crush or break down (as by a severe blow or by pressure against a hard surface) ⟨be careful not to ~ the tender tobacco leaves⟩ ⟨~ enough berries for a pint of juice⟩ **4** : WOUND, INJURE; *esp* : to inflict psychological hurt on ⟨a human spirit that has been *bruised* by the brutalities of the world —J.C.Powys⟩ ~ *vi* **1** : to inflict a bruise ⟨hailstones are likely to ~⟩ **2** : to bear or show the effects of a bruise : be susceptible to bruising ⟨tomatoes ~ readily unless carefully handled⟩ ⟨she ~*s* easily⟩

²**bruise** \"\ *n* -s [ME *bruse* fr. *brusen*, v.] **1** : an injury esp. produced by a blow or collision that does not break the surface it injures: as **a** : an injury transmitted through unbroken skin to underlying tissue causing rupture of small blood vessels and escape of blood into the tissue with resulting discoloration : CONTUSION **b** : a similar injury to a plant or fruit **2** : an abrasion or scratch on a surface (as of leather or rock) **3** : an injury or hurt (as to the feelings or the pride) **syn** see WOUND

bruis·er \-zə(r)\ *n* -s **1** *slang* : a professional boxer : PUGILIST **2** : a big husky man; *esp* : one somewhat coarse and beefy

bruisewort \'ˌ=\ *n* [ME *brisewort*, fr. OE *brȳsewyrt*, fr. *brȳsan* to bruise + *wyrt* wort — more at BRUISE, WORT] : any plant supposed to heal bruises: as **a** : DAISY 1a **b** : SOAPWORT **c** : COMFREY 1

bruising *adj* : forceful and compelling esp. in a brutal way : CRUSHING ⟨civilians at home . . . protected from the ~ facts of battle —John Mason Brown⟩

¹**bruit** \'brüt, *for 2* -üē\ *n* -s [ME *bruit, brute*, fr. MF *bruit*, fr. OF, noise, din, fr. past part. of *bruire* to make a din, to roar, fr. (assumed) VL *brugere*, prob. blend of (assumed) VL *bragere* to yell, roar, make a noise and L *rugire* to roar; akin to OE *rēoc* wild, Goth *inrauhtjan* to become angry, Gk *erygmēlos* bellowing, MIr *rucht* roar, howl, OSlav *rŭžetŭ* he neighs, and prob. to L *rumor* noise, rumor — more at BRAY, RUMOR] **1** *archaic* **a** : NOISE, CLAMOR, DIN **b** : report or rumor esp. when favorable **2** [F, fr. *bruit* noise, fr. MF] : any of several generally abnormal sounds heard on auscultation

²**bruit** \-üt\ *vt* -ED/-ING/-s **1** : to noise abroad : REPORT — often used with *about* **2** : to make celebrated by general mention : PUBLICIZE, TOUT ⟨the much ~*ed* superiority of the male —*Saturday Rev.*⟩

bru·ja \'brü,hä, -,kä\ *n* -s [Sp, of non-IE origin; akin to the source of Pg *bruxa* witch, Catal *bruixa*] : WITCH, SORCERESS

bru·jo \-,hō, -,kō\ *n* -s [Sp, fr. *bruja*] : SORCERER, WITCH DOCTOR; *esp* : one that works black magic

bru·lé \(ˈ)brüˈlā, ˈbrül(ē)\ *n, pl* **brulé** *or* **brulés** *usu cap* [CanF, fr. F *brûlé*, past part.] : an Indian people constituting a subdivision of the Teton Dakotas

brû·lée *also* **brû·lé** \(ˈ)brüˈlā, brüˈlā\ *n* -s [CanF *brûlé*, fr. F, past part. of *brûler* to burn, fr. OF *bruller*, perh. blend of OHG *brennen* + L *ustulare*, fr. *ustus*, past part. of *urere* — more at BURN, EMBER] : a piece of burned-over woodland

brul·yie \'brül(y)ē, -rəl-\ *n* -s [MF *brouillis* quarrel, trouble, disturbance, fr. *brouiller* to mix, confuse — more at BROIL] *Scot & Irish* : DISTURBANCE, ROW, SCUFFLE

bru·mal \'brüməl\ *adj* [L *brumalis*, fr. *bruma* winter + *-alis* -al — more at BRUME] *archaic* : indicative of or occurring in the winter ⟨the bears . . . were sunk in the ~ sleep —Vance Randolph⟩

bru·ma·lia \brüˈmālēə, -lyə\ *n pl, cap* [L, fr. neut. pl. of *brumalis*] : a pagan festival held at the winter solstice from which some features of the celebration of Christmas seem to have originated

brum·by \'brəmbē\ *n* -ES [prob. native name in Queensland, Australia] *Austral* : WILD HORSE : OUTLAW

brume \'brüm\ *n* -s [F, mist, winter, fr. MF, fr. OProv *bruma*, fr. L, winter, fr. *brevis* short; fr. the short days — more at BRIEF] : MIST, FOG, VAPOR ⟨the valleys faint with ~ —Christopher Fry⟩

¹**brum·ma·gem** \'brəmǝjəm\ *adj* [fr. *Brummagem*, alter. of *Birmingham*, England] **1** *usu cap* : of or belonging to Birmingham, England — sometimes taken to be offensive **2** [fr. the fact that in the 17th cent. notorious counterfeit groats were coined in Birmingham and that in the 19th cent. various cheap and flimsy articles were manufactured there] : showy and cheap

: PHONY, SHAM ⟨her extraordinary beauty, caustic wit, and ~ royalty —G.H.Genzmer⟩
[2]**brummagem** \"\ *n* -s : something cheap or inferior : TINSEL, COUNTERFEIT
brum·my \ˈbrəmi\ *adj* [by shortening & alter.] *chiefly Brit* : BRUMMAGEM
bru·mous \ˈbrüməs\ *adj* [F *brumeux*, fr. *brume* fog — more at BRUME] : FOGGY, MISTY ⟨the ~ October gloaming —John Galsworthy⟩
brum·stone \ˈbrümztən, -rəm-, -mst\ *dial Brit var of* BRIMSTONE
brunch \ˈbrənch\ *n* -ES [*breakfast* + *lunch*] : a meal served usu. in the late morning : a late breakfast, an early lunch, or a combination of the two
brunch coat *n* : a woman's short housecoat or wraparound dress
brun do·ré \ˌbrəndəˌrā, -ˌdȯ-\ *n, pl* **brun do·rés** *or* **bruns dorés** \-nd . . . āz\ [F, lit., golden brown] : OLIVE WOOD
brune \ˈbrün, ˈbrüen\ *n* -s [F — more at BRUNET] : BRUNET
bru·nel·lia \brüˈnelēə, -lyə\ *n, cap* [NL, fr. G. *Brunelli*, 18th cent. Ital. botanist + NL *-ia*] : a small genus (coextensive with the family Brunelliaceae of the order Ranales) of tropical American trees having unisexual panicled apetalous flowers and follicular fruits
[1]**bru·net** *or* **bru·nette** \(ˈ)brüˈnet, *usu* -ed·+V\ *adj* [F *brunet*, masc. & *brunette*, fem, brownish, fr. OF, fr. *brun* brown, fr. ML *brunus*, of Gmc origin; akin to OHG *brūn* brown — more at BROWN] : of or marked by dark or relatively dark pigmentation: **a** *of hair and eyes* : BROWN, BLACK **b** *of skin* : BROWN, OLIVE
[2]**brunet** *or* **brunette** \"\ *n* -s [F *brunet*, masc., & *brunette*, fem., fr. *brunet*, *brunette*, adj.] : a person with brunet hair or skin or both
brun·fel·sia \brünˈfelzēə\ *n, cap* [NL, fr. Otto *Brunfels* †1534 Ger. botanist + NL *-ia*] : a genus of tropical American shrubs (family Solanaceae) that have alternate entire leaves and a fleshy fruit like a berry and that are commonly grown in greenhouses for their flowers
brung *substand past of* BRING
bru·ni·zem \ˈbrünəˌzem\ *n* -s [origin unknown] : a soil of the prairies developed from loess and occurring extensively in Iowa
brun·ne·ous \ˈbrənēəs\ *or* **brun·nes·cent** \(ˈ)brəˈnesᵊnt\ *adj* [irreg. fr. ML *brunus* brown + E *-ous* or *-escent* — more at BRUNET] : dark brown — used chiefly scientifically
brun·ner's gland \ˈbrünə(r)z-\ *n, usu cap B* [after Johann C. *Brunner* †1727 Swiss anatomist] : any of certain compound racemose glands in the submucous layer of the duodenum secreting alkaline mucus and a potent proteolytic enzyme
brun·nich·ia \(ˌ)brəˈnikēə\ *n, cap* [NL, fr. M.T.*Brünnich* †1827 Dan. naturalist + NL *-ia*] : a small genus of herbaceous vines (family Polygonaceae) having climbing tendrils, broad leaves, and inconspicuous racemose flowers — see BUCKWHEAT VINE
brün·nich's murre *also* **brünnich's guillemot** \ˈbriniks-\ *n, usu cap B* [after M.T.*Brünnich*] : THICK-BILLED MURRE
brünn race \ˈbrin-, -rœn-\ *n, usu cap B* [fr. *Brünn* (now Brno), Czechoslovakia] : an Upper Paleolithic people related to the Cro-Magnons but differing in having shorter stature, narrower face and head, and heavier brow ridges, orig. based on skeletal material found associated with Solutrean artifacts at Brno and Predmost, Czechoslovakia, and subsequently recognized in fossil finds in other parts of Europe, in No. Africa, and in western Asia and as a component in modern man
brunn's membrane \ˈbrünz-\ *n, usu cap B* [after Albert von *Brunn* †1895 Ger. anatomist] : the part of the nasal mucous membrane that serves as an organ of smell
bru·no man \ˈbrü(ˌ)nō-\ *n* [*Bruno* (*shovel*), a hand shovel used to move loose ore] : a worker who uses a hand shovel to move loose ore (as to an ore car)
bru·no·nia \brüˈnōnēə, -ōnyə\ *n, cap* [NL, irreg. fr. Robert *Brown* †1858 Scot. botanist + NL *-ia*] : a genus (coextensive with the family Brunoniaceae of the order Campanulales) of Australian herbs with radical leaves and a long-stalked globular head of showy blue flowers
bruns·wick \ˈbrənz(ˌ)wik, -ˌwēk\ *adj, usu cap* [fr. Brunswick (Braunschweig), Germany] : of or from the city of Brunswick, Germany : of the kind or style prevalent in Brunswick
brunswick black *n, often cap 1st B* [trans. of G *Braunschweiger schwarz*] : a black varnish usu. similar in composition to black japan
brunswick blue *n, often cap 1st B* [trans. of G *Braunschweiger blau*] **1** : a pigment consisting of a mixture of an iron blue with a large amount of barium sulfate **2** : PRUSSIAN BLUE 2
brunswick green *n, often cap B* [trans. of G *Braunschweiger grün*] **1 a** : a green pigment consisting of a copper salt (as a basic copper chloride or a basic copper carbonate) — called also *old Brunswick green* **b** : CHROME GREEN 1b **2** : any of three greens: **a** : DEEP BRUNSWICK GREEN **b** : MIDDLE BRUNSWICK GREEN **c** : LIGHT BRUNSWICK GREEN
brunswick stew *n, often cap B* [fr. *Brunswick* county, Va., where it originated] **1** : a hunter's stew made with squirrel or rabbit and onion **2** : a stew of two or more meats with vegetables (as game and chicken with corn, okra, and tomatoes)
[1]**brunt** \ˈbrənt\ *n* -s [ME] **1** *obs* **a** : a forceful onset : a sudden or violent assault ⟨the garrison withstood the ~ of the castle⟩ **b** : a sudden outburst or effort **2** : the main force, shock, or stress : the impact, strain, or violence calling for greatest resistance ⟨employees in the textile and metal trades exposed to the full ~ of foreign competition —J.A.Hobson⟩ ⟨the ~ of the struggle with the German army fell upon the Russians —Walter Lippmann⟩ **syn** see IMPACT
[2]**brunt** \ˈbrənt, -rənt\ *dial Brit past of* BURN
[1]**brush** \ˈbrəsh\ *n* -ES *often attrib* [ME *brusch*, fr. MF *broce*, fr. OF, perh. of Celt origin; akin to OIr *froech* heather — more at BRIER] **1** : BRUSHWOOD **2 a** : scrub vegetation **b** : land covered with scrub vegetation : BRUSHLAND — often used with *the* ⟨helped work cattle in the Florida ~ —F.B.Gipson⟩ **3** *chiefly Austral* : a dense growth of forest and undergrowth

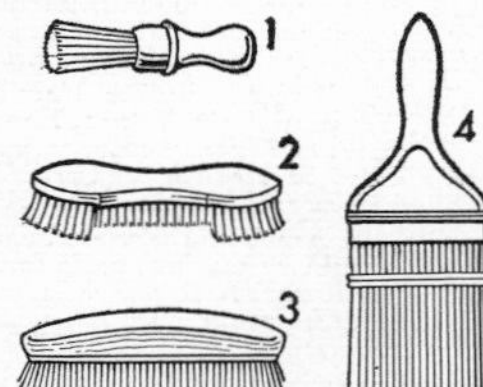

brushes: *1* shaving brush, *2* scrubbing brush, *3* clothes brush, *4* paintbrush

[2]**brush** \"\ *vt* -ED/-ING/-ES **1** : to clear (land) of brush and undergrowth ⟨~ the back forty⟩ **2** : to use cut-off branches as supports for (vines and plants) ⟨peas should be ~*ed*⟩
[3]**brush** \"\ *n* -ES [ME *brusshe*, fr. MF *broisse*, fr. OF *broce* brushwood] **1 a** : a hand-operated or power-driven tool or device composed of bristles set into a back or a handle or attached to a roller and designed or adapted for such uses as sweeping, scrubbing, painting, and smoothing ⟨a floor ~⟩ ⟨a wire ~⟩ **b** : one of a pair of long slender devices of this kind with flexible wire bristles used for making soft rhythmic hissing sounds on a cymbal or snare drum esp. in a dance band **2** : something resembling or suggesting a brush ⟨a thick ~ of wavy hair⟩: as **a** : a heavily haired bushy tail (as that of a fox or squirrel or of certain dogs or cats) ⟨the fox had a handsome red ~⟩ **b** (1) : an herb (*Lepachys columnifera*) of the western U.S. resembling a coneflower (2) : the young strobile or gynoecium of the hop (3) : a tuft of hairs (as on the tip of the wheat kernel) (4) : the inflorescence of the broomcorn **c** : a feather tuft worn on a hat ⟨a cock-green Tyrolean ~ in my hat —Saul Bellow⟩ **3 a** : an electrical conductor commonly in the form of a bundle of copper strips or wire gauze or a block of carbon serving as a means of connection by sliding contact between a stationary and a moving part of an electric circuit (as between line and armature of a generator or a motor) **b** : BRUSH DISCHARGE **4** [[4]*brush*] **a** : an act or instance of brushing ⟨he gave his old suit a quick ~⟩ **b** : a quick light touch : a fleeting momentary contact ⟨she felt the ~ of his coat as he hurried by⟩ **c** (1) : a light stroke with one foot, toe, or heel along the floor in any direction in dancing (2) : a low ballet kick in which the sole of the foot strikes the floor **d** *slang* : a quiet and decisive rejection or dismissal : BRUSH-OFF

[4]**brush** \"\ *vb* -ED/-ING/-ES [ME *brusshen*, fr. *brusshe*, n.] *vt* **1 a** : to apply a brush to or use a brush on ⟨she was ~*ing* her hair⟩ ⟨take the bread from the oven and ~ the loaves with butter⟩ **b** : to apply with a brush ⟨the paint must be ~*ed* carefully onto the porous surface⟩ **2 a** : to remove with a brush or by an act similar to brushing ⟨~ the dust from your shoes⟩ ⟨he . . . ~*ed* the ash from his cigarette —Nevil Shute⟩ **b** : to push or force esp. in the course of physical motion ⟨two men ~*ed* their way through the crowd⟩ ⟨~ obstacles aside⟩ **c** : to dispose of in an offhand way : dismiss or reject summarily or perfunctorily — usu. used with *aside* or *away* ⟨impatiently ~*ed* aside the thought —Kathleen Freeman⟩ ⟨~*ed* our thanks away —Thomas Wood †1950⟩ **3 a** : to pass lightly over or across : touch gently against in passing ⟨my left hand ~*ed* the wall and found the doorknob —Hartley Howard⟩ **b** : AFFECT, TOUCH ⟨the spirit of compromise which responsibility brings has not ~*ed* him —*Time*⟩ **4** : to beat (fibers) lightly to cause fraying or roughening rather than cutting in papermaking **5** *dial chiefly Eng* : TRIM, CLIP ⟨~*ing* the shrubbery⟩ ~ *vi* **1** : to make the contact or motion or perform the action of brushing something ⟨other stewards and messmen were scouring, scrubbing ~*ing*, mopping —*Nation's Business*⟩ **2** *of a horse* : to interfere slightly so as to produce abrasion
[5]**brush** \"\ *adj* [[3]*brush*] : resembling a brush esp. in being bristly or cut relatively short and of even length ⟨a ~ haircut⟩ ⟨a ~ mustache⟩
[6]**brush** \"\ *vb* -ED/-ING/-ES [ME *bruschen* to rush, drive (influenced in meaning by [3] & [4] *brush*), fr. MF *brosser* to dash through underbrush, fr. *broce*, *brosse*, *broisse* underbrush] *vi* : to move so lightly or deftly as to be scarcely perceptible : move so as to graze, skim over, or sweep something ⟨~ past people quickly without hitting them carelessly with your umbrella —Agnes M. Miall⟩ ~ *vt* : to force (a horse) to top speed over a short distance
[7]**brush** \"\ *n* -ES [ME *brusche* rush, hostile collision (influenced in meaning by [3] & [4] *brush*), fr. *bruschen* to rush, drive] **1** : a brief or fleeting encounter; *usu* : one that involves an element of risk or contention ⟨he had several ~*es* with the law⟩ ⟨a ~ with enemy troops⟩ **2** : a usu. short often impromptu race ⟨the two horses came side by side and their riders decided to have a ~⟩
brush·a·bil·i·ty \ˌbrəshəˈbilədē\ *n* -ES : the behavior characteristic of a liquid (as paint) when applied by brush
brush apple *n* [[1]*brush*] : BLACK APPLE
brush arbor *n* [[1]*brush*] *South & Midland* : an arbor made of brushwood esp. as a place for a camp meeting
brush block *n* [[6]*brush*] : a football maneuver in which an offensive player makes light contact with an opponent and continues downfield for secondary blocking
brush bloodwood *n* [[1]*brush*] : BLOODWOOD a(2)
brush border *n* [[3]*brush*] : a striated border on the cells forming the membrane proper in certain epithelial membranes (as in that of the proximal convoluted tubule of the kidney) that is usu. regarded as associated with absorptive phenomena
brush box *n* [[1]*brush*] : an Australian tree (*Tristania conferta*) that has evergreen foliage and is cultivated for shade — called also *Brisbane box*
brush bronzewing *n* [[1]*brush*] : a bronzewing (*Phaps elegans*) that is bronze-brown above and largely bluish gray below
brush broom *n* [[1]*brush*] *South & Midland* : a broom made of small twiggy branches or corn husks tied together and used for outdoor sweeping ⟨the paths swept with a *brush broom* —Ellen Glasgow⟩
brush burn *n* : an injury of the skin due to intense friction ⟨there were also *brush burns* showing that she had been dragged —M.G.Bishop⟩
brush cherry *n* [[1]*brush*] **1** : an Australian timber tree (*Eugenia myrtifolia*) — called also *native myrtle* **2** : the edible fruit of the brush cherry — called also *rose apple* **3** : an Australian shrub (*Trochocarpa laurina*)
brush coating *n* [[3]*brush*] : a paper-coating process in which the wet coating mixture is smoothed on the surface by means of brushes
brush country *n* : an extensive area of land on which the characteristic plant forms are low shrubby growths — compare CHAPARRAL, THICKET
brush cut *n* [[3]*brush*] : a very short even haircut often in a flat plane on top so that the hair stands out and suggests a brush
brush dampener *n* [[3]*brush*] : a machine for spattering water onto paper by means of rotary brushes
brush discharge *n* [[3]*brush*] : a faintly luminous relatively slow electrical discharge having no spark
[1]**brushed** \ˈbrəsht\ *adj* [[1]*brush* + *-ed*] : [2]BRUSHY
[2]**brushed** \"\ *adj* [fr. past part. of [4]*brush*] *of a woven or knitted fabric* : finished with a nap ⟨a ~ rayon bed jacket⟩
[1]**brush·er** \ˈbrəshə(r)\ *n* -s [[4]*brush* + *-er*] : one that brushes by hand or by machine esp. as a vocation
[2]**brusher** \"\ *n* -s [[1]*brush* + *-er*] **1** : a worker who cuts and burns small trees and brush **2** : LIMBER **3** : WHITE BISKOP
brushes *pl of* BRUSH, *pres 3d sing of* BRUSH
brush fire *n* [[1]*brush*] : a fire involving scrub trees, brush, or other growth that is heavier than grass but not of full tree size
brush–fire \ˈ≈,≈\ *adj* [*brush fire*] *of warfare* : limited in scale or in area ⟨a mobile striking force, always on the ready, to fight *brush-fire* wars —*Newsweek*⟩
brush harrow *n* [[1]*brush*] : a crude light harrow made of short tough tree branches (as hawthorn) fastened to one side of a pole and used chiefly to cover seeds
brush hook *n* [[1]*brush*] : BUSH HOOK
brushier *comparative of* BRUSHY
brushiest *superlative of* BRUSHY
brushing *n* -s [fr. gerund of [4]*brush*] : a finishing process for fabrics usu. used to produce a thick nap
brushings *n pl* [fr. gerund of [4]*brush*] : material removed and collected by brushing
brush·ite \ˈbrəˌshīt\ *n* -s [George J. *Brush* †1912 Am mineralogist + E *-ite*] : a nearly colorless mineral $CaHPO_4 \cdot 2H_2O$ consisting of calcium hydrogen phosphate in slender crystals or massive
brush kangaroo *n* [[1]*brush*] : a large wallaby
brushland \ˈ≈,≈\ *n* [[1]*brush* + *land*] : an area characterized by scrub growth
brush·less \ˈbrəshləs\ *adj* [[3]*brush* + *-less*] **1** : lacking a brush **2** : designed for use without a brush ⟨~ shaving cream⟩
[1]**brush·man** \-mən\ *n, pl* **brushmen** [[3]*brush* + *man*] **1** : one who uses a brush esp. as a vocation: as **a** : a worker who assists in cleaning the outside of a building by brushing a previously scoured surface with a chemical cleaner **b** : one who applies coats of finish with a brush **c** : a worker who roughens new concrete pavement with a stiff brush — called also *broom man* **2** : a painter esp. skilled in brushwork
[2]**brushman** \"\ *n, pl* **brushmen** [[1]*brush* + *man*] : one who cuts and burns brush
brush mouse *n* [[1]*brush*] : a common white-footed mouse (*Peromyscus boylii*) of the western U.S.
brush–off \ˈ≈,≈\ *n* -s [*brush off*, v.] **1** : a quietly curt or disdainful dismissal ⟨she gave him the *brush-off*⟩ **2** : an offensive maneuver used by basketball and lacrosse players to get rid of an opponent by running him into a teammate
brush ore *n* [[3]*brush*] : an iron ore in stalactitic forms resembling a brush
brushout \ˈ≈,≈\ *n* -s [*brush out*, v.] : a sample application of paint usu. for testing
brush–pen \ˈ≈,≈\ *n* [[3]*brush*] : a pen with a fibrous point
brushpopper \ˈ≈,≈≈\ *n* -s [[1]*brush* + *popper*] *West* : COWBOY; *esp* : one working in brushy country
brush rabbit *n* [[1]*brush*] : a small short-legged brownish rabbit (*Sylvilagus bachmani*) found on the Pacific coast
brush scythe *n* [[1]*brush*] : BUSH SCYTHE
brushstroke \ˈ≈,≈\ *n* : the configuration given to thick paint (as oil paint) by contact with the bristles of a brush; *also* : the paint left on a surface by a single application of a loaded brush or palette knife
brush–tailed porcupine *or* **brush–tail porcupine** *n* : any of certain Old World porcupines that constitute the genus *Atherurus* and have a tuft of large beaded bristles on the tail
brush–tongued \ˈ≈,≈\ *adj* [[3]*brush*] : having the tongue papillae long and slender, forming an organ resembling a brush ⟨the *brush-tongued* lorikeets⟩
brush–tongued parrot *n* : LORIKEET

brush–treat \ˈ≈,≈\ *vt* : to apply preservatives to with a brush ⟨*brush-treat* the floorboards⟩
brush turkey *n* [[1]*brush*] : MEGAPODE; *esp* : a large megapode (*Alectura lathami*) of the wooded regions of eastern Australia
brush turpentine *n* [[1]*brush*] : either of two Australian trees (*Rhodamia trinerva* and *Syncarpia leptopetala*) of the family Myrtaceae used as a source of timber
brush up *vt* **1** : to polish up or improve by eliminating small imperfections ⟨spent their off time in *brushing up* their act⟩ **2** : to refresh one's memory of : renew one's skill in or knowledge of ⟨*brush up* your Shakespeare⟩ ⟨*brushed up* his piano technique⟩ ~ *vi* : to refresh one's memory : renew one's skill or knowledge — used with *on* ⟨*brushing up* on his golf⟩ ⟨*brushing up* on their understanding of the accepted maritime law —F.L.Paxson⟩ ⟨*brush up* on the significant dates before the history exam⟩
brushup \ˈ≈,≈\ *n* -s [*brush up*] **1 a** : review or practice with the intent of refreshing the memory or polishing up a skill ⟨the orchestra needed a good deal of ~ before the performance⟩ ⟨a special ~ course⟩ ⟨a little instructive ~ on English history —Mollie Panter-Downes⟩ **b** : a period of such review or practice ⟨the play had a two-week ~ before opening in New York⟩ **2** : a fixing up of something that has begun to show signs of age or wear or that shows slight imperfections ⟨the painters . . . had been doing some ~ work in the halls —E.D.Radin⟩
brush wheel *n* [[3]*brush*] **1** : a wheel used formerly to turn another wheel by the friction of bristles fixed in the outer rim **2** : a circular revolving brush used for polishing
brush wolf *n* [[1]*brush*] : COYOTE
brushwood \ˈ≈,≈\ *n* [[1]*brush* + *wood*] **1** : the wood of small branches esp. when cut or broken **2** : a thicket composed of shrubs and small trees
brushwork \ˈ≈,≈\ *n* [[3]*brush* + *work*] **1** : work done with a brush (as in painting) **2** : the distinctive and characteristic use of the tools and equipment of an art (as of a brush by a painter or words by a writer) : TECHNIQUE
[1]**brushy** \ˈbrəshē, -shi\ *adj* -ER/-EST [[3]*brush* + *-y*] : resembling a brush; *also* : SHAGGY, ROUGH
[2]**brushy** \"\ *adj* -ER/-EST [[1]*brush* + *-y*] : covered with or abounding in brush or brushwood
brusque *also* **brusk** \ˈbrəsk *sometimes* -rüsk *or* -rü-\ *adj* -ER/-EST [F *brusque*, fr. It *brusco*, fr. ML *bruscus* butcher's-broom, perh. blend of L *ruscus* butcher's-broom and LL *brucus* heather — more at BRIER] : markedly short and abrupt : tending to be brisk, sharp, and often somewhat harsh or lacking gentleness **syn** see BLUFF
brusque·ly *also* **brusk·ly** *adv* : in a brusque manner
brusque·ness *n* -ES : the quality or state of being brusque
brus·que·rie \ˌbrəskəˈrē *sometimes* ¦brüs- *or* ¦brüs-\ *n* -s [F, fr. *brusque* + *-erie* -ery] : the quality or state of being brusque
brus·sels \ˈbrəsəlz\ *adj, usu cap* [fr. *Brussels*, Belgium] : of or from Brussels, the capital of Belgium : of the kind or style prevalent in Brussels
brussels brown *n, often cap 1st B* : NEW BRONZE
brussels carpet *n, usu cap B* **1** : a carpet made of variously colored worsted yarns first fixed in a foundation web of strong linen thread and then drawn up in loops to form the pattern — called also *body Brussels*; see WILTON **2** : an inexpensive substitute for Brussels carpet that is made of a single-colored yarn varied in color by dyeing at intervals or of undyed yarn with a printed pattern — called also *tapestry Brussels*
brussels classification *n, usu cap B* : UNIVERSAL DECIMAL CLASSIFICATION
brussels griffon *n, usu cap B & sometimes cap G* : a shaggy reddish brown wire-haired griffon (sense 1)
brussels lace *n, usu cap B* **1** : any of various fine needlepoint or bobbin laces with floral designs made orig. in or near Brussels **2** : a machine-made net of hexagonal mesh
brussels sprout *n, often cap B* **1** : any of the edible small green heads resembling diminutive cabbages and borne in the lower axils of the stem of a plant (*Brassica oleracea gemmifera*) closely related to the cabbage and cauliflower **2** : the plant that bears Brussels sprouts — usu. used in pl.

Brussels sprouts

brust \ˈbrüst, -rəst\ *dial Brit var of* [1]BURST
brus·tle \ˈbrəsəl, -rüs-\ *dial var of* BRISTLE
[1]**brut** \ˈbrüt\ *n* -s *cap* [MW, fr. MF *Brut*, legendary settler of Britain, fr. ML *Brutus*] : any of several medieval chronicles of Britain tracing the history and legend of the country from the exploits of mythical Brutus, descendant of Aeneas
[2]**brut** \ˈbrüet\ *adj* [F, lit., rough — more at BRUTE] *of champagne* : very dry : usu. containing less than 1.5 percent sugar by volume : drier than extra sec
[1]**bru·ta** \ˈbrüd·ə\ *n pl, cap* [NL, fr. L, neut. pl. of *brutus* heavy — more at BRUTE] *in former classifications* : an order of mammals comprising the edentates, elephants, and walruses
[2]**bruta** \"\ [NL, fr. L] *syn of* EDENTATA
bru·tage \brüˈtäzh, brüetäzh\ *n* -s [F, fr. *brut* rough + *-age* — more at BRUTE] : BRUTING
bru·tal \ˈbrüd·ᵊl, -ütᵊl\ *adj, sometimes* -ER/-EST [ME, fr. MF or ML; MF, fr. ML *brutalis*, fr. *brutus* brute, animal + L *-alis* -al — more at BRUTE] **1** *archaic* : of, belonging to, or typical of beasts or animals as distinguished from man : ANIMAL ⟨thee, Serpent . . . to me so friendly grown above the rest of ~ kind —John Milton⟩ **2** : befitting or resembling a brute: as **a** : stemming from or based on crude animal instincts : grossly ruthless ⟨a ~ attack⟩ **b** : devoid of mercy or compassion : cruel and cold-blooded ⟨blunt and occasionally ~, but . . . never niggling and peevish —Cleanth Brooks⟩ **c** : harsh and severe : unpleasant to a degree that is nearly unbearable ⟨another summer of ~ heat⟩ ⟨two ~ winters in a row⟩ **d** : unpleasantly accurate and incisive : undeniable but harsh ⟨the ~ truth⟩ ⟨the ~ facts must be faced and action taken⟩
syn BRUTISH, BESTIAL, FERAL, BEASTLY, BRUTE: BRUTAL stresses sensuality, coarse cruelty, or crude grossness, always without the alleviation of normal human moderation, reticence, sympathy, mercy, or consideration of others ⟨Constance Kent was rather a beauty—a nice girl with an engaging air; yet she cut her little brother's throat in a thoroughly *brutal* manner —W.H. Wright⟩ ⟨*brutal* Ode and St. Dunstan force their rude way into the quiet room, and hurl coarse insults at the sweet-faced queen —J.K.Jerome⟩ BRUTISH stresses either gross sensuality completely unchecked or utter animal stupidity unenlightened by even faint human intelligence ⟨in the mines and factories an indiscriminate sexual intercourse of the most *brutish* kind was the only relief from the tedium and drudgery of the day —Lewis Mumford⟩ ⟨it requires wisdom to liberate ourselves from natural *brutish* stupidity and enslaving passions —M.R. Cohen⟩ BESTIAL usu. indicates either a complete lack of human intelligence and refinement or an utter lustful depravity ⟨they were much impressed with the size and *bestial* ferocity of the niggers whom they had now learned to call "Paythans" —Rudyard Kipling⟩ ⟨he is a thief, a murderer, a defiler, a *bestial*, lecherous dog —Rafael Sabatini⟩ FERAL stresses wild fury and ferocity like a wild beast's ⟨her wrath, savage and *feral*, utterly possessed her. She was like a wild animal, cornered and conscious of defeat —W.H.Wright⟩ BEASTLY may imply beastlike indelicacy, cruelty, or sensuality ⟨some woman, coarse and low and vulgar, some *beastly* creature in whom all the horror of sex is blatant —W.S.Maugham⟩ ⟨systematic mutilation of the body rendered the crime particularly *beastly* —Earl of Birkenhead b. 1907⟩ Often it simply implies irritation or disgust on the speaker's part ⟨she can't eat the soup—no more can I. It's *beastly*. —W.M.Thackeray⟩ BRUTE may connote cruelty or stupidity ⟨the *brute* mentality of the clods who constitute the parish —A.J.Cronin⟩ ⟨murdered, along the coast of Lincolnshire, out of *brute* spite —Charles Kingsley⟩
bru·tal·i·tar·i·an \(ˌ)brüˌtaləˈterēən, *attrib* ˈ *or* (ˈ)brüˈtalə,t-\ *adj* [*brutality* + *-arian* (as in *humanitarian*; prob. newly coined in the 30s or construed as a blend of *brutal* and *totalitarian*] : advocating or practicing brutality ⟨a ~ regime⟩ — **bru·tal·i·tar·i·an·ism** \(ˌ)brüˌtaləˈterēəˌnizəm\ *n* -s
bru·tal·i·ty \brüˈtaləd·ē, -ətē, -i\ *n* -ES **1** : the quality or state of being brutal ⟨impulse without sensitiveness spells ~ —A.N.

Whitehead⟩ **2 :** a brutal act or course of action ⟨the ~ of war⟩

bru·tal·i·za·tion \ˌbrüd·ᵊlə'zāshən, -üt²l-, -ᵊlˌī'z-\ *n* -s **:** the act or process of brutalizing **:** the state of being brutalized ⟨the ~ that comes from indifference to the hardships of others —J.R.Ellingston⟩

bru·tal·ize \'brüd·ᵊlˌīz, -üt²l-\ *vt* -ED/-ING/-S [*brutal* + *-ize*] **1 a :** to make brutal, unfeeling, or inhuman ⟨perhaps . . . we shall ~ ourselves sufficiently to make regret impossible —E.W. Griffiths⟩ **b :** to alter (as by distorting) so as to lessen or destroy the essential or aesthetic value of **c :** to make less sensitive or humane ⟨the experience of war *brutalized* him somewhat⟩ ⟨in his lower moments *brutalizing* . . . noble legends into farce —O.W.Holmes †1935⟩ **2 :** to treat brutally ⟨man *brutalizing* man on the indifferent earth —I.L.Salomon⟩

bru·tal·ly \'brüd·ᵊlē, -üt²lē, -li\ *adv* **:** in a brutal manner **:** to an extent considered brutal

bru·tal·ness \-ᵊlnəs\ *n* -ES **:** the quality or state of being brutal

¹brute \'brüt, *usu* -üd·+V\ *adj* [ME, fr. MF *brut* rough, brutish, fr. L *brutus* stupid, irrational, lit., heavy; akin to L *gravis* heavy — more at GRIEVE] **1 :** of, relating to, or typical of animals, brutes, or beasts **:** not possessed of human rational powers ⟨the same kind of service for the ~ world that the study of genealogy has rendered to human history —*Encyc. Americana*⟩ **2 :** having neither life nor soul **:** not conscious or animate ⟨as we left the harbor, the North Atlantic, ~ gray, heckled the ship with its strength —Saul Bellow⟩ **3 :** resembling an animal in quality, action, or instinct **:** BRUTAL: as **a :** dull, stupid, and unreasoning **b :** cruel and savage **:** utterly lacking in sensitivity or higher feelings **c :** coarse and grossly sensual ⟨the ~ instinct that prompted the crime⟩ **4 :** purely physical **:** involving no mental exertion or effort ⟨by ~ strength they broke the heavy door⟩ **5 :** not influenced or governed by human intelligence **:** utterly insensible and unaffected by reason **6 :** rough, crude, and unrefined **:** unrelieved and unmodified ⟨the ~ facts with which . . . we have to come to terms —Aldous Huxley⟩ **syn** see BRUTAL

²brute \"\ *n* -s [ML *brutus*, fr. L *brutus*, adj.] **1 a :** an animal other than man of the class of mammals or certain other vertebrates **:** BEAST **b** *chiefly dial* **:** a male bovine animal **:** BULL **2 :** one that is brutal; *esp* **:** a coarse, insensate, unfeeling, crude, or cruel man ⟨he was a drunken loutish ~⟩

³brute \"\ *obs var of* BRUIT

⁴brute \"\ *vt* -ED/-ING/-S [back-formation fr. *bruting*] **:** to shape (a diamond) by rubbing or grinding with another diamond or a diamond chip

brute·ly *adv* **:** in the manner of a brute

brute·ness *n* -ES **:** the quality or state of being brute

brut·ing \'brüd·iŋ\ *n* -s [modif. (influenced by E *-ing*) of F *brutage* — more at BRUTAGE] **:** the process of bruting a diamond

brut·ish \'brüd·ish, -üt|, |ēsh\ *adj* [ME *brutisshe*, fr. ¹*brute* + *-isshe* -ish] **1 :** of or relating to animals as opposed to man **:** resembling or typical of a brute or beast ⟨~ form rather than human —John Milton⟩ **2 a :** strongly and grossly sensual **:** utterly without sensitivity or delicacy **b :** marked by very little intelligence or rationality ⟨an insensitive and ~ reaction to any reasonable suggestion⟩ ⟨~ aesthetic apathy —Cyril Connolly⟩ **c :** stupidly cruel ⟨plantations where slavery was . . . ~ —Allan Nevins & H.S.Commager⟩ **syn** see BRUTAL

brut·ish·ly *adv* **:** in a brutish manner

brut·ish·ness *n* -ES **:** the quality or state of being brutish

brut·ter \'brəd·ə(r)\ *n* -s [origin unknown] **1 :** BALLHOOTER **2 :** LIMBER

brux·el·lois \brēseIwä\ *n, pl* **bruxellois** *cap* [F, fr. *Bruxelles* (Brussels), Belgium] **:** a native or resident of Brussels, Belgium

brux·ism \'brəkˌsizəm\ *n* -s [irreg. (Gk *υ* & *χ* being transliterated respectively as *u* & *x* instead of *y* & *ch*) fr. Gk *brychein* to gnash the teeth + E *-ism;* akin to OIr *brōn* trouble, W *brwyn* stabbing pain, Lith *gráužti* to gnaw, OSlav *grysti*] **:** the habit of unconsciously gritting or grinding the teeth esp. in situations of stress or during sleep

bruxo·mania \ˌbrəksō+\ *n* -s [NL, irreg. fr. Gk *brychein* to gnash the teeth + NL *-o-* + *-mania*] **:** BRUXISM

bru·yère \brüēyeer\ *n* -s [F — more at BRIER] **:** ²BRIER

bry- *or* **bryo-** *comb form* [NL, moss, fr. Gk *bryo-* moss, catkin, fr. *bryon;* perh. akin to OHG *krūt* herb, cabbage — more at SAUERKRAUT] **:** moss ⟨*Bryaceae*⟩ ⟨*bryology*⟩

brya \'brīə\ *n, cap* [NL, fr. L, tamarisk, fr. Gk] **:** a genus of prickly shrubs and small trees (family Leguminosae) of the Caribbean region that yield a very durable hard wood — see GRANADILLA TREE

bry·a·ce·ae \brī'āsēˌē\ *n pl, cap* [NL, fr. *Bryum*, type genus + *-aceae*] **:** a family of acrocarpous mosses (order Eubryales) having symmetrical often pendent capsules with a double peristome, the inner one being ciliate — compare BRYUM — **bry·a·ceous** \(')brīˌāshəs\ *adj*

bry·a·les \brī'ā(ˌ)lēz\ *n pl, cap* [NL, fr. *Bryum* + *-ales*] *in some classifications* **:** an order or subclass of Musci comprising the mosses that have the spore case separated from the capsule wall by a hollow cylindrical intercellular space — compare EUBRYALES

bry·an·ite \'brīəˌnīt\ *n* -s *usu cap* [William O'*Bryan* †1868 Eng. preacher + E *-ite*] **:** a member of a Methodist body formerly called Bible Christians founded in England by William O'Bryan in 1815

bry·an·thus \brī'an(t)thəs\ *n* [NL, fr. *bry-* + *-anthus*] **1** *cap* **:** a genus of Old World prostrate mat-forming evergreen heaths (family Ericaceae) with 4-parted flowers in racemes that was formerly included in *Phyllodoce* **2** *pl* **bryanthuses** \-thəsəz\ *also* **bryan·thi** \-nˌthī\ **:** any plant of the genus *Bryanthus* or sometimes of the genus *Phyllodoce*

bryn·za \'brinzə\ *n* -s [Romanian *brînză*] **:** a ewe's-milk cheese made in central Europe and Asia Minor

bry·o·bia mite \(')brī¦ōbēə-\ *n* [NL *Bryobia* genus of mites, fr. *bry-* + *-bia*] **:** CLOVER MITE

bry·o·log·i·cal \ˌbrīə¦läjəkəl\ *adj* **:** of or relating to bryology

bry·ol·o·gist \brī'äləjəst\ *n* -s **:** a specialist in bryology

bry·ol·o·gy \-jē\ *n* -ES [ISV *bry-* + *-logy*] **1 a** *obs* **:** the science of mosses **b :** a branch of botany that deals with the bryophytes **2 a :** moss life (as of a region) ⟨the ~ of Wales⟩ **b :** the properties and life phenomena exhibited by a moss or moss type ⟨the ~ of sphagnum⟩

bry·o·nia \brī'ōnēə\ *n* [NL, fr. L, bryony, fr. Gk *bryōnia*, *bryōnē;* akin to *bryon* moss — more at BRY-] **1** *cap* **:** a small genus of perennial Old World herbaceous tendril-bearing vines (family Cucurbitaceae) having large leaves and small dioecious flowers with the staminate borne in racemes — see BRYONY **2** -s **:** the dried root of bryony (*Bryonia alba* or *B. dioica*) used as a cathartic

bry·o·ny *also* **bri·o·ny** \'brīənē, -ni\ *n* -ES [L *bryonia*] **1 :** a plant of the genus *Bryonia* (esp. *B. alba* or *B. dioica*) **2 :** BRYONIA 2

¹bryo·phyl·lum \ˌbrīə'filəm\ [NL, fr. *bry-* + *-phyllum*] *syn of* KALANCHOE

²bryophyllum \"\ *n* -s [NL, fr. *bry-* + *-phyllum*] **:** a succulent plant (*Kalanchoe pinnata*) with oblong simple or pinnate leaves

bry·oph·y·ta \brī'äfəd·ə\ *n pl, cap* [NL, fr. *bry-* + *-phyta*] **:** a division of nonflowering plants comprising the mosses and liverworts characterized by rhizoids rather than true roots, by little or no organized vascular tissue, by multicellular archegonia and antheridia in which only some of the cells are sporogenous, and by a clear-cut alternation of generations, the sporophyte being without chlorophyll and remaining attached to and nourished by the gametophyte — see HEPATICAE, MUSCI

bry·o·phyte \'brīəˌfīt\ *n* -s [NL *Bryophyta*] **:** a plant of the Bryophyta — **bry·o·phyt·ic** \¦==¦fid·ik\ *adj*

bry·op·si·da·ce·ae \(ˌ)brīˌäpsə'dāsēˌē\ *n pl, cap* [NL, fr. *Bryopsid-*, *Bryopsis*, type genus + *-aceae*] **:** a family of marine green algae (order Siphonales) having the characteristics of the genus *Bryopsis*

bry·op·sis \brī'äpsəs\ *n, cap* [NL, fr. *bry-* + *-opsis*] **:** a genus (the type of the family Bryopsidaceae) of marine green algae that occur in warmer seas and have nonseptate filaments forming a rhizomatous prostrate base and an upright pinnately branched portion

bryo·zoa \ˌbrīə'zōə\ *n pl, cap* [NL, fr. *bry-* + *-zoa*] **1 :** a small phylum of aquatic animals that reproduce by budding, that usu. form branching, flat, or mosslike colonies permanently attached on stones or seaweeds and enclosed by an external cuticle soft and gelatinous or rigid and chitinous or calcareous, and that consist of complex zooids each having an alimentary canal with distinct mouth and anus surrounded by a true coelom and associated with a protrusible lophophore — see AVICULARIUM, VIBRACULUM; BUGULA; ENTOPROCTA, GYMNOLAEMATA, PHYLACTOLAEMATA **2** *in some classifications* **:** a class or other division of Molluscoidea comprising the Bryozoa and the Entoprocta

¹bryo·zo·an \ˌbrīə'zōən\ *or* **bryo·zo·on** \-ōˌän\ *adj* [NL *bryozoon*, fr. *bry-* + *-zoon*] **:** of or relating to the Bryozoa

²bryozoan \"\ *or* **bryozoon** \"\ *n, pl* **bryozoans** \-ōənz\ *or* **bryo·zoa** \-ōə\ **1 :** an individual zooid of a bryozoan colony **2 :** an animal of the phylum Bryozoa

bryo·zoologist \ˌbrīə+\ *n* -s [blend of NL *Bryozoa* and E *zoologist*] **:** a specialist on the Bryozoa

bryth·on \'briˌthän\ *n* -s *cap* [W] **1 :** a member of the British branch of Celts **:** BRITON **2 :** a speaker of one of the Brythonic languages — compare GOIDEL

¹bry·thon·ic \bri'thänik\ *adj, usu cap* [*Brython* + *-ic*] **1 :** of, relating to, or characteristic of the Brythons **2 :** of, relating to, or characteristic of the division of the Celtic languages that includes Welsh, Cornish, and Breton — compare GOIDELIC

²brythonic \"\ *n* -s *cap* **:** the Brythonic branch of the Celtic languages — see INDO-EUROPEAN LANGUAGES table

bry·um \'brīəm\ *n, cap* [NL, alter. of L *bryon* moss, fr. Gk — more at BRY-] **:** a genus (the type of the family Bryaceae) of mosses containing species distinguished by mostly erect and tufted gametophytes and symmetrical short-necked capsules — compare MNIUM

brz *abbr* bronze

BS *or* **BSc** *abbr or n* -s Bachelor of Science

BS *abbr* **1** balance sheet **2** bill of sale **3** bill of store **4** bishop suffragan **5** bottom settlings **6** British standard

b's *or* **bs** *pl of* B

bsc *abbr* basic

b-scope *n, usu cap B* **:** a radarscope on which signals appear as bright spots that by their vertical or horizontal displacement indicate the angle and range of the target — compare A-SCOPE

bsh *abbr* bushel

b sharp \'=¦=\ *n, usu cap B* **:** the tone a half step above B and sounding enharmonically the same as C in the tempered scale

bskt *abbr* basket

bsmt *abbr* basement

BSt *abbr* bill of sight

b-stage resin \'=ˌ=-\ *n, usu cap B* **:** RESITOL

b star *n, usu cap B* **:** a star of spectral type B — see SPECTRAL TYPE table

b station *n, usu cap B* **:** a radio station aboard a ship

b switchboard *n, usu cap B* **:** a switchboard in a telephone exchange for receiving and completing trunk calls that originate in another exchange

bt *abbr* **1** baronet **2** bent **3** boat **4** bought **5** brevet

BT *abbr* **1** basic training **2** berth terms **3** board of trade

btn *abbr* battalion

btr *abbr* better

BTU *abbr* **1** board of trade unit **2** British thermal unit

btwn *abbr* between

bty *abbr* battery

bu \'b(y)ü\ *n, pl* **bu** [Jap] **1 :** an old Japanese rectangular coin orig. made of gold and from 1830 to 1870 of silver; *also* **:** a corresponding unit of value ⟨¼-*bu* and 2-*bu* pieces were issued⟩ **2 :** either of two Japanese units of measure: **a :** a unit of length equal to 0.1 inch **b :** TSUBO

bu *abbr* **1** blue **2** bulletin **3** bureau **4** bushel

bual \'bwäl, bü'äl\ *n* -s *usu cap* [Pg *boal*, a kind of white grape] **:** a rich golden-colored Madeira wine

bu·ang \'büˌäŋ\ *n, pl* **buang** *or* **buangs** *usu cap* **1 :** a Papuan people of the Morobe district, North-East New Guinea **2 :** a member of the Buang people

bu·at \'büət\ *var of* BOUET

bua·ze \'bwäzē\ *n* -s [Nyanja *bwazi*] **:** an African woody vine (*Securidaca longipedunculata*) of the family Polygalaceae yielding a fiber that resembles flax

¹bub \'bəb\ *n* -s [perh. short for *bubble*] *archaic* **:** strong malt liquor

²bub \"\ *n* -s [short for ²*bubby*] **:** BROTHER, LAD, BOY — used chiefly as a term of address and with an implication of superiority to the one addressed ⟨come on, ~, make it snappy⟩

¹bu·ba·line \'byübəˌlīn, -ˌlən\ *adj* [NL *Bubalis* + E *-ine*] **:** like, relating to, or being one of certain large African antelopes of *Alcelaphus* and related genera that were formerly regarded as forming a subfamily (Bubalinae) of Bovidae

²bubaline \"\ *adj* [NL *Bubalus* + E *-ine*] **:** of, like, or relating to *Bubalus* or a related genus

¹bu·ba·lis \'byübələs\ [NL, fr. Gk *boubalis*, *boubalos*, an African antelope] *syn of* ALCELAPHUS

²bubalis \"\ *or* **bu·bal** *also* **bu·bale** \'byübəl\ *n, pl* **bubalises** *or* **bubals** *also* **bubales :** the northern hartebeest

bu·ba·lus \'byübələs\ *n, cap* [NL, fr. LGk *boubalos* buffalo, fr. Gk, an African antelope, prob. fr. *bous* head of cattle — more at cow] **:** a genus of Bovidae comprising the nearly hairless mud-wallowing buffaloes of Asia, certain large extinct relatives, and in some classifications the buffaloes of Africa

bubbies *pl of* BUBBY

¹bub·ble \'bəbəl\ *vb* **bubbled**; **bubbled**; **bubbling** \'bəb(ə)liŋ\ **bubbles** [ME *bublen*, *bobelen*, prob. of imit. origin like D *bobbelen* to bubble, MLG *bubbeln*, Lith *bubséti*] *vi* **1 a :** to form or produce bubbles ⟨soup *bubbling* in the kettle⟩ **b :** to move upward or rise in or as if in bubbles ⟨gases *bubbling* from the mud⟩ — often used with *up* ⟨cool water *bubbling* up from the ground⟩ ⟨these questions ~ up from time to time⟩ **2 :** to flow out or pour out with a gurgling sound suggesting the forming and rising of bubbles ⟨a clear fountain *bubbling* in the shade⟩ **3 :** to suggest bubbling water: **a :** to make gurgling or warbling sounds ⟨a nightingale softly *bubbling* in the shrubbery⟩ ⟨her carefree laughter *bubbled* behind us⟩ **b :** to utter as though giving off bubbles either with sparkle and effervescence ⟨songs that ~ with wit and grace⟩ or with persistent monotonous repetition ⟨they ~ of Marx or Disraeli to their dying day —*Times Lit. Supp.*⟩ **c :** to be or become lively or effervescent (as with joy) **:** bubble over ⟨he looked like a good soldier and *bubbled* with natural joyousness —Alan Sullivan⟩ **d** *Scot* **:** BLUBBER, SNIVEL **e :** to be in agitated movement or activity **:** rise into consciousness usu. unexpectedly **:** CHURN, STIR — used chiefly of intangibles ⟨such contacts soon set his brain to *bubbling* with new ideas⟩ ~ *vt* **1 :** to utter (as words) bubblingly **:** express in bubbles or as if in giving off bubbles ⟨she *bubbled* questions —R.A.W. Hughes⟩ ⟨dozens of birds *bubbling* their joy to the clearing sky⟩ **2 a :** to cause to bubble ⟨~ cocoa and sugar together in a little water —*Better Homes & Gardens*⟩ **b :** BURP **3** *archaic* **:** CHEAT, DECEIVE, DELUDE **4 :** to pass (as gas) through some medium in the form of discrete bubbles

²bubble \"\ *n* -s *often attrib* **1 :** a small globule typically hollow and light: as **a :** a small body of air or gas within a liquid ⟨~*s* rising in champagne⟩ **b :** a thin film of liquid inflated with air or gas ⟨soap ~*s*⟩ **c :** a hollow globule of blown glass (as a small floating bead formerly used for testing the strength of spirits) **d :** a globule (as of air) in a transparent solid ⟨windowpanes marred with ~*s* and wavy patches⟩; *broadly* **:** such globules constituting an imperfection in glass and resulting from the trapping of air or gas during the melting process **e :** the globule of air in the tube of a spirit level; *sometimes* **:** the tube and its contents **f :** BUBBLE SHELL **g** *Scot* **:** mucus from the nose **h :** BUBBLE CANOPY **2 a :** something that lacks firmness, solidity, or reality **:** a false show ⟨a dream of what thou wast . . . a breath, a ~ —Shak.⟩ **b :** a delusive scheme **:** a dishonest speculation ⟨the South sea ~⟩ **3** *archaic* **:** one readily deceived or tricked **:** DUPE, GULL **4 a :** a bubbling as of boiling or flowing water ⟨we'll not be long, the kettle's just at the ~⟩ **b :** a sound like that of bubbling **:** a gurgling or warbling song ⟨the cadenced ~ of certain bird songs⟩

bubble and squeak *n* [so called fr. the sounds made in cooking the dish] **:** a dish consisting of potatoes and cabbage or esp. formerly potatoes, cabbage, and meat fried together

bubble bath *n* **1 :** a liquid or granular perfumed preparation that foams in water **2 :** a bath prepared with bubble bath

bubble bowl *n* **:** a somewhat spherical bowl usu. of clear glass and with a small lipless opening used chiefly for ornamental display (as of floating short-stemmed flowers)

bubble canopy *n* **:** an airplane-cockpit canopy that is usu. transparent, nearly hemispherical, seamless, and without bracing or supports

bubble cap *n* **:** a device (as a metal cup with notches or slots around the edge) that is inverted over a hole in a plate in a bubble tower for effecting contact of vapors rising from the plate below and liquid already on the plate

bubble chamber *n* **:** a chamber in which a superheated liquid is produced so that an ionizing particle passing through the liquid initiates boiling along its path, the strings of bubbles so produced being photographed and indicating the behavior of the ionizing particle

bubble dance *n* **:** a solo dance act performed in or as if in the nude, the dancer using one or more balloons for covering — compare FAN DANCE

bubble disease *n* **:** a disease of mushrooms caused by a fungus (*Mycogone perniciosa*) that grows over infected mushrooms in a white mat causing deformation and sometimes the deposition of brownish drops on the injured surface

bubble fountain *n* **:** a bubbler drinking fountain

bubble glass *n* **:** glass in which bubbles have been induced during manufacture for artistic effect

bubble gum *n* **:** a chewing gum that can be blown into large bubbles

bub·ble·less \'bəbəl(l)əs\ *adj* **:** being without bubbles

bub·ble·ment \'bəbəlmənt\ *n* -s **:** an effervescent state or condition

bubble nest *n* **:** a collection of bubbles made by certain fishes as a place in which to deposit their eggs

bubble octant *n* **:** an octant using the same principle as a bubble sextant

bubble over *vi* **:** to be so filled with something (as with emotion, an idea, or information) as to be unable to restrain it from escaping as if in bubbles ⟨she came back *bubbling over* with news⟩; *esp* **:** to give vent to emotion in a series of impulses ⟨he frisked around her *bubbling over* with joy —Nathaniel Hawthorne⟩

bub·bler \'bəb(ə)lə(r)\ *n* -s **1 :** FRESHWATER DRUM **2 a** (1) **:** DRINKING FOUNTAIN (2) **:** the spout of a drinking fountain **b :** any of several devices in which air or gas is bubbled through liquid

bubble sextant *n* **:** a sextant used esp. in aerial navigation in which the image of the heavenly body being observed is brought to the edge of a bubble instead of to the sea horizon, the bubble appearing in its proper position in the field of view only when the sextant is held so that its zero plane is the observer's horizontal plane

bubble shell *or* **bubble snail** *n* **1 :** any of a number of marine gastropod mollusks (order Opisthobranchia) having the shell comparatively thin and small with the body whorl enveloping the other whorls (as members of the Akeridae or of the genus *Bulla*) — see HAMINOEA **2 :** a freshwater snail of *Physa* or a related genus

bub·blet \'bəb(ə)lət\ *n* -s [blend of *bubble* and *-let*] **:** a small bubble

bubble tower *n* **:** a tower in which gas or vapor is bubbled through liquid; *specif* **:** a plate tower (as for fractionating petroleum distillates) in which the plates are provided with bubble caps

bubble tube *n* **:** the glass tube containing the liquid and bubble in a spirit level

bubbling *adj* **:** CHURNING, EFFERVESCENT, EFFUSIVE — **bub·bling·ly** *adv*

¹bub·bly \'bəb(ə)lē, -li\ *adj* -ER/-EST [²*bubble* + *-y*] **1 :** full of bubbles **:** BUBBLING, EFFERVESCENT **2 :** resembling a bubble ⟨buildings with ~ domes⟩

²bubbly \"\ *n* -ES *chiefly Brit* **:** CHAMPAGNE

bub·bly-jock \ˌbəbli¦jäk, ¦büb-\ *n* -s [¹*bubbly* (fr. its cry) + *Jock* (rustic, clown)] *chiefly Scot* **:** a male turkey

¹bub·by \'bəbē *also* 'bübē\ *n* -ES [perh. imit. of the noise made by a sucking infant] **:** BREAST — now often considered vulgar

²bub·by \'bəbē\ *n* -ES [prob. baby talk alter. of ¹*brother*] **:** little boy **:** BROTHER — used chiefly as a familiar or affectionate term of address

bubbybush \'==ˌ=\ *or* **bubby-blossom** \'==ˌ==\ *also* **bubby** *or* **bubby-flower** *or* **bubby-shrub** *n* [¹*bubby;* prob. fr. the red flowers compared to human nipples] **:** CAROLINA ALLSPICE

bu·be \'büˌbā\ *or* **bu·bi** \-(ˌ)bē\ *n, pl* **bube** *or* **bubes** *or* **bubi** *or* **bubis** *usu cap* **1 a :** a Bantu-speaking people of the island of Fernando Po, West Africa **b :** a member of such people **2 :** a Bantu language of the Bube people

bu·binga \bü'biŋ(g)ə\ *n* -s [Bantu] **1 :** any of several large leguminous trees of tropical West Africa (esp. *Didelotia africana* and members of the genera *Copaifera* and *Brachystegia*) **2 :** the wood of a bubinga; *esp* **:** the hard heavy heartwood of a bubinga that is similar in appearance to rosewood and is used for veneers — called also *African rosewood*

¹bu·bo \'b(y)ü(ˌ)bō\ *n* -ES [ML, fr. Gk *boubōn* groin, gland, bubo] **1 :** an inflammatory swelling of a lymph gland esp. in the groin that is due to the absorption of infective material (as in gonorrhea, syphilis, or the plague) **2 :** LYMPHOGRANULOMA

²bubo \"\ *n, cap* [NL, fr. L, horned owl; akin to Gk *byas*, *byza* owl, Arm *bu*, *bueč*, Per *bum*] **:** a nearly cosmopolitan genus of large horned owls including the eagle owls — see GREAT HORNED OWL

bu·bon·ic \(')b(y)ü¦bänik, -nēk\ *adj* [ML *bubon-*, *bubo* + E *-ic*] **:** of or attended with buboes

bubonic plague *n* **:** plague in which the formation of buboes is a prominent feature — compare PNEUMONIC PLAGUE

bu·bon·i·dae \b(y)ü'bänəˌdē\ *n pl, cap* [NL, fr. *Bubon-*, *Bubo*, type genus + *-idae*] *syn of* STRIGIDAE — used in place of Strigidae as usu. restricted when Strigidae replaces Tytonidae

bu·bon·o·cele \-nəˌsēl\ *n* -s [Gk *boubōnokēlē*, fr. *boubōn* groin + *-o-* + *-kēlē* -cele] **:** an inguinal hernia; *esp* **:** a hernia in which the hernial pouch descends only as far as the groin and forms a swelling there like a bubo

bubs *pl of* BUB

bubu *var of* BOO-BOO

bu·buk·le \'b(y)üˌbəkəl\ *n* -s [blend of ¹*bubo* and *carbuncle*] *archaic* **:** a large red blemish or pimple — **bu·buk·led** \-kəld\ *adj, archaic*

bucan *var of* BUCCAN

bu·ca·re \'bükəˌrā, -ˌrē, bü'kärē\ *n* -s [Sp *búcare*, *bucare*] **:** a spiny Peruvian tree (*Erythrina poeppigiana*) widely planted for shading coffee and cacao plantations in the West Indies

bucayo *var of* BUKAYO

¹buc·ca \'bəkə\ *n* -s [L — more at POCK] **:** CHEEK; *specif* **:** the part of the insect head wall adjoining and sometimes including the mouth

²bucca \"\ *n* -s [Corn, hobgoblin, scarecrow; akin to W *bwgan* bogey] *dial Eng* **:** SCARECROW

buc·cal \'bəkəl\ *adj* [L *bucca* cheek + E *-al*] **1** *of an oral structure* **:** directed toward the cheek ⟨the ~ aspect of the gum⟩ **2 :** of, relating to, or involving the cheeks ⟨a large ~ ganglion⟩ **3 :** of, relating to, involving, or lying within the mouth **:** ORAL ⟨~ organs⟩ ⟨a strong ~ capsule⟩

buccal gland *n* **1 :** any of the small racemose mucous glands in the mucous membrane lining the cheeks **2 :** any of the lymphatic glands situated near the buccinator muscle

buc·cal·ly \-kəl(l)ē\ *adv* **:** toward the cheek

buccal mass *n* **:** the mouthparts in mollusks other than bivalves and the muscles by which they are operated and with which they generally form a more or less compact mass

¹buc·can \(ˌ)bə'kan, 'bəkən\ *or* **bu·can** *or* **bou·can** \(')bü¦kan, -kän\ *vt* -ED/-ING/-S [MF *boucaner*, fr. *boucan*] **:** to expose (meat) in strips to fire and smoke upon a buccan

²buccan \"\ *or* **bucan** *or* **boucan** \"\ *n* -s [MF *boucan*, of Tupian origin; akin to Tupi *mukém* buccan] **1 :** a wooden frame or grid for roasting, smoking, or drying meat over fire **2 :** buccaned meat

¹buc·ca·neer \ˌbəkə¦ni(ə)r, -iə\ *n* -s [F *boucanier* French woodsman of the 17th century in the West Indies, pirate, fr. *boucaner* to buccan; fr. their typical manner of conserving meat] **1 :** a person who dries and smokes flesh or fish after the manner of the Indians — orig. used of the French settlers in Haiti who hunted wild cattle and swine **2 :** one of the freebooters preying upon Spanish ships and settlements esp. in the West Indies in the 17th century; *broadly* **:** PIRATE **3 :** a dark reddish orange that is deeper and slightly redder than average lacquer red, redder, stronger, and slightly darker than ocher red, and redder and deeper than burnt sienna **4 :** an unscrupulous adventurer esp. in politics or business ⟨railroad ~*s* —Owen Lattimore⟩ ⟨financial ~*s* —John Dos Passos⟩

²**buccaneer** \"\ *vi* ED/-ING/-S **:** to act or live as a buccaneer

buc·che·ro \'bükə,rō\ *n* -S [It, fr. Sp *búcaro* clay vase, prob. fr. Pg — more at BOCCARO] **:** an ancient unglazed and unpainted gray, red, or black pottery often ornamented with designs in relief that is found in Tuscany, Italy

buc·ci·na \'bəksənə\ *also* **buc·cin** \-sən\ *n, pl* **bucci·nae** \-,nē\ *also* **buccins** [L *buccina, bucina,* fr. *bu-* (fr. *bov-, bos* head of cattle) + *-cina* (fr. *canere* to sing, play) — more at COW, CHANT] **:** a Roman military trumpet shaped like the letter C

buc·ci·na·tor \'bəksə,nād·ə(r)\ *n* -S [NL, fr. L *bucinator, buccinator* trumpeter, fr. *bucinatus, buccinatus* (past part. of *bucinare, buccinare* to sound the trumpet, fr. *bucina, buccina* trumpet) + *-or*] **:** a thin broad muscle forming the wall of the cheek and serving to compress the cheek against the teeth and to retract the angle of the mouth — **buc·ci·na·to·ry** \-,nə-,tōrē,-,nād·ərē\ *adj*

buc·cin·i·dae \,bək'sinə,dē\ *n pl, cap* [NL, fr. *Buccinum,* type genus + *-idae*] **:** a family of marine gastropod mollusks (suborder Stenoglossa) — see WHELK

buc·ci·num \'bəksənəm\ *n, cap* [NL, fr. L *buccinum, bucinum* trumpet, a shellfish, fr. *buccina, bucina* trumpet] **:** a genus (the type of the family Buccinidae) of marine gastropod mollusks comprising the typical whelks

bucco *var of* BUCHU

bucco- *comb form* [prob. fr. NL, fr. L *bucca* cheek — more at POCK] **:** buccal and ⟨*bucco*gingival⟩ ⟨*bucco*lingual⟩

buc·con·i·dae \(,)bə'känə,dē\ *n pl, cap* [NL, fr. *Buccon-, Bucco,* type genus (fr. L, babbler, blockhead, fr. *bucca* cheek, mouth) + *-idae* — more at POCK] **:** a family of large-headed insectivorous tropical American birds (order Piciformes) having long heavy bills and comprising the puffbirds

buccra *var of* BUCKRA

buc·cu·la \'bəkyələ\ *n, pl* **buccu·lae** \-,lē, -,lī\ [NL, fr. L, small cheek, dim. of *bucca* cheek] **:** one of the elevated plates or ridges beneath the head on either side of the rostrum of members of the Heteroptera

buc·cu·la·trix \,bəkyə'lā·triks\ *n, cap* [NL, fr. L *buccula* + *-trix*] **:** a genus of small moths (family Lyonetiidae) having larvae that feed in or on leaves and spin fusiform ribbed cocoons — see APPLE BUCCULATRIX

bu·cel·las \b(y)ü'seləs\ *n* -ES *usu cap* [Pg, fr. *Bucellas,* village near Lisbon, Portugal, where it is made] **:** a Portuguese white wine

bu·ceph·a·la \byü'sefələ\ *n, cap* [NL, fr. Gk *boukephalē,* fem. of *boukephalos* bullheaded, fr. *bous* bull, ox, head of cattle + *kephalē* head — more at COW, CEPHALIC] **:** a genus of ducks consisting of the goldeneyes and the buffleheads

bu·ce·phal·i·dae \,byüsə'falə,dē\ *n pl, cap* [NL, fr. *Bucephalus,* type genus + *-idae*] **:** a family of atypical digenetic trematodes that parasitize the intestines of various fishes and that have the mouth in the middle of the ventral surface, a saccular intestine, a single anterior sucker, and a posterior genital pore

¹**bu·ceph·a·lus** \byü'sefələs\ *n, pl* **bucephaluses** \-ləsəz\ *or* **bucepha·li** \-,lī\ [after *Bucephalus,* horse of Alexander the Great †323B.C. king of Macedon, fr. L, fr. Gk *Boukephalos*] *archaic* **:** a riding horse esp. if spirited and mettlesome — often used ironically

²**bucephalus** \"\ *n, cap* [NL, fr. Gk *boukephalos* bullheaded — more at BUCEPHALA] **:** a genus of small digenetic trematodes having the mouth near the center of the ventral surface and the intestine saclike and not bifurcated and comprising intestinal parasites of carnivorous fishes

bu·ce·ros \'byüsə,räs\ *n, cap* [NL, fr. Gk *boukerōs* with horns like a head of cattle, fr. *bous* head of cattle + *keras* horn — more at HORN] **:** the type genus of Bucerotidae comprising a number of typical hornbills — see BUCEROTES

bu·ce·ro·tes \,byüsə'rōd·(,)ēz\ *n pl, cap* [NL, fr. pl. of *Bucerot-, Buceros*] **:** a suborder (coextensive with the family Bucerotidae) of Coraciiformes comprising the hornbills

bu·cha·rest \'bükə,rest, ,=='= *also* -byü-\ *adj, usu cap* [fr. *Bucharest,* capital of Romania] **:** of or from Bucharest, the capital of Romania **:** of the kind or style prevalent in Bucharest

buch·ite \'bü,kīt\ *n* -S [G *buchit,* fr. Baron Christian L. von *Buch* †1853 Ger. mineralogist + G *-it* -ite] **:** a vitreous metamorphic rock produced by the contact action of basalt or by friction metamorphism

bu·chloë \'byüklə,wē\ *n, cap* [NL, fr. Gk *bous* head of cattle + *chloē* young grass; akin to Gk *chloos* light green — more at COW, GLOW] **:** a genus of perennial stoloniferous grasses (family Gramineae) having pistillate and staminate spikelets borne on the same or separate plants, the pistillate in sessile capitate clusters and the staminate in elongated one-sided racemes — see BUFFALO GRASS

buch·man·ism \'bükmə,nizəm, 'bək-\ *n* -S *cap* [Frank N.D. *Buchman* b1878 Am. evangelist, its founder + E *-ism*] **:** OXFORD GROUP MOVEMENT

buch·man·ite \-,nīt\ *n* -S *usu cap* [F. *Buchman* + E *-ite*] **:** a member of the Oxford Group movement **:** a follower of the religious reformer Frank Buchman or his teachings

buch·nera \'bəknərə, 'bük-\ *n, cap* [NL, after J.G.*Buchner,* 18th cent. Ger. botanist] **:** a genus of herbs (family Scrophulariaceae) chiefly of warm regions with mostly opposite leaves and showy white or bluish purple flowers in bracted spikes — see BLUEHEARTS

büch·ner funnel \'büknə(r), 'bɛkn-\ *n, usu cap B* [after Ernst *Büchner* *fl*1888 Ger. chemist, its inventor] **:** a cylindrical often porcelain filtering funnel that has a perforated plate on which the filter paper is placed and that is used usu. with a vacuum

bu·chu \'b(y)ü(,)k(y)ü\ *also* **buc·co** \'bə(,)kō\ *or* **bucku** \'bə(,)k(y)ü\ *n* -S [Zulu *bucu*] **1 :** the dried leaves of certain plants of the genera *Barosma* and *Diosma* used as a diuretic and diaphoretic: as **a :** those of either of two short-leafed plants (*B. setulina* and *B. crenulata*) — called also *oval buchu, short buchu* **b :** those of a long-leafed plant (*B. serratifolia*) — called also *long buchu* **2 :** a plant of the genera *Barosma* and *Diosma*

buchu camphor *n* **:** DIOSPHENOL

¹**buck** \'bək\ *n* -S *see senses 1&3, often attrib* [ME *buck, bucke,* fr. OE *buc, bucca* he-goat, stag; akin to OHG *boc* he-goat, ON *bukkr,* MIr *bocc* he-goat, Arm *buz* lamb] **1** *or pl* **buck :** a male animal: **a :** a male deer or antelope — not usu. used of the male elk or moose or technically of the male red deer; compare BULL, STAG **b :** a male of any of several other four-footed mammals (as the goat, sheep, hare, rabbit, guinea pig, or rat); *specif* **:** RAM **c :** a male of some game fishes (as the salmon or shad) **2 :** a male human being **:** MAN: **a :** a dashing fellow **b :** a male Indian or Negro — often used disparagingly **3** *or pl* **buck :** ANTELOPE — often used in combination ⟨bush*buck*⟩ ⟨spring*buck*⟩ **4 a** [by shortening] **:** BUCKSKIN; *often* **:** an article (as a shoe) made of buckskin **b** *archaic* **:** a deerskin regarded as a unit of exchange in early dealings with American Indians **c** *slang* **:** DOLLAR 4a **5** [short for *sawbuck*] **:** SAWHORSE **6 a :** a supporting rack or frame: as (1) **:** a heavy square framework used in the glazing of leather (2) **:** a rack for plate glass (3) **:** a frame on which a clay model is built up (4) **:** a large jig used esp. in aircraft assembly operations **b :** a rough doorframe placed in a wall or partition during construction and used as a support to which the finished frame is made fast **c :** the padded usu. horizontal part of a pressing machine on which clothes are placed for pressing — compare SHOE **d :** a short thick leather-covered block for gymnastic vaulting usu. without pommels and adjustable for height — **go to buck** *of female rabbits and hares* **:** COPULATE

²**buck** \"\ *vb* -ED/-ING/-S [¹*buck,* influenced in some meanings by *butt,* v.] *vi* **1** *of a horse or mule* **:** to spring with a quick plunging leap arching the back and descending with the forelegs rigid and the head held as low as possible **2 :** to meet head on as if in butting: **a :** to charge an obstruction under power ⟨the plows . . . ~*ed* day and half the night to keep the roads open —Helen Rich⟩ **b :** to act, move, or stand firm in opposition ⟨East Bay legislators ~*ed* in vain —*Fortnight*⟩ — often used with *against* ⟨salmon ~*ing* against the stiff current⟩ ⟨you're the one who has ~*ed* against your churchmen —Zane Grey⟩ **c :** to oppose one electric potential or field to another so that there is counteraction or neutralization **3 a :** to move or react jerkily or erratically ⟨the vehicles ~*ed* in and out of the obstructions —Darrell Berrigan⟩ ⟨the way those early outboard motors would ~ and die on you —*Newsweek*⟩ **b :** to refuse to submit or agree **:** BALK; *sometimes* **:** to become resentful **4 :** to strive diligently for advancement or reward sometimes without regard to ethical behavior or the rights or interests of others — usu. used with *for* ⟨~*ing* for sergeant's stripes⟩ ~ *vt* **1 :** to throw or dislodge (as a rider) by bucking ⟨the pinto sunfished and ~*ed* Charley over the paddock fence⟩ — often used with *off* ⟨leaned all his weight on it as the pressure of the water tried to ~ him off the hose —C.D.Lewis⟩ **2 a** *archaic* **:** ¹BUTT **b :** to move in opposition to ⟨was ~*ing* sleet and snow all the way⟩ **c :** to act in opposition to **:** fight against **:** OPPOSE, RESIST ⟨there's no point in ~*ing* a well-established trend⟩; *sometimes* **:** to compete with ⟨the show occupied one of the toughest spots of the week . . . ~*ing* the fantastically popular Charlie McCarthy at the same hour —Charles Jackson⟩ **d :** to play or gamble against ⟨~*ing* the odds⟩ **e :** to hold a tool against (a rivet) in order to resist the force of hammering — often used with *up* ⟨the man who ~*s* up the rivets has a hot difficult job⟩ **f :** to carry, move, or load (heavy or troublesome objects) esp. with mechanical equipment **3 :** to charge into (the opponents' line in football) **4 :** to buck up — usu. used in passive ⟨Jumbo was greatly ~*ed* over it —*Time*⟩ **5 :** to restrain (a person) by tying the wrists together, passing the arms over the bent knees, and putting a stick across the arms and through the angle formed by the knees; *usu* **:** to punish (as a soldier) by so restraining **6 :** to pass esp. from one person to another **:** hand on ⟨it was easier to ~ the heavy sacks down the line than to carry them one by one⟩ ⟨the Post Office department ~*ed* the question on to Postmaster Pafford —*Time*⟩ — **buck the board :** to work as an employee of a railroad on the extra board or roster for part-time employment — **buck the tiger :** to play against the faro bank

³**buck** \"\ *n* -S **:** the act or an instance of bucking ⟨he gave easily to the first excited ~*s* of his pony —Rudyard Kipling⟩; *esp* **:** a charge by the ball carrier into the opposing line in football

⁴**buck** *adj* [prob. fr. ¹*buck* (man)] *slang* **:** being of the lowest grade within the military category to which one belongs ⟨a ~ private⟩ ⟨a ~ general⟩

⁵**buck** \"\ *vt* -ED/-ING/-S [prob. fr. ¹*buck* (sawhorse)] **1 :** to saw (felled trees) into logs or small pieces (as with a bucksaw) **2 :** BRING, CARRY ⟨~ water⟩ **3 :** to split (a stick of timber) into two crossties

⁶**buck** \'bək, 'bük\ *vt* -ED/-ING/-S [ME *bouken;* akin to MHG *büchen* to wash with lye, OHG *buohha* beech tree — more at BEECH] **1** *dial chiefly Brit* **:** to soak, steep, or boil in lye or suds **2** *dial chiefly Brit* **:** to wash (clothes) in lye or suds or by beating on stones in running water

⁷**buck** \"\ *n* -S **1** *dial chiefly Brit* **:** lye or suds in which cloth or yarn is soaked or boiled in bleaching or in which clothes are washed **2** *dial chiefly Brit* **:** the cloth or clothes soaked or washed in buck **:** WASH ⟨a jolly brown wench, a-washing of her ~ —Thomas D'Urfey⟩

⁸**buck** \'bək\ *vt* -ED/-ING/-S [D *beuken* (fr. MD *bōken, bōken*) or LG *bōken* to strike, fr. MLG *bōken;* akin to MHG *bocken, pochen* to strike, beat — more at POKE] **:** to break up **:** PULVERIZE ⟨~ ore samples⟩

⁹**buck** \"\ *n* -S [origin unknown] *Brit* **:** a basket for catching eels; *sometimes* **:** a frame supporting a group of such baskets

¹⁰**buck** \"\ *n* -S [short for earlier *buckhorn knife*] **1 :** an object formerly used in poker to mark the next player to deal or to deal a jackpot, the winner of each jackpot placing the buck in front of him; *esp* **:** a buckhorn-handled knife used for this purpose — see PASS **2 :** a token used as a mark or reminder in a gambling game (as one used to designate a player's point in a dice game) **3 :** a small object (as a silver token) used to mark the place of the officer who is to be served first in a naval wardroom

¹¹**buck** \"\ *var of* BUKH

¹²**buck** \"\ *adv* [origin unknown] *South & Midland* **:** STARK, COMPLETELY — usu. used in the phrase *buck naked*

buck ague *also* **buck ager** *n* [¹*buck*] **:** BUCK FEVER

buck-and-wing \,==='=\ *n* **:** a solo tap dance with sharp foot accents, springs, leg flings, and heel clicks that was adapted to the stage from a blend of Negro and Irish clog dancing

buck arm *n* **:** a crossarm placed parallel to line wires usu. to afford a takeoff for a branch circuit

buck·a·roo *or* **buck·e·roo** \'bəkə,rü, ,=='=\ *n* -S [by folk etymology fr. Sp *vaquero,* fr. *vaca* cow, fr. L *vacca* — more at VACCINE] **1 :** COWBOY 3a **2 :** BRONCOBUSTER

buckass \'=,=\ *adj* [⁴*buck* + *ass* (buttocks)] *slang* **:** LOW-DOWN ⟨a ~ private who does just what he's told —James Jones⟩

buck basket *n* [⁷*buck* (clothes) + *basket*] **:** CLOTHES BASKET ⟨conveyed me into a *buck basket* —Shak.⟩

buckbean \'=,=\ *n* [trans. of D *boksboon*] **:** a plant (*Menyanthes trifoliata*) that grows in bogs in Europe and America and has racemes of white or purplish flowers and trifoliolate intensely bitter leaves — called also *bogbean, bog myrtle, marsh trefoil*

buckbean family *n* **:** MENYANTHACEAE

buck·ber·ry \'bək- — *see* BERRY\ *n* [¹*buck* + *berry*] **1 :** a huckleberry (*Gaylussacia ursina*) of the southern U.S. having black insipid fruit eaten by deer **2 :** a deerberry (*Vaccinium stamineum*)

buck·board \'bək+,-\ *n* [obs. E *buck* body of a wagon + *board*] **:** a 4-wheeled driving vehicle having an elastic platform fastened without springs directly to the rear axle and the bolster of the front axle usu. with a seat above it often mounted on springs

buckboard

buckbrush \'=,=\ *n* [¹*buck* + *brush*] **:** any of various shrubby No. American plants that furnish browse for sheep, deer, and other animals: as **a :** either of two plants of the genus *Ceanothus* (*C. velutinus* and *C. sanguineus*) **b :** BUTTONBUSH **c :** a low much-branched shrub (*Purshia tridentata*) of the Rocky mountain region **d :** a shrub (*Cornus femina*) of eastern No. America with white flowers and fruit **e :** BUCKBUSH 1

buckbush \'=,=\ *n* [¹*buck*] **1 a :** WOLFBERRY 1 **b :** CORALBERRY 1 **2 :** BUCKBRUSH d

¹**bucked** \'bəkt\ *adj* [fr. past part. of ²*buck*] **:** PLEASED, ENCOURAGED **:** bucked up

²**bucked** \"\ *adj* [¹*buck* + *-ed*] *of teeth* **:** somewhat protuberant

bucked shin *n* [fr. past part. of ²*buck*] **:** stiffness of the leg of a horse due to muscular strain

¹**buck·een** \,bə'kēn\ *n* -S [¹*buck* + *-een*] *chiefly Irish* **:** a rather shabby young dandy ⟨after college he lived for some years the life of a ~ —W.M.Thackeray⟩

²**buckeen** \"\ *n* -S [D *bokkin,* fem. of *bok* male Indian (trans. of E *buck*), buck, fr. MD *boc;* akin to OHG *boc* he-goat — more at BUCK] *in Guiana* **:** an Indian woman

¹**buck·er** \'bəkə(r)\ *n* -S [²*buck* + *-er*] **:** one that bucks: as **a :** a bucking horse ⟨rodeo owners, who search all over the country for good ~*s* —Mary Elting⟩ **b :** a workman who cuts felled trees into shorter lengths — called also *crosscutter* **c :** a person who carries or moves something (as water or wood); *esp* **:** a worker who uses mechanical equipment to handle material (as bales) and load it **d :** one that bucks rivets — called also *bucker-up, dollyman* **e :** a miner that shovels coal down a chute or into a bin or mine car **f :** one that saws logs in making a fireguard **g :** one that lifts bales of hay onto a wagon or truck **h :** one that loads filled vegetable or fruit sacks in the field **i :** one that cuts staves for kegs **j :** a football player who bucks the line of scrimmage

²**bucker** \"\ *n* -S [⁸*buck* + *-er*] **:** one that bucks ore samples; *also* **:** a broad-headed hammer used in bucking ore

buckeroo *var of* BUCKAROO

bucker-up \'==,=, ,=='=\ *n, pl* **buckers-up** *or* **bucker-ups 1 :** ¹BUCKER d ⟨the *bucker-up,* who holds the red-hot rivet in place with a combination of iron bars and brute strength —*San Francisco Chronicle*⟩ **2 :** BUCKING BAR

¹**buck·et** \'bəkət, *usu* -əd·+V\ *n* -S [ME, fr. AF *buket,* fr. OE *būc* pitcher, belly; akin to OHG *būh* belly, ON *būkr* trunk of the body, Latvian *buga* hornless cow, Skt *bhūri* abundant — more at BOAST] **1 a :** a typically round and wooden vessel for drawing up water from a well **b :** any comparable vessel (as of wood, metal, or plastic) for catching, holding, or carrying liquids or solids **:** PAIL — often used in combination with a term suggesting the function ⟨ice ~⟩ ⟨fire ~⟩ ⟨lunch ~⟩ **2 a :** a vessel (as a tub or scoop) for hoisting and conveying material (as coal, ore, grain, gravel, mud, or concrete) **b :** the dipper or scoop at the end of the arm of a bucket dredge **c :** one of the receptacles on the rim of a water wheel into which the water rushes causing the wheel to revolve **d :** a float or paddle of a water wheel or of a boat's side wheel or stern wheel **e :** one of the containers of an endless-belt type of conveyor **f :** one of the vanes of a turbine rotor upon which the force of the steam or gas is exerted to cause rotation **g :** a frame covered with canvas that is sometimes used as a signal for boats **3 :** the quantity that a bucket contains; *often* **:** a very or unexpectedly large quantity ⟨the rain came down in ~*s*⟩ ⟨I could drink a ~ right now⟩ **4 :** a leather socket for holding a whip, lance, or carbine **5 :** a curved surface designed to deflect flowing water gradually and to prevent shock and erosion (as between the overflow face and apron of a dam) **6** *slang* **:** a means of conveyance (as an automobile); *esp* **:** a slow old ship — usu. used disparagingly **7** *slang* **:** JAIL, PRISON **8 :** a part of a basketball court keyhole bounded by the free-throw lane and the free-throw line — **in the bucket** *baseball* **:** drawn back from the plate ⟨left foot *in the bucket* so that he is half facing the pitcher —*Time*⟩ **:** with the foot nearest the pitcher drawn back from the plate ⟨batting *in the bucket*⟩ **:** so that one foot is in such a position ⟨step *in the bucket* while batting⟩

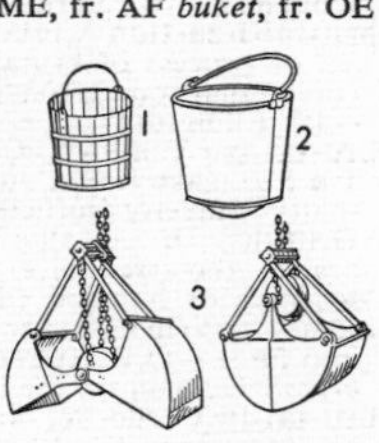

buckets: *1* wooden bucket, *2* fire bucket, *3* clamshell automatic bucket for excavating, open and closed

²**bucket** \"\ *vb* -ED/-ING/-S *vt* **1 :** to draw or lift in or as if in buckets ⟨~*ing* water from the well⟩ — often used with *out* or *up* ⟨you can ~ out the slops before dark⟩ **2** *Brit* **a :** to ride (a horse) hard **b :** to drive (as a car) hurriedly or roughly ⟨~*ed* his car down the drive and pulled up . . . with a savage jerk —Ngaio Marsh⟩ **3 :** to deal with (an order to buy or sell stocks) in or as if in a bucket shop ~ *vi* **1 :** to drive or progress rapidly **:** HUSTLE, HURRY ⟨the ship was ~*ing* through the heavy seas —Joyce Cary⟩ ⟨they ~*ed* into their household chores⟩ **2 :** to do a bucket-shop business **3 a :** to move haphazardly without a well-defined objective or without restraint ⟨you can't let such a valuable horse ~ about the pasture at his own good pleasure⟩ ⟨hordes of people go ~*ing* all over the shop —G.F.T.Ryall⟩ ⟨jaunty ladies who ~ around foreign parts —*New Yorker*⟩ **b :** to move roughly or jerkily ⟨the jeep ~*ed* over the rocky road⟩ ⟨as we jolted, jerked, ~*ed* along —Nancy Hale⟩

bucket brigade *n* **1 :** a chain of persons acting to suppress a fire by passing buckets of water from hand to hand **2 :** any chain (as of persons) acting to meet an emergency

bucket conveyor *n* **:** CONVEYER 2a(6)

bucket dredge *or* **bucket dredger** *n* **:** a dredge that excavates and raises material either by a series of closely connected scoops or buckets or with a single bucket operated by a boom

bucket elevator *n* **:** an endless-chain elevator having buckets

buck·et·er *or* **buck·e·teer** \'bəkəd·ə(r\ *or* \,bəkə'ti(ə)r\ *n* -S **:** a broker who conducts a bucket shop **:** one that buckets orders

buck·et·ful \'bəkət,fu̇l\ *n, pl* **bucketfuls** \-lz\ *or* **buckets·ful** \-t,sfu̇l\ **:** ¹BUCKET 3

bucketing *n* -S **1 :** the operation of a bucket shop **2 :** the practice of a broker who buckets orders or takes the other side of customers' trades

bucketline \'==,=\ *n* **:** the train of buckets in a bucket conveyor, bucket elevator, or similar device

bucket loader *n* **1 :** a mobile bucket conveyor for loading loose materials into trucks or railway cars **2 :** a tractor with a bucket mounted on the front used for digging and truck loading

bucket pump *n* **1 :** a vertical-piston usu. duplex pump whose valves are in the piston or pistons **2 :** CHAIN PUMP **3 :** a hand-operated force pump commonly used for spraying with liquids contained in a bucket

buckets *adv* [fr. pl. of ¹*bucket*] **:** in great quantity — used with an intransitive verb ⟨it's raining ~⟩

bucket seat *n* **:** a low separate seat that is designed for one person and that has a rounded back, is often hinged for tipping or folding forward, and is used chiefly in autos and planes

bucket shop *n* [fr. *bucket shop* "low ginmill where alcoholic beverages were dispensed in small amounts in buckets"; fr. the small speculations that originally took place there] **1 :** a dishonest brokerage house operating in securities or commodities that does not execute orders placed on margin by customers, anticipating a profit from market fluctuations adverse to the customer's interests **2 :** a gambling establishment in which wagers are made in the form of orders or options at current prices for securities or commodities without real intention to purchase or deliver, losses or gains being computed on the basis of changes in market quotations

bucket trap *n* **:** a contrivance to let air and condensed water out of steam pipes and radiators with but little escape of steam

bucket wheel *n* **:** a wheel having buckets attached to its rim or to a rope or chain passing over it (as for raising water)

¹**buckeye** \'=,=\ *n* -S [¹*buck* + *eye*] **1** [so called fr. the appearance of the seed] **a :** any No. American shrub or tree of the genus *Aesculus; esp* **:** OHIO BUCKEYE **b :** the large nutlike seed of one of these plants — called also *horse chestnut* **c :** a shrub or small tree (*Ungnadia speciosa*) of the southwestern U.S. and Mexico having pink flowers resembling those of the buckeyes and reputedly poisonous seeds — called also *Mexican buckeye* **2** *usu cap* **:** OHIOAN — used as a nickname **3 :** BUGEYE **4 :** a No. and So. American butterfly (*Precis lavinia*) having dark brown wings, each with 2-ringed eyespots and larvae that feed on plantain, snapdragon, and related plants **5 :** a small cigar-manufacturing unit often operated in a private home

²**buckeye** \"\ *adj* **:** naively flamboyant **:** CORNY ⟨a thoroughly ~ illustration⟩ **:** SLAPDASH, HAPHAZARD

buckeyed \"+d\ *adj* [¹*buckeye* + *-ed*] **:** poisoned by buckeye (sense 1a) or one of its products (as seeds or honey)

buckeye rot *n* [¹*buck* + *eye;* fr. the resemblance of the rotten spot to a buck's eye] **:** a fungous rot of tomato fruit caused by a phycomycete (*Phytophthora parasitica*) that causes a gray= green or brown discoloration usu. with darker zonate bands at the blossom end of the fruit

buck·ey-wrack \'bəkē+,-\ *n* [alter. of Sc *boxie-wrack,* fr. Sc *boxie* (dim of *box*) + *wrack;* fr. the form of the air capsules] **:** BLADDER WRACK

buck fever *n* [¹*buck*] **1 :** the nervous excitement of an inexperienced hunter at the sight of game **2 :** extreme tension or nervousness accompanying initial or unexpected exposure to some new situation or responsibility that requires positive action — compare STAGE FRIGHT

buck hook *n* [³*buck*] *West* **:** a blunt upcurved projection on the frame of a spur that is thrust into the cinch to hold a rider on a bucking horse

buckhorn \'=,=\ *n* [ME, fr. *buck* + *horn*] **1 :** the horn of a buck; *often* **:** the substance of such a horn ⟨knives with ~ handles⟩ **2 :** DEERHORN 2 **3 a :** CINNAMON FERN **b** *also* **buckhorn plantain :** any of several plantains having leaves that suggest a buck's horn in shape: as (1) **:** a European plantain (*Plantago coronopus*) (2) **:** a common No. American plantain (*P. aristata*) (3) **:** a ribgrass (*Plantago lanceolata*)

buckhorn brake *or* **buckhorn fern** *n* **:** ROYAL FERN

buckhorn sight *also* **buckhorn** *n* **:** a rear sight with a deep curved notch used on some rifles

buckhound \'=,=\ *n* [¹*buck* + *hound*] **:** a dog used for coursing deer

¹**buck·ie** \'bəkē\ *n* -S [perh. modif. of L *buccinum, bucinum,* a shellfish used in dyeing purple, fr. *bucina, buccina* trumpet,

shell used as a trumpet — more at BUCCINA] *chiefly Scot* **:** a spiral-shelled marine gastropod or its shell; *esp* **:** RED WHELK

²buckie \"\ *n* -S [perh. modif. of L *buccinum*] *Scot* **:** a perverse intractable person

³buckie \"\ *n* -S [origin unknown] *NewEng* **:** ALEWIFE 1a; *esp* **:** an alewife smoked for food

buckier *comparative of* BUCKY

buckiest *superlative of* BUCKY

bucking *n* -S [ME *bouking*, fr. gerund of *bouken* to buck — more at BUCK] **1** *obs* **:** liquid used in bucking clothes or fabric **2** *archaic* **:** a quantity of clothes or fabric bucked at one time

bucking bar *n* [fr. pres. part. of ²*buck*] **:** a steel block serving to back up a rivet while it is being headed and clinched

bucking board *or* **bucking plate** *n* [fr. pres. part. of ⁸*buck*] **:** a flat plate usu. of chilled steel upon which ore is pulverized with a hand-operated bucking hammer

bucking hammer *or* **bucking iron** *n* [fr. pres. part. of ⁸*buck*] **:** a heavy iron instrument shaped like a pestle with a wooden handle attached hammer fashion and operated by hand on a bucking board

buck·ing·ham·shire \ˈbəkiŋəm,shi(ə)r, *US also* -ŋ,ham-\ *or* **buckingham** *adj, usu cap* [fr. *Buckinghamshire* or *Buckingham* county, England] **:** of or from the county of Buckingham, England **:** of the kind or style prevalent in Buckingham

bucking plate *var of* BUCKPLATE

bucking roll *n* [fr. pres. part. of ²*buck*] **:** a usu. leather pad that is fastened on either side of the pommel of a saddle to help a rider hold his seat on a bucking horse

bucking transformer *n* [fr. pres. part. of ²*buck*] **:** a transformer connected to oppose partly or wholly the voltage from a second transformer

buck·ish \ˈbəkish\ *adj* [¹*buck* + *-ish*] **1 :** DANDIFIED, FOPPISH **2 :** lively and vigorous; *also* **:** IMPETUOUS — **buck·ish·ly** *adv*

buck·ism \ˈbə,kizəm\ *n* -S [¹*buck* + *-ism*] *archaic* **:** DANDYISM

buckjump \ˈ=,=\ *vb* [²*buck* + *jump*] **1** *of a horse or other equine* **:** BUCK **2 :** to leap or leap on like a bucking horse

buckjumper \"+ə(r)\ *n* **:** a bucking horse

buck knee *n* [³*buck*] **:** a knee (as of a horse) inclining inwards — usu. used in pl. — **buck-kneed** \ˈ=ˈ=\ *adj*

buck lateral *n* [³*buck*] **:** a football play in which the back who receives the pass from center either (1) bucks into the line with the ball after faking a hand-off to a teammate who in turn fakes a pitchout or (2) fakes a buck into the line after giving the ball to a teammate who in turn may lateral the ball, hand it off, keep it and run with it, or drop back and pass

buck law *n* [¹*buck*] **:** a game law or regulation that limits the hunter to taking only male deer

¹buck·le \ˈbəkəl\ *n* -S [ME *bocle*, fr. MF *bocle, boucle* boss of a shield, buckle, fr. L *buccula* small cheek, dim. of *bucca* cheek — more at POCK] **1 :** a fastening for two loose ends (as of a belt or strap) attached to one and holding the other by a catch **2 :** an ornamental device that suggests a buckle in form but often does not act as a fastening and that is used esp. on women's garments and shoes **3** *archaic* **a :** a curl esp. when crisp **b :** the state of being in curl **4 :** one of the thin openwork plates of lead sometimes shaped like buckles that are exposed to the action of carbon dioxide in the manufacture of white lead **5** *or* **buckle joint :** CLAMP CONNECTION

²buckle \"\ *vb* **buckled; buckled; buckling** \-k(ə)liŋ, -lēŋ\ **buckles** [ME *boclen*, fr. MF *boucler*, fr. *boucle*] *vt* **1 a :** to fasten or make fast with a buckle — often used with *on* ⟨he *buckled* on his spurs⟩ **b :** to fasten the buckle of ⟨be sure to ~ your belt⟩ **2 :** to prepare (as oneself) for action **:** apply intensively and with vigor ⟨Redworth *buckled* himself to the task —George Meredith⟩ **3** *chiefly Scot* **:** MARRY **4 :** to cause to bend, give way, or crumple ⟨changing stresses *buckled* the land surface into a series of ridges that now form the main coastal range⟩ ⟨*buckled* the car fender⟩ **5 :** to make (hair) curly **:** CRIMP ~ *vi* **1 a :** to equip oneself or make ready for a contest or undertaking by or as if by buckling on armor **b :** to apply oneself ardently or with vigor **:** STRIVE — often used with *down* ⟨he'll finish if he ~s down to the job⟩ ⟨they were advised to ~ down⟩ **2** *obs* **:** to join in combat **:** CONTEND, GRAPPLE — often used with *with* **3** *chiefly Scot* **:** MARRY **4 :** to close or become confined with a buckle ⟨this dress won't ~⟩ **5 :** to bend, heave, warp, or kink usu. under the influence of some external agency ⟨the pavement *buckled* in the heat⟩ ⟨his knees *buckled* with exhaustion⟩ — often used with *up* ⟨the floor *buckled* up under the weight of so many people⟩ **6 :** to become altered or distorted usu. permanently by buckling ⟨the panels did not ~ under pressure⟩; *broadly* **:** to fall to pieces or into a heap **:** CRUMBLE, CRUMPLE, COLLAPSE ⟨the balloon *buckled* together⟩ ⟨the *buckling* imperialisms of western Europe —C.W. de Kiewiet⟩ — often used with *up* **7 a :** to give way **:** YIELD — usu. used with *under* ⟨less devout creatures . . . would have *buckled* under this severe test of faith —Paul Willen⟩ **b** *now dial Eng* **:** to be or become subservient **:** CRINGE

³buckle \"\ *n* -S **1 :** a product of buckling **:** BEND, WARP, FOLD, KINK: as **a :** a small fold in land **b :** one of the wrinkles that develop at the top edge of the leaves of a book near the backbone margin during folding **c :** a depression or flaw on the surface of a casting caused by fault or failure of the mold (as from inadequate venting) **2 :** a machine for folding printed sheets of paper

buckle chain *n* **:** SWIVEL CHAIN

buckled *adj* **:** BENT, CRINKLED, WARPED, WAVY

buck·le·less \ˈbəkəl(l)əs\ *adj* **:** being without a buckle

buckle plate *or* **buckled plate** *n* **:** a slightly arched steel plate used as a floor plate to give rigidity

¹buck·ler \ˈbəklə(r)\ *n* -S [ME *bocler*, fr. OF, shield with a boss, fr. *bocle* boss — more at BUCKLE] **1 a :** a small shield generally round and held by a handle at arm's length and used not to cover the body but to stop or parry blows **b :** a shield of varying shape and size usu. worn on the left arm to protect the front of the body **2 :** something or someone that shields and protects **3 :** a crab whose shell is sufficiently firm to give only slightly under the fingers **4 :** a cover of wood or metal made to fit a hawsehole or other opening on a ship **5 :** the anterior shield of the shell of a trilobite **6 :** one of the large bony external plates found on many ganoid fishes

²buckler \"\ *vt* -ED/-ING/-S **:** to shield or defend with or as if with a buckler

buckler fern *n* **:** SHIELD FERN

buckler mustard *n* **:** a plant of the genus *Biscutella* (family Cruciferae) with yellow flowers like those of mustard and pods with open valves that resemble bucklers

buck·leya \ˈbəklēə, ˈ=ˈ==\ *n, cap* [NL, after Samuel B. *Buckley* †1883 Am. naturalist] **:** a small genus of Asiatic and American partly parasitic shrubs (family Santalaceae) with opposite leaves, small greenish flowers, and an oily nutlike drupe

¹buck·ling \ˈbək(ə)liŋ, -lēŋ\ *n* -S [fr. gerund of ²*buckle*] **:** an act or instance of bending or of being distorted by bending or crumpling; *specif* **:** failure (as of a column) when subjected to a compressive stress in excess of its elastic limit

²buck·ling \ˈbəkliŋ, -lēŋ\ *n* -S [¹*buck* + *-ling*] **:** a male goat between one and two years of age

buck moth *n* [so called fr. its prevalence in the deer season] **:** a large autumn-flying saturniid moth (*Hemileuca maia*) of the eastern U.S. with smoky translucent wings crossed by a white band and a spiny larva that feeds on oak foliage

bucko \ˈbə(,)kō\ *n* -ES [¹*buck* + *-o*] **1 :** one who is domineering and bullying — used esp. of officers on sailing ships who maintained control of their crews by free resort to physical violence **2** *chiefly Irish* **:** young fellow **:** LAD, CHAP — often used as a term of address ⟨and as for you, my ~⟩

buck passer *n* [¹⁰*buck*] **:** a person that habitually evades responsibility — **buck-passing** \ˈ=ˌ==\ *n*

buckplate \ˈ=,=\ *or* **bucking plate** *n* [⁸*buck* + *plate*] **:** BUCKING BOARD

buckpot \ˈ=,=\ *n* [¹*buck* (Indian) + *pot*] **:** a clay cooking pot of British Guiana

buck·ra *also* **buc·cra** \ˈbəkrə\ *n* -S [Ibibio and Efik *mba*¹*ka*²*ra*², lit., master] **1** *chiefly South* **:** a white man or a person of predominantly white as opposed to Negro blood — used chiefly by Negroes and often disparagingly **2** *chiefly South* **:** BOSS, MASTER

buck rake *n* [²*buck* (to charge against, push)] **:** a wide horse-drawn or tractor-mounted long-toothed rake for gathering hay from a windrow and carrying it — called also *go-devil, hay sweep*

¹buck·ram \ˈbəkrəm\ *n* -S [ME *bukeram, bokeram*, fr. OF *boquerant, bouquerant*, fr. OProv *bocaran*, fr. *Bokhara, Bukhara*, city of central Asia (now in Uzbekistan, U.S.S.R.) whence it was imported] **1** *archaic* **:** a fabric of fine linen or cotton formerly used for church vestments and wearing apparel **2 a :** a stiff-finished heavily-sized fabric of cotton or linen used for interlinings in garments and stiffening in millinery and in bookbinding **b :** a similar fabric made by plying together with glue two or more layers of open-weave cotton cloth **3** *archaic* **:** stiffness of manner or reaction **:** precise formality **:** RIGIDITY; *also* **:** a precise or starchy person **4 :** BUCKLER 3

²buckram \"\ *adj* **:** suggesting buckram esp. in stiffness, formality, and rigidity ⟨in translation the flow of his prose took on a ~ quality⟩ ⟨a ~ pretense prevented the world from piercing to his hollowness —G.D.Brown⟩

³buckram \"\ *vt* -ED/-ING/-S **1 :** to strengthen with or as if with buckram **2** *archaic* **:** to make pretentious **:** give a false appearance of strength, worth, or beauty to

bucks *pl of* BUCK, *pres 3d sing of* BUCK

buck sail *n* [part modif., part trans. of Afrik *bokseil*, fr. *bok* beam of a wagon + *seil* sail, sailcloth — more at BUCKWAGON] *Africa* **:** CANVAS, TARPAULIN; *esp* **:** one used to cover a buckwagon

bucksaw \ˈ=,=\ *n* [¹*buck* (sawhorse) + *saw*] **:** a saw set in a usu. H-shaped frame that is used for sawing wood on a sawbuck

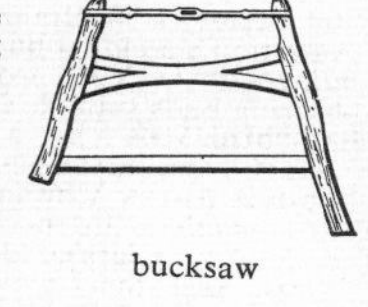

bucksaw

buck scraper *n* [²*buck* (to charge against, push)] **:** a modified drag scraper having two runners to lift the scoop from the ground when filled

buck's extension \ˈbəks-\ *n, usu cap B* [after Gurdon *Buck* †1877 Am. surgeon] **:** an apparatus for extension of a fractured limb by the application of a weight controlled by a rope and pulley; *also* **:** the traction so applied

buck's-eye \ˈ=,=\ *n, pl* **buck's-eyes** [¹*buck*] *archaic* **:** BUCKEYE 1a

buck·shee \ˌbəkˈshē\ *n* -S [Hindi *bakhśiś*, fr. Per *bakhshīsh* — more at BAKSHEESH] *Brit* **:** GRATUITY, WINDFALL; *esp* **:** extra rations — used chiefly in military circles

buck's horn *n* [¹*buck*] **1** *also* **buck's horn plantain :** BUCKHORN 3b **2 :** SWINE CRESS **3 :** BRASS BUTTONS

buckshot \ˈ=,=\ *n, pl* **buckshot** *or* **buckshots** [¹*buck* + *shot*] **1 :** a coarse lead shot manufactured in sizes ranging from a quarter to a third of an inch in diameter and used in shotgun shells for hunting and police purposes **2 a** *also* **buckshot soil** *or* **buckshot land :** a soil that contains or that on drying breaks into pellets resembling buckshot (as certain heavy clays of the Mississippi delta area and some sandy alluviums of Australia) **b :** one of the pellets of such soil

buckskin \ˈ=,=\ *n, often attrib* [ME, fr. ¹*buck* + *skin*] **1 a :** the skin of a buck **b :** a soft pliable usu. suede-finished leather made from deer or elk skins and used chiefly for gloves and shoe uppers **c :** any leather resembling buckskin (as certain goat and sheepskin leathers) — not used technically in the leather trade **2 a buckskins** *pl* **:** a garment of buckskin; *esp* **:** buckskin breeches **b** *archaic* **:** a person dressed in buckskin garments; *often* **:** a backwoodsman or countrified person of the earlier periods of American settlement **3** *chiefly West & Southwest* **:** a horse of a light yellowish dun color and usu. with a dark stripe down the back and dark mane and tail **4 a :** a heavy thick cotton fabric with a smooth face, napped back, and satin weave used for outerwear **b :** a durable woolen cloth for outerwear made in satin weave and napped and sheared for a smooth face **5 a :** a leathery scurfy condition of the skin of grapefruit and sometimes of sweet oranges caused by attacks of the citrus rust mite **b :** a virus disease of cherry, peach, and other stone fruit characterized by small pointed fruits that remain green and underdeveloped and shrivel prior to ripening, the affected cherry trees having also a lusterless leathery-skinned pale fruit **6 :** a log with bark removed or lost

buck-skinned \"+d\ *adj* **:** dressed in buckskin

buck slip *n* [prob. fr. ¹⁰*buck*] **:** a routing slip used esp. in military offices to indicate the persons to whom the attached material is to go and usu. the kind of action to be taken with such material

buckstay \ˈ=,=\ *also* **buckstave** \ˈ=,=\ *n* -S [¹*buck* (steel support) + *stay* or *stave*] **:** either of two connected girders used one on each side of the masonry structure of a furnace or flue to take the thrust of an arch; *also* **:** any girder similarly used as a stay

bucktail \ˈ=,=\ *n* [¹*buck* + *tail*] **1** [so called fr. the fact that members wore deer tails in their hats on certain occasions] *archaic* **:** a member of the Tammany political society during the period from about 1817–26; *also* **:** an opponent of Governor DeWitt Clinton of New York State of about the same period **2 a :** an artificial angler's fly made of hairs from the tail of a deer or a similar material **b :** a fishing lure used in saltwater angling with a similar dressing and a weighted head — see LURE illustration

buckthorn \ˈ=,=\ *n* [trans. of It *spino cervino* & NL *cervi spina*] **1 :** a shrub or tree of the genus *Rhamnus* sometimes having thorny branches and often containing purgative principles in bark or sap and producing fruits sometimes used as a source of yellow and green dyes or pigments — see CASCARA BUCKTHORN **2 :** a shrub or tree of the genus *Bumelia* — usu. used in combination; see SOUTHERN BUCKTHORN **3 :** a prickly shrub (*Ceanothus seriedatus*) of the California chaparral

buckthorn aphid *n* **:** an aphid (*Aphis nasturtii*) common in eastern No. America and a destructive pest of potatoes in some areas

buckthorn berries *n pl* **:** the dried unripe berries of various buckthorns a powder or extract of which is used to dye mordanted wool and cotton — called also *yellow berries*

buckthorn brown *n* **:** a strong yellowish brown that is stronger, slightly yellower, and darker than centennial brown and yellower, less strong, and slightly lighter than orange rust — called also *chamoline, sumac*

buckthorn family *n* **:** RHAMNACEAE

buckthorn fencing *n* **:** fencing of a steel band or ribbon with sawtooth barbs

buckthorn weed *also* **buckthorn** *n* **:** FIDDLE-NECK 2

bucktooth \ˈ=,=\ *n, pl* **buckteeth** [¹*buck*] **:** a large projecting front tooth — **buck-toothed** \ˈ=ˈ=\ *adj*

bucku *var of* BUCHU

buck up *vb* [²*buck*] *vi* **:** to become encouraged or cheerful **:** brace up ~ *vt* **1 :** IMPROVE, SMARTEN **2 :** to cheer up **:** give a lift to **:** raise the morale of ⟨mountain air *bucked* her up⟩

buck·wagon \ˈbək+,-\ *n* [part modif., part trans. of Afrik *bokwa*, fr. *bok* beam of a wagon, stand, tripod, male goat (fr. MD *boc* male goat) + *wa* wagon; akin to OHG *boc* male goat — more at BUCK] **:** a large strong wagon with the frame projecting over the wheels that is used in southern Africa for hauling loads

buckwash \ˈ=,=\ *vt* [⁶*buck* + *wash*] *archaic* **:** BUCK

buckwheat \ˈ=,=\ *n, often attrib* [part. modif., part trans. of D *boekweit*, fr. MD *boecweit* (akin to MLG *bōkwēte*), fr. *boec-* (akin to OHG *buohha* beech tree) + *weit* wheat; fr. the similarity of the seeds to beechnuts — more at BEECH] **1 :** an herb of the genus *Fagopyrum*, characterized by alternate hastate or cordate leaves and clusters of pink-tinged white dimorphous flowers rich in nectar; *esp* **:** either of two species (*F. esculentum* and *F. tataricum*) long cultivated as cereal plants — see COMMON BUCKWHEAT, TARTARIAN BUCKWHEAT **2 :** the triangular seed of buckwheat containing somewhat less protein than wheat and used as animal feed or cracked or ground for flour or cereal for human consumption **3 :** WILD BUCKWHEAT 2

buckwheat cake *n* **:** a griddlecake that is made with buckwheat flour

buckwheat coal *also* **buckwheat** *n* **:** anthracite coal in any one of five small sizes — see ANTHRACITE table

buck·wheat·er \-ēd·ə(r), -ētə-\ *n* -S *slang* **:** a novice at lumbering

buckwheat family *n* **:** POLYGONACEAE

buckwheat honey *n* **:** a dark strongly flavored honey produced from buckwheat esp. in parts of the northeastern U.S.

buckwheat note *n* **:** SHAPE NOTE

buckwheat tree *n* **:** TITI 1a

buckwheat vine *n* **:** a high-climbing woody vine (*Brunnichia cirrhosa*) with ovate leaves cordate or truncate at the base, the lower flower spikes solitary and axillary and the upper ones in a loose panicle

bucky \ˈbəkē\ *adj* -ER/-EST [¹*buck* + *-y*] **:** like a buck or like that of a buck; *esp* **:** exhibiting characteristics of an entire male ⟨some discount is usual on ~ lambs⟩

bu·co·li·ast \byüˈkōlē,ast, -,əst\ *n* -S [Gk *boukoliastēs*, fr. *boukoliazesthai* to sing or write pastorals, fr. *boukolos* cowherd] *obs* **:** a pastoral poet

¹bu·col·ic \(ˈ)byüˈkälik\ *also* **bu·col·i·cal** \-ləkəl\ *adj* [L *bucolicus*, fr. Gk *boukolikos*, fr. *boukolos* cowherd (fr. *bous* head of cattle + *-kolos*; akin to L *colere* to cultivate) + *-ikos* -ic, -ical — more at COW, WHEEL] **1 :** of or relating to shepherds or herdsmen **:** PASTORAL ⟨~ poetry⟩ **2 a :** relating to or typical of rural life **:** RUSTIC ⟨a pleasant ~ scene⟩ **b :** countrified and unsophisticated or unaffected **:** natural and without artful elaboration ⟨his calm ~ writings⟩ — **bu·col·i·cal·ly** \-lək(ə)lē\ *also* **bu·col·ic·ly** \-lə̇klē\ *adv*

²bucolic \"\ *n* -S [L *bucolicum*, fr. neut. of *bucolicus*] **1 :** a pastoral poem **:** ECLOGUE, IDYL — usu. used in pl. ⟨the *Bucolics* of Theocritus⟩; compare GEORGIC **2 :** a bucolic person or condition; *sometimes* **:** RUSTIC, BUMPKIN

bucolic caesura *or* **bucolic diaeresis** *n* **:** a diaeresis after the fourth foot in a dactylic hexameter esp. common in pastoral poetry

bu·cor·vus \byüˈkȯrvəs\ *n, cap* [NL, fr. *bu-* (fr. *Buceros*) + *Corvus*] **:** a genus of African birds (family Bucerotidae) consisting of the ground hornbills — compare BUCEROS

bu·cra·ni·um \byüˈkrānēəm\ *also* **bu·crane** \(ˈ)byüˈkrān\ *n, pl* **bucra·nia** \byüˈkrānēə\ *also* **bucranes** [L, fr. Gk *boukranion* ox head, fr. *bous* ox, head of cattle + *kranion* skull — more at COW, CRANIUM] **:** a sculptured ornament (as on a Roman Ionic or Corinthian frieze) composed of an ox skull adorned with ribbons or garlands

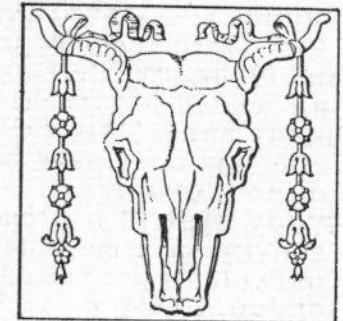

bucranium

¹bud \ˈbəd\ *n* -S [ME *budde*; akin to OE *budda* beetle, D *bot* bud, MLG *buddich* swollen, OHG *būtil* bag, MHG *butzen* to swell, Icel *budda* purse, Skt *bhūri* abundant — more at BOAST] **1 :** a small lateral or terminal protuberance on the stem of a plant consisting of an undeveloped shoot made up of rudimentary foliage leaves or floral leaves or both overarching a growing point and often protected by specialized bud scales or by a coating of resin or hairs or by both — see FLOWER BUD, LEAF BUD, MIXED BUD **2 :** something not yet mature or attained to full growth and development: as **a :** an incompletely opened flower ⟨the ~s are getting full of color⟩ — often used in combination ⟨one red rose*bud*⟩ **b** *dial Eng* **:** a yearling calf **c :** a young girl just entering social life **d :** CHILD, YOUTH — compare ³BUD **e :** an outgrowth from the body of an organism that differentiates into a new individual **:** GEMMA; *also* **:** a primordium having potentialities for growth and development into a definitive structure ⟨an embryonic limb ~⟩ ⟨a horn ~⟩ **f :** an initial phase of development ⟨raised havoc with the first ~s of a contemporary and a functional architecture in Dixie —M.W.Fishwick⟩ **3 :** state of budding **:** INCIPIENCE — used esp. in the phrase *in the bud* ⟨the plot was nipped in the ~⟩ **4 :** something likened to or suggestive of a bud esp. in shape: as **a :** an anatomical structure resembling a bud (as a tactile corpuscle); *esp* **:** NIPPLE **b :** a small somewhat conical morsel of sweet chocolate

²bud \"\ *vb* **budded; budded; budding; buds** [ME *budden*, fr. *budde*, n.] *vi* **1** *of a plant or its parts* **a :** to set buds ⟨the plant will not ~ well without heavy fertilizing⟩ **b :** to commence growth from buds **:** break dormancy ⟨spring is here, all the trees are *budding*⟩ — often used with *out* ⟨the leaves have *budded* out almost overnight⟩ **2 a :** to be like a bud in youth and freshness or in the unfolding of growth and promise **b :** to develop like a plant part through the unfolding of a bud ⟨new antlers ~ during the summer⟩ **c :** to arise like a bud from some precursor — often used with *off* ⟨a number of sects have *budded* off from the early churches of the Reformation⟩ **3 :** to reproduce asexually; *specif* **:** to produce a new cell (as in yeasts) by pinching off a small part of the parent cell **4 :** to perform the operation of budding a plant **5** *of a bird* **:** to feed on buds ~ *vt* **1 :** to produce or develop (as leaves) from buds ⟨some honeysuckles ~ their leaves very early in the spring⟩ — often used with *off* or *out* ⟨some zoophytes ~ off young at regular intervals⟩ **2 :** to cause (as a plant) to bud — often used with *out* ⟨warm weather will ~ out trees⟩ **3 :** to insert a bud from a plant of one kind into an opening in the bark of (a plant of another kind) usu. in order to propagate a desired variety — compare GRAFT *vt* 1 **4 :** to produce (as young) by gemmation — often used with *out*

³bud \"\ *n* [short for ²*buddy*] **:** BROTHER, BUDDY — often used in informal address ⟨say ~, have you got the right time⟩

bu·da·pest \ˈbüdə,pest *also* ˈbu̇d- *or* ˈbyüd- *or* ,==ˈ= *or* -esht *sometimes* -esh\ *adj, usu cap* [fr. *Budapest*, Hungary] **:** of or from Budapest, the capital of Hungary **:** of the kind or style prevalent in Budapest

budbreak \ˈ=,=\ *n* **:** initiation of growth from a bud ⟨~ may be delayed after pruning in hot dry weather⟩

bud brush *n* [so called fr. its clusters of leaves and flowers that resemble buds] **:** a half-shrubby perennial (*Artemisia spinescens*) valuable as sheep forage in the western U.S.

bud cutting *n* **:** a plant cutting containing a single bud

bud·da *also* **bud·dah** \ˈbədə\ *n* -S [native name in Australia] **:** a hoary Australian forage shrub (*Pholidia mitchelli* or *Eremophila mitchelli*) of the family Myoporaceae with alternate leaves, 2-lipped corolla, and globular drupaceous fruits

bud·der \ˈbədə(r)\ *n* -S **:** one that buds; *esp* **:** a person who inserts buds in plant stocks

bud·dha \ˈbüdə, ˈbu̇-\ *n* -S [Skt *buddha* awakened, enlightened, fr. *bodhati* he awakes, understands — more at BID] **1** *usu cap* **:** a person who has attained Buddhahood **2** [after Gautama *Buddha* †*ab* 483 B.C. Indian philosopher who founded Buddhism] **:** a representation of the philosopher Gautama Buddha

buddha 2

buddha-field \ˈ==,=\ *n, usu cap B* **:** a paradisiacal sphere beyond the conditions of historical existence and under the beneficent control of a Buddha

bud·dha·hood \-,hu̇d\ *n* -S *usu cap* **:** a state of enlightenment or religious salvation characterized negatively as release from the earthly fetters of suffering, sorrow, and illusion and positively as the state of perfect spiritual fulfillment

buddha-nature \ˈ==ˈ==\ *n, usu cap B* **:** the essence of and potency to attain Buddhahood

buddha's-hand \ˈ==ˈ=\ *n, pl* **buddha's-hands** *usu cap B* **:** a citron (*Citrus medica* var. *sarcodactylis*) that is cultivated in eastern Asia as an ornamental and for its very fragrant fruit which is split into several usu. pulpless sections

bud·dhi \ˈbüdē, ˈbu̇-\ *n* -S [Skt, lit., understanding, fr. *bodhati* he awakes, understands — more at BUDDHA] **:** the faculty of intuitive discernment or direct spiritual awareness in the beliefs of Hinduism and Buddhism

bud·dhism \-,dizəm\ *n* -S [Gautama *Buddha* + E *-ism*] **1** *usu cap* **:** the teaching ascribed to Gautama Buddha holding that suffering is inherent in life and that one can escape it into nirvana by mental and moral self-purification — see EIGHTFOLD PATH, FOUR NOBLE TRUTHS **2** *cap* **:** a religion of eastern and central Asia growing out of the teaching of Gautama Buddha and comprising widely differing sects — see HINAYANA, MAHAYANA

1bud·dhist \-.dəst\ *n* -s *usu cap* [Gautama *Buddha* + E *-ist*] **:** an adherent of Buddhism

2buddhist \"\ *or* **bud·dhis·tic** \(')ˌ≈ˈdistik\ *also* **bud·dhis·ti·cal** \-təkəl\ *adj, usu cap* **:** of or relating to Buddha or Buddhism — **bud·dhis·ti·cal·ly** \-tək(ə)lē\ *adv, usu cap*

bud·dho·log·i·cal \ˌbüdəˈläjəkəl, ˌbu̇-, -dᵊlˈä-\ *adj, usu cap* **:** of, relating to, or contained in Buddhology

bud·dhol·o·gy \büˈdäləjē, bu̇-\ *n* -ES *usu cap* [Gautama *Buddha* + E *-ology* (as in *theology*)] **:** the theology of the deified Buddha

budding *adj* [fr. pres. part. of 2*bud*] **:** beginning to make one's way or to come into notice ⟨a ~ diplomat⟩

budding yeast *n* **:** a yeast that buds off daughter cells smaller than the parent cell — compare FISSION YEAST

1bud·dle \ˈbüdᵊl, ˈbu̇d-,ˈbəd-\ *n* -s [origin unknown] *dial Eng* **:** CORN MARIGOLD

2bud·dle \ˈbədᵊl, ˈbu̇d-\ *n* -s [origin unknown] **:** an apparatus (as an inclined trough or platform) on which crushed ore is concentrated by running water which washes out the lighter and less valuable portions

3buddle \"\ *vt* -ED/-ING/-S **:** to wash (ore) on a buddle

bud·dle·ia \ˈbədlēə, ˌ≈ˈ≈≈\ *n* [NL, fr. Adam *Buddle* †1715 Eng. botanist + NL *-ia*] **1** *cap* **:** a genus of showy shrubs or trees (family Loganiaceae) of warm regions with opposite leaves and terminal clusters of yellow or violet flowers **2** *also* **bud·dle·ja** \"\ -s **:** a plant of the genus *Buddleia*

bud·dler \ˈbəd(ᵊ)lə(r), ˈbu̇d-\ *also* **bud·dle·man** \-dᵊlmən\ *n, pl* **buddlers** *also* **buddlemen :** one that buddles

1bud·dy \ˈbədē, -di\ *adj* -ER/-EST [1*bud* + *-y*] **:** full or suggestive of buds

2buddy \"\ *also* **bud·die** \"\ *n, pl* **buddies** [prob. baby talk alter. of 1*brother*] **1 :** little boy — used chiefly in address **2 a :** COMPANION, PARTNER; *esp* **:** fellow soldier **b :** an intimate friend **c :** one of two persons paired off in the buddy system **3 :** FELLOW — used in informal address ⟨hey, ~, when's the next bus leave⟩

3buddy \"\ *vi* -ED/-ING/-ES **:** to become friendly — often used with *up* ⟨he *buddied* up with the other corporal⟩

buddy-buddy \ˈ≈≈ˌ≈≈\ *adj* [redupl. of 2*buddy*] *slang* **:** closely associated **:** INTIMATE

buddy sap *n* [1*buddy*] **:** a late run of sugar-maple sap gathered after the buds have begun to swell and usu. producing syrup of poor quality

buddy system *n* [2*buddy*] **:** an arrangement (as for military activity or engagement in hazardous sports) in which two individuals are paired for mutual assistance or protection

1budge \ˈbəj\ *n* -s [ME *bugee, bogey,* fr. AF *bogee*] **:** a fur formerly prepared from lambskin dressed with the wool outward

2budge \"\ *vb* -ED/-ING/-S [MF *bouger,* fr. OF *bougier,* fr. (assumed) VL *bullicare,* fr. L *bullire* to boil — more at BOIL] *vi* **:** MOVE, SHIFT; *esp* **:** to give way **:** YIELD — usu. used with an expressed or implied negative ⟨the mule refused to ~⟩ ~ *vt* **:** to start or cause to move ⟨the door was stuck fast, I couldn't ~ it⟩; *often* **:** to move (someone) to make a new decision **:** cause (a person) to change his mind ⟨once he decided to stay no one could ~ him⟩

3budge \"\ *adj* [origin unknown] *archaic* **:** austere or stiff in manner **:** POMPOUS, SOLEMN

4budge *n* -s [origin unknown] *obs slang* **:** THIEF

5budge \ˈbəj\ *n* [origin unknown] *slang* **:** intoxicating liquor

bud·ger·ee \ˈbəjərē\ *adj* [native name in Australia] *Austral* **:** GOOD, FINE, PRETTY

bud·ger·i·gar \ˈbəjərēˌgär, ˌgä(r\ *also* **bud·ger·ee·gah** *or* **bud·ger·y·gah** \-gä,-gä\ *n* -s [native name in Australia] **:** a small Australian parrot (*Melopsittacus undulatus*) that is usu. light green with black and yellow markings in the wild but that under domestication has been bred in many colors and has become a favored cage and show bird — called also *grass parrakeet, lovebird, shell parrakeet*

bud·ger·ow \ˈbəj(ə),rō\ *n* -s [Hindi *bajrā*] **:** a large cumbrous barge without a keel used on the Ganges river

1bud·get \ˈbəjət, *usu* -əd.+V; *chiefly dial* ˈbu̇j-\ *n* -s [ME *bowgette,* fr. MF *bougette,* dim. of *bouge* leather bag, fr. L *bulga,* fr. Gaulish; akin to MIr *bolg* bag, OE *bælg* bag, skin — more at BELLY] **1 a** *now dial* **:** a usu. leather pouch or wallet; *often* **:** a pack to be carried on the back **b** *archaic* **:** a leather or skin bottle — compare WATER BOUGET **c :** PACKAGE, BUNDLE, COLLECTION — now dial. except of written or printed matter ⟨grandma made me up a snack in a ~⟩ ⟨a neatly stacked ~ of letters⟩ **2 :** STOCK, SUPPLY, QUANTITY ⟨building up her ~ of complaints⟩ ⟨he was a ~ of foibles and contradictions⟩; *sometimes* **:** a quantity (as of energy or water) involved in, available for, or assignable to a particular situation ⟨the A-bomb . . . yields its ~ of energy . . . in a fraction of a second —*Scientific American Reader*⟩ **3 a :** a statement of the financial position of a sovereign body (as of a nation) for a definite period of time based on detailed estimates of planned or expected expenditures during the period and proposals for financing them — used orig. of such a statement presented annually by the chancellor of the exchequer to the British House of Commons **b :** a plan for the coordination of resources (as of money or manpower) and expenditures ⟨a good family ~ keeps something in reserve for emergencies⟩; *esp* **:** such a plan covering a definite period of time **c :** the amount of money available, required, or assigned to a particular purpose in or as if in a budget ⟨a minimum weekly ~ for a family of five⟩ ⟨trying to operate efficiently on a ~ of less than $3000⟩

2budget \"\ *vb* -ED/-ING/-S *vt* **1 a :** to put or allow for in a budget ⟨funds ~*ed* by the administration for navigation⟩ ⟨I doubt that we can ~ a new car this year⟩ **b :** to put on a budget ⟨~*ed* shoppers⟩ **2a :** to plan expenditures for (as an enterprise) in a budget ⟨the new municipal hospital became a major undertaking and over a million was ~*ed* for it⟩ **b :** to plan or provide for the use of in detail ⟨in the present tight labor market manpower must be ~*ed* carefully⟩ ⟨the wise man ~*s* his time⟩ ~ *vi* **:** to formulate or draw up a budget — usu. used with *for* ⟨in case you're ~*ing* for an auto trip —Richard Joseph⟩ ⟨he actually ~*ed* for a trifling £1,000,000 —*Melbourne (Australia) Herald*⟩

3budget \"\ *adj* **:** suitable for one using or adhering to a budget esp. in cheapness ⟨several attractive ~ dresses⟩ ⟨~ cuts of meat usu. require slow cooking⟩

bud·get·ary \ˈbəjə,terē, -ri\ *adj* **1 :** of, relating to, involved in, or provided for a budget ⟨~ plans⟩ ⟨~ accounts⟩ ⟨~ expenditures⟩ **2 :** involving or exercised through a budget ⟨~ control of production⟩ ⟨~ questions in the assembly⟩

bud·ge·teer \ˌbəjəˈti(ə)r, -iə\ *or* **bud·get·er** \ˈbəjəd·ə(r), -ətə-\ *n* -s **:** a person who prepares or uses a budget

budg·ie \ˈbəjē\ *n* -s [by alter. and shortening] **:** BUDGERIGAR

bud grafting *n* **:** the grafting of a plant by budding

bud gum *n* **:** the sticky exudation covering a plant bud

bud·less \ˈbədləs\ *adj* **:** being without a bud

bud·let \ˈbədlət\ *n* -s **:** a young, small, or secondary bud ⟨some yeasts form several ~*s* on their primary buds before breaking up⟩

bud·ling \-liŋ\ *n* -s **:** the shoot that develops from the scion bud in bud grafting

bud·mash \ˈbəd,mäsh\ *n* -ES [Per *badmaʻāsh* immoral, fr. *bad* bad (fr. MPer *vat*) + *maʻāsh* living, life, fr. Ar] *India* **:** a bad character **:** a worthless person

bud mite *n* **:** any of a number of minute phytophagous mites that attack the young buds of plants and commonly cause failure of normal development of infested buds

bud moth *n* **:** any of certain moths which in the larval state are destructive to buds of fruit trees; *esp* **:** EYE-SPOTTED BUD MOTH

bud mutation *n* **:** bud variation resulting from local genetic alteration and producing a permanent modification that usu. can be perpetuated by grafting ⟨the navel orange is a notable product of *bud mutation*⟩

bu·dong monkey \ˈb(y)ü,dȯŋ-\ *n* [prob. native name in Ceylon] **:** PURPLE-FACED LANGUR

bu·dor·cas \byüˈdȯrkəs\ *n, cap* [NL, fr. Gk *bous* head of cattle + *dorkas* gazelle — more at COW, DORCAS GAZELLE] **:** a genus of heavy-coated Asiatic bovines comprising the takins

bud rot *n* **:** a plant disease or symptom of disease involving decay of the buds: as **a :** COCONUT BUD ROT **b :** a disease of carnations caused by an imperfect fungus (*Sporotrichum poae*) that is carried by mites and produces a rotting of the petals while yet in the bud

buds *pl of* BUD, *pres 3d sing of* BUD

bud sage *also* **bud sagebrush** *n* **:** BUD BRUSH

bud scale *or* **bud sheath** *n* **:** one of the leaves resembling scales that form the external covering of a plant bud and are often densely coated with hair, gum, or resin

bud sport *n* **:** a product of bud mutation or bud variation ⟨a red-flowered branch on a white-flowering plant is a typical *bud sport*⟩ — compare BUD VARIETY

bud stick *n* **:** a shoot usu. of the current year's growth which is cut from a tree and from which buds are removed for budding

budtime \ˈ≈,≈\ *n* **:** the season of budding **:** SPRING

bu·du·kha \bəˈdükə\ *n, pl* **budukha** *or* **budukhas** *usu cap* [Russ *Budukhi, Budugi*] **1 :** a Lezghian people dwelling in the Caucasus **2 :** a member of the Budukha people

bu·du·ma \bəˈdümə\ *n, pl* **buduma** *or* **budumas** *usu cap* **1 :** a Negroid people dwelling on the shores and islands of Lake Chad **2 :** a member of the Buduma people

bud variation *n* **1 :** marked deviation from the normal in the development of a plant shoot from a bud — see BUD MUTATION **2 :** a product of bud variation **:** a shoot or clone originating from a single bud unlike other buds of the parent plant — see BUD SPORT, BUD VARIETY

bud variety *n* **:** a strain or variety of plant originating by bud variation **:** a clonal bud variation — compare BUD SPORT

budwood \ˈ≈,≈\ *n* **:** wood consisting of strong young shoots bearing buds suitable for use in budding

budworm \ˈ≈,≈\ *n* **:** a larval moth that feeds on the buds of plants — see BLACK-HEADED BUDWORM, SPRUCE BUDWORM

bue·nos ai·res \ˌbwānəˈs\|a(ə)rēz, \|er-,\|ir-, -riz *also* ˌbōn- *or* -rōs *sometimes* ˌbwen- *or* -nōˈz\| *or* \|är- *or* \|ār- *or* \|a(ə)rz *or* \|e(ə)rz *or* \|a(ə)z *or* \|eəz\ *adj, usu cap B&A* [fr. *Buenos Aires,* Argentina] **:** of or from Buenos Aires, the capital of Argentina **:** of the kind or style prevalent in Buenos Aires

buen re·ti·ro \ˌbwänrəˈtē(,)rō, ˌbwen-\ *n* [Sp, lit., good retreat] **1 :** a resting place or retreat **2** *usu cap B&R* [fr. *Buen Retiro,* near Madrid, Spain, where it was manufactured] **:** a soft-paste porcelain produced during the latter half of the 18th century in the private manufactory of the king of Spain

buer·ger's disease \ˈbərgərz-, ˈbu̇r-\ *n, usu cap B* [after Leo *Buerger* †1943 Am. physician] **:** THROMBOANGIITIS OBLITERANS

buetsch·li·ite *also* **bütsch·li·ite** \ˈbüchlē,īt\ *n* -s [Otto *Bütschli* (*Buetschli*) †1920 Ger. zoologist + E *-ite*] **:** a mineral $K_6Ca_2(CO_3)_5.6H_2O$ consisting of hydrous carbonate of potassium and calcium

1buett·ne·ri·a·ce·ae \(ˌ)byüt,nirēˈāsē,ē\ [NL, fr. *Buettneria,* type genus (fr. David S. A. *Buettner* †1768 Ger. botanist + NL *-ia*) + *-aceae*] *syn of* STERCULIACEAE

2buettneriaceae \"\ [NL, fr. *Buettneria,* type genus + *-aceae*] *syn of* CALYCANTHACEAE

bu·fa·gin \ˈbyüfəjən\ *n* -s [ISV *bufag-* (fr. NL *Bufo agua* agua toad) + *-in*] **:** a crystalline toxic steroid genin $C_{24}H_{34}O_5$ obtained from the poisonous secretion of a skin gland on the back of the neck of the agua toad and like digitalis in biological action; *also* **:** any of several similar genins from secretions of other toads — see BUFOTOXIN

1buff \ˈbəf\ *n* -s [ME *buffe,* fr. MF, of imit. origin] *now chiefly dial* **:** BUFFET, BLOW ⟨a ~ on the head⟩

2buff \"\ *vt* -ED/-ING/-S *chiefly Scot* **:** STRIKE, BEAT

3buff \"\ *adv, archaic* **:** FIRMLY, STURDILY — used in the phrase *to stand buff*

4buff \"\ *n* -s [MF *buffle,* fr. OIt *bufalo* — more at BUFFALO] **1 :** a buffalo or other wild ox **2 a :** BUFF LEATHER **b :** a garment made of buff leather; *esp* **:** a buff leather uniform or military garment **3 :** the bare skin **4 a :** a moderate orange yellow **b :** a light to moderate yellow **5** [6*buff*] **:** any of various devices employed in buffing: as **a :** BUFF STICK **b :** a device (as a stick or block) having a soft absorbent surface (as of cloth or velvet) by which polishing material is applied (as to the fingernails) **c :** BUFFING WHEEL **6 :** a country cattlehide weighing 45 to 60 pounds untrimmed **7 a** [so called fr. the buff overcoats worn by volunteer firemen in New York City *ab*1820] **:** an enthusiast about going to fires **b :** FAN, ENTHUSIAST, DEVOTEE ⟨theater ~*s* of all sorts⟩ ⟨twelve-year-old history ~*s* should have a fine time with this big volume —Katharine T. Kinkead⟩

5buff \"\ *adj* **1 :** made of or like buff leather **2 :** of the color buff

6buff \"\ *vt* -ED/-ING/-S **1 :** to polish with a buff; *broadly* **:** POLISH, SHINE ⟨shoes freshly ~*ed*⟩ ⟨~*ing* her nails on her sleeve⟩ **2 :** to give a buff or velvety surface to (leather) **3 :** to color or stain buff (as willow rods)

7buff \"\ *n* -s [origin unknown] *Scot* **:** silly talk **:** NONSENSE

8buff \"\ *vi* -ED/-ING/-S [back-formation fr. 3*buffer*] **:** to act as a buffer in preventing contact or deadening the shock of contact

buf·fa \ˈbüfə, -(ˌ)fä\ *n, pl* **buf·fe** \-(ˌ)fā\ [It, fem. of *buffo* — more at BUFFO] **1 :** a woman singer of comic roles in opera **2 :** OPERA BUFFA

buff·a·bil·i·ty \ˌbəfəˈbiləd·ē\ *n* -ES **:** the capability of being polished by buffing

buff·able \ˈbəfəbəl\ *adj* [6*buff* + *-able*] **:** capable of being buffed

1buf·fa·lo \ˈbəfə,lō *also* -f(ˌ)lō\ *n, pl* **buffalo** *or* **buffaloes** *also* **buffalos** [It *bufalo* & Sp *búfalo,* fr. LL *bufalus,* alter. of L *bubalus* buffalo, African gazelle, fr. Gk *boubalos* African gazelle, irreg. fr. *bous* ox, cow — more at COW] **1 :** any of several wild oxen: as **a :** the water buffalo (*Bubalus bubalis*) orig. from India but now domesticated, developed into several breeds, and used as draft and milch animals in most of the warmer countries of Asia and adjacent islands, being larger and less docile than the common ox and fond of marshy places and rivers **b :** CAPE BUFFALO **c :** a member of the genus *Bison; esp* **:** a large shaggy-maned No. American wild ox (*B. bison*) having short horns and heavy forequarters with a large muscular hump formed by the withers and prolonged spinal processes of the ribs — called also *bison* **d :** ANOA **2 :** something derived from the American buffalo: **a :** a coverlet or rug of buffalo skin **b :** a horn (as for powder) made from the horn of a buffalo **3 :** BUFFALO FISH **4 :** a large heavily armored and armed amphibious military vehicle **5 :** a tap-dance step suggestive of a buffalo's pawing

2buffalo \"\ *vt* -ED/-ING/-ES **:** BAMBOOZLE, BEWILDER, OVERAWE, BAFFLE ⟨he tried to ~ me at first meeting but I soon caught on to his tricks⟩

3buffalo \"\ *adj, usu cap* [fr. *Buffalo,* N.Y.] **:** of or from the city of Buffalo, N.Y. ⟨*Buffalo* factories⟩ **:** of the kind or style prevalent in Buffalo

buffalo bean *or* **buffalo apple** *n* **1** [so called fr. its location in buffalo country] **:** GROUND PLUM **2 :** any of certain African climbing legumes (genus *Stizolobium*) having a velvety seed pod and hairs which cause intolerable itching when they come in contact with the skin

buffalo berry *n* [so called fr. its location in buffalo country] **1** *or* **buffalo bush :** either of two shrubs (*Shepherdia argentea* and *S. canadensis*) of the western U.S. having silvery foliage — called also *bullberry, rabbitberry* **2 :** the edible scarlet berry of the buffalo berry

buffalo bug *or* **buffalo carpet beetle** *n* [so called fr. its appearance] **:** CARPET BEETLE

buffalo bunchgrass *n* [so called fr. its location in buffalo country] **:** a densely tufted perennial fescue (*Festuca scabrella*) of western No. America with usu. scabrous culms and narrow or involute leaf blades

buffalo bur *n* [so called fr. its being frequently entangled in the hair of buffalo] **:** a No. American nightshade (*Solanum rostratum*) with prickly foliage and racemose yellow flowers

buffalo chips *n pl* **:** dry dung of buffalo or of livestock esp. when used as fuel

buffalo cholera *or* **buffalo disease** *n* **:** BARBONE

buffalo cloth *n* [so called fr. its shaggy appearance] **:** a woolen fabric with a shaggy pile

buffalo clover *n* [so called fr. its location in buffalo country] **1 :** either of two clovers (*Trifolium reflexum* and *T. stoloniferum*) of the western U.S. **2 :** BLUEBONNET 3b

buffalo cod *n* **:** LINGCOD

buffalo currant *n* [so called fr. its location in buffalo country] **1 :** an ornamental hardy currant (*Ribes odoratum*) of the western U.S. with fragrant yellow flowers and black fruit **2 :** GOLDEN CURRANT 1

buffalo dance *n* **:** a ritual group dance of No. American Indians imitative of the buffalo for cure, for success in the hunt, or as part of the sun-dance ceremony

buffalofish *n* **:** any of several large suckers (family Catostomidae) mostly found in the Mississippi valley, some being important food fishes: as **a :** BIGMOUTH BUFFALO **b :** BLACK BUFFALO 1 **c :** SMALLMOUTH BUFFALO

buffalo fly *n* **:** a small gray biting muscid fly (*Siphona exigua*) widespread in Indo-Malaysia and Australia where it is a major pest of water buffalo and other domestic animals

buffalo gnat *n* **1 :** BLACKFLY a **2 :** HORN FLY

buffalo gourd *n* [so called fr. its location in buffalo country] **:** CALABAZILLA

buffalo grass *n* **1 :** either of two No. American grasses: **a :** a low-growing dioecious grass (*Buchloë dactyloides*) very common on former feeding grounds of the American buffalo and sometimes used to establish permanent sod in droughty areas **b :** GRAMA **2** *Austral* **:** SAINT AUGUSTINE GRASS **3 :** any of several African grasses; *esp* **:** a hairy guinea grass (*Panicum maximum* var. *hirsutissimum*)

buffalo gun *n* **:** a large-caliber rifle used primarily in hunting the American buffalo

buffalo hump *n* **:** fat pads localized on the back of the neck that produce a resemblance to the hump of a bison and constitute one of the clinical features of Cushing's disease

buffalo indian *n, usu cap B&I* **:** PLAINS INDIAN

buffalo leather *n* **:** leather produced from the hides of Old World buffalo (as the water buffalo)

buffalo moth *n* [so called fr. its appearance] **:** the larva of the carpet beetle

buf·fa·lo·nian \ˌbəfəˈlōnēən, -nyən\ *n* -s *cap* [blend of *Buffalo,* N.Y. and E *-onian* (as in *Oxonian*)] **:** a native or resident of Buffalo, N.Y.

buffalo nut *n* **1 :** the oily drupaceous fruit of rabbitwood — called also *elk nut, oil nut* **2 :** RABBITWOOD

buffalo pea *n* [so called fr. its location in buffalo country] **1 :** GROUND PLUM **2 :** AMERICAN VETCH

buffalo robe *n* **:** the hide of an American buffalo dressed with the hair on, commonly trimmed to rectangular shape, lined on the skin side with fabric, and used as a carriage robe, rug, or article of bedding

buffalo rye *n* [so called fr. its growing in buffalo country] **:** LYME GRASS

buffalos *pl of* BUFFALO

buffalo soldier *n* **:** a Negro soldier serving in the western U.S. after the Civil War

buffalo thorn *n* **:** a low tree (*Acacia latronum*) of western India that is shaped like an umbrella and covered with long straight spines borne in pairs and connected at the base

buffalo tree *n* **:** RABBITWOOD

buffalo treehopper *n* [so called fr. its horned prothorax] **:** a bright green treehopper (*Stictocephala bubalus*) that has two lateral horns on the prothorax, is common throughout the U.S., and damages fruit and other trees by laying its eggs in the bark of the twigs

buffalo wallow *n* **:** a shallow undrained depression occurring on the Great Plains, often containing water in wet seasons, and generally thought to have been produced or deepened by the rolling and wallowing of herds of buffalo in mud and dust

buffalo weaver *n* [so called fr. the massive and rough appearance of its nest] **:** any of several gregarious African weavers constituting a subfamily of Ploceidae and being distinguished from other weavers by their bulky untidy nests that are placed on rather than suspended from branches

buffalo weed *n* **:** GREAT RAGWEED

buffalo wolf *n* [so called fr. its former abundance in the buffalo country] **:** the gray wolf of central and western U.S.

buff–backed heron \ˈ≈,≈-\ *n* **:** CATTLE EGRET

buff·bar \ˈbəf,bär\ *n, usu cap* [*buff* Orpington + *barred* Rocks] **:** a breed of buff or golden autosexing fowls developed by interbreeding barred Rocks and buff Orpingtons

buff–bare \ˈ≈ˌ≈\ *adj* [4*buff*] **:** completely unclothed **:** stark naked

buff–breasted sandpiper \ˈ≈,≈≈-\ *n* **:** a small stocky sandpiper (*Tryngites subruficollis*) having uniformly buff underparts and yellowish legs, breeding on the northwest coast of No. America, wintering in Argentina, and migrating chiefly by the central flyway or to the east coast of Canada and over the Atlantic

buffcoat \ˈ≈,≈\ *n* [4*buff* + *coat*] **1 a :** a coat of buff leather; *specif* **:** a close short-sleeved military coat worn for defense in the 17th century **b** *archaic* **:** SOLDIER **2 :** BUFFY COAT

buffe *pl of* BUFFA

buffed *adj* [6*buff* + *-ed*] **:** SMOOTH, POLISHED

buf·fel grass \ˈbəfəl-\ *n* [part trans. of Afrik *buffelgras,* fr. *buffel* buffalo (fr. MD, fr. MF *buffle*) + *gras* grass — more at BUFF] **:** an erect tussock-forming perennial bur grass (*Pennisetum cenchroides*) used esp. in Australia and southern Africa for pasture and forage

buffelhead *var of* BUFFLEHEAD

1buff·er \ˈbəfə(r)\ *n* -s [obs. E *buff* to bark (of imit. origin) + *-er*] *archaic slang* **:** DOG 1

2buf·fer \"\ *n* -s [origin unknown] **1** *slang* **:** FELLOW, GUY; *esp* **:** DUFFER — often used with *old* **2** *slang Brit* **:** a chief boatswain's mate

3buff·er \"\ *n* -s *often attrib* [2*buff* + *-er*] **1 :** any of various devices, apparatus, or pieces of material designed primarily to reduce shock due to contact: as **a :** an apparatus on the end of a railway car to close the space between adjoining cars and to absorb shocks incident to car coupling and movement **b** *Brit* **:** a bumper-type shock absorber usu. installed in pairs on the ends of railway cars in Europe **2 :** a means or device used as a cushion against the shock of fluctuations in business or financial activity **3 :** something that serves to separate two items: as **a :** BUFFER STATE **b :** a person who shields another esp. from trivial and annoying routine matters that would interfere with more important activities **c :** an electronic device (as a circuit) used to isolate two radio circuits to avoid undesired reactions between them **d :** an animal that by serving as food for predators cuts down the predation losses of another animal (as a game bird) more desired in a community **e :** a member of a complex of multiple factors that tends to modify the expression of a major gene and reduce the variability of its response to environment **f :** an intermediate storage unit in an electronic computer that accepts signals at high rates and delivers them at lower rates **4 a :** a substance or mixture of substances (as acid salts of weak acids or amphoteric substances) that in solution is capable of neutralizing within limits both acids and bases and thus acts to maintain the original hydrogen-ion concentration of the solution, various of such substances playing fundamental roles in natural processes (as bicarbonates and proteins in biological fluids or clay and organic matter in soils) **b :** BUFFER SOLUTION

4buff·er \"\ *vt* -ED/-ING/-S **1 :** to modify the effect of **:** lessen the impact of **:** CUSHION ⟨the canopy likewise ~*s* the burning sun —*Newsweek*⟩ **2 :** to treat (as an acid solution) with a buffer

5buff·er \"\ *n* -s [6*buff* + *-er*] **1 :** a worker who buffs a particular thing or material (as shoes or leather) or who uses a particular buffing device (as a buffing wheel) **2 :** any of various devices used in buffing: as **a :** BUFFING WHEEL **b :** a horseshoer's tool with a chisel blade to remove heads of nails and a point or prod to drive the nails out **c :** a padded device for polishing fingernails

buffer solution *n* [3*buffer*] **:** a solution that usu. contains on the one hand either a weak acid (as carbonic acid) together with one of the salts of this acid or at least one acid salt of a weak acid or on the other hand a weak base (as ammonia) together with one of the salts of the base and that by its resistance to changes in hydrogen-ion concentration on the addition of acid or base is useful in many chemical, biological, and technical processes

buffer state *n* [3*buffer*] **:** a small neutral state lying between two or more larger potentially rival powers and serving as a military barrier and a means of preventing friction between such powers

buffer stock *n* : a stock of a basic commodity (as tin) acquired (as by a cartel) in a period of low or unstable prices and distributed in a period of high prices to stabilize the market

buffer stop *n* [3*buffer*] *Brit* : a bumping post placed at the end of a track in train sheds or at stations as an emergency stop for incoming trains and locomotives

buffer strip *n* [3*buffer*] : a grassed strip between strips of cropland subject to erosion

1**buf·fet** \'bəfət, *usu* -əd·+V\ *n* -s [ME, fr. MF, fr. OF, dim. of *buffe* blow — more at BUFF] **1** : a blow with the hand : SLAP, CUFF **2 a** : a blow from any source ⟨recurrent ~s of fate⟩ **b** : something that affects like a blow (as the violence of wind or wave) **c** : the shaking and vibrating of an airplane when forced to a speed greater than that for which it was designed — see BUFFETING

2**buffet** \"\ *vb* -ED/-ING/-S [ME *buffeten*, fr. OF *buffeter*, fr. *buffet*] *vt* **1** : to strike with or as if with the hand : CUFF, SLAP **2 a** : to strike repeatedly : POMMEL, BATTER ⟨the wind ~*ed* him as he climbed the slope⟩ **b** : to contend against : strive with ⟨~*ing* the billows⟩ **3** : to drive, force, or move by or as if by repeated blows — often used with *about* ⟨he was ~*ed* about by his somber thoughts⟩ ⟨~*ed* about by one failure after another⟩ ~ *vi* **1** : STRIVE, CONTEND, STRUGGLE **2 a** : to progress or make one's way esp. under conditions of stress or difficulty or by or as if by physical struggle ⟨the . . . child as he ~*s* back and forth between mother with lovers and father with . . . mistresses —James Kelly⟩ ⟨the milk train ~*ing* along through the valley⟩ **b** *of an airplane* : to undergo or become subjected to buffeting **syn** see BEAT

3**buf·fet** \,bə'fā, (')bü¦fā, ,bə'fā *sometimes* (')bu̇¦fā; *Brit usu* 'bu̇(,)fā *for sense 3b and often* 'bəfit *for senses 1 & 2; sense 4 is* 'bəfi(t)\ *n* -s [F] **1** : a sideboard often without a mirror **2** : a cupboard or set of shelves either movable or fixed to a wall for the display of tableware **3 a** : a counter for refreshments **b** *chiefly Brit* : a restaurant operated in conjunction with some other enterprise and primarily as a public convenience (as in a railway station or theater); *specif* : BUFFET CAR **c** : a meal at which persons help themselves to food set out on a buffet or a table and eat while standing or sitting but not at a formally arranged table ⟨a ~ luncheon⟩ **4** *usu* **buffet stool** *chiefly Scot* : FOOTSTOOL, HASSOCK

buffet car *n* [3*buffet*] *chiefly Brit* : a railway passenger car having facilities for preparing and serving light meals or snacks usu. in combination with other facilities (as for sleeping or lounging); *also* : DINING CAR

buf·fet·ing \'bəfəd·iŋ, -ət|, |ēŋ\ *n* -s [fr. gerund of 2*buffet*] : repeated alteration of the aerodynamic forces acting on any part of an airplane in flight due to unsteady air flow that originates in a disturbance set up by some other part of the airplane; *often* : irregular oscillation of the airplane or its parts resulting from such buffeting

buffi *pl of* BUFFO

buffier *comparative of* BUFFY

buffiest *superlative of* BUFFY

1**buffing** *n* -s [fr. gerund of 6*buff*] **1 a** : the action of a buffer **b** : the process by which something (as leather) is buffed **2** : material removed by a buffing machine — usu. used in pl.

2**buffing** *n* -s [4*buff* + *-ing*] : a thin sheet of leather split from a hide and commonly used for bookbinding

buffing head *n* : a frame supporting a spindle with means for revolving it and attaching a buffing wheel

buffing wheel *n* : a wheel (as a bob) covered with buff leather, muslin, felt, bristle brushes, or comparable material and used in polishing

buff jerkin *n* [4*buff* & 5*buff*] : a buff-leather jacket formerly worn by soldiers under the corselet; *sometimes* : a buff-colored jacket or waistcoat

buf·fle \'bəfəl\ *n* -s [MF — more at BUFF] *archaic* : BUFFALO

buff leather *n* [4*buff*] : a strong supple oil-tanned leather usu. rather light in color and with a velvety surface that is now produced chiefly from cattle hides

buffle duck *n* [*bufflehead*] : BUFFLEHEAD

bufflehead \'⸗⸗,⸗\ *n* **1** *now dial* : BLOCKHEAD, FOOL **2** *also* **buf·fel·head** \"\ : a small No. American diving duck (*Bucephala albeola*) that in general resembles the goldeneye but is distinguished by the lobed hind toe and by the very densely feathered head of the male with a white patch behind the eye — called also *butterball, spirit duck*

bufflehead

buffle-headed \'⸗⸗¦⸗⸗\ *adj, now chiefly dial* : STUPID, FOOLISH

buf·fle·horn \'bəfəl-,hȯrn\ *n* [trans. of Afrik *buffelhoring*] : a small African tree (*Burchellia capensis*) of the family Rubiaceae that has very hard tough wood and scarlet flowers

buf·fler \'bəflə(r)\ *n* -s [by alter.] *dial* : BUFFALO

buff nor stye *n* [7*buff* + *stye*, origin unknown] *Scot* : head nor tail : one thing or another ⟨couldn't make *buff nor stye* of his letter⟩

1**buf·fo** \'bü(,)fō\ *n, pl* **buffos** \-ōz\ *also* **buf·fi** \-fē\ [It, fr. *buffone* buffoon — more at BUFFOON] : CLOWN, BUFFOON; *specif* : a male singer of comic roles in opera

2**buffo** \"\ *adj* **1 a** : of, relating to, or suitable for an operatic buffo ⟨a fine ~ aria⟩ **b** : adapted to or competent in buffo singing ⟨a noted ~ tenor⟩ **2** : COMIC, FARCICAL ⟨a ~ character⟩

1**buf·foon** \,bə'fün, ,bə'f-\ *n* -s *often attrib* [MF *bouffon*, fr. OIt *buffone*, fr. ML *bufon-, bufo*, fr. L, toad — more at BUFO] **1 a** : a man professionally engaged in entertaining others by tricks, gestures, or comic pantomime : JESTER, MERRY-ANDREW, CLOWN; *broadly* : COMEDIAN **b** : a person who strives for comical effects **2** : a gross and clownish person; *esp* : one ill-educated or stupid — **buf·foon·ish** \-nish, -nēsh\ *adj*

2**buffoon** \"\ *vb* -ED/-ING/-S *vt* : to treat with buffoonery : RIDICULE, BURLESQUE ~ *vi* : to play the buffoon : behave like a buffoon

buf·foon·ery \(,)bə'fün(ə)rē, -ri\ *n* -ES [F *bouffonnerie*, fr. *bouffon* + *-erie* -ery] : the practices of a buffoon; *esp* : coarse loutish behavior

buffs *pl of* BUFF, *pres 3d sing of* BUFF

buff stick *n* [6*buff*] : a strip of wood covered with buff leather or chamois and used in polishing

buff stop *n* [9*buff*] : a partially damping or muffling device on a harpsichord or piano

buff-tip \'⸗,⸗\ *or* **buff-tipped moth** \'⸗,⸗-\ *n* [5*buff*] : a European moth (*Phalera bucephala*) having violet-gray forewings with creamy tips and caterpillars that feed on the leaves of elm, beech, birch, oak, and fruit trees

buff top *n* [6*buff*] : a style of cut of certain gemstones in which the top is cut cabochon and the bottom is step-cut

buff·y \'bəfē\ *adj, often* -ER/-EST [4*buff* + *-y*] **1** : of the color buff **2** *slang* : INTOXICATED

buffy coat *n* : the superficial layer of yellowish or buff coagulated plasma from which the red corpuscles have settled out in slowly coagulated blood

bu·fo \'b(y)ü(,)fō\ *n* [NL, fr. L, toad; perh. akin to OS *quappa* tadpole, MLG *quappe*, Dan *kvabbe* burbot, OPruss *gabawo* toad, OSlav *žaba* frog] **1** *cap* : a large genus (the type of the family Bufonidae) of toads that contains the common toads of America and Europe and the agua toad and is represented on all the continents except Australia **2** -s : any toad of the genus *Bufo*

bu·fo·gen·in \,byüfə'jenən, byü'fäjənən\ *n* [NL *Bufo* + E *-gen* + *-in*] : BUFAGIN

bu·fo·nid \'byüfənəd, -,nid\ *n* -s [NL *Bufonidae*] : a toad of the family Bufonidae

bu·fon·i·dae \byü'fänə,dē\ *n pl, cap* [NL, fr. *Bufon-, Bufo*, type genus + *-idae*] : a large family of toads (suborder Procoela) including all the typical toads that are distinguished by an incompletely fused shoulder girdle and dilated or cylindrical transverse sacral processes

bu·fo·nite \'byüfə,nīt\ *n* -s [L *bufon-, bufo* toad + E *-ite*] : a fossil consisting of the petrified teeth and palatal bones of pycnodont fishes — see TOADSTONE

bu·fo·tal·in \,byüfə'talən, -tāl-\ *n* -s [ISV *bufo-* (fr. NL *Bufo*, genus name of *Bufo vulgaris*) + *digitalin*] : a crystalline bufagin $C_{26}H_{36}O_6$ obtained esp. from the poisonous secretion of the skin glands of the common European toad (*Bufo vulgaris*)

bu·fo·ten·ine \,byüfə'te,nēn, -,nən\ *n* -s [ISV *bufo-* (fr. NL *Bufo*) + *-ten-* (origin unknown) + *-ine*] : a crystalline toxic alkaloid $C_{12}H_{16}N_2O$ derived from indole that is obtained from poisonous secretions of toads and is like epinephrine in biological action

bu·fo·tox·in \,byüfə'täksən\ *n* [ISV *bufo-* (fr. NL *Bufo*, genus name of *Bufo vulgaris*) + *toxin*] : a crystalline toxic steroid $C_{40}H_{60}N_4O_{10}$ obtained from the poisonous secretion of skin glands of the common European toad (*Bufo vulgaris*) that is like digitalis in biological action and that yields bufotalin and suberyl-arginine on hydrolysis; *also* : any of several similar steroids from the secretions of other toads that yield a bufagin and suberylarginine on hydrolysis

1**bug** \'bəg\ *n* -s [ME *bugge* scarecrow; akin to G dial. *bögge* piece of dried nasal mucus, hobgoblin, Norw dial. *bugge* important man — more at BOAST] **1** *obs* : BOGEY, BUGBEAR **2 a** : an insect or other creeping or crawling invertebrate (as a spider or small crustacean) — not used technically **b** : any of certain insects commonly considered esp. obnoxious: as (1) : BEDBUG (2) : COCKROACH (3) : HEAD LOUSE **c** : an insect of the order Hemiptera; *esp* : a member of the suborder Heteroptera **3** : an unexpected defect, fault, flaw, or imperfection (as in a plan, a mechanism, or a piece of legislation) — used esp. of such items as are regarded as capable of alteration or ready improvement ⟨there are still some ~*s* to iron out but the new motor will do the job⟩; compare JOKER **4 a** : a disease-producing germ or other microorganism **b** : a disease caused by such bugs ⟨probably caused by a ~ . . . as yet unknown —Horace Sutton⟩; *esp* : any of various respiratory conditions of virus origin (as influenza or grippe) ⟨stricken with a virus ~⟩ **5 a** : FAD, CRAZE, HOBBY ⟨bitten by the miniature-golf ~⟩ ⟨got the trailer ~ on a vacation trip⟩ **b** : enthusiasm, concern, or deep interest esp. in respect to some particular matter or objective ⟨I have rather a ~ about learning in class —Jean Nison⟩ **c** : a person notably concerned with, enthusiastic about, or efficient at a specified interest or activity ⟨he's a ~ on proper training of young shooters⟩ ⟨she was a ~ at languages —*Newsweek*⟩ ⟨a perfect ~ for detail⟩ **d** : HOBBYIST ⟨camera ~*s*⟩ ⟨ski ~*s*⟩ **e** : a crazy person; *esp* : FIREBUG **6 a** *archaic* : a vain or self-important person **b** : a person of prominence or high social standing ⟨we'll have all the ~*s* to lunch⟩ — see BIG BUG **7** *poker* : the joker when considered wild only for the purpose of filling straights or flushes or of acting as an ace **8** *slang* **a** : an alarm system (as a burglar alarm) **b** : a concealed microphone **c** : a device for wiretapping **d** : a high-speed telegrapher's key that makes repeated dots or dashes automatically and saves motion of the operator's hand **9** [so called fr. its designation by an asterisk on race programs] : the 5-pound weight allowance given apprentice jockeys **10** *slang* : NUMBERS GAME **11** : a light usu. two-seater stripped-down automobile **12** : a fishing plug felt to resemble a large insect

2**bug** \"\ *vb* **bugged**; **bugged**; **bugging**; **bugs** *vt* **1** : to rid (as plants) of insects ⟨we'll have to ~ the potatoes again next week⟩ **2** *slang* : BOTHER, ANNOY, IRRITATE; *sometimes* : to drive (a person) crazy **3** *slang* **a** : to equip with a burglar alarm **b** : to plant a concealed microphone in : WIRETAP ⟨~ a meeting⟩ ~ *vi* : to hunt for or collect bugs

3**bug** \"\ *also* **bug light** *n* -s [prob. fr. (*lightning*) *bug*] **1** : a small channel or harbor light with intermittent flash **2** : FLASHLIGHT b

4**bug** \'bəg, 'bu̇g\ *adj* [perh. of Scand origin; akin to Norw *bugge* important man] *dial Eng* : CONCEITED, STUCK-UP

5**bug** \'bəg\ *vb* **bugged**; **bugged**; **bugging**; **bugs** [prob. alter. (influenced by 1*bug*) of *bulge*] *vi, of the eyes* : PROTRUDE, BULGE — often used with *out* ~ *vt* : BULGE, PROTRUDE ⟨his eyes were *bugged* with horror⟩

bug·a·boo \'bəgə,bü *sometimes* 'bu̇g-\ *n* -s [alter. of earlier *buggybow*] **1** : an imaginary object of fright : BUGBEAR, BOGEY ⟨they scurried home, seeing goblins and ~*s* in every shadow⟩ **2** : a source of concern ⟨the ~ of inbreeding —W.L.McAtee⟩; *esp* : something that causes fear or distress often out of proportion to its actual importance in a situation ⟨the old ~ of insufficient purchasing power . . . is real enough to warrant deep study and careful planning—Nathan Robertson⟩

bu·ga·ku \bü'gä(,)kü\ *n* -s *usu cap* [Jap, lit., dancing, music] : a stately classical Japanese dance orig. introduced from China

bu·gala \bü'galə\ *n* -s [Ar *baqlah*] : a large dhow used chiefly in the Red sea

bu·gan \'bu̇gən, 'büg-, 'bəg-\ *n* -s [W *bwgan* hobgoblin, fr. MW, perh. fr. ME *bugge* — more at BUG] *dial Eng* : a hobgoblin or ghost

bu·gara \bü'garə\ *n* -s [origin unknown] : RAINBOW PERCH

bugbane \'⸗,⸗\ *n* **1** : a plant of the genus *Cimicifuga*; *esp* : a perennial herb (*C. racemosa*) with flowers reputed to be distasteful to insects — called also *snakeroot* **2** : AMERICAN HELLEBORE

bug·bear \'bəg,ba(ə)(ə)r, -,be(ə)r, -,ba(a)ə, -,beə\ *n* -s [1*bug* (goblin) + *bear*] **1** : an imaginary goblin or specter used to excite needless fear (as in children) **2 a** : an object or source of dread or abhorrence ⟨the French tendency to make a ~ of Germany is exactly what the Russians want —*New Yorker*⟩ **b** : PROBLEM; *esp* : a continuing source of irritation or annoyance ⟨their biggest ~ has been the cross-filing system that California adopted a generation ago —Gladwin Hill⟩

bugbite \'⸗,⸗\ *n* : a bite or sting by an insect

bug boy *n* [1*bug* (weight allowance)] *slang* : an apprentice jockey

bug dust *n* : fine coal produced in mining with a cutting machine

bug-eater \'⸗,⸗⸗\ *n, usu cap B* [fr. *bug-eater*, a species of goatsucker common in Nebraska] : NEBRASKAN — a nickname

bugeye \'⸗,⸗\ *n* : a small shallow-draft flat-bottomed boat with a centerboard and two raked masts carrying jib and triangular sails that is largely used by oystermen and others in Chesapeake Bay

bug-eyed \'⸗¦⸗\ *adj* : having the eyes bulging (as with astonishment)

bugfish \'⸗,⸗\ *n* [so called fr. a parasite that often adheres to the roof of its mouth] : MENHADEN

bugged *past of* BUG

1**bug·ger** \'bu̇gə(r), 'bəg-\ *or* **boog·er** \'bu̇g-\ *n* -s [ME *bougre* heretic, sodomite, fr. MF, fr. ML *Bugarus, Bulgarus*, lit., Bulgarian; fr. the adherence of the Bulgarians to the Eastern Church considered heretical] **1** : one that commits buggery **2 a** : a worthless person : GUY, FELLOW — a generalized term of abuse **b** : ROGUE, RASCAL, SCAMP — often used affectionately esp. of children or animals

2**bugger** \"\ *vb* -ED/-ING/-S *vt* **1** : to commit buggery with — usu. considered vulgar **2** *slang* : DAMN, BLAST, DARN ⟨I'll be ~*ed*⟩ **3** *slang* : to wear out : EXHAUST ⟨we had tramped for hours and were completely ~*ed*⟩ ~ *vi, slang Brit* : to go away : LEAVE, SCRAM — usu. used with *off*

3**bugger** *var of* BOOGER

bug·ger·man \'bu̇gə(r),man, -maa(ə)n *sometimes* 'bəg- *or* 'büg-\ *var of* BOOGEYMAN

bugger up *vt* [2*bugger*] : to mix up : put into disorder : CONFUSE

bug·gery \'bu̇gərē, 'bəg-, -ri\ *n* -ES [ME *bugerie*, fr. MF *bougrerie* heresy, sodomy, fr. *bougre* bugger + *-erie* -ery — more at BUGGER] : unnatural sexual intercourse : SODOMY

bug·gi·ness \'bəgēnəs, -gin-\ *n* -ES : the quality or state of being buggy

bugging *pres part of* BUG

1**bug·gy** \'bəgē, -gi\ *adj* -ER/-EST [1*bug* + *-y*] **1 a** : infested with bugs **b** : of, relating to, or suggestive of bugs ⟨a ~ odor⟩ **2** *slang* **a** : lacking restraint or good judgment : SILLY, BATTY ⟨she's ~ about horses⟩ **b** : INSANE, DEMENTED

2**buggy** \"\ *n* -ES [origin unknown] **1** : a light one-horse carriage made with two wheels in England and with four wheels in the U.S. **2** : a small wagon or truck used for short transportations of heavy materials (as coal in a mine or ingots in a steel mill); *specif* : a 2-wheeled cart used for transporting freshly mixed concrete short distances on construction jobs **3** *slang* : CABOOSE; *sometimes* : OBSERVATION CAR **4** : any of various vehicles: as **a** *slang* : AUTOMOBILE **b** : BABY CARRIAGE **c** : MARSH BUGGY

American buggy

3**buggy** \"\ *adj* -ER/-EST [5*bug* + *-y*] *of the eyes* : BULGING

buggy cultivator *n* [2*buggy*] : a sulky cultivator

bug·gy·man \'bəgēmən, -gim-, -,man\ *n, pl* **buggymen** [2*buggy* + *man*] : a worker who handles a barrow or buggy for the transportation of bulk material (as coal, ore, concrete, or slag)

buggy plow *n* [2*buggy*] : a sulky plow

bughead \'⸗,⸗\ *n* [so called fr. a parasite that adheres to the roof of its mouth] : MENHADEN

1**bughouse** \'⸗,⸗\ *n* [1*bug* (crazy person) + *house*] *slang* : an insane asylum

2**bughouse** \'⸗,⸗\ *adj, slang* : mentally deranged : INSANE, CRAZY

bught *Scot var of* BOUGHT

bu·gi \'bügē\ *or* **bu·gis** \-gəs\ *n, pl* **bugi** *or* **bugis** *usu cap* [Malay *Bugis*] : BUGINESE

bu·gia \'b(y)üj(ē)ə\ *n* -s [NL, fr. ML *candela Bugiae, candela de Bugia* candle from Bougie, seaport town in northeastern Algeria from which they were exported, trans. of MF *chandelle de Bougie*] : a low candlestick with a short handle

bu·gi·nese \¦bügə¦nēz, -ēs\ *n, pl* **buginese** *or* **bugineses** *usu cap* [D *Boeginees*, fr. Malay *Bugis*] **1 a** : an Indonesian people of the southern part of Celebes island, Indonesia **b** : a member of such people **2** : the language of the Buginese people

bu·gin·vil·laea *or* **bu·gin·vil·lea** *syn of* BOUGAINVILLAEA

bug juice *n, slang* : inferior whiskey or other strong liquor

1**bu·gle** \'byügəl\ *n* -s [ME, fr. OF, fr. LL *bugula*] : a plant of the genus *Ajuga*; *esp* : a low European annual (*A. reptans*) with spikes of blue flowers that is now naturalized in parts of the U.S.

2**bugle** \"\ *n* -s [ME, fr. OF, fr. L *buculus, boculus* young steer, dim. of *bos* head of cattle — more at COW] **1** *obs* : a wild ox; *esp* : BUFFALO **2** : a signal horn; *esp* : one made of an animal's horn **3 a** : a brass instrument with a cupped mouthpiece like the trumpet but having a shorter and more conical tube and now chiefly for military and parade use ⟨drum and ~ corps⟩ **b** : one of a family of valved brass instruments of sizes grading from flügelhorns to tubas now chiefly used in brass bands — compare EUPHONIUM, SAXHORN

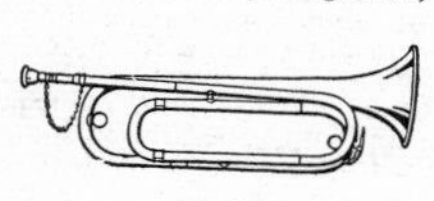

bugle

3**bu·gle** \"\ *vb* **bugled**; **bugled**; **bugling** \-g(ə)liŋ\ **bugles** *vt* : to sound or summon by or as if by a bugle call ~ *vi* **1** : to sound a bugle **2** *of bull elks or certain other large deer* : to utter a prolonged cry that suggests the sound of a bugle and is the characteristic rutting call

4**bugle** \"\ *adj, of a hunting dog* : having a strong deep melodious bay

5**bugle** \"\ *or* **bugle bead** *n* -s [perh. fr. 2*bugle*; fr. its resemblance to a trumpet] : a small cylindrical bead of glass or plastic used for trimming esp. on women's clothing

6**bugle** \"\ *adj* **1** : like a bugle; *esp* : jet-black like most early glass bugles **2** : trimmed or fashioned with bugles ⟨a band of dainty ~ work about the neckline⟩

bugle horn *n* [2*bugle*] : BUGLE 2

bu·gler \'byüglə(r)\ *n* -s [2*bugle* + *-er*] : a person who plays on or signals with a bugle

bu·glet \'byüglət\ *n* -s [2*bugle* + *-et*] : a small bugle

bugleweed \'⸗⸗,⸗\ *n* **1** *also* **buglewort** : a mint of the genus *Lycopus*; *esp* : a mildly narcotic and astringent herb (*L. virginicus*) **2** : INDIGO BROWN **3** : BUGLE

bug light *var of* 3BUG

bu·gloss \'byü,gläs, -lȯs\ *n* -ES [MF *buglosse*, fr. L *buglossa*, irreg. fr. Gk *bouglōssos, bouglōsson*, fr. *bous* head of cattle + *-glōssos, -glōsson* (fr. *glōssa* tongue) — more at COW, GLOSS] **1** : a plant of the genus *Anchusa* (esp. *A. officinalis*) sometimes cultivated for its delicate usu. blue flowers — called also *alkanet* **2** : GERMAN MADWORT **3** : a European hawkweed (*Picris echioides*) with yellow flowers that is now naturalized in the eastern U.S. **4** : a very bristly annual European herb (*Lycopsis arvensis*) naturalized in eastern No. America

bugloss cowslip *n* : LUNGWORT 2 a

bug·ol·o·gist \,bə'gäləjəst\ *n* -s : ENTOMOLOGIST — not used technically

bug·ol·o·gy \-jē\ *n* -ES [1*bug* + *-ology* (as in *entomology*)] : ENTOMOLOGY — not used technically

bugong moth *var of* BOGONG MOTH

bug out \¦bəg\ *vi* [prob. short for 2*bugger*] : to retreat during a military action; *esp* : to flee in panic or without orders

bugout \'⸗,⸗\ *n* -s [*bug out*] : unauthorized flight from a military action : desertion esp. when under fire; *also* : DESERTER

bu·gre \'bügrə\ *n* -s [Pg. fr. F *bougre* bugger — more at BUGGER] : a Brazilian Indian — usu. taken to be offensive

1**bugs** *pl of* BUG, *pres 3d sing of* BUG

2**bugs** \'bəgz\ *adj* [fr. pl. of 1*bug* (craze)] *slang* : CRAZY — used in the predicate ⟨the man was totally ~ and thought he was Napoleon⟩

bugseed *or* **bugweed** \'⸗,⸗\ *n* : an herb of the genus *Corispermum* of the family Chenopodiaceae; *esp* : a fleshy annual (*C. hyssopifolium*) with flat oval seeds that is a common weed in north temperate regions

bu·gu·la \'byügyələ\ *n, cap* [NL, fr. LL, bugle (plant)] : a common and widespread genus (the type of the family Bugulidae) of marine shallow-water branching bryozoans that sometimes cause fouling of ships

bug word *also* **bug's word** *n* [1*bug*] **1** *obs* : a word to terrify **2** *obs* : threatening language — usu. used in pl.

bu·hid \bü'(h)ēd\ *also* **bu·id** \-'ēd\ *or* **bu·kid** \-'kēd\ *n, pl* **buhid** *or* **buhids** *usu cap* [Buhid *Buhid, Buid, Bukid*] **1** : a predominantly pagan people inhabiting southern Mindoro, Philippines **2** : a member of the Buhid people

buhl *var of* BOULLE

buhl and counter *n* : decorative work in which a material is divided into two parts by sawing out a pattern and each part is made complete again by inlay

buhr \'bər\ *n* -s [by shortening] : BUHRSTONE 2; *also* : one of the projections resembling teeth on such a stone

buhrmill \'⸗,⸗\ *n* : a mill that uses buhrstones for grinding grain

buhrstone *also* **burrstone** *or* **burstone** \'⸗,⸗\ *n* [*buhrstone*, alter. of *burrstone*, *burstone*, prob. fr. *burr, bur* + *stone*] **1** : a siliceous rock used as a material for millstones **2** : a millstone cut from buhrstone

buik \'byük, 'biēk\ *Scot var of* BOOK

1**build** \'bild\ *vb* **built** \-lt\ *or archaic* **builded** \-ldəd\ **built** *or archaic* **builded**; **building**; **builds** [ME *bilden*, fr. OE *byldan*, denominative fr. the root of *bold* house; akin to ON *bōl* abode, farm, OE *būan* to dwell — more at BOWER] *vt* **1 a** : to construct for a dwelling ⟨birds ~*ing* their nests⟩ ⟨they *built* a snug little cottage beside the stream⟩ **b** : to form by ordering and uniting materials by gradual means into a composite whole — used esp. with reference to comparatively large or massive structures ⟨they *built* churches and roads and power lines⟩ ⟨he is making a model of the boat his father *built*⟩ **2** : to cause to be constructed : be responsible for the building of ⟨some contractors ~ hundreds of houses every year⟩; *esp* : to be the source of the money for building ⟨sugar and cotton *built* the gracious plantation houses⟩ **3** : to fashion or develop according to a systematic plan, by a definite process, or on a particular base ⟨~*ing* security for the future⟩ ⟨an argument *built* on solid facts⟩: as **a :** to give form **:** CREATE — used passively and of human or other living bodies ⟨a horse *built* for speed⟩ **b :** to give an inherent tendency **:** orient fundamentally — usu. used passively ⟨he was *built* to fight for what he believed in⟩ ⟨I'm not *built* that way⟩ **c :** MAKE, CONSTRUCT, FORM: as (1) **:** to arrange the combustibles for and usu. to light (a fire) (2) **:** TAILOR ⟨vest pockets are cut and *built* much in the same way —Clarence Poulin⟩ (3) **:** to cook up (a dish) ⟨Grandma will ~ one of her famous fruitcakes⟩ (4) *dial* **:** ROLL ⟨~ a cigarette⟩ (5) **:** to produce (a work of art or literature) ⟨~*ing* a new book⟩ esp. as an elaboration or exposition of a particular basis or theme ⟨a recurring phrase . . . upon which this whole book seems to be *built* —Richard Sullivan⟩ (6) **:** to make the blank parts of (a wax mold) higher by adding molten wax to ensure that the corresponding areas of the finished electrotype will be well below the face — often used with *up* **d :** ENLARGE, INCREASE ⟨~ an inventory⟩; *esp* **:** to improve the status of **:** ENHANCE, EXALT ⟨~ a candidate⟩ — usu. used with *up* ⟨his scholarly interpretation *built up* the role⟩ **e :** to bring into being **:** develop through deliberate effort ⟨beginning to ~ some understanding . . . of health practices among these people —Roger Angell⟩ ⟨~*ing* a society without extremes of poverty and wealth —Maurice Cranston⟩ **f** (1) *casino* **:** to put together (a numerical combination of cards) to be taken in by a card of that value (2) *in word games* **:** to form (a word) by assembling letters **4 a :** to employ so as to produce a structure ⟨they *built* the stones into sturdy fences⟩ **b :** to use as material from which to form or formulate something ⟨you could ~ these arguments into a whole new philosophy⟩ **5 :** to improve the cleansing action of (as soap) by the addition of a builder **~** *vi* **1 :** to perform the act, exercise the art, or practice the business of building ⟨you can trust his work, he's been ~*ing* for 30 years⟩ **2 :** to be in the course of construction — usu. used as a present participle ⟨ships ~*ing* in the docks⟩ ⟨the road turned west and *built* slowly across Dakota —R.A.Billington⟩ **3 :** to reach or progress towards a peak (as of intensity or interest) ⟨the wind began to ~ and the sleet to blow about⟩ ⟨a good boxing card ~*s* from the first minute of the first bout⟩

syn BUILD, CONSTRUCT, ERECT, FRAME, RAISE, REAR: these all have in common the sense of to form a structure or something comparable to a structure. BUILD stresses the fitting together of parts or materials to form the thing desired ⟨*build* a cathedral⟩ ⟨*build* a nest⟩ ⟨*build* a road⟩ ⟨*build* a city⟩ CONSTRUCT, very close in meaning to BUILD, usu. lays stress upon the problem, or intricacy of the process, of fitting the parts together often implying more skill and intelligence than BUILD ⟨*construct* a railroad⟩ ⟨*construct* a plan⟩ ⟨*construct* a poem⟩ ERECT, true to its etymology, carries the idea of putting up something that is upright ⟨*erect* a flagpole⟩ ⟨*erect* a building⟩ FRAME usu. emphasizes the forming or fashioning to suit a preconceived design, an intention, a purpose, or certain unavoidable facts, applying generally to intangibles ⟨*frame* an answer⟩ ⟨*frame* a financial report⟩ ⟨*frame* a constitution⟩ RAISE and REAR, interchangeable with ERECT, usu. apply to things that are upright or that have or imply height ⟨*raise* a wall⟩ ⟨*raise* a building of several stories⟩ ⟨*rear* a tower⟩ ⟨*rear* a complex philosophic and metaphysical construction⟩

— **build a fire under :** to stimulate (someone or something) to vigorous action — **build around :** to fashion, construct, or develop (a whole) in orientation to some constituent factor ⟨usually a sponsor buys a show *built around* a star —Arthur Godfrey⟩ ⟨their lives are *built around* their house and garden⟩ — **build into :** to make an integral part of something ⟨quality is *built into* our product⟩ — **build on 1 :** to use as a foundation ⟨*built on* early experiences⟩ ⟨Scott has renewed the literature of his people by *building on* this ancient balladry —Van Wyck Brooks⟩ **2 :** to rely upon ⟨he did not *build on* these promises —J.D.Beresford⟩

²build \"\ *n* -s **1 a :** form or mode of structure (as of a ship) **:** MAKE **b :** the bodily conformation of a person or lower animal **:** PHYSIQUE, MAKEUP ⟨a man of heavy ~⟩ ⟨a horse of good ~⟩ **c :** the structural arrangement of a landmass (as an island) or country ⟨the ~ of the country . . . explains the sites of . . . the towns —J.M.Mogey⟩ **d** *of a coating* **:** capacity to form a relatively substantial continuous film ⟨some of the resins have excellent ~⟩ **2 :** a combination (as of playing cards) formed by building **3 :** a vertical joint in masonry **4 :** a mounting state of intensity or of steady progress toward a climax ⟨the author . . . neglected to give the continuous ~ that the more complex literary situation demands —Virgil Thomson⟩ ⟨a good actor instinctively gives ~ to an important scene⟩ **syn** see PHYSIQUE

build·able \-ləbəl\ *adj* **:** suitable for building; *esp* **:** capable of being built or built from without excessive outlay (as of money, time, or materials) ⟨designs for attractive ~ benches⟩ ⟨a very ~ sketch for a cottage⟩

builded *archaic past of* BUILD

build·er \-ldə(r)\ *n* -s [ME *bilder*, fr. *bilden* + *-er*] **1 :** one that builds: as **a :** a worker (as a carpenter, shipwright, or mason) whose occupation is to build **b :** a person who supervises and usu. has a financial interest in building operations and the arts and trades involved in their progress — compare CONTRACTOR **c :** a person or organization that creates something (as a business or a railroad); *esp* **:** one that is a pioneer organizer or developer (as of a country) ⟨the empire ~*s*⟩ **2 :** a substance (as a sodium polyphosphate or sodium carbonate) added to soaps or synthetic detergents or used with them to increase their cleansing action (as by softening hard water or controlling the hydrogen-ion concentration of the bath) **3 :** a man in backgammon that can be moved without leaving a blot **4** *or* **builder motion :** the mechanism in a textile mill that distributes yarn or roving onto a bobbin, spool, or other holder to form a package **5 :** a worker who builds up (as wax molds for electrotype plates) or assembles (as tires or parts of tires)

builders' hardware *n* **:** articles of hardware (as hinges, locks, catches, sash lifts) that are used in the construction of buildings

builder's iron *n* **:** BUILDING IRON

builder's jack *n* **1 a :** a bracket that rests on a windowsill and projects outside for a worker to stand or sit upon in repairing a window **b :** a bracket fastened to a wall to support a scaffold **2 :** a jack (as a jackscrew) used by builders

builder's knot *n* **:** CLOVE HITCH

builder's risk insurance *n* **:** insurance on an increasing-value basis against loss by fire and related hazards covering buildings or ships in course of construction

build·er-up·per \ˌbildə(r)ˈəpə(r)\ *n* **:** one that builds up ⟨an occasional change is a great *builder-upper* of morale⟩

build in *vt* **1 :** to enclose or fill in by building ⟨the open fields are now entirely *built in*⟩ **2 :** to construct (as furniture) as an integral part of something ⟨I want the carpenter to *build in* chests, cabinets, everything⟩ ⟨our children will get a sort of *built-in* balance wheel —Sidonie M. Gruenberg⟩

build·ing \ˈbildiŋ, -dēŋ\ *n* -s [ME *bilding*, fr. gerund of *bilden* to build] **1 :** a thing built: as **a :** a constructed edifice designed to stand more or less permanently, covering a space of land, usu. covered by a roof and more or less completely enclosed by walls, and serving as a dwelling, storehouse, factory, shelter for animals, or other useful structure — distinguished from structures not designed for occupancy (as fences or monuments) and from structures not intended for use in one place (as boats or trailers) even though subject to occupancy **b :** a portion of a house occupied as a separate dwelling **:** APARTMENT, TENEMENT — used only in some legal statutes **2 :** the act or practice of making, erecting, or establishing; *specif* **:** the art or business of assembling materials into a structure — sometimes distinguished from *architecture* and *construction* as involving relatively simple artistic and engineering problems **3** *archaic* **:** a flock of rooks **:** ROOKERY

building and loan association *n* **:** SAVINGS AND LOAN ASSOCIATION

building block *n* **:** BLOCK 1d, 1f (7), 1l

building carpenter *n* **:** a person in charge of a stage building crew that prepares scenery for theatrical productions

building code *n* **:** a collection of regulations adopted by a city to govern the construction of buildings

building drain *n* **:** HOUSE DRAIN

building iron *n* **:** a tool with which wax is melted and applied in building an electrotype mold

building lease *n* **:** a lease of land for a long term of years in consideration of the payment of rent and of a covenant of the lessee to erect or alter a building or other improvement thereon — called also *ground lease*

build·ing·less \-ləs\ *adj* **:** being without a building

building line *n* **:** a line usu. set with respect to the frontage of a plot of land which is fixed by statute or by deed or contract and beyond which the owner of the land may not build

building lot *n* **:** a surveyed and bounded plot of land that is set aside for a building — compare SUBDIVISION

building paper *n* **:** paper used for insulation (as in walls, roofs, and between floors)

building sewer *n* **:** HOUSE SEWER

building slip *or* **building berth** *n* **:** the inclined structure on which a vessel is built

building superintendent *n* **:** one who is responsible for the cleaning and maintenance of a building and its equipment — called also *custodian*

building trades *n pl* **:** trades (as carpentry, bricklaying, plumbing) that are essential to and chiefly practiced in connection with building construction

building trap *n* **:** HOUSE TRAP

build on *vt* **:** to add (a new part) to an existent structure ⟨we plan to *build on* a porch⟩

builds *pres 3d sing of* BUILD, *pl of* BUILD

build up *vt* **1 a :** to construct or erect gradually, little by little, piece by piece, or layer by layer **b :** to construct (a whole, as a wheel) of separate parts **2 a :** to obstruct or close by building ⟨they *built up* the door between the two houses⟩ **b :** to obstruct or fill with buildings ⟨the fields where we played are all *built up* now⟩ **3 :** to develop, increase, or improve esp. by successive increments ⟨he *built up* his business by good service and attention to detail⟩ ⟨anyone can *build up* his constitution by heeding a few simple rules⟩: as **a :** to add fuel to and freshen (a fire) **b :** to enhance the prominence of ⟨she had a talent for *building up* minor roles⟩; *esp* **:** to give favorable publicity to ⟨they *built* him *up* with a series of articles and broadcasts⟩ **c :** to increase the voltage or current of (an electric generator or circuit) **d :** to stimulate or arouse the interest or emotions of (as a team) esp. with a particular aim in view ⟨the coach *built* the team *up* to a fighting pitch⟩ **~** *vi* **:** to increase esp. by successive increments — used chiefly of pressure

buildup \ˈ=,=\ *n* [*build up*] **1 :** the act of building up **2 :** something produced by building up: **a :** a quantity (as of pressure or water) so produced **b :** a marked or excessive increase in a natural population usu. resulting from progressively altered ecological relations **c :** something intended to enhance the popularity or prestige of an individual, product, or organization; *esp* **:** excessively favorable publicity designed to sway public opinion often without regard to the merits of the case ⟨his last employer gave him a good ~ but he was not up to the job here⟩

¹built *adj* [fr. past part. of ¹*build*] **1 :** FORMED, SHAPED, CONSTRUCTED, MADE — usu. used with a qualifying word ⟨a Clyde-*built* vessel⟩ ⟨a well-*built* house⟩ **2 :** composed of pieces or parts joined systematically **:** BUILT-UP; *esp* **:** LAMINATED

²built *n* -s [irreg. fr. ¹*build*] *obs* **:** SHAPE, BUILD

¹built-in \ˈ=ˈ=\ *adj* **1 :** forming an integral part of a structure ⟨a *built-in* range finder⟩; *esp, of furnishings* **:** constructed as or in a recess in a wall ⟨I want *built-in* bookcases next to the fireplace⟩ **2 :** present by reason of the nature or makeup of some other relevant matter **:** INHERENT, CONSTITUTIONAL ⟨the *built-in* safeguards that our constitution provides against tyranny⟩ ⟨release of the atom's *built-in* energy —Stuart Chase⟩

²built-in \ˈ=,=\ *n* -s [¹*built-in*] **:** a piece of built-in furniture

built-up \ˈ=ˈ=\ *adj* **1 :** made of several sections or layers fastened together ⟨a *built-up* girder⟩ ⟨*built-up* roofing⟩ **2** *of a land area* **:** having many buildings **:** covered with buildings **3 :** THICKENED, ENLARGED ⟨a *built-up* heel of a shoe⟩ **:** piled higher by gradual accumulation ⟨*built-up* slag⟩ ⟨*built-up* land where the old town dump was⟩; *often* **:** filled in **:** WIDENED ⟨a *built-up* neckline on her dress⟩

built-up fraction *n* **:** PIECE FRACTION

built-up gun *n* **:** a gun whose parts are formed separately and then so united as to utilize to the best advantage the elastic qualities of the metals

built-up mast *n* **:** a mast made of several pieces bound together

buird \ˈbü(ə)rd\ *Scot var of* BOARD

buird·ly \ˈbœ̄r(d)li, ˈbür-\ *adj* [prob. alter. of ¹*burly*] *Scot* **:** stalwart and husky **:** well built ⟨a ~ lad for twelve⟩

buis·son \bwēˈsōⁿ, *F* bwᵉsōⁿ\ *n* -s [F, lit., bush, of Gmc origin; akin to OHG *busc* bush — more at BUSH] **:** a fruit tree with a very short stem and a closely pruned head

bu·ka \ˈb(y)ükə\ *n* -s [prob. modif. of Zulu *bucu*] **:** BUCHU

bu·kaua \büˈkaüə\ *n, pl* **bukaua** *or* **bukauas** *usu cap* **1 a :** a people inhabiting the Huon gulf region of Morobe, Northeast New Guinea **b :** a member of such people **2 :** the Austronesian language of the Bukaua people

bu·ka·yo *also* **bu·ca·yo** \büˈkī(ˌ)ō\ *n* -s [Tag *bukayò*] **:** a Philippine sweetmeat of grated coconut fried in brown sugar

bu·ke·yef \büˈkā(y)əf\ *n pl, usu cap* [Russ *Bukeyevskoi* (pl.)] **:** a subdivision of the Kazak living between the Ural and the Volga rivers

bukh \ˈbu̇k\ *vi* [Hindi *bak*] *India* **:** PRATE, TALK

bukhara *often cap, var of* BOKHARA

¹bu·kha·ran \büˈkärən, -karə\ *or* **bo·kha·ran** \bō'-\ *adj, usu cap* [*Bukhara* or *Bokhara*, city and state in Russian central Asia + E *-an*] **1 :** of, relating to, or characteristic of Bukhara in central Asia **2 :** of, relating to, or characteristic of the people of Bukhara

²bukharan \"\ *or* **bokharan** \"\ *n* -s *cap* **:** a native or resident of Bukhara

bukid *usu cap, var of* BUHID

bu·kid·non \büˈkid,nän\ *n, pl* **bukidnon** *or* **bukidnons** *usu cap* [Bisayan *Bukidnon* hill people, fr. *búkid* mountain + *-non* people] **1 a :** a predominantly pagan people inhabiting central northern Mindanao, Philippines **b :** a member of such people **2 :** an Austronesian language of the Bukidnon people — called also *Binokid*

buksha *var of* BOGSHA

buk·shee *or* **buk·shish** \ˈbək,shēsh, ˌ=ˈ=\ *var of* BAKSHEESH

buk·shi \ˌbəkˈshē\ *n* -s [Per *bakhshī*, lit., giver, fr. *bakhshīdan* to give — more at BAKSHEESH] *India* **:** a military paymaster

bul \ˈbül\ *n* -s *usu cap* [Heb *būl*, fr. Canaanite] **:** the 8th month of the ancient Hebrew calendar, corresponding to Heshvan

¹bulb \ˈbəlb, ˈbəu̇b\ *n* -s [L *bulbus* onion, bulb, fr. Gk *bolbos* bulbous plant; akin to Arm *bołk* radish and perh. to Skt *balbaja* yard grass (*Eleusine indica*)] **1 :** a mass of overlapping membranous or fleshy leaves on a short stem base enclosing one or more buds that may develop under suitable conditions into new plants and constituting the resting stage of many plants (as lily, onion, hyacinth, tulip) — distinguished from *corm*, *rhizome*, *tuber* **2 a :** a fleshy tuber, corm, or other plant structure resembling a bulb in appearance ⟨a dahlia ~⟩ ⟨a crocus ~⟩ — not used technically **b** *Brit* **:** a fleshy bulbous root ⟨beet and turnip ~*s*⟩ **3 :** a plant having or developing from a bulb ⟨spring-flowering ~*s*⟩ **4 :** a protuberance resembling a plant bulb: as **a :** a rounded dilatation or expansion of something cylindrical ⟨the ~ of a thermometer⟩; *esp* **:** a rounded or pear-shaped enlargement on a small base ⟨the ~ of an eyedropper⟩ **b :** the thickened edge characteristic of certain construction elements (as a bulb angle or bulb bar) **c :** a rounded or pear-shaped glass envelope enclosing the light source of an incandescent or other electric lamp; *broadly* **:** such an envelope together with the light source it encloses ⟨a fluorescent ~⟩ — see INCANDESCENT LAMP illustration **5 :** a rounded part: as **a :** a rounded enlargement of one end of a part ⟨the ~ of the urethra⟩ — see END BULB, OLFACTORY BULB **b :** MEDULLA OBLONGATA; *broadly* **:** the rhombencephalon exclusive of the cerebellum **c :** the upper portion of the heel of a horse's hoof **d :** a thick-walled muscular enlargement of the pharynx of certain nematode worms **e :** the modified tarsal tip of a male spider that contains the coiled seminal receptacle, is often highly complex, and constitutes a character of taxonomic importance **6** [so called fr. the pneumatic bulb sometimes used to control the shutter] **:** a camera setting that indicates that the shutter can be opened by pressing on the release and closed by ending the pressure and that is used in making short time exposures and flashlight exposures — abbr. *B.*

bulb of meadow lily

²bulb \"\ *vi* -ED/-ING/-S **1 :** to assume a bulbous form **:** SWELL **2** *of a plant* **:** to produce bulbs ⟨the onions ~*ed* poorly in this cold wet season⟩

bulb- *or* **bulbo-** *comb form* [MF & L; MF *bulb-*, fr. L, fr. *bulbus*] **1 :** bulb ⟨*bulb*ar⟩ ⟨*Bulbo*codium⟩ **2 :** bulbar and — esp. in terms referring to the medulla oblongata or to the bulb of the penis or urethra ⟨*bulbo*spinal⟩ ⟨*bulbo*rectal⟩

bul·ba·ceous \ˌbəlˈbāshəs\ *adj* [L *bulbaceus*, fr. *bulbus* + *-aceus* -aceous] **:** producing or growing from bulbs

bulb angle *n* **:** an angle iron with one edge thickened out into a bulbous rib

bul·bar \ˈbəlbə(r), -l,bär, -l,bȧ(r\ *adj* [¹*bulb* + *-ar*] **:** of or relating to a bulb; *specif* **:** involving the medulla oblongata

bulbar paralysis *n* **:** destruction of nerve centers of the medulla oblongata and paralysis of the parts innervated from the medulla with interruption of their functions (as swallowing or speech), usu. encountered as a symptom of pseudorabies in cattle or of botulism in fowls

bulb bar *n* **:** a rolled bar of iron or steel that is thickened along one edge so as to have a cross section bulbous at that edge

bulbed \ˈbəlbd\ *adj* **1 :** shaped like a bulb **:** BULBOUS **2 :** having a bulb

bulb eelworm *or* **bulb nematode** *n* **:** a plant-parasitic nematode (*Ditylenchus dipsaci*) of the family Tylenchidae that infests bulbs and leaves of numerous plants and is esp. destructive to narcissus

bulberry *var of* BULLBERRY

bulb fly *n* **1 :** NARCISSUS BULB FLY 1 **2 :** LESSER BULB FLY

bulbi *pl of* BULBUS

bul·bil \ˈbəlbəl, -l,bil\ *or* **bul·bel** \-lbəl, -l,bel\ *n* -s [F *bulbille*, dim. of *bulbe* bulb, fr. L *bulbus* — more at BULB] **1 a :** a small or secondary plant bulb; *esp* **:** one produced on the aerial part of the plant and capable when separated of producing a new plant — called also *brood bud bulblet*, **b :** an underground node of algae of the genus *Chara* **2 :** any of the small resting few-celled masses produced in great numbers by certain fungi

bulb·less \ˈbəlbləs\ *adj* **:** being without a bulb

bulb·let \ˈbəlblət\ *n* **1 :** BULBIL 1a **2 :** CORMEL

bulblet fern *n* **:** a No. American bladder fern (*Cystopteris bulbifera*) often bearing bulbils on the rachis near the base of the pinnae

bulb mite *n* **:** a cosmopolitan mite (*Rhizoglyphus echinopus* or related species) that burrows in lily and other bulbs

bul·bo·cap·nine \ˌbəlbōˈkap,nēn, -pnən\ *n* [ISV *bulbocapn-* (fr. NL *Bulbocapnos*, in some esp. former classifications a genus of herbs now included in the genus *Corydalis*, from a species of which it was extracted, fr. *bulb-* + Gk *kapnos* smoke) + *-ine* — more at COVET] **:** a crystalline alkaloid $C_{19}H_{19}NO_4$ that induces catalepsy and that is obtained from the roots of plants of the genus *Corydalis* and from squirrel corn

bul·bo·cav·er·no·sus \ˌbəl(ˌ)bō,kavə(r)ˈnōsəs\ *n, pl* **bulbocaverno·si** \-ō,sī, -ō,sē\ [NL, fr. *bulb-* + L *cavernosus* hollow — more at CAVERNOUS] **:** a muscle in the male surrounding and compressing the bulb of the penis and the bulbar portion of the urethra and in the female divided into lateral halves that extend from immediately behind the clitoris along either side of the vagina to the central tendon of the perineum and serve to compress the vagina — called also in the female *sphincter vaginae*

bul·bo·cav·er·nous \-ˈkavə(r)nəs\ *adj* [NL *bulbocavernosus*] **:** of, relating to, or located near the bulb of the penis

bulbocavernous gland *n* **:** COWPER'S GLAND

bul·bo·chae·te \ˌbəlbōˈkēd·ē\ *n, cap* [NL, fr. *bulb-* + Gk *chaitē* flowing hair — more at CHAET-] **:** a genus of freshwater green algae (family Oedogoniaceae) having much-branched filaments with each cell bearing a long hair with a bulbous base

bul·bo·co·di·um \ˌbəlbəˈkōdēəm\ *n* [NL, fr. *bulb-* + Gk *kōidion* small sheepskin, fleece, dim. of *kōas* sheepskin] **1** *cap* **:** a monotypic genus of bulbous herbs (family Melanthaceae) native to the Mediterranean region and having purple flowers that resemble crocuses **2** -s **:** any plant of the genus *Bulbocodium*

bulb of percussion *archeol* **:** a cone-shaped bulge on a fractured surface of flint that is made by a blow applied at an angle

bulb of the penis : the proximal expanded part of the corpus cavernosum of the male urethra

bul·bose \ˈbəl,bōs\ *adj* [L *bulbosus* — more at BULBOUS] **:** BULBOUS

bul·bo·urethral \ˌbəl(ˌ)bō+\ *adj* [*bulb-* + *urethral*] **:** of or relating to the bulb of the penis and the urethra

bulbourethral gland *n* **:** COWPER'S GLAND

bul·bous \ˈbəlbəs\ *adj* [MF & L; MF *bulbeux*, fr. L *bulbosus*, fr. *bulbus* bulb + *-osus* -ose — more at BULB] **1 :** like or being a plant bulb ⟨a thick ~ root⟩ ⟨~ and tuberous structures⟩ **2 a :** bearing or producing bulbs **b :** growing from a bulb ⟨~ plants⟩ **3 :** resembling or suggesting a bulb esp. in roundness or in the gross enlargement of a part ⟨thick ~ fingers⟩ ⟨an oak table mounted on a ~ pedestal⟩

bulbous begonia *n* **:** a tuberous begonia with a tuber resembling a bulb

bulbous bluegrass *n* **:** an erect tufted perennial grass (*Poa bulbosa*) used in the U. S. for pasture, lawns, and golf courses

bulbous bow *n* **:** a form of entrance in high-speed ships designed for the avoidance of wavemaking at high speeds, the stem being sharp at and below the waterline but expanding into a pear-shaped form as it nears the keel, the displacement necessary at this section of the hull thus being transferred in part to the vicinity of the keel where it becomes subject to the laws governing a totally submerged body

bulbous buttercup *or* **bulbous crowfoot** *n* **:** a common European herb (*Ranunculus bulbosus*) having a bulbous base and naturalized in No. America

bulbous fumitory *n* **:** MOSCHATEL

bulbous iris *n* **:** any of certain irises having a rootstock formed like a bulb

bul·bous·ly *adv* **:** in a bulbous manner

bulb plate *n* **:** a structural metal plate reinforced by a thickening on one edge

bulbs *pl of* BULB, *pres 3d sing of* BULB

bulb scale *n* **:** one of the leaves of a bulb (as of the lily)

bulb-tee \ˈ=ˌ=\ *adj, of a T bar or beam* **:** having the web thickened into a bulbous rib at its edge

bul·bul \ˈbu̇l,bu̇l\ *n* -s [Per, fr. Ar] **1 a :** a Persian songbird frequently mentioned in poetry that is prob. a nightingale (*Luscinia golzii*) **b :** any of a group of gregarious arboreal passerine birds (family Pycnonotidae) of Asia and Africa that feed on fruits, berries, and insects — see CHLOROPSIS, GREEN BULBUL **2 :** a maker or singer of sweet songs

bul·bus \ˈbəlbəs\ *n, pl* **bul·bi** \-l,bī, -l,bē\ [NL, fr. L, bulb of a plant — more at BULB] **:** BULB 5

bulbus ar·te·ri·o·sus \-(ˌ)är,tirēˈōsəs\ *also* **bulbus aor·tae** \-āˈōr,tē\ *n* [NL *bulbus arteriosus*, lit., arterial bulb & *bulbus aortae*, lit., bulb of the aorta] **:** the dilated part of the aorta just in front of the heart from which the aortic arches arise in vertebrate embryos and in the adult of many lower vertebrates

bule \ˈb(y)ül\ *var of* ²BOOL

¹bul·gar \ˈbəl,gär, ˈbu̇l-, -gȧ(r\ *n* -s *cap* [ML *Bulgarus*] **1 a :** a people native to or inhabiting Bulgaria **b :** a member of such people **2 :** the Slavic language of the Bulgar people

²bulgar \"\ *n* -s [fr. *Bolgar*, *Bolghar*, former kingdom on the Volga river around Kazan] **:** a Russian leather orig. from Bolgar

bul·gar·ia \ˌbəlˈga(a)rēə, (ˈ)bu̇l-, -ger-, -gär-\ *adj, usu cap* [fr. *Bulgaria*, country in southeastern Europe] **:** of or from Bulgaria **:** of the kind or style prevalent in Bulgaria **:** BULGARIAN

¹bul·gar·i·an \-ēən\ *n* -s *cap* [*Bulgaria* + E *-an*] **1 :** one of the people of modern Bulgaria speaking a southern Slavic language and orig. being Finno-Ugrians living along the Volga **2 :** the language of the Bulgarians written in a modified Russian alphabet

²bulgarian \"\ *adj, usu cap* **:** of or relating to Bulgaria, the Bulgarians, the language of the Bulgarians, or the Bulgarian Orthodox church autonomously governed by a synod with an exarch as head and now in full communion with all Eastern Orthodox churches

bulgarian milk *n, usu cap B* **:** a fermented milk; *esp* **:** YOGURT

bul·gar·ic \-¦garik *also* -gər-\ *adj, usu cap* [*Bulgar* + *-ic*] **:** BULGARIAN

bul·ga·rize \'bəlgə,rīz, 'bu̇l-\ *vt* -ED/-ING/-S *often cap* [*Bulgar* + *-ize*] **:** to bring under Bulgar domination or influence

¹bulge \'bəlj, 'bu̇lj\ *vb* -ED/-ING/-S [prob. alter. of ²*bilge*] *vt* **1** *archaic* **:** to stave in (as a ship's bottom) **2 :** to cause to bulge ~ *vi* **1** *archaic, of a ship* **:** BILGE **2 a :** to jut out **:** SWELL **b** *of a structure under pressure* **:** to bend outward ⟨the wall buckled and *bulged*⟩ **c :** to become protuberant ⟨his eyes will ~ when he sees what we've brought him⟩ **3 :** to enter hastily, clumsily, or unexpectedly — usu. used with *in* or *into* ⟨he *bulged* into the road ahead of me⟩ **4** *of a fish* **:** to cause bulges of the overlying water while feeding (as in pursuing insect nymphs and larvae) **5 :** to become filled to overflowing — used with *with* ⟨notebook *bulged* with ideas⟩ ⟨a big new market *bulging* with sales potential —*Printers' Ink*⟩ **syn** PROTUBERATE, JUT, STICK OUT, PROTRUDE, PROJECT, OVERHANG, BEETLE: BULGE and the now uncommon PROTUBERATE may suggest a swelling out, sometimes abnormally, through defect, imperfection, or unwholesome condition ⟨above her boots . . . the calves *bulged* . . . out —Arnold Bennett⟩ ⟨cans so imperfectly sealed that their contents ferment and *bulge* the can noticeably —Emily Holt⟩ ⟨houses that *bulged* with the tumors and warts of the ornamental architecture of the jigsaw period —W.A.White⟩ JUT and STICK OUT may indicate the fact of position, situation, or arrangement whereby something extends out from a surface ⟨a window that *jutted* out and looked up the narrow street —Willa Cather⟩ ⟨a tiny platform that *jutted* out over the side of the carrier —J.A. Michener⟩ ⟨a square block of stone that *jutted* from the floor —Liam O'Flaherty⟩ PROTRUDE may suggest an unexpected or unusual thrusting out ⟨the jacket slipped to the ground and from the inner pocket he saw the white tops of three envelopes *protruding* —Victor Canning⟩ ⟨Bill March was carried out, a naked white foot *protruding* from beneath the white sheet —Robert Tallant⟩ PROJECT may apply to a throwing or pressing forward or outward or to something comparable to the results of such an action ⟨the young man *projected* from the side of the car like the figurehead of a ship —Ernest Hemingway⟩ ⟨a long spit of land covered with pine trees *projecting* out from the shore —Frank Gibney⟩ ⟨Sullivan was always obliged to think far ahead of its progress. He must *project* himself hours ahead, a thousand miles beyond the horizon —E.K.Gann⟩ OVERHANG and BEETLE imply a jutting out over a support, the latter sometimes suggesting ominousness or precariousness ⟨the booths where goods were exposed to sale projected far into the streets and were *overhung* by the upper stories —T.B.Macaulay⟩ ⟨the limestone bluff rolls closer to the water's edge, *overhanging* the road with cedar —*Amer. Guide Series: Mich.*⟩ ⟨a small dark courtyard above which *beetled* the walls of the castle —John Buchan⟩ ⟨he half arose from his chair and *beetled* over her. His face was full of the surreptitious joy of having trapped her —Augusta Walker⟩

²bulge \"\ *n* -S [prob. alter. of ¹*bilge*] **1 :** BILGE 1, 2 **2** [prob. fr. ¹*bulge*] **:** a swelling or protuberant part: as **a :** an outward bend produced by pressure ⟨a ~ in the wall⟩ **b :** a landmass projecting beyond the general contour of the body of which it is a part ⟨the ~ of Brazil⟩ **c :** a part of a military front that is advanced beyond the general line of the front **:** SALIENT **d :** the rounded fill of a well-packed container of fresh produce **3 :** ADVANTAGE, UPPER HAND — often used in the phrase *get the bulge on* **4 :** an upward trend or movement esp. when relatively abrupt, limited in extent, and transitory in nature ⟨the usual seasonal ~ in inventories⟩: as **a :** a rippling of the surface of water; *esp* **:** one caused by the movement of feeding fish below the surface **b :** a rise in prices **c :** an increase in numbers ⟨using schools in the summer could help provide essential space for the growing ~ in the youth population —W.H.Gaumnitz⟩; *esp* **:** one associated with a particular social phenomenon

bulge hoop *n* **:** the hoop nearest the middle of a cask

bulg·er \-jə(r)\ *n* -S **:** one that bulges; *specif* **:** a wooden golf club with a convex face

bulg·i·ly \-jəlē, -li\ *adv* **:** in a bulgy manner

bul·gur \(')bu̇l¦gu̇(ə)r\ *n* -S [Turk] **:** parched crushed wheat as prepared and used as a dietary staple in Turkey and adjacent regions

bulgy \'bəljē, 'bu̇l-, -ji\ *adj* -ER/-EST **:** BULGED, BULGING; *esp* **:** PROTUBERANT

-bu·lia \'byüelēə\ *also* **-bou·lia** \'bü-\ *n comb form* -S [NL *-bulia*, fr. Gk *-boulia*, fr. *boulē* will; prob. akin to Gk *ballein* to throw — more at DEVIL] **:** condition of having (such) will ⟨hyper*bulia*⟩

-bu·lic \¦byülik\ *also* **-bou·lic** \¦bü-\ *adj comb form* [ISV, fr. NL *-bulia* + ISV *-ic*] **:** of, relating to, or characterized by a (specified) state of the will

bu·lim·ia \byü'limēə\ *also* **bou·lim·ia** \bü-\ *n* -S [NL, fr. Gk *boulimia* great hunger, fr. *bous* head of cattle + *limos* hunger, famine + *-ia* — more at LESS] **:** an abnormal and constant craving for food

bu·lim·i·dae \byü'limə,dē\ *n pl, cap* [NL, fr. *Bulimus*, type genus + *-idae*] **:** a family of operculate snails (order Pectinibranchia) that includes numerous intermediate hosts of medically and economically important flukes

bu·li·moid \'byülə,mȯid\ *adj* [NL *Bulimus* + E *-oid*] **:** resembling the land snails of the family Bulimulidae esp. in having ovate somewhat elongate shells with an ovate aperture

bu·li·mu·li·dae \,byülə'myülə,dē\ *n pl, cap* [NL, fr. *Bulimulus*, type genus (dim. of *Bulimus*) + *-idae*] **:** a family of land snails many of which are large and beautifully colored — see BULIMOID

bu·li·mus \byü'līməs\ *n, cap* [NL, prob. fr. L, great hunger, fr. Gk *boulimos*, fr. *bous* head of cattle + *limos* hunger — more at COW, LESS] **1 :** a genus of small freshwater snails that is the type of the family Bulimidae and includes a species (*B. fuchsianus*) that is the chief intermediate host of the Chinese liver fluke **2** *in former classifications* **:** a genus of land snails somewhat equivalent to the family Bulimulidae

bu·li·my \'byüləmē\ *n* -ES [alter. of ME *bolisme*, *bolismus*, fr. MF & ML; MF *bolisme*, fr. ML *bolismus*, alter. of L *bulimus* — more at BULIMUS] **:** an insatiable appetite; *esp* **:** BULIMIA

¹bu·li·nus \byü'līnəs\ *n, cap* [NL, perh. irreg. fr. L *bulla* bubble + *-inus* -ine — more at POLL (head)] **:** a genus (the type of the family Bulinidae) of small sinistral freshwater pulmonate snails including a number that are intermediate hosts of flukes of domestic animals

²bulinus \"\ *n, cap* [NL, alter. of *Bulimus*] *in some classifications* **:** a genus coextensive with *Bulimus* — used chiefly in medical literature

¹bulk \'bəlk, 'bu̇lk, 'bau̇k\ *n* -S [ME *bulke*, fr. ON *bulki* cargo; prob. akin to OE *blāwan* to blow — more at BLOW] **1 a** *obs* **:** HEAP, PILE **b :** one of the long stacks in which salted fish are layered for curing **c :** a large pile of tobacco arranged for fermentation **d** *archaic* (1) **:** the cargo of a ship (2) **:** the whole quantity of a commodity **2 a :** spatial dimension **:** MAGNITUDE, VOLUME; *esp* **:** great extent ⟨his industry was proven by the ~ of his accomplishment⟩ **b** *archaic* **:** POWER, MIGHT **c :** thickness of paper: (1) **:** thickness of a book exclusive of its cover (2) thickness of a specified number of sheets of paper or board (as of leaves in a book) (3) **:** thickness of a sheet of paper or board in relation to its weight ⟨of two sheets of equal weight the thicker is said to be of higher ~⟩ **d :** MASS 1c(1) **e :** material (as fibrous residues of food) that forms a mass in the intestine and is usu. felt to promote intestinal motility **3 a :** the body of a man or lower animal whether living or dead; *esp* **:** TRUNK — now usu. used of human bodies and with an implication of largeness or corpulence ⟨he hauled his black-clad ~ out of the armchair —Herman Wouk⟩ **b :** an organized structure **:** BODY; *esp* **:** one considered primarily as a mass of material substance ⟨the dark ~s of stalled cars —Raymond Chandler⟩ ⟨the giant ~ of Mt. Katahdin — Jackson Rivers⟩ **c :** a large mass **4 a :** the main or greater part ⟨the ~ of his work was finished before supper⟩ ⟨the ~ of our property is in bonds⟩ **b :** MAJORITY ⟨the ~ of the citizens agreed⟩ — often used with adjectives of magnitude ⟨the great ~ of the population⟩ — **in bulk :** in a mass **:** not divided into parts or packaged in separate units ⟨unmilled grains are shipped *in bulk*⟩

²bulk \"\ *vb* -ED/-ING/-S *vt* **1 a :** to cause to swell or bulge **:** STUFF — often used with *out* ⟨a dozen petticoats ~*ing* out her figure⟩ **b :** to add bulk to ⟨any inert innocuous material can be used to ~ the trace-element mixture⟩ **2 :** to gather into a mass ⟨she ~*ed* up her hair with one hand as she reached for the shears with the other⟩: as **a :** to pile (fish or tobacco) in bulks — often used with *down* **b :** to mix (as tea of different lots or grades) in order to secure a uniform product **c :** to assemble (as funds) in aggregates ⟨baggage is often ~*ed* for the determination of charges⟩ **3 :** to have a bulk of **:** amount to ⟨the Hoover Dam ~*s* about 4,400,000 cubic yards — Joseph Bryan⟩ ~ *vi* **1 :** SWELL, EXPAND — often used with *up* ⟨the loaf ~*ed* up and browned nicely⟩ **2 a :** to have bulk **:** present a bulky appearance **:** LOOM ⟨a dark mass that ~*s* on the horizon⟩ **b :** to be weighty, significant, or impressive ⟨the factor that ~*s* largest in the present discussion⟩ **c** *of sheets of paper or board* **:** to reach a certain thickness ⟨the pages of your book ~ 400 to the inch⟩ **3 a :** to form into a cohesive mass ⟨esparto paper pulp ~*s* well⟩ **b** *of sewage sludge* **:** to form into masses that will not concentrate normally

³bulk \"\ *adj* **1 :** in bulk ⟨~ cement⟩ ⟨~ cargoes⟩ **2 :** dealing with or involving materials in bulk ⟨a ~ buyer⟩ ⟨the ~ window at the post office⟩

⁴bulk \"\ *n* -S [perh. fr. ON *bālkr* partition; akin to ON *bjalki* beam — more at BALK] *archaic* **:** a small structure projecting from a building (as a shop or booth) — compare BULKHEAD

bulked \¦bəlkt, ¦bu̇lk-\ *adj* [ME, fr. *bulke* + *-ed*] **1 :** having bulk — usu. used in combination ⟨big-*bulked* rugged frame⟩ **2 :** handled in bulk ⟨~ wheat⟩

¹bulker *n* -S [perh. fr. ⁴*bulk* + *-er*] **1** *obs* **:** a pickpocket's helper **2** *archaic* **:** STRUMPET, PROSTITUTE

²bulk·er \'bəlkə(r), 'bu̇l-\ *n* -S [²*bulk* + *-er*] **:** one that bulks; *esp* **:** a worker who bulks tobacco

bulk eraser *n* **:** a device for erasing previous recordings on an entire reel of magnetic tape

¹bulk·head \'bəl,ked, 'bu̇l-, -lk,hed\ *n* -S [⁴*bulk* + *head*] **1 :** an upright partition separating compartments; *esp* **:** such a partition separating compartments on a ship **2 :** a stone, wood, or concrete structure or partition designed to resist pressure or to shut off water, fire, or gas; *esp* **:** the retaining wall along a waterfront **3 a** *chiefly NewEng* **:** a projecting framework with a sloping door giving access to a cellar stairway or a shaft **b :** PENTHOUSE 2a

bulkhead 3a

²bulkhead \"\ *vt* **:** to enclose, separate, or support with bulkheads — used with *off* ⟨~ off part of the hold and make twenty bunks for the crew —Ken Leuty⟩

bulkhead deck *n* **:** the uppermost continuous deck of a ship to which all main transverse watertight bulkheads are carried

bulk·head·ed \-edəd\ *adj* **:** equipped with bulkheads or partitioned off by a bulkhead

bulkhead line *n* **:** a line marking the limit to which piers or wharves may project along a waterfront

bulk·i·ly \-kəlē, -li\ *adv* **:** in a bulky manner

bulk·i·ness \-kēnəs, -kin-\ *n* -ES **:** the quality or state of having bulk or being bulky

bulking power *n* **:** the relative capacity of a textile fiber to build up a bulk of material ⟨wool has high *bulking power*⟩

bulking value *n* **:** the relative capacity of a pigment or other ingredient to add volume to a paint

bulk-line system *n* **:** a system of fixing prices sufficiently high to cover the costs of marginal producers so as to stimulate production

bulk mail *n* **:** second-class, third-class, or fourth-class mail consisting of identical pieces mailed under permit in quantity and paid for as one lot

bulk modulus *n* **:** the ratio of the intensity of stress to the volume strain produced by stress — used of an elastic medium subjected to volume compression

bulk-pile \'⸗¦⸗\ *vt* **:** to pile (as seasoned lumber) closely esp. without cross strips

bulk process *n* **:** CHARMAT PROCESS

bulks *pl of* BULK, *pres 3d sing of* BULK

bulk-sales law *n* **:** a statute regulating the sale of stocks of goods in bulk where creditors may be prejudiced

bulky \'bəlkē, 'bu̇l-, -ki\ *adj* -ER/-EST **1 a :** having bulk; *esp* **:** large of its kind ⟨a ~ volume⟩ **b :** STOUT, CORPULENT — used of the human body **2 :** occupying overmuch space **:** CLUMSY, UNWIELDY ⟨a ~ ill-packed load⟩; *esp* **:** having great bulk in proportion to weight ⟨a pound of feathers is *bulkier* than a pound of lead⟩ **3** *of explosives* **:** having considerable bulk in proportion to disruptive power **syn** see MASSIVE

bulk yarn *n* **:** synthetic staple-fiber yarn containing a proportion of stretched fiber that will contract and crimp during wet finishing, used in knitted and woven fabrics for a full well-covered appearance

bulky color *n* **:** any partly or wholly transparent color perceived as filling a space in three dimensions — compare FILM COLOR

¹bull \'bu̇l\ *n* -S [ME *bule*, fr. OE *bula*; akin to OE *bulluc* young bull, MLG *bulle* bull, ON *boli* bull, OE *blāwan* to blow — more at BLOW] **1 a :** a sexually mature uncastrated male of any wild or domesticated animal of the genus *Bos* **b :** a male esp. when sexually mature of any of various other large mammals (as of the elephant, moose, elk, whale, or seal) **c :** any of certain other large male animals (as a male terrapin or alligator) **2 a :** one who operates on a stock, commodity, or produce exchange in expectation of a rise in the price of securities or commodities or in order to effect such a rise — compare BEAR **b :** a person with an optimistic attitude as to the course of events, esp. as to business **3 :** one that resembles or is likened to a bull (as in size, strength, or loud roaring): as **a :** a large powerful often somewhat stolid and clumsy person **b :** an elephant whether male or female — used chiefly of elephants semidomesticated in circuses and zoos **c** *or* **bull of the woods :** FOREMAN, STRAW BOSS, SUPERVISOR — used esp. of a working foreman in a lumber camp **d :** an ox or steer esp. when used for draft **4** *slang Brit* **:** a crown piece **5** [by shortening] **a :** BULL'S-EYE 5 **b :** BULLDOG **6** *slang* **:** POLICEMAN, DETECTIVE

²bull \"\ *adj* [ME *bule*, fr. *bule*, n.] **1 :** MALE ⟨a ~ calf⟩ **2 a :** of or relating to a bull ⟨tough ~ beef⟩ **b :** like or like that of a bull ⟨a strong ~ back⟩ **3 a :** large of its kind ⟨a ~ ladle⟩ ⟨a ~ lathe⟩ **b :** COARSE, HARSH ⟨a ~ screen⟩ ⟨a heavy ~ voice⟩ **4 a** *of markets* **:** RISING; *esp* **:** marked by the activities of bulls **b :** acting as a bull in the markets ⟨a ~ pool of speculators⟩

³bull \"\ *vb* -ED/-ING/-S [ME *bulen*, fr. *bule*, n.] *vi* **1** *of a cow or heifer* **:** to be in heat **:** take the bull **2 a :** to behave like a bull; *esp* **:** to press on or advance vigorously **b :** to advance in price — used esp. of stocks and speculative commodities or of markets dealing in these ~ *vt* **1** *of a bull* **:** to serve (a cow or heifer) **2 :** to try to raise the market price of (as stocks or bonds); *sometimes* **:** to try to raise prices in (a market) **3 a :** to enforce or bring into existence against opposition — usu. used with *through* ⟨they had decided to ~ through a demand for outright repeal —Helen Fuller⟩ **b :** to act on with or as if with the physical violence of a bull ⟨he ~*ed* his opponent all over the ring⟩ — **bull one's way :** to move forward against opposition by or as if by the exertion of physical violence **:** PUSH, SHOVE ⟨he *bulled his way* homeward through the storm⟩

⁴bull \"\ *n* -S [ME *bulle*, fr. ML *bulla*, fr. L *bulla* bubble, amulet — more at POLL (head)] **1 :** BULLA 2 **2 :** a papal letter distinguished from other apostolic letters by being sealed with a bulla or with a red-ink imprint of the device on the bulla, by being written on parchment and in the third person, by opening with the pope's name and the formula "Bishop, servant of the servants of God", and by significance of subject matter **3 :** an edict (as of the Holy Roman Empire) or other formal and supposedly authoritative statement ⟨~s issued by certain groups of professional educators —H.J.Fuller⟩

⁵bull \"\ *n* -S [perh. fr. obs. *bull* to make fun of, mock, prob. fr. MF *bouler* to deceive, cheat, roll, fr. *boule* ball — more at BOWL] **1** *obs* **:** an absurd jest **2 a :** a grotesque blunder in language (as in "his brother and sister are much alike, esp. his sister"); *esp* **:** IRISH BULL **b :** a serious error **:** a bad or sometimes ludicrous blunder **3** *slang* **a :** trivial and commonly boastful and inaccurate talk ⟨sat there shooting the ~⟩ **b :** something regarded as undesirable, superfluous, or incorrect ⟨that's ~, I'll tell you the whole story⟩ ⟨this business of sending flowers and things like that is the ~ —Jerome Weidman⟩ **syn** see ERROR

⁶bull \"\ *vb* -ED/-ING/-S *vi* **1** *slang* **:** to talk bull **:** BLOW **2 :** to act blunderingly; *sometimes* **:** BALK ~ *vt, slang* **:** to fool or bemuse esp. by fast talking and bull

⁷bull \"\ *n* -S [origin unknown] **:** a weak drink made by pouring water into an emptied spirit cask or rinsing out a sugar bag

⁸bull \"\ *or* **bull board** *n* -S [origin unknown] **:** a game that resembles quoits and is often played on shipboard

bull *abbr* bulletin

bul·la \'bu̇lə\ *n, pl* **bul·lae** \-,lē, -,lī, *esp in sense 2* -,lau̇\ [L, bubble, boss, amulet — more at POLL (head)] **1 :** a small case of leather or of metal usu. lenticular in shape, designed to contain amulets, and suspended by a cord around the neck by ancient Romans; *broadly* **:** a rounded ornament used as a pendant, boss, knob, or stud in Roman costume or architecture **2** [ML, fr. L] **:** a seal appended to a document; *esp* **:** the round usu. lead seal attached to the papal bulls that has on one side a representation of St. Peter and St. Paul and on the other the name of the pope who uses it **3** [NL, fr. L] **:** a hollow thin-walled rounded bony prominence (as that situated beneath the opening of the ear of many mammals) **4** [NL, fr. L] **:** a large vesicle or an elevation of the cuticle usu. containing serum **:** a large blister — compare BLEB **5** [NL, fr. L] **:** a transparent or weakly chitinized spot in the wing vein of certain insects

bul·lace \'bu̇ləs\ *n* -S [ME *bolace*, fr. MF *beloce*, fr. ML *bolluca*, *bulluga*] **1 :** a small wild or half-domesticated European plum (*Prunus domestica insititia*) related to the damson and having small ovoid fruit in clusters **2 :** BALATA 2 **3** *or* **bullace grape :** MUSCADINE

bul·la·ma·cow *or* **bul·la·ma·cau** \¦bu̇ləmə¦kau̇\ *n* -S [Pidgin English, prob. modif. of E *bull* + *cow*] **1** *Pacific Islands* **:** tinned beef **:** canned meat **2** *Pacific Islands* **:** cattle in general

bul·lar·i·um \bu̇'la(a)rēəm\ *or* **bul·la·ry** \'bu̇lərē\ *n, pl* **bullar·ia** \-a(a)rēə\ *or* **bullaries** [ML *bullarium*, fr. *bulla* seal, papal bull + L *-arium* -ary] **:** a collection of papal bulls

bul·late \'bu̇,lāt\ *or* **bul·lat·ed** \-ād·əd\ *adj* [NL *bulla* + E *-ate*, *-ated*] **1 :** appearing as if blistered **:** PUCKERED ⟨a ~ leaf⟩ — compare RUGOSE **2 :** like or having a bulla ⟨a ~ tympanic bone⟩

bullbaiting \'⸗,⸗⸗\ *n* -S **:** the former practice of baiting bulls with dogs

bull band *also* **bull banding** *n* -S *Midland* **:** CHARIVARI

bullbat \'⸗,⸗\ *n* -S [so called fr. their roaring sound in flight] **:** NIGHTHAWK 1a; *esp, South* **:** a nighthawk (*Chordeiles minor*)

bull bay *n* **:** EVERGREEN MAGNOLIA

bull·beg·gar \'bu̇l,begə(r)\ *n* [perh. blend of obs. E *bullbear* (alter. of *bugbear*) + *beggar*, by folk etymology fr. *boggard*, *boggart*] *dial Brit* **:** GOBLIN, BUGBEAR

bull·ber·ry \'bu̇l- —*see* BERRY\ *also* **bul·ber·ry** \"\ *n* [¹*bull* + *berry*] **:** BUFFALO BERRY

bull birch *n, NewZeal* **:** BEECH 4

bull bit *n* **:** a single-edged rock-drilling bit

bull block *n* **1 :** a perforated block or die through which wire is drawn to reduce its size **2 :** a large wide-throated pulley block used in yarding logs

bullboat \'⸗,⸗\ *n* [so called fr. its construction of bull or buffalo skins] **:** a shallow-draft skin boat shaped like a tub and formerly used (as by Indians) in the Great Plains area

bullbrier \'⸗,⸗⸗\ *n* **:** any of several American plants of the genus *Smilax* with large farinaceous rootstocks formerly used as food by the Indians — compare GREENBRIER

bull bucker *n, slang* **:** the man in charge of the fallers and buckers in a lumber camp

bull cane *n* **:** a thick vigorous grape cane that usu. bears inferior fruit

bull chain *n* **1 :** a heavy chain to which are attached short chains having each a hook on one end and dogs on the other that is used for drawing logs **2 :** JACK CHAIN 2

bull cook *n* [so called fr. his job of caring for oxen once used in logging camps] **:** a handyman in a camp (as of loggers); *esp* **:** one who does caretaking chores and acts as cook's helper

bull ditcher *n* **:** a large heavy plow that has a double moldboard and is used in ditching

¹bulldog \'⸗,⸗\ *n* [¹*bull* + *dog*] **1 :** a compact muscular short-haired dog of a breed developed in England and used orig. in bull baiting but now usu. kept as a domestic pet, being noted equally for its vigor and sagacity and for its equable disposition, having the forelegs set widely apart and the lower jaw longer than the upper so that its grip is very powerful against resistance, and being usu. white, brindle, or a combination of brindle and white — see BOSTON TERRIER, FRENCH BULLDOG **2 :** a pistol or a revolver; *esp* **:** one of large caliber and short barrel **3 :** a proctor's attendant at Oxford and Cambridge **4 a :** BULLDOG ANT **b** *or* **bulldog fly :** HORSEFLY **5 :** a refractory material used as a furnace lining that is obtained by calcining mill cinder **6 :** any of several devices designed to obtain a firm and steady grip **7** *or* **bulldog pipe :** a tobacco pipe with a square shank and squat bowl, the latter having two grooves cut around its widest circumference **8 :** BULLDOG EDITION

²bulldog \"\ *adj* **1 :** of, relating to, or characteristic of a bulldog ⟨the mechanism of the ~ jaw⟩ **2 a :** like or suggestive of a bulldog (as in courage or stubbornness) **b :** having a powerful grip ⟨~ clips⟩ ⟨a ~ wrench⟩ **c :** having an excessively or abnormally undershot jaw ⟨~ bats⟩ **d** *of cattle* **:** affected with a destructive mutation of which such a jaw is a characteristic

³bulldog \"\ *vt* **1 :** to behave like a bulldog toward esp. in attacking with fierceness and vigor or in proceeding with methodical deliberation **2** *West* **:** to throw (a steer) by seizing the horns and twisting the neck

bulldog ant *n* **:** any of the large pugnacious fiercely biting Australian ants of the genus *Myrmecia*

bulldog bat *n* **:** MASTIFF BAT

bulldog edition *n* **:** the earliest edition of a morning or Sunday newspaper usu. appearing the evening before

bull·dog·ged \'bu̇l,dȯgəd *sometimes* -dāg-\ *adj* [blend of ¹*bulldog* and *dogged*] **:** stubbornly tenacious — **bull·dog·ged·ness** *n* -ES

bull·dog·ger \-gə(r)\ *n* [³*bulldog* + *-er*] **1** *West* **:** one that bulldogs cattle **2 :** ROUGHER

bull·dog·gish \-gish\ *adj* **:** BULLDOG; *esp* **:** BULLDOGGED

bull·dog·gy \-gē\ *adj* **:** BULLDOGGED

bulldog spear *n* [so called fr. its grasping ability] **:** a fishing tool for recovering well pipe or casings

bulldog toe *n* **:** a high bulging box toe

shoe with a bulldog toe

bull donkey *n* [*donkey* (engine)] **:** a large donkey engine fitted with drum and cable for hauling logs

bull·doze \'bu̇l,dōz\ *vb* -ED/-ING/-S [perh. fr. ¹*bull* + alter. of *dose*] *vt* **1 :** to coerce, restrain, or intimidate esp. by overt or implicit threats (as of violence) **:** BULLY **2 :** to break (boulders of rock or ore) by secondary blasting (as by mudcapping or blockholing) **3 :** to move, clear, gouge out, or level off by pushing with a bulldozer **4 :** BULLDOG 2 **5 :** to force (as one's way) or push out of the way (as obstructions) as if by using a bulldozer ~ *vi* **1 :** to operate a bulldozer **2 :** to engage in bulldozing **:** BULLY **syn** see INTIMIDATE

bull·doz·er \-zə(r)\ *n* -s **1 :** one that bulldozes: as **a :** BULLY, INTIMIDATOR **b :** PISTOL, REVOLVER **c :** an operator of a machine for bulldozing **2 :** an upsetting machine (as a forging or bending press) in which the ram slides in a horizontal path and is actuated by a pair of powerful cranks and connecting rods **3 :** a tractor-driven machine having a broad blunt horizontal blade or ram for clearing land, road building, or comparable activities; *also* **:** the blade or ram of such a machine

bulldozer 3

bull driver *n* **:** a driver of cattle **:** an ox driver **:** DROVER
bulldust \ˈ=,=\ *n, Austral* **:** coarse dust or silt
bull earing *n* **:** an earing fixed to the yard instead of to the sail — see SAIL illustration
bulled \ˈbu̇ld\ *adj* [¹*bull* + *-ed*] **:** THICKENED, STRENGTHENED — used esp. of the neck
¹bul·len \ˈbu̇lən\ *or* **bullen nail** *n* -s [alter. of earlier *bullion-nail*, fr. *bullion* (boss on harness) + *nail*] **:** a nail with a round head and short shank, tinned and lacquered
²bullen \ˈ"\ *n* -s [origin unknown] **:** a device for catching large turtles consisting essentially of a metal ring that settles over the turtle and an attached net in which it becomes entangled
¹bul·ler \ˈbələr, ˈbēl-, ˈbül-\ *vi* -ED/-ING/-S [ME *bulleren* to bubble, boil, prob. of Scand origin; akin to Icel *bulla* to boil, Sw *bullra* to make a noise — more at BULLER (to roar)] *Scot* **:** BOIL, SEETHE
²buller \ˈ"\ *n* -s [ME, bubble, fr. *bulleren*, v.] *Scot* **:** WHIRLPOOL
³buller \ˈ"\ *vi* -ED/-ING/-S [prob. of Scand origin; akin to Sw *bullra* to make a noise, Dan *buldra*, OE *bellan* to roar — more at BELLOW] *Scot* **:** ROAR, BELLOW
⁴bull·er \ˈbu̇lə(r)\ *n* -s [³*bull* + *-er*] **:** a cow or heifer constantly in heat **:** a bovine nymphomaniac
⁵bull·er \ˈ"\ *n* -s [*bulldog* + *-er*] **:** BULLDOG
¹bul·let \ˈbu̇lət, *usu* -əd·+V\ *n* -s [MF *boulette* small ball, small missile & *boulet* cannonball, missile, diminutives of *boule* ball — more at BOWL] **1** *archaic* **a :** CANNONBALL **b :** a small round mass **c :** a missile for a sling **2 a :** a missile (as of lead, steel, or lead with a steel casing) that is round or elongated and designed to be fired from a rifle, musket, or pistol; *broadly* **:** CARTRIDGE 1a **3 :** something suggesting or likened to a bullet esp. in form or vigor of action: as **a** *slang* **:** an ace of a deck of cards **b :** a hollow hemispherical iron shell filled with pitch and used to hold small objects during metalcraft tooling **c :** a large solid dot so placed in printed matter as to call attention to a particular passage **d :** a conical part or structure; *esp* **:** an electric lamp enclosed in a cone-shaped metal case that is usu. supported by a flexible shaft **e :** something (as a neutron) that can be bombarded against an atomic nucleus to induce fission

S B
revolver cartridge showing *S* shell, *B* bullet

²bullet \ˈ"\ *adj* **:** relating to or resembling a bullet (as in form, in speed of action, or in producing a single impact)
³bullet \ˈ"\ *vi* -ED/-ING/-S **:** to move fast ⟨the car ~*ed* toward him⟩
bullet bolt *n* **:** a bolt contracted or extended by the turning of a knob or handle — compare SPRING BOLT
bullet catch *also* **bullet latch** *n* **:** a catch having a bullet bolt
bullet hawk *n* **:** ACCIPITER 2
bullethead \ˈ==,=\ *n* **1 :** a head that is round or shaped like a bullet **2 :** a pigheaded person — **bullet-headed** \ˈ==ˈ==\ *adj*
¹bul·le·tin \ˈbu̇lətᵊn, -ətən,-əd·ən\ *n* -s [F, fr. It *bullettino*, dim. of *bulla* papal edict, fr. ML, papal edict, document, seal — more at BILL (document)] **:** a brief or condensed public notice or announcement usu. concerning a matter of marked current interest and issuing from a source that might reasonably be considered authoritative: as **a :** a brief statement from an official source concerning the current status of a source of prolonged interest (as of a war or the health of a sovereign) **b :** an announcement of future plans; *esp* **:** a college or university catalog **c :** a brief monograph; *esp* **:** one issued by a public agency to provide popular information on a subject ⟨the state college issued several ~s on local plants⟩ **d :** a brief statement of news considered to be of outstanding importance or interest and made public at the earliest possible moment (as by last-minute insertion on the front page of a newspaper or by interruption of a radio program) — compare FLASH
²bulletin \ˈ"\ *vt* -ED/-ING/-S **:** to make public by means of or in the form of a bulletin
bulletin board *n* **:** a board on which bulletins or other notices are posted
bul·le·tin·ize \-ᵊn,īz, -ə,nīz\ *vt* -ED/-ING/-S **:** to approach or notify by means of a bulletin ⟨we will ~ the whole membership⟩
bullet jacket *n* **:** the outer metal casing of a bullet
bul·let·less \ˈbu̇lətləs\ *adj* **:** being without a bullet
bullet money *n* **:** an old Siamese money in the form of bullet-shaped lumps of gold and silver that was valued in divisions and multiples of the tical
¹bulletproof \ˈ==ˈ=\ *adj* **1 :** impenetrable to bullets ⟨~ glass⟩ **2 :** not subject to correction, alteration, or modification ⟨a ~ argument⟩
²bulletproof \ˈ"\ *vt* -ED/-ING/-S [¹*bulletproof*] **:** to make impenetrable to bullets ⟨~ a car⟩
bullet trap *n* **:** a backstop for small-arms firing that acts as a target frame and that serves to deflect and arrest bullets safely by means of its heavy steel sides
bul·let tree \ˈbu̇lət-\ *n* [by folk etymology fr. AmerSp *balata* — more at BALATA] **1 :** a bully tree (esp. *Manilkara bidentata*) **2 :** a tree (*Terminalia buceras*) of Central America and the West Indies with brownish gray very close-grained wood
bulletwood \ˈ==,=\ *n* **1 :** the wood of a bully tree **2 :** a bully tree (*Manilkara bidentata*)
bul·lety \ˈbu̇ləd·ē\ *adj* **:** like a bullet in shape or hardness
bull-eye \ˈ=ˈ=\ *n* **:** an eye (as of a pigeon) having both iris and pupil dark in color
bull fiddle *n* **:** CONTRABASS — **bull fiddler** *n*
bullfight \ˈ=,=\ *n* -s **:** a Spanish, Portuguese, and Latin-American spectacle in which a bull is ceremonially fought and usu. killed in an arena by a matador assisted by picadors and banderilleros — called also *corrida*
bullfighter \ˈ=,==\ *n* **:** one that fights bulls; *esp* **:** TORERO
bullfighting \ˈ=,==\ *n* **:** the activity of a bullfight; *also* **:** the custom of presenting bullfights
¹bullfinch \ˈ=,=\ *n* [prob. so called fr. the thick neck] **1 :** a finch of the genus *Pyrrhula*; *esp* **:** a European finch (*P. pyrrhula*) that is often kept as a cage bird and taught to whistle various airs, the male having rose-red underparts, blue-gray back, black cap, chin, tail, and wings, and white rump, the female being chiefly pinkish brown below, grayish brown above **2 :** any of several other finches that resemble the European bullfinch (as a pyrrhuloxia or grosbeak)
²bullfinch \ˈ"\ *n* [fr. earlier *bullfinch* (*fence*)] **:** a hedge too high for a mounted hunter to leap
bull·fist *or* **bull·fice** \ˈbu̇l,fis(t)\ *n* -s [*bullfist* fr. ¹*bull* + *fist* flatus, fr. ME; *bullfice* alter. of *bullfist* — more at FEIST] **:** GIANT PUFFBALL
bullfoot *var of* BULL'S-FOOT
bullfrog \ˈ=,=\ *n* [so called fr. its size and its bull-like croak] **:** FROG; *esp* **:** any of numerous large heavy-bodied deep-voiced frogs chiefly of the genus *Rana* (esp. *R. catesbeiana*)
bull gang *n* [*bullwork*] **:** a crew of unskilled laborers
bull gear *n* **:** a bull wheel having gear teeth
bull·gine \ˈbu̇l,jīn\ *n* -s [¹*bull* + *engine*] *dial* **:** ENGINE — used specif. of steam locomotives
bull grape \ˈbu̇l+,-\ *n* [*bullace grape*] **:** MUSCADINE
bull grass *n* **1 :** SOFT CHEAT **2 :** PRAIRIE CORDGRASS
bull-grip \ˈ=,=\ *n* **:** any of several prickly plants of the genus *Smilax* (esp. *S. rotundifolia*)
bull grunter *n* **:** a silvery dark-dotted marine percoid fish (*Pomadasys multimaculatus*) of the east coast of southern Africa highly regarded for food and sport
bull gun *n* **:** a heavy-barreled target rifle
bullhead \ˈ=,=\ *n* **1 :** any of numerous large-headed fishes: as **a :** any of several scorpaenid fishes: as (1) **:** MILLER'S-THUMB 1 (2) **:** FATHER-LASHER (3) **:** SEA POACHER (4) **:** SCULPIN **b :** any of several catfishes (genus *Ameiurus*) abundant in fresh waters of No. America **c :** a marine sciaenid food fish (*Laumus fasciatus*) of the southern U.S. **d :** a small primitive brown shark (*Heterodontus japonicus*) of Australasia **2 :** a stupid person; *esp* **:** one stupidly headstrong and stubborn **3 a :** BLACK-BELLIED PLOVER **b :** GOLDEN PLOVER **c :** AMERICAN GOLDENEYE **4 :** a deformed or atrophied flower; *esp* **:** one that is abnormally double **5 :** a head (as of a rivet or a rail) of approximately bulbous section; *also* **:** a bullhead rail **6 :** a caltrop (*Tribulus terrestris*) of the southwestern U.S. **7** *also* **bullhead clam :** a freshwater mussel (*Plethobasis cyphus*) of the upper Mississippi drainage with a nacreous shell used for making buttons
bullheaded \ˈ=ˈ==\ *adj* [*bull* + *headed*] **1 :** having a massive head suggesting that of a bull **2 :** stupidly stubborn **:** HEADSTRONG, OBSTINATE **3 a :** having a bullhead **b** *of railway rails* **:** being double-headed with one bulbous end larger than the other, the small end being designed to fit in a chair **syn** see OBSTINATE
bull·head·ed·ly *adv* **:** in a bullheaded manner **:** OBSTINATELY
bull·head·ed·ness *n* -ES **:** OBSTINACY
bull header *n* **:** a header brick laid on its edge; *also* **:** a brick having one of its corners rounded, laid with one of its ends exposed, and serving as the sill under and beyond a window frame, as a quoin, or as a part of the masonry around a doorway
bullhead lily *n* [¹*bull* + *head*] **:** SPATTERDOCK
bullhead shark *n* [¹*bull* + *head*] **:** a shark of the family Heterodontidae — see HETERODONTUS
bullhoof \ˈ=,=\ *n, Jamaica* **:** a West Indian passionflower (*Passiflora murucuja*) with leaves like a cloven hoof
bullhorn \ˈ=,=\ *n* **:** a loudspeaker esp. on naval vessels
bull-horn acacia *n* [so called fr. the shape of the thorns] **:** any of several hollow-thorned trees of the genus *Acacia*; *esp* **:** a large-thorned chiefly Central American tree (*A. cornigera*) the thorns of which are inhabited by ants
bul·li·dae \ˈbu̇lə,dē\ *n pl, cap* [NL, fr. *Bulla*, type genus (fr. L, bubble) + *-idae* — more at POLL (head)] **:** a family of gastropod mollusks (order Opisthobranchia) including a number of typical bubble shells
bullied *past of* BULLY
bullier *comparative of* BULLY
bullies *pl of* BULLY, *pres 3d sing of* BULLY
bulliest *superlative of* BULLY
bul·li·form \ˈbu̇lə,fȯrm\ *adj* [L *bulla* bubble + E *-iform*] **:** shaped like a bubble **:** BULLATE — used chiefly of plant structures
bulliform cell *n* **:** one of the large thin-walled apparently empty cells that occur in the epidermis of many grass leaves and that by their turgor changes cause rolling and unrolling of the leaves thus regulating water loss — called also *hygroscopic cell, motor cell*
bullimong *n* -s [ME *bulimong, bolymong*, prob. fr. *bule* bull + *imong* mixture, fr. OE *gemong, gemang* mixture, mingling, crowd — more at BULL, AMONG] *dial Eng* **:** a mixture of various grains and forage plants sown together
bull in a china shop : a person notably clumsy or ill-adapted to the situation in which he finds himself
bull index *n* **:** a measure of the relative ability of a dairy bull to transmit desirable qualities to his daughters obtained by comparing the productivity of a certain number of daughters with that of their dams
bulling *n* -s [fr. gerund of ³*bull*] **:** the dislodging of rock by exploding blasting charges in fissures
bulling bar *n* **:** a bar used to ram clay into cracks before blasting
bulling heifer *n* [fr. pres. part. of ³*bull*] *Brit* **:** a heifer unbred but of an age for breeding usu. from 15 months to the first service
bul·lion \ˈbu̇lyən\ *n* -s [ME *bullioun* gold or silver as metal measurable by weight, fr. AF *bullion* mint, prob. fr. MF *bouillir, boillir* to boil — more at BOIL] **1 a :** gold or silver considered merely as so much metal without regard to any value imparted to it by its form ⟨the ~ contained in a silver dollar⟩; *specif* **:** uncoined gold or silver in the shape of bars, ingots, or comparable masses **b :** metal in the mass ⟨lead ~⟩ **2** *obs* **:** a place where precious metals are tested, minted, or exchanged **3** *obs* **:** an ornamental metal boss used on harness, jewelry, or other objects **4 a :** lace of gold or silver threads used esp. formerly in church vestments, robes of state, or other formal costumes **b :** cord with a core usu. of wire or cotton covered with textile or metal threads of gold, silver, or other color and used esp. to form braids or twisted fringes (as for military insignia or ornamentation); *also* **:** braid or fringe so made **5 :** BULL'S-EYE 4a
bullion balance *n* **:** a sensitive beam balance of heavy construction that is used for weighing bullion and specie
bul·lioned \-nd\ *adj* **:** trimmed or finished with bullion
bul·lion·ism \-,nizəm\ *n* -s **:** the principles and practices advocated by a bullionist
bul·lion·ist \-nəst\ *n* -s **1 :** an advocate of a metallic medium of exchange **2 :** a believer in the prohibition of the export of specie and in the regulation of trade so as to insure an import of bullion preferably after each transaction — used esp. in ref. to early mercantilist doctrine **3 :** one who holds that a premium on bullion is indicative of bank-note depreciation — used esp. in ref. to the English currency controversies of the early 19th century
bul·lion·less \-yənləs\ *adj* **:** being without bullion
bullion point *n* **1 :** GOLD EXPORT POINT **2 :** GOLD IMPORT POINT
bullion stitch *or* **bullion knot** *n* **:** a decorative stitch similar to the French knot forming very short bars
bull·ish \ˈbu̇lish, -lēsh\ *adj* **1 :** of, relating to, or suggestive of a bull; *esp* **:** obstinate as a bull **2 a :** inclined to bull the market ⟨speculators are feeling ~⟩ **b :** characterized by a trend toward rising prices ⟨a ~ market⟩ **c :** looking toward a rise in prices ⟨a ~ report⟩ ⟨~ commitments for the new year⟩ **d :** marked by hopefulness for the future **:** OPTIMISTIC — **bull·ish·ly** *adv*
bul·li soil \ˈbu̇,lī-\ *also* **bulli** *n* -s *usu cap B* [fr. *Bulli*, town in New South Wales, Australia, whence it comes] **:** a black soil used as a topdressing to produce a hard surface (as of a cricket pitch)
bull kelp *n* **:** any of certain large brown Pacific seaweeds (division Phaeophyta) esp. of the genus *Nereocystis*
bull mastiff *n* [*bulldog* + *mastiff*] **:** a large powerful dog of an English breed developed from crossings of the bulldog and mastiff that is brindled or fawn with black mask and is used esp. in South Africa as a watch or guard dog
bull moose \ˈ=ˈ=\ *also* **bull moos·er** \ˈ"+ə(r)\ *n, usu cap B&M* [*bull moose*, the emblem of the Progressive party formed in 1912 by Theodore Roosevelt †1919 Am. president] **:** a follower of Theodore Roosevelt in the U.S. presidential campaign of 1912
bullneck *in senses 1 & 3* ˈ=,=, *in sense 2* ˈ=ˈ=\ *n* **1 :** leather made from the neck hide of a bull **2** *usu* **bull neck a :** a thick short powerful neck **b :** a swelling of the neck in severe diphtheria filling and distending the space beneath the jaw from ear to ear **3 :** any of several American wild ducks: as **a :** CANVASBACK **b :** RUDDY DUCK **c :** RING-NECKED DUCK
bullnecked \ˈ=ˈ=\ *adj* **:** having a bull neck
bull nettle *n* **1 :** HORSE NETTLE **2 :** SPURGE NETTLE
bullnose *in sense 3* ˈ=,=, *in other senses* ˈ=ˈ=\ *n* **1** *or* **bullnosed plane :** a small plane with the iron set near the fore end of the stock **2 :** BULL'S-NOSE **3 :** a necrobacillosis arising in facial wounds of swine and characterized by swelling of the face, nose, and mouth and sloughing of the tissues **4** *slang* **:** the front drawbar of a locomotive

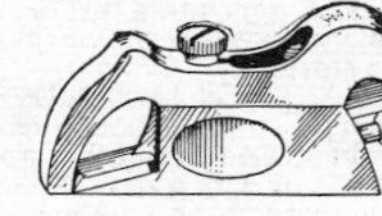
bullnose 1

bullnose pepper *n* **:** SWEET PEPPER
bullnose tool *n* **:** a tool that is shaped like a roundnose tool but has a wider and stronger point and that is used for taking heavy roughing cuts (as on a lathe or planer)
bullnut \ˈ=,=\ *n* **:** MOCKERNUT
bull oak *n* [prob. by folk etymology fr. *beloh*] **:** any of several Australian trees of the genus *Casuarina* (esp. *C. equisetifolia, C. glauca*, and *C. luehmanni*)
¹bull·ock \ˈbu̇lək\ *n* -s [ME *bullok*, fr. OE *bulluc* — more at BULL] **1 :** a young bull **2 :** a castrated bull **:** OX, STEER, STAG **3 :** a domestic bovine **:** COW, ZEBU
²bullock \ˈ"\ *vb* -ED/-ING/-S *vt* [prob. influenced in meaning by ³*bully*] *dial Brit* **:** BULLY **~** *vi, Austral* **:** to work hard; *esp* **:** to do heavy manual labor
bullock block *n* **:** a large iron-strapped gin block fitted under the topmast crosstrees to take the topsail tyes
bull·ock·ing \-kiŋ\ *adj* [¹*bullock* + *-ing*] **1** *Austral* **:** resembling a bullock in size or strength ⟨a big ~ fellow⟩ **2** *Austral, of work* **:** HARD, ARDUOUS
bul·lock·ite \ˈbu̇lə,kīt\ *n* -s *usu cap* [Jeremiah *Bullock*, 19th cent. Am. leader of the sect + E *-ite*] **:** one of three Freewill Baptist groups
bul·lock oriole \ˈbu̇lək-\ *or* **bul·lock's oriole** \-ks-\ *n, usu cap B* [after William *Bullock* fl1827 Eng. naturalist] **:** a common black and yellow oriole (*Icterus bullockii*) of western No. America
bullock's-heart *also* **bullock heart** \ˈ=,=ˈ=\ *n* [so called fr. its size and appearance] **:** a light green to yellow slightly bristly and somewhat acid tropical fruit that turns brown when fully ripe, is closely related to the soursop and sweetsop, and is produced on a small tree (*Annona reticulata*) native to tropical America but widely cultivated
bul·lock's lungwort \ˈbu̇ləks-\ *n* **1 :** MULLEIN **2 :** LUNGWORT 2a
¹bull·ocky \ˈbu̇ləkē\ *n* -ES *Austral* **:** a bullock-team driver
²bullocky \ˈ"\ *adj* **1** *Austral* **:** relating to or concerned with the driving or management of cattle ⟨~ lore⟩ **2 :** like that of a bullock ⟨thick ~ shoulders⟩
bull of the bog [so called fr. its booming cry] **:** the common bittern (*Botaurus stellaris*) of Europe
bull of the woods : ¹BULL 3c
bul·lous \ˈbu̇ləs\ *also* **bul·lose** \-,lōs\ *adj* [NL *bulla* + E *-ous* or *-ose*] **:** resembling or characterized by bullae **:** VESICULAR ⟨a ~ lesion⟩
bullpates \ˈ=,=\ *n pl but sing in constr* [¹*bull* + *pates*, pl. of *pate*] **:** TUFTED HAIR GRASS 2
bull peep *n* **1 :** WHITE-RUMPED SANDPIPER **2 :** SANDERLING
bullpen \ˈ=,=\ *n* [¹*bull* + *pen*] **1 a** *archaic* **:** an enclosure (as of logs) used as a temporary place of confinement **b :** a prison, guardhouse, or other place of confinement; *esp* **:** a large detention cell (as in a police station or courthouse) where prisoners are held until brought into court **2 :** a place on a baseball field where relief pitchers warm up during a game; *sometimes* **:** the relief pitchers ⟨got good support from the ~⟩ **3 :** any of certain places in which a number of people congregate for a common purpose: as **a :** DORMITORY, BUNKHOUSE **b :** a business office that is not divided into individual compartments **c :** a place designed for the comfort and relaxation of employees; *esp* **:** a designated smoking area in a plant where smoking is not generally permitted
bull pine *n* **1 :** PONDEROSA PINE **2 :** any of several pines (as the Digger pine, loblolly, pond pine, Jeffrey pine, and limber pine)
bull-point *also* **bull-prick** \ˈ=,=\ *n* **:** a pointed steel bar usu. driven with a sledge for making drill holes in soft rock
bull·pout \ˈbu̇l,pau̇t\ *n, pl* **bullpout** *also* **bullpouts** [*bullhead* + *pout*] **:** the brown bullhead or a related catfish
bull pump *n* **:** a direct single-acting pumping engine with the steam cylinder placed above the pump, the return stroke being effected by gravity
bullpup \ˈ=ˈ=\ *n* -s **:** a rifle whose barrel is bedded well back on the stock so that the end of the receiver is very close to the heel of the butt
bull quartz *n* **:** BASTARD QUARTZ
bull rattle *n* **1 :** BLADDER CAMPION **2 :** WHITE CAMPION a
bull redfish *n* **:** CHANNEL BASS
bullring \ˈ=,=\ *n* **1 a :** an arena for bullfights **b :** a ring passed through the septal cartilage of the nose of a bull and used in directing and controlling him **2 :** a T-section ring usu. shrunk on a piston, the ring acting as a carrier and distance ring to support and separate two split piston rings
bull riveter *n* **:** a large stationary riveter operated by a ram
bull-roarer \ˈ=ˈ==\ *n* **:** a slat of wood tied to the end of a thong and making an intermittent roaring sound when whirled that is used esp. by Australian aborigines in religious rites or among western peoples as a children's toy
bull rope *n* [*bull* (*wheel*)] **:** a strong fiber or wire rope: **a :** a rope working through a bull's-eye; *esp* **:** one used in securing a light yard or mast **b :** the rope that drives a bull wheel
bull runner *n* [*bull* (*ladle*)] **:** a foundry worker who pours molten metal from a bull ladle into molds
bullrush *var of* BULRUSH
bulls *pl of* BULL, *pres 3d sing of* BULL
bull screen *n* **:** a coarse screen for separating knots and unground material from freshly ground wood pulp
bull session *n* [⁵*bull*] **:** an informal discursive group discussion ⟨evening *bull sessions* where the talk moved roughly from women to football and back again —Millard Lampell⟩
bull set *n* **:** a small hammer for breaking stone often used with a sledge hammer
bull's-eye \ˈ=,=\ *n, pl* **bull's-eyes 1 a :** a small circular or oval wooden block without sheaves having a groove around it and a hole through it **b :** a round usu. margined spot or opening **2 :** a small thick disk of glass inserted (as in a deck, roof, floor) to let in light — compare DEADLIGHT **3 :** a very hard globular candy **4 a :** a lump left on glass by the end of the blowpipe — see CROWN GLASS **b :** a raised circular design on glass **c :** a white glass marble with a dark center **5 a :** the center of a target; *also* **:** something regarded as central or crucial **b :** a shot that hits the bull's-eye; *broadly* **:** anything that precisely attains a desired end **6 a :** a simple lens of large numerical aperture for concentrating rays of light **b :** a lantern with a bull's-eye lens **:** DARK LANTERN — see LANTERN illustration **7 :** a circular or oval opening (as in a wall) for air or light **8 :** DAISY 2 **9** *usu* **bullseye :** a reddish small-scaled Australian food fish (*Priacanthus macracanthus*)

b bull's-eye 5a

bull's-eye rot *n* **:** a disease of apples characterized by spots resembling eyes on the fruit and caused by either of two fungi (*Neofabraea malicorticis* and *Gloeosporium perennans*)
bull's-eye window *n* **:** a circular window or a window filling a bull's-eye
bull's feather *n, obs* **:** HORN 4b
bull's-foot *or* **bullfoot** \ˈ"\ *n, pl* **bull's-foots** *or* **bullsfoots :** COLTSFOOT a
¹bullshit \ˈ=,=\ *n* [¹*bull* + *shit*] **:** NONSENSE; *esp* **:** foolish insolent talk — usu. considered vulgar
²bullshit \ˈ"\ *vi* **:** to talk bullshit — usu. considered vulgar
bull's-horn thorn *n* **:** BULL-HORN ACACIA
bull's mouth *n* **:** a large handsome helmet shell (*Cypraecassis rufa*) that is reddish brown externally with a brilliant orange-red lining and is common throughout the Indo-Pacific area
bull snake *n* **:** any of several large harmless colubrid snakes widely distributed in No. America, feeding chiefly on rodents, and constituting a genus *Pituophis* — called also *gopher snake, pine snake*
bull's noon *n, dial Eng* **:** MIDNIGHT
bull's-nose \ˈ=,=\ *n, pl* **bull's-noses** *archit* **:** an external angle when obtuse or rounded
bull stag *n* **:** a bull castrated when full-grown
bull stick *n* [*bull* (*wheel*)] **:** a lever used in lieu of a bull wheel to swing a derrick into position to pick up its load
bull stretcher *n* **:** a stretcher brick laid on edge; *also* **:** a brick with one corner rounded and laid with the face exposed (as in a quoin)
bullsucker \ˈ=,==\ **:** any of several West Indian cacti of the genus *Opuntia* with prickly flat joints
bulls·wool \ˈ=,=\ *n, Austral* **:** STRINGYBARK 1, 2

bull team *n* : OXTEAM

bullterrier \'ˌ=ˌ==\ *n* [*bulldog* + *terrier*] : a short-haired terrier of a breed originated in England by crossing the bulldog with terriers to develop a dog of speed, hardihood, and powerful bite for use in dog fights, dogs of this breed having great courage and strength but being built on the trim lines of a terrier

bull thistle *n* **1** : a European thistle (*Cirsium lanceolatum*) with rather large heads and prickly leaves that is extensively naturalized as a weed in the U.S. **2** : HORSE NETTLE

bull tongue *n* : a shovel or wide tooth attached to a cultivator or plow to stir the soil, kill weeds, or mark furrows; *also* : an instrument fitted with such an attachment

bull train *n* : a train of ox-drawn wagons that was used esp. for haulage in western U.S. before establishment of the railroads

bull trout *n* **1** *Brit* : SEA TROUT; *esp* : a large old sea trout **2** : DOLLY VARDEN 2

bull–voiced \'ˌ=ˌ=\ *adj* : having a loud deep voice

bullweed \'ˌ=ˌ=\ *n* [ME *bulwed*, prob. fr. *bule* bull + *wed* weed] : KNAPWEED

[1]**bullwhack** \'bu̇l,(h)wak\ *n* [back-formation fr. *bullwhacker*] *chiefly West* : a long heavy whip with short handle used esp. when driving teams of four or more animals

[2]**bullwhack** \"\ *vb* [back-formation fr. *bullwhacker*] *vt*, *chiefly West* : to drive (as an ox team) using a whip rather than a goad ~ *vi*, *chiefly West* : to drive a team (as of oxen) using a whip rather than a goad

bullwhacker \'ˌ=ˌ=\ *n* [[1]*bull* + *whacker*] **1** *chiefly West* : a driver of an ox wagon or other heavy freight wagon esp. in the early settlement of the West **2** *chiefly West* : BULLWHACK

bull wheel *n* **1** : the main driving wheel or gear of a machine, usu. the largest and strongest wheel in the train of mechanism, in some machines (as a shaper) transmitting the power received by the machine to the various mechanisms, in others (as a tractor) delivering to the driving wheels the power transmitted to it from the motor **2** : a drum on which a rope is wound for hauling or lifting (as logs or well-boring tools) **3** : a wheel attached to the boom of a derrick at the base and used to swing the boom about a vertical axis

bullwhip \'ˌ=ˌ=\ *n* [[1]*bull* + *whip*] : a rawhide whip with plaited lash 15 to 25 feet long

bullwork \'ˌ=ˌ=\ *n* : hard manual labor

[1]**bul·ly** \'bu̇lē, -li\ *n* -ES [prob. modif. of D *boel* lover, fr. MD *boele*, fr. MHG *buole*, prob. alter. (baby talk) of *bruoder* brother — more at BROTHER] **1** *archaic* **a** : SWEETHEART, DARLING — used of either sex **b** : a good fellow : a fine chap **2 a** *archaic* : a man of outstanding physical powers **b** : a blustering fellow more insolent than courageous : one given to hectoring, browbeating, and threatening; *esp* : one habitually threatening, harsh, or cruel to others weaker or smaller than himself **c** : the protector of a prostitute : PIMP, PANDER **3 a** : a hired ruffian : BRAVO **b** *dial Brit* : a fellow workman : MATE **c** : KEELBOATMAN **d** : the boss of a logging camp **4 a** : any of several blenniod fishes **b** : any of several gobies

[2]**bully** \"\ *adj*, *sometimes* -ER/-EST **1** *of a person* : JOVIAL, DASHING, GALLANT — used esp. in *bully boy*, a term of familiar address **2** : of the best quality : EXCELLENT, FIRST-RATE ⟨what a ~ car⟩ ⟨that's a ~ idea⟩ **3** : like, characteristic of, or in the manner of a bully ⟨don't try your ~ tricks around here⟩

[3]**bully** \"\ *vb* -ED/-ING/-ES *vt* : to intimidate by an overbearing swaggering demeanor or by threats : act the part of a bully toward : DOMINEER ~ *vi* : to act as a bully : BLUSTER **syn** see INTIMIDATE

[4]**bully** \"\ *interj* [[2]*bully*] — used to express satisfaction, congratulation, or pleasure

[5]**bully** \"\ *adv* [[2]*bully*] : VERY, EXTREMELY, OUTSTANDINGLY ⟨a ~ good dinner⟩

[6]**bully** \"\ *or* **bully beef** *n* -ES [prob. modif. of F (*bœuf*) *bouilli* boiled beef, fr. *bouilli*, past part. of *bouillir* to boil — more at BOIL] : pickled or canned usu. corned beef

[7]**bully** \"\ *n* -ES [origin unknown] : a procedure of putting the ball in play in field hockey in which two opposing players face one another and alternately strike the ground and the opponent's stick three times after which the ball may be played

[8]**bully** \"\ *vb* -ED/-ING/-ES *vt* : to put (a field hockey ball) in play with a bully ~ *vi* : to put a field hockey ball in play with a bully

bullyboy \'ˌ=ˌ=\ *n* [[1]*bully* + *boy*] : a swaggering overbearing tough; *esp* : one associated with or acting as an agent of a political faction

bullyhuff \'bu̇lē,həf\ *n* [[1]*bully* + *huff*] *archaic* : a bragging bully

bullying *adj* : OVERBEARING, BLUSTERING — **bul·ly·ing·ly** *adv*

bul·ly·ism \'bu̇lē,izəm\ *n* -S : bullying behavior or practice

bully–off \'ˌ=ˌ=\ *n* -S [[8]*bully*] *Brit* : [7]BULLY

bul·ly·rag \'bu̇lē,rag\ *or* **bal·ly·rag** \'bal-\ *vt* [modif. of earlier *balarag*] **1** : to intimidate by bullying : BULLDOZE **2** : to abuse, scold, harass, or vex with teasing or complaining words; *broadly* : BADGER, BAIT, TORMENT

bullyrook *also* **bullyrock** \'ˌ=ˌ=\ *n* [*bullyrook* fr. [1]*bully* + *rook* (cheat, simpleton); *bullyrock* by folk etymology fr. *bullyrook*] *archaic* : BULLY 1b, 3a

bul·ly tree \'bu̇lē-\ *or* **bul·let tree** \-lət-\ *n* [by folk etymology fr. AmerSp *balata* — more at BALATA] : any of several hard-wooded tropical American trees of the family Sapotaceae; *esp* : a large tree (*Manilkara bidentata*) of the West Indies and northern So. America that yields balata gum and a heavy red timber — called also *balata*, *beefwood*

bul·oke \'bu̇,lōk\ *n* -S [by alter.] : BELAH 1

bul·rush *also* **bull·rush** \'bu̇l,rəsh\ *n* [ME *bulrysche*, *bolrysche*, perh. fr. *bule* bull + *rysche*, *roysche*, *rusche* rush — more at BULL, RUSH] **1** : any of several large rushes growing in wet land or water: as **a** : a sedge of the genus *Scirpus* (esp. *S. lacustris*) **b** *Brit* : either of two cattails (*Typha latifolia* and *T. angustifolia*) **c** : a common American rush (*Juncus effusus*) **2** *in the Old Testament* : PAPYRUS — **bulrushy** \-shē\ *adj*

bulrush millet *n* : PEARL MILLET; *esp* : a type widely grown in Africa and the Orient and commonly referred to a distinct species (*Pennisetum typhoideum*)

buls *pl of* BUL

bulse \'bəls\ *n* -S [Pg *bolsa*, lit., purse, fr. ML *bursa* — more at PURSE] : a purse or bag in which to carry or measure valuables (as diamonds or gold dust); *broadly* : a parcel of jewels

bult \'bəlt\ *n* -S [Afrik, fr. MD; akin to OE *bold* house — more at BUILD] *Africa* : a rocky outcropping : ridge of land : HILLOCK

bult·fon·tein·ite \ˌbəlt(ˌ)fän·'tā,nīt, -ˌfən\ *n* -S *usu cap* [*Bultfontein*, village in Cape Province, Union of So. Africa + E *-ite*] : a mineral $Ca_2SiO_2(OH,F)_2$ consisting of calcium silicate with hydroxyl or fluoride that is found at Bultfontein, So. Africa

bulti *var of* BOLTI

bul·to \'bu̇l(ˌ)tō, 'bül-\ *n* -S [Sp, image, bulk, form, body, statue, fr. L *vultus*, *voltus* countenance, expression, shape; perh. akin to Goth *wulthus* glory, W *gweled* to see] **1** : an image of a saint carved in wood and polychromed made in the southwestern U.S. and Latin America in the 18th and 19th centuries **2** : a bundle esp. of fibers for rope making

bul·tow \'bu̇l(ˌ)tō\ *n* -S [origin unknown] : LONGLINE; *esp* : SETLINE

bu·lu \'bü(ˌ)lü\ *n*, *pl* **bulu** *or* **bulus** *usu cap* **1** : a Bantu language of the southern Cameroons **2** : a people of the southern Cameroons who speak the Bulu language **3** : a member of the Bulu people

[1]**bul·wark** \'bu̇l,wə(r)k; 'bu̇l,wərk, -ˌwōk, -ˌwəik; 'bu̇l,wȯrk, -ȯ(ə)k; 'bu̇l,wärk, -wák; *also* 'bəl,wə(r)k *or* 'bəl,wərk *or* 'bəl,wəik\ *n* -S [ME *bulwerke*, fr. MD, fr. MHG *bolwerc*, fr. *bole* plank + *werc* work, fr. OHG; akin to ON *bolr* tree-trunk — more at BOLE, WORK] **1 a** : a solid wall-like structure raised for defense usu. not too high for the defenders to fire over : RAMPART, PARAPET **b** : BREAKWATER, SEAWALL **2** : something that offers strong support or protection in danger **3** : a powerful means of defense : an imposing safeguard ⟨a strong representative government is a ~ of liberty⟩ **3** : the side of a ship above the upper deck — usu. used in pl.; see SHIP illustration

[2]**bulwark** \"\ *vt* -ED/-ING/-S [ME *bulwerken*, fr. *bulwerke*, n.] : to fortify, secure, or reinforce with or as if with a bulwark : PROTECT ⟨ability to ~ a moral choice —Margaret Mead⟩ ⟨trying to ~ the country against internal disorder⟩

bulwark plating *n* : the light plating that projects above the hull plating of a ship and serves as a bulwark

bul·wer's petrel \'bu̇lwə(r)z-\ *n*, *usu cap B* [after James *Bulwer* †1879 Brit. clergyman and fellow of the Linnaean society] : a small sooty black petrel (*Bulweria bulwerii*) with a gray chin and pinkish feet

[1]**bum** \'bəm\ *n* -S [ME *bom*] *chiefly Brit* : BUTTOCKS — often considered vulgar

[2]**bum** \'bəm, 'bu̇m\ *vi* **bummed**; **bummed**; **bumming**; **bums** [ME *bumben*, of imit. origin] *dial chiefly Brit* : to make a droning or murmuring sound : HUM ⟨hear the bagpipes ~⟩

[3]**bum** \'bəm\ *n* -S *chiefly Scot* : a constant humming noise : DIN ⟨the ~ and bustle of the street⟩

[4]**bum** \'bəm\ *vt* **bummed**; **bummed**; **bumming**; **bums** [prob. imit.] : BEAT, POUND

[5]**bum** \'bəm\ *n* -S [by shortening] : BUMBAILIFF

[6]**bum** \'bəm\ *vb* **bummed**; **bummed**; **bumming**; **bums** [prob. back-formation fr. *bummer*] *vi* : to go around in the manner of a bum: **a** : LOAF ⟨he had been *bumming* around the house all day⟩ **b** : to wander esp. like a tramp ⟨he had *bummed* through the far West⟩ ~ *vt* : MOOCH, CADGE ⟨he tried to ~ a ride home⟩ ⟨she was always *bumming* cigarettes⟩

[7]**bum** \'bəm\ *n* -S [prob. short for *bummer*] **1 a** : LOAFER, VAGRANT; *esp* : one who drinks heavily ⟨a ~ from down on skid row⟩ **b** : a lazy indolent person; *esp* : one inclined to sponge off others and avoid work — often a generalized expression of disparagement ⟨Mickey . . . dwells in a black-and-white world where a guy is either your pal or probably a ~ —Hal Boyle⟩ **c** : HOBO, TRAMP ⟨hallelujah, I'm a ~⟩ **d** : one who travels around pursuing a particular activity and working only enough to keep going — usu. used with a qualifying noun ⟨the fruit ~s followed the peach harvest north from Georgia⟩: as (1) : a nonprofessional so enthusiastic about a sport that he lives on what he can earn in temporary jobs or on what he can sponge and devotes most of his time to the sport ⟨tennis ~s trying to keep their amateur status⟩ (2) : a person so enthusiastic about a sport that he devotes most of his leisure to it ⟨a train loaded with ski ~s off for a weekend⟩ **2** : an empty mail sack **3** : a lamb whose mother has died or deserted it **syn** see VAGABOND

[8]**bum** \'bəm\ *adj* **1** : of poor quality or nature : not good : INVALID, INFERIOR ⟨a ~ check⟩ **2 a** : not in working order or condition **b** *of a part of the body* : permanently or frequently stiff, sore, lame, or otherwise disabling ⟨a ~ knee from an old football injury⟩

[9]**bum** \'bəm\ *n* -S [prob. fr. [6]*bum*] : a drinking spree : BENDER ⟨a terrific 2-day ~⟩ — **on the bum** *adv* (*or adj*) **1** : footloose and wandering around the country in the manner of a tramp : in the manner or role of a vagrant ⟨he would go back *on the bum* awhile and try some other city —James Jones⟩ ⟨travel across country *on the bum*⟩ **2** : SPONGING, CADGING ⟨when his money ran out he always came to me *on the bum*⟩ **3** : in poor order or condition ⟨my wrists are a bit *on the bum* —Sinclair Lewis⟩ : in a state of depression ⟨the old days in the States before everything was *on the bum* there —Ernest Hemingway⟩

bum·bai·liff \ˌbəm'bālə̇f\ *n* -S [[1]*bum* + *bailiff*; fr. his close pursuit of debtors] *Brit* : BAILIFF — usu. used contemptuously ⟨a confounded, pettifogging ~ —W.M.Thackeray⟩

bum ball *n* [by alter.] : BUMP BALL

bumbalo *var of* BUMMALO

bumbass \'ˌ=ˌ=\ *n* -ES [prob. fr. [3]*bum* + *bass* (musical instrument)] **1** : BLADDER-AND-STRING **2** : [1]DRONE 3a

bumbast *obs var of* BOMBAST

bumbaste \ˌ=ˌ=\ *vt* -ED/-ING/-S [[1]*bum* + *baste*] *dial Eng* : to beat on the buttocks : THRASH

bum·baze \ˌbəm'bāz\ *vt* -ED/-ING/-S [perh. alter. of Sc *baze* to dismay, fr. ME *baisen*, *baishen* to dismay, be dismayed, fr. MF *baissier* to lower, abase, fr. (assumed) VL *bassiare* to lower — more at ABASE] *chiefly Scot* : BEWILDER, PERPLEX

bumbee \'ˌ=ˌ=\ *n* -S [[2]*bum* + *bee*] *chiefly Scot* : BUMBLEBEE

bum·ber·shoot \'bəmbə(r),shüt\ *n* -S [*bumber-* (alter. of *umbr-* in *umbrella*) + *-shoot* (alter. of *-chute* in *parachute*)] *slang* : UMBRELLA ⟨a bowler and ~ to go with his tidy, official face —*Time*⟩

[1]**bum·ble** \'bəmbəl\ *vi* **bumbled**; **bumbled**; **bumbling** \-mb(ə)liŋ\ **bumbles** [ME *bomblen* to boom, of imit. origin] **1** : to make a humming sound : BUZZ ⟨the June bugs *bumbled* foolishly against the window screens —Jean Stafford⟩ **2** : to make a low hollow sound : RUMBLE ⟨we *bumbled* across the trestle into the city —Grace H. Flandrau⟩

[2]**bumble** \"\ *vb* **bumbled**; **bumbled**; **bumbling** \-mb(ə)liŋ\ **bumbles** [prob. alter. (influenced by [1]*bumble*) of *bungle*] *vi* **1** : BUNGLE, BLUNDER ⟨someone *bumbled* and the advantage was lost⟩; *specif* : to speak ineptly, stuttering and faltering ⟨he *bumbled* through his speech⟩ **2** : to move or proceed unsteadily : STUMBLE ⟨*bumbling* along absent-mindedly on rope-soled shoes —Sybille Bedford⟩ ~*vt* : BUNGLE

[3]**bumble** \"\ *n* -S **1 a** : JUMBLE, SNARL **b** : BUNGLE, BOTCH **2** *chiefly Scot* : BUNGLER, BLUNDERER

[4]**bum·ble** \'bəm(b)əl, 'bu̇m-\ *n* -S [short for *bumblebee*] **1** *dial Eng* : BUMBLEBEE **2** *chiefly Scot* : IDLER, LOAFER **3** ([1]*bumble*) *dial Eng* : BITTERN

[5]**bum·ble** \'bu̇məl\ *n* -S [origin unknown] *dial Eng* : BULRUSH

[6]**bum·ble** \'bəmbəl\ *n* -S [after *Bumble*, a parish beadle in the novel *Oliver Twist* (1837-9) by Charles Dickens †1870 Eng. novelist] *Brit* : a pompous self-important minor official; *esp* : BEADLE

bum·ble·bee \'bəmbəl,bē\ *n* [[1]*bumble* + *bee*] : any of numerous large robust hairy social bees of the genus *Bombus* that form small annual colonies and like the honeybees store up honey in their underground nests, often using for this purpose the cells vacated by the young

bumblebee buzzer *or* **bumblebee coot** *n* : RUDDY DUCK

bumblebee hawkmoth *n* : a day-flying clearwing hawkmoth (*Hemaris diffinis* or related species) of the U.S., Europe, and Asia having the body largely yellow and resembling a bumblebee when in flight

bumblebee root *n* : PURPLE TRILLIUM

bum·ble·dom \'bəmbəldəm\ *n* -S *often cap* [*Bumble*, a parish beadle in *Oliver Twist* + E *-dom*] : the actions and mannerisms of pompous but inefficient government officials ⟨a strain of mild obstinacy exquisitely calculated to infuriate the self-important ~ of that time —G.M.Trevelyan⟩

bumble flower beetle *n* [prob. fr. [4]*bumble*] : a hairy yellowish brown black-marked beetle (*Euphoria inda*) that may sometimes become a pest by feeding on corn ears and certain fruits

bumblefoot \'ˌ=ˌ=\ *n* [[3]*bumble*] **1** *dial Eng* : a misshapen foot; *specif* : CLUBFOOT **2** : a disease of poultry characterized by a swelling on the ball of the foot with or without abscess formation

bum·ble·kite \'bu̇məl,kīt\ *n* -S [[1]*bumble* + *kyte*; fr. a belief that blackberries cause flatulence] *dial Eng* : BLACKBERRY

bum·ble·pup·py \'bəmbəl,pəpē\ *n* [[2]*bumble* + *puppy*] **1** : the old game of nineholes **2** : whist played poorly or without regard for rules

[1]**bum·bler** \'bəm(b)(ə)lə(r), 'bu̇m-\ *n* -S [[1]*bumble* + *-er*] *dial* : BUMBLEBEE

[2]**bum·bler** \'bəmb(ə)lə(r)\ *n* -S [[2]*bumble* + *-er*] : one that bumbles : BLUNDERER, BUNGLER

[1]**bumbling** *n* -S [fr. gerund of [2]*bumble*] : stupid and awkward blundering ⟨a story of military fatuity, of pompous ~, of reckless waste of lives —J.H.Powers⟩

[2]**bumbling** *adj* [fr. pres. part. of [2]*bumble*] **1 a** : blundering and awkward : likely to make foolish mistakes ⟨a kindly, ~ ne'er-do-well who had lately lost his job —Dixon Wecter⟩ **b** : ineffective as a speaker (as because of faltering and stuttering) ⟨animated and splendidly communicative one evening and ~ the next —R.H.Rovere⟩ **2** : marked by conspicuous blundering, inefficiency, ineffectiveness, and lack of organization ⟨the ~ policies of the administration led to its downfall⟩

[1]**bum·bo** \'bəm(ˌ)bō\ *also* **bom·bo** \'bäm-\ *n* -S [perh. fr. It (baby-talk) *bombo* drink, of imit. origin] : an alcoholic drink usu. made with rum or gin, sugar, water, and sometimes spices

[2]**bumbo** \"\ *n* -S [of West African origin; prob. akin to Mende *bogbo*, a tree whose fruit is used for vegetable sauce] : a West African leguminous tree (*Daniella thurifer*) that is the chief West African source of copal and has a soft pleasant-scented and damp-resistant wood

bum·boat \'bəm+,-\ *n* [prob. fr. LG *bumboot*, fr. *bum*, *bōm* tree + *boot* boat, fr. ME; akin to OHG *boum* tree — more at BEAM, BOAT] : a boat that brings provisions and commodities for sale to larger ships in port or offshore ⟨I bought a bunch of the tiny Azores bananas from a ~ under the side —F.M Ford⟩ ⟨Nelson's sailors had their ~ women who used to swarm aboard by rope's end and anchor chains —H.W.Baldwin⟩

bum·clock \'bəm,kläk\ *n* -S [[2]*bum* + *clock* (beetle)] *Scot* : DORBEETLE

bu·me·lia \byü'mēlēə\ *n* [NL, fr. L, ash, fr. Gk *boumelia*] **1** *cap* : a genus of tough spiny American trees and shrubs (family Sapotaceae) that bear edible berries **2** -S : any plant of the genus *Bumelia*

bumf \'bəm(p)f\ *n* -S [short for *bumfodder*, fr. [1]*bum* + *fodder*] **1** *slang Brit* : TOILET PAPER **2** *slang Brit* : documents and official papers — usu. used disparagingly

bumfeg *vt* **bumfegged**; **bumfegged**; **bumfegging**; **bumfegs** [[1]*bum* + obs. *feague*, *fegue* to beat, prob. fr. D *vegen*, lit., to sweep, fr. MD *vēghen*; akin to OS *fegon* to sweep, MHG *vegen* to sweep, clean, OE *fæger* beautiful — more at FAIR] *obs* : THRASH

bumfreezer \'ˌ=ˌ=\ *n* [[1]*bum*] *Brit* : a boy's short jacket; *esp* : ETON JACKET

bum·fuz·zle \ˌbəm'fəzəl\ *vt* -ED/-ING/-S [prob. alter. of E dial. *dumfoozle*, prob. alter. of E *dumfound*] *chiefly dial* : CONFUSE, PERPLEX, FLUSTER

bum·icky \'bəməkē\ *n* -ES [origin unknown] : a mixture of cement and powdered stone used for filling crevices in building stones

bumkin *var of* BUMPKIN

bum·ma·lo *or* **bum·ma·low** *or* **bum·me·lo** \'bəmə,lō\ *also* **bum·ba·lo** \-mbə-\ *n* -S [prob. modif. of Marathi *bombilā*, oblique case form of *bombīl*] : BOMBAY DUCK

bummed *past of* BUM

[1]**bum·mel** *or* **bum·mle** \'bəməl\ *vi* -ED/-ING/-S [by alter.] *chiefly Scot* : [1]BUMBLE

[2]**bummel** *or* **bummle** \"\ *n* -S [by alter.] *chiefly Scot* : [4]BUMBLE 1, 2

[3]**bum·mel** \'bəməl\ *vi* **bummeled** *or* **bummelled**; **bummeled** *or* **bummelled**; **bummeling** *or* **bummelling**; **bummels** [G *bummeln* to loaf] : to go or wander around at a leisurely pace : STROLL, SAUNTER

bum·mer \'bəmə(r)\ *n* -S [prob. modif. of G *bummler* loafer, tramp, fr. *bummeln* to loaf, dangle] **1** : one that bums; *specif* : one that subsists by cadging **2** : PLUNDERER, MARAUDER — used esp. of looting soldiers during the Civil War **3** : a low 2-wheeled logging truck or tracked cart for skidding logs **4** : the workman in charge of the conveyors in a mine or quarry

bumming *pres part of* BUM

bum·mler \'bəm(ə)lər\ *n* -S [[1]*bummel* + *-er*] *chiefly Scot* : one that bumbles: **a** : BUMBLEBEE **b** : BUNGLER, BLUNDERER

[1]**bump** \'bəmp\ *vb* -ED/-ING/-S [imit.] *vt* **1 a** : to strike or knock typically with a degree of force or violence and making a thudding impact and usu. with a degree of injury or damage ⟨he ~*ed* his head on the low ceiling⟩ **b** *chiefly Brit* : SMASH **c** *chiefly Brit* : NIP **2** : to meet with or come up against forcibly (as an obstruction, buffer, or guard rail) ⟨the front fender was crushed as it ~*ed* the stone wall⟩ **3 a** : to displace, dislodge, or move from a position by bumping : knock out of place ⟨the passenger was ~*ed* out of his seat by the impact⟩ **b** : to oust (another) from a job or position and fill it oneself usu. by virtue of seniority rights ⟨he was ~*ed* from his job as a switchman by an older railroader⟩ **c** : to deprive (another) of travel accommodations esp. on an airplane by virtue of higher priority or rank or greater need ⟨he was ~*ed* at the airport to make room for a top-ranking army officer⟩ **d** : to demote in rank usu. suddenly : BUST ⟨he was ~*ed* from colonel to major⟩ **e** : to oust or dismiss from membership ⟨a move to ~ the senator from the committee⟩ **4 a** : to approach or attain to in a manner suggesting irregular jolting and forceful progress ⟨prices began ~*ing* officially approved limits⟩ **b** : to increase or raise with suddenness or force — usu. used with *up* ⟨demand has ~*ed* up prices⟩ **5 a** : to apply pressure to (sheet or plate metal) so as to make or remove a concavity or convexity **b** : to raise a low area of (a printing plate) esp. by hammering on the back or by interlaying — often used with *up* ~ *vi* **1** : to strike or knock against something with a forceful thud or jolt — often used with *into* or *against* ⟨the car ~*ed* into the light pole⟩ **2** : to travel or proceed in or as if in a series of bumps — often followed by an adverb or a preposition ⟨~*ed* over the dirt road⟩ ⟨the jeep turned and ~*ed* back onto the highway —Donald Stokes⟩ **3** : to encounter usu. forcibly or somewhat unpleasantly something that is an obstacle, hindrance, or threat — usu. used with *into* or *against* ⟨expected to ~ against serious opposition —Ned Russell⟩ **4** : to boil suddenly and sometimes with explosive violence (as of water covered with a layer of oil and rapidly heated) **5** *of a bowled cricket ball* : to rise to an unusual height after pitching **6** : to thrust the hips forward with a quick, convulsive, or suggestive motion in or as if in a burlesque striptease ⟨the strippers still ~ and grind in the clubs, although with modifications —*Time*⟩

syn CLASH, COLLIDE, CONFLICT: BUMP indicates forceful knocking or running against, typically with thudding impact ⟨the ferry *bumped* into the mooring post⟩ ⟨he *bumped* his foot on the stove⟩ It may suggest encountering an obstacle or difficulty ⟨the builder *bumped* up against the problem of shoring up the wall⟩ CLASH may suggest hitting, knocking, or dashing together or against with sharp force and jangling metallic din ⟨the swords *clashed*⟩ ⟨where ignorant armies *clash* by night —Matthew Arnold⟩ or sharp, although sometimes short-lived, variance, incompatibility, or opposition ⟨Cavour and Victor Emmanuel *clashed* sharply, and on these occasions it was usu. the King who won —*Times Lit. Supp.*⟩ ⟨when the new demands of our changing economic life *clash* with the old dogmas —M.R.Cohen⟩ COLLIDE suggests a more or less direct running together or against with a certain force or shock ⟨the tanker sank after it *collided* with the freighter⟩ It also indicates a forceful direct disagreement or opposition ⟨an English East India Company was using the Portuguese route around Africa and *colliding* with the Portuguese in India —Stringfellow Barr⟩ CONFLICT, archaic in senses involving physical contact, indicates variance, incompatibility, or opposition ⟨*conflicting* testimony by two witnesses⟩ ⟨to stand up amid *conflicting* interests —William Wordsworth⟩

— **bump into** : to encounter or meet with esp. by chance ⟨just happened to *bump into* him at the meeting⟩

[2]**bump** \"\ *n* -S **1 a** : a somewhat forceful, sudden, thudding, or jolting blow or impact : the action, the effect, or the noise of such a blow ⟨the freight cars came together with a ~⟩ ⟨the ~ of a chestnut falling —Sylvia Stallings⟩ ⟨a ~ that still hurts⟩: as (1) : a jolt experienced in an airplane in flight that is caused by local ascending or descending air currents (2) : a sudden shock or rock concussion sometimes accompanying rock subsidence in and around mines **b** : displacement to a lower position : DEMOTION ⟨a ~ to the bottom of his class⟩ **2** : a relatively abrupt convexity or protuberance on a surface: as **a** : a swelling of tissue usu. resulting from a bump ⟨a week later she still had a bad ~ on her forehead⟩ **b** : a protuberance on the body: as (1) : BREAST ⟨a young girl beginning to mature and show ~s⟩ (2) : a cranial protuberance associated in phrenology with one of various faculties or personal qualities **c** (1) : a sudden rise in a road surface likely to jolt a passing vehicle (2) : any marked unevenness in a road surface likely to cause such a jolt ⟨an old pavement now full of ~s and holes⟩ **d** : a hill or other bulky rounded protuberance typically somewhat isolated geographically ⟨the lone ~ of hill that stands on the Jersey flats —Horace Sutton⟩ **3 a** : an obstruction giving sudden check or pause ⟨help people over the ~s of defeat —L.C.May⟩; *also* : the abrupt perception of an obstruction or difficulty ⟨Mrs. Miniver remembered with a ~, felt dismayed —Jan Struther⟩ **b** : OBSTACLE, DIFFICULTY ⟨the ~s he encountered on his way to success⟩ **4** : natural endowment : FACULTY, QUALITY ⟨has need of a big ~ of irreverence —John Raymond⟩ ⟨possessing a ~ of skepticism and a bent toward rationality —C.J.Rolo⟩ ⟨children with big ~s of curiosity⟩ **5** : an action of thrusting the hips forward with abrupt suggestive motion typically in a burlesque striptease act — compare GRIND **syn** see IMPACT

bump ball *n* **:** a ball hit (as by a batsman in cricket) so that it strikes the ground and then rises ⟨a fielder caught a *bump ball* and mistakenly thought he had caught the batsman out⟩

¹bump·er \'bəmpə(r)\ *n* -s [prob. fr. ¹*bump* (in obs. sense, to bulge, be protuberant) + -*er*] **1 :** a cup or glass filled to the brim or till the liquor runs over esp. in drinking a toast **2 :** something unusually large **3 :** a fish (*Chloroscombrus chrysurus*) of the family Carangidae of the southern U.S. and West Indies

²bumper \"\ *vb* -ED/-ING/-S *vt* **1 :** to fill to the brim (as a wineglass) and empty by drinking **2 :** to toast with a bumper ~ *vi* **:** to drink bumpers of wine or other alcoholic beverages

³bumper \"\ *adj* **1 :** unusually large ⟨a ~ crop of wheat⟩ **2 :** very good, fine, or successful ⟨going to be a ~ winter on TV — probably the best ever —*Glasgow Sunday Post*⟩

⁴bumper \"\ *n* -s [¹*bump* + -*er*] **1 :** one that bumps or operates a machine or device that bumps: as **a :** a bumping-die press operator **b :** one who backs up a riveting dolly with another hammer **c :** one who molds handmade bricks **d :** one that hammers sheet metal into shape by hand or machine: (1) **:** one who removes dents from automobile bodies and fenders or from sheet-metal parts of airplanes — called also *dingman* (2) **:** one who straightens damaged ship plates by a heating and cooling process **e :** an engraver's assistant in the making of textile printing rolls **f :** a bowled ball in cricket that bumps **g** *chiefly Brit* **:** a smashing machine in bookbinding; *also* **:** the operator of such a machine **h** (1) **:** a hand canceler for canceling stamps on second, third, and fourth-class mail; *also* **:** a hand canceler for use on registered mail (2) **:** a cancellation mark made by such a canceler **i :** a worker who bumps broomcorn fibers up and down on a table to even them prior to measuring and cutting **2 :** a device or attachment (as on a vehicle) for absorbing shock and lessening or preventing damage in collision or impact with another object: as **a :** a metal bar or metal bars attached to either end of an automobile or other powered transportation vehicle to prevent damage to the body **b :** a buffer (as a log or a bundle of rope) suspended down the side of a ship or boat or suspended or floating alongside a landing or docking place **c** *also* **bumper beam :** a timber or casting across the frame ends of a railroad engine, tender, or car **d :** BUMPING POST **e :** a usu. rubber-tipped doorstop attached to a wall behind a door to keep the door from hitting the wall **f :** a protective cornerpiece (as on a suitcase) made of metal, leather, or other durable material **g :** a rubber or plastic guard running around the base portion of a vacuum cleaner as a protection to furniture **h :** a protective pad designed to fit around the inside of a baby's crib **3 :** a flat metallic disk in or on the pavement that is used in some traffic signaling systems and that may be run over without being injured and without damaging the vehicle **4 :** a woman's hat with a narrow brim fashioned like a tube or padded roll; *also* **:** an imitation of this style **5** *Austral* **:** a cigarette butt

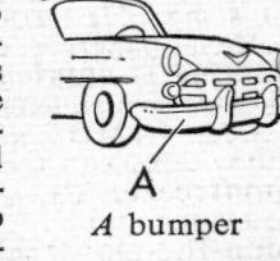

A bumper

⁵bumper \"\ *adj* **:** having a curved armless end or ends — used of an upholstered divan or unit of one ⟨a ~ sofa⟩ ⟨sofas fitted with ~ units⟩

bumper guard *n* **:** either of two vertical shoes attached to the bumper of an automobile to prevent the locking of bumpers with other cars and to facilitate pushing

bumper jack *n* **:** a jack designed to lift an automobile by its bumper

¹bump·e·ty *or* **bump·i·ty** \'bəmpəd·ē, -pətē, -i\ *or* **bumpety-bump** *or* **bumpity-bump** \ˌ⁼⁼⁼ˌ⁼\ *adv* [*bumpety & bumpity* irreg. fr. ¹*bump*; *bumpety-bump* & *bumpity-bump* redupl. of ¹*bump*] **:** in a bumping, thudding, or jolting way ⟨he felt his heart go ~⟩

²bumpety *or* **bumpity** \"\ *adj* [irreg. fr. *bumpy*] **:** JOLTING, BUMPY ⟨a ~ ride in a wagon over rough roads⟩

bumpety-bump *or* **bumpity-bump** *see* ¹BUMPETY\ *or* **bumpety-bumpety** *or* **bumpity-bumpity** \ˌ⁼⁼⁼ˌ⁼⁼⁼\ *n* [redupl. of ²*bump*] **:** an uneven jolting, thudding, or beating ⟨the *bumpety-bump* of the wagon over the cobblestones⟩ ⟨the nervous *bumpety-bumpety* of his heart⟩

bumph \'bəm(p)f\ *var of* BUMF

bump·i·ly \'bəmpəlē, -li\ *adv* **:** in a bumpy manner

bump·i·ness \-pēnəs, -pin-\ *n* -ES **:** the quality or state of being bumpy

bumping *pres part of* BUMP

bumping conveyor *or* **bumping trough** *n* **:** a suspended chute or trough along which broken ore or coal is conveyed by a longitudinal reciprocating action that terminates on the forward stroke with a bump

bumping die *n* **:** a die designed to form sheet-metal tubing

bumping hammer *n* **:** a usu. power-driven hammer with two broad flat faces on a narrow head used in bumping sheet metal

bumping post *n* **:** a post placed as a buffer at the end of a spur of railroad track

bumping race *n* **:** a rowing race in certain English universities in which the boats start at a fixed distance behind one another and each boat endeavors to overtake and bump the boat ahead of it so as to take its place in the following race if successful

bumping table *n* **:** a vibrating table upon which heavy minerals in a stream of water are separated from the lighter particles

bump joint *n* **:** a pipe-and-flange joint in which the end of the pipe or tubing is driven into a recess in the flange

¹bump·kin \'bəm(p)kən\ *n* -s [perh. fr. Flem *bommekijn* small cask, fr. MD, fr. *bomme* cask + -*kijn* -kin] **:** a typically awkward blockish and utterly unsophisticated rustic ⟨they gawked up at the tall buildings like ~*s*⟩ **syn** see BOOR

²bump·kin *or* **bum·kin** \'bəm(p)kən\ *also* **boom·kin** \'bümk-\ *n* -s [prob. fr. Flem *boomken* little tree, fr. *boom* tree (fr. MD) + -*ken*, dim. suffix, fr. MD -*kijn*; akin to OHG *boum* tree — more at BEAM, -KIN] **:** a projecting boom: as **a :** one projecting from each bow of a ship to haul the foretack to — called also *tack bumpkin* **b :** one from each quarter for the main-brace blocks — called also *brace bumpkin*; see SHIP illustration **c :** a small outrigger over the stern of a ship to extend the mizzen

bump·kin·ly \'bəm(p)kənlē\ *adj* [¹*bumpkin* + -*ly*] **:** like or suggesting a bumpkin

bump off *vt* [¹*bump* + *off*] *slang* **:** KILL; *esp* **:** to murder with crude and brutal violence ⟨two hoodlums were *bumped off* by a rival gang⟩

bump-off \'⁼ˌ⁼\ *n* [*bump off*] *slang* **:** MURDER

bump·ol·o·gist \ˌbəm'päləjəst\ *n* -s [*bumpology* + -*ist*] **:** PHRENOLOGIST — usu. used disparagingly

bump·ol·o·gy \-jē\ *n* -ES [²*bump* + -*o-* + -*logy*] **:** PHRENOLOGY — usu. used disparagingly

bump·om·e·ter \ˌbəm'päməd·ə(r)\ *also* **bump meter** \'bəmpˌmēd·ə(r)\ *n* [*bumpometer* fr. ²*bump* + -*o-* + -*meter*; *bump meter* fr. ²*bump* + *meter* (measurer)] **:** a device that indicates irregularities in a pavement or roadbed

bumps *pl of* BUMP, *pres 3d sing of* BUMP

bump supper *n*, *Brit* **:** a usu. riotous celebration by a college making a certain number of bumps or retaining its first-place position in a bumping race

bump·tious \'bəm(p)shəs\ *adj* [¹*bump* + -*tious* (as in *fractious*)] **:** presumptuously, obtusely, and often noisily self-assertive **:** somewhat arrogantly self-confident **:** OBTRUSIVE ⟨the least ~ and aggressive and the one least given to self-serving publicity —R.H.Rovere⟩ ⟨every ~ adventurer and fluent charlatan —G.B.Shaw⟩ ⟨the police keep crowds from becoming ~ —L.C.Stevens⟩ ⟨our ~, prodigal days are nearly ended —Russell Lord⟩ — **bump·tious·ly** *adv* — **bump·tious·ness** *n* -ES

bumpy \'bəmpē, -pi\ *adj* -ER/-EST [²*bump* + -*y*] **1 a :** having or covered with bumps ⟨a ~ road⟩ **:** NUBBY ⟨a ~ book cover⟩ **:** exhibiting protuberances ⟨a ~ face⟩ **b :** PROTUBERANT ⟨~ muscles⟩ **2 a :** causing or giving bumps or jolts ⟨a ~ ride⟩ ⟨the plane ran into ~ air⟩ **b :** rhythmically choppy **:** somewhat unpleasantly irregular ⟨an especially ~ kind of short-winded prose —S.E.Fitzgerald⟩ **c :** full of difficulties ⟨an unusually ~ life for a man of reflection —P.R.Levin⟩

bumpy ash *n* **:** BUNJI-BUNJI

bum rap *n* [⁸*bum*] *slang* **:** a false charge or conviction of crime esp. resulting in a prison term **:** FRAME-UP ⟨a bookie who has done five years . . . on a *bum rap* and is once more on the loose —John McCarten⟩

bums *pl of* BUM, *pres 3d sing of* BUM

bum's rush *n* [⁷*bum*] *slang* **1 :** forcible eviction or dismissal ⟨they gave him the *bum's rush*⟩ **2 :** any compulsion applied against one's will or before one can consider the significance or consequences of an action

bum steer *n* [⁸*bum*] *slang* **:** an instance of false or misleading information or directions esp. when purposely so ⟨a man who got himself a *bum steer* . . . and was attempting to brazen it out rather than admit his error —R.H.Rovere⟩

bumtrap *n* [¹*bum*] *slang* **:** BAILIFF

bum·wood \'bəm+ˌ-\ *n* [prob. fr. ⁸*bum*] **:** POISONWOOD 1

¹bun \'bən, 'bůn\ *n* -s [ME *bune, bunne*, fr. OE *bune* reed; akin to ON *buna* jet of water, clumsy leg] *dial Eng* **:** a hollow stem or stalk **:** STUBBLE

²bun \'bən\ *chiefly Scot var of* BOUND

³bun \'bən\ *n* -s [ME *bunne*, prob. fr. (assumed) MF *bugne* (whence F dial. *bugne* pancake), fr. MF *bugne* bump on the head, prob. of non-IE origin; akin to the source of Catal *bony* bump on the head] **1 a :** any of a variety of sweet or plain breads that are leavened with yeast or baking powder and shaped in a variety of forms **b :** a usu. round or oblong roll **2 :** a knot or coil of hair (as at the nape of the neck) used in dressing women's long hair

⁴bun \'bən, 'bůn\ *n* -s [ScGael, root, stump, bottom; akin to MIr *bun* bottom, W *bôn* trunk, stump] **1** *chiefly dial* **:** the hind part or tail esp. of a squirrel or rabbit **2** *chiefly dial* **a :** SQUIRREL **b :** RABBIT

⁵bun \'bən\ *n* -s [perh. alter. of E dial. (chiefly Sc) *bung, bungie* intoxicated] *slang* **:** a drunken condition **:** JAG ⟨arrive at a party with a ~ on⟩

Bu·na \'b(y)ünə\ *trademark* — used for synthetic rubber and rubberlike materials

bunce \'bən(t)s\ *n* -s [origin unknown] *slang Brit* **:** unexpected gain **:** GRAVY, BONUS; *also* **:** unexpected luck

¹bunch \'bənch\ *n* -ES [ME *bunche*; perh. akin to D *bonk* bone, mass (as of flesh), cluster (of fruits), OHG *bungo* tuber, ON *bunki* cargo, *bunga* hump, Gk *pachys* thick — more at PACHY-] **1 :** PROTUBERANCE, HUMP, SWELLING **2 a :** AGGREGATE, CLUSTER, TUFT ⟨a ~ of odds and ends out of the attic⟩ ⟨a ~ of grapes⟩ ⟨pull up a ~ of grass⟩; *esp* **:** an aggregate of things of the same kind existing as a natural group or considered together ⟨a ~ of cattle⟩ ⟨a ~ of liberals⟩ **b :** a group of friends bound together by intimate social or cultural ties ⟨he was the handiest with tools in our ~ —John O'Hara⟩ **3 :** a small irregular ore body **4 :** the filler and binder of a cigar without the wrapper **5 a :** a proposal in various card games that the current deal be called off for a new deal **b :** an alternative name for any game in which this proposal is permitted; *esp* **:** such a form of auction pitch

²bunch \"\ *vb* -ED/-ING/-ES [ME *bunchen*, fr. *bunche* protuberance] *vi* **1 :** to swell into a protuberance **:** PROTRUDE — usu. used with *out* ⟨his shoulder and arm muscles ~*ed* out with the effort of lifting⟩ **2 :** to gather into clusters, tufts, or groups — often used with *up* **3 :** to throw in playing cards for a new deal in a card game **:** assemble the cards for shuffling and dealing — compare ¹BUNCH 5 ~ *vt* **1 :** to form into a bunch: as **a :** to group together **:** ASSEMBLE ⟨~*ing* cattle preparatory to shipment⟩ ⟨more than 2000 saloons that were ~*ed* at the southern end of Manhattan —John Lardner⟩ **b :** to make into a cluster or tuft ⟨onions sent to West Indian ports were always strung or ~*ed* —*Amer. Guide Series: Conn.*⟩ **c :** to fill out **:** make protuberant ⟨a raised chair that was ~*ed* out with cushions —V.S.Pritchett⟩ **d :** to form or pull or squeeze into a small compact unit ⟨I wish you wouldn't ~ the paper so —A.J.Cronin⟩ ⟨all his fingers ~*ed* together on his chest —Richard Llewellyn⟩ **e :** to make into a usu. compact pile — usu. used with *up* ⟨~*ing* up haycocks and pitching them into wagons —Christopher Rand⟩ **2 :** to assemble (railroad cars) for loading or unloading in excess of the number ordered or of the number which can be handled at one time with available loading and unloading facilities

³bunch \", 'bůn-\ *vt* -ED/-ING/-ES [ME *bunchen*, perh. of imit. origin] *dial Brit* **:** to strike esp. with the foot **:** KICK

bunch bean *n* **:** KIDNEY BEAN

bunch·ber·ry \'bənch-—*see* BERRY\ *n* **1 :** DWARF CORNEL **2 :** the fruit of the stone bramble

bunch·er \'benchə(r)\ *n* -s [²*bunch* + -*er*] **:** one that bunches: as **a :** one who makes bunches (sense 4) by rolling filler tobacco in binder leaves — called also *binder* **b :** the velocity-modulating element that effects the electron bunching in a klystron — compare CATCHER 4, RHUMBATRON

bunch evergreen *n* **:** any of several club mosses of erect bushy habit (esp. *Lycopodium obscurum*)

bunchflower \'⁼ˌ⁼⁼\ *n* **:** a plant of the genus *Melanthium*; *esp* **:** a tall summer-blooming herb (*M. virginicum*) of the eastern and southern U.S. bearing a panicle of small greenish flowers

bunchflower family *n* **:** MELANTHACEAE

bunch grape *n* **:** SUMMER GRAPE

bunchgrass \'⁼ˌ⁼\ *n* **:** any of several grasses chiefly of the western U.S. which grow in tufts (as *Sporobolus aeroides, Elymus condensatus, Andropogon scoparius, Oryzopsis hymenoides* and various grasses of the genus *Stipa*)

bunch·i·ly \'bənchəlē\ *adv* **:** in a bunchy manner ⟨knee-length coat, cocoon-shaped through the middle and wrapping ~ —Lois Long⟩

bunching *n* -s [fr. gerund of ²*bunch*] **:** the velocity modulation of an orig. steady electron beam in a klystron in such a way that the electrons travel in uniformly spaced concentrations or bunches

bunch light *n* **1 :** an open-faced metal hood in which a group of low-wattage lamps is used **2 :** a single light-source unit

bunch oyster *n* **:** COON OYSTER

bunch peanut *n* **:** a peanut having upright bushy growth with the pods clustered about the base — compare RUNNER PEANUT

bunch pink *n* **:** SWEET WILLIAM

bunch plum *n* **:** DWARF CORNEL

bunchy \'bənchē, -chi\ *adj* -ER/-EST [¹*bunch* + -*y*] **1 a :** protruding or swelling out in a bunch or in bunches **:** showing protuberances ⟨women in ~ cotton dresses—Nadine Gordimer⟩ ⟨a round ~ face —Mary Carter Roberts⟩ **b :** growing in bunches **:** resembling a bunch **:** marked by tufts ⟨the scanty and ~ nature of the grass cover —G.R.Stewart⟩ **2** *of a mine or a vein* **:** yielding irregularly: here rich, there poor ⟨a ~ vein of silver⟩

bunchy top *n* **:** any of various plant diseases esp. caused by viruses which produce shortening of the internodes and crowding of the twigs and leaves at the shoot apex ⟨banana *bunchy top*⟩

¹bun·co *or* **bun·ko** \'bəŋ(ˌ)kō\ *n* -s [perh. alter. of Sp *banca* bench, banking business, bank in gambling (or, a card game), fr. It, bank, bench — more at ⁴BANK] **1 :** swindling by misrepresentation (as in a confidence game) **2 :** any of various games (as card games) in which the person who proposes the game expects to win by virtue of an opponent's ignorance, lack of skill, or naiveté

²bunco *or* **bunko** \"\ *vt* -ED/-ING/-S **:** to swindle by a bunco game or scheme **:** cheat or victimize in any similar way ⟨knew when he was being ~*ed* but there was not much he could do —H.A.Sinclair⟩

buncombe *var of* BUNKUM

bunco steerer *or* **bunko steerer** *n* **:** a confidence man **:** SWINDLER

¹bund \'bən(d)\ *dial Brit var of* BOUND

²bund \'bənd\ *n* -s [Hindi *band*, fr. Per; akin to Skt *bandha* fetter — more at ¹BAND] **1 :** an embankment used esp. in India to control the flow of water (as on a river or on irrigated land) **2 :** an embanked thoroughfare along a river or the sea esp. in the Far East

³bund \"\ *vt* -ED/-ING/-S *Far East* **:** to construct a bund (as for the control of flowing water) **:** EMBANK

⁴bund \'bůnd, 'bənd, 'bunt\ *n* -s *often cap* [G, fr. MHG *bunt*; akin to MD *bont* league, MLG *bunt*, OS *gibund* bundle, OE *byndel* — more at BUNDLE] **:** FEDERATION, LEAGUE, CONFEDERACY, ASSOCIATION; *esp* **:** a politically oriented association of people

bun·da·bun·da \'bəndəˌbəndə\ *var of* BANDY-BANDY

bun·de·li \'bůndə(ˌ)lē\ *n* -s *cap* [Hindi *bundelī*] **:** the dialect of Western Hindi spoken in Bundelkhand

bunder *var of* BANDAR

bun·der boat \'bəndə(r)-\ *n* [Hindi *bandar* harbor, landing-place, fr. Per] **:** a coastal and harbor boat in the Far East

bun·des·rat \'bůndəsˌrät, *G* -rääṭ\ *n* -s *usu cap* [G, fr. *bundes* (gen. of *bund* federation) + *rat* council, advice, fr. OHG *rāt* advice; akin to *rātan* to advise — more at READ] **:** a federal council esp. having legislative or executive functions: as **a :** the upper house of the German and Austrian parliaments composed of members selected by the state governments **b :** the chief executive authority of Switzerland consisting of members elected by the Federal Assembly

bun·des·staat \-dəs(h)ˌshtät, *G* -tääṭ\ *n* -s *usu cap* [G, fr. *bundes* (gen. of *bund*) + *staat* state, fr. MHG *stat* condition, fr. L *status* condition, position — more at STATE] **:** a federated state **:** FEDERATION 2a — contrasted with *Staatenbund*

bun·des·tag \-dəˌstäk, *G* -tääk\ *n* -s *usu cap* [G, fr. *bundes* (gen. of *bund* federation) + -*tag* (fr. MHG, prob. fr. *tagen* to hold court, to hold a meeting, fr. *tag*-, *tac* day, fr. OHG *tag*) — more at DAY] **:** an assembly of representatives of a bund (as the assembly of the German Confederacy of 1815 or the lower house of parliament of the Federal Republic of Germany)

bundies *pl of* BUNDY

bund·ist \'bůndəst, 'bən-\ *n* -s *often cap* [⁴*bund* + -*ist*] **:** a member of a bund; *esp* **:** a member of a pro-Nazi bund

¹bun·dle \'bəndᵊl\ *n* -s [ME *bundel*, fr. MD *bundel, bondel*; akin to OE *byndel* bundle, OHG *gibuntilī* bundle, *bintan* to tie — more at BIND] **1 a :** a number of things fastened together into a mass or bunch convenient for handling or conveyance ⟨a ~ of sticks⟩ ⟨a ~ of shirts⟩ **b :** PACKAGE; *often* **:** a loose package esp. wrapped in paper **:** PARCEL, ROLL ⟨make up soiled clothes into a ~⟩ ⟨a ~ of groceries⟩ **c :** a number or group of things considered as a unit **:** LOT, COLLECTION ⟨a large ~ of mistakes⟩ ⟨a ~ of contradictions⟩ ⟨a ~ of energies⟩ **d :** a group of isoglosses running close together in the same general direction whether coinciding, diverging, converging, or crossing each other — called also *fascicle* **2 :** the amount contained in a bundle esp. as fixed for a certain commodity and sometimes used as a unit of quantity: as **a :** a board measure unit equalling 50 pounds that is used in papermaking **b :** a shipping unit of about 125 pounds that is used in papermaking **3 :** a small band or group of mostly parallel fibers (as of nerves or muscles) **:** FASCICULUS, TRACT **4 :** VASCULAR BUNDLE **5** *slang* **:** a sizable sum of money ⟨left a fortune of half a million bucks — quite a ~ for that day —Pete Martin⟩

²bundle \"\ *vb* **bundled; bundled; bundling** \-nd(ᵊ)liŋ, ÷nliŋ\ **bundles** *vt* **1 a :** to tie or bind in a bundle **:** assemble in a bundle **b :** to make into a roughly rounded loose unit ⟨he *bundled* the coat into a human outline⟩ **c :** to compress (book sections) in groups after the folding operation in bookbinding **2 :** to hustle or hurry unceremoniously often by shoving or throwing ⟨*bundled* the children off to school⟩ ⟨he *bundled* his possessions into an empty carriage —David Garnett⟩ ~ *vi* **1 a :** to prepare for departure **b :** to set off or go in a hurry or without ceremony **:** HURRY ⟨a group of servants came *bundling* from the kitchen —Charlotte Brontë⟩ **2 :** to practice bundling

bundle boy *n* **:** a boy employed by a store or market to carry articles purchased to a wrapping counter or a shipping room or sometimes outside to the purchaser's automobile

bundle branch *n*, *anat* **:** either of the parts of the atrioventricular bundle passing respectively to the right and left ventricles

bundle branch block *n* **:** heart block due to a lesion in one of the bundle branches

bundle browning *n* **:** a symptom of disease consisting of browning or necrosis of the vascular bundles in stems or tubers (as of the potato)

bundle burial *n* **:** the burial of the dead with arms and legs flexed; *also* **:** a secondary burial in a bundle of the bones only

bundle of his \-'his\ *usu cap H* [trans. of G *hissches bündel*, after Wilhelm *His* †1934 Ger. anatomist] **:** ATRIOVENTRICULAR BUNDLE

bundle pillar *n* **:** a clustered column or pillar

bun·dler \'bənd(ᵊ)lə(r), ÷nlə-\ *n* -s **:** one that bundles; *esp* **:** one whose vocation is to bundle material or products for ease of handling

bundle sheath *n* **:** a compact layer of commonly parenchymatous cells forming a sheath around a vascular bundle

bundle up *vb* **:** to dress warmly or cumbrously ⟨the man *bundled up* in a sweater and heavy coat⟩ ⟨the woman *bundled up* her children in heavy jackets and woollen underwear⟩

bundle work *n* **:** commercial laundry work done by the bundle instead of by the piece

bundling *n* -s [fr. gerund of ²*bundle*] **:** the custom of unmarried couples' occupying the same bed without undressing, practiced chiefly in earlier days esp. during courtship in some British and American communities

bun·do·bust \'bəndəˌbəst\ *n* -s [Hindi *band-o-bast*, lit., tying and binding, fr. Per] *India* **:** arrangement or settlement of details

bundocks *var of* BOONDOCKS

bun·dweed \'bənˌ(d)wēd, 'bůn-\ *n* [alter. of earlier *bunweed*, fr. ME *bunwed*, perh. fr. *bune* hollow stalk + *wed*, *weed* weed — more at ¹BUN, WEED] *dial Eng* **:** any of various weedy plants (as the knapweed, ragwort, scabious, or cow parsnip)

¹bun·dy \'bəndē\ *n* -ES [origin unknown] **:** a small often crooked Australian tree (*Eucalyptus elaeophora*) with pendulous branches

²bundy \"\ *n* -ES [prob. fr. *Bundy*, alter. of *Bundaberg*, seaport town in Queensland, Australia] *Austral* **:** TIME CLOCK

bune·most \'bünˌmōst, 'büen-, -ˌməst\ *adj* [E dial. *bunemost*, *boonmost*, fr. E dial. *boon* above (short for E dial. *aboon*) + E -*most* — more at ABOON] *dial Brit* **:** UPPERMOST, HIGHEST

bun-fight \'⁼ˌ⁼\ *n* [³*bun*] *slang Brit* **:** TEA PARTY

bun foot *n* [³*bun*] **:** a slightly flattened ball foot on a piece of furniture

¹bung \'bəŋ\ *n* -s [ME *bunge*, fr. MD *bonghe*, alter. of *bonne*, fr. LL *puncta* puncture, fr. L, fem. of *punctus*, past part. of *pungere* to prick — more at POINT] **1 :** the stopper in the bunghole of a cask; *also* **:** BUNGHOLE **2 a :** ANUS — used esp. of a domestic or game animal **b :** the cecum of a slaughter animal; *also* **:** a sausage casing made from this **3 :** a stack of ceramic ware in a sagger; *also* **:** a stack of filled saggers in a kiln

²bung \"\ *vt* -ED/-ING/-S **1 a :** to stop (as a bunghole) with a bung **:** close (as a cask); *also* **:** to enclose (as in a cask) — usu. used with *up* **b** *slang* **:** FILL, PLUG ⟨by the time the furniture was unloaded and moved in, the house was ~*ed* up to the attic⟩ **2** *slang* **:** THROW, HEAVE, TOSS ⟨~*ing* rocks through a neighbor's window⟩ ⟨in a position to ~ a spanner into the works —P.G.Wodehouse⟩ **3** *slang* **:** to bung up

³bung *n* -s [origin unknown] *obs slang* **:** PURSE; *also* **:** PICKPOCKET

⁴bung \'bəŋ\ *adj* [prob. fr. a native word in Australia] *Austral* **:** out of commission: **a :** DEAD **b :** BANKRUPT — usu. used in the phrase *go bung*

bun·ga \'bəŋgə\ *n* -s *usu cap* [Xhosa *i-Bunga*, fr. *bunga*, *bungana* to meet in council] **:** a native council in the Transkeian Territories, Union of So. Africa, having limited power to consider and act upon native interests generally

bun·ga·loid \'bəŋgəˌlȯid\ *adj* [*bungalow* + -*oid*] **:** resembling or suggesting a bungalow ⟨when the prairie house was a pink ~ rash on the great open spaces —*Times Lit. Supp.*⟩ **:** characterized by constructions resembling bungalows ⟨depressed by the uglier and drearier parts of the town, or alarmed by its ~ outskirts —William Plomer⟩ — usu. used disparagingly

bun·ga·low \'bəŋgəˌlō\ *n* -s [Hindi *baṅglā*, lit., (house) in the Bengal style] **1 :** a lightly built low-sweeping single-story house or cottage of the Far East (as in India) that is usu. thatched or tiled and surrounded by a veranda **2 a :** a quite solidly constructed house for permanent residence that is usu. one but sometimes one and a half stories high and that preserves the low sweeping lines and wide veranda, usu. on the front only, of the bungalow **b :** a cottage intended chiefly for summer occupancy

bun·ga·rum \ˌbəŋ'gārəm\ *n* -s [modif. of Telugu *baṅgāru*] **:** one of several venomous snakes of the genus *Bungarus*; *esp* **:** KRAIT

bun·ga·rus \-rəs\ *n*, *cap* [NL, fr. Telugu *baṅgāru*, fr. *baṅgāramu* gold, fr. Skt *bhṛṅgāra*] **:** a genus of exceedingly venom-

BUTTERFLIES AND MOTHS

MONARCH
ZEBRA SWALLOWTAIL
PIPEVINE SWALLOWTAIL
BANDED PURPLE
RED-SPOTTED PURPLE
VICEROY
RED ADMIRAL
GOATWEED EMPEROR
RUDDY COPPER
LONG-TAILED SKIPPER
PURPLE HAIRSTREAK
MOURNING CLOAK
PROMETHEA MOTH
SULPHUR
REGAL MOTH
LESSER VINE SPHINX
BUCKEYE
ACHEMON SPHINX
IO MOTH
IMPERIAL MOTH
UNDERWING
CECROPIA MOTH
TIGER MOTH
BUCK MOTH
LUNA MOTH

ous Asiatic snakes including the krait and related to the cobra but with shorter fangs and without a dilatable hood

bun·gee \ˈbənjē\ *n* -s [origin unknown] **:** an auxiliary spring device esp. on the movable controls of an airplane designed to make the movement of the controls easier and to limit their motion; *also* **:** an elasticized cord used as a fastening or shock-absorbing device esp. for planes on the deck of a carrier

bun·ger·some \ˈbəŋgə(r)səm\ *adj* [*bunger-* (prob. alter. of *bungle*) + *-some*] *dial* **:** AWKWARD, CLUMSY

bung-eyed \ˈbəŋ,īd\ *adj* [perh. fr. ⁴*bung*] **:** having an eye swollen; *also* **:** BUG-EYED

bung-full \ˈ≈,≈\ *adj* [¹*bung* + *full*] **:** very or completely full **:** CHOCK-FULL ⟨an auto *bung-full* of children⟩ ⟨zealots who are *bung-full* of schemes —A.J.Nock⟩

bung head *n* [perh. fr. ¹*bung*] **:** a tapered square head on a bolt or screw

bunghole \ˈ≈,≈\ *n* [¹*bung*] **:** an opening usu. in the bilge of a cask for filling it with or emptying it of liquids — see BARREL illustration

¹**bun·gle** \ˈbəŋgəl\ *vb* **bungled; bungled; bungling** \-g(ə)liŋ\ **bungles** [perh. of Scand origin; akin to Sw dial. *bangla* to work ineffectually, Icel *banga* to hammer — more at BANG] *vi* **:** to act or work in a clumsy and awkward manner ⟨officials said and did stupid things and inexperience led to *bungling* —*Saturday Rev.*⟩ **~** *vt* **:** to do, make, perform, or handle clumsily or badly **:** MISHANDLE, BOTCH ⟨the job of cleaning up the slums was *bungled* badly by incompetent and venal administrators⟩

²**bungle** \ˈ"\ *n* -s **:** a clumsy or inadequate performance **:** BOTCH, BLUNDER ⟨a bureaucratic ~⟩

bun·gler \-g(ə)lə(r)\ *n* -s **:** a clumsy and awkward workman ⟨could not think with calmness of the possibility of appearing in the light of a ~ and an incompetent —J.C.Kirkpatrick⟩ ⟨muddleheaded ~s —C.W.M.Hart⟩

bun·gle·some \-gəlsəm\ *adj* **:** bungling or tending to lead to bungling ⟨a tedious and ~ enterprise⟩ ⟨carrying a load of ~ paraphernalia with him⟩

¹**bungling** *adj* [fr. pres. part. of ¹*bungle*] **:** UNSKILLFUL, AWKWARD, CLUMSY ⟨a ~ workman⟩ ⟨~ diplomacy —Stuart Portner⟩ — **bun·gling·ly** *adv*

²**bungling** *n* -s [fr. gerund of ¹*bungle*] **:** unskillful or clumsy handling, acting, or performing **:** MISHANDLING ⟨a piece of ~ due to hot heads —H.J.Laski⟩

bun·go \ˈbəŋ(,)gō\ *also* **bon·go** \ˈbäŋ-\ *n* -s [Sp *bongo*] **:** a large canoe or dugout of the southwestern U.S. and parts of Central and So. America

¹**bungs** *pl of* BUNG, *pres 3d sing of* BUNG

²**bungs** \bəŋz\ *n pl but sing in constr* [prob. fr. pl. of ¹*bung*] **1** *slang* **:** a ship's cooper **2** *slang* **:** a dock worker who repairs boxes and cases

bung starter *n* **:** a wooden mallet used for loosening the bung of a cask

bung·town \ˈbəŋ,taůn\ *n* -s [prob. fr. *Bungtown* (now Barneysville), Rehoboth, Massachusetts, where it was manufactured] **:** a copper token resembling an English halfpenny that circulated in the U.S. in the 18th and 19th centuries

bung up *vt* [²*bung*] **1** *slang* **:** BRUISE, BATTER, LACERATE ⟨his eyes and face were all *bunged up* from the fistfight⟩ **2 :** to damage or dent considerably ⟨an automobile body pretty *bunged up* from an accident⟩

bungy *n* -s [Hindi *bhaṅgī* — more at BHANGI] **:** BHANGI

bu·ni·na·wa *or* **bu·ni·na·hua** \,bünəˈnäwə\ *n, pl* **buninawa** *or* **buninawas** *or* **buninahua** *or* **buninahuas** *usu cap* [native name] **1 :** a people that constitute a branch of the Cashibo **2 :** a member of the Buninawa people

bun·ion \ˈbənyən\ *n* -s [prob. irreg. fr. *bunny* (swelling)] **1 :** an enlargement of the first joint of the great toe resulting from excessive growth of bone at the joint margin associated with a bursal sac filled with fluid **2 :** the egg mass on a berried female blue crab

bun·ji-bun·ji \,bənjēˈbənjē\ *n* -s [native name in Australia] **:** an Australian tree (*Flindersia schottiana*) closely related to the flindosa and having bark that contains a poison

¹**bunk** \ˈbəŋk\ *n* -s [perh. fr. Ar, an odoriferous root] **1 :** CHICORY **2 :** POISON HEMLOCK

²**bunk** \ˈ"\ *n* -s [prob. short for *bunker*] **1 a :** a built-in frame that usu. has low sides and a canvas, mesh, or spring bottom and that serves as a bed or sleeping place (as on a ship or in a camp) and often is one of a series in tiers **b :** a sleeping place **:** BED **2 a :** a heavy timber or crossbeam on a logging sled or car on which the logs rest **b :** a log car or log truck **3 a :** a long usu. wood or concrete trough or manger for feeding cattle — called also *feed bunk*

³**bunk** \ˈ"\ *vb* -ED/-ING/-S *vi* **1 :** to occupy a bunk or bed ⟨~ in the attic⟩ **:** share a bed ⟨having no hotel room, he ~*ed* with a friend for the night⟩ **2 :** to stay the night **:** occupy sleeping quarters **:** put up ⟨~ at a neighbor's house for a couple of days⟩ **~** *vt* **1 :** to place (logs) on bunks **2 :** to provide with a bunk, bed, or sleeping quarters ⟨I don't know where the exec means to ~ you so we can't move you into a stateroom just yet —Wirt Williams⟩

⁴**bunk** \ˈ"\ *vi* -ED/-ING/-S [perh. fr. ³*bunk* (in the phrase *to bunk across* to go across by ship)] *slang Brit* **:** to go away esp. as an escape **:** LEAVE, SCRAM ⟨suddenly got frightened and ~*ed* —Margery Allingham⟩

⁵**bunk** \ˈ"\ *n* -s *slang chiefly Brit* **:** a hurried departure usu. in escaping something — used in the phrase *do a bunk* ⟨the pranksters did a ~ before the police arrived⟩

⁶**bunk** \ˈ"\ *n* -s [short for *bunkum*] *slang* **:** BUNKUM, NONSENSE

⁷**bunk** \ˈ"\ *vt* -ED/-ING/-S *slang* **:** FOOL, DECEIVE, MISLEAD ⟨on both sides of the Senate aisle there are men . . . who will go down to defeat before they will try to ~ the people —Blair Moody⟩

⁸**bunk** \ˈ"\ *vi* -ED/-ING/-S [prob. alter. of ¹*bump*] **:** BUMP, RUN ⟨~ into a post⟩ ⟨~ into a friend on the street⟩

bunk bed *n* **:** a bed for two people with one sleeping place above the other in the manner of tiered bunks

bunk car *n* [²*bunk*] **:** CAMP CAR

¹**bun·ker** \ˈbəŋkə(r)\ *n* -s [alter. of earlier Sc *bonker*, perh. alter. of E *banker* covering for a bench — more at BANKER] **1 a** *Scot* **:** a chest or box often used as a window seat **b :** a large bin or other storage place: as (1) **:** a large compartment on shipboard for storing the ship's coal or oil (2) **:** metal containers in a refrigerator railroad car for ice or other refrigerants (3) **:** a coal bin in a locomotive terminal; *also* **:** a coal receptacle at the rear of a tank engine **c :** a fortification chamber mostly below ground level built of reinforced concrete or similar material and usu. provided with embrasures; *also* **:** a dugout that is reinforced (as with logs or bags of sand) and usu. has firing slits **2 a** *chiefly Scot* **:** a small sand hole or pit **b :** a sand trap or embankment with soil exposed constituting a hazard on a golf course **c :** OBSTACLE, DIFFICULTY

bunk bed

²**bunker** \ˈ"\ *vb* **bunkered; bunkered; bunkering** \-k(ə)riŋ\ **bunkers** *vi* **:** to fill a ship's bunker with coal or oil **~** *vt* **1 :** to put (as oil or coal) into a bunker ⟨the flattop . . . will ~ oil to refuel its protective screen of ships —*Newsweek*⟩ **2 a :** to hit (a golf ball) into a bunker **b :** to stop the advance or progress of; *also* **:** to entangle in difficulties **3 :** to provide or protect with bunkers ⟨a well-*bunkered* golf course⟩ ⟨the ~*ed* Japanese position —*Infantry Jour.*⟩

³**bunker** \ˈ"\ *n* -s [by shortening] **:** MOSSBUNKER

bun·ker·age \ˈbəŋk(ə)rij\ *n* -s **1 :** the filling of a bunker (as of a ship) with oil or coal ⟨~ service⟩ **2 :** the facilities for the storing of oil or coal ⟨an oil ~ that consisted of two huge tanks⟩

bunker charge *n* **:** the charge for loading coal or oil into a ship's bunker

bunker coal *n* **:** coal on a collier for its own use

bunker fuel *or* **bunker oil** *n* **:** any of various fuel oils used esp. on ships

bunker suit *or* **bunker clothes** *n* [³*bunk* + *-er*] **:** fire fighters' apparel that consists of trousers or overalls tucked into a pair of boots and is designed for dressing quickly when answering an alarm

bunk fatigue *n, slang* **:** sleeping or resting in bed esp. during the daytime

bunkhouse \ˈ≈,≈\ *n* **:** a rough simple building providing sleeping quarters usu. with bunks (as for workers on construction projects or for logging crews, ranch hands, or harvest crews)

bunk·ie \ˈbəŋkē\ *n* -s [²*bunk* + *-ie*] **:** BUNKMATE

bunk in *vi* [³*bunk*] **:** stay in one's bed or bunk ⟨don't think you can *bunk in* late —L.M.Uris⟩

bunkload \ˈ≈,≈\ *n* [²*bunk*] **:** a load of logs not over one log in depth

bunkmate \ˈ≈,≈\ *n* **:** a person occupying the same sleeping quarters as oneself or as another esp. in one of the armed services; *esp* **:** such a person occupying the next bunk or bed

bunko *var of* BUNCO

bunko steerer *var of* BUNCO STEERER

bunks *pl of* BUNK, *pres 3d sing of* BUNK

¹**bun·kum** *or* **bun·combe** \ˈbəŋkəm\ *n* -s [*Buncombe* County, N.C.; fr. a remark made by Felix Walker *fl*1820, U.S. representative from the Congressional district including this county, who explained a seemingly irrelevant speech in Congress by the statement that he was speaking to Buncombe] **:** insincere public talk or action **:** NONSENSE, CLAPTRAP, FOOLISHNESS

²**bunkum** \ˈ"\ *adj* [perh. fr. CanF *le buncum sa* (F *il est bon comme ça*) it is good as it is] **1** *dial* **:** of outstanding quality **:** very fine ⟨these are ~ apples⟩ **2** *dial* **:** in good health **:** well and strong ⟨I don't feel so ~⟩

bun·nia \ˈbənyə\ *n* -s [Hindi *baniyā* — more at BANYAN] **:** BANYAN 1a

bun·ning \ˈbəniŋ\ *n* -s [origin unknown] **:** a timber shelf or platform in a mine working on which stones and other waste material are deposited

¹**bun·ny** \ˈbəni, ˈbůni\ *n* -ES [ME *bony*, prob. fr MF *bugne* bump on the head — more at BUN] *dial Eng* **:** SWELLING; *specif* **:** a swelling on an animal's joint

²**bun·ny** \ˈbənē, -ni\ *n* -ES [⁴*bun* + *-y*] **1** *also* **bunny rabbit** **:** RABBIT; *esp* **:** a young rabbit — often used as a pet name **2 :** BISMARCK BROWN

bunny cat *n* [²*bunny*] **1 :** ABYSSINIAN CAT **2 :** a bobtail cat

bunny hop *n* **:** a short leap in figure skating often to gain speed that is made by hopping from a forward edge to the toe point of the free foot and stepping off immediately onto the forward edge of the take-off foot

bunny hug *n* [²*bunny*] **:** an American ballroom dance in ragtime rhythm in which the couple hold each other closely and which was esp. popular at the early part of this century

bun ochra *n* -s [¹*bun* + *ochra* (alter. of *okra*)] *India* **:** the bast fiber of the Caesar weed

¹**bu·no·dont** \ˈbyünə,dänt\ *adj* [NL *Bunodonta*] **:** having tubercles on the crown of the molar teeth — opposed to *lophodont*

²**bunodont** \ˈ"\ *n* -s [NL *Bunodonta*] **:** one of the Bunodonta

bu·no·don·ta \,byünəˈdäntə\ *n pl, cap* [NL, fr. *bun-* (fr. Gk *bounos* mound, hill) + *-odonta*; fr. the tuberculated molar teeth] *in some classifications* **:** a division of the Artiodactyla including the hogs and hippopotami

bu·no·loph·o·dont \,byünəˈläfə,dänt\ *adj* [*bun-* (fr. Gk *bounos*) + *-o-* + *loph-* + *-odont*] **1** *of teeth* **:** having the outer cusps blunt cones and the inner cusps modified to form transverse ridges (as in the tapirs) **2** *of an animal* **:** having bunolophodont teeth

¹**bu·no·mas·to·dont** \-ˈmastə,dänt\ *adj* [NL *Bunomastodontidae*] **:** of or relating to the Bunomastodontidae

²**bunomastodont** \ˈ"\ *n* -s [NL *Bunomastodontidae*] **:** one of the Bunomastodontidae

bu·no·mas·to·don·ti·dae \,≈≈≈ˈdäntə,dē\ *n pl, cap* [NL, fr. *bun-* (fr. Gk *bounos*) + *-o-* + *mast-* + *-odont-*, *-odon* + *-idae*] *in former classifications* **:** a family of extinct mastodons with trefoils or conelets of enamel in the valleys between the main crests of the molars that is now considered invalid because it is based on no type and is replaced in modern taxonomy by the family Gomphotheriidae

bu·no·se·le·no·dont \,byünōsəˈlēnə,dänt\ *adj* [ISV *bun-* (fr. Gk *bounos*) + *-o-* + *selen-* + *-odont*] **1** *of teeth* **:** having inner cusps that are blunt cones and outer ones modified into longitudinal crescents (as in the extinct titanotheres) **2** *of an animal* **:** having bunoselenodont teeth

bu·nos·to·mum \byüˈnästəməm\ *n, cap* [NL, fr. *bun-* (fr. Gk *bounos*) + *-o-* + *-stomum*] **:** a genus of nematode worms including the hookworms of sheep and cattle

buns *pl of* BUN

bun·sen burner \ˈbən(t)sən-*sometimes* ˈbůnzən-*or* ˈbůn(t)sən-\ *n, usu cap 1st B* [after Robert Wilhelm *Bunsen* †1899 Ger. chemist who invented it] **:** a burner used esp. in the laboratory that consists typically of a straight tube four or five inches long with a gas orifice and holes near the bottom for admission of air, the mixture of gas and air formed burning at the top with a feebly luminous but intensely hot flame

bun·sen·ite \-ə,nīt\ *n* -s [Robert Wilhelm *Bunsen* + E *-ite*] **:** a mineral NiO consisting of nickel monoxide occurring in green octahedrons

Bunsen burner: *1* gas inlet, *2* barrel, *3* air inlet, *4* movable collar

bun·sen-kirch·hoff law \-ənˈkir,kōf-, -rk-, -hōf-\ *n, usu cap B&K* [after Robert Wilhelm *Bunsen* and Gustav Robert *Kirchhoff* †1887 Ger. physicist, its formulators] **:** a statement in spectroscopy: each chemical element has an emission spectrum of bright lines and an absorption spectrum of dark lines which are characteristic of the element

¹**bunt** \ˈbənt\ *n* -s [perh. fr. LG *bunt* bundle, fr. MLG; akin to OE *byndel* bundle — more at BUNDLE] **1 :** the middle part of a square sail; *also* **:** the part of a furled square sail which is gathered up in a bunchy roll at the center of the yard **2 :** the central or bagging portion of a fishing net; *also* **:** something resembling this

²**bunt** \ˈ"\ *n* -s [origin unknown] **:** a destructive kernel smut of wheat caused by either of two fungi (*Tilletia caries* or *T. foetida*) and characterized by replacement of the normal grains with considerably smaller greasy masses of fishy smelling smut spores — called also *stinking smut*

³**bunt** \ˈ", ˈbůnt\ *n* -s [prob. alter. of ⁴*bun*] *dial Brit* **:** a rabbit tail

⁴**bunt** \ˈbənt\ *vb* -ED/-ING/-S [alter. of *butt* (to strike)] *vt* **1 a :** to strike or push with the horns or head; BUTT ⟨the goat ~*ed* the small boy so that he sat down with a jolt⟩ **b :** to strike or push (a railroad car) without coupling to the striking car or locomotive **2 :** to block or push (the ball) in a game of baseball within the infield by meeting with a loosely held bat and no swing **~** *vi* **:** to bunt something ⟨the team coach instructed the next batter to ~⟩ ⟨a goat very good at ~*ing*⟩

⁵**bunt** \ˈ"\ *n* -s **1 :** a push or shove esp. with the head **2 :** the act of bunting in a baseball game; *also* **:** a bunted ball — see DRAG BUNT

⁶**bunt** \ˈ"\ *n* -s [origin unknown] **:** a prehistoric stone arrowhead or spearhead having a blunt straight or curved tip

bun·tal \bůnˈtäl, ˈbəntᵊl\ *n* -s [Tag *buntál* talipot palm fiber, hat made of talipot palm fiber] **:** a very fine white Philippine fiber obtained from the stalks of unopened leaves of the talipot palm and used in making hats

bunt·ed \ˈbəntəd\ *adj* [²*bunt* + *-ed*] **:** affected with bunt ⟨~ wheat⟩

bun·ter \ˈbůntə(r), ˈbən-\ *adj, usu cap* [G *bunter* (*sandstein*) mottled sandstone] **:** of or relating to the lowest division of the European Triassic — see GEOLOGIC TIME table

bunt·er dog \ˈbəntə(r)-\ *also* **bunter** *n* -s [*bunter* (fr. ⁴*bunt* + *-er*) + *dog* (holding device)] **:** a gripping device for a planing machine consisting of a piece having a hook end to engage in the T slot of the table and a setscrew

¹**bun·ting** \ˈbəntiŋ, -tēŋ\ *n* -s [ME *buntynge*] **1 :** any of various stout-billed birds of *Emberiza* and related genera usu. included in the finch family (Fringillidae) and distinguished from typical finches by their more angular gape and often by a bony knob on the palate — see INDIGO BUNTING, REED BUNTING **2 a :** COWBIRD **b :** BOBOLINK

²**bunting** \ˈ"\ *n* -s [perh. fr. gerund of E dial. *bunt* to sift (meal), fr. ME *bonten*] **1 a :** a lightweight loosely woven fabric of plain weave used chiefly for flags and festive decorations and draperies **b :** FLAGS **2 :** festive decorations made of bunting or sometimes of paper; *esp* **:** such decorations in the colors of the national flag or the national coat of arms for patriotic occasions

³**bunting** \ˈ"\ *n* -s [*bunting* (term of endearment in the nursery rhyme "Bye, baby bunting"), perh. alter. of ²*bunny*] **1 :** a thickly napped fabric of natural or synthetic fiber used esp. for infant wear **2 :** an outdoor garment for infants consisting of a large envelope with attached hood

bunting crow \ˈ"-\ *n* [part modif. (influenced by E ¹*bunting*), part trans. of D *bonte kraai*, lit., pied crow] **:** HOODED CROW 1

bunting iron \ˈ"-\ *n* [by folk etymology (influence of *bunting*, gerund of ⁴*bunt*) fr. *punty-iron* punty, fr. *punty* + *iron*] **1 :** BLOWPIPE 4 **2 :** a flat piece of metal against which molten glass is bunted to stop its elongation in the forming period

bunt·line \ˈbənt,līn, -,lən\ *n* [¹*bunt* + *line*] **:** one of the ropes attached to the foot of a square sail to haul the sail up to the yard for furling — see SAIL illustration

bunting 2

buntline cloth *n* **:** a strengthening piece of canvas on the forward part of a square sail from foot to bellyband where the strain and chafe of the buntlines is greatest

buntline hitch *n* **:** a knot consisting of two half hitches used to secure the buntlines to the foot of a square sail

bun·ton \ˈbəntᵊn\ *or* **bun·ting** \ˈ", -tən,-tiŋ\ *n* -s [E dial. *bunting* piece of squared timber] **:** DIVIDER 3

bunts *pl of* BUNT, *pres 3d sing of* BUNT

¹**bun·ty** \ˈbəntē\ *n* -ES [E dial. *bunty* tailless fowl, perh. fr. ¹*bunt* + *-y*] **:** RING-NECKED DUCK

²**bunty** \ˈ"\ *adj* -ER/-EST **:** short and stout **:** STUMPY ⟨the little ~ streetcars on the long, single track —Booth Tarkington⟩

bu·ñu·e·lo \,bünyəˈwā(,)lō\ *n* -s [Sp; akin to Catal *bunyol* buñuelo, *bony* bump on the head — more at BUN] **:** a flat semisweet cake made mainly of eggs, flour, and milk fried in deep fat and usu. served with sugar and cinnamon or cane syrup

bun·ya bun·ya \,bənyəˈbənyə\ *or* **bunya** *or* **bunya pine** *n* -s [Australian *bunya bunya*, *bunya*, perh. fr. *bunya* shade] **:** an Australian coniferous tree (*Araucaria bidwillii*) bearing seeds about two inches long which have the flavor of roasted chestnuts when ripe and are a staple food of the aborigines among whom the tree is hereditary property and is protected by law

bun·yan·esque \,bənyəˈnesk\ *adj, usu cap* [John *Bunyan* †1688 Eng. preacher and writer + E *-esque*] **1 :** resembling or suggesting the allegorical writings of John Bunyan (as *Pilgrim's Progress*) ⟨*Bunyanesque* names like Sir Adroit and Cunning and The Dragon Evasive⟩ **2** [Paul *Bunyan*, legendary giant lumberjack associated with Canada and the northern and northwestern U.S.] **:** of or befitting the tales of Paul Bunyan ⟨such *Bunyanesque* characters as Babe the Blue Ox and Big Joe the Cook⟩; *esp* **:** of fantastically large size ⟨if all of a year's consumption were brewed in a *Bunyanesque* retort and decanted into the Niagara river —*Time*⟩

bun·yip \ˈbən,yip\ *n* -s [native name in Australia] **1** *Austral* **:** a legendary wild animal usu. described as a monstrous swamp-dwelling man-eater **2** *Austral* **:** IMPOSTOR, PHONY

buon fres·co \bwȯnˈfre(,)skō\ *n* [It, lit., good fresco] **:** FRESCO 1a(1)

¹**buoy** \ˈbüi, ˈbȯi, ˈbȯi — ˈbȯi *is usual in pronunc of* "*life buoy*"\ *n* -s [ME *boye*, fr. (assumed) MF *boie* (whence MF & F *bouée* buoy), of Gmc origin; akin to OHG *bouhhan* sign — more at BEACON] **1 :** ¹FLOAT 4; *esp* **:** an object floating in a body of water and moored to the bottom to mark a channel or to point out the position of something beneath the water (as an anchor, rock, or shoal) **2 :** LIFE BUOY

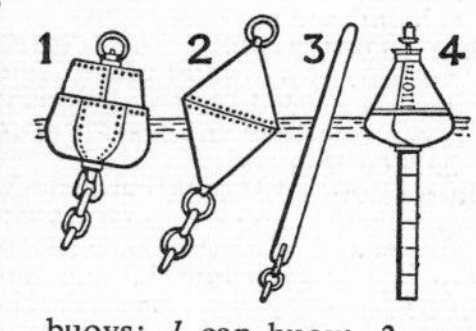

buoys: *1* can buoy; *2* nun buoy; *3* spar buoy; *4* whistling buoy

²**buoy** \ˈ"\ *vb* -ED/-ING/-S [in sense *vt* 1, fr. ¹*buoy*; in other senses, prob. fr. Sp *boyar* to float, fr. *boya* buoy, fr. (assumed) MF *boie*] *vt* **1 :** to provide with or mark by a buoy ⟨~ an anchor⟩ ⟨~ a channel⟩ **2 a :** to keep afloat on a liquid **:** keep from sinking — usu. used with *up* ⟨the raft was ~*ed* up by airtight oil drums⟩; *also* **:** to keep floating in the air — usu. used with *up* ⟨for a moment the falling leaf was ~*ed* up by a rising air current⟩ **b :** SUPPORT, SUSTAIN — usu. used with *up* ⟨with a patience ~*ed* only by the stimulus of a great idea —Waldemar Kaempffert⟩ ⟨~*ed* up during the trying period by high hopes of recovery⟩ ⟨an economy ~*ed* by the dramatic postwar growth of industry —*Time*⟩ **3 a** *archaic* **:** RAISE, LIFT — usu. used with *up* **b :** to raise the spirits of **:** make happier (as after a period of emotional depression) — usu. used with *up* ⟨the waltz ~*ed* her up —Scott Fitzgerald⟩ **~** *vi* **1** *obs* **:** to swell up **:** flood up — usu. used with *up* **2 :** to come to the surface of a liquid ⟨bound and thrown into the water . . . they ~*ed* up like a cork —*Amer. Guide Series: Conn.*⟩

buoy·age \ˈbüi-ij, ˈbüi(·i)j, ˈbȯi-ij\ *n* -s **1 a :** BUOYS **b :** a system of buoys (as for marking a channel) **2 :** the fee for the use of a buoy for mooring a boat

buoy·an·cy \ˈbȯiənsē, ˈbüyən-, ˈbüiən-, ˈbȯiyən-, ˈbüin-\ *also* **buoy·ance** \-n(t)s\ *n, pl* **buoyancies** *or* **buoyances** [*buoyancy* fr. *buoyant* + *-cy*; *buoyance* fr. *buoyancy*, after such pairs as E *elegancy*: *elegance*] **1 a :** the property of floating on the surface of a liquid or in a fluid **:** the tendency of a body to float or to rise when submerged in a fluid being dependent upon the excess of the specific gravity of the fluid over that of the body **b :** the property of a fluid by which it exerts an upward force on a body placed in it; *specif* **:** the upward force exerted on a lighter-than-air craft due to the air which it displaces **2 a :** resilience of spirit **:** the ability to emerge from or to elude depression **:** LIGHTHEARTEDNESS, SPRIGHTLINESS **:** the ability to recover quickly from discouragement **b :** generating or resulting in such lightheartedness or recovery ⟨a novel of great ~ and optimism⟩ **3 :** LIGHTNESS, SPRINGINESS ⟨walking with amazing ~ considering his increasing age⟩ **4 :** the property (as of prices or business activity) of maintaining a satisfactorily high level ⟨the future of the fund depends on the ~ of national wealth —*Meet New Zealand*⟩ ⟨the ~ of bank deposits —*Economist*⟩

buoyancy tank *n* **:** an airtight tank fitted into the stern or bow of a small boat (as a lifeboat) to keep it afloat if it fills with water or capsizes

buoy·ant \-nt\ *adj* [prob. fr. Sp *boyante*, fr. pres. part. of *boyar*] **1 :** having the quality or property of buoyancy ⟨iron is ~ in mercury⟩ ⟨held up by the ~ water⟩ ⟨floating in midair in the ~ gas⟩ ⟨a person cheerful of face and ~ of spirits⟩ ⟨a ~ stock market⟩ ⟨walking with a ~ step⟩ **2 :** light and floating ⟨a wonderfully delicate and ~ evening gown⟩ **syn** see ELASTIC

buoyant force *n* **:** the upward force exerted by any fluid upon a body placed in it — compare ARCHIMEDES' PRINCIPLE

buoy·ant·ly *adv* **:** in a buoyant manner ⟨go at a hard task cheerfully and ~⟩

buoy·ant·ness *n* -ES **:** the quality or state of being buoyant

buph·thal·mic \(ˈ)b(y)üfˈthalmik, ˌbəf-\ *adj* [ISV *buphthalm-* (fr. NL *buphthalmos*) + *-ic*] **:** of, relating to, or affected with buphthalmos

buph·thal·mos \b(y)üfˈthalməs, ˌbəf-, -ˌmäs\ *also* **buph·thal·mia** \-mēə\ *n, pl* **buphthalmos·es** \-məsəz, -ˌmäsəz\ *also* **buphthalmi·as** \-mēəz\ [*buphthalmos* fr. NL, fr. Gk *bo-* (fr. *bous* cow, ox) + *ophthalmos* eye; *buphthalmia* fr. NL, fr. *buphthalm-* (fr. *buphthalmos*) + *-ia* — more at COW, OPHTHALMIA] **:** marked enlargement of the eye usu. congenital and attended by symptoms of glaucoma

buph·thal·mum \-lməm\ *n, cap* [NL, fr. Gk *bouphthalmon* oxeye (flower), fr. *bo-* (fr. *bous*) + *-ophthalmon* (fr. *ophthalmos*)] **:** a genus of Eurasian perennial herbs (family Compositae) sometimes cultivated in gardens for their bright yellow-rayed flower heads — see OXEYE

bu·pleu·rum \byüˈplůrəm\ *n, cap* [NL, fr. L *bupleuron* hare's ear (*Bupleurum rotundifolium*), alter. of Gk *boupleuros*, fr. *bou-* (fr. *bous*) + *-pleuros* (fr. *pleura* rib) — more at PLEURISY] **:** a genus of widely distributed herbs (family Umbelliferae) having simple often stem-clasping leaves and greenish yellow flowers

bu·plev·er \-ˈplevə(r)\ *n* -s [F *buplèvre* hare's-ear, fr. L *bupleuron*] : a plant of the genus *Bupleurum*

¹bu·pres·tid \-ˈprestəd\ *adj* [NL *Buprestidae*] : of or relating to the Buprestidae

²buprestid \"\ *n* -s [NL *Buprestidae*] : a beetle of the family Buprestidae

bu·pres·ti·dae \-tə,dē\ *n pl, cap* [NL, fr. *Buprestis*, type genus + *-idae*] : a large family of beetles having rather short serrate antennae, an elongate form usu. sharply tapering behind, and an exceedingly hard thick integument often of brilliant metallic colors and producing larvae that are fleshy legless grubs that usu. bore in wood and are often destructive to trees

bu·pres·tis \-təs\ *n, cap* [NL, fr. L, poisonous beetle causing cattle that ate it in the grass to swell up and die, fr. Gk *bouprēstis*, fr. *bou-* (fr. *bous*) + *-prēstis* (fr. *prēthein* to blow up) — more at FROTH] : the type genus of the family Buprestidae

bur *var of* BURR

bur *abbr* **1** bureau **2** buried

bu·ran \bü'rän\ *n* -s [Russ, of Turkic origin; akin to Turk & Kazan Tatar *buran*, Kirghiz *boran*] : a northeasterly wind of gale force in Russia and central Asia usu. identified with sandstorms in summer and blizzards in winter; *also* : a sandstorm or blizzard of this kind — compare PURGA

burbark \ˈ=,=\ *n* -s [*burr* (prickly envelope) + *bark*] **1** : the bark of certain tropical shrubs of the genus *Triumfetta* (esp. *T. rhomboidea* and *T. semitriloba*) that yield a fiberlike jute **2** : a plant that yields burbark

Bur·ber·ry \ˈbərbərē, -,berē\ *trademark* — used for various usu. wool fabrics used esp. for coats for outdoor wear

¹bur·ble \ˈbər|bəl, ˈbə̄|, ˈbəi|\ *vb* **burbled; burbled; burbling** \ |b(ə)liŋ\ **burbles** [ME *burblen*, prob. of imit. origin] *vi* **1** : to make a bubbling sound : GURGLE ⟨brooks . . . that ~ past our own home windows —Gladys B.Stern⟩ **2** : to talk incessantly and usu. with enthusiasm : PRATTLE ⟨passengers who ~ on about how small . . . the world has become —Richard Thruelsen⟩ **3** : to separate from the surface of an airfoil and break up into eddies : become turbulent ⟨an angle at which the air no longer flows smoothly away under the trailing edge of the wing, but ~s up to fill the partial vacuum above the wing, thus spoiling the lift —Mary Chapin⟩ ~ *vt* **1** *Scot* : CONFUSE, MUDDLE **2** : to utter with unrestrained enthusiasm : GUSH

²burble \"\ *n* -s [ME *burble* bubble, fr. *burblen*, v.] **1** *Scot* : DISORDER, TROUBLE **2** : a bubbling noise; *esp* : burbling talk **3** : the breaking up into eddies of the streamline flow of air about a body (as an airplane wing)

burble point *n* : the angle of attack of an airfoil at which the first signs of burble appear

bur·bler \|b(ə)lə(r)\ *n* -s : one that burbles

bur·bly \|b(ə)lē\ *adj, sometimes* -ER/-EST [ME, fr. *burble* bubble + *-y*] : BURBLING, BUBBLING ⟨a novel, told in ~, panting tones —*New Yorker*⟩

bur·bot \ˈbərbət\ *n, pl* **burbot** *also* **burbots** [ME *borbot*, fr. MF *bourbotte*, *bourbete*, fr. *bourbeter* to burrow in the mud, fr. OF, fr. *bourbe* mud, prob. of Celt origin; akin to MIr *berbaim* I boil, W *berwi* to boil, Gaulish *Borvo*, deity associated with medicinal springs; akin to L *fervēre* to boil — more at BURN] : a freshwater fish (*Lota lota*) that is related to the cod, has two small barbels on the nose and a larger one on the chin, and is usu. held to exist in distinct forms in the northern parts of the Old World and the New, that of the latter being recognized as a subspecies (*Lota lota maculosa*) — called also *eelpout*; see LAWYER, LING

bur bristlegrass *n* [*burr* (prickly envelope) + *bristle grass*] : a Eurasian annual grass (*Setaria verticillata*) that is naturalized as a weed in No. America esp. in the northeastern states, is often tufted in appearance, and has spikelets with backward-barbed bristles

bur·chell's zebra \ˈbərchəlz-\ *n, usu cap B* [after William J. *Burchell* †1863 Eng. naturalist] : a zebra (*Equus burchelli*) of the plains of central or eastern Africa with stripes continuing onto the belly but the legs nearly or wholly unstriped — see CHAPMAN'S ZEBRA, GRANT'S ZEBRA

bur chervil *n* : WILD CHERVIL 1

bur clover *or* **burr clover** *n* : any of several clovers of the genus *Medicago* (esp. *M. denticulata*) having prickly seed pods

bur cucumber *n* **1** : a herbaceous vine (*Sicyos angulatus*) of the U.S. naturalized in Europe **2** : GHERKIN 1

¹burd \ˈbərd\ *n* -s [ME *bird, byrd, burde*, perh. alter. of OE *brȳd* bride — more at BRIDE] *chiefly Scot* : a young woman

²burd \"\ *Scot var of* BIRD

burd–alane \ˌbərdəˈlān\ *adj* [prob. fr. Sc *burd, bird* bird + *alane* alone — more at ALANE] *Scot* : all alone : SOLITARY ⟨she died and left us *burd-alane*⟩

bur·de·kin duck \ˈbərdəkən-\ *n, usu cap B* [*Burdekin* river, Queensland, Australia] : a white-headed sheldrake (*Tadorna radjah*) of tropical Australia and islands to the north

burdekin plum *n, usu cap B* **1** : an Australian tree (*Pleiogynium solandri*) of the family Anacardiaceae **2** : the edible red fruit of the Burdekin plum

burdekin vine *n, usu cap B* : an Australian vine (*Vitis opaca*) bearing large edible tubers

¹bur·den \ˈbərdᵊn, ˈbə̄d-,ˈbəid-\ *n* -s [ME *burden, burthen*, fr. OE *byrthen*; akin to OS *burthinnia* burden, OHG *burdī*, ON *byrthr*, Goth *baurthei*; derivatives fr. the root of OE *beran* to carry — more at BEAR] **1 a** : something that is carried : LOAD ⟨a donkey hidden under his ~ of firewood⟩ ⟨a ~ of dust carried by the wind⟩ ⟨images carry the ~ of the poem's effect⟩ **b** *obs* : a child in the womb **c** : something that is borne as a duty, obligation, or responsibility often with labor or difficulty ⟨the ~ of empire⟩ ⟨executive ~s⟩ ⟨tax ~s⟩ **d** : the aggregate load of instruments supplied with current by an instrument transformer in proration usu. downward from the actual load in the circuit being metered **2** : something that weighs down, oppresses, or causes worry ⟨she came with little but her ~ of fear⟩ : ENCUMBRANCE ⟨to have the ~ of a foreign tongue removed was . . . an inexpressible relief —William Black⟩ **3** : LADING — usu. used in the phrases *beast of burden, ship of burden* **4** *dial* : something the soil bears : CROP ⟨a good ~ of grass⟩ **5** : the capacity of a ship for carrying cargo ⟨a ship of a hundred tons ~⟩ **6** *Scots law* : an obligation, restriction, or encumbrance upon a person or property **7** : the proportion of ore and flux in relation to the coke or other fuel in the charge of an iron blast furnace **8** : the part of the cost of manufacturing that does not contribute directly to production : OVERHEAD; *specif* : all manufacturing costs other than direct labor and materials **9 a** : OVERBURDEN 2 **b** (1) : the resistance that an explosive charge must overcome in breaking the rock adjacent to a drill hole in mining (2) : the material that must be moved by the blast **10** : the degree of infestation of an animal body esp. with parasitic worms

²burden \"\ *vt* **burdened; burdened; burdening** \-d(ᵊ)niŋ\ **burdens** **1** : to load with or as if with something heavy, grievous, unwieldy, difficult, or unmanageable ⟨the numerous pretty things . . . which ~ the tables —Herbert Spencer⟩ ⟨~*ed* his men with endless labors⟩ **2** : to trouble, vex, or afflict with nonmaterial burdens ⟨I will not ~ you with a lengthy account⟩ : CHARGE ⟨~*ing* his conscience with a grave moral responsibility⟩ **3** *archaic* : BLAME, CHARGE **4** : to regulate the ratio of ore and flux to fuel in charging an iron blast furnace

syn ENCUMBER, CUMBER, WEIGH, WEIGHT, LOAD, LADE, SADDLE, CHARGE, TAX: BURDEN stresses the fact of bearing a heavy or grievous weight, often figuratively, sometimes literally ⟨men *burdened* with such intellectual tasks as theirs —H.O.Taylor⟩ ENCUMBER is likely to suggest cumbersome and unwieldy burdens making progress difficult, literally or figuratively ⟨*unencumbered* with luggage they would soon overtake the coach —Charles Dickens⟩ ⟨the overheavy richness and *encumbered* gait of the Asiatic style —Matthew Arnold⟩ CUMBER suggests what is unwieldy, bulky, and cluttering but is less likely to stress motion than ENCUMBER ⟨beyond the power of Rome, *cumbered* already with so many duties —John Buchan⟩ ⟨the whole Palace had been burnt in 1698, and its roofless walls still *cumbered* the river bank —G.M.Trevelyan⟩ Usu. figurative, WEIGH in such phrases as *weigh on one* or *weigh one down* suggests the depressing effect of some burden carried over a long period ⟨the tyranny at Bulaire *weighed* so heavily on the countryside —T.B.Costain⟩ ⟨for nearly a century the Dutch problem had *weighed* on Spain —Stringfellow Barr⟩ WEIGHT now often suggests a tendency to inclination, bias, slanting, often through a contrived arrangement ⟨there is no doubt that the new magazine will be heavily *weighted* on the American side —Crane Brinton⟩ ⟨those who fear that such planning councils . . . will be nothing but a further addition to an already *weighted* bureaucracy are in error —Norman Thomas⟩ LOAD is likely to suggest a full or more than adequate supply ⟨her hands . . . *loaded* with rings —Victoria Sackville-West⟩ and may suggest a packing with significance or perhaps the slanting associated with WEIGHT ⟨the discoverers of a new theory . . . may have *loaded* a useful notion with more than it can bear —B.N.Cardozo⟩ ⟨his absolutism *loaded* legality in his favor —Francis Hackett⟩ LADE, more common in the past participle *laden* than in other uses, is occas. used in situations involving burdens or grief ⟨with grief my heart is *laden* —A.E.Housman⟩ SADDLE may suggest an inescapable oppressive burden or responsibility lasting over a long period ⟨the reason being that . . . the abbeys were *saddled* with multitudes of statutory masses —G.G.Coulton⟩ ⟨the indemnity for the Opium War . . . *saddled* the Chinese government with an international debt —Owen & Eleanor Lattimore⟩ CHARGE in this series may refer to either heavy responsibilities or packed or loaded significances ⟨I *charge* myself with him; let him remain with me —Charles Dickens⟩ ⟨all the perennial, elemental processes of nature . . . were *charged* for psalmist and prophet with spiritual significance —J.L.Lowes⟩ TAX indicates continuing heavy demands ⟨the labor of calculating and recording would have *taxed* energy beyond endurance —Edward Clodd⟩

³burden \"\ *n* -s [by folk etymology (influence of ¹*burden*) fr. *bourdon*] **1** *archaic* : a bass or accompanying part : DRONE ⟨I would sing my song without a ~; thou bringest me out of tune —Shak.⟩ **2** : the verse repeated in a song or the return of the theme at the end of each stanza : CHORUS, REFRAIN **3 a** : a recurring or emphasized idea or theme : central topic : GIST ⟨the ~ of the argument⟩ ⟨words of praise are fraught with that desire to hear lost laughter which is the ~ of every century's lament —Agnes Repplier⟩

burdened *adj* [fr. past part. of ²*burden*] : responsible by the nautical rules of the road to keep clear of another ship ⟨a sailboat on the port tack is ~⟩ — contrasted with *privileged*

bur·den·less \-dᵊnləs\ *adj* : being without a burden

bur·den·man \-mən, -,man\ *n, pl* **burdenmen** [¹*burden* + *man*] : CRANE FOLLOWER

burden of proof [trans. of L *onus probandi*] : the duty of proving a disputed assertion or charge ⟨the *burden of proof* is upon the critic⟩; *specif* : the duty of proving a particular position in a court of law under penalty against the party on whom the duty is imposed

burdenous *adj, obs* : BURDENSOME

burdens *pl of* BURDEN, *pres 3d sing of* BURDEN

bur·den's grass \ˈbərdᵊnz-, ˈbə̄d-,ˈbəid-\ *n, usu cap B* [prob. fr. the name *Burden*] : REDTOP 1

bur·den·some \-ᵊnsəm\ *adj* : difficult or distressing to carry or to bear : OPPRESSIVE ⟨a ~ load⟩ ⟨a ~ responsibility⟩ **syn** see ONEROUS

bur·den·some·ly *adv* : in a burdensome manner

bur·den·some·ness *n* -ES : the quality or state of being burdensome

burd·ie \ˈbərdē\ *n* -s [¹*burd* + *-ie*] *Scot* : GIRL, WOMAN ⟨the bonnie ~ —Robert Burns⟩

burdock \ˈ=,=\ *n* -s [*burr* (prickly envelope) + *dock*] **1** : any plant of the genus *Arctium* **2** : COCKLEBUR 1

burds *pl of* BURD

¹bure \ˈbür\ *Scot var of* BORE

²bu·re \ˈbü(,)rā\ *n* -s [Fijian] : a large house or temple in the Fiji islands

³bure \ˈbyü(ə)r, ˈbu̇e̅r\ *n* -s [F, coarse woolen cloth] : a moderate yellowish brown that is redder, lighter, and stronger than Bismarck brown, bronze, or maple sugar and lighter, stronger, and slightly redder than cinnamon brown

bu·reau \ˈbyü(,)rō, ˈbyü- *also esp when no pause follows* -,rə\ *n, pl* **bureaus** *also* **bureaux** [F, office, desk, cloth covering for desks or tables, coarse woolen cloth, fr. OF *burel* coarse woolen cloth, fr. (assumed) OF *bure* coarse woolen cloth (whence MF *bure*), fr. (assumed) VL *bura*, alter. of LL *burra* shaggy cloth, prob. of non-IE origin; akin to the source of Gk *berberion* shabby garment] **1 a** *Brit* : a writing desk; *esp* : one having drawers and a slant top — called also *writing bureau* **b** : a low chest of drawers with a mirror for use in a bedroom — compare CHIFFONIER, DRESSER **2 a** : a specialized administrative unit ⟨the university testing ~⟩; *esp* : a subdivision of an executive department of a government ⟨the Internal Revenue *Bureau* of the Department of the Treasury⟩ **b** : a usu. commercial agency that serves as a clearinghouse or intermediary for exchanging information, making contacts, or coordinating cooperative activities ⟨credit ~⟩ ⟨speakers' ~⟩ ⟨farm ~⟩ **c** : a branch of a newspaper, newsmagazine, or wire service in an important news center ⟨the Washington ~ of the Associated Press⟩ **3** : an executive committee or small directing body: as **a** : the small body of officers in each chamber of the French parliament that controls proceedings in its chamber **b** [Russ *byuro*, fr. F *bureau*] : the policy-forming committee of the Communist party of the U.S.S.R. **4** *or* **bureau print** *usu cap B* : a postage stamp precanceled by the U.S. Bureau of Engraving and Printing

bureau 1b

bu·reauc·ra·cy \byu̇ˈräkrəsē, byu̇'-,byə'- *sometimes* ÷bə'- *or* -rōk-\ *n* -ES [F *bureaucratie*, fr. *bureau* + *-cratie* -cracy] **1 a** (1) : the whole body of nonelective government officials ⟨criticized the growth of the ~⟩ (2) : a particular group of government officials ⟨Uncle Sam's vast overseas ~ —Carter Henderson⟩ **b** : the administrative policy-making group in any large organization ⟨a cleavage between the ~ and the working membership of the unions⟩ **2** : systematic administration characterized by specialization of functions, objective qualifications for office, action according to fixed rules, and a hierarchy of authority **3 a** : a system of administration marked by constant striving for increased functions and power, by lack of initiative and flexibility, by indifference to human needs or public opinion, and by a tendency to defer decisions to superiors or to impede action with red tape ⟨inveighed against the evils of ~⟩ **b** : the body of officials that gives effect to such a system ⟨caught in the meshes of a timid and heartless ~⟩

bu·reau·crat \ˈbyu̇rə,krat, ˈbyü-, -rō,-, *usu* -ad·+V\ *n* -s [F *bureaucrate*, fr. *bureau* + *-crate* -crat] : an official of a bureau or a member of a bureaucracy; *esp* : a government official confirmed in a narrow rigid formal routine or established with great authority in his own department

bu·reau·crat·ic \ˌ==ˈkrad·ik, -at|, |ēk\ *adj* [F *bureaucratique*, fr. *bureau* + *-cratique* -cratic] : of, relating to, or resembling a bureaucrat or a bureaucracy — **bu·reau·crat·i·cal·ly** \ |ək(ə)lē, |ēk-, -li\ *adv*

bu·reau·crat·ism \ˈ== *as at* BUREAUCRAT + ,krad·,izəm *or* -a,ti-; =ˈ= *as at* BUREAUCRACY + ,krə,tizəm\ *n* -s : a bureaucratic system : BUREAUCRACY

bu·reauc·ra·ti·za·tion \byu̇,räkrəd·əˈzāshən, byu̇,-,byə,-, -krə,tīˈz- *sometimes* ÷bə,- *or* -,rōk-\ *n* -s : the action or result of bureaucratizing ⟨~ of economic life and the growth of the octopus state —David Dubinsky⟩

bu·reauc·ra·tize \=ˈ=rə,tīz\ *vt* -ED/-ING/-S [F *bureaucratiser*, fr. *bureaucratie* bureaucracy + *-iser* -ize] : to make bureaucratic : subject to bureaucracy

bureau print *n, usu cap B* : BUREAU 4

bur·el \ˈbərəl\ *var of* BORREL

bu·re·lage \ˌbu̇rəˈläzh\ *n* -s [F, fr. *burèle, burelle* barrulet (back-formation fr. *burelé* barruly) + *-age*] : a fine network or allover pattern of lines or dots printed on the face or back of stamp paper as a protection against fraudulent changes — compare MOIRÉ

bu·re·lé \ˌbu̇rəˈlā\ *adj* [F, lit., barruly, fr. OF] : having a burelage ⟨~ paper⟩ ⟨~ pattern⟩

bu·rel·ly *or* **bu·re·ly** \ˈb(y)u̇rəlē\ *also* **bu·ru·lée** \-r(y)ə,lā\ *or* **bu·ru·ly** \-r(y)əlē\ *adj* [OF *burelé*, prob. fr. *burel* coarse woolen cloth — more at BUREAU] : BARRULY

bures *pl of* BURE

bu·rette \byu̇ˈret\ *n* -s [F, fr. MF, cruet esp. for sacramental wine, alter. of *buirette* cruet, fr. *buire* pitcher (fr. OF, alter. of *buie*, of Gmc origin and akin to OE *būc* pitcher, belly) + *-ette* — more at BUCKET] **1** *or* **bu·ret** : a laboratory apparatus consisting typically of a graduated glass tube with a small aperture and stopcock and used for delivering measured quantities of liquid or for measuring the liquid or gas received or discharged **2** : a cruet esp. for sacramental wine

bu-rette 1

burfish *var of* BURRFISH

burg \ˈbərg\ *n* -s [OE *burg, burh* — more at BOROUGH] **1** : an ancient or medieval fortress or walled town **2 a** : CITY, TOWN ⟨mushroomed . . . into a booming ~ of 36,000 —*Newsweek*⟩ **b** : a village typically unimportant and out of the way ⟨little mountain ~s not down on the map —*Boston Sunday Herald*⟩

burg *abbr* **1** burgess **2** burgomaster

bur·gage \ˈbu̇rgij\ *n* -s [ME, property held by burgage tenure, fr. MF *bourgage*, lit., burgage, fr. OF, fr. *bourg, borc* town + *-age* — more at BOURG] **1** : a tenure by which real property in English boroughs was held of the king or other lord for a certain yearly rent — compare SOCAGE **2** : a tenure by which real property in Scottish royal burghs was held directly of the king for the service of watching and warding — compare FEU

bur·gall \ˈbər,gȯl\ *n* -s [origin unknown] : CUNNER b

bur·ga·mot \ˈbərgə,mät, -,mət, *usu* -d·+V\ *var of* BERGAMOT

bur·gao *also* **bur·gau** \bərˈgau̇\ *or* **bur·go** \-gō\ *n* -s [AmerSp & F & Pg; AmerSp *burgao* & F *burgau*, fr. Pg *burgó, burgão*, fr. Tupi *perigoá*] : a common top shell (*Livona pica*) of the West Indies whose flesh is esteemed as food and whose shell is used in making buttons and ornamental novelties

bur·gee \,bərˈjē, ˈ=,=\ *also* **bou·gee** \büˈjē, ˈ=,=\ *n* -s [perh. fr. F dial. (Jersey) *bourgeais* shipowner, fr. MF *borjois, borgeis* shipowner, master of the house, freeman of a borough, fr. OF, master of the house, freeman of a borough] **1** : a swallow-tailed flag used esp. by ships for signals and house flags **2** : the usu. triangular identifying flag of a yacht club flown by the boats of members

burgee command pennant *n* : a personal command pennant flown by U.S. Naval vessels to denote an officer below flag rank commanding a division of warships or a major subdivision of an aircraft wing — compare BROAD COMMAND PENNANT

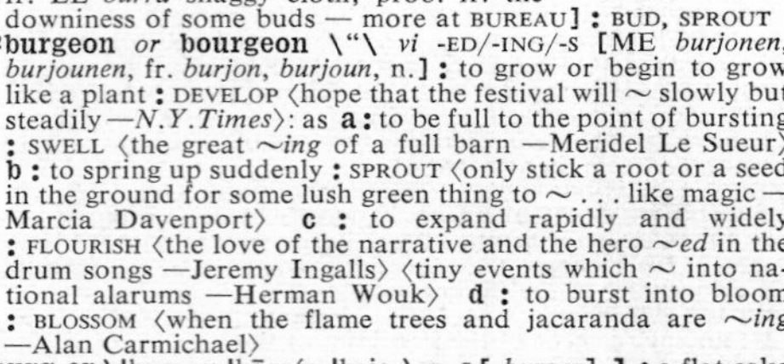

burgees

¹bur·geon *or* **bour·geon** \ˈbərjən, ˈbə̄j-, ˈbəij-\ *n* -s [ME *burjon, bourjon* bud, fr. OF *burjon*, fr. (assumed) VL *burrion-, burrio*, fr. LL *burra* shaggy cloth; prob. fr. the downiness of some buds — more at BUREAU] : BUD, SPROUT

²burgeon *or* **bourgeon** \"\ *vi* -ED/-ING/-S [ME *burjonen, bourjounen*, fr. *burjon, bourjon*, n.] : to grow or begin to grow like a plant : DEVELOP ⟨hope that the festival will ~ slowly but steadily —*N.Y.Times*⟩: as **a** : to be full to the point of bursting : SWELL ⟨the great ~*ing* of a full barn —Meridel Le Sueur⟩ **b** : to spring up suddenly : SPROUT ⟨only stick a root or a seed in the ground for some lush green thing to ~ . . . like magic —Marcia Davenport⟩ **c** : to expand rapidly and widely : FLOURISH ⟨the love of the narrative and the hero ~*ed* in the drum songs —Jeremy Ingalls⟩ ⟨tiny events which ~ into national alarums —Herman Wouk⟩ **d** : to burst into bloom : BLOSSOM ⟨when the flame trees and jacaranda are ~*ing* —Alan Carmichael⟩

burg·er \ˈbərgər; ˈbə̄gə(r, ˈbəig-\ *n* -s [*-burger*] **1** : a flat cake of ground or chopped meat or meat substitute fried or grilled and served between slices of bread **2** : a sandwich containing a burger; *esp* : HAMBURGER

-burg·er \,==\ *n comb form* -s [*hamburger*] **1 a** : patty of a (specified) kind of food usu. meat or a meat substitute ⟨pork*burger*⟩ ⟨nut*burger*⟩ **b** : sandwich made of such a patty ⟨pork*burger*⟩ **2** : sandwich with a filling consisting of a hamburger patty topped with a (specified) food ⟨cheese*burger*⟩

bur·gess \ˈbərjəs, ˈbə̄j-,ˈbəij-\ *n* -ES [ME *burgeis*, fr. OF *borjois, borgeis*, fr. *borc* town, fr. L *burgus* fortified place] **1 a** : a citizen of a British borough ⟨the plaintiff was a ~ of Aylesbury and as such entitled to vote for two Members of Parliament —T.E.May⟩ **2** : a magistrate or member of the governing body of a town or borough; *specif* : the chief executive officer of a borough in Pennsylvania **3 a** : a representative of a borough, corporate town, or university in the British Parliament — now called *Member of Parliament* **b** : a representative in the popular branch of the legislatures of colonial Maryland and Virginia

burgh *like* BOROUGH\ *n* -s [ME — more at BOROUGH] **1** *archaic* : BOROUGH **2** : CITY, TOWN; *specif* : an incorporated town in Scotland possessing a charter and having local jurisdiction of certain services — see PARLIAMENTARY BURGH, POLICE BURGH

burgh·al \ˈbərgəl\ *adj* : of or relating to a burgh or municipal corporation : URBAN

bur·gher \ˈbərgər; ˈbə̄gə(r, ˈbəig-\ *n* -s [G *bürger* & D *burger*; G *bürger* fr. MHG *burgære, burger* freeman of a borough, fr. OHG *burgāri* inhabitant of a town or city, fr. *burg* fortified place, city; D *burger* fr. MD *burgher* freeman of a borough, fr. MHG *burgære, burger*] **1 a** : a resident of a town : TOWNSMAN **b** : a member of the middle class : a prosperous solid citizen ⟨shock the Boston ~s out of their staid decorum —Van Wyck Brooks⟩ **2** *usu cap* : a member of the party in the Scottish Secession Church that held it permissible for members to take an oath requiring acceptance of the authorized religion of the realm **3 a** *usu cap* : a Ceylonese of mixed blood; *specif* : one of Dutch descent **b** [Afrik *burger*, fr. D] : a citizen of the former Dutch republics of So. Africa

bur·gher·hood \-,hu̇d\ *n* -s : the status or condition of a burgher

bur gherkin *n* [*burr* (prickly envelope) + *gherkin*] : GHERKIN 1

bur·gher·ly *adj* : of or relating to a prosperous solid citizen

burgh·master \ˈbə·rə+,-\ *n* [by folk etymology (influence of *burgh*) fr. earlier *bargh-master* — more at BARMASTER] *Brit* : BARMASTER

¹bur·glar \ˈbərglər; ˈbə̄glə(r, ˈbəig-\ *n* -s [AF *burgler*, fr. ML *burglator*, prob. alter. of *burgator*, fr. *burgatus*, past part. of *burgare* to commit burglary, fr. L *burgus* fortified place, of Gmc origin; akin to OHG *burg* fortified place — more at BOROUGH] : one who commits burglary

²burglar \"\ *vb* -ED/-ING/-S *Brit* : BURGLARIZE

burglar alarm *n* : a device for automatically giving an alarm in case of burglary

bur·glar·i·ous \ˌbərˈgla(a)rēəs\ *adj* [*burglary* + *-ous*] **1** : of, involving, or resembling burglary ⟨a ~ entry⟩ ⟨no adequate notification was given to the Indians of this ~ measure —H.L.Ickes⟩ **2** : of or suitable for the use of a burglar ⟨~ tools⟩ — **bur·glar·i·ous·ly** *adv*

bur·glar·ize \ˈbərglə,rīz, ˈbə̄g-,ˈbəig-\ *vb* -ED/-ING/-S *vt* : to break into and steal from ~ *vi* : to commit burglary **syn** see ROB

burglarproof \ˌ==ˈ=\ *adj* : proof against burglars or burglary

bur·gla·ry \ˈbərglərē, ˈbə̄g-,ˈbəig-, -ri\ *n* -ES [AF *burglarie*, fr. *burgler* + *-ie* -y] : the act of breaking into a building illegally esp. with intent to steal; *specif* : the act of breaking into and entering the dwelling house of another at night with felonious intent — see THEFT; compare HOUSEBREAKING

burglary insurance *n* : insurance against loss or damage resulting from or following the unlawful breaking and entering of designated premises or places of safekeeping

bur·gle \ˈbərgəl\ *vb* **burgled; burgled; burgling** \-g(ə)liŋ\ **burgles** [back-formation fr. *burglar*] : BURGLARIZE

burgo *var of* BURGAO

bur·go·master \ˈbərgə, ˈbə̄gə, ˈbəigə+\ *also* **bur·gher·master** \-R -gə(r), -R -gə+\ *n* -s [part modif., part trans. of D *burgemeester*, fr. *burg* town (fr. MD *burch*) + *meester* master; akin to OHG *burg* fortified place, town, city] **1** : the chief magistrate of a town in certain European countries : MAYOR **2** : GLAUCOUS GULL

bur·go·net \ˈbərgənət, ˌ==ˈnet\ *n* -s [modif. of MF *bourguig-*

notte, fr. *bourguignon* Burgundian, fr. *Bourgogne* Burgundy; fr. its use by Burgundian soldiers] **:** either of two 16th century helmets: **a :** a light helmet resembling a morion but having cheekpieces and sometimes a nosepiece **b :** a visored helmet resembling an armet

bur·goo \'bər,gü, (,)bər'gü\ *n* -s [origin unknown] **1 :** oatmeal gruel **2 :** hardtack and molasses cooked together **3 a :** a savory highly seasoned stew or thick soup containing several kinds of meat and vegetables orig. served at political rallies, barbecues, picnics, and community occasions **b :** a picnic at which burgoo is served

bur grass *n* [*burr* (prickly envelope) + *grass*] **:** a grass of the genus *Cenchrus*

bur·grave \'bər,grāv\ *n* -s *often cap* [modif. of G *burggraf*, fr. MHG *burcgrāve*, fr. *burc* fortress, town (fr. OHG *burg* fortified place) + *grāve* count, fr. OHG *grāvo*, *grāvio* count, overseer; akin to OFris *grēva* overseer, MD *grave*, *greve*, MLG *grēve*, and perh. to Goth *gagrefts* decree] **1 :** the military governor of a German city in the 12th and 13th centuries **2 :** a noble ruling by hereditary right a German castle or town and its adjacent lands — compare LANDGRAVE, MARGRAVE

burgs *pl of* BURG

[1]**bur·gun·di·an** \bə(r)'gəndēən, ,bər'-,bə̄'-,bəi'-\ *n* -s *usu cap* [*Burgundy* + E *-an*, n. suffix] **1 :** a member of a Germanic people that entered Gaul early in the 5th century A.D. and established the kingdom of Burgundy **2 :** a native or inhabitant of the prerevolutionary French province of Burgundy — called also *Bourguignon*

[2]**burgundian** \bə(r)'g-, ,bər¦g-,(')bə̄¦g-,(')bəi¦g-\ *adj, usu cap* [*Burgundy* + E *-an*, adj. suffix] **:** of or relating to Burgundy or the Burgundians

bur·gun·dy \'bərgəndē, 'bə̄g-,'bəig-\ *n* -ES [*Burgundy*, region in east central France] **1** *usu cap* **a :** any of the red or white table wines from vineyards in the departments of Côte d'Or, Yonne, and Saône-et-Loire, France, usu. possessing stronger flavor and heavier body than Bordeaux wines **b :** a table wine that resembles the red Burgundy of France but is produced elsewhere and that is usu. darker red and heavier-bodied than claret (sense 1b) though sometimes made from the same grapes **2** *often cap* **a :** a variable color averaging a dark grayish reddish brown that is redder and slightly stronger than carbuncle and redder and duller than average brown mahogany **b :** a blackish purple that is redder and less strong than average eggplant

burgundy mixture *n, usu cap B* **:** a fungicide similar to Bordeaux mixture but containing sodium carbonate instead of lime

burgundy pitch *n, usu cap B* [trans. of F *poix de Bourgogne*] **1 :** a yellowish brown or reddish brown hard viscous resin obtained as an exudation from the Norway spruce and used esp. formerly in medicinal plasters **2 :** resin from any of various pines or firs sometimes mixed with other substances (as turpentine)

burgundy violet *n, often cap B* **:** MANGANESE VIOLET

burhead \'=,=\ *n* [*burr* (prickly envelope) + *head*] **1 :** CLEAVERS **2 :** a plant of the genus *Echinodorus*

burh·el \'bərəl\ *var of* BHARAL

bu·rhin·i·dae \byü'rinə,dē\ *n pl, cap* [NL, fr. *Burhinus*, type genus + *-idae*] **:** a family (coextensive with the superfamily Burhenoidea of the Charadrii) of large long-legged wading birds that resemble the plovers and comprise the stone curlews

bu·rhi·nus \byü'rīnəs\ *n, cap* [NL, fr. Gk *bou-* (fr. *bous* cow, ox) + NL *-rhinus;* fr. an incorrect illustration showing a broad bill — more at COW] **:** the type genus of Burhinidae including a number of typical stone curlews — see THICK-KNEE

bu·ri \'bü'rē, 'bürē\ *n* -s [Tag *buri*] **1 :** TALIPOT PALM **2 :** BUNTAL

buri·al \'berēəl\ *n* -s *often attrib* [ME *berial*, alter. (influenced by *-al*, n. suffix) of *beriel*, *buryel*, back-formation fr. *beriels*, *buryels* tomb (taken as a plural), fr. OE *byrgels;* akin to OS *burgisli* tomb; derivative fr. the root of OE *byrgan* to bury — more at BURY] **1 :** a place of interment **:** GRAVE, TOMB ⟨artifacts occurring in ~s were few —G.W.Hewes⟩ **2 a** (1) **:** the act or ceremony of burying ⟨the ~ took place yesterday⟩ (2) **:** the process of being buried ⟨~ of the deposits by sediment⟩ **b :** the act or process of irrevocably dismissing, abandoning, or putting away **:** LOSS, ABANDONMENT ⟨the ~ of dangerous illusions —*N.Y.Times*⟩ **3 :** an interred human body or its remains — see PRIMARY BURIAL, SECONDARY BURIAL

burial case *n* **:** CASKET 3

burial ground *n* **:** a piece of land used for burying the dead **:** CEMETERY

burial mound *n* **:** a mound erected over the dead; *esp* **:** one constructed by the Indian Mound Builders of No. America

buriat *usu cap, var of* BURYAT

bu·ri·dan's ass \'byürəd°nz-, -dənz-\ *n, usu cap B* [after Jean Buridan †*ab*1358 Fr. philosopher, who is reputed to have posed the problem] **:** a hypothetical dilemma in which a person is postulated as presented with two equally attractive and attainable alternatives and therefore loses freedom of choice

buried *past of* BURY

buried hill *n* **:** an elevation on an ancient land surface now concealed by younger sedimentary rocks

buried suture *n* **:** a surgical stitch not appearing above the skin

buried valley *n* **:** a depression in an ancient land surface now concealed by younger deposits

bur·i·er \'berēə(r)\ *n* -s [ME *buryere*, fr. OE *byrgere*, fr. *byrgan* + *-ere* -er] **:** one that buries

buries *pres 3d sing of* BURY, *pl of* BURY

bu·rin \'byürən, 'bərən\ *n* -s [F, perh. fr. Catal *buri*, perh. of Celt origin; akin to MIr *bern*, *berna* gap, chasm; akin to OE *borian* to bore — more at BORE] **1 :** an engraver's tool having a tempered steel shaft ground obliquely to a sharp point at one end and inserted into a handle at the other — called also *graver* **2 :** a flint tool with a point like that of a chisel found chiefly in upper Paleolithic sites of western Europe and in Mesolithic sites of Siberia

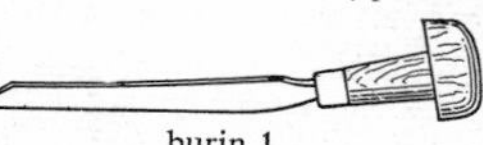
burin 1

bu·rin·ist \-nəst\ *n* -s **:** ENGRAVER

bu·ri·on \'byürēən, bür'yōn\ *n* -s [MexSp *burrión*, perh. alter. of Sp *gorrión* sparrow] *Southwest* **:** HOUSE FINCH

buri palm *n* **:** TALIPOT PALM

buri straw *n* **:** BUNTAL

bu·ri·ti *or* **bu·ri·ty** \,bürə¦tē\ *n, pl* **buritis** *or* **burities** [Pg *buriti* — more at MURITI PALM] **:** MURITI PALM

[1]**bur·ka** \'bürkə\ *n* -s [Russ, prob. fr. *buryĭ* dark brown (of a horse), prob. of Turkic origin; akin to Turk *bur* red like a fox; the Turkic word prob. fr. Per *bōr* reddish brown; akin to Skt *babhru* reddish brown — more at BROWN] **:** a coarse cloak worn esp. in Russia

[2]**bur·ka** *or* **bur·kha** *or* **bour·kha** \"\ *n* -s [Hindi *burqa'*, fr. Ar *burqu'*] **:** a loose enveloping garment with usu. veiled eyeholes that is worn in public by Muslim women esp. of India and Pakistan

burke \'bərk\ *vt* -ED/-ING/-S [after William *Burke* †1829 Ir. criminal, executed for this crime] **1 :** to murder by suffocation or strangulation in order to obtain a body to be sold for dissection **2 a :** to suppress quietly or indirectly **:** hush up ⟨she had never believed such a thing as the *burking* of the enquiry into the raid possible —H.W.Nevinson⟩ **b :** to set aside without consideration or decision **:** BYPASS, AVOID ⟨~ the issue⟩

burk·ean \'bərkēən\ *adj, usu cap* [Edmund *Burke* †1797 Brit. statesman + E *-an*] **:** of, relating to, or resembling Edmund Burke or his political philosophy

burke·ite \'bər,kīt\ *n* -s [William Edmund *Burke* *b*1880 Am. chemical engineer + E *-ite*] **:** a mineral $Na_6(CO_3)(SO_4)_2$ consisting of a carbonate-sulfate of sodium

bur·kun·daz \¦bərkən¦däz\ *n* -ES [Hindi *barqandāz*, fr. Per, fr. *barq* lightning (fr. Ar) + *andāz* thrower] **:** an armed guard or policeman of 18th and 19th century India

burk·wood viburnum \'bər,kwüd-\ *n, usu cap B* [after Albert *Burkwood* *b*1890 and Arthur *Burkwood* *b*1888 Brit. nurserymen] **:** a nearly evergreen shrub (*Viburnum burkwoodii*) having leaves with shiny upper and gray tomentose lower surface and heads of pink-flushed flowers

[1]**burl** \'bərl, 'bə̄l, 'bəil, *esp bef pause or cons* 'bər·əl\ *n* -s [ME *burle*, fr. (assumed) MF *bourle* tuft of wool (fr. OF *burle*), fr. (assumed) VL *burrula*, dim. of LL *burra* shaggy cloth — more at BUREAU] **1 :** a knot or lump in thread or cloth **2 a :** a hard woody growth often of a flattened hemispherical form that occurs on the trunks or branches of trees usu. in association with adventitious buds and is used to make bowls and veneers **b :** veneer made from such burls **c :** a mottled figure in the grain produced by cutting through such burls

[2]**burl** \"\ *vt* -ED/-ING/-S [ME *burlen*, fr. *burle*, n.] **:** to finish (cloth) by inspecting and repairing usu. by hand any imperfections (as loose threads and knots)

[3]**burl** \"\ *n* -s [prob. alter. (influenced by *birl*) of *whirl* (in the expression *give it a whirl*)] *Austral* **:** ATTEMPT, TRY ⟨give it a ~⟩

bur·la \'bürlə, -(,)lä\ *n, pl* **bur·le** \-(,)lā\ *or* **burlas** [It, joke] **1 :** a musical composition or movement of a humorous or playful and often boisterous character **2 :** an interpolated comic episode in the commedia dell' arte usu. involving a practical joke — compare LAZZO

bur·la·de·ro \,bürlə'de(,)rō\ *n* -s [Sp, fr. *burlar* to deceive, make fun of, fr. *burla* joke] **:** a wooden shield set parallel to and a little distance out from the barrera behind which bullfighters can take shelter if pursued ⟨safe behind a ~ . . . he found that his fever to fight bulls had all drained away —Tom Lea⟩

[1]**bur·lap** \'bər,lap, 'bə̄,-, 'bəi,-\ *n* -s [alter. of earlier *borelap*, perh. fr. [2]*bore* (of a cannon) + *lap* (rag)] **1 :** a coarse heavy plain-woven fabric usu. of jute or hemp used for bagging and wrapping and in furniture and linoleum manufacture — called also *gunny*, *hessian* **2 :** a material resembling burlap but of lighter weight used in interior decoration and for clothing

[2]**burlap** \"\ *vt* **burlapped; burlapped; burlapping; burlaps :** to wrap in or cover with burlap ⟨a balled and *burlapped* evergreen⟩

bur·lap·per \-pə(r)\ *n* -s **:** one that puts burlap coverings on cloth for shipment

burlaw *var of* BYRLAW

bur·le·cue *or* **bur·ley·cue** \'bərlē,kyü, 'bə̄l-,'bəil-\ *n* -s [by alter.] **:** [2]BURLESQUE 3

burled \'bər(-ə)ld, 'bə̄ld, 'bəild\ *adj* [[1]*burl* + *-ed*] **:** having a burl figure ⟨a humidor of ~ walnut⟩

burl·er \'bərlər; 'bə̄lə(r, 'bəil-\ *n* -s [[2]*burl* + *-er*] **1 :** one that removes loose threads, knots, and other imperfections from cloth **2 :** one that inspects rugs before the finishing process, mends dropped stitches on the back, and pulls matching yarn into spots where tufts are missing or shearing is uneven

bur·les·ca \bür'leskə, ,bər-\ *n* -s [It, fem. of *burlesco*] **:** BURLA 1

[1]**bur·lesque** \¦bər¦lesk, (')bə̄¦l-, (')bəi¦l-, bə(r)'l-\ *adj* [F, fr. It *burlesco*, fr. *burla* joke, fr. Sp, prob. modif. of LL *burra* trifle, bit of nonsense, perh. fr. *burra* shaggy cloth — more at BUREAU] **1** *archaic* **:** DROLL, JOCULAR, ODD **2 :** marked by an effect of comic or grotesque imitation or exaggeration usu. with the intent of mocking or making ridiculous **:** derisively imitative ⟨a ~ account of the adventures of a knight errant⟩ ⟨a ~ version of the heroic epic⟩ ⟨a favorite bulldog, whose . . . great corpulence gave it a ~ resemblance to its master —Sir Walter Scott⟩ **3 :** of, relating to, or having the characteristics of burlesque entertainment ⟨a ~ house⟩ ⟨~ jokes⟩ ⟨jolt the chorus regulars out of their usual sloppy, tawdry, ~ style —Flora Lewis⟩ — **bur·lesque·ly** *adv*

[2]**burlesque** \"— '=,= *is esp freq for sense 3*\ *n* -s **1 a :** literary composition or dramatic representation that ridicules something, usu. the serious and dignified (as Samuel Butler's *Hudibras*) but sometimes the trivial and commonplace (as Alexander Pope's *Rape of the Lock*) by means of grotesque exaggeration or comic imitation ⟨the literature of ~⟩ **b :** a work (as a play or novel) of this kind ⟨a first-class ~ in response . . . to Scott's "Ivanhoe" —Harvey Breit⟩ **2 :** a grotesque likeness or exaggerated imitation **:** CARICATURE ⟨he has become a perversion of its ideals and a ~ of his own earlier hopes —J.W.Aldridge⟩ **3** *also* **bur·lesk** \"\ **:** theatrical entertainment of a broadly humorous often earthy character consisting of comic skits, striptease acts, and songs and dances performed by soloists or a chorus **syn** see CARICATURE

[3]**burlesque** \"\ *vb* -ED/-ING/-S *vt* **:** to make ridiculous by burlesque **:** make the subject of a burlesque **:** MOCK ⟨each of the three dancers *burlesqued* his own style —John Martin⟩ ⟨the act that ~s a magician sawing a person in half —Henry La Cossitt⟩ ~ *vi* **:** to employ burlesque **syn** see COPY

bur·lesqu·er \-kə(r)\ *n* -s **:** one that burlesques; *specif* **:** an actor in burlesque

burlet *n* -s [ME, fr. MF *bourrelet*, fr. OF *borrelet*, fr. *borrel*, *bourel* cushion (dim. of *borre*, *bourre* padding, fr. LL *burra* shaggy cloth) + *-et* — more at BUREAU] **:** a padded roll of cloth formerly used for decoration on a child's cap or a woman's headdress

bur·let·ta \bür'led·ə, ,bər-\ *n* -s [It, dim. of *burla* joke] **:** a usu. entirely musical comic opera popular in England in the latter half of the 18th century

[1]**bur·ley** \'bərlē, 'bə̄l-,'bəil-, -li\ *n* -s *often cap* [prob. fr. the name *Burley*] **:** a thin-bodied air-cured tobacco varying in color from buff to chocolate, high in content of alkaloids and nitrogenous constituents, grown mainly in Kentucky and neighboring states, and used in cigarettes and to a lesser extent in plugs and smoking mixtures

[2]**burley** \"\ *or* **bur·ly** \"\ *n, pl* **burleys** *or* **burlies** [by shortening & alter.] **:** BURLESQUE

bur·li·ly \-lə̇lē, -li\ *adv* **:** in a burly manner

bur·li·ness \-lēnə̇s, -lin-\ *n* -ES **:** the quality or state of being burly

burling *pres part of* BURL

burls *pl of* BURL, *pres 3d sing of* BURL

[1]**bur·ly** \'bərlē, 'bə̄l-,'bəil-, -li\ *adj, usu* -ER/-EST [ME *burly*, *borlich;* prob. akin to OE *borlīce* extremely, excellently, OHG *burlīh* lofty; derivative fr. the root of OE *beran* to carry — more at BEAR] **1 :** strongly built **:** STOUT, STURDY ⟨~ 205-pound . . . blocking quarterback —Eddie Beachler⟩ ⟨his ~ ship slashed through 4-foot-thick ice —R.E.Byrd⟩ **2 :** heartily frank or direct esp. in manner **:** ROUGH-AND-READY, BLUFF, FORTHRIGHT ⟨an evocative story less ~ than the real thing but entertaining —E.A.Weeks⟩

[2]**burly** \"\ *n* -ES **:** one of burly frame; *specif* **:** TRAMP

bur·ma \'bərmə, 'bə̄mə, 'bəimə\ *adj, usu cap* [fr. *Burma*, country in southeast Asia] **:** of or from Burma **:** of the kind or style prevalent in Burma **:** BURMESE

burma mahogany *n, usu cap B* **:** the hard heavy wood of a Burmese tree (*Pentace burmanica*) of the family Tiliaceae — called also *thitka*

[1]**bur·man** \-mən\ *also* **bir·man** \"\ *n* -s *cap* [*Burma* (formerly also *Birma*) + E *-an*] **:** BURMESE; *specif* **:** a member of the Mongolian ethnic group in Burma

[2]**burman** *also* **birman** \"\ *adj, usu cap* **:** of or relating to Burma or the Burmans **:** BURMESE

bur·man·nia \(,)bər'manēə\ *n, cap* [NL, fr. Johannes *Burmann* †1779 Du. botanist + NL *-ia*] **:** a genus (the type of the family Burmanniaceae) of slender herbs native to warm regions and having leaves resembling scales and flowers with a 3-angled or 3-winged perianth

bur·man·ni·a·ce·ae \(,)bər,manē'āsē,ē\ *n pl, cap* [NL, fr. *Burmannia*, type genus + *-aceae*] **:** a family (order Orchidales) of chiefly tropical herbs having the leaves basal or arranged like bracts along the flower stalk and small flowers — **bur·man·ni·a·ceous** \-āshəs\ *adj*

burma padauk *n, usu cap B* **1 :** a tree (*Pterocarpus macrocarpus*) of India and Burma that yields a wood resembling mahogany **2 :** the wood of the Burma padauk

bur marigold *or* **burr marigold** *n* [*burr* (prickly envelope) + *marigold*] **:** any plant of the genus *Bidens* — called also *beggar-ticks*

[1]**bur·mese** \¦bər¦mēz, (')bə̄¦m-, (')bəi¦m-, -ēs *sometimes* ,bər'm-\ *adj, usu cap* [*Burma* + E *-ese*] **:** of or relating to Burma

[2]**burmese** \"\ *n, pl* **burmese** **1** *cap* **:** a native or inhabitant of Burma **2** *cap* **:** the language of the Burmans **3** *usu cap* **:** a late 19th century American opaque glassware of graduated color shading from yellow to pink **4** *usu cap* **:** BURMESE CAT

burmese cat *n, usu cap B* **1 :** a breed of cat resembling the Siamese but of solid and darker color and with orange rather than blue eyes **2 :** a cat of the Burmese breed

burmese lacquer *n, usu cap B* **:** a thick grayish liquid from the black-varnish tree (*Melanorrhoea usitata*) used as a varnish

burmese rosewood *n, usu cap B* **:** BURMA PADAUK

burmese ruby *n, often cap B* **:** PEONY 2

bur·mite \'bər,mīt\ *n* -s [*Burma*, its locality + E *-ite*] **:** a dark brown variety of amber found in Upper Burma

bur·mo-chinese \¦bər(,)mō +\ *adj, cap B&C* [*Burmo-* (fr. *Burma*) + *Chinese*] **:** of, relating to, or being the subregion of the Oriental biogeographic region that includes southeast Asia east of the Indian subregion except the Malay peninsula

[1]**burn** \'bərn, 'bə̄n\ *n* -s [ME *burn*, *bourne* — more at BOURN] **1** *Brit* **:** STREAM, BROOK, RIVULET **2** *chiefly Scot* **:** WATER; *esp* **:** water used in brewing

[2]**burn** \'bərn, 'bə̄n, 'bəin\ *vb* **burned** \-nd\ *or* **burnt** \-nt\ *or archaic* **brent** *or dial Brit* **brunt; burned** *or* **burnt** *or archaic* **brent** *or dial Brit* **brunt; burning; burns** [ME *birnen*, *brinnen*, *brennen*, *barnen*, fr. OE *byrnan* (intransitive), *bærnan* (transitive); akin to OHG *brinnan* to burn (intransitive), *brennen* to burn (transitive), ON *brenna*, *brinna* (intransitive), *brenna* (transitive), Goth *brinnan* (intransitive), *-brannjan* (transitive), L *fervēre* to boil, Gk *porphyrein* to surge, Skt *bhurati* he quivers] *vi* **1 a** (1) *of fire* **:** to consume fuel and give off light, heat, and gases ⟨a small fire ~s on the hearth⟩ (2) *of a light source* **:** to give off light ⟨headlights ~*ing* bright⟩ **b** *of fuel* **:** to be on fire **:** undergo combustion ⟨even green ash ~s well⟩ **c :** to contain a fire — used of stoves, furnaces, or other devices in which fire is customarily shielded ⟨the stove is ~*ing* brightly⟩ **2 a :** to be hot as if on fire ⟨the sand ~*ing* under the torrid sun⟩ **b :** to become excited by a specified emotion or feeling ⟨~*ing* with curiosity⟩: as (1) **:** to yearn ardently ⟨he ~*ed* to tell the story⟩ ⟨~*ing* to get out into the country⟩ (2) **:** to become excited sexually ⟨better to marry than to ~ —1 Cor 7:9 (AV)⟩ — often used with *for* (3) **:** to be or become very angry or utterly disgusted ⟨when I heard what he had done I really ~*ed*⟩ — usu. used with *up* ⟨they ~*ed* up for fair over his statement⟩ **3 a :** to appear as if on fire **:** glow brightly ⟨windows that ~ in the setting sun⟩ ⟨zinnias ~*ing* along the fence⟩ **b :** to produce a sensation of heat ⟨the blood ~*ed* in her cheeks⟩ **c :** to produce or undergo discomfort suggestive of the pain accompanying a burn ⟨iodine ~s so⟩ ⟨the old scar throbbed and ~*ed*⟩; *sometimes* **:** STING, TINGLE ⟨our ears are ~*ing* with the cold⟩ ⟨my arm ~*ed* where her softness had passed —Herbert Gold⟩ **4 a :** to become altered by the action of fire or heat ⟨coal ~*ing* in the stove⟩; *esp* **:** to become charred, scorched, seared, or consumed by excessive heat ⟨the potatoes ~*ed* to a crisp⟩ **b :** to become affected as if by fire: as (1) *of the skin* **:** to become reddened or irritated by or as if by exposure to sun or wind (2) *of herbage* **:** to become desiccated or withered (3) *of crop plants* **:** to wither or discolor as a result of chemical damage due to excessive or improper use of fertilizers or sprays and dusts (4) *of a rubber compound* **:** SCORCH **5 a :** to die by fire esp. through execution by burning **b :** to die in the electric chair **c :** to become damned **6 :** to force or make a way by or as if by burning — used with *into* ⟨her words ~*ed* into his memory⟩ **7 :** to be hot in search of an answer or object **8** *of a chemical element* **:** to undergo fission or fusion ⟨uranium ~s by absorption of neutrons⟩ ⟨hydrogen ~s to form helium⟩ ~ *vt* **1 a** *of fire* **:** to consume as fuel in burning — often used with adverbs or phrases of degree or direction ⟨their house was ~*ed* down last Saturday⟩ ⟨if lightning strikes, the haystack will be ~*ed* up in no time⟩ **b :** to cause to undergo combustion ⟨~ iron in oxygen⟩ **c :** to employ as a source of light or heat ⟨we shall ~ oil this year⟩ ⟨this hotel ~s gas for all cooking and heating⟩ **d** *of fires or firing devices* **:** to require or use as fuel ⟨this stove ~s coal or wood⟩ ⟨the new system ~s cheap heavy oils⟩ **2 :** to produce by the action of fire or heat ⟨you'll ~ a hole in your sleeve⟩ ⟨supplementing their income by ~*ing* charcoal for the smelters⟩ **3 a :** to subject to the action of or cause to be consumed by fire ⟨we ~*ed* up all the rubbish⟩ ⟨pile and ~ the brush as you go⟩: as (1) **:** to execute by burning ⟨heretics ~*ed* by the church⟩; *broadly, slang* **:** ELECTROCUTE (2) **:** to make an offering of (as incense) by burning (3) **:** to mark (as a criminal) by branding (4) *slang* **:** DAMN ⟨well, I'll be ~*ed*⟩ **b :** to injure by fire or heat **:** alter a property of by undue exposure to fire or heat **:** SCORCH, SCALD, BLISTER, SEAR, SINGE, CHAR ⟨~ steel in the forging⟩ ⟨grass ~*ed* brown by the sun⟩ ⟨the cook ~*ed* the roast⟩ ⟨look out, you'll ~ your fingers⟩ **c** (1) **:** to produce a comparable effect upon by an agent other than fire or heat (as by certain radiations, chemicals, or friction) ⟨the sun ~*ed* his shoulders badly⟩ ⟨overfertilization may ~ the plants⟩ ⟨his face chapped and ~*ed* by the wind⟩ (2) *of a rubber compound* **:** SCORCH **d :** to subject to the action of fire or heat for some economic purpose (as for the alteration or elimination of undesired qualities); *specif* **:** to transform by the action of controlled fire or heat ⟨~ clay to bricks⟩ ⟨~ wood into charcoal⟩ — compare CALCINE **4 a** *obs* **:** to inflame with emotion or passion **b** *slang* **:** IRRITATE, ANNOY ⟨the constant bickering ~*ed* her⟩ — usu. used with *up* ⟨he ~s me up⟩ **c** *slang* **:** CHEAT, BEFOOL, DO ⟨he surely *burnt* me over that deal⟩ **5 a :** to wear out **:** DIMINISH, EXHAUST ⟨his anger is ~*ing* him up⟩ **b :** WASTE, SQUANDER, DISSIPATE — usu. used as an infinitive ⟨money to ~⟩ **c :** to traverse or cause to traverse at high speed — usu. used with *up* ⟨~ up the road⟩ ⟨~*ed* up the international cables —Cameron Hawley⟩ **6 a :** to touch or move (a piece) in a manner forbidden by the rules of a game **b :** to expose and then turn (a playing card) face up on the bottom of the pack **c :** to throw (as a baseball) very hard ⟨he ~*ed* a fast one over the plate⟩ **7 :** to join (pieces of metal) by flowing molten metal through or over the joint to be fused until adjacent surfaces soften and unite with the added metal — often used with *in*, *on*, or *together;* compare LEAD-BURN **8 :** to cause (a plating) to become dark or rough because of change in physical or chemical character usu. by exposure to excessive current **9 :** to cause (a chemical element) to burn

syn CHAR, SEAR, SCORCH, SINGE: BURN is a general term usable in any situation in which fire or heat has had a positive destructive effect and consequently interchangeable with any of the following except SINGE in some of its uses. CHAR indicates a burning that reduces to carbon or to cinder ⟨only a few *charred* planks remaining after the conflagration⟩ ⟨a third-degree burn occurs when the flesh is *charred*⟩ SEAR typically indicates burning through quick exposure to high heat, with resulting cauterizing, closing of tissues, deadening, branding, or unforgettably impressing ⟨*searing* the tissues with an electric needle⟩ ⟨the roast was first *seared*, then cooked slowly⟩ ⟨the *searing* effect of the first atomic bombs⟩ SCORCH indicates superficial burning of exposed surface or area, burning which changes color or texture without consuming ⟨the paint on the garage was *scorched* by the bonfire⟩ ⟨the potatoes at the bottom *scorched* when the pan went dry⟩ SINGE implies quick passing over or otherwise exposing to a flame with extremely superficial burning, often with burning only of an integument like hair or feathers ⟨some of the coats on the rack were *singed*⟩ ⟨his hair was *singed* when the gas flared up⟩ ⟨to *singe* a chicken before cooking it⟩

— **burn a hole in one's pocket** *of money* **:** to get itself spent quickly — **burn daylight** *archaic* **:** to make a light before it is dark; *also* **:** to waste time or energy — **burn one's bridges** *also* **burn one's boats :** to cut off all means of retreat — **burn one's ears** *slang* **:** to rebuke strongly **:** call down **:** BLISTER — **burn one's fingers :** to get into unexpected trouble, embarrassment, or distress (as by interfering in the affairs of others or by an injudicious or rash venture) — **burn the books :** to act as a suppressive force esp. by withholding knowledge that would affect the actions of others — **burn the candle at both ends :** to be unreasonably prodigal with one's material or physical resources — **burn the midnight oil :** to work or study far into the night — **burn the water :** to spear salmon by torchlight — **burn the wind :** to go speedily; *also* **:** dissipate rapidly

[3]**burn** \"\ *n* -s **1 :** an injury, damage, or effect produced by burning (as with fire): **a :** bodily injury resulting from exposure to heat, caustics, electricity, or certain radiations, marked by varying degrees of skin destruction and hyperemia often with the formation of watery blisters and in severe cases by charring of the tissues, and classified according to the extent and degree of the injury as first degree, second degree, or third degree **b** (1) **:** BRAND 3a(1) (2) **:** BRANDING IRON **c :** a burned area ⟨a ~ on the table top⟩; *esp* **:** an area denuded of vegetation by burning produced deliberately (as in land-

clearing) or by chance ⟨poplars coming in on an old ~⟩ **d** : an abrasion (as of the skin) having the appearance of a burn ⟨friction ~s⟩ ⟨cold ~⟩ ⟨a floor marred by rubber ~⟩ **e** : a burning sensation or appearance ⟨the ~ of iodine on a cut⟩ ⟨the ruddy ~ of her hair⟩ **2 a** : the process, operation, or result of burning ⟨bricks properly baked have a good ~⟩ **b** : an instance of burning; *specif* : burning of vegetation from the surface of land ⟨the rate of deterioration after a severe ~ was about the same for spruce, balsam, and jackpine —*Biol. Abstracts*⟩ **3** : the capacity of ignited tobacco to continue burning without producing a flame **4** : a worn place on a railroad rail caused by the friction of spinning engine drivers **5** *slang* : ANGER; *esp* : increasing fury — used chiefly in the phrase *slow burn*

burn·able \-nəbəl\ *adj or n* : COMBUSTIBLE

burn away *vi* : to dissipate as though consumed by fire ⟨the haze has *burned away*⟩ ~ *vt* : to eliminate by or as if by burning ⟨his style *burns away* overlocalized fact —*Saturday Rev.*⟩

burn·beat \'bərn,bēt, -,bāt\ *vt* [2*burn* + *beat* (turf)] : to pare off and burn the sod or turf from in order to improve (sour or soggy land) for cultivation

burn blue *n* : a pale blue to purplish blue

burned *past of* BURN

burned-out *or* **burnt-out** \'=ˌ=\ *adj* [fr. past part. of *burn out*] **1** : debilitated or excessively worn by excessive consumption of energy or physical resources **2** *of a negative or a print* : overexposed so that detail is lacking in the highlights

burned-over *also* **burnt-over** \'=ˌ==\ *adj, of land* : freed of vegetation by fire

burn·er \'bərnər; 'bənə(r, 'bəin-\ *n* -s [ME *brennere*, fr. *brennen* to burn + *-ere* -er — more at BURN] **1** : one that burns: **a** : a person whose occupation involves burning or the use of heat in the preparation or production of some desired product: as (1) : a worker in charge of a kiln in which brick or tile is burned — called also *baker* (2) *also* **burner man** : a worker who burns a mineral substance (as lime, ground stone, or filter clay) to alter its properties in some desired manner (3) : a worker who cuts metals with a flame-cutting torch **b** : a device for burning some particular material: as (1) : the part of a lamp, gas stove, or other fluid-burning device where the flame is produced; *broadly* : a device for consuming fluid fuel including accessories concerned with such matters as firing, fuel distribution, and vaporization and being typically a compact unit attached to or incorporated in a boiler, stove, furnace, or engine (2) : INCINERATOR (3) : a blowtorch or other device used for softening old paint to facilitate its removal (4) : an ornamental vessel usu. of clay, porcelain, or metal in which incense is burned **2** : a furnace for burning sulfur or a sulfide ore (as pyrite) to produce sulfur dioxide and other gases (as for making sulfuric acid or sulfite pulp)

burner man *n* : a worker who burns or heats something: as **a** : one that burns up sawmill waste **b** : one in charge of the mobile kettle in which asphalt paving material is kept soft by an oil flame — called also *kettleman* **c** : BURNER 1a(2)

bur·net \'bərˈnet, bər'net, 'bərnət\ *n* -s [ME, fr. OF *burnete*, *brunete*, fr. *brun* brown — more at BRUNET] **1** : black or brown woolen fabric used for clothing from the 13th to the 16th century **2 a** : BURNET SAXIFRAGE **b** : any plant of the genus *Sanguisorba*: as (1) : a New World herb (*S. canadensis*) (2) : SALAD BURNET **3** : BURNET MOTH

burnet bloodwort *n* : SALAD BURNET

burnet moth *n* : any of numerous moths of the family Zygaenidae; *esp* : a diurnal European moth (*Zygaena filipendula*) with crimson spots on the wings

burnet rose *n* : SCOTCH ROSE

burnet saxifrage *n* : a European herb (*Pimpinella saxifraga*) with pinnate leaves and white flowers and an aromatic root

bur·nett·ize \(,)bər'ned·,īz, (')bərnə,tīz\ *vt* -ED/-ING/-S [Sir William *Burnett* †1861 Scot. physician, inventor of the process + E *-ize*] : to impregnate (as wood or fabrics) with zinc chloride solution under pressure to prevent decay

bur·nett salmon \'bərˈnet, bər'net, 'bərnət\ *n, usu cap B* [*Burnett* river, Queensland, Australia] : BARRAMUNDA a

bur·ne·win \'bərnə,win\ *var of* BURN-THE-WIND

burn·ie \'bərnē\ *n* -s [1*burn* + *-ie*] *Scot* : a little stream

burnier *comparative of* BURNY

burniest *superlative of* BURNY

burn in *vt* **1** : to heat (a metal photoengraving plate) after development of the printed image until the enamel carbonizes and becomes acid-resisting **2** : to increase the density of (certain areas of a photographic print) during enlarging by giving extra exposure — compare DODGE

1burning *adj* [ME *brenninge*, fr. pres. part. of *brennen* to burn] **1 a** : on fire : ALIGHT, AFLAME, IGNITED ⟨the house is ~⟩ **b** : excessively hot : FIERY, ARDENT, SHINING, GLOWING ⟨under a ~ sun⟩ ⟨a ~ and dedicated spirit drove her⟩ **2 a** : affecting with or as if with heat : HEATING ⟨a ~ fever⟩ **b** : INFLAMING, EXCITING ⟨a ~ enthusiasm⟩; *also* : INTENSE ⟨~ wrath⟩ **c** : of fundamental and immediate import : URGENT ⟨a ~ need⟩ ⟨the ~ issue of the day⟩ **d** *of sensations* : like that produced by a burn ⟨a ~ sensation on the tongue⟩ **3** : prominently in view : GLARING, SHOCKING — used esp. of unpleasing states or conditions ⟨a ~ shame⟩ ⟨a ~ disgrace to his family⟩

2burning *n* -s [ME *brenninge*, fr. gerund of *brennen*] **1 a** : a consuming or being consumed by fire or heat **b** : the state or sensation of being on fire, as if on fire, or excessively heated **2** : subjection to the action of heat or of an agent that burns : COMBUSTION: as **a** : the calcining esp. of limestone or ore **b** : the heating of ores without access to air preparatory to smelting **c** : a firing of ceramic materials (as for maturing, glazing, fixing colors) **d** : the sterilizing of soil for tobacco beds by burning piles of brush and wood on the area **3** : the effect produced on something by subjection to the action of heat or of an agent that burns: as **a** : the cutting or wearing caused by friction (as from blown sand); *esp* : the roughening or discoloration of material from heat produced in machining or abrasive finishing **b** : vulcanization by heat **c** : a withered brownish appearance of foliage (as in hopperburn or tipburn) **4** *obs* : an inflammatory disease; *esp* : a venereal disease

burning bush *n* [so called fr. the bush in Exod 3:2 that was on fire but was not consumed] : any of several plants: as **a** : 2WAHOO a **b** : FRAXINELLA **c** : ARTILLERY PLANT **d** : SUMMER CYPRESS

burning ghat *n* : the space in a ghat (as at the head) where the Hindus cremate their dead

burning glass *n* : a positive lens for producing intense heat by converging the sun's rays approximately to the principal focus of the lens the point of convergence being a very small image of the sun

burning index *n* : a number which is determined from the moisture content of a forest, wind speed, and other factors that affect burning conditions and from which ease of ignition and behavior of a forest fire may be estimated

burn·ing·ly *adv* [ME *brenningly*, fr. *brenning*, *brenninge* burning + *-ly* — more at BURNING] : in a burning manner : with heat : ARDENTLY

burning mountain *n* : VOLCANO

burning nettle *n* **1** : SMALL NETTLE **2** : ROMAN NETTLE

burning oil *n* : an oil used for burning; *specif* : KEROSENE

burning point *n* : FIRE POINT

burning time *n* : the time during which the propellant charge of a rocket engine is fully consumed

burning torch *n* : a gas torch with an intensely hot oxidizing flame that is used for cutting metal by burning

burning-wood \'==ˌ=\ *n* : LEATHERWOOD 1b

1bur·nish \'bərnish, 'bən-, 'bəin-, -nēsh, *esp in pres part* -nəsh\ *vb* -ED/-ING/-ES [ME *burnischen*, fr. MF *bruniss-*, stem of *brunir* to make brown, burnish, fr. OF, fr. *brun* brown, shining, fr. ML *brunus*, of Gmc origin; akin to OHG *brūn* brown, shining — more at BROWN] *vt* **1** : to make shiny or lustrous : POLISH; *specif* : to polish by friction with something hard and smooth ⟨~ metal⟩ ⟨*burnished* leather⟩ **2** *of a deer* : to rub (as the head) so as to remove the dead velvet and polish the antlers **3** : to rub with a burnisher: as **a** : to fix with a burnisher ⟨~ a glass into a metal rim⟩ **b** : to make an area of (a halftone printing plate) darker by rubbing down the dots and thus enlarging them ~ *vi* : to take a polish : become lustrous under burnishing

2burnish \"\ *n* -ES : a polished surface : superficial luster; *also* : POLISH 4

burnished *adj* [ME *burnisched*, fr. past part. of *burnischen*] : having a surface like that produced by burnishing : LUSTROUS ⟨the ~ light of the evening sun —F. Tennyson Jesse⟩

burnished gold *n* : a dark orange yellow to strong yellowish brown — called also *pinchbeck brown*

burnished straw *n* : a light brown that is yellower and deeper than blush, deeper and yellower than alesan, and redder and deeper than cork

bur·nish·er \-shə(r)\ *n* -s **1** : a worker employed in burnishing ⟨a shoe ~⟩ **2** : a tool, variously shaped, with a hard smooth rounded end or surface (as of steel, ivory, or agate) used in smoothing, polishing, turning an edge, or other manipulation by rubbing

burnishing die *n* : one of a set of cutting dies whose matrix is a little smaller at the bottom than at the cutting edge so that the edge of the work forced through the die becomes burnished

burn off *vb* [2*burn* + *off*] *vt* **1** : to clear up : break away : DISSIPATE — used of weather phenomena (as fog, dew, clouds) that are regarded as adverse and particularly subject to the sun's warmth and often with *it* as an indefinite nominative ⟨it will *burn off* before noon⟩ **2 a** : to remove (as debris on a surface) by burning ⟨I want to *burn off* the rest of the brush this fall⟩ **b** : to free (a piece of land) of unwanted vegetation or plant residues ⟨we'll *burn off* the north field the next time it rains⟩ ~ *vi, of the sun* : to cause watery vapor (as clouds or fog) to dissipate

burn-off \'=ˌ=\ *n* -s [*burn off*] : an act or process of removing unwanted material (as old paint or superfluous metal) by burning; *sometimes* : material so removed

bur·nous *or* **bur·noose** \(,)bər'nüs, '=ˌ=\ *n, pl* **burnouses** *or* **burnooses** [F *burnous*, fr. Ar *burnus*, fr. Gk *birros* cloak with a hood, fr. (assumed) L *birrus* (whence LL *birrus*) — more at BIRETTA] **1 a** : a long loose flowing hooded cloak of wool woven in one piece and worn by Arabs and Moors **2** : an outer garment for women based on the design of the burnous

burnous 1

burn out *vb* [2*burn* + *out*] *vt* **1** : to destroy or obliterate by fire or heat ⟨we found that we had *burned out* a bearing⟩ **2** : to drive out or destroy the property of by fire — usu. passive ⟨we were *burnt out* just before Christmas⟩ ⟨the store was completely *burnt out*⟩ **3 a** : to cause to fail, wear out, or become exhausted by making excessive demands on energy, strength, or resources ⟨he will *burn* himself *out* unless he gets more sleep⟩ **b** : to spoil the condition of (livestock) esp. for breeding by too rich feeding or overfeeding ~ *vi* **1** : to cease to be in a condition to perform a normal function by reason of usu. prolonged exposure to fire or heat ⟨the bulb in the kitchen light just *burned out*⟩ ⟨the grate in the furnace is nearly *burned out*⟩ **2** : to fail, wear out, or become exhausted by reason of excessive demands on energy, strength, or resources ⟨at this rate you'll *burn out* before you're 30⟩ ⟨the best soil *burns out* under constant heavy cropping⟩

burnout \'=ˌ=\ *n* -s [*burn out*] **1** : a fire that consumes all the flammable contents (as of a building); *broadly* : a large and destructive fire **2** : a breakdown of an electrical circuit caused by fusion or combustion (as of a conducting element or insulation) resulting from abnormal increase in temperature **3** : an area of soil from which the organic material has been removed by fire or other agency leaving usu. a distinct depression of unfertile mineral soil **4** : the moment at which a jet or rocket motor exhausts its fuel

burn-out *var of* BURNT-OUT

burnover \'=ˌ==\ *n* -s [*burn over*, v., fr. 2*burn* + *over*] : an imperfectly burned brick that requires reburning

burns *pl of* BURN, *pres 3d sing of* BURN

1burns·ian \'bərnzēən\ *adj, usu cap* [Robert *Burns* †1796 Scot. poet + E *-ian*] : of, relating to, or like the poet Robert Burns or his writings

2burnsian \"\ *n* -s *usu cap* : a devotee of the poet Burns

burnside \'=ˌ=\ *n* [ME, fr. 1*burn* + *side*] *Brit* : BROOKSIDE

burn·sides \'bərn,sīdz, 'bən-, 'bəin-\ *n pl* [after Ambrose E. *Burnside* †1881 Am. general, who wore them] : SIDE WHISKERS; *esp* : full muttonchop whiskers

burns meter *or* **burns stanza** \'bərnz-, 'bənz-, 'bəinz-\ *n, cap B* : a stanza often used by Robert Burns and other Scottish poets consisting of six lines rhyming *aaabab* of which the fourth and sixth are regularly iambic dimeters and the others iambic tetrameters

burnt *adj* [fr. past part. of 2*burn*] : consumed or altered by or as if by fire or heat: as **a** *of iron or steel* : rendered crumbly and unfit for welding or otherwise damaged by excessive heat **b** *of colors* : giving a somewhat dull appearance as though scorched ⟨~ carnelian⟩ **c** *of gems* : altered in color by heating

burnt almond *n* **1** : roasted sweet almond — usu. used in pl. **2** : COCONUT BROWN

burnt alum *n* : alum that has been dried at 200° C and powdered, being a caustic used to remove dead tissues — called also *dried alum*

burnt brass *n, obs* : COPPER SULFATE

burnt carmine *or* **burnt crimson lake** *or* **burnt lake** *n* : a moderate to deep red that is slightly bluer than cadmium purple — called also *old red*, *purple lake*

burn-the-wind \'=ˌ=ˌ=\ *n, chiefly Scot* : BLACKSMITH

burnt iron *n* : iron that has been subjected in the Bessemer or the open-hearth process to excessive oxidation following the removal of impurities

burnt italian earth *or* **burnt italian ocher** *n, often cap I* : BURNT SIENNA 2

burnt lime *n* : LIME 2a

burnt ocher *n* **1** : a brown-red pigment made by calcining yellow ocher **2** : a moderate reddish orange that is yellower and duller than crab apple and yellower and darker than flamingo — called also *light red*

burnt offering *or* **burnt sacrifice** *n* : a sacrifice offered to a deity and burned typically on or at an altar

burnt orange *n* : a moderate reddish orange that is yellower and duller than crab apple, yellower and darker than flamingo, yellower than burnt ocher, and deeper than average persimmon (sense 3a)

1burnt-out *var of* BURNED-OUT

2burnt-out \'=ˌ=\ *or* **burn-out** \'=ˌ=\ *adj* [*burnt-out* fr. past part. of *burn out*; *burn-out* fr. *burn out*] **1** *of machine-made laces* : made by embroidering on a sheer foundation cloth that is later destroyed by chemicals **2** *of fabrics with two different yarns* : having patterns formed by the destruction of one yarn by chemicals

burnt-over *var of* BURNED-OVER

burnt roman ocher *n, often cap R* : OCHER ORANGE

burnt rose *n* : POMPEII

burnt russet *n* : WALLFLOWER 4

burnt sienna *n* **1** : a yellowish red to reddish brown pigment made by calcining raw sienna and used esp. in stains and glazes and as an artist's color **2** : a dark reddish orange that is yellower and less strong than average lacquer and yellower and slightly lighter than ocher red — called also *burnt Italian earth*

burnt terre verte *n* : VANDYKE BROWN

burnt umber *n* **1** : a dark brown pigment made by calcining raw umber and used esp. in stains and paints and as an artist's color **2** : a moderate brown that is yellower, lighter, and stronger than bay or tobacco, yellower and deeper than toast brown, redder, lighter, and stronger than coffee, and stronger and slightly redder than chestnut brown — called also *manganese velvet brown*, *umber*, *velvet brown*

burntweed \'=ˌ=\ *n* [so called fr. its growing in burned-over areas] **1** : FIREWEED **2** : HART'S-TONGUE 1

burnt work *n* : PYROGRAPHY

burnup \'=ˌ=\ *n* -s [fr. *burn up*, v.] **1** : the amount of fuel destroyed (as in a nuclear reactor) ⟨uranium ~⟩ ⟨a fuel ~ of five percent —Richard Stephenson⟩ **2** : the heating and vaporization of a rocket or satellite due to air resistance

burnut \'=ˌ=\ *n* -s [*burr* (prickly envelope) + *nut*; fr. its spiny fruit] : any plant of the genus *Tribulus*

burnwood \'=ˌ=\ *n* : LEATHERWOOD 1b

burny \'bərnē\ *adj* -ER/-EST [2*burn* + *-y*] : inclined to burn ⟨a ~ liqueur⟩ : suggestive of burning ⟨a ~ odor⟩

1bu·ro *like* BUREAU, *or* ='rō\ *n* -s [Russ *byuro*, fr. F *bureau* — more at BUREAU] : BUREAU 3b

2bu·ro \'bü(,)rō\ *n* -s [Tag] : a Philippine dish of fish prepared with boiled rice, salt, and spicy seasonings

bur oak *or* **burr oak** *n* : a useful and ornamental oak (*Quercus macrocarpa*) of central and eastern No. America with ovoid acorns enclosed in very large fringed cups and tough close-grained durable wood — called also *mossy-cup oak*

bu·row's solution \'bü(,)rōz-\ *n, usu cap B* [after Karl A. *Burow* †1874 Ger. surgeon] : a solution of aluminum acetate used as an antiseptic and astringent

1burp \'bərp, 'bəp, 'bəip\ *n* -s [imit.] : BELCH

2burp \"\ *vb* -ED/-ING/-S *vi* : BELCH ~ *vt* : to help (a baby) expel gas from the stomach esp. by patting or rubbing the back

bur parsley *n* : a spreading hairy Old World annual herb (*Anthriscus neglecta*) that is closely related to wild chervil

burp gun *n* : MACHINE PISTOL

bur·qa \'bu̇rkə\ *n* -s [Hindi *burqa'* — more at BURKA] : BURKA

1burr \'bər, +V 'bər-; 'bə, +V 'bər- *also* 'bər\ *n* -s [ME *burre*; akin to OSw *borre* bur, OE *byrst* bristle — more at BRISTLE] **1** *usu* **bur a** : any rough or prickly envelope of a fruit whether a pericarp, a persistent calyx, or an involucre: as (1) : the husk of a chestnut (2) : the hull of a mature cotton boll (3) : the cone of a hop plant at the time of flowering **b** : any weed that bears burs **c** : plant debris in raw wool **2 a** : something that resembles a bur (as in sticking or clinging) ⟨a ~ in the throat⟩ **b** : HANGER-ON ⟨hang off thou cat, thou ~ —Shak.⟩ **3** [ME *burwhe* circle, perh. alter. of *burgh* borough — more at BOROUGH] **a** *obs* : a broad iron ring on a tilting lance fixed just below the grip to prevent slipping of the hand **b** : a small washer put on the end of a rivet before swaging it down **c** : a disk or cylinder of metal punched from a sheet **d** : NUT 3 **4** : the external part of the ear; *esp* : the irregular inner part of the pinna of the ear (as of a dog) **5** : the circular boss at the base of an antler or horn **6 a** : any rounded knot or excrescence on a tree : BURL **b** : lumber or veneer cut from such a burr **7** : a thin ridge or area of roughness produced in cutting or shaping metal (as in drilling, turning, or blanking): as **a** : the fin left on a casting at the mold junctions; *also* : a thin protrusion of excess metal on a newly cast slug or piece of type **b** : edges of metal raised above the face of an engraved plate by the graving tool **8 a** : a trilled uvular *r* as used by some speakers of English esp. in northern England and in Scotland **b** : a tongue-point trill that is the usual Scottish *r* **c** : a pronunciation regarded as odd and uncouth **9 a** *usu* **bur** : a small rotary cutting tool often with fluted edges arranged spirally that is used on a powered apparatus (as a dental drill) **b** : a small circular saw **c** *or* **burr chisel** : a chisel with three cutting edges that is used to clear the burrs from machine-cut corners **d** : a wheel with projections for forming loops between needles in a circular knitting machine **10** : a rough humming sound : WHIR, BIRR

2burr \"\ *vb* -ED/-ING/-S *vi* **1** : to speak with a burr **2** : to make a whirring sound ~ *vt* **1** : to pronounce with a burr ⟨~*ed* his *r*'s⟩ **2 a** : to form into a projecting edge **b** : to remove burrs from (a hole or sharp edge)

3burr \"\ *also* **bur** \"\ *n* -s [perh. fr. 1*burr*; fr. its roughness] **1** : BUHRSTONE **2** : a knob or boss of siliceous rock in softer formations **3** : WHETSTONE **4** : 1CLINKER 2a, 2b

4burr \"\ *also* **bur** \"\ *n* -s [Hindi *bar*, fr. Prakrit *vaḍa*, fr. Skt *vṛta* covered, surrounded, fr. *vṛṇoti* he covers, surrounds — more at WEIR] *India* : BANYAN 2

bur·ra \bə(,)rä\ *adj* [Hindi *baṛā*, fr. Skt *vṛddha*, fr. *vardhate* he increases — more at ORTH-] *India* : GREAT — used chiefly in phrases as a title of respect and specif. to designate a father or elder brother or a chief officer ⟨~ sahib⟩

bur·rage \'bərij\ *n* -s [ME *borage* — more at BORAGE] *archaic* : BORAGE

bur-ragweed \'=ˌ=ˌ=\ *n* [1*burr* + *ragweed*] : FRANSERIA 2

burr artichoke *n* : ARTICHOKE 1

bur·ra·wang \'bərə,waŋ\ *n* -s [prob. after Mt. *Burrawang*, New South Wales, Australia] : an Australian plant of the genus *Macrozamia* (esp. *M. spiralis*)

burr clover *var of* BUR CLOVER

burred \'bərd, 'bəd\ *adj* [1*burr* + *-ed*] **1** : rough and prickly ⟨a ~ edge of metal⟩ **2** : enclosed in a bur ⟨~ fruits⟩

bur reed *n* : any plant of the genus *Sparganium* having elongated linear leaves and globose fruits resembling burs

bur-reed family *n* : SPARGANIACEAE

burr·er \'bər·ə(r) *also* 'bərə(r\ *n* -s : a worker who removes burr or burrs from textile fibers or metal objects

burrfish *also* **burfish** \'=ˌ=\ *n* : a spiny globefish : PORCUPINE FISH

burrhel *var of* BHARAL

burrier *comparative of* BURRY

bur·ri·er's oak \'bərēə(r)z-\ *n, usu cap B* [prob. fr. the name *Burrier*] : BARTRAM OAK

burriest *superlative of* BURRY

burring *n* -s [fr. gerund of 2*burr*] : the mechanical removal of burs from wool during processing

burrio *n* -ES [MF *bourreau*, prob. fr. *bourrer* to mistreat, beat — more at BOURRÉE] *obs Scot* : EXECUTIONER

bur·ri·to \bə'rēd·(,)ō\ *n* -s [AmerSp, fr. Sp, little donkey, dim. of *burro*] : any of several small grunts of tropical American waters

burrknot \'=ˌ=\ *n* : a rough excrescence often present on the trunk or roots of certain trees and characteristic of some varieties that was formerly thought to be a form of crown gall but is now believed to be nonpathogenic

burrlike \'=ˌ=\ *adj* : like a burr (as in being prickly)

burr marigold *var of* BUR MARIGOLD

burr medic *n, Austral* : a bur clover (*Medicago denticulata*) with serrated leaf margins

burr mill *n* : a mill (as a coffee mill) that grinds by means of a steel burr resembling in principle the old-fashioned millstone

bur·ro \'bər·(,)ō, 'bə·(,)rō, -ər·ə,-ə·rə *also* 'bu̇(,)rō *or* -u̇rə, *often* -r·əw *or* -·rəw+V\ *n* -s [Sp, irreg. fr. *borrico* donkey, fr. LL *burricus* small horse] : DONKEY; *esp* : a small donkey used as a pack animal or that is feral in the southwestern U.S. and adjacent Mexico

burr oak *var of* BUR OAK

burro-back \'=ˌ=ˌ=\ *adv* : on the back of a burro

burrobrush \'=ˌ=ˌ=\ *n* : a spreading-branched composite shrub (*Hymenoclea monogyra*) with filiform leaves and numerous small unisexual flower heads in mixed panicles that is common on rangeland in the western U.S. — called also *arrowwood*

burrobush \'==ˌ=\ *n* [*burro* + *bush*; fr. its use as food by donkeys] : BUR SAGE

burro deer *n* : MULE DEER

burro grass *n* : a tufted grass (*Scleropogon brevifolius*) of semiarid plains and open valleys of the southwestern U.S. with wiry stolons, leaves that are flat and crowded at the base, and spikelets with long twisted awns

1burrough *obs var of* BOROUGH

2burrough *obs var of* BURROW

1bur·row \'bər·(,)ō, 'bə·(,)rō, -ər·ə,-ə·rə, *often* -ər·əw *or* -ə·rəw +V\ *n* -s [ME *borugh*, *borow*, perh. fr. *borugh* borough — more at BOROUGH] **1** : a hole in the ground made by certain animals (as rabbits) for shelter and habitation **2** : PASSAGE, GALLERY; *esp* : one formed in or under the skin by the warble or a parasite (as the mite of scabies or a foreign hookworm) **3** : a miserable dwelling : HOVEL, HOLE

2burrow \"\ *vb* -ED/-ING/-S *vt* **1** *archaic* : to hide (as oneself) in or as if in a burrow — usu. passive **2** : to produce like a burrow : construct by digging and tunneling ⟨~*ed* a dwelling in the side of the hill⟩ ⟨he can ~ passages underneath a river bed —F.M.Godfrey⟩ **3** : to pass or extend like a burrow ⟨the tunnel ~*ed* its way under the mountain⟩ **4** : to make a motion suggestive of burrowing with : SNUGGLE, NESTLE ⟨she ~*s* her grubby hand into mine⟩ ~ *vi* **1** : to conceal oneself in or lodge in a mean abode — used chiefly of persons **2 a** *of an animal* : to dig a burrow ⟨rats ~*ing* in the wall⟩ **b** : TUNNEL, DELVE, DIG ⟨he ~*ed* into his records⟩ ⟨~*ing* through the mass of reports⟩ **3 a** *of an animal* : to progress through the earth by means of digging movements ⟨many worms ~ freely in the surface soil⟩ **b** : to form and move along a tunnel in a specified direction ⟨they ~*ed* under the wall⟩ **c** : to enter into as though through a hidden burrow ⟨Communists ~*ing* into the labor unions⟩ **4** : to make a motion suggestive of burrowing : SNUGGLE, NESTLE ⟨~*ed* against his back for warmth⟩

³burrow \"\ *n* -S [ME *borough, borgh,* prob. alter. of *bergh* barrow — more at BARROW] *archaic* **:** BARROW, HILLOCK

bur·ro·weed \ˈ==,=\ *n* [*burro* + *weed*] **1 :** a weed (*Suaeda moquini*) of the family Chenopodiaceae growing on alkaline lands in the southwestern U.S. **2 :** IODINE BUSH **3 :** BUR SAGE **4 :** any of several rayless goldenrods

bur·row·er \ˈbərəwə(r), ˈbə·rəw-; ˈbərōə(r), ˈbə·rō-\ *n* -S **:** one that burrows; *specif* **:** an animal that makes a hole underground and lives in it

burrower bug *also* **burrowing bug** *n* **:** any of numerous largely subterranean usu. dark-colored small bugs constituting the family Cydnidae and resembling beetles

burrowing anemone *n* **:** any of various sea anemones that burrow in muddy or sandy sea bottoms

burrowing nematode *n* **:** a soil nematode (*Radopholus similis*) attacking the roots of sugarcane in Hawaii

burrowing owl *n* **:** a small chiefly terrestrial owl (*Speotyto cunicularia*) of western No. America, Florida, and So. America living in burrows (as those abandoned by prairie dogs)

burrowing shrimp *n* **:** GHOST SHRIMP

bur·row–town *also* **bur·rows–town** \ˈbə·rə(z),tün\ *n* [*burrow-town* fr. ME *borwtown,* fr. *borw, borugh* borough (fr. OE *burg, burh* fortress) + *town; burrows-town* fr. ME (northern dial.) *borowstown,* prob. fr. *borows* (gen. of *borow* borough, fr. OE *burg, burh*) + *town* — more at BOROUGH] *Scot* **:** BOROUGH

burrs *pl of* BURR, *pres 3d sing of* BURR

burrstone *var of* BUHRSTONE

bur·ry \ˈbər\|ē, \|i *also* ˈbər\|\ *adj* -ER/-EST [ME, fr. *burre* + *-y* — more at BURR] **1 :** abounding in or containing burs ⟨~ wool⟩ **2 :** like a bur **:** PRICKLY **3** *of speech* **:** characterized by a burr

¹bur·sa \ˈbərsə\ *n, pl* **bursas** \-səz\ *or* **bur·sae** \-,sē, -,sī\ [NL, fr. ML *bursa* bag, purse — more at PURSE] **1 :** a pouch-shaped bodily cavity **:** SAC: as **a :** any of the small serous sacs enclosing viscid fluid and being interposed between moving parts (as tendons and bony prominences) where they lessen friction effects **b :** BURSA COPULATRIX **2 :** a residence hall for students at a medieval university

²bur·sa \(ˈ)bu̇rˈsä, ˈbu̇rsə\ *adj, usu cap* [fr. *Bursa, Turkey*] **:** of or from the city of Bursa, Turkey **:** of the kind or style prevalent in Bursa

bursa cop·u·la·trix \-,käpyəˈlā·triks\ *n* [NL, fr. *bursa* + *copulatrix* of copulation, fr. LL, she that unites, fem. of *copulator* he that unites, fr. L *copulatus,* past part. of *copulare* to bind, join, unite — more at COPULATE] **1 :** a pouch receiving spermatozoa during copulation (as in certain insects) **2 :** a thin fan or bell-shaped expansion of the cuticle of the tail of many male nematode worms that functions as a clasper during copulation

bur sage *n* [¹*burr* + *sage*] **:** a plant of the genus *Franseria*; *esp* **:** a low spiny shrub (*F. dumosa*) having the leaves densely covered with whitish hairs and being widely distributed in desert regions of the southwestern U.S. and adjacent Mexico

bur·sal \ˈbərsəl\ *adj* [NL *bursa* + E *-al*] **:** of, relating to, or affecting a bursa

bursa of fa·bri·cius \-fəˈbrish(ē)əs\ *usu cap F* [trans. of NL *bursa Fabricii,* fr. *bursa* + *Fabricii,* gen. of *Fabricius* (Johan C. *Fabricius* †1808 Dan. entomologist)] **:** a blind glandular sac that opens into the cloaca of birds and functions in immunoglobulin production

bur·sar \ˈbərsər, -,sär; ˈbəsə(r, ˈbəis-, -,sä(r\ *n* -S [ML *bursarius,* fr. *bursa* purse + L *-arius* -ary, n. suffix] **1 :** an administrative officer (as of a monastery or college) in charge of funds **:** TREASURER, PURSER; *sometimes* **:** an officer or other agent supervising material as distinguished from intellectual or spiritual matters **2** *chiefly Scot* **:** a student receiving a scholarship **3 :** a student living in a bursa

bur·sar·i·al \(ˈ)bərˈsa(a)rēəl\ *adj* [ML *bursarius* + E *-al*] **:** of or relating to a bursar or bursary

bur·sar·ship *pronunc at* BURSAR+,ship\ *n* -S **:** BURSARY 2

bur·sa·ry \ˈbərsərē, ˈbəs-, ˈbəis-\ *n* -ES [ML *bursaria,* fr. *bursa* + L *-aria* -ary, n. suffix] **1 :** the treasury of a college or monastery **2 :** a sum of varying amount granted to a needy student at a British college or university

bur·sate \ˈbər,sāt\ *adj* [NL *bursa* + E *-ate*] **:** having a bursa ⟨a ~ worm⟩

bur·sa·ti *also* **bur·sat·tee** \bə(r)ˈsäd·ē\ *n* -S [Hindi *barsātī* of the rainy season, fr. *barsāt* the rainy season, fr. Skt *varṣārātri,* fr. *varṣati* it rains; akin to Gk *arrhēn* male — more at ARRHENATHERUM] **1 :** East Indian cutaneous habronemiasis of the horse esp. prevalent in the rainy season **2** *India* **:** a waterproof cloak or coat

burse \ˈbərs\ *n* -S [MF *bourse,* fr. ML *bursa* bag, purse — more at PURSE] **1** *obs* **:** EXCHANGE, BOURSE **2 a :** PURSE **b** *obs* **:** a covering resembling a purse (as a vesicle, pod, or hull) **c :** a square pocket or case used in some Christian liturgies to carry the communion cloth

burse 2c

burseed \ˈ=,=\ *n* **:** STICKSEED

bur·sera \ˈbərsərə\ *n, cap* [NL, after Joachim *Burser* †1649 Ger. botanist] **:** the type genus of Burseraceae comprising a number of tropical and subtropical American shrubs and trees that have flowers with three to five petals and fleshy capsular fruit and including some that are valuable sources of timber and resins

bur·ser·a·ce·ae \,bərsəˈrāsē,ē\ *n pl, cap* [NL, fr. *Bursera,* type genus + *-aceae*] **:** a family of resinous or aromatic chiefly tropical shrubs or trees (order Geraniales) with alternate pinnately compound leaves, small greenish usu. panicled flowers, and drupaceous fruit — see BURSERA, ELEMI — **bur·ser·a·ceous** \ˌbərsəˈrāshəs\ *adj*

bur·si·cle \ˈbərsəkəl\ *n* -S [NL *bursicula,* dim. of ML *bursa* bag, purse — more at PURSE] *bot* **:** a pursed or pouched receptacle

bur·sic·u·late \ˌbərˈsikyələt\ *adj* [NL *bursicula* + E *-ate*] **:** shaped like a small pouch or purse

bur·si·form \ˈbərsə,fȯrm\ *adj* [ML *bursa* bag, purse + E *-iform* — more at PURSE] **:** shaped like a pouch

bur·si·tis \,bərˈsīd·əs, bə̄ˈ-, bəiˈ-, ,bə(r)ˈ-, -ītəs\ *n* -ES [NL, fr. *bursa* + *-itis*] **:** inflammation of a bursa; *esp* **:** a painful inflammation involving bursae of the shoulder or elbow

¹burst \ˈbərst, ˈbəst, ˈbəist\ *vb* **burst** \"\ *or* **burst·ed** \-təd\ *or archaic* **brast** \ˈbrast\ **burst** *or* **bursted** *or archaic* **brast; bursting; bursts** [ME *bersten, bresten,* fr. OE *berstan;* akin to OHG *brestan* to burst, ON *bresta* to burst, MIr *brosc* noise, and perh. to Lith *braškėti* to make a cracking noise] *vi* **1 :** to break or fail by breaking when subjected to tension ⟨the rope ~ in two as they pulled⟩; *specif* **:** to splinter on impact — used esp. of manual weapons (as swords or lances) **2 a** *of a boil or similar lesion* **:** to rupture and discharge its contents ⟨the pain will ease when the abscess ~s⟩ **b :** to break to pieces esp. from pressure from within **:** EXPLODE ⟨the shell ~ overhead⟩ ⟨if you eat any more you will ~⟩; *broadly* **:** to give way suddenly, explosively, or unexpectedly ⟨the dam ~ under the pressure of flood waters⟩ ⟨he was ready to ~ with disgust⟩ **3 a :** to pass from one place to another esp. with great vigor against obstacles or on release from some restraint ⟨he ~ into the room⟩ ⟨~*ing* free from the clinging mud⟩ ⟨the water ~ through the break in the dam⟩ **b :** to appear or disappear suddenly or unexpectedly — usu. used with words expressing direction (as *forth, out, away, into, through*) ⟨the sun ~ through⟩ ⟨the valley ~ into view⟩ **c :** to make or undergo an abrupt change: as (1) **:** to pass from a less to a more vigorous, ardent, or glowing state ⟨the smoldering logs ~ into flame⟩ ⟨the whole slope will ~ into bloom in another month⟩ (2) **:** to come into bloom **:** OPEN, UNFOLD ⟨buds are ~*ing* on all the trees⟩ **4 a :** to give or receive sudden or unexpected release or expression (as of a cry previously repressed) ⟨he let his fear ~ out in a babble of meaningless chatter⟩ ⟨they ~ out laughing at the sight of us⟩ **b :** to make an abrupt beginning **:** LAUNCH, PLUNGE — usu. used with *into* and esp. of expressions of emotion ⟨he ~ into song⟩ ⟨~*ing* into a furious rage⟩ ⟨he ~ into print without adequate preparation⟩ **5 a :** to be full to the point of breaking open or overflowing ⟨barns ~*ing* with grain⟩ ⟨streams ~*ing* after the late thaw⟩ **b :** to be at the point of giving way to suppressed emotion ⟨he was like to ~ with fury⟩ **6 :** to make a play in forty-one pool that scores more than 41 points ~ *vt* **1 a** *obs* **:** BREAK, SHATTER **b :** to break, rend, or shatter by or as if by violent action or by strain or pressure esp. from within ⟨a blow that nearly ~ his skull⟩ ⟨the ever-increasing number of children who are constantly ~*ing* the walls of outmoded buildings —*Saturday Rev.*⟩ **2 a :** to force open (as a door) or open (as a way) by sudden or vigorous action ⟨he ~ his way through the underbrush⟩ ⟨open up or we'll ~ the door⟩ **b :** to produce (as an opening) by an act or through the effect of bursting ⟨~ a hole through the wall⟩ **3 :** to cause to burst ⟨this warm weather will ~ the buds in a hurry⟩ **syn** see BREAK — **burst at the seams** *also* **burst one's seams :** to be very full or crowded; *esp* **:** to be larger, fuller, or more crowded than could reasonably have been anticipated

²burst \"\ *n* -S **1 a :** a sudden intense outbreak (as of sound or light) ⟨a ~ of flames coming through the roof⟩ ⟨one great ~ of thunder⟩; *esp* **:** a vehement outburst (as of emotion) ⟨a ~ of furious rage⟩ **b :** EXPLOSION, ERUPTION ⟨a ~ of violence⟩; *esp* **:** the explosion of a projectile ⟨the devastating effect of ground ~s⟩ **c :** a brief, intense, or violent effort or exertion ⟨reaching 102 miles per hour in one sustained ~ —A.W. Baum⟩ **:** SPURT ⟨put on a final ~ of speed and crossed the line first⟩; *sometimes* **:** a hard fast ride on horseback **d :** a series of shots fired from an automatic weapon by one pressure of the trigger; *also* **:** the period covered by such a series ⟨a 10-second ~⟩ **2 a :** an act of bursting ⟨beech buds were near the ~ —George Meredith⟩ **b :** a sudden and often unexpected breaking forth, expressing, or manifesting ⟨in a ~ of confidence he told me⟩ ⟨a wild ~ of sobbing⟩ **3 :** a result of bursting: **a :** a flaw or break (as in a water pipe) produced by bursting **b :** a visible puff accompanying the blast of an antiaircraft shell **c :** an intense ionization caused by cosmic rays or by particles resulting from spallation and seen in a cloud chamber or photographic emulsion as a figure resembling a bursting artillery shell **d :** a sudden increase in signal strength of radio waves being received by ionospheric reflection that is believed to be caused by a disturbance of the ionosphere meteors **4 :** a sudden unfolding to view **:** an expanse made visible ⟨a fine ~ of country —Jane Austen⟩ **5 :** a play in the game of forty-one pool that scores more than 41 points and requires the player to begin again with no points **6** *chiefly Brit* **:** SPREE, BLOWOUT

³burst \"\ *also* **bursted** \"\ *adj* **:** that has broken esp. by reason of tension or stress ⟨a ~ bubble⟩ ⟨~ seams⟩

burst·en \-tən\ *adj* [ME, fr. past part. of *bersten* to burst — more at BURST] *archaic* **:** ³BURST

burst·er \-tə(r)\ *n* -S **:** one that bursts: as **a :** a workman who breaks up stone with a light hammer **b :** an explosive charge used to break open and scatter the contents of chemical shells, bombs, and mines **c :** a heavy southerly gale accompanied by a sharp fall in temperature that occurs chiefly along the east coast of Australia **d :** an abnormally double flower (as of the carnation) in which the calyx splits or fragments

bursting charge *n* **:** a charge of explosive designed to burst a projectile

bursting heart *n* [so called fr. its dehiscent red capsules] **:** ²WAHOO

bursting point *n* **:** the point at which emotional control esp. of oneself is lost

bursting strength *n* **:** the capacity of a material (as a paper or textile) or object (as a metal pipe) to maintain its continuity when subjected to pressure; *broadly* **:** the pressure often expressed in pounds per square inch required to rupture such a material or object under rigidly controlled conditions

burstone *var of* BUHRSTONE

burstwort \ˈ=,=\ *n* [²*burst* + *wort;* fr. the belief that it cured ruptures] **:** RUPTUREWORT

bur·su·la \ˈbərsələ\ *n, pl* **bursu·lae** \-,lē, -,lī\ [NL, dim. of *bursa*] **:** a small anatomical bursa

bur·then \ˈbərt͟hən\ *var of* BURDEN

bur·then·some \-səm\ *archaic var of* BURDENSOME

¹bur·ton \ˈbərtᵊn\ *n* -S [origin unknown] **1 :** any of several arrangements of hoisting tackle; *usu* **:** one with a single and a double block **2 :** stowage (as of casks) athwartships in the hold of a ship

²burton \"\ *n* -S [fr. *Burton* on Trent, county borough, Staffordshire, England, the locality of the water orig. used] **:** a strong dark ale

burton-ail \"+,āl\ *n, usu cap B* [prob. after Glenn W. *Burton* *b*1910 Am. agronomist] *in N. H.* **:** cobalt deficiency disease of cattle and sheep **:** PINE

bur·ton·ing \ˈbərt(ᵊ)niŋ\ *n* -S [¹*burton* + *-ing*] **:** a system of handling a ship's cargo by means of a sling rigging between two derricks or masts

bur·ton·ize \ˈbərtᵊn,īz\ *vt* -ED/-ING/-S *often cap* [*Burton* on Trent, England, + *-ize*] **:** to harden (water used in brewing) by adding gypsum or certain salts esp. for the purpose of approximating the flavor of burton

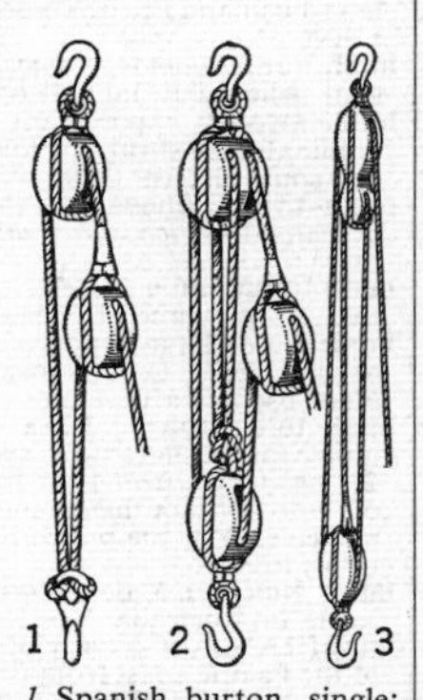

1 Spanish burton, single; *2* Spanish burton, double; *3* top burton

burulée *or* **buruly** *var of* BURELLY

bu·run·di \bu̇ˈründē, bə-,bü-, -ˈrün-,-ˈrən-\ *adj, usu cap* [fr. *Burundi,* country in east central Africa] **:** of or from the country of Burundi **:** of the kind or style prevalent in Burundi

bu·run·di·an \-dēən\ *n* -S *cap* [*Burundi,* Africa + E *-an*] **:** a native or inhabitant of Burundi — **burundian** *adj, usu cap*

burunduki *var of* BARONDUKI

bu·ru·shas·ki \,bu̇rəˈshäskē\ *n* -S *usu cap* **:** a language of unknown affinity spoken in northwestern Kashmir, India

bu·rut *or* **bou·rout** \bəˈrüt\ *n* -S *usu cap* **:** KARA KIRGHIZ

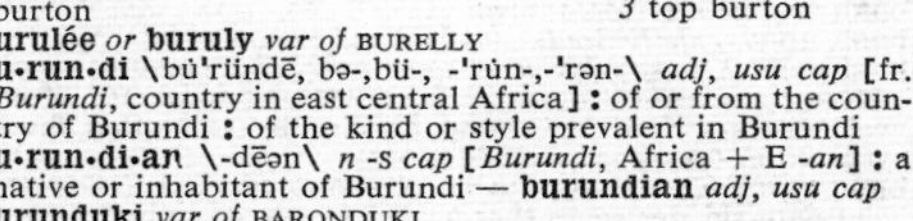

burweed \ˈ=,=\ *n* **:** any of certain plants having the fruit enclosed in a bur: as **a :** COCKLEBUR **b :** BURDOCK **c :** any of certain plants of the genera *Galium, Triumfetta,* or *Amsinckia*

burweed marsh elder *n* **:** a tall annual marsh elder (*Iva xanthifolia*) that is common in moist rich soil in central No. America, causes contact dermatitis in many people, and produces much pollen that is a major cause of hay fever where the plant occurs — called also *false ragweed*

¹bury \ˈberē, -ri\ *vb* -ED/-ING/-ES [ME *berien, burien,* fr. OE *byrgan;* akin to OE *beorgan* to preserve, defend, *borgian* to borrow, OHG *bergan* to shelter, hide, ON *bjarga* to save, Goth *bairgan* to keep, save, Russ *berech'* to look after, save] *vt* **1 a :** to dispose of (a corpse) by depositing in the earth, a grave, or a tomb, by consigning to the water, or by cremation ⟨they *buried* the victims where they fell⟩ ⟨he was *buried* at sea⟩; *esp* **:** to inter with appropriate funeral ceremonies ⟨they *buried* him with full military honors⟩ **b :** to perform the burial rites of ⟨the priest that *buried* my father⟩ **c :** to lose by death ⟨she has *buried* three husbands⟩ **d :** to be or become responsible for the burial costs of ⟨he left nothing, the town had to ~ him⟩ **2 :** to cover esp. with earth ⟨like a dog ~*ing* his bone⟩: as **a :** to dispose of by covering out of sight in the earth ⟨a wise camper *buries* his garbage every day⟩ — used esp. when the object dealt with is regarded as permanently abandoned **b :** to conceal by or as if by covering with earth ⟨~*ing* treasures in the sand⟩ **c :** to cover from view ⟨she *buried* her face in her hands⟩ **3 :** to put irrevocably or completely out of sight or mind: as **a :** to consign to oblivion **:** have done with **:** give up ⟨finally ~*ing* their differences⟩ **b :** to conceal in obscurity **:** remove from the world of action or affairs (as by remoteness) ⟨*buried* his family in the country⟩ ⟨*buried* herself in the cloister⟩; *often* **:** to render negligible by depriving of proper prominence ⟨*buried* the retraction among the classified ads⟩ **c :** SUBMERGE, ENGROSS — usu. used with *in* ⟨had necessarily *buried* himself in his books⟩ ⟨*buried* in grief and despair⟩ **d** *in card games* **:** to put (one or more cards) permanently or temporarily out of play (as by placing an exposed card in or under the dealer's pack or by covering a card in certain solitaire games) ~ *vi* **:** to become buried; *specif* **:** to thrust the bow of a ship under water **syn** see CONCEAL — **bury the hatchet :** to settle a disagreement **:** make peace

²bury \"\ *n* -ES **1 :** a dugout or pit in the earth in which potatoes or other vegetables are protected against freezing; *often* **:** a heap or quantity of produce stored in a bury **:** CLAMP **2 :** the depth at which something is buried beneath a surface ⟨in milder regions a ~ of two feet will protect the pipes⟩

³bury \ˈbəri\ *n* -ES [alter. of ¹*burrow*] *dial Brit* **:** ¹BURROW 1

bur·yat *also* **bur·iat** \(ˈ)bu̇rˈyät, ˈbu̇rēˈät\ *n, pl* **buryat** *or* **buryats** *also* **buriat** *or* **buriats** *usu cap* [Russ *buryat,* fr. Mongolian *burijad*] **1 a :** a Mongol people of eastern Siberia **b :** a member of such people **2 :** the language of the Buryat people

¹burying *n* -S [ME *berying, burying,* fr. gerund of *berien, burien* to bury — more at BURY] **:** a funeral and interment ⟨the country preacher who took charge of the ~s⟩

²burying *adj* [fr. pres. part. of ¹*bury*] **:** used for or concerned with burying **:** BURIAL ⟨a ~ lot⟩ ⟨~ places near small towns⟩

burying beetle *n* **:** any of various carrion beetles of *Necrophorus, Silpha,* and related genera that bury small dead animals by digging away the earth beneath them, thus feeding their larvae on the fly maggots that develop in such carcasses

burying ground *n* **:** a plot of land set aside for burying the dead

¹bus \ˈbəs\ *n, pl* **bus·es** *or* **bus·ses** \-səz\ *often attrib* [short for *omnibus*] **1 a :** a large motor-driven vehicle designed to carry passengers usu. according to a schedule along a fixed route but sometimes under charter for a special trip (as by a social group or an athletic team) ⟨sightseeing ~⟩ ⟨~ station⟩ ⟨the ~ is usu. on time⟩ **b :** any vehicle either publicly owned or privately owned and operated for compensation used for transporting children to or from school **c :** any of various conveyances resembling a bus (as in carrying passengers or traveling a fixed route according to a schedule) ⟨up the Grand Canal by water ~ —Nigel Balchin⟩ ⟨a horse ~⟩ ⟨a milk ~⟩ **d** *slang* **:** AUTOMOBILE ⟨not a bad old ~ —A.J.Cronin⟩ **e :** a hand-pushed usu. 4-wheeled vehicle used typically for carrying dishes in a restaurant **2 :** BUSBOY **3** *or* **bus bar :** an assembly of conductors usu. bare but supported on insulators for collecting electric currents from sources and distributing them to outgoing feeders

²bus \"\ *vb* **bused** *or* **bussed** \ˈbəst\ **bused** *or* **bussed** \"\ **busing** *or* **bussing** \ˈbəsiŋ\ **buses** *or* **busses** \ˈbəsəz\ *vi* **1 :** to travel by bus **2 :** to work as a busboy or bus girl ~ *vt* **:** to move or transport by bus ⟨~ children to school⟩

³bus \ˈbəs\ *var of* BAS

bus *abbr* business

busaun *obs var of* POSAUNE

bus·boy \ˈbəs,bȯi\ *n* **:** a boy or man who cleans up restaurant tables for reuse, removes dirty dishes, keeps ready a supply of needed items (as dishes, silver, napkins), and helps clean up the place **:** a waiter's assistant ⟨he has been all through the mill, from counterman in a hash house to ~ to banquet waiter —Dwight Macdonald⟩

bus·by \ˈbəzbē\ *n* -ES [prob. fr. the name *Busby*] **1 :** a large bushy wig **2 :** a military full-dress hat made of fur with a bag usu. of cloth and of the color of the facings of the regiment hanging from the top on the right **b :** the bearskin worn by British guardsmen

busby 2

buscarle *n* -S [alter. of OE *butsecarl,* fr. (assumed) ON *būzukarl,* fr. ON *būza* buss (ship) + *karl* man — more at BUSS, CARL] *archaic* **:** MARINER

bus driver *n* **:** one that drives a bus and usu. serves also as conductor

bus duct *n* **:** an electric conduit prefabricated in sections and containing heavy conductors for transmission of large currents at relatively low voltage

bus girl *n* **:** a female busboy

¹bush \ˈbu̇sh\ *n* -ES *often attrib* [ME *bush, busk, bosk;* akin to MD *busch, bosch* bush, forest, OHG *busc,* OSw *buske* bush] **1 a :** SHRUB; *esp.* **:** a low densely branched shrub suggesting a single plant ⟨a blueberry ~⟩ **b :** a close thicket of shrubs ⟨~*es* suitable for a hedge⟩ **c** *dial Eng* **:** THORN **2 a** (1) **:** common uncultivated usu. undesirable bushes ⟨a field overgrown with ~⟩ (2) **:** the mixed plant growth typical of an uncleared or uncultivated area esp. when other than grass or trees ⟨part of the land once cultivated has been abandoned, to the sea, to flood waters, or to ~ —W.A.Lewis⟩ (3) **:** FOREST, WOODS, JUNGLE ⟨in the dense ~ . . . creepers of many kinds and of every size, from huge cables to thin cords, loop from tree to tree, pushing up to the sunlight and knotting the undergrowth into impenetrable thickets —C.D.Forde⟩ **b :** a large uncleared or uncultivated area usu. scrub-covered or heavily forested **:** WILDERNESS ⟨all this property . . . was ~ where last year nothing thrived but zebra and impala, wildebeest and bad snakes —Basil Davidson⟩ **c :** a usu. vast sparsely settled area **:** BACKCOUNTRY ⟨~ doctor⟩ ⟨~ flying⟩ ⟨~ airline⟩ — usu. used with *the* when not attributive ⟨in the lonely ~ —Henry Lawson⟩ ⟨boys from the ~ —Esther Warner⟩; *specif* **:** any of certain vast and sparsely settled geographical areas esp. in New Zealand, Australia, Africa, and Canada **3 a** (1) *archaic* **:** a bunch or branch of ivy formerly hung outside a tavern to indicate wine for sale (2) *obs* **:** TAVERN **b :** ADVERTISING — used esp. with *need* ⟨good wine needs no ~ —Shak.⟩ ⟨good essays need no ~ —*Yale Review*⟩ **4 :** something resembling or felt to resemble a bush ⟨the ermine ~ of feathers that formed the crest —W.H.St. John Hope⟩ ⟨~*es* of black smoke —Barrett McGurn⟩ ⟨a ~ of hair —Roger Senhouse⟩ **5 :** SUGAR BUSH **6** [by shortening] **:** BUSH LEAGUE — usu. used in pl. ⟨finally decided to ship him back to the ~*es* —*Scholastic Coach*⟩

²bush \"\ *vb* -ED/-ING/-ES *vt* **1 :** to support (as a plant) with bushes ⟨the birch he said I could have to ~ my peas —Robert Frost⟩ **2 :** to mark (as a route) with bushes ⟨a logging road across the river was ~*ed* where the ice was safe⟩ **3 :** to protect (land or game) from net poachers by placing obstacles (as bushes) to prevent effective use of a net ~ *vi* **:** to extend like a bush **:** have the appearance of a bush ⟨his eyebrows ~*ed* together⟩ ⟨he looked about 30 but surprising gray hair ~*ed* out of his fore-and-aft cap —Richard Llewellyn⟩ — **bush it** *Austral* **:** to live in the bush

³bush \"\ *n* -ES [D *bus* bushing, box, fr. MD *busse* box, fr. LL *buxis* — more at BOX] **1 :** BUSHING **2 :** a threaded socket flush with a surface of a camera or projector for attachment to a tripod

⁴bush \"\ *vt* -ED/-ING/-ES **:** to furnish with a bushing

⁵bush \"\ *vt* -ED/-ING/-ES [by shortening] **:** BUSHHAMMER

bush baby *n* **:** any of several small African lemurs of the genus *Galago*

bush basil *n* **:** a small cultivated annual herb (*Ocimum minimum*) with nearly entire leaves

bush bean *n* **:** any of various low-growing cultivated beans that have short internodes, form compact bushy plants, show no tendency to vine, and are usu. considered to constitute a variety (*Phaseolus vulgaris humilis*) of the kidney bean

bush·beat \ˈbu̇sh,bēt, *usu* -ēd·+V\ *vi* [back-formation fr. *bushbeater*] **:** to beat the bushes

bush·beat·er \"+ə(r)\ *n* [¹*bush* + *beater*] **:** one that beats the bushes; *esp* **:** a scout esp. for promising young actors or ballplayers

bushberry \ˈbu̇sh- —*see* BERRY\ *n* **:** any of various berries or fruits resembling berries borne on bushes (as raspberries, gooseberries, currants)

bushboy \ˈ=,=\ *n* **:** BUSHMAN

bushbuck \ˈ=,=\ *n, pl* **bushbuck** *or* **bushbucks** [trans. of Afrik *bosbok*] **:** a small southern African harnessed antelope (*Strepsiceros scriptus* or *Tragelaphus scriptus*) having spirally twisted horns and frequenting forests; *also* **:** any of several related species — called also *boschbok*

bush canary *n* **:** a small New Zealand bird (*Mohua ochrocephala*) having a yellow head and breast

bush cat *n* **1 a :** SERVAL **b :** any of various small Asiatic and African cats **2 :** an Asiatic civet cat

bush cinquefoil *n* **:** a much-branched shrub (*Potentilla fruticosa*) with compound leaves and yellow flowers common through the north temperate zone often as a weed

bush clover *n* **:** any of certain usu. shrubby lespedezas (as bicolor lespedeza)

bush cow *n* **1 :** the short-horned buffalo of West Africa sometimes regarded as a separate species (*Syncerus nanus*) **2 :** TAPIR

bushcraft \ˈ⸗,⸗\ *n* **:** the skill gained by or necessary for living in bush country

bush disease *n* **:** [1]PINE 3

bush doe *n* **:** the female of the bushbuck

bush dog *n* **1 :** a small wild dog (*Speothos venadictus* syn. *Icticyon venaticus*) of northern So. America **2 :** POTTO

bushed \ˈbu̇sht\ *adj* [[1]*bush* + *-ed*] **1 :** covered with or as if with a bushy growth ⟨we had to land the boat on a steep, densely ~ bank⟩ **2** *chiefly Austral* **a :** lost in the bush ⟨he said it would be dangerous for me to go up without him; I was bound to get ~ and he was too busy to be bothered having to waste a day hunting for me —F.S.Anthony⟩ **b :** AMAZED, BEWILDERED ⟨adapting his language to my ~ comprehension —Henry Lawson⟩ **3 :** TIRED, EXHAUSTED ⟨I heard a noise, and yells, but I was too ~ to worry —Christopher Morley⟩

[1]**bush·el** \ˈbu̇shəl\ *n* -S [ME *busshel, boyschel*, fr. OF *boissel*, fr. (assumed) OF *boisse* one sixth of a bushel (whence MF *boisse*), of Celt origin; akin to MIr *boss, bass* palm of the hand] **1 :** any of various units of capacity: as **a :** a unit of dry capacity used in the U.S. equal to 2150.42 cubic inches **:** WINCHESTER BUSHEL **b :** a British unit of dry and liquid capacity equal to 8 imperial gallons or 2219.36 cubic inches — see MEASURE table **2 a :** a container used as a bushel measure ⟨nor do men light a lamp and put it under a ~, but on a stand —Mt 5:15 (RSV)⟩ **b :** something that conceals by or as if by covering ⟨razzle-dazzle journalism continued to be a *Times* specialty, albeit one well hidden under the ~ of its solemn thoroughness —*Newsweek*⟩ **3 :** a large quantity **:** LOTS, LOADS ⟨~*s* of fun⟩ ⟨didn't do anything wrong, except tell a ~ of cockeyed lies —Calder Willingham⟩ ⟨~*s* of love letters —G.B.Shaw⟩ ⟨pamphlets mailed out by the ~⟩

[2]**bushel** \"\ *vt* **busheled** *also* **bushelled**; **busheled** *also* **bushelled**; **busheling** *also* **bushelling** \-sh(ə)liŋ\ **bushels** **1 :** to hide under or as if under a bushel ⟨don't ~ your light in the city⟩ ⟨~*ed* information⟩ **2** [so called fr. the fact that scrap iron was formerly sold by the bushel] **:** to heat (scrap iron) to a welding temperature esp. in a reverberatory furnace

[3]**bushel** *vb* **busheled** *also* **bushelled**; **busheled** *also* **bushelled**; **busheling** *also* **bushelling** \-sh(ə)liŋ\ **bushels** [prob. fr. G *bosseln* to do poor work, to do odd jobs, to patch, fr. MHG *bōzeln* to beat, freq. of *bōzen*, fr. OHG *bōzan* — more at BEAT] *vt* **:** ALTER, FINISH, REPAIR ⟨~*s* men's suits⟩ ~ *vi* **:** to alter, finish, or repair garments, esp. men's suits

bush·el·age \ˈbu̇shəlij\ *n* -S [[1]*bushel* + *-age*] **:** amount in bushels

bush·el·er \-sh(ə)lə(r)\ *n* -S [prob. fr. G *bossler*, fr. *bosseln* + *-er*] **:** one that bushels

bush·el·ful \-shəl,fu̇l\ *n* -S **:** as much as a bushel will hold

bush·el·man \-shəlmən\ *n, pl* **bushelmen** [[3]*bushel* + *man*] **:** BUSHELER

bush·er \ˈbu̇shə(r)\ *n* -S [[1]*bush* + *-er*] **1 :** SWAMPER **2 :** BUSH LEAGUER ⟨who gave you a ticket to get into the game, ~⟩

bushes *pl of* BUSH, *pres 3d sing of* BUSH

bushfelling \ˈ⸗,⸗⸗\ *n* -S *Austral* **:** the cutting of timber in bush country

bushfighter \ˈ⸗,⸗⸗\ *n* **:** one that engages in bushfighting

bushfighting \ˈ⸗,⸗⸗\ *n* **1 :** warfare in or as if in the bush **:** hard fighting that involves a resourceful dodging, hiding, or moving warily and surreptitiously among trees, rocks, and undergrowth **2 :** a hard skirmishing between resourceful opponents

bush fly *n* **:** any of several small flies related to the housefly that are often extremely abundant in pastoral parts of Australia and that swarm over cattle and other animals

bush forest *n* **:** CHAPARRAL

bush fowl *n* **:** MEGAPODE

bush fruit *n* **1 :** a small fruit growing on a woody bush (as the currant and gooseberry) **2 :** a plant producing bush fruit — compare CANE FRUIT

bush goat *n* [trans. of Afrik *bosbok*] **:** BUSHBUCK

bush grape *n* **1 :** SAND GRAPE **2 :** a shrubby wild grape (*Vitis acerifolia*) of the southern U.S. having leaves permanently pilose beneath and fruit with persistent heavy bloom

bushgrass \ˈ⸗,⸗\ *n* **:** a stout erect perennial Eurasian grass (*Calamagrostis epigejos*) having spikelets with a profusion of basal silky hairs longer than the lemmas

[1]**bush·hammer** \ˈbu̇sh+,-\ *n* [modif. of G *bosshammer*, fr. obs. G *bossen* to beat (fr. OHG *bōzan*) + G *hammer*, fr. OHG *hamar* — more at BEAT, HAMMER] **:** a hammer with a serrated face for dressing stone and concrete

[2]**bushhammer** \"\ *vt* **:** to dress (stone or concrete) with a bushhammer

bushhammer

bush harrow *n* **:** BRUSH HARROW

bush-harrow \ˈ⸗,⸗(,)⸗\ *vb* [*bush harrow*] **:** to till with a brush harrow

bush hawk *n* **:** a small falcon (*Falco novaeseelandiae*) of New Zealand that resembles the kestrel

bush honeysuckle *n* **1 :** a plant of the genus *Diervilla; esp* **:** a shrub (*D. lonicera*) of the northeastern U.S. having opposite leaves and fragrant yellow flowers **2 :** any of several shrubby honeysuckles of the genus *Lonicera* (esp. *L. tatarica*)

bush hook *n* **:** a short stout hooked blade fitted to an ax handle and used for cutting bushes — called also *bush scythe*

bush hook

bush huckleberry *n* **:** a low shrub (*Gaylussacia dumosa*) of eastern No. America with rather watery and tasteless black fruit

bu·shi·do \ˌbüshēˌdō, ˌbu̇sh-, ⸗ˈ⸗(,)⸗, *Jap approximately* ˈbu̇shˈdō\ *n* -S *usu cap* [Jap *bushidō*, fr. *bushi* warrior (fr. *bu* military + *shi* man) + *dō* doctrine] **:** a traditional specif. feudal-military Japanese code of behavior emphasizing loyalty, benevolence, bravery, self-control, and the valuing of honor above life

bushier *comparative of* BUSHY

bushies *pl of* BUSHY

bushiest *superlative of* BUSHY

bush·i·ly \ˈbu̇shəlē, -li\ *adv* **:** in a bushy manner

bush·i·ness \ˈbu̇shēnəs, -shin-\ *n* -ES **:** the quality or state of being bushy

bush·ing \ˈbu̇shiŋ, -shēŋ\ *n* -S [fr. gerund of [4]*bush*] **1 :** a usu. removable lining or sleeve of metal or other material that is inserted or screwed into an opening (as of a mechanical part) to limit its size, resist wear or erosion, or serve as a guide **2 :** an insulating sleeve inserted in an opening in a metal plate or case (as of a microphone or electric clock) to protect a through conductor from abrasion and possible short circuit **3 :** an internally and externally threaded plug for connecting a pipe or fitting with another of different size

bush jacket *n* **:** a long cotton jacket like a shirt with four patch pockets, self belt, and notched collar worn esp. in rough country

bushland \ˈ⸗,⸗\ *n* **:** BUSH 2b

bush lark *n* **:** any of several larks (genus *Mirafra*) of the Old World frequenting bushy and wooded places

bush lawyer *n* **1 :** NEW ZEALAND BRAMBLE **2** *Austral* **:** a person pretending to have considerable legal knowledge

bush league *n* **:** a minor league esp. in baseball **:** a sports league of low classification or poor quality ⟨a good catcher but not a great one, he was tricky and tough enough to move up through the *bush leagues* into the big time —*Time*⟩

bush-league *adj* [*bush league*] **:** belonging to an inferior class or group of its kind **:** MINOR, MEDIOCRE ⟨a *bush-league* demagogue⟩ ⟨a *bush-league* college⟩ **:** INADEQUATE ⟨a *bush-league* carrier and three 4-stack destroyers too old for anything else —Wirt Williams⟩

bush leagu·er \ˈbu̇shˈlēgə(r)\ *n* **1 :** someone in a bush league; *esp* **:** a player in such a league **2 :** an incompetent performer or small-time operator — called also *busher*

bush lespedeza *n* **:** BUSH CLOVER

bush·less \ˈbu̇shləs\ *adj* **:** being without a bush

bush lima *n* **:** a lima bean that grows as a bush bean rather than as a vine

bush·man \ˈbu̇shmən\ *n, pl* **bushmen** [modif. (influenced by [1]*bush*) of obs. Afrik *boschjesman*, fr. *boschjes* (gen. of obs. *boschje*, dim. of *bosch* forest — now *bos*) + *man*, fr. MD; akin to OHG *man* person, man — more at BOSCHBOK, MAN] **1** *usu cap* **:** one of a race of nomadic hunters of southern Africa now chiefly confined to the Kalahari desert that are of short stature and have leathery yellow skin, a flat triangular face, often excessive development of fat on the buttocks esp. of females, and low cranial capacity **2** *usu cap* **:** a Khoisan language of the Bushmen **3** [[1]*bush* + *man*] *chiefly Austral* **a :** one that lives in the bush **b :** one skilled in bushcraft **c :** FARMER, RUBE, HICK

bushman grass *n* **:** any of a number of southern African grasses; *specif* **:** a perennial forage grass (*Stipa dregeana*) of the arid veld

bush·man·oid \-,nȯid\ *adj, usu cap* **:** resembling the Bushman people or their artifacts

bushmanship \-mən,ship\ *n* -S **:** BUSHCRAFT

bushman's poison *n, pl* **bushman's poisons :** ORDEAL TREE 3

bush maple *n* **1 :** MOUNTAIN MAPLE **2 :** STRIPED MAPLE

bush marrow *n* **:** a squash with a bushy habit

bushmaster \ˈ⸗,⸗⸗\ *n* **:** the largest of the New World pit vipers (*Lachesis mutus*) sometimes reaching a length of 12 feet, producing immense quantities of venom, and being widely distributed in tropical American forests and of notably irritable aggressive disposition

bush meeting *n* **:** a religious gathering held in a woods — compare CAMP MEETING

bush metal *n* [[3]*bush*] **:** an alloy that is similar in composition to gun metal and used for bushings

bush monkey *n* **:** a logger who piles tanbark into ricks

bush monkeyflower *n* **:** a low shrubby plant (*Mimulus longiflorus*) of California with evergreen viscid foliage and showy light yellow to salmon flowers

bush morning-glory *n* **:** MAN-OF-THE-EARTH

bush negro *n, usu cap B&N* [trans. of D *bosneger*] **:** one of a people of African ancestry descended from runaway slaves and inhabiting the interior of the Guianas in So. America

bush nut *n* **1 :** MACADAMIA 2a **2 :** MACADAMIA NUT

bush oak *n* **:** a scrub oak (*Quercus ilicifolia*)

bu·shon·go \büˈshäŋ(,)gō\ *n, pl* **bushongo** *or* **bushongos** *usu cap* **:** [2]KUBA

bush out *vt* **:** to clear or make (as a path or road) through bush country

bush parole *n, slang* **:** escape from prison

bush pea *n* **:** a plant of the genus *Thermopsis*

bush pepper *n* **:** BIRD PEPPER

bushpig \ˈ⸗ˌ⸗\ *n* [trans. of D *bosvark*] **:** an African wild swine (*Koiropotamus koiropotamus* or *Potamochoerus koiropotamus*) having a reddish coat that turns gray with age, white cheek patches, and a white erectile crest

bush pilot *n* **:** an airplane pilot who flies over uninhabited country (as in Canada or Alaska) esp. off regular commercial lanes ⟨a frontier still penetrated only by river barge, dog team, tractor train, and *bush pilot* — W.C.Gilman⟩

bush poppy *n* **:** a California evergreen shrub (*Dendromecon rigida*) of the family Papaveraceae with yellowish green foliage often cultivated for its long-stalked golden-yellow flowers

bush pumpkin or **bush squash** *n* **:** any of various cultivated pumpkins derived from the variety *Cucurbita pepo melopepo* and having the internodes of the plant axis greatly shortened so that the whole plant forms a compact bushy growth with no tendency to vine

bushranger \ˈ⸗ˌ⸗⸗\ *n* **1 :** FRONTIERSMAN, WOODSMAN **2** *Austral* **:** an outlaw living in the bush

bush rat *n* **1 :** WOOD RAT **2 :** YUNGAS **3 :** DEGU

bush robin *n* **:** any of several small Oriental birds related to the American robin but resembling the European robin

bushrope \ˈ⸗ˌ⸗\ *n* **:** LIANA

bush scythe *n* **:** any of several implements: **a :** a scythe that has a short thick heavy blade and a stout handle and is used for cutting brush and bushes **b :** BUSH HOOK **c :** BILLHOOK

bush shirt *n* **:** BUSH JACKET

bush shrike *n* **:** any of various African thicket-dwelling shrikes

bush sickness *n* [so called fr. its occurrence in the New Zealand bushland] **:** cobalt deficiency disease of cattle and sheep **:** PINE

bush soul *n, among some primitive peoples* **:** a man's second soul believed to inhabit a wild animal of the bush

bush swamp *n* **:** a plant association found in wet places, dominated by shrubs or low trees, and common in Europe and the southeastern U.S.

bush-tailed opossum \ˈ⸗,⸗-\ *n* **:** a common Australian marsupial (*Trichosurus vulpecula*) with thick woolly grizzled fur

bush tamarind *n* **:** an African tree (*Machaerium schomburgkii*) that is the source of tigerwood

bush tea *n* **1 :** a southern African plant (*Cyclopia subternata*) of the family Leguminosae **2 :** the leaves of the bush-tea plant used as a beverage

bush telegraph *n* **1 :** a means whereby the natives of a jungle or bush rapidly spread news from person to person **2 :** *chiefly Austral* **:** an informal but well-organized system of word-of-mouth communication transmitting plans and movements of the police **:** GRAPEVINE **3 :** unofficial information **:** RUMOR

bush tick *n* **:** a tick (*Haemaphysalis bispinosa*) common on cattle in Australia

bushtit \ˈ⸗,⸗\ *n* -S **:** any of several titmice (genus *Psaltriparus*) of the Pacific coast from British Columbia to Lower California and inland and southward to Wyoming, Texas, and Guatemala usu. considered varieties of a single species (*P. minimus*)

bush trefoil *n* **:** TICK TREFOIL

bush up *vi, chiefly South and Midland* **:** HIDE

bush·veld \ˈbu̇sh,felt\ *n* -S *sometimes cap* [modif. of obs. Afrik *boschveld* — more at BOSCHVELD] **:** southern African veld characterized by abundant shrubby and often thorny vegetation (as of acacias and aloes)

bush vetch *n* **:** a European purple-flowered vetch (*Vicia sepium*) with slender stems that occurs as a weed in hedgerows

bush·wa *or* **bush·wah** \ˈbu̇sh(,)wä, -wȯ\ *n* -S [prob. euphemism for *bullshit*] **:** BALONEY, HOOEY, BULL ⟨there it was again: the ~, the sloganeering, being poured out to him with no regard for the truth —David Driscoll⟩

bush warbler *n* **:** any of various chiefly tropical warblers (family Sylviidae) of open or brushy country

bush·whack *also* **bush·wack** \ˈbu̇sh,(h)wak\ *vb* -ED/-ING/-S [back-formation fr. *bushwhacker, bushwacker*] *vi* **1 a :** to clear a path through thick woods esp. by chopping down bushes and low branches **b :** to propel a boat by pulling on bushes along the bank **2 a :** to make repeated emphatic gestures while speaking specif. in a manner felt to resemble the chopping of bushes **b :** to make a speech accompanied by such gestures **3 a :** to hide out in the woods **b :** to travel through thick woods (as in making a thorough search) **4 :** to fight as a bushwhacker ~ *vt* **1 :** to propel (a boat) by pulling on bushes along the bank **2 :** to fight or attack as a bushwhacker **:** AMBUSH

bush·whack·er *also* **bush·wack·er** \-kə(r)\ *also* **bushwhack** \-k\ *n* -S [*bushwhacker* fr. [1]*bush* + *whacker; bushwacker & bushwack*, alter. of *bushwhacker*] **:** one that bushwhacks: as **a :** a person who clears away the bush (as in preparing land for grazing); *also* **:** an implement for this **b :** one that lives in or frequents the woods **:** WOODSMAN **c :** a Confederate soldier who engaged in guerrilla warfare in the Civil War **d :** one that fires from ambush **:** SNIPER **e :** a deserter or draft dodger who became an outlaw esp. during and after the Civil War **f :** BUSHFIGHTER, RAIDER, GUERRILLA **g :** OUTLAW, BANDIT

bush willow *n* **:** any of a number of southern African trees of the genus *Combretum:* as **a :** a small deciduous tree (*Combretum apiculatum*) 15 to 20 feet high that is a common constituent of the Transvaal bushveld **b :** a small tree (*Combretum erythrophyllum*) bearing 4-winged fruits and usu. growing on the banks of streams

bushwood *n* **:** BRUSHWOOD, UNDERGROWTH; *specif* **:** a woodland in which shrubs predominate

[1]**bushy** \ˈbu̇shē, -shi\ *adj* -ER/-EST [ME, fr. [1]*bush* + *-y*] **1 :** full of or overgrown with bushes ⟨~ country⟩ ⟨a ~ garden⟩ **2 :** resembling a bush; *esp* **:** thick and spreading ⟨~ eyebrows⟩ ⟨a ~ tail⟩

[2]**bushy** \"\ *n* -ES [by shortening & alter.] **:** BUSHMAN 3

bushy aster *n* **:** a stiff perennial herb (*Aster dumosus*) of the eastern U.S. having small linear leaves and numerous tiny white flower heads

bushy gerardia *n* **:** a conspicuous yellow-flowered perennial herb (*Aureolaria pedicularia*) of the family Scrophulariaceae of eastern No. America with divided sticky foliage

bushy stunt *n* **:** a virus disease of tomato causing yellowing and purpling of the foliage, necrotic lesions, and a dwarfed much-branched growth habit

bushy-tailed rat \ˈ⸗⸗,⸗-\ *n* **:** CLOUD RAT

busied *past of* BUSY

busier *comparative of* BUSY

busies *pres 3d sing of* BUSY

busiest *superlative of* BUSY

bus·i·ly \ˈbiz(ə)lē, -li\ *adv* [ME *bisily*, fr. *bisy* busy + *-ly* — more at BUSY] **:** in a busy manner **:** INDUSTRIOUSLY, ACTIVELY, BRISKLY ⟨his tongue wagged ~ —Dorothy Sayers⟩ **:** INTENTLY ⟨studying ~⟩

bu·sine \büˈzēn\ *or* **bo·zine** \bōˈz-\ *n* -S [ME *bosyne*, fr. MF *buisine, busine, bosine*, fr. L *bucina* — more at BUCCINA] **:** a medieval straight trumpet

busi·ness \ˈbiznəs, -nəz, *rapid or substand* ˈbidnə- *or* ˈbinə-; *sometimes* ÷ ˈbizᵊnə-\ *n* -ES *often attrib* [ME *bisinesse*, fr. *bisy* busy + *-nesse* -ness] **1 a** (1) *archaic* **:** purposeful activity **:** activity directed toward some end ⟨the greatest master of parliamentary tactics and political ~ in his generation —Walter Bagehot⟩ (2) **:** an activity engaged in as normal, logical, or inevitable and usu. extending over a considerable period of time **:** ROLE, FUNCTION ⟨formal study is the primary ~ of a college student⟩ ⟨how the human mind went about its ~ of learning —H.A.Overstreet⟩ (3) **:** an activity engaged in toward an immediate specific end and usu. extending over a limited period of time **:** TASK, CHORE, MISSION, ASSIGNMENT ⟨what is your ~ here at this hour⟩ ⟨a mob of a thousand people may lynch a Negro on the slightest provocation and apparently enjoy the dirty ~ —C.C.Furnas⟩ ⟨this knife will do the ~⟩ **b** (1) **:** a usu. commercial or mercantile activity customarily engaged in as a means of livelihood and typically involving some independence of judgment and power of decision ⟨the ~ of a printer being generally thought a poor one —Benjamin Franklin⟩ and sometimes contrasted with the arts ⟨but in a sick world it is not literature, it becomes simply the writing ~ —Francis Hackett⟩ or professions ⟨there was none . . . who did more to raise it from the dull routine of a ~ to something approaching a profession —R.R.Rowe⟩ or sport ⟨hunting and fishing were favorite pastimes but the abundance of game and its use as food made these amusements less sport than ~ or slaughter —*Amer. Guide Series: N.C.*⟩ or other activity considered less practical, serious, respectable, or mundane ⟨he changed the processing and marketing of petroleum from a gamble to a ~ —Marquis James⟩ ⟨the way therefore to avoid public comment is to avoid the speech of affection and to use that of ~ —R.M.Weaver⟩ **:** OCCUPATION, POSITION, TRADE, LINE (2) **:** a commercial or industrial enterprise ⟨he's in ~ for himself⟩ ⟨he sold out his ~⟩; *collectively* **:** such enterprises ⟨the city is a ~ center⟩ ⟨~ does not act as a unit⟩ (3) **:** a place where such an enterprise is carried on ⟨the explosion broke windows in ~*es* several blocks away⟩ (4) **:** transactions, dealings, or intercourse of any nature ⟨they were far away from the Zidonians and had no ~ with any man —Judg 18:7 (AV)⟩ but now esp. economic (as buying and selling) ⟨~ as usual⟩ ⟨you can't do ~ with that heel⟩ ⟨the company did more ~ than ever⟩; *esp* **:** PATRONAGE ⟨how's ~⟩ ⟨I'll take my ~ somewhere else⟩ (5) **:** the procedures and techniques of such enterprises ⟨a strong ~ sense⟩ ⟨he supervised the manufacturing while his brother handled the ~⟩ **c :** serious activity that requires time and effort and usu. the avoidance of distracting influences ⟨Kate at once got down to ~. "Well, you wanted to walk with us: what for?" she asked sharply —Sherwood Anderson⟩ **:** JOB, DUTY, WORK ⟨~ before pleasure⟩ ⟨she means ~⟩ **d :** a particular field of endeavor ⟨the best comedian in the ~⟩ ⟨that jockey really knows his ~⟩ **2 a :** AFFAIR, MATTER ⟨the ~ of people being able to feed themselves is fundamentally . . . a local matter —S.A.Cain⟩ ⟨I'm sick of this stupid ~⟩ **b :** a difficult or complicated matter **:** PROJECT ⟨getting her down the mountain next day was a ~ —*Time*⟩ **3 :** something that is so put together as to be not easily classified or felt not worth classification: **a :** CONCOCTION, CREATION ⟨one of the slinky printed cotton dresses here, a halter neck ~ —*New Yorker*⟩ **b :** DEVICE, GADGET ⟨assistant laundressing is another merry game. Instead of a washboard they use a patent ~ —Sinclair Lewis⟩ **4 a :** a movement or action (as sitting down, lighting a cigarette, or winding a clock) by an actor intended esp. to establish atmosphere, reveal character, or explain a situation ⟨stage ~ is often written into the script by the playwright . . . but just as often it is introduced by the director —F.H.O'Hara & Margueritte Bro⟩ **b :** all such movements and acting esp. in the performance of one dramatic work or the portrayal of one dramatic role ⟨generally speaking the composer and original producer have conferred during the first rehearsals of a new opera and the stage ~ has therefore become a tradition . . . altered by successive producers and artists —Warwick Braithwaite⟩ **5 a :** something felt to be one's particular concern or responsibility ⟨none of your ~⟩ **b :** something felt to be one's right — usu. used in the negative ⟨you had no ~ hitting her⟩ **6 :** everything possible (as all-out effort) applied toward a desired end or enough of something (as trickery) to bring it about **:** WORKS: as **a :** all that one is capable of **:** utmost effort ⟨I wish you'd give it the old ~ today. One of the big shots is coming through —Mary J. Ward⟩ **b :** HARM, INJURY, DAMAGE, ABUSE; *esp* **:** something that disables or destroys ⟨that quarterback really got the ~. They carried him off on a stretcher⟩ **c :** a setback or rebuke usu. deserved **:** COMEUPPANCE ⟨he thought he was the hero of the outfit until the sarge gave him the ~⟩ **d :** a good tongue-lashing **:** a hard time ⟨a witness has given him the ~ such as I've never heard a senator take before —F.C.Othman⟩ **e :** DOUBLE CROSS ⟨he's been giving his partner the ~ for years⟩ **f :** a bowel movement **syn** see WORK

business agent *n* **:** one that handles business affairs for another; *esp* **:** a paid official of a union local who administers union business with its members and with the employer

business car *n* **:** a private railroad car usu. equipped with office and living accommodations for the use of railway officials while traveling

business card *n* **:** a card that bears information (as the name, address, type of business) about a business or business representative

business cycle *n* **:** a recurring succession of business conditions loosely divisible into periods of prosperity, crisis, liquidation, depression, and recovery

business double *n* **:** a double in bridge made with the purpose of increasing penalties

business education *n* **:** education designed for use in business: **a :** training in subjects (as business administration, finance) useful in developing general business knowledge **b :** training in subjects (as accounting, shorthand) useful in developing commercially useful skills

business end *n* **:** the end at, from, or through which a thing's function is fulfilled ⟨the *business end* of the broom⟩

business english *n, cap E* **1 :** English as used in business; *specif* **:** the study and practice of composition with emphasis on correctness, propriety, spelling, punctuation, and the forms of business correspondence **2 :** English as taught in non-English-speaking countries in courses that emphasize its commercial rather than its cultural importance and that are normally designed to produce conversational fluency within a limited vocabulary

business income *n* **:** the income of a business from current production as sometimes distinguished from incidental or extraneous income (as from the investments of a manufacturer)

business interruption insurance *n* **:** insurance against loss of net profits and continuing fixed charges during a period of total or partial suspension of business activity because of damage to described premises from specified perils

business life insurance *n* **1 :** insurance on the life of a member of a partnership or upon an officer or stockholder in a corporation payable so as to finance purchase by surviving owners of the insured's interest at his death **2 :** insurance on the life of a sole proprietor payable so as to finance the purchase of the business by an outside interest at the owner's death **3 :** insurance on the life of a key employee for the benefit of a business concern

businesslike \'⸗⸗,⸗\ *adj* **:** characterized by or exhibiting qualities felt to be common or advantageous in business: as **a :** EFFICIENT, PRACTICAL, SYSTEMATIC ⟨a ~ administration⟩ ⟨she went about her housework in a ~ way⟩ **b :** SERIOUS, PURPOSEFUL ⟨a ~ rain⟩ ⟨got off and went to her waiting father with a firm ~ air —Sherwood Anderson⟩ **c :** competent but lacking in enthusiasm, imagination, or emotion ⟨always the skillful pianist, attending to the music in a ~ manner, frequently turning a phrase with spirit but never showing any great identification with the musical style —*N.Y.Times*⟩

business machine *n* **:** a machine (as a computor or tabulator) designed esp. to facilitate clerical operations common in business or industrial firms

busi·ness·man \'⸗⸗,man, -,maa(ə)n *sometimes* -ˌmən\ *n, pl* **businessmen :** a man who transacts business; *esp* **:** a business executive

business paper *n* **:** COMMERCIAL PAPER

business pass *n* **:** a pass in bridge to avoid interfering with a partner's double

business reply card *n* **:** a postcard for enclosure with a mailed communication bearing indicia stating that postage for its use in making reply will be paid by the one requesting the reply; *also* **:** a double postcard

business reply envelope *n* **:** an envelope bearing indicia like those on a business reply card

business suit *n* **:** a man's suit for business wear consisting of matching coat and trousers and sometimes a vest of the same material

business trust *n* **:** MASSACHUSETTS TRUST

business unionism *n* **:** the theory and practice of trade unionism esp. associated with Samuel Gompers that is directed toward the attainment of practical limited material advantages (as better wages, hours, and working conditions) through collective bargaining within the framework of capitalism rather than toward the achievement of extensive social changes or reforms

busi·ness·wom·an \'⸗⸗,wu̇mən\ *n, pl* **businesswom·en** \-,wimən\ **:** a woman active in business

[1]**busing** *pres part of* BUS

[2]**bus·ing** \'bəsiŋ\ *n* -S [[1]*bus* + *-ing*] **:** an assembly of bus bars

[1]**busk** \'bəsk, 'bu̇sk\ *n* -S [ME — more at BUSH] *dial Brit* **:** [1]BUSH 1

[2]**busk** \"\ *vb* -ED/-ING/-S [ME *busken*, fr. ON *būask* to prepare oneself, get ready, fr. *būa* to prepare, make ready, dwell + *-sk* oneself, fr. *sik* (accus.) oneself — more at BOWER, SUICIDE] *vt* **1** *dial Brit* **:** to make ready **:** PREPARE ⟨they're ~*ing* the *Covenant* for sea —R.L.Stevenson⟩ **2** *dial Brit* **:** to dress up **:** ADORN ⟨cowslips ~ the brae⟩ **3** *dial Brit* **:** to dress (flies) on hooks for fishing **~** *vi, dial Brit* **:** to make oneself ready esp. hastily **:** hurry up

[3]**busk** \'bəsk\ *n* -S [MF *busc*, prob. fr. OIt *busco* stick, mote, of Gmc origin; akin to MHG *būsch* cudgel — more at BEASTINGS] **:** a thin rigid strip (as of metal, whalebone, or wood) inserted in the front of a bodice or corset for stiffening and support used from the 16th to the 19th centuries

[4]**busk** \"\ *n* -S [Creek *púskita* fast, fasting] **:** a Creek Indian festival of first-fruits and purification that was celebrated when the first green corn was edible and that marked the beginning of the new year

[5]**busk** \"\ *vi* -ED/-ING/-S [origin unknown] *Brit* **:** to entertain esp. by singing or reciting on the street or in a pub

busk·er \'bəskə(r)\ *n* -S [[5]*busk* + *-er*] **:** one who busks; *esp* **:** an itinerant entertainer ⟨as a ~ along the Bowery and then as a singing waiter —*Nation*⟩

bus·kin \'bəskən\ *n* -S [perh. modif. of Sp *borcegui* (OSp also *borzeguina*), of non-IE origin; prob. akin to the source of MF *broissequin*, a sometimes fawn-colored cloth, ML *brucequinus* buskin] **1 :** a strong thick-soled laced foot covering with a legging reaching halfway or more to the knee **2 a :** COTHURNUS **b :** TRAGEDY ⟨they witnessed 10 new plays in 12 days, which is plenty of sock and a lot of ~ —*Newsweek*⟩; *esp* **:** tragedy felt to resemble that of the ancient Greek drama in style or spirit — compare SOCK 3b **3 :** a woman's low-cut house shoe in leather or fabric having a piece of elastic goring at the instep **4 buskins** *pl* **:** gold-threaded silk stockings worn by a Roman Catholic bishop at a pontifical mass

bus·kined \-nd\ *adj* **:** of, relating to, or befitting tragedy; *esp* **:** in the manner of tragic drama

busky \'bəskē\ *adj* [[1]*busk* + *-y*] *obs* **:** BOSKY

bus line *n* **1 :** TRAIN LINE 1 **2 a :** a route over which a bus regularly travels **b :** a company operating such buses

busload \'⸗¦⸗\ *n* **:** a load that fills a bus ⟨a ~ of school children⟩ **:** bus capacity

bus·man \'bəsmən, -,sman, -,smaa(ə)n\ *n, pl* **busmen :** an operator of a bus

busman's holiday *n* **:** a holiday spent in following or observing the practice of one's usual occupation

bus-mile \'⸗¦⸗\ *n* **:** a statistical unit denoting one mile traveled by one bus — compare CAR-MILE, TON-MILE

bus rod *n* **:** BUS BAR

[1]**buss** \'bəs\ *n* -ES [ME *busse*, fr. MF, fr. ON *būza*, fr. ML *bucia*] **:** a rugged square-sailed boat formerly used esp. in herring fishery

[2]**buss** \"\ *n* -ES [prob. of imit. origin like G *buss* kiss, Sw *puss* kiss, MIr *bus*, *pus* lip, Lith *bučiuoti* to kiss] **:** KISS

[3]**buss** \"\ *vt* -ED/-ING/-ES **:** KISS ⟨we ~ our wantons but our wives we kiss —Robert Herrick †1674⟩ ⟨when the tumult stilled, the doctor had ~*ed* his wife heartily —A.J.Cronin⟩

[4]**buss** \"\ *n* -ES [ME (northern dial.) *bus*, alter. of *busk* — more at BUSH] *chiefly Scot* **:** [1]BUSH

[5]**buss** \"\ *vt* -ED/-ING/-ES [by alter.] *chiefly Scot* **:** [2]BUSK

bussed *past of* BUS

busses *pl of* BUS, *pres 3d sing of* BUS

bussing *pres part of* BUS

bus·sock \'bu̇|sək, 'bə|, |zək\ *n* -S [origin unknown] *dial Eng* **:** DONKEY

bus stop *n* **:** a point (as a street corner) on a bus route at which buses stop and which is often marked by an overhead sign

bus·su \bə'sü\ *n* -S [Pg *bussú*, fr. Tupi *ubu-ussu*, fr. *ubu* leaf + *ussu* big] **:** a low palm (*Manicaria saccifera*) of Central and So. American tidal swamps having enormous undivided oblong leaves often used in thatching, spathes like sacs, and a very large fruit — see TROOLIE

bussy \'bəsē\ *n* -ES [[2]*buss* + *-y*] *dial* **:** SWEETHEART

[1]**bust** \'bəst\ *n* -S [F *buste*, fr. It *busto*, fr. L *bustum* tomb, crematory, prob. short for *ambustum*, neut. of *ambustus*, past part. of L *amburere* to burn up, consume, fr. *ambi-* on both sides, around + *urere* to burn — more at AMBI-, EMBER] **1 a :** a sculptured representation of the upper part of the human figure including the head and neck and usu. part of the shoulders and breast **b :** a pictorial representation (as in a painting or on a coin) of this part of the human figure **2 a :** the upper portion of the human torso between neck and waist; *esp* **:** the breasts of a woman **b :** a measure around the female body marking the maximum projection of the breasts ⟨a 36-inch ~⟩ **c :** the part of a woman's garment covering the bust

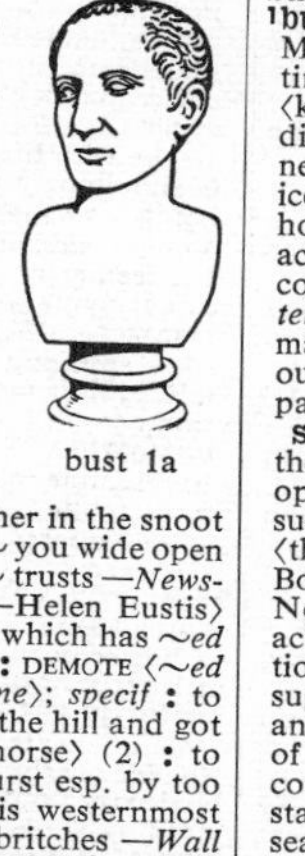

bust 1a

[2]**bust** \"\ *vb* **busted** *also* **bust; busted** *also* **bust; busting; busts** [alter. of *burst*] *vt* **1 :** HIT, PUNCH, SLUG ⟨he and his instructor had an overpowering compulsion to ~ each other in the snoot —H.H.Martin⟩ **2 a :** to break open ⟨going to ~ you wide open —Erle Stanley Gardner⟩ or break up ⟨helped ~ trusts —*Newsweek*⟩; *specif* **:** FRACTURE ⟨~ his arm trying —Helen Eustis⟩ **b :** to break financially ⟨the game of cheaters, which has ~*ed* more men than blackjack —Arthur Mayse⟩ **c :** DEMOTE ⟨~*ed* them to the bottom of the seniority list —*Time*⟩; *specif* **:** to reduce in military grade or rank ⟨he went over the hill and got ~*ed* —Mack Morriss⟩ **d** (1) **:** BREAK ⟨~ a horse⟩ (2) **:** to throw (as a steer) by roping the legs **3 :** to burst esp. by too much or too sudden swelling or growth ⟨this westernmost province . . . is beginning to ~ its industrial britches —*Wall Street Jour.*⟩ **~** *vi* **1 :** to burst esp. from too much or too sudden swelling or growth ⟨laughing fit to ~⟩ ⟨the book winds up with hell ~*ing* loose —Marshall Sprague⟩ **2 :** to break down completely while making an all-out effort ⟨engineers . . . busy making sure that the world shall be convenient if they ~ doing it —E.B.White⟩ **3 :** to fail financially **:** go broke ⟨they threw their sudden money around and ~*ed* —Noel Houston⟩ **4 a :** to fail to complete a straight or a flush in poker usu. by one card **b :** to lose at cards by exceeding a limit (as the count of 21 in blackjack) **syn** see BREAK

[3]**bust** \"\ *n* -S **1** *slang* **:** PUNCH, SOCK ⟨a good ~ on the nose —J.T.Farrell⟩ **2 a :** FAILURE ⟨we think he's going to be either a genius or a ~ —Josephine Pinckney⟩ **b :** a very weak hand in cards **3 a :** BENDER, BINGE, SPREE ⟨he could get more action in El Paso or Juarez when he went on a ~ —Ross Santee⟩ **b :** a drinking bout ⟨a beer ~⟩ **4 :** a reduction in military grade **5 a :** a sudden break and sharp decline in business activity, prices, and employment **b :** a severe recession or a depression ⟨boom and ~⟩

[4]**bust** \"\ *or* **bust·ed** \-təd\ *adj* [*bust*, alter. of *busted; busted* fr. gerund of [2]*bust*] **:** BANKRUPT, BROKE ⟨her father, before he went ~, had owned a drygoods store —Saul Bellow⟩ ⟨to play roulette side by side with a *busted* . . . duke —David Dodge⟩

bu·sta·men·te furnace \¦büstə¦mentē-\ *n* [after Juan Alonso de *Bustamante*, 18th cent. Span. metallurgist] **:** a shaft furnace for roasting quicksilver ores that has aludels for condensing the vapors — called also *aludel furnace*

bu·sta·mite \'büstə,mīt\ *n* -S [Anastasio *Bustamente* †1853 Mexican general + E *-ite*] **:** a mineral $CaMnSi_2O_6$ consisting of a calcium manganese pyroxene

bus·tard \'bəstə(r)d\ *n* -S [ME *bustarde*, modif. (perh. influenced by MF *oustarde* bustard, fr. L *avis tarda*) of MF *bistarde*, fr. OIt *bistarda*, fr. L *avis tarda*, lit., slow bird, fr. *avis* bird + *tarda* fem. of *tardus* slow — more at AVIARY] **:** any of a family (Otididae) of large chiefly terrestrial game birds of the Old World and Australia that are related both to the cranes and plovers and that frequent grassy steppes and cultivated areas, being somewhat slow and stately on the ground but capable of powerful swift flight when alarmed — see GREAT BUSTARD, KORHAAN, PLAIN TURKEY

bustard quail *n* **:** BUTTON QUAIL

bus·tee *or* **bus·ti** \'bə,stē\ *n* -S [Hindi *bastī*, fr. *basnā* to dwell, fr. Skt *vasati* he dwells — more at WAS] **1** *India* **:** a small village **2** *India* **:** a group of poor huts **:** SLUM

bust·er \'bəstə(r)\ *n* -S [[2]*bust* + *-er*] **1 a :** a person who is extraordinary (as in size, energy, or ability) **:** an esp. male child who is healthy and full of life ⟨a tough little ~, square-chinned and full of fight —John & Ward Hawkins⟩ **b** *often cap* **:** FELLOW — usu. used as a noun of address ⟨they shoot deserters, ~ —Martin Dibner⟩ **2 :** one that breaks or breaks up ⟨tank ~⟩: as **a :** PLOW — compare LISTER **b** [short for *broncobuster*] **:** one that breaks horses ⟨sometimes a contract ~ goes from ranch to ranch breaking horses at so much a head —S.E.Fletcher⟩ **3** *Austral* **:** a sudden violent wind often coming from the south — called also *southerly buster* **4 :** a crab or other decapod after the shell has split but before it is shed — compare SHEDDER 2a **5** *slang* **:** a bad fall ⟨he took a ~ that jarred the ground —F.B.Gipson⟩

buster brown \¦⸗⸗¦ brau̇n\ *adj, usu cap both Bs* [after *Buster Brown*, boy comic strip character pictured with wide-brimmed sailor hat, Lord Fauntleroy suit, and pageboy haircut, created by Richard F. Outcault †1928 Am. artist] **:** resembling or suggestive of Buster Brown (as in style of clothing or haircut) ⟨he felt the pinch and chafe of the *Buster Brown* collar as he turned to watch the minister —Charles Jackson⟩

busthead \'⸗,⸗\ *n* [[2]*bust* + *head*] **1** *dial* **:** MOONSHINE WHISKEY **2** *dial* **:** HEADACHE

bustian *n* -S [ME *busteyne*] *obs* **:** a cotton fabric formerly used in clothing (as vestments, waistcoats)

bus·tic \'bəstik\ *n* -S [origin unknown] **:** a tree (*Dipholis salicifolia*) of the family Sapotaceae of southern Florida and the West Indies with hard wood, shining lanceolate leaves, and white flowers

busting *pres part of* BUST

[1]**bus·tle** \'bəsəl\ *vb* **bustled; bustled; bustling** \'bəs(ə)liŋ\ **bustles** [prob. alter. of obs. *buskle* to prepare, bustle about, freq. of [2]*busk*] *vi* **1 a :** to move energetically and often with apparent purpose but usu. noisily or inefficiently ⟨she never ~*s* but she is constantly busy —*Time*⟩ **b :** HURRY, HUSTLE ⟨the head waiter *bustled* up, full of apologies —Ian Bevan⟩ **2** *obs* **:** STRUGGLE, CONTEND **3 :** TEEM, CRAWL ⟨all the river landings *bustled* with colorful activity —*Amer. Guide Series: Minn.*⟩ **~** *vt* **:** to cause to bustle **:** HURRY, HUSTLE

[2]**bustle** \"\ *n* -S **1 :** a stir or commotion of bustling **:** noisy or energetic activity ⟨the hustle and ~ of the city⟩ **2** *archaic* **:** STRUGGLE, SCUFFLE **syn** see STIR

[3]**bustle** \"\ *n* -S [origin unknown] **:** a framework (as of metal, whalebone, crinoline) or a padded cushion that expands and supports the fullness and drapery of the back of a woman's skirt in some former fashions; *also* **:** a recurrent fashion adapted from this

bus·tled \'bəsəld\ *adj* [[3]*bustle* + *-ed*] **:** wearing a bustle

bustle pipe *n* [[1]*bustle*] **:** the outside pipe that supplies the blast to the tuyeres in a blast furnace

bus·tler \'bəs(ə)lə(r)\ *n* -S **:** one that bustles **:** HUSTLER

bustle

bustling *adj* **:** making a bustle **:** given to or full of bustle ⟨he had the ~ ways of an amateur nurse —Stephen Crane⟩ — **bus·tling·ly** *adv*

bus·to \'bə(,)stō, 'bü(-\ *n, pl* **bustos** *or* **bustoes** [It — more at BUST] *archaic* **:** [1]BUST 1a

bust out *vi* **:** to fail to attain in a school or training program the minimum grades required for continuing **:** flunk out **~** *vt* **1** *dial* **:** to plough out **2 :** to drop (as from a school or training program) usu. because of failure to maintain minimum grades or other standards **:** flunk out ⟨sooner or later he must be *busted out* —A.Q.Maisel⟩

bust-out man \'⸗,⸗-\ *n* **:** one skilled at switching crooked dice in and out of a game

bust peg *n* [[1]*bust*] **:** a post fixed to a flat base and used as a support for the clay or wax a bust is modeled from

bustrophedon *or* **bustropheidon** *var of* BOUSTROPHEDON

busts *pl of* BUST, *pres 3d sing of* BUST

bust-up \'⸗,⸗\ *n* -S [*bust up*, v.] **1 :** a breaking up or apart ⟨the *bust-up* of camp⟩ ⟨the *bust-up* of their marriage⟩ **2 :** a big party or celebration ⟨there'll be an awful crowd — a regular *bust-up* —Norman Douglas⟩

busty \'bəstē, -ti\ *adj, usu* -ER/-EST [[1]*bust* + *-y*] **:** having a large bust ⟨a ~ actress⟩

bus·way \'⸗,⸗\ *n* **:** BUS DUCT

[1]**busy** \'bizē, -zi\ *adj* -ER/-EST [ME *bisy*, fr. OE *bisig;* akin to MD & MLG *besich* busy] **1 :** engaged in something requiring time or attention **:** not idle or at leisure **:** OCCUPIED, ENGAGED ⟨keeping the American front ~ while Howe and his other divisions were moving —F.V.W.Mason⟩ **2 :** full of business activity **:** ACTIVE, BUSTLING ⟨a ~ seaport⟩ ⟨the snow and ice melted . . . and Mount Vernon was soon ~ with its old hospitality —H.E.Scudder⟩ **3 :** foolishly or intrudingly active **:** OFFICIOUS, MEDDLING ⟨a ~, fussy sort of man much concerned with regulating everything —A.M.Young⟩ **4** *of a telephone line* **:** being used **5 :** having intricate details or many separate parts that are not coordinated into a harmonious whole — used esp. of an artistic design ⟨a ~ floral wallpaper⟩

syn INDUSTRIOUS, DILIGENT, ASSIDUOUS, SEDULOUS: BUSY, the most general of these words, mainly stresses activity as opposed to idleness ⟨always *busy*, making it a point never to suspend for one moment his occupation —John Burroughs⟩ ⟨the merchants of Charleston and Portsmouth, Norfolk and Boston with their *busy* offices full of bustling clerks —Allan Nevins & H. S. Commager⟩ The word may connote purposive activity ⟨this man of action wanted to get *busy* on the proposition without loss of time —Upton Sinclair⟩ INDUSTRIOUS may suggest habitual or continual earnest enterprise ⟨a vigorous and *industrious* girl, who, single-handed, kept the farm in a sort of order —Dorothy Sayers⟩ DILIGENT may stress care, constancy, attentiveness, and thoroughness ⟨when we came to start, the Yankee's boots were missing, and after a *diligent* search were not to be found —Herman Melville⟩ ⟨the young investigator becomes a *diligent* student of literature and laboriously examines the relevant passages —Havelock Ellis⟩ ASSIDUOUS suggests constant, unremitting effort ⟨he inherited the strict and severe piety of his father; he was *assiduous* in his attendance on religious services whether by night or day —J.R.Green⟩ ⟨even the most *assiduous* critic can scarcely hope to keep abreast of the growing flood of translated books —*Times Lit. Supp.*⟩ SEDULOUS connotes careful painstaking attentiveness ⟨too prolonged and heated and discursive to interest any but the most *sedulous* reader —H.G.Wells⟩ ⟨this man who, after weeks of *sedulous* and disheartening analysis, eventually ferreted out the source —W.H.Wright⟩

[2]**busy** \"\ *vb* -ED/-ING/-ES [ME *bisien*, fr. OE *bisgian*, fr. *bisig*, adj.] *vt* **:** to make busy ⟨the faithful servant *busied* himself about the room —Winston Churchill⟩ **:** ENGAGE, OCCUPY ⟨I have need to ~ my heart with quietude —Rupert Brooke⟩ **~** *vi* **:** to get or keep busy ⟨I *busied* about and I made him two good-sized sandwiches —Edwin Corle⟩

[1]**busybody** \'⸗⸗,⸗⸗\ *n* [[1]*busy* + *body*] **1 :** one who concerns himself with affairs not his own **:** SNOOPER, MEDDLER **2 :** a device consisting typically of three mirrors mounted in a metal frame usu. attached to the side of an upper window and used to enable a person indoors to see places not ordinarily within his view ⟨with her ~ she could see both doors from her favorite chair⟩

[2]**busybody** \"\ *vi* -ED/-ING/-ES **:** to behave like a busybody — usu. used in the form *busybodying* ⟨~*ing* about —Nathaniel Burt⟩ — **busy·body·ism** \-,izəm\ *n* -S

bu·sy·con \byü'sī,kän\ *n, cap* [NL, fr. Gk *bousykon*, a large fig, fr. *bous* head of cattle + *sykon* fig] **:** a genus of large marine snails of the family Buccinidae — see WINKLE

busy·ness \'bizēnəs, -zin-\ *n* -ES [[1]*busy* + *-ness*] **:** the quality or state of being busy ⟨his presence caused a marked increase in ~ on the staff —J.G.Cozzens⟩; *often* **:** the condition or appearance of busily engaging in some trivial, unproductive, or meaningless labor or activity ⟨sterile ~ . . . has crept into the colleges and universities —Robert Ulich⟩ ⟨his main object in life was to combine an elaborate obstructionist policy with an appearance of intense ~ and affability —J.B.D.Cotter⟩ ⟨ceremonial and vacuous ~ —Mary McCarthy⟩

busywork \'⸗⸗,⸗\ *n* **:** work that usu. appears productive or of intrinsic value but actually only keeps one occupied ⟨freshmen know perfectly well that most of the writing assigned to them is pedagogical ~ —Mary P. Keeley⟩

[1]**but** \(')bət, *usu* -əd·+V\ *conj* [ME, conj. & prep., fr. OE *būtan*, *būte*, conj. & prep., without, except, outside; akin to OS *būtan*, *biūtan* without, except, OHG *būzan*, *biūzan;* all fr. a prehistoric WGmc compound whose first and second constituents respectively are the preposition represented by OE *be*, *bī* by and the adverb represented by OE *ūtan* outside, from outside, OHG *ūzana*, *ūzan*, ON *ūtan*, Goth *ūtana;* derivative fr. the root of OE *ūt* out — more at BY, OUT] **1 a :** except for the fact — used to introduce a dependent clause ⟨he would have protested ~ that he was afraid⟩ **b :** THAT — sometimes used more or less tautologically with *that;* used after negatives ⟨there is no doubt ~ he was killed in the wreck⟩ ⟨he did not question ~ that he would win⟩ ⟨it is 10 to 1 ~ the challenger will lose⟩ **c :** without the concomitant that ⟨it never rains ~ it pours⟩ ⟨you cannot look into the index ~ you will find the word⟩ **d :** if not **:** UNLESS ⟨may I die ~ she is right⟩ **:** if it were not true that ⟨~ my noble Moor is true of mind . . . it were enough to put him to ill thinking —Shak.⟩ **e :** that . . . not ⟨there was never a new plan ~ someone objected to it⟩ ⟨he was not so stupid ~ he could drive a hard bargain⟩ ⟨it was impossible ~ he should notice it⟩ ⟨a pity ~ we knew more about him⟩ **f** (1) *archaic* **:** WHEN, BEFORE **:** at the time that (2) *now substand* **:** THAN — used after *no sooner* ⟨no sooner started ~ it stopped again⟩ **2 a :** on the contrary **:** on the other hand **:** in opposition **:** NOTWITHSTANDING — used to connect coordinate elements ⟨not peace ~ a sword⟩ ⟨not Smith ~ Smyth⟩ ⟨not with haste ~ with caution⟩ ⟨he was called ~ he did not answer⟩ **b :** YET ⟨he was commonly thought to be wealthy ~ he had no money⟩ — sometimes used at the beginning of a separate sentence ⟨the rebels' cause looked hopeless. *But* they received help from the provinces⟩ and sometimes interpreted as an adverb when so used **c :** EXCEPT **:** with the exception of — used before a word often taken to be the subject of a clause ⟨whence all ~ he had fled —Felicia D. Hemans⟩ ⟨none ~ the brave deserve the fair —John Dryden⟩ **d** — used with little meaning as a formal connective ⟨all men are mortal ~ he is a man⟩ **e** — used in connection with interjectional expressions to express a degree of restraining, countering, or modifying ⟨heavens, ~ it rains⟩ — **but and** *archaic Scot* **:** and also **:** in addition — **but what 1 :** but that ⟨not . . . such an opprobrious nickname *but what* kings have been so nicknamed —E.C.Smith⟩ **2 :** that . . . not — used to indicate possibility or uncertainty ⟨I don't know *but what* I will go⟩

[2]**but** \"\ *prep* [ME, conj. & prep.] **1** *Scot* **a :** WITHOUT, LACKING ⟨touch not the cat ~ a glove —*Motto of the Mackintoshes*⟩ **b :** to or into the outer room of **:** OUTSIDE ⟨go ~ the house⟩ **2 :** EXCEPT: **a :** EXCLUDING, BARRING **:** with the exception of ⟨there was no one left ~ me —R.L.Stevenson⟩ ⟨wanting nothing ~ a little time⟩ ⟨what could he do ~ protest⟩ — see [1]BUT 2c **b :** other than **:** otherwise than **:** anything else than ⟨this letter is nothing ~ an insult⟩ ⟨who could fill the position ~ this man⟩ ⟨how would he look ~ haggard⟩ ⟨nothing would please him ~ that we go along⟩

[3]**but** \"\ *adv* [ME, fr. *but*, conj. & prep.] **1 :** ONLY: **a** (1) **:** no other or no more than indicated ⟨he is ~ a child⟩ (2) **:** more than ⟨I never heard of ~ one man that survived such an experience⟩ — often considered substand. **b :** without alternative **:** with no other choice ⟨we could ~ listen to his plea⟩ **c :** no longer ago than ⟨it happened ~ yesterday⟩ ⟨he was here ~ five minutes ago⟩ **d :** MERELY ⟨the presence of ~ a little poisonous gas⟩ **2** *Scot* **:** to or into the outer room or kitchen of a house **:** OUTSIDE, WITHOUT — opposed to *ben* **3 :** to the contrary — usu. used with *that* beginning a following clause ⟨who knows ~ that he may succeed⟩ **4 :** DEFINITELY, POSITIVELY, STRONGLY, THOROUGHLY **:** to a degree precluding doubt or reservation ⟨get there ~ fast⟩

[4]**but** \"\ *pron* [[1]*but*] **:** that not **:** who not ⟨nobody ~ has his fault —Shak.⟩ ⟨nothing indeed ever entered that little country ~ came out rejuvenated and clarified —Norman Douglas⟩

[5]**but** \"\ *adj* [[3]*but*] *Scot* **:** in the outer room or kitchen of a house **:** OUTER

[6]**but** \"\ *n* -S *Scot* **:** the outer apartment of a house; *esp* **:** the kitchen of a but-and-ben

[7]**but** *var of* BUTT

but- *or* **buto-** *comb form* [ISV, fr. *butyric*] **:** containing a group of four carbon atoms ⟨*but*ane⟩ ⟨*but*ene⟩ ⟨*buto*pyronoxyl⟩

bu·ta-bu·ta \¦büd·ə¦büd·ə\ *n* -S [Malay] **:** a tree (*Excoecaria agallocha*) of the family Euphorbiaceae that is native along the coastal regions in southern Asia and has a poisonous milky juice and flowers in axillary spikes

bu·ta·caine \'byüd·ə,kān, ,⸗⸗'⸗\ *n* -S [*buta*ne + *-caine* (as in *cocaine*)] **:** a local anesthetic $NH_2C_6H_4COO(CH_2)_3NH(C_4H_9)_2$ that is an ester of *para*-aminobenzoic acid and is applied in the form of its white crystalline sulfate to mucous membranes

bu·ta·di·ene \,byüd·ə'dī,ēn, ,⸗⸗,⸗'⸗\ *n* -S [ISV *buta*ne + *di-* + *-ene*] **:** a flammable gaseous diolefin $CH_2{=}CHCH{=}CH_2$ very reactive and polymerizing readily that is made by several processes (as by catalytic dehydrogenation of normal butane or normal butylenes at high temperatures) and is used chiefly in making synthetic rubbers (as GR-S and nitrile rubbers) — called also *bivinyl*, *1,3-butadiene*

bu·tal·de·hyde \byü'taldə,hīd\ *n* -S [by alter.] **:** BUTYRALDEHYDE

bu·ta·nal \'byüd·ə,nal, -üt[ə]n,al\ *n* -S [*butane* + *-al*] **:** normal butyraldehyde

but and ben \¦bət[ə]n¦ben\ *adv* [Sc [3]*but* (out) + *ben* (in)] *Scot* **1 :** back and forth **:** in and out; *specif* **:** from one part of a house to the other **2 :** on opposite sides or at opposite ends of (a house, a corridor) ⟨we lived *but and ben* with them⟩

but-and-ben \"\ *n, Scot* **:** a 2-roomed cottage

bu·tane \'byü,tān, ⸗'⸗\ *n* -S [ISV *but-* + *-ane*] **:** either of two isomeric flammable easily liquefiable gaseous paraffin hydrocarbons C_4H_{10} obtained usu. from petroleum or natural gas and occurring in gasoline and in liquefied petroleum gas: **a :** the normal compound $CH_3CH_2CH_2CH_3$ used chiefly in making butadiene and as a fuel gas — called also *n-butane*, *normal butane* **b :** ISOBUTANE

bu·tane·di·ol \'byü(ˌ)tān(ˌ)dīˌȯl, -ˌōl\ *n* -s [*butane* + *-diol*] **:** any of four isomeric glycols $C_4H_8(OH)_2$: as **a :** a hygroscopic liquid $CH_3CHOHCH_2CH_2OH$ made usu. by hydrogenation of aldol and used chiefly as a humectant and plasticizer — called also *1,3-butanediol, 1,3-butylene glycol* **b :** a viscous liquid $CH_2OHCH_2CH_2CH_2OH$ made from acetylene, formaldehyde, and hydrogen and used chiefly in making polyurethane resins — called also *1,4-butanediol, 1,4-butylene glycol, tetramethylene glycol* **c :** a hygroscopic viscous liquid or crystalline solid $CH_3CHOHCHOHCH_3$ known in four optically different forms, obtained usu. by fermentation (as of grains or molasses), and used chiefly in organic synthesis — called also *2,3-butanediol, 2,3-butylene glycol*

bu·ta·no·ic acid \ˌbyüd·ə¦nōik-\ *n* [*butane* + *-o-* + *-ic*] **:** BUTYRIC ACID a — used in the system of nomenclature adopted by the International Union of Pure and Applied Chemistry

bu·ta·nol \'byüd·ənˌōl, -nȯl; -üt°nˌōl, -nˌōl\ *n* -s [ISV *butane* + *-ol*] **:** either of the two butyl alcohols derived from normal butane and distinguished as 1-butanol and 2-butanol; *esp* **:** BUTYL ALCOHOL a

bu·tan·o·lide \byü'tanəˌlīd, -ˌləd\ *n* -s [ISV *butanol* + *-ide*] **:** BUTYROLACTONE

bu·ta·none \'byüd·əˌnōn, -üt°nˌōn\ *n* -s [ISV *butane* + *-one*; prob. orig. formed in F] **:** METHYL ETHYL KETONE

¹butch \'bu̇ch, 'bəch\ *vt* -ED/-ING/-ES [back-formation from ¹*butcher*] **1** *dial* **:** BUTCHER, SLAUGHTER **2** *dial* **:** to make a clumsy job of **:** BOTCH

²butch \'bu̇ch\ *n* -ES [perh. fr. *Butch*, a nickname for boys, esp. tough boys; fr. the close-cropped appearance of some stereotype ruffians] **:** a close haircut **:** CREW CUT

¹butch·er \'bu̇chə(r), *dial sporadically* 'büch- *also* 'bəch-\ *n* -s [ME *bocher*, fr. OF *bochier, bouchier*, fr. *bouc* he-goat, prob. of Celt origin; akin to MIr *bocc* he-goat, W *bwch* — more at BUCK] **1 :** one who slaughters animals or dresses the flesh of animals, fish, or poultry for market; *also* **:** a dealer in meat **2 :** one that kills ruthlessly or brutally or bloodily ⟨oh pardon me . . . that I am meek and gentle with these ~*s* —Shak.⟩ **3 :** an unskillful or careless workman **:** BOTCHER **4 :** a hog suitable for slaughter for general table purposes usu. as distinguished from light porkers and from very heavy hogs chiefly fit for the sausage trade **5 :** a vendor esp. on trains or in theaters ⟨candy ~⟩

²butcher \"\ *vt* **butchered; butchered; butchering** \-ch(ə)riŋ\ **butchers 1 :** to slaughter and dress (meat, fish, and poultry) for market **2 :** to kill in a bloody, barbarous, or cruel manner **3 :** BOTCH ⟨~ a text⟩ ⟨~ a musical composition⟩

³butcher \"\ *adj* [²*butcher*] *of animals* **:** suitable for butchering

butcher-bird \'==ˌ=\ *n* [so called fr. their habit of impaling their prey on thorns] **:** any of various shrikes: as **a :** a member of the genus *Lanius* (esp. the common European species *L. exubitor* and in America the northern shrike *L. borealis*) **b :** any of several pied birds (genus *Cracticus*) widely distributed in Australia

butcher-bird

butch·er·er \-ch(ə)rə(r)\ *n* -s **:** one that butchers

butcher knife *n* **:** a heavy-duty knife usu. 6 to 8 inches long having a broad rigid blade that curves slightly at the tip

butch·er·less \-chə(r)ləs\ *adj* **:** being without a butcher

butcher linen *also* **butcher's linen** *also* **butcher rayon** *n* **:** a strong heavy linen of plain weave used orig. for butchers' aprons; *also* **:** a similar fabric for clothing made of rayon staple or cotton with a finish like linen

butch·er·ly \-chə(r)lē, -li\ *adj* **:** like a butcher: as **a :** without compunction **:** SAVAGE, BLOODY **b :** CLUMSY, UNSKILLFUL ⟨~ mob⟩

butcher paper *n* **:** a strong wrapping paper resistant to the penetration of blood and meat fluids

butcher's-broom \'==ˌ=\ *n, pl* **butcher's-brooms :** a European leafless plant (*Ruscus aculeatus*) that bears stiff-pointed cladophylls and is often cultivated for its twigs which are used for ornament and for whisk brooms

butch·ery \-ch(ə)rē, -ri\ *n* -ES [ME *bocherie*, fr. MF *bocherie, boucherie*, fr. *bochier, bouchier* butcher + *-ie* -y — more at BUTCHER] **1** *now chiefly Brit* **:** a place where slaughtered meat is cut up **:** SLAUGHTERHOUSE **2 :** the process or business of preparing meat for sale **3 :** violent, cruel, or bloody slaughter **:** MASSACRE, CARNAGE **4 :** BOTCH, BUNGLE

bu·tea \'byüd·ēə\ *n, cap* [NL, after John Stuart, 3d earl of *Bute* †1792 Scot. statesman and scholar] **:** a genus of East Indian trees or shrubs (family Leguminosae) having 3-flowered racemes and a downy bracted calyx — see DHAK

butea gum *n, often cap B* **:** the dried juice of the dhak tree obtained as reddish or dark translucent masses and used as an astringent — called also *Bengal kino*

bu·te·in \'byüd·ēən\ *n* -s [ISV *bute-* (fr. NL *Butea*, genus name of *Butea frondosa*) + *-in*] **:** a yellow crystalline coloring matter $C_{15}H_{12}O_5$ derived from chalcone that is obtained esp. from the flowers of the dhak tree

bu·tene \'byüd·ēn, -ü(ˌ)tēn\ *n* -s [ISV *but-* + *-ene*] **:** BUTYLENE 1a, 1b

bu·te·nyl \'byüt°nəl\ *n* -s [ISV *butene* + *-yl*] **:** any of three univalent radicals C_4H_7 derived from the two butenes by removal of one hydrogen atom — see CROTYL

bu·teo \'byüd·ēō\ *n* [NL, fr. L, a falcon or hawk — more at BUZZARD] **1** *cap* **:** a genus of hawks that have broad rounded wings and fan-shaped tails and that soar and wheel high in the air **2** -s **:** a hawk of the genus *Buteo* (as the rough-legged hawks and red-shouldered hawks); *also* **:** a hawk resembling a member of this genus in appearance or habits of flight

¹bu·te·o·nine \'byüd·ēəˌnīn, -ˌnən; byü'tē-\ *adj* [NL *Buteon-, Buteo* + E *-ine*] **:** of or relating to the genus *Buteo* or to the short-winged hawks — compare ACCIPITRINE, CATHARTINE

²buteonine \"\ *n* -s **:** BUTEO 2

bute·shire \'byütshi(ə)r\ *or* **bute** \'byüt\ *adj, usu cap* [fr. *Buteshire* or *Bute* county, Scotland] **:** of or from the county of Bute, Scotland **:** of the kind or style prevalent in Bute

bu·thi·dae \'byüthəˌdē\ *n pl, cap* [NL, fr. *Buthus*, type genus + *-idae*] **:** a widely distributed family of scorpions having a large triangular sternum with the sides strongly convergent anteriorly

bu·thus \'byüthəs\ *n, cap* [NL] **:** the type genus of Buthidae containing a number of dangerous scorpions of warm regions of the Old World

bu·tine \'byüˌtīn\ *archaic var of* BUTYNE

but·ler \'bətlə(r)\ *n* -s [ME *buteler, boteler*, fr. OF *bouteillier* bottle bearer, fr. *bouteille* bottle — more at BOTTLE] **1 :** a manservant having charge of the wines and liquors **2 :** an officer of a royal household who was orig. the supplier of wines **3 :** the chief servant of a household who has charge of other employees, receives guests, performs personal services as requested, and serves or directs the serving of meals **4 :** a receptacle used for collecting, carrying, holding, or serving esp. food or drinks ⟨silent ~⟩

but·ler·age \-lərij\ *n* -s [ME *botelerage*, fr. *boteler, buteler* + *-age*] **1 :** a former duty on wine imported into England payable to the king's butler — compare PRISAGE **2 :** the part of a household's management under a butler's charge

butler finish *n* [so called fr. the fact that silver polishing is a traditional task of butlers] **:** a satin finish produced on silver by first buffing bright and then dulling to simulate the appearance of old silver

but·ler·ite \'bətləˌrīt\ *n* -s *usu cap* [Dean G. M. *Butler* b1881 Am. geologist and mineralogist + E *-ite*] **:** a mineral $Fe(SO_4)(OH).2H_2O$ consisting of hydrous basic sulfate of iron

butler's pantry *n* **:** a pantry for the use of a butler **:** a service room between kitchen and dining room

butler's tray *n* **1 :** an oval wooden tray whose four sides are hinged to fold out flat when set down **2 :** a tray with attached and usu. folding legs

but·lery \'bətlərē, -ri\ *n* -ES [ME *botelerie*, fr. OF *bouteillerie* wine cellar, fr. *bouteille* bottle + *-erie* -ery — more at BOTTLE] **:** BUTTERY

bu·to·ma·ce·ae \ˌbyüd·ə'māsēˌē\ *n pl, cap* [NL, fr. *Butomus*, type genus + *-aceae*] **:** a small family of monocotyledonous water or marsh herbs (order Naiadales) distinguished chiefly by the many ovules and the dehiscent carpels of the fruit — compare WATER POPPY — **bu·to·ma·ceous** \ˌ==¦māshəs\ *adj*

bu·to·mus \'byüd·əməs\ *n, cap* [NL, fr. Gk *boutomos, boutomon* sedge] **:** a genus (the type of the family Butomaceae) of bog herbs having leaves ensiform and 3-angled at the base and flowers in umbels

bu·to·py·ro·nox·yl \ˌbyüd·əˌpīrə'näksəl\ *n* -s [*but-* + *pyrone* + *oxyl*] **:** a yellow to reddish brown liquid $C_{12}H_{18}O_4$ used as an insect repellent

bu·tox·ide \byü'täkˌsīd, -ˌsəd\ *n* -s [*but-* + *oxide*] **:** a binary compound of butoxyl; *esp* **:** a base formed from a butyl alcohol by replacement of the hydroxyl hydrogen ⟨sodium ~⟩

bu·toxy \byü'täksē\ *adj* [*butoxy-*] **:** of, relating to, or containing butoxyl

butoxy- *comb form* [ISV, fr. *butoxyl*] **:** containing butoxyl

bu·tox·yl \byü'täksəl\ *n* -s [blend of *butyl* and *oxy-*] **:** a univalent radical $C_4H_9O—$ composed of butyl united with oxygen; *esp* **:** the radical corresponding to normal butyl

buts *pl of* BUT

bütschliite *var of* BUETSCHLIITE

butsudan \'bu̇tsəˌdän\ *n, pl* **butsudan** *or* **butsudans** [Jap, fr. *butsu* Buddha + *dan* platform, altar] **:** a small household Buddhist altar shelf found in many Japanese homes and bearing typically the image of the principal family deity and ancestral name tablets

¹butt \'bət, *usu* -əd·+V\ *vb* -ED/-ING/-S [ME *butten*, fr. OF *boter, bouter*, of Gmc origin; akin to OHG *bōzan* to beat — more at BEAT] *vi* **1 :** to thrust or push head foremost **:** strike with the head or horns ⟨~*ing* and kicking⟩ ⟨~*ing* against the fence⟩ **2** *of gears* **:** to mesh improperly so that only the tips of the teeth touch ~ *vt* **:** to strike or shove with the head or horns ⟨~*ed* his opponent heavily in the ribs⟩ **:** drive by striking or pushing with the head ⟨~*ed* him through the gate and out of the yard⟩

²butt \"\ *n* -s **:** a blow or thrust with the head or horns **:** an act of butting

³butt \"\ *or* **but** \"\ *n* -s [ME *butte*, fr. MD *but, butte* or MLG *but*; akin to MD *bot* blunt, LG *butt*, ON *būtr* log, OHG *bōzan* to beat — more at BEAT] **:** FLOUNDER, FLATFISH; *esp* **:** HALIBUT

⁴butt \"\ *n* -s [ME *but, butte*, partly fr. MF *but* goal, target, of Gmc origin (akin to ON *būtr* log); partly prob. fr. MF *bute* mound of earth serving as backstop for a target, fr. *but* target] **1 a :** a mound, bank, or other backstop for catching arrows shot at a target **b :** TARGET **c :** a mound or bank that catches rifle bullets or other projectiles (as for protecting men operating targets on a target range) **d butts** *pl* **:** RANGE 5a(3) **e :** a stand concealed by a parapet or thicket or sunk in the ground and used for shooting birds **2 a** *obs* **:** LIMIT, BOUND, GOAL **b** *archaic* **:** the object of one's efforts **:** END, AIM **3 a :** a person at whom ridicule or jokes are directed **:** LAUGHINGSTOCK ⟨a favorite ~ of the village wits⟩ **b :** an object of criticism, abuse, contempt, or swindling **:** VICTIM, MARK ⟨the ~ of a propaganda attack⟩ ⟨cardsharpers and their ~*s*⟩

⁵butt \"\ *vb* -ED/-ING/-S [partly fr. ⁴*butt*, partly fr. ⁶*butt*] *vi* **:** to meet or adjoin at the end **:** ABUT — used with *on* ⟨the crofts are usually long and narrow, one end ~*ing* on the fields —M.W.Beresford⟩ or *against* ⟨the plate ~*s* against the end stop secured on the front end of the planer —J.M.Walter⟩ ~ *vt* **1** *obs* **:** to lay out the limits of **:** BOUND **2 a :** to place (as a beam) end to end with another **:** set (two pieces) together with the ends meeting but not overlapping **b :** to trim or otherwise cause to meet or be joined along the edges (as strips of wallpaper) **3 a :** to place end to end (as two type slugs to make a longer line than can be cast in one piece) **b :** to fit corner to corner (as border rules to make a box) **c :** to position (two printing plates) so close together that the printing surfaces meet **4 :** to trim or square off the end of (as a log or a shoulder of meat) **5 a :** to strike (a fish) by depressing the butt of the rod so as to obtain a sudden tension of the line **b :** to set (as a ladder) on the bottom end **6 :** to reduce (as a cigarette) to a butt by stubbing or stamping ⟨hastily ~*ed* their cigarettes and came to attention⟩

⁶butt \"\ *n* -s [ME *but, butte*, prob. of native origin and akin to OE *buttuc* end, piece of land, ME *buttok* buttock, LG *butt* blunt — more at BUTT (fish)] **1 a** *slang* **:** BUTTOCKS **b** (1) **:** the large end of a beef loin (2) **:** the body end of a pork shoulder **c :** the thicker or handle end of a tool or weapon ⟨the ~ of a spear⟩ ⟨the ~ of a whip⟩ ⟨the ~ of an arrow⟩ **d** (1) **:** the end of a rifle stock that is placed against the shoulder when fired **:** the end of a rifle opposite the muzzle (2) **:** the bottom of the grip of a pistol **e :** the base section of a fishing rod upon which the reel is mounted **f :** the end of a connecting rod or similar link in a machine, enlarged and squared off (as for the attachment of an adjacent link) **g** *of the hand* **:** the heel or part nearest the wrist **h :** BUTT HINGE **2 a :** the end of a plant from which the roots spring (as the base of a tree trunk) **:** the big end of a log; *also* **:** the end of a stalk or twig opposite to the flowering end ⟨the ~ of a cornstalk⟩ ⟨asparagus ~*s*⟩ **b :** the thick end of a plank, plate, bar, board, or shingle **c :** the heavy or bottom end of a ladder **d** (1) **:** a fitting that serves as a coupling at the end of a line of hose (2) **:** the end of a hose **3 a :** a tree stump; *specif* **:** a walnut stump **b :** an unused or unburned end (as of a candle or a cigarette or cigar) **c** *slang* **:** CIGARETTE **d** *slang* **:** a remaining part ⟨two more years and a ~ of a prison term⟩ **e** *obs* **:** a strip of plowed land shortened by abutting against some object (as a river, a highway, or a neighboring furlong) **:** SELION **4 a :** the part of a hide or skin corresponding to the animal's back and sides after trimming off shoulders and belly, containing the thickest and stoutest leather, and used for harness, belting, soles of shoes — see HIDE illustration **b :** the thickest part of a leaf spring where the leaves have not been thinned by tapering or drawing **5 :** a place where a stratum of rock to be quarried is cut off by other rock **6 :** the posterior end of the dubbing of an artificial fly — see FLY illustration

⁷butt \"\ *n* -s [ME, fr. MF *botte*, fr. OProv *bota*, fr. LL *buttis*, perh. of non-IE origin; akin to the source of Gk *pytinē*, a kind of wine bottle, Gk dial. (Tarentum) *bytinē* chamber pot] **1 :** a large cask esp. for wine, beer, or water or formerly for salmon and shrimps **2 :** any of various units of liquid capacity: as **a :** a measure equal to 108 imperial gallons (2 hogsheads of 54 gallons each) **b :** a Spanish unit for wine equal to 140 U. S. gallons or 116.57 imperial gallons

⁸butt \"\ *n* -s [ME *but, butt* ridge of ground between two furrows, fr. ML *butta, buttis*, perh. fr. LL *buttis* cask] *now dial* **:** a small piece of ground separated or set out in any way from the surrounding land

butt block *n* [⁶*butt*] **:** a block of hardwood to which the ends of adjoining planks of a ship's frames are fastened

butt chain *n* [⁶*butt*] **:** a chain to attach the end of a trace to a singletree in a harness

butt chisel *n* [⁶*butt*] **:** a short woodworking chisel suitable for fitting hinges or strike plates

butt cut *n* [⁶*butt*] **1 :** the log next above the stump — called also *butt log* **2 :** tanbark taken from the lower part of a tree before felling it for subsequent further peeling

butte \'byüt, usu -üd·+V\ *n* -s [F, knoll, hillock, fr. MF *bute* mound of earth serving as backstop for a target — more at BUTT (mound)] **:** an isolated hill or small mountain with steep or precipitous sides and a top variously flat, rounded, or pointed that may be a residual mass isolated by erosion (as at Butte, Montana), a volcanic cone (as East Butte, Idaho), or an exposed volcanic neck (as Ship Rock, New Mexico) and that usu. has a smaller summit area than a mesa

butted *past of* BUTT

butt end *n* [⁶*butt*] **1 :** the thicker or handle end **2 :** an unused or remaining portion **:** FAG END

¹but·ter \'bəd·ə(r), 'bətə-\ *n* -s [ME, fr. OE *butere*; akin to OFris & OHG *butera* butter; all fr. a prehistoric WGmc word borrowed fr. L *butyrum* butter, fr. Gk *boutyron*, fr. *bou-* (fr. *bous* cow) + *-tyron* (fr. *tyros* cheese); akin to Av *tūiri-* whey and perh. to L *tumēre* to swell — more at COW, THUMB] **1 :** an important food consisting of a solid emulsion mainly of fat globules, air bubbles, and water droplets made to coalesce by churning the cream obtained from milk and used esp. as a spread on bread and in cooking **2 :** a substance resembling butter esp. in consistency: as **a :** an inorganic chloride — not now used technically ⟨~ of zinc⟩ **b :** any of various fatty oils remaining nearly solid at ordinary temperatures ⟨vegetable ~*s*⟩ **c :** a smooth food spread made from fruit, nuts, or other food ⟨anchovy ~⟩ ⟨apple ~⟩ **d :** dairy butter mixed with a savory food or food product ⟨parsley ~⟩ ⟨garlic ~⟩ **3 :** BUTTER DISH **4 :** FLATTERY, CAJOLERY

²butter \"\ *vt* **buttered; buttered; buttering** \'bəd·əriŋ, 'bət(ə)riŋ\ **butters** [ME *butteren*, fr. OE *buterian* to butter, fr. *butere*, n.] **1 :** to cover or spread with butter **2 :** to beguile or cover with lavish or fulsome flattery or praise — usu. used with *up* **3 :** to spread the surface of (as a brick or tile) with a plastic material (as mortar) before setting in place

butter-and-egg man \ˌbəd·ə(r)'neg-, -ə(r)n'deg-\ *n, slang* **:** a free spender or wealthy investor **:** a naive prosperous businessman

butter-and-eggs \ˌbəd·ə(r)'negz, -ə(r)n'degz\ *n pl but sing or pl in constr* **:** any of several plants having flowers of two shades of yellow: as **a :** TOADFLAX **b :** OWL'S CLOVER

butterball \'==ˌ=\ *n* **1 :** a fat chubby person **2 :** any of certain ducks: as **a :** BUFFLEHEAD **b :** RUDDY DUCK

butter basket *n* **:** GLOBEFLOWER

butter bean *n* **1 :** WAX BEAN **2 :** LIMA BEAN: as **a** *chiefly South & Midland* **:** a large dried lima bean **b :** SIEVA BEAN **3 :** a green shell bean; *also* **:** a shell bean as opposed to snap bean

butterbill \'==ˌ=\ *n* **:** AMERICAN SCOTER

butterboat \'==ˌ=\ *n* **:** a small gravy boat

butterboat-bill *or* **butterboat-billed coot** \'==ˌ=ˌ=-\ *n* **:** SURF SCOTER

butterbread \'==ˌ=\ *n* [trans. of PaG *budderbrot* & G *butterbrot*] *dial* **:** a piece of bread and butter ⟨hey ma, can I have a ~⟩

but·ter·bump \'bətə(r)ˌbəmp\ *n, dial Eng* **:** the common European bittern (*Botaurus stellaris*)

but·ter·bur \'bəd·ərˌbər\ *n* -s **:** any of certain composite plants of the genus *Petasites* (esp. *P. hybridus*) with broad leaves and purplish rayless flowers

butterbush \'==ˌ=\ *n* **:** a plant of the genus *Pittosporum*; *esp* **:** POISONBERRY TREE

butter cake *n* **:** a cake made with shortening as distinguished from sponge cake — see GOLD CAKE, WHITE CAKE

butter chip *n* **:** an individual dish for butter

butter clam *n* **:** either of two species (*Saxidomus nuttallii* or *S. giganteus*) of large delicately flavored clams (family Veneridae) of the Pacific coast of No. America

butter color *n* **:** a yellow dye (as annatto) used to impart the desired color to butter and butter substitutes

buttercream \'==ˌ=\ *n* **1 :** fondant to which butter is added before creaming **2 :** a cake filling or frosting made by creaming butter, cream, and powdered sugar to which a desired flavoring may be added

buttercup \'==ˌ=\ *n* [so called fr. its yellow cup-shaped flowers] **1 :** a plant of the genus *Ranunculus* (esp. *R. acris* and *R. bulbosus*) with bright yellow flowers — called also *butterflower, goldcup, kingcup*; see TALL BUTTERCUP **2 :** a variable color averaging a vivid yellow that is redder and deeper than dandelion (sense 3b) or goldenrod (sense 2a) — compare BUTTERCUP YELLOW **3 a** *usu cap* **:** a breed of medium-sized fowls of Italian origin distinguished by a comb with a cup-shaped blade **b** *sometimes cap* **:** a bird of this breed, the male being orange-red with black tail, the female golden buff spangled with buff

buttercup family *n* **:** RANUNCULACEAE

buttercup primrose *n* **:** an Asiatic primrose (*Primula floribunda*) grown in greenhouses for its golden yellow bloom

buttercup squash *n* **:** a turban squash with flesh resembling sweet potato in flavor

buttercup yellow *n* **1 :** a grayish yellow that is paler and slightly redder than chamois and redder, lighter, and stronger than old ivory — compare BUTTERCUP 2 **2 :** ZINC YELLOW

butter dish *n* **:** a round or rectangular dish often with a drainer and a cover for holding butter at table

butter dock *n* **1 :** BUTTERBUR **2 :** CURLED DOCK **3 :** BITTER DOCK

butter duck *n* **:** any of several American ducks: as **a :** RUDDY DUCK **b :** BUFFLEHEAD **c :** SHOVELER

buttered *past of* BUTTER

buttered joint *n* **:** a thin masonry joint made by applying the mortar to one end and on the four edges of the bottom of the brick before it is laid

butterfat \'==ˌ=\ *n* **:** the natural fat of milk and the chief component of butter that consists essentially of a mixture of glycerides derived from lower fatty acids (as butyric acid) as well as from higher fatty acids and has a melting range low enough that the fat becomes liquid in the mouth, the amount of fat in dairy products serving as one of the main criteria of their quality

butterfingered \¦==¦==\ *adj* **:** apt to let things fall or slip through the fingers **:** CLUMSY, CARELESS

butterfingers \'==ˌ==\ *n pl but sing in constr* **:** a butterfingered person

butterfish \'==ˌ=\ *n* **:** any of numerous fishes esp. of the family Stromateidae and the suborder Percoidea that have a distinctly slippery mucus coating: as **a :** a small, deep-bodied marine food fish (*Poronotus triacanthus*) of the east coast of the U.S. **b :** GUNNEL **c :** CONEY 5a **d** *Austral* **:** MULLOWAY

butterflower \'==ˌ==\ *n* **:** BUTTERCUP 1

¹but·ter·fly \'bəd·ə(r)ˌflī, -ətə-\ *n* [ME *butterflie*, fr. OE *buterflēoge*, fr. *butere* butter + *flēoge* fly, perh. fr. the belief that butterflies or witches in the shape of butterflies stole milk and butter — more at BUTTER, FLY] **1 :** any of certain slender-bodied diurnal insects forming the division Rhopalocera of the order Lepidoptera that have very large broad wings which are often strikingly colored and patterned and are usu. held vertically over the back or expanded when at rest and slender usu. somewhat club-shaped antennae sometimes hooked near the ends — distinguished from *moth* **2 a :** a person who dresses gaudily or extravagantly **b :** a person chiefly occupied with the pursuit of pleasure ⟨a social ~⟩ **3 :** something resembling a butterfly in shape or motion: as **a :** BUTTERFLY VALVE **b :** an auxiliary support like a cross attached to a sculptor's armature **c :** a roof distinguished by a pitch that rises to the eaves leaving a valley **d** *slang* **:** a usu. weighted note thrown from a moving train **e :** a gauze-covered frame for diffusing light in motion-picture photography **f :** a marking in butterfly shape on an animal **g** (1) *also* **butterfly breaststroke :** a swimming stroke not now used in competition that is executed in a prone position with both arms extended and moving simultaneously in a circular motion and being out of the water during the recovery half of the cycle, the kick consisting of one breaststroke kick to each arm cycle (2) *also* **butterfly dolphin :** a competitive swimming stroke with this same arm motion but with a kick consisting of a simultaneous up-and-down action of the feet, two kicks being executed to each complete arm cycle — called also *dolphin, dolphin butterfly, dolphin fishtail* **4 butterflies** *pl* **:** a feeling of hollowness or queasiness esp. caused by emotional or nervous tension or anxious anticipation ⟨the paratrooper got *butterflies* in his stomach before the jump⟩ **5 :** a rope spinning stunt in which a loop is spun vertically and moved in front of the body from left to right without interruption

²butterfly \"\ *adj* **:** resembling a butterfly: **a :** cut or shaped to resemble the outlines of a butterfly ⟨~ collar⟩ **b** *in cookery* **:** resembling a butterfly in form by being partially split and spread apart ⟨a ~ steak⟩ ⟨~ fillet⟩ **c** *of a dog's nose* **:** PARTI-COLORED

³butterfly \"\ *vt* -ED/-ING/-ES **:** to split almost entirely and spread apart in such a way as to resemble the spread wings of a butterfly ⟨a *butterflied* steak⟩

butterfly banners *n pl* **:** DUTCHMAN'S-BREECHES

butterfly bat *n* [so called fr. its fluttery flight] **:** any of several small delicate African bats (genus *Glauconycteris*) with translucent pearly or amber-bronze wings

butterfly bomb *n* **:** a small antipersonnel bomb fitted with two folding wings that flutter and arm the fuze as the bomb falls

butterfly bush *n* [so called fr. its flowers that attract butterflies] **:** a shrub of the genus *Buddleia*

butterfly chair *n* [so called fr. the resemblance of the cloth

sling to the outspread wings of a butterfly] **:** a lounging chair consisting of a cloth sling supported by a frame of metal tubing or bars
butterfly clam *or* **butterfly mussel** *n* **:** a freshwater mussel (*Plagiola securis*) found in the Ohio and Illinois rivers and reported to produce pearls of fine quality
butterfly cod *n* [so called fr. the winglike fins] **:** a percoid fish (*Pterois volitans*) of tropical coral reefs having vertical scarlet stripes on a creamy ground and the dorsal and pectoral fins greatly enlarged and shaped like a fan
butterfly crab *n* [so called fr. the resemblance of its shell to the outspread wings of a butterfly] **:** a small shallow-water crab (*Cryptolithodes typicus*) of the Pacific coast of No. America
butterfly dam *n* [so called fr. its opening like the wings of a butterfly] **:** a movable steel dam pivoted at top and bottom and opened and closed by a rack-and-pinion mechanism and electric motor
butterfly damper *n* **:** BUTTERFLY VALVE 2
butterfly dolphin *n* **:** [1]BUTTERFLY 3g(2)
butterfly fish *n* **1 :** any of various fishes having variegated colors, broad expanded fins, or both: as **a :** OCELLATED BLENNY **b :** FLYING GURNARD **c :** a flying fish (*Exocoetus volitans*) of the Atlantic **d :** any of numerous small brilliantly colored carnivorous spiny-finned fishes of tropical seas that constitute the family Chaetodontidae and have narrow deep bodies and fins partly covered with scales **e :** a small brown fish (*Pantodon buchholzi*) of the streams of western Africa that has elongate lacy pectoral fins suggestive of wings and is often kept in the tropical aquarium **f :** BUTTERFLY COD **2 :** CHITON 2
butterfly flower *n* **:** a flower of the genus *Schizanthus*
butterfly hinge *n* **:** a decorative hinge that has the appearance of a butterfly when the leaves are spread flat
butterfly knot *n* **:** a knot used by mountain climbers to form a middle loop in the climbing rope — called also *lineman's loop knot*
butterfly lily *n* **1 :** a plant of the genus *Hedychium* often cultivated for the white, yellow, or red irregular flowers **2 :** MARIPOSA LILY
butterfly net *n* **:** a conical net for catching insects that is made of light cheesecloth or muslin and held open by a metal ring attached at the end of a wooden handle
butterfly nut *n* **:** WING NUT
butterfly orchid *also* **butterfly orchis** *n* **1 :** either of two European terrestrial orchids of the genus *Platanthera* (*P. bifolia* and *P. chlorantha*) **2 :** a Mexican epiphytic orchid (*Epidendrum venosum*) often cultivated **3 :** BUTTERFLY PLANT **4 :** an orchid of the genus *Gymnadenia*
butterfly pea *n* **:** any of several large-flowered wild peas of the closely related genera *Clitoria* and *Centrosema*: as **a :** a common twining vine (*Clitoria mariana*) of the southeastern and central U.S. with pale blue 2-inch flowers having very large standards **b :** a weakly twining to prostrate vine (*Centrosema virginianum*) occurring from New Jersey to tropical eastern No. America and sometimes cultivated for its purple and white flowers
butterfly plant *n* **1 :** ONCIDIUM 2 **2 :** an East Indian orchid (*Phalaenopsis amabilis*) having spikes of white-and-yellow flowers
butterfly ray *n* [so called fr. the winglike shape of the pectoral fins] **:** any of several short-tailed broad-finned sting rays
butterfly shell *n* **:** a shell suggestive of a butterfly: as **a :** BRACHIOPOD **b :** one of the plates of a chiton
butterfly table *n* **:** a usu. small drop-leaf table with splayed legs, oval top, and leaves supported by brackets shaped like a butterfly's wings

butterfly table

butterfly tulip *n* **:** MARIPOSA LILY
butterfly valve *n* [so called fr. the winglike clappers] **1 :** a double clack valve (as in a lift-pump piston) consisting of two semicircular clappers hinged to a cross rib **2 :** a damper or throttle valve in a pipe consisting of a disk turning on a diametral axis
butterfly weed *n* **1 :** an orange-flowered showy milkweed (*Asclepias tuberosa*) of eastern No. America — called also *pleurisy root* **2 :** a prairie plant (*Gaura coccinea*) of western No. America with irregular scarlet flowers
butterfly window *n* [so called fr. its winglike shape and manner of opening] **:** a small usu. 3-cornered portion of the front window of an automobile that is independently hinged on a vertical axis
butterhead \ˈ==ˌ=\ *or* **butterheading** \ˈ==ˌ==\ *adj, of lettuce* **:** forming a substantial but soft head of delicate-flavored tender leaves that tend to bleach at the heart to a clear yellow
butterier *comparative of* BUTTERY
butteries *pl of* BUTTERY
butteriest *superlative of* BUTTERY
but·ter·i·ness \ˈbəd·ərēnəs, -ətər-, -ri-\ *n* -ES **:** the quality or state of being buttery
buttering *pres part of* BUTTER
but·ter·is \ˈbəd·ərəs, -ət(ə)rəs\ *n* -ES [alter. of ME *buttyr*, fr. MF *boutoir*, fr. *bouter* to thrust, strike — more at BUTT (thrust)] **:** a steel instrument for paring the hoofs of horses

butteris

butter knife *n* **1 :** a usu. silver knife for cutting butter from a butter dish **2 :** BUTTER SPREADER
butter leaves *n pl* [so called fr. their use in packing butter] **1 :** GARDEN ORACH **2 :** BEET **3 :** ALPINE DOCK
but·ter·less \ˈbəd|ərləs, ˈbət|, -R |əl- *or* |ᵊl-\ *adj* **:** being without butter
but·ter·man \ˈbəd·ə(r)ˌman, -ətə-, -ˌmaa(ə)n, -ˌmən\ *n, pl* **buttermen :** one whose chief work is making, selling, or dealing in butter
buttermilk \ˈ==ˌ=\ *n* **1 :** the fluid remaining after the solids in cream have coalesced into butter in the churning process **2 :** cultured milk made by the addition of certain organisms to sweet milk
butter muslin *n* [so called fr. its use in butter making] *Brit* **:** CHEESECLOTH
butternose \ˈ==ˌ=\ *n* **:** AMERICAN SCOTER
butternut \ˈ==ˌ=\ *n* [so called fr. the oil in the nut] **1 a :** the sweet-flavored edible nut of an American tree (*Juglans cinerea*) that is distinguished from the black walnut by being ellipsoid and pointed **b :** the tree that bears butternuts — called also *white walnut;* see TREE illustration **2 :** SOUARI NUT **3 a** (1) **:** coarse homespun cloth or jean of a brown color dyed with an extract from the butternut tree (2) **butternuts** *pl* **:** an outer garment (as trousers or overalls) made of this cloth **b** *slang* **:** a soldier or partisan of the Confederacy during the Civil War
butternut squash *n* [so called fr. its color] **:** a smooth somewhat bottle-shaped straight-necked winter squash that is buff to yellow in color and has fine textured orange to yellow flesh
butter of antimony [trans. of NL *butyrum antimonii;* fr. its softness] **:** ANTIMONY CHLORIDE a
butter of tin [prob. trans. of NL *butyrum stanni;* fr. its softness] **:** stannic chloride or its pentahydrate
butter oil *n* **:** butterfat melted and clarified (as for use in making process butter) — compare GHEE
butter paper *n* **:** greaseproof paper that is used for wrapping butter or lard
butter pat *n* **:** a piece of butter formed into a ball or other ornamental shape for table use or an individual square cut from a quarter-pound stick of commercial butter
butter pear *n* **:** AVOCADO
butter plate *n* **1 :** BUTTER DISH **2 :** BREAD-AND-BUTTER PLATE
butter print *n* **1 :** a piece of carved wood used to mark molds of butter; *also* **:** the impress made by it **2 :** INDIAN MALLOW 1
butt·er-rigged \ˈbəd·ə(r)ˌrigd, -ətə-\ *adj* [[5]butt + -er; fr. the topgallant yard's being butted against the topsail yard when the sails are furled] *of a topsail schooner* **:** having the topgallant yard hoisted with halyards rather than fixed by lifts
butter-rose \ˈ==ˌ=\ *n* **:** BUTTERCUP

butters *pl of* BUTTER, *pres 3d sing of* BUTTER
butter sauce *n* **:** a sauce made of butter, water or broth, and seasonings, thickened with flour, and used also as a basis for the making of other sauces (as caper sauce or shrimp sauce) by the addition of special ingredients
butterscotch \ˈ==ˌ=\ *n, often attrib* [prob. fr. [1]butter + Scotch] **1 :** a hard candy made by boiling together brown sugar, corn syrup, and water **2 :** the flavor of brown sugar and butter cooked together **3 a :** a dark orange yellow that is yellower, stronger, and slightly lighter than average topaz and duller than average amber (sense 3b) **b :** a moderate brown to yellowish brown
butter spreader *n* **:** a small knife with rounded blade used for buttering bread at table
butter tree *n* **:** any of various trees the seeds of which yield a substance similar to butter: as **a :** SHEA TREE **b :** a Himalayan tree (*Madhuca butyracea*) related to the illipi tree **c :** a tropical African tree (*Combretum butyrosum*)

butter spreader

butterweed \ˈ==ˌ=\ *n* **:** any of several plants having yellow flowers or smooth soft foliage: as **a :** HORSEWEED 1 **b :** INDIAN MALLOW 1 **c :** an American wild lettuce (*Lactuca canadensis*) **d :** any of several plants of the genus *Senecio; esp* **:** an American ragwort (*Senecio glabellus*) **e :** FIREWEED a
butter weight *n* **1 :** a pound weight once used for butter equal to 18 or more ounces **2** *obs* **:** OVERWEIGHT **:** good measure
butterwort \ˈ==ˌ=\ *n* [so called fr. the mucilage secreted by the leaves] **:** a plant of the genus *Pinguicula*
[1]**but·tery** \ˈbəd·ərē, -ət(ə)rē, -ri\ *n* -ES [ME *boterie*, fr. MF, alter. of *bouteillerie* — more at BUTLERY] **1 :** a storeroom for liquors **2 a** *now dial* **:** PANTRY, LARDER **b :** a room where ale, wine, and other provisions are kept for sale to students (as in an English college)
[2]**buttery** \"\ *adj, sometimes* -ER/-EST [ME, fr. [1]butter + -y] **1 a :** having the qualities, consistency, or appearance of butter **b :** containing or spread with butter **2 :** FLATTERING, WHEEDLING
buttery bar *n* [[1]buttery] **:** a serving bar on a buttery hatch
butter yellow *n* **1 :** OIL YELLOW 1b **2 :** a brilliant yellow that is greener and paler than lemon chrome — called also *jasmine yellow;* compare JASMINE
buttery hatch *n* [[1]buttery] **:** a half door between a buttery and the hall
buttes *pl of* BUTTE
butt gauge *n* [[6]butt] **:** a gauge usu. with three independent cutters used chiefly for marking the outlines of mortises for door butts or strike plates
butt·gen·bach·ite \ˈbətgənˌbaˌkīt, ˈbu̇t-\ *n* -S [F, fr. Henri J. F. *Buttgenbach* b1874 Belg. mineralogist + F *-ite*] **:** a mineral composed of a hydrous copper nitrate with chlorine occurring in mattes of light-blue acicular crystals
butt-headed \ˈ=ˌ==\ *adj* [[6]butt] *dial, of an animal* **:** without horns **:** MULEY
butt hinge *n* [[6]butt] **:** a hinge applied on and usu. mortised flush into the edge of a door and the face of the casing against which this edge of the door butts when closed

butt hinges: *1* loose-pin butt, *2* fast-pin butt, *3* double-acting spring butt

butties *pl of* BUTTY
butt in *vi* [[1]butt] **:** to thrust oneself upon others **:** INTRUDE, INTERFERE, MEDDLE ⟨*butting in* on other people's private affairs⟩
butt-in \ˈ=ˌ=\ *n* -S [*butt in*] **1 :** one who butts in **2** *Brit* **:** the first bid in contract bridge made by a member of the side that did not open the bidding **:** OVERCALL
butt·ing \ˈbəd·iŋ, -ətiŋ\ *n* -S [fr. gerund of [5]butt] **:** ABUTTAL, BOUNDARY
butt·in·sky \bəd·ˈinskē\ *n* -ES [*butt in* + *-sky* (last element in many Slavic names)] *slang* **:** one given to butting in **:** a troublesome meddler **:** PEST
butt joint *n* [[6]butt] **:** a joint made by fastening the parts together end-to-end and in wood usu. perpendicular to the grain or edge-to-edge without overlap and often strengthened (as with a strap)
butt knuckle *n* [[6]butt] **:** a projection shaped like a knuckle usu. of metal and designed to receive pressure (as from a window pole)
but·tle \ˈbəd·ᵊl, -ətᵊl\ *vi* **buttled; buttled; buttling** \-əd·ᵊliŋ, -ət(ᵊ)liŋ\ **buttles** [back-formation fr. *butler*] *substand* **:** to serve or act as butler
butt log *n* [[6]butt] **:** BUTT CUT 1
[1]**but·tock** \ˈbəd·ək, -ətək\ *n* -S [ME *buttok* — more at BUTT (end)] **1 a** (1) **:** either of the two rounded prominences separated by a median cleft that form the lower part of the back in man and consist largely of the gluteus muscles (2) **:** the lower part of the back made up of these prominences **:** SEAT — usu. used in pl. **b buttocks** *pl* **:** the corresponding part of a quadruped **:** RUMP **2 a :** the convex aftermost part of a ship above the water line **:** COUNTER — usu. used in pl. **b** *or* **buttock line :** a line of intersection of a longitudinal vertical plane with the hull of a ship or the body or float of an aircraft **3** *chiefly Brit* **:** a maneuver in which a wrestler gets his opponent across his back and throws him over his head
[2]**buttock** \"\ *vt* -ED/-ING/-S **:** to throw with a buttock ⟨~*ed* his opponent onto the mat⟩
[1]**but·ton** \ˈbətᵊn\ *n* -S *often attrib* [ME *boton*, fr. MF *boton*, *bouton*, fr. OF, fr. *boter, bouter* to strike, thrust — more at BUTT (to thrust)] **1 a :** a disk, ball, or device of other shape having holes or a shank by which it is sewn or secured to an article (as of clothing or upholstery) and that is used as a fastener by passing it through a buttonhole or loop or as a trimming and is made of glass, shell, bone, wood, leather, or cloth ⟨on Fortune's Cap, we are not the very *Button* —Shak.⟩ **b :** an ornament or badge of similar shape often of metal with a stamped design or of plastic with a slogan imprinted on the face **c :** a thing of slight value ⟨not worth a ~⟩ **d :** a unit of one inch used in determining length of gloves and measured from base of thumb towards wrist ⟨a 12-*button* glove reaches nearly to the elbow⟩ **e buttons** *pl but sing in constr* [so called fr. the buttons on his livery] *now chiefly Brit* **:** PAGE, BELLBOY **2 :** any of various parts or growths of plants resembling buttons: as **a :** BUD **b :** the fruit of a rose or the flower head of one of the Compositae ⟨a ~ chrysanthemum⟩ **c :** a small round seed vessel **d :** an immature whole mushroom; *esp* **:** one just before expansion of the pileus **e :** an abnormally small fruit **f :** an onion bulb or a garlic clove **3 :** a small knob or piece resembling a button in shape: as **a :** an incipient or stunted growth of horn (as in the calf or stag) — see SCUR **b buttons** *pl* **:** dung esp. of a sheep **c :** the terminal segment of a rattlesnake's rattle **d :** a uterine cotyledon **e :** a small mass or globule of metal remaining after fusion (as at the bottom of a crucible or cupel) **4** *West* **:** YOUNGSTER, BOY **5 :** a device suggestive of a button: as **a :** an oblong or elongated piece of wood or metal turning on a nail, pin, or screw (as to fasten a door or window) **b :** a leather washer for a nail or screw **c :** PUSH BUTTON **d :** the knob in the end block to which the tailpiece of a stringed instrument (as a violin) is anchored **e :** a marker in the pavement indicating a proper pivoting point for traffic or one of a set marking vehicle or pedestrian lanes **f :** a leather ring running along the reins of a bridle for tightening or loosening it **g :** a guard on the tip of a fencing foil **h :** one of the push buttons on a musical instrument (as an accordion) **i :** the earpiece of a hearing aid **6** *slang* **:** the point of the chin esp. as the target for a knockout blow ⟨the next punch landed square on the ~⟩ **7 :** a small white spot on the throat or chest of a solid-colored cat **8 buttons** *pl, slang* **:** WITS ⟨hasn't got all his ~*s*⟩ — **on the button :** on the dot **:** PRECISELY
[2]**button** \"\ *vb* **buttoned; buttoned; buttoning** \ˈbət(ᵊ)niŋ\ **buttons** [ME *botenen*, fr. MF *botoner*, fr. OF, fr. *boton*, n., button] *vt* **1 :** to furnish or decorate with buttons **2 a :** to pass (a button) through a buttonhole or loop **b :** to fasten, secure, or close with a button — often used with *up* ⟨~ up your overcoat⟩ ⟨he ~*ed* his brother's jacket⟩ **3 :** to close (the lips) to prevent speech ⟨keep your lip ~*ed* about this business⟩ ~ *vi* **1 :** to have buttons for fastening ⟨this jacket ~*s* at the side⟩ **2 a** *of fruit* **:** to form buttons **b :** to head prematurely (as of cauliflower)
button aster *n* **:** an herb (*Aster multiflorus*) resembling the bushy aster but having smaller flowers and spiny-tipped involucral bracts
buttonball \ˈ==ˌ=\ *n* **1 :** *also* **buttonball tree** *chiefly North* **:** SYCAMORE 3a **2 :** BUTTONBUSH
buttonboard \ˈ==ˌ=\ *n* [so called fr. its use in making buttonmolds] **:** a hard stiff paperboard
buttonbur \ˈ==ˌ=\ *n* -S **:** COCKLEBUR
buttonbush \ˈ==ˌ=\ *n* **:** a No. American shrub (*Cephalanthus occidentalis*) with globular flower heads
button cactus *n* **:** a small cactus (*Epithelantha micromeris*) of Texas and adjacent Mexico shaped like a globe and having flattish tubercles, white spines, and edible fruits
button chrysanthemum *n* **:** a garden chrysanthemum with numerous small heads in profuse clusters
button clover *n* **:** an annual European forage plant (*Medicago orbicularis*) introduced into the U.S. that has sharply toothed leaflets and greenish yellow flowers
button day *n, chiefly Austral* **:** TAG DAY
button-down \ˈ==ˌ=\ *adj* [*button down*, v.] **:** fastened down with buttons ⟨a *button-down* collar on a man's shirt⟩
button ear *n* **:** a dog's ear which falls forward and completely hides the inside — called also *drop ear* — **button-eared** \ˈ==ˌ=\ *adj*
buttoned *adj* **1 :** furnished with or decorated with buttons — usu. used in combination with adjective or noun ⟨pearl-*buttoned*⟩ **2 :** closed or secured with or as if with buttons
but·ton·er \ˈbət(ᵊ)nə(r)\ *n* -S **1 :** one that buttons; *specif* **:** BUTTONHOOK **2 a :** one who sews on buttons **b :** a worker who buttons articles (as shoes or shirts) prior to packaging
button flower *n* **:** a tropical tree or shrub of the genus *Gomphia* (family Ochnaceae)
button grass *n* **1 :** TALL OAT GRASS **2 :** any of several Australian grasses: **a :** a crab grass (*Digitaria sanguinalis*) **b :** any of several grasses (genus *Dactyloctenium*) that are used to some extent for hay and pasture
[1]**buttonhead** \ˈ==ˌ=\ *adj, of a bolt, rivet, or screw* **:** having a head with a spherical exposed surface and plane shoulder, the height of the head being usu. less than a hemisphere
[2]**buttonhead** \"\ *n* **:** a buttonhead bolt, screw, or rivet — see RIVET illustration
buttonhold \ˈ==ˌ=\ *vt* [back-formation fr. *buttonholder* one who buttonholes a person, fr. [1]button + holder] *archaic* **:** [3]BUTTONHOLE
[1]**buttonhole** \ˈ==ˌ=\ *n* **1 :** a bound or stitched slit or a loop through which a button is passed **2** *chiefly Brit* **:** BOUTONNIERE **3 :** HART'S-TONGUE 1
[2]**buttonhole** \"\ *vt* **:** to furnish with buttonholes or to work with buttonhole stitch
[3]**buttonhole** \"\ *vt* [alter. of *buttonhold*] **:** to hold by or as if by the buttonhole in order to detain in conversation ⟨be *buttonholed* by a bore —Virginia Woolf⟩ ⟨peddlers of gossip who ~ each other —Carl Sandburg⟩ ⟨ready to ~ members as they leave an executive session and to find out what has just happened —F.L.Mott⟩ **:** catch the attention of ⟨a voice from our radio *buttonholed* us —E.B.White⟩
buttonholer \ˈ==ˌ==\ *n* **1 :** one that makes buttonholes by hand or machine **2 :** a sewing-machine attachment for making buttonholes
buttonhole stitch *n* **:** an embroidery stitch made by drawing the needle and thread from the upper through the lower edge of the design and out over the lower thread of a preceding stitch held in place with a thumb, the stitches being repeated to form a firm line of closely spaced loops at the lower edge of the design

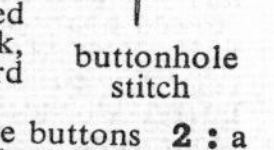

buttonhole stitch

buttonhook \ˈ==ˌ=\ *n* **1 :** a hook for drawing small buttons through buttonholes **2 :** a forward-pass play in football in which the intended receiver runs straight toward a defensive back, then stops and pivots or doubles back toward the passer
buttoning *n* -S **1 :** a closing with two or more buttons **2 :** a decorative method of fastening padded upholstery
button lac *n* **:** lac formed into cakes shaped like buttons by melting and solidifying
but·ton·less \-tᵊnləs\ *adj* **:** being without a button
button mangrove *n* **:** BUTTON TREE 1
buttonmold *also* **buttonmould** \ˈ==ˌ=\ *n* **:** a disk (as of wood or metal) to be made into a button by covering with cloth
button-on \ˈ==ˌ=\ *adj* [fr. *button on*, v.] **:** attached with buttons ⟨a child's *button-on* waist⟩
button onion *n* **:** an onion picked before it has reached full size and used esp. for pickling or as a garnish
button pearl *var of* BOUTON PEARL
button pink *n* **:** a much-branched pink having flowers in clusters of two to four surrounded by bracts and being considered as a hybrid between the sweet william and the China pink or as a distinct species (*Dianthus latifolius*)
button quail *n* **:** any of various small terrestrial birds that resemble quails, are widely distributed in the Old World, and constitute a family (Turnicidae) of the order Gruiformes distinguished by the absence of a hind toe — called also *bustard quail, hemipode*
buttons *pl of* BUTTON, *pres 3d sing of* BUTTON
button sage *n* **:** BLACK SAGE 3
button-seal \ˈ==ˌ=\ *n* **:** a stamp seal of the Near East (including Egypt) that is flat and resembles a button
button sedge *n* **:** a sedge of the genus *Kyllinga* (family Cyperaceae)
button shell *n* **:** any of several somewhat flattened gastropod mollusks: as **a :** a large Australian top shell (*Trochus niloticus*) **b :** the marine pulmonate snail (*Gadinia reticulata*) of the California coast that resembles a limpet
button shoe *n* **:** a shoe fastened with buttons
button snakeroot *n* **1 :** a plant of the genus *Liatris* **2 :** any of several plants of the genus *Eryngium; esp* **:** a coarse prickly plant (*E. aquaticum*) of the southern U.S. with compact umbels and aromatic roots
button snakeweed *n* **:** a very spiny plant (*Eryngium leavenworthii*) of the central U.S. with palmately divided leaves and heads of flowers resembling thistles
button spider *n* [prob. trans. of Afrik *knopiespinnekop*] **:** either of two venomous spiders (*Latrodectus indistinctus* and *L. geometricus*) of southern Africa closely related to the American black widow and resembling it in appearance and habits
button stick *n* **:** a strip of metal or wood slotted in such a way that it will pass over a row of buttons (as on a military tunic) allowing each button to appear through a slit so that the buttons may be polished without soiling the cloth
button strike *n* **:** a strike called by a union to compel members to pay dues and to prevent employment of workers without union buttons
button test *n* **:** a test of the fusibility of enamel frits made by heating button-shaped masses
button thistle *n* **:** BULL THISTLE 1
button tree *n* **1 :** a shrub or tree of the genus *Conocarpus* having hard tough fruits like buttons **2 :** SYCAMORE 3a
button up *vt* **1 :** to close tightly and securely ⟨a tank *buttoned up* and ready for action⟩ **2 :** to carry to completion (as an order or assignment) **3 :** to bring to complete and final decision or irrevocable settlement ~ *vi* **:** to become mum
buttonweed \ˈ==ˌ=\ *n* **1 :** a small troublesome weed (*Diodia teres*) with linear leaves and small flowers and fruits resembling buttons **2 :** any of several plants of the genus *Spermacoce* (family Rubiaceae) of similar appearance to buttonweed **3 :** INDIAN MALLOW 1 **4 :** KNAPWEED **5 :** CLUSTERED BLUET
button willow *n* **:** BUTTONBUSH
buttonwood \ˈ==ˌ=\ *n* **1** *chiefly North* **:** SYCAMORE 3a **2 :** BUTTONTREE 1 **3 :** WHITE MANGROVE 1 **4 :** BUTTONBUSH
buttonwood shrub *n* **:** BUTTONBUSH
but·tony \ˈbət(ᵊ)nē, -ni\ *adj* **1 :** ornamented with many buttons **2 :** like a button ⟨~ eyes⟩
butt plate *n* [[6]butt] **:** the usu. metal plate on the butt end of a gunstock

1but·tress \'bətrəs\ *n* -ES [ME *butres, boterace,* fr. MF *bouterez,* fr. OF *boterez,* fr. *boter, bouter* to thrust — more at BUTT] **1 :** a projecting structure of masonry or wood for supporting or giving stability to a wall or building (as to resist lateral pressure or strain acting at a particular point in one direction) but sometimes serving chiefly for ornament **2 :** any of various things that resemble a buttress in appearance: **a :** COUNTERFORT **b :** a projecting part of a mountain or hill **c :** a horny protuberance on a horse's hoof at the heel where the wall bends inward and forward **d :** the broadened basal portion of a tree trunk or a thickened vertical part of it **3 :** something that supports, strengthens, or helps to defend ⟨a ~ of the cause of peace⟩ **4 :** an abutment built from a river bank to prevent logs in a drive from injuring the bank or jamming

buttress 1

2buttress \"\ *vt* -ED/-ING/-ES **1 :** to furnish or support with a buttress ⟨~*ing* the bridge piers⟩ **:** shore up **:** PROP, SUSTAIN ⟨the present river system ~*ed* now with . . . good levees —A.W. Baum⟩ **2 :** SUPPORT, SUSTAIN, STRENGTHEN ⟨arguments ~*ed* by solid facts⟩ ⟨measures to ~ the national economy against the stresses of war⟩ **syn** see SUPPORT

3buttress \"\ *adj, of a saw blade* **:** having widely separated teeth with one edge perpendicular and the other oblique to the direction of motion

but·tress·less \-ləs\ *adj* **:** being without a buttress

buttress pier *n* **1 :** a pier serving wholly or in part as a buttress **2 :** the part of a buttress above the point of thrust **3 :** the pier receiving the thrust of a flying buttress

buttress root *n* **:** an adventitious root serving as an added support to a tree (as in the banyan and ceiba) — compare KNEE

buttress thread *n* **:** a screw thread in which the driving face is made perpendicular to the axis of the screw (as in a square thread) while the back face makes an angle with the axis (as in a V thread) in order to combine efficiency in the transmission of power with strength

buttress tower *n* **:** a tower at either side of an archway (as for defense of a gate wall)

butt rot *n* [6*butt*] **:** a fungous decay of the basal portion of a tree trunk generally involving primarily the heartwood and caused by polypores (as species of *Fomes*)

butts *pres 3d sing of* BUTT, *pl of* BUTT

butts and bounds *n pl* [4*butt*] **:** abuttals and boundaries of a property — compare METES AND BOUNDS

butt saw *or* **butting saw** *n* [6*butt*] **:** a circular or band saw for crosscutting logs or lumber **:** CUTOFF SAW

butt seam *n* [6*butt*] **:** a seam in a shoe affixing edges that are brought together edge to edge with a zigzag or straight stitch

butt shaft *n* [4*butt*] **:** a target arrow

butt sling *n* [7*butt*] **:** a sling for suspending casks consisting of a rope looped round one end by means of an eye and round the other end with two half hitches

buttstock \'ˌ=ˌ=\ *n* [6*butt* + *stock*] **:** the stock of a firearm in the rear of the breech mechanism — compare TIPSTOCK

butt strap *n* [6*butt*] **:** a strap or plate covering a butt joint and secured to both pieces

butt-strap \'=ˌ=\ *vt* [*butt strap*] **:** to fasten by butt straps

butt veneer *n* [6*butt*] **:** veneer cut from roots of trees (as walnut) to show a curly figure resulting from intertwined fibers

butt weld *n* [6*butt*] **:** a butt joint made by welding

butt-weld \'=ˌ=\ *vt* [6*butt*] **:** to unite by a butt weld — **butt welding** *n*

buttwood \'=ˌ=\ *n* [6*butt* + *wood*] **:** STUMP WOOD

but·ty \'bəd·ē, -ətē, |i\ *n* -ES [origin unknown] **1** *dial Brit* **:** a fellow workman **:** CHUM, PARTNER **2** *also* **buttyman** \-man\ *pl* **buttymen :** a worker or middleman who takes an allotment of work by contract at so much per ton of coal or ore for execution as an individual or foreman of a gang ⟨~ collier⟩ ⟨~ system⟩ **3** [prob. fr. 4*butt* + -*y*] **:** an archer's shooting companion at the butts

butty boat *n* **:** a boat or barge towed by another boat; *esp* **:** a towed boat used in cruising on canals and rivers in England

butty lark *n* [so called fr. the cuckoo's laying eggs in its nest] *dial Eng* **:** MEADOW PIPIT

bu·tyl \'byüd·ᵊl, -üt ᵊl, -ü,til\ *n* -S [ISV *but-* + *-yl*] **:** any of four isomeric alkyl radicals C_4H_9 derived from butane and isobutane: **a :** the normal radical $CH_3CH_2CH_2CH_2$— — called also *n-butyl* **b :** the secondary radical $CH_3CH_2CH(CH_3)$— — called also *sec-butyl* **c :** the tertiary radical $(CH_3)_3C$— — called also *tert-butyl* **d :** ISOBUTYL

Butyl \"\ *trademark* — used for any of a class of synthetic rubbers that are made by polymerizing isobutylene with a small proportion usu. of isoprene at a low temperature (as −140°F) with aluminum chloride as catalyst, that are characterized by low permeability to gases and good resistance to oxygen, ozone, and many chemicals, and that are used esp. in inner tubes for tires

butyl acetate *n* **:** a colorless liquid ester $CH_3COOC_4H_9$ of acetic acid that has a fruity odor and is used as a solvent esp. in cellulose nitrate lacquers — called also *n-butyl acetate, normal butyl acetate*

butyl alcohol *n* **:** any of four flammable liquid alcohols C_4H_9OH derived from the butanes and used chiefly in organic synthesis and as solvents often in the form of their esters: **a :** the normal alcohol $CH_3CH_2CH_2CH_2OH$ made by bacterial fermentation of molasses or grain or synthetically (as by dehydration and reduction of aldol); 1-butanol — called also *n-butyl alcohol* **b :** the secondary alcohol $CH_3CH_2CH(OH)CH_3$ known in three optically different forms and made by hydration of 1-butene; 2-butanol — called also *sec-butyl alcohol* **c :** the tertiary alcohol $(CH_3)_3COH$ made by hydration of isobutylene; 2-methyl-2-propanol — called also *tert-butyl alcohol, trimethylcarbinol* **d :** ISOBUTYL ALCOHOL

butyl aldehyde *n* **:** BUTYRALDEHYDE

bu·tyl·a·mine \ˌbyüd·ᵊlə'mēn, -üt ᵊl-, -lˌamən\ *n* -S [ISV *butyl* + *amine*] **1 :** any of four flammable liquid bases $C_4H_9NH_2$; *esp* **:** the normal amine $CH_3CH_2CH_2CH_2NH_2$ used chiefly in organic synthesis **2 :** any amine in which butyl is attached to the nitrogen atom

butyl aminobenzoate *n* **:** a white odorless crystalline ester $C_{11}H_{15}NO_2$ used as a local anesthetic; *n*-butyl *para*-aminobenzoate

1bu·tyl·ate \'byüd·ᵊl,āt, -üt ᵊl-, -lət, *usu* -d·+V\ *n* -S [*butyl* + -*ate*] **:** BUTOXIDE

2butylate \-lāt, *usu* -d·+V\ *vt* -ED/-ING/-S **:** to introduce the butyl group into (a compound) — **bu·tyl·a·tion** \ˌbyüd·ᵊl'āshən\ *n* -S

butyl chloral hydrate *n* **:** a bitter crystalline compound $CH_3CHClCCl_2CH(OH)_2$ obtained as a by-product in the manufacture of chloral hydrate and used similarly

bu·tyl·ene \'byüd·ᵊl,ēn, -üt ᵊl-\ *n* -S [ISV *butyl* + *-ene*] **1 :** any of three isomeric flammable easily liquefiable gaseous hydrocarbons C_4H_8 of the ethylene series obtained usu. by the cracking of petroleum and converted into gasoline by polymerization: **a :** the normal compound $CH_2{=}CHCH_2CH_3$ used in making butadiene — called also *alpha-butylene, 1-butene* **b :** the normal symmetrical compound $CH_3CH{=}CHCH_3$ occurring in cis and trans forms used in making butadiene — called also *beta-butylene, 2-butene* **c :** ISOBUTYLENE **2 :** any of four isomeric alkylene radicals C_4H_8 (as tetramethylene) derived from normal butane

butylene glycol *n* **:** BUTANEDIOL

butyl phthalate *n* **:** a butyl ester of phthalic acid; *usu* **:** DIBUTYL PHTHALATE

Bu·tyn \'byüt ᵊn, -ü,tin\ *trademark* — used for butacaine

bu·tyne \'byü,tīn\ *n* -S [ISV *but-* + *-yne, -ine*] **:** either of two isomeric hydrocarbons C_4H_6 of the acetylene series: **a :** an easily condensable gas $CH{\equiv}CCH_2CH_3$ — called also *1-butyne, ethylacetylene* **b :** a volatile liquid $CH_3C{\equiv}CCH_3$ of strong odor — called also *2-butyne, dimethylacetylene*

butyr- *or* **butyro-** *comb form* [ISV, fr. *butyric*] **:** butyric **:** related to butyric acid or butyraldehyde ⟨*butyr*aldol⟩ ⟨*butyro*nitrile⟩

bu·tyr·a·ceous \ˌbyüd·ə¦rāshəs\ *adj* [L *butyrum* butter + E *-aceous*] **:** having the qualities of butter **:** resembling butter; *also* **:** yielding or containing a substance like butter

bu·tyr·al \'byüd·ə,ral, -ˌrəl\ *n* -S [*butyr-* + *-al*] **:** an acetal of butyraldehyde ⟨~ resins⟩

bu·tyr·aldehyde \¦byüd·ər +\ *n* -S [ISV *butyr-* + *aldehyde*] **:** either of the two aldehydes C_3H_7CHO corresponding to the two butyric acids; *esp* **:** normal butyric aldehyde $CH_3CH_2CH_2CHO$ obtained as a pungent flammable liquid by partial hydrogenation of crotonaldehyde or by dehydrogenation of normal butyl alcohol and used chiefly in making polyvinyl butyral resins for safety glass and condensation products (as with aniline) for rubber accelerators

bu·tyr·ate \'byüd·ə,rāt\ *n* -S [*butyr-* + *-ate*] **1 :** a salt or ester of butyric acid **2 :** CELLULOSE ACETATE BUTYRATE

1bu·tyr·ic \(')byü¦tirik\ *adj* [F *butyrique*, fr. L *butyrum* butter + F *-ique* -ic — more at BUTTER] **:** relating to or producing butyric acid ⟨~ fermentation⟩

2butyric \"\ *n* -S **:** a microorganism that engages in butyric fermentation

butyric acid *n* **:** either of two isomeric fatty acids C_3H_7COOH **: a :** the normal acid $CH_3CH_2CH_2COOH$ found esp. in butter in the form of glycerides and in rancid butter as the free acid, obtained as a colorless liquid of unpleasant odor usu. by oxidation of normal butyl alcohol or butyraldehyde or by fermentation (as of molasses), and used chiefly in making esters (as simple esters for use as flavoring materials or esters of cellulose for use as plastics) — called also *butanoic acid, n-butyric acid* **b :** ISOBUTYRIC ACID

butyric fermentation *n* **:** fermentation occurring in putrefaction and apparently in the digestion of herbivorous mammals in which butyric acid is produced by certain chiefly anaerobic bacteria acting upon various organic substances (as lactic acid or butter)

bu·tyr·in \'byüd·ərən\ *n* -S [alter. (influenced by L *butyrum* butter) of earlier *butirine*, fr. F, fr. *butir-* butyr- (irreg. fr. L *butyrum*) + *-ine*] **:** any of the three liquid glycerides of butyric acid; *esp* **:** TRIBUTYRIN

bu·tyr·in·ase \-nās,-,nāz\ *n* -S [*butyrin* + *-ase*] **:** an enzyme occurring esp. in blood serum and capable of hydrolyzing any butyrin

bu·tyr·o·lactone \¦byüd·ə(,)rō, -ə,rə +\ *n* -S [*butyr-* + *lactone*] **:** a mobile liquid lactone $C_4H_6O_2$ made usu. by dehydrogenation of 1,4-butanediol and used chiefly as a solvent for resins (as polymers of acrylonitrile) — called also *butanolide*

bu·tyr·om·e·ter \ˌbyüd·ə'rämәd·ə(r)\ *n* -S [ISV *butyr-* + *-meter*] **:** an instrument for determining the amount of butterfat in dairy products (as milk) — **bu·tyr·o·met·ric** \¦byüd·ə(,)rō¦me·trik, -ˌrə¦m-\ *adj*

bu·tyr·one \'byüd·ə,rōn\ *n* -S [ISV *butyr-* + *-one*] **:** a liquid ketone $(C_3H_7)_2CO$ obtained by heating calcium butyrate and used as a solvent — called also *dipropyl ketone*

bu·tyr·ous \-rəs\ *adj* [L *butyrum* butter + E *-ous* — more at BUTTER] **:** BUTYRACEOUS

bu·tyr·yl \'byüd·ərəl\ *n* -S [ISV *butyr-* + *-yl*] **:** the radical $CH_3CH_2CH_2CO$— of normal butyric acid

bu·vette \bü'vet, bü've-\ *n* -S [F, fr. MF *beuvette, buvette*, fr. *beuv-, buv-* (stem of *beivre* to drink) + *-ette* — more at BEVERAGE] **:** TAPROOM, BAR, TAVERN

buwayhid *also* **buwaihid** *usu cap, var of* BUYID

bux·a·ce·ae \bək'sāsē,ē\ *n pl, cap* [NL, fr. *Buxus*, type genus + *-aceae*] **:** a small family of widely distributed shrubs, trees, or sometimes herbs (order Sapindales) having evergreen foliage and flowers with no corolla and a 3-loculed ovary — **bux·a·ceous** \(')bək¦sāshəs\ *adj*

bux·bau·mia \ˌbəks'bōmēə\ *n, cap* [NL, after J. C. *Buxbaum* †1730 Ger. botanist + NL *-ia*] **:** a genus of mosses (order Buxbaumiales) having a capsule which is placed obliquely on the erect stalk and resembles a small bug

bux·bau·mi·a·les \ˌbəks,bōmē'ā(,)lēz\ *n pl, cap* [NL, fr. *Buxbaumia* + *-ales*] **:** a small order of minute atypical mosses often isolated in a distinct subclass of Musci and characterized by a reduced gametophore consisting of a few leaves which die shortly after fertilization leaving an asymmetrical capsule

bux·om \'bəksəm\ *adj, sometimes* -ER/-EST [ME *buhsum, buxsum*, fr. (assumed) OE *būhsum*, fr. OE *būgan* to bend, bow + *-sum* -some — more at BOW] **1** *archaic* **:** marked by obedience **:** TRACTABLE, COMPLIANT ⟨are disposed to be ~ and obedient to the customs and laws of the republic —George Borrow⟩ **2** *obs* **:** physically flexible **:** PLIANT, UNRESISTING ⟨wing silently the ~ air —John Milton⟩ **3** *archaic* **:** full of gaiety **:** BLITHE, LIVELY ⟨how jovial it is and ~ —Andrew Marvell⟩ **4 a :** vigorously or healthily plump **:** sturdily formed ⟨a ~ warm friendly woman —Burl Ives⟩ **b :** FULL-BOSOMED ⟨~ blondes⟩ — **bux·om·ly** *adv*

bux·om·ness *n* -ES [ME *buhsumnesse* obedience, submissiveness, fr. *buhsum* + *-nesse* -ness] **:** the quality or state of being buxom

bux·us \'bəksəs\ *n, cap* [NL, fr. L, box (shrub) — more at BOX] **:** a genus (the type of the family Buxaceae) of evergreen shrubs and small trees having opposite entire leaves and capsular fruit

1buy \'bī\ *vb* **bought** \'bȯt, *usu* -ȯd· +V\ **bought; buying; buys** [ME *byen* (past *boughte*, past part. *bought, ybought*) fr. OE *bycgan* (past *bohte*, past part. *boht, geboht*); akin to OS *buggean* to buy (past part. *giboht*), Goth *bugjan* (past *bauhta*, past part. *-bauhts*), and perh. to OHG *biogan* to bend — more at BOW] *vt* **1 :** to get possession or ownership of by giving or agreeing to give money in exchange **:** PURCHASE — opposed to *sell* **2 :** to obtain at a price of sacrifice ⟨~*ing* peace at the sacrifice of sovereignty⟩ ⟨fame is dearly *bought* at the cost of honor⟩ **3 :** to pay the price for so as to free **:** redeem esp. by a ransom — used chiefly in a theological sense ⟨He that *bought* us with his blood⟩ **4 :** to gain the support or obedience of by an inducement **:** BRIBE, HIRE ⟨~ a public official⟩ — often used with *over* ⟨whether they would go to jail or ~ over the jury when the Act began to operate —H.J.Laski⟩ **5 :** to be the purchasing equivalent of ⟨$2000 will ~ this land⟩ ⟨the dollar ~*s* less than it used to⟩ **6 :** to obtain for cash or other consideration the rights to the services of **:** to take over the contract of ⟨if a baseball club cannot get players in trades it must ~ them⟩ **7** *card games* **:** to obtain (a specified card or cards) by drawing or from a widow **8** *slang* **:** BELIEVE ⟨I won't ~ any part of that explanation⟩ **:** ACCEPT, APPROVE ⟨whether Britain . . . would ~ that compromise . . . remained to be seen —*Time*⟩ ~ *vi* **:** to perform the act of buying something ⟨the ~*ing* public⟩ ⟨the advantages of catalog ~*ing*⟩ — **buy it** *also* **buy a packet** *slang Brit* **:** to get killed **:** DIE — **buy on a scale :** to buy usu. on a falling market at intervals in order to average the costs more advantageously than would be possible with a purchase made at the beginning at a single price

2buy \"\ *n* -S **1 :** an act of buying **:** PURCHASE ⟨make a ~ of wheat⟩ **2 :** a thing bought or to be bought **:** something of value at a favorable price; *esp* **:** BARGAIN ⟨this stock is a good ~ at the current asking price⟩

buy boat *n* **:** a boat operated to buy the catch (as of shellfish) from fishing boats at sea and bring it in to market

buy·er \'bīə(r)\ *n* -S [ME *byer*, fr. *byen* to buy + *-er* — more at BUY] **1 :** PURCHASER ⟨let the ~ beware⟩; *specif* **:** PURCHASING AGENT **2 :** one that has charge of the selection, purchasing, pricing, and display of the goods of a department of a retail store ⟨hat ~⟩ **3 :** BUY BOAT

buyers' market *n* **:** a market in which goods are plentiful, buyers have a wide range of choice, and prices tend toward costs — contrasted with *sellers' market*

buyer's option *n* **:** an option allowed to one who contracts to buy stocks at a certain future date and at a certain price to demand instead the delivery of the stock (giving one day's notice) at any previous time at the market price

bu·yid \'büyəd\ *or* **bu·way·hid** *also* **bu·wai·hid** \'büwā,hid\ *n, pl* **buyids** \'büyədz\ *or* **bu·yides** \", -,yīdz\ *or* **buwayhids** \'büwā,hidz\ *or* **buway·hides** \-,hīdz\ *usu cap* [Abu Shaja *Buya* or *Buwayha* or *Buwaiha fl* A.D. 932 founder of the dynasty + E *-id*] **:** a member of a Persian Shi'ite dynasty that arose in A.D. 932 and extended its authority into Baghdad and reduced the caliphs to puppets before being overthrown by the Seljuk sultans in 1055

buy in *vt* **1 :** to buy a number or quantity of (as stock in a fund or partnership) **2 :** to buy (undelivered securities or commodities) according to the rules of the exchange by claiming against the original seller the difference in price and expense of broker's commissions **3 :** to buy for oneself (what one has offered to sell at auction) ~ *vi* **1 :** to buy a place in a stock company or regiment **2 :** to cover a commodity or security contract previously sold short

buying option *n* **:** 2CALL 3d

buying power *n* **:** PURCHASING POWER

buy into *vt* **:** to obtain a place, footing, or interest in by purchase

bu·yo \'büyō\ *n* -S [Sp, fr. Bisayan *buyò*] *Philippines* **:** a masticatory consisting of betel leaf, the areca nut, lime, and often tobacco — compare 5PAN

buy off *vt* **1 :** to induce to refrain (as from prosecution) by a payment or other consideration ⟨the police were *bought off* with several well-placed gifts⟩ **2 :** to free (as from military service) by payment

buy out *vt* **1 :** to purchase the share or shares of in a stock, fund, or partnership so that the seller is separated from the company and the purchaser takes his place **2 :** to purchase the entire stock in trade and the good will of (a business) or the entire holdings in real estate of (a group) **3 :** to buy off

buys *pres 3d sing of* BUY, *pl of* BUY

buys bal·lot's law \'bīsbə'läts-\ *n, usu cap both Bs* [after C.H.D. *Buys Ballot* †1890 Dutch meteorologist] **:** a law in meteorology: when the observer has his back to the wind the lower barometric pressure is to his left in the northern hemisphere and to his right in the southern hemisphere owing to rotation of the earth

buy up *vt* **1 :** to buy freely or extensively ⟨*buying up* land right and left⟩ **2 :** to buy the entire available stocks of ⟨the government *bought up* the whole domestic rubber crop⟩

bu·zain \bü'zän, bə'z-, -zan\ *n* -S [prob. modif. of G *posaune* — more at POSAUNE] **:** POSAUNE 2

1buzz \'bəz\ *vb* -ED/-ING/-ES [ME *bussen*, of imit. origin] *vi* **1 :** to make a steady rasping low-pitched sound like that made by a flying insect ⟨flies darted and ~*ed* above the sorry nags —Kenneth Roberts⟩ **2** *archaic* **:** to speak in a muttering or half-whispering way esp. so as to irritate or incite one ⟨disturbers of our peace ~ in the people's ears —Shak.⟩ **3 :** to make a confused sibilant noise of many people talking at once ⟨the village ~*ed* with excitement at the news⟩ **4 a :** to move about like or with the sound of flying insects ⟨delegates ~*ing* about in a convention⟩ **b :** to go quickly **:** DART, WHIZZ — often used with *off* ⟨~*ing* off to New York for a weekend⟩ **c :** to act in an ineffectually busy or agitated manner ⟨the forest seemed a vast hive of men ~*ing* about in frantic circles —Stephen Crane⟩ **d :** to move or travel with the steady rapidity of a motor ⟨~*ing* along superhighways⟩ **5 :** to make a signal with a buzzer ⟨~*ed* for his secretary⟩ ~ *vt* **1 a :** to tell with an air of suppressed excitement, secrecy, or urgency **:** to spread as gossip or rumor ⟨I will ~ abroad such prophecies —Shak.⟩ **b :** to express with buzzing ⟨the committee ~*ed* its indignation⟩ **2 a :** to cause to buzz ⟨a fly ~*ed* its wings⟩ **b :** to summon or signal by buzzing ⟨~*ed* the control room to make his report⟩ **c** *slang* **:** to call on the telephone ⟨I'll ~ you in the morning⟩ **3** *dial chiefly Eng* **:** to throw violently **:** FLING **4** *dial Eng* **:** to drink to the last drop **:** finish the contents of ⟨get some more port whilst I ~ this bottle —W.M. Thackeray⟩ **5 :** to cut with a buzz saw **6 :** to dive and fly low and fast over ⟨two U.S. Air Force planes ~*ed* the crowd to add glory to the ceremony —T.H.White b.1915⟩ **7 :** to ask questions of **:** INTERVIEW

2buzz \"\ *n* -ES **1 :** the insistent rasping sound characteristic of flying insects **:** a sound produced by very fast irregular pulsations **:** a sibilant hum ⟨the angry ~ of a bluebottle fly⟩ **2 :** a noisy vibration or very rapid flutter esp. of a poorly functioning mechanical part ⟨a badly-tracking phonograph needle will make a ~⟩ ⟨a ~ developing in the ailerons of a plane at high speed⟩ **3 a :** a confused sibilant murmuring of many voices esp. in suppressed excitement ⟨a ~ went through the crowded courtroom⟩ **b :** a sound of busy activity **:** STIR **:** continuous bustle **4 :** RUMOR, GOSSIP, NEWS **5** *phonetics* **a :** the friction that characterizes the utterance of a fricative consonant; *also* **:** the combined sound of friction and of vocal-cord vibration that characterizes a voiced fricative **b :** a fricative esp. when voiced; *specif* **:** \z\ — compare HISS **6** *slang* **:** a call on the telephone ⟨I'll give you a ~ some time tomorrow⟩ **7 :** a game in which players quickly count round in turn, a player whose turn comes at a number containing 7 or at a multiple of 7 being required to say "buzz" instead of the number **8** *or* **buzz step :** a square-dance step in which one foot is kept firmly on the floor and the other is used for a series of pushes to effect the in-place pivot used in swinging one's partner **9** *slang* **:** a reaction from alcohol or narcotics ⟨had a good ~ on⟩; *also* **:** pleasurable excitement ⟨the kids will love this toy and adults will get a ~ out of it too⟩

3buzz \"\ *n* -ES [perh. alter. of *burrs*, pl. of 1*burr*] **1** *dial Eng* **:** the bur of a plant **2 :** a bushy fishing fly

1buzzard \'bəzə(r)d\ *n* -S [ME *busard*, fr. OF *busard, buisard*, alter. (influenced by OF *-ard*) of *buison* buzzard, fr. L *buteon-, buteo*; prob. akin to L *bubo* horned owl — more at BUBO] **1** *chiefly Brit* **:** BUTEO 2; *esp* **:** the common European short-winged hawk (*Buteo buteo*) that is rich dark brown above and mottled with white on the underparts **2 :** any of various birds of prey: as **a :** TURKEY BUZZARD **b :** HONEY BUZZARD **c :** CONDOR **3 :** a person exhibiting rapacity or disgusting habits — used often as a generalized expression of disapproval ⟨the old ~ won't sell his land⟩ ⟨a cranky old ~⟩ **4 :** a golf score of two strokes over par on a hole

2buzzard \"\ *n* -S [1*buzz* + *-ard*] *dial Eng* **:** a buzzing insect (as a cockchafer or dorbeetle)

buzzard cult *n, often cap B&C* [so called fr. the symbol of the eagle on artifacts of its members] **:** SOUTHERN CULT

buzzard curlew *n* **:** LONG-BILLED CURLEW

buzzard eagle *n* **:** any of several buteos somewhat resembling eagles: **a :** a member of a genus (*Butastur*) of Africa and eastern Asia **b :** one of a So. American genus (*Geranoaetus*)

buzzard hawk *n* **:** BUTEO 2

buzzard's-berry \'==ˌ==\ *n, pl* **buzzard's-berries :** BEARBERRY c

buzz bomb *n* **:** ROBOT BOMB

buzzed *adj, slang* **:** somewhat drunk

buzz·er \'bəzə(r)\ *n* -S **1 :** one that buzzes: as **a :** the interrupter of an induction coil **b :** an electric signal device producing a buzzing sound **c :** a miniature spark generator of which the principal element is a small vibrator actuated by an electromagnet **2** *Brit* **:** a textile burrer **3** *slang* **:** a detective's or policeman's badge

buzzes *pres 3d sing of* BUZZ, *pl of* BUZZ

buzzing *pres part of* BUZZ

buzz·ing·ly *adv* **:** in a buzzing manner

buzz planer *n* **:** a wood-planing machine consisting of a revolving horizontal cutter projecting slightly above a slot in the surface of a flat table

buzz saw *n* **:** CIRCULAR SAW

buzz stick *n* **:** a wooden rod fitted with two metal prongs like forks and used for testing suspension insulators on a high-tension transmission line

buzz-track \'=ˌ=\ *n* **:** a motion-picture film that contains a special sound track and is used for testing alignment of the optical system in a reproducer

buzz wig *n* [perh. fr. 3*buzz*] **:** a large bushy wig

buzz·wig \'bəˌzwig\ *n* [*buzz wig*] **:** a person wearing a buzz wig; *specif* **:** BIGWIG

buzzy \'bəzē, -zi\ *adj* -ER/-EST **1 :** making a buzz **:** filled with a buzz **2 :** GOSSIPY, TALKATIVE

BV *abbr* **1** [LL *Beata Virgo*] Blessed Virgin **2** book value

B.V.D. \ˌbē,vē'dē\ *trademark* — used for underwear

BVM *abbr* [LL *Beata Virgo Maria*] Blessed Virgin Mary

bvt *abbr* brevet; brevetted

BW *abbr* **1** bacteriological warfare; biological warfare **2** black and white **3** board of works **4** bonded warehouse **5** bread and water

bwa·na \'bwänə\ *n* -S [Swahili, fr. Ar *abūna* our father] *Africa* **:** MASTER, BOSS

bwd *abbr* backward

BWD *abbr* bacillary white diarrhea

BWG *abbr* Birmingham wire gauge

bx *abbr* box

bxd *abbr* boxed

1by \'bī *also esp bef cons* bə\ *prep* [ME, prep. & adv., fr. OE *be, bī*, prep., & *bī*, adv., by, near; akin to OHG *bī* by, near, Goth *bi* by, about, at, L *ambi-, amb-* on both sides, around, Gk *amphi* around, Skt *abhi* to, toward] **1 a :** in proximity to **:** in the immediate neighborhood of — used of place or position: (1) **:** at the side or edge of **:** NEAR ⟨the tree ~ the fence⟩ ⟨a cottage ~ the sea⟩ ⟨sat ~ him on the train⟩ (2) **:** close to or on (one's person) **:** within easy reach of **:** ABOUT ⟨kept the rabbit's foot ~ him day and night⟩ **b :** in the general region of ⟨they commonly commanded both ~ sea and land —John & William Langhorne⟩ **2 a :** ALONG, OVER, THROUGH ⟨the family drove to the farm ~ the old highway⟩ ⟨came from the garden ~ a path⟩ ⟨entered the house ~ the back door⟩: (1) **:** along the surface or through the medium of ⟨went to Europe ~ water and returned ~ air⟩ (2) **:** in passing along ⟨was cozened ~ the way and lost all my money —Shak.⟩ **b** (1) *now dial* **:** at or to the home of ⟨am going ~ Grandma for a week⟩ (2) **:** at or into (as another's house) on passing ⟨he came ~ the house for a few minutes yesterday⟩ **c :** in the direction of **:** TOWARD — used esp. of points of the compass ⟨sailed north ~ east⟩ **d :** into the presence of **:** close to ⟨we are not to stay together but to come ~ him where he stands —Shak.⟩ **e :** into the vicinity of and beyond **:** PAST ⟨drove rapidly ~ the church⟩ ⟨went ~ him without saying a word⟩ **3 a :** during the course of **:** within the period of ⟨worked ~ day and studied ~ night⟩ **b** *archaic* **:** for a specified period of time — used esp. in the phrase *by the space of* ⟨~ the space of three years I ceased not to warn everyone —Acts 20:31 (AV)⟩ **c :** not later than (a specified time) **:** at or before ⟨expected to arrive ~ two o'clock⟩ ⟨ought to be here ~ now⟩ **d** *dial Eng* **:** AFTER ⟨seventeen minutes ~ noon⟩ **4 a :** through the means or instrumentality of ⟨put to death ~ the sword⟩ ⟨a town taken ~ force⟩ **b :** through the direct agency of ⟨put to death ~ the executioner⟩ ⟨ordered ~ the captain to stand guard⟩ ⟨a poem written ~ Keats⟩ **c :** through the medium of (an indirect or subordinate agent) ⟨represented ~ his deputy⟩ ⟨votes ~ proxy⟩ **d :** through the work or operation of (as natural agencies) ⟨changes wrought ~ time⟩ ⟨eaten away ~ corrosion⟩ ⟨came to the right house ~ luck⟩ **e** (1) **:** born or begot of ⟨had two sons ~ his first wife⟩ ⟨children ~ her second husband⟩ (2) *in animal breeding* **:** sired by **f :** in consequence of **:** as a result of **:** THROUGH ⟨blunders of foreign policy ~ which Austria declined . . . from a great and stable power to a satellite —Hugh Seton-Watson⟩ **g** — used as a function word to indicate something that forms an accompanying setting or condition ⟨ate ~ candlelight⟩ or that constitutes a manner ⟨began ~ criticizing the style of the poem⟩ often with an added sense of means ⟨the case went ~ default⟩ **5 :** with the witness or sanction of **:** in the presence of — used esp. in oaths ⟨~ heaven I'll know thy thoughts —Shak.⟩ ⟨swear ~ all that is holy⟩ **6 a :** in conformity or harmony with (as a standard of action) ⟨judged them ~ our customs⟩ ⟨he plays ~ the rules⟩ **b :** according to — used esp. with verbs of calling and naming ⟨call him ~ whatever name you choose⟩ **c :** according to (as a unit of measurement) ⟨sold beef ~ the pound⟩ ⟨works ~ the hour⟩ ⟨workers paid ~ the piece⟩ **7 a :** on behalf of — used esp. to indicate direction of effort ⟨did his duty ~ his country⟩ ⟨did his best ~ his family⟩ **b :** on the basis of (as a distinction or classification) **:** in the matter of **:** with respect to ⟨a Kansan ~ birth⟩ ⟨a lawyer ~ profession⟩ **8 a :** in or to the amount or extent of — used in expressions involving comparison to indicate an amount or degree of excess or increase or of deficiency or decrease esp. in space, time, quantity, or weight ⟨won the race ~ two yards⟩ ⟨missed the train ~ five minutes⟩ ⟨carried his ward ~ 80 votes⟩ ⟨lighter ~ six pounds⟩ ⟨better ~ far⟩ **b** *now chiefly Scot* **:** in comparison with **:** BESIDE ⟨was but as a fly ~ an eagle —Shak.⟩ **9** — used as a function word to indicate a succession of units or groups of the same class ⟨they left the party two ~ two⟩ ⟨the snow fell flake ~ flake⟩ ⟨count ~ 5s to 100⟩ ⟨he succeeded little ~ little⟩ **10 a** *chiefly Scot* **:** in addition to **:** over and above **:** BESIDES ⟨few folks ken o' this place . . . there's just twa living ~ myself —Sir Walter Scott⟩ **b** *now chiefly Scot* **:** outside the range or sphere of **:** BEYOND — often used in combination with an adjective or adverb ⟨my father was a man of *by*-ordinary mildness —Margaret Oliphant⟩ **11 a** *now chiefly Scot* **:** contrary to **:** DESPITE ⟨I could not deny him but was forced ~ myself to give —Samuel Pepys⟩ **b** *obs* **:** AGAINST ⟨for I know nothing ~ myself —1 Cor 4:4 (AV)⟩ **12 a** — used as a function word in multiplication to connect multiplicand and multiplier ⟨multiply 15 ~ 12⟩ **b** — used as a function word to indicate two or more dimensions in measurements ⟨a room 20 feet ~ 12⟩; compare ⁴X **13 :** in the opinion of **:** from the point of view of ⟨it's O.K. ~ me⟩ — **by oneself 1 :** apart from others **:** ALONE ⟨we left them *by themselves* for a few hours⟩ **2 :** through the agency of oneself **:** without help **:** INDEPENDENTLY ⟨the boy finished the job *by himself*⟩ **3** *chiefly Scot* **:** out of one's mind — **by the bye** *or* **by the by** *adv* **:** INCIDENTALLY ⟨*by the by* have you seen my father —Anthony Trollope⟩

²by \ˈbī\ *adv* [ME, prep. & adv.] **1 a :** near at hand **:** in the immediate neighborhood ⟨they live close ~⟩ — often used in combination with a noun ⟨others of the . . . *by*-sitters put various questions —Nathaniel Hawthorne⟩ **b :** at or to another's home ⟨he stopped ~ for a few minutes yesterday⟩ **2 :** to and beyond a point near at hand **:** PAST ⟨the parade had gone ~ when I reached the corner⟩ — often used in combination with a noun ⟨each window has blinds to prevent the *by*-passers from looking in —Robert Southey⟩ **3 a :** off to one side **:** ASIDE, AWAY ⟨put her sewing ~ when he came in⟩ **b :** in reserve for future use **:** in store ⟨had laid enough ~ for his old age⟩ **4** *archaic* **:** over and above **:** BESIDES **5 :** in the past ⟨in days gone ~⟩

³by \ˈ"\ *or* **bye** \ˈ"\ *adj* [ME *by*, fr. *by*, adv.] **1 :** aside esp. in position or direction **:** out of the way **:** off the beaten track ⟨the mule preferred the high road to the ~ one —Robert Southey⟩ ⟨nothing can be more ~ and unfrequented —Samuel Richardson⟩ — often used in combination with a noun ⟨would slip into the next shop or *by*-passage to avoid them —John Dryden⟩ **2 :** aside esp. in purpose or importance **:** INCIDENTAL, SECONDARY ⟨the ~ effect may be unfavorable —William Paley⟩ ⟨too serious a work to be undertaken in a ~ way —John Ruskin⟩ — often used in combination with a noun ⟨the *by*-productions of a busy man —J.R.Lowell⟩ **3** *chiefly Scot* **:** done with **:** PAST, OVER

⁴by *or* **bye** \ˈ"\ *n, pl* **byes :** something of secondary importance **:** a side issue — now used chiefly in the phrase *by the by*

⁵by \ˈ"\ *vi* **byed; byed; bying; bys** \ˈbīz\ [prob. fr. *by*, adv.] **:** PASS 12a(1)

⁶by \ˈ"\ *n, pl* **bys** \ˈbīz\ [prob. fr. *by*, adv.] **:** a pass in certain card games (as bridge)

⁷by *or* **bye** [by shortening] **:** GOOD-BYE — used interjectionally often with *now* ⟨~ now⟩

by-alley \ˈ=,==\ *n* **:** a side alley

by-altar \ˈ=,==\ *n* **:** a side altar **:** a secondary altar

by and by \ˌbīən(d)ˈbī, (ˈ)bīn(d)ˈbī, (ˈ)bīmˈbī, ˌbīəmˈbī, ˌbəmˈbī\ *adv* [²*by*] **1** *obs* **:** at once **:** IMMEDIATELY ⟨the end is not *by and by* —Lk 21:9 (AV)⟩ **2 :** in a little while **:** before long **:** SOON ⟨*by and by* he discovered that the black night had changed to gray —Zane Grey⟩

by-and-by \ˈ"\ *n* [*by and by*] **:** a future time or occasion ⟨in the sweet *by-and-by* we shall meet on that beautiful shore —S.F.Bennett⟩

by and large \ˌbīən(d)ˈ=\ *adv* [²*by*] **1 :** alternately close-hauled and free — used of sailing a ship ⟨they soon found out one another's rate of sailing *by and large* —*Fraser's Mag.*⟩ **2 :** on the whole **:** in general ⟨*by and large* he gave us a lot of trouble —Mary R. Rinehart⟩

by-bidder \ˈ=,==\ *n* **:** one who bids at an auction in behalf of the auctioneer or owner in order to run up the price

byb·lis \ˈbibləs\ *n, cap* [NL, fr. L *Byblis*, a nymph, fr. Gk] **:** a small genus of low Australian shrubs with a superficial resemblance to the sundews that in some classifications is isolated in a monotypic family but is more commonly included in Droseraceae

by-blow \ˈ=,=\ *n* **1 :** an indirect or incidental blow ⟨pass these incidents off as *by-blows* and as being of no real consequence —*Springfield (Mass.) Daily News*⟩ **2 :** an illegitimate child **:** BASTARD ⟨they were obviously gentlemen and, it is hinted, *by-blows* of some nobleman —C.R.Anderson⟩

by-by *var of* BYE-BYE

by-channel \ˈ=,==\ *n* **:** a stream at one side of the main stream

by-child \ˈ=,=\ *n, dial Eng* **:** an illegitimate child

by·cok·et \(ˈ)bīˈkäkət\ *or* **aba·cot** \ˈabəˌkät\ *also* **abo·cock·et** \ˌabəˈkäkət\ *n* -s [ME *bycoket*, fr. ME, fr. MF *bicoquet*; *abacot*, *abococket* alter. of *a bycoket*, fr. ²*a* + *bycoket*] **:** a hat with a high crown and a wide brim turned up in back and coming to a point like a beak in front worn esp. in the 15th century

by-corner \ˈ=,==\ *n* **:** an out-of-the-way corner

by-day \ˈ=,=\ *n* **:** an off day

byd·goszcz \ˈbidˌgōsh(ch)\ *adj, usu cap* [fr. *Bydgoszcz*, Poland] **:** of or from the city of Bydgoszcz, Poland **:** of the kind or style prevalent in Bydgoszcz

by dint of *prep* **:** through the force or power of ⟨he succeeded *by dint of* hard work⟩

by-drinking \ˈ=,==\ *n, archaic* **:** a drinking between meals

¹bye *var of* BY

²bye \ˈbī\ *interj* [ME *by*, of unknown origin] — used to lull a child ⟨~ baby bunting⟩

³bye \ˈ"\ *n* -s [alter. of ²*by*] **1 :** a run made on a bowled ball that passes without touching or being touched by the batsman in cricket — compare LEG BYE, WIDE **2 :** the position of a participant in a tournament who has no opponent after pairs are drawn and advances to the next round without playing ⟨drew a first-round ~ in the tennis tournament⟩

⁴bye \ˈ"\ *n* -s [by shortening & alter.] **:** BY-WATER

¹bye-bye *or* **by-by** \(ˈ)bīˈbī\ *interj* [baby-talk redupl. of *goodbye*] — used to express farewell

²bye-bye *or* **by-by** \ˈ"\ *adv* **:** out esp. for a walk or ride — used with the verb *go* ⟨if he wants to go *bye-bye* the baby may pat his head to indicate his desire for a hat —A.L.Gesell & Frances Ilg⟩

³bye-bye *or* **by-by** \ˈ"\ *n* [redupl. of ²*bye*] **:** BED, SLEEP ⟨lie down . . . and go to *bye-bye* —Rudyard Kipling⟩

⁴bye-bye *or* **by-by** \ˈ"\ *adv* **:** to bed or sleep — used with the verb *go* ⟨I'll run in and read for just a second . . . and then perhaps I'll go *bye-bye* —Sinclair Lewis⟩

by-effect \ˈ=,=,=\ *n* **:** an additional effect **:** an unintended effect

bye hole *n* [¹*bye*] **:** a small opening in the side of a glass furnace for withdrawing samples of molten glass, heating the punty, or reheating small articles

by-election *also* **bye-election** \ˈ==,==\ *n* **:** a special election held between regular elections in order to fill a vacancy

byelorussian *cap, var of* BELORUSSIAN

bye·man \ˈbīmən\ *n, pl* **byemen** [¹*bye* + *man*] **:** a worker underground in a mine

by-end \ˈ=,=\ *n* **1 :** a subordinate end; *esp* **:** a selfish motive ⟨they are all for *by-ends*, the whole clan of them —R.L. Stevenson⟩ **2 :** FRAGMENT, SNATCH ⟨*by-ends* of old rhymes —J.B.Cabell⟩

by·er·ite \ˈbī(ə)ˌrīt\ *n* -s [William N. Byers †1903 Am. surveyor and pioneer + E *-ite*] **:** bituminous coal resembling albertite

byes *pl of* BY *or of* BYE

by-fellow \ˈ=,==\ *n* **:** a fellow of one of the colleges of Cambridge University holding a secondary often nominal fellowship — **by-fellowship** \ˈ=,==,=\ *n*

by-form \ˈ=,=\ *n* **:** a parallel and sometimes less important form ⟨certain expressions have slurred and shortened *by-forms* in which the phonetic pattern is lost —Leonard Bloomfield⟩

bygane \(ˈ)bīˌgān\ *chiefly Scot var of* BYGONE

by·go·ing \ˈbīˌgōiŋ\ *n* **:** the action of passing by — **in the bygoing :** in passing **:** INCIDENTALLY

¹by·gone \ˈbīˌgȯn\ *adj* [ME (Sc dial.) *bygane*, fr. ²*by* + *gane*, var. of *gon*, past part. of *gon* to go — more at GO] **1 :** that is past **:** gone by **:** FORMER ⟨the music of a ~ day⟩ **2 a :** of or relating to the past **:** OUTMODED ⟨current fashions . . . are revivals of ~ styles —P.M.Gregory⟩ **b :** no longer living **:** DEAD, EXTINCT ⟨circles of burned and broken stone remain as evidence of its popularity with ~ tribes —*Amer. Guide Series: Mich.*⟩ ⟨~ species of animals —Weston LaBarre⟩

²bygone \ˈ"\ *n* -s **1 :** something that is past; *esp* **:** a past grievance — usu. used in pl. ⟨a gesture to show that ~*s* are ~*s* —William Walton⟩ ⟨let ~*s* be ~*s*⟩ **2 :** one that belongs to the past ⟨to them he is a ~ —*Bookman*⟩ ⟨a museum in search of ~*s* —H.V.Morton⟩

by-hour \ˈ=,==\ *n* **:** a leisure hour

bying *pres part of* BY

by-interest \ˈbī+,-\ *n* **:** an additional esp. private interest

by-job \ˈ=,=\ *n* **:** an odd job

byke *chiefly Scot var of* ¹BIKE 1

by-lane \ˈ=,=\ *n* **:** a side lane

bylaw *or* **byelaw** \ˈ=,=\ *n* [ME *bilage*, *bilawe*, prob. fr. (assumed) ON *bȳlǫg*, fr. ON *bȳr* town (fr. *būa* to live) + *lǫg* law — more at BE, LAW] **1 a :** the local law esp. of a vill or manor **b :** an ordinance made by a court leet or court baron **2 :** a law, ordinance, or regulation made by a public or private corporation or an association or unincorporated society for the regulation of its own local or internal affairs and its dealings with others or for the government of its members **3** [influenced in meaning by ²*by*] **:** a secondary or subordinate law

by·law·man \ˈbīˌlȯmən\ *n, pl* **bylawmen** [by folk etymology] **:** BYRLAWMAN

by-lead \ˈbīˌlēd\ *n* **:** BY-WASH

by·li·na \bəˈlēnə\ *n, pl* **byli·ny** \-nē\ *or* **bylinas** \-nəz\ [Russ, fr. *bylina* what has been, fr. *byl* was, past of *bit'* to be; akin to Skt *bhavati* he is — more at BE] **:** a Russian folk epic or ballad

¹by-line \ˈ=,=\ *n* **1 :** a secondary line **:** SIDELINE **2 a :** a line at the head of a newspaper or magazine article giving the writer's name **b :** something resembling such a by-line ⟨his calm "This is London" was one of the war's most famous *by-lines* —*Newsweek*⟩

²by-line \ˈ"\ *vt* **:** to write under a by-line ⟨has *by-lined* numerous magazine pieces —*Publishers' Weekly*⟩

byliner \ˈ=,==\ *n* -s **:** a journalist who writes under a by-line

by means of *prep* **:** through the agency or instrumentality of

bymeby *var of* BIMEBY

by-motive \ˈ=,==\ *n* **:** a hidden motive

byname \ˈ=,=\ *n* [ME, fr. ²*by* + *name*] **1 :** a secondary name (as a cognomen or surname) **2 :** NICKNAME

by·on \ˈbīˌän, -ēən\ *n* -s [prob. native name in Burma] **:** a clayey gem-bearing earth of Burma

¹byous \ˈbīəs\ *adj* [²*by* + *-ous*] *Scot* **:** EXTRAORDINARY

²byous \ˈ"\ *adv, Scot* **:** EXTREMELY, MARKEDLY

byp *abbr* bypass

¹bypass \ˈ=,=\ *n* [²*by* + *pass*] **1 :** a passage to one side; *esp* **:** a passage providing an alternative deflected route (as a road to carry traffic around a congested district or a channel to deflect flood water) **2 a :** an auxiliary passage (as a channel or pipe) through which a fluid passes around a particular place or part and returns to the main passage **:** a passage forming a secondary outlet for a fluid **b :** a path for shunting part or all of an electric current around one or more elements of a circuit

²bypass \(ˈ)=ˈ=\ *vt* **1 :** to make a circuit or detour around ⟨the new highway ~*es* the city⟩ **:** avoid by means of a bypass ⟨we ~*ed* most congested areas on our trip⟩ **2 :** to make (as a fluid or gas) follow a bypass ⟨incoming air was ~*ed* through the intercoolers in the intake air line⟩ **3 :** to neglect or ignore usu. intentionally ⟨critics have tended to ~ this side of his work —L.A.G.Strong⟩ ⟨these problems cannot be ~*ed* —Walter Terry⟩ **:** get around **:** EVADE ⟨men seek to ~ the law —H.J. Laski⟩ **4 :** to go around and beyond (an enemy) without attempting to attack

bypass condenser *n* **:** a capacitor providing a path for alternating current around some part of a circuit through which the current cannot so readily pass

bypasser \ˈ"+ə(r)\ *n* **:** PASSERBY

bypass valve *n* **:** a valve placed to control the flow of fluid through a bypass

bypast \(ˈ)=ˈ=\ *adj* [ME (Sc dial.), fr. ²*by* + *past*] **:** BYGONE

bypath \ˈ=,=\ *n* [ME, fr. ²*by* + *path*] **:** BYWAY

by-place \ˈ=,=\ *n* **:** an out-of-the-way place **:** an odd corner

by-play \ˈ=,=\ *n* **:** action engaged in on the side while the main action proceeds ⟨one bit of ~ unnoticed by the seconds —Joseph Conrad⟩; *specif* **:** incidental stage business

by-plot \ˈ=,=\ *n* **:** a subordinate plot (as in a play)

by-product \ˈ=,==\ *n* **1 :** a secondary or additional product **:** something produced (as in manufacturing) in addition to the principal product ⟨glycerol is principally obtained as a *by-product* of soap manufacture —P.O.Powers⟩ **2 :** a secondary and sometimes unexpected or unintended result of an action or process ⟨pleasure is a very important *by-product* of education —Agnes Repplier⟩

by-product coke *n* **:** coke made in a by-product oven, usu. obtained in various sizes, and when made by high-temperature carbonization having great structural strength and being esp. suitable for use in blast furnaces and cupola furnaces

by-product oven *n* **:** a coke oven consisting typically of rows of long narrow coking chambers that alternate with flues in which fuel gas is burned, used esp. for high-temperature and medium-temperature carbonization of coal, and having provision for recovery of volatile products (as gas, ammonia, light oils, and tar)

byre \ˈbī(ə)r, ˈbīə\ *n* -s [ME, fr. OE *bȳre*; akin to OE *būr* cottage, dwelling — more at BOWER] *chiefly Brit* **:** a stable for cows

by-reaction \ˈ==ˈ==\ *n* **:** an accompanying reaction (as in a chemical process)

byre·man \ˈbī(ə)rmən, ˈbīəm-\ *n, pl* **byremen** *chiefly Brit* **:** COWMAN

byre·woman \ˈbī(ə)r, ˈbīə+,-\ *n, pl* **byrewomen** *chiefly Brit* **:** a woman that tends cows

byr·lady \(ˌ)bī(ə)r, ˌbīə+\ *interj* [contr. of *by our Lady*] — a mild oath

byrlakin *interj* [contr. of *by our Ladykin*] *obs* — a mild oath

byr·law \ˈbirˌlȯ, ˈbiəˌlȯ *or* **bur·law** \ˈbərˌlȯ, ˈbəˌlȯ\ *n* -s [ME *birelage*, *birlawe*, perh. fr. (assumed) ON *bȳjar lǫg*, fr. ON *bȳjar* (gen. of *bȳr* town) + *lǫg* law — more at BYLAW] **:** the local custom or law of a vill, township, or rural district in the north of England or in Scotland that governs disputes relating esp. to boundaries, dates of plowing, and use of common land; *also* **:** a particular custom or law established by common consent of the landholders of such a district

byr·law·man \ˈbirˌlȯmən, ˈbiəˌl-\ *n, pl* **byrlawmen** [ME, fr. *birlawe* + *man*] **:** a local officer appointed at a court leet in northern England or in Scotland to perform such duties as framing byrlaws and administering petty justice

byr·nie \ˈbərnē\ *n* -s [ME *brinie*, fr. ON *brynja*; akin to OE *byrne* coat of mail, OHG *brunia*, *brunna*, Goth *brunjo*, and prob. to OIr *bruinne* breast] **:** a coat of mail **:** HAUBERK

byroad \ˈ=,=\ *n* **:** a road that is little traveled ⟨wander along the ~*s* . . . soaking up atmosphere from the out-of-the-way hamlets —Richard Joseph⟩; *specif* **:** SIDE ROAD ⟨to the right a ~ suddenly branched off —George Bellairs⟩

by·ron·ic \(ˈ)bīˈränik\ *adj, usu cap* [George N. Gordon, Lord Byron †1824 Eng. poet + E *-ic*] **:** of, relating to, or having the characteristics of the poet Byron or his writings ⟨with despair and *Byronic* misanthropy —W.M.Thackeray⟩ ⟨his attitude, his smile were *Byronic*, at once world-weary and contemptuous —Aldous Huxley⟩ — **by·ron·i·cal·ly** \-nək(ə)lē, -li\ *adv, usu cap*

by·ron·ics \bīˈräniks\ *n pl, usu cap* **:** Byronic behavior or utterances ⟨was not to be taken in by any *Byronics* —*Times Lit. Supp.*⟩

by·ron·ism \ˈbīrəˌnizəm\ *n* -s *usu cap* [Lord *Byron* + E *-ism*] **:** the characteristics of the poet Byron or his writings ⟨he's got a streak of his father's *Byronism* —John Galsworthy⟩

by-room \ˈ=,=\ *n* **:** a side or private room

byrrus *var of* BIRRUS

byr·son·i·ma \bərˈsänəmə\ *n, cap* [NL, irreg. fr. Gk *byrseuein* to tan + *onoma* useful] **:** a large genus of tropical American trees or shrubs (family Malpighiaceae) having entire leaves, yellow flowers, and fleshy edible fruits — see NANCE

bys *pres 3d sing of* BY, *pl of* BY

by-sitter \ˈ=,==\ *n* **:** one sitting nearby **:** ONLOOKER

bys·ma·lith \ˈbizməˌlith\ *n* -s [Gk *bysma* plug + E *-lith*] **:** a modified laccolith in which the roof has been lifted in part by peripheral faulting

bys·sa·ceous \bəˈsāshəs\ *adj* [NL *byssus* + E *-aceous*] **:** like a byssus

bys·sal \ˈbisəl\ *adj* [NL *byssus* + E *-al*] **:** of or relating to a byssus ⟨the ~ gland⟩

bys·sif·er·ous \bəˈsif(ə)rəs\ *adj* [NL *byssus* + E *-i-* + *-ferous*] **:** having a byssus

bys·sine \ˈbisən\ *adj* [L *byssinus*, fr. Gk *byssinos*, fr. *byssos* byssus + *-inos* -ine] **:** made of byssus

bys·si·no·sis \ˌbisəˈnōsəs\ *n, pl* **byssino·ses** \-ˌsēz\ [NL, fr. LL *byssinum* linen garment (fr. neut. of L *byssinus*) + NL *-osis*] **:** a chronic industrial disease associated with the inhalation of cotton dust over a long period of time and characterized by chronic bronchitis sometimes complicated by emphysema or asthma — called also *mill fever*

bys·soid \ˈbiˌsȯid\ *adj* [NL & L *byssus* + E *-oid*] **1 :** BYSSACEOUS **2 :** COTTONY 1

bys·so·lite \ˈbisəˌlīt\ *n* -s [F, fr. Gk *byssos* flax, linen + F *-lite* — more at BYSSUS] **:** a mineral consisting of an olive-green fibrous amphibole

bys·sus \ˈbisəs\ *n, pl* **byssuses** \-səz\ *or* **bys·si** \-ˌsī, -ˌsē\ [L *byssus*, fr. Gk *byssos* flax, linen, of Sem origin; akin to Heb *būṣ* linen cloth] **1 :** a fine cloth of ancient times believed to have been made of linen, cotton, or silk **2** [NL, fr. L] **:** a tuft of long tough filaments secreted by a gland in a groove of the foot of certain bivalve mollusks (as those of the genera *Pinna* and *Mytilus*), issuing from between the valves, and serving as the means whereby the mollusk attaches itself to rocks or other foreign bodies

by-stake \ˈ=,=\ *n* **:** a rod serving as an upright framing rod in a basket — see BASKET illustration

bystander \ˈ=,==\ *n* -s **:** one present but not taking part **:** a chance spectator ⟨there are no ~*s* in modern warfare —A.M. Sullivan⟩

bystreet \ˈ=,=\ *n* **:** a street off a main thoroughfare **:** a side street ⟨the wanderer passed into a ~ comparatively deserted —E.A.Poe⟩

by-stroke \ˈ=,=\ *n* **:** a subtle and indirect action as a means to an end

bys·trom·ite \ˈbistrəˌmīt\ *n* -s [prob. fr. the name *Byström* + E *-ite*] **:** a mineral $MgSb_2O_6$ consisting of a magnesium antimony oxide

by-talk \ˈ=,=\ *n* **:** SMALL TALK

by-term \ˈ=,=\ *n* **:** a term at Cambridge University that is not the usual one for entering or for taking a degree

by the way *adv* **1 :** along or near the side of the road **2 :** in the course of a journey **3 :** by way of incident or digression **:** in passing **:** INCIDENTALLY

¹by-the-way \ˌ==ˈ=\ *adj* [*by the way*] **:** CASUAL, OFFHAND ⟨asked in a *by-the-way* fashion about his army service —J.N. Hall⟩

²by-the-way \ˈ"\ *n* -s [*by the way*] **:** an incidental remark **:** a casual comment

by-thing \ˈ=,=\ *n* **:** a thing of little importance

by·thin·ia \bəˈthinēə\ [NL, irreg. fr. *Bithynia*, ancient province of Asia Minor, fr. L, fr. Gk] *syn of* BULIMUS

by-time \ˈ=,=\ *n* **:** a leisure interval

by·tom \ˈbiˌtȯm\ *adj, usu cap* [fr. Bytom, Poland] **:** of or from the city of Bytom, Poland **:** of the kind or style prevalent in Bytom

by·town·ite \ˈbī(ˌ)taủˌnīt, =ˈ=,=\ *n* -s [*Bytown* (now Ottawa), Canada + E *-ite*] **:** a plagioclase feldspar consisting of 10 to 30 percent albite and 90 to 70 percent anorthite

by-track \ˈ=,=\ *n* **:** a little-used track

by-trail \ˈ=,=\ *n* **:** a side trail

by virtue of *prep* **:** by reason of **:** as a result of ⟨they survive through adaptive change and *by virtue of* their natural boundaries —A.L.Locke⟩

bywalk \ˈ=,=\ *n* **:** a secluded or private walk **:** BYWAY

by-wash \ˈ=,=\ *n* **:** a spillway or weir made to permit the escape of surplus water (as from a dam or reservoir)

by-water \ˈ=,==\ *n* **:** a diamond of yellowish tint

byway \ˈ=,=\ *n* [ME, fr. ²*by* + *way*] **1 :** a secluded, roundabout, or little traveled road **:** SIDE ROAD ⟨along the stretch of sandy creek-road and thence by the rough ill-tended county ~ to the main road —Elizabeth M. Roberts⟩ — contrasted with *highway* **2 :** a secondary or little known aspect or field ⟨has explored with great skill this ~ in the development of political theory —Gordon Wright⟩

by·wo·ner \ˈbīˌvōnə(r), ˈbāˌvə-\ *n* -s [Afrik, fr. *by* with, at (fr. MD *bī*) + *woner* dweller (fr. *woon* to dwell — fr. MD *wōnen* — + *-er*); akin to OHG *bī* with, at, and to OHG *wonēn* to dwell — more at BY, WONT] *southern Africa* **:** a laborer or farmer working another person's land: **a :** SQUATTER **b :** SHARECROPPER

byword \ˈ=,=\ *n* [ME, fr. OE *bīword*, fr. *bī* by + *word* — more at BY, WORD] **1 :** a proverbial saying **:** PROVERB ⟨the old ~ of necessity being the mother of invention —A.L.Kroeber⟩ **2 a :** one that is proverbial as a type of specified characteristics ⟨John Henry has become a ~ with them, a synonym for superstrength and superendurance —G.B.Johnson⟩ ⟨the mountain view from its spacious glassed-in porches is a White Mountain ~ —E.W.Smith⟩ **b :** an object of scorn or derision ⟨we ourselves shall become a reproach and ~ down to future ages —Benjamin Franklin⟩ **3 :** EPITHET; *esp* **:** a scornful epithet **4 :** a word or phrase frequently used by a particular person **:** a favorite expression ⟨we called him "the Deacon" because of his favorite ~ "Praise be" —H.A.Chippendale⟩

bywork \'=,=\ *n* **:** work done on the side **:** work done in intervals of leisure ⟨won popular fame . . . by a piece of ~ —*Times Lit. Supp.*⟩

by-your-leave \¦==¦=\ *n* **:** a request for permission ⟨look over one's correspondence without so much as a *by-your-leave* —Frances Towers⟩

byzant *var of* BEZANT

[1]**by·zan·tian** \bə̇'zansh(ē)ən, -zantēən, -tyən\ *n* -S *usu cap* [*Byzantium*, ancient city on the site of İstanbul, Turkey + E *-an*] **:** BYZANTINE

[2]**byzantian** \"\ *adj, usu cap* **:** BYZANTINE ⟨*Byzantian* civilization⟩

[1]**byz·an·tine** \¦bizən¦tēn *also* -¦tīn *sometimes* ¦bīz-; 'bizəntə̇n; bə̇'zan,tēn, -zaan,-, *also* -,tīn, -‗tə̇n *sometimes* bī'z-\ *n* -S [LL *Byzantinus* native of Byzantium, fr. *Byzantium* + L *-inus* -ine] **1 :** BEZANT **2** *usu cap* **:** a native or inhabitant of the ancient city of Byzantium

[2]**byzantine** \"\ *adj, usu cap* [LL *Byzantinus*, adj. & n.] **1 a :** of, relating to, or characteristic of the ancient city of Byzantium **b :** of, relating to, or characteristic of the Eastern Roman Empire **2 a :** of, relating to, or having the characteristics of a style of architecture developed in the Byzantine Empire esp. in the 5th and 6th centuries and having as its central structural feature the dome carried on pendentives over a square and as its chief decorative feature the incrustation of walls, vault faces, and spandrels with marble veneering and with richly colored mosaic on grounds of gold **b :** of, relating to, or having the characteristics of a school of painting that originated in the Byzantine Empire, was influential until the 14th century throughout western Europe esp. in Italy, and survived until recent times esp. in Bulgaria and Russia and that was characterized by formality of design, by absence of shadow and of the appearance of relief, and by the free use of gilding in the background **3 :** of or relating to the Eastern Orthodox Church ⟨*Byzantine* monks⟩ ⟨the *Byzantine* rite⟩ **4 :** of, relating to, or marked by Byzantinism

byzantine speedwell *n, usu cap B* **:** a Eurasian annual herb (*Veronica persica*) having long-stalked blue flowers and being widely distributed as a weed

by·zan·tin·esque \bə̇¦zantə̇¦nesk\ *adj, usu cap* **:** in the Byzantine style

by·zan·tin·ism \bə̇'zantə,nizəm\ *n* -S *usu cap* **1 :** the political principles, social patterns, manner, style, and spirit characteristic of Byzantine life esp. when manifested in architecture, art, or literature **2 :** the doctrine or system of state supremacy in ecclesiastical affairs — compare CAESAROPAPISM, ERASTIANISM

by·zan·ti·nist \-tənə̇st\ *n* -S *usu cap* **:** a student of Byzantine culture

by·zan·tin·ize \-tə̇,nīz\ *vt* -ED/-ING/-S *often cap* **:** to make Byzantine

by·zen *also* **bi·zen** \'bīzən, 'bēz-\ *n* -S [ME *bysen* example, disgraceful spectacle, fr. OE *bisen*, *bysen* example; akin to ON *bȳsn* marvel, Goth an*abusns* command, OE *bēodan* to command — more at BID] *dial Eng* **:** a disgraceful spectacle or example

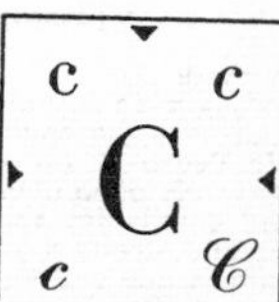

[1]c \'sē\ *n, pl* **c's** *or* **cs** \'sēz\ *often cap, often attrib* **1 a :** the third letter of the English alphabet **b :** an instance of this letter printed, written, or otherwise represented **c :** a speech counterpart of orthographic *c* (as hard *c* in *cat* or soft *c* in *cell*) **2 a :** one hundred — see NUMBER table **b** *slang* **:** a sum of $100 **3 a :** the keynote of C major or C minor **b :** the tone C **4 :** a printer's type, a stamp, or some other instrument for reproducing the letter *c* **5 :** someone or something arbitrarily or conveniently designated *c* esp. as the third in order or class ⟨A deeded land to B and *C* together⟩ **6 a :** a grade assigned by a teacher or examiner rating a student's work as fair, average, or mediocre in quality ⟨pass Latin with a *C*⟩ **b :** one graded or rated with a C ⟨a *C* student⟩ ⟨the movie was a *C*⟩ ⟨your quiz papers are all *C's*⟩ **7 :** something having the shape of the letter C

[2]**c** *abbr, often cap* **1** calm **2** calorie **3** Canadian **4** canceled **5** candle **6** canon **7** capacitance; capacity **8** cape **9** captain **10** caput **11** carat **12** cargo **13** case **14** castle **15** catcher **16** cathode **17** Catholic **18** caught **19** cause **20** Celsius **21** cent **22** cental **23** centavo **24** center **25** centi- **26** centigrade **27** centime **28** centimeter **29** centum **30** century **31** chairman **32** chancellor; chancery **33** chapter **34** chief **35** child **36** church **37** circa; circiter; circum **38** circuit **39** circumference **40** clearance **41** clockwise **42** cloudy **43** cobalt **44** cocaine **45** codex **46** coefficient **47** cognate **48** cold **49** college **50** color **51** colt **52** combat **53** commander **54** common meter **55** common time **56** companion **57** condemned **58** conductor **59** confessor **60** confidential **61** congius **62** congregation **63** congress **64** conservative **65** constable **66** consul **67** contact **68** continental **69** contra **70** contraction **71** contralto **72** copper **73** copy **74** copyright **75** cord **76** cordoba **77** corps **78** correct **79** cost **80** coulomb **81** count **82** coupon **83** court **84** cousin **85** created **86** crowned **87** cubic **88** cum **89** cup **90** currency **91** current **92** cycle **93** cylinder

[3]**c** *symbol* **1** 4/4 time — used after the clef sign on a musical staff **2** *cap* carbon **3** copyright — often enclosed in a circle **4 a** cipher — used as a subscript ⟨$F_p = T_c$ means that the plaintext letter F has the cipher substitute T⟩ **b** *cap* the numerical value of a cipher letter when the cipher component is serially numbered from 0 to 25 ⟨P+K=C is the Vigenère keying method⟩ **5** *cap* consonant

ca *abbr* **1** cable **2** candle **3** case **4** cathode **5** centare **6** circa

CA *abbr* **1** capital account **2** chartered accountant **3** chief accountant **4** chronological age **5** claim agent **6** coast artillery **7** cold air **8** [It *coll'arco*] with the bow **9** commercial agent **10** controller of accounts **11** [F *cor anglais*] English horn **12** cost accountant **13** council accepted **14** court of appeal **15** credit account **16** crown agent **17** current account

Ca *symbol* calcium

ca' \'kȯ, 'kä\ *Scot var of* CALL

caaba *usu cap, var of* KAABA

caa·ing whale *also* **ca'·ing whale** \'kȯiŋ, 'kä·iŋ, 'kä·-\ *n* [*caaing, ca'ing,* gerund of *ca'* to call, drive (whales into shallow water)] **:** a blackfish (*Globicephala melaena*) of the north Atlantic — called also *pilot whale*

caam \'käm, -ām\ *n* -s [D *kam,* lit., comb, fr. MD *cam;* akin to OE *camb* comb — more at COMB] **:** the heddles of a loom

caa·ma \'kämə\ *n* -s [of African origin; akin to Vai *ka'ma³* elephant] **1** *also* **ca·ma fox** \'kä-\ **:** a southern African fox (*Vulpes chama*) **2 :** CAPE HARTEBEEST

caam·ing \'kämiŋ, -'ä-\ *n* -s [*caam* + *-ing*] **:** the setting of the reed in weaving by the proper placing of the threads of the warp

caa·pi \'käpē\ *n* -s [Pg, fr. Tupi] **1 :** a vine (*Bannisteria caapi*) of the family Malpighiaceae of northwestern So. America **2 :** the rhizome and roots of the caapi vine used in preparing a stimulating native beverage

caa·tin·ga \kä'tiŋgə, kə-\ *n* -s [Pg, modif. of Tupi *caá-tinga* white forest, fr. *caá* forest + *tinga* white] **:** stunted rather sparse forest that is leafless in the dry season and is widespread in areas of small rainfall in northeastern Brazil

[1]**cab** *or* **kab** \'kab, -äb\ *n* -s [Heb *qabh*] **:** an ancient Hebrew unit of capacity equal to about two quarts

[2]**cab** \'käb\ *vt* **cabbed; cabbed; cabbing; cabs** [short for *cabbage* (steal)] *slang Scot* **:** PURLOIN

[3]**cab** \'kab, -aa(ə)b\ *n* -s [short for *cabriolet*] **1 :** a horse-drawn carriage: as **a :** CABRIOLET **b :** a similar light closed carriage (as a hansom) **c :** any carriage for hire whether closed or open and drawn by one or two horses **:** a hackney carriage **2** [by shortening] **:** TAXICAB **3** [short for *cabin*] **a :** the part of a locomotive that houses the engineer, fireman, and operating controls **b :** a shelter for operator and controls of a power-driven vehicle, tractor, or hoisting apparatus: as (1) **:** an enclosed compartment on a motor truck or trailer truck having a windshield at the front and a seat for the driver (2) **:** a suspended control compartment for the operator of a traveling crane or monorail tractor (3) **:** the car or cage of an elevator **c :** CABIN 4d

[4]**cab** \"\ *vi* **cabbed; cabbed; cabbing; cabs :** to travel in a cab

[5]**cab** \"\ *n* -s [perh. alter. of *gob* (lump)] *dial* **:** something sticky or dirty

[6]**cab** \"\ *n* -s [by shortening] **:** CABOCHON

cab *abbr* **1** cabin **2** cabinet **3** cable

ca·ba \kə'bä\ *n* -s [F *cabas,* fr. OProv, prob. fr. (assumed) VL *capacium,* fr. L *capere* to take, contain — more at HEAVE] **:** a woman's workbasket or handbag

[1]**ca·bal** \kə'bal *also* -'ä- *or* -'à-\ *n* -s [F *cabale,* fr. ML *cabala, cabbala,* fr. Heb *qabbālāh* received or traditional lore, fr. *qābal* to receive] **1** *obs* **:** CABALA 2a **2 a :** a number of persons secretly united and using devious and undercover means to bring about an overturn or usurpation esp. in public affairs or to undermine and cause the downfall of a person in a position of authority **b :** the artifices and intrigues of such a group **c :** a coterie in artistic circles **syn** see PLOT

[2]**cabal** \"\ *vi* **caballed; caballed; caballing; cabals :** to unite in or form a cabal

cab·a·la *or* **cab·ba·la** *or* **cab·ba·lah** *or* **kab·a·la** *or* **kab·ba·la** *or* **kab·ba·lah** *also* **qab·ba·la** *or* **qab·ba·lah** \'kabələ; kə'bälə, -'à-\ *n* -s *often cap* [ML — more at CABAL] **1 :** a system of occult theosophy or mystical interpretation of the Scriptures orig. developed orally among Jewish rabbis in the Geonic period and transmitted to certain medieval Christians, holding such tenets as creation through emanation, supremacy of man's spirit over his desires, Messianic restoration of the world to a perfect state, and laying stress on hidden senses in the Scriptures and occult means of interpretation even to foretelling events by these methods **2 a :** a traditional, esoteric, occult, or secret matter **b :** esoteric doctrine or mysterious art ⟨of the several ~s the most prominent are the mystic and the psychoanalytic, while the Marxist method . . . itself at times threatens to expand to the nebulousness of a ~ —Charles Neider⟩

cab·a·las·sou \,kabə'la(,)sü\ *n* -s [perh. alter. of *cabassou*] **:** GIANT ARMADILLO

cab·a·let·ta \,kabə'led·ə, -äb-\ *n* -s [It, prob. alter. of *cobolетta* stanza, dim. of *cobola* stanza, couplet, fr. OProv *cobla* couplet, fr. L *copula* bond — more at COUPLE] **1 :** an operatic song or a short melodious instrumental composition in a simple popular style characterized by uniform rhythm in the accompaniment **2 :** the lively bravura conclusion of an aria or duet

cabalic *adj, often cap* [*cabala* + *-ic*] *obs* **:** learned in cabala

cab·a·lism \'kabə,lizəm\ *n* -s [*cabala* + *-ism*] **1** *often cap* **:** esoteric doctrine or interpretation according to the Jewish cabala **2 :** adherence to some fundamental theological interpretation or tenets ⟨the "key verse" and "key word" theory is a form of ~ based on a fundamental misconception of the nature of the Biblical material —J.C.Swaim⟩

[1]**cab·a·list** \'kabələst\ *n* -s [ML *cabbalista,* fr. *cabbala, cabala* + L *-ista* -ist] **1** *often cap* **:** a student, interpreter, or devotee of the Jewish cabala **2 :** one skilled in esoteric doctrine or mysterious art

[2]**cabalist** *n* -s [prob. fr. F *cabaliste,* fr. *cabale* cabal + *-iste* -ist — more at CABAL] *obs* **:** an adherent to a cabal

cab·a·lis·tic \¦kabə¦listik, -ēk\ *adj* **1** *sometimes cap* **:** belonging, according, or relating to the Jewish cabala ⟨a ~ explanation of an Old Testament text⟩ ⟨~ asceticism⟩ **2 :** having an occult, mystical, or esoteric meaning **:** MAGIC, MYSTERIOUS ⟨a few ~ words from our guide —Herman Melville⟩ ⟨the potency of certain ~ signs over the lintel⟩ ⟨by describing with the hands certain ~ patterns on the air and uttering at the same time the proper Sanskrit formulas it was believed that goblins and demons . . . could be exorcised —J.B.Noss⟩ — **cab·a·lis·ti·cal·ly** \-tək(ə)lē, -ēk-, -li\ *adv*

ca·ba·lla·da \,kavə'yädə, -abə-, -ē'y-\ *n* -s [Sp, fr. *caballo* horse (fr. L *caballus*) + *-ada* -ade — more at CAVALCADE] *West* **:** REMUDA

ca·bal·ler \kə'balə(r) *also* -'ä- *or* -'à-\ *n* -s [[2]*cabal* + *-er*] **:** one that cabals or intrigues

ca·bal·le·ro \,kabə'le(ə)(,)rō, -ə'ye-, *Cast* kȧbȧ'lyārō\ *n* -s [Sp, knight, horseman, fr. LL *caballarius* groom, hostler — more at CAVALIER] **1 :** KNIGHT, CAVALIER **2** *chiefly Southwest* **:** HORSEMAN

cab·al·line \'kabə,līn, -ən\ *adj* [ME *caballin,* fr. L *caballinus,* lit., of a horse, fr. *caballus* horse, nag + *-inus* -ine; fr. the ancient belief that the Muses' spring Hippocrene came from a hoofprint of the winged horse Pegasus — more at CAVALCADE] *of a fountain* **:** imparting poetic inspiration

caballine aloes *n pl but sing or pl in constr* **:** impure aloes formerly used in veterinary practice

ca·ba·lli·to \,kabə'yē(,)tō\ *n* -s [AmerSp, short for *caballito del mar,* lit., little sea horse, fr. *caballito* (dim. of *caballo* horse) + *del mar* of the sea] **:** a small fishing boat made of reeds and used off the coast of Peru

ca·ba·llo \kə'bī(,)ō\ *n* -s [Sp, fr. L *caballus* nag] *Southwest* **:** HORSE

cabals *pres 3d sing of* CABAL, *pl of* CABAL

caban *var of* CAVAN

ca·bana \kə'ban(y)ə\ *n* -s [Sp *cabaña,* fr. ML *capanna* — more at CABIN] **1 :** a tentlike often portable shelter with a projecting canopy over an open side facing a beach or swimming pool **2 :** a lightweight cabinlike structure with living facilities providing recreation quarters

ca·bane \kə'ban, -ān\ *n* -s [F, lit., cabin — more at CABIN] **1 :** a framework supporting the wings of an airplane at the fuselage **2 :** the system of trussing for supporting overhang in an airplane wing

[1]**cab·a·ret** \¦kabə¦rā\ *n* -s [F, fr. ONF, prob. irreg. fr. LL *camera* chamber — more at CHAMBER] **1** *archaic* **:** a shop having wines and liquors for sale **2 :** a porcelain coffee, tea, or chocolate service of 18th century manufacture with tray decorated with painted figures **3 :** a restaurant serving liquor and providing entertainment, usu. singing or dancing **4 :** the floor show at a cabaret

[2]**cabaret** \"\ *vi* -ED/-ING/-s **:** to attend or frequent a cabaret

cab·a·rine red MB \'kabə,rēn-\ *n, usu cap C&R* [origin unknown] **:** an organic pigment — see DYE table I (under *Pigment Red 55*)

cabas *pl of* CABA

ca·ba·sa \kə'bäsə\ *n* -s [AmerSp, fr. Pg *cabaça,* lit., gourd, fr. OPg *calabaço;* akin to Sp *calabaza* gourd, Catal *carbassa*] **:** a percussion instrument made of a hollow gourd enclosed in a net of threaded beads for use in a Cuban band

cab·as·set \¦kabə¦sā\ *n* -s [F, dim. of *cabas* — more at CABA] **:** a morion of small size

ca·bas·sou \kə'ba(,)sü, ¦kabə¦sü\ *n* -s [F, prob. fr. Galibi *capaçou*] **:** TATOUAY

ca·bas·so·us \kə'basəwəs, ,kabə'sōəs\ *n, cap* [NL, fr. F *cabassou*] **:** a genus of short-tailed armadillos having the third front claw very large and falcate and including only the tatouay

cabazone *var of* CABEZONE

[1]**cab·bage** \'kabij, -ēj\ *n* -s *often attrib* [ME *caboche,* fr. ONF, head, perh. fr. *boche* swelling, bump; akin to OF *boce* bump — more at BOSS] **1 :** a leafy garden plant (*Brassica oleracea capitata*) derived from a wild European plant (*B. oleracea*) and distinguished by a short stem upon which is crowded a mass of leaves usu. green but in some varieties red or purplish forming a dense globular head that is used as a vegetable **2 :** a terminal bud of certain palm trees that resembles a head of cabbage and is eaten as a vegetable **3 :** CABBAGE PALMETTO ⟨~ woods⟩ **4** *slang* **:** paper money or bank notes

[2]**cabbage** \"\ *vt* -ED/-ING/-s **:** to compress (loose sheet-metal scrap) into a form convenient for handling and remelting

[3]**cabbage** \"\ *n* -s [perh. by folk etymology fr. MF *cabas* cheating, theft, lit., basket — more at CABA] *Brit* **:** cloth remaining after the cutting out of a garment and traditionally said to be appropriated by the tailor as a perquisite

[4]**cabbage** \"\ *vb* -ED/-ING/-s *vt* **:** to take surreptitiously **:** STEAL, FILCH ⟨they also *cabbaged* our bats, balls, and gloves —H.L. Mencken⟩ ~ *vi* **:** to take something surreptitiously — sometimes used with *onto*

cabbage aphid *also* **cabbage aphis** *n* **:** a widely distributed and destructive grayish green plant louse (*Brevicoryne brassicae*) that lives on cabbage leaves and other cruciferous plants

cabbage bark *or* **cabbage–bark tree** *n* [*cabbage (palm)* + *bark*] **:** an angelim (*Andira inermis*) widely distributed in tropical America and western Africa having a shaggy unpleasant-smelling toxic bark that has been used together with the seeds as a purgative, vermifuge, and narcotic and yielding a hard strong durable wood variable in color and susceptible of a fine polish — called also *cabbage tree*

cabbage butterfly *n* **:** any of several largely white butterflies (family Pieridae) the green larvae of which are cabbageworms: as **a :** a small cosmopolitan form (*Pieris rapae*) — called also *small white* **b :** a larger Old World form (*P. brassicae*) — called also *large white* **c :** a common No. American form (*P. protodice*) — called also *southern cabbage butterfly*

cabbage curculio *n* **:** a small weevil (*Ceutorhynchus rapae*) that feeds within the stems and on the leaves of cabbage and other cruciferous plants

cabbage family *n* **:** CRUCIFERAE

cabbage fly *n* **:** the adult cabbage maggot

cabbage green \'==,=\ *n* **:** a greenish gray that is bluer and deeper than hathi gray and slightly bluer and less strong than artemisia green

cabbage gum *n* [prob. so called fr. the fleshy leaves] **:** any of certain Australian gum trees (esp. *Eucalyptus pauciflora* and *E. virgata*) with very soft wood and thick leaves

cabbagehead \'==,=\ *n* **1 :** the compact head formed by the leaves of a cabbage **2 :** a thick-witted person **3 :** an abnormal growth in rutabagas caused by the larvae of a gall midge (*Contarinia nasturtii*) feeding in the basal part of the stalks

cabbage–leaf miner *n* **:** a small fly (*Phytomyza rufipes*) whose maggot is injurious to cabbages and related plants

cabbage lettuce *n* **:** HEAD LETTUCE

cabbage looper *n* **:** a pale green white-striped measuring worm (*Trichoplusia ni*) that is the larva of a moth of the family Noctuidae and that feeds on the leaves of cabbage and other cruciferous plants

cabbage maggot *n* **:** a small white maggot (*Hylemya brassicae*) that feeds in the roots and stems of cabbage and other cruciferous plants and becomes as an adult a grayish fly resembling a small housefly

cabbage moth *n* **:** DIAMONDBACK MOTH

cabbage palm *n* **1 :** a palm whose terminal bud is eaten like cabbage as a vegetable: as **a :** CABBAGE PALMETTO **b :** a tall West Indian palm (*Roystonea oleracea*) **c :** CABBAGE TREE 1a **2 :** ASSAI PALM **3 :** a palm of the genus *Areca*

cabbage palmetto *n* **:** a fan-leaved palm (*Sabal palmetto*) native to the southern U.S. near the coast and to the Bahamas

cabbage–root fly *n* **:** the adult of the cabbage maggot; *broadly* **:** any stage of this pest

cabbage rose *n* **:** a fragrant garden rose (*Rosa centifolia*) with upright branches and large full white or pink flowers

cabbages *pl of* CABBAGE, *pres 3d sing of* CABBAGE

cabbage seedpod weevil *n* **:** a small grayish black weevil (*Ceutorhynchus assimilis*) related to the cabbage curculio but smaller and feeding on and destroying the developing seeds of cabbage and other cruciferous plants

cabbage snake *n* **:** a nematode worm of the family Mermithidae

cabbage tree *n* **1 :** any of several palms having an edible terminal bud: **a :** an Australian palm of the genus *Livistona* (esp. *L. australis*) **b** *NewZeal* **:** TI 1 **c :** CABBAGE PALMETTO **2 :** any of certain trees resembling in some respect a cabbage palm: as **a :** CABBAGE BARK **b :** any of several African araliaceous trees (genus *Cussonia*) with soft spongy wood and sparse angular branches that terminate in tufted foliage or in a spikelike inflorescence

cabbage–tree hat *n* **:** an Australian broad-brimmed hat plaited from the fibrous leaves of the cabbage tree

cabbage webworm *n* **:** a widely distributed webworm (*Hellula undalis*) native to southern Europe or Asia that injures cabbages and other vegetables in the Gulf states

cabbage white \'==,=\ *n* **:** CABBAGE BUTTERFLY

cabbage wilt *n* **:** CABBAGE YELLOWS

cabbagewood \'==,=\ *n* [*cabbage (tree)* + *wood*] **1 :** ACAPU 1b **2 :** CEIBA 2a **3 :** PRIVET 1a(1)

cabbageworm \'==,=\ *n* **:** any of numerous insect larvae that feed on cabbages: **a :** the green larva of the cabbage butterflies that is a destructive pest eating the leaves of cabbages and related plants and being toxic to animals that consume the infested foliage — see IMPORTED CABBAGEWORM **b :** the larva of the cabbage moth **c :** CUTWORM

cabbage yellows \'==,==\ *n pl but sing in constr* **:** a destructive disease of cabbage caused by a fungus (*Fusarium conglutinans*) and characterized by yellowing and dwarfing

cabbaging *pres part of* CABBAGE

cabbaging press *n* **:** a packing press for cabbaging loose sheet-metal scrap

cab·bagy \'kabəjē, -i\ *adj* **1 :** having the odor, taste, or color of cabbage **2 :** like or suggestive of a cabbage

cabbala *or* **cabbalah** *var of* CABALA

cabbed *past of* CAB

cab·ber \'kabə(r), -aab-\ *n* -s [[3]*cab* + *-er*] **:** CAB HORSE

cabbing *pres part of* CAB

cab·by *or* **cab·bie** \'kabē, -aabē, -i\ *n, pl* **cabbies** [[3]*cab* + *-y*] **:** CABDRIVER

cabdriver \'=,==\ *n* **:** a driver of a taxicab or a horse-drawn cab

ca·be·car \,kabə'kär\ *n, pl* **cabecar** *or* **cabecars** *usu cap* [Sp *cabécar,* of AmerInd origin] **1 a :** a Chibchan people of eastern Costa Rica **b :** a member of such people **2 :** the language of the Cabecar people

ca·be·ce·ra \,kabə'serə\ *n* -s [Sp, fr. *cabeza* head — more at CABEZON] **:** the chief city of a province or district in a Spanish-speaking country

ca·be·cu·do \,kabə'sü(,)dō\ *n* -s [Pg *cabeçudo,* fr. *cabeçudo* big-headed, fr. *cabeça* head, fr. (assumed) VL *capitia* — more at CABEZON] **:** OURICURY

cabeiri *usu cap, var of* CABIRI

ca·ber \'kābə(r), -āb-, -ab-\ *n* -s [ScGael *cabar*] **1** *Scot* **:** [1]RAFTER **2 :** a young tree trunk used in a Scottish sport in which it is raised vertically in the hands and tossed across a line

ca·ber·net \¦kabə(r)¦nā\ *n* -s *usu cap* [F] **:** a dry red California table wine like claret with medium body and fruity flavor

ca·bes·tro \kə'be(,)strō; -bre(,)stō, -,tə\ *n* -s [AmerSp, fr. Sp, halter, fr. L *capistrum,* fr. *capere* to take — more at HEAVE] *Southwest* **:** a rope of hair used esp. as a lasso or tether

cab·ette \(')ka¦bet\ *n* -s **:** a woman who drives a taxicab

ca·be·za \kə'bāzə\ *n* -s [Sp] **1** *Southwest* **:** the head of a person or animal **2 :** a headman of a Philippine group of families

cab·e·zone *also* **cab·e·zon** \'kabə,zōn, ,==',=\ *n* -s [Sp *cabezón,* aug. of *cabeza* head, fr. (assumed) VL *capitia,* fr. L *capit-, caput* — more at HEAD] **1** *also* **cab·a·zone a :** a large green-fleshed edible sculpin (*Scorpaenichthys marmoratus*) of the Pacific coast of No. America **b :** a smaller related fish (*Leptocottus armatus*) of southern California **2 :** a croaker (*Larimus breviceps*) of the West Indies and southwest Atlantic ocean having a short thick head and a nearly vertical mouth

cab horse *n* **1 :** a horse used for drawing a cab **2 :** a horse of moderate weight and size with ability to draw a fair load at a moderate speed

ca·bil·do \kə'bil(,)dō\ *n* -s [Sp, fr. ML *capitulum,* fr. L, small head — more at CHAPTER] **1** *chiefly Southwest* **:** the chapter house of a cathedral or collegiate church **2 :** a town council or a town hall in a country formerly a Spanish colony

[1]**cab·in** \'kabən\ *n* -s [ME *cabane,* fr. MF, fr. OProv *cabana,* fr. ML *capanna*] **1** *obs* **a :** a prison or convent cell **b :** an individual study cubicle **2 a :** a small room on a ship providing private accommodations for one or a few persons — see CABIN CLASS **b :** a compartment below deck for passengers or crew on a small boat **c :** a closed airplane compartment for cargo, crew, or passengers **d :** an accommodation compartment in an airship **3** *obs* **:** a temporary shelter (as one made of boughs or a soldier's tent) or a structure of stakes with withes woven between them and a roof of thatch **4 :** a small one-story low-roofed dwelling usu. of plain construction: as **a :** a 4-sided dwelling of logs built as a home by early settlers of the western frontier of No. America or by mountain folk **b :** a similar structure serving as the home of the family of a servant or plantation hand in the South **c :** a dwelling used during a vacation esp. for hunting and fishing **d :** a small typically one-room house suitable for overnight lodging for tourists; *also* **:** a unit in a block of apartments belonging to a motel ⟨10 ~s in each building⟩ **5 a :** an interlocking or block station on a railroad **b** *chiefly Brit* **:** [3]CAB 3a **c** *Brit* **:** [3]CAB 3b(1) **d** *Brit* **:** [3]CAB 3b(2) **e :** a passenger cage of an aerial tram **f :** a glassed-in shelter on top of a lookout tower **g :** the part of a passenger trailer used for living quarters **6** *obs* **a :** COT, LITTER **b :** BENCH **7** *obs* **:** a cabinet advisory to a sovereign **8 :** a shelved container

cabin 4

[2]**cabin** \"\ *vb* -ED/-ING/-s *vi* **:** to live or lodge in a cabin or within narrow confines ~ *vt* **:** to lodge or confine in a cabin or within a narrow space or limits

cabin boy *n* **:** a boy acting as servant to the officers and cabin passengers of a ship

cabin car *n* **:** CABOOSE

cabin class *n* **:** a class of accommodations on a passenger ship superior to tourist class and inferior to first class

cabin court *n* **:** MOTEL

cabin cruiser *n* **:** CRUISER 3

ca·bin·da \kə'bində\ *n, pl* **cabinda** *or* **cabindas** *usu cap* [Pg] **1 :** a Bantu people north of the lower Congo skilled in boatbuilding **2 :** a member of the Cabinda people

cab·in·eer \¦kabə¦ni(ə)r\ *n* -s **:** one that occupies a cabin

[1]**cab·i·net** \'kab(ə)nət\ *n* -s *often attrib* [MF, dim. of ONF *cabine* gambling house, gambling booth] **1 :** a box for storing chiefly small articles usu. closed by a hinged or sliding door, fitted with shelves or drawers, and suitably finished as an item of home, office, or laboratory furniture: **a :** an upright case or cupboardlike repository for utensils, materials, or documents conveniently accessible for use ⟨a bathroom wall ~ for medicines, bandages, and toilet articles⟩ ⟨cards alphabetically arranged in rows of file ~s⟩ ⟨installation of a ~ sink in the kitchen⟩ **b :** a similar repository for specimens of a biological, mineralogical, numismatic, antiquarian, or curio collection usu. ordered for display; *also* **:** a collection of specimens regarded independently of the repository ⟨original owner of the ~ that was the basis of a classical work in the field⟩ **c :** an enclosed framework for printers' cases or material **d :** an upright case housing a radio or television receiver **:** CONSOLE **e :** a box having a tight-closing door and containing an ovenlike chamber in which a desired temperature, humidity, and circulation of air may be maintained for humidification, sterilization, or evaporation or for incubation of biological samples **f :** a small box containing both writing paper and envelopes **g :** a cupboardlike compartment usu. of steel with a swinging door used to house an electric panelboard **2 a** [prob. influenced by *cabin*] *archaic* **:** a small room providing seclusion (as for study or reading) **b :** a room for the safekeeping and exhibition of treasured art works or art objects; *specif* **:** a small exhibition room in a museum **c :** a small enclosed space or stall for a person performing some action ⟨a shower ~ installed in the bathroom⟩ **3** *obs* **a :** a bower in a garden **b :** a retreat or shelter **4 a** *archaic* (1) **:** the private room serving as council chamber of the chief councilors or ministers of a sovereign, in England orig. of the members of the privy council (2) **:** the consultations and actions of these councilors **b** *often cap* **:** a body of advisers of a sovereign or head of a state: (1) **:** an executive or policy-making body consisting of a prime minister

and the ministers in charge of the principal departments of government whose members take the leadership of all legislation and are by custom responsible for it to parliament ⟨a constitutional monarchy with a ~ system⟩ ⟨the ~ consists of about twenty members appointed nominally by the governor-general but really by the prime minister —F.A.Magruder⟩ — compare MINISTRY 7a (2) **:** an advisory council of a president composed of the heads of the executive departments of the government whose members have been appointed by the president and who are responsible only to him ⟨the ~ of the president of the U.S.⟩ ⟨at present the civil service commissioner, the director of the budget, and the chief U.S. delegate to the U.N. are also de facto ~ members —Ernest Maass⟩ (3) **:** a similar advisory council of a national chief executive (as a chancellor) (4) **:** a similar advisory council of a governor of a state or a mayor in the U.S. **c** *Brit* **:** a meeting of a cabinet **d** *Brit* **:** GOVERNMENT 8c (1) **5 :** the advisory or executive council of an organization (as religious, fraternal, academic)

²**cabinet** \"\ *adj* **1 :** suitable by reason of small size for a private compartment or by reason of attractiveness and antique character or perfection as a specimen for preservation and display in a cabinet ⟨~ painting is a defunct art —Herbert Read⟩ ⟨porcelain ~ plates with figural centers⟩ **2 :** belonging to a governmental cabinet ⟨~ ministers⟩ ⟨the new post carries ~ rank⟩ **3 a :** used or adapted for cabinetmaking ⟨mahogany, walnut, and other fine ~ woods⟩ **b :** done, made, or used by a cabinetmaker

³**cab·i·net** \'kab(ə)nət, -bə,net\ *vt* **cabineted** *or* **cabinetted; cabineted** *or* **cabinetted; cabineting** *or* **cabinetting; cabinets 1** *archaic* **:** to put in a cabinet **2** *archaic* **:** to lock up **:** SHUT

cabinet ball *n* **:** a game played on a volleyball court by two teams usu. of nine players each using a small medicine ball and scoring points by errors in either catching or throwing

cabinet beetle *n* **:** DERMESTID

cabinet bench *n* **:** a steel cabinet with doors or drawers and a flat top that is used as a workbench

cabinet cherry *n* **:** BLACK CHERRY 2

cabinet council *n, archaic* **:** the English cabinet; *also* **:** a session of it

cab·i·ne·teer \¦kab(ə)nə¦ti(ə)r\ *n* -s *slang* **:** a member of a government cabinet

cabinet file *n* [so called fr. its use in cabinetmaking] **:** a thin woodworking file with coarse teeth that is flat on one side and convex on the other

cabinet finish *n* **:** interior building finish in hardwoods framed, paneled, molded, and varnished or polished like cabinetwork as distinguished from that in softwoods nailed together and usu. painted

cabinet government *n* **:** a government in which the real executive power rests with a cabinet of ministers who are individually and collectively responsible to the legislature

cabinetmaker \'=(=)=,==\ *n* [¹*cabinet* (furniture) + *maker*] **:** a skilled woodworker who cuts, shapes, and assembles high-grade articles of furniture calling for fine finish (as decorative cabinets, desks, and chairs, store fixtures, office equipment)

cabinetmaking \'=(=)=,==\ *n* -s **:** the occupation or art of the cabinetmaker

cabinet organ *n* [so called fr. its shape] **:** a reed organ having pedal-operated bellows and mounted in a case about the size and shape of an upright piano

ca·bi·net par·ti·cu·lier \kàbēnāpàrtēkülyā\ *n, pl* **cabinets particuliers** \-nāp...lyā\ [F] **:** a small private room for guests in a restaurant

cabinet photograph *n* **:** a photograph in a mount about four by six inches

cabinet piano *n* **:** a small upright piano

cabinet projection *n* **:** an oblique projection in mechanical drawing in which dimensions parallel to the third axis of the object are shortened one half to overcome apparent distortion

cabinet pudding *n* **:** a pudding of bread or cake, candied or dried fruit, milk, and eggs often molded and usu. served hot with a tart sauce

cab·i·net·ry \'kab(ə)nətrē, -i\ *n* -ES **1 :** CABINETMAKING **2 :** CABINETWORK

cabinets *pl of* CABINET, *pres 3d sing of* CABINET

cabinet saw *n* **:** a short broad-bladed saw with parallel edges, one sharpened for ripping and the other for crosscutting

cabinet scraper *n* **:** a scraper with the blade clamped in a single-handled or double-handled frame for smoothing wood

cabinet system *n* **:** CABINET GOVERNMENT

cab·in·ette \,kabə¦net\ *n* -s **:** a small cabin

cabinet trim *n* **:** CABINET FINISH

cabinet ware *n* **:** CABINETWORK

cabinet wine *n* [trans. of G *kabinettwein*] **1 :** a bottled German Rhine wine usu. representing the vintner's choice of his best wine **2 :** any wine of excellent quality

cabinetwork \'=(=)=,=\ *n* **:** finished woodwork made by a cabinetmaker — compare MILLWORK 2

cabinetworn \'=(=)=,=\ *adj* **:** slightly worn from frequent removal from dealers' cabinets for display to customers ⟨a ~ coin⟩

cabin fever *n* **:** extreme irritability and combativeness resulting from the boredom of living in a remote region alone or with only a few companions

cabin hook *n* **:** a small hook and eye for use on cabinet doors

cabin house *n* **:** the part of a cabin that projects above deck (as on a small yacht)

cabining *pres part of* CABIN

cabin passenger *n* **1** *obs* **:** a passenger on a ship privileged to dine or lounge in the captain's cabin **2 :** a passenger on a ship who pays for and is allotted the use of a cabin or part of a cabin, the minimum allotted space for each such passenger being fixed by law

cabins *pl of* CABIN, *pres 3d sing of* CABIN

cabin supercharger *n* **:** a supercharger used to pressurize a cabin of an airplane

ca·bio \kə'bī(,)ō, -ēō\ [Bisayan *kabayo*, fr. Sp *caballo* horse, fr. L *caballus* — more at CAVALCADE] *var of* COBIA

ca·bi·ri *or* **ca·bei·ri** \kə'bīrē, -bī,rī\ *n pl, usu cap* [L *Cabiri*, *Cabeiri*, fr. Gk *Kabiroi*, *Kabeiroi*] **:** a group of ancient Greek deities of Phrygian prob. chthonic origin whose mysteries of Samothrace were second in repute only to the Eleusinian mysteries

¹**ca·ble** \'kābəl\ *n* -s *often attrib* [ME, fr. ONF, fr. ML *capulum* lasso, fr. L *capere* to take — more at HEAVE] **1 a :** a strong rope; *esp* **:** a rope 10 or more inches in circumference **b :** a cable-laid rope **c :** a wire rope or metal chain of great strength used esp. for hauling, for securing a ship to an anchor, or for supporting the rods and roadway of a suspension bridge **d :** a wire or wire rope by means of which force is exerted to control or operate a mechanism ⟨ailerons operated by control ~*s*⟩ **2 :** CABLE LENGTH **3 a :** a ropelike usu. stranded assembly of electrical conductors or of groups of two or more conductors insulated from each other but laid up together usu. by being twisted around a central core, the whole usu. heavily insulated by outside wrappings; *specif* **:** a submarine cable — see TELEGRAPH CABLE **b** [by shortening] **:** CABLEGRAM **c :** CABLE TRANSFER **4 a :** something resembling or fashioned like a cable ⟨creepers of many kinds and of every size, from huge ~*s* to thin cords, loop from tree to tree —C.D. Forde⟩ ⟨a ~ motif⟩ **b :** a convex molding that occupies a flute of a column or pilaster usu. in the lower part of the shaft **c** *also* **cable stitch :** a knitting stitch that produces a pattern resembling the twist of a 2-ply cable ⟨a ~ on a sweater⟩

cross section and view of suspension-bridge cable showing arrangement of strands

²**cable** \"\ *vb* **cabled; cabled; cabling** \'kāb(ə)liŋ\ **cables** *vt* **1 :** to fasten with or as if with a cable **2 :** to ornament with something resembling a cable **3 :** to telegraph by a submarine cable **4** *archit* **:** to fill (flutes) with cables **5 :** to make into a cable or into a form resembling a cable; *specif* **:** to twist together (two or more strands, plied yarns, or threads) ~ *vi* **1 :** to communicate by a submarine cable ⟨~ for immediate delivery of goods⟩ **2 :** to make a cable stitch

cable address *n* **:** the address for a cable message esp. when condensed into a code word

cable bend *n* **1 :** a small rope used for lashing the end of a cable into a loop for securing an anchor **2 :** the clinch by which an anchor is secured to its cable

cable buoy *n* **:** a float used to support a submarine cable (as over a rocky bottom)

cable car *n* **:** a car used on a cable railway or overhead cableway

cable chain *n* **:** a heavy chain having links with a crossbar across the inside of each link usu. used as a ship's cable **:** CHAIN CABLE

cable desk *n* **:** a department or section of a newspaper or news bureau where overseas news esp. as received by cable is edited

cable driller *n* **:** a supervisor of the setup and operation of a cable-drilling rig for drilling oil and gas wells

cable drilling *n* **:** ROPE DRILLING

cable engineer *n* **:** an engineer who plans and directs the laying and repair of undersea cable lines

ca·ble·gram \'kābəl,gram, -aa(ə)m\ *n* -s [¹*cable* + *-gram*] **:** a message sent by a submarine telegraph cable

cable grip *n* **:** the grip of a cable car

cablehead \'==,=\ *n* -s **:** a terminal for cable or radio circuits to and from foreign countries

cable holder *or* **cable lifter** *n* **:** WILDCAT 4

cable-laid \'==¦=\ *adj* **:** composed of three ropes laid together left-handed with each containing three strands twisted together ⟨*cable-laid* rope⟩

cable length *n* **:** a maritime unit of length based on the length of a ship's cable and variously reckoned as equal to 100 fathoms, 1/10 of the nautical mile of 6080 ft., or 120 fathoms

ca·ble·less \'kābəlləs\ *adj* **:** being without a cable

ca·ble·man \-lmən, -,man, -,maa(ə)n\ *n, pl* **cable·men** \-lmən, -,men\ **1 :** a worker who installs and repairs conduit systems transmitting electric power **2 :** a worker who lays out cables used in electrical prospecting for petroleum-bearing formations **3 :** a worker who installs aerial and underground cables used for communication and signaling **4 :** a worker who installs engine-control equipment in airplane fuselages and wings

cable net *n* **:** coarse-meshed cotton net used for curtains

cable paper *n* **:** a strong paper used as insulation around electric cables

ca·bler \'kāblə(r)\ *n* **:** one that cables

cable railway *n* **:** a railway on which the cars grip and are moved by an endless cable that is sometimes laid underground and that is driven by a stationary engine — see FUNICULAR RAILWAY

cable rate *n* **:** the charge per unit of currency for a cable transfer

cable release *n* **:** a flexible wire moving within a sheath and used to trip a camera shutter — called also *antinous release*

cable rope *n* **:** CABLE 1

cables *pl of* CABLE, *pres 3d sing of* CABLE

ca·blese \,kābə¦lēz, -ēs\ *n* -s [¹*cable* + *-ese*] **:** the language of a cablegram or language resembling that of a cablegram characterized by the omission of connectives and by the use of special combinations, abbreviations, and code symbols ⟨in my memorandum book wrote a reminder in ~, "Uplook kids" —W.L.White⟩

cable ship *n* **:** a ship fitted for laying and repairing submarine cables

cable's length *n, pl* **cables' lengths :** CABLE LENGTH

cable stitch *n* **:** CABLE 4c

cable stopper *n* **:** a device to hold an anchor cable so as to prevent the anchor from running out or to relieve the strain at the inboard end

cable system *n* **1 :** a system of propelling cars, plows, or other working units from a stationary source by means of an esp. endless cable and accessory tackle **2 :** ROPE DRILLING

ca·blet \'kāblət\ *n* -s [¹*cable* + *-et*] **:** a small cable; *specif* **:** a cable-laid rope less than 10 inches in circumference

cable tank *n* **:** a large cylindrical watertight iron tank used for storing or testing submarine telegraph cable

cable tier \-,ti(ə)r, -iə\ *n* **:** the part of a ship where cables and spare rigging are stowed **:** CHAIN LOCKER

cable tool *n* **:** a tool of the set used in rope drilling

cable transfer *n* **:** the transfer of credit between persons or firms in different countries by means of cable, radio, or transoceanic telephone

cable vault *n* **:** a manhole giving access to underground electrical cables and their connections

cableway \'==,=\ *n* **:** a transporting system typically consisting of a cable suspended between elevated supports so as to constitute a track along which carriers can be pulled

cable wheel *n* **:** a drum of a windlass or capstan on which cable is wound **:** WILDCAT

cabling *n* -s **1 :** CABLE 1 **2 :** a cable or cables used in decoration ⟨~ running down the front of a knitted sweater⟩ ⟨~ on the lower part of a pilaster⟩

cab·man \'ka(a)bmən\ *n, pl* **cabmen :** CABDRIVER

cabnt *abbr* cabinet

cabob *var of* KABOB

ca·bo·ceer \,kabə¦si(ə)r, -bō-, -iə\ *n* -s [Pg *cabeceira*, fr. *cabeça* head, fr. (assumed) VL *capitia* — more at CABEZON] **:** a West African native chief

caboched *var of* CABOSHED

¹**cab·o·chon** \'kabə,shän\ *n* -s [MF, aug. of ONF *caboche* head — more at CABBAGE] **1 :** an uncut gem somewhat polished **2 a :** a gem or bead cut in convex form, highly polished, but not faceted — see CUT illustration **b :** this style of cutting gems or other ornaments

²**cabochon** \"\ *adv* **:** in cabochon ⟨a stone cut ~⟩

ca·bo·clo \kə'bō(,)klü, -'ō-\ *n* -s [Pg, fr. Tupi *caboco*, *caboculo*, *caboclo*] **1 a :** an acculturated pure-blooded Brazilian Indian **b :** a Brazilian of mixed Indian and white blood — compare MAMELUCO **2 :** a So. American rural half-breed

ca·bom·ba \kə'bämbə\ *n, cap* [NL, fr. Sp *cabomba*, a So. American aquatic plant] **:** a small genus of American aquatic plants (family Nymphaeaceae) comprising the water shield and having minute white or yellow flowers and submerged dissected leaves as well as peltate floating ones

ca·bom·ba·ce·ae \,ka,bäm'bāsē,ē\ *n pl, cap* [NL, fr. *Cabomba*, type genus + *-aceae*] *in some classifications* **:** a small family of aquatic plants comprising those members of the family Nymphaeaceae that constitute the genera *Cabomba* and *Brasenia* and have flowers with three or four persistent sepals and petals and distinct coriaceous carpels

ca·boo·dle \kə'büd³l\ *n* -s [prob. fr. *ca-* (alter. or earlier spelling of *ker-*) + *boodle*] *slang* **:** COLLECTION, LOT — often used with *whole* ⟨sell the whole ~⟩; compare BOODLE 1, ¹KIT 3

ca·book \kə'bu̇k\ *n* -s [prob. modif. of Pg *cavouco* quarry, irreg. fr. *cavo* hollow, concave, fr. L *cavus* — more at CAVE] **:** laterite as used as building material in Ceylon

¹**ca·boose** \kə'büs\ *n* -s [prob. fr. D *kabuis*, *kombuis*, fr. MLG *kabūse*] **1** *also* **cam·boose** \kam'b-\ **a :** a deckhouse where cooking is done **:** a ship's galley **b :** an open-air cooking oven **2** *dial* **:** HUT **3 :** a freight-train car usu. attached to the rear of a train mainly for the use of trainmen in the performance of their duties although sometimes used to transport passengers, esp. livestock caretakers

²**caboose** \"\ *n* -s [by contraction] *slang* **:** CALABOOSE

ca·boshed \kə'bäsht\ *also* **ca·bossed** \-äst\ *or* **ca·boched** \-äsht\ *adj* [fr. past part. of obs. *caboche* to behead (a deer) close behind the horns, fr. ME *cabochen*, fr. ONF *caboche* head — more at CABBAGE] *heraldry* **:** borne affronté without the neck showing — used of an animal's head

ca·bot \kə'bō\ *n* -s [F dial.] **:** a unit of capacity in the Channel islands (Jersey) equal to ½ bushel

cab·o·tage \'kabə,täzh, -äzh, -,tij\ *n* -s [F, fr. *caboter* to sail along the coast (prob. fr. Sp *cabo* cape, promontory, fr. L *caput* head) + F *-age* — more at HEAD] **1 :** trade or transport in coastal waters or between two points within a country esp. by other than domestic carriers **2 a :** the right to engage in cabotage **b :** restriction of the right of cabotage to domestic carriers

cab·o·ti·nage \¦kabətə¦näzh\ *n, pl* **caboti·nages** \"\ [F, fr. *cabotin* strolling actor, charlatan (fr. Cabotin, 17th cent. Fr. actor) + *-age*] **:** behavior befitting a second-rate actor **:** obvious playing to the audience **:** THEATRICALITY

cab·ot's ring \'kabəts-\ *or* **cab·ot ring** \-ət·'r-\ *n, usu cap C* [after Richard C. *Cabot* †1939 physician] **:** a ringlike body present in many immature red blood cells that stains with nuclear dyes and may represent remains of the nuclear membrane

cabot's tern *n, usu cap C* [prob. fr. the name *Cabot*] **:** SANDWICH TERN

ca·bou·ca \kə'bükə\ *n* -s [AmerF] **:** LAZY CRAB

cab-over \'=,==\ *or* **cab-over-engine** \¦=,=='==\ *n* -s **:** an automotive vehicle with a cab at the front end over the engine

ca·bra·lea \kə'brālēə, -'ä-\ *n, cap* [NL, fr. Pedro A. *Cabral* †*ab*1526 Portuguese navigator] **:** a genus of trees of southern tropical America (family Meliaceae) noted chiefly for their wood which resembles cedar but is firmer and stronger and which is used for construction, joinery, furniture, and sculpture

cab rank *n* **1** *Brit* **:** a row of cabs at a cabstand **2** *Brit* **:** TAXI STAND

ca·bree *also* **ca·bri** *or* **ca·brie** *or* **ca·brit** \kə'brē, 'kabrē\ *or* **ca·bret** \'kabrē\ *n* -s [LaF *cabri*, fr. F, kid, fr. OProv *cabrit*, fr. LL *capritus*, fr. L *capr-*, *caper* goat — more at CAPRIOLE] **:** PRONGHORN

ca·bret·ta \kə'bredˑə\ *n* -s [modif. (influenced by It *-etta*, fem. dim. suffix) of Pg and Sp *cabra* goat] **:** leather tanned from hair sheepskins and used for gloves, garments, and shoe uppers

ca·bre·u·va \kabrē'üvə\ *n* -s [Pg *cabriúva*, fr. Tupi *cabreúva*, *cabureíba*] **:** either of two timber trees (*Myrocarpus frondosus* and *M. fastigiatus*) of the family Leguminosae of southern Brazil and Argentina whose wood is brownish, strong, and hard, takes a high polish, and yields a balsam

ca·bri·lla \kə'brē(y)ə, -rilə\ *n* -s [Sp, fr. dim. of *cabra* goat, fr. L *capra* she-goat, fem. of L *caper* he-goat] **:** any of various sea basses of the Mediterranean, the coast of California, and the warmer parts of the western Atlantic **:** as **a :** RED HIND 1 **b :** ROCK BASS

cab·ri·ole \'kabrē,ōl, (*esp sense 2*) kàbrēōl\ *n* -s [F, leap, caper; fr. its resemblance to the foreleg of a capering animal] **1 :** a form of Queen Anne and Chippendale furniture leg frequent in Queen Anne and Chippendale furniture that curves outward from the structure which it supports and then descends in a tapering reverse curve terminating in an ornamental foot **2 :** a ballet leap in which one leg is extended in mid-air and the other struck against it

cabrioles 1: *A* early 18th century; *B* mid-18th century; *C* early Georgian; *D* second half of 18th century

cab·ri·o·let \¦kabrē¦ō¦lā\ *n* -s [F, dim. of *cabriole*, *capriole* leap, caper; fr. its skipping lightness — more at CAPRIOLE] **1 :** a light 2-wheeled one-horse carriage with a single seat, a folding leather hood, a large rigid apron, gracefully upward-curving shafts, and usu. a rear platform between the C springs for a groom **2 :** an automobile resembling a coupe in appearance and capacity but with a folding top **:** a convertible coupe

ca·bri·to \kə'brē,tō\ *n* -s [Sp, dim. of *cabro* male goat, fr. L *capr-*, *caper* — more at CAPRIOLE] *southwest* **:** the flesh of a young kid roasted or stewed

cabs *pl of* CAB, *pres 3d sing of* CAB

cab signal *n* **:** a visual signal in the cab of a locomotive used in conjunction with interlocking signals and in conjunction with or in lieu of block signals to provide continuous data for the engineman on conditions affecting train or engine movement

cabstand \'=,=\ *n* **:** a place where cabs may stand awaiting hire

cab system \'kab-, 'kaa(ə)b-\ *n* [command bids + *a*pproach bids + *B*aron *system*] **:** a system of bidding at contract bridge popular in England

ca·bu·ya *also* **ca·bu·ja** *or* **ca·bu·lla** \kə'büyə\ *n* -s [Sp, fr. Taino] **1 :** any of several hard fibers (as sisal, cajun, or Mauritius hemp) **2 :** a plant yielding cabuya — see GIANT CABUYA

cac- *or* **caco-** *comb form* [NL, fr. Gk *kak-*, *kako-*, fr. *kakos* bad — more at CACK] **1 :** bad ⟨*caco*nym⟩ **:** incorrect ⟨*caco*epy⟩ **:** unpleasant ⟨*caco*phonous⟩ **2 :** diseased ⟨*caco*chylia⟩

cac·a·fue·go \,kakə'fyü(,)gō, -fwā(-\ *also* **cac·a·fu·go** \-fyü(-\ *n* -s [Sp *Cacafuego*, name of a ship captured in 1579 by Sir Francis Drake, fr. L *cacare* to void as excrement + Sp *fuego* fire, fr. L *focus* hearth — more at CACK, FOCUS] *obs* **:** a swaggering braggart or boaster

ca·ca·jao \¦kakə¦jau̇, ,kakə¦jä(,)ō\ *n, cap* [NL, fr. Pg *cacajão*, fr. Tupi *cacajao*] **:** the genus consisting of the ouakaris

ca·ca·lia \kə'kālyə, -lēə\ *n* [NL, fr. L, a plant, fr. Gk *kakalia*, *kakkalia*] **1** *cap* **:** a genus of tall smooth herbs (family Compositae) with alternate often petioled leaves and large heads in flat corymbs — see MESADENIA **2** -s **:** any plant of the genus *Emilia*

¹**ca' can·ny** \'kȯ'kanē, 'kä'-, 'kȧ'-, -i\ *vi* [*ca'* + *canny*] **1** *Scot* **:** to proceed cautiously **:** go slow **2** *Brit* **:** to work slowly in order to prolong work

²**ca' canny** \"\ *n, Brit* **:** a deliberate slackening by workmen in the rate of work or quantity produced **:** SLOWDOWN

ca·cao \kə'kau̇, -'kä(,)ō, -'kā(,)ō\ *n* -s [Sp, fr. Nahuatl *cacahuatl* cacao beans] **1** *or* **cacao bean** *or* **cocoa bean :** the dried and usu. partly fermented seed of the cacao tree used chiefly in the preparation of cocoa, chocolate, and cocoa butter **2 :** any of several trees of the genus *Theobroma*; *esp* **:** a tree (*T. cacao*) native to So. America and now extensively cultivated (as in the West Indies, Mexico, Central America) that bears on the trunk or the old branches flowers with a pink calyx and yellowish corolla succeeded by fleshy yellow pods six or more inches long and three or four inches in diameter containing numerous seeds — called also *chocolate tree* **3 :** ANTIQUE BRONZE

cacao brown *n* **:** a strong brown that is paler and slightly yellower than rust, rust brown, or average russet and very slightly paler and redder than gold brown

cacao butter *var of* COCOA BUTTER

cacao moth *n* **:** TOBACCO MOTH

cacao nib *or* **cocoa nib** *n* **:** a piece of a cacao bean that has been roasted, dried, dehusked, and degermed — usu. used in pl.

cacao thrips *n* **:** RED-BANDED THRIPS

ca·ca·tua \,kakə'tüə, -ə'tyüə\ [NL, fr. D or Malay; D *kakatoe*, fr. Malay *kokatua* — more at COCKATOO] *syn of* KAKATOE

ca·cax·te \kə'kästē\ *n* -s [AmerSp *cacaxtle*, *cacaxte*, fr. Nahuatl *cacaxtli* small ladder for carrying things on the back] **:** a square wooden packing frame or crate that has four legs and a net cover and is carried on the back esp. by Guatemalan Indians with the help of a tumpline

cac·cia \'kä(,)chä\ *n, pl* **cac·ce** \-(,)chā\ *or* **caccias** \-(,)chäz\ [It, lit., hunt, chase, fr. *cacciare* to chase, fr. (assumed) VL *captiare* — more at CATCH] **:** a part song in canon form portraying the hunt or village scenes and usu. employing such sounds as the cries of beggars and vendors and the barks of dogs

cac·cia·to·re \,kächə'tōrē\ *also* **cac·cia·to·ra** \-rə\ *or* **cac·cia·to·ri** \-rē\ *adj* [It *cacciatore*, lit., hunter, fr. *cacciato* (past part. of *cacciare*) + *-ore* -or] **:** simmered or stewed with herbs and other seasonings ⟨chicken ~⟩

-ca·ce \kə,sē\ *n comb form* -s [Gk *kakē* badness, fr. *kakos* bad — more at CACK] **:** diseased or vitiated condition of a (specified) bodily part ⟨arthro*cace*⟩ ⟨carpo*cace*⟩

cacha *n* -s [Bengali *kaṣāy* or Marathi *kāṣāy*, fr. Skt *kaṣāya* yellowish red, brownish red] *obs* **:** AUBURN

cach·a·lot \'kashə,lät, -'aa-,-'ai-, -,lō\ *n* -s [F, fr. F dial. (Bayonne, 17th cent.) *cachalut*] **:** SPERM WHALE

ca·char \'kä,chär\ *n* -s *usu cap* [fr. *Cachar*, district in India where it is produced] **:** any of several teas of India

ca·cha·ri \'kächərē, kə'chärē\ *n, pl* **cachari** *or* **cacharis** *usu cap* **:** BODO

ca·cha·za \kə'chäsə, -äsə\ *n* -s [Sp] **:** PRESS CAKE a

¹**cache** \'kash, -aa-,-ai-\ *n* -s [F, hiding place, fr. *cacher* to hide, fr. (assumed) VL *coacticare* to press together, fr. L *coactare* to compel, fr. *coactus*, past part. of *cogere* to drive together, compel — more at COGENT] **1 a :** a hiding place; *esp* **:** one used by settlers, explorers, or campers for concealing and preserving provisions or implements **b :** a secure place of storage **2 a :** something that is hidden or stored in a cache **b :** a group of artifacts occurring alone or with a burial **3 a :** the hibernation place of a group of insects (as a hole in the ground) **b :** the mass of insects hibernating in such a place

²**cache** \"\ *vt* -ED/-ING/-S **:** to place in a cache **:** place or store in safety or concealment ⟨~ camp supplies by a lake⟩ ⟨coins *cached* in a teapot⟩ **syn** see CONCEAL

ca·chec·tic \ka'kektik, kə-\ *adj* [F *cachectique*, fr. L *cachecticus*, fr. Gk *kachektikos*, fr. *kak-* cac- + *hektikos* habitual, constitutional, fr. *hekt-* (stem of *echein* to have) + *-ikos* -ic — more at SCHEME] **1 :** relating to cachexia **2 :** having the symptoms of cachexy; *esp* **:** thin or emaciated of body

cache-peigne \'kash,pān\ *n* -s [F, lit., comb hider, fr. *cacher* to hide + *peigne* comb, fr. L *pecten* — more at CACHE, PECTINATE] **:** trimming on the back part of a woman's hat either placed under the brim or attached to the edge

cache·pot \'kash,pät, -,pō\ *n* -s [F, lit., pot hider, fr. *cacher* to hide + *pot*, fr. (assumed) VL *pottus* — more at POT] **:** an ornamental receptacle to hold and usu. to conceal a flowerpot

cache-sexe \-¦seks\ *n* -s [F, lit., sex hider, fr. *cacher* to hide + *sexe* sex, fr. L *sexus* — more at SEX] **:** a small garment (as a loincloth) worn to cover the genitals

¹ca·chet \(')ka¦shā\ *n* -s [MF, fr. *cacher* to press, hide] **1 a :** a seal or stamp that is used esp. as a mark of official approval **b :** an indication or sign of approval usu. carrying with it great prestige ⟨the president placed his ~ upon the project⟩ **2 a :** a characteristic feature or quality conferring prestige or distinction or inspiring respect ⟨regarded the possession of . . . land as a ~ of respectability —G.W.Johnson⟩ **b :** high status **:** PRESTIGE ⟨being a guard gave you a certain ~ —*New Yorker*⟩ ⟨few read them but those who do acquire ~ —Bernard De Voto⟩ **3 :** two circles of wafer sheet sealed together with powdered medicine between them to form a dose that can be easily swallowed after being dipped in water — called also *wafer capsule* **4 a :** a picture, design, or inscription stamped or printed on an envelope to commemorate some postal or philatelic event **b :** a pictorial or slogan advertisement on a piece of mail as part of a postal meter impression — called also *postmark ad* **c :** a motto or slogan included in a postal cancellation on a piece of mail

²cachet \"\ *vt* -ED/-ING/-S **:** to put a cachet on ⟨a ~*ed* envelope⟩

ca·chex·ia \ka'keksēə, kə-\ *also* **ca·chexy** \'ka,keksē; ka'keksē, kə-\ *n, pl* **cachexias** *also* **cachexies** [LL *cachexia*, fr. Gk *kachexia* bad condition of body, fr. *kak-* cac- + *-hexia* (fr. *hexis* possession, condition, fr. *echein* to have) — more at SCHEME] **1 :** a general physical wasting and malnutrition caused by a chronic disease (as tuberculosis or cancer) **2** *usu cachexy* **:** a chronic debased condition esp. of mind or outlook

ca·chi·mi·lla \,kächə'mē(y)ə, -,a-\ *also* **ca·cha·ni·lla** \-'nē(y)ə\ *n* -s [MexSp] **:** a shrub (*Pluchea sericea*) of the family Compositae of southwestern U.S. and adjacent Mexico whose slender tough stems are used to make arrows, birdcages, and baskets

cachina *var of* KACHINA

cach·in·nate \'kakə,nāt\ *vi* -ED/-ING/-S [L *cachinnatus*, past part. of *cachinnare*; prob. of imit. origin like OE *ceahhetan* to laugh loudly, OHG *kachazzen*, Gk *kachazein* to laugh loudly, Skt *kakhati* he laughs] **:** to laugh usu. loudly or convulsively ⟨*cachinnated* till his sides must have ached —John Burroughs⟩ — **cach·in·na·tion** \,kakə'nāshən\ *n* -s

cach·o·long \'kashə,lȯŋ\ *n* -s [F, prob. fr. a native name in Kalmuck, U.S.S.R.] **:** an opaque bluish white or pale yellow variety of opal containing a little alumina

ca·chou \ka'shü, kə-; 'ka,shü, -'aa-, -'ai-\ *n* -s [F, fr. Pg *cachu*, fr. Malayalam *kāccu*] **1 :** CATECHU **2 :** an aromatic pill or pastille made of licorice, various aromatics, and gum and used to sweeten the breath **3 :** CACHOU DE LAVAL **4 :** AUBURN

ca·chou de la·val \-dələ'val\ *n, usu cap C&L* [F, fr. *Laval*, city in France, place of its first manufacture] **:** a direct dark brown dye for cotton obtained as the first sulfur dye by heating organic materials (as sawdust or bran) with sulfur and sodium sulfide — see DYE table I (under *Sulfur Brown 1*)

ca·chua \kə'chüə, 'käch(,)wä\ *also* **ka·shua** \kə'shüə, 'käsh(,)wä\ *or* **ka·swa** \'käs(,)swä\ *n* -s [AmerSp *cachúa*] **1 :** a Peruvian dance in rapid unsyncopated 2/4 time **2 :** the music for a cachua

ca·chu·cha \kə'chüchə\ *also* **ca·chu·ca** \-ükə\ *n* -s [Sp, small boat, cap, cachucha, prob. fr. *cacho* shard, piece, prob. fr. (assumed) VL *cacculus* pot, alter. of L *caccabus*, fr. Gk *kakkabos*, of Sem origin; akin to Assyr *kukubu* vessel] **:** a gay Andalusian solo dance in triple time done with castanets

ca·ci·cus \kə'sēkəs\ *n, cap* [NL, fr. AmerSp *cacique*] **:** a genus of tropical American orioles (family Icteridae) — see CACIQUE 2

ca·cio·ca·val·lo \¦kächōkə'va(,)lō\ *or* **caciocavallo cheese** *n* -s [It *caciocavallo*, lit., horse cheese, fr. *cacio* cheese (fr. L *caseus*) + *cavallo* horse, fr. L *caballus* nag — more at CHEESE, CAVALCADE] **:** a cheese originating in southern Italy and made from matted curd worked in hot water or whey and often molded into the shape of an Indian club or tenpin

ca·cique \kə'sēk\ *or* **ca·zique** \-'z-\ *n* -s [Sp *cacique*, of Arawakan origin; akin to Taino *cacique* chief, Arawak *kassequa*] **1 a :** a native Indian chief in areas dominated primarily by a Spanish culture, esp. the West Indies and Central and So. America **b :** a local political boss in Spain and Latin America **2** [AmerSp, fr. Sp] **:** any of numerous tropical American orioles, some black in plumage, others conspicuously colored, of *Cacicus* or related genera, having the base of the bill expanded into a frontal shield **3** [PhilSp, fr. Sp] **:** a powerful landowner in the Philippines, usu. Spanish or of Spanish descent

ca·ciqu·ism \-ē,kizəm\ *n* -s [Sp *caciquismo*, fr. *cacique* + *-ismo* -ism] **:** domination by caciques ⟨economic and administrative ~ —C.A.Buss⟩

ca·ci·quis·mo \,käsē'kēz(,)mō\ *n* -s [Sp] **:** CACIQUISM

¹cack \'kak, -ä-\ *vi* -ED/-ING/-S [ME *cakken*, fr. L *cacare*; akin to Gk *kakkan* to void excrement, MIr *cacc* dung, and perh. to Gk *kakos* bad] **1** *dial* **:** to discharge excrement **2** *dial* **:** VOMIT

²cack \"\ *n* -s *dial* **:** DUNG, MUCK

³cack \'kak\ *n* -s [origin unknown] **:** a baby's heelless shoe with a soft leather sole

¹cack·le \'kakəl\ *vi* **cackled; cackled; cackling** \'kak(ə)liŋ\ **cackles** [ME *cakelen*, of imit. origin] **1 :** to make the sharp broken noise or cry characteristic of or resembling that of a goose or of a hen after laying **2 :** to laugh with a broken somewhat harsh noise suggestive of a hen's cackle **3 :** to converse in a silly noisy way **:** CHATTER

²cackle \"\ *n* -s **1 :** the action or noise of cackling ⟨a hen's ~⟩ ⟨there should be no ~ of voices at your elbow —R.L.Stevenson⟩ **2 :** idle chatter **:** pointless conversation ⟨the constant ~ at a club meeting⟩

cack·ler \'kak(ə)lə(r)\ *n* -s **:** one that cackles; *specif* **:** BABBLER 2

cackling goose *n* **:** a goose of a western variety (*Branta canadensis minima*) of the Canada goose resembling but much smaller than the white-cheeked goose

caco- —see CAC-

caco·chy·my \'kakō,kīmē\ *n* -ES [NL *cacochymia*, fr. Gk *kakochymia*, fr. *kak-* cac- + *-chymia* (fr. *chymos* juice, fr. *chein* to pour) — more at FOUND] *obs* **:** an unhealthy condition of the humors of the body, esp. of the blood

caco·de·mon *also* **caco·dae·mon** \¦kakə¦dēmən\ *n* -s [Gk *kakodaimōn*, fr. *kak-* cac- + *daimōn* demon — more at DEMON] **:** an evil spirit **:** DEVIL, DEMON — opposed to *eudaemon* — **caco·de·mon·ic** *also* **caco·dae·mon·ic** \¦kakədē¦mänik\ *adj*

caco·de·mo·nia \,kakədē'mōnēə\ *or* **caco·de·mo·no·ma·nia** \-,dēmənō'mānēə\ *n* -s [*cacodemonia* fr. NL, fr. Gk *kakodaimonia* possession by an evil spirit, fr. *kakodaimōn*, *kakodaimōn*; *cacodemonomania* fr. NL, fr. Gk *kakodaimōn*, *kakodaimōn* + NL *-o-* + *mania*] **:** insanity in which the patient has the delusion of being possessed by an evil spirit

caco·doxy \'kakə,däksē\ *n* -ES [LGk *kakodoxia* heretical opinion, fr. Gk *kak-* cac- + *-doxia* (fr. *doxa* opinion, fr. *dokein* to seem) — more at DECENT] **:** perverse teachings **:** HETERODOXY

cac·o·dyl \'kakə,dil\ *n* -s [ISV *cacod-* (fr. Gk *kakōdēs* ill-smelling, fr. *kak-* cac- + *-ōdēs*, akin to *ozein* to smell) + *-yl*; orig. formed as G *kakodyl* — more at ODOR] **1 :** an arsenical radical $As(CH_3)_2$ whose compounds are noted for their vile smell and poisonous properties **2 :** a colorless poisonous liquid compound $As_2(CH_3)_4$ consisting of two cacodyl radicals and having an offensive odor

cac·o·dyl·ate \,kakə'di,lāt\ *n* -s [ISV *cacodylic* + *-ate*] **:** a salt of cacodylic acid

cac·o·dyl·ic acid \¦kakə¦dilik-\ *n* [part trans. of G *kakodylsäure*, fr. *kakodyl* + *säure* acid] **:** a crystalline deliquescent compound $(CH_3)_2AsOOH$ obtained by oxidizing cacodyl oxide and used in medicine in the form of its salts; dimethyl-arsinic acid — compare SODIUM CACODYLATE

cacodyl oxide *n* [ISV *cacodyl* + *oxide*; orig. formed as G *kakodyloxyd*] **:** a heavy oily liquid $(AsC_2H_6)_2O$ that has a repulsive odor and is obtained by distilling arsenic trioxide with potassium acetate

caco·epy \'kakə,wepē; ka'kōəpē, kə-\ *n* -ES [*cac-* + *-epy* (as in *orthoepy*)] **:** bad pronunciation — opposed to *orthoepy*

cac·o·ë·thes \,kakə'wē(,)thēz\ *n* [L, fr. Gk *kakoēthes* wickedness, fr. neut. of *kakoēthēs* malignant, fr. *kak-* cac- + *-ēthēs* (fr. *ēthos* custom) — more at ETHICAL] **:** a habitual and uncontrollable desire **:** MANIA, ITCH

cacoëthes scri·ben·di \-skrə'bendē, -,dī\ *n* [L] **:** an uncontrollable urge to write ⟨his book tempts us to encourage him in a senile *cacoëthes scribendi* — *Spectator*⟩

caco·gen·e·sis \,kakə'jenəsəs\ *n* [NL, fr. *cac-* + *genesis*] **1 :** inability to produce hybrids that are both viable and fertile **2 :** racial deterioration esp. when due to the retention of inferior breeding stock

caco·gen·ic \¦kakə¦jenik\ *adj* [*cac-* + *-genic* (as in *eugenic*)] **1 :** DYSGENIC **2 :** of or relating to cacogenesis

caco·gen·ics \,==¦=iks\ *n pl but usu sing in constr* [*cac-* + *-genics* (as in *eugenics*)] **1 :** DYSGENICS **2 :** CACOGENESIS 2

ca·cog·ra·phy \ka'kägrəfē, kə-\ *n* -ES [*cac-* + *-graphy*] **1 :** bad handwriting — opposed to *calligraphy* **2 :** bad spelling — opposed to *orthography*

ca·col·o·gy \ka'käləjē, kə-\ *n* -ES [prob. fr. F *cacologie*, fr. *cac-* + *-logie* -logy] **:** bad diction or pronunciation

cac·o·mis·tle \'kakə,misəl\ *also* **cac·o·mixl** *or* **cac·o·mix·le** \-i(k)səl\ *n* -s [MexSp *cacomistle*, *cacomixtle*, fr. Nahuatl *tlacomiztli*, fr. *tlaco* half + *miztli* mountain lion] **1 :** a slender carnivorous mammal (*Bassariscus astutus*) of the southwestern U. S. and Mexico related to the raccoons but distinguished by the long bushy black-and-white ringed tail — called also *civet cat*, *ringtail* **2 :** the fur or pelt of the cacomistle

cac·onym \'kakə,nim\ *n* -s [*cac-* + *-onym*] **:** a taxonomic name that is objectionable for linguistic reasons — **cac·onym·ic** \¦kakə¦nimik\ *adj*

ca·coon \ka'kün, kə-\ *n* -s [perh. of African origin; akin to Twi *kankua*, a tree and its fruit] **1** *West Indies* **:** SNUFFBOX BEAN **2 :** a tropical American plant (*Fevillea cordifolia*) of the family Cucurbitaceae with seeds which have cathartic qualities

caco·phon·ic \¦kakə¦fänik\ *adj* [*cacophony* + *-ic*] **:** CACOPHONOUS — **caco·phon·i·cal·ly** \-nək(ə)lē\ *adv*

ca·coph·o·nist \ka'käfənəst, kə-\ *n* -s [*cacophony* + *-ist*] **:** a composer of cacophonous or atonal music — usu. used disparagingly

ca·coph·o·nous \-ənəs\ *adj* [Gk *kakophōnos*, fr. *kak-* cac- + *-phōnos* (fr. *phōnē* sound); akin to Gk *phanai* to say — more at BAN] **:** marked by cacophony **:** harsh-sounding ⟨as ~ as a henyard —John McCarten⟩ ⟨whose writing is . . . uniformly ~ —Brand Blanshard⟩ ⟨a ~ melody⟩ ⟨ ~ laughter⟩ — **ca·coph·o·nous·ly** *adv*

ca·coph·o·ny \-ənē, -i\ *n* -ES [F & NL; F *cacophonie* & NL *cacophonia*, fr. Gk *kakophōnia*, fr. *kak-* cac- + *-phōnia* -phony] **1 :** harsh or discordant sound **:** DISSONANCE ⟨marshes sent forth the multitudinous ~ of song and croak and trill and call and scream —D.C.Peattie⟩; *specif* **:** harshness in the sound of words or phrases ⟨the subtle blending of vowels and consonants so as to avoid even the suspicion of ~ —Irving Babbitt⟩ —opposed to *euphony* **2 :** an instance of cacophony ⟨wooden wheels screeching a ~ —*Amer. Guide Series: Minn.*⟩

ca·coth·e·line \kə'käthə,lēn, ka-, -lən\ *n* -s [ISV *cacothel-* (fr. LGk *kakothelēs* malevolent, fr. Gk *kak-* cac- + *-thelēs*, fr. *thelein* to wish, will) + *-ine*; orig. formed as F *cacothéline* — more at MONOTHELETE] **:** a poisonous base $C_{21}H_{21}N_3O_7$ obtained as the orange-yellow crystalline nitrate by heating brucine with nitric acid

ca·cox·e·nite \kə'käksə,nīt, ka-\ *also* **ca·cox·ene** \kə'käk,sēn, ka-\ *n* -s [G *kakoxen* cacoxenite (fr. *kak-* cac- + *-xen* -xene) + E *-ite*] **:** a mineral $Fe_4(PO_4)_3(OH)_3.12H_2O$ consisting of a hydrous iron phosphate occurring in yellow or brownish radiated tufts

cac·ta·ce·ae \kak'tāsē,ē\ *n pl, cap* [NL, fr. *Cactus*, type genus + *-aceae*] **:** a family of plants (order Opuntiales) that are nearly all American and common in desert areas and characterized chiefly by fleshy stems and branches on which the foliage leaves are much reduced or early deciduous being usu. replaced by spines, scales, or hairs borne in areoles — see CACTUS 1 — **cac·ta·ceous** \(')kak¦tāshəs\ *adj*

cac·ta·les \kak'tā(,)lēz\ [NL, fr. *Cactus*, type genus + *-ales*] *syn of* OPUNTIALES

cac·to·blas·tis \,kaktə'blastəs\ *n* [NL, fr. *cactus* + *-o-* + *-blastis* -blast] **1** *cap* **:** a genus of small moths (family Phycitidae) native to So. America including the cactus moth (*C. cactorum*) which has been introduced into Australia to control prickly-pear infestation **2** *pl* **cactoblas·tes** \-,tēz\ **:** CACTUS MOTH

cac·tus \'kaktəs\ *n* [NL, fr. L, cardoon, fr. Gk *kaktos*] **1** *cap, in some classifications* **:** a genus of globose spiny plants (family Cactaceae) now referred to several other genera (as *Melocactus* and *Coryphantha*) **2** *pl* **cac·ti** \-,tī, -(,)tē\ *or* **cactuses** \-,təsəz\ **:** any plant of the family Cactaceae — see CARNEGIEA, ECHINOCACTUS, MESCAL, OPUNTIA

cactus alkaloid *n* **:** ANHALONIUM ALKALOID

cactus coral *n* **:** any of various corals (family Mussidae) related to the brain corals but distinguished by well-developed walls between the polyp grooves

cactus dahlia : any of various dahlias having flower heads with the rays revolute wholly or in part and resembling the flowers of cacti of the genus *Cereus*

cactus fig *n* **:** INDIAN FIG 2

cactus moth *n* **:** a moth having a larva that feeds on cactus; *specif* **:** a small whitish or yellowish moth (*Cactoblastis cactorum*) with dusky markings the larva of which is an orange-red gregarious borer that invades and consumes prickly pear — see CACTOBLASTIS

cactus mouse *n* **:** a white-footed mouse (*Peromyscus eremicus*) of desert areas of southwestern No. America

cactus woodpecker *n* **:** a small desert woodpecker (*Dryobates scalaris cactophilus*) of the southwestern U. S. with the back barred black and white

cactus wren *n* **:** a large harsh-voiced wren (*Heleodytes brunneicapillus*) occurring in several varieties or subspecies in southwestern No. America

ca·cu·mi·nal \ka'kyümənᵊl, kə-\ *adj* [ISV *cacumin-* (fr. L *cacumin-*, *cacumen* top, point) + *-al*] **:** RETROFLEX

¹cad \'kad, -aa(ə)d\ *n* -s [short for ¹*caddie*] **1** *dial Eng* **:** an assistant who does tasks which call for no special talent **:** HELPER ⟨a bricklayer's ~⟩ **2** *obs* **:** an omnibus conductor **3** *Brit* **:** a town boy or townsman as distinguished from a student at a local school **4 :** a person without gentlemanly instincts **:** one that deliberately and callously violates the code of decent responsible behavior esp. in relations with women

²cad \'kad, -ä-\ *n* -s [by shortening] *dial Eng* **:** CADDISWORM

cad *abbr* **1** cadenza **2** cadet

cad·a·lene \'kadᵊl,ēn\ *n* -s [*cadinene* + naphth*alene*] **:** a colorless liquid hydrocarbon $C_{15}H_{18}$ obtained by dehydrogenating cadinene and other sesquiterpenes; 4-isopropyl-1,6-dimethyl-naphthalene

ca·dang-ca·dang \'kä,däŋ'kä,däŋ\ *n* -s [Iloko *kadang-kadang* stilts; fr. the appearance of the palm affected by the disease] **:** an infectious chlorotic disease of the coconut palm particularly destructive in the Philippines and characterized by yellow-bronzing esp. of the older lower leaves

ca·das·tral \kə'dastrəl\ *adj* [F, fr. *cadastre* + *-al*] **1 :** of or relating to the records of a cadastre **:** concerned with assembling or keeping the records necessary to a cadastre **2** *of a map or survey* **:** showing or recording property boundaries, subdivision lines, buildings, and other details — **ca·das·tral·ly** \-rəlē\ *adv*

ca·das·tre \kə'dastə(r)\ *n* -s [F, fr. It *catastro*, alter. of OIt (Venetian dial.) *catastico*, fr. LGk *katastichon* notebook, fr. Gk *kata-* cata- + *stichos* line — more at DISTICH] **:** an official register of the quantity, value, and ownership of real estate used in apportioning taxes

ca·dav·er \kə'davə(r) *also* -ȧv- *or* -äv- *or* -āv-\ *n* -s [L, fr. *cadere* to fall — more at CHANCE] **1 :** a dead human or animal body usu. intended for dissection **:** CORPSE — compare CARCASS **2 :** a sculptured representation of a human corpse usu. emaciated or in a state of partial decomposition made as part of a funerary monument

ca·dav·er·ic \kə'dav(ə)rik\ *adj* [F *cadavérique*, fr. *cadavre* cadaver + *-ique* -ic] **:** of or relating to a cadaver ⟨~ rigidity⟩ — compare CADAVEROUS

ca·dav·er·ine \kə'davə,rēn, -v(ə)rən\ *n* -s [ISV *cadaver* + *-ine*; orig. formed as G *kadaverin*] **:** a syrupy nontoxic ptomaine $H_2N(CH_2)_5NH_2$ formed esp. in putrefaction of flesh—called also *pentamethylenediamine*

ca·dav·er·ous \kə'dav(ə)rəs\ *adj* [F or L; F *cadavéreux*, fr. L *cadaverosus*, fr. *cadaver* + *-osus* -ous] **1 a :** of or relating to a corpse ⟨a peculiar, fetid, ~ odor —W.H.Lowe⟩ **b :** suggestive of corpses or tombs ⟨in that ~ library —Ngaio Marsh⟩ **2 a** *of a complexion* **:** like that of a corpse **:** PALLID, LIVID ⟨the deputy's face looked ~ in the light of the green-shaded table lamp —C.D.Lewis⟩ **b :** GAUNT, EMACIATED — **ca·dav·er·ous·ly** *adv*

cad·bait \'kad,bāt, -'ä-\ *n* [alter. of *codbait*] *dial Eng* **:** CADDISWORM

¹cad·die *or* **cad·dy** *or* **cad·ie** \'kadē, -i\ *n, pl* **caddies** *or* **cadies** [F *cadet* — more at CADET] **1** *Scot* **:** a military cadet **2** *Scot* **:** one that waits about for odd jobs; *specif* **:** an 18th century Edinburgh commissionaire **3** *Scot* **:** young fellow **:** LAD **4 a :** one that assists a golf player esp. by carrying his clubs around the course during play **b :** CADDIE CART **c :** any small cartlike device for conveying things inconvenient to carry by hand

²caddie *or* **caddy** \"\ *vi* **caddied; caddied; caddying; caddies :** to serve as a caddie

caddie cart *n* **:** a long-handled 2-wheeled cart (as for carrying upright a golf bag and clubs on a golf course)

caddies *pl of* CADDY

¹cad·dis *or* **cad·dice** \'kadəs, -'ä-\ *n, pl* **caddises** *or* **caddices** [ME *cadas*, prob. fr. MF *cadaz*, *cadarce*, fr. OProv *cadarz*, perh. fr. Gk *akathartos* unclean, fr. *a-* ²a- + *-kathartos* cleansed (fr. *kathairein* to cleanse) — more at CATHARTIC] **1** *dial Brit* **a :** FLOSS, COTTON WOOL, LINT **b :** shreds esp. of cloth **2 :** worsted yarn **:** CREWEL; *specif* **:** a worsted ribbon or binding often used for garters **3** [MF *cadis*, fr. OProv] **a :** a heavy woolen twill used by the clergy in France **b :** a cheap sergelike woolen used in Scotland

²cad·dis *or* **cad·dice** \'kadəs\ *n, pl* **caddises** *or* **caddices** [by shortening] **:** CADDISWORM

caddis fly *n* [²*caddis*] **:** any of numerous insects constituting the order Trichoptera or sometimes included among the Neuroptera, having four membranous wings more or less densely hairy, vestigial mouth parts, and slender many-jointed antennae — see CADDISWORM

caddis fly

cad·dish \'kadish, -aad-, -ēsh\ *adj* **:** like a cad **:** ILL-BRED — **cad·dish·ness** *n*

cad·dis·worm \'kadə,swərm, -wōm\ *n* [prob. alter. of obs. *cadworm*, alter. of *codworm*] **:** the wormlike aquatic larva of a caddis fly that is often used as bait and lives in and carries around a cylindrical sometimes spiral case of silk covered externally with pieces of shell, fine gravel, wood, or straw

¹cad·dle \'kadᵊl\ *vb* -ED/-ING/-S [perh. alter. of *caudle*] *vt, dial* **:** CONFUSE, ANNOY, TEASE ~ *vi, dial* **:** PUTTER, LOAF, GOSSIP

²caddle \"\ *n* -s **1** *dial* **:** confused mess **:** CONFUSION **2** *dial* **:** WORRY, TROUBLE, FUSS

¹cad·do \'kad(,)dō\ *n, pl* **caddo** *or* **caddos** *usu cap* [prob. modif. of Caddo *Kädohädächo* (name of a leading tribe in the confederacy), lit., real chiefs] **1 :** a group of Indian peoples of Arkansas, No. and So. Dakota, Kansas, Nebraska, Louisiana, Oklahoma, and Texas, comprising the Hasinai, Kadohadacho, and Natchitoches confederacies and the Adai, Arikara, Eyeish, Kichai, Pawnee, Wichita, and other tribes **2 :** a member of the Caddo group of peoples

²caddo \"\ *or* **cad·do·an** \'kadəwən\ *adj, usu cap* **:** of or relating to an ancient culture of the lower Mississippi valley characterized by pottery having decoration engraved on the polished surface after firing

cad·do·an \'kadəwən\ *n* -s *usu cap* **:** a language family comprising the Caddo languages

¹cad·dow \'ka(,)dō\ *n* -s [ME *cadaw*, *cadowe*, prob. fr. (northern dial.) *ca* enough + *daw*, *dawe* jackdaw — more at KAE, DAW] *now dial Eng* **:** JACKDAW

²caddow \"\ *n* -s [perh. alter. of ¹*caddis*] *dial* **:** a coarse woolen quilt or covering

¹caddy *var of* CADDIE

²cad·dy \'kadē, -i\ *n* -ES [modif. of Malay *kati*] **1 a :** a small box, can, or chest esp. to keep tea in **b :** a paper, wood, or metal case used to package or display (as cookies or plugs of tobacco) **2 :** any container or device for storing or holding frequently used things (as clothes or tools) when they are not in use

³caddy *var of* KADY

caddying *pres part of* CADDIE

¹cade \'kād\ *n* -s [ME, fr. L *cadus* jar, bottle, fr. Gk *kados*, of Sem origin; akin to Heb *kadh* water jar] **:** BARREL, CASK, KEG; *esp* **:** a small barrel for 500 herrings or 1000 sprats

²cade \"\ *n* -s [ME *cad* pet lamb] *dial* **:** a pet animal; *esp* **:** a pet lamb

³cade \"\ *adj* **1** *of an animal* **:** left by the mother and reared by hand **:** PET ⟨a ~ lamb⟩ **2 :** PETTED, INDULGED

⁴cade \"\ *n* -s [MF, fr. OProv, fr. ML *catanus*] **:** a European juniper (*Juniperus oxycedrus*) with angled branchlets, awl-shaped needles in alternate whorls of three, and a reddish brown berry

-cade \¦kād\ *n comb form* -s [¹*cavalcade*] **:** procession ⟨motorcade⟩ **:** spectacle ⟨aquacade⟩

cadee *obs var of* CADET

ca·delle \kə'del\ *n* -s [F, fr. Prov *cadello*, fr. L *catella*, fem. of *catellus* little dog, whelp; akin to MHG *hatele* goat, ON *hathna* young she-goat, L *catulus* young of an animal, Russ *kotit' sya* to bear young] **:** the larva or adult of a small cosmopolitan black beetle (*Tenebroides mauritanicus*) destructive to stored grain and sometimes preying on other insects — compare GRAIN BEETLE

¹ca·dence \'kādᵊn(t)s\ *n* -s [ME, fr. OIt *cadenza*, fr. *cadere* to fall (fr. L) + *enza* -ence; in senses other than 1, prob. mostly fr. MF or F *cadence*, fr. OIt *cadenza* — more at CHANCE] **1 a :** a rhythmic sequence or flow of sounds in language; *specif* **:** a particular rhythmic sequence distinctive of an individual author or literary composition ⟨the grand ~ of his poetry⟩ **b :** the beat, time, measure, or sequence of any rhythmical motion or activity (as marching, dancing, rowing) **c :** a sequence of motions, colors, or events ⟨the ~ of glittering ripple and moving leaf—Richard Jefferies⟩ ⟨slower ~ of life—*Irish Digest*⟩ **2 a :** a falling inflection of the voice in reading or speaking (as at the end of a sentence) **b :** a concluding and usu. falling strain; *specif* **:** a musical chord sequence moving to a harmonic close or point of rest and giving a sense of partial or total harmonic completion **3 a :** the modulated and rhythmic recurrence of any sound, esp. the sounds of nature (as of waves or wind) **b :** the general or a characteristic rhythmic modulation of the voice ⟨the ~ of the countryman's speech⟩ **4 :** the characteristic unit of the harmonic structure of tonal music consisting of a musical progression from harmonic stability to suspension and back to stability **5 a :** the rising or falling order of strong, long, or stressed syllables and weak, short, or unstressed syllables ⟨ris-

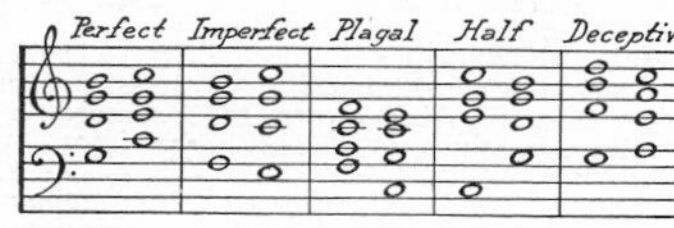

cadence 2b

ing ~) ⟨iambic ~⟩ — compare ARSIS, IONIC, METER **b :** an unmetrical or irregular arrangement of stressed and unstressed syllables in prose or free verse based on natural stress groups **syn** see RHYTHM

²cadence \"\ *vt* -ED/-ING/-S : to put into cadence or rhythm

ca·denced \'kād³n(t)st\ *adj* : marked by cadence : RHYTHMICAL ⟨the ~ crunch of GI shoes on cinder —Alan Surgal⟩ ⟨in verse or ~ prose —John Gassner⟩

ca·den·cy \'kād³nsē, -i\ *n* -ES **1 :** CADENCE **2 a** (1) **:** the status of being a younger son or brother or of belonging to a younger branch of a family (2) **:** the status of being one (as an heir apparent or a cadet) whose proper coat of arms is a differenced version of that to which the head of the family is entitled **b :** the status of being a younger branch of a family

cadency mark *n* **:** an addition to a coat of arms to mark the position of the bearer with respect to a present or former head of the family — called also *mark of cadency*; compare DIFFERENCE; ANNULET, CRESCENT, CROSS MOLINE, DOUBLE QUATREFOIL, FLEUR-DE-LIS, LABEL, MARTLET, MULLET, ROSE; BORDURE

ca·dent \'kād³nt\ *adj* [L *cadent-, cadens*, pres. part. of *cadere* to fall — more at CHANCE] **1** *archaic* **:** FALLING **2 :** having rhythmic fall

ca·den·tial \kā'denchəl\ *adj* [fr. ¹*cadence*, after such pairs as E *essence*: *essential*] **:** of or relating to a cadence, esp. a concluding cadence

ca·den·za \kə'denzə\ *n* -S [It — more at CADENCE] **1 a :** a parenthetic flourish in the course of an aria or other solo piece commonly just before the final or other important cadence **b :** a technically brilliant sometimes improvised solo passage toward the close of a concerto in which the main themes of the preceding movement are given further development **2 :** an episodic departure from the main theme of a larger musical work

cade oil *n* [⁴*cade*] **:** a dark thick oily liquid that has a tar odor and is obtained by destructive distillation of the wood of the cade and used locally in skin diseases — called also *juniper-tar oil*

cades *pl of* CADE

-cades *pl of* -CADE

¹ca·det \kə'det, *usu* -ded·+V, *West Point slang* 'kā,d-\ *n* -S *often attrib* [F, fr. F dial. (Gascon) *capdet* chief, captain, fr. LL *capitellum* small head, dim. of L *capit-, caput* head — more at HEAD] **1 a :** a younger brother or son **b :** the youngest son **c :** a younger branch of a family ⟨a ~ of a royal line⟩ **d :** a member of such a younger branch **2 a :** a gentleman who enlisted in a military regiment for the purpose of acquiring military skill and eventually a commission **b :** one in training for military or naval service as a commissioned officer in the armed forces; *specif* **:** a pupil in a national military school **c :** a trainee working to gain a merchant-marine license (as for third mate) **d :** a member of the armed forces assigned as a student in a special-service school to train for a commission ⟨an aviation ~⟩ **e :** a student in a private military academy **f :** one undergoing training for officership in the Salvation Army **3 a :** a junior in a business or occupation who is engaged principally in learning ⟨entered the civil service as a ~⟩ ⟨a ~ teacher⟩ **b** *Austral* **:** an apprentice on a sheep or cattle farm **4** *slang* **:** PIMP **5 :** a grayish blue that is redder and paler than electric, redder and duller than copenhagen, and less strong and very slightly redder than Gobelin

²ca·det \kə'det, *usu* -ded·+V\ *n* -S *usu cap* [Russ *Kadet*, by shortening & alter. (influenced by *kadet* young soldier) fr. *Konstitutsionno-Demokraticheskaya* (*Partiya*) Constitutional Democratic Party] **:** a member of the former Constitutional Democratic party of Russia

cadet blue *n* **1 :** a variable color averaging a grayish blue that is redder and paler than electric, greener and slightly paler than copenhagen, and redder, lighter, and stronger than Gobelin **2 :** a moderate blue that is redder and duller than average copen and redder and deeper than azurite blue or Dresden blue

cadet cloth *n* **:** a heavy firm bluish gray woolen fabric often used for uniforms in military schools

cadet gray *n* **:** a variable color averaging a pale blue that is redder and duller than average powder blue, redder, less strong, and slightly darker than Sistine, and redder and deeper than old blue

ca·det·ship \-,ship\ *n* -S **:** the position, rank, or commission of a cadet

¹cadge \'kaj, -aa(ə)j\ *vb* -ED/-ING/-S [back-formation fr. *cadger*] *vt* **1** *dial Brit* **:** CARRY ⟨~ a burden⟩ **2 :** to get by begging esp. habitually or as a means of livelihood **:** SPONGE ⟨*cadging* dimes from passers-by⟩ ⟨~ a meal from a chance acquaintance⟩ ~ *vi* **:** to cadge food or money **:** SPONGE ⟨no men loitering around the hotels from whom he could ~ —J.A. Lee⟩ ⟨you have *cadged* on me for your keep —F.M.Ford⟩ ⟨a footsore tramp *cadging* for a meal⟩

²cadge \"\ *n* -S [prob. alter. of *cage*] **:** a wooden frame on which live hawks are carried

cadg·er \'kajə(r), -aaj-\ *n* -S [ME *cadgear*, fr. *caggen, cagen* to tie + *-ear, -er* -er; perh. fr. the hitching of the horse used for transporting wares] **1** *chiefly Scot* **:** CARRIER; *esp* **:** a dealer who takes dairy produce to the towns and town wares to the country **2** *chiefly Scot* **:** an itinerant huckster or street seller **3 :** one that cadges ⟨a most celebrated ~ of drinks —Allan Temko⟩ **4** [²*cadge* + *-er*] **:** one that carries hawks on a cadge

cadg·i·ly \-jəlē, -i\ *adv, dial* **:** in a cadgy manner

cadgy \'kajē, -aaj-, -i\ *adj* [origin unknown] **1** *chiefly Scot* **:** CHEERFUL, MERRY **2** *dial* **:** sexually excited **:** in rut **:** AMOROUS

cadi *var of* QADI

cadie *var of* CADDIE

cad·i·nene \'kad³n,ēn\ *n* -S [ISV *cadin-* (fr. NL *cadinus* of cade, fr. F *cade* + L *-inus* -ine) + *-ene* — more at CADE] **:** an oily hydrocarbon $C_{15}H_{24}$ of the sesquiterpene class found as the chief constituent in cade oil and in many essential oils

Cá·diz *or* **Ca·diz** \kə'diz *also* kā'diz *or* kə'diz *or* kā'diz *or* -'dēz *or* 'kādəz *or* 'kādəz *or* 'kadəz; *Sp* 'kāthēth *or* -ēs\ *adj, usu cap* [fr. *Cádiz*, Spain] **:** of or from the city of Cádiz, Spain **:** of the kind or style prevalent in Cádiz

cadj·an *also* **ca·jan** \'kājən, jän\ *or* **ca·jang** \-jäŋ\ *n* -S [Malay *kajan*] **1 :** interwoven coco-palm leaves for thatching **2 :** a strip of fan-palm leaf (as of the talipot) used as writing material; *also* **:** a document written on a palm leaf

cad·me·an *or* **cad·mae·an** \(')kad¦mēən, 'kad,m-\ *adj, usu cap* [L *Cadmeus* (fr. Gk. *Kadmeios*, fr. *Kadmos* Cadmus, mythical founder of Thebes and introducer of the alphabet from Phoenicia into Greece) +E *-an*] **:** of, relating to, associated with, or derived from Cadmus

cadmean victory *n, usu cap C* [trans. of Gk *Kadmeia nikē*; fr. the mutual slaughter of all but five of the armed men who sprang from dragon's teeth sown by Cadmus] **:** a victory obtained only at great or ruinous cost to the victor — compare PYRRHIC VICTORY

cad·mic \'kadmik\ *adj* [ISV *cadm-* (fr. NL *cadmium*) + *-ic*; orig. formed as F *cadmique*] **:** of, relating to, or derived from cadmium

cad·mif·er·ous \(')kad¦mif(ə)rəs\ *adj* [ISV *cadmi-* (fr. NL *cadmium*) + *-ferous*] **:** containing cadmium

cad·mi·um \'kadmēəm\ *n* -S [NL, fr. L *cadmia* calamine (fr. Gk *kadmeia*, fr. fem. of *Kadmeios* Cadmean) + NL *-ium*; fr. the occurrence of its ores together with calamine] **:** a tin-white malleable ductile toxic bivalent metallic element capable of a high polish and emitting a crackling sound when bent, occurring in greenockite and also in small amounts in ores of zinc from which it is separated as a by-product, and used chiefly in the protective electroplating of iron and steel and in the manufacture of bearing metals — symbol *Cd*; see ELEMENT table

cadmium blende *n* **:** GREENOCKITE

cadmium carmine *n* **:** GOYA

cadmium cell *n* **:** a Weston cell

cadmium green *n* **:** a strong green that is bluer and paler than primitive green and bluer, lighter, and stronger than mintleaf —called also *Empire*

cadmium lamp *n* **:** a vapor lamp in which the fluorescence of cadmium vapor produces red light whose wavelength taken as 6438.4696 international angstroms is used as a standard of length

cadmium lemon *n* **:** a brilliant to vivid greenish yellow — called also *Mutrie yellow*

cadmium lithopone *n* **:** a pigment analogous to lithopone consisting essentially of cadmium yellow or cadmium red and containing barium sulfate — called also *cadmopone*

cadmium ocher *n* **:** GREENOCKITE

cadmium orange *n* **1 :** an orange-hued cadmium-yellow pigment **2 :** a strong orange that is yellower, lighter, and stronger than pumpkin, redder, stronger, and slightly darker than cadmium yellow, and yellower, lighter, and stronger than mandarin orange — called also *marigold*

cadmium purple *n* **:** a moderate to deep red that is slightly yellower than burnt carmine

cadmium red *n* **1 :** a pigment consisting of a mixture of cadmium sulfide, cadmium selenide, and often barium sulfate and varying in hue from light red to maroon **2 :** FRENCH VERMILION

cadmium sulfate *n* **:** a colorless salt $CdSO_4$ ordinarily crystallizing with $2\frac{2}{3}$ molecules of water

cadmium sulfide *n* **:** a compound CdS occurring naturally as greenockite and obtained as a bright-yellow precipitate by the action of hydrogen sulfide on solutions of cadmium salts — see CADMIUM YELLOW

cadmium vermilion *n* **:** BLOOD RED

cadmium yellow *n* **1 :** a pigment consisting of cadmium sulfide and barium sulfate with or without zinc sulfide and varying in hue from lemon yellow to orange — called also in its orange hues *cadmium orange* **2 :** a strong orange that is yellower and paler than pumpkin, yellower, less strong, and slightly lighter than cadmium orange, and yellower and paler than mandarin orange — called also *aurora yellow, daffodil yellow, nasturtium yellow, orient yellow, radiant yellow*

cad·mo·pone \'kadmə,pōn\ *n* -S [NL *cadmium* + *-o-* + *-pone* (as in *lithopone*)] **:** CADMIUM LITHOPONE

cad·re \'kadrē *also* -'ā- *or* -'à- *or* -(,)drā *or* -,dri *or* -,drə; *Brit often* 'kādr³ *or* -də\ *n* -S [F, fr. It *quadro*, fr. L *quadrum* square — more at QUARREL] **1 :** FRAME, FRAMEWORK **:** SCHEME **:** skeletal organization ⟨the current specialisms and ~s of our university curricula —H.M.McLuhan⟩ **2 a :** a nucleus or core group esp. of trained personnel or active members of an organization who are capable of assuming leadership or of training and indoctrinating others ⟨a highly skilled ~ of technicians and workers —*Economist*⟩ ⟨only a ~ of maintenance men worked here in the winter —T.W.Duncan⟩ ⟨the permanent ~ of the Indian Civil Service —H.N.Brailsford⟩: as (1) **:** a group of key officers and enlisted men assigned to a new unit as a nucleus for its formation, administration, and training (2) [prob. fr. Russ *kadr*, fr. F *cadre*] **:** a cell of indoctrinated leaders active in promoting the interests of a revolutionary party ⟨a ~ of dedicated men ready to initiate any violence the party demanded⟩ **b** [prob. fr. Russ *kadr*, fr. F *cadre*] **:** a member of a cadre, esp. a political cadre ⟨do not want a conflict . . . before their own ~s are already —*New Republic*⟩

cad·re·man \-mən,-,man,-,maa(ə)n\ *n, pl* **cadremen :** a member of a military cadre

cads *pl of* CAD

ca·du·ca·ry \kə'd(y)ükərē\ *or* **ca·du·ci·ary** \-üs(h)ē,erē, -üshərē\ *adj* [L *caducarius*, fr. *caducus* caducous + *-arius* -ary] **:** relating to or transferred by escheat, lapse, or forfeiture

ca·du·ce·an \kə'd(y)üsēən, -üshən\ *adj* [*caduceus* + *-an*] **:** of or relating to a caduceus

ca·du·ce·us \kə'd(y)üs(h)ēəs\ *n, pl* **ca·du·cei** \-s(h)ē,ī\ [L *caduceus, caduceum*, modif. of Gk (Dor) *karykeion* (Attic *kērykeion*) herald's staff, fr. *karyx* (Attic *kēryx*) herald; akin to OE *hrēth* glory, OHG *hruod-*, ON *hrōthr* praise, Goth *hrotheigs* triumphant, Skt *carkṛti* praise] **1 :** the symbolic staff of a herald; *specif* **:** a conventionalized representation of a staff with two snakes curled around it and with two wings at the top **2 :** an insignia consisting of or bearing a caduceus: as **a :** one of the symbols of a physician — compare STAFF OF AESCULAPIUS **b :** the emblem of a medical corps or department of the armed services (as of the U.S. Army)

caduceus 1

ca·du·ci·ary \kə'd(y)üs(h)ē,erē, -üshərē\ *n* -ES [modif. (influenced by E *fiduciary*) of L *caducarius* — more at CADUCARY] **:** a caducary estate or subject of property

ca·du·ci·branch \kə'd(y)üsə,braŋk\ *adj* [NL *Caducibranchiata*] **:** of or relating to the Caducibranchiata

ca·du·ci·bran·chi·a·ta \kə¦d(y)üsə,braŋkē'ād·ə, -'ād·ə\ *n pl, cap* [NL, fr. *caduci-* (fr. L *caducus* falling) + L *branchiae* gills + NL *-ata*; akin to Gk *bronchos* throat — more at CRAW] **1** *in former classifications* **:** a division of tailed amphibians whose gills are lost in adult life **2 :** THALIACEA

ca·du·ci·bran·chi·ate \¦=¦=¦braŋkēət, -ē,āt\ *adj* [NL *Caducibranchiata*] **:** CADUCIBRANCH

ca·du·ci·corn \kə'd(y)üsə,kȯrn\ *adj* [*caduci-* (fr. L *caducus* falling) + *-corn*] **:** having deciduous horns ⟨~ deer⟩

ca·du·ci·ty \kə'd(y)üsəd·ē\ *n* -ES [F *caducité*, fr. *caduc* falling, decrepit (fr. L *caducus*) + F *-ité* -ity] **1 :** PERISHABLENESS, TRANSITORINESS **2 a :** feebleness from age **:** SENILITY **b :** old age ⟨the housebound old man...in his peaceable ~ —Christopher Morley⟩ **3 :** LAPSE ⟨the ~ of a legacy⟩ ⟨the ~ of a treaty may also be declared when...the causes which originated it have disappeared —*Havana Convention on Treaties*⟩

ca·du·cous \kə'd(y)ükəs\ *adj* [L *caducus* falling, inclined to fall, fr. *cadere* to fall — more at CHANCE] **1 :** falling off easily or before the usual time — used esp. of floral organs and opposed to *persistent* ⟨the ~ calyx of a poppy⟩; compare DECIDUOUS, FUGACIOUS **2** *law* **:** subject to caducity **:** LAPSED

ca·du·veo \,kädü'vā(,)ō\ *n* -S *usu cap* [Sp or Pg. of AmerInd origin] **:** GUAICURU

cad·wal·a·der·ite \kad'wälədə,rīt\ *n* -S [Charles B.M. *Cadwalader* b1885 Am. mineralogist + E *-ite*] **:** a mineral $Al(OH)_2Cl.4H_2O$ consisting of a hydrous basic aluminum chloride

cady *var of* KADY

caec- *or* **caeci-** *or* **caeco-** — see CEC-

caecal *var of* CECAL

cae·ci·dae \'sēsə,dē, -ēkə-\ *n pl, cap* [NL, fr. *Caecum*, type genus (fr. L, neut. of *caecus* blind) + *-idae* — more at CAECUM] **:** a family of minute marine gastropod mollusks (order Pectinibranchia) having the shells initially spiral but ultimately cylindrical and comprising the blind shells

¹cae·cil·i·an *or* **coe·cil·i·an** \sē'silyən, sə-, -'sēl-, -lēən\ *adj* [NL *Caecilia* + E *-an*] **:** of or relating to the Caeciliidae

²caecilian *or* **coecilian** \"\ *n* -S **:** an amphibian of the family Caeciliidae

cae·ci·li·idae \,sēsə'līə,dē\ *n pl, cap* [NL, fr. *Caecilia*, type genus (fr. L *caecilia*, a lizard, fr. *caecus* blind) + *-idae*; fr. the small eyes — more at CAECUM] **:** a family (type genus *Caecilia*) of small slender wormlike burrowing amphibians that is coextensive with the order Gymnophiona

caecum *var of* CECUM

caed·mo·nian \(')kad¦mōnēən\ *also* **caed·mon·ic** \-mänik\ *adj, usu cap* [*Caedmon fl* A.D.670 English Christian poet + E *-an* or *-ic*] **:** of or relating to the poet Caedmon

¹caen- *or* **caeno-** — see ²CEN-

²caen- *or* **caeno-** — see CEN-

cae·nag·nath·i·for·mes \¦sē,nag,nathə'fȯr,mēz, ¦kīn-\ *n pl, cap* [NL, fr. ¹*caen-* + *agnath-* (fr. *a-* ²a- + Gk *gnathos* jaw) + *-iformes* — more at GNATH-] **:** an order of Canadian Cretaceous birds (Neognathae) known from a single immense jaw and believed to be related to the ostriches though in some respects the jaw resembles that of a toothless dinosaur

caenobium *var of* COENOBIUM

caenogenesis *var of* CENOGENESIS

cae·no·les·tes \,sēnə'le(,)stēz, ,kīn-\ *n, cap* [NL, fr. ¹*caen-* + Gk *lēistēs* robber; akin to L *lucrum* gain — more at LUCRE] **:** a genus (the type of the family Caenolestidae) of small carnivorous diprotodont marsupials comprising the opossum rats

¹cae·no·les·tid \¦=¦=¦lestəd\ *adj* [NL *Caenolestidae*] **:** of or relating to the Caenolestidae

²caenolestid \"\ *n* -S **:** a member of the Caenolestidae

cae·no·les·ti·dae \,=='lestə,dē\ *n pl, cap* [NL, fr. *Caenolestes*, type genus + *-idae*] **:** a family of diprotodont marsupials that includes all recent diprotodonts occurring outside the Australian region and many extinct related forms — see CAENOLESTES

cae·no·les·toi·dea \,=nə(,)le'stȯidēə\ *n pl, cap* [NL, fr. *Caenolestes*, type genus + *-oidea*] **:** a superfamily of diprotodont marsupials comprising the opossum rats and extinct related forms

cae·no·pi·the·cus \,sēnōpə'thēkəs, ,kīn-, -ō'pithikəs\ *n, cap* [NL, fr. ¹*caen-* + *-pithecus*] **:** a genus of primates (family Adapidae) of the Eocene of Switzerland in some respects intermediate between tarsioids and the higher primates

cae·no·sty·lic \¦=nə¦stīlik\ *adj* [¹*caen-* + *-stylic*] **:** having the first two visceral arches without gills but attached to the cranium and serving in taking food — used of sharks, chimaeras, and amphibians — **cae·no·sty·ly** \'==,stīlē\ *n* -ES

caenozoic *usu cap, var of* CENOZOIC

caenozoology *var of* CENOZOOLOGY

caen stone \'käⁿ-, 'kān-\ *n, usu cap C* [*Caen*, city in Normandy, France, near which it is found] **1 :** a yellowish limestone marked with a rippled figure **2 :** FREESTONE 3

cae·o·ma \sē'ōmə, kī-\ *n* [NL, irreg. fr. Gk *kaiein* to burn; fr. its fiery red color — more at CAUSTIC] **1** *cap* **:** a form genus of rust fungi that produce an aecium without a peridium **2** -S **:** an aecium without a peridium

caer·nar·von·shire \kär'närvən,shi(ə)r, kə(r)'närv-, -,shər\ *or* **caernarvon** *adj, usu cap* [fr. *Caernarvonshire* or county of *Caernarvon*, Wales] **:** of or from the county of Caernarvon, Wales **:** of the kind or style prevalent in Caernarvon

caerulean *var of* CERULEAN

caes·al·pin·ia \,se,zal'pinēə, ,sē-\ *n, cap* [NL, fr. Andrea Cesalpino (Andreas *Caesalpinus*) †1603 Ital. botanist + NL *-ia*] **:** a genus of usu. small spiny tropical trees (family Leguminosae) having evenly bipinnate leaves and small whitish, green, yellow, or reddish flowers in showy racemes — see BRAZILWOOD

caes·al·pin·i·a·ce·ae \-,pinē'āsē,ē\ *n pl, cap* [NL, fr. *Caesalpinia*, type genus + *-aceae*] *in some classifications* **:** a large family of chiefly tropical shrubs and trees having a regular or slightly irregular corolla, the petals imbricated in the bud, and the fruit a legume, important genera being *Caesalpinia, Cassia, Bauhinia, Tamarindus*, and *Copaifera* — **caes·al·pin·i·a·ceous** \-'āshəs\ *adj*

cae·sar \'sēzə(r)\ *n* -S [after Gaius Julius *Caesar* †44 B.C. Roman general and statesman] **1** *often cap* **:** a Roman emperor succeeding Augustus Caesar **2 a** *often cap* **:** a powerful ruler **:** EMPEROR **:** AUTOCRAT, DICTATOR ⟨there were ~s before Caesar —H.D.Scott⟩ ⟨no tyrant of history, neither khan nor ~ nor czar —*Time*⟩ **b** *usu cap* [so called fr. the reference in Mt 22:21 (RSV)] **:** the civil power **:** a temporal ruler ⟨a dual loyalty — a loyalty to *Caesar* and a loyalty to God —J.H. Hallowell⟩ **3 :** TOMTATE

¹cae·sar·e·an *or* **cae·sar·i·an** \sē'za(a)rēən, -zer-,-zär-\ *adj, usu cap* [L *caesareus, caesarianus*, fr. *Caesar*] **:** of or relating to Julius or Augustus Caesar or to one of the Caesars who succeeded Augustus Caesar as Roman emperor

²caesarean *or* **caesarian** *often cap, var of* CESAREAN

cae·sar·ism \'sēzə,rizəm\ *n* -S *usu cap* **:** imperial authority or system **:** political absolutism **:** DICTATORSHIP ⟨he feared the coming of *Caesarism* and of military autocracy —Ernest Barker⟩

cae·sar·ist \-rəst\ *n* -S *usu cap* **:** an advocate of or adherent to Caesarism

cae·sa·ro·pa·pism \¦sēzə(,)rō'pā,pizəm\ *n* -S *often cap* [*caesar* + *-o-* + LL *papa* pope + E *-ism* — more at POPE] **1 :** exercise of supreme authority over ecclesiastical matters by a secular ruler **2 :** government in which the church is subordinate to the state or a secular ruler — compare BYZANTINISM, ERASTIANISM

caesar's agaric *or* **caesar's mushroom** *n, usu cap C* [after Gaius Julius *Caesar* — more at CAESAR] **:** ROYAL AGARIC

caesar substitution *also* **caesar shift** *n, usu cap C, cryptography* **:** the replacement of each letter in a text by the one at a certain constant distance in the alphabet, esp. a normal alphabet — compare JULIUS CAESAR CIPHER

caesar weed *n, usu cap C* **:** a tropical shrub (*Urena lobata*) valued for its strong bast fiber

cae·si·ous \'sēzēəs, 'kī-\ *adj* [L *caesius*; prob. akin to L *caelum* sky — more at CELESTIAL] **:** having a blue color very low in chroma

caesium *var of* CESIUM

caes·pi·tose *also* **ces·pi·tose** \'sespə,tōs\ *adj* [NL *caespitosus*, fr. L *caespit-, caespes* turf + *-osus* -ose] **:** arranged or combined in a thick mat or clumps **:** TUFTED: as **a :** having low stems forming a dense turf or sod **b :** growing in clusters ⟨the ~ spore fruits of some fungi⟩

caestus *var of* CESTUS

cae·su·ra *also* **ce·su·ra** \sē'z(h)ùrə, sə̇, ¦ü- *also* ¦z'y\ *n, pl* **caesuras** \-rəz\ *or* **caesu·rae** \-(,)rē\ [L, cutting off, fr. *caedere* to cut — more at CONCISE] **1** *in Greek and Latin prosody* **a :** a break in the flow of sound in a verse caused by the ending of a word within a foot (arma vi¦rumque ca¦no¦ Tro¦jae qui¦ primus ab¦oris) — symbol ||; usu. distinguished from *diaeresis*; see HEPHTHEMIMERAL CAESURA, PENTHEMIMERAL CAESURA, TRITHEMIMERAL CAESURA **b** *obs* **:** a lengthening of the last syllable of a word by the break in the verse **c :** DIAERESIS — see BUCOLIC CAESURA **2** *in modern prosody* **:** a break in the flow of sound in a line of verse occasioned usu. by a rhetorical pause and occurring usu. at about the middle of the verse (of man's | first dis¦obe¦dience || and | the fruit) — see EPIC CAESURA, FEMININE CAESURA, MASCULINE CAESURA **3 :** STOP, BREAK, INTERRUPTION ⟨the ~ between vol. I and vol. II —Erich Dinkler⟩ ⟨it was a ~, a pause between the last classes and the afternoon exercises —Nathaniel Burt⟩ ⟨the trenchant ~ which occurs between the apprehension of data and the judgment —Mary W. Hess⟩ **4 :** a pause marking a rhythmic point of division in a melody

cae·su·ral \-rəl\ *adj* **:** of or relating to a caesura

caeteris paribus *var of* CETERIS PARIBUS

CAF *abbr, often not cap* **1** clerical, administrative, and fiscal **2** cost and freight **3** cost, assurance, and freight

ca·fard \kȧfär\ *n* -S [F, lit., cockroach, fr. MF, cockroach, hypocrite, modif. of Ar *kāfir* infidel — more at KAFFIR] **:** severe depression or apathy — used esp. of white men in the tropics

ca·fé *also* **ca·fe** \(')ka¦fā, kə'fā\ *n* -S *often attrib* [F *café*, fr. Turk *kahve* — more at COFFEE] **1 a :** a room for coffee and light refreshments **:** COFFEEHOUSE ⟨they went into the ~ for a cup or two of something hot —Richard Llewellyn⟩ **b :** COFFEE **2 a :** RESTAURANT ⟨enjoy your dinner in a hotel dining room or ~ —Helen E.Stiles⟩ ⟨the dining room was not yet open, but he knew that there were several all-night ~s near the station —Hamilton Basso⟩ ⟨glass windows of a . . . ~ full of sugary cakes —Barbara Beecher⟩ **b :** an open-air eating place often partly on the sidewalk ⟨sat at the table in front of the big ~ —R.H.Newman⟩ ⟨a ~ with tables in the street . . . surrounded by a shallow fence of dark-green creeper —William Sansom⟩ **3 :** BARROOM, SALOON ⟨speakeasies, some of which have survived as legitimate saloons, nightclubs, or ~s —D.W.Maurer⟩ **4 :** CABARET, NIGHTCLUB

ca·fé au kirsch \¦ka,fā(,)ō'ki(ə)rsh\ *n, pl* **cafés au kirsch** \¦ka,fā(,)zō-\ [F, coffee with kirschwasser] **:** a drink consisting of black coffee, kirschwasser, white of egg, and sugar shaken with cracked ice and served in a glass

ca·fé au lait \¦ka,fā(,)ō'lā\ *n, pl* **cafés au lait** \¦ka,fā(,)zō-\ [F, coffee with milk] **1 :** coffee with esp. hot milk in about equal portions **2 :** the color of coffee with milk **:** ALESAN

ca·fé brû·lot \¦ka,fā,brü'lō\ *n, pl* **café brûlots** \-lōz\ [AmerF (La.), lit., burned-brandy coffee] **:** a drink prepared with black coffee, cognac that is ignited and allowed to burn briefly, sweetening, and flavoring (as lemon peel, cloves, cinnamon, vanilla)

ca·fe car \ka'fā-, kə-\ *n* **:** a railroad passenger car having a kitchen, usu. in the center, and one end equipped to serve meals or beverages, the other end being fitted for other uses (as coach, lounge, parlor, smoking room)

ca·fé chan·tant \kȧfāshäⁿtäⁿ\ *n, pl* **café chantants** *or* **cafés chantants** \"\ [F, lit., singing café] **:** a café where singers or musicians entertain the patrons **:** CABARET

ca·fé con·cert \kȧfākōⁿser\ *n, pl* **cafés concerts** \"\ [F, lit., concert café] **:** a café offering a program of light music

ca·fé crème \¦ka,fā'krem\ *n, pl* **café crèmes** \-mz\ [F, coffee with cream] **:** SUEDE 3

ca·fe curtain \ka'fā-, kə-\ *n* **:** a plain straight-hanging curtain usu. hung in pairs on a pole by loops or rings and used to cover the lower part of a window or door

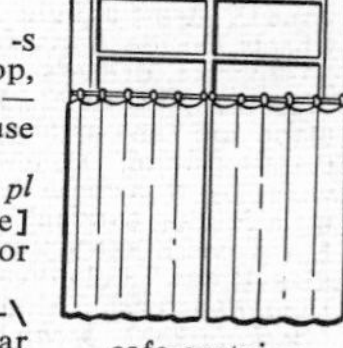
cafe curtains

ca·fe·neh *or* **ca·fe·net** \'kafə,nä\ *n* -s [Turk *kahvane, kahvehane* coffee shop, café, fr. *kahve* coffee + *hane* house — more at COFFEE] **:** a Turkish coffeehouse or inn

ca·fé noir \'ka,fān(ə)'wär, -ár\ *n, pl* **cafés noirs** \"\ [F, black coffee] **1 :** black coffee **:** coffee without milk or cream; *also* **:** DEMITASSE **2 :** MUSK 4

ca·fé society \'ka,fā- *also* ka'fā *or* kə'-\ *n* **:** society of persons who are regular patrons of fashionable cafés

ca·fe·tal \,käfā'täl\ *n, pl* **cafeta·les** \-ä(,)lās\ [Sp, fr. *café* coffee, fr. F & It; F, fr. It *caffè* — more at COFFEE] **:** a Spanish-American coffee plantation

caf·e·te·ria \,kafə'tirēə, -ēr-\ *n* -s *often attrib* [AmerSp *cafeteria* retail coffee store, fr. Sp *café* coffee] **1 :** a self-service restaurant or lunchroom **2 a :** a feeding regime for domestic animals in which varied foodstuffs are kept before them at all times **:** FREE-CHOICE FEEDING **3 :** something so arranged and presented that one can freely make his own choice of individual items ⟨an educational ~⟩ ⟨a ~ questionnaire⟩

cafeteria car *n* **:** a railroad passenger car having facilities for preparing and serving food or beverages cafeteria style

caf·e·to·ri·um \,kafə'tōrēəm\ *n* -s [blend of *cafeteria* and *auditorium*] **:** a large room (as in a school building) designed for use both as a cafeteria and an auditorium

caff \'kaf, 'käf\ *n* -s [ME, fr. OE *ceaf* — more at CHAFF] *dial Brit* **:** [1]CHAFF

caf·fa \'kafə\ *n* -s [Ar dial. *kaffa, kaffīyah* (literary Ar *kūfīyah*), fr. al-*Kufah* Al Kufa, town in Iraq where it was made] **1 :** a rich silk cloth with printed or woven designs popular in the 16th century **2 :** a painted cotton cloth formerly made in India

caf·fè \kä'fā\ *n* -s [It — more at COFFEE] **:** CAFÉ

caf·fe·ate \'kafē,āt\ *n* -s [ISV *caffeic* + *-ate;* prob. orig. formed as F *caféate*] **:** a salt or ester of caffeic acid

caf·fe·ic acid \(')ka¦fēik-, -fē,ēk-\ *n* [*caffeic* ISV *caffe-* (fr. F *café* coffee) + *-ic*] **:** a yellow crystalline acid $C_6H_3(OH)_2$-$CH{=}CHCOOH$ obtained by hydrolysis of chlorogenic acid; 3,4-dihydroxy-cinnamic acid

caf·feine \(')ka¦fēn\ *also* 'kafēən\ *also* **caf·fei·na** \ka'fēnə; ,kafē'ēnə, -'ī-\ *n* -s [G *kaffein* (now usu. *koffein*, after NL *coffea*), fr. *kaffee* coffee (fr. F *café*) + *-in* -ine — more at CAFÉ] **:** a feebly basic bitter crystalline compound $C_8H_{10}N_4O_2$ that occurs in coffee, tea, maté, guarana, and kola nuts, is synthesized by methylation of theobromine, and acts as a stimulant of the central nervous system and as a diuretic; 1,3,7-trimethyl-xanthine

caffeine citrate *n* **:** CITRATED CAFFEINE

caf·fein·ic \(')ka¦fēnik, ¦kafē¦inik\ *adj* **:** of or containing caffeine

caf·fe·ol \'kafē,ōl, -ōl\ *also* **caf·fe·one** \-ē,ōn\ *n* -s [G *kaffeol*, fr. *kaffee* coffee + *-ol*] **:** a fragrant oil produced by roasting coffee

caffer *or* **caffre** *usu cap, var of* KAFFIR

caf·fe·tan·nin \¦kafə¦tanən, -fē-\ *or* **caf·fe·tan·nic acid** \-anik-\ *n* -s [*caffetannin* fr. *caffeic* + *tannin; caffetannic* fr. *caffetannin* + *-ic*] **:** a crystalline substance obtained from coffee berries and other plant products and consisting chiefly of chlorogenic acid

caf·fle \'kafəl\ *vi* -ED/-ING/-S [alter. of [1]*cavil*] *dial Eng* **:** WRANGLE, ARGUE

caffre cat *or* **caffer cat** *usu cap 1st C, var of* KAFFIR CAT

ca·fi·la \'kafələ, 'kä-\ *n* -s [Ar *qāfilah*] **:** a company of travelers esp. in Arabia, Iran, or the Indian subcontinent

caf·tan \'kaftən, -,tan, kaf'tan\ *n* -s [Russ *kaftan*, fr. Turk, fr. Per *qaftān*] **:** an ankle-length coatlike garment, usu. of cotton or silk, often striped, with very long sleeves and a sash fastening, common throughout the Levant

ca·fu·so \kə'fü(,)zō\ *n* -s [Pg, perh. of African origin; akin to Hausa *ka³fur³chi¹* heathenism, *ka³fu¹ri²* heathen] *in Brazil* **:** ZAMBO

[1]**cag** \'kag, -aa(ə)-,-ai-\ *dial var of* KEG 1

[2]**cag** \"\ *vt* **cagged; cagged; cagging; cags** [origin unknown] *dial Eng* **:** OFFEND, INSULT

cá·ga·ba \'kägəbə\ *n, pl* **cágaba** *or* **cágabas** *usu cap* [Sp, of AmerInd origin] **1 a :** a Chibcha people of northern Colombia **b :** a member of such people **2 :** the language of the Cágaba people

ca·ga·yan \,kägə¦yän, -gē¦än\ *n, pl* **cagayan** *or* **cagayans** *usu cap* [Sp *cagayán*, fr. Río Grande del *Cagayán*, river in northern Luzon, Philippines, on the banks of which they reside] **:** IBANAG

[1]**cage** \'kāj\ *n* -s [ME, fr. OF, fr. L *cavea* cavity, cage, fr. *cavus* hollow — more at CAVE] **1 :** a box or enclosure having some openwork (as of wires or bars) esp. for confining or carrying birds or animals **2 a :** a barred cell for confining prisoners **b :** a strongly fenced area for prisoners of war **3 :** a framework serving as support ⟨the ~ of a staircase⟩ ⟨the steel ~ of a skyscraper⟩ ⟨the ~ of a field gun⟩ **4 :** a small enclosing or sheltering structure designed (as by the use of openwork, glass, or windows) to admit air or light or to allow visibility or accessibility from outside ⟨bank teller's ~⟩; as **a :** the car of an elevator **b :** a chapel or chantry in a church formed by partitioning off a section with a screen of open tracery **5 :** a drum on which the rope is wound in a hoisting whim **6 :** an enclosing or containing screen or strainer; as **a :** a wirework strainer on an intake pipe **b :** a wire shield enclosing electrical apparatus **c :** a revolving drum of wire netting for shaking dust out of furs or cotton **7 a :** a frame to limit the motion of a loose part (as of a ball valve) **b :** the frame for holding bearings in place around a shaft journal — see ROLLER BEARING illustration **8 :** CADGE **9 a :** a movable screen placed behind home plate to stop baseballs during batting practice **b :** a goal structure consisting of goalposts or a goal frame with a net attached (as in ice hockey) **c :** a basketball basket **10 :** a large building with unobstructed area for practicing outdoor sports and often adapted for indoor events — compare FIELD HOUSE

[2]**cage** \"\ *vt* -ED/-ING/-S **1 :** to place in a cage **:** confine, shut in, keep in or as if in a cage **:** enclose in or with a strong structure to prevent escape ⟨~ circus animals⟩ ⟨*caged* birds⟩ **2 :** to put (as a puck) into a cage and score a goal **3 :** to inactivate (a gyroscopic instrument) esp. in an airplane (as by means of a control knob) **syn** see ENCLOSE

cage antenna *n* **:** an antenna whose conductor consists of parallel wires stretched between two hoops and arranged as elements of the curved surface of a cylinder

cage bird *n* **:** a bird adaptable to being kept in a cage

cage construction *n* **:** SKELETON CONSTRUCTION

caged *adj* **1 :** confined in or as if in a cage **2 :** like a cage or prison ⟨the ~ cloister —Shak.⟩

cage·ful \'kāj,fu̇l\ *n* -s **:** the number held in a cage

cage·less \-jlə̇s\ *adj* **:** being without a cage

cage·ling \'kājliŋ, -ēŋ\ *n* -s [*cage* + *-ling*] **:** a caged bird

cage·man \'kājmən, -,man, -,aa(ə)n\ *n, pl* **cagemen 1 :** CAGER 1a **2 :** HOISTMAN **3 :** a basketball player

cage mast *n* **:** BASKET MAST

cag·er \'kājə(r)\ *n* -s [[1]*cage* + *-er*] **1 a :** a workman who loads and unloads cages and gives hoisting signals — called also *cageman, cage tender, onsetter, skip tender* **b :** a mechanical apparatus for pushing cars on or off a cage **2 :** a basketball player

cage tender *n* **:** CAGER 1a

cagework \'‑,‑\ *n* **:** OPENWORK

[1]**ca·gey** *also* **ca·gy** \'kājē, -i\ *adj* **cagier; cagiest** [origin unknown] **1 :** reluctant to act or speak in a direct or open manner **:** hesitant about committing oneself ⟨the speaker was ~ about giving a ruling —B.A.Young⟩ **2 :** wary of being taken advantage of or deceived ⟨a ~ buyer⟩ **:** SHREWD ⟨a ~ lawyer⟩ **:** FORESIGHTED — **ca·gey·ness** *or* **ca·gi·ness** *n* -ES

[2]**cagey** \"\ *dial var of* CADGY

cagged *past of* CAG

cagging *pres part of* CAG

ca·gi·ly \'kājəlē, -i\ *adv* **:** in a cagey manner

ca·glia·ri \'kälyərē\ *adj, usu cap* [fr. *Cagliari*, Sardinia, Italy] **:** of or from the city of Cagliari, Sardinia, Italy **:** of the style or kind prevalent in Cagliari

cag·mag \'kag,mag\ *n* -s [origin unknown] **1** *dial Eng* **:** inferior meat **2** *dial Eng* **:** something inferior

ca·gou·lard \¦kagü¦lär\ *n, pl* **cagoulards** \-är(z)\ *usu cap* [F, fr. *cagoule* hood, cowl (fr. LL *cuculla* monk's cowl) + *-ard* — more at COWL] **:** a member of a secret reactionary revolutionary French organization suppressed in 1937-38

cags *pl of* CAG, *pres 3d sing of* CAG

ca·hens·ly·ism \kə'henzlē,izəm, -n(t)sl-\ *n* -s *usu cap* [Peter P. *Cahensly fl* 1891 Ger. parliamentarian who proposed the plan + E *-ism*] **:** a movement to divide the foreign-born Roman Catholic population of the U.S. for ecclesiastical purposes according to European nationalities and to appoint bishops and priests of the same national origin and language as the majority of the members of a diocese or parish

ca·hier \ka'yā, kä-,kä-\ *n* -s [F, signature (section of a bound book), written statement presented to the sovereign by a representative body of the state, fr. L *quaterni* four each, by fours — more at QUIRE] **1 :** a report or memorial embodying resolutions or instructions concerning policy esp. of a parliamentary body; *specif* **:** one of the memorials prepared by the French States-General before the revolution of 1789 **2 :** a number of sheets of paper put together for binding or bound loosely together to form a notebook or pamphlet

ca·hin·ca root \kə'hiŋkə-\ *also* **ca·in·ca root** \kə'ī-\ *n* [Pg *cahinca, cainca*, fr. Tupi] **1 :** the root of a tropical American shrub (*Chiococca alba*) used medicinally as a purgative and diuretic **2 :** the root of a So. American shrub (*Chiococca anguifuga*) used as an antidote for snake poison

ca·hin·nio \kə'hinē,ō\ *n, pl* **cahinnio** *or* **cahinnios** *usu cap* [Caddo] **1 :** a Caddoan people of the Kadohadacho confederacy **2 :** a member of the Cahinnio people

ca·hi·ta \kə'hēd·ə\ *n, pl* **cahita** *or* **cahitas** *usu cap* [Sp, prob. fr. *Cahita*, lit., nothing] **1 a :** a Taracahitian people of southwestern Sonora and northwestern Sinaloa, Mexico, the only survivors being the Mayo and Yaqui **b :** a member of such people **2 :** the language of the Cahita people

cahn·ite \'kä,nīt\ *n* -s [Lazard *Cahn* †1940 Am. mineral collector who first recognized it + E *-ite*] **:** a mineral $Ca_2B(OH)_4(AsO_4)$ consisting of hydrous calcium boroarsenate occurring in white sphenoidal crystals

ca·hoot \kə'hüt\ *n* -s [perh. fr. F *cahute* hut, cabin, modif. (prob. influenced by *cabane* hut, cabin) of *hutte* — more at CABIN, HUT] **1 :** PARTNERSHIP — usu. pl. ⟨in ~s with the devil⟩ ⟨go into ~s with someone⟩ **2 :** COLLUSION, CONNIVANCE **:** secret agreement — usu. pl. ⟨officials in ~s with the underworld⟩

ca·hot \kä(h)ō\ *n* -s [F] *chiefly Canad* **:** THANK-YOU-MA'AM

ca·houn palm \kə'hün-\ *n* [by alter.] **:** COHUNE

ca·how *or* **co·how** *or* **co·howe** \kə'hau̇\ *n* -s [imit.] **:** a brown-and-white earth-burrowing nocturnal edible petrel (*Pterodroma cahow*) formerly abundant in Bermuda but now nearly extinct

ca·hua·pa·na \,käwə'pänə\ *n, pl* **cahuapana** *or* **cahuapanas** *usu cap* [Sp *cahuapana, caguapana*, of AmerInd origin] **1 a :** a people of northern Peru **b :** a member of such people **2 :** the language of the Cahuapana people constituting with Chébero the Cahuapana language family

ca·hui·lla \kə'wēə\ *n, pl* **cahuilla** *or* **cahuillas** *usu cap* [Sp, of AmerInd origin] **1 a :** a Shoshonean people of southeastern California **b :** a member of such people **2 :** the language of the Cahuilla people

cai·a·ra·ra \,kīə'rärə\ *n* -s [Pg, fr. Tupi & Guarani, fr. *caí* monkey + *arára* macaw] **:** a large-headed arboreal monkey (*Cebus gracilis*) of the Amazon valley

ca·id *or* **qa·id** \kä'ēth, 'kīth\ *n* -s [Sp *caíd, caid*, fr. Ar *qā'id*] **1 :** ALCAIDE **2 a :** a Muslim local administrator, judge, and tax collector in Algeria, Morocco, and Tunisia **b :** a chief esp. of the Berber tribal communities of the Atlas region

cail·ce·dra \kīl'sēdrə, -'e-\ *n* -s [origin unknown] **:** an African mahogany (*Khaya senegalensis*)

cai·lin \(')kä¦lēn\ *Irish var of* COLLEEN

cail·leach *also* **cail·liach** \'käl,yək, 'käl,(y)ək\ *n* -s [ScGael & IrGael *cailleach*, fr. OIr *caillech* nun, fr. *caille* veil, fr. L *pallium* cloak — more at PALL] *Irish & Scot* **:** an old woman **:** CRONE, HAG

cai·man \kā'man, kī-, -maa(ə)n, '‑,‑, 'kāmən\ *n* [Sp *caimán* caiman, alligator, prob. fr. 16th cent. Carib *caymán*] **1** *or* **cay·man** \"\ *n* -s **:** any of several Central and So. American crocodilians fundamentally similar to alligators but differing in ventral armor and often superficially resembling crocodiles — called also *jacare;* see SPECTACLED CAIMAN **2** *cap* [NL, fr. Sp *caimán*] **:** a genus of crocodilians comprising most of the caimans

cai·mi·til·lo \,kīmə'tē(,)(y)ō\ *n* -s [Sp, dim. of *caimito*] **:** a tropical American timber tree (*Chrysophyllum oliviforme*) with dark hard heavy wood — called also *satinleaf*

cai·mi·to \kī'mēd·(,)ō, -ē,tō\ *n* -s [Sp, fr. Taino *caymito*] **:** STAR APPLE

[1]**cain** \'kān\ *n* -s *usu cap* [after *Cain*, the eldest son of Adam and the first murderer, described in Gen 4, fr. Heb *Qayin*] **:** TROUBLE, DISTURBANCE, UPROAR — used chiefly in the phrase *raise Cain* ⟨the children were raising *Cain* upstairs⟩ ⟨if I'm late again the boss will raise *Cain*⟩

[2]**cain** \"\ *n* -s [ME *cane*, fr. ScGael *cāin* rent; akin to MIr *cāin* law, prob. fr. LL *canon* decree, tribute, fr. L, model — more at CANON] *Scot* **:** animals or produce of the land paid as a rent in kind

cainca root *var of* CAHINCA ROOT

cain-colored \'kān,-\ *adj, usu cap 1st C* [after *Cain*, son of Adam; fr. the supposed red color of Cain's hair] **:** reddish yellow

-caine \¦kān\ *n comb form* -s [G *-kain*, fr. *kokain* cocaine] **:** synthetic alkaloid anesthetic ⟨*dibucaine*⟩ ⟨*procaine*⟩

cain·gang \'kīn,gaŋ\ *n, pl* **caingang** *or* **caingangs** *usu cap* [Pg, of AmerInd origin] **1 a :** the non-Guarani-Indian peoples of southern Brazil comprising a number of distinct but related groups **b :** a member of any such people **2 a :** a language of any Caingang people **b :** a language family of the Ge stock comprising the several Caingang languages

caingin *or* **caiñgin** [Sp, fr. Tag *kaingin*] *var of* KAINGIN

cain·gi·ne·ro *also* **caiñ·gi·ne·ro** \,kīnjə'ne(,)rō\ *n* -s [Sp, fr. *caingin* + *-ero* -er] *Philippines* **:** one that makes and cultivates a kaingin

cain·gua \'kīŋ,gwä\ *n, pl* **caingua** *or* **cainguas** *usu cap* [Sp, fr. a native name, lit., inhabitants of the forest] **:** CAYUÁ

ca'ing whale *var of* CAAING WHALE

cain·ite \'kā,nīt\ *n* -s *usu cap* [*Cain*, son of Adam + E *-ite* — more at CAIN] **1 :** a descendant of Cain, one of the sons of Adam **2** [LL *Cainita*, fr. *Cain* + L *-ita* -ite] **:** a member of a gnostic sect that regarded the Old Testament as an account of the work of a demiurge and a distortion of the true nature of such men as Cain, whom they honored

cain·it·ic \(')kā¦nid·ik\ *adj, usu cap* **:** of or relating to the Cainites

cainozoic *usu cap, var of* CENOZOIC

cains *pl of* CAIN

cai·po·to·ra·de \,kīpətə'rädē\ *n, usu cap* [Sp *caipatorade, caipotade*, of AmerInd origin] **:** a dialect of the Zamuco people

[1]**ca·ique** \kä'ēk, kī'ēk, 'kīk\ *n* -s [alter. (influenced by F *caïque*, fr. Turk *kayık*) of earlier *caik*, fr. Turk *kayık*] **1 :** a light skiff used on the Bosporus **2 :** a Levantine sailing vessel

[2]**ca·i·que** \kä'ē(,)kä, kī'-, -ēkə\ *n, pl* **ca·i·ques** \-äz, -əz\ *or* **ca·i·que·nes** \,kä·ē'kä(,)nās, kī'k-\ [Sp or Pg] **:** any of various small stocky often brightly colored parrots native to northeastern So. America

ca·ique·jee \kä'ēk(,)jē, kī'ē-, 'kīk-(\ *n* -s [alter. (influenced by *caique*) of earlier *caikjee*, fr. Turk *kayıkçı* boatman, fr. *kayık* boat + *-cı* (occupational suffix)] **:** a rower of a caique

[1]**caird** \'kā(ə)rd\ *Scot var of* CARD

[2]**caird** \"\ *n* -s [ScGael *ceard* tinker; akin to OIr *cerd* smith, poet, W *cerdd* music, Gk *kerdos* profit, and perh. to OE *horsc* wise, OHG *horsk* quick, ON *horskr* wise] **1** *Scot* **:** a traveling tinker **2** *Scot* **:** TRAMP, VAGRANT, GYPSY

[1]**cai·rene** \'kī,rēn, ‑'‑\ *adj, usu cap* [*Cairo*, Egypt + E *-ene* (as in *Nazarene*)] **:** of or relating to Cairo, Egypt

[2]**cairene** \"\ *n* -s *cap* **:** a native or resident of Cairo, esp. Cairo, Egypt

cairn \'ka(a)(ə)rn, 'ke(ə)rn\ *also* **carn** \'kärn\ *n* -s [ME *carne*, fr. ScGael *carn;* akin to OIr & W *carn* cairn and perh. to OE *heard* hard — more at HARD] **:** a rounded or pyramidal heap of stones made as a monument or memorial or as a landmark or trail marker for explorers, surveyors, or hikers — **cairned** \-nd\ *adj*

cairn·gorm \‑,gȯrm\ *or* **cairngorm stone** *n* -s [fr. *Cairngorm*, mountain in Scotland, its locality] **:** a yellow or smoky-brown variety of crystalline quartz — called also *smoky quartz*

cairn's ash *or* **cairn's hickory** \'ka(a)(ə)rnz-, 'ke(ə)rnz-\ *n, usu cap C* [prob. fr. *Cairns*, seaport in Queensland, Australia] **:** QUEENSLAND HICKORY

cairn terrier *n* [so called fr. its use in hunting among cairns] **:** a small compactly built hard-coated terrier of a breed originating in Scotland

cai·ro \'kī(,)rō\ *adj, usu cap* [fr. *Cairo*, Egypt] **:** of or from Cairo, the capital of Egypt **:** of the kind or style prevalent in Cairo **:** CAIRENE

cais·son \'kā,sän, -,sᵊn, *Brit often* kə'sün\ *n* -s [F, aug. of *caisse* box, fr. OProv *caisa*, fr. L *capsa* small box — more at CASE (box)] **1 a :** a chest packed with explosives so that it can be laid in the way of an enemy and exploded on his approach **b :** a chest to hold ammunition **c :** a 2-wheeled vehicle for artillery ammunition attachable to a horse-drawn limber for marching **2 a :** a watertight chamber used in construction work under water (as in a harbor or river) or as a foundation — see BOX CAISSON, OPEN CAISSON, PNEUMATIC CAISSON; compare COFFERDAM **b :** a large cistern used to float forward materials of construction during the work of extending a canal over lower ground **c :** a float for raising a sunken vessel **:** CAMEL **d :** a hollow floating box or a boat used as a floodgate for a dock or basin **3 :** COFFER 4a

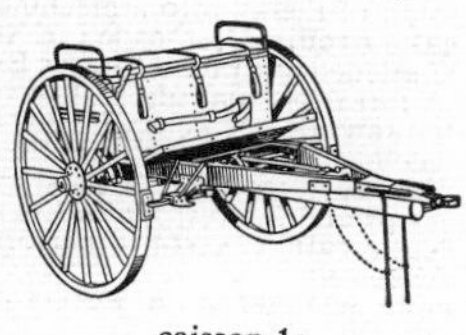
caisson 1c

caisson crib *n* **:** a platform of heavy timbers on which rests the caisson used in construction of an underwater pier or foundation

caisson disease *n* **:** a sickness induced by too rapid decrease in air pressure after a stay in compressed atmosphere (as in a caisson, diving bell, or tunnel) and caused by nitrogen bubbles forming in blood and tissues — called also *bends, chokes, staggers;* see AEROEMBOLISM

caith·ness \'kāth,nes\ *adj, usu cap* [fr. county of *Caithness*, Scotland] **:** of or from the county of Caithness, Scotland **:** of the kind or style prevalent in Caithness

[1]**cai·tiff** \'kād·əf, -ātəf\ *adj* [ME *caitif*, fr. ONF, captive, miserable, vile, fr. L *captivus* captive — more at CAPTIVE] **1** *obs* **:** CAPTIVE **2 :** BASE **:** wicked and mean **:** COWARDLY, DESPICABLE

[2]**caitiff** \"\ *n* -s [ME *caitif*, fr. *caitif*, adj.] **1** *obs* **a :** CAPTIVE, PRISONER **b :** a wretched or unfortunate man **2 :** a base despicable person **:** a mean and wicked man

cai·xi·nha \kī'shēnyə\ *n* -s [Pg, fr. dim. of *caixa* box, fr. L *capsa* — more at CASE (box)] **:** a box rattle used in Brazilian dance orchestras

[1]**cajan** *or* **cajang** *var of* CADJAN

[2]**cajan** *cap, var of* CAJUN

[3]**ca·jan** \'kājən, -,jän\ [NL] *syn of* CAJANUS

ca·ja·nus \kə'jānəs, -än-\ *n, cap* [NL, prob. fr. *Cajan*, fr. Malay *kachang* bean, pea] **:** a genus of woody herbs of the family Leguminosae including solely the pigeon pea

caj·e·put \'kajəpət, -,pu̇t\ *n* -s [Malay *kayu puteh*, fr. *kayu* wood, tree + *puteh* white] **1** *or* **caj·a·put** *or* **caj·u·put** \'kajə-\ **:** an East Indian tree (*Melaleuca leucadendron*) that yields a pungent oil — called also *paperbark* **2 :** CALIFORNIA LAUREL

caj·e·put·ene *or* **caj·u·put·ene** \-,pə,tēn\ *n* -s [ISV *cajeput* or *cajuput* (*Melaleuca leucadendron*) + *-ene*] **:** DIPENTENE

cajeput oil *or* **cajuput oil** *n* **:** a pungent essential oil obtained from cajeput and certain other plants of the genus *Melaleuca* and used chiefly as a local application in skin disease and as a stimulating expectorant

caj·e·put·ol *or* **caj·u·put·ol** \-,pə,tōl, -ōl\ *n* -s [*cajeput* or *cajuput* (*Melaleuca leucadendron*) + *-ol*] **:** CINEOLE

ca·ji \kə'hē, kä-\ *n* -s [AmerSp *cají*] **:** SCHOOLMASTER 3

ca·jole \kə'jōl\ *vt* -ED/-ING/-S [F *cajoler* to chatter like a jay, cajole, prob. blend of MF *gaioler* to chatter like a jay in a cage (fr. ONF *gaiole* birdcage, fr. LL *caveola*, dim. of L *cavea* cage) and MF *cage* — more at CAGE] **1 a :** to persuade with deliberate flattery esp. in the face of reasonable objection or reluctance **:** COAX ⟨lulled into . . . repose or *cajoled* into specious reconciliation —Havelock Ellis⟩ **b :** to obtain (an object or a favor) from someone by cajoling **:** WHEEDLE ⟨~ an autograph from him —H.T.Moore⟩ **2 :** to deceive with soothing words or false promises ⟨*cajoled* himself with thoughts of escape —Robertson Davies⟩

ca·jole·ment \-mənt\ *n* -s **:** CAJOLERY **:** a means of cajoling

ca·jol·ery \-l(ə)rē, -i\ *n* -ES [F *cajolerie*, fr. *cajoler* + *-ie* -y] **:** the act or practice of cajoling **:** use of delusive enticements

ca·jol·ing·ly *adv* **:** in a cajoling manner

ca·jón \kə'hōn\ *n, pl* **cajo·nes** \-ō(,)nās, -ōnēz\ [AmerSp, fr. Sp, big box, aug. of *caja* box, fr. L *capsa* — more at CASE] **1** *Southwest* **:** a narrow gorge with vertical sides **:** BOX CANYON **2** [Sp] **:** a Spanish and Spanish-American method of construction in which walls are made of mud rammed into a narrow boxlike frame and allowed to harden

[1]**ca·jun** *also* **ca·jan** *or* **ca·jin** \'kājən\ *n* -s *usu cap* [alter. of *Acadian* (native of Acadia)] **1 :** ACADIAN 2 — sometimes taken to be offensive **2** *usu cajan* **:** one of a people of mixed white, Indian, and Negro ancestry in southwest Alabama and adjoining sections of Mississippi

[2]**ca·jun** \kə'hün\ *n* -s [AmerSp *cajún, cajum*, fr. Maya] **:** a West Indian fiber plant (*Furcraea cubensis*)

cajuput *var of* CAJEPUT

cajuputene *var of* CAJEPUTENE

cajuputol *var of* CAJEPUTOL

cak·chi·quel *also* **cak·chi·kel** \¦käkchə¦kel\ *n, pl* **cakchiquel** *or* **cakchiquels** *usu cap* [Sp *cakchiquel, cachiquel*, of AmerInd origin] **1 a :** an Indian people of south central Guatemala **b :** a member of such people **2 :** a Mayan language of the Cakchiquel people

[1]**cake** \'kāk\ *n* -s [ME, fr. ON *kaka;* akin to OE *cœcil* small cake, OHG *kuocho* cake, and prob. to Lith *guoge* cabbage-head, head] **1 a :** any of a variety of breads usu. small in size and typically round and flat in shape: as (1) **:** a flat mass of dough, sometimes unleavened, shaped round or oval by hand, and baked with a crust on both sides (2) *Scot* **:** a thin hard-baked bread of oatmeal (3) **:** a thin flat bread (as a griddlecake) made from batter fried on a griddle or other utensil (4) **:** biscuit dough enriched with shortening and eggs and baked and served hot with fruit or meat (as shortcake) **b :** any of a variety of fancy sweetened breads: as (1) **:** a loaf baked in a variety of forms and sizes, made from a sweet dough or batter of flour and other ingredients, and often coated with an icing (2) **:** a usu. small mass of firm dough variously shaped, leavened with yeast or baking powder, and cooked in deep fat (as a friedcake) **c :** a flattened usu. round mass of food (as potato, hashed meat, fish) baked or fried **2 a :** a block of compacted or congealed matter ⟨a ~ of soap⟩ ⟨an ice ~⟩ **b :** a hard or brittle layer or deposit **:** CRUST ⟨the ~ formed in a pipe⟩ **c :** a hollow cylinder of yarn produced by the spinning process for viscose rayon **3 :** OIL CAKE, FILTER CAKE

[2]**cake** \"\ *vb* -ED/-ING/-S *vt* **:** to cover (a surface) with a crust **:** ENCRUST ⟨his jacket was *caked* with dust⟩ **:** fill (a space) with a packed mass ⟨*caked* fingernails⟩ ~ *vi* **1 :** to form or harden into a mass ⟨coral is formed by the *caking* of minute shells into stone⟩ — see CAKED BREAST **2 :** to fuse (as of coal) into a pasty mass when heated

cakebread \'‑,‑\ *n, now dial Brit* **:** bread made in cakes or of a quality like cake

cake cooler *n* **:** a wire-mesh rack on which cakes or cookies are placed to cool

caked breast *n* **:** a localized hardening in one or more segments of a lactating breast caused by accumulation of blood in dilated veins and milk in obstructed ducts — compare BLUE BAG, BOVINE MASTITIS

caked udder *n* **:** BOVINE MASTITIS

cake–eater \'=,==\ *n, slang* **:** an effeminate party-going dandy **:** TEA HOUND

cake flour *n* **:** flour ground from soft wheat to a highly refined texture

cake former *n* **:** an operator of a machine for wrapping crushed and steam-cooked cottonseed kernels and shaping into cloth-wrapped cakes prior to the expression of oil

cake makeup *n* **:** a tinted cosmetic base usu. in semimoist cake form used as a foundation for face powder

cake mill *n* **:** a machine for crushing stock-feed cake

cake puller *n* **:** a worker who pulls pressed cottonseed cakes from the press and trucks them to a cake stripper — called also *knocker*

cakes and ale *n* **:** the good things of life **:** PLEASURE, ENJOYMENT ⟨dost thou think because thou art virtuous, there shall be no more *cakes and ale* —Shak.⟩

cake stripper *n* **:** one that feeds cottonseed cakes after expression of the oil into a machine that strips off the press cloth

cake urchin *n* [so called fr. the disklike shape] **:** a strongly flattened sea urchin (order Exocycloida): as **a :** SAND DOLLAR **b :** KEYHOLE URCHIN

[1]**cakewalk** \'=,=\ *n* **1 :** an American Negro entertainment having a cake as the prize for the most accomplished steps and figures in walking **2 :** a stage dance developed from walking steps and figures; *typically* **:** a high prance with backward tilt

[2]**cakewalk** \"\ *vi* **:** to perform, dance, or walk in or as if in a cakewalk

cake wringer *n* **:** a worker who centrifuges cakes of rayon thread

cak·ey *or* **caky** \'kākē, -i\ *adj* **cakier; cakiest :** having or tending to form crusts or lumps ⟨~ face powder⟩

cak·i·le \'kakə,lē\ *n, cap* [NL, fr. Ar *qāqulla*] **:** a small genus of annual succulent herbs (family Cruciferae) found along sandy shores of No. America and Europe and having opposite fleshy leaves and cruciform flowers — see SEA ROCKET

caking *pres part of* CAKE

cakra *var of* CHAKRA

cal \'kal\ *n* -s [prob. fr. OCorn *cal* cunning, sly, fr. L *callidus*; fr. its presence in tin ore, considered by the miners an impish intrusion of a worthless substance — more at CALLIDITY] *Cornwall* **:** WOLFRAMITE

cal *abbr* **1** calando **2** calendar **3** calends **4** caliber; calibrate **5** calorie

[1]**ca·la** \kə'lä\ *n* -s [of African origin; akin to Vai *ko¹lo³* uncooked rice, Bambara *kala* stalk of a cereal] **:** a Creole fried cake made mainly of rice

[2]**cala** \'kalə\ *or* **cali** \'kalē\ *n* -s [short for *California ham*] **:** PICNIC HAM

ca·la·ba \kə'läbə\ *n* -s [Sp, of Cariban origin; akin to Galibi *calaba, carapa* oil, Calinago *kalapa*] **:** SANTA MARIA TREE

cal·a·bar bean \'kalə,bär-, -bà-\ *n, usu cap C* [fr. *Calabar*, Nigeria] **:** the dark brown highly poisonous seed of a tropical African woody vine (*Physostigma venenosum*) of the family Leguminosae serving as a source of physostigmine and as an ordeal bean in native witchcraft trials

calabar potto *n, usu cap C* **:** ANGWANTIBO

calabar swelling *n, usu cap C* **:** a transient subcutaneous swelling marking the migratory course of the adult filarial eye worm through the tissues — compare LOAIASIS

[1]**cal·a·bash** \'kalə,bash, -aa(ə)-,-ai-\ *n* -ES *often attrib* [F & Sp; F *calebasse* gourd, fr. Sp *calabaza*, prob. fr. Ar *qar'ah yābisah* dry gourd, fr. *qar'ah* gourd + *yābisah* dry] **1 :** GOURD; *esp* **:** the common bottle gourd **2 a** *or* **calabash tree :** a tropical American tree (*Crescentia cujete*) **b :** the hard globose fruit of the calabash **3 a :** a utensil (as a dipper, bottle, kettle) made from the shell of a calabash **b :** a noise-making device made from the calabash gourd **4 :** BAOBAB **5 :** MEDAL BRONZE **6 :** a usu. curved-stemmed tobacco pipe made from the calabash gourd

[2]**calabash** \"\ *adj* [perh. so called fr. the fact that close friends ate from the same calabash] *Hawaii* **:** related by ties of affection rather than blood

calabash curare *n* **:** curare obtained from a So. American woody vine (*Strychnos toxifera*)

calabash nutmeg *n* **1 :** the fruit of a tropical shrub (*Monodora myristica*) of the family Annonaceae about the size of an orange and containing many aromatic seeds that are used like nutmegs **2 :** the shrub that bears calabash nutmegs

ca·la·ba·za \,kalə'bäzə, -sə\ *n* -s [Sp, gourd] **:** CALABASH

cal·a·ba·zi·lla \,kaləbə'zē(y)ə\ *or* **cal·a·ba·ci·lla** \-'sē-\ *n* -s [MexSp *calabacilla*, fr. Sp, squirting cucumber, dim. of *calabaza*] *Southwest* **:** PRAIRIE GOURD

cal·a·ber *or* **cal·a·bar** \'kaləbə(r)\ *n* -s [ME *calabre*, fr. MF, fr. *Calabria*, region in Italy] **1 :** a deep-brown Calabrian squirrel fur **2 :** the gray fur of a Siberian squirrel

cal·a·boose \'kalə,büs\ *n* -s [modif. of Sp *calabozo* dungeon] *dial* **:** JAIL; *esp* **:** the local jail

cal·a·bo·zo \,kalə'bō(,)zō, -ōzə\ *or* **cal·a·bo·za** \-ōzə\ *n* -s [Sp] *Southwest* **:** JAIL

cal·a·bra·sel·la \,kalabrə'zelə, -'s-\ *n* -s [It *calabresella*, fr. *calabrese* Calabrian, fr. *Calabria* + *-ese*] **:** an Italian card game for three players played with a 40-card pack

cal·a·bre·se \,kalə'brāzē, -sē\ *n* -s [It, Calabrian] **:** a broccoli (*Brassica oleracea italica*) having a greenish terminal head and similar lateral heads that develop after the terminal one is cut

[1]**ca·la·bri·an** \kə'lābrēən, -'ä-\ *also* **cal·a·brese** \¦kalə¦brēz, -ēs\ *adj, usu cap* [*Calabrian* fr. *Calabria*, region in Italy + E *-an; Calabrese* fr. It *Calabrese*, fr. *Calabria* + It *-ese*] **:** of or relating to Calabria, Italy

[2]**calabrian** \"\ *also* **calabrese** \"\ *n, pl* **calabrians** *also* **calabrese** *cap* **:** a native or inhabitant of Calabria, Italy

calabrian manna *n* -s *usu cap C* **:** MANNA 2

cal·a·bur tree \'kalə,bu̇(ə)r-, -(,)bər-\ *n* [NL *calabura*] **:** a tropical American shrub or small tree (*Muntingia calabura*) of the family Elaeocarpaceae whose bark yields a silky fiber used in cordage and whose wood is valuable for staves — called also *capulin, Jamaica cherry, silkwood*

ca·la·di·um \kə'lādēəm\ *n* [NL, fr. Malay *kĕladi*, any of a number of aroids including taro] **1** *cap* **:** a small genus of tropical American plants (family Araceae) with variously colored usu. peltate arrow-shaped leaves and a boat-shaped spathe **2** -s **:** any plant of the genus *Caladium* (as *C. bicolor* often cultivated as a pot plant for its foliage)

calaite *n* -s [F *calaïte* (now usu. *callaïte*), fr. L *callaïs* (fr. Gk *kalaïs, kallaïs*) + F *-ite*] *obs* **:** TURQUOISE

cal·a·lu \¦kalə¦lü\ *n* -s [AmerSp *calalú*] **:** a tropical American plant (*Xanthosoma hastifolium*) whose leaf is used as a vegetable in the West Indies

calam- *or* **calami-** *or* **calamo-** *comb form* [NL, fr. Gk *kalam-, kalamo-*, fr. *kalamos* reed — more at HAULM] **:** reed **:** reedlike ⟨*Calam*agrostis⟩ ⟨*calami*ferous⟩ ⟨*Calamo*dendron⟩

cal·a·ma·gros·tis \,kaləmə'grästəs\ *n, cap* [NL, fr. *calam-* + L *agrostis* couch grass, fr. Gk *agrōstis* dog's-tooth grass, perh. fr. *agros* field — more at ACRE] **:** a genus of tall mostly perennial grasses having single-flowered spikelets, the lemmas entire, and the rachillae usu. extending beyond the palet into a hairy bristle or stalk — see BLUEJOINT 1

cal·a·man·co *also* **cal·i·man·co** \,kalə'maŋ(,)kō\ *n* -ES *often attrib* [perh. modif. of Sp *calamaco*, modif. of LL *calamaucus* felt cap, skullcap] **1 :** a glossy woolen fabric of satin weave with striped or checkered designs manufactured from the 16th to the 19th centuries **2 :** a garment made of calamanco

cal·a·man·der \'kalə,mandə(r), ,==¦==\ *or* **calamander wood** *n* -s [prob. fr. D *kalamander-* (in *kalamanderhout* calamander wood), perh. modif. of *Coromandel* (in *Coromandel Coast*, southeast India)] **:** the wood of any of several East Indian trees of the genus *Diospyros* (esp. *D. quaesita*) colored a mottled hazel brown striped with black and used in furniture manufacturing

cal·a·mar·i·a·ce·ae \,kalə,merē'āsē,ē\ *n pl, cap* [NL, fr. L *calamarius* of a writing reed (fr. *calamus* reed, fr. Gk *kalamos*) + NL *-aceae* — more at HAULM] **:** a family of Paleozoic horsetaillike pteridophytes having *Calamites* as its principal genus and being variously considered as belonging to the order Equisetales or in some classifications as coextensive with a separate order — **cal·a·mar·i·a·ceous** \¦==,==¦āshəs\ *adj* — **cal·a·mar·i·an** \,==¦merēən\ *n* -s

cal·a·mary \'kalə,merē\ *or* **cal·a·mar** \-,mär\ *n, pl* **calamaries** *or* **calamars** [L *calamarius*] **:** SQUID; *esp* **:** GIANT SQUID

cal·am·bac \'kaləm,bak\ *or* **cal·am·bour** \-,bu̇(ə)r\ *n* -s [F, fr. Pg *calambac, calambuco*, fr. Malay *kĕlĕmbak, kĕlambak*] **:** AGALLOCH

calami *pl of* CALAMUS

calami- — see CALAM-

cal·a·mine \'kalə,mīn, ˌmən\ *n* -s *often attrib* [F, fr. ML *calamina*, alter. of L *cadmia*, Gk *kadmeia*, lit., Cadmean (earth), Theban (earth)] **1** *obs* **a** *Brit* **:** SMITHSONITE **b :** HEMIMORPHITE **c :** HYDROZINCITE **2 :** an alloy of zinc, lead, and tin formerly used for coating iron to prevent oxidation **3 :** a pink powder consisting of a mixture of zinc oxide with a small amount of ferric oxide used in lotions, liniments, and ointments in skin treatment

calamine blue *n* **:** a light greenish blue that is greener, lighter, and stronger than average robin's-egg blue (sense 1), bluer and deeper than average aqua, and bluer and lighter than average turquoise blue

cal·a·mint \'kalə,mint\ *or* **calamint balm** *n* -s [alter. (influenced by E *mint* [plant] and by LL *calaminthe*, fr. Gk *kalaminthē*) of ME *calament*, fr. OF, fr. ML *calamentum*, modif. of Gk *kalaminthē*] **:** a mint of the genus *Satureja* (esp. *S. calamintha*) — called also *basil thyme*

cal·a·mis·trum \,kalə'mistrəm\ *n, pl* **calamis·tra** \-rə\ [L, curling iron, irreg. fr. Gk *kalamis*, fr. *kalamos* reed — more at HAULM] **:** a spinose comb on the hind metatarsi of a cribellate spider that aids in organizing silk spun from the cribellum

cal·a·mi·ta·ce·ae \,kalə,mī'tāsē,ē, -,mə't-\ *n pl, cap* [NL, fr. *Calamites*, type genus + *-aceae*] **:** a family of fossil plants coextensive with Calamariaceae — used by strict adherents to the International Rules of Botanical Nomenclature

cal·a·mite \'kalə,mīt\ *n* -s [NL *Calamites*] **:** any fossil of the genus *Calamites* or related genera — **cal·a·mit·ean** \¦kalə¦mīd·ēən, -,mī'tē-\ *adj*

cal·a·mi·tes \,kalə'mīd·(,)ēz\ *n, cap* [NL, fr. LGk *kalamitēs* reedlike, fr. Gk, of a reed, fr. *kalamos* reed] **:** a genus of Paleozoic fossil plants (family Calamariaceae) having large grooved and jointed stems bearing verticillate branches at the nodes

cal·a·mi·toid \¦kalə¦mī,tȯid\ *adj* [NL *Calamites* + E *-oid*] **:** resembling a calamite

ca·lam·i·tous \kə'lamәd·əs, -ətəs\ *adj* [MF *calamiteux*, fr. L *calamitosus*, fr. *calamitas* calamity + *-osus* -ous] **1 :** marked by distress, affliction, or disaster: **a :** constituting or causing calamity **:** bringing distress ⟨the ~ disregard of mine-safety regulations⟩ **b :** concerned with or relating to disaster ⟨this ~ catalog of serious problems —J.M.McCloy⟩ **2** *obs* **:** involved personally in calamity **:** suffering disaster or misery ⟨the distress of these ~ persons⟩ — **ca·lam·i·tous·ly** *adv*

ca·lam·i·ty \-əd·ē, -ətē, -i\ *n* -ES [MF *calamité*, fr. L *calamitat-, calamitas*; akin to L *incolumis* unharmed, Gk *kolobos* docked — more at HALT (lame)] **1 :** a state of deep distress or misery ⟨life is neither a pleasure nor a ~ —Agnes Repplier⟩ **2 :** an extraordinarily grave event marked by great loss and lasting distress and affliction ⟨*calamities* of nature such as flood and drought — *Notes & Queries on Anthropology*⟩ **syn** see DISASTER

calamity howler *n* **:** one that makes dismal predictions of impending disaster

calamo- — see CALAM-

cal·a·mo·den·dron \,kaləmō'dendrən\ *n, cap* [NL, fr. *calam-* + *-dendron*] **:** a form genus of fossil plants based on remains of stems only

cal·a·mon·din \¦kalə¦mändən\ *n* -s [Tag *kalamunding*] **1 :** a small spiny citrus tree (*Citrus mitis*) native to the Philippines **2 :** the small very acid loose-skinned fruit of the calamondin

cal·a·moph·y·ton \,kalə'mäfə,tän\ *n, cap* [NL, fr. *calam-* + Gk *phyton* plant — more at PHYT-] **:** a genus (the type of the family Calamophytaceae) of sphenopsid plants from the Middle Devonian of Germany that have bifurcated leaves and naked pendulous sporangia and are the earliest indubitable sphenopsids

cal·a·mos·ta·chys \,kalə'mästəkəs\ *n, cap* [NL, fr. *calam-* + Gk *stachys* ear of grain; akin to OE *stingan* to sting — more at STING] **:** a genus of Carboniferous fossil plants (family Calamariaceae) with cone-shaped fructifications and peltate sporophylls

cal·a·mus \'kaləməs\ *n* [L, fr. Gk *kalamos* — more at HAULM] **1** *pl* **cala·mi** \-,mī, -ē\ **a** *obs* **:** REED, CANE **b :** a reed pen ⟨a manuscript that was written with a ~⟩ **2** *pl* **calami :** SWEET FLAG **3** *pl* **calami :** the aromatic peeled and dried rhizome of the calamus used as a carminative and tonic **4** *cap* [NL, fr. L] **:** a genus of tropical Asian tufted pinnate-leaved palms whose hooked petioles enable them to climb over tall trees and from whose light tough stems rattan canes are made with one species (*C. rotang*) being used for Malacca canes **5** *pl* **calami :** the barrel of a feather **:** QUILL

calamus oil *n* **:** a yellow aromatic essential oil obtained from the underground parts of the sweet flag and used as a flavor and perfume

ca·lan·do \kä'län(,)dō\ *adj (or adv)* [It, fr. L *calandum*, gerund of *calare* to slacken, let down, fr. Gk *chalan*; perh. akin to Skt *jahāti* he leaves, abandons — more at GO] **:** diminishing in rapidity and loudness **:** dying away — used as a direction in music

ca·lan·dra \kə'landrə\ *n, cap* [NL, fr. F *calandre* weevil] *in some classifications* **:** a genus of weevils (family Curculionidae) equivalent to *Calendra* or to *Sitophilus* of other classifications and sometimes made the type of a separate family

calandra lark \"-\ *also* **ca·lan·der** \kə'landə(r)\ *n* -s [MF *calandre*, fr. OProv *calandra*, fr. LGk *kalandros*, prob. fr. Gk *charadrios*, a bird — more at CHARADRIUS] **:** a large European lark (*Melanocorypha calandra*) noted for its ability to mimic the songs of other birds and sometimes kept as a cage bird

[1]**ca·lan·dria** \kə'landrēə\ *n* -s [Sp, lit., calandra lark] **:** a heating element of an evaporator; *esp* **:** a part of a vacuum evaporating system in which the liquid to be concentrated rises through tubes surrounded by steam and descends through a central well

[2]**calandria** \"\ *n* -s [AmerSp, fr. Sp, calandra lark, fr. (assumed) VL, modif. of LGk *kalandros*] **:** a black-headed So. American mockingbird (*Mimus modulator* or *M. orpheus*) often kept as a cage bird

cal·an·drin·ia \,kalən'drinēə\ *n, cap* [NL, after Jean Louis *Calandrini* †1758 Swiss botanist] **:** a large genus of mostly So. American and Australian succulent herbs of the family Portulacaceae that have basal or alternate leaves and purplish ephemeral flowers in bracted racemes or panicles — see ROCK PURSLANE

calangall *var of* GALINGALE

[1]**cal·a·nid** \'kalənəd, -(,)nid\ *adj* [NL *Calanidae*, fr. *Calanus*, type genus + *-idae*] **:** of or relating to the genus *Calanus* or the family Calanidae

[2]**calanid** \"\ *n* -s **:** a calanid copepod

ca·lanque \kə'läŋk\ *n* -s [F, fr. Prov *calanco, calanca*] **:** a cove or inlet esp. on the Mediterranean coast of France

calantas [Sp *calantás*, fr. Tag *kalantas*] *var of* KALANTAS

ca·lan·the \kə'lan(t)thē\ *n* [NL, fr. *cal-* + Gk *anthē* blossom; akin to Gk *anthos* flower — more at ANTHOLOGY] **1** *cap* **:** a large and widely distributed genus of terrestrial showy orchids having white, rose-colored, or yellow flowers and broad leaves folded lengthwise **2** -s **:** any plant or flower of the genus *Calanthe*

cal·a·nus \'kalənəs\ *n, cap* [NL, after *Calanus* (Kalanos) †*ab* 325 B.C. Indian Brahman] **:** a genus (the type of the family Calanidae) of reddish marine copepods widely distributed in northern seas where they are a major food for herring, mackerel, and the bowhead

ca·lao \kə'lau̇\ *n* -s [Sp, fr. Tag *kalaw*] **:** a very large Philippine hornbill (*Buceros hydrocorax*) with a large red bill and casque, rufous head and neck, dull black breast, brown back and wings, and a white tail often stained yellowish buff — called also *rufous hornbill*

calapooya *or* **calapuya** *usu cap, var of* KALAPOOIA

ca·lap·pa \kə'lapə\ *n, cap* [NL] **:** a genus (the type of the family Calappidae) of brachyuran crustaceans of tropical seas that includes a number of typical box crabs

calas *pl of* CALA

ca·la·scio·ne \,kalə'shōnē\ *n* -s [It, prob. fr. (assumed) VL *calassium* basket, irreg. fr. Gk *kalathos*] **:** a guitar with two or three strings used esp. in southern Italy

ca·lash \kə'lash, -'aa(ə)-,-'ai-\ *n* -ES [F *calèche*, fr. G *kalesche*, fr. Czech *kolesa* wheels, carriage; akin to OSlav *kolo* wheel, Gk *kyklos* — more at WHEEL] **1 a :** a light carriage with small wheels, inside seats for four passengers, a separate driver's seat, and a folding top **b :** CALÈCHE 2 **2 a :** a large hood made on an arrangement of hoops to permit folding far back on the head and worn by women in the late 18th century **b :** a folding carriage top **3 :** a seaman of Far Eastern extraction

calash 2a

cal·a·thea \,kalə'thēə\ *n* [NL, irreg. fr. L *calathus* basket shaped like a flower, fr. Gk *kalathos*] **1** *cap* **:** a genus of chiefly tropical American herbs (family Marantaceae) having showily marked basal leaves and small flowers in clusters on short stems and used as foliage plants **2** -s **:** any plant of the genus *Calathea*

cal·a·thos \'kalə,thäs, -,thəs\ *or* **cal·a·thus** \-,thəs\ *n, pl* **cala·thi** \-,thī, -ē\ [L & Gk; L *calathus*, fr. Gk *kalathos*; perh. akin to Gk *klōthein* to spin] **:** a flared fruit basket borne on the head as a symbol in Greek and Egyptian art of fruitfulness

calavance *var of* GARAVANCE

cal·a·ver·as warbler \¦kalə¦verəs-\ *n, usu cap C* **:** the Pacific coast subspecies (*Vermivora ruficapilla ridgwayi*) of the Nashville warbler

cal·a·ver·ite \,kalə've,rīt\ *n* -s [*Calaveras* county, California, its locality + E *-ite*] **:** a yellowish mineral having a metallic luster and consisting of gold telluride and variable minor amounts of silver (hardness 2.5, sp. gr. 8.35)

calc *abbr* calculate

calc- *or* **calci-** *or* **calco-** *comb form* [L *calc-, calx* lime — more at CHALK] **:** calcium **:** calcium salts ⟨*calc*ite⟩ ⟨*calci*meter⟩ ⟨*calco*spherite⟩

cal·ca·ne·al \(')kal¦kānēəl\ *also* **cal·ca·ne·an** \-ēən\ *adj* [LL *calcaneus* heel + E *-al* or *-an*] **1 :** relating to the heel **2 :** relating to the calcaneus

calcaneo- *comb form* [*calcaneum*] **:** calcaneal and ⟨*calcaneo*astragalar⟩ ⟨*calcaneo*cuboid⟩

cal·ca·neo·cu·boid ligament \kal¦kānē(,)ō¦kyü,bȯid-\ *n* **:** either of two ligaments of the tarsus connecting the calcaneus and the cuboid

cal·ca·ne·um \kal'kānēəm\ *n, pl* **calca·nea** \-nēə\ [L, heel, fr. *calc-, calx* — more at CALK] **1 :** CALCANEUS **2 :** a process of the back upper part of the tarsometatarsal bone of birds prob. not homologous to the calcaneum of mammals

cal·ca·ne·us \kal'kānēəs\ *n, pl* **calca·nei** \-nē,ī\ [LL, heel, alter. of L *calcaneum*] **:** one of the bones of the tarsus which in man forms the great bone of the heel homologous to the fibulare of certain lower vertebrates

[1]**cal·car** \'kal,kär\ *n, pl* **calcar·ia** \kal'ka(a)rēə\ [L, spur, fr. *calc-, calx* heel] **:** a spur or spurlike prominence: as **a :** a clawlike process on the leg or wing of a bird that is not the termination of a digit **b :** a process of the calcaneum of a bat helping to support the web between the leg and tail — see BAT illustration **c :** a spur at the end of the tibia of an insect **d :** PREHALLUX

[2]**calcar** \"\ *n* -s [It *calcara*, fr. LL *calcaria* limekiln, fr. L *calc-, calx* lime — more at CHALK] **:** an oven or reverberatory furnace used in early glassmaking processes for calcination of the batch into frit

cal·ca·rate \'kalkə,rāt\ *also* **cal·ca·rat·ed** \-rād·əd\ *adj* [[1]*calcar* + *-ate* or *-ate* + *-ed*] *bot* **:** SPURRED

calcar avis \-'āvəs, -'ä-\ *n, pl* **calcaria avi·um** \-vēəm\ [NL, lit., bird's spur] **:** a curved ridge on the medial wall of the posterior horn of each lateral ventricle of the brain opposite the calcarine fissure

cal·car·ea \kal'ka(a)rēə\ *n pl, cap* [NL, alter. of L *calcaria*, neut. pl. of *calcarius* of lime] *in some classifications* **:** CALCISPONGIAE

cal·ca·re·nite \,kalkə'rē,nīt\ *n* -s [*calc-* + L *arena* sand + E *-ite* — more at ARENA] **1 :** a detrital carbonate rock formed of particles of sand-grain size **2 :** a consolidated lime sand

calcareo- *comb form* [*calcareous*] **:** calcareous ⟨*calcareo*corneous⟩ ⟨*calcareo*sulfurous⟩

cal·car·e·ous *also* **cal·car·i·ous** \kal'ka(a)rēəs, -ker-,-kär-\ *adj* [*calcareous* alter. (influenced by *-eous*) of *calcarious*, fr. L *calcarius* of lime, fr. *calc-, calx* lime + *-arius* -ary — more at CHALK] **1 a :** like calcite or calcium carbonate esp. in hardness **b :** consisting of or containing calcium carbonate **c :** containing calcium or any calcium compound **d :** relating to rocks containing calcium carbonate **2 :** growing on limestone or in soil impregnated with lime ⟨a ~ plant⟩ — **cal·car·e·ous·ly** *adv* — **cal·car·e·ous·ness** *n* -ES

calcareous sinter *n* **:** TRAVERTINE

calcareous spar *n* **:** CALCITE

calcaria *pl of* [1]CALCAR, CALCARIUM

cal·ca·rine \'kalkə,rīn\ *adj* [L *calcar* spur + E *-ine* — more at CALCAR] **1 :** shaped like a spur **2 :** belonging to or situated near the calcar avis

calcarine fissure *n* **:** a fissure in the mesial surface of the occipital lobe of the cerebrum

cal·car·i·um \kal'ka(a)rēəm\ *n, pl* **calcar·ia** \-rēə\ [NL, fr. [1]*calcar* + *-ium*] **:** [1]CALCAR

calced \'kalst\ *adj* [back-formation fr. *discalced*] **:** SHOD — used of religious who wear shoes; compare DISCALCED

calcedony *var of* CHALCEDONY

cal·ce·i·form \'kalsēə,fȯrm, kal'sē-\ *adj* [*calcei-* (fr. L *calceus* shoe) + *-form*] **:** shaped like a slipper ⟨the ~ lip in the flowers of certain orchids⟩

cal·ce·o·lar·ia \,kalsēə'la(a)rēə\ *n* [NL, fr. L *calceolus* small shoe (dim. of *calceus* shoe, fr. *calc-, calx* heel) + NL *-aria* — more at CALK] **1** *cap* **:** a large genus of tropical American plants (family Scrophulariaceae) with highly irregular 2-parted showy flowers having a small upper lip and a large inflated slipper-shaped lower lip **2** -s **:** any garden plant of the genus *Calceolaria* — called also *slipperwort*

cal·ce·o·late \'kalsēə,lāt\ *adj* [L *calceolus* + E *-ate*] **:** CALCEIFORM — **cal·ce·o·late·ly** *adv*

calces *pl of* CALX

cal·ce·us \'kalsēəs\ *n, pl* **cal·cei** \-sē,ī,-sē,ē\ [L *calceus, calcius*] **:** an ancient Roman ankle-length shoe usu. of leather

cal·cha·qui \,kalchə'kē\ *n, pl* **calchaqui** *or* **calchaquis** *usu cap* [Sp *calchaquí*, fr. *Calchaquí* valley in Argentina] **1 a :** an ancient Indian people of northwest Argentina and northern Chile — called also *Diaguita* **b :** a member of such people **2 :** the language of the Calchaqui of unknown affinity

cal·cha·qui·an \-ən\ *adj, usu cap* **:** of or relating to an American Indian language family formerly occupying a large area in northwest Argentina and including the language of the Calchaquis

calci- — see CALC-

cal·cic \'kalsik\ *adj* [ISV *calc-* + *-ic*] **:** derived from or containing calcium or lime **:** rich in calcium

cal·ci·coat·er \'kalsə,kōd·ə(r)\ *n* -s **:** a flat paint that is usu. made with lime-treated oils and that gives a uniform appearance when applied to porous surfaces

cal·ci·cole \'kalsə,kōl\ *n* -s [fr. *calcicole*, adj.] **:** a plant that grows solely or predominantly in an alkaline medium rich in calcareous matter (as a limestone soil) — called also *calciphile*; compare CALCIFUGE

cal·cic·o·lous \(')kal¦sikələs\ *or* **calcicole** *adj* [*calcicolous* fr. F *calcicole* + E *-ous*; *calcicole*, fr. F, fr. *calci-* + *-cole* -colous] **:** growing or living in an alkaline medium rich in calcareous matter

cal·ci·co·sis \,kalsə'kōsəs\ *n, pl* **calcico·ses** \-,sēz\ [NL, fr. *calc-* + *-cosis* (as in *silicosis*)] **:** a lung disease caused by inhalation of limestone dust; *sometimes* **:** pneumonoconiosis so caused

cal·cif·er·ol \kal'sifə,rȯl, -ōl\ *n* -s [*calciferous* + *ergosterol*] **:** VITAMIN D_2

cal·cif·er·ous \(')kal¦sif(ə)rəs\ *adj* [*calc-* + *-ferous*] **1 :** bearing, producing, or containing calcium, calcium carbonate, or calcite **2** *cap* [so called fr. its calciferous sandstone] *geol* **:** of or relating to a subdivision of the Ordovician in New York and elsewhere

calciferous gland *n* **:** one of a series of glands that open into the esophagus of various oligochaete worms, that secrete calcium carbonate, and that are believed to assist in adjusting the pH of the food material

cal·cif·ic \(ˈ)kal¦sifik\ *adj* [*calcify* + *-ic*] **:** involving or caused by calcification

cal·ci·fi·ca·tion \ˌkalsəfəˈkāshən\ *n* -s [fr. *calcify*, after such pairs as E *ossify: ossification*] **1 :** impregnation with calcareous matter: as **a :** deposition of calcium salts within the matrix of cartilage often as the preliminary step in the formation of bone — compare OSSIFICATION **b :** abnormal deposition of calcium salts within tissue ⟨~ of a tuberculosis focus in the lung⟩ **c :** accumulation or deposition of calcium and magnesium carbonates at a level in the soil profile approximating the depth to which most of the water percolates **2 :** a calcified structure or part ⟨the lung X rays clearly showed the ~⟩

¹cal·ci·fuge \ˈkalsəˌfyüj\ *or* **cal·cif·u·gous** \(ˈ)kal¦sifyəgəs\ *adj* [*calcifuge* fr. F, fr. *calc-* + *-fuge* (fr. L *fugere* to flee); *calcifugous* fr. F *calcifuge* + E *-ous* — more at FUGITIVE] **:** growing or living in an acid medium that is poor in calcareous matter

²calcifuge \"\ *n* -s **:** a plant that grows solely or predominantly in an acid medium that is poor in calcareous matter ⟨heathers are well-known ~s⟩ — compare CALCICOLE

cal·ci·fy \ˈkalsəˌfī\ *vb* -ED/-ING/-ES [*calc-* + *-fy*] *vt* **1 :** to make calcareous by deposit or secretion of calcium salts **2 :** to make inflexible or unchangeable **:** FIX ⟨~ the state of things as they are — *Fortune*⟩ ~ *vi* **1 :** to become calcareous **2 :** to become inflexible and changeless **:** become fixed **:** HARDEN

cal·ci·lu·tite *or* **cal·ci·lu·tyte** \ˌkalsəˈlüˌtīt\ *n* -s [*calc-* + L *lut*um mud + E *-ite* or *-yte* — more at POLLUTE] **:** a consolidated lime mud

cal·cim·e·ter \kalˈsimədə(r)\ *n* -s [ISV *calc-* + *-meter*] **:** an instrument for liberating and measuring carbon dioxide (as in limestone or soil) and for estimating the amount of lime in soils

¹cal·ci·mine *or* **kal·so·mine** \ˈkalsəˌmīn\ *n* -s *often attrib* [*calcimine*, alter. (influenced by *calc-*) of *kalsomine; kalsomine*, origin unknown] **:** a typically white but sometimes tinted wash made by mixing clear glue, whiting or zinc white, and water and used mainly on plastered surfaces

²calcimine *or* **kalsomine** \"\ *vt* -ED/-ING/-S **:** to paint or wash with calcimine

cal·ci·min·er \-nə(r)\ *n* -s **:** one that calcimines ceilings or walls

cal·ci·nate \ˈkalsəˌnāt\ *vt* -ED/-ING/-S [back-formation fr. *calcination*] **:** CALCINE

cal·ci·na·tion \ˌkalsəˈnāshən\ *n* -s [ME *calcinacioun*, fr. MF *calcination*, fr. *calciner* + *-ation*] **:** the action or process of calcining **:** state of being calcined

¹cal·cine \(ˈ)kal¦sīn\ *vb* -ED/-ING/-S [ME *calcenen, calcynen*, fr. MF *calciner*, fr. L *calc-, calx* lime — more at CHALK] *vt* **:** to heat (as inorganic materials) to a high temperature but without fusing in order to effect useful physical and chemical changes: as **a :** to convert to a powder or to a friable state by heating **b :** to heat in order to drive off volatile matter (as carbon dioxide from limestone, ores, or concentrates, or chemically combined water from clay) and thus usu. to disintegrate (as bones) — compare BURN *vt* 3d **c :** to heat under oxidizing conditions (as for producing metal oxides) — compare ROAST *vt* 2 ~ *vi* **:** to undergo calcination

²cal·cine \ˈkalˌsīn\ *n* -s **:** a product (as a metal oxide) of calcination or roasting

calcined gypsum *n* **:** gypsum partially dehydrated by heat; *specif* **:** PLASTER OF PARIS

cal·cin·er \(ˈ)kal¦sīnə(r)\ *n* -s **:** one that calcines: as **a :** BURNER 1a(2) **b :** a furnace or kiln that calcines (as for converting coal to coke or sodium bicarbonate to soda ash)

cal·ci·no \kalˈchē(ˌ)nō, kälˈ-\ *n* -s [It, fr. L *calc-, calx* lime — more at CHALK] **:** a disease of silkworms and other larval moths caused by a fungus (*Beauveria bassiana* or a related species) and marked by a mummified chalky appearance of the larva after death

cal·ci·no·sis \ˌkalsəˈnōsəs\ *n, pl* **calcino·ses** \-ōˌsēz\ [NL, fr. *calc-* + connective *-n-* + *-osis*] **:** the abnormal deposition of calcium salts in the skin, subcutaneous tissues, or other parts of the body

calcio- *comb form* [*calcium*] **:** calcium — used chiefly in names of minerals ⟨*calcio*biotite⟩

cal·cio·fer·rite \¦kalsē(ˌ)ōˈfeˌrīt\ *n* -s [ISV *calcio-* + L *ferr*um iron + ISV *-ite;* orig. formed as G *kalkoferrit* — more at FARRIER] **:** a mineral consisting of a hydrous calcium iron phosphate occurring in yellow to green nodular masses

cal·cio·vol·borth·ite \¦kalsē(ˌ)ōˈvōlˌbórˌthīt, -väl-\ *n* -s [ISV *calcio-* + *volborthite;* orig. formed as G *kalkvolborthit*] **:** a mineral $CuCa(VO_4)(OH)$ consisting of a basic vanadate of calcium and copper

cal·cip·e·tal \(ˈ)kal¦sipədᵊl\ *adj* [*calci-* + *-petal*] **:** CALCICOLOUS

¹cal·ci·phile \ˈkalsəˌfīl\ *or* **cal·ci·phil·ic** \¦kalsə¦filik\ *also* **cal·ciph·i·lous** \(ˈ)kal¦sifələs\ *adj* [*calci-* + *-phile, -philic, -philous*] **:** CALCICOLOUS

²calciphile \"\ *n* -s **:** CALCICOLE

cal·ci·phobe \ˈkalsəˌfōb\ *n* -s [fr. *calciphobe*, adj.] **:** CALCIFUGE

cal·ci·pho·bic \¦kalsə¦fōbik\ *or* **cal·ci·phobe** \ˈkalsəˌfōb\ *also* **cal·ciph·o·bous** \(ˈ)kal¦sifəbəs\ *adj* [*calci-* + *-phobic, -phobe, -phobous*] **:** CALCIFUGE

cal·ci·sponge \ˈkalsəˌspənj\ *n* -s [NL *Calcispongiae*] **:** one of the Calcispongiae

cal·ci·spon·gi·ae \ˌkalsəˈspənjēˌē, -ˈä-\ *n pl, cap* [NL, fr. *calci-* + *-spongiae*] **:** a class of Porifera comprising marine sponges with a skeleton of calcareous spicules commonly divided into orders Asconosa and Syconosa on the basis of the complexity of the canal system

cal·cite \ˈkalˌsīt\ *n* -s [ISV *calc-* + *-ite;* orig. formed as G *kalzit*] **:** a mineral consisting of calcium carbonate crystallized in hexagonal form, cleaving readily into rhombohedrons, and including besides common limestone chalk, marble, dogtooth spar, Iceland spar, stalactites, and stalagmites (hardness 3, sp. gr. of crystals 2.71) — distinguished from *aragonite* — **cal·cit·ic** \(ˈ)kal¦sid·ik\ *adj*

cal·ci·trate \ˈkalsəˌtrāt\ *vb* -ED/-ING/-S [L *calcitratus*, past part. of *calcitrare* to kick, fr. *calc-, calx* heel — more at CALK] *archaic* **:** KICK — **cal·ci·tra·tion** \ˌkalsəˈtrāshən\ *n* -s

cal·ci·um \ˈkalsēəm\ *n* -s *often attrib* [NL, fr. L *calc-, calx* lime + NL *-ium* — more at CHALK] **1 :** a silver-white rather soft bivalent metallic element of the alkaline-earth group that quickly tarnishes in air and when heated burns with a brilliant light, used chiefly in alloys and in various metallurgical processes, often as a scavenger, and never occurring native but very common in combination in certain minerals and rocks, esp. as a carbonate (as in limestone), sulfate, or phosphate, in practically all natural waters, and in most animals and plants as an essential constituent — symbol *Ca;* see ELEMENT table **2 a :** a very strong white light source given by lime heated to incandescence in an oxyhydrogen flame — compare LIMELIGHT **b :** the flame of acetylene gas generated by reaction of calcium carbide with water

calcium aluminate *n* **:** any of various compounds of lime and alumina (as monocalcium aluminate $CaO.Al_2O_3$ and tricalcium aluminate $3CaO.Al_2O_3$) important as constituents of hydraulic cements

calcium arsenate *n* **:** an arsenate of calcium [as the normal tricalcium arsenate $Ca_3(AsO_4)_2$ or a basic salt $3Ca_3(AsO_4)_2.Ca(OH)_2$]; *esp* **:** a commercial mixture obtained as a white powder usu. by heating arsenic pentoxide and calcium hydroxide in water and used as an insecticide esp. in the form of a dust

calcium bisulfite *n* **:** acid calcium sulfite $Ca(HSO_3)_2$ obtained as a yellowish solution usu. containing free sulfur dioxide by reaction of sulfur dioxide with limestone in the presence of water or with calcium hydroxide and used in the sulfite process for making wood pulp and as a disinfectant and antichlor — called also *bisulfite of lime, calcium hydrogen sulfite*

calcium carbide *n* **:** a crystalline compound CaC_2 that is colorless when pure but usu. varying from dark gray to brown made commercially by heating lime and carbon together in an electric furnace and used for the generation of acetylene and for making calcium cyanamide

calcium carbonate *n* **:** a salt $CaCO_3$ found in nature as calcite (as in limestone, chalk, and marble) and aragonite and in plant ashes, in bones, and in many shells, obtained also as a white precipitate by passing carbon dioxide into a suspension of calcium hydroxide in water, and used chiefly as a pigment, pigment extender, and filler, in dentifrices and pharmaceuticals esp. as an antacid, and in making lime and portland cement — compare CHALK 1, LIMESTONE, ²WHITING 2

calcium chloride *n* **:** a deliquescent salt $CaCl_2$ obtained chiefly as a by-product in making soda ash and other chemicals, appearing in its anhydrous state as a white porous solid used as a drying and dehumidifying agent and in a more or less hydrated state as a solid, as colorless flakes, or in water solution used for controlling dust and ice on roads, for freezeproofing, in freezing mixtures and refrigeration brine, and with concrete as an accelerator or aid in curing

calcium cloud *n* **:** a patch of ionized calcium vapor in the sun's atmosphere

calcium cyanamide *also* **calcium cyanamid** *n* **:** a compound $CaCN_2$ obtained in impure cokelike form by passing dry nitrogen over calcium carbide at about 1100° C and used chiefly as a fertilizer, as a weed killer, in the defoliation of crops (as cotton), and as a source of other nitrogen compounds — called also *lime nitrogen, nitrolim*

calcium cyanide *n* **:** a compound $Ca(CN)_2$ that gives off hydrogen cyanide on exposure to air, is made usu. in impure black or gray flakes, powder, or cast blocks by heating crude calcium cyanamide in the presence of salt in an electric furnace, and is used chiefly as an insecticide and rodenticide and in making hydrogen cyanide and ferrocyanides — called also *black cyanide*

calcium fluoride *n* **:** a salt CaF_2 that is colorless when pure and is found in nature chiefly as the mineral fluorite

calcium gluconate *n* **:** a white crystalline or granular powdery salt $[HOCH_2(CHOH)_4COO]_2Ca.H_2O$ used in medicine as a source of calcium

calcium hydrate *n* **:** HYDRATED LIME — used chiefly commercially

calcium hydride *n* **:** a saltlike compound CaH_2 that is white and crystalline when pure but is usu. obtained in gray to grayish brown lumps and that is used chiefly as a reducing agent in the preparation of powdered metals, as a portable source of hydrogen, and as a drying agent — called also *hydrolith*

calcium hydrogen sulfite *n* **:** CALCIUM BISULFITE

calcium hydroxide *n* **:** a strong alkali $Ca(OH)_2$ commonly sold as a white powder or in water solution — see HYDRATED LIME, LIMEWATER

calcium hypochlorite *n* **:** any hypochlorite of calcium: as **a :** the normal anhydrous salt $Ca(ClO)_2$ that is white and relatively stable when pure **b :** a commercial product usu. containing 70 to 75 percent available chlorine and used as a bleaching agent, disinfectant, bactericide, and deodorant — called also *high-test hypochlorite*

calcium iodobehenate *n* **:** a white or yellowish-white powder $(C_{21}H_{42}ICOO)_2Ca$ used in medicine in place of inorganic iodides

calcium lactate *n* **:** a white almost tasteless crystalline salt $(CH_3CHOHCOO)_2Ca.5H_2O$ made by the action of lactic acid on calcium carbonate and used chiefly in medicine as a source of calcium and in foods (as in baking powder)

calcium levulinate *n* **:** a white powdery salt $(CH_3COCH_2CH_2COO)_2Ca.2H_2O$ used in medicine as a source of calcium

calcium light *n* **:** LIMELIGHT 1a, 1b

calcium nitrate *n* **:** a colorless crystalline deliquescent salt $Ca(NO_3)_2$ occurring often in natural waters and soil and as the mineral nitrocalcite, made by reaction of nitric acid or nitrogen oxides with lime or calcium carbonate, and used as a fertilizer

calcium oxalate *n* **:** a colorless crystalline salt $CaC_2O_4.H_2O$ noted for its insolubility, normally deposited in many plant cells, and in animals sometimes excreted in urine or retained in the form of urinary calculi

calcium oxide *n* **:** a caustic solid CaO that is white when pure and that is the chief constituent of lime

calcium pantothenate *n* **:** a white powdery salt $(C_9H_{16}NO_5)_2Ca$ made synthetically and used as a source of pantothenic acid for animals

calcium phosphate *n* **1 :** an orthophosphate of calcium: as **a :** one of the three simple orthophosphates, white or colorless when pure, usu. prepared by reaction of phosphoric acid or phosphorus pentoxide with lime, hydrated lime, or limestone: (1) **:** the primary phosphate $CaH_4(PO_4)_2$ or its monohydrate $CaH_4(PO_4)_2.H_2O$ used in the form of superphosphate as a fertilizer and in pure form as an acid ingredient in baking powder, prepared flours, and bakery products — called also *calcium dihydrogen phosphate, monobasic calcium phosphate, monocalcium phosphate* (2) **:** the secondary phosphate $CaHPO_4$ or its dihydrate $CaHPO_4.2H_2O$ found in nature as monetite or brushite respectively and used as a mineral supplement in pharmaceutical preparations and animal feeds and as a polishing agent in tooth powders and pastes — called also *calcium hydrogen phosphate, dibasic calcium phosphate, dicalcium phosphate* (3) **:** the tertiary phosphate $Ca_3(PO_4)_2$ found in nature as whitlockite and made by fusion of phosphorus pentoxide and lime or by fusion and defluorination of phosphate rock or phosphate sand for use as a fertilizer — called also *tribasic calcium phosphate, tricalcium phosphate* **b** (1) **:** a naturally occurring apatite (2) **:** an industrial product consisting essentially of hydroxylapatite usu. prepared by adding phosphoric acid to a lime slurry and used chiefly in ceramics, in making enamels and milk glass, as a noncaking agent esp. in salt and sugar, and as a source of calcium and phosphorus in pharmaceutical preparations — called also *tertiary calcium phosphate, tribasic calcium phosphate, tricalcium phosphate* **2 :** a phosphate of calcium (as calcium metaphosphate, calcium pyrophosphate) other than an orthophosphate

calcium-phosphorus ratio *n* **:** the proportional relation existing between calcium and phosphorus in the form of phosphate in body fluids and bone that in man is normally about 2.2 to 1

calcium resinate *n* **:** a yellowish-white powder or lumpy solid obtained by treating rosin with hydrated lime and used chiefly in varnishes, paints, and printing inks and in core oils and binders for foundry cores — called also *limed rosin*

calciums *pl of* CALCIUM

calcium silicate *n* **:** any of several silicates of calcium: as **a :** tricalcium silicate Ca_3SiO_5 found as an essential constituent of portland cement **b :** dicalcium silicate Ca_2SiO_4 also found as an essential constituent of portland cement **c :** calcium metasilicate $CaSiO_3$ found in nature as wollastonite

calcium stearate *n* **:** a white powder consisting essentially of calcium salts of stearic acid and palmitic acid and used chiefly in waterproofing, in paints (as flat-finish coatings), and in printing inks

calcium sulfate *n* **:** a white salt $CaSO_4$ known best in the hydrated forms gypsum and plaster of paris but also found as the anhydrous mineral anhydrite, obtained as a by-product in chemical processes, and used in its anhydrous form chiefly in Keene's cement, in composite pigments, as a filler (as in paper), and as a drying agent

calcium sulfite *n* **:** either of the two sulfites of calcium: **a :** the normal salt $CaSO_3$ prepared as a white powder and used as a disinfectant, preservative, and antichlor **b :** CALCIUM BISULFITE

calcium tungstate *n* **:** a white crystalline salt $CaWO_4$ found in nature as scheelite and used chiefly in screens for radiography, in luminous paint, and in fluorescent lamps

cal·cla·cite \ˈkalkləˌsīt\ *n* -s [ISV *cal*cium + *Cl* (symbol for *chlorine*) + *acetate* + *-ite;* orig. formed in F] **:** calcium chloride acetate $CaCl(C_2H_3O_2).5H_2O$ found as an efflorescence on museum specimens (as of calcareous rocks and fossils)

calco- — see CALC-

cal·co·sphe·rite *or* **cal·co·sphae·rite** \ˌkal(ˌ)kōˈsfiˌrīt\ *n* -s [ISV *calc-* + *spher-* or *sphaer-* + *-ite;* prob. orig. formed as F *calcosphérite*] **:** a granular or laminated deposit of calcium salts in the fat body or Malpighian tubules of certain insects

cal·crete \ˈkalˌkrēt\ *n* -s [*calcium* + *-crete* (as in *concrete*, n.)] **:** a limestone formed by the cementation of soil, sand, gravel, shells, by calcium carbonate deposited by evaporation, or by the escape of carbon dioxide from vadose water **:** CALICHE

calc–sin·ter \ˈkalk¦sintə(r)\ *n* -s [G *kalksinter*, fr. *kalk* lime (fr. OHG) + *sinter* — more at CHALK, SINTER] **:** calcareous sinter **:** TRAVERTINE

calc·spar \-ˌspär, -ä(r\ *n* -s [part trans. of Sw *kalkspat*, fr. *kalk* lime (fr. OSw *kalker*, fr. MLG *kalk*) + *spat* spar — more at CHALK] **:** CALCITE

calc–tu·fa \ˈkalk¦tüfə\ *or* **calc–tuff** \-ˌtəf, -üf\ *n* -s [G *kalk* + E *tufa* or *tuff*] **:** calcareous tufa — compare TRAVERTINE, TUFA

cal·cu·la·bil·i·ty \ˌkalkyələˈbiləd·ē\ *n* -ES **:** the quality of being calculable

cal·cu·la·ble \ˈkalkyələbəl\ *adj* [*calcul*ate + *-able*] **1 :** capable of being calculated **:** ascertainable by calculation **2 :** that may be counted on or depended on **:** DEPENDABLE, PREDICTABLE ⟨a systematic man, as ~ as the stars⟩ — **cal·cu·la·ble·ness** *n* -ES — **cal·cu·la·bly** *adv*

cal·cu·late \ˈkalkyəˌlāt, ˈkau̇k-, *usu* -ād·+V; *chiefly dial* ˈkalk(ə)ˌlā- *or* ˈkau̇k(- *or* ˈka(l)ˌlā-\ *vb* -ED/-ING/-S [L *calculatus*, past part. of *calculare*, fr. *calculus* pebble, small stone used in reckoning, dim. of *calc-, calx* stone used in gaming, limestone, lime — more at CHALK] *vt* **1 a :** to ascertain or determine by mathematical processes esp. of some intricacy ⟨~ atomic weights⟩ **b :** to reckon by exercise of practical judgment rather than by strict mathematical process **:** ESTIMATE **c :** to solve the significance of **:** probe the meaning of **:** figure out **:** INTERPRET ⟨trying to ~ his expression —Hugh MacLennan⟩ **2 :** to plan the nature of beforehand **:** think out **:** FRAME **3 :** to design, prepare, or adapt by forethought or careful plan **:** fit or prepare by appropriate means — used chiefly as past part. with complementary infinitive ⟨*calculated* to succeed⟩ **4** *chiefly North* **a :** to judge to be true or probable on the basis of evidence at hand **:** SUPPOSE, BELIEVE, THINK ⟨I ~ it's money well spent⟩ **b :** INTEND, PURPOSE, PLAN ~ *vi* **1 a :** to make a calculation **:** form an estimate **b :** to make a judgment about the future **:** forecast consequences **2 :** to count or rely — used with *on* or *upon* ⟨my uncle was *calculating* on the thing as concluded —Charles Lever⟩

syn COMPUTE, RECKON, ESTIMATE: CALCULATE is usu. preferred in ref. to more complex, difficult, and lengthy mathematical processes executed with precision and care ⟨*calculate* the velocity of light⟩ ⟨in 1920 it was *calculated* that in the twenty years . . . Gulf coast hurricanes caused $105,642,000 damage —A.F.Harlow⟩ COMPUTE is often used for simpler mathematical processes, esp. arithmetical ones, and with less abstruse and problematical questions ⟨*compute* interest due⟩ ⟨*compute* time in hours or days⟩ ⟨one half the children born, it is *computed*, die before the age of manhood —Adam Smith⟩ RECKON, an informal and familiar term, usu. suggests the simplest arithmetical processes ⟨*reckon* up a small grocery bill⟩ ⟨eighteen pence a day may be *reckoned* the common price of labor in London and its neighborhood —Adam Smith⟩ ESTIMATE may suggest the degree of complexity of any of the foregoing, but is likely to be used in situations in which data or figures are incomplete, guessed at, or unverified, and with processes perhaps simplified, to attain usable but tentative and approximate results ⟨experts now *estimate* the Easter island gaunt stone faces to be less than 800 years old —R.W.Murray⟩ Often it is used in connection with computing in advance, before the acquisition of sure data ⟨*estimate* next year's rainfall⟩

calculated *adj* **1 a :** worked out by calculation **:** computed mathematically ⟨~ tables⟩ **b :** ascertained or estimated by calculation ⟨the ~ velocity of a bullet⟩ **c :** engaged in, undertaken, or displayed after reckoning or estimating the statistical probability of success or failure — see CALCULATED RISK **2 :** planned or contrived so as to accomplish a purpose or achieve an effect **:** thought out in advance **:** deliberately planned ⟨his ways are not ~; he considers himself as honest as noonday —G.W.Brace⟩ ⟨that political justice is attainable only by a nicely ~ system of checks and balances —V.L.Parrington⟩ **3 :** brought about or brought into existence as a consequence of deliberate intent and planning **4 :** LIKELY — used with complementary infinitive ⟨a circumstance ~ to excite strong suspicion —W.E.Gladstone⟩ ⟨not ~ to be soft on such a subject —A.H.Vandenberg †1951⟩ **5 :** SUITED, FITTED, ADAPTED **:** of such a nature as — used with complementary infinitive ⟨she was perfectly ~ to convince the sisters that times had worsened —Arnold Bennett⟩ — **cal·cu·lat·ed·ly** *adv*

calculated risk *n* **1 :** a hazard or chance of failure whose degree of probability has been reckoned or estimated before some undertaking is entered upon **2 :** an undertaking or the actual or possible product of an undertaking whose chance of failure has been previously estimated

calculating *adj* **1 :** performing calculations **2 a :** marked by the performance of calculation or by prudent and deliberate analysis ⟨examining his hurts with a ~ eye —Jack London⟩ **b :** marked by coldhearted calculation as to what will most promote self-interest **:** SHREWD, SCHEMING ⟨to Kate, ~ and cold, the most important thing was power —Ruth Randall⟩

syn see CAUTIOUS

cal·cu·lat·ing·ly \ˈ==ˌ===, ˌ=ˈ===\ *adv* **:** in a calculating manner

calculating machine *n* **:** a machine for performing arithmetical operations (as multiplication) that are usu. more complex than can be done on an adding machine — called also *calculator;* compare COMPUTER

calculating punch *n* **:** a calculating machine into which problems or data are fed on punched cards and which presents its output in the form of similarly punched cards — compare PUNCHED CARD

cal·cu·la·tion \ˌkalkyəˈlāshən, ˌkau̇k-\ *n* -s [ME *calculacioun*, fr. LL *calculation-, calculatio*, fr. L *calculatus* (past part. of *calculare* to calculate) + *-ion-, -io* -ion] **1 a :** the action or process of calculating **b :** an instance of such action **:** an act of calculating **c :** the result of an act of calculating **:** a conclusion reached by reckoning or estimation sometimes accompanied by a verbal or written statement of the steps by which the conclusion has been reached **2 a :** deliberate prudent studied care in analyzing, planning, or contriving **b :** cold heartless planning to promote self-interest **:** SHREWDNESS ⟨by every effort of subterfuge and ~ —Hilaire Belloc⟩

cal·cu·la·tion·al \¦==¦=shənᵊl, -shnəl\ *adj* **:** CALCULATORY

cal·cu·la·tive \ˈ==ˌlād·iv, -ātiv, -ēv\ *adj* **1 :** of or relating to calculation **2 :** involving calculation **3 :** given to calculation

cal·cu·la·tor \-ˌlād·ə(r), -ātə-\ *n* -s [ME, fr. L, fr. *calculatus* + *-or*] **1 :** one that calculates: as **a :** CALCULATING MACHINE **b :** a person who operates a calculating machine esp. in checking figures in financial or statistical papers **c :** a computing clerk and supervisor of a mutuel department who calculates the amounts due to patrons holding parimutuel tickets on the leading horses in each race **2 :** a set or book of tables for facilitating computations **:** READY RECKONER

cal·cu·la·to·ry \-ləˌtōrē, -ˌȯ-\ *adj* [LL *calculatorius*, fr. L *calculatus* + *-orius* -ory] **:** of or relating to calculation ⟨how the Maya carried out their ~ operations —A.L.Kroeber⟩

cal·cu·li·form \-ləˌfórm\ *adj* [ISV *calcul-* (fr. L *calculus* pebble) + *-iform*] **:** shaped like a pebble

cal·cu·lo·sis \ˌkalkyəˈlōsəs\ *n, pl* **calculo·ses** \-ōˌsēz\ [NL, fr. *calculus* + *-osis*] *med* **:** the formation of or the condition of having a calculus or calculi

cal·cu·lous \ˈkalkyələs, ˈkau̇k-\ *adj* [F or L; F *calculeux*, fr. L *calculosus*, fr. *calculus* pebble + *-osus* -ous] **1 :** caused or characterized by the presence of a calculus **2 :** affected with gravel or stone

cal·cu·lus \ˈkalkyələs, ˈkau̇k-\ *n, pl* **calcu·li** \-ˌlī, -ē\ *also* **calcu·lus·es** \-ləsəz\ [L, pebble, stone in the bladder or kidneys, stone used in calculating, act of calculating — more at CALCULATE] **1 a :** a solid concretion usu. composed of mineral salts, formed around organic material, and found mainly in hollow organs, ducts, passages, and cysts ⟨renal *calculi*⟩ ⟨a small ~ was eliminated from the bladder⟩ — see GALLSTONE, RENAL CALCULUS, URINARY CALCULUS **b :** a concretion on teeth **:** TARTAR **2** *archaic* **:** CALCULATION, COMPUTATION **3 :** a method or process of reasoning by computation of symbols: as **a :** a branch of mathematics (as the infinitesimal calculus) involving calculation **b :** any one of the commonly distinguished divisions of symbolic logic **4** *pl* **calculuses :** a book or treatise on infinitesimal calculus

calculus of classes : ALGEBRA OF CLASSES

calculus of enlargement : a method in the calculus of finite differences of finding analytical expansions by means of *E* and other operators, where $E.f(x) = f(x + 1)$

calculus of finite differences : a branch of mathematics that interprets variation as a succession of small increments but permits those increments to be finite instead of infinitesimally small

calculus of individuals : a branch of symbolic logic designed to avoid the terminological platonism inherent in an algebra of classes by recourse to the notion of individuals esp. in their relationships of overlapping, discreteness, and being a part

calculus of relations or **calculus of relatives** : ALGEBRA OF RELATIONS

calculus of variations : a branch of infinitesimal calculus whose fundamental notion is the variation of a curve and whose problem is to find the form of curve that will make a definite integral of a given function along the curve have a stationary value, the curve playing the role of the independent variable in ordinary differential calculus

[1]**cal·cut·ta** \(')kal¦kəd·ə, -ətə\ *adj, usu cap* [fr. *Calcutta*, India] : of or from the city of Calcutta, India : of the kind or style prevalent in Calcutta

[2]**calcutta** \"\ *n* -s **1** [short for *Calcutta cane*] : a fishing rod made from a single piece of bamboo cane **2** or **calcutta pool** *usu cap C* [fr. the *Calcutta* sweepstakes, famous auction pool held in Calcutta, India] : a form of auction pool in which each contestant esp. in golf and bridge tournaments is sold at a fixed price but at a handicap established by bidding in an auction

calcutta hemp *n, usu cap C* [fr. *Calcutta*, India] : JUTE

cal·de·ra \kal'derə, -dirə\ *n* -s [Sp, lit., caldron, fr. LL *caldaria*] : a crater whose diameter is many times that of the volcanic vent because of the collapse or subsidence of the central part of a volcano or because of explosions of extraordinary violence

cal·dron *also* **caul·dron** \'kòldrən\ *n* -s [ME, alter. (influenced by L *caldus, calidus*) of *caudron*, fr. ONF, dim. of *caudiere*, fr. LL *caldaria*, fr. L, warm bath, fr. fem. of *caldarius* suitable for warming, fr. *caldus, calidus* warm, fr. *calēre* to be warm — more at LEE] **1** : a large kettle or boiler **2** : something resembling a boiling caldron or its contents (as in being a mixture of elements or forces in a state of unrest or upheaval) ⟨from this witches' ~ of politics, race, language . . . arose fierce . . . hatred —A.L.Guérard⟩ **3** : MOROCCO RED

ca·le·an \¦kalē¦ān\ *n* -s [Per *qalyān*] : a Persian water pipe

ca·leb·ite \'kālə,bīt\ *n* -s *usu cap* [*Caleb fl ab* 1200 B.C. Israelite who participated in the conquest of Canaan + E *-ite*] : a member of a clan that traces its descent to the biblical Caleb and was once a part of the tribe of Judah

ca·lèche or **ca·leche** \kə'lesh\ *n* -s [F *calèche* — more at CALASH] **1** : CALASH 1a **2** : a 2-wheeled horse-drawn vehicle with or without a folding top and with a driver's seat on the splashboard that is used in Quebec, Canada **3** : CALASH 2a

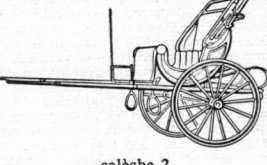

calèche 2

[1]**cal·e·do·ni·an** \¦kalə¦dōnēən, -nyən\ *adj, usu cap* [NL *Caledonia* Scotland (fr. L, province of ancient Britain) + E *-an*] **1** : of or relating to Scotland : SCOTTISH, SCOTS, SCOTCH **2** : of or relating to mountain-making movements of the European Paleozoic era — see GEOLOGIC TIME table

[2]**caledonian** \"\ *n* -s **1** *cap* : a native or inhabitant of Scotland : SCOTSMAN **2 caledonians** *pl but sing in constr, usu cap* : a square dance for eight resembling the quadrille

caledonian brown *n, usu cap C* **1** : a permanent natural pigment that consists chiefly of hydrated oxides of manganese and iron and is ruddy brown when raw but nearly black when burnt **2** : GYPSY 4

cal·e·do·nite \,kalə'dō,nīt\ *n* -s [F *calédonite*, fr. L *Caledonia* Scotland, its locality + F *-ite*] : a mineral $Cu_2Pb_5(SO_4)_3(CO_3)(HO)_6$ consisting of basic copper lead sulfate occurring in minute green crystals

cal·e·don jade green \'kalə,dän-, -əd°n-\ *n, usu cap C, often cap J&G* [*caledon*, prob. modif. of NL *Caledonia*] : VAT JADE GREEN

[1]**cal·e·fa·cient** \¦kalə¦fāshənt\ *adj* [L *calefacient-, calefaciens*, pres. part. of *calefacere* to warm — more at CHAFE] : making warm : HEATING

[2]**calefacient** \"\ *n* -s : a calefacient remedy

cal·e·fac·tion \¦kalə¦fakshən\ *n* -s [ML *calefaction-, calefactio*, fr. L *calefactus* (past part. of *calefacere*) + *-ion-, -io* -ion] **1** : WARMING **2** : the state of being warmed

[1]**cal·e·fac·to·ry** \¦kalə¦fakt(ə)rē\ *n* -ES [ML *calefactorium*, fr. LL, neut. of *calefactorius*] : a monastery room warmed and used as a sitting room

[2]**calefactory** \"\ *adj* [LL *calefactorius*, fr. L *calefactus* + *-orius* -ory] : making hot : producing or communicating heat

cal·e·fy \'kalə,fī\ *vb* -ED/-ING/-ES [ML *calificare*, *calificare* to heat, fr. L *calēre* to be warm — more at LEE] *vt* : to make warm ~ *vi* : to become warm

ca·lem·bour \¦kaləm¦bù(ə)r\ *n* -s [F] : PUN

calenda *var of* CALINDA

[1]**cal·en·dar** \'kaləndə(r)\ *n* -s [ME *calender*, fr. AF or ML; AF *calender*, fr. ML *kalendarium*, fr. L, moneylender's account book, fr. *kalendae* calends — more at CALENDS] **1** : a system by which the beginning, length, and divisions of the civil year are fixed and by which days and longer divisions of time (as weeks, months, and years) are arranged in a definite order — see GREGORIAN CALENDAR, JULIAN CALENDAR; MONTH table, YEAR table **2 a** : a tabular register of days according to a system usu. covering one year, referring the days of each month to the days of the week, often giving also important astronomical data, and sometimes indicating the dates of ecclesiastic festivals, holidays, and other events connected with particular days **b** : ALMANAC; *esp* : one giving agricultural information (as dates most suitable for planting a particular crop) **3** *obs* : an example to be followed : MODEL **4** : an orderly list of persons, things, or events: as **a** : a chronological register of documents with a brief summary of the contents of each, made to serve as an index to the documents of a period **b** : a list of cases to be tried in court or of prisoners to be tried with the time and reason for their commitment **c** : a list of bills, resolutions, or other items in the order in which they are reported out of committee for consideration by a legislative assembly **d** : a list of events or activities giving dates and details of planned events ⟨the college ~ begins with Freshman Week⟩; *also* : a list of events or the series of events scheduled for a particular period or time ⟨many new offerings of corporate securities on the ~ this week⟩ ⟨parades, parties, concerts, dances make up a full ~ for the weekend⟩ **e** : the whole range of possible variations in any type or category ⟨wanted for murder . . . and almost every other crime in the ~ —James Thurber⟩ **5** *Brit* : a university catalog

[2]**calendar** \"\ *vt* **calendared; calendared; calendaring** \-d(ə)riŋ\ **calendars** **1** : to enter (as a name or event) in a calendar or list **2** : to enter an analysis or summary of (as a book or document) in a catalog or index **3** : to assign a date to ⟨~*ed* predictions⟩

calendar art *n* : pictures of widely popular appeal displayed on wall calendars distributed esp. as advertisements ⟨have no more vitality or originality than *calendar art* —Elizabeth Hardwick⟩

calendar clock *n* : a clock that shows the days of the week and month, phases of the moon, and sometimes other phenomena in addition to hours, minutes, and seconds

calendar day *n* : a civil day : the time from midnight to midnight

cal·en·dar·i·al \¦==¦da(a)rēəl\ *adj* [[1]*calendar* + *-ial*] : CALENDRICAL

cal·en·dar·ic \¦==¦darik\ *adj* [[1]*calendar* + *-ic*] : CALENDRICAL

cal·en·dar·ist \'kaləndərəst\ *n* -s : one devoted to the study or making of calendars

calendar month *n* **1** : one of the months as named in the calendar **2** : the period from a day of one month to the corresponding day of the next month if such exists or if not to the last day of the next month (as from Jan. 3 to Feb. 3 or from Jan. 31 to Feb. 29)

calendar quarter *n* : one of the four periods of three months each of a calendar year

calendar round *n* : a period of fifty-two 365-day years after which the combinations of day names, day numbers, and month positions repeat in the Maya or Aztec calendars

calendar stone *n* : a stone with an inscription elucidating an ancient time-reckoning system ⟨the Aztec *calendar stone*, 12 feet in diameter, is preserved at Mexico City⟩

calendar watch *n* : a watch that shows the days of the week and month and sometimes other phenomena as well as hours, minutes, and seconds

calendar wednesday *n, usu cap C&W* : the Wednesday of each week that committees of the U.S. House of Representatives may bring unprivileged bills before that house

calendar week *n* : a week beginning with Sunday and ending with Saturday

calendar year *n* **1** : a period of a year beginning and ending with the dates which are conventionally accepted as marking the beginning and end of a numbered year (as Jan. 1 and Dec. 31 in the Gregorian calendar) **2** : a period of time equal in length to that of the year in the calendar conventionally in use (as in the Gregorian calendar 365 days or when a Feb. 29 is included 366 days)

[1]**cal·en·der** \'kaləndə(r)\ *archaic var of* CALENDAR

[2]**calender** \"\ *vt* **calendered; calendered; calendering** \-d(ə)riŋ\ **calenders** [MF *calandrer*, fr. *calandre*] : to press (as cloth, rubber, paper) between rollers or plates in order to make smooth and glossy or glazed or to thin into sheets — see SUPERCALENDER, [2]WATER 5c

[3]**calender** \"\ *n* -s [F *calandre* machine for calendering, modif. of Gk *kylindros* cylinder — more at CYLINDER] **1** *archaic* : CALENDERER **2** : a machine for calendering cloth, rubber, or paper by passing it between rollers or plates — see FRICTION CALENDER, SUPERCALENDER **3** : a machine for giving tubular knitted fabric the desired width by applying steam and stretching

[4]**calender** \"\ *n* -s [Per *qalandar*, fr. Ar, fr. Per *kalandar* uncouth man, perh. fr. *kaland* pickax, shovel] : one of a Sufic order of wandering mendicant dervishes

cal·en·der·er \-dərə(r)\ *n* -s [ME *calenderar*, fr. MF *calendrer* to calender + ME *-ar* (var. of *-er*)] : one that calenders

calender man *n* : CALENDERER; *also* : a worker who processes plastics or rubber sheets or fabrics in rolling or embossing machines

ca·len·dra \kə'lendrə\ *n, cap* [NL, modif. of F *calandre* weevil] : a genus of weevils (family Curculionidae) including a number of pests (as the maize billbug) of Indian corn and other field crops

ca·len·dri·cal \kə'lendrəkəl, ka-\ *also* **ca·len·dric** \-rik\ *adj* [*calendr-* (alter. of *calendar*) + *-ical* or *-ic*] **1** : of, relating to, characteristic of, or used in a calendar **2 a** : serving to measure time in calendar units or to record the calendar time or sequence of events ⟨~ inscriptions⟩ ⟨~ systems⟩ : serving the purposes of chronologizing **b** : having to do with or relating to the measuring and recording of calendar units of time or recording the calendar time or sequence of events ⟨solstice is a time of ~ importance⟩ **3** : occurring on special days as marked in a calendar ⟨~ festivals⟩

cal·en·dry \'kaləndrē\ *n* -ES [[3]*calender* + *-ry*] : a place for calendering

cal·ends or **kal·ends** \'kalən(d)z\ *n pl but sometimes sing in constr* [ME *kalendes*, fr. L *kalendae*; akin to L *calare* to call, proclaim — more at LOW] : the first day of the ancient Roman month from which days were counted backward to the ides — compare NONES; see GREEK CALENDS

ca·len·du·la \kə'lenjələ\ *n* [NL, fr. ML, fr. L *calendae*, *kalendae* calends + *-ula*; perh. fr. its use in folk medicine against menstrual disorders] **1** *cap* : a small genus of herbs (family Compositae) native to temperate regions and having alternate simple oblong to oblong-ovate leaves and large heads of yellow-rayed flowers with a naked receptacle and incurved achenes — see POT MARIGOLD **2** -s : any plant of the genus *Calendula* **3** : the dried florets of plants of the genus *Calendula* (esp. *C. officinalis*) sometimes used as a mild aromatic and diaphoretic

ca·len·du·lin \-lən\ *n* -s [ISV *calendul-* (fr. NL *Calendula*) + *-in*; orig. formed as G *kalendulin*] : a yellowish pigment found in the pot marigold

cal·en·ture \'kalən,chù(ə)r\ *n* -s [earlier *calentura*, fr. Sp, fever, fr. *calentar* to heat, fr. L *calent-, calens*, pres. part. of *calēre* to be warm — more at LEE] **1 a** : a fever formerly supposed to affect sailors in the tropics causing them to imagine the sea a green field and to leap into it **b** : any fever supposedly caused by heat **2** : PASSION, ARDOR, ZEAL

ca·le·sa \kə'lāsə\ *n* -s [Sp, fr. F *calèche* — more at CALASH] : a small 2-wheeled calash used in the Philippines

ca·le·sín \¦kalə¦sēn\ *n* -s [Sp, dim. of *calesa*] : a small one-horse hooded chaise or gig having a seat behind for the driver and used in the Philippines

ca·ley pea \'kālē-\ *n, usu cap C* [prob. fr. the name *Caley*] : SINGLETARY PEA

[1]**calf** \'kaf, -aa(ə)-, -ai-, -á-, -ä-\ *n, pl* **calves** \|vz\ *also* **calfs** \|fs\ *often attrib* [ME, fr. OE *cealf*; akin to OHG *kalb* calf, ON *kālfr*, Goth *kalbo*, ON *kalfi* calf of the leg, Gaulish *galba* fat man, L *galla* gall on a tree — more at GALL (excrescence)] **1** : the young of the domestic cow or of certain other larger members of the Bovidae **2** : the young of the domestic cow when past the vealer stage but not yet mature enough to be considered a beef **3** : the young of the elephant, rhinoceros, hippopotamus, moose, whale, or various other large animals **4** *pl calfs* **a** : the fur or skin of the young of the domestic cow **b** : leather made of the skin of the calf; *esp* : a fine light-colored bookbinder's leather made from the skin of a calf **5** : an awkward or silly boy or youth **6** : a small mass of ice set free from a coast glacier or from an iceberg or floe — **in calf** : PREGNANT — used of a cow

[2]**calf** \"\ *n, pl* **calves** [ME, fr. ON *kalfi*] : the fleshy hinder part of the leg below the knee

calfbound \'=,=\ *adj, of a book* : bound in calfskin

calf diphtheria *n* : necrobacillosis of the mouth and pharynx of calves and young cattle commonly passing into pneumonia or generalized septicemia and terminating in death

calf·hood \-,fùd,-f,hùd\ *n* -s : the state or time of being a calf ⟨~ vaccination⟩ ⟨~ disease⟩

calf·kill \'=,kil\ *n* -s **1** : any of several plants whose foliage is poisonous to cattle: as **a** : MOUNTAIN LAUREL **b** : SHEEP LAUREL **c** : an evergreen shrub (*Leucothoë catesbaei*) of the southeastern U.S. cultivated for ornament **2** : VELVET GRASS

calf knee *n* : BUCK KNEE—**calf-kneed** \'=¦=\ *adj*

calf·less \-fləs\ *adj* : being without a calf

calf love *n* : transitory affection felt by a boy or a girl for one of the opposite sex ⟨the ambiguous ardors of *calf love* — H.M.Kallen⟩ — called also *puppy love*

calf rope *n, dial*—a cry of surrender ⟨they punched him until he hollered *calf rope*⟩

calf's-foot jelly \-vz,-,-f,s-\ *n* : jelly made from gelatin obtained by boiling calves' feet

calf·skin \'=,=\ *n* -s : leather made of the skin of a calf

calf's-mouth \-vz,-,-f,s-\ *n, pl* **calf's-mouths** : SNAPDRAGON 1 a

calf's-tongue molding \-vz,-,-f,s-\ *n, archit* : a molding bearing in relief a series of tonguelike members

calf ward *n, Scot* : a small enclosure for calves

calf wheel *n* [so called fr. its resemblance to a bull wheel] : a drum for raising and lowering heavy strings of well casing

calfy \-fē\ *adj* : in calf

cal·ga·ry \'kalgərē, -ri\ *adj, usu cap* [fr. *Calgary*, Alberta, Canada] : of or from the city of Calgary, Alberta : of the kind or style prevalent in Calgary

Cal·gon \'kal,gän\ *trademark* — used for a sodium phosphate glass that approximates a sodium metaphosphate in composition and is used chiefly in water softening, in detergents, in tanning leather, and in deflocculating suspensions

[1]**ca·li** \'kälē\ *adj, usu cap* [fr. *Cali*, Colombia] : of or from the city of Cali, Colombia : of the kind or style prevalent in Cali

[2]**cali** *var of* CALA

cali- — see CALLI-

[1]**ca·lia·na** \kal'yänə\ *n, pl* **caliana** or **calianas** *usu cap* [Sp, of AmerInd origin] **1 a** : an Indian people of Venezuela **b** : a member of such people **2** : the language of the Caliana people constituting a language family

[2]**ca·lia·ná** \¦kalyə¦nä\ *n, pl* **calianá** or **calianás** *usu cap* [Pg, of AmerInd origin] **1 a** : a Tupi-Guaranian people of northeastern Brazil **b** : a member of such people **2** : the language of the Calianá people

cal·i·ban \'kalə,ban *also* -,bən\ *n* -s *usu cap* [after *Caliban*, a brutal and deformed slave in Shakespeare's *Tempest*] : a person or thing that is or is felt to be slavish, brutal, monstrous, or deformed

calibash *obs var of* CALIPASH

cal·i·ber or **cal·i·bre** \'kaləbə(r), *Brit also* kə'lēb-\ *n* -s [MF *calibre*, fr. OIt *calibro*, fr. Ar *qālib* shoemaker's last, prob. fr. Gk *kalapous*, fr. Gk *kalon* wood (fr. *kaiein* to burn) + *pous* foot — more at CAUSTIC, FOOT] **1 a** : the bore diameter of the barrel of a weapon (as a firearm) measured in rifled arms from land to land — compare LAND DIAMETER **b** : the diameter of the projectile fired from such a weapon **c** : the land-to-land diameter of the bore of a piece of ordnance used as a unit of measurement for stating the length of the tube of the piece — now used only of naval and coastal defense guns ⟨a 3″/50 gun is 3″ in bore and 50 ~*s* or 150″ long⟩ **2** : the diameter of a round or cylindrical body; *esp* : the internal diameter of a tube or hollow cylinder **3** *obs* : degree of importance or station in society : RANK **4 a** : degree in personal qualities (as mental capacity or breadth of knowledge) or moral qualities ⟨a man of high intellectual ~⟩ **b** : degree of excellence or importance : QUALITY ⟨the ~ of instruction⟩ **5** : the model number given to a watch movement by the factory **syn** see QUALITY

caliber compass *n* : CALIPERS

caliber rule *n, obs* : a gunmaker's calipers

cal·i·bo·gus *also* **cal·li·bo·gus** \,kalə'bōgəs\ *n* -ES [origin unknown] : a drink consisting of rum, spruce beer, and molasses

cal·i·brate \'kalə,brāt, *usu* -ād·+V\ *vt* -ED/-ING/-S [*caliber* + *-ate*] **1 a** *obs* : to ascertain the caliber of (as a thermometer tube) **b** : to determine or mark the capacity or the graduations of or to rectify the graduations of (as a graduated measuring instrument) **c** : to standardize (as a measuring instrument) by determining the deviation from standard esp. so as to ascertain the proper correction factors **2** : to determine by actual firing the corrections in range or elevation settings required to make (a piece of artillery) fire uniformly with a standard or reference piece

calibrated airspeed *n* : the reading (of an airspeed indicator) corrected for instrumental and installation errors

cal·i·bra·tion \,kalə'brāshən\ *n* -s **1** : the act or process of calibrating : state of being calibrated **2** : a set of graduations marked to indicate values — usu. used in pl. ⟨pressure ~*s* on steam gauges⟩

cal·i·bra·tor or **cal·i·brat·er** \'kalə,brād·ə(r), -ātə-\ *n* -s : one that calibrates: as **a** : an instrument for measuring the caliber of any passage **b** : an instrument that measures variable quantities or elements (as frequency or capacity) in electronic equipment

calibre *var of* CALIBER

caliceal *var of* CALYCEAL

calices *pl of* CALIX

ca·li·che \kə'lēchē\ *n* -s [AmerSp, fr. Sp, pebble in a brick, flake of lime, fr. *cal* lime, fr. L *calx* — more at CHALK] **1** : the nitrate-bearing gravel or rock of the sodium nitrate deposits of Chile and Peru **2** : a crust or succession of crusts of calcium carbonate that forms within or on top of the stony soil of arid or semiarid regions

ca·lic·i·form \kə'lisə,fórm\ *adj* [ISV *calic-* (fr. L *calic-*, *calix* cup) + *-iform* — more at CHALICE] : shaped like a calyx or bell; *specif* : of or relating to a type of pottery of the late neolithic and early bronze age found in France, Spain, England, and central Europe

cal·i·cle \'kaləkəl\ *n* -s [L *caliculus*, dim. of *calic-*, *calix* cup] : CALYCULUS

[1]**cal·i·co** \'kalə,kō, -lē-\ *n, pl* **calicoes** or **calicos** [fr. *Calicut*, city in India from which it was first imported] **1 a** *obs* : cotton cloth usu. figured imported from India **b** : any of various cotton stuffs of European make **c** *Brit* : a plain white cotton fabric that is heavier than muslin **d** : any of various cheap cotton fabrics with figured patterns **2** : any of several plant diseases usu. of virus origin characterized by leaf variegation: as **a** : the mosaic disease of tobacco; *also* : a plant affected with this disease **b** : a virus disease of the potato **c** : a virus disease of celery **3** : a blotched or spotted animal: as **a** : a horse with calico markings : PIEBALD **b** : BLACK CRAPPIE **c** : a goldfish of any fancy breed having thin transparent scales and a pigmented skin showing spots and blotches **4** *slang* : GIRL, WOMAN

[2]**calico** \"\ *adj* **1** : made of calico **2** : resembling calico in appearance : MULTICOLORED; *specif* : marked with well-defined patches of color (as on a tortoiseshell cat)

calico ash *n* [[2]*calico*] : lumber from a white ash (*Fraxinus americana*) esp. from the southern U.S.

calico bass *n* [[2]*calico*] **1** : BLACK CRAPPIE **2** : KELP BASS

calico bean *n* [[2]*calico*] **1** : KIDNEY BEAN **2** : SIEVA BEAN

calico bird *n* [[2]*calico*] : TURNSTONE

calico bush *n* [[2]*calico*] : MOUNTAIN LAUREL

calico corn *n* [[2]*calico*] : Indian corn having red, yellow, and brownish red striping and mottling of the kernels

calico crab *n* [[2]*calico*] **1** : LADY CRAB **2** : a shallow-water crab (*Hepatus epheliticus*) brilliantly spotted with red and occurring along the coast from Maryland to Cuba and Texas

cal·i·coed \-,kōd\ *adj* : dressed in calico

calico flower *n* [[2]*calico*] **1** : MOUNTAIN LAUREL **2** : a Brazilian vine (*Aristolochia elegans*) often cultivated for its brownish-purple beautifully veined flowers somewhat resembling a bent pitcher in shape **3** : FIVE-SPOT

calico marble *n* [[2]*calico*] : a brecciated limestone conglomerate found in Maryland and used as a decorative stone

calico plover or **calico snipe** *n* [[2]*calico*] : TURNSTONE

calico printing *n* [[1]*calico*] : the process of making fast-color designs on cotton fabrics, esp. calico

calico salmon *n* [[2]*calico*; fr. its variegated color in summer] : DOG SALMON

calico scale *n* [[2]*calico*] : a scale (*Lecanium cerasorum*) that is brown mottled with yellow and attacks various fruit and ornamental trees in California

calico tree *n* [[2]*calico*] : MOUNTAIN LAUREL

calico wood *n* [[2]*calico*] **1** : the wood of the silver bell **2** : SILVER BELL

calicular *var of* CALYCULAR

caliculate *var of* CALYCULATE

cal·i·cut \'kaləkət\ *adj, usu cap* [fr. *Calicut*, India] : of or from the city of Calicut, India : of the kind or style prevalent in Calicut

cal·id \'kaləd\ *adj* [L *calidus* — more at CALDRON] *archaic* : WARM, HOT, BURNING

cal·i·duct \'kalə,dəkt\ *n* -s [L *calidus* hot + E *-duct* (as in *aqueduct, ventiduct*)] : a duct to convey hot air, hot water, or steam for heating

calif *var of* CALIPH

califate *var of* CALIPHATE

cal·i·for·nia \¦kalə¦fórnyə, -ō(ə)n-, -nēə\ *adj, usu cap* [fr. *California*, state in the western U.S., fr. Sp, prob. fr. the name of an island in the romance *Las Sergas de Esplandián* (1510), by García Ordóñez de Montalvo, 15th cent. Span. writer] : of or from the state of California : of the kind or style prevalent in California : CALIFORNIAN ⟨*California* weather⟩

california barberry *n, usu cap C* : OREGON GRAPE

california bayberry *n, usu cap C* : a Pacific coast shrub or small tree (*Myrica californica*) with waxy resinous fruit

california bay tree *n, usu cap C* : CALIFORNIA LAUREL

california bearberry *n, usu cap C* : CALIFORNIA COFFEE 2

california blackberry *n, usu cap C* : an evergreen prostrate or semierect shrub (*Rubus vitifolius*) with oblong black fruit

california black oak *n, usu cap C* : a Pacific coast deciduous tree (*Quercus kelloggii*) with deeply parted bristle-tipped leaves

california black walnut *n, usu cap C* : a medium-sized tree (*Juglans californica*) with somewhat aromatic compound leaves and channeled or smooth edible nuts

california blight *n, usu cap C* : a fungous disease of peaches,

apricots, plums, and cherries caused by an imperfect fungus (*Coryneum carpophilum*) and producing shot holes, pustular spots on the leaf and fruit, cankers, and bud and twig blight
california bluebell *n, usu cap C* **:** a desert herb (*Phacelia minor*) of the western U.S. having blue or purple tubular flowers in one-sided clusters
california bluegrass *n, usu cap C* **:** MUTTON GRASS
california box elder *n, usu cap C* **:** a Pacific coast maple that is a variety (*Acer negundo* var. *californicum*) of the box elder having fruits that are crimson when young and white when mature
california brown pelican *n, usu cap C* **:** a Pacific coast pelican that is a variety (*Pelecanus occidentalis californicus*) of the brown pelican and has a creamy head and bright red gular pouch
california buckeye *n, usu cap C* **:** a shrub or small tree (*Aesculus californica*) with palmately compound leaves and fragrant white or rose-colored flowers
california buckthorn *n, usu cap C* **:** CALIFORNIA COFFEE 2
california bulrush *n, usu cap C* **:** a tall marsh sedge (*Scirpus californicus*) with 3-sided or nearly round almost leafless stems used for packing and as thatch for haystacks
california bur clover *n, usu cap 1st C* **:** an aggressive adventive clover (*Medicago hispida*) from Europe now widespread in southwestern U.S. and distinguished esp. by the double row of hooked spines on the spiral ridges of the seed pod
california buttercup *n, usu cap C* **:** a common herb (*Ranunculus californicus*) of moist foothills and canyons with twice-divided leaves and large showy yellow flowers
california calycanth *n, usu cap 1st C* **:** SPICEBUSH 2
california clapper rail *n, usu cap 1st C* **:** a large short-tailed clapper rail (*Rallus obsoletus*) of the Pacific coast of No. America from Puget Sound to Lower California
california coffee *n, usu cap 1st C* **1 :** CASCARA BUCKTHORN **2 :** a buckthorn (*Rhamnus californica*) with alternate but scattered dark green leaves, small greenish flowers, and reddish black berries
california color *n, usu cap 1st C* **:** a moderate brown that is yellower, lighter, and stronger than auburn, bay, or chestnut brown and redder, lighter, and stronger than coffee
california condor *n, usu cap 1st C* **:** a very large nearly extinct No. American vulture (*Gymnogyps californianus*) related to the condor of So. America and sometimes larger though of lighter build, chiefly dull black with some white and with a bare head and neck

California condor

california coneflower *n, usu cap 1st C* **:** a stiff hairy perennial herb (*Rudbeckia californica*) of the Pacific coast with coarse hispid foliage and long-stalked heads of yellow flowers
california cress *n, usu cap 1st C* **:** a hedge mustard (*Sisymbrium officinale*)
california dandelion *n, usu cap C* **:** CAT'S-EAR 1
california day lily *n, usu cap C* **:** DESERT LILY
california everlasting *n, usu cap C* **:** a stout biennial weedy plant (*Gnaphalium decurrens californicum*) with white woolly foliage that becomes green in age
california fan palm *n, usu cap C* **:** WASHINGTON PALM
california feverbush *n, usu cap C* **:** BEAR BRUSH
california flying fish *n, usu cap C* **:** a large flying fish (*Cypselurus californicus*) of the open seas off the coast of southern California and adjacent Mexico
california fuchsia *n, usu cap C* **:** a plant of the genus *Zauschneria* (esp. *Z. californica*) with brilliant scarlet flowers
california geranium *n, usu cap C* **:** a Mexican groundsel (*Senecio petasitis*) having leaves like those of a garden geranium and a much-branched cluster of yellow flower heads
california golden bells *n pl but sing or pl in constr, usu cap C* **:** CALIFORNIA YELLOW BELLS
california greasewood *n, usu cap C* **:** IODINE BUSH
california green *n, usu cap C* **:** a dark grayish yellow that is greener, less strong, and slightly darker than honey or yellowstone and redder and less strong than olivesheen
california ground squirrel *n, usu cap C* **:** a grizzled brown-and-gray burrowing squirrel (*Citellus beecheyi*) widely distributed in California and important as a vector of endemic plague and as a destructive pest on cultivated land
california gull *n, usu cap C* **:** a large gull (*Larus californicus*) resembling the herring gull in color and breeding in the plains region of the western U.S. where it is important as a consumer of noxious insects
california halibut *n, usu cap C* **:** a large greenish brown or grayish brown flatfish (*Paralichthys maculosus*) of the southern Californian and Mexican coasts important as a food fish and sport fish
california harebell *n, usu cap C* **:** a slender herb (*Campanula prenanthoides*) of the Pacific coast having a much-branched leafy stem and showy racemes of blue flowers with narrow corolla segments and long exserted style
california hazel *n, usu cap C* **:** a Pacific coast hazel that is a variety (*Corylus cornuta californica*) of the beaked hazel having velvety foliage and finely fringed nut beaks
california holly *n, usu cap C* **:** TOYON
california indigo bush *n, usu cap C* **:** MOCK LOCUST
california jack *n, usu cap C&J* **:** a two-handed card game that is a variety of high-low jack in which the winner of each trick draws first from the top of the stock which is kept face up
california jay *n, usu cap C* **:** a crestless jay (*Aphelocoma californica*) of the Pacific coast with blue to brownish gray above and white underneath
california job case *n, usu cap 1st C* **:** a job case widely used in the U.S. and typically having capitals on the right

California job case showing typical lay of type

california juniper *n, usu cap C* **:** a dense much-branched shrub or sometimes an erect tree (*Juniperus californica*) with ashy-gray shredding bark and reddish or brownish sweet berries covered with a dense whitish bloom
california laurel *n, usu cap C* **:** a Pacific coast tree (*Umbellularia californica*) of the laurel family having hard tough wood, very aromatic evergreen foliage, and small umbellate flowers succeeded by fleshy drupes resembling olives — called also *California bay tree, mountain laurel, Oregon myrtle, pepperwood, sassafras laurel, spice tree*
california lilac *n, usu cap C* **:** BLUEBLOSSOM
california lion *n, usu cap C* **1 :** an extinct very large lionlike cat (*Felis atrox*) of California **2 :** COUGAR
california live oak *n, usu cap C* **:** COAST LIVE OAK
california maidenhair *n, usu cap C* **:** a delicate California fern (*Adiantum emarginatum*) resembling the common maidenhair but having broadly fan-shaped pinnules
california maybush *n, usu cap C* **:** TOYON
california mountain holly *n, usu cap C* **:** REDBERRY 2c
california mussel *n, usu cap C* **:** an edible mussel (*Mytilus californianus*) sometimes responsible for mussel poisoning

¹cal·i·for·ni·an \ˌkaləˈfȯrnyən, -ō(ə)n-, -nēən\ *adj, usu cap* **1 :** of, relating to, or characteristic of the state of California **2 :** of, relating to, or characteristic of Californians
²californian \"\ *n* **1** -s *cap* **:** a native or resident of California **2** *usu cap* **:** a breed of domestic rabbits that is white with black points and developed by intercrossing large commercial breeds with the Himalayan
california newt *n, usu cap C* **:** GIANT NEWT
california nutmeg *n, usu cap C* **:** a California evergreen tree (*Torreya californica*) having a fleshy fruit resembling a nutmeg but with a strong turpentine flavor
california oakworm *n, usu cap C* **:** the larva of a small brownish California moth (*Phryganidia californica*) that feeds on the leaves of and frequently defoliates various oaks
california onyx *n, usu cap C* **:** an amber-and-brown variety of aragonite
california orange *n, usu cap C* **:** an orange grown in California; *specif* **:** NAVEL ORANGE
california pepper tree *n, usu cap C* **:** PEPPER TREE 1
california pitcher plant *n, usu cap C* **:** a marsh or bog herb (*Darlingtonia californica*) of the family Sarraceniaceae having leaves formed into a curved hood, the circular orifice at one side of the hood being covered by a 2-forked appendage
california pocket mouse *n, usu cap C* **:** a small mouselike rodent (*Perognathus californicus*) related to the ground squirrel
california pompano *n, usu cap C* **:** a Pacific coast butterfish (*Palometa simillima*) highly esteemed as food
california poppy *n, usu cap C* **1 :** a yellow-flowered plant of the genus *Eschscholtzia* (esp. *E. californica*) widely cultivated in varieties ranging in color from creamy yellow to dark red and often bicolored **2 :** WESTERN POPPY **3 :** CREAMCUPS 1
california poppy tree *n, usu cap C* **:** BUSH POPPY
california privet *n, usu cap C* **:** a Japanese privet (*Ligustrum ovalifolium*) used for hedges and having deciduous or half-evergreen foliage
california process *n, usu cap C* **:** a process of shoe construction in which the upper and the sock lining are stitched together, a platform cover is stitched to the upper, the platform is pressed into place, and the sole attached by cementing or vulcanizing — compare SLIP-LASTED
california quail *n, usu cap C* **:** a quail (*Lophortyx californica*) having an erectile black crest, the back brownish gray, the throat black bordered by white, the breast bluish, and the belly and flanks marked with black, white, and chestnut; *esp* **:** a member of the typical subspecies (*L. c. californica*) inhabiting the humid coast region of Oregon and California — compare VALLEY QUAIL
california red fir *n, usu cap C* **:** the largest of the native American true firs (*Abies magnifica*) having 4-angled leaves and purplish brown cones 6 to 9 inches long
california red scale *n, usu cap C* **:** a common California armored scale (*Aonidiella aurantii*) that is a major pest of citrus in California and that resembles but is somewhat larger than the San Jose scale and has a transparent covering shield so that the red or yellow body shows through
california rose *n, usu cap C* [prob. so called fr. a belief that it came from California] **:** an Asiatic bindweed (*Convolvulus japonicus*) naturalized in the eastern U.S. and having pink much-doubled sterile flowers
california rosebay *n, usu cap C* **:** a usu. pink-flowered rhododendron (*Rhododendron macrophyllum*) of the Pacific coast
california sage *or* **california sagebrush** *n, usu cap C* **:** a low ashy-gray California shrub (*Artemisia californica*) having finely divided leaves and long loose racemes of yellowish flowers
california sardine *n, usu cap C* **:** a sardine (*Sardinops caerulea*) of the Pacific coast — called also *pilchard*
california sassafras *n, usu cap C* **:** CALIFORNIA LAUREL
california scrub oak *n, usu cap C* **:** a low evergreen shrub (*Quercus dumosa*) of the California chaparral valuable for its resistance to and recovery from fire and intense drought
california sea trout *n, usu cap C* **:** a common greenling (*Hexagrammos decagrammus*) of the Pacific coast that is brownish or grayish in color, the males often being tinged with blue or copper and having sky-blue spots about the head
california skullcap *n, usu cap C* **:** a slightly hairy herb (*Scutellaria californica*) with oval leaves and yellowish white flowers
california slippery elm *n, usu cap C* **:** FLANNELBUSH
california soaproot *n, usu cap C* **:** SOAPPLANT a
california strawberry shrub *also* **california sweetshrub** *n, usu cap C* **:** SPICEBUSH 2
california sycamore *n, usu cap C* **:** a tall tree (*Platanus racemosa*) having deciduous bark, large alternate palmately lobed leaves, and ball-like clusters of greenish flowers without petals or sepals
california tea *n, usu cap C* **:** an erect herb (*Psoralea physodes*) that has greenish purple flowers and whose herbage can be dried and used as tea
california thistle *n, usu cap C* [prob. so called fr. a belief that it came from California] **:** CANADA THISTLE
california thrasher *n, usu cap C* **:** the common thrasher (*Toxostoma redivivum*) of California that is brown above and unstriped buffy below
california tokay *n, usu cap C&T* **:** TOKAY 2
california towhee *n, usu cap C* **:** a chiefly dull-brown towhee (*Pipilis fuscus crissalis*)
california tree poppy *n, usu cap C* **:** MATILIJA POPPY
california vetch *n, usu cap C* **:** a very slender almost prostrate herb (*Vicia exigua*) with compound leaves and long-stalked clusters of white or purplish flowers
california vine disease *n, usu cap C* **:** PIERCE'S DISEASE
california vulture *n, usu cap C* **:** CALIFORNIA CONDOR
california white oak *n, usu cap C* **:** a tall graceful tree (*Quercus lobata*) native to California and much planted as a shade tree having deep-lobed leaves dark green above and whitish beneath and nearly sessile long-conical acorns — called also *roble, valley oak, valley white oak*
california white pine *n, usu cap C* **:** PONDEROSA PINE
california wild grape *n, usu cap C* **:** a woody vine (*Vitis californica*) that climbs on and often smothers trees and that has a fragrant dense white bloom and purple fruit
california wild rose *n, usu cap C* **:** a prickly shrub (*Rosa californica*) of the Pacific coast with pink flowers in leafy-bracted clusters
california wine *n, usu cap C* **:** a complex of wines produced in California, some resembling in varying degree Old World Burgundy, Chablis, Chianti, claret, Marsala, muscatel, port, Riesling, sauterne, sherry, and vermouth and others having distinctive characteristics not duplicated elsewhere but made from the grapes of an imported vine (*Vinis vinifera*)
california woodpecker *n, usu cap C* **:** a common woodpecker (*Melanerpes formicivora bairdi*) of the Pacific states noted for its habit of storing acorns in little holes which it digs in the bark of trees
california yellow bells *n pl but sing or pl in constr, usu cap C* **:** a California annual plant (*Emmenanthe penduliflora*) of the family Hydrophyllaceae with pendulous yellow flowers — called also *whispering bells*
california yellowtail *n, usu cap C* **:** a yellowtail (*Seriola dorsalis*) of the California coast and southward that reaches a length of three feet and is an esteemed sport fish
california yew *n, usu cap C* **:** PACIFIC YEW
cal·i·for·nio \ˌkaləˈfȯrn(ˌ)yō, -ō(ə)n-, -nēˌō\ *n* -s *cap* [Sp, fr. *California*] **1 :** CALIFORNIAN 1 **2 :** one of the original Spanish colonists of California or their descendants
cal·i·for·nite \-ˌnīt\ *n* -s [*California*, its locality + E *-ite*] **:** a compact variety of idocrase of an olive-green or grass-green color closely resembling jade
cal·i·for·ni·um \-ˌnēəm, -nyəm\ *n* -s [NL, fr. *California* + NL *-ium*] **:** a radioactive element discovered by bombarding curium 242 with alpha particles — symbol *Cf;* see ELEMENT table
cal·i·ga \ˈkaləgə\ *n, pl* **cali·gae** \-ləˌgī, -əˌjē\ [L] **1 a :** a heavy-soled Roman military shoe or sandal worn by all ranks up to and including centurions **2** [ML, fr. L] **:** a stocking worn by bishops — compare BUSKIN 4
ca·lig·i·nous \kəˈlijənəs\ *adj* [MF or L; MF *caligineux*, fr. L *caliginosus*, fr. *caligin-, caligo* darkness + *-osus* -ous; akin to L *columba* dove — more at COLUMBINE] **:** MISTY, DARK, OBSCURE
ca·li·go \kəˈlē(ˌ)gō, -ˈī-\ *n* [NL, fr. L, darkness, dimness of sight] **1** *cap* **:** a genus of very large butterflies of tropical America that are related to the morphos and satyrs and have wings richly but somberly colored above and with eyespots and intricate lines below **2** *pl* **caligos** *or* **caligoes :** a butterfly of the genus *Caligo*
caligraphy *var of* CALLIGRAPHY
calimanco *var of* CALAMANCO
ca·lim·er·is \kəˈlimərəs\ *n, cap* [NL, fr. *cali-* + Gk *meris* part; akin to L *merēre* to deserve — more at MERIT] **:** a small genus of Asiatic herbs (family Compositae) resembling the genus *Aster* but differing in having the bracts of the involucre scarious-margined
cal·i·myr·na fig \ˌkaləˈmərnə-, -mōnə-\ *n, usu cap C* [fr. *Calimyrna*, a trademark] **:** the Smyrna fig when grown in California
ca·lin \ˈkālaⁿ\ *n* -s [F, fr. Pg *calaim*, fr. Ar *qala'ī*] **:** an alloy apparently of lead and tin of which the Chinese make tea canisters and other utensils
ca·li·na·go \ˌkaləˈnä(ˌ)gō\ *n* -s *usu cap* [Sp, fr. Carib *karinako*, lit., brave men, fr. *kari-* (fr. *ka* sky, spirit) + *-na* group + *-ko* (group pl.)] **1 :** a Carib of the Lesser Antilles **2 :** ISLAND CARIB
ca·lin·da \kəˈlində\ *or* **ca·len·da** \-ˈe-\ *n* -s [AmerSp] **:** a Negro ceremonial dance of the West Indies and formerly of the U.S.
ca·line \ˈkāˌlēn\ *n* -s [origin unknown] **:** the complex of hormones or hormonelike factors not including auxin that are involved in the formation of roots, stems, and leaves
cal·i·nut \ˈkaləˌnət\ *n* -s [of African origin; akin to Mende *kale* seed, stone of a fruit, Bambara, a kind of plant] **:** the flattened brown circular seed of a tropical African woody vine (*Physostigma cylindrosperma*)
cal·i·pash \ˈkaləˌpash, -ˌa(ə)-, -ai-, ˌ=ˈ=\ *n* -ES [origin unknown] **:** the fatty gelatinous dull-greenish substance found under the upper shell of a turtle and esteemed as a delicacy
cal·i·pee \ˈkaləˌpē, ˌ=ˈ=\ *n* -s [origin unknown] **:** the fatty gelatinous light-yellow substance found immediately over the lower shell of a turtle and esteemed as a delicacy
¹cal·i·per *or* **cal·li·per** \ˈkaləpə(r)\ *n* -s [alter. of *caliber*] **1 a :** a measuring instrument having two legs or jaws that can be adjusted to determine thickness, diameter, caliber, and distance between surfaces — usu. used in pl. and often with *pair* ⟨a pair of ~*s*⟩; see HERMAPHRODITE CALIPER, INSIDE CALIPER, MICROMETER CALIPER, ODD-LEG CALIPER, OUTSIDE CALIPER, VERNIER CALIPER **b :** an instrument consisting of a graduated beam and at right angles to it a fixed arm and a movable arm which slides along the beam to measure the diameter of logs and trees **c :** a watchmaker's tool with adjustable female center points for holding a wheel while it is being trued **d :** CALIPER SPLINT **2 :** thickness esp. of paper, paperboard, or a tree — compare POINT 16e

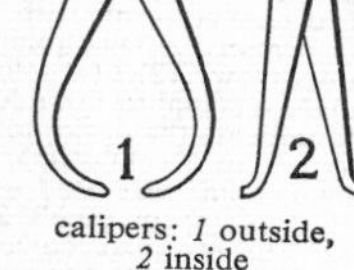

calipers: *1* outside, *2* inside

²caliper *or* **calliper** \"\ *vt* **calipered** *or* **callipered; calipered** *or* **callipered; calipering** *or* **callipering** \-p(ə)riŋ\ **calipers** *or* **callipers :** to measure by or as if by calipers
³caliper *var of* CALIBER
caliper compass *n* **:** a divider or a hermaphrodite caliper
caliper gauge *n* **1 :** a gauge of fixed size for calipering **2 :** VERNIER CALIPER
caliper rule *n* **:** a rulelike scale with one fixed and one adjustable jaw
caliper splint *n* **:** a support for the leg consisting of two metal rods extending between a foot plate and a padded thigh band and worn so that the weight is borne mainly by the hipbone
caliper square *n* **:** a caliper consisting of jaws placed at right angles to a graduated beam, one or both jaws being adjustable
ca·liph *or* **ca·lif** \ˈkāləf *also* -ˈa-\ *n* -s [ME *caliphe, califfe*, fr. MF *calife*, fr. Ar *khalīfah* successor, fr. *khalafa* to succeed] **1 :** a successor of Muhammad as temporal and spiritual head of the community and religious faith of Islam — used primarily in historical reference following Turkey's abolition of the caliphate on March 23, 1924 **2 :** a Muslim political leader claiming rightful succession to the caliphate
ca·liph·al \-əl\ *adj* **:** of or relating to a caliph
ca·liph·ate *also* **ca·lif·ate** \-ˌfāt, -fət, *usu* -d·+V\ *n* -s [F *califat*, fr. ML *caliphatus*, fr. *calipha* caliph (fr. Ar *khalīfah*) + *-atus* -ate] **:** the office, term, or dominion of a caliph
ca·lip·pus \kəˈlipəs\ *n, cap* [NL, irreg. fr. *cali-* + *-hippus*] **:** a genus of dwarf horses of the Pliocene of No. America prob. not directly ancestral to modern horses
ca·lir·oa \kəˈlirəwə\ *n, cap* [NL, alter. of L *Callirrhoe*, a water nymph — more at CALLIRRHOË] **:** a genus of sawflies (family Tenthredinidae) including the pear slugs
cal·i·saya bark \ˌkaləˈsīə-\ *n* [Sp *calisaya*, perh. fr. *Calisaya*, 17th cent. Indian who revealed the properties of quinine to the Spaniards] **:** cinchona bark obtained from either of two cinchonas (*Cinchona calisaya* and *C. ledgeriana*) or from a hybrid of either of these with other cinchonas — called also *yellow cinchona*
cal·is·then·ic \ˌkaləsˈthenik, -ēk\ *also* **cal·is·then·i·cal** \-əkəl, -ēk-\ *adj* [*cali-* + Gk *sthenos* strength + E *-ic* or *-ical* — more at ASTHEN-] **:** of or relating to calisthenics ⟨well-planned ~ periods —*Athletic Jour.*⟩
cal·is·then·ics \ˌ==ˈ=niks, -ēks\ *n pl but sometimes sing in constr* [*cali-* + Gk *sthenos* strength + E *-ics*] **1 :** systematic exercises performed usu. in rhythm and often in a group without apparatus or with light hand apparatus to improve the strength, suppleness, balance, and health of the body **2** *usu sing in constr* **:** the art or practice of calisthenics
cal·is·the·ni·um \ˌ==ˈthēnēəm, -en-\ *n* -s [*calisthenics* + *-ium* (as in *gymnasium*)] **:** a gymnasium for calisthenics
calithump *var of* CALLITHUMP
cal·i·ver \ˈkaləvə(r)\ *n* -s [modif. of MF *calibre* caliber] **:** an early handgun like a harquebus
ca·lix \ˈkāliks, -ēks *also* -ˈa-\ *n, pl* **cali·ces** \-ləˌsēz\ [L — more at CHALICE] **:** CUP; *esp* **:** an ecclesiastical chalice
¹ca·lix·tin \kəˈlikstən\ *or* **ca·lix·tine** \", -ˌtēn, -ˌtīn\ *n* -s *usu cap* [F *calixtin*, fr. ML *calixtinus*, fr. L *calix* cup] **:** a member of a Hussite body that maintained that the laity should receive the cup as well as the bread in the Eucharist
²calixtin \"\ *or* **calixtine** \"\ *n* -s *usu cap* [Georg *Calixt* (Latinized as Georgius Calixtus) †1656 Ger. theologian + E *-in* or *-ine*] **:** a follower of Georgius Calixtus — compare SYNCRETISM 1
¹calk *var of* CAULK
²calk *or* **caulk** \ˈkȯk\ *n* -s [prob. back-formation fr. *calkin* (taken as a pl. or a verbal n.), fr. ME *kakun*, fr. MD or ONF; MD *calcoen* horse's hoof, fr. ONF *calcain* heel, fr. L *calcaneum*, fr. *calc-, calx;* akin to Lith *kulnis* heel, Skt *kaṭi* hip, Gk *kōlon* limb, OHG *scelah* squinting, crooked — more at CYLINDER] **1 :** a tapered wedge or cone-shaped piece of iron or steel projecting downward on the shoe of a draft animal to prevent slipping — called also *calkin* **2 :** a pointed metal piece or a device with sharp points worn on the shoe of a person or boot to prevent slipping

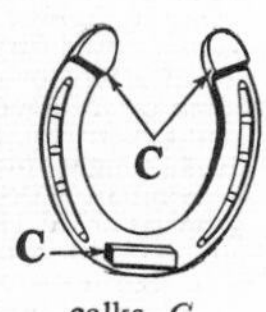

calks, *C*

³calk *or* **caulk** \"\ *vt* -ED/-ING/-s **1 :** to furnish with calks to prevent slipping ⟨~ the shoes of a horse⟩ **2 :** to wound with a calk ⟨the lame horse had ~*ed* himself⟩
¹calker *var of* CAULKER
²calk·er \ˈkȯkər\ *Scot var of* ²CALK 1
cal·kin *also* **caul·ken** \ˈkȯkən, ˈkalk-\ *n* -s [ME *kakun* — more at CALK] **:** ²CALK 1
calking *var of* CAULKING
calking roll *n* [*calking*, fr. pres. part. of ³*calk*] **:** ³BOOT 3b
¹call \ˈkȯl\ *vb* -ED/-ING/-s [ME *callen*, prob. fr. ON *kalla;* akin to OE hildecalla battle herald, CHG *kallōn* to talk loudly, MIr *gall* swan, OSlav *glasŭ* voice] *vi* **1 a :** to speak in a loud distinct voice so as to be heard at a distance esp. in

order to attract the attention of, summon, or make a request of another : CRY, SHOUT ⟨~ for help⟩ **b** : to make a request, appeal, or demand ⟨~ upon all nations to keep the peace⟩ ⟨he ~*ed* for an investigation of the facts⟩ **c** *of an animal* : to utter a characteristic note or cry ⟨the thrush ~*s*⟩ **d** : to communicate with or try to get into communication with a person by telephone — often used with *up* **e** *card games* (1) : to make a demand (as by requesting or signaling for a particular card or suit to be played) (2) *bridge* : to make a declaration (sense 4) (3) *poker* : to make one's total bet equal to that of the last preceding bettor **f** : to give the calls for a square dance — often used with *off* **2** *Scot* : to become driven : DRIVE — usu. used in the form *ca'*; compare CA' CANNY **3** : to make a brief stop or visit at a place ⟨~ to pay your respects⟩ ⟨only one ship a year ~*s* at the island⟩ — often used with *on* ⟨a salesman ~*ing* on his customers⟩ ~ *vt* **1 a** (1) : to utter in a loud distinct voice : SHOUT, CRY — often used with *out* ⟨~ out a number⟩ (2) : to announce or read out loudly or authoritatively ⟨~ the roll⟩ ⟨~ a halt⟩ — often used with *off* ⟨~ off a row of figures⟩ **b** (1) : to command or request (as by an utterance) to come or be present ⟨I can ~ spirits from the vasty deep—Shak.⟩ : SUMMON ⟨~*ed* to testify in court⟩ ⟨~ off the dogs⟩ (2) : to cause to come : BRING ⟨~ a new principle into operation⟩ ⟨~ to mind the words of his brother⟩ **c** (1) : to summon to a particular activity, employment, or office ⟨~*ed* to the presidency of the university⟩ ⟨~*ed* to active duty in the army⟩ (2) : to move or impel (as by divine influence) to a particular condition or activity ⟨America is ~*ed* to greatness —A.E.Stevenson b.1900⟩ (3) : to summon (a Jewish male) to read a benediction or a set portion of the Torah before the congregation at public worship in the synagogue **d** : to invite or command (a group) to meet : CONVOKE ⟨~ a meeting⟩ **e** : to rouse from sleep or summon to get up by a call **f** : to give the order for : bring into action ⟨~ a case in court⟩ ⟨~ a strike⟩ **g** (1) *bridge* : to make a demand for (a particular card or suit to be played) (2) *poker* : to make one's total bet equal to (the preceding bet) or equal to the bet of (the preceding bettor) (3) : to challenge (a person) to make good on a statement ⟨if he is not telling the truth someone should ~ him⟩ (4) : to charge with or censure for an offense — often used with *on* ⟨they ~*ed* him on his sloppy dress⟩ **h** : to decoy (game) by imitating the characteristic cry **i** : to halt (a baseball game or other public event) because of unsuitable conditions (as rain or darkness) **j** : to rule on the status of (as a played ball or a player's action) ⟨~ a tennis serve out⟩ ⟨~ a base runner safe⟩ **k** : to give the calls for (a square dance or a square-dance figure) — often used with *off* **l** (1) : to communicate with or try to get in communication with (a person) by telephone — sometimes used with *up* ⟨~ me up tomorrow⟩ (2) : to deliver (a message) by telephone (3) : to make a signal to (an addressee as by transmitting his call sign) to indicate the desire to transmit a message — often used with *up* ⟨~ up the flagship⟩; compare CQ **m** : to suspend (playing time) ⟨time was ~*ed* while the field was cleared⟩ **n** *cricket* (1) : to inform (one's fellow batsman) that it is safe to run (2) : to inform (a bowler) that a delivery is unfair — used of an umpire **o** (1) : to demand payment of esp. by formal notice ⟨directors ~*ed* an assessment of 10 percent⟩ (2) : to demand presentation of (an issue of bonds) for redemption and payment ⟨the bonds could be ~*ed* 10 years after issue⟩ **2 a** : to speak of or address by a specified name ⟨they ~ her Kitty⟩ : give a name to : NAME ⟨forces . . . which Empedocles ~*s* love and hate —Arnold Toynbee⟩ **b** (1) : to give a descriptive name to (the actual price at which any commodity is commonly sold is ~*ed* its market price —Adam Smith⟩ : regard as or characterize as of a certain kind : describe as : CONSIDER ⟨you don't ~ this keeping what belongs to you —Lillian Hellman⟩ ⟨a world where nothing can be ~*ed* unknowable —W.R.Inge⟩ (2) : ESTIMATE : reckon to be ⟨how far would you ~ it to town⟩ : consider for purposes of an estimate or for convenience ⟨99 cents, ~ it an even dollar⟩ **c** *dial Eng* : SCOLD, REVILE **d** *dial* : to announce or publish as an official notice of intention ⟨when our names have been ~*ed* in church we can be married⟩ **e** *South & Midland* : MENTION, SPEAK ⟨~*ed* the loved name⟩ ⟨carefully refrained from ~*ing* his name —Ellen Glasgow⟩ **f** : to describe correctly in advance of or without knowledge of the event ⟨he ~*ed* the upward trend of the market in February⟩ : name or describe in advance : PREDICT, GUESS ⟨~ the toss of a coin wrongly⟩ **3** *chiefly Scot, usu* **ca'** \ˈkȯ\ **a** : DRIVE ⟨~ an animal to market⟩ **b** : to drive into place : KNOCK, HAMMER **c** : PROPEL, RUN ⟨~ some machinery⟩ : USE ⟨~ an instrument⟩ **4** : to pay a brief visit to ⟨I'll ~ you at your house —Shak.⟩ — **call a spade a spade** : to give a thing its plain name even if considered offensive : speak plainly or bluntly without elaboration or euphemism — **call cousin** : to claim relationship ⟨*call cousin* with the mayor⟩ — **call for 1** : to call (as at one's house) to get ⟨I'll *call for* you at 8 o'clock⟩ **2** : to require as necessary or appropriate ⟨lifting the box *called for* all her strength⟩ : make necessary ⟨more business *calls for* more judges —S.D.Bailey⟩ **3** : to give an order for : DIRECT ⟨legislation *calling for* the establishment of two new schools⟩ : provide for ⟨the design *calls for* three windows⟩ — **call in question** *or* **call in doubt 1** : to cast doubt upon : challenge the soundness of : IMPUGN ⟨standards of value which are never *called in question* —F.R.Leavis⟩ **2** *obs* : to make inquiry into — **call it a day** : to stop at least for the present whatever one has been doing — **call it quits 1** : call it a day **2** : to cease efforts (as of both parties of a rivalry, strife, or competition) ⟨neither side having a clear advantage, they decided to *call it quits*⟩ — **call names** : to address or speak of a person or thing with contemptuous or offensive names — **call on** : to call upon — **call one's bluff** : to challenge and expose an empty pretense or threat — **call one's shot** : to declare from a knowledge of the alignment of sights at the instant of firing a rifle or pistol the spot which a bullet should strike on the target; *also* : to predict in any game or sport the result of a shot — **call the shots** : call the tune — **call the tune** : to be in charge or control : MANAGE : determine policy or procedure ⟨the secretary *called the tune* all through the meeting⟩ — **call the turn 1** *in faro* : to name the order in which the last three cards in the dealing box will appear on the last turn of the deal **2** : CALL *vt* 2f **3** : call the tune — **call to account** : to hold responsible : REPRIMAND ⟨*called to account* for violation of the rules⟩ — **call to order** : to request to come to order: as **a** : to open (a meeting) for business **b** : to warn or restrain (a person transgressing the rules of debate) — **call to the bar** : to admit as a barrister — **call to the colors** : to summon for active military duty — **call upon** : REQUIRE, OBLIGE ⟨may be *called upon* to do several jobs⟩ : make a demand upon : depend on ⟨universities are *called upon* to produce trained men⟩ — **call within the bar** : to appoint as king's or queen's counsel

²call \"\ *n* -S [ME, fr. *callen*, v.] **1 a** : a loud vocal utterance (as in addressing or summoning) : SHOUT, CRY ⟨a ~ for help⟩ **b** : an imitation of the cry of a bird or other animal made to decoy it **c** *obs* : a decoy bird **d** : an instrument (as a whistle or pipe) used for calling ⟨a boatswain's ~⟩ ⟨a duck ~⟩ **e** : the cry of a bird or other animal **2 a** : a request or command to come or to assemble : SUMMONS, INVITATION ⟨the council met at the ~ of the president⟩ **b** : a summons or signal esp. on a drum, bugle, or pipe ⟨bugle ~*s* were heard in the distance⟩ — compare HUNT'S-UP, REVEILLE **c** : admission to the bar as a barrister **d** (1) : an invitation to become the minister of a church; *also* : the official written form of such an invitation usu. signed by members of the congregation (2) : an invitation to accept a professional appointment ⟨he accepted a ~ to the state university⟩ **e** (1) : a divine vocation or prompting to a special service or duty (2) : a strong inner prompting to undertake a particular course of action or to enter a particular type of vocation **f** : a summons, invitation, or appeal to undertake a particular course of action ⟨a ~ for the restoration of spiritual values⟩ **g** : a summoning (as by a posted notice) of actors to rehearsal or members of a film unit to a rehearsal or a take ⟨the ~ is for 11 o'clock⟩; *also* : REHEARSAL **h** : a signal summoning firemen and apparatus into action ⟨a fire ~⟩ ⟨a drill ~⟩; *also* : the response of men and equipment to such a call **i** : the attraction or appeal of a particular activity, condition, or place ⟨islanders feel strongly the ~ of the sea⟩ **j** : an announcement issued by the national committee of a political party concerning a nominating convention to be held, its date and place, and the rules governing the choosing and apportionment of delegates to it **k** : CALL OF NATURE **l** : an order specifying the number of men to be inducted into the armed services during a specified period ⟨the November ~ is for 10,000 men⟩ **m** : an order left at a hotel desk setting a specified hour for being wakened ⟨leave a ~ for 7:30⟩ **3 a** : DEMAND, REQUIREMENT ⟨maintaining order makes the greatest ~ on his energies⟩ : CLAIM ⟨the aircraft industry continues to have first ~ on aluminum production —*American Annual*⟩ **b** : NECESSITY, OBLIGATION, OCCASION, JUSTIFICATION ⟨there is no ~ for the federal government to apologize for the views of a private citizen —J.L.Teller⟩ **c** : a demand for payment of money: as (1) : a notice by the U.S. Treasury to depository banks to transfer a part of its deposit balance to the Federal Reserve bank (2) : a notice to a stockholder or subscriber to pay an assessment or an installment of subscription to capital **d** : an option to buy a certain amount of stock, grain, or other commodity at a fixed price at or within a certain time — compare ²PUT 3 **e** : an instance of asking for something : REQUEST ⟨the library has many ~*s* for Christmas stories⟩ **4** *obs* : CALLING 4 **5** : a roll call (as to discover absentees or to take the ayes and noes) ⟨the speaker ordered a ~ of the house⟩ **6** : a short usu. formal visit ⟨pay a ~ on a neighbor⟩ : a brief stop in passing (as to conduct business or make a delivery) ⟨a salesman making his ~*s*⟩ **7** : the name or thing called or indicated by calling ⟨his ~ was heads; mine was tails⟩ **8** : the act or an instance of calling in a card game **9** : a reference in a land survey or grant to an object, a measurement, or other descriptive detail requiring a corresponding physical detail on the land **10** : the act or an instance of calling on the telephone **11 a** : CALL SIGN **b** : a signal (as a letter or combination of letters) sent by a caller to inform an addressee that the caller has a message to transmit to him — compare CQ **12** : the solo or recitative part of a folk song or rhyme; *esp* : the stanza answered by the refrain ⟨the standard West African song pattern of ~ and response, by a leader and chorus —Roger Angell⟩ **13** : the score at any given time while a tennis game is in progress ⟨what's the ~, please⟩ **14** : a direction or a succession of directions for the next movement or figure of a square dance chanted or rhythmically called to the dancers by a caller **15** : a decision or ruling made by an official of a sports contest — **at call** *or* **on call 1** : available for use : at the service of ⟨thousands of men *at his call*⟩ : ready to respond to a summons or command ⟨a doctor *on call* at any hour⟩ **2** : subject to demand for payment or return without previous notice ⟨money lent *at call*⟩ ⟨cotton bought *on call*⟩ — compare CALL LOAN — **have the call** : to be in the leading position or in greatest demand — **within call** : within hearing or reach of a summons : subject to summons

cal·la \ˈkalə\ *n* [NL, modif. of Gk *kallaia* rooster's wattles, perh. fr. *kallos* beauty — more at CALLI-] **1** *cap* : a genus of bog herbs (family Araceae) with ovate cordate leaves and a spreading spathe with white upper surface and a short cylindrical spadix — see WATER ARUM **2** -S **a** *or* **calla lily** : a familiar house plant or greenhouse plant (*Zantedeschia aethiopica*) with a flowerlike inflorescence consisting of a pure white showy spathe and yellow spadix **b** : any of various plants resembling but not necessarily related to the calla — see BLACK CALLA, GOLDEN CALLA, PINK CALLA

call·a·ble \ˈkȯləbəl\ *adj* : capable of being called : liable to be called; *specif* : subject to a demand for presentation for payment before maturity ⟨a ~ bond⟩

calla green *n* : a moderate yellow green that is greener and deeper than average moss green, yellower and darker than average pea green, yellower and duller than apple green (sense 1), and greener and darker than box green

cal·la·is \ˈkaləəs\ *n, pl* **cal·la·i·des** \kəˈlāə,dēz\ [L, fr. Gk *kalaïs, kallaïs*] : an ancient green stone, prob. turquoise

calla lily begonia *n* : a wax begonia the youngest leaves of which are white and somewhat resemble the calla lily flower

cal·lant \ˈkälən(t)\ *or* **cal·lan** \-ən\ *n* -S [D or ONF; D *kalant* customer, fellow, fr. ONF *calland* customer, fr. L *calent-, calens*, pres. part. of *calēre* to be warm — more at LEE] *chiefly Scot* : BOY, LAD, FELLOW

cal'·late \ˈka(l),lāt\ *vt* [by contraction] *dial* : CALCULATE 4

callathump *var of* CALLITHUMP

call–back \ˈ=,=\ *n* -S **1** : a return call on a customer to transact unfinished business or give repair or maintenance service on goods sold **2 a** : a recall of an employee to work after a lay-off **b** : a summons back to work after regular working hours

call–back pay *n* : guaranteed minimum payment to a worker called back for work after completing his regular shift and leaving the plant

call bell *n* : a bell used to summon an attendant or give an alarm or notice

call bird *n* : a bird used to lure others : a decoy bird

call–board *n* : BULLETIN BOARD: as **a** : a backstage bulletin board on which rehearsal calls and notices to the company are posted **b** : a board on which train times and the assignments of train crews are posted

call box *n* **1** : a post-office box from which the renter can get his mail only by calling for it at a delivery window **2** *Brit* : a public telephone booth **3** : a street telephone for police communications or for reporting fires

callboy \ˈ=,=\ *n* **1 a** : a page who gives periodic warning calls before curtain time and individual warnings to actors when time for their appearance on stage is approaching **b** : a page who notifies sleeping railroad train-crew members in time for duty — called also *caller* **2** : a hotel employee who pages guests and delivers messages

call button *n* : a push button to operate a call bell or other summoning device

call card *n* : CALL SLIP

call change *n* : a change rung on bells according to the directions of the conductor or according to written instructions

call down *vt* **1** : to cause or entreat to descend : bring or draw down : INVOKE ⟨*call down* a blessing on the crops⟩ ⟨*call down* upon himself the displeasure of the village⟩ **2** : to reprimand or scold for an offense ⟨she *called* me *down* for coming in late⟩

call–down \ˈ=,=\ *n* -S : REPRIMAND

call duck *n* : a breed of very small domestic ducks consisting of a gray variety like the mallard and a pure white variety, both often used by hunters as decoys

called *past of* CALL

called strike *n* : a pitched ball not swung at by a baseball batter but ruled by the umpire to have passed through the strike zone

call·ee \(ˈ)kȯˈlē\ *n* -S [¹*call* + *-ee*] : one that is called

ca·lle·jón \kälʸeˈhōn\ *n, pl* **calle·jo·nes** \-hōnās\ [Sp, lit., narrow lane, narrow pass, aug. of *calleja* small street, lane, dim. of *calle* street, fr. L *callis* path] : the narrow passageway between the shoulder-high barrier around a bullring and the wall of the grandstand

¹cal·ler \ˈkälər\ *adj* [ME *callour*, prob. alter. of *calvur*] **1** *Scot* : FRESH ⟨~ fish⟩ ⟨~ herrings⟩ **2** *Scot* : COOL, REFRESHING ⟨blessed by the ~ upland air —R.P. Kennedy⟩

²call·er \ˈkȯlə(r)\ *n* -S : one that calls: as **a** : one that makes the calls for a square dance **b** : one that announces train departures and arrivals in a railroad waiting room **c** : CALLBOY **d** : an announcer of winning numbers in a gambling establishment — called also *floorman*

cal·let \ˈkalət\ *n* -S [perh. fr. MF *caillette* frivolous person, after *Caillette fl* 1500 Fr. court fool] **1** *now Scot* : TRULL, PROSTITUTE **2** *now dial Eng* : SCOLD, SHREW

call–fire \ˈ=,=\ *n* : naval artillery support supplied to ground troops as called for

call forth *vt* : to bring into being or action : ELICIT ⟨these events *call forth* great emotions⟩

call game *n* : a game of pocket billiards in which a player before shooting calls the ball he intends to make and the pocket in which he intends to drop it

call girl *n* : a prostitute who may be called by telephone to visit male customers

call house *n* : a house or apartment where call girls may be procured

calli *pl of* CALLUS

calli– *or* **callo–** *or* **cali–** *or* **calo–** *comb form* [*calli-* fr. L, fr. Gk *kalli-*, fr. *kallos* beauty; akin to Gk *kalos* beautiful, Skt *kalya* healthy; *calo-* fr. ML, fr. Gk *kalo-*, fr. *kalos*; *callo-* & *cali-* fr. blending of other forms] : beautiful ⟨calligraph⟩ ⟨*Callorynchus*⟩ ⟨*Calimeris*⟩ : white ⟨*calomel*⟩ : beauty ⟨*Calliphora*⟩

cal·li·a·nas·sa \,kalēəˈnasə\ *n, cap* [NL, fr. *calli-* + Gk *anassa* queen, fem. of *anax* lord] : a genus (the type of the family Callianassidae) of marine burrowing crustaceans (order Decapoda) having the chelipeds very unequal in size — **cal·li·a·nas·sid** \,=ˌ=ˈnasəd\ *adj or n*

cal·li·an·dra \,kalēˈandrə\ *n, cap* [NL, fr. *calli-* + *-andra*] : a genus of tropical pinnate-leaved trees and shrubs (family Leguminosae) with clustered flowers having conspicuous stamens

callibogus *var of* CALLIBOGUS

cal·li·car·pa \,kaləˈkärpə\ *n, cap* [NL, fr. *calli-* + *-carpa* (fem. of *-carpus* -carpous)] : a genus of widely distributed shrubs and trees (family Verbenaceae) with small 4-parted flowers some of which are cultivated for their attractive red or purple berrylike fruit — see FRENCH MULBERRY

cal·li·ce·bus \,kaləˈsēbəs\ *n, cap* [NL, fr. *calli-* + Gk *kēbos*, a long-tailed monkey — more at CEBUS] : a genus of So. American monkeys containing the titis

cal·lich·thy·idae \,ka,likˈthīə,dē\ *n pl, cap* [NL, fr. *Callichthys*, type genus (fr. Gk *kallichthys*, a sea fish, fr. *kalli-* calli + *ichthys* fish) + *-idae* — more at ICHTHUS] : a family of So. American armored catfishes (type genus *Callichthys*) including several species sometimes kept in the tropical aquarium

cal·lid·i·ty \kaˈlidəd·ē, kə-\ *n* -ES [L *calliditas*, fr. *callidus* crafty, shrewd (fr. *callēre* to have a thick skin, be witty, experienced) + *-itas* -ity; akin to L *callum* thick skin — more at CALLOUS] : CRAFTINESS, CUNNING, SHREWDNESS

cal·lier quotient \ˈkal,yā-\ *n, cap C* [after A. *Callier fl* 1909 Fr. photography expert] : the ratio of specular density to diffuse density — called also *Q factor*

cal·li·gram \ˈkalə,gram *n* -S [*calli-* + *-gram*] : a design in which the letters of a word (as a name) are rearranged so as to form a decorative pattern or figure (as for a seal) — compare MONOGRAM

cal·lig·ra·pha \kəˈligrəfə, ka-\ *n* -S [NL, genus of beetles, fr. *calli-* + *-grapha* (fr. Gk *graphein* to write) — more at CARVE] : a beetle of a genus (*Calligrapha*) of brightly marked foliage-eating beetles — see ELM CALLIGRAPHA

cal·lig·ra·pher \-fə(r)\ *n* -S [*calligraphy* + *-er*] **1** : one that writes a beautiful, ornamental, or stylized hand : a handwriting artist **2** : one that writes : PENMAN ⟨a fair ~⟩ **3** : a professional copyist or engrosser

cal·li·graph·ic \ˌkaləˈgrafik\ *adj* [MGk *kalligraphikos*, fr. Gk *kalligraphos* calligrapher + *-ikos* -ic] **1** : of or relating to calligraphy: as **a** *of writing or hand-lettering* : elaborate or ornamental in style **b** *of a document* : written by hand esp. in an elaborate or ornamental style **2 a** : consisting of or ornamented with lines resembling the flourishes of ornate or decorated handwriting or hand-lettering ⟨~ scrolls⟩ ⟨a ~ figure⟩ **b** : printed, engraved, or otherwise produced in a style imitative of ornamental handwriting, hand-lettering, or freehand drawing ⟨a printed ~ title⟩ ⟨engraved ~ ornament⟩ **c** : bearing writing or a representation of writing that is regarded as being in itself a source of aesthetic pleasure — used esp. of works of art displaying Chinese characters or one of the ornamental types of Arabic script **3** : drawn, painted, or formed in the manner of calligraphy (sense 3) ⟨a wiry arabesque of swift ~ line —Eric Newton⟩ — **cal·li·graph·i·cal·ly** \-ək(ə)lē\ *adv*

cal·lig·ra·phist \kəˈligrəfəst, ka-\ *n* -S : CALLIGRAPHER

cal·lig·ra·phy *also* **ca·lig·ra·phy** \-əfē, -i\ *n* -ES [F or Gk; F *calligraphie*, fr. Gk *kalligraphia*, fr. *kalli-* calli- + *-graphia* -graphy] **1 a** : fair or elegant writing or penmanship — opposed to *cacography* **b** : the art or profession of producing fair or elegant writing **2** : HANDWRITING, PENMANSHIP **3** : ornamental line in drawing or painting; *esp* : drawn or painted line having the variety, flexibility, expressiveness, and characteristic feeling of rapid execution of brilliant penmanship

cal·li·mi·co \,kaləˈmē(,)kō\ *n* [NL, fr. *calli-* + Pg & Sp *mico*, a kind of marmoset — more at MICO] **1** *cap* : a genus of small marmosetlike monkeys of the Amazon basin related to the spider monkeys and howlers but usu. considered to constitute a separate subfamily of Cebidae **2** -S : any monkey of the genus *Callimico*

cal·lim·o·mid \kəˈlimə,mid\ *adj* [NL *Callimomidae*] : of or relating to the Callimomidae

cal·li·mom·i·dae \,kaləˈmämə,dē\ *n pl, cap* [NL, fr. *Callimome*, type genus (irreg. fr. Gk *kallimos* beautiful, fr. *kallos* beauty) + *-idae* — more at CALLI-] : a large family (type genus *Callimome*) of minute brilliantly iridescent parasitic or seed-infesting chalcidoid wasps

call in *vt* **1** : to order to return or to be returned: as **a** : to withdraw from an advanced position ⟨*call in* a battalion's outposts⟩ **b** : to withdraw from circulation ⟨*call in* bank notes and issue new ones⟩ **c** : CALL *vt* 1o (2) **2** : to summon to one's aid or for consultation ⟨*call in* a mediator to settle the dispute⟩

cal·li·nec·tes \,kaləˈnek(,)tēz\ *n, cap* [NL, fr. *calli-* + *-nectes*] : a genus of swimming crabs (family Portunidae) comprising the New World blue crabs

call·ing \ˈkȯliŋ, -ēŋ\ *n* -S [ME, fr. gerund of *callen* to call] **1** *obs* : NAME, APPELLATION **2** : a strong inner impulse toward a particular course of action or duty ⟨a conflict between outer pressure and inner ~ —Siegfried Kracauer⟩; *specif* : such an impulse accompanied by conviction of divine influence **3** *obs* : station or position in life : RANK ⟨let every man abide in the same ~ wherein he was called —1 Cor 7:20 (AV)⟩ **4** : the activity in which one customarily engages as a vocation or profession ⟨when literature and journalism were not yet distinct ~*s* —A.B.Faust⟩ **5** : the characteristic cry of the female cat during heat; *also* : the period of heat **syn** see WORK

calling card *n* : VISITING CARD

calling crab *n* [so called fr. the apparently beckoning position of its larger claw] : FIDDLER CRAB

calling hare *n* [so called fr. its cry] : PIKA

call–in pay \ˈ=,=-\ *n* **1** : REPORTING PAY **2** : payment of not less than an agreed amount to a worker called in for work at a time other than that of his regular shift ⟨four hours' *call-in pay*⟩

cal·li·o·nym·i·dae \,kalēōˈnimə,dē\ *n pl, cap* [NL, fr. *Callionymus*, type genus (fr. Gk *kalliōnymos* stargazer, fr. *kalli-* calli- + *-ōnymos*, fr. *onyma*, *onoma* name) + *-idae* — more at NAME] : a family of percomorph fishes widely distributed in shallow seas and comprising the dragonets

cal·li·o·pe \kəˈlīə(,)pē, *+* ˈkalē,ōp\ *n* -S [fr. *Calliope*, chief of the Muses, fr. L, fr. Gk *Kalliopē*] **1** : a musical instrument consisting of a series of crude steam or air whistles used on riverboats and in circuses and carnivals **2** *also* **calliope hummingbird** [NL, fr. L *Calliope*] : a tiny hummingbird (*Stellula calliope*) of California and adjacent regions that is golden-green above and white below and marked with reddish brown and lavender **3** *slang* : a steam locomotive

cal·li·o·pe·an \kəˌlīəˈpēən, ÷ˌkalēˈōp-\ *adj* : resembling the sound of a calliope : loud and piercing

cal·li·op·sis \,kalēˈäpsəs\ *n* [NL, fr. *calli-* + *-opsis*] **1** *cap, in some classifications* : a genus of plants comprising chiefly the annual members of the genus *Coreopsis* **2** *pl* **calliopsis** : COREOPSIS 2; *esp* : a cultivated annual plant of the genus *Coreopsis*

callipash *var of* CALIPASH

calliper *var of* CALIPER

cal·liph·o·ra \kəˈlif(ə)rə\ *n, cap* [NL, fr. *calli-* + *-phora*] : a genus (the type of the family Calliphoridae) of large bluebottle flies — see BLOWFLY — **cal·liph·o·rine** \-fə,rīn\ *adj*

¹cal·liph·o·rid \-fərəd\ *adj* : of or relating to the family Calliphoridae

²calliphorid \"\ *n* -S [NL *Calliphoridae*] : a fly of the family Calliphoridae : BLOWFLY

cal·li·phor·i·dae \,kaləˈfȯrə,dē\ *n pl, cap* [NL, fr. *Calliphora*, type genus + *-idae*] : a family of large usu. hairy metallic blue or green calyptrate flies comprising the blowflies and a few related forms with parasitic larvae — compare BLUEBOTTLE

cal·li·pyg·i·an \ˌkaləˈpij(ē)ən\ *also* **cal·li·py·gous** \-ˈpīgəs\ *adj* [*callipygian* fr. Gk *kallipygos* callipygian (fr. *kalli-* calli- + *-pygos*, fr. *pygē* buttocks) + E *-ian*; *callipygous* fr. Gk *kallipygos* — more at FOG] : having shapely buttocks

cal·lir·rhoë \kəˈlirə,wē\ *n* [NL, fr. L *Callirrhoe*, a water nymph, daughter of the river Achelous and wife of Alcmeon, fr. Gk *Kallirrhoē*] **1** *cap* **:** a small genus of No. American herbs (family Malvaceae) having usu. red or purple flowers, truncate petals, and beaked carpels **2** *-s* **:** any plant of the genus *Callirrhoë*, several species of which are cultivated — called also *poppy mallow*

cal·li·sau·rus \ˌkalə'sȯrəs\ *n, cap* [NL, fr. *calli-* + *-saurus*] **:** a small genus of lizards (family Iguanidae) having stripes around the tail, seven species occurring in the southwestern U.S. — see GRIDIRON-TAILED LIZARD

cal·lis·te green \kə'listē-\ *n* [prob. fr. Gk *kallistē*, fem. superl. of *kalos* beautiful — more at CALLI-] **:** a moderate to strong yellow green

cal·li·ste·mon \ˌkalə'stēmən\ *n, cap* [NL, fr. *calli-* + Gk *stēmōn* warp, thread — more at STAMEN] **:** a genus of Australian trees and shrubs of the family Myrtaceae having brushlike spikes of showy flowers — see BOTTLEBRUSH

cal·lis·te·phus \kə'listəfəs\ *n, cap* [NL, fr. *calli-* + Gk *stephos* crown, fr. *stephein* to encircle, bewreath] **:** a genus of erect Asiatic herbs (family Compositae) having ovate alternate leaves of which the upper become narrow and spatulate, leafy reflexed outer involucral bracts, and showy solitary flower heads that are two to five inches across — see CHINA ASTER

cal·li·thric·id \ˌkalə'thrisəd\ *n* *-s* [NL *callithricidae*] **:** a monkey of the family Callithricidae

cal·li·thric·i·dae \-sə,dē\ *n pl, cap* [NL, alter. of *Callitrichidae*] **:** a family of So. American monkeys comprising the marmosets and the tamarins

[1]**cal·li·thrix** \'kalə,thriks\ *n, cap* [NL, fr. L, an ape, fr. Gk *kallithrix* beautiful-haired, fr. *kalli-* calli- + *thrix* hair] **:** a genus consisting of the true marmosets

[2]**callithrix** \"\ [NL, fr. L, an ape] *syn of* CALLICEBUS — a prior name invalid as a homonym of [1]*Callithrix*

cal·li·thump *or* **cal·la·thump** *also* **cal·li·thump** \'kalə,thəmp\ *n* *-s* [back-formation fr. *callithumpian, callathumpian, callithumpian*, adj., alter. of E dial. (Dorsetshire & Devonshire) *gallithumpian* disturber of order at elections in 18th century, perh. fr. *galli-* (alter. of *gallows*) + *thump* + *-ian*] **1 :** a noisy boisterous parade **2** *chiefly NewEng* **:** SHIVAREE — **cal·li·thump·i·an** \ˌ==;=pēən\ *adj*

callithumpian duck *n, dial* **:** OLD-SQUAW

cal·lit·ri·cha·ceous \kə¦li·trə¦kāshəs, ¦kalə-·-\ *adj* [NL *Callitriche* + E *-aceous*] **:** of or relating to the genus *Callitriche*

cal·lit·ri·che \kə'li·trə,kē\ *n, cap* [NL, modif. of LGk *kallitrichos* beautiful-haired, fr. Gk *kalli-* calli- + LGk *-trichos*, fr. Gk *trich-, thrix* hair — more at TRICHINA] **:** a genus (the type of the family Callitrichaceae of the order Geraniales) comprising widely distributed aquatic herbs having opposite linear leaves and minute monoecious flowers — see WATER STARWORT

cal·li·trich·i·dae \ˌkalə'trikə,dē\ *or* **cal·li·tric·i·dae** \-risə-\ [NL, fr. *Callitrich-* or *Callitric-, Callithrix*, type genus + *-idae*] *syn of* CALLITHRICIDAE

cal·li·tris \'kalə·trəs\ *n, cap* [NL, irreg. fr. Gk *kalli-*] **:** a genus of African and Australasian evergreen trees (family Pinaceae) with small scalelike leaves — see SANDARAC TREE

cal·li·tro·ga \ˌkalə'trōgə\ *n, cap* [NL, fr. *calli-* + *-troga* (fr. Gk *trōgein* to gnaw) — more at TERSE] **:** a genus of No. American blowflies (family Calliphoridae) having larvae that are screwworms and including two serious pests of domestic animals, the common screwworm (*C. hominivorax*) and the secondary screwworm (*C. macellaria*)

call letters *n pl* **:** CALL SIGN

call loan *n* **:** a loan payable on demand of either party and usu. secured by stock or bond collateral and used chiefly by stock-exchange brokers to finance margin purchases

call man *n* **:** a man subject to call; *specif* **:** a part-time fireman available for emergency call at an hourly wage

call market *n* **:** the market for call loans

call money *n* **:** money loaned or ready to be loaned on call

call note *n* **:** a note used by a bird or other animal to call another (as its mate or young)

call number *or* **call mark** *n* **:** a combination of characters assigned to a library book to indicate its place on the shelf relative to other books — compare PRESSMARK

callo- — see CALLI-

call off *vt* **1 :** to draw away **:** DIVERT ⟨her attention was *called off* by a new arrival⟩ **2 :** to give up (an undertaking or planned activity) **:** CANCEL ⟨*call off* a baseball game⟩ ⟨*call* the trip *off*⟩

call office *n, Brit* **:** PAY STATION

call of nature : the need to expel body wastes

cal·lop \'kaləp\ *n* *-s* [native name in Australia] **:** an edible serranid fish (*Plectroplites ambiguus*) of inland waters of Australia — called also *golden perch*

cal·lo·phis \'kaləfəs\ *n, cap* [NL, fr. *callo-* + *-ophis*] **:** a genus comprising the Indian coral snakes

cal·lo·rhi·nus \ˌkalə'rīnəs\ *n, cap* [NL, fr. *callo-* + *-rhinus*] **:** a genus consisting of the No. Pacific fur seals

cal·lo·ryn·chus \ˌkalə'riŋkəs\ *n, cap* [NL, fr. *callo-* + *-rynchus* (alter. of *-rhynchus*)] **:** a genus (coextensive with the family Callorynchidae) of chimaeralike fishes comprising the elephant fishes, found in south temperate seas, and having the snout elongated and provided with a pendent tactile organ

cal·lo·sal \(')ka¦lōsəl, kə'l-\ *adj* [NL *callosum* + E *-al*] **:** of, relating to, or adjoining the corpus callosum

callosal convolution *n* **:** a convolution of the mesial surface of the cerebrum curving around the corpus callosum from which it is separated by a callosal fissure

cal·lo·sci·u·rus \ˌkalō,sī'(y)ürəs\ *n, cap* [NL, fr. *callo-* + *Sciurus*] **:** a genus of squirrels of southeastern Asia comprising the red-bellied squirrels

[1]**cal·lose** \'ka,lōs\ *adj* [ISV *call-* (fr. L *callum* hard skin) + *-ose*; orig. formed in F — more at CALLOUS] **:** having protuberant hardened spots ⟨~ leaves⟩

[2]**callose** \"\ *n* *-s* [L *callosus* callous] **:** a carbohydrate component of cell walls that is readily stained by aniline blue and is found esp. on sieve plates where it forms the callus

cal·los·i·ty \ka'läsəd·ē, kə-, -ətē, -i\ *n* *-ES* [MF *callosité*, fr. L *callositas*, fr. *callosus* + *-itas* -ity] **1 :** the condition or quality of being callous: as **a :** abnormal hardness and thickness (as of the skin) **b :** lack of feeling or capacity for emotion **2 :** a hard or thickened area or protuberance esp. on the skin or on the bark of a plant **:** CALLUS

cal·lo·so·bru·chus \kə,lōsə'brükəs\ *n, cap* [NL, fr. L *callosus* hard-skinned + LL *bruchus* a kind of locust, fr. Gk *bronchos, bronkos* locust; perh. akin to Russ *brukat'* to kick out with the hind legs, Slovenian *brkniti, brkati* to kick, to propel with the fingers, Lith *briankšt, brūkšt* a cry made during throwing] **:** a small genus of weevils (family Bruchidae) closely related to the bean weevil and including the cowpea weevil

callosum *n, pl* **callosa** [NL, fr. L, neut. of *callosus*] **:** CORPUS CALLOSUM

[1]**cal·lous** \'kaləs\ *adj* [MF *calleux*, fr. L *callosus*, fr. *callum, callus* callous skin; akin to Skt *kiṇa* callosity, OIr *calath* hard] **1 :** hardened and thickened ⟨~ skin on the heel⟩ ⟨~ plant bark⟩ **:** having callouses ⟨with labouring ~ hands —William Congreve⟩ **2 a :** hardened in sensibility **:** feeling no emotion ⟨piety . . . is made ~ and inactive by kneeling too much —W. S.Landor⟩ **b :** feeling no sympathy for others **:** without regard for the feelings or welfare of others **:** indifferent to the suffering of others ⟨a ~ disregard for human rights —W.O. Douglas⟩ — **cal·lous·ly** *adv* — **cal·lous·ness** *n* *-ES*

[2]**callous** \"\ *vt* *-ED/-ING/-ES* **:** to make callous

[3]**callous** *var of* CALLUS

cal·loused \'kaləst\ *adj* **:** having calluses **:** CALLOUS

call out *vt* **1 :** to summon or order into action ⟨*call out* troops to control rioting⟩ **:** call forth ⟨danger *called out* the best in him⟩ **2 :** to challenge to fight a duel **3 :** to order to go on strike ⟨*call out* the steelworkers⟩

call–over \'=,==\ *n* *-s* *Brit* **:** a meeting of bookmakers at which a list of entries in a coming race is read, odds are offered, and bets are made

[1]**cal·low** \'ka(,)lō, -lə; -ləw,-lō+V\ *adj, sometimes* *-ER/-EST* [ME *calu, calewe* bald, fr. OE *calu*; akin to OHG *kalo* bald, OSlav *golŭ* naked] **1 a** *of a bird* **:** lacking feathers **:** UNFLEDGED **b :** characteristic of or indicating immaturity ⟨the ~ down began to clothe my chin —John Dryden⟩ **2 :** marked by lack of adult sophistication, experience, perception, or judgment ⟨a troop of newly arrived students, very young, pink and ~, followed nervously . . . at the director's heels —Aldous Huxley⟩ **3 a** *dial Eng, of land* **:** BARE **b** *Irish* **:** LOW-LYING **:** MARSHY — used esp. of a meadow **syn** see RUDE

[2]**callow** \"\ *n* *-s* **1** *Irish* **:** a low-lying or marshy meadow **2** *dial Eng* **:** the layer of soil above the subsoil **:** the top or rubble bed of a quarry **3 :** a freshly transformed insect not yet fully colored

cal·low·ness \-ōnəs, -ən-\ *n* *-ES* **:** the quality or state of being callow

call pay *n* **:** payment made to a worker who reports upon schedule but finds no work for him to do

call price *n* **:** the price required by the terms of a bond to be paid if the bond is called before maturity

call rate *n* **:** the interest rate charged on call loans

calls *pres 3d sing of* CALL, *pl of* CALL

call sheet \'=,=\ *n* **:** a summons to a film actor or technician to report for a take often specifying costume or properties

call sign *n* **:** the combination of identifying letters or letters and numbers assigned to an operator, office, activity, or station for use in communication (as in the address of a message sent by radio)

call slip *n* **:** a form filled out by a library patron for a book that he wishes to see or borrow — called also *call card*

call to quarters : a bugle call usu. shortly before taps that summons soldiers to their quarters

call to worship : the opening sentences or prayer often including a congregational response in a worship service

cal·lu·na \kə'l(y)ünə\ *n, cap* [NL, irreg. fr. Gk *kallynein* to beautify, sweep clean, fr. *kallos* beauty; fr. its use in making brooms — more at CALLI-] **:** a genus of low shrubs (family Ericaceae) included by some in the genus *Erica* but distinguished by opposite leaves and sepals which are much longer than the petals — see HEATHER

call up *vt* **1 :** to bring to mind or recollection **:** RECALL, EVOKE ⟨the music *calls up* other times and emotions⟩ **2 :** to summon before an authority or tribunal ⟨*called up* by the investigating committee⟩ **3 :** to summon together or collect (as for a united effort) ⟨*call up* all his forces for the attack⟩ **4 :** to summon for active military duty **:** DRAFT **5 :** to bring forward for consideration or action ⟨*call up* a bill for senate approval⟩

call–up \'=,=\ *n* *-s* **:** an order to report for military service; *also* **:** DRAFT 13c

call–up–a–storm \,=(,)==ˈ=\ *n, NewEng* **:** COMMON LOON

[1]**cal·lus** *or* **cal·lous** \'kaləs\ *n, pl* **callus·es** \-ləsəz\ *or* **callous·es** *also* **cal·li** \-,lī\ [*callus* fr. L; *callous*, alter. (influenced by *callous*, adj.) of *callus* — more at CALLOUS (adj.)] **1 a** *usu callous* **:** a thickening of the horny layer of the epidermis as a result of friction or pressure **:** CALLOSITY 1a **b** *usu callous* **:** an area of skin so thickened **:** CALLOSITY 2 **c :** the soft parenchymatous tissue from which new roots form in cuttings and which develops from the phloem or cortex or more frequently from the cambium itself over any cut or wounded surface of a stem or root, the outer cells usu. becoming suberized or covered by a periderm **d :** a thickened area or protuberance on the surface of a plant **:** CALLOSITY; *specif* **:** the hard often hairy swelling from which the lemma and palea arise in grasses **e :** a growth of shelly material within or about the umbilicus of a gastropod shell **f :** a cuticular swelling on the body of an insect; *esp* **:** one serving as a point of articulation for a wing **2 :** a substance that is exuded around the ends of a broken bone and that by conversion into true bone bridges the gap and restores the continuity of the bone **3** *usu callous* **:** a protective condition of mental or emotional insensitivity ⟨beneath my defensive ~ of belligerence, I was filled with feelings of guilt —*Harper's*⟩ **4** *bot* **:** an accumulation of callose formed first as cylinders around the protoplasmic strands passing through the sieve plate and developing toward the end of the functional period of the sieve tube as a cushion or pad on each surface of the sieve plate

[2]**callus** \"\ *vb* *-ED/-ING/-ES* *vi* **:** to form callus ~ *vt* **:** to cause callus to form on (as a cutting)

callused *adj* [[1]*callus* + *-ed*] **:** having calluses **:** covered with callus

[1]**calm** \'kälm, 'kȧ| *also* |lm; *sporadic & old-fash* 'kam\ *n* *-s* [ME *calme*, fr. MF *calme*, fr. OIt *calma*, fr. LL *cauma* heat, fr. Gk *kauma* burning heat, heat of the day, fr. *kaiein* to burn — more at CAUSTIC] **1 a :** a period or condition of freedom from storms, high winds, or rough activity **:** STILLNESS, QUIETUDE ⟨gradual sinks the breeze into a perfect ~ —James Thomson †1748⟩ **b :** complete lack of wind ⟨a sailing ship motionless in the ~⟩ **c :** complete absence of wind or presence of wind having a speed no greater than one mile per hour — see BEAUFORT SCALE table **2 :** a state or condition of repose and freedom from turmoil, disturbance, or marked activity or from agitation, tension, or vexation ⟨the bustle subsides and relative ~ is resumed —*Amer. Guide Series: N.C.*⟩ ⟨the majesty of artistic contemplation, looking in sacred ~ upon all this world . . . itself unmoved —Josiah Royce⟩

[2]**calm** \"\ *adj, usu* *-ER/-EST* [ME *calme*, fr. *calme*, n.] **1 :** marked by calm **:** STILL **:** without rough motion, storminess, or agitated activity ⟨the sea was ~, save for a heavy but smooth ground swell —Jack London⟩ **2 :** marked by quiet unruffled freedom from agitation, passion, excitement, hurry, or disturbance ⟨we men are all in a fever of excitement, except Harker, who is ~ —Bram Stoker⟩ ⟨be rational . . . consider, and make a cool, ~ choice —T.L.Peacock⟩ **3 a :** COOL, DELIBERATE, ASSURED ⟨a ~ liar⟩ **b :** SELF-ASSURED, BRAZEN **:** unmoved by any delicate or lofty feeling ⟨a ~ scoundrel⟩

syn TRANQUIL, SERENE, PLACID, PEACEFUL, HALCYON: CALM suggests simple quietude, sometimes quietude in the face of disaster ⟨when winds that move not its *calm* surface sweep the azure sea —P.B.Shelley⟩ ⟨the senate, surprised but *calm* and energetic as usual, hushed up the news of these many defeats —H. W. Van Loon⟩ TRANQUIL may suggest a somewhat deeper, more settled or composed quietude with less notion of previous agitation dispelled ⟨on the balmy zephyrs *tranquil* rest the silver clouds —John Keats⟩ ⟨with footsteps quiet and slow at a *tranquil* pace —Elinor Wylie⟩ ⟨all unhappiness, all discontent, seemed banished, giving way to a *tranquil* content —Charles Nordhoff & J.N.Hall⟩ ⟨a *tranquil* trust in God amid tortures and death too horrible to be related —J.L.Motley⟩ SERENE suggests sheer and utter peace, lofty, happy, and quite unruffled ⟨gliding o'er ocean, smooth, *serene*, and even —P.B.Shelley⟩ ⟨the large fair face . . . was neither clouded nor ravaged, but finely *serene* —Henry James †1916⟩ ⟨his [Washington's] unflagging patriotism, his calm wisdom, his *serene* moral courage, because in the gloomiest hours he never lost his dignity, poise, or decision —Allan Nevins & H.S. Commager⟩ It is occasionally used in situations involving an enervating absence of challenge ⟨his marriage had relapsed into the *serene* monotony that so often wears the aspect of happiness —Ellen Glasgow⟩ PLACID may stress utter lack of agitation more strongly than the positive fact of peace and composure ⟨the *placid* gleam of sunset after storm —Alfred Tennyson⟩ ⟨a plump and *placid* figure...[she] received the invasion with competent tranquillity —Dorothy Sayers⟩ In derogation it may imply stupidity ⟨no teasing worried Una; she was as *placid* as a young cow —Rose Macaulay⟩ PEACEFUL, which has less suggestion than the others in this group, stresses the fact of undisturbed repose unlikely to change ⟨now sleeping in those *peaceful* groves —William Wordsworth⟩ ⟨I am grown *peaceful* as old age tonight —Robert Browning⟩ HALCYON suggests magic or golden stillness ⟨the brightest hour of unborn spring...the *halcyon* morn —P.B.Shelley⟩ ⟨change into such *halcyon* days the winter of the world, that the birds . . . may have their nests in peace —John Ruskin⟩

[3]**calm** \"\ *vb* *-ED/-ING/-S* [ME *calmen*, prob. fr. *calme*, adj.] *vi* **:** to become calm **:** subside or abate from storm or agitation — usu. used with *down* ⟨the tempest ~*ed*⟩ ⟨the madman ~*ed* down⟩ ~ *vt* **1 :** to make calm **:** still, abate, or reduce the force or activity of ⟨~ the tempest —John Dryden⟩ **2 :** to make peaceful **:** induce quietude and repose in in place of agitation, passion, or excitement — often used with *down* ⟨~ feelings excited by civil war —T.M.Whitfield⟩ ⟨~ him down; get him to be reasonable —S.H.Adams⟩ **3** *obs* **:** BECALM

syn COMPOSE, QUIET, QUIETEN, STILL, LULL, SOOTHE, SETTLE, TRANQUILIZE are here treated only as they relate to persons and their feelings and moods. CALM may indicate return to inner quietude aided by judgment, fortitude, or faith ⟨Christian faith *calmed* in his soul the fear of change and death —William Wordsworth⟩ ⟨her also I with gentle dreams have *calmed* —John Milton⟩ COMPOSE, often reflexive, may heighten suggestions of conscious effort, resolution, and fortitude ⟨my child, if ever you were brave and serviceable in your life . . . you will *compose* yourself now —Charles Dickens⟩ ⟨a most *composed* invincible man, in difficulty and distress knowing no discouragement —Thomas Carlyle⟩ QUIET and QUIETEN may connote a temporary external calmness in speech or demeanor rather than lasting inner calm ⟨the most unreasonable of Franklin's impulses had now been *quieted* by this most reasonable of marriages —Carl Van Doren⟩ These words are likely to be used in indicating the effect of actions of persons in authority on others ⟨threats to the physical well-being of the unborn baby can *quieten* a noisy and uncooperative patient in labour —*Lancet*⟩ STILL, now somewhat literary or poetic, stresses the fact of cessation of agitation ⟨flattened, silenced, *stilled* —Virginia Woolf⟩ ⟨a voice *stilled* by death⟩ It may suggest more peremptory action than others in this list, connoting a return to quietude induced by power, authority, or awe ⟨the debate was *stilled* by the crash of guns⟩ ⟨it was Mary who *stilled* the hideous bawling of Peter —H.G.Wells⟩ LULL is the only word in this group that does not imply noticeable previous agitation or excitation. It connotes the somnolence of *lullaby*, to which it is related ⟨Aiken has *lulled* the reader with a seductive music and has transported him into the dreamworld of Freudian fantasy —F.O.Matthiessen⟩ It often suggests sleepy relaxation into repose, complacence, unawareness, or apathy when one should be vigilant ⟨we must not let a year or two of prosperity *lull* us into a false feeling of security —H.S.Truman⟩ SOOTHE suggests bland, gentle mitigation, assuagement, or solace ⟨it [the weather] cool'd their fever'd sleep, and *soothed* them into slumbers full and deep —John Keats⟩ ⟨when they [babies] wake screaming and find none to *soothe* them —Charles Lamb⟩ SETTLE stresses the subsiding of swirling agitation ⟨I'll read a bit before supper to *settle* my mind —Agnes S. Turnbull⟩ ⟨if I can't *settle* my brains, your next news of me will be that I am locked up —Mary W. Montagu⟩ TRANQUILIZE, more than the others in this group, stresses the depth of peace achieved ⟨when contemplation . . . sends deep into the soul its *tranquilizing* power —William Wordsworth⟩

[4]**calm** \'käm\ *n* *-s* [origin unknown] *now chiefly Scot* **:** a mold or frame esp. as used for casting metal

[5]**calm** \'käm\ *var of* CAME

calm·ant \'kä(l)mənt, -ä(l)m-, -alm-\ *n* *-s* [F, fr. *calmer* to calm, fr. *calme* calm] **:** CALMATIVE

calm·a·tive \-məd·iv\ *n or adj* [[3]*calm* + *-ative* (as in *sedative*)] **:** SEDATIVE

cal·ma·to \käl'mä,tō\ *adj (or adv)* [It, past part. of *calmare* to calm, fr. *calma* calm] **:** TRANQUIL, CALM — used as a direction in music

cal·me·cac \¦kälmä¦käk\ *n* *-s* [Sp, fr. Nahuatl] **:** an Aztec school that prepared the sons of nobles in the duties of priests and chiefs — distinguished from *telpuchcalli*

calm·ing·ly *adv* **:** in a calming manner

calm·ly *adv* **:** in a calm manner **:** with calm

calm·ness *n* *-ES* **:** the quality or state of being calm

calms *pres 3d sing of* CALM, *pl of* CALM

calmuck *var of* KALMUCK

calmy *adj, usu* *-ER/-EST* [[1]*calm* + *-y*] *archaic* **:** CALM

ca·ló \kə'lō\ *n* [Sp, fr. Romany, gypsy] **:** a language spoken by Spanish gypsies and widely influencing the argots of the Spanish-speaking underworld and of bullfighting

calo- — see CALLI-

cal·o·car·pum \ˌkalə'kärpəm\ *n, cap* [NL, fr. *calo-* + *-carpum* (irreg. fr. Gk *karpos* fruit) — more at HARVEST] **:** a genus of tropical American trees (family Sapotaceae) having obovate to oblanceolate leaves clustered towards the branch ends, nearly sessile white flowers with densely imbricated sepals and filamentous staminodia, and a berrylike fruit — see MARMALADE TREE

cal·o·chor·tus \ˌkalə'kȯrd·əs\ *n, cap* [NL, fr. *calo-* + Gk *chortos* fodder, grass, farmyard — more at YARD] **:** a large genus of western No. American leafy-stemmed herbs (family Liliaceae) having flowers with three sepals and three petals

ca·lom·ba \kə'lämbə\ *n* *-s* [native name in New South Wales, Australia] **:** an Australian annual cloverlike plant (*Trigonella suavissima*) with yellow flowers and fragrant foliage valued as forage

calombo *var of* CALUMBA

cal·o·mel \'kaləməl, -ə,mel\ *n* *-s* [prob. fr. (assumed) NL *calomelas*, fr. *calo-* + Gk *melas* black — more at MULLET] **:** a white tasteless salt Hg_2Cl_2 found in nature as a sectile tetragonal mineral (hardness 1.5, sp. gr. 7.15), obtained as a heavy powder by precipitation from solution or by sublimation of a mixture of mercury and chlorine, and used as a cathartic, fungicide, and insecticide — called also *mercurous chloride*

calomel electrode *n* **:** a reference electrode consisting of mercury, calomel, and potassium chloride solution

cal·o·mor·phic \¦kalə¦mȯrfik\ *adj* [*calo-* (fr. *calcium*, influenced by *halo-*) + *-morphic*] **:** of or relating to intrazonal soils characterized by a high content of available calcium in the parent material — compare HALOMORPHIC, HYDROMORPHIC

cal·o·neu·ro·dea \ˌkalōn(y)ü'rōdēə\ *n pl, cap* [NL, fr. *calo-* + *neur-* + *-odea* (alter. of *-oidea*)] **:** a small order of neopterous insects with two similar pairs of wings and with legs adapted for running that appeared in the Upper Pennsylvanian and became extinct after the Permian — **cal·o·neu·ro·de·an** \-dēən\ *n* *-s*

ca·lon–sé·gur \kȧlōⁿsāgüer\ *n* *-s* *usu cap C&S* [F, fr. the Château *Calon-Ségur*, Gironde dept., France, where it is produced] **:** a dry red table wine from Bordeaux, France, made from the Médoc grape

cal·o·nyc·ti·on \ˌkalə'niktē,än\ *n, cap* [NL, fr. *calo-* + Gk *nyktion*, neut. of *nyktios* of the night, fr. *nykt-, nyx* night — more at NIGHT] **:** a small genus of tropical American vines (family Convolvulaceae) having a salverform corolla with a long cylindrical tube and with a pointed capsular fruit — see MOONFLOWER

ca·lool \kə'lül\ *n* *-s* [native name in New South Wales] **:** an Australian kurrajong (*Sterculia quadrifida*)

caloosa *cap, var of* CALUSA

cal·o·phyl·lum \ˌkalə'filəm\ *n, cap* [NL, fr. *calo-* + *-phyllum*] **:** a genus of tropical trees (family Guttiferae) having thick shiny feather-veined leaves, clustered white flowers, aromatic resinous juice, and oily seeds — see SANTA MARIA TREE, TACAMAHAC

cal·o·po·gon \ˌkalə'pō,gän\ *n, cap* [NL, fr. *calo-* + *-pogon*] **:** a small genus of American bulbous orchids having grasslike leaves and spikelike racemes of pink bearded flowers — see GRASS PINK

cal·o·res·cence \ˌkalə'resᵊn(t)s\ *n* *-s* [L *calor* heat + E *-escence*] **:** the incandescence of a body produced by the incidence upon it of infrared rays which are thus converted indirectly into radiant energy of shorter wavelength — **cal·o·res·cent** \-ᵊnt\ *adj*

calori- *comb form* [L, fr. *calor*] **:** heat ⟨*calori*meter⟩

[1]**ca·lor·ic** \kə'lȯrik, -'lär-, 'kalər-, -ēk\ *n* *-s* [F *calorique*, fr. L *calor* heat (fr. *calēre* to be warm) + F *-ique* -ic — more at LEE] **1 :** a supposed fluid form of matter to which the phenomena of heat and combustion were ascribed according to an obsolete concept of heat **2** *archaic* **:** HEAT

[2]**caloric** \"\ *adj* **1 :** of or relating to heat **2 :** of or relating to calories ⟨comparison of foods on a ~ basis⟩ — **ca·lor·i·cal·ly** \=ˈ=ək(ə)lē, -ēk-, -li\ *adv*

caloric engine *n* **:** HOT-AIR ENGINE

cal·o·ric·i·ty \ˌkalə'risəd·ē\ *n* *-ES* [F *caloricité*, fr. L *calor* heat + F *-icité* (fr. L *-icus* -ic + F *-ité* -ity)] **:** physiological ability to develop and maintain bodily heat

caloric punsch *or* **caloric punch** *n* **:** SWEDISH PUNSCH

cal·o·rie *also* **cal·o·ry** \'kal(ə)rē, -i\ *n, pl* **calories** [F *calorie*, fr. L *calor* heat + F *-ie* -y — more at CALORIC] **:** any of several thermal units: **a :** the amount of heat required at a pressure of one atmosphere to raise the temperature of one gram of water one degree centigrade esp. from 15° to 16° — abbr. *cal;* called also *gram calorie, small calorie* **b** *cap* (1) **:** the amount of heat required to raise the temperature of one kilogram of water one degree centigrade **:** 1000 gram calories or 3.968 Btu — abbr. *Cal;* called also *kilogram calorie, large calorie* (2) **:** a unit expressing a heat-producing or energy-producing value in food that when oxidized in the body is capable of releasing one large calorie of energy (3) **:** an amount of food (as in a diet) having an energy-producing value of one large calorie **c :** 1/100 of the amount of heat required to raise the temperature of one gram of water from 0° to 100° C — called also *mean calorie*

ca·lor·i·fa·cient \kə¦lȯrə¦fāshənt, -är-, ¦kalərə-\ *adj* [*calori-* + *-facient*] **:** heat-producing — usu. used of foods

cal·o·rif·ic \¦kalə¦rifik\ *adj* [F or L; F *calorifique*, fr. L *calorificus*, fr. *calori-* + *-ficus* -fic] **:** of or relating to heat or to calories **:** productive of heat ⟨the ~ properties of various fuels⟩

calorific value *or* **calorific power** *n* **:** the heat produced by the combustion of a unit weight of a fuel

calorific wool *n* **:** CAPSICUM WOOL

ca·lor·i·fi·er \kə'lȯrə,fī(ə)r, -'är-\ *n* -S [L *calor* heat + E *-ify* + *-er* — more at CALORIC] **:** an apparatus for heating a fluid (as water) by circulating it past usu. steam-filled heating coils

ca·lor·i·gen·ic \kə¦lȯrə¦jenik, -är-, ¦kalərə-\ *adj* [*calori-* + *-genic*] **:** generating heat or energy ⟨the ~ action of carbohydrates⟩

cal·o·rim·e·ter \,kalə'rimәd·ə(r)\ *n* -S [ISV *calori-* + *-meter*; orig. formed as F *calorimètre*] **:** any of several apparatuses for measuring quantities of absorbed or evolved heat or for determining specific heats by means of (1) the change in temperature of a solid (as copper or silver), (2) the heat of combustion (as of coal) in a chamber consisting of a strong steel shell, (3) the continuous flow through a heat exchanger of a fluid whose specific heat is being measured, (4) the melting of a known mass of ice, (5) the condensation of a known mass of steam, (6) the change in temperature of a known mass of water or other liquid — called also respectively (1) *aneroid calorimeter*, (2) *bomb calorimeter*, (3) *flow calorimeter*, (4) *ice calorimeter*, (5) *steam calorimeter*, (6) *water calorimeter*; see RESPIRATION CALORIMETER

ca·lo·ri·met·ric \¦kalərə¦me·trik; kə¦lȯrə¦-, -är-\ *or* **ca·lo·ri·met·ri·cal** \-ə̇kəl\ *adj* [*calorimetry* + *-ic* or *-ical*] **:** of or relating to calorimetry — **ca·lo·ri·met·ri·cal·ly** \-ə̇k(ə)lē\ *adv*

cal·o·rim·e·try \,kalə'rimə·trē\ *n* -ES [F *calorimétrie*, fr. *calori-* + *-métrie* -metry] **:** measurement of quantities of heat

ca·lo·ris \kə'lōrə̇s\ *n, pl* **caloris·es** \-rəsəz\ [irreg. fr. L *calor* heat — more at CALORIC] **:** SUMMER SORES

cal·o·rist \'kalərə̇st\ *n* -S [*calori-* + *-ist*] **:** one that holds to the caloric theory of heat

ca·lor·i·za·tor *or* **ca·lor·i·sa·tor** \kə'lȯrə,zād·ə(r), -'ä-, -,sā-\ *n* -S [fr. (assumed) *calorize* to heat (fr. L *calor* heat + E *-ize*) + *-ator*] **:** an apparatus used in beet-sugar factories to heat juice in order to aid the diffusion of sugar

cal·o·rize \'kalə,rīz\ *vt* -ED/-ING/-S [L *calor* + E *-ize*] **:** to treat by a process for coating metal (as iron or steel) with aluminum in which the metal is heated in a reducing atmosphere in a closed retort with a mixture containing finely divided aluminum that alloys with the metal to a depth dependent on the length of the treatment — compare SHERARDIZE

calory *var of* CALORIE

cal·o·so·ma \,kalə'sōmə\ *n* [NL, fr. *calo-* + *-soma*] **1** *cap* **:** a genus of large predaceous ground beetles (family Carabidae) that are green, black, or bronze in color and that feed on injurious caterpillars **2** -S **:** any beetle of the genus *Calosoma*

ca·lot \kə'lät\ *n* -S [modif. of F *calotte*] **:** a close-fitting cap without visor or brim; *also* **:** a woman's or child's cap of this basic design

calotermes *syn of* KALOTERMES

calotermitid *var of* KALOTERMITID

calotermitidae *syn of* KALOTERMITIDAE

cal·o·thrix \'kalə,thriks\ *n, cap* [NL, fr. *calo-* + *-thrix*] **:** a genus of blue-green algae (family Rivulariaceae) with free non-mucilaginous simple or falsely branched filaments

ca·lot·ro·pis \kə'lä·trəpə̇s\ *n, cap* [NL, fr. *calo-* + Gk *tropis* keel; akin to Gk *trepein* to turn — more at TROPE] **:** a genus of Asiatic or African shrubs or trees (family Asclepiadaceae) having bell-shaped flowers with showy keel-shaped hoods and used as fiber plants — see MUDAR

ca·lotte \kə'lät\ *n* -S [F] **1 a :** CALOT, SKULLCAP **b :** ZUCCHETTO **2 a :** an ice cap or a large glacier not confined to a single valley **b :** a snow-capped summit or dome **3 a :** CALVA **b** *zool* **:** a cap or a part likened to a cap **4 a :** a caplike architectural construction; *esp* **:** the interior of a small cupola or a cup-shaped vault

cal·o·type \'kalə,tīp\ *n* -S [*calo-* + *type*] **1 :** an early photographic-negative process in which paper is sensitized with silver iodide, brushed over with a solution of silver nitrate and acetic and gallic acids, and after exposure developed in a gallic acid-silver nitrate solution **2 :** a positive print made from a calotype negative — **cal·o·typ·ic** \¦==¦tipik\ *adj* — **cal·o·typ·ist** \'==,tīpə̇st\ *n* -S

ca·loy·er \kə'lȯiə(r), -ȯyə-, 'ka,l-; 'kaləyə-\ *n* -S [It & F; F *caloyer*, fr. obs. It *caloiero*, fr. MGk *kalogēros* venerable, lit., having a beautiful old age, fr. *kalo-* calo- + *-gēros* (fr. Gk *gēras* old age) — more at CORN] **:** a monk of the Eastern Church

cal·pac *or* **cal·pack** \'kal,pak, =¦=\ *n* -S [Turk *kalpak*] **:** a high-crowned cap usu. of sheepskin or felt that is worn in Turkey, Iran, and neighboring countries

cal·pul·li \kal'pülē\ *also* **cal·pol·li** \-'ō-\ *or* **cal·pul** \'kal,pül\ *n, pl* **cal·pul·li** \-ülē\ *also* **cal·pul·lec** \-ü(,)lek\ [Nahuatl *calpulli*, lit., big house, aug. of *calli* house] **:** a clan or ward constituting the fundamental unit of Aztec society

calque \'kalk, -äk\ *n* -S [F, lit., copy, fr. *calquer* to trace, fr. It *calcare* to trace, trample, fr. L, to trample — more at CAULK] **1 :** a linguistic borrowing that consists of the imitation in one language of some part of the peculiar range of meaning of a particular word in another language ⟨English *foot* meaning a metrical unit is a ~ from Latin *pes*⟩ **2 :** LOAN TRANSLATION

cal·tha \'kalthə\ *n, cap* [NL, fr. L, pot marigold] **:** a small genus of marsh or aquatic herbs (family Ranunculaceae) growing in arctic and temperate regions and having rounded and cordate or reniform leaves and apetalous flowers with yellow, white, or pink showy sepals — see MARSH MARIGOLD

cal·throps \'kalthrəps, -'ō-\ *n pl but usu sing in constr* [var. of *caltrop*] **:** a tetraxon sponge spicule in which the rays are equal or nearly equal in length

cal·trap \'kal·trəp, -'ō-\ *or* **galtrap** *n* -S [var. of *caltrop*] **:** a heraldic representation of a military caltrop

cal·trop \'kal·trəp, -'ō-\ *also* **cal·throp** \-thrəp\ *n* -S [ME *calketrappe*, a plant, fr. OE *coltetræppe*, *calcatrippe*, fr. ML *calcatrippa*, prob. fr. (assumed) *calcitrappa*, fr. *calci-* (fr. L *calc-*, *calx* heel) + *trappa* trap, of Gmc origin; akin to OE *træppe* trap — more at CALK, TRAP] **1 :** any of several plants having stout spines on the fruit or flower heads: as **a :** STAR THISTLE **b :** a plant of either of two genera (*Tribulus* and *Kallstroemia*) of the family Zygophyllaceae **c :** WATER CHESTNUT **2 a :** a device with four metal points so arranged that when any three are on the ground the fourth projects upward as a hazard to the hoofs of horses or to pneumatic tires — see CALTRAP **b :** a calk on a horseshoe

caltrop 2a

ca·lum·ba *also* **co·lum·ba** \kə'ləmbə\ *or* **co·lom·bo** *or* **co·lum·bo** *or* **ca·lom·bo** \kə'ləm(,)bō\ *n* -S [perh. of African origin, akin to Hausa *ka'lu'mbo*] **:** a small tree] **:** the root of an African plant (*Jatrorrhiza palmata*) of the family Menispermaceae that contains the bitter principle columbin and is used as a tonic

cal·u·met \'kalyə,met, ==¦=, '==,mə̇t\ *n* -S *often attrib* [AmerF, fr. F dial., straw, fr. LL *calamellus* little reed, dim. of L *calamus* reed — more at CALAMUS] **:** a highly ornamented ceremonial pipe of the No. American Indians that was smoked at sacrifices and other magical or religious rites and on state occasions

calumet

calumet dance *n* **1 :** a ritual dance with a plumed calumet originated by Indians of the Great Plains as an invocation by pipe and later combined with mimicry of the eagle **2** *among the Iroquois* **:** EAGLE DANCE

ca·lum·ni·ate \kə'ləmnē,āt, *usu* -ād+V\ *vt* -ED/-ING/-S [L *calumniatus*, past part. of *calumniari*, fr. *calumnia* calumny] **1 :** to utter false statements, charges, or imputations in order to impair the public reputation of ⟨it provides an always welcome opportunity to ~ the masses —R.W.Brown b.1925⟩ **2 :** to injure or impair the public reputation of by calumny ⟨trying to ~ the leaders of the opposition⟩ ⟨gallantly defended the sage . . . against those who sought to ~ his memory —A.L. Sachar⟩ **syn** see MALIGN

ca·lum·ni·a·tion \kə,ləmnē'āshən\ *n* -S [LL *calumniation-*, *calumniatio*, fr. L *calumniatus* + *-ion-*, *-io* -ion] **1 :** the act of calumniating **:** SLANDERING ⟨the constant ~ engaged in by the courtiers⟩ **2 :** a slanderous report **:** CALUMNY

ca·lum·ni·a·tor \kə'ləmnē,ād·ə(r), -ātə-\ *n* -S [MF or L; MF *calomniateur*, fr. L *calumniator*, fr. *calumniatus* + *-or*] **:** one that calumniates

ca·lum·ni·ous \-nēəs\ *adj* [MF or LL; MF *calomnieux*, fr. LL *calumniosus* full of trickery, fr. L *calumnia* trickery, calumny + *-osus* -ous] **:** given to calumny ⟨~ backbiting rivals⟩ **:** constituting or marked by calumny ⟨hurt by ~ reports⟩ **:** SLANDEROUS

ca·lum·ni·ous·ly *adv* **:** in a calumnious manner

calumnize *vt* -ED/-ING/-S [*calumny* + *-ize*] *obs* **:** CALUMNIATE

cal·um·ny \'kal(y)əmnē, -ni\ *n* -ES [MF & L; MF *calomnie*, fr. L *calumnia*, fr. *calvi* to deceive; akin to OE *hōl* calumny, OHG *huolen* to deceive, ON *hōl* flattery, Goth *holon* to accuse falsely, Gk *kēlein* to beguile] **1 :** the act of uttering false charges or misrepresentations maliciously calculated to damage another's reputation ⟨a circle of false friends spending their time in *calumnies*⟩ **2 :** a false charge or misrepresentation intended to blacken one's reputation **:** SLANDER ⟨this publication was felt to be a ~ on the innocence of the nursery —Ernest Jones⟩ ⟨there are always such *calumnies* about rebels —H.F.West⟩ **syn** see DETRACTION

calumpang *var of* KALUMPANG

calumpit *var of* KALUMPIT

ca·lu·sa *also* **ca·loo·sa** \kə'lüsə\ *n, pl* **calusa** *or* **calusas** *usu cap* [perh. modif. of Sp *Carlos* (Charles V †1558 Holy Roman emperor)] **1 :** a people of southern Florida of uncertain, perhaps Muskogean, relationship **2 :** a member of the Calusa people

ca·lu·sar \kə,lü'shär\ *n, pl* **calusa·ri** \-ärē\ *sometimes cap* [Romanian *călușar*, fr. *căluș* hobbyhorse] **:** a Romanian hobbyhorse dance done by members of a sworn brotherhood in wild steps and fierce mock combat

cal·u·tron \'kalyə,trän\ *n* -S [*Cal*ifornia *U*niversity + E *-tron*] **:** an electromagnetic apparatus for separating isotopes according to their masses on the principle of the mass spectrograph

cal·va \'kalvə\ *n, pl* **calvas** \-vəz\ *or* **cal·vae** \-,vē, -,ī\ [NL, fr. L, scalp without hair — more at CALVARIUM] **:** the upper part of the human cranium — compare CALVARIUM

cal·va·dos \¦kalvə¦dōs, -ōs, -äs\ *n* -ES *often cap* [F, fr. *Calvados* dept., Normandy, France, where it originated] **:** a dry fruity brown brandy distilled esp. from apples grown in Auge and Bessin in the department of Calvados

cal·vaire \kal'va(a)(ə)r\ *n* -S [F, fr. LL *Calvaria*] **:** CALVARY

cal·var·ia \kal'va(a)rēə\ *n* -S [L, skull] **:** CALVARIUM

cal·var·i·al \-ēəl\ *adj* [NL *calvarium* + E *-al*] **:** of or relating to the calvarium

cal·var·i·um \-ēəm\ *n, pl* **calvar·ia** \-ēə\ [NL, alter of L *calvaria* skull, fr. *calva* scalp without hair, fr. fem. of *calvus* bald; akin to Skt *atikulva* completely bald] **:** an incomplete skull: **a :** a skull lacking the lower jaw **b :** a skull lacking the lower jaw and facial portion **c :** CALVA

cal·va·ry \'kalv(ə)rē, -ri\ *n* -ES *sometimes cap* [fr. *Calvary*, the hill near the ancient city of Jerusalem where Jesus was crucified, fr. ME *Calvarie*, fr. OE, fr. LL *Calvaria* (fr. L, skull), trans. of Gk *kranion*, trans. of Aram *gūlgaltā*] **1 :** a cross with the figure of the crucified Christ typically flanked by two other crosses with figures of thieves and set out of doors as a shrine **2 :** experience of intense suffering **:** TRIAL, ORDEAL ⟨penury and financial dependency constituted a veritable ~ for Michelangelo —*Publ's Mod. Lang. Assoc. of Amer.*⟩

calvary clover *n, usu cap 1st C* **:** a prickly-fruited medic (*Medicago echinus*) of the Mediterranean region

calvary cross *n, usu cap 1st C* **:** a Latin cross set upon three steps or upon a mount — called also *cross Calvary*, *cross of Calvary*

cal·va·tia \kal'vāsh(ē)ə\ *n, cap* [NL, irreg. fr. L *calvus* bald] **:** a genus of fungi (family Lycoperdaceae) including the giant puffball (*C. gigantea*) that have outer casings whose upper parts break at maturity into angular pieces to expose the spores

Calvary cross

¹calve \'kav, 'kaf, -aa(ə)-,-ai-,-á-,-ä-\ *vb* -ED/-ING/-S [ME *calven*, fr. OE *cealfian*, fr. *cealf* calf — more at CALF] *vi* **1 a :** to give birth to a calf — sometimes used with *down* **b :** to bear young **:** produce offspring **2** *of an ice mass* **:** to separate or break so that a part becomes detached ~ *vt* **1 :** to produce by birth **2 :** *of an ice mass* **:** to let break off and become detached ⟨the glacier *calved* a large iceberg⟩

²calve \'kȧv, -ō-\ *vi* -ED/-ING/-S [prob. fr. Flem *inkalven* to cave in, fr. *in* + *kalven* to bear a calf, to calve (said of a glacier); akin to OE *cealfian*] *dial Eng, of an earth or rock mass* **:** to fall esp. from undermining **:** CAVE — used with *in*

calved *adj* [fr. past part. of ¹*calve*] **:** having produced a calf — often used with *down* ⟨a *calved*-down heifer⟩

calv·er \'kavə(r), -afə-, -aa-,-ai-,-á-,-ä-\ *n* -S [¹*calve* + *-er*] **:** a pregnant cow

calves *pl of* CALF, *pres 3d sing of* CALVE

cal·vin·ism \'kalvə,nizəm\ *n* -S *cap* [John *Calvin* (Jean Chauvin or Caulvin) †1564 Fr. theologian + E *-ism*] **:** the theological system or distinguishing tenets of the Christian reformer John Calvin and his followers; *esp* **:** the theological doctrines that emphasize the sovereignty of God in the bestowal of grace and that specif. include election or predestination, limited atonement, total depravity, irresistibility of grace, and the perseverance of saints — compare ARMINIANISM

¹cal·vin·ist \-nə̇st\ *n* -S *usu cap* **:** a follower of John Calvin **:** an adherent of Calvinism

²calvinist \"\ *or* **cal·vin·is·tic** \¦==¦nistik, -ēk\ *also* **cal·vin·is·ti·cal** \-ə̇kəl, -ēk-\ *adj, usu cap* **:** of, relating to, or characteristic of Calvinism or Calvinists — **cal·vin·is·ti·cal·ly** \-ə̇k(ə)lē, -ēk-, -li\ *adv, usu cap*

calvinistic baptist *n, usu cap C&B* **1 :** PARTICULAR BAPTIST **2 :** a Baptist holding Calvinistic doctrinal views

calvinistic methodist *n, usu cap C&M* **:** a member of a British religious body following the Calvinistic opinion of George Whitefield and antedating the Arminian form of Methodism

cal·vin·ize \'kalvə,nīz\ *vb* -ED/-ING/-S *often cap* [John *Calvin* + E *-ize* — more at CALVINISM] *vi* **:** to follow Calvinism ~ *vt* **:** to convert to Calvinism **:** imbue with Calvinism

cal·vi·ti·es \kal'vishē,ēz, -ishēz\ *n, pl* **calvities** [L, baldness, fr. *calvus* bald — more at CALVARIUM] **:** BALDNESS

¹calx \'kalks\ *n, pl* **calxes** \-lksə̇z\ *or* **cal·ces** \-l,sēz\ [ME *cals* powder produced by calcining a mineral, fr. L *calx* lime — more at CHALK] **:** the friable residue (as a metal oxide) left when a mineral or metal has been subjected to calcination or roasting **:** CALCINE

²calx \"\ *n, pl* **cal·ces** \-l,sēz\ [L — more at CALK] **:** HEEL

calyc- *or* **calyco-** *comb form* [NL, fr. Gk *kalyk-*, *kalyko-*, fr. *kalyk-*, *kalyx* — more at CHALICE] **:** calyx ⟨*calyc*oid⟩ ⟨*Calyc*ophora⟩

cal·y·canth \'kalə,kan(t)th\ *n* -S [NL *Calycanthus*] **:** a plant of the genus *Calycanthus*

cal·y·can·tha·ce·ae \,kalə̇(,)kan'thāsē,ē\ *n pl, cap* [NL, fr. *Calycanthus*, type genus + *-aceae*] **:** a family of shrubs (order Ranales) of the eastern U. S. and eastern Asia having opposite simple leaves, aromatic bark, and large solitary flowers — see CALYCANTHUS — **cal·y·can·tha·ceous** \¦==(,)¦thāshəs\ *adj*

cal·y·can·the·my \,==¦kan(t)thəmē\ *n* -ES [*calyc-* + Gk *anthemon* flower + E *-y* — more at ANTHEMION] **:** abnormal development of calyx parts into petals or petallike structures

cal·y·can·thine \-'kan,thēn, -an(t)thə̇n\ *n* -S [NL *Calycanthus* + E *-ine*] **:** a bitter and poisonous crystalline alkaloid $C_{22}H_{26}N_4$ that is obtained from seeds of plants of the genus *Calycanthus*

cal·y·can·thus \-n(t)thəs\ *n* [NL, fr. *calyc-* + *-anthus*] **1** *cap* **:** a small genus (the type of the family Calycanthaceae) of American shrubs having aromatic bark, opposite entire leaves, and purple or red flowers — see CAROLINA ALLSPICE **2** -ES **:** CAROLINA ALLSPICE

ca·ly·cate \'kālə,kāt, -'a-, -,kə̇t\ *adj* [NL *calycatus*, fr. *calyc-* + *-atus* -ate] *bot* **:** having a calyx

cal·y·ce·al *or* **cal·i·ce·al** \¦kalə¦sēəl, ¦kā-\ *also* **ca·ly·cal** \'kālə̇kəl, -'a-\ *adj* [*calyc-* + *-eal* or *-al*] **:** of or relating to a calyx

cal·y·ce·ra·ce·ae \,kaləsə'rāsē,ē\ *n pl, cap* [NL, fr. *Calycera*, type genus (irreg. fr. *calyc-* + Gk *keras* horn) + *-aceae* — more at CEREBRAL] **:** a family of So. American herbs or subshrubs (order Campanulales) having flowers in heads like the composites but differing in the variable number of perianth lobes and the more or less distinct anthers — **cal·y·ce·ra·ceous** \¦===¦rāshəs\ *adj*

calyces *pl of* CALYX

calyci- *comb form* [L *calyc-*, *calyx*] **:** calyx ⟨*calyci*ferous⟩ ⟨*calyci*floral⟩

ca·ly·cine \'kālə,sīn, -'a-\ *also* **ca·lyc·i·nal** \kə'lis^ənᵊl\ *adj* [*calycine* fr. *calyc-* + *-ine*; *calycinal* fr. *calycine* + *-al*] **:** relating to or resembling a calyx

cal·y·cle *sense 1* 'kalə̇kəl *or* -'a-, *sense 2* -'a-\ *n* -S [modif. of F *calicule*, fr. L *calyculus* small flower bud, calyx, dim. of *calyc-*, *calyx* — more at CALYX] **1 :** EPICALYX **2** [alter. of *calicle*] **:** CALYCULUS

ca·ly·cled \-kəld\ *adj* **:** having a calycle **:** CALYCULATE

calyco- — see CALYC-

ca·ly·coid \'kālə,kȯid, -'a-\ *also* **ca·ly·coi·de·ous** \¦==¦dēəs\ *adj* [*calyc-* + *-oid*] **:** like a calyx in form, color, or appearance

ca·ly·coph·o·ra \,kālə'käfərə, -al-\ *n pl, cap* [NL, fr. *calyc-* + *-phora*] **:** a suborder of Siphonophora containing forms having a long stem with the zooids arranged along it and one or more swimming bells but no air sac near its upper end — **ca·ly·coph·o·ran** \¦==¦==rən\ *adj or n* — **ca·ly·co·phore** \'==lə̇kə,fō(ə)r\ *n* -S

ca·ly·coph·o·rae \,==¦käfə,rē\ *syn of* CALYCOPHORA

ca·ly·co·phyl·lum \,=lə̇kō'filəm\ *n, cap* [NL, fr. *calyc-* + *-phyllum*] **:** a genus of tropical American trees (family Rubiaceae) of medium to large size characterized by smooth shiny reddish or brown shredding bark — see DAGAME

ca·ly·co·zoa \-kə'zōə\ [NL, fr. *calyc-* + *-zoa*] *syn of* STAUROMEDUSAE

ca·ly·co·zo·an \¦===¦zōən\ *adj or n* [NL *Calycozoa* + E *-an*] **:** STAUROMEDUSAN — **ca·ly·co·zo·ic** \-ōik\ *adj*

ca·lyc·u·lar *also* **ca·lic·u·lar** \kə'likyələ(r)\ *adj* [*calycular* fr. L *calyculus* small flower bud + E *-ar*; *calicular* fr. F *calicule* calycle + E *-ar* — more at CALYCLE] **:** of the nature of or relating to a calycle or calyculus

ca·lyc·u·late *also* **ca·lic·u·late** \-,lāt, -,lə̇t\ *adj* [*calyculate* fr. L *calyculus* + E *-ate*; *caliculate* fr. F *calicule* + E *-ate*] **1 :** having a calycle **2 :** having the surfaces pitted

ca·lyc·u·lus \-,ləs\ *n, pl* **calycu·li** \-,lī, -ē\ [NL, modif. (influenced by E *calycle* and L *calyculus* small flower bud, calyx) of E *calicle*, fr. L *caliculus* small cup, dim. of *calic-*, *calix* cup — more at CHALICE] **:** a small cup-shaped structure (as a taste bud, an optic cup, or a cavity of a coral containing a polyp)

cal·y·do·ni·an \¦kalə¦dōnēən, -ōnyən\ *adj, usu cap* [*Calydon*, ancient city of Aetolia, Greece (fr. L, fr. Gk *Kalydōn*) + E *-ian*] **:** of or relating to Calydon

ca·lym·e·ne \kə'limə(,)nē\ *n, cap* [NL, modif. of Gk *kekalymmenē*, fem. of *kekalymmenos*, perf. pass. part. of *kalyptein* to cover, conceal — more at HELL] **:** a genus of trilobites of the Ordovician, Silurian, and Devonian periods

ca·lym·ma \kə'limə\ *n* -S [NL, fr. Gk *kalymma* covering, fr. *kalyptein*] **:** the matrix of a chromosome

ca·lym·ma·to·bacterium \kə¦limәd·ō+\ *n, cap* [NL, fr. Gk *kalymmat-*, *kalymma* covering + NL *-o-* + *Bacterium*] **:** a genus of pleomorphic nonmotile bacterial rods (family Brucellaceae) that includes solely the causative organism of human granuloma inguinale — see DONOVAN BODY

¹ca·lyp·so \kə'lip(,)sō\ *n* [NL, prob. fr. L *Calypso*, island nymph who detained Odysseus 7 years on his journey home from Troy, fr. Gk *Kalypsō*] **1** *cap* **:** a genus of delicate bulbous bog herbs (family Orchidaceae) of northern Europe and No. America **2** -S **:** any plant of the genus *Calypso* or its single flower which is white variegated with purple, pink, and yellow

²calypso \"\ *n* -S *sometimes cap* [prob. after *Calypso*, island nymph] **:** a balladlike improvisation in African rhythm usu. satirizing current events first composed and sung in competition in the British West Indies

¹ca·lyp·so·ni·an \kə,lip'sōnēən, ¦ka(,)lip¦s-\ *n* -S *sometimes cap* [²*calypso* + connective *-n-* + *-ian*] **:** a composer and singer of calypso songs

²calypsonian \"\ *adj* **:** of, relating to, or characteristic of calypso music

ca·lyp·ter \kə'liptə(r), 'kaləp-\ *n, pl* **ca·lyp·ters** \-ə(r)z\ *or* **cal·yp·te·res** \,kaləp'ti(ə)(,)rēz\ [NL, fr. Gk *kalyptēr* sheath, fr. *kalyptein* to cover, conceal — more at HELL] **1 :** the alula of a two-winged fly esp. when large enough to cover the halter **2 :** CALYPTRA

ca·lyp·te·rae \kə'liptə,rē\ *syn of* CALYPTRATAE

ca·lyp·to·blas·tea \kə,liptō'blastēə\ [NL, fr. Gk *kalyptos* covered (fr. *kalyptein*) + *blastos* shoot, bud + NL *-ea* (neut. pl. of L *-eus*) — more at -EAE] *syn of* LEPTOMEDUSAE

ca·lyp·to·blas·tic \¦==¦=¦tik\ *adj* [Gk *kalyptos* + E *-blastic*] **1 :** having the gonophores in a gonotheca — used of hydroids of the order Leptomedusae **2** *also* **ca·lyp·to·blas·te·an** \-tēən\ **:** LEPTOMEDUSAN

ca·lyp·to·pis \kə'liptəpə̇s\ *or* **cal·yp·top·sis** \,kaləp'täpsə̇s\ *n, pl* **calypto·pes** \-,pēz\ *or* **calyptop·ses** \-(,)sēz\ [NL, fr. Gk *kalyptos* + NL *-opis* or *-opsis*] **:** a modified zoea larva typical of euphausiid crustaceans

ca·lyp·to·rhyn·chus \kə,liptə'riŋkəs\ *n, cap* [NL, fr. Gk *kalyptos* + NL *-rhynchus*] **:** a genus of chiefly black Australian insectivorous cockatoos

ca·lyp·tra \kə'liptrə\ *n* -S [NL, fr. Gk *kalyptra* veil, fr. *kalyptein*] **1 :** the archegonium of a liverwort or moss when distended and modified by the growth of the enclosed sporophyte; *esp* **:** such an archegonium when forming a thin membranous hood over the capsule of a moss **2 :** a caplike covering of a flower or fruit (as the calyx of plants of the genus *Eschscholtzia*) **3 :** ROOT CAP

cal·yp·trae·i·dae \,kaləp'trēə,dē\ *n pl, cap* [NL, fr. *Calyptraea*, type genus (irreg. fr. Gk *kalyptra*) + *-idae*] **:** a family (order Pectinibranchia) of limpetlike marine gastropod mollusks having a curved internal lamina in the shell — see CUP-AND-SAUCER LIMPET

cal·yp·tran·thes \,kaləp'tran(,)thēz\ *n, cap* [NL, fr. *calyptra* + *-anthes*] **:** a large genus of tropical American aromatic shrubs or trees of the family Myrtaceae with evergreen leathery leaves and small flowers in which the top of the calyx falls away like a calyptra — see WHITE STOPPER

cal·yp·tra·ta \,kaləp'träd·ə, -'ā-\ [alter. (influenced by NL *-ata*) of NL *Calyptratae*] *syn of* CALYPTRATAE

cal·yp·tra·tae \-'ād·,ē, -ād-\ *n pl, cap* [NL, fr. *calyptr-* (fr. *calypter*) + *-atae* (fem. pl. of *-atus* -ate)] **:** a group of dipterous flies (suborder Schizophora) including in recent classifications the Muscidae and related families distinguished by the large calypters

¹ca·lyp·trate \kə'lip,trāt, -,trə̇t, 'kaləp,trāt\ *adj* [NL *calyptra* + E *-ate*] **1** *bot* **:** having a calyptra **2 a** [²*calyptrate*] **:** of or relating to the Calyptratae **b** [NL *calyptr-* (fr. *calypter*) + E *-ate*] **:** furnished with calypters

²calyptrate \"\ *n* -S [NL *Calyptratae*] **:** one of the Calyptratae

calyptri- *or* **calyptro-** *comb form* [NL *calyptra*] **:** calyptra **:** hood **:** cap ⟨*calyptri*form⟩ ⟨*calyptro*gen⟩

ca·lyp·tro·gen \kə'liptrəjən, -,jen\ *n* -S [ISV *calyptro-* + *-gen*] **:** the layer of cells from which the root cap originates

cal·yp·trog·y·ne \,kaləp'träjə(,)nē\ *n, cap* [NL, fr. *calyptro-* + Gk *gynē* woman — more at QUEEN] **:** a small genus of almost stemless tropical American palms with pinnate almost stalkless leaves and small flowers half hidden by the spadix

ca·lys·so·zoa \kə,lisə'zōə\ [NL *calysso-* (prob. alter. of *calyc-*) + *-zoa*] *syn of* ENTOPROCTA

cal·y·ste·gia \,kalə'stējē·ə\ *n, cap* [NL, irreg. fr. *calyx* + Gk *stegē* roof (fr. *stegein* to cover) + NL *-ia* — more at THATCH] **:** a small genus of twining or prostrate perennial herbs closely related to and by some included in *Convolvulus* but distinguished by the large bracts below the calyx

ca·lyx \ˈkāliks, -ēks *also* ˈka-\ *n, pl* **calyx·es** \-ksə̇z\ *or* **caly·ces** \-lə,sēz\ [L, fr. Gk *kalyx* — more at CHALICE] **1 :** the outer set of floral leaves making up the external part of the flower and consisting of separate or fused sepals that are usu. green and foliaceous but often colored like the corolla — see COROLLA, PERIANTH **2 :** a cuplike division of the pelvis of the kidney surrounding one or more of the renal papillae **3 :** any of various more or less cup-shaped zoological structures (as the body or the test of a crinoid or the calyculus of a coral)

calyx, C

calyx spray *n* **:** a pesticidal spray applied to fruit trees (as apple and pear) just after the petals fall but before the calyx closes — called also *petal fall spray, shuck spray*

calyx tooth *n* **:** a tip of a calyx lobe or division

calyx tube *n* **1 :** the lower tubular or cup-shaped portion of a gamosepalous calyx **2 :** HYPANTHIUM

cal·zo·ne·ras *or* **cal·zo·ne·ros** \,kalzəˈnerəs\ *n pl* [MexSp *calzoneras*, fr. Sp *calzón* pants, fr. *calza* stocking, fr. ML *calcea*, fr. L *calceus* shoe] *Southwest* **:** trousers buttoned at the sides and usu. slit at the bottom

¹cam *dial Brit past of* COME

²cam \ˈkam\ *adv* [prob. fr. W, crooked] *dial* **:** CROOKEDLY, AWRY, ASKEW

³cam \ˈ"\ *adj* [prob. fr. W; akin to OIr *camm* crooked — more at CHANGE] *dial* **:** CROOKED, TWISTED, PERVERSE

⁴cam \ˈkam, -aa(ə)m\ *n* -s [perh. fr. F *came*, fr. G *kamm*, lit., comb, fr. OHG *kamb* — more at COMB] **1 :** a rotating or sliding piece of machinery (as a wheel or a projection on a wheel) that imparts motion to a roller moving against its edge or to a pin free to move in a groove on its face or that receives motion from such a roller or pin **2 :** a curved wedge movable about an axis and used for forcing or clamping two pieces together

⁵cam \ˈ"\ *vt* **cammed; cammed; camming; cams 1 :** to move or control the movement of with a cam **2 :** to shape into a cam (as by grooving) — often used with *out*

needlebar cam, *A;* heart cam, *B;* cam wheel, *C*

cam *abbr* camouflage

cam·a·ca *also* **cam·a·ka** \ˈkaməkə\ *n* -s [ME, *also*, fr. MF *camocas* or ML *camoca*, fr. Ar & Per *kamkha, kimkha*] **:** a medieval fabric prob. of silk and camel's hair used for draperies and garments

ca·ma·chi·le \,kämə'chilē\ *n* -s [AmerSp *camachile, cuamóchil, guamúchil*, fr. Nahuatl *cuauh-mochitl*] **:** a common tropical American tree (*Pithecolobium dulce*) yielding good timber, a yellow dye, a mucilaginous gum, and a widely used edible fruit — called also *huamuchil;* see MANILA TAMARIND

cam·a·du·la seed \,kamə'düla-\ *n* [origin unknown] **:** the seed of the adlay

cama fox *var of* CAAMA

ca·ma·gon \ˈkamə,gän\ *n* -s [Sp *camagón*, fr. Tag *kamagóng*] **1 :** a timber tree (*Diospyros discolor*) of the Philippines that yields an edible fruit **2 :** the wood of the camagon noted for its dark color

ca·ma·güey *or* **ca·ma·guey** \,kamə'gwā\ *adj, usu cap* [fr. *Camagüey*, Cuba] **:** of or from the city of Camagüey, Cuba **:** of the kind or style prevalent in Camagüey

ca·ma·ïeu \kämäyœ\ *n, pl* **camaïeux** \-yœ\ [MF; akin to It *cammeo* — more at CAMEO] **1** *obs* **:** CAMEO **2 :** MONOCHROME 1

ca·mail \kə'māl\ *n* -s [F, fr. OProv *capmalh*, perh. fr. *cap* head (fr. L *caput*) + *malha* mesh, ring of mail, fr. L *macula* spot, mesh — more at HEAD, MAIL] **:** a hood or neck guard of chain mail usu. hanging from the basinet

ca·mal·do·lese \kä,maldə'lēz, -ēs\ *n, pl* **camaldolese** *usu cap* [It, fr. *Camaldoli*, monastery in So. Italy where the order was founded + It *-ese*] **:** a member of a barefooted order of hermit Benedictines founded in 1012 by St. Romuald

ca·ma·lig \kə'mälig\ *n* -s [Tag *kamalig*] **1** *Philippines* **:** STOREHOUSE **2** *Philippines* **:** HUT

¹ca·ma·lo·te \,kamə'lōd·ē\ *n* -s [AmerSp] **:** WATER LILY

²camalote \"\ *n* -s [AmerSp, perh. alter. of Sp *camelote*, camlet, fr. MF *camelot* — more at CAMLET] **:** any of several coarse grasses of tropical America (esp. *Echinochloa crus-galli, Gynerium sagittatum*, and *Hymenachne amplexicaulis*)

ca·man \kə'mōn\ *n* -s [IrGael *camān*, fr. OIr *camm* crooked — more at CHANGE] *Irish & Scot* **:** CAMMOCK

cam·a·nay \,kamə'nī\ *n* -s [AmerSp] **:** BLUE-FOOTED BOOBY

ca·man·cha·ca \,kamən'chäkə\ *n* -s [AmerSp] **:** a thick fog on the coasts of Peru and Chile

ca·man·si *or* **ka·man·si** \kə'män(t)sē\ *n* -s [Sp, fr. Tag *kamansi*] *Philippines* **:** BREADFRUIT 1

cam·a·ra \ˈkamərə, ,kamə'rä\ *n* -s [Pg *camará*, fr. Tupi] **1 :** the hard and durable wood of the tonka-bean tree and other plants of the genus *Dipteryx* **2 :** the camara nutmeg tree **3 :** a tropical American shrub (*Lantana camara*) having showy yellow-orange tubular flowers

ca·ma·ra·de·rie \,kam(ə)'radərē, -äm-; ,käm(ə)'räd-, ,kåm(ə)-'räd-, -am-; *also* ,=(=),==ˈ=\ *n* -s [F, fr. *camarade* comrade + *-erie* -ery — more at COMRADE] **:** the spirit of friendly familiarity and goodwill that exists between comrades **:** GOOD-FELLOWSHIP ⟨a greater spirit of tolerance and ~ among the drivers —Priscilla Hughes⟩ ⟨a great deal of affection on both sides, but little ~ —A.C.Benson⟩

camara nutmeg *n* [perh. fr. Pg *camará*] **:** the fruit of a tree (*Licaria camara*) of the family Lauraceae of Guiana somewhat resembling the nutmeg

cam·a·ra·sau·rus \ˈkamərə'sȯrəs\ *n, cap* [NL, fr. Gk *kamara* vaulted chamber + NL *-saurus* — more at CHAMBER] **:** a genus of American Jurassic dinosaurs (order Sauropoda) with the orbits and nares large and situated high on the head suggesting adaptation to an amphibious mode of life

cam·a·ril·la \,kamə'rilə, -rē(y)ə\ *n* -s [Sp, lit., small room, dim. of *cámara* room, fr. LL *camara, camera* — more at CHAMBER] **:** a group of unofficial often secret and usu. scheming advisers esp. of one in power (as a king or premier) **:** CABAL, CLIQUE ⟨a vivid picture of the sycophantic timeservers who constituted the Kaiser's court ~ —L.P.Lochner⟩

cam·as \ˈkaməs\ *also* **cam·ash** \-mish\ *or* **cam·ass** \-məs\ *or* **quam·ash** \ˈkwämish\ *n* -ES [Chinook Jargon *kamass*, fr. Nootka *chamas* sweet] **1 :** an American plant of the genus *Camassia* (esp. *C. quamash*) of the western U.S. **2 :** a plant of the genus *Zigadenus* — see DEATH CAMAS

camas rat *n* **:** a large dark pocket gopher (*Thomomys bulbivorus*) of the northwestern U.S. that feeds on the camas

ca·mas·sia \kə'masēə\ *n, cap* [NL, fr. E *camass* + NL *-ia*] **:** a genus of scapose herbs (family Liliaceae) mostly of western No. America having edible bulbs, basal linear leaves, and racemes of blue, purple, or white flowers — see CAMAS

ca·ma·ta \kə'mäd·ə\ *n* -s [origin unknown] **:** the almost unripe acorns and cups of the valonia oak gathered from the ground, dried, and used for tanning — compare CAMATINA

ca·ma·ti·na \,kamə'tēnə\ *n* -s [*camata* + *-ina* (It dim. suffix)] **:** the unripe acorns and cups of the valonia oak picked from the tree, dried, and used for tanning — compare CAMATA

ca·mau·ro \kə'maü(,)rō\ *n* -s [It, prob. fr. ML *camaurum*] **:** a red velvet cap bordered with ermine formerly used by popes

cam·bar \ˈkam,bär\ *n, usu cap* [*Campine* + *barred* Rock] **:** a breed of autosexing domestic fowls with the male chicks pale gray striped with brown and the females much darker that was developed in England from crosses of barred rocks and golden Campines

cam·ba·rus \ˈkambərəs\ *n, cap* [NL, alter. (influenced by LL *gambarus*, alter. of L *cammarus*) of L *cammarus* sea crab, lobster, fr. Gk *kammaros;* akin to ON *humarr* lobster, Skt *kamaṭha* tortoise, and prob. to L *camur* curved — more at CHAMBER] **:** a genus of crayfishes (family Astacidae) lacking pleurobranchiae, having a specialized sperm receptacle, and including the common large crayfishes of eastern No. America some of which (esp. *C. limosus*) are used as food

cam·baye \(ˈ)kam¦bā\ *n* -s [earlier *cambaya*, prob. fr. Pg. *cambaia*, fr. *Cambaia* (Cambay) India] **:** a coarse cotton cloth made in India

¹cam·ber \ˈkambə(r), -aam-\ *vb* -ED/-ING/-S [F *cambrer*, fr. MF *cambre* curved] *vi* **:** to bend or curve upward toward the middle ~ *vt* **:** to cut, bend, or fashion to a slight convex curve **:** arch slightly ⟨above and athwartships ran a narrow platform, heavily ~*ed* and naked to the weather —Thomas Wood †1950⟩

²camber \"\ *n* -s [obs. *camber*, adj., curved, fr. obs. F *cambre*, fr. L *camur* — more at CHAMBER] **1 a :** a slight convexity, arching, or curvature (as of a beam, a deck, or a road) **b :** the greatest perpendicular distance in a semielliptical spring from an imaginary line drawn through the centers of the spring eyes to the top of the master leaf or to the bottom of the short plate **c :** the convexity or rise of the curve of an airfoil from its chord **:** the ratio of the maximum departure of this curve from the chord to the length of the chord **2 :** a setting of the front wheels of an automotive vehicle closer together at the bottom than at the top ⟨excessive ~ prevents the tire from having correct contact with the road —Joseph Heitner⟩ **3 :** a superficial geological structure induced during erosion, the strata dipping downward from hilltops toward adjacent valleys

camber angle *n* **1 :** the angle between two joined plane surfaces with a camber at the joining point or edge **2 :** the angle between the center line of the front wheel of an automotive vehicle and the vertical

camber arch *n* **:** an arch having a straight horizontal extrados and a slightly arched intrados

camber beam *n* **:** a beam that cambers

camber–keeled \ˈ= =¦=\ *adj, of a ship* **:** having the keel cambered but not actually hogged

camber piece *or* **camber slip** *n* **:** a piece or frame of wood cambered for use as a center in building camber arches

cam·ber·well beauty \ˈkambə(r),wel-, -,wəl-\ *n, usu cap C* [fr. *Camberwell*, formerly parish of Surrey, England, now metropolitan borough of London] **:** MOURNING CLOAK

cam·bi·al \ˈkambēəl\ *adj* [NL *cambium* + E *-al*] **:** of, relating to, or functioning as cambium

cam·bi·a·ta \,kambē'äd·ə\ *n* -s [It, fem. of *cambiato*, past part. of *cambiare* to change, fr. L, to exchange — more at CHANGE] **:** a nonharmonic note of a melody reached by a skip of a third and resolved by a step

cam·bi·form \ˈkambə,fȯrm\ *adj* [ISV *cambi-* (fr. NL *cambium*) + *-form;* prob. orig. formed as G *kambiform*] **:** of the form or character of the cambium or cambium cells

cam·bio \ˈkambē,ō\ *n* -s [It, fr. *cambiare* to exchange, fr. L — more at CHANGE] **:** a money exchange esp. in a Latin country

cam·bism \ˈkam,bizəm\ *n* -s [fr. *cambist*, after such pairs as E *journalist : journalism*] **:** the theory and practice of exchange in commerce

cam·bist \-,bə̇st\ *n* -s [F *cambiste*, fr. It *cambista*, fr. *cambio* + *-ista* -ist] **1 :** one who deals in bills of exchange or who is skilled in the science and practice of exchange **2 :** a table or manual giving the exchange values of moneys, weights, and measures of various countries

cam·bist·ry \-trē\ *n* -ES [*cambist* + *-ry*] **:** the science of exchange esp. in its international aspects

cam·bi·um \ˈkambēəm\ *n, pl* **cambiums** \-ēəmz\ *or* **cam·bia** \-ēə\ [NL, fr. ML, exchange, fr. L *cambiare* to exchange — more at CHANGE] **:** a formative layer one cell thick occurring between the xylem and phloem of most vascular plants, being persistently capable of giving rise to new cells, often for many years in woody plants, and being responsible for secondary growth — compare MERISTEM, PHELLOGEN

camblet *var of* CAMLET

cam·bo·dia \(ˈ)kam¦bōdēə\ *adj, usu cap* [fr. *Cambodia*, Indochina] **:** of or from Cambodia **:** of the kind or style prevalent in Cambodia **:** CAMBODIAN

¹cam·bo·di·an \(ˈ)kam¦bōdēən\ *adj, usu cap* [*Cambodia*, Indochina + E *-an*] **:** of or relating to the independent state of Cambodia resulting from the breakup of French Indochina after World War II and situated in the lower Mekong river valley

²cambodian \"\ *n* -s *cap* **1 :** a native or resident of Cambodia **2 :** the language of the Cambodians, which is of Mon-Khmer origin

¹camboge *var of* GAMBOGE

²cam·bo·gé \,kambō¦zhā\ *n* -s [origin unknown] **:** pierced concrete block used to make brise-soleils in Latin-American architecture ⟨achieve ventilation and decoration at the same time by the skillful insertion of ~ —*House Beautiful*⟩

cam·bo·gia \kam'bōjə\ *n* -s [NL, alter. of *cambugia, cambugium* — more at GAMBOGE] **:** GAMBOGE 1

camboose *var of* CABOOSE

cam·brel \ˈkam(b)rəl\ *dial Eng var of* GAMBREL 1, 2

¹cam·bri·an \ˈkambrēən, -ˈā-\ *adj, usu cap* [*Cambria* Wales (fr. ML *Cambria, Cumbria*, perh. fr. — assumed — OW *combrog* fellow countryman, Welshman) + E *-an* — more at CYMRY] **1 :** of or relating to Cambria **:** WELSH **2** *or* **cambric** \-brik, -ēk\ **:** of or relating to the earliest geologic period of the Paleozoic era and the lowest system of Paleozoic rocks whose formations (as conglomerates, sandstones, shales, and limestones) indicating conditions of shallow sea water, a far from uniform climate, and a period of great duration show scarcely recognizable plant fossils but record every great animal type except the vertebrate, trilobites being one of the most characteristic groups — see GEOLOGIC TIME table

²cambrian \"\ *n* -s **1** *cap* **:** a native or resident of Cambria **:** WELSHMAN **2** *usu cap* **:** the Cambrian period or system of rocks

¹cam·bric \ˈkāmbrik, -ēk\ *n* -s [alter. of earlier *cameryk*, fr. obs. Flem *Kameryk* Cambrai, city of France (formerly of Flanders), where it was first made] **1 :** a fine thin closely woven plain white linen fabric **2 :** a cotton fabric that resembles cambric, is usu. white or piece-dyed, and is made with a glossy or glazed finish for clothing and with various finishes for industrial uses

²cam·bric \ˈkambrik, -ām-, -ēk\ *usu cap, var of* CAMBRIAN

cambric grass \-ām-\ *n* [prob. so called fr. the use of its fibers in making cloth] **:** RAMIE

cambric tea \-ām-\ *n* [so called fr. its being thin and white] **:** a hot drink made of water, milk, sugar, and often a very small portion of tea that is usu. given to children as a tea substitute

cam·bridge \ˈkāmbrij, -rēj\ *adj, usu cap* [fr. the place name *Cambridge*] **1** [fr. *Cambridge*, England] **:** of or from the municipal borough of Cambridge, England **:** of the kind or style prevalent in Cambridge, England **:** CANTABRIGIAN **2** [fr. *Cambridge* University, England] **:** of, relating to, or characteristic of Cambridge University **3** [fr. *Cambridge*, Mass.] **:** of or from the city of Cambridge, Mass. ⟨a *Cambridge* street⟩ **:** of the kind or style prevalent in Cambridge, Mass.

cambridge blue *n, often cap C* [fr. *Cambridge*, England, seat of Cambridge University] **:** ETON BLUE

cambridge platonist *n, usu cap C&P* [fr. *Cambridge* University, England, a center of the movement] **:** one of a group of 17th century Christian philosophers who united in opposition to empiricism and Hobbesian mechanism and who sought to reconcile science and religion within a Neoplatonic framework

cambridge red *n, often cap C* **:** a grayish to moderate red that is bluer and lighter than dianthus

cam·bridge·shire \-,shi(ə)r,-,shiə,-,shə(r)\ *or* **cambridge** *adj, usu cap* [fr. *Cambridgeshire* or the county of *Cambridge*, England] **:** of or from the county of Cambridge, England **:** of the kind or style prevalent in the county of Cambridge

cam·bril \ˈkam(b)rəl\ *dial Eng var of* GAMBREL 1, 2

cam·den \ˈkamdən, -aam-\ *adj, usu cap* [fr. *Camden*, N.J.] **:** of or from the city of Camden, N.J. ⟨*Camden* schools⟩ **:** of the kind or style prevalent in Camden

¹came *past of* COME

²came \ˈkām\ *also* **calm** \ˈkäm\ *n* -s [origin unknown] **:** a slender grooved rod of cast lead used to hold together panes of glass in a window esp. with latticework or stained glass

cam·eist \ˈkamēə̇st\ *n* -s [*cameo* + *-ist*] **1 :** a maker of cameos **2 :** a collector or connoisseur of cameos

cam·el \ˈkaməl\ *n* -s [ME *camel* (fr. OE & ONF) & *chamel*, fr. OF; all fr. L *camelus*, fr. Gk *kamēlos*, of Sem. origin; akin to Heb & Phoenician *gāmāl* camel, Ar *jamal*] **1 a :** either of two large ruminant mammals used as draft and saddle animals in desert regions esp. of Africa and Asia and peculiarly adapted to desert life in their ability to live on tough thorny plants, in their capacity to conserve water in the body, and in their highly modified feet with broad thick calloused soles and small hoofs situated at the end of the toes: (1) **:** the Arabian camel (*Camelus dromedarius*) with a single large hump on the back **:** DROMEDARY (2) **:** the Bactrian camel (*C. bactrianus*) with two humps **b :** any member of the family Camelidae **2 :** a watertight structure (as a large box or cylinder) used esp. to lift submerged ships by being sunk, attached to the object to be raised, and then pumped free of water **3 a :** a variable color averaging a light yellowish brown that is slightly redder and very slightly less strong than khaki, yellower and less strong than cinnamon, and yellower and duller than walnut brown **b :** a brownish gray that is lighter than average chocolate, redder, lighter, and stronger than taupe (sense 1) or castor, and redder than mouse gray **4 :** a wooden float used as a fender esp. to fend ships off piers

Bactrian camel

¹camelback \ˈ= =,=\ *n* **1 :** the back of a camel ⟨crossed the desert on ~⟩ **2 :** a back (as of a dog) that is slightly curved upward **:** ROACH BACK — opposed to *swayback* **3** *or* **camelback locomotive :** a steam locomotive with the cab astride the boiler **4** *or* **camelback house :** a house one story high at the front and two stories high in the rear **5** [so called fr. the shape of one kind of retread made with it] **:** an uncured compound of rubber made chiefly of reclaimed or synthetic rubber and used for retreading or recapping pneumatic tires

²camelback \"\ *adj* **:** having a back slightly curved upward — opposed to *swaybacked*

³camelback \"\ *adv* **:** on camelback

camel bird *n* **:** OSTRICH

camel cricket *n* **:** CAVE CRICKET

cam·el·eer \¦kamə¦li(ə)r, -iə\ *or* **cam·el·teer** \-məl¦ti-\ *n* -s [*cameleer* fr. *camel* + *-eer; camelteer* alter. (influenced by *muleteer*) of *cameleer*] **:** a driver and tender of a camel

cameleon *var of* CHAMELEON

camel grass *or* **camel hay** *n* [so called fr. its serving as feed for camels] **:** any sweet-scented Asiatic grass of the genus *Cymbopogon* (esp. *C. schoenanthus*)

camel hair *var of* CAMEL'S HAIR

camelia *var of* CAMELLIA

ca·mel·i·dae \kə'melə,dē\ *n pl, cap* [NL, fr. *Camelus*, type genus + *-idae*] **:** a small family of ruminant mammals (order Artiodactyla) comprising camels, llamas, and extinct related forms all having long limbs with two toes and fused but distally divergent metapodials, a 3-chambered stomach, and oval red blood cells

cam·e·li·na \,kamə'līnə, -lē-; kə'melənə\ *n, cap* [NL, fr. ML *camelina, chamaelinum*, alter. of L *chamaemelinus* of chamomile, fr. *chamaemelon* chamomile — more at CHAMOMILE] **:** a small genus of Old World herbs (family Cruciferae) distinguished by their ovoid flaxlike seed pods — see FALSE FLAX, GOLD OF PLEASURE, SMALL-SEEDED FALSE FLAX

cam·e·line \ˈkamə,lēn, -m(ə)lən\ *n* -s [ME *camelyn*, fr. MF *camelin*, fr. ML *camelinum*, fr. L, neut. of *camelinus* of a camel, fr. *camelus* camel — more at CAMEL] **1 :** a twilled camel's-hair fabric **2 :** a garment made of cameline

cam·e·line oil \ˈkamə,lin-, -ēn-\ *n* **:** a pungent yellow semidrying oil obtained from the seeds of gold of pleasure — called also *dodder oil, German sesame oil*

camelion *obs var of* CHAMELEON

¹ca·mel·lia \kə'mēlyə, -lēə *also* -el-\ *n* [NL, fr. Georg Josef Kamel (Georgius Josephus *Camellus*) †1706 Moravian Jesuit missionary + NL *-ia*] **1** *cap* **:** a genus of tropical Asiatic evergreen shrubs or small trees (family Theaceae) having alternate elliptic short-petioled leaves and solitary usu. reddish or white flowers with stamens that are connate at the base **2** *also* **ca·me·lia** \-ēl-\ -s **:** any of several shrubs or trees of the genus *Camellia; esp* **:** an ornamental greenhouse shrub (*C. japonica*) with glossy evergreen leaves and showy roselike flowers **3** -s **:** a moderate to strong red that is bluer and lighter than blood red

²camellia \"\ [NL] *syn of* THEA

ca·mel·li·a·ce·ae \=,=lē'āsē,ē\ [NL, fr. *Camellia*, type genus + *-aceae*] *syn of* THEACEAE

cam·el·oid \ˈkamə,lȯid\ *adj* [*camel* + *-oid*] **:** like a camel

ca·mel·o·pard \kə'melə,pärd, -pȧd *also* ˈkamə(,)lō,p-\ *n* -s [ML *camelopardus*, alter. of L *camelopardalis*, fr. Gk *kamēlopardalis*, fr. *kamēlos* camel + *pardalis* leopard — more at PARD] **:** GIRAFFE

ca·mel·o·par·da·lis \kə,melə'pärdᵊləs, ,kamə(,)lō'-\ [NL, fr. L] *syn of* GIRAFFA

cam·el·ry \ˈkaməlrē\ *n* -ES [*camel* + *-ry* (as in *cavalry*)] **:** troops mounted on camels ⟨a column of ~ moved in from the north —*Time*⟩

camel's hair *n* **1** *also* **camel hair a :** the hair of a camel **b :** a substitute for camel's hair (as hair from the tail of a squirrel) **2** *also* **camel hair :** cloth made of camel's hair or a mixture of camel's hair and wool usu. light tan and soft and silky to the touch **3 :** the color deer

camel's hay *n* **:** CAMEL GRASS

camel spin *n* **:** an arabesque spin executed by a skater with back humped instead of arched

camelteer *var of* CAMELEER

camel thorn *also* **camel's thorn** *n* [so called fr. the use of its seed as feed for camels] **1 a :** a low spiny shrub (*Alhagi camelorum*) of the Arabian desert that yields manna **b :** a related shrub (*A. maurorum*) **2 :** an East Indian spiny shrub (*Zizyphus nummularius*) used as fodder for sheep and goats **3 :** any of several southern African acacias; *esp* **:** a browse plant (*Acacia giraffae*) of the veld

ca·me·lus \kə'mēləs\ *n, cap* [NL, fr. L, camel] **:** a genus comprising the true camels and a number of extinct related animals

cam·em·bert *or* **camembert cheese** \ˈkaməm,be(ə)r, -,a(a)(ə)r, -,eə, -,a(a)ə, ,==ˈ=\ *n* -s *usu cap 1st C* [F *camembert*, fr. *Camembert*, town in Normandy, France, where it was first made] **:** a soft unpressed cheese having a characteristic odor and flavor produced by the presence of a blue mold (*Penicillium camemberti*) and usu. covered with a feltlike rind inside which the cheese softens progressively toward the center

cam engine *n* [⁴*cam*] **:** an engine in which the reciprocating motion of the piston is converted into rotary motion by means of a cam and roller instead of the more usual crank

¹cam·eo \ˈkamē,ō\ *n* -s *often attrib* [It *cammeo, cameo;* akin to MF *camaieu*, ML *camahutus, camaeus*] **1 a :** a gem carved in relief; *esp* **:** a small piece of sculpture on a stone (as onyx or sardonyx) or on a shell having layers of different colors, the figure being cut in relief in one layer and another serving as background — compare INTAGLIO **b :** a small medallion usu. simulating stone or shell with a profiled head in relief **2 :** a carving or sculpture made in the manner of a cameo **3 :** any of several colors varying in hue from purplish red to bluish green, in chroma from low to moderate, and in lightness from medium to very high — see CAMEO BLUE, CAMEO BROWN, CAMEO GREEN, CAMEO PINK, CAMEO YELLOW **4 :** a usu. brief literary or dramatic piece that brings into delicate or sharp relief the character of a person, place, or event ⟨his ~*s* and short commentaries on men and manners —R.T.Dunlop⟩

²cameo \"\ *vt* -ED/-ING/-S **1 :** to make into or as if into a cameo ⟨polished basalt ~*ed* upon malachite —Amy Lowell⟩

2 : to treat in cameo form ⟨the North American College . . . has never been properly ~ed for history —J.P.Boland⟩

cameo blue *n* : a light to very light bluish green

cameo brown *n* : a grayish red to light reddish brown

cameo glass *n* : glass consisting of layers of different colors and cut after the manner of a cameo

cam·eo·graph \'kamē(,)ō,graf\ *n* -s [blend of *cameo* & *photograph*] : an image in relief produced largely mechanically from photographs

cam·e·og·ra·phy \,kamē'ägrəfē\ *n* -ES [blend of *cameo* & *photography*] : the art or process of producing cameographs

cameo green *n* : a pale green to light yellowish green — called also *hazy blue, mist blue*

cameo paper *n* : a clay-coated paper having an ivory tint and a dull finish used by artists for making pencil drawings

cameo pink *n* : a grayish purplish pink that is redder and deeper than average orchid mist and bluer and stronger than dawn pink

cameo shell *also* **cameo conch** *n* : a large gastropod shell used for cameos: as **a** : QUEEN CONCH **b** : a large king conch

cameo ware *n* **1** : a fine ware decorated with relief figures on a different-colored ground (as Wedgwood ware) **2** : a highly glazed shell-tinted ware usu. pink shading into white

cameo yellow *n* : a pale yellow that is greener, stronger, and slightly darker than ivory and deeper and slightly greener than cream

cam·era \'kam(ə)rə, 'kaamrə\ *n* -s *often attrib* [LL, chamber, room — more at CHAMBER] **1** *pl also* **cam·er·ae** \'kamə,rē, -ī\ : a chamber, room, or small hall: as **a** : a room having a vaulted or domical ceiling **b** : a judge's chamber **2** : the treasury department of the papal curia **3 a** [NL, by shortening] : CAMERA OBSCURA **b** : a lightproof box fitted with a lens through the aperture of which the image of an object is recorded on a light-sensitive material **c** : the part of a television transmitting apparatus in which the image to be televised is formed for conversion into electrical impulses — **in camera 1** : in the judge's chamber ⟨the trial was held *in camera*⟩ **2** : in private : PRIVATELY, SECRETLY — **on camera** : before a live televising camera ⟨at the studio for rehearsals by 5 and *on camera* from 7 to 10 —*Newsweek*⟩

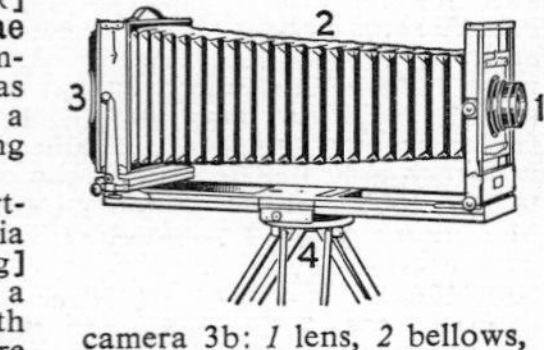

camera 3b: *1* lens, *2* bellows, *3* plateholder, *4* tripod

camera–eye \'=(=)=,=\ *n* **1** : the capacity for reporting that is as detailed and detached as a photograph ⟨does not pretend that his is the impartial *camera-eye* —Robert Graves⟩ **2** : observation or reporting that is detached and photographic in detail ⟨*camera-eye* reportage —Angus Wilson⟩

cam·er·al \'kam(ə)rəl, 'kaamrəl\ *adj* [G *kameral-*, fr. ML *cameralis*, fr. *camera* treasury (fr. L, arched roof) + L *-alis* -al — more at CHAMBER] **1** : of or relating to a legislative or judicial chamber **2** : CAMERALISTIC ⟨the ~ sciences⟩

cam·er·a·lism \-ə,lizəm\ *n* -s [*cameral* + *-ism*] : the theories and practices of the cameralists

cam·er·a·list \-ələst\ *n* -s [G *kameralist*, fr. NL *cameralista*, fr. ML *cameralis* + L *-ista* -ist] **1** : a public administrative servant of continental rulers of the 17th and 18th centuries who was a mercantilist and advocated economic policies tending to strengthen the position of the ruler **2** : an economist who strongly emphasizes political factors in recommending economic policy

cam·er·a·lis·tic \'=(=)=¦listik\ *adj* [G *kameralistisch*, fr. *kameralist* + *-isch* -ic] **1** : of or relating to public finance **2** : of or relating to cameralism

cam·er·a·lis·tics \-ks\ *n pl but usu sing in constr* [G *kameralistik*, fr. *kameralist* + *-ik* -ics] : the science of public finance

camera lu·ci·da \¦=(=)=¦lüsədə\ *n, pl* **camera lucidas** [NL, lit., light chamber] : an instrument that by means of a prism of a peculiar form or an arrangement of mirrors and often a microscope causes a virtual image of an external object to appear as if projected upon a plane surface (as of paper or canvas) so that an outline may be traced

camera·man \'=(=)=,man, -,mən, -,maa(ə)n\ *n, pl* **camera·men 1** : one that operates a camera: as **a** : a news photographer **b** : an operator of a motion-picture or television camera — compare CINEMATOGRAPHER **2** : one who sells photographic equipment

camera ob·scu·ra \¦=(=)=əbz'kyu̇rə, -(,)äb-, -b'sk-\ *n, pl* **camera obscuras** [NL, lit., dark chamber] : a darkened box or boxlike enclosure having an aperture usu. provided with a lens through which light from external objects enters to form an image of the objects on the opposite surface used esp. for making exact drawings or for taking photographs

camera rehearsal *n* : a dress rehearsal of a television show

camera script *n* : a cue sheet indicating the various camera positions to be used in a telecast

cam·er·a·ta \,kamə'räd·ə, -'ā-\ *n pl, cap* [NL, fr. L, neut. pl. of *cameratus*, past part. of *camerare* to arch, fr. *camera* arched roof — more at CHAMBER] : the largest order of crinoids including all Paleozoic species that have the lower brachial plates included in the cup and the mouth and food grooves closed

¹**cam·er·ate** \'kamə,rāt, -(ə)rət\ *adj* [NL *cameratus*, fr. LL *camera* chamber + L *-atus* -ate] **1** *or* **cam·er·at·ed** \-mə,rād·əd\ : divided into chambers ⟨a ~ shell⟩ ⟨a ~ eye⟩ **2** [NL *Camerata*] : of or relating to the Camerata

²**camerate** \"\ *n* -s : one of the Camerata

cam·er·a·tion \,kamə'rāshən\ *n* -s [¹*camerate* + *-ion*] : division into chambers

camera tube *n* : the television vacuum tube that by means of scanning converts the image into electrical impulses

cam·er·i·na \,kamə'rīnə, -'ē-\ [NL, fr. LL *camera* chamber, room + NL *-ina* — more at CHAMBER] *syn of* NUMMULITES

cam·er·in·i·dae \,kamə'rinə,dē\ [NL, fr. *Camerina*, type genus + *-idae*] *syn of* NUMMULITIDAE

cam·er·ist \'kam(ə)rəst\ *n* -s : PHOTOGRAPHER

cam·er·len·go \,kamə(r)'leŋ(,)gō\ *also* **cam·er·lin·go** \-'i-\ *n* -s *often cap* [It *camarlingo, camerlingo*, of Gmc origin; akin to OHG *chamaling* chamberlain — more at CHAMBERLAIN] : the cardinal who heads the Apostolic Camera and administers papal affairs when there is no pope

¹**cam·er·o·ni·an** \,kamə'rōnyən, -nēən\ *n* -s *usu cap* [Richard *Cameron* †1680 Scottish religious leader + E *-ian*] : one that holds the ecclesiastical and political doctrines of Richard Cameron and his followers who refused to recognize any civil government that did not explicitly admit that it derived its power from Jesus Christ, who were called Scottish Covenanters after 1680, and who later formed the Reformed Presbytery that in time became the Reformed Presbyterian Church

²**cameronian** \¦==¦=(=)=\ *adj, usu cap* : of or relating to Richard Cameron or the Cameronians

¹**cam·er·oon** \¦kamə¦rün\ *or* **cam·er·oons** \-nz\ *n, pl* **cameroons** [perh. fr. *Cameroon, Cameroons*, W. Africa] : a dice game played with five dice in which the object is to make certain combinations in several casts

²**cameroon** *adj, usu cap* **1** *or* **cameroons** \-ünz\ [fr. *Cameroon, Cameroons*, W. Africa] : of or from the Cameroons region : of the kind or style prevalent in the Cameroons **2** *or* **cam·er·oun** \-ün\ [fr. *Cameroon, Cameroun*, republic in W. Africa] : of or from the Republic of Cameroon : of the kind or style prevalent in Cameroon

cam·er·oon·ian *or* **cam·er·oun·ian** \¦kamə¦rünēən\ *n* -s *cap* [*Cameroon, Cameroun*, republic in W. Africa + E *-ian*] : a native or inhabitant of the Republic of Cameroon or the Cameroons region — **cameroonian** *or* **camerounian** *adj, usu cap*

cam·er·o·stome \'kam(ə)rə,stōm\ *n* -s [NL *camerostoma*, fr. *camero-* (fr. LL *camera* chamber) + *-stoma* — more at CHAMBER] : the anterior marginal depression of the body wall of a tick in which its capitulum lies

cam follower *n* [⁴*cam*] : the peg or roller which follows the curvature of a cam and to which the motion of the cam is thereby directly communicated

camias *var of* KAMIAS

cam·i·knick·ers \'kamə,nikə(r)z\ *n pl* [*camisole* + *knickers*] *Brit* : a woman's one-piece undergarment similar to a chemise but usu. shorter and more fitted

ca·mi·no re·al \kə¦mē(,)nōrā'äl\ *n, pl* **caminos re·a·les** \-nō(s)rā'ä(,)lās\ *or* **camino reals** \-'älz\ [Sp, highway, lit., royal road] : a main highway; *esp* : a highway orig. existing during the period of Spanish rule in the Southwest, Mexico, and Central America ⟨wagons will not travel along that *camino real* beyond Vao Colorao —Oliver La Farge⟩

ca·mion \kȧmyō"\ *n* -s [F] **1** : a low wagon : DRAY **2** : MOTORTRUCK, BUS

ca·mi·o·nette \¦kamyə¦net, -mēə-\ *n* -s [F *camion* cart, wagon + *-ette*] : a small truck or bus

camis *or* **camus** *n* -ES [prob. modif. of Sp *camisa*] *obs* : a light loose robe

ca·mi·sa \kə'mēsə\ *n* -s [Sp, fr. LL *camisia* — more at CHEMISE] **1** : a shirt or undershirt for men or women **2** : a woman's embroidered blouse with loose sleeves

cam·i·sa·do \,kamə'sä(,)dō, -'z-, -'ā-\ *also* **cam·i·sade** \-'ād, -'äd\ *n* -s [*camisado* prob. fr. obs. Sp *camisada*, fr. *camisa* shirt; *camisade* prob. fr. MF, prob. fr. OSp *camisada*] *archaic* : an attack by night ⟨on march all night, intending a night attack or ~ —Thomas Carlyle⟩

cam·i·sard \¦kamə¦zärd, *Fr* kȧmēzȧär\ *n* -s *usu cap* [F, fr. F dial. *camiso* shirt (fr. LL *camisia*) + F *-ard*; fr. the peasants' smocks that the Camisards wore] : one of the French Protestant insurgents of the Cévennes who early in the 18th century rebelled against Louis XIV on account of the persecutions that followed the revocation of the Edict of Nantes

ca·mise \kə'mēz, -ēs\ *n* -s [Ar *qamīṣ*, fr. LL *camisia* — more at CHEMISE] : a light loose long-sleeved shirt, gown, or tunic sometimes worn as an undergarment

cam·i·sole \'kamə,sōl\ *n* -s [F, prob. fr. OProv *camisolla*, fr. *camisa* shirt, fr. LL *camisia*] **1** : a jacket or jersey with sleeves formerly worn by men **2** : a short negligee jacket for women **3 a** : an underwaist usu. with straight top and shoulder straps and often elaborately trimmed and worn orig. to cover a corset but now esp. with sheer clothing to camouflage underwear **b** : a woman's blouse without sleeves but often with shoulder straps and a low neckline **4** : a long-sleeved straitjacket

¹**cam·let** \'kamlət\ *also* **cam·blet** \-m(b)l-\ *n* -s *often attrib* [ME *cameloit*, fr. MF *camelot*, fr. Ar *ḥamlat* woolen plush] **1 a** : a medieval Asiatic fabric of camel's hair or Angora wool **b** : a European imitation of this fabric of silk and wool **c** : a fine lustrous woolen of plain weave usu. dyed bright red **2** : a garment made of camlet

²**camlet** *vt* -ED/-ING/-S *obs* : to mark with wavy lines like those of watered cloth

cam·le·teen *also* **cam·le·tine** \¦kamlə¦tēn\ *n* -s [prob. fr. ¹*camlet* + *-een*] : a worsted cloth in imitation of camlet

¹**cammed** \'kamd\ *adj* [alter. (influenced by *-ed*) of ³*cam*] **1** *dial Eng* : CROOKED, AWRY **2** *dial Eng* : ILL-TEMPERED

²**cammed** *past of* CAM

camming *pres part of* CAM

cam·mock \'kamək\ *n* -s [ME *cambok*, fr. ML *cambuca*, of Celt origin; akin to W *camog* bent stick, ScGael *camag* curl, crook, OIr *camm* crooked — more at CHANGE] **1** *Scot* : a curved or crooked stick; *esp* : a field-hockey stick **2** *Scot* : FIELD HOCKEY

ca·mog \kə'mōg\ *n* -s [IrGael, fr. *cam* crooked, fr. OIr *camm*] *Irish* : a stick similar to a cammock

ca·mo·gie \kə'mōgē\ *n* -s [*camog* + *-ie*] : a team sport similar to hurling played with camogs by women in Ireland

camomile *var of* CHAMOMILE

ca·moo·di *also* **ca·moo·die** *or* **ca·mou·die** \kə'müdē\ *n* -s [Arawak *kamudu*] : any large tropical American constricting snake ⟨some huge ~, able to crush my bones like brittle twigs in its constricting coils —W.H.Hudson †1922⟩

ca·mor·ra \kə'mȯrə, -'ä-\ *n* -s [It] : a group of persons united for dishonest or dishonorable ends ⟨the ~ of Welsh and Scotch political scoundrels —H.L.Mencken⟩

ca·mor·ris·ta \,kä,mȯ'rēstə, ,mə-\ *also* **ca·mor·rist** \kə'mȯrəst, -'ä-\ *n, pl* **camorris·ti** \-ēstē\ *also* **camorrists** \-əs(t)s\ [It *camorrista*, fr. *camorra* + *-ista* -ist] **1** : a member of a camorra **2** *often cap* : a member of an Italian secret organization engaged esp. in extortion ⟨like a true *Camorrista* he never lost an opportunity of showing that he could do what he pleased with everybody —Norman Douglas⟩

ca·mo·te \kə'mōd·ē\ *n* -s [AmerSp, fr. Nahuatl *camotli* yam] : SWEET POTATO

camote de ra·ton \-dərə'tōn\ *n* [MexSp *camote de ratón*, lit., mouse yam] : an herb (*Hoffmanseggia densiflora*) of the family Leguminosae found in alkaline areas of the desert of southern U. S. having orange-red flowers and glandular-dotted chiefly basal tufted leaves with several pairs of leaflets

¹**cam·ou·flage** \'kamə,fläzh, -,äj *also* -äm- *or* -ȧm- *or* |j\ *n* -s *often attrib* [F, fr. *camoufler* to disguise (modif. of It *camuffare*) + F *-age*] **1 a** : the disguising of an installation, vehicle, gun position, or ship with paint, garnished nets, or foliage to reduce its visibility or conceal its actual nature or location from the enemy **b** : the disguise so applied or utilized ⟨battleship-gray paint is an effective ~ on a cloudy day⟩ **2 a** : concealment by means of disguise ⟨a totally different means of ~ is used by the spider crab —W.H.Dowdeswell⟩ **b** : a disguise, behavior, or expedient adopted or designed to deceive or hide ⟨behind this undistinguished ~ of "everyman" resides a subtle and confusing individuality —C.L.Sulzberger⟩

²**camouflage** \"\ *vb* -ED/-ING/-S *vt* : to conceal or disguise by camouflage ⟨guns that had been *camouflaged* with green saplings —Edmund Wilson⟩ ⟨his carriage flanked by detectives thinly *camouflaged* in tall hats and frock coats —J.J.Horgan⟩ ⟨they wanted to prevent and correct their mistakes, not ~ them —Milton Silverman⟩ ~ *vi* : to practice camouflage ⟨you can ~ all you want to —Sinclair Lewis⟩

camouflage discipline *n* : discipline (as enforcement of the proper methods of movement within, into, and out of a camouflaged area) necessary to maintain a military camouflage

ca·mou·flet \¦kamə¦flā\ *n* -s [F, lit., smoke blown into a sleeper's face from lighted paper] **1** : a mine so charged and placed that its detonation will destroy enemy mining tunnels **2 a** : an underground or subsurface explosion of a bomb or shell that leaves a sealed pocket of smoke and gas **b** : a pocket formed in this way

ca·mou·fleur \¦kamə¦flər, +V -ər-\ *n* -s [F, fr. *camoufler* to disguise + *-eur* -or] : a person employed in camouflaging or skilled in the techniques of camouflage

¹**camp** \'kamp, -aa(ə)-, -ai-\ *n* -s *often attrib* [MF, prob. fr. ONF or OProv, fr. L *campus* plain, field; akin to OHG *hamf* crippled, Goth *hamfs* maimed, Gk *kampē* bend, turning, Lith *kampas* corner, region; basic meaning: bend; hence, concavity, depression] **1** : a place of temporary shelter, lodging, or residence often at a distance from urban areas or the tents, cabins, or other buildings used for such shelter, lodging, or residence: **a** : the ground on which tents or buildings are erected for shelter or usu. temporary residence (as for troops, prisoners, or vacationers) **b** : the group of tents, cabins, or buildings either temporary or permanent in construction or location erected on such ground ⟨an army ~⟩ ⟨fishing ~*s* are located all along the river⟩ **c** : a town usu. new and often temporary sprung up esp. in an isolated lumbering or mining region ⟨the well-known gold ~*s* of Canada —A.M.Bateman⟩ **d** *Austral* : a place of rest, lodging, or assembly; *specif* : a place where cattle or other livestock are rounded up **e** (1) : a place provided with tents or cabins usu. in mountain or lake areas designed for rest or recreation esp. for children during the summer ⟨the boys went to ~ every July⟩ (2) : the institution of going or sending children to such a camp ⟨~ during the summer gets children away from the hot cities⟩ **2 a** : a company or body of persons (as soldiers) encamped or moving in a group **b** (1) : a group or body of persons acting unanimously: *esp* : a group engaged in promoting or defending a given theory or doctrine ⟨testified that the world was divided into two ~*s*, the exploiting capitalists and the proletariat —Eleanor Davis & Valentine Ughet⟩ (2) : an ideological position usu. strongly defended ⟨had unexpectedly gone over to the rival ~⟩ **3 a** : the scene of military service ⟨the soldier's conduct was all right for ~ but was not acceptable in polite society⟩ **b** : MILITARY SERVICE : life in the military service ⟨the recreations of ~ and court⟩ **4** *Austral* : a camping expedition (as for hunting) **5** : a lodge or local chapter of a society or league ⟨addressed the veteran ~*s* throughout the state⟩ **6** *southern Africa* : a large field usu. used for pasture ⟨the farm was divided into a dozen ~*s*⟩ **7** : a shack used for permanent habitation **8** : a military post that is not a permanent installation

²**camp** \"\ *vb* -ED/-ING/-S [MF *camper*, fr. *camp*, n.] *vi* **1 a** : to pitch or occupy a camp ⟨he had ~*ed* under a tree . . . and slept until dawn —Irwin Shaw⟩ ⟨you drive down the hill . . . where Rochambeau's army ~*ed* —Gladys Taber⟩ **b** : to live usu. temporarily in a camp or outdoors esp. for recreation — often used with *out* ⟨it had been a cold time of year to ~ out —H.L.Davis⟩ **2 a** : to take up one's quarters : LODGE ⟨it was in a modest little flat . . . that he now ~*ed* whenever the claims of scholarship brought him to town —Aldous Huxley⟩ **b** : to occupy quarters that are unsuitable or temporarily uncomfortable ⟨the whole family ~*ed* on the first floor of the unfinished house⟩ **3 a** : to take up one's position : settle down ⟨they ~*ed* around the room, talking idly among themselves and waiting —Maeve Brennan⟩ **b** : to settle down to or as if to a siege or pursuit ⟨reporters ~*ed* upon his doorstep day and night —H.L.Mencken⟩ ⟨they ~*ed* on his trail for 20 miles⟩ **4** *Austral* : SLEEP, NAP, REST ~ *vt* **1 a** : to put into or station in a camp : establish a camp for ⟨all his host ~*ed* themselves in Willingham field —Charles Kingsley⟩ **b** : to provide with temporary shelter or accommodations ⟨it was necessary to ~ the refugees on the wall —Nora Waln⟩ **2** *Southern Africa* : to divide into camps ⟨the farm is fenced and ~*ed*⟩

cam·pa \'kämpə\ *n, pl* **campa** *or* **campas** *usu cap* [Sp, prob. of AmerInd origin] **1 a** : an Arawakan people of the upper valley of the Ucayali river in eastern Peru **b** : a member of such people **2** : the language of the Campa people

-cam·pa \'kampə, -'aa-, -'ai-\ *n comb form* [NL, fr Gk *kampē*; prob. akin to Gk *kampē* bend, turning — more at CAMP] : caterpillar — in generic names of insects ⟨*Lasiocampa*⟩ ⟨*Taeniocampa*⟩

cam·pa·gnol \¦kampə¦nyȯl, -ōl\ *n* -s [F, fr. *campagne* plain] : the European field vole or a related species

¹**cam·paign** \(')kam¦pān, -aam-\ *n* -s *often attrib* [F *campagne*, prob. fr. ONF or OProv, fr. LL *campania* level country, fr. L *Campania*, the level country about Naples, fr. *campus* field — more at CAMP] **1** *obs* : a tract of open country : PLAIN **2** [F *campagne*, prob. fr. It *campagna*, fr. LL *campania*] **a** *obs* : the time during which an army is in the field **b** : a connected series of military operations forming a distinct phase of a war **3** *obs* : a trip or excursion into the country esp. in summer **4** : a connected series of determined operations or systematic efforts designed to bring about a particular result ⟨an advertising ~⟩ ⟨a ~ against tuberculosis⟩ ⟨a ~ to combat crime⟩; *specif* : a series of operations or efforts designed to influence the public to support a particular political candidate, ticket, or measure ⟨a presidential ~⟩ ⟨the manager of the governor's ~⟩ **5** : a period of activity usu. continuous and often competitive esp. in any seasonal occupation or industry ⟨the football team ended its ~ with an unexpected defeat⟩ **6 a** : the working life of a blast-furnace lining **b** : the working life of a melting unit in glass manufacturing

²**campaign** \"\ *vb* -ED/-ING/-S *vi* : to go on, engage in, or conduct a campaign ⟨they ~*ed* vigorously against the zoning laws⟩ ~ *vt* : to race (a horse) in a series of major races ⟨was at that time ~*ing* a big steeplechase stable —A.H.Higginson⟩

cam·paign·er \-ə(r)\ *n* -s **1** : one that goes on, engages in, or conducts a campaign ⟨an effective ~ for slum clearance⟩ **2** : one that has taken part in many campaigns; *esp* : a veteran in any field or vocation who takes pleasure in his activities ⟨that stout, battle-scarred old ~ —Frank Yerby⟩

campaign hat *n* : a broad-brimmed felt hat having a high crown with four dents worn by U. S. Army and Marine Corps personnel

campaign ribbon *n* : a narrow ribbon-covered bar or strip of ribbon whose distinctive coloring indicates a military campaign in which the wearer has taken part

campaign wig *n* : a wig worn for traveling in the late 17th and early 18th centuries having a twisted lock on each side and curls about the forehead

cam·pa·na \kam'panə, -'ä-, -'ā-\ *n* -s *often attrib* [LL, bell, fr. L, fem. of *campanus* Campanian, fr. *Campania*, the level country about Naples; fr. the use of Campanian metal in making bells] : BELL, GUTTA — usu. used of shape in decoration

cam·pa·na·rio \,kampə'närē,ō\ *n* -s [Sp, fr. *campana* bell (fr. LL) + *-ario* (fr. L *-arius* -ary)] : CAMPANILE

cam·pa·ne·ro \,kampə'ne(,)rō\ *n* -s [Sp, lit., bellman, fr. *campana* bell + *-ero* -er] : the bellbird of So. America

campania *n* -s [LL] *obs* : CAMPAIGN

cam·pan·i·form \(')kam¦panə,fȯrm\ *adj* [LL *campana* + E *-iform*] : shaped like a bell

cam·pa·ni·le \,kampə'nēlē, -aam-, -äm-\ *n, pl* **campaniles** \-lēz\ *or* **campani·li** \-lē\ [It, fr. *campana* bell, fr. LL] : a bell tower usu. freestanding — compare BELFRY

cam·pa·nil·la \,kampə'nilə, -nē(y)ə\ *n* -s [Sp, lit., small bell, dim. of *campana* bell, fr. LL] **1** : FLORIPONDIO **2** : a West Indian morning glory (*Ipomoea triloba*) with showy white or pink flowers **3** *Philippines* : a plant of the genus *Allamanda* (esp. *A. cathartica*)

cam·pa·nist \'kampənəst\ *n* -s [LL *campana* bell + E *-ist*] : CAMPANOLOGIST, CARILLONNEUR — **cam·pa·nis·tic** \¦==¦nistik\ *adj*

cam·pa·no·log·i·cal \¦kampənō¦läjəkəl, -m,pan°¦ä-\ *adj* [*campanology* + *-ical*] : of or relating to campanology

cam·pa·nol·o·gist \,kampə'näləjəst\ *n* -s [*campanology* + *-ist*] : one that practices or is skilled in campanology

cam·pa·nol·o·gy \-jē\ *n* -ES [NL *campanologia*, fr. LL *campana* + NL *-o-* + *-logia* -logy] **1** : the science of making bells **2** : the art of bell ringing — compare CARILLON, CHANGE RINGING

campanile

cam·pan·u·la \kam'panyələ\ *n, cap* [NL, dim. of LL *campana*] : a large genus (the type of the family Campanulaceae) of widely distributed herbs with a regular bell-shaped corolla, separate anthers, and laterally dehiscent capsule — see BELLFLOWER, CANTERBURY BELL

campanula blue *n* [NL *Campanula*] : a light purplish blue that is redder and deeper than lupine and bluer and slightly darker than average periwinkle

cam·pan·u·la·ce·ae \(,)kam,panyə'lāsē,ē\ *n pl, cap* [NL, fr. *Campanula*, type genus + *-aceae*] : a large family of dicotyledonous plants (order Campanulales) including herbs, shrubs, trees, and some climbers and having an acrid mostly milky juice, alternate leaves, and rather showy usu. regular flowers — **cam·pan·u·la·ceous** \¦=,==¦lāshəs, =,==¦===\ *adj*

cam·pan·u·la·les \(,)kam,panyə'lā(,)lēz\ *n pl, cap* [NL, fr. *Campanula* + *-ales*] : an order comprising dicotyledonous plants with a tubular 5-lobed corolla and five stamens with the anthers connivent and often partly or wholly united and including the Campanulaceae, Lobeliaceae, Cucurbitaceae, Goodeniaceae, Stylidiaceae, Calyceraceae, and Compositae

cam·pan·u·lar·i·ae \(,)kam,panyə'la(a)rē,ē\ *n pl, cap* [NL, pl. of *Campanularia*, genus of polyps, fr. *campanula* bell-shaped part (dim. of LL *campana* bell) + *-aria*] *in some classifications* : a division of Hydroida comprising forms in which each polyp is able to retract into a bell-shaped hydrotheca — used as more or less exactly equivalent to Leptomedusae

¹**cam·pan·u·lar·i·an** \¦=,==¦rēən, =,==¦===\ *adj* [NL *Campanulariae* + E *-an*] : of or relating to the Campanulariae

²**campanularian** \"\ *n* -s : a campanularian hydroid

cam·pan·u·la·ri·i·dae \(,)kam,panyələ'rīə,dē\ *n pl, cap* [NL, fr. *Campanularia*, type genus + *-idae*] : a large family of marine hydrozoan polyps (suborder Leptomedusae) having globular manubria and comprising forms with free medusae (as those of the genus *Obelia*) and others with the medusae replaced by sessile gonophores (as in the type genus *Campanularia*)

cam·pan·u·la·tae \(,)kam,panyə'läd·(,)ē, -'ā-\ *n pl, cap* [NL, fr. *Campanula* + L *-atae* (fem. pl. of *-atus* -ate)] *syn of* CAMPANULALES

cam·pan·u·late \(')kam¦panyələt, -,lāt\ *or* **cam·pan·u·lat·ed**

\-ˌlād·əd\ *also* **cam·pan·u·lar** \-lə(r)\ *or* **cam·pan·u·lous** \-ləs\ *adj* [NL *campanula* bell-shaped part (dim. of LL *campana* bell) + E *-ate* or *-ate* + *-ed* or *-ar* or *-ous* — more at CAMPANA] **:** shaped like a bell

campanula violet *or* **campanula purple** *n* [NL *Campanula*] **:** a grayish reddish purple that is redder and duller than heather (sense 2 a) and paler than livid purple

campas *pl of* CAMPA

camp bed *n* **:** a small portable bed **:** COT

camp·bell·ism \ˈkam(b)əˌlizəm, -ambə-\ *n* -S *usu cap* [Alexander *Campbell* + *-ism*] **:** the doctrines or practices of the Campbellites

¹camp·bell·ite \-ˌlīt\ *n* -S *usu cap, often attrib* [Alexander *Campbell* †1866 Am. theologist, the founder + E *-ite*] **1 :** a follower of Alexander Campbell who founded the denomination called the Disciples of Christ — often taken to be offensive **2** [so called fr. its supposed similarity, as a fish that does not keep well when out of water, to a member of the Disciples of Christ, who emphasize the saving power of baptism by immersion] *Midland* **:** WHITE CRAPPIE

²campbellite \"\ *n* -S *usu cap* [John McLeod *Campbell* †1872 Scotch theologian + E *-ite*] **:** a follower of John McLeod Campbell who was ejected from the Church of Scotland because of his views on the atonement

camp car *n* **:** a car equipped for feeding and housing construction and maintenance employees of a railroad — called also *bunk car, outfit car*

camp ceiling *n* [alter. (influenced by *camp*) of earlier *cant ceiling*, fr. *cant* + *ceiling*] **:** a ceiling common in top stories and attics that consists of a plane horizontal central surface joined at two sides by inclined surfaces which meet the side walls

camp chair *n* **:** a light folding chair

camp circle *n* **:** a circle or a series of concentric circles of tepees arranged by the Plains Indians in a definite order in accordance with their tribal custom

camp cot *n* **:** a light portable folding cot

campcraft \ˈ=ˌ=\ *n* -S **:** skill and practice in the activities that relate to camping

cam·pea·chy hat \(ˈ)kamˈpēchē-\ *n, sometimes cap C* [fr. *Campeche*, city & state in Mexico] **:** a broad-brimmed hat formerly worn in the southern U.S. in hot weather

campeachy wood *n* [fr. *Campeche*, Mexico] **:** LOGWOOD

camped *past of* CAMP

cam·pe·phag·i·dae \ˌkampəˈfajəˌdē\ *n pl, cap* [NL, fr. *Campephaga*, type genus (fr. Gk *kampē* caterpillar + NL *-phaga*) + *-idae* — more at -CAMPA] **:** the family of passerine birds consisting of the cuckoo shrikes — **cam·peph·a·gine** \(ˈ)kamˈpefəˌjīn\ *adj*

cam·peph·i·lus \kamˈpefələs\ *n, cap* [NL, fr. Gk *kampē* caterpillar + NL *-philus*] **:** a genus of birds (family Picidae) including some of the largest woodpeckers (as the ivory-billed woodpecker, the imperial woodpecker, and related tropical American species)

camp·er \-pə(r)\ *n* -S **1 a :** one that lives temporarily in a tent or lodge or outdoors without shelter esp. for recreation **b :** one that occupies a lodge, cabin, or summer residence in a vacation area only during the summer season or part of it **c :** one that attends a summer camp esp. for boys or girls **d :** one that lives in a work camp and participates in an outdoor work program **2 :** one that attends or participates in a camp meeting

cam·per·down elm \ˈkampə(r)ˌdau̇n-\ *n, usu cap C* [prob. fr. *Camperdown*, seat of the earls of Camperdown, Dundee, Scotland] **:** an elm (*Ulmus glabra camperdownii*) derived from the wych elm and having long drooping branches

cam·per·nelle jonquil *also* **campernelle** \ˌkampə(r)ˈnel\ *n* -S *often cap C* [prob. fr. the name *Campernelle*] **:** a bulbous plant (*Narcissus odorus*) similar to the common jonquil but having a crown at least half as long as the perianth segments

camp·er·ship \ˈ==ˌship\ *n* -S [*camper* (fr. ²*camp* + *-er*) + *-ship* (as in *scholarship*)] **:** a grant to a boy or girl to aid him in attending a summer camp

cam·pe·si·no \ˌkampəˈsē(ˌ)nō\ *n* -S [Sp, fr. *campo* country, field, fr. L *campus* field — more at CAMP] **:** a native of a Latin-American rural area; *esp* **:** a Latin-American Indian farmer or farm laborer

cam·pes·tral \(ˈ)kamˈpestrəl\ *adj* [L *campestr-, campester* of the fields (fr. *campus* field) + E *-al*] **:** of or relating to fields or open country **:** RURAL ⟨living in secluded ~ concentration in his country house —Janet Flanner⟩

camp fever *n* **:** TYPHUS

campfight \ˈ=ˌ=\ *n* -S [prob. trans. of ML *pugna campi*] **:** trial by fighting; *esp* **:** the decision of a case by duel

campfire \ˈ=ˌ=\ *n* -S **1 :** a fire usu. built outdoors (as in a camp or on a picnic) for cooking, heat, or illumination; *esp* **:** such a fire designed to serve as the focal point of a social gathering ⟨his conduct was the one topic of discussion around ~*s* —W.E. Woodward⟩ **2 :** a social gathering of the members of a lodge or local chapter of a society or league ⟨cheery ~*s* in the hall of George H. Thomas post —Meredith Nicholson⟩

camp fire girl *n* [fr. *Camp Fire Girls*, Inc., founded in 1912] **:** a member of a national organization for girls from 7 to 18 years old that conducts activities combining recreation with the development of responsible citizenship and the acquisition of various skills; *specif* **:** such a member aged 10 to 14

camp follower *n* **1 :** a civilian that follows or takes up lodging near a military unit for the purpose of attending or exploiting military personnel; *specif* **:** PROSTITUTE ⟨she behaved more like a *camp follower* than a land girl —Ralph Hammond-Innes⟩ **2 :** one that is a disciple or follower (as of a group or theory) but is not of the main body of members or adherents; *esp* **:** one that follows with little understanding or for the purpose of personal gain ⟨a new dogmatism spread by the *camp followers* of science —N.E.Nelson⟩ ⟨and then those *camp followers* of the arts, those delicious Bohemians —Aldous Huxley⟩

campground \ˈ=ˌ=\ *n* -S **:** the area or place (as a field or grove) used for a camp, for camping, or for a camp meeting

camph- *or* **campho-** *comb form* [NL *camphora*] **:** camphor ⟨*camph*ane⟩ ⟨*campho*carboxylic⟩

cam·phane \ˈkamˌfān\ *n* -S [*camph-* + *-ane*] **:** BORNANE

cam·pha·nyl \ˈkam(p)fəˌnil, -ēl\ *n* -S [*camphane* + *-yl*] **:** BORNYL

cam·phene \ˈkamˌfēn, =ˈ=\ *n* -S [ISV *camph-* + *-ene*] **:** any of several terpenes related to camphor; *specif* **:** a colorless crystalline terpene $C_{10}H_{16}$ found in three optically different forms in several essential oils, made synthetically from pinene as a step in synthesizing camphor, and used in making insecticides (as toxaphene); 3,3-dimethyl-2-methylene-norbornane

cam·phine *or* **cam·phene** \ˈkamˌfēn, =ˈ=\ *n* -S [ISV *camph-* + *-ine* or *-ene*] **:** oil of turpentine or a mixture of oil of turpentine and alcohol used as an illuminant

¹cam·phire \ˈkamˌfī(ə)r\ *now dial var of* CAMPHOR

²camphire \"\ *n* -S [ME *camphire, caumfre* camphor — more at CAMPHOR] **:** HENNA ⟨a cluster of ~ —Song of Sol 1:14 (AV)⟩

campho- — see CAMPH-

cam·phoid \ˈkamˌfȯid\ *n* -S [*camph-* + *-oid*] **:** a solution of pyroxylin in an alcoholic solution of camphor used as a substitute for collodion

cam·phol \ˈkamˌfȯl, -ōl\ *n* -S [ISV *camph-* + *-ol;* orig. formed in F] **:** BORNEOL

cam·pho·lide \ˈkam(p)fəˌlīd\ *n* -S [ISV *camphol* + *-ide*] **:** either of two crystalline isomeric lactones $C_{10}H_{16}O_2$ distinguished as α and β and made indirectly from camphoric acid

cam·pho·lyt·ic acid \ˌkam(p)fəˈlid·ik-\ *n* [*camph-* + *electrolytic;* fr. the acid's having been first obtained by electrolysis] **:** either of two unsaturated acids $C_8H_{13}COOH$ distinguished as α and β and made indirectly from camphoric acid

cam·phor \ˈkam(p)fə(r), -aam-\ *n* -S [alter. (influenced by ML & NL *camphora*) of ME *caumfre*, fr. AF, fr. ML *camphora*, fr. Ar *kāfūr*, fr. Malay *kāpūr*, prob. of Austroasiatic origin (whence Skt *karpūra* camphor); akin to Khmer *kāpōr* camphor] **1 :** a tough gumlike crystalline terpenoid ketone $C_{10}H_{16}O$ existing in three optically different forms all of which have the same qualities of volatility, fragrance, and taste; 2-keto-bornane: (1) the dextrorotatory form obtained esp. from the wood and bark of the camphor tree and used chiefly as a carminative and stimulant in medicine, as a plasticizer in cellulose nitrate plastics (as celluloid and photographic films), and as an insect repellent; (2) the levorotatory form found in some essential oils (as that of feverfew); and (3) the inactive form found in the oil of an Asiatic chrysanthemum or made synthetically from certain terpenes and their derivatives (as α-pinene, camphene, isoborneol) and used similarly to dextrorotatory camphor — called also respectively (1) *d-camphor, dextro-camphor, Formosa camphor, gum camphor, Japan camphor, laurel camphor* (2) *l-camphor, levo-camphor, matricaria camphor* (3) *dl-camphor, racemic camphor*, and, when synthetized, *synthetic camphor* **2 :** any of several compounds similar in properties to camphor (as certain terpene alcohols and ketones): **a :** dextrorotatory borneol **b :** levorotatory menthol

cam·pho·ra·ceous \ˌ=fəˈrāshəs\ *adj* [*camphor* + *-aceous*] **:** being or having the properties of camphor ⟨~ odor⟩

¹cam·phor·ate \ˈ=fəˌrāt, *usu* -ād· + V\ *vt* -ED/ -ING/ -S [*camphor* + *-ate*] **:** to treat or impregnate with camphor

²camphorate \", -ˌrə-\ *n* -S [ISV *camphoric* + *-ate*] **:** a salt or ester of camphoric acid

camphorated oil *n* **:** a solution of about 20 percent camphor in cottonseed oil used as a counterirritant — called also *camphor liniment*

cam·phor·ene \-fəˌrēn\ *n* -S [ISV *camphor* + *-ene*] **:** a liquid diterpene $C_{20}H_{32}$ derived from cyclohexene and obtained from camphor oil

cam·phor·ic \(ˈ)kamˈfȯrik, -aam-, -är-, -ēk\ *adj* [ISV *camphor* + *-ic*] **:** of, relating to, derived from, or containing camphor

camphoric acid *n* **:** a white crystalline acid $C_8H_{14}(COOH)_2$ existing in three optically different forms, esp. the dextrorotatory form obtained by the oxidation of dextrorotatory camphor and used in pharmaceuticals; *cis*-1,2,2-trimethyl-1,3-cyclopentane-dicarboxylic acid

camphor ice *n* **:** a cerate made chiefly of camphor, white wax, spermaceti, and castor oil

cam·phor·ize \ˈkam(p)fəˌrīz, -aam-\ *vt* -ED/ -ING/ -S **:** CAMPHORATE

camphor liniment *n* **:** CAMPHORATED OIL

camphor oil *n* **:** an essential oil obtained by distilling the wood and other parts of the camphor tree; *esp* **:** that portion of the oil left after removing part or all of the camphor usu. separated into safrole and various fractions of oils often distinguished by color (as white or red) or volatility (as light or heavy) and used as a solvent, flavoring agent, and technical perfume (as in soap)

cam·phor·one \ˈkam(p)fəˌrōn, -aam-\ *n* -S [ISV *camphor* + *-one*] **:** a liquid ketone $C_9H_{14}O$ obtained by distilling calcium camphorate; 2-isopropylidene-5-methyl-cyclopentanone

cam·phor·on·ic acid \ˌ==ˈränik-\ *n* [ISV *camphor* + *-one* (fr. Gk *-ōnē*, suffix denoting a female descendant) + *-ic*] **:** a crystalline tribasic acid $C_6H_{11}(COOH)_3$ obtained by the oxidation of camphor or camphoric acid

cam·phor·o·yl \kamˈfȯrəˌwil, -aam-, -ēl\ *n* -S [*camphoric* + *-oyl* (as in *benzoyl*)] **:** the bivalent radical $C_8H_{14}(CO)_2$ of camphoric acid

camphor scale *n* **:** a scale (*Pseudaonidia duplex*) native to eastern Asia but now established in the southern U. S. where it is sometimes destructive to citrus and various ornamental plants

cam·phor·sul·fon·ic acid \ˌkam(p)fə(r)ˌsəlˈfänik-, -aam-, ˈ= =ˈ=,= =-\ *n* **:** a white crystalline acid $C_{10}H_{15}OSO_3H$ made by reaction of camphor with sulfuric acid and acetic anhydride and used esp. in the form of salts as a stimulant (as in heart failure, shock, or some types of poisoning) — called also *beta-camphorsulfonic acid*

camphor tree *or* **camphor laurel** *n* **:** a large evergreen tree (*Cinnamomum camphora*) prob. native to China but now grown in most warm countries which has lax smooth branches and shining triple-nerved lanceolate leaves and from which camphor is collected by steaming the chips and subliming the product so obtained

camphor water *n* **:** a saturated solution of camphor in distilled water

camphor weed *n* **:** any of several aromatic herbs: as **a :** BLUE CURLS **b :** a ragweed (*Ambrosia bidentata*) of the prairie region of the U. S., with hairy stiff stems, sessile leaves, and 4-angled spiny fruits

camphorwood \ˈ===ˌ=\ *n* **1 a :** the wood of the camphor tree **b :** the wood of the tree that produces Borneo camphor **2 :** any of several Australian cypress pines; *esp* **:** DARK PINE

cam·phor·yl \ˈkam(p)fəˌril, -aam-, -ēl\ *n* -S [ISV *camphor* + *-yl*] **1 :** any of six univalent radicals $C_{10}H_{15}O$ of which camphor is the hydride **2 :** CAMPHOROYL

camp hospital *n* **:** STATION HOSPITAL

campi *pl of* CAMPUS

cam·pi·da·nese \ˌkämpədəˈnäsē, -äzē\ *n* -S *usu cap* [It, fr. *Campidano*, lowland in southeast Sardinia + It *-ese*] **:** the dialect of southern Sardinia

cam·pi·gnian \(ˈ)kamˈpēnyən\ *adj, usu cap* [*Campigny*, town in No. France + E *-ian*] **:** of or relating to a late Mesolithic or early Neolithic culture characterized by coarse pottery, hewn stones, milling stones, and some indication of plant raising and domestic animals

campilan *var of* KAMPILAN

cam·pim·e·ter \kamˈpimәd·ə(r)\ *n* -S [ISV *campi-* (fr. L *campus* field) + *-meter* — more at CAMP] **:** an instrument for testing indirect or peripheral visual perception of form and color

cam·pi·nas \kamˈpēnəs\ *adj, usu cap* [fr. *Campinas*, Brazil] **:** of or from the city of Campinas, Brazil **:** of the kind or style prevalent in Campinas

cam·pine \(ˈ)kamˈpēn, -äm-\ *n, usu cap* [fr. *Campine*, district in northern Belgium, where it was developed] **:** a European breed of gold-colored or silver-colored domestic fowls that resemble the Hamburgs but that have a single comb

camping *pres part of* CAMP

cam·pi·ni engine \(ˈ)kamˈpēnē-\ *n, usu cap C* [after Campini, 20th cent. Ital. airplane engine designer] **:** an aircraft propulsion system consisting of a reciprocating-engine-driven compressor, a burner, and an exhaust nozzle from which the stream of air passing through the compressor is ejected to the rear with increased momentum

cam·pi·on \ˈkampēən\ *n* -S [prob. fr. obs. *campion* champion, fr. ME, fr. ONF, fr. ML *campion-, campio* — more at CHAMPION] **1 :** a plant of the genus *Lychnis* **2 :** any of several species of *Silene*: as **a :** ALPINE CAMPION **b :** BLADDER CAMPION

cam·ple \ˈkampəl\ *vi* -ED/ -ING/ -S [freq. of obs. *camp* to wrangle, fight, fr. ME *campen* to fight, fr. OE *campian*, fr. *camp* war, combat; akin to OHG *kamph* combat, ON *kapp* war, contest, energy; all fr. a prehistoric NGmc-WGmc word borrowed fr. L *campus* field, battlefield — more at CAMP] *dial Eng* **:** to speak angrily or sharply **:** SCOLD, WRANGLE

camp·man \ˈ=mən, -ˌman, -ˌmaa(ə)n\ *n, pl* **campmen :** a building-maintenance man in a logging camp

campmaster \ˈ=ˌ= =\ *n* [trans. of MF *maistre de camp*] **:** a 16th century or 17th century military officer corresponding to a colonel

camp meat *n, North* **:** illegal venison ⟨they had one legal buck on the fender and the trunk full of *camp meat*⟩

camp meeting *n* **:** a meeting conducted usu. by an evangelical denomination in the open air (as in a field or grove) or in a tent and attended by families who bring provisions and often stay more than one day to hear preaching and exhortation and to participate in worship services

cam·po \ˈkam(ˌ)pō, -ˈä-\ *n* -S [AmerSp (Argentina), fr. Sp, field, countryside, fr. L *campus* plain, field — more at CAMP] **:** a grassland plain in So. America having scattered perennial herbs and in some places stunted trees **:** SAVANNA — compare LLANO, PAMPA, PRAIRIE

cam·po·dea \kamˈpōdēə\ *n, cap* [NL, fr. Gk *kampē* caterpillar + NL *-odea* (modif. of Gk *-ōdēs* -ode) — more at -CAMPA] **:** a genus of wingless elongated insects (order Entotrophi) lacking eyes, having the abdomen ending in two long filaments, and regarded as illustrating a generalized form from which many insects are descended — **cam·po·de·id** \-ēəd\ *n or adj* — **cam·po·de·oid** \-ēəˌd\ *adj*

cam·po·de·i·form \-ēəˌfȯrm\ *adj* [NL *Campodea* + E *-iform*] **:** having the shape of a bristletail of the genus *Campodea* — used esp. of larvae of some beetles and other higher insects

campong *var of* KAMPONG

cam·po·no·tus \ˌkampəˈnōd·əs\ *n, cap* [NL, fr. *campo-* (fr. Gk *kampē* bend) + *-notus* — more at CAMP] **:** a genus of ants represented by many species throughout the world — see CARPENTER ANT, SUGAR ANT

cam·poo·dy \kamˈpüdē\ *n* -ES [Paiute, fr. Sp *campo* camp, field, fr. L *campus* field] *Southwest* **:** an Indian village

cam·po·ree \ˌkampəˈrē, -aam-\ *n* -S [¹*camp* + *jamboree*] **:** a gathering of boy scouts or girl scouts or a gathering of scouts from a given geographic area, usu. in a camp, for purposes of contests or exhibitions in scoutcraft or campcraft — compare JAMBOREE

cam·po san·to \ˌkam(ˌ)pōˈsan(ˌ)tō, -äm(ˌ)pōˈsän-\ *n, pl* **campos santos** \-pōs...tōs\ *or* **cam·pi san·ti** \ˌkämpēˈsäntē\ [It & Sp, lit., holy field] *chiefly Southwest* **:** burial ground **:** CEMETERY

camp-out \ˈ=ˌ=\ *n* -S [²*camp* + *out*] **:** an occasion on which a group camps out

cam press *n* [⁴*cam*] **:** a punch press in which power is applied to the ram by means of a cam

camp robber *n* **:** CANADA JAY

camps *pl of* CAMP, *pres 3d sing of* CAMP

camp·shed \ˈkampˌshed\ *or* **camp·shot** \-ät\ *n* -S [by folk etymology fr. earlier *camp shede, campshide*, prob. fr. ¹*camp* + *shede, shide* — more at SHIDE] *Brit* **:** a facing of piles and planking usu. along the bank of a river used to protect or keep up the side of a bank

camp·sis \ˈkam(p)səs\ *n, cap* [NL, fr. Gk *kampsis* bending; fr. the curved stamens; akin to Gk *kampē* bend, turn — more at CAMP] **:** a genus of deciduous woody vines (formerly included in *Bignonia* or *Tecoma*) climbing by aerial roots and having opposite odd-pinnate toothed leaves and large orange or scarlet flowers in showy clusters

campsite \ˈ=ˌ=\ *n* [*camp* + *site*] **:** a place suitable for or used as the site of a camp ⟨we surveyed our ~ and contemplated the time at our disposal —Mary R. Zimmer⟩

campstool \ˈ=ˌ=\ *n* **:** a small portable folding backless stool

camp stove *n* **:** a small portable stove for cooking or heating used esp. by campers or picnickers

campto- *comb form* [NL, fr. Gk *kamptos* flexible; akin to Gk *kampē* bend — more at CAMP] **:** bent **:** curved ⟨*campto*drome⟩ ⟨*Campto*sorus⟩

camp·to·cor·mia \ˌkam(p)təˈkȯrmēə\ *n* -S [NL, fr. *campto-* + *-cormia* (fr. Gk *kormos* tree trunk + NL *-ia*) — more at CORMUS] **:** an hysterical condition marked by forward bending of the trunk and sometimes accompanied by lumbar pain

campstool

camp·to·drome \ˈkam(p)təˌdrōm\ *adj* [prob. fr. NL *camptodromus*, fr. *campto-* + *-dromus* -dromous] **:** having a bent course — used of a form of leaf venation in which the secondary veins curve forward before reaching the margin of the leaf, anastomosing in arches

camp·ton·ite \ˈkam(p)təˌnīt\ *n* -S [G *camptonit*, fr. *Campton (Falls)*, N.H., its locality + G *-it* -ite] **:** a dark porphyritic lamprophyric rock occurring in dikes

camp·to·saur \ˈkam(p)təˌsȯ(ə)r\ *n* -S [NL *Camptosaurus*] **:** any dinosaur of the genus *Camptosaurus*

camp·to·sau·rus \ˌ==ˈsȯrəs\ *n, cap* [NL, fr. *campto-* + *-saurus*] **:** a genus of small unspecialized bipedal duck-billed dinosaurs (order Ornithischia) that were widely distributed in Upper Jurassic and Early Cretaceous formations of Europe and No. America

camp·to·so·rus \-ˈsōrəs, -ȯr-\ *n, cap* [NL, fr. *campto-* + *-sorus*] **:** a genus of ferns (family Polypodiaceae) having lanceolate fronds that root at the tips — see WALKING FERN

¹cam·pus \ˈkampəs, -ˈaa-,-ˈai-\ *n, pl* **campuses** \-pəsəz\ *also* **cam·pi** \-ˌpī, -ē\ *often attrib* [L, plain, field — more at CAMP] **1 a :** the grounds and buildings of a university, college, or school ⟨visitors crowded the ~ on graduation day⟩ **b :** a particular part of such grounds and buildings; *esp* **:** the open grassy area in the center or in a central part of the grounds of a university, college, or school ⟨he left the library and walked out on the ~⟩ **c :** a geographically separate part of a university ⟨the new laboratory is equidistant from the east and west ~*es*⟩ **d :** a college, school, or division of a university that is complete in itself in having its own faculty and physical facilities but that is linked to the university by a common president and policy-making body ⟨the University of California has a number of ~*es*⟩ **2 :** university, college, or school considered as an educational, social, or spiritual entity **:** the academic world ⟨these critics have exerted considerable influence on the American ~⟩ **3 :** any grounds that resemble a campus ⟨the Maine camp has a ~ that includes the adjacent mainland —R.M. Hodesh⟩

²campus \"\ *vt* -ED/-ING/-ES **:** to punish by confinement to a university, college, or school campus or dormitory usu. after a certain hour in the evening ⟨a student ~*ed* for a month⟩

cam·pyl·o·drome \kamˈpiləˌdrōm, ˈkampə(ˌ)lō,-\ *adj* [Gk *kampylo-* (fr. *kampylos* bent, curved) + E *-drome;* akin to Gk *kampē* bend — more at CAMP] **:** ACRODROME

cam·py·lot·ro·pous \ˌkampəˈlä·trəpəs\ *also* **cam·py·lot·ro·pal** \-pəl\ *adj* [ISV *campylo-* (fr. Gk *kampylo-*) + *-tropous* or *-tropal;* orig. formed as F *campylotrope*] *bot* **:** having the ovule curved so that the micropyle is located near the base — compare AMPHITROPOUS, ANATROPOUS, ORTHOTROPOUS

cams *pl of* CAM, *pres 3d sing of* CAM

camshaft \ˈ=ˌ=\ *n* -S [⁴*cam* + *shaft*] **:** a shaft to which a cam is fastened or of which a cam forms an integral part

cam·stea·ry *or* **cam·stee·ry** \kämˈstārē, -ˈē-\ *adj* [perh. fr. Sc & E dial. ³*cam* + Sc *steery* busy, fr. *steer* (var. of E *stir*) + E *-y*] *Scot* **:** PERVERSE, STUBBORN, REFRACTORY, WILLFUL

cam·stone \ˈkämzˌtōn, -mˌst-\ *or* **cam·stane** \-ān\ *n* -S [Sc *cam* pipeclay (fr. ME *calm* limestone) + E *stone* or Sc *stane*, var. of E *stone*] **1** *Scot* **:** a limestone containing much clay **2** *Scot* **:** pipe clay used to whiten hearths or doorsteps

cam switch *n* [⁴*cam*] **:** a switch actuated by a cam

camuning *var of* KAMUNING

¹cam·us \ˈkaməs\ *adj* [ME *camuse*, fr. MF *camus*] **1** *of the nose* **:** short and flat or concave **2 :** having a camus nose **:** PUG-NOSED

²camus *var of* CAMIS

cam wheel *n* [⁴*cam*] **:** a wheel set or shaped so that it acts as a cam — see CAM illustration

cam·wood \ˈkamˌwu̇d\ *n* -S [Temne *k'am* camwood + E *wood*] **1 :** the hard red wood of an African tree (*Baphia nitida*) used as a dyewood **2 :** BARWOOD

¹can \kən, (ˌ)kan; *esp after a stressed vowel* ˌkᵊn; *esp in NewEng* (ˌ)ke(ə)n; *esp dial* (ˌ)kin\ *vb, past* **could** \kəd, (ˌ)ku̇d\ *or archaic 2d sing* **couldst** \kətst; (ˌ)ku̇dzt, -u̇dst, -u̇tst\ (with *thou*) *pres sing & pl* **can** *or archaic 2d sing* **canst** \kənzt, (ˌ)kan-, -n(t)st\ (with *thou*) [ME, know, know how, am able (1st & 3d sing. pres. indic. of *cunnen*, past *coude, couthe*), fr. OE *can, con* (infin. *cunnan*, past *cūthe*); akin to OHG *kan* know, am able (infin. *kunnan*), ON *kann* (infin. *kunna*), Goth *kann* know (infin. *kunnan*), OE *cnāwan* to know — more at KNOW] *vt* **1** *obs* **:** KNOW, UNDERSTAND ⟨most of the inhabitants ~ no word of Cornish —Richard Carew⟩ **2 :** to be able to do, make, or accomplish ⟨the will of Him who all things ~ —John Milton⟩ ~ *vi, archaic* **:** to have knowledge or skill — used with following *of* ⟨thou *canst* well of woodcraft —Sir Walter Scott⟩ ~ *verbal auxiliary* **1 a :** know how to **:** have the skill to ⟨he ~ read⟩ ⟨she ~ play the piano⟩ **b :** be physically or mentally able to ⟨he ~ lift 200 pounds⟩ ⟨I ~ tell red from green⟩ **c :** may perhaps **:** may possibly ⟨do you think he ~ still be living⟩ ⟨it *could* be true⟩ **d :** have the necessary courage or resolution to ⟨he ~ accept defeat without complaining⟩ **e :** be permitted by conscience or feeling ⟨you ~ hardly blame him⟩ ⟨I ~ forgive anything but that⟩ **f :** be made possible or probable by circumstances to ⟨he ~ hardly have meant that⟩ ⟨I *could* cry for shame⟩ **g :** be inherently able or designed to ⟨everything that money ~ buy⟩ ⟨this car ~ hold five persons⟩ **h :** be logically or axiologically able to ⟨2 + 2 ~ also be written 3 + 1⟩ ⟨we ~ reasonably conclude from this that such is the case⟩ **i :** be enabled by law, agreement, or custom to **:** have a right to ⟨only the House ~ originate financial measures⟩ **j :** have permission to — used interchangeably with *may* ⟨you ~ go now if you like⟩; see COULD **2** *dial* **:** to be able to — used as infinitive ⟨I may ~ go⟩ ⟨he'll ~ tell us —Alexander Wardrop⟩

2can \'kan, -aa(ə)n\ *n* -s [ME *canne*, fr. OE; akin to OHG *channa*, ON *kanna*; all perh. fr. a prehistoric NGmc-WGmc word borrowed from LL *canna*, a vessel, fr. L, reed; fr. the long thin spout of certain ancient vessels — more at CANE] **1 :** a receptacle (as for holding liquids) usu. cylindrical in shape: **a :** a vessel for holding or carrying water, wine, beer, or other liquids ⟨I have brought thee in this ~ fresh water from the brook —William Wordsworth⟩; *specif* **:** a drinking vessel ⟨in his hand did bear a boozing ~ —Edmund Spenser⟩ — compare CANNIKIN **b :** a cylindrical metal receptacle usu. with an open top, often with a removable cover, and sometimes with a spout or side handles (as for holding milk, oil, coffee, tobacco, ashes, or garbage) **c :** a single-trip tinplate container in which perishable foods or other products are hermetically sealed for preservation until use — called also *tin* **d :** a glass or earthenware jar with an airtight cover used for packing or preserving fruit or vegetables in the home ⟨we put up a dozen ~s of tomatoes last fall⟩ **e :** a small usu. cylindrical container made of paper or paper compound — compare COMPOSITE CAN, FIBER CAN **2 a :** a steam-heated hollow metal cylinder over which cloth is passed to be dried **b :** a hollow cylindrical combustion chamber of an airplane engine **c :** an air cleaner for a carburetor **3** *slang* **:** JAIL **4 :** TOILET **5** — not often in formal use **5** *slang* **:** BUTTOCKS, SEAT **6 :** DEPTH CHARGE **7 :** DESTROYER 2 — **in the can** *of a motion picture* **:** filmed, edited, and ready for release

can 1b : ash can, *A;* milk can, *B;* oilcan, *C;* sprinkling can, *D*

3can \'kan, -aa(ə)n\ *vt* **canned; canned; canning; cans** **1 a :** to put in a can **:** preserve by sealing in airtight cans or jars **b :** to hit (a golf ball) into the cup **:** HOLE **2** *slang* **:** to expel esp. from school **:** discharge esp. from employment ⟨they *canned* him within a month of his arrival⟩ **3** *slang* **:** to put a stop or end to **:** refrain from ⟨~ the chatter⟩ **4 a :** to enclose completely (as a pump or motor) in a housing **b :** to seal hermetically (as an oil tank or a package enclosed in metal foil) **5 :** to record (as a singing voice) on discs or tape ⟨he wouldn't let me ~ his voice —J.A.Lomax⟩ ⟨laughter *canned* for comedy programs⟩

4can \(ˌ)kan\ *verbal auxiliary* [ME, alter. of *gan*, past of *ginnen* to begin — more at GIN] *obs* **:** DID ⟨with gentle words he ~ her fairly greet —Edmund Spenser⟩

5can *obs var of* KHAN

6can \'kan, -aa(ə)n\ *n* -s [by shortening] **:** CANVASBACK DUCK

can *abbr* **1** canceled; cancellation **2** canon **3** canto **4** cantoris

ca·naan \'kānən\ *n* -s *usu cap* [LL *Chanaan* Canaan, the part of Palestine west of the Jordan, considered by the ancient Israelites as a land promised to them by God, fr. Gk *Chanaan*, *Kanaan*, fr. Heb *Kĕna'an*] **1 :** a promised land **:** place of rest, reward, or fulfillment **2 :** the region beyond death **:** HEAVEN

1ca·naan·ite \'kānəˌnīt\ *n* -s *usu cap* [Gk *Kananitēs*, fr. *Kanaan*, *Chanaan* + *-itēs* -ite] **1** *in the Bible* **a :** a member of a pre-Israelite people of Palestine which dwelt in the lowlands of Canaan — distinguished from *Amorite* **b :** any pre-Israelite inhabitant of Palestine **:** AMORITE 1b **2 a :** a member of a Semitic people which settled in Palestine and Syria subsequent to the Amorites, dwelt in various independent cities each of which had its separate Baal cult, and were ultimately absorbed by the Israelites and Aramaeans **b :** the Semitic language spoken by this people, closely allied to Phoenician, and known principally from glosses in the Tell el-'Amarna letters of approximately 1400 B.C. **3 :** the various languages of the Canaanitic subgroup of the Semitic subfamily sometimes regarded as constituting merely dialects of a single language

2canaanite \"\ *adj, usu cap* **:** of or relating to Canaan, any of the peoples known as Canaanites, or the Canaanite language

3canaanite \"\ *n* -s *usu cap* [Gk *Kananitēs*] **:** CANANAEAN

1ca·naan·it·ic \ˌkānəˈnid·ik\ *adj, usu cap* **1 :** 2CANAANITE **2 :** constituting or belonging to a subdivision of the Northwest Semitic languages that includes Canaanite, Phoenician, Hebrew, and various allied languages

2canaanitic \"\ *n* -s *usu cap* **:** the Canaanitic subdivision of languages

ca·naan·it·ish \'ˌ-ˌnīd·ish\ *adj, usu cap* **:** 1CANAANITIC

ca·na bra·va \ˌkänyəˈbrävə\ *n* [Sp *caña brava* wild cane] **:** either of two tall grasses of tropical America: **a :** a bamboo (*Bambusa vulgaris*) **b :** UVA GRASS

ca·na·cuas \kəˈnäkwəs\ *n pl but sing or pl in constr* [MexSp, pl. of *canacua*] **:** a wedding dance of Tarascan Indian girls wearing crowns of flowers

1can·a·da \'kanədə\ *adj, usu cap* [fr. dominion of *Canada*, country in No. America] **:** of or from the dominion of Canada **:** of the kind or style prevalent in Canada **:** CANADIAN ⟨*Canada* wheat⟩

2canada \"\ *usu cap, var of* CANADA GOOSE

3ca·ña·da \kənˈyädə, -adə\ *n* -s [Sp, fr. *caña* cane, long hollow object, fr. L *canna* — more at CANE] **1** *chiefly West* **a :** a small canyon **:** GLEN **b :** an open valley **2** *chiefly West* **:** a small stream of fresh water **:** CREEK

canada anemone *n, usu cap C* **:** a common woodland herb (*Anemone canadensis*) with palmately parted leaves and flowers having waxy white sepals and no petals

canada balsam *n, usu cap C* **:** an oleoresin exuded by the balsam fir as a viscous yellowish to greenish liquid, solidifying to a transparent mass, and used as a transparent cement esp. in microscopy for mounting specimens and in optical instruments — called also *Canada turpentine*

canada birch *n, usu cap C* **:** SWEET BIRCH

canada blueberry *n, usu cap C* **:** a low shrub (*Vaccinium myrtilloides*) of northeastern No. America having hairy foliage, white flowers, and sweet bluish black fruit

canada bluegrass *n, usu cap C* **:** WIRE GRASS a

canada buffalo berry *n, usu cap C* **:** a buffalo berry (*Shepherdia canadensis*)

canada field pea *n, usu cap C* **:** FIELD PEA

canada fleabane *n, usu cap C* **:** HORSEWEED 1

canada ginger *n, usu cap C* **:** WILD GINGER 2a

canada goose *also* **canada** *n, pl* **canada geese** *also* **canadas** *usu cap C* **:** the common wild goose (*Branta canadensis*) of No. America that is chiefly gray and brownish with black head and neck and a white patch from the sides of the head under the throat and represented by several varieties differing chiefly in size and details of coloring — see CACKLING GOOSE, HUTCHINS'S GOOSE, WHITE-CHEEKED GOOSE

Canada goose

canada hare *n, usu cap C* **:** the varying hare of No. America

canada hemp *n, usu cap C* **:** INDIAN HEMP 1

canada jay *n, usu cap C* **:** a jay (*Perisoreus canadensis*) having gray and sooty plumage and no crest, widely distributed in northern and western No. America, ranging southward in the Rocky mountains, and noted for its boldness in stealing provisions from hunters' camps — called also *camp robber*, *moose-bird*, *whiskey jack*; see ROCKY MOUNTAIN JAY

canada lily *n, usu cap C* **:** MEADOW LILY

canada lyme grass *n, usu cap C* **:** a wild rye (*Elymus canadensis*)

canada lynx *n, usu cap C* **:** a No. American lynx (*Lynx canadensis*) that is distinguished from the bobcat by larger size, longer ear tufts, heavier looser coat, large padded paws, and wholly black tail tip and that is now largely restricted to Canada though formerly widely distributed in forested eastern and central U.S.

canada mayflower *n, usu cap C* **:** FALSE LILY OF THE VALLEY

canada mint *n, usu cap C* **:** a common wild American mint (*Mentha canadensis*) that has whorled flowers in the upper axils

canada moonseed *n, usu cap C* **:** a woody vine (*Menispermum canadense*) of eastern No. America with large oval leaves, small white flowers, and black fruits

canada pea *n, usu cap C* **:** TUFTED VETCH

canada pitch *n, usu cap C* **:** the resinous exudation of the hemlock spruce — called also *hemlock pitch*

canada plum *n, usu cap C* **:** a native plum (*Prunus nigra*) of northeastern No. America with oblong orange-red fruit

canada porcupine *n, usu cap C* **:** the porcupine (*Erethizon dorsatus*) of northeastern No. America being about two feet long with barbed spines largely concealed in the coarse fur, feeding chiefly on bark and leaves, and sometimes causing considerable damage to isolated buildings which it gnaws for the salt and grease accumulated in their substance

canada rockrose *n, usu cap C* **:** FROSTWEED a

canada root *n, usu cap C* [prob. so called fr. a belief that it is esp. prevalent in Canada] **:** BUTTERFLY WEED

canada snakeroot *n, usu cap C* **:** WILD GINGER 2a

canada sweet gale *n, usu cap C* **:** SWEET FERN 2

canada tea *n, usu cap C* [so called fr. the use of its leaves as a substitute for tea] **:** WINTERGREEN 2a

canada thistle *n, usu cap C* **:** a European thistle (*Cirsium arvense*) naturalized in the U.S. and Canada where it is a pernicious weed

canada turpentine *n, usu cap C* **:** CANADA BALSAM

canada violet *n, usu cap C* **:** a leafy-stemmed No. American perennial herb (*Viola canadensis*) with heart-shaped pointed leaves and white flowers streaked with violet

canada warbler *n, usu cap C* **:** a common warbler (*Wilsonia canadensis*) of northern No. America that is blue-gray above and yellow below and has a necklace of black streaks below the throat

canada wild rye *n, usu cap C* **:** a wild rye (*Elymus canadensis*)

canada wormwood *n, usu cap C* **:** an aromatic weedy herb (*Artemisia canadensis*) with divided leaves and a terminal raceme of greenish flower heads found chiefly in Canada

canada yew *n, usu cap C* **:** GROUND HEMLOCK

ca·na de am·bar \ˌkänyəthəˈämˌbär\ *n* [Sp *caña de ámbar*, lit., amber cane] **:** a butterfly lily (*Hedychium coronarium*)

can·a·der \'kanədə(r)\ *n* -s [*Canada* + *-er*] *Brit* **:** CANOE

1ca·na·di·an \kəˈnādēən *also* -dyən\ *adj, usu cap* [F *canadien*, fr. *Canada* + F *-ien* -ian] **1 :** of, relating to, or characteristic of the dominion of Canada **2 :** of, relating to, or characteristic of the people of Canada **3 :** relating to or being a biogeographic zone extending across No. America including the northern tier of states of the U.S., and parts of Canada, the northern tier of states of the U.S., and certain mountain slopes and summits farther south and comprising the southern part of the coniferous forest region between the Hudsonian and Transition zones — compare BOREAL **4 :** of or relating to the earliest major subdivision of the Ordovician period in America — see GEOLOGIC TIME table

2canadian \"\ *n* -s *cap* **:** a native or inhabitant of Canada

canadian bacon *n, usu cap C* **:** bacon cut from the loin of a pig

canadian burnet *n, usu cap C* **:** a common herb (*Sanguisorba canadensis*) of eastern No. America

canadian football *n, usu cap C* **:** a game resembling both American and Rugby football played between two 12-man teams on a field 110 x 65 yards

canadian-french *adj, usu cap C&F* **:** FRENCH-CANADIAN

canadian french *n, usu cap C&F* **:** the language of the French Canadians

canadian goldenrod *n, usu cap C* **:** a large goldenrod (*Solidago canadensis*) of eastern No. America with 3-nerved leaves and large flower clusters

canadian goose *n, usu cap C* **:** CANADA GOOSE

canadian hemlock *n, usu cap C* **:** EASTERN HEMLOCK

canadian hemp *n, usu cap C* **:** INDIAN HEMP 1

canadian holly *n, usu cap C* **:** MOUNTAIN HOLLY 1

ca·na·di·an·ism \-ˌnizəm\ *n* -s *usu cap* **1 :** a quality distinctive of Canadians **2 :** allegiance to or pride in Canada **3 :** a characteristic feature of English as used in Canada

ca·na·di·an·ize \-ˌnīz\ *vt* -ED/-ING/-S *see -ize in Explan Notes, often cap* **:** to make Canadian **:** assimilate to a pattern of life and interests distinctive of Canadians

canadian moonseed *n, usu cap C* **1 :** CANADA MOONSEED **2 :** YELLOW PARILLA 2

canadian pondweed *n, usu cap C* **:** WATERWEED a

canadian red pine *n, usu cap C* **:** RED PINE 1

canadian rig *n, usu cap C* **:** an oil-well rig with slender wooden poles joined end to end instead of a cable or rope

canadian small reed *n, usu cap C* **:** BLUEJOINT 1

canadian warbler *n, usu cap C* **:** CANADA WARBLER

canadian waterleaf *n, usu cap C* **:** a woodland perennial herb (*Hydrophyllum canadense*) with purplish white flowers

can·a·dine \'kanəˌdēn, -dən\ *n* -s [ISV *canad-* (fr. NL *canadensis*, specific epithet of the goldenseal, *Hydrastis canadensis*, fr. *Canada*, country in No. America) + *-ine*] **:** a crystalline alkaloid $C_{20}H_{21}NO_4$ found in the root of the goldenseal

can·a·dol \'kanəˌdōl, -ōl\ *n* -s [G *kanadol*, fr. *Kanada* Canada + G *-ol* (fr. L *oleum* oil); fr. its having been obtained by fractional distillation of Canadian petroleum — more at OIL] **:** a light ligroin

ca·na dul·ce \ˌkänyəˈdülsē\ *n* [MexSp *caña dulce*, fr. Sp, sugar cane] **:** the seeds of the cana dulce tree (*Licania arborea*) of Mexico that yield an oil used for illumination and in soapmaking

ca·na es·pi·na \ˌkänyəeˈspēnə\ *n* [Sp *caña espina*, lit., spiny cane] **:** a valuable bamboo (*Bambusa spinosa*) of tropical Asia grown in the Philippines and used in building

ca·na·fis·tu·la \ˌkänyəˈfis(h)chələ\ *also* **ca·na·fis·to·la** \-stōlə\ *n* -s [Sp *cañafístula*, fr. *caña* cane (fr. L *canna*) + *-fístula* prob. fr. obs. *casiafistula*, fr. ML *cassia fistula*) — more at CANE, CASSIA FISTULA] **1 a :** DRUMSTICK TREE **b :** CASSIA FISTULA **2 :** a tropical American tree (*Cassia grandis*) related to the drumstick tree — called also *horse cassia*

ca·nai·gre \kəˈnīgrē\ *n* -s [MexSp] **:** a large dock (*Rumex hymenosepalus*) of the southwestern U.S. and northern Mexico having a root rich in tannin

ca·naille \kəˈnā(ə)l, -ˈnī\ *n* -s [F, fr. It *canaglia*, fr. *cane* dog, fr. L *canis* — more at HOUND] **:** MOB, RABBLE, RIFFRAFF ⟨the shoeblacks and linkboys and all the idling ~ of Dublin —Malachy Hynes⟩

can·a·jong \'kanəˌjoŋ, -äŋ\ *n* -s [perh. fr. Tasmanian] *Austral* **:** BEACH APPLE

canakin *var of* CANNIKIN

1ca·nal \kəˈnal\ *n* -s [ME, fr. L *canalis* pipe, channel, fr. *canna* reed — more at CANE] **1** *obs* **:** a pipe esp. for conveying liquids **2 a :** CHANNEL, WATERCOURSE; *esp* **:** STRAIT **b** *obs* **:** a long narrow ornamental pond **3 a :** a tubular passage or channel either in bone (as the haversian canals) or formed by soft tissues (as the alimentary canal or inguinal canal) **:** DUCT **b :** a groove which prolongs the shell aperture and in which the siphon of certain snails rests **4 :** an artificial waterway designed for navigation or for draining or irrigating land ⟨the Panama ~⟩ **5** *obs* **:** a means of communication **6 :** a groove or channel in an architectural member; *specif* **:** the recess or drip in the undersurface of a corona **7 :** a narrow arm of the sea usu. extending far inland and approximately uniform in width ⟨Lynn ~⟩ **8** [It *canale* channel, fr. L *canalis*] **:** any of various faint narrow markings on the planet Mars

2canal \"\ *vt* **canalled** *or* **canaled; canalled** *or* **canaled; canalling** *or* **canaling; canals** **1 :** to construct a canal through or across **:** provide with canals **2 :** CANALIZE ⟨they can ~ the natural forces —Elizabeth Bowen⟩

3ca·nal \kəˈnäl\ *n, pl* **cana·les** \-ä(ˌ)lās\ [Sp, fr. L *canalis*] *Southwest* **:** WATERSPOUT, EAVES TROUGH

canalboat \-ˈ-ˌ-\ *n* **:** a boat for use on a canal; *esp* **:** a long narrow boat having a bluff nearly vertical bow and stern that give it large freight capacity

canal-built \-ˈ-ˌ-\ *adj* **:** built for canal navigation

canal cell *n* [trans. of G *kanalzelle*] *bot* **:** one of the single row of cells constituting the axial row within the neck of an archegonium — compare NECK CELL

can·a·lete \ˌkanᵊlˈedē\ *also* **can·a·let·ta** \-edə\ *n* -s [AmerSp *canalete*] **:** PRINCEWOOD 1

can·a·lic·u·lar \ˌkanᵊlˈikyələ(r)\ *adj* [NL *canalicularis*, fr. L *canaliculus* + *-aris* -ar] **:** relating to, like, or provided with a canaliculus

can·a·lic·u·late \-lət, -ˌlāt\ *also* **can·a·lic·u·lat·ed** \-ˌlād·əd\ *adj* [L *canaliculatus* channeled, fr. *canaliculus* + *-atus* -ate] **:** grooved or channeled longitudinally ⟨the ~ leafstalk of certain palms⟩

can·a·lic·u·la·tion \ˌkanᵊlˌikyəˈlāshən\ *also* **can·a·lic·u·li·za·tion** \-yələˈzāshən, -ˌlīˈz-\ *n* -s **:** the formation of canaliculi

can·a·lic·u·lus \ˌkanᵊlˈikyələs\ *n, pl* **canaliculi** \-ˌlī, -ē\ [L, dim. of *canalis* channel — more at CANAL] **:** a minute canal in a bodily structure: as **a :** one of the hairlike channels ramifying an haversian system in bone and linking the lacunae with one another and with the haversian canal **b :** one of the narrow spaces between cells in the cell cords that make up a liver lobule

can·a·lif·er·ous \ˌkanᵊlˈif(ə)rəs\ *adj* [1*canal* + *-iferous*] **:** having canals or canaliculi

can·a·line \'kanᵊlˌēn, -ən\ *n* -s [irreg. fr. NL *Canavalia* + E *-ine*] **:** a crystalline amino acid $NH_2OCH_2CH_2CH(NH_2)COOH$ obtained from canavanine by enzymatic hydrolysis

ca·na·lis \kəˈnaləs, -ˈä-\ *n, pl* **cana·les** \-a(ˌ)lēz, -ä(ˌ)lās\ [L — more at CANAL] **1** *anat* **:** CANAL **2 :** the slightly convex or concave area between the fillets of an Ionic volute

ca·nal·i·za·tion \ˌkanᵊləˈz-, -lˌīˈz-\ *n* -s [F *canalisation*, fr. *canaliser* + *-ation*] **1 :** the act of canalizing: **a :** the construction or formation of canals **b :** the providing of a channel or an outlet **c :** the direction into a channel or groove **2 a :** a system of canals or conduits conveying or distributing gas, electricity, water, or steam **b :** the conveyance or distribution esp. of gas or water **3 a :** surgical formation of holes or canals for drainage without tubes **b :** natural formation of new channels in tissue (as formation of new blood vessels through a blood clot) **c :** establishment by repeated passage of nerve impulses of new pathways in the central nervous system

ca·nal·ize \kəˈnaˌlīz, ˈkanᵊlˌīz\ *vb* -ED/-ING/-S *see -ize in Explan Notes* [F *canaliser*, fr. *canal* (fr. L *canalis*) + *-iser* -ize] *vt* **1 a :** to provide with canals **:** build a canal through or across **b :** to make into or like a canal; *specif* **:** to make navigable or improve the navigation of by constructing canals **2 :** to provide with an outlet or a channel of expression **:** facilitate the discharge of (as an emotion) ⟨rituals both arouse and ~ emotion⟩ **3 :** to direct into certain channels **:** give a fixed or limited character, scope, or direction to ⟨*canalizing* such energies as he had towards the business of ruling —Hilaire Belloc⟩ **4 :** to drain (a wound) by forming channels without the use of tubes ~ *vi* **1 :** to flow in or into a channel **2 :** to develop new channels (as new capillaries in a blood clot)

ca·nal·ler *also* **ca·nal·er** \kəˈnalə(r)\ *n* -s [*canal* + *-er*] **1 :** one that works on canal transportation esp. on a canal or a canalboat **2 :** CANALBOAT

canalling *n* -s **1 :** canal construction or work **2 :** travel or commerce by canal **:** canal traffic

canal of schlemm \-ˈshlem\ *usu cap S* [trans. of G *schlemmscher kanal*, after Friedrich *Schlemm* †1858 Ger. anatomist] **:** SCHLEMM'S CANAL

canal ray *n* [trans. of G *kanalstrahl*; fr. the openings in the cathode through which the ions pass] **:** POSITIVE RAY

canals *pl of* CANAL, *pres 3d sing of* CANAL

canal system *n* **:** a system of passages connecting various cavities of the animal body (as in corals and sponges)

ca·na·nae·an *or* **ca·na·ne·an** \ˌkānəˈnēən, -ˌaˈ-\ *n* -s *usu cap* [LL *Cananaeus* (fr. Gk *Kananaios*, fr. Aram *qan'ānā* zealot) + E *-an*] **:** a member of a Jewish sect that bitterly opposed the Roman domination of Palestine **:** ZEALOT

ca·nan·ga \kəˈnaŋgə\ *n* [NL, fr. Malay *kĕnanga*, a tree of the genus *Canangium*] *syn of* CANANGIUM

cananga oil *n* **:** a yellow essential oil obtained from the flowers of the ilang-ilang tree and characterized by a less fragrant odor than ilang-ilang oil

ca·nan·gi·um \kəˈnanjēəm\ *n, cap* [NL, fr. Malay *kĕnanga* + NL *-ium*] **:** a small genus of Malayan trees (family Annonaceae) distinguished by the simple alternate leaves and linear sepals and petals and including the ilang-ilang tree

ca·nao *also* **kan·yaw** \kənˈyaů\ *n* -s [Sp *cañao*, fr. Iloko *kanyaw* sacred or ritual sanction] **:** a pagan religious feast in the mountain regions of the Philippines

ca·na·pé \ˈkanəpē, -ˌpā *also* ˌkanəˈpā\ *n* -s [F, lit., sofa, fr. ML *canapeum*, *canopeum* mosquito net; fr. the conception that the bread is a seat for the delicacy — more at CANOPY] **1 :** an appetizer consisting of a piece of bread or toast or a cracker topped with caviar, anchovy, or other savory food — compare HORS D'OEUVRE **2 :** SOFA ⟨a Louis XV ~ of carved walnut and needlepoint⟩

ca·na·pi·na \ˌkanəˈpēnə\ *n* -s [AmerSp, fr. It *canapino* hempen, fr. *canapa* hemp, fr. LL *canapis*, *cannapis*, fr. L *canabis*, *cannabis*, prob. fr. Gk *kannabis* — more at HEMP] **:** the fine silky strong fiber of the Indian mallow

ca·nard *senses 1 & 3* kəˈnärd, ka-, -nȧd; *sense 2* kȧnär\ *n, pl* **canards** *senses 1 & 3* -dz; *sense 2* -är\ [F, duck, fr. OF *quanart* drake, fr. *caner* to cackle (of imit. origin) + *-art* -ard; in sense 1, F, fr. the expression MF *vendre des canards à moitié* to cheat, deceive, lit., to half-sell ducks] **1 a :** a false or unfounded report or story; *esp* **:** a fabricated report (as by a newspaper) **b :** a groundless rumor or belief **2** *cookery* **:** DUCK 1b **3 :** an airplane having the horizontal stabilizing and control surfaces in front of the main supporting surfaces

canarese *usu cap, var of* KANARESE

canari *var of* KANARI

1ca·nar·i·an \kəˈnerēən, -ˈa(a)-,-ˈä-\ *also* **ca·nar·i·ote** \-rēˌōt, -ēət\ *adj, usu cap* [*Canary* Islands + E *-an* or *-ote*] **:** of or relating to the Canary Islands

2canarian \"\ *n* -s *cap* **:** a native or inhabitant of the Canary Islands; *esp* **:** one of the ancient Guanches

ca·nar·i·um \-rēəm\ *n, cap* [NL, fr. Malay *kĕnari* Java almond + NL *-ium*] **:** a large genus of tropical Asiatic and African trees (family Burseraceae) having compound leaves, panicled flowers, and triangular drupaceous often edible fruits and yielding balsamic resins — see BLACK DAMMAR, ELEMI, JAVA ALMOND

1ca·nary \kəˈnerē, -ˈeə-,-ˈa(a)(ə)-,-ˈä-, -ri\ *n* -ES *often attrib* [in sense 1, fr. MF *canarie*, *canaries*, fr. OSp *canario*, fr. *Islas Canarias* Canary Islands, group in the Atlantic ocean southwest of Spain, fr. LL *Canariae insulae*, lit., dog islands; in other senses, fr. *Canary* Islands, *Canaries*, fr. Sp *Islas Canarias*] **1 :** a lively court dance of the 16th century **2 :** a Canary Islands usu. sweet wine similar to Madeira and once popular in England **3** *or* **canary bird a :** a small finch (*Serinus canarius*) that is native to the Canary Islands, that is greenish with brown streaks above and yellowish below with many variations in size, form, and color, and that is now extensively bred as a cage bird and singer — see CHOPPER, 2ROLLER 2 **b :** any of various small birds of different countries most of which are largely yellow in color (as some American warblers of the genus *Dendroica*, some of the African weaverbirds, and the American goldfinch) **4** *slang* **a** (1) **:** SOPRANO; *esp* **:** a coloratura singer (2) **:** a woman singer with a dance band **b :** INFORMER, SQUEALER **5** *or* **canary yellow** [so called fr. the color of the canary bird] **a :** a light to moderate greenish yellow **b :** a moderate yellow **6 :** a diamond of a pale-yellow color **7** *or* **canary bird a :** a device for detecting gases in mines **b :** GAS MASK

2canary \"\ *vi* -ED/-ING/-ES *obs* **:** to dance nimbly (as in the canary dance)

canary banana *n, usu cap C* [fr. *Canary* Islands] **:** DWARF BANANA

canary bellflower *n, usu cap C* [fr. *Canary* Islands] **:** a tall Canary Islands herb (*Canarina campanula*) of the family Campanulaceae with yellow flowers

canarybird flower *n* **1** *also* **canarybird vine :** a climbing plant (*Tropaeolum peregrinum*) with canary-colored flowers **2 :** BIRD PLANT

canary broom *n, usu cap C* [fr. *Canary* Islands] **:** a much-branched yellow-flowered shrub (*Cytisus canariensis*) native to the Canary Islands — called also *genista*

canary cedar *n, usu cap 1st C* [fr. *Canary* Islands] **:** an evergreen tree (*Juniperus cedrus*) that has pendulous branches, bluish foliage, and orange-brown fruit and is endemic in the Canary Islands

canary creeper *n* **:** CANARYBIRD FLOWER 1

canary fly *n* **:** the Australian apple leafhopper

canary glass *n* [so called fr. its color] **:** glass colored with oxide of uranium

canary grass *n* [fr. *Canary* Islands] **1 :** a Canary Islands grass (*Phalaris canariensis*) the seeds of which are used as food for cage birds **2 :** a plant of the genus *Lepidium* of which the pods are sometimes fed to tame birds

canary island bellflower *n, usu cap C&I* **:** CANARY BELLFLOWER

canary island date palm *n, usu cap C&I* **:** a date palm (*Phoenix canariensis*) indigenous in the Canary Islands, larger and more graceful than the common date palm, and often used for ornament

canary island juniper *n, usu cap C&I* **:** CANARY CEDAR

canary island pine *n, usu cap C&I* **:** CANARY PINE

canary ivy *n, usu cap C* [fr. *Canary* Islands] **:** ALGERIAN IVY

canary pine *n, usu cap C* [fr. *Canary* Islands] **:** a tall evergreen tree (*Pinus canariensis*) of the Canary Islands with reddish bark, long drooping needles, and ovoid cones — called also *blue pine*

canary pox *n* **:** a virus disease of canaries closely related to fowl pox

canary seed *n* [fr. *Canary* Islands] **1 :** seed of the canary grass used as food for cage birds — compare BIRDSEED **2 :** seed of the common plantain (*Plantago major*)

canary stone *n* [so called fr. its color] **:** a yellow species of carnelian

canary vine *n* [so called fr. the color of the flowers of *Tropaeolum peregrinum*] **1 :** CANARYBIRD FLOWER 1 **2 :** CLIMBING FUMITORY

canary wood *n* [fr. *Canary* Islands] **1 :** the wood of various trees: as **a :** that of either of two laurels (*Persea indica* and *P. canariensis*) of Madeira and the Canary Islands **b :** that of the Indian mulberry **c :** that of an Australian tree (*Eucalyptus hemiphloia*) **d :** that of Leichhardt's pine **2** *Brit* **:** the wood of a tulip tree

canary yellow *n* **:** CANARY 5

ca·nas·ta \kə'nastə, -'äs-, -'aa-, -'ȧ-\ *n* -s [Sp, lit., basket, prob. back-formation fr. *canastillo* wicker tray, fr. LL *canistellum*, dim. of L *canistrum* basket — more at CANISTER] **1 :** a card game that is a form of rummy played usu. as a 2-hand or as a 4-hand partnership game using two full decks plus four jokers, all jokers and deuces being wild, red threes having special scoring value, and black threes having special value in play, the object being to meld groups but not sequences of cards esp. of seven or more of the same rank which earn large bonuses — called also *basket rummy;* compare BOLIVIA, SAMBA **2 :** a combination of at least seven cards of the same rank melded in the game of canasta and related games

ca·nas·ter \kə'nastə(r)\ *n* -s [D *kanaster*, fr. Sp *canastro* basket, prob. fr. Gk *kanastron;* fr. its being shipped from South America in baskets — more at CANISTER] **:** a smoking tobacco made of the dried leaves coarsely broken

can·a·val·ia \,kanə'valyə, -'äl-, -'ȧ-\ *n, cap* [NL] **:** a small genus of tropical twining herbs (family Leguminosae) having long tough pods with large seeds that are sometimes used for food but more often to adulterate coffee — see JACK BEAN

can·a·val·in \,==='=lən, kə'navələn\ *n* -s [NL *Canavalia* + E -*in*] **:** a globulin found in the jack bean

can·a·van·ine \,kanə'va,nēn, -'ä-, -'a-; kə'navə,n-\ *n* -s [ISV *canavan-* (irreg. fr. NL *Canavalia*) + *-ine*] **:** an amino acid $NH_2C(:NH)NHOCH_2CH_2CH(NH_2)COOH$ occurring in the jack bean

ca·nawl·er \kə'nȯlə(r)\ *substand var of* CANALLER

can·ber·ra \'kan,berə, -,bərə\ *adj, usu cap* [fr. *Canberra*, Australia] **:** of or from Canberra, the capital of Australia **:** of the kind or style prevalent in Canberra

can buoy *n* **:** a truncated buoy having a flat top — see BUOY illustration

can·can \'kan,kan, 'kaan,kaa(ə)n\ *n* -s *often attrib* [F, prob. fr. (baby talk) *cancan* duck, of imit. origin or alter. of *canard;* fr. the resemblance of some of the movements to those of a duck — more at CANARD] **:** a woman's dance of French origin characterized by high kicking usu. while holding up the front of a full ruffled skirt

¹can·cel \'kan(t)səl, -'aa-, -'ai-\ *vb* **canceled** *or* **cancelled; canceling** *or* **cancelling** \-s(ə)liŋ\ **cancels** [ME *cancellen*, fr. MF *canceller*, fr. LL *cancellare*, fr. L, to make like a lattice, fr. *cancelli* lattice, dim. of *cancer* lattice, alter. of *carcer* prison] *vt* **1 a :** to mark or strike out for omission or deletion typically with lines crossed latticewise over the passage in question or by a line through the symbols involved ⟨~ an offensive passage⟩ ⟨a section ~*ed* as unimportant⟩ **b** (1) **:** OMIT ⟨~ matter set in type and not yet printed⟩ ⟨~ sheets printed but not yet bound⟩ (2) **:** to remove (a leaf) from a book (3) **:** to remove (a blank leaf) from a printed sheet before binding **2 :** to remove from significance or effectiveness: as **a :** to destroy the force, effectiveness, or validity of **:** REVOKE, ANNUL, INVALIDATE ⟨~ an order⟩ ⟨~*ing* a magazine subscription⟩ **b :** to bring to nothingness **:** DESTROY, RUIN ⟨~*ing* more material and labor with the same weight of explosives —Harland Manchester⟩ **c :** to remove from need for consideration **:** reduce or vitiate to the point of insignificance ⟨was slavery so deep an evil that it ~*ed* out all other political rights and interests —Herbert Agar⟩ **d :** to match or nullify in force or effect **:** COUNTERBALANCE, NEUTRALIZE, OFFSET — often used with *out* ⟨his irritability ~*ed* out his natural kindness —Osbert Sitwell⟩ **e :** to cease from planning or expecting **:** call off usu. without expectation of conducting or performing at a later time **:** DROP, RELINQUISH ⟨~ a trip⟩ ⟨a football game ~*ed* because of heavy snow⟩ **3 a :** to remove (a common divisor) esp. from numerator and denominator **b :** to remove (equivalents) on opposite sides of an equation or account **c :** BALANCE ⟨~ an equivalent of opposite sign⟩ — often used with *out* **4 :** to counteract the effect of (a previous sharp or flat) by inserting in musical notation a natural sign **5 a :** to deface (a postage or revenue stamp) esp. with a set of parallel lines, a postmark, or a series of cuts or slits to invalidate for reuse **b :** to deface the stamps on (a piece of mail) **~** *vi* **1 :** to neutralize each other's strength or effect **:** become counterbalanced or offset — often used with *out* ⟨the various pressure groups to a large degree ~*ed* out —J.B.Conant⟩ **2 :** to admit of being dropped together as equal or equivalent ⟨the two x's on each side of the equation ~⟩ **syn** see ERASE — **cancel to order :** to cancel (a stamp) as an indication of sale to a collector rather than passage through the mails

²cancel \"\ *n* -s **1 :** CANCELLATION **:** the act of annulling or rescinding ⟨an order quickly followed by a ~⟩ **2 a :** a written part or passage suppressed or deleted **b :** a passage or page from which something has been suppressed and to which new matter has been added in its place **:** the leaf containing matter so replaced — called also *cancelland* **c :** a new leaf, sheet, or pasted-in slip substituted for or emending matter already printed as part of a book — called also *cancellans* **d :** blank pages removed from a printed sheet before binding **3 :** a canceling direction in music **:** NATURAL **4 :** a postal cancellation **5 :** a punch for canceling tickets — usu. used in pl. and often with *pair* ⟨a pair of ~*s*⟩

can·cel·able *or* **can·cel·lable** \-sələbəl\ *adj* **:** that can be canceled

canceled *adj* [fr. past part. of *cancel*] **:** represented or cast with a slant line across the face ⟨a ~ arabic numeral⟩

can·ce·leer *or* **can·ce·lier** \,kan(t)sə'li(ə)r\ *n* -s [ONF *canceler* to waver, totter, fr. LL *cancellare* to cross the legs, fr. L, to make like a lattice — more at CANCEL] **:** the turn of a hawk in flight made before seizing or after missing the prey

can·cel·er *or* **can·cel·ler** \'kan(t)s(ə)lə(r), -'aa-, -'ai-\ *n* -s **:** one that cancels; *esp* **:** a machine for canceling postage stamps

can·cel·land \'kan(t)sə'land\ *or* **can·cel·lan·dum** \,=='=dəm\ *n, pl* **cancellands** \-n(d)z\ *or* **cancellan·da** \-ndə\ [LL *cancellandum*, neut. of *cancellandus*, gerundive of *cancellare* to strike or cross out — more at CANCEL] **:** ²CANCEL 2b

can·cel·lans \'=='=lanz\ *n, pl* **cancellans·es** \-nzəz\ *or* **cancellan·tia** \,=='=nchēə\ [LL, pres. part. of *cancellare*] **:** ²CANCEL 2c

can·cel·la·re·sca cor·si·va \(,)kän,chelə'reskə(,)kȯr'sēvə\ *also* **cancellaresca** *n* [*cancellaresca corsiva*, modif. of It *cancelleresca corsiva* cursive cancellaresca; *cancellaresca*, modif. of It *cancelleresca*, prob. short for *lettera cancelleresca* chancellery handwriting, fr. *lettera* handwriting + *cancelleresca*, fem. of *cancelleresco* of a chancellery, fr. *cancelleria* chancellery (fr. F *chancellerie*) + *-esco* -esque — more at CHANCELLERY] **:** a style of cursive manuscript handwriting that had its origin at the Vatican in the 15th century

can·cel·lar·ia \,kan(t)sə'la(a)rēə\ *n, cap* [NL, fr. L *cancelli* bars, lattice + NL *-aria* — more at CANCEL] **:** the type genus of Cancellariidae comprising the nutmeg shells that are nearly cosmopolitan in warm seas

can·cel·la·ri·idae \(,)kan,selə'rīə,dē\ *n pl, cap* [NL, fr. *Cancellaria*, type genus + *-idae*] **:** a family of herbivorous marine snails (order Pectinibranchia) having nonoperculate oval shells strongly sculptured with axial ribs and spiral ridges forming a latticelike pattern — see CANCELLARIA

can·cel·late \'kan(t)sə,lāt, -'aa-, -,lət\ *or* **can·cel·lat·ed** \-,lād·əd\ *adj* [L *cancellatus*, past part. of *cancellare* to make like a lattice — more at CANCEL] **1 :** marked with numerous crossing lines or ridges **:** RETICULATE ⟨~ leaves⟩ **2 :** divided into small spaces by laminae **:** CANCELLOUS

can·cel·la·tion *also* **can·ce·la·tion** \,kan(t)sə'lāshən, -,aa-, -,ai-\ *n* -s [*cancel* + *-ation*] **1 a :** the act of canceling, of deleting, or of nullifying or invalidating ⟨the ~ of the faulty passage⟩ ⟨~ of the town ordinance⟩ **b** (1) **:** the calling off of an arrangement (as for travel) (2) **:** the accommodation released ⟨was lucky to get a late ~ for the trip to Chicago⟩ **2 :** the result of canceling: as **a :** the set of marks on a piece of mail made in the process of canceling the stamp **b :** the marks applied to the stamp itself as distinct from the postmark **3 :** the termination by the insured or the insurer or both of insurance in accordance with the specified terms of a policy

cancelled *past of* CANCEL

can·cel·li \kan'se,lī, -(,)lē, *in sense 1 also* kän'chelē\ *n pl* [L, lattice — more at CANCEL] **1 :** screens or rails typically of latticework or stone grating used to enclose or separate a part of a church; *specif* **:** the partitions between the nave of a church and the altar or choir — compare CHANCEL **2** [NL, fr. L] **a :** the intersecting osseous plates and bars of which cancellous bone is composed **b :** the interstices between such plates and bars

cancelling *pres part of* CANCEL

can·cel·lous \'kan(t)sələs\ *adj* [NL *cancelli* + E *-ous*] **:** having a spongy or porous structure **:** made up of intersecting plates and bars that form small cavities or cells — used of the bony tissue near the ends of long bones and elsewhere where both rigidity and lightness are essential

can·cel·lus \kan'seləs\ *sing of* CANCELLI

cancels *pres 3d sing of* CANCEL, *pl of* CANCEL

can·cer \'kan(t)sə(r), -'aa-, -'ai-\ *n* [ME, Cancer (sign of the zodiac), fr. L, crab, cancer; akin to Gk *karkinos* crab, cancer, Skt *karkaṭa* crab, *karkara* hard — more at HARD] **1** -s *usu cap* **:** the 4th sign of the zodiac — see SIGN table **2** -s **a :** a mass of tissue cells possessed of potentially unlimited growth that serves no useful function in the body, robs the host of nutrients necessary for survival, expands locally by invasion and systemically by transmission of cells along lymphatic and blood pathways, and unless recognized early and removed kills the host and that is usu. considered due to a combination of carcinogens and predisposing factors (as heredity, age, trauma, or chronic irritation), cancer itself never being directly inherited though a predisposition to certain forms may be heritable — compare CARCINOMA, SARCOMA; NEOPLASM, TUMOR; METASTASIS **b :** an abnormal condition characterized by the presence of a cancer or cancers **3** -s **:** an often malignant source of spreading and corroding destructive evil ⟨a man who offends in this way should be removed at once as a ~ in the body politic —Robert Graves⟩ **4** -s **a :** an enlarged tumorlike growth (as that typical of crown gall) **b :** a disease characterized by such growths **5** *cap* [NL, fr. L] **:** a genus of crabs almost cosmopolitan in distribution both in deep water and alongshore containing important edible crabs and common shore crabs (as the Dungeness crab, the rock crabs, and the Jonah crab) and being the type of the family Cancridae

can·cer·ate \-ə,rāt, *usu* -ād.+V\ *vi* -ED/-ING/-S [LL *canceratus* cancerous, fr. L *cancer* + *-atus* -ate] **:** to become cancerous **:** develop into a cancer

cancer eye *n* **:** a malignant epithelioma originating in the mucous membranes of the eye of cattle, common in regions of intense sunlight, chiefly affecting animals with white or light-colored skin about the eyes, and ultimately destroying the eye and adjacent bony structures and metastasizing widely

can·cer·ism \'= =,rizəm\ *n* -s [ISV *cancer* + *-ism*] **:** a hypothetical tendency to develop cancer

can·cer·i·za·tion \,= =,rə'zāshən, -,rī'z-\ *n* -s [ISV *cancer* + *-ize* + *-ation*] **:** transformation into cancer ⟨~ of a wart⟩ or from a normal to a cancerous state ⟨epithelial ~⟩

cancer jalap *n* [perh. so called fr. a belief in folk medicine that it was effective against cancer] **:** POKEBERRY

can·cer·o·ci·dal \,= =,rō'sīdᵊl\ *adj* [*cancer* + *-o-* + *-cidal*] **:** destructive of cancer cells

can·cer·o·gen·ic \,= =,rō'jenik\ *or* **can·cer·i·gen·ic** \-,rə-\ *adj* [*cancer* + *-o-* or *-i-* + *-genic*] **:** CARCINOGENIC

can·cer·ol·o·gist \,= ='räləjəst\ *n* -s [*cancerology* + *-ist*] **:** a cancer specialist

can·cer·ol·o·gy \-əjē\ *n* -ES [*cancer* + *-o-* + *-logy*] **:** the study of cancer

can·cer·o·lyt·ic \'= =,ō'lid·ik\ *adj* [*cancer* + *-o-* + *-lytic*] **:** CARCINOLYTIC

can·cer·ous \'kan(t)s(ə)rəs, -'aa-, -'ai-\ *adj* [*cancer* + *-ous*] **1 :** affected with cancer ⟨a ~ lung⟩ ⟨a leprous or ~ man —J.G.Frazer⟩ **2 :** of or relating to cancer **:** constituting a cancer ⟨a ~ indication⟩ ⟨a ~ tumor⟩ **3 :** like a cancer ⟨the months of spreading ~ distrust —Jean Stafford⟩ ⟨if we consider only the sordid aspects of urban life the American city of the period seems a ~ growth —A.M.Schlesinger b. 1888⟩ — **can·cer·ous·ly** *adv*

can·cer·pho·bia \'kan(t)sə(r)'fōbēə\ *or* **can·cer·o·pho·bia** \-(t)sərō'f-\ *n* -s [NL, fr. L *cancer* + *-phobia*] **:** an abnormal dread of cancer

cancerroot \'= =,=\ *n* [*cancer* + *root;* prob. fr. its use in folk medicine as a cancer remedy] **:** any of several root parasites of the family Orobanchaceae (as the squawroot)

cancers *pl of* CANCER

cancer virus *n* **:** TUMOR VIRUS

cancerweed \'= =,=\ *n* [so called fr. its use in folk medicine as a cancer remedy] **1 :** a rattlesnake root (*Prenanthes alba*) of which the root has bitter tonic properties **2 :** a sage (*Salvia lyrata*) of the eastern U. S.

can·cer·wort \'= =,wərt, -,ȯ-\ *n* -s [perh. so called fr. a belief in folk medicine that it was effective against cancer] **:** either of two European plants (*Kickxia spuria* and *K. elatine*) of the family Scrophulariaceae

canch \'kanch\ *n* -ES [origin unknown] **1** *dial Eng* **:** a sloping slice removed from the roof or floor of a mine roadway to adjust the gradient between adjacent workings **2** *dial Eng* **:** a small stack or pile **:** a small quantity

can·cha \'känchə\ *n* -s [Sp, fr. Quechua] **1** *Southwest* **:** an enclosed yard; *esp* **:** a yard used for cockfights or games **2 :** a jai alai court

can·cha·la·gua \,känchə'lägwə\ *n* -s [Sp, alter. of *cachanlaguen*, modif. of Araucan *cachanlahuen*, fr. *cachan* pain in the side + *lahuen* medicinal herb] **:** a bitter tonic herb of the genus *Centaurium* (esp. *C. chilensis* of Chile and *C. venustum* of California)

can·cion *also* **can·ción** *AmerSp* kȧn'syōn, *Cast* -n'thyōn\ *n, pl* **cancio·nes** \-yōnās\ [Sp, *canción*, fr. L *cantion-, cantio* song — more at CANZONE] **:** SONG; *esp* **:** a popular song of Spain or Spanish America

can·cio·ne·ro \,känchō'ne(,)rō\ *or* **can·cio·nei·ro** \", -'ā-\ *n* -s [*cancionero* fr. Sp, *canción* + *-ero* -ary; *cancioneiro* fr. Pg, fr. Sp *cancionero*] **:** a Spanish or Portuguese collection of songs and poems usu. by several authors

cancln *abbr* cancellation

¹can·crid \'kaŋkrəd\ *adj* **:** of or relating to the Cancridae

²cancrid \"\ *n* -s [NL *Cancridae*] **:** a crab of the family Cancridae

can·cri·dae \'kaŋkrə,dē\ *n pl, cap* [NL, fr. *Cancri-, Cancer*, type genus + *-idae*] **:** a large family of crabs (tribe Brachyura) that are nearly cosmopolitan in distribution and include many of the best-known edible crabs — see CANCER 5

can·cri·nite \-,nīt\ *n* -s [G *cancrinit*, fr. Count Georg *Cancrin* †1845 Russian statesman + G *-it* -ite] **:** a mineral $(Na_2,Ca)_4(AlSiO_4)_6CO_3.nH_2O$ consisting of an aluminosilicate and carbonate of sodium and calcium occurring in igneous rocks usu. as transparent to translucent masses of various colors (hardness 5–6, sp. gr. 2.42–2.5)

can·criv·o·rous \(')kaŋ'krivərəs, -aŋ'-\ *adj* [NL *cancrivorus*, fr. *cancr-, cancer* crab + *-i-* + *-vorus* -vorous — more at CANCER] **:** feeding on crustaceans

can·cri·zans \'kaŋkrə,zanz, -ank-\ *adj* [ML, pres. part. of *cancrizare* to go backwards, fr. L *cancr-, cancer* crab + LL *-izare* -ize] *music* **:** having the theme or subject repeated backwards note for note ⟨a ~ canon⟩ ⟨a 12-tone composition that is ~⟩ — compare CRAB FORM

¹can·croid \'kaŋ,krȯid, -an,-\ *adj* [L *cancr-, cancer* crab + E *-oid* — more at CANCER] **1 :** resembling a crab ⟨a ~ spider⟩ **2** [F *cancroïde*, fr. L *cancr-, cancer* crab, cancer + F *-oïde* -oid] **:** like a cancer ⟨a ~ tumor⟩

²cancroid \"\ *n* -s [F *cancroïde*, fr. L *cancr-, cancer* + F *-oïde* -oid] **:** a skin cancer of low or moderate malignancy

can·crum oris \'kaŋkrə'mōrəs, -ȯr-,-'är-\ *n, pl* **can·cra oris** \-rə'ō-, -'ȯ-,-'ä-\ [NL, lit., canker of the mouth] **:** NOMA

cand \'kand\ *n* -s [prob. modif. of Corn *can* brightness, whiteness, fluorite; prob. akin to L *candidus* white, bright — more at CANDID] **:** FLUORITE

can·da·reen *also* **can·da·rin** \'kandə'rēn\ *n* -s [Malay *kĕndĕri*, fr. Tamil *kunri* Indian licorice (*Abrus precatorius*); fr. the use of its berries as weights] **1 :** a Chinese unit of weight equivalent to 1/100 tael **2 :** a Chinese unit of value equivalent to 1/100 tael of silver

C and D *abbr* collection and delivery

can·de·la \kan'dēlə, -'ā-\ *n* -s [L, candle] **:** CANDLE 4b

can·de·la·bra \,kandə'läbrə, -aan-, -ab-,-äb-,-ab-\ *n* -s [L, pl. (taken as sing.) of *candelabrum*] **:** CANDELABRUM ⟨four silver ~s holding great waxen torches — Sir Walter Scott⟩ ⟨a solid-brass ~⟩

can·de·la·brum \-brəm\ *n, pl* **candela·bra** \-brə\ *also* **candelabrums** \-brəmz\ [L, fr. *candela* candle — more at CANDLE] **1 a :** a large candlestick or a lamp usu. ornamented and having several arms or branches ⟨taking a ~ with no less than six tapers in it —Hervey Allen⟩ ⟨oil for the eight-branched ~ —Maurice Samuel⟩ ⟨on the left . . . we found two fine *candelabra* —Arthur Milton⟩ — compare CHANDELIER **b :** a usu. ornate and often heavy and large standard supporting a candlestick or lamp **2 a :** a small decorated modified column or columnlike rib of molded profile **b :** a design of which such a candelabrum forms the center

candelabrum

candelabrum tree *n* **:** a tropical African shrub or tree (*Pandanus candelabrum*) with a huge spreading head of foliage — called also *chandelier tree*

can·de·li·lla \,kandə'lē(y)ə, *attrib* '= =\ *n* -s [AmerSp, fr. Sp, little candle, dim. of *candela* candle, fr. L — more at CANDLE] **1 :** a wax-coated shrub (*Euphorbia antisyphilitica*) of northern Mexico and southwestern U. S. **2 a :** any of several Mexican euphorbias **b :** a related plant (*Pedilanthus pavonis*)

candelilla wax *n* **:** a hard yellowish to brown wax composed chiefly of hydrocarbons that is found as a coating on candelilla shrubs and used similarly to carnauba wax

can·dent \'kandənt\ *adj* [L *candent-, candens*, pres. part. of *candēre* to shine — more at CANDID] **:** white or glowing usu. from great heat

can·des·cence \kan'desᵊn(t)s\ *n* -s **:** a candescent state or condition **:** dazzling clear whiteness ⟨the ~ of the new moon⟩

can·des·cent \(')kan'desᵊnt\ *adj* [L *candescent-, candescens*, pres. part. of *candescere*, incho. of *candēre* to shine] **:** glowing or dazzling often from great heat ⟨a ~ meteorite⟩

C and F *abbr* cost and freight

C and I *abbr* cost and insurance

can·di·ci·din \,kandə'sīdᵊn\ *n* -s [NL *Candida* + E *-cide* + *-in*] **:** an antibiotic elaborated by a streptomyces and active against certain molds of the genus *Candida*

¹can·did \'kandəd *also* -'aa-\ *adj, sometimes* -ER/-EST [F & L; F *candide*, fr. L *candidus* white, bright, fr. *candēre* to shine, be white; akin to LGk *kandaros* ember, Skt *candra* shining, moon] **1 :** WHITE ⟨a welding blast of ~ flame —E.C.Stedman⟩ **2 :** free from bias, prejudice, or malice **:** marked by concern for truth and justice **:** fairly disposed **:** DISINTERESTED, FAIR, JUST ⟨in the back of his ~ mind he knew that . . . the charges against him were true —Irwin Edman⟩ **3** *archaic* **:** free from stain **:** CLEAR, PURE ⟨a ~ completely unblemished reputation⟩ **4 a :** marked by honest sincere expression **:** uttered or given out as fair and unbiased **:** free from expedient reservation and modification ⟨to tell you my private and ~ opinion . . . I think he's a man from the other camp —James Joyce⟩ **b :** indicating or suggesting sincere honesty and absence of deception and duplicity ⟨his ~ eyes took on an expression of genuine sympathy —Archibald Marshall⟩ **c :** performed, expressed, or acknowledged without concealment or reservation ⟨her eyes burning with a ~ excitement —Edith Wharton⟩ **d :** disposed to criticize severely **:** BLUNT, FORTHRIGHT ⟨as a leader . . . I have never lacked ~ critics in my own ranks —Clement Attlee⟩ **5 :** relating to photography or other presentation or recording of subjects acting naturally, informally, or spontaneously without being posed, rehearsed, or inhibited ⟨a ~ picture⟩ ⟨a ~ microphone interview⟩ — see CANDID CAMERA **syn** see FRANK

²candid \"\ *n* -s [by shortening] **:** a candid photograph

can·di·da \'kandədə\ *n, cap* [NL, fr. L, fem. sing. of *candidus* white, bright] **:** a genus of parasitic yeastlike imperfect fungi (order Moniliales) producing small amounts of mycelium — see MONILIA, THRUSH

can·di·da·cy \'kan(d)ədəsē, -aandə-, -i\ *n* -ES [fr. ¹*candidate*, after such pairs as E *magistrate: magistracy*] **:** the quality or state of being a candidate **:** standing as a candidate

¹can·di·date \'kan(d)ə,dāt, -aandə-; *esp freq in S* -,dət; *rapid also* -n,dāt, -ndət; *usu* -ād.,-əd.+V\ *n* -s [L *candidatus*, fr. *candidatus* clothed in white, fr. *candidus* white + *-atus* -ate; fr. the white toga worn by candidates for office in ancient Rome — more at CANDID] **1 :** one that presents himself or is presented by others often formally or officially as suitable for and aspiring to an office, position, membership, right, or honor — usu. used with *for* ⟨a ~ for governor⟩ ⟨a ~ for the board of directors⟩ ⟨~*s* for admission to the club⟩ **2 :** one that is likely or worthy to gain a post, position, or distinction or to come to a certain place, end, or fate **:** CHOICE ⟨I am not ambitious of ridicule — not absolutely a ~ for disgrace —Edmund Burke⟩ ⟨a ~ for the penitentiary⟩ ⟨this play is a ~ for the prize⟩ **3 :** a student taking a course of study leading to a degree; *esp* **:** one in the process of meeting final requirements ⟨a ~ for the Ph.D⟩

²candidate \"\ *vi* -ED/-ING/-S **:** to be a candidate; *esp* **:** to preach on invitation in a church preparing to call a new minister

³candidate *adj* [L *candidatus*] *obs* **:** dressed in white

can·di·da·ture \-,də,chü(ə)r, -üə *also* -dəchə(r) *or* ,dāchə(r)\ *n* -s [F, fr. *candidat* (fr. L *candidatus*) + *-ure*] *chiefly Brit* **:** CANDIDACY

candid camera *n* **1 :** a usu. small camera equipped with a fast lens and used for taking informal photographs of unposed subjects often without their knowledge **2 :** MINIATURE CAMERA

can·di·di·a·sis \,kandə'dīəsəs\ *n, pl* **candidia·ses** \-,sēz\

[NL, fr. *Candida* + *-iasis*] **:** infection with or disease caused by a fungus of the genus *Candida* — compare MONILIASIS, THRUSH

can·did·ly *adv* **:** in a candid manner

can·did·ness *n* -ES **:** the quality or state of being candid

candied *adj* [fr. past part. of *candy*] **1 :** encrusted or coated with sugar or with a sugarlike or candylike substance ⟨~ fruits⟩ **2 :** cooked esp. by baking with sugar or syrup until translucent ⟨~ sweet potatoes⟩

candies *pl of* CANDY, *pres 3d sing of* CANDY

¹can·di·ote \'kandē,ōt, -ēət\ *or* **can·di·ot** \-ēət,-ē,ät\ *adj, usu cap* [F *candiote*, fr. *candiote*, n.] **:** of or relating to Candia **:** CRETAN

²candiote \"\ *or* **candiot** \"\ *n* -s *cap* [prob. fr. F *candiote*, fr. *Candie* Candia (Crete, island south of the mainland of Greece) + F *-ote*] **:** a native or inhabitant of the island of Crete **:** CRETAN

can·di·ru \ˌkandəˈrü\ *n* -s [Pg *candirú*, fr. Tupi *candirú*, *canderú*] **:** a minute bloodsucking catfish (*Vandellia cirrhosa*, family Pygidiidae) of the Amazon that commonly parasitizes the gill chambers of freshwater fishes but may enter orifices of human or other animal bodies from which it is dislodged only with great difficulty due to the erectile spines on its gill covers

can·dite \'kan,dīt\ *n* -s [*Candy* (now *Kandy*), Ceylon + E *-ite*] **:** a blue spinel

C and LC *abbr* capitals and lower case

¹can·dle \'kandᵊl, -'aa-\ *n* -s *often attrib* [ME *candel*, fr. OE, fr. L *candela*, fr. *candēre* to shine — more at CANDID] **1 :** a long slender cylindrical mass typically of tallow or wax containing a wick of loosely twisted linen or cotton threads made by dipping or by casting in a metal mold and burned to give light **2 :** something that gives light; *specif* **:** a heavenly body ⟨he that can count the ~s of the sky —Richard Linche⟩ **3 :** a medicated candle or pastille used for fumigation **4 a :** an international unit of luminous intensity equal to the luminous intensity of five square millimeters of platinum at its solidification point of 1773.5°C — called also *international candle* **b :** a similar unit equal to one sixtieth of the luminous intensity of one square centimeter of a blackbody surface at the solidification point of platinum **:** a unit about 98.1 percent of a candle (sense 4 a) — called also *candela, new candle* **5 :** FILTER 1b **6 :** a device for emitting thick colored smoke for various military purposes — **by the candle :** with a time limit determined by the burning of a candle

²candle \"\ *vt* **candled; candled; candling** \-d(ᵊ)liŋ\ **candles :** to examine by holding between the eye and a light; *esp* **:** to test (eggs) in this way for staleness, blood clots, fertility, and growth

candle alder *n* **:** SMOOTH ALDER

candle anemone *n* **:** a silky-haired herb (*Anemone cylindrica*) of temperate No. America having divided leaves, white petalless flowers, and cylindrical silky fruits

candlebark \'ˌ==ˌ=\ *or* **candlebark gum** *n* **:** a ribbon gum (*Eucalyptus rubida*)

candlebeam \'==ˌ=\ *n* [ME *candelbem*, fr. *candel* candle + *bem* beam] **1 :** a hanging wooden or metal lighting fixture holding several candles **2 :** a horizontal beam or rail used to hold liturgical or votive candles in old churches

candleberry \'==ˌ==\ *n* **1** *also* **candleberry tree a** [so called fr. the use of the nuts as candles by natives in the So. Pacific] **:** CANDLENUT **b** [so called fr. the wax obtained from its berries, formerly used to make candles] **:** WAX MYRTLE **2 :** the fruit of either the candlenut or the wax myrtle

candleberry bark *n* **:** BAYBERRY BARK

candleberry myrtle *n* **:** WAX MYRTLE

candle board *n* **:** a small shelf or ledge usu. fitted below a table top and used to hold a candlestick

candlebranch \'==ˌ=\ *n* **:** CHANDELIER

candle burner *n* **:** a protective metal tip placed on the wick end of a candle to protect the flame against drafts and to help the candle burn evenly and cleanly

candle cactus *n* **1 :** CANDLEWOOD 1a **2 :** CANE CACTUS

candle coal \-n(d)ᵊl-\ *var of* CANNEL COAL

candle dance *n* **:** a dance that requires manipulation of lighted candles

candlefish \'=dᵊl,fish\ *n* [so called fr. the use of the fish as a candle by Am. Indians] **1 :** a marine fish (*Thaleichthys pacificus*) of the north Pacific coast related to the smelt, highly esteemed as a food fish, and so oily that when dried its body may be equipped with a wick and used as a candle — called also *eulachon* **2 :** SABLEFISH **3** *southern Africa* **:** HALFBEAK

candle fly *n* **:** LANTERN FLY

candle–foot \'=ˌ=\ *n, pl* **candle–feet :** FOOTCANDLE

candle hour *n* **:** a unit of light or luminous energy equal to the total luminous energy emitted in one hour by a source having a luminous intensity of one candle

candle larkspur *n* **:** any of several perennial hybrid larkspurs having tall spikelike racemes of showy flowers and usu. assigned to *Delphinium elatum* but sometimes grouped under the name *D. cultorum*

candlelight \'= =ˌ=\ *n, often attrib* [ME *candel-liht*, fr. OE *candel-lēoht*, fr. *candel* candle + *lēoht* light] **1 a :** the light of a candle or candles ⟨sat by ~ in his study meditating on the eight years that had passed —C.G.Bowers⟩ **b :** any soft artificial light **2** *also* **candlelighting :** the time for lighting up **:** TWILIGHT, DUSK ⟨meet in the courthouse Saturday evening at early ~ —Carl Sandburg⟩

candlelighter \'= =ˌ= =\ *n* [*candle* + *lighter*] **:** an ecclesiastical implement made with a long handle surmounted by a wick on one side and a bell-like candlesnuffer on the other and used for the ceremonial lighting and extinguishing of candles

candlelighter

candlemaker \'= =ˌ= =\ *n* **:** one that performs one or more of the operations in making candles

can·dle·mas \'kandᵊlməs, -'aa- *also* -ˌmas \ *n, pl* **candlemases** *usu cap, often attrib* [ME *candelmasse*, fr. OE *candelmæsse*, fr. *candel* candle + *mæsse* mass, feast; fr. the candles blessed and carried in procession in celebration of the feast — more at MASS] **1 a :** the church feast celebrated on February 2 in commemoration of the presentation of Christ in the temple **b :** this feast commemorating additionally in the Roman Catholic Church the purification of the Virgin Mary **c :** this feast commemorating additionally in the Eastern Orthodox Church the meeting with Simeon and Anna **2** *or* **candlemas day** *usu cap C & D* **:** GROUNDHOG DAY

candlemas term *n, usu cap C* **:** the second of the three terms of the academic year in Scottish universities

candle–meter \'= =ˌ= =\ *n* **:** LUX

candlenut \'==ˌ=\ *n* **1 :** the oily seed of a tropical tree used locally to make candles and commercially as a source of oil — see CANDLENUT OIL **2 :** a large tree (*Aleurites moluccana*) that is probably native to southeast Asia but is now widely distributed in tropical regions, produces candlenuts, and is closely related to the tung — called also *varnish tree*

candlenut oil *n* **:** a drying oil obtained from candlenut seeds and used in paints and soap — called also *kekune oil, kukui oil, lumbang oil*

candlepin \'= =ˌ=\ *n* **1 :** a slender nearly cylindrical bowling pin tapering toward top and bottom **2 candlepins** *pl but sing in constr* **:** a bowling game using candlepins and differing from tenpins in that a smaller ball is used, three balls per frame are bowled, and fallen pins are left on the alley

candle plant *n* **1 :** a southern African succulent plant (*Kleinia articulata*) with white flowers **2 :** MULLEIN 1

candlepower *n* **:** luminous intensity (as of an electric lamp) expressed in candles ⟨a flare which produced 800,000 ~ for six minutes —Stanley Frank⟩ — see CANDLE 4

can·dler \-d(ə)lə(r)\ *n* -s **:** one that candles

candle rent *n, obs* **:** rent derived from houses and consequently liable to diminution through loss or deterioration

candles *pl of* CANDLE, *pres 3d sing of* CANDLE

candle snuff *n* **:** a burnt wick of a candle

candlesnuffer \'= =ˌ= =\ *n* **1 :** an instrument for snuffing candles **2 :** an attendant in charge of the candles (as formerly in a theater)

candlestand \'= =ˌ=\ *n* **1 :** an iron tripod fitted with candlesticks **2 :** a small wooden stand or table

candlestick \'= =ˌ=\ *n* [ME *candlestikke*, fr. OE *candelsticca*, fr. *candel* candle + *sticca* stick — more at STICK] **:** a plain or ornate utensil with a spike or socket for holding a candle

candlestick lily *n* [prob. so called fr. its erect flower clusters] **:** a Siberian herb (*Lilium dauricum*) with terminal clusters of spotted red flowers

candlestick tulip *n* **:** LADY TULIP

candle tree *n* **1 :** WAX MYRTLE **2 :** a tree (*Parmentiera cerifera*) of Panama having a long yellow candlelike pod **3 :** a catalpa (*Catalpa bignonioides*) that has a long slender pod

candlewaster *n, obs* **:** one that consumes candles by late study

candlewick \'= =ˌ=\ *n* **1 :** the wick of a candle **2 :** CATTAIL **3** [so called fr. the downy leaves and stalks, formerly used for making candlewicks] **:** MULLEIN **4** *or* **can·dle·wick·ing** \-iŋ\ **a :** a soft cotton yarn of loosely twisted threads used for embroidery **b :** embroidery made with this yarn usu. in tufts or French knots and often on unbleached muslin in making bedspreads

candlestand

candlewood \'= =ˌ=\ *n* [so called fr. its use for illumination] **1 :** any of several trees or shrubs chiefly of resinous character: as **a :** a plant of the genus *Fouquieria*; *esp* **:** OCOTILLO 1 **b :** a torchwood (*Amyris balsamifera*) **c :** a So. American tree (*Diporidium guianense*) **d :** a So. American shrub (*Panax capitatum*) **e :** a West Indian tree (*Dacryodes excelsa*) of the family Burseraceae yielding a fine lustrous brown wood **2 :** slivers and fine pieces of resinous wood burned for light

candlewood pine *n* **:** OCOTE

candling *pres part of* CANDLE

can·dock \'kan,däk\ *n* -s [³*can* + *dock* (plant); fr. its dock-like leaves and flagon-shaped capsules] **:** any of several water lilies: as **a :** a yellow-flowered European water lily (*Nuphar luteum*) **b :** the common white-flowered European water lily (*Nymphaea alba*) **c :** SPATTERDOCK 1 **d :** WATER CHINQUAPIN

¹can·dol·lea \kan'dälēə, -'ō-\ [NL, fr. Augustin Pyrame de *Candolle* †1841 Swiss botanist + L *-a* (fem. nom. sing. adj. ending)] *syn of* STYLIDIUM

²candollea *n* -s [NL] **:** a plant of the genus *Stylidium*

can·dol·le·a·ce·ae \(ˌ)=ˌ=ē'āsē,ē\ [NL, fr. *Candollea*, type genus + *-aceae*] *syn of* STYLIDIACEAE

can·dol·le·a·ceous \ˌ=ˌ= =ˌ'ā-shəs, =ˌ= =ˌ'ā-\ *adj* [NL *Candolleaceae* + E *-ous*] **:** of, relating to, or like the Stylidiaceae

can·dom·blé \ˌkan,dōm'blā\ *n* -s [Pg] **:** a Brazilian Negro matriarchal fetish cult combining African, Indian, and Roman Catholic elements; *specif* **:** the ceremony or dance connected with this cult

can·dor \'kandə(r), -'aa- *also* -ˌdȯr *or* -ˌdȯ(ə)\ *n* -s *see -or in Explan Notes* [F & L; F *candeur*, fr. L *candor*, fr. *candēre* to shine, be white — more at CANDID] **1 a :** WHITENESS, BRILLIANCE ⟨the sun poured with a more golden ~ —Christopher Morley⟩ **b** *obs* **:** unstained purity and innocence ⟨a young prince of valor and ~⟩ **2 :** disposition to open-mindedness **:** freedom from bias, prejudice, and malice **:** FAIRNESS, IMPARTIALITY ⟨a heavy accusation . . . from a gentleman of your talents, liberality, and ~ —Noah Webster⟩ **3** *archaic* **:** KINDLINESS ⟨~ in pardoning errors⟩ **4 :** unreserved, honest, or sincere expression **:** FRANKNESS, CANDIDNESS ⟨the ~ with which he acknowledged a weakness in his own case —Aldous Huxley⟩ ⟨~ and courtesy, the desire to please and perfect openness, are mutually inimical —W.C.Brownell⟩

cands *pl of* CAND

C and SC *abbr* capital and small capitals

¹can·dy \'kandē, -'aa-, -di *also* -'ai-\ *n* -ES *often attrib* [short for *sugar candy*, fr. ME *sugre candy*, part trans. of MF *sucre candi*, part trans. of OIt *zucchero candi*, fr. *zucchero* sugar + Ar *qandī* candied, fr. *qand* cane sugar, prob. of Dravidian origin (whence Skt *khaṇḍaka* candy); akin to Tamil *kaṇṭu* candy, *kaṭṭu* to harden, condense] **1 a :** crystallized sugar formed by boiling down sugar syrup **b :** a confection of crystallized sugar **c :** the density at which boiling syrup will form candy ⟨boil to a ~⟩ **2 a :** a food made of a sugar paste or syrup often enriched and varied with coloring and flavoring (as chocolate) and filling (as fruits or nuts) and shaped into various attractive forms **b :** a piece of this food **3 a :** doughy bee food of sugar and honey **:** boiled sugar prepared as food for bees

²candy \"\ *vb* -ED/ -ING/ -ES [perh. fr. It *candire*, back-formation fr. *candito* (in *zucchero candito*), alter. of *candi* (in *zucchero candi*)] *vt* **1 :** to encrust in or coat with sugar often by cooking down in a heavy syrup ⟨ ~ fruits⟩ **:** saturate with syrup **:** coat with sugar by rolling or pressing ⟨~ dates⟩ **2 :** to make seem pleasant and attractive **:** SUGAR, SWEETEN ⟨~*ing* up the duke's reputation⟩ **3 :** to crystallize into sugar, candy, or a candy-like substance ⟨excessive boiling *candies* jelly⟩ **~** *vi* **:** to become coated or encrusted with sugar crystals **:** become crystallized into sugar

³candy \"\ *n* -ES [Marathi *khaṇḍī* & Tamil-Malayalam *kaṇṭi*, prob. fr Skt *khaṇḍa* piece, portion, prob. of Proto-Munda origin, akin to Santali *guṇḍa* pieces, small parts] **:** any of various units of weight used in India, Burma, and Ceylon usu. equal to between 500 and 600 pounds

candy grass *n* [so called fr. its sweet secretion] **:** MOLASSES GRASS

candy kitchen *n* **:** an establishment for making and selling candy at retail

candymaker \'= =ˌ= =\ *n* **:** one that makes candy **:** CONFECTIONER

candy pink *n* **:** a deep yellowish pink that is yellower and paler than tigerlily

candy pull *n also* **candy pulling :** a party at which taffy or molasses candy is made

can·dys \'kandəs\ *n* -ES [Gk *kandys*] **:** a long loose wide-sleeved woolen outer gown worn by the Medes and Persians

candy stripe *n* [so called fr. the similarity of the design to that of some stick candy] **:** a design consisting usu. of bright-colored stripes of one color against a plain background esp. in textiles ⟨his shirts . . . were silk with *candy stripes* —Joseph Mitchell⟩ — **can·dy-striped** \'=ˌ=ˈstrīpt\ *adj*

can·dy·tuft \'= =ˌtəft\ *n* [obs. *Candy* (now *Candia*) Crete, Greek island + E *tuft*] **:** a cultivated plant of the genus *Iberis* (as the perennial *I. sempervirens* and the annuals *I. amara* and *I. umbellata*)

candyweed \'= =ˌ=\ *n* [¹*candy* + *weed*] **:** ORANGE MILKWORT

¹cane \'kān\ *n, pl* **canes** *or* **cane** *often attrib* [ME, fr. MF, fr. OProv *cana*, fr. L *canna*, fr. Gk *kanna*, of Sem origin; akin to Ar *qanāh* hollow stick, reed, Heb *qāneh*, Assyr *qanū*] **1 :** a hollow or pithy jointed stem that is usu. slender and more or less flexible **2** *obs* **:** PIPE, TUBE; *esp* **:** a slender glass tube **3 a :** a slender jointed stem used as a walking stick **b :** a short staff used as an aid in walking **:** WALKING STICK **c :** a rod or stick used for flogging **4 :** a slender rod or cylinder (as of solid glass or sulfur) **5 a :** RATTAN; *esp* **:** split rattan used in chair seats and wicker articles **b** (1) **:** the stem of any one of various bamboolike grasses esp. of the genus *Arundinaria* (2)**:** any plant of this genus **c** (1) **:** SUGARCANE (2) **:** the stems of sugarcane **d :** SORGHUM; *esp* **:** SORGO **6 :** one of the stems of certain plants; *esp* **:** a shoot directly from the base (as in the raspberry, grape, or rose) **7 :** a warp in handweaving

²cane \"\ *vt* -ED/ -ING/ -S **1 :** to punish by whacking or beating with a cane ⟨he sat in a professor's chair and *caned* sophomores for blowing spitballs —H.L.Mencken⟩ **2 :** to weave or furnish with cane (as seats or backs of chairs)

³cane \"\ *n* -s [origin unknown] *Brit* **:** WEASEL; *esp* **:** a small female weasel

cane apple \'kā,napəl\ *n* [modif. of IrGael *caithne* strawberry tree + E *apple*] **:** a strawberry tree (*Arbutus unedo*)

cane ash *n* [¹*cane* + *ash* (tree); perh. fr. its use in making walking sticks] **:** WHITE ASH 1a

cane blight *n* **:** a disease affecting the canes of various bush fruits (as currants, where it is caused by the fungus *Botryosphaeria ribis*, and raspberries, where it is caused by the fungus *Leptosphaeria coniothyrium*)

cane borer *n* **:** any of various insects having larvae that bore into the pith and destroy the stalks of certain plants — see RASPBERRY CANE BORER, SUGARCANE BORER

cane·brake *also* **cane·break** \'kān,brāk\ *n* -s [¹*cane* + *brake* or *break* (thicket)] **:** a thicket of canes; *esp* **:** a dense growth of the giant cane

canebrake rattler *or* **canebrake rattlesnake** *n* **:** a rattlesnake that is a southern variety (*Crotalus horridus atricaudatus*) of the American timber rattlesnake

cane cactus *n* **:** any of several cylindrical-stemmed cacti of the genus *Opuntia*

cane chair *n* **:** a chair having cane in the seat or back

canecutter \'=ˌ= =\ *n, South* **:** SWAMP RABBIT

cane–cutter's cramp *n* **:** HEAT CRAMPS

cane fruit *n* **:** a fruit (as the blackberry) growing on canes

cane grass *n* **:** any of several grasses; *esp* **:** an Australian grass (*Glyceria ramigera*) having wax-coated stems and used for thatching and making chair seats

cane killer *n* **:** an annual plant (*Melasma melampyroides*, family Scrophulariaceae) that is parasitic on sugar-cane roots

cane knife *n* **:** a heavy wide-bladed hooked knife used for cutting sugarcane

canel *var of* CANNEL

ca·nel·la \kə'nelə\ *n* [ML, dim. of L *canna* reed; fr. the shape of the rolls of prepared bark — more at CANE] **1** *also* **canela** -s **:** CINNAMON **2** *cap* [NL, fr. ML, cinnamon] **:** a monotypic genus of trees (order Parietales) having alternate simple entire leathery gland-dotted leaves and flowers with three sepals and producing a berry **3** *or* **canella al·ba** \-'albə *also* -'ȯ-\ *or* **canella bark** *also* **ca·ne·lo** \-'ne(ˌ)lō, -'ā-\ -s [*canella* fr. NL *canella; canella alba* fr. NL *Canella alba*, syn. of *Canella winterana; canelo* fr. AmerSp, fr. Sp, cinnamon tree, fr. *canela* cinnamon, fr. ML *canella*] **:** the highly aromatic orange-colored inner bark of a tree (*Canella alba* or *C. winterana*) used as a condiment and in medicine as a tonic — called also *white cinnamon* **4** *also* **ca·nela** \-'nelə, -'ā-\ *or* **canelo** -s [*canella* fr. NL *canella; canela* fr. AmerSp, fr. Sp, cinnamon; *canelo*, fr. AmerSp, fr. Sp, cinnamon tree] **:** any of various trees of the family Lauraceae

¹ca·ne·lo \kə'ne(ˌ)lō, -'ā-\ *n, pl* **canelo** *or* **canelos** *usu cap* [Sp, of American Indian origin] **1 :** a Quechua-speaking Indian people of central Ecuador **2 :** a member of the Canelo people

²canelo *var of* CANELLA

can·e·phore \'kanə,fō(ə)r, -ȯ(ə)r *also* **can·e·phor** \-ȯ(ə)r\ *or* **ca·neph·o·ra** \kə'nefərə\ *or* **ca·neph·o·ros** \=ˈ=ərəs, -ˌräs\ *or* **ca·neph·o·rus** \=ˈ=ərəs\ *n, pl* **can·e·phores** \'= =ˌ=\ *also* **ca·neph·o·rae** \=ˈ= =ˌrē, -ˌrī\ *or* **ca·neph·o·ri** \=ˈ= =ˌrī, -ˌrē\ [L *canephoros, canephora*, fr. Gk *kanēphoros*, fr. *kaneon* reed basket (fr. *kanna* reed) + *-phoros* -phorous — more at CANE] **1 :** a maiden bearing a basket on her head in an early Greek religious festival **2 :** a caryatid supporting a basket-like member that serves as a capital

ca·ne·pin \'kanəpən, *F* kȧnpaⁿ\ *n, pl* **canepins** \-pənz, -paⁿ\ [F] **:** a fine leather made from the skins of kids, lambs, and chamois

can·er \'kānə(r)\ *n* -s **:** one that weaves cane seats and backs of chairs

cane rat *n* [so called fr. its feeding on sugarcane] **1 :** a large ratlike African rodent (*Thryonomys swinderianus* or related species) that is related to the porcupine — called also *ground pig* **2 :** HUTIA

cane rust *n* **1 :** any of several diseases of the stems of blackberries and raspberries (as orange rust) **2 :** a disease of roses caused by a rust (*Earlea speciosa*)

canes *pl of* CANE, *pres 3d sing of* CANE

ca·nes·cent \kə'nesᵊnt\ *adj* [L *canescent-, canescens*, pres. part. of *canescere*, incho. of *canēre* to be gray, be white, fr. *canus* white, hoary — more at HARE] **1 :** growing white, whitish, or hoary ⟨the ~ moon⟩ **2** *bot* **:** having a fine grayish white pubescence **:** HOARY, GLAUCOUS

cane sugar *n* **:** sucrose from sugar cane

cane trash *n* **:** refuse of sugar cane **:** BAGASSE

caneware \'=ˌ=\ *n* -s [so called fr. its color] **:** a buff or yellowish stoneware developed by Wedgwood

canework \'=ˌ=\ *n* -s **:** interwoven split cane used for the seats and backs of chairs

can·field \'kan,fēld\ *n* -s *usu cap* [after Richard A. *Canfield* †1914 Am. gambling-house proprietor] **1 :** KLONDIKE 2 **2 :** a form of solitaire in which the player deals a reserve pile of 13 cards, lays out 4 face-up cards as a tableau, and turns up the remaining cards one or three at a time, the object being to build additional piles of each suit in ascending sequence

can·field·ite \'kan,fēl,dīt\ *n* -s [F.A. *Canfield* †1926 Am. mining engineer, + E *-ite*] **:** a mineral Ag_8SnS_6 consisting of silver thiostannate isomorphous with the germanium mineral argyrodite that occurs in black metallic octahedrons (sp.gr. 6.28)

can frame *n* **:** a machine used in spinning for forming the rove and delivering it into cans

can·ful \'=ˌfu̇l\ *n, pl* **can·fuls** *also* **cans·ful :** the quantity a can holds

can·gia \'kanj(ē)ə\ *n* -s [It & Ar; It *cangia*, fr. Ar *qanjah*] **:** a long light sailboat used on the Nile

can·gle \'kaŋgəl\ *vi* -ED/ -ING/ -S [perh. alter. of *jangle*] *chiefly Scot* **:** WRANGLE

¹cangue *also* **cang** \'kaŋ, -'ai-\ *n* -s [F *cangue*, fr. Pg *canga* yoke, perh. of Celt origin; akin to OIr *camm* crooked — more at CHANGE] **:** a wooden collar three or four feet square used in Oriental countries for confining the neck and sometimes also the hands for punishment

cangue

²cangue \"\ *vt* -ED/ -ING/ -S **:** to compel to wear a cangue

can hook *n* [prob. fr. ²*can* "barrel"] **:** a device that consists of a short rope or jointed bar with flat hooks at each end and that is used for hoisting casks or barrels by the ends of the staves

ca·ni·cha·na \ˌkānē'chānə\ *n, pl* **canichana** *or* **canichanas** *usu cap* [Sp, of American Indian origin] **1 :** an Indian people of northern Bolivia **2 :** a member of the Canichana people

ca·nic·o·la fever \kə'nikələ-\ *n* [NL *canicola* (specific epithet of *Leptospira canicola*), fr. L *canis* dog + NL *-cola* inhabitant (fem. of *-colus* -colous) — more at HOUND, -COLOUS] **:** an acute febrile disease in man and dogs characterized by gastroenteritis and mild jaundice and caused by a spirochete (*Leptospira canicola*) — compare STUTTGART DISEASE

ca·nic·u·lar \kə'nikyələ(r)\ *adj* [ME, fr. LL *canicularis*, fr. *canicula* Sirius, lit., small bitch, dim. of *canis* dog — more at HOUND] **1 :** immediately preceding and following the heliacal rising of the Dog Star ⟨the days ~ —Edith Sitwell⟩ **2 :** of or relating to the dog days ⟨the ~ heat of the Deep South⟩

can·i·cule \'kanə̇,kyül\ *n* -s [F, dog days, Sirius, fr. L *canicula* Sirius] **:** DOG DAYS ⟨the ~ of 1825⟩

can·id \'kanə̇d, -'ā-\ *n* -s [NL *Canidae*] **:** a member of the family Canidae

can·i·dae \'kanə̇,dē\ *n pl, cap* [NL, fr. *Canis*, type genus + *-idae*] **:** a cosmopolitan family comprising digitigrade carnivorous mammals (superfamily Arctoidea) that in many respects resemble members of the Felidae but that have in general longer coarser fur, comparatively long limbs with strong nonretractile claws, head rounded to elongated with well-developed often somewhat pointed muzzle and jaws, ears erect or drooping, and eyes with rounded pupils and that are commonly more diurnal and social in habits, often hunting in packs, running down rather than stalking their prey and taking it with their jaws rather than claws, and including the dogs, wolves, jackals, foxes, and extinct related animals

canier *comparative of* CANY

caniest *superlative of* CANY

canikin *var of* CANNIKIN

¹ca·nine \'kā,nīn *also* -'a-\ *adj* [L *caninus*, fr. *canis* dog + *-inus* -ine — more at HOUND] **1 :** of or relating to dogs or to the family Canidae ⟨the most graceful of the ~ race⟩ **2 :** resembling that of a dog ⟨she had followed him with a kind of ~ devotion through his senior year —Robert Carson⟩

²canine \"\ *n* -s **1** *also* **canine tooth :** a conical pointed tooth: **a :** such a tooth situated between the lateral incisor

and the first premolar on each side of each jaw in man and many mammals — see DENTITION illustration **b :** one of the conical teeth in the front part of the jaw in some fishes **2 a :** DOG **b :** a member of the family Canidae
canine chorea *n* **:** chorea in dogs that is believed to be caused by a virus
canine eminence *n* **:** a prominence on the surface of the superior maxillary bone caused by the socket of the canine tooth
canine fossa *n* **:** a depression external to and somewhat above the canine eminence
canine hysteria *n* **:** an epileptic condition of dogs usu. considered due to toxic elements in the food in which the affected dog may suddenly run or bark senselessly, hide without cause, or undergo spasms or convulsions — called also *fright disease, running fits*
canine letter *n* **:** DOG'S LETTER
canine madness *n* **:** RABIES
canine muscle *n* **:** CANINUS
canine typhus *n* **:** CANICOLA FEVER
caning *pres part of* CANE
ca·ni·ni·form \(ˈ)kā¦nīnə,fȯrm, -¦nin-, kəˈn-\ *adj* [²*canine* (tooth) + *-iform*] **:** having the form of a typical canine tooth
ca·nin·i·ty \kāˈninəd·ē, kə-\ *n* -ES [*canine* + *-ity*] **1 :** canine quality or nature ⟨only now did Nip emerge into his full ~ —Israel Zangwill⟩ **2 :** the canine race ⟨a lover of ~⟩
ca·ni·nus \kāˈnīnəs, kə-\ *n, pl* **cani·ni** \-ī,nī\ [NL, fr. L, adj., canine] **:** a muscle that elevates the corner of the mouth
can·ions \ˈkanyənz\ *n pl* [Sp *cañones*, pl. of *cañón*, lit., tube, pipe, fr. *caña* reed, fr. L *canna* — more at CANE] **:** close-fitting usu. ornamental kneepieces joining the upper and lower parts of the leg covering and worn by men esp. in Elizabethan and Jacobean England
ca·nis \ˈkānəs, -ˈa-,-ˈä-\ *n, cap* [NL, fr. L, dog — more at HOUND] **:** the chief and type genus of the dog family including the domestic dogs, the wolves and jackals, and sometimes in older classifications the foxes
can·is·tel \¦kanə¦stel\ *n* -S [AmerSp *canistel, canisté*] **:** the ovoid orange-yellow mealy sweet fruit of a tropical tree (*Pouteria campechiana* var. *nervosa*) of Florida and the West Indies — called also *eggfruit*
can·is·ter *also* **can·nis·ter** \ˈkanəstə(r)\ *n* -S [L *canistrum* basket, fr. Gk *kanastron*, fr. *kanna* reed — more at CANE] **1** *archaic* **:** a small basket for holding bread, fruit, or flowers **2 a :** a cylindrical or rectangular container usu. of lightweight metal, plastic, or laminated pasteboard used for holding a dry product (as tea, crackers, flour, matches) **b :** any of various cylindrical metal receptacles usu. with a removable close-fitting top **3 a :** encased shot for close-range artillery fire consisting of a large number of balls in a light cylindrical case fitting the gun's bore and bursting by the force of the firing charge **b :** a metal drum or cylindrical barrel ⟨~s of TNT dropped by a destroyer⟩ **4 :** a light perforated metal box that contains material to adsorb, filter, or detoxify poisons and irritants in the air and is used with gas masks — see GAS MASK illustration

canisters 2a

²**canister** \"\ *vt* -ED/-ING/-S **:** to place or enclose in a canister
ca·ni·ti·es \kəˈnishē,ēz, -ishēz\ *n, pl* **canities** \"\ [L, fr. *canus* white, hoary — more at HARE] **:** grayness or whiteness of the hair
can·i·tist \ˈkanətəst\ *n* -S [*canities* + *-ist*] **:** one who dyes or tints hair esp. in a beauty shop
¹**can·ker** \ˈkaŋkə(r), -ˈai-\ *n* -S [ME *canker, cancre*, fr. ONF *cancre* & OE *cancer*, fr. L *cancer* crab, cancer — more at CANCER] **1** *obs* **:** a spreading sore that corrupts and eats away body tissues **:** GANGRENE **2** *archaic* **:** a caterpillar destructive of buds and leaves of plants **3** *now dial* **a :** RUST **b :** VERDIGRIS 3 **4 a :** an area of necrotic tissue in a woody stem or sometimes other plant organ caused by various agents (as fungi, bacteria, or toxic substances) and marked by shrinkage, cracking, and sloughing of tissue that leave an open wound surrounded by zones of callus often girdling and killing the affected stem **b :** POWDERY SCAB **c :** POTATO WART **5 :** a center and source of spreading corruption, debasement, or enfeeblement ⟨the metropolis was the ~ of a continent and the wickedest city since Gomorrah —Herbert Asbury⟩ **6** *now dial* **:** DOG ROSE **7 a :** an obstinate chronic inflammation of the ear in dogs, cats, or rabbits; *esp* **:** a localized form of mange **b :** a chronic and progressive inflammation of the deep horn-producing tissues of the frog and sole of the hoofs of horses resulting in softening and destruction of the horny layers **c :** FOWL POX **d :** pigeon trichomoniasis
²**canker** \"\ *vb* **cankered; cankered; cankering** \-k(ə)riŋ\ **cankers** *vt* **1** *obs* **:** to infect with a spreading sore **2** *now dial* **:** to corrode with rust **3 :** to corrupt with a malignancy of mind or spirit ⟨God help that country, ~*ed* deep by doubt —Archibald MacLeish⟩ ⟨~*ed* by a persecution complex⟩ ~ *vi* **1** *obs* **:** to become rusty **2 :** to become infested with canker ⟨blighted stems often ~⟩ **3 :** to undergo corruption and disintegration
cankerberry \ˈ==,=\ *n* **1 :** the fruit of the dog rose **2 a :** the red berry of a West Indian soft prickly herb (*Solanum bahamense*) **b :** the West Indian herb bearing the cankerberry
cankered *adj* **1 a :** affected with canker **b :** eaten by a cankerworm **2 :** debased by slow moral corruption **3 :** cantankerous from deep-seated bitterness **:** malicious from ill temper **:** CRABBED, SPITEFUL — **can·kered·ly** \-kə(r)dlē\ *adv* — **can·kered·ness** *n* -ES
canker lettuce *n* [prob. so called fr. a belief that it cures canker] **:** FALSE WINTERGREEN
can·ker·ous \ˈkaŋk(ə)rəs, -ˈai-\ *adj* **1 a** *obs* **:** having the effect of a spreading sore **b :** eating into and corrupting the flesh **2 :** that spreads corruption of mind or spirit ⟨his firmness of mind soon relapsed into a ~ intolerance —Maurice Cranston⟩ **3 :** affected with or caused by canker ⟨a ~ stem disease⟩
cankerroot \ˈ==,=\ *n* [so called fr. the use of the roots in folk medicine as a cure for canker] **:** any of several plants with astringent roots: as **a :** SEA LAVENDER 1 **b :** GOLDTHREAD 1
canker rose *n* **1 :** DOG ROSE **2 :** CORN POPPY
cankers *pl of* CANKER, *pres 3d sing of* CANKER
canker sore *n* **:** a mouth sore of unknown cause that develops as one or more vesicles which rupture and leave a small ulcer
canker stain *n* **:** a disease of plane trees caused by a fungus (*Endoconidiophora fimbriata platani*) and marked by bluish black or reddish brown discoloration which forms a radial pattern beneath elongate blackened cankers on the trunk and less frequently on the branches
cankerweed \ˈ==,=\ *n* **1 :** TANSY RAGWORT **2 :** RATTLESNAKE ROOT a
cankerworm \ˈ==,=\ *n* **:** any of various insect larvae that injure plants esp. by feeding on buds and foliage — see FALL CANKERWORM, SPRING CANKERWORM
can·ker·wort \ˈ==,wərt, -,ȯ-\ *n* **:** DANDELION 1
can·kery \ˈkaŋk(ə)rē, -ˈai-\ *adj* **1 :** affected with canker ⟨a ~ root⟩ **2** *dial* **:** RUSTY **3** *Scot* **:** CRABBED, ILL-NATURED
cann \ˈkan, -aa(ə)n\ *n* -S [ME — more at CAN (vessel)] **:** a drinking cup; *esp* **:** a bulbous mug
¹**can·na** \ˈkanə\ *n* [NL, fr. L, reed — more at CANE] **1** *cap* **:** a genus (coextensive with the family Cannaceae of the order Musales) of tropical perennial herbs having simple stems, large alternate broad entire leaves, and a terminal spike or spikelike cluster of very irregular flowers with the four staminodia forming the enlarged and colored portion **2** -S **:** any plant of the genus *Canna* including many hybrid cultivated forms — see INDIAN SHOT **3** -S **:** ANTIQUE RED
²**can·na** \ˈkänə\ *dial Brit var of* CANNOT
can·nab·ic \kəˈnabik, kaˈ-\ *adj* [L *cannabis* + E *-ic*] **:** of, relating to, or derived from hemp
can·na·bi·di·ol \¦kanəbəˈdī,ōl, -,ȯl\ *n* -S [NL *Cannabis* (genus name of *Cannabis sativa*) + E *-diol*] **:** a crystalline diphenol $C_{21}H_{28}(OH)_2$ that is obtained from the resin of the hemp plant and is physiologically inactive but is rearranged by acids into tetrahydro-cannabinol which has a high marihuana activity
can·na·bin \ˈkanəbən\ *n* -S [L *cannabis* + E *-in*] **:** a greenish black resin that is extracted from the dried leaves and flowering tops of the pistillate hemp plants and contains the physiologically active principles of cannabis — compare CHARAS
can·na·bi·nol \ˈkanəbə,nōl, kəˈnab-, -ōl\ *n* -S [*cannabin* + *-ol*] **:** a crystalline phenol $C_{21}H_{25}O(OH)$ that is obtained from the resin of the hemp plant and is physiologically inactive
can·na·bis \ˈkanəbəs\ *n* [NL, fr. L, hemp, fr. Gk *kannabis* — more at HEMP] **1** *cap* **:** a genus of tall rough annual herbs (family Moraceae) having erect stems, leaves with three to seven elongate leaflets, and pistillate flowers in spikes along the leafy stems — see HEMP **2** -ES **:** the dried flowering spikes of the pistillate plants of the hemp — compare GANJA, HASHISH, MARIHUANA
cannabis in·di·ca \-bəˈsindikə\ *n, pl* **cannabes indicae** \-,bēˈzində,sē, -,bāˈsində,kī\ [NL, Indian hemp] **:** a variety of cannabis (sense 2) obtained in India — used esp. in pharmacy
can·na·bism \ˈkanə,bizəm\ *n* -S [*Cannabis* + *-ism*] **1 :** narcotic habituation to cannabis **2 :** chronic poisoning from excessive smoking or chewing of cannabis
can·na·ble \ˈkanəbəl, -ˈaa-\ *adj* **:** suitable for canning
can·na·ceous \(ˈ)ka¦nāshəs\ *adj* [NL *Cannaceae*, monotypic family containing the genus *Canna* (fr. *Canna* + *-aceae*) + E *-ous*] **:** of or relating to the genus *Canna*
cannach *n* -S [ScGael *canach*; akin to MIr *canach* sedge] *Scot* **:** COTTON GRASS
canna–down \ˈ==,=\ *n* -S [so called fr. the soft bristles of the perianth] **:** either of two sedges (*Eriophorum vaginatum* and *E. callitrix*) of temperate regions
canned *adj* **1 :** sealed in cans usu. after sterilization and esp. for commerce ⟨~ peaches⟩ **2 :** transcribed (as on a phonograph record or magnetic tape) for reproduction esp. over a radio or television system ⟨his major points were that live TV had spontaneity and topicality that ~ shows did not have —F.N. Karmatz⟩ **3 a :** prepared in identical form for wide or repeated use **:** SYNDICATED ⟨~ editorials for country newspapers⟩ **b :** having a stereotyped cast **:** HACKNEYED, CUT-AND-DRIED ⟨the salesman's ~ phrases⟩ **4** *slang* **:** DRUNK
canned heat *n* **:** a fuel (as solidified alcohol) furnished in small containers for use esp. with chafing dishes and portable stoves
¹**cannel** *or* **canel** *n* -S [ME *canel*, fr. OF *canele*, fr. ML *canella* — more at CANELLA] *obs* **:** CINNAMON
²**cannel** *n* -S [ME *canel* channel, gutter, fr. ONF *canel* channel, fr. L *canalis* — more at CANAL] *obs* **:** a gutter in a road
³**cannel** *var of* CANNEL COAL
cannel bone *n* [ME *canel-bon*, fr. *canel* neck, channel + *bon* bone] *obs* **:** CLAVICLE
can·nel coal *also* **cannel** \ˈkanᵊl\ *or* **candle coal** \ˈka(a)n-(d)ᵊl-\ *n* -S [prob. fr. E dial. *cannel* candle, fr. ME *candel* — more at CANDLE] **:** a bituminous coal of fine texture and little luster containing much volatile matter and burning with a bright flame
can·nel·lat·ed *or* **can·ne·lat·ed** \ˈkanᵊl,ād·əd\ *adj* [modif. (influenced by E *-ated*, as in past participles of verbs in *-ate*) of F *cannelé*, fr. *cannelé*, past part. of *canneler* to flute, fr. MF, irreg. fr. *cannelature*] **:** FLUTED
can·nel·oid \ˈkanᵊl,ȯid\ *adj* [*cannel* + *-oid*] **:** resembling cannel coal
can·ne·lon \ˈkanᵊl,än\ *n* -S [prob. fr. It *cannellone* tubular noodle for soup, aug. of *cannello* segment of a stalk of cane, small tube, fr. *canna* cane, reed, fr. L — more at CANE] **1 :** a hollow roll or cone of baked puff paste usu. stuffed with a savory filling as an appetizer or with cream as a dessert **2 :** a roll of highly seasoned minced meat baked or fried
can·nel·lo·ni \,kanᵊlˈōnē\ *n pl* [It, pl. of *cannellone*] **:** CANNELONS
can·ne·lure \ˈkanᵊl,(y)u̇(ə)r\ *or* **chan·ne·lure** \ˈcha-\ *n* -S [F *cannelure*, alter. of MF *cannelature*, fr. OIt *cannellatura*, prob. fr. *cannella* small tube, cinnamon, fr. ML *canella* — more at CANELLA] **1 :** a groove running lengthwise on the surface of a cylinder or column **2 a :** a groove around the cylinder of an elongated bullet for small arms to contain a lubricant **b :** a groove around a bullet into which the edge of the cartridge case is crimped **c :** a groove around the rotating band of a gun projectile to lessen the resistance offered to the rifling **d :** a groove around the base of a cartridge where the extractor takes hold
can·ner \ˈkanə(r), -ˈaa-\ *n* -S **1 :** one engaged in or making a business of canning food **2 :** an animal (as a steer) whose meat is fit only for canned products **3 :** a vessel for holding cans or jars of food in the process of canning; *specif* **:** PRESSURE COOKER
can·nery \ˈkan(ə)rē, -ˈaa-, -i\ *n* -ES **:** a factory or other place for the canning of foods
can·nery·man \-,man,-,mən,-,maa(ə)n\ *n, pl* **cannerymen :** a worker in or owner of a cannery
can·ne·tille \¦kanə¦tē(l), *F* kántēy\ *n* -S [F, fr. It *cannutiglia, canutiglia*, fr. Sp *cañutillo*, lit., small tube, dim. of *cañuto* tube, pipe, fr. Ar dial. (Spain) *qannūt*, fr. (assumed) VL *cannutus*, fr. L *canna* cane — more at CANE] **:** a fine gold or silver thread twisted spirally that is used in embroidery and often made into lace for vestments or into military braid
can·ni·bal \ˈkanəbəl\ *n* -S *often attrib* [NL *canibalis* Carib, fr. Sp *canibal, caribal*, fr. 15th cent. Arawakan *caniba, carib* (forms recorded by Columbus in Cuba and Haiti respectively), of Cariban origin; akin to Carib *calina, calinago, galibi* Caribs, lit., strong men, brave men] **1 :** a human being that eats human flesh — called also *anthropophagite* **2 :** an animal that devours its own kind **3 :** one that cannibalizes machines for replacement parts
can·ni·bal·ic \¦==ˈbalik\ *adj* **1 :** rapaciously savage **:** CRUEL, SANGUINARY **2 :** like that of a cannibal **3 :** marked by barbarity traditionally suggestive of cannibals
can·ni·bal·ism \ˈkanəbə,lizəm\ *n* -S **1 :** the eating of human flesh by a human being seldom done for nutritional purposes but among cannibals done in conjunction with religious or sacramental rites and usu. including the eating of certain organs believed to be the seat of desired virtues or powers — compare ENDOCANNIBALISM **2 a :** the eating of the flesh or the eggs of any animal by its own kind **b :** the eating of human flesh by a lower animal **3 :** the pecking and tearing of the live flesh of its own members in a domestic poultry flock — compare PECK ORDER **4 :** the act or practice of weakening or destroying a competitor or rival ⟨threatened only from time to time by the incursions of political or economic ~ —Paul Schrecker⟩ **5 :** CANNIBALIZATION **6 :** oral sadism
can·ni·bal·is·tic \¦kanəbə¦listik, -ēk\ *adj* **1 :** addicted or inclined to cannibalism among humans or animals ⟨an inherent ~ tendency in poultry⟩ **2 a :** analogous with or suggestive of the voracity of cannibalism ⟨~ impulses attendant on teething⟩ ⟨a mother's ~ fixation on a son⟩ **b :** derived from or akin to cannibalism ⟨the ~ principle of an acquisitive society⟩ **3 :** given to or exhibiting cannibalism among associates in civilized society ⟨a school of ~ novelists⟩ ⟨a view of business as ~⟩ ⟨a chronic and ~ appetite for personalities —Aldous Huxley⟩ **4 :** performed or involved in the process of cannibalization **5 :** orally sadistic **:** ORAL
can·ni·bal·is·ti·cal·ly \-tək(ə)lē, -tēk-, -i\ *adv* **:** in a cannibalistic manner **:** toward, in, or through the practice of cannibalism
can·ni·bal·i·ty \,kanəˈbaləd·ē\ *n* -ES **:** CANNIBALISM; *esp* **:** ANTHROPOPHAGY
can·ni·bal·i·za·tion \,kanəbələˈzāshən, -,līˈz-\ *n* -S **:** the action of cannibalizing an operating unit or enterprise
can·ni·bal·ize \ˈkanəbə,līz\ *vb* -ED/-ING/-S *vt* **1 :** to eat the flesh of (a live animal) **2 a :** to dismantle (as a new or usable airplane, vehicle, or other machine) for parts to be used as replacements in other machines of the same make **b :** to strip (a disabled or outmoded machine) of salvageable parts for repair or for assembling into a serviceable machine **c :** to deprive or strip (a combat group) of manpower or equipment for reinforcing or building up the striking power of another group **3 :** to deprive or strip of integral parts or essential tools, equipment, or personnel for rehabilitating or strengthening another facility or enterprise of the same kind ⟨war plants *cannibalized* by peacetime buyers⟩ ~ *vi* **1 :** to practice cannibalism **2 :** to cannibalize one operating unit or enterprise for building up another of the same kind
can·ni·bal·ly \-bəlē\ *adv* **:** according to the nature or practice of a cannibal
cannier *comparative of* CANNY
canniest *superlative of* CANNY
can·ni·kin *also* **can·a·kin** *or* **can·i·kin** \ˈkanəkən, -ˈaa-, -nēk-\ *n* -S [prob. fr. obs. D *kanneken*, fr. MD *canneken*, dim. of *canne* can (akin to OE *canne*) + *-ken* -kin — more at CAN (vessel)] **1 :** a small can or drinking vessel **2** *NewEng* **:** a wooden bucket
can·ni·ly \ˈkanᵊlē, -i\ *adv* [*canny* + *-ly*] **:** in a canny manner: as **a :** KNOWINGLY, SHREWDLY **b :** CAREFULLY, CAUTIOUSLY
can·ni·ness \ˈkanēnəs, -nin-\ *n* -ES [*canny* + *-ness*] **:** a canny propensity or trait: as **a :** PRUDENCE, WARINESS **b :** CLEVERNESS, SHREWDNESS **c :** FORESIGHTEDNESS, SAGACITY
canning *n* -S [fr. gerund of ⁴*can*] **:** a method of food preservation in which packed cans or jars are subjected to temperatures high enough to sterilize the containers and their contents — compare COLD-PACK METHOD, HOT-PACK METHOD
cannister *var of* CANISTER
can·ni·za·ro reaction \¦kanə¦zä(,)rō-, -nət¦sä-\ *n, usu cap C* [after Stanislao *Cannizzaro* †1910 Ital. chemist] **:** a reaction of aldehydes with caustic alkali in which one molecule of aldehyde is reduced to the corresponding alcohol and another molecule is oxidized to the salt of the corresponding acid
¹**can·non** \ˈkanən\ *n, pl* **cannons** *or* **cannon** [MF *canon*, fr. It *cannone*, lit., large tube, aug. of *canna* reed, tube, fr. L, reed — more at CANE] **1** *pl usu* **cannon a :** a weapon consisting of a metal tube now usu. steel and either cast in one piece or built up from a series of forgings, supported by a carriage or mount, and used for firing projectiles — compare GUN **b :** a heavy-caliber automatic aircraft gun firing explosive shells **2 a :** *also* **cannon bit :** a smooth round horse bit **b :** the straight portion of the mouthpiece of certain bits **3** *or* **can·on :** the projecting part of a bell by which it is hung **:** EAR **4** *also* **cannon curl :** a cylindrical curl of hair worn in a horizontal position **5** *Brit* **a :** *also* **canon :** a carom in billiards and bagatelle **b :** bagatelle played with only three balls and sometimes without cups **c :** a rebound after colliding **:** CAROM **6** *Brit* **:** a hollow spindle or shaft containing another spindle having an independent motion **7 :** the part of the leg where the cannon bone is situated **:** SHANK — see HORSE illustration **8** *slang* **a :** PICKPOCKET **b :** PISTOL, REVOLVER **9 :** a blackish green that is yellower and deeper than ultramarine green

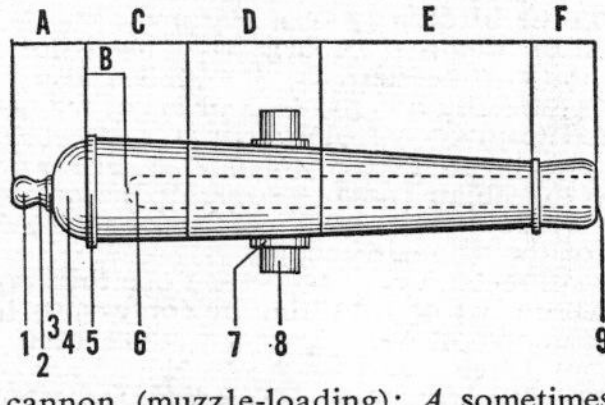

cannon (muzzle-loading): *A* sometimes called cascabel; *B* breech; *C* first reinforce; *D* second reinforce; *E* chase; *F* swell of muzzle; *1* knob; *2* neck; *3* fillet; *4* base of breech; *5* base ring; *6* chamber; *6-9* bore; *7* rimbase; *8* trunnion; *9* face of the piece

²**cannon** \"\ *vb* -ED/-ING/-S [prob. fr. MF *canonner*, fr. *canon*] *vi* **1 :** to discharge cannon **2 a** *Brit* **:** to carom in billiards **b** *chiefly Brit* **:** to bump violently so as to rebound **:** rebound after colliding ~ *vt* **1 :** CANNONADE **2** *Brit* **a :** to cause to rebound by violent collision **b :** to carom into
¹**can·non·ade** \¦kanə¦nād\ *n* -S [MF *canonnade* cannon shot, modif. of It *cannonata*, fr. *cannone* cannon + *-ata* -ade] **1 :** a firing of artillery in considerable quantity for an appreciable length of time **2 :** a loud noise like a cannonade of artillery **:** a noisy bombardment (as of questions)
²**cannonade** \"\ *vb* -ED/-ING/-S *vt* **:** to attack with artillery **:** batter with artillery fire ~ *vi* **1 :** to deliver artillery fire **2 :** to make a noise like that of artillery fire **3 :** ²CANNON 2b
¹**cannonball** \ˈ==,=\ *n* **1 a :** a round solid missile made for firing from a cannon **b :** a missile of any solid or hollow shape made for cannon **2 a :** a jump into the water made with the arms holding the knees tight against the chest **b :** a hard tennis service with a virtually flat trajectory **3 :** a fast train; *esp* **:** EXPRESS TRAIN
²**cannonball** \"\ *vi* -ED/-ING/-S **:** to travel with a speed like that of a cannonball
cannonball tree *n* **1 :** a So. American tree (*Couroupita guianensis*) of the family Lecythidaceae bearing a large globose fruit with a hard woody rind **2 :** an East Indian tree (*Xylocarpus granatum*) of the family Meliaceae bearing a hard woody fruit and yielding a hard useful wood
cannon bit *n* **:** CANNON 2a
cannon bone *n* [F *canon*, lit., cannon — more at CANNON] **:** a bone in hoofed mammals that supports the leg from the knee or hock joint to the fetlock; *esp* **:** the enlarged metacarpal or metatarsal of the third digit in the horse — compare METACARPUS
cannon cracker *n* **:** a large firecracker
cannon curl *n* **:** CANNON 4
can·non·eer *also* **can·non·ier** \¦kanə¦ni(ə)r, -iə\ *n* -S [MF *canonnier*, fr. *canon* cannon + *-ier* -eer — more at CANNON] **:** an artilleryman assigned to the care and use of a gun
cannon fodder *n* [trans. of G *kanonenfutter*] **:** soldiers wounded or killed by artillery fire
can·non·ism \ˈkanə,nizəm\ *n* -S *usu cap* [Joseph G. *Cannon* †1926 Am. politician + E *-ism*] **:** concentration of the means of control over the procedure and business of the U.S. House of Representatives in the hands of its speaker
cannon metal *n* **:** GUNMETAL
cannon pinion *n* **:** a small steel tube having at the lower end teeth that mesh with the teeth of the minute wheel of a timepiece and at the upper end the minute hand which is mounted on the arbor of the center wheel friction-tight so as to allow hand-setting
can·non·ry \ˈkanənrē, -i\ *n* -ES **1 :** CANNONADING **2 :** ARTILLERY
cannons *pl of* CANNON, *pres 3d sing of* CANNON
cannon–shot \ˈ==,=\ *n* **:** the range of a cannon
cannon stove *n* **:** a cast-iron stove resembling a cannon set up on its breech
can·not \ˈka(,)nät, kəˈnät, kaˈnät, ˈkanət, ˈka(n)ˈnät, *usu* -d·+V\ [ME, fr. ¹*can* + *not*] **:** can not — **cannot but 1 :** to be inescapably constrained to (as out of a sense of fitness or rightness) **:** be left with no alternative than to ⟨an obsequiousness one *cannot but* feel aversion to⟩ **2 :** to be bound to **:** be sure to **:** MUST ⟨his personality *cannot but* come through in his letters⟩ **3 :** to be unable to do otherwise than to ⟨the outsider *cannot but* be struck by the frequent reluctance of the learned world to recognize important discoveries —Edmund Wilson⟩ — compare ²BUT 2b
can·nu·la *also* **can·u·la** \ˈkanyələ\ *n, pl* **cannulas** \-ləz\ *or* **cannu·lae** \-,lē\ [NL, fr. L *cannula* small reed, dim. of *canna* reed — more at CANE] **:** a small tube made for insertion into a body cavity (as for drainage) or into a duct or vessel and sometimes fitted with a trocar during the act of insertion
can·nu·lar \-lə(r)\ *adj* [NL *cannula* + E *-ar*] **:** having the form of a cannula **:** TUBULAR
can·nu·late \-,lāt\ *vt* -ED/-ING/-S [*cannula* + *-ate*] **:** to insert a cannula into
can·nu·la·tion \,kanyəˈlāshən\ *n* -S **:** the act or process of cannulating
can·nu·lize \ˈkanyə,līz\ *vt* -ED/-ING/-S [NL *cannula* + E *-ize*] **:** CANNULATE
¹**can·ny** \ˈkanē, -i\ *adj* -ER/-EST [¹*can* + *-y*] **1 a :** FORESIGHTED, KNOWING, WISE **b :** CAUTIOUS, PRUDENT, WARY **c :** CLEVER, CUNNING, SLY **d :** FRUGAL, THRIFTY **e :** shrewd in worldly affairs **:** SHARP-WITTED **:** watchful for self-interest **2** *Scot* **a :** FORTUNATE, LUCKY **b :** free from weird qualities or unnatural powers **:** safe to deal with — used in a negative constr. ⟨the glen looked like something not ~⟩ **c :** wise in supernatural affairs **:** having occult powers ⟨a ~ woman⟩ **3 a** *Scot* **:** CAREFUL, GENTLE, STEADY ⟨walking in a ~ way like a horse on a slippery slope⟩ **b** *Scot* **:** COMFORTABLE, COZY, QUIET, SNUG **c** *dial Brit* **:** agreeable to the eyes or perception **:** PLEASANT, WORTHY — used as a general term of approbation **d** *dial Eng* **:** considerable esp. in extent, number, or amount
²**canny** \"\ *adv, Scot* **:** in a canny manner: as **a :** CAREFULLY, CAUTIOUSLY **b :** GENTLY, QUIETLY — compare CA' CANNY
canny moment *n, archaic Scot* **:** the moment of childbirth
ca·noa \kəˈnōə\ *n* -S [Pg, canoe, fr. Sp] **:** a sloop-rigged fishing boat common in the Amazon delta

[1]ca·noe \kə'nü\ n -s often attrib [alter. (prob. influenced by MF canoue, MF & F canoe, fr. Sp canoa) of earlier canoa, canow, fr. NL canoa, fr. Sp, fr. 15th cent. Arawakan canoa (form recorded by Columbus), of Cariban origin; akin to Galibi canaoua, Chayma & Cumanagoto canagua, canahua, Carib & Macusi canaoa] 1 : a long and narrow boat that is sharp at both ends, has curved sides, is usu. built of lightweight materials (as bark, hide, canvas, light wood, or light metal), and is usu. propelled by hand-driven paddles although sometimes mounting a sail or sails 2 : a synchronized swimming stunt executed with arched back, head and heels above water, and hands at hip level propelling the body forward by sculling

canoe

[2]canoe \"\ vb **canoed; canoed; canoeing; canoes** vi 1 : to paddle a canoe : manage a canoe 2 : to go or travel in a canoe ⟨~ across the lake⟩ ~ vt : to transport in a canoe ⟨munitions being canoed across the river⟩
canoe birch n : PAPER BIRCH
canoe cedar n : a large valuable arborvitae (Thuja plicata) of the northwestern U. S. — called also red cedar
ca·noe·ing n -s : the act or art of managing a canoe
ca·no·ei·ro \,kanə'wā(,)rō\ n -s usu cap, often attrib [Pg, lit., canoeman, fr. canoa canoe (fr. Sp) + -eiro -er] 1 a : a Tupi-Guaranian Indian people of the central part of the state of Goiaz, Brazil b : a member of such people 2 : the language of the Canoeiro people
ca·noe·ist \kə'nüəst\ n -s : one that canoes
canoe tilting n : tilting by contestants in canoes
canoewood \=ˈ=,=\ n 1 : TULIP TREE 2 : the wood of the tulip tree
can·oid \'ka,nȯid, -'ā-\ adj [NL Canoidea] : of or relating to the Arctoidea
ca·noi·dea \kə'nȯidēə\ [NL, fr. Canis + -oidea] syn of ARCTOIDEA
[1]can·on \'kanən\ n -s often cap [ME canoun, canon, fr. OE & OF canon, fr. LL, fr. L, model, standard, fr. Gk kanōn rod, measuring line, standard; akin to Gk kanna reed — more at CANE] 1 : a decree, decision, regulation, code, or constitution made by ecclesiastical authority; specif : a law or rule of doctrine or discipline enacted by a council and confirmed by highest ecclesiastical authority 2 [ME, prob. fr. OF, fr. LL] a : a fundamental and relatively unchangeable part of the Roman Catholic mass containing the fixed rule according to which the sacrifice of the mass is to be offered; specif : the part of the mass beginning after the sanctus with the prayer "Te igitur" and ending just before the paternoster or with the consummation of the eucharistic elements b : a book containing the canon and ordinary used at pontifical mass 3 [ME, fr. LL] a : a collection or authoritative list of books accepted as holy scripture: as (1) : books forming the accepted Hebrew list of the Holy Scriptures collected under the divisions of the Law, the Prophets, and the writings accepted by Protestant Christians as the original and definitive canon of the Old Testament but supplemented by Roman Catholics with additional books drawn from the Septuagint (2) : books forming the Christian New Testament (3) : books forming the Old and New Testaments and constituting the Christian Bible b : an accepted or sanctioned list of books ⟨established in the ~ of literature⟩ c : the authentic works of a writer ⟨the Chaucer ~⟩ 4 archaic : a general mathematical rule, formula, or table 5 a : a basic general principle or rule commonly accepted as true, valid, and fundamental ⟨I accept Plato's well-known ~ that only the perfectly real can be perfectly known —W.R.Inge⟩ b : a norm, criterion, model, or standard for evaluating, judging, testing, or criticizing ⟨Novalis . . . set up the fairy tale as the ~ of art —Irving Babbitt⟩ c : a body of principles, rules, standards, or norms (as in the normative sciences) ⟨according to newspaper ~ . . . a big story calls for a lot of copy —A.J. Liebling⟩ d [G kanon, fr. L canon or Gk kanōn] in Kant : the totality of fundamental a priori principles for the correct use of our capacities for knowledge e in Mill : any one of the five methods for induction — compare INDIRECT METHOD OF DIFFERENCE, METHOD OF AGREEMENT, METHOD OF CONCOMITANT VARIATIONS, METHOD OF DIFFERENCE, METHOD OF RESIDUES 6 [LGk kanōn, fr. Gk] : a contrapuntal musical composition in two or more voice parts in which the melody is imitated exactly and completely by the successively entering voices though not always at the same pitch and which either ends with a coda or begins over again — see CIRCULAR CANON; compare CATCH 5, ROUND 7 [LL] a : a fixed annual or customary payment or tribute (as to the church) : QUITRENT b : the annual rent payable under a Roman emphyteusis 8 [F; prob. fr. having been used in printing the canon of the mass] : a type of either about 44 point or about 48 point which is the largest size having a specific name 9 [ML, list, fr. LL, catalog of saints, fr. Gk kanōn table (as of dates)] a : a list (as of clergy, deaconesses, or those receiving charity) in the early church b : a catalog of recognized saints 10 : a liturgical sequence of the Eastern Orthodox Church consisting normally of nine odes each comprising several troparia sung as an integral part of matins and also at certain other offices (as at compline during the first week of Lent) ⟨the Canon of the Holy Fathers⟩ ⟨the Great Canon of St. Andrew of Crete⟩ 11 : a dance in which certain dancers follow the patterns previously set by others who then change to new patterns **syn** see LAW

Aa

canon type

[2]canon \"\ n -s [ME canoun, fr. AF canunie, fr. LL canonicus one living under a rule, fr. L canonicus according to rule, fr. Gk kanonikos, fr. kanon-, kanōn rod, rule + -ikos -ic — more at [1]CANON] 1 : one of the clergy of a medieval cathedral or large church living as a community under a rule 2 : a clergyman belonging to the chapter or the staff of a cathedral or collegiate church — compare HONORARY CANON, MINOR CANON 3 : CANON REGULAR 2
[3]canon var of CANNON
[4]ca·non \kə'nōn\ var of CANUN
[5]ca·ñon \'kanyən\ var of CANYON
canon cancrizans n : CRAB CANON
can·on·ess \'kanənəs\ n -ES [[2]canon + -ess] 1 : a woman living with others in a community or college under a rule but not under a perpetual vow 2 : a woman holding a canonry in a conventual chapter
[1]ca·non·ic \kə'nänik, -ēk\ adj [LL canonicus one living under a rule — more at CANON (clergyman)] 1 : CANONICAL ⟨~rights⟩ 2 : of, relating to, or resembling a musical canon ⟨tonal balance is important in all ~ writing —Walter Piston⟩
[2]canonic \"\ n -s [LL canonicus belonging to the canon of Scripture, fr. L, according to rule — more at CANON (clergyman)] 1 : a system of philosophical or logical canons; esp : Epicurean logic 2 : a person in canonical orders
ca·non·i·cal \-ə̇kəl, -ēk-\ adj [[1]canonic + -al] 1 a : of, relating to, established by, or conforming to a canon b : of or relating to canon law 2 : like or conforming to a general rule : accorded wide acceptance : SANCTIONED, ORTHODOX, AUTHORITATIVE ⟨the ~ code of the party⟩ ⟨the drinking of cocktails was as ~ a rite as the mixing —Sinclair Lewis⟩ 3 : belonging to or accepted as forming a canon ⟨a ~ book⟩ ⟨~ scriptures⟩ 4 : of or relating to a clergyman (as a canon) or to an ecclesiastical chapter ⟨a ~ house⟩ 5 : relating to various of the simplest and most significant forms or schemata to which general equations, statements, or expressions may be reduced without loss of generality : STANDARD, BASIC ⟨the ~ equations of dynamics⟩ — compare NORMAL FORM — **ca·non·i·cal·ly** \-k(ə)lē, -i\ adv
canonical age n : the age at which an individual may in accordance with the canons of a particular church become liable to certain obligations (as fasting) or eligible for certain privileges (as ordination)
canonical hour n 1 : any of certain stated times of the day appointed by various churches for the offices of prayer and devotion — see COMPLINE, LAUD, MATINS, NONE, PRIME, SEXT, TIERCE, VESPER 2 : any of the hours of the period from 8 a.m. to 3 p.m. before and after which marriage cannot be legally performed in any parish church in England 3 : an appropriate or climactic hour or time
canonical purgation n [trans. of ML purgatio canonica; fr. its use in the ecclesiastical courts] : purgation by means of oath helpers — compare COMPURGATION, VULGAR PURGATION
ca·non·i·cals \-kəlz\ n pl : the vestments prescribed by canon to be worn by an officiating clergyman of certain churches
canonical sin n : a sin (as idolatry, murder, adultery, heresy) for which excommunication or public penance was decreed by the canons of the early church
ca·non·i·cate \kə'nänə̇kə̇t, -ēk-, -,kāt\ n -s [ML canonicatus, fr. canonicus canon (fr. LL, one living under a rule) + -atus -ate] : the office of a canon : CANONRY
can·on·ic·i·ty \,kanə'nisəd-ē, -ətē, -i\ n -ES [F canonicité, fr. canonique canonical, authoritative (fr. LL canonicus, fr. L, according to rule) + -ité -ity — more at CANON (clergyman)] 1 : the status or character of belonging within the biblical canon 2 : canonical acceptability, authority, or genuineness
ca·non·ics \kə'näniks, -ēks\ n pl but usu sing in constr : a division of theology that deals with the origin, history, or authority of the biblical canon
can·on·ist \'kanənə̇st\ n -s [MF canoniste, fr. canon (fr. LL) + -iste -ist — more at CANON (rule)] : one skilled in canon law
can·on·is·tic \,kanə'nistik, -ēk\ adj 1 : pertinent to or characteristic of a canonist 2 : relating to canon law
can·on·i·za·tion \,kanənə̇'zāshən, -,nī'z-\ n -s [F canonization, fr. ML canonization-, canonizatio, fr. canonizatus (past part. of canonizare to canonize) + L -ion-, -io -ion] : the act of canonizing or the state of being canonized; specif : the final process or decree by which the name of a deceased person is placed in the catalog of saints and commended to perpetual veneration and invocation
can·on·ize \'kanə,nīz\ vt -ED/ -ING/ -S [ME canonizen, fr. ML canonizare, fr. LL canon — more at CANON (rule)] 1 : to declare (a deceased person) a saint : put in the catalog of saints : SAINT — compare BEATIFY 2 : to include in a canon esp. of Scripture : make canonical 3 : to sanction or ratify by or as if by ecclesiastical authority 4 archaic : to make into a god or into something divine : APOTHEOSIZE 5 : to regard as sanctioned, rightly and securely established, or sacrosanct ⟨canonized as dean of drama critics⟩ ⟨his mother had canonized all his timidities as common sense —Scott Fitzgerald⟩
canon law n [alter. of ME lawe canoun, prob. trans. of MF droit canonel] 1 : a body of ecclesiastical law for the government of a Christian church; esp : a codified body of rules and regulations as distinguished from other noncodified forms of church law 2 : a body of religious law governing the conduct of members of a particular faith ⟨the canon law of Islam⟩
canon lawyer n : CANONIST
ca·non oak \'kanyən-\ n : CANYON LIVE OAK
can·on regular \'kanən-\ n, pl **canons regular** 1 : one of the clergy of a cathedral organized as a monastic community under a rule 2 : a priest of the Roman Catholic Church belonging to an order or congregation bound by the vows of religion, living in community under usu. the Augustinian rule, and formerly monastic but in modern times being largely engaged in parish, educational, or hospital work
can·on·ry \'kanənrē, -i\ n -ES [[2]canon + -ry] 1 : the prebend or office of a canon or canoness 2 : a body of canons
canons pl of CANON
ca·noo·dle \kə'nüd°l\ vb **canoodled; canoodled; canoodling** \-d(°)liŋ\ **canoodles** [perh. fr. E dial. canoodle, n., donkey, fool, silly lovemaker, perh. alter. of noodle (blockhead)] vi : PET, CARESS, FONDLE ⟨the best way of dealing with lovers . . . found canoodling in church doors —Bruce Marshall⟩ ~ vt : to persuade by or as if by caresses
can opener n : a device for opening cans
ca·no·pic \kə'nōpik, -äp-\ adj, usu cap [L canopicus, fr. Canopus, city in ancient Egypt (fr. Gk Kanōbos, Kanōpos) + L -icus -ic] : of or relating to Canopus
canopic jar or **canopic vase** n, often cap C : a jar in which the ancient Egyptians preserved the viscera of a deceased person usu. for burial with the mummy
[1]can·o·py \'kanəpē, -i\ n -ES [ME canope, canape, fr. ML canopeum, canapeum mosquito net, fr. L conopeum, conopium, fr. Gk kōnōpion, fr. kōnōps mosquito, gnat] 1 : a covering usu. for shelter or protection ⟨from midships aft she was covered with a vast ~ of solid construction —C. S. Forester⟩: a : a covering usu. of cloth suspended from the four high posts of a bed b : a covering typically of cloth carried on poles above an exalted personage or sacred object : BALDACHIN c : SKY ⟨the wild blue ~ above⟩ d : a temporary or permanent cover providing shelter and decoration (as over a door or window) e : a formation of branches affording a cover of foliage ⟨the fabulous avenue . . . covered with a ~ of chestnut trees —Horace Sutton⟩; specif : the uppermost spreading branchy layer of a forest — see UNDERSTORY f : an awning or marquee often stretching from doorway to curb or covering a section of grandstand 2 a : the rooflike construction above the stage of an Elizabethan theater b : a curtained recess at the back of such a stage 3 : an ornamental rooflike structure that provides or suggests shelter and that projects from a wall or is supported by columns 4 : a metal covering used to enclose wiring where an electric fixture protrudes (as from a ceiling) 5 a : the transparent enclosure over an airplane cockpit b : the lifting or supporting surface of a parachute

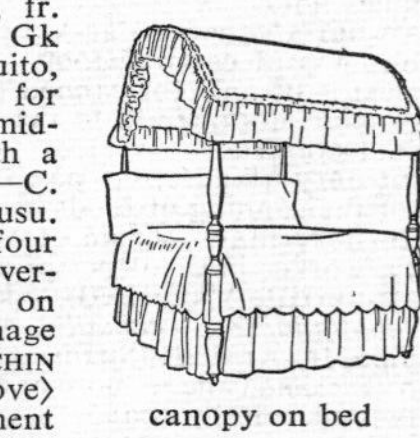
canopy on bed

[2]canopy \"\ vt -ED/ -ING/ -ES : to cover with or as if with a canopy ⟨the streets were quiet as churches and canopied by stately trees —Hugh MacLennan⟩
canopy stringer n : one of a pair of workers who thread shroud lines through holes down the panel seams of a parachute canopy to connect with the harness
canopy switch n : a small compact electric switch installed in the canopy of a ceiling fixture for direct control of the light at the fixture and usu. operated by a cord or chain
ca·no·rous \kə'nōrəs, -'ȯ-; 'kanər-\ adj [L canorus, fr. canor melody, fr. canere to sing — more at CHANT] : marked by or suggestive of melody or song, often full loud swelling song ⟨the ~ noise of the revelers⟩ — **ca·no·rous·ly** adv
ca·nos·sa \kə'näsə, -'ȯsə\ n -s usu cap [fr. Canossa, village in northern Italy where Emperor Henry IV made humble submission to Pope Gregory VII in 1077] : a place or occasion of submission, humiliation, or penance — often used with go to ⟨he went to his Canossa when he reversed his policy⟩
can·o·tier \,kanə;tyā\ n -s [F, sailor, sailor's hat, fr. MF, sailor, fr. canot small boat, alter. of canoe, canoa canoe — more at CANOE] : SAILOR 4
cans pl of CAN, pres 3d sing of CAN
cansful pl of CANFUL
can·so \'kan,sō\ also **can·zo** \-,zō\ n -s [Prov, fr. L cantion-, cantio song — more at CANZONE] : a troubadour's love song usu. in stanza form
canst archaic pres 2d sing of CAN
canstick n [by contr.] obs : CANDLESTICK
[1]cant \'kant\ adj [ME, prob. fr. (assumed) MLG kant (whence LG kant)] dial Eng : LIVELY, VIGOROUS, CHEERFUL
[2]cant \'kant, -aa(ə)-, -ai-\ n -s [ME, prob. fr. MD or ONF; MD, edge, fr. ONF, fr. L cantus, canthus iron ring round a carriage wheel, perh. of Celt origin; akin to W cant rim, Bret cant circle; akin to Gk kanthos corner of the eye, Russ kut corner] 1 obs : CORNER, NOOK, NICHE 2 : an outer or external angle (as of a building) 3 a : a frame joined obliquely to the keel of a ship b : a segment forming a sidepiece in the head of a cask 4 [prob. modif. of D kanthout, fr. kant edge + hout wood; akin to OE holt wood — more at HOLT] : a log slabbed on one or more sides 5 a : a sudden thrust producing a bias b : the bias so given ⟨to give a beam a ~⟩ 6 : an oblique or slanting surface (as of a polygon, a buttress, or a bank) 7 : an inclination from a horizontal, vertical, or other given line : SLOPE, BEVEL, TILT ⟨the ~ of a gun barrel⟩ ⟨~ of a helm⟩
[3]cant \"\ vb -ED/ -ING/ -S vt 1 : to give a cant or oblique edge to : cut off an angle from (as the head of a bolt) : BEVEL — often used with off ⟨~ off a corner⟩ 2 : to slab (a log) thereby producing cants 3 : to set at an angle : tip or tilt up or over : SLOPE, SLANT, INCLINE ⟨~ a cask⟩ ⟨~ a ship⟩ 4 : to turn completely : turn upside down — often used with over ⟨~ over a net⟩ 5 : to turn or throw off or out by tilting or rotating ⟨~ a rifle⟩ 6 chiefly Brit : to give a sudden turn or new direction to : pitch esp. by an unexpected lurch : throw with a sudden jerk : TOSS ⟨~ round a piece of timber⟩ ~ vi 1 : to pitch to one side : LEAN, TILT ⟨the ~ing deck of a destroyer⟩ : TURN — often used with over ⟨the ship ~ed over⟩ 2 : to have a sloping position : SLANT, SLOPE ⟨a ~ing yardarm⟩ 3 of a ship : to move into or assume a position oblique to a defined direction or course : change direction or swing from a position — sometimes used with round or across
[4]cant \"\ adj 1 : having canted corners or sides ⟨a ~ molding⟩ 2 : inclined from a perpendicular or other given straight line : SLOPING, SLANTING, CANTING, CANTED ⟨a ~ buttress⟩
[5]cant \"\ vb -ED/ -ING/ -S [prob. fr. ONF canter to tell, say, lit., to sing, chant, fr. L cantare to sing — more at CHANT] vi 1 : to speak in a whining voice or an affected singsong tone : BEG ⟨bade me ~ and whine in some other place —Samuel Johnson⟩ 2 : to use or speak in cant (as that of thieves or gypsies) or technical terms 3 dial Eng : TALK, GOSSIP 4 : to talk with an affectation of piety : use religious or solemn language insincerely to gain a reputation for goodness or piety : practice hypocrisy ⟨~ about brotherly love⟩ ⟨let them jabber and ~ —Rose Macaulay⟩ ~ vt 1 : to speak or utter as cant or in a manner suggestive of cant esp. of a particular subject, school, or specialty 2 dial Eng : WHEEDLE, INDULGE
[6]cant \"\ n -s often attrib 1 : affected singsong speech ⟨a beggar's ~⟩ 2 a : ARGOT 1 b obs : the phraseology peculiar to a religious class or sect c : [1]JARGON 3a 3 a obs : a set form of words b : a set or stock phrase : SLANG ⟨a ~ phrase⟩ 4 : the expression or repetition of conventional, trite, or unconsidered ideas, opinions, or sentiments; esp : the insincere use of pious phraseology 5 obs : a user of religious cant : HYPOCRITE 6 chiefly Scot : GOSSIP **syn** see DIALECT
[7]cant \'kant\ n -s [modif. of MF encant, inquant, fr. ML incantum, inquantum, fr. in quantum for how much, fr. L in + quantum, accus. neut. of quantus how much — more at IN, QUANTITY] 1 chiefly Irish : AUCTION 2 civil law : a mode of partitioning property held in common by sale at auction
[8]cant \"\ vt -ED/ -ING/ -S chiefly Irish : to sell by auction
can't \'kant, -aa(ə)-, -ai-; esp S -ā-; esp NewEng & Brit -a-, -ä-; sporadically -e-\ [by contr.] : can not
can·tab \'kan,tab\ n -s usu cap [by shortening] : CANTABRIGIAN
can·ta·bank \'kantə,baŋk\ n -s [modif. of It cantambanco, cantimbanco, fr. cantare to sing (fr. L) + in on, in (fr. L) + banco bench, fr. a Gmc word akin to E bench — more at CHANT, [1]IN] : a singer from benches or platforms : a ballad singer
[1]can·ta·bi·le \kän·'täbə,lā, kan·'ta-, kən·'tä-, kən·'t-, -,lē\ adj (or adv) [It, fr. LL cantabilis worthy to be sung, fr. L cantare to sing] : in a singing manner : MELODIOUS, FLOWING ⟨a smooth ~ tone⟩ — often used as a direction in music
[2]cantabile n -s 1 : cantabile style — used esp. of instrumental music in distinction from recitative or parlando or from the marked rhythm of dance music 2 : a piece or passage in cantabile style ⟨Schumann's passionate and pleading ~s —Abram Chasins⟩
[1]can·ta·brig·i·an \,kantə'brij(ē)ən\ n -s cap [ML Cantabrigia Cambridge + E -an] 1 a : a native or resident of Cambridge, England b : a student or graduate of Cambridge University 2 a : a native or resident of Cambridge, Mass. b : a student or graduate of Harvard University
[2]cantabrigian \"\ adj, usu cap 1 : of, relating to, or characteristic of Cambridge, England, or its university 2 : of, relating to, or characteristic of Cambridge, Mass. or Harvard University
can·tal \kän'täl\ n -s often cap [F, fr. Cantal, department in France where it is made] : a hard Cheddar-type cheese made in the south of France
can·ta·la \kan·'tälə\ n -s [origin unknown] : a hard fiber produced from the leaves of an agave (Agave cantala) grown esp. in the Philippines and used for coarse twines (as binder twine) — called also Cebu maguey, maguey, manila maguey
can·ta·loupe also **can·ta·loup** or **can·te·lope** \'kant°l,ōp, -'aa-, -tə,lōp also -üp\ n -s [fr. Cantalupo, former papal villa near Rome, Italy, where it was first grown in Europe] 1 : a muskmelon (Cucumis melo cantalupensis) grown chiefly in Europe and having a hard ridged or warty rind and reddish orange flesh that is eaten raw as a fruit 2 : any of several muskmelons resembling the cantaloupe; broadly : MUSKMELON
can·tan·do \kän·'tän(,)dō\ adj (or adv) [It, fr. L cantandum, gerund of cantare to sing — more at CHANT] : CANTABILE — used as a direction in music
can·tan·ker·ous \(')kan·;ta(i)ŋk(ə)rəs, -aan·;taŋ-, kən·'t-\ adj [perh. irreg. (influence of cankerous, rancorous) fr. obs. conteck, contack contention (fr. ME contek, contak, fr. AF contek) + -ous] 1 of a person : marked by ill humor, irritability, and determination to disagree ⟨a ~ and venomous-tongued old lady —Dorothy Sayers⟩ 2 of an animal or thing : difficult and irritating to deal with or use ⟨a ~ burro⟩ ⟨a ~ pump⟩ **syn** see CONTRARY
can·tan·ker·ous·ly adv : in a cantankerous manner
can·tan·ker·ous·ness n -ES : the quality or state of being cantankerous
can·tar var of KANTAR
can·ta·rist \'kantərəst\ n -s [ML cantarista, fr. cantaria chantry (fr. L cantare to sing) + L -ista -ist] : a chantry priest
can·ta·ta \kən·'täd-ə, -ä|, ka(a)-,kä-,ká-, |ta\ n -s [It, fr. cantare to sing, fr. L — more at CHANT] 1 : a narrative poem set to recitative or alternate recitative and melody for a single voice accompanied by one or more instruments 2 : a sacred or secular choral composition comprising choruses, solos, recitatives, and interludes, usu. accompanied by organ, piano, or orchestra, and arranged in a somewhat dramatic manner but not intended to be acted
can·ta·to·ry \'kantə,tōrē\ adj [L cantatus + E -ory] : of or relating to singing or song, esp. chanting
can·ta·trice \,käntə'trēchē; ;kän°tə;trēs, -änt-\ n, pl **cantatrices** \-trēchēz,-trēs(əz)\ or **can·ta·tri·ci** \,käntə'trēchē\ [It & F; F, fr. It, fr. LL cantatric-, cantatrix, fem. of L cantator singer, fr. cantatus (past part. of cantare) + -or] : a woman singer; esp : an opera singer
cant block n [[2]cant] : either block of a cant purchase
cantboard \'=,=\ n [[2]cant + board] 1 : a board that slopes (as one placed to shed or divert water) 2 : a board showing the curved outline of a carriage body
cant body n [[2]cant] : a part of the body of a ship in which the frames run obliquely to the keel to form the bow or stern — compare SQUARE BODY
cant dog n [[2]cant] : PEAVEY
canted adj [fr. past part. of [3]cant] : placed at or given a cant : ANGLED, SLANTED
can·teen \(')kan·'tēn, -kaa-\ n -s [F cantine bottle case, canteen (the shop), fr. It cantina wine cellar, fr. canto corner, fr. L cantus iron ring round a carriage wheel — more at CANT (angle)] 1 a : a sutler's shop connected with a military post for supplying to enlisted men extra provisions, tobacco, or liquors b : POST EXCHANGE — formerly used as the official designation c chiefly Brit : a restaurant or refreshment bar provided by an industrial or commercial concern for employees (as in an office building) d : a place of refreshment and recreation maintained by civilians for servicemen e : a temporary or mobile restaurant ⟨~s were set up in the flooded areas⟩ 2 a : a partitioned chest or box for holding cutlery b : a soldier's mess kit 3 : a flask typically cloth-jacketed for carrying water or other liquids (as by soldiers or campers)
can·te hon·do or **cante jon·do** \,käntā'kondō, -;ā-, -'hō-\ n [Sp, lit., deep song] : FLAMENCO
cantelope var of CANTALOUPE
[1]cant·er \'kantə(r), -'aa-,-'ai-\ n -s [[5]cant + -er] : one that cants : one that uses cant: as a : BEGGAR, VAGABOND b : one that uses professional or religious cant — used esp. in the 17th century as a nickname for a Puritan ⟨the days when he was a ~ and a rebel —T.B.Macaulay⟩
[2]can·ter \"\ vb **cantered; cantered; cantering** \-ntəriŋ, -ntriŋ\ **canters** [prob. short for obs. canterbury to canter,

fr. *canterbury*, n.] *vi* **1 :** to move at or as if at a canter (as of a horse) **:** LOPE **2 :** to ride or go on a cantering horse (as of a rider) ~ *vt* **:** to cause to go at a canter **:** make canter

³can·ter \"\ *n* -s **1 a :** a 3-beat gait resembling but smoother and slower than the gallop **b :** a ride at such a gait **:** a brisk ride or other progression **2 :** a waltz step in which the same foot leads at each repetition

⁴cant·er \"\ *n* -s [³*cant* + *-er*] **:** an overhead log-turning device in a sawmill that is used in making cants

can·ter·bu·ri·an \ˌkantə(r)ˈbyu̇rēən, ˈkaan-\ *adj, usu cap* [*Canterbury*, city in England + E *-an*] **:** of, relating to, or characteristic of Canterbury, esp. its archbishopric

¹can·ter·bury *R* ˈkantə(r)ˌberē, -ˈaa-, -i, –*R* -tə,b-\ *adj, usu cap* [fr. *Canterbury*, city in England] **1 :** of or from the city of Canterbury, England **:** of the kind or style prevalent in Canterbury **:** CANTERBURIAN **2 :** of or from the provincial district of Canterbury, New Zealand **:** of the kind or style prevalent in Canterbury provincial district

²canterbury \"\ *n* -ES **1** *usu cap* [fr. the supposed gait of horses ridden by pilgrims to the shrine of Thomas à Becket in Canterbury] *archaic* **:** a moderate and easy gait like a gallop **:** ³CANTER **2** *often cap* **:** a stand with divisions for music, magazines, or loose papers

canterbury bell *n, usu cap C* [fr. *Canterbury*, city in England; prob. fr. the resemblance of the flowers to the small bells on the horses of pilgrims going to Canterbury] **1 :** any of several plants of the genus *Campanula* (esp. *C. medium*, *C. trachelium*, and *C. glomerata*) having blue, pink, or white bell-shaped flowers **2 :** CUCKOOFLOWER 1

canterbury palm *n, usu cap C* [fr. *Canterbury*, provincial district of New Zealand] **:** UMBRELLA PALM 1

canterbury tale *or* **canterbury story** *n, usu cap C* [fr. *The Canterbury Tales*, literary work by Geoffrey Chaucer †1400 Eng. poet, consisting mostly of narrative poems which he puts into the mouths of persons on a pilgrimage to Canterbury] **1 :** a cock-and-bull story **:** YARN, FABLE ⟨a *Canterbury tale* of a leg and an eye and heaven knows what —George Colman †1794⟩ **2 :** a long tedious tale ⟨it grows into a long *Canterbury tale* of two hours —Richard Steele⟩

cant file *n* [²*cant*] **:** a fine-toothed file that is isosceles-triangular in cross section, tapered to a point, and used for sharpening saw teeth

cant frame *n* [*cant* (*body*)] **:** the frame of the cant body of a ship

canth- *or* **cantho-** *comb form* [NL, fr. *canthus*] **:** canthus **:** canthal ⟨*canth*itis⟩ ⟨*cantho*lysis⟩

can·thal \ˈkan(t)thəl\ *adj* [NL *canthus* + E *-al*] **:** belonging to a canthus

can·tha·rel·lus \ˌkan(t)thəˈreləs\ *n, cap* [NL, dim. of L *cantharus* drinking vessel — more at CANTHARUS] **:** a genus of fungi (family Agaricaceae) distinguished from other white-spored agarics by the low ridgelike and sometimes forked gills of the pileus and including the chanterelle

¹can·thar·i·dae \kanˈtharəˌdē\ [NL, fr. *Cantharis*, type genus + *-idae*] *syn of* MELOIDAE

²cantharidae \"\ *n pl, cap* [NL, fr. *Cantharis*, type genus + *-idae*] **:** a family of nonluminescent elongated soft-bodied beetles (as the soldier beetles) related to and in some classifications including the Lampyridae

can·thar·i·dal \-rədᵊl\ *adj* [*cantharides* + *-al*] **:** relating to or containing cantharides ⟨a ~ plaster⟩

can·thar·i·date \-rəˌdāt\ *vt* -ED/-ING/-S [*cantharides* + *-ate*] **:** to treat or impregnate with cantharides

cantharides *pl of* CANTHARIS

cantharides cerate *n* **:** BLISTERING CERATE

can·tha·rid·i·an *or* **can·tha·rid·e·an** \ˌkan(t)thəˈridēən, ˈkaan-\ *adj* [*cantharides* + *-ian* or *-ean* (var. of *-ian*)] **:** composed of or containing cantharides

can·thar·i·din \kanˈtharədᵊn, kaan-, -dən\ *n* -s [F *cantharidine*, fr. L *cantharid-*, *cantharis* + F *-ine* -in] **:** a bitter crystalline compound $C_{10}H_{12}O_4$ constituting the active vesicating principle of cantharides

can·thar·i·dism \-ˌdizəm\ *n* -s [*cantharides* + *-ism*] **:** poisoning due to misuse of cantharides

can·thar·i·dize \-ˌdīz\ *vt* -ED/-ING/-S [*cantharides* + *-ize*] **:** to treat with cantharides

¹can·tha·ris \ˈkan(t)thərəs, ˈkaan-\ *n* [alter. (influenced by L *cantharis*) of ME *cantharide*, fr. L *cantharid-*, *cantharis*, fr. Gk *kantharis*] **1** *pl* **can·thar·i·des** \kanˈtharəˌdēz, kaan- *also* -ˈe-\ **:** SPANISH FLY 1 **2 cantharides** *pl but sing or pl in constr* **:** a preparation of dried beetles (as Spanish flies) used as a counterirritant and formerly as an aphrodisiac but highly toxic when taken internally — called also *Spanish fly* **3** *cap* [NL, fr. L] **:** the type genus of Cantharidae

²cantharis \"\ [NL, fr. L] *syn of* LYTTA

can·tha·rus \ˈkan(t)thərəs\ *or* **kan·tha·ros** \-ˌräs\ *n, pl* **can·tha·ri** \-ˌrī, -ē\ *or* **kan·tha·roi** \-ˌȯi\ [L & Gk; L *cantharus*, fr. Gk *kantharos*] **1 :** a deep cup of ancient Greece with a high stem and loop-shaped handles continuing the curve of the bottom of the body and rising above the brim **2 :** a stoup for holy water

cantho- — see CANTH-

cant hook *n* [²*cant*] **:** a wooden lever resembling a peavey but having a blunt end often with a toe ring and lip instead of a sharp spike

cant hook

can·thus \ˈkan(t)thəs\ *n, pl* **can·thi** \-ˌnˌthī, -ē\ [LL, fr. Gk *kanthos* — more at CANT (angle)] **:** either of the angles formed by the meeting of the upper and lower eyelids **:** one of the corners of the eye

canthus ros·tra·lis \-räˈstraləs, -ˈā-,-ˈä-\ *n, pl* **canthi rostra·les** \-(ˌ)lēz\ [NL, lit., rostral canthus] **:** the more or less angular ridge from the anterior border of the eye to the nostril in reptiles and amphibians

can·ti·cle \ˈkantəkəl, -ˈaa-, -ēk-\ *n* -s [ME, fr. L *canticulum* little song, dim. of *canticum* song, fr. *cantus*, past part. of *canere* to sing — more at CHANT] **:** SONG, POEM, HYMN; *specif* **:** one of the biblical hymns or songs of praise (as the Benedicite, the Magnificat, and the Nunc Dimittis) used in church services

can·ti·co \ˈkantəˌkō\ *n* -s [modif. of Del *kǝntka* to dance] **1 :** a ceremonial dance of the Algonquian Indians of the Atlantic seaboard **2 :** a lively social gathering **:** a dancing party **:** DANCE

can·ti·ga \kanˈtēgə\ *n* -s [Sp & Pg; Sp, prob. fr. Pg, prob. of Celt origin; akin to OIr *canim* I sing; akin to L *canere* to sing — more at CHANT] **:** a Portuguese or Spanish folk song usu. having love or religion as its theme

can·til \kanˈtēl, kä-\ *n, pl* **canti·les** \-ē(ˌ)lās\ [AmerSp] **:** a dark-colored Mexican moccasin snake (*Agkistrodon bilineatus*) having a pair of white or yellow lines on each side of the head and the body markings outlined in white

can·ti·le·na \ˌkantᵊlˈēnə, -ˈē-\ *n* -s [It, fr. L, song, fr. *cantus*] **1 :** a brief simple melody often repeated (as in a lullaby or folk song) **2 :** sustained melody **:** CANTABILE

¹can·ti·le·ver \ˈkantᵊlˌēvə(r), -ˈaa-, -təˌlē- *also* -ˌe-\ *n* -s *often attrib* [perh. fr. ²*cant* + *-i-* + *lever*] **:** a projecting beam or member supported at only one end (as by being built into a wall or a pier): as **a :** a bracketlike member supporting a balcony or a cornice — compare BRACKET **b :** either of the two beams or trusses that project from piers toward each other and that when joined directly or by a suspended connecting member form a span of a cantilever bridge

cantilever a

²cantilever \"\ *vt* -ED/-ING/-S **:** to build or project as a cantilever

cantilever arch *n* **:** an archlike spanning structure made by corbeling opposed surfaces **:** a corbel arch

cantilever bridge *n* **1 :** a bridge whose span consists of two cantilever trusses that project toward each other and that are usu. joined by a suspended connecting member — see BRIDGE illustration **2 :** a dental bridge having one end attached to a natural tooth and the other resting unattached in a tooth depression

cantilever spring *n* **:** a flat spring supported at one end and fastened to its load at the center and the other end; *specif* **:** a leaf spring so used in the rear suspension of an automobile

cantilever truss *n* **:** a horizontal truss supported at the middle and sustaining a load at one end or both ends (as in a cantilever bridge)

can·til·late \ˈkantᵊlˌāt\ *vt* -ED/-ING/-S [L *cantillatus*, past part. of *cantillare* to sing low, hum, fr. *cantare* to sing — more at CHANT] **:** to recite with musical usu. improvised tones (as in synagogues and highly liturgical churches) **:** CHANT, INTONE

can·til·la·tion \ˌ==ˈāshən\ *n* -s [L *cantillatus* + E *-ion*] **:** liturgical chanting **:** INTONATION

cant·i·ly \ˈkantəlī, -ˈä-\ *adv* [*canty* + *-ly*] *Scot* **:** CHEERFULLY

can·ti·na \kanˈtēnə\ *n* -s [AmerSp, fr. Sp, lunch box, canteen (the shop), wine cellar, fr. It, wine cellar — more at CANTEEN] *Southwest* **1 :** a pouch or bag at the pommel of a saddle ⟨put the mail into his ~s and rode off⟩ **2** [AmerSp, fr. Sp, canteen (the shop)] **:** a small barroom **:** SALOON

cant·ing \ˈkantiŋ, -ˈaa-,-ˈai-, -ēŋ\ *adj* [fr. pres. part. of ⁵*cant*] **1 :** affectedly pious **:** HYPOCRITICAL ⟨a ~ moralist⟩ **2 :** ALLUSIVE; *esp* **:** alluding in the manner of a rebus to the name of the bearer or owner — used of heraldic bearings, figures on bookplates, and other emblems ⟨the three castles of the Castletons are ~ bearings⟩

canting quoin *or* **canting coin** *n* [fr. pres. part. of ³*cant*] **:** a triangular block for steadying stowed casks in a ship

can·ti·no \kanˈtē(ˌ)nō, kä-\ *n* -s [It, fr. *canto* song — more at CANTO] **:** ²CHANTERELLE

cantion *n* -s [L *cantion-*, *cantio* — more at CANZONE] *obs* **:** SONG

¹can·tle \ˈkantᵊl, -ˈaa-,-ˈai-\ *n* -s [ME *cantel*, fr. ONF, dim. of *cant* edge, corner — more at CANT (angle)] **1 :** a segment or slice cut off or out from something (as from a piece of land or a cheese) **:** PART, PORTION ⟨cutting off . . . a solid ~ of high land from the rest of Yorkshire —Richard Blackmore⟩ **2 :** the upwardly projecting rear part of a saddle — compare POMMEL; see STOCK SADDLE illustration **3** *Scot* **:** the crown of the head

²can·tle *vt* -ED/-ING/-S *obs* **:** to divide into cantles **:** PORTION

cant·let \ˈkantlət\ *n* -s [¹*cantle* + *-et*] **:** a small cantle **:** PIECE, FRAGMENT ⟨a ~ of cold custard pudding —Charlotte Brontë⟩

cantline *var of* CONTLINE

cant·ly \ˈkantlē, -ˈaa-,-ˈai-, -i\ *adv* [⁶*cant* + *-ly*] **:** in canting terms **:** SLANGILY

cant molding *n* [²*cant*] **:** a beveled molding

can·to \ˈkan(ˌ)tō, -ˈä-,-ˈaa-,-ˈá-\ *n* -s [It, fr. L *cantus* song — more at CHANT] **1 :** one of the major divisions of a long poem **2 :** the melody in choral or instrumental music **3** *slang* **:** one of the divisions of a sports contest (as an inning of baseball)

can·to fer·mo \ˈkän(ˌ)tōˈfer(ˌ)mō\ *n* [It, lit., firm song, trans. of ML *cantus firmus*] **:** CANTUS FIRMUS

¹can·ton \ˈkantᵊn, -ˈaa-, -ntən; ˈka(a)nˌtän, (ˈ)=ˈ=\ *n* -s [MF, fr. OProv, fr. *cant* edge, fr. L *cantus*, *canthus* iron ring round a carriage wheel — more at CANT (angle)] **1** *obs* **:** DIVISION, PART, SECTION; *esp* **:** CORNER **2** [MF, fr. It *cantone*, fr. *canto* corner, fr. L *cantus*, *canthus*] **a :** a small territorial division of a country **b :** a district or local governing unit: as (1) **:** one of the states of the Swiss confederation (2) **:** a division of a French arrondissement **3 a :** the area in the upper inner corner of a flag; *specif* **:** a rectangular division occupying the upper inner corner of a flag, usu. comprising one fourth or less of its surface, and usu. containing the national or other device — compare UNION 4 **b :** any one of the four quarters of the surface of a flag **4 a** (1) **:** a rectangular division of a heraldic field usu. placed in the dexter chief (2) **:** the dexter chief region of a heraldic field **b :** any one of the spaces left in the four corners of a heraldic field by a cross; *specif* **:** the dexter chief canton

canton 4a(1)

²can·ton *vb* -ED/-ING/-S *vt* **1** \"\ **:** to divide into parts **:** PORTION; *specif* **:** to divide into cantons or districts — often used with *out* **2** \(ˈ)ka(a)nˌtōn, -tän, kən-ˈt- *also* ˈka(a)ntᵊn *or* -ntən; *Brit usu, US sometimes* (ˈ)ka(a)nˌtün *or* kən-ˈt-\ [F *cantonner*, fr. *canton* part of a country] **:** to allot quarters to (as to a body of troops) **:** QUARTER ~ *vi* *pronounced like vt 2*\ *of troops* **:** to take up quarters

³can·ton \ˈkanˌtän, -ˈaa-, =ˈ=\ *adj, usu cap* [fr. *Canton*, city in S.E. China] **:** of or from the city of Canton, China **:** of the kind or style prevalent in Canton **:** CANTONESE

⁴can·ton \ˈkantᵊn, -ˈaa-, -tən\ *adj, usu cap* [fr. *Canton*, city in Ohio] **:** of or from the city of Canton, Ohio ⟨a *Canton* product⟩ **:** of the kind or style prevalent in Canton

⁵canton *like* ³CANTON\ *n* -s *often cap* [prob. fr. *Canton*, city in S.E. China] **:** HOLLAND BLUE

can·ton·al \ˈka(a)ntᵊnəl, -tən-, (ˈ)ka(a)nˈtän-\ *adj* [F, fr. *canton* + *-al*] **:** of or relating to a canton — **can·ton·al·ism** \-ˌlizəm\ *n* -s

canton crepe \ˈka(a)nˌtän-\ *n, often cap 1st C* [fr. *Canton*, China] **:** a soft thick dress crepe made of silk or rayon in plain weave with fine crosswise ribs

cantoned *adj* [fr. past part. of ²*canton*] **1** *of a heraldic cross* **:** having a charge in each of the four cantons or angular spaces between the branches ⟨a cross ~ with four martlets⟩ **2 :** having the angles or exterior corners provided or decorated with projecting members (as moldings or small columns) ⟨a ~ pier⟩

¹can·ton·ese \ˌka(a)ntᵊnˈēz, -ntəˈn-, -ēs\ *adj, usu cap* [*Canton*, China + E *-ese*] **:** of or relating to Canton, China, its inhabitants, or their dialect

²cantonese \"\ *n, pl* **cantonese** *cap* **1 :** a native or inhabitant of Canton, China **2 :** the dialect of Chinese spoken in and around Canton

canton flannel \ˈka(a)nˌtän-\ *n, often cap C* [fr. *Canton*, China] **:** FLANNEL 1b (2)

canton ginger \"-\ *n, usu cap C* [fr. *Canton*, China] **:** a fine grade of crystallized or preserved ginger

can·ton·i·za·tion \ˌka(a)ntᵊnəˈzāshən, (ˌ)ka(a)nˌtän-\ *n* -s **:** the process of cantonizing

can·ton·ize \ˈka(a)ntᵊnˌīz\ *vt* -ED/-ING/-S [¹*canton* + *-ize*] **:** CANTON 1

can·ton·ment \kanˈtōnmənt, kaan-ˌkən-, -tän- *also* ˈka(a)ntᵊn- *or* -ntən- *or* -nˌtän-; *Brit usu, US sometimes* ka(a)nˈtün- *or* kən-\ *n* -s [F *cantonnement*, fr. *cantonner* to canton (troops) — more at CANTON] **1 :** the quartering of troops **2 a :** a group of more or less temporary structures for housing troops ⟨all hands now set to work to prepare a winter ~ —Washington Irving⟩ **b** *India* **:** a permanent military station

cantons *pl of* CANTON, *pres 3d sing of* CANTON

can·ton's phosphorus \ˈka(a)ntᵊnz-, -ntənz-\ *n, usu cap C* [after John *Canton* †1772 Eng. physicist, its discoverer] **:** phosphorescent calcium sulfide CaS

canton ware \ˈka(a)nˌtän-, (ˈ)=ˈ=-\ *n, usu cap C* [fr. *Canton*, China, whence it was imported] **:** ceramic ware exported from China esp. during the 18th and 19th centuries mostly by way of Canton and including blue-and-white and enameled porcelain and various ornamented stonewares

can·tor \ˈkantə(r), -ˈaa-,-ˈai-\ *n* -s [L, singer, fr. *cantus* (past part. of *canere* to sing) + *-or* — more at CHANT] **1 :** a choir leader **:** PRECENTOR ⟨the ~ of the church intones the Te Deum —H.H.Milman⟩ **2 :** a synagogue official who sings or chants liturgical music and leads the congregation in prayer — called also *hazan*

can·tor·ate \-ərət,-əˌrāt\ *n* -s **1 :** the office or tenure of office of a cantor **2 :** the body of cantors

can·to·ria \ˌkantəˈrēə\ *n, pl* **cantori·as** \-ˈrēəz\ *or* **canto·rie** \-ˈrēˌā\ [It, fr. *cantore* singer (fr. L *cantor*) + *-ia* -y] **:** a balcony for singers; *specif* **:** the choir gallery in an Italian church

can·to·ri·al \(ˈ)ka(a)nˌtōrēəl, -ˈȯ-\ *or* **can·tor·al** \ˈka(a)ntərəl, -ˈai-\ *also* **can·tor·ous** \ˈ==rəs\ *adj* [*cantor* + *-ial* or *-al* or *-ous*] **1 :** of or being the ecclesiastical north side of the choir of a cathedral or church — contrasted with *decanal* **2 :** of or relating to a cantor ⟨a ~ position⟩

can·to·ris \(ˈ)kanˌtōrəs, -aan-, -ȯr-\ *adj* [L, gen. of *cantor*] **:** CANTORIAL

cantos *pl of* CANTO

cant purchase *n* [²*cant*] **:** a powerful tackle used to cant a whale in the operation of flensing

can·tred \ˈkanˌtred\ *or* **can·tref** \-ev\ *n* -s [ME *cantrede*, *candrede* fr. ML *cantredus*, *candredus*, modif. (prob. influenced by ML *hundredus* hundred, division of an English county) of MW *cantref*, fr. *cant* hundred + *tref* home, town; akin to L *centum* hundred and to OE *thorp* village] **:** an obsolete Welsh territorial unit composed of a hundred trefs **:** HUNDRED

can·trip *also* **can·trap** *or* **can·traip** \ˈkänˌtrəp\ *n* -s *often attrib* [prob. alter. of *caltrop*] *chiefly Scot* **:** SPELL **:** a witch's trick **:** a mischievous or extravagant act

cants *pl of* CANT, *pres 3d sing of* CANT

cant·saw file \ˈ=ˌ=\ *n* [²*cant* + *saw*] **:** a file similar to the cant file but slightly thicker and not tapered

cant spar *n* [prob. fr. *cant* "frame joined obliquely to the keel" — more at ²CANT] **:** a small pole suitable for a small mast, yard, or boom

cant strip *n* [²*cant*] **1 :** a beveled strip placed in the angle between a roof and a wall against which the roof abuts so as to avoid a sharp bend in the roofing material **2 :** a strip used under the lower edge of the lowest row of tiles on a roof to give this row the same slope as the rows above it

cant timber *n* [²*cant*] **:** a timber of a cant frame of a ship

can·tua \kanˈtüə\ *n, cap* [NL, fr. Sp *cantú* cantuta, fr. Quechua *ccantu*] **:** a genus of shrubs or small trees (family Polemoniaceae) having crowded, simple, short-stalked or sessile leaves, flowers in close terminal clusters, and a corolla with a slender tube much exceeding the calyx — see CANTUTA

can·tus \ˈkantəs, -ˈaa-\ *n, pl* **cantus** [L, song — more at CHANT] **1 :** CANTUS FIRMUS **2 :** the principal melody or voice

cantus fir·mus \-ˈfirməs, -ˈfər-\ *n* [ML, lit., fixed song] **1 :** the plainchant or simple Gregorian melody that was orig. sung in unison and prescribed as to form and use by ecclesiastical tradition **2 :** a melodic theme or subject; *esp* **:** one for contrapuntal treatment

cantus ge·mel·lus \-jəˈmeləs, -gəˈ-\ *n* [ML, lit., twin song] **:** GYMEL

cantus men·su·ra·bi·lis \-ˌmen(t)səˈräbələs, -nchə-, -ab-\ *n* [ML, lit., measurable song] **:** MEASURED MUSIC 2

cantus pla·nus \-ˈplänəs, -ˈā-\ *n* [ML, lit., plain song] **:** CANTUS FIRMUS 1

can·tu·ta \kanˈtüd·ə\ *also* **can·tut** \-üt\ *n* -s [Sp, *cantuta*, var. of *cantú* — more at CANTUA] **:** a shrub or small tree (*Cantua buxifolia*) used as an ornamental in the southwestern U. S. and having a showy yellow-striped pink or red flower — called also *Inca magic flower*

cant window *n* [²*cant*] **:** a projecting window with angles — sometimes distinguished from *bow window*

canty \ˈkanti, -ˈä-\ *adj* [¹*cant* + *-y*] *dial Brit* **:** CHEERFUL, SPRIGHTLY, LIVELY

ca·nuck \kəˈnək\ *n* -s *cap, often attrib* [prob. alter. of ²*Canadian*] **1 :** CANADIAN **2** *chiefly Canad* **:** FRENCH CANADIAN **3 :** CANADIAN FRENCH — usu. used disparagingly

canula *var of* CANNULA

ca·nun \kä'nün\ *or* **ca·non** \-ˈnōn\ *n* -s [Turk & Ar; Turk *kānun*, fr. Ar *qānūn*, fr. Gk *kanōn* monochord, measuring line, standard — more at CANON] **:** ZITHER

can·u·til·lo \ˌkan(y)əˈtē(ˌ)ō\ *n* -s [MexSp, fr. Sp *canutillo*, *cañutillo* little tube, dim. of *canuto*, *cañuto* tube, pipe, section of cane, fr. Ar dial. (Spain) *qannūt*, fr. (assumed) VL *cannutus* of cane, fr. L *canna* cane — more at CANE] **:** MORMON TEA

¹can·vas *also* **can·vass** \ˈkanvəs, -ˈaa-\ *n* -ES *often attrib* [ME *canevas*, fr. ONF, fr. (assumed) VL *cannabaceus* hempen, fr. L *cannabis* hemp, fr. Gk *kannabis* — more at HEMP] **1 :** a firm closely woven cloth of plain weave made in various weights usu. of linen, hemp, or cotton and used esp. for clothing, sails, tarpaulins, and awnings — compare ⁴DUCK **2 :** a set of sails **:** SAIL ⟨sailing under full ~⟩ ⟨under light ~⟩ **3 :** a piece of canvas used for a particular purpose: as **a :** a covering over the end of a racing boat to keep out water **b :** APRON 4a **4 :** a tent or a group of tents: as **a :** CIRCUS, CARNIVAL ⟨the lure of the ~⟩ **b :** a military or camping tent ⟨sleeping under ~⟩ **5 a** (1) **:** a cloth surface prepared to receive an oil painting (2) **:** the painting on such a surface **b :** the background, setting, or scope of an historical or fictional account or narrative ⟨the crowded ~ of history⟩ **c :** PICTURE 9a **6 :** a stiff material with coarse even meshes woven usu. of hard-twisted yarns in a plain weave often with drawable threads for tapestry and embroidery **7 :** a linen or hair-and-wool canvas with a soft or sized finish used as an interlining or foundation to give body to some part of a garment, esp. a coat front **8 :** the floor of a boxing or wrestling ring — **on the canvas :** knocked down **:** close to defeat

²canvas \"\ *vt* **canvased** *or* **canvassed; canvased** *or* **canvassed; canvasing** *or* **canvassing; canvases** *or* **canvasses** **:** to cover, line, or furnish with canvas ⟨the door had been nailed up and ~*ed* over —Charles Dickens⟩

³canvas *var of* CANVASS

can·vas·back \ˈ=ˌ=\ *also* **canvasback duck** *n* [so called fr. its color] **:** a No. American wild duck (*Aythya valisineria*) formerly abundant in Chesapeake Bay and somewhat resembling the redhead in plumage but differing in the longer deeper bill and in the duller reddish brown head of the male which has the back finely vermiculated with gray and white

canvas board *n* **1 :** a board having a textured surface often stamped or molded in imitation of canvas to receive an artist's painting **2 :** CANVAS PANEL

can·vas·man \-ˌman, -mən, -ˌmaa(ə)n\ *n, pl* **canvasmen** **1 :** a circus employee who assists in the pitching and taking down of tents **2 :** BRATTICER

canvas panel *n* **:** a surface composed of canvas mounted on stiff board and prepared to receive an artist's painting

¹can·vass *also* **can·vas** \ˈkanvəs, -ˈaa-\ *vb* -ED/-ING/-ES [¹*canvas*] *vt* **1** *obs* **:** to toss in or as if in a canvas sheet by way of sport or punishment ⟨I'll ~ thee between a pair of sheets —Shak.⟩ **2 a** *obs* **:** to knock about **:** BEAT, TROUNCE **b** *archaic* **:** to lash with criticism or invective **:** CASTIGATE ⟨the ribald style in which Martin Marprelate ~*ed* the bishops —E.K.Chambers⟩ **3 a :** to examine in detail **:** subject to scrutiny or investigation; *specif* **:** to examine (votes) officially for authenticity **b :** DISCUSS, DEBATE ⟨~*ed* all the items on the agenda⟩ **4** *archaic* **:** to strive after (as approval) ⟨kings sometimes ~*ed* that title for themselves —Oliver Goldsmith⟩ **5 a :** to go through (a district) or go to (persons) to solicit orders, subscriptions, or advertising **b :** to cover (a district) or go to (persons) to solicit political support or to try to ascertain the probable vote before an election ⟨the candidate is ~*ing* the farm belt this week⟩ **c :** to determine the opinions or sentiments of (as the members of a club or the staff of an institution) esp. by informal questioning **:** POLL ⟨the faculty was ~*ed* on its preferences in teaching schedules⟩ **6** *chiefly Brit* **a :** to put forward (as a plan or an idea) **b :** SPREAD, CIRCULATE ⟨~*ing* rumors⟩ ~ *vi* **1 :** DEBATE, DISCUSS **2 a :** to seek orders, contributions, support, subscriptions, or advertising **:** SOLICIT ⟨~ for a newspaper⟩ ⟨~ in behalf of a charity⟩ **b :** to solicit votes or seek political support in an election campaign ⟨~ for a seat in Parliament⟩

²canvass \"\ *n* -ES **1 a :** a detailed examination esp. by means of discussion or debate **:** full discussion ⟨learned ~*es* of the deep points of divinity —Joseph Hall⟩ **b :** a scrutiny or recount of votes ⟨a ~ of the election returns⟩ **2 :** the act or action of canvassing ⟨a house-to-house ~⟩: as **a :** the personal solicitation of votes **b :** a survey to ascertain the probable vote before an election

³canvass *var of* CANVAS

can·vass·er \-sə(r)\ *n* -s **:** one that canvasses: as **a :** one that takes or counts votes **b :** a solicitor esp. for funds or subscriptions **:** a campaign worker **c :** a door-to-door salesman

canvas shoe *n* **:** a light shoe with a canvas upper and a rubber, leather, or fiber sole **:** TENNIS SHOE

canvas work *n* **:** embroidery worked usu. in cross-stitch or tent stitch on canvas or by the aid of canvas — compare PETIT POINT

cany \ˈkānē\ *adj, sometimes* -ER/-EST [¹*cane* + *-y*] **1 :** made of cane **2 :** abounding in canes **3 :** characterized by canebrakes

¹can·yon *also* **ca·ñon** \ˈkanyən\ *n* -s [AmerSp *cañón*, prob. alter. of obs. Sp *callón*, aug. of *calle* street, fr. L *callis* footpath; akin to Czech *klanec* mountain pass] **1 a :** a deep narrow valley with precipitous sides characteristic of regions where downward cutting of the streams greatly exceeds weathering **:** GORGE **b :** a long deep steep-sided depression in the ocean floor typically on the continental shelf and opening out in a deep basin — called also *submarine canyon*; compare DEEP, TRENCH, TROUGH **c :** a city street bordered on both sides by lofty buildings ⟨the ~*s* of the financial district⟩ **2 :** PLUM VIOLET

[2]**canyon** *also* **cañon** \"\ *vb* -ED/-ING/-S *vt* **:** to make a canyon in **:** pierce with canyons ~ *vi* **:** to enter or flow into a canyon (as of a stream) **:** narrow into a canyon (as of a valley)
canyon gooseberry *n* **1 :** the globose bristly fruit of a low shrub (*Ribes menziesii*) of the western U. S. **2 :** the shrub yielding the canyon gooseberry
canyon grape *n* **:** a grape (*Vitis arizonica*) of Texas and Arizona yielding inferior black fruit
canyon live oak *or* **canyon oak** *n* **:** a California evergreen oak (*Quercus chrysolepis*) with oblong leathery often spiny-edged leaves covered on the under side with a yellow tomentum — called also *iron oak, maul oak*
canyon mouse *n* **:** a white-footed mouse (*Peromyscus crinitus*) widely distributed in rocky areas of the western U. S.
can·yon·side \ˈ==,=\ *n* **:** the steeply sloping side of a canyon
canyon wren *n* **:** a common wren (*Catherpes mexicanus*) having a white breast and rusty belly and occurring in several local races in the southwestern U. S.
canzo *var of* CANSO
canzon *n* -S [It *canzone*] *archaic* **:** SONG
can·zo·ne \kanˈzōnē, käntˈsō(,)nä\ *also* **can·zo·na** \-ōnə\ *n, pl* **canzo·ne** \-ō(,)nä\ *also* **canzonas** \-ōnəz\ *or* **canzo·ni** \-ō(,)nē\ *or* **canzones** \-ōnēz, -ō(,)näz\ [It, fr. L *cantion-, cantio* song, fr. *cantus* (past part. of *canere* to sing) + *-ion-, -io* -ion — more at CHANT] **1 a :** a medieval Italian or Provençal lyric poem in stanzaic form **b :** an elaborately constructed ode suited to musical setting **2 a :** the melody of a canzone **b :** a setting of a canzone in polyphonic style resembling that of the madrigal **c :** an instrumental composition in similar style
can·zo·net \ˌkanzəˈnet\ *also* **can·zo·net·ta** \ˌkanzəˈned·ə\ *n, pl* **canzonets** \-ets\ *also* **canzonettas** \-ed·əz\ *or* **canzo·net·te** \-ed·ē\ [It *canzonetta*, dim. of *canzone*] **1 :** a short canzone **:** a part-song resembling but less elaborate than a madrigal **2 :** a light and graceful song
CAO *abbr* chief administrative officer
ca·o·ba \käˈōbə\ *n* -S [Sp, fr. Taino *caoban*] **1 :** MAHOGANY 3a **2 :** QUIRA
cao dai \(ˈ)kaùˈdī\ *n, pl* **cao dai** *cap C&D* [Vietnamese] **:** CAODAISM
cao·da·ism \(ˈ)kaùˈdī,izəm\ *n* -S *cap* [Vietnamese *Cao Dai*, lit., great palace + E *-ism*] **:** an Indo-Chinese religion originating in Cochin China in 1926, consisting of an amalgamation of elements from Buddhism, Taoism, Confucianism, Christianity, and spiritualism, and having its clergy headed by a pope who as the direct representative of its supreme deity exercises both spiritual and temporal power
cao·da·ist \-ˈīəst\ *n* -S *usu cap* **:** an adherent of Caodaism
caoine \ˈkēn\ *n* -S [IrGael] *Irish* **:** [5]KEEN
caou·tchouc \(ˈ)kaùˈchük, -ük, kəˈch-, *F* käùchü\ *n* -S [F, fr. obs. Sp *cauchuc* (now *caucho*), fr. Quechua *cauchu, caucho, cauchuc*] **:** [1]RUBBER 2a
caoutchouc tree *n* **:** PARA RUBBER
[1]**cap** \ˈkap\ *n* -S *often attrib* [ME *cappe*, fr. OE *cæppe*, fr. LL *cappa* head covering, cloak, perh. irreg. fr. L *caput* head — more at HEAD] **1 :** a covering for the head typically fairly tight-fitting, brimless, and relatively simple: as **a :** one with a full crown and a ruffled edge gathered on or held by a ribbon band and worn formerly by women **b :** one of fabric, yarn, rubber, or leather, without brim, with or without visor, chin strap, or earflaps, and with a crown ranging from shallow to deep and from soft to stiff **c :** HELMET, HEADPIECE **d :** a man's or boy's cap typically with a visor of some stiffness **e :** one without a brim, fitting close to the crown of the head, made usu. of fabric, often elaborately trimmed, and worn by women

caps 3, *A*

2 : something that covers naturally **:** a natural cover or top: as **a :** an overlying rock layer or stratum usu. hard to penetrate: as (1) **:** an impervious layer immediately over the oil-producing or gas-producing formation in an oil pool (2) **:** dense usu. limestone or anhydrite rock immediately above the salt in a salt dome (3) *or* **cap rock :** a bed of resistant rock, boulders, or gravel at the summit of a mesa, hill, or cliff **b** (1) **:** PILEUS (2) **:** CALYPTRA **c :** KNEECAP, PATELLA **d :** WHITECAP **e :** POLAR CAP, ICE CAP **f** (1) **:** the whole top of a bird's head from the base of the bill to the nape of the neck (2) **:** a patch of distinctively colored feathers on the head of many birds **g :** the wax covering for the individual cell made by bees in sealing up honey or pupae in the comb **h** *Northeast* **:** CORNHUSK **3 :** something that serves as a cover or protection esp. for a tip, knob, or end **:** something designed to cover and to protect, preserve, or close (as over a camera lens, fountain pen, automobile hub, or narrow-mouthed bottle): **a :** the separate piece of leather commonly attached to the vamp at the toe of a shoe as a covering — called also *tip* **b :** a fitting for closing the end of a tube (as a water pipe or electric conduit); *esp* **:** an internally threaded cup-shaped part that screws on **c :** a covering of tarred canvas for the end of a rope **d :** a readily removable protective cover or plate over a lock (as on a door) or latch **e :** the part of an electrical attachment plug or cord connector to which a flexible conductor is attached **f :** a paper covering placed over the gold edges of fine books until they are bound **g :** a sheet-steel cone placed over the end of a log to facilitate its being skidded esp. by steam power **h :** a layer of new rubber fused onto the worn surface of a pneumatic tire **i :** a blunt nose that is fitted onto an armor-piercing projectile (as a shell) **4** *archaic* **:** a respectful doffing of one's cap ⟨he that will give a ~ and make a leg in thanks —Thomas Fuller⟩ **5 :** a cap as a token or symbol: as **a :** a cardinal's biretta **b :** a cap worn by students and officers of schools, colleges, and universities typically tight-fitting and having a flat projecting square top with a tassel — see MORTARBOARD **c** *Brit* (1) **:** a cap awarded to an athlete (as a soccer player) in recognition of membership on a national or other representative team ⟨he gained his county ~⟩ (2) **:** a player awarded a cap ⟨a new ~ was brought in to replace the halfback⟩ **d :** a white cap worn by graduate nurses or by student nurses after a probationary period **6 :** an overlaying or covering structure **:** something that is placed or constructed above ⟨the galleried ~ of the old water tower is sometimes open to visitors⟩: **a :** the uppermost of any assemblage of architectural parts esp. of a column, door, or molding (as a capital, lintel, cornice, or coping) **b** (1) **:** a horizontal support typically of heavy timber for the roof of a mine working (2) **:** the narrowing of an ore vein by contraction at its upper part **c :** CAPSHEAF **7 :** a device for joining together masts or spars consisting either of a thick wood block with two large holes or of a metal collar — see SHIP illustration **8 a :** a paper or metal container holding an explosive charge **:** such a device used to detonate another charge **b :** a firearm primer **c :** a minute explosive charge sealed between the layers of a paper strip for use in a toy gun **d :** a BB or CB cap **9 :** a blue tip on a safety-lamp flame that shows the presence of firedamp **10** *Brit* **:** the collection taken at a fox hunt esp. from nonsubscribers — **cap in hand :** RESPECTFULLY, SUBMISSIVELY, OBSEQUIOUSLY
[2]**cap** \"\ *vb* **capped; capped; capping; caps** [ME *cappen*, fr. *cappe*, n.] *vt* **1 :** to provide with a cap **:** put a cap on **:** cover, protect, or close with or as if with a cap **:** cover the top or end of ⟨Corinthian columns *capped* by Grecian spans of Bedford limestone —*Amer. Guide Series: Texas*⟩: as **a :** to give a cap to as a symbol of honor or rank: (1) *Scot* **:** to confer a university degree on (2) **:** to invest (a student nurse) with a cap as an indication of completion of a probationary period of study **b :** to cover (a diseased or exposed part of a tooth) with a protective substance (as a paste) **c :** to seal off (an oil or gas well) by clamping a cap over the end of a casing **d :** to seal (a cell of a honeycomb) with wax **e** (1) **:** to put a cap on the nipple of (a percussion lock) (2) **:** to seat a cap or primer in the recess in the base of (a cartridge case) **2** *archaic* **:** to salute by tipping one's cap to ⟨you would not ~ the pope's commissioner —Alfred Tennyson⟩ **3** *dial* **:** SURPRISE, PUZZLE, PERPLEX **4 :** to form a cap over **:** CROWN, COVER, OVERLAY ⟨limestone ledges a few feet in thickness ~ the hills —*Amer. Guide Series: La.*⟩ ⟨the mountains were *capped* with mist —John Buchan⟩ **5 a :** to follow with something more noticeable or more significant **:** proffer as better or more extreme **:** OUTDO, SURPASS, EXCEL ⟨*capped* the comment with a remark still more immodest —Dorothy Sayers⟩ **b :** to provide with a high point, zenith, or acme **:** CLIMAX ⟨suppose he ~*s* his studies by marrying one of the doctor's daughters —William Black⟩ ⟨St. Thomas ~*s* his ethical system with a doctrine of salvation —Frank Thilly⟩ **c :** to reply to in order with an appropriate answer or quotation according to set rules (as calling for a verse beginning with the initial or final letter of what has been previously offered) ⟨I'll ~ verses with him —John Dryden⟩ ⟨a group of farmers *capping* alliterative sentences with one another —F.M.Stenton⟩ **6 :** to take the cap off or away from ⟨~ a bottle⟩ ⟨~ a comb of honey⟩ ~ *vi* **:** to take off one's cap in respectful salute ⟨they ~ when they pass the dean⟩ — **cap the climax :** to exceed a plausible climax **:** pass the limits of what might be expected
[3]**cap** *vt* **capped; capped; capping; caps** [prob. fr. ONF *caper* to seize, prob. fr. *cape* cloak with hood, fr. LL *cappa* head covering, cloak — more at CAP (head covering)] *obs* **:** ARREST, SEIZE
[4]**cap** \ˈkap\ *n* -S [alter. of earlier Sc *cop*, fr. ME, cup, bowl, fr. OE *copp* cup; akin to OHG *kopf* cup, ON *koppr*; all fr. a prehistoric NGmc-WGmc word borrowed fr. LL *cuppa* — more at CUP] *Scot* **:** a shallow wooden bowl often with two handles
[5]**cap** \ˈkap\ *n* -S *often attrib* [by shortening] **:** a capital letter ⟨the names of places written in ~*s*⟩
[6]**cap** \"\ *vt* **capped; capped; capping; caps** [by shortening] **:** CAPITALIZE
[7]**cap** \"\ *n* -S [by shortening] **:** a handicap race
[8]**cap** \"\ *n* -S [by shortening] **:** a capsule esp. of heroin
cap *abbr* **1** capacity **2** \ˈkap\ capital **3** capitulum **4** captain **5** caput
ca·pa \ˈkäpə\ *n* -S [Sp, fr. LL *cappa* hooded cloak — more at CAP (head covering)] **1 a :** a circular mantle or cloak **b :** a bullfighter's cape **2** [AmerSp, fr. Sp, cloak] **:** a fine grade of Cuban tobacco used largely for wrappers
ca·pa·bil·i·ty \ˌkāpəˈbiləd·ē, -ətē, -i\ *n* -ES [LL *capabilis* + E *-ity*] **1 :** the quality or state of being capable physically, intellectually, morally, or legally **:** CAPACITY, ABILITY ⟨participating in sports according to their *capabilities*⟩ ⟨developed the *capabilities* that made him a nationally known mining engineer⟩ **2 :** a feature or faculty capable of development or likely to improve **:** a latent usu. valuable characteristic **:** POTENTIALITY ⟨there were great *capabilities* in the scenery —T.L.Peacock⟩ **3 :** the quality or state of being susceptible to action or treatment as indicated ⟨the ~ of a metal to be fused⟩
ca·pa·ble \ˈkāpəbəl, *rapid* -pb-\ *adj, sometimes* -ER/-EST [MF or LL; MF *capable*, fr. LL *capabilis*, irreg. fr. L *capere* to take, contain — more at HEAVE] **1** *archaic* **a :** able to take in, contain, receive, or accommodate ⟨a room ~ of 20 people⟩ ⟨a harbor ~ of the largest ships⟩ **b :** able to perceive or comprehend ⟨an ear ~ of faint sounds⟩ ⟨when he became ~ of ordinary occurrences she detailed all —James Stephens⟩ **2 :** constituted, situated, or characterized as susceptible or open to being affected — used postpositively with following *of* ⟨such as we, not ~ of death or pain —John Milton⟩ ⟨an order ~ of execution⟩ ⟨a passage ~ of misinterpretation⟩ ⟨a formal doctrine ~ of being expressed in a few catchwords —Lewis Mumford⟩ **3** *obs* **:** INCLUSIVE, COMPREHENSIVE ⟨a ~ and wide revenge —Shak.⟩ **4 :** having sufficient power, prowess, intelligence, resources, strength, or other needed attributes to perform or accomplish — usu. used postpositively with *of* followed by a gerund or actional noun ⟨a highly intelligent man, ~ of close application of mind —Charles Dickens⟩ ⟨children are not ~ of looking after their own interests —Bertrand Russell⟩ ⟨ships ~ of facing the heavy seas —J.A.Froude⟩ **5 :** marked by or possessed of a predisposition to **:** having characteristics or personality traits conducive to or admitting of — used postpositively with *of* ⟨all who are ~ of absorption in an inward passion —Bertrand Russell⟩ ⟨this woman is ~ of murder by violence —Robert Graves⟩ ⟨a grace and dexterity of which no common maid is ~ —Lafcadio Hearn⟩ **6 :** possessed of or marked by general efficiency and ability and by adequate resourcefulness, skill, and reliability ⟨~ pilots⟩ ⟨the ~ direction of the play⟩ ⟨the ~ fashioning fingers of the artist —W.S.Maugham⟩ ⟨still composed, still ~, still mistress of herself and any emergency —Ellen Glasgow⟩ **7** *obs* **:** having legal qualification or right to own, enjoy, or perform ⟨of my land. . . to make thee ~ —Shak.⟩ **syn** see ABLE
ca·pa·ble·ness \-bəlnəs\ *n* -ES **:** CAPABILITY
ca·pa·bly \-blē, -li\ *adv* **:** in a capable manner
ca·pa·cious \kəˈpāshəs\ *adj* [L *capac-, capax* capacious (fr. *capere* to take, contain) + E *-ious* — more at HEAVE] **1** *obs* **:** having size or scope enough to contain — used with *of* or an infinitive ⟨a jar ~ of six gallons⟩ **2 a :** able to contain a great deal **:** affording much space **:** LARGE, COPIOUS ⟨his ~ pockets contained a pruning knife and twine —John Buchan⟩ ⟨a colonial fireplace ~ enough to roast an ox —*Amer. Guide Series: Pa.*⟩ **b :** not narrow or constricted **:** marked by ample scope **:** INCLUSIVE ⟨the rule did not tie men of quick and ~ minds —R.W.Southern⟩ **3** *archaic* **:** fitted or disposed to receive or entertain ⟨a mind ~ of such interests⟩ **syn** see AMPLE
ca·pa·cious·ly \-slē, -li\ *adv* **:** in a capacious manner
ca·pa·cious·ness \-snəs\ *n* -ES **:** the quality or state of being capacious
ca·pac·i·tance \kəˈpasətən(t)s, -əd·ən-\ *n* -S [[1]*capacity* + *-ance*] **1 :** the property of an electric nonconductor that permits the storage of energy as a result of electric displacement when opposite surfaces of the nonconductor are maintained at a difference of potential (as in a capacitor), its measure being the ratio of the charge on either surface to the potential difference between the surfaces and its value for a capacitor being the sum of the combined values of its several dielectric plates — called also *capacity* **2 :** a part of a circuit or network that possesses capacitance
ca·pac·i·tate \kəˈpasə,tāt\ *vt* -ED/-ING/-S [[1]*capacity* + *-ate*] **:** to make capable **:** QUALIFY ⟨by this instruction we may be *capacitated* to observe those errors —John Dryden⟩
ca·pac·i·ta·tion \kə,pasəˈtāshən\ *n* -S **:** the act of capacitating **:** QUALIFICATION
ca·pac·i·tive \kəˈpasəd·iv\ *also* **ca·pac·i·ta·tive** \-sə,tād·iv\ *adj* [*capacitive* fr. [1]*capacity* + *-ive; capacitative* fr. *capacitate* + *-ive*] **:** of or relating to capacitance — **ca·pac·i·tive·ly** *adv*
capacitive coupling *n* **:** a coupling in which the two circuits have a common capacitor
capacitive reactance *n* **:** reactance due to the presence of capacitance in an alternating-current circuit
ca·pac·i·tiv·i·ty \kə,pasəˈtivəd·ē\ *n* -ES **:** DIELECTRIC CONSTANT
ca·pac·i·tor \kəˈpasəd·ə(r), -ətə-\ *n* -S [[1]*capacity* + *-or*] **:** a device giving large capacitance or desired values of capacitance usu. consisting of conducting plates or foils separated by thin layers of dielectric (as air, paraffin paper, or mica), the plates on opposite sides of the dielectric layers being oppositely charged by a source of voltage and the electrical energy of the charged system being stored in the polarized dielectric with the capacitance proportional to the area and dielectric constant of the dielectric layer and inversely proportional to its thickness — called also *condenser*

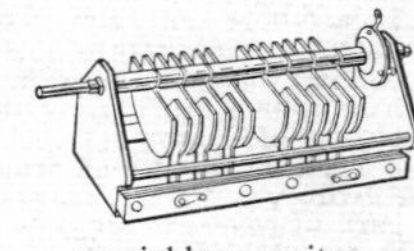
variable capacitor

capacitor motor *n* **:** a single-phase alternating-current motor having a main winding that receives energy directly from the power line and a second usu. auxiliary winding that receives energy through a capacitor, the currents in the two windings differing in phase and producing torque
[1]**ca·pac·i·ty** \kəˈpasəd·ē, -s(ə)tē, -ˈaa-, -i\ *n* -ES [ME *capacite*, fr. MF *capacité*, fr. L *capacitat-, capacitas*, fr. *capac-, capax* capacious, capable + *-itat-, -itas -ity* — more at CAPACIOUS] **1 a :** the power or ability to hold, receive, or accommodate ⟨had our great palace the ~ to camp this host, we all would sup together —Shak.⟩ **b** *obs* **:** an empty space **:** a hollowed-out area **:** CAVITY **c :** a containing space **:** a measure of content for gas, liquid, or solid **:** the amount held **:** the measured ability to contain **:** VOLUME ⟨a tank with a ~ of 20 gallons⟩ ⟨the air ~ of a normal lung⟩ ⟨one modern cement elevator has a storage ~ of 114,000 barrels —*Amer. Guide Series: Minn.*⟩ **d :** the ability to absorb ⟨the ~ of warm air for moisture⟩ **e :** the ability to accommodate people **:** the size or number of accommodations **:** the condition of maximum service with all accommodations used ⟨an auditorium with a seating ~ of 5000⟩ ⟨taxing the *capacities* of nearby hospitals⟩ ⟨the stadium was filled to ~⟩ **f :** the ability to store, process, treat, manufacture, or produce **:** an instrumentality or facility for production **:** maximum processing, production, or output ⟨a flood of war orders that strained the ~ of factories long idle —Oscar Handlin⟩ ⟨the largest spruce mill in the world, with a ~ of 400,000 board feet every eight hours —*Amer. Guide Series: Oregon*⟩ ⟨steel mills operating at ~⟩ ⟨a generating ~ measured in kilovolt amperes⟩ **g :** the ability to yield and to sustain ⟨ranchers considering the carrying ~ of the range lands⟩ **h** (1) **:** CAPACITANCE (2) **:** the quantity of electricity that a battery can deliver under specified conditions **i :** the ability of a stream to transport detritus as measured by the quantity carried past a point in a certain time — compare COMPETENCE **j :** potentiality for production or use **:** maximum potentiality **:** facilities for production or service **2 :** legal qualification, competency, power, or fitness **3 a :** ABILITY, CALIBER, STATURE **b :** mental power, capability, and acumen blended to enable one to grasp ideas, to analyze and judge, and to cope with problems **:** maximum potential mental ability ⟨inexpressibly ordinary, yet giving an impression of ~ —G.K.Chesterton⟩ ⟨not a philosophical treatise but a work intended for the ~ of the popular mind —S.F.Mason⟩ **c :** blended power, strength, and ability ⟨encourage physical activity to the limit of the child's ~ —Morris Fishbein⟩ ⟨the *capacities* of present-day rockets —*Time*⟩ **d :** capability or faculty for executing, considering, appreciating, or experiencing — used with *for* or an infinitive ⟨with all her ~ for violence, Lola possessed also a strong ~ for affection —Margaret Mead⟩ ⟨a ~ for delicate discrimination —J.L.Lowes⟩ ⟨the ~ of American idealism to survive a major disillusionment —Archibald MacLeish⟩ **4 a** *archaic* **:** a situation enabling or making capable ⟨a ship in a ~ to begin the battle⟩ **b :** a position, character, or role either duly assigned or assumed without sanction ⟨in his ~ as legal adviser⟩ ⟨served the government in several *capacities*⟩ — **at capacity :** in service or production with all facilities utilized **:** at maximum production
[2]**capacity** \"\ *adj* **:** attaining to or equaling maximum capacity ⟨a ~ crowd⟩ ⟨~ production of electricity⟩
capacity coupling *n* **:** CAPACITIVE COUPLING
capacity factor *n* **:** the ratio of the average load carried by a power station or system for a given period to the rated capacity of the station or system for the same period — compare LOAD FACTOR
cap-and-ball *adj* **:** having a lock that utilizes a percussion cap to fire a separately loaded charge
cap and bells *n, pl* **caps and bells 1 :** a cap with bells attached worn by a court fool or professional jester **2 :** a fool's bauble **:** MAROTTE
cap and gown *n, pl* **caps and gowns :** the cap and gown that together constitute academic costume
capape *obs var of* CAP-A-PIE
cap-a-pie *or* **cap-à-pie** \ˌkapəˈpē\ *adv* [MF (*de*) *cap a pé* from head to foot, fr. OProv *de cap a pe*] **:** from head to foot **:** at all points ⟨he was armed *cap-a-pie* —W.H.Prescott⟩
ca·pa pri·eto \kəˈpäprēˈäd·(,)ō\ *n, pl* **capa prietos** [AmerSp *capá prieto*, lit., black capá (tree of the genus *Cordia*)] **:** SPANISH ELM
[1]**ca·par·i·son** \kəˈparəsən, -əzən *also* -ˈe-\ *n* -S [MF *caparaçon*, fr. OSp *caparazón*] **1 a :** an ornamental covering for a horse **b :** decorative trappings and harness **2 :** rich clothing **:** ADORNMENT, DECORATION
[2]**caparison** \"\ *vt* -ED/-ING/-S **1 :** to cover with a caparison **:** deck out with ornamental trappings **2 :** to dress richly **:** ADORN ⟨the trees stood majestically ~*ed*, with their innumerable leaves gilt —Virginia Woolf⟩

caparison 1a, 13th century

capas *pl of* CAPA
ca·pa·taz \ˌkapəˈtäz\ *also* **ca·pa·tas** \-äs\ *n, pl* **capata·ces** \ˌkapəˈtäˌsās\ [Sp *capataz*, irreg. fr. L *caput* head — more at HEAD] **:** BOSS, FOREMAN, OVERSEER ⟨behaved very well under their ~ —Joseph Conrad⟩
cap board *n* **:** paperboard used in circular stoppers of bottles
cap bolt *n* **:** TAP BOLT
capcase *n* -S [perh. fr. [1]*cap* + *case*] **1** *obs* **:** a small traveling case or bag **2** *obs* **:** CHEST 1
cap cloud *n* **:** a small cloud surmounting a mountain peak
[1]**cape** \ˈkāp\ *n* -S *often attrib* [ME *cap*, fr. MF, fr. OProv, fr. L *caput* head — more at HEAD] **1 :** a point or extension of land jutting out into water either as a peninsula ⟨*Cape* Cod⟩ or as a projecting point ⟨*Cape* Hatteras⟩ — compare HEADLAND, PROMONTORY **2** *usu cap* [fr. *Cape* of Good Hope] **a :** a product of the Cape of Good Hope Province or of another part of So. Africa ⟨a *Cape* diamond⟩ **b :** leather produced from a So. African hair sheepskin; *broadly* **:** a sheepskin or lambskin glove or garment leather with natural grain retained — compare CAPESKIN **c :** a triangular postage stamp issued by the Cape of Good Hope Colony from 1853 to 1864
[2]**cape** \"\ *n* -S [prob. fr. Sp *capa* cloak, fr. LL *cappa* head covering, cloak — more at CAP (head covering)] **1 a :** a sleeveless outer garment of fabric or fur that fits closely at the neck, hangs loosely from the shoulders, and is made in all lengths **b :** an attached collarlike part of a garment **2 :** the short feathers covering the shoulders of a fowl below the hackle — see COCK illustration **3 :** the pelt from the head, neck, and forepart of the shoulders of an animal esp. for mounting as a trophy **4 :** a red cloak used by a bullfighter or capeador to attract a bull and direct its charge
[3]**cape** \"\ *vt* -ED/-ING/-S [trans. of Sp *capear*] **:** to attract and direct the charge of (a bull) by flourishing a cape
ca·pe·ador \kəpāəˈthȯr\ *n, pl* **capeadors** \-thȯrz\ *or* **capeado·res** \-thōräs\ [Sp, fr. *capear* to play tricks on the bull with one's cloak, fr. *capa* cloak — more at CAPE] **:** a bullfighter's aide who uses a capa to distract or excite the bull
cape aloe *n, usu cap C* [fr. *Cape* of Good Hope, Union of South Africa] **:** a much-branched southern African plant (*Aloe ferox*) with reddish prickly succulent leaves
cape anteater *n, usu cap C* [fr. *Cape* of Good Hope] **:** AARDVARK
cape armadillo *n, usu cap C* [fr. *Cape* of Good Hope] **:** the scaly anteater (*Manes temminckii*) of southern Africa that like the true armadillo rolls into a ball when alarmed — compare PANGOLIN
cape ash *n, usu cap C* [fr. *Cape* of Good Hope] **1 :** a southern African tree (*Ekebergia capensis*) of the family Meliaceae **2 :** the tough wood of the Cape ash
cape asparagus *n, usu cap C* [fr. *Cape* of Good Hope] **:** LATTICE PLANT
cape baboon *n, usu cap C* [fr. *Cape* of Good Hope] **:** CHACMA
cape beech *n, usu cap C* [fr. *Cape* of Good Hope] **1 :** a southern African hardwood tree (*Myrsine melanophleos*) **2 :** the wood of the Cape beech
cape bladder senna *n, usu cap C* [fr. *Cape* of Good Hope] **:** a scarlet-flowered southern African shrub (*Sutherlandia frutescens*) cultivated in California
cape bonnet *n* [[2]*cape*] **:** a bonnet with a projecting front edge and a deep ruffle on the bottom
cape box *or* **cape boxwood** *n, usu cap C* [fr. *Cape* of Good Hope] **:** a southern African timber tree (*Buxus macowani*)
cape buffalo *n, usu cap C* [fr. *Cape* of Good Hope] **:** a large powerful often very savage buffalo (*Syncerus caffer*) of southern Africa having the horns joined at the bases to form a heavy frontal casque
cape bulb *n, usu cap C* [fr. *Cape* of Good Hope] **:** any of various bulbs or bulbous plants from southern Africa esp. of the genus *Ixia* or *Sparaxis* — compare DUTCH BULB

cape cart *n, usu cap 1st C* [fr. *Cape* of Good Hope] *Africa* : a 2-wheeled vehicle usu. seating four, drawn by two horses, and having a bowed canvas or leather hood
cape cat *n, usu cap 1st C* [*Cape* Cod, Mass., where it originated + E *cat*boat] : a catboat for fishing and pleasure sailing
cape chestnut *n, usu cap 1st C* [fr. *Cape* of Good Hope] : an ornamental southern African evergreen tree (*Calodendrum capense*) of the family Rutaceae having large panicles of white or flesh-colored flowers
cape chincherinchee *n, usu cap 1st C* [fr. *Cape* of Good Hope] : CHINCHERINCHEE
cape chisel *n* [perh. fr. ¹*cape*] : a cold chisel that has a long taper on the top and bottom of the cutting end and a narrow edge and is used for cutting keyways and similar flat grooves

cape chisel

cape cobra *n, usu cap 1st C* [fr. *Cape* of Good Hope] : an aggressive partly arboreal cobra (*Naja nivea*) of southern Africa that is extremely variable in coloring, being predominantly yellow, reddish, brown, or black — called also *yellow cobra*
cape cod cottage \(ˈ)kāp¦käd-\ *also* **cape cod** \=ˈ=\ *n, usu cap 1st & 2d Cs* [fr. *Cape Cod*, Mass.; fr. the frequent occurrence there of this type of house] : a compact rectangular dwelling of one or one-and-a-half stories usu. with a central chimney and a steep gable roof and with the main entrance on one of the long sides
cape cod lighter *n, usu cap both Cs* : a lump of porous material fixed upon a handle and soaked with kerosene for use in lighting fires
cape cod turkey *n, usu cap both Cs* : CODFISH
cape colored *n, pl* **cape colored** *or* **cape coloreds** *usu cap both Cs* [fr. *Cape* of Good Hope] : a native or inhabitant of So. Africa of mixed European and African or Malayan descent
cape cotton *n, usu cap 1st C* [fr. *Cape* of Good Hope] : a shrub (*Gomphocarpus fruticosus*) native to Africa but now found elsewhere often as a troublesome weed
cape cowslip *n, usu cap 1st C* [fr. *Cape* of Good Hope] : a southern African bulb or plant of the genus *Lachenalia* bearing bell-shaped flowers
cape crawfish *or* **cape crayfish** *n, usu cap 1st C* [fr. *Cape* of Good Hope] : the common spiny lobster (*Jasus lalandii*) of the coast of southern Africa valued as food and shipped canned or frozen to the U. S. — see ROCK LOBSTER
cape dagga *n, usu cap C* [fr. *Cape* of Good Hope] : DAGGA
cape diamond *n, usu cap C* [fr. *Cape* of Good Hope] : a diamond of yellowish tinge
cape doctor *n* [fr. *Cape* of Good Hope; fr. the belief that it carries germs out to sea] *Africa* : a strong southeast wind
cape dutch *n, cap C & D* [fr. *Cape* of Good Hope] : AFRIKAANS
cape ebony *n, usu cap C* [fr. *Cape* of Good Hope] **1** : an African timber tree (*Euclea pseudebenus*) **2** : the valuable hard wood of the Cape ebony
cape elk *n, usu cap C* [fr. *Cape* of Good Hope] : ELAND
cape fennel *n, usu cap C* [fr. *Cape* of Good Hope] : a southern African herb (*Foeniculum capense*) having a thick aromatic edible root
cape foot *n, usu cap C* [fr. *Cape* of Good Hope] : a unit of measure of the Union of So. Africa equal to 1.033 English feet
cape forget-me-not *n, usu cap C* [fr. *Cape* of Good Hope] : either of two southern African anchusas (*Anchusa capensis* and *A. riparia*)
cape fox *n, usu cap C* [fr. *Cape* of Good Hope] : CAAMA 1
cape fuchsia *n, usu cap C* [fr. *Cape* of Good Hope] : a southern African shrub (*Phygelius capensis*) of the family Scrophulariaceae often cultivated for its tubular scarlet flowers like those of a fuchsia
cape fur seal *n, usu cap C* [fr. *Cape* of Good Hope] : CAPE SEAL
cape gooseberry *n, usu cap C* [fr. *Cape* of Good Hope; fr. its extensive cultivation in So. Africa] : any of several groundcherries (esp. *Physalis peruviana*) bearing edible acid berries
cape grape *n, usu cap C* [fr. *Cape* Cod, Mass., where it was developed] : a tuberous-rooted grapelike vine (*Cissus capensis*) having very long forked tendrils and red-black glossy fruit in short clusters and used esp. in southwestern U. S. as an ornamental
cape gum *n, usu cap C* [fr. *Cape* of Good Hope] **1 a** : a gum arabic obtained from various southern African acacias (esp. *Acacia horrida* and *A. giraffae*) — see KARROO BUSH **2** : a tree yielding Cape gum
cape hare *n, usu cap C* [fr. *Cape* of Good Hope] : a large swift long-legged hare (*Lepus capensis*) that resembles the American cottontail rabbit and is widely distributed in arid southern African grasslands
cape hartebeest *n, usu cap C* [fr. *Cape* of Good Hope] : a large reddish hartebeest (*Alcelaphus caama*) with black-marked face, limbs, and tail and white underparts
cape hen *n, usu cap C* [fr. *Cape* of Good Hope] : any of several sea birds of southern seas; *esp* : a large white-chinned petrel (*Procellaria aequinoctialis*)
cape holly *n, usu cap C* [fr. *Cape* of Good Hope] : a southern African timber tree (*Elaeodendron croceum*)
cape honeysuckle *n, usu cap C* [fr. *Cape* of Good Hope] : a southern African evergreen woody vine (*Tecomaria capensis*) of the family Bignoniaceae with orange-red flowers in dense terminal clusters
cape horn·er \kāˈpȯrnər, kāpˈhȯ-\ *n, usu cap C&H* [*Cape Horn*, southern extremity of So. America + E *-er*] : a ship that voyages around Cape Horn
cape hunting dog *n, usu cap C* [fr. *Cape* of Good Hope] : AFRICAN HUNTING DOG
cape hyacinth *n, usu cap C* [fr. *Cape* of Good Hope] : SUMMER HYACINTH
cape hyrax *n, usu cap C* [fr. *Cape* of Good Hope] : DASSIE 1
cape ivy *n, usu cap C* [fr. *Cape* of Good Hope] : GERMAN IVY
cape jasmine *or* **cape jessamine** *n, usu cap C* [fr. *Cape* of Good Hope; fr. its having been found in So. Africa] : an Asiatic shrub (*Gardenia jasminoides*) long cultivated for its fragrant white flowers
cape jumping hare *n, usu cap C* [fr. *Cape* of Good Hope] : JUMPING HARE
cape lancewood *n, usu cap C* [fr. *Cape* of Good Hope] : ASSEGAI 2
cape·let \ˈkāplət\ *n* -s [²*cape* + *-let*] : a small cape usu. covering the shoulders
cape lily *n, usu cap C* [fr. *Cape* of Good Hope] : a southern African bulbous herb (*Crinum longifolium*) with showy pinkish red flowers
cap·e·lin *also* **cap·e·lan** \ˈkap(ə)lən\ *or* **cap·lin** \-plən\ *or* **cap·ling** \-pliŋ, -lən\ *n* -s [CanF *capelan*, fr. F, codfish, fr. OProv *capelan*, *cappellan* chaplain, codfish, fr. ML *cappellanus* chaplain — more at CHAPLAIN] : a small salmonoid marine fish (*Mallotus villosus*) related to and resembling the smelts that is very abundant off Greenland, Iceland, Newfoundland, and Alaska and is used as food and as bait for the cod
cap·e·line \ˈkapə,lēn, -,lən\ *n* -s [ME *capleyne*, fr. MF *capeline*, fr. OProv *capelina*, fr. *capa* cloak, fr. LL *cappa* head covering, cloak — more at CAP] **1** : a small skullcap of steel or iron worn by foot soldiers in medieval times **2** [F, fr. MF] : a cap-shaped or hood-shaped bandage for the head, the shoulder, or the stump of an amputated limb **3** [F, woman's hat, woman's hood, fr. MF] : a woman's hat with a small crown and a wide soft brim
cape lion *n, usu cap C* [fr. *Cape* of Good Hope] : a large black-maned lion formerly abundant in southern Africa but extinct since about 1850
ca·pel·la \kəˈpelə\ *n, cap* [NL, fr. L, she-goat, star in the constellation Auriga, dim. of *caper* goat — more at CAPRIOLE] : a genus of birds (family Scolopacidae) comprising the snipes
capelle *often cap, var of* KAPELLE
cape lobster *n, usu cap C* [fr. *Cape* of Good Hope] **1** : CAPE CRAWFISH **2** : a small lobster (*Homarus capensis*) from the Cape of Good Hope
cape marigold *n, usu cap C* [fr. *Cape* of Good Hope] : a daisylike plant of the genus *Dimorphotheca* often cultivated for ornament
cape may goody \(ˈ)kāp¦mā-\ *n, usu cap C&M* [*Cape May*, New Jersey, near which it is found + E *goody* (fish)] : ¹SPOT 7
cape may warbler *n, usu cap C&M* [fr. *Cape May* county, New Jersey, where it was first identified] : an American warbler (*Dendroica tigrina*) that is olive green with dark streaks above and yellow with black streaks on the underparts
cape merchant *n* [prob. fr. It *capo* leader, lit., head, or MF *cap* (fr. OProv), fr. L *caput* head — more at HEAD] **1** *obs* : SUPERCARGO 1 **2** *obs* : the head merchant in a trading post
cape mole rat *n, usu cap C* [fr. *Cape* of Good Hope] : MOLE RAT C
cape otter *n, usu cap C* [fr. *Cape* of Good Hope] : a large clawless otter (*Aonyx capensis*) of southern Africa
cape periwinkle *n, usu cap C* [fr. *Cape* of Good Hope] : PERIWINKLE 1c
cape pigeon *n, usu cap C* [fr. *Cape* Horn, southern extremity of So. America] : a pigeon-sized black-and-white petrel (*Daption capense*) of southern seas breeding chiefly in southern So. America
cape polecat *n, usu cap C* [fr. *Cape* of Good Hope] : MUISHOND
cape pondweed *n, usu cap C* [fr. *Cape* of Good Hope] : a southern African aquatic plant (*Aponogeton distachyus*) with long-petioled floating leaves and emersed fragrant flower spikes — called also *water hawthorn*
cape primrose *n, usu cap C* [fr. *Cape* of Good Hope] : an herb of the genus *Streptocarpus* cultivated for its primroselike flowers
¹**ca·per** \ˈkāpə(r)\ *n* -s *often attrib* [back-formation fr. earlier *capers*, taken as a plural, fr. ME *caperis*, *capres*, fr. L *capparis*, fr. Gk *kapparis*] **1** : a plant of the genus *Capparis*; *esp* : a low prickly shrub (*C. spinosa*) of the Mediterranean region cultivated in Europe for its buds — see CAPPARIS **2 capers** *pl* **:** the greenish flower buds and young berries of the caper plant pickled and used as a condiment in sauces and dressings **3** : a marsh marigold (*Caltha palustris*)
²**caper** \"\ *vi* **capered; capered; capering** \-p(ə)riŋ\ **capers** [prob. by shortening & alter. fr. *capriole*] : to leap about, prance, or cavort in a gay frolicsome way : prance, frisk, or gambol playfully or wildly ⟨lambs ~*ing* in the meadow⟩ ⟨~*ing* like a witch doctor among African natives —Geoffrey Household⟩
³**caper** \"\ *n* -s [prob. by shortening & alter. fr. *capriole*] **1 a** : a gay unrestrained bounding leap : SKIP, JUMP ⟨the skip of the lamb and the ~ of the kid —Douglas Kennedy⟩ **b** : a leaping or cavorting dance motion ⟨the couples jigging in from opposite corners, performing ~*s* and shuffles —H.L.Davis⟩ **2 a** : a capricious or madcap escapade : PRANK, ANTIC ⟨lead in all kinds of pranks and ~*s* —W.A.White⟩ **b** : PERFORMANCE, ACTIVITY, PURSUIT **3** *slang* : an illegal or questionable escapade : criminal action : CRIME ⟨an improbable jewel robbery called a ~ in the jungle patois —Robert Hatch⟩ **4** : three quick jumps in morris dancing followed by a leap with one leg forward and the other back
⁴**caper** *n* -s [D *kaper*, fr. *kapen* to privateer, fr. *kaap* privateering, prob. fr. Fris, fr. OFris *kāp* trade; akin to OHG *kouf* trade — more at CHEAP] **1** *archaic* : PRIVATEER **2** *archaic* : PIRATE
⁵**ca·per** \ˈkāpər, -ˈä-\ *n* -s [ScGael *ceapaire*, prob. fr. *ceap* shoemaker's last, clog on an animal's foot, pair of stocks, akin to MIr *cepp* block, fr. L *cippus* stake, post — more at CEPE] *chiefly Scot* : a piece of buttered bread usu. with cheese on it
caper berry *n* [¹*caper*] : the small berrylike fruit of the caper
caperbush \ˈ==,=\ *n* : ¹CAPER 1
cap·er·cail·lie \,kapə(r)ˈkāl(y)ē, ,kāp-\ *or* **cap·er·cail·zie** \-ālzē\ *n* -s [modif. of ScGael *capalcoille*, lit., horse of the woods, fr. *capall* mare, horse (akin to OIr *capall* horse, fr. L *caballus*) + *coille* forest; akin to MIr *caill* forest, Gk *klados* branch — more at CAVALCADE, GLADIATOR] : a large true grouse (*Tetrao urogallus*) found in many wooded areas of Europe and Asia and in parts of Britain to which it has been reintroduced after being exterminated and where it feeds on fruits and small invertebrates and esp. in winter on pine shoots which give the flesh a strong flavor, the dark-gray and black male being the size of a wild turkey and the mottled female much smaller — called also *cock of the wood*
caper family *n* [¹*caper*] : CAPPARIDACEAE
ca·per·ing·ly *adv* : in a capering manner
ca·per·na·ite \kəˈpərnē,īt\ *n* -s *usu cap* [*Capernaum*, city in ancient Palestine + E *-ite*] **1** : a native or inhabitant of Capernaum **2** : one who believes in transubstantiation; *specif* : one who interprets literally Jesus' discourse at Capernaum on the bread of life (Jn 6:26–58) — usu. used disparagingly
cap·er·noi·ted \,kapərˈnȯitəd\ *adj* [perh. fr. *capernaite* (believer in transubstantiation) + *-ed*] **1** *Scot* : PEEVISH **2** *Scot* : MUDDLEHEADED, TIPSY
cap·er·noi·tie \-tē\ *n* -s [origin unknown] *Scot* : HEAD, NODDLE
cape robin *n, usu cap C* [fr. *Cape* of Good Hope] : a southern African songbird (*Caffrornis caffra*) of the family Turdidae that is dusky brown above fading to brownish red on the tail with an orange throat patch and pale or whitish underparts and that is common in settled areas where it feeds on insects and berries
cape rock lobster *n, usu cap C* [fr. *Cape* of Good Hope] : CAPE CRAWFISH
capers *pl of* CAPER, *pres 3d sing of* CAPER
caper spurge *n* [¹*caper*] : a poisonous European spurge (*Euphorbia lathyrus*) that is adventive in America and has seeds that yield a purgative oil — called also *mole plant*
caper tree *n* [¹*caper*] : the common cultivated caper (*Capparis spinosa*); *also* : a related shrub (*C. cynophallophora*) of Florida and the West Indies
cape ruby *n, usu cap C* [fr. *Cape* of Good Hope] : a ruby-colored garnet : PYROPE
ca·per·wort \ˈkāpər,wərt, -,ȯ-\ *n* -s [¹*caper* + *wort*] : a plant of the family Capparidaceae
capes \ˈkāps\ *n pl* [perh. fr. pl. of ²*cape*] **1** *dial Brit* : ears of grain broken off in threshing **2** *dial Brit* : grain that threshing has not removed the husks from
cape salmon *n, usu cap C* [fr. *Cape* of Good Hope] **1** : GEELBEC 2 **2** *Africa* : TENPOUNDER 1
cape seal *or* **cape sea lion** *n, usu cap C* [fr. *Cape* of Good Hope] : a fur seal (*Arctocephalus pusillus*) inhabiting islands off the coast of southern Africa
capeskin \ˈ=,=\ *n, often attrib* [*Cape* of Good Hope + E *skin*] **1** : a hair sheepskin from southern Africa **2** : glove or garment leather made from capeskin
cape sparrow *n, usu cap C* [fr. *Cape* of Good Hope] : a very dark southern African sparrow (*Passer melanurus*) common in settled areas
cape spiny lobster *n, usu cap C* [fr. *Cape* of Good Hope] : CAPE CRAWFISH
cape·stane \ˈkāp,stān\ *Scot var of* COPESTONE
cape teal *or* **cape widgeon** *n, usu cap C* [fr. *Cape* of Good Hope] : a small rather drably colored duck (*Nototenna capensis*) of southern and eastern Africa
¹**ca·pe·tian** \kəˈpēshən, kā-\ *adj, usu cap* [F *capétien*, fr. Hugh (Hugues) *Capet* †996 Fr. king, founder of the dynasty + F *-ien* -ian] : of or relating to the French dynasty founded in 987 and with its collateral branches reigning until 1848 except during the years 1795–1814
²**capetian** \"\ *n* -s *usu cap* : a member of the Capetian dynasty; *esp* : a Capetian king
cape·to·ni·an \kāpˈtōnēən\ *n* -s *cap* [irreg. (influence of such words as *Newtonian*, *Bostonian*) fr. *Cape Town*, Union of So. Africa + E *-ian*] : a native or inhabitant of Cape Town, Union of So. Africa
cape town \ˈkāp,tau̇n\ *adj, usu cap C&T* [fr. *Cape Town*, city in the Union of So. Africa] : of or from Cape Town, the legislative capital Union of So. Africa : of the kind or style prevalent in Cape Town
ca·pette \(ˈ)kāˈpet\ *n* -s [*capon* + *-ette*] : CAPONETTE
cape tulip *n, usu cap C* [fr. *Cape* of Good Hope] **1** : BLOOD LILY **2** : a plant of the genus *Homeria*
capeweed \ˈ=,=\ *n, often cap* [*Cape* Verde islands, Portuguese colony off West Africa + E *weed*] **1** : an African lichen (*Roccella tinctoria*) abundant in the Cape Verde islands **2** [*Cape* of Good Hope + E *weed*] : a low-growing yellow-flowered composite herb (*Cryptostemma calendulacea*) that is native to southern Africa but introduced into Australia and New Zealand where it is usu. considered a troublesome weed **3** [*Cape* of Good Hope + E *weed*] : CAT'S-EAR
cape wine *n, usu cap C* [fr. *Cape* of Good Hope] : wine made in the Cape Province region of So. Africa
cape wolf snake *n, usu cap C* [fr. *Cape* of Good Hope] : a small wolf snake (*Lycophidion capense*) of tropical and southern Africa
capework \ˈ=,=\ *n* [²*cape* + *work*] : the art of the bullfighter in working a bull with the cape
cape yellowwood *n, usu cap C* [fr. *Cape* of Good Hope] : SOUTH AFRICAN YELLOWWOOD
cap-flash \ˈ=,=\ *vt* [¹*cap* + *flash*] : to construct with one flashing superimposed on another to protect against leakage of water
cap flashing *n* [¹*cap* + *flashing*] : COUNTERFLASHING
cap·ful \ˈkap,fu̇l\ *n* -s : a light puff ⟨a ~ of wind⟩
cap gun *n* [¹*cap* (explosive)] : CAP PISTOL
caph *var of* KAPH
ca·phar·na·um \kəˈfärnēəm\ *n* -s [F, fr. *Capharnaum*, Aram form of *Capernaum*, ancient city of Palestine; fr. the crowd before the house where Jesus preached (Mk 2:2)] : a confused jumble : a place marked by a disorderly accumulation of objects
caph·to·rim \ˈkaftə,rim\ *or* **caph·to·rims** \-mz\ *n pl, cap* [Heb *Kaphtōrīm* (pl.), fr. *Kaphtōr* Caphtor, biblical name of the land of origin of the Philistines] : the people of biblical Caphtor, prob. present-day Crete
ca·pi·as \ˈkāpēəs\ *n* -ES [ME, fr. L, you should seize, 2d pers. sing. pres. subj. of *capere* to take, seize — more at HEAVE] : a legal writ or process commanding the officer to arrest the person named in it
capibara *var of* CAPYBARA
cap·il·la·ceous \¦kapə¦lāshəs\ *adj* [L *capillaceus*, fr. *capillus* hair + *-aceus* -aceous] **1** : having filaments ⟨a ~ leaf⟩ **2** : like a hair
cap·il·laire \¦kapə¦la(a)(ə)r\ *n* -s [F, fr. LL (*herba*) *capillaris*, fr. L *capillaris* of hair, fr. *capillus* hair + *-aris* -ary] **1** : MAIDENHAIR **2** : CREEPING SNOWBERRY **3 a** : a syrup prepared from the maidenhair **4** : a syrup flavored with orange flowers
ca·pi·lla ma·yor \kəˈpē(ly)ə,mīˈō(ə)r\ *n* [Sp, lit., larger chapel] : a main chapel or chancel in churches of Spanish architecture
cap·il·lar·ec·ta·sia \ˈkapə,lerekˈtāzh(ē)ə, -lär-\ *n* -s [NL, fr. L *capillaris* capillary + NL *ectasia*] : TELANGIECTASIA
cap·il·lar·ia \,kapəˈla(a)rēə\ *n* [NL, fr. L *capillus* hair + NL *-aria*] **1** *cap* : a genus of slender white nematode worms (family Trichuridae) that includes serious pathogens of the alimentary tract of fowls and certain tissue and organ parasites of mammals one of which (*C. hepatica*) is common in rodents and occas. invades the human liver sometimes with fatal results **2** -s : a worm of the genus *Capillaria* — **cap·il·lar·id** \-rəd, kəˈpilərəd\ *n* -s
ca·pil·la·ri·a·sis \kə,piləˈrīəsəs\ *also* **cap·il·lar·i·o·sis** \,kapə,lerēˈōsəs\ *n, pl* **capillaria·ses** \-ə,sēz\ *also* **capillario·ses** \-ōsēz\ : infestation with or disease caused by nematode worms of the genus *Capillaria*
cap·il·lar·i·ty \,kapəˈlarəd-ē, -ətē, -i, *also* -ˈe-\ *n* -ES [F *capillarité*, fr. *capillaire* capillary (fr. L *capillaris* of hair) + *-ité* -ity] **1** : the quality or state of being capillary **2** : the action by which the surface of a liquid where it is in contact with a solid is elevated or depressed depending upon the relative attraction of the molecules of the liquid for each other and for those of the solid and being esp. observable in capillary tubes where it determines the elevation or depression of the liquid above or below the level of the liquid in which the tube is dipped — compare SURFACE TENSION
cap·il·la·rized \ˈkapələ,rīzd, kəˈpilə-\ *adj* [²*capillary* + *-ize* + *-ed*] : infiltrated with or divided into capillaries
cap·il·lar·o·scope \,kapəˈlarə,skōp, -ˈe-\ *n* -s [ISV *capillary* + *-o-* + *-scope*; orig. formed as G *kapillaroskop*] : a microscope that permits visual examination of the living capillaries in nail beds, skin, and conjunctiva
cap·il·la·ros·co·py \,kapələˈräskəpē\ *also* **cap·il·lar·i·os·co·py** \,lerēˈäskəpē, -la(a)r-\ *n* -ES [ISV *capillar-* (fr. *capillary*) or *capillary* + *-o-* + *-scopy*; orig. formed as G *kapillaroskopie*] : diagnostic examination of capillaries, esp. of the nail beds, with a microscope
¹**cap·il·lary** \ˈkapə,lerē, -ri, *Brit usu* kəˈpiləri\ *adj* [F or L; F *capillaire*, fr. L *capillaris*, fr. *capillus* hair + *-aris* -ary] **1** : belonging or relating to hair ⟨~ growth⟩ **2** : resembling a hair : FINE, MINUTE, SLENDER; *esp* : having a very small or thin bore usu. permitting capillarity ⟨a ~ tube⟩ **3** : involving or held by capillary action ⟨~ water⟩ : resulting from surface tension in the soil ⟨~ capacity is a measure of the ability of a soil to hold water in the surface layers against the action of gravity⟩ **4 a** : showing or suggesting an arrangement of capillaries ⟨a ~ network⟩ **b** : relating to capillarity or to an apparatus employing it ⟨~ action⟩
²**capillary** \"\ *n* -ES : a minute thin-walled vessel of the body; *esp* : any of the smallest constituent vessels of the blood-vascular system connecting arterioles with venules so as to form networks practically throughout the body, averaging ½ millimeter in length and at their widest being not many times the diameter of a blood corpuscle, and being walled by a single layer of endothelial cells that permits ready exchange of nutrients and metabolic wastes between the tissues and the circulating blood — see ROUGET CELL
capillary analysis *n* : analysis by chromatography (as paper chromatography)
capillary attraction *n* : the force of adhesion between a solid and a liquid in capillarity
capillary bed *n* : the whole system of capillaries of a body, part, or organ
capillary chemistry *n* : a branch of physical chemistry that is concerned with phenomena in very small pores sometimes including adsorption, absorption, catalysis, and colloid chemistry
capillary electrometer *n* : an electrometer for measuring small electric potential differences based upon change of surface tension between mercury and an electrolytic solution in a capillary tube with change of potential difference between the liquids
capillary potential *n* **1** : the work done in bringing a unit mass of liquid from a level liquid surface to any point within a capillary region **2** : the driving force that causes moisture to move in soil by capillarity
capillary pyrites *n* : MILLERITE
capillary water *n* : water that remains in the soil after gravitational water is drained out, that is subject to the laws of capillary movement, and that is in the form of a film around the soil grains
ca·pil·li·cul·ture \kəˈpilə,kəlchə(r)\ *n* -s [ISV *capilli-* (fr. L *capillus* hair) + *culture*; prob. orig. formed in F] : treatment to cure or prevent baldness
ca·pil·li·form \kəˈpilə,fȯrm\ *adj* [ISV *capilli-* (fr. L *capillus* hair) + *-form*] : having the form of a hair : like a hair
cap·il·li·tial \¦kapə¦lishəl\ *adj* [NL *capillitium* + E *-al*] : of or belonging to a capillitium
cap·il·li·ti·um \,kapəˈlishēəm\ *n, pl* **capilli·tia** \-ēə\ [NL, fr. L, hair (collectively), fr. *capillus*] : an assemblage or network of simple or branched noncellular strands formed of waste materials cast off in elongate vacuoles during cleavage of the spores in the sporangium of many slime molds and within the fruiting body of certain gasteromycetes
ca·pil·lus \kəˈpiləs\ *n, pl.* **capil·li** \-i,lī, -(,)lē\ [L] **1** : a hair esp. of the head **2** [NL, fr. L] : the bore of a capillary tube
cap·i·lo·tade \¦kapəlō¦täd, keˈpilə¦t-\ *n* -s [F *capilotade*, *capirotade*, fr. Sp *capirotada* sauce containing herbs, eggs, and garlic, fr. *capirote* hood, fr. *capa* cloak — more at CAPE] : a stew often of several minced meats
ca·pim gor·du·ra \kəˈpim(,)gōrˈdu̇(ə)rə\ *n* [Pg, lit., fatness grass] : a hardy forage grass (*Melinis minutiflora*) much used in Brazil for fattening cattle and introduced into the southern U.S.
caping *pres part of* CAPE
cap iron *n* [¹*cap*] : a stiffening plate fastened to the upper side of the cutter of a carpenter's plane
capita *pl of* CAPUT
¹**cap·i·taine** \ˈkapə¦tān\ *n* -s [F, lit., captain — more at CAPTAIN] **1** : NILE PERCH **2** : an African fish (*Lates microlepis*) closely related to the Nile perch
²**capitaine** *var of* CAPITAN

¹**cap·i·tal** \ˈkapəd·ᵊl, -p(ə)tᵊl\ *adj* [ME, fr. L *capitalis*, fr. *capit-, caput* head — more at HEAD] **1** *obs* **:** of or relating to the head ⟨his ~ bruise —John Milton⟩ **2 a** *archaic* **:** DEADLY, FATAL ⟨an inexorable ~ enemy⟩ ⟨a plague ~ to many⟩ **b :** punishable by death **:** involving execution ⟨a ~ crime⟩ ⟨a ~ verdict⟩ ⟨put to death a ~ offender —John Milton⟩ **c :** involving or punishable by loss of legal personality **d :** most serious **:** fatally detrimental **:** EGREGIOUS ⟨a ~ error⟩ ⟨the ~ folly of cutting herself off from her family —Arnold Bennett⟩ **3 a** *obs* **:** standing at the beginning of a page, passage, or line ⟨the illumination of the ~ words in the manuscript⟩ **b** *of a letter* **:** comparatively large, clear, or elegant in form and in print like the majuscule letters of ancient inscriptions and consequently regarded as esp. fit for use in initial position **:** of or conforming to the series A, B, C, etc. rather than a, b, c, etc. **4 a** *archaic* **:** having authority or preeminence **:** most important **:** CHIEF ⟨the ~ lords of the realm⟩ — used of a person **b :** above comparable matters in importance, significance, worth, or influence **:** PROMINENT, PREDOMINANT, MAJOR, MAIN ⟨whatever is ~ and essential in Christianity should be clearly and strenuously affirmed —Isaac Taylor⟩ ⟨the ~ importance of criticism in the work of creation itself —T.S.Eliot⟩ **5** *of a city* **:** most important; *specif* **:** being the seat of government ⟨London is the ~ city of England⟩ **6** [²*capital*] **a :** consisting of, serving as, or intended as capital **b :** accruing to or from capital **c :** carried on or conducted by means of capital **d :** of or having to do with capital **7 :** highly meritorious **:** most enjoyable **:** EXCELLENT, FIRST-RATE ⟨a ~ essay, still diverting after three quarters of a century —H.L.Mencken⟩ ⟨~ dinners they give at those crack hotels —George Meredith⟩ **syn** see CHIEF — **with a capital :** EMPHATICALLY, CERTAINLY — used with a following relevant capital letter ⟨not an accident but murder *with a capital M*⟩

²**capital** \ˈ"\ *n* -s [F or It; F, fr. It *capitale*, fr. *capitale*, adj., principal, fr. L *capitalis*] **1 a** *or* **capital goods** *or* **capital account :** a stock of accumulated goods esp. at a specified time and in contrast to income received during a specified period **b :** the value of these accumulated goods **c** *or* **capital goods :** accumulated goods devoted to the production of other goods **:** facilities or goods utilized as factors of production ⟨~ is not money but means of production —Bertrand Russell⟩ ⟨the employer who could set ~ and land and labor to work —G.B.Shaw⟩ **d :** any accumulated factors of production capable of being owned ⟨working ~ in the form of plow beasts, heavy plows, and slaves —F.M.Stenton⟩ **e :** the proprietary claim in a business **f :** the principal of a loan as contrasted with interest **g :** NET ASSETS **:** excess of assets over liabilities **h :** CAPITAL STOCK **i :** accumulated possessions calculated to bring in income ⟨a thousand acres of haying land meant a ~ as reliable as government bonds —Margaret Deland⟩ **j :** accumulated assets, resources, sources of strength, or advantages utilized to aid in accomplishing an end or furthering a pursuit ⟨the accumulated scientific and mathematical ~ on which our technology flourishes —W.F.Albright⟩ **k :** available money ⟨walking into Hollisburg on a ~ of twenty cents —Elmer Davis⟩ **l :** persons holding capital **:** investors, potential or actual ⟨troubled international conditions have made ~ reluctant to invest heavily —*Amer. Guide Series: Ark.*⟩ **m :** asset, gain, or profit through utilization of an adventitious characteristic or development ⟨to make poetic ~ out of the suffering of others —C.D.Lewis⟩ ⟨a keen and wary ruler who made ~ of his weakness —Agnes Repplier⟩ **2** [¹*capital*] **a :** a capital letter; *esp* **:** an initial capital letter **b :** a letter belonging to a style of alphabet modeled upon and departing in form relatively little from the style customarily used in inscriptions — see ROMAN CAPITAL, RUSTIC CAPITAL, SQUARE CAPITALS; compare CURSIVE, HALF UNCIAL, MINUSCULE, UNCIAL **3** [¹*capital*] **a :** the chief city of a country or region ⟨Scranton . . . ~ of the anthracite basin —*Amer. Guide Series: Pa.*⟩ **b :** a city serving as a seat for the government of a larger area or as a seat of a government branch (as of sovereign, legislature, or administration) ⟨Washington is the ~ of the U. S.⟩ **c :** a city preeminent or dominant in some special activity — used with a specifying attributive ⟨had once been considered the world's diamond ~⟩ ⟨Paris reigned as the fashion ~ of the world⟩ ⟨San Antonio, a veritable cattle ~ —*Amer. Guide Series: Texas*⟩

³**capital** \ˈ"\ *n* -s [ME *capitale*, by folk etymology (influence of ¹*capital*) fr. ONF *capitel*, fr. LL *capitellum* small head, top of column, dim. of L *capit-, caput* head — more at HEAD] **1 :** the head or uppermost member of a column or pilaster crowning the shaft and taking the weight of the entablature — see COLUMN illustration **2 :** the head or cap esp. of a chimney or a crucible

capitals 1: *1* Doric, *2* Ionic, *3* Corinthian

capital account *n* **1 a :** an account representing ownership in a business: as (1) **:** a proprietor's account (2) **:** a partner's account **b :** any corporation account classified as part of net worth: as (1) **:** a capital stock account (2) **:** a surplus account **c :** ²CAPITAL 1 a **2 :** a capital assets account

capital assets *n pl* **:** long-term assets either tangible or intangible (as land, buildings, patents, or franchises); *specif* **:** any assets so designated by statute or governmental regulation (as the U.S. Internal Revenue Code) — contrasted with *current assets*

capital budget *n* **:** a financial statement of estimated capital expenditures for a period of time usu. including proposed methods for financing

capital coefficient *n* **:** the ratio of the value of capital to the value of output

capital expenditure *n* **:** an expenditure for long-term additions or betterments properly chargeable to a capital assets account

capital gain *n* **:** the excess over market or book value at purchase or other acquisition realizable or realized from the sale of a capital asset; *specif* **:** a gain so designated by statute or governmental regulation (as the U.S. Internal Revenue Code) — compare LONG-TERM, SHORT-TERM

capital goods *n pl* **:** ²CAPITAL 1a, 1c

capital grant *n* **:** a contribution usu. by a government to an independent governmental body or authority to cover part of the cost of the latter's facilities (as federal grants for highways or public housing) — compare GRANT-IN-AID

capital investment *n* **:** the amount of money invested or required to be invested in an enterprise or undertaking

cap·i·tal·ism \ˈ⸗(⸗)⸗ˌlizəm, *Brit also* kəˈpitᵊlˌi-\ *n* -s [²*capital* (wealth) + *-ism*] **:** an economic system characterized by private or corporation ownership of capital goods, by investments that are determined by private decision rather than by state control, and by prices, production, and the distribution of goods that are determined mainly in a free market — compare INDUSTRIALISM, LIBERALISM, SOCIALISM

capital issue *n* **:** stocks or bonds issued by a corporation or government

¹**cap·i·tal·ist** \ˈ⸗(⸗)⸗ləst, *Brit also* kəˈpitᵊl-\ *n* -s [F, D, or G; F *capitaliste* fr. D or G; D *kapitalist*, fr. G, fr. *kapital* capital + *-ist*] **:** a person who has capital esp. invested or to be invested in business ⟨spare money is called capital; its owner is called a ~ —G.B.Shaw⟩; *broadly* **:** a person of wealth **:** PLUTOCRAT

²**capitalist** \ˈ"\ *adj* **1 :** owning capital ⟨the ~ class⟩ **2 a :** practicing capitalism **:** adhering to or defending capitalism ⟨~ nations⟩ **b :** marked by capitalism ⟨the modern ~ period of history from 1815 to 1914 —Norman Thomas⟩

cap·i·tal·is·tic \¦⸗(⸗)⸗¦listik, -ēk, *Brit also* kəˌpitᵊl¦i-\ *adj* [¹*capitalist* + *-ic*] **1 :** existing or accomplished under capitalism ⟨~ production⟩ **:** typical of or according with capitalism ⟨~ methods and incentives⟩ **2 :** practicing, favoring, or furthering capitalism ⟨~ nations⟩ ⟨~ propaganda⟩ — **cap·i·tal·is·ti·cal·ly** \-ək(ə)lē, -ēk-, -li\ *adv*

cap·i·tal·i·za·tion \ˌkapəd·ᵊləˈzāshən, -p(ə)tᵊl-, -ˌlīˈz-, *Brit also* kəˌpitᵊl-\ *n* -s [F *capitalisation*, fr. *capitaliser* + *-ation*] **1 a :** the act or process of capitalizing **b :** a sum resulting from a process of capitalizing **c :** the total liabilities of a business including both ownership capital and borrowed capital **d :** the total par value or the stated value of issues of no par value of the authorized capital of a company — called also *capital stock* **e :** the bonds and capital stock of a company **f :** the act or process of recording capital expenditures **2** [*capitalize* + *-ation*] **:** the use of a capital letter in writing or printing ⟨the ~ of proper nouns⟩

cap·i·tal·ize *also* **cap·i·tal·ise** \ˈkapəd·ᵊlˌīz, -p(ə)tᵊl-, *Brit also* kəˈpitᵊl-\ *vb* -ED/-ING/-S [F *capitaliser*, fr. *capital* + *-iser* -ize] *vt* **1 a** [²*capital* (letter) + *-ize*] **:** to write or print with an initial capital letter ⟨days of the week are usu. *capitalized*⟩ **b :** to write or print in capital letters ⟨abbreviations like B.A. and M.D. are usu. *capitalized*⟩ **2 :** to convert into capital **:** arrange for use in acquiring capital ⟨~ the company's reserve funds⟩ **3 :** to profit by **:** utilize gainfully **:** turn to one's advantage ⟨the producer and his designer assistant ~ the curiosity and vanity of their customers —Edward Sapir⟩ **4 a :** to compute, appraise, or estimate the present value of (an income extended over a period of time) ⟨*capitalized* earnings⟩ **b :** to convert (a periodic payment) into an equivalent capital sum ⟨*capitalized* annuity⟩ **5 a :** to charge (an expenditure) to a capital assets account **b :** to fix or determine the amount of capital stock to be authorized or issued by (a company) **6 :** to supply capital for **:** arrange available capital for the operation of ⟨some troubles in *capitalizing* the new venture⟩ ~ *vi* **:** to gain by opportune use of the adventitious **:** PROFIT — used with *on* or *upon* ⟨Lee hoped to ~ on his victory by pressing a further invasion —Horace Sutton⟩ ⟨unscrupulous industrialists and politicians, ever ready to ~ on baseless popular superstitions —M.F.A.Montagu⟩

capital justiciar *n* **:** JUSTICIAR 2

capital levy *n* **:** a levy on personal or industrial capital in addition to income tax and other taxes **:** a general property tax

capital liability *n* **1 :** the capital stock of a company representing the ownership interest for which the company is answerable to its stockholders even though a debtor and creditor relationship does not exist **2 :** a fixed liability (as a bond or mortgage) representing borrowed capital

capital loss *n* **:** the excess of book value or cost over the amount realized from the sale of a capital asset; *specif* **:** a loss so designated by statute or governmental regulation (as the U. S. Internal Revenue Code)

cap·i·tal·ly \ˈkapəd·ᵊlē, -p(ə)tᵊlē, -li\ *adv* **1 :** with a procedure or in a manner involving or likely to involve the death sentence ⟨punish ~⟩ ⟨try ~⟩ **2 :** in a capital manner ⟨she talks ~⟩

cap·i·tal·ness \-ᵊlnəs\ *n* -ES **:** the quality or state of being capital

capital punishment *n* **:** the death penalty for crime

capitals *pl of* CAPITAL

capital ship *n* **:** a warship of the first rank in size and armament **:** a major surface ship (as a battleship, cruiser, aircraft carrier)

capital sin *n* **:** DEADLY SIN

capital stock *n* **1** *or* **capital :** the outstanding shares of a joint-stock company considered as an aggregate ⟨the control of a majority of the *capital stock*⟩ **2 :** CAPITALIZATION 1d **3 :** the ownership element of a corporation divided into shares and represented by certificates

capital sum *n* **:** the amount specified for maximum injury or damage in an insurance policy

capital surplus *n* **:** the portion of the surplus of a business arising from sources other than earnings **:** all surplus other than earned surplus usu. including amounts received from sale or exchange of capital stock in excess of par or stated value, profits on resale of treasury stock, donations to capital by stockholders or others, or increment arising from revaluation of fixed or other assets

ca·pi·tan \ˌkapəˈtan, -ˈän\ *or* **ca·pi·taine** \-ˈān\ *n* -s [*capitan* fr. AmerSp *capitán*, fr. Sp, captain, fr. (assumed) VL *capitanus*; *capitaine* prob. fr. AmerFr, fr. AmerSp *capitán*] **:** HOGFISH 1 a

ca·pi·ta·nia \ˌkapətəˈnēə\ *n* -s [Pg, fr. Sp *capitanía* captaincy, company of soldiers, military district, fr. *capitán* + *-ia* -ia] **:** a territorial division in colonial Brazil **:** PROVINCE

ca·pi·ta·no \ˌkapəˈtä(ˌ)nō\ *n, pl* **capita·ni** \-ä(ˌ)nē\ *or* **capitanos** [It, lit., captain, fr. (assumed) VL *capitanus* foremost, chief, fr. L *capit-, caput* head] **:** a vainglorious and cowardly soldier esp. appearing as a stock character in the commedia dell' arte

cap·i·tate \ˈkapəˌtāt\ *adj* [L *capitatus* headed, fr. *capit-, caput* head + *-atus* -ate — more at HEAD] **1** *also* **cap·i·tat·ed** \-ād·əd\ *bot* **:** forming a head ⟨~ inflorescence⟩ ⟨~ flowers⟩ **2** *biol* **:** abruptly enlarged and globose ⟨a ~ stigma⟩ ⟨a ~ antenna⟩ — see ANTENNA illustration

cap·i·ta·tim \ˌkapəˈtād·əm, -ˈtä-\ *adj* [NL, fr. L *capit-, caput* head + NL *-atim* (as in ML *verbatim*)] **:** levied or granted at so much per head ⟨a ~ tax⟩

cap·i·ta·tion \ˌkapəˈtāshən\ *n* -s *often attrib* [LL *capitation-, capitatio* poll tax, fr. L *capit-, caput* head + *-ation-, -atio* -ation] **1 a :** a direct uniform tax imposed upon each head or person **:** POLL TAX **b :** the amount of tax so levied **2 :** a uniform payment payable on a per capita basis: as **a :** an annual fee paid a doctor or medical group for each patient enrolled under a health plan **b :** a payment by a subordinate body (as a local union) of a prescribed amount per member to a parent body

capitation grant *n* **:** a grant of a definite sum per person

cap·i·ta·tum \ˌkapəˈtād·əm, -ˈä-\ *n, pl* **capita·ta** \-d·ə\ [NL, fr. L, neut. of *capitatus* headed — more at CAPITATE] **:** the largest bone of the wrist articulating with the third metacarpal

cap·i·tel·late \ˌkapəˈteləṫ, -ˌlāt\ *adj* [NL *capitellum* + E *-ate*] **1** *bot* **:** having a very small knoblike termination **2** *bot* **:** collected into small capitula

¹**cap·i·tel·lid** \ˌkapəˈteləd\ *n* -s [NL *Capitellidae*] **:** a capitellid worm

²**capitellid** \¦⸗⸗¦⸗⸗\ *adj* **:** of or relating to the Capitellidae

cap·i·tel·li·dae \ˌkapəˈteləˌdē\ *n pl, cap* [NL, fr. *Capitella*, type genus (alter. of LL *capitellum* small head) + *-idae*] **:** a widely distributed family of polychaete worms that resemble the terrestrial oligochaetes in the simplicity of their structure

cap·i·tel·lum \ˌkapəˈteləm\ *n, pl* **capitel·la** \-elə\ [NL, fr. LL, small head, dim. of L *capit-, caput* head — more at HEAD] **1 :** a knoblike protuberance esp. at the end of a bone ⟨the ~ of the humerus⟩ **2 :** CAPITULUM

ca·pi·tis de·mi·nu·tio \ˈkapəd·əs,deməˈn(y)üshēˌō, ˈkä . . . -ˌdāməˈnüd·ēˌō\ *n, pl* **capitis deminuti·o·nes** \-ˌn(y)üshēˈō-(ˌ)nēz, -ˌnüd·ēˈō(ˌ)nās\ [L, lit., diminution of life] *Roman law* **:** impairment of legal status or civil capacity before the strict law through loss of freedom, citizenship, or family membership

cap·i·to \ˈkapəˌtō\ *n, cap* [NL, fr. L, large-headed one, fr. *capit-, caput* head] **:** the type genus of Capitonidae comprising most of the So. American and Central American barbets

cap·i·tol \ˈkapəd·ᵊl, -p(ə)tᵊl\ *n* -s *often attrib* [L *Capitolium* temple of Jupiter at Rome on the Capitoline hill] **:** the building in which a legislative body meets **:** STATEHOUSE ⟨many state ~s have gilded domes⟩ ⟨the national Capitol in Washington⟩

cap·i·to·line \ˈkapəd·ᵊlˌīn, -ətᵊl-, *Brit usu* kaˈpitəˌlīn\ *adj, usu cap* [L *capitolinus*, fr. *Capitolium* + *-inus* -ine] **:** belonging or relating to the smallest of the seven hills of Rome, to the ancient temple on it, or to the gods worshiped there

cap·i·ton·i·dae \ˌkapəˈtänəˌdē\ *n pl, cap* [NL, fr. *Capiton-, Capito*, type genus + *-idae*] **:** a family of stocky chiefly tropical arboreal birds (order Piciformes) with large stout bills swollen at the base and usu. with brilliantly colored plumage including a number of New and Old World barbets and sometimes esp. formerly the honey guides

cap·i·toph·o·rus \ˌkapəˈtäfərəs\ *n, cap* [NL, fr. L *capit-, caput* head + *-o-* + NL *-phorus* — more at HEAD] **:** a genus of aphids including the widespread currant aphid (*C. ribis*) and the strawberry aphid (*C. fragaefolii*)

capitula *pl of* CAPITULUM

ca·pit·u·lant \kəˈpichələnt\ *n* -s [F, pres. part. of *capituler* to capitulate, fr. ML *capitulare* to distinguish by heads or chapters — more at CAPITULATE] **:** one that capitulates

¹**ca·pit·u·lar** \-lər, -ˌlär\ *adj* [ML *capitularis*, fr. *capitulum* ecclesiastical chapter, meeting place of canons — more at CHAPTER] **1 :** of or relating to an ecclesiastical chapter **:** CAPITULARY ⟨~ estates⟩ **2** [NL *capitulum* + E *-ar*] **:** of or relating to a capitulum

²**capitular** \ˈ"\ *n* -s **1 :** CAPITULARY 1 **2** [ML *capitulare*, lit., document divided into sections] **:** a law or canon of a chapter or council **3 :** a member of a chapter

¹**ca·pit·u·lary** \-ˌlerē\ *n* -ES [ML *capitulare*, lit., document divided into sections, fr. LL *capitulum* section, chapter, fr. L, small head — more at CHAPTER] **1 a :** a civil or ecclesiastical ordinance esp. of the Frankish kings **b :** a collection of ordinances — usu. used in pl. **2 :** a member of a chapter, esp. an ecclesiastical chapter **:** CAPITULAR **3** [ML *capitularium*, fr. LL *capitulum* section, chapter] **:** a book containing an index of first and last words of portions of the Bible read in the liturgy of the Roman Catholic Church

²**capitulary** \ˈ"\ *adj* [ML *capitularis* — more at CAPITULAR] **:** belonging or relating to a chapter, esp. an ecclesiastical or masonic chapter **:** CAPITULAR

¹**ca·pit·u·late** \kəˈpichəˌlāt, *usu* -ād· + V\ *vb* -ED/-ING/-S [ML *capitulatus*, past part. of *capitulare* to distinguish by heads or chapters, fr. LL *capitulum* section, chapter, fr. L, small head] *vi* **1** *archaic* **a :** to arrange for bargaining and parleying **:** TREAT, NEGOTIATE ⟨magistrates . . . *capitulated* with the . . . agricultural rioters —Robert Southey⟩ **b :** to assent to terms arranged or proposed **:** AGREE ⟨two gentlemen ~ to fight on horseback —William Segar⟩ **2 a :** to surrender often according to terms agreed on **:** YIELD ⟨the Continentals, outnumbered, fled to Forty Fort, which *capitulated* on July 4 —F.E. Ross⟩ **b :** to cease withholding, resisting, or contending **:** ACQUIESCE ⟨I always tip for special services rendered but I will not ~ before sheer impertinence —Joseph Wechsberg⟩ ~ *vt, archaic* **:** to arrange in or as if in chapters **:** draw up under or as if under heads or articles ⟨sadly the wise youth *capitulated* Berry's words —George Meredith⟩ **syn** see YIELD

²**ca·pit·u·late** \-lət, -ˌlāt\ *adj* [NL *capitulatus*, fr. L, having a small head, fr. *capitulum* small head + *-atus* -ate — more at CAPITULUM] **:** CAPITELLATE

ca·pit·u·la·tion \⸗ˌ⸗⸗ˈlāshən\ *n* -s [MF, fr. *capituler* to capitulate (fr. ML *capitulare*) + *-ation* -ation] **1 :** a listing of the main headings of a subject **:** ENUMERATION **2 a :** a set of terms or articles constituting an agreement (as a treaty or convention) between governments **b :** an agreement by which specified stipulations (as the granting of special privileges and rights of extraterritoriality) exacted by one government of another **c :** one of the articles or terms of such an agreement **3 a :** the act or agreement of one that surrenders to an enemy upon stipulated terms ⟨the ~ of the defenders of the besieged town⟩ **b :** the instrument setting forth the terms of such an agreement **4 :** a giving way **:** a ceasing to resist **:** YIELDING ⟨~ to jealousy —Marcia Davenport⟩

ca·pit·u·la·tor \⸗ˈ⸗⸗ˌlād·ə(r), -ātə-\ *n* -s [¹*capitulate* + *-or*] **:** one that capitulates

ca·pit·u·la·to·ry \⸗ˈ⸗⸗ləˌtōrē, -ōrē, -i\ *adj* [¹*capitulate* + *-ory*] **:** of, relating to, or established by capitulation **:** EXTRATERRITORIAL ⟨the claims of U.S. ~ rights —*Current History*⟩

ca·pit·u·li·form \-ˈləˌfȯrm\ *adj* [ISV *capituli-* (fr. NL *capitulum*) + *-form*; prob. orig. formed as F *capituliforme*] **:** resembling a capitulum

ca·pit·u·lum \kəˈpichələm\ *n, pl* **capitu·la** \-lə\ [LL, fr. L, small head, dim. of *capit-, caput* head — more at HEAD] **1 :** a passage or reading from the Bible **2** [NL, fr L] **:** a rounded usu. terminal protuberance of a part: as **a :** the knob at the end of a bone or cartilage **b :** the enlarged tip of the proboscis of a fly **c :** the enlarged end of a halter of a fly **d :** the end of a capitate antenna **e :** the beak of a tick composed of the mouthparts and palpi **f :** the body of a barnacle as distinguished from the peduncle **3** [NL, fr. L] **a :** one of the rounded cells borne upon the manubrium in the antheridium of plants of the family Characeae **b :** a simple racemose inflorescence in which the primary axis is shortened and dilated forming a rounded or flattened cluster of sessile flowers (as in the buttonbush and in all composite plants) — called also *head*

capitulum of the buttonbush

capivara *var of* CAPYBARA

ca·pi·vi \kəˈpēvē, -ˈpī-\ *n* -s [modif. of Sp & Pg *copaiba* — more at COPAIBA] **:** COPAIBA 1

caple *n* -s [ME *capel, capul*, prob. of Celt origin; akin to OIr *capall* horse, ScGael, mare, horse, fr. L *caballus* nag — more at CAVALCADE] *archaic* **:** HORSE

cap·less \ˈkapləs\ *adj* **:** being without a cap

caplin *or* **capling** *var of* CAPELIN

caplock \ˈ⸗,⸗\ *n* -s **:** a muzzle-loader fired by a percussion cap

cap·mint \ˈkap,mint\ *n* -s [prob. alter. of *catmint*] **:** CALAMINT

-cap·nia \ˈkapnēə\ *n comb form, pl* **-capni·as** \-nēəz\ *or* **-capni·ae** \-nēˌē\ [NL, fr. Gk *kapnos* smoke + NL *-ia*; akin to L *cupere* to desire — more at COVET] **:** carbon dioxide in the blood ⟨hyper*capnia*⟩ ⟨hypo*capnia*⟩

cap·no·di·a·ce·ae \(ˌ)kapˌnōdēˈāsēˌē\ *n pl, cap* [NL, fr. *Capnodium*, type genus + *-aceae*] **:** a family of ascomycetous fungi that includes most of the sooty molds, is usu. placed in the order Dothideales but sometimes in Perisporiales, and is characterized by dark-colored mycelium and a dark massive brittle stroma

cap·no·di·um \kapˈnōdēəm\ *n, cap* [NL, fr. Gk *kapnōdēs* smoky, dark (fr. *kapnos* smoke) + NL *-ium* — more at COVET] **:** a genus of sooty molds that is the type of the family Capnodiaceae and includes some fungi that attack economic plants (as citrus, coffee, and olive)

cap nut *n* **:** BOX NUT

ca·po \ˈkä(ˌ)pō\ *n* [by shortening] **:** CAPOTASTO

capoc *var of* KAPOK

ca·po·col·lo \ˌkapəˈkōlə, -ăp-, -ōl-, -(ˌ)lō\ *n, pl* **capocol·li** \-(ˌ)lē\ *or* **capocollos** [It, fr. *capo* head of an animal (fr. L *caput* head) + *collo* neck, fr. L *collum* — more at HEAD, COLLAR] **:** a cured and smoked pork product cased like a sausage

ca·po di mon·te \ˌkä(ˌ)pōdēˈmäntē\ *n, usu cap C&M* **:** an 18th century soft paste porcelain produced at Capodimonte, Italy, under patronage of the King of Naples

cap of liberty : LIBERTY CAP

cap of maintenance *also* **cap of dignity** *or* **cap of estate** **1 :** a cap formerly worn as a symbol of office or high rank and still used as the cap of state borne before the British sovereign on certain ceremonial occasions and in modified form as the lining of British royal crowns and peers' coronets **2 :** the fur hat worn by the city sword-bearer or borne before the mayor on ceremonial occasions in several cities in England and Ireland **3 :** a heraldic cap showing a fur lining turned up about the bottom and split at the back sometimes borne as a charge and often used instead of a wreath to support the crest — called also *chapeau*

cap of maintenance 3

capolin *var of* CAPULIN

ca·po·mo \kəˈpō(ˌ)mō\ *n* -s [MexSp] **:** a breadnut tree (*Brosimum alicastrum*) whose fruits and leaves are fed to cattle

¹**ca·pon** \ˈkāˌpän *also* -ˌpən\ *n* -s [ME, fr. OE *capūn*, prob. fr. ONF *capon*, fr. L *capon-, capo*; akin to Gk *koptein* to smite, cut off, *skaptein* to dig, Lith *skopti* to hollow out with a knife, Russ *shchepat'* to split, OSlav *kopati* to dig, *skopiti* to castrate] **1 :** a castrated male chicken — compare POULARDE **2 :** a castrated male rabbit

²**capon** \ˈ"\ *vt* -ED/-ING/-S **:** CASTRATE, CAPONIZE

ca·pon·ette *also* **ca·pon·et** \¦kāpə¦net\ *n* -s [*capon* + *-ette* or *-et*] **:** a chemically castrated fowl **:** a capon produced by use of diethylstilbestrol

ca·pon·i·za·tion \ˌkāpənəˈzāshən, -ˌnīˈz-\ *n* -s **:** castration esp. of a fowl

ca·pon·ize \ˈkāpəˌnīz\ *vt* -ED/-ING/-S [*capon* + *-ize*] **:** CASTRATE — compare POULARDIZE

ca·pon·iz·er \-zə(r)\ *n* -s **:** one that caponizes

capon's-feather \ˈ⸗(ˌ)⸗,⸗⸗ *or* **capon's-tail** \ˈ⸗(ˌ)⸗,⸗\ *n, pl* **capon's-feathers** *or* **capon's-tails :** the common columbine (*Aquilegia vulgaris*)

capon's-grass \ˈ⸗(ˌ)⸗,⸗\ *or* **capon's-tail grass** \ˈ⸗(ˌ)⸗,⸗¦⸗\ *n, pl* **capon's-grasses** *or* **capon's-tail grasses :** RATTAIL FESCUE

ca·poor cutch·ery \kəˌpu(ə)rˈkəchərē\ *n* [Hindi *kapūr-kacarī*, fr. *kapūr* camphor (fr. Skt *karpūra*) + *kacarī* (*Hedychium spicatum*) — more at CAMPHOR] **:** the dried root of an East Indian plant (*Hedychium spicatum*)

[1]**cap·o·ral** \'kap(ə)rəl *also* ¦kapə¦ral *or* -äl\ *n* -s [F, lit., corporal — more at CORPORAL] : a coarse tobacco

[2]**cap·o·ral** \¦kapə¦ral, -äl\ *n* -s [Sp, foreman, fr. It *caporale* corporal — more at CORPORAL] *Southwest* : a foreman or assistant manager on a stock ranch

[1]**ca·pot** \kə'pät, -'pō\ *n* -s [F, adj., not having made a trick at piquet, fr. *capot* hooded cloak] : the winning of all the tricks in piquet and other games

[2]**ca·pot** \kə'pō\ *n* -s [F, hooded cloak, fr. MF *cape* cloak, fr. LL *cappa* head covering, cloak — more at CAP] **1** : CAPOTE **2** : an old large worthless bud or fruit of the caper

ca·po·ta·sto \,käpō'tä(,)stō\ *n, pl* **capotastos** \-(,)stōz\ *or* **ca·pi·ta·sti** \,käpē'tä(,)stē\ [It, lit., chief key, fr. *capo* head, chief (fr. L *caput* head) + *tasto* key of a musical instrument, fr. *tastare* to feel, touch, fr. (assumed) VL *tastare* — more at HEAD, TASTE] : a bar or movable nut attached to the fingerboard of a guitar or other fretted instrument to uniformly raise the pitch of all the strings

ca·pote \kə'pōt\ *n* -s [F, fr. *cape* cloak, fr. MF] **1 a** : a usu. long and hooded cloak or overcoat of rough cloth worn esp. by travelers and soldiers **b** : a Levantine long cloak of coarse fur **c** : a rain cape made of vegetable fibers **d** : a long mantle worn by women **e** : a bullfighter's cape **2** : a small Victorian bonnet with tie strings and varied trimmings

cap·pa \'käpə, -'a-\ *n, pl* **cap·pae** \'kä(,)pā, 'ka(,)pē\ *or* **cappas** [LL — more at CAP] : a cape esp. as part of ecclesiastical or academic garb

[1]**cap·pa·do·ci·an** \,kapə'dōsh(ē)ən\ *adj, usu cap* [*Cappadocia*, ancient country in extreme eastern Asia Minor + E *-an*] : of or relating to Cappadocia, its people, or their language

[2]**cappadocian** \¦==¦=(=)=\ *n* -s *cap* **1** : a native or inhabitant of Cappadocia **2** : the ancient language of the Cappadocians

cap·pagh brown *or* **cap·pah brown** \'kapə-\ *n, usu cap C* [fr. *Cappagh*, near Cork, Ireland, its locality] **1** : a natural pigment consisting chiefly of hydrated oxides of manganese and iron and having a hue of reddish brown that heating makes richer **2** : RUSSIAN CALF

cap·pa ma·gna \¦käpə'mänyə\ *n* [ML, lit., large cope] : a flowing long-trained ceremonial vestment with ermine or silk hood worn by cardinals, bishops, and a few other prelates

cap·pa·ri·da·ce·ae \,kapərə'dāsē,ē, kə,par-\ *n pl, cap* [NL, irreg. fr. *Capparis*, type genus + *-aceae*] : a family of herbs, shrubs, and trees (order Rhoeadales) distinguished from the related Cruciferae by a one-celled capsule — **cap·pa·ri·da·ceous** \¦===¦dāshəs, =¦==-\ *adj*

cap·pa·ris \'kapərəs\ *n, cap* [NL, fr. L, caper, fr. Gk *kapparis*] : a genus (the type of the family Capparidaceae) of shrubs or small trees widely distributed in warm regions, sometimes climbing by stipular thorns, and having simple leaves and showy flowers with four sepals, four petals, and numerous stamens — see [1]CAPER

capped *adj* [fr. past part. of [2]*cap* "to cause to swell"] : affected with a bursal swelling tending to become a hard fibrous mass resulting from pressure or repeated injury — used chiefly of leg affections of horses ⟨~ hock⟩ ⟨~ knee⟩ ⟨~ elbow⟩

capped dice *n pl* : crooked dice covered on one or more sides with resilient faces

capped macaque *n* : BONNET MONKEY

capped pawn *n* : a chess handicap in which a player undertakes to give checkmate with a specified pawn

cap·pe·len·ite \'kap(ə)lə,nīt\ *n* -s [G or Sw *cappelenit*, fr. D. *Cappelen fl* 1885 Norwegian scientist + G or Sw *-it* -ite] : a rare yttrium-barium borosilicate in greenish brown hexagonal crystals

cap·pel·let·ti \,kapə'led·ē\ *n pl* [It, pl. of *cappelletto*, dim. of *cappello* hat, fr. ML *cappellus*, *capellus* cap, dim. of LL *cappa* head covering, cloak — more at CAP] : small cases of dough usu. filled with meat or cheese — compare RAVIOLI

cap·per \'kapə(r)\ *n* -s [ME, fr. *cappe* cap + *-er*] **1** : a maker or seller of caps **2** : one that caps: as **a** : an operator or a machine that applies the closure or cap to bottles, jars, cans, or tubes **b** : one that presses a paper disk into the top of a paper cup **3** : a device for applying a percussion cap **4 a** : one that bids up prices artificially at auctions **b** : a lure, decoy, or steerer esp. in some illicit or questionable activity : SHILL **5** : a worker who withdraws cylinders of curved window glass from the blowing machine and cuts them into desired lengths — called also *corker*, *sealer* **6** : a worker who impregnates log piling at the butt end with preserving chemicals

cap·pie \'kapi\ *n* -s [[4]*cap* + *-ie*] *Scot* : a small wooden drinking vessel

capping *n* -s **1** : something that caps: as **a** : rock overlying the mineral body of a mine **b** : a fore-and-aft finishing piece at the frame heads in an open boat **2** : the architectural member that serves as a cap **3** : the wax that covers honey or cells in a comb **4** : the action of one that caps

capping plane *n* : a plane for working the upper surface of staircase rails

cap pistol *n* [[1]*cap* (explosive)] : a toy pistol that fires caps

cap plate *n* : HEADPLATE

cap·po \kə'pō\ *n* -s [modif. of F *capote*] : CAPOTE 1a

cap·py \'kapē\ *adj, often* -ER/-EST **1** : like a cap ⟨a ~ hairdo⟩ **2** *of dairy products* : having a tallow taste because of butterfat oxidation

cap·ra \'kaprə\ *n, cap* [NL, fr. L, she-goat, fem. of *caper* goat — more at CAPRIOLE] : a genus of ruminant mammals (family Bovidae) consisting of the goats, the ibex, and related animals

cap·ral·de·hyde \ka'praldə,hīd\ *n* -s [*capric* + *aldehyde*] : DECANAL

cap·rate \'ka,prāt\ *n* -s [ISV *capric* + *-ate;* orig. formed in F] : a salt or ester of capric acid

ca·prel·la \kə'prelə\ *n, cap* [NL, dim. of L *capra* — more at CAPRA] : a genus of small amphipod crustaceans that are found chiefly on seaweeds and that have a grotesque form suggestive of the praying mantis

ca·pre·o·line \kə'prēə,līn, 'kapr-\ *adj* [NL *Capreolus* + E *-ine*] : of or belonging to the genus *Capreolus*

ca·pre·o·lus \kə'prēələs\ *n, cap* [NL, fr. L, wild goat — more at CAPRIOLE] : a genus consisting of the roe deer

ca·pret·to \kə'pred·(,)ō\ *n, pl* **caprettos** \-ōz\ *or* **ca·pret·ti** \-(,)ē\ [It, kid, dim. of *capra* goat, fr. L, she-goat, fem. of *capr-*, *caper* goat, male goat] : the meat of a kid

ca·pri \ka'prē, kə-; 'kä(,)prē, -'a-\ *n* -s *often cap* [fr. *Capri*, island in the Bay of Naples] **1** : a pale dry wine made orig. on the island of Capri and now also on the island of Ischia and in the vicinity of Naples **2** : a strong greenish blue that is bluer and deeper than grotto, greener and duller than cobalt, and greener and deeper than average cerulean blue (sense 1a)

capri- *comb form* [L, fr. *capr-*, *caper*] : goat ⟨*Capri*corn⟩

capri blue *n, often cap C* [fr. *Capri*, island in the Bay of Naples, Italy; prob. fr. the famous blue grotto on the island] **1** : a vivid blue that is greener and slightly less strong than Ch'ing and greener and duller than Cleopatra or ultramarine — compare CAPRI 2 **2** : a blue oxazine dye

cap·ric \'kaprik\ *adj* [*capri-* + *-ic*] : of or relating to a goat

capric acid *n* [ISV *capri-* + *-ic;* fr. its goatlike odor; orig. formed as F *caprique*] : a low-melting crystalline fatty acid $CH_3(CH_2)_8COOH$ occurring in fats and oils often along with caproic acid — called also *decanoic acid*

capric aldehyde *n* : DECANAL

ca·pric·ciet·to \,kaprə'ched·(,)ō, -äp-, kə,prēchē'ed-\ *n, pl* **capricciettos** \-ōz\ *or* **capricciet·ti** \-(,)ē\ [It *capriccetto*, dim. of *capriccio*] : a short musical capriccio

ca·pric·cio \kə'prē(,)chō, -'i-, -,chē,ō\ *n, pl* **capriccios** \-ōz\ *also* **capric·ci** \-(,)chē\ [It] **1** : a sudden apparently unmotivated turn of mind : FANCY, WHIMSY ⟨notwithstanding his excellences . . . Lamb could be guilty of ~ —John Mason Brown⟩ **2** : a sudden sportive motion or action : CAPER, PRANK ⟨magnificent were thy ~*s* on this globe of earth —Charles Lamb⟩ **3 a** : a composition or adornment (as in sculpture) showing unrestrained fancy ⟨a neobaroque monument covered with decorative forms which . . . are intended as ~*s* —J.T.Soby⟩ **b** : an instrumental piece in free form usu. lively in tempo and brilliant in style — called also *caprice*

ca·pric·ci·o·so \kə,prēchē'ō(,)sō, -ich-\ *adj* [It, fr. *capriccio* + *-oso* -ous] : free and impulsive — used chiefly as a direction in music

ca·price \kə'prēs *also* ka-\ *n* -s [F, fr. It *capriccio* caprice, shiver, fr. *capo* head (fr. L *caput*) + *riccio* hedgehog, fr. L *ericius;* basic meaning: head with hair standing on end, hence, horror, shivering, then (after It *capra* goat), whim — more at HEAD, URCHIN] **1 a** : a sudden impulsive apparently unmotivated change of mind : WHIM, FANCY ⟨a gang of unruly children whose ~*s* may be tolerated —Kenneth Tynan⟩ ⟨she sang a verse of it, merely out of ~ —William Black⟩ **b** : any sudden change or series of changes or vicissitudes hard to predict or explain ⟨the large and small ~*s* of the weather —C.C. Furnas⟩ ⟨between unchanging custom and the legitimate ~ of custom which is fashion —Edward Sapir⟩ **2** : a disposition to change one's mind suddenly, impulsively, or without apparent motive : WHIMSICALITY ⟨his owners worked him sorely and with the ~ of Indians alternately . . . tortured him and treated him as one of themselves —Bernard DeVoto⟩ **3 a** : a fanciful work of art **b** : CAPRICCIO 3b

ca·pri·cious \kə'prishəs, -ēsh- *also* ka-\ *adj* [It *capriccioso*] **1** : marked or guided by caprice : given to changes of interest or attitude according to whims or passing fancies : not guided by steady judgment, intent, or purpose ⟨he judged her to be ~ and easily wearied of the pleasure of the moment —Edith Wharton⟩ ⟨the editing of these papers is so ~ and so wholly without any consistent and discriminating standards —C.P. Aiken⟩ **2** : lacking a standard or norm : marked by variation or irregularity : lacking predictable pattern or law : CHANGEABLE, ERRATIC, WHIMSICAL ⟨the revenue of government from the taxes was not regular but ~ and exceptional —Hilaire Belloc⟩ ⟨the demand for fur felt provided a steadier, less ~ market —D.G.Creighton⟩ **syn** see INCONSTANT

ca·pri·cious·ly \-lē, -i\ *adv* : in a capricious manner

ca·pri·cious·ness \-snəs\ *n* -ES : the quality or state of being capricious

cap·ri·corn \'kaprə,kȯrn, -rē,k-, -ȯ(ə)n\ *n* -s *usu cap* [ME *capricorne*, a southern zodiacal constellation, fr. L *capricornus* (trans. of Gk *aigokerōs*, lit., goat-horned), fr. *capri-* + *-cornus* (fr. *cornu* horn) — more at HORN] : the 10th sign of the zodiac — see SIGN table; ZODIAC illustration

capricorn beetle *n* [earlier *capricorn*, prob. fr. (assumed) NL *capricornus*, fr. L; fr. the hornlike antennae] : any of various beetles of the family Cerambycidae

cap·ri·cor·nis \¦==¦=nəs\ *n, cap* [NL, fr. *capri-* + *-cornis* (irreg. fr. *cornu* horn) — more at HORN] : the genus (family Bovidae) consisting of the serow

[1]**cap·rid** \'kaprəd\ *adj* : of or relating to Capridae or goats

[2]**caprid** \"\ *n* -s [NL *Capridae*] : one of the Capridae; *esp* : GOAT

cap·ri·dae \'kaprə,dē\ *n pl, cap* [NL, fr. *Capra*, type genus + *-idae*] *in former classifications* : a family of Artiodactyla comprising the sheep, goats, and related forms now usu. included in Bovidae

cap·ri·fi·cate \'kaprəfə,kāt, kə'prif-\ *vt* -ED/-ING/-S [back-formation fr. *caprification*] : to subject to caprification

cap·ri·fi·ca·tion \,kaprəfə'kāshən\ *n* -s [L *caprification-*, *caprificatio*, fr. *caprificatus*, past part. of *caprificare* to ripen figs by caprification, fr. *caprificus* wild fig, fr. *capri-* + *ficus* fig — more at FIG] : a horticultural operation in which flowering branches of the caprifig are hung in fig trees so as to facilitate pollination by the fig wasp which carries pollen from the flower of the caprifig to that of the edible fig

cap·ri·fig \'kaprə,fig\ *n* -s [ME *caprifige*, part trans. of L *caprificus*] **1** : a wild fig (*Ficus carica sylvestris*) of southern Europe and Asia Minor used in most fig-raising countries for pollination of the edible fig — see CAPRIFICATION **2** : the fruit of the caprifig

caprifoil *or* **caprifole** *n* -s [modif. of ML *caprifolium*] *obs* : HONEYSUCKLE

cap·ri·fo·li·a·ce·ae \,kaprə,fōl 'āsē,ē\ *n pl, cap* [NL, fr. *Caprifolium*, type genus + *-aceae*] : a large family of plants (order Rubiales) characterized by opposite usu. exstipulate leaves and flowers with calyx tube adnate to the ovary

cap·ri·fo·li·um \-'fōlēəm\ *n* [NL, fr. ML, honeysuckle, fr. L *capri-* + *folium* leaf — more at BLADE] **1** *cap, in some esp former classifications* : a genus of plants that is the type of the family Caprifoliaceae but is now usu. considered a subgenus of *Lonicera* **2** -s : a plant of the family Caprifoliaceae (as a honeysuckle)

cap·ri·fy \'kaprə,fī\ *vt* -ED/-ING/-ES [ME *caprifien*, fr. L *caprificare* — more at CAPRIFICATION] **1** : to induce the formation of fig fruits in (a tree) by caprification **2** : to induce the development of parthenocarpic fig fruits in (a tree) by the use of chemical growth regulators

cap·ri·mul·gid \,kaprə'məljəd, -lg-\ *n* -s [NL *Caprimulgidae*] : one of the Caprimulgidae : GOATSUCKER

cap·ri·mul·gi·dae \-ə,dē\ *n pl, cap* [NL, fr. *Caprimulgus*, type genus (fr. L, milker of goats, goatsucker, fr. *capri-* + *-mulgus*, fr. *mulgēre* to milk) + *-idae* — more at MILK] : a family of birds with a deeply cleft broad bill comprising the goatsuckers and constituting with the frogmouths a suborder of the order Caprimulgiformes

cap·ri·mul·gi·for·mes \,==,=ə'fȯr,mēz\ *n pl, cap* [NL, fr. *Caprimulgus*, type genus + *-iformes*] : an order of long-winged nonpasserine birds comprising the goatsuckers, frogmouths, and oilbirds — see CAPRIMULGIDAE

cap·rin \'kaprən\ *n* -s [ISV *capric* + *-in;* prob. orig. formed as F *caprine*] : glycerol tri-caprate

cap·rine \'ka,prīn\ *adj* [L *caprinus*, fr. *capr-*, *caper* + *-inus* -ine] **1** : being a goat : belonging to a group typified by the goat ⟨a ~ creature⟩ ⟨~ antelopes⟩ **2** : like or suggestive of a goat : like that of a goat ⟨a ~ voice⟩ **3** : developing or thriving in a goat ⟨a ~ strain of virus⟩

ca·prin·ic \kə'prinik, (')ka¦p-\ *adj* [prob. fr. G *kaprin-* (prob. modif., influenced by L *caprinus* caprine, of F *caprique* capric) + E *-ic*] : CAPRIC

[1]**cap·ri·ole** \'kaprē,ōl\ *vi* -ED/-ING/-S [prob. fr. It *capriolare*, fr. *capriola*] : to perform a capriole

[2]**capriole** \"\ *n* -s [MF or OIt; MF *capriole*, fr. OIt *capriola*, fr. *capriolo* roebuck, fr. L *capreolus* roebuck, wild goat, fr. *capr-*, *caper* goat; akin to OE *hæfer* goat, ON *hafr*, Gk *kapros* wild boar] **1** *dancing* **a** : CAPER **b** : CABRIOLE **2** *of a trained horse* : a vertical leap with a backward kick of the hind legs at the height of the leap

ca·pri·ote \'kaprē,ōt, 'kä-, -ēət\ *n* -s *cap* [*Capri*, island in the Bay of Naples, Italy + E *-ote*] : a native or inhabitant of Capri

cap·ro·al·de·hyde \¦ka(,)prō'aldə,hīd\ *n* -s [*caproic* (in *caproic acid*) + *aldehyde*] : HEXANAL

cap·ro·ate \'kaprə,wāt\ *n* -s [*caproic* + *-oate*] : a salt or ester of caproic acid

cap rock *n* : [1]CAP 2a(3)

ca·pro·ic acid \kə'prōik-, (')ka¦p-\ *n* [ISV *capr-* (fr. L *capr-*, *caper* goat) + *-oic;* orig. formed as F *caproïque* — more at CAPRIOLE] : a liquid fatty acid $CH_3(CH_2)_4COOH$ that is found in the form of its glycerol ester in fats and oils (as butter and coconut oil) or made synthetically and used in synthesizing pharmaceuticals and flavors — called also *hexanoic acid*

cap·ro·in \'kaprəwən\ *n* -s [ISV *caproic* + *-in*] : glyceryl caproate

cap·ro·lac·tam \,kaprō'lak,tam, ¦==,lak'tam\ *n* -s [ISV *caproic* + *lactam*] : a white crystalline cyclic amide $C_6H_{11}NO$ that yields epsilon-amino-caproic acid on hydrolysis and is used chiefly in making one type of nylon — called also *epsilon-caprolactam*

cap·ro·yl \'kaprə,wil, -ēl\ *n* -s [ISV *caproic* + *-yl*] : the radical $C_5H_{11}CO-$ of caproic acid — called also *hexanoyl*

cap·ryl \'kaprəl\ *n* -s [ISV *capric* + *-yl*] **1** : the radical $C_9H_{19}CO-$ of capric acid — called also *decanoyl* **2** : the univalent radical $CH_3(CH_2)_5CH(CH_3)-$ derived from 2-octanol; 1-methyl-heptyl

cap·ryl·al·de·hyde \,kaprə'laldə,hīd\ *n* -s [ISV *capryl* + *aldehyde*] : OCTANAL

cap·ry·late \'kaprə,lāt\ *n* -s [ISV *caprylic* + *-ate*] : a salt or ester of caprylic acid

ca·pryl·ic \kə'prilik, (')ka¦p-\ *adj* [ISV *capryl* + *-ic*] **1** : relating to caprylic acid **2** [*capri-* + *-yl* + *-ic*] *of an odor* : suggesting an animal body in rank pungency

caprylic acid *n* : a liquid fatty acid $CH_3(CH_2)_6COOH$ having a rancid odor and occurring in fats and oils often along with caproic acid — called also *octanoic acid*

cap·ry·lin \'kaprələn, -(,)lin; kə'prilən, ka-\ *n* -s [ISV *caprylic* + *-in*] : glycerol caproate

cap·ry·lyl \'kaprə,lil; kə'prilal, ka-\ *n* -s [ISV *capryl* + *-yl*] : the radical $C_7H_{15}CO-$ of caprylic acid—called also *octanoyl*

caps *pl of* CAP, *pres 3d sing of* CAP

caps *abbr* capsule

cap·sa·i·cin \kap'sāəsən\ *n* -s [alter. (perh. influenced by L *capsa* box) of *capsicine* "an extract from cayenne pepper", fr. NL *Capsicum* + E *-in*] : a colorless crystalline phenolic amide $C_9H_{17}CONHCH_2C_6H_3(OCH_3)OH$ that is a powerful irritant and the pungent principle of cayenne pepper

cap·san·thin \kap'san(t)thən\ *n* -s [ISV *caps-* (fr. NL *Capsicum*) + *anth-* + *-in*] : a carmine red crystalline carotenoid pigment $C_{40}H_{58}O_3$ found in paprika

cap screw *n* : TAP BOLT

cap scuttle *n* : a ship scuttle having a cap set closely over coamings into a rabbet

cap·sel·la \kap'selə\ *n, cap* [NL, fr. L *capsa* box, case + NL *-ella* — more at CASE] : a genus of widely distributed weeds of the family Cruciferae with basal tufted leaves, small white racemose flowers, and notched markedly flattened pods—see SHEPHERD'S PURSE

capsheaf \'=,=\ *n, pl* **capsheaves** **1** : the top sheaf of a shock or stack of grain **2** : the crowning point : most extreme instance : dominant element : CLIMAX, ACME ⟨insulting his benefactor was the ~ of folly⟩

capshore \'=,=\ *n* -s [[1]*cap* + *shore*] : a support under the fore part of the cap of a lower mast

cap·si·an \'kapsēən\ *adj, usu cap* [F *capsien*, fr. *Capsa* (L name for Gafsa, town & oasis in W. cen. Tunisia, near where prehistoric remains were found) + F *-ien* -ian] : of or relating to a paleolithic culture of northern Africa and southern Europe characterized by microlithic stone implements in geometric forms and rock paintings of hunting scenes, the early period being regarded as contemporaneous with the Aurignacian and the later with the Solutrean-Magdalenian

cap·si·cum \'kapsəkəm\ *n* [NL, prob. fr. L *capsa* box + *-icum* (neut. sing. of *-icus* -ic) — more at CASE] **1** *cap* : a genus of chiefly tropical perennial shrubby plants (family Solanaceae) that are widely grown as annuals for their fruits which under cultivation occur as many-seeded berries with a thickened usu. fleshy integument and vary greatly in size, shape, color, and pungency — see BIRD PEPPER, CAYENNE PEPPER, HOT PEPPER, SWEET PEPPER **2** -s : any plant of the genus *Capsicum* **3** -s : the dried-ripe fruit of any of certain plants of the genus *Capsicum* (esp. *C. frutescens*) containing capsaicin and used as a gastric and intestinal stimulant and as a rubefacient

capsicum wool *n* : cotton impregnated with oleoresin of capsicum — called also *calorific wool*

cap·sid \'kapsəd\ *n* -s [NL *Capsidae*] : any of several small to moderate-sized delicate-bodied active bugs constituting a family (Miridae) and including certain destructive pests of cultivated plants some of which are important vectors of plant diseases as well as predaceous forms that are important in the biological control of insect pests

cap·si·dae \'kapsə,dē\ [NL, fr. *Capsus*, type genus (irreg. fr. Gk *kapsis* gulping, fr. *kaptein* to gulp down) + *-idae* — more at HEAVE] *syn of* MIRIDAE

cap·size \'kap,sīz, ='=\ *vb* -ED/ -ING/ -S [origin unknown] *vt* **1** : to turn over; *specif* : to cause to keel over or upset from a safe or accustomed level position to one involving danger or loss ⟨ ~ a canoe⟩ **2** : COLLAPSE ~ *vi* **1** : to turn over : become overturned : UPSET ⟨the ship *capsized* in the storm⟩ **2** : to fold down : COLLAPSE **syn** see OVERTURN

cap sleeve *n* : a sleeve cut in one piece with the bodice and usu. covering only the cap of the shoulder

cap spinning *n* : a method of spinning by means of a cap on the spindle used in the production of Bradford-spun worsted

cap·stan \'kapstən\ *n* -s *often attrib* [ME] **1** : a machine for moving or raising heavy weights (as in warping a ship or hoisting an anchor) by winding cable (as a chain or hawser) around a vertical spindle-mounted drum which is rotated manually by bars fitted into sockets in the drumhead or driven by steam or electric power, pawls at the foot of the drum permitting rotation in one direction only — compare WINCH 2, WINDLASS **2** : a flangeless pulley used to control the motion of magnetic tape through a recorder

capstan 1

capstan lathe *n* : TURRET LATHE

capstan nut *n* : a nut resembling the head of a capstan and operated by a bar inserted in one of several holes about its periphery

capstan screw *or* **capstan bolt** *n* : a screw that has a head resembling a capstan and that is capable of being turned by a bar inserted in one of several radial holes in the head

capstern *or* **capstorm** *obs var of* CAPSTAN

capstone \'=,=\ *n* -s [[1]*cap* + *stone*] **1 a** : a coping stone : COPING **b** : the horizontal topmost stone of a dolmen **2** : the crowning point : most important element : decisive factor : CLIMAX, ACME ⟨a system of primary and secondary schools . . . with the university the ~ — *Amer. Guide Series: Va.*⟩

cap strip *n* : a continuous strip of material on the outer edge of an airplane wing rib for adding strength and providing increased area for the attachment of wing-covering material

capsul- *or* **capsuli-** *or* **capsulo-** *comb form* [NL, fr. *capsula*] : capsule ⟨*capsul*itis⟩ ⟨*capsuli*form⟩ ⟨*capsulo*lenticular⟩

cap·su·la \'kapsələ\ *n, pl* **capsu·lae** \-,lē, -ī\ [NL, fr. L, small box — more at CAPSULE] : CAPSULE

cap·su·lar \'kapsələ(r) *also* -syə-\ *adj* [NL *capsularis*, fr. *capsula* capsule + *-aris* -ar] **1** : of, relating to, or like a capsule **2** : CAPSULATE

capsular ligament *n* : a ligamentous sac surrounding the articular cavity of a freely movable joint and attached to the bones thus completely enclosing the joint

capsulary *adj* [NL *capsularius*, fr. *capsula* + *-arius* -ary] *obs* : CAPSULAR

cap·su·late \'kapsə,lāt, -,lət *also* -syə-\ *or* **cap·su·lat·ed** \-ād·əd\ *adj* [*capsulate* fr. NL *capsulatus*, fr. *capsula* + L *-atus* -ate; *capsulated* fr. NL *capsulatus* + E *-ed*] : enclosed in a capsule

cap·su·la·tion \,=='lāshən\ *n* -s [[1]*capsule* + *-ation*] : enclosure in a capsule : ENCAPSULATION

[1]**cap·sule** \'kapsəl, -(,)sül *also* -ps(,)yül *or* -psyəl\ *n* -s [F, fr. L *capsula* small box, dim. of *capsa* chest, case — more at CASE] **1 a** : a membrane or saclike structure enclosing a part or organ ⟨the ~ of the kidney⟩ ⟨an insect egg ~⟩ **b** : either of two layers or laminae of white matter in the cerebrum: (1) : a layer that consists largely of fibers passing to and from the cerebral cortex and that lies internal to the lenticular nucleus — called also *internal capsule* (2) : one that lies between the lenticular nucleus and the claustrum — called also *external capsule* **2** : a closed container bearing spores or seeds: **a** *in seed plants* : a dry dehiscent usu. many-seeded fruit composed of two or more carpels and releasing its seed at maturity through pores or by breaking into valves — compare POD; see FRUIT illustration **b** : the spore sac of the sporogonium of a moss — called also *theca*, *pyxidium* **3 a** *obs* : an earthenware saucer for roasting or melting samples of ores : SCORIFIER **b** : a small shallow cup or boat (as of porcelain, platinum, or glass) used in chemical manipulation to hold a substance being heated **4 a** : a gelatin shell enclosing medicine **b** : any similar gelatin container **5** : a metal seal over the cork of a bottle **6** *biol* : a viscous or gelatinous often polysaccharide envelope surrounding certain microscopic organisms (as the pneumococcus or many plantlike flagellates) **7 a** : an extremely brief condensation : OUTLINE, SURVEY ⟨ ~*s* of information too small to contain extended discussion —William Bridgwater⟩ **b** : a small quantity or amount : a little dose ⟨ ~*s* of history given to students⟩ **8** : a compact usu. detachable receptacle ⟨watches operating on energy ~*s*⟩ **9** : a small pressurized compartment for an aviator or astronaut for high-altitude flight, space flight, or emergency escape

capsules 2: *1* datura, *2* poppy, *3* gentian

[2]**capsule** \"\ *vt* -ED/ -ING/ -S **1** : to equip with or enclose in a capsule ⟨a *capsuled* bottle of wine⟩ **2** : to condense into or formulate in a very brief compact form ⟨*capsuled* the news⟩

³capsule \"\ *adj* **1 :** extremely brief and condensed ⟨a ~ biography⟩ ⟨~ coverage of the news⟩ **2 :** small and very compactly arranged and equipped ⟨a ~ submarine⟩

cap·sul·ec·to·my \,kapsə'lektəmē *also* -syə-\ *n* -ES [ISV *capsul-* + *-ectomy*] **:** excision of a capsule (as of a joint, kidney, or lens)

capsule of bow·man \-'bōmən\ *usu cap B* **:** BOWMAN'S CAPSULE

capsule of glis·son \-'glisᵊn\ *usu cap G* **:** GLISSON'S CAPSULE

capsule of te·non \-tə'nōⁿ\ *usu cap T* **:** TENON'S CAPSULE

capsuli- — see CAPSUL-

cap·sul·ize \'kapsə,līz *also* -syə-\ *vt* -ED/-ING/-S **:** CAPSULE ⟨a *capsulized* account of the news⟩

capsulo- — see CAPSUL-

cap·su·min \'kapsəmən\ *n* -S [ISV *capsum-* (irreg. fr. NL *Capsicum*) + *-in*; orig. formed as G *kapsumin*] **:** a red crystalline carotenoid pigment in a Guinea pepper (*Capsicum annuum*)

¹cap·tain \'kaptən, *rapid or before a name sometimes* -pᵊm\ *n* -S [ME *capitane, captein*, fr. MF *capitaine, capitain*, fr. LL *capitaneus* foremost, chief, fr. L *capit-, caput* head — more at HEAD] **1 :** a person having authority over and responsibility for a group or unit **:** CHIEF, LEADER: as **a :** the commander of a body of troops or of a military establishment (as a fortress) **b :** an officer entrusted with a command under a sovereign or general **c :** a ranking naval or maritime officer: (1) **:** an officer in charge of a warship (2) **:** an officer in charge of any ship and responsible for its navigation and for direction of its operations regardless of official rank — often used as a courtesy title (3) **:** a senior naval officer ranking just below a rear admiral or commodore and above a commander **d :** an army, marine, or air-force officer ranking below a major and above a first lieutenant **e :** a distinguished or highly skilled military leader **f** *chiefly Eng* **:** a mine superintendent or manager **g** *obs* **:** an Indian chief **h** *chiefly Eng* **:** a leader of a student group **:** HEAD BOY **i :** a leader in charge of the personnel of a train, caravan, or airplane: as (1) **:** a railroad conductor in charge of a freight or passenger train (2) **:** a pilot of a plane in flight; *esp* **:** a pilot of an air-force plane **j :** a leader of a side or team in a sports contest or similar activity **k :** a fire or police department officer usu. ranking between a chief and a lieutenant **l :** a party officer charged with organizing voters in a ward, precinct, or electoral district **m** (1) **:** a restaurant functionary in charge of waiters **:** HEADWAITER (2) **:** a hotel functionary in charge of bellboys — called also *bell captain* **n** *chiefly South* **:** BOSS — sometimes used as a generalized term of respect **o :** a Salvation Army officer ranking above a first lieutenant and below a senior captain **p :** the player in chouette who plays against the man in the box — abbr. *capt.* **2 :** a dominant figure **:** a person of importance and influence ⟨~*s* of commerce⟩

²captain *adj, obs* **:** CHIEF, HEAD

³cap·tain \'kaptən\ *vt* -ED/-ING/-S **:** to be captain of **:** fill the role of captain of **:** LEAD

captain ball *n* **:** a game similar to basketball played on an area marked with six circles by teams of seven or more players who try to pass the ball to the player stationed in the end circle

cap·tain·cy \'kaptənsē, -i\ *n* -ES **1 :** a captain's post, rank, or commission ⟨promoted to a ~⟩ **2 :** the caliber of a captain's actions **:** CAPTAINSHIP ⟨neither diplomatic statesmanship nor military ~⟩ **3 :** an administrative district under a captain

captaincy general *n, pl* **captaincies general :** the office, power, territory, or jurisdiction of a captain general

cap·tain·ess \'kaptənəs\ *n, pl* **captainesses** \-nəsəz, -,nes-\ [ME *captenesse*, fr. *captein* captain + *-esse* -ess] **:** a female captain

captain general *n, pl* **captains general** *or* **captain generals** **1 :** the commander in chief of an army **2 :** the commander in chief of the militia of a colony or state **3 :** the military governor of a colony, esp. a Spanish colony

cap·tain–gen·er·al·cy \,ₛₛ'ₛ(ₛ)sē\ *n* **:** CAPTAINCY GENERAL

cap·tain·ly *adv* **:** in the manner of a captain

captain of fortune : ADVENTURER

captain of industry : the head of a great industrial enterprise **:** ENTREPRENEUR

captain of numbers : the archery contestant making the highest score

captain of the fleet : a British naval officer of the rank of captain serving on the staff of a flag officer and in charge of staff work pertaining to maintenance of material

cap·tain·ry \'kaptənrē\ *n* -ES **:** CAPTAINCY

captain's chair *n* **:** an armchair with a low curved back with vertical spindles and a saddle seat

cap·tain·ship \-tən,ship\ *n* -S **1 :** condition, rank, post, or authority of a captain **2 :** skill as a military leader **3 :** CAPTAINCY 3

captain's chair

captain's mast *n* **:** a disciplinary proceeding at which the commanding officer of a naval vessel hears and disposes of cases against members of his command charged with an offense — called also *mast*

captain's walk *n* **:** WIDOW'S WALK

cap·ta·tion \kap'tāshən\ *n* -S [L *captation-, captatio*, fr. *captatus* (past part. of *captare* to chase, strive to seize) + *-ion-, -io* -ion — more at CATCH] **1 :** an attempt to achieve or acquire something (as favor or applause) esp. artfully ⟨the candidate's obvious ~⟩ **2 :** the making of an ad captandum appeal

¹cap·tion \'kapshən\ *n* -S [ME *capcioun*, fr. L *caption-, captio*, fr. *captus*, past part. of *capere* to take — more at HEAVE] **1 a** *archaic* **:** act of taking or seizing **:** SEIZURE **b** *chiefly Scots law* **:** arrest by legal process **2 :** CAVIL, QUIBBLE ⟨a mere ~ unworthy of answer⟩ **3 :** the part of a legal instrument (as a commission, indictment, or deposition) that shows where, when, and by what authority it was taken, found, or executed **4** [influenced in meaning by L *caput* head] **a :** the heading or title of an article, story, document, chapter, or other composition or of a page or section **b :** the explanatory comment or designation accompanying a pictorial illustration usu. as an underline or overline **c :** a motion-picture subtitle

²caption \"\ *vt* **captioned; captioned; captioning** \-sh(ə)niŋ\ **captions :** to furnish with a caption **:** ENTITLE

caption code *n* **:** a code book in which phrases are listed under their important words rather than alphabetized by their first words

cap·tious \'kapshəs\ *adj* [ME *capcious*, fr. MF or L; MF *captieux*, fr. L *captiosus*, fr. *captio* act of taking, deception, fallacious argument + *-osus* -ous] **1 :** calculated to confuse, entrap, or entangle in argument **:** likely to perplex or discomfit ⟨a ~ question demanding a careful answer⟩ **2 :** marked by an inclination to stress faults and raise often trivial objections **:** perversely hard to please esp. because overstrict or capricious ⟨it is perhaps ~ when one is given so much, to wish for more —Bergen Evans⟩ ⟨never willfully unjust, but . . . too often ~ in his justice, fond of legal chicanery —J.R.Green⟩ **syn** see CRITICAL

cap·tious·ly \-lē, -li\ *adv* **:** in a captious manner

¹cap·ti·vate \'kaptə,vāt, *usu* -ād·+V\ *vt* -ED/-ING/-S [LL *captivatus*, past part. of *captivare*, fr. L *captivus* captive] **1** *archaic* **:** take or hold as prisoner or prize **:** SEIZE, CAPTURE ⟨our prize, *captivated* from the British in a fair fight —P.L. Ford⟩ **2 :** to influence and dominate by some special charm, art, or trait and with an irresistible appeal precluding considered reservation ⟨every charm of person and address that can ~ a woman —Jane Austen⟩ ⟨*captivated* the delegates with his patriotic speech⟩ **syn** see ATTRACT

²captivate *adj* [LL *captivatus*] *obs* **:** CAPTIVATED

captivating *adj* **:** CHARMING, WINNING **:** showing ability to captivate ⟨a prose ~ in its music⟩ — **cap·ti·vat·ing·ly** *adv*

cap·ti·va·tion \,kaptə'vāshən\ *n* -S [LL *captivation-, captivatio*, fr. *captivatus* + L *-ion-, -io* -ion] **1 :** act of captivating **2 :** state of being captivated

cap·ti·va·tor \'ₛₛ,vād·ə(r)\ *n* -S **:** one that captivates

¹cap·tive \'kaptiv, -ēv\ *n* -S [ME, fr. L *captivus*, fr. *captivus*, adj.] **1 :** one captured **:** PRISONER **:** one taken and held usu. in confinement and esp. by an enemy in war **2 :** one captivated, dominated, or controlled ⟨a ~ to love⟩ ⟨the politician seemed a ~ of hidden interests⟩

²captive \"\ *adj* [ME, fr. L *captivus*, fr. *captus* (past part. of *capere* to take, seize) + *-ivus* -ive — more at HEAVE] **1 a :** taken and held as prisoner esp. by an enemy in war ⟨~ knights⟩ **b :** CONFINED **:** kept within bounds **:** CAGED ⟨a ~ bird⟩ **:** fenced in ⟨~ herds⟩ **c :** checked from free activity or course ⟨a ~ balloon riding on its cable⟩ ⟨~ waters impounded by the dam⟩ **2 :** indicative of or relative to a captive **:** making captive ⟨~ hours⟩ ⟨~ chains⟩ **3 :** CAPTIVATED, CHARMED, ENCHANTED ⟨her woman's heart ~ to his blandishments⟩ ⟨writing that holds the mind ~⟩ **4 a :** owned or controlled by another concern and operated according to its needs or demands rather than for an open market ⟨a ~ coal mine⟩ ⟨~ railroads⟩ **b :** dominated by a state, government, or philosophy alien to one's own often despite ostensible autonomy ⟨~ states on the boundaries of the empire⟩ **:** controlled by others despite semblance of independence ⟨a ~ candidate⟩ **5 :** in a situation making departure or inattention difficult **:** obliged to stay within hearing of a speech or demonstration ⟨a ~ audience⟩

³captive \"\ *vt* -ED/-ING/-S [ME *captiven*, fr. LL *captivare*, fr. L *captivus*] **1** *archaic* **:** CAPTURE **2** *archaic* **:** CAPTIVATE

captive bolt *n* **:** a gunlike instrument that when fired projects from the barrel an attached plunger used in slaughtering animals

cap·tiv·i·ty \kap'tivəd·ē, -ətē, -i\ *n* -ES [ME *captivite*, fr. MF *captivité*, fr. L *captivitas*, fr. *captivus* captive + *-itas* -ity] **1 a :** state or condition of being held captive esp. in war **:** subjection to a captor ⟨troops remaining in ~ years after the war⟩ **b :** state of being kept caged or fenced in ⟨some birds thrive in ~⟩ **2 :** domination by or subjection to another **:** oppressive control by another ⟨the ~ of science and invention by business —W.H.Hamilton⟩ **3** *archaic* **:** a group of captives ⟨they delivered up the whole ~ to Edom —Amos 1:9 (AV)⟩

cap·tor \'kaptə(r), -,tȯr, -,tō(ə)\ *n* -S [LL, catcher of animals, fr. L *captus* + *-or*] **:** one that has captured a person or thing

cap·to·rhi·no·morph \,kaptə'rīnə,mȯ(ə)rf\ *n* -S *sometimes cap* [NL *Captorhinomorpha*] **:** one of the Captorhinomorpha

cap·to·rhi·no·mor·pha \,ₛₛₛ,ₛₛ'mȯrfə\ *n pl, cap* [NL, fr. *Captorhinus*, type genus + *-o-* + *-morpha*] **:** a suborder of Cotylosauria comprising reptiles of the Carboniferous and Lower Permian which are sometimes held to be generalized forms ancestral to most later reptiles and to mammals and birds though possessing distinctly specialized dentition

cap·tress \'kaptrəs\ *n* -ES [*captor* + *-ess*] **:** a female captor

¹cap·ture \'kapchə(r), -psh-\ *n* -S [MF, fr. L *captura*, fr. *captus* (past part. of *capere* to take, seize) + *-ura* -ure — more at HEAVE] **1 a :** the act of catching and holding by force, show of strength, stratagem, or guile often despite attempt to resist or to escape ⟨the ~ of the town by the enemy⟩ ⟨the ~ of an escaped convict⟩ ⟨snares, traps, gins, and pitfalls for the ~ of men by women —G.B.Shaw⟩ **b :** the act of winning, seizing, gaining control, or coming to dominate ⟨the ~ of the party by extremists⟩ ⟨the ~ of one's fancy by a piece of music⟩ **2 :** one that has been seized or taken; *esp* **:** a prize ship **3 :** the natural diversion of one stream into the channel of another — called also *stream piracy* **4 :** the act of moving so as to take one of an opponent's chessmen or one or more of his checkers **5 :** the coalescence of an atomic nucleus with an elementary particle (as a neutron or electron) that may result in an emission (as of gamma rays) from the nucleus or in fission of the nucleus

²capture \"\ *vb* **captured; captured; capturing** \-pchəriŋ -psh(ə)r-\ **captures** *vt* **1 :** to take, seize, or catch esp. as captive or prize by force, surprise, stratagem, craft, or skill: as **a :** to subdue into surrender and loss of independence ⟨*captured* prisoners⟩ **b :** to seize and occupy ⟨the king's forces *captured* the city⟩ **c :** to get control or secure domination of **:** WIN, GAIN ⟨making plans to enter the highest finance and to ~ the banking of the country —Hilaire Belloc⟩ **d :** to circumscribe, hold, or preserve in or as if in some pattern, medium, record, or other relatively permanent form ⟨at any such moment as a photograph might ~ —C.E.Montague⟩ **e :** to influence as though captive **:** captivate and hold the interest of ⟨*captured* their imagination⟩ **2 :** to take (as a piece in chess or a trick in cards) according to rules of a game **3** *of a stream* **:** to divert (another stream) into its own channel usu. by a process of erosion — compare BEHEAD 2 **4 :** to bring about the capture of (an elementary particle) ⟨the uranium 238 nucleus may ~ a slow-moving neutron to form uranium 239⟩ — see ¹CAPTURE 5 ~ *vi* **:** to take an opponent's checker or chessman from the board **syn** see CATCH

cap·u·an \'kapyəwən\ *adj, usu cap* [*Capua* ancient city of Italy known for its luxury (fr. L) + E *-an*] **:** of, relating to, or having the characteristics of Capua; *esp* **:** LUXURIOUS ⟨found the *Capuan* comforts he expected in Virginia —Henry Adams⟩

ca·puche \kə'püch, -üsh\ *n* -S [It *cappuccio*, fr. *cappa* cloak, fr. LL, head covering, cloak — more at CAP] **:** HOOD; *esp* **:** the cowl of a Capuchin friar

cap·u·chin \'kapyə|shən, kə'p(y)ü|, |ch-\ *n* -S *often attrib* [MF *capuchin, capucin*, fr. OIt *cappuccino*, fr. *cappuccio* hood + *-ino* -ine] **1** *usu cap* **:** a Franciscan friar of the austere branch established in 1526 by Matteo di Bassi in Italy **2** *also* **cap·u·chine** \", 'kapyə,shēn, -,ch-\ **:** a hooded cloak for women that resembles the habit of a Capuchin friar **3** [so called fr. its resemblance to the hoodlike appearance of the hair at the back of the head] **a :** a long-tailed So. American monkey (*Cebus capucinus*) having the forehead naked and wrinkled with the hair on the crown reflexed and resembling a friar's cowl **b :** a monkey of the genus *Cebus* **4** [so called fr. the hoodlike tuft of feathers on the head and neck] **:** a variety of the domestic pigeon

capuchin cross *n, usu cap 1st C* [prob. so called fr. its resemblance to a pilgrim's staff, an important tenet of the Capuchin order being that men are but pilgrims and strangers on earth] **:** a cross pommée

ca·pu·chin·ess \kə'p(y)üshənəs, -üch-\ *n* -ES *usu cap* **:** a member of an austere order of Franciscan nuns under Capuchin rule

cap·u·cine \'kapyə,sēn\ *n* -S [F, fr. *capucin* Capuchin; fr. the resemblance of the flower to a hood] **:** QUINCE YELLOW

capucine buff *n* **:** a pale orange yellow that is slightly yellower, lighter, and stronger than sunset and redder and stronger than freestone

capucine lake *n* **:** a moderate reddish orange that is yellower and lighter than flamingo and yellower and paler than crab apple

capucine madder *n* **:** a moderate orange that is yellower and slightly less strong than honeydew and less strong and slightly lighter than Persian orange

capucine orange *n* **:** a moderate orange that is yellower and slightly lighter and stronger than honeydew and yellower and paler than Persian orange

capucine red *n* **:** a vivid yellowish pink to strong reddish orange that is very slightly yellower than Chinese orange

capucine yellow *n* **:** a moderate orange that is yellower, stronger, and slightly lighter than honeydew and yellower and lighter than Persian orange

capul *var of* CAPLE

ca·pu·lin \'käpə,lēn\ *also* **ca·pu·li** \-lē\ *or* **ca·po·lin** \-pə,lēn\ *n* -S [AmerSp *capulín, capulí*, fr. Nahuatl *capulin*] **1 :** a Mexican tree (*Prunus capuli*) that is sometimes considered to be a form of black cherry (*P. serotina*) and that yields a sap used in native remedies and has edible cherries of which the kernels of the pits furnish a flour **2 :** a tropical American tree (*Trema micrantha*) the bark of which yields a strong fiber **3 :** a ground cherry (*Physalis pubescens*) **4 :** a Mexican timber tree (*Condalia obovata*) whose hard wood furnishes a blue dye **5 :** CALABUR TREE

ca·put \'kä,pu̇t, -pət; 'kapət, -'ā-\ *n, pl* **ca·pi·ta** \'käpə,tä, 'kapəd·ə\ [L, head — more at HEAD] **1 :** a knoblike protuberance (as of a bone or muscle) **2 :** a university council **3** *Roman law* **:** legal status or civil capacity embracing the status of being a free man, a Roman citizen, and a member of a Roman family

caput mor·tu·um \-'mȯrchəwəm\ *n, pl* **capita mor·tua** \-wə\ [NL, lit., dead head] **1** *alchemy* **:** the residuum after distillation or sublimation **2 :** DROSS **:** worthless residue **3** *or* **caput mortuum vi·tri·o·li** \-,vi·trē'ō,lē, -ī\ **:** a red iron-oxide pigment made by calcining iron sulfate

caput suc·ce·da·ne·um \-,səksə'dānēəm\ *n, pl* **capita succeda·nea** \-nēə\ [NL, lit., substituted head] **:** a swelling formed upon the presenting part of the fetus during labor

capy *abbr* capacity

cap·y·bara *also* **cap·i·bara** \,kapə'barə, -ärə\ *or* **cap·i·vara** \-'v-\ *n* -S [Pg *capibara*, fr. Tupi] **:** an edible So. American rodent (*Hydrochoerus capybara*) that reaches in maturity over four feet in length and is the largest rodent in existence, is largely aquatic in habit having partly webbed feet, has no tail, has coarse fur, and somewhat resembles the guinea pig to which it is related

capybara

ca·que·tío \,käkə'tē(,)ō\ *n, pl* **caquetío** *or* **caquetí·os** *usu cap* [Sp *caquetío, caquetio*, of AmerInd origin] **1 a :** an extinct Arawakan people of the coast of Venezuela **b :** a member of this people **2 :** the language of the Caquetío people

¹car \'kär, 'kȧ(r\ *n* -S [ME *carre*, fr. AF, fr. L *carra*, pl. of *carrum*, alter. of *carrus*, of Celt origin; akin to OIr & MW *carr* vehicle, Bret *karr* — more at CURRENT] **1 :** a vehicle moving on wheels: **a** *archaic* **:** CARRIAGE, CART, WAGON **b :** a chariot of war or of triumph **:** a vehicle of splendor, dignity, or solemnity **c :** a vehicle adapted to the rails of a railroad or street railway and used for carrying passengers and mail, baggage, freight, or other things — in British usage usu. applied only to city tramways not railroads; compare CARRIAGE, COACH, TRUCK, VAN, WAGON **d :** AUTOMOBILE; *esp* **:** a private passenger automobile as distinguished from a bus or truck **2 :** the cage of an elevator **3 :** the portion of an airship or balloon that is intended to carry the power plant, personnel, cargo, or equipment **4** [by folk etymology fr. *corf*] **:** a large live-box for keeping fish or lobsters alive

²car \'kär\ *adj* [ScGael *cearr*] **1** *chiefly Scot* **:** LEFT-HANDED **2** *chiefly Scot* **a :** AWKWARD **b :** WRONG, SINISTER, PERVERSE

car *abbr* **1** carat **2** cargo

¹ca·ra \'kärə\ *n,pl* **cara** *or* **caras** *usu cap* [Sp, of AmerInd origin] **1 a :** an ancient Indian people possibly Barbacoan people of northern Ecuador conquered by the Incas in the 15th century **b :** a member of this people **2 :** the language of the Cara people

²ca·rá \kə'rä\ *n* -S [Pg] **:** CUSH-CUSH

car·ab \'karəb\ *or* **carab beetle** *n* -S [F, L, or Gk; F *carabe*, fr. L *carabus*, fr. Gk *karabos* — more at CARAVEL] **:** a beetle of the family Carabidae

car·a·bao \,karə'bau̇, ,kä-\ *n, pl* **carabao** *or* **carabaos** [PhilSp, fr. Eastern Bisayan (Samar-Leyte) *karabáw*] **1** *chiefly Philippines* **:** BUFFALO 1a **2** *also* **carabao mango :** a highly prized and widely planted Philippine variety of the mango

car·a·been \'karə,bēn\ *n* -S [native name in New South Wales] **:** an Australian tree (*Sloanea woollsii*)

car·a·bid \'karəbəd\ *n* -S [NL *Carabidae*] **:** a beetle of the family Carabidae **:** GROUND BEETLE

ca·rab·i·dae \kə'rabə,dē\ *n pl, cap* [NL, fr. *Carabus*, type genus + *-idae*] **:** a large family of beetles comprising the ground beetles which are usu. shining black or metallic in color, have long antennae and 5-jointed tarsi, are mostly of active, predaceous, and largely terrestrial habits, and destroy many injurious insects — compare BOMBARDIER BEETLE — **ca·rab·i·dan** \kə'rabədᵊn\ *adj or n* — **car·a·bid·e·ous** \,karə'bidēəs\ *adj*

car·a·bin \'karəbən\ *n* -S [MF — more at CARBINE] *archaic* **:** CARABINEER

car·a·bi·neer *or* **car·a·bi·nier** \,karəbə'ni(ə)r\ *or* **car·bi·neer** \,kärbə'ni(ə)r, ,käb-\ *n* -S [F *carabinier*, fr. *carabine* carbine + *-ier* -eer — more at CARBINE] **:** a soldier armed with a carbine

car·a·bi·ner *or* **kar·a·bi·ner** \,karə'bēnə(r)\ *n* -S [G *karabiner*, short for *karabinerhaken* carbine hook, fr. *karabiner* carbine (modif. of F *carabine*) + *haken* hook; fr. its original use to fasten carbines to bandoleers — more at CARBINE] **:** an oblong ring that snaps to the eye or link of a piton to hold a freely running rope

car·a·bi·ne·ro \,karəbə'ne(,)rō\ *n* -S [Sp, fr. *carabina* carbine (fr. F *carabine*) + *-ero* -er] **1 :** a member of a Spanish national police force serving esp. as frontier guards **2 :** a customs or coast-guard officer in the Philippines

ca·ra·bi·nie·re \,karəbə'nyerē, -e(,)rā\ *n, pl* **carabinie·ri** \-erē\ [It, fr. F *carabinier*] **:** a member of the Italian national police

car·a·boid \'karə,bȯid\ *adj* [NL *Caraboidea*] **1 :** of or relating to the Caraboidea **2** *of a beetle larva* **:** active and predacious with well-developed thoracic legs and considerable chitinization

car·a·boi·dea \,karə'bȯidēə\ *n pl, cap* [NL, fr. *Carabus*, type genus + *-oidea*] **:** a superfamily coextensive with the suborder Adephaga comprising beetles that have the eyes entire and the antennae slender and elongated

car·a·bus \'karəbəs\ *n* [NL, fr. Gk *karabos* horned beetle — more at CARAVEL] **1** *cap* **:** a genus (the type of the family Carabidae) of large ground beetles **2** -ES **:** an insect of the genus *Carabus*

car·a·cal \'karə,kal, ,ₛₛ'ₛ\ *n* -S [F, fr. Sp, fr. Turk *karakulak*, lit., black-ear, fr. *kara* black + *kulak* ear] **1 :** a cat (*Felis*, or *Caracal*, or *Lynx, caracal*) of Africa and parts of Asia that is somewhat larger than a fox and has reddish brown fur, black ears, and long lynxlike ear tufts **2 :** the fur or pelt of the caracal

car·a·cara \,karə'karə, -əkə'rä\ *n* -S [Sp *caracara* & Pg *caracará*, fr. Tupi *caracará*, of imit. origin] **:** any of certain large mostly So. American hawks of vulturelike habits having rather long legs and able to run well on the ground — see AUDUBON'S CARACARA

ca·ra·cas \kə'rakəs, -äk-\ *adj, usu cap* [fr. *Caracas*, city in Venezuela] **:** of or from Caracas, the capital of Venezuela **:** of the kind or style prevalent in Caracas

car accounting *n* **:** the record of the movement of cars from one railroad system to another and of the debits and credits thereby created

carack *or* **carac** *var of* CARRACK

car·a·co \'karə,kō\ *n* -S [F, perh. fr. Turk *kerrake* alpaca coat] **:** a woman's short coat or jacket usu. about waist length

¹car·a·cole \'karə,kōl\ *n* -S [F, fr. Sp *caracol* snail, spiral stair, caracole (of a horse), perh. modif. of L *conchylium* shellfish — more at COCKLE] **1 :** a staircase in a spiral form **2 a :** a half turn either to the right or the left executed by a horseman **b :** a turning, wheeling, prancing, or capering movement ⟨his dog . . . came around the corner . . . with a ~ —Paul Horgan⟩

²caracole \"\ *vb* **caracoled** *also* **caracolled; caracoled** *also* **caracolled; caracoling** *also* **caracolling; caracoles** [F *caracoler*, fr. *caracole*] *vi* **1 :** to perform a caracole or move in caracoles **2 :** to ride a caracoling horse ~ *vt* **:** to cause to caracole

car·a·co·li \,karəkə'lē\ *n* -S [AmerSp *caracolí*, of Cariban origin; akin to Oyana *caracoulí* silver, Carib *caracolis* trinkets, gold] **:** ESPAVÉ

car·a·co·lite \,karə'kō,līt\ *n* -S [G *caracolit*, fr. *Caracoles*, town in Chile, its locality + G *-it* -ite] **:** a rare mineral occurring as a colorless crystalline incrustation and consisting of lead sulfate together with chlorine and sodium

car·a·core \'karə,kō(ə)r\ *also* **car·a·co·ra** \,ₛₛ'kōrə\ *or* **car·a·coa** \,ₛₛ'kōə\ *n* -S [F, fr. Malay *kurakura*] **:** a proa used by Moro peoples

¹caract *n* -S [ME *carecte, caracte*, fr. MF, fr. L *character* mark, sign — more at CHARACTER] *obs* **:** MARK, SIGN, CHARACTER

²caract *obs var of* CARAT

¹caracul *var of* KARAKUL

²car·a·cul \'karəkəl *also* -er-\ *n* -S **:** the pelt of a karakul lamb after the curl begins to loosen — compare BROADTAIL, PERSIAN LAMB

caracul cloth *n* **:** a heavy fabric woven in imitation of caracul

ca·rafe \kə'raf, -aa(ə)f,-aif,-äf\ *n* -S [F, fr. It *caraffa*, fr. Ar *gharrāfah*, fr. *gharafa* to dip up water] **:** a bottle usu. made of glass with a narrow neck and spherical body and used to hold water or beverages ⟨a water ~ on the desk⟩

car·a·ga·na \,karə'gänə,-anə,-ānə\ *n* [NL, of Turkic origin; akin to Kirghiz *karaghan* Siberian pea tree] **1** *cap* **:** a large genus of Asiatic shrubs or small trees (family Leguminosae) having even-pinnate leaves with small leaflets and solitary or clustered mostly yellow flowers and bearing seeds in a linear pod — see CHINESE PEA TREE, SIBERIAN PEA TREE **2** -S : any plant of the genus *Caragana* shrubby members of which are extensively used in dry parts of the central U. S. for hedges and in shelter belts

caragcen *var of* CARRAGEEN

¹car·a·gua·ta \ˌkarəgwəˈtä\ *n* -S [AmerSp *caraguatá*, fr. Pg, fr. Tupi *caragoatá, caraquatá*, lit., which scratches those walking] **1** : a plant (*Bromelia argentina*) of Argentina and Paraguay with leaves that yield a long silky fiber **2** : the fiber yielded by the caraguata

²caraguata \"\, ˌkarəˈgwäd·ə\ [NL, fr. Sp or Pg *caraguatá*] *syn of* GUZMANIA

car·a·ibe \ˌkarəˈēb, kəˈrīb\ *n* -S [prob. fr. F *caraïbe* Carib, modif. of Sp *caribe* — more at CARIB] : BROWN SUGAR 2

¹ca·rai·pi *or* **ca·rai·pe** \kəˈrīpē\ *n* -S [Pg *caraipe*] : POTTERY TREE

²ca·rai·pi \ˌkarəˈpē\ *or* **ca·rai·pe** \-ˈpā\ *n* -S [Pg *caraipé*, fr. Tupi] : any of several Brazilian timber trees of the genus *Caraipa* (family Guttiferae) yielding a strong hard valuable wood

ca·ra·já \ˌkarəˈhä\ *also* **ca·ra·ya** \-ˈyä\ *n, pl* **carajá** *or* **carajás** *also* **caraya** *or* **carayas** *usu cap* [Sp & Pg, fr. *Carajá*, lit., great people] **1 a** : a people or group of peoples of eastern Brazil **b** : a member of such people **2** : the language of the Carajá people constituting a language family

car·a·ju·ra \ˌkarəˈzhürə\ *also* **car·a·ju·ru** \-ˌzhəˈrü\ *or* **ca·ra·ja·ra** \-ˈzhärə\ *n* -S [Pg *carajura, carajurú*, fr. Tupi *carajurú*, perh. of Cariban origin; akin to Galibi *caraerú, cariarú*] **1** : a Brazilian plant (*Bignonia chica*) that is the source of a red dye **2** : the red pigment extracted from the leaves of the carajura — called also *chica*

car·am·bo·la \ˌkarəmˈbōlə\ *n* -S [Pg, fr. Marathi *karambal*] **1** : an East Indian tree (*Averrhoa carambola*) widely cultivated in the tropics **2** : the green to yellow usu. somewhat acid fruit of the carambola that is much used in Chinese cookery

¹car·am·bole \ˈkarəmˌbōl\ *n* -S [Sp *carambola*, lit., carambola (the fruit), fr. Pg] **1** *obs* : CAROM **2** *obs* : a shot in billiards in which the cue ball strikes more than one cushion before completing a carom

²carambole \"\ *vi* -ED/-ING/-S : CAROM

¹car·a·mel \ˈkarəməl, ˈkerə-, ÷ˈkärməl, ÷ˈkäm- *also* ˈkarəˌmel *or* ˈkerə- *or* ÷kärˈmel *or* ÷käˈm-\ *n* -S [F, fr. Sp *caramelo*, fr. Pg, icicle, caramel, fr. LL *calamellus* small reed — more at SHAWM] **1** : an amorphous brittle brown and somewhat bitter substance obtained as a porous mass by heating sugar to about 170–180° C that is usu. made commercially by heating dextrose with a small amount of ammonia or ammonium salts and used as a coloring agent (as in carbonated beverages, bakery products, confections, and liquors) **2 a** : a firm chewy usu. caramel-flavored candy often containing fruits and nuts and typically cut in small blocks **b** : a piece of this candy **3** : a brownish orange to light brown that is lighter than sorrel or tawny and redder and lighter than raw sienna

²caramel \"\ *vb* -ED/-ING/-S : CARAMELIZE

caramel brown *n* : a moderate to dark brown

car·a·mel·iza·tion \ˌkarəmələˈzāshən, -er-, -ˌmel-, -ˌmaˌlīˈz-; ÷ˌkärmələˈzāshən, ÷ˌkäm-, -əˌlīˈz-\ *n* -S : the process of caramelizing

car·a·mel·ize \ˈkarəməˌlīz, ÷ˈkärm-,÷ˈkäm- *also* ˈkerəm-\ *vb* -ED/-ING/-S [¹*caramel* + *-ize*] *vt* **1** : to change (sugar or the sugar content of a food) into caramel **2** : to change (as a carbohydrate) to a brown caramellike color ~ *vi* : to change to caramel or a caramellike substance or color

car·a·mel·like \-əmәlˌlīk\ *adj* : resembling caramel

car·a·mous·sal \ˌkarəməˈsal\ *n* -S [Turk *karamürsel, karamusal*, perh. fr. *kara* black + *mürsel* envoy, apostle] : a high-pooped Turkish or Moorish merchant ship esp. of the 17th century

ca·ran·cha \kəˈranchə, -ˈän-\ *or* **ca·ran·cho** \-(ˌ)chō\ *n* -S [AmerSp *carancho*, fr. Quechua *caranchi*] : any of several So. American caracaras (esp. *Polyborus plancus*)

ca·ran·dá \ˌkaranˈdä\ *n* -S [AmerSp, of Guaranian origin; akin to Guarani *caranday*] **1** : a tropical palm (*Copernicia australis*) that yields a wax similar to carnauba **2** : CARNAUBA

ca·ran·das \kəˈrandəs\ [NL, fr. Malayalam *karaṇṭa*] *syn of* CARISSA

car·an·day \ˌkaranˈdī\ *n* -S [AmerSp, fr. Guarani] : CARNAUBA

¹ca·ran·gid \kəˈranjəd\ *adj* [NL *Carangidae*] : of or relating to the Carangidae

²carangid \"\ *n* -S : a fish of the family Carangidae

ca·ran·gi·dae \-jəˌdē\ *n pl, cap* [NL, fr. *Carang-, Caranx*, type genus + *-idae*] : a large family of marine percoid fishes containing the pompanos, amberfishes, cavallas, and a number of other narrow-bodied food fishes with widely forked tail chiefly of warm seas

¹ca·ran·gin \-jən\ *adj* [²*carangin*] : of or relating to the genus *Caranx*

²carangin \"\ *n* -S [NL *Carang-, Caranx* + E *-in*] : a fish of the genus *Caranx*

ca·ran·goid \kəˈraŋˌgȯid\ *adj* [prob. fr. NL *Carang-, Caranx* + E *-oid*] : like or belonging to the Carangidae

²carangoid \"\ *n* -S : CARANGID

ca·ran·gus \kəˈraŋgəs\ [NL, fr. F *carangue* shad, horse mackerel — more at CARANX] *syn of* CARANX

ca·ran·na \kəˈranə\ *or* **caranna gum** *also* **ca·ra·na** \", -anyə\ *or* **ca·rau·na** \-rȯnə\ *n* -S [Sp *caraña*, prob. fr. a native name in Venezuela] : a dark resinous medicinal gum obtained from any of several So. American trees (*esp. Protium carana, P. altissimum*, and *Pachylobus hexandrus*)

ca·ranx \ˈkaˌraŋks, ˈkäˌ-\ *n* [NL, fr. F *carangue* shad, horse mackerel, fr. Sp *caranga, carangue*] **1** *cap* : the type genus of Carangidae — see CAVALLA **2** *pl* **caranx** : any fish of the genus *Caranx*

ca·rapa \kəˈrapə\ *n* [NL, fr. Galibi *carapa, krapa*, lit., oil] **1** *cap* : a small genus of tropical trees (family Meliaceae) having abruptly pinnate leaves and flowers with four or five petals and monadelphous stamens **2** *also* **ca·rap** \kəˈrap\ *or* **crab** \ˈkrab\ -S [*carap*, short for *carapa*; *crab*, by folk etymology fr. *carapa*] : any tree of the genus *Carapa* ⟨*carap* wood⟩ ⟨*crab* nut⟩ — see CRABWOOD

car·a·pace \ˈkarəˌpās\ *n* -S [F, fr. Sp *carapacho*] **1 a** : a bony or chitinous case or shield covering the back or part of the back of an animal (as the upper shell of a turtle, the shell of an armadillo, or the shell of a crab) **b** : the entire shell of a turtle comprising the carapace and the plastron **2 a** : a hard superficial crust ⟨the ~ of a lava flow⟩ **b** : any hard protective outer covering; *specif* : a manner, attitude, or state of mind (as indifference or hostility) serving to protect or isolate from external influence ⟨their ~ of incuriosity —William Sansom⟩

car·a·pa·cial \ˌkarəˈpāshəl\ *adj* : of or relating to a carapace

carapato *var of* CARRAPATO

car·a·pax \ˈkarəˌpaks\ *n* -ES [by alter.] : CARAPACE 1a

ca·rap·i·dae \kəˈrapəˌdē\ *n pl, cap* [NL, fr. *Carapus*, type genus + *-idae*] : a small family of percomorph fishes related to the brotulids and comprising the pearl fishes — see CARAPUS

ca·rap nut \kəˈrap-\ *n* : the seed of the carapa (esp. of *Carapa procera* and *C. guianensis*) yielding a bitter oil or fat that is used as a protective against vermin and insects

car·a·pus \ˈkarəpəs\ *n, cap* [NL, fr. Pg *carapó*] : a genus (the type of the family Carapidae) of small slender fishes living as inquilines in the alimentary canal of large holothurians or between the valves of large bivalve mollusks — see PEARLFISH 1

ca·ra·que·ño \ˌkarəˈkān(ˌ)yō\ *n* -S *cap* [Sp, fr. *Caracas*, Venezuela + Sp *-eño* (suffix denoting an inhabitant)] : a man or boy of Caracas; *broadly* : a native or inhabitant of Caracas

ca·rara \kəˈrarə, -ˈä-\ [NL] *syn of* CORONOPUS

¹caras *pl of* CARA

²carás *pl of* CARÁ

ca·ra spo·sa \ˌkärəˈspōzə\ *n* [It] : a dear wife

¹carat *var of* KARAT

²car·at \ˈkarət *also* -er-\ *n* -S [prob. fr. ML *carratus*, fr. Ar *qīrāṭ* bean or pea pod, weight of four grains, carat, fr. Gk *keration* carob bean, small weight, carat, lit., small horn, dim. of *kerat-, keras* horn — more at HORN] **1** : any of various units of weight for precious stones (as diamonds and pearls): as **a** : a unit equal to 205.3 milligrams used in the U.S. before 1913 **b** : an international unit equal to 200 milligrams that had already been adopted in most European countries and in Japan when it was made standard in the U.S. in 1913 — abbr. *c*; called also *international carat, metric carat* **2** *obs* : WORTH, VALUE, ESTIMATE ⟨of too good ~ to be left so without a guard —Ben Jonson⟩

ca·ra·te \kəˈräd·ē\ *n* -S [Sp] : a disease endemic in tropical America that is characterized by the presence of white, brown, blue, red, or violet spots on the skin and caused by a spirochete (*Treponema carateum*)

carat grain *n* : a unit of weight equal to ¼ carat used esp. for pearls — called also *pearl grain*

carauna *var of* CARAVANCE

ca·raun·da \kəˈraündə, -ˌdä\ *n* -S [Hindi *karaṇdā*, fr. Skt *karamardaka*] : an East Indian evergreen shrub or small tree (*Carissa carandas*) having a somewhat acid fruit that is pickled green or eaten ripe

¹car·a·van \ˈkarəˌvan, -aa(ə)n *also* -er- *or* -ˌvən; *Brit often* ˌ==ˈvan\ *n* -S [It *caravana, carovana*, fr. Per *kārwān*] **1 a** : a company of travelers, pilgrims, or merchants on a long journey through desert or hostile regions : a train of pack animals **b** : a group of vehicles proceeding or traveling together in a file ⟨a ~ of buses⟩ **2** *obs* **a** : a Russian or Turkish fleet esp. of merchant ships with convoy **b** : a sea campaign against the Muslims obligatory upon each member of the Knights of Malta **3** : a covered vehicle : VAN: as **a** : a covered wagon or motor truck equipped as traveling living quarters or office **b** *Brit* : TRAILER 4e

²caravan \"\ *vb* **caravaned** *or* **caravanned**; **caravaned** *or* **caravanned**; **caravaning** *or* **caravanning**; **caravans** *vt* : to convey in a caravan ~ *vi* : to travel in a caravan

caravance *var of* GARAVANCE

car·a·van·sa·ry \ˌkarəˈvan(t)sərē\ *or* **car·a·van·se·rai** \-səˌrī\ *n, pl* **caravansaries** *or* **caravanserais** *or* **caravanserai** [modif. of Per *kārwānsarāī*, fr. *kārwān* caravan + *sarāī* palace, large house, inn; akin to Av *thrāya-* to protect] **1** : an inn in eastern countries where caravans rest at night that is commonly a large bare building surrounding a court ⟨stopped for food and shelter at an unpromising ~ situated on a small oasis—L.C.Douglas⟩ **2** : HOTEL, INN ⟨a ~ for cosmopolitans with more money than sense —Frank Clune⟩

car·a·vel \ˈkarəˌvel, -ˌvəl\ *n* -S [MF *caravelle, carvelle*, fr. OPg *caravela*, dim. of *cáravo*, a ship, fr. LL *carabus* coraclelike boat, fr. L, a sea crab, fr. Gk *karabos*, a sea crab, a horned beetle; prob. akin to Gk *karis*, a sea crab — more at -CARIS] : any of several sailing vessels: as **a** : a small vessel of the 15th and 16th centuries with broad bows, high narrow poop, three or four masts, and usu. lateen sails on the two or three aftermasts ⟨the ~s of Columbus⟩ **b** : a Portuguese vessel of 100 to 150 tons burden **c** : a small fishing boat used on the French coast **d** : a Turkish man-of-war

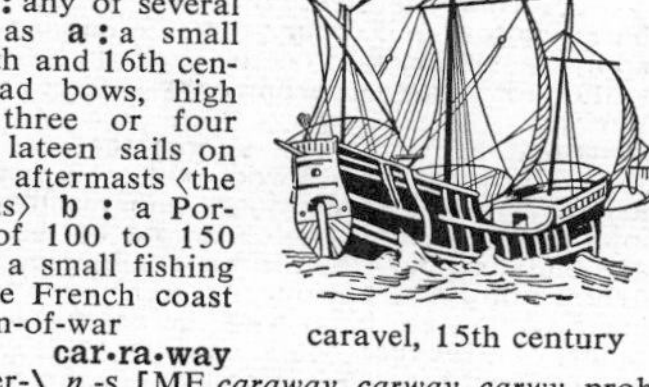

caravel, 15th century

car·a·way *also* **car·ra·way** \ˈkarəˌwā *also* -er-\ *n* -S [ME *caraway, carway, carwy*, prob. fr. ML *carvi*, fr. Ar *karawyā*, fr. Gk *karon*] **1** : a perennial usu. white-flowered herb (*Carum carvi*) **2** *or* **caraway seed** : the aromatic pungent-tasting fruit of the caraway used in cookery and confectionery, in the manufacture of certain beverages, and as a source of an oil **3** *obs* : a cake or sweetmeat containing caraway seeds

caraway oil *n* : an essential oil obtained from caraway seeds and used in pharmaceuticals and as a flavoring agent in foods and liqueurs

caraya *cap, var of* CARAJÁ

carb \ˈkärb, -äb\ *n* -S [by shortening] *slang* : CARBURETOR

carb- *or* **carbo-** *comb form* [F, fr. *carbone* — more at CARBON] : carbon : carbonic : carbonyl : carboxyl ⟨*carb*odiimide⟩ ⟨*carbo*hydrazide⟩ ⟨*carbo*hydrate⟩

car·ba·chol \ˈkärbəˌkōl, -ōl\ *n* -S [*carba*moyl-*choline*] : a synthetic drug $C_6H_{15}ClN_2O_2$ used as a cholinergic agent in the treatment of urinary retention and abdominal distention and topically in glaucoma : carbamoyl-choline chloride

carb·ac·i·dom·e·ter \(ˌ)kärˌbasəˈdäməd·ər\ *n* -S [ISV *carbonic* + *acid* + *-o-* + *-meter*; orig formed as G *karbazidometer*] : an instrument for determining the percentage of carbon dioxide in the air

carb·alk·oxy \ˌkärˌbalˈkäksē\ *adj* [*carbalkoxy-*, fr. *carbalkoxyl*] : relating to or containing carbalkoxyl

carb·alk·ox·yl \ˌ==ˈ=səl\ *n* -S [*carb-* + *alkoxyl*] : a radical —COOR consisting of carbonyl combined with alkoxyl

car·ba·mate \ˈkärbəˌmāt, kärˈbaˌmāt\ *n* -S [ISV *carbamic* + *-ate*] : a salt or ester of carbamic acid — see URETHANE

car·bam·ic acid \(ˈ)kärˈbamik-\ *n* [ISV *carb-* + *amide* + *-ic*] : an acid NH_2COOH known in the form of its salts (as ammonium carbamate) and esters (as urethan) : the half amide of carbonic acid

car·bam·ide \kärˈbaˌmīd, -ˌməd; ˈkärbəˌm-\ *n* -S [ISV *carb-* + *amide*] : UREA

carb·am·i·do- \kärˈbaməˌdō, ¦kärbə¦mē(ˌ)dō\ *comb form* [*carbamide*] : UREIDO- ⟨5-*carbamido*hydantoin⟩

carb·am·i·no \kärˈbaməˌnō, ¦kärbə¦mē(ˌ)nō\ *adj* [ISV *carb-* + *amino-*; orig. formed as G *karbamino-*] : relating to any carbamic acid derivative formed by reaction of carbon dioxide with an amino acid or a protein (as hemoglobin)

car·bam·o·yl \kärˈbaməˌwil, -ēl\ *or* **car·ba·myl** \ˈkärbəˌmil, -ēl\ *n* -S [*carbamoyl* fr. *carbamic* (in *carbamic acid*) + *-o-* + *-yl*; *carbamyl* fr. *carbamic* + *-yl*] : the radical NH_2CO— of carbamic acid

car·ba·nil \ˈkärbəˌnil\ *n* -S [ISV *carb-* + *anil*] : PHENYL ISOCYANATE

car·ba·nil·ate \ˌkärbəˈniˌlāt, -lət; kärˈbanᵊlˌāt, -ət\ *n* -S [*carbanilic* (in *carbanilic acid*) + *-ate*] : a salt or ester of carbanilic acid

car·ba·nil·ic acid \¦kärbə¦nilik-\ *n* [ISV *carbanil* + *-ic*] : an acid $C_6H_5NHCOOH$ known in the form of its salts and esters — called also *phenylcarbamic acid*

car·ba·nil·ide \ˌkärbəˈniˌlīd, -ˌləd, kärˈbanᵊlˌīd, -ˌəd\ *n* -S [ISV *carb-* + *anilide*] : a silky crystalline compound $(C_6H_5NH)_2CO$ obtained by heating aniline with urea and in other ways — called also *symmetrical diphenyl-urea*

carb·an·i·on \kärˈbaˌnīən *also* -īˌän\ *n* -S [*carb-* + *anion*] : an organic ion carrying a negative charge at a carbon location (as methyl carbanion or butenyl carbanion) — compare CARBONIUM

carbarn \ˈ=ˌ=\ *n* -S [¹*car* + *barn*] : a building that houses the cars of a street railway or the buses of a bus system

car·bar·sone \kärˈbärˌsōn\ *n* -S [*carbanilic* + *-arsone* (fr. *arsonic*)] : a white powder $NH_2CONHC_6H_4AsO_3H_2$ used in treating amebic dysentery; *p*-ureido-benzene-arsonic acid

car·ba·sus \ˈkärbəsəs\ *n* -ES [L, fine linen; prob. akin to Gk *karpasos* fine flax, Skt *karpāsa* cotton] *archaic* : surgical gauze : LINT

car·baz·ic acid \(ˈ)kärˈbazik-\ *n* [*carb-* + *az-* + *-ic*] : an acid $NH_2NHCOOH$ known chiefly in the form of its esters and derivatives (as amino-carbamic acid, hydrazine-carboxylic acid)

car·ba·zide \ˈkärbəˌzīd, kärˈba-, -zəd\ *n* -S [ISV *carb-* + *az-* + *-ide*] **1** : CARBOHYDRAZIDE **2** : a crystalline explosive compound $CO(N_3)_2$ made by the action of nitrous acid on carbohydrazide : the azide of carbonic acid

car·ba·zole \ˈkärbəˌzōl, kärˈba-\ *n* -S [ISV *carb-* + *az-* + *-ole*] : a white crystalline feebly basic cyclic compound $C_{12}H_9N$ occurring in crude anthracene and constituting the parent of a number of dyes — called also *diphenylenimine*

carbazole blue R *n, usu cap C&B* : a vat dye — see DYE table I (under *Vat Blue 43*)

carb·azot·ic acid \¦kärbə¦zäd·ik-, -zōl\ *n* [*carb-* + *azotic*] : PICRIC ACID

car·been \ˈkärˌbēn\ *n* -S [native name in Australia] : an Australian eucalypt (*Eucalyptus tessellaris*) yielding a white crystalline kino

car·bene \ˈkärˌbēn\ *n* -S [*carb-* + *-ene*] : one of the components of bitumen soluble in carbon disulfide but insoluble in carbon tetrachloride — usu. used in pl.; compare ASPHALTENE

car·be·ni·um \kärˈbēnēəm\ *n* -S [NL, by alter.] : CARBONIUM

carb·eth·oxy \ˌkärˌbeˈthäksē\ *adj* [*carbethoxy-*] : relating to or containing carbethoxyl

carbethoxy- \"\ *comb form* [ISV, fr. *carbethoxyl*] : containing carbethoxyl ⟨*carbethoxy*alanine⟩

carb·eth·ox·yl \ˌ=ˌ=ˈ=səl\ *n* -S [blend of *carboxyl* and *ethyl*] : the radical $—COOC_2H_5$ consisting of the ethyl ester of carboxyl — called also *ethoxycarbonyl*

carb·eth·ox·yl·a·tion \ˌ=ˌ=ˌ=səˈlāshən\ *n* -S [*carbethoxyl* + *-ation*] : the introduction of carbethoxyl into an organic compound

carb·he·mo·glo·bin \ˈkärb¦h-\ *or* **car·bo·he·mo·glo·bin** \ˈkär(ˌ)bō¦h-\ *n* -S [ISV *carb-* + *hemoglobin*] : a compound of hemoglobin with carbon dioxide

car·bide \ˈkärˌbīd, ˈkäˌb-\ *n* -S [ISV *carb-* + *-ide*] : a binary compound of carbon with a more electropositive element: as **a** : CALCIUM CARBIDE **b** : a very hard material made by cementing together with a binder or by means of powder metallurgy a mixture of powdered carbides of heavy metals (as tungsten and titanium) and used in metal-cutting tools — called also *cemented carbide*

car·bi·mide \ˈkärbəˌmīd, kärˈbi-; kärˈbiməd\ *n* -S [ISV *carb-* + *imide*] : ISOCYANIC ACID

car·bin·a·mine \kärˈbinəˈmēn\ *n* -S [ISV *carbin-* (fr. obs. G *karbin* methyl) + *amine* — more at CARBINOL] : METHYLAMINE — used in the names of derivatives; *also* : any amine derived from methylamine

car·bine \ˈkärˌbīn, ˈkäˌb-, -ēn *also* -ˌbən\ *n* -S [F *carabine* carbine, carabineer, fr. MF *carabin* harquebusier, carabineer, prob. alter. of *escarrabin, scarrabin* preparer of plague corpses for burial, prob. alter. of *scarabée* dung beetle — more at SCARAB] **1 a** : a short-barreled shoulder firearm used by cavalry **b** : any short-barreled lightweight rifle **2** : a light automatic or semiautomatic military rifle using ammunition of relatively low power and often issued to troops that are not primarily riflemen

carbineer *var of* CARABINEER

car·bi·nette \ˌkärbəˈnet\ *n* -S [origin unknown] : KINGFISH 1a (2)

car·bi·nol \ˈkärbəˌnōl, -ōl\ *n* -S [ISV *carbin-* (fr. obs. G *karbin* methyl, fr. *karb-* carb- + *-in*) + *-ol*; orig. formed as G *karbinol*] **1** : METHANOL — used esp. in the names of alcohols derived from methanol ⟨phenyl-acetyl-*carbinol*⟩ **2** : an alcohol derived from methanol

car·bi·nyl \ˈkärbəˌnil\ *n* -S [prob. fr. obs. G *karbin* + E *-yl*] **1** : METHYL — used esp. in the names of derivatives of methyl ⟨triphenyl-*carbinyl*⟩ **2** : the univalent radical corresponding to any carbinol ⟨a ~ chloride⟩

car bit *n* [so called fr. its being originally used in car building] : a long auger bit for use in boring deep holes

Car·bi·tol \ˈkärbəˌtōl, -ōl\ *trademark* — used for a high-boiling ether-alcohol used esp. as an organic solvent

car·bo \ˈkärˌbō\ *n* -S [L, charcoal, ember — more at CARBON] : CHARCOAL

carbo- — see CARB-

carbo a·ni·ma·lis \-ˌanəˈmaləs, -äl-, -āl-\ *n* [NL, lit., animal charcoal] : charcoal prepared from bone : BONE BLACK, IVORY BLACK

car·bo·ben·zoxy \¦kär(ˌ)bō¦benˈzäksē\ *or* **car·bo·ben·zy·loxy** \ˌ==ˌbenzəˈläksē\ *adj* [*carbobenzoxy-* or *carbobenzyloxy-*] : relating to or containing the radical $—COOCH_2C_6H_5$ ⟨~ synthesis of peptides⟩

carbobenzoxy- \"\ *or* **carbobenzyloxy-** \"\ *comb form* [ISV, fr. *carb-* + *benzoxy-* or *benzyloxy-*] : containing the univalent radical $—COOCH_2C_6H_5$ composed of a benzyloxy radical united with carbonyl ⟨*carbobenzyloxy*glycine⟩

car·bo·cer \ˈkärbə(ˌ)sər\ *n* -S [*carb-* + NL *cerium*] : a mineral consisting of a carbonaceous, ocherous, or pitchy substance containing rare-earth elements

car·bo·cy·a·nine \¦kär(ˌ)bōˈsīəˌnēn, -ˌnən\ *or* **carbocyanine dye** *n* -S [ISV *carb-* + *cyanine*; orig. formed as G *karbozyanin*] : any of a class of cyanine dyes in whose structure the two heterocyclic rings are joined by a three-carbon chain (as =CH—CH=CH—); *specif* : any such dye containing two quinoline rings — called also *trimethine*

car·bo·cy·clic \¦kärbō¦sīklik, -si-\ *adj* [ISV *carb-* + *cyclic*] : relating to or characterized by a ring composed of carbon atoms — used esp. of organic compounds classed as alicyclic or aromatic

car·bo·di·i·mide \¦kär(ˌ)bōˈdīəˌmīd, -ōˌdīˈiˌm-, -ˌməd\ *n* -S [ISV *carb-* + *di-* + *imide*; prob. orig. formed in F] : a tautomeric form of cyanamide NH=C=NH known in the form of its derivatives

Car·bo·frax \ˈkärbōˌfraks\ *trademark* — used for an acid-resisting refractory cement

carbohemoglobin *var of* CARBHEMOGLOBIN

car·bo·hy·drase \ˌkärbōˈhīˌdrās\ *n* -S [ISV *carbohydrate* + *-ase*] : any of a group of enzymes (as invertase or an amylase) that hydrolyze disaccharides and more complex carbohydrates

car·bo·hy·drate \ˌkärbōˈhīˌdrāt, -bə-, -drət\ *n* -S [*carb-* + *hydrate*; fr. the former classification of such compounds as hydrates of carbon] : any of a group of neutral compounds composed of carbon, hydrogen, and oxygen including the sugars, starches, dextrans, glycogens, celluloses, and pentosans some of which are formed by all green plants and used immediately for growth or stored for future use and which as a whole constitute a major class of animal foods characterized chemically as hydroxy aldehydes, hydroxy ketones, or compounds hydrolyzing to hydroxy aldehydes or ketones and classified into monosaccharides, disaccharides, trisaccharides, and polysaccharides on the basis of the number of aldehyde or ketone groups present in one molecule

car·bo·hy·drat·u·ria \ˌ==ˌ=drəd·əˈyürēə, -ˌdrāt-; ˌ==ˌ=drə-ˈt(y)ürēə\ *n* -S [NL, fr. ISV *carbohydrate* + NL *-uria*] : GLYCOSURIA

car·bo·hy·dra·zide \ˌkärbōˈhīdrəˌzīd, -zəd\ *n* -S [ISV *carb-* + *hydrazide*; orig. formed as G *karbohydrazid*] : a crystalline compound $CO(NHNH_2)_2$: the hydrazide of carbonic acid

carbol- *comb form* [ISV *carb-* + L *oleum* oil; orig. formed as G *karbol-* — more at OIL] : carbolic acid ⟨*carbol*uria⟩ ⟨*carbol*xylol⟩ ⟨*carbol*ate⟩

¹car·bo·late \ˈkärbəˌlāt\ *n* -S [*carbol-* + *-ate*] : a salt of carbolic acid : PHENOXIDE 1

²carbolate \"\ *vt* -ED/-ING/-S : PHENOLATE

car·bol·fuch·sin \ˌkärˌbälˈfyüksən, -bōl- *also* -ˈfyüshən *or* -ˈfüksən\ *n* -S [*carbol-* + *fuchsin*] : a mixture of aqueous solution of phenol and alcoholic solution of fuchsine used as a stain in microscopy esp. in staining bacteria

carbolfuchsin paint *n* : a solution containing boric acid, phenol, resorcinol, and fuchsine in acetone, alcohol, and water and applied externally in the treatment of fungous infections of the skin — called also *Castellani's paint*

car·bol·ic acid \(ˈ)kär¦bälik-, käˈb-, -ēk\ *also* **carbolic** *n* -S [ISV *carb-* + L *oleum* oil + ISV *-ic*] : PHENOL 1 — not used technically

carbolic oil *n* : a fraction obtained in coal-tar distillation that contains chiefly tar acids and sometimes naphthalene — called also *middle oil*

car·bo lig·ni \ˌkär(ˌ)bōˈligˌnē, -gˌnī\ *n* [NL, lit., charcoal of wood] : charcoal prepared from soft wood and used as an adsorbent

Car·bo·lin·e·um \ˌkärbəˈlinēəm\ *trademark* — used for a heavy oily substance distilled from an anthracene-oil or creosote-oil fraction of coal tar and used as a wood preservative, disinfectant, or insecticide

car·bo·lize \ˈkärbəˌlīz\ *vt* -ED/-ING/-S [*carbol-* + *-ize*] : PHENOLATE

Car·bo·loy \ˈkärbəˌlȯi\ *trademark* — used for a hard metallic substance that consists essentially of a cemented carbide of tungsten with cobalt or nickel as a binder, is produced by powder metallurgy, and is used in metal-cutting tools

car·bom·e·ter \kärˈbäməd·ər\ *n* -S [ISV *carb-* + *-meter*] : an instrument for measuring the carbon content of steel

car·bo·meth·oxy \¦kär(ˌ)bōmə¦thäksē\ *adj* [*carbomethoxy-*] : relating to or containing carbomethoxyl

carbomethoxy- \"\ *comb form* [ISV, fr. *carbomethoxyl*] : containing carbomethoxyl ⟨*carbomethoxy*glycine⟩

car·bo·meth·ox·yl \ˌ=(ˌ)==ˈ=səl\ *n* -S [blend of *carboxyl* and *methyl*] : the radical $—COOCH_3$ consisting of the methyl ester of carboxyl — called also *methoxycarbonyl*

car·bo·my·cin \ˌ==ˈmīsᵊn\ *n* -S [*carb-* + *-mycin*] : a colorless crystalline basic antibiotic $C_{42}H_{67}NO_{16}$ produced by an actinomycete (*Streptomyces halstedii*) and active esp. in inhibiting the growth of gram-positive bacteria

¹car·bon \'kärbən, 'kȧb- *also* -‚bän; *rapid sometimes* -bᵊm\ *n* -S *often attrib* [F *carbone*, fr. L *carbon-, carbo* ember, charcoal — more at HEARTH] **1 :** a nonmetallic chiefly tetravalent element occurring native (as in the diamond and graphite) and forming a constituent of coal, petroleum, and asphalt, of limestone and other carbonates, and of all organic compounds and also obtained artificially in varying degrees of purity esp. as carbon black, lampblack, activated carbon, charcoal, and coke and used in these and other forms (as baked carbon and resin-impregnated impervious carbon and graphite) chiefly as a pigment, adsorbent, fuel, electrode material, structural material, and reducing agent (as for metal oxides) — symbol *C;* see ELEMENT table; CARBON FOURTEEN, CARBON THIRTEEN **2 a :** a sheet of carbon paper **b :** CARBON COPY **3 a :** a carbon rod used in an arc lamp **b :** a plate or piece of carbon used as one of the elements in a voltaic cell **4 :** ³CARBONADO **5 :** CARBON TRANSFER

²carbon \"\ *vt* -ED/-ING/-S **1 :** to deposit carbon upon (as a cylinder or spark plug) **2 :** to make a carbon copy of (as a letter)

car·bo·na \kär'bōnə\ *n* -S [prob. irreg. fr. ¹*carbon;* fr. the frequently black color of the ore] *Brit* **:** an irregular deposit of tin ore consisting of many reticulating veinlets **:** STOCKWORK

car·bo·na·ceous \¦kärbə¦nāshəs, ¦kȧb-\ *adj* [¹*carbon* + *-aceous*] **1 :** rich in carbon **:** COALY ⟨~ sandstone⟩ **2 :** relating to, containing, or composed of carbon **3** *bot* **:** CARBONOUS

¹car·bo·na·do \‚kärbə'nā(‚)dō\ *n, pl* **carbonados** *or* **carbonadoes** [obs. *carbonado*, n., scored and broiled piece of meat, fr. Sp *carbonada*, fr. *carbón* charcoal, coal, cinder] *archaic* **:** a broiled or grilled piece of meat scored before cooking

²carbonado \"\ *vt* -ED/-ING/-S **1** *archaic* **:** to make a carbonado of **2** *archaic* **:** to cut, hack, or slash esp. with a sword

³carbonado \"\ *n* -S [Pg, lit., carbonated, fr. *carbone* carbon, fr. F — more at CARBON] **:** an impure opaque dark-colored and fine-grained aggregate of diamond particles held together in a matrix composed mainly of diamond that is valuable for its superior toughness resulting from the fine-grained structure and absence of planes of cleavage — called also *black diamond, carbon diamond*

carbon arc *n* **1 :** an arc lamp having carbon electrodes **2 :** an arc between carbon electrodes or between a carbon electrode and another material (as the parent metal in welding by carbon arc)

car·bo·na·ri \‚kärbə'närē\ *n pl, usu cap* [It, pl. of *Carbonaro*, fr. It dial. *carbonaro* charcoal burner or seller, fr. L *carbonarius* charcoal burner, fr. *carbon-, carbo* charcoal, ember + *-arius* -ary — more at HEARTH] **:** the members of a secret political association organized in the early 19th century in Italy to establish a republic

carbon assimilation *n* **:** PHOTOSYNTHESIS

car·bon·a·ta·tion \‚kärbənə'tāshən\ *n* -S [ISV ¹*carbonate* + *-ation*] **:** CARBONATION

¹car·bon·ate \'kärbə‚nāt, 'kȧb-, -ənət, *usu* -d.+V\ *n* -S [F, fr. *carbone* carbon + *-ate*] **1 :** a salt or ester of carbonic acid **2 :** an ore containing a large proportion of lead carbonate

²car·bon·ate \-‚nāt, *usu* -ād.+V\ *vt* -ED/-ING/-S [¹*carbon* + *-ate*] **1** *obs* **:** to burn to carbon **:** CARBONIZE **2 :** to convert into a carbonate **3 a :** to impregnate with carbon dioxide; *specif* **:** to impregnate (a beverage) with carbon dioxide to infuse with freshness and sparkle **b :** to make lively, pungent, or sparkling ⟨*carbonated* prose⟩

³car·bon·ate \-‚nət\ *adj* [¹*carbonate*] **1 :** of or relating to a carbonate **2 :** composed of one or more members of the calcite, dolomite, and aragonite groups of minerals

carbonate-apatite *n* **:** apatite containing a considerable amount of carbonate: as **a :** apatite in which the calcium phosphate carbonate predominates over other components **b :** calcium phosphate carbonate of uncertain formula prob. $Ca_{10}(PO_4)_6(CO_3)(H_2O)$ — called also *dahllite*

carbonated water *n* **:** SODA WATER 2a

carbonated wine *n* **:** artificially carbonated wine — distinguished from *sparkling wine*

carbonate of lime : CALCIUM CARBONATE

carbonate of potash : POTASSIUM CARBONATE

carbonate of soda : SODIUM CARBONATE

car·bon·a·tion \‚kärbə'nāshən, ‚kȧb-\ *n* -S [ISV ²*carbonate* + *-ion*] **:** the process of carbonating

car·bon·a·tite \kär'bänə‚tīt\ *n* -S [¹*carbonate* + *-ite*] **:** a carbonate rock of intrusive origin

car·bon·at·i·za·tion \‚kärbə‚nād.ə'zāshən\ *n* -S [²*carbonate* + *-ization*] **:** conversion into a carbonate

car·bon·a·tor \'kärbə‚nād.ər\ *n* -S [²*carbonate* + *-or*] **:** one that carbonates

carbon bisulfide *n* **:** CARBON DISULFIDE — used chiefly commercially

carbon black *n* **:** any of various colloidal black substances consisting wholly or principally of carbon obtained usu. as soot by partial combustion of hydrocarbons and used chiefly as reinforcing agents in automobile tires, as extremely black pigments of high hiding power in paint, printing ink, and carbon paper, and in electric resistors; *esp* **:** FURNACE BLACK — see CHANNEL BLACK, THERMAL BLACK; compare BONE BLACK, LAMPBLACK, VEGETABLE BLACK

carbon copy *n* **1 :** a copy made by use of carbon paper **2 :** an exact duplicate **:** REPLICA

carbon cycle *n* **1 :** a cycle of thermonuclear reactions that involves the synthesis of four hydrogen atoms into a helium atom with the release of nuclear energy and is held to be the source of most of the energy radiated by the sun and stars **2 :** the cycle of carbon in living beings consisting of the uptake and fixing of carbon dioxide by photosynthesis, its consumption in carbohydrate, protein, and fat by animals and plants lacking photosynthesis (as in plant tissues eaten or organic matter absorbed), and its return to the inorganic state through respiratory processes and the decay of plant and animal bodies

carbon diamond *n* **:** ³CARBONADO

carbon dichloride *n* **:** TETRACHLOROETHYLENE

carbon dioxide *n* **:** a heavy colorless gas CO_2 that does not support combustion, that dissolves in water to form carbonic acid, that is formed esp. by the action of acids on carbonates, by the fermentation of liquors, and by the combustion and decomposition of organic substances (as in animal respiration, in the decay of animal and vegetable matter, and in the explosion of firedamp in mines), that is absorbed from the air by plants in the first step in photosynthesis, and that is used in the gaseous and liquefied forms chiefly in the carbonation of beverages, in fire fighting, in therapeutical work, in mining operations, in the chemical industry, and as a source of power (as in spray painting and inflating life rafts) and in the solidified form as dry ice — called also *carbonic acid gas;* see AFTERDAMP, BLACKDAMP

carbon disulfide *n* **:** a colorless flammable poisonous liquid CS_2 of high refractive power made usu. by reaction of sulfur vapor with charcoal or hydrocarbons at high temperature and used chiefly in the manufacture of viscose rayon, cellophane, xanthates, carbon tetrachloride, and rubber accelerators, as a solvent esp. for rubber, and as a fumigant for rodents and insects

carboned *past of* CARBON

carbon flame *n* **:** the white flame produced by burning carbon

carbon 14 *n* **:** a heavy radioactive isotope of carbon having the mass number 14 that is formed by the action of cosmic rays on nitrogen in the atmosphere and made artificially by bombardment of nitrogen compounds with neutrons and is valuable in tracer studies in chemistry and biology and in dating archaeological and geological materials — symbol C^{14} or ^{14}C; called also *radiocarbon*

carboni- *comb form* [L *carbon-, carbo* ember, charcoal — more at CARBON] **:** coal ⟨*carboni*ferous⟩ ⟨*carboni*genous⟩

car·bon·ic \(')kär¦bänik, -ȧ¦b-, -ēk\ *adj* [F *carbonique*, fr. *carbone* carbon + *-ique* -ic — more at CARBON] **1 :** of, relating to, or derived from carbon, carbonic acid, or carbon dioxide **2** *usu cap* **:** CARBONIFEROUS 2

carbonic acid *n* **:** a weak dibasic acid H_2CO_3 known only in solution, decomposing readily into water and carbon dioxide, and reacting with bases to form carbonates

carbonic acid gas *n* **:** CARBON DIOXIDE

carbonic anhydrase *n* **:** a zinc-containing enzyme occurring in living tissues (as red blood cells) that accelerates in either direction the reversible hydration of carbon dioxide to carbonic acid and thereby aids carbon-dioxide transport from the tissues and its release from the blood in the lungs

carbonic anhydride *n* **:** CARBON DIOXIDE

carbonic oxide *n* **:** CARBON MONOXIDE

¹car·bon·if·er·ous \¦kärbə¦nif(ə)rəs, ¦kȧb-\ *adj* [*carboni-* + *-ferous*] **1 :** producing or containing carbon or coal **2** *usu cap* **a :** of or relating to the period of the Paleozoic geologic era between the Devonian and the Permian — see GEOLOGIC TIME table **b :** of or relating to the system of rocks formed in the Carboniferous period

²car·bon·if·er·ous \"\ *n* -ES *usu cap* **:** the Carboniferous period or system of rocks

car·bon·i·fi·ca·tion \(‚)kär‚bänəfə'kāshən\ *n* -S [*carboni-* + *-fication*] **:** conversion of vegetable matter to coal

car·bon·i·mide \kär'bänə‚mīd, ‚kärbə'ni‚m-, -‚məd\ *n* -S [ISV ¹*carbon* + *imide*] **:** ISOCYANIC ACID

carboning *pres part of* CARBON

car·bon·ite \'kärbə‚nīt\ *n* -S [ISV ¹*carbon* + *-ite;* orig. formed as G *karbonit*] **1 :** a blasting explosive varying greatly in formula but containing among its ingredients a carbonaceous substance (as oak bark), a nitrate, and now usu. nitroglycerin **2** [¹*carbon* + *-ite*] **:** a natural coke usu. resulting from contact of coal deposits with igneous rock intrusions

¹car·bo·ni·tride \‚kärbō'nī‚trīd, -‚trəd\ *n* -S [*carb-* + *nitride*] **:** a compound with carbon and nitrogen

²carbonitride \"\ *vt* -ED/-ING/-S **:** to treat (an iron alloy) by heating in a gaseous atmosphere of such composition that carbon and nitrogen are absorbed and then cooling in such a way as to produce case hardening

car·bo·ni·trile \-'nī‚trəl; -‚trēl, -‚trīl\ *n* -S [*carb-* + *nitrile*] **:** NITRILE

car·bo·ni·um \kär'bōnēəm\ *n* -S [*carb-* + *-onium*] **:** an organic ion (as triphenylmethyl carbonium) carrying a positive charge at a carbon location owing to an electron deficiency — compare CARBANION

car·bon·i·za·tion \‚kärbənə'zāshən, ‚kȧb-, -‚nī'z-\ *n* -S [F *carbonisation*, fr. *carbone* carbon + *-isation* -ization — more at CARBON] **:** the process of carbonizing; *esp* **:** destructive distillation (as of coal, lignite, or peat)

car·bon·ize \'kärbə‚nīz, 'kȧb-\ *vb* -ED/-ING/-S [F *carboniser*, prob. back-formation fr. *carbonisation*] *vt* **1 :** to convert into carbon or a residue of carbon (as by the action of heat or some corrosive agent) **2 :** CARBURIZE 1 **3 :** to remove (vegetable matter) from wool fleece or fabric by chemically reducing the burrs, cotton, and other vegetable impurities to dust **4 :** to apply carbon black to (as the back of a printed form) in preparation for making a carbon copy ~ *vi* **:** to become carbonized **:** CHAR

car·bon·iz·er \-zə(r)\ *n* -S **:** one that carbonizes: as **a :** a worker who carbonizes wool fabrics **b :** one that fills retorts

carbon knock *n* **:** preignition with resultant knocking in an internal-combustion engine caused by the overheating of an accumulation of carbon in the combustion chambers

carbon lamp *n* **1 :** an incandescent lamp with a carbon filament **2 :** an arc lamp with the arc formed between carbon points esp. for therapeutic use

car·bon·less \-bənləs\ *adj* **:** being without carbon

carbon microphone *n* **:** a microphone whose operation depends on the alteration of the electrical resistance of carbon contacts

carbon monoxide *n* **:** a colorless odorless very toxic gas CO that burns to carbon dioxide with a blue flame, that is formed as a product of the incomplete combustion of carbon (as in water gas and producer gas, in the exhaust gases from internal-combustion engines, and in the gases from the detonation of explosives), and that is used chiefly in the synthesis of carbonyls (as nickel carbonyl in the refining of nickel), phosgene, and many organic compounds (as hydrocarbons for fuels, methanol and higher alcohols, aldehydes, and formates) — see CARBONYLHEMOGLOBIN

carbon-nitrogen cycle *n* **:** CARBON CYCLE 1

carbon oil *n, Midland* **:** KEROSINE

car·bon·ous \'kärbənəs, 'kȧb-\ *adj* [¹*carbon* + *-ous*] **1 :** derived from, containing, or resembling carbon **2 :** brittle and dark or almost black in color

carbon oxide *n* **:** any of the three oxides of carbon: **a :** CARBON DIOXIDE **b :** CARBON MONOXIDE **c :** CARBON SUBOXIDE

carbon oxychloride *n* **:** PHOSGENE

carbon paper *n* **1 :** a thin paper having a waxy pigmented coating on the face and used in making duplicate copies by being placed face down between two sheets of paper so that the pressure of writing or typing on the top sheet causes a transfer of the pigment to the bottom sheet **2 :** gelatin-coated paper used in the carbon process

carbon pencil *n* **:** a small stick of carbon or charcoal containing a small amount of niter that on being lighted is used for cracking glass

carbon process *n* **:** a photographic printing process in which a sheet of paper coated with bichromated gelatin mixed with a pigment is exposed under the negative and transferred to a support, the image then being developed by washing away the unexposed gelatin

carbons *pl of* CARBON, *pres 3d sing of* CARBON

carbon silicide *n* **:** SILICON CARBIDE

carbon spot *n* **:** a black spot in the body of a diamond

carbon steel *n* **:** steel that derives its physical properties (as strength and hardness) chiefly from the presence of carbon, other alloying elements (as manganese, silicon, and phosphorus) being present only in unimportant amounts — contrasted with *alloy steel*

carbon suboxide *n* **:** a gas having an extremely unpleasant odor and having the structure of a ketene O=C=C=C=O prepared by pyrolysis of biacetyl-tartaric anhydride or by dehydration of malonic acid

carbon sulfochloride *n* **:** THIOPHOSGENE

carbon tetrachloride *n* **:** a colorless mobile nonflammable toxic liquid CCl_4 with a chloroformlike odor made usu. by chlorination of carbon disulfide or hydrocarbons and used chiefly as a solvent (as in dry cleaning), in extinguishing small fires, and in medicine as an anthelmintic

carbon 13 *n* **:** a heavy isotope of carbon having the mass number 13, constituting about 1/70 of natural carbon, and used in tracer studies in chemistry and biology — symbol C^{13} or ^{13}C

carbon tissue *n* **:** CARBON PAPER 2

carbon transfer *n* **:** a photographic print made by the carbon process

car·bon·yl \'kärbə‚nil, -ēl\ *n* -S [ISV ¹*carbon* + *-yl*] **1 :** the bivalent radical CO occurring in aldehydes, ketones, carboxylic acids, esters, acid halides, and amides **2 :** a compound of the carbonyl radical with a metal (as chromium *carbonyl*) — **car·bon·yl·ic** \¦kärbə¦nilik\ *adj*

car·bon·yl·ate \kär'bänᵊl‚āt\ *vt* -ED/-ING/-S [*carbonyl* + *-ate*] **:** to introduce the carbonyl group into (an organic compound) — **car·bon·yl·a·tion** \(‚)kär‚bänᵊl'āshən\ *n* -S

carbonyl chloride *n* **:** PHOSGENE

car·bon·yl·he·mo·glo·bin \‚kärbə‚nil¦h-, -ēl-\ *n* -S [*carbonyl* + *hemoglobin*] **:** a very stable pinkish red combination of hemoglobin and carbon monoxide formed in the blood when carbon monoxide is inhaled with resulting loss of ability of the blood to combine with oxygen — called also *carbon monoxide hemoglobin, carboxyhemoglobin*

car·bo·ra \kär'bōrə\ *n* -S [native name in Australia] **1** *Austral* **:** KOALA **2** *Austral* **:** a wood-boring worm that destroys timber in tidal rivers

Car·bo·run·dum \‚kärbə'rəndəm, ‚kȧb-\ *trademark* — used for various abrasives

carbos *pl of* CARBO

car·bo·ther·mic \¦kärbō¦thərmik\ *also* **car·bo·ther·mal** \-məl\ *adj* [*carb-* + *thermic* or *thermal*] **:** relating to a process for producing magnesium by reduction of magnesia with carbon at high temperatures

Car·bo·wax \'kärbō‚waks\ *trademark* — used for any of a series of liquid and solid polyethylene glycols

carboxy- *or* **carbox-** *comb form* [ISV, fr. *carboxyl*] **:** carboxyl ⟨*carbox*amide⟩ ⟨*carboxy*phenyl⟩

car·boxy·he·mo·glo·bin \(')kär¦bäksē¦h-\ *n* -S [ISV *carboxy-* + *hemoglobin*] **:** CARBONYLHEMOGLOBIN

car·box·yl \(')kär¦bäksəl\ *n* -S [ISV *carb-* + *ox-* + *-yl*] **:** the univalent radical —COOH characteristic of the largest class of organic acids including formic, acetic, and benzoic acids

car·box·yl·ase \kär'bäksə‚lās\ *n* -S [ISV *carboxyl* + *-ase*] **:** an enzyme of either of two groups that catalyze decarboxylation or carboxylation: **a :** any enzyme that accelerates the removal of carbon dioxide from a carboxyl group esp. in alpha-keto acids; *specif* **:** an enzyme first recognized in yeast that converts pyruvic acid to acetaldehyde and carbon dioxide in living cells and in alcoholic fermentation — see COCARBOXYLASE **b :** any enzyme that accelerates the addition of carbon dioxide to form a carboxyl group (as in the conversion of pyruvic acid to oxalacetic acid) — usu. distinguished from *decarboxylase*

¹car·box·yl·ate \-‚lāt, -lət\ *n* -S [*carboxyl* + *-ate*] **:** a salt, ester, or acylal of a carboxylic acid

²car·box·yl·ate \-‚lāt\ *vt* -ED/-ING/-S [*carboxyl* + *-ate*] **:** to introduce carboxyl or carbon dioxide into (a compound) with formation of a carboxylic acid — **car·box·yl·a·tion** \(‚)kär‚bäksə'lāshən\ *n* -S

car·box·yl·ic \¦kär‚bäk¦silik\ *adj* [*carboxyl* + *-ic*] **:** of, relating to, or containing carboxyl

carboxylic acid *n* **:** an organic acid (as acetic acid, benzoic acid, phthalic acid) characterized by the presence of one or more carboxyl groups

car·box·y·meth·yl cellulose \(‚)kär‚bäksē¦methəl-\ *n* [*carboxymethyl*, the univalent radical $HOOCCH_2$—, fr. *carboxyl* + *methyl*] **:** an acid ether derivative of cellulose best known in the form of its sodium salt — see SODIUM CARBOXYMETHYL CELLULOSE

car·box·y·pep·ti·dase \-'peptə‚dās\ *n* -S [ISV *carboxy-* + *peptidase;* orig. formed as G *karboxypeptidase*] **:** an enzyme (as obtained in crystalline form from the pancreas) that hydrolyzes peptides and esp. polypeptides by splitting off the amino acids containing free carboxyl groups

car·boy \'kär‚bȯi, 'kȧ‚b-\ *n* -S [Per *qarāba*, fr. Ar (Iraq) *qarrābah* demijohn, carboy] **:** a cylindrical container of about 5 to 15 gallons capacity for corrosive or pure liquids (as strong acids or drinking water) made of glass, plastic, or metal with a neck and sometimes a pouring tip and cushioned in a wooden box, wicker basket, or special drum — compare DEMIJOHN

carboy

car·bro \'kär‚brō\ *or* **carbro process** *n* -S [blend of *carb-* and *bro-* (in *bromide*)] **:** a photographic process of making either a carbon transfer or color print from a developed silver image by soaking in a bichromate bleach solution a gelatin-coated tissue containing either carbon particles or color pigments and then placing the tissue in contact with a wet silver-bromide print, after which the unhardened parts of the gelatin are washed away leaving a carbon image that is then transferred to another support

car·bro·mal \kär'brōməl\ *n* -S **:** a white crystalline compound $(C_2H_5)_2CBrCONHCONH_2$ used as a sedative and hypnotic; (2-bromo-2-ethyl-butyryl)-urea

carbs *pl of* CARB

car·bun·cle \'kär‚bəŋkəl, 'kȧ‚b-\ *n* -S [ME, fr. MF, fr. L *carbunculus* small coal, dark red precious stone, tumor, dim. of *carbon-, carbo* ember — more at CARBON] **1 a** *obs* **:** any of several red precious stones (as the ruby) **b :** the garnet cut cabochon **c :** ESCARBUNCLE **2 a :** a painful local inflammation of the skin and deeper tissues esp. of the back of the neck and trunk characterized by hardness, formation of openings for the discharge of pus from multiple pockets, breakdown of the surface skin and sloughing of dead tissue, usu. accompanied by fever **b** *obs* **:** a pimple or red spot (as on the face) believed to be due to intemperance **3 :** a dark grayish reddish brown that is duller and slightly redder than average brown mahogany and yellower and slightly less strong than average Burgundy (sense 2a) — called also *London brown*

car·bun·cled \-əld\ *adj* **1 :** set with carbuncles **2 :** affected with a carbuncle

car·bun·cu·lar \(')kär¦bəŋkyələr, -ȧ¦b-, -lə\ *adj* [L *carbunculus* + E *-ar*] **:** related to or resembling a carbuncle **:** afflicted with a carbuncle **:** RED, INFLAMED

car·bun·cu·lo·sis \(‚)kär‚bəŋkyə'lōsəs\ *n, pl* **carbunculo·ses** \-ō‚sēz\ [NL, fr. L *carbunculus* + NL *-osis*] **:** a condition marked by the formation of many carbuncles simultaneously or in rapid succession

car·bun·gi \kär'bənjē\ *n* -S [native name in Australia] **:** a narrow-leaved cattail (*Typha angustifolia*) of Australia — see MURRAY DOWN

car·bu·ran \'kärbyə‚ran\ *n* -S [Russ *karburan*, fr. *karb-* carb- + *uran* uranium, fr. G, fr. *Uranus* (the planet) — more at URANIUM] **:** a pitchlike hydrocarbon containing uranium

car·bu·rant \'kärb(y)ərənt\ *n* -S [prob. fr. F, fr. *carburant* containing a hydrocarbon, fr. *carbure* carbide (fr. *carb-* + *-ure* binary chemical compound) + *-ant* — more at -URET] **:** a substance (as oil gas) used to carburet a gas (as water gas)

car·bu·rate \'kärb(y)ə‚rāt, 'kȧb-\ *vt* -ED/-ING/-S [back-formation fr. *carburation*] **:** CARBURET

car·bu·ra·tion \‚==ˈrāshən\ *n* -S [F, fr. *carbure* + *-ation*] **:** CARBURETION

car·bu·ra·tor \'==‚rād.ə(r), -ātə-\ *n* -S **:** CARBURETOR

¹car·bu·ret \'kärbyə‚ret, 'kȧb-\ *n* -S [*carb-* + *-uret*] *archaic* **:** CARBIDE

²car·bu·ret \-byə‚ret; *with reference to gasoline engines, usu* -b(y)ə‚rāt *by nonchemists; usu* -d.+V\ *vt* **carbureted** *also* **carburetted; carbureted** *also* **carburetted; carbureting** *also* **carburetting; carburets 1 :** to combine chemically with carbon **2 :** to enrich (a gas) by mixing with volatile carbon compounds (as hydrocarbons) — see CARBURETED WATER GAS

car·bu·ret·ant \-etᵊnt, -ät-\ *n* -S **:** CARBURANT

carbureted hydrogen *n, archaic* **:** any of several gaseous compounds of carbon and hydrogen (as methane)

carbureted water gas *n* **:** water gas enriched by mixing with hydrocarbon gases (as oil gas) of high fuel value

car·bu·re·tion \‚==b(y)ə'rāshən *also* -esh-\ *n* -S [alter. (influenced by *carburetor*) of *carburation*] **:** the act or process of carbureting; *specif* **:** the process of mixing usu. in a carburetor the vapor of a flammable hydrocarbon (as gasoline) with air to form an explosive mixture esp. for use in vapor-type internal-combustion engines

car·bu·re·tor *also* **car·bu·ret·er** *or chiefly Brit* **car·bu·ret·ter** *or* **car·bu·ret·tor** \'kärb(y)ə‚rād.ər, 'kȧb(y)ə‚rād.ə, -ātə(r), *Brit usu & US rarely* -re-\ *n* -S [²*carburet* + *-or*] **1 :** an apparatus for supplying an internal-combustion engine with vaporized fuel mixed with air in an explosive mixture commonly by means of an atomizer discharging the fuel into an air stream produced by the suction of the engine pistons **2 :** the part of an apparatus for manufacturing carbureted water gas in which the enriching oil is vaporized and cracked

diagram of an early type (Maybach) carburetor: gasoline inlet pipe, *A;* mixing chamber, *B;* spray nozzle or jet, *C;* float, *D;* gasoline adjusting screw, *E;* main air inlet, *F;* float needle valve, *G*

car·bu·ri·za·tion \‚kärbyərə'zāshən, ‚kȧb-, -‚rī'z-\ *n* -S **:** the process of carburizing

car·bu·rize \'kärbyə‚rīz, 'kȧb-\ *vt* -ED/-ING/-S [¹*carburet* + *-ize*] **1 :** to combine or impregnate (a metal) with carbon; *specif* **:** to introduce carbon into (a solid ferrous alloy) by heating the metal in contact with a solid, liquid, or gaseous carbonaceous material to a sufficiently high temperature and holding at that temperature — see CASE HARDEN 1; compare CEMENTATION 2 a **2 :** ²CARBURET 2

car·bu·riz·er \-zə(r)\ *n* -S **1 :** one that carburizes **2 :** a substance used as a source of carbon in carburizing

car·byl \'kärbəl, -(‚)bil\ *n* -S [ISV *carb-* + *-yl*] **:** a carbon atom acting as a bivalent radical

car·byl·a·mine \‚kär‚bilə'mēn, =ˈ==‚=\ *n* -S [ISV *carb-* + *-yl* + *amine;* orig. formed in F] **:** ISOCYANIDE ⟨phenylcarbylamine C_6H_5NC⟩

car·byl·ox·ime \ˌkärbəˈläkˌsēm, -ˌsəm\ *n* -s [*carbyl* + *oxime*] : FULMINIC ACID

carbyl sulfate *n* : ETHIONIC ANHYDRIDE

car·ca·jou \ˈkärkəˌjü, -ˌzhü\ *n* -s [CanF, fr. Algonquian Montagnais *karkajou* wolverine — more at QUICKHATCH] : WOLVERINE

car·ca·net \ˈkärkənət, -ˌnet\ *also* **car·can** \-kən\ *n* -s [*carcanet* fr. MF *carcan* + E *-et; carcan* fr. MF, iron collar for criminals, ornamental collar or necklace, fr. ML *carcannum* collar for criminals] *archaic* : an ornamental gold or jeweled chain, necklace, collar, or headband

car card *n* **1** : a small cardboard placard for advertising or other display esp. in or on streetcars and buses **2** : cardboard coated on one side only

car·case \ˈkäkəs\ *Brit var of* CARCASS

¹car·cass \ˈkärkəs, ˈkäk-\ *n* -ES [MF *carcasse*, alter. of OF *carcois*, perh. fr. *carquois, carquais* quiver, alter. of *tarquais*, fr. ML *tarcasius*, fr. Ar *tarkāsh*, fr. Per *tīrkash*, fr. *tīr* arrow (fr. OPer *tigra* pointed) + *-kash* bearing (fr. *kashīdan* to pull, draw, fr. Av *karsh-*); akin to Gk *stizein* to tattoo and to Skt *karṣati* he pulls, draws — more at STICK] **1 a** : a dead body of a human being or an animal : CORPSE **b** *of a slaughtered animal* : the trunk after the hide, head, limbs, edible organs, and offal have been removed : the dressed body **2** : the living, material, or physical body **3 a** : the decaying or corroding remains (as the framework or skeleton) of a structure ⟨~*es* of old cars lay rusting among the trees —Calvin Kentfield⟩ **b** : a thing from which vitality, soul, or essence is gone : SHELL, HUSK ⟨the mere ~ of nobility —William Shenstone⟩ **4** : the framework about which or upon which a structure is built: as **a** : the shell of a building **b** : an uncovered, undecorated, or unfinished framework (as of a piece of furniture) **c**(1) : the foundation structure of a pneumatic tire consisting of several superimposed layers of cord fabric insulated in rubber (2) : a worn rubber tire still capable of useful service when recapped **d** : the cover or the cover and bladder of an inflated or inflatable ball **5** : a hollow case or shell filled with combustibles and thrown from a mortar or howitzer and formerly used to set fire to buildings, ships, or fortifications

²carcass \"\ *vt* -ED/-ING/-ES : to erect the framework of (a structure)

car·cass·less \-ləs\ *adj* : being without a carcass

car·ca·vel·los *also* **car·ca·ve·los** \ˌkärkəˈveləs\ *n, usu cap* [Pg *carcavelos*, fr. *Carcavelos*, village near Lisbon, Portugal] : a sweet Portuguese wine usu. white

car·ce·ag \ˈkärsēˌag\ *n* -s [Romanian] : babesiasis of the sheep

car·cel \ˈkärsəl\ *n* -s [Sp *cárcel*, fr. L *carcer*] *Southwest* : JAIL, PRISON

car·cer \ˈkär,ke(ə)r, -rsər\ *n, pl* **carce·res** \ˈkärkəˌrās, -rsəˌrēz\ [L, lit., prison] : one of the stalls at the starting point of the racecourse of a Roman circus

car·cha·rhin·i·dae \ˌkärkəˈrinəˌdē\ *n pl, cap* [NL, fr. *Carcharhinus*, type genus + *-idae*] : a large cosmopolitan family comprising sharks with no spines in the dorsal fin and with the last gill opening above the pectoral fin and including the dangerous tiger shark and the economically important soupfin shark

car·cha·rhi·nus \-ˈrīnəs\ *n, cap* [NL, fr. Gk *karcharos* sawlike + NL *-rhinus*] : the type genus of Carcharhinidae

car·char·i·as \kärˈka(a)rēəs\ *n, cap* [NL, fr. Gk *karcharias*, a shark, fr. *karcharos* sawlike, jagged; akin to Skt *khara* harsh, rough] **1** : the type and sole recent genus of Carcharidae that comprises the common sand sharks **2** *in some classifications* : a genus of sharks variously limited; *esp* : one coextensive with the genus *Carcharhinus*

car·cha·ri·idae \ˌkärkəˈrīəˌdē\ *n pl, cap* [NL, fr. *Carcharias*, type genus + *-idae*] : a family of sharks that has existed at least since Lower Cretaceous times and as now understood contains *Carcharias* and various extinct genera but formerly included many other genera (as *Galeorhinus* and *Mustelus*) and in some classifications was coextensive with Carcharhinidae

car·cha·ri·nus \-īnəs\ *syn of* CARCHARHINUS

car·char·o·don \kärˈkarəˌdän\ *n, cap* [NL, fr. Gk *karcharodōn*] : a genus of sharks (family Lamnidae) comprising the man-eater and a number of extinct related forms having carcharodont teeth

car·char·o·dont \-ˌdänt\ *adj* [Gk *karcharodont-, karcharodōn* having jagged teeth, fr. *karcharos* jagged + *odont-, odōn* tooth — more at TOOTH] : of, belonging to, or resembling the man-eater shark; *esp* : having teeth of sharp triangular flattened form with finely serrate edges like those of this shark

car checker *n* **1** : one that reports and records the identifying numbers on cars in a freight yard **2** : a worker who inspects new automobiles before delivery to customers

carcin- *or* **carcino-** *comb form* [Gk. *karkin-, karkino-*, fr. *karkinos* — more at CANCER] **1** : crab ⟨*carcino*logy⟩ **2** : tumor ⟨*carcino*genic⟩ : cancer ⟨*carcin*emia⟩ ⟨*carcino*sarcoma⟩

car·cin·i·des \kärˈsinəˌdēz\ *n, cap* [NL, fr. *Carcinus* + *-ides* (pl. of *-is* -id)] : a genus of swimming crabs (family Portunidae) including only the common edible green crab (*C. maenas*) — commonly replaced by the older but invalid name *Carcinus*

car·ci·noe·ci·um \ˌkärsəˈnēs(h)ēəm\ *n, pl* **carcinoe·cia** \-s(h)ēə\ [NL, fr. *carcin-* + *-oecium* (fr. Gk *oikion* house, nest, dim. of *oikos* house) — more at VICINITY] : a colony of zoanthidean anemones (genus *Epizoanthus*) enclosing a hermit crab after dissolving the shell in which the crab lodged

car·cin·o·gen \kärˈsinəjən, ˈkärsᵊnəˌjen\ *n* -s [*carcin-* + *-gen*] : a substance or agent producing or inciting cancerous growth — compare LEUKEMOGEN

car·ci·no·gen·e·sis \ˌkärsᵊn(ˌ)ōˈjenəsəs\ *n* [NL, fr. *carcin-* + L *genesis*] : the production of cancer

car·ci·no·gen·ic \ˌ==(ˌ)=ˈjenik\ *adj* [*carcin-* + *-genic*] : producing or tending to produce cancer — **car·ci·no·ge·nic·i·ty** \ˌ==(ˌ)=jəˈnisəd·ē\ *n* -ES

car·ci·noid \ˈkärsᵊnˌȯid\ *n* -s *often attrib* [*carcin-* + *-oid*] : a benign but potentially malignant tumor of the stomach and intestine having cells that resemble those of carcinoma

car·ci·no·log·i·cal \ˌkärsᵊnōˈläjəkəl\ *adj* : of or relating to carcinology

car·ci·nol·o·gist \ˌkärsᵊnˈäləjəst\ *n* -s : a specialist in carcinology

car·ci·nol·o·gy \-jē\ *n* -ES [ISV *carcin-* + *-logy*; prob. orig. formed as F *carcinologie*] : a branch of zoology that treats of the Crustacea

car·ci·no·lyt·ic \ˌkärsᵊnōˈlid·ik\ *adj* [ISV *carcin-* + *-lytic*; prob. orig. formed as G *karzinolytisch*] : destructive of cancer cells

car·ci·no·ma \ˌkärsᵊnˈōmə, ˌkäs-\ *n, pl* **carcinomas** \-ōməz\ *or* **carcinoma·ta** \-ōməd·ə, -ətə\ [L, fr. Gk *karkinōma* cancer, fr. *karkinos*] : a malignant tumor consisting of epithelial cells lying within the connective tissue framework of an organ or other structure of a human or an animal body — compare CANCER, SARCOMA

carcinoma in situ *n* [NL] : carcinoma in the stage of development when the cancer cells are still within their site of origin; *specif* : such a carcinoma in the uterine cervix

car·ci·nom·a·toid \ˌ==ˈäməˌtȯid, -ōm-\ *adj* [L *carcinomat-, carcinoma* + E *-oid*] : resembling a carcinoma

car·ci·no·ma·to·sis \-ˌōməˈtōsəs\ *n, pl* **carcinomato·ses** \-ōˌsēz\ [NL, fr. L *carcinomat-, carcinoma* + NL *-osis*] : a condition in which carcinomas are developing simultaneously in many parts of the body as a result of dissemination from a primary source

car·ci·nom·a·tous \ˌ==ˈäməd·əs, -ōm-, -ətəs\ *adj* [L *carcinomat-, carcinoma* + E *-ous*] : being of or relating to carcinoma ⟨a ~ lesion⟩

car·ci·no·mor·phic \ˌ==ōˈmȯrfik\ *adj* [*carcin-* + *-morphic*] : resembling a crab

car·ci·no·ne·mer·tes \ˌ===ōˈmərd·ēz\ *n, cap* [NL, fr. *carcin-* + *Nemertes*, genus of worms, fr. Gk *Nēmertēs* daughter of Nereus] : a genus of nemertine worms (order Hoplonemertea) with rudimentary proboscis and a single stylet that are parasitic on the gills and eggs of crabs

car·ci·no·sar·co·ma \ˌkärsᵊn(ˌ)ōˌsärˈkōmə\ *n, pl* **carcinosarcomas** \-ōməz\ *or* **carcinosarcoma·ta** \-ōməd·ə\ [NL, fr. *carcin-* + *sarcoma*] : a malignant tumor combining elements of carcinoma and sarcoma

car·ci·no·sis \ˌkärsᵊnˈōsəs\ *n, pl* **carcino·ses** \-ōˌsēz\ [NL, fr. *carcin-* + *-osis*] : dissemination of carcinomatous growths in the body : CARCINOMATOSIS

car·ci·nus \ˈkärsᵊnəs\ [NL, fr. Gk *karkinos* crab — more at CANCER] *syn of* CARCINIDES

car·coon \(ˈ)kärˈkün\ *n* -s [Marathi *kārkūn*, fr. Per *kārkun* manager, fr. *kār* work, business + *-kun* doer] *India* : CLERK

car cooper *n* : one that makes minor repairs to the bodies of freight cars to prepare them for hauling of such bulk commodities as grain

¹card \ˈkärd, ˈkȧd\ *vt* -ED/-ING/-S [ME *carden*, fr. MF *carder*, fr. *carde*] **1** : to cleanse, disentangle, and collect together (as animal or vegetable fibers) by the use of a card preparatory to spinning, the process being used to prepare fibers of relatively short length — compare COMB *vt* 1b **2** *obs* : to stir together and mix as if by combing together with a card **3** : to torture by drawing a wool card or similar instrument over the bare back or other part of the body

²card \"\ *n* -s [ME *carde*, fr. MF, fr. LL *cardus* thistle, fr. L *carduus* — more at CHARD] **1** : an implement (as a wire brush) for raising a nap on cloth **2 a** : a hand instrument for cleaning, disentangling, and ordering animal or vegetable fibers preparatory to spinning usu. consisting of bent wire teeth set closely in rows in a thick piece of leather fastened to a back **b** : CARDING MACHINE

³card \"\ *n* -s [ME *carde*, modif. of MF *carte*, prob. fr. OIt *carta*, lit., leaf of paper, fr. L *charta* leaf of papyrus, fr. Gk *chartēs*] **1 a** : PLAYING CARD **b** : a playing card considered in terms of its rank, value, or function ⟨a high ~⟩ ⟨a trump ~⟩; *esp* : a relatively high or valuable card ⟨they had all the ~*s*⟩ ⟨I didn't hold a ~⟩ **2 cards** *pl but sometimes sing in constr* **a** : a game played with cards : card playing ⟨lose a fortune at ~*s*⟩ **b** : the winning of a majority of the cards in certain games (as casino) ⟨give three points for ~*s*⟩ **c** : playing cards used for fortunetelling or to reveal what is destined to be ⟨read the ~*s* correctly⟩ — used esp. with *in* or *on* ⟨it is not in the ~*s* for him to win the election⟩ **3** : something compared to a valuable playing card in one's hand : an act, fact, force, or means advantageous to the attainment of an object ⟨hold strong ~*s* in the negotiations⟩ **4** : an amusing person : one given to freakish, clownish, or uninhibited behavior : an amateur comedian : WAG **5 a** *obs* : CHART ⟨a ~ of the sea⟩ **b** : COMPASS CARD **6 a** : a flat stiff piece of paper or thin paperboard suitable for writing or printing, typically small and rectangular, and carrying (1) a communication for transmission by mail (as a postcard), (2) an invitation or announcement ⟨wedding ~⟩ ⟨graduation ~⟩, (3) a person's or firm's name or name and address (as a visiting card), (4) a certification of membership, reference, or credential (as in a labor union or political party), (5) a record (as a unit in a system of filing or sorting) ⟨the information was punched on ~*s*⟩ **b** : a piece of paper or thin paperboard having any of a variety of shapes and formats and bearing a greeting or a message of sentiment, sympathy, or congratulation ⟨birthday ~⟩ **c** : PROGRAM; *esp* : a sports program ⟨racing ~⟩ ⟨boxing ~⟩ **d** : a tally sheet (as for a player's golf score) : SCORECARD **e** : a wine list : MENU **f** : STORE CARD **g** : a number of articles attached to a piece of stiff paper or bound together in a flat sheet to be sold as a unit ⟨a ~ of buttons⟩ ⟨a ~ of matches⟩ **h** : CARDBOARD **7** : a published note (as in a newspaper) containing a brief statement, request, or advertisement **8** : any of the perforated boards or plates in a dobby or a jacquard loom for operating the successive combinations of wires that move the warp threads **9** *slang* : a single portion of a narcotic drug

⁴card \"\ *vb* -ED/-ING/-S *vi, archaic* : to play cards — sometimes used with *it* ⟨~ it all night —Henry Fielding⟩ ~ *vt* **1** : to place or fasten on or by means of a card ⟨his name was ~*ed* upon three staterooms —E.A.Poe⟩ **2** : to provide with a card : attach a card to **3** : to enter or list on a card **4** *sports* : SCORE; *specif* : to record (a score) upon a scorecard ⟨golfers who ~*ed* 80 on an 18-hole course⟩ **5** : SCHEDULE ⟨~ a train⟩ **6** : ⁵SLIP 2

card *abbr, usu cap* cardinal

car·dam·i·ne \kärˈdaməˌ(ˌ)nē\ *n* [NL, fr. Gk *kardaminē* water cress, fr. *kardamon* garden peppergrass] **1** *cap* : a large genus of mostly perennial glabrous herbs (family Cruciferae) growing in temperate regions and having flat pods and wingless seeds **2** -s : a plant of the genus *Cardamine*

car·da·mom \ˈkärdəməm *also* -ˌmäm\ *also* **car·da·mum** \-məm\ *or* **car·da·mon** \-mən *also* -ˌmän\ *n* -s [L *cardamomum*, fr. Gk *kardamōmon*, blend of *kardamon* garden peppergrass & *amōmon*, an Indian spice plant] **1 a** : the aromatic capsular fruit of an East Indian herb (*Elettaria cardamomum*) the seeds of which are used as a condiment and in medicine as an adjuvant to other aromatics and stomachics **b** : a similar fruit of certain related plants (as members of the genus *Amomum*) that are sometimes used as adulterants **2** : a plant that produces cardamoms

cardamom oil *n* : a colorless or pale-yellow essential oil with a camphoraceous odor and pungent taste distilled from cardamom seeds and used in pharmaceutical preparations and as a flavoring for foods

car·dan \ˈkärˌdan\ *or* **cardan joint** *n* -s *usu cap C* [after Jerome *Cardan* (Geronimo Cardano) †1576 Ital. mathematician, its inventor] : a universal joint that transmits motion unchanged

car·da·nol \ˈkärdᵊnˌōl, -ōl\ *n* -s [*card-* (fr. NL *Anacardium*, genus name of *Anacardium occidentale*) + *-an* + *-ol*] : a nonvesicant oily liquid that is composed chiefly of monohydroxy phenols, obtained from cashew nutshell liquid or anacardic acid, and used esp. in making phenolic resins

cardan shaft *n, usu cap C* [after Jerome *Cardan*, its inventor] **1** : a shaft that has a universal joint at one or both ends enabling it to rotate freely when in varying angular relation to another shaft or shafts to which it is joined **2** : a shaft (as on a motor vehicle) that transmits power

car·dan suspension \ˈkärˌdan-\ *or* **car·dan·ic suspension** \(ˈ)kärˈdanik-\ *n, usu cap C* [after Jerome *Cardan*] : a support in which an instrument (as a chronometer) is hung on gimbals

¹cardboard \ˈ=ˌ=\ *n* -s [³*card* + *board*] : a stiff moderately thick paperboard sometimes coated and of a quality suitable for signs or printed matter — compare ¹BOARD 6a

²cardboard \"\ *adj* **1** : made of or as if of cardboard : FLAT : TWO-DIMENSIONAL ⟨~ Spanish ironwork —Cyril Connolly⟩ **2** : UNREAL, UNLIFELIKE : STIFF : STEREOTYPED ⟨the detective story is partial to ~ characters and notoriously fatal to any real emotion —J.P.Bishop⟩

card catalog *n* [³*card*] : a catalog (as of books) the entries in which are on cards

card clothier *also* **card clother** \-ˌklōt͟hə(r)\ *n* [²*card*] : one that removes and replaces the card clothing of carding machines

card clothing \-ˌklōt͟hiŋ\ *n* [²*card*] : material consisting of leather or cloth in which teeth are set that is used esp. for covering the cylinders of carding machines

card cutter *n* [³*card*] : one that perforates a card in a pattern to be woven in a jacquard loom

car·de·cu \ˈkärdəˌkyü\ *n* -s [F *quart d'écu* quarter of an ecu] : an old French silver coin equal to ¼ ecu that was first issued by Henry III

¹carded *adj* [fr. past part. of ¹*card*] : prepared by the action of a card or carding machine ⟨~ wool⟩

²carded *adj* [fr. past part. of ⁴*card*] **1** : entered on a card : PROGRAMMED **2** : mounted on a card

carded silk *n* [¹*carded*] : waste silk or silk from imperfect cocoons carded for making into spun silk

carded yarn *n* [¹*carded*] : yarn of any fiber spun from carded stock — compare COMBED YARN

car·del \ˈkärˌdel, -ˌdᵊl\ *n* -s [D *kardeel*, prob. modif. of MF *quartel, cartel*, dim. of *quart* fourth — more at QUART] : a cask used by Dutch whalers

card·er \ˈkärdər, ˈkȧdə\ *n* -s [ME, fr. *carden* to card (comb) + *-er*] : one that cards: as **a** : CARDING MACHINE **b** : one that attaches articles (as jewelry, needles, hairpins) to cards for display or sale

card field *n* [³*card*] : a particular group of columns, rows, or punching positions in a punched card

card grinder *n* [²*card*] : a textile worker who cleans and sharpens the wire teeth of a carding or napping machine

cardholder \ˈ=ˌ==\ *n* [³*card* + *holder*] **1** : one whose membership in a union or political party is attested by a membership card **2** : a person who has a card issued by a library entitling him to borrow books **3** : one of two metal ears in front of the line scale on a typewriter that when raised to a vertical position help to hold cards or envelopes in place during typing

cardhouse \ˈ=ˌ=\ *or* **cardcastle** \ˈ=ˌ==\ *n* -s *often attrib* [³*card* + *house* or *castle*] : a structure or situation felt to resemble a construction built of playing cards in being insubstantial, unsound, or in constant danger of collapse ⟨a ~ plan that collapsed at the first test⟩ — called also *house of cards*

cardi- *or* **cardio-** *comb form* [Gk. *kardi-, kardio-*, fr. *kardia* — more at HEART] **1** : heart : cardiac ⟨*cardi*agra⟩ ⟨*cardio*aortic⟩ ⟨*cardio*ptosis⟩ ⟨*cardio*puncture⟩ **2** : heart action ⟨*cardio*gram⟩

car·dia \ˈkärdēə, ˈkȧd-\ *n, pl* **cardi·ae** \-dēˌē\ *or* **cardias** \-dēəz\ [NL, fr. Gk *kardia* heart, upper orifice of the stomach] **1 a** : the opening of the esophagus into the stomach **b** : the part of the stomach adjoining this opening **2** : the enlarged anterior portion of the ventriculus of some insects (as sucking insects that lack a proventriculus)

-cardia \"\ *n comb form* -s [NL, fr. Gk. *kardia*] **1** : heart action or location (of a specified type) ⟨dextro*cardia*⟩ ⟨tachy*cardia*⟩ **2 a** : animal or animals having a (specified) type of heart ⟨Diplo*cardia*⟩ ⟨Lepto*cardia*⟩ **b** : heart-shaped animal — esp. in generic names of mollusks

¹car·di·ac \ˈkärdēˌak, ˈkȧd-\ *adj* [L *cardiacus*, fr. Gk *kardiakos*, fr. *kardia* heart] **1 a** : of, relating to, or acting on the heart : situated near the heart — see CARDIAC MUSCLE **b** : of or relating to the cardia or sometimes to the whole stomach except the narrow part near the pyloric end **2** : of or relating to heart disease ⟨~ patient⟩ ⟨~ clinic⟩

²cardiac \"\ *n* -s : a person with heart disease

cardiac arrest *n* : temporary or permanent cessation of the heartbeat

cardiac asthma *n* : asthma due to heart disease (as heart failure) that occurs in paroxysms usu. at night and is characterized by difficult wheezing respiration, pallor, and anxiety — called also *paroxysmal dyspnea*

cardiac cycle *n* : the complete sequence of events in the heart from the beginning of one beat to the beginning of the following beat : a complete heartbeat including systole and diastole

car·di·a·cea \ˌkärdēˈāsh(ē)ə\ *n pl, cap* [NL, fr. *Cardium*, type genus + *-acea*] : a suborder of Eulamellibranchia comprising the cockles and related mollusks — **car·di·a·cean** \ˌ==ˈāshən\ *adj or n*

cardiac failure *n* : HEART FAILURE

cardiac gland *n* : any of the branched tubular mucus-secreting glands of the cardia of the stomach; *also* : one of the similar glands of the esophagus

cardiac impulse *n* : the wave of cardiac excitation passing from the sinoatrial node to the atrioventricular node and along the atrioventricular bundle and initiating the cardiac cycle; *broadly* : HEARTBEAT

cardiac jelly *n* : a layer of resilient jellylike material lying between the cardiac endothelium and the epimyocardium in the early development of the vertebrate heart

cardiac muscle *n* : the principal muscle tissue of the vertebrate heart made up of striated extensively branched fibers in cytoplasmic continuity and adapted to long-continued rhythmic contraction

cardiac nerve *n* : any of the nerves connecting the cervical ganglia of the sympathetic system with the cardiac plexus

cardiac neurosis *n* : a condition marked by shortness of breath, fatigue, rapid pulse, and heart palpitation sometimes with extra beats that occurs chiefly with exertion and is not due to physical disease of the heart — called also *effort syndrome, irritable heart, neurocirculatory asthenia, soldier's heart*

cardiac orifice *n* : CARDIA 1 a

cardiac plexus *n* : a plexus of nerves derived from the sympathetic and vagus and supplying the heart and neighboring structures

cardiac sphincter *n* : the somewhat thickened muscular ring surrounding the opening between esophagus and stomach

cardiac tamponade *n* : mechanical compression of the heart by large amounts of fluid or blood within the pericardial space that limits the normal range of motion and function of the heart

cardiac vein *n* : any of the veins returning the blood from the tissues of the heart that open into the right auricle either directly or through the coronary sinus

car·di·al·gia \ˌkärdēˈalj(ē)ə\ *n* -s [NL, fr. Gk *kardialgia*, fr. *kardia* heart + *-algia* — more at HEART] **1** : HEARTBURN **2** : pain in the heart

car·di·a·zol \kärˈdīəˌzōl, -ōl, ˈkärdēə-\ *also* **car·di·a·zole** \-ōl\ *n* -s [fr. *Cardiazol*, a trademark] : PENTYLENETETRAZOL

car·di·ec·to·my \ˌkärdēˈektəmē\ *n* -ES [ISV *cardi-* (fr. NL *cardia*) + *-ectomy*] : excision of the cardiac portion of the stomach

car·diff \ˈkärdəf\ *adj, usu cap* [fr. *Cardiff*, county borough in Wales] : of or from the county borough of Cardiff, Wales : of the kind or style prevalent in Cardiff

car·di·form \ˈkärdəˌfȯrm\ *adj* [²*card* + *-iform*] : arranged like a series of combs or wool cards (as the teeth of certain fishes)

¹car·di·gan \ˈkärdəgən, ˈkȧd-, -ēg-\ *n* -s *often attrib* [after James Thomas Brudenell, 7th Earl of *Cardigan* †1868 Eng. soldier] : a sweater or jacket that opens the full length of the center front and usu. has a round or V-shaped collarless neck

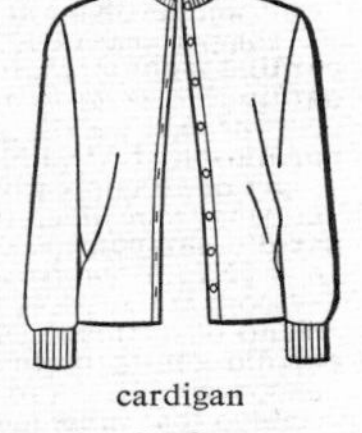
cardigan

²cardigan \"\ *n* -s *usu cap* [fr. *Cardigan*, county in Wales] : a Welsh Corgi of a variety characterized by rounded ears, slightly bowed forelegs, and long tail

car·di·gan·shire \-ˌshi(ə)r, -iə, -ˌshə(r)\ *or* **cardigan** *adj, usu cap* [fr. *Cardiganshire*, or the county of *Cardigan*, Wales] : of or from the county of Cardigan, Wales : of the kind or style prevalent in Cardigan

car·di·i·dae \kärˈdīəˌdē\ *n pl, cap* [NL, fr. *Cardium*, type genus + *-idae*] : a family of marine bivalve mollusks (order Eulamellibranchia) that have an equivalve ribbed shell with prominent umbones, a large foot adapted for creeping over sandy bottoms, and much-folded gills and that include the true cockles

¹car·di·nal \ˈkärd(ᵊ)nəl, ˈkȧd-\ *adj* [ME, fr. OF, fr. LL *cardinalis*, fr. L, of a hinge, fr. *cardin-, cardo* hinge + *-alis* -al; akin to OE *hratian* to rush, hasten, MHG *scherzen* to leap for joy, jest, ON *hrata* to stagger, fall, Gk *kradan* to shake, brandish, *kordylē* bump, swelling, *skairein* to gambol, Skt *kūrdati* he leaps; basic meaning: to spring, turn] **1** : of basic importance : central, basic, or critical to any system, construction, organization, or framework of thought ⟨might ask for the return of the German colonies, but this was evidently not ~ —Sir Winston Churchill⟩ ⟨the ~ element in the plan was speed⟩ : of principal importance : CHIEF, PRIMARY ⟨progress had been elevated into a ~ doctrine of the educated classes —Lewis Mumford⟩ ⟨a ~ symptom in diagnosis⟩ **2 a** : of or relating to the hinge of a bivalve shell **b** : of or relating to the cardo of an insect **3** : of a cardinal red color **syn** see ESSENTIAL

²cardinal \"\ *n* -s [ME, fr. ML *cardinalis*, fr. LL *cardinalis*, adj., principal] **1** : a high ecclesiastical official taking precedence over every other dignitary of the Roman Catholic Church below papal rank who is appointed by the pope to assist him as a member of the college of cardinals **2** : CARDINAL NUMBER — usu. used in pl. **3** : a woman's short hooded cloak orig. of scarlet cloth **4** [so called fr. the color of a cardinal's robes] *or* **cardinal red** : a variable color averaging a vivid red that is yellower and duller than madder crimson or carmine, bluer and duller than scarlet or Castilian red, and duller than apple red **5** [so called fr. its red color, compared with that of a cardinal's robes] *also* **cardinal bird** : any of several American songbirds (genus *Richmondena*) of the family Fringillidae of the southern and middle U.S., the male being bright red with a black face, pointed crest, and loud song and the female being much duller in color — see ARIZONA CARDINAL

cardinal archbishop *n* [trans. of ML *cardinalis archiepiscopus*] : a cardinal who governs an archdiocese — not used as a canonical title

car·di·nal·ate \-ələt, -,lāt\ *n* -S [F *cardinalat*, fr. ML *cardinalatus*, fr. *cardinalis* + L *-atus* -ate] **1 :** the office, rank, or dignity of a cardinal **2 :** CARDINALS

cardinal bishop *n* [trans. of ML *episcopus cardinalis*] **:** a member of the first order of cardinals holding until 1932 one of the suburbicarian sees of Rome

cardinal climber *n* [²*cardinal*] **:** an annual vine (*Quamoclit sloteri*) resembling the cypress vine

cardinal deacon *n* [trans. of ML *diaconus cardinalis*] **:** a member of the third order of cardinals who is also titular chief officer of a Roman diaconia

cardinal dean *n* [trans. of ML *diaconus cardinalis*] **:** the senior cardinal bishop of the college of cardinals at Rome

cardinal fish *n* [²*cardinal*; fr. its color, compared with that of a cardinal's robes] **:** a fish of the genus *Apogon* or family Apogonidae related to the family Percidae and commonly red in color; *esp* **:** the common European cardinal fish (*Apogon imberbis*)

cardinal flower *n* [²*cardinal*] **1 :** the brilliant red flower of a No. American herb (*Lobelia cardinalis*) **2 :** the plant bearing the cardinal flower

car·di·nal·i·tial \¦kärd(ᵊ)nə¦lishəl\ *also* **car·di·nal·i·tian** \-shən\ *adj* [irreg. fr. It *cardinalizio* cardinalitial (fr. *cardinale* cardinal, fr. ML *cardinalis*) + E *-al* or *-an* — more at CARDINAL] **:** of or relating to a cardinal

car·di·nal·ly \'⸗d(ᵊ)nəlē, -i\ *adv* **:** in a cardinal manner or degree **:** PREEMINENTLY

cardinal number *or* **cardinal numeral** *n* [¹*cardinal*] **:** a primary number used in simple counting **:** a number (as one, two, three) answering the question "how many?" — distinguished from *ordinal number;* see NUMBER table

cardinal point *n* [¹*cardinal*] **1 a :** one of the four principal points of the compass **:** north, south, east, or west **b** *in magical ritual* **:** one of the four principal directional points of the compass or one of the additional points zenith, nadir, and center **2** *of a lens or lens system* **:** one of the two principal foci, the two principal points, or the two nodal points — called also *Gauss point*

cardinal points of the ecliptic : the two equinoctial and the two solstitial points

cardinal priest *n* [trans. of ML *presbyter cardinalis*] **:** a member of the second order of cardinals orig. but now only titularly in charge of a parish church at Rome

cardinal process *n* [¹*cardinal*] **:** a projection in the shells of many brachiopods at the posterior edge of the dorsal valve to which the muscles that open the shell are attached — see BRACHIOPOD illustration

cardinal red *n* **:** CARDINAL 4

cardinals *pl of* CARDINAL

cardinal sauce *n* [²*cardinal*; fr. its color, compared with that of a cardinal's robes] **:** a white sauce variously flavored and colored red

cardinal's hat *n* [²*cardinal*] **:** a red hat with low crown and broad brim symbolic of the dignity of a cardinal — called also *red hat*

car·di·nal·ship \-,ship\ *n* -S [²*cardinal* + *-ship*] **:** CARDINALATE

cardinal sign *n* [¹*cardinal*] **:** one of the four zodiacal signs Aries, Cancer, Libra, and Capricorn corresponding to cardinal points of the ecliptic

cardinal tooth *n* [¹*cardinal*] **:** a tooth of the hinge of a bivalve mollusk's shell situated just under the umbo and often relatively large — compare LATERAL TOOTH

coat of arms showing cardinal's hat

cardinal vein *also* **cardinal sinus** *n* [¹*cardinal*] **:** any of four longitudinal veins of the vertebrate embryo running anteriorly and posteriorly along each side of the vertebral column with the pair on each side meeting at and discharging blood to the heart through the corresponding duct of Cuvier

cardinal virtue *n* [¹*cardinal*] **:** one of a group of preeminent virtues: as **a** *among the ancients and in scholasticism* **:** one of the natural virtues prudence, justice, temperance, or fortitude **b :** one of seven virtues including in addition to the natural virtues the three theological virtues faith, hope, and charity

cardinal vowel *n* [¹*cardinal*] **:** one of a series of 16 invariable vowel sounds set up as a standard for describing the quality of the vowels of any language or speaker

cardinal wind *n* [¹*cardinal*] **:** one of the winds that blow from the cardinal points of the compass

card index *n* [³*card*] **:** an index having the entries on cards

card–in·dex \'⸗¦⸗,⸗\ *vt* **1 :** to list in a card index **:** CATALOG **2 :** to analyze or categorize elaborately and systematically

cardines [L] *pl of* CARDO

carding *n* -S [fr. gerund of ¹*card*] **1 :** a roll of wool or other fiber from a carding machine **2** [by shortening] **:** CARDING MACHINE

carding engine *n, Brit* **:** CARDING MACHINE

carding leather *n* **:** a cattlehide leather produced for use on cards of textile machinery

carding machine *n* **:** a machine for carding wool, cotton, or other fiber consisting of cylinders having intermeshing wire teeth and revolving at different speeds or in opposite directions — compare BREAKER 2c(1), COMBING MACHINE

carding wool *n* **:** CLOTHING WOOL 1

cardio- *in words below,* ¦⸗⸗ = ¦kärdēō *or* ¦kȧd- *or* -ēə, ¦⸗⸗(,)⸗ = " *or* -ē,ō, ,⸗⸗'⸗ = ,kärdē'ä *or* ,kȧd-\ — see CARDI-

car·dio·blast \'⸗⸗⸗,blast\ *n* -S [*cardi-* + *-blast*] *of an insect* **:** any of certain early embryonic cells occurring segmentally in pairs from which the heart develops

car·dio·car·pon \,⸗⸗⸗'kär,pän\ *also* **car·dio·car·pum** \-,pəm\ *n* -S [NL, fr. *cardi-* + *-carpon, -carpum* (fr. Gk *karpos* fruit) — more at HARVEST] **:** any of certain nutlike fruits or seeds of plants of the fossil genus *Cordaites*

car·dio·gen·ic plate \¦⸗⸗⸗¦jenik-\ *n* **:** an area of splanchnic mesoderm anterior to the head process of the early mammalian embryo that subsequently gives rise to the heart

car·dio·gram \'⸗⸗⸗,gram, -aa(ə)m\ *n* -S [ISV *cardi-* + *-gram*] **:** the curve or tracing made by a cardiograph

car·dio·graph \-,graf, -aa(ə)f, -äf\ *n* -S [ISV *cardi-* + *-graph;* orig. formed as F *cardiographe*] **:** an instrument that registers graphically the heart's movements — **car·di·og·ra·pher** \,⸗⸗'⸗grəfə(r)\ *n* -S — **car·dio·graph·ic** \¦⸗⸗⸗¦grafik, -ēk\ *adj*

car·di·og·ra·phy \,⸗⸗'⸗grəfē, -i\ *n* -ES [ISV *cardiograph* + *-y*] **:** the use of the cardiograph **:** examination by cardiograph

¹**car·di·oid** \'kärdē,ȯid\ *n* -S [*cardi-* + *-oid*] **:** a heart-shaped closed curve traced by a point on the circumference of a circle as it rolls completely around an equal fixed circle and forms an epicycloid of one cusp and one loop, the polar equation with cusp as pole being $r = a\ (1 - \cos\theta)$, where *a* is the diameter of either circle

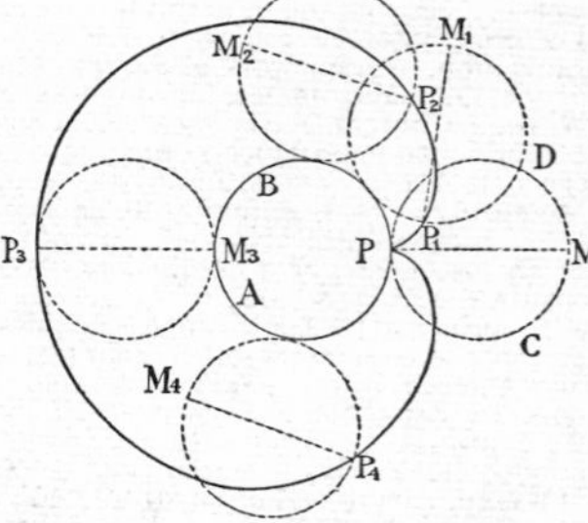

cardioid: *ABP* fixed circle; *PCD* first position of rolling circle; *P* tracing point; *PM* diameter through *P*; P_1, P_2, P_3, P_4 various positions of *P*; P_1M_1, P_2M_2, P_3M_3, P_4M_4 various positions of *PM*

²**cardioid** \"\ *adj* **:** connected with or relating to a cardioid

cardioid condenser *n* **:** a substage condenser that may be used with a microscope to give illumination approximating that obtained with the ultramicroscope

cardioid microphone *n* **:** a microphone having approximately uniform response over 180 degrees in front and minimum response in back, a polar curve representing its directional response being a cardioid

car·dio·in·hib·i·to·ry \¦⸗⸗(,)⸗-\ *adj* [*cardi-* + *inhibitory*] **:** interfering with or slowing the normal sequence of events in the cardiac cycle ⟨the ~ center of the medulla⟩

car·dio·lip·in \,⸗⸗⸗'lipən\ *n* -S [*cardi-* + *lip-* + *-in*] **:** a phosphatide obtained esp. from beef heart and used in antigens for diagnostic blood tests for syphilis

car·dio·log·ic \¦⸗⸗⸗¦läjik\ *adj* [ISV *cardiology* + *-ic*] **:** relating to the study of the heart — **car·dio·log·i·cal** \-ə̇kəl\ *adj*

car·di·ol·o·gist \,⸗⸗'⸗ləjə̇st\ *n* -S **:** a specialist in cardiology

car·di·ol·o·gy \-jē, -i\ *n* -ES [ISV *cardi-* + *-logy*] **:** the study of the heart and its action and of the diagnosis and therapy of its diseases

car·di·om·e·ter \,⸗⸗'⸗məd·ə(r)\ *n* -S [*cardi-* + *-meter*] **:** an instrument used in measuring the force of the heart's action — **car·dio·met·ric** \¦⸗⸗⸗¦me·trik\ *adj* — **car·di·om·e·try** \,⸗⸗'⸗mə·trē\ *n* -ES

car·dio·path \'⸗⸗⸗,path\ *n* -S [back-formation fr. *cardiopathy*] **:** a person having heart disease

car·di·op·a·thy \,⸗⸗'⸗pəthē\ *n* -ES [prob. fr. NL *cardiopathia*, fr. *cardi-* + *-pathia*] **:** a disease of the heart

car·dio·pho·bia \,⸗⸗⸗'fōbēə\ *n* -S [NL, fr. *cardi-* + *phobia*] **:** abnormal fear of heart disease

car·dio·pul·mo·nary machine \¦⸗⸗(,)⸗-\ *n* [ISV *cardi-* + *pulmonary*] **:** HEART-LUNG MACHINE

car·dio·res·pi·ra·to·ry \¦⸗⸗(,)⸗-\ *adj* [*cardi-* + *respiratory*] **:** relating to the heart and lungs and their functions

car·di·or·rha·phy \,⸗⸗'ȯrəfē\ *n* -ES [ISV *cardi-* + *-rrhaphy*] **:** a surgical operation of suturing the heart muscle (as in the repair of a stab wound)

car·dio·scope \'⸗⸗⸗,skōp\ *n* -S [*cardi-* + *-scope*] **1 :** an instrument that permits direct visual inspection of the interior of the heart **2 :** an instrument that permits continuous electrocardiographic observation of the heart's action during an operation **3 :** an instrument equipped with a screen on which tracings of the heart's action and sounds can be demonstrated

car·dio·spasm \'⸗⸗⸗,spazəm\ *n* -S [ISV *cardi-* + *spasm*] **:** failure of the cardiac sphincter to relax during swallowing with resultant esophageal obstruction — compare ACHALASIA — **car·dio·spas·tic** \¦⸗⸗⸗¦spastik\ *adj*

car·dio·sper·mum \,⸗⸗⸗'spərməm\ *n, cap* [NL, fr. *cardi-* + *-spermum* (neut. of *-spermus* -spermous)] **:** a large genus of tropical American herbaceous vines (family Sapindaceae) having alternate biternate leaves, coarsely serrate leaflets, small white flowers, and an inflated capsular fruit — see BALLOON VINE

car·dio·ta·chom·e·ter \¦⸗⸗(,)⸗-\ *n* -S [*cardi-* + *tachometer*] **:** a device for prolonged graphic recording of the heartbeat

car·di·ot·o·my \,⸗⸗'⸗d·əmē\ *n* -ES [ISV *cardi-* + *-tomy*] **1 :** surgical incision of the heart **2 :** surgical incision of the cardia of the stomach

¹**car·dio·ton·ic** \¦⸗⸗⸗¦tänik\ *adj* [ISV *cardi-* + *-tonic*] **:** tending to increase the tonus of heart muscle

²**cardiotonic** \"\ *n* -S **:** a cardiotonic substance

car·dio·vas·cu·lar \¦⸗⸗(,)⸗-\ *adj* [ISV *cardi-* + *vascular*] **:** of, relating to, or involving the heart and blood vessels ⟨~ disease⟩ ⟨~ system⟩

car distributor *n* **1 :** one that directs the distribution of railroad cars and equipment to points where they are required for loading or other use **2 :** MOTOR BOSS

car·di·ta \kär'dīd·ə, -ēə\ *n* [NL, fr. Gk *kardia* heart + L *-ita* -ite] **1** *cap* **:** a genus (the type of the family Carditidae) of marine lamellibranch mollusks resembling the cockles but lacking siphons and having a short foot **2** -S **:** any mollusk of the genus *Cardita*

car·dite \'kär,dīt\ *n* -S [F, fr. NL *Cardita*] **:** CARDITA 2

car·di·tis \kär'dīd·ə̇s\ *n* -ES [NL, fr. *cardi-* + *-itis*] **:** inflammation of the heart muscle **:** MYOCARDITIS — see ENDOCARDITIS, PERICARDITIS

car·di·um \'kärdēəm, 'kȧd-\ *n, cap* [NL, fr. Gk *kardia* heart + NL *-ium;* fr. its shape] **:** the type genus of Cardiidae including a number of cockles esteemed as food

-car·di·um \"\ *n comb form, pl* **-car·dia** \-ēə\ [NL, fr. Gk *-kardion,* fr. *kardia* — more at HEART] **:** heart ⟨endo*cardium*⟩ ⟨meso*cardium*⟩

cardium clay *n, cap 1st C* **:** a Pleistocene glacial clay of northern Europe characterized by fossil shells of the genus *Cardium*

car·do \'kär,dō\ *n, pl* **car·di·nes** \-,dᵊn,ēz, -,äs\ [L, hinge — more at CARDINAL] **:** a basal or proximal part (as the basal joint of the insect maxilla or the hinge of a bivalve shell)

¹**cardon** *var of* CARDOON

²**car·don** \'kär,dän, ⸗'⸗\ *n* -S [AmerSp *cardón,* fr Sp, teasel, fr. LL *cardon-, cardo* thistle] **1** *also* **car·do·na** \kär'dōnə\ **:** any of several large columnar cacti esp. of the genus *Cereus* that have a woody skeleton sometimes used for lumber (as in furniture making), may attain a height of 60 feet, and often form forestlike stands from Lower California to Chile and in Venezuela **2 :** any of several cactuslike plants of the genus *Euphorbia* of Central America and the West Indies

car·don·ci·llo \,kärdᵊn'sē(,)(y)ō\ *n* -S [MexSp, fr. Sp, milk thistle (*Silybum marianum*), dim. of *cardón* teasel] **:** a cactus (*Wilcoxia papillosa*) of tropical America used for food and fuel

car·doon \(')kär¦dün, -kȧ¦d-\ *or* **car·don** \-ōn\ *n* -S [F *cardon,* fr. LL *cardon-, cardo* thistle, fr. *cardus,* fr. L *carduus* thistle, artichoke — more at CHARD] **:** a large thistlelike plant (*Cynara cardunculus*) related to the artichoke, the blanched leaves and stalks and the thick main roots being used as food

card page *also* **card plate** *n* [³*card*] **:** a page in a book on which are listed other works by the same author or publisher

cardplayer \'⸗,⸗⸗\ *n* [³*card* + *player*] **:** one that plays cards

card punch *n* [³*card*] **:** a machine or hand tool that punches coded information onto cards — compare PUNCHED CARD

cardroom \'⸗,⸗\ *n* -S **1 :** a room in which gambling with playing cards is carried on **2 :** a room equipped for pastime card playing ⟨a game of bridge in the ~ of the club —Raymond Paton⟩ **3 :** a room equipped for cloth carding

cards *pl of* CARD, *pres 3d sing of* CARD

cards and spades *n pl* **:** a liberal handicap ⟨could give him *cards and spades* and still beat him at his own game⟩

card setter *n* [²*card*] **:** a machine for setting the wire teeth in making card clothing

cardsharper \'⸗,⸗⸗\ *or* **cardsharp** \'⸗,⸗\ *n* -S [³*card* + *sharper* (cheat) *or sharp*] **:** one that consistently seeks to win at card games by cheating

card strip *n* [²*card*] **:** cotton waste consisting of cleanings from a carding machine

card stripper *n* [²*card*] **:** one that cleans accumulated fiber from the teeth of a carding or doffing drum

card table *n* [³*card*] **:** a table for playing cards: **a :** a table with folding top that can be placed against a wall like a console when not in use **b :** a square table with folding legs

card teasel *n* [²*card;* fr. its use in dressing cloth] **:** WILD TEASEL

card tender *n* [²*card*] **:** a worker who feeds lap into one or more textile or asbestos carding machines and removes slivers — called also *winder*

card thistle *n* [²*card;* fr. its use in dressing cloth] **:** TEASEL

car·du·a·ce·ae \,kärjə'wāsē,ē\ *n pl, cap* [NL, fr. *Carduus,* type genus + *-aceae*] *in some classifications* **:** a family of plants comprising all the composites (as thistles and asters) that have syngenesious stamens and flower heads containing tubular flowers or both tubular and ligulate flowers but not ligulate flowers alone — **car·du·a·ceous** \¦⸗⸗¦wāshəs\ *adj*

car·du·e·line \,kärjə'wēlən\ *adj* [NL *Carduelis* + E *-ine*] **:** of or relating to the genus *Carduelis*

car·du·e·lis \-ləs\ *n, cap* [NL, fr. L, goldfinch, fr. *carduus* thistle] **:** the genus of birds (family Fringillidae) containing the European goldfinch and often the siskins, redpolls and linnets, and related birds — compare SPINUS

car·du·us \'kärjəwəs\ *n, cap* [NL, fr. L, thistle — more at CHARD] **:** a genus of annual or perennial prickly thistles (family Compositae) having the bristles of the pappus not plumose and being native to the Old World — compare CIRSIUM; see MUSK THISTLE

card voting *n* [³*card*] **:** a system of voting (as in some European trade unions) by which one vote is cast by a person bearing a card that specifies the number of voters he represents

¹**care** \'ke(ə)r, 'keə, 'ka(a)(ə)r, 'ka(a)ə\ *n* -S [ME, fr. OE *caru, cearu;* akin to OHG *kara* lament, Goth *kara* care, L *garrire* to chatter, talk, Gk *gērys* voice, Ossetic *zar* song] **1 :** suffering of mind **:** GRIEF, SORROW ⟨a *care*-marked face⟩ **2 a :** a burdened or disquieted state of blended preoccupation, uncertainty, apprehension or fear, and consideration of expedients ⟨oppressed by sickness, grief, or ~ —William Wordsworth⟩ **b :** a cause for such state **3 :** serious attention; *esp* **:** attention accompanied by caution, pains, wariness, personal interest, or responsibility ⟨his gentlemen conduct me with all ~ to some securest lodging —John Keats⟩ **4 :** regard coming from desire or esteem **:** INCLINATION, WISH — usu. used with *of* or *for* ⟨a ~ for the common good⟩ **5 :** CHARGE, SUPERVISION, MANAGEMENT **:** responsibility for or attention to safety and well-being ⟨under a doctor's ~⟩ ⟨the ~ of all the churches —2 Cor 11:28 (AV)⟩ **:** CUSTODY **:** temporary charge — used esp. in the phrase *care of* or *in care of* on mail sent to a person through another person or other agency ⟨I addressed him ~ of general delivery⟩; abbr. *c/o* **6 :** a person or thing that is an object of attention, anxiety, or solicitude ⟨the flower garden was her special ~⟩

syn SOLICITUDE, CONCERN, WORRY, ANXIETY: CARE designates a troubled, preoccupied, or oppressed mental condition induced by responsibilities and duties or by doubts and apprehensions ⟨the king . . . most sovereign slave of *care* —H.D.Thoreau⟩ ⟨she was free . . . to go where she liked and do what she liked. She had no responsibilities, no *cares* —Arnold Bennett⟩ SOLICITUDE designates an apprehensive or thoughtful protectiveness, attentiveness, or regard for well-being or success, usu. another's ⟨with motherly *solicitude,* he insisted that Tom get to his feet —Sherwood Anderson⟩ ⟨no amount of parental *solicitude* can give a boy or girl the same advantages at home as are to be enjoyed in a good school —Bertrand Russell⟩ CONCERN, the antonym of *indifference,* means primarily an interest in one's well-being or safety but is likely to suggest apprehension or doubt about difficulties, dangers, or failures ⟨but your friends, Señora, would feel less *concern* for your safety if you kept them [valuables] further from your person —Mary Austin⟩ ⟨she really did feel *concern* for her fellow creatures, for the rural poor upon whom it was not the custom of Church or State to waste sympathy or help —Agnes Repplier⟩ WORRY suggests troubled fretting about adverse developments from uncertain conditions ⟨thought that now all the *worries* were over . . . a most soothing certitude —Joseph Conrad⟩ ⟨alternating *worry* with quiet qualms —Robert Browning⟩ ANXIETY adds a strong suggestion of dread and distress in the expectation of an evil issue or outcome ⟨I shut my eyes, but *anxiety* forced me to open them again . . . we were not twenty yards from the rocks —Frederick Marryat⟩ ⟨when the child told her first lie her foster-mother was nearly sick with dismay and *anxiety* —Margaret Deland⟩

²**care** \"\ *vb* -ED/-ING/-S [ME *caren,* fr. OE *carian,* fr. *caru, cearu,* n.] *vi* **1 a :** to feel trouble or anxiety ⟨*cared* for his safety⟩ **b :** to feel interest, concern, or solicitude ⟨~ about freedom⟩ ⟨did not much ~ about her children's hunger⟩ **:** feel resentment or irritation ⟨the child doesn't ~ if his toy is taken away⟩ **:** consider as a matter of relevance or interest or as having a bearing on the issue or event ⟨I do not ~ about what you believe; I am certain I am right⟩ — usu. used with a negative and with *for* or *about* **2 a :** to give care (as to the safety, well-being, or maintenance of a charge) **:** provide for or attend to needs or perform necessary personal services (as for a patient or a child) ⟨~ for the sick⟩ **:** give proper use and maintenance ⟨know how to ~ properly for a car⟩ — used with *for* **b :** to afford accommodation ⟨parking space to ~ for all the cars that come⟩ **3 a :** to have a liking, fondness, or taste ⟨never *cared* for a human creature before —Margaret Deland⟩ ⟨doesn't ~ for ice cream⟩ **:** have regard or respect ⟨I *cared* for what he had to say —Edna S.V.Millay⟩ **b :** to have an inclination, wish, or disposition — usu. used with a complementary infinitive ⟨few men *cared* to contradict him⟩ or with *for* ⟨would you ~ for some apples⟩ **~** *vt* **1** *dial* **:** to take care of **2 a :** to be concerned about ⟨nobody ~*s* what I do⟩ **b :** to be concerned to the extent of ⟨~ a damn⟩ **3 :** to long for **:** WISH ⟨if you ~ to go⟩ — **not care :** to be willing **:** have no objection **:** be pleased — usu. used in response to an invitation ⟨I *don't care* if I do, thanks⟩

¹**ca·reen** \kə'rēn\ *n* -S [MF *carène* keel, fr. OIt *carena,* fr. L *carina* keel, nutshell; akin to Gk *karyon* nut, Skt *karkara* hard — more at HARD] *archaic* **:** the act or process of careening **:** the state of being careened — used chiefly in the phrase *on the careen*

²**careen** \"\ *vb* -ED/-ING/-S *vt* **1 a :** to cause (a boat) to lean over on one side (as on a beach) making the other side accessible for repairs below the waterline **b :** to clean, calk, or repair (a boat in this position) **2 :** to cause to heel over ⟨high waves ~*ed* the ship⟩ **~** *vi* **1 a :** to perform the operation of careening a boat **b :** to clean, calk, or repair a boat in a careened position ⟨orders were to ~ and refit⟩ **c :** to undergo this process ⟨the ship is ~*ing* at that port⟩ **2 :** to heel over (as of a ship under a breeze) **3 :** to sway from side to side **:** LURCH ⟨the taxi ~*ed* west toward the main avenue⟩

ca·reen·age \-ij\ *n* -S [F *carénage,* fr. *caréner* to careen (fr. *carène* keel) + *-age*] **1 :** the expense of careening **2** *also* **ca·re·nage** \kə'rēnij\ **:** a harbor suitable for careening

¹**ca·reer** \kə'ri(ə)r, -iə\ *n* -S *often attrib* [MF *carrière,* fr. OProv *carriera* street, fr. ML *carraria* road for vehicles, fr. L *carrus* wheeled vehicle — more at CAR] **1 a :** COURSE, PASSAGE ⟨the sun's ~ across the sky⟩ ⟨the ~ of armed steeds —P.B.Shelley⟩ **b :** SPEED **:** full speed or exercise of activity — used esp. in the phrase *in full career* or *in the full career* ⟨he was now in the full ~ of conquest —T.B.Macaulay⟩ **2 a** *of a horse* **:** a short gallop or run at full or great speed — used esp. in the phrase *to pass career* or *to pass a career* **b :** CHARGE **:** an encounter esp. in a tournament **c :** the way or route over which one passes **3 :** a course of continued progress (as in the life of a person or nation) **:** a field for or pursuit of consecutive progressive achievement esp. in public, professional, or business life ⟨Washington's ~ as a soldier⟩ ⟨~*s* open to educated men⟩ **4 :** a profession for which one undergoes special training and which is undertaken as a permanent calling ⟨a ~ diplomat⟩ ⟨ambassadorships were . . . treated as ~ posts —*Wall Street Jour.*⟩ **:** an occupation or profession engaged in as a lifework ⟨~ girl⟩

²**career** \"\ *vb* -ED/-ING/-S *vi* **1 a :** to make a short gallop **:** CHARGE **b :** to turn to one side and another in running **:** PRANCE, CARACOLE **2 a :** to go, drive, or run at top speed esp. in a headlong or reckless manner ⟨sightseers had gathered in clumps to watch the cars ~*ing* homeward —James Joyce⟩ ⟨mobs ~*ing* through the streets —Kenneth Roberts⟩ **b :** to go or run rapidly with veering or sidelong rocking **~** *vt* **:** to cause (as a horse) to career **syn** see RUN

ca·reer·ing·ly *adv* **:** in a careering manner

ca·reer·ism \kə'ri(ə),rizəm\ *n* -S **:** the policy or practice of advancing one's career (as in the arts and professions) often at the cost of professional or personal integrity **:** career building as a deliberate aim

ca·reer·ist \-rə̇st\ *n* -S **:** one that engages in careerism

careers master *n, Brit* **:** vocational adviser

carefree \'⸗,⸗\ *adj* **:** free from care: as **a :** having no worries **:** HAPPY, LIGHT-HEARTED ⟨the ~ joys of childhood⟩ **b :** IRRESPONSIBLE, INCAUTIOUS **:** neglectful of consequences ⟨~ with his money⟩ — **care·free·ness** \'⸗¦⸗⸗\ *n* -ES

care·ful \'⸗fəl, *-R also* 'kaf-\ *adj, sometimes* **carefuller** \-f(ə)lə(r)\ *sometimes* **carefullest** \-f(ə)ləst\ [ME, fr.OE *carful, cearful,* fr. *caru, cearu* care + *ful* or *full* full — more at CARE, FULL] **1** *archaic* **a :** full of care **:** SOLICITOUS, TROUBLED ⟨be ~ for nothing —Phil 4:6(AV)⟩ **b :** filling with care or solicitude **:** causing or exposing to concern, anxiety, or trouble ⟨by Him that raised me to this ~ height —Shak.⟩ **2 :** exercising thoughtful supervision or making solicitous provision **:** taking good care — usu. used with *for* or *of* ⟨~ of a child's welfare⟩ **3 :** marked by care: as **a :** marked by attentive concern and solicitude ⟨a sad accident! He will need very ~ watching —Bram Stoker⟩ **b :** marked by wary caution or prudence ⟨be very ~ of the moving blades⟩ ⟨the perpetual fear which prompts ~ stepping —Herbert Spencer⟩ **c :** marked by painstaking effort to avoid errors or omissions ⟨a ~, sober, and accurate description of the events⟩ ⟨~ of detail, laborious, methodical —J.R.Green⟩ — often used with *of* or with an infinitive ⟨~ of money⟩ ⟨~ to adjust the machine⟩

syn METICULOUS, PUNCTILIOUS, SCRUPULOUS, PUNCTUAL: CAREFUL indicates a varying blend of attentiveness and caution ⟨Oh, I intend being very *careful* —Jack London⟩ ⟨have given the matter very *careful* attention —J.P.Marquand⟩ ⟨a *careful* search conducted by three young ladies and the postmaster in question —Dorothy Sayers⟩ METICULOUS describes extreme attentiveness to detail or timorous caution about minutiae ⟨the *meticulous* care with which the operation in Sicily was planned has paid dividends. For our casualties . . . have been low —F.D.Roosevelt⟩ ⟨McKinley . . . was too polite, too *meticulous* in his observation of the formalities of the political Sanhedrin —W.A.White⟩ PUNCTILIOUS describes extreme attention to fine points ⟨lecture scripts, every one of them marked with *punctilious* care for emphasis, accent, and pause —A.T.Quiller-Couch⟩ ⟨the *punctilious* honor of the Spanish gentleman —George Santayana⟩ SCRUPULOUS describes painstaking attention to the proper and fitting, the fair and ethical, or the exact and true ⟨it's simply that I owe my city the most *scrupulous* performance of duty in safeguarding it from disease —Sinclair Lewis⟩ ⟨more zealous about the triumph of their righteous cause than *scrupulous* about the justice of their arguments —M.R.Cohen⟩ Once a synonym of PUNCTILIOUS, PUNCTUAL now stresses fidelity to agreed-on times, as for appointments or payments ⟨I made Mr. Middleditch *punctual* before he died, though when he married me he was known far and wide as a man who could not be up to time —Compton Mackenzie⟩

care·ful·ly \-f(ə)lē, -i\ *adv* [ME, fr. OE *carfullīce*, fr. *carful* + *-līce* -ly] **:** in a careful manner **:** with care **:** with attention to precision or to details **:** CAUTIOUSLY

care·ful·ness \'==fəlnəs\ *n* -ES [ME, fr. OE *carfulnes*, fr. *carful* + *-nes* -ness] **:** the quality of being careful **:** close or steady attention (as to a task) **:** CAUTION, HEED, FORESIGHT

¹care·less \kə'les\ *also* **-R** *also* 'kal-\ *adj* [ME *careles*, fr. OE *carlēas*, fr. *caru* care + *-lēas* -less] **1 a :** free from care, anxiety, or responsibility ⟨~ infancy⟩ **b :** having no concern or interest **:** UNCONCERNED, UNMINDFUL ⟨raise all kinds of hope, ~ of the disillusionment that will certainly follow —Granville Hicks⟩ **2 :** not taking ordinary or proper care **:** NEGLECTFUL, HEEDLESS, INATTENTIVE, REGARDLESS ⟨my brother was too ~ of his charge —Shak.⟩ ⟨~ of hardship⟩ **3 :** not receiving or exhibiting care: **a** *obs* **:** not attended to or cared for **b :** done, made, or caused without attention to rule or system **:** UNSTUDIED, SPONTANEOUS ⟨her ~ refinement of manner —G.B. Shaw⟩ **c :** done, said, or written without due care **:** NEGLIGENT, HEEDLESS, SLOVENLY ⟨writing that is ~ and full of errors⟩ — **care·less·ly** *adv* — **care·less·ness** *n* -ES

²careless \"\ *also* **careless weed** *n* -ES [*careless* (uncared for)] **1 :** any of several herbs of the genus *Amaranthus* (esp. *A. palmeri*) **2 :** BURWEED MARSH ELDER

carelian *usu cap, var of* KARELIAN

carenage *var of* CAREENAGE

car·ene \'ka,rēn\ *n* -S [*Carum* (genus name of the caraway *Carum carvi*) + *-ene* — more at CARUM] **:** either of two liquid bicyclic terpenes $C_{10}H_{16}$ found esp. in some turpentine oils and pine oils and in the oil of an East Indian grass (*Cymbopogon iwarancusa*) and distinguished as 3-(or Δ^3-)carene and 4-(or Δ^4-)carene

cares *pl of* CARE, *pres 3d sing of* CARE

¹ca·ress \kə'res\ *n* -ES [F *caresse*, fr. It *carezza*, fr. *caro* dear, fr. L *carus* — more at CHARITY] **1 :** an act or expression of kindness or affection **:** ENDEARMENT ⟨he exerted himself to win by indulgence and ~*es* the hearts of all who were under his command —T.B.Macaulay⟩ **2 a :** a light stroking, rubbing, or patting **b :** KISS

²caress \"\ *vt* -ED/-ING/-ES [F *caresser*, fr. It *carezzare*, fr. *carezza* caress] **1 :** to treat with tokens of fondness, affection, or kindness **:** CHERISH ⟨the regiment was fed and ~*ed* at station after station —Stephen Crane⟩ **2 a :** to touch or stroke in a loving or endearing manner **:** FONDLE, EMBRACE, PET ⟨left hand . . . ~*es* the boy's face —Henry Adams⟩ **b :** to touch or affect as if with a caress ⟨echoes that ~ the ear⟩

caressing *adj* **:** touching with or as if with a caress ⟨the doctor's voice, soothing, ~, infinitely consoling —Ellen Glasgow⟩ — **ca·ress·ing·ly** *adv*

ca·ress·ive \kə'resiv\ *adj* **1 :** like a caress **:** CARESSING ⟨diminutives have a ~ character⟩ **2 :** given to caresses ⟨childishly ~⟩ — **ca·ress·ive·ly** *adv*

¹car·et \'karət *also* -'aa-, -'aə-, -'e(ə)-, -'ā-\ *n* -S [L, there is lacking, 3d pers. sing. pres. indic. of *carēre* to lack, be without — more at CASTE] **:** a mark made on written or printed matter to indicate the place where something is inserted or is to be inserted **:** an inverted v placed below the line or in the margin

²caret \"\ *vt* **careted** *or* **caretted**; **careted** *or* **caretted**; **careting** *or* **caretting**; **carets :** to indicate with a caret the place at which to insert (new matter) — usu. used with *in* or *into* ⟨~*ed* the revision into the manuscript⟩

caretaker \'=,==\ *n* -S **1 :** one that is placed usu. as occupant in charge of the upkeep, repairs, and protection of the house, estate, or farm of an owner who may be absent **2 :** one fulfilling the functions of office on a temporary or provisional basis ⟨a ~ government⟩

caretaking \'=,==\ *n* -S [*caretaker* + *-ing*] **:** the act or occupation of serving as a caretaker

ca·ret·ta \kə'red·ə\ *n, cap* [NL, fr. F *caret* hawksbill turtle, fr. Sp *carey*, fr. Taino] **:** a genus of marine turtles (family Chelonidae) comprising all the loggerhead turtles or in some classifications solely the common loggerhead (*C. caretta*)

ca·ret·to·che·lyd·i·dae \kə¦red·(,)ōkə'lidə,dē\ *n pl, cap* [NL, fr. *Carettochelyd-, Carettochelys*, type genus (fr. *caretta* + *-o-* + Gk *chelys* tortoise) + *-idae* — more at CHELYS] **:** a family of pleurodiran freshwater turtles including a New Guinea turtle (*Carettochelys insculpta*)

careworn \'=,=\ *adj* **:** showing the effect of grief or anxiety ⟨a ~ face⟩

car·ex \'ka(a),reks\ *n* [NL, fr. L, sedge; perh. akin to L *carrere* to card — more at CHARD] **1** *cap* **:** a genus of perennial grasslike herbs (family Cyperaceae) of very wide distribution and distinguished by having the seedlike achenes enclosed in a sac in the axil of a bract — see SEDGE **2** *pl* **car·i·ces** \'karə,sēz\ **:** any plant of the genus *Carex*

ca·rey \kə'rā\ *n* -S [AmerSp, fr. Sp, fr. Taino] **1 :** HAWKSBILL TURTLE **2 :** the tortoiseshell obtained from the hawksbill turtle

carf \'kärf\ *dial var of* KERF

carfare \'=,=\ *n* -S **:** fare for carrying a passenger on a streetcar or railroad

car·fax \'kär,faks, -ä,f-\ *n* -ES [ME *carfouk, carfuks*, modif. of AF *querrefourc*, fr. LL *quadrifurcum*] *Brit* **:** a place where four or more roads meet — used chiefly in place names

car ferry *n* **:** a ferry of special design for the transportation of railroad cars by water

car float *n* **:** a barge equipped with tracks on which railroad cars are moved in harbors and inland waterways

carfour *n* -S [MF *carrefour*, fr. LL *quadrifurcum*, neut. of *quadrifurcus* having four forks, fr. L *quadr-* + *-furcus* (fr. *furca* fork) — more at FORK] *obs* **:** CARFAX

¹car·fuf·fle \kär'fəfəl, kər-\ *vt* -ED/-ING/-S [Sc *car-* (fr. ScGael *car* turn, twist) + *fuffle*, v.] *Scot* **:** DISORDER, DISARRANGE, RUFFLE

²carfuffle \"\ *n* -S *Scot* **:** RUFFLE, AGITATION, DISORDER, FLURRY

car·ga \'kärgə\ *n* -S [Sp, lit., load] **:** a unit of weight usu. of a value about equal to 300 lbs. used in Mexico and certain other Spanish-American countries

car·ga·dor \¦kärgə¦dō(ə)r\ *n, pl* **cargado·res** \,==='dōrēz, -ōr-\ [AmerSp, fr. Sp, fr. *cargar* to load] **1 :** PORTER **2 :** STEVEDORE

cargason *or* **cargazon** *n* -S [Sp *cargazón*, aug. of *cargo*] *obs* **:** CARGO

car·go \'kär(,)gō, 'kå(,)-\ *n, pl* **cargoes** *or* **cargos** [Sp *cargo, carga* load, burden, charge, fr. *cargar* to load, fr. LL *carricare* — more at CHARGE] **:** the lading or freight of a ship, airplane, or vehicle **:** the goods, merchandise, or whatever is conveyed **:** LOAD, FREIGHT — usu. used of goods only and not of live animals or persons

cargo cult *n, often cap both Cs* **:** a religiopolitical movement among natives of various So. Pacific islands characterized by the messianic expectation of the return of their ancestors in ships or planes carrying cargoes of the products of modern civilization that will suffice for all native needs, render work unnecessary, and free natives from white control

cargo liner *n* **1 :** a ship that carries general cargo and usu. follows a fixed schedule **2 :** a transport plane that carries freight

cargo mill *n* **:** a sawmill with dockage facilities for direct loading on ships

car·hop \'kär,häp, 'kå,h-\ *n* -S [¹*car* + *-hop* (as in *bellhop*)] **:** a waiter at a drive-in who serves customers in their cars

car·i·ama \,karē'amə\ *n* [NL, fr. Pg, seriema, modif. of Tupi *çariama* — more at SERIEMA] **1** *cap* **:** a genus of long-legged So. American birds (order Gruiformes) having as sole recent representative the Brazilian cariama **2** -S **:** a bird (*Cariama cristata*) of southern Brazil or a closely related bird (*Chunga burmeisteri*) of northern Argentina, both being large long-legged birds with short wings and limited powers of flight that feed on berries, insects, and to some extent snakes and lizards and that are usu. regarded as related to the cranes and bustards though formerly sometimes included with the birds of prey — called also *seriema*; see CHUNGA, CRESTED CARIAMA

¹car·i·an \'ka(a)rēən, -er-, -ar-\ *n* -S *usu cap* [*Caria*, ancient division of SW Asia Minor (fr. L, fr. Gk *Karia*) + E *-an*] **1 :** a native or inhabitant of ancient Caria, a division of southwest Asia Minor **2 :** the ancient language of the Carians

²carian \"\ *adj, usu cap* **1 a :** of, relating to, or characteristic of Caria **b :** of, relating to, or characteristic of the people of Caria **2 :** of, relating to, or characteristic of the language of the Carians

car·ib \'karəb\ *n, pl* **carib** *or* **caribs** *usu cap* [NL *Caribes* (pl.), fr. Sp *caribe*, fr. 15th cent. Arawakan *caribe* (form recorded by Columbus in Haiti) — more at CANNIBAL] **1 a :** an Indian people of northern Brazil, the Guianas, Venezuela, Colombia, the Lesser Antilles, and the Caribbean coast of Honduras, Guatemala, and British Honduras **b :** a member of such people **2 :** the language of the Caribs

car·ib·al \'karəbəl\ *adj, usu cap* [prob. fr. Sp *caribal* — more at CANNIBAL] **:** of or relating to the Caribs

cari·ban \'karəbən, -,ban; kə'rēb-\ *n* -S *usu cap* [Sp *caribán*, fr. *caribe* Carib] **1 a :** a group of Amerindian peoples of northern So. America, the Lesser Antilles, and the Caribbean coast of Honduras, Guatemala, and British Honduras **b :** a member of any such peoples **2 :** the language family comprising the languages of the Cariban peoples

¹carib·be·an \¦karə¦bēən *also* ¦ker- *or* kə'ribē-\ *adj, usu cap* [NL *Caribaeus, Caribbaeus* (fr. *Caribes*) + E *-an*] **1 :** of, relating to, or characteristic of the Caribs **2 a :** of, relating to, or characteristic of the eastern and southern West Indies **b :** of, relating to, or characteristic of the Caribbean sea, which lies between the West Indies and Central America

²caribbean \"\ *n, pl* **caribbean** *or* **caribbeans** *usu cap* **:** CARIB 1

caribbean pine *n, usu cap C* **:** a timber tree (*Pinus caribaea*) of Florida, the Bahamas, and Cuba, having two or three very long leaves in each fascicle and cones with thick-edged scales tipped with slightly recurved prickles

car·ib·bee *or* **car·i·bee** \'karə(,)bē\ *n, pl* **caribbee** *or* **caribbees** *or* **caribee** *or* **caribees** *usu cap* [Sp or Pg *caribe*] **:** CARIB 1

ca·ri·be \kə'rēbē, -(,)bā\ *n* -S [AmerSp, fr. Sp, cannibal, Carib — more at CARIB] **:** any of several So. American freshwater fishes of the genus *Serrasalmus* (family Characidae) remarkable for their voracity, in spite of their small size often attacking and inflicting dangerous wounds upon men and large animals — called also *piranha*

carib grass *n, usu cap C* **:** a native West Indian grass (*Eriochloa polystachya*) grown in Florida and Texas for forage and resembling Para grass but finer-stemmed and leafier

car·i·bou \'karə,bü *also* -'e-\ *n, pl* **caribou** *or* **caribous** [CanF, of Algonquian origin; akin to Micmac *khalibu* caribou, lit., pawer, scratcher, Quinnipiac *maccarib*] **:** any of several large deer (genus *Rangifer*) of northern No. America that are related to the Old World reindeer and have large palmate antlers in both sexes, broad flat hooves, a heavy double coat, and short ears and tail — see BARREN GROUND CARIBOU, WOODLAND CARIBOU

caribou eskimo *n, usu cap C&E* [so called fr. the fact that they live chiefly from caribou] **:** an Eskimo of the Barren Grounds of northern Canada

caribou moss *n* **:** REINDEER MOSS

caric- *or* **carico-** *comb form* [NL *Caric-, Carex*] **:** carex **:** sedges ⟨*caricetum*⟩ ⟨*caricology*⟩

car·i·ca \'karəkə\ *n, cap* [NL, fr. L, a dried fig, fr. fem. of *caricus* Carian, fr. Gk *karikos*, fr. *Karia*, ancient division of Asia Minor + Gk *-ikos* -ic] **:** a genus (the type of the family Caricaceae) of chiefly tropical American trees — see PAPAYA

car·i·ca·ce·ae \,karə'kāsē,ē\ *n pl, cap* [NL, fr. *Carica*, type genus + *-aceae*] **:** a family of trees (order Parietales) native to tropical and subtropical America and Africa having milky juice, a rarely branched trunk, and large palmately lobed leaves and including the papaya and a few related plants — **car·i·ca·ceous** \¦==¦kāshəs\ *adj*

car·i·ca·tur·a·ble \¦karəkə¦chürəbəl\ *adj* **:** suitable for caricature **:** having features easily caricatured

car·i·ca·tur·al \-ü(ə)rəl\ *adj* **:** like or having the characteristics of caricature

¹car·i·ca·ture \'karəkə,chü(ə)r, -üə, -rēk- *also* 'ker- *or* -,t(y)ü- *or* -kəchə(r)\ *n* -S [earlier *caricatura*, fr. It, affectation, caricature, lit., a loading, fr. *caricare* to load, fr. LL *carricare* — more at CHARGE] **1 a :** exaggeration by means of deliberate simplification and often ludicrous distortion of parts or characteristics ⟨the art of ~⟩ **b :** an instance of such caricature ⟨in her rambling and her idleness she might only be a ~ of herself, but in her silence and sadness she was the very reverse of all that she had been before —Jane Austen⟩ **2 :** a representation esp. in literature or art that has the qualities of caricature ⟨a series of satirical ~*s* of the faculty of a progressive college for women —Orville Prescott⟩ **3 :** a distortion so gross as to seem like caricature ⟨the kangaroo court a ~ of justice⟩

syn BURLESQUE, PARODY, TRAVESTY all indicate kinds of grotesque and exaggerated imitation. CARICATURE suggests ludicrous distortion of a peculiar feature ⟨*caricature* is a very special kind of portraiture, permitting extravagance and enunciating the awkward and uncomplimentary —*Christian Science Monitor*⟩ ⟨his *caricature* of the "gentleman" . . . is a biting sarcasm of the respectable, gentle, and polite bourgeois —*Commonweal*⟩ BURLESQUE is likely to imply humor sought or attained in imitation of the dignified, heavy, or grand ⟨ridiculing follies with a *burlesque* as riotous as that in *The Innocents Abroad* —Carl Van Doren⟩ ⟨he whipped off his old slouch hat with an air of gallantry which reminded Dorinda of the *burlesque* of some royal cavalier —Ellen Glasgow⟩ PARODY, like CARICATURE, involves the heightening of a peculiar feature and, like BURLESQUE, is likely to aim at humor. It may differ from the first in attempting less obvious and pictorial and more sustained and subtle imitation, from the second in aiming at a quieter, less boisterous effect ⟨Dryden's method here is something very near to *parody;* he applies vocabulary, images, and ceremony which arouse epic associations of grandeur —T.S.Eliot⟩ ⟨played in the manner of a *parody*, an intention which . . . cannot possibly be recognized by any hearer who has not previously been warned of it —Eric Blom⟩ TRAVESTY is perhaps the strongest word in the group. It may apply to any palpably extravagant imitation designed to mock and consistently sustained, esp. in stylistic matters ⟨in producing *Androcles and the Lion* his motion picture executor has already managed to make a public *travesty* of his work —*New Republic*⟩ All these terms may be used in reference to a situation that contains grotesque distortion ⟨a *caricature* of the truth⟩ ⟨a *burlesque* on religious observations⟩ ⟨a *parody* of justice⟩ ⟨a *travesty* on decent marriage⟩

²caricature \"\ *vt* -ED/-ING/-S **:** to make or draw a caricature of **:** represent in caricature ⟨he could draw an ill face or ~ a good one —George Lyttelton⟩

caricature plant *n* [so called fr. the yellowish leaf blotches, often suggesting a human profile] **:** an East Indian ornamental foliage plant (*Graptophyllum pictum*) of the family Acanthaceae

car·i·ca·tur·ist \¦===chü(ə)rəst *also* -¦t(y)ü-\ *n* -S **:** one that makes caricatures

carices *pl of* CAREX

carico- — see CARIC-

car·id \'karəd\ *n* -S [NL *Carides*] **:** a crustacean of the tribe Carides

ca·ri·da \¦kə'rīdə, 'karədə\ *or* **ca·rid·ea** \kə'ridēə\ *syn of* CARIDES

ca·rid·e·an \kə'ridēən\ *adj* **:** of or relating to the Carides ⟨~ prawn⟩

car·i·deer \'karə,di(ə)r\ *n, pl* **carideer** [*cari*bou + rein*deer*] **:** a hybrid between the caribou and the reindeer

car·i·des \kə'rī(,)dēz, 'karə,dēz\ *n pl, cap* [NL, fr. L, pl. of *carid-, caris*] **:** a tribe of decapod crustaceans (suborder Natantia) containing most shrimps, prawns, and related forms in which the lateral plates of the second abdominal segment overlap those of the first — **car·i·doid** \'karə,dȯid\ *adj or n*

car·ies \'ka(ə)rēz, -e(ə)r-,-aa-,-är-, -riz *also* -rē,ēz\ *n, pl* **caries** [L, decay; akin to Gk *kēr* death, Skt *śṛṇāti* he breaks, crushes] **:** the decay of animal tissues: **a :** ulceration and destruction of bone ⟨~ of the spine⟩ **b :** tooth decay; *specif* **:** the pathological process of localized destruction of tooth tissue by microorganisms

car·i·gnane \¦karə¦nyan, -än, 'karə̇gən\ *n* -S *usu cap* [F, fr. *Carignan*, town near Bordeaux, France] **:** a French red wine produced from a grape grown primarily in the departments of Hérault and Pyrénées-Orientales

car·i·jo·na \,karə'hōnə\ *n, pl* **carijona** *or* **carijonas** *usu cap* [Sp, fr. Carib *carihona* people] **1 a :** a Cariban people of southeastern Colombia **b :** a member of such people **2 :** the language of the Carijona people

car·il·lon \'karə,län *also* -er- *or* -ələn *or* -rē,yän *or* kårēyōn *or (esp Brit)* kə'rilyən\ *n* -S [F, alter. of OF *quarregnon*, fr. LL *quaternion-, quaternio* set of four; prob. fr. its consisting in early times of four bells — more at QUATERNION] **1 a :** a set of fixed bells pitched in chromatic series of at least two octaves and sounded by hammers controlled by a keyboard, each bell being tuned to harmonize with the others — compare CHIME **b :** a mixture stop in a pipe organ imitating a carillon **c :** an instrument imitating a carillon by electronically amplifying the sounds made by striking small variously shaped metallic bodies — called also *electronic carillon* **2 a :** a composition for the carillon **b :** a composition suggesting the sound of bells **3 :** BELL TOWER, CAMPANILE

car·il·lon·ic \¦karə¦länik\ *adj* **:** of, produced by, or imitating a carillon

car·il·lon·is·tic \¦karə(,)lä¦nistik, -lə¦- *also* kə¦rilyə¦n-\ *adj* **:** having the characteristics of, suitable for, or produced by a carillon

car·il·lon·neur *also* **car·il·lo·neur** \¦karə(,)lä¦nər, -ələ¦- *also* ¦karē(,)yä¦- *or* kə¦rilyə¦-\ *n* -S [F *carillonneur*, fr. *carillon* + *-eur* -er] **:** a carillon player — called also *bellmaster*

ca·ri·na \kə'rīnə, -'rē-\ *n, pl* **carinas** \-nəz\ *or* **cari·nae** \-'rī,nē -'rē,nī\ [NL, fr. L, keel — more at CAREEN] **:** any of various keel-shaped anatomical structures, ridges, or processes: as **a :** a ridge on the lower surface of the fornix of the brain — called also *carina fornicis* **b :** the ventral distal part of the vagina — called also *carina urethralis, carina vaginae* **c :** the part of a papilionaceous flower that encloses the stamens and pistil and consists of two commonly united petals **d :** the median ridge on the breastbone of most birds **:** KEEL **e :** a thickened ridge on the median dorsal plate of a barnacle **f :** any of several reinforcing ridges on the exoskeleton of an insect

carina c: carina and calyx of bristly locust (standard and wings removed)

ca·ri·nal \kə'rīnᵊl, -'rē-, 'karən-\ *adj* [NL *carina* + E *-al*] **:** relating to or resembling a carina

carinal canal *n* **:** LACUNA 2c (2)

car·i·nar·ia \,karə'na(a)rēə\ *n, cap* [NL, fr. L *carina* + NL *-aria*; fr. the shape of the shell] **:** a genus of oceanic heteropod mollusks having a thin glassy bonnet-shaped shell covering only the nucleus and gills

car·i·na·tae \,karə'nād·,ē, -ād-\ *n pl, cap* [NL, fr. *carina* + L *-atae* (fem. pl. of *-atus* -ate)] *in old classifications* **:** a division of Aves including all the Neognathae together with the tinamous or with these and the penguins

¹car·i·nate \'karə,nāt, -,nət\ *also* **car·i·nat·ed** \-,nād·əd\ *adj* [L *carinatus*, fr. *carina* keel + *-atus* -ate] **:** shaped like the keel or prow of a ship **:** KEELED, RIDGED ⟨a ~ sepal⟩ ⟨a ~ scale⟩ — compare RATITE

²carinate \"\ *n* -S [NL *Carinatae*] **:** a bird with a keeled breastbone **:** one of the Carinatae

carinate fold *n* **:** a closely compressed almost isoclinal anticline or syncline

car·i·na·tion \,karə'nāshən\ *n* -S **1 :** the quality or state of being carinate **2 :** a carinate formation

caring *pres part of* CARE

ca·rin·i·a·na \kə,rinē'ānə, -'a-, -'ā-\ *n, cap* [NL, irreg. fr. L *carina* keel — more at CAREEN] **:** a genus of tropical So. American timber trees (family Lecythidaceae) having small flowers, the lid of the fruit joined with the woody column, and seeds with one long lateral wing — see COLOMBIAN MAHOGANY, JEQUITIBA

ca·rin·i·form \kə'rinə,fȯ(ə)rm\ *adj* [NL *carina* + E *-iform*] **:** having the form of a carina

ca·rin·thi·an \kə'rin(t)thēən\ *adj, usu cap* [*Carinthia*, province in Austria + E *-an*] **:** of or relating to the Austrian province of Carinthia

ca·rin·u·la \kə'rinyələ\ *or* **car·i·nule** \'karə,n(y)ül\ *n* -S [NL *carinula*, dim. of *carina*] **:** a small carina — **ca·rin·u·late** \kə'rinyə,lāt, -,lət\ *adj*

cario- *comb form* [*caries*] **:** caries ⟨*cariogenic*⟩ ⟨*cariostatic*⟩

car·i·o·ca \,karē'ōkə *also* -er-\ *n* -S [Pg, fr. Tupi, fr. *cari* white + *oca* house] **1** *usu cap* **:** a native or resident of Rio de Janeiro **2 a :** the samba adapted to ballroom dancing **b :** the music for such a dance

car·i·o·gen·ic \¦ka(a)rēō¦jenik\ *adj* [*cario-* + *-genic*] **:** conducive to the development of caries

car·i·ole *or* **car·ri·ole** \'karē,ōl\ *n* -S [F *carriole*, fr. OProv *carriola* small two-wheeled carriage, dim. of *carri* chariot, fr. (assumed) VL *carrium*, fr. L *carrus* vehicle — more at CAR] **1 :** a light four-wheel open or covered one-horse carriage **2 :** a light covered cart **3 :** a dog-drawn toboggan

car·i·ous \'ka(a)rēəs, -'er-, -'är-\ *adj* [L *cariosus*, fr. *caries* decay + *-osus* -ous — more at CARIES] **1 :** relating to or affected with caries ⟨a ~ tooth⟩ **2 :** ROTTING, DECAYING ⟨~ timbers⟩

car·i·pu·na \,karə'pünə\ *n, pl* **caripuna** *or* **caripunas** *usu cap* [prob. fr. Carib *karipona*, fr. *kari-* (fr. *ka* sky, spirit) + *-po* at + *-na* group] **1 a :** a Panoan people of Brazil and Bolivia **b :** a member of such people **2 :** the language of the Caripuna people

car·i·ri \,karə¦rē\ *n, pl* **cariri** *or* **cariris** *usu cap* [Pg, of AmerInd origin] **1 a :** an Indian people of eastern Brazil **b :** a member of such people **2 :** the language of the Cariri people

-car·is \'ka(a)rəs, -e(ə)r-, -aar-, -är-\ *n comb form* [NL, fr. L *caris*, a kind of sea crab, fr. Gk *karis*; perh. akin to Gk *kara* head — more at CEREBRAL] **:** shrimp **:** prawn — in generic names of crustacea ⟨Echino*caris*⟩

ca·ris·sa \kə'risə\ *n* [NL] **1** *cap* **:** a large genus of spiny shrubs (family Apocynaceae) found in tropical Africa, Asia, and Australia **2** -S **:** any plant of the genus *Carissa* **3** *also* **carissa plum** -S **:** the plumlike fruit of a plant of the genus *Carissa* — see NATAL PLUM

car·i·tas \'karə,tas, 'kärə,täs\ *n* [LL — more at CHARITY] **:** CHARITY 1

car·i·ta·tive \'karə,tād·iv, -ətətiv\ *adj* [ML *caritativus*, fr. LL *caritat-, caritas* + L *-ivus* -ive] **:** charitable in nature or tendency ⟨the ~ principle of Christianity⟩

car·i·tive \'karəd·iv\ *adj* [L *caritus* (past part. of *carēre* to be without) + E *-ive* — more at CASTE] **:** ABESSIVE

ca·ri·us method \'kärēəs-, -a(a)r-\ *n, usu cap C* [after G. Ludwig *Carius* †1875 Ger. chemist] **:** a method for determining halogens, sulfur, and phosphorus in organic compounds by heating them in sealed glass tubes with fuming nitric acid in a special furnace, the glass tubes being enclosed in iron tubes to avoid danger from explosion

¹cark \'kärk\ *vb* -ED/-ING/-S [ME *carken*, lit., to load, burden, fr. ONF *carquier*, fr. LL *carricare* — more at CHARGE] *vt* **:** to burden with care or anxiety **:** VEX, WORRY, TROUBLE ⟨fate had not smiled on him . . . he was beset by ~*ing* troubles and anxieties —Max Beerbohm⟩ **~** *vi* **1 :** to be anxious or troubled **:** FRET ⟨a covetous man . . . ~*ing* about his bags —Isaac Barrow⟩ **2 :** to labor anxiously ⟨why for sluggards ~ and moil? —Charles Kingsley⟩

²cark \"\ n -s [ME, lit., load, burden, fr. ONF *carque*, fr. *carquier*, v.] **1 :** something that burdens the spirit **:** TROUBLE ⟨its artless advocacy of freedom from ~ and care —*Harper's*⟩ **2 :** a troubled state of mind **:** DISTRESS ⟨by ~ and care deranged —Robert Browning⟩

car knocker *n* **:** one that taps or knocks the wheels of a railroad car to check their soundness **:** one that checks the running gear of a train **:** a car inspector **:** a car repairman

¹carl *or* **carle** \'kärl, -rəl\ *n* -s [ME, fr. OE *-carl*, fr. ON *karl* man, man of the common people; akin to OE *ceorl* man, man of the common people — more at CHURL] **1 :** a man of the common people **:** WORKER, FARMER, CRAFTSMAN **2** *now dial* **:** a base or lowbred fellow **:** CHURL, BOOR — used as a term of contempt **3** *now Scot* **:** a niggardly man **:** PINCHPENNY **4** *chiefly Scot* **:** FELLOW, LAD

²carl *vi* -ED/-ING/-S [prob. fr. ¹*carl*] *obs* **:** to behave churlishly **:** SNARL

carlacue *var of* CURLICUE

car·let \'kärlət\ *n* -s [F *carrelet*, dim. of OF *carrel*, *quarrel* square-headed arrow for an arbalest — more at QUARREL] **:** a 3-square single-cut file used by combmakers

carl·ie \'kärli\ *n* -s [¹*carl* + *-ie*] *Scot* **:** a man of small stature

¹car·lin \'kärlən\ *or* **car·line** \", -,lēn\ *or* **car·li·no** \kär'lē(,)nō\ *n, pl* **carlins** *or* **carlines** \-nz\ *or* **car·li·ni** \-(,)nē\ [It *carlino*, after Charles (*Carlo*) of Anjou] **1 a :** a small silver coin of the kingdom of the Two Sicilies first struck in the 13th century **b :** any of several old Italian coins **2 :** a unit of value equivalent to a carlin

²carlin *var of* CARLING

car·li·na \kär'līnə, -ēnə\ *n* [NL, fr. ML, carline thistle, prob. fr. OIt — more at CARLINE THISTLE] **1** *cap* **:** a genus of herbs (family Compositae) of the Mediterranean region differing from the true thistles in having the outer involucral scales leaflike and spiny-toothed and the inner ones colored, raylike, and longer than the flowers **2** *pl* **carli·nae** \-ī(,)nē, -ē,nī\ **:** a plant of the genus *Carlina*

¹car·line *or* **car·lin** \'kärlən\ *n* -s [ME *kerling*, fr. ON, fr. *karl* man — more at CARL] *chiefly Scot* **:** WOMAN; *esp* **:** an old woman — often used contemptuously or disparagingly (as of a witch)

²carline *var of* CARLING

car line *n* **:** a street railway line

car·line thistle \'kärlən-, -,līn-\ *n* [MF *carline*, fr. OIt *carlina*, prob. irreg. fr. *cardo* thistle, fr. LL *cardus*, fr. L *carduus* — more at CHARD] **:** a plant of the genus *Carlina* (esp. *C. acaulis* or *C. vulgaris*)

¹car·ling \'kärliŋ, -lən\ *also* **car·lin** *or* **car·line** \-lən\ *n* -s [F *carlingue*, fr. ONF *calingue*, fr. ON *kerling*, lit., old woman — more at CARLINE] **:** a fore-and-aft member supporting a deck of a ship or framing a deck opening where the beams have been cut — usu. used in pl.

²carling *pres part of* CARL

car·lings *or* **car·lins** \'kärlənz\ *n pl* [*Care* (*Sunday*), the fifth Sunday in Lent, when they were traditionally eaten in the north of England + *-ling*] *dial Eng* **:** parched peas

carlino *var of* CARLIN

carl·ish \'kärlish\ *adj* [ME, fr. ¹*carl* + *-ish*] **:** CHURLISH

car·lisle \(')kär¦līl, -ä¦l-, kə(r)'l-, -īəl\ *n* -s *usu cap* [short for *Carlisle hook*, prob. fr. the name *Carlisle*] **:** a fishhook of short-curved pattern — see FISHHOOK illustration

carlisle table *n, usu cap C* [fr. *Carlisle*, England, where the statistics were gathered] **:** a mortality table for the years 1779–87

car·lism \'kär,lizəm\ *n* -s *usu cap* [Sp *carlismo*, fr. Don *Carlos* María Isidro de Borbón †1855 pretender to the throne of Spain + Sp *-ismo* -ism] **:** adherence to Don Carlos of Spain or his successors or to Carlist principles, plans, or claims

car·list \'kärləst\ *n* -s *usu cap* [Sp *carlista*, fr. Don *Carlos* + *-ista* -ist] **:** a supporter of Don Carlos or his successors whose claims to the Spanish throne were annulled by repeal of the Salic law of succession in 1829

carload \'=,=\ *n* **1 :** a load that fills a car, esp. a freight car **2 :** the minimum number of tons required for shipping at carload rates — abbr. *CL*

carloading \'=,==\ *n* -s **:** the amount of freight loaded into freight cars during a specified period — usu. used in pl. ⟨~*s* increased during October⟩

carload rate *n* **:** a rate per hundred pounds or per ton for large shipments lower than that quoted for less-than-carload lots of the same class

¹carlot *n* -s [dim. of ¹*carl*] *obs* **:** CHURL, BOOR

²carlot \'=,=\ *n* -s [¹*car* + *lot*] **:** a shipment of freight of the minimum amount required to secure the carload rate

car·lo·vin·gi·an \¦kärlō¦vinj(ē)ən, -äl-, -lə-\ *adj, usu cap* [F *carlovingien*, prob. blend of obs. F *carlien* Carolingian (irreg. fr. ML *Carolus* Charles) and F *mérovingien* Merovingian] **:** CAROLINGIAN

car·low \'kär(,)lō\ *adj, usu cap* [fr. *Carlow*, county in Ireland] **:** of or from County Carlow, Ireland **:** of the kind or style prevalent in County Carlow

car·lo·witz \'kärlə,wits\ *n* -ES *usu cap* [G *karlowitzer*, fr. *Karlowitz* (now *Karlovci Sremski*), town in Yugoslavia where it is made] **:** a strong sweet red wine

¹carls \'kär(ə)lz\ *n pl* [by shortening] *dial Eng* **:** CARLINGS

²carls *pl of* CARL, *pres 3d sing of* CARL

carl·ton table \'kärltᵊn-, -tən-\ *n, usu cap C* [fr. *Carlton* House, onetime London residence of the prince of Wales, for which it was designed] **:** a writing table with compartments and drawers on the top

car·lu·do·vi·ca \¦kär,lüdə'vēkə, -īkə\ *n, cap* [NL, after Charles IV (*Carolus*) †1819 king of Spain, and María Luisa (*Ludovica*) †1819 his queen] **:** a genus of tropical American erect or climbing palmlike plants (family Cyclanthaceae) differing from the palms in having tetramerous flowers and many-seeded fruit — see JIPIJAPA

¹car·lyl·e·an *also* **car·lyl·i·an** *or* **car·lyle·i·an** \(')kär¦līlēən, -ä¦l-, kə(r)'l-, -īlyən\ *adj, usu cap* [Thomas *Carlyle* + E *-an* or *-ian*] **:** of, relating to, or resembling Thomas Carlyle or his writings — compare CARLYLISM

²carlylean *also* **carlylian** *or* **carlyleian** \"\ *n* -s *usu cap* **:** a student of Thomas Carlyle or a follower of his beliefs

car·lyl·ese \(¦)kär,lī¦lēz, -ä,l-, -ēs, kär'lī,l-, kä'l-; kə(r)¦lī|-\ *n, usu cap* [Thomas *Carlyle* + E *-ese*] **:** Carlylean use of language — often used of style imitative of Carlyle's literary excesses

car·lyl·ism \(')kär¦lī,lizəm, -ä¦l-, kə(r)'l-\ *n* -s *usu cap* [Thomas *Carlyle* †1881 Scot. essayist and historian + E *-ism*] **1 :** the characteristic teachings, ideas, or opinions of Thomas Carlyle who arraigned modern society and emphasized the need for strong leaders **2 :** the literary style or a literary mannerism characteristic of Thomas Carlyle whose writings are marked by long and irregular sentence constructions, neologisms, and Germanisms

car·ma·gnole \¦kärman¦yōl\ *n* -s [F, fr. F dial. (Dauphiné) *carmagnola* jacket worn by peasants on festive occasions, fr. *Carmagnola*, town in northwestern Italy where the jacket presumably originated] **1 :** a lively song popular at the time of the first French Revolution **2 :** a street dance in a meandering course to the tune of the carmagnole

carm·al·um \kär'maləm\ *n* -s [*carminic* + *alum*] **:** a stain composed of carminic acid, alum, and water for use in microscopy

car·man \'kärmən, 'käm-\ *n, pl* **carmen 1 :** one who drives or conveys goods in a car or cart **:** CARTER **2 :** a motorman or conductor on an electric railway **3 :** a worker who handles or guides the handling of materials conveyed in cars (as in a mine, mill, or factory) **4 :** a skilled workman who performs one or more operations in the building, repairing, dismantling, maintaining, and inspection of railroad cars at a station, shop, or yard

car·ma·ni·an \kär'mānēən, -nyən\ *n* -s *usu cap* [L *Carmanus* Carmanian (fr. Gk *Karmanos*) + E *-ian*] **:** a member of an ancient people that prob. lived north of the Persian gulf

car·mar·then·shire \kär'märthən,shi(ə)r, -,shər\ *or* **car·marthen** *adj, usu cap* [fr. *Carmarthenshire*, or the county of *Carmarthen*, Wales] **:** of or from the county of Carmarthen, Wales **:** of the kind or style prevalent in Carmarthen

carmathian *usu cap, var of* QARMATIAN

car·mel·ite \'kärmə,līt, 'kám-, *usu* -īd· + V\ *n* -s *usu cap, often attrib* [ME, fr. ML *carmelita*, fr. *Carmel* (*Mons*) Mount Carmel, Palestine, where the order was founded + L *-ita* -ite] **:** a member of the Roman Catholic mendicant Order of Our Lady of Mount Carmel founded in the 12th century **:** WHITE FRIAR

car·men \'kärmən\ *n, pl* **carmi·na** \-mənə\ [L, fr. *canere* to sing — more at CHANT] **:** SONG, POEM, INCANTATION

car·met·ta \kär'med·ə\ *n* -s [¹*carmine* + It *-etta* (dim. suffix)] **:** vermilion or a color resembling it

car-mile \'=¦=\ *n* **:** a statistical unit denoting one mile traveled by one railroad car and used in comparing freight earnings or costs — compare BUS-MILE

car mileage *n* **1 :** car-miles used as a basis by which a railroad reimburses another railroad or private car owner for the use of a car **2 :** the amount paid for the use of a car on a mileage basis — compare PER DIEM

¹car·min·a·tive \kär'minəd·iv, 'kärmə,nād·-\ *adj* [F *carminatif*, fr. L *carminatus* (past part. of *carminare* to card, fr. *carrere* to card) + F *-if* -ive — more at CHARD] **:** expelling gas from the alimentary canal **:** relieving colic, griping, or flatulence

²carminative \"\ *n* -s **:** a carminative agent

¹car·mine \'kärmən, 'kám-, -,mīn *also* -,mēn\ *n* -s [F *carmin*, fr. ML *carminium*, irreg. fr. Ar *qirmiz* kermes + L *minium* — more at CRIMSON, MINIUM] **1 a :** a vivid red lake consisting essentially of an aluminum salt of carminic acid made from cochineal usu. by treatment with alum and used as a biological stain and as coloring in foods, drugs, and cosmetics — see DYE table I (under *Natural Red 4*) **b :** any of certain other coloring matters (as indigo carmine) **2** *or* **carmine lake :** a vivid red that is bluer and darker than apple red, bluer and duller than pimento or Castilian red, bluer and less strong than madder crimson, and bluer and darker than scarlet — called also *animal rouge, lake, Munich lake, Roman lake, Venetian lake, Vienna lake*

²carmine \"\ *vt* -ED/ -ING/ -S **:** to make carmine in color **:** add or apply carmine to

car·mi·nette \¦kärmə¦net\ *n* -s [¹*carmine* + *-ette*] **:** CARMETTA

car·min·ic \(')kär¦minik\ *adj* [ISV *carmine* + *-ic*] **:** relating to or derived from carmine

carminic acid *n* [ISV *carminic* + *acid*] **:** a red crystalline anthraquinone dye $C_{22}H_{20}O_{13}$ best known as the essential coloring matter of cochineal and used chiefly as a biological stain

car·min·ite \'kärmə,nīt\ *n* -s [*carmine* + *-ite*] **:** a mineral $PbFe_2(AsO_4)_2(OH)_2$ consisting of a carmine arsenate of lead and iron

car·moi·sin \¦kärm,wä¦zēn, (')kär¦mȯizᵊn\ *n* -s [prob. fr. G *karmoisin* carmine, alter. (influenced by F *cramoisi* crimson) of *karmesin*, fr. obs. It *carmesino*, modif. of Ar *qirmizī* kermes-colored, fr. *qirmiz* kermes — more at CRIMSON] **:** AZO RUBINE

car movement *n* **:** the total number of miles traveled by cars on a given railroad system during a given period expressed in car-miles

carn *var of* CAIRN

car·na·cian \(')kär¦nāshən\ *adj, usu cap* [*Carnac*, town in Brittany, France, the locality of its type station + E *-ian*] **:** of or relating to a late period in neolithic culture characterized by many-chambered dolmens

car·nage \'kärnij, 'kán-, -nēj\ *n* -s [MF, fr. ML *carnaticum* tribute consisting of animals or meat, fr. L *carn-*, *caro*] **1 :** the flesh of slain animals or men **:** a heap of dead bodies ⟨a multitude of dogs came to feast on the ~ —T.B.Macaulay⟩ **2 :** great destruction of life (as in battle) **:** great bloodshed **:** SLAUGHTER, BUTCHERY, MASSACRE ⟨appeals to put a stop to the ~ of war⟩

car·nal \'kärnᵊl, 'kán-\ *adj* [ME, fr. ONF or LL; ONF, fr. LL *carnalis* (trans. of Gk *sarkikos*), fr. L *carn-*, *caro* flesh; akin to Gk *keirein* to cut — more at SHEAR] **1 a :** BODILY, CORPOREAL ⟨armed against ghostly as well as ~ attack —Bram Stoker⟩ ⟨~ interment⟩ **b :** consanguineous and bodily in relationship ⟨the ~ mother of Christ⟩ **c** *obs* **:** BLOODTHIRSTY **2 a :** marked by sexuality that is often frank, crude, and unrelieved by higher emotions ⟨~ infatuation —T.S.Eliot⟩ **b :** relating to or given to crude bodily pleasures ⟨gluttony and other ~ traits⟩ **3 :** UNSPIRITUAL: **a :** TEMPORAL ⟨the superiority of the spiritual and eternal over the ~ —H.O.Taylor⟩ **b :** WORLDLY ⟨should abstain from singing vain and ~ ballads —Charles Kingsley⟩ **c :** FLESHY, SENSUAL ⟨with red and bloated cheeks and ~ eyes —Nathaniel Hawthorne⟩

syn FLESHLY, SENSUAL, ANIMAL: CARNAL, once equivalent to *bodily* or *physical*, now refers almost exclusively to sexual or other sensual actions or interests ⟨Barbara Villiers . . . is the most unpleasant of Charles II's mistresses . . . he was besotted by her purely *carnal* attractions —*Times Lit. Supp.*⟩ FLESHLY is close to CARNAL in meaning but less severe and sometimes a little apologetic in suggestion ⟨punishments were set for the *fleshly* sins of monks and nuns and clergy —H.O.Taylor⟩ SENSUAL may simply indicate gratification of any bodily desire or pleasure ⟨his feet and hands were always cold and there was for him an almost *sensual* satisfaction to be had from . . . letting the hot sun beat down on him —Sherwood Anderson⟩ Usu. it indicates concentration on bodily satisfaction and absence of anything intellectual or spiritual ⟨it ceases to be sensuous and becomes *sensual*. This isolation of sense is not characteristic of esthetic objects but of such things as narcotics, sexual orgasms, and gambling —John Dewey⟩ Often it implies gross sexuality ⟨a coarse heavy face, loose-featured, red, and *sensual* —Thomas Wolfe⟩ ANIMAL, often without derogation, simply indicates bodily or sentient characteristics common to both man and animal or traits resembling those found in animals rather than man ⟨the state in his view is not merely a convenient machinery that raises a man above his *animal* wants —G. L. Dickinson⟩ ⟨he taught the boy boxing . . . and superintended the direction of his *animal* vigor —George Meredith⟩

carnal abuse *n* **:** genital contact between a male and a female minor with or without penetration and with or without the consent of the female; *broadly* **:** rape esp. of a female child

car·nal·ist \-nᵊləst\ *n* -s **:** one given to sensual esp. sexual pleasures

car·nal·i·ty \kär'nalədē, kä'n-, -ətē, -i\ *n* -ES [ME *carnalite*, fr. LL *carnalitas*, fr. L *carnalis* carnal + *-itas* -ity] **1 :** the quality or state of being flesh ⟨matter is not intrinsically corrupt, and ~ is not a sin in Hebrew thought —O.J.Baab⟩ **2 :** fleshly lust or its indulgence **:** SENSUALITY **3 :** indulgence of the senses **:** WORLDLINESS ⟨he looked upon my . . . fight for flesh-colored silk stockings as a form of incomprehensible feminine ~ —Hannah Smith⟩ **4 :** a carnal act; *specif* **:** SEXUAL INTERCOURSE ⟨dancing has often been denounced as disposing to ~⟩

car·nal·ize \'kärnᵊl,īz, 'kán-\ *vt* -ED/ -ING/ -S **:** to make carnal **:** SENSUALIZE

carnal knowledge *n* **:** SEXUAL INTERCOURSE — usu. used of acts involving a female child, the precise legal interpretation varying with different jurisdictions

car·nall·ite \'kärnᵊl,īt\ *n* -s [G *carnallit*, fr. Rudolf von *Carnall* †1874 Ger. mining engineer + G *-it* -ite] **:** a mineral $KMgCl_3.6H_2O$ consisting of a hydrous potassium-magnesium chloride occurring commonly as white or reddish deliquescent masses and useful as a source of potassium

car·nal·ly \-nᵊlē, -i\ *adv* **:** in a carnal manner

car·nal·ness \-nᵊlnəs\ *n* -ES **:** CARNALITY

car·nap·tious \(')kär¦napshəs, kər'n-\ *adj* [perh. fr. *ker-* + *knap* (to bite) + connective *-t-* + *-ious*] *dial chiefly Brit* **:** bad-tempered

car·nar·ia \kär'na(a)rēə\ *n pl, cap* [NL, fr. L *carn-*, *caro* flesh + NL *-aria*] *in old classifications* **:** an order of mammals including the Carnivora, Insectivora, Chiroptera, and carnivorous marsupials

¹car·nas·si·al \(')kär¦nasēəl\ *adj* [modif. (influenced by *-al*) of F *carnassier* carnivorous, fr. (assumed) OProv *carnassier* (whence Prov *carnassie*), fr. *carnasso* meat in plenty, fr. *carn* flesh, fr. L *carn-*, *caro*] **:** of, relating to, or being teeth of a carnivorous mammal that are larger and longer than adjacent teeth and adapted for cutting rather than tearing **:** SECTORIAL ⟨the last premolars of the upper jaw and first true molars of the lower constitute the ~ teeth of most carnivores⟩

²carnassial \"\ *n* -s **:** a carnassial tooth

car·nate \'kär,nāt, -,nət\ *adj* [by shortening] **:** INCARNATE

car·na·tion \kär'nāshən, kä'n-, *attrib* (')=¦=\ *n* -s [MF, color or complexion of a person, fr. OIt *carnagione*, fr. *carne* flesh, fr. L *carn-*, *caro* — more at CARNAL] **1 a :** the variable color of human flesh averaging the color seed pearl **b :** CARNATION RED **2 :** any of the numerous cultivated usu. double-flowered varieties of the clove pink (*Dianthus caryophyllus*) orig. flesh-colored but now found in many color variations — compare ²BIZARRE, ²FLAKE 3, PICOTEE, PINK **3 :** PRIDE OF BARBADOS

carnation 2

car·na·tioned \(')=¦=shənd\ *adj* **:** made red or ruddy ⟨her cheeks ~ by the wind —Thomas Hardy⟩

carnation red *n* **:** a moderate red that is bluer and paler than cerise, claret (sense 3a), average strawberry (sense 2a), Turkey red, or Harvard crimson (sense 1)

carnation rose *n* **:** a strong pink that is bluer and less strong than coral (sense 3c), bluer and stronger than rose d'Althaea, and bluer, lighter, and stronger than sea pink

carnation rust *n* **:** a disease of carnations caused by a rust fungus (*Uromyces caryophyllinus*) characterized by discoloration and spotting of the leaves and the production of chocolate-brown powdery spore masses

car·nau·ba \kär'nȯbə, ,kärnə'übə *also* kär'nübə *or* -'naübə\ *n* -s [Pg] **1 :** a fan palm (*Copernicia cerifera*) of Brazil that has an edible root and is the source of a useful leaf fiber and a brittle yellowish wax **2 :** CARNAUBA WAX

carnauba wax *n* **:** a yellowish to dark-brownish gray hard brittle high-melting wax obtained from the surface of leaves of the carnauba palm and used chiefly in polishes (as for floors, furniture, and shoes), in coatings for paper (as carbon paper), in phonograph records, and in pharmaceutical and cosmetic preparations

car·nau·bic acid \(')=¦=bik-, ¦==¦übik-\ *n* [ISV *carnaubic* (fr. *carnauba* + *-ic*) + *acid*; orig. formed as G *karnaubasäure*] **:** a crystalline fatty acid that is found as esters and esp. in carnauba wax and wool fat and that may be a mixture of acids

car·neau \(')kär¦nō\ *n, pl* **car·neaux** \-ō(z)\ *also* **carneaus** \-ōz\ *usu cap* [F] **:** a pigeon of a popular stocky close-feathered utility breed producing large squabs freely, the preferred colors being reddish and white

car·ne·giea \kär'negēə\ *n, cap* [NL, fr. Andrew *Carnegie* †1919 Am. industrialist and humanitarian] **:** a monotypic genus of cacti consisting of the saguaro

car·ne·gie·ite \'kärnəgē,īt, kär'neg-\ *n* -s [Andrew *Carnegie* + E *-ite*; fr. the fact that it was synthesized at the Carnegie Institution of Washington, D.C., founded by Andrew Carnegie] **:** an artificial mineral $NaAlSiO_4$ consisting of sodium aluminum silicate and related to feldspar

car·ne·gie unit \'kärnə¦gē-, -ān- *also* (')kär¦negē- *or* -ä¦n- *or* kə(r)'n-\ *n, usu cap C* [so called fr. the fact that it was first defined by the Carnegie Foundation for the Advancement of Teaching, founded by Andrew Carnegie] **:** the credit given for the successful completion of a year's study of one subject in a secondary school — called also *unit*

car·ne·lian \kär'nēlyən, kä'n-\ *n* -s [alter. (prob. influenced by L *carn-*, *caro* flesh) of *cornelian*; fr. its flesh-red color] **1 :** a chalcedony that has a clear deep red, flesh red, or reddish white color, that polishes well, and that being hard and tough is much used for seals **2 :** COPPER 5a

carnelian red *n* **:** a moderate reddish orange that is yellower and lighter than flamingo and yellower and paler than crab apple

car·ne·ol *or* **car·ne·ole** \'kärnē,ōl, -ōl\ *n* -s [prob. fr. ML *carneolus*, prob. fr. LL *carneus*, fr. *carn-*, *caro* flesh — more at CARNAL] **:** CARNELIAN 1

car·net \(')kär¦nā\ *n* -s [F, lit., notebook, fr. MF *quernet*, fr. L *quaterni* group of four — more at QUIRE] **1 a :** a card issued to an aviator by the Fédération Aéronautique Internationale and designed to eliminate the necessity for his having a passport **b :** an international credit card for aviation fuel **2 :** a customs pass permitting an automobile free passage across national boundaries

¹car·ney *or* **car·ny** \'kärnē\ *vb* **carneyed** *or* **carnied**; **carneyed** *or* **carnied**; **carneying** *or* **carnying**; **carneys** *or* **carnies** [origin unknown] *Brit* **:** CAJOLE, WHEEDLE

²carney *var of* CARNY

carnie *var of* CARNY

car·ni·fex \'kärnə,feks\ *n, pl* **carnifexes** \-ksəz\ *or* **car·nif·i·ces** \kär'nifə,sēz, -ə,kās\ [L, fr. *carni-* (fr. *carn-*, *caro* flesh) + *-fex* (fr. *facere* to make) — more at CARNAL, DO] **:** EXECUTIONER; *specif* **:** the public executioner in ancient Rome

car·ni·fi·ca·tion \,kärnəfə'kāshən\ *n* -s [*carnify* + *-fication*] **1 :** the process by which lung tissue becomes converted into fibrous tissue as a result of unresolved pneumonia **2 :** the conversion of bread into flesh through transubstantiation

car·ni·fi·cial \¦kärnə¦fishəl\ *adj* [L *carnific-*, *carnifex* + E *-ial*] **:** of or relating to an executioner or a butcher ⟨a ~ knife⟩

car·ni·fy \'kärnə,fī\ *vb* -ED/-ING/-ES [*carni-* (fr. L *carn-*, *caro* flesh) + *-fy* — more at CARNAL] *vt* **:** to make or turn into flesh ~ *vi* **:** to undergo carnification

car·ni·o·lan \¦kärnē¦ōlən, (')kärn¦yō-\ *adj, usu cap* [*Carniola*, region in Yugoslavia + E *-an*] **:** of or relating to the former Austro-Hungarian crownland of Carniola or its later subdivisions

carniolan bee *n, usu cap C* [*Carniola*, region in southern Europe northeast of the head of the Adriatic sea + E *-an*] **:** a honeybee of a race characterized by grayish color, quiet disposition, and high honey production with minimal production of propolis and marked by a strong tendency to swarm

car·ni·tine \'kärnə,tēn\ *n* -s [ISV *carn-* (fr. G *karnin*, basic substance isolated fr. meat extract) + *-ite*, + *-ine*; orig. formed as G *karnitin*] **:** a white betaine $(CH_3)_3N^+CH_2CH(OH)CH_2COO^-$ that is found esp. in muscle tissue and is an essential food factor for certain insect larvae (as the mealworm) — called also *vitamin B_T*

car·ni·val \'kärnəvəl, 'kán-\ *n* -s *often attrib* [It *carnevale*, *carnovale*, alter. of OIt *carnelevare*, lit., removal of meat, fr. *carne* flesh (fr. L *carn-*, *caro*) + *levare* to raise, take away, fr. L — more at CARNAL, LEVER] **1 :** the season or festival of merrymaking and revelry before Lent observed esp. by Roman Catholics and orig. extending from the feast of the Epiphany to Ash Wednesday but now usu. confined to a few days just before Lent **:** SHROVETIDE — compare MARDI GRAS **2 a :** any merrymaking, feasting, or masquerading ⟨in a ~ mood⟩ **b :** a time of exuberance or of riotous excesses ⟨the ~ of spring⟩ **3 a :** a traveling enterprise consisting of such amusements as sideshows, games of chance, Ferris wheels, merry-go-rounds, and shooting galleries **:** CIRCUS **b :** an organized program of entertainment or exhibition **:** FESTIVAL ⟨a winter ~⟩ ⟨a book ~⟩

car·ni·val·esque \¦===¦esk\ *adj* [It *carnivalesco*, fr. *carnivale* + *-esco* -esque] **:** like or suggestive of a carnival ⟨Venice . . . is like a museum with ~ overtones —Truman Capote⟩

car·niv·o·ra \kär'niv(ə)rə\ *n pl* [NL, fr. L, neut. pl. of *carnivorus* carnivorous — more at CARNIVOROUS] **1** *cap* **:** an order of eutherian mammals that are believed to have arisen from generalized insectivores during the Paleocene and are mostly carnivorous in habit having teeth adapted for flesh eating, a simple stomach and short intestine, feet with four or more usu. clawed toes, a well-developed brain, clavicles wanting or vestigial, and a zonary deciduate placenta — compare CREODONTA, FISSIPEDA, PINNIPEDIA **2 :** carnivorous animals; *esp* **:** members of the Carnivora

car·ni·vore \'kärnə,vō(ə)r, 'kán-, -vȯ(ə)r,-vōə,-vȯ(ə)\ *n* -s [NL *Carnivora*] **1 :** a flesh-eating animal; *esp* **:** one of the Carnivora **2** [F, fr. *carnivore* carnivorous, fr. L *carnivorus*] **:** an insectivorous plant

car·niv·o·ri \kär'nivə,rī, -,rē\ *syn of* CARNIVORA

car·nivo·rism \kär'nivə,rizəm, 'karnə,vōr,iz-\ *n* -s [*carnivorous* + *-ism*] **:** the consuming or digesting of insects by plants

car·ni·vor·i·ty \,kärnə'vȯrəd·ē\ *n* -ES [ISV *carnivorous* + *-ity*] **:** the quality or state of being carnivorous

car·niv·o·rous \(')kär¦niv(ə)rəs, -ä¦n-\ *adj* [L *carnivorus*, fr. *carni-* (fr. *carn-*, *caro* flesh) + *-vorus* -vorous — more at CARNAL] **1** *of an animal* **:** eating flesh ⟨the dog is a typical ~ mammal⟩ **:** subsisting or feeding on animal tissues ⟨many larval insects are ~⟩ **:** ZOOPHAGOUS ⟨the ~ hunting spiders⟩ — compare HERBIVOROUS, OMNIVOROUS **2** *of a plant* **:** subsisting on nutrients obtained from the breakdown of animal protoplasm — compare PHYTOPHAGOUS **3 :** of or relating to the Carnivora **4** *anthrop* **:** having a slender body build and a short small intestine — opposed to *herbivorous* and nearly equivalent to *ectomorphic* — **car·niv·o·rous·ly** *adv* — **car·niv·o·rous·ness** *n* -ES — **car·niv·o·ry** \ˈ=ˈvərē\ *n* -ES

car·no·sau·ria \ˌkärnəˈsȯrēə\ *n pl, cap* [NL, fr. L *carn-, caro* flesh + NL *-o-* + *-sauria*] **:** a group of moderate to large-sized carnivorous saurischian dinosaurs that had recurved daggerlike teeth and were widely distributed in the Upper Triassic and Jurassic — compare ALLOSAURUS, CERATODUS

car·nose \ˈkär,nōs\ *adj* [L *carnosus*, fr. *carn-, caro* + *-osus* -ose] **1 :** like or relating to flesh **:** FLESHY **2 :** of a fleshy consistence — used of succulent parts of plants

car·no·sine \ˈkärnə,sēn, -sən\ *n* -S [ISV *carnos-* (fr. L *carnosus* fleshy) + *-ine*; orig. formed as G *karnosin*] **:** a colorless crystalline dipeptide $C_9H_{14}N_4O_3$ occurring in the muscles of most mammals; β-alanyl-histidine

car·not cycle \(ˈ)kärˈnō-\ *or* **car·not's cycle** \-ōz-\ *n, usu cap 1st C* [trans. of F *cycle de Carnot*, after N.L.S. *Carnot* †1832 Fr. physicist] **:** an ideal heat-engine cycle in which the working substance goes through the four successive operations of isothermal expansion to a desired point, adiabatic expansion to a desired point, isothermal compression, and adiabatic compression back to its initial state

carnot engine *n, usu cap C* **:** an ideal reversible heat engine esp. as postulated in the statement of Carnot's principle of engine efficiency

car·no·tite \ˈkärnə,tīt\ *n* -S [F, fr. M. A. *Carnot* †1920 Fr. inspector general of mines + F *-ite*] **:** a mineral $K_2(UO_2)_2(VO_4)_2.3H_2O$ consisting of a hydrous strongly radioactive vanadate of uranium and potassium that occurs as a powder or in loosely coherent masses of a canary-yellow color at various points in western Colorado and is a source of radium and uranium

car·not's law \(ˈ)kärˈnōz-\ *n, usu cap C* [after N.L.S. *Carnot* †1832, Fr. physicist] **:** a statement in physics: the specific heat of a gas at constant pressure minus the specific heat at constant volume multiplied by the mechanical equivalent of heat equals the gas constant for the gas in question

carnot's theorem *or* **carnot's principle** *n, usu cap C* [trans. of F *principe de Carnot*, after N.L.S. Carnot, its formulator] **:** a principle in thermodynamics: an engine working in a reversible cycle is at least as efficient as any other engine working between the same limits of temperature, the efficiency of such an engine being a function of the two limiting temperatures and not dependent on the mechanical design or the working substance of the engine

[1]**carny** *var of* CARNEY

[2]**car·ny** *or* **car·ney** *or* **car·nie** \ˈkärnē\ *n, pl* **carnies** *or* **carneys** *often attrib* [short for *carnival*] **1 :** CARNIVAL 3a **2 :** one who works with a carnival

ca·roa \ˌkarəˈwä\ *n* -S [Pg *caroá*, fr. Tupi] **1 :** a Brazilian plant (*Neoglaziovia variegata*) related to the pinguin **2 :** the silky resistant leaf fiber of the caroa plant used esp. locally in making cordage, coarse cloth, and paper

car·ob \ˈkarəb\ *n* -S [MF *carobe, caroube*, fr. ML *carrubium*, fr. Ar *kharrūbah*] **1** *also* **carob bean a** *or* **carob tree :** a leguminous tree (*Ceratonia siliqua*) of the Mediterranean region having evergreen pinnate leaves and apetalous flowers in small red racemes **b :** one of the long pods of this tree containing a sweetish pulp, having small seeds that are formerly employed as standards of weight, and used as food for humans and livestock — called also *algarroba, locust bean, locust pod, St.-John's-bread* **2** [alter. of *caroba*] **:** any of several So. American timber trees of the genus *Jacaranda*

ca·ro·ba \kəˈrōbə\ *n* -S [Pg, caroba tree, fr. Tupi *caa-roba*] **1 :** the leaflets of any of certain trees of the family Bignoniaceae (esp. *Jacaranda procera* and *Cybistax antisyphilitica*) used in Brazil as a remedy for syphilis **2 :** CAROB 2

carob brown *n* **:** RUSSIAN CALF

carob flour *n* **:** a powder extracted from the fruit of the carob tree and used in the pharmaceutical, textile, and food industries as a thickener, stabilizer, and sizing agent — called also *locust bean gum powder*

carob gum *n* **:** a gummy substance made from carob flour

ca·roche \kəˈrōch, -ōsh\ *n* -S [MF *carroche*, fr. OIt *carroccio*, aug. of *carro* vehicle, fr. L *carrus* — more at CAR] **:** a luxurious or stately carriage for persons

[1]**car·ol** \ˈkarəl *also* -er-\ *n* -S [ME *carole*, fr. OF, modif. of LL *choraula* choral song, fr. L, one that accompanies a chorus on a reed instrument, alter. of *choraules*, fr. Gk *choraulēs*, fr. *choraulein* to accompany a chorus on a reed instrument, fr. *choros* chorus + *aulein* to play a reed instrument, fr. *aulos* reed instrument like an oboe — more at CHORUS, ALVEOLUS] **1** *or* **car·ole** \"\ **:** an old round dance with singing by couples associated orig. with May-day celebrations of western Europe **2 :** a song of joy, exultation, or mirth ⟨I float this ~ with joy —Walt Whitman⟩ ⟨the ~ of a bird —Lord Byron⟩ **3 a :** a song of praise or devotion **:** a popular song or ballad of religious joy ⟨a Christmas ~⟩ ⟨an Easter ~⟩ ⟨sing your ~ of high praise —John Keble⟩ **b :** the music of such a song

[2]**carol** \"\ *vb* **caroled** *or* **carolled; caroled** *or* **carolled; caroling** *or* **carolling; carols** [ME *carolen*, fr. OF *caroler*, fr. *carole*, n.] *vi* **1 :** to sing esp. in a joyful manner ⟨he used to ~ cheerfully in the morning, locked in the single bathroom —H.S. Canby⟩ ⟨a wren on a tree stump ~*ed* clear —John Masefield⟩ **2 :** to sing carols; *specif* **:** to go about outdoors in a group singing Christmas carols on Christmas Eve ⟨gone ~*ing*⟩ ~ *vt* **1 :** to praise in or as if in song ⟨the shepherds . . . ~ her goodness loud in rustic lays —John Milton⟩ ⟨the union's star salesman . . . has been ~*ing* its glories for many a year —*Newsweek*⟩ **2 :** to sing esp. in a cheerful manner ⟨the robin . . . ~*s* from the treetops his loud, hearty strain —John Burroughs⟩ ⟨they ~*ed* nothing but love ditties —J.D.Hart⟩

carolean *var of* CAROLINE

car·ol·er *or* **car·ol·ler** \ˈkarələ(r) *also* -er-\ *n* -S **:** one that carols

caroli *pl of* CAROLUS

car·o·lin \ˌkarəˈlēn\ *n, pl* **carolins** \-nz\ *or* **caroli·ner** \ˌ==ˈlēnə(r)\ [Sw *karolin*, fr. NL *carolinus* of Charles, fr. ML *Carolus* Charles (after Charles XI †1697, Charles XII †1718 & Charles XIV †1844, kings of Sweden) + L *-inus* -ine] **1 :** any of several coins issued under Swedish kings named Charles **2** *or* **kar·o·lin** \ˌkarəˈlēn\ [G *karolin*, fr. NL *carolinus*, fr. ML *Carolus* (after Charles Albert †1745 prince of Bavaria) + L *-inus* -ine] **a** (1) **:** an old gold coin of Bavaria first struck in the 18th century (2) **:** any of several similar coins of southern German states, esp. Württemberg **b :** a unit of value equivalent to a German carolin ⟨half-*carolin* and ¼-*carolin* coins⟩ **3** [modif. of It *carlino*] **:** [1]CARLIN

car·o·li·na \ˌkarəˈlīnə *also* ˌker-; *chiefly in substand speech* kə(r)ˈl-\ *adj, usu cap* [fr. *Carolina*, English colony from which No. & So. Carolina were formed — more at CAROLINIAN] **:** of or from the state of No. Carolina or the state of So. Carolina **:** of the kind or style prevalent in No. Carolina or So. Carolina **:** CAROLINIAN

carolina allspice *n, usu cap C* **:** a shrub of the genus *Calycanthus* — called also *strawberry shrub*

carolina anemone *n, usu cap C* **:** a prairie herb (*Anemone caroliniana*) with a solitary showy purplish white flower found in the central and southern U.S.

carolina ash *n, usu cap C* **:** a water ash (*Fraxinus caroliniana*)

carolina bay *n, usu cap C* **:** any of various shallow often oval depressions in the coastal plain of the southeastern U.S. ranging from a few hundred feet to several miles long and being usu. marshy and rich in humus, heavily forested, and covered with a pure stand of trees (as cypress, bay, or black gum) different from the dominant tree (as pine) of surrounding areas

carolina bean *n, usu cap C* **:** SIEVA BEAN

carolina beechdrops *n pl but often sing in constr, usu cap C* **:** a rare purple or purplish brown American herb (*Monotropsis odorata*) with pink flowers

carolina box tortoise *n, usu cap C* **:** the common box tortoise (*Terrapene carolina*)

carolina buckthorn *n, usu cap C* **1 :** YELLOW BUCKTHORN **2 :** SOUTHERN BUCKTHORN

carolina chickadee *n, usu cap C* **:** a chickadee (*Penthestes carolinensis carolinensis*) of the southeastern U.S. resembling but smaller than the black-capped chickadee

carolina duck *n, usu cap C* **:** WOOD DUCK 1

carolina grasshopper *or* **carolina locust** *n, usu cap C* **:** a large dark-colored grasshopper (*Dissosteira carolina*) common throughout the U.S. that has the edge of the wing bordered with bright yellow

carolina hemlock *n, usu cap C* **:** a hemlock (*Tsuga caroliniana*) of the southeastern U.S. having wide spreading leaves and widely divergent cone scales

carolina horsenettle *n, usu cap C* **:** HORSENETTLE

carolina ipecac *n, usu cap C* **:** IPECAC SPURGE

carolina jessamine *or* **carolina jasmine** *n, usu cap C* **:** YELLOW JESSAMINE 2

carolina junco *n, usu cap C* **:** a slaty-gray junco (*Junco hyemalis carolinensis*) of the higher Allegheny mountains

carolina moonseed *n, usu cap C* **:** a woody vine (*Cocculus carolinus*) of the southern U.S. resembling the common moonseed (*Menispermum canadense*) but having red fruits

carolina parakeet *or* **carolina paroquet** *n, usu cap C* **:** an extinct parakeet (*Conuropsis carolinensis*) having a long tail and mostly green plumage but with yellow head, red face, and blue and yellow on the wings and being the only parrot whose range extended far into the U.S.

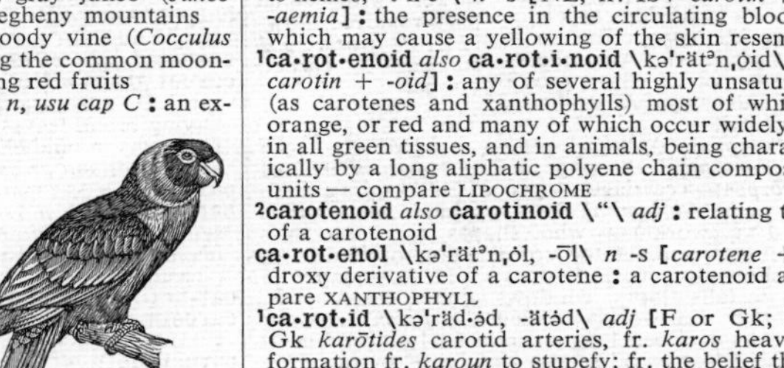

Carolina parakeet

carolina pink *n, usu cap C* **1 :** a wild pink (*Silene caroliniana*) **2 :** PINKROOT a

carolina pompano *n, usu cap C* **:** a pompano (*Trachynotus carolinus*)

carolina poplar *n, usu cap C* **1 a :** a common cottonwood (*Populus deltoides*) **b :** a hybrid resulting from crosses involving this species and also two other poplars (*P. nigra italica* and *P. canadensis amoena*) **2 :** BALSAM POPLAR

carolina rail *n, usu cap C* **:** SORA

carolina rhododendron *n, usu cap C* **:** an evergreen shrub (*Rhododendron carolinianum*) of the southeastern U.S. cultivated for its showy pale rose-purple flowers

carolina rose *n, usu cap C* **:** SWAMP ROSE

carolina tea *n, usu cap C* **:** a yaupon (*Ilex vomitoria*)

carolina vanilla *n, usu cap C* **:** WILD VANILLA

carolina water shield *n, usu cap C* **:** FANWORT

carolina whiting *n, usu cap C* **:** KING WHITING

carolina wild woodbine *n, usu cap C* **:** YELLOW JESSAMINE 2

carolina wren *n, usu cap C* **:** a large wren (*Thryothorus ludovicianus*) familiar as a loud songster

[1]**car·o·line** \ˈkarə,līn, -,lən *also* -er-\ *or* **car·o·le·an** \ˌ==ˈlēən\ *adj, usu cap* [*caroline* fr. NL *carolinus*, fr. ML *Carolus* Charles + L *-inus* -ine; *carolean* alter. (influenced by *jacobean*) of *caroline*] **:** of or relating to Charles — used esp. with ref. to Charles I and Charles II of England or their times

[2]**caroline** \"\ *or* **caroline hat** *n* -S *chiefly Irish* **:** STOVEPIPE HAT

caroline minuscule *n, usu cap C* [[1]*caroline*] **:** the Carolingian script

caroling *pres part of* CAROL

Caroline

Caroline minuscule

car·o·lin·gi·an \ˌkarəˈlinj(ē)ən *also* -er-\ *adj, usu cap* [F *carolingien*, fr. ML *karolingi* French people (prob. fr. assumed OHG *karling, kerling* Frenchman — whence MHG *kerlinc* — fr. *Karl* Charles + OHG *-ing*) + F *-ien* -ian] **1 :** of or relating to a Frankish family that was founded about A.D. 613 and including among its members the rulers of France from 751 to 987, of Germany from 752 to 911, and of Italy from 774 to 961 **2 :** being a script developed in France in the 8th century and combining characteristics of cursive and half uncial

[2]**carolingian** \"\ *n* -S *usu cap* **:** a member of the Carolingian dynasty

[1]**car·o·lin·ian** \ˌkarəˈlinyən, -nēən *also* -er- *or* -lē-; *chiefly substand* kə(r)ˈl-\ *adj, usu cap* [*Carolina*, English colony from which No. and So. Carolina were formed, after Charles I (*Carolus*) †1649 king of England + E *-ian*] **1 :** of, relating to, or characteristic of the state of No. Carolina or of So. Carolina or of both **2 :** of, relating to, or characteristic of the people of No. Carolina or of So. Carolina or of both **3 :** of, relating to, or being the part of the Upper Austral life zone that lies east of the 100th meridian, has a northern mean daily temperature of 71.6°F during the 6 hottest weeks and a similar southern mean daily temperature of 78.8°F, extends from southern New England to Georgia, and forms the humid division of the Upper Austral zone **4 :** [[1]*caroline* + *-ian*] **:** CAROLINGIAN 1 **5** [[1]*caroline* + *-ian*] **:** CAROLINE

[2]**carolinian** \"\ *n* -S *cap* **:** a native or resident of No. Carolina or So. Carolina

[3]**carolinian** \"\ *n* -S *cap* [*Caroline* (*islands*), archipelago in west Pacific + E *-ian*] **1 :** a native or inhabitant of the Caroline islands **2 :** any or all of the closely related Micronesian languages spoken by the native inhabitants of the Caroline islands

carolins *pl of* CAROLIN

carolled *past of* CAROL

caroller *var of* CAROLER

carolling *pres part of* CAROL

carols *pl of* CAROL, *pres 3d sing of* CAROL

car·o·lus \ˈkarələs\ *n, pl* **caroluses** \-ləsəz\ *or* **caro·li** \-,lī, -,lē\ [NL, Charles, fr. ML] **:** any of various coins issued under monarchs called Charles: as **a :** an English gold coin of the reign of Charles I orig. worth 20 shillings **b** *or* **carolus dollar** *usu cap C* **:** a Spanish-American peso or piece of eight issued by Charles III (1759-1788) and Charles IV (1788-1808) of Spain

car·o·lyt·ic *or* **car·o·lit·ic** \ˌkarəˈlid·ik\ *adj* [modif. of F *corollitique*, fr. *corolle* corolla (fr. L *corolla*) + *-itique* -itic] *of a column* **:** having a foliated shaft

[1]**car·om** *also* **car·rom** \ˈkarəm *also* -er-\ *n* -S [by shortening & alter. fr. [1]*carambole*] **1 :** a shot in billiards in which the cue ball strikes each of two object balls **2 :** a rebounding esp. at an angle **:** a glancing off **3** [fr. *Carroms*, a trademark] **a caroms** *pl but sing in constr* **:** a game played by two or four persons with round wooden counters on a large square board having corner pockets **b :** a counter used in caroms

[2]**carom** *also* **carrom** \"\ *vb* -ED/-ING/-S *vi* **1 :** to make a carom **2 :** to strike and rebound **:** GLANCE **:** rebound or glance after striking ⟨his drive hit a tree and ~*ed* off into a roadway —*Time*⟩ **3 :** to proceed by or as if by caroms ⟨she tried to ~ from my corner of the room to the bar —Henry Miller⟩ ~ *vt* **:** to make (an object) bounce off something ⟨place an object ball on the table and try to ~ the cue ball from it —Willie Hoppe⟩

carom ball *n* **:** the second ball hit by the cue ball in making a carom in billiards

carom billiards *n pl but usu sing in constr* **:** any of several games of billiards played with a cue and three balls on a pocketless table, points being scored by a player's causing the cue ball to caroom from one object ball to another — compare BALKLINE, POOL, STRAIGHT RAIL, THREE-CUSHION BILLIARDS

ca·ro·ny bark \kəˈrōnē-\ *n, usu cap C* [fr. *Caroni*, river in Venezuela, where it is found] **:** ANGOSTURA BARK

caroome *n* -S [perh. irreg. fr. [1]*car*] **:** a license to keep a cart granted by the lord mayor of London

ca·ro's acid \ˈkä(,)rō'z-\ *n, usu cap C* [trans. of G *Caro'sche säure*, after Heinrich *Caro* †1910 Ger. chemist] **:** PERMONOSULFURIC ACID

car·o·sel·la \ˌkarəˈselə, -ˈz-\ *n* -S [It] **:** a fennel (*Foeniculum vulgare peperitum*) grown for its edible young stems which are used in salads — called also *Italian fennel*

carot *var of* CAROTTE

car·o·tene \ˈkarə,tēn *also* -er-\ *also* **car·o·tin** \-ətᵊn, -tən\ *or* **car·ro·tene** *or* **car·ro·tin** *n* -S [ISV *carot-* (fr. LL *carota* carrot) + *-ene* or *-in*; prob. orig. formed as G *karotin* — more at CARROT] **:** any of several orange or red crystalline pigments of the class of carotenoid hydrocarbons commonly occurring in the chromoplasts of plants and in the fatty tissues of plant-eating animals: as **a :** a mixture of three such pigments $C_{40}H_{56}$ convertible in the animal body to vitamin A, obtained esp. from various plant sources (as carrots and alfalfa), and used as a precursor of vitamin A and as a color for foods **b :** any of the three pigments $C_{40}H_{56}$ convertible in the animal body to vitamin A, characterized chemically by one or two unsaturated rings terminating a long aliphatic polyene chain, and distinguished according to the number and nature of these rings as α-, β-, and γ-*carotene*; *specif* **:** the dark-red β-carotene that is the most widely distributed carotenoid and the principal pigment of carrots, that is also made synthetically, and that is the most active provitamin A since its molecule contains two rings of the type present in the vitamin A molecule

car·o·ten·emia *or* **car·o·ten·aemia** *also* **car·o·tin·emia** \ˌ==təˈnēmēə, -tᵊnˈē-\ *n* -S [NL, fr. ISV *carotin* + NL *-emia* or *-aemia*] **:** the presence in the circulating blood of carotene which may cause a yellowing of the skin resembling jaundice

[1]**ca·rot·enoid** *also* **ca·rot·i·noid** \kəˈrätᵊn,ȯid\ *n* -S [*carotene, carotin* + *-oid*] **:** any of several highly unsaturated pigments (as carotenes and xanthophylls) most of which are yellow, orange, or red and many of which occur widely in plants, esp. in all green tissues, and in animals, being characterized chemically by a long aliphatic polyene chain composed of isoprene units — compare LIPOCHROME

[2]**carotenoid** *also* **carotinoid** \"\ *adj* **:** relating to or consisting of a carotenoid

ca·rot·enol \kəˈrätᵊn,ȯl, -ōl\ *n* -S [*carotene* + *-ol*] **:** a hydroxy derivative of a carotene **:** a carotenoid alcohol — compare XANTHOPHYLL

[1]**ca·rot·id** \kəˈräd·əd, -ätəd\ *adj* [F or Gk; F *carotide*, fr. Gk *karōtides* carotid arteries, fr. *karos* heavy sleep, back-formation fr. *karoun* to stupefy; fr. the belief that pressure on these arteries causes stupor; akin to Gk *kara* head — more at CEREBRAL] **:** belonging to or situated near a carotid artery

[2]**carotid** \"\ *or* **carotid artery** *n* -S **:** either of the two main arteries that supply blood to the head, the left in man arising from the arch of the aorta, the right by bifurcation of the innominate artery, each passing along the corresponding anterolateral aspect of the neck and dividing opposite the upper border of the thyroid cartilage into an external branch supplying the face, tongue, and external parts of the head and an internal branch supplying the brain, eye, and other internal parts of the head

ca·rot·id·al \-ədᵊl\ *or* **ca·rot·i·de·an** \kəˌräd·əˈdēən, -ätə-, ˌkarəˈtid·ē-\ *adj* [ISV *carotid* + *-al* or *-ean*] **:** CAROTID

carotid body *or* **carotid gland** *n* **:** a small body of highly vascular chromaffin tissue adjoining the carotid sinus and serving as a chemoreceptor sensitive to changes of the oxygen tension in blood and mediating reflex changes in respiratory activities

carotid canal *n* **:** the canal by which the internal carotid artery enters the skull

carotid plexus *n* **:** a network of nerves of the sympathetic system surrounding the internal carotid artery

carotid sinus *n* **:** the slight enlargement of the common carotid artery at the point where it divides into external and internal carotid arteries, being richly supplied with sensory nerve endings and playing a major part in the mechanism regulating heart rate and blood pressure

carotin *var of* CAROTENE

carotinemia *var of* CAROTENEMIA

carotinoid *var of* CAROTENOID

car·o·tol \ˈkarə,tōl, -ōl\ *n* -S [LL *carota* + E *-ol*] **:** a liquid sesquiterpenoid alcohol $C_{15}H_{25}OH$ found in the essential oil of carrots

ca·rotte *also* **ca·rot** \kəˈrät\ *n* -S [F, *carotte*, lit., carrot — more at CARROT] **:** a cylindrical roll of tobacco

ca·rou·bi·er \kəˈrübē,ā\ *n* -S [F, carob tree, fr. *caroube* — more at CAROB] **:** RUSSIAN CALF

[1]**ca·rous·al** \kəˈrauzəl\ *n* -S [by folk etymology (influence of [2]*carouse*)] **:** CARROUSEL 1

[2]**carousal** \"\ *n* -S [[2]*carouse* + *-al*] **:** CAROUSE 2 ⟨the spirit of continual carnival and ~ —Carleton Beals⟩

[1]**ca·rouse** \kəˈrauz\ *n* -S [MF *carrousse, carroux*, fr. *carous, carroux*, adv., all out (in *boire carous* to empty the cup), modif. of G *garaus* (in *garaus trinken* to empty the cup), fr. *gar* quite, entirely (fr. OHG *garo*, fr. *garo*, adj., ready, complete) + *aus* out (fr. OHG *ūz*) — more at YARE, OUT] **1** *archaic* **:** a large draft of liquor **:** a cupful drunk up **:** TOAST ⟨drank a deep ~ to the queen's health —John Milton⟩ **2 :** a drinking bout **:** a drunken revel ⟨drowning care in a perpetual ~ —R.L.Stevenson⟩

[2]**carouse** \"\ *vb* -ED/-ING/-S *vi* **1 :** to drink deeply or freely and repeatedly (as in compliment) ⟨he had been aboard *carousing* to his mates —Shak.⟩ **2 :** to take part in a carouse ⟨the sailors went ashore to ~⟩ ~ *vt, obs* **:** to drink up **:** QUAFF

carousel *var of* CARROUSEL

ca·rous·er \kəˈrauzə(r)\ *n* -S **:** one that carouses **:** REVELER

ca·rous·ing·ly *adv* **:** in a carousing manner

[1]**carp** \ˈkärp, ˈkāp\ *vb* -ED/-ING/-S [ME *carpen*, of Scand origin; akin to Icel *karpa* to dispute, wrangle, ON *karp* arrogance, boasting; akin to OFris *kerp* dispute, ON *korpr* raven] *vi* **:** to find fault ill-naturedly, complain querulously, or cavil sharply ⟨perhaps it would be wise not to ~ or criticize —W.S.Gilbert⟩ — often used with *at* ⟨ancient critics were never at a loss for something to ~ at —E.S.McCartney⟩ ~ *vt* **:** to complain esp. in a censorious or peevish manner ⟨lest anyone ~ that such conditions are too ancient to mean anything —Eugene Burr⟩

[2]**carp** \"\ *n, pl* **carp** *or* **carps** [ME *carpe*, fr. MF, fr. LL *carpa*, prob. of Gmc origin; akin to MD *carpe* carp, MLG *karpe*, OHG *karpfo*, ON *karfi*] **1 a :** a soft-finned freshwater fish (*Cyprinus carpio*) that inhabits ponds and sluggish streams feeding chiefly on vegetable matter, attaining a large size, and sometimes living to a great age and that is indigenous to Asia but was early introduced into Europe where it is extensively reared in artificial ponds and esteemed as food and later into America where it has escaped into natural waters and in many areas has become a pest destroying the growth of water plants and crowding out more valued fishes — see LEATHER CARP, MIRROR CARP **b :** any of a number of other fishes of the family Cyprinidae — see CRUCIAN CARP **2 :** any of several somewhat carplike fishes that do not belong to the family Cyprinidae (as the carpsucker and the European sea bream)

carp *abbr* carpenter

[1]**carp-** *or* **carpo-** *comb form* [F & NL, fr. Gk *karp-, karpo-*, fr. *karpos* fruit — more at HARVEST] **:** fruit ⟨*Carp*oidea, *carpo*logy⟩

[2]**carp-** *or* **carpo-** *comb form* [NL, fr. Gk *karp-, karpo-*, fr. *karpos* wrist — more at WHARF] **:** carpus ⟨*carp*itis⟩ **:** carpus and ⟨*carpo*metacarpus⟩ **:** carpal and ⟨*carpo*pedal⟩

-carp \ˌkärp, ˌkāp\ *also* **-car·pi·um** \ˈkärpēəm, -āp-\ *n comb form, pl* **-carps** \-ps\ *also* **-car·pia** \-pēə\ [NL *-carpium*, fr. Gk *-karpion*, fr. *karpos* fruit] **1 :** part of a fruit ⟨peri*carp*⟩ **:** fruit ⟨schizo*carp*⟩ ⟨amphi*carpium*⟩ **2** [NL *-carpus*, fr. Gk *-karpos* -carpous, fr. *karpos*] **:** plant having fruit (in a specified place) ⟨acro*carp*⟩ ⟨pleuro*carp*⟩

car·pa·ine \ˈkärpə,ēn\ *n* -S [ISV *carpa-* (irreg. fr. NL *Carica papaya*, species name of the papaya, fr. *Carica* + *papaya*, fr. Sp) + *-ine*; orig. formed as D *carpain* — more at CARICA, PAPAYA] **:** a crystalline alkaloid $C_{14}H_{25}NO_2$ obtained esp. from the leaves, fruit, and seeds of the papaya

[1]**car·pal** \ˈkärpəl, -āp-\ *adj* [NL *carpalis*, fr. [2]*carp-* + L *-alis* -al] **:** relating to the carpus

[2]**carpal** \"\ *n* -S **:** a carpal element

car·pa·le \kärˈpā(,)lē\ *n, pl* **carpa·lia** \-ālēə\ [NL, neut. of *carpalis* carpal] **:** a carpal bone; *esp* **:** one of the distal series articulating with the metacarpals

car park *n, chiefly Brit* **:** an area set apart for the parking of motor vehicles **:** PARKING LOT

[1]**car·pa·thi·an** \(ˈ)kärˈpāthēən *also* -th-\ *adj, usu cap* [prob. fr. G *Karpathen* Carpathian mts. (fr. L *Carpatus*, fr. Gk *Karpatos*) + E *-ian*] **:** situated in or relating to the Carpathian mountains of central Europe

[2]**carpathian** \"\ *adj, usu cap* [*Carpathus* (now usu. *Karpathos*) Greek island between Rhodes & Crete (fr. L, fr. Gk *Karpathos*) + E *-ian*] **:** of or relating to the island of Karpathos

car·pa·tho-rus·sian \kärˈpā(,)thō;rəshən *also* -th-\ *n, cap C & R* [*Carpatho-Russia*, former name of Carpathian Ruthenia (fr. *Carpathian* mts. + *-o-* + *Russia*) + E *-an*] **:** RUTHENIAN

carp dropsy *n* [[2]*carp*] **:** a bacterial disease of carps and suckers marked by intense inflammation of the skin, fins, and body cavity

car·pe di·em \ˌkärpēˈdē,em, -(,)pā-; ˌkärpēˈdī-\ *n, pl* **carpe diems** [L, enjoy the day!] **:** the enjoyment of the pleasures of the moment without concern for the future

car·pel \'kärpəl, 'kȧp- *also* -,pel\ *n* -s [F & NL; F *carpelle* & NL *carpellum*, fr. NL ¹*carp-* + F *-elle* & NL *-ellum* -el] **:** one of the structures in a seed plant comprising the innermost whorl of a flower, functioning as megasporophylls, and collectively constituting the gynoecium — compare PISTIL

flower with some parts removed showing: *1* petal, *2* stamen, *3* carpel, *4* sepal

car·pel·lary \-,pə,lerē, -i\ *adj* [NL *carpellum* + E *-ary*] **:** belonging to, forming, or containing carpels

car·pel·late \-,pə,lāt, -,lət\ *adj* [NL *carpellum* + E *-ate*] **:** having carpels

car·pen·tar·i·an \,kärpən'terēən\ *n* -s *cap* [Gulf of *Carpentaria*, Australia + E *-an*] **:** a member of an ethnic group native to north and central Australia — compare MURRAYIAN

¹**car·pen·ter** \'kärpəntə(r), 'kȧp-, -pᵊmt-\ *n* -s [ME, fr. ONF *carpentier*, fr. L *carpentarius* carriage maker, fr. *carpentarius* of a carriage, fr. *carpentum* carriage, wagon, of Celt origin; akin to Gaulish place name *Carbantia*] **1 :** a workman who builds with wood: **a :** a workman who shapes and assembles structural woodwork esp. in the construction of buildings, stage settings, ships, tunnels, and mines **b :** a workman who cuts, fits, and installs floors, windows, doors, baseboards, cabinets, and other trim work — called also *finish carpenter* **c :** one who works at a bench in an industrial establishment making and assembling wood sections of boxes or furniture according to blueprints — called also *bench carpenter* **2 a :** a petty officer on merchant ships who attends to repairs not made by engineers **b :** a warrant officer in the U.S. Navy whose chief shipboard duties are hull maintenance and damage control

²**carpenter** \"\ *vb* **carpentered; carpentered; carpentering** \-pəntəriŋ, -n·triŋ, -pᵊmt(ə)riŋ\ **carpenters** *vi* **:** to do carpentry **:** follow the trade of a carpenter ⟨he ~*ed* in his youth, then graduated to heavy construction work —John Kobler⟩ ~ *vt* **1 :** to make by or as if by carpentry ⟨a doctor ~*ed* a splint for the broken arm —Frederick Way⟩ **2 :** to put together often in a mechanical manner ⟨I've ~*ed* dozens of scripts but this is cabinetmaking —Clemence Dane⟩ **:** CONSTRUCT ⟨is well ~*ed*, easily written, and well calculated to shorten a train ride —*Time*⟩

carpenter ant *n* **:** an ant (as American members of the genus *Camponotus*) that gnaws galleries in wood esp. when dead or partially decayed and constructs its nest in them

carpenter bee *n* **:** any of various large solitary bees (family Xylocopidae) that gnaw long galleries in sound timber — see GREAT CARPENTER BEE

carpenter bird *n* **:** CALIFORNIA WOODPECKER

carpenter frog *n* **:** a frog (*Rana virgatipes*) of the southeastern U. S. having a loud hammerlike call and large vocal sacs that when fully inflated resemble water wings

carpenter grass *or* **carpenter's grass** *n* [so called fr. its supposed power to cure wounds inflicted by carpenter tools] **:** a yarrow (*Achillea millefolium*)

car·pen·te·ria \,kärpən'tirēə\ *n*, *cap* [NL, fr. William M. *Carpenter* †1848 Am. physician + NL *-ia*] **:** a genus of California evergreen shrubs (family Saxifragaceae) comprising a single species (*C. californica*) having opposite leaves and showy fragrant white flowers in few-flowered terminal clusters

carpentering *n* -s [fr. gerund of ²*carpenter*] **:** the act, occupation, or work of a carpenter **:** CARPENTRY

carpenter moth *n* **:** the adult of the carpenterworm or a related moth (family Cossidae) — called also *goat moth*

carpenter's clamp *n* **:** a bar with adjustable jaws that can be spread to hold cabinets, doors, and similar large pieces

carpenter's level *n* **1 :** PLUMB LEVEL **2 :** a straight bar (as of aluminum or wood) with a small spirit level embedded in it

carpenter's scene *or* **carpenter scene** *n* **:** a scene played on the forepart of the stage to give the stage carpenters opportunity to construct a scene behind the backdrop

carpenter's square *n* **1 :** a usu. steel square used by carpenters **2 :** either of two plants of the genus *Scrophularia:* **a :** the common figwort (*S. nodosa*) of Europe **b :** a related American species (*S. marylandica*)

carpenter's square 1

carpenter weed *also* **carpenter's herb** *n* [so called fr. its supposed power to heal wounds inflicted by carpenter tools] **:** SELF-HEAL

car·pen·ter·worm \'ˌˌˌ,ˌ\ *n* [so called fr. its wood boring] **:** the wood-boring larva of the American goat moth (*Prionoxystus robiniae*) that bores large galleries in living trees and is esp. destructive to oaks and locusts

car·pen·try \'kärpən·trē, 'kȧp-, -pᵊmt-, -i\ *n* -ES [ME *carpentrie*, fr. ONF *carpenterie*, fr. *carpentier* carpenter] **1 :** the art or trade of a carpenter; *specif* **:** the art of shaping and assembling structural woodwork (as in constructing buildings) **2 :** timberwork constructed by a carpenter; *specif* **:** an assemblage of pieces of timber connected by being framed together (as in a roof) **3 :** the form or manner of putting together the parts (as of a literary or musical composition) **:** STRUCTURE, ARRANGEMENT ⟨as neat a piece of interlocking dramatic ~ as can be imagined —Peter Forster⟩

carp·er \'kärpər, 'kȧpə-\ *n* -s [ME, fr. *carpen* to carp, talk + *-er*] **:** one that carps; *esp* **:** a perverse faultfinder ⟨vast and general discontent . . . not only among professional ~*s* —Joel Carmichael⟩

¹**car·pet** \'kärpət, 'kȧp-, *usu* -əd· + V\ *n* -s *often attrib* [ME *carpete*, fr. MF *carpite*, fr. OIt *carpita*, fr. *carpire* to pluck, modif. of L *carpere* — more at HARVEST] **1 :** a heavy woven or felted fabric usu. made of wool: as **a :** a floor covering made in breadths to be sewed together and tacked to the floor — see ORIENTAL RUG; compare RUG **b** *obs* **:** a thick wrought fabric used for covering tables or beds; *specif* **:** an altar covering **c** *archaic* **:** a luxurious floor covering found esp. in boudoirs — now used only attributively to convey the notion of effeminacy ⟨a ~ poet⟩; see CARPET KNIGHT **2 a :** a surface resembling or suggesting a carpet (as in smoothness or softness) ⟨the grassy ~ of this plain —Shak.⟩ **b :** the surface of a cricket field ⟨a ~ drive⟩ **3 a :** a thin skin of boards laid as a wearing surface on a floor **b** *chiefly Brit* **:** a thin layer of resurfacing material (as asphalt) covering a previously paved roadway — **on the carpet** *adv (or adj)* **1 :** under consideration or deliberation ⟨he nodded and asked was there something fresh *on the carpet* —F.W.Crofts⟩ **2 :** before an authority for censure or reproof ⟨called a salesman *on the carpet* and reprimanded him for not reaching his quota —W.J. Reilly⟩

²**carpet** \"\ *vt* -ED/-ING/-S **1 a :** to furnish with a carpet **:** spread with carpets ⟨the floors were ~*ed* —Al Spiers⟩ **b :** to cover as if with a carpet ⟨flowers ~ the streets —Claudia Cassidy⟩ **2** *chiefly Brit* **:** to take to task **:** REPRIMAND ⟨if the chap's a casualty and anything happens, we might be ~*ed* —Richard Llewellyn⟩

¹**carpetbag** \'ˌˌ,ˌ\ *n* [so called fr. its having been originally made of carpet] **1 :** a traveling bag often made in the style of the Boston bag and esp. common in the U.S. in the 19th century **2 :** any traveling bag

²**carpetbag** \"\ *adj* **:** following the practices of carpetbaggers **:** of or characteristic of carpetbaggers ⟨~ adventurers⟩ ⟨a ~ government⟩

³**carpetbag** \"\ *vi* **1 :** to travel with little luggage **2 :** to act in the manner characteristic of carpetbaggers ~ *vt* **:** to infest or oppress with carpetbaggers

car·pet·bag·ger \-ə(r)\ *n* -s [²*carpetbag* + *-er*] **1 :** one that travels with a carpetbag or has all of his property with him in a carpetbag: **a :** a promoter of wildcat banks or stocks in the western U.S. in the 19th century **b :** a Northerner in the South after the American Civil War esp. seeking private gain under the reconstruction governments **2 :** STRANGER, OUTSIDER, TRANSIENT; *esp* **:** a nonresident who meddles in politics — **car·pet·bag·gery** \-(ə)rē, -i\ *n* -ES

car·pet·bag·gism *or* **car·pet·bag·ism** \-,gizəm\ *n* -s **:** carpetbag practices

carpet bedding *n* **:** a patterned arrangement of low or clipped herbaceous and usu. varicolored foliage plants — distinguished from *design bedding*

carpet beetle *n* **:** any of several small beetles having larvae that feed in and damage materials of animal origin (as woolen carpets): as **a :** a small black, red, and white dermestid beetle (*Anthrenus scrophulariae*) having such habits — called also *buffalo carpet beetle* **b :** a related solid-black beetle (*Attagenus piceus*) — called also *black carpet beetle*

carpet bomb *vt* **:** to drop bombs on (an area) so as to cover as if by a carpet ⟨and *carpet bombed* the . . . front with 400 tons —*Newsweek*⟩ — see AREA BOMBING

carpet cut *n* **:** a long narrow slot near the front of a stage into which the edge of a stage carpet is dropped and made secure

carpet dance *n* **:** a dance on the carpet instead of on a prepared floor **:** an informal dance

carpeted *past of* CARPET

carpet grass *n* [so called fr. the carpetlike smoothness of its turf] **1 :** a tropical American pasture grass (*Axonopus affinis*) having broad leaves and flat prostrate stems and being useful for lawns in mild climates and also as a sand binder — called also *Louisiana grass* **2 :** SMUT GRASS

carpeting *n* -s **:** material for carpets; *also* **:** CARPETS

carpet knight *n* [so called fr. the carpet's having been a symbol of luxury and effeminacy] **:** a knight who has spent his time in ease and luxury **:** a man devoted to idleness and pleasure

car·pet·less \-pətləs\ *adj* **:** being without a carpet

carpetmonger \'ˌˌ,ˌˌ\ *n* -s *obs* **:** a frequenter of boudoirs **:** GALLANT ⟨a whole bookful of these quondam ~*s* —Shak.⟩

carpet moth *n* **:** a moth (*Trichophaga tapetzella*) of the family Tineidae whose larva feeds on carpets and woolen goods

carpet pink *n* **:** MOSS CAMPION

carpet rod *n* **:** STAIR ROD

carpets *pl of* CARPET, *pres 3d sing of* CARPET

carpet shark *n* **:** a shark (*Orectolobus barbatus*) of the western Pacific having a flattened body and mottled skin; *also* **:** any related species

carpet shell *n* **:** any of several marine clams (family Veneridae); *esp* **:** the common hard clam (*Protothaca*, or *Paphia, staminea*) of the Pacific coast of the U.S.

carpet slipper *n* [so called fr. its having been originally made of carpet] **:** HOUSE SLIPPER

carpet snake *n* [perh. so called fr. its variegated coloring] **1 :** a rather large Australian constricting snake (*Python variegatus* or *spilotes*) chiefly pale brown with a mottled pattern — see DIAMOND SNAKE **2** *in Tasmania* **:** a pale form of the tiger snake **3 :** a common Indian wolf snake (*Lycodon aulicus*)

carpet strip *n* **:** the molding used between the baseboard and the floor; *also* **:** a piece attached to the floor under a door

carpet sweeper *n* **:** one that sweeps carpets; *specif* **:** a long-handled implement with a revolving brush pushed along on and rotated by wheels on a containing box

carpet tack *n* **:** a short wire tack having a flat disk-shaped head that is used esp. to nail down carpets

carpet viper *n* [perh. so called fr. its variegated coloring] **:** SAW-SCALED VIPER

carpetweed \'ˌˌ,ˌ\ *n* [so called fr. its matted appearance] **:** a prostrate annual weed (*Mollugo verticillata*) of No. America — called also *Indian chickweed;* see AIZOACEAE

carpetweed family *n* **:** AIZOACEAE

carpet wool *n* **:** coarse rough wool of a low grade

car·phi·oph·i·ops \,kärfē'äfē,äps\ [NL, fr. Gk *karphos* dry stalk, stick + NL *ophi-* + *ops*] *syn of* CARPHOPHIS

car·pho·lite \'kärfə,līt\ *n* -s [G *karpholith*, fr. Gk *karphos* dry stalk + G *-lith* -lite] **:** a fibrous mineral $MnAl_2Si_2O_6(OH)_4$ consisting of a hydrous aluminum manganese silicate and occurring in straw-yellow tufts (sp. gr. 2.93)

car·phol·o·gy \kär'fäləjē\ *also* **car·pho·lo·gia** \,kärfə'lōj(ē)ə\ *n, pl* **carphologies** *also* **carphologi·as** [NL *carphologia*, fr. LL, twitching of blankets, picking of straws from mud walls, fr. Gk *karphologia*, fr. *karphos* dry stalk, stick + *-logia* gathering — more at -LOGY] **:** an aimless semiconscious plucking at the bedclothes observed in conditions of exhaustion or stupor or in high fevers

car·pho·phis \'kärfəfəs, -(,)fis, kär'fäfəs\ *n, cap* [NL, fr. Gk *karphos* dry stalk, stick + NL *-ophis* — more at HARP] **:** a monotypic genus of small No. American colubrid snakes that are brownish black to glossy black above and pinkish below, have narrow flat heads, and feed chiefly on earthworms — see WORM SNAKE

car·pho·sid·er·ite \,kärfō'sidə,rīt\ *n* -s [G *karphosiderit*, fr. Gk *karphos* dry stalk + *sidēros* iron + G *-it* -ite] **:** a mineral consisting of a basic hydrous iron sulfate occurring in yellow masses and crusts

carpi *pl of* CARPUS

-carpia *pl of* -CARPIUM

-carpic *adj comb form* [prob. fr. NL *-carpicus*, fr. Gk *karpos* fruit + L *-icus* -ic] **:** -CARPOUS ⟨eucarpic⟩

-carpies *pl of* -CARPY

car pincher *n* **:** a mine worker who by means of a pinch bar moves railroad cars under or away from loading chutes (as at a tipple) — called also *spotter*

car·pin·cho *also* **car·pin·choe** \kär'pin(,)chō, 'kärpən,-\ *n* -s [AmerSp *carpincho*, prob. fr. Tupi *caapim* grass + *súú* to bite, eat] **1 :** CAPYBARA **2 a :** the hide of the capybara **b :** a fine soft-grained leather prepared from this hide and resembling pigskin

carping *adj* [ME, fr. pres. part. of *carpen* to carp — more at CARP] **:** likely to carp **:** characterized by frequent ill-natured, querulous, or disgruntled faultfinding ⟨Eliza's nagging and ~ attack —Thomas Wolfe⟩ **syn** see CRITICAL

carp·ing·ly \-lē, -i\ *adv* **:** in a carping manner

car·pi·nus \kär'pīnəs, -ēn-\ *n, cap* [NL, fr. L, hornbeam; akin to Lith *skirpstus* copper beech and prob. to Gk *karpos* fruit — more at HARVEST] **:** a genus of small trees (family Corylaceae) of the northern hemisphere having smooth fluted beechlike bark, straight-veined leaves, fruit that is a nut in the axil of a leaflike lobed bract, and very hard strong wood

car·pi·o·des \kär'pīə,dēz\ *n, cap* [NL, fr. *carpio* (specific epithet of the carp *Cyprinus carpio*, fr. ISV *carp*) + *-odes*] **:** the genus comprising the carpsuckers

car·pi·tis \kär'pīd·əs\ *n* -ES [NL, fr. ²*carp-* + *-itis*] **:** arthritis of the carpal joint in domestic animals

-carpium — see -CARP

carp louse *n* [²*carp* + *louse*] **:** any of the members of the copepod genus *Argulus* (order Branchiura) all of which are parasites on the skin or gills of fish — see FISH LOUSE

carpo- *below* ¦ˌˌ = ¦kärpə *or* -äp- *or* -pō, ˌ'ˌ = kär'pä *or* kȧ'pä\ — see CARP-

car·po·cap·sa \,ˌˌ'kapsə\ *n, cap* [NL, fr. ¹*carp-* + *-capsa* (modif. of Gk *kapsis* act of gulping down, fr. *kaptein* to gulp down) — more at CAPSIDAE] **:** a genus of moths (family Tortricidae) including the codling moth

car·po·ceph·a·lum \,ˌˌ'sefələm\ *n, pl* **carpocepha·la** \-lə\ [NL, fr. ¹*carp-* + *cephal-* + *-um*] **:** the sporogonial receptacle in certain liverworts (as members of the genus *Marchantia*)

car·po·cra·tian \,kärpə'krāshən\ *n* -s *usu cap* [ML *Carpocratianus*, fr. Gk *Karpokratianos*, fr. *Karpokratēs* Carpocrates, 2d cent. A.D. Alexandrian Gnostic + *-ianos* -ian] **:** a follower of Carpocrates who taught that men can attain to a higher degree of illumination than that of Jesus — compare GNOSTICISM

car·pod·a·cus \ˌ'ˌdəkəs\ *n, cap* [NL, fr. ¹*carp-* + Gk *dakos* biting animal, fr. *daknein* to bite — more at TONGS] **:** a genus of finches including the purple finch and house finch

car·pod·e·tus \ˌ'ˌdəd·əs\ *n, cap* [NL, fr. ¹*carp-* + *-detus* (irreg. fr. Gk *dein* to bind); fr. the fact that the fruit is surrounded by the calyx — more at DIADEM] **:** a genus of shrubs or trees (family Escalloniaceae) with marbled leaves, small fragrant flowers in broad axillary cymes, and black berrylike fruit — see WHITE MAPAU

car·pog·e·nous \ˌ'ˌjənəs\ *or* **car·po·gen·ic** \¦ˌˌ¦jenik\ *adj* [¹*carp-* + *-genous* or *-genic*] **:** producing fruit — used of those cells of the procarp forming the carpogonium of red algae

car·po·gone \'ˌˌ,gōn\ *n* -s [by alter.] **:** CARPOGONIUM

car·po·go·ni·al \¦ˌˌ¦gōnēəl\ *adj* [NL *carpogonium* + E *-al*] **:** of or relating to a carpogonium

car·po·go·ni·um \,ˌˌ'gōnēəm\ *n, pl* **carpogo·nia** \-ēə\ [NL, fr. ¹*carp-* + *-gonium*] **1 a :** the flask-shaped egg-bearing portion of the female reproductive branch in some thallophytes (as the red algae) in which fertilization occurs and which usu. terminates in an elongate receptive trichogyne **b :** PROCARP **2 :** ASCOGONIUM

car·poi·dea \kär'pȯidēə\ *n pl, cap* [NL, fr. ¹*carp-* + *-oidea*] **:** a small class (formerly an order of Cystoidea) of widely distributed Paleozoic echinoderms having a movable tail or stalk, a bilaterally compressed body, and no evident traces of radial symmetry

car·po·lite \'ˌˌ,līt\ *or* **car·po·lith** \-,lith\ *n* -s [prob. fr. NL *carpolithus*, fr. ¹*carp-* + *-lithus* -lite] **:** a fossil fruit, nut, or seed

car·pol·o·gy \ˌ'ˌləjē\ *n* -ES [ISV ¹*carp-* + *-logy*] **:** a branch of plant morphology dealing with the structure of fruit and seeds

¹**car·po·meta·car·pal** \'ˌˌ¦med·ə,kärpəl\ *adj* [²*carp-* + *metacarpal*] **:** relating to a carpus and metacarpus or to the carpometacarpus of birds

²**carpometacarpal** \'ˌˌ,ˌˌ\ *n* -s [NL *carpometacarpus* + E *-al*] **:** a carpometacarpal bone

car·po·met·a·car·pus \'ˌˌ¦ˌˌ,ˌpəs\ *n, pl* **carpometacar·pi** \'ˌˌ,ˌ'ˌ,pī\ [NL, fr. ²*carp-* + *metacarpus*] **:** the fused distal carpal and metacarpal bones of birds or the portion of the wing supported by these bones

car pool *n* **:** a joint arrangement by a group of private automobile owners or drivers in which each in turn drives his own car and takes the other passengers; *also* **:** the group entering into such an arrangement

car·po·ped·al spasm \¦ˌˌ¦pedᵊl-, -ēd-\ *n* [ISV *carpopedal* (fr. ²*carp-* + *pedal*) + *spasm*] **:** a spasmodic contraction of the muscles of the hands and feet or esp. of the wrists and ankles in disorders such as alkalosis and tetany

car·poph·a·gous \(')kär'päfəgəs\ *adj* [Gk *karpophagos*, fr. *karp-* ¹carp- + *-phagos* -phagous] **:** feeding on fruits

car·po·phore \'ˌˌ,fō(ə)r\ *n* -s [prob. fr. NL *carpophorum*, fr. ¹*carp-* + *-phorum* -phore] **1 a :** the stalk of a fruiting body in fungi **b :** the entire fruiting body (as in many mushrooms) **2 :** a slender often forked prolongation of a receptacle or pistil or both which develops as the fruit ripens and from which the ripened carpels are suspended (as in members of the genus *Geranium* and in the Umbelliferae)

car·po·phyll *also* **car·po·phyl** \'ˌˌ,fil\ *n* -s [prob. fr. NL *carpophyllum*, fr. ¹*carp-* + *-phyllum* -phyll] **:** CARPEL

car·po·phyte \'ˌˌ,fīt\ *n* -s [¹*carp-* + *-phyte*] **1 :** a thallophyte that forms a sporocarp after fertilization (as the red seaweeds and the ascomycetous fungi) **2 :** PHANEROGAM

car·po·po·dite \kär'päpə,dīt\ *n* -s [*carp-* + Gk *pod-*, *pous* foot + E *-ite* — more at FOOT] **:** CARPUS 2 — **car·pop·o·dit·ic** \¦kär,päpə¦did·ik, kär¦p-\ *adj*

carport \'ˌ,ˌ\ *n* **:** an open-sided roofed automobile shelter that is usu. formed by extension of the roof from the side of a building

car·po·sperm \'ˌˌ,spərm\ *n* -s [¹*carp-* + *sperm*] **:** the egg of a red alga or of any alga after fertilization

car·po·spo·ran·gi·al \¦ˌˌspə¦ranjēəl\ *adj* [NL *carposporangium* + E*-al*] **:** of or relating to a carposporangium

car·po·spo·ran·gi·um \,ˌˌˌ'jēəm\ *n, pl* **carposporan·gia** \-jēə\ [NL, fr. ¹*carp-* + *sporangium*] **:** one of the sporangia forming the cystocarp in the red algae and containing carpospores

car·po·spore \'ˌˌ,spō(ə)r\ *n* -s [¹*carp-* + *spore*] **:** a diploid spore of a red alga that is produced terminally by a gonimoblast that germinates to produce the diploid tetrasporic plant — compare TETRASPORE

car·po·spor·ic \¦ˌˌ¦spōrik\ *also* **car·pos·po·rous** \ˌ'ˌspərəs\ *adj* **1 :** of, relating to, or resembling a carpospore **2 :** having carpospores

car·po·stome \'ˌˌ,stōm\ *n* -s [¹*carp-* + *-stome*] **:** the opening in the red algae through which a cystocarp discharges its spores

-car·pous \¦kärpəs, ¦kȧp-\ *adj comb form* [NL *-carpus*, fr. Gk *-karpos*, fr. *karpos* fruit — more at HARVEST] **:** fruited **:** having (such) fruit or (so many) fruits ⟨syncarpous⟩ ⟨monocarpous⟩ — **-car·py** \,kärpē, ,kȧp-, -i\ *n comb form* -ES

car·po·xe·nia \,ˌˌ'zēnēə, -nyə\ *n* -s [NL, fr. ¹*carp-* + *xenia*] **:** the direct effect of pollen on the carpel tissue — compare METAXENIA, XENIA

carps *pl of* CARP, *pres 3d sing of* CARP

-carps *pl of* -CARP

carpsucker \'ˌ,ˌˌ\ *n* [²*carp* + *sucker*] **:** any of several No. American suckers of the family Catostomidae and genus *Carpiodes* (as *C. carpio*) — compare BUFFALO FISH

car puller *n* **:** a vehicle or mechanical device for moving a freight car short distances

car·pus \'kärpəs, 'kȧp-\ *n, pl* **car·pi** \-,pī, -,pē\ [NL, fr. Gk *karpos* wrist — more at WHARF] **1 a :** the wrist or the part of the forelimb between the antebrachium and the metacarpus **b :** the group of bones supporting the wrist comprising in man a proximal row which contains the navicular, lunatum, triquetrum, and pisiform that articulate with the radius and a distal row which contains the trapezium, trapezoid, capitatum, and hamatum that articulate with the metacarpals, the number being modified in many specialized forelimbs (as those of birds) by disappearance or fusion of certain of the bony elements or by addition of a bone between the two rows — compare CENTRALE **2 :** the fifth segment from the base of a generalized appendage of a crustacean (as one of the walking legs of a lobster)

-car·pus \¦kärpəs, -äp-\ *n comb form* [NL, fr. Gk *-karpos* -carpous] **:** plant having (such) fruit — in generic names ⟨*Corynocarpus*⟩ ⟨*Thysanocarpus*⟩

carr \'kär\ *n* -s [ME *ker*, of Scand origin; akin to ON *kjarr* underbrush, Sw *kärr* marsh — more at CHARE] **1** *Brit* **:** FEN, MARSH **2** *Brit* **:** an alder grove

carr *abbr* **1** carriage **2** carrier

car·rack *also* **car·ack** *or* **car·ac** \'karək\ *n* -s [ME *carryk*, *carrake*, fr. MF *caraque*, fr. OSp *carraca*, fr. Ar *qarāqīr*, pl. of *qurqūr* merchant vessel] **:** a large Mediterranean merchant ship sometimes fitted for fighting **:** GALLEON

car·ra·geen *or* **car·ra·gheen** *also* **car·a·geen** \'karə,gēn, ,ˌˌ'ˌ\ *n* -s [fr. *Carragheen*, near Waterford, Ireland] **1 :** a dark purple branching cartilaginous seaweed (*Chondrus crispus*) found on the coasts of northern Europe and No. America — compare IRISH MOSS **2 :** CARRAGEENIN

car·ra·gee·nin *or* **car·ra·ghee·nin** \,ˌˌ'ˌnən\ *n* -s [*carrageen* or *carragheen* + *-in*] **:** a colloidal extractive of carrageen and other red algae (as *Gigartina mammillosa*) composed of a mixture of sodium, potassium, calcium, and magnesium salts of an acid sulfate of a galactose-containing polysaccharide and used chiefly as a suspending agent in foods, pharmaceuticals, cosmetics, and industrial liquids, as a clarifying agent for beverages, and in controlling crystal growth in frozen confections — called also *Irish moss extractive*

car·ra·pa·to *or* **car·a·pa·to** \,karə'päd·(,)ü, -(,)ō\ *n* -s [Pg] **:** any of several So. American ticks (genus *Amblyomma*) including pests of man and domestic animals, some being implicated as disease vectors

car·ra·ra marble *also* **carrara** \kə'rärə, -'ȧ-\ *n, usu cap C* [fr. *Carrara* (now part of Apuania), Italy, where it is found] **:** a white statuary marble — **car·ra·ran** \-rən\ *adj, usu cap*

carraway *var of* CARAWAY

car·re·four \¦karə¦fü(ə)r\ *n* -s [MF — more at CARFOUR] **1 :** CROSSROADS ⟨he was not much on maps and drove too fast to read the signs at ~*s* —A.J.Liebling⟩ **2 :** SQUARE, PLAZA ⟨the farmers . . . preferred the open ~ for their transactions —Thomas Hardy⟩

car·rel *also* **car·rell** \'karəl *also* -er-\ *n* -s [alter. of ME *carole* round dance, carol, ring — more at CAROL] **:** a small enclosure or alcove designed for individual study or reading in the stack room of a library — called also *cubicle, stall*

car·rel–da·kin solution \kə'rel/'dākən-, 'karəl- *also* 'kerəl-\ *n, usu cap C&D* **:** Dakin's solution in which sodium bicarbonate replaces the boric acid

carrel–dakin treatment *n, usu cap C&D* [after Alexis *Carrel* †1944 Fr. surgeon and biologist, and Henry Drysdale *Dakin* †1952 Eng. chemist] **:** an antiseptic treatment of wounds in World War I consisting of regular intermittent irrigation through surgically placed rubber tubes to obviate infection in contaminated wounds and to hasten asepsis in suppurating wounds — compare CARREL-DAKIN SOLUTION, DAKIN'S SOLUTION

car·re·ta \kə'red·ə\ *n* -s [Sp, fr. *carro* cart, fr. L *carrus* wheeled vehicle — more at CAR] *Southwest* **:** a two-wheeled cart

car·riage \'karij, -ēj *also* -er-\ *n* -s *often attrib* [ME *cariage*, fr. ONF, fr. *carier* to transport in a vehicle — more at CARRY]

1 : the act of carrying **:** TRANSPORT, CONVEYANCE ⟨the ~ of weapons inside the . . . town —P.A.Rollins⟩ ⟨impassable to any other ~ but a mule —Tobias Smollett⟩ **2 a** *archaic* **:** moral or social behavior **:** DEPORTMENT ⟨her very prudent ~ —Lord Byron⟩ **b :** manner of bearing the body **:** POSTURE ⟨that slender unrigid erectness and the fine ~ of head —Willa Cather⟩ **3** *archaic* **:** the act or manner of conducting measures or projects **:** MANAGEMENT, EXECUTION, ADMINISTRATION ⟨the passage and whole ~ of this action —Shak.⟩ **4 :** the price or expense of carrying **5** *obs* **:** something that is carried **:** BURDEN, LOAD, BAGGAGE **6** *obs* **:** IMPORT, SENSE ⟨missed the whole ~ of the former chapter⟩ **7 :** means of conveyance **:** VEHICLE: **a** *obs* **:** any means of carrying or conveying (as a litter, wheelbarrow, or barge) **b :** a wheeled vehicle for people; *esp* **:** a horse-drawn vehicle designed for private use and for comfort or elegance **c** *Brit* **:** a railway passenger coach **8 :** a wheeled support carrying a burden ⟨a gun ~⟩ ⟨a log ~ in a sawmill⟩ **9 :** a movable part of a machine for supporting or carrying some other movable object or part ⟨the ~ on a lathe⟩ ⟨a typewriter ~⟩ **10 a :** a frame in or on which something is carried or supported **b :** the wheeled supporting framework of a carriage or other vehicle **:** RUNNING GEAR **11** *obs* **:** a hanger for a sword **12 :** the timber or iron joist supporting a wooden staircase **13 :** CHAIR 5a

car·riage·a·ble \-jəbəl\ *adj* **1 :** PORTABLE **2 :** passable by carriages

carriage band *n* **:** DRAWBAND

carriage bolt *n* **:** a square-necked threaded bolt with a snaphead

carriage bolt

carriage boot *n* **1 :** a fur-trimmed boot for winter wear made usu. of fabric with a fur or felt lining **2 :** [3]BOOT 5a

carriage bow *n* **:** a shooting bow made in jointed sections for convenience in carrying

carriage dog *n* **:** COACH DOG

carriage folk *n pl* **:** people wealthy enough to keep carriages

carriage forward *adv, Brit* **:** with charges to be paid on delivery **:** COLLECT ⟨the parcels were sent *carriage forward*⟩

carriage guard *n* **:** CRAMP IRON 2

carriage horse *n* **:** a horse esp. adapted for carriage use by appearance and stylish action

carriage piece *n* **:** ROUGHSTRING

carriage porch *n* [prob. intended as trans. of F *porte-cochère*] **:** a roofed structure that extends from the entrance of a building over an adjacent driveway and that shelters callers as they get in or out of their vehicles

carriage rail *n* **:** a track along which the carriage of a typewriter moves by means of ball or roller bearings

carriage return *n* **:** LINE SPACE LEVER

carriage rod *n* **:** a round rod along which the carriage of a typewriter moves

carriage starter *n* **:** one that directs the flow of vehicles taking on passengers at the curbside — compare DOORMAN

carriage trade *n* **1 :** trade from the well-to-do or the wealthy **2 :** people of wealth and social position **:** upper-class people ⟨a sophisticated, elegantly equipped shop for the *carriage trade* —Welden Reynolds⟩

carriageway \'⸗⸗,⸗\ *n, Brit* **:** a roadway used by vehicular traffic **:** HIGHWAY ⟨walk on the right of the ~ —*English Highway Code*⟩; *specif* **:** LANE 3c ⟨these roads are 150 feet wide with two 22-foot ~*s* —S.P.B.Mais⟩

car·rick bend \'karik-\ *n* [*carrick* prob. fr. obs. E *carrick* carrack, fr. ME *carryk* — more at CARRACK] **:** a knot used to join the ends of two large ropes or hawsers

carrick bend

carrick bitts *n pl* **:** heavy upright pieces of timber supporting each end of the windlass of a ship

car·rick·ma·cross \'karikmə,krȯs\ *or* **carrickmacross lace** *n, usu cap C* [fr. *Carrickmacross,* Ireland, where it is made] **:** a guipure or appliqué lace of Irish origin usu. having floral or foliage designs

carried *adj* [fr. past part. of *carry*] *dial Brit* **:** RAPT, ABSTRACTED, LIGHT-HEADED, VAIN

car·ri·er \'karēə(r) *also* 'ker-\ *n* -s [ME *cariere,* fr. *carien* to carry + *-ere* -er] **1 :** one that carries **:** BEARER, MESSENGER ⟨the air is but . . . a ~ of the sounds —Francis Bacon⟩ **2 a :** an individual, partnership, corporation, or any organization engaged in transporting passengers or goods for hire by land, water, or air; *specif* **:** COMMON CARRIER **b :** a transportation line holding a government contract for carrying mail between post offices **c :** a postal employee who delivers or collects mail ⟨a rural ~⟩ **d :** a worker who transfers materials, equipment, or products from one part of an establishment to another — called also *distributor* **e :** one that delivers newspapers to subscribers on a specified route — called also *newsboy* **3 :** CARRIER PIGEON **4 :** a device for holding something while it is carried: as **a :** a conduit or drain for conveying liquids or gases **b :** a receptacle made of wood, metal, or paperboard used to ship small containers (as baskets for fruits and vegetables) — compare CRATE **c :** a frame or a box attached to a vehicle (as a bicycle or automobile) for carrying objects securely or conveniently **d :** a device or machine part that carries or drives another part: as (1) **:** CONVEYER 2a (2) **:** DOG 3d **e** *railroading* (1) **:** a grooved roller that works in a stand and that supports and permits the longitudinal movement of a signal pipeline (2) **:** a device for supporting and guiding a wire line used in signaling **5 a :** a boat that takes the catch from a fishing fleet to market **b :** AIRCRAFT CARRIER **6** *usu cap* **a :** an Athapaskan people of south-central British Columbia **b :** a member of such people **7** *usu cap* **:** the language of the Carrier people **8 a :** a person, animal, or plant that harbors and disseminates the specific microorganism or other agent causing an infectious disease from which it has recovered or to which it is immune and that may therefore become a spreader of a disease ⟨~ of typhoid fever⟩ ⟨~ of plant viruses⟩ — compare RESERVOIR, VECTOR **b :** an individual possessing a specified gene and capable of transmitting it to offspring but not of showing its typical expression; *esp* **:** one that is heterozygous for a recessive factor **9 :** a usu. inactive substance used in association with an active substance esp. for aiding in the application of the active substance: as **a :** a support for a catalyst **b :** an insoluble substance used in the preparation of certain pigments as a base upon which to precipitate the coloring matter **c :** a dyeing assistant that penetrates the textile fibers and aids diffusion and absorption of the dye **d :** a chemical element (as a stable isotope) or a compound associated with a radioactive element (as for giving a ponderable quantity for use in reactions) **e :** a vehicle serving esp. as a diluent (as for an insecticide or a drug) **10 a :** a substance (as a catalyst) by whose agency some element or group is transferred from one compound to another ⟨iron is a ~ of oxygen⟩ **b :** a fertilizer or fertilizer component considered as a source of a plant nutrient ⟨ammonium nitrate is a nitrogen ~⟩ **11 :** CARRIER'S STAMP **12 a :** a spool or bobbin holder in a braiding machine **b :** a yarn feeder in a machine knitting full-fashioned hosiery **13** *or* **carrier current** *or* **carrier wave :** an electric wave or alternating current whose modulations are used as signals in radio, television, telephonic, or telegraphic transmission **14 :** an organization acting as an underwriter or insurer

carrier pigeon *n* **1 :** a pigeon used to carry messages; *specif* **:** one of a fancy chiefly English breed of pigeons of large size having long wings and body, much bare skin about the eyes, and a greatly developed carunculated cere **2 :** HOMING PIGEON

carrier shell *n* **:** the carrier snail or its shell

carrier's lien *n* **:** a common-law lien for freight conferring the right to retain the property only until the claim is paid

carrier snail *n* **:** a marine snail of the genus *Xenophora*

carrier's option *n* **:** the option allowed to a carrier of fixing freight charges on the basis of either the weight of the goods or the space occupied

carrier's stamp *n* **:** a stamp issued in the U.S. from 1842 to 1861 by a government or private carrier or by a postmaster to pay for delivery of mail from post office to addressee, government service being limited to carriage between post offices — compare POSTMASTER'S STAMP

carrier suppression *n* **:** a method of signal transmission in which the power associated essentially with the carrier frequency is not transmitted

carries *pres 3d sing of* CARRY, *pl of* CARRY

carriole *var of* CARIOLE

car·ri·on \'karēən *also* -er-\ *n* -s *often attrib* [ME *carion, caroine,* fr. AF *caroine,* fr. (assumed) VL *caronia,* irreg. fr. L *carn-, caro* flesh — more at CARNAL] **1** *obs* **:** a dead body **:** CARCASS, CORPSE ⟨croaking like so many ravens about a ~ —Charles Johnstone⟩ **2 :** the dead and putrefying flesh of an animal **:** flesh that is unfit for food ⟨we killed a tiger and a wolf; but God be thanked, we were not so reduced as to eat ~ —Daniel Defoe⟩ **3 a :** a scavenging animal ⟨enemy dead were left to rot or be eaten by ~⟩ **b :** a worthless or noxious animal **:** VERMIN **4 :** something that is corrupt, vile, or rotten ⟨Roman fashionable society hated Caesar, and any ~ was welcome to them which would taint his reputation —J.A.Froude⟩

carrion beetle *n* **:** any of numerous beetles of the genera *Necrophorus* and *Silpha* (family Silphidae) that feed chiefly on dead animals though a few (as *S. bituberosa*) attack economic plants — see SPINACH CARRION BEETLE

carrion buzzard *n* **:** an American vulture of the family Cathartidae

carrion crow *n* **:** the common European black crow (*Corvus corone*)

carrion flower *n* **1 :** an American catbrier (*Smilax herbacea*) whose flowers smell like carrion **2 :** a plant of the genus *Stapelia*

carrion fly *n* **:** a fly that lays its eggs in decaying flesh; *specif* **:** a widespread and destructive blowfly (*Phormia terrae-novae*)

carrion fungus *n* **:** STINKHORN

carrion hawk *n* **:** CARACARA

carrion poisoning *n, Austral* **:** botulism of sheep

car·ri·on's disease \¦karē¦ōnz-\ *n, usu cap C* [after Daniel A. *Carrión* †*ab*1886 Peruvian medical student, who voluntarily contracted the disease and died from it] **:** BARTONELLOSIS

car·ritch \'karich, -ij\ *n* -ES [back-formation fr. *carritches,* taken as pl., alter. of [1]*catechise*] *Scot* **:** CATECHISM — often used in pl. but sing. in constr.

car·ri·witch·et \,karə'wichət, '⸗⸗,⸗⸗\ *or* **car·witch·et** \kär-'w-, '⸗,⸗⸗\ *n* -s [origin unknown] **:** a hoaxing or riddling question

car·ri·zo \kə'rē(,)zō, -(,)sō\ *n* -s [Sp, irreg. fr. L *caric-, carex* reed grass, sedge — more at CAREX] **:** a reed grass of the genus *Phragmites*

car·roc·cio \kə'rȯ(,)chō, -ȯchē,ō\ *n, pl* **carroc·ci** \-ȯ(,)chē\ [It — more at CAROCHE] **:** a large wheeled vehicle bearing a standard and used in medieval times esp. by Italian free cities to serve as a rallying point for an army in battle

car·roll·ite \'karə,līt\ *n* -s [*Carroll* co., Maryland, its locality + E *-ite*] **:** a mineral $CuCo_2S_4$ consisting of a light steel-gray copper cobalt sulfide

carrom *var of* CAROM

car·ro·ma·ta \,karə'mäd·ə\ *n* -s [PhilSp, alter. of Sp *carromato* horse-drawn covered cart, fr. It *carromatto* low 4-wheeled cart without sides, fr. *carro* cart, vehicle (fr. L *carrus*) + *matto* mad, crazy, fr. L *mattus* stupid, drunk — more at CAR, MAT] *Philippines* **:** a light 2-wheeled boxlike passenger vehicle usu. drawn by a single native pony

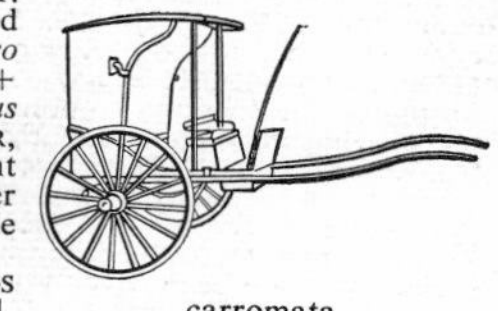
carromata

car·ron·ade \¦karə¦nād\ *n* -s [*Carron,* village in Scotland, where it was first made + E *-ade*] **:** an obsolete short light iron cannon differing from guns and howitzers in having no trunnions and used on ships to throw heavy shot at close quarters and on shore as a howitzer

car·ron oil \'karə,n-\ *n* [fr. *Carron,* Scotland; fr. its use in treating the burns of workmen in the ironworks there] **:** a lotion of equal parts of linseed oil and limewater formerly applied to burns and scalds — called also *lime liniment*

car·ros·se·rie \kȧrōsrē\ *n, pl* **carrosseries** \-rē(z)\ [F, fr. *carrosse* carriage (fr. It *carrozza,* fr. *carro* cart, vehicle, fr. L *carrus*) + *-erie* -ery — more at CAR] **:** the carriage body of an automobile — compare CHASSIS

[1]**car·rot** \'karət *also* -er, *usu* -əd·+V\ *n* -s [MF *carotte,* fr. LL *carota,* modif. of Gk *karōton;* prob. akin to Gk *kara* head — more at CEREBRAL] **1 a :** a biennial plant (*Daucus carota*) having a yellow or orange-red tapering root that is used as a vegetable **b :** the root of this plant **2 :** something felt to resemble a carrot in shape or color: **a :** a spindle-shaped bundle of rolled and twisted tobacco leaves **b :** a red-haired person **3 :** a chemical agent used in producing hatter's felt from fur **4** [so called fr. the traditional method of urging a donkey on by holding a carrot in front of him] **:** a promised often illusory reward or advantage used esp. as a political enticement ⟨failed to offer the community either the ~ of private enterprise or the stick of compulsion —D.B.Copland⟩

[2]**carrot** \"\ *vt* -ED/-ING/-S [so called fr. the color of fur so treated] **:** to treat (fur) with a chemical agent (as a solution of mercuric nitrate) to improve the felting property — **car·rot·er** \-əd·ə(r)\ *n* -s

carrot aphid *n* **:** an aphid (*Cavariella aegopodii*) of Australia and Tasmania that is highly destructive to carrots, parsnips, and celery

carrot beetle *n* **:** a large reddish or dark brown beetle (*Ligyrus gibbosus*) of the family Scarabaeidae that in the adult stage injures carrots by attacking the roots

carrotene *or* **carrotin** *var of* CAROTENE

carrot family *n* **:** UMBELLIFERAE

carrot oil *or* **carrot-seed oil** *n* **:** either of two oils obtained from seeds of the carrot: **a :** a light-yellow essential oil having a spicy odor and used in liqueurs, flavors, and perfumes **b :** a golden yellow fatty oil that is rich in vitamin A and that is used in coloring butter and margarine

carrot red *n* **1 :** the color of the carrot **:** a moderate to strong orange that is lighter than Mars yellow and redder and darker than zinc orange or sunburst **2 :** a moderate reddish orange that is yellower and duller than crab apple or flamingo

carrot rust fly *also* **carrot fly** *n* **:** a small two-winged fly (*Psila rosae*) whose larva burrows in the roots of the carrot

carrot soft rot *n* **:** a soft rot of carrots caused by a bacterium (*Erwinia carotovora*)

carrottop \'⸗⸗,⸗\ *n, slang* **:** a red-haired person

carrotweed \'⸗⸗,⸗\ *n* [so called fr. the resemblance of the leaves to those of the carrot] **:** a ragweed (*Ambrosia elatior*)

carrotwood \'⸗⸗,⸗\ *n* [so called fr. the color of the fruit] **:** a wood derived from an Australian tree (*Blighia anacardioides*) of the family Sapindaceae having compound leaves and white flowers in axillary racemes

car·roty \-əd·ē, -ətē, -i\ *adj, sometimes* -ER/-EST **1 :** resembling carrots in color ⟨~ hair⟩ **2 :** having hair the color of carrots

car·rou·sel *or* **car·ou·sel** \,karə'sel, '⸗⸗,⸗ *also* -er- *or* -zel\ *n* -s [F *carrousel,* fr. It *carosello* tourney in which the contestants threw balls of clay at each other, prob. fr. It dial. (Neapolitan) *carusello* ball of clay, fr. *caruso* shorn head, boy] **1 a :** a tournament in which troops of horsemen execute various evolutions **b :** a riding exhibition performed to music in dancelike patterns by a group on horseback **2 a :** MERRY-GO-ROUND **b :** a conveyer (as for assembly-line work) on which objects are placed and carried around a complete circuit on a horizontal plane

carrow *n* -s [IrGael *cearrbhach;* akin to ScGael *cearrach* gambler, dexterous] *Irish* **:** an itinerant gambler

carr-price reaction \'kär'prīs-\ *n, usu cap C&P* [fr. the names *Carr & Price*] **:** a reaction of antimony trichloride and vitamin A in chloroform solution that gives a blue color and is used for the identification and assay of vitamin A

[1]**car·ry** \'karē, -i *also* -er-\ *vb* -ED/-ING/-ES [ME *carien,* fr. ONF *carier* to transport in a vehicle, fr. *car* vehicle, fr. L *carrus* — more at CAR] *vt* **1 :** to move while supporting (as in a vehicle or in one's hands or arms) **:** move an appreciable distance without dragging **:** sustain as a burden or load and bring along to another place ⟨gas, oil, water, and food [are] available at desert hamlets, but extra supplies should be *carried* —*Amer. Guide Series: Calif.*⟩ ⟨her legs refused to ~ her further —Ellen Glasgow⟩ **2 :** CONVEY ⟨~ the news⟩ ⟨~ a message⟩ **:** TAKE ⟨*carried* his complaint to the president⟩ **3** *chiefly dial* **:** CONDUCT, ESCORT, LEAD, GUIDE ⟨he *carried* her to the party⟩ ⟨~ the cow through the gate⟩ **4 :** to lead along or influence by mental or emotional appeal **:** MOVE, SWAY ⟨~ an audience with one⟩ **5 :** to get possession or control of (as in a contest or by effort or force) **:** WIN, CAPTURE ⟨~ a town by storm⟩ ⟨~ off the prize⟩ **6 :** to transfer from one place (as a book or column) to another ⟨~ an account to the ledger⟩ ⟨~ a number in adding⟩ **7 :** CHANNEL, CONDUCT **:** contain and direct the course of ⟨the canal *carries* the water⟩ ⟨the drain *carries* sewage⟩ **8 a :** to hold, wear, or have upon one's person ⟨he *carries* a watch⟩ **b :** to be burdened or ladened with **:** bear upon or within one ⟨~ an unborn child⟩ **9 :** to hold or contain without apparent effort or discomposure ⟨he knows how to ~ his liquor⟩ **10 :** to have as a mark, attribute, or property ⟨~ a scar⟩ **:** IMPLY, INVOLVE ⟨the crime *carried* a heavy penalty⟩ **11 :** to hold (the body or some part of it) as if well-supported ⟨he *carries* his head high⟩ **12 :** to behave (oneself) in a specified manner **:** DEMEAN ⟨~ himself proudly⟩ **13 :** to sustain the weight or burden of **:** BEAR ⟨pillars ~ an arch⟩ **14 :** to bear as a crop **:** SUPPORT, MAINTAIN ⟨~ livestock⟩ — usu. used of land **15 a :** to sing with reasonable correctness of pitch ⟨he can ~ a tune⟩ **b :** SING, PLAY ⟨only two men to ~ the violins⟩ ⟨he *carried* the tenor⟩ **16 a :** to keep in stock **:** maintain on hand for sale ⟨a department store *carries* hardware⟩ **b :** to have or maintain on a list or record ⟨~ a person on a payroll⟩ **17 :** to maintain and cause to continue through financial support or personal effort ⟨he has *carried* the magazine single-handedly⟩ **18 :** to extend, prolong, or continue in space, time, or degree ⟨~ the chimney through the roof⟩ ⟨~ the war into Africa⟩ ⟨~ a principle too far⟩ **19 a :** to gain victory for (a principle or a candidate); *esp* **:** to secure the adoption or passage of (a motion or bill) **b :** to succeed in (an election) **:** win a majority of votes in (as a legislative body or a state) ⟨the bill *carried* the Senate⟩ **20** *archaic* **:** MANAGE, CONDUCT, PROSECUTE **21 :** PUBLISH ⟨newspapers ~ weather reports⟩ **:** BROADCAST ⟨the committee's proceedings were *carried* on a network⟩ **22 a :** to bear the charges (as interest or insurance) of holding or having (as stocks or merchandise) from one time to another ⟨a packing house *carries* meat for future export⟩ **b** (1) **:** to keep on one's books as a debtor **:** await payment by ⟨a merchant *carries* a customer⟩ (2) **:** to keep on one's books as a debt ⟨~ an account⟩ **c :** to hold (issues of new securities) in anticipation of a rise in price **23** *hunting* **a :** to keep and follow ⟨the dog could not ~ the scent⟩ **b :** SUPPORT ⟨this land will ~ a scent⟩ **24 :** to hold (the staff of a color or a guidon) at the carry **25 :** to hoist and maintain (a sail) in use ⟨the ship *carried* too much sail⟩ **26 :** to cover (a distance) or pass (an object) at a single stroke in golf ⟨his drive *carried* the bunker⟩ **27 a :** to propel and control (a puck) along the playing surface with a hockey stick **:** DRIBBLE **b** *basketball* **:** [2]PALM c **28 a** *of a student* **:** to be enrolled in (as a course) ⟨~ both French and Spanish this semester⟩ **b** *of a teacher* **:** TEACH ⟨~ a class⟩ ⟨no instructor will be asked to ~ more than three sections of freshman English⟩ **29 a :** to allow (an opponent) to make a good showing by lessening one's opposition **b :** to perform with sufficient ability to make up for the poor performance of (a partner or teammate) ~ *vi* **1 :** to act as a bearer **:** convey something — often used in the phrase *fetch and carry* **2 a :** to reach or penetrate to a distance **:** sustain flight ⟨voices ~ well over water⟩ ⟨a golf drive will not ~ against the wind⟩ **b :** to project itself to a distance with full effect — usu. used of a work of art **c :** to convey itself to a reader or audience **:** get across — usu. used of a literary or dramatic work **3 :** to undergo or admit of carriage in a specified way ⟨a load that *carries* easily⟩ **4** *of a horse* **:** to hold head and neck properly esp. when in action **5** *hunting* **a** (1) *of a running animal* **:** to collect mud on the feet ⟨a hare *carries* on wet plowland⟩ (2) *of soft ground* **:** to stick to the feet of a running animal **b** *of a hunting dog* **:** to keep and follow the scent **6** *falconry* **:** to fly away with the quarry **7** *of a goalkeeper* **:** to take more than the legal number of steps while in possession of the soccer ball **8 :** to win adoption (as in a legislative body) ⟨the motion *carried* by a vote of 71 to 25⟩

syn BEAR, CONVEY, TRANSPORT, TRANSMIT: CARRY indicates moving to a location some distance away while supporting or maintaining off the ground. Orig. indicating movement by car or cart, it is a natural word to use in ref. to cargoes and loads on trucks, wagons, planes, ships, or even beasts of burden. It has spread widely from its original meaning and may be substituted in most situations for the following words. BEAR in this sense may more strongly suggest maintaining or holding aloft the weight involved, more incidentally the fact of its being moved. It may also suggest some special kind of carrying or carriage, for instance, one attended by ceremony ⟨over his head was *borne* a rich canopy —Samuel Johnson⟩ ⟨two boats were lowered; one . . . *bore* the captain —B.N.Cardozo⟩ CONVEY may be used of passage or carriage in which the nature of the sustaining and moving agency is less significant, noteworthy, definite, or individual ⟨irrigation water *conveyed* from rivers⟩ ⟨he looked white and tired and listless, even his bristling hair and mustache *conveyed* his depression —H.G.Wells⟩ TRANSPORT refers to carriage in bulk or number over an appreciable distance and, typically, by a customary or usual carrier agency ⟨how many merchants and carriers . . . must have been employed in *transporting* the materials from some of those workmen to others who often live in a very distant part of the country —Adam Smith⟩ TRANSPORT is also used to signify the carrying of persons into very distant or strange spheres, esp. by unusual instrumentalities ⟨the astrophysicist with the aid of his spectroscope *transports* himself through millions of miles to worlds incredibly terrifying and beautiful —Waldemar Kaempffert⟩ TRANSMIT is sometimes used as a synonym for *send* or *ship* in reference to tangible things ⟨*transmit* baggage⟩ but it is now much more commonly used in reference to agencies that impart or communicate more intangible items ⟨the typewriter has become the direct means of *transmitting* even poetry to the page —T.S.Eliot⟩ ⟨such a youth has come into an inheritance of illusions as important and perhaps as valuable as anything else which his ancestors have *transmitted* to him —J.W.Krutch⟩ — **carry a torch** *or* **carry the torch 1 :** CRUSADE **2 :** to be in love esp. without success or return **:** cherish a longing or a devotion ⟨she still *carries a torch* for him even though their engagement is broken⟩ — **carry one's bat** *of a cricket batsman* **:** to be not out at the close of play or of one's side's innings — **carry the ball :** to perform or assume the chief role **:** bear the major portion of work or responsibility — **carry the banner :** to be destitute

[2]**carry** \"\ *n* -ES **1 :** a vehicle, receptacle, or contrivance used for carrying; *specif, dial Brit* **:** a 2-wheeled barrow **2 :** the range of a gun or projectile or of a struck or thrown ball **:** carrying power **3** *chiefly Scot* **a :** the drift of the clouds **b :** CLOUDS, SKY **4 a :** the act or method of carrying ⟨fireman's ~⟩ ⟨one-hand ~⟩ **b :** a portage esp. between two bodies of navigable water **5 :** the position assumed by a color bearer or guidon bearer with color staff or guidon in position for marching **6 :** [4]RUSH 4 **7 :** the holding of securities with borrowed money esp. to secure a higher rate of return than the interest paid for the money borrowed

car·ry·all \'karē,ȯl *also* -er-\ *n* -s [by folk etymology fr. F *carriole* — more at CARIOLE] **1 a :** a light covered carriage having four wheels and seats for four or more persons and usu. drawn by one horse **b :** a passenger automobile having a closed body and two facing seats along the sides **2** [[1]*carry* + *all*] **:** a capacious bag or case **3 :** a carrier with a scraperlike self-loading device drawn by a tractor, pushed by a bulldozer, or self-propelled and used esp. for hauling earth and crushed rock

carry away *vt* **1 :** to cause the death of **:** carry off **2 :** to break off **:** DEMOLISH ⟨the gale *carried away* the foremast⟩ **3 :** to drive or draw out of the control of reason and judgment (as by passion, flattery, or charm) ⟨the girl was *carried away* by her pity —Winston Churchill⟩ ~ *vi* **1 :** to break off (as of a mast) **:** become swept away ⟨the bridge *carried away*⟩ **2 :** to lose rigging ⟨the ship *carried away* in the storm⟩

carry back *vt* **:** to deduct (a loss or an unused credit) from taxable income of a prior period ⟨*carry back* an unused excess-profits-tax credit⟩

carry–back \'⸗⸗,⸗\ *n* -s **:** a loss sustained or a portion of a credit not used in a given period that may be deducted from taxable income of a prior period ⟨showed operating losses in 1946 despite heavy tax *carry-backs* allowed by the government —*Newsweek*⟩

carry bag *n* **:** a deep bag made typically of heavy paper, having handles, and used for carrying small purchases

carry forward *vt* **1 :** to transfer (an amount) to the succeeding column, page, or book relating to the same account **2 :** to carry over (sense 2)

carry–forward \ˈ⸗⸗ˌ⸗⸗\ *n* -s **1 :** CARRY-OVER **2** *Brit* **:** the accumulated undivided profits of a corporation after provision has been made for reserves and dividends

carrying *pres part of* CARRY

carrying capacity *n* **:** the population (as of one species of animal) that a given area (as of water or pasture) will support without undergoing deterioration ⟨when deer herds are allowed to exceed the *carrying capacity*, permanent damage to woodland results⟩ ⟨a *carrying capacity* of one sheep per acre⟩ — compare BIOTIC POTENTIAL 1

carrying charge *n* **1 :** expense incident to the continued ownership or use of property (as taxes on real estate); *specif* **:** a charge made for carrying a debtor (as interest charged on a margin account with a broker) **2 :** a charge added to the price of merchandise sold on the installment plan

carrying–on \ˈ⸗⸗⸗ˈ⸗\ *n, pl* **carryings–on :** foolish, excited, or improper behavior; *also* **:** an instance of such behavior ⟨scandalous *carryings-on*⟩

carrying place *n* **:** PORTAGE 4b

carrying trade *n* **:** trade or commerce consisting in transporting goods (as from one country to another)

carrying value *n* **:** BOOK VALUE

carry–log \ˈ⸗⸗ˌ⸗\ *n* [¹*carry* + *log*] **:** a high-wheeled cart for hauling logs suspended from the axle

carry off *vt* **1 :** to cause the death of ⟨the plague *carried off* thousands⟩ **2 :** to perform easily or successfully **3 :** to make acceptable ⟨her charm *carried off* her husband's fiery temper⟩ **4 :** to brave out **:** face out

carry on *vt* **:** CONDUCT, MANAGE ⟨*carry on* the new enterprise⟩ ~ *vi* **1 :** to behave in a foolish, excited, or improper manner: as **a :** to frolic noisily or destructively **b :** to rage in anger or in grief **c :** to act indiscreetly or immorally **2 :** to continue one's course or activity; *esp* **:** to persevere unfalteringly in spite of hindrance or discouragement **3 :** to carry sail up to or beyond the limits of prudence **:** spread the utmost extent of canvas possible

carry out *vt* **1 :** to put into execution **2 :** to bring to a successful issue **3 :** to continue to an end or stopping point

carry over *vt* **1 a :** to hold over (as goods) for another season **b :** to transfer (an amount) to the succeeding column, page, or book relating to the same account **c** *on the London stock exchange* **:** to carry (a customer) until the next settlement **:** extend (the date of settlement for stock) until the end of the next account — compare CONTANGO **2 :** to deduct (a loss or an unused credit) from taxable income of a subsequent period ~ *vi* **:** to persist from one stage to another or from one sphere of activity to another

carry–over \ˈ⸗⸗ˌ⸗⸗\ *n* -s **1 :** the act or process of carrying over **2 :** something that is carried over

carrytale \ˈ⸗⸗ˌ⸗\ *n* **:** GOSSIP, TALEBEARER

carry through *vt* **:** to carry out ~ *vi* **1 :** to bring to completion or carry out a task or obligation ⟨they *carried through* on the agreement⟩ **2 :** PERSIST, SURVIVE ⟨feelings that *carry through* to the present⟩

cars *pl of* CAR

carse \ˈkärs\ *n* -s [ME *cars, kerss,* perh. fr. *kerres,* pl. of *ker* carr] *Scot* **:** low fertile land usu. along a river

car service *n* **1 :** the work performed by a railroad car **2 :** the supply of cars and subsidiary equipment by one railroad carrier to another or to a shipper

carshop \ˈ⸗ˌ⸗\ *n* **:** a group of workshops for the construction, maintenance, and repair of railroad equipment (as rolling stock) — usu. used in pl.

carshuni *usu cap, var of* KARSHUNI

carsick \ˈ⸗ˌ⸗\ *adj* **:** affected with car sickness

car sickness *n* **:** motion sickness experienced when riding in vehicles, esp. automobiles

car·son city \ˌkärsᵊnˈ⸗ˈ⸗\ *adj, usu cap both Cs* [fr. *Carson City,* city in Nevada] **:** of or from Carson City, the capital of Nevada ⟨a *Carson City* street⟩ **:** of the kind or style prevalent in Carson City

car·stone \ˈkärˌstōn\ *n* [by folk etymology fr. *quernstone*] **:** a firmly cemented ferruginous sandstone found in the British isles; *esp* **:** one of Cretaceous age used as a building stone

¹cart \ˈkärt, ˈkȧt, *usu* -d·+V\ *n* -s [ME *carte, cart,* prob. fr. ON *kartr;* akin to OE *cræt* cart, OHG *kranz* wreath, Lith *grandis* hoop, OE *cradol* cradle — more at CRADLE] **1** *obs* **:** CHARIOT **2 :** a heavy 2-wheeled vehicle without springs used for the ordinary purposes of farming or for transporting freight — compare WAGON **3 :** any lightweight 2-wheeled vehicle drawn by a horse, pony, or dog: as **a :** a light vehicle for delivery (as by bakers or butchers) **b :** an open 2-wheeled pleasure carriage **c :** SULKY **4 :** any small wheeled vehicle (as for groceries, golf clubs, or tea service) — **cart before the horse :** two things in illogical, improper, or unnatural order ⟨his emphasis on method at the expense of content puts the *cart before the horse*⟩ — **in the cart** *adv (or adj), slang Brit* **:** in an embarrassing position (as from deception or defeat)

cart 2

²cart \ˈ"\ *vb* -ED/-ING/-s [ME *carten,* fr. *cart,* n.] *vt* **1 :** to carry or convey in or as if in a cart ⟨buses to ~ the kids to and from school —L.S.Gannett⟩; *specif, archaic* **:** to carry publicly in or drag behind a cart as a punishment ⟨suspected, tried, condemned, and ~*ed* in a day —George Crabbe⟩ **2 :** to take or drag (a person) away without ceremony or by force — usu. used with *off* ⟨they ~*ed* him off to jail⟩ ~ *vi* **:** to drive a cart esp. in transporting freight **:** follow the business of a carter

cart·age \ˈkärd·ij, ˈkȧt, |tij, -ēj\ *n* -s [ME, fr. *cart* or *carten* + *-age*] **1 :** the act of carrying by cart or truck usu. within a city **:** HAULING **2 :** the rate charged for carting or hauling

car·ta·ge·na \ˌkärd·əˈjēnə, -ˈgänə, -ˈhänə\ *adj, usu cap* [fr. *Cartagena,* city in Spain] **1 :** of or from the city of Cartagena, Spain **:** of the kind or style prevalent in Cartagena, Spain **2 :** of or from the city of Cartagena, Colombia **:** of the kind or style prevalent in Cartagena, Colombia

cartagena bark *n, usu cap C* [fr. *Cartagena,* seaport in Colombia] **:** a cinchona bark derived from a Colombian tree (*Cinchona lancifolia*)

cartagena ipecac *n, usu cap C* [fr. *Cartagena,* seaport in Colombia where it is exported] **:** ipecac derived from a Brazilian tree (*Cephaelis acuminata*) — called also *Panama ipecac*

cart–driver \ˈ⸗ˌ⸗⸗\ *n* **:** a widely distributed active yellowish burrowing shore crab (*Ocypode gaudichaudii*) of the western coast of Central and So. America

carte *n* -s [ME, charter, playing card, fr. MF — more at CARD] **1** \ˈkärt, -e-\ *Scot* **a :** PLAYING CARD **b :** a game of cards — usu. used in pl. **2** *obs* **:** CHART, MAP ⟨the distance . . . when measured on the ~ does not exceed 90 miles —Tobias Smollett⟩

carte blanche \ˈkärtˈbläⁿsh, ˈkȧt-, -änch\ *n, pl* **cartes blanches** \-t...sh(əz), -ch(əz)\ [F] **1 :** a blank document signed in advance by one party to an agreement and given to the other with permission to fill in what conditions he pleases **2 :** full discretionary power **:** unlimited delegated authority ⟨the architect was given *carte blanche* to build, landscape, and furnish the house⟩ **3 :** a hand of cards (as in piquet) containing no king, queen, or jack but having special value

carted *adj, of a deer* **:** brought to the scene of the hunt and released in order to be tracked down but not killed

carte d'en·trée \ˌkärt‚däⁿ-ˈtrā, ˈkȧt-, -dän-\ *n, pl* **cartes d'entrée** \ˈ"\ [F] **:** card of admission **:** TICKET

carte de vi·site \ˌ⸗də̇vēˈzēt, -vē-\ *n, pl* **cartes de visite** \ˈ"\ [F] **1 :** VISITING CARD **2 :** a close-trimmed portrait photograph approximately 2¼x3¾ in. intended as a substitute for a visiting card

carte du jour \-dəˈzhu̇(ə)r, -u̇ə\ *n, pl* **cartes du jour** \ˈ"\ [F, lit., the day's menu] **:** MENU

car·tel \(ˈ)kärˈtel, -ˈt-\ *n* -s [MF, fr. OIt *cartello* letter of defiance, placard, fr. *carta* card, leaf of paper — more at CARD] **1 :** a letter of defiance or challenge (as to single combat) **2 a :** a written agreement between belligerent nations esp. for the treatment and exchange of prisoners and the regulation of nonbelligerent relations **b :** an exchange of prisoners **c :** CARTEL SHIP **3 :** a card or paper bearing writing or printing ⟨he ordered a ~ with some Greek verses —Horace Walpole⟩ **4** [G *kartell,* lit., written agreement between opposing belligerents, fr. F *cartel,* lit., letter of defiance] **:** a voluntary often international combination of independent private enterprises supplying like commodities or services that agree to limit their competitive activities (as by allocating customers or markets, regulating quantity or quality of output, pooling returns or profits, fixing prices or terms of sale, exchanging techniques, trademarks, or patents, or by other methods of controlling production, price, or distribution) **5** [G & F; G *kartell,* fr. F *cartel*] **:** a combination of or an agreement between political groups for common action — compare BLOC

cartel clock \ˈ⸗ˈ⸗ˌ⸗\ *n* [F *cartel* decorative scrollwork, dial case of a clock, framed hanging clock, fr. It *cartella* frieze or slab with space for an inscription, leaflet, ticket, dim. of *carta*] **:** a hanging wall clock of French origin usu. of gilt bronze and asymmetrical in design

carte–let·tre \kȧrtəletr(ᵊ), -et(rə)\ *n, pl* **carte–lettres** \-trᵊ, -t(rə)\ [F, fr. *carte* card + *lettre* letter — more at CARD, LETTER] **:** LETTERCARD

car·tel·ism \kärˈte‚lizəm, kȧˈ-\ *n* -s **:** the practice of forming cartels **:** CARTELIZATION

¹car·tel·ist \-ˈləst\ *n* -s **:** one that belongs to or favors a cartel

²cartelist \ˈ"\ *or* **car·tel·is·tic** \ˌkärd·ᵊlˈistik, ˌkȧd-, ˌ⸗ˌteˈli-\ *adj* **:** relating to, favoring, or characterized by cartelization

car·tel·i·za·tion *or* **car·tel·li·za·tion** \(ˌ)kärˌteləˈzāshən, (ˌ)kȧ-; ˌ⸗ d·ᵊləˈzāshən, -ˌīˈz-\ *n* -s **:** organization into cartels ⟨~ of the chemical industry⟩

car·tel·ize \kärˈteˌlīz, kȧˈ-, ˈ⸗ d·ᵊlˌīz\ *vb* -ED/-ING/-s *vt* **:** to form into a cartel **:** bring under the control of a cartel ~ *vi* **:** to form a cartel

cartel ship *n* **:** a ship commissioned in time of war to sail under a safe-conduct for the exchange of prisoners or conveyance of proposals between belligerents

cart·er \ˈkär|d·ə(r), ˈkȧ|, |tə-\ *n* -s [ME, fr. ¹*cart* + *-er*] **:** one that drives a cart or a truck **:** one engaged in vehicle transport **:** TEAMSTER

car·ter grass \ˈ"-\ *n, usu cap C* [prob. fr. the name *Carter*] **:** NAPIER GRASS

carterly *adj, obs* **:** resembling a carter **:** BOORISH

carter process *n, usu cap C* [after Levi *Carter fl*1885 Am. industrial chemist] **:** a process for making white lead by treating powdered lead in water suspension with acetic acid and carbon dioxide

cartes *pl of* CARTE

¹car·te·sian \(ˈ)kärˈtēzhən, -ˈt-\ *adj, usu cap* [NL *cartesianus,* fr. *Cartesius* (René Descartes) †1650 Fr. scientist and philosopher + *-anus* -an] **:** of or relating to Descartes, his writings, theories, or methods — see CARTESIANISM

²cartesian \ˈ"\ *n* -s *usu cap* **:** a follower of Descartes **:** an adherent of Cartesian philosophy

cartesian coordinate *n, usu cap 1st C* **1 :** either of two coordinates for locating a point on a plane being the distances of the point from each of two infinite intersecting straight-line axes of reference usu. designated as X and Y measured in each case parallel to the other axis and each coordinate being given arbitrarily an algebraic sign according to the direction in which it extends from the reference axis to the point **2 :** any one of three coordinates for locating a point in space being the distances from each of three intersecting coordinate planes measured in each case parallel to that one of three straight-line axes that is the intersection of the other two planes — compare RECTANGULAR COORDINATE

Cartesian coordinates in a plane: P point in a plane; *x′,x* and *y′,y* straight-line axes intersecting at O; UP,SP Cartesian coordinates

cartesian diver *n. usu cap C* **:** a small hollow glass figure placed in a vessel of water that has an elastic cover so arranged that by an increase of pressure the water can be forced into the figure producing the effects of suspension, sinking, and floating as the pressure varies

cartesian equation *n, usu cap C* **:** an equation of a curve or surface in which the variables are the Cartesian coordinates of a point on the curve or surface

car·te·sian·ism \⸗ˈ⸗⸗ˌnizəm\ *n, usu cap* [¹*Cartesian* + *-ism*] **:** the philosophy of René Descartes and his followers deriving its chief significance from its reaction to scholastic subtleties, its utilization of radical doubt and of the postulate of cogito as its starting point, its proclamation of mathematical certitude as an ideal in metaphysical demonstration, and its dualistic distinction between thought and extension or mind and matter

¹car·tha·gin·i·an \ˌkärthəˈjinēən, -äth-, -nyən\ *adj, usu cap* [L *Carthagin-, Carthago* Carthage, ancient city of northern Africa + E *-ian*] **1 :** of, relating to, or characteristic of Carthage **2 :** of, relating to, or characteristic of the people of Carthage

²carthaginian \ˈ"\ *n* -s *usu cap* **:** a native or inhabitant of Carthage

carthaginian peace *n, usu cap C* **:** a treaty of peace so severe that it means the virtual destruction of the defeated contestant

car·tha·min \ˈkärthəmən\ *also* **car·thame** \-ˌthām\ *or* **car·tham·ic acid** \(ˈ)kärˈthamik-\ *n* -s [*carthamin,* ISV *cartham-* (fr. NL *Carthamus tinctorius,* species name of the safflower) + *-in; carthame* fr. F, fr. NL *Carthamus; carthamic* fr. NL *Carthamus* + E *-ic*] **:** a red crystalline glucoside $C_{21}H_{22}O_{11}$ constituting the coloring matter of the safflower

car·tha·mus \ˈkärthəməs\ *n, cap* [NL, fr. Ar (colloq.) *qarṭam* safflower] **:** a genus of Eurasian herbs (family Compositae) resembling the members of the genus *Centaurea* but distinguished by their spiny leaves and spreading outer involucral scales — see SAFFLOWER

carthamus red *or* **carthamus rose** *n, often cap C* **:** a vivid red that is yellower, lighter, and slightly stronger than apple red, yellower, lighter, and stronger than carmine, and lighter, stronger, and slightly bluer than scarlet — called also *artillery, leaf red, Lincoln red, Portuguese red, rose Carthame, rouge vegetal, safflor, safflower red, vegetable red, vegetable rouge*

cart horse *n* **:** a large strong horse bred or used for drawing heavy loads

¹car·thu·sian \kärˈth(y)üzhən, kȧˈ-\ *n* -s *usu cap* [modif. (perh. influenced by *charterhouse* or ME *charthous* Carthusian) of ML *cartusiensis,* irreg. fr. OF *Chartrouse, Chartrose* (now *Grande Chartreuse*), mother house of the Carthusian order, mountainous region near Grenoble in southeast France where that house was founded] **:** a member of an austere religious order founded by St. Bruno in 1084

²carthusian \(ˈ)⸗ˈ⸗⸗\ *adj, usu cap* **:** of or relating to the Carthusians

cartier *comparative of* CARTY

cartiest *superlative of* CARTY

car·ti·lage \ˈkär|d·ᵊlij, -ȧ|, |tᵊl-; |tlij, |tlēj\ *n* -s [L *cartilago;* akin to L *cratis* wickerwork — more at HURDLE] **1 :** a translucent elastic tissue that composes most of the skeleton of the embryos and very young of vertebrates and is for the most part converted into bone in the higher forms but remains through life the chief constituent of the skeleton of primitive forms (as the sturgeons and elasmobranchs) **:** GRISTLE — see CHONDRIN, ELASTIC CARTILAGE, FIBROCARTILAGE, HYALINE CARTILAGE **2 :** a part or structure composed of cartilage (as a piece of a cartilaginous skeleton or an articular cartilage)

cartilage bone *n* **:** a bone formed by ossification of cartilage — distinguished from *membrane bone*

cartilage glottis *n* **:** WHISPER GLOTTIS

cartilage of ja·cob·son \-ˈjākəbsən, -əps-\ *usu cap J* **:** JACOBSON'S CARTILAGE

cartilage of san·to·ri·ni \-ˌsantəˈrēnē\ *usu cap S* [after G.D. *Santorini* †*ab*1737 Ital. physician and anatomist] **:** CORNICULATE CARTILAGE

cartilage of wris·berg \-ˈrizˌbərg, *G* -ˈvrisˌberk\ *usu cap W* [trans. of G *Wrisberger knorpel,* after Heinrich A. *Wrisberg* †1808 Ger. anatomist] **:** a cuneiform cartilage

cartilage pit *n* **:** one of the concave or spoon-shaped depressions in the valves of mollusks of the class Lamellibranchia fitted to receive the ligament

car·ti·la·gin·e·ous \ˌkärd·ᵊləˈjinēəs, -nyəs\ *adj* [L *cartilagineus,* fr. *cartilagin-, cartilago* cartilage + *-eus* -eous] **:** CARTILAGINOUS

car·ti·lag·i·noid \ˌkärd·ᵊlˈajəˌnȯid\ *adj* [L *cartilagin-, cartilago* + E *-oid*] **:** resembling cartilage

car·ti·lag·i·nous \ˌkär|d·ᵊlˈajənəs, -ȧ|, |tᵊl-\ *adj* [MF *cartilagineux,* fr. L *cartilaginosus,* fr. *cartilagin-, cartilago* cartilage + *-osus* -ous] **:** composed of or relating to cartilage **:** firm and tough like cartilage **:** GRISTLY

cartilaginous fish *n* **:** any of the fishes having the skeleton wholly or largely composed of cartilage **:** one of the Cyclostomi or Chondrichthyes

carting *pres part of* CART

cart ladder *or* **cart leather** *n* [¹*cart* + *ladder* or *leather,* E dial. var. of *ladder*] **:** a framework attached to a cart to increase its carrying capacity

cartload \ˈ⸗ˌ⸗\ *n* **1 :** as much as will fill or load a cart; *sometimes* **:** an indefinitely large amount ⟨collected by the ~⟩ **2 :** one third of a cubic yard (as of dirt)

cart·man \-mən\ *n, pl* **cartmen :** CARTER, TEAMSTER

car toad *n, slang* **:** a railroad-car repairman

car·to·bib·li·og·ra·phy \ˌkärd·ō-\ *n* -ES [*carto-* (as in *cartography*) + *bibliography*] **:** a history or description of printed maps

car·to·gram \ˈkärd·əˌgram\ *n* -s [F *cartogramme,* fr. *carto-* + *-gramme* -gram] **:** a map showing geographically diagrammatic statistics of various kinds usu. by the use of shades, curves, or dots

car·to·graph \-ˌgraf\ *n* -s [back-formation fr. *cartographer* and *cartography*] **:** MAP, CHART; *specif* **:** an illustrated map

car·tog·ra·pher \kärˈtägrəfər, kȧˈt-, -fə\ *n* -s [*cartography* + *-er*] **:** one that makes maps

car·to·graph·ic \ˌkär|d·əˈgrafik, -ȧ|, |tə-, -ēk\ *or* **car·to·graph·i·cal** \-ə̇kəl, -ēk-\ *adj* [F *cartographique,* fr. *cartographie* + *-ique* -ic, -ical] **:** of or relating to cartography

cartographic unit *n* **:** rock that is represented on a geologic map by a single color or pattern

car·tog·ra·phy \kärˈtägrəfē, kȧˈt-, -i\ *n* -ES [F *cartographie,* fr. *carto-* (fr. *carte* map, card) + *-graphie* -graphy — more at CARD] **:** the science or art of making maps

car·to·man·cy \ˈkärd·əˌman(t)sē\ *n* -ES [F *cartomancie,* fr. *carto-* (fr. *carte* card) + *-mancie* -mancy] **:** fortune-telling by means of playing cards

¹car·ton \ˈkärtᵊn, ˈkȧt-\ *n* -s [F, fr. It *cartone* pasteboard] **1 a :** a cardboard box or container; *esp* **:** a relatively small container that when filled with merchandise is enclosed in a larger and stronger container for shipping **b :** cardboard or a piece of cardboard suitable for making cartons **2 :** a material like pasteboard or papier-mâché made by insects (as certain wasps or termites) of chewed vegetable matter often mixed with soil for use in building their nests

²carton \ˈ"\ *vb* **cartoned; cartoned; cartoning** \-t(ᵊ)niŋ\ **cartons** *vt* **:** to pack or enclose in a carton ~ *vi* **:** to shape cartons from cardboard sheets ⟨a ~*ing* machine⟩

car·ton·er \ˈkärt(ᵊ)nər, -ȧt-, -nə\ *n* -s **:** one that cartons; *specif* **:** a machine that opens a folding carton, inserts a packaged product, and closes the carton ends

car·ton·nage \ˌkärtᵊnˈäzh\ *n* -s [F, fr. *carton* pasteboard + *-age*] **:** the material of which many Egyptian mummy cases are made consisting of linen or papyrus glued together in many thicknesses and usu. coated with stucco; *also* **:** a mummy case made of such material

car·ton pierre \ˈkärˌtōⁿˈpye(ə)r, -ⁿ pēˈe-\ *n* [F *carton-pierre,* lit., stone pasteboard, fr. *carton* pasteboard + *pierre* stone, fr. L *petra,* fr. Gk, rock] **:** a papier-mâché made to imitate stone or bronze and usu. used for statuary and architectural ornaments

¹car·toon \(ˈ)kärˈtün, -ˈt-\ *n* -s [It *cartone* pasteboard, cartoon, aug. of *carta* card — more at CARD] **1 :** a preparatory design, drawing, or painting (as for a fresco, painting, mosaic, or tapestry); *esp* **:** a drawing in full size usu. on paper which is traced or copied on a surface to be used for a final work ⟨tapestry weaves that closely follow the modeling in the ~⟩ **2 a :** a drawing that is often symbolic and usu. intended as humor, caricature, or satire and comment on public and usu. political matters ⟨a political ~⟩ **b :** COMIC 3a **3 :** ANIMATED CARTOON

²cartoon \ˈ"\ *vb* -ED/-ING/-s *vt* **1 :** to make a cartoon or preparatory sketch of **2 :** to make simple outline drawings of **3 :** to caricature pictorially ~ *vi* **:** to make a cartoon

car·toon·ery \⸗ˈ⸗nə)rē, -i\ *n* -ES **:** the art or practice of cartooning

car·toon·ist \⸗ˈ⸗nəst\ *n* -s **:** one who draws cartoons

cartoon set *n* **:** a television studio set with a background consisting of a large line drawing

cartop \ˈ⸗ˌ⸗\ *adj* **:** suitable in size and weight for carrying on top of an automobile ⟨~ canoe⟩

car·touche *or* **car·touch** \(ˈ)kärˈtüsh, -ˈt-\ *n, pl* **cartouches** [F, fr. It *cartoccio,* fr. *carta* card, paper — more at CARD] **1 :** a gun cartridge having a paperboard case **2 a** *obs* **:** a scroll-shaped architectural ornament or member sometimes used for inscriptions **:** MODILLION **b :** an ornamental enframement (as for an inscription, a monogram, a map title, or a coat of arms) often in a baroque or rococo style **c :** an ornately framed ornamental tablet often bearing a design or an inscription **3 :** an oval shield sometimes used for the display of heraldic bearings (as of women or of ecclesiastics) **4 :** an oval or oblong figure (as on ancient Egyptian monuments) enclosing a sovereign's name **5 :** a contour (as of a table top) based on the superimposition of an oval and a rectangle **6 :** a moderate brown that is yellower, lighter, and stronger than auburn, lighter, stronger, and slightly redder than chestnut brown, and redder, lighter, and stronger than coffee — called also *Durango, mesa*

cartouche 3

cartouse *obs var of* CARTOUCHE

cart path *n, North* **:** a narrow unimproved road **:** LANE

car·tridge \ˈkär·trij, ˈkȧ-, -ēj, *chiefly dial & old-fash* ˈka-\ *n* -s *often attrib* [alter. of earlier *cartage,* modif. of MF *cartouche*] **1 a :** a tube of metal, paper, or a combination of both containing a complete charge for a firearm and in modern ammunition usu. containing a cap or other initiating device — compare FIXED AMMUNITION **b :** a case containing an explosive charge for blasting **2 :** a usu. replaceable or refillable case containing loose material and designed to permit ready insertion into a larger mechanism, apparatus, or installation **:** CAPSULE ⟨a filter ~⟩ ⟨a ~ of compressed gas⟩ **3 :** a pointed metal cylinder attachment to a mole plow which is pulled through the soil at the drain depth and forms the drainage passage **4 :** a roll of light-protected film ready to be inserted in a camera for exposure **5 a :** a small removable case in a pickup on a phonograph containing the needle and the mechanism for translating stylus motion into an electrical voltage **b :** a small case containing a reel of magnetic tape or wire, a take-up reel, and suitable guides that allows use of tape or wire without the necessity of threading through heads and guides

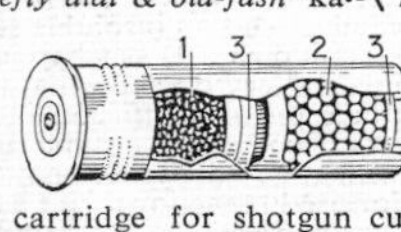

cartridge for shotgun cut away to show: *1* powder, *2* shot, *3* wad

cartridge bag *n* **:** a cloth bag for holding a cannon charge

cartridge belt *n* **:** a belt having loops or pockets that is usu. worn around the waist and used to carry ammunition (as cartridges for small arms) and other equipment (as a canteen)

cartridge box *n* **:** a usu. leather case attached to a belt or strap and used to carry cartridges

cartridge brass *n* **:** a wrought brass containing usu. about 70 percent copper and 30 percent zinc and having sufficient ductility and other properties to stand the severe mechanical treatment necessary in making cartridge cases

cartridge buff *n* **:** SEED PEARL 2

cartridge fuse *n* **:** an electric fuse in which the link is enclosed in a cartridge

cartridge heater *n* **:** an electric heating coil enclosed in a metal case shaped like a cartridge

cartridge paper *n* **1 :** a strong durable paper used for making cartridges **2 :** a strong hard paper sometimes with a rough finish suitable for printing by offset lithography **3 :** a cheap drawing paper

cartridge pleat *n* **:** one of a series of small rounded standaway folds of cloth so stitched to a foundation cloth as to resemble the webbing for cartridges on a cartridge belt and used decoratively (as on clothes or curtains)

cartridge starter *n* **:** a starter for gasoline engines that consists of a cartridge containing an explosive which on being electrically detonated forces the piston forward and starts the engine — called also *combustion starter*

cart rope *n* [ME, rope for a cart, fr. ¹*cart* + *rope*] **:** rope strong enough for drawing a heavy load

carts *pl of* CART, *pres 3d sing of* CART

cart–track plant *n* **:** BROAD-LEAVED PLANTAIN 1

car·tu·lary \ˈkärchə,lerē\ *n* -ES [ML *cartularium, chartularium*, fr. L *chartula* little paper + *-arium* -ary — more at CHARTER] **:** a collection or register of charters; *esp* **:** a book containing duplicates of the charters and title deeds relating to an estate (as a monastery)

car–tunnel kiln *n* **:** CONTINUOUS KILN

cartway \ˈ=,=\ *n* [ME *cart-way*, fr. *cart* + *way*] **:** a road for carts **:** a rough unimproved road

¹**cartwheel** \ˈ=,=\ *n* [ME, fr. ¹*cart* + *wheel*] **1 :** the wheel of a cart **2 :** a large coin: as **a :** a silver dollar **b :** CROWN 8a **c :** one of the penny and twopenny copper coins issued in England in 1797 **3 a :** a rolling or spinning motion suggesting that of a turning wheel; *specif* **:** a lateral handspring with arms and legs extended ⟨they stood on their heads and turned ~s down the garden path —Evelyn R. Sickels⟩ **b :** a figure performed in baton twirling in which the baton describes a circle alternately on each side of the body **4 :** a shallow-crowned hat with a wide stiff brim

²**cartwheel** \"\ *vi* -ED/-ING/-S **:** to move like a turning wheel; *specif* **:** to turn cartwheels

cart whip *n* **:** a heavy short-handled horsewhip

cartwhip \ˈ=,=\ *vt* **:** to flog with a cart whip

cart·wright \ˈkärt·,rīt\ *n* -S [ME, fr. ¹*cart* + *wright*] **:** one that makes carts

carty \ˈkärd·ē\ *adj* -ER/-EST **:** resembling a cart horse

carucage *n* -S [ML *carrucagium*, fr. *carruca* plow, fr. L, coach, of Celtic origin; akin to OE *carr* vehicle — more at CAR] *Old Eng law* **:** a tax on every plow or plowland

carucate *n* -S [ME, fr. ML *carrucata*, fr. *carruca* plow] **:** any of various old English units of land area that in the counties of Suffolk, Norfolk, York, Lincoln, Derby, Nottingham, and Leicester corresponded to the hide; *esp* **:** a unit equal to 120 acres

car·um \ˈka(a)rəm\ *n, cap* [NL, fr. Gk *karon* caraway — more at CARAWAY] **:** a large genus of biennial aromatic herbs (family Umbelliferae) having fusiform or tuberous roots, pinnate leaves, and white or yellow flowers in compound umbels having few or no bracts — see CARAWAY

car·un·cle \ˈka,rəŋkəl, kəˈr-\ *n* -S [modif. of obs. F *caruncule*, fr. L *caruncula* little piece of flesh, dim. of *caro* flesh — more at CARNAL] **1 a :** a naked fleshy outgrowth (as a bird's wattle or comb or as on certain caterpillars) **b :** COTYLEDON 1 **2 :** an outgrowth on a seed developed by proliferation of integumentary tissue adjacent to the micropyle **3 :** a small fleshy growth; *specif* **:** a reddish growth situated at the urethral meatus in women causing pain and bleeding

ca·run·cu·la \kəˈrəŋkyələ, ka-\ *n, pl* **caruncu·lae** \-,lē, -ī\ [L] **:** CARUNCLE

ca·run·cu·lar \kəˈrəŋkyələ(r), ka-\ *also* **ca·run·cu·lous** \-ləs\ *adj* [L *caruncula* + E *-ar* or *-ous*] **1 :** like a caruncle **2 :** CARUNCULATE

ca·run·cu·late \-ət, -,lāt\ *also* **ca·run·cu·lat·ed** \-,lād·əd\ *adj* [prob. fr. NL *carunculatus*, fr. L *caruncula* + NL *-atus* -ate] **:** having a caruncle

car·va·crol \ˈkärvə,krōl, -ōl\ *n* -S [ISV *carv-* (fr. NL *carvi*, specific epithet of the caraway *Carum carvi*, fr. ML *carvi* caraway) + L *acr-*, *acer* sharp + ISV *-ol* — more at CARAWAY, EDGE] **:** a liquid phenol $CH_3C_6H_3(C_3H_7)OH$ found in the essential oils of various plants of the mint family (as origanum and thyme) and used as an antiseptic; 2-methyl-5-isopropylphenol

car·va·cryl \-,kril\ *n* -S [*carvacrol* + *-yl*] **:** the univalent radical $C_{10}H_{13}$ of which carvacrol is the hydroxide

carve \ˈkärv, -äv\ *vb* -ED/-ING/-S [ME *kerven*, fr. OE *ceorfan*; akin to MHG *kerben* to notch, Gk *graphein* to scratch, write] *vt* **1 :** to cut (as with knife or chisel) with deliberate care or practiced precision ⟨*carved* fretwork⟩ **2 :** to cut or hew out ⟨~ a path⟩ **:** make or get by or as if by cutting — often used with *out* ⟨~ out a fortune⟩ **3 :** to cut into pieces or slices (as meat at table) **:** divide or cut off for distribution or apportionment **4 :** to cut up (as a county into districts) **:** SUBDIVIDE ~ *vi* **1 :** to cut up **:** cut up and serve ⟨~ for all the guests⟩ **2 :** to practice the trade of a sculptor or engraver **syn** see CUT

carved rug *n* **:** a rug having a pattern produced by cutting the pile to different levels

car·vel \ˈkärvəl, -,vel\ *n* -S [ME *carvile*, fr. MF *carvelle* — more at CARAVEL] **:** CARAVEL a

carvel–built \ˈ=(,)=,=\ *adj* [prob. fr. D *karveel* caravel (in compounds such as *karveelwerk* carvel-built construction), fr. MF *carvelle*] *of a ship* **:** built with the planks meeting flush at the seams instead of overlapping — compare CLINKER-BUILT

carvel joint *n* **:** a flush joint of the planks of a ship

carvel–planked \ˈ=(,)=,=\ *adj* **:** CARVEL-BUILT

carv·en \ˈkärvən, -äv-\ *adj* [alter. of ME *corven*, past part. of *kerven* to carve] **:** wrought or ornamented by carving **:** CARVED

car·vene \ˈkär,vēn\ *n* -S [prob. fr. F *carvène*, fr. *carvi* caraway (fr. Ar *karawyā*) + *-ène* -ene — more at CARAWAY] **:** dextrorotatory limonene

carv·er \ˈkärvər, ˈkåvə\ *n* -S [ME *kerver*, fr. *kerven* to carve + *-er* — more at CARVE] **:** one that carves or produces by carving: as **a :** one that carves meat at table **b :** one that carves designs or figures on or in wood, stone, or metal **c :** CROPPER c **d** (1) **:** a knife for carving or slicing meat (2) **:** either one of a knife and fork set ⟨a pair of ~s⟩

car·ver chair \"-\ *n, usu cap 1st C* [after John Carver †1621 first governor of Plymouth Colony; fr. a specimen belonging to him] **:** a heavy turned chair having three vertical and three horizontal spindles in the back

Carver chair

car·ves·trene \kärˈve,strēn, ˈkärvə,s-\ *n* -S [blend of ISV *carvol* carvone (fr. ML *carvi* caraway + *-ol*) and *sylvestrene*; orig. formed as G *karvestren* — more at CARAWAY] **:** inactive sylvestrene

carving *n* -S [ME *kerving*, fr. gerund of *kerven* to carve — more at CARVE] **1 :** the act or art of one who carves **2 :** carved work **:** decorative sculpture **:** a design or figure made by carving

carving set *n* **:** a table set comprised of a carving knife, two-tined fork with finger guard, and usu. a sharpening steel — called also *roast set*

car·vol \ˈkär,vōl, -ōl\ *n* -S [ISV *carv-* (fr. ML *carvi* caraway) + *-ol*] **:** CARVONE

car·vo·men·thene \,kärvōˈmen,thēn\ *n* -S [ISV *carvone* + *menthene*] **:** a colorless oily hydrocarbon $C_{10}H_{18}$; 1-*p*-menthene

car·vo·men·thol \-,thōl, -ōl\ *n* -S [*carvo-* (fr. ML *carvi* caraway) + *menthol*] **:** an oily terpenoid alcohol $C_{10}H_{19}OH$ made synthetically (as by reducing carvomenthone)

car·vo·men·thone \-,thōn\ *n* -S [*carvo-* + *menthone*] **:** a colorless oily terpenoid ketone $C_{10}H_{18}O$ occurring with carvotanacetone in some essential oils

car·vone \ˈkär,vōn\ *n* -S [prob. fr. G *karvon*, fr. ML *carvi* caraway + G *-on* -one — more at CARAWAY] **:** an oily liquid terpenoid ketone $C_{10}H_{14}O$ having a characteristic odor of caraway, found in many essential oils (as caraway, dill, or spearmint) and used as a flavoring agent and perfume

car·vo·ta·nac·e·tone \,kär(,)vōtəˈnasə,tōn\ *n* -S [*carvo* + *tanacetone*] **:** an oily terpenoid ketone $C_{10}H_{16}O$ found in the essential oils of some plants of the genus *Blumea*

car wash *n* **:** an establishment equipped to wash automobiles

car whacker *n, slang* **:** CAR KNOCKER

carwitchet *var of* CARRIWITCHET

cary \ˈka(a)rē\ *n* -S *usu cap* [fr. *Cary*, Ill.] **:** a substage of the Wisconsin glacial stage; *also* **:** its drift

cary- *or* **caryo-** — see KARY-

car·ya \ˈka(a)rēə\ *n, cap* [NL, fr. Gk *karya* nut tree, fr. *karyon* nut — more at CAREEN] **:** a genus of No. American hardwood trees (family Juglandaceae) with the husk of the fruit dehiscent and the nuts angular — see BITTERNUT, HICKORY, PECAN, PIGNUT; compare JUGLANS

car·y·at·ic \¦karē¦ad·ik\ *adj* [*caryatid* + *-ic*] **:** of, relating to, or using a caryatid ⟨~ order⟩

car·y·at·id \,karēˈad·əd, ˈkarēə,tid, kəˈrīətəd\ *n, pl* **caryatids** \-ədz,-idz\ *or* **caryat·i·des** \,karēˈad·ə,dēz\ [L *Caryatides*, pl., fr. Gk *Karyatides*, lit., priestesses of Artemis at Caryae (Gk *Karyai*) in Laconia] **:** a draped female figure supporting an entablature in the place of a column or pilaster — compare ATLAS

car·y·at·id·al \¦karē¦ad·əd³l\ *or* **car·y·at·i·de·an** \,==,==ˈdēən; ¦karēə¦tid-, kə¦rīə¦t-\ *or* **car·y·a·tid·ic** \¦karēə¦tidik, kə¦rīə¦-\ *adj* [*caryatid* + *-al* or *-ean* or *-ic*] **:** of or resembling a caryatid

caryatid from a Greek temple

car·y·i·nite \ˈkarēə,nīt, kəˈrīə-\ *n* -S [ISV *caryin-* (fr. Gk *karyinos* nut-brown, fr. *karyon* nut) + *-ite* — more at CAREEN] **:** a mineral $(Ca,PbNa)_5(Mn,Mg)_4(AsO_4)_5$ consisting of a rare calcium manganese arsenate containing other elements

cary·o·car \kəˈrīə,kär, ˈkarēō,-\ *n, cap* [NL, fr. *cary-* + Gk *kar* head; fr. the size of the fruit; akin to Gk *kara* head — more at CEREBRAL] **:** a genus (the type of the family Caryocaraceae) of So. American trees having strong fine-grained wood useful for furniture and shipbuilding and bearing edible seeds — see SOUARI NUT

car·y·o·ca·ra·ce·ae \¦karē(,)ōkəˈrāsē,ē\ *n pl, cap* [NL, fr. *Caryocar*, type genus + *-aceae*] **:** a family of tropical So. American trees (order Parietales) differing from Theaceae in having coherent petals and separate styles — **car·y·o·ca·ra·ceous** \-kə¦rāshəs\ *adj*

car·y·o·my·ia \,karēōˈmī(y)ə\ *n, cap* [NL, fr. *cary-* + *-myia*] **:** a genus of gallflies (family Cecidomyiidae) including the hickory midges

car·y·oph·a·na·les \,karē,äfəˈnā(,)lēz\ *n pl, cap* [NL, fr. *Caryophanon* + *-ales*] **:** a small order of filamentous bacteria that occur in water, decaying organic matter, and the alimentary canal and have in general the characteristics of members of the genus *Caryophanon*

car·y·oph·a·non \,karēˈäfə,nän\ *n, cap* [NL, fr. *cary-* + Gk *phanon*, neut. of *phanos* bright, fr. *phaos* light — more at FANCY] **:** a genus (coextensive with the family Caryophanaceae) of large filamentous or bacillary bacteria of oral mucous membranes and the alimentary tract of various mammals that are closely related to the chlamydobacteria though usu. placed in a separate order and are distinguished by well-defined nuclei comparable to isolated chromosomes, peritrichous or no flagella, and absence of spores

car·y·o·pnyl·la·ce·ae \¦karē(,)ōfəˈlāsē,ē\ *n pl, cap* [NL, fr. ²*Caryophyllus*, type genus + *-aceae*] **:** a large widely distributed family of herbs or occas. subshrubs (order Caryophyllales) usu. with stems swollen at the nodes and opposite linear leaves and with symmetrical pentamerous or tetramerous flowers that have distinct stamens as numerous or twice as numerous as the sepals

car·y·o·phyl·la·ceous \-¦lāshəs\ *adj* [NL *Caryophyllaceae* + E *-ous*] **1 :** of or relating to the Caryophyllaceae **2 :** having long-clawed petals enclosed in a tubular calyx

car·y·o·phyl·lae·i·dae \-ˈlēə,dē\ *n pl, cap* [NL, fr. *Caryophyllaeus*, type genus (alter. of *Caryophyllus*, fr. *cary-* + *-phyllus* -phyllous) + *-idae*] **:** a family that contains monozootic tapeworms infesting the intestine of fishes and that is placed in the Pseudophyllidea or with related forms in a separate order

car·y·o·phyl·la·les \-ˈlā(,)lēz\ *n pl, cap* [NL, fr. ²*Caryophyllus*, type genus + *-ales*] **:** an order of dicotyledonous herbs and shrubs distinguished by a superior unilocular ovary and a generally coiled or curved embryo, important member families being the Chenopodiaceae, Amaranthaceae, and Caryophyllaceae

car·y·o·phyl·lene \,===ˈfi,lēn\ *n* -S [ISV *caryophyll-* (fr. NL ²*Caryophyllus*) + *-ene*] **:** a liquid sesquiterpene $C_{15}H_{24}$ obtained from various essential oils (as clove oil) as a mixture of stereoisomers distinguished as α-, β-, and γ-caryophyllene — compare HUMULENE

car·y·o·phyl·lid \-ˈfiləd\ *adj* [NL *Caryophyllidae*, family of worms, fr. *Caryophyllus*, type genus + *-idae* — more at CARYOPHYLLAEIDAE] **:** of or relating to the family Caryophyllaeidae

car·y·o·phyl·lin \-ˈfilən\ *n* -S [ISV *caryophyll-* + *-in*] **:** OLEANOLIC ACID

¹**car·y·o·phyl·lus** \-ˈfiləs\ *n* [NL, modif. of Gk *karyophyllon* clove — more at GILLYFLOWER] *syn of* JAMBOS

²**caryophyllus** \"\ *n* [NL, modif. of Gk *karyophyllon*] *syn of* DIANTHUS

car·y·op·sis \,karēˈäpsəs\ *n, pl* **caryop·ses** \-p,sēz\ *or* **caryop·si·des** \-psə,dēz\ [NL, fr. *cary-* + *-opsis*] **:** a small one-seeded dry indehiscent fruit with a thin membranous pericarp adhering so closely to the seed that fruit and seed are incorporated in one body forming a single grain (as in wheat, barley, Indian corn, and other grasses) — see FRUIT illustration

car·y·op·ter·is \-ˈäptərəs\ *n* [NL, fr. *cary-* + *-pteris* (irreg. fr. Gk *pteron* wing); fr. the wings on the carpels — more at FEATHER] **1** *cap* **:** a genus of Asiatic shrubs (family Verbenaceae) with a 5-lobed corolla, four exserted stamens, and a fruit of 4-winged nutlets — see ³BLUEBEARD **2** *pl* **caryop·terides** \-äpˈterə,dēz\ **:** any plant of the genus *Caryopteris*

car·y·o·ta \,karēˈōd·ə\ *n, cap* [NL, fr. L *caryota* nut-shaped date, modif. of Gk *karyōtis* date, fr. *karyon* nut — more at CAREEN] **:** a small genus of East Indian palms having bipinnate leaves with wedge-shaped divisions and including several species that are cultivated — see FISHTAIL PALM, JAGGERY PALM; compare KITTUL

cas *abbr* **1** casing **2** castle **3** casualty

ca·sa \ˈkäsə, -ä-, -ȧ-, -ȧ-\ *n* -S [Sp & It, fr. L, hut, cabin; prob. akin to L *catena* chain — more at CHAIN] *Southwest* **:** DWELLING HOUSE

ca·sa·ba *or* **cas·sa·ba** \kəˈsäbə, -ȧ-\ *n* -S *also* **casaba melon** *or* **cassaba melon** *n* -S [fr. *Kasaba* (now Turgutlu), Turkey, whence it was introduced] **:** any of several long-keeping winter melons having a yellow rind and sweet flesh

ca·sa·be \kəˈsäbē\ *n* -S [Sp] **:** ¹BUMPER 3

ca·sa·blan·ca \¦kasə¦blaŋkə, ¦käzə-, -läŋ-; ¦käsə¦bläŋ-, ¦käzə-\ *adj, usu cap* [fr. *Casablanca*, city in Morocco] **:** of or from Casablanca **:** of the kind or style prevalent in Casablanca

ca·sa·gha pine \kəˈsägə-\ *n* [modif. of Singhalese *kasagaha*, fr. Skt *kaśā* whip + *gaccha* tree] **:** a beefwood (*Casuarina equisetifolia*)

ca·sa·le process \kəˈsälē-\ *n, usu cap C* [after Luigi *Casale* †1927 Ital. chemist] **:** a method of synthesizing ammonia similar in principle to the Haber process

cas·al·ty \ˈkazəltē, -as-\ *adj* [alter. of *casualty*] **1** *dial Eng* **:** susceptible to chance or accident **:** UNCERTAIN, UNRELIABLE **2** *dial Eng* **:** INSECURE, SHAKY, INFIRM

cas·a·no·va \,kazəˈnōvə, -as-\ *n* -S *usu cap* [after Giovanni Jacopo *Casanova* †1798 Ital. adventurer] **:** LOVER; *esp* **:** a man who is a promiscuous and unscrupulous lover

ca·saque \kəˈzak\ *n* -S [F, fr. MF, cassock — more at CASSOCK] **:** a kind of woman's blouse

ca·sa·sia \kəˈsāzh(ē)ə, -ˈa-\ *n, cap* [NL, fr. Luis de las Casas y Arargorri †1800 Span. soldier + NL *-ia*] **:** a small genus of tropical American shrubs or trees (family Rubiaceae) having opposite leathery leaves and white or yellow flowers with a salverform corolla

casava *var of* CASSAVA

cas·bah *or* **kas·bah** *also* **kas·ba** \ˈkaz,bä, -äz-, -äz- -,bə,-,bä\ *n* -S *usu cap* [F, fr. Ar dial. (No. Africa) *qaṣbah, qaṣabah*] **1 :** a No. African castle or fortress **2 :** the native section of a No. African city surrounding the castle or fortress; *specif* **:** a section containing nightclubs and houses of prostitution

cas·ca·bel \ˈkaskə,bel\ *n* -S [Sp, lit., small spherical bell like a sleigh bell, fr. OProv *cascavel*, fr. ML *cascabellus*, dim. of *cascabus* cooking pot, alter. of L *caccabus*, fr. Gk *kakkabos*, *kakkabē*, of Sem origin; akin to Assyr *kukubu* vessel] **1 :** a knoblike projection, sometimes in the form of a loop, behind the breech of a muzzle-loading cannon; *also* **:** all the rear part of the cannon behind the base ring — see CANNON illustration **2 :** a vicious So. and Central American rattlesnake (*Crotalus durissus terrificus*) that has a powerful neurotoxic venom and is the only rattlesnake of eastern So. America **3 :** a small hollow perforated spherical bell enclosing a loose pellet which causes it to jingle when moved — called also *jingle bell*

¹**cas·cade** \(ˈ)kaˈskād\ *n* -S [F, fr. It *cascata*, fr. *cascare* to fall, fr. (assumed) VL *casicare*, fr. L *casus*, past part. of *cadere* to fall — more at CHANCE] **1 :** a fall of water over steeply slanting rocks (as in a river or brook); *esp* **:** a small fall or one of a series **2 a :** something arranged, formed, or piled up in a series of steps or ranks ⟨the ~s of the Deville glacier⟩ **b :** SERIES 8 **c :** a fall of material (as lace) that is so arranged in folds at the upper edge that the lower edge hangs in a zigzag line and that is used esp. in clothing and draperies **d :** a succession of stages (as in a process or in the arrangement of the parts of an apparatus) in which each stage derives from or acts, sometimes cumulatively, upon the product or output of the preceding ⟨relays in ~⟩ ⟨a ~ amplifier⟩ ⟨a distillation column is a ~ with each plate representing a stage —Richard Stephenson⟩ **e :** a series of equally spaced and similarly oriented airfoils or hydrofoils that direct the flow of a fluid (as the stator blades direct the flow of air in a compressor) **3 a :** something falling or rushing forth in quantity ⟨a ~ of sound so great that you cannot hear a word anyone says —Douglas Brown⟩ **b :** an arrangement of flowers fastened together so that an extended part or strip trails down from the main body

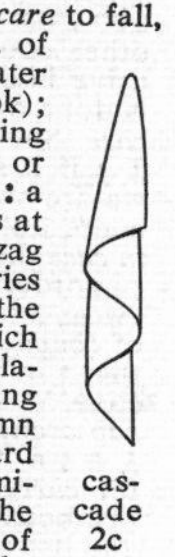
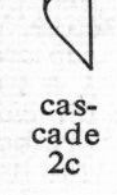
cascade 2c

²**cascade** \"\ *vb* -ED/-ING/-S *vi* **1 :** to fall or pour in or as if in a cascade ⟨the price *cascaded* to 140 —F.L.Allen⟩ ⟨*cascaded* down a flight of steps and spilled into the street —Truman Capote⟩ **2** *dial* **:** VOMIT ~ *vt* **1 :** to cause to fall like a cascade **2** *also* **cascade–connect :** to connect in cascade (as an electric circuit) **3 :** to carry out (as a manufacturing process) in a number of stages

cascade amplification *n* **:** multistage amplification **:** the use of two or more electron tubes each amplifying the output of the preceding

cascade fir *n, usu cap C* [fr. *Cascade* range, Washington, Oregon, and northern California] **:** SILVER FIR 1b(1)

cascade shower *n* **:** a cosmic-ray shower in which a high-energy electron produces one or more photons that convert into electrons and positrons, these secondary electrons producing the same effect as the primary, the shower thus building up until the level of energy becomes so low that photon emission and pair production cannot occur

cascade transformer *n* **:** a high-voltage source consisting of a limited number of step-up transformers with their secondaries in series, the primary of each after the first being supplied from a pair of taps on the secondary of the preceding

cas·ca·di·an \(ˈ)ka¦skādēən\ *adj, usu cap* [*Cascadian* (revolution, a group of earth movements that uplifted the mountain ranges of the Pacific coast of No. America, fr. *Cascadia*, hypothetical land mass along western border of No. America (fr. *Cascade* Range) + E *-an*] **:** of or relating to mountain-making movements in the Cenozoic era — see GEOLOGIC TIME table

cascading glacier *n* **:** a glacier that because of its steep and uneven bed is much broken by crevasses and suggestive in appearance of a cascading stream

cas·ca·do \kaˈskä(,)dō, -ˈā-\ *n* -S [Sp, cracked, broken, fr. past part. of *cascar* to crack, break — more at CASCARA] **:** a verminous crustated dermatitis of cattle caused by a nematode (*Stephanofilaria dedoesi*) and occurring esp. in Indonesia but reported also in the U. S.

cas·ca·du·ra \,kaskəˈdu̇rə\ *n* -S [AmerSp, fr. Sp, breaking, fr. *cascado* + *-ura* -ure] **:** an armored catfish of the family Callichthyidae

cas·ca·lo·te \,kaskəˈlōd·ē\ *n* -S [MexSp *cascalote*, *nacascolote* divi-divi, fr. Nahuatl *nacazcolotl*, lit., twisted ear, fr. *nacaztli* ear + *colotl* twisted] **1 :** any of several tropical American trees that yield extracts rich in tannin: **a :** a West Indian tree (*Croton cascarilla*) **b :** either of two Mexican trees (*Caesalpinia cacalaco* and *C. coriaria*) closely related to the divi-divi **2 :** HUISACHE

cas·cara \kaˈskarə *also* -ˈe- *or* -ˈä- *or* ˈkaskərə\ *n* -S [Sp *cáscara* bark, fr. *cascar* to crack, break, fr. (assumed) VL *quassicare* to shake, break, fr. L *quassare* — more at QUASH] **1 :** CASCARA BUCKTHORN **2 :** CASCARA SAGRADA

cascara amar·ga \-əˈmärgə\ *n* [AmerSp *cáscara amarga*, lit., bitter bark] **:** the dried bark of a tropical American tree (*Picramnia antidesma*) formerly used in treatment of syphilis and skin diseases — called also *Honduras bark*

cascara buckthorn *n* **:** a buckthorn (*Rhamnus purshiana*) of the Pacific coast of the U.S. yielding cascara sagrada — called also *bearberry, bearwood, coffeeberry*

cascara sa·gra·da \-səˈgrädə\ *n* [AmerSp *cáscara sagrada*, lit., sacred bark] **:** the dried bark of cascara buckthorn used as a mild laxative — called also *chittam bark*

cas·ca·ril·la \,kaskəˈrilə, -ˈrēə-\ *n* -S *or* **cascarilla bark** *n* -S [Sp, dim. of *cáscara* bark] **1 :** the aromatic bark of a West Indian shrub (*Croton eluteria*) used for making incense and as a tonic — called also *eleuthera bark, sweetwood bark* **2 :** the shrub that yields cascarilla bark

cascarilla oil *n* **:** a pale-yellow essential oil with a spicy odor obtained from cascarilla bark and used in perfumes

cas·ca·ron \,kaskəˈrōn\ *n, pl* **cascaro·nes** \-ōnēz\ [AmerSp *cascarón*, fr. Sp, eggshell, aug. of *cáscara* bark] *Southwest* **:** an eggshell filled with confetti and thrown by revelers and dancers at balls or carnivals

cas·ca·vel \ˈkaskə,vel\ *n* -S [AmerSp *cascabel*, fr. Sp, small spherical bell — more at CASCABEL] **:** CASCABEL 2

cas·co \ˈka(,)skō\ *n* -S [Sp, potsherd, ship's hull — more at CASK] **:** a long almost rectangular barge or lighter sometimes with sails used in the Philippines

¹**case** \ˈkās\ *n* -S [ME *cas*, fr. OF, fr. L *casus* fall, event, chance, fr. *casus*, past part. of *cadere* to fall — more at CHANCE] **1 a :** a special set of circumstances or conditions **:** a peculiar situation or series of developments; *esp* **:** the circumstances and situation of a particular person, thing, or action ⟨he lost not a single life in any ~ where the men were under his personal control —W.J.Ghent⟩ **b :** a set of circumstances constituting a problem **:** a matter for consideration or decision: as (1) **:** a circumstance or situation (as a crime) requiring investigation or action by the police or other agency (2) **:** one that is the object of investigation, consideration, or attention ⟨the man is a relief ~⟩ **2 a :** the state of being or of affairs **:** the condition with respect to welfare or success ⟨the critic of fiction is in no worse ~ than the critic of verse —C.H.Rickword⟩; *specif* **:** the condition of body or mind ⟨cows, red of hide and in good ~ —Llewelyn Powys⟩ **b :** a condition of readiness **:** a suitable state of mind ⟨I am in ~ to justle a constable —Shak.⟩ **c :** the order (sense 2d) of leaf tobacco **3** [ME *cas*, fr. MF, fr. L *casus*, trans. of Gk *ptōsis*, lit., fall; fr. the idea that cases other than the nominative are like deviations fr. a perpendicular line — more at PTOSIS] *of a noun, adjective, or pronoun* **a :** an inflectional form indicating the sense relation (as that of subject, object, possessor, thing possessed) to another word in the context **b :** a sense relation to another word in the context of a kind that may be but is not necessarily indicated by a particular inflectional form ⟨the subject of a verb is in the nominative ~⟩ **c :** the characteristic of having inflectional forms indicating the sense relation to another word or words in the context ⟨a Latin noun has gender, number, and ~⟩ **4 :** what actually exists or happens **:** the existing situation **:** FACT — used with *the* ⟨advance was slower than had ever been the ~ before⟩ **5 a** (1) **:** the matters of fact or conditions involved in a suit **:** a suit or action in law or equity **:** CAUSE (2) **:** the printed

report of the decision of a case at law **b** (1) **:** the body of evidence tending to support a conclusion or judgment ⟨the ~ for an industrialized Oxford lies in its ideal geographical position —S.P.B.Mais⟩ (2) **:** a statement of the evidence or arguments relevant to a proposition **:** ARGUMENT; *esp* **:** an apparently valid or convincing argument ⟨make a ~ for the privately endowed college⟩ **6 a :** an instance of disease or injury ⟨10 ~*s* of pneumonia⟩; *also* **:** a patient under treatment **b :** an instance or example of a particular type ⟨Napoleon is the supreme ~ of reason in the novel —E.K.Brown⟩ ⟨a ~ of a sacred marriage was reported —J.G.Frazer⟩ **c :** a person who is peculiar or extraordinary in some way **:** CHARACTER ⟨the rustlers were hard ~*s*⟩ **7 :** ²CRUSH 6 **8** *mapping* **:** the position of the plane of projection relative to a point on the sphere ⟨polar ~⟩ ⟨oblique ~⟩ ⟨equational ~⟩ **syn** see INSTANCE — **in any case :** without regard to or in spite of other considerations ⟨a scandal which, *in any case*, would drive him out of public life —S.H.Adams⟩ **:** whatever else is done or is the case ⟨you could not have caught her *in any case*. She sailed two days ago —Pearl Buck⟩ — ¹**in case** *conj* **1 :** if it should happen that **:** supposing that **:** IF ⟨*in case* we are surprised, keep by me —Washington Irving⟩ **2 :** as a precaution against the event that ⟨people still carry guns *in case* they need them —*N. Y. Herald Tribune*⟩ — ²**in case** *adv* **:** in order to provide against any chance event or circumstance ⟨wear a raincoat just *in case*⟩ — **in case of** *prep* **:** in the event of ⟨*in case of* trouble, yell⟩ — **in case that** *conj* **:** in the event that **:** in case

²**case** \ "\ *n* -s *often attrib* [ME *cas*, fr. ONF *casse*, fr. L *capsa* chest, case, fr. *capere* to take, hold — more at HEAVE] **1 a :** a box or receptacle to contain or hold something (as for carrying, shipping, or safekeeping) ⟨a silver cigarette ~⟩ ⟨12 bottles in a ~⟩ ⟨display ~ in a meat market⟩ **b :** a box and its contents **:** the quantity contained in a box ⟨three ~*s* of eggs⟩ **c :** SET ⟨a ~ of instruments⟩; *specif* **:** PAIR, BRACE ⟨a ~ of pistols⟩ **d :** a compartmented box or rack for sorting or classification: as (1) **:** a shallow tray divided into boxes for holding printing type; *also* **:** any similar container for auxiliary material (as leads, slugs, or accents) — see JOB CASE, LOWER CASE, UPPER CASE (2) **:** a rack used in the postal service for sorting mail **e** (1) **:** the fourth card of any denomination left in the dealing box in faro ⟨~ card⟩ (2) **:** the remaining card of a denomination or suit of which the other cards have been played or dealt ⟨a ~ king⟩ **2 a :** an outer protective covering, sheath, or housing ⟨a watch*case*⟩ ⟨a pillow*case*⟩ ⟨seed*case*⟩ **b** *obs* **:** the skin, hide, or pelt of an animal **c :** CASE SHOT **d :** the carcass of a building or of a piece of furniture **e** (1) **:** a book cover that is made complete before it is affixed to a book (2) **:** SLIPCASE **f :** a large triangular cavity in the upper anterior part of the head of a sperm whale formed by the transverse crest of the skull and the lateral crests of the maxillary bones; *also* **:** the fluid mixture of spermaceti and oil that it contains **g :** the hardened surface layer of case-hardened iron or steel ⟨a ~ of 0.040 inch⟩ **h :** the metal or paper and metal tube into which the components of a round of ammunition are loaded — compare CARTRIDGE 1a **3 :** the enclosing frame in which a door or window is set **:** CASING **4** *slang* **:** DOLLAR ⟨a 5-*case* note⟩ **5 :** a form in plaster made from a block mold and used for making the working molds in ceramics **6 :** a flat metal plate having on one side a layer of wax that when impressed forms a mold for an electrotype — **down to cases** **:** to the point **:** to the actual matter concerned ⟨get right *down to cases* without any preliminaries⟩

³**case** \ "\ *vt* -ED/-ING/-S **1 a :** to enclose or put in a case or casing **:** cover or protect with or as if with a case **:** ENCASE ⟨the man who, *cased* in steel, had passed whole days and nights in the saddle —W.H.Prescott⟩ **b** *building* **:** to cover with a facing of different material usu. of a better grade ⟨~ a brick wall with stone⟩ **c :** to apply an overlay of glass to — compare CASING 1b **d :** to affix (a book) in a case by adhering the pastedowns to the inside of the covers — usu. used with *in*; compare BIND **e :** to lay (new type) **f :** to sort (mail) into a case **2 :** to strip the skin from specif. by making a single slit along the hind legs from heel to heel rather than along the belly **3 :** to line (a shaft or well) with supporting material (as metal pipe) **4 :** to order (tobacco leaf) **5** *slang* **a :** to inspect or study esp. with a view to the commission of a crime ⟨the bank was carefully *cased* before the robbery⟩ **b :** to inspect or examine closely **:** CANVASS **6 :** to cover the compost in (a mushroom bed) with a thin layer of soil to induce fruiting after the mycelium from the spawn has penetrated the bed **7 :** to keep track of (cards played)

case- *or* **caseo-** *comb form* [casein] **:** casein ⟨*case*ase⟩ ⟨*caseo*lysis⟩

ca·se·ar·ia \ˌkasēˈa(a)rēə, ˌkā-\ *n, cap* [NL, fr. Johannes *Casearius* †1678 Dutch clergyman + NL *-ia*] **:** a large genus of cosmopolitan tropical trees (family Flacourtiaceae) having alternate toothed leaves, apetalous flowers, and capsular fruits and including some plants of which the leaves and bark are medicinal and others of which the fruit is used as a fish poison

¹**ca·se·ate** \ˈkāsēˌāt\ *vi* -ED/-ING/-S [L *case*us cheese + E *-ate* — more at CHEESE] *med* **:** to become cheesy **:** undergo caseation

²**caseate** \ "\ *n* -s [*case-* + *-ate*] **:** CASEINATE

ca·se·a·tion \ˌkāsēˈāshən\ *n* -s [²*caseate* + *-ion*] **:** necrosis with conversion of damaged tissue into a soft cheeselike substance occurring particularly in the lesions of tuberculosis

case bay *n* [²*case*] **:** a bay or division of a roof or floor, except a tail bay, comprising two principals with the joists or purlins between them

casebearer \ˈ=,==\ *n* **:** any of various insect larvae; *specif* **:** a moth larva that forms a protective case of silk or of fragments of leaves or other substances and is often a serious pest of cultivated plants — see CIGAR CASEBEARER, PISTOL CASEBEARER

case binding *n* [²*case*] **:** a process of bookbinding in which the book is fastened into a case

casebook \ˈ=,=\ *n* [¹*case* + *book*] **:** a book containing records of cases illustrative of general principles or typifying significant situations that is used for reference and instruction (as in law, medicine, sociology, or psychiatry)

case bottle *n* [²*case*] **:** a bottle fitting into a case, sometimes with others

case-bound \ˈ=,=\ *adj* [²*case*] **:** produced by case binding

casebox \ˈ=,=\ *n* [³*case* + *box*] **:** a frame resembling an abacus with miniature cards at the end of each rod for marking the denomination of the cards as they are withdrawn from the dealing box in faro

case count *n* [²*case*] **:** a count of items to the case irrespective of quality — used in the buying of ungraded eggs

cased frame *n* **:** BOX FRAME

cased glass *also* **case glass** *n* **:** glass consisting of two or more fused layers of different colors often decorated by cutting so that the inner layers show through

case goods *n pl* [²*case*] **1** *also* **case furniture a :** furniture (as buffets, bureaus, bookcases, or vanities) that serves principally to provide interior space for storage (as by drawers or shelves) **b :** dining-room and bedroom furniture sold as sets **2 :** any of a number of products (as whiskey or canned milk) often sold by the case

case gun *n* [²*case*] **:** a gun of a caliber greater than one inch using ammunition with the powder charge in a metallic case — formerly called *rapid-fire gun*

case harden *vb* [²*case* (covering) + *harden*] *vt* **1 :** to harden (a ferrous alloy) so that the surface layer is made considerably harder than the interior (as by carburizing and quenching, cyaniding, carbonitriding, or nitriding) **2 :** to make callous or insensible **3 a :** to harden superficially, producing a hard, durable, or inflexible surface; *specif* **:** to affect (lumber) with case hardening **b :** to temper (glass) **~** *vi* **:** to become affected by the process of case hardening

case-hardened \ˈ=,==\ *adj* **:** not easily moved or affected **:** INSENSIBLE, CALLOUS ⟨people are more *case-hardened* to sensation —E.D.Canham⟩ **:** set in a pattern of thought or behavior **:** resistant to change ⟨boys and girls are not yet *case-hardened* —*Canadian Forum*⟩

case hardening *n* **1 :** a condition in lumber in which too rapid drying and setting of the surface results in the shrinkage being inhibited by the still moist interior, the subsequent drying and shrinking of which sets up opposing stresses in the wood **2 :** the hardening and darkening of the surface of certain foods caused by too rapid evaporation during dehydration

case history *n* [¹*case*] **1 :** a record of an individual's personal and family history and environment for use in analyzing his case or as an instructive illustration of a type ⟨a *case history* of the patient⟩ **2 :** a genetic description of a single concrete case esp. as illustrative of a type ⟨the study is a *case history* of the . . . bogging down of a great reform movement —R.L. Strout⟩ **3 :** the history of a case ⟨trace the *case history* of a storm —Jerome Namias⟩ **4 :** a typical example **:** a significant illustration **:** TYPE ⟨a *case history* in corrupt municipal government —M.D.Hirsch⟩

ca·sein \kāˈsēn, ˈkāˌsēn, ˈkāsēən\ *n* -s *often attrib* [prob. fr. F *caséine*, fr. L *caseus* cheese + F *-ine* -in — more at CHEESE] **:** any of various phosphoproteins characteristic of the milk of mammals: as **a :** the phosphoprotein occurring as a colloidal suspension in milk — called also *caseinogen* **b :** the phosphoprotein that is precipitated as a cream-colored to light yellow curd from milk (as skim milk from a cow) by heating with an acid (as sulfuric acid) or by the action of lactic acid formed in the milk by souring and that is used chiefly in coating paper, in making cold-water and emulsion paints, adhesives, and synthetic fibers, and as an emulsifying and stabilizing agent — called also *acid casein* **c :** the phosphoprotein produced when milk is curdled by rennet and precipitated as a calcium compound in the form of a cream-colored curd that constitutes the principal protein of cheese and is used also in making casein plastics — called also *paracasein, rennet casein*

ca·sein·ate \kāˈsēˌnāt, ˈkāsēəˌn-\ *n* -s [*casein* + *-ate*] **:** a compound of casein with a metal ⟨calcium ~⟩

casein glue *n* **:** a water-resistant adhesive made from casein and usu. hydrated lime and mixed with cold water for use esp. in making plywood and furniture

ca·sein·o·gen \kāˈsēnəjən, ˌkāsēˈin-\ *n* -s [ISV *casein* + *-o-* + *-gen*] **:** CASEIN a

casein paint *n* **:** a paint having as its vehicle an alkaline solution of casein

casein plastic *n* **:** any of certain tough hard hornlike substances obtained from powdered casein, usu. rennet casein, with water as the usual plasticizer, hardened after molding by the action of formaldehyde or some other agent, and used chiefly in making buttons and buckles

casekeeper \ˈ=,==\ *n* [²*case* + *keeper*] **1 :** CASEBOX **2 :** the person in charge of the casebox

case knife *n* [²*case*] **1 :** a knife carried or kept in a sheath and formerly often used at table **2 :** a table knife; *esp* **:** one with a wooden handle

case law *n* [¹*case*] **:** law established by legal precedent or by judicial decision in particular cases **:** judge-made law

case·less \ˈkāsləs\ *adj* **:** being without a case

case liner *n* [²*case*] **:** a moisture-resistant and oil-resistant paper bag or other covering used to line a shipping case

case load *n* [¹*case* + *load*] **:** the number of cases handled in a particular period (as by a court, welfare agency, or clinic)

cas·el·ty *var of* CASALTY

case made *n* [¹*case*] **:** a statutory mode of procedure, often briefer than at common law, for making an appeal to a higher court and often including matters which do not appear in the record at common law and sometimes presenting only certain points of law sought to be reviewed **:** a case reserved for consideration of an appellate court in the manner provided for by statute

casemaker \ˈ=,==\ *n* **1 :** one that makes cases; *specif* **:** a worker or machine that makes cases for books **2 :** one that assembles and pastes pieces of leather for later sewing to make articles such as pocketbooks

casemaking clothes moth \ˈ=,==-\ *n* **:** a common clothes moth (*Tinea pellionella*) having a larva that makes and lives in a tube of its food material fastened with silk which it spins

case·mate \ˈkāˌsmāt, *usu* -ād·+V\ *n* -s [MF, fr. OIt *casamatta*, prob. fr. *casa* house + *matta*, fem. of *matto* mad, crazy, fr. L *mattus* stupid, drunk — more at CASA, MAT] **1 :** a fortified usu. masonry position or chamber in which cannon or other guns may be placed to fire through embrasures **2 :** an armored enclosure for a gun on a warship and with an embrasure for firing through

case·mat·ed \-ād·əd\ *adj* **:** furnished with, protected by, or built like a casemate

case·ment \ˈkāsmənt, *older Brit* -āzm-\ *n* -s [ME, prob. modif. of ONF *encassement* frame, fr. *encasser* to enchase, frame, fr. *casse* case — more at CASE (box)] **1 :** a hollow molding similar to a cavetto or scotia **2 a :** a window sash that opens on hinges fastened to the upright side of the frame **b** *or* **casement window :** a window with such a sash or sashes **c :** WINDOW **d :** CASEMENT CLOTH

casement 2b

casement cloth *n* **:** a plain or figured fabric in a sheer weave used for window draperies

case·ment·ed \-məntəd, -ˌmen-\ *adj* **:** having a casement

case method *n* [¹*case*] **1 :** CASE SYSTEM **2 :** a method of instruction used esp. in colleges and universities that presents for observation and analysis actual recorded or current instances of the problem under study and often calls upon the student to render practical help

case moth *n* [*caseworm*] *Austral* **:** any of several moths having larvae that are caseworms

caseo- — see CASE-

case of first impression [¹*case*] **:** a case presenting a novel question of law for which no controlling precedent can be found

case oil *n* [²*case*] **:** kerosene contained in 5-gallon tin cans packed by twos in wooden cases

ca·se·o·lyt·ic \ˌkāsēōˈlid·ik\ *adj* [*case-* + *-lytic*] **:** capable of breaking down casein; *broadly* **:** PROTEOLYTIC ⟨~ bacteria⟩

case on appeal [¹*case*] **:** the statement which an appellant lays before the court for the prosecution of his appeal as the presentation of the facts on which the appeal is based

ca·se·ous \ˈkāsēəs\ *adj* [L *case*us cheese + E *-ous* — more at CHEESE] **:** characterized by caseation

caseous lymphadenitis *n* **:** a chronic infectious disease of sheep and goats characterized by caseation of the lymph glands and occas. of parts of the lungs, liver, spleen, and kidneys that is caused by a bacterium (*Corynebacterium pseudotuberculosis*) — called also *pseudotuberculosis*

case-phrase \ˈ=,=\ *n* [¹*case*] **:** a prepositional phrase indicating sense relations of a kind that may also be indicated by a case form (as head *of a cow* compared with *cow's* head)

case piece *n* [²*case*] **:** a piece of case goods

cas·er \ˈkāsə(r)\ *n* -s [² and ³*case* + *-er*] **1 :** one that cases or that makes, packs, or works with cases or casings **2 :** a pottery worker who makes block, case, and working molds of plaster of paris — called also *blocker* **3 :** one that applies casing to tobacco leaves or lump tobacco **4 :** a shoe-factory worker who selects and bundles paired soles from stock according to orders from the lasting and bottoming departments

case reserved *n* [¹*case*] **:** a statement of facts and of the points of law arising thereon drawn up by counsel and certified by the trial judge as the basis for argument and determination before the full bench

ca·sern *or* **ca·serne** \kəˈzərn, -ze(ə)rn\ *n* -s [F *caserne*, fr. MF, small room for the night watch, fr. OProv *cazerna* group of four persons, modif. of L *quaterni* four each — more at QUATERNARY] **:** a military barracks in a garrison town

cases *pl of* CASE, *pres 3d sing of* CASE

case shot \ˈkās(h),shät\ *n* [²*case*] **:** an artillery projectile consisting of a number of balls or metal fragments enclosed in a case — see CANISTER 3

case spring *n* [²*case*] **:** one of two springs controlling the hinged cover of a hunting watch, a lock spring that keeps it closed and a lift spring that causes it to open when the lock spring is released by pressure on the crown

case stated *n* [¹*case*] **:** an agreed statement of facts made for presentation to a court in order to obtain a decision of law upon the facts stated

case study *n* [¹*case*] **1 :** an intensive analysis of an individual unit (as a person, social group, institution, community, or culture) stressing developmental factors in relation to environment ⟨the *case study* of a juvenile delinquent⟩ ⟨a *case study* of capitalism⟩ **2 :** CASE HISTORY; *specif* **:** a detailed analysis of the personal and social history of an individual pupil used esp. in student counseling

case study method *n* **:** a method of research used esp. in sociology by which accumulated case histories are analyzed with a view toward formulating general principles

case system *n* [¹*case*] **:** a system of teaching law in which the instruction is chiefly on the basis of leading or selected cases as primary authorities instead of from textbooks

caseweed \ˈ=,=\ *n* [²*case* + *weed*] **:** SHEPHERD'S PURSE

casewood \ˈ=,=\ *n* [²*case* + *wood*] **:** wood for making case furniture

¹**casework** \ˈ=,=\ *n* [²*case* + *work*] **1** *bookbinding* **:** the making of cases **2** *printing* **:** HAND COMPOSITION

²**casework** \ "\ *n* [¹*case* + *work*] **:** social work involving direct consideration of the problems, needs, and adjustments of the individual case (as a person or family)

caseworker \ˈ=,==\ *n* [¹*case* + *worker*] **:** a worker (as in a social welfare agency) who investigates, diagnoses, and often assists in individual cases (as of persons or families in need of financial or psychiatric aid)

caseworm \ˈ=,=\ *n* [²*case* + *worm*] **:** an insect larva (as a caddisworm or a casebearer) that makes a case for its body

¹**cash** \ˈkash, -aa(ə)-, -ai-\ *n* -ES *often attrib* [modif. of MF or OIt; MF *casse* money box, fr. OIt *cassa* box, money box, fr. L *capsa* chest, case — more at CASE] **1** *obs* **:** a money box or chest **:** TILL **2 a :** ready money (as coin, specie, paper money, an instrument, token, or anything else being used as a medium of exchange) ⟨a check made payable to "cash" will be paid in ~ to the bearer⟩; *broadly* **:** bank deposits and certain readily negotiable paper (as checks, drafts, notes, bearer bonds, coupons) **b :** money or its equivalent paid immediately or promptly after purchasing ⟨sell goods for ~⟩ ⟨a ~ sale⟩ **3** *obs* **:** an amount of money **:** SUM ⟨keep a large ~ on hand⟩ — **cash on the nail** *or* **cash on the barrelhead :** CASH 2b ⟨my price is 10 dollars *cash on the nail*⟩

²**cash** \ "\ *n, pl* **cash** [Pg *caixa*, fr. Tamil *kācu*, a small copper coin, fr. Skt *karṣa*, a weight of gold or silver; akin to OPer *karsha-*, a weight] **1 :** any of various coins of small value in China and southern India: as **a :** any of several usu. copper coins formerly issued in the Madras States of British India, in French India, and Danish Tranquebar **b :** a Chinese coin usu. of copper alloy that is about the size of a U.S. quarter, has a square hole in the center, and was formerly issued by both the central and provincial governments **2 :** a unit of value equivalent to one cash coin

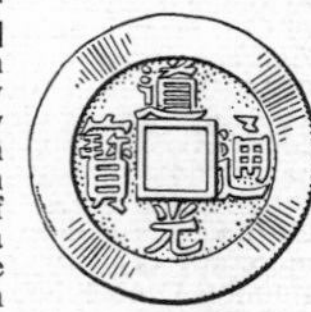

cash 1b

³**cash** \ "\ *vt* -ED/-ING/-ES [¹*cash*] **1 :** to pay or obtain cash for (as a check or bond) **:** exchange for money ⟨the store will ~ your check⟩ ⟨~ your check at the bank⟩ **2 :** to lead and win a bridge trick with (a card that is the highest remaining card of its suit) — **cash in one's chips :** DIE

⁴**cash** \ "\ *adj* [¹*cash*] **:** to be delivered and paid for within a specified period ⟨~ grain⟩

cash *abbr* cashier

cash account *n* **1 :** an account in which money transactions are recorded **2** *Scot* **:** bank credit

¹**cash-and-carry** \ˈ=¦=¦==\ *adj* **:** sold for cash and without delivery service

²**cash-and-carry** \ "\ *n* [¹*cash-and-carry*] **:** selling or the policy of selling cash-and-carry

cash assets *n pl* **:** assets consisting of cash and items readily convertible to cash (as marketable securities or life insurance)

¹**cashaw** *var of* CUSHAW

²**ca·shaw** \kəˈshȯ\ *n* -s [of African origin; akin to Yoruba *ka²shā²*, a running plant, Bobangi *nkasa*, a tree] *Jamaica* **:** MESQUITE 1a

cash basis *n* **:** a method of keeping accounts that includes as income only what has been received in cash and as expenses only those paid in cash — compare ACCRUAL BASIS

cashbook \ˈ=,=\ *n* **:** a book of original entry in which record is kept of all cash receipts and disbursements **:** a cash journal

cashbox \ˈ=,=\ *n* **:** a box or other receptacle for keeping cash — see BOX illustration

cashboy \ˈ=,=\ *n* **1 :** a store messenger given the job of carrying customers' money from the salesperson to a cashier and bringing back change **2 :** a general helper and errand boy at the exchange desk of a retail store

cash budget *n* **:** a projection of the future receipts and expenditures of a business

cash carrier *n* **:** a device (as a pneumatic tube) for conveying cash to and from a cashier

cash contract *n* **:** a sale on a stock exchange requiring cash settlement by a certain time on the day the contract is made

cash credit *n, in Scottish banking* **:** credit given to a depositor for an overdraft allowed by agreement up to a specified sum

cash crop *n* **:** a crop produced or gathered primarily for the market and readily salable (as cotton, tobacco, or vegetables)

cash customer *n* **:** a customer that pays cash for purchases

cash discount *n* **:** a discount granted in consideration of immediate payment or payment within a prescribed time

cash·el \ˈkashəl\ *n* -s [IrGael *caiseal*, fr. MIr *caisel* castle, fr. L *castellum* — more at CASTLE] **:** the ancient circular wall found in Scotland and Ireland enclosing a group of ecclesiastical buildings

cash·ew \ˈka(ˌ)shü, -ˈaa-, -ˈai-; kəˈshü\ *n* -s [Pg *cajú*, *acajú*, fr. Tupi *acajú*] **1 :** a tropical American tree (*Anacardium occidentale*) naturalized in all warm countries and important chiefly for its nut but yielding also a gum **2 a :** CASHEW NUT **b :** CASHEW APPLE

cashew apple *n* **:** the pear-shaped edible receptacle on which the cashew nut is borne

cashew family *n* **:** ANACARDIACEAE

cashew lake *n* **:** AUBURN

cashew nut *n* **1 :** the kidney-shaped fruit of the cashew borne at the apex of a fleshy receptacle and rendered edible by expelling the caustic oil from the shell by roasting **2 :** SEDGE 3

cashew nutshell liquid *n* **:** a phenolic oily liquid obtained from the double shell of the cashew nut and used chiefly in making phenolic resins notable for their flexibility and alkali resistance

cashgirl \ˈ=,=\ *n* **:** a girl having the duties of a cashboy

ca·shi·bo \kəˈshē(ˌ)bō\ *n, pl* **cashibo** *or* **cashibos** *usu cap* [Sp, perh. fr. Pano, lit., vampire (orig. an insult)] **1 a :** a Panoan people of eastern Peru **b :** a member of such people **2 :** the language of the Cashibo people

¹**ca·shier** \(ˈ)kaˈshi(ə)r, -kaa-, -kai-, -iə\ *vt* -ED/-ING/-S [modif. of D *casseren*, fr. MF *casser* to discharge, annul — more at QUASH] **1 :** to dismiss from service; *esp* **:** to dismiss summarily, ignominiously, and formally from a military or state position ⟨a court-martial sentenced him to two years' hard labor and ordered him ~*ed* —*Time*⟩ **2 :** to discard or reject **:** do away with ⟨~ the literal express sense of the words —Robert South⟩ **syn** see DISMISS

²**cash·ier** \ "\ *n* -s [modif. of D or MF; D *kassier*, fr. MF *cassier*, fr. *casse* merchandise box, money box — more at CASH] **:** one that has charge of money: as **a :** one of the higher officers in a bank or trust company responsible for moneys received (as for discounts, interest, dividends) and for moneys expended (as for operating expenses, letters of credit); *sometimes* **:** the chief executive officer of a bank charged with the management of its property and business in the ordinary way **b :** an officer usu. of the treasurer's department of a company who has responsibility for receipt, disbursement, and cash on hand **c :** a clerical worker in any business who handles and keeps records of cash transactions, receipts, and disbursements **d :** one that handles customer payments for goods or services rendered, either at the time (as one that takes money at a ticket window) or for bills previously rendered (as one that receives payments on credit accounts)

cashier's check *n* **:** a check drawn by a bank upon its own funds and signed by the cashier

cash in *vt* **:** to convert into cash ⟨*cashed in* all his bonds⟩ ~ *vi* **1 a :** to cash in one's chips in a gambling game (as poker) **:** retire from a gambling game **b :** to settle accounts and withdraw from a business arrangement; *also* **:** to withdraw from any involvement **2 :** to obtain monetary profit or other advantage ⟨the rise in the market will enable investors to *cash in*⟩ — often used with *on* ⟨politicians *cashed in* on the people's apathy⟩ **3 :** DIE

cash letter *n* **:** a deposit slip or list mailed by the transit department of a bank to a correspondent bank together with items to be credited immediately upon receipt

cash·mere *or* **kash·mir** \ˈkazh,mi(ə)r, -aizh-, -iə; -ash-, -aa-,-ai-\ *n* -s [fr. *Cashmere, Kashmir*, region in the northern part of the Indian subcontinent] **1 a :** fine soft light wool from the undercoat of the Kashmir goat of the Himalayan regions **b :** a fine yarn made of this wool alone or in a blend and used for sweaters and overcoatings **2 a :** a fine soft twilled fabric handloomed orig. from the underwool of Kashmir goats but imitated now on jacquard looms and used esp. for shawls with brilliant coloring and embroidery **b :** a soft lightweight clothing fabric of twill weave usu. of wool but often of other fibers or blends of fibers

cashmere goat *n, usu cap C* [fr. *Cashmere*, region] **:** KASHMIR GOAT

cashmere stag *n, usu cap C* [fr. *Cashmere*, region] **:** a deer (*Cervus cashmirianus*) of the northern Indian subcontinent that is similar to but larger than the red deer

cash·mer·ette \ˌ=₌məˈret\ *n* -s [*cashmere* + *-ette*] **:** a clothing fabric of cotton or of wool and silk made with a soft and glossy surface to imitate cashmere

cashmiri *usu cap, var of* KASHMIRI

cash money *n, South & Midland* **:** money in cash

cash nexus *n* **:** an agglomerate of impersonal monetary factors specif. considered as the basis for human relations

cash on delivery *adj* (*or adv*) **:** collect on delivery — abbr. *COD*

cash refund annuity *n* **:** a refund annuity payable in cash to a beneficiary upon the annuitant's death

cash register *n* **:** a business machine that records the amount of money received (as in running daily sales), that usu. has a money drawer, that exhibits the amount of each sale, and that often performs related operations (as totaling receipts, counting particular operations, certifying sales slips, or punching coded data on tape for later recording in ledgers or analysis sheets)

cash tenant *n* **:** a tenant who pays a money rent for a farm — compare SHARE-TENANT

cash value *n* **:** the amount available to the owner of a life insurance policy upon termination before maturity, being the reserve held by the company against the policy less the surrender charge if any

casimire *var of* CASSIMERE

cas·i·mi·roa \ˌkazəməˈrōə, -ˈmirəwə\ *n, cap* [NL, fr. *Casimiro* Gómez Ortega †1810 Span. botanist] **:** a small genus of tropical American evergreen trees and shrubs (family Rutaceae) having alternate digitately compound leaves and small greenish yellow flowers

casinet *var of* CASSINETTE

cas·ing \ˈkāsiŋ, -ēŋ\ *n* -s [fr. gerund of ³*case*] **1 :** something that encases **:** material for encasing **:** a case esp. for ornament, protection, or support: as **a :** an enclosing frame; *specif* **:** the wide molding used around door and window openings **b :** a thin layer of glass fused upon glass of a different kind or color **c :** a metal pipe used to case a well **d :** TIRE 2c **e :** a skinlike case for processed meat (as sausage) usu. made of the cleaned intestines of cattle, hogs, or sheep or of cellulose **f :** ²CASE 2e(1) **g :** the layer of soil with which a mushroom bed is cased **2 :** the layer of rock enclosing a vein, usu. modified by contact with the intruded ore **3 :** an opening or pocket between two parallel lines of stitching through at least two layers of cloth into which something (as a rod, string, or bone) may be inserted for supporting, gathering, or stiffening and which is used esp. in curtains and clothing **4 :** a solution of flavoring materials in either water or alcohol that is applied to cigarette blends, chewing plugs, and smoking mixtures during manufacture

casing dog *also* **casing spear** *n* **:** a tool for removing sections of casing from a drilled or bored well

casinghead \ˈ=₌,=\ *n* **:** a fitting at the top of the casing of an oil or gas well to allow pumping, cleaning, and the separation of gas from oil

casinghead gas *n* **:** natural gas rich in hydrocarbon vapors that is taken without processing from an oil well

casinghead gasoline *n* **:** NATURAL GASOLINE

casing nail *n* **:** a wire nail that has a small slightly flared head and is used for finish work

casing shoe *n* **:** a cylinder or ring of hard steel with a cutting edge attached to the bottom of a string of well casing

ca·si·no \kəˈsē(,)nō\ *n* -s [It, fr. *casa* house — more at CASA] **1 :** a building or room used for social meetings and public amusements (as dancing); *specif* **:** a building or room for gambling **2 a :** a small usu. decoratively designed Italian country house **b :** SUMMERHOUSE **3** *also* **cas·si·no :** a card game played by two or more persons in which each player wins cards by matching or combining cards exposed on the table with cards from his hand — see BIG CASINO, LITTLE CASINO; ROYAL CASINO, SPADE CASINO

casino pink *n* **:** MADDER ROSE

ca·si·ta \kəˈsēd·ə\ *n* -s [Sp, dim. of *casa* house — more at CASA] **:** a small house

¹**cask** \ˈkask, -aa(ə)-,-ai-,-á-\ *n* -s [Sp *casco* potsherd, skull, helmet, cask, fr. *cascar* to crack, break — more at CASCARA] **1 :** any barrel-shaped vessel made of staves, headings, and hoops usu. closely fitted together so as to hold liquids — see BUTT, HOGSHEAD, KEG, PIPE, TUN **2 a** *archaic* **:** CASKET **b** *obs* **:** CASE, SHELL **3 :** a cask and its contents ⟨a ~ of wine⟩; *also* **:** the quantity contained in a cask

²**cask** \"\ *vt* -ED/-ING/-S **:** to put or store in a cask

¹**cas·ket** \ˈkaskət, -aa-,-ai-,-á-, *usu* -əd·+V\ *n* -s [ME, modif. of MF *cassette* — more at CASSETTE] **1 :** a small usu. ornamental chest or box (as for jewels or other valuables) **2 :** something regarded as a repository ⟨the individual is only the ~ of the continuing race —J.S.Huxley⟩ **3 :** a usu. ornamented and lined rectangular box or chest for a corpse to be buried in — compare COFFIN

²**casket** \"\ *vt* -ED/-ING/-S **:** to put into or enclose in a casket

cask shell *n* **:** TUN SHELL

cas·par·i·an dot \(ˈ)kaˈspa(a)rēən-, (ˈ)käˈspär-\ *n, usu cap C* **:** the Casparian strip viewed in cross section

casparian strip *n, usu cap C* [Robert *Caspary* †1887 Ger. botanist + E *-an*] **:** a secondary thickening in many endodermal cells in the form of a continuous band or strip on the radial and transverse walls — compare ENDODERMIS

cas·pi·an \ˈkaspēən, -ˈaa-\ *adj, usu cap* [L *caspius* (fr. Gk *kaspios*) + E *-an*] **:** of, relating to, or characteristic of the Caspian sea

caspian languages *n pl, usu cap C* **:** a group of Iranian languages or dialects spoken chiefly in the Caspian provinces of Persia but distinct from Persian and including Tat, Talishi, Gilaki, Mazanderani, and Samnani

caspian tern *n, usu cap C* **:** a large scarlet-billed tern (*Sterna caspia* or *Hydropygne caspia*) widely distributed in the northern hemisphere with one subspecies occurring in much of northern No. America

casque \ˈkask, -aa(ə)-,-ai-,-á-\ *n* -s [alter. (influenced by F *casque*, fr. Sp *casco*) of *cask*] **1 :** a piece of armor for the head **:** a helmet or military headpiece of any kind **2 :** a helmet-shaped hat or headdress **3 :** a process or structure suggestive of a helmet: as **a :** the process of the bill of a hornbill **b :** the frontal shield of a coot or gallinule **c :** the covering of bony plates enclosing the head of certain extinct fishes

light casque, 15th cent.

casqued \-skt\ *adj* **:** provided with a casque **:** wearing a casque

cas·quet \ˈkaskət, -ˈaa-,-ai-,-á-\ *n* -s [F or Sp; F, fr. Sp *casquete*, fr. *casco* helmet] **:** CASQUE; *also* **:** a light open headpiece

cas·que·tel \ˌ=skəˈtel\ *n* -s [*casquet* + *-el*] **:** a light open helmet without beaver or visor

cas·quette \(ˈ)=ˈket\ *n* -s [F, dim. of *casque* helmet — more at CASQUE] **:** a cap with visor

cass *vt* -ED/-ING/-ES [ME *cassen*, fr. MF *casser* — more at QUASH] **1** *Scots law, obs* **:** to render useless or void **:** QUASH, ANNUL **2** *obs* **:** DISCHARGE, CASHIER

cassaba *var of* CASABA

cas·sa·ba·nana \ˌkasəbəˈnanə\ *n* -s [origin unknown] **:** a tropical vine (*Sicana odorifera*) of the family Cucurbitaceae that is often cultivated for its ornamental slender fruit similar to the vegetable marrow — called also *curuba, musk cucumber*

cas·san·dra \kəˈsandrə, -ˈaan-\ *n* -s *usu cap* [after *Cassandra*, daughter of King Priam of Troy, renowned as a prophetess of evil, fr. L, fr. Gk *Kassandra*] **1 :** one who prophesies misfortune or disaster **2** [NL, fr. L] **:** LEATHERLEAF 1

cas·san·dran \-rən\ *or* **cas·san·dri·an** \-rēən\ *adj, usu cap* [*Cassandra* + E *-an* or *-ian*] **:** prophetic of misfortune

cas·sa·pan·ca \ˌkasəˈpaŋkə\ *n* -s [It *cassapanca, cassabanca*, fr. *cassa* box (fr. L *capsa*) + *panca, banca* bench — more at CASE, BANK] **:** a cassone with wooden back and arms added to form a settee

cas·sa·reep \ˈkasə,rēp\ *n* -s [alter. of earlier *casserepo*, of Cariban origin; akin to Galibi *kaseripu*, Akawai *cassiripo*] **:** a flavoring agent orig. made in the West Indies by boiling the juice of the bitter cassava to a thick syrup

cassate *vt* -ED/-ING/-S [LL *cassatus*, past part. of *cassare*] *obs* **:** CASS

¹**cas·sa·tion** \kaˈsāshən, kə-\ *n* -s [ME *cassacioun*, fr. MF *cassation*, fr. *casser* to annul + *-ation* — more at QUASH] **:** the act of annulling, canceling, or quashing **:** ABROGATION ⟨a general ~ of their constitutions —J.L.Motley⟩ — see COURT OF CASSATION

²**cassation** \"\ *n* -s [G *kassation*, fr. G dial. (orig. students' slang) *kassation, gassation* serenade, fr. *kassaten, gassaten* (in the phrase *kassaten gehen, gassaten gehen, gassatim gehen* to roam the streets at night serenading ladies or looking for love affairs or fights), fr. G *gasse* street, fr. OHG *gazza* — more at GATE] **:** an 18th century instrumental composition in several short movements that is similar in style to the serenade and often performed outdoors

cas·sa·va *also* **ca·sa·va** \kəˈsävə, -ˈá-\ *n* -s [Sp *cazabe* cassava bread, fr. Taino *caçábi*] **1 :** any of several plants of the genus *Manihot* having fleshy rootstocks yielding a nutritious starch and cultivated throughout the tropics where it provides a staple food — called also *manioc, tapioca plant;* see BITTER CASSAVA, CASSAREEP, CASSIRI, SWEET CASSAVA **2 :** the rootstock of the cassava plant used in making tapioca, cassava bread, and starch

casse \ˈkas\ *n* -s [F, lit., breakage, fr. *casser* to break — more at QUASH] **:** a disorder that sometimes occurs in wine usu. due to the formation of colloidal complexes of metals resulting from the use of metallic utensils

cas·se·grain·i·an telescope \ˌkasəˈgrānēən-\ *n, usu cap C* [N. *Cassegrain* 17th cent. Fr. physician who invented it in 1672 + E *-ian*] **:** a reflecting telescope that has a paraboloidal primary mirror and hyperboloidal secondary mirror, is equivalent in its optical effects to a telephoto lens, and usu. has the light brought to a focus through a perforation in the center of the primary mirror

cassel *usu cap, var of* KASSEL

cas·sel brown *or* **cas·sel earth** \ˈkasəl-, -ˈä-\ *n, often cap C* [fr. *Cassel* (*Kassel*), Germany] **:** VANDYKE BROWN

cassel green *n, often cap C* **:** MANGANESE GREEN

cas·sel·mann's green \ˈkasəlmənz-, -ˈä-\ *n, usu cap C* [prob. trans. of G *Casselmanns grün*, after *Casselmann fl* 1890 Ger. chemist, its discoverer] **:** a basic copper sulfate used as a pigment

cas·sel yellow \ˈkasəl-, -ˈä-\ *n, often cap C* **1 :** an oxychloride of lead approximately $PbCl_2.7PbO$ used as a pigment — called also *mineral yellow, Turner's yellow* **2 :** LEMON YELLOW 1b

cas·se·na \kəˈsēnə\ *n* -s [earlier *casseena*, fr. Timucua] **:** a yaupon (*Ilex vomitoria*)

¹**cas·se·role** \ˈkasə,rōl, ˈkaas- *also* ˈkaz-\ *n* -s [F, saucepan, fr. MF, irreg. fr. *casse* ladle, dripping pan, fr. OProv *cassa* ladle, saucepan, fr. ML *cattia* dipper, modif. of Gk *kyathion* small ladle, dim. of *kyathos* ladle — more at CYATHUS] **1 :** a deep round usu. porcelain dish with a handle used for heating substances in the laboratory **2 :** a vessel of earthenware, glass, or metal usu. having a cover and a handle or a separable holder of metal and in which food may be baked and served **3 :** a dish cooked and served in a casserole **4 :** RUSTIC BROWN

casserole 1

²**casserole** \"\ *vt* -ED/-ING/-S **:** to cook in a casserole

casses *pres 3d sing of* CASS

cas·sette \kəˈset, ka-\ *n* -s [F, fr. MF, dim. of ONF *casse* box, case — more at CASE] **1 :** CASKET **2 :** SAGGER 1a **3 :** a lighttight magazine for holding sensitized film or plates for use in a camera; *specif* **:** one for holding the intensifying screens and film in X-ray photography

cas·sia \ˈkashə, -ˈaa-,-ˈai- *also, esp in sense 2*, -sēə\ *n* [ME, fr. OE, fr. L *casia, cassia*, fr. Gk *kasia, kassia*, of Sem origin; akin to Heb *qĕṣîʿāh* cassia] **1** -s **:** any of the coarser varieties of cinnamon bark — see CHINESE CINNAMON **2** *cap* [NL, fr. L cassia bark] **:** a genus of herbs, shrubs, and trees (family Leguminosae) that are native to warm regions and have even-pinnate leaves sometimes much reduced and nearly regular flowers with calyx teeth equal and usu. longer than the corolla — see RINGWORM BUSH, SENNA **3** -s **:** CASSIA FISTULA

cassia bark *n* **:** CHINESE CINNAMON

cassia bud *n* **:** the dried flower bud of any of several plants of the genus *Cinnamomum* (esp. *C. cassia*)

cas·si·a·ce·ae \ˌkasēˈāsē,ē\ [NL, fr. *Cassia*, type genus + *-aceae*] *syn of* CAESALPINIACEAE

cassia fis·tu·la \-ˈfis(h)chələ\ *n* [ME, fr. ML, lit., fistulous (spongy) cassia] **:** the dried pods of the drumstick tree the sweet pulp of which is a mild laxative — called also *purging cassia*

cassia flask *n* **:** a small volumetric flask with a long graduated neck used in pharmacy for determining cinnamaldehyde in cassia bark and other forms of cinnamon

cassia lig·nea \-ˈlignēə\ *n, pl* **cassia ligne·as** [ME, fr. ML lit., ligneous (woody) cassia] **:** Chinese cinnamon in thick flat pieces taken from wild trees

cassia oil *n* **:** a yellowish or brownish essential oil that contains chiefly cinnamaldehyde, is obtained from the leaves and young twigs of Chinese cinnamon (*Cinnamomum cassia*), and is used chiefly as a flavor and in medicine — called also *Chinese cinnamon oil, cinnamon oil*

cassia pulp *n* **:** the sweet pulp of cassia fistula

cas·sic acid \ˈkasik-\ *n* [NL *Cass*ia (genus name of *Cassia reticulata*) + E *-ic*] **:** RHEIN

cas·sid·e·ous \kəˈsidēəs, ka-\ *adj* [L *cassid-, cassis* helmet + E *-eous*] **:** bot **:** shaped like a helmet

cas·sid·i·dae \kəˈsidə,dē, ka-\ *n pl, cap* [NL, fr. *Cassid-, Cassis*, type genus + *-idae*] **:** a family of usu. large marine gastropod mollusks (order Pectinibranchia) having thick heavy shells of which many are used for making cameos — see HELMET SHELL

¹**cas·sie** \ˈkāzē, ˈkasē\ *n* -s [Orkney Islands Norse *kassi;* akin to Icel *kassi, kass* box, creel, ON *kjarr* underbrush — more at CHARE] *Scot* **:** a basket made of twisted straw

²**cas·sie** \ˈkasē\ *n* -s [F, fr. Prov *cacio*, short for *acacio* acacia, fr. L *acacia* — more at ACACIA] **:** HUISACHE

cas·sie paper \ˈkasē-\ *n* [part modif., part trans. of F *papier cassé*, lit., broken paper, fr. *papier* paper + *cassé*, past part. of *casser* to break — more at QUASH] **:** the top and bottom sheets of packaged paper when damaged (as in transportation) — compare RETREE

cas·si·mere *also* **cas·i·mire** \ˈkazə,mi(ə)r, -asə-,-aasə-\ *n* -s [fr. *Cassimere* (now usu. *Kashmir*), region in northern part of the Indian subcontinent] **:** a smooth twilled suiting fabric usu. made of wool; *also* **:** any of various fancy woolen clothing fabrics

cas·si·na *or* **cas·si·ne** \kəˈsēnə\ *n* -s [*cassina* fr. Timucua *cassiné; cassine* fr. MF *casiné*, fr. Timucua] **:** a yaupon (*Ilex vomitoria*)

cas·si·nese \ˌkasᵊnˈēz, -ēs\ *adj, usu cap* [It, fr. Monte *Cassino*, Italy, site of the monastery from which the Benedictine rule spread + It *-ese*] **1 :** of or relating to a congregation of Benedictine monasteries organized in the 15th century to promote the primitive observance of the Benedictine rule **2 :** of or relating to the American Cassinese congregation established in 1855 and including a majority of the Benedictine abbeys in the U. S.

cas·si·nette *also* **cas·i·net** \ˌkasᵊnˈet\ *n* -s [perh. irreg. fr. *cassimere*] **:** a lightweight twilled trousering usu. with cotton warp and wool filling

cas·sin finch \ˈkasᵊn-, -sin-\ *n, usu cap C* [after John *Cassin* †1869 Am. ornithologist] **:** a large finch (*Carpodacus cassinii*) of the Rocky mountain region the male being rosy red with dusky-brown shoulders, wings, and tail and the female drab and sparrowlike

cassing *pres part of* CASS

cassino *var of* CASINO

cas·sin's auklet \ˈkasᵊnz-, -sinz-\ *n, usu cap C* [after John *Cassin*] **:** a very small chubby auklet (*Ptychoramphus aleuticus*) common along the Pacific coast of No. America

cassin's kingbird *n, usu cap C* **:** a kingbird (*Tyrannus vociferans*) of southwestern No. America that is largely gray with a sulfur-yellow abdomen and has in the male an orange-red tuft of feathers on the crown

cas·sio·ber·ry \ˈkashə,berē\ *n* -ES [*cassina* + *-o-* + *berry*] **1 :** a yaupon (*Ilex vomitoria*); *also* **:** its fruit **2 :** a shrub (*Viburnum obovatum*) of the southern U.S.; *also* **:** its fruit **3 :** a winterberry (*Ilex laevigata*); *also* **:** its fruit

cas·si·o·pe \kəˈsīə(,)pē\ *n, cap* [NL, fr. L *Cassiope, Cassiopea*, mythical queen of Ethiopia and mother of Andromeda, fr. Gk *Kassiopē, Kassiopeia, Kassiepeia*] **:** a genus of low tufted shrubs of the family Ericaceae with mosslike foliage and nodding white or pink flowers found in the colder parts of the north temperate zone

cas·si·o·pe·ian \ˌkasēəˈpē(y)ən\ *adj, usu cap* [*Cassiopeia*, a northern constellation between Andromeda and Cepheus (fr. L *Cassiopeia, Cassiepeia*, fr. Gk *Kassiopeia, Kassiepeia*) + E *-an*] **:** of or relating to the constellation Cassiopeia

cas·si·ri \ˌkasəˈrē\ *n* -s [Carib *cassiri*, of Tupian origin; akin to Tupi *cassiri, caxiri* cassiri] **:** a drink resembling beer made by allowing cassava juice to ferment

¹**cas·sis** \ˈkasəs\ *n, cap* [NL, fr. L, helmet — more at HOOD] **:** a genus (the type of the family Cassididae) of mollusks comprising forms (as the cameo shell) with the body whorl very large and the shell more or less globular

²**cas·sis** \kaˈsēs\ *n* -ES [F, fr. L *cassia* — more at CASSIA] **1 :** a black currant (*Ribes nigrum*) of Europe **2 :** a syrupy liquor of low alcoholic strength made from black currants and used chiefly as a flavoring and sweetening agent with vermouth, water, or spirits — see VERMOUTH CASSIS

cassite *usu cap, var of* KASSITE

cas·sit·er·ite \kəˈsid·ə,rīt\ *n* -s [F *cassitérite*, fr. Gk *kassiteros* tin + F *-ite*] **:** a brown or black mineral that consists of tin dioxide SnO_2, is the chief source of metallic tin, and occurs in tetragonal crystals of brilliant adamantine luster and also in massive forms sometimes (1) compact with concentric fibrous structure resembling wood and sometimes (2) in rolled or pebbly fragments (hardness 6–7, sp. gr. 6.8–7.1) — called also respectively (1) *wood tin* (2) *stream tin*

cassius purple *n, usu cap C* **:** PURPLE OF CASSIUS

cas·sock \ˈkasək, -ˈaa-\ *n* -s [MF *casaque*, fr. Per *kazhāghand* padded jacket, fr. *kazh, kaj* raw silk + *āghand* stuffed] **1 :** a long loose coat or gown formerly worn by men and women; *specif* **:** a long coat formerly worn by soldiers **2 a :** a long close-fitting garment reaching to the feet that is worn by the clergy of certain churches often during divine service under a surplice or vestments and by choristers under a surplice or cotta and by vergers as an outer garment **b :** a shorter light double-breasted coat or jacket usu. of black silk that is worn under the Geneva gown **c :** an apronlike garment worn under vestments at outdoor ceremonies esp. by Anglican clergymen — called also *skirt cassock* **3 a :** the clerical or priestly office **b :** CLERGYMAN, PRIEST

cas·so·lette \ˌkasəˈlet\ *n* -s [F, fr. MF, fr. OProv *casoleta* small saucepan, dim. of *casola* saucepan, fr. *cassa* ladle, saucepan — more at CASSEROLE] **1 :** a vessel often with a perforated cover in which perfumes may be kept or burned **2 :** a small casserole in which an individual portion of food is cooked and served

cas·son \ˈkasᵊn, -zᵊn\ *n* -s [earlier *casen*, prob. of Scand origin; akin to ON *kös* heap, Dan *kokase* cow dung; akin to ON *kasta* to throw — more at CAST] *dial Eng* **:** dried dung of cattle used for fuel — usu. used in pl.

cas·so·ne \kəˈsōnē, -ˌnā\ *n, pl* **casso·ni** \-(,)nē\ [It, aug. of *cassa* box — more at CASH] **:** a large Italian chest having a hinged lid and often decorated with carving or painting

cas·soon \kəˈsün\ *n* -s [It *cassone* — more at CAISSON] **1 :** CAISSON 1 **2 :** COFFER 5a

cas·sou·let \ˌkasəˈlā\ *n* -s [F, fr. F dial., lit., stone dish (where this food is prepared), dim. of *cassolo* bowl, dim. of *casso* ladle; akin to OProv *cassa* ladle — more at CASSEROLE] **:** a casserole of beans baked with herbs and pork sausage and sometimes other meats

cas·so·wary \ˈkasə,werē\ *n* -ES [Malay *kĕsuari*] **:** any of several large ratite birds of New Guinea, Australia, the Aru islands, and Ceram closely related to the emu and constituting a genus and family of the order Casuariiformes and having the claw of the inner toe elongated, a horny casque on the head, wattles on the neck, slender hairlike feathers of dark color with the aftershaft as large as the main portion, and wing quills reduced to a few stout barbless shafts

cassubian *cap, var of* KASHUBIAN

cas·sy·tha \kəˈsīthə, -thə\ *n, cap* [NL, modif. of LGk *kasytas* dodder, of Sem origin; akin to Syr *kisōthō*, Aram *kĕsāthā*] **:** a genus of widely distributed tropical climbing parasites (family Lauraceae) which form masses of leafless threadlike stems on branches of trees and shrubs — see DODDER LAUREL

¹**cast** \ˈkast, -aa(ə)-,-ai-,-á-\ *vb* **cast; cast; casting; casts** [ME *casten*, fr. ON *kasta*; akin to ON *kös* heap and perh. to L *gerere* to bear, wage, cherish] *vt* **1 a** (1) **:** to cause to move by throwing **:** send forth by throwing **:** impel with force **:** THROW ⟨~ dice⟩ ⟨~ myself on my grass bed —W.H.Hudson †1922⟩ (2) **:** to throw out (a bait) by means of a fishing rod ⟨~ a plug into the surf⟩ **:** throw out (a net) **:** fish (an area) by casting **b** (1) **:** DIRECT ⟨~ a glance⟩ ⟨~ her mind back in an effort to remember⟩ (2) **:** to put forth ⟨the fire ~s a warm glow⟩ **:** project or send forth esp. in a particular direction ⟨his words ~ new light on the problem⟩ (3) **:** to place or propel as if by throwing ⟨~ another burden on the reader⟩ ⟨~ doubt upon their reliability⟩ ⟨the player ~ a spell on the audience⟩ (4) *obs* **:** to cause to enter or begin a state or activity (5) **:** to deposit (a ballot) formally or officially **:** give (a vote) **c** (1) **:** to throw off or away (as something lost, outworn, or no longer wanted) **:** get rid of **:** DISCARD ⟨the horse ~ a shoe⟩ — often used with *off, away, aside* ⟨~ off all restraint⟩ (2) *now dial Brit* **:** VOMIT (3) **:** to reject or dismiss as unfit or disqualified **:** CASHIER, CULL ⟨the state cannot with safety ~ him —Shak.⟩ — now used chiefly of farm animals ⟨ewes were ~ for age at five years⟩ (4) *Brit* **:** to bring forth, bear, or drop prematurely **:** SLINK *vt* 1 ⟨an infected cow may ~ its calf at the sixth month⟩ (5) **:** SHED, MOLT ⟨~ feathers⟩ ⟨~ leaves⟩ (6) *of honeybees* **:** to throw off (a swarm) (7) **:** to bring forth **:** BEAR, YIELD **d** (1) **:** to throw to the ground **:** overthrow esp. in wrestling **:** throw (an animal) down ⟨the cow was ~ and her legs tied⟩ (2) **:** to defeat in a lawsuit (3) *archaic* **:** CONVICT, CONDEMN ⟨she was ~ to be hanged —Francis Jeffrey⟩ **e** *now dial Brit* **:** to dig or shovel up (as earth or sod) ⟨they were *~ing* the peats⟩; *also* **:** to form by digging or throwing up earth ⟨~ a ditch⟩ ⟨~ a mound⟩ **2 a** (1) **:** to perform arithmetical operations on **:** compute or reckon (as accounts) **:** ADD ⟨~ the page of entries in an account book⟩ — often used with *up* ⟨~ up a row of figures⟩ (2) **:** to calculate by means of astrology ⟨~ a person's horoscope⟩ (3) *archaic* **:** to examine (urine) to diagnose disease (4) *printing* **:** to cast off **b** (1) **:** CONTRIVE, DEVISE, PLAN ⟨~ a cheap way how they may be all destroyed —Francis Beaumont & John Fletcher⟩ (2) *archaic* **:** DECIDE, INTEND ⟨we ~ to dine there⟩ (3) *now dial Brit* **:** to meditate on **:** CONSIDER, PONDER ⟨~ no more doubts —Christopher Marlowe⟩ — now often used with *over* **3 a :** to dispose or arrange into parts or into a suitable order **:** DEVISE ⟨I shall ~ what I have to say under two principal heads —*Tatler*⟩ **b :** to arrange or dispose (as ele-

ments or details in a painting) ⟨~ the draperies in a graceful arrangement⟩ **c :** to assign (as a part in a play) to an actor ⟨~ the leading part⟩ : assign the parts of (a dramatic production) to actors ⟨~ the play⟩ **:** assign to a role or part ⟨~ him as Othello⟩ ⟨the president and Congress have been ~ for opposite parts —W.E.Binkley⟩ **4 a** (1) **:** to give a particular shape to (a substance) by pouring in liquid or plastic form into a mold and letting or causing to harden without pressure ⟨~ steel⟩ **:** form by this process ⟨~ machine parts⟩ ⟨~ concrete pillars⟩ ⟨toys ~ from plastic⟩ (2) **:** to make a stereotype, electrotype, or other printing plate from (letterpress matter) **:** PLATE **:** make (as type, slugs, rules, stereotypes) by forcing hot metal into a matrix or mold **b :** to give form to **:** ARRANGE ⟨the book is ~ in the form of an autobiography⟩ **:** establish or create in a particular form ⟨those who were *~ing* the new Protestant state of England and Scotland —Padraic Colum⟩ **:** EXPRESS, FORMULATE ⟨*~ing* of morality in terms of economic gain —Abraham Edel⟩ **5 :** TURN ⟨~ the scale slightly⟩ **:** DECIDE ⟨~ the balance between the outward advantages and disadvantages —J.H.Newman⟩ **6 :** to make into a knot or stitch ⟨~ a square knot⟩ ⟨~ a stitch⟩ **7 :** TWIST, WARP ⟨a beam ~ by age⟩ **8 :** to cause (a dog or a pack) to make a cast **:** put (a dog) on the scent **~** *vi* **1 a :** to throw or project something; *specif* **:** to throw out a lure or bait with a fishing rod **b** *now dial Brit* **:** VOMIT **c** *dial Eng* **:** to bear fruit **:** YIELD ⟨the wheat *~s* well⟩ **2 a :** to perform addition ⟨~ and balance at a desk —Alfred Tennyson⟩ **b** *obs* **:** ESTIMATE, CONJECTURE ⟨~ beyond ourselves in our opinions —Shak.⟩ **3 :** WARP ⟨lumber *~s*⟩ **4 :** to make a cast — used of hunting dogs or trackers **5** *of a boat* **:** to turn the bow from the wind so as to bring it on the desired side (as when getting under way from a mooring) **:** VEER **6 a :** to undergo the process of shaping in a mold **:** take form in a mold ⟨overheated metal may ~ badly⟩ **b** *printing* **:** to produce a cast ⟨the safety device will not permit a loose line of matrices to ~⟩ **syn** see DISCARD, THROW — **cast anchor :** to let drop an anchor to keep a ship at rest **:** ANCHOR — **cast in one's teeth :** to reproach or reproach with ⟨*cast* his cowardice *in his teeth*⟩ — **cast loose :** to untie or unfasten (as a boat) **:** UNLASH — **cast lots :** to draw or use lots to determine a matter by chance — **cast one's lot with** *or* **cast in one's lot with :** to associate oneself with for good or ill **:** share the fortunes of ⟨leaving home he *cast in his lot with* the trappers⟩ **:** take the side of **:** align oneself with ⟨*cast his lot with* the Republicans⟩ — **cast out nines :** to check the results obtained in multiplication, division, addition, and subtraction of integral numbers by a series of divisions by the factor 9 and comparison of the remainders obtained, the operation in multiplication being as follows: (1) divide each factor by 9, (2) divide the products of the remainders obtained by 9, (3) divide the number being checked by 9, the result being prob. correct if the remainders in operations (2) and (3) are equal — **cast the lead :** to make a sounding with the lead — **cast the withers** *of cattle* **:** to evert the uterus after calving due to failure of normal contraction

²cast \"\ *n* -s [ME, fr. *casten* to cast] **1 :** an act or the action or process of casting **2 a :** an act of casting a throw (as of a missile) **b :** something that happens as a result of chance **:** a stroke of fortune **:** CHANCE, FATE, VENTURE ⟨his future depended on this ~⟩ **c :** a throw of dice ⟨a seven on the first ~⟩; *also* **:** the number of spots showing or counted in a single throw of dice ⟨a ~ of seven⟩ **d** (1) **:** a throw of a line (as a fishing line or lariat) or net (as a fishing net or butterfly net) (2) **:** a place for casting **:** a fishing place ⟨a good ~ near the bridge⟩ **3 a :** the form in which a thing is constructed ⟨forcing argument to the ~ of rhyme —Karl Shapiro⟩ **b** (1) **:** the set of actors assigned parts in a dramatic production (2) **:** a descriptive list of these parts (3) **:** the set of characters in a narrative **c :** the arrangement or disposition of draperies in a painting **4 :** the distance to which a thing can be thrown; *specif* **:** the distance a bow can shoot **5 a :** a turning of the eye in a particular direction **:** GLANCE, LOOK; *also* **:** EXPRESSION ⟨this freakish, elfish ~ came into the child's eye —Nathaniel Hawthorne⟩ **b :** a twist or turn to one side; *specif* **:** a slight strabismus **6 :** something that is thrown or the quantity thrown: as **a :** the number (as a couple) of hawks released by a falconer at one time **b :** the number (as of herrings, crabs, or oysters) that can be thrown into a vessel at one time by hand **:** WARP **c** *Brit* **:** a length of silkworm gut or nylon used to connect a fish lure or fly to the line **:** LEADER **d :** the quantity of metal cast at a single operation **7 a :** something that is formed by casting in a mold or form: as (1) **:** a reproduction or copy (as of a work of art) in metal or plaster **:** CASTING (2) **:** a fossil reproduction of the external details of a natural object produced by infiltration of a mold of the object by water-borne minerals (as lime salts) — compare PETRIFACTION **b :** an impression taken from an object by covering its surface with a liquid or plastic substance that when hardened retains form and detail of the original and can serve as a mold for reproduction **c :** a rigid dressing usu. made from gauze or crinoline impregnated with plaster of paris or other material used for immobilizing a diseased, deformed, or broken part **8 :** a forecast or conjecture concerning future events or conditions ⟨to make a long ~ ahead⟩ **9 :** the quality of elastic resilience in a bow that determines its ability to propel an arrow ⟨improving the ~ of a bow⟩ **10** *archaic* **:** a specimen intended to show the quality of the whole **:** EXAMPLE ⟨showing us a ~ of his logic⟩ — used esp. in the phrase *a cast of one's office* **11 a :** an overspread of a color or modification of the appearance of a substance by a trace of some added hue **:** SHADE ⟨the rock itself had a deep purplish ~ —Willa Cather⟩ ⟨gray with a greenish ~⟩ **b :** a trace of a particular quality **:** TINGE, SUGGESTION ⟨had a small ~ of the coxcomb —Laurence Sterne⟩ ⟨a ~ of bitterness in his words —Walter O'Meara⟩ **12 a :** a ride on one's way in a vehicle **:** LIFT ⟨a wagoner gave him a ~ as far as the town⟩ **b** *Scot* **:** HELP, ASSISTANCE ⟨if we had the ~ of a cart to bring it —Sir Walter Scott⟩ **13 a :** physical form or character **:** SHAPE, APPEARANCE ⟨the delicate ~ of his features⟩ **b :** characteristic quality ⟨Russia, the culture of which has as definite a ~ as that of France —Edward Sapir⟩ **:** NATURE, CHARACTER, BENT ⟨his mental habits . . . were always of a Quakerish ~ —H.S.Canby⟩ **:** TYPE, KIND ⟨Madison, Washington, and others of that ~ —J.C.Miller⟩ **c :** BENT, COMPLEXION ⟨~ of mind⟩ ⟨a mind of scientific ~⟩ **14 :** something that is thrown out or off, shed, or ejected: as **a** *of honeybees* **:** an afterswarm, esp. the first **b :** the excrement of an earthworm **c :** PELLET 1e **d :** a mass of plastic matter formed by effusion in cavities of certain usu. diseased organs and subsequently discharged from the body — see RENAL CAST **e :** the skin of an insect **15 :** the right to shoot first in an archery match given to the winner of the last shot — used with *the* **16 :** the ranging over the field in search of a trail by a dog, hunting pack, or tracker ⟨the setter made a wide ~⟩

³cast *adj* [ME, fr. L *castus* — more at CASTE] *obs* **:** CHASTE

⁴cast *obs var of* CASTE

⁵cast \'kast, -aa(ə)-,-ai,-à-\ *adj* [fr. past part. of ¹*cast*] *of an animal* **:** down or on its back and unable to get up

cast·a·ble \-əbəl\ *n* -s **:** a refractory material that has a bonding agent added and can be mixed with water and poured in a mold to set

cast about *vt* **:** to lay plans concerning **:** CONSIDER, CONTRIVE ⟨*cast about* how he was to go⟩ **~** *vi* **1 a :** to turn one's course **b** *of a ship* **:** to go about **2 :** to seek here and there **:** look around **:** SEARCH ⟨*cast about* for means of amusement —Rudyard Kipling⟩ ⟨*casting about* for something he is likely to be able to do best —G.N.Shuster⟩

¹cas·ta·lia \ka'stālyə, -lēə\ *or* **cas·ta·lie** \'kastəlē\ *n* -s *usu cap* [fr. *Castalia*, spring on Parnassus sacred to the Muses, fr. L, fr. Gk *Kastalia*] **:** a source of poetic inspiration

²castalia \"\ *n* [NL, fr. *Castalia* (spring)] *syn of* NYMPHAEA

cas·ta·li·an \(')ka¦stālyən, -lēən\ *adj, usu cap* [*Castalia* + E *-an*] **:** of or relating to the spring Castalia

cas·ta·na \ka'stan(y)ə\ *n* -s [Pg *castanha*, lit., chestnut, fr. L *castanea*] **1 a :** BRAZIL NUT **b :** the Brazil-nut tree **2** [AmerSp *castaña*, fr. Sp, chestnut, fr. L *castanea*] *Puerto Rico* **:** BREADFRUIT

cas·ta·nea \ka'stānēə\ *n, cap* [NL, fr. L, chestnut — more at CHESTNUT] **:** a small genus of rough-barked trees or shrubs (family Fagaceae) native to temperate regions and characterized by having four bud scales on each bud, unlobed leaves, and staminate flowers in stiff cylindrical catkins, the fruit ripening in one season and being a single nut or group of two or three nuts within a 2- to 4-valved scaly prickly involucre — see CHESTNUT; compare QUERCUS

cas·ta·ne·an *or* **cas·ta·ni·an** \(')ka¦stānēən\ *adj* [NL *Castanea* + E *-an*] **:** of or belonging to the genus *Castanea*

cas·ta·ne·ous \-nēəs\ *adj* [L *castanea* + E *-ous*] **:** of the color chestnut

cas·ta·net \¦kastə¦net, -aas-,-ais-, *usu* -ned·+V\ *n* -s [modif. of Sp *castañeta* fr. *castaña* chestnut, fr. L *castanea*] **:** a rhythm instrument used esp. by dancers that consists of two small shells of ivory, hard wood, or plastic which are fastened together to hang from the thumb by a double loop and are clicked together by the other fingers — usu. used in pl.

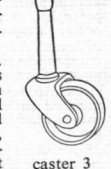

castanets

cas·ta·nop·sis \,kastə'näpsəs\ *n, cap* [NL, fr. *Castanea* + *-opsis*] **:** a small genus of trees (family Fagaceae) that contains one or two species in the Pacific coastal U.S. and a number in Asia and is closely related to *Castanea* but whose members are distinguished by having numerous bud scales on each bud, persistent leaves, a 3-celled ovary, and a fruit consisting of a nut that ripens at the end of the second season — see CHINQUAPIN

cas·ta·no·sper·mum \¦kastənō'spərməm\ *n, cap* [NL, fr. *castano-* (fr. *Castanea*) + *-spermum*] **:** a genus of Australian trees (family Leguminosae) having pinnate leaves, orange-yellow flowers, and chestnutlike seeds borne in large thick almost woody pods — see BEAN TREE a

cast around *vi* **:** cast about (sense 2)

cast away *vt* **1 :** to waste wantonly **:** SQUANDER ⟨*cast* his life *away*⟩ **2 :** WRECK ⟨*cast away* a ship⟩ **:** throw upon the shore as a survivor of a shipwreck ⟨a man *cast away* on a desert island⟩

¹castaway \'ₛₛ,ₛ\ *adj* [fr. past part. of *cast away*] **1 :** cast off as of no value **:** thrown away **:** REJECTED **2 a :** cast adrift or cast ashore as a survivor of a shipwreck **b :** thrown out or left without friends or resources **:** OUTCAST

²castaway \"\ *n* -s **1 :** one who has been cast away, cast off, or rejected ⟨~*s* from God —E.F.Burr⟩ **2** *archaic* **:** a disqualified person ⟨I keep under my body, and bring it into subjection: lest that by any means, when I have preached to others, I myself should be a ~ —1 Cor 9:27 AV⟩ **3 :** one cast away at sea **:** a shipwrecked person **4 :** one cast out by society **:** OUTCAST

cast back *vt, obs* **:** to drag back **:** IMPEDE **~** *vi* **:** to go back, search back, or refer back (as in history or in the memory) ⟨he *casts back* to the fiction of his own region for a helpful analogy —Katharine F. Gerould⟩

cast behind *vt, archaic* **:** to leave behind **:** OUTRUN

cast coating *n* [²*cast*] **:** a process for making paper with a fine glossy surface in which the coating of the paper while still soft is pressed against a highly polished heated cylinder until dry

¹cast down *vt* **:** to bring down (as from high position) **:** ABASE, DESTROY, DEMOLISH ⟨the proud will be *cast down*⟩

²cast down *adj* **:** DOWNCAST

caste \'kast, -aa(ə)-,-ai-,-à-\ *n* -s *often attrib* [in sense 1, fr. Sp *casta* race, breed, lineage, fr. *casta*, fem. of *casto* chaste, fr. L *castus*; in other senses, fr. Pg *casta*, lit., race, breed, lineage, fr. *casta*, fem. of *casto* chaste, fr. L *castus* pure, chaste; akin to L *carēre* to be without, Gk *keazein* to split, Skt *śasati* he cuts to pieces; basic meaning: to cut] **1** *obs* **:** a race, stock, or breed of men or animals **2 :** one of the hereditary classes into which the society of India is divided in accordance with a system fundamental in Hinduism, reaching back into distant antiquity, and dictating to every orthodox Hindu the rules and restrictions of all social intercourse and of which each has a name of its own and special customs that restrict the occupation of its members and their intercourse with the members of other castes — see BRAHMAN, KSHATRIYA, SUDRA, VAISYA, VARNA **3 a :** a division or class of society comprised of persons within a separate and exclusive order based variously upon differences of wealth, inherited rank or privilege, profession, occupation ⟨the tinkers then formed an hereditary ~ —T.B.Macaulay⟩ ⟨his sturdy brown legs were tattooed in blue to the thighs, indicating his high ~ —Robert Trumbull⟩; *broadly* **:** CLASS **b :** the position conferred by caste standing **:** PRESTIGE, FACE — used esp. in the phrase *lose caste* ⟨art and religion have lost ~ —F.L.Baumer⟩ **4 :** a system of social stratification more rigid than a class and characterized by hereditary status, endogamy, and social barriers rigidly sanctioned by custom, law, or religion **5 :** a form of polymorphic social insects (as ants, bees, and termites) that carries out a particular function in the colony ⟨worker ~⟩ ⟨soldier ~⟩

caste·less \-ləs\ *adj* **1 :** not divided into rigid social classes ⟨there is no leisure class in that ~ country⟩ **2** *India* **:** outside the caste system and thus having no place or status in society ⟨the foreigner was a ~ person⟩

cas·te·let *or* **cas·tel·let** \¦kas(t)ə¦let\ *n* -s [ME, fr. ONF, dim. of *castel* — more at CASTLE] **:** a small castle

cas·tel·lan \'kastələn, -,lan, ka'stelən\ *n* -s [alter. (influenced by L *castellanus*) of ME *castelleyn*, fr. ONF *castelain*, fr. L *castellanus* occupant of a castle, fr. *castellanus*, adj., of a castle, fr. *castellum* castle — more at CASTLE] **:** a governor or warden of a castle or fort

cas·tel·la·ni's paint \¦kastə¦lānēz-\ *n, usu cap C* [after Aldo *Castellani* b1875 Ital. physician & bacteriologist] **:** CARBOL-FUCHSIN PAINT

cas·te·lla·no \,kastə'l(y)ä(,)nō\ *n* -s [Sp, lit., *Castilian* — more at CASTILIAN] **1 :** an ancient Spanish gold coin bearing the Castilian arms; *esp* **:** one weighing 1/50 of a mark **2 :** an ancient Spanish unit of weight equivalent to 1/50 of a mark

cas·tel·lany \'kastə,lanē, -,lā-,-lə-, ka'stelənē\ *n* -ES [ML *castellania*, fr. *castellanus* castellan (fr. L, occupant of a castle) + L *-ia* -y] **:** the office or jurisdiction of a castellan **:** the extent of land and jurisdiction appertaining to a castle

cas·tel·lar \(')ka¦stelə(r), 'kastəl-\ *adj* [L *castell*um castle + E *-ar*] **:** belonging to or suggestive of a castle ⟨mansions of a ~ style⟩

cas·tel·late \'kastə,lāt, *usu* -ād·+V\ *vb* -ED/-ING/-S [back-formation fr. *castellated*] *vt* **:** to build like a castle **:** build or furnish with battlements **~** *vi* **:** to take the form of a castle ⟨*castellating* clouds⟩

cas·tel·lat·ed \-ād·əd\ *adj* [ML *castellatus* (past part. of *castellare* to fortify, fr. L *castellum* castle) + E *-ed*] **1 :** built or formed like a castle **:** having battlements or parts resembling battlements ⟨~ country houses⟩ ⟨~ cliffs⟩: as **a :** having a design or decoration resembling a line of battlements ⟨a ~ cornice⟩ ⟨a ~ band of velvet⟩ **b** *of clouds* **:** of the type altocumulus castellatus **2 :** CASTLED 1 **3 :** lodged in a castle **:** securely established in a position of strength ⟨~ power and wealth —*No. Amer. Rev.*⟩

castellated nut *n* **:** a nut with radial grooves in its upper face to receive a split pin passed through a hole in the bolt to prevent the nut from turning

cas·tel·la·tion \,kastə'lāshən\ *n* -s [ML *castellation-, castellatio*, fr. *castellatus* + *-ion-, -io* -ion] **1 :** the act of castellating **2 :** a castellated structure **3 a :** BATTLEMENT **b :** a groove or recess in a castellated structure (as a nut) ⟨a cotter pin passing through the ~ and the hole in the bolt⟩

cas·tel·la·tus \,ₛₛ'lād·əs, -'lä-\ *adj* [ML] *of a cloud formation* **:** shaped like a turret or a row of turrets — see ALTOCUMULUS CASTELLATUS

caste mark *n* **1 :** a mark or symbol that is worn on the forehead esp. in India and denotes the wearer's caste **2 :** a distinguishing characteristic or trait that identifies a member of a particular class or group ⟨the *caste mark* of the intellectual⟩

¹cast·er \'kastə(r), -'aa-,-'ai-,-'à-\ *n* -s [ME, fr. *casten* to cast + *-er*] **1 a :** one that casts: as (1) **:** a worker who shapes (as in a mold) molten metal, semiliquid clay, or other plastic material into finished products or bodies to be finished esp. in founding, jewelry making, brickmaking, tilemaking, or the making of hat blocks — compare MOLDER, POURER (2) **:** a machine that casts type **b** *also* **caster plate :** a plate (as an electrotype) used as a master printing surface for the molding of other plates — called also *master, pattern plate;* compare WORKER **2** *also* **cas·tor** \-tə(r)\ **a :** a cruet, sifter, or other small container for condiments used at the table **b :** a stand for holding a set of casters **3** *also* **castor** [¹*cast* (turn) + *-er, -or*] **:** a wheel or set of wheels mounted in a frame free to swivel about an axis perpendicular to the axis of the wheel or set and used for supporting furniture, trucks, and various portable machines or inverted on the upper ends of posts for handling plate and sheet metal in rolling mills **4 :** the slight usu. backward tilt of the upper end of the knuckle pin of an automotive vehicle employed as a means of giving directional stability to the front wheels

caster 3

²caster *also* **castor** \"\ *vb* -ED/-ING/-S [¹*caster* (wheel)] *vt* **1 :** to mount (as an airplane wheel) so as to permit to swivel freely ⟨~*ed* nosewheel⟩ **2 :** to equip (as table legs) with casters **~** *vi* **:** to swivel freely ⟨~*ing* and steerable nosewheel —*Flying*⟩

castering landing gear *n* **:** an airplane landing gear having means to permit castering of the wheels about substantially vertical axes during crosswind landings

cast·er·less \-ləs\ *adj* **:** lacking casters

castes *pl of* CASTE

cas·ti·gate \'kastə,gāt, -aas-, *usu* -ād·+V\ *vt* -ED/-ING/-S [L *castigatus*, past part. of *castigare* to correct, punish — more at CHASTEN] **1 a :** to punish or subdue by punishment ⟨~ thy pride —Shak.⟩ **b :** to reprove for error or criticize with drastic severity ⟨those poems in which he ~*s* man's general inhumanity and lack of sincerity —J.G.Southworth⟩ ⟨not even the ablest critic can ~ an artless generation into repentance and creative vigor —A.J.Barnouw⟩ **2 :** to correct or revise (a literary text) **3** *obs* **:** to tone down or subdue in intensity or boldness **syn** see PUNISH

cas·ti·ga·tion \,ₛₛ'gāshən\ *n* -s [ME *castigacioun*, fr. L *castigation-, castigatio*, fr. *castigatus* + *-ion-, -io* -ion] **1 a :** severe punishment **:** CHASTISEMENT **b :** severe reproof or criticism **2 :** revision or correction (of a literary text)

cas·ti·ga·tor \'ₛₛ,gād·ə(r), -ātə-\ *n* -s [L, fr. *castigatus* + *-or*] **:** one that castigates

¹cas·ti·ga·to·ry \-gə,tōrē\ *adj* [L *castigatorius*, fr. *castigatus* + *-orius* -ory] **:** of or concerned with castigation **:** PUNITIVE

²castigatory *n* -ES *obs* **:** an instrument for castigation; *specif* **:** CUCKING STOOL

cas·ti·glia·no's theorem \¦käst°l¦yä(,)nōz-, ¦kas-\ *n, usu cap C* [after Carlo Alberto *Castigliano* †1884 Ital. engineer] **:** a theorem in structural mechanics: when an external force is applied at any point of a structure composed of rigidly connected elastic members the resulting internal work throughout the structure is equal to the product of the force by the displacement of the point of application in the direction of the force and the derivative of the internal work with respect to either factor thereof is equal to the other factor

cas·tile *or* **castile soap** \(')ka¦stēl, -kaa-,-kai-\ *n* -s *often cap C* [fr. *Castile*, region of Spain where it was orig. made] **1 :** a fine hard bland soap usu. white or cream-colored but sometimes marbled or green that is made from olive oil and sodium hydroxide — called also *olive-oil castile soap* **2 :** any of various hard soaps (as a white neutral toilet soap) made partly from olive oil together with other fats or oils (as coconut oil) or wholly from other fats and oils

¹castilian *n* -s [modif. of L *castellanus* — more at CASTELLAN] *obs* **:** one of the garrison of a castle

²cas·til·ian \ka'stilyən *also* kə-\ *n* -s *cap* [modif. of Sp *castellano*, fr. *castellano*, adj., Castilian, fr. L *castellanus* of a castle, fr. *castellum* castle — more at CASTLE] **1 :** a native or inhabitant of the central Spanish provinces of Old and New Castile or of the former kingdom of Castile; *broadly* **:** SPANIARD **2 a :** the dialect of Castile **b :** the official and literary language of Spain based on this dialect **:** standard Spanish

³castilian \(')ka¦stilyən *also* kə's-\ *adj, usu cap* [modif. of Sp *castellano*] **1 :** of, relating to, or characteristic of the Spanish province of Castile or its inhabitants **:** native to Castile; *broadly* **:** SPANISH **2 :** of, relating to, or characteristic of the standard Spanish language

castilian brown *n, usu cap C* **:** a moderate reddish brown that is yellower than roan and redder and slightly lighter and stronger than mahogany — called also *brown madder, Columbian red, madder brown, old cedar, Tanagra*

cas·til·ian·ism \ₛ'ₛₛ,nizəm\ *n* -s *usu cap* [modif. of Sp *castellanismo*, fr. *castellano* + *-ismo* -ism] **:** a characteristic feature of the Castilian dialect or of Castilian Spanish occurring in another language or dialect

castilian red *n, usu cap C* **:** a vivid red that is lighter, slightly yellower, and stronger than apple red, yellower, lighter, and stronger than carmine, yellower and lighter than madder crimson, bluer and lighter than pimento, and bluer, lighter, and stronger than scarlet — called also *cochineal, Dutch scarlet, fire scarlet, goblin scarlet*

cas·til·la \ka'stilə, -tē(y)ə\ [NL, after Juan *Castillo* y López] *syn of* CASTILLOA

cas·til·le·ia *also* **cas·til·le·ja** \,kastə'lē(y)ə\ *n, cap* [NL, irreg. (influence of Sp *-eja*, dim. suffix) fr. Juan *Castillo* y López] **:** a large genus of root-parasitic herbs (family Scrophulariaceae) abundant in western No. America and characterized by irregular hooded flowers in dense spikes usu. with brightly colored bracts — see INDIAN PAINTBRUSH

cas·til·loa \,kastə'lōə, ka'stiləwə\ *n, cap* [NL, fr. Juan *Castillo* y López †1793 Span. botanist] **:** a genus of tropical American trees (family Moraceae) of which some yield caucho and all are characterized by the development of long slender deciduous twigs which bear large showy usu. densely hairy leaves

casting *n* -s [ME, fr. gerund of *casten* to cast] **1 :** the act of one that casts: as **a :** the act or process of making casts or impressions or of shaping in a mold (as in making pottery or forming metal objects by pouring molten metal into a mold) **b :** the throwing of a fishing line by means of a rod and reel — see BAIT CASTING, FLY CASTING, SURF CASTING **c :** the assignment of parts and duties to actors or performers ⟨insight into the workings of an opera house, its ~, its repertory and its general management —Harriett Johnson⟩ **2 :** something that is cast in a mold; *specif* **:** an object (as of metal, plaster or glass) so cast **3 :** something that is cast out or off (as skin, feathers, or excrement): as **a :** WORMCAST **b :** PELLET 1e

casting bottle *n* **:** a bottle for sprinkling perfumes

casting box *n* **:** the matrix-holding receptacle into which hot metal is poured in casting a stereotype

casting director *n* **:** one that supervises the casting of plays, operas, or other dramatic performances

casting glass *n, obs* **:** CASTING BOTTLE

casting man *n* **1 :** one who backs electrotype shells **2 :** one who casts stereotypes **3 :** a stock clerk who issues castings and other mechanical equipment used in textile-machine repair

casting net *var of* CAST NET

casting sheet *n* **:** a list containing descriptions of the types of actors needed for a particular play or other dramatic work

casting slip *n, pottery* **:** a slurry of clay and additives mixed to a creamy consistency in water with deflocculating agents and ready to pour into a plaster mold

casting table *or* **casting plate** *n* **:** a table with raised edges and polished metal surface used as a mold for casting plate glass

casting vote *or* **casting voice** *n* [fr. pres. part. of ¹*cast* (decide)] **:** a deciding vote cast by a presiding officer or judge to break a tie or sometimes to create a tie

casting wax *n* **:** any clean free-flowing wax out of which the pattern or matrix for a casting (as of a metal) is made

cast iron *n* [fr. past part. of ¹*cast*] **:** a commercial alloy of iron, carbon, and silicon cast in a mold, being hard, brittle, nonmalleable, and incapable of being hammer-welded but more easily fusible than steel, containing usu. 2.0 to 4.5 percent carbon and 1 to 4 percent silicon, and having a melting point of 1200 to 1250°C and a weight per cubic foot of 425 to 475 pounds (sp. gr. 7.0–7.6)

cast-iron \'ₛ'ₛₛ\ *adj* **1 :** made of cast iron **2 :** resembling cast iron: as **a :** capable of withstanding great hardship or strain ⟨a *cast-iron* stomach⟩ **b :** not admitting change, adaptation, or exception **:** RIGID, STRICT ⟨a man of *cast-iron* will⟩

cast-iron front \'ₛ,ₛ'ₛ\ *n* **:** a type of usu. commercial architecture employing large windows and columns and spandrels of cast iron

cast-iron plant \'ₛ'ₛ,ₛ\ *n* [so called fr. its hardiness] **:** a commonly cultivated foliage plant (*Aspidistra elatior*)

¹cas·tle \'kasəl, -'aa-,-'ai-,-'á-\ *n* -s [ME *castel,* fr. OE, fr. ONF & LL; ONF *castel* castle and LL *castellum* village, fr. L *castellum* castle, dim. of *castrum* fortified place; akin to L *castrare* to castrate — more at CASTRATE] **1 a :** a large fortified building or set of buildings, (as of a prince or nobleman) built orig. in medieval times as a single donjon often surrounded by inferior buildings (as stables), a palisaded enclosure, and a moat and later often having more elaborate accessory buildings (as a great hall and a chapel), courtyards, surrounding defensive walls, and a drawbridge over the moat **b :** a large dwelling that has served as a fortress **c :** a large dwelling that has replaced a fortress **d :** a large building; *esp* **:** a massive or imposing house or mansion **2 :** a retreat or stronghold safe against intrusion or invasion ⟨a man's house is his ~⟩ **3 :** a raised structure on the deck of an early sailing ship or galley **4 :** ³ROOK **5** [trans. of D *kasteel* castle, stronghold] **:** a fortified place or village of an Indian tribe in the northeastern U.S. **6 :** a heraldic representation of a castle or of a portion of an embattled wall often having a gateway and crowned with usu. three towers **7 :** CASTLE IN THE AIR — usu. used in pl.

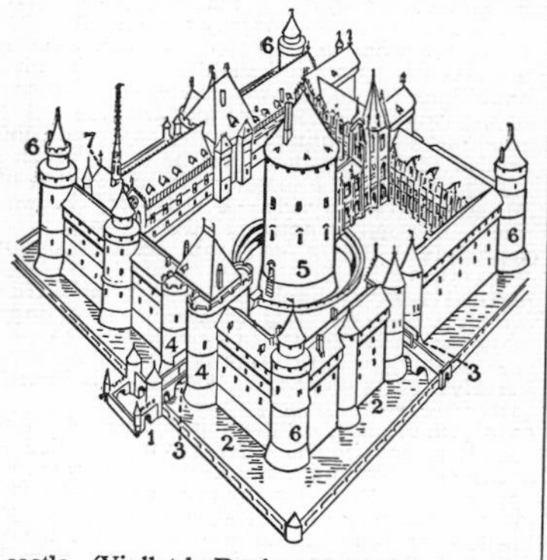

castle (Viollet-le-Duc's restoration of the Louvre in Paris before 1527) showing: *1* fortified approach; *2* moat; *3* drawbridge; *4* tower flanking main entrance; *5* donjon, or keep, encircled by fosse; *6* angle tower for defense of outer wall; *7* chapel

²castle \"\ *vb* **castled; castled; castling** \-s(ə)liŋ\ **castles** *vt* **1** *obs* **:** to enclose (as a water conduit) in stone walls **2 :** to establish in a secure position in or as if in a castle ⟨*castled* up in his mountain retreat⟩ **3** *chess* **:** to move (the king) in castling ~ *vi* **:** to move the king two squares toward a rook and then, in the same move, the rook to the square next past the king; *also, of the king* **:** to be moved in this way — usu. designated in notation by 0-0 (king's side) or 0-0-0 (queen's side)

castle–builder \'==,==\ *n* **:** one that builds castles in the air or forms visionary schemes

castle–building \'==,==\ *n* **:** building castles in the air **:** DAYDREAMING

castled *adj* **1 :** having a castle ⟨a ~ village⟩ **:** supporting a castle ⟨a ~ height⟩ **2 :** CASTELLATED

castle earth *n* [alter. of *cassel earth*] **:** CASSEL BROWN

castle–guard \'==,=\ *n* **1 :** a feudal knight service of the tenant to defend the lord's castle; *also* **:** the tenure of such service **2 :** a tax or charge now mostly fallen into desuetude that was orig. imposed in lieu of castle-guard

castle in the air *also* **castle in spain** *usu cap S* **:** a visionary project **:** DAYDREAM

castle nut *n* [so called fr. the resemblance of its grooves to the crenels of a battlement] **:** CASTELLATED NUT

cas·tle·ry \-səlrē\ *n* -ES [*castle* + *-ry*] **:** a territory subject to a feudal castle and organized for its maintenance and defense

castles *pl of* CASTLE, *pres 3d sing of* CASTLE

cas·tlet \'kaslət, ¦kasə¦let\ *n* -s [alter. (influenced by *castle*) of *castelet*] **:** a small castle

castle walk *n, usu cap C* [after Vernon Blythe *Castle* †1918 Eng. dancer who originated it] **:** a ballroom dance consisting basically of a straight forward walk with reach and lift, one step to each musical beat

cas·tle·ward \'==,wȯ(ə)rd\ *n* **:** CASTLE-GUARD

¹castling *pres part of* CASTLE

²cast·ling \'kastliŋ, -slən\ *n* -s [*cast* (past part. of ¹*cast*) + *-ling*] **1** *now dial Eng* **:** an offspring brought forth prematurely **:** ABORTION **2** *obs* **:** CAST 14a

cast·ner cell \'kastnə(r)-\ *n, usu cap 1st C* [after H.Y.*Castner* †1899 Am. chemist] **1 :** a rocking cell with a layer of mercury on the bottom for making sodium hydroxide and chlorine by electrolysis of sodium chloride solution **2 :** a cell for making metallic sodium and hydrogen by electrolysis of fused sodium hydroxide

cast net *also* **casting net** *n* **:** a circular or conical weighted net designed to be cast mouth downward by hand and withdrawn by lines attached to its margin — compare DIP NET, SETNET

ca·stock \'kä,stök, -,stōk\ *n* -s [alter. of ME *calstok,* fr. ME *cal* kale + *stok* stock, stem — more at KALE, STOCK] *chiefly Scot* **:** a cabbage stalk

cast off *vt* **1 :** LOOSE, SLIP ⟨*cast off* a hunting dog⟩ **2 :** UNFASTEN, UNHITCH ⟨*cast off* a boat⟩ **:** let go **:** UNTIE ⟨*cast off* a line⟩ **:** loose from a mooring **3 :** to bind off **4 :** to measure (copy or set type) to determine the amount of printed matter that will be made or the space that will be occupied when set or reset in a particular face, size, and measure ~ *vi* **1 :** to unfasten or untie a boat or a line **2 :** to turn from one's partner in a country or square dance and pass around the outside of the set and back

cast–off \'=,=\ *adj* [*cast off,* past part. of *cast off*] **:** thrown away or aside **:** worn out **:** DISCARDED ⟨wearing his brother's *cast-off* clothing⟩

cast·off \"\ *n* -s **1 :** a person or thing that has been cast off ⟨dressed in his older brother's ~*s*⟩ **2 :** the lateral offset of the stock of a shotgun that enables the shooter's eye to be brought in line with the sights **3 :** an estimate of typographical space made by casting off

cast on *vt* **:** to place (stitches) on a knitting needle for beginning or enlarging knitted work

¹cas·tor \'kastə(r), -'aa-,-'ai-,-'á-\ *n* [ME, fr. L, fr. Gk *kastōr,* fr. *Kastōr* Castor, one of the Dioscuri (the other being L *Pollux,* Gk *Polydeukēs*), twin heroes or demigods of Greek mythology] **1 a** -s **:** BEAVER 1 **b** *cap* [NL, fr. L] **:** the type genus of Castoridae comprising the beavers **2** -s **:** a creamy orange-brown substance with strong penetrating odor and bitter taste that consists of the dried perineal glands of the beaver and their secretion or an extract of this and is used by perfumers as a fixative and by professional trappers to scent bait — called also *castoreum* **3** -s **a :** a beaver or other hat made often of fur in imitation of a beaver **b :** the skin of a beaver **c :** a glove leather with a soft finish made by grinding off or suede-finishing the grain surface of goatskins or certain sheepskins **4** -s **:** a brownish gray that is yellower and slightly lighter than taupe, yellower and paler than chocolate, and duller and slightly yellower than mouse gray **5** -s **:** MADE-BEAVER

²castor \"\ *var of* CASTER

³castor \"\ *var of* CASTORITE

⁴castor \"\ *n* -s [origin unknown] **:** CHESTNUT 5

⁵castor \"\ *n* -s [by shortening] **:** CASTOR-OIL PLANT

castor bean *also* **castor–oil bean** *n* [*castor* (*oil*) + *bean*] **1 :** the seed of the castor-oil plant from which castor oil is extracted — see RICIN **2 :** CASTOR-OIL PLANT

castor–bean tick *n* **:** a widely distributed tick (*Ixodes ricinus*) that resembles the castor-bean seed in color and shape, lives on various mammals, and is a vector of piroplasmosis and certain virus diseases of domestic animals

cas·tor·ette \¦kastə¦ret\ *n* -s [¹*castor* (beaver) + *-ette*] **:** rabbit fur sheared and dyed to simulate beaver

cas·to·re·um \ka'stōrēəm\ *n* -s [ME *castorium,* fr. L *castoreum,* fr. *castor* beaver — more at CASTOR] **:** ¹CASTOR 2

castor gray *n* [prob. fr. ¹*castor*] **:** a dark greenish gray that is bluer and paler than sagebrush green and yellower and slightly less strong than muscovite

cas·tor·i·dae \ka'stȯrə,dē\ *n pl, cap* [NL, fr. *Castor,* type genus + *-idae*] **:** a family of rather large heavy-skulled sciuromorph rodents comprising the beavers and extinct related forms

cas·tor·ite \'kastə,rīt, -'aa-,-'ai-,-'á-\ *or* **cas·tor** \-tə(r)\ *n* -s [*castorite* fr. G *kastor* (fr. *Kastor* mythological personage, fr. L *Castor*) + E *-ite; castor* fr. G *kastor;* fr. its appearance with pollucite (previously called *pollux*)] **:** a mineral consisting of a variety of petalite occurring in transparent crystal

cas·to·roi·des \,kastə'rȯi(,)dēz\ *n, cap* [NL, fr. *Castor* + *-oides* -oid] **:** a genus of extinct giant beavers of the Pleistocene of the eastern and southern U.S.

castor oil *n* [¹*castor* + *oil;* prob. fr. a supposed connection with the substance castor] **:** a colorless to amber or greenish viscous nondrying fatty oil expressed or extracted from castor beans and used chiefly as a cathartic and usu. after processing as a lubricant and drying oil — called also *ricinus oil;* see TURKEY-RED OIL

castor–oil plant *n* **:** a tropical African and Asiatic herb (*Ricinus communis*) naturalized in all tropical countries and growing as an annual in temperate regions, having large palmate bronze-green leaves, small apetalous flowers, and spiny capsules containing beanlike mottled seeds that yield castor oil and are poisonous because of the presence of ricin — called also *palma Christi;* see CASTOR BEAN

castor pomace *or* **castor cake** *n* [*castor* (*bean*)] **:** a pomace produced by the extraction of oil from castor beans and used as a fertilizer and soil conditioner

castors *pl of* CASTOR

castor seed *n* **:** CASTOR BEAN

castor sugar *n* [²*castor*] *chiefly Brit* **:** finely granulated or powdered white sugar that can be shaken through the perforated top of a caster

castor ware *n, usu cap C* [fr. *Castor,* Peterborough, England, where it was found] **:** an ancient Roman pottery having ornaments and animal forms laid in white slip on a dark ground

castory *n* -ES [ME, castoreum, modif. of L *castoreum*] *obs* **:** a reddish brown coloring material from castoreum

cast out *vt* **:** to drive out **:** BANISH, EXPEL ~ *vi, chiefly Scot* **:** to fall out **:** QUARREL ⟨he *cast out* with his brother⟩

castra *pl of* CASTRUM

cas·tra·me·ta·tion \,kastrəmə'tāshən\ *n* -s [F, fr. ML *castrametation-, castrametatio,* fr. L *castra metatus* (past part. of *castra metari* to pitch a camp, fr. *castra* camp — pl. of *castrum* fortified place — + *metari* to measure out) + *-ion-, -io* -ion; akin to L *munire* to fortify — more at CASTLE, MUNITION] **:** the making or laying out of a military camp

¹cas·trate \'ka,strāt, -'aa-, *esp Brit* =ˈ=; *usu* -ād.+V\ *vt* -ED/-ING/-s [L *castratus,* past part. of *castrare;* akin to Skt *śasati* he cuts to pieces — more at CASTE] **1 a :** to deprive of the testes **:** EMASCULATE, GELD **b :** to deprive of the ovaries **:** SPAY **2 :** to deprive of vigor or vitality ⟨intelligence is *castrated* —John Dewey⟩ **:** weaken by removal of the most effective or forceful elements **:** EMASCULATE ⟨the bill was *castrated* by removal of the enforcement provisions⟩ **3 :** to delete a part of (a text) so as to render innocuous; *esp* **:** EXPURGATE ⟨~ a text⟩ **4 :** to remove the stamens from (a flower)

²castrate \'=,=\ *adj* [L *castratus*] **:** of a castrate **:** CASTRATED

³castrate \"\ *n* -s [L *castratus,* past part.] **:** a castrated individual

cas·trat·er *or* **cas·tra·tor** \'=,=d·ə(r), -tə(r), =ˈ==\ *n* -s **:** one that castrates

cas·tra·tion \ka'strāshən, kaa'-\ *n* -s [ME *castracioun,* fr. L *castration-, castratio,* fr. *castratus* + *-ion-, -io* -ion] **1 a :** the removal of testes or ovaries **:** GELDING, SPAYING **b :** inhibition of the function or development of the gonads (1) by inadequate nutrition in worker bees, (2) by the action of certain parasites, or (3) by the use of synthetic hormones in domestic animals — called also respectively (1) *alimentary castration,* (2) *parasitic castration,* (3) *chemical castration* **2 :** a depriving of vigor **:** WEAKENING ⟨mass persecution of most eminent scientists, a ~ of science —A.G.Mazour⟩ **3 :** the deletion of a part of (a text) esp. for purposes of expurgation; *also* **:** a part deleted **4 :** the removal of the stamens of a flower

castration complex *n* **:** a child's fear or delusion of genital injury at the hands of the parent of the same sex as punishment for unconscious guilt over oedipal strivings; *broadly* **:** the often unconscious fear or feeling of bodily injury or loss of power at the hands of authority

cas·tra·tive \'ka,strād·iv, 'kaa-, =ˈ==\ *adj* [*castrate* + *-ive*] **:** of, relating to, or tending to produce castration

cas·tra·to \ka'sträd·(,)ō\ *n, pl* **castra·ti** \-d·(,)ē\ [It, fr. L *castratus*] **:** a singer castrated in boyhood to preserve the soprano or contralto range of his voice

cas·tren·sian \(')kas¦trenchən\ *adj* [L *castrensis* (fr. *castra* camp — pl. of *castrum* fortified place — + *-ensis* -ese) + E *-an*] **:** of or relating to a camp

cas·trum \'kastrəm\ *n, pl* **cas·tra** \-rə\ [L — more at CASTLE] **1 :** an old Roman fortress **2** *castra pl* **:** a Roman encampment

casts *pres 3d sing of* CAST, *pl of* CAST

cast shadow *n* **:** a shadow cast by an object or figure in a painting or other picture

cast stone *n* [fr. past part. of ¹*cast* (mold)] **:** building stone made from concrete so as to resemble natural stone

cast up *vt* **1** *dial* **:** to bring up or say by way of reproach ⟨*casting up* to her that she had failed⟩ **2 a :** to measure (set type) usu. in ems pica in order to determine the cost or charge to be made **b :** to lay out (tabular matter) before setting in type **3 :** to add up (figures) in making an accounting ~ *vi, chiefly Scot* **:** to turn up esp. unexpectedly

cast ware *n* [fr. past part. of ¹*cast*] **:** ware formed in ceramics by pouring slip into a plaster mold that absorbs water and causes a suitably thick layer of clay body to form on the mold wall, the excess slip being poured out

cast–weld \'=,=\ *vt* [²*cast*] **:** to join (parts) by placing together in a mold and pouring molten metal between or around

¹ca·su·al \'kazhəwəl *also* -zhəl\ *adj* [ME *casuel, casual,* fr. MF & LL; MF *casuel,* fr. LL *casualis,* fr. L *casus* fall, chance — more at CASE] **1 a :** subject to or produced as a result of chance ⟨where ~ fire had wasted woods —John Milton⟩ **:** without design **:** not resulting from plan ⟨not merely ~ but a part of one great plan⟩ **b :** occurring, appearing, or singled out by chance or without calculated intent ⟨seek help from ~ passers-by⟩ **:** without specific motivation, special interest, or constant purpose ⟨an unusual ability to interest ~ students —John Gillin⟩ ⟨most comment, whether ~ or deliberate —Felix Frankfurter⟩ **c :** without foresight, plan, or method **:** not considered **:** HAPHAZARD ⟨information collected by ~ methods and in their spare time⟩ **2 a :** occurring, encountered, acting, or performed without regularity or at random **:** OCCASIONAL ⟨~ kindnesses⟩ ⟨exhausted firemen were getting ~ soup and sleep on the floors —Christopher Morley⟩ **b** *Brit* (1) **:** of the class of poor persons receiving occasional relief as distinguished from those receiving regular relief or being permanent inmates of workhouses ⟨the ~ poor⟩ (2) **:** of or for those poor persons or vagrants who are not residents of the place where they receive public aid or work — see CASUAL WARD **c** *of a workman* **:** having no steady employment but engaged for irregular periods esp. at an hourly or daily rate and at jobs requiring little training **3** *obs* **:** subject to accident **:** UNCERTAIN, PRECARIOUS ⟨the body is frail and ~⟩ **4 a :** feeling or showing little concern or interest **:** not giving close attention **:** INDIFFERENT, NONCHALANT ⟨tried to look ~ . . . but it was the handsomest house he had ever entered —Sinclair Lewis⟩ **b** (1) **:** without ceremony or formality **:** UNSTUDIED, INFORMAL ⟨referring to dear friends by their Christian names in a ~ and familiar way —Havelock Ellis⟩ **:** free from constraint **:** not showing effort or strain **:** NATURAL, EASY ⟨a difficult feat performed with ~ mastery⟩ (2) **:** suited by simplicity, comfort, and informality of design for everyday wear or use or for any occasion other than formal ⟨a ~ coat for town or country wear⟩ **c :** of little interest, concern, or importance **:** without significance **:** UNIMPORTANT ⟨subjects homely, slight, and ~ —E.J.Banfield⟩ **syn** see ACCIDENTAL, RANDOM

²casual \"\ *n* -s **1 a :** a casual or migratory worker **b** *Brit* **:** VAGRANT; *esp* **:** one who receives relief in a casual ward **2 :** an officer or enlisted man who is not assigned or attached to a unit and is awaiting assignment or who is awaiting transportation to his unit **3 :** an article of dress for casual wear **4 :** an essay written in a familiar often humorous style

casual ejector *n, Eng law* **:** a fictitious person alleged to have ousted the lessee of the plaintiff in the old action of ejectment, the real defendant being substituted for him after notice

ca·su·al·ism \-,lizəm\ *n* -s [*casual* + *-ism*] **1 :** a condition of things in which chance rules **2 :** the theory that all things exist or are controlled by chance — compare TYCHISM

casuality *n* -ES [alter. (prob. influenced by MF *casualité* or ML *casualitas*) of *casualty*] *obs* **:** CASUALTY 1, 2, 3

ca·su·al·ly \'kazhəlē, -zhəwəlē, -i\ *adv* **:** in a casual manner

ca·su·al·ness \-lnəs\ *n* -ES **:** the quality or state of being casual

¹ca·su·al·ty \'kazhəltē, -i *also* -zhəwəl-\ *n* -ES [ME *casuelte,* fr. *casuel* casual + *-te* -ty] **1** *archaic* **:** CHANCE, FORTUNE ⟨losses that befall them by mere ~ —Walter Raleigh⟩ **2 a :** an unfortunate occurrence **:** MISCHANCE ⟨yielding to the *casualties* of trade —H.S.Canby⟩ **b :** serious or fatal accident **:** DISASTER ⟨*casualties* at sea during the storm⟩ ⟨losses from fire, storm, or other ~ —J.S.Seidman⟩ **3** [trans. of ML *casualitas*] **a :** a casual charge or payment **b** *Scots law* **:** a payment demandable by a superior from his tenant upon the happening of various uncertain events as distinguished for example from a payment at a certain time (as rent) **4 :** a person lost to a command through death, wounds, injury, sickness, internment, capture, or through being missing in action ⟨*casualties* were heavy⟩ **5 a :** injury or death from accident **b :** one injured or killed (as by an accident) ⟨the dog was a traffic ~⟩ **6 :** a person or thing that has failed, been injured, lost, or destroyed as a result of uncontrollable circumstance or of some action **:** VICTIM ⟨the ex-senator was a ~ of the last election⟩ ⟨the factory was a ~ of the recession⟩

²ca·su·al·ty \'kazəltē, -asə-\ *var of* CASALTY

casualty insurance *n* **:** insurance against loss from accident (as automobile, burglary, liability, accident and health, and workmen's compensation insurance and corporate suretyship) consisting in the U.S. of all forms of insurance written commercially except life insurance and the forms of property insurance written by fire and marine companies

casual ward *n* [²*casual*] *Brit* **:** a ward in which vagrants seeking temporary public relief are detained for brief specified periods

casual water *n* [¹*casual*] **:** a temporary accumulation of water not forming a regular hazard of a golf course

ca·su·ari·ifor·mes \,kazhə,wa(a)rēə'fȯr,mēz\ *n pl, cap* [NL, fr. *Casuarius,* type genus + *-iformes*] **:** an order of large ostrichlike birds (superorder Neognathae) comprising the cassowaries and the emus

ca·su·a·ri·na \,kazhə(wə)'rēnə\ *n* [NL, fr. Malay (*pohon*) *kĕsuari* cassowary tree (fr. *pohon* tree + *kĕsuari* cassowary) + NL *-ina* (fem. of L *-inus* -ine); fr. the resemblance of its twigs to the cassowary's feathers] **1** *cap* **:** a genus (coextensive with the family Casuarinaceae and order Casuarinales) of dicotyledonous trees and shrubs now widely naturalized and used for hedge and ornamental work in southern No. America and the West Indies and characterized by jointed horsetaillike stems with whorls of scalelike leaves, some species yielding heavy hard wood — see BEEFWOOD, SHE-OAK **2** -s **:** a tree of the genus *Casuarina*

ca·su·ar·i·na·les \,kazhə,warə'nā(,)lēz\ *n pl, cap* [NL, fr. *Casuarina* + *-ales*] **:** an order of chiefly Australian woody plants comprising the casuarinas

ca·su·ar·i·us \,kazhə'wa(a)rēəs\ *n, cap* [NL, fr. D *kasuarisboom* cassowary tree, fr. Malay *kĕsuari* + D *boom* tree] **:** a genus (the type and sole representative of the family Casuariidae) of ratite birds comprising the cassowaries

casubian *cap, var of* KASHUBIAN

ca·su·ist \'kazhəwəst\ *n* -s [prob. fr. Sp *casuista,* fr. L *casus* fall, chance, case + Sp *-ista* -ist — more at CASE] **:** one skilled in or given to casuistry

ca·su·is·tic \¦kazhə¦wistik, -ēk\ *adj* [L *casus* + E *-istic*] **:** of or based upon actual cases or case histories

ca·su·is·ti·cal \-tȯkəl, -tēk-\ *or* **ca·su·is·tic** \-tik,-tēk\ *adj* [*casuist* + *-ical, -ic*] **:** using or marked by casuistry ⟨~ argument⟩ — **ca·su·is·ti·cal·ly** \-k(ə)lē, -i\ *adv*

ca·su·ist·ry \'kazhəwəstrē, -i\ *n* -ES [*casuist* + *-ry*] **1 a :** the study of or the doctrine that deals with cases of conscience **b :** the reasoning about or resolution of questions of right or wrong in conduct through the application of religious or secular ethical principles and rules **2 :** sophistical, equivocal, or specious reasoning **:** false application of principles specif. in regard to law or morals ⟨no ingenious ~ will convince us that this loss is really a victory⟩

ca·su·la \'käsù,lä\ *n* -s [LL & ML, prob. fr. L, little hut, dim. of *casa* hut, cabin — more at CASA] **:** CHASUBLE

ca·sus bel·li \¦käsəs'be,lē, ¦kāsəs'be,lī\ *n, pl* **casus belli** \"\ [NL, occasion of war] **1 :** an event, circumstance, or action that justifies the making of war (as interference with the exercise of a nation's rights or injury to a nation's vital interest or national honor) **2 :** a cause or occasion for war or other strife **:** an excuse for declaring war ⟨greeting an oil embargo as a *casus belli* —John Gunther⟩

casus foe·de·ris \-'fēdərəs -'fed-,-'fēd-\ *n, pl* **casus foederis** \"\ [NL, case of the treaty] **:** a case or event covered by the provisions or stipulations of a treaty or compact ⟨the *casus foederis* had arisen. When Italy attacked Ethiopia . . . no one could doubt . . . that . . . it had been in breach of the clearest obligations of the Covenant —Robert Cecil †1958⟩

casus for·tu·i·tus \-(,)fȯr'tüəd·əs, -'tyü-\ *n, pl* **casus fortui·ti** \-üə,tē, -ī\ [NL, fortuitous event] **:** an accident or chance **:** an inevitable accident — compare ACT OF GOD

casus omis·sus \-ō'misəs\ *n, pl* **casus omis·si** \-,sē, -ī\ [NL] **:** a case omitted or not provided for (as by a statute) and therefore governed by the common law

cas·well·ite \'kazwə,līt\ *n* -s [John H. *Caswell,* 19th cent. Am. mineralogist + E *-ite*] **:** a mineral from Franklin, N.J., consisting of an altered biotite

¹cat \'kat, *usu* -ad.+V\ *n* -s *often attrib* [ME *cat, catte,* fr. OE *catt, catte;* akin to OFris *katte,* OHG *kazza,* ON *köttr;* all fr. a prehistoric NGmc-WGmc word prob. borrowed fr. LL *cattus, catta,* perh. of Hamitic origin; akin to Berber *kaddiska* cat, Nubian *kadīs*] **1 a :** a long-domesticated carnivorous mammal that is usu. regarded as a distinct species (*Felis catus* syn. *F. domestica*) though probably ultimately derived by selection from among the hybrid progeny of several small Old World wildcats (as the Kaffir cat and the European wildcat), that occurs in several varieties distinguished chiefly by length of coat, body form, and presence or absence of tail, and that makes a pet valuable in controlling rodents and other small vermin but tends to revert to a feral state if not housed and cared for — see ABYSSINIAN CAT, ANGORA CAT, MANX CAT, PERSIAN CAT, SIAMESE CAT **b :** a member of the family Felidae (as a lion, leopard, jaguar, or wildcat) **c :** an animal that in appearance or behavior resembles any member of the family Felidae — usu. used with a qualifying term ⟨bear ~⟩ ⟨toddy ~⟩ ⟨polecat⟩ ⟨native ~⟩ **d :** the fur or pelt of the domestic cat **2 :** a person felt to resemble a cat: as **a :** a malicious woman; *esp* **:** one given to making catty remarks about other women **b :** a timid person — used with a modifier ⟨a scared ~⟩ **3 :** a low movable defensive structure used in medieval warfare as a means of approaching fortifications **4 a :** the tapered peg used in tipcat **b** [by shortening] **:** TIPCAT **5 :** a strong tackle used to hoist an anchor to the cathead of a ship **6 a :** a seagoing ship with a narrow stern, projecting quarters, and deep waist formerly used in England in the coal and timber trade **b :** an old-fashioned 3-masted Deal lugger **c** [by shortening] **:** CATBOAT **7** [by shortening] **:** CAT-O'-NINE-TAILS **8** [by shortening] **:** CATFISH — usu. used with a qualifying term ⟨channel ~⟩ ⟨blue ~⟩ ⟨mud ~⟩ **9 :** a double tripod that rests on three of its legs however it is set down and is usu. used as a stand near or over an open fireplace **10 :** ONE OLD CAT **11** *slang* **a :** SKAT **b :** ³KITTY 2c **12 :** the part of the first coat of plaster going between laths **13 a :** BIG CAT **b :** LITTLE CAT **14** *slang* **a :** a player or a devotee of hot jazz **:** HEPCAT **b :** GUY, PERSON, CHARACTER **15 :** the heraldic representation of a European wildcat or a domestic cat

²cat \"\ *vb* **catted; catted; catting; cats** *vt* **1 :** to bring (the anchor) up to a ship's cathead **2 :** to flog with a cat-o'-nine-tails ~ *vi* **1** *Brit* **:** VOMIT **2 :** to search for a sexual mate — usu. used in the phrase *go catting;* usu. considered vulgar

³cat *var of* KAT

cat *abbr* **1** catalog **2** catalyst **3** cataplasm **4** catechism

Cat \"\ *trademark* — used for a Caterpillar tractor

cata– *or* **cat–** *or* **cath–** *prefix* [Gk *kata-, kat-, kath-,* fr. *kata* down; akin to OW *cant* with, along, Hitt *katta* under, with,

L *com-* with, together — more at CO-] **1 :** down ⟨*cat*ion⟩ ⟨*cata*biotic⟩ **2 :** against ⟨*cata*baptist⟩

cata·bap·tist \ˌkad·əˈ==\ *n* -s [prob. fr. NL *catabaptista,* fr. LGk *katabaptistēs,* fr. Gk *kata-* cata- + *baptistēs* baptizer — more at BAPTIST] **:** one who opposes baptism

catabasis *var of* KATABASIS

cata·bi·o·sis \ˌkad·əˌbīˈōsəs, -ˌbē'-\ *n, pl* **catabio·ses** \-ōˌsēz\ [NL, fr. *cata-* + *biosis*] **:** the degenerative biological changes accompanying cellular senescence

cata·bi·ot·ic \ˌkad·əˌbīˈäd·ik, -ˌbē'-\ *adj* [*cata-* + *biotic*] **:** of, relating to, or exhibiting catabiosis

cat·a·bol·ic \ˌ==ˈbälik, -ēk\ *adj* [Gk *katabolē* + E *-ic*] **:** relating to or characterized by catabolism

ca·tab·o·lism *or* **ka·tab·o·lism** \kəˈtabəˌlizəm\ *n* -s [Gk *katabolē* throwing down (fr. *kataballein* to throw down, fr. *kata-* cata- + *ballein* to throw) + E *-ism* — more at DEVIL] **:** destructive metabolism involving release of energy and resulting in true excretion products although certain new substances may be formed in metabolic processes that are mainly catabolic — opposed to *anabolism*

ca·tab·o·lite \-ˌlīt\ *n* -s [*catabol*ism + *-ite*] **:** a substance (as nectar) produced in catabolism; *esp* **:** a waste product so produced

ca·tab·o·lize \-ˌlīz\ *vb* -ED/-ING/-S [fr. *catabolism,* after E *metabolism: metabolize*] *vt* **:** to subject to catabolism; *specif* **:** OXIDIZE ~ *vi* **:** to undergo catabolism

cata·caus·tic \ˌkad·əˈkȯstik\ *adj* [*cata-* + *caustic*] **:** relating to a caustic curve or caustic surface formed by reflection — compare DIACAUSTIC

cat·a·chre·sis \ˌ==ˈkrēsəs\ *n, pl* **catachre·ses** \-ēˌsēz\ [L, fr. Gk *katachrēsis* misuse, fr. *katachrēsthai* to use up, misuse, fr. *kata-* cata- + *chrēsthai* to use — more at CHRESTOMATHY] **:** the misuse of words: as **a :** the use of the wrong word for the context **b :** the use of a forced figure of speech, esp. one that involves or seems to involve strong paradox (as *blind mouths*)

cat·a·chres·tic \ˌ==ˈkrestik, *esp Brit* -ēs-\ *or* **cat·a·chres·ti·cal** \-əkəl\ *adj* [Gk *katachrēstikos,* fr. *katachrēsthai* + *-ikos* -ic] **:** constituting, characterized by, or given to catachresis — **cat·a·chres·ti·cal·ly** \-ək(ə)lē\ *adv*

catachromasis *var of* KATACHROMASIS

cata·cla·sis \ˌkad·əˈklāsəs; kəˈtakləsəs, kaˈ-\ *n, pl* **catacla·ses** \-ˌsēz\ [NL, fr. Gk *kataklasis,* fr. *kata-* cata- + *klasis* breaking — more at -CLASIA] **:** the crushing or fracturing of rocks and minerals during metamorphism — compare BRECCIA, CRUSH BRECCIA

cat·a·clasm \ˈkad·əˌklazəm\ *n* -s [irreg. (after Gk *klasma* fragment, fr. *klan* to break) fr. Gk *kataklan* to break down, fr. *kata-* cata- + *klan* to break — more at GLADIATOR] **:** a breaking down **:** DISRUPTION — **cat·a·clas·mic** \ˌ==ˈklazmik\ *adj*

cata·clas·tic \ˌ==ˈklastik\ *adj* [prob. modif. of Norw *kataklastisk,* fr. Gk. *kataklastos* broken down (fr. *kataklan*) + Norw *-isk* -ish] **1 :** of, relating to, or caused by cataclasis ⟨a pronounced ~ texture⟩ **2 :** having the granular fragmental texture induced in rocks by mechanical crushing ⟨~ structures⟩

cata·cli·nal \ˌ==ˈklīnᵊl\ *adj* [*cata-* + *-clinal*] **:** descending in the same direction as that of the dip of the geological strata ⟨a ~ valley⟩ ⟨a ~ river⟩ — opposed to *anaclinal*

cat·a·clysm \ˈkad·əˌklizəm, -atə-\ *n* -s [F *cataclysme,* fr. L *cataclysmos,* fr. Gk *kataklysmos,* fr. *kataklyzein* to inundate, fr. *kata-* cata- + *klyzein* to wash — more at CLYSTER] **1 :** a surging flood of water **:** DELUGE **2 :** a violent geologic change involving sudden and extensive alterations of the earth's surface **:** CATASTROPHE **3 :** a momentous and violent event or series of events marked by overwhelming upheaval and demolition (as of a political or social order) ⟨if all future world organization were rent asunder and if new ~*s* . . . destroyed all that is left —Sir Winston Churchill⟩ **syn** see DISASTER

cat·a·clys·mic \ˌ==ˈklizmik, -ēk\ *or* **cat·a·clys·mal** \-məl\ *adj* **:** of, relating to, or having the characteristics of a cataclysm ⟨a ~ nuclear war⟩ — **cat·a·clys·mi·cal·ly** \-ək(ə)lē, -ēk-, -li\ *adv*

cat·a·clys·mist \ˈ==ˌ=məst, ˌ==ˈ=\ *n* -s **:** CATASTROPHIST

cat·a·comb \ˈkad·əˌkōm, -atə-, *Brit also* -üm\ *n* -s [MF *catacombe,* prob. fr. OIt *catacomba,* fr. LL *catacumbae,* pl., prob. alter. of (assumed) VL *cata tumbas* near the tombs, fr. *cata* near, by (fr. Gk *kata* down, against, opposite) + *tumbas,* accus. pl. of *tumba* tomb — more at CATA-, TOMB] **1 :** a subterranean cemetery consisting of galleries or passages with side recesses for tombs — usu. used in pl. ⟨the ~*s* at Rome⟩ **2 :** a place like a catacomb: as **a :** a subterranean passageway or vault or a group of such passageways or vaults used esp. for storing the bones of the dead ⟨the underground stone quarries which form the ~*s* of Paris⟩ **b :** a complex set of interrelated passageways or rooms ⟨the sulphurous ~*s* of Liverpool Street Station in London —Fred Majdalany⟩

catacorner *or* **cata-cornered** *var of* CATERCORNER

cata·di·op·tric \ˌkad·əˌdīˈäptrik\ *also* **cata·di·op·tri·cal** \-trəkəl\ *adj* [*cata-* + *dioptric* or *dioptrical*] **:** belonging to, produced by, or involving both the reflection and the refraction of light ⟨~ prisms⟩

cata·drom·ic \ˌ==ˈdrämik\ *adj* [NL *catadromus* + E *-ic*] *bot* **:** having the lowest interior segment of a pinna nearer the rachis than the lowest superior one

ca·tad·ro·mous \kəˈtadrəməs, kaˈ-\ *adj* [prob. fr. NL *catadromus,* fr. *cata-* + *-dromus* -dromous] **1 :** living in fresh water and going to the sea to spawn ⟨the eel is ~⟩ — compare ANADROMOUS **2 :** CATADROMIC

catadupe *n* -s [L *Catadupa* (pl.), first cataract of the Nile, near Aswân, Egypt, fr. Gk *Katadoupoi* (pl.)] *obs* **:** CATARACT, WATERFALL

cat·a·falque \ˈkad·əˌfalk, ˈkatə-, -fȯ(l)k\ *also* **cat·a·fal·co** \ˌ==ˈfal(ˌ)kō\ *n, pl* **catafalques** *also* **catafalcoes** [It *catafalco,* fr. (assumed) VL *catafalicum* scaffold, irreg. fr. *cata-* + L *fala* siege tower] **1 :** an ornamental sometimes very elaborate structure used in many churches in solemn funerals for the lying in state of the body **2 :** a pall-covered coffin-shaped structure used at requiem masses celebrated after burial **3 :** HEARSE

catafalque 2

cata·gen·e·sis \ˌkad·əˈjenəsəs\ *n, pl* **catagene·ses** \-ˌsēz\ [NL, fr. *cata-* + *genesis*] **:** regressive evolution

cata·ge·net·ic \ˌkad·əjəˈned·ik\ *adj* [fr. NL *catagenesis,* after E *genesis: genetic*] **:** of or relating to catagenesis

cat·a·hou·la hog dog \ˌkad·əˈhülə-\ *n, usu cap C* [fr. *Catahoula,* parish in Louisiana] **:** a large vigorous speckled houndlike dog of the southern U.S. used in hunting and in herding wild hogs

cataian *n* -s *usu cap* [ML *Cataya* Cathay + E *-an* — more at CATHAY] **1** *obs* **:** a native of Cathay **2** [so called fr. the reputation for thievery given to the Chinese by early travelers] *obs* **:** SHARPER, SCOUNDREL

¹cat·a·lan \ˈkad·ᵊlən, -atᵊl-; -lˌan, -ˌaa(ə)n, ˌ==ˈ=\ *n, cap* [Sp *catalán*] **1 :** a native or inhabitant of Catalonia, an eastern region of Spain **2 a :** the Romance language of Catalonia, Valencia, and the Balearic islands **b :** a speaker of this language

²catalan \"\ *adj, usu cap* [Sp *catalán*] **1 a :** of, relating to, or characteristic of Catalonia **b :** of, relating to, or characteristic of the Catalans **2 :** of, relating to, or characteristic of the Catalan language

catalan ass *n, usu cap C* **:** CATALONIAN ASS

catalan forge *or* **catalan furnace** *n, usu cap C* **:** a bloomery that produces wrought iron from ore and that has a siliceous bottom lined with charcoal and a tuyere inclining downwards, the front being piled with ore and the back with charcoal and the whole covered with fine mixed ore and charcoal dust moistened with water

cat·a·lan·ist \-nəst\ *n* -s *usu cap* [Sp *catalanista,* fr. *catalán* + *-ista* -ist] **:** one who favors regional autonomy for Catalonia

cat·a·lase \ˈkad·ᵊlˌās\ *n* -s [*catalysis* + *-ase*] **:** a red crystalline enzyme widely distributed in plant and animal cells (as red blood cells) and consisting of a protein complex with hematin groups that catalyzes the decomposition of hydrogen peroxide into water and oxygen and the oxidation by hydrogen peroxide of alcohols to aldehydes and is held to function in tissues as an oxidative catalyst — compare PEROXIDASE — **cat·a·lat·ic** \ˌ==ˈad·ik\ *adj*

¹cat·a·lec·tic \ˌkad·ᵊlˈektik\ *adj* [LL *catalecticus,* fr. Gk *katalēktikos* incomplete, fr. *katalēgein* to leave off, fr. *kata-* cata- + *lēgein* to leave off, stop — more at SLACK] **:** lacking a syllable at the end or terminating in an imperfect foot

²catalectic \"\ *n* -s **:** a catalectic line of verse

cat·a·lep·sy \ˈkad·ᵊlˌepsē, -atᵊl-, -si\ *n* -ES [alter. (influenced by ML, LL, and/or Gk) of earlier *catalency,* modif. of ME *cathalempsia,* modif. of ML *catalepsia,* modif. of LL *catalepsis,* fr. Gk *katalēpsis,* lit., act of seizing, fr. *katalambanein* to seize, fr. *kata-* cata- + *lambanein* to take, seize; akin to OE *læccan* to seize — more at LATCH] **1 :** a condition of suspended animation and loss of voluntary motion associated with hysteria and schizophrenia in man and with organic nervous disease in animals and characterized by a trancelike state of consciousness and a posture in which the limbs hold any position they are placed in **2 :** CATAPLEXY

¹cat·a·lep·tic \ˌ==ˈeptik, -ēk\ *adj* [LL *catalepticus,* fr. Gk *katalēptikos* able to check, fr. *katalambanein*] **:** of, having the characteristics of, or affected with catalepsy ⟨a ~ state⟩ ⟨a ~ person⟩ — **cat·a·lep·ti·cal·ly** \-ək(ə)lē, -ēk-, -li\ *adv*

²cataleptic \"\ *n* -s **:** one affected with catalepsy

cat·a·lep·ti·form \ˌ==ˈeptəˌfȯrm\ *adj* [*cataleptic* + *-form*] **:** CATALEPTOID

cat·a·lep·toid \ˌ==ˈepˌtȯid\ *adj* [*cataleptic* + *-oid*] **:** resembling catalepsy

cat·a·lex·is \ˌkad·ᵊlˈeksəs\ *n, pl* **catalexes** \-ˌsēz\ [NL, fr. Gk *katalēxis* close of a rhetorical period, fr. *katalēgein* to leave off — more at CATALECTIC] **:** omission or incompleteness in the last foot of a line or other unit in metrical verse **:** terminal truncation

Cat·a·lin \ˈkad·ᵊlən\ *trademark* — used for a thermosetting plastic made of a cast phenol-formaldehyde resin and marked by high compressive strength and ready machinability

cat·a·li·na \ˌkad·ᵊlˈēnə, -atᵊl-\ *n* -s [fr. Santa *Catalina* Island, Calif.] **:** a synchronized swimming stunt executed from a back-floating position in which one leg is raised and held vertically while the body rolls over and submerges, the legs being brought together before submersion is complete

catalina cherry \ˌ==ˈ==-\ *n, usu cap 1st C* **:** an evergreen shrub or tree (*Prunus lyonii*) found on islands off the coast of California

catalina ironwood *n, usu cap C* **:** a tree (*Lyonothamnus floribundus*) of the family Rosaceae found on the islands off southern California and having thin brown shredding bark and opposite long-stalked leaves some of which are simply toothed and others irregularly compound

cat·a·li·neta \ˌkad·ᵊlˈnedˌə\ *n* -s [AmerSp, dim. of Sp *Catalina* Catherine (fem. prop. name), modif. of ML *Katharina,* by folk etymology (influence of Gk *katharos* pure) fr. *Katerina,* modif. of LGk *Aikaterinē*] **1 :** any of several angelfishes (esp. *Holacanthus tricolor*) **2 :** PORKFISH

cat·a·li·nite \ˌkad·ᵊlˈēˌnīt\ *n* -s [Santa *Catalina* Island, Calif., its locality + E *-ite*] **:** an agate beach pebble used as a gem

cat·al·lac·tics \ˌkad·ᵊlˈaktiks\ *n pl but sing in constr* [Gk *katallakt-* (fr. *katallassein* to exchange, fr. *kata-* cata- + *allassein* to change, fr. *allos* other) + E *-ics* — more at ELSE] **:** political economy as the science of exchanges

catalo *var of* CATTALO

¹cat·a·log *or* **cat·a·logue** \ˈkad·ᵊlˌȯg, -atᵊl-, -ˌäg\ *n* -s [ME *cateloge,* fr. MF *catalogue,* fr. LL *catalogus,* fr. Gk *katalogos* list, fr. *katalegein* to list, enumerate, fr. *kata-* cata- + *legein* to gather, speak — more at LEGEND] **1 a :** a detailed enumeration **:** LIST, REGISTER ⟨the narrative is broken by a ~ of kings⟩ ⟨it does not pretend to be a ~ of past achievements —Mortimer Graves⟩ **b :** a group of similar or related things often standing or succeeding in order **:** SERIES ⟨began to recapitulate items in the ~ of his escapades —H.G.Wells⟩ ⟨gave little support to the long-believed ~ of disorderly and brutal private crimes —F.L.Paxson⟩ **2 a :** a complete enumeration of items (as of books for sale or courses of instruction in a college) arranged systematically in a pamphlet or a book often alphabetically and with descriptive details (as of price or content) accompanying each item — see CARD CATALOG **b :** a pamphlet or book that contains such a list often with other related matter ⟨a mail-order ~⟩ ⟨a ~ of secondhand books⟩ ⟨a college ~⟩ ⟨a museum ~⟩ **c :** the material in such a list (as the works of a composer or author) ⟨his ~ of more than 300 numbers in active use today includes overtures, operatic selections, solos —*Baton*⟩ **3 :** the price quoted for a particular article in a stamp or coin catalog ⟨that stamp sold under ~⟩ ⟨this coin has a high ~⟩

²catalog *or* **catalogue** \"\ *vb* **cataloged** *or* **catalogued; cataloged** *or* **catalogued; catalog·ing** *or* **catalogu·ing; catalogs** *or* **catalogues** *vt* **1 :** to make a catalog of ⟨~ a collection of books⟩ ⟨~ items for sale at auction⟩ **2 :** to enter the name of or appropriate information about in a catalog; *esp* **:** to describe the physical format of and classify (books or other library material) ~ *vi* **1 :** to make or work on a catalog **2 :** to become listed in a stamp or coin catalog at a specified price ⟨this stamp ~*s* at two dollars⟩

cat·a·log·er *or* **cat·a·logu·er** \-gə(r)\ *n* -s **:** one that catalogs; *esp* **:** a person engaged in cataloging material for a library

cat·a·lo·gia \ˌkad·ᵊlˈōj(ē)ə\ *n* -s [NL, fr. *cata-* + *-logia*] **:** VERBIGERATION

cat·a·log·ic \ˌkad·ᵊlˈäjik, -ēk\ *adj* **:** having the characteristics of or belonging to a catalog ⟨much of the volume is, in spite of the lightness of touch, ~ —*Times Lit. Supp.*⟩

cataloging *or* **cataloguing** *n* -s **:** the science or the profession of classifying books or other library material and making out appropriate entries for library catalogs

cat·a·log·ize *or* **cat·a·logu·ize** \ˈ==ˌōˌgīz, -ˌä,-\ *vt* -ED/-ING/-S *archaic* **:** CATALOG

catalog paper *n* **:** a lightweight paper of good printing quality suitable for use in mail-order catalogs or telephone directories

catalogue rai·son·né \-ˌrāzᵊnˈā, -ez-\ *n, pl* **catalogues raisonnés** \-g(z)ˌr...nˈā\ [F, lit., reasoned catalog] **:** a systematic catalog with critical or descriptive notes; *esp* **:** a critical bibliography arranged according to subject

cat·a·lo·ni·an \ˌkad·ᵊlˈōnēən, ˌkatᵊl-, -nyən\ *adj or n, usu cap* [*Catalonia,* region of Spain + E *-an*] **:** CATALAN

catalonian ass *n, usu cap C* **:** an ass of a Spanish breed noted for its style, quality, and black or brown color with light or mealy points — called also *Catalan ass*

catalonian jasmine *n, usu cap C* **:** SPANISH JASMINE 1

ca·tal·pa \kəˈtalpə *also* -ȯl-\ *n* [NL, fr. E, fr. Creek *kutuhlpa,* lit., head with wings; fr. the shape of its flowers] **1** *cap* **:** a small genus of American and Asiatic trees (family Bignoniaceae) having broad cordate leaves, large white or mottled flowers in terminal panicles, and long terete pods — see HARDY CATALPA, INDIAN BEAN **2** -s [Creek *kutuhlpa*] **:** a tree of the genus *Catalpa*

catalpa sphinx *n* **:** a large American hawk moth (*Ceratomia catalpae*) having a larva that feeds on leaves of the catalpa and in some areas is highly regarded as fish bait

catalpa worm *n* **:** the green and black larva of the catalpa sphinx

cat·a·lu·fa \ˌkad·ᵊlˈüfə\ *n* -s [AmerSp, fr. Sp, variegated material used in making carpets, fr. OIt *cataluffa,* a cloth made in Venice] **:** any of various brightly colored carnivorous marine percoid fishes (family Priacanthidae) of tropical seas; *esp* **:** a fish (*Priacanthus arenatus*) of the western Atlantic and West Indies

ca·tal·y·sis \kəˈtaləsəs\ *n, pl* **cataly·ses** \-əˌsēz\ [Gk *katalysis,* fr. *katalyein* to dissolve, fr. *kata-* cata- + *lyein* to loosen, release — more at LOSE] **1 :** the change in the rate of a chemical reaction brought about by often small amounts of a substance that is unchanged chemically at the end of the reaction; *specif* **:** acceleration of a reaction (as the oxidation of sulfur dioxide to sulfur trioxide in the presence of platinized asbestos) — compare AUTOCATALYSIS, CONTACT CATALYSIS, NEGATIVE CATALYSIS **2 :** an action or reaction between two or more persons or forces provoked or precipitated by a separate agent or force, esp. by one that is essentially unaltered by the reaction ⟨a representative list of questions . . . valuable for the ~ of class discussions —B.S.Meyer & D.B.Anderson⟩ ⟨George Washington wrote friends of the powerful ~ that "Common Sense" was working —Eric Goldman⟩

cat·a·lyst \ˈkad·ᵊləst, -atᵊl-\ *n* -s [fr. *catalysis,* prob. after E *analysis: analyst*] **1 :** a substance that brings about catalysis and that may or may not actually take part chemically in the reaction; *broadly* **:** any substance (as an enzyme) that initiates a reaction and enables it to take place under milder conditions (as at a lower temperature) than in the absence of the catalyst — compare BIOCATALYST **2 :** an agent that provokes or precipitates catalysis ⟨the housing program is intended to become the ~ of the new French economy —Edmond Taylor⟩ ⟨the major ~ in his writing life has been the Mississippi countryside —C.H.Baker⟩ ⟨he was rumored to be the ~ in a native uprising —H.W.Wind⟩

cat·a·lyte \-ˌīt\ *n* -s [prob. back-formation fr. *catalytic*] **:** CATALYST

¹cat·a·lyt·ic \ˌ==ˈid·ik, -itik, -ēk\ *adj* [Gk *katalytikos,* fr. *katalysis* + *-ikos* -ic] **:** causing, involving, or relating to catalysis ⟨a ~ agent⟩ ⟨a ~ reaction⟩ ⟨a ~ function⟩ ⟨a ~ personality⟩ — **catalytically** *adv*

²catalytic \"\ *n* -s **:** CATALYST ⟨duty is sometimes still offered as a ~ —Irwin Edman⟩

catalytic cracker *n* **:** the unit in a petroleum refinery in which catalytic cracking is carried out — called also *cat cracker*

catalytic cracking *n* **:** cracking of petroleum oils (as gas oils or diesel oils) esp. for the production of high-octane gasoline in the presence of a catalyst (as clay) in various forms (as pellets or beads either stationary in a fixed bed or moving through the oil or as a fine powder fluidized by a stream of air or hydrocarbon vapors) — distinguished from *thermal cracking*

cat·a·lyze \ˈ==ˌīz\ *vt* -ED/-ING/-S [prob. fr. F *catalyser,* fr. *catalyse* catalysis, fr. E *catalysis*] **1 :** to bring about the catalysis of (a chemical reaction); *specif* **:** to speed up (a chemical reaction) **2 :** to produce (a substance) by means of chemical catalysis **3 :** to bring about **:** PROVOKE, PRECIPITATE, INSPIRE ⟨religious faith which alone ~*s* important sacred art —Janet Flanner⟩ ⟨his vigorous efforts to ~ us into activity —Harrison Brown⟩ **4 :** to transform or alter significantly by catalysis ⟨innovations in basic chemical theory that have *catalyzed* the field and its technology —*Newsweek*⟩ ⟨take over the proletarian formula, revolution and all, and ~ it into one of the epics of the twentieth century —Leo Gurko⟩

cat·a·lyz·er \-zə(r)\ *n* -s **:** CATALYST

cat·a·ma·ran \ˌkad·əməˈran, -atə-, -raa(ə)n\ *n* -s [modif. of Tamil *kaṭṭumaram,* fr. *kaṭṭu* to tie + *maram* tree, timber] **1 :** a raft or float consisting of two or more logs or pieces of wood lashed together, propelled by paddles or sails, and used esp. as a surfboat on the coasts of India, the East Indies, the West Indies, and So. America **2 :** a boat with twin hulls or planing surfaces side by side; *esp* **:** a fast pleasure boat having two hulls joined by a framework that supports the mast or motor **3 :** an early 19th century fire raft **4 :** a raft with windlass and grapple used in logging **5 :** a raft that consists of a rectangular platform attached to two parallel cylindrical floats and is used in lifesaving or for work alongside a ship **6 :** an ill-natured quarrelsome person; *esp* **:** a faultfinding woman

cat·a·me·nia \ˌkad·əˈmēnēə, -nyə\ *n pl but sing or pl in constr* [NL, fr. Gk *katamēnia,* neut. pl. of *katamēnios* monthly, fr. *kata-* cata- + *mēn* month — more at MOON] **:** MENSES — **cat·a·me·ni·al** \ˌ==ˈ=nēəl, -nyəl\ *adj*

cat·a·mite \ˈkad·əˌmīt, ˈkatə-, *usu* -īd-+V\ *n* -s [L *catamitus,* fr. *Catamitus* Ganymede, cupbearer of the gods, fr. Etruscan *Catmite,* fr. Gk *Ganymēdēs*] **:** a boy kept for purposes of sexual perversion

cat·am·ne·sis \ˌkad·ˌamˈnēsəs\ *n, pl* **catamne·ses** \-ēˌsēz\ [NL, fr. *cata-* + *-mnesis* memory (as in *anamnesis*)] **:** the follow-up medical history of a patient — compare ANAMNESIS — **cat·am·nes·tic** \ˌ=ˌ=ˈnestik\ *adj*

catamorphism *var of* KATAMORPHISM

cat·a·mount \ˈkad·əˌmau̇nt\ *n* -s [short for *cat-a-mountain*] **:** any of various wild animals of the cat family: as **a :** COUGAR **b :** LYNX

cat-a-mountain \ˌkad·əˈ==\ *n, pl* **cat-a-mountains** *or* **cats-a-mountain** [alter. of ME *cat of the mountaine*] **:** any of various wild animals of the cat family: as **a :** the European wildcat **b :** LEOPARD

ca·tan *or* **cat·tan** \kəˈtän\ *n* -s [Sp *catán,* fr. Jap *katana*] **:** a Japanese sword resembling a broad cutlass

cat·a·nan·che \ˌkad·əˈnaŋ(ˌ)kē\ *n* [NL, modif. of L *catanance,* plant used in love potions, fr. Gk *katananankē,* lit., means of compulsion, fr. *kata-* cata- + *anankē* force, compulsion — more at ANANKE] **1** *cap* **:** a genus of Mediterranean herbs (family Compositae) having linear or lanceolate leaves crowded toward the base of the stem and ligulate blue or yellow flowers in long-stalked heads **2** -s **:** a plant of the genus *Catananche*

cat and clay *n* [Sc *cat* wisp of straw, perh. fr. E *cat*] **:** straw and clay worked together to form a building or chinking material

cat-and-dog \ˌ=ˌ=ˈ=\ *adj* **1 :** resembling or having the character of the proverbial antagonism of dogs and cats: **a :** QUARRELSOME, INHARMONIOUS ⟨they led a *cat-and-dog* life together —Ellen Glasgow⟩ **b** *of a fight* **:** malicious and incessant ⟨the *cat-and-dog* fight among the early wire companies —F.L.Mott⟩ **2 :** being or consisting of cheap or questionable securities **:** highly speculative ⟨*cat-and-dog* stocks are swinging through sensational gyrations — rising 100 percent in ten days, then collapsing —Sylvia F. Porter⟩

cat-and-mouse \ˌ=ˌ=ˈ=\ *adj* **1 :** consisting of constant torment prior to destruction or defeat ⟨the *cat-and-mouse* technique of handling an opponent⟩ **2 :** consisting of constant pursuit, near captures, and repeated escapes ⟨a . . . *cat-and-mouse* kind of thriller with the hunter and the hunted occasionally switching roles —Martin Levin⟩ **3 :** consisting of watchful waiting for the best opportunity to attack or strike an opponent ⟨a *cat-and-mouse* mood⟩

cat and mouse *or* **cat and rat** \ˌ=ˌ=ˈ=\ *n* **:** a children's game in which players in a circle raise their joined hands to let one player in and out of the circle and lower them to bar a second player who chases the first

ca·ta·nia \kəˈtänyə, -tān-\ *adj, usu cap* [fr. *Catania,* city in Italy] **:** of or from the city of Catania, Italy **:** of the kind or style prevalent in Catania

cat·a·pan \ˈkad·əˌpan\ *n* -s [ML *catapanus, catipanus,* fr. MGk *katapanos,* modif. of OIt *capitano* leader, commander, fr. (assumed) VL *capitanus* foremost, chief, fr. L *capit-, caput* head — more at HEAD] **:** the governor of Calabria and Apulia under the Byzantine emperors

cata·pha·sia \ˌkad·əˈfāzh(ē)ə\ *n* -s [NL, fr. *cata-* + *-phasia*] **:** VERBIGERATION

cata·pho·re·sis \ˌkad·əfəˈrēsəs\ *n, pl* **cataphore·ses** \-ēˌsēz\ [NL, fr. *cata-* + *-phoresis*] **:** ELECTROPHORESIS — **cata·pho·ret·ic** \ˌ==ˈred·ik\ *adj* — **cata·pho·ret·i·cal·ly** \-ək(ə)lē\ *adv*

cata·phor·ic \ˌkad·əˈfȯrik\ *adj* [Gk *kataphorein* to carry down, wash downstream (fr. *kata-* cata- + *phorein* to carry, freq. of *pherein*) + E *-ic*] **:** of or relating to cataphoresis

cat·a·phract \ˈkad·əˌfrakt\ *n* -s [L *cataphractes,* fr. Gk *kataphraktēs,* fr. *kataphraktos* covered, armored, fr. *kataphrassein* to protect, fortify, fr. *kata-* cata- + *phrassein* to enclose — more at FARCE] **1 :** a suit of armor for the whole body **:** COAT OF MAIL **2** [L *cataphractus,* lit., armored, fr. Gk *kataphraktos*] **:** a soldier wearing a cataphract

cat·a·phrac·ta \ˌ==ˈ=tə\ *n, pl, cap* [NL, fr. L, neut. pl. of *cataphractus* armored] *in former classifications* **:** a division of reptiles including the crocodilians, chelonians, and sometimes others

cat·a·phrac·ti \ˌ==ˈ=ˌtī, -ˌtē\ [NL, fr. L, pl. of *cataphractus*] *syn of* SCLEROPAREI

cata·phre·nia \ˌ==ˈfrēnēə\ *n* -s [NL, fr. *cata-* + *-phrenia*] **:** a dementia from which the sufferer usu. recovers — **cata·phren·ic** \ˌ==ˈfrenik\ *adj*

cata·phyll \ˈkad·əˌfil\ *n* -s [*cata-* + *-phyll;* intended as trans. of G *niederblatt,* lit., lower leaf] **:** a rudimentary scalelike leaf (as a bud scale) that precedes the foliage leaves of a plant — compare HYPSOPHYLL — **cata·phyl·la·ry** \ˌ==ˈfiləˌrē\ *adj*

cata·pla·sia \ˌkad·əˈplāzh(ē)ə\ *n* -s [NL, fr. *cata-* + *-plasia*] **:** regressive biological change in cells or tissues **:** reversion to more primitive character — **cata·plas·tic** \ˌ==ˈplastik\ *adj*

cat·a·plasm \ˈkad·əˌplazəm\ *n* -s [MF *cataplasme,* fr. L *cataplasma,* fr. Gk *kataplasma,* fr. *kataplassein* to plaster over fr. *kata-* cata- + *plassein* to form, mold — more at PLASTIC] **:** POULTICE

cataplasm of kaolin : a paste made of purified clay, glycerin, boric acid, thymol, methyl salicylate, and oil of peppermint and used like a poultice

cat·a·plec·tic \ˌkad·ə¦plektik\ *adj* [fr. *cataplexy*, after such pairs as E *apoplexy: apoplectic*] **:** of, relating to, or affected with cataplexy

cat·a·plei·ite \ˌkad·ə'plī,īt\ *n* -S [G *katapleiit*, fr. Gk *kata* in the region of, down + *pleiōn* more + G *-it* -ite; fr. its occurrence together with other rare minerals — more at CATA-, PLEONASM] **:** a rare mineral $(Na_2,Ca)ZrSi_3O_9.2H_2O$ consisting of hydrous silicate of sodium, calcium, and zirconium occurring in thin tabular yellow or yellowish brown crystals (hardness 6, sp. gr. 2.8)

cat·a·plexy \'kad·ə,pleksē\ *n* -ES [G *kataplexie*, modif. of Gk *kataplēxis* fixation (of the eyes), fr. *kataplēssein* to strike down, terrify, fr. *kata-* cata- + *plēssein* to strike — more at PLAINT] **:** sudden loss of muscle power in animals and man following a strong emotional stimulus (as fright, anger, or shock) characterized by clear consciousness but loss of muscular control and in animals sometimes associated with narcolepsy

¹**cat·a·pult** \'kad·ə,pəlt, -atə-, -ůlt\ *n* -S [MF or L; MF *catapulte*, fr. L *catapulta*, modif. of Gk *katapaltēs*, *katapeltēs*, fr. *kata-* cata- + *-paltēs*, *-peltēs* (fr. *pallein* to hurl) — more at POLEMIC] **1 :** an ancient military device used for hurling heavy missiles (as stones) or for hurling other missiles (as spears, arrows) with extreme force; *esp* **:** ONAGER 2 **2** *Brit* **:** SLINGSHOT **3 a :** any of various mechanical devices utilizing the recoil of a spring (as for hurling grenades or bombs) **b :** a device for launching an airplane at flying speed (as from an aircraft carrier) usu. consisting of a carriage accelerated on a track by the explosion of powder, by hydraulic pressure, or by steam pressure

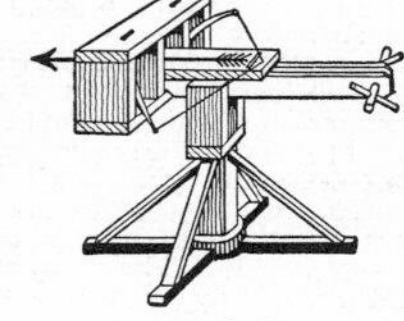

catapult 1

²**catapult** \"\ *vb* -ED/-ING/-S *vt* **1 :** to throw, drive, discharge, move, or launch by or as if by means of a catapult ⟨he is . . . ~*ed* some fifteen to twenty feet before his flight is stayed —Henry LaCossitt⟩ ⟨factors which ~*ed* him into absolute power —Andrew Gyorgy⟩ ⟨the question ~*s* us at once into . . . highly technical controversy —Bernard Brodie⟩ **2** *Brit* **:** to shoot or shoot at with a slingshot ⟨might be stealing shell eggs somewhere or ~*ing* farmers, shepherds, or sheep —Rose Macaulay⟩ ~ *vi* **1 :** to become catapulted ⟨the plane ~*ed* from the carrier deck⟩ ⟨the flier ~*ed* from the cockpit of the damaged plane⟩ **2 :** to move with a suddenness or force as if propelled by a catapult ⟨the stream ~*ing* down from the gray, cold boulders —Curtis Zahn⟩ ⟨the turmoil which ~*ed* through him —Marcia Davenport⟩

¹**cat·a·ract** \'kad·ə,rakt, -atə-\ *n* -S [ME *cataracte* floodgate, fr. L *cataracta*, *catarractes* waterfall, portcullis, floodgate, fr. Gk *kataraktēs*, *katarrhaktēs*, lit., sheer, abrupt, fr. *katarassein* to dash down, fr. *kata-* cata- + *arassein* to strike, smash] **1** *obs* **:** FLOODGATE — used in pl. ⟨the rain descended for forty days, the ~*s* . . . of heaven being opened —John Milton⟩ **2** [MF or ML; MF *cataracte*, fr. ML *cataracta*; perh. fr. its likeness to a portcullis in constituting an obstruction] **:** a clouding of the lens of the eye or of its capsule varying in degree from slight to complete opacity and obstructing the passage of light **3** [L *cataracta*, *catarractes* waterfall] **a** *obs* **:** WATERSPOUT **b :** WATERFALL; *esp* **:** a great fall of water over a precipice — compare CASCADE 1 **c :** steep rapids in a large river ⟨the ~*s* of the Nile⟩ **d :** an overwhelming downpour or rush **:** FLOOD ⟨~*s* of rain poured down —C.S.Forester⟩ ⟨his ~ of eloquence —Herman Wouk⟩ — **cat·a·ract·al** \¦==¦=tᵊl\ *adj*

²**cataract** \"\ *vb* -ED/-ING/-S *vt* **:** to cause to fall like a cataract ⟨the . . . rotor ~*s* water over the top of the case —*Flow Quarterly*⟩ ~ *vi* **:** to fall like a cataract ⟨rain ~*ing* down the windowpanes⟩

cataract bird *n, Austral* **:** ROCK WARBLER

cat·a·ract·ous \¦==¦=təs\ *adj* **:** of, relating to, or affected with an eye cataract

catarhina *syn of* CATARRHINA

catarhine *var of* CATARRHINE

cata·rhi·ni \ˌkad·ə'rī,nī\ *syn of* CATARRHINA

ca·tar·ia \kə'ta(a)rēə\ *n* -S [NL (specific epithet of the catnip *Nepeta cataria*), fr. LL *cattus*, *catus* cat + NL *-aria* (fr. L, fem. of *-arius* -ary) — more at CAT] **:** CATNIP

cat·a·ri·nite \ˌkad·ə'rē,nīt\ *n* -S [F, fr. Santa *Catarina*, state of Brazil, its locality + F *-ite*] **:** a class of iron meteorites remarkable for high percentage of nickel

ca·tarrh \kə'tär, -tå(r\ *n* -S [MF or LL; MF *catarrhe*, fr. LL *catarrhus*, fr. Gk *katarrhous*, *katarrhoos*, fr. *katarrhein* to flow down, fr. *kata-* cata- + *rhein* to flow — more at STREAM] **1 :** inflammation of a mucous membrane in man or animals characterized by congestion and secretion of mucus ⟨gastrointestinal ~ of the horse⟩; *specif* **:** such inflammation when chronically affecting the human nose and air passages **2 :** COMMON COLD — not used technically — **ca·tarrh·al** \kə'tärəl, -år-\ *adj* — **ca·tarrh·al·ly** \-əlē, -li\ *adv*

catarrhal fever *n* **:** any of several diseases of livestock (as influenza of the horse, pasteurellosis of sheep and cattle, or bluetongue and carceag of sheep) marked by edema of the respiratory tract and adjacent tissues

catarrhal jaundice *n* **:** INFECTIOUS HEPATITIS

catarrhal pneumonia *n* **:** BRONCHOPNEUMONIA

cat·ar·rhi·na \ˌkad·ə'rīnə\ *n pl, cap* [NL, fr. Gk *katarrhina*, neut. pl. of *katarrhin* hooknosed, fr. *kata-* cata- + *rhin-*, *rhis* nose — more at RHIN-] *in many classifications* **:** a division of Anthropoidea comprising the Old World monkeys, higher apes, and man, all having the nostrils close together and directed downward, 32 teeth, often cheek pouches and ischial callosities, and the tail if present never prehensile — **cat·ar·rhin·i·an** \¦==¦rinēən\ *adj*

¹**cat·ar·rhine** *also* **cat·a·rhine** \'kad·ə,rīn\ *adj* **:** of or relating to the Catarrhina

²**catarrhine** *also* **catarhine** \"\ *n* -S [NL *Catarrhina*] **:** a monkey of the division Catarrhina

cat·ar·rhi·ni \,==ˈrī,nī\ *syn of* CATARRHINA

ca·tarrh·ous \kə'tärəs, -år-\ *adj* [F *catarrheux*, fr. *catarrhe* + *-eux* -ous] *archaic* **:** CATARRHAL

cat·a·sar·ka \ˌkad·ə¦särkə\ *n* -S [MGk *katasarka*, fr. Gk *kata sarka* next to the skin, fr. *kata* next to, down + *sarka*, accus. of *sarx* flesh — more at CATA-, SARCASM] **:** the second of three altar cloths in the Eastern Church

cata·se·tum \ˌkad·ə'sēd·əm\ *n, cap* [NL, fr. *cata-* + L *seta*, *saeta* bristle + NL *-um*; fr. the appendages of the column — more at SINEW] **:** a genus of tropical American orchids having globose expanded flowers in racemes and the column provided with a sensitive appendage that when touched releases the pollen suddenly from the stamens — see JUMPING ORCHID

ca·tas·ta·sis \kə'tastəsəs\ *n, pl* **catasta·ses** \-ə,sēz\ [Gk *katastasis* settlement, establishment, fr. *kathistanai* to set in order, fr. *kata-* cata- + *histanai* to set, place — more at STAND] **1 :** the dramatic complication immediately preceding the climax of a play **2 :** the climax of a play — compare CATASTROPHE, EPITASIS, PROTASIS

cata·state \'kad·ə,stāt\ *n* -S [*catabolism* + *-state*] **:** CATABOLITE — **cata·stat·ic** \¦==¦stad·ik\ *adj*

ca·tas·tro·phe \kə'tastrə(,)fē, -aas-,-ais-\ *n* -S [Gk *katastrophē*, fr. *katastrephein* to overturn, fr. *kata-* cata- + *strephein* to turn — more at STROPHE] **1 a :** the final action that completes the unraveling of the plot in a play, esp. a tragedy **:** DENOUEMENT ⟨pat he comes like the ~ of the old comedy —Shak.⟩ ⟨the need for some element of reconciliation in a tragic ~ —A.C.Bradley⟩ **b :** a similar action in a novel or story ⟨the novel's ~ did not occur until the closing scene⟩ **2 :** a momentous tragic usu. sudden event marked by effects ranging from extreme misfortune to utter overthrow or ruin **:** DISASTER ⟨the ~ of war⟩ ⟨what ~ had overwhelmed them —Willa Cather⟩ **3** *Scot* **:** broken pieces (as of china) — usu. used in pl. **4 :** a violent and sudden change in a feature of the earth — compare CATASTROPHISM 1 **5 :** utter failure **:** FIASCO ⟨monuments, most of them artistic ~*s* —Robert O'Brien⟩ **6 :** death (as from an inexplicable cause) before, during, or after an operation **syn** see DISASTER

cat·a·stroph·ic \ˌkad·ə¦sträfik, -atə-, -ēk *also* -ōf-\ *also* **cat·a·stroph·i·cal** \-äfəkəl, -ēk-\ *or* **ca·tas·tro·phal** \kə'tastrəfəl\ *adj* **1 :** of, relating to, resembling, or resulting in catastrophe ⟨a time of ~ history —Herbert Agar⟩ ⟨he has ~ energy —H.M.Robinson⟩ ⟨a ~ depression —T.W.Arnold⟩ ⟨lawsuits are rare and ~ experiences —B.N.Cardozo⟩ **2** *of an illness* **:** financially ruinous — **cat·a·stroph·i·cal·ly** \ˌkad·ə¦sträfək(ə)lē, -atə-, -ēk-, -li *also* -ōf-\ *adv*

ca·tas·tro·phism \kə'tastrə,fizəm\ *n* -S **1 a :** the doctrine that changes in the earth's crust have in the past been brought about suddenly by physical forces operating in ways that cannot be observed today — compare UNIFORMITARIANISM **b :** a similar doctrine concerning the changes in the earth's fauna and flora **2 :** the theory that the millennium or a particular historical condition will be ushered in by a catastrophic event

ca·tas·tro·phist \-fəst\ *n* -S **:** a believer in the doctrine or theory of catastrophism — called also *cataclysmist*

catathermometer *var of* KATATHERMOMETER

cata·thy·mic crisis \ˌkad·ə¦thīmik-\ *n* [*cata-* + Gk *thymos* spirit + E *-ic* — more at FUME] **:** an unexpected explosive outburst of impulsive often destructive behavior understandable only in terms of unconscious motivation

cata·to·nia \ˌkad·ə'tōnēə\ *also* **cata·to·ny** \'==,tōnē, kə'tatᵊnē\ *n, pl* **catatonias** *also* **catatonies** [NL, fr. G *katatonie*, fr. *kata-* cata- + *-tonie* -tonia] **1 :** CATALEPSY **2 :** CATATONIC SCHIZOPHRENIA

¹**cata·ton·ic** \ˌkad·ə¦tänik\ *adj* [NL *catatonia* + E *-ic*] **:** of, relating to, or marked by catatonia

²**catatonic** \"\ *n* -S **:** a catatonic person

catatonic schizophrenia *n* **:** schizophrenia characterized by negativism, mutism, catalepsy, and an underlying thinking disorder and often accompanied by hallucinations and delusions of omnipotence and occas. by a state of violence

cat·a·wam·pous·ly \ˌkad·ə¦wämpəslē -ad·ē¦- *also* -ôm-\ *adv*, *dial* **:** FIERCELY, EAGERLY

¹**cat·a·wam·pus** \,==¦=pəs\ *n* -ES [prob. alter. of *catamount*] *dial* **:** an imaginary fierce wild animal **:** BOGEY

²**catawampus** *also* **cat·a·wam·pous** \¦==¦=pəs\ *adj* [prob. by folk etymology fr. *catercorner*] **1** *dial* **:** FIERCE, SAVAGE, DESTRUCTIVE **2** *dial* **:** ASKEW, AWRY, CATER-CORNERED

ca·taw·ba \kə'tȯbə\ *n* -S *see sense 1* [Choctaw *Katápa*, lit., separated] **1** *or pl* **catawba** *usu cap* **a :** a Siouan people of No. Carolina and So. Carolina **b :** a member of such people **2** *usu cap* **:** the language of the Catawba people **3** [fr. *Catawba* river, No. & So. Carolina] *usu cap* **:** a white wine usu. dry and either still or sparkling produced from a native American grape grown extensively in Ohio and New York **4** *often cap* **a :** a very dark to blackish red **b** *of textiles* **:** a dark purplish red that is bluer and paler than dahlia purple and bluer and duller than pansy purple

catawba rhododendron *n* **:** a pink-flowered rhododendron (*Rhododendron catawbiense*) of the southern Allegheny mountains

catawba tree *n* [by folk etymology fr. *catalpa*] **:** either of two American catalpas (*Catalpa bignonioides* and *C. speciosa*)

cat back *n* [*cat* (*block*)] **:** a lanyard sometimes fastened to the hook of a cat block to aid in hooking the ring of the anchor

cat bear *n* **:** PANDA

catberry \'=,==\ *n* **:** MOUNTAIN HOLLY

catbird \'=,=\ *n* [so called fr. the fact that one of its calls resembles that of a cat] **1 :** an American songbird (*Dumetella carolinensis*) dark gray in color with black cap and reddish under tail coverts related to the mockingbird but having a weaker and less varied song **2** *Austral* **a :** any of several birds (genus *Ailuroedus*) closely related to the bowerbirds but building no bowers and having a mewing catlike call **b :** APOSTLE BIRD

catbird grape *n* **:** MISSOURI GRAPE

catbird seat *n* **:** a position of great prominence or advantage ⟨sitting in the *catbird seat*⟩

catbite fever *n* [so called fr. the cat's being a carrier of the disease] **:** RAT-BITE FEVER

cat block *n* [²*cat*] **:** a heavy iron-strapped block with a large hook used in catting an anchor

catboat \'=,=\ *n* **:** a sailboat having a cat rig and usu. a centerboard and being of light draft and broad beam

catboat

catbrier \'=,==\ *n* [¹*cat* + *brier*; fr. its prickles] **:** any of several plants of the genus *Smilax* (esp. *S. rotundifolia*)

cat-built \'=,=\ *adj* **:** built like a catboat

cat burglar *n* **:** a burglar who enters by way of upper-story windows or skylights — called also *cat man*

¹**catcall** \'=,=\ *n* **1 a :** a small instrument for producing a sound like the cry of a cat formerly used esp. in theaters to express disapproval or contempt **b :** the sound made by this instrument **c :** a similar sound made by the human voice **2 :** a loud or raucous cry expressing disapproval (as at a political gathering)

²**catcall** \"\ *vt* **:** to deride or assail with catcalls **:** express disapproval of by catcalls ~ *vi* **:** to sound catcalls (as at a theater) ⟨the audience booed and ~*ed*⟩

¹**catch** \'kach, -e-\ *vb* **caught** \'kȯt\ *or now chiefly dial* **catched** \'kecht *also* -a-\ **caught** *or now chiefly dial* **catched; catching; catches** [ME *cacchen* to chase, catch, fr. ONF *cachier* to hunt, fr. (assumed) VL *captiare*, alter. of L *captare* to chase, strive to seize, fr. *captus*, past part. of *capere* to take, seize — more at HEAVE] *vt* **1 a :** to capture or seize esp. after pursuit or attempts to capture ⟨~ a thief⟩ **b :** TRAP, ENSNARE, ENTANGLE ⟨~ fish in a net⟩ ⟨*caught* in a tangle of confusion —F.V.W.Mason⟩ **c :** DECEIVE ⟨he could at times be *caught* by the second-rate —F.A.Swinnerton⟩ **d :** to discover unexpectedly or by surprise **:** FIND, DETECT ⟨~*es* his wife out, or so he thinks —Howard M. Jones⟩ ⟨~ a man in the act of stealing⟩ **e :** to check (oneself) suddenly esp. in the act of speaking ⟨he started to say the wrong thing but quickly *caught* himself⟩ **f :** to get in marriage esp. after pursuit ⟨there is nobody so likely to ~ me at last as yourself —Fanny Burney⟩ **g :** to take or come on unprepared ⟨the storm *caught* them before they reached shelter⟩ **h :** to become suddenly aware of **:** notice unexpectedly or suddenly ⟨you can ~ yourself entertaining habitually certain types of ideas —A.N.Whitehead⟩ ⟨sometimes I would ~ her looking at Dorothea —Lloyd Alexander⟩ **2 :** to take hold of esp. suddenly or forcibly **:** GRASP: **a :** to clasp suddenly **:** SEIZE ⟨tentacles to ~ and pass the food to the mouth —W.E.Swinton⟩ ⟨the mother *caught* her child to her⟩ **b :** to affect esp. as if by grasping suddenly — used of an affliction or an emotion ⟨the disease *caught* the youth before he was twenty⟩ ⟨sorrow *caught* the bereaved mother⟩ ⟨fear *caught* the victim's throat⟩ **c :** SNATCH, INTERCEPT ⟨~ a forward pass⟩ ⟨~ a high fly to center field⟩ ⟨an instrument to ~ cosmic rays⟩ **d :** to avail oneself of (as an opportunity) **:** TAKE ⟨~ the first chance of a ride to town⟩ **e :** to obtain esp. through active effort **:** GET ⟨~ a ride⟩ **f** *of fire* **:** to fasten upon **:** spread to ⟨the flames *caught* the wooden shingles of the roof⟩ **g :** to get (as a coattail or a heel) suddenly and accidentally held, hooked, snagged, impeded, or entangled ⟨~ her coat in a door⟩ ⟨~ a foot on the top step and fall headlong⟩ ⟨~ a sleeve on a projecting nail⟩ **3 :** to be affected by: **a :** TAKE, CONTRACT ⟨~ the measles⟩ ⟨~ pneumonia⟩ ⟨~ trouble⟩ **b :** to become imbued with by sympathetic reaction ⟨~ the enthusiasm of the group⟩ ⟨~ the spirit of an occasion⟩ **c :** to take or get the impact of (as a blow) **:** be struck by ⟨*caught* a piece of shrapnel in his right leg —Gilbert Millstein⟩ ⟨the flag above the grandstand *caught* the last of the sun —Maurice Duggan⟩ ⟨outside the breakwater the squadron *caught* the full sweep of a rising southeast wind —Joseph Millard⟩ **d :** to get or suffer from (as a punishment for misdoing) ⟨~ a spanking⟩ ⟨~ hell⟩ **4 a :** to seize and hold; *esp* **:** to take in and retain ⟨a barrel to ~ rain water⟩ **b :** to grip or hold against one's will; *esp* **:** to make immovable or vulnerable by placing between equally undesirable alternatives ⟨the branches *caught* the deer's antlers⟩ ⟨a ship *caught* between fire from shore batteries and sea attack⟩ **c :** to cause to be seized and held **:** FASTEN ⟨~ down a loose edge of a dress⟩ ⟨~ back a curtain⟩ **5 :** to take or get usu. momentarily, quickly, or for a brief intervening period ⟨~ a glimpse of a friend⟩ ⟨~ a nap⟩ ⟨catching a cup of coffee between trains⟩ **6 a** *obs* **:** GAIN, ATTAIN ⟨torment myself to ~ the English crown —Shak.⟩ **b :** to come up with **:** OVERTAKE ⟨~ the man before he had a chance to go a mile⟩ **c :** to meet and get aboard (as a train or plane) **:** get to in time for ⟨~ a plane⟩ ⟨the last bus home⟩ **d :** to be in time for ⟨~ an early show with minutes to spare⟩ **7 :** to attract and hold **:** ARREST ⟨the idea of cooperation did not ~ general attention —W.C.Allee⟩ ⟨one of the guests who *caught* his fancy —Abram Kardiner⟩ **8 a :** STRIKE ⟨his fist shot out and *caught* the small man directly on the mouth —Sherwood Anderson⟩ **b :** to make contact with ⟨a searchlight . . . *caught* and held them in its glare —Nevil Shute⟩ ⟨her high notes ~ the microphone —Edward Sackville-West & Desmond Shawe-Taylor⟩ **9 a :** to grasp or apprehend with the senses or the mind ⟨his ears open to ~ all the night noises —W.F.Davis⟩ ⟨from their pages we ~ something of the philosophy of the men and women —C.R. Woodward⟩ **b :** to apprehend and fix by artistic means ⟨~ a person's likeness⟩ ⟨the writer ~*es* the atmosphere of the 17th century court⟩ **10 a :** to catch out in cricket **b :** to serve as catcher for in baseball ⟨*caught* both ends of the doubleheader⟩ ⟨*caught* the lefthander⟩ **11 :** to deal with in some fitting fashion (as by picking, tapping, or slaughtering) ⟨the cowslips are good *caught* early —Meridel Le Sueur⟩ ⟨the pig had been *caught* early before it lost flesh —Pearl Buck⟩ ⟨they *caught* the maple trees too early in the season⟩ **12 :** to see or listen to (as a play or sports event) ⟨~ the first part of the evening's performance⟩ ~ *vi* **1** *of fire* **:** to take hold ⟨the flame *caught* in the chimney⟩ **2 :** to grasp by a hasty motion or make a hasty motion to grasp or as if to grasp — used with *at* ⟨~ at someone's coat as he passes⟩ ⟨~ at the first opportunity that comes up⟩ **3 a :** to become held or impeded esp. by entanglement or an obstruction ⟨the kite *caught* in the tree branches⟩ ⟨the boy's foot *caught* on the edge of the step⟩ **b** *of the breath* **:** to become involuntarily drawn in in a quick gasp ⟨make your breath ~ with suspense —Bernard De Voto⟩ **4 :** to take and retain hold ⟨the hook does not ~⟩ **5** *of a sail or sailing boat* **:** to catch the wind **6 a :** to catch fire **b** *of a gasoline engine* **:** to begin to function by the regular igniting and exploding of gasoline vapor in the cylinders **7** *dial, of water* **:** to freeze slightly — usu. used with *over* **8** *of a domestic mammal* **:** CONCEIVE **9** *of a plant* **:** to sprout and become established ⟨the clover *caught* well at the first sowing⟩ **10 :** to play the position of catcher on a baseball team **11** *slang* **:** to catch on (sense 2) **12 :** to begin to burn and stick to the pan ⟨the water boiled away and the potatoes *caught*⟩

syn CAPTURE, TRAP, ENTRAP, SNARE, ENSNARE, BAG: all these words indicate taking or seizing and their ramifications. They are likely to connote the hunter's craft or strength in taking or seizing. CATCH is a general term and in its first senses may often substitute for any of the other words on this list ⟨the hunters *caught* the fox⟩ ⟨the police *caught* the killer⟩ ⟨it may have seemed to Augustus an easy way of filling his treasury and it *caught* the imagination of the Roman poets —John Buchan⟩ CAPTURE is narrower in range than CATCH in often implying somewhat greater magnitude or importance of the thing caught, longer duration of the capture, and less necessary constriction or confinement during that period ⟨he *captured* 27 prizes in the *Comet* —R.G.Albion⟩ ⟨the business of the major parties is to *capture* control of the government —H.S.Commager⟩ ⟨no artist can set out to *capture* charm —A.C.Benson⟩ TRAP suggests craft or guile on the pursuer's part or unwariness on the quarry's. It stresses the existence of an adverse situation from which escape is unlikely, but may leave open the possibility, while CAPTURE indicates finality of seizure ⟨*trap* wild animals⟩ ⟨the Texans *trapped* in the Alamo⟩ ⟨his reliance on feeling . . . frequently *trapped* him into absurdities —F.B. Millett⟩ The verb SNARE differs from the verb TRAP as the noun SNARE from the noun TRAP. SNARE may suggest entanglement as in a net in contrast to the clamping stricture of TRAP ⟨folks who are still *snared* in the toils of mortal compulsions —R.P.Warren⟩ ENSNARE and ENTRAP are interchangeable with SNARE and TRAP most of the time but may occasionally suggest greater subtlety of contrivance and more entanglement and complexity in the victim's situation ⟨as if he would clear away some entanglement which had *entrapped* his thought —Louis Bromfield⟩ ⟨sympathetic to the regime that *ensnared* them in its monstrous net —*Saturday Rev.*⟩ BAG implies what is implicit in a hunter's putting game in his bag, that is, unquestioned success in seizing a difficult quarry by a hunter's arts ⟨Victor Weybright, of the American branch, *bagged* the British rights to John Hersey's *Hiroshima* while other English publishers were asleep —Bennett Cerf⟩

— **catch a crab 1 :** to fail to raise the oar clear of the water on the recovery **2 :** to miss the water completely when making a stroke with an oar — **catch fire 1 :** to become ignited ⟨the barn roof is thought to have *caught fire* from flying sparks from a passing locomotive⟩ **2 :** to become fired with enthusiasm ⟨the poet *caught fire* from the philosopher's talk⟩ **3 :** to increase greatly in scope, interest, or effectiveness ⟨the movie really *catches fire* —*Time*⟩ ⟨his imagination *caught fire* —Dorothy C. Fisher⟩ — **catch it** *slang* **:** to get a scolding or a punishment — **catch one's breath 1 :** to take in a short involuntary gasp of air ⟨make you *catch your breath* in excitement —H.J.Laski⟩ **2 :** to rest long enough to restore normal breathing ⟨they let the horses *catch their breath* at the top of the long hill⟩ — **catch the wind :** to fill with wind (as of a sail)

²**catch** \"\ *n* -ES [ME *cacche*, fr. *cacchen*, v.] **1 :** something that is caught; *esp* **:** the total quantity caught at one time ⟨the ~ of valuable native fur —F.S.Cohen⟩ ⟨a good ~ of fish⟩ **2 :** the act, action, or fact of catching: **a :** the act of catching fish **b :** a momentary audible impeding (as of the breath or voice) ⟨a sudden ~ in the speaker's voice⟩ **c :** the act of catching the ball esp. before it touches the ground ⟨a good running ~⟩ **d :** a game for two or more people in which a ball is thrown and caught **e :** the initial force and application of an oar or a swimmer's hand to the water **3 a :** something that checks or holds immovable **b :** a device (as a rod, bar, or hook) for temporarily holding immovable an otherwise moving or movable part or mechanism: as (1) **:** a latch esp. on a door, window, or trunk (2) **:** the fastening mechanism on a brooch, decorative pin, or belt **4 :** one that is worth catching or acquiring ⟨another important ~ of the patrol was a submarine⟩; *esp* **:** one particularly desirable as a husband or wife ⟨he was an excellent ~⟩ **5 :** a round for three or more unaccompanied voices written out as one continuous melody with each succeeding singer taking up a part in turn; *specif* **:** a ludicrous or coarse round **6 :** FRAGMENT, SNATCH ⟨young men . . . sing ~*es* of a traditional Genoese melody as they mend their sails —J.V.Taberner⟩ **7 :** an unsuspected or trickily concealed consideration or difficulty designed esp. to take advantage of the unwary ⟨there must be a ~ in it somewhere⟩ **8 :** the germination of a field crop esp. to such an extent that replanting is unnecessary — compare ²STAND 12 **9 :** GLOTTAL STOP

³**catch** \"\ *adj* [¹*catch*] **:** CATCHY ⟨a ~ question⟩

cat chain *n* [²*cat*] **:** a small chain that reeves through a block at the cathead or at a davit head and is used with the ground chain to cat an anchor in ships with ram bows

catchall \'=,=\ *n* -S **:** something designed or serving to catch, hold, account for, or include a variety of odds and ends ⟨the third room . . . was a ~ for harness and tools and implements —Margaret I. Ross⟩ ⟨the docks act as a ~ for the overflow from other trades and for the failures and misfits from all walks of life —E.P.Hohman⟩ ⟨a ~ statute is one which covers a multitude of sins —R.V.Sherwin⟩

¹**catch-as-catch-can** \,==,==\ *n* -S **:** a style of wrestling in which all holds are permitted except those that may be barred by mutual consent and in which a fall is gained by the contestant who pins his opponent's shoulders to the ground

²**catch-as-catch-can** \"\ *adj* **:** utilizing or exploiting any

available means or method : UNPLANNED, UNSYSTEMATIC ⟨a *catch-as-catch-can* existence begging and running errands —*Time*⟩

catch basin *n* **1 :** a cistern located at the point where a street gutter discharges into a sewer and designed to catch and retain matter that would not pass readily through the sewer **2 :** a reservoir or well into which surface water may drain off

catch boom *n* **:** a boom used in logging to prevent logs from floating downstream

catch colt *n* **:** WOODS COLT

catch crop *n* **:** a crop grown between two crops in ordinary sequence, between the rows of a main crop, or as a substitute for a staple crop that has failed — compare COVER CROP — **catch cropping** *n*

catchcry \'=,=\ *n* **:** a distinctive word or expression (as a catchword or slogan) serving to attract attention or rally support

catch dog *n, dial* **:** a large dog used for catching and holding something (as livestock)

catched *now chiefly dial past of* CATCH

catch·er \'kachə(r), -ech-\ *n* -s [ME *caccher*, fr. *cacchen* to catch + *-er*] **1 :** one that catches: as **a :** the baseball or softball player stationed behind home plate to catch pitched balls and to defend the plate and the area around it **b :** a member of a flying-trapeze act who hanging head down from a trapeze catches the flier **c** *or* **catcher arm :** a movable metal arm on railway post-office cars used to pick up mail pouches from trackside cranes while the train is in motion **2 a :** a worker in the tobacco, woodworking, or paper-goods industry who removes materials or products from the delivery end of conveyors or machines **b :** a laundry worker who removes flatwork from an ironing machine **c :** a basketry worker who keeps the splitting machine free of rattan, reeds, dust, and fiber particles **3 :** a small boat accompanying a whaling boat and specif. intended for the pursuit and catching of sighted whales **4 :** the element in a klystron that resonates to the beam of bunched electrons and then generates the oscillator output — compare BUNCHER, BUNCHING, RHUMBATRON

catcher-off \'==,=\ *n, pl* **catchers-off :** one that catches laces as they come through the cutting machine, cuts them to even lengths by hand, and bundles them

catcher pouch *n* **:** a mail sack used in transferring mail to and from small stations and moving trains

catches *pres 3d sing of* CATCH, *pl of* CATCH

catchfly \'=,=\ *n* **:** any of various plants having on the stems or inflorescence a viscid secretion to which small insects adhere; *esp* **:** any of various members of the genera *Lychnis* and *Silene*

catchfly grass *n* **:** a marsh grass (*Leersia lenticularis*) of the southern U. S.

catchier *comparative of* CATCHY

catchiest *superlative of* CATCHY

catch·ing \'kachiŋ, -ech-\ *adj* [ME *cacching*, fr. pres. part. of *cacchen* to catch] **1 :** INFECTIOUS, CONTAGIOUS ⟨colds are ~⟩ ⟨her laughter was the most ~ I ever heard —W.S.Maugham⟩ **2 :** CAPTIVATING, ALLURING, CATCHY ⟨she had such a ~ way with her⟩ ⟨their rhyme . . . is abundant and ~ —H.O.Taylor⟩ — **catch·ing·ly** *adv*

catching bargain *n* **:** an entrapping or overreaching bargain; *specif* **:** one made with an heir expectant for the purchase of his expectancy at an inadequate price

catch-letter \'=,==\ *n* **:** a faint letter written in the margin of a manuscript as a guide for the rubricator in filling in the required initial

catchlight \'=,=\ *n* -s **:** a small spot of light reflected from a shiny surface (as from an eye in portraiture or from metal or glass in photography)

catch line *n* **1 a :** a line containing a catchword **b :** a short line (as of less important words in a title or display advertisement) between lines that are longer and sometimes larger **c :** an identification line (as on a printer's proof or a manuscript) **2 :** a phrase or sentence designed to catch attention esp. in an advertisement or as a heading or title of a story, article, or newspaper item **3 :** a line in a theatrical production expected to cause a laugh and often repeated as a gag

catch·man \-,man, -mən\ *n, pl* **catchmen :** one who sorts floating logs according to owner's mark by deflecting them with a pike pole

catch·ment \'kachmənt, -ech-\ *n* -s **1 :** the act or action of catching water ⟨water conservation and ~ —W.B.Fisher⟩ **2 a :** something that catches water ⟨a separate house . . . set in a waste as sheer as a rain ~ —Jean Stafford⟩ **b :** CATCHMENT AREA **3 :** the amount of water that is caught

catchment area *or* **catchment basin** *n* **:** the entire area from which drainage is received by a body of water (as a reservoir, lake, or river) **:** WATERSHED

catch on *vi* **1 :** to seize hold **:** attach oneself ⟨the swimmer *caught on* to the back of the boat⟩ **2 :** UNDERSTAND, LEARN, TUMBLE ⟨the police *caught on* to what he was doing⟩ ⟨you can *catch on* to the job in two or three days⟩ **3 :** to become popular ⟨this movement has already *caught on* in other states —Bernard Smith⟩ **4 :** to get a job ⟨he finally *caught on* as a chore boy with an outfit in New Mexico —Ross Santee⟩

cat-chop \'=,=\ *n* [1*cat* + *chop* (jaw)] **:** a fig marigold (*Mesembryanthemum felinum*) having pointed teeth on the leaf margins

catch out *vt* **1 :** to put out (a cricket player) by catching a batted ball before it touches the ground **2 :** to detect in error or wrongdoing ⟨he watched carefully in the hope of *catching* one of the dishonest employees *out*⟩

1**catchpenny** \'=,==\ *adj* [1*catch* + *penny*] **1 :** designed esp. to make a ready appeal to the ignorant or unwary through sensationalism or cheapness ⟨for his countless miscellaneous pieces any ~ subject would do —Douglas Bush⟩ **2 :** aiming at making even the smallest sum of money quickly by almost any expedient ⟨caused the fly-by-night ~ boomers to move out, taking their quick money with them —*Amer. Guide Series: Texas*⟩ **3 :** popular but ill-considered and superficial ⟨clever ~ critical objections —J.C.Powys⟩

2**catchpenny** \"\ *n* -ES **:** something that is catchpenny ⟨you know already by the title that it is no more than a ~ —Washington Irving⟩

catchphrase \'=,=\ *n* **:** a phrase that is or has become a catchword ⟨are apt to take fiction for reality, to fool ourselves and others with ~*s* and make-believe —Wilhelm Roepke⟩

catch·pole *or* **catch·poll** \'kach,pōl, -ech-\ *n* -ES [ME *cacchepol*, fr. OE *cæcepol*, fr. (assumed) ONF *cachepol*, lit., chicken chaser, fr. *cachier* to hunt, chase + *poul*, *pol* rooster, fr. L *pullus* young animal, young fowl — more at CATCH, PULLET] **1 :** a sheriff's deputy; *esp* **:** one who makes arrests for debt **2 :** DEPUTY, REPRESENTATIVE ⟨hires out to other private citizens to go about as a sort of ~ on Sunday —W.J.Gaynor⟩

catch ring *n* **:** a wooden hoop that holds the staves of a slack barrel in place after the head hoop is removed

catch-rope \'=,=\ *n* **:** LARIAT

catch-roper \'=,rōpə(r)\ *n* **:** LASSOER

catch-roping \'=,rōpiŋ\ *n* **:** lassoing esp. as a rodeo event

catch stitch *n* **1 :** KETTLE STITCH **2 :** a large cross-stitch of uneven proportions used esp. on bulky materials for finishing and hemming — called also *catstitch*

catch-stitch \'=¦=\ *vt* [*catch stitch*] **:** to sew with a catch stitch

catch the ten *n* **:** a card game in which the chief object is to catch the ten of trumps — called also *Scotch whist*

catch title *n* **1 :** a distinguishing abbreviation of or a short substitute for a full title used esp. in book lists and catalogs **2 :** the often abbreviated titles of the first and last entries or articles appearing on the spine of any volume of a multivolume set **3 :** a faintly written title in the margin of a manuscript page intended as a guide for the rubricator

catch up *vt* **1 a :** to pick or lift up often abruptly ⟨a thief *caught* the purse *up* and ran⟩ **b :** ENSNARE, ENTANGLE ⟨*caught up* in the trivia of everyday things —Honor Tracy⟩ **c :** to involve often against the will ⟨the firms have been *caught up* in a revolution —Percy Winner⟩ **d :** ENTHRALL ⟨*caught up* in the ecstasy of *Vanity Fair* —Bernard De Voto⟩ **2 :** to adopt or take over (as an expression) ⟨*catch up* all the new fads and slang terms⟩ **3 :** to interrupt (a speaker) usu. to question or criticize what is being said ⟨you *catch* me *up* so very short —Charles Dickens⟩ **4** *Brit* **:** OVERTAKE ⟨*catch* a friend *up* before he gets out of sight⟩ **5 :** to provide with the latest information ⟨*catch* me *up* on what's happening at the office⟩ ~ *vi* **1 a :** to travel fast enough to join company ⟨*catch up* with an advance battalion⟩ **b :** to bring about arrest for illicit activity — used with *with* ⟨the police *caught up* with the thieves⟩ **c :** to have the expected ill effect or result — used with *with* ⟨his evil ways *caught up* with him at last and he died a poverty-stricken and miserable man⟩ **2** *West* **:** to prepare horses, mules, or oxen for travel ⟨we were told to *catch up* and begin the march at daybreak⟩ **3 a :** to bring something to an end or to a final state — used with *on* ⟨*catch up* on your bookkeeping⟩ **b :** to acquire belated information ⟨*catch up* on what's happening in the news⟩

catchup *var of* CATSUP

catch-up \'ka,chəp, 'ke,-\ *n* -s [*catch up*] **1 :** an activity or move intended to catch up to a theoretical norm (as a level of production or supply) esp. following a period of curtailment of such activity ⟨postwar *catch-up* in construction work was rapid⟩ **2 :** the fact of catching up to a theoretical norm esp. in industrial production ⟨the *catch-up* in quantity —*Wall Street Jour.*⟩

catchwater \'=,==\ *or* **catchwater drain** *n* **:** a ditch to catch water on sloping land designed to divert the flow or to irrigate the soil — called also *catchwork*

catchweed \'=,=\ *n* [so called fr. the hooked bristles covering the stem] **:** a rough-stemmed plant of the genus *Galium*

1**catchweight** \'=,=\ *n* [1*catch* + *weight*] **:** the weight of a contestant in a sports event as he happens or chooses to be instead of as fixed by an agreement or by rule ⟨many interesting bouts at ~*s* —John Lardner⟩

2**catchweight** \"\ *adv* **:** without restriction or artificial handicap as to the weight of contestants in a sports event ⟨to fight ~⟩

catchword \'=,=\ *n* **1 :** an identifying or distinguishing word: as **a :** a word standing under the right-hand side of the last line of text on a book page that repeats the first word of text on the following page — called also *direction word* **b :** either one of the pair of terms placed to right and left of the head of a page of an alphabetical reference work (as a dictionary) indicating the alphabetically first and last entries or articles on the page — called also *guide word* **2 a :** a usu. sloganlike and telling word or expression caught up and repeated so that it becomes representative of a political party or belief, a school of thought, or a point of view ⟨worlds of contemporary controversy with their ~*s*, their insensitive condemnations, and their callow proofs —*Times Lit. Supp.*⟩ **b :** a word or phrase distinctive of a subject, scheme of thought, or point of view used esp. for effect by one having only superficial acquaintance with the subject or scheme of thought ⟨the freeing of mankind from labels and ~*s* —*Times Lit. Supp.*⟩ **c :** a catchy word or phrase devised esp. for advertising purposes

catchword entry *or* **catchword title** *n* **1 :** a title entry (as of a book) in a catalog, list, or index beginning with a significant or an easily remembered word in the title ⟨"Architecture, A history of" is a *catchword entry*⟩ **2 :** the method of entry in a catalog, list, or index that uses catchword entries

catchwork \'=,=\ *n* **:** CATCHWATER

catchy \'kachē, -ech-, -chi\ *adj* -ER/-EST **1 a :** having the power or tending to catch the interest or attention ⟨a ~ idea⟩ ⟨a ~ title⟩ **b :** easily retained in the memory ⟨a ~ melody⟩ **2** *of a question* **:** tending to mislead the unwary **:** TRICKY ⟨the examiner asked several purposely ~ questions⟩ **3 :** FITFUL, IRREGULAR ⟨a ~ wind⟩ ⟨~ breathing⟩ **4** *dial* **:** CAPTIOUS

catclaw *var of* CAT'S-CLAW

catclaw acacia *n* **:** a cat's-claw (*Acacia greggii*)

cat-clover \'=,==\ *n* **:** a bird's-foot trefoil (*Lotus corniculatus*)

cat cracker \'kat,==\ *n* [by shortening] **:** CATALYTIC CRACKER

cat davit *n* [*cat*head] **:** the forward bow davit of a ship for hoisting the stock end of the anchor — compare FISH DAVIT

cat distemper *n* **:** PANLEUCOPENIA

cate \'kāt\ *n* -s [ME, short for *acate*, fr. ONF *acat* purchase, fr. *acater* to buy, fr. (assumed) VL *accaptare* to buy, procure, fr. L by folk etymology (influence of L *captare* to chase) fr. L *acceptare* to accept — more at ACCEPT] **1 a** *obs* **:** an article of food bought as distinguished from that prepared at home — usu. used in pl. **b** *archaic* **:** an article of food **:** VIAND — usu. used in pl. **2 :** a dainty or choice food **:** DELICACY

cat·e·che·sis \,kad·ə'kēsə̇s, -atə-\ *n, pl* **cateche·ses** \-ē,sēz\ [LL, fr. Gk *katēchēsis* instruction, fr. *katēchein* to teach — more at CATECHIZE] **1 :** oral instruction of catechumens **:** CATECHIZING **2 :** a discourse marked by catechesis; *esp* **:** a formal discourse sometimes committed to writing ⟨the *catecheses* of St. Cyril of Jerusalem⟩

cat·e·chet·i·cal \¦==¦ked·|ə̇kəl, -et|, |ēk-\ *also* **cat·e·chet·ic** \-ik,-ēk\ *adj* [*catechetical* fr. NL *catecheticus* (fr. LL *catechesis*, after such pairs as LL *haeresis* heresy: LL *haereticus* heretical) + E *-al; catechetic* fr. NL *catecheticus*] **1 :** of, relating to, or associated with catechesis or catechetics **2 :** of, relating to, or conforming to a church catechism **3 :** using questions and answers ⟨the ~ method of Socrates⟩; *esp* **:** using set questions and answers (as in a church catechism) — **cat·e·chet·i·cal·ly** \-ə̇k(ə)lē, -ēk-, -li\ *adv*

catechetical school *n* **:** any of certain early Christian schools (as at Alexandria and at Antioch) in which both sacred and secular studies were pursued

cat·e·chet·ics \,=='=iks, -ēks\ *n pl but usu sing in constr* [G *katechetik*, fr. NL *catechetica*, fem. sing. or neut. pl. of *catecheticus*] **:** practical theology dealing with catechesis

cat·e·chin \'kad·əchə̇n, -əsh-,-ək-\ *n* -s [G *katechin*, fr. *katechu* catechu (fr. E) + *-in* — more at CATECHU] **1 :** a white crystalline phenol-alcohol $C_{15}H_{14}O_6$ related chemically to the flavones and found as the dextrorotatory form in catechu — called also *catechol* **2 :** PYROCATECHOL

1**cat·e·chise** *or* **cat·e·chis** \'käd·ə,jiz, -,chis\ *n, pl* **catechis·es** \-,jizə̇z,-,chisə̇z\ [*catechise*, modif. of F *catéchèse*, fr. MF, fr. LL *catechesis; catechis*, prob. short for *catechism*] *now dial* **:** CATECHISM

2**cat·e·chise** \'kad·ə,kīz, -atə-\ *var of* CATECHIZE

cat·e·chism \'kad·ə,kizəm, -atə-\ *n* -s [LL *catechismus*, prob. fr. *catechizare* to catechize, after such pairs as LL *christianizare* to profess Christianity: *christianismus* Christianity] **1 :** oral instruction ⟨teaches his history class and interrupts his ~ only with random thoughts on the boys —W.P.Jones⟩ **2 :** a manual or guide for catechizing (as for moral and religious instruction) sometimes in the form of a comprehensive summary of doctrine and often in the form of questions and answers **3 a :** a series of questions with officially correct answers; *esp* **:** a set of formal questions with such answers put as a test **b :** a series of questions

cat·e·chis·mal \¦==¦kizməl\ *adj* **:** of, relating to, or using a catechism ⟨~ responses⟩ ⟨a ~ exercise⟩ ⟨~ schools⟩

cat·e·chist \'=ə̇kə̇st\ *n* -s [LL *catechista*, prob. fr. *catechizare* to catechize, after such pairs as LL *baptizare* to baptize: *baptista* baptizer] **:** one that catechizes: as **a :** a teacher of catechumens **b** *in some mission churches* **:** a Christian native who teaches

cat·e·chis·tic \¦=ə¦kistik, -ēk\ *or* **cat·e·chis·ti·cal** \-ə̇kəl, -ēk-\ *adj* **:** of or relating to a catechist or a catechism ⟨a ~ examination⟩ ⟨a ~ method⟩ ⟨a ~ school⟩ — **cat·e·chis·ti·cal·ly** \-ə̇k(ə)lē, -ēk-, -li\ *adv*

cat·e·chi·za·tion \,=ə̇kə̇'zāshən, -ə,kī'z-\ *n* -s [*catechize, catechise* + *-ation*] **:** the act of catechizing or being catechized ⟨the teacher's ~ of the students⟩ ⟨the lawyer was present at the prisoner's ~⟩

cat·e·chize \'=ə,kīz\ *vb* -ED/-ING/-S *see -ize in Explan Notes* [LL *catechizare*, fr. Gk *katēchein* to teach, instruct in the elements of religion (fr. *kata-* cata- + *ēchein* to sound, fr. *ēchē* sound) + LL *-izare* -ize — more at ECHO] *vt* **1 :** to instruct systematically esp. by asking questions, receiving answers, and offering explanations and corrections; *specif* **:** to give religious instruction in such a manner ⟨he preached informally in homes and hospitals, *catechized* children —K.S.Latourette⟩ **2 :** to question systematically or searchingly in order to determine the extent of one's knowledge or the probity of opinions or conduct or to call forth inconsistent or self-condemning answers ⟨he *catechized* Randall to the last detail about every toy that John was to receive —Marcia Davenport⟩ ~ *vi* **:** to give oral instruction esp. in religion ⟨preach and ~ —J.C. Brauer⟩ **syn** see ASK

cat·e·chiz·er \-zə(r)\ *n* -s **:** one that catechizes **:** CATECHIST

cat·e·chol \'kad·ə,chōl, -ə,sh-, -ə,k-, -ōl\ *n* -s [*catechu* + *-ol*] **1 :** CATECHIN **2 :** PYROCATECHOL

cat·e·chu \'kad·ə,chü, -,shü, -,kyü\ *n* -s [prob. modif. of Malay *kachu*, of Dravidian origin; akin to Tamil & Kanarese *kācu*, Malayalam *kāccu*] **1 :** any of various dry, earthy, or resinous astringent substances obtained by extraction and evaporation from the wood, leaves, or fruits of various tropical Asiatic plants: as **a :** an extract of the heartwood of an East Indian acacia that is used for dyeing, tanning, preserving fish nets and sails, and formerly in medicine — called also *black catechu* **b :** GAMBIER — see DYE table I (under *Natural Brown 3*) **c :** 1CUTCH 2 **2 :** an East Indian spiny tree (*Acacia catechu*) that has twice-pinnate leaves, yellow flowers, and flat pods and is the source of catechu **3 :** a variable color averaging auburn — called also *cutch*

cat·e·chu·men \¦kad·ə¦kyümə̇n, -atə-\ *n* -s [alter. (influenced by LL *catechumenus*) of ME *cathecumyn*, fr. MF *cathecumine*, fr. LL *catechumenus*, fr. Gk *katēchoumenos*, pres. pass. part. of *katēchein* to teach, instruct in the elements of religion — more at CATECHIZE] **1 :** one receiving instruction in doctrines, discipline, and morals preliminary to admission among the faithful of the early church **2 :** one receiving rudimentary instruction in the doctrines of Christianity **:** NEOPHYTE

cat·e·chu·men·al \-nᵊl\ *or* **cat·e·chu·men·i·cal** \-(,)kyü¦menə̇kəl\ *adj* **:** of or relating to a catechumen — **cat·e·chu·men·i·cal·ly** \-(,)kyü¦menə̇k(ə)lē\ *adv*

cat·e·chu·men·ate \,=='kyümə̇,nāt, -nə̇t\ *n* -s **1 a :** the status of a catechumen **b :** the duration of this status **2 :** the body of catechumens **3 :** the institution by which catechumens are prepared for church membership through a course of religious instruction

cat·e·chu·tan·nic acid \'kad·ə,chü¦tanik-, -ə,shü-, -ə,kyü-\ *n* [prob. part trans. of G *katechugerbsäure*, fr. *katechu* catechu + *gerbsäure* tannic acid] **:** the tannin of catechu obtained as a reddish brown amorphous powder

cat·e·go·rem \'kad·ə̇gə,rem, kə'tegərəm\ *n* -s [Gk *katēgorēma* predicate] **:** a categorematic expression

cat·e·gor·e·mat·ic \¦kad·ə,gȯrə¦mad·ik\ *adj* [F *catégorématique*, fr. Gk *katēgorēmat-*, *katēgorēma* predicate (fr. *katēgorein* to predicate) + F *-ique* -ic — more at CATEGORY] **:** capable of standing alone as the subject or predicate of a logical proposition **:** expressing a complete substantive meaning ⟨*man* is a ~ word⟩ — opposed to *syncategorematic*

cat·e·go·ri·al \¦kad·ə¦gōrēəl\ *adj* [*category* + *-al*] **:** of, dealing with, or involving a category **:** A PRIORI ⟨a ~ system⟩ — **cat·e·go·ri·al·ly** \-ēəlē\ *adv*

1**cat·e·gor·i·cal** \¦kad·ə¦gȯrə̇kəl, -atə-, -är-,-ōr-, -ēk-\ *also* **cat·e·gor·ic** \-rik, -ēk\ *adj* [*categorical* fr. LL *categoricus* (fr. Gk *katēgorikos*, fr. *katēgoria* category) + E *-al; categoric* fr. LL *categoricus*] **1 a :** ABSOLUTE, UNQUALIFIED — distinguished from *conditional* and *hypothetical* **b :** marked by clear certain positive statement or effect without qualifying, reserving, temporizing, or obscuring ⟨asked for a ~ answer —Allan Nevins & H.S.Commager⟩ ⟨a ~ no⟩ **2 :** CATEGORIAL **syn** see EXPLICIT

2**categorical** \"\ *n* -s **:** a categorical proposition or judgment

categorical imperative *n* [trans. of G *kategorischer imperativ*] **:** a moral obligation or command that is unconditionally and universally binding — contrasted with *hypothetical imperative*

cat·e·gor·i·cal·ly \-ə̇k(ə)lē, -ēk-, -li\ *adv* **:** in a categorical way: **a :** without qualification or reservation **:** ABSOLUTELY **b :** DIRECTLY, EXPLICITLY **c :** CATEGORIALLY

categorical proposition *n* **:** a proposition having the verbal form of direct assertion or denial

categorical syllogism *n* **:** a syllogism with all the propositions categorical

cat·e·go·rist \'==,gōrə̇st\ *n* -s [*category* + *-ist*] **:** one that categorizes

cat·e·go·ri·za·tion \¦=ə̇gərə̇'zāshən, -,rī'z-; -ə,gōrə̇'z-, -ȯr-\ *n* -s **:** the act of categorizing or the state of being categorized **:** CLASSIFICATION

cat·e·go·rize \'=ə̇gə,rīz; -ə,gōr,īz, -,gȯ,rīz\ *vt* -ED/-ING/-S [*category* + *-ize*] **:** to put into a category or class **:** CLASSIFY

cat·e·go·ry \'kad·ə,gōrē, -atə-, -ȯr-, -ri\ *n* -ES [LL *categoria*, fr. Gk *katēgoria*, fr. *katēgorein* to accuse, affirm, predicate, fr. *kata-* cata- + *-agorein* to speak publicly, fr. *agora* assembly — more at GREGARIOUS] **1 :** one of the most abstract and universal terms, concepts, or notions: **a** *in Aristotle* (1) **:** one of the major forms of predication (2) **:** one of the most ultimate modes of being (as substance, quantity, quality, relation, place, time, position, possession, action, affection) **b** *in Kant* **:** one of the pure a priori forms of the understanding ⟨the ~ of quantity (unity, plurality, universality)⟩ ⟨the ~ of quality (relation, negation, limitation)⟩ ⟨the ~ of relation (substantiality, causality, reciprocity)⟩ ⟨the ~ of modality (possibility, actuality, necessity)⟩ **c** *in post-Kantian philosophy* **:** any major fundamental conception or general class of concepts ⟨*categories* — that is, controlling conceptions of inquiry —John Dewey⟩ **2 :** a class, group, or classification of any kind: as **a :** one of several groupings of related soils in the international classification developed by the U.S. Department of Agriculture **b :** a division of the dependent population whose needs are attended to by specific government measures ⟨the aged, the blind, dependent children are in separate relief *categories*⟩ **3 categories** *n pl but sing in constr* **:** a game in which the players decide on a keyword and a list of categories (as cities, animals, tools) and then try within a time limit to fill in under each letter of the keyword a name beginning with that letter to fit each category — called also *guggenheim* **syn** see CLASS

cat·elec·tro·ton·ic \¦kad·ə,lektrə¦tänik, -d·ᵊl,e-\ *adj* [NL *catelectrotonus* + E *-ic*] **:** of, relating to, or caused by catelectrotonus

cat·elec·trot·o·nus \,==,='trätᵊnəs\ *n* [NL, fr. *cata-* + *electrotonus*] **:** the local depolarization and increased irritability of a nerve in the region of the negative electrode or cathode; *also* **:** the passage of a current of electricity through it — compare ANELECTROTONUS

ca·te·na \kə'tēnə, -tā-\ *n, pl* **cate·nae** \-ē(,)nē, -ā,nī\ *or* **cate·nas** \-nəz\ [ML & L; ML, extract from patristic writings, fr. L, chain — more at CHAIN] **1 :** a connected series of related things ⟨a ~ of passages which indicates a kind of amoral determinist attitude —S.G.F.Brandon⟩: as **a :** a series of extracts from patristic writings serving to expound some portion of scripture **b :** a group of closely associated soils within a given geographic zone or region that originated from the same or similar parent material but that developed differing characteristics of the solum because of local variations in relief or drainage **2 a :** a bast fiber found in any of several Mexican trees of the genus *Heliocarpus* **b** [NL, fr. L] **:** a tree of the genus *Heliocarpus* in which catena is found

cat·e·nar·in \,kad·ə'na(a)rə̇n\ *n* -s [ISV *catenar-* (fr. NL *catenarium* — specific epithet of *Helminthosporium catenarium* —, fr. L, neut of *catenarius*) + *-in;* orig. formed as G *katenarin*] **:** a red pigment $C_{15}H_{10}O_6$ produced as a metabolic product of certain fungi (as *Helminthosporium catenarium*); 1,4,5,7-tetrahydroxy-2-methyl-anthraquinone

1**cat·e·nary** \'kad·ə,nerē, -atə,ne-,-atᵊn,e-, -ri, *esp Brit*

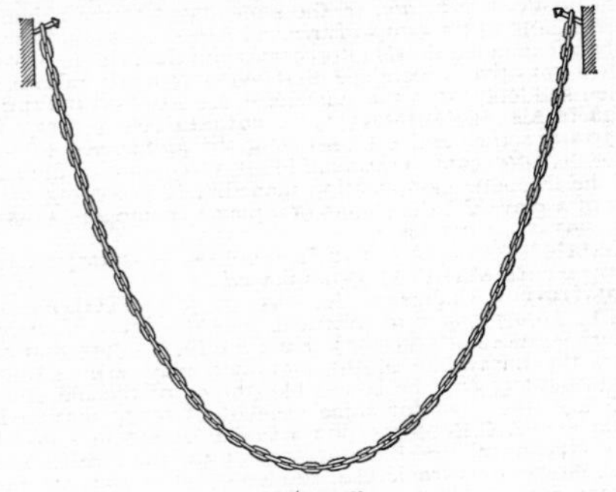

catenary

kə'tēnər-\ *n* -ES [NL *catenaria*, fr. L, fem. of *catenarius*, fr. *catena* + *-arius* -ary] **1 :** the curve assumed by a perfectly flexible inextensible cord of uniform density and cross section hanging freely from two fixed points **2 :** something having or being in the form of a catenary or a series of catenaries: as **a :** a cable suspended between two points (as in a suspension bridge) **b :** a length of cordage secured to or in a piece of fabric in the form of such a curve

2catenary \"\ *adj* [L *catenarius*] **1 :** being or belonging to a catenary **2 :** like or belonging to a catenary

1cat·e·nate \ˈkad·əˌnāt, -atə-, -tᵊnˌāt\ *vt* -ED/-ING/-S [L *catenatus*, past part. of *catenare*, fr. *catena* chain — more at CHAIN] **:** to connect in a series of links or ties **:** form into a catena **:** LINK

2catenate \"\ *adj* [L *catenatus*] **:** CATENULATE

cat·e·na·tion \ˌ==ˈnāshən, ˌ=ᵊnˈā-\ *n* -S [*1catenate* + *-ion*] **:** connection, arrangement, or succession in a regular or connected series (as in a chain): as **a :** a formation in meiosis by chromosomes that have undergone reciprocal translocation, of rings or chains due to the tendency of the homologous portions of chromatin to attain synapsis **b :** linkage between atoms of the same chemical element (as carbon or silicon) — compare CONCATENATION

1cat·e·noid \ˈ=əˌnȯid, ˈ=ᵊnˌȯid\ *n* -S [L *catena* + E *-oid*] **:** the surface described by the rotation of a catenary about its axis

2catenoid \"\ *adj* [L *catena* + E *-oid*] **:** chain-shaped **:** FILIFORM — used esp. of the colonies of certain protozoans

ca·ten·u·late \kəˈtenyələt, -ˌlāt\ *adj* [ISV *catenula* (fr. LL, little chain, dim. of L *catena* chain) + *-ate*] **:** having a chainlike form ⟨~ bacterial cell colonies⟩ ⟨the ~ color marks or indentations on butterflies' wings⟩

1cater *n* -S [ME *catour*, short for *acatour*, fr. AF, fr. *acater* to buy — more at CATE] *obs* **:** a buyer of provisions often for a large household

2ca·ter \ˈkād·ə(r), -ātə-\ *vb* **catered; catered; catering** \-əriŋ *also* ˈkā·triŋ\ **caters** *vi* **1 :** to provide a supply of usu. prepared food **:** act as caterer ⟨~ for a large banquet⟩ ⟨~ to local parties and entertainments⟩ **2 a :** to supply what is required or desired ⟨carry a good supply of charts so as to ~ for such emergencies —Peter Heaton⟩ ⟨too many movies, novels, and comic books ~ to an appetite for violence —J.P.Sisk⟩ **b :** to act with special consideration ⟨~ to a very sick boy⟩ **~** *vt* **:** to provide prepared food and service for ⟨the full-course dinner will be ~*ed* by a local firm⟩

3ca·ter \ˈkād·ə(r), -id-, -ad-\ *vb* -ED/-ING/-S [obs. *cater*, n., four-spot of cards or dice, fr. ME, fr. MF *quatre* four, fr. L *quattuor* — more at FOUR] *vt, dial* **:** to place, move, or cut across diagonally **~** *vi, dial* **:** to move or cut diagonally

cat·er·an \ˈkad·ərən, ˈka·trən\ *n* -S [alter. of ME *ketharan*, prob. fr. ScGael *ceathairneach* freebooter, robber; akin to MIr *cethern* band of soldiers — more at KERN] **1 :** a military irregular of the Scottish Highlands **2 :** MARAUDER, BRIGAND

cat·er·cor·ner *or* **cat·er·cor·nered** *or* **cata·cor·ner** *or* **cata·cor·nered** *or* **cat·ty·cor·ner** *or* **cat·ty·cor·nered** *or* **kit·ty·cor·ner** *or* **kit·ty·cor·nered** \ˈkad·ē¦-, -id·ˌ|-at-|,-it|, |i- *also* |ə-\ *adv* (*or adj*) [*catercorner, cater-cornered* fr. obs. *cater* four-spot + *corner, cornered*; *catty-corner, catty-cornered* & *kitty-corner, kitty-cornered* by folk etymology fr. *catercorner, cater-cornered*] **:** in a diagonal or oblique position or on a diagonal or oblique line ⟨situated *catercorner* to each other on opposite sides of Bradford Island —*Time*⟩ ⟨the ship had come down *catercorner* across two roofs —*Reader's Digest*⟩ ⟨walking *cater-cornered* through the field —A.J. Liebling⟩ ⟨sailing *catty-cornered* across the bay —Louisa W. Peat⟩ ⟨the house stood *catercorner* across the square⟩ ⟨told the movers to place the divan *catercorner* at the end of the long room⟩

ca·ter-cous·in \ˈkād·ə(r)¦-\ *n* [perh. fr. *1cater*] **:** an intimate friend

ca·ter·er \ˈkād·ərə(r), -ātə-\ *n* -S [prob. fr. *2cater* + *-er*] **:** one that caters: as **a :** one whose business is to arrange for and supervise all the details as to food and service for any social affair (as at a club or private house) **b :** a worker in a hotel or restaurant who solicits, promotes, and arranges for social functions to be held there

ca·ter·ess \ˈkād·ərəs, -ātər-, -ā·tr-\ *n* -ES [*caterer* + *-ess*] **:** a female caterer

cat·er·pil·lar *R* ˈkad·ə(r)ˌpilər, -*R* ˈkad·əˌpilə; -atə-\ *n* -S *often attrib* [ME *catyrpel*, modif. of ONF *catepelose*, lit., hairy cat, fr. *cate* female cat (fr. LL *catta*) + *pelose, pelouse*, fem. of *pelous* hairy, fr. L *pilosus*, fr. *pilus* hair — more at CAT, PILE] **1 a :** the elongated wormlike larva of a butterfly or moth that has strong biting jaws, short antennae, three pairs of true legs, several pairs of abdominal prolegs armed with hooks, and often a somewhat complete coat of fine bristles or coarse shining hairs and that is almost exclusively vegetarian, feeding on leaves, fruit, or other succulent parts of plants — called also *worm* esp. in combination (as *armyworm, cutworm*, or *silkworm*) **b :** any of various other insect larvae (as those of sawflies or scorpion flies) that resemble true caterpillars **2** *archaic* **:** a rapacious person preying on the community **3 :** a machine (as an army tank) traveling on two endless belts consisting of series of flat treads with one belt on each side of the machine and the belts kept in motion by toothed driving wheels so that the machine moves forward or backward with the revolution of the belts **4 :** an amusement-park device consisting of a series of connected cars equipped with an enclosing canopy and running on a circular undulating track

Caterpillar \"\ *trademark* — used for a tractor made for use on rough or soft ground and moved on two endless metal belts

caterpillar-eater \ˈ===,==,=\ *n* **:** TRILLER

caterpillar fungus *n* **:** a fungus of the genus *Cordyceps*

caterpillar hunter *n* **:** any of various beetles of the family Carabidae that feed largely upon caterpillars

caterpillar tread *n* **:** the endless chain belt on which a caterpillar-type vehicle runs

ca·ters *or* **qua·ters** \ˈkād·ə(r)z, -ad-\ *n pl but usu sing in constr* [prob. fr. F *quatre* four — more at CATER] **:** a system of ringing changes on nine bells in which four pairs of bells interchange at each permutation

1cat·er·waul \ˈkad·ə(r)ˌwȯl, -atə-\ *vi* -ED/-ING/-S [alter. (influenced by *wawl*) of earlier *caterwawe*, fr. ME *caterwawen*, *caterwrawen*, perh. fr. (assumed) MD *katerwrauwen*, fr. MD *cāter* tomcat (akin to OE *catt* cat) + *wrauwen* to wail, of imit. origin — more at CAT] **1 a** *of a cat* **:** to make a harsh cry at rutting time — compare CALLING 5 **b :** to cry as cats do in rutting time **:** make a harsh offensive noise ⟨the continuous ~*ing* of the . . . street bands —H.A.Sinclair⟩ **c :** to quarrel noisily like cats ⟨government can . . . degenerate into a ~*ing* of hatred and venom —*New Republic*⟩ **2 :** to be lecherous **:** go in lecherous pursuit of women

2caterwaul \"\ *n* -S **1 :** the cry of cats at rutting time **:** CATERWAULING ⟨the ~ of an alley-cat —Marcia Davenport⟩ **2 :** a sound resembling a caterwaul ⟨the Great Eastern sailed in a mass ~ from the banks —James Dugan⟩

cates *pl of* CATE

cates·baea \kāts'bēə, ˈ===\ *n, cap* [NL, fr. Mark Catesby (*Catesbaeus*) †1749 Eng. naturalist and traveler] **:** a genus of West Indian spiny shrubs or trees (family Rubiaceae) having small crowded leaves and solitary white flowers

cat-eyed \ˈ=,=\ *adj* **1 :** having eyes like a cat **2 :** able to see in the dark

catface \ˈ=,=\ *n* **:** a partially healed scar on a tree or log

cat·fac·ing \ˈkatˌfāsiŋ\ *also* **cat·face** \-ās\ *n* **:** a disfigurement or malformation of fruit suggesting a cat's face in appearance (as that caused in peaches by punctures of various sucking insects or in tomatoes by unsatisfactory water balance in the plant)

catfall \ˈ=,=\ *n* [*1cat* (tackle) + *fall* (rope, chain)] **:** a rope or chain used in hoisting an anchor to a cathead

cat family *n* **:** FELIDAE

cat fever *n* [short for *catarrhal fever*] **:** a respiratory infection accompanied by fever

catfight \ˈ=,=\ *n* **:** a bitter and usu. intensely personal dispute ⟨there'll be questions from the floor and a general ~ —Helen Howe⟩

catfish \ˈ=,=\ *n* [so called fr. the catlike appearance of the head] **:** any of the numerous fishes comprising the suborder Siluroidea of the order Ostariophysi, being mostly stout-bodied, large-headed, and voracious with long tactile barbels, some being marine but most inhabiting lakes and streams esp. in the tropics, generally lurking close to the bottom, often attaining a large size, and some being important food fishes though their flesh is not of the finest quality — see ARMORED CATFISH, BULLHEAD, ELECTRIC CATFISH, NAKED CATFISH, SEA CATFISH

catfit \ˈ=,=\ *n* **:** CONNIPTION

cat flea *n* **:** a common flea (*Ctenocephalides felis*) that breeds chiefly on cats, dogs, and rats and is often a pest where these animals are harbored

catfoot \ˈ=,=\ *n* -S [prob. so called fr. the shape of the leaves] **:** a biennial cudweed (*Gnaphalium obtusifolium*) with linear lanceolate leaves that are decurrent as wings down the stem

cat foot *n* **:** a short round compact foot like a cat's ⟨a hound with a good *cat foot* —A.J.Liebling⟩

cat-foot \ˈ=,=\ *vi* **:** to move in a manner suggesting a cat (as stealthily or silently) ⟨the butler came *cat-footing* back along the hall —Raymond Chandler⟩

cat-foot·ed \ˈ=¦==\ *adj* **1 :** having cat feet ⟨~ dogs⟩ **2 :** soft-footed like a cat **:** stealthy or noiseless in walking

cat grape *n* [short for *catbird grape*] **:** MISSOURI GRAPE

cat·gut \ˈ=ˌgət *also* -ˌgət\ *n* -S [*1cat* + *gut*] **1 :** a tough cord that is made from the intestines of certain animals (as sheep) and that is used for strings of musical instruments, for sports rackets, or for sutures in closing wounds — called also *gut* **2 :** a heavy linen or cotton fabric that has an open plain weave and is used for stiffening in clothes and for embroidery **3 a :** an almost prostrate herb (*Tephrosia virginiana*) of eastern No. America with yellowish purple flowers — called also *goat's rue, wild sweet pea* **b :** the strong wiry root of this herb which is the only known significant No. American native source of rotenone

cath- — see CATA-

cath *abbr* **1** cathedral **2** cathode

catha \ˈkathə\ *n, cap* [NL, fr. Ar *qāt* kat] **:** a genus of African evergreen shrubs (family Celastraceae) characterized by thick leaves, small white flowers in axillary cymes, and seed with a white aril at the base

cat-hair \ˈkatˌha(a)(ə)r\ *n, dial* **:** BOIL, SORE

cat ham *n* **:** a thin flat thigh

cat-hammed \ˈ=,=\ *adj* **:** having cat hams with an incurving of the rear line of the thigh — used of cattle or horses

cath·ar \ˈkaˌthär\ *n, pl* **cath·a·ri** \-thəˌrī, -ē\ *or* **cath·ars** \-ˌthärz\ *usu cap* [LL *catharus*, fr. LGk *katharos*, fr. Gk, adj., pure] **:** a member of any of various widely distributed sects found in medieval Europe; *specif* **:** a member of a sect that interpreted Christianity from a dualistic Manichaean point of view and that practiced rigorous asceticism

catharine wheel *var of* CATHERINE WHEEL

cath·a·rism \ˈkathəˌrizəm, -aˌthäˌr-\ *n* -S *usu cap* **:** the doctrines and practices of the Cathari

cath·a·rist \-rəst\ *n* -S *usu cap* [LL & ML *Catharista*, fr. *Cathar* + *-ista* -ist] **:** CATHAR

cath·a·ris·tic \¦=(ˌ)=¦ristik\ *adj, usu cap* **:** of or relating to the Cathari or their doctrines and practices

ca·thar·sis \kəˈthärsəs, -thás-\ *n, pl* **cathar·ses** \-ˌsēz\ [NL, fr. Gk *katharsis*, fr. *kathairein* to clean, purify, fr. *katharos* pure] **1 :** PURGATION 1 **2 a :** the purification or purgation of the emotions (as pity and fear) primarily through art ⟨leaves the spectator "as empty, as changed, and as sad" as any other tragic ~ —Carlos Baker⟩ — used by Aristotle in his description of the effect of tragedy **b :** any purification or purgation that brings about a spiritual renewal or a satisfying release from tension ⟨these drawings served as a ~, relieving him of his burden of terrible memories, at the same time releasing hidden creative forces —Eva Michaelis-Stern⟩ **3 a :** the process of bringing repressed ideas and feelings into consciousness esp. by the technique of free association as employed in psychoanalysis, drugs or hypnosis sometimes being used as adjuvants — compare HYPNOTHERAPY, NARCOANALYSIS **b :** ABREACTION

ca·thar·tae \kəˈthärdˌē\ *n pl, cap* [NL, fr. *Cathartes*] **:** the suborder of Falconiformes comprising the New World vultures and related extinct birds — see CATHARTIDAE

ca·thar·tes \-d·(ˌ)ēz\ *n, cap* [NL, fr. Gk *kathartēs* cleanser, fr. *kathairein* to clean] **:** the type genus of Cathartidae comprising the New World turkey vultures and related extinct birds

1ca·thar·tic \kəˈthär|d·ik, -thȧ|, |tik, -ēk\ *also* **ca·thar·ti·cal** \-ekəl, -ēk-\ *adj* [LL or Gk; LL *catharticus*, fr. Gk *kathartikos*, fr. (assumed) Gk *kathartos* (verbal of Gk *kathairein*) + Gk *-ikos* -ic, -ical] **:** of, relating to, or having the effect of catharsis **:** CLEANSING, PURIFYING ⟨argument as to how Aristotle thought the ~ process worked —Hunter Mead⟩ ⟨cold, ~ rain —R.P.Warren⟩; *specif* **:** cleansing the bowels — **ca·thar·ti·cal·ly** \-ək(ə)lē, -ēk-, -li\ *adv*

2cathartic \"\ *n* -S [LL or Gk; LL *catharticum*, fr. Gk *kathartikon*, fr. neut. of *kathartikos*] **:** a cathartic medicine **:** PURGATIVE

ca·thar·tid \kəˈthärd·əd\ *n* -S [NL *Cathartidae*] **:** NEW WORLD VULTURE

ca·thar·ti·dae \kəˈthärd·əˌdē\ *n pl, cap* [NL, fr. *Cathartes*, type genus + *-idae*] **:** a family of American carnivorous birds constituting with a few extinct related forms the suborder Cathartae of Falconiformes and comprising the New World vultures (as the condor, turkey buzzard, or king vulture), all differing from the Old World vultures in many points of structure (as in having pervious nostrils, no ceca, and no syringeal muscles) but resembling them in general appearance and habits and like them feeding chiefly on carrion

1ca·thar·tine \kəˈthärd·ˌīn, ˈkathərˌtīn\ *adj* [NL *Cathartes* + E *-ine*] **:** of or relating to the genus *Cathartes* or to the typical vultures ⟨the distinctive features of the ~ head⟩ — compare ACCIPITRINE, BUTEONINE

2cathartine \"\ *n* -S **:** a bird of the genus *Cathartes*; *broadly* **:** a vulture or vulturelike member of the family Cathartidae

cat-haul \ˈ=,=\ *vt* **:** to punish by forcibly dragging a cat along the bare back ⟨*cat-haul* a slave for a misdemeanor⟩

ca·thay \kaˈthā, kaˈ-\ *n, often cap* [Cathay China, fr. ML *Cataya, Kitai*, of Turkic origin; akin to Kazan Tatar *Kytai* China, Old Turk *Qytan* Khitan] **:** FRENCH YELLOW

ca·thay·an \-āən\ *adj, usu cap* [*Cathay* + E *-an*] **:** of or relating to the Tatar race in northern China in the 10th and 11th centuries; *broadly* **:** CHINESE

1cathead \ˈ=,=\ *n* [*1cat* (tackle) + *head*] **1 :** a projecting piece of timber or iron near the bow of a ship to which the anchor is hoisted and secured **2** *dial Eng* **:** a nodule of ironstone **3 :** a sleeve clamped around a noncylindrical piece of lathe-work to make suitable contact with the steady rest **4 :** a winch forming part of the drawworks of an oil-well rig

2cathead \"\ *vt* **:** CAT ⟨~ an anchor⟩

cathead line *n* **:** CATLINE

ca·thect \kəˈthekt, ka-\ *vt* -ED/-ING/-S [back-formation fr. *cathectic*] **:** to invest with libidinal energy

ca·thec·tic \kəˈthektik, (ˈ)ka¦th-\ *adj* [fr. NL *cathexis*, after Gk *kathexis* holding: *kathektikos* capable of holding; intended as trans. of G *besetzt*, lit., occupied] **:** of or relating to cathexis **:** libidinally invested

ca·thec·tion \kəˈthekshən, ka-\ *n* -S **:** CATHEXIS

ca·the·dra \kəˈthēdrə *also* ˈkathədrə *or* kəˈthēdrə *or* ˈkätəˌdrä\ *n* -S [L, chair — more at CHAIR] **:** the official throne of a bishop in the principal church of his diocese

1ca·the·dral \kəˈthēdrəl\ *adj* [ME, fr. LL *cathedralis*, fr. L *cathedra* + *-alis* -al] **1 :** of, relating to, or containing a cathedra **:** of, relating to, or being a bishop's church ⟨a ~ church⟩ **2 :** emanating from the chair of office or authority (as of a bishop) **:** OFFICIAL, AUTHORITATIVE ⟨a ~ pronouncement⟩ **3 :** fit for or suggestive of a cathedral ⟨great elms forming ~ arches above its roads —Phyllis Duganne⟩

2cathedral \"\ *n* -S [LL *cathedralis*, prob. short for (assumed) *ecclesia cathedralis* cathedral church] **1 a :** a church that contains a cathedra and that is officially the principal church of a diocese ⟨the *Cathedral* of St. John the Divine in New York⟩ **b :** a church that was once a bishop's church **c :** any of various large or important nonepiscopal churches **2 a :** something that resembles or suggests a cathedral esp. in its proportions or architectural features ⟨a Broadway cinema ~⟩ ⟨that red-brick secular ~, Memorial Hall —A.N. Whitehead⟩ ⟨elms that turn those streets into great ~*s* in summer —Maxwell Mays⟩ **b :** the chapter house of a Scottish rite consistory **3 :** PLUM PURPLE

cathedral bells *n pl, often cap C* **:** a plant of the genus *Cobaea*; *specif* **:** an herb (*C. scandens*) — called also *cup-and-saucer vine*

cathedral ceiling *n* **:** a ceiling left open to expose the underside of a peaked roof

cathedral chimes *n pl* **:** bell-metal tubes of different lengths hung vertically and played by striking the upper ends with a mallet, the tones produced closely resembling distant church bells

cathedral glass *n* **:** translucent sheet glass made by casting and rolling but without polishing

cathedras *pl of* CATHEDRA

cath·e·drat·ic \ˌkathəˈdrad·ik\ *adj* [ML *cathedraticus*, fr. *cathedraticum*] **:** of or relating to an episcopal see; *specif* **:** AUTHORITATIVE

cath·e·drat·i·cum \ˌ==ˈ=əkəm\ *n, pl* **cathedrati·ca** \-kə\ [ML, fr. L *cathedra* + *-aticum* -age] **:** an annual sum paid by a Roman Catholic parish for the support of the bishop

ca·thep·sin \kəˈthepsən, ka-\ *n* -S [Gk *kathepsein* to boil down, digest (fr. *kata-* cata- + *hepsein* to boil) + E *-in*; akin to Arm *epem* I boil] **:** any of a class of proteases present in most animal tissues (as in kidney, liver, and spleen) that aid in autolysis in certain diseased conditions and after death — **ca·thep·tic** \-tik\ *adj*

cath·er·ine wheel \ˈkath(ə)rən-\ *n, often cap C* [after St. *Catherine* of Alexandria † *ab* 307 Christian martyr; fr. the attempt made to torture her on a spiked wheel] **1 a** *also* **cathar·ine wheel :** a wheel with spikes projecting from the rim **b :** a representation of such a wheel used esp. in heraldry **2 :** WHEEL WINDOW **3 :** PINWHEEL 2b **4 :** CARTWHEEL 2a

catherine wheel 1b

cath·e·ter \ˈkathəd·ə(r), -ətə-, *rap.* -thtə-\ *n* -S [LL, fr. Gk *kathetēr*, fr. *kathienai* to send down, fr. *kata-* cata- + *hienai* to send — more at JET] **:** any of various tubular medical devices designed for insertion into canals, vessels, passageways, or body cavities so as to permit injection or withdrawal of fluids or substances or to maintain the openness of a passageway

catheter fever *n* **:** fever ascribed to the passage of a urethral catheter and associated with infection of the bladder

cath·e·ter·i·za·tion \ˌ=(=)=rəˈzāshən, -ˌrīˈz-\ *n* -S **:** the use or insertion of a catheter (as into the bladder, the trachea, or the heart)

cath·e·ter·ize \ˈ=(=)=ˌrīz\ *vt* -ED/-ING/-S [*catheter* + *-ize*] **:** to introduce a catheter into

catheterized *adj* **:** obtained by catheterization ⟨~ urine specimens —*Science*⟩

cath·e·tom·e·ter \ˌkathəˈtäməd·ə(r)\ *n* -S [ISV *catheto-* (fr. Gk *kathetos* vertical height, perpendicular line, fr. *kathetos* let down, fr. *kathienai*) + *-meter*] **:** an instrument for accurate measurement of small differences in height (as of columns of mercury or other fluids) consisting of a telescopic leveling apparatus that slides up or down a perpendicular standard with a finely graduated scale — **cath·e·to·met·ric** \ˌkathəd·əˈmeˌtrik\ *adj*

ca·thex·is \kəˈtheksəs, ka-\ *n, pl* **cathex·es** \-kˌsēz\ [NL, fr. Gk *kathexis* holding, fr. *katechein* to hold fast, occupy, fr. *kata-* cata- + *echein* to have, hold; intended as trans. of G *besetzung*, lit., act of occupying — more at SCHEME] **1 :** the investment of libidinal energy in a person, object, idea, or activity **2 :** libidinal energy that is either invested or being invested

cathisma *var of* KATHISMA

cath·ode \ˈkaˌthōd\ *n* -S [Gk *kathodos* way down, descent, fr. *kata-* cata- + *hodos* way; fr. the belief that the electric current passes from east to west — more at CEDE] **1 :** the electrode at which electrons enter a device from the external circuit — opposed to *anode* **2 a :** the negative terminal of an electrolytic cell **b :** the positive terminal of a primary cell or of a storage battery that is delivering current **c :** the electron-emitting electrode (as a tungsten filament or an oxide-coated metal) of an electron tube

cathode current *n* **:** the current consisting of the total emission of electrons from the cathode of a vacuum tube expressed usu. in milliamperes

cathode dark space *n* **:** CROOKES DARK SPACE

cathode follower *n* **:** an electronic amplifier circuit in which the input is applied between the grid and the remote end of the cathode circuit and the output taken between the cathode and ground, producing an unusually low output impedance

cathode glow *n* **:** a thin layer of luminosity immediately surrounding the cathode in a Crookes tube

cathode ray *n* [part trans. of G *kathodenstrahl*, fr. *kathode* cathode + *strahl* ray] **1 :** one of the high-speed electrons (as a thermion) projected in a stream from the heated cathode of a vacuum tube under the propulsion of a strong electric field **2 :** a stream of cathode-ray electrons

cathode-ray oscillograph *n* **:** an oscillograph in which the moving element is a vibrating beam of cathode rays — compare OSCILLOSCOPE

cathode-ray oscilloscope *n* **:** OSCILLOSCOPE

cathode-ray tube *n* **:** a vacuum tube in which cathode rays usu. in the form of a slender beam are projected upon a fluorescent screen that serves as an anticathode where the rays produce a luminous spot

cathode spot *n* **1 :** a small area of the anticathode of an X-ray tube upon which the cathode rays are focused and from which proceed the X rays **2 :** a small area on the mercury cathode of a mercury-arc rectifier where the arc strikes it and liberates electrons

cath·od·ic \(ˈ)kaˈthädik, -ōd-, kəˈthä-\ *adj* **1 a :** of, at, or relating to a cathode ⟨~ deposition of metals⟩ — opposed to *anodic* **b** *of a chemical element* **:** tending to form a cathode in an electrochemical cell in relation to another element, often hydrogen ⟨copper is ~ to zinc⟩ **2** *or* **kathodic :** turned away — used of that half of a leaf which is turned away from the course of the genetic spiral; compare ANODIC — **cath·od·i·cal·ly** \-ək(ə)lē\ *adv*

cathodic protection *n* **:** the control of the electrolytic corrosion of an underground or underwater metallic structure (as a pipeline) by the application of an electric current in such a way that the structure is made to act as the cathode instead of anode of an electrolytic cell

cath·o·do·flu·o·res·cence \ˈkathəˌdō-\ *n* -S [*cathode* + *-o-* + *fluorescence*] **:** fluorescence due to exposure to cathode rays

cath·o·do·lu·mi·nes·cence \ˈkathəˌdō-\ *n* -S [*cathode* + *-o-* + *luminescence*] **:** luminescence produced when a substance is bombarded with cathode rays — **cath·o·do·lu·mi·nes·cent** \¦==,=¦=¦=\ *adj*

cathole \ˈ=,=\ *n* **1 :** a small opening (as in a door) for a cat to go through **2 :** any small opening that allows passage

1cath·o·lic \ˈkath(ə)lik, -ēk, *esp Brit also* ˈkȧ-\ *n* -S *usu cap* [ME *catholike*, fr. MF *catholique*, fr. *catholique*, adj.] **1 :** a person who belongs to the universal Christian church **2 :** a member of a Catholic church: as **a :** a member of the Roman Catholic Church **b :** a member of an Eastern Orthodox church ⟨a Greek *Catholic*⟩ **c :** a member of an Anglican or Episcopal church ⟨an Anglo-*Catholic*⟩ **d :** a member of an Old Catholic church **e :** a member of a national Catholic church ⟨Polish National *Catholics*⟩

2catholic \"\ *adj* [MF & LL; MF *catholique*, fr. LL *catholicus*, fr. Gk *katholikos* universal, general, fr. *katholou* in general, fr. *kata* down, concerning + *holou*, gen. neut. of *holos* whole — more at CATA-, SAFE] **1** [prob. fr. Gk *katholikos*] **:** WIDESPREAD: **a** *obs* **:** universally prevalent ⟨a ~ legal system⟩ **b** *obs* **:** universally applicable ⟨a ~ remedy⟩ **2** [prob. fr. Gk *katholikos*] **:** general, universal, or inclusive in human affairs: **a :** affecting people generally **:** concerning or influencing all or much of mankind **b :** comprehensive or very broad in sympathies, understanding, appreciation, or interest **:** not narrow, isolative, provincial, or partisan ⟨a much more ~ appreciation of different styles and points of view than the 18th century allowed —Edmund Wilson⟩ **3** *usu cap* **a :** of, relating to, or being the church universal ⟨a truly *Catholic*, ecumenical church⟩ **b :** of, relating to, or being the ancient undivided Christian church **c :** of, relating to, or being a body of Christians belonging to any of various churches claiming historical

continuity from the ancient undivided Christian Church — see 1CATHOLIC 2 **4** *usu cap* : of, relating to, or constituting one of a number of usu. clericalist political parties arising in the late 19th and early 20th centuries principally in continental European countries and characterized by basic principles drawn chiefly from the social and economic teachings of the Roman Catholic Church ⟨European countries with solidly organized *Catholic* parties are Switzerland, Belgium . . . and Austria —C.J.Friedrich⟩ ⟨selection of a *Catholic* chancellor⟩
syn see UNIVERSAL

ca·thol·i·cal·ly \kəˈthälə̇k(ə)lē\ *or* **cath·o·lic·ly** \-lə̇klē, -kli\ *adv* : in a catholic manner

catholic apostolic *adj, usu cap C&A* : of or relating to the body of premillenarian Christians founded about 1832 on the teachings of those they regard as inspired prophets that call their religious body the Catholic Apostolic Church, that observe a highly ritualistic and symbolic form of worship, that have an elaborate hierarchy of apostles and prophets, that emphasize the existence in modern times of the miraculous and prophetic element in early Christianity, and that are commonly known as Irvingites

ca·thol·i·cate \kəˈthälə,kāt, -lə̇kə̇t\ *n* -s [ML *catholicatus*, fr. *catholicus* catholicos + *-atus* -ate] : the see of a catholicos

catholic creditor *n, Scots law* : a creditor whose debt is a lien or charge on two or more items of the debtor's property

catholic existentialism *n, usu cap C* : CHRISTIAN EXISTENTIALISM 1

catholic frog *n, usu cap C* : a toad (*Notaden bennetti*) of eastern Australia with a mark like a cross on its back

ca·thol·i·cism \kəˈthälə,sizəm, kaˈ-\ *n* -s *usu cap* [prob. fr. F *catholicisme*, fr. *catholique* catholic + *-isme* -ism] **1** : the faith, practice, or system of the Catholic church : adherence to the Catholic church ⟨by *Catholicism* is meant that traditional faith expressed in the days of "the undivided Church" —W.N. Pittenger⟩ ⟨Greek, Roman, and Anglican *Catholicism*⟩ **2** : the faith, practice, or system of a Catholic church, specif. the Roman Catholic Church : CATHOLICITY 1a **3** : a peculiarity or characteristic of a Catholic **4** : a political philosophy derived chiefly from the doctrines of the Roman Catholic Church and constituting the primary basis of the principles and policies of Catholic political parties ⟨*Catholicism* inclines toward socialism on many economic questions⟩

cath·o·lic·i·ty \,kathəˈlisəd·ē, -ətē, -i\ *n* -ES [prob. fr. F *catholicité*, fr. *catholique* + *-ité* -ity] **1** *usu cap* **a** : the character of belonging to or being in conformity with a Catholic church, esp. the Roman Catholic Church **b** : CATHOLICISM 1 **2** [1*catholic* + *-ity*] **a** : liberality esp. of sentiments or views ⟨~ of viewpoint —W.V.O'Connor⟩ **b** : UNIVERSALITY ⟨any church . . . which lays prophetic claim to ~ —W.L.Sperry⟩ **c** : comprehensively wide range : INCLUSIVENESS ⟨better to err on the side of ~ than of exclusiveness —C.D.Lewis⟩ ⟨the ~ of subjects represented by the press's trade list —*Current Biog.*⟩

ca·thol·i·ci·za·tion \kə,thäləsəˈzāshən, -,sīˈz-\ *n* -s *usu cap* : the process of making or becoming Catholic

ca·thol·i·cize \kəˈthälə,sīz\ *vb* -ED/-ING/-s *often cap* [2*catholic* + *-ize*] *vt* : to make Catholic; *specif* : ROMANIZE ~ *vi* : to become Catholic; *specif* : ROMANIZE

cath·o·lic·ness \-liknə̇s, -lēk-\ *n* -ES : CATHOLICITY

ca·thol·i·con \kəˈthälə,kän\ *n* -s [F or ML; F, fr. ML, fr. Gk *katholikon*, neut. of *katholikos* universal — more at CATHOLIC] : CURE-ALL, PANACEA ⟨less inclined to look upon this technique as the ~ it appeared to represent —T.M.Pryor⟩

ca·thol·i·cos \kəˈthäləkəs, -ə,käs\ *also* **ca·thol·i·cus** \-əkəs\ *n, pl* **catholi·cos·es** \-əkəsə̇z, -ə,käsə̇z\ *or* **catholi·coi** \-ə,koi\ *also* **catholi·ci** \-ə,sī, -ə,kē\ *often cap* [LGk *katholikos*, fr. Gk *katholikos*, adj. — more at CATHOLIC] : any of the heads of certain independent Eastern churches (as the Armenian Church) ⟨manuscripts written for the ~ Nerses the Gracious⟩ — used only in the non-Greek churches orig. as an honorary title given certain exarchs or primates ranking below a patriarch but above a metropolitan

catholics *pl of* CATHOLIC

cath·o·lyte \ˈkathə,līt\ *n* -s [ISV *cath*ode + electro*lyte*] : the portion of the electrolyte in the immediate vicinity of the cathode in an electrolytic cell — opposed to *anolyte*

cat hook *n* : a hook attached to a ship's cat block

cat-hop \ˈkat,häp\ *n* -s : the situation in faro in which two of the three cards left in the dealing box for the last turn are of the same denomination

cathouse \ˈ=,=\ *n* : BROTHEL 2

ca'·thro *or* **ca'·throw** \ˈkȯ,thrō, ˈkä-, -rü\ *n* -s [Sc *ca'thro'*, v., to work hard, lit., drive through, fr. *ca'* + *thro'*] *Scot* : DISTURBANCE, COMMOTION

cat ice *n* : thin often milky ice from under which the water has receded : SHELL ICE

1cat·i·li·nar·i·an \ˌkad·ᵊlə̇ˈnerēən\ *adj, usu cap* [L *Catilinarius* Catilinarian (fr. Lucius Sergius *Catilina* (Catiline) †62 B.C. Roman politician) + E *-an*] : of, relating to, or like Catiline, who conspired against the government; *specif* : CONSPIRATORIAL ⟨a *Catilinarian* existence⟩

2catilinarian \"\ *n* -s *usu cap* : CONSPIRATOR; *specif* : a participant in Catiline's conspiracy ⟨Cicero had written to Pompey about the suppression of the *Catilinarians* —J.H.Taylor⟩

ca·tin·ga *var of* CAATINGA

cat·ion \ˈkad·,īən *also* -,ī,än *or* ˈka,tī-\ *n* -s [Gk *kation*, neut. of *katiōn*, pres. part. of *katienai* to go down, fr. *kata-* cata- + *ienai* to go — more at ISSUE] **1** : a positively charged ion (as a hydrogen, calcium, or ammonium ion) — opposed to *anion* **2 a** : the ion in an electrolyzed solution that migrates to the cathode and is there discharged and liberated or deposited **b** : a positive gaseous ion

cation-active \ˈ=,=(,)=ˈ==\ *adj* : CATIONIC 2

cation exchange *n* : ion exchange in which one cation (as sodium or hydrogen) is substituted for one or more other cations (as calcium and magnesium in hard water) — called also *base exchange*

cation exchanger *n* : a cation-exchange agent that can exchange its cation with the cation or cations of a solution passed through it and that consists of an insoluble saltlike or acidic substance: as **a** : a natural or synthetic zeolite **b** : a sulfonated coal **c** : a synthetic organic resin containing sulfonic or carboxylic acid groups

cat·ion·ic \ˌkad·,īˈänik, -a,tī-, -ēk\ *adj* **1** : relating to or consisting of cations **2** *of a chemical compound* : characterized by an active cation, esp. by a surface-active cation (as a large hydrophobic organic group) ⟨~ germicide⟩ ⟨~ surface-active agent⟩ — **cat·ion·i·cal·ly** \-ə̇k(ə)lē, -ēk-, -li\ *adv*

cationic detergent *n* : any of a class of synthetic detergents usu. consisting essentially of a quaternary ammonium salt (as cetyl-trimethyl-ammonium chloride $[C_{16}H_{33}N(CH_3)_3]^+Cl^-$) with 12 to 24 carbon atoms in the organic groups attached to the nitrogen atom in the cation and valuable as a wetting and emulsifying agent in acid or neutral solutions or as a germicide or fungicide — called also *invert soap*

cat·ion·oid \(ˈ)=ˈ=ə,nȯid\ *adj* [*cation* + *-oid*] : ELECTROPHILIC

cat·ion·o·trop·ic \ˈ=,=,änəˈträpik\ *adj* [*cationotropy* + *-ic*] : of or relating to cationotropy

cat·ion·ot·ro·py \ˈ=,=əˈnä·trəpē\ *n* -ES [*cation* + *-o-* + *-tropy*] : tautomerism involving migration of a cation, the best-known type being prototropy — compare *anionotropy*

ca·ti·vo \kəˈtē(,)vō, -,və\ *also* **cau·ti·vo** \kau̇ˈ-\ *n* -s [modif. of AmerSp *cativa*, fr. Sp, fem. of *cativo* captive, miserable, fr. L *captivus* captive — more at CAPTIVE] : a large tree (*Prioria copaifera*) of the family Leguminosae of Panama

ca·tjang \ˈkä,chäŋ\ *or* **catjang pea** *n* -s [D *katjang*, fr. Malay & Sundanese *kachang* bean, pea] : PIGEON PEA

cat·kin \ˈkatkə̇n\ *n* -s [trans. of obs. D *katteken* catkin, kitten; fr. its resemblance to a cat's tail] : an ament esp. long and densely crowded with bracts — **cat·kin·ate** \-ə,nāt\ *adj*

cat·la \ˈkätlə, -,lä\ *n* -s [Bengali *kātlā*] : either of two very large cyprinid fishes extensively used as food in southeast Asia: **a** : an Indian fish (*Catla catla*) often cultivated in ponds and attaining a length of six feet **b** : a fish (*C. siamensis*) that is most common in Thailand and that may exceed nine feet in length

catlap \ˈ=,=\ *n* -s [prob. fr. *cat* + *lap* (something lapped up)] *chiefly Scot* : weak drink fit only for a cat to lap

catlike \ˈ=,=\ *adj* : resembling, suggestive of, or having the characteristics of a cat : STEALTHY, NOISELESS

catline \ˈ=,=\ *n* [1*cat* (tackle) + *line*] : a heavy line used for general hoisting in oil-well drilling — called also *cathead line*

cat·ling \ˈkatliŋ\ *n* -s [1*cat* + *-ling*] **1** : a small cat : KITTEN **2** : a catgut string for a musical instrument **3** : the smallest string on a stringed instrument (as a lute) **4** *also* **cat·lin** \-lə̇n\ : a long double-edged sharp-pointed knife used in amputations to divide tissues between close-lying bones

cat·lin·ite \ˈkatlə̇,nīt\ *n* -s [George *Catlin* †1872 Am. artist + E *-ite*] : a red indurated clay from the upper Missouri region used by Indians for tobacco pipes : PIPESTONE

cat·lin mark \ˈkatlə̇n-\ *n, usu cap C* [fr. *Catlin*, name of a family in which this fenestration is typical] : bilateral fenestration of the parietal bones of the skull occurring as a congenital anomaly that was orig. known from primitive human skulls and thought to be the result of trephining

cat louse *n* : a biting louse (*Felicola subrostratus*) of the family Trichodectidae common on cats esp. in warm regions

cat·mal·i·son \ˈkat,maləsən, -əzən\ *n* -s [1*cat* + *malison*; prob. fr. the fact that the cat cannot get in] *dial Eng* : a cupboard in or near the ceiling

cat man *n* **1** : the member of a circus staff responsible for the care and training of lions, tigers, and other large members of the cat family **2** : CAT SKINNER **3** : CAT BURGLAR

catmint \ˈ=,=\ *n* [alter. of ME *cattesminte*, fr. *cattes* (gen. of 1*cat*) + *minte* mint — more at MINT] : CATNIP

1catnap \ˈ=,=\ *n* : a very short light nap ⟨didn't go to bed for two days and nights but caught ~s at my desk —Ralph Ellison⟩

2catnap \"\ *vi* [1*catnap*] : to take a catnap : DOZE

cat·nip \ˈkat,nip\ *also* **cat·nep** \-,nep, -,nəp\ *n* -s [1*cat* + *nip*] : a strong-scented herb (*Nepeta cataria*) that has whorls of small dull-white purple-dotted flowers in a terminal spike, was often used in the past as a domestic remedy, and is much relished by cats — called also *catmint*

cato- *prefix* [Gk *katō-*, fr. *katō* downwards, fr. *kata* down — more at CATA-] : down : lower ⟨*cato*gene⟩ ⟨*Cato*stomus⟩

ca·toc·a·la \kəˈtäkələ; ˌkad·əˈkālə, -ˈkalə\ *n* [NL, fr. *cato-* + *-cala* (irreg. fr. Gk *kalos* beautiful); fr. the red or yellow hind wings — more at CALLI-] **1** *cap* : a widely distributed genus of large moths (family Noctuidae) having the fore wings dull and the hind wings larger and brightly colored **2** *also* **ca·toc·a·lid** \-lə̇d\ -s : a moth of the genus *Catocala* : UNDERWING 2

ca·toc·tin \kəˈtäktə̇n\ *n* -s [fr. *Catoctin* Mountain, Maryland & Virginia] : a residual hill or ridge that rises above a peneplain and preserves on its summit a remnant of an older peneplain

cat·o·met·o·pa \ˌkad·əˈmed·əpə\ *n pl, cap* [NL, fr. *cato-* + L *metopa* metope — more at METOPE] *in former classifications* : a division of crabs comprising the grapsoid members of Brachyrhyncha — **cat·o·met·ope** \-ˈmed·,ōp, -e,tōp\ *n* -s

ca·to·nian \kāˈtōnēən, -nyən\ *or* **ca·ton·ic** \kāˈtänik\ *adj, usu cap* [*catonian* fr. L *catonianus*, fr. *Caton-*, *Cato* (Marcus Porcius *Cato* †149 B.C. Roman statesman, or Marcus Porcius *Cato* †46 B.C. Roman Stoic philosopher, both celebrated for austerity) + L *-ianus* -ian; *catonic* fr. L *Caton-*, *Cato* + E *-ic*] : AUSTERE, HARSH

cat-o'-nine-tails \ˌkad·əˈnīn,tālz, ˌkatˈnī-, ˌkatəˈnī-\ *n, pl* **cat-o'-nine-tails** [so called fr. a comparison of its blows to the scratches of a cat] **1** : a whip made of usu. nine knotted lines or cords fastened to a handle and used for flogging **2** : CATTAIL

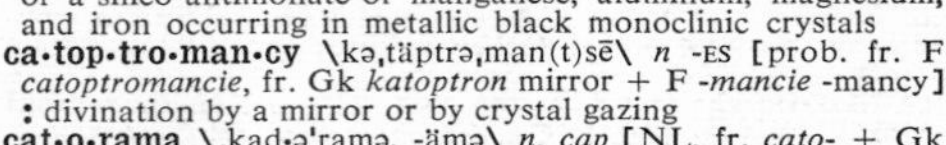
cat-o-nine-tails

ca·top·tric \kəˈtäptrik\ *also* **ca·top·tri·cal** \-ə̇kəl\ *adj* [*catoptric* fr. Gk *katoptrikos*, fr. *katoptron* mirror (fr. *katopsesthai* to be going to observe — fr. *kata-* cata- + *opsesthai* to be going to see — + *-tron*) + *-ikos* -ic; *catoptrical* fr. Gk *katoptrikos* + E *-al* — more at OPTIC] : of or relating to a mirror or reflected light : produced by or based on reflection — **ca·top·tri·cal·ly** \-ə̇k(ə)lē\ *adv*

ca·top·trite *or* **ka·top·trite** \kəˈtäp,trīt, ˈkad·əp,-\ *n* -s [Sw *katoptrit*, fr. Gk *katoptron* + Sw *-it* -ite; fr. its mirrorlike cleavage surfaces] : a mineral consisting of a silico-antimonate of manganese, aluminum, magnesium, and iron occurring in metallic black monoclinic crystals

ca·top·tro·man·cy \kə,täptrə,man(t)sē\ *n* -ES [prob. fr. F *catoptromancie*, fr. Gk *katoptron* mirror + F *-mancie* -mancy] : divination by a mirror or by crystal gazing

cat·o·rama \ˌkad·əˈramə, -ˈämə\ *n, cap* [NL, fr. *cato-* + Gk *horama* that which is visible, fr. *horan* to see] : a genus of deathwatch beetles (family Anobiidae) including some that are pests of stored grain

ca·tos·to·mid \kəˈtästəmə̇d\ *n* -s [NL *Catostomidae*] : a fish of the family Catostomidae : SUCKER

cat·o·stom·i·dae \ˌkad·əˈstämə,dē\ *n pl, cap* [NL, fr. *Catostomus*, type genus + *-idae*] : a family of freshwater fishes (order Ostariophysi) consisting of the suckers and being closely related to and sometimes included in the Cyprinidae — **ca·tos·to·moid** \kəˈtästə,mȯid\ *adj or n*

ca·tos·to·mus \kəˈtästəməs\ *n, cap* [NL, fr. *cato-* + *-stomus*] : a large genus (the type of the family Catostomidae) of suckers

ca·touse \kəˈtau̇s, -au̇z\ *n* -s [origin unknown] *North* : UPROAR, COMMOTION

cat owl *n* : an owl having ear tufts (as the great horned owl, long-eared owl, or screech owl)

cat pea *n* : TUFTED VETCH

catpiece \ˈ=,=\ *n* : a stick with holes at regular intervals into which uprights fastened in floating booms are fitted so as to regulate the width of a logging sluiceway entrance

cat pine *n* : WHITE SPRUCE 1a

cat plague *n* : PANLEUCOPENIA

cat rig *n* : a rig consisting of a single mast placed far forward and carrying a single large sail extended by a long boom

cat-rigged \ˈ=,=\ *adj* : having a cat rig

cats *pl of* CAT, *pres 3d sing of* CAT

1cats and dogs *adv* : in great quantities : very hard — used with an intransitive verb, esp. *rain* ⟨it was raining *cats and dogs*⟩

2cats and dogs *n pl* **1** *slang* : speculative securities of dubious standing or little value **2** *slang* : ODDS AND ENDS; *esp* : miscellaneous merchandise usu. sold at or below cost

cat schooner *n* : a cat-rigged 2-masted boat formerly used for inshore fishing

cat's-claw *or* **catclaw** \ˈ=,=\ *n, pl* **cat's-claws** *or* **catclaws** **1 a** : a climbing shrub (*Doxantha unguis-cati*) with hooked tendrils **b** : an erect shrub (*Pithecolobium unguis-cati*) with curved pointed pods and black shining seeds **2** : any of several prickly shrubs (as *Acacia greggii* or *Mimosa biuncifera*)

cat's cradle *n* **1** : a game in which an endless string looped in a cradlelike pattern on the fingers of one person's hands is transferred to the hands of another in such a way as to form a different symmetrical figure at each transfer — compare STRING FIGURE **2 a** : any of the figures formed with string in the game of cat's cradle **b** : something resembling one of these figures esp. in intricacy ⟨trees . . . latticed and knitted and strung together by a *cat's cradle* of lianas and creepers —Nadine Gordimer⟩

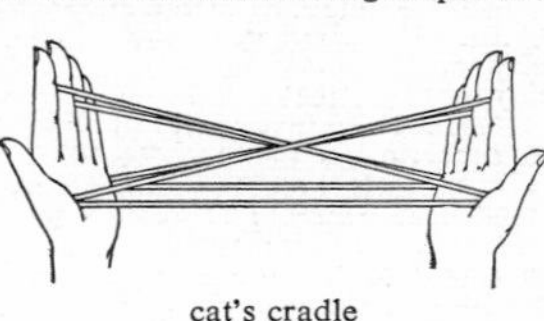
cat's cradle

cat's-cradle \ˈ=,==\ *n, pl* **cat's-cradles** : RIBGRASS

cat scratch disease *n* : an illness that is characterized by chilliness, slight fever, and swelling of the lymph glands and is assumed to be caused by a virus infection starting in a scratch or other skin lesion

cat's-ear \ˈ=,=\ *n, pl* **cat's-ears** **1** : a European weed (*Hypochaeris radicata*) now widely naturalized in No. America that has yellow flower heads and leaves resembling a cat's ear — called also *California dandelion, capeweed, gosmore* **2** : any of various plants with soft hairy blossoms or leaves (as the cudweed or the hawkweed) **3** *West* : a plant of the genus *Calochortus*

cat's-eye \ˈ=,=\ *n, pl* **cat's-eyes** : any of various things resembling the eye of a cat: as **a** : any of various gems (as a chrysoberyl or a chalcedony) usu. cut cabochon exhibiting opalescent reflections from within **b** : a child's marble (as an agate) light in color (as yellow) or with eyelike concentric circles **c** : the operculum of various turban shells of the Pacific islands and adjoining seas that is externally convex with a lustrous brightly colored central area surrounded by zones of white, ivory, and brown and is sometimes used for ornamentation **d** : a small reflector (as a thick lens backed by polished metal) that is used esp. in signs along highways and is usu. placed so as to reflect beams from automobile headlights

cat's-foot \ˈ=,=\ *n, pl* **cat's-feet** **1** : GROUND IVY **2** : any of several plants of the genus *Antennaria* (esp. *A. neodioica*)

cat shark *n* **1** : any of several small mottled sharks comprising the galeoid family Scyliorhinidae **2** : LEOPARD SHARK **3** : any of several small sharks (genus *Parascyllium*) related to and resembling the carpet sharks

catskin \ˈ=,=\ *n* **1** : the skin of a cat esp. when used for fur clothing **2** *archaic slang* : an inferior silk hat

cat skinner *n* : an operator of a Caterpillar tractor — called also *cat man*

catslide \ˈ=,=\ *n* [1*cat* + *slide* (inclined plane)] : a side of a roof that slopes very low and often nearly to the ground (as in a saltbox house)

cat sloop *n* : a catboat on which a bowsprit may be rigged in order to carry a jib

cat snake *n* [so called fr. its manner of stalking lizards] **1** : a back-fanged terrestrial snake (*Tarbophis fallax*) of southern Europe and Syria **2** : a member of the genus *Boiga* which includes various green-eyed nocturnal arboreal Old World back-fanged snakes

catso *n* -s [It *cazzo*, lit., penis, perh. modif. of ML *cattia* dipper — more at CASSEROLE] *obs* : BLACKGUARD, RASCAL

cat's-paw \ˈ=,=\ *n, pl* **cat's-paws** **1** : a light air that ruffles the surface of the water in irregular patches during a calm **2** [so called fr. the fable of the monkey that used a cat's paw to draw roasting chestnuts from the fire] : one used by another to accomplish his purposes : DUPE, TOOL ⟨had no intention of becoming a *cat's-paw* for either belligerent —F.L. Paxson⟩ **3** : a hitch in the bight of a rope so made as to form two eyes into which a tackle may be hooked **4** : CAT'S-FOOT

cat's paw 3

cat spruce *n* : WHITE SPRUCE 1a

cat's purr *n* : a vibratory murmur heard on auscultation or a vibratory fremitus felt on palpation in some cases of valvular disease of the heart

cat squirrel *n* **1** : a reddish-coated fox squirrel found in the eastern part of its range **2** : the common European squirrel **3** : CACOMISTLE **4** : GRAY SQUIRREL

1cat's-tail \ˈ=,=\ *also* **cat's-tail grass** *n, pl* **cats'-tails** [ME *cattestail*, a kind of plant, prob. mullein, fr. *cattes* (gen. of 1*cat*) + *tail*] : any of several grasses of the genus *Phleum*; *esp* : TIMOTHY

2cat's-tail *var of* CATTAIL

catstep \ˈ=,=\ *n* -s : one of a succession of small terracelike forms created on a steep hillside by the slumping of the soil — usu. used in pl.

catstick \ˈ=,=\ *n* [1*cat* (pointed stick) + *stick*] : a stick or club used as a bat in tipcat or trapball

cat·stitch \ˈkat,stich\ *n* [by alter.] : CATCH STITCH

cat·sup *or* **catch·up** *or* **ketch·up** *or* **kat·sup** \ˈkechəp, ˈkachəp *also* ˈkatsəp\ *n* -s [*catsup*, *catchup*, *katsup* by folk etymology fr. *ketchup*; *ketchup* fr. Malay *kĕchap* spiced fish sauce] **1** : a seasoned sauce of puree consistency the principal ingredient of which is usu. tomatoes but sometimes another foodstuff (as mushrooms or walnuts) **2** *usu catchup* : a moderate red that is yellower and slightly lighter than cerise, yellower than claret (sense 3 a), yellower and very slightly lighter than average strawberry (sense 2 a), and yellower and lighter than Turkey red

cat swamper *n* : one that clears logging trails for tractors

cat's whisker *var of* CAT WHISKER

cattail \ˈ=,=\ *n* [alter. of *cat's-tail*] **1** *or* **cat's-tail** *or* **cattail flag** : a plant of the genus *Typha*; *esp* : a tall marsh plant (*T. latifolia*) with long flat leaves used for making mats and chair seats — called also *reed mace* **2** : MUSK 4

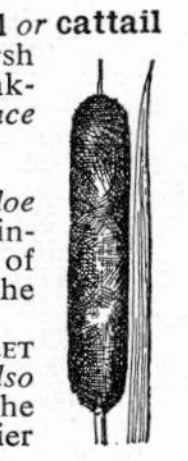
cattail (*Typha latifolia*)

cattail family *n* : TYPHACEAE

cattail fungus *n* : an ascomycetous fungus (*Epichloe typhina*) of the family Hypocreaceae forming cylindrical whitish or gray stromata around the stems of certain grasses and often affecting development of the inflorescence — see CHOKE 5

cattail millet *n* **1** : FOXTAIL MILLET **2** : PEARL MILLET

cat·ta·lo \ˈkad·ᵊl,ō\ *n, pl* **cattaloes** *or* **cattalos** *also* **cattalo** [*cattle* + *buffalo*] : a hybrid between the American buffalo and domestic cattle that is hardier than the latter

cattan *var of* CATAN

cat tapeworm *n* : a common tapeworm (*Taenia taeniaeformis* or *T. crassicollis*) of cats who ingest the cysticercus from various rodents in whose livers this larva forms conspicuous tumors

1catted *past of* CAT

2cat·ted \ˈkad·ə̇d\ *adj* [*cat* (plaster) + *-ed*] : built up or bonded with clay or cat and clay ⟨a ~ chimney⟩

cat·tery \ˈkad·ərē\ *n* -ES : a place for the breeding, raising, or care of cats

cat thyme *n* : a low-growing germander (*Teucrium marum*) formerly used in cosmetics that has tiny hairy or woolly leaves and reddish purple flowers and is attractive to cats — called also *marum*

cattier *comparative of* CATTY

cat·tier·ite \kəˈtē,rīt\ *n* -s [fr. *Cattier*, railroad workshops in Leopoldville province, Congo + E *-ite*] : a mineral CoS_2 consisting of cobalt sulfide and belonging to the pyrite group

catties *pl of* CATTY

cattiest *superlative of* CATTY

cat·ti·ly \ˈkad·|ᵊlē, -at|, |ᵊlē, -li\ *adv* : in a catty manner

cat·ti·ness \ˈkad·ēnə̇s, -atē-\ *n* -ES : the quality or state of being catty

catting *pres part of* CAT

cat·tish \ˈkad·ish, -ati-, -ēsh\ *adj* **1** : like a cat : like that of a cat : FELINE ⟨he had a ~ secrecy and serenity —Esther Forbes⟩ **2** : SPITEFUL, CATTY — **cat·tish·ly** *adv*

cat·tle \ˈkad·ᵊl, ˈkatᵊl\ *n, pl* **cattle** *usu pl in constr, often attrib* [ME *catel*, fr. ONF, personal property, fr. ML *capitale*, fr. L, neut. of *capitalis* of the head — more at CAPITAL] **1 a** : live domesticated quadrupeds (as sheep, horses, swine) held as property or raised for some use; *specif* : bovine animals (as cows, bulls, steers) kept on a farm or ranch **b** : domesticated or feral animals of the genus *Bos* comprising the many breeds of the common ox that have arisen either from the urus with some admixture of zebu blood by crossbreeding and selection among strains or according to some authorities from the Celtic ox (*B. longifrons*) — see BEEF BREED, DAIRY BREED, DUAL-PURPOSE BREED **2** : human beings especially en masse — usu. used derogatorily

cattlebush \ˈ==,=\ *n* : an Australian tree (*Atalaya hemiglauca*) of the family Sapindaceae that is often used for fodder in droughts

cattle cake *n, chiefly Brit* : a concentrated ration for cattle processed in the form of blocks or cakes

cattle egret *n* [so called fr. its habit of feeding on insects on or in the vicinity of cattle] : a small white buff-backed egret (*Bubulcus ibis*) native to Africa, southern Europe, and southwestern Asia but now occurring also in northern So. America and intermittently in the eastern U. S.

cattle farcy *n* : FARCY 2

cattle fever *n* **1** : TEXAS FEVER **2** : bovine pasteurellosis

cattle fly *n* : HORN FLY

cattle grid *n, Brit* : CATTLE GUARD

cattle grub *n* **1** : the maggot of a warble fly **2** : the adult warble fly

cattle guard *n* **1** : a device consisting of a shallow ditch across which ties or rails are laid far enough apart to prevent livestock from crossing that is often used instead of a gate at a fence opening ⟨where the *cattle guard* barred the entrance to horses, he dismounted —Oliver La Farge⟩ **2** : an opening in a fence where a cattle guard has been laid

cattlehide \ˈ==,=\ *n* : leather made from the hides of mature bovines — contrasted with *calfskin, kip*

cat·tle·less \'==ləs\ *adj* **:** being without cattle

cattle louse *n* **:** a louse infesting cattle — see CATTLE RED LOUSE, LONG-NOSED CATTLE LOUSE, SHORT-NOSED CATTLE LOUSE

cat·tle·man \'==mən, -,man, -,aa(ə)n\ *n, pl* **cattlemen 1 :** one who tends cattle **2 :** a rancher who raises beef cattle on the open range

cattle pass *n* **:** a passageway for livestock; *esp* **:** one under a highway or railroad

cattle plague *n* [trans. of G *rinderpest*] **:** RINDERPEST

cattle red louse *n* **:** the common bird louse (*Trichodectes bovis*) of domestic cattle that feeds chiefly on the hair

cattle tick *n* **:** a tick (*Boophilus annulatus*) infesting cattle in the warmer parts of the U.S. and in tropical America and transmitting the parasite that causes Texas fever; *broadly* **:** any of several other ticks attacking cattle esp. in Australia

cattle-tick fever *n* **:** TEXAS FEVER

cat·tleya \'katlēə, ='==; kat'lāə\ *n* [NL, fr. William *Cattley* †1832 Eng. patron of botany] **1** *cap* **:** a genus of tropical American epiphytic orchids the flowers of which are among the showiest known and are characterized by a hood-shaped 3-lobed lip enclosing the column **2** -s **:** a plant of the genus *Cattleya* **3** -s **:** a moderate purple that is redder and paler than heliotrope (sense 4a), bluer and paler than average amethyst, and paler and slightly bluer than manganese violet

cattleya fly *n* **:** a small black chalcid fly (*Eurytoma orchidearum*) the larvae of which live in and damage and deform the shoots of orchids

cattle yard \'==,=\ *n* **1 :** a barnyard used by cattle **2 :** STOCKYARD

cat·tley guava \'katlē-\ *n* [after William *Cattley*] **:** STRAWBERRY GUAVA

cat train *n* [¹*cat* (caterpillar) + train] **:** a train of large connected sleds drawn by a tractor and used for transportation in arctic areas

cat twist *n* **:** a tumbling and trampolining stunt consisting of a full or partial twisting of the shoulders and hips in the air with the body usu. in pike position

¹cat·ty \'kad·ē, -atē, -i\ *n* -ES [Malay *kati*] **:** any of various units of weight used in China and southeast Asia varying around 1⅓ pounds or 600 grams; *also* **:** a Chinese unit according to a standard set up in 1929 equal to 1.1023 pounds or 500 grams

²cat·ty \"\ *adj, usu* -ER/-EST [¹*cat* + *-y*] **1 :** having characteristics resembling those of a cat ⟨writes of its problems with a ~ aloofness charmingly disguised as sympathy —Lewis Mumford⟩: as **a :** STEALTHY ⟨a noiseless ~ walk⟩ **b :** AGILE ⟨three of the *cattiest* men who ever rode a log —S.H.Holbrook⟩ **c :** slyly spiteful ⟨a ~ remark⟩ **d :** given to malicious gossip ⟨a ~ woman⟩ **2 :** of, relating to, or like a cat ⟨a ~ smell in the house⟩

catty-corner *or* **catty-cornered** *var of* CATERCORNER

cat typhoid *n* **:** PANLEUCOPENIA

cat·ty·wam·pus *var of* CATAWAMPUS

ca·tul·li·an \kə'təlēən\ *adj, usu cap* [L *catullianus,* fr. Gaius Valerius *Catullus* †54 B.C. Roman poet + L *-ianus* -ian] **:** of, relating to, or like Catullus or his lyric poems, which are marked by facility of language, perfection of form, and intensely personal subject matter

cat wagon \'=,==\ *n* [¹*cat* (caterpillar) + *wagon*] **:** a truck trailer on caterpillar treads used esp. on soft ground

catwalk \'=,=\ *n* **:** a narrow walkway allowing passage over or around areas not otherwise traversable or giving access to places otherwise inaccessible: as **a :** a raised gangway that runs the length of a tanker and gives passage forward and aft when the upper deck is awash **b :** a high narrow steel platform over the engine room or stokehold of a ship **c :** a narrow footway along the keel of a rigid airship **d :** a walkway along the roof of a railway freight car **e :** a narrow footway along a bridge

cat whisker *or* **cat's whisker** *n* **:** a fine wire making contact with the crystal in the crystal detector or mixer of certain types of radio or electronic circuits

cat willow *n* **:** FALSE INDIGO 1a

cat·wort \'kat,wərt, -ȯrt\ *n* [ME, fr. *cat, catte* + *wort*] **:** CATNIP

cat yawl *n* **:** a yawl without headsails and with the mainmast set forward

catydid *var of* KATYDID

catzerie *n* -s [prob. fr. *catso* + *-ery*] *obs* **:** KNAVERY

cau·been \(')kȯ¦bēn\ *n* -s [IrGael *cāibīn,* dim. of *cāba* cape, prob. fr. ML *capa* cope — more at COPE] *Irish* **:** a man's hat

¹cau·ca·sian \(')kȯ¦kāzhən *also* -azh- *or* -aizh-\ *adj, usu cap* [*Caucasus* or *Caucasia,* region between the Black & Caspian seas (fr. L *Caucasus,* fr. Gk *Kaukasos*) + E *-ian* or *-an*] **1 :** of or relating to the Caucasus or its inhabitants **2 :** CAUCASIC 2 **3 :** of or relating to the Caucasian race

²caucasian \"\ *n* -s **1** *cap* **:** a member of one of various native peoples of the Caucasus (as the Abkhas, Georgians, Mingrelians, Circassians, Kartvelians, Chechens, and Lezghians) most of whom are racially white but linguistically isolated **2** *cap* **a :** a member of the white race of mankind as opposed by classification according to physical features (as skin color, hair form, or body and skeletal characteristics) but without regard to language or culture to members of the Negroid, Mongoloid, or other putative races of mankind **b :** a member of the white race as defined by law (as in California or So. Africa); *specif* **:** a descendant of European, No. African, or southwest Asian immigrants **c** *chiefly Southwest* **:** a person of white race or European descent as opposed to those of other ethnic affiliation or descent (as certain Mexicans, Indians, Negroes, Orientals) **:** ANGLO **3** *usu cap* **:** a rug of any of the types woven in the Caucasus mountains and the adjacent plains to the north and south

caucasian walnut *n, usu cap C* **:** a tall often forked tree (*Pterocarya fraxinifolia*) native to the Caucasus and distinguished from other walnuts by its 2-winged fruit

cau·cas·ic \(')kȯ¦kasik, -zik\ *adj, usu cap* [*Caucasus* + E *-ic*] **1 :** CAUCASIAN, CAUCASOID **2 :** of or relating to the languages of the Caucasus region that are not Indo-European or Altaic

¹cau·ca·soid \'kȯkə,sȯid\ *adj, usu cap* [*Caucasian* + *-oid*] **:** of, resembling, or related to the Caucasian race

²caucasoid \"\ *n* -s *cap* **:** CAUCASIAN 2a

cauch \'kȯch\ *n* -ES [modif. of Corn *caugh* dung; akin to MIr *cacc* dung — more at CACK] *dial Eng* **:** MESS

cau·che·ro \kau̇'che(,)rō\ *n* -s [AmerSp, fr. Sp *caucho* + *-ero* -er] **:** one who gathers rubber sap

cau·chi·llo \kau̇'chē(,)(y)ō\ *n* -s [AmerSp] **:** a tropical American timber tree (*Lecythis ollaria*) yielding a valuable reddish brown wood and bearing fruits with seeds resembling Brazil nuts — see CREAM NUT

cau·cho \'kau̇(,)chō, -)shü\ *n* -s [Sp — more at CAOUTCHOUC] **:** RUBBER; *specif* **:** the wild rubber obtained from a Brazilian tree (*Castilloa ulei*) or from a Central American tree (*C. elastica*) — see CASTILLOA

¹cau·cus \'kȯkəs *also* -'ä-\ *n* -ES *often attrib* [earlier *corcas,* prob. of Algonquian origin; akin to *caucauasu* elder, counselor (in some Algonquian language of Virginia), Abnaki *kakesoman* to encourage, arouse, Natick *kogkahtimau* he gives advice to] **1 a :** a conference of party or organization leaders (as legislators) to decide on policies, plans, appointees, and candidates **b :** a local or regional meeting of party members to choose candidates or delegates **c** *chiefly West* **:** an open meeting to nominate township candidates **2 :** a system of party organization by representative committees that determine and implement policies **3** *Austral* **:** a party that uses caucus procedures to make decisions binding its members

²caucus \"\ *vi* -ED/-ING/-ES **:** to hold a caucus **:** meet in a caucus

caud- *or* **caudi-** *or* **caudo-** *comb form* [L *cauda*] **:** tail **:** caudal vertebrae **:** caudal ⟨*caud*ad, *caudi*form, *caudo*dorsal⟩

cau·da \'kau̇də, 'kȯdə\ *n, pl* **cau·dae** \'kau̇,dī, 'kȯ,dē\ [L, tail — more at COWARD] **1 :** a taillike appendage **:** TAIL **2 :** TAIL 16, CODA

cau·dad \'kȯ,dad\ *adv* [L *cauda* tail + E *-ad*] *anat* **:** toward the tail or posterior end — opposed to *cephalad*

cauda equi·na \'kau̇dəe'kwēnə, 'kȯdəe'kwīnə\ *n, pl* **cau·dae equi·nae** \'kau̇,dīe'kwē,nī, 'kȯ,dēe'kwī,nē\ [NL, fr. L, horse's tail] **:** the roots of the upper sacral nerves which are of great length because the spinal cord does not extend beyond the first lumbar vertebra and which form a bundle of filaments within the spinal canal

cau·da he·li·cis \¦kau̇də'heləkəs, ¦kȯdə'heləsəs\ *n, pl* **cau·dae helicis** \'kau̇,dī-, 'kȯ,dē-\ [NL, lit., tail of the helix] **:** the lower posterior part of the helix of the external ear

¹cau·dal \'kȯdᵊl\ *adj* [NL *caudalis,* fr. L *cauda* tail + *-alis* -al — more at COWARD] **1 :** constituting, belonging to, or relating to a tail ⟨~ appendage⟩ ⟨~ veins⟩ **2 :** situated in or directed toward the hind part of the body or the part from which the tail arises **:** POSTERIOR ⟨a ~ nerve⟩ ⟨the ~ end of the body⟩ — **cau·dal·ly** \-dᵊlē, -li\ *adv*

²caudal \"\ *n* -s **:** a caudal part (as a fin or scale)

caudal anesthesia *or* **caudal analgesia** *n* **:** loss of pain sensation below the umbilicus produced by injection of an anesthetic into the caudal portion of the spinal canal

caudal artery *n* **:** the portion of the dorsal aorta of a vertebrate that passes into the tail

caudal fin *n* **:** the terminal fin of a fish — called also *tail fin;* see FISH illustration

caudal peduncle *n* **:** the narrow region of the body of a fish immediately in front of the caudal fin

caudal vesicle *n* **:** the posterior part of certain larval tapeworms into which the scolex and neck may be retracted — compare CYSTICERCOID

cau·da·ta \kȯ'dād·ə, kau̇'däd·ə\ *n pl, cap* [NL, fr. ML, neut. pl. of *caudatus* caudate] **:** an order of Amphibia containing the salamanders, newts, congo snakes, and related forms and having long bodies, long tails retained through life, short weak limbs, and feebly ossified crania

¹cau·date \'kȯ,dāt, *usu* -ād·+V\ *also* **cau·dat·ed** \-ād·əd\ *adj* [It & NL; It *caudato,* fr. ML (& NL) *caudatus,* fr. L *cauda* tail + *-atus* -ate — more at COWARD] **:** having a tail or a taillike appendage or termination **:** TAILED — **cau·da·tion** \kȯ'dāshən\ *n* -s

²caudate \"\ *n* -s [NL *Caudata*] **:** one of the Caudata **:** a tailed amphibian

caudate lobe *n* **:** a lobe of the liver bounded on the right by the inferior vena cava, on the left by the fissure of the ductus venosus, and connected with the right lobe by a narrow prolongation

caudate nucleus *n* **:** a mass of gray matter in the corpus striatum of the brain forming part of the floor of the lateral ventricle and separated from the lenticular nucleus by the internal capsule

cau·da·to·len·tic·u·lar \kȯ¦dād·(,)ō,len¦tikyələ(r)\ *adj* [¹*Caudate* + *-o-* + *lenticular*] **:** relating to the caudate and lenticular nuclei of the corpus striatum

cau·dex \'kȯ,deks\ *n, pl* **caudi·ces** \-də,sēz\ *or* **caudex·es** \-,deksəz\ [L — more at CODE] **:** the main axis including both stem and root of a plant: **a :** the stem of a palm or tree fern covered with persistent leaf bases or marked with their scars **b :** the woody base of a perennial plant

caudi- — see CAUD-

cau·di·cle \'kȯdəkəl\ *n* -s [prob. fr. NL *caudicula,* dim. of L *cauda* tail — more at COWARD] **:** the slender stalklike appendage of the pollen masses in orchids

cau·di·form \'kȯdə,fȯrm\ *adj* [L *cauda* tail + E *-iform*] **:** having the shape of a tail

cau·di·llis·mo \,kau̇t͟hē(l)'yēz(,)mō\ *n* -s [Sp, fr. *caudillo* + *-ismo* -ism] **:** the doctrine or practice of a caudillo **:** DICTATORSHIP

cau·di·llo \kau̇'t͟hē(l)(,)yō\ *n* -s [Sp, fr. LL *capitellum* small head — more at CADET] **:** a military leader (as in a Latin-American country) usu. of guerrilla or irregular forces loyal to him personally; *specif* **:** a political boss with his own military following

¹cau·dle \'kȯdᵊl\ *n* -s [ME *caudel,* fr. ONF, fr. *caud-, caut* warm, fr. L *caldus, calidus* warm — more at CALDRON] **:** a drink made usu. of warm ale or wine mixed with bread or gruel, eggs, sugar, and spices and often taken medicinally

²caudle \"\ *vt* **caudled; caudled; caudling** \-d(ᵊ)liŋ\ **caudles :** to serve a caudle to

caudle cup *n* **:** a small 2-handled cup having a bulbous body, contracted neck, and usu. a top, made typically of silver, and esp. popular in the late 17th century

caudle of hempseed *obs* **:** a hangman's rope

caudo- — see CAUD-

cauf \'kȯf\ *Scot var of* CHAFF

caugh·na·wa·ga \,kägnə'wägə\ *n* -s *cap* [Mohawk *Gahnawa'ge,* lit., at the rapids] **:** a native or inhabitant of Caughnawaga, a settlement founded by the French near Montreal, Canada, for Mohawk converts to Christianity

¹caught *past of* CATCH

²caught *past part of* CATCH — **caught dead :** publicly known even though dead and impervious to criticism **:** DISCOVERED, FOUND ⟨I wouldn't be *caught dead* wearing that shirt⟩ — **caught short 1 :** taken unawares **:** found ill-prepared, inadequately equipped, or poorly supplied ⟨he was *caught short* by the blunt question⟩ **2 :** inopportunely seized with a need to relieve oneself

³caught *adj* [²*caught*] **:** PREGNANT — often used in the phrase *get caught*

¹cauk \'kȯk, -äk-\ *n* -s [ME (northern dial.) *calke,* fr. OE (northern dial.) *calc* (in other dialects *cealc*) — more at CHALK] *dial Brit* **:** CHALK, LIMESTONE

²cauk \"\ *vt* -ED/-ING/-S *Scot* **:** CHALK

³cauk \"\ *dial Brit var of* ¹CAWK

⁴cauk \'käk, -ȯk-\ *vt* -ED/-ING/-S [prob. alter. of *cock* (to cog)] **:** to secure by a tenon

¹caul \'kȯl\ *n* -s [ME *calle,* fr. MF *cale,* perh. back-formation fr. *calotte* skullcap] **1 :** a covering network: **a** *archaic* **:** a woman's netted close-fitting cap **b** *obs* **:** a net used to enwrap **c** *obs* **:** a net foundation for a wig **d :** the network at the back of a woman's cap **2 :** an enclosing or investing membrane: **a :** GREATER OMENTUM **b :** the inner fetal membrane of higher vertebrates esp. when unruptured or covering the head at birth **:** AMNION

²caul \"\ *n* -s [F *cale* chock, shim, modif. of G *keil* wedge, fr. OHG *kil;* akin to OE *cīth* sprout, *cīnan* to gape, crack, OHG *kīmo* sprout, *kīnan* to sprout, ON *kill* inlet, Goth *keinan* to germinate, sprout, Lith *žydėti* to bloom] **:** a usu. heated sheet of metal or other material used to equalize pressure in making plywood and in shaping veneer to a surface

³caul \"\ *var of* CAWL

caul- *or* **cauli-** *or* **caulo-** *comb form* [*cauli-* fr. L *caulis; caul-, caulo-* fr. NL, fr. Gk. *kaul-, kaulo-,* fr. *kaulos* — more at HOLE] **:** stem **:** stalk ⟨*caul*ome⟩ ⟨*cauli*flory⟩

¹cauld \'käl(d), -ȯ-\ *chiefly Scot var of* COLD

²cauld \"\ *n* -s [origin unknown] *chiefly Scot* **:** WEIR

cauld·rife \'käl(d)rif, -ȯl-, -,(d)rīf\ *adj* [¹*cauld* + *rife*] **1** *Scot* **a :** COLD, CHILLING **b :** susceptible to cold **2** *Scot, of a person* **:** COLD, CHEERLESS

caul·dron \'kȯldrən\ *var of* CALDRON

cauldron subsidence *n* **:** the sinking of part of the roof of a magma chamber usu. involving downward movement along circumferential faults

cau·ler·pa \kȯ'lərpə\ *n, cap* [NL, fr. *caul-* + *-erpa* (fr. Gk *herpein* to creep) — more at SERPENT] **:** a genus (coextensive with the family Caulerpaceae) of green algae of the order Siphonales occurring on tropical sea bottoms, having a thallus composed of a single coenocyte differentiated into a long creeping stemlike portion that forms rhizoids below and variously shaped foliose expansions above, and reproducing asexually by detached vegetative shoots — **cau·ler·pa·ceous** \¦kȯ(,)lər¦pāshəs\ *adj*

cau·les·cent \(')kȯ¦lesᵊnt\ *adj* [ISV *caul-* + *-escent;* orig. formed in F] *bot* **:** having a stem evident above ground — opposed to *acaulescent*

caul fat *n* [¹*caul*] **:** fat from the visceral cavity of a slaughtered animal

cauli- — see CAUL-

cau·li·cle \'kȯləkəl\ *n* -s [L *cauliculus,* dim. of *caulis* stem, stalk — more at COLE] **:** a rudimentary stem; *specif* **:** the stem of an embryo or young seedling

cau·li·cole \'kȯlə,kōl\ *also* **cau·li·co·lo** \kau̇'lēkə,lō\ *n, pl* **cau·li·coles** \-,kōlz\ *or* **cau·li·co·li** \-,kə,lē\ [F & It; F *caulicole,* fr. It *caulicolo,* fr. L *cauliculus,* lit., little stalk, dim. of *caulis* stalk — more at HOLE] **:** one of the eight stalks rising out of the leafage in a Corinthian capital and ending in leaves that support the volutes

cau·lic·o·lous \(')kȯ¦likələs\ *adj* [ISV *caul-* + *-colous;* prob. orig. formed as F *caulicole*] **:** growing on the stems of other plants ⟨many fungi are ~⟩

cau·li·cule \'kȯlə,kyül\ *n* -s [L *cauliculus*] **:** CAULICLE

cau·li·flo·rous \¦kȯlə¦flōrəs\ *adj* [ISV *caul-* + *-florous*] **:** producing flowers from the main stem or older branches ⟨the redbud, chocolate tree, and many tropical trees are ~⟩ — **cau·li·flo·ry** \'==,=rē\ *n* -ES

¹cau·li·flow·er \'kȯlə, 'käl-, -lē *also* 'kəl-+,-\ *n* -s *often attrib* [alter. (influenced by L *caulis* cabbage and E *flower*) of earlier *colieflorie,* modif. of It *caoli fiori,* pl. of *cavolfiore,* lit., cabbage flower, fr. *cavolo* cabbage (fr. LL *caulus,* alter. of L *caulis*) + *fiore* flower, fr. L *flor-, flos* — more at COLE, FLOWER] **1 a :** a garden plant (*Brassica oleracea capitata*) that is closely related to the cabbage and is grown for its edible head of greatly modified and compacted white or purplish undeveloped flowers — see BROCCOLI **2 :** the flower cluster of the cauliflower used as a vegetable **3 :** something resembling a cauliflower; *esp* **:** a cloud shaped like a cauliflower cluster

cauliflower 2

²cauliflower \"\ *vt* -ED/-ING/-S **:** to disfigure (an ear) esp. by repeated blows in boxing

cauliflower disease *n* **1 :** an eelworm disease of the strawberry characterized by clustered, malformed, and puckered leaves **2 :** a disease of the strawberry and other plants caused by a bacterium (*Corynebacterium fascians*)

cauliflower ear *n* **:** an ear deformed from injury (as by repeated blows in boxing) and excessive growth of reparative tissue

cauliflower growth *n* **:** a wartlike growth of tissue that is usu. a condyloma but sometimes a stage of cancer and resembles a cauliflower

cau·line \'kȯ,līn\ *adj* [prob. fr. NL *caulinus,* fr. L *caulis* stem + *-inus* -ine] *bot* **:** belonging to or growing on a stem; *specif* **:** growing on the upper portion of a stem — contrasted with *radical*

cauline bundle *n* **:** a vascular bundle remaining within a stem and having no connection with leaves — compare COMMON BUNDLE

¹caulk *or* **calk** \'kȯk\ *vb* -ED/-ING/-S [ME *caulken, calken,* fr. ONF *cauquer* to trample, fr. L *calcare,* fr. *calc-, calx* heel — more at CALK] *vt* **1 a :** to stop up and make watertight the seams of (a boat or ship) by driving in tarred oakum or cotton twist or wicking and filling up with a waterproofing compound **b :** to stop up and make tight against leakage (as the seams of a boat, the cracks in a window frame, or the joints of a pipe) by forcing in a sealing substance **c :** to tighten (a joint formed by overlapping or abutting metal plates) by driving the edge of one plate into closer contact with the surface of the other or by driving the edges of abutting plates together **2 :** to shape (the insole of a shoe) closely to the surface contours of the sole of the foot **~** *vi, slang* **:** to take a nap **:** SLEEP — used with *off*

²caulk *or* **calk** \"\ *n* -s [origin unknown] *slang* **:** a short sleep **:** NAP

³caulk *var of* CALK

caulk·en *var of* CALKIN

caulk·er *or* **calk·er** \'kȯkə(r)\ *n* -s [ME *calker,* fr. *calken* + *-er*] **1 :** a worker who forces sealing matter into seams or joints with a caulking tool to make them watertight **2 :** a tool for caulking; *specif* **:** a caulking iron operated by compressed air **3** *slang* **:** a drink of liquor **:** DRAM

caulking *or* **calking** *n* -s [ME *calking,* fr. gerund of *calken*] **1 :** the action of one that caulks **2 :** the material used to caulk

caulking iron *also* **caulking chisel** *or* **caulking tool** *n* **:** a chisellike tool used for caulking seams or joints; *specif* **:** a chisellike tool with a concave edge for receiving a caulking yarn and driving it into a seam

caulking mallet *n* **:** a wooden mallet with a very long head used for driving a caulking iron

caulk weld *n* **:** a weld that seals a joint

caulk-weld \'=,=\ *vt* **:** to unite by a caulk weld

caulo- — see CAUL-

cau·lo·bac·ter \'kȯlō,baktə(r)\ *n, cap* [NL, fr. *caul-* + *-bacter*] **:** a genus (the type of the family Caulobacteraceae) of gram-negative aquatic bacteria that are motile by polar flagella when young but later fixed to the substrate by a stalk and that multiply by transverse binary fission — **cau·lo·bac·te·ri·um** \¦==,=¦tirēəm\ *n*

cau·lo·bac·te·ra·ce·ae \¦==,=,tirə'āsē,ē\ *n pl, cap* [NL, fr. *Caulobacter,* type genus + *-aceae*] **:** a family of nonfilamentous free-living aquatic bacteria that form stalks or zoogleal masses of ferric hydroxide or gum and that are now usu. placed in the order Pseudomonadales though they are sometimes esp. in former classifications included in Enbacteriales or isolated in a separate order — see CAULOBACTER, CAULOBACTERALES

cau·lo·bac·te·ra·les \¦==,=tə'rā(,)lēz\ *n pl, cap* [NL, fr. *Caulobacter* + *-ales*] *in some classifications* **:** an order of bacteria coextensive with the family Caulobacteraceae

cau·lo·bac·te·ri·a·les \¦==,=,tirē'ā(,)lēz\ [NL, fr. *Caulobacter* + *-i-* + *-ales*] *syn of* CAULOBACTERALES

cau·lo·ca·line \,==¦kā,lēn\ *n* -s [*caul-* + *caline*] **:** a hormone or hormonelike factor distinct from auxin that is held to play a role in the formation of plant stems — compare RHIZOCALINE

cau·lo·car·pic \¦==¦kärpik\ *also* **cau·lo·car·pous** \-pəs\ *adj* [ISV *caul-* + *-carp* + *-ic* or *-ous*] **:** having stems that bear flowers and fruit year after year

cau·loid \'kȯ,lȯid\ *adj* [*caul-* + *-oid*] **:** resembling a stem

cauloid theory *n* **:** a theory of the origin of the sporophyte of vascular plants that proposes that the plant body has been differentiated from a primeval axis or stem — compare PROTOCORM THEORY

cau·lo·lat·i·lus \,==lad·ᵊləs\ *n, cap* [NL, fr. *caul-* + *latilus,* fr. L *latus* broad] **:** a genus of percoid fishes (family Branchiostegidae) including the ocean whitefish and other important food fishes — compare BLANQUILLO

cau·lome \'kȯ,lōm\ *n* -s [ISV *caul-* + *-ome;* prob. orig. formed as G *kaulom*] **:** a stem structure or stem axis of a plant — **cau·lo·mic** \(')kȯ¦lōmik, -äm-\ *adj*

cau·lo·phyl·line \,=='fi,lēn, -,lən\ *n* -s [NL *Caulophyllum* + E *-ine*] **:** a crystalline alkaloid $C_{12}H_{16}N_2O$ found in the root of the blue cohosh; methyl-cytisine

cau·lo·phyl·lum \,=='=,ləm\ *n, cap* [NL, fr. *caul-* + *-phyllum*] **:** a genus of herbs (family Berberidaceae) of eastern Asia and the eastern U.S. having a single sessile triternate basal leaf and a raceme of yellowish flowers succeeded by blue berries — see BLUE COHOSH

cau·lop·ter·is \kȯ'läptərəs\ *n* [NL, fr. *caul-* + *-pteris*] **1** *cap* **:** a genus of fossil tree ferns (family Marattiaceae) **2** *pl* **caulopter·es** \-,rēz\ **:** any fossil trunk of certain tree ferns

caulp *n* -s [ME *cawp,* prob. modif. of ScGael *colpach* heifer] **:** a fee or gift formerly given to the head of a Scottish clan for his maintenance and protection or exacted by him out of one's estate after death

cauls *pl of* CAUL

caup \'käp, -ȯ-\ *var of* ⁴CAP

cauponate *vt* -ED/-ING/-S [L *cauponatus,* past part. of *cauponari,* fr. *caupon-, caupo* huckster, innkeeper + *-atus* -ate — more at CHEAP] *obs* **:** to traffic in **:** HAWK

cau·qui \'kau̇(,)kē\ *n, pl* **cauqui** *or* **cauquis** *usu cap* [Sp, of AmerInd origin] **1 a :** an Indian people of central Peru **b :** a member of such people **2 :** the language of the Cauqui

caure \'kär, -ȯ-\ *n pl* [alter. of (assumed) ME *calver,* pl. fr. OE *calfur, cealfru,* pl. of *cealf* calf] *Scot* **:** CALVES

cauri *var of* CHOWRIE

cau·sa \'kau̇sə, -,zä, -,sä,-,zə; 'kȯzə\ *n, pl* **cau·sae** \'kau̇,sī, -,zī; 'kȯ,zē\ [L — more at CAUSE] **:** CAUSE — used in various Latin phrases

caus·a·ble \'kȯzəbəl\ *adj* **:** capable of being caused

¹caus·al \'kȯzəl\ *adj* [LL *causalis,* fr. L *causa* + *-alis* -al — more at CAUSE] **1 :** expressing or indicating cause **:** CAUSATIVE ⟨a ~ conjunction⟩ **2 :** of, relating to, or dealing with a cause ⟨the ~ part of the exposition⟩ **3 a :** constituting or acting as a cause ⟨whether any one of the factors is so predominant that it is the ~ force —John Dewey⟩ **b :** containing or involving cause or a cause **:** marked by cause and effect ⟨the relationship . . . was not one of ~ antecedence so much as one of analogous growth —H.O.Taylor⟩ **c :** arising from a cause **:** ensuing according to cause ⟨a ~ development⟩ — **caus·al·ly** \-əlē, -li\ *adv*

²causal \"\ *n* -s **:** a causal word or form

cau·sal·gia \kȯˈzalj(ē)ə, -ˈsa-\ *n* -s [NL, fr. Gk *kausos* fever + NL *-algia*; akin to Gk *kaiein* to burn — more at CAUSTIC] **:** a constant usu. burning pain resulting from injury to a peripheral nerve — **cau·sal·gic** \(ˈ)ˌ=ˈ=ˌ=\ *adj*

cau·sal·i·ty \kȯˈzaləd·ē, -ətē, -i\ *n* -ES [F *causalité,* fr. MF, fr. *causal* (fr. LL *causalis*) + *-ité* -ity] **1 :** a causal quality or agency ⟨the ~ of the divine mind —William Whewell⟩ **2 :** the relation of cause and effect or between certain regularly correlated events or phenomena: as **a :** a necessary connection or intrinsic bond embedded in the very nature of things **b :** the regular sequence of events that the mind connects from habit, innate disposition, or experience or that it correlates on the basis of scientifically elaborated theories

causal necessity *n* **:** NECESSITY 1d(2)

cau·sa·tion \kȯˈzāshən\ *n* -s [ML *causation-, causatio,* fr. *causatus* (past part. of *causare* to cause, fr. L *causa*) + L *-ion-, -io* -ion] **1 a :** the act or process of causing ⟨scientific ~ means that nothing happens arbitrarily but always as the result of a definite chain of causes —H.P.Becker⟩ **b :** the act or agency by which an effect is produced ⟨in a complex situation ~ is likely to be multiple —W.O.Aydelotte⟩ **2 :** the relation of cause and effect **:** CAUSALITY ⟨the law of ~ . . . is but the familiar truth that invariability of succession is found by observation to obtain between every fact in nature and some other fact which has preceded it —J.S.Mill⟩

cau·sa·tion·al \-shənᵊl, -shnəl\ *adj* **:** of or relating to causes, causation, or the doctrine of causation

cau·sa·tion·ism \-shəˌnizəm\ *n* -s **:** the principle or law of universal causation

cau·sa·tion·ist \-sh(ə)nəst\ *n* -s **:** a believer in causationism

¹caus·a·tive \ˈkȯzəd·iv, -ətiv\ *adj* [ME, fr. LL *causativus,* fr. L *causa* + *-atus* -ate + *-ivus* -ive] **1 :** effective or operating as a cause or agent **:** CAUSING ⟨poverty as a ~ factor in crime⟩ **2** *of a linguistic form or set of linguistic forms* **:** expressing cause ⟨~ case⟩ ⟨~ mood⟩; *specif* **:** indicating that the subject of a verb causes an act to be performed or a condition to come into being ⟨the ~ verb *fell,* meaning "cause to fall"⟩ ⟨the ~ suffix *-en* in *darken,* meaning "cause to be dark"⟩ — **caus·a·tive·ly** *adv* — **caus·a·tiv·i·ty** \ˌkȯzəˈtivəd·ē, -ətē, -i\ *n* -ES

²causative \"\ *n* -s **:** a causative word or form

cau·sa·tum \kau̇ˈzäd·əm, kȯˈzād-\ *n, pl* **causa·ta** \-d·ə\ [ML, neut. of *causatus,* past part. of *causare* to cause — more at CAUSATION] **:** something that is caused **:** EFFECT

¹cause \ˈkȯz\ *n* -s [ME, fr. OF, fr. L *causa;* perh. akin to L *cudere* to beat — more at HEW] **1 a :** a person, thing, fact, or condition that brings about an effect or that produces or calls forth a resultant action or state ⟨it should be obvious that it is the conditions producing the end effects which must be regarded as the efficient ~s of them —M.F.A.Montagu⟩ ⟨trying to find the ~ of the accident⟩ **b :** a reason or motive for an action or condition ⟨a ~ for celebrating⟩ ⟨~ for regret⟩ **c :** a good or adequate reason **:** a sufficient activating factor ⟨an employee discharged for ~⟩ **2 a** (1) **:** a ground of legal action (2) **:** a legal process (as a suit or action in court) by which a party endeavors to obtain his claim or what he regards as his right **:** CASE **b :** the presupposition or underlying fact of a transaction in civil law **3 a :** something that occasions or effects a result **:** the necessary antecedent of an effect **:** something that determines any motion or change or produces a phenomenon — see EFFICIENT CAUSE, FINAL CAUSE, FORMAL CAUSE, MATERIAL CAUSE; FIRST CAUSE; IMMANENT CAUSE, TRANSIENT CAUSE; OCCASIONAL CAUSE **b :** an event or set of events that on the basis of scientific methods and laws has been established as the invariant antecedent or concomitant necessary for the occurrence of another event or set of events — compare REGULARITY THEORY **4 :** a charge or accusation brought against one ⟨what was thy ~? adultery? —Shak.⟩ **5 a** *now dial* **:** a matter occupying one's attention **:** CONCERN, AFFAIR, PURSUIT ⟨now to our French ~s —Shak.⟩ **b** *obs* **:** INTENT, PURPOSE, END — see FINAL CAUSE **6 :** a principle or movement supported militantly or zealously **:** a belief advocated or upheld ⟨God befriend us, as our ~ is just —Shak.⟩ ⟨the insurgents' ~⟩ ⟨he served the ~ of truth less devotedly than the ~ of party —V.L.Parrington⟩ **7** *obs* **:** DISEASE

syn REASON, DETERMINANT, OCCASION, ANTECEDENT: CAUSE indicates a condition or circumstance or combination of conditions and circumstances that effectively and inevitably calls forth an issue, effect, or result or that materially aids in that calling forth ⟨there was more in it than a struggle for wages. The unrest in the towns had deeper *causes* —G.M.Trevelyan⟩ REASON is often interchangeable with CAUSE, but it may add to CAUSE notions of that which explains, clarifies, or justifies or that which suggests a conditioning by human action, consideration, or thought ⟨they admire the rich and titled for the good *reason* that the rich and titled are themselves —Aldous Huxley⟩ ⟨the *reason* why the distinguished chairman of the committee feels that the conference report should not be debated —*Congressional Record*⟩ DETERMINANT indicates that factor which determines or shapes the nature of an outcome, issue, or result rather than indicating that which calls it forth or causes it ⟨so habituated have most persons become to believing . . . that moral forces are the ultimate *determinants* of the rise and fall of all human societies —John Dewey⟩ ⟨asserts that the final *determinant* of the lawyer's thought and activity is now the maxim of the best fee —R.D.Mack⟩ OCCASION refers to a time or situation at which underlying causes may be manifested or activated or, loosely, to an immediate or ostensible factor ⟨in 1837 Baxley became the *occasion,* if not the cause, of the temporary disruption of the University of Maryland Medical School —C.R.Bardeen⟩ ⟨there exists, not as the *occasion* of this war but as the cause of a series of wars in which we are engaged, a desire, shared by all peoples, to redefine the concepts of freedom and order —*Times Lit. Supp.*⟩ ANTECEDENT refers to that which has preceded or gone before or which may or may not be a cause or determinant of something following ⟨it is certainly true that these twelfth-century windows break the French tradition. They had no *antecedent* and no fit succession —Henry Adams⟩ ⟨the *antecedents* of emperor worship lay far back in history —John Buchan⟩

²cause \"\ *vt* -ED/-ING/-S [ME *causen,* prob. fr. *cause, n.*] **1 :** to serve as cause or occasion of **:** bring into existence **:** MAKE ⟨careless driving ~s accidents⟩ ⟨trying to find what *caused* the fire⟩ ⟨~ the water to flow into the new channel⟩ **2 :** to effect by command, authority, or force ⟨the president *caused* the ambassador to protest⟩

'cause \(ˈ)kȯz, (ˌ)kəz\ *conj* [by shortening] **:** BECAUSE

cause cé·lè·bre \ˌkȯzsāˈlebr(ᵊ), ˌkōz-, -eb(rə)\ *n, pl* **causes célèbres** \-br(ᵊ), -b(rəz)\ [F] **1 :** a celebrated legal case **:** a case whose resolutions excite widespread interest **2 :** a notorious incident or episode **:** a situation attracting much attention ⟨the paper made the controversy a *cause célèbre* —S.H. Adams⟩

cause·less \ˈkȯzləs\ *adj* **1 :** having no cause or no apparent cause **:** FORTUITOUS **:** inexplicable by natural causes ⟨a ~ miracle⟩ **2 :** having no justifying reason or motive ⟨a senseless, ~ murder⟩ ⟨~ war that never had an aim —William Morris⟩ — **cause·less·ly** *adv*

cause list *n* **:** a legal calendar

cause of action : the ground on which the plaintiff's case is based

caus·er \ˈkȯzə(r)\ *n* -s **:** one that causes ⟨a ~ of disease⟩

cau·se·rie \ˌkōz(ə)ˈrē, ˈkōzəˌrē\ *n* -s [F, fr. *causer* to chat, fr. L *causari* to plead, discuss, debate, fr. *causa* cause — more at CAUSE] **1 :** an informal light conversation **:** CHAT **2 :** a short familiar composition in informal style ⟨~s and light sketches⟩

cau·seur \kōˈzər\ *n* -s [F, fr. *causer* + *-eur* -or] **:** a fluent and often witty talker or conversationalist

cau·seuse \kōˈzə(r)z, -zə̄z\ *n* -s [F, lit., talkative woman, fem. of *causeur*] **:** a small sofa for two persons **:** TÊTE-À-TÊTE

¹cause·way \ˈkȯzˌwā\ *n* [alter. of ME *cauciwey,* fr. *cauci,* cause causey + *wey* way — more at WAY] **1 :** a way of access or raised road typically across marshland or water ⟨for access to the mainland they depended on a ~, flooded at high tide —F.M.Stenton⟩ **2 :** CAUSEY; *esp* **:** a paved or corduroy highway ⟨the Roman ~s of early Britain⟩

²causeway \"\ *vt* -ED/-ING/-S **1 :** to pave with cobblestones or pebbles ⟨the ~*ed* streets of the village⟩ **2 :** to provide with a causeway **:** make a causeway through or over ⟨a ~*ed* swamp⟩

¹cau·sey \ˈkȯz|ē, *dial Brit also* -ōs| *or* |ä *or* |ə\ *n* -s [ME *cauci, cause,* fr. ONF *caucie, caucíée,* fr. ML *calciata* paved highway, fr. *calciata,* fem. of *calciatus* paved with limestone, fr. L *calc-, calx* limestone, lime + *-atus* -ate — more at CHALK] **1** *obs* **:** a mound retaining water **:** an earth dam **2 :** a raised way of access (as a road or sidewalk) typically across wet land or water **:** CAUSEWAY **3 a** *dial* **:** a paved way (as a street or sidewalk) **b** *dial Brit* **:** an area (as part of a farmyard) paved with cobblestones **4** *obs* **:** HIGHWAY; *esp* **:** a highway of or like those of ancient Roman construction in Britain

²causey \"\ *vt* -ED/-ING/-S *dial* **:** to pave esp. with stones or logs

causing *pres part of* CAUSE

causse \ˈkōs\ *n* -s [F, fr. Prov, fr. (assumed) VL *calcinus* of limestone, fr. L *calc-, calx* + *-inus* -ine] **:** a small limestone plateau deeply pitted with sinkholes common in south-central France

¹caus·tic \ˈkȯstik, -ēk\ *adj* [L *causticus,* fr. Gk *kaustikos,* fr. *kaustos* (verbal of *kaiein* to burn) + *-ikos* -ic; akin to Lith *kulė̃* smut of plants] **1 :** capable of destroying the texture of anything or eating away its substance by chemical action **:** CORROSIVE: as **a :** capable of destroying animal or other organic tissue ⟨silver nitrate and sulfuric acid are ~ agents⟩ **b :** strongly alkaline ⟨~ liquors⟩ ⟨~ lyes⟩ **2 :** marked by or indicative of tart sharpness; *specif* **:** characterized by incisive wit ⟨a ~ reply⟩ ⟨a bitter, ~, and backbiting humor —Sir Walter Scott⟩ ⟨a ~ and disillusioned satirist, trenchant, arrogant —J.L.Lowes⟩ — **caus·ti·cal·ly** \-tək(ə)lē, -ēk-, -li\ *or* **caus·tic·ly** \-klē, -kli\ *adv* — **caus·tic·ness** \-tiknəs, -tēk-\ *n* -ES

²caustic \"\ *n* -s **1 :** a caustic agent: as **a :** a substance or means that can burn, corrode, or destroy animal or other organic tissue by chemical action **:** ESCHAROTIC **b :** CAUSTIC ALKALI **2 a :** CAUSTIC CURVE **b :** CAUSTIC SURFACE

caustic alcohol *n* **:** SODIUM ETHOXIDE

caustic alkali *n* **:** a strong corrosive alkali; *esp* **:** a hydroxide of an alkali metal (as caustic soda or caustic potash)

caustic ammonia *n* **:** ammonia esp. in water solution

caustic baryta *n* **:** BARIUM HYDROXIDE — used esp. commercially

caustic creeper *n* [so called fr. the caustic quality of fresh latex] **:** an Australian euphorbia (*Euphorbia drummondii*) — called also *milk plant*

caustic curve *n* **:** a plane section through the cusp of a caustic surface that is visible on a plane surface where light has been reflected from a smooth concave surface (as the inside of a metal ring)

caus·tic·i·ty \kȯˈstisəd·ē, -ətē, -i\ *n* -ES [F *causticité,* fr. L *causticus* + F *-ité* -ity] **1 :** the quality or state of being caustic **:** CORROSIVENESS ⟨the ~ of potash⟩ **2 :** dry tart sharpness esp. of biting wit ⟨the ~ of his retort⟩

caus·ti·ci·za·tion \ˌkȯstəsəˈzāshən, -ˌsīˈz-\ *n* -s **:** the process of causticizing

caus·ti·cize \ˈkȯstəˌsīz\ *vt* -ED/-ING/-S [*caustic* + *-ize*] **1 :** to make caustic; *esp* **:** to convert (alkaline carbonate) into a hydroxide by the use of lime **2 :** to treat (textiles) with caustic alkali — compare MERCERIZE

caus·ti·ciz·er \-zə(r)\ *n* -s **1 :** a chemical worker who makes caustic soda by controlling chemical reactions of soda ash and milk of lime in a dissolving tank and a reactor **2 :** one who makes caustic liquor for digesting wood chips into pulp by mixing and heating lime, soda ash, and water in a wooden vat

caustic lime *n* **:** LIME 2a

caustic man *or* **caustic mixer** *n* [²*caustic*] **:** a worker who mixes caustic-soda solution for use in cloth-finishing or yarn-finishing processes

caustic potash *n* **:** POTASSIUM HYDROXIDE — used esp. commercially

caustic soda *n* **:** SODIUM HYDROXIDE — used esp. commercially

caustic surface *n* **:** the cusped surface of maximum brightness that is sometimes observed when light is refracted or reflected by a curved mirror or interface and is geometrically the envelope of the system of refracted or reflected rays

caustic vine *or* **caustic plant** *n* **:** an Australian vine (*Sarcostemma australe*) of the family Asclepiadaceae that is poisonous to cattle

cau·sus \ˈkȯzəs, -ōsəs\ *n, cap* [NL, fr. Gk *kausos* fever, heat, fr. *kaiein* to burn — more at CAUSTIC] **:** a genus of nocturnal venomous African snakes (family Viperidae) comprising the night adders

cautel *n* -s [ME, fr. MF *cautele,* fr. L *cautela* caution, precaution, fr. *cautus,* past part. of *cavēre* to be on one's guard — more at SHOW] **1** *obs* **a :** TRICK **b :** TRICKERY ⟨no soil nor ~ doth besmirch the virtue of his will —Shak.⟩ **2** *obs* **a :** CAUTION **b :** PRECAUTION

cautelous *adj* [ME, fr. MF *cauteleux, cautileus,* fr. *cautele* + *-eux, -eus* -ous] **1** *archaic* **:** CRAFTY, CUNNING **2** *archaic* **:** CAUTIOUS, WARY — **cautelously** *adv, archaic*

cau·ter \ˈkȯd·ə(r)\ *n* -s [earlier *cautere,* fr. MF *cautère,* fr. L *cauterium* — more at CAUTERY] **:** an iron for cauterizing **:** CAUTERY

¹cau·ter·ant \ˈkȯd·ərənt\ *n* -s [*cauter-* + *-ant*] **:** a cauterizing substance

²cauterant \"\ *adj* **:** CAUTERIZING

cau·ter·i·za·tion \ˌkȯd·ərəˈzāshən, -ōtər-, -ˌrīˈz-\ *n* -s [MF *cautérisation,* fr. *cautériser* + *-ation*] **1 :** the act of searing abnormal or injured tissue by a cautery **2 :** the effect of cauterization

cau·ter·ize \ˈkȯd·əˌrīz, -ōtə-\ *vt* -ED/-ING/-S [MF *cautériser,* fr. LL *cauterizare* to brand, fr. L *cauterium* + LL *-izare* -ize] **1 :** to burn or sear with a cautery or caustic ⟨~ a wound⟩ **2** *obs* **:** BRAND **3 :** to make insensible **:** DEADEN

cau·tery \-ərē, -ri\ *n* -ES [L *cauterium* cautery, branding iron, fr. Gk *kautērion* branding iron, fr. *kaiein* to burn — more at CAUSTIC] **1 :** a burning or searing (as of abnormal or injured tissue) with a hot iron or caustic **2 :** the hot iron, caustic, or other agent used to burn, sear, or destroy tissue

cau·tio \ˈkōshēˌō, ˈkau̇d·ēˌō\ *n, pl* **cauti·o·nes** \-shēˈōˌnēz, -d·ēˈōˌnās\ [L] *Roman, Scots, & civil law* **:** an oral or written agreement to indemnify **:** GUARANTY: **a :** a written assurance given as evidence of the receipt of money or as an acknowledgment of the making of a promise or of an existing state of affairs **b :** an agreement by one furnishing security, a pledge, or a mortgage **c :** an agreement often imposed by a judge or magistrate whereby one guarantees to protect another from loss or harm caused by the guarantor or a third person for whom the guarantor is responsible or whereby one guarantees payment or performance of an obligation of another

¹cau·tion \ˈkȯshən\ *n* -s [ME *caucioun,* fr. OF *caution,* fr. L *caution-, cautio,* fr. *cautus,* past part. of *cavēre* to be on one's guard) + *-ion-, -io* -ion — more at SHOW] **1 a :** security for the performance of an obligation (as bail, a guarantee, or a pledge) **b :** the person giving such security **:** SURETY — called also *cautionary* **2** *obs* **:** a contingent provision **:** RESERVATION, SAVING CLAUSE ⟨with the ~ that the procedure be found legal⟩ **3 :** a warning or admonishment esp. in counseling vigilance, due attention or consideration, safety, or reservation ⟨the first ~ which we shall do well to bear in mind is that religion is not always true or good —W.R.Inge⟩ **4 :** the action of taking heed **:** PRECAUTION ⟨a surgeon taking the ~ of sterilizing his equipment⟩ **5 :** heedful prudent forethought to minimize risk or danger **:** provident care about the results of an action or course **:** careful avoidance of undue risk **:** reserve in acceptance ⟨my dear Percy's wonderful ~ . . . a thing that no mere reckless woman can hope to emulate —Rose Macaulay⟩ ⟨a difficult climb, safe but requiring ~ —*Amer. Guide Series: Calif.*⟩ **6 :** a preparatory warning of a maneuver or direction given prior to a decisive command (as *forward* preceding the command *march*) **7 a :** one that arouses alarm or astonishment or commands attention or interest **:** an extreme or grotesque example ⟨a fun-loving life of the party, a real ~⟩ **b :** an incident or example that startles and may serve as a check, admonition, or incentive ⟨the way he drove was a ~⟩

²caution \"\ *vt* **cautioned; cautioned; cautioning** \-sh(ə)niŋ\ **cautions :** to advise caution to **:** admonish or put on guard typically against danger, carelessness, imprudence, or excess ⟨we . . . while experience ~s us in vain, grasp seeming happiness and find it pain —William Cowper⟩ **syn** see WARN

¹cau·tion·ary \ˈkȯshəˌnerē, -ri\ *adj* **1 :** of, relating to, or constituting a cautio or a caution **2** *archaic* **:** characterized by caution **:** CAUTIOUS, WARY **3 :** having the characteristics of, serving as, or offering a caution **:** ADMONITORY ⟨a warmly human story rather than the usual mere ~ tale intended to warn us —J.W.Krutch⟩

²cautionary \"\ *n* -ES **:** SECURITY, SURETY, CAUTION

cau·tion·er \ˈkȯsh(ə)nə(r)\ *n* -s [¹*caution* + *-er*] **:** SURETY, GUARANTOR

cautiones *pl of* CAUTIO

caution money *n* **:** money deposited by a student on entering a British university typically as security for possible damages (as to laboratory equipment)

cau·tion·ry \ˈkȯshənrē\ *n* -ES [*caution* + *-ry*] **:** SURETYSHIP

cau·tious \ˈkȯshəs\ *adj* [¹*caution* + *-ous*] **:** marked by caution, by careful prudence in reducing risk or danger, and by reluctance to proceed or advance rashly ⟨~ in all his movements, always acting as if surrounded by invisible spies—W.H. Hudson †1922⟩ ⟨too ~ and too conservative to seek any revolutionary end —V.L.Parrington⟩

syn CIRCUMSPECT, WARY, CHARY, CALCULATING: CAUTIOUS may suggest limited objectives, prudence and forethought in proceeding, and fear of failure, danger, or harm ⟨meek, humble, timid persons . . . , who are *cautious,* prudent, and submissive, leave things very much as they find them —A.C. Benson⟩ ⟨we were *cautious* in keeping to windward of them, their sense of smell and hearing being . . . extremely acute —Herman Melville⟩ ⟨*cautious,* deliberate, methodical, he was in no danger, she felt, of plunging precipitately into marriage —Ellen Glasgow⟩ Without connoting fear, as CAUTIOUS does, CIRCUMSPECT stresses prudence, discretion, vigilance, and consideration of consequences ⟨the packages were examined by the police and found to contain bombs . . . for the next few days people in high station were very *circumspect* about undoing brown paper packages —F.L.Allen⟩ ⟨they do not live very happy lives, for they even more than the others are restricted in their movements, and they must live the most *circumspect* of lives —John Steinbeck⟩ WARY implies suspicious alertness to danger, difficulty, or loss, and cunning in escaping or evading it ⟨a *wary* old rabbit stealing out at dawn with quivering nose and oscillating ears —Kenneth Roberts⟩ ⟨we must always be *wary* of those who with sounding brass and tinkling cymbal preach the 'ism' of appeasement —F.D. Roosevelt⟩ ⟨girls like her . . . , wild and lost and lonely, full of distrust, letting him approach with a *wary* look in their eyes as if they would dash away before he could touch them —Katherine A. Porter⟩ CHARY stresses hesitancy, reserve, and discretion in proceeding ⟨the high priests were *chary* of adding tumult to tumult, and they did not dare to take action against Reb Jacob —Maurice Samuel⟩ ⟨contempt for the chattering fool runs through the *Edda.* Let a man be *chary* of speech —H.O.Taylor⟩ ⟨my business experience has taught me to be *chary* of committing anything of a confidential nature to any more concrete medium than speech —William Faulkner⟩ CALCULATING stresses very deliberate and careful planning ⟨Aunt Ella, ostensibly meek, confused, helpless, and self-effacing, has actually a steel core of *calculating* purposiveness and a genius for devious expedients; under the appearance of tender sisterly devotion she fights by methods of sly sabotage a lifelong duel —Wilson Follett⟩ Sometimes this word connotes not care and caution but a cold-blooded objectivity approaching disdain of and even cruelty to others ⟨that selfish and *calculating* principle has taken . . . the form of a national and racial egoism that has turned a continent into a shambles —J.L.Lowes⟩

cau·tious·ly *adv* **:** in a cautious manner

cau·tious·ness *n* -ES **:** the quality or state of being cautious

cautivo *var of* CATIVO

cav *abbr* **1** cavalier **2** cavalry **3** caveat **4** cavity

¹ca·va \ˈkävə, ˈkä-,ˈkā-\ *n, pl* **ca·vae** \ˈkäˌvē, ˈkā-, -ˌvī; ˈkāˌvē\ **:** VENA CAVA — **ca·val** \-vəl\ *adj*

²cava *var of* KAVA

³cava *pl of* CAVUM

¹cav·al·cade \ˌkavəlˈkād\ *n* -s [MF, ride on horseback, fr. OIt *cavalcata,* fr. *cavalcare* to go on horseback, fr. LL *caballicare,* fr. L *caballus* horse, nag; akin to Gk dial. (Black sea) *kaballeion* horse-drawn vehicle, OSlav *kobyla* horse; all perh. of eastern European origin; akin to the source of Finn *hepo* horse] **1 a :** a procession of riders or carriages **:** a company in procession **b :** a train, procession, or sequence of vehicles or ships **2 :** a dramatic sequence or pageant **:** PROCESSION, SERIES ⟨the ~ of years⟩ ⟨the ~ of scientific research⟩

²cavalcade \"\ *vi* -ED/-ING/-S **:** to take part in a cavalcade ⟨horsemen *cavalcading* along⟩

¹cav·a·lier \ˌkavəˈli(ə)r, -iə\ *n* -s [MF, fr. OIt *cavaliere,* fr. OProv *cavalier,* fr. LL *caballarius* groom, hostler, fr. L *caballus* + *-arius* -ary] **1 :** a raised fortified structure usu. rising from the middle of a bastion but sometimes erected by besiegers and designed to command the enemy's works **2 :** a gentleman trained in arms and manege **:** a gallant courtly soldier **3 :** a mounted soldier of rank, often colorful and with romantic appeal **:** KNIGHT **4** *usu cap* **a :** an adherent of Charles I of England as contrasted with a supporter of parliament **:** ROYALIST **b :** a Southerner of the plantation-owning class; *specif* **:** VIRGINIAN **5 :** a lady's escort or dancing partner **:** GALLANT

²cavalier \"\ *vi* -ED/-ING/-S **1 :** to play the cavalier **2 :** to act in a cavalier manner

³cavalier \"\ *adj* **1 :** insouciant and debonair **2 :** marked by lofty disregard of others' interests, rights, or feelings **:** high-handed and arrogant or supercilious **:** given to airy dismissal of things worthy of attention ⟨~ in his methods, too lordly over appointments and forgotten promises —F.Tennyson Jesse⟩ ⟨~ ignoring of his arguments⟩ **3 a** *usu cap* **:** of or relating to the party of Charles I of England **:** ROYALIST ⟨an old *Cavalier* family⟩ **b :** marked by colorful self-confident affluence **:** ARISTOCRATIC ⟨older middle-class Virginia . . . being superseded by a ~ Virginia —V.L.Parrington⟩ **c** *usu cap* **:** of, relating to, or resembling the work of the English Cavalier poets of the mid-17th century **:** valuing courtliness, urbanity, and polish **d :** imitative of the flaring ornamental dress of the Cavaliers ⟨a ~ cuff⟩ — **cav·a·lier·ness** *n* -ES

ca·va·lie·re \ˌkavəlˈyerē\ *n, pl* **cavalieres** \-rēz\ *or* **cava·lie·ri** \-rē\ [It] **1 :** CAVALIER **2 :** CAVALIER SERVENTE

cav·a·lier·ism \ˌkavəˈlirizəm\ *n* -s *often cap* **:** the practice or principles of cavaliers, esp. of the 17th century Cavaliers

cav·a·lier·ly \ˌ=ˈ=ˈli(ə)rlē, -iəl-, -li\ *adv* **:** in a cavalier manner

ca·va·lier ser·vant \kävälyāserväⁿ, ˌkavəˌli(ə)rˈsərvənt\ *n* [trans. of It *cavalier servente*] **:** CAVALIER SERVENTE

ca·va·lier ser·ven·te \ˌkävälˈye(ə)rsərˈventē, ˌkav-\ *or* **ca·va·lie·re servente** \-ˌyerēsər-\ *n, pl* **cavalie·ri serven·ti** \-ˌyerē...ntē\ [It, lit., serving cavalier] **:** LOVER, GALLANT

ca·va·lier seul \kävälyāsœl\ *n, pl* **cavaliers seuls** [F, lit., gentleman alone] **:** a quadrille figure performed in turn by each man of two opposite couples while the other man and the women face him

ca·val·la \kəˈvalə, -ˈvīə\ *n, pl* **cavalla** *or* **cavallas** [Sp *caballa,* a fish, fr. LL, mare, fem. of L *caballus* horse — more at CAVALCADE] **1 :** CERO **2** *also* **ca·val·ly** -ES **:** any of various fishes of *Caranx* or other closely related genera — compare CREVALLE

cavalla (*Caranx hippos*)

ca·val·let·ti \ˌkavəˈled·ē\ *n* -s [It *cavalletti,* pl. of *cavalletto,* lit., little horse, dim. of *cavallo* horse, fr. L *caballus*] **:** a series of timber jumps that are adjustable in height for schooling horses

cavallo *var of* CABALLO

cav·al·ry \'kavəlrē, -ri\ *n* -ES *often attrib* [It *cavalleria* cavalry, chivalry, fr. *cavaliere* cavalier + *-ia* -y — more at CAVALIER] **1 a** *obs* : HORSEMANSHIP ⟨the art of ~⟩ **b** *obs* : KNIGHTHOOD ⟨the ~ of the court⟩ **c** : HORSEMEN ⟨a thousand ~ in flight⟩ **2 a** (1) : the component of an army that maneuvers and fights on horseback (2) : a similar component that maneuvers on horseback but fights on foot **b** : the component of an army mounted on horseback or moving in motor vehicles and having combat missions (as reconnaissance and counterreconnaissance) that require great mobility **3** : DEEP CHROME YELLOW

cavalry bone *n* : RIDER'S BONE

cav·al·ry·man \-mən, -,man, -,maa(ə)n\ *n, pl* **cavalrymen** : a cavalry soldier

cavalry twill *n* : a sturdy suiting usu. woolen or worsted but sometimes cotton or rayon, woven of tightly twisted yarns in a steep double twill, and similar to elastique but with a coarser raised cord effect

1ca·van \kə'vän\ *or* **ca·ban** \-'b-\ *n, pl* **cavans** \-änz\ *or* **cava·nes** *or* **caba·nes** \-ä,näs\ [PhilSp *caván, cabán,* fr. Tag *kabán,* lit., trunk, coffer] : a Philippine unit of dry measure equal to 2.13 bushels

2cav·an \'kavən\ *adj, usu cap* [fr. *Cavan,* county in Ireland] : of or from County Cavan, Ireland : of the kind or style prevalent in County Cavan

ca·va·qui·nho \,kavə'kē(,)nyü\ *n* -S [Pg, dim. of *cavaco* piece of wood, fr. *cavar* to dig out, hollow out, fr. L *cavare* to hollow out] : a Brazilian stringed musical instrument somewhat smaller than a ukulele

cav·a·scope \'kavə,skōp\ *n* -S [*cava-* (fr. L *cavus* hollow) + *-scope*] : an instrument for illuminating bodily cavities (as the throat)

ca·vate \'kā,vāt\ *adj* [L *cavatus,* past part. of *cavare* to hollow out] : cut in soft rock : EXCAVATED ⟨~ cliff dwelling⟩

cav·a·ti·na \,kavə'tēnə, ,kä-\ *n* -S [It, fr. *cavata* production of sound, fr. *cavare* to extract, dig out, fr. L, to hollow out, fr. *cavus* hollow] **1** : an operatic solo that is simpler and briefer than an aria **2** : a sustained melody

cav·a·yard \'kavə,yärd\ *or* **cavy·yard** \-vē,y-\ *n* -S [modif. of Sp *caballada,* fr. *caballo* horse (fr. L *caballus*) + *-ada* -ade — more at CAVALCADE] *West* : REMUDA

1cave \'kāv\ *n* -S *often attrib* [ME, fr. OF, fr. L *cava,* fr. *cavus* hollow; akin to OE *hyse* young man, ON *hūnn* bear cub, Gk *koilos* hollow, *kyein* to be pregnant, Skt *śvayati* he swells, *śāva* young of an animal; basic meaning: hollow, swelling] **1** : a hollowed-out chamber in the earth or in the side of a cliff or hill : CAVERN; *esp* : a natural underground chamber (as one produced in limestone by running water) with an opening to the surface **2 a** : an underground chamber or recess for storage or safety; *esp* : an outdoor cellar dug or natural ⟨if she had bacon in the ~ —Willa Cather⟩ **b** : a cached supply ⟨selling the ~s of wine⟩ **3** *Brit* **a** : the act of secession from a political party **b** : a group of persons seceding from a political party — compare ADULLAMITE **4** : a tunnel under a glass furnace used for raking the fire, removing ashes, or regulating heat **5** : a heavily shielded enclosure for radioactive experiments controlled and observed from outside

2cave \"\ *vb* -ED/-ING/-S [prob. fr. MF *caver,* fr. L *cavare*] *vt* : to form a cave in or under : HOLLOW, UNDERMINE ⟨the waters *caving* the banks⟩ ~ *vi* : to explore caves

3cave \"\ *vt* -ED/-ING/-S [ME (northern dial.) *caven,* fr. *caf* chaff (in other dialects *chaf, chef*) — more at CHAFF] *now dial* : to separate (as grain) from chaff

4cave \"\ *vb* -ED/-ING/-S [perh. fr. ON *kafa* to dive — more at BAPTIZE] *vi* **1** *dial Brit* : OVERTURN **2** *Midland* : to be noisily and demonstratively angry ~ *vt* **1** *dial Brit* : to tilt over **2** *dial Brit* : to give a toss to (the head) **3** *dial Brit* : PLUNGE

5cave \"\ *vb* -ED/-ING/-S [prob. alter. (influenced by ²*cave*) of *calve*] *vi* **1** : to fall in or down esp. from being undermined — usu. used with *in* ⟨the road *caved* in above the old mine⟩ **2** : to collapse esp. from exhaustion — usu. used with *in* ⟨the challenger *caved* in during the seventh round⟩ **3** : to cease to resist : become forceless or disorganized : admit defeat or culpability : SUBMIT — usu. used with *in* ⟨the defenders *caved* in and surrendered⟩ ~ *vt* **1** : to cause to fall or collapse — usu. used with *in* ⟨the floodwaters *caved* in the retaining wall⟩ **2** : to smash in or down — usu. used with *in* ⟨a car with its fenders *caved in*⟩

6cave \"\ *n* -S [⁵*cave*] : the action of caving in or being caved in

7cave *adj* [MF & L; MF, fr. L *cavus* hollow] *obs* : CONCAVE, HOLLOW

ca·vea \'kāvēə, 'kā-\ *n, pl* **cave·ae** \'kāvē,ī, 'kāvē,ē\ [L — more at CAGE] : the tiered semicircular seating space of an ancient theater

caveare *obs var of* CAVIAR

cave art *n* : the art of Paleolithic man represented by drawings and paintings on the walls of caves esp. in Europe

1ca·ve·at \'kāvē,at, 'kāvē,ät, -ēət, *often* -d·+V\ *n* -S [L, let him beware, 3d pers. sing. pres. subj. of *cavēre* to be on one's guard — more at SHOW] **1** : CAUTION: **a** : a warning enjoining one from certain acts or practices ⟨a ~ against unfair practices⟩ **b** : a cautionary explanation to prevent misinterpretation ⟨to enter a ~ about the sense in which a word is used⟩ **2** : a legal notice given by an interested party to some officer not to do a certain act until the party is heard in opposition ⟨a ~ entered in a probate court to stop the proving of a will⟩

2caveat \"\ *vi* ED/-ING/-S : to enter a caveat

ca·ve·a·tee \¦==¦tē\ *n* -S [²*caveat* + *-ee*] : one against whose interest a caveat is entered or filed

caveat emp·tor \¦==,ad·'em(p)tər, -,äd--,-,əd--, -,tȯ(ə)r\ *n* [NL, let the buyer beware] : a warning principle in trading: the purchaser should be alert to see that he gets the quality and the quantity he is paying for

ca·ve·at·or \'==,ad·ər, -,äd·ər, ¦==¦tȯ(ə)r\ *n* -S [²*caveat* + *-or*] : one that enters or files a caveat

cave bat *n* : any of various cave-dwelling bats; *esp* : a member of a No. American genus (*Antrozous*)

cave bear *n* : a very large extinct bear (*Ursus spelaeus*) known from remains in caves in Europe and England and believed to be contemporaneous with Paleolithic man

cave beetle *n* : any of various cave-inhabiting beetles without eyes or with degenerate eyes

cave cricket *n* : any of several wingless cricketlike grasshoppers (family Stenopelmatidae) found in caves or other dark moist places — compare STONE CRICKET

caved *past of* CAVE

cave dweller *n* **1** : one that dwells in a cave; *esp* : a prehistoric man whose remains and utensils have been discovered in ancient caves **2** : a city dweller

cave earth *n* : the residual accumulation of insoluble materials on the floor of a cave, many of such deposits being covered with a layer of stalagmite and some of them containing remains of extinct animals

cave fish *n* : any of various fishes found in cave waters having usu. vestigial and functionless eyes — compare BLINDFISH

cave hunter *n* : a caveman subsisting by hunting rather than by agriculture

cave hyena *n* : an extinct hyena whose remains are found abundantly in British caves and now usu. regarded as a large variety of the living African spotted hyena

cave–in \'=,=\ *n* -S **1** : the action of caving in : ⁶CAVE **2** : a place where earth has caved in

1cav·el \'kavəl, -ev-,-äv-\ *n* -S [ME, fr. MD *kavele;* akin to ON *kefli* stick of wood — more at KEVEL] *dial Brit* : a lot determined by a cast

2cavel \"\ *vt* **cavelled; cavelled; cavelling** \-v(ə)liŋ, -ləŋ\ **cavels** *dial Brit* : to allot or apportion according to lots cast ⟨the working positions *cavelled* by the miners⟩

3cavel *n* -S [ME *kevell,* perh. fr. ON *kefli* stick of wood] *obs* : a mean fellow

4cavel *var of* KEVEL

cave lion *n* : a lion known from remains found in European and English caves and believed to be an extinct variety of the existing lion

cave locust *n* : WETA

cave·man *in senses 1 & 2* 'kāv,man *or* -aa(ə)n, *in senses 3 & 4* " *or* -,mən\ *n, pl* **cavemen** **1** : a cave dweller esp. of the Stone Age — compare PALEOLITHIC MAN **2** : a man who acts with rough violent directness **3** *Brit* : one who clears the cave of a furnace **4** : an explorer of caves : SPELEOLOGIST

cav·en·dish \'kavən(,)dish\ *n* -ES [prob. fr. the name *Cavendish*] : leaf tobacco softened, sweetened, and pressed into plugs or cakes

cavendish banana *n, usu cap C* : DWARF BANANA

cavendish experiment *n, usu cap C* [after Henry *Cavendish* †1810 Eng. chemist and physicist who first performed it] : measurement of gravitation constant by a sensitive torsion balance

cave of adul·lam \-ə'dələm\ *usu C&A* [fr. *Adullam,* biblical cave where David fled to escape Achish, king of Gath, & where he was joined by other discontented people (1 Sam 22:1-2)] : a group of seceders from a particular political or intellectual position

cave onyx *n* : a fine-grained banded calcite aragonite found in caves

cave pearl *n* : a small smooth round concretion of carbonate of lime found in limestone caves

cav·er \'kāvə(r)\ *n* -S : one that studies or explores caves

1cav·ern \'kavə(r)n\ *n* -S *often attrib* [ME *caverne,* fr. MF, fr. L *caverna,* fr. *cavus* hollow — more at CAVE] **1** : an underground chamber often large or indefinite in extent : CAVE ⟨~s attracting tourist trade⟩ ⟨Carlsbad *Caverns*⟩ **2** : a large dark recess ⟨his eye sockets were dark ~s —Kenneth Roberts⟩ ⟨the ~s of his memory —Earl Birney⟩ **3** : a cavity (as in the lung) caused by disease

2cavern \"\ *vt* -ED/-ING/-S **1** : to place or enclose in or as if in a cavern **2** : to form a cavern of : hollow out — used with *out*

cav·er·ni·cole \ka'vərnə,kōl, kə'-, 'kavərnə,-\ *n* -S [F, fr. *cavernicole,* adj., fr. *caverne* cavern + *-i-* + *-cole* -colous] : a cavernicolous animal

cav·er·nic·o·lous \¦kavər¦nikələs\ *adj* [*cavern* + *-i-* + *-colous*] : inhabiting caverns ⟨a ~ fauna⟩

cav·er·no·ma \,kavə(r)'nōmə\ *n, pl* **cavernomas** \-məz\ *or* **cavernoma·ta** \-məd·ə\ [NL, fr. L *caverna* cavern + NL *-oma*] : a vascular tumor or angioma containing hollow spaces

cav·er·nos·to·my \-'nästəmē\ *n* -ES [L *caverna* cavern, cavity + E *-o-* + *-stomy*] : incision and drainage of a tuberculous cavity

cav·ern·ous \'kavə(r)nəs\ *adj* [ME, fr. L *cavernosus,* fr. *caverna* + *-osus* -ous] **1 a** : having many caverns ⟨a ~ limestone area⟩ **b** : having many cavities or interstices ⟨a ~ substance⟩ **c** : productive of caverns ⟨~ weathering⟩ **2 a** : constituting or suggesting a cavern : deep, vast, and commodious ⟨the chilly ~ chambers, hollowed out of carboniferous limestone —*Amer. Guide Series: Calif.*⟩ ⟨a ~ cellar⟩ ⟨a ~ mind⟩ **b** : of or relating to a cavern ⟨ill-smelling ~ waters⟩ **3** *of animal tissue* : composed of vascular sinuses intercalated between afferent arteries and efferent veins and capable of becoming dilated with blood to bring about the erection of a body part — **cav·ern·ous·ly** *adv*

cavernous body *n* [trans. of NL *corpus cavernosum*] : CORPUS CAVERNOSUM

cavernous plexus *n* : a nerve plexus of the sympathetic system lying below and internal to the carotid artery at each side of the sella turcica

cavernous respiration *n* : a peculiar blowing respiratory sound heard over abnormal lung cavities

cavernous sinus *n* : either of a pair of large venous sinuses situated in a groove at the side of the body of the sphenoid bone in the cranial cavity and opening behind into the petrosal sinuses

ca·ver·nu·lous \ka'vərnyələs, kə-\ *adj* [L *cavernula* (dim. of *caverna* cavern) + E *-ous*] : full of little cavities

caves *pl of* CAVE, *pres 3d sing of* CAVE

cav·es·son *or* **cav·e·son** \'kavəsən\ *n* -S [modif. of It *cavezzone* halter with noseband, aug. of *cavezza* halter, irreg. fr. L *capitium* opening in tunic for head to go through, fr. *capit-, caput* head — more at HEAD] **1** : a noseband made of metal or other stiff material well padded and used on horses esp. during breeding or training **2** : a halter or bridle with a cavesson

ca·vet·to \kə'ved·(,)ō\ *n, pl* **cavet·ti** \-d·ē\ *or* **cavettos** \-d·(,)ōz\ [It, fr. *cavo* hollow, fr. L *cavus* — more at CAVE] : a concave molding having a curve that roughly approximates a quarter circle — see MOLDING illustration

cavi *pl of* CAVUS

ca·via \'kāvēə\ *n, cap* [NL, modif. of obs. Pg *çaviá* (now *saviá*), fr. Tupi *sawiya* rat] : the type genus of Caviidae consisting of the guinea pigs and a few related forms

cav·i·ar *or* **cav·i·are** \'kavē,är, -,á(r *also* -äv- *or* -áv- *or* ,==¦=\ *n* -S [alter. (prob. influenced by F *caviar*) of earlier *caviari, cavery,* fr. OIt *caviari,* pl. of *caviaro* caviar, fr. Turk *havyar*] **1** : processed salted roe of the sturgeon and certain other large fish prepared as an appetizer **2** : a choice product or production too delicate or lofty for mass appreciation ⟨this play will be ~ to the general public⟩ **3** [so called fr. the resemblance of the blotch to caviar] : a passage canceled by a censor

cav·i·ary \'kavē,erē\ *n* -ES [¹*cavy* + *-ary* (as in *aviary*)] : a place for keeping or raising cavies

cav·i·corn \'kavə,kȯrn\ *adj* [NL *Cavicornia*] : having hollow horns ⟨~ members of the family Bovidae⟩

cav·i·cor·nia \,==¦=nēə, -nyə\ *n* [NL, fr. *cavi-* (fr. L *cavus* hollow) + *-cornia* (fr. L, neut. pl. of *-cornis* -corn) — more at CAVE] *syn of* BOVOIDEA

ca·vie *also* **cavey** \'kāvē\ *n* -S [obs. D or obs. Flem *kavie,* fr. MD *cavie;* akin to OS & OHG *kevia* cage; all fr. a prehistoric D-LG-HG word borrowed fr. L *cavea* cage — more at CAGE] *Scot* : a coop or cage for hens

cavies *pl of* CAVY

ca·vi·i·dae \kə'vīə,dē, kə-\ *n pl, cap* [NL, fr. *Cavia,* type genus + *-idae*] : a family of more or less tailless rodents having but three toes on each hind foot — see CAVY

1cav·il \'kavəl, *Brit often* -vil\ *vb* **caviled** *or* **cavilled; caviled** *or* **cavilled; caviling** *or* **cavilling** \-v(ə)liŋ, -vil-\ **cavils** [L *cavillari* to jest, mock, cavil, fr. *cavilla* raillery, sophistry; prob. akin to L *calvi* to deceive — more at CALUMNY] *vi* : to raise captious and frivolous objection : object or criticize adversely for trivial reasons — usu. used with *at, about,* or *with* ⟨mere captiousness . . . that ~s at a whetstone because it's not a sword blade —J.L.Lowes⟩ ~ *vt* : to raise picayune objections to : cavil at ⟨~ the conditions of the agreement⟩

2cavil \"\ *n* -S **1** : a captious frivolous picayune objection : QUIBBLE ⟨accept without ~ whatever he was told —Samuel Butler †1902⟩ **2** : tendency to cavil : susceptibility to cavils ⟨the general standard of the judicature is above reproach or ~ —Ernest Barker⟩

cav·il·er *or* **cav·il·ler** \-əl(ə)r, -il-\ *n* -S : one that cavils

caviling *or* **cavilling** *adj* : disposed to cavil : inclined to find fault and raise picayune ill-grounded objections ⟨~ pettifoggers and quibbling pleaders —Edmund Burke⟩ **syn** see CRITICAL

cav·il·ing·ly *adv* : in a caviling manner

cav·il·ing·ness *n* -ES : the quality or state of being caviling

cav·il·la·tion \,kavə'lāshən, -vi'-\ *n* -S [ME *cavillacioun,* fr. MF *cavillation,* fr. L *cavillation-, cavillatio,* fr. *cavillatus,* (past part. of *cavillari* to cavil) + *-ion-, -io* -ion] **1** *archaic* : CAVIL ⟨sophistical ~⟩ **2** *archaic* : the raising of cavils

cav·il·lous \'==ləs\ *adj* : given to cavil : CAVILING

ca·vi·na \kə'vēnyə\ *n, pl* **cavina** *or* **cavinas** *usu cap* [Sp *caviña,* of AmerInd origin] **1 a** : a Tacanan people of northwest Bolivia and adjacent Brazil **b** : a member of such people **2** : the language of the Cavina people

cav·ing \'kāviŋ, -vēŋ\ *n* -S **1** : a falling or hollowing in **2** : the exploring of caves

cav·ings \-ŋz, -vēnz\ *n pl* [fr. gerund of *cave* (to separate from chaff)] *dial Brit* : chaff and refuse esp. of threshed grain

cav·i·tar·i·ly \¦kavə¦terəlē\ *adv* : in a cavitary manner

cav·i·tary \'kavə,terē\ *adj* [*cavity* + *-ary*] : characterized by cavitation

cav·i·tate \-,tāt\ *vi* -ED/-ING/-S [back-formation fr. *cavitation*] **1** : to form a partial vacuum by cavitation **2** : to form a cavity (as in cavitation)

cav·i·ta·tion \,==¦tāshən\ *n* -S [*cavity* + *-ation*] **1 a** : the formation of partial vacuums in a liquid esp. as a result of the passage through it of a swiftly moving solid body (as a propeller blade) or of high-frequency sound waves **b** : the pitting and wearing away of solid surfaces (as metal or concrete) as a result of the collapse of these vacuums **2** : the formation of one or more cavities in an organ or tissue (as in the brain, lung, spinal cord, or teeth) esp. as a result of disease **3** : a cavity formed by cavitation

ca·vi·te·no \,kavə'ten(,)yō, -ān-\ *n* -S *cap* [PhilSp *caviteño,* fr. *Cavite,* province & city of SW Luzon, Philippines] : a Spanish-based pidgin language spoken around Cavite, Philippines

cav·i·tied \'kavəd·ēd, -vət|ēd, |id\ *adj* : having cavities

cav·i·to·ma \,kavə'tōmə\ *n* -S [NL, fr. L *cavitas* + NL *-oma*] : a series of changes in cotton fiber involving loss of strength and resulting from the activities of microorganisms — **cav·i·to·mic** \¦==¦tōmik, -äm-\ *adj*

cav·i·ty \'kavəd·ē, -ətē, -i\ *n* -ES [MF *cavité,* fr. LL *cavitas* hollowness, fr. L *cavus* hollow + *-itas* -ity — more at CAVE] : a three-dimensional discontinuity in the substance of a mass or body : a space within a mass ⟨a water-filled ~ in limestone⟩; *also* : a space hollowed out (as by decay) ⟨teeth full of *cavities*⟩ ⟨an old ~ excavated by a woodpecker —John Burroughs⟩

cavity oscillator *n* : an ultrahigh-frequency oscillator whose frequency is controlled by means of a cavity resonator

cavity resonator *n* : an electronic device consisting of a space usu. enclosed by metallic walls within which resonant electromagnetic fields may be excited and extracted for use in microwave systems

cavity wall *n* : a usu. masonry wall built in two thicknesses separated by an air space that provides thermal insulation

cav·i·u·na wood \¦kavē¦ünə-, kə'vyü-\ *n* [Pg *cabiuna,* prob. fr. Tupi *caa- biuna*] : BRAZILIAN ROSEWOOD

ca·vo–re·lie·vo *or* **ca·vo–ri·lie·vo** \¦kä(,)vōrē'lē(,)vō, ¦kā-, ¦ká-; ¦kä(,)vōrēl'yā-, ¦ká-, -ye-\ *n, pl* **cavo–relievos** \-vōz\ *or* **ca·vi–ri·lie·vi** \¦kä(,)vērēl'yā(,)vē, ¦ká-, -ye-\ [It *cavo rilievo*] : SUNK RELIEF

ca·vort \kə'vȯ(ə)rt, -ō(ə)t\ *vi* -ED/-ING/-S [perh. alter. of *curvet*] **1** : to bound, prance, or frisk about ⟨the forest ponies kicking up their heels and ~*ing* . . . in sheer delight of living —S.P.B.Mais⟩ **2** : to engage in any agile frisky extravagant showy behavior ⟨lads . . . ~*ed* with the buxom lassies in the reel and barn dance —A.D. Graeff⟩

CAVU *abbr* ceiling and visibility unlimited

ca·vum \'kāvəm, 'kä-\ *n, pl* **ca·va** \-və\ [L, cavity, fr. neut. of *cavus* hollow — more at CAVE] : RECESS, HOLLOW: as **a** : the lower part of the concha of the ear adjoining the origin of the helix **b** : the nasal cavity

cav·vy *or* **cavy** \'kavē\ *n* -ES [short for *cavayard*] *West* : REMUDA

ca·vy \'kāvē\ *n* -ES [NL *Cavia*] **1** : any of several short-tailed rough-haired So. American rodents constituting the family Caviidae; *specif* : GUINEA PIG **2** : any of several rodents (as the paca and agouti) related to the Caviidae

cavyyard *var of* CAVAYARD

1caw \'kȯ\ *Scot var of* CALL

2caw \"\ *vi* -ED/-ING/-S [imit.] : to utter a harsh raucous cry; *typically, of a crow, raven, or rook* : to utter its natural call ⟨the crows ~ above the wood —John Burroughs⟩

3caw \"\ *n* -S : a harsh raucous throaty outcry; *typically* : the natural call of the crow, raven, or rook

4caw \"\ *var of* ²COE

ca·wa·hib \'käwə,hēb\ *n, pl* **cawahib** *or* **cawahibs** *usu cap* [Cawahib, perh. fr. *kab, kāwa* wasp] **1 a** : a Tupian people including the Cawahib proper and the Parintintin of the Tapajoz river area in northern Brazil **b** : a member of such people **2** : the language of the Cawahib people

caw·die \'kädē\ *Scot var of* CADDIE

1cawk \'kȯk\ *n* -S [ME *calke* chalk, limestone — more at CAUK] **1** : an opaque compact variety of barite **2** : BARITE

2cawk \"\ *vi* -ED/-ING/-S [ME *cauken,* fr. ONF *cauquer,* fr. L *calcare* to tread] *of hawks* : MATE

cawky \'kȯkē\ *adj* -ER/-EST : containing cawk : like cawk

cawl \'kȯl\ *n* -S [OE *cawl, ceawl* basket, fr. ML *cavellum,* fr. L *cavus* hollow — more at CAVE] *dial Brit* : a wooden basket with handholes instead of handles used esp. in Cornwall to carry fish

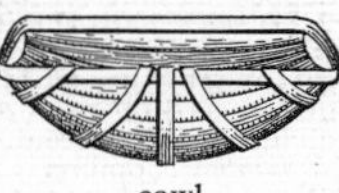
cawl

cawn·pore \'kȯn,pō(ə)r, =¦=\ *or* **kan·pur** \'kän,pu̇(ə)r, =¦=\ *adj, usu cap* [fr. *Cawnpore,* city in India] : of or from the city of Cawnpore, India : of the kind or style prevalent in Cawnpore

caw·quaw \'kȯ,kwȯ\ *n* -S [Cree *kaakwa*] : CANADA PORCUPINE

cax·on \'kaksən\ *n* -S [perh. fr. the name *Caxon*] : WIG; *esp* : a much-worn wig

cax·to·nian \(')kak¦stōnēən, -nyən\ *adj, usu cap* [William *Caxton* †1491 Eng. printer & translator + E *-ian*] : of or relating to William Caxton or his work

1cay \'kē (*usual in W Indies*), 'kā\ *n* -S [Sp *cayo* — more at KEY] : a small low island or emergent reef of sand or coral : ISLET, KEY — used esp. in the West Indies

2cay \'kī\ *n* -S [AmerSp *cay, caí,* fr. Guarani *caí,* lit., bashful; fr. its habit of hiding its face in its hands] : a monkey of the genus *Cebus* : CAPUCHIN

ca·ya·bi \¦käyə¦bē, ¦kīə¦-\ *n, pl* **cayabi** *or* **cayabis** *usu cap* [Pg, of AmerInd origin] **1 a** : a Tupian people of the Tapajoz river area in northern Brazil **b** : a member of such people **2** : the language of the Cayabi people

cayak *var of* KAYAK

ca·ya·pa \kə'yäpə, kī'äpə\ *n, pl* **cayapa** *or* **cayapas** *usu cap* [Sp, of AmerInd origin] **1 a** : a Barbacoan people of the province of Esmeraldas in northwestern Ecuador **b** : a member of such people **2** : the language of the Cayapa people

ca·ya·po \¦käyə¦pō, ¦kīə¦-\ *n, pl* **cayapo** *or* **cayapos** *usu cap* [Pg *Cayapó,* of AmerInd origin] **1 a** : a Gesan people of the state of Mato Grosso in Brazil **b** : a member of such people **2** : the language of the Cayapo people

1cay·enne \(')kī¦en, -kā- *also* (')kī¦an\ *n* -S *sometimes cap* **1** : CAYENNE PEPPER **2** : a small reddish marine surface-swimming copepod that is a food of whales and certain fishes

2cayenne \"\ *also* **cayenne whist** *n* -S [fr. *Cayenne,* city and island in French Guiana] : a card game in which the dealer may designate the trump suit; *also* : the turned-up card that affects the scoring values in this game

cayenne cherry *n, usu cap 1st C* : SURINAM CHERRY 2

cayenne linaloe oil *n, usu cap C* : BOIS DE ROSE OIL

cayenne pepper *n, sometimes cap C* [alter. (influenced by *Cayenne,* city and island in French Guiana) of earlier *cayan, chian, kayan,* modif. of Tupi *kyinha, quiynha*] **1** : a very hot and pungent powder made by drying and grinding the whole fruits or the seeds of several hot peppers (as the long pepper) **2** : HOT PEPPER 2; *often* : any of several cultivated peppers derived from one variety (*Capsicum frutescens longum*) and characterized by very long twisted pungent red fruits **3** : the fruit of a cayenne pepper

cayman *var of* CAIMAN

cay·o·mi·to \,kīə'mēd·(,)ō\ *var of* CAIMITO

cay·to·nia \kā'tōnēə, -nyə\ *n, cap* [NL, fr. *Cayton,* England + NL *-ia*] : a genus (the type of the family Caytoniaceae and the order Caytoniales) of fossil gymnospermous plants of the Mesozoic era having seeds enclosed in a carpellike case that suggests their ancestry to the angiosperms

ca·yuá \¦käyə¦wä, ¦kīə¦-\ *n, pl* **cayuá** *or* **cayu·ás** *usu cap* [Sp *cayuá* & Pg *caiuá,* of AmerInd origin] **1 a** : a non-Christian Guarani people of southwestern Brazil and northern Paraguay **b** : a member of such people **2** : the language of the Cayuá people

ca·yu·co \kä'yü(,)kō, kī'(y)ü-\ *or* **ca·yu·ca** \-,kə\ *n* -S [AmerSp] : a small native fishing dugout of Central and So. America

ca·yu·ga \kē'ügə, 'kyü-; kā'(y)ü-, kī'(y)ü-, *attrib* (')=¦=\ *n, pl* **cayuga** *or* **cayugas** *usu cap* [prob. modif. of Mohawk *Kweñiógwē'* (place name), lit., place where locusts were taken out] **1 a** : an Iroquois people of New York state **b** : a member of such people **2** : the language of the Cayuga people

cayuga duck *n, usu cap C* : an American breed of ducks resembling but slightly smaller than the Pekin ducks and having greenish black plumage

ca·yu·gan \-ügən\ *adj, usu cap* [*Cayuga* lake, N. Y. + E *-an*] : of or relating to the uppermost major division of the American Silurian — see GEOLOGIC TIME table

cay·use \'kī,(y)üs, =¦=\ *n, pl* **cayuse** *or* **cayuses** **1** *usu cap* **a** : a Wailatpuan people of Washington and Oregon **b** : a member of such people **2** : the language of the Cayuse people **3** *pl cayuses, West* : a native range horse; *esp* : INDIAN PONY — compare BRONCO, MUSTANG

ca·yu·va·va \ˌkäyəˈvävə, ˌkīə'-\ *also* **ca·yu·ba·ba** \-ˈbäbə\ *n, pl* **cayuvava** *or* **cayuvavas** *also* **cayubaba** *or* **cayubabas** *usu cap* [Sp, of AmerInd origin] **1 a :** a people of northern Bolivia **b :** a member of such people **2 :** the language of the Cayuvava people

ca·yu·va·van \-vən\ *also* **ca·yu·ba·ban** \-bən\ *n* -s *usu cap* **:** a language family of northern Bolivia comprising only the Cayuvava

ca·za \kəˈzä\ *n* -s [Turk *kaza* district, judgment, sentence, fr. Ar *qaḍā'* decision, judging, fr. *qaḍā* to decide, judge] **:** a subdivision of a Turkish vilayet

caz·can \(ˈ)käˌskän\ *n, pl* **cazcan** *or* **cazcans** *usu cap* [Sp *cazcán*, fr. Nahuatl] **1 :** a Nahuatlan people of southern Zacatecas and northern Jalisco, Mexico **2 :** a member of the Cazcan people

cazique *var of* CACIQUE

cb *abbr* centibar

Cb *abbr* cumulonimbus

CB *abbr* **1** cashbook **2** [It *col basso*] with the bass **3** confined to barracks **4** construction battalion **5** contrabass **6** currency bond

Cb *symbol* columbium

cbal *abbr* counterbalance

c battery *n, usu cap C* **:** a battery used to maintain the potential of a grid-controlled electron tube at a desired value, constant except for signals superposed upon it

CBC *abbr* contraband control

cb cap *n, usu cap 1st C & B* **:** a .22-caliber rimfire cartridge similar to a BB cap but with a larger bullet

CBD *abbr* cash before delivery

c-bias \ˈ=,=\ *n, usu cap C* **:** the voltage applied to the control grid of a vacuum tube to make it negative with respect to the cathode

cbn *abbr* carbine

CBR *abbr* chemical, bacteriological, and radiological

cbt *abbr* cabinet

cby *abbr* carboy

cc *abbr* **1** centuries **2** chapters **3** copies **4** cubic centimeter

CC *abbr* **1** carbon copy **2** cash credit **3** cashier's check **4** chamber of commerce **5** chess club **6** chief clerk **7** circuit court **8** city council **9** civil commotion **10** combat command **11** common carrier **12** common council **13** company commander **14** confined to camp **15** connecting carrier **16** continuation clause **17** contra credit **18** council of churches **19** counterclockwise **20** country club **21** county council **22** county court **23** cricket club **24** crown colony **25** cubic contents **26** current cost **27** cycling club

CCA *abbr* circuit court of appeals

cckw *abbr* counterclockwise

c-clamp \ˈ=,=\ *n, cap 1st C* **:** a C-shaped general-purpose clamp that clamps between the open ends of the C by means of a long flat-ended screw that threads through one end and presses the clamped material against the other

c clef *n, usu cap 1st C* **:** a movable clef indicating middle C by its placement on one of the five lines of the staff — see ALTO CLEF, SOPRANO CLEF, TENOR CLEF; CLEF illustration; compare F CLEF, G CLEF

C-clamp

CCP *abbr* court of common pleas

CCS *abbr* **1** casualty clearing station **2** combined chiefs of staff

ccw *abbr* counterclockwise

cd *abbr* **1** candela **2** canned **3** card **4** cataloged **5** command **6** commissioned **7** condemned **8** cord **9** could

CD *abbr* **1** carried down **2** cash discount **3** certificate of deposit **4** chief of division **5** civil defense **6** coast defense **7** [It *colla destra*] with the right hand **8** commercial dock **9** completely denatured **10** confidential document **11** congressional district **12** consular declaration **13** contagious disease **14** [F *corps diplomatique*] diplomatic corps **15** cum dividend **16** current density

Cd *symbol* cadmium

CDD *abbr* certificate of disability for discharge

cde *abbr* code

cdg *abbr* commanding

cdl *abbr* cardinal

cdr *abbr* commander

cdre *abbr* commodore

CDS *abbr* cash on delivery service

cdt *abbr* commandant

ce *var of* CEE

CE *abbr or n* -s civil engineer

CE *abbr* **1** *often not cap* caveat emptor **2** Christian Era **3** Common Era **4** counterespionage **5** customs and excise

Ce *symbol* cerium

ce·a·no·thus \ˌsēəˈnōthəs\ *n, cap* [NL, fr. Gk *keanōthos*, a thistle] **:** a large genus of American vines, shrubs, and small trees (family Rhamnaceae) distinguished by having the calyx disk adherent to the ovary which develops into a dry fruit that splits into three carpels — see NEW JERSEY TEA

ce·a·rá rubber \ˌsāəˈrä-, ˌsēə-\ *n, usu cap C* [fr. *Ceará*, state in Brazil] **:** wild rubber obtained from any of certain So. American trees of the genus *Manihot* (esp. *M. glaziovii*)

¹cease \ˈsēs *sometimes* ˈsez\ *vb* -ED/-ING/-S [ME *cesen, cessen*, fr. OF *cesser*, fr. L *cessare* to delay, be idle, fr. *cessus*, past part. of *cedere* to withdraw — more at CEDE] *vt* **1 :** to leave off **:** bring to an end **:** DISCONTINUE, TERMINATE ⟨his efforts had no . . . chance of success, and he had made up his mind to ~ them —Arnold Bennett⟩ ⟨the resort hotel *ceased* to function after the fire⟩ **2** *obs* **:** to put a stop to **:** HALT ⟨he *ceased* her fears⟩ ⟨~ the rioters' noise⟩ ~ *vi* **1 a :** to come to an end **:** break off or taper off to a stop ⟨these demonstrations *ceased* as suddenly as they had broken out —Charles Dickens⟩ ⟨the squealing which became slower and fainter and at last *ceased* —Jean Stafford⟩ **b :** to give over or bring to an end an activity or action **:** DISCONTINUE ⟨rock for hours before the fire without *ceasing*⟩ — often used with *from* ⟨the admonition that men ~ from their wickedness —*Amer.Scholar*⟩ **2** *obs* **:** to die out **:** become extinct ⟨the poor will never ~ out of the land —Deut 15:11 (RSV)⟩ **syn** see STOP

²cease \ˈ"\ *n* -s [ME *ces*, fr. MF *ces, cesse*, fr. *cesser*, v.] **:** CESSATION — usu. used with *without* ⟨I kept an eye upon her without ~ —R.L.Stevenson⟩

cease and desist order *n* **:** an order by an administrative agency to refrain from a method of competition or a labor practice found by the agency to be unfair

cease-fire \ˈ=ˌ=\ *n* -s **1 :** a military order to cease firing **2 :** a suspension of active hostilities ⟨the armistice, which was never more than an imperfect *cease-fire* —A.J.Liebling⟩

cease·less \-ləs\ *adj* **:** continuing without pause, check, or interruption **:** CONSTANT, CONTINUAL ⟨paying ~ attention to the lecturer⟩ ⟨the ~ tinny tumult of the jukebox —John McNulty⟩ ⟨a ~ stream of newspaper articles —J.F.Golay⟩ — **cease·less·ly** *adv* — **cease·less·ness** *n* -ES

cebadilla *var of* SABADILLA

ceb·a·tha \ˈsebəthə\ *n* -s [NL, fr. Ar *kebath*, a plant] *syn of* COCCULUS

ce·bell \səˈbel\ *n* -s [origin unknown] **:** an old English dance similar to the gavotte

ce·bid \ˈsēbəd, ˈseb-\ *n* -s [NL *Cebidae*] **:** a monkey of the family Cebidae

ceb·i·dae \ˈsebəˌdē\ *n pl, cap* [NL, fr. *Cebus*, type genus + *-idae*] **:** a family of platyrrhine monkeys comprising all the New World monkeys except the marmosets and tamarins, having one more pair of molar teeth in each jaw than the marmosets and usu. a long prehensile tail, and constituting with the marmosets a superfamily that includes all the New World monkeys — compare PLATYRRHINA — **ce·boid** \ˈsēˌbȯid\ *adj*

ce·bil \səˈbēl\ *n* -s [AmerSp] **:** the So. American tree that yields angico gum

ce·bol·lite \(ˈ)sēˈbȯi,(y)īt, ˈsebə,līt\ *n* -s [*Cebolla* Creek, Gunnison county, Colo. + E *-ite*] **:** a mineral $H_2Ca_4Al_2Si_3O_{16}$ consisting of hydrous calcium aluminum silicate occurring in greenish to white fibrous aggregates (hardness 5, sp. gr. 3)

ce·bu \säˈbü, sə'-\ *adj, usu cap* [fr. *Cebu*, Philippines] **:** of or from the city of Cebu, Philippines **:** of the kind or style prevalent in Cebu

ce·bu·an \-üən\ *also* **ce·bua·no** \säbˈwä(ˌ)nō\ *n, pl* **cebuan** *or* **cebuans** *usu cap* [Sp *cebuano*, fr. *Cebú*, island & province of the Philippines + Sp *-ano* -an] **1 a :** a Bisayan people inhabiting Cebu **b :** a member of such people **2 :** the Austronesian language of the Cebuans — called also *Sugbuhanon*

ce·bu hemp *n, usu cap C* [fr. *Cebu*, island in the Philippines] **:** ABACA

cebu maguey *n, usu cap C* **:** CANTALA

ce·bus \ˈsēbəs\ *n, cap* [NL, fr. Gk *kēbos, kēpos* long-tailed monkey, prob. fr. Egypt *gjf*, an East African ape] **:** a genus (the type of the family Cebidae) that comprises medium-sized monkeys with well-developed thumbs and fully haired prehensile tails — see CAPUCHIN

cec- *or* **ceci-** *or* **ceco-** *or* **caec-** *or* **caeci-** *or* **caeco-** *comb form* [NL, fr. *cecum*] **:** cecum ⟨cecectomy⟩ ⟨ceciform⟩ ⟨cecitis⟩ ⟨cecocolic⟩

ceca *pl of* CECUM

ce·cal *or* **cae·cal** \ˈsēkəl\ *adj* [NL *caecum* + E *-al*] **:** of or like a cecum — **ce·cal·ly** *or* **cae·cal·ly** \-əlē\ *adv*

cecal coccidiosis *n* **:** a destructive infectious disease of the domestic fowl caused by a protozoan (*Eimeria tenella*) that develops in the cecal tissue producing acute hemorrhagic diarrhea frequently fatal in young birds

cecal fluke *n* **:** a digenetic trematode (*Postharmostomum gallinum*) infesting the ceca of chickens and causing severe hemorrhages

cecal worm *n* **:** a worm parasitizing the cecum; *specif* **:** a nematode worm (*Heterakis gallinae*) of gallinaceous birds that serves as an intermediate host and transmitter of the blackhead organism

cecchine *obs var of* CHEQUEEN

ce·cec·to·mized \sēˈsektəˌmīzd\ *adj* **:** surgically deprived of the cecum

ce·cec·to·my \-ˌmē\ *n* -ES [*cec-* + *-ectomy*] **:** excision of all or part of the cecum

čech *usu cap, var of* CZECH

ce·cid·i·ol·o·gy \səˌsidēˈäləjē\ *n* -ES [NL *cecidium* + E *-o-* + *-logy*] **:** a branch of biology that treats of the galls produced on plants by insects, mites, and fungi

ce·cid·i·um \səˈsidēəm, sē'-\ *n, pl* **cecid·ia** \-ēə\ [NL, fr. Gk *kēkidion*, dim. of *kēkid-, kēkis* anything gushing out, dye, oak gall; akin to OE *hengest* stallion, OHG *hengist*, ON *hestr*, W *caseg* mare, Lith *šokti* to leap, dance] **:** GALL; *esp* **:** one caused by insects or mites — used esp. in combinations ⟨acarocecidium⟩ ⟨zoocecidium⟩

cec·i·dog·e·nous \ˌsesəˈdäjənəs\ *adj* [Gk *kēkid-, kēkis* + E *-o-* + *-genous*] **:** producing galls on plants ⟨~ insects⟩

cec·i·dol·o·gy \ˌ==ˈdäləjē\ *n* -ES [by alter.] **:** CECIDIOLOGY

cec·i·do·my·ia \ˌsesədōˈmī(y)ə\ *n* [NL, fr. Gk *kēkid-, kēkis* oak gall + NL *-o-* + *-myia*] **1** *cap* **:** a very large genus (the type of the family Cecidomyiidae) of gall-forming midges **2** -s **:** a midge of the genus *Cecidomyia; broadly* **:** GALL MIDGE

cec·i·do·my·id \-ˈī(y)əd\ *var of* CECIDOMYIID

cec·i·do·my·iid \-ī(y)əd\ *n* -s [NL *Cecidomyiidae*] **:** an insect of the genus *Cecidomyia* or family Cecidomyiidae **:** GALL MIDGE

cec·i·do·my·i·i·dae \ˌsesə(ˌ)dōməˈīəˌdē, -ˈmīə-\ *n pl, cap* [NL, fr. *Cecidomyia*, type genus + *-idae*] **:** a family of small mosquitolike nematocerous flies comprising the gall midges

ce·cil \ˈsesəl\ *n* -s *usu cap* [fr. *Cecil* county, Maryland, its locality] **:** a series of reddish soils derived from material weathered from metamorphic and igneous rocks and found chiefly in the southern and central parts of the Piedmont plateau region of the U. S.

ce·ci·tis \sēˈsīd·əs\ *n* -ES [NL, fr. *cec-* + *-itis*] **:** inflammation of the cecum

ce·ci·ty \ˈsēsəd·ē\ *n* -ES [MF *cécité*, fr. L *caecitat-, caecitas*, fr. *caecus* blind + *-itat-, -itas* -ity — more at CECUM] **:** BLINDNESS

ce·cos·to·my \sēˈkästəmē\ *n* -ES [*cec-* + *-stomy*] **:** the surgical formation of an opening into the cecum to serve as an artificial anus

ce·cot·o·my \sēˈkäd·əmē\ *n* -ES [*cec-* + *-tomy*] **:** incision of the cecum

ce·cro·pia \səˈkrōpēə, sē'-\ *n, cap* [NL, fr. L, fem. of *Cecropius* Athenian, Attic, fr. Gk *Kekropios*, fr. *Kekrop-, Kekrops*, mythical first king of Athens] **:** a large genus of tropical American trees (family Moraceae) that have stems hollow between the nodes and peltate deeply lobed rough leaves usu. whitish beneath and clustered at the ends of the branches and that yield a bast fiber used for cordage, a bark used in tanning, and caoutchouc from their milky juice — see TRUMPETWOOD

cecropia moth \ˈ"-\ *also* **cecropia** *n* -s *sometimes cap C* [NL *cecropia* (specific epithet of *Samia cecropia*), fr. L *Cecropia*, fem. of *Cecropius*, adj.] **:** a large silkworm moth (*Hyalophora cecropia*) that is the largest moth native to the eastern U. S., that is represented by related species in the West, and that has larvae which feed on and are sometimes serious defoliators of many forest and fruit trees

ce·cum *or* **cae·cum** *also* **coe·cum** \ˈsēkəm\ *n, pl* **ce·ca** *or* **cae·ca** *also* **coe·ca** \-kə\ [NL, fr. L *intestinum caecum*, fr. *intestinum* intestine + *caecum*, neut. of *caecus* blind; akin to Goth *haihs* one-eyed, OIr *caech*, one-eyed, Skt *kekara* squint-eyed] **:** a cavity open at one end (as the blind end of a duct); *esp* **:** the blind pouch in which the large intestine begins and into which the ileum opens from one side — called also *blind gut*; see DIGESTION illustration

ce·dar \ˈsēdə(r)\ *n* -s *often attrib* [ME *cedre*, fr. OF, fr. L *cedrus*, fr. Gk *kedros* cedar, juniper; akin to Lith *kadagys* juniper, and perh. to OSlav *kaditi* to fumigate, Skt *kadru* tawny] **1 a :** CEDAR OF LEBANON; *broadly* **:** a tree of the genus *Cedrus* (as a deodar) — called also *true cedar* **b :** any of numerous coniferous trees chiefly of temperate or subtropical regions that are felt to resemble the true cedars esp. in the fragrance and durability of their wood: as (1) **:** a tree of the genus *Juniperus; esp* **:** RED CEDAR (2) **:** a tree of the genus *Chamaecyparis; esp* **:** SOUTHERN WHITE CEDAR (3) **:** a tree of the genus *Thuja* (as western red cedar) (4) **:** a tree of the genus *Libocedrus* (as incense cedar or kaikawaka) **c :** any of various chiefly tropical trees of the family Meliaceae having typically a reddish aromatic wood: as (1) **:** a tree of the genus *Cedrela* (as Spanish cedar or toon) (2) **:** MAHOGANY 3a, 3b **d :** any of several tropical American trees of the genera *Tabebuia* and *Tecoma; esp* **:** a medium-sized West Indian tree (*Tabebuia pallida*) with compound leaves and showy pink or white flowers **e** *Austral* **:** SILKY ASH **2 a :** CEDARWOOD **b :** any of various woods that are felt to resemble cedarwood esp. in fragrance, durability, or color — not used technically without a qualifying term **3 :** a variable color averaging a grayish red that is yellower and duller than bois de rose or appleblossom, yellower and less strong than blush rose, and duller than Pompeian red

cedar apple *also* **cedar ball** *n* **:** a hard brown more or less spherical excrescence on cedar trees of the genus *Juniperus* formed by various rusts (genus *Gymnosporangium*) during their telial stage — compare APPLE RUST

cedar-apple rust *n* **:** APPLE RUST

cedarbird \ˈ=ˌ=\ *n* **:** CEDAR WAXWING

cedar camphor *n* **:** CEDROL

cedar elm *n* **:** an elm (*Ulmus crassifolia*) of the southern U. S. and Mexico having spreading pendulous corky branches and yielding valuable timber

cedar green *n* **:** a moderate olive green that is lighter, stronger, and slightly yellower than forest green (sense 2), yellower, lighter, and stronger than cypress, and stronger and slightly greener and lighter than Lincoln green

cedarleaf oil \ˈ==ˌ-\ *n* **:** THUJA OIL

cedar mahogany *n* **:** MAHOGANY 1b(2)

cedar man *n* **:** one who grades cedar poles according to size, length, and specified standards

cedar moss *n* **:** a hornwort (*Ceratophyllum demersum*) found as a submerged aquatic plant throughout No. America and grown in aquariums for its feathery foliage and as an aerator

ce·darn \ˈsēdə(r)n\ *adj* [*cedar* + *-n* (fr. *-en*)] *archaic* **:** made or suggestive of cedar ⟨carved ~ doors—Alfred Tennyson⟩

cedar nut *n* **:** the seed of the Swiss pine (*Pinus cembra*) — called also *cembra nut*

cedar of atlas *usu cap A* **:** ATLAS CEDAR

cedar of goa \-ˈgōə\ *cap G* [prob. trans. of Pg *cedro de Goa*, fr. *Goa*, Portuguese possession in India; prob. fr. a belief that it was introduced into Portugal from there] **:** MEXICAN CYPRESS

cedar of leb·a·non \-ˈlebənən\ *cap L* [fr. *Lebanon*, mountain range in the Republic of Lebanon; trans. of LL *cedrus Libani*, trans. of Heb *arzē hallĕbhānōn* (Ps 29: 5), *arzē lĕbhānōn* (Ps 104: 16)] **:** an evergreen tree (*Cedrus libani*) having short fascicled leaves and erect cones and attaining a great age and height

cedar pencil *n, dial* **:** an unpainted pencil

cedar rose *n* **:** a grayish red that is bluer and paler than bois de rose, yellower, lighter, and stronger than blush rose, and bluer and slightly paler than Pompeian red

cedar rust *n* **:** APPLE RUST

cedar waxwing *n* [prob. so called fr. its feeding on the berries of the red cedar (*Juniperus virginiana*)] **:** a waxwing (*Bombycilla cedrorun*) that is widely distributed over temperate No. America — see WAXWING

cedarwood \ˈ==ˌ=\ *n* **:** the wood of various cedars, esp. of a red cedar (*Juniperus virginiana*), used as a source of cedarwood oil and because it repels insects for lining wardrobes and closets

cedarwood oil *n* **:** a colorless to yellow essential oil obtained from the heartwood of various cedars (as red cedar) and used in soaps and perfumes and with immersion lenses in microscopy

cede \ˈsēd\ *vb* -ED/-ING/-S [F or L; F *céder*, fr. L *cedere* to go, proceed, withdraw, yield; prob. akin to L *cis* on this side and to Gk *hodos* way, journey, OSlav *chodŭ* gait, Skt *āsad* to arrive at, L *sedēre* to sit — more at HE, SIT] *vt* **1 :** to give up, give over, grant, or concede typically by treaty or negotiated pact ⟨the territory *ceded* by France, under the name of Louisiana —R.B.Taney⟩ **2 :** ASSIGN, TRANSFER ⟨~ his stock holdings to his children⟩ **3 :** to transfer by reinsurance (all or part of one's liability as insurer under an insurance policy) to some other insurer ~ *vi* **:** to give way **:** yield precedence — used with *to* **syn** see RELINQUISH

ce·dent \ˈsēdᵊnt\ *n* -s [L *cedent-, cedens*, pres. part. of *cedere* to yield] **1** *also* **ce·dens** -ES \ˈsēˌdenz\ **:** an assignor of a debt or claim **2** *Scots law* **:** an assignor of property or claims by a deed of conveyance

ced·er \ˈsēdə(r)\ *n* -s **:** one that cedes

ce·dil·la \səˈdilə, sē'-\ *n* -s [Sp, the obs. letter *ç* (actually a medieval form of the letter *z*), cedilla, fr. dim. of *ceda, zeda* the letter *z*, fr. LL *zeta* — more at ZED] **:** a mark or diacritic ̧ placed under a letter or symbol to indicate a sound different from that which the unmodified character bears in certain or all situations (as under *c* in French and in Portuguese before *a, o*, or *u* to indicate a pronunciation\s\ rather than \k\)

ced·or \ˈsēdə(r)\ *n* -s [*cede* + *-or*] **:** CEDENT 1

ce·drat *or* **ce·drate** \ˈsēdrət\ *also* **ce·dra** \-rə\ *n* -s [F *cédrat*, fr. It *cedrato*, fr. *cedro* citron, fr. L *citrus* — more at CITRON] **:** CITRON

ce·dre \ˈsēdə(r), ˈsedrᵊ, ˈsedrə\ *n* -s [F *cèdre* cedar — more at CEDAR] **:** CEDAR GREEN

ce·dre·la \səˈdrēlə\ *n, cap* [NL, modif. of Sp *cedrelo*, dim. of *cedro* cedar, fr. L *cedrus* — more at CEDAR] **:** a small genus of large tropical American timber trees (family Meliaceae) that are characterized by bipinnate leaves and flowers with a 5-celled ovary which produces winged seeds and that yield ornamental wood used for furniture — see SPANISH CEDAR

ce·drene \ˈsēˌdrēn\ *n* -s [ISV *cedr-* (fr. L *cedrus* cedar) + *-ene*] **:** a sesquiterpene $C_{15}H_{24}$ occurring in cedarwood oil and oils of other conifers

ced·ri·ret \ˌsed(r)əˈret\ *n* -s [G *zedriret*, fr. L *cedrium* cedar oil (fr. Gk *kedrion*, fr. *kedros* cedar) + *rete* net; fr. the netlike pattern of the crystals on a filter — more at CEDAR, RETINA] **:** CERULIGNONE

ce·dro \ˈse(ˌ)drō, ˈsā-\ *n* -s [Sp & Pg, lit., cedar, fr. L *cedrus* — more at CEDAR] **:** any of several reddish cedarlike woods (as of Spanish cedar and other species of *Cedrela*)

ce·drol \ˈsēˌdrōl, -ōl\ *n* -s [ISV *cedr-* (fr. L *cedrus*) + *-ol*] **:** a colorless crystalline sesquiterpenoid alcohol $C_{15}H_{25}OH$ found in cedarwood oil and oils of other conifers and used in perfumes

ce·dron \səˈdrōn\ *n* -s [AmerSp *cedrón*, fr. Sp *cedro* cedar, fr. L *cedrus*] **1 :** a tropical American tree (*Simaba cedron*) **2 :** the fruit of the cedron

ce·drus \ˈsēdrəs\ *n, cap* [NL, fr. L, cedar — more at CEDAR] **:** a small genus of Old World evergreen trees (family Pinaceae) having erect cones and leaves clustered as in the larches but persistent

ce·du·la \ˈsāthəˌlä, ˈthāth-\ *n* -s [Sp *cédula*, fr. LL *schedula* — more at SCHEDULE] **1 :** any of various official documents or certificates in Spain, Latin America, or the Philippines: as **a :** a permit or order issued by the government **b :** a personal registration tax certificate in the Philippines **c :** any of certain securities issued by some of the So. and Central American governments or banks **2 :** a Philippine personal registration tax

cee *also* **ce** \ˈsē\ *n* -s **1 :** the letter *c* **2 :** something having the shape of the letter C

cee spring *n* **:** C SPRING

cei·ba \ˈsābə\ *n* [NL, fr. Sp, prob. of Arawakan origin; akin to Taino *ceyba*] **1** *cap* **:** a large genus of tropical American trees (family Bombacaceae) with palmately compound leaves and showy bell-shaped flowers **2** -s [Sp *ceiba*] **a** *or* **ceiba tree :** a massive tree (*Ceiba pentandra*) widely cultivated in the tropics having a trunk of large size with buttresslike ridges and bearing large pods filled with seeds invested with a silky floss that yields in the cultivated state the fiber kapok — called also *Bombay ceiba, God tree, silk-cotton tree* **b :** KAPOK

cei·bo \ˈsā(ˌ)bō\ *n* -s [AmerSp, ceibo, ceiba tree, fr. Sp. *ceiba*] **1 :** a So. American shrub or small tree (*Erythrina crista-galli*) with crimson and scarlet flowers **2 :** KAPOK

ceil \ˈsēl, -ēəl\ *vt* -ED/-ING/-S [ME *celen, cylen*, prob. fr. (assumed) MF *celer* (OF *celé, cielé* provided with an ornate ceiling), fr. L *caelare* to carve, engrave, fr. *caelum* chisel, graver, fr. *caedere* to cut, hew — more at CONCISE] **1 a** *obs* **:** to overlay (as a wall) with a covering (as of thin boards or plaster) **b :** to line the bottom and sides of (a wooden ship) with planking **2 a :** LINE ⟨~ a roof⟩ **b :** to furnish with a ceiling

ceiled \ˈsēld, -ē(ə)ld\ *adj* [ME *cyled*, fr. past part. of *cylen, celen* to ceil] **1 :** having a ceiling **2 :** finished with wainscot

cei·lidh *also* **cei·lidhe** \ˈkālē\ *n* -s [IrGael *céilidhe* & ScGael *cèilidh*, fr. MIr *célide*, fr. OIr *céle, céile* companion, husband; akin to L *civis* citizen — more at CEMETERY] **1** *Irish & Scot* **:** a friendly call **:** VISIT **2** *Irish & Scot* **:** an evening entertainment usu. with storytelling and singing or dancing

ceil·ing \ˈsēliŋ, -ēŋ\ *n* -s *often attrib* [ME *celing*, fr. *celen* to ceil + *-ing* — more at CEIL] **1 a** *obs* **:** woodwork lining the roof or walls of a room **:** WAINSCOTING **b** *obs* **:** a wall hanging or tapestry **c :** the overhead inside lining of a room **:** the underside of the floor above **d :** planking that lines the inside and bottom of a wooden ship or that covers the inner bottom of a steel ship — see SHIP illustration **e :** material used to ceil a wall or roof of a room; *esp* **:** narrow beaded matchboards used for wainscoting **f :** an uppermost surface of a cavity or chamber **2 :** something thought of as an overhanging shelter or lofty canopy ⟨above the gulls was a ~ of terns —Llewellyn Howland⟩ ⟨an incredible ~ of stars —M.P. O'Connor⟩ **3 a :** the height above the ground from which prominent objects on the ground can be seen and identified **b :** the height above the ground of the base of the lowest layer of clouds when over half of the sky is obscured **4 a :** ABSOLUTE CEILING **b :** SERVICE CEILING **5 :** the maximum height to which a projectile rises upon being fired from a gun **6** *or* **ceiling frame :** a canvas-covered frame suspended horizontally over a theater set to close it off on top **7 a :** an upper limit imposed by an authoritative ruling above which a particular quantity or rate is not to be allowed to rise ⟨a ~ on prices, wages, rents, profits, new construction⟩ ⟨asking Congress to raise the debt ~⟩ ⟨a 4-million manpower ~ on the armed forces⟩ **b :** an uppermost limit determined by conditions and circumstances of a particular situation ⟨the speed ~ of a helicopter⟩ **c :** a top level determined by economic factors ⟨today's stock market averages broke through all previous ~s⟩ **d :** any deliberately prescribed limit on increase in amount or quantity **e :** a barrier against potential rise in status or prestige **f :** an upper limit of ability or capability ⟨a low ~ of tolerance⟩

ceiling climbing *n, slang* **:** playing high notes for display of virtuosity in jazz improvization
ceil·inged \'sēlind, -ēŋd\ *adj* **:** provided with a ceiling ⟨the studio was high-*ceilinged* —Winifred Bambrick⟩ ⟨the large, beam-*ceilinged* living room —John McDowell⟩
ceiling floor *n* **:** the framework of a room receiving a ceiling framed separately from the floor of the story above
ceiling hook *n* **:** a wood screw with head formed of a loop left open at its base to serve as a down-hanging hook
ceiling joist *n* **:** one of a series of small joists supporting the lath and plaster of a ceiling
ceiling note *n* **:** a note of spectacularly high pitch (as made by a jazz trumpet)
ceiling plate *n, in the theater* **:** a metal plate with ring attached that is bolted to a ceiling frame for use in fastening or flying it
ceiling unlimited *n* **:** a cloudless or nearly cloudless sky **:** a sky less than half obscured by clouds at levels lower than an arbitrary fixed altitude, often 9750 feet
ceil·om·e·ter \sē'lämәd·ә(r), sә'-\ *n* -s [*ceiling* + *-o-* + *-meter*] **:** a photoelectric instrument for determining the height of the cloud ceiling above the earth by indicating the angular elevation of a spot of light formed where a strong modulated beam of light meets the cloud so that the height may be computed automatically by triangulation
cein·ture \'sānchә(r), *F* saⁿtüer\ *n* -s [F, fr. L *cinctura* — more at CINCTURE] **1 :** a girdle or belt for the waist **2 a :** a connected series of fortifications around a city **b :** a railroad encircling a city
ce·ja \'sā,hä, 'sāә\ *n* -s [Sp, lit., eyebrow, fr. L *cilia*, pl. of *cilium*] *Southwest* **:** a jutting edge along the top of a mesa or upland plain
cel *or* **cell** \'sel\ *n* -s [short for *celluloid*] **:** one of the transparent sheets of celluloid on which objects or sections of objects are drawn or painted in the making of animated cartoons for motion pictures and television
cel *abbr, usu cap* Celsius
cel- — see COEL-
cel·a·don \'selә,dän, -dᵊn\ *or* **cé·la·don** \sālädōⁿ\ *n* -s [F *céladon*, fr. *Céladon*, Astrée's lover in Honoré d'Urfé's romance *L'Astrée* (1610)] **1 :** a grayish yellow green that is paler and slightly yellower than average sage green, yellower and lighter than palmetto, and greener and lighter than mermaid **2 :** a reduction-fired iron-containing ceramic glaze originated in China that ranges from putty colored or greenish brown or gray to true green or bluish green and is used esp. in the Orient on various stonewares and porcelains; *also* **:** an article or ware with a celadon glaze **3 :** a monochrome glaze
celadon gray *n* **:** a pale green that is yellower and very slightly lighter and stronger than bayberry gray and yellower and duller than spray green
celadon green *or* **sel·a·don green** *n* [*celadon* fr. F *céladon*; *seladon* fr. G] **:** a variable color averaging a grayish yellow green that is yellower and paler than average sage green, greener and stronger than mermaid, yellower, lighter, and stronger than palmetto, and yellower and deeper than celadon
cel·a·don·ite \'seləd°n,īt\ *n* -s [prob. fr. G *seladonit*, fr. *seladon* celadon green (fr. F. *céladon*) + *-it* -ite] **:** a soft green earthy mineral consisting of silicate of iron, magnesium, and potassium
celadon tint *n* **:** a very pale green that is yellower and paler than tourmaline, yellower and duller than emerald tint, and yellower and slightly less strong than microcline green
cel·an·dine \'selәn,dīn *also* -,dēn\ *n* -s [ME *salendyne, celidoine*, fr. MF *celidoine*, fr. L *chelidonia*, fr. fem. of *chelidonius* of the swallow, fr. Gk *chelidonios*, fr. *chelidon-, chelidōn* swallow; akin to OE *giellan* to yell — more at YELL] **1 a :** a perennial herb (*Chelidonium majus*) of the family Papaveraceae with a branched woody stock and bright yellow flowers — called also *swallowwort* **2 :** LESSER CELANDINE **3 :** a variable No. American jewelweed (*Impatiens capensis*) sometimes cultivated as an ornament in Europe
celandine green *n* **:** a pale to grayish green
celandine poppy *n* **:** a yellow-flowered herb (*Stylophorum diphyllum*) of the family Papaveraceae of the eastern U.S. resembling the celandine but with flowers having a long style and a hirsute capsule
cel·as·tra·ce·ae \,selәs'trāsē,ē\ *n pl, cap* [NL, fr. *Celastrus*, type genus + *-aceae*] **:** a family of trees, shrubs, and woody vines (order Sapindales) having simple leaves, small regular flowers, and usu. brightly colored fruit with arillate seeds
cel·as·tra·ceous \¦==¦=shәs\ *adj* [NL *Celastraceae* + E *-ous*] **:** belonging to the Celastraceae
ce·las·trus \sә'lastrәs\ *n, cap* [NL, fr. Gk *kēlastros* holly] **:** a genus (the type of the family Celastraceae) of woody vines and erect shrubs native chiefly to Asia and Australia and having alternate deciduous leaves, flowers in panicles or racemes, and fruit a 3-valved orange or yellow capsule — see BITTERSWEET
ce·la·tion \sә'lāshәn, sē-\ *n* -s [L *celatus* (past part. of *celare* to conceal) + E *-ion* — more at HELL] **:** CONCEALMENT; *esp* **:** concealment of pregnancy or childbirth
cel·a·ture \'selә,chu̇(ә)r\ *n* -s [ME, fr. L *caelatura*, fr. *caelatus* (past part. of *caelare* to engrave) + *-ura* -ure; — more at CEIL] **:** embossed work or figures **:** EMBOSSING
¹-cele \,sēl\ *n comb form* -s [MF, fr. L, fr. Gk *kēlē* tumor; akin to OE *hēala* hydrocele, hernia, OHG *hōla* hernia, ON *haull*, OSlav *kyla*] **:** tumor **:** hernia ⟨cystocele⟩ ⟨gastrocele⟩
²-cele \"\ — see -COELE
ce·leb \sә'leb\ *n* -s [by shortening] *slang* **:** CELEBRITY 3
cel·e·be·sian \¦selә¦bēzhәn\ *adj, usu cap* [*Celebes*, island in the Malay archipelago + E *-ian*] **:** of, relating to, or characteristic of Celebes
cel·e·brant \'selәbrәnt\ *n* -s [F & L; F *célébrant*, fr. L *celebrant-, celebrans*, pres. part. of *celebrare*] **1 :** one who celebrates a public religious rite; *esp* **:** the officiating priest in the celebration of the Eucharist or mass as distinguished from his assistants **2 a :** one who takes part in ceremonious or convivial festivities celebrating a special occasion **b :** one who participates in any noisy party (as one at which there is a good deal of drinking) **3 :** one who sedulously exalts or extols a particular theme esp. in literary or art form ⟨a ~ of city life⟩
¹celebrate *adj* [ME *celebrat*, fr. L *celebratus*] *obs* **:** CELEBRATED
²cel·e·brate \-,brāt, *usu* -ād·+V\ *vb* -ED/-ING/-S [L *celebratus*, past part. of *celebrare* to frequent, celebrate, fr. *celebr-, celeber* much frequented, famous; akin to L *celer* swift — more at CELERITY] *vt* **1 :** to perform (a sacrament or solemn ceremony) publicly and with appropriate rites **:** SOLEMNIZE ⟨~ the mass⟩ ⟨~ a marriage⟩ **2 a :** to honor (as a holy day or feast day) by conducting or engaging in religious, commemorative, or other solemn ceremonies or by refraining from ordinary business **b :** to demonstrate grateful and happy satisfaction in (as an anniversary or event) by engaging in festivities, indulgence, merrymaking, or other similar deviation from accustomed routine ⟨as though he had had a drink or two — which indeed he might have had in reality, to ~ the occasion —Joseph Conrad⟩ **3 :** to proclaim or broadcast for the attention of a wide public ⟨that bloody nationalism which *celebrated* itself on so large a scale in 1914-1918 —Francis Hackett⟩ **4 a :** to portray with a high valuation and usu. in enhanced or poetic form or in exalted interpretation in a way to contribute to public awareness, edification, or enjoyment **:** hold up or play up for public acclaim or homage **:** EXTOL, GLORIFY ⟨verses *celebrating* the personal idiosyncrasy of the Yankee farmer⟩ ⟨American fiction had regularly *celebrated* the American village as the natural home of the pleasant virtues —Carl Van Doren⟩ **b :** to commemorate in appreciative interpretation for posterity esp. in some literary or art form ⟨his birthplace, *celebrated* by him in his early poetry —Padraic Colum⟩ ⟨the sort of beauty that is *celebrated* by the heroic male sculptures in the fountains of Rome —Tennessee Williams⟩ **~** *vi* **1 :** to observe a holiday, perform a religious ceremony, or take part in a festival ⟨in an Eastern liturgy several priests may ~ together⟩ ⟨in the Western mass, the priests ~ in the Latin fashion⟩ **2 a :** to observe the occasion of an achievement, reunion, anniversary, or other notable occasion with gaiety **b :** to engage in hilarious festivities usu. including drinking **syn** see KEEP
celebrated *adj* **:** widely or commonly known and often referred to because of some memorable quality or association **:** NOTED ⟨a ~ physician⟩ ⟨~ for its marble quarries⟩ ⟨one of the most ~ cases in the annals of crime⟩ — **cel·e·brat·ed·ness** *n* -ES
cel·e·brat·er \-,brād·ә(r), -ātә-\ *archaic var of* CELEBRATOR
cel·e·bra·tion \,selә'brāshәn\ *n* -s [MF & L; MF *célébration*, fr. L *celebration-, celebratio*, fr. *celebratus*, past part. of *celebrare* + *-ion-, -io* -ion] **1 :** the act or process of celebrating ⟨the ~ of a wedding anniversary⟩ ⟨a rowdy Saturday night ~⟩ ⟨moving ~ of an intricately human marriage —Robert Phelps⟩; *specif* **:** the performance of a public religious ceremony or of a sacred rite ⟨the ~ of the Eucharist⟩ **2** *obs* **:** RENOWN
cel·e·bra·tive \'selә,brād·iv, -,brәd-·\ *adj* **:** designed or set apart for celebrating
cel·e·bra·tor \-,brād·ә(r), -ātә-\ *n* -s [L, fr. *celebratus* + *-or*] **:** one that celebrates
cel·e·bra·to·ry \'selәbrә,tōrē\ *adj* **:** used or intended for use in celebrating a solemn or festive occasion
cel·e·bret \'selә,bret\ *n* -s [L, let him celebrate, 3d sing. pres. subj. of *celebrare* to celebrate — more at CELEBRATE] **:** a letter from a Roman Catholic bishop or religious superior testifying that the bearer is a priest and asking that he be permitted to say mass in dioceses other than his own
ce·leb·ri·ous \sә'lebrēәs\ *adj* [L *celebr-, celeber* + E *-ious*] **1** *obs* **:** THRONGED **2 :** FESTIVE **3 :** FAMOUS
ce·leb·ri·ty \sә'lebrәd·ē, -әtē, -i\ *n* -ES [MF & L; MF *célébrité*, fr. L *celebritat-, celebritas*, fr. *celebr-, celeber* famous + *-itat-, -itas* -ity — more at CELEBRATE] **1** *obs* **:** a solemn celebration **2 :** the state of being celebrated, acclaimed, or widely known on account of specific accomplishments ⟨that was in the spring of 1820, and the season of ~ was often quite as short then as it is today —H.V.Gregory⟩ ⟨made a sensational debut as a pianist at the age of six . . . but by adolescence, her ~ was finished —Roul Tunley⟩ **3 :** a celebrated or widely known person **:** one popularly honored for some signal achievement ⟨a visiting ~⟩ **syn** see FAME
celebrous *adj* [L *celebr-, celeber* + E *-ous*] *obs* **:** CELEBRATED
celenteron *var of* COELENTERON
ce·ler·i·ac \sә'lerē,ak, -ir-\ *n* -s [irreg. fr. *celery*] **:** a celery of a variety (*Apium graveolens rapaceum*) grown for its thickened turniplike edible root — called also *celery root, knob celery, root celery, turnip-rooted celery*
ce·ler·i·tous \sә'lerәd·әs\ *adj* [*celerity* + *-ous*] **:** swift-moving
ce·ler·i·ty \-әd·ē, -әtē, -i\ *n* -ES [ME *celerite*, fr. MF *célérité*, fr. L *celeritat-, celeritas*, fr. *celer* swift + *-itat-, -itas* -ity; akin to Goth *haldan* to feed, tend (animals), Gk *kellein* to beach (a ship), Skt *kalayati* he drives] **:** rapidity of motion or action: **a :** PROMPTNESS, ALACRITY ⟨disposing of the parsnip wine with a ~ which might have been due to eagerness —Dorothy Sayers⟩ ⟨the human brain, we are reminded, acts at times with extraordinary ~ —B.N.Cardozo⟩ **b :** SWIFTNESS, SPEED ⟨reptiles swim with astonishing ~⟩
cel·ery \'sel(ә)rē, -ri\ *n* -ES [prob. fr. It dial. (Lombardy) *seleri*, pl. of *selero*, modif. of LL *selinon*, fr. Gk] **1 :** a European herbaceous plant (*Apium graveolens*); *specif* **:** one of a cultivated variety (*A. graveolens dulce*) the leafstalks of which are eaten raw or cooked **2** *also* **celery grass :** TAPE GRASS
celery blight *n* **:** early blight, late blight, or bacterial blight of celery or a combination of these
celery cabbage *n* **:** CHINESE CABBAGE
celery calico *n* **:** a virus disease of celery and certain other plants (as delphinium) characterized by conspicuous green and yellow, orange, or amber mottling usu. on the older leaves
celery family *n* **:** UMBELLIFERAE
celery fly *n* **1 :** a small brown-winged green-eyed European fly (*Trypeta*, or *Acidia, heraclei*) whose larvae are leaf miners in celery, parsnips, and uncultivated related plants **2 :** an Australian agromyzid fly whose larvae mine celery stalks
celery leaf ti·er \-,tī(ә)r\ *n* **:** a small pale reddish brown European moth (*Udea rubigalis*) of the family Pyralididae that is widespread in No. America and whose yellowish green larvae are a major pest on the leaves of celery and greenhouse crops
celery–leaved buttercup \-,lēvd-\ *n* **:** CURSED CROWFOOT
celery mosaic *n* **:** a mosaic disease of celery producing stiff bushy growth
celery pine *n* **:** CELERY-TOPPED PINE
celery root *n* **:** CELERIAC
celery salt *n* **:** a mixture of ground celery seed and salt
celery seed *n* **:** minute seedlike fruits of a widely cultivated celery plant (*Apium graveolens*) that are dried for use as a condiment
celery–seed oil *or* **celery oil** *n* **:** a colorless or yellowish essential oil with a celery odor and taste obtained from celery seeds and used chiefly as a flavoring agent
celery–topped pine \-,täpt-\ *or* **celery top pine** *n* **:** an Australasian coniferous tree of the genus *Phyllocladus* (esp. *P. rhomboidalis* and *P. trichomanoides*) of the family Taxaceae cultivated for the graceful heads of celerylike foliage composed of rhombic phyllodes borne in the axils of scaly leaves
celery yellows *n pl but sing in constr* **:** a disease of celery caused by a fungus of the genus *Fusarium* and characterized by yellowing and stunting
-celes *pl of* -CELE
ce·les·ta \sә'lestә, *or* chә'- *as if from It*\ *n* -s [F *célesta*, irreg. fr. *céleste*] **:** a keyboard instrument having an action like that of a piano with hammers that strike steel plates suspended above wooden resonance boxes, producing a tone similar to that of a glockenspiel, and having a range of four octaves sounding an octave higher than the notes indicate

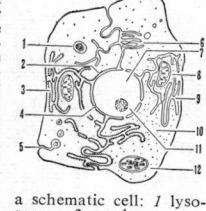

celesta

ce·leste \sә'lest\ *n* -s [F *céleste*, lit., heavenly, fr. L *caelestis*] **1 :** a grayish blue to pale purplish blue **2 a :** VOIX CÉLESTE **b :** a pedal that mutes the strings of a piano by interposing a muffling strip between the hammers and the strings
¹ce·les·tial \sә'les(h)chәl *sometimes* -estēәl\ *adj* [ME, fr. MF, fr. L *caelestis* celestial (fr. *caelum* sky, heaven, atmosphere, temperature) + MF *-al* — more at -HOOD] **1 a :** of or relating to heaven ⟨~ hosts⟩ ⟨the gods of the ~ regions⟩ **b :** felt to resemble or as if proceeding from something divine ⟨a ~ brightness . . . on her face —H.W.Longfellow⟩ **2 :** of or relating to the sky; *specif* **:** representing the visible bodies in the sky ⟨a ~ map⟩ ⟨a ~ globe⟩ **3 a :** ETHEREAL, OTHERWORLDLY ⟨the ~ quiet of an autumn snow⟩ **b :** OLYMPIAN, SUPREME ⟨the ~ impudence of the boy —Leonard Bacon⟩ **4 :** of the color celestial **5** [fr. *Celestial* Empire, old name for China, trans. of Chin *T'ien¹ Ch'ao²*] *usu cap* **:** of or relating to a native of China, the Chinese, or the Chinese nation — **ce·les·tial·ly** \-әlē, -li\ *adv* — **ce·les·tial·ness** *n* -ES
²celestial \"\ *n* -s **1 :** a heavenly or mythical being ⟨the ~s instructed the Indian maid to summon her people to council⟩ **2** *usu cap* **:** a native of China **3** *or* **celestial blue :** SKY BLUE
celestial blue *n* **:** a pale iron-blue pigment usu. containing a large amount of barium sulfate — compare CELESTIAL 3
celestial body *n* **:** an aggregation of matter in the universe that constitutes a unit (as a planet, nebula) for astronomical study
celestial coordinate *n* **:** a member of any system of coordinates used for locating a point on the celestial sphere — compare ECLIPTIC COORDINATE, EQUATOR SYSTEM OF COORDINATE, GALACTIC COORDINATE, HORIZON COORDINATE
celestial crown *n* **:** a heraldic crown having rays like an antique crown but with a star at the end of each ray
celestial equator *n* **:** the great circle on the celestial sphere midway between the celestial poles
celestial glory *n* **:** the highest of the three Mormon degrees or kingdoms of glory attainable in heaven — compare TELESTIAL GLORY, TERRESTIAL GLORY

celestial crown

celestial hierarchy *n* **:** a hierarchy of angels based upon interpretations of various scriptural references and ranked from those nearest to God into nine orders (as seraphim, cherubim, thrones; dominions, virtues, powers; principalities, archangels, angels)
celestial horizon *n* **:** the great circle on the celestial sphere midway between the zenith and the nadir
ce·les·tial·ize \-,līz\ *vt* -ED/-ING/-S **:** to make divine or spiritual in quality or appearance **:** ETHEREALIZE ⟨the *celestialized* figure of a saint⟩ ⟨a face *celestialized* with joy⟩
celestial latitude *n* **:** latitude in the ecliptic system of celestial coordinates
celestial lily *n* **:** a plant of the genus *Nemastylis*
celestial longitude *n* **:** longitude in the ecliptic system of coordinates measured eastward from the March equinox
celestial marriage *n* **:** marriage for eternity solemnized in a Mormon temple
celestial mechanics *n pl but sing or pl in constr* **:** the application of the methods of analytic mechanics to the determination of the motions of the celestial bodies under the action of gravitation — called also *gravitational astronomy*
celestial meridian *n* **:** a great circle of the celestial sphere passing through the celestial poles and the zenith
celestial navigation *n* **:** navigation in which the observed positions of celestial bodies at exact instants of time are employed by a navigator to determine his position
celestial pole *n* **:** one of the two points on the celestial sphere around which the diurnal rotation of the stars appears to take place — compare NORTH POLE, SOUTH POLE
celestial sphere *n* **:** an imaginary sphere of infinite radius against which the celestial bodies appear to be projected and of which the apparent dome of the visible sky forms half
celestial teacher *n, usu cap C&T* [trans. of Chin (Pek) *T'ien¹ Shih¹*] **:** HEAVENLY PRECEPTOR
celestial telescope *n* **:** a variety of telescope goldfish in which the eye pupils are directed upward
celestical *adj* [L *caelestis* + E *-ical* — more at CELESTIAL] *obs* **:** CELESTIAL
celestify *vt* -ED/-ING/-ES [*celestial* + *-ify*] *obs* **:** to make like heaven
¹cel·es·ti·na \,selә'stēnә, ,che-\ *n* -s [It, fem. of *celestino* heavenly, fr. *celeste*, fr. L *caelestis* — more at CELESTIAL] **:** a 4-foot organ stop of flute quality
²cel·es·ti·na \"\ *n* -s [prob. irreg. fr. L *caelestis* heavenly] **:** a largely experimental keyboard musical instrument producing sustained tones by means of a usu. rosined-silk wheel that is made to rub against a tuned string or bar during the depression of each key
¹cel·es·tine *or* **coel·es·tine** \'selә,stēn, -īn; sә'lestәn\ *n* -s [G *zölestin* — more at CELESTITE] **:** CELESTITE
²ce·les·tine \¦selә¦stēn\ *adj* [F *célestine* (in *à la célestine* in the Celestine manner) Celestine ("of an order of monks"), after Pope Celestine (F *Célestine*) V (Pietro di Murrone or Morone) †1296, its founder] *of food* **:** garnished with finely shredded pancakes — usu. used postpositively ⟨consommé ~⟩
cel·es·tite \'selә,stīt, sә'le,-\ *n* -s [G *zölestin* (fr. L *caelestis* celestial + G *-in* -ine) + E *-ite*; fr. its blue color] **:** a mineral $SrSO_4$ consisting of native strontium sulfate commonly white and occas. of a delicate blue color and occurring in orthorhombic crystals and in compact massive and fibrous forms
celi- — see COELI-
¹celiac *var of* COELIAC
²ce·li·ac \'sēlē,ak\ *adj* [*celiac* (*disease*)] **:** belonging to or prescribed for celiac disease ⟨the ~ syndrome⟩ ⟨a ~ diet⟩
celiac disease *n* [¹*celiac*] **:** a chronic nutritional disturbance in young children that is characterized by defective digestion and utilization of fats and by abdominal distention, diarrhea, and fatty stools
cel·i·ba·cy \'selәbәsē, -si\ *n* -ES [L *caelibatus* celibacy + E *-cy*] **:** the state of not having a spouse **:** single life ⟨~ can usu. be tolerated as a state favorable to education —*New Statesman & Nation*⟩ **:** abstention from sexual intercourse **:** CHASTITY; *specif* **:** the obligation (as of certain priests) not to marry
cel·i·ba·tar·i·an \¦selәbә¦ta(a)rēәn\ *adj* [¹*celibate* + *-arian*] **:** favoring or marked by celibacy
¹cel·i·bate \'selәbәt\ *n* -s [L *caelibatus*, fr. *caelib-, caelebs* unmarried + *-atus* -ate; akin to Skt *kevala* alone and to Goth *liban* to live — more at LIVE] **1 :** CELIBACY ⟨the ~ of priests⟩ **2** [²*celibate*] **:** one who lives a single life (as a bachelor)
²celibate \"\ *adj* [L *caelib-, caelebs* + E *-ate*] **:** of or relating to celibacy
celio- — see COELI-
ce·li·ot·o·my \,sēlē'äd·әmē\ *n* -ES [ISV *celio-* + *-tomy*] **:** surgical incision of the abdomen
ce·lite \'sē,līt\ *n* -s [ISV *ce-* (fr. *c*) + *-lite*; fr. its being considered as third in a group including also alite and belite] **:** a constituent of portland-cement clinker now identified as brownmillerite
Celite \"\ *trademark* — used for any of a series of diatomaceous silica and perlite products including filter material and fillers
¹cell \'sel\ *n* -s [ME *celle*, fr. OF, fr. L *cella*; akin to L *celare* to hide — more at HELL] **1 :** a small religious house dependent on and at some distance from a monastery or convent **2 a :** a dwelling of one room occupied by a solitary person (as a hermit) **b :** a single room usu. housing only one person within a building having numerous similar rooms (as in a convent or in a prison) **c :** a small abode or enclosure (as the den of a wild animal) **d :** GRAVE ⟨each in his narrow ~ for ever laid —Thomas Gray⟩ **3 :** a compartment, hollow receptacle, or compartmentlike demarcation: as **a :** one of the compartments of a honeycomb **b :** a ring-shaped enclosure in which an object is secured for observation under a microscope **c :** the entire structure of the wings and wing trussing in an airplane on one side of the fuselage or between fuselages or nacelles when there is more than one **d :** a bag containing aerostatic gas in a balloon or airship **4 a** (1) **:** the bounding walls of a cell (sense 5) that has lost its living content — used esp. of cavities in cork before the discovery of the protoplast (2) **:** a calyculus enclosing a zooid in hydroids and corals **b :** a membranous area bounded by veins in the wing of an insect **c** (1) **:** one of the cavities or compartments into which a compound ovary is partitioned or the whole interior of a monocarpellary ovary (2) **:** THECA 1b **5 :** a small usu. microscopic mass of protoplasm bounded externally by a semipermeable membrane, usu. including one or more nuclei and various nonliving products of its activities (as ergastic granules or rigid external walls), and being capable alone or interacting with other cells of performing all the fundamental functions of life **:** the least structural aggregate of living matter capable of functioning as an independent unit **:** a protoplast with its derivative structures **6 :** a cup, jar, or other vessel or a division of a compound vessel containing electrodes and an electrolyte either for generating electric currents by chemical action or for use in electrolysis — see PRIMARY CELL, SECONDARY CELL, STANDARD CELL, STORAGE CELL **7 a :** CELLA **b :** a space between ribs in a vaulted roof **c :** a compartment of a frame or truss **d :** an air space introduced into a piece of building material (as a cement block or hollow tile) for thermal insulation **8 a :** a unit of a statistical array comprising a group of individuals and formed by the intersection of a column and a row **b :** an aggregate of points in one-to-one correspondence with an aggregate in a euclidean space of any number of dimensions ⟨a circle is a ~ with respect to its interior⟩ **9 :** a small group dedicated to the study and development of a social, religious, or political program; *esp* **:** the smallest organizational unit of a proscribed political party often located within and made up of employees of a particular business, industry, or school **10 :** the oblong arrangement of braille dots in two vertical rows of three high and two wide which in various combinations represent letters, figures,

a schematic cell: *1* lysosome, *2* nuclear membrane, *3* endoplasmic reticulum with associated ribosomes, *4* nuclear pore, *5* intrusion of cell membrane, *6* Golgi apparatus, *7* nucleus, *8* mitochondrion, *9* endoplasmic reticulum, *10* cytoplasm and ribosomes, *11* nucleolus, *12* chloroplast

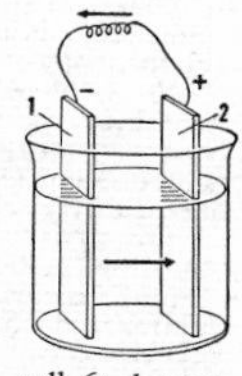

cell 6: *1* negative pole (zinc plate); *2* positive pole (carbon plate)

punctuation marks, and other characters **11 :** any portion of the atmosphere from a few cubic feet to many thousands of cubic miles in volume that moves or behaves as a unit despite varying conditions of temperature, humidity, and air movement inside of it and that takes part in a systematic circulation **12 :** a single unit in a device for converting radiant energy into electrical energy or for varying the intensity of an electric current in accordance with radiation

²cell \"\ *vb* -ED/-ING/-S *vi* **:** to live in a cell ⟨the anchorite ~*ed* underground⟩ ⟨the embezzler ~*ed* with two other prisoners⟩ ~ *vt, of bees* **:** to store (honey) in a comb

³cell *var of* CEL

cell- *or* **cello-** *comb form* [¹*cellulose*] **:** cellulose ⟨*Cell*falcicula⟩ ⟨*cello*biose⟩

cel·la \ˈselə\ *n, pl* **cel·lae** \-ˌlē\ [L — more at CELL] **:** the frequently hidden inner part of a Greek or Roman temple that housed the image of the deity; *also* **:** the corresponding part of a modern building of similar design — called also *naos*

¹cel·lar \ˈselə(r)\ *n* -s [ME *celer*, fr. AF, fr. L *cellarium*, fr. *cella* small room, storeroom — more at CELL] **1 a** *now dial* **:** an above-ground storeroom for foodstuff or produce (as a pantry or granary) **b :** a room or set of rooms below the ground often used for storage and for protecting the building above from ground dampness and sometimes not possessing a finished interior — sometimes distinguished from *basement* **c :** an underground room (as one partitioned off in a basement or one dug in the earth and often roofed over with sod) used to store provisions (as vegetables) or as a refuge — see CYCLONE CELLAR **d :** the bottommost stage or rank ⟨their spirits were in the ~⟩; *esp* **:** the lowest place in the standings of an athletic league or conference **2 :** a stock of wine ⟨a ~ depleted by festivities⟩ **3** *obs* **:** a case esp. for holding bottles

²cellar \"\ *vt* -ED/-ING/-S **:** to put into a cellar (as for storage)

³cellar \"\ *n* -s [by shortening] **:** SALTCELLAR

cel·lar·age \ˈselərij\ *n* -s **1 a :** CELLAR 1 b **b :** a storage cellar or connected group of storage cellars **2 :** charge for storage in a cellar or storehouse **3 :** region resembling cellarage as in its relative position or in what it comprises ⟨comment lifted out of the ~ at the foot of various pages and spread over the upper levels of print —V.L.O.Chittick⟩ ⟨had driven that down into the ~ of his mind, and had almost forgotten it —Robertson Davies⟩ ⟨the murder and the rats and decay in the ~ of the novel —Lionel Trilling⟩

cellar club *n* **:** a social club made up of young men in a poor urban area

cel·lar·er \ˈselərə(r)\ *n* -s [ME *celerer*, fr. OF *celerer*, *celerier*, fr. LL *cellariarius*, fr. L *cellarium* storeroom] **:** an official (as in a monastery) in charge of procuring, storing, and distributing provisions

cel·lar·ess \-ərəs\ *n* -ES [*cellarer* + -*ess*] **:** a member of a religious community of women who is officially in charge of the procuring, storing, and distributing of provisions

cel·lar·ette *also* **cel·lar·et** \ˌseləˈret\ *n* -s [¹*cellar* + -*ette*, -*et*] **:** a case or sideboard designed to hold a few bottles of wine or liquor

cellar hole *n* **:** an excavation intended for a cellar or the exposed cellar area where a house has once stood

cel·lar·less \ˈselə(r)ləs\ *adj* **:** having no cellar ⟨a low-lying city of ~ houses⟩

cel·lar·man \-mən\ *n, pl* **cellarmen 1 :** a stock clerk in a hotel or restaurant who handles the alcoholic-beverage supply **2 :** one who clarifies wine before it is filtered

cellar pipe *n* **:** a fire-fighting device consisting of a hose nozzle at the end of a tube designed to be inserted into a burning area (as a cellar or ship's hold) and so controlled from without that it can direct a spray toward any area within

cellarway \ˈ==,=\ *n* **:** a way leading through or into a cellar or cellars

cellblock \ˈ=,=\ *n* **:** a group of cells constituting a subdivision of a prison

cell–blockade phenomenon *n* **:** INTERFERENCE PHENOMENON

cell body *n* **:** a living cell proper exclusive of its processes

cell bridge *n* **:** PLASMODESMA

cell count *n* **:** a count of cells esp. of the blood or other body fluid in a standard volume (as a cubic millimeter)

cell division *n* **:** the process by which cells multiply (as by involving fission of nucleus and cytosome to produce new individuals) — see AMITOSIS, MITOSIS

celled \ˈseld\ *adj* **:** containing a cell — usu. used with a qualifying adverb or attributive noun ⟨many-*celled*⟩ ⟨nerve-*celled*⟩

cel·le·por·i·dae \ˌseləˈpȯrəˌdē\ *n pl, cap* [NL, fr. *Cellepora*, type genus (irreg. fr. L *cella* cell + NL -*pora*) + -*idae*] **:** a family of bryozoans resembling coral, having tubular calcareous zooecia with terminal openings, and forming erect or encrusting colonies

cell·fal·cic·u·la \ˌsel,falˈsikyələ\ *n, cap* [NL, fr. *cell-* + LL *falcicula* small sickle, dim. of L *falc-, falx* sickle — more at FALCHION] **:** a genus of motile gram-negative monotrichous soil bacteria (family Spirillaceae) that oxidize cellulose to oxycellulose and thus cause disintegration of vegetable fiber, appearing as short rods with pointed ends and containing metachromatic granules — compare CELLVIBRIO

cell house *n* **:** a prison building having a number of separate cells each ordinarily designed for one occupant

cel·lif·er·ous \(ˈ)seˈlif(ə)rəs\ *adj* [¹*cell* + -*i-* + -*ferous*] **:** bearing or producing cells

cel·lif·u·gal \(ˈ)seˈlif(y)əgəl\ *or* **cel·lu·lif·u·gal** \ˌselyəˈli-\ *adj* [ISV ¹*cell* or *cellul-* + -*i-* + -*fugal*; prob. orig. formed as G *zellulifugal*] **:** conducting or conducted away from a cell body — used chiefly of nerve-cell processes and nerve impulses

celling *pres part of* CELL

cel·lip·e·tal \(ˈ)seˈlipəd·əl\ *or* **cel·lu·lip·e·tal** \ˌselyəˈli-\ *adj* [ISV ¹*cell* or *cellul-* + -*i-* + -*petal*; prob. orig. formed as G *zellulipetal*] **:** conducting or conducted toward a cell body — used chiefly of nerve-cell processes and nerve impulses

cel·list \ˈchelə̇st\ *n* -s [¹*cello* + -*ist*] **:** one that plays the cello — called also *violoncellist*

cell–lethal \ˈ=ˌ==\ *n* -s **:** a chromosome deficiency that induces death of the cell in which it occurs

cell lineage *n* **:** the developmental history of a cell from the first cleavage division until its ultimate fate is determined

cell membrane *n* **1 :** PLASMA MEMBRANE **2 :** CELL WALL

¹cel·lo \ˈche(ˌ)lō\ *n, pl* **cellos** \-ōz\ *also* **cel·li** \(ˌ)lē\ [short for *violoncello*] **:** the bass member of the violin family tuned an octave below the viola and played from a sitting position with the instrument held almost vertically on the floor — compare CONTRABASS

cello

²cel·lo \ˈse(ˌ)lō\ *adj* [short for *cellophane*] **1 :** made of cellophane ⟨a ~ bag⟩ **2 :** wrapped in cellophane ⟨a dozen carrots, ~⟩

cello– — see CELL-

cel·lo·bi·ose \ˌselōˈbīˌōs\ *n* -s [ISV *cell-* + *biose*; orig. formed as G *zellobiose*] **:** a white crystalline faintly sweet-tasting sugar $C_{12}H_{22}O_{11}$ of the disaccharide class obtained by partial hydrolysis of cellulose; 4-β-glucosyl-glucose — called also *cellose*

cel·lo·bi·u·ron·ic acid \ˌselō,bīyəˈränik-\ *n* [*cell-* + *bi-* + *uronic*] **:** an aldobiuronic acid obtained by partial hydrolysis of a specific polysaccharide of pneumococci and yielding glucose and glucuronic acid on hydrolysis

cel·lo·cut \ˈselō,kət, -lə,-\ *n* -s [²*cello* + *cut*] **1 :** an artist's print made from a plastic plate in which a design determined by the use of liquid plastics has been cut in relief; *also* **:** the plate from which such a print is made **2 :** the art of making and printing from cellocuts

cel·lo·dex·trin \ˌseləˈdekstrən\ *n* [*cell-* + *dextrin*] **:** a polysaccharide obtained by partial hydrolysis of cellulose

cell of clau·di·us \-ˈklau̇dēəs, -ōd-\ *usu cap 2d C* [after Friedrich Matthias *Claudius* †1869 Austrian anatomist] **:** one of the low cuboidal cells covering the outermost part of the basilar membrane of the organ of Corti

cell of cor·ti \-ˈkȯrd·ē\ *usu cap 2d C* [after Alfonso *Corti* †1876 Ital. anatomist] **:** a hair cell in the organ of Corti

cell of dei·ters \-ˈdīd-ə(r)z, -)s\ *usu cap D* [after Otto Friedrich Karl *Deiters* †1863 Ger. anatomist] **:** one of the slender cells that end in rigid filaments terminated by platelike structures and that are placed among and support and separate the outer hair cells of the organ of Corti

cell of golgi *usu cap G* **:** GOLGI CELL

cell of leydig *usu cap L* **:** LEYDIG CELL

cell of purkinje *usu cap P* **:** PURKINJE CELL

cell of schwann *usu cap S* **:** SCHWANN'S CELL

cell of sertoli *usu cap S* **:** SERTOLI CELL

cel·loi·din \(ˈ)seˈlȯidᵊn\ *n* -s [ISV *cell-* + -*oid* + -*in*; prob. orig. formed as G *zelloidin*] **:** a purified form of pyroxylin obtained from collodion by precipitation and used chiefly in microscopy for embedding

cel·lo·phane \ˈseləˌfān\ *n* -s [ISV *cell-* + -*phane* (as in *diaphane*); orig. formed in F] **:** a transparent sheet or tube of regenerated cellulose highly impermeable to dry gases, grease, and bacteria made by extruding alkaline viscose solution through a narrow straight or circular die into an acid bath, usu. moisture-proofed by thin coatings and sometimes dyed, and used chiefly as wrappers or bags for packaging food and merchandise, window envelopes, or bags for dialysis

cel·lose \ˈseˌlōs\ *n* -s [ISV *cell-* + -*ose*; orig. formed as G *zellose*] **:** CELLOBIOSE

Cel·lo·solve \ˈselə,sälv\ *trademark* — used for a colorless mobile liquid ether-alcohol used chiefly as a solvent (as for lacquers and varnishes) and component of hydraulic fluids

cell plasm *n* **:** CYTOPLASM

cell plate *n* **:** a disk formed in the phragmoplast of a dividing plant cell, marking the beginning of separation into two daughter cells, developing gradually from the center toward the parent cell, and eventually forming the true middle lamella of the wall between the daughter cells

cells *pl of* CELL, *pres 3d sing of* CELL

cell sap *n* **1 :** the liquid content of the vacuole of a plant cell consisting of an aqueous solution of organic acids and their salts as well as pigments, proteins, tannins, emulsified fats, and other complex compounds chiefly in the colloidal state **2 :** the more fluid part of protoplasm **:** KARYOLYMPH, HYALOPLASM

cell theory *n* **:** either of two theories in biology: (1) the cell is the fundamental unit of living matter, and (2) the organism is a mosaic of autonomous cells, its properties being the sum of those of the constituent cells

Cel·lu·cot·ton \ˈselyə,kätᵊn\ *trademark* — used for a soft absorbent creped cellulose used in surgical dressings

¹cellul- *or* **celluli-** *or* **cellulo-** *comb form* [NL, fr. *cellula*] **1 :** plant or animal cell ⟨*celluli*cidal⟩ ⟨*cellulo*toxic⟩ **2 :** cellular and ⟨*cellulo*fibrous⟩

²cellul- *or* **cellulo-** *also* **cellu-** *comb form* [¹*cellulose*] **:** cellulose ⟨*cellu*loid, *cellu*lolytic⟩

cel·lu·la \ˈselyələ\ *n, pl* **cellu·lae** \-ˌlē\ [NL, fr. L, small storeroom] **:** a small cell **:** CELLULE

cel·lu·lar \-lə(r)\ *adj* [NL *cellularis*, fr. *cellula* living cell, fr. L, small storeroom, dim. of *cella* small room — more at CELL] **1 :** characterized by, consisting of, or dealing with cells ⟨~ structure⟩ ⟨~ physiology⟩ **2 a :** containing cavities **:** POROUS ⟨~ rubber⟩ **b** *of igneous rock* **:** having a porous texture produced by the expansion of gases within the fluid lava ⟨~ basalt⟩ **3 :** consisting of or employing separate semi-independent sections or units ⟨a ~ plan of defense⟩ ⟨the ~ structure of medieval society⟩; *specif* **:** using or marked by the use of cell-like rooms or living quarters ⟨~ confinement⟩ — **cel·lu·lar·ly** *adv*

cellular cryptogam *or* **cellular plant** *n* **:** a cryptogamous plant possessing little or no vascular tissue (as algae, fungi, lichens, and mosses) — compare VASCULAR CRYPTOGAM

cellular glass *n* **:** a lightweight glass of spongelike appearance widely used as a heat and sound insulator

cel·lu·lar·i·ty \ˌselyəˈlarəd·ē\ *n* -ES **:** the quality or state of being cellular

cellular kite *n* **:** BOX KITE

cellular tissue *n* **1 :** areolar connective tissue **2** *bot* **:** tissue entirely parenchymatous

cel·lu·lase \ˈselyə,lās\ *n* -s [ISV ²*cellul-* + -*ase*] **:** any of a group of enzymes that are found in various fungi, bacteria, insects, and lower animals and that hydrolyze cellulose

cel·lu·late \-āt\ *vt* -ED/-ING/-S [¹*cellul-* + -*ate*] **:** to provide with cells ⟨glass *cellulated* in manufacture⟩

cel·lu·la·tion \ˌselyəˈlāshən\ *n* -s **:** division into cells; *esp* **:** division of a syncytium into cells

cel·lule \ˈsel(ˌ)yül\ *n* -s [F or L; F, monk's cell, fr. L *cellula* small storeroom — more at CELLULAR] **1** *archaic* **:** a small receptacle (as a pigeonhole) **2 :** a minute cavity **:** INTERSTICE, CELL

celluli– — see CELLUL-

cellulifugal *var of* CELLIFUGAL

cel·lu·lin \ˈselyələn\ *n* -s [²*cellul-* + -*in*] **:** a cellulose like carbohydrate chiefly of animal origin but found also in certain fungi (as Leptomitales)

cellulipetal *var of* CELLIPETAL

cel·lu·li·tis \ˌselyəˈlīd·əs\ *n* -ES [NL, fr. ¹*cellul-* + -*itis*] **:** diffuse and usu. subcutaneous or intrapelvic spreading inflammation of connective tissue

cellulo– — see CELLUL-

¹cel·lu·loid \ˈselyəˌlȯid *also* -eləˌl- *or* ˌ==ˈ=\ *n* -s [*Celluloid*] **:** motion-picture film ⟨the story was on ~ in a year⟩; *broadly* **:** MOTION PICTURES ⟨the picture was as funny as ~ can get⟩ ⟨banned foreign ~s⟩

²celluloid \"\ *adj* **:** of or relating to the motion pictures **:** CINEMATIC

Cel·lu·loid \"\ *trademark* — used for a tough highly flammable but not usu. explosive synthetic thermoplastic composed essentially of cellulose nitrate and camphor or other plasticizer and used in the manufacture of toilet articles (as combs and brushes), novelties, and photographic films

cel·lu·lo·lyt·ic \ˌselyəlōˈlid·ik\ *adj* [²*cellul-* + -*lytic*] **:** having the capacity to hydrolyze cellulose — used of certain bacteria and protozoans

cel·lu·lo·mo·nas \ˌselyəˈlämənəs, -ˌnas\ *n, cap* [NL, fr. ²*cellul-* + -*monas*] **:** a genus of short peritrichous gram-negative rod-shaped soil-inhabiting bacteria (family Corynebacteriaceae) that digest cellulose

cel·lu·los·an \ˌselyəˈlōsᵊn, ˌselyəˌlōˈsan\ *n* -s [¹*cellulose* + -*an*] **:** any of several carbohydrates (as xylan and mannan) that occur in close association with cellulose in cell walls (as in wood) and are sometimes classed as hemicelluloses

¹cel·lu·lose \ˈselyəˌlōs\ *n* -s [F, fr. *cellule* living cell (fr. NL *cellula*) + -*ose* — more at CELLULAR] **1 :** any of several fibrous substances constituting the chief part of the cell walls of plants and of many fibrous products (as paper, cotton, linen) — see HEMICELLULOSE, LIGNIN, MICELLE **2 a :** a complex polymeric carbohydrate $(C_6H_{10}O_5)_x$ having the same percentage composition as starch and also yielding only glucose on complete hydrolysis by acid but consisting of a long chain of beta-glucosidic residues linked through the 1,4-positions **b :** the portion of a cellulosic material that does not dissolve in a 17.5 to 18 percent sodium hydroxide solution and constitutes the most abundant form of cellulose — called also *alpha cellulose* **c :** the portion of a cellulosic material that dissolves in an alkaline solution and is precipitated on acidification — called also *beta cellulose* **d :** the portion of a cellulosic material that dissolves in an alkaline solution and is not precipitated on acidification — called also *gamma cellulose* **e :** the white fibers obtained from vegetable matter (as wood or cotton linters) by purification (as by treatment with acid sulfite or dilute alkali) that usu. consist chiefly of alpha cellulose and are used esp. in making regenerated cellulose products (as rayon and cellophane) and cellulose derivatives (as cellulose esters and cellulose ethers) — called also *chemical cellulose*

²cellulose \"\ *vt* -ED/-ING/-S **:** to coat or treat with some cellulose preparation (as with cellulose acetate)

³cellulose \"\ *adj* **:** containing or made from cellulose or a derivative of cellulose ⟨~ plastic⟩ ⟨~ sponge⟩ ⟨~ tape⟩

cellulose acetate *n* **:** any of several esters that are obtained by the partial or complete acetylation of cellulose (as cotton linters or wood) usu. with acetic anhydride, acetic acid, and concentrated sulfuric acid, that are soluble in acetone, thermoplastic, and less flammable than cellulose nitrates, and that are used chiefly in making acetate fibers and tough plastics (as films, molded articles, and foamed insulation) — called also *acetate*

cellulose acetate butyrate *n* **:** any of several mixed esters that are formed by acylation of cellulose with a mixture of acetic and butyric acids and anhydrides and an acid catalyst, that are thermoplastic like cellulose acetates but have a wider range of solubility and are more moisture-resistant, and that are used in molded and extruded plastics and in lacquers

cellulose acetate propionate *n* **:** any of several mixed esters of cellulose and acetic and propionic acids that are similar to cellulose acetate butyrates in method of manufacture, properties, and uses

cellulose ester *n* **:** an ester of cellulose (as cellulose nitrate or cellulose acetate) with an inorganic or organic acid

cellulose ether *n* **:** an ether (as ethyl cellulose or sodium carboxymethyl cellulose) made usu. by etherification of alkali cellulose

cel·lu·lose·like \ˈselyə,lō,slīk\ *adj* **:** resembling cellulose

cellulose nitrate *n* **1 :** any of several esters that are obtained as white fibrous flammable solids by the nitration of cellulose (as cotton linters or wood) usu. with a mixture of nitric and sulfuric acids — called also *nitrocellulose* **2 a :** a low-nitrated plastics grade of cellulose nitrate containing less than 12.5% nitrogen that is soluble in a variety of organic solvents (as mixtures of ether and alcohol) and is used chiefly in making photographic films, lacquers and other coatings (as for automobiles, furniture, and fabrics simulating leather), tough thermoplastic materials, and adhesives — see PYROXYLIN **b :** a high-nitrated ballistics grade of cellulose nitrate containing 12.5 to 13.5 percent nitrogen that is insoluble in most organic solvents and is used in explosives — see GUNCOTTON, SMOKELESS POWDER

cellulose propionate *n* **:** any of several esters made by the action of propionic anhydride on cellulose and used as thermoplastics for making tough molded products (as frames for eyeglasses and goggles, pens, and flashlight housings)

cellulose xanthate *n* **:** any of several colorless esters obtained usu. as alkali salts in the form of orange-colored crumbs by xanthation of alkali cellulose with carbon disulfide as a step in the manufacture of viscose

¹cel·lu·los·ic \ˌselyəˈlōsik\ *adj* **:** of, containing, or made from cellulose ⟨~ fibers⟩

²cellulosic \"\ *n* -s [¹*cellulosic*] **:** a substance (as a plastic or fiber) made from cellulose or a derivative of cellulose

cell·vib·rio \(ˈ)selˈvibrē,ō\ *n, cap* [NL, fr. cell- + *Vibrio*] **:** a genus of long slender slightly curved monotrichous motile rod-shaped bacteria (family Spirillaceae) with rounded ends that oxidize cellulose to oxycellulose and cause disintegration of vegetable fiber — compare CELLFALCICULA

cell wall *n* **1 :** the somewhat rigid permeable wall typical of plant cells (as the cellulose or celluloselike layers secreted by the cytoplasm in most plants) at first thin and delicate but modified in extent, thickness, and chemical nature as it develops and matures — compare CUTINIZATION, LIGNIFY, PRIMARY WALL **2 :** a membrane bounding an animal cell; *usu* **:** PLASMA MEMBRANE

celo– — see COEL-

celom *var of* COELOM

ce·lo·nav·i·ga·tion \ˈsē(ˌ)lō-, ˈse-\ *n* [*celestial* + -*o-* (as in *geonavigation*) + *navigation*] **:** CELESTIAL NAVIGATION

ce·lo·sia \seˈlōzh(ē)ə\ *n, cap* [NL, irreg. fr. Gk *kēleos* burning or LGk *kēlos* dry; akin to Gk *kaiein* to burn — more at CAUSTIC] **:** a large genus of tropical annual herbs (family Amaranthaceae) having alternate leaves and showy flowers in spikes which in cultivated forms are often fasciated and form compact often feathery clusters — see COCKSCOMB 2b

cels *pl of* CEL

cels *abbr, usu cap* Celsius

cel·sia \ˈselsēə, -lsh(ē)ə\ *n, cap* [NL, fr. Olaf *Celsius* †1756 Swed. botanist + NL -*ia*] **:** a genus of mostly European herbs (family Scrophulariaceae) with large yellow flowers resembling snapdragons — see CRETAN BEAR'S TAIL, CRETAN MULLEIN

cel·si·an \ˈselsē,an\ *n* -s [prob. fr. Anders *Celsius* + E -*an*] **:** a mineral $BaAl_2Si_2O_8$ that consists of a barium feldspar and is isomorphous with orthoclase

celsitude *n* -s [prob. fr. L *celsitudo* loftiness, fr. *celsus* high, lofty — more at HILL] *archaic* **:** HEIGHT, ALTITUDE, EXALTATION

cel·si·us \ˈselsēəs, -lshəs\ *adj, usu cap* [after Anders *Celsius* †1744 Swed. astronomer who invented the centigrade scale] **:** CENTIGRADE ⟨a *Celsius* thermometer⟩ ⟨10° *Celsius*⟩ — abbr. *C, Cels*

¹celt \ˈselt, ˈke-\ *also* **kelt** \ˈke-\ *n* -s *cap* [F *Celte*, sing. of *Celtes*, fr. L *Celtae*] **1 a :** a member of a division of the early Indo-European peoples in Iron-Age Europe and pre-Roman Europe whose subdivisions had a range of distribution from the British Isles and Spain to Asia Minor and were in part absorbed into the Roman Empire as Britons, Gauls, Boii, Galatians, or Celtiberians **b :** a descendant of these people who has somewhere in his background a native knowledge of a Celtic language **2 :** a modern Gael, Highland Scot, Irishman, Welshman, Cornishman, or Breton

²celt \ˈselt\ *n* -s [LL *celtis* chisel] **:** a prehistoric implement shaped like a chisel or ax head made of polished stone in neolithic times and later of metal

¹celt·ibe·ri·an \ˌseltəˈbirēən, ˌke-, -lˌtī,ˈ-\ *adj, usu cap* [L *Celtiberia* (fr. *Celtiberi* Celtiberians, fr. *Celtae* Celts + *Iberi* Iberians) + E -*an*] **1 :** of, relating to, or characteristic of Celtiberia, a mountainous district of ancient Spain **2 :** of, relating to, or characteristic of the people of Celtiberia

²celtiberian \"\ *n* -s *cap* **:** one of the Celts of Iberian intermixture that inhabited ancient Celtiberia

¹celt·ic \ˈseltik, ˈke-, -ēk\ *or* **kelt·ic** \ˈke-\ *adj, usu cap* [L *Celticus*, fr. *Celtae* Celts + L -*icus* -ic] **1 :** of or relating to the Celts, their language, civilization, or abode **2 :** of or relating to certain ancient strains of European domestic animals — see CELTIC HORSE, CELTIC OX

²celtic \"\ *or* **keltic** \"\ *n* -s *cap* **:** a group of languages closely akin to the Italic and now confined to Brittany, Wales, western Ireland, and the Scottish Highlands, usu. subdivided into Brythonic and Goidelic, and possessed of a copious medieval prose and verse literature — see INDO-EUROPEAN LANGUAGES table

celtic cross *n, usu cap 1st C* **:** a cross having essentially the form of a Latin cross with a ring about the intersection of the crossbar and upright shaft; *also* **:** something having the form of such a cross (as a monument, badge, emblem)

Celtic cross

celtic fringe *n, usu cap C* **:** the portion of the population of the British Isles which is of Celtic origin or the land to which such people are native

celtic horse *or* **celtic pony** *n, usu cap C* **:** a small shaggy large-headed horse of northwestern Europe and Iceland of which the Shetland pony is an improved breed

celt·i·cism \-tə,sizəm\ *n* -s *usu cap* **:** a Celtic custom, expression, or idiom ⟨the *Celticisms* within modern English⟩

celt·i·cist \-sə̇st\ *n* -s *usu cap* **:** a specialist in Celtic languages or cultures

cel·tic·i·ty \(ˌ)selˈtisəd·ē, -sətē, -i\ *n* -ES *usu cap* **:** the quality or state of being Celtic

celt·i·cize \-ˌsīz\ *vt* -ED/-ING/-S *sometimes cap* **:** to make Celtic in language practices, culture, or customs ⟨the upper end of the island has been thoroughly *celticized* —*American*⟩

celtic ox *n, usu cap C* [so called fr. its occurrence in Alpine regions where Celts lived in early historical times] **:** a small prehistoric European ox (*Bos longifrons*) having a high forehead and short horns and considered by some to be the ancestor or an ancestor of domestic cattle

cel·tis \ˈseltə̇s\ *n, cap* [NL, fr. L, an African lotus] **:** a large genus of widely distributed trees and shrubs (family Ulmaceae) characterized by a berrylike fruit and leaves predominantly 3-veined at the base — see HACKBERRY

celt·ist \ˈseltə̇st, ˈke-\ *n* -s *usu cap* [F *celtiste*, fr. F *Celte* Celt + -*iste* -ist] **:** CELTICIST

cel·ti·um \ˈselshēəm, -ltēəm\ *n* -s [NL, fr. L *Celtae* Celts + NL -*ium*] **:** HAFNIUM

celts *pl of* CELT

cel·tuce \ˈseltə̇s\ *n* -s [*cel*ery + let*tuce*] **:** a celerylike vegetable that is derived from lettuce and has edible stalks and leaves that combine the flavors of celery and lettuce

BLUE PERSIAN
RED TABBY PERSIAN
(PEKE-FACED)
BLACK PERSIAN
STRIPED MANX
DOMESTIC
SHORT-HAIR
BLUE POINT SIAMESE
SEAL POINT SIAMESE
BURMESE
ABYSSINIAN
KAFFIR CAT

cem *abbr* **1** cement **2** cemetery

cem·bal d'a·mo·re \'chem,bäldə'mōrē, 'chäm-\ *n, pl* **cemba·li d'amore** \-,bə(,)lēdə-\ [It, lit., clavichord of love] **:** a clavichord with double-length strings

cem·ba·list \'chembələst, -äm-\ *n* -s [*cembalo* + *-ist*] **1 :** a player on the harpsichord **2 :** a player of any keyboard instrument in an orchestra

cem·ba·lo \-,lō\ *n, pl* **cemba·li** \-(,)lē\ *or* **cembalos** [It, clavichord, tambourine, fr. L *cymbalum* cymbal — more at CYMBAL] **1 :** DULCIMER **2** [short for *clavicembalo*] **:** HARPSICHORD **3 :** the manual as distinguished from the pedal part of early organ music **4 :** the continuo part of a concerto

cembalon *var of* CIMBALOM

cem·bra nut \'sembrə-\ *n* **:** CEDAR NUT

cembra pine \"-\ *or* **cem·bran pine** \-brən-\ *n* [*Cembra* fr. NL (specific epithet of the Swiss pine *Pinus cembra*), modif. of G dial. *zember, zimber* timber, fr. OHG *zimbar* wood; *cembran* fr. NL *cembra* + E *-an* — more at TIMBER] **:** SWISS PINE

¹ce·ment \sə'ment, sē'- *sometimes* 'sē,m-\ *n* -s [ME *sement, siment*, fr. OF *ciment*, fr. L *caementum* rough unhewn stone, marble chips used in making mortar, fr. *caedere* to cut, hew — more at CONCISE] **1 a :** a powder made from alumina, silica, lime, iron oxide, and magnesia burned together in a kiln and finely pulverized which when mixed with water to form a plastic mass hardens by chemical combination and by gelation and crystallization and is used as an ingredient of mortar and concrete; *esp* **:** PORTLAND CEMENT — see ALUMINA CEMENT, NATURAL CEMENT **b :** a material in which mainly cement is used **:** CONCRETE, MORTAR **2 :** a binding element or agency: as **a :** any fabricated substance to make objects adhere to each other (as asphalt, glue, gypsum, lime, paste, or plaster) **b :** any of various secretions chiefly produced by special glands of invertebrates that harden rapidly when exposed to air or water and are used to fasten objects together (as an animal to its substrate, sand grains into the wall of a test, or nits to hairs) **c :** a notion or feeling serving to unite firmly **:** any agency making for lasting union ⟨the States, on their part, lacking the ~ of national feeling —Percival Spear⟩ **3 :** CEMENTUM **4 :** a plastic composition usu. made of zinc, copper, or silica for filling dental cavities **5 :** the fine-grained groundmass or glass of a porphyry **:** residual uncrystallized material

²cement \"\ *vb* -ED/-ING/-S [ME *simenten*, fr. *siment*, n.] *vt* **1 :** to join, unite, or cause to adhere by or as if by means of a cement ⟨layers ~*ed* together with glue⟩ ⟨sand particles being ~*ed* in strata⟩ **2 a :** to bind together, unite firmly, unify **:** exert a marked cohesive influence on ⟨~ scattered groups from all the northern states into a national party —*Amer. Guide Series: Pa.*⟩ **b :** to stop or end disruptive tendencies and ensure the continuation of (as an association or friendship) **:** establish firmly ⟨in ~*ing* a more stable Pan-American union —R.W.Murray⟩ **3 :** to overlay with concrete ⟨~ a cellar floor⟩ **4 :** to subject to cementation ⟨~*ed* steel⟩ ~ *vi* **:** to become cemented **:** unite firmly or solidify as if into cement **:** COHERE, STICK ⟨the snow . . . compacting and ~*ing* until the streams are spanned —John Muir †1914⟩

³cement \"\ *adj* [¹*cement*] **1 :** of or relating to cement **2 :** obtained by cementation ⟨~ steel⟩ ⟨~ copper⟩

ce·ment·al \sə'mentᵊl, (')sē¦m-\ *adj* **:** of or relating to cement

ce·men·ta·tion \,sē,men'tāshən\ *n* -s **1 :** the act or process of cementing **:** the state of being cemented ⟨~ of sand into stone⟩ **2 a :** a process that consists in surrounding a solid body with the powder of other substances and heating the whole to a degree not sufficient to cause fusion, the physical properties of the body being changed by chemical combination with the powder ⟨iron becomes steel by ~ with charcoal⟩ ⟨green glass becomes porcelain by ~ with sand⟩ **b :** the process of obtaining a metal from a solution of one of its compounds by precipitation with another metal (as the obtaining of copper from a solution of copper sulfate by means of metallic iron)

ce·ment·a·to·ry \sə'mentə,tōrē, sē'-\ *adj* [²*cement* + *-atory* (as in *separatory*)] **:** cementing firmly **:** tending to unify

cement block *n* **:** CONCRETE BLOCK

cement clinker *n* **:** the glassy clinkerlike product of fusing together clay and limestone as the first stage in the manufacture of portland cement

cement disease *n* **:** pneumonia in young pigs kept on cold damp concrete floors

cemented shoe *or* **cement shoe** *n* **:** a shoe in which the outsole, upper, and insole are cemented together instead of being sewed

ce·ment·er \-ə(r)\ *n* -s **1 :** one that cements or makes cement **2 a :** GLUER **b :** a shipworker who applies cement on ships' bottoms, in crevices, or in any joints to make them watertight **c :** CEMENT FINISHER **d :** one who directs and assists workers in cementing the space between the sidewalls and steel casings of an oil or gas well to provide protection and control for underground operations **e :** a vulcanizer of breaks and holes in pneumatic tires — called also *patcher* **f :** a repairer of broken concrete structural parts and equipment — called also *cement mason*

cement finisher *n* **:** one that makes a cement surface of specified texture by using hand tools (as trowels)

cement gland *n* **:** a gland that secretes an adhesive substance (as those in the foot of many rotifers that produce secretions to anchor the animals to the substrate or as those associated with the female reproductive system of many insects)

cement gravel *n* **:** gravel consolidated by clay, calcium carbonate, silica, or some other binding material

ce·ment·i·cle \sə'mentəkəl, sē-\ *n* -s [NL *cementum* + E *-icle* (as in *clavicle*)] **:** a calcified body formed in the periodontal membrane of a tooth

ce·ment·i·fi·ca·tion \≈,≈təfə'kāshən\ *n* -s [¹*cement* + *-i-* + *-fication*] **:** the process by which cementum of a tooth is formed

ce·men·tin \≈'≈tᵊn\ *n* -s [¹*cement* + *-in*] **:** intercellular material uniting the borders of squamous endothelial cells

ce·ment·ite \≈'≈,tīt\ *n* -s [¹*cement* + *-ite*] **:** a hard brittle iron carbide Fe_3C occurring in steel, cast iron, and nearly all iron-carbon alloys

ce·men·ti·tious \¦sē,men¦tishəs\ *adj* [¹*cement* + *-itious*] **:** having the properties of cement **:** like or relevant to cement ⟨the adhesion of ~ materials⟩

ce·ment·less *pronunc at* ¹CEMENT + ləs\ *adj* **:** lacking cement **:** bonded without cement

cement mixer *n* **1 :** one that produces a thin rubber cement by mixing latex or raw rubber with a solvent **2 :** one that produces slurry for cement by mixing clay or shale with powdered limestone and water — called also *boxman* **3 :** CONCRETE MIXER

cement mortar *n* **:** mortar of portland cement and sand sometimes with a little lime to make it more plastic

ce·ment·o·blast \sə'mentə,blast, sē- -ntō,-\ *n* -s [NL *cementum* + E *-o-* + *-blast*] **:** one of the specialized osteoblasts of the dental sac that produce cementum

ce·ment·o·gen·e·sis \≈,≈≈'jenəsəs\ *n, pl* **cementogene·ses** \-ə,sēz\ [NL, fr. *cementum* + *-o-* + L *genesis*] **:** formation or development of the cementum of a tooth

ce·men·to·ma \,sē,men'tōmə\ *n, pl* **cementomas** \-ōməz\ *or* **cementoma·ta** \-ōməd·ə\ [NL, fr. *cementum* + *-oma*] **:** a tumor resembling cementum in structure

cement organ *n* **:** ADHESIVE ORGAN

cement plaster *n* **1 :** a gypsum plaster with certain impurities present or added in the calcining process mixed with sand or wood fiber and water to form a mortar for plastering interior surfaces — called also *hard wall plaster, patent plaster* **2 a :** a mortar consisting of portland cement, sand, and water used for plastering interior surfaces of a building **b :** STUCCO

cement rock *or* **cement stone** *n* **:** a clayey limestone having approximately the ratio of alumina, lime, and silica in cement

cement rod *n* **:** the rod to one end of which a gem is cemented while being cut **:** DOP STICK

cements *pl of* CEMENT, *pres 3d sing of* CEMENT

cement stucco *n* **:** STUCCO

cement substance *n* **1 :** the intercellular substance in certain tissues (as endothelium) **2 :** the substance binding together the enamel rods in the teeth

cement–temper \≈'≈¦≈≈\ *vt* **:** to mix (a lime plaster) with portland cement to improve its strength and durability

ce·men·tum \sə'mentəm, sē'-\ *n, pl* **cemen·ta** \-tə\ [NL, fr. L *caementum* rough stone — more at CEMENT] **:** the specialized external bony layer covering the dentin of the part of a tooth normally within the gum — see TOOTH illustration

ce·me·te·ri·al \¦semə¦tirēəl\ *adj* [*cemetery* + *-ial*] **:** of or belonging to a cemetery or burial

ce·me·tery \'semə,terē, -ri\ *n* -ES [ME *cimitery*, fr. MF *cimitere, cimetière*, fr. LL *cimiterium, coemeterium*, fr. Gk *koimētērion* sleeping chamber, burial place, fr. *koiman* to put to sleep; akin to L *cunae* cradle, Gk *keisthai* to lie, Skt *śete* he lies, sleeps] **:** an area for burial or entombment: **a :** a Roman catacomb **b :** a consecrated churchyard **c :** any burial ground, typically a large one **:** GRAVEYARD

CEMF *abbr* counter electromotive force

¹cen- *or* **ceno-** see COEN-

²cen- *or* **ceno-** *or* **caen-** *or* **caeno-** *comb form* [Gk *kain-, kaino-*, fr. *kainos* new — more at RECENT] **1 :** recent ⟨*cenozoic*⟩ **2 :** novel ⟨*cenogenesis*⟩

¹cé·na·cle \sānäkl(ᵊ), -k(lə)\ *n, pl* **cénacles** \"\ [F, lit., room where Christ and his apostles had the Last Supper, fr. LL *cenaculum*, fr. L, dining room, fr. *cena* dinner; akin toGk *keirein* to cut — more at SHEAR] **:** a philosophical, literary, or artistic group **:** COTERIE

²cen·a·cle \'senəkəl\ *n* -s [fr. *The Society of Our Lady of the Cenacle*, congregation of nuns founded in France in 1826 to direct retreats for women] **:** a retreat house; esp **:** one under the direction of the Society of Our Lady of the Cenacle

cen·chrus \'seŋkrəs\ *n, cap* [NL, fr. Gk *kenchros* millet; prob. akin to L *frendere* to grind — more at GRIND] **:** a genus of grasses having spikelets enclosed in ovoid spiny involucres that form burs, the plants providing good forage before the bur develops

cendal *var of* SENDAL

cen·dre \'sä(ⁿ)ⁿdr(ᵊ), -d(rə)\ *n, pl* **cendres** \"\ [F, lit., ash, fr. L *cinis* — more at INCINERATE] **:** AZURITE BLUE

-cene \,sēn\ *adj comb form* [Gk *kainos* new — more at RECENT] **:** recent — in names of geologic periods ⟨*eocene*⟩; compare CENOZOIC

cenesthesia *var of* COENESTHESIA

ce·ni·zo \sə'nē(,)zō, -sō\ *n* -s [AmerSp, fr. Sp, white goosefoot, prob. fr. *ceniza* ashes, fr. (assumed) VL *cinisia*, irreg. fr. L *cinis* — more at INCINERATE] **1** *Southwest* **:** SHAD SCALE **2** *West Indies* **:** any of a variety of shrubs and herbs with silver-gray foliage

cenobe *var of* COENOBE

ce·no·bi·an \sə'nōbēən, sē-\ *adj* [*cenoby* + *-an*] **:** relating to a cenoby **:** MONKISH, MONASTIC

cenobiar *var of* COENOBIAR

cen·o·bite *or* **coe·no·bite** \'senə,bīt, *usu* -īd·+V; *Brit usu* -sēn-\ *n* -s [LL *coenobita*, fr. *coenobium* cenoby + *-ita* -ite] **:** a member of a religious group living in common — opposed to *hermit*

cen·o·bit·ic \¦≈≈¦bid·ik\ *or* **cen·o·bit·i·cal** \-d·əkəl\ *or* **coe·no·bit·ic** \¦≈≈¦bid·ik\ *or* **coe·no·bit·i·cal** \-d·əkəl\ *adj* [*cenobitic, coenobitic*, fr. F *cénobitique* fr. MF, fr. *cénobite* + *-ique* -ic; *cenobitical, coenobitical*, fr. F *cénobitique* + E *-al*] **:** of or relating to cenobites or cenobitism — **cen·o·bit·i·cal·ly** \-d·ək(ə)lē\ *adv*

cen·o·bit·ism \'≈≈,bīd·,izəm\ *n* -s [*cenobite* + *-ism*] **:** the state, system, or practices of cenobites

cenobium *var of* COENOBIUM

cen·o·by *or* **coen·o·by** \'senəbē, *Brit usu* 'sēn-\ *n* -ES [ME *cenobie*, fr. LL *coenobium*, fr. LGk *koinobion*, fr. Gk, neut. of *koinobios* living in community, fr. *koin-* coen- + *bios* life — more at QUICK] **:** a conventual establishment or religious community

ce·no·genesis *or* **coe·no·genesis** *also* **cae·no·genesis** \¦sēnə, ¦senə +\ *n* [G *zänogenesis*, fr. *zän-* ²cen- + L *genesis* birth — more at GENESIS] **:** introduction during development of adaptive characters or structures that are absent from the earlier phylogeny of a strain (as addition of the placenta to the common vertebrate pattern in mammalian evolution) — opposed to *palingenesis*

ce·no·genetic *or* **coe·no·genetic** *also* **cae·no·genetic** \"+\ *adj* [G *zänogenetisch*, fr. *zäno-* ²cen- + *genetisch* genetic] **:** of or relating to cenogenesis — **ce·no·genetically** *or* **coe·no·genetically** *also* **cae·no·genetically** \"+\ *adv*

ce·nog·o·nous *or* **coe·nog·o·nous** \sē'nägənəs\ *adj* [¹*cen-* + *-gonous* (fr. Gk *gonos* generation); akin to Gk *genea* race, family — more at KIN] **:** oviparous at one season of the year and ovoviviparous at another —used esp. of certain aphids

cen·o·ma·nian \¦senə¦mānēən, -nyən\ *adj, usu cap* [F *cénomanien*, fr. ML *Cenomania* Le Mans, city in northwestern France, fr. L *Cenomani*, a Celtic tribe of northern Italy] **:** of or relating to the division of the European Upper Cretaceous between the Albian and the Turonian — see GEOLOGIC TIME table

cen·o·site \'senə,sīt\ *n* -s [modif. (influenced by E ²cen-) of Sw *kainosit*, fr. Gk *kainos* new + Sw *-it* -ite — more at RECENT] **:** a yellowish brown mineral composed of hydrous silicate and carbonate of calcium and rare earths

ce·no·species *or* **coenospecies** \¦sēnə, ¦senə +\ *n* [*coen-* + *species*] **1 :** the sum of the possible expressions of a complex genotype **2 :** a group of biological units (as varieties, subspecies, and ecospecies) that is capable by reason of closely related genotypes of essentially free gene interchange between units, is rarely capable of such interchange with units not part of the group, and is typically more or less equivalent to the taxonomic subgenus or superspecies in scope

cen·o·taph \'senə,taf, -taa(ə)f,-taif,-täf\ *n* -s [F *cénotaphe*, fr. L *cenotaphium*, fr. Gk *kenotaphion*, fr. *keno-* (fr. *kenos* empty) + *-taphion* (fr. *taphos* funeral rites, tomb); akin to Arm *sin* empty — more at EPITAPH] **:** a tomb or a monument erected in honor of a person whose body is elsewhere ⟨his remains were removed . . . and a ~ was placed at the original grave —*Amer. Guide Series: N.C.*⟩

ce·no·te \sə'nōd·ē\ *n* -s [Sp, fr. Maya *tzonot*] **:** a deep sinkhole esp. in Central America and the Yucatán peninsula formed by the collapse of strata overlying solution cavities in limestone and having a pool at the bottom fed by the water table; *esp* **:** such a natural well into which sacrificial offerings were thrown in Mayan ceremonies

¹ce·no·zo·ic *or* **cae·no·zo·ic** \¦sēnə¦zōik, ¦sen-\ *also* **cai·no·zo·ic** *or* **kai·no·zo·ic** \¦kīnə-, ¦kānə-\ *adj, usu cap* [²*cen-* + *-zoic*] **:** of or relating to a grand division of geological history including the entire interval from the beginning of the Tertiary period to the present time marked by a rapid evolution of mammals and birds and of grasses, shrubs, and higher flowering plants and by little change in the invertebrates — see GEOLOGIC TIME table

²cenozoic *or* **caenozoic** \"\ *also* **cainozoic** *or* **kainozoic** \"\ *n* -s *usu cap* **:** the Cenozoic era or system of rocks

ce·no·zoology *also* **cae·no·zoology** \¦sēnə, ¦senə +\ *n* -ES [²*cen-* + *zoology*] **:** the zoology of existing animals disregarding those extinct

cens \sä(ⁿ)ⁿs\ *n, pl* **cens** [F, fr. LL *census* land tax, fr. L, valuation of property for the purpose of imposing taxes — more at CENSUS] *French & Canadian law* **:** a payment or service reserved to an owner of an estate as a recognition of his title

¹cense \'sen(t)s\ *vt* -ED/-ING/-S [ME *censen*, prob. short for *encensen* to incense — more at INCENSE] **:** to perfume (as in a religious ritual by swinging a censer of burning incense) ⟨*censing* the area around the altar⟩

²cense *n* -s [MF, irreg. fr. L *census*] **1** *obs* **:** CENSUS **2** *obs* **:** RANK, RATING

³cense *vt* -ED/-ING/-S [obs. F *censer*, fr. L *censēre* — more at CENSOR] *obs* **:** ESTIMATE, ASSESS

cen·ser \'sen(t)sə(r)\ *n* -s [ME *censer, senser*, fr. OF *censier*, *senser*, short for *encensier*, fr. ML *incensarium*, fr. LL *incensum* incense — more at INCENSE] **:** a vessel for burning incense; *esp* **:** a covered incense burner swung on chains in a religious ritual **:** THURIBLE

censer

cen·si·taire \sä(ⁿ)ⁿsēteer\ *n, pl* **censitaires** \-r(z)\ [F, irreg. fr. *cens* — more at CENS] **1 a :** one who paid a quitrent to his feudal lord **b :** one who paid the dues required to qualify as an elector in certain jurisdictions **2** *Canad* **:** one who renders cens

cen·sive \sä(ⁿ)ⁿsēv\ *adj* [F *censif*, fr. *cens*] **:** relating to or held by cens

cen·so \'sen(t)sō, -n,sō\ *n* -s [Sp, fr. LL *census* land tax — more at CENS] *Spanish law* **:** ANNUITY; *esp* **:** GROUND RENT

¹cen·sor \'sen(t)sə(r)\ *n* -s [L, fr. *censēre* to assess, tax; akin to Skt *śaṁsati* he recites, praises] **1 :** one of two magistrates of early Rome who acted as census takers, assessors, and inspectors of morals and conduct **2 :** a supervisor or inspector esp. of conduct and morals: **a :** an official empowered to examine written or printed matter (as manuscripts of books or plays) in order to forbid publication, circulation, or representation if it contains anything objectionable **b :** one having authority to guide and supervise students in English colleges and universities **c :** one of a council, since abolished, in some states of the U.S. (as Vermont and Pennsylvania) responsible for ensuring constitutional government and for inquiring into the conduct of state officials **d :** an officer or official charged with scrutinizing communications to intercept, suppress, or delete material harmful to his country's or organization's interests **e :** one who lacking official sanction but acting ostensibly in society's interests scrutinizes communications, compositions, and entertainments to discover anything immoral, profane, seditious, heretical, or otherwise offensive **3** *archaic* **:** CRITIC; *esp* **:** a faultfinding or severe critic ⟨moderating both eulogists and ~*s*⟩ **4** [G *zensur* censorship, fr. L *censura* — more at CENSURE] **:** the agency which represses or veils unacceptable notions before they reach the level of consciousness

²censor \"\ *vt* **censored; censored; censoring** \-n(t)s(ə)riŋ\ **censors :** to subject to a censor's examination; *often* **:** to alter, delete, or ban completely after examination ⟨~ out risqué passages⟩ ⟨slanted news officially ~*ed*⟩

cen·sor·a·ble \-n(t)s(ə)rəbəl\ *adj* **:** subject to being censored; *specif* **:** likely to be expunged or objected to by a censor ⟨~ dialogue⟩

cen·sor·ate \'sen(t)s(ə)rət, -n(t)sə,rāt\ *n* -s [¹*censor* + *-ate*] **:** a body of censors **:** a department for censoring

censored *adj* **:** subjected to a censor's actions: **a :** deleted or suppressed **b :** approved as acceptable after scrutiny

cen·so·ri·al \(')sen¦sōrēəl, -ȯr-\ *adj* [F, fr. L *censorius* of a censor (fr. *censor*) + F *-al*] **:** belonging or relating to a censor **:** exercising a censor's function

cen·so·ri·an \-ēən\ *adj* [¹*censor* + *-ian*] **:** CENSORIAL

cen·so·ri·ous \(')sen¦sōrēəs, -ȯr-\ *adj* [L *censorius* of a censor, fr. *censor* — more at CENSOR] **:** marked by or given to censure or an inclination to discover and severely condemn esp. social, moral, or artistic errors ⟨one who thus berated pope and clergy might be ~ of princes —H.O.Taylor⟩ ⟨even the most ~ could find nothing to complain of —Samuel Butler †1902⟩ **syn** see CRITICAL

cen·so·ri·ous·ly *adv* **:** in a censorious manner

cen·so·ri·ous·ness *n* -ES **:** the quality or state of being censorious

cen·sor·ship \'sen(t)sə(r),ship\ *n* -s **1 :** the institution, system, or practice of censoring **:** the actions or practices of censors or censorates; *esp* **:** censorial control exercised repressively ⟨~ that has . . . permitted a very limited dispersion of facts —Philip Wylie⟩ **2 :** the office, power, or term of a Roman censor ⟨during the ~ of Claudius⟩ **3 :** the process of excluding from consciousness those ideas and feelings that would be intolerable in other than symbolic form

censos *pl of* CENSO

cen·su·al \'sen(t)səwəl, -nchəw-\ *adj* [LL *censualis*, fr. L *census* — more at CENSUS] **:** relating to a census **:** containing or constituting a census roll

cen·sur·a·ble \'sench(ə)rəbəl\ *adj* **:** deserving or open to censure **:** BLAMABLE, REPREHENSIBLE

¹cen·sure \'senchə(r) *sometimes* -n,shu̇(ə)r *or* -ùə, *chiefly substand* -n(t)s(ə)r\ *n* -s [L *censura*, fr. *censēre* to assess — more at CENSOR] **1 :** a judgment involving condemnation: **a :** spiritual chastisement by an ecclesiastical agency ⟨acts receiving public ~ of the church⟩ **b :** sentence of punishment by civil or military authority ⟨awaiting the ~ of the ruling council⟩ **2 :** CENSORSHIP **3** *archaic* **:** OPINION, JUDGMENT ⟨will you go to give your ~*s* in this weighty business —Shak.⟩ **4 :** adverse judgment **:** the act of blaming, finding fault with, or condemning sternly ⟨heads turning all along the block in discreet ~ of his unsabbatical behavior —Mary Austin⟩ **5 :** critical recension **6 :** expression of official disapproval ⟨army letters of ~⟩; *often* **:** a resolution by a legislative body expressing disapproval of a government official

²censure \"\ *vb* **censured; censured; censuring** \-nch(ə)riŋ, *chiefly substand* -n(t)s(ə)riŋ\ **censures** *vt* **1** *obs* **:** ESTIMATE, JUDGE **:** to form or pronounce an opinion on **2 a :** to find fault with and criticize adversely as blameworthy esp. with stern judgment **:** disapprove of or dispraise ⟨appraisements imply censures and it is not one writer's business to ~ others —F.M.Ford⟩ **b :** to express official censure of ⟨a resolution on the floor to ~ the senator⟩ **3** *obs* **:** to condemn by judicial sentence ~ *vi, obs* **:** JUDGE — used with *of* or *on* **syn** see CRITICIZE

cen·sur·er \'sench(ə)rə(r), *chiefly substand* -n(t)s(ə)rə(r)\ *n* -s **:** one that censures

cen·sure·less *pronunc at* ¹CENSURE + ləs\ *adj* **:** free from censure

¹cen·sus \'sen(t)səs\ *n* -ES *often attrib* [L, fr. *censēre* to assess, tax — more at CENSOR] **1** *archaic* **:** POLL TAX **2 :** a count of the, esp. male, population and a property evaluation held every fifth year in early Rome **3 :** an official enumeration of the population of a country, city, or other administrative district generally including vital statistics and other classified information relating to the social and economic conditions ⟨~ returns⟩ ⟨~ bureau⟩ **4 :** a count, list, or tally typically concerning items not easy to count and conducted with care and thoroughness ⟨a ~ of manufacturing establishments⟩ ⟨a ~ of deer in a game refuge⟩ ⟨a ~ of extant copies of a first edition⟩ **5** *civil law* **:** a ground rent or rent charge

²census \"\ *vt* -ED/-ING/-ES **:** to take a census of **:** count in a census ⟨~ the game birds of an area⟩

census taker *n* **:** one who goes from house to house to obtain data for a census

census tract *n* **:** an administrative district used in collating census data

cent \'sent\ *n* -s [MF, hundred, fr. L *centum* — more at HUNDRED] **1 a :** a unit of value equal to 1/100 part of some basic monetary unit (as in the U.S. and Canada 1/100 dollar, in Ceylon 1/100 rupee, in British East Africa 1/100 shilling, in the Netherlands 1/100 guilder, in Indonesia 1/100 rupiah) — see MONEY table **b :** a coin or token, often of copper or some copper alloy, representing one cent **c :** a note representing one cent; *specif* **:** a Hong Kong note representing 1/100 Hong Kong dollar **d :** a coin similar to a cent (as to the U.S. or Canadian cent) but not equal to 1/100 unit of value (as in the British West Indies a halfpenny) **e :** a smallest unit of money **:** a petty sum of money **:** MITE ⟨didn't make a ~ on the deal⟩ ⟨haven't got a ~⟩ **2 :** an old card game similar to piquet — called also *sant* **3 :** the interval between two pure tones whose frequency ratio is the 1200th root of 2 or the 100th root of the tempered semitone interval — **cent per cent 1 :** a hundred for every hundred **2 :** without exception

cent *abbr* **1** cental **2** center; central **3** centiare **4** centigrade **5** centime **6** centum **7** century

cen·tage \'sentij\ *n* -s [*cent* + *-age*] **:** PERCENTAGE

cen·tal \'sentᵊl\ *n* -s [L *centum* hundred + E *-al* (as in *quintal*)] *chiefly Brit* **:** SHORT HUNDREDWEIGHT

cen·tare \'sen,ta(a)(ə)r, -tär\ *or* **cen·ti·are** \'sentē,a(a)(ə)r, 'sän-, -ē,är, ≈≈'≈, *F* sä(ⁿ)ⁿtyär\ *n* -s [F *centiare*, fr. *centi-* + *are*] **:** a metric unit of area equal to 1/100 of an are **:** SQUARE METER — see METRIC SYSTEM table

cen·tas \'sen,täs\ *n, pl* **cen·tai** \-tī\ [Lith, fr. E *cent*] **:** a Lithuanian unit of value equivalent to 1/100 of a litas; *also* **:** a coin representing this value

centaur \'sen,tȯ(ə)r, -tär, -tō(ə), -tá(ə)r\ *n* -s [ME *Centaur*, *Centaurus*, fr. L *Centaurus*, fr. Gk *Kentauros*] **:** one of an ancient mythical Greek race dwelling in the mountains of Thessaly and imagined as men with the bodies of horses and half-bestial natures

cen·tau·rea \sen'tȯrēə\ *n, cap* [NL, fr. ML, centaury (*Chlora perfoliata* or *Centaurium umbellatum*) — more at CENTAURY] **:** a large genus of plants (family Compositae) including the cornflower and the knapweed native chiefly to the Old World but now widely cultivated and characterized by flower heads composed entirely of tubular florets, the outer ones often sterile and enlarged so as to simulate ray florets

cen·tau·ri·um \sen·ˈtȯrēəm\ *n, cap* [NL, fr. L *centaureum, centaurion* centaury — more at CENTAURY] **:** a genus of low-growing herbs (family Gentianaceae) distinguished by flowers with exserted spirally twisted anthers

cen·tau·ro·mach·ia \(ˌ)sen·ˌtȯrōˈmakēə\ *n* -s [Gk *kentauromachia*, fr. *Kentauros* Centaur + *-machia* (fr. *machē* battle)] **:** a battle in which centaurs take part

cen·tau·ry \ˈsen·ˌtȯrē, -ārē\ *n* -ES [ME *centaure*, fr. MF *centaurée*, fr. ML *centaurea*, fr. L *centaureum* & LL *centauria*, fr. Gk *kentaureion, kentauriē*, fr. *Kentauros* centaur; fr. the belief that its medicinal properties were discovered by the centaur Chiron] **1 :** a plant of the genus *Centaurium; esp* **:** an Old World herb (*Centaurium umbellatum*) formerly used as a tonic **2 :** AMERICAN CENTAURY **3 :** any of several plants of the genus *Centaurea; esp* **:** KNAPWEED

¹cen·ta·vo \sen·ˈtä(ˌ)vō, -vō\ *n* -s [Sp, lit., hundredth part, fr. L *centum* hundred — more at HUNDRED] *in the monetary systems of some Spanish-American countries and the Philippines* **:** CENT: **a :** a unit equal to 1/100 peso (as in Argentina, Colombia, Cuba, Dominican Republic, Mexico, the Philippines), 1/100 boliviano (Bolivia), 1/100 sucre (Ecuador), 1/100 colon (El Salvador), 1/100 quetzal (Guatemala), 1/100 lempira (Honduras), 1/100 cordoba (Nicaragua), or 1/100 sol (Peru) — see MONEY table **b :** a coin representing one centavo

²cen·ta·vo \sen·ˈtä\ *n* -s [Pg, fr. Sp] **:** a Portuguese or Brazilian cent: **a :** a unit equal to 1/100 escudo (Portugal) or 1/100 cruzeiro (Brazil) — see MONEY table **b :** a coin representing one centavo

¹cen·te·nar·i·an \ˌsentᵊnˈerēən, -ntəˈne-, -a(a)r-, -ār-\ *adj* [L *centenarius* + E *-an*] **1 :** marked by 100 years **:** 100 years old or older **2 :** of or pertinent to a centenary

²centenarian \"\ *n* -s **:** one that is 100 years old or older

cen·te·nar·i·an·ism \-ˌnizəm\ *n* -s **:** the state of being a centenarian

¹cen·ten·a·ry \sen·ˈtenərē, -ri; ˈsentᵊnˌer-, -ntəˌne-; *Brit often* sen·ˈtēn-\ *n* -ES [LL *centenarium, centenarius*, fr. L *centenarius*, adj.] **1** *obs* **:** a weight of 100 pounds **2 :** a period, space, or age of 100 years **:** CENTURY **3 :** a commemoration or celebration of an event that occurred 100 years before **:** CENTENNIAL **4 :** the governor of a county hundred

²centenary \"\ *adj* [L *centenarius* of a hundred, fr. *centeni* one hundred each, fr. *centum* hundred — more at HUNDRED] **1 :** being 100 years later **:** marking a duration of 100 years **:** lasting 100 years **:** measured by hundred-year spans **:** CENTENNIAL ⟨a ~ celebration⟩ ⟨a ~ practice⟩ **2 :** belonging or relating to a county hundred

cen·te·nier \ˌsentᵊnˌi(ə)r, -iə\ *n* -s [ME *centener*, fr. (assumed) OF *centenier* (whence MF *centenier*), fr. LL *centenarius*, fr. L *centenarius* of a hundred] **:** a police officer in the island of Jersey

¹cen·ten·nial \(ˈ)sen·ˈtenēəl, sən·ˈt-, -nyəl\ *adj* [L *centum* hundred + E *-ennial* (as in *biennial*)] **1 :** of or relating to a period of 100 years or its completion **:** completing 100 years **2 :** relating to or associated with the commemoration of an event that happened 100 years before ⟨a ~ exhibition⟩ **3 :** lasting or aged 100 years ⟨~ pines⟩ — **cen·ten·nial·ly** \-əlē, -əli\ *adv*

²centennial \"\ *n* -s **1 :** a 100th anniversary or its celebration ⟨the ~ of the U.S. in 1876⟩ **2 :** a dice game in which two players throw three dice to get singly or in combination sequences from 1 to 12 and then 12 to 1

centennial brown *n* **:** a strong yellowish brown less strong and slightly redder and lighter than buckthorn brown and yellower and paler than orange rust — called also *Pygmalion*

¹cen·ter \ˈsentə(r)\ *n* -s *see -er in Explan Notes, often attrib* [ME *centre*, fr. MF, fr. L *centrum*, fr. Gk *kentron* sharp point, stationary point of a drawing compass, center of a circle, fr. *kentein* to prick, goad; akin to OHG *hantag* pointed, ON *hannarr* skillful, Goth *handugs* wise, Latvian *sīts* hunting spear] **1 a :** the point around which a circle or sphere is described **:** the point equidistant from all points on a circumference; *broadly* **:** MIDDLE **:** the point at an average distance from the exterior angles, points, or lines of a figure or body **b** *archaic* **:** the middle point of the earth **2 :** a point around which things revolve; *often* **:** a focal point for attraction, concentration, or activity **:** a point, area, person, or thing that is most important or pivotal in relation to an indicated activity, interest, or condition ⟨St. Thomas and his God placed man in the ~ of the universe and made the sun and stars for his uses —Henry Adams⟩: **a :** PIVOT, AXIS **:** cardinal point ⟨the ~ from which the spokes branch out⟩ **b :** a point, area, person, or thing upon which attention, feeling, or action converges **:** FOCUS ⟨the old school was the ~ of our lives somehow: dances, socials, Sunday services, political meetings —E.A. McCourt⟩ ⟨the . . . Abilene region . . . has been the ~ of considerable controversy —R.W.Murray⟩ **c :** a place, area, person, group, or concentration marked significantly or dominatingly by an indicated activity, pursuit, interest, or appeal ⟨a railroad ~⟩ ⟨a tobacco ~⟩ ⟨a ~ for textile research⟩ ⟨the landing . . . is usually the ~ of much activity, because of the constant ferrying —*Amer. Guide Series: R.I.*⟩ ⟨the Emperor Napoleon was the real ~ of French sympathy for the South —A.L.Churchill⟩ **d :** a source or point of origin for an influence, force, process, action, or effect **:** HEART **:** a vital or stimulating factor ⟨intensive propaganda from the ~ —Alex Comfort⟩ **e :** a group of nerve cells having a common function ⟨the respiratory ~⟩ ⟨the visual or motor ~⟩ **f :** a region showing concentration of population **:** a large city **g :** a group of activities of the military each under its own commander but all having closely related functions and an overall commander ⟨medical ~⟩ ⟨separation ~⟩ **h :** a concentration of requisite facilities for an activity, pursuit, or interest along with various likely adjunct conveniences ⟨shopping ~⟩ ⟨medical ~⟩ ⟨amusement ~⟩ **i :** the ultimate head of an endocentric construction **3 :** middle part in contrast to sides, boundaries, outskirts, circumference, or peripheral features **:** middle area **:** MIDST ⟨the crown or arching ~ of the road —Thomas De Quincey⟩ ⟨at the ~ of the battle⟩ **:** a person or persons stationed or acting at or near the middle **:** a thing placed at the middle **:** a shot or stroke toward the middle: **a :** CORE, NUCLEUS **:** material constituting a middle part ⟨chocolates with hard ~s⟩ **b :** the middle element laterally of a military formation **c** *sometimes cap* **:** legislators and other political figures holding moderate views esp. between those of conservatives and liberals; *esp.* **:** legislators holding moderate views and occupying seats in the middle of a chamber between the right and the left **d** *sometimes cap* **:** a position marked by moderation of political, economic, social, or religious views; *also* **:** adherents of moderate views **e :** the middle part of a theater stage **:** the most prominent part **f :** a part of a ballet practice floor away from the bar ⟨ballet exercises are easier done at the bar than in the ~⟩ **4 :** ¹CENTERING **5 a :** a player position in the middle of a playing surface or of a line of player positions: (1) **:** the position in the line in football between the guards, the lineman in this position having the extra duty of handing or passing the ball to a back to start each of his team's downs (2) **:** the position in basketball in the center circle at the start of play, the player of this position engaging in the center jump (3) **:** the position in hockey and lacrosse in the mid-area facing circle, the player of this position engaging in the initial face-off (4) **:** CENTER THREE-QUARTER **b :** the player of this position **6 a :** a pass of a puck or ball in hockey or lacrosse from either side to or toward the middle of the playing surface **b :** the handing or passing of a football by the center from his position in the line of scrimmage to one of the backs ⟨his bad ~ sailed over the fullback's head⟩ **c :** the starting point of a skating figure **7 a :** one of two tapered metal rods that support work in a lathe or grinding machine and about or with which the work revolves **b :** a conical recess in the end of work (as a shaft) for receiving such a center

syn MIDDLE, MIDST, FOCUS, NUCLEUS, HEART, CORE, HUB: in the meaning of that around which a circumference or periphery exists and in the metaphorical extensions of this, these words are often interchangeable and are often used together ⟨the very *center* and *focus* of literary education —F.N.Robinson⟩ ⟨the true *center* of the book is its *core* of irony —Dayton Kohler⟩ ⟨the mark that Sunday school what it ought to have been . . . the *heart* and *focus* of the parochial life —Compton Mackenzie⟩ In its geometrical sense CENTER suggests more exactness than MIDDLE. The latter word may be used for considerations of time ⟨in the *middle* (but not the *center*) of the night⟩ or of a sequence ⟨the *middle* of a series⟩ CENTER differs further from MIDDLE in being able to suggest capacity for acting, influencing, effecting. Contrast "he was the *center* of the conflict" and "he was in the *middle* of the conflict". MIDST suggests location well within a perimeter or situation of being surrounded or beset by matters important, demanding, or threatening ⟨the small democratic island in the *midst* of the European sea of dictatorship —*Books Abroad*⟩ ⟨we were in the *midst* of the foam, which boiled around us —Frederick Marryat⟩ FOCUS may suggest a center to which lines converge or on which forces act ⟨gold — the *focus* of desire —Bernard De Voto⟩ ⟨the *focus* of religious life was the church building —H.S.Bennett⟩ NUCLEUS suggests a center likely to grow, increase, undergo accretion, acquire surrounding or additional matter, force, or numbers ⟨not primarily boarding schools but rather day schools with a *nucleus* of boarders —J.B.Conant⟩ ⟨these two institutions have provided our Army and our Navy with the *nucleus* of their corps of officers —C.T.Lanham⟩ HEART indicates a center which either gives an essential nature to the whole or serves as a vital, positive, or motivating part ⟨sense knowledge cannot therefore be genuine knowledge, for it does not . . . get at the *heart* of reality —Frank Thilly⟩ ⟨the industrial northeast, widening westward, became the ruling region, the economic *heart*; the plantation South and the agrarian West became colonies —Roger Burlingame⟩ CORE may add to the ideas of NUCLEUS and HEART the idea of resistant firmness in which reliability may be placed and imply that peripheral matters are unimportant and adventitious ⟨the *core* or the *nucleus* upon which all the other civilized democracies of Europe . . . can one day rally —Sir Winston Churchill⟩ ⟨the *core* of the book, to wit, the allegory —J.L.Lowes⟩ HUB may contrast with FOCUS and suggest a center whence lines or influences radiate out, a center on which matters peripheral may depend ⟨the *hub* of roads fanning out to the four points of the compass —*N.Y. Times*⟩ ⟨some activities . . . are relatively isolated; other activities such as those at Pearl Harbor are grouped together to form a vast naval *hub* —*All Hands Magazine*⟩

²center \"\ *vb* **centered; centered; centering** \-ntəriŋ, -n·triŋ\ **centers** *see -er in Explan Notes*, *vt* **1 a :** to place or fix at a center or central area or position ⟨~ a typewriter carriage⟩ ⟨~ a picture on a wall⟩ ⟨the shaft is ~*ed* in a city square —*Amer. Guide Series: Minn.*⟩ **b :** to place near a center **:** cluster near a focal point ⟨a hamlet that was ~*ed* around the church⟩ **2 :** to gather to or around a center, fixed point, or pivot **:** draw together within a limit **:** COLLECT, CONCENTRATE, FOCUS ⟨a story to tell, ~*ed* around the political development of a great state —J.T.Adams⟩ ⟨everything had prepared the Boston mind to ~ its thoughts on history —Van Wyck Brooks⟩ ⟨all work on the plantation was ~*ed* on raising foodstuffs —A.W.Long⟩ ⟨more scholarship than is usual was ~*ed* around the main problems⟩ **3 :** to constitute a center of or for **:** serve as center or centerpiece for **:** occupy or adorn the center of **:** give, form, or shape a center for ⟨the business square, neat and compact, ~*s* the village —*Amer. Guide Series: Vt.*⟩ ⟨a bowl of white flowers ~*ed* the table⟩ **4 a :** to rig up between centers (as in a lathe) **b :** to form a recess or indentation in (work) for the reception of a center (as in a lathe) **5 a :** to adjust (lenses, mirrors, or other elements in an optical system) so that the axes coincide **b :** to grind the periphery of (a lens or mirror) to make optical center coincide with geometrical center **6 a :** to pass (a ball or a puck) from either side to or toward the middle of the playing area **b :** to play center on (a team) **c :** to hand or pass (a football) backward between one's legs from a position on the ground to a back **7 a :** to perforate (a stamp) so that all four margins are of equal width **b :** to place (a stamp) in relation to the perforations ⟨a stamp may be ~*ed* to the right or left⟩ ⟨a stamp well ~*ed*⟩ ~ *vi* **1** *obs* **:** to rest on as a cardinal point ⟨our hopes ~*ing* on his success⟩ **2 a :** to have a center **:** cluster or be concentrated **:** FOCUS **:** pivot or revolve — used with *in, at, on, upon, about,* or *around* ⟨the community ~*s* around a small circular park —*Amer. Guide Series: Ark.*⟩ ⟨many legends ~ about him⟩ ⟨the tribal organization ~*ed* in the chief⟩ **b :** to be primarily concerned **:** have a dominant theme or climax — used with *in, at, on, about,* or *around* ⟨another trilogy . . . would have ~*ed* in the battle of Gettysburg —Carl Van Doren⟩ ⟨series of discussions ~*ing* successively about such subjects as the weather, the house, the farm —M.L. Hanley⟩

³center \"\ *adj, see -er in Explan Notes* **:** CENTRAL **:** constituting a center **:** occupying or occurring at a center **:** MIDDLE ⟨a ~ table⟩ ⟨a ~ panel⟩ ⟨a ~ seat in a theater⟩ ⟨the ~ aisle⟩

center back *n* **:** the volleyball or water polo player stationed in the middle of the back line — see VOLLEYBALL illustration

center bet *n* **:** a crapshooter's bet placed in the center of the playing surface for fading

center bit *n* **:** a bit with a sharp conical or threaded center spur for guiding it, a scorer for marking the circumference of the hole, and a lip for cutting away the wood inside the circumference

centerboard \ˈ--ˌ-\ *n* -s [¹*center* + *board*] **1** *in a shallow-draft sailing vessel* **:** a device (as a broad board or slab of wood or metal pivoted at its forward lower corner) in a casing or trunk amidships so that it may be raised either in shallow water or when the vessel is beached or lowered to increase the area of lateral resistance and prevent leeway when the vessel is working to windward or sailing wind abeam — called also *drop keel, sliding keel* **2** *also* **center boarder** [short for *centerboard boat*] **:** a boat with a centerboard

section of boat showing *1* trunk, *2* centerboard

center circle *n* **:** the circle marked at the center of a playing surface (as in basketball, hockey, lacrosse, or soccer) where a center jump, face-off, or kickoff takes place

center down *vi* **1 :** to achieve steadiness, sobriety, and concentration **:** amend habits of flighty irresponsibility **2** *in Quaker worship* **:** to turn one's attention in reverent silence toward the religious meaning of life

center draw *n* **:** the face-off in lacrosse at the center circle following a score or beginning a quarter

center drill *n* **:** a small twist drill used to make centers in a piece of work about to be turned

cen·tered \ˈsentə(r)d\ *adj* **1 :** having a center; *specif* **:** having a center of curvature ⟨the ~ arc of a circle⟩ ⟨a 3-*centered* arch⟩ or center of figure ⟨a ~ crystal⟩ **2 :** placed in the center: **a :** having equal bordering areas ⟨an off-*centered* postage stamp⟩ **b** *of periods, points, or dots* **:** at hyphen level and placed equidistant from characters to left and right

cen·ter·er \ˈsentərə(r)\ *n* -s **:** one that works with a centering apparatus

center field *n* **1 :** the sector of the outfield beyond second base and between right field and left field in baseball or softball **2 :** the player position for defending this area

center fielder *n* **:** the baseball or softball player stationed in center field — see BASEBALL illustration

center-fire *also* **central-fire** \ˈ--ˌ-\ *adj* **1** *of a cartridge* **:** fired by the striking of a hammer or firing pin upon a cap or primer at the center of the base — distinguished from *rimfire* **2 :** designed for or adapted to the use of center-fire cartridges ⟨a *center-fire* rifle⟩

center forward *n* **:** the player position in the middle of the attacking line in soccer, field hockey, volleyball, or water polo; *also* **:** the player who plays this position — see VOLLEYBALL illustration

center gauge *n* **:** a gauge for testing angles (as of lathe centers, screw threads, or the points of cutting tools) or for testing the setting of a thread-cutting tool with reference to work under way

center halfback *n* **:** the player position in the center of the middle line in soccer, speedball, or field hockey; *also* **:** the player who plays this position

center ice *n* **:** the zone between the blue lines in hockey

¹centering *n* -s [¹ and ² *center* + *-ing*] **:** a usu. timber falsework used to support the parts of a masonry arch during construction

²centering *adj* [fr. pres. part. of ²*center*] *of a diphthong or triphthong* **:** concluded with the tongue in the position for the central vowel \ə\ (as \ˈiə\, one pronunciation of *ear*)

centering machine *n* **:** a machine like a small speed lathe used esp. to drill and countersink work to be turned on lathe centers

centering: *1* bearers, *2* bearing strips, *3* stiffening pieces, *4* braces, *5* wedges

center jam *n* **:** STREAM JAM

center jump *n* **:** a jump ball by the centers in basketball

cen·ter·less grinder \ˈsentə(r)-ləs-\ *n* **:** a grinder for production of cylindrical work in which centers are replaced by a work-supporting member and two abrasive wheels one of which grinds work while the other regulates the speed of its rotation — **centerless grinding** *n*

center line *n* **1 :** a straight or curved line that continuously bisects a plane figure (as a building plan, a machine-work layout, or the surface of a paved highway or playing field) **2 :** AXIS 1

cen·ter·man \-tə(r)mən, -ˌman\ *n, pl* **centermen :** a worker who uses plumb bobs to locate the center line of underground mine openings and marks them so that the openings (as entries, rooms, and haulageways) can be driven in a straight line

cen·ter·most \-tə(r)ˌmōst, *esp Brit also* -ˌməst\ *adj* [³*center* + *-most*] **:** MIDDLEMOST, MIDMOST

center of action : any of several large oval areas where the average seasonal or annual barometric pressure is distinctly low or high

center of area : the point of a plane figure that would coincide with the center of mass of a thin uniform distribution of matter over the area of the figure — compare CENTER OF FIGURE

center of buoyancy *or* **center of displacement :** the center of mass of the fluid displaced by a floating or submerged body (as a ship, submarine, or balloon)

center of curvature : the center of the osculating circle at a given point of a curve

center of effort : the point on a sail at which application of the whole propelling force of the wind would produce an effect identical with that produced by its distribution over the whole sail

center of figure : the center of area of a plane figure or the center of volume of a 3-dimensional figure

center of flotation : the center of gravity of the water plane of a vessel

center of gravity [prob. trans. of F *centre de gravité*, trans. of Gk *kentron bareos*] **1 :** CENTER OF MASS **2 :** the single point in a body (as a homogeneous sphere) toward which every particle of matter external to the body is gravitationally attracted **3 :** the point or area of greatest concentration, significance, or interest **:** a predominating or controlling situation **:** FOCAL POINT ⟨a shifting of the industrial *center of gravity* is taking place —Lewis Mumford⟩

center of inversion : the point *O* from which the distances of two points *P* and *P′* which correspond to one another in an inversion are measured, the inversion being characterized by the fact that the product *OP·OP′* is constant

center of mass *or* **center of inertia :** the point that represents the mean position of the matter in a body

center-of-mass system *n* **:** a system of polar coordinates used in describing processes involving moving swarms of particles (as cosmic-ray bursts) with the moving common center of mass as origin and the path of that center as polar axis

center of origin : an area in which extensive and often rapid speciation has taken place within a natural group

center of oscillation : a point in a pendulum at which if the mass were concentrated the period would be unchanged — compare CENTER OF SUSPENSION

center of ossification : a point within a developing bone at which ossification begins within the preexistent cartilaginous matrix

center of percussion : the point in a body free to move about a fixed axis at which the body may be squarely struck without jarring the axis

center of pressure 1 *of an airfoil section* **:** the point in the chord (prolonged if necessary) that is at the intersection of the chord and the line of action of the resultant air force **2 :** the point of a surface exposed to external pressure (as of a fluid) at which a single force must be applied to equal or counterbalance the pressure forces acting on the whole surface

center of projection : PROJECTION AREA

center of similitude : a point in which concur all lines joining corresponding points in two similar figures similarly or oppositely placed and which divides all such lines in a fixed ratio that is direct or inverse according as the division is outside of or between the points

center of suspension : the point about which a pendulum oscillates — compare CENTER OF OSCILLATION

center of symmetry 1 : a point within a crystal with respect to which similar planes and edges are symmetrical in opposite pairs **2 :** the property exhibited by some crystals whereby every direction (as AB) through the crystal is alike in both senses (AB and BA) with respect to all characteristics

center of volume : the point of a 3-dimensional figure that would coincide with the center of mass of a homogeneous material body having the same boundaries — compare CENTER OF FIGURE

centerpiece \ˈ--ˌ-\ *n* [³*center* + *piece*] **:** an object occupying a central or most conspicuous position; *specif* **:** an adornment in the center of a table ⟨a bowl of roses for a ~⟩

centerplate \ˈ--ˌ-\ *n* **:** a metal centerboard

center punch *n* **:** a machinist's hand punch consisting of a short steel bar with a hardened conical point at one end used for marking the centers of holes to be drilled

centerpuncher \ˈ--ˌ--\ *n* **:** one that punches indentations in metal to indicate where holes are to be drilled or punched

center rest *n* **:** STEADY REST

centers *pl of* CENTER, *pres 3d sing of* CENTER

center-sawed \ˈ--ˈ-\ *adj* **:** QUARTERSAWED

cen·ter·scope \ˈsentə(r)ˌskōp\ *n* -s **:** a device to magnify layout lines for accurate placing of center-punch marks for drilling

center seal *n* **:** a compound hydraulic valve used in gas manufacturing for regulating the passage of the gas through a set of purifiers so as to cut out each in turn for renewal of the lime

center-second \ˈ--ˈ--\ *n* **:** SWEEP-SECOND

center spread *n* **:** a unit of printed matter usu. without columnar division and largely pictorial on the two center facing pages of typical magazine format — compare DOUBLE TRUCK

center square *n* **:** a combination of straightedge and sliding square used for finding the center of a circle

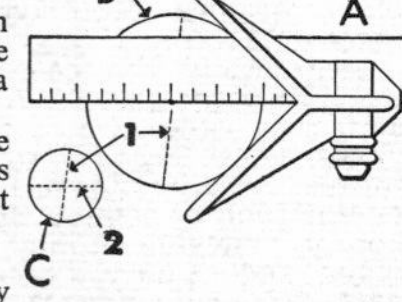

A center square with circle *B* in position for ruling the diameter, two such rulings (*1* and *2*) giving its center as in *C*

center staff *n* **:** the arbor upon which are mounted the minute hand and cannon pinion of a timepiece

center strap *n* **:** a band on the center of a tennis net that anchors to the ground to keep the net secure

center tester *n* **:** CENTER GAUGE

center three-quarter *n* **:** a rugby three-quarter positioned next to a wing three-quarter; *also* **:** the position of such a player

cen·ter·velic \ˌsentə(r)+\ *n* -s [*center* + *velic*] **:** CENTER OF EFFORT

center wheel *n* **:** the first wheel in the going train of a timepiece driving the wheels leading to the escapement and having a pinion post on which the minute hand is carried

cen·tes·i·mal \(ˈ)sen·ˈtesəməl\ *adj* [L *centesimus* hundredth (fr. *centum* hundred) + E *-al* — more at HUNDRED] **1 :** marked by division into hundredths ⟨a ~ or centigrade thermometer⟩ **2 :** relating to marking in hundredths or to devices using it

cen·tes·i·mate \sen'tesə,māt\ *vt* -ED/-ING/-S [LL *centesimatus,* past part. of *centesimare,* fr. L *centesimus* hundredth + *-atus* *-ate*] **:** to punish or execute every hundredth man of (a group) ⟨the legion being *centesimated* on account of mutinous tendencies⟩

¹cen·te·si·mo \chen'tezə,mō\ *n, pl* **centesi·mi** \-(,)mē\ [It *centesimo,* lit., hundredth, fr. L *centesimus*] **:** an Italian cent: **a :** a unit of value equal to $\frac{1}{100}$ lira — see MONEY table **b :** a coin representing one centesimo

²cen·te·si·mo \sen'tesə,mō\ *n* -S [Sp *centésimo,* fr. L *centesimus*] **1 :** a unit of value equal to $\frac{1}{100}$ balboa (Panama) or $\frac{1}{100}$ escudo (Chile) or $\frac{1}{100}$ peso (Uruguay) — see MONEY table **2 :** a coin representing one centesimo

cen·te·sis \sen'tēsəs\ *n, pl* **cente·ses** \-ē,sēz\ [NL, fr. Gk *kentēsis* act of pricking, fr. *kentein* to prick — more at CENTER] **:** surgical puncture (as of a tumor or membrane) — usu. used in compounds ⟨para*centesis*⟩ ⟨thora*centesis*⟩

cen·te·tes \sen'tēd·,ēz\ [NL, fr. LGk *kentētēs* piercer, fr. Gk *kentein* to prick; fr. the spines on the back — more at CENTER] *syn of* TENREC

cen·tet·i·dae \-ted·ə,dē\ [NL, fr. *Centetes,* type genus + *-idae*] *syn of* TENRECIDAE

cent·ge·ner \'sentjənə(r)\ *n* -S [L *centum* hundred + *gener-, genus* birth, race — more at KIN] **1 :** a large number of plants or animals having a common parentage; *esp* **:** 100 plants (as of wheat) derived from a single parent and so planted (as in plots or rows) that the value of the breed may be determined **2 :** a device for planting 100 seeds equally spaced and at a uniform depth

centi- *comb form* [F & L; F, hundredth, fr. L, hundred, fr. *centum* hundred — more at HUNDRED] **1 :** hundred ⟨*centi*pede⟩ **2 :** hundredth part ⟨*centi*meter⟩ ⟨*centi*normal⟩ — chiefly in terms belonging to the metric system

centiare *var of* CENTARE

cen·ti·bar \'sentə,bär\ *n* -S [ISV *centi-* + *bar;* orig. formed as G *zentibar*] **:** a unit of atmospheric pressure equal to $\frac{1}{100}$ bar — abbr. *cb*

cen·ti·day \-,dā\ *n* -S [*centi-* + *day*] **:** a period of 14 minutes 24 seconds used esp. in the study of plant growth

¹cen·ti·grade \'sentə,grād *also* 'sän-\ *adj* [F, fr. *centi-* + *grade* degree, grade — more at GRADE] **:** relating to, conforming to, or having a thermometric scale on which the interval between the two standard points, the freezing point and the boiling point of water, is divided into 100 degrees, 0° representing the freezing point and 100° the boiling point ⟨10° ~⟩ ⟨a ~ instrument⟩ — abbr. *C*

²centigrade \"\ *n* -S **1 :** a centigrade thermometer **2 :** a centigrade scale

cen·ti·gram \-,gram, -aa(ə)m\ *n* -S [F *centigramme,* fr. *centi-* + *gramme* gram — more at GRAM] **:** a unit of mass and weight equal to $\frac{1}{100}$ gram — see METRIC SYSTEM table

cen·tile \'sen,tīl\ *n* -S [L *centum* hundred + E *-ile* — more at HUNDRED] **:** PERCENTILE

cen·ti·liter \'sentə, 'sän- +,-\ *n* -S [F *centilitre,* fr. *centi-* + *litre* liter — more at LITER] **:** a unit of liquid capacity equal to $\frac{1}{100}$ liter — see METRIC SYSTEM table

cen·til·lion \sen'tilyən\ *n* -S *often attrib* [L *centum* hundred + E *-illion* (as in *million*)] — see NUMBER table

cen·time \'sän,tēm, 'sen-, ='=\ *n* -S [F, fr. *cent* hundred, fr. L *centum* — more at HUNDRED] **1 :** a monetary unit equivalent to $\frac{1}{100}$ franc or $\frac{1}{100}$ gourde — see MONEY table **2 :** a coin representing one centime

cen·ti·meter \'sentə *also* 'sän-+,-\ *n* -S [F *centimètre,* fr. *centi-* + *mètre* meter — more at METER] **:** a unit of length equal to $\frac{1}{100}$ meter — see METRIC SYSTEM table

centimeter dyne *n* **:** ERG

centimeter-gram-second *adj* **:** of, relating to, or being a system of units based upon the centimeter as the unit of length, the gram as the unit of mass, and the mean solar second as the unit of time — abbr. *cgs*

cen·ti·mo \'sentə,mō\ *n* -S [Sp *céntimo,* modif. of F *centime*] **1 :** a unit of value equal to $\frac{1}{100}$ Spanish peseta or Venezuelan bolivar or Costa Rican colon or Paraguayan guarani — see MONEY table **2 :** a coin representing one centimo

cen·ti·molar \¦sentə *also* ¦sän- +\ *adj* [*centi-* + *molar*] **:** $\frac{1}{100}$ molar

cen·ti·normal \¦sentə, -tē +\ *adj* [*centi-* + *normal*] *of a chemical solution* **:** having $\frac{1}{100}$ of normal strength

cen·ti·pede \'sentə,pēd\ *n* -S [L *centipeda,* fr. *centi-* + *-peda* (fr. *ped-, pes* foot) — more at FOOT] **1 :** any of various flattened elongated arthropods constituting the class Chilopoda, having a single posterior genital aperture and the body divided into a number of segments each bearing one pair of legs of which the foremost pair is modified into poison fangs, and being active, predaceous, and chiefly nocturnal animals useful as destroyers of noxious insects — compare MILLIPEDE **2 :** a rope with short crosspieces that runs the length of a jib boom and is used in stowing jibs in port

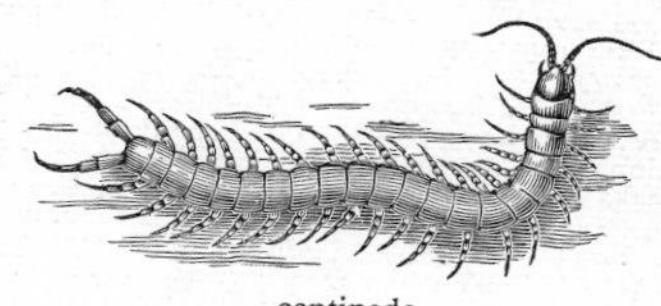
centipede

centipede grass *n* [prob. so called fr. the appearance of the creeping stolons] **:** a grass (*Eremochloa ophiuroides*) introduced into the southern U.S. from China esp. for lawn use

centipede plant *n* **:** an erect shrub (*Homalocladium platycladum*) of the islands of the Pacific with flat ribbonlike jointed stems and with leaves only on the young branches — called also *ribbon bush, tapeworm plant*

cen·ti·poise \'sentə,pȯiz\ *n* -S [*centi-* + *poise*] **:** a unit of viscosity equal to $\frac{1}{100}$ poise

cen·ti·stoke \'sentə,stōk, -tē,-\ *n* -S [*centi-* + *stoke*] **:** a unit of kinematic viscosity equal to $\frac{1}{100}$ stoke

cent·ner \'sentnə(r) *also* 'tse- *with reference to Germany*\ *n* -S [prob. fr. LG; akin to MD *centenaer,* OHG *centenāri;* all fr. a prehistoric D-LG-HG word borrowed fr. L *centenarius* of a hundred — more at CENTENARY] **:** any of various units of weight: as **a :** a unit used in Germany and Scandinavia usu. equal to 110.23 pounds **b :** a unit used in the U.S.S.R. equal to 220.46 pounds **:** METRIC CENTNER

cen·to \'sen,tō, -ntō\ *n, pl* **cento·nes** \sen'tō(,)nēz\ *or* **centoes** *or* **centos** \'sen,tōz, -ntōz\ [L; akin to OHG *hadara* rag, Skt *kanthā* patched garment] **1** *obs* **:** a garment of patches **2 :** an often poetic patchwork composition of parts from other works

cen·ton·i·cal \(')sen¦tänəkəl\ *adj* [L *centon-, cento* + E *-ical*] **:** of, like, or constituting a cento

cen·to·nism \'sentə,nizəm\ *also* **cen·to·ni·za·tion** \,sentənə'zāshən\ *n* -S [L *centon-, cento* + -E *-ism* or *-ization*] **:** the act or practice of composing centos

centr- *or* **centro-** *comb form* [Gk *kentr-, kentro-,* fr. *kentron* center, sharp point] **1 :** center ⟨*centr*oid⟩ **:** central and ⟨*centro*dorsal⟩ **2 :** spiny ⟨*centr*archid⟩ ⟨*centro*sema⟩

centra *pl of* CENTRUM

¹cen·trad \'sen,trad\ *adv (or adj)* [*centr-* + *-ad*] **:** toward the center (as of the body) ⟨~ to the epidermis⟩

²centrad \"\ *n* -S [*cent-* (fr. *centi-*) + *radian*] **:** a unit of angular measure equal to $\frac{1}{100}$ of a radian or about 0.57 degrees

¹cen·tral \'sentrəl\ *adj, sometimes* -ER/-EST [L *centralis,* fr. *centrum* center — more at CENTER] **1 :** containing or constituting a center **:** relevant or pertinent to a center ⟨the sun having a ~ place in the solar system⟩ ⟨the ~ areas⟩ **2 :** belonging to the center as most important part **:** BASIC, ESSENTIAL, PRINCIPAL, DOMINANT **:** not peripheral or incidental **:** cardinally related ⟨these efforts have been marginal and not ~ —Max Lerner⟩ ⟨ethical values ~ to the democratic way of life —Sidney Hook⟩ ⟨the ~ virtues . . . courage, honor, faithfulness, veracity, justice —Walter Lippmann⟩ ⟨a notion ~ to his beliefs⟩ **3 a :** situated at, in, or near the center **:** occupying a center **:** proceeding from a center ⟨the ~ block of the city⟩ ⟨the ~ part of the state⟩ **b :** placed at a center and accessible from all outlying points without undue or disproportionate difficulty ⟨a new theater in a ~ location⟩ **4 a :** centrally placed and superseding or eliminating separate scattered units ⟨~ heating⟩ ⟨~ offices⟩ **b :** controlling or directing local or branch activities **:** constituting a governing or administrative center ⟨decided by the ~ committee⟩ **5 :** holding to a middle course or position between extremes **:** MODERATE, CENTER **6 a :** of or concerning the centrum of a vertebra **b :** of, relating to, or indicating the part of the nervous system comprising the brain and spinal cord — distinguished from *peripheral* **7** *of a vowel* **:** articulated at a point in the oral passage between front and back

²central \"\ *n* -S **1** *sometimes cap* **a :** a telephone exchange **b :** a telephone operator — now usu. called *operator* ⟨ask ~ to cancel the call⟩ **2 :** CENTRALE **3 :** a central office or bureau usu. controlling or dominating others ⟨~ ran the various branches⟩ **4** *usu cap* **:** a branch of the Niger-Congo language family including Bantu, Ekoi, Ibibio, and Tiv

³cen·tral \sen'träl\ *n, pl* **centrals** \-lz\ *or* **centra·les** \-lä(,)lās\ [AmerSp, fr. Sp *central,* adj., fr. L *centralis*] *in Spanish America & the Philippines* **:** a mill for making raw sugar out of cane

central african *n, cap C & A* **:** a native or inhabitant of the Central African Republic — **central african** *adj, usu cap C & A*

central algonquian *n, usu cap C&A* **:** a subdivision of the Algonquian language stock including Cree, Ojibwa, Fox, Menomini, Potawatomi, Illinois, and Shawnee

¹central american \¦==¦===\ *adj, usu cap C&A* [*Central America* + E *-an*] **1 :** of or relating to Central America **2 :** of, relating to, or being the subregion of the Nearctic region that includes tropical America north of Panama

²central american \"\ *n, cap C&A* **:** a native or inhabitant of Central America

central american cedar *n, usu cap 1st C&A* **:** SPANISH CEDAR

central apparatus *n* **:** the centrosome or centrosomes including usu. a surrounding area of differentiated cytoplasm — called also *cytocentrum;* compare MICROCENTRUM

central bank *n* **:** a bank that deals mainly with other banks and the government and assumes broad responsibilities in the interests of the national economy apart from the earning of profits (as by regulating the volume, character, and cost of outstanding bank credit)

central basin *adj, usu cap C&B* [prob. so called fr. sites in the Illinois river valley in central Illinois] **:** of or relating to a phase of Woodland culture preceding and related to Hopewell and characterized by small habitation sites, flexed burials, and incised and stamped grit-tempered pottery

central body *n* **1 :** CENTROSOME 1 **2 :** the colorless inner portion of the protoplasm in the cells of blue-green algae and of certain bacteria that is assumed by some to be a primitive nucleus lacking nucleoli and nuclear membrane — called also *centroplasm;* compare CHROMATOPLASM

central canal *n* **:** a minute canal running through the gray matter of the whole length of the spinal cord and continuous anteriorly with the ventricles of the brain

central cell *n* **1 :** CHIEF CELL 1 **2 :** the cell in the venter of the archegonium whose division produces the egg and usu. also the ventral canal cell (as in cycads)

central convolution *n* **:** any of the gyri bordering the central sulcus in the brain

central cylinder *n* **:** STELE

cen·tra·le \sen'trā(,)lē, -al(,)ē, -'tä(,)lē\ *n, pl* **centra·lia** \-'lēə\ [NL, fr. L, neut. of *centralis* central] **:** a bone in the carpus or tarsus situated between the proximal and distal rows of bones, in man that of the carpus usu. fusing with the navicular and that of the tarsus being replaced by the navicular

central eclipse *n* **1 :** a solar eclipse at the point when the centers of the sun and moon are in line with the observer **2 :** a lunar eclipse in which the moon passes through the center of the earth's shadow

cen·tra·les \sen'trä(,)lēz\ *n pl, cap* [NL, fr. L *centrum* center + NL *-ales*] **:** an order of diatoms having cylindrical disklike or even-angular cells always lacking a raphe or pseudoraphe and having radial markings and often spines — compare PENNALES

central-fire *var of* CENTER-FIRE

central force *n* **:** a force of attraction toward or of repulsion from a fixed or moving definite point

cen·tral·id \'sentrələd, -,lid\ *n* -S *usu cap* [*central* + *-id*] **:** an early American Indian of a physical type characterized by broad high-vaulted head and relatively broad face and found primarily in southwestern U.S. and the northern Mississippi valley — compare PACIFID, SYLVID

cen·tral·ism \'sentrə,lizəm\ *n* -S **:** CENTRALIZATION **:** disposition to centralize **:** a system marked by centralization esp. in government

¹cen·tral·ist \-,ləst\ *n* -S [Sp *centralista,* fr. *central* (fr. L *centralis*) + *-ista* -ist, fr. L — more at CENTRAL] **:** an advocate of centralization esp. in government

²centralist \"\ *adj* **:** advocating centralization — **cen·tral·is·tic** \¦==¦listik, -tēk\ *adj*

cen·tral·ite \-,līt\ *n* -S [fr. *Centralite,* a trademark] **:** a dialkyl derivative of carbanilide (as diethyl-diphenyl-urea) used as a stabilizer for smokeless powder

cen·tral·i·ty \sen'tralad·ē, -atē, -i\ *n* -ES **:** the quality or state of being central **:** tendency to remain in or at the center

cen·tral·i·za·tion \,sentrələ'zāshən, -,lī'z-\ *n* -S [F *centralisation,* fr. *centraliser* + *-ation*] **1 :** the act or process of centralizing **:** the state of being centralized **2 :** concentration of the powers and agencies of government in the central or national organization **:** concentration of authority and power into the hands of a few ⟨he believed in strong ~ — the concentration of power in a few hands, the strict regimentation —H.L.Mencken⟩

cen·tral·ize \'sentrə,līz\ *vb* -ED/-ING/-S *see -ize in Explan Notes* [F *centraliser,* fr. *central* + *-iser* -ize] *vi* **:** to form a center **:** to cluster around a center ⟨a tendency of the whirling particles to ~⟩ ~ *vt* **1 :** to serve as center for **:** draw to a central point **:** gather about a center ⟨the post office *centralizing* the town⟩ **2 :** to concentrate by placing power and authority in a center or central organization ⟨I urge upon the Congress the desirability of *centralizing* these functions in a single agency —H.S.Truman⟩

cen·tral·iz·er \-zə(r)\ *n* -S **1 :** an advocate or agent of centralization **2 :** one that centralizes

cen·tral·la·site \sen'tralə,sīt\ *n* -S [*centr-* + Gk *allassein* to change + E *-ite*] **:** a mineral composed of a hydrous silicate of calcium, probably $Ca_4Si_7O_{18}.5H_2O$

central lobe *n* **:** ISLAND OF REIL

cen·tral·ly \'sentrəlē, -li\ *adv* [³*central* + *-ly*] **:** in a central position **:** at, near, or toward a center **:** according to a central role or function

central nervous system *n* **:** the part of the nervous system which in vertebrates consists of brain and spinal cord, to which sensory impulses are transmitted and from which motor impulses pass out, and which supervises and coordinates the activity of the entire nervous system — compare AUTONOMIC NERVOUS SYSTEM

cen·tral·ness *n* -ES **:** CENTRALITY

central quadric *n* **:** a second-degree surface possessing a center about which there is a symmetrical figure (as an ellipsoid, 1-sheeted or 2-sheeted hyperboloid, or cone)

central reserve city *n* **:** a major financial center in which banks are usu. subject to higher legal reserve requirements than those in other cities — compare COUNTRY BANK, RESERVE CITY

centrals *pl of* CENTRAL

central school *n* **:** CONSOLIDATED SCHOOL

central staging *n* **:** ARENA THEATER

central station *n* **1 :** a central electric-power-generating plant **2 :** a communications center esp. on a warship

central sudanic *n, cap C&S* **:** a branch of the Chari-Nile language family including Bagirmi, Efe, Lendu, Lugbara, Moru, Madi, and Mangbetu that is spoken in northeastern Congo, southern Republic of Sudan, and westward toward Lake Chad

central sulcus *n* **:** the sulcus separating the frontal lobe of the cerebral cortex from the parietal — called also *fissure of Rolando*

central symmetry *n, math* **:** symmetry with respect to a point

central tendency *n* **:** a value (as the mean or median) representative of an entire statistical distribution

central time *or* **central standard time** *n, often cap C* **:** the time of the sixth time zone west of Greenwich based on the 90th meridian and used in east central Canada, central U.S., Mexico, and Central America — abbr. *CT, CST*

cen·tranth \'sen,tran(t)th\ *n* -S [NL *Centranthus* (genus name), fr. *centr-* + *-anthus*] **:** a plant of a genus (*Centranthus*) of the family Valerianaceae; *esp* **:** RED VALERIAN

cen·trar·chid \sen'trärkəd, -ák-, -,kid\ *n* -S [NL *Centrarchidae*] **:** a fish of the family Centrarchidae

cen·trar·chi·dae \-,kə,dē\ *n pl, cap* [NL, fr. *centrarchus,* type genus (fr. Gk *kentron* sharp point + *archos* rectum) + *-idae* — more at CENTER] **:** a family of No. American carnivorous percoid freshwater fishes containing the sunfishes, crappies, black basses, and others valuable as food and game — **cen·trar·choid** \-,kȯid\ *adj or n*

cen·tra·tion \sen'trāshən\ *n* -S [*centr-* + *-ation*] **:** the act of centering

cen·trax·o·nia \,sen,trak'sōnēə\ *n pl, cap* [NL, fr. *centr-* + *axonia*] *biol* **:** organisms having a median axis regarded as a group — **cen·trax·o·ni·al** \¦=,=¦=nēəl\ *adj*

cen·tre \'sentə(r)\ *chiefly Brit var of* CENTER

cen·trech·i·noi·da \(,)sen,trekə'nȯidə\ *n pl, cap* [NL, fr. *Centrechinus* + *-oida*] **:** a large order of sea urchins having peristomial gills, sphaeridia, and an apically located anus — compare CIDAROIDA, EXOCYCLOIDA

cen·tre·chi·nus \,sen,trē'kīnəs\ *n, cap* [NL, fr. *centr-* + *Echinus*] **:** a widely distributed genus of tropical reef-dwelling black sea urchins having slender poisonous spines

cen·tred \'sentə(r)d\ *chiefly Brit var of* CENTERED

cen·tre·man \-tə(r)(,)m-\ *n, pl* **centremen** *Brit* **:** CENTER 5b

centri- *comb form* [NL, fr. L CENTRUM] **:** center ⟨*centri*fugal⟩ ⟨*centri*ole⟩

cen·tric \'sen·trik, -rēk\ *adj* [Gk *kentrikos* of the center, fr. *kentron* center, sharp point] **1 :** located in or at a center **:** CENTRAL ⟨a ~ point⟩ **2 a :** having a center **:** having parts grouped around or directed to a center ⟨a ~ activity⟩ **b :** tending to cluster around a center **:** marked by concentration on something as of central importance ⟨~ ideas⟩ **3 :** of or relating to a nerve center **4 a** *of leaves* **:** CYLINDRICAL, TERETE **b :** of or concerning the order Centrales **c** *of a diatom* **:** having the surface markings radially arranged (as in members of the order Centrales) **5** [trans. of G *zentrisch*] *of a rock* **:** having a texture (as oolitic, ocellar) in which the constituents are grouped about a center **6 :** possessing or relating to a centromere **7** *of dental occlusion* **:** involving spatial relationships such that all teeth of both jaws meet in a normal manner and forces exerted by the lower on the upper jaw are perfectly distributed in the dental arch

-cen·tric \¦sen·trik, -rēk\ *adj comb form* [ME *-sentrik* (in *consentrik* concentric), fr. ML *-centricus* (in *concentricus* concentric, *eccentricus* eccentric) — more at ECCENTRIC] **:** having (such) a center or (such or so many) centers ⟨hetero*centric*⟩ ⟨homo*centric*⟩ ⟨poly*centric*⟩ **:** having (something specified) as its center ⟨anthropo*centric*⟩ ⟨helio*centric*⟩

cen·tri·cae \'sen·trə,sē\ *n pl, cap* [NL, fem. pl. of *centricus* centric, fr. Gk *kentrikos*] *in some classifications* **:** a group of diatoms equivalent to the order Centrales

cen·tri·cal \'sen·trəkəl\ *adj* **:** CENTRAL, CENTRIC ⟨in the ~ part of town⟩ — **cen·tri·cal·ly** \-rək(ə)lē\ *adv*

cen·tric·i·ty \sen'trisəd·ē, -ətē, -i\ *n* -ES [*centric* + *-ity* (as in *eccentricity*)] **:** the quality or state of being centric ⟨concentrated its religious and cultural emphasis upon the ~ of the home —L.F.Wood⟩

centries *pl of* CENTRY

¹cen·trif·u·gal \(')sen¦trifyəgəl, -fə\|g-, -fē\|g-, \|k-, *Brit also* \|sen·trə·¦fyüg-\ *adj* [NL *centrifugus* (fr. *centri-* + *-fugus,* fr. L *fugere* to flee) + E *-al* — more at FUGITIVE] **1 :** moving, proceeding, or acting in a direction away from a center or axis — opposed to *centripetal* ⟨~ acceleration of a body⟩ **2 a :** using or acting by centrifugal force ⟨a ~ compressor⟩ **b :** separated or freed from (as liquid) by centrifugal force ⟨~ flotation of solids from liquids⟩ **3 a :** developing and expanding successively outward and downward from the center or summit — used of the flowers of an inflorescence **b :** having the radicle turned toward the sides of the fruit **4 :** passing outward (as from a nerve center to a muscle or gland) **:** EFFERENT **5 :** tending away from centralization **:** SEPARATIST ⟨a balance between the expansive or ~ forces which make for diversity and adventure, and the constraining or centripetal forces which make for organization and safety —M.R.Cohen⟩ ⟨~ tendencies in modern society —David Riesman⟩

²centrifugal \"\ *n* -S **1 a :** a centrifugal machine **b :** a drum in such a machine **2 :** CENTRIFUGAL SUGAR — often used in pl.

centrifugal blower *n* **:** a blower that operates on the principle of a centrifugal pump

centrifugal casting *n* **:** the casting of metal in a rapidly revolving mold — used esp. of the casting of pipe in which a rotating tube serves as mold

centrifugal clutch *n* **:** an automatic friction clutch in which contact between driving and driven parts is established and maintained through centrifugal force commonly against the action of springs that break the contact when the driving part slows down

centrifugal compressor *n* **:** an air or gas compressor utilizing a centrifugal pump

centrifugal field *n* **:** a space in which centrifugal forces may be detected (as in a rotating centrifuge or in a vehicle rounding a curve)

centrifugal force *n* **:** the force that a material particle moving along a curve exerts on the body constraining the motion and that is directed outwardly along the radius of the curve **:** the reaction to the centripetal force ⟨a stone whirled about on the end of a string exerts *centrifugal force* on the string⟩ — compare CENTRIPETAL FORCE

centrifugal governor *n* **:** a governor (sense 4a) operated by centrifugal force

cen·trif·u·gal·i·za·tion \(,)=,===lə'zāshən, -,lī'z-\ *n* -S **:** the process of being centrifuged or otherwise submitted to centrifugal force

cen·trif·u·gal·ize \='===,līz\ *vt* -ED/-ING/-S [¹*centrifugal* + *-ize*] **:** CENTRIFUGE

cen·trif·u·gal·ly \='==gəlē, -li\ *adv* **:** in a centrifugal manner or direction **:** by or as if by centrifugal force

centrifugal machine *n* **:** a machine (as a blower, compressor, fan, filter, or separator) acting by centrifugal force

centrifugal pump *n* **:** a pump having vanes that rotate in a casing and whirl the fluid around so that it acquires sufficient momentum to discharge from the extremities into a volute casing which surrounds the impeller and in which the fluid is conducted to the discharge pipe

centrifugal separator *n* **:** a machine that separates two mixed substances of different density (as cream and milk or oil and sludge) by centrifugal force

centrifugal sugar *n* **:** sugar freed from liquid by a centrifugal machine

¹cen·trif·u·gate \sen'trif(y)ə,gāt, *usu* -ād·+V\ *vt* -ED/-ING/-S [¹*centrifugal* + *-ate*] **:** to drive out centrifugally **:** CENTRIFUGE

²cen·trif·u·gate \-,gət, -,gāt, *usu* -d·+V\ *n* -S **:** the denser material separated by centrifugal action

cen·trif·u·ga·tion \(,)sen,trif(y)ə'gāshən\ *n* -S **:** the process of centrifuging

¹cen·tri·fuge \'sen·trə,fyüj *also* 'sän-\ *n* -S [F, fr. *centrifuge* centrifugal, fr. NL *centrifugus* — more at CENTRIFUGAL] **1 :** a machine for whirling fluids rapidly to separate substances of different densities by centrifugal force (as cream from milk, sediment from oil) **2 :** a centrifugal machine that produces artificial gravity

²centrifuge \"\ *vt* -ED/-ING/-S **:** to subject to centrifugal action; *esp* **:** to whirl in a centrifuge

cen·trif·u·gence \sen'trif(y)əjən(t)s, -əgən(t)s; ¦sen·trə·¦fyüjə-\ *n* -S [NL *centrifugus* + E *-ence*] **:** centrifugal force, tendency, or action

cen·tring \'sentriŋ, -n·triŋ\ *chiefly Brit var of* CENTERING

cen·tri·ole \'sen·trē,ōl\ *n* -S [ISV *centri-* + *-ole;* orig. formed as G *zentriol*] **1 :** a minute body forming the center of a centrosome **2 :** CENTRAL APPARATUS **3 :** CENTROSOME

cen·trip·e·tal \(ˈ)senˈtripəd·ᵊl, -pətᵊl, *esp Brit also* ˌsen·trəˈpēt·\ *adj* [NL *centripetus* (fr. *centri-* + *-petus*, fr. L *petere* to go toward, seek) + E *-al* — more at FEATHER] **1** : moving, proceeding, or acting in a direction toward a center or axis ⟨~ acceleration of a body⟩ — opposed to *centrifugal* **2 a** : developing and expanding successively upward and inward toward the summit or center — used of the flowers of an inflorescence **b** : having the radicle turned toward the axis of the fruit — used of an embryo **3** : passing inward (as from a sense organ to the brain or spinal cord) : AFFERENT **4** : tending toward centralization : UNIFYING, INTEGRATIVE, CENTRALIZING ⟨the ~ force for union was barely superior to the centrifugal force for state independence —H.E.Scudder⟩

centripetal force *n* : the force that constrains a material particle to follow a curved path and that acts inwardly toward the center of curvature of the path causing centripetal acceleration (as a railroad train is prevented from leaving the track on a curve by the force exerted on the flanges of the outer wheels by the outer rail) — compare CENTRIFUGAL FORCE

cen·trip·e·tal·ism \-ˌlizəm\ *n* -S : the tendency to centralize

cen·trip·e·tal·ly \-ᵊlē, -ᵊli\ *adv* : in a centripetal manner or direction : by or as if by centripetal force

cen·tris·ci·dae \senˈtrisəˌdē\ *n pl, cap* [NL, fr. *Centriscus*, type genus + *-idae*] : a family (order Solenichthyes) of tropical marine fishes comprising the shrimpfishes

¹**cen·tris·cus** \senˈtriskəs\ *n, cap* [NL, fr. Gk *kentriskos*, a fish] : the type genus of Centriscidae

²**centriscus** \"\ [NL, fr. Gk *kentriskos*, a fish] *syn of* MACRORHAMPHOSUS

cen·trist \ˈsen·trəst\ *n* -S [*centr-* + *-ist*] **1** *often cap* : a member of a center party : one who holds views between those of the left and the right **2** : one who holds moderate views between extremes : MODERATE

cen·tro \ˈsen·(ˌ)trō\ *n* -S [modif. of NL *Centrosema*] : a twining perennial (*Centrosema pubescens*) used as a forage and pasture plant esp. in Australia

cen·tro- *in pronunciations below*, ˈ=(ˌ)= = ˈsen·(ˌ)trō or -ˌtrə\ — see CENTR-

cen·tro·ac·i·nar \ˈ=(ˌ)=ˈasənər, -ˌnär\ *or* **cen·tro·ac·i·nose** \-ˌnōs\ *adj* [*centr-* + *acinus* + *-ar* or *-ose*] : relating to or being certain specialized cells in the central part of glandular acini (as in the pancreas) of some animals

cen·tro·bar·ic \-ˈbarik\ *adj* [LGk *kentrobarikos*, fr. Gk *kentron bareos* center of gravity (fr. *kentron* center + *bareos*, gen. of *baros* weight) + Gk *-ikos* -ic — more at GRIEVE] **1** : relating to the center of gravity or to the process of finding it **2** : having a center of gravity

cen·tro·blepharoplast \ˈ=(ˌ)=+\ *n* -S [ISV *centrosome* + *blepharoplast*] : a body that combines the function of basal granule and centrosome in certain flagellates

cen·tro·clinal \-ˈklīnᵊl\ *adj* [*centr-* + *-clinal*] *of geologic strata* : dipping toward a common point or center — opposed to *quaquaversal*

cen·tro·des·mose \-ˈdezˌmōs\ *n* -S [modif. of NL *centrodesmus*] : a fibril connecting the intranuclear centrioles during mitosis esp. in certain protozoans — compare PARADESMOSE

cen·tro·des·mus \-zməs\ *n* -ES [NL, fr. *centr-* + Gk *desmos* bond, band — more at DIADEM] : CENTRODESMOSE

cen·tro·dorsal \ˈ=(ˌ)=+\ *adj* [*centr-* + *dorsal*] : central and dorsal ⟨the ~ median aboral plate of certain crinoids⟩ — **cen·tro·dorsally** \ˈ=(ˌ)=+\ *adv*

cen·tro·gen·ic \-ˈjenik\ *adj* [*centr-* + *-genic*] : originating in the central nervous system ⟨~ factors in the control of respiration⟩

cen·troid \ˈsen·ˌtrȯid\ *n* -S [*centr-* + *-oid*] **1 a** : CENTER OF MASS **b** : CENTER OF FIGURE **2** *prosody* : the central peak or crest of intensity of utterance in a stress-group : the nuclear syllabic in a word or stress-group : a primary or quasi-primary stress

cen·troi·dal \(ˈ)senˈtrȯidᵊl\ *adj* : of or relating to a centroid; *esp* : passing through the centroid

cen·tro·lec·i·thal \ˌsen·(ˌ)trōˈlesəthəl\ *adj* [*centr-* + Gk *lekithos* yolk of an egg + E *-al*] *of arthropod eggs* : having the yolk massed centrally and surrounded by a thin layer of clear cytoplasm

cen·tro·lep·i·da·ce·ae \-ˌlepəˈdāsēˌē\ *n pl, cap* [NL, fr. *Centrolepid-*, *Centrolepis*, type genus (fr. Gk *kentron* sharp point + NL *-lepis*) + *-aceae* — more at CENTER] : a small family (order Xyridales) of plants resembling sedges or mosses, occurring in the southern hemisphere (as in Australia) and comprising the bristleworts — **cen·tro·lep·i·da·ceous** \-ˈdāshəs\ *adj*

cen·tro·lin·e·ad \-ˈlinēˌad, -ēəd\ *n* -S [irreg. fr. *centr-* + L *linea* line — more at LINE] : a long ruler that has two adjustable arms fastened to one end of it by wing nuts and is used for drawing convergents toward inaccessible vanishing points in perspective

cen·tro·mere \ˈsen·trəˌmi(ə)r\ *n* -S [ISV *centr-* + *-mere*; orig. formed as G *zentromer*] : a specialized portion of a chromosome to which a spindle fiber apparently attaches in mitosis — **cen·tro·mer·ic** \ˈ=(ˌ)=ˈmirik, -mer-\ *adj*

cen·tro·plasm \ˈ=(ˌ)=ˌplazəm\ *n* -S [ISV *centr-* + *-plasm*] **1** : the protoplasm of the central apparatus **2** : CENTRAL BODY

cen·tro·plast \ˈ=(ˌ)=ˌplast\ *n* -S [*centr-* + *-plast*] : CENTRIOLE

cen·tro·pom·i·dae \ˌ=(ˌ)=ˈpäməˌdē\ *n pl, cap* [NL, fr. *Centropomus*, type genus (fr. Gk *kentron* sharp point + *pōma* lid) + *-idae* — more at POMACENTRIDAE] : a family of percoid fishes (type genus *Centropomus*) comprising the snooks

centros *pl of* CENTRO

cen·tro·se·ma \ˌ=(ˌ)=ˈsēmə\ *n, cap* [NL, fr. Gk *kentron* spur, sharp point + *sēma* sign — more at SEMANTICS] : a genus of chiefly tropical American vines (family Leguminosae) having trifoliate leaves and large lilac or white flowers and including the butterfly pea

cen·tro·some \ˈsen·trəˌsōm\ *n* -S [G *zentrosom* (trans. of F *corpuscule central*), fr. *zentr-* centr- + *-som* -some] **1** : a minute protoplasmic body found in the cytoplasm, less often in the nucleus, of many animal and some plant cells that takes an important part in mitosis, being regarded by many as the center of the dynamic activity manifested in that process, and that comprises one or two centrioles surrounded by a centrosphere and when active in mitosis by an aster — called also *central body*; compare MITOSIS **2** : CENTRIOLE **3** : CENTROSPHERE — **cen·tro·so·mic** \ˈ=ˈsōmik, -äm-, -ēk\ *adj*

cen·tro·sper·mae \ˌsen·(ˌ)trōˈspərˌmē\ [NL, fr. *centr-* + *-spermae*] *syn of* CARYOPHYLLALES

cen·tro·sphere \ˈ=(ˌ)=+\ *n* -S [ISV *centr-* + *sphere*; orig. formed as G *zentrosphäre*] **1 a** : the differentiated layer of cytoplasm surrounding the centriole within the centrosome **b** : CENTRAL APPARATUS **2** : the central part of the earth composed of very dense material and having a radius of about 2200 miles

cen·tro·symmetric \ˈ=(ˌ)=+\ *or* **cen·tro·symmetrical** \ˈ=(ˌ)=+\ *adj* **1** : symmetric with respect to a center : radially symmetric **2** : having no polar direction

cen·tro·symmetry \ˌ=(ˌ)=+\ *n* -ES [*centr-* + *symmetry*] : the quality or state of being centrosymmetric

cen·tro·tus \senˈtrōd·əs\ *n, cap* [NL, fr. Gk *kentrōtos* spiky, fr. *kentron* sharp point — more at CENTER] : a common genus of treehoppers (family Membracidae) comprising many bizarrely shaped forms

cen·trum \ˈsen·trəm\ *n, pl* **centrums** \-rəmz\ *or* **cen·tra** \-rə\ [L — more at CENTER] **1** : the body of a vertebra **2 a** : the central air space in hollow-stemmed plants esp. of the horsetails (genus *Equisetum*) **b** *in fungi* : the tissue within the hard rind of many perithecia including the asci — called also *core* **3** : CENTROSOME **4** : the point, line, or place within the earth from which an earthquake wave is propagated

cen·tru·roi·des \ˌsen·trəˈrȯi(ˌ)dēz\ *n, cap* [NL, prob. fr. *Centrurus*, genus of arachnids (fr. *centr-* + *-urus*) + *-oides* -oid] : a genus of scorpions containing the only forms dangerously virulent to man that occur in the U.S.

¹**centry** *n* -ES [alter. of *center*] **1** *obs* : CENTER **2** *archaic* : CENTERING

²**centry** *obs var of* SENTRY

cents *pl of* CENT

¹**cen·tum** \ˈsentəm\ *n* -S [L — more at HUNDRED] : HUNDRED — used instead of *cent* in phrases ⟨~ per ~⟩

²**cen·tum** \ˈkentəm, -nˌtu̇m\ *adj* [L, hundred; fr. the fact that the initial sound of L *centum* (pronounced approximately \ˈkenˌtu̇m\) represents an IE palatal stop — more at HUNDRED] : belonging to or constituting that part of the Indo-European language family in which the palatal stops did not in prehistoric times become palatal or alveolar fricatives — opposed to *satem*

cen·tum·vir \senˈtəmvər, kenˈtu̇mˌvi(ə)r\ *n, pl* **cen·tum·vi·ri** \-əmvəˌrī, -u̇mvəˌrē\ [L, *centumviri*, pl. fr. *centum viri* hundred men, fr. *centum* hundred + *viri*, pl. of. *vir* man — more at VIRILE] : one of orig. about 100 judges or jurors of a Roman court for civil suits

¹**cen·tu·ple** \ˈsen·t(y)əpəl, =ˈ==; ˈsentəp-\ *adj* [F, fr. LL *centuplus*, fr. L *centum* hundred + *-plus* multiplied by — more at HUNDRED, DOUBLE] : HUNDREDFOLD

²**centuple** \"\ *vt* **centupled; centupled; centupling** \-p(ə)liŋ\ **centuples** : CENTUPLICATE

cen·tu·pli·cate \senˈt(y)üpləˌkāt\ *vt* -ED/-ING/-S [L *centuplicatus*, past part. of *centuplicare*, fr. *centuplic-*, *centuplex* hundredfold, fr. *centum* hundred + *-plex* (as in *duplex*)] : to make 100 times as much or as many : CENTUPLE

cen·tu·ri·al \(ˈ)senˈt(y)u̇rēəl\ *adj* [L *centurialis*, fr. *centuria* century + *-alis* -al] : relating to 100 years : marking or beginning a century ⟨the ~ years 1600 and 1700⟩

cen·tu·ri·ate \=ˈ==ət, -ˌāt\ *adj* [L *centuriatus*, past part. of *centuriare* to divide into hundreds, fr. *centuria* group of one hundred — more at CENTURY] **1** : of or relating to centuries or hundreds ⟨~ assemblies⟩ **2** : divided into centuries or hundreds ⟨~ lands⟩

cen·tu·ri·a·tion \(ˌ)=ˌ==ˈāshən\ *n* -S [L *centuriation-*, *centuriatio*, fr. *centuriatus* + *-ion-*, *-io* -ion] : division into hundreds

cen·tu·ri·a·tor \=ˈ==ˌād·ə(r)\ *n* -S [NL, fr. L *centuriatus* (past part. of *centuriare* to divide into hundreds) + *-or*] : a historian who distinguishes time by centuries

cen·tu·ried \ˈsench(ə)rēd, -id\ *adj* : having lasted for a century or centuries ⟨a ~ castle⟩ ⟨~ traditions which gave stability to peasant life⟩

cen·tu·ri·on \senˈt(y)u̇rēən, -ür-\ *n* -S [ME *centurioun*, *centurio*, fr. L & MF; MF *centurion*, fr. L *centurion-*, *centurio*, fr. *centuria*] **1** : an officer commanding a Roman century **2** : an officer commanding a hundred men

¹**cen·tu·ry** \ˈsench(ə)rē, -ri\ *n* -ES *often attrib* [L *centuria*, irreg. fr. *centum* hundred — more at HUNDRED] **1 a** : a subdivision of the Roman legion **b** : a unit of 100 men **2 a** : a group, sequence, or series of 100 like things ⟨a ~ of sonnets⟩ : a score of 100 or more runs by one batsman in one innings of a cricket match : a work of 100 units : a division into hundreds **b** : 100 pounds or a hundred-pound note **c** : $100 or a hundred-dollar bill **3** : a Roman voting unit constituted according to property qualifications **4** : a period of 100 years ⟨did a detailed study of the way people lived two *centuries* ago⟩; *specif* : one of the 100-year divisions of the Christian era or of the preceding period ⟨the 19th ~⟩ ⟨the fourth ~ B.C.⟩ **5** : a race over a distance of 100 units (as yards or miles)

²**century** \"\ *adj* : CENTENNIAL

century plant *n* [so called fr. its reaching maturity and flowering only after many years] : any plant of the genus *Agave*; *esp* : the commonly cultivated Mexican plant (*A. americana*) having fleshy leaves in a massive rosette, maturing and flowering only once in many years, then dying, and being perpetuated by suckers at its base

ceorl \ˈchāˌȯr(ə)l\ *n* -S [OE — more at CHURL] : a freeman of the lowest rank in Anglo-Saxon England

cep \(ˈ)sep\ *prep* [by shortening] *chiefly dial* : EXCEPT

cepe \ˈsēp, ˈsep\ *also* **cep** \ˈsep\ *n* -S [F *cèpe*, fr. F dial. (Gascon) *cep* tree trunk, mushroom, cepe, fr. L *cippus* stake, post; akin to Alb *thep* sharp rock, Skt *śepa* tail, penis, and prob. to OHG *sciba* disk — more at SHEAVE] : an edible mushroom of the genus *Boletus* (esp. *B. edulis*)

ceph·a·e·line \seˈfāəˌlēn, -ələn\ *n* -S [ISV *cephael-* (fr. NL *Cephaelis*, genus name of ipecac + *-ine*] : a colorless crystalline alkaloid $C_{28}H_{38}N_2O_4$ extracted from ipecac root

cepha·elis \ˌsefəˈēləs, -fāˈē-\ *n, cap* [NL, irreg. fr. *cephal-* + Gk *eilein* to compress; perh. akin to L *vulgus* common people — more at VULGAR] : a large genus of tropical shrubs and trees (family Rubiaceae) with small tubular flowers crowded into dense bracteate heads — see IPECAC

cephal- *or* **cephalo-** *comb form* [L, fr. Gk *kephal-*, *kephalo-*, fr. *kephalē* head — more at CEPHALIC] **1** : head ⟨*cephal*itis⟩ ⟨*cephalo*meter⟩ **2** : cephalic and ⟨*cephalo*facial⟩

cephala *pl of* CEPHALON

-cephala *pl of* -CEPHALUS

¹**ceph·a·lad** \ˈsefəˌlad\ *adv* [*cephal-* + *-ad*] : toward the head or anterior end of the body — opposed to *caudad*

²**cephalad** \"\ *adj* : located cephalad

ceph·a·lal·gia \ˌsefəˈlalj(ē)ə\ *n* -S [L, fr. Gk *kephalalgia*, fr. *kephal-* cephal- + *-algia*] : HEADACHE

ceph·a·las·pid \-ˈlaspəd\ *n* -S [NL *Cephalaspid-*, *Cephalaspis*]

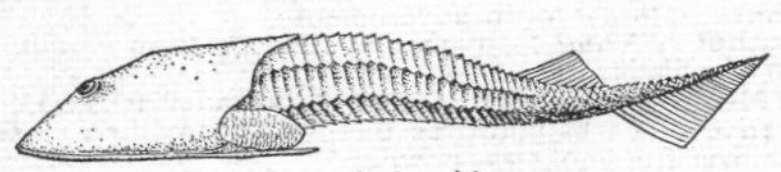

cephalaspid

: any ostracoderm of the genus *Cephalaspis*, family Cephalaspidae, or class Cephalaspida

ceph·a·las·pi·da \-pədə\ *n pl, cap* [NL, fr. *Cephalaspis* + *-ida*] : a class or lesser division of primitive extinct vertebrates including *Cephalaspis* and a few related genera of Devonian ostracoderms

ceph·a·las·pis \-pəs\ *n, cap* [NL, fr. *cephal-* + *-aspis*] : a genus (the type of the family Cephalaspidae) of Devonian ostracoderms having the head covered by a flattened shield rounded in front and prolonged into posteriorly directed lateral points and the eyes close together in the middle of the head shield — see CEPHALASPIDA

ceph·a·late \ˈsefələt, -ˌlāt, *usu* -d.+V\ *or* **ceph·a·lat·ed** \-ˌlād·əd\ *adj* [*cephal-* + *-ate*] *zool* : having a head or an enlargement suggesting a head

ceph·a·leu·ros \ˌsefəˈlürəs\ *n, cap* [NL, fr. *cephal-* + Gk *eurōs* mold, mustiness; perh. akin to L *operire* to cover — more at WEIR] : a genus of epiphytic and parasitic green algae (family Trentepohliaceae) that includes the causative organism of red rust

-cephali *pl of* -CEPHALUS

ce·phal·ic \səˈfalik, -lēk *also* se-, *Brit often* k-\ *adj* [MF *cephalique*, fr. L *cephalicus*, fr. Gk *kephalikos*, fr. *kephalē* head + *-ikos* -ic; akin to OHG *gebal* skull, *gibil* housetop, gable, ON *gafl* gable, Goth *gibla* pinnacle, Toch A *śpāl*- head] **1** : of or relating to the head; *esp* : directed toward or situated on or in or near the head **2** : CEREBRAL 3a — **ce·phal·i·cal·ly** \-lək(ə)lē, -ēk-, -li\ *adv*

-cephalic \ˈ=ˈ==\ *adj comb form* [NL *-cephalus*, F *-céphale*, E *-cephalous* + E *-ic*] : -headed : having (such) a head or (so many) heads ⟨brachy*cephalic*⟩ ⟨disco*cephalic*⟩ ⟨bi*cephalic*⟩ — **-ceph·a·lism** \ˈsefəˌlizəm\ *n comb form* -S — **-ceph·a·ly** \-fəlē, -li\ *n comb form* -ES

cephalic index *n* : the ratio multiplied by 100 of the maximum breadth of the head to its maximum length — compare CRANIAL INDEX; see BRACHYCEPHALIC, DOLICHOCEPHALIC, MESATICEPHALIC

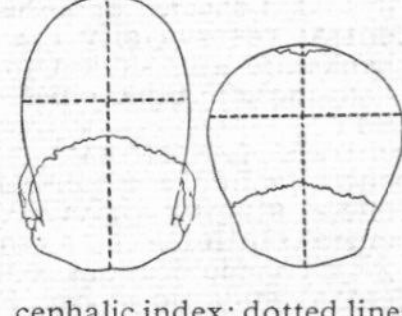

cephalic index: dotted lines in the brachycephalic (right) and dolichocephalic (left) skulls above indicate measurements taken

cephalic module *n* : an anthropological measure of absolute head size obtained by averaging the length, breadth, and auricular height of the head

cephalic vein *n* [prob. trans. of MF *veine céphalique* — prob. fr. a former practice of opening it to relieve ailments of the head] : any of certain superficial veins of the arm; *specif* : a large vein of the upper arm lying along the outer edge of the biceps muscle and emptying into the axillary vein

¹**ceph·a·lin** \ˈsefələn\ *n* -S [NL *Cephalina*] : a gregarine trophozoite complete with epimerite and usu. attached to the cells of the host — compare SPORADIN

²**cephalin** \"\ *n* -S [ISV *cephal-* + *-in*; orig. formed as G *kephalin*] : any of various acidic phosphatides that are similar to lecithins but contain ethanolamine, serine, or inositol instead of choline and are widely distributed in living tissues (as nervous tissue in the brain) and have a marked thromboplastic activity

ceph·a·li·na \ˌsefəˈlīnə, -lē-\ *n pl, cap* [NL, fr. *cephal-* + *-ina*] : a tribe of gregarines comprising forms with septate trophozoites that do not undergo schizogony and are inhabitants of the alimentary tract of arthropods and other invertebrates — **ceph·a·line** \ˈsefəˌlīn, -ēn\ *adj*

ceph·a·li·za·tion \ˌsefələˈzāshən, -ˌlīˈz-\ *n* -S [*cephal-* + *-ize* + *-ation*] **1** : specialization of the anterior part of the animal body resulting in localization and concentration of sensory and neural organs in an anterior head **2** : the tendency to cephalization as a factor in evolution

ceph·a·lo- \ *in pronunciations below*, ˈ==(ˌ)= = ˈsefə(ˌ)lō *or* -ələ\ — see CEPHAL-

ceph·a·lob \ˈsefəˌlōb, -äb\ *n* -S [modif. of NL *Cephalobidae*] : a member of the family Cephalobidae

ceph·a·lo·bi·dae \ˌsefəˈlōbəˌdē\ *n pl, cap* [NL, fr. *Cephalobus*, type genus (prob. irreg. fr. *cephal-* + *-lobus*) + *-idae*] : a family of rhabditoid nematode worms that are saprophagous or associated with the roots of plants — compare VINEGAR EEL — **ceph·a·lo·boid** \ˈ==ˌ=ˌbȯid\ *adj*

ceph·a·lo·cereus \ˌ==(ˌ)=+\ *n, cap* [NL, fr. *cephal-* + *Cereus*] : a large genus of tropical American cacti (family Cactaceae) having usu. columnar erect stems topped with white wool, no leaves, and showy nocturnal flowers and including the old-man cactus

ceph·a·lo·chord \ˈ==(ˌ)=ˌkȯrd\ *n* -S [NL *Cephalochorda*] : one of the Cephalochorda : LANCELET

ceph·a·lo·chor·da \ˌ==(ˌ)=ˈkȯrdə\ *n pl, cap* [NL, fr. *cephal-* + *-chorda* (neut. pl. of *-chordus* having such a chorda, fr. *chorda*)] : a subphylum or other division of Chordata consisting of the lancelets in which the notochord extends to the anterior as well as the posterior end of the body — **ceph·a·lo·chor·dal** \ˈ==(ˌ)=ˈdᵊl\ *adj*

ceph·a·lo·chor·da·ta \-ˌkȯrˈdäd·ə, -ˈād·ə\ [NL, fr. *cephal-* + *chorda* + *-ata*] *syn of* CEPHALOCHORDA

ceph·a·lo·dis·cus \ˌ==(ˌ)=ˈdiskəs\ *n, cap* [NL, fr. *cephal-* + *-discus*] : a genus of colonial Pterobranchia with the zooids inhabiting a common gelatinous tube or test

ceph·a·lo·di·um \ˌsefəˈlōdēəm\ *n, pl* **ceph·a·lo·dia** \-ēə\ [NL, fr. Gk *kephalōdēs* like a head (fr. *kephal-* cephal- + *-ōdēs* -ode) + NL *-ium*] : an irregular internal or external gall-like growth in lichens that differs from an isidium in having an algal component other than that natural to the lichen

ceph·a·loid \ˈsefəˌlȯid\ *adj* [*cephal-* + *-oid*] : CAPITATE

ceph·a·lo·mere \ˈ==(ˌ)=ˌmi(ə)r, -miə\ *n* -S [*cephal-* + *-mere*] : one of the somites that make up the arthropod head

ceph·a·lom·e·ter \ˌsefəˈlämәd·ə(r)\ *n* -S [ISV *cephal-* + *meter*; prob. orig. formed as F *céphalomètre*] : an instrument for measuring the living head

ceph·a·lo·met·ric \ˈ===ˈme·trik, -ēk\ *adj* [ISV *cephal-* + *-metric*; prob. orig. formed as F *céphalométrique*] : of or relating to cephalometry

ceph·a·lom·e·try \ˌsefəˈlämə·trē, -i\ *n* -ES [ISV *cephal-* + *-metry*; prob. orig. formed as F *céphalométrie*] : the science of measuring the head esp. for determining the dimensions and proportions characteristic of a particular race, sex, or somatotype or for determining the relation of a fetal head to the maternal pelvic outlet — distinguished from *craniometry*

ceph·a·lon \ˈsefəˌlän, -ələn\ *n, pl* **cepha·la** \-ələ\ [NL, irreg. fr. Gk *kephalē* head — more at CEPHALIC] **1** : HEAD 1 **2** : the anterior shield of a trilobite

ce·phal·o·phine \səˈfaləˌfīn\ *adj* [NL *Cephalophus* + E *-ine*] : of or relating to the duikers

ceph·a·lo·pho·lis \ˌ==(ˌ)=ˈfōləs\ *n, cap* [NL, fr. *cephal-* + *Pholis*, genus of fishes, fr. Gk *phōlis*, a sea fish that hides in mud; akin to Gk *phōleos* den and perh. to OE *būan* to dwell — more at BOWER] : a genus of groupers (family Serranidae) including the coney (*C. fulvus*) and other food fish

ce·phal·o·phus \səˈfaləfəs\ *n, cap* [NL, irreg. fr. *cephal-* + Gk *lophos* crest] : a genus of small alert African antelopes comprising the typical duikers some of which are no larger than hares

¹**ceph·a·lo·pod** \ˈsefələˌpäd\ *adj* [NL *Cephalopoda*] : of or belonging to the Cephalopoda

²**cephalopod** \"\ *n* -S : one of the Cephalopoda

ceph·a·lop·o·da \ˌsefəˈläpədə\ *n pl, cap* [NL, fr. *cephal-* + *-poda*] : the highest class of Mollusca containing the squids, cuttlefishes, octopuses, nautiluses, ammonites, and related forms all having around the front of the head a group of elongated muscular arms usu. furnished with prehensile suckers or hooks, a highly developed head with large well-organized eyes showing remarkable resemblance to the vertebrate eye, usu. a cartilaginous brain case, a pair of powerful horny jaws shaped like a parrot's beak, and in most existing forms a bag of inklike fluid which they can eject from the siphon, the higher forms (as the cuttlefishes and squids) being able to swim rapidly by ejecting a jet of water from the tubular siphon beneath the head — **ceph·a·lop·o·dan** \ˈ==ˈ=dᵊn\ *adj or n* — **ceph·a·lo·pod·ic** \ˈ=(ˌ)lōˈpädik\ *adj*

ceph·a·lop·ter·us \ˌsefəˈläptərəs\ *n, cap* [NL, fr. *cephal-* + *-pterus*] : a genus of birds of the family Cotingidae including the umbrella bird and its related forms that are remarkable for their development of crests and wattles

ceph·a·lo·spo·ri·um \ˌ==(ˌ)=ˈspōrēəm\ *n, cap* [NL, fr. *cephal-* + *-sporium*] : a form genus of imperfect fungi with conidia held together by a slimy secretion in more or less spherical heads at the ends of the fertile branches

ceph·a·lo·thecium \ˌ==(ˌ)=+\ [NL, fr. *cephal-* + *thecium*] *syn of* TRICHOTHECIUM

ceph·a·lo·thorax \ˈ==(ˌ)=+ˈ-\ *n* [ISV *cephal-* + *thorax*; prob. orig. formed as F *céphalothorax*] : the united head and thorax of arachnids and higher crustaceans

ceph·a·lo·tus \ˌsefəˈlōd·əs\ *n, cap* [NL, fr. Gk *kephalōtos* headed, fr. *kephalē* head — more at CEPHALIC] : a monotypic genus (coextensive with the family Cephalotaceae of the order Rosales) of Australian perennial herbaceous marsh plants having some leaves modified to saclike pitchers with lids and thickened rims and comprising the Australian pitcher plant

-ceph·a·lous \ˈsefələs\ *adj comb form* [Gk *-kephalos*, fr. *kephalē* — more at CEPHALIC] : -CEPHALIC

-ceph·a·lus \"\ *n comb form* [NL, fr. Gk *-kephalos*] **1** *pl* **-cephali** : cephalic abnormality (of a specified type) ⟨micro*cephalus*⟩ ⟨hydro*cephalus*⟩ **2** *pl* **-cepha·li** \-ˌlī\ *or* **-ceph·a·la** \-lə\ : organism having a (specified) type of head ⟨Ichthyo*cephali*⟩ ⟨Phanero*cephala*⟩

-cephaly — see -CEPHALIC

ceph·a·ran·thine \ˌsefəˈranˌthīn, -ˌthən\ *n* -S [*cepharanth-* (fr. NL *cepharantha*, specific epithet of *Stephania cepharantha*) + *-ine*] : an alkaloid $C_{37}H_{38}N_2O_6$ obtained from the tubers of roots of a Formosan plant (*Stephania cepharantha*) and used experimentally in the treatment of tuberculosis

ce·phe·id \ˈsēfēəd *also* ˈsef-\ *or* **cepheid variable** *n* -S *usu cap C* [ISV *cephe-* (fr. L *Cepheus*, a northern constellation, fr. *Cepheus*, mythical king of Ethiopia and father of Andromeda, fr. Gk *Kēpheus*) + *-id*] : one of a class of pulsating stars whose intrinsic light variations are very regular, occurring in periods up to two months

ce·phe·no·my·ia \səˌfēnəˈmī(y)ə, ˌsefənōˈ-\ *n* [NL, fr. Gk *kēphēn* drone bee + NL *-o-* + *-myia*] **1** *cap* : a genus of large gray-brown beelike botflies (family Oestridae) chiefly attacking the nostrils and pharyngeal cavity of members of the deer family and being among the fastest moving living things, reputedly attaining speeds in excess of 800 miles per hour **2** -S : any insect of the genus *Cephenomyia*

ce·phus \ˈsēfəs\ *n, cap* [NL, irreg. fr. Gk *kēphēn* drone bee] : a genus (the type of the family Cephidae) of small sawflies having larvae that bore in the stems of plants and including serious pests esp. of cereal grasses — see WHEAT STEM SAWFLY

ce·pol·i·dae \səˈpäləˌdē, -pōl-\ *n pl, cap* [NL, fr. *Cepola*, type genus + *-idae*] : a family of elongated marine percoid fishes having the dorsal and anal fins elongated and confluent at the end of the pointed tail — see RIBBONFISH 1b

cer- *or* **cero-** *comb form* [Gk *kēr-, kēro-,* fr. *kēros* — more at CEREUS] **:** wax ⟨*cerophilous*⟩ ⟨*cerotype*⟩

-cera \sərə\ *n comb form, pl* **-cera** [NL, fr. Gk *keras* horn — more at CEREBRAL] **:** horned one **:** horned ones — in taxonomic names in zoology ⟨*Acrocera*⟩ ⟨*Cladocera*⟩ ⟨*Nematocera*⟩

ce·ra al·ba \ˌsirəˈalbə\ *n* [NL] **:** bleached beeswax

ce·ra·ceous \səˈrāshəs\ *adj* [L *cera* wax + E *-aceous* — more at CEREUS] **:** like wax **:** WAXY

ce·ra fla·va \ˌsirəˈflāvə, -ävə\ *n* [NL] **:** yellow unbleached beeswax

ce·ram·al \səˈraməl\ *n* -s [¹*ceramic* + *alloy*] **:** CERMET

¹**ce·ram·by·cid** \səˈrambəsəd, -(ˌ)sid\ *adj* [NL *Cerambycidae*] **:** of or relating to the Cerambycidae

²**cerambycid** \"\ *n* -s [NL *Cerambycidae*] **:** a beetle of the family Cerambycidae

cer·am·byc·i·dae \ˌserˌamˈbisəˌdē, -rəm-\ *n pl, cap* [NL, fr. *Cerambyc-, Cerambyx,* type genus (fr. Gk *kerambyx,* a horned beetle, fr. *keras* horn) + *-idae*] **:** a large family of beetles comprising the long-horned beetles, including large oblong or somewhat cylindrical beetles with antennae often longer than the body, and having larvae that usu. bore in the roots or wood of trees or shrubs, some (as the locust borer and twig pruner) doing great damage — **ce·ram·by·coid** \səˈrambəˌkȯid\ *n or adj*

ce·ram·i·a·ce·ae \səˌramēˈāsēˌē, -rām-\ *n pl, cap* [NL, fr. *Ceramium,* type genus + *-aceae*] **:** a family of delicate filamentous red algae (order Ceramiales) branched dichotomously or unilaterally pinnate and found in nearly all seas — see FAVELLA — **ce·ram·i·a·ceous** \ˌ=ˌ==ˈāshəs\ *adj*

ce·ram·i·a·les \səˌramēˈā(ˌ)lēz, -rām-\ *n pl, cap* [NL, fr. *Ceramium* + *-ales*] **:** an order of red algae characterized by having the auxiliary cell formed after fertilization — compare CERAMIACEAE, RHODYMENIALES

¹**ce·ram·ic** \səˈramik, -mēk\ *adj* [Gk *keramikos,* fr. *keramos* potter's clay, pottery] **1 :** of or relating to the art of fashioning clay into useful or ornamental objects and hardening them by firing at high temperatures **2 a :** of or relating to the manufacture of any product (as earthenware, porcelain, tile, brick, glass, vitreous enamels, cement, plaster refractories) made essentially from a nonmetallic mineral by firing at high temperatures — in Brit. use not usu. extended to include glassmaking **b :** of, relating to, or consisting of such a product

²**ceramic** \"\ *n* -s [prob. fr. F *céramique,* fr. *céramique* ceramic, fr. Gk *keramikos*] **1 ceramics** *pl but usu sing in constr* **a :** the art or process of making useful or ornamental articles from clay by shaping and then firing at high temperatures **b :** the industry concerned with making any ceramic product **:** the technology of ceramic manufacturing and processing **2 :** a product of ceramic art or manufacture **3 :** AZURITE BLUE

ceramic aggregate *n* **1 :** an ornamental portland-cement concrete containing ceramic products in the form of lumps or fragments and usu. coloring ingredients **2 :** concrete containing bloated clay to reduce weight

ceramic bond *n* **:** mechanical strength in a body developed by heating earthy materials and thus producing glass or effective crystallization; *esp* **:** a bond used in abrasive wheels and shapes

ceramic engineering *n* **:** a branch of engineering dealing with the treatment of earthy nonmetallic minerals by fire or heat and the design and operation of plant and equipment for ceramic production

ceramic glaze *n* **:** a mixture of powdered materials that often includes a premelted glass made into a slip and applied to a ceramic body by spraying or dipping and capable of fusing to a glassy coating when dried and fired

ce·ram·i·cite \səˈraməˌsīt\ *n* -s **:** a porcelainlike pyrometamorphic rock consisting of basic plagioclase and cordierite with accessory hypersthene and a groundmass of glass

ceramic mosaic *n* **:** mosaic formed by setting small glazed or unglazed tiles in cement

ce·ram·ist \səˈramәst *also* ˈserəm-\ *or* **ce·ram·i·cist** \səˈraməsəst\ *n* -s [F *céramiste,* fr. *céramique,* n. + *-iste* -ist] **:** one who engages in ceramic arts, manufacturing, or technology

ce·ram·i·um \səˈramēəm, -rām-\ *n, cap* [NL, fr. Gk *keramion* earthen vessel, fr. *keramos* potter's clay, pottery] **:** a genus (the type of the family Ceramiaceae) of delicate red algae comprising the rosetangles

cer·a·mog·ra·phy \ˌserəˈmägrəfē\ *n* -ES [ISV ¹*ceramic* + *-o-* + *-graphy*] **:** the description or study of ceramics

ce·rar·gy·rite \səˈrärjəˌrīt\ *n* -s [F *kérargyre* cerargyrite (fr. Gk *keras* horn + *argyros* silver), trans. of Sw *hornsilver* + E *-ite* — more at CEREBRAL, ARGENT] **1 :** a white to pale-yellow or gray mineral consisting of silver chloride AgCl and darkening on exposure to light **2 :** a group of isomorphous silver halides that includes mainly cerargyrite, bromyrite, and embolite

cer·as \ˈserəs, ˈk-\ *n, pl* **cera·ta** \-rəd·ə\ [NL, fr. Gk *keras* horn] **:** one of the often brightly colored and branching integumentary papillae that serve as gills and occur on the backs of nudibranchs and certain related mollusks

-cer·as \sərəs\ *n comb form* [NL, fr. Gk *keras*] **:** horned one — in generic names of plants and animals ⟨*Cyrtoceras*⟩ ⟨*Dinoceras*⟩

¹**ce·ras·tes** \səˈras(ˌ)tēz\ *n, pl* **cerastes** [ME, fr. L, fr. Gk *kerastēs* cerastes, horned, fr. *keras* horn — more at HORN] **:** HORNED VIPER

²**cerastes** \"\ [NL, fr. L] *syn of* ASPIS

ce·ras·ti·um \səˈraschēəm, -stē-\ *n, cap* [NL, fr. Gk *kerastēs* horned + NL *-ium*] **:** a large genus of low herbs (family Caryophyllaceae) containing the mouse-ear chickweed and the field chickweed and having small white flowers with bifid petals and cylindrical often curved capsules

cer·a·sus \ˈserəsəs\ *n, cap* [NL, fr. L, cherry tree — more at CHERRY] *in some classifications* **:** a genus of shrubs or trees comprising the cherries and now included in the genus *Prunus*

cerat- *or* **cerato-** *also* **kerat-** *or* **kerato-** *comb form* [NL, fr. Gk *kerat-, kerato-,* fr. *keras* horn] **:** horn **:** horny ⟨*Ceratodus*⟩ ⟨*keratiasis*⟩ ⟨*Ceratosaurus*⟩

¹**ce·rate** \ˈsirˌāt, -ˌət, *usu* -d·+V\ *n* -s [L *ceratum* wax salve, fr. *cera* wax + *-atum* -ate — more at CEREUS] **:** an unctuous preparation for external application consisting essentially of wax (sometimes resin or spermaceti) mixed with oil, lard, and medicinal ingredients and having a melting point above body temperature

²**cerate** \"\ *n* -s [*cerium* + *-ate*] **:** a compound having an anion containing cerium in the tetravalent state

ce·rat·ed \-ād·əd\ *adj* [L *ceratus,* past part. of *cerare* to wax, fr. *cera* wax] **:** covered with wax

cer·a·ti·i·dae \ˌserəˈtīəˌdē\ *n pl, cap* [NL, fr. *Ceratias,* type genus (fr. Gk *keratias* horned, fr. *kerat-, keras* horn) + *-idae* — more at HORN] **:** a family of deep-sea fishes (order Pediculati) comprising the black sea devils and related to the anglers but black in color and often having luminous organs, the males in several species being diminutive and carried in the gill cavity or attached to the body or head of the female

ceratin *var of* KERATIN

¹**cer·a·ti·oid** \ˌserəˈtīˌȯid\ *adj* [NL *Ceratioidea*] **1 :** resembling the Ceratiidae **2 :** of or relating to the Ceratioidea

²**ceratioid** \"\ *n* -s [NL *Ceratioidea*] **:** a ceratioid fish

cer·a·ti·oi·dea \-ˌtīˈȯidēə\ *n pl, cap* [NL, fr. *Ceratias* (fr. Gk *keratias* horned) + *-oidea*] **:** a suborder of Pediculati comprising oceanic anglers that lack pelvic fins and usu. have a luminous tip on the illicium

cer·a·tite \ˈserəˌtīt\ *n* -s [NL *Ceratites*] **:** a fossil of the genus *Ceratites*

cer·a·ti·tes \ˌserəˈtīd·ēz\ *n, cap* [NL, fr. *cerat-* + *-ites* -ite] **:** a genus (the type of the large family Ceratitidae) of Triassic ammonites having the septa with simple rounded saddles and finely denticulated lobes — **cer·a·tit·ic** \ˌserəˈtid·ik\ *adj* — **cer·a·ti·toid** \ˌserəˈtīˌtȯid\ *adj or n*

cer·a·ti·tis \ˌserəˈtīd·əs\ *n, cap* [NL, fr. Gk *keratitis* horned, fr. *kerat-, keras* horn] **:** a genus of acalyptrate flies (family Trypetidae) including the Mediterranean fruit fly

ce·ra·ti·um \səˈrāshēəm\ *n, cap* [NL, fr. Gk *keration,* dim. of *kerat-, keras* horn] **:** a genus of marine and freshwater flagellates (order Dinoflagellata) certain species of which form an important part of the plankton of northern seas

¹**cer·a·to·branchial** \ˌserə(ˌ)tō+\ *adj* [ISV *cerat-* + *branchial*] **:** belonging to the segment next below the epibranchial in a branchial arch

²**ceratobranchial** \"\ *n* -s **:** a ceratobranchial bone or cartilage

cer·a·to·con·junc·ti·vi·tis *var of* KERATOCONJUNCTIVITIS

cer·a·to·cricoid \ˌserə(ˌ)tō+\ *adj* [*cerat-* + *cricoid*] **:** belonging to or associated with the inferior horn of the thyroid and the cricoid cartilages

ce·rat·o·dus \səˈrad·əd·əs\ *n* [NL, fr. *cerat-* + *-odus*] **1** *cap* **:** a

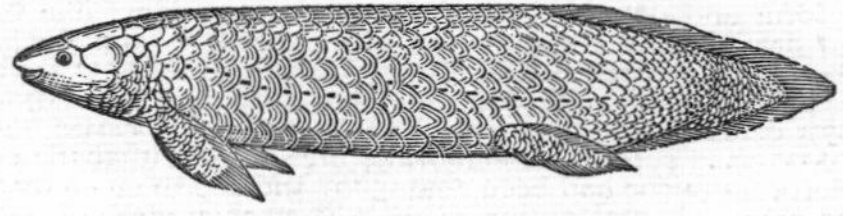

a fish of the genus *Ceratodus*

genus (the type of the family Ceratodontidae) comprising dipnoan fishes that have archipterygial pectoral and pelvic fins and dental plates with radiating ridges, being orig. based on and now usu. restricted to fossil forms from the Mesozoic but in some esp. former classifications including the surviving Australian lungfish — see BARRAMUNDA **2** -ES **:** any fish or fossil of *Ceratodus* or a closely related genus

¹**cer·a·to·glos·sal** \ˌserə(ˌ)tōˈgläsəl, -ȯs-\ *adj* [NL *ceratoglossus* + E *-al*] **:** belonging or relating to the cornua of the hyoid bone and the tongue

²**ceratoglossal** \"\ *n* -s **:** the ceratoglossus muscle

cer·a·to·glos·sus \-səs\ *n, pl* **ceratoglos·si** \-ˌsī, -(ˌ)sē\ [NL, fr. *cerat-* + *-glossus* (fr. Gk *glōssa* tongue) — more at GLOSS] **:** the part of the hyoglossus muscle attached to the greater cornu of the hyoid

cer·a·to·hy·al \ˌserə(ˌ)tōˈhīəl\ *or* **cer·a·to·hy·oid** \-ˌīˌȯid\ *n* -s [*ceratohyal* ISV *cerat-* + *hyoid* + *-al; ceratohyoid* fr. *cerat-* + *hyoid*] **:** a horn or cartilage lying below the epihyal and forming a segment of the hyoid arch, in man being the small horn of the hyoid

cer·a·to·mandibular \ˌserə(ˌ)tō+\ *adj* [*cerat-* + *mandibular*] **:** belonging to the horns of the hyoid and the mandible

cer·a·to·mor·pha \ˌserətōˈmȯrfə\ *n pl, cap* [NL, fr. *cerat-* + *-morpha*] *in some classifications* **:** a suborder of perissodactylous mammals comprising tapirs, rhinoceroses, and extinct related forms

cer·a·to·phyl·la·ce·ae \ˌserə(ˌ)tōfəˈlāsēˌē\ *n pl, cap* [NL, fr. *Ceratophyllum* + *-aceae*] **:** a family of aquatic plants that is coextensive with the genus *Ceratophyllum* and is usu. included in the order Ranales

cer·a·to·phyl·lum \-ˈfiləm\ *n, cap* [NL, fr. *cerat-* + *-phyllum*] **:** a cosmopolitan genus of rootless thin-stemmed aquatic herbs that occur in quiet freshwaters and that have flowers with a sepaloid perianth and a single carpel — see CERATOPHYLLACEAE, HORNWORT

cer·a·to·phyl·lus \-ləs\ *n, cap* [NL, prob. irreg. fr. *cerat-* + Gk *phyllon* leaf — more at PHYLL-] **:** a genus of fleas formerly coextensive with the family Dolichopsyllidae but now restricted to certain parasites of birds — see EUROPEAN CHICKEN FLEA, WESTERN CHICKEN FLEA

cer·a·to·po·gon \ˌserətōˈpōˌgän\ *n, cap* [NL, fr. *cerat-* + *-pogon*] **:** the type genus of the family Ceratopogonidae

¹**cer·a·to·po·go·nid** \ˌ===ˈpōgənəd\ *adj* [NL *Ceratopogonidae*] **:** of or relating to the Ceratopogonidae

²**ceratopogonid** \"\ *n* -s [NL *Ceratopogonidae*] **:** one of the Ceratopogonidae

cer·a·to·po·gon·i·dae \ˌserə(ˌ)tōpəˈgänəˌdē\ *n pl, cap* [NL, fr. *Ceratopogon* + *-idae*] **:** a large family of tiny long-legged nematocerous two-winged flies that have piercing mouthparts, that comprise the biting midges which attack man, various other mammals, and birds, and that include various vectors of filarial worms

cer·a·tops \ˈserəˌtäps\ *n, cap* [NL, fr. *cerat-* + *-ops*] **:** the type genus of the family Ceratopsidae

cer·a·top·sia \ˌserəˈtäpsēə\ *n pl, cap* [NL, fr. *Ceratops* + *-ia*] **:** a group of large dinosaurs, usu. made a suborder of the order Ornithischia, known chiefly from the Upper Cretaceous of No. America and Mongolia, and comprising animals of robust build that walked on all four feet and had an enormously developed skull, long horns, and a sharp horny beak — see TRICERATOPS — **cer·a·top·si·an** \ˌ==ˈ=sēən\ *adj or n*

¹**cer·a·top·sid** \ˌ==ˈ=səd\ *adj* [NL *Ceratopsidae*] **:** of or relating to the Ceratopsidae

²**ceratopsid** \"\ *n* -s [NL *Ceratopsidae*] **:** a dinosaur or fossil of the family Ceratopsidae

cer·a·top·si·dae \ˌserəˈtäpsəˌdē\ *n pl, cap* [NL, fr. *Ceratops,* type genus + *-idae*] **:** a large family of American dinosaurs (suborder Ceratopsia) that includes *Triceratops*

cer·a·top·te·ris \ˌserəˈtäptərəs\ *n, cap* [NL, fr. *cerat-* + *-pteris*] **:** a genus of aquatic ferns (family Parkeriaceae) having leaves in rosettes, the sterile floating or emergent, the fertile more erect and with margins revolute over the sporangia

¹**cer·a·to·rhine** \ˈserətəˌrīn\ *n* -s [NL *Ceratorhinus* (proposed genus name), fr. *cerat-* + *-rhinus*] **:** any of a group of 2-horned rhinoceroses having well-developed lower canine teeth (as the Sumatran rhinoceros)

²**ceratorhine** \"\ *adj* **:** belonging to or like a ceratorhine

cer·a·to·sa \ˌserəˈtōsə, -ōzə\ [NL, fr. neut. pl. of (assumed) *ceratosus* keratose] *syn of* KERATOSA

cer·a·to·sau·rus \ˌserətōˈsȯrəs\ *n, cap* [NL, fr. *cerat-* + *-saurus*] **:** a genus of American Jurassic carnivorous dinosaurs nearly 20 feet long that had a bony horn core on the united nasal bones

ceratose *var of* KERATOSE

cer·a·to·spon·gi·ae \ˌserə(ˌ)tōˈspənjēˌē, -pän-\ [NL, fr. *cerat-* + *-spongiae*] *syn of* KERATOSA

cer·a·to·spon·gi·da \-jədə\ [NL, fr. *cerat-* + *Spongida*] *syn of* KERATOSA

cer·a·tos·to·ma·ta·ce·ae \ˌserəˌtästəməˈtāsēˌē, ˌserə(ˌ)tōˌstōmə-\ *n pl, cap* [NL, fr. *Ceratostomat-, Ceratostoma,* type genus (fr. *cerat-* + *-stoma*) + *-aceae*] **:** a family of fungi (order Sphaeriales) characterized by carbonous perithecia with long necks

cer·a·tos·to·mel·la \ˌserəˌtästəˈmelə, ˌserə(ˌ)tōstə-\ *n, cap* [NL, fr. *Ceratostoma* + *-ella*] **:** a genus of fungi (family Ceratostomataceae) forming continuous hyaline spores — see BLUE ROT, DUTCH ELM DISEASE

cer·a·to·the·ca \ˌserətōˈthēkə\ *n, pl* **ceratothe·cae** \-ēˌsē\ [NL, fr. *cerat-* + *theca*] **:** the part of the integument of an insect pupa that covers the antenna — **cer·a·to·the·cal** \ˌ====ˌkəl\ *adj*

cer·a·to·za·mia \ˌserətōˈzāmēə\ *n, cap* [NL, fr. *cerat-* + *Zamia*] **:** a small genus of Mexican cycads (family Cycadaceae) having short scaly woody trunks, fernlike foliage, and woody cones

ceraun- *or* **cerauno-** *comb form* [Gk *keraun-, keraunо-,* fr. *keraunos* thunderbolt; akin to Gk *kēr* death — more at CARIES] **:** thunder ⟨*ceraunograph*⟩ ⟨*ceraunophone*⟩

ce·rau·no·gram \səˈrȯnəˌgram\ *n* -s [*ceraun-* + *-gram*] **:** the record obtained by a ceraunograph

ce·rau·no·graph \-ˌgraf\ *n* -s [*ceraun-* + *-graph*] **:** an instrument for recording chronologically by sound the occurrence of thunder and lightning

cer·be·re·an \(ˌ)sə(r)ˈbirēən, ˌsər'-, sə̄'-; ˈsərbəˈrēən, ˈsə̄b-\ *adj, usu cap* [L *cerbere*us of Cerberus (fr. *Cerberus*) + E *-an*] **:** of, relating to, or like Cerberus

cer·ber·us \ˈsərb(ə)rəs, ˈsə̄b-\ *n, pl* **cerberuses** \-rəsə̇z\ *or* **cer·beri** \-bəˌrī\ [L *Cerberus,* three-headed dog guarding the entrance to Hades, fr. Gk *Kerberos;* akin to Skt *śabara, śabala* spotted (used as name of one of the two dogs of Yama, god of the dead)] **1** *sometimes cap* **:** WATCHDOG, GATEKEEPER, CUSTODIAN **2** [NL, fr. L] *cap* **:** a genus of East Indian water snakes (family Homalopsidae) related to and sometimes including *Hurria*

cerc- *or* **cerco-** *comb form* [NL, fr. Gk *kerk-, kerko-,* fr. *kerkos* tail] **:** tail **:** tailed ⟨*cercaria*⟩ ⟨*cercopod*⟩

cerc·aër·tus \ˌsərkēˈərd·əs\ *n* [NL, fr. *cerc-* + *-aertus* (fr. Gk *aertan, aertazein* to lift up)] **:** a genus of marsupials consisting of the dormouse opossums

cer·cal \ˈsərkəl, -ōk-\ *adj* [*cerc-* + *-al*] **:** of or relating to a tail

-cer·cal \ˈsərkəl, -ōk-\ *adj comb form* [F *-cerque* (fr. Gk *kerkos* tail) + E *-al*] **:** tailed ⟨*homocercal*⟩ ⟨*isocercal*⟩

cer·car·ia \(ˌ)sərˈka(a)rēə\ *n, pl* **cercari·ae** \-rēˌē\ [NL, fr. *cerc-* + *-aria*] **:** a tadpole-shaped larval trematode worm produced in the molluscan host by a redia and later freed into water to encyst as a metacercaria or to actively penetrate a suitable definitive host — **cer·car·i·al** \-ēəl\ *adj* — **cer·car·i·an** \-ēən\ *adj or n* — **cer·car·i·form** \-karəˌfȯrm\ *adj*

1 2 3 4 5 6

cercaria of Fasciola: *1* oral sucker, *2* pharynx, *3* intestine, *4* spherules in nephridia, *5* acetabulum, *6* nephridium in tail

cer·car·i·ae·um \(ˌ)sərˌkarēˈēəm\ *n, pl* **cercari·aea** \-ēˈēə\ [NL, irreg. fr. *cercaria*] **:** a tailless cercaria usu. remaining in the snail host until eaten by the proper definitive host

cercarial dermatitis *n* **:** an itching inflammation caused by infestation of the skin by cercariae and usu. acquired when wading or swimming in infested waters

cercelée *var of* SARCELLY

cerci *pl of* CERCUS

cer·cis \ˈsərsə̇s\ *n, cap* [NL, fr. Gk *kerkis* Judas tree, weaver's shuttle, perh. fr. *kerkos* tail; fr. the movement of its leaves] **:** a small genus of widely distributed shrubs or low trees (family Leguminosae) having irregular pink to reddish flowers borne on the old wood — see JUDAS TREE, REDBUD

cer·cle \ˈserkl(ᵊ), -k(lə)\ *n, pl* **cercles** \"\ [F — more at CIRCLE] **:** a French administrative district; *esp* **:** an administrative subdivision in a French colony

cerco- — see CERC-

cer·co·ce·bus \ˌsərkōˈsēbəs\ *n, cap* [NL, fr. *cerc-* + Gk *kēbos,* a long-tailed monkey — more at CEBUS] **:** a genus of long-tailed monkeys of western Africa comprising the mangabeys and having prominent ischial callosities and white upper eyelids

cer·col·a·bes \(ˌ)sərˈkäləˌbēz\ [NL, fr. *cerc-* + *-labes* (irreg. fr. Gk *lambanein* to take, seize); akin to OE *læccan* to seize — more at LATCH] *syn of* COENDOU

cer·com·o·nas \(ˌ)sərˈkämənəs\ *n, cap* [NL, fr. *cerc-* + *-monas*] **:** a genus of commensal or coprophilous flagellated protozoans (order Protomonadina) having two anterior flagella, one of which is trailing

¹**cer·co·pid** \ˈsərkəpəd, -ˌpid\ *adj* [NL *Cercopidae*] **:** of or relating to the Cercopidae

²**cercopid** \"\ *n* -s **:** one of the Cercopidae **:** FROGHOPPER

cer·cop·i·dae \(ˌ)sərˈkäpəˌdē\ *n pl, cap* [NL, fr. *Cercopis,* type genus (prob. modif. of Gk *kerkōpē* long-tailed cicada, alter. of *kerkōps,* a long-tailed ape & *Kerkōps,* one of a pair of malicious brothers captured by Herakles, fr. *kerk-* cerc- + *ōps* eye, face) + *-idae* — more at OPTIC] **:** a family of insects (suborder Homoptera) including the froghoppers that suck the juices of plants and live in a mass of froth which they secrete

cer·co·pith \ˈsərkəˌpith\ *n* -s [modif. of NL *Cercopithecidae*] **:** a monkey of the family Cercopithecidae

cer·co·pi·the·ci·dae \ˌsərkōpə̇ˈthēsəˌdē, -ēkə-\ *n pl, cap* [NL, fr. *Cercopithecus,* type genus + *-idae*] **:** an anthropoid family that includes all the Old World monkeys except the anthropoid apes and is coextensive with a superfamily (Cercopithecoidea) — compare CATARRHINA — **cer·co·pith·e·coid** \-ˈpithəˌkȯid, -ˌpə̇ˈthēˌk-\ *adj or n*

cer·co·pi·the·cus \ˌ==pə̇ˈthēkəs, -ˈpithə̇kəs\ *n, cap* [NL, fr. L, a long-tailed ape, fr. Gk *kerkopithēkos, kerk-* cerc- + *pithēkos* ape — more at BEBUNG] **:** a genus (the type of the family Cercopithecidae) of slender long-tailed African monkeys comprising the guenons and related forms and having cheek pouches and ischial callosities

cer·co·pod \ˈsərkəˌpäd\ *n* -s [*cerc-* + *-pod*] **:** CERCUS

cer·cos·po·ra \(ˌ)sərˈkäspərə\ *n, cap* [NL, fr. *cerc-* + *-spora*] **:** a form genus of imperfect fungi (family Dematiaceae) that are leaf parasites with long slender multiseptate spores

cercospora leaf spot *n, usu cap C* **:** any of several leaf spots caused by fungi of the genus *Cercospora* (as sigatoka, beet leaf spot, and early blight of celery) — compare GRAY MOLD

cer·cos·po·rel·la \(ˌ)sərˌkäspəˈrelə\ *n, cap* [NL, fr. *Cercospora* + *-ella*] **:** a form genus of imperfect fungi (family Moniliaceae) distinguished from the genus *Cercospora* and other members of the family Dematiaceae mainly by the lack of pigment in the conidiophores and spores — see FROSTY MILDEW

cer·cos·po·ri·o·sis \(ˌ)sərˌkäspərēˈōsə̇s\ *n, pl* **cercosporioses** \-ˌōˌsēz\ [NL, fr. *Cercospora* + *-i-* + *-osis*] **:** a disease of plants caused by fungi of the genus *Cercospora*

cer·cus \ˈsərkəs, ˈker-\ *n, pl* **cer·ci** \ˈsərˌsī, ˈkerˌkē\ [NL, fr. Gk *kerkos* tail] **:** either of a pair of simple or segmented appendages believed to be sensory in function situated at the posterior end of many insects and certain other arthropods

-cer·cy \ˌsər|sē, -s|, -kē, -i\ *n comb form* -ES [ISV *-cercal* + *-y;* prob. orig. formed as F *-cerquie*] **:** tail formation (of a specified type) ⟨*diphycercy*⟩

¹**cere** \ˈsi(ə)r\ *vt* -ED/-ING/-S [ME *ceren, seren,* fr. MF *cirer,* fr. L *cerare,* fr. *cera* wax — more at CEREUS] **1** *obs* **:** to smear or cover with or as if with wax **2 :** to wrap in or as if in a cerecloth

²**cere** \"\ *n* -s [ME *sere,* fr. MF *cire, cere,* fr. ML *cera,* fr. L, wax] **:** a protuberance or tumid area at the base of the bill of a bird; *specif* **:** a soft swollen mass through which the nostrils open at the base of the upper mandible and which occurs esp. in birds of prey and parrots and in the latter is often feathered

ce·rea flex·i·bil·i·tas \ˈsirēəˌfleksəˈbiləˌtas\ *n* [NL, lit., waxen flexibility] **:** the capacity to maintain the limbs or other bodily parts in whatever position they have been placed (as in catalepsy)

¹**ce·re·al** \ˈsirēəl, ˈsēr-\ *adj* [F or L; F *céréale,* fr. L *cerealis* of Ceres, of agriculture, of grain, fr. *Ceres,* goddess of grain; akin to L *crescere* to grow — more at CRESCENT] **:** relating to grain or to the plants that produce it **:** made of grain ⟨a ~ beverage⟩

²**cereal** \"\ *n* -s **1 :** a plant (as a grass) yielding farinaceous seeds suitable for food (as wheat, maize, rice); *also* **:** the seeds or grain so produced either in their original state or commercially prepared **2 :** a prepared foodstuff of grain (as oatmeal or cornflakes) used esp. as a breakfast food

ce·re·a·lian \ˌ==ˈālyən, -lēən\ *also* **ce·re·al·ic** \-ˈalik\ *adj* [²*cereal* + *-ian* or *-ic*] **:** of or relating to cereals

ce·re·al·ist \ˈ==ələst\ *n* -s [²*cereal* + *-ist*] **:** a specialist in the study of cereals

cer·e·bel \ˈserəˌbel\ *n* -s [ML *cerebellum*] **:** CEREBELLUM

cerebell- *or* **cerebelli-** *or* **cerebello-** *comb form* [*cerebellum*] **1 :** cerebellum ⟨*cerebell*itis⟩ **2 :** cerebellar **:** cerebellar and ⟨*cerebello*cortex⟩ ⟨*cerebello*spinal⟩

cer·e·bel·lar \ˌserəˈbelə(r)\ *adj* [*cerebell*um + *-ar*] **:** of or relating to the cerebellum

cerebellar artery *n* **:** a branch of the basilar and vertebral arteries supplying the cerebellum

cerebellar peduncle *n* **:** any of three large bands of nerve fibers that join each hemisphere of the cerebellum with the parts of the brain below and in front

cer·e·bel·lo·ru·bral \ˌserəˌbelōˈrübrəl\ *adj* [*cerebell-* + L *rubr-, ruber* red + E *-al* — more at RED] **:** of or relating to the cerebellum and red nucleus

cer·e·bel·lum \ˌserəˈbeləm\ *n, pl* **cerebellums** \-ləmz\ *or* **cerebel·la** \-lə\ [ML, fr. L, small brain, dim. of *cerebrum* brain] **:** a large dorsally projecting part of the brain esp. concerned with the coordination of muscles and the maintenance of bodily equilibrium, anterior to and above the medulla which it partly overlaps and consisting in man of two lateral lobes and a median lobe connected with the other parts of the brain by three pairs of peduncles, the superior connecting it with the cerebrum, the middle with the pons, and the inferior with the medulla, the surface of the cerebellum exhibiting transverse sulci of varying depth and consisting of gray matter, the interior consisting chiefly of white matter which extends into the laminae formed by the sulci, branching in such a way that in an anteroposterior section it has a treelike appearance — see ARBORVITAE, BRAIN illustration

cerebr- *or* **cerebri-** *or* **cerebro-** *comb form* [*cerebrum*] **1 :** brain **:** cerebrum ⟨*cerebr*itis⟩ ⟨*cerebri*form⟩ ⟨*cerebro*scope⟩ **2 :** cerebral **:** cerebral and ⟨*cerebro*spinal⟩

cerebra *pl of* CEREBRUM

ce·re·bral \səˈrēbrəl, ˈserəb-\ *adj* [F *cérébral,* fr. L *cerebrum* brain + F *-al;* akin to OHG *hirni* brain, ON *hjarni,* Gk *kara* head, keras horn, Skt *śiras* head — more at HORN] **1 a :** of or relating to the brain or the intellect **b :** of, relating to, or being the cerebrum or the hemispheres of the brain **2 a :** appealing to intellectual and critical rather than emotional appreciation : demanding thought for perception of subtleties ⟨~ music⟩ ⟨~ drama⟩ **b :** characterized by the usu. subtle use of the mind : primarily intellectual in nature ⟨a ~ poet⟩ **3** [trans. of Skt *mūrdhanya*, lit., of the head] **a :** articulated with or involving the participation of the tongue tip curled up and back until its under surface touches the hard palate — used esp. of various consonants in Asiatic-Indian languages **b :** RETROFLEX **syn** see MENTAL

²cerebral \"\ *n* -s **1 :** a cerebral speech sound **2 :** a cerebral anatomical element (as an artery)

cerebral accident *n* **:** a sudden damaging occurrence (as of hemorrhage) within the cerebrum — compare APOPLEXY

cerebral apophysis *n* **:** PINEAL BODY

cerebral aqueduct *n* **:** AQUEDUCT OF SYLVIUS

cerebral artery *n* **:** any of the arteries supplying the cerebral cortex, the anterior and middle arising from the internal carotid and the posterior bifurcating from the basilar

cerebral cortex *n* **:** the superficial layer of gray matter overlying the cerebral hemispheres and functioning chiefly in coordination of higher nervous activity

cerebral dominance *n* **:** dominance in development and functioning of one of the cerebral hemispheres

cerebral fossa *n* **:** CRANIAL FOSSA

cerebral ganglion *n* **:** one of a pair of ganglia situated in the head or anterior part of the body in many invertebrates in front of or dorsal to the esophagus; *also* **:** a median ganglion formed by the fusion of such a pair

cerebral hemisphere *n* **:** either of the two lateral halves of the cerebrum

cerebral hemorrhage *n* **:** the bleeding into the tissue of the brain, esp. of the cerebrum, from a ruptured blood vessel — compare APOPLEXY

cere·bral·ism \sə'rēbrə,lizəm, 'serəb-\ *n* -s [*cerebral* + *-ism*] **1 :** the theory that consciousness is merely a function or product of the brain **2 :** a tendency to emphasize or to place undue stress upon cerebral, intellectual, or abstract ideas

cere·bral·ly \-brəlē, -li\ *adv* **:** in a cerebral manner

cerebral palsy *n* **:** a disability that results from direct or indirect damage to the motor centers of the brain before or during birth and is outwardly manifested according to the degree and area of injury by muscular incoordination (as in walking) and speech disturbances — compare SPASTIC PARALYSIS

cerebral peduncle *n* **:** either of two large bundles of nerve fibers passing from the pons forward and outward to form the main connection between the cerebral hemispheres and the spinal cord

cerebral thrombosis *n* **:** the formation within a cerebral artery of a blood clot preventing the circulation of blood in the blocked area of brain tissue

cerebral vesicle *n* **:** one of the divisions or dilatations into which the developing brain of vertebrates is marked off by incomplete transverse constrictions

cer·e·brate \'serə,brāt\ *vi* -ED/-ING/-S [back-formation fr. *cerebration*] **:** to use the mind **:** THINK ⟨legal helpers should do their *cerebrating* in their offices —Clarence Woodbury⟩

cer·e·bra·tion \,serə'brāshən\ *n* -s [*cerebr-* + *-ation*] **:** the act or the product of cerebrating **:** mental activity **:** THOUGHT

cer·e·brat·u·lus \,serə'brachələs\ *n, cap* [NL, irreg. fr. L *cerebrum* brain; prob. fr. the resemblance of its coils to the convolutions of the brain — more at CEREBRAL] **:** a genus of marine burrowing nemertine worms usu. of flattened form and often many feet long

cerebri- — see CEREBR-

cere·bric \sə'rēbrik, -eb-, -ēk, 'serəbrik\ *adj* [ISV *cerebr-* + *-ic*] **:** of, relating to, or derived from the brain or cerebrum

cere·bri·form \sə'rēbrə,fȯrm, -eb-, 'serəb-\ *adj* [ISV *cerebr-* + *-iform*; orig. formed as F *cérébriforme*] **:** like the brain in form or structure **:** CONVOLUTED

cer·e·brip·e·tal \¦serə¦bripəd·ᵊl\ *adj* [*cerebr-* + *-petal*] *of nerve fibers or impulses* **:** AFFERENT

cere·bro- *in pronunciations below*, ≈≈≈ = sə¦rēbrō *or* -brə *or* ¦serə(,)brō\ — see CEREBR-

cere·bro·ganglion \≈≈≈ *at* CEREBRO- +\ *n, pl* **cerebroganglia** [*cerebr-* + *ganglion*] **:** the cerebral ganglion of invertebrates — **cere·bro·ganglionic** \"+\ *adj*

cer·e·broid \'serə,brȯid\ *adj* [ISV *cerebr-* + *-oid*] **:** resembling or analogous to the cerebrum or brain

cer·e·bron·ic acid \¦serə¦brānik-\ *n* [ISV *cerebron*, a substance derived from brain tissue (fr. *cerebr-* + *-on*) + *-ic*] **:** a hydroxy fatty acid obtained from phrenosin by hydrolysis — called also *phrenosinic acid*

cere·bro·pedal \≈≈≈ *at* CEREBRO- +\ *adj* [*cerebr-* + *pedal*] **:** relating to or connecting the cerebral ganglion and pedal ganglia in mollusks

cer·e·brose \'serə,brōs *also* -ōz\ *n* -s [*cerebr-* + *-ose*] **:** GALACTOSE

cer·e·bro·side \'serəbrō,sīd\ *n* -s [*cerebrose* + *-ide*] **:** any of a group of white waxlike basic glycolipides found esp. in the brain and other nerve tissue that on hydrolysis yield sphingosine, a fatty acid, and a sugar (as galactose)

cere·bro·spinal \≈≈≈ *at* CEREBRO- +\ *adj* [*cerebr-* + *spinal*] **:** of or relating to the brain and spinal cord

cerebrospinal axis *n* **:** a primary bodily axis consisting of the brain and spinal cord **:** CENTRAL NERVOUS SYSTEM

cerebrospinal fluid *n* **:** a liquid comparable to serum but containing less dissolved material and in health no floating cells that is secreted from the blood into the lateral ventricles of the brain by the choroid plexus, circulates through the ventricles to the spaces between the meninges about the brain and spinal cord, and is resorbed into the blood through the subarachnoid sinuses, serving chiefly to maintain uniform pressure within the brain and spinal cord but also assisting in the metabolic exchanges

cerebrospinal meningitis *or* **cerebrospinal fever** *n* **:** inflammation of the membranes enveloping the brain and spinal cord in man or animals; *specif* **:** an infectious epidemic febrile disease caused by the meningococcus, producing severe headaches, vomiting, muscular spasm esp. of the neck, and delirium, often marked by a skin eruption of petechial or purpuric spots, and often ending fatally

cerebrospinal nervous system *n* **:** the portion of the nervous system in vertebrates comprising the brain, cranial nerves, spinal cord, and the spinal nerves concerned with transmission of impulses from sense organs to the voluntary muscles — compare AUTONOMIC NERVOUS SYSTEM

cere·bro·to·nia \"+'tōnēə\ *n* -s [NL, fr. *cerebr-* + *-tonia*] **:** a pattern of temperament typical of the ectomorphic individual marked by predominance of intellectual over social or physical factors and by exhibition of restraint, introversion, and shyness

¹cere·bro·ton·ic \"+¦tänik\ *adj* [NL *cerebrotonia* + E *-ic*] **:** exhibiting cerebrotonia

²cerebrotonic \"\ *n* -s **:** a cerebrotonic person **:** ECTOMORPH

cere·bro·vascular \≈≈≈ *at* CEREBRO- +\ *adj* [*cerebr-* + *vascular*] **:** of or involving the cerebrum and the blood vessels supplying it ⟨~ accident⟩ ⟨~ disease⟩

cere·bro·visceral \"+\ *adj* [*cerebr-* + *visceral*] **:** belonging to or connecting cerebral and visceral ganglia in mollusks

cere·brum \sə'rēbrəm, 'serəb-\ *n, pl* **cerebrums** \-rəmz\ *or* **cere·bra** \-rə\ [L, brain — more at CEREBRAL] **1 a :** BRAIN 1a — now used chiefly figuratively or affectedly **b :** an enlarged anterior or upper part of the brain: (1) **:** all the brain anterior to the isthmus **:** the forebrain and midbrain with their derivatives (2) **:** FOREBRAIN 1b (3) **:** the two cerebral hemispheres — see BRAIN illustration **2 :** the chief cephalic ganglion of an invertebrate **:** SUPRA-ESOPHAGEAL GANGLION

¹cere·cloth \'si(ə)r+,-\ *n* -s [alter. of earlier *cered cloth*, fr. *cered* (past part. of *cere*) + *cloth*] **1 :** cloth or a cloth smeared or impregnated with melted wax or with gummy or glutinous matter and formerly used esp. as a waterproof or protective material for wrapping a dead body or as a plaster in medicine **2 :** a covering for an altar table that is placed under the altar cloths

²cerecloth \"\ *vt* -ED/-ING/-S *obs* **:** to cover with a cerecloth

cered *past of* CERE

Ce·re·lose \'sirə,lōs *also* -ōz\ *trademark* — used for dextrose

cere·ment \'serəmənt, 'si(ə)rm-\ *n* -s [*cere* + *-ment*] **:** a usu. waxed winding-sheet — usu. used in pl. ⟨the corpses of royal children . . . wrapped up in ~s of gold —J.C.Powys⟩

¹cer·e·mo·nial \¦serə¦mōnēəl, -nyəl\ *adj* [ME *cerimonial*, fr. MF, fr. LL *caerimonialis*, fr. L *caerimonia* ceremony + *-alis* -al] **1 :** marked by, involved in, or belonging to a ceremony **:** marked by careful, full, and often elaborate attention to form and detail **:** RITUAL ⟨grave ~ occasions, like birth and death and the assumption of manhood —John Buchan⟩ ⟨the highly colored ~ life of the Greek court —H.O.Taylor⟩ ⟨~ paraphernalia⟩ **2** *obs* **:** observant of forms **:** CEREMONIOUS **syn** CEREMONIOUS, FORMAL, CONVENTIONAL, SOLEMN: CEREMONIAL may suggest an elaborate, prescribed, ritualistic code of procedure ⟨he had been among the Indians so much that he had acquired some notion of their *ceremonial* ideas of politeness, which demand a decent interval of light conversation before any important announcement is made —C.B.Nordhoff & J.N.Hall⟩ CEREMONIOUS also suggests elaborate procedures, perhaps punctilious and dignified ⟨the gay throngs of the people moved . . . outside the huge many-moated castle of the Shogun . . . but had no lot in the *ceremonious* existence within them —Laurence Binyon⟩ CEREMONIOUS is more likely than CEREMONIAL to refer to people ⟨the Zuñi are a *ceremonious* people . . . their interest is centered upon their rich and complex *ceremonial* life —Ruth Benedict⟩ FORMAL indicates accordance with a set procedure and may suggest stiffness, restraint, or old-fashioned custom ⟨his air was grave and stately, and his manners were very *formal* —Jane Austen⟩ ⟨"I kiss your hand, Miss", said Mr. Lorry, with the manners of an earlier date, as he made his *formal* bow again —Charles Dickens⟩ CONVENTIONAL indicates accord with general custom or usage ⟨when she herself had been seriously sick or in danger they uttered a *conventional* word of sympathy at the news, and forgot all about it immediately —Thomas Hardy⟩ ⟨your *conventional* morality is stronger than you. You are the slave to the opinions which have credence among the people you have known and have read about —Jack London⟩ CONVENTIONAL may suggest stodgy lack of originality ⟨I discovered . . . that the right people were often the most tiresome and the most *conventional* —A.C.Benson⟩ SOLEMN, in this sense now applicable mostly to religious, legalistic, or state procedures, stresses attention to all forms and details ⟨a *solemn* rite⟩

²ceremonial \"\ *n* -s [ME *cerimonial*, fr. *cerimonial*, adj.] **1 :** a system of formal rules and ceremonies enjoined by law, protocol, or custom for observance in religious worship, social affairs, or courtly procedure **2 :** a ceremonial usage or formality **:** a standardized rite, ceremony, or ritual ⟨the magic and religious ~s of primitive cultures⟩ **syn** see FORM

cer·e·mo·nial·ism \,serə'mōnēə,lizəm, -nyə,l-\ *n* -s **1 :** observance of or adherence to ceremonies esp. of religion **2 :** the addiction to or particular fondness for ceremonies

cer·e·mo·nial·ist \-ləst\ *n* -s **:** one who favors an emphasis on ceremonial forms esp. in religious affairs **:** RITUALIST

ceremonial law *n* **:** law prescribing the ceremonies of religion (as those of the Jewish religion contained in the Old Testament)

cer·e·mo·nial·ly \¦serə¦mōnēəlē, -nyəlē, -li\ *adv* **1 :** in a ceremonial manner **2 :** in regard to ceremonial law

cer·e·mo·nial·ness \,≈≈'mōnēəlnəs, -nyəl-\ *n* -ES **:** the quality or state of being ceremonial

ceremonial tea *n* [so called fr. its use in chanoyu] **:** a Japanese green tea cured by steaming, drying, and powdering selected shade-grown leaves and used in chanoyu

cer·e·mo·ni·ar·i·us \,serə,mōnē'a(a)rēəs\ *n, pl* **ceremoniarii** \-rē,ī\ [NL, fr. L *caerimonia* sacred rite + *-arius* -ary] **:** MASTER OF CEREMONIES b

cer·e·mo·nious \¦serə¦mōnēəs, -nyəs\ *adj* [MF *cérimonieux*, *cérémonieux*, fr. *cérimonie*, *cérémonie* + *-eux* -ous] **1 :** CEREMONIAL **2 :** devoted to forms and ceremony **:** punctilious about ceremony and formal procedure ⟨~ courtiers⟩ ⟨it was evidently to be a ~ occasion, for . . . he found his dress clothes put out for him —Compton Mackenzie⟩ **3 :** in accord with esp. stiff or formal usage or prescribed procedures ⟨the mere ~ salutation attending his entrance —Jane Austen⟩ ⟨that kind of ~ devotion punctually observed by a gentleman of the old school —Washington Irving⟩ **4 :** marked by ceremony, esp. by full, elaborate, and often showy observance of prescribed forms ⟨a ~ procession⟩ ⟨his ~ diction wore the aspect of pomposity —Sir Winston Churchill⟩ **syn** see CEREMONIAL

cer·e·mo·nious·ly *adv* **:** in a ceremonious manner

cer·e·mo·nious·ness *n* -ES **:** the quality or state of being ceremonious

cer·e·mo·ny \'serə,mōnē, -ni, *Brit usu & US sometimes* -əmən-\ *n* -ES [ME *cerimonie*, *ceremonie*, fr. MF *cérimonie*, *cérémonie*, fr. L *caerimonia*, perh. of Etruscan origin; akin to *Caere*, Etruscan city near Rome] **1 :** a formal act or series of acts typically conducted elaborately, solemnly, and as prescribed by the ritual or protocol of religious, state, courtly, social, or tribal procedure ⟨after the death of a king, a solemn ~ of purification was performed by a princess —J.G Frazer⟩ ⟨the marriage ~⟩ ⟨a religious ~⟩ ⟨the new republic was formally proclaimed with elaborate *ceremonies* —*Collier's Yr. Bk.*⟩ **2 a :** a conventional act or gesture of politeness or etiquette esp. when done elaborately ⟨the ~ of introductions completed, the party resumed⟩ **b :** an action performed with formality but lacking deep significance, force, or effect ⟨the drift towards conformity revealed itself . . . in the emphasis upon gestures and *ceremonies* of loyalty —H.S.Commager⟩ **c :** a commonplace routine action performed with elaboration, pomp, or punctiliousness ⟨the weekly ~ of giving out the wages to the help⟩ **3 a** *obs* **:** a symbol or device used in an elaborate ritual procedure **b :** pomp or display associated with such a procedure **c** *obs* **:** PORTENT, OMEN **4 a :** prescribed procedures **:** USAGES, OBSERVANCES ⟨the ~ attending the inauguration⟩ **b :** accordance with or observance of an established code of civility or politeness ⟨the door of Major Post's small office . . . opened without ~ and a young flight officer strode in —J.G.Cozzens⟩ **c :** a special occasion or function (as a parade, review, or escort) performed according to prescribed regulations **syn** see FORM

ce·ren·kov radiation *or* **che·ren·kov radiation** \chə'reŋkəf, chər'ye-\ *n, usu cap C* [after P.A.*Cherenkov* b. 1904 Russ. physicist, its discoverer] **:** polarized light produced by charged particles (as electrons) traversing pure solids or liquids at a speed greater than that of light in the same medium

cereous *adj* [L *cereus*, fr. *cera* wax] *obs* **:** like wax **:** WAXEN

¹ceres *pl of* CERE, *pres 3d sing of* CERE

²ce·res \'sir(,)ēz, 'sē(,)rēz\ *n* -ES *often cap* [L *Ceres*, goddess of grain] **:** a moderate orange that is slightly yellower and paler than honeydew and redder and paler than Persian orange

cer·e·sin \'serəsən\ *also* **cer·e·sine** \'serə,sēn, -,sən\ *n* -s [ISV *ceres-* (irreg. fr. L *cera* wax) + *-in*, *-ine*] **:** a white or yellow hard brittle wax made by purifying ozokerite and used as a substitute for beeswax; *also* **:** a petroleum wax (as paraffin wax) having similar physical properties

ce·re·us \'sirēəs\ *n, cap* [NL, fr. L, wax candle, fr. *cera* wax, prob. fr. Gk *kēros*; akin to Lith *korys* honeycomb] **:** a genus of cacti of the western U.S. and tropical America including mostly erect and columnar much-branched forms with spiny ribs and large elongated nocturnal flowers usu. borne singly along the ribs — compare NIGHT-BLOOMING CEREUS, SAGUARO

ce·re·za \sə'rāzə, -āsə, -re-\ *n* -s [AmerSp, fr. Sp, cherry, fr. LL *ceresia* — more at CHERRY] **1** *in tropical America* **a :** any of several plants having fruits resembling cherries (as *Malpighia glabra*, *M. coccigera*, and various species of *Cordia*) **b :** the fruit of these plants **2** *in Mexico* **:** CAPULIN 1

ce·ria \'sirēə\ *n* -s [NL, fr. *cerium* + *-a*] **:** the cerium oxide CeO_2

ce·ri·an·thar·ia \,sirē,an'tha(a)rēə\ *n pl, cap* [NL, fr. *Cerianthus*, type genus (fr. Gk *kērion* honeycomb — fr. *kēros* wax — + NL *-anthus*) + *-aria* — more at CEREUS] *in some classifications* **:** an order of Anthozoa coextensive with Cerianthidae and usu. included in Actiniaria — **ce·ri·an·thar·i·an** \¦≈≈¦≈'rēən\ *adj or n*

ce·ri·an·thid \,sirē'an(t)thəd\ *n* -s [NL *Cerianthidae*] **:** any actinian of the family Cerianthidae

ce·ri·an·thi·dae \-thə,dē\ *n pl, cap* [NL, fr. *Cerianthus*, type genus + *-idae*] **:** a family of elongated tube-building Actiniaria comprising the vestlets and related forms

ce·ri·an·thid·ea \,sirē,an'thidēə\ [NL, fr. *Cerianthus* + *-idea*] *syn of* CERIANTHARIA

ce·ric \'sirik, 'ser-\ *adj* [ISV *cer-* (fr. NL *cerium*) + *-ic*] **:** of, relating to, or containing cerium in the tetravalent state

ceric oxide *n* **:** the cerium oxide CeO_2

ce·ride \'sir,īd, -,əd\ *also* **ce·rid** \-,əd\ *n* -s [*cer-* + *-ide*, *-id*] **:** any of the simple lipides that are esters of higher monohydroxy alcohols and fatty acids esp. of higher molecular weight — compare WAX

ce·ri·llo \sə'rē(,)(y)ō\ *n* -s [AmerSp, hog gum (*Symphonia globulifera*), princewood (*Exostema caribaeum*), cogwood, zapatero, wax taper, match, alter. of Sp *cerilla* wax taper, fr. *cera* wax, fr. L — more at CEREUS] **1 :** ZAPATERO 2 **2 :** PRINCEWOOD 2

ceri·man \¦serə¦man, -ān\ *n* -s [AmerSp *cerimán*] **:** a plant of the genus *Monstera*; *esp* **:** a tropical American vine (*M. deliciosa*) with hanging cordlike roots

ce·rin \'sirən\ *n* -s [ISV *cer-* + *-in*; orig. formed in G] **1 :** a crystalline triterpenoid $C_{30}H_{50}O_2$ that is extracted from cork **2 :** CEROTIC ACID

ce·rine \'sir,ēn, -,ən\ *n* -s [ISV *cer-* (fr. NL *cerium*) + *-ine*] **1 :** ALLANITE **2 :** CERITE 1

cering *pres part of* CERE

ce·rin·the \sə'rin(t)thē\ *n, cap* [NL, fr. L *cerinthe*, *cerintha* honeywort, fr. Gk *kērinthē*, prob. fr. *kērinthos* beebread, perh. fr. *kēros* wax — more at CEREUS] **:** a genus of Eurasian herbs of the borage family with alternate leaves and yellow flowers — see HONEYWORT 1

¹ce·rin·thi·an \-ēən\ *adj, usu cap* [*Cerinthus*, 1st cent. A.D. Syrian heresiarch + E *-ian*] **:** relating to Cerinthus or his doctrine of adoptionist Christology

²cerinthian \"\ *n* -s *usu cap* **:** a follower of Cerinthus

ce·ri·om·e·try \,sirē'ämə·trē\ *or* **ce·rim·e·try** \sə'rim-\ *n* -ES [NL *cerium* + E *-ometry* (fr. *-o-* + *-metry*) or *-metry*] **:** volumetric chemical analysis by the use of a ceric compound [as ceric sulfate $Ce(SO_4)_2$]

ce·ri·on \'sirē,än\ *n* [NL, fr. Gk *kērion* honeycomb, fr. *kēros* wax] **1** *cap* **:** a genus (family Cerionidae) of pupa-shaped land snails that are confined to the West Indies and the southern tip of Florida **2** -s **:** any mollusk of the genus *Cerion* **:** PUPA SHELL

cerion

ce·ri·on·i·dae \,sirē'änə,dē\ *n pl, cap* [NL, fr. *Cerion*, type genus + *-idae*] **:** a family (order Pulmonata) of land snails coextensive with the genus *Cerion*

ce·ri·ops \'sirē,äps\ *n* -ES [NL, perh. fr. Gk *kērion* honeycomb + *ōps* eye, face — more at OPTIC] **:** an East Indian mangrove (*Ceriops tagal*) that is the source esp. in the Philippines of a valuable tanning extract

ceriph *var of* SERIF

ce·rise \sə'rēs *also* -ēz\ *n* -s [F, lit., cherry, fr. LL *ceresia* — more at CHERRY] **:** a moderate red that is slightly darker than claret (sense 3a), slightly lighter than Harvard crimson (sense 1), very slightly bluer and duller than average strawberry (sense 2a), and bluer and very slightly lighter than Turkey red

ce·rite \'sir,īt\ *n* -s [Sw *cerit*, fr. NL *Ceres*, an asteroid + Sw *-it* -ite] **1 :** a mineral consisting of a hydrous silicate of cerium and allied metals occurring generally in brownish masses (hardness 5.5, sp. gr. 4.86) **2** [Sw *cerin* allanite (fr. *cerium* + *-in* -ine) + E *-ite*] **:** ALLANITE

cer·i·thid·ea \,serə'thidēə\ *n, cap* [NL, prob. irreg. fr. *Cerithium*] **:** a genus of brackish-water snails (family Cerithiidae) having a long usu. dark brown or blackish spiral shell, common on tidal mud flats, and including intermediate hosts of the intestinal fluke (*Heterophyses heterophyes*)

cer·i·thi·idae \,serə'thīə,dē\ *n pl, cap* [NL, fr. *Cerithium*, type genus + *-idae*] **:** a family of slender elongated spirally coiled gastropod mollusks (order Pectinibranchia) comprising the horn shells of fresh and brackish waters — **ce·rith·i·oid** \sə'rithē,ȯid\ *adj*

cerithium \sə'rithēəm\ *n, cap* [NL, modif. of Gk *keration*, dim. of *kerat-*, *keras* horn — more at HORN] **:** the type genus of Cerithiidae

ce·ri·um \'sirēəm\ *n* -s [NL, fr. *Ceres*, an asteroid (fr. L *Ceres*, goddess of grain) + *-ium* — more at CEREAL] **:** the most abundant element of the rare-earth group that occurs combined in monazite, cerite, and other rare-earth minerals, that resembles iron in color and luster but is soft and malleable and ductile, and that emits sparks when scratched with steel and forms pyrophoric iron alloys used as flints (as for lighters) — symbol *Ce*; see ELEMENT table

cerium metal *n* **:** any of a group of rare-earth metals separable as a group from other metals occurring with them and in addition to cerium including lanthanum, praseodymium, neodymium, promethium, samarium, and sometimes europium

cerium oxalate *n* **1 :** a yellowish white crystalline salt $Ce_2(C_2O_4)_3.9H_2O$ **2 :** a mixture of the oxalates of cerium metals prepared as a white or pinkish powder and formerly used to allay gastric irritation

cerium oxide *n* **:** an oxide of cerium; *esp* **:** the dioxide CeO_2 obtained as a colorless to yellow heavy powder usu. by igniting a cerium compound (as the oxalate) and used as a polishing agent and esp. in the hydrated form as a decolorizer for glass

cer·met \'sər,met\ *n* -s [¹*ceramic* + *metal*] **:** a strong alloy of a heat-resistant compound (as titanium carbide) and a metal (as nickel) used esp. for turbine blades and other objects made by powder metallurgy — called also *ceramal*

cern \'sərn\ *vi* -ED/-ING/-S [L *cernere*, lit., to sift — more at CERTAIN] *Roman law* **:** to resolve to enter upon an inheritance; *also* **:** to make known the determination formally

cer·ni·ture \'sərnə,chu̇(ə)r\ *n* -s [L *cernitus* (past part. of *cernere*) + E *-ure*] *Roman & civil law* **:** a formal acceptance of an inheritance

cer·nu·ous \'sərnyəwəs\ *adj* [L *cernuus* with the face turned toward the earth; akin to L *cerebrum* brain — more at CEREBRAL] *of a plant* **:** inclining or nodding **:** PENDULOUS, DROOPING

cero \'se(,)rō\ *n, pl* **cero** *or* **ceros** [modif. of Sp *sierra* saw, sawfish. cero — more at SIERRA] **:** either of two large mackerel-like food and sport fishes (*Scomberomorus cavalla* and *S. regalis*) of the warmer parts of the western Atlantic ocean — called also *cavalla*, *kingfish*, *pintado*

cero- — see CER-

ce·ro·graph \'sirə,graf\ *n* -s [back-formation fr. *cerography*] **:** a writing or engraving on wax

ce·rog·ra·phy \sə'rägrəfē\ *n* -ES [Gk *kērographia*, fr. *kēr-* cer- + *-graphia* -graphy] **:** the art of making characters or designs in or with wax

ce·roid \'si,rȯid\ *n* -s [*cer-* + *-oid*] **:** a yellow to brown pigment found esp. in the liver in cirrhosis and brought about by various experimental diets

cero·lite \'sirə,līt, 'ser-\ *n* -s [G *kerolith*, fr. *ker-* cer- + *-lith* -lite] **:** a hydrous magnesium silicate like serpentine occurring in yellow or greenish waxlike masses

ce·ro·ma \sə'rōmə\ *n* -s [NL, fr. L, cerate, fr. Gk *kērōma*, fr. *kēros* wax — more at CEREUS] **:** the cere of a bird

ce·ro·man·cy \'sirə,man(t)sē, 'ser-\ *n* -ES [prob. fr. F *céromancie*, fr. *cér-* cer- + *-mancie* -mancy] **:** divination from figures formed by melted wax in water

ceroon *var of* SEROON

ce·ro·plastic \¦sirō, ¦serō+\ *adj* [Gk *kēroplastikos*, fr. *kēr-* cer- + *plastikos* plastic] **1 :** relating to the art of modeling in wax **2 :** modeled in wax

ce·ro·plastics \"+\ *n pl* [Gk *kēroplastikē*, fr. fem. of *kēroplastikos*] **1** *sing in constr* **:** the art of modeling in wax **2** *sometimes sing in constr* **:** WAXWORKS

ce·ro·tate \'sirə,tāt, 'ser-\ *n* -s [ISV *cerotic* + *-ate*] **:** a salt or ester of cerotic acid

ce·ro·tic acid \sə'rōd·ik, -räd·-\ *n* [L *cerotum*, a pomade, fr. Gk *kērōton* (fr. *keros* wax) + E *-ic*] **:** a solid fatty acid $C_{25}H_{51}COOH$ occurring usu. as an ester in most waxes (as Chinese wax, beeswax, montan wax) and some fats

cer·ous \'sirəs\ *adj* [ISV *cer-* (fr. NL *cerium*) + *-ous*] **:** of or relating to or containing cerium in the trivalent state

ce·rox·y·lon \sə'räksə,län, -lən\ *n, cap* [NL, fr. *cer-* + *-xylon*] **:** a small genus of tall So. American palms — see WAX PALM

cer·ris \'serəs\ *n, pl* **cerris** [NL, alter. of L *cerrus*] **:** the European Turkey oak

cer·ro green \'ser(,)ō-\ *n* [perh. fr. Sp *cerro* hill, fr. L *cirrus* curl, ringlet, tuft of hair on an animal — more at CIRRUS] **:** a moderate yellow green that is greener and deeper than average moss green and yellower and deeper than average pea green or apple green (sense 1)

cert \'sərt, 'sə̄t\ *n* -s [short for *certainty*] *slang Brit* **:** a sure thing **:** CERTAINTY

cert *abbr* **1** certificate; certified **2** certiorari

[1]**cer·tain** \'sərtᵊn, 'sə̄t-, 'səit- *sometimes* -tən\ *adj, sometimes* **certainer** \-t(ᵊ)nə(r)\ *sometimes* **certainest** \-t(ᵊ)nəst\ [ME *certain, certein*, fr. OF *certain*, fr. (assumed) VL *certanus*, fr. L *certus* determined, fixed, certain, fr. *cernere* to sift, discern, understand, decide; akin to OE *hriddel* sieve, OHG *rītera* sieve, *hreini* clean, pure, ON *hreinn*, Goth *hrains*, Gk *krinein* to separate, decide, Lith *krijas* hoop around a sieve, Gk *keirein* to cut — more at SHEAR] **1 a :** FIXED, SETTLED, STATED ⟨guaranteed a ~ percentage of the profit⟩ ⟨where an agency such as a board of education has by law been granted ~ powers —M.R.Cohen⟩ ⟨fair play means ~ definite things —Margaret Mead⟩ —sometimes used as a postpositive modifier ⟨a rent ~ in money —Adam Smith⟩ **b :** EXACT, PRECISE ⟨I could not find the ~ reasons for thinking the modern society was destitute of its normal humanity —J.C.Ransom⟩ **c** *of a statement* **:** proved to be either logically or factually correct **:** thoroughly confirmed **:** believed without reservation or doubt **2 a :** PARTICULAR **:** of a character difficult or unwise to specify —used to distinguish a person or thing not otherwise distinguished or not distinguishable in more precise terms ⟨he telephoned a ~ Mr. Smith⟩ ⟨~ people would like him to speak⟩ ⟨the comfortable-looking houses . . . along the tree-lined streets give it a ~ charm —*Amer. Guide Series: Md.*⟩ **b :** small but tangible **3 :** SURE, DEPENDABLE: **a :** entirely reliable ⟨no ~ early likeness of him survives —Carl Van Doren⟩ ⟨a ~ remedy for the disease⟩ **b :** not to be doubted as a fact **:** INDISPUTABLE ⟨it is ~ that we exist⟩ **4 a :** INEVITABLE ⟨the ~ advance of age and decay⟩ **b :** incapable of failing **:** DESTINED —used with a following infinitive ⟨he is ~ to see her⟩ ⟨he is ~ to be a success⟩ **5 a :** given to or marked by complete assurance and conviction, lack of doubt, reservation, suspicion, or wavering through or as if through infallible knowledge or perception **b :** firm and assured as though practiced **:** without hesitation, wavering, or diffidence ⟨I am sure that he was candid . . . I am ~ that he had no guile —W.A.White⟩ **6** *obs* **:** STEADFAST **syn** see SURE —**of a certain age :** past youth but yet not old ⟨a lady *of a certain age* —Crabb Robinson⟩

[2]**certain** \"\ *n* -s [ME *certain, certein*, fr. *certain, certein*, adj.] **:** CERTAINTY, CERTITUDE—**for certain** *adv* **:** ASSUREDLY **:** as a certainty ⟨never knew *for certain* how it happened —*Time*⟩

[3]**certain** \"\ *adv* [ME *certain, certein*, fr. *certain, certein*, adj.] *now dial* **:** CERTAINLY

[4]**certain** \"\ *pron, pl in constr* [[1]*certain*] **:** certain ones ⟨~ of my generation —W.B.Yeats⟩

cer·tain·ly *adv* [ME, fr. [1]*certain* + *-ly*] **1 :** in a manner that is certain **:** with certainty **:** without fail **:** INFALLIBLY **:** with assurance **2 :** without doubt **:** UNQUESTIONABLY ⟨~ innocent⟩

cer·tain·ness \-n(n)əs\ *n* -ES **:** CERTAINTY

cer·tain·ty \-ntē, -i\ *n* -ES [ME *certeinte*, fr. AF *certeinté*, fr. *certein, certain* + *-té* -ty] **1 :** something that is certain **2 :** the quality or state of being certain—**for a certainty** *also* **of a certainty** *or* **to a certainty :** CERTAINLY, ASSUREDLY **:** beyond doubt

cer·ta·tion \(,)sər'tāshən\ *n* -s [L *certation-, certatio* contest, fr. *certatus*, past part. of *certare* to fight, contend, settle something by a contest, fr. *certus* certain—more at CERTAIN] **:** competition between male elements of different genotype for opportunity to fertilize available female elements esp. as manifested by differential growth of pollen tubes

certes \'sərd·ēz, -r(,)tēz, 'sərts\ *adv* [ME, fr. OF, fr. *cert* certain, fr. L *certus*—more at CERTAIN] *archaic* **:** CERTAINLY **:** in truth

cer·thia \'sərthēə\ *n, cap* [NL, alter. of *certhius* tree creeper, fr. Gk *kerthios*] **:** a genus (the type of the family Certhiidae) of small songbirds with a slender more or less decurved bill and stiff pointed tail feathers serving as props in climbing trees — see CREEPER 4

cer·thi·i·dae \(,)sər'thīə,dē\ *n pl, cap* [NL, fr. *Certhia*, type genus + *-idae*] **:** a family (suborder Passeres) of small Old World and New World birds including the typical creepers

cer·tie \'sərti\ *n* -s [prob. back-formation fr. *certes*, taken as a plural] *chiefly Scot* **:** FAITH, TROTH — usu. used in exclamation

cer·ti·fi·a·ble \'sərd·ə,fīəbəl, 'sə̄|, 'səi|, |tə-, ₌₌'₌₌₌\ *adj* **1 :** capable of being certified **2 a :** fit to be certified as insane ⟨the very real increase in the number of ~ defectives —*Times Lit. Supp.*⟩ **b :** befitting an insane person ⟨a ~ urge to torture⟩ — **cer·ti·fi·a·bly** \-blē, -bli\ *adv*

[1]**cer·tif·i·cate** \sə(r)'tifəkət, ,sər't-, ,sə̄'t-, ,səi't-, -fēk-, *usu* -kəd· + V\ *n* -s [ME *certificat*, fr. MF, fr. ML *certificatum*, fr. LL, neut. of *certificatus*, past part. of *certificare* to certify — more at CERTIFY] **1 :** a document containing a certified and usu. official statement **:** a signed, written, or printed testimony to the truth of something (as a personal claim) ⟨he must present a ~ that he has never been arrested —Ernest Hemingway⟩; *esp* **:** a document issued by a school, a state agency, or a professional organization certifying that one has satisfactorily completed a course of studies, has passed a qualifying examination, or has attained professional standing in a given field and may officially practice or hold a position in that field ⟨a teacher's ~⟩ **2 :** something resembling or serving the same end as a certificate **:** CERTIFICATION ⟨a mood which she could surely take as a ~ that all was well —Rebecca West⟩ ⟨describes a pilgrimage thither as a ~ of patriotism —A.M.Young⟩ **3 :** a document evidencing ownership or debt ⟨stock ~⟩ ⟨~ of deposit⟩ **4 :** a document issued by a qualified officer of an organization asserting that a person is a member in good standing, holds a given rank or office, or has attained a specified honor; *also* **:** a blank form for such a document **5 :** a contract issued in place of an insurance policy by an insurer to one insured as evidence of membership in an insurance or pension plan

[2]**cer·tif·i·cate** \-fə,kāt, *usu* -ād· + V\ *vt* -ED/-ING/-S **:** to testify to, furnish with, authorize, or license by a certificate; *esp* **:** to certify by means of a certificate showing adequate training or competence to practice a particular trade or profession ⟨the *certificated* airlines —*Air Transportation*⟩ ⟨a *certificated* parachute technician —C.A.Zweng⟩ ⟨~ a physician⟩

certificated stock *n* **:** a quantity of a commodity available in a warehouse and certified by a commodity exchange as deliverable on future contracts — usu. used in pl.

certificate of age : an official certificate permitting the employment of a minor

certificate of convenience and necessity : a certificate from a public board or commission required by federal or state statute before engaging in certain public undertakings or services to protect existing franchises against injurious competition

certificate of deposit 1 : a receipt issued by a bank for an interest-bearing time deposit coming due at a specified future date **2 :** a negotiable receipt issued by a trust company for bonds or stocks deposited under a recapitalization or reorganization or other plan or agreement

certificate of incorporation : an instrument authorized by existing law and regulation and serving as evidence of the creation of a corporation — compare CHARTER

certificate of indebtedness : a short-term negotiable promissory note issued by a government or a corporation as evidence of a floating indebtedness

certificate of mailing : a certificate issued by a post office on special request and for a small fee attesting the nature, destination, and date of mailing of a particular piece of mail

certificate of necessity : a document issued by a certifying government agency under authority of which the internal revenue service allows deductions from taxable income for accelerated amortization of all or a part of the cost of emergency facilities

certificate of participation 1 : a certificate issued by some forms of investment trust evidencing a proportionate equitable interest of the holder in securities held by the issuing concern **2 :** a certificate of membership in a pension plan issued by the trustee who holds the policies as issued by the insuring company

certificate of public convenience and necessity : CERTIFICATE OF CONVENIENCE AND NECESSITY

cer·ti·fi·ca·tion \,sərd·əfə'kāshən, ,sə̄|, ,səi|, |tə-; (*certificating*) sə(r),tifə'k-, ,sər,t-, ,sə̄,t-, ,səi,t-\ *n* -s [ME *certificacioun*, fr. MF or ML; MF *certification*, fr. ML *certification-, certificatio*, fr. LL *certificatus*, past part. of *certificare* to certify + *-ion-, -io* -ion —more at CERTIFY] **1 :** the act of certifying or certificating or the state of being certified or certificated **2 :** a certified statement **:** CERTIFICATE **3** *Scots law* **:** a notice certifying to a party to a suit the consequences of his default in the matters specified as required of him **4 :** guarantee of the genuineness of the signature on a check by an authorized bank official **5 :** an authorization of a labor union by an appropriate public agency to act as a bargaining agent for all employees in a bargaining unit

cer·tif·i·ca·to·ry \(,)sər'tifəkə,tōrē, *Brit sometimes* -,kātəri\ *adj* [ML *certificatorius*, fr. LL *certificatus* + L *-orius* -ory] **:** serving to certify **:** constituting or of the nature of a certificate

certified *adj* **:** endorsed authoritatively **:** guaranteed or attested as to quality, qualifications, fitness, or validity

certified check *n* **:** a check certified to be good by the bank upon which it is drawn by the signature of usu. the cashier or paying teller with the word *certified* or *accepted* across the face of the check

certified mail *n* **:** first class mail for which proof of delivery is secured but no indemnity value is claimed — compare REGISTERED MAIL

certified milk *n* **:** pasteurized or unpasteurized milk produced in dairies which operate under the rules and regulations of an authorized medical milk commission

certified public accountant *n* **:** an accountant usu. in professional public practice who has met the requirements of a state law and has been granted a state certificate — abbr. *C.P.A.*; compare CHARTERED ACCOUNTANT

certified seed *n* **:** seed of good quality and established identity verified by an official agency after inspection

certified transfer *n* **:** MARKED TRANSFER

cer·ti·fi·er \'sərd·ə,fī(ə)r, 'sə̄|,'səi|, |tə-, -īə\ *n* -s **:** one that certifies

cer·ti·fy \-,fī\ *vb* -ED/ -ING/ -ES [ME *certifien*, fr. MF *certifier*, fr. LL *certificare*, fr. L *certi-* (fr. L *certus* certain) + L *-ficare* -fy — more at CERTAIN] *vt* **1 :** to attest esp. authoritatively or formally: **a :** CONFIRM ⟨cards ~*ing* me as a member of the . . . Civil Defense Corps —Wilder Hobson⟩ ⟨she is not permitted aboard a plane unless a doctor *certifies* the trip is necessary —Henry La Cossitt⟩ ⟨*certifies* his dramatic talent as the assassin in a nerve-thrumming piece —*Newsweek*⟩ **b :** to present in formal communication, esp. in a document under hand or seal ⟨the judges shall ~ their opinion to the chancellor —William Blackstone⟩ **c :** to confirm or attest often by a document under hand or seal as being true, meeting a standard, or being as represented ⟨the director . . . has *certified* about 140 acres as meeting the conditions presented in the statute —H.S.Truman⟩ ⟨they could ~ on their honor that their extract contained no salicylic acid —V.G.Heiser⟩ ⟨a *certified* copy of the record⟩ ⟨a *certified* agent of the law⟩ **d :** to attest officially to (a person's) insanity ⟨a *certified* mental case⟩ ⟨*certified* defectives⟩ **2 :** to inform with certainty **:** ASSURE ⟨it does not, of course, ~ us of the truth of any event in the past or future —W.R.Inge⟩ **3 :** to guarantee (a personal check) as to signature and amount by so indicating on its face — see CERTIFIED CHECK **4 a :** to designate as having met the requirements for pursuing a certain kind of study or work ⟨~ a student for college⟩ **b :** CERTIFICATE, LICENSE ⟨~ a teacher⟩ ⟨~ a physician⟩ ~ *vi* **:** to attest by a certificate ⟨five year program leading to examination by the American Board which *certifies* in that specialty —*Bull. of Meharry Med. Coll.*⟩ **syn** see APPROVE

cer·tio·ra·ri \,sərsh(ē)ə'rerē, -'rer,ī, -'rärē\ *n* -s [ME, fr. L, to be informed, be shown, pass. infin. of *certiorare* to inform, fr. *certior* more certain, compar. of *certus* certain; fr. the use of the word *certiorari* in the Latin form of the writ — more at CERTAIN] **:** a writ issuing out of a superior court to call up the records of an inferior court or a body acting in a quasi-judicial capacity (as commissioners and assessors of taxes) in order that the party may have more sure and speedy justice or that errors and irregularities may be corrected

certiorate *vt* -ED/-ING/-S [L *certioratus*, past part. of *certiorare*] *archaic* **:** CERTIFY, APPRISE, ASSURE

cer·ti·tude \'sərd·ə,tüd, 'sə̄|,'səi|, |tə-, -ə,tyüd\ *n* -s [ME, fr. LL *certitudo*, fr. L *certus* certain — more at CERTAIN] **1 :** the state of being certain of the truth or rightness of something **:** freedom from doubt **:** CONFIDENCE ⟨~ is not the test of certainty —O.W.Holmes †1935⟩ **2 :** accuracy, precision, or unfailingness of act or event ⟨the objective moral ~s have dissolved —Walter Lippmann⟩ ⟨demonstrate the absolute ~ of its conclusions —J.W.Krutch⟩

cer·to·si·na \,cherd·ə'sēnə\ *n* -s [It *certosino* Carthusian, fr. *certosa*] **:** a Renaissance Italian style of elaborate inlay of bone, ivory, light-colored wood, metal, or other material in stylized designs against a dark background

certs *pl of* CERT

cer·ty \'sərti\ *var of* CERTIE

[1]**ce·ru·lean** *also* **cae·ru·lean** \sə'rülēən, sē-, -lyən\ *adj* [L *caeruleus* dark blue (prob. fr. *caelum* sky) + E *-an* — more at CELESTIAL] **1 :** somewhat resembling the blue of the sky **2 :** of the color sky blue

[2]**cerulean** \"\ *n* -s **:** the color of the sky on a bright cloudless day **:** deep blue or azure

cerulean blue *n* **1 a :** a variable color averaging a strong greenish blue that is bluer and duller than grotto or cobalt blue and bluer and lighter than indigo carmine **b :** a strong blue that is greener and stronger than Sèvres and greener, lighter, and stronger than Victoria blue — called also *coelin* **2 :** a stable light greenish blue pigment consisting essentially of oxides of cobalt and tin and used as an artist's color

cerulean warbler *n* **:** an eastern U. S. wood warbler (*Dendroica cerulea*) mostly blue above and white below that migrates to northern So. America in winter

cerulein *var of* COERULEIN

ce·ru·le·ite \sə'rülē,īt\ *n* -s [F *céruléite*, fr. *cérulé* cerulean (fr. L *caeruleus*) + *-ite*] **:** a mineral $CuAl_4(AsO_4)_2(OH)_8.4H_2O$ consisting of a hydrous copper aluminum arsenate occurring in turquoise-blue microcrystalline masses (sp. gr. 2.80)

ce·ru·le·um \-lēəm\ *n* -s [L *caeruleum*, fr. neut. of *caeruleus*] **:** CERULEAN BLUE 2

ce·ru·lig·nol *also* **coe·ru·lig·nol** \,sē(,)rü'lig,nōl, -ōl\ *n* -s [*ceru-* (fr. L *caeruleus*) + L *lignum* wood + E *-ol*; prob. fr. the color which its alcoholic solution gives with barium hydroxide — more at LIGNEOUS] **:** a colorless oily phenol $C_{10}H_{14}O_2$ of burning taste obtained from wood-tar oils

ce·ru·lig·none *also* **coe·ru·lig·none** \-;nōn\ *n* -s [ISV *ceru-* (fr. L *caeruleus*) + L *lignum* + ISV *quinone*; orig. formed as G *zörulignon*] **:** a dark blue crystalline quinone $C_{16}H_{16}O_6$ obtained from beechwood tar

ce·ru·men \sə'rümən, sē'-\ *n* -s [NL, irreg. fr. L *cera* wax — more at CEREUS] **1 :** the yellow waxlike secretion from the glands of the external ear — called also *earwax* **2 :** a mixture of wax, resin, and sometimes earth that is used in place of pure wax in the building activities of stingless bees

ce·ru·mi·nous \-mənəs\ *also* **ce·ru·mi·nal** \-nᵊl\ *adj* [NL *cerumin-, cerumen* + E *-ous, -al*] **:** relating to or secreting cerumen

ceruminous gland *n* **:** one of the modified sweat glands of the ear that produce earwax

-ce·rus \sərəs\ *n comb form* [NL, fr. Gk *-kerōs*, fr. *keras* horn — more at HORN] **:** horned one — in generic names of insects ⟨*Tetracerus*⟩

ce·ruse \sə'rüs, 'sir,üs, -üz\ *n* -s [ME, fr. MF *céruse*, fr. L *cerussa*, perh. fr. (assumed) Gk *kēroessa* waxen, fr. *kēros* wax — more at CEREUS] **1 :** white lead used as a pigment **2 :** a cosmetic containing white lead

ce·rus·site \sə'rəs,īt\ *also* **ce·ru·site** \-rü,sīt, -ü,z-\ *n* -s [G *zerussit*, fr. L *cerussa* + G *-it* -ite] **:** native lead carbonate $PbCO_3$ occurring in colorless white or yellowish transparent crystals and also massive

cer·van·tite \sə(r)'van,tīt\ *n* -s [*Cervantes*, town in northwestern Spain, its supposed locality + E *-ite*] **:** a mineral $Sb^{III}Sb^{V}O_4$ composed of an antimony oxide occurring in yellow or white crystals and also massive

cer·ve·lat \'sərvə,lat; -,lä, 'servə,lä\ *n* -s [obs. F *cervelat* (now *cervelas*) — more at SAVELOY] **1** *also* **cer·ve·las** \'sərvə,lä, 'ser-\ -ES **:** sausage of several regional kinds made of varying proportions of pork and beef with added fat and spices, stuffed into casings, and smoked **2** *also* **cer·va·let** \'sərvə,lā, 'ser-\ **:** RACKETT

cer·ve·lière \,servəl'ye(ə)r\ *n* -s [F, fr. *cervelle* brain, irreg. fr. L *cerebellum* small brain — more at CEREBELLUM] **:** a close-fitting steel cap sometimes worn under a hood of mail or a helmet in medieval and later armor

cervi- *comb form* [F & NL, fr. L *cervus* — more at HART] **:** deer ⟨*Cervi*capra⟩

cervic- *or* **cervici-** *or* **cervico-** *comb form* [L *cervic-, cervix* neck] **:** neck ⟨*cervicodynia*⟩ **:** cervix of an organ ⟨*cervicectomy*⟩ **:** cervical and ⟨*cervicofacial*⟩

[1]**cer·vi·cal** \'sərvəkəl, 'sə̄v-,'səiv-, -vēk- *esp Brit also* ,sər'vīk- *or* sə̄'v-\ *adj* [prob. fr. NL *cervicalis*, fr. L *cervic-, cervix* neck + *-alis* -al — more at CERVIX] **:** of or relating to a neck or cervix or to a part like a neck

[2]**cervical** \"\ *n* -s **:** a cervical vertebra, nerve, or artery

cervical canal *n* **:** the passage through the cervix uteri

cer·vi·cale \,sərvə'kal(,)ē, -ā(,)lē, -ä(,)lē\ *n* -s [NL, fr. neut. of *cervicalis*] **:** the tip of the dorsal spine of the seventh cervical vertebra

cervical flexure *n* **:** a ventral bend in the neural tube of the vertebrate embryo marking the point of transition from brain to spinal cord

cervical ganglion *n* **:** one of the sympathetic ganglia of the neck, being in man usu. three in number on each side

cervical nerve *n* **:** one of the spinal nerves of the cervical region, being eight on each side in man and most mammals

cervical plexus *n* **:** a plexus formed by the anterior divisions of the four upper cervical nerves

cervical plug *n* **:** a mass of tenacious secretion by glands of the uterine cervix present during pregnancy and tending to close the uterine orifice

cervical rib *n* **:** a supernumerary rib sometimes found in the neck above the usual first rib

cer·vi·cap·ra \,sərvə'kaprə\ [NL, fr. *cervi-* + L *capra* she-goat, fr. *capr-, caper* goat — more at CAPRIOLE] *syn of* REDUNCA

cer·vi·cap·rine \-p,rīn\ *adj* [NL *Cervicapra* + E *-ine*] **:** of or relating to the reedbucks

cer·vi·ci·tis \,sərvə'sīd·əs\ *n* -ES [NL, fr. *cervic-* + *-itis*] **:** inflammation of the cervix uteri

cer·vi·co·facial nerve \;sərvə(,)kō+-\ *n* **:** a branch of the facial nerve supplying the lower part of the face and upper part of the neck

cer·vi·corn \'sərvə,kȯrn\ *adj* [ISV *cervi-* + *-corn*; prob. orig. formed as F *cervicorne*] **1 :** branching like antlers **2 :** bearing antlers

cer·vi·cum \'sərvəkəm\ *n* -s [NL, irreg. fr. *cervic-*] **:** the flexible intersegmental region joining the insect head and thorax

cer·vid \'sərvəd\ *n* -s [NL *Cervidae*] **:** one of the Cervidae **:** DEER, MOOSE, ELK

cer·vi·dae \-və,dē\ *n pl, cap* [NL, fr. *Cervus*, type genus + *-idae*] **:** a large family of ruminant mammals (order Artiodactyla) that are distinguished from the related Bovidae by possession of solid deciduous antlers and that include deer, elk, moose, and related forms — compare ANTLER — **cer·void** \-,vȯid\ *adj or n*

cer·vine \-,vīn\ *adj* [L *cervinus* of a deer, fr. *cervus* + *-inus* -ine] **:** belonging to or resembling deer

cer·vix \'sərviks, 'sə̄v-,'səiv-, -vēks\ *n, pl* **cer·vi·ces** \-və,sēz; ,sər'vī(,)s-, sə̄'vī-,səi'vī-\ *or* **cervixes** [L, neck; prob. akin to L *cerebrum* brain and to L *vincire* to bind, tie — more at CEREBRAL, VETCH] **1 :** NECK; *esp* **:** the back part of the neck **2 :** a constricted portion of an organ or part: as **a** *also* **cervix ute·ri** \-'yüd·ə,rī\ **:** the narrow lower or outer end of the uterus **b** *also* **cervix cor·nu** \-'kȯr,n(y)ü\ **:** the constricted cementoenamel junction on a tooth

cer·voi·dea \(,)sər'vȯidēə\ *n pl, cap* [NL, fr. *Cervus* + *-oidea*] **:** a superfamily of ruminants coextensive with the family Cervidae

cer·vu·lus \'sərvyələs\ [NL, dim. of *Cervus*] *syn of* MUNTIACUS

cer·vus \'sərvəs\ *n, cap* [NL, fr. L, stag, deer — more at HART] **:** a genus (the type of the family Cervidae) formerly including all the deers but now limited to the larger forms (as the red deer and elk)

ce·ryl alcohol \'sirəl-\ *n* [ISV *cer-* + *-yl*] **:** a white crystalline alcohol $C_{26}H_{53}OH$ occurring as an ester in waxes (as Chinese wax and beeswax)

ces *pl of* CE

[1]**ce·sar·e·an** *or* **ce·sar·i·an** *also* **cae·sar·e·an** *or* **cae·sar·i·an** \sē'za(a)rēən, sə'-, -zer-,-zär-\ *adj, often cap* [alter. of earlier *caesarean*] **:** having to do with abdominal delivery

[2]**cesarean** *or* **cesarian** *also* **caesarean** *or* **caesarian** \"\ *n* -s *often cap* [by shortening & alter. fr. earlier *caesarean section*, prob. trans. of ML *sectio caesaria*; fr. the belief that Julius Caesar was so brought into the world] **:** a surgical operation through the walls of the abdomen and uterus for the purpose of delivering the young of a human or animal

ce·sar·e·vich \sə'zarə,vich, -zär-\ *n* -ES *often cap* [Russ *tsesarevich*, fr. *tsesar'* emperor (fr. L *caesar*) + *-evich* (patronymic suffix) — more at CZAR] **1 :** the eldest son of the czar **2 :** the heir to the Russian throne — compare CZAREVITCH

ce·sa·ro·lite \,chäzə'rō,līt\ *n* -s [F, fr. G.R.P.*Cesaro* †1939 Italian-Belgian mineralogist + F *-lite*] **:** a mineral $H_2PbMn_3O_8$ occurring in spongy steel-gray masses and supposed to be a hydrous lead manganate (hardness 4.5, sp. gr. 5.3)

ce·si·um *also* **cae·si·um** \'sēzēəm *sometimes* 'sēzhē- *or* 'sēsē- *or* 'kīsē-\ *n* -s [NL, fr. L *caesius* bluish gray + NL *-ium*; fr. two blue lines in its spectrum — more at CAESIOUS] **:** a silver-white soft ductile metallic element of the alkali metal group that is the most electropositive element known, found usu. with rubidium and lithium (as in pollucite), and used esp. in the form of its compounds and alloys in electron tubes and photoelectric cells — symbol *Cs*; see ELEMENT table

cespitose *var of* CAESPITOSE

[1]**cess** \'ses\ *vt* -ED/-ING/-ES [ME *cessen, sessen*, short for *assessen* — more at ASSESS] *Brit* **:** TAX

[2]**cess** \"\ *n* -ES **1 :** ASSESSMENT, LEVY, TAX: **a** *now dial Brit* **:** a local tax **b** *Scot* **:** the land tax **c** *India* **:** a tax esp. upon a commodity or for a special purpose ⟨a tea ~⟩ ⟨a road ~⟩ ⟨an education ~⟩ **2 :** an exaction of provisions at a fixed price for the supply of the household and soldiers of the lord lieutenant of Ireland; *broadly* **:** a military exaction or imposition — **out of all cess** *obs* **:** beyond measure **:** in the extreme

[3]**cess** \"\ *n* -ES [prob. short for *success*] *chiefly Irish* **:** LUCK — used chiefly in the phrase *bad cess to* ⟨wish bad ~ to all his enemies⟩

ces·sa·tion \se'sāshən, sə'-\ *n* -s [ME *cessacioun*, fr. MF *cessation*, fr. L *cessation-, cessatio* delay, idleness, fr. *cessatus*, past part. of *cessare* to delay, be idle + *-ion-, -io* -ion — more at CEASE] **1 :** a temporary or final ceasing or discontinuance (as of action) **:** STOP ⟨the ~ of hostilities⟩ ⟨the ~ of relief activities⟩ ⟨the ~ of pain⟩ **2** *obs* **:** INACTIVITY, IDLENESS

ces·sa·tive \'sesəd·iv *also* se'säd· - *or* 'se,säd· -\ *adj* [L *cessatus* + E *-ive*] *of a verb form* **:** expressing cessation

ces·ser \'sesə(r)\ *n* -s [MF, fr. *cesser*, v. — more at CEASE] *law* **:** CEASING: **a :** a neglect of a tenant to perform due services or make payment for two years **b :** a ceasing of liability **c** *obs* **:** a ceasing to hold office

ces·sio \'ses(h)ē,ō\ *n* -s [L] *civil law* **:** act of ceding **:** CESSION; *specif* **:** CESSIO BONORUM

cessio bo·no·rum \-bə'nōrəm\ *n* [L, lit., cession of goods] *Roman & civil law* **:** a voluntary assignment by a debtor of all his property to his creditors by which he escapes the more painful penalties of insolvency (as liability to arrest and imprisonment) but is not generally discharged from liability for the debts **:** VOLUNTARY BANKRUPTCY

cessio in ju·re \-,in'jürē, -'yü-\ *n* [NL, cession in law] **:** IN JURE CESSIO

ces·sion \'seshən\ *n* -s [ME, fr. MF, fr. L *cession-, cessio*, fr. *cessus*, past part. of *cedere* to withdraw, yield + *-ion-, -io* -ion — more at CEDE] **1 :** a yielding (as of property or territory or rights) to another **:** act of ceding **:** CONCESSION ⟨no territorial ~s in the west were envisaged —Vera M. Dean⟩ ⟨his ~ to her of every right of judgment in the home —Mary Austin⟩ **2** *obs* **:** a yielding to physical or moral force, persuasion, or temptation **:** COMPLIANCE ⟨they shall prevail by ~, by sweetness and counsel —Jeremy Taylor⟩ **3** *civil law* **:** an assignment to another of the rights of a creditor or of ownership of a right of action or a claim **4** *ecclesiastical law* **:** the vacating of a

benefice by becoming a bishop or by accepting another without proper dispensation **5** *international law* **:** a transfer usu. evidenced by a treaty of sovereignty over territory by one sovereign state to another apparently willing to accept it
ces·sio·naire \ˌseshəˈna(a)(ə)r\ *n* -s [F *cessionnaire*, fr. *cession*] *civil law* **:** CESSIONARY
ces·sio·nar·i·us \ˌ≈≈ˈna(a)rēəs\ *n, pl* **cessionarii** [ML, fr. LL, adj., ceding, fr. L *cession-, cessio* + *-arius* -ary] *Roman law* **:** CESSIONARY
ces·sion·ary \ˈseshəˌnerē\ *n* -ES [ML *cessionarius*] *civil & Scots law* **:** an assignee or grantee of property, a claim, or a debt under a deed of conveyance
ces·sion·ee \ˌseshəˈnē\ *n* -s [*cession* + *-ee*] *Scots law* **:** CESSIONARY
cess·pit \ˈses,pit\ *n* -s [*cesspool* + *pit*] **1 :** a pit for the disposal of sewage and other refuse **2 :** something resembling or suggesting a cesspit ⟨a ~ of vice⟩
cess·pool \-ˌpül\ *n* -s [by folk etymology fr. earlier *cesperalle*, alter. of *suspiral* vent, pipe leading to a conduit, cesspool, fr. ME, fr. MF *souspirail* air hole, ventilator, fr. *soupirer* to sigh, breathe, fr. L *suspirare* — more at SUSPIRE] **1 :** an underground catch basin that is used where there is no sewer and into which household sewage or other liquid waste is drained to permit leaching of the liquid into the surrounding soil **2 :** a receptacle of filth ⟨~ of crime⟩
cest \ˈsest\ *n* -s [MF *ceste*, fr. L *cestus* — more at CESTUS] *archaic* **:** [1]CESTUS
ces·ta \ˈsestə\ *n* -s [Sp, lit., basket, fr. L *cista* — more at CHEST] **:** a narrow curved wicker basket used to catch and propel the ball in jai alai
cesti *pl of* CESTUS
ces·ti·da \ˈsestədə\ *n pl, cap* [NL, fr. *Cestus* + *-ida*] **:** a small order of ctenophores (class Tentaculata) comprising a single family (Cestidae) characterized by a greatly flattened and elongated body
[1]**ces·to·da** \seˈstōdə\ [NL, alter. (influenced by NL *-odes*) of *Cestoidea*] *syn of* [1]CESTOIDEA
[2]**cestoda** \"\ *n pl, cap* [NL, alter. of *Cestoidea*] **:** the subclass of Cestoidea comprising the tapeworms — **ces·to·dan** \(ˈ)sesˈtōdᵊn\ *adj* — **ces·tode** \ˈses,tōd\ *adj or n* — **ces·toid** \-ˌtȯid\ *adj or n*
ces·to·dar·i·a \ˌsestəˈda(a)rēə\ *n pl, cap* [NL, fr. [1]*Cestoda* + *-aria*] **:** a subclass of Cestoidea comprising intestinal parasites of primitive fishes that differ from the tapeworms in possession of a 10-hooked embryo and in the lack of strobilation — **ces·to·dar·i·an** \ˌ≈≈ˈrēən\ *adj or n*
ce·sto·des \seˈstō(ˌ)dēz\ [NL, fr. *Cestus* + *-odes*] *syn of* [2]CESTODA
ces·to·di·a·sis \ˌsestəˈdīəsəs\ *n, pl* **cestodia·ses** \-əˌsēz\ [NL, fr. *Cestoda* + *-iasis*] **:** infestation with tapeworms
[1]**ces·toi·dea** \seˈstȯidēə\ *n pl, cap* [NL, fr. *Cestus* + *-oidea* — more at CESTUS] **:** a class of Platyhelminthes comprising dorsoventrally flattened nonciliated parasitic flatworms typically consisting of a differentiated scolex and a chain of proglottides each including a complete more-or-less mature set of reproductive organs — see [2]CESTODA, CESTODARIA — **ces·toi·de·an** \(ˈ)sesˈtȯidēən\ *adj or n*
[2]**cestoidea** \"\ [NL, fr. *Cestus* + *-oidea*] *syn of* CESTIDA
ceston *n* -s [modif. (prob. influenced by Gk *-on*, neut. ending) of L *cestus* — more at CESTUS, -ON] *obs* **:** [1]CESTUS
ces·tra·ci·on \seˈstrāshēˌän\ [NL, fr. Gk *kestra* a kind of fish, hammer + *kiōn* pillar, uvula, division of the nostrils; akin to Arm *siun* pillar] *syn of* HETERODONTUS
[1]**ces·tra·ci·ont** \-nt\ *adj* [NL *Cestraciontidae*] **:** of or relating to the genus *Heterodontus*
[2]**cestraciont** \"\ *n* -s **:** a shark of the genus *Heterodontus*
ces·tra·ci·on·tes \(ˌ)ses,trāshēˈänˌtēz\ *n pl, cap* [NL, pl. of *Cestraciont-, Cestracion*, type genus] *in some classifications* **:** an order of primitive sharks
ces·tra·ci·on·ti·dae \-ntəˌdē\ [NL, fr. *Cestraciont-, Cestracion*, type genus + *-idae*] *syn of* HETERODONTIDAE
[1]**ces·tri·an** \ˈsestrēən\ *adj, usu cap* [OE *Cester, Ceaster* Chester + E *-ian*] **1 :** of, relating to, or characteristic of Chester or Cheshire, England **2 :** of, relating to, or characteristic of the people of Chester or Cheshire
[2]**cestrian** \"\ *n* -s *cap* **:** a native or resident of Chester or Cheshire, England
ces·trum \ˈsestrəm\ *n, cap* [NL, fr. Gk *kestron* betony] **:** a large genus of fragrant tropical American shrubs (family Solanaceae) having red, yellow, or white fragrant clustered tubular flowers — see DAY JESSAMINE, NIGHT JASMINE
ces·tui \ˈsed·ē, ˈsestwē\ *n* -s [MF, fr. OF, dat. of *cist* that one, fr. VL *ecce iste*, fr. L *ecce* behold + *iste* this, that; L *ecce* akin to Gk *ekeinos* that one, OSlav *jedinŭ* one, Skt *asau* that one, and to L *cis* on this side; L *iste* akin to L *is* he and to Gk *to* (neut.) the — more at HE, ITERATE, THAT] **:** BENEFICIARY
cestui que trust \-(ˌ)kēˈtrəst, -ˌkwe·ˈ-\ *n, pl* **cestuis que trust** [AF, lit., he for whom (the) trust (is held)] **:** a person who has the equitable and beneficial interest in property the legal interest in which is vested in a trustee
cestui que use \-ˈyüz\ *n, pl* **cestuis que use** [AF, lit., he for whose use (something is held)] **:** a person for whose use land or other property is legally held by another
cestui que vie \-ˈvē\ *n, pl* **cestuis que vie** [AF, lit., he for whose lifetime (something is held)] **1 :** the person whose life measures the duration of an estate **2 :** the person on whose life an insurance policy is written
ces·tum \ˈsestəm\ *n, cap* [NL, alter. of L *cestus* girdle] **:** a genus of ctenophores (order Cestida) including the Venus's-girdle
[1]**ces·tus** \ˈsestəs\ *n, pl* **ces·ti** \-ˌtī\ [L, girdle, belt, fr. Gk *kestos*, fr. *kestos* stitched, embroidered; akin to Gk *kentron* point — more at CENTER] **:** a woman's belt; *esp* **:** a symbolic one worn by a bride
[2]**ces·tus** \"\ [NL, fr. L] *syn of* CESTUM
[3]**ces·tus** \"\ *also* **caes·tus** \",ˈkīs-\ *n, pl* **cestus** *or* **caestus** [L *caestus*, fr. *caedere* to strike — more at CONCISE] **:** a boxer's hand covering in ancient Rome made of leather bands and often loaded with lead or iron

cestus

cestuy *obs var of* CESTUI
cesura *var of* CAESURA
cesure *n* -s [MF *césure*, fr. L *caesura*] *obs* **:** CAESURA
cet- *or* **ceto-** *comb form* [F *cét-, céto-*, NL *cet-, ceto-*, fr. L *cetus* — more at CETE] **:** whale ⟨*cetyl*⟩ ⟨*cetotolite*⟩ ⟨*Cetorhinus*⟩
ce·ta·cea \sēˈtāshēə\ *n pl, cap* [NL, fr. neut. pl. of *cetaceus* cetaceous] **:** an order of completely aquatic mammals consisting of the whales, dolphins, porpoises, and related forms, all having a very large head, a tapering body like a fish and nearly devoid of hair, forelimbs like paddles, no hind limbs, a tail ending in a broad horizontal fin, a large brain, a complex stomach of four or more chambers, and two mammae posterior in position
[1]**ce·ta·cean** \-shən\ *adj* [NL *Cetacea* + E *-an*] **:** of or relating to the Cetacea
[2]**cetacean** \"\ *n* -s **:** an animal of the order Cetacea
ce·ta·ceous \-shəs\ *adj* [NL *cetaceus*, fr. *cet-* + L *-aceus* -aceous] **:** CETACEAN
ce·ta·ce·um \-s(h)ēəm\ *n* -s [NL, fr. neut. of *cetaceus* cetaceous] **:** SPERMACETI
ce·tane \ˈsē,tān\ *n* -s [*cet-* + *-ane*; fr. its belonging to the cetyl series] **:** a colorless oily hydrocarbon $C_{16}H_{34}$ found in petroleum; normal hexadecane
cetane number *or* **cetane rating** *n* **:** a measure of the ignition value of a diesel fuel oil **:** the percentage by volume of cetane in a mixture of cetane and 1-methylnaphthalene that gives the same ignition lag as the oil being tested
[1]**cete** \ˈsēt\ *n* -s [L *cetus*] **:** WHALE
[2]**ce·te** \ˈsē,tē\ [NL, fr. L (pl. of *cetus* whale), fr. Gk *kētē* (pl. of *kētos* sea monster, whale)] *syn of* CETACEA
[3]**cete** \ˈsēt\ *n* -s [perh. fr. L *coetus* coming together, assembly, fr. *coitus*, past part. of *coire* to come together, fr. *co-* + *ire* to go — more at ISSUE] *of badgers* **:** GROUP, COMPANY
ce·tene \ˈsē,tēn\ *n* -s [ISV *cet-* + *-ene*; orig. formed as F *cétène*; fr. its being derived from spermaceti] **:** an oily hydrocarbon $C_{16}H_{32}$ of the ethylene series obtained by dehydrating cetyl alcohol — called also *1-hexadecene*

cet·er·ach \ˈsed·əˌrak\ *n* [ML *ceterah*, fr. Ar *shītaraj*, fr. Per *shītarakh*] **1** -s **:** SCALE FERN **2** *cap* [NL, fr. ML *ceterah*] **:** a small genus of mainly Old World ferns (family Polypodiaceae) typified by the scale fern
ce·te·ris pa·ri·bus *also* **cae·te·ris pa·ri·bus** *or* **coe·te·ris pa·ri·bus** \ˌkād·ərəˈsparəbəs, ˈse-, ˌchā-, -əˌrē¦s-, -ˌbüs\ *adv* [NL, other things being equal] **:** if all other relevant things (as factors or elements) correspond or remain unaltered ⟨staple-growing states are, *ceteris paribus*, more favorable to slave labor than manufacturing states —Joseph Dorfman⟩
ce·tin \ˈsētᵊn\ *n* -s [ISV *cet-* + *-in*; orig. formed as F *cétine*] **:** a crystalline fat $C_{32}H_{64}O_2$ constituting the chief component of spermaceti **:** cetyl palmitate
ce·ti·o·sau·rus \ˌsēd·ē(ˌ)ōˈsȯrəs, ˌsēshē-\ *n, cap* [NL, fr. Gk *kēteios* of sea monsters, monstrous (fr. *kētos* sea monster, whale) + NL *-saurus*] **:** a genus of primitive generalized sauropod dinosaurs found in the Jurassic of England
cet·ole·ic acid \ˌsēd·+...-\ *n* [*cet-* + *oleic*] **:** a crystalline unsaturated fatty acid $C_{21}H_{41}COOH$ occurring in the form of esters in many fish oils (as those from sharks' livers)
ce·tol·o·gy \sēˈtäləjē\ *n* -ES [ISV *cet-* + *-logy*] **:** a branch of zoology dealing with the whales
ce·to·mi·mid \ˌsēd·əˈmīməd\ *n* -s [NL *Cetomimidae*] **:** a fish of the family Cetomimidae
ce·to·mim·i·dae \-ˈmiməˌdē\ *n pl, cap* [NL, fr. *Cetomimus*, type genus (fr. *cet-* + *-mimus*) + *-idae*] **:** a family of small feeble deep-sea fishes (order Iniomi) resembling whales in shape and in having smooth black skin
ce·to·mor·pha \-ˈmȯrfə\ *n pl, cap* [NL, fr. *cet-* + *-morpha*] **:** a formerly recognized subdivision of Mammalia consisting of the Sirenia and Cetacea — **ce·to·mor·phic** \ˌ≈≈¦≈fik\ *adj*
ce·to·ni·an \səˈtōnēən, -nyən\ *adj* [NL *Cetonia* + E *-an*] **:** of or relating to the Cetoniidae
ce·to·ni·i·dae \ˌsēd·əˈnīəˌdē\ *n pl, cap* [NL, fr. *Cetonia*, type genus (irreg. fr. Gk *kētos* sea monster) + *-idae*] **:** a family of rather large brightly colored diurnal beetles comprising the sap chafers, having the mandibles thin and feeble and the mouth parts adapted to soft or liquid food, and being closely related to and often included as a subfamily of the Scarabaeidae — see GOLIATH BEETLE
ce·to·rhi·nus \-ˈrīnəs\ *n, cap* [NL, fr. *cet-* + *-rhinus*] **:** a genus that includes the basking shark as its only living species and is commonly placed in the family Lamnidae or sometimes made the type of a separate family (Cetorhinidae)
ce·to·there \ˈsēd·ə,thi(ə)r\ *n* -s [NL *Cetotherium*] **:** one of the Cetotheriidae — **ce·to·the·re·an** \ˌ≈≈ˈthirēən\ *adj*
ce·to·the·ri·i·dae \ˌsēd·ōthəˈrīəˌdē\ *n pl, cap* [NL, fr. *Cetotherium*, type genus (fr. *cet-* + *-therium*) + *-idae*] **:** a family of extinct whalebone whales
cet·oto·lite \sēˈtōd·ᵊlˌīt\ *n* -s [*cet-* + *otolite* "ear bone"] **:** a fossil bone of a whale; *usu* **:** one of the often detached and well-preserved tympanic or petrosal bones
ce·trar·ia \səˈtra(a)rēə\ *n, cap* [NL, fr. L *caetra, cetra* short Spanish shield + NL *-aria*; fr. the shape of the apothecia] **:** a genus of foliose lichens (family Parmeliaceae) chiefly of northern latitudes — see ICELAND MOSS — **ce·trar·ic** \-ˈtrarik\ *adj*
cetraric acid *n* [ISV *cetrar-* (fr. NL *Cetraria*) + *-ic*] **:** a bitter crystalline acid that is obtained from lichens (esp. *Cetraria islandica*)
ce·tyl \ˈsēd·ᵊl *also* ˈse-\ *n* -s [ISV *cet-* + *-yl*; fr. the occurrence of some of its compounds in spermaceti] **:** a univalent radical $C_{16}H_{33}$ compounds of which occur in waxes (as beeswax, spermaceti) **:** normal hexadecyl
cetyl alcohol *n* **:** a waxy crystalline solid alcohol $C_{16}H_{33}OH$ found in the form of its palmitic ester in spermaceti and used in pharmaceutical and cosmetic preparations (as creams and lotions) and in making detergents — called also *1-hexadecanol*
ce·tyl·pyridinium chloride \"+...-\ *n* [*cetyl* + *pyridinium*] **:** a white powder consisting of a quaternary ammonium salt $C_{21}H_{38}ClN.H_2O$ and used as a cationic detergent and antiseptic
ceu·to·rhyn·chus \ˌsüd·əˈriŋkəs\ *n, cap* [NL, fr. *ceuto-* (irreg. fr. Gk *keuthein* to hide) + *-rhynchus* — more at HIDE] **:** a large nearly cosmopolitan genus of weevils (family Curculionidae) including a number of forms very destructive to cruciferous plants
ce·va·dil·la \ˌsevəˈdilə, -dē(y)ə\ *n* -s [Sp *cebadilla* — more at SABADILLA] **:** SABADILLA
ce·va·dine \ˈsevəˌdēn, -dən\ *n* -s [*cevadilla* + *-ine*] **:** a poisonous crystalline alkaloid $C_{32}H_{49}NO_9$ found in sabadilla seeds and green hellebore — called also *crystalline veratrine*
ce·va's theorem \ˈchāvəz-, -ev-\ *n, usu cap C* [after Giovanni *Ceva* †ab 1734 Ital. mathematician, its formulator] **:** a theorem in geometry: if three lines from a point *O* to the vertices *A*, *B*, and *C* of a triangle meet the opposite sides in *A′*, *B′*, and *C′* respectively then $AB'.BC'.CA'+AC'.BA'.CB' = 0$ and conversely if this relation holds the three lines *AA′*, *BB′*, *CC′* meet in a point
ce·vi·an \ˈchāvēən, -ev-\ *n* -s *often cap* [Giovanni *Ceva* + E *-ian*] **:** a straight line drawn through a vertex of a triangle or of a tetrahedron and intersecting the opposite side or face
ce·vi·che \səˈvēchē\ *n* -s [AmerSp] **:** a dish or appetizer made essentially of fish (as corvina) marinated in lime or lemon juice
ce·vine \ˈsevˌēn, ˈsēˌvēn\ *n* -s [ISV *cevadine*] **:** a crystalline alkaloid $C_{27}H_{43}NO_8$ found in sabadilla seeds and formed from cevadine by hydrolysis
ce·vi·tam·ic acid \ˌsēˌvīˈtamik-\ *n* [*ce-* (fr. *c*) + *vitamin* + *-ic*] **:** ASCORBIC ACID
cewa *usu cap, var of* CHEWA
cey·lon \səˈlän, sē-, sā-\ *adj, usu cap* [fr. *Ceylon*, island south of India] **:** of or from Ceylon **:** of the kind or style prevalent in Ceylon **:** CEYLONESE
ceylon bowstring hemp *n, usu cap C* **:** a bowstring hemp (*Sansevieria zeylanica*)
ceylon cinnamon *n, usu cap 1st C* **:** the bark of a Ceylonese tree (*Cinnamomum zeylanicum*)
ceylon cinnamon oil *n, usu cap 1st C* **:** CINNAMON-BARK OIL
ceylon creeper *n, usu cap 1st C* **:** IVY-ARUM
[1]**cey·lon·ese** \ˌsäləˈnēz, ˌsē-, -ēs; ˌsēˌlä¦n-, ˌsā-; səˌlä¦n-, sē-,sā-\ *adj, usu cap* [*Ceylon* + E *-ese*] **1 :** of, relating to, or characteristic of Ceylon **2 :** of, relating to, or characteristic of the people of Ceylon
[2]**ceylonese** \"\ *n, pl* **ceylonese** *cap* **:** a native or inhabitant of Ceylon; *esp* **:** SINHALESE
ceylon gooseberry *n, usu cap C* **:** KETEMBILLA
cey·lon·ite *also* **cey·lan·ite** \səˈläˌnīt, sē-, sā-\ *n* -s [earlier *ceylanite*, fr. F, fr. *Ceylan* Ceylon, its locality + F *-ite*] **:** a dark-colored spinel — called also *pleonaste*
ceylon lily *n, usu cap C* **:** a large Asiatic bulbous herb (*Crinum zeylanicum*) of the amaryllis family having white flowers striped with red
ceylon moss *n, usu cap C* **:** an East Indian red alga (*Gracilaria lichenoides*) that is one of the chief sources of agar
ceylon oak *n, usu cap C* **:** KUSAM
ceylon pearl oyster *n, usu cap C* **:** a small pearl oyster (*Pinctada vulgaris*) widely distributed in the Indian ocean
ceylon tea *n, usu cap C* **:** a pekoe tea produced in Ceylon
ceylon tea tree *n, usu cap C* **:** a tropical Asiatic tree (*Elaeodendron glaucum*) of the family Celastraceae having leaves like those of the tea plant
ceys·sa·tite \ˈsāsəˌtīt\ *n* -s [F, fr. *Ceyssat*, France, its locality + F *-ite*] **:** RANDANNITE
cf *abbr* **1** calf **2** *pronounced like* COMPARE *also* (ˈ)sē¦ef *sometimes* kənˈfər *or* -fə\ [L *confer*, imp. of *conferre* to compare — more at CONFER] compare
CF *abbr* **1** cannot find **2** [ML *cantus firmus*] plain chant **3** carried forward **4** center field **5** center forward **6** *often not cap* centrifugal force **7** corresponding fellow **8** cost and freight
Cf *symbol* californium
CFH *abbr, often not cap* cubic feet per hour
CFI *abbr, sometimes not cap* cost, freight, and insurance
c fiber *n, usu cap C* **:** an unmyelinated nerve fiber esp. of the autonomic system
c flat \ˈ≈¦≈\ *n, usu cap C* **1 :** the keynote of C-flat major **2 :** the tone a half step below C
c-flat major \ˈ≈,≈¦≈≈\ *n, usu cap C* **:** the major musical key having a signature of seven flats
CFM *abbr, often not cap* cubic feet per minute

CFO *abbr* canceling former order
CFS *abbr, often not cap* cubic feet per second
cg *abbr* centigram
CG *abbr* **1** captain general **2** *sometimes not cap* center of gravity **3** coast guard **4** combat group **5** commanding general **6** commissary general **7** complete games **8** comptroller general **9** consul general
CGA *abbr* **1** certified general accountant **2** cargo's proportion of general average
cge *abbr* carriage
cgm *abbr* centigram
cgo *abbr* **1** cargo **2** contango
CGS *abbr* **1** *usu not cap* centimeter-gram-second **2** chief of general staff
ch *abbr* **1** chain **2** chairman **3** chaldron **4** *usu cap C* champion **5** chancellor; chancery **6** chaplain **7** chapter **8** check **9** checkered **10** chervonets **11** chest **12** chestnut **13** chief **14** child **15** choice **16** choir organ **17** choke **18** chromogenic **19** church
CH *abbr* **1** case-hardened **2** central heating **3** clearing house **4** compass heading **5** courthouse **6** customhouse
chaac *or* **chac** \ˈchäk\ *n* -s *sometimes cap* [Sp *chaac, chac*, fr. Maya] **:** one of the Mayan gods of rain and fertility — usu. used in pl.
cha·ba·ka·no \ˌchäbəˈkä(ˌ)nō\ *n, usu cap* [PhilSp *chabacano*, fr. Sp, insipid, tasteless, crude, awkward] **:** a Spanish-based pidgin language spoken in and around Zamboanga, Philippines
chab·a·zite *or* **chab·a·site** \ˈkabəˌzīt\ *n* -s [G *chabasit*, fr. F *chabasie* (fr. LGk *chabazios*, MS var. of *chalazios* precious stone resembling a hailstone, fr. Gk *chalazios* of hail, fr. *chalaza* hailstone) + G *-it* -ite — more at CHALAZA] **:** a zeolite $CaAl_2Si_4O_{12}.6H_2O$ consisting of a hydrous silicate of calcium and aluminum that occurs in glassy rhombohedral crystals, varies in color from white to yellow or red, and is used in some water softeners (hardness 4–5, sp. gr. 2.08–2.16)
chaber *n, pl* **chaberim** *var of* HAVER
cha·ber·tia \shəˈberd·ēə, -bər-\ *n, cap* [NL, fr. Philibert *Chabert* †1814 Fr. veterinary + NL *-ia*] **:** a genus of nematode worms (family Strongylidae) infesting the colon of sheep and other ruminants and causing a bloody diarrhea
cha·blis \ˈsha(ˌ)blē, shäˈblē\ *n, pl* **chablis** \-lēz\ *usu cap* [F, fr. *Chablis*, France, where it is made] **1 :** a dry white Burgundy table wine of a straw-gold to pale amber color produced in the department of Yonne, France **2 :** a wine resembling Chablis and retailed under the name Chablis usu. with the addition of its geographical designation ⟨California *Chablis*⟩
cha·bu·tra *or* **cha·boo·tra** \chəˈbü·trə, -ü·,trä\ *n* -s [Hindi *cabūtrā*] *India* **:** a raised platform **:** TERRACE, DAIS
cha·ca·te \chəˈkäd·ē\ *n* -s [MexSp, fr. Nahuatl *chacatl*] **:** a small shrub (*Krameria grayi*) of Mexico and the southwestern U.S. the bark of which furnishes a brownish red dye
[1]**chace** *var of* CHASE
[2]**chace** \ˈshäs\ *n, pl* **chaces** \-äs(əz)\ [MF *chace, chasse*, lit., chase — more at CHASE] **:** a 14th century French part-song in the form of a canon at the unison
[1]**cha-cha** \ˈshäˌshä\ *n* -s *usu cap 1st C & often cap 2d C* [origin unknown] **:** one of a group of poor whites of French ancestry in the Virgin islands
[2]**cha-cha** \ˈchäˌchä\ *also* **cha-cha-cha** \¦chä,chä¦chä\ *n* -s [AmerSp (Cuba) *cha-cha-cha*] **:** a fast rhythmic ballroom dance originating in Latin America
cha·cha·la·ca \ˌchächəˈläkə\ *n* -s [Sp, fr. Nahuatl. twittering of a bird, of imit. origin] **:** any of several large chiefly arboreal guans of *Ortalis* and related genera that somewhat resemble wild turkeys but are longer legged and have a well-developed feathered crest, that are native to Central America and Mexico with one variety (*O. vetula macalli*) extending into southern Texas, and that are highly regarded as game birds
chachamim *or* **chachomim** *pl of* CHOCHEM
cha·cha·poya \ˌchächəˈpȯiə\ *n, pl* **chachapoya** *or* **chachapoyas** *usu cap* [Sp, of AmerInd origin] **1 :** an unusually light-skinned Indian people of the Chinchaisuyu group **2 :** a member of the Chachapoya people
chack \ˈchak\ *n* -s [Sc *chack* to snap with the teeth, bite, of imit. origin] *chiefly Scot* **:** a bite or small portion of food **:** SNACK
chack·le \ˈchakəl\ *vi* -ED/-ING/-S [prob. blend of [1]*chatter* and [1]*cackle*] *dial Eng* **:** CACKLE, RATTLE
chac·ma \ˈchakmə\ *n* -s [Hottentot] **:** a large brownish black baboon (*Papio comatus*) of southern Africa often a serious pest of cultivated crops
chac·mool *or* **chac·mol** \ˈchäkˌmōl\ *n* -s *usu cap* [Maya *Chac*, a god + *mool* paw] **:** a reclining figure with flexed knees found in the prehistoric remains of Mexico and Central America, esp. in Yucatan
cha·co·bo \chäˈkō(ˌ)bō\ *n, pl* **chacobo** *or* **chacobos** *usu cap* [Sp, of AmerInd origin] **1 a :** a Panoan people of northern Bolivia **b :** a member of such people **2 :** the language of the Chacobo people
cha·conne *also* **cha·con** \shäˈkȯn, sha-,shə-,shä-, -än,-ən,-ōn\ *or* **cha·co·na** \chäˈkōnə\ *n* -s [F & Sp; F *chaconne*, fr. Sp *chacona*, prob. of imit. origin; fr. the sound of castanets used in the dance] **:** an old orig. Spanish dance in moderate three-quarter measure resembling the slower passacaglia; *also* **:** a musical composition with stress on the second beat and consisting typically of continuous variations based on a repeated succession of chords
cha·cra \ˈchäkrə\ *n* -s [AmerSp, fr. Quechua *chakra*] *in So. America* **:** a small farm or ranch
[1]**chad** \chəd, (ˈ)chad\ [alter. of ME *ich hadde*] *dial Eng* **:** I had
[2]**chad** \ˈchad, -aa(ə)d\ *n* -s [prob. alter. of *shad*] **:** a young European sea bream
[3]**chad** \"\ *n* -s [perh. fr. Sc. gravel] **:** one of the small disks produced in cutting code perforations on tape used sometimes in transmitting by code or in some code-actuated office machines
[4]**chad** \"\ *n* -s *usu cap* **:** a branch of the Afro-Asiatic language family comprising a large number of languages of northern Nigeria and Cameroons — see AFRO-ASIATIC LANGUAGES table
[5]**chad** \"\ *adj, usu cap* [fr. *Chad*, republic formerly part of French Equatorial Africa] **:** of or relating to Chad **:** of the kind or style prevalent in Chad
chadarim *pl of* CHEDER
chad·ian \ˈchadēən\ *n* -s *cap* [*Chad*, country in central Africa + E *-ian*] **:** a native or inhabitant of Chad — **chadian** *adj, usu cap*
chadlock *var of* CHARLOCK
cha·dor *or* **cha·dar** *or* **chud·dar** *or* **chud·der** *also* **chad·dar** \ˈchədə(r)\ *n* -s [Hindi *caddar*, fr. Per *chaddar*] **:** a large cloth used as a combination head covering, veil, and shawl usu. by women among Muslim and Hindu peoples esp. in India and Iran
chae·nac·tis \kēˈnaktəs\ *n, cap* [NL, fr. Gk *chainein* to gape + *aktis* ray; akin to L *hiare* to gape — more at YAWN, ACTIN-] **:** a genus of herbs (family Compositae) found in the western U.S. and characterized by entire or pinnately lobed leaves and long peduncled heads of white or yellow flowers
chae·no·me·les \ˌkēnəˈmē(ˌ)lēz\ *n, cap* [NL, fr. *chaeno-* + *-meles* (irreg. fr. Gk *mēlon* apple, fruit) — more at MALUS] **:** a genus of Asiatic shrubs (family Rosaceae) comprising the flowering quinces and having alternate serrate leaves, 5-petaled flowers, and many seeds in each cell of the ovary — see JAPANESE QUINCE
chae·ro·pus \ˈkirəpəs\ *n, cap* [NL, fr. *chaer-* (irreg. fr. Gk *choiros* pig) + *-pus*; fr. the resemblance of the forefeet to those of a pig; akin to L *horrēre* to bristle — more at HORROR] **:** a genus of marsupial mammals consisting of the pig-footed bandicoots
chaet- *or* **chaeto-** *comb form* [NL, fr. Gk *chaitē*] **:** bristle **:** hair ⟨*Chaetodon*⟩ ⟨*chaeto*phorous⟩
chae·ta \ˈkēd·ə\ *n, pl* **chae·tae** \-ˌē,tē, -ēd·(ˌ)ē\ [NL, fr. Gk *chaitē* long flowing hair; akin to MIr *gaīset* bristle, Av *gaēsa* curly hair] **:** SPINE, BRISTLE, SETA
-chae·ta \ˈkēd·ə, -ētə\ *n comb form* [NL, fr. Gk *-chaitēs* -haired, fr. *chaitē*] **1** *also* **-chae·tes** \ˈkēd·(ˌ)ēz, -ē,tēz\ *or* **-chae·tus** \ˈkēd·əs, -ētəs\ **:** haired one **:** hairlike one — in generic names ⟨*Spirochaeta*⟩ ⟨*Connochaetes*⟩ **2** *pl* **-chae·tae** \ˈkēd·(ˌ)ē, -ē,tē\ **:** bristle (of a specified type) ⟨*microchaeta*⟩
chae·tal \ˈkēd·ᵊl, -ētᵊl\ *adj* [NL *chaeta* + E *-al*] **:** of or relating to bristles or setae

chae·te·tes \kē'tēd·ēz\ *n, cap* [NL, irreg. fr. Gk *chaitē* long flowing hair] **:** a genus (the type of the large extinct family Chaetetidae) of fossil corals that have the skeleton composed of slender closely contiguous tubes and are common in the Carboniferous limestones — **chae·te·tid** \-tēd·əd\ *adj or n*

chae·tig·er·ous \kē'tij(ə)rəs\ *adj* [NL *chaeta* + E *-i-* + *-gerous*] **:** bearing bristles or setae

chae·to·cer·cus \,kēd·ō'sərkəs\ *n, cap* [NL, fr. *chaet-* + Gk *kerkos* tail] **:** a genus of Australian desert-dwelling marsupial mice

chae·to·dip·ter·us \-'diptərəs\ *n, cap* [NL, fr. *chaet-* + Gk *dipteros* two-winged — more at DIPTEROUS] **:** a genus of spadefishes (family Ephippidae) found in warm seas along both coasts of America and distinguished by protractile premaxillaries and dorsal spines of unequal length

chae·to·don \'⁼⁼,dän\ *n* [NL, fr. *chaet-* + *-odon*] **1** *cap* **:** the type genus of Chaetodontidae **2** -s **:** any fish of the genus *Chaetodon*

chaetodon

chae·to·don·ti·dae \,⁼⁼'däntə,dē\ *n pl, cap* [NL, fr. *Chaetodont-, Chaetodon*, type genus + *-idae*] **:** a large family of percoid tropical marine fishes common about coral reefs that includes the butterfly fishes

chae·to·gas·ter \'⁼⁼,gastə(r), ,⁼⁼'⁼⁼\ *n, cap* [NL, fr. *chaet-* + *-gaster*] **:** a common widely distributed genus of small transparent oligochaete worms (family Naididae) that are parasites on gastropods or free-living in fresh water

¹chae·tog·nath \'kēd·,äg,nath, -d·əg-\ *n* -s [NL *Chaetognatha*] **:** one of the Chaetognatha **:** ARROWWORM

²chaetognath \"\ *adj* **:** of or relating to the Chaetognatha

chae·tog·na·tha \kē'tägnəthə\ *n pl, cap* [NL, fr. *chaet-* + *-gnatha*] **:** a group of small active transparent marine worms of uncertain systematic position with horizontal lateral and caudal fins and a row of movable curved spines at each side of the mouth and comprising the arrowworms — see SAGITTA, SPADELLA — **chae·tog·na·than** \-thən\ *adj* — **chae·tog·na·thous** \-thəs\ *adj*

chae·to·mi·um \kē'tōmēəm\ *n, cap* [NL, fr. Gk *chaitōma* plume (fr. *chaitē* hair) + NL *-ium* — more at CHAETA] **:** a genus (the type of the family Chaetomiaceae) of ascomycetous fungi that are characterized by long straight, curled, or branched hairs on the usu. dull-colored perithecia esp. on their upper surfaces and that include several fungi destructive to paper and other materials and to some plastics

chae·toph·o·ra \-'täph(ə)rə\ *n, cap* [NL, fr. *chaet-* + *-phora*] **:** the type genus of Chaetophoraceae

chae·toph·o·ra·ce·ae \⁼,⁼ə'rāsē,ē\ *n pl, cap* [NL, fr. *Chaetophora*, type genus + *-aceae*] **:** a large family of widely distributed green algae (order Ulotrichales) — see CHAETOPHORALES — **chae·toph·o·ra·ceous** \⁼;⁼⁼;⁼shəs\ *adj*

chae·toph·o·ra·les \-(,)lēz\ *n pl, cap* [NL, fr. *Chaetophora* + *-ales*] *in some classifications* **:** a large order of green algae that includes the families Chaetophoraceae, Trentepohliaceae, Coleochaetaceae, and related forms and sometimes embraces the Ulotrichaceae and related families and also the Oedogoniaceae and that is characterized by a plant body typically consisting of two systems of branching filaments one of which is prostrate and attached to the substratum and the other upright and often possessing hairs or bristles — compare ULOTRICHALES

chae·toph·o·rous \kē'täf(ə)rəs\ *adj* [*chaet-* + *-phorous*] **:** CHAETIGEROUS

chae·to·pod *or* **che·to·pod** \'kēd·ə,päd\ *n* -s [NL *Chaetopoda*] **:** one of the Chaetopoda

chae·top·o·da \kē'täpədə\ *n pl, cap* [NL, fr. *chaet-* + *-poda*] *in many classifications* **:** a major division (usu. a class) of annelid worms containing the Polychaeta and Oligochaeta as subdivisions — **chae·top·o·dan** \-dən, -dᵊn\ *adj* — **chae·top·o·dous** \-dəs\ *adj*

chae·top·ter·us \⁼'⁼tərəs\ *n, cap* [NL, fr. *chaet-* + *-pterus*] **:** a genus (the type of the small family Chaetopteridae) of large marine polychaete worms that inhabit parchmentlike U-shaped tubes open at both ends, are highly bioluminescent, and have one pair of large lateral appendages and several broad fanlike membranous folds by which they maintain a current of water within the tube

chae·to·tac·tic \,kēd·ō¦taktik\ *adj* [*chaet-* + *-tactic*] **:** of or relating to chaetotaxy

chae·to·taxy \'kēd·ō,taksē\ *n* -ES [*chaet-* + *-taxy*] **1 :** the arrangement or pattern of bristles on an arthropod (as a mosquito, mite, or larva) **2 :** the study of chaetotaxy

chae·tu·ra \kē'türə, kē'tyü-\ *n, cap* [NL, fr. *chaet-* + *-ura*] **:** a genus of swifts having stiff spinelike projecting shafts to the tail feathers and including the chimney swift

chaetura black *n, often cap C* **:** a nearly neutral slightly olive black that is very slightly darker and more neutral than London smoke

chaetura drab *n, often cap C* **:** BEAR 6

-chaetus — see -CHAETA

¹chafe \'chāf, *esp dial* -af\ *vb* -ED/-ING/-S [ME *chaufen* to warm, fr. MF *chaufer*, fr. (assumed) VL *calfare*, alter. of L *calefacere*, fr. *calēre* to be warm + *facere* to make — more at CALDRON, DO] *vt* **1** *obs* **:** to make warm (as the emotions) **:** EXCITE ⟨~ the blood and spirits⟩ **2 :** IRRITATE, ANNOY, VEX ⟨the noise of the children playing *chafed* her⟩ **3 :** to warm by rubbing esp. with the hands ⟨*chafing* his hands together as though they were cold —Elizabeth Bowen⟩ **4 a :** to rub so as to wear away **:** ABRADE ⟨the schooner *chafed* her sides against the dock⟩ **b :** to irritate or make sore by or as if by rubbing ⟨the tight collar *chafed* his neck⟩ ~ *vi* **1 :** to feel irritation or discontent **:** be impatient (as with restraint or restriction) **:** FRET ⟨he *chafed* at the forced inaction —F.Tennyson Jesse⟩ **2 :** to rub with such pressure (as of one body against another) that much wear or irritation is caused ⟨a rope weakened by *chafing* against the rail⟩ **3 :** to dash or toss violently (as of the sea) **:** press or strain esp. against restraint ⟨the river ~s against the rocky shore⟩

²chafe \"\ *n* -s **1 :** a state of vexation **:** PASSION, RAGE ⟨the cardinal in a ~ sent for him —William Camden⟩ **2 :** injury or wear caused by friction; *also* **:** RUBBING, FRICTION **3 :** the usu. leather shield that covers the ring of a saddle cinch to prevent it from chafing the horse

chafe iron *n* **:** CRAMP IRON 2

¹cha·fer \'chāfə(r), -af-, -aif-\ *n* -s [ME *cheaffer*, fr. OE *ceafor*; akin to OHG *kevar* beetle, OE *ceafl* jowl — more at JOWL] **:** any of various beetles of Scarabaeidae and closely related families esp. of large or medium size, clumsy in flight, and slow in movement (as the june beetle, the rose chafer, and esp. the cockchafer)

²chafer *n* -s [ME *chaufour*, modif. of MF *chaufoire*, fr. *chaufer* to warm — more at CHAFE] *obs* **:** a portable grate **:** CHAFING DISH

³chaf·er \'chāfə(r)\ *n* -s [¹*chafe* + *-er*] **:** a strip of rubberized fabric covering the bead of a tire as a protection from chafing against the rim

chafe·wax \'chāf,waks\ *or* **chaff·wax** \-af-\ *n* [¹*chafe* (to heat) + *wax*; trans. of F *chauffe-cire*] **:** the holder of a now abolished English chancery office whose duty was to prepare wax for sealing documents

¹chaff \'chaf, -aa(ə)f,-aif,-áf\ *n* -s [ME *chaf, chef*, fr. OE *ceaf*; akin to MD *caf* chaff, OHG *cheva* husk] **1 :** the glumes, husks, or other seed coverings or small pieces of stems or leaves (as of grains and grasses) separated from the seed in threshing or processing **2 :** straw or hay cut up fine for the food of cattle **3 :** something comparatively light and worthless **:** a worthless or useless product of an endeavor ⟨in the book are a few practical suggestions; all else is ~⟩ **4 :** the scales borne on the receptacle among the florets in the heads of many composite plants **5 :** WINDOW 4

²chaff \"\ *vt* -ED/-ING/-S **:** to cut into chaff

³chaff \"\ *archaic var of* CHAFE

⁴chaff \"\ *n* -s [prob. fr. ¹*chaff*] **:** light jesting talk **:** BANTER, TEASING, RAILLERY ⟨no end of ~ about my way of speaking —G.B.Shaw⟩

⁵chaff \"\ *vb* -ED/-ING/-S [prob. fr. ⁴*chaff*] *vt* **:** to make fun of in a good-natured way **:** tease good-naturedly ⟨they ~*ed* me for leaving so early —Lucien Price⟩ ~ *vi* **:** to make fun of or joke about someone or something **:** JEST, BANTER

chaffcutter \'⁼,⁼⁼\ *n* **:** a machine for cutting up straw or hay for fodder

¹chaf·fer \'chafə(r), -aif-\ *n* -s [ME *chaffare, cheffare, cheapfare*, fr. *chep* trade, bargaining + *fare* journey — more at CHEAP, FARE] **1** *obs* **a :** buying and selling **:** TRADE **b :** articles of merchandise **:** WARES **2** *archaic* **:** a haggling about price **:** BARGAINING

²chaffer \"\ *vb* **chaffered; chaffered; chaffering** \-f(ə)riŋ\ **chaffers** [ME *chaffaren*, fr. *chaffare*, bargain, n.] *vi* **1** *obs* **:** to buy and sell **:** do business **:** TRADE **2 :** to discuss terms **:** haggle esp. over a price **:** BARGAIN ⟨the . . . ruffian with whom he had ~*ed* to move in the piano —Marcia Davenport⟩ ⟨~ over the price of the room —C.S.Forester⟩ **3** *Brit* **:** to exchange small talk **:** CHAT, CHATTER ~ *vt* **1** *obs* **a :** to buy or sell **:** deal in trading ⟨~ high offices of state⟩ **b :** EXCHANGE, BARTER ⟨~ honor for gold⟩ **2 :** to bargain for **:** alter (as a price) by bargaining — often used with *down* ⟨slash prices in half and ~ them down to nothing —*Johannesburg Sunday Express*⟩

³chaff·er \'chafə(r), -aaf-, -aif-, -áf-\ *n* -s [¹*chaff* + *-er*] **:** a usu. adjustable sieve at the rear end of the grain pan of a threshing machine

chaff–flower \'⁼,⁼⁼\ *n* [¹*chaff*] **:** a tropical herb (*Achyranthes aspera*) having slender chaffy somewhat prickly flower spikes

chaf·finch \'cha(,)finch\ *n* -ES [ME *chaffynche*, fr. OE *ceaffinc*, fr. *ceaf* chaff + *finc* finch] **:** a common Old World finch (*Fringilla coelebs*) often kept as a cage bird and having in the male a reddish breast plumage and a cheerful but not much varied song

chaff·ing·ly *adv* **:** in a chaffing manner

chaff·less \'⁼ləs\ *adj* **:** being without chaff

chaffron *or* **chafron** *var of* CHAMFRON

chaff scale *n* **1 :** a chaffy or chafflike scale **:** PALEA **2 :** a small pale rounded scale insect (*Parlatoria pergandii*) injurious to citrus and other cultivated plants

chaffseed \'⁼,⁼\ *n* [¹*chaff* + *seed*] **:** a leafy maritime herb (*Schwalbea americana*) of the family Scrophulariaceae that is native to eastern No. America, has irregular yellowish purple flowers in showy sparse spikes, and produces chaffy seeds

chaffwax *var of* CHAFEWAX

chaffweed \'⁼,⁼\ *n* [¹*chaff* + *weed*] **:** a low glabrous weedy branching herb (*Centunculus minimus*) of the family Primulaceae having short dry chafflike leaves — called also *bastard pimpernel, false pimpernel*

chaffy \'chafē, -aaf-,-aif-,-áf-, -fi\ *adj* -ER/-EST [¹*chaff* + *-y*] **1 a :** abounding in or covered with chaff **b :** consisting of or resembling chaff **2 a :** LIGHT, WORTHLESS ⟨an empty ~ book by a foolish ~ fellow⟩ **b :** having a bantering quality **:** CHAFFING ⟨teasing in a ~ tone⟩ **3 a :** like paleae **b :** covered with scales

chafing *n* -s **:** inflammation on opposing skin surfaces resulting from friction

chaf·ing dish \'chāfiŋ-\ *n* [ME, fr. *chafing*, fr. pres. part. of *chafen, chaufen* to warm — more at CHAFE] **1** *archaic* **:** a dish holding burning coals used esp. for cooking or warming food **2 :** a cooking utensil supplied with a source of heat (as electricity or an alcohol lamp) and used to cook food at the table

chafing dish 2

chafing gear *n* **:** a usu. rope or canvas covering placed on a line or spar to protect it from chafe

chaft \'chaft\ *n* -s [ME, prob. fr. ON *kjaptr* — more at JOWL] *dial Brit* **:** JAW, CHAP

cha·ga *or* **chag·ga** \'chägə\ *n, pl* **chaga** *or* **chagas** *or* **chagga** *or* **chaggas** *usu cap* **1 a :** a tall agricultural Negro people of the slopes of Mt. Kilimanjaro, Tanganyika **b :** a member of such people **2 :** a Bantu language of the Chaga people

cha·gas' disease \'shägəs(əz)-, -ag-\ *n, usu cap C* [after Carlos *Chagas* †1934 Braz. physician who described it] **:** a trypanosomiasis of tropical America marked by prolonged high fever, edema, and enlargement of spleen, liver, and lymph nodes and caused by a flagellate (*Trypanosoma cruzi*) which is transmitted by reduviid bugs and occurs in flagellated form in the blood and as leishmanial reproductive forms in tissue (as heart muscle)

chagigah *var of* HAGIGAH

cha·go·ma \shə'gōmə\ *n, pl* **chagomas** \-məz\ *or* **chago·ma·ta** \-məd·ə\ [NL, fr. Carlos *Chagas* + NL *-oma*] **:** a tumorlike swelling that appears at the site of infection in Chagas' disease

cha·gres fever \'chägrəs-, -ag-\ *n, usu cap C* [fr. *Chagres* river, Panama, where it occurs] **:** a malignant malarial fever occurring along the Chagres river in Panama

¹cha·grin \shə'grin, *Brit usu* 'shagrin *or* shə'grēn\ *n* -s [F, fr. *chagrin*, adj.] **1** *obs* **:** disturbance of mind resulting from care or anxiety **:** WORRY **:** depression of spirits **:** MELANCHOLY **2 a :** vexation, disquietude, or distress of mind brought on by humiliation, hurt pride, disappointment, or consciousness of failure or error ⟨the unhappy defects of her family, a subject of yet heavier ~ —Jane Austen⟩ **b chagrins** *pl, archaic* **:** circumstances causing chagrin **:** TROUBLES, VEXATIONS ⟨so many additional inconveniences and ~s —Alexander Pope⟩

²chagrin *adj* [F, sad] *obs* **:** CHAGRINED

³cha·grin \shə'grin, *Brit usu* shə'grēn *or* 'shagrin\ *vt* **chagrined** *also* **chagrinned; chagrined** *also* **chagrinned; chagrining** *also* **chagrinning; chagrins** [prob. fr. F *chagriner*, fr. *chagrin*, adj.] **1** *archaic* **:** to cause to feel anxiety **:** TROUBLE, GRIEVE **2 :** to vex through humiliation, hurt pride, or disappointment ⟨their increasing neglect of his welfare ~s him⟩

chagrined *adj* **:** feeling or made to feel chagrin **:** DISAPPOINTED, MORTIFIED ⟨you are ~ at having lost that dowry —Willa Cather⟩ **syn** see ASHAMED

cha·gual gum \(')chä¦gwäl-\ *n* [AmerSp *chagual*] **:** gum obtained in Chile from various plants of the genus *Puya*

cha·guar \(')chä¦gwär\ *n* -s [AmerSp *chaguar, cháguar, chagual*, prob. fr. Quechua *ch'ahuar* vegetable fiber] **:** CARAGUATA

cha·gul *or* **cha·gal** \'chägəl\ *n* -s [Hindi *chāgal*, fr. Skt *chāgala* coming from a goat, fr. *chāga* he-goat] **:** a leather water bag of goatskin used in India

chahar \(')chä¦här\ *n, pl* **chahar** *or* **chahars** *usu cap* **:** a Mongol people inhabiting the Inner Mongolian steppes northwest of Peking

chahi *var of* SHAHI

chai·ma *or* **chay·ma** \'chīmə\ *n, pl* **chaima** *or* **chaimas** *or* **chayma** *or* **chaymas** *usu cap* [Sp *chaima*, of AmerInd origin] **1 a :** a Cariban people of the coast of Venezuela **b :** a member of such people **2 :** the language of the Chaima people

¹chain \'chān\ *n* -s [ME *cheyne*, fr. OF *chaeine*, fr. L *catena* chain, brace; akin to L *cassis* net and perh. to OE *heathor* confinement, ON *hadda* chain of rings] **1 a** (1) **:** a series of usu. metal links or rings connected to or fitted into one another so as to move freely, forming a flexible ligament used for various purposes (as support, restraint, or transmission of mechanical power), and made in many forms and sizes, the size usu. being designated by the thickness of the links (as a half-inch chain made of bar metal half an inch in diameter) ⟨cable ~⟩ ⟨bicycle ~⟩ ⟨a bridle with a ~ snaffle⟩ ⟨a harness with a ~ trace⟩ — see BICYCLE illustration (2) **:** a mesh of interconnected rods and plates that is often in the form of a belt and is used esp. for transmission of power or as a conveyor **b :** a series of links used or worn as an ornament or insignia **:** COLLAR 1g ⟨he wore a gold ~ of office around his neck⟩ **c** (1) **:** a measuring instrument that consists of 100 links joined together by rings and is used in surveying — see ENGINEER'S CHAIN, GUNTER'S CHAIN; compare TAPE 2c (2) **:** a unit of length equal to 66 feet — see GUNTER'S CHAIN **d :** TIRE CHAIN — **e :** a chain 10 yards in length used for measuring the first-down distance in football **2 a :** a chain used as an obstruction to the passage of traffic (as in a street, river, or harbor entrance) — compare ²BOOM 6 **b :** something that confines, restrains, or secures **:** BOND, FETTER ⟨ignorance is . . . a ~ on your mind —Lyman Bryson⟩ **c chains** *pl* **:** manacles or fetters linked with chain; *also* **:** IMPRISONMENT, CAPTIVITY ⟨wept with me when I returned in ~s —Alfred Tennyson⟩ **d :** DOOR CHAIN **3 a :** a continuous series of things, events, or conceptions in which each succeeding member depends upon (as for causal agency or motive impulse), derives from, or interrelates with the preceding ⟨a vast ~ of creatures stretching down from . . . the Deity . . . to the grades of men, animals, plants, and minerals —S.F.Mason⟩ ⟨~ of events⟩ ⟨~ of thought⟩ ⟨~ reasoning in which the conclusion of one argument is used in the premise of the next⟩ **b :** a continuous line or series of things connected or adjacent to one another: as (1) **:** a range of mountains (2) **:** a series of events in a temporal order usu. connected causally ⟨a ~ of strikes in the steel industry⟩ (3) **:** a diagonal arrangement of connected pawns in chess (4) **:** a line of dancers with hands linked (5) **:** LADIES CHAIN **c** (1) **:** a group of enterprises, establishments, institutions, or constructions of the same kind or function linked together into a single system usu. under a single ownership, management, or control ⟨a ~ of 100 grocery stores⟩ ⟨a ~ of weather stations⟩ ⟨a ~ of highways⟩ (2) **:** NETWORK 5a **d :** a number of atoms united like links in a chain; *esp* **:** OPEN CHAIN — see BRANCHED CHAIN, SIDE CHAIN, STRAIGHT CHAIN; compare ¹RING 18 **e :** a system of rigid links (sense 2c) pivoted or otherwise movably connected each to one or more others in such a way that their motions are interdependent **4 chains** *pl* **:** the structure composed of channels, chain plates, and deadeyes to which the shrouds of a mast are fastened and in which the leadsman stands in making a cast of the lead — see SHIP illustration **5 :** ¹WARP 1a

²chain \"\ *vb* -ED/-ING/-S [ME *cheynen*, fr. *cheyne*, n.] *vt* **1 :** to fasten, bind, or connect with a chain **:** fetter or restrain with a chain **:** put in chains **2 a :** to bind, fasten, or hold fast as if with a chain ⟨the audience, ~*ed* to their seats by terror⟩ **b :** to hold back, repress, or restrict the movement, function, or change of ⟨you may ~ the law down with all manner of clamps and bonds —B.N.Cardozo⟩ **:** make or hold captive **:** CONFINE ⟨buried now and lost in silent pools, now in strong eddies ~*ed* —William Wordsworth⟩ **3 :** to obstruct or protect (as a harbor) by a chain **4 :** to measure with a surveying chain **5 :** to make a series of (chain stitches) in crocheting —abbr. *ch* ~ *vi* **1 :** to form or join in a chain **2 :** to perform a ladies chain in square dancing

³chain \"\ *adj* [¹*chain*] **1 :** performed, occurring, or acting in a connected series ⟨~ reader of murder mysteries —Louise Mace⟩ **2 :** gathering force or increasing with each successive step **:** CUMULATIVE ⟨~ effects that may ultimately affect the whole country⟩ **3 :** characterized by uniformity **:** STEREOTYPED ⟨stereotyped ~ thinking and acting —Harlow Shapley⟩

chain armor *n* **:** CHAIN MAIL

chain banking *n* **:** the possession of stock control of two or more banks by one or a few individuals

chain bearer *n* **:** CHAINMAN 4

chain belt *n* **:** a belt constructed of links of metal or other material (as leather) and used in chain gearing or as a conveyor

chain block *n* **:** CHAIN HOIST

chain bolt *n* **:** a bolt with a chain attached for drawing it out

piece of a chain belt

chain bond *n* **:** a bond formed in masonry by building in a tie (as a metal chain, bar, or strap) or a timber

chain boom *n* **:** ²BOOM 6

chain break *n* **:** a brief radio or television commercial given during one of the station-identification intervals in a network program

chain bridge *n* **:** a suspension bridge suspended from chains

chain cable *n* **:** an anchor chain

chain conveyor *n* **:** CONVEYER 2a(3)

chain coral *n* **:** a fossil coral (genus *Halysites*) common in the upper Ordovician and Silurian rocks having tubular corallites of oval section united by their narrow sides and looking like links of chain

chain course *n, masonry* **:** a bond course of stone headers fastened together continuously by cramps

chain discount *n* **:** a series of discounts allowed from the list price of an article of merchandise

chain drive *n* **:** a mechanical drive consisting of chain gears and a driving chain ⟨an automotive *chain drive*⟩ — called also *chain transmission*

chain–driven \'⁼;⁼⁼\ *adj* **:** having a chain drive

chaî·né \she'nā, shā-\ *n* -s [F, fr. past part. of *chaîner* to chain, fr. *chaîne*, n., fr. L *catena* — more at CHAIN] **:** a series of small regular turns by which a ballet dancer moves across the stage

chained *adj* **:** furnished, fitted, or adorned with a chain

chain envelope *n* **:** a business envelope usu. for interdepartmental use that may be readdressed and reused many times

chain·er \'chānə(r)\ *n* -s [¹*chain* + *-er*] **1 :** CHOKERMAN **2 :** a clipper in a coal mine **3 :** one that arranges the pattern chain on a dobby loom **4 :** a worker who ties skeins of yarn into a continuous chain for processing

chain feed *vt* **:** to feed (as envelopes) into a typewriter so that each successive piece is held in place by the preceding one

chain fern *n* **:** a fern having the sori in chainlike rows (as members of the genus *Woodwardia*)

chain gang *n* **1 :** a gang of convicts chained together esp. as an outside working party **2** *slang* **:** one of two or more railroad train crews taking turns in the operation of extra trains in addition to regular trains

chain gear *or* **chain gearing** *n* **:** a gear through which motion is transmitted by a chain that runs in a groove or engages the cogs of a sprocket wheel

chain–grate stoker *n* **:** a wide endless traveling chain that feeds and supports the fuel in a boiler furnace

chain harrow *n* **:** a harrow made of linked chainwork

chain hoist *also* **chain fall** *n* **:** a tackle employing an endless chain instead of a rope and operated esp. in workshops from an overhead track for hoisting heavy weights — called also *chain block*

chain gears: grooved wheel with chain, *A*; sprocket wheels with chain, *B*

chain hook *n* **:** a hook used for dragging or lifting cables

chaining *pres part of* CHAIN

chain isomerism *n* **:** isomerism involving atoms in a chain (as in butane and isobutane)

chain knot *n* **:** a knot resembling a chain or a link of a chain

chain·less \'chānləs\ *adj* **:** being without a chain

chain·let \'chānlət\ *n* -s [¹*chain* + *-let*] **:** a small chain

chain letter *n* **:** a letter sent to a number of recipients requesting each to write similar letters to an equal number of recipients and often employed as a moneymaking scheme by the inclusion with each letter of a list of persons to whom money is to be sent

chain lightning *n* **:** lightning that appears to move very rapidly in a long angular, zigzag, or forked course

chain line *or* **chain mark** *n* **:** one of the wider-spaced parallel watermark lines in a laid paper made by the chain wires and running with the grain — compare LAID LINE

chain link fence *n* **:** a fence of heavy steel wire woven in continuous spirals so that when the spirals are integrated with each other a diamond-shaped mesh is formed

chain locker *n* **:** a forward compartment in the lower part of a ship for stowing the chain cable

chain mail *n* **:** flexible armor of interlinked metal rings — called also *chain armor*

chain·man \'chānmən, -,man\ *n, pl* **chainmen** [*chain* + *man*] **1 :** one who searches tax and assessment records in order to compile lists of mortgages, deeds, contracts, and other instruments pertaining to real-estate titles **2 :** a sawmill worker who removes lumber from a conveyor and sorts and stacks it according to grade markings **3 :** CHOKERMAN **4 :** a surveyor's assistant who measures distances, marks measuring points, and performs related duties — called also *lineman, rodman, tapeman*

chain of being : a hierarchical order of all entities; *esp* **:** an uninterrupted hierarchy of all beings arranged according to an order of perfection

chain of causation 1 : a series of events or situations interrelated and leading to a particular effect **2** *often cap both Cs, Buddhism* **:** the chain of cause and effect leading in 12 stages from ignorance of the vanity of existence to suffering

chain of command : a series of executive positions or of officers and subordinates in order of authority esp. with respect to the passing on of orders, responsibility, reports, or requests from higher to lower or lower to higher

chain of title : the succession of conveyances from some accepted starting point whereby the present holder of real property derives his title

chain·o·mat·ic \ˌchānəˈmad·ik\ *adj* [fr. *Chainomatic*, a trademark] *of a balance or scale* **:** having suspended from the beam an adjustable fine chain the length of which is measured to determine minute weights

chain pickerel *also* **chain pike** *n* **:** a large greenish black pickerel (*Esox niger*) with dark chainlike markings along the sides that is common in quiet waters of eastern No. America

chain pin *n* **:** ARROW 2c

chain pipe *n* **:** the pipe through which the cable chain passes from the windlass to the chain locker

chain plate *n* **:** a metal plate which is bolted to the channels or to the side of a ship and to which the shrouds are fastened by means of a deadeye or turnbuckle — see ¹CHAIN 4

chain pump *n* **:** a pump consisting of a sprocket-operated endless chain fitted at close intervals with disks that lift the water by moving rapidly through a pipe in the direction of the desired flow

chain-react \ˈ=ˌ=ˈ=\ *vi* [back-formation fr. *chain reaction*] **:** to take part in or undergo chain reaction

chain-reacting pile *n* **:** REACTOR

chain reaction *n* **1 :** a series of events so related to each other that each one initiates the succeeding one esp. in such a manner as to produce a cumulative effect ⟨the employee with more retention points can and does bump the employee with fewer points, setting off a costly *chain reaction* down the line —Sam Stavisky⟩ **2 :** a chemical reaction (as polymerization) that once started can maintain itself by interaction of the starting materials with transitory reactive products (as atoms or free radicals), more of the transitory products being formed as they are consumed **3 :** a self-propagating fission of atomic nuclei continued by the further action of one of the products (as in the fission of a uranium nucleus by a neutron that causes the release of more neutrons that cause further fissions and so on)

chain reactor *n* **:** REACTOR

chain reflex *n, psychol* **:** a series of responses each serving as a stimulus that evokes the next response

chain riveting *n* **:** riveting in which the rivets in rows along the seam are set one behind the other

chains *pl of* CHAIN, *pres 3d sing of* CHAIN

chain saw *n* **:** a portable power saw that has teeth linked together to form an endless chain and is usu. used for the cutting of timber

chain saw

chain scale *n* **:** an engineer's or draftsman's scale graduated in inches that are subdivided by 10 and multiples of 10

chain shot *n* **:** a cannon shot consisting of two balls or half balls united by a short chain and formerly used in naval warfare to cut a ship's rigging; *also* **:** a discharge of such shot

chainsmith \ˈ=ˌ=\ *n* **:** a smith who makes chains

chain-smoke *vi* **:** to smoke cigarettes or cigars continually esp. by lighting each from the previous one ⟨*chain-smoked* all during the conference⟩ ~ *vt* **:** to smoke (as cigarettes) almost without interruption ⟨rolled cigarettes and *chain-smoked* them all afternoon out of nervousness⟩ — **chain smoker** *n*

chain snake *n* **:** KING SNAKE

chain splice *n* **:** a splice for joining a rope to the end link of a chain

chain stitch *n* **1 :** an ornamental stitch that resembles the links of a chain and is used in crocheting, sewing, and embroidery **2 :** a stitch in machine sewing in which the looping of the thread forms a chain on the underside of the work

chain stopper *n* **:** a device (as a hook) that secures the anchor chain (as when the anchor is raised) thus taking the strain from the windlass

chain store *n* **:** a retail store that is a unit of a chain

chain timber *n* **:** a timber used to form a chain bond

chain tongs *n pl* **:** tongs for turning large pipe that consist of a lever with notched head whose teeth engage the pipe and an adjustable short chain which encircles the pipe and whose ends are secured to the head

chain transmission *n* **:** CHAIN DRIVE

chain vise *n* **:** a vise in which round work (as a pipe) is held in a V-shaped support by a chain clamped tightly around the work

chain·wale \ˈchānˌwāl, ˈchanᵊl\ *n* -S [¹*chain* + *wale*] **:** ³CHANNEL

chain wire *n* **:** any of the wires running around the circumference of a dandy roll — compare LAID WIRE

chainwork \ˈ=ˌ=\ *n* **1 :** work consisting of esp. metal units looped or linked together in the manner of a chain **2 :** a decorative pattern of links and loops resembling a chain; *specif* **:** CHAIN STITCH

chain wrench *n* **:** CHAIN TONGS

¹chair \ˈche(ə)r, -a(a)(ə)r, -eə,-a(ə)ə\ *n* -S [ME *chayere*, fr. OF *chaiere*, fr. L *cathedra*, fr. Gk *kathedra*, fr. *kata-* cata- + *hedra* seat, fr. *hezesthai* to sit — more at SIT] **1 a :** a usu. movable seat that is designed to accommodate one person and usu. has four legs and a back and often has arms **b :** something used to serve as such a seat or to support in the manner of such a seat ⟨lower a rope ~ over the side of the ship to bring up the captain's wife⟩ ⟨made a ~ of their clasped hands to carry the lame hiker⟩ **c :** ELECTRIC CHAIR **d :** a glassworker's bench with two extended arms on which the blowpipe is rolled back and forth while the glass is being fashioned **e :** one of the suspended seats on a chair lift **2 a :** an official seat or a seat of authority, state, or dignity (as of a chief magistrate, a judge, a professor, or a bishop) **b :** an office or position of authority or dignity (as of a bishop, a mayor of an English corporate town, a professor, or one who presides on a committee or at a meeting) **:** MAYORSHIP, PROFESSORSHIP, CHAIRMANSHIP ⟨the gubernatorial ~⟩ ⟨the ~ of comparative literature at the university⟩ **c** *obs* **:** PULPIT **d :** CHAIRMAN ⟨it is polite to address the ~ in a large meeting⟩ **3 a :** SEDAN CHAIR **b :** a formerly popular light one-horse carriage (as a chaise or gig) **4 a :** an office in a society (as a fraternal organization) **b :** a position of employment usu. of one occupying a chair or desk ⟨a ~ as editorial writer⟩; *specif* **:** the position of a player in an orchestra or band ⟨the first viola ~⟩ ⟨auditioning for the drum ~⟩ **5 :** one of a number of devices that hold up or support: as **a :** a support or carriage of a railroad rail; *specif* **:** an iron or steel block or plate forming a kind of socket or clutch supporting a rail or securing it to a sleeper or tie **b :** a supporting block or socket for a pipe where it passes over a wall or pier **c :** a support for holding reinforcing bars in position while concrete is being placed, the supports and bars becoming part of the permanent structure **6 :** a team of three or more glassworkers who make glass by hand — see FOOTMAKER, GAFFER, SERVITOR

²chair \"\ *vt* -ED/-ING/-S **1 a :** to place in a chair **b :** to install formally in a chair of office or honor; *specif* **:** to install the successful competitor at a Welsh eisteddfod in a chair of honor **2 a** (1) **:** to carry in or as if in a chair (2) *chiefly Brit* **:** to carry orig. in a chair, now usu. on the shoulders of several members of a group as an expression of acclaim ⟨the time you won your town the race we ~*ed* you through the market place —A.E. Housman⟩ **b :** to wheel in a chair **3 :** to provide with a chair or chairs **4 :** to act as presiding officer of (a meeting or program) **5 :** to be the chief officer of (a committee or any group whose chief officer is customarily called *chairman*)

³chair \"\ *n* -S [alter. (influenced by ¹*chair*) of ME *chare*, fr. OF *char*, fr. L *carrus* — more at CAR] **:** CHARIOT

chairback \ˈ=ˌ=\ *n* **:** TIDY 1a

chairbed \ˈ=ˌ=\ *n* **:** a living-room chair convertible into a bed usu. by means of a retractable seat extension and a back that may be lowered

chairborne \ˈ=ˌ=\ *adj* [blend of ¹*chair* and *airborne*] *slang* **:** assigned to a desk job **:** not serving in the field or esp. in combat — used orig. and esp. of military officers

chair car *n* **1 :** a railroad passenger car having pairs of chairs with individually adjustable backs on each side of the aisle **2 :** PARLOR CAR

chair desk *n* **:** a chair with an arm whose top surface is made wide enough to serve as a writing table or small table or with board attachment usu. for one of the arms to serve the same purpose

chaired *adj* [¹*chair* + *-ed*] **:** seated in a chair

chair form *n* **:** one of the stereochemical conformations of a strainless 6-membered ring (as a cyclohexane ring) in which two atoms directly opposite each other in the ring are outside the plane containing the other four atoms, one of the two atoms being above the plane and the other below the plane — compare BOAT FORM

chairlady \ˈ=ˌ=\ *n* **:** a female chairman **:** CHAIRWOMAN

chair lift *n* **:** a power-driven conveyor consisting of seats hung from an endless cable for carrying skiers and sightseers up or down a mountain slope

chairmaker's rush \ˈ=ˌ==\ *n* **:** a tall coarse sedge (*Scirpus americanus*) used for making chair bottoms

¹chair·man \ˈ=mən\ *n, pl* **chairmen 1 :** one who occupies a chair: as **a :** the presiding officer of a meeting or assembly **b :** the head officer of an organization or committee who is entitled to preside at its meetings and usu. to exercise some authority in carrying on its affairs; *specif* **:** CHAIRMAN OF THE BOARD **c :** a professor or instructor who is chief officer of a department of instruction; *often* **:** one who has relatively little power to determine policy and exercise authority except with the approval of his colleagues or of a committee of them — distinguished from *head* **2 a :** one who serves as a carrier of a sedan chair **b :** one who wheels an invalid's chair **3 :** one in charge **:** SUPERVISOR, DIRECTOR ⟨~ of refreshments for a club meeting⟩ ⟨hospitality ~⟩ ⟨legislative ~⟩ ⟨~ of freshman history courses⟩ **4 :** a master of ceremonies of music-hall entertainments

²chairman \"\ *vt* **chairmaned** *or* **chairmanned; chairmaned** *or* **chairmanned; chairmaning** *or* **chairmanning; chairmans** [¹*chairman*] **1 :** to act as chairman of (a meeting or assembly) **2 :** to be chairman of (an organization or committee)

chairman of the board : the presiding officer of the board of directors of a corporation chosen to provide the board with leadership (1) by bringing forward for discussion and action problems arising from conflict of interest, problems stressing financial stewardship, policy questions growing out of operating decisions and (2) by setting up sound board procedures and securing competent board members

chair·man·ship \-ˌship\ *n* -S **:** the office or status of a chairman

chair·o·plane \ˈ=rəˌplān\ *n* -S [blend of ¹*chair* and *aeroplane*] **:** an amusement park device usu. for children consisting of a high revolving wheel from which seats hang on chains that swing out when the wheel revolves

chair organ *n* [perh. so called fr. the fact that such organs often formed the back of the organist's seat] **1** *obs* **:** a second organ added to the great organ **2 :** CHOIR ORGAN

chair post *n* **:** a chair leg

chair rail *n* **:** a wooden molding on a wall around a room to protect the wall from being damaged by the backs of chairs

chairs *pl of* CHAIR, *pres 3d sing of* CHAIR

chair swing *n* **:** a swing for young children that has a back, arms, and a protective bar across the front

chair table *n* **:** a table convertible into a chair or settle by raising the hinged top to form the back of a chair whose seat lies between the upright supports

chair table

chairwarmer \ˈ=ˌ==\ *n, slang* **:** one who habitually lounges in a chair **:** LOAFER: **a :** a person (as one not registered as a guest) who sits for prolonged periods in hotel lobbies **b :** an employee (as one in a sedentary occupation) who is superfluous or who makes little effort to apply himself to his work ⟨the seniority rule . . . discourages ability and efficiency, and encourages the ~ —S.T.Williamson & Herbert Harris⟩

chairway \ˈ=ˌ=\ *n* [*chair* + *-way* (as in *tramway*)] **:** CHAIR LIFT

chairwoman \ˈ=ˌ==\ *n, pl* **chairwomen :** a female chairman

chaise \ˈshāz\ *n* -S [F, chair, sedan chair, chaise, fr. MF, chair, alter. of *chaire*, fr. OF *chaiere* — more at CHAIR] **1 :** any of various traveling or pleasure carriages usu. of a chair-backed type: as **a :** a 2-wheeled carriage for one or two persons with a calash top and the body hung on leather straps or thoroughbraces and usu. drawn by one horse **b :** a similar 4-wheeled pleasure carriage **c :** POST CHAISE **2 :** any light carriage or pleasure cart **3 :** CHAISE LONGUE

chaise 1a

chaise longue \(ˈ)shāzˈlȯŋ, -ez-\ *or* **chaise lounge** \(ˈ)shāzˈlau̇nj, (ˈ)chās-\ *n, pl* **chaise longues** \-ŋz\ *or* **chaise loung·es** \-njəz\ *also* **chaises longues** \-zˈlȯŋz\ [*chaise longue* fr. F, lit., long chair; *chaise lounge* by folk etymology fr. F *chaise longue*] **:** an elongated couchlike seat with a raised back support at one end — called also *chaise*

chait \ˈchīt\ *or* **chai·tra** \-ī·trə\ *n* -S *usu cap* [Hindi *Cait*, fr. Skt *Caitra*] **:** a month of the Hindu year — see MONTH table

chait·ya \ˈchītyə, -īchə\ *n* -S [Skt *caitya*, fr. *citā* funeral pile, fr. *cinoti* he piles up; akin to Gk *poiein* to make, do — more at POET] *India* **:** a sacred place **:** SHRINE, MONUMENT — compare DAGOBA, STUPA, TOPE

cha·ja \chəˈhä, chäˈ-\ *n* -S [Sp *chajá*, prob. fr. Guarani *chahá*] **:** the largest of the crested screamers (*Chauna torquata*) native to southern Brazil and Argentina

cha·kar \ˈchäkə(r)\ *n* -S [Hindi *cākor*, fr. Per *chākar*] *India* **:** a person in domestic service or in clerical employment **:** SERVANT

cha·ka·ri \ˈchäkə(ˌ)rē\ *n* -S [Hindi *cākarī*, fr. Per *chākarī*, fr. *chākar*] *India* **:** domestic or more commonly clerical service

chak·dar \(ˌ)chəkˈdär, ˈchək,d-\ *n* -S [Panjabi *cakdār*, fr. *cak* tenure (fr. Skt *cakra*) + Per *-dār* having] **:** a native land tenant of India intermediate in position between the proprietor and the cultivator

chak·ra *also* **cak·ra** \ˈchəkrə\ *n* -S [Skt *cakra*, lit., wheel — more at WHEEL] **1 :** a disk representing the sun and sovereignty **2 a :** a sharp-edged circular missile weapon carried as an attribute by Vishnu **b :** such a weapon used by the Sikhs

chak·ram *also* **chuck·ram** *or* **chuck·rum** \ˈchəkrəm\ *n* -S [Malayalam *cakram*, fr. Skt *cakra* wheel] **1 :** a very small silver coin formerly issued by the state of Travancore, southern India **2 :** the value of one chakram **:** a unit of value equivalent to 1/32 of a rupee or 1/4 of a fanam

chak·ra·var·tin \ˌchəkrəˈvärtᵊn\ *n* -S [Skt *cakravartin*, fr. *cakra* wheel + *-vartin* one who turns, fr. *vartate* he turns — more at WORTH] *India* **:** a universal sovereign **:** an ideal ruler

cha·la·co \chəˈlä(ˌ)kō\ *n* -ES [AmerSp, perh. aug. of Sp *chala* cornhusk, fr. Quechua] **:** a goby (*Dormitator maculatus*) of eastern So. America extensively used in mosquito control

cha·lan \ˈchəlan\ *n* -S [Hindi *calan*] *India* **:** VOUCHER, INVOICE

chal·a·ra \ˈkalərə\ *n, cap* [NL, fr. fem. sing. of Gk *chalaros* slack, loose, fr. *chalan* to loosen, relax; akin to Gk *kichanein* to attain, reach — more at GO] **:** a genus of imperfect fungi (family Dematiaceae) that reproduce by terminally discharged endospores, one species (*C. quercina*) causing the destructive oak wilt disease

chal·a·rop·sis \ˌkaləˈräpsəs\ *n, cap* [NL, fr. Gk *chalaros* slack, loose + NL *-opsis*] **:** a genus of imperfect fungi (family Dematiaceae) one species of which (*C. thielavioides*) causes black mold of rose grafts

cha·las·to·gas·tra \kəˌlastəˈgastrə\ *n pl, cap* [NL, fr. LGk *chalastos* loose + NL *-gastra* (fr. Gk *gastr-*, *gastēr* belly) — more at GASTRIC] **:** a suborder of Hymenoptera including the sawflies and horntails and characterized by the caterpillar-like larvae and by having the abdomen attached to the thorax by a broad base

cha·la·za \kəˈlāzə\ *n, pl* **chala·zae** \-ˌzē\ *or* **chalazas** [NL, fr. Gk, hailstone, hard lump, chalazion; akin to OSlav *žlědica* frozen rain, Per *zhāla* hail] **1 :** either of a pair of spiral bands of thickened albuminous substance in the white of a bird's egg that extend out from opposite sides of the yolk to the ends of the egg and are there attached to the lining membrane — called also *treadle;* see EGG illustration **2 :** the region at the base of an ovule where the seed stalk is attached and from which the integuments arise — **cha·la·zi·an** \-ˈzēən\ *adj*

cha·la·zal \-zəl\ *adj* [NL *chalaza* + E *-al*] **:** of or relating to the chalaza; *specif* **:** located or facing toward the chalaza of a seed

chal·a·zif·er·ous \ˌkaləˈzif(ə)rəs\ *adj* [ISV *chalaz-* (fr. NL *chalaza*) + *-i-* + *-ferous*] **:** having chalazas

cha·la·zi·on \kəˈlāzēən, -ēˌän\ *n, pl* **chala·zia** \-zēə\ [NL, fr. Gk *chalazion* small lump, chalazion, dim. of *chalaza* hailstone, hard lump, chalazion — more at CHALAZA] **:** a small circumscribed tumor of the eyelid formed by retention of the Meibomian-gland secretions and sometimes accompanied by inflammation

chal·a·zog·a·my \ˌkaləˈzägəmē\ *n* -ES [ISV *chalaz-* (fr. NL *chalaza*) + *-o-* + *-gamy;* prob. orig. formed as F *chalazogamie*] **:** a process of fertilization in which the pollen tube penetrates to the embryo sac through the tissue of the chalaza

chal·a·zoid·ite \ˈkaləˌzȯiˌdīt, ˌ==ˈ==\ *n* -S [Gk *chalaza* hailstone + E *-oid* + *-ite*] **:** a spherical body formed during some volcanic eruptions by concentric accretion of pumiceous dust upon a pellet of mud blown into the air from the volcano

chalc- *or* **chalco-** *also* **chalk-** *or* **chalko-** *comb form* [F & L, fr. Gk *chalk-*, *chalko-*, fr. *chalkos* copper, prob. akin to Lith *geležis* iron, Russ *zhelezo*] **:** copper **:** brass **:** bronze ⟨*chalco*menite⟩ ⟨*chalco*mancy⟩

chal·can·thite \kalˈkanˌthīt, ˈkalkan-\ *n* -S [G *chalkanthit*, fr. L *chalcanthum* copper sulfate solution (fr. Gk *chalkanthon*, fr. *chalk-* chalc- + *-anthon*, fr. *anthos* flower) + G *-it* -ite — more at ANTHOLOGY] **:** a mineral $CuSO_4.5H_2O$ consisting of native copper sulfate — called also *cyanose*

chal·ce·don *or* **chalcedon butterfly** \(ˈ)kalˈsedᵊn, ˈkalsəˌdän\ *n* -S [NL *chalcedona* (specific epithet of *Euphydryas chalcedona*), prob. irreg. fr. LL *chalcedonius* chalcedony — more at CHALCEDONY] **:** a common butterfly (*Euphydryas chalcedona*) of western No. America having black wings speckled with yellow and brownish orange

¹chal·ce·do·ni·an \ˌkalsəˈdōnēən, -nyən\ *adj, usu cap* [*Chalcedon*, ancient city (now *Kadıköy*) in Asia Minor opposite Byzantium (fr. L, fr. Gk *Chalkēdōn*) + E *-ian*] **:** of or relating to Chalcedon, the ecumenical council held there in A.D. 451, or the teachings of the council

²chalcedonian \"\ *n* -S *usu cap* **:** one who adheres to the doctrinal decisions of the ecumenical council held in Chalcedon in A.D. 451; *esp* **:** a non-Monophysite orthodox Christian

chal·ce·don·ic \ˌkalsəˈdänik\ *also* **chal·ced·o·nous** \(ˈ)kalˈsedᵊnəs\ *adj* [*chalcedony* + *-ic* or *-ous*] **:** of or relating to chalcedony

chal·ced·o·ny *also* **cal·ced·o·ny** \kalˈsedᵊnē, -ni\ *n* -ES [ME *calcedonie*, a precious stone, fr. LL *chalcedonius*, fr. Gk *chalkēdōn*] **:** a cryptocrystalline translucent mineral constituting a variety of quartz and commonly of a pale blue or gray color, uniform tint, and nearly waxlike luster — see AGATE, CARNELIAN, CHRYSOPRASE, ONYX

chal·ce·don·yx \ˌkalsəˈdäniks, kalˈsedᵊniks\ *n* -ES [*chalced*ony + *onyx*] **:** a mineral consisting of onyx in which the bands are white to gray and valued as a semiprecious stone

chalcedony yellow *n* **:** a pale to light greenish yellow — called also *reed yellow*

chal·chi·huitl \ˌchälchēˈwēd·ᵊl\ *n* -S [Nahuatl] **:** CHALCHUITE

chal·chu·ite \ˌchälchəˈwēd·ē\ *n* -S [AmerSp *chalchihuite*, fr. Nahuatl *chalchihuitl*] **:** a blue or green turquoise

¹chal·cid \ˈkalsəd\ *adj* [NL *Chalcid-*, *Chalcis*] **:** of or relating to the Chalcididae

²chalcid \"\ *n* -S **:** CHALCID FLY

chal·ci·dae \ˈkalsəˌdē\ [NL, fr. *Chalcis*, type genus + *-idae*] *syn of* CHALCIDIDAE

chalcid fly *or* **chalcid wasp** *n* **:** a usu. minute insect of a large superfamily (Chalcidoidea) of Hymenoptera, a few being gall wasps or seed infesters but most being in their larval state parasitic on the eggs, larvae, or pupae of other insects, some living within and others upon the bodies of their hosts, feeding on their juices and tissues, and thus benefiting man by destroying many injurious insects — see CLOVER SEED CHALCID

¹chal·cid·i·an \kalˈsidēən\ *n, usu cap* [L *Chalcid-*, *Chalcis*, city on Euboea Island, Greece (fr. Gk *Chalkid-*, *Chalkis*) + E *-ian*] **:** a native or inhabitant of the city of Chalcis, Greece

²chalcidian \(ˈ)=ˈ===\ *adj, usu cap* **:** of or relating to the city of Chalcis ⟨*Chalcidian* culture⟩ ⟨*Chalcidian* colonies⟩

chalcidian alphabet *n, usu cap C* **:** any of the non-Ionic Greek alphabets

chal·cid·i·cum \kalˈsidəkəm\ *or* **chal·cid·ic** \-dik\ *n, pl* **chalcidi·ca** \-əkə\ *or* **chalcidics** [L *chalcidicum*, fr. neut. of *Chalcidicus* Chalcidian, fr. *Chalcid-*, *Chalcis* + L *-icus* -ic] **1 a :** a porch of entrance esp. to a Roman basilica **b :** a vestibule of a Christian basilica **:** NARTHEX **2 :** a building attached to a Roman basilica **3 :** a large Roman building for judicial functions

chal·cid·i·dae \-əˌdē\ *n pl, cap* [NL, fr. *Chalcid-*, *Chalcis*, type genus + *-idae*] **:** a family of chalcid flies now restricted to certain typical forms but formerly somewhat coextensive with the superfamily Chalcidoidea

¹chal·ci·doid \ˈkalsəˌdȯid\ *n* -S [NL *Chalcidoidea*] **:** one of the Chalcidoidea **:** CHALCID FLY

²chalcidoid \"\ *adj* **:** of or relating to Chalcidoidea **:** resembling a chalcid fly

chal·ci·doi·dea \ˌkalsəˈdȯidēə\ *n pl, cap* [NL, fr. *Chalcid-*, *Chalcis* + *-oidea*] **:** a superfamily of Hymenoptera comprising the chalcid flies

chal·cis \ˈkalsəs\ *n, cap* [NL, irreg. fr. Gk *chalkos* copper; fr. the metallic color of insects of this genus — more at CHALC-] **:** the type genus of Chalcididae comprising chalcid flies with the abdomen sessile and the hind femora greatly swollen and toothed below

chalcis fly *n* [NL *Chalcis*] **:** CHALCID FLY

chalco- — see CHALC-

chal·co·al·u·mite \ˌkal(ˌ)kōˈ—\ *n* -S [*chalc-* + *alumite*] **:** a turquoise-green to pale blue mineral $CuAl_4(SO_4)(OH)_{12}.3H_2O$ consisting of a hydrous basic sulfate of copper and aluminum

chal·co·cite \ˈkalkəˌsīt\ *n* -S [irreg. fr. F *chalcosine* chalcocite + E *-ite* — more at CHALCOSINE] **:** a black or dark gray mineral Cu_2S of metallic luster consisting of native cuprous sulfide occurring in orthorhombic crystals or massive (hardness 2.5–3, sp. gr. 5.5–5.8)

chal·co·cy·a·nite \ˌkal(ˌ)kō-\ *n* -S [ISV *chalc-* + *cyanite;* orig. formed as It *calcocianite*] **:** a mineral $CuSO_4$ consisting of anhydrous sulfate of copper

chal·co·gen \ˈkalkəjən, -ˌjen\ *n* -S [ISV *chalc-* + *-gen*] **:** any of the four elements oxygen, sulfur, selenium, and tellurium forming part of group VI of the periodic table

chal·co·gen·ide \ˈkalkəjəˌnīd, kalˈkäjə-\ *n* -S [*chalcogen* + *-ide*] **:** a binary compound of a chalcogen with a more electropositive element or radical **:** OXIDE, SULFIDE, SELENIDE, TELLURIDE

chal·co·lite \ˈkalkəˌlīt\ *n* -S [G *chalkolith*, fr. *chalk-* chalc- + *-lith* -lite] **:** TORBERNITE

chal·co·lith·ic \ˌkalkəˈlithik\ *adj, usu cap* [*chalc-* + *-lithic*] **:** AENEOLITHIC

chal·co·me·nite \ˌkalkəˈmēˌnīt\ *n* -S [F *chalcoménite*, fr. *chalc-* + Gk *mēnē* moon + F *-ite;* fr. its being a compound of selenium, which is named for the moon — more at MOON] **:** a mineral $CuSeO_3.2H_2O$ consisting of copper selenite occurring in blue crystals

chal·cone *also* **chal·kone** \ˈkalˌkōn\ *n* -S [G *chalkon*, fr.

chalk- chalc- + *-on* -one; fr. its use in producing reddish yellow dyestuffs] **:** a yellow crystalline ketone C_6H_5CH-$CHCOC_6H_5$ made by the condensation of benzaldehyde and acetophenone; *also* **:** any of various derivatives of this compound, several of which are plant pigments related to the flavones

chal·coph·a·nite \kal'käfə,nīt\ *n* -s [*chalc-* + *phan-* (fr. Gk *phainein* to show) + *-ite*; fr. its change to a copper color when heated] **:** a mineral $(Zn,Mn,Fe)Mn_2O_5.nH_2O$ consisting of black hydrous manganese and zinc oxide and having a metallic luster

chal·co·phile \'kalkə,fīl\ *adj* [*chalc-* + *-phile*] **:** having such an affinity for sulfur that in a molten mass the greatest concentration (as of an element) is found in the sulfide phase

chal·co·phyl·lite \,kalkō'fi,līt\ *n* -s [G *chalkophyllit*, fr. *chalk-* chalc- + *phyll-* + *-it* -ite] **:** a highly basic arsenate and sulfate of copper and aluminum $Cu_{18}Al_2(AsO_4)_3(SO_4)_3$-$(OH)_{27}.33H_2O$ of various shades of green that occurs in tabular crystals or foliated masses

chal·co·py·rite \-'pī,rīt\ *n* -s [NL *chalcopyrites*, fr. *chalc-* + L *pyrites* sulfide of metallic appearance — more at PYRITES] **:** a bright brass-yellow mineral $CuFeS_2$ consisting of copper-iron sulfide that crystallizes in the tetragonal system but usu. occurs massive and that is one of the most important ores of copper (hardness 3.5–4, sp. gr. 4.1–4.3)

chal·co·sid·er·ite \¦kal(,)kō'sidə,rīt\ *n* -s [G *chalkosiderit* fr. *chalk-* chalc- + *sider-* + *-it* -ite] **:** a mineral $Cu(Fe, Al)_6$-$(PO_4)_4(OH)_8.4H_2O$ consisting of a hydrous basic green phosphate of copper, iron, and aluminum, closely related to turquoise, and containing more iron than aluminum

chal·co·sine \'kalkə,sēn\ *n* -s [F, fr. Gk *chalkos* + F *-ine* — more at CHALC-] **:** CHALCOCITE

chal·co·stib·ite \,kalkō'sti,bīt\ *n* -s [G *chalkostibit*, fr. *chalk-* chalc- + *stib-* + *-it* -ite] **:** a lead-gray mineral $CuSbS_2$ consisting of antimony copper sulfide (sp. gr. 4.75–3.0)

chal·co·trich·ite \,kalkō'tri,kīt, kal'kätrə,kīt\ *n* -s [G *chalkotrichit*, fr. *chalk-* chalc- + *trich-* + *-it* -ite] **:** a mineral consisting of a capillary variety of cuprite

chal·dae-pah·la·vi \¦kal,dē'pälə,(,)vē\ *n* -s *usu cap C&P* [*Chaldaean* + *Pahlavi*] **:** the variety of Pahlavi using an alphabet found only on inscriptions

chal·da·ic \(')kal¦dāik\ *adj or n, usu cap* [L *Chaldaicus*, fr. Gk *Chaldaïkos*, fr. *Chaldaia* + Gk *-ikos* -ic] **:** CHALDEAN

[1]**chal·de·an** *also* **chal·dae·an** \kal'dēən\ *n* -s *usu cap* [L *Chaldaeus* Chaldean, astrologer (fr. Gk *Chaldaios*, fr. *Chaldaia* Chaldea, region of ancient Babylonia) + E *-an*] **1 a :** one of an ancient Semitic people that orig. occupied the low alluvial land about the estuaries of the Tigris and Euphrates and that gradually became the dominant people of Babylonia **b :** the original Semitic language of the Chaldeans — called also *neo-Babylonian* **2 :** a person versed in the occult arts (as astrology and sooth-saying) **3 :** a member of a Uniate church in Iraq and Iran converted from Nestorianism in the 16th century

[2]**chaldean** *also* **chaldaean** \(')=¦==\ *adj, usu cap* **:** of or belonging to Chaldea or to the language, culture, or occult arts of the Chaldeans

chal·dee \'kal,dē *also* (')kal'dē\ *n* -s *usu cap* [ME *Caldey*, prob. fr. MF *chaldée*, fr. L *Chaldaicus*] **:** the Aramaic vernacular that was the original language of some parts of the Bible (as passages in Daniel, Ezra, and Jeremiah) and that superseded Hebrew among the Jews of Palestine and Babylon

chal·der \'chòdər, -àd-\ *n* -s [ME *chaldre*, fr. MF *chaldere*, *chaudière* kettle, pot, fr. LL *caldaria* — more at CALDRON] **1 :** a unit of capacity for dry measure formerly used in Scotland equal to 12 quarters or about 96 Winchester bushels **2 :** CHALDRON

chal·dron \'chòldrən, 'chád-\ *n* -s [alter. (influenced by *caldron*) of earlier *chawdron*, fr. MF *chauderon*, fr. *chaudere*, *chaudière* kettle, pot] **:** any of various old units of measure (as for coal and lime) varying from 32 to 72 imperial bushels; *esp* **:** a unit of measure for coal equal to 36 bushels or 25½ hundredweight

cha·let \'sha,lā, sha'lā *sometimes* 'shalē\ *n* -s [F, fr. F dial. (Switzerland and Savoy); akin to OProv & Catal *cala* cove, inlet; basic meaning: sheltered place] **1 :** a remote herdsman's hut in the Alps **2 a :** a Swiss dwelling characterized by unconcealed structural members that are emphasized by decorative carving, a roof with a wide overhang at the front and sides, and balconies and an exterior staircase under the eaves **b :** a cottage or house built in the style of such a dwelling

chalet 2a

chal·ice \'chaləs\ *n* -s [ME, fr. AF, fr. L *calix* cup; akin to Gk *kalyx* calyx of a flower, Skt *kalaśa* pot, and prob. to Gk *skallein* to hoe — more at SHELL] **1 :** a drinking cup **:** GOBLET; *esp* **:** the cup used in the sacrament of the Lord's supper **2 :** FLOWER CUP 2

chalice 1

chalice cell *n* **:** GOBLET CELL

chal·iced \'chaləst\ *adj, of a flower* **:** having a cup-shaped blossom

chalice vine *n* **:** a climbing strong-branching shrub (*Solandra guttata*) of the family Solanaceae having elliptic-oblong leaves and large solitary terminal funnelform fragrant yellow flowers with purple-brown ridges in the throat

chal·i·co·sis \,kalə'kōsəs\ *n, pl* **chalico·ses** \-ō,sēz\ [NL, fr. Gk *chalik-*, *chalix* pebble, gravel + NL *-osis* — more at CHALK] **:** a pulmonary affection occurring among stonecutters that is caused by inhalation of stone dust

chal·i·co·there \'kalə,kō,thi(ə)r\ *n* -s [NL *Chalicotherium*] **:** one of the Chalicotheriidae

chal·i·co·the·ri·idae \,kalə,kōthə'rīə,dē\ *n pl, cap* [NL, fr. *Chalicotherium*, type genus (fr. Gk *chalik-*, *chalix* gravel + NL *-therium*) + *-idae*] **:** a family, coextensive with Chalicotherioidea, of Tertiary perissodactyls of worldwide distribution having cleft clawlike toes

chal·i·co·the·ri·oi·dea \¦kalə,kō,thirē'òidēə\ *n pl, cap* [NL, fr. *Chalicotherium* + *-oidea*] **:** the Ancylopoda regarded as a superfamily of the Perissodactyla — see CHALICOTHERIIDAE

cha·li·na \kə'līnə, -ēnə\ *n, cap* [NL, modif. of Gk *chalinos* bridle, strap] **:** a genus (the type of the family Chalinidae) of sponges that includes the finger sponge and dead-man's-fingers

[1]**chalk** \'chȯk\ *n* -s [ME, fr. OE *cealc*; akin to OHG & MLG *kalk* lime; all fr. a prehistoric WGmc word borrowed fr. L *calc-*, *calx* limestone, lime, fr. Gk *chalix* small stone, pebble; akin to Gk *skallein* to hoe — more at SHELL] **1 a :** a soft friable limestone of marine origin earthy in texture and white, gray, or buff in color, found widely distributed in Europe and America chiefly in the Cretaceous system, and composed for the most part of the minute shells of Foraminifera — compare CALCIUM CARBONATE, WHITING 2 **b :** chalk or a chalky material in prepared form (as for filler or for marking or drawing purposes) ⟨one twirl or whisk of the ~ is enough —*Billiard Player*⟩ ⟨hand ~ to keep your hands dry —Margery Shaughnessy⟩ ⟨apply liquid ~ to white canvas shoes⟩ ⟨rub a cord with ~ to mark a line⟩ — sometimes used in pl. ⟨some colored ~*s* by the blackboard —Adrian Bell⟩ ⟨only white and transparent ~*s* should be used on a garment fabric —Evelyn A. Mansfield⟩ **2 a :** a mark or line made with chalk ⟨cut a plank to the ~⟩ **b** *Brit* **:** a point scored in a game ⟨winning with 30 ~*s* more than any other player⟩ **3 a :** a drawing done in chalk **b :** a line on a tennis court ⟨the drive hit the ~⟩ **4** *usu cap* **:** the Chalk stage **5 :** the late odds of a horse race, often posted in chalk; *also* **:** a favorite as indicated by such posting — **by a long chalk** *Brit* **:** by any means — usu. used after a negative ⟨that isn't the last of our financial problems *by a long chalk*⟩

[2]**chalk** \"\ *vb* -ED/-ING/-S *vt* **1 :** to treat, process, or prepare with chalk: as **a :** to rub or mark with chalk; *specif* **:** to apply chalk to (the tip of a billiard cue) to prevent slippage **b** *Brit* **:** to fertilize (land) with chalk **2 a :** to write, draw, sketch, or outline with chalk ⟨~ one's name on a wall⟩ **b :** to mark with a sign, number, label, or symbol with or as if with chalk ⟨warehouse goods ~*ed* for export⟩ **3 a :** to delineate roughly with or as if with chalk **:** OUTLINE — usu. used with *out* ⟨~ out a plan of attack⟩ **b :** to set down, add up, or record with or as if with chalk — usu. used with *up* ⟨~*ing up* his good points and ticking off the bad —Hamilton Basso⟩; see CHALK UP **~** *vi* **:** to become chalky; *specif, of paint* **:** to develop a powdery surface due to disintegration of binder — **chalk the door** *Scots law* **:** to make a chalk mark on a door as a notice (as in warning out a tenant)

[3]**chalk** \"\ *adj* **1 :** CHALKY ⟨in the ~ earth of our garden — Clare Leighton⟩ **2** *usu cap* **:** of or belonging to the Upper Cretaceous of Britain and western Europe

chalk- *or* **chalko-** — see CHALC-

chalk blue *n* **:** a pale blue that is lighter than average powder blue, greener and paler than Sistine, and greener, lighter, and stronger than average cadet gray

chalkboard \'=,=\ *n* **:** BLACKBOARD

chalk·er \'chȯkə(r)\ *n* -s **1 :** a worker who applies liquid chalk or wax to shoe parts to prevent their sticking during the lasting process **2 :** a worker who sprinkles chalk over the surface of white leather to improve its appearance

chalkland \'=,=\ *n* **:** an area underlain by chalk

chalklike \'=,=\ *adj* **:** resembling chalk

chalk line *n* **:** a cord rubbed with chalk and used for marking a guide line (as on cement work or on a board); *also* **:** the line marked by such a cord

chalk manner *n* **:** CRAYON MANNER

chalk maple *n* **:** a shade tree (*Acer leucoderme*) of the southeastern U.S. distinguished by its light gray bark

chalk mixture *n* **:** an antacid preparation of chalk, bentonite magma, saccharin sodium, cinnamon water, and distilled water used to combat some diarrheal conditions

chal·kog·ra·phy \kal'kägrəfē\ *n* -ES [G *chalkographie*, fr. Gk *chalkos* copper, anything made of metal + G *-graphie* -graphy — more at CHALC-] **:** the study of opaque minerals under the microscope by means of incident light

chalkone *var of* CHALCONE

chal·ko·si·der·ic \¦kal(,)kō,sī¦derik, -ōsə¦-\ *adj, usu cap* [*chalk-* + *sider-* + *-ic*] **:** of or belonging to the transitional period between the Bronze and Iron ages

chalk pink *n* **:** a moderate pink that is yellower and duller than arbutus pink, yellower and less strong than blossom pink, and deeper than hydrangea pink

chalk plant *n* **:** BABY'S BREATH 1a

chalks *pl of* CHALK, *pres 3d sing of* CHALK

chalkstone \'=,=\ *n* **:** a chalklike concretion mainly of urate of sodium found esp. in and about the small joints of persons suffering from gout **:** TOPHUS

chalk stream *n* **:** a brook or river flowing across or among beds of chalk

chalk stripe *n* **:** a textile design consisting of fine white lines against a dark background

chalk-surfaced paper *n* **:** CHALKY PAPER

chalk-talk \'=,=\ *n* **:** a talk usu. illustrated by impromptu pictures ⟨a *chalk-talk* on malaria control⟩ ⟨a *chalk-talk* for children given by a cartoonist⟩; *specif* **:** a talk designed to brief a group for concerted action ⟨before the attack all noncoms were given *chalk-talks*⟩

chalk up *vt* **1 :** ASCRIBE, CREDIT ⟨why the invasion was not launched still puzzles the field marshal, but he *chalks* it *up* to . . . grudging fondness for the English —*Time*⟩ **2 :** ATTAIN, ACHIEVE ⟨the company will *chalk up* enormous profits⟩ ⟨*chalk up* a record score⟩

chalkware \'=,=\ *n* **:** cheap painted plaster ornamental figures (as of animals, birds, or fruit) made in the 19th century after Staffordshire prototypes

chalky \'chȯkē, -ki\ *adj, often* -ER/-EST **1 :** consisting of, abounding in, or characterized by chalk **:** CRETACEOUS ⟨~ soil⟩ **2 :** having the consistency of chalk **:** POWDERY ⟨~ bread⟩ **3 a :** having the color of chalk ⟨a ~ complexion⟩ **b :** *photog* **:** having excessive contrast and lacking detail in the highlights ⟨~ prints⟩ — compare CONTRASTY

chalky paper *n* **:** a coated paper used in some issues of postage stamps, its sensitive surface making impossible the removal of cancellation marks without removal of the design — called also *chalk-surfaced paper*

challah *n, pl* **challoth** *or* **challot** *or* **challahs** *var of* HALLAH

[1]**chal·lenge** \'chalənj, -enj\ *vb* -ED/-ING/-S [ME *challenge*, *calengen* to accuse, claim, fr. OF *chalengier* & ONF *calengier*, fr. L *calumniari* to accuse falsely — more at CALUMNIATE] *vt* **1** *obs* **:** to bring a charge against **:** ACCUSE ⟨~ the enemy to be the aggressor⟩ **2 a** *obs* **:** to assert a right, title, or claim to ⟨he *challenged* half the ransom⟩ **b :** to call for, often as if possessing a natural right **:** REQUIRE, DEMAND ⟨an event that ~*s* explanation⟩ ⟨Homer of all Greek poets ~*s* first place⟩ — often used of an attitude, ability, or psychological response ⟨survival in enemy territory ~*s* skill⟩ **3 a :** to call into question esp. for verification, explanation, or justification **:** QUESTION, EXAMINE ⟨I have constantly *challenged* my own principles —A.L.Guérard⟩ ⟨by *challenging* the opinions current among young people —M.R.Cohen⟩ **b** *of a sentry* **:** HALT ⟨~ an unknown person⟩ **4 a :** to dispute esp. as being unjust, invalid, or outmoded **:** take exception to **:** IMPUGN ⟨with recent discoveries *challenging* our former notions not only of the Neanderthal . . . fossils but of *Homo sapiens* as well —R.W.Murray⟩ **b :** to question formally the legality or legal qualifications of (as a vote or voter during elections, a juror or member of a court) **5 a :** to summon boldly or defiantly **:** DARE — used with the infinitive ⟨~ an opponent to show his evidence⟩ **b :** to summon to fight or duel, often in answer to an affront **c :** to invite into competition ⟨the Australian team *challenged* the Americans to meet them next summer⟩ ⟨Germany *challenged* the world in science and then, alas, in arms —G.C.Sellery⟩ **6 :** AROUSE ⟨new ideas to ~ your interest⟩ **:** STIMULATE, EXCITE ⟨temptation ~*s* them at every turn⟩ ⟨we must bring the discussion back to . . . where once again it ~*s* the imagination —A.E.Stevenson b. 1900⟩ **7 :** to administer a challenge (sense 6) to (a person) **:** test (immunity) by administration of infective material **~** *vi* **1** *of a hound* **:** to give tongue on finding scent **2 :** to make, present, or appear as a challenge ⟨when the appropriate moment *challenged*, he was capable of . . . leadership —C.H. Driver⟩ **3 :** to take legal exception **:** OBJECT **syn** see FACE

[2]**challenge** \"\ *n* -s [ME *chalenge*, *calenge* claim, accusation, challenge, fr. OF *chalenge* & ONF *calenge*, fr. OF *chalengier* & ONF *calengier*, v.] **1** *obs* **:** the act or action of accusing **:** REPROACH, OBJECTION **2** *obs* **:** a demand of a right **:** CLAIM **3 a :** a calling to account or into question (as to obtain justification, verification, or information) ⟨a ~ to the chairman to explain a ruling⟩ **:** EXCEPTION, PROTEST ⟨a ~ to unauthorized use of public funds⟩ **b :** a formal exception taken to a juror or jurors arrayed for the trial of a cause but before they are sworn; *also* **:** a similar exception to a member of a court-martial **c :** words or distinctive sounds used by a sentry to cause an unidentified individual to halt and establish identity **d :** an exception taken to a voter or vote at the polls as not being legally qualified or valid **4 a :** a summons often threatening, provocative, stimulating, or inciting ⟨an unholy ~ to peace and security⟩ ⟨a ~ to uphold the spirit of democracy⟩; *specif* **:** a summons to a duel esp. as answer to an affront **b :** an invitation to compete esp. in a sport ⟨a ~ tennis match⟩ **c :** the crying of a hound when first scenting game **5 :** something that is to be striven for ⟨the ~ today is not merely to improve the material standards of living, but actually to maintain existing standards —S.G.Hanson⟩ **6** *immunol* **:** TEST; *specif* **:** a test of immunity by exposure to virulent infective material after specific immunization

challenge cup *or* **challenge trophy** *n* **:** a cup that must be competed for more than once before passing into the permanent possession of a winner

chal·leng·er \-jə(r)\ *n* -s [ME *chalenger*, fr. *chalengen* + *-er*] **:** one that challenges; *specif* **:** a contender for a championship (as in boxing)

challenging *adj* **1 :** arousing interest, thought, or action that is often contentious or competitive ⟨a ~ hypothesis⟩ ⟨a ~ divergence of opinion⟩ **2 :** inviting often alluringly or enticingly **:** pleasingly or disturbingly provocative **:** FASCINATING ⟨a ~ smile⟩ ⟨a ~ personality⟩

chal·leng·ing·ly *adv* **:** in a challenging manner **:** so as to be challenging

chal·lis \'shalē, *esp Brit* -ləs\ *also* **chal·lie** \-lē\ *n, pl* **chal·lises** \'shalēz, *esp Brit* -ləsəz\ *also* **challies** \-lēz\ [prob. fr. the name *Challis*] **:** a lightweight soft clothing fabric made of cotton, wool, or synthetic yarns in a plain or twill weave in solid colors or small floral prints

challoth *or* **challot** *pl of* CHALLAH

chal·mer \'chámər, -òm-\ *n* -s [ME *chalmer*, *chamer*, alter. of *chambre* chamber — more at CHAMBER] *Scot* **:** CHAMBER

chal·mers·ite \'chalmə(r),zīt\ *n* -s [G *chalmersit*, fr. G. *Chalmers* fl1902 superintendent of the Brazilian mine where it was found + G *-it* -ite] **:** CUBANITE

chal·one \'ka,lōn\ *n* -s [Gk *chalōn*, pres. part. of *chalan* to slacken — more at CALANDO] **:** an internal secretion that depresses activity — compare HORMONE

cha·loupe \shə'lüp\ *n* -s [F; perh. akin to OProv *calup* small boat] **:** a small French boat (as a ship's boat or harbor craft); *specif* **:** an obsolete French lug-rigged fishing boat

chaluka *or* **chalukah** *var of* HALUKKAH

cha·lu·kya \'chäləkyə\ *n, pl* **chalukya** *or* **chalukyas** *usu cap* [Skt *Cālukya*] **:** either of two dynasties of Central India: Early Chalukya, 6th century to A.D. 753, and Later Chalukya, A.D. 973 to the 11th century

cha·lu·kyan \-yən\ *adj, usu cap* **:** of or belonging to the Chalukya or to their architectural styles

cha·lu·meau \¦shalə¦mō\ *n, pl* **chalu·meaux** \-ōz\ [F, fr. LL *calamellus* little reed — more at CALUMET] **1 a :** a medieval wind instrument consisting of an upright tube surmounted by a small tube in which was fixed a double reed **:** SHAWM **b :** an obsolete single-reed wind instrument of varying size that after progressive modifications became the clarinet **2 :** CHANTER 3 **3 :** the lowest register of the clarinet — often used as a direction to play a passage an octave lower **4 :** a reed organ pipe usu. of 8-foot pitch and of clarinetlike tone — called also *schalmei*

chalutz *var of* HALUTZ

chalutziut *var of* HALUTZIUT

chal·y·be·an \¦kalə¦bēən, kə'libēən\ *adj, usu cap* [L *Chalybes* (fr. Gk) + E *-an*] **:** of or belonging to the Chalybes

[1]**cha·lyb·e·ate** \kə'libēət, -lēb-\ *adj* [prob. fr. NL *chalybeatus*, irreg. fr. L *chalybs* steel (fr. Gk *chalyb-*, *chalyps*, fr. *Chalybes*) + *-atus* -ate] **:** impregnated with salts of iron **:** having a taste due to iron ⟨a ~ spring⟩

[2]**chalybeate** \"\ *n* -s **:** a chalybeate liquid or medicine

cha·lyb·e·ous \-ēəs\ *adj* [L *chalybeius* of steel, fr. Gk *chalybeios*, fr. *chalyb-*, *chalyps* steel] **:** bluish black with a steely luster

chal·y·bes \'kalə,bēz\ *n pl, usu cap* [L, fr. Gk] **:** an early people living in northeastern Asia Minor and known to the ancient Greeks as ironworkers

chal·y·bite \-,bīt\ *n* -s [G *chalybit*, fr. L *chalyb-*, *chalybs* steel + G *-it* -ite] **:** SIDERITE

[1]**cham** \'cham\ *vt* **chammed**; **chammed**; **chamming**; **chams** [ME *chammen*, perh. of imit. origin] *dial Eng* **:** CHEW, BITE

[2]**cham** *var of* KHAN

[3]**cham** \chəm, (¦)cham\ [alter. of ME *ich am*] *dial Eng* **:** I am

[4]**cham** \'chăm\ *or* **chi·am** \'chē,ăm\ *n, pl* **cham** *or* **chams** *or* **chiam** *or* **chiams** *usu cap* **1 a :** a people of an ancient kingdom in the central coastal part of Annam that reached its peak of power in the 7th and 8th centuries and was absorbed by Annam in 1471 **b :** a member of such people **2 a** (1) **:** a people in central coastal Annam linguistically related to the Cambodians (2) **:** a member of such people **b :** the language of the Cham people

[1]**cha·ma** \'kāmə\ *n* [NL, fr. L *chama*, *chema* cockle, fr. Gk *chēmē*; akin to Gk *chaskein* to yawn, gape, L *hiare* — more at YAWN] **1** *cap* **:** a genus (the type of the family Chamidae) of eulamellibranchiate bivalve mollusks of warm or tropical seas having fixed massive irregular inequivalve shells and comprising the rock oysters and extinct related forms **2** -s **:** a member of the genus *Chama* **:** ROCK OYSTER

[2]**cha·ma** \'chämə\ *n, pl* **chama** *or* **chamas** *usu cap* [Sp, of AmerInd origin] **1 a :** a Panoan people of northeastern Peru **b :** a member of such people — called also *Chuncho* **2 :** the language of the Chama people

cha·ma·co·co \,chämə¦kō(,)kō\ *n, pl* **chamacoco** *or* **chamacocos** *usu cap* [Sp, of AmerInd origin] **1 a :** a Zamuco people of Bolivia **b :** a member of such people **2 :** the language of the Chamacoco people

cha·made \shə'mäd\ *n* -s [F, prob. fr. Pg *chamada*, fr. *chamar* to call, fr. L *clamare* to cry out — more at CLAIM] **:** a drum or trumpet signal for a parley with the enemy

chamae- *or* **chame-** *in pronunciations below*, ¦== = ¦kamē *or* -mə\ *comb form* [NL, fr. Gk *chamai* on the ground — more at HUMBLE] **:** low **:** ground ⟨*Chamaerops*⟩ ⟨*Chamaesaura*⟩ — used chiefly in generic names of plants and animals

cham·ae·ba·tia \,==¦bash(ē)ə\ *n, cap* [NL, fr. Gk *chamaibatos* blackberry (fr. *chamai-* chamae- + *batos* blackberry) + NL *-ia*] **:** a small genus of low heavy-scented California evergreen shrubs of the family Rosaceae with fernlike foliage and white flowers in loose terminal cymes

cham·ae·ce·phal·ic \¦==sə¦falik\ *adj* [ISV *chamae-* + *cephalic*] *anthrop* **:** having a flattened receding head with a length-height index of 70 or less — **cham·ae·ceph·a·ly** \,=='sefəlē\ *n* -ES

cham·ae·conch \'==,käŋk, -änch\ *adj* [*chamae-* + *-conch* (fr. L *concha* shell) — more at CONCH] *anthrop* **:** having low wide orbits with an orbital index of less than 83 — **cham·ae·con·chy** \-äŋkē,-änchē\ *n* -ES

cham·ae·cra·ni·al \¦==¦krānēəl\ *adj* [G *chamäkran* chamaecranial (fr. *chamä-* chamae- + Gk *kranion* cranium) + E *-ial* — more at CRANIUM] *anthrop* **:** having a low flat skull with a length-height index of less than 70 — **cham·ae·cra·nic** \-¦krānik\ *adj* — **cham·ae·cra·ny** \'==,krānē\ *n* -ES

cham·ae·cris·ta \,=='kristə\ *n, cap* [NL, fr. *chamae-* + *crista* (fr. *crista pavonis*, lit., peacock's crest, the pre-Linnaean name of a certain plant of the family Leguminosae) — more at CREST] *in some classifications* **:** a genus of herbs or low shrubs characterized by sensitive leaves and suddenly and forcibly dehiscing pods, now included in the genus *Cassia*

cham·ae·cyp·a·ris \,=='sipərəs\ *n, cap* [NL, fr. *chamae-* + *-cyparis* (fr. Gk *kyparissos* cypress) — more at CYPRESS] **:** a small genus of important timber trees of the family Pinaceae native to No. America and Japan — see SOUTHERN WHITE CEDAR

cha·mae·leon \kə'mēlyən, -lēən\ *n, cap* [NL, fr. L, chameleon — more at CHAMELEON] **:** a large genus (the type of the family Chamaeleontidae) of lizards including most of the Old World chameleons — compare RHIPTOGLOSSA

cha·mae·le·on·i·da \kə,mēlē'änədə\ *or* **cha·mae·le·on·tes** \-'än(,)tēz\ [*Chamaeleonida* fr. NL *Chamaeleon* + *-ida*; *Chamaeleontes* fr. NL, fr. L *chamaeleontes*, pl. of *chamaeleont-*, *chamaeleon* chameleon] *syn of* RHIPTOGLOSSA

cham·ae·lir·i·um \,kamə'lirēəm\ *n* [NL, fr. *chamae-* + Gk *leirion* lily — more at LILY] **1** *cap* **:** a genus of plants (family Melanthaceae) of eastern No. America with flowers in a spikelike raceme **2** *pl* **chamaelir·ia** \-rēə\ **:** HELONIAS

cham·ae·ne·ri·on \,=='nirē,än, -ēən\ *n, cap* [NL, fr. *chamae-* + Gk *nērion* oleander] *in some classifications* **:** a small genus of herbs of the family Onagraceae that is usu included in the genus *Epilobium*

cham·ae·phyte \'kamə,fīt\ *n* -s [*chamae-* + *-phyte*] **:** a perennial plant that bears its over-wintering buds above the surface of but within a few inches of the soil — compare GEOPHYTE, PHANEROPHYTE

cham·ae·pro·so·pic \¦==prə¦sōpik, -äpik\ *adj* [G *chamäprosop* (fr. *chamä-*chamae- + Gk *prosōpon* face) + E *-ic* — more at PROSOP-] *anthrop* **:** having a low broad face with a facial index of 90 or below — **cham·ae·pros·o·py** \,==-'präsəpē, -,prə'sōpē\ *n* -ES

cha·mae·rops \kə'mē,räps\ *n, cap* [NL, fr. L, fr. Gk *chamairōps* wall germander, fr. *chamai-* chamae- + *rhōps* shrub, bush; akin to Gk *rhabdos* rod — more at VERVAIN] **:** a genus of dwarf fan palms of the Mediterranean region having petioles with long straight teeth on their margins usu. for their whole length — see HEMP PALM

cham·aer·rhine \'kamə,rīn\ *adj* [ISV *chamae-* + *-rrhine*; orig. formed as G *chamärrhin*] *anthrop* **:** having a short broad nose with a nasal index of 51–57.9 on the skull, of 85–99.9 on the living — **cham·aer·rhi·ny** \-īnē\ *n* -ES

cham·ae·sau·ra \,kamē'sȯrə, -mə-\ *n, cap* [NL, fr. *chamae-* + *-saura*] **:** a genus of African snakelike lizards (family Cordylidae) without limbs or with one or both pairs of limbs reduced to scaly vestiges

cham·ae·si·phon \-'sīfən, -,fän\ *n, cap* [NL, fr. *chamae-* +

Gk *siphōn* tube] **:** a genus (the type of the family Chamaesiphonaceae) of one-celled blue-green algae characterized by epiphytic habit and formation of endospores that are released by early breakdown of the cell wall at the apex and by successive abstriction

cham·ae·sy·ce \\‚==ˈsī(‚)sē\\ *n, cap* [NL, fr. L, fr. Gk *chamaisykē*, fr. *chamai-* chamae- + *sykē* fig tree, fr. *sykon* fig — more at FIG] *in some classifications* **:** a genus of herbs or shrubs (family Euphorbiaceae) now usu. included in the genus *Euphorbia*

cha·ma fox \\ˈkämə-\\ *n* [part trans. of NL *Vulpes chama*, fr. *Vulpes* + *chama*, modif. of E *caama*] **:** CAAMA 1

[1]**cha·mar** \\chəˈmär\\ *n* -S *often cap* [Hindi *camār*, fr. Skt *carmakāra* leather worker, fr. *carman* skin, leather + *-kāra* worker, fr. *kṛnoti* he does, makes; akin to L *corium* leather — more at CUIRASS, KARMA] **:** a member of a low Indian caste whose caste occupation is leatherworking

[2]**cha·mar** \\ˈchəmə(r)\\ *n* -S [Hindi *camar*, fr. Skt *camara*] **:** a fan, typically made of a yak's tail or peacock feathers, used in the Indian subcontinent as a mark of royalty or in temples

chamas *pl of* CHAMA

[1]**cham·ber** \\ˈchāmbə(r)\\ *n* -S [ME *chambre*, fr. OF, fr. LL *camera*, fr. L, arched roof, fr. Gk *kamara* vault; akin to L *camur* curved, Av *kamarā* girdle] **1 :** a room usu. in a house and typically with some special feature or distinguishing characteristic: **a :** a private room: as (1) **:** BEDROOM (2) **:** a room situated above the ground floor of a house **b** *chiefly Brit* **:** a suite of rooms **:** APARTMENT — used in pl. ⟨he lived in ~*s* which had once belonged to his deceased partner —Charles Dickens⟩ **c** *South* **:** a ground-floor sitting room usu. furnished with a bed **d :** *chiefly New Eng* **:** a storage room on an upper floor of a house or barn **e :** the upper level of the inner stage of an Elizabethan playhouse typically used to represent a room of intimate or domestic character — compare STUDY **2 :** an enclosed or compartmented space within the body of an animal ⟨anterior and posterior ~*s* of the eye⟩ **3 :** an often large room devoted to some special or unusual purpose ⟨the reception hall, a magnificent ~ two stories high . . . executed in a manner that could be called palatial —Lewis Mumford⟩: **a :** a hall for the meetings of a deliberative, legislative, or judicial body or assembly ⟨senate ~⟩ ⟨council ~⟩ **b :** a chamberlain's office **:** a treasury or room where government moneys are received and kept **c :** a room to which a judge retires for consultation (as with opposing counsel) or for official proceedings that may be conducted out of court — usu. used in pl. ⟨Judge Winters reentered the courtroom from his ~*s* —Erle Stanley Gardner⟩ **d :** the reception room of a person of high rank or authority ⟨the king's audience ~⟩ **4 a :** a legislative or judicial body; *esp* **:** either of the houses of a bicameral legislature **b :** a voluntary board or council (as for some business purpose) **5 a** *obs* **:** a detached plug containing the charge inserted at the breech of heavy firearms **b** *obs* **:** a short cannon that stood on its breech and that was used for celebrations and in the theater **c :** the part of the bore of a gun that holds the charge — see CANNON illustration **d :** the part of a firearm tooled to receive the cartridge: as (1) **:** any of the barrels containing the cartridge in an old revolver (2) **:** a compartment in the cartridge cylinder of a revolver **6 :** an enclosed or compartmented space designed for some special purpose ⟨a dyeing ~⟩ ⟨a gear ~⟩ **7 :** a canal lock **8 :** CHAMBER POT — **chambered** *adj*

[2]**chamber** \\"\\ *vt* **chambered; chambered; chambering** \\-b(ə)riŋ\\ **chambers** [ME *chambren*, fr. *chambre*, n.] **1 :** to place in or as if in a chamber **:** SHELTER, HOUSE, CONFINE ⟨~*ed* in a narrow cave⟩ **2 :** to furnish with a chamber ⟨~*ed* corridors⟩ **3 :** to serve as a chamber for; *esp* **:** to accommodate in the chamber of a firearm ⟨a rifle that will ~ short, long, or long-rifle cartridges⟩ **4 :** to enlarge the bottom of (a drill hole) by one or more light preliminary shots so that a sufficient blasting charge may be loaded for the final shot

[3]**chamber** \\"\\ *adj* [[1]*chamber*] **1 :** conducted with or marked by privacy or secrecy ⟨personal ~ studies⟩ ⟨the king's ~ council⟩ **2 :** intended for performance by a few musicians for a small audience **:** INTIMATE ⟨~ works⟩ ⟨~ opera⟩

chamber acid *n* [*chamber (process)*] **:** sulfuric acid made by the chamber process; *esp* **:** the acid of less than 70 percent strength as it leaves the lead chambers before being concentrated

chamber composer *n* [*chamber (music)*] **:** a musician attached to a noble household to compose and direct music

chamber crystals *n* [*chamber (process)*] **:** nitrosylsulfuric acid formed as crystals in the chamber process of making sulfuric acid

chamberdeacon *n* -S [ME *chambredeken*, fr. *chambre* chamber + *deken* deacon] **:** any of certain impoverished Irish scholars at a 15th century English university

chambered nautilus *n* **:** NAUTILUS 1a

[1]**chamberer** *n* -S [ME *chamberere*, *chambrier*, fr. MF *chamberiere*, fem. of *chamberier* chamberlain, fr. LL *camerarius*, fr. LL *camera* + L *-arius* -er] *obs* **:** CHAMBERMAID

[2]**chamberer** *n* -S [ME, chamberlain, fr. MF *chamberier*] *archaic* **:** GALLANT, LOVER, CAVALIER

chamber filter *n* **:** a filter press in which the spaces for the filter cake are formed by raised edges on the plates

cham·be·ri \\ˈchämbərē\\ *n, pl* **chamberi** *or* **chamberis** *usu cap* **:** TCHAMBULI

cham·ber·ing \\ˈchāmb(ə)riŋ\\ *n* -S [ME *chambring*, fr. gerund of *chambren*] **:** WANTONNESS, FORNICATION

chamber kiln *n* **:** a kiln with chambers heated separately

cham·ber·lain \\ˈchāmbə(r)lən\\ *n* -S [ME *chamberleyn*, fr. OF *chamberlenc*, *chamberlayn*, of Gmc origin; akin to OHG *chamarling* chamberlain, fr. *chamara* chamber (fr. LL *camera*) + *-ling* (akin to OE *-ling*) — more at CHAMBER] **1 :** a bedchamber attendant for royalty or nobility **2 a :** a chief officer in the household of a king or nobleman **b :** one in charge of moneys **:** TREASURER ⟨the town ~⟩ **3** *archaic* **:** an inn attendant in charge of bedchambers

cham·ber·land filter \\ˈchāmbə(r)lən(d)-, *F* shä^{n}berlä^n-\\ *n, usu cap C* [after Charles-Édouard *Chamberland* †1908 Fr. scientist, its inventor] **:** a candle-shaped porcelain filter used chiefly to filter out microorganisms (as from culture media)

chamber lye *n* [*chamber (pot)*] *now dial* **:** URINE

chambermaid \\ˈ==‚=\\ *n* [[1]*chamber* + *maid*] **1 :** a maid who makes beds and does general cleaning of bedrooms and bathrooms in a home, hotel, or motel **2** *obs* **:** a lady's maid

cham·ber·man \\ˈ==mən, -‚man\\ *n, pl* **chambermen** [*chamber (process)* + *man*] **:** a skilled worker engaged in the making of sulfuric acid by the chamber process

chamber music *n* [trans. of It *musica da camera*] **:** art music, usu. instrumental, intended for performance in a private room or small audience hall **:** intimate music as distinguished esp. from operatic and symphonic music

chamber of commerce : an association of businessmen to promote the commercial and industrial interests of a community, state, or nation — compare BOARD OF TRADE

chamber of deputies : the lower or popular branch of certain legislatures

chamber of horrors 1 : a hall in which various things of macabre interest (as relics of criminals and instruments of torture) are exhibited; *also* **:** a collection of such exhibits **2 :** an assemblage of things of macabre interest

chamber orchestra *n* [*chamber (music)*] **:** a small orchestra usu. with one player for each instrumental part **:** SINFONIETTA

chamber organ *n* **:** a small pipe organ

chamber pot *n* **:** a bedroom vessel for urine or other waste

chamber practice *n* **:** the part of the practice of lawyers that is conducted in their offices as distinguished from that involved in appearing in court

chamber process *n* **1 :** a process of making sulfuric acid in which sulfur dioxide is oxidized by moist air with nitrogen oxides as catalyst in a series of lead-lined chambers — see GAY-LUSSAC TOWER, GLOVER TOWER **2 :** a process of making basic carbonate white lead in which lead strips are exposed to carbon dioxide, moist air, and acetic acid vapor in brick chambers

chambers *pl of* CHAMBER, *pres 3d sing of* CHAMBER

chamber sonata *n* [trans. of It *sonata da camera*] **:** SONATA DA CAMERA

cham·ber·tin \\shä^{n}bertа^n\\ *n* -S *usu cap* [F, fr. *Chambertin*, vineyard near Dijon, France, where it is produced] **:** a red Burgundy wine

chamberwoman \\ˈ==‚==\\ *n* **:** CHAMBERMAID

cham·bé·ry \\shä^{n}bārē\\ *n* -ES *usu cap* [fr. *Chambéry*, France, where it is made] **:** a dry vermouth

chamblet *obs var of* CAMLET

cham·bray \\ˈsham‚brā, -‚brē, shamˈbrā, -aam-\\ *n* -S [irreg. fr. *Cambrai*, city of France] **:** a lightweight clothing fabric of plain weave made of cotton, silk, linen, or synthetic yarns and having a frosted appearance due to the interweaving of colored warp and white filling yarns

chame- — see CHAMAE-

cha·me·leon *also* **ca·me·leon** \\kəˈmēlyən, -lēən *sometimes* shə-\\ *n* -S *often attrib* [modif. (influenced by L *chamaeleon*) of ME *camelion*, fr. MF *camelion*, fr. L *chamaeleon*, fr. Gk *chamaileōn*, fr. *chamai-* chamae- + *leōn* lion — more at LION] **1 :** any of a group (Rhiptoglossa) of specialized slow-moving Old World acrodont lizards that have a laterally compressed body with the skin covered with small granules, a prehensile tail, opposed digits, very large independently movable eyeballs behind eyelids partially fused to leave only a small central opening, and an extremely elastic extensible tongue which can be shot out nearly the length of the animal to take the insects on which it feeds, and that display unusual ability to change the color of the skin in response to both external stimuli and internal factors **2 a :** a fickle person; *esp* **:** a person given to expedient or facile change in ideas or character ⟨he was a ~ and his rare capacity for recognizing what was required of him . . . was equalled only by his capacity for becoming it —Anthony West⟩ **b :** something subject to quick or frequent change esp. in appearance ⟨his goodness was a ~ that changed its hue to the hue of the situation in which he found himself —Peggy Bennett⟩ **3 :** any of various American lizards capable of changing their color; *esp* **:** any of several members of the common genus *Anolis*

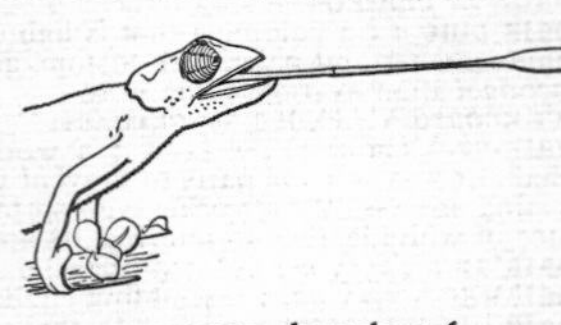

common chameleon 1

cha·me·le·on·ic \\kə¦mēlē¦änik\\ *adj* **:** like a chameleon in changeability **:** assuming varying hues **:** INCONSTANT

chameleon tree frog *n* **:** TREE TOAD

chametz *var of* HAMETZ

[1]**cham·fer** \\ˈcham(p)fə(r), -aam-, -mpə(r)\\ *n* -S [modif. of MF *chanfrein*, alter. of *chanfreint* beveled edge, fr. past part. of *chanfraindre* to bevel, fr. *chant* edge (fr. L *canthus* iron ring round a carriage wheel) + *fraindre* to break, fr. L *frangere* — more at CANT, BREAK] **1 :** a small groove **:** FURROW **2 :** the surface formed by cutting away the angle at the intersection of two faces of a piece of timber, stone, or metal **:** a beveled edge

[2]**chamfer** \\"\\ *vt* **chamfered; chamfered; chamfering** \\-f(ə)riŋ, -p(ə)r-\\ **chamfers 1 a :** to cut a furrow in (as in a column) **:** GROOVE, CHANNEL, FLUTE **b :** to cut off corners or edges (as of timber columns and beams) **2 :** to make a chamfer on **:** cut or reduce (as an angle) to a chamfer **:** BEVEL

chamfer angle *n* **:** the angle between a chamfered surface and one of the original surfaces from which the chamfer is cut

chamfer bit *n* **:** a bit formed to bevel the edge of a hole

cham·fer·er \\-m(p)fərə(r), -mpər-\\ *n* -S **:** one that chamfers

chamfer plane *n* **:** a carpenter's plane having a V-grooved bottom and used for chamfering the edges of woodwork

chamfron *also* **chaffron** *or* **chafron** *or* **chamfrain** *or* **chanfron** *n* -S [ME *shamfron*, fr. MF *chanfrein*, fr. OF, irreg. fr. *chafresner* to subdue, make obedient, fr. *chief* head (fr. L *caput*) + *frener* to bridle, fr. L *frenare*, fr. *frenum* bridle — more at HEAD, REFRAIN] **:** the headpiece of a horse's bard

cha·mi·cu·ro \\‚chäməˈkürō\\ *also* **cha·mi·cu·ra** \\-ü(ə)‚rō\\ *n, pl* **chamicura** *or* **chamicuras** *also* **chamicuro** *or* **chamicuros** *usu cap* [Sp *chamicuro*, of AmerInd origin] **1 a :** a people of northern Peru considered by some Americanists to be Panoan **b :** a member of such people **2 :** the language of the Chamicura people

cham·i·sal \\¦shamə¦sal\\ *n* -S [AmerSp, fr. *chamiso*] **:** a California chaparral of chamiso

cha·mi·so \\shəˈmē(‚)sō, ch-, -ēsə\\ *or* **cha·mise** \\-ēs\\ *also* **cha·mi·sa** \\-ēsə\\ *n* -S [AmerSp *chamiso*, *chamis*, alter. of Sp *chamizo* half-burned wood, fr. Pg *chamiço* stick, wood, fr. *chamiça* small dry pieces of wood — more at CHAMIZA] **1 :** a California shrub (*Adenostoma fasciculatum*) that forms a dense chaparral — see CHAMISAL **2 :** TOYON **3** *Puerto Rico* **:** AKEAKE 1 **4** *Southwest* **:** CHAMIZA

cha·mite \\ˈkā‚mīt\\ *n* -S [NL *Chama* + E *-ite*] **:** a fossil shell of the genus *Chama* or a related genus

cha·mi·za \\shəˈmēzə, ch-\\ *n* -S [MexSp, fr. Sp, a grass used in thatching, brushwood, fr. Pg *chamiça* small dry pieces of wood, a cane, a heather, fr. *chama* flame, fr. L *flamma*; akin to L *flagrare* to burn] **:** a semidesert evergreen shrub (*Atriplex canescens*) that has greenish gray foliage and is important as a browse plant in the southern U.S. — called also *chamiso*

chamlet *obs var of* CAMLET

cham·ma \\ˈshamə\\ *n* -S [Amharic *shamma*] **:** a cotton togalike usu. white garment worn in Ethiopia

chammed *past of* CHAM

chamming *pres part of* CHAM

[1]**cham·ois** \\ˈshamē, -mi, *in sense 1 also* (ˈ)sham¦wä\\ *n, pl* **cham·ois** *also* **cha·moix** *in sense 1* -ē(z) *or* -i(z) *or* -wä(z); *in other senses* -ēz *or* -iz\\ [MF, fr. LL *camox*, prob. of non-IE origin; akin to the source of OHG *gamiza* chamois] **1 :** a small agile goatlike antelope (*Rupicapra rupicapra*) that lives on the loftiest mountain ridges of Europe and in the Caucasus and is a favorite quarry of hunters **2** *also* **cham·my** *or* **sham·my** *or* **sha·moy** \\ˈshamē, -mi\\ **a :** a soft pliant leather prepared from the skin of the chamois **b :** an oil-tanned suede-finished leather prepared from the flesher of sheepskins **3** *or* **shammy** -ES **:** a piece of chamois; *esp* **:** a cloth used for washing or polishing **4** *or* **chamois yellow** *also* **chamois skin :** a grayish yellow that is redder, stronger, and slightly lighter than crash, lighter, stronger, and slightly redder than old ivory, and stronger and slightly redder than flax

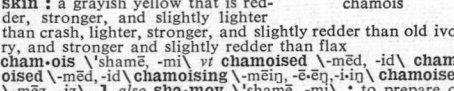

chamois

[2]**cham·ois** \\ˈshamē, -mi\\ *vt* **chamoised** \\-mēd, -id\\ **chamoised** \\-mēd, -id\\ **chamoising** \\-mēiŋ, -ēəŋ, -iiŋ\\ **chamoises** \\-mēz, -iz\\ **1** *also* **sha·moy** \\ˈshamē, -mi\\ **:** to prepare or dress like chamois **2** *or* **sham·my** \\ˈshamē, -mi\\ **:** to clean or polish with a chamois

chamois cloth *n* **:** a soft cloth fabric made in imitation of chamois leather

cham·o·line \\ˈshamə‚lēn, ‚==ˈ=\\ *n* -S [perh. irreg. fr. *chamois*] **:** BUCKTHORN BROWN

cham·o·mile *or* **cam·o·mile** \\ˈkamə‚mīl, -ī(ə)l *also* -ēl *or* -ē(ə)l\\ *n* -S [ME *camemille*, fr. ML *camomilla*, fr. LL *chamomilla*, modif. of L *chamaemelon*, fr. Gk *chamaimēlon*, fr. *chamai-* chamae- + *mēlon* apple; fr. the applelike smell of its flower — more at MALUS] **1 a :** a plant of the genus *Anthemis* (esp. the common European *A. nobilis*) having strong-scented foliage and flower heads that contain a bitter medicinal principle used as an antispasmodic or a diaphoretic **b :** a plant of the related genus *Matricaria* (esp. *M. chamomilla*) having foliage and flower heads that contain the bitter principle found in plants of the genus *Anthemis* **2 :** the dried flower heads of either of two plants of the genera *Anthemis* and *Matricaria* (*A. nobilis* and *M. chamomilla*) used as aromatic bitters

chamomile oil *n* **:** a blue aromatic essential oil obtained from the flower heads of either of two plants: **a :** such an oil obtained from the common European chamomile and used in perfumes and in medicine — called also *Roman chamomile oil* **b :** such an oil obtained from a related plant (*Matricaria chamomilla*) and used in perfumes — called also *German chamomile oil*

cha·mor·ro \\chəˈmȯ(‚)rō\\ *n, pl* **chamorro** *or* **chamorros** *usu cap* [Sp, lit., man with a shorn head, perh. of Iberian origin; akin to Basque *samur*, *samurr* tender] **1 a :** a people of the Mariana islands **b :** a member of such people **2 :** the language of the Chamorro people

cham·o·site \\ˈshamə‚zīt\\ *or* **cham·oi·site** \\-m(w)ə‚z-\\ *n* -S [F, fr. *Chamoson*, *Chamoison*, Valais canton, Switzerland, its locality + F *-ite*] **:** a mineral consisting of a greenish gray or black silicate (sp. gr. 3–3.4) — **cham·o·sit·ic** \\¦==¦zidik\\ *adj*

cha·motte \\shəˈmät\\ *n* -S [prob. fr. F, fr. G *schamotte*] **:** GROG 2

[1]**champ** \\ˈchamp, -aa(ə)-,-ai-\\ *vb* -ED/-ING/-S [perh. imit.] *vt* **1 a :** to chew on with noisy vigor ⟨~*ing* his food with the gusto of a healthy young animal —*MacLean's Mag.*⟩ **b :** to bite on repeatedly or grind the teeth forcefully against ⟨~*ing* the stem of his pipe in his teeth —Marcia Davenport⟩ **2 :** to press, open and close with force and noise **:** GNASH ⟨a green crab . . . ~*ing* enormous claws —I.L.Idriess⟩ **3 :** MASH, TRAMPLE ⟨~*ing* soil and water into mud⟩ ~ *vi* **1 :** to make biting or gnashing movements or gestures **:** BITE ⟨a race horse ~*ing* behind a barrier —Upton Sinclair⟩ ⟨little caterpillars . . . ~*ing* on leaves —Peggy Bennett⟩ **2 :** to show restive impatience of delay or restraint ⟨for years industrial psychologists had been ~*ing* to apply scientific methods —W.H.Whyte⟩ — **champ at the bit** *or* **champ the bit 1** *of a horse* **:** to bite or gnash a bit in unruliness or impatience ⟨the mustang snorted and *champed the bit* . . . ready to bolt —Zane Grey⟩ **2 :** to be impatient of restraint or inactivity ⟨Gaul may *champ the bit* and foam in fetters —Lord Byron⟩

[2]**champ** \\"\\ *n* -S **:** the act or action of champing

[3]**champ** *adj* -ER/-EST [origin unknown] *dial Eng* **:** FIRM, HARD

[4]**champ** \\"\\ *n* -S [by shortening] **:** CHAMPION

[5]**champ** \\"\\ *n* -S [by shortening] **:** CHAMPAC

cham·pa \\ˈchampə\\ *n, pl* **champa** *or* **champas** *usu cap* **1 :** a Tibetan people of eastern Kashmir **2 :** a member of the Champa people

cham·pac *also* **cham·pak** \\ˈcham‚pak, -əm(‚)pək\\ *or* **cham·pa·ca** *or* **cham·pa·ka** \\-pəkə\\ *n* -S [Hindi & Skt; Hindi *campak*, fr. Skt *campaka*, of Dravidian origin; akin to Tamil *canpakam*, *cenpakam*] **:** an East Indian tree (*Michelia champaca*) the yellow flowers of which yield an oil used as a perfume

cham·pa·col \\ˈchampə‚kōl, -ōl\\ *n* -S [*champac* + *-ol*] **:** GUAIOL

cham·pagne \\(ˈ)sham¦pān, -aam-\\ *n* -S *often attrib* [F, fr. *Champagne*, region (formerly province) of northeastern France where it was first produced, fr. LL *campania* level country] **1 :** a white sparkling wine that undergoes one fermentation in a cask and a second fermentation in a bottle, the latter generating carbon dioxide that makes the wine sparkle **2 :** a wine of the champagne type; *broadly* **:** an effervescent white wine **3 :** a pale orange yellow to light grayish yellowish brown — called also *belleek*

champagne cider *n* **:** a sparkling cider that is matured in vats and then fermented in bottles to produce effervescence

champagne cocktail *n* **:** a cocktail consisting of champagne flavored with sugar and bitters, garnished with a twist of lemon peel, and usu. served in a saucer champagne glass

champagne d'ar·gent \\-‚därˈzhä^n, *F* shä^{n}pan^{y}dàrzhä^n\\ *n, usu cap C&A* [F, lit., silver champagne] **:** a French breed of large hardy productive domestic rabbits having silvery blue fur

cham·pagn·i·za·tion \\(‚)sham‚pānəˈzāshən\\ *n* -S **:** the process of making a wine sparkling

cham·pagn·ize \\shamˈpā‚nīz\\ *vt* -ED/-ING/-S [F *champagniser*, fr. *champagne* + *-iser* -ize] **:** to make (a wine) sparkling by retaining the carbon dioxide generated during fermentation

[1]**cham·paign** *often* ˈcham‚pān *during its floruit; today prob usu* (ˈ)sham¦p-\\ *n* -S [ME *champayne*, fr. MF *champagne*, fr. LL *campania* level country — more at CAMPAIGN] **1 a :** an expanse of level open country **:** PLAIN ⟨the wide ~ around the city⟩ **b :** level open country ⟨traversing the ~ and avoiding the mountains⟩ **2** *archaic* **:** an area of army operations **:** BATTLEGROUND **3 a :** an open expanse ⟨the ~ of the broad sea⟩ **b :** an encompassed expanse **:** FIELD ⟨the ~ of science⟩

[2]**champaign** \\"\\ *adj* **1 :** flat and open like a champaign **:** constituting a champaign ⟨a ~ region⟩ **2 :** occurring in a champaign ⟨~ sports⟩ **:** of a champaign ⟨~ scenery⟩

champed *past of* CHAMP

cham·per·tor \\ˈchampə(r)d·ə(r)\\ *n* -S [earlier *champartour*, *champertour*, fr. MF *champarteor*, fr. *champart* + *-eor* -or] **:** one that engages in champerty

cham·per·tous \\-d·əs\\ *adj* [*champerty* + *-ous*] **:** of, relating to, or involving champerty ⟨a ~ contract⟩

cham·per·ty *also* **cham·par·ty** \\-d·ē\\ *n* -ES [ME *champartie*, modif. (prob. influenced by ME *partie* part) of MF *champart* field rent, fr. *champ* field (fr. L *campus*) + *part* portion — more at CAMP, PART] **:** a proceeding, illegal in many jurisdictions, by which a person not a party in a suit bargains to aid in or carry on its prosecution or defense by furnishing money or personal services in consideration of his receiving a share of the matter in suit **:** maintenance with the addition of an agreement to divide the thing in suit

champest *superlative of* CHAMP

champian *n or adj* [by alter.] *obs* **:** CHAMPAIGN

cham·pi·gnon \\shamˈpinyən, -pē- *also* ch-; *F* shä^{n}pē^{ny}ō^n\\ *n* -S [MF, alter. of *champigneul*, fr. *champagne* level country — more at CHAMPAIGN] **1** *obs* **:** FUNGUS **2 :** an edible fungus; *esp* **:** the common meadow mushroom **3 :** a fairy ring (*Marasmius oreades*)

champing *pres part of* CHAMP

[1]**cham·pi·on** \\ˈchampēən, -aam-,-aim-, *chiefly dial or substand* (ˈ)=¦pēn\\ *n* -S [ME *champioun*, fr. OF *champion*, fr. ML *campion-*, *campio*, of WGmc origin; akin to OE *cempa* warrior, soldier, OHG *kempho* — more at KEMP] **1 :** WARRIOR, FIGHTER, COMBATANT ⟨~*s* arming for battle⟩ **2 :** a militant advocate or defender ⟨a royalist, always a ~ of his king⟩ **3 :** one that fights, often in single formal combat, for another's rights, honor, or fame ⟨the lady's ~ entered the lists⟩ **4 a :** one whose supremacy or superiority is formally acknowledged esp. after a test, contest, or series of tests or contests ⟨individual and team ~*s* at the Olympics⟩ ⟨the conference ~*s*⟩ ⟨the world's chess ~⟩ **b :** a show animal that has won a certain number of points in open competition ⟨this collie puppy is already a ~⟩ **c :** a plant or plant part (as a fruit or flower) that has received a first prize in a competitive exhibit ⟨these tomatoes are ~*s*⟩ **d :** one showing a marked superiority ⟨a ~ at telling tall tales⟩ **5** *or* **champion oak :** RED OAK 1a

[2]**champion** \\"\\ *vt* -ED/-ING/-S **1** *archaic* **:** CHALLENGE, DEFY ⟨~*ing* one to speak⟩ **2 :** to protect or fight for as a champion ⟨~*ing* his lady in the lists⟩ **3 :** to act as militant supporter of **:** DEFEND, UPHOLD, ADVOCATE ⟨faithful to Jefferson's principles, ~*ed* states' rights —*Amer. Guide Series: Va.*⟩

[3]**champion** \\"\\ *adj* **1 :** acknowledged as supreme over contestants or rivals ⟨the ~ team of the league⟩ ⟨the ~ speller of the class⟩ **2 a :** FIRST-RATE, SPLENDID ⟨if you'll drop me at the next corner, my lord, that'll do me ~ —Dorothy L. Sayers⟩ **b :** FOREMOST, UNSURPASSED ⟨the ~ liar of the club⟩

[4]**champion** *obs var of* CHAMPAIGN

cham·pi·on·less \\-ləs\\ *adj* **:** being without a champion

cham·pi·on·ship \\-‚ship\\ *n* -S *often attrib* **1 :** the position of a champion **:** acknowledged supremacy; *specif* **:** the title of champion in a competitive sport or game ⟨won four ~*s* in five years⟩ **2 :** the act of championing **:** ADVOCACY, DEFENSE, SUPPORT ⟨his ~ of the new theory⟩ ⟨~ of the small nations against the Big Four —Vera M. Dean⟩ **3 :** a contest held to determine a champion ⟨colleges represented in the NCAA ~*s*⟩

champion tooth *n* **:** a form of double tooth for crosscut saws

cham·plain·ian \\(ˈ)sham¦plānēən\\ *adj, usu cap* [Lake *Champlain*, N. Y. + E *-ian*] **:** of or relating to a subdivision of the No. American Ordovician — see GEOLOGIC TIME table

[1]**champ·le·vé** \\¦shä^{n}lə¦vā\\ *adj* [F, fr. past part. of *champlever* to engrave depressions in a smooth surface, fr. *champ* field, ground of an engraving (fr. L *campus* field) + *lever* to raise, remove — more at CAMP, LEVER] **:** having the metal ground engraved, cut out, or depressed and the resultant spaces filled in with enamel pastes and fired — used of enamel work; compare CLOISONNÉ

[2]**champlevé** \\"\\ *n* -S **1 :** a piece of champlevé enamel **2 :** the art or process of making champlevé work

champ·ney rose \\ˈchampnē-\\ *n, usu cap C* [after John *Champney* fl1801 Am. horticulturist who developed it] **:** NOISETTE ROSE

champs *pl of* CHAMP, *pres 3d sing of* CHAMP
chams *pres 3d sing of* CHAM, *pl of* CHAM
chamsin *var of* KHAMSIN
ch'an \'chän\ *n* -s *usu cap* [prob. fr. Chin *ch'an²* meditation] **:** a Chinese school of Mahayana Buddhism founded in the 6th century A.D. by the Indian teacher Bodhidharma that emphasizes meditation and higher contemplation as a method of salvation — the Chinese equivalent of the Japanese *Zen* or the Indian *Dhyana*
chan *abbr* channel
cha·ná \chə'nä, chä'-\ *n, pl* **chaná** or **chanás** *usu cap* [Sp, of AmerInd origin] **:** one of a number of groups of Indian peoples of various language affiliation: **a :** the Charrua peoples of Uruguay **b :** some Arawakan peoples; *esp* **:** LAYANÁ **c :** some Tupi-Guaranian peoples
cha·ña·bal \,chänyə'bäl\ *also* **cha·ne·abal** \", -nēə;-\ *n, pl* **chañabal** \-äl\ *or* **chañaba·les** \-ä(,)läs\ *or* **chañabals** \-älz\ *usu cap* [Sp *chaneabal, chañabal,* of AmerInd origin] **:** TOJOLABAL
cha·nar \chän'yär\ *n, pl* **chana·res** \-ä(,)räs\ [Sp *chañar*] **:** a thorny shrub or small tree (*Geoffraea decorticans*) of the family Leguminosae common in central Argentina which bears sweet edible berries
chanc *abbr* chancellor; chancery
¹chance \'chan(t)s, -aa(ə)-,-ai-,-á-\ *n* -s [ME, fr. OF *cheance, chance,* fr. (assumed) VL *cadentia* fall, fr. L *cadent-, cadens,* pres. part. of *cadere* to fall; akin to Skt *śad* to fall and prob. to W *cesair* hailstones] **1 a :** something that happens unpredictably without any discernible human intention or direction and in dissociation from any observable pattern, causal relation, natural necessity, or providential dispensation ⟨this is a strange ~ that throws you and me together —Charles Dickens⟩ ⟨when the ~*s* of war make him again the spokesman of the majority —B.N.Cardozo⟩ **b** *archaic* **:** such a happening or happenings affecting human well-being in a particular way ⟨hard ~ they had, and lots of 'em died, I guess —Sarah O. Jewett⟩ **c :** the assumed impersonal purposeless determiner of such unaccountable happenings and of the outcome of uncertain situations involving alternatives unavailable to human choice **:** LUCK ⟨whatever be my ~ or my mischance —Robert Browning⟩ ⟨sane persons who by ~ or by evil design have been confined in a lunatic asylum —C.H.Grandgent⟩ ⟨my experience as a historian is that more documents survive by ~ than by intention —Robert Graves⟩ ⟨games in which ~ predominates over skill are used for gambling⟩ **d :** the fortuitous or incalculable element in phenomenal existence **:** CONTINGENT — compare TYCHISM **2 :** a circumstantial situation affording the possibility of effectuating some objective **:** OPPORTUNITY: **a :** an opportunity typically offering problematical success if taken and afforded either by luck or accident or by an equitable arrangement ⟨a ~ for the community to take a hand in punishing a somewhat contemptible malefactor —Agnes Repplier⟩ ⟨the feeling that the system under which we live deprives the majority of the ~ of a decent life —C.D.Lewis⟩ **b :** an opening for a try, venture, or grasp ⟨10 years after his death historians will get a ~ at his personal file⟩ **c :** a suitable space of time or set of conditions for allowing some process to take place **:** OPPORTUNITY ⟨the people had not had a ~ to become indoctrinated⟩ ⟨giving the wound a ~ to heal⟩ **d :** an opportunity given by a batsman to a fielder in cricket to put the batsman out **e :** a fielding opportunity in baseball ⟨the shortstop fumbled on a hard ~⟩; *specif* **:** any play by a player on defense that is scored as a put-out, assist, or error ⟨handling 200 ~*s* without an error⟩ **3 a** (1) **:** the possibility of an indicated or a favorable outcome in an uncertain situation (2) **:** the measure or strength of possibility or degree of likelihood of such an outcome ⟨what ~ has he of pulling through⟩ ⟨we have practically no ~ of winning⟩ — often used in pl. ⟨dubious of his ~*s* on the lottery ticket⟩ — compare PROBABILITY 3 **b :** a possibility that an indicated or likely future happening, condition, or combination of circumstances will come to pass ⟨until I thought I had eliminated all ~ of error —David Fairchild⟩ ⟨and if you guarantee a ~, it is no longer a ~; it is a sinecure —C.W.Mills⟩ ⟨go ahead with the printing on the ~ that no major correction may prove necessary⟩ **c :** at least a tenuous possibility of experiencing a favorable outcome or an escape from a hazard ⟨well, no matter what they think they have on me, I stand a ~ in court —William Faulkner⟩ **d :** ground for hope or expectation **:** PROSPECT ⟨to me, the best ~ for future society lies through apathy, uninventiveness, and inertia —E.M.Forster⟩ **e chances** *pl* **:** the more likely or weighty indications issuing from an overall estimate of the various possible outcomes or facts eventually to emerge — often used without the definite article ⟨the ~*s* are that no one who opens the book will skip a page⟩ ⟨~*s* are he has already heard the news⟩ **4 :** a gamble or risk of a looked-for or a favorable but quite indeterminable outcome of a hazardous situation entered voluntarily or involuntarily — usu. following the verb *take* ⟨a man bold enough to take his ~*s* —F.B.Gipson⟩ ⟨they took a long ~, and they made it —Shine Philips⟩; *esp* **:** such a risk voluntarily undertaken in a gambling game ⟨lost his money taking ~*s* in local lotteries⟩ **5** *Midland* **a :** a quantity, number, or distance usu. specified as large ⟨a right smart ~ of corn⟩ **b :** SAMPLE, SPECIMEN **6 a :** a forest location suitable for a logging operation **b :** a unit of such operation

syn FORTUNE, LUCK, HAP, HAZARD, ACCIDENT: CHANCE is a general term indicating the force that governs issues unpredictably, unanalyzably, without being determined by strict causes or by causes determined by human intent or consideration ⟨we may say that two or more phenomena are conjoined by *chance* . . . meaning that they are in no way related by causation —J.S.Mill⟩ CHANCE may stress blind, random, utter unpredictability ⟨he had felt no will to resist, but had let *chance* take its way —Willa Cather⟩ ⟨the gun . . . wavered as he raised it and fired, but *chance* came to his assistance —Sherwood Anderson⟩ FORTUNE in this sense may be associated with the notion of the goddess Fortuna, a subdeity who capriciously and inconsistently apportioned men's differing allotments of wealth and power ⟨not only, to carry out Bacon's conception, does a man who marries give hostages to *fortune,* but also he who accumulates objects of value; for each affords occasions for Fortune's malice —Herbert Spencer⟩ LUCK is quite similar to FORTUNE in this sense; it differs mainly in being less formal and bookish than FORTUNE and, sometimes, in being more applicable to one specific situation ⟨*luck* operates in most departments of human affairs . . . Read the autobiographies of businessmen and gather from those who are frank their examples of the lucky break —Lydia Strong⟩ Without modification, LUCK is likely to indicate a favoring force, a beneficial one ⟨with *luck* and the help of atomic research, our children may be safe from this grim disease —A.E.Stevenson b. 1900⟩ HAP, now rare, is rather colorless and neutral, and is limited in its use to reference to things past ⟨we had the good *hap* to meet with some young deer, a thing we had long wished for —Daniel Defoe⟩ HAZARD indicates either more or less pure chance ⟨the choice has been determined more by the *hazards* of my recent reading than by anything else —Aldous Huxley⟩ or chance involving much risk or danger ⟨it is much more difficult for small business to survive the *hazards* which come from trade recessions and widespread unemployment —H.S.Truman⟩ ACCIDENT stresses lack of essential cause; it may differ from CHANCE in suggesting an occurrence or event rather than the blind force motivating it ⟨only an occasional *accident,* such as the discovery of some chemically preserved textiles —*Amer. Guide Series: Ind.*⟩ **syn** see in addition OPPORTUNITY
— by chance *adv* **:** unaccountably, without premeditation, prearrangement, or any sign of motivation and without observable causal relation to attendant circumstances **:** FORTUITOUSLY ⟨*by chance* the moment of his entrance was also a big moment in the life of the man he had come to see —Sherwood Anderson⟩ **:** in the casual, undirected, haphazard course of events ⟨did you *by chance* see my fountain pen⟩
²chance \"\ *vb* -ED/-ING/-S [ME *chancen,* fr. *chance,* n.] *vi* **1 a :** to take place or come about by chance without intention or direction **:** HAPPEN ⟨it *chanced* that the winter of 1783–84 was a very severe one —H.E.Scudder⟩ **b :** to be found or to prove by chance or fortuitous occurrence ⟨let me know if there should ~ to be another book with the same title⟩ **c :** to have the luck, the ill fortune, or the indifferent fortune ⟨a mumbled conversation I *chanced* to hear in the subway⟩ **d** *obs* **:** to come about — used after interrogative *how* ⟨how ~ this was not done before —Christopher Marlowe⟩ **2 :** to come or light by chance esp. casually and unexpectedly — used with *upon* ⟨Shakespeare *chanced* upon the best time and country in which to live —G.M.Trevelyan⟩ **~** *vt* **1 :** to leave to chance the outcome, disposal, or ordering of ⟨I know the course has dangerous curves but I'll ~ one descent⟩ **2 a :** to accept whatever may through chance eventuate from (an action or choice) ⟨hesitant whether to ~ commitment to a world government⟩ **b** *Brit* **:** to accept the uncertainties of (one's luck) **3 :** to accept the hazard of **:** RISK ⟨it was decided to withdraw rather than ~ defeat in enemy territory —T.R. Hay⟩ **syn** see HAPPEN, VENTURE — **chance one's arm** *Brit* **:** to take a position involving possible or probable disastrous loss
³chance \"\ *adv* [prob. by shortening] *archaic* **:** by chance
⁴chance \"\ *adj* [¹*chance*] **:** happening, made, experienced, or encountered by chance, without forethought, plan, or intention **:** ACCIDENTAL, CONTINGENT ⟨by a charming accident he had disposed of them to a ~ buyer in Bainbridge —Arnold Bennett⟩ ⟨living on the ~ presents of his friends —Anthony Trollope⟩ **syn** see RANDOM
chance·a·ble \-əbəl\ *adj* [²*chance* + *-able*] *archaic* **:** FORTUITOUS, CASUAL, ACCIDENTAL
chance child *n* **:** an illegitimate child
chance·ful \-fəl\ *adj* **1 a** *archaic* **:** dependent on chance **:** CASUAL **b** *obs* **:** HAZARDOUS **2 :** full of chance or chances — **chance·ful·ly** \-fəlē\ *adv*
chan·cel \'chan(t)səl, -aan-,-ain-,-án-\ *n* -s [ME, fr. MF, chancel, lattice separating the chancel from the nave, fr. LL *cancellus* lattice in front of the altar, fr. L *cancelli* lattice — more at CANCEL] **1 :** the part of a church in which is located the altar or communion table, pulpit, and lectern, which is occupied by the clergy and usu. the choir during religious services, and which is customarily on a higher level than the nave and separated from it by steps **2 :** a section similar to a chancel in a building other than a church
chan·ce·lade man \,shäⁿsə'läd, (')shäⁿs;l-\ *n, usu cap C* [trans. of F *homme de Chancelade,* fr. *Chancelade,* France, where remains were unearthed] **:** a short-statured long-nosed late paleolithic man known from a skeleton found associated with Magdalenian artifacts and having some affinities with modern Eskimos
chance·less \'=ləs\ *adj* **:** giving or receiving no chance
chan·cel·lery *or* **chan·cel·lory** \chan(t)s(ə)lərē, -aan-,-ain-, -án-, -sələrē, -ri\ *n* -ES [*chancelier* fr. ME *chancellerie,* fr. OF, fr. *chancelier* chancellor + *-ie* -y, *chancellory,* alter. (influenced by *-ory*) of *chancellery*] **1 a :** the position, court, or department of a chancellor **b :** the building or room where a chancellor has his office **2 :** the office of secretary of the court of a person high in authority **3 a :** the office and official residence of a diplomatic minister at a foreign seat of government or the office where a consul conducts business **b :** the official personnel of an embassy or consulate ⟨mounting tension among the *chancelleries* of Europe⟩
chan·cel·lor \-s(ə)lə(r)\ *n* -s [ME *chanceler,* fr. OF *chancelier,* fr. LL *cancellarius* doorkeeper, secretary, fr. *cancellus* lattice, fr. L *cancelli*] **1 a** *obs* **:** a secretary esp. of a nobleman, prince, or king; *specif* **:** the chief secretary of the king of England **b :** the lord chancellor of Great Britain **c :** an official esp. in England who keeps a record of proceedings and does other official acts in a chapter of an order of knighthood **d :** one of four chief dignitaries of Anglican cathedrals of the old foundation some of whose duties are to arrange services, to lecture in theology, and to keep the books **e :** CHARTOPHYLAX **f** *Brit* **:** the chief secretary of an embassy **g :** a Roman Catholic priest in the U.S. appointed by a bishop to take charge of a chancery **h :** an officer in some fraternal or sororal orders having any of varying duties, responsibilities, or privileges **2 :** a university officer of high rank: **a :** the titular head of a British university **b :** PRESIDENT **c :** the chief executive officer of some state systems of higher education **d :** an officer in charge of a certain branch or certain administrative functions of a university **3 a :** a clerical or lay law officer of a bishop or diocese in the Church of England or Protestant Episcopal Church who acts for a bishop esp. in cases relating to ecclesiastical law **b :** a judge in a court of chancery or equity in various states of the U.S.; *specif* **:** the presiding judge in such a court as distinguished from the vice-chancellors **4 :** the chief minister of state in any of certain European countries who is charged with responsibilities corresponding to those of a prime minister **5 :** the foreman of a jury in Scotland
chan·cel·lor·ate \-s(ə)lə,rāt, -,rət\ *n* -s **:** CHANCELLORSHIP
chan·cel·lor·ism \-s(ə)lə,rizəm\ *n* -s **:** government with a chancellor as responsible head
chancellor of the exchequer *often cap C&E* **:** a member of the British cabinet who, as the highest finance minister of the government, is in charge of the public income and expenditure, submitting to Parliament an annual budget with proposals to extend or curtail taxation
chan·cel·lor·ship \-s(ə)lə(r),ship\ *n* -s [ME *chancelershipe,* fr. *chanceler* chancellor + *-shipe* -ship] **:** the office or the term of a chancellor
chancel organ *n* **:** a division of a pipe organ for accompanying a choir
chan·cel·ry \-səlrē\ *archaic var of* CHANCELLERY
chancels *pl of* CHANCEL
chancel table *n* **:** a communion table
chance·man \'=,man\ *n, pl* **chancemen :** a regular member of certain police forces who does only auxiliary or emergency police duty
chance–med·ley \'=;medlē\ *n* [AF *chance medlée* mingled chance, fr. MF *chance* + *medlée,* fem. of *medlé,* past part. of *medler* to mix, mingle — more at CHANCE, MEDDLE] **1 a :** the killing of another in self-defense in a sudden and unpremeditated encounter **b :** any accidental homicide in a sudden encounter where the killer is partly at fault but where there was no premeditation or evil intent — see CHAUD-MEDLEY **2 :** HAPHAZARDNESS ⟨abandoning himself to the *chance-medley* of carnival revelry⟩
chance–met \'=;=\ *adj* **:** having met or been met with by chance
chance process \'chan(t)s-, -aa-,-ai-,-á-\ *n, usu cap C* [after Thomas M. *Chance* b1887 Am. mining engineer] **:** a method of cleaning coal by using a fluid mixture of sand and water which floats off a clean coal product but allows slate and other impurities to sink
¹chan·cer \-sə(r)\ *vt* -ED/-ING/-S [prob. back-formation fr. *chancery*] **:** ABATE, REDUCE, TAX, ADJUST ⟨~ a bill of costs⟩ ⟨~ an account⟩ **:** make an equitable settlement of (an obligation)
²chanc·er \"\ *n* -s [¹*chance* + *-er*] *Africa* **:** a transient job seeker from another country intent on quick profit
chance–ridden \'=;==\ *adj* **:** ruled by chance
¹chan·cery \'chan(t)s(ə)rē, -aan-,-ain-,-án-, -ri\ *n* -ES [ME *chancerie,* alter. of *chancellerie* chancellery] **1 a** *usu cap* **:** a former high court having jurisdiction in England and Wales over causes in equity and various common-law functions and now forming the Chancery Division of the High Court of Justice with jurisdiction over causes in equity **b :** a court of equity in the American judicial system **c :** the principles and practice of judicial administration of cases on grounds of conscience and equity where strict law cannot afford relief **d** *obs* **:** a judicial adjustment (as a curtailment) on grounds of equitability of a claim, bond, or similar matter of dispute **2 :** a record office orig. for issuance and preservation of a sovereign's diplomas, charters, and bulls and later for the collection, arrangement, and safekeeping of public archives and ecclesiastical, legal, or diplomatic proceedings ⟨the papal ~⟩ ⟨organize a ~ for a consulate⟩ ⟨the various *chanceries* of the orders of knighthood —F.J.Grant⟩ **3 a :** a chancellor's court or office or the building in which he has his office **b :** an office or department of the Roman curia now charged mainly with the sending of bulls for consistorial benefices and new dioceses **c :** the office in which the business of a diocese is transacted and recorded **d :** the office of a foreign embassy **:** CHANCELLERY 3 **4 :** a style of cursive handwriting used by papal secretaries from the middle of the 15th century and imitated in early italic type **5 :** a wrestling hold that imprisons the head or encircles the neck **:** STRANGLEHOLD — **in chancery 1 :** in litigation in a court of chancery; *also* **:** under the superintendence of the lord chancellor ⟨a ward *in chancery*⟩ **2 :** caught in a chancery hold in boxing or wrestling **3 :** in an inextricable predicament
²chancery *vt* -ED/-ING/-ES *obs* **:** CHANCER
chances *pl of* CHANCE, *pres 3d sing of* CHANCE
chance·wise \'=,=\ *adv* **:** by chance **:** in a random manner
chan·chi·to \chän'chēd·(,)ō\ *n* -s [AmerSp, dim. of *chancho* pig] **:** a small black-banded yellow cichlid fish (*Cichlasoma facetum*) of the Plata river that is often kept in an aquarium
chanc·i·ly \'chan(t)sələ̇, -aan-,-ain-,-án-, -li\ *adv* [*chancy* + *-ly*] **:** without avoiding chance perils **:** HAZARDOUSLY, RISKILY, VENTURESOMELY
chanc·i·ness \-sēnəs, -in-\ *n* -ES **:** uncertainty or risk due to chance **:** FORTUITOUSNESS
chancing *adj* **:** relying on or inviting the risks of chance
chan·co \'chaŋ(,)kō, -äŋ-\ *n* -s [Lepcha *chaṅk'u* wolf] **:** an Asiatic wolf closely related to or possibly a variety of the common wolf
chan·cre \'shaŋkə(r), -aiŋ-\ *n* -s [F, chancre, canker, cancer, fr. L *cancer* — more at CANCER] **:** the primary sore or ulcer formed at the site of entry of an infecting organism in some diseases (as tularemia); *specif* **:** the initial lesion of syphilis
chan·cri·form \'shaŋkrə,fȯrm\ *adj* [ISV *chancre* + *-i-* + *-form;* prob. orig. formed as F *chancriforme*] **:** resembling a chancre
chan·croid \'shaŋ,krȯid\ *n* -s [F *chancroïde,* fr. *chancre* + *-oïde* -oid] **:** a venereal sore resembling a chancre in its seat and some external characters but differing from it in being the starting point of a purely local process and never a systemic disease and in being caused by a different microorganism (*Hemophilus ducreyi*) — called also *soft chancre* — **chan·croi·dal** \(')=;krȯid³l\ *adj*
chan·crous \'shaŋkrəs, -aiŋ-\ *adj* [F *chancreux,* fr. MF, fr. *chancre* + *-eux* -ous] **:** of the nature of a chancre **:** having chancres
chancy *also* **chanc·ey** \'chan(t)sē, -aan-,-ain-,-án-, -si\ *adj* **chancier; chanciest** [¹*chance* + *-y*] **1** *Scot* **:** bringing good luck **:** AUSPICIOUS — often used with a negative ⟨whistling maidens and crawing hens were ne'er very ~ —*Henderson's Scottish Proverbs*⟩ **2 a :** marked by uncertainty of outcome or prospect **:** open to unpredictable developments or contingencies or to eventualities entirely subject to chance ⟨a ~ appeal, at best, to the shifting and unguessable sympathies of their readers —Robert Morse⟩ **b :** showing erratic inconsistent traits **:** unpredictable or capricious in decisions and actions **:** given to taking chances ⟨she was a brilliant, if ~ player —Rose Macaulay⟩ **c :** attended with doubtful or adverse chances **:** RISKY, HAZARDOUS ⟨virgin country, untamed forest, no road but a ~ track —Thomas Wood †1950⟩ **syn** see RANDOM
chan·da·la \(,)chən'dälə\ *n* -s [Skt *caṇḍāla*] **:** an Indian of low caste **:** OUTCAST, UNTOUCHABLE; *esp* **:** the son of a Sudra by a Brahman woman
chan·de·lier \,shandə'li(ə)r, -aan-, -iə *sometimes* ;ch-\ *n* -s [F, lit., candlestick, modif. of L *candelabrum* — more at CANDELABRUM] **:** a lighting fixture suspended from the ceiling and having two or more usu. upcurving arms bearing lights, orig. candles, or two or more pendent lights

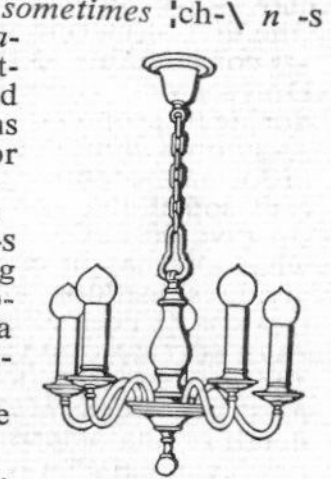
chandelier

chandelier tree *n* **:** CANDELABRUM TREE
¹chan·delle \(')shan;del, -än;-, -äⁿ;-\ *n* -s [F, lit., candle] **:** an abrupt climbing turn of an airplane in which the momentum of the plane is used to attain a higher rate of climb than would be possible in unaccelerated flight
²chandelle \"\ *vi* -ED/-ING/-S **:** to execute a chandelle
chan·dler \'chandlə(r), -aan-,-án-, *rap.* -nl-\ *n* -s [ME *chandeler,* fr. MF *chandelier,* fr. OF, fr. *chandelle* candle, fr. L *candela* — more at CANDLE] **1 :** a maker or seller of tallow or wax candles and usu. soap **2 :** a retail dealer in provisions and usu. supplies, equipment, and knickknacks esp. of a specified kind ⟨a chart of tides obtainable from any yacht ~⟩ ⟨a series of cheap lodgings, laundries, lunches, tattoo parlors, and small trinket ~*s* —Christopher Morley⟩ — compare CORN CHANDLER, SHIP CHANDLER
chan·dler–chaft·ed \-;chaftəd\ *adj* [Sc *chandler* candlestick, lantern (fr. ME *chandeler* candlestick, fr. MF *chandelier*) + *chaft* + E *-ed* — more at CHANDELIER] *Scot* **:** LANTERN JAWED
chan·dler·ess \-lərəs\ *n* -ES **:** a female chandler
chan·dler·ing \-ləriŋ\ *or* **chan·dling** \-liŋ\ *n* -s **:** the business of a chandler
chan·dlery \-lərē, -ri\ *n* -ES [*chandler* + *-y*] **1 :** a place where candles are kept **2 :** the business of a chandler **3 :** commodities sold by a chandler — often used in pl.
chan·du *also* **chan·doo** \'chən(,)dü\ *n* -s [Hindi *caṇḍū*] **:** prepared opium in India and China
chan·dul \'chənd³l, -än-\ *n* -s [origin unknown] **:** a fiber derived from the inner bark of the upas tree (*Antiaris toxicaria*) used for making sacking
cha·né \'chä(,)nā, *in sense 1* " *or* 'shänə\ *n, pl* **chané** *or* **chanés** *usu cap* [Sp & Pg, of AmerInd origin] **1 :** ²GUANÁ **2 a :** an Arawakan people of the Paraná river valley **b :** a member of such people **3 :** the language of the Chané people
chaneabal *usu cap, var of* CHAÑABAL
chanfron *var of* CHAMFRON
¹chang \'chaŋ\ *n* -s [imit.] *dial Brit* **:** a loud confused noise (as of talk or complaint) **:** UPROAR
²chang \'chaŋ, -äŋ\ *n* -s [Tibetan *chaṅ* beer, wine] **:** a Tibetan beer made from malted barley or rice
³chang \"\ *n, pl* **chang** *or* **changs** *usu cap* **1 :** a Naga people in the southern part of the Naga hills in the India-Burma frontier region **2 :** a member of the Chang people
chan·ga \'chaŋgə, -äŋ-\ *n* -s [AmerSp] **:** a large brown mole cricket (*Scapteriscus vicinus*) native to So. America but now widely distributed in the West Indies and southeastern U. S. where it is a destructive pest of many cultivated crops, feeding on crowns and stems and damaging roots by its burrowing
chang·chun \'chäŋ;chün, -ún\ *adj, usu cap* [fr. *Changchun,* Manchuria] **:** of or from Changchun, a city of Manchuria **:** of the kind or style prevalent in Changchun
¹change \'chānj\ *vb* -ED/-ING/-S [ME *changen,* fr. OF *changier,* fr. L *cambiare* to exchange, of Celt origin; akin to OIr *camm* crooked; akin to Gk *skambos* crooked and prob. to Sw *skimpa* to hop, Lith *kibti* to hook on] *vt* **1 :** to make different: **a :** to make different in some particular but short of conversion into something else **:** ALTER, MODIFY ⟨on advice of counsel she never bothered to ~ the will —Alan Hynd⟩ ⟨can the Ethiopian ~ his skin, or the leopard his spots —Jer 13: 23 (AV)⟩ ⟨sorrow has *changed* him in mental attitude⟩ **b :** to make over to a radically different form, composition, state, or disposition **:** TRANSFORM, CONVERT ⟨the airplane simply ~*s* the map of a territory as vast and as little built up as the Congo —Tom Marvel⟩ ⟨you can't ~ human nature⟩ ⟨he is not moved . . . he is not *changed* by his experience —Herbert Read⟩; *specif* **:** to lead (a person) to religious conversion **c :** to dispose of or give up toward the substituting of something roughly equivalent — used with *into* ⟨she had to ~ the family jewels into land⟩ ⟨~ a monarchy into a republic⟩ **d :** to give a different position, status, course, or direction to ⟨*changing* residence from Switzerland to Portugal⟩ ⟨the electrolytic refining process that was to ~ aluminum from a scientific curiosity to a widely used material —*Amer. Guide Series: Ark.*⟩ ⟨he seldom ~*s* his itinerary⟩ ⟨*changed* our thinking about parole⟩ **e :** to shift or transfer in position — used with *to* ⟨Netta *changed* her weight from one foot to the other —Stuart Cloete⟩ ⟨he was *changed* from KP to guard duty⟩ **f :** to give a contrary character or trend to **:** REVERSE ⟨~ one's vote⟩ ⟨*changed* his stand⟩ ⟨abruptly *changing* his policy⟩ **g :** CASTRATE, SPAY ⟨our cat has been *changed*⟩ **2 :** to substitute another or others in place of (something under consideration) **:** make substitution for or among: **a :** to replace with another or others of the same kind or class **:** remove, discard, or withdraw and replace with another ⟨*changing* the school's name⟩ ⟨the movie made of the novel ~*s* the ending⟩ ⟨let's ~ the subject⟩ ⟨intended for the

law, he *changed* plans before graduation⟩ ⟨frequently *changing* hands in turning the crank⟩ **b** : to switch to another ⟨he *changed* his seat⟩ ⟨official permission to ~ occupation⟩ ⟨the right to hold or ~ faith⟩ ⟨not till you ~ your attitude⟩ ; make a shift from one to another of two ⟨forced to ~ planes by bad weather⟩ ⟨one does not ~ parties as he ~s tailors⟩ ⟨weakly *changing* sides in the argument⟩ **c** : to give or receive an equivalent sum in bank notes or coins of other (as smaller) denomination or of a different national currency in return for ⟨~ a 20-dollar bill⟩ **d** : to undergo a loss or modification of (some property or aspect) ⟨we arrived in time to find the foliage rapidly *changing* color⟩ ⟨when confronted with the photograph the accused *changed* countenance⟩ **e** : to put a fresh covering on to replace that or those in use (as a diaper on a baby, garments on a bed patient, covers on a bed) **3 a** : to give (something) to another, taking in return something corresponding : give and receive reciprocally : INTERCHANGE — now used chiefly in colloquial applications ⟨wilt thou ~ fathers? I will give thee mine —Shak.⟩ ⟨this chamber ~ for one more holy —E.A.Poe⟩ ⟨I wouldn't ~ places with him⟩ ⟨let's ~ seats⟩ ⟨he and I *changed* shifts so he could attend his son's graduation⟩ **b** : to give up, taking in return something of a different kind : EXCHANGE, TRADE — used with *for* ⟨'tis a fault I will not ~ for your best virtues —Shak.⟩ ⟨for a new name . . . to ~ the honors of abandoned Rome —P.B.Shelley⟩ ⟨~ a uniform for mufti⟩ ⟨unwilling to ~ independence for the comforts of wealth⟩ ~ *vi* **1** : to become different in one or more respects without becoming something else : **a** : to lose or to acquire some characteristic, property, or tendency : ALTER ⟨the *changing* foliage of autumn⟩ ⟨with the threat of war the popular mood *changed*⟩ ⟨racial relations seem to be *changing* for the better⟩ **b** (1) : to pass from one form, appearance, position, state, or stage to another : SHIFT ⟨the country has survived *changing* governments⟩ ⟨wait till the light ~s⟩ ⟨*changing* world conditions⟩ ⟨fashions ~ like the weather⟩ (2) *obs* : to pale or blush ⟨how they ~! Their cheeks are paper —Shak.⟩ **c** : to increase or decrease ⟨prices ~ overnight⟩ **d** : to adopt different customs, methods, attitudes ⟨people don't like to ~ —J.P.Blank⟩; *specif* : to experience a religious conversion **e** *of the moon* : to pass from one phase to another; *specif* : to pass through the phase of new moon **f** *chiefly dial* : to turn sour : become tainted **g** : to shift one's means of conveyance : TRANSFER ⟨there we *changed* to a local train⟩ **h** *of the voice* : to shift to lower register : BREAK **i** *Brit* : to shift gears **2** : to turn into or become something materially different from before : **a** : to undergo transformation or conversion — used with *into* ⟨but the truth is that after a certain point quantity of money does indeed ~ into a quality of personality —Lionel Trilling⟩ **b** : to pass over from one character or state : undergo transition — used with *to* ⟨winter *changed* to spring⟩ ⟨the terrain *changed* gradually from rolling farm land to rugged mining country⟩ ⟨the chilly sensations ~ to discomfort and the acuity of touch sensations and muscular reactions are dulled —H.G. Armstrong⟩ **c** : to undergo substantial substitution or replacement or to be wholly replaced ⟨external circumstances may ~ catastrophically, as during a war —Aldous Huxley⟩ ⟨the diet of marine species is generally very varied, and often ~s considerably as the animals grow older and larger —W.H. Dowdeswell⟩ ⟨how the objects of a war may ~ completely during its progress —Zechariah Chafee⟩ **3** : to disrobe and rearray oneself more suitably esp. in clothes suitable for a social or formal occasion ⟨prepared to ~ for dinner⟩ **4 a** *obs* : to accept something else in return ⟨but might I of Jove's nectar sip I would not ~ for thine —Ben Jonson⟩ **b** *obs* : to give up what one has in exchange— used with *for* **c** : to engage in giving something and receiving something in return : EXCHANGE ⟨I need a lighter ax; I'll ~ with you⟩

syn ALTER, MODIFY, VARY: CHANGE is wide in use and meaning and may be used in place of any of the others in this set on most occasions. ALTER may suggest changes only in a single detail or characteristic, without an ensuing loss of identity or new essential character ⟨he looked . . . with clouded eyes and with an *altered* manner of breathing —Charles Dickens⟩ ⟨Tockwotton House, the grounds of which, somewhat *altered* with the passing years, now form Tockwotton Park —*Amer. Guide Series: R. I.*⟩ MODIFY may indicate a change away from an extreme or a minor change made in the interest of adapting to a new use, function, or significance ⟨Boner, refusing to *modify* his politics, found all doors closed to him in his own state —Tremaine McDowell⟩ ⟨all of these have their respiratory organs *modified* to suit their mode of respiration —Joyce Allan⟩ VARY stresses a breaking away from sameness, from identity, duplication, exact repetition ⟨this is not a proceeding which may be *varied* . . . but is a precise course accurately marked out by law and is to be strictly preserved —John Marshall⟩ ⟨tasks may be *varied* slightly, as when a worker in a cigarette factory is shifted from the job of feeding tobacco into a machine to the job of packing and weighing —Aldous Huxley⟩ — **change color** : to undergo a blanching or a diffusion of color in one's face usu. revealing a sudden emotion (as pallor from fear, a blush of shame or embarrassment, or a flush of anger) — **change ends** *of a hunting dog* : to reverse direction in scent-following — **change gears** *Brit* : to shift gears — **change hands** : to pass from the possession of one person or owner to another or from one of two contesting teams or armies to the other — **change one's feet** *Scot* : to put on other shoes or other shoes and stockings — **change step** : to reverse the order in which the feet are advanced in walking esp. by bringing one foot almost up to the other and then stepping off with the foot that is in advance — **change the leg** *of a horse* : to change gait

2change \"\ *n* -s [ME, fr. OF, fr. *changier*, v. — more at 1CHANGE] **1** : the action of making something different in form, quality, or state : the fact of becoming different : introduction of novelty ⟨~ consists in realizing a potentiality that is not real already —W.T.Harris⟩ ⟨things and processes are the sort of entities of which ~ is predicable —Arthur Pap⟩ ⟨in other words, ~ is concomitant variation in time and some other respect —Nelson Goodman⟩ — used often without implication as to bettering or worsening and often with an implication of undirection or haphazardness **2 a** : an instance of making or becoming different in some particular : a departure from a norm : a deviation from established character, sequence, or condition : a divergence from uniformity or constancy in any quality, quantity, or degree : ALTERATION, MODIFICATION, VARIATION, MUTATION ⟨but in the daily routine of their business there was little ~ —Thomas Hardy⟩ ⟨for while there have been several clear and distinct ~s in the pattern, the essence of the university tradition has through all the years remained constant —J.B.Conant⟩ ⟨quite clearly, there is no ~ in phenomenal any more than in physical time —Nelson Goodman⟩ **b** : a passing from one state to another marked by radically different makeup, character, or operation, whether by sudden mutation or gradually by evolution : TRANSFORMATION, CONVERSION ⟨there is always the danger that people who are impatient when ~ comes too slowly will attempt violent solutions —P.E.James⟩ ⟨the semantics of functional ~⟩ ⟨since the beginning of the 20th century, however, the time span of social ~ is shorter than a human life —Maurice Graney⟩ ⟨another kind of evidence for the ubiquitousness of ~ in culture can be drawn from our own everyday experience as well as from nonliterate societies —M.J.Herskovits⟩ **c** : a shift in relation to surroundings (as to a different place, situation, course level) ⟨prices are subject to ~ without notice⟩ **d** : a switch to contrasting character or trend : REVERSAL **e** : CHANGE OF LIFE **f** *obs* : INCONSTANCY ⟨it is the woman's part . . . ambitions, covetings, ~ of prides, disdain, nice longing, slanders, mutability . . . for even to vice they are not constant —Shak.⟩ **g** : a religious or moral conversion **h** : any step in the manufacture of soap by boiling including drawing off and addition of liquid (as lye or brine) ⟨strong ~⟩ ⟨salt ~⟩ **3** : the action of replacing something with something else of the same kind or with something that serves as a substitute : SUBSTITUTION ⟨beware of sudden ~ in any great point of diet —Francis Bacon⟩ ⟨but ~ of air changes not the mind —John Milton⟩: **a** : a replacing of some agent, method, means, material, or other subject of regard with a different one ⟨wore out four ~s of horses as he galloped all night —Dorothy C. Fisher⟩ ⟨striking for ~s in working conditions⟩ **b** : a shift from some mode of personal action or disposition or matter of concern to a different one ⟨American expansion into the Pacific and into the Caribbean, however, represented a ~ in American thinking —Carol L. Thompson⟩ **c** (1) : the passage of the moon from one monthly revolution to another (2) : the coming of the new moon (3) : the passage of the moon from one phase to another (as crescent to quarter) **d** : a spare or reserve outfit of clothing or article of wear to replace one in use; *also* : the act of making a transfer from one of these to the other ⟨management supplies each worker with three ~s a week⟩ ⟨time for a quick ~ before dinner⟩ **e** : a succeeding or superseding of some activity, condition, circumstance, or other phenomenon or relationship by a different one ⟨on the occasion of her recent tour it was, for a ~, a beautiful summer evening —G.W.Talbot⟩ **f** : a transfer from one point to another in time, space, or measure ⟨a ~ of venue to an adjoining county⟩ ⟨sudden ~s of temperature⟩ **g** : a shift of weight from one foot to the other in dancing **4 a** *obs* : reciprocal giving and receiving : EXCHANGE **b** *Brit* : something that is due or obtained in return (as by way of retaliation, by way of advantage over another, or by way of desired cooperation or disclosure) **5** *Brit* : a place where merchants, brokers, bankers meet to transact business — used with a prefixed apostrophe as if an abbreviation of *exchange* ⟨with sensational press campaigns and stocks and shares on '*change* —William Irvine⟩ **6 a** : the equivalent in money of small denominations of a sum of money in higher denominations or the equivalent in money of one currency of a sum in another currency ⟨to get ~ at a bank to facilitate cash sales⟩ ⟨supplying ~ for a tourist's dollars⟩ **b** : money returned to one making a payment consisting of the difference between the amount of money given in payment and the amount due ⟨to receive 11 cents in ~⟩ ⟨a cashier quick at making ~⟩ **c** : coins esp. of low denominations ⟨jingling a pocketful of ~⟩ **d** *slang* : money in hand : DOUGH **7** : any order in which a set of bells is struck in change ringing properly other than that of the diatonic scale but loosely including it ⟨in ringing the ~s a bell may shift one place in position or keep its position⟩ **8 a** (1) : FIGURE 13a (2) *in square dancing* : a dancing of the figure around the set **b** : CALL 14

3change \"\ *adj* [1*change*] *archaic* : serving or held ready to serve as a substitute

change·abil·i·ty \ˌchānjəˈbilədˌē, -ətē, -i\ *n* [ME *changeabilite*, fr. *changeabil, changeable* changeable + *-ite* -ity] : the capacity of being changeable or changed : CHANGEABLENESS

change·able \ˈchānjəbəl\ *adj* [ME, fr. MF, fr. OF, fr. *changier* to change + *-able*] **1** : liable to change; *specif* : having a marked tendency to change esp. as a property (as in form, quality, action) : fluctuating in direction or tendency : MUTABLE, VARIABLE **2** : capable of being changed : subject to change : ALTERABLE ⟨a provision ~ at will⟩ **3** : given or prone to change esp. as a characteristic : erratic in disposition : CAPRICIOUS, FICKLE, INCONSTANT, MERCURIAL, UNSTABLE **4** : varying in color with the change of light or point of view; *specif* : having such a color effect produced in certain fabrics (as taffeta) by weaving contrasting colors in warp and weft

change·able·ness \-nəs\ *n* -ES [ME *changeablenesse*, fr. *changeable* + *-nesse* -ness] : the quality or state of being changeable

change·ably \-əblē, -li\ *adv* [ME, alternately, fr. *changeable* + *-ly*] **1** *obs* : in exchange **2** *obs* : in alternation **3** *archaic* : with the possibility of changing or being changed ⟨events scheduled ~ depending on weather conditions⟩ **4** : with frequent changing or shifting : VARIABLY, INCONSTANTLY ⟨the instrument needle flicking ~⟩ ⟨~ disposed on successive ballots⟩ **5** : with changing shades or hues ⟨feathers on the drake's neck glinting ~⟩

change·about \ˈ=,=,=\ *n* -s [2*change* + *about*, adv.] : a reversal esp. in position or direction

change bowler *n* [3*change*] : a relief bowler in cricket

changed *past of* CHANGE

change·ful \-fəl\ *adj* : given to or full of frequent changes — **change·ful·ly** \-fəlē\ *adv*

change gear *n* **1** : a gear by means of which the speed of a mechanism or of a vehicle may be changed while the speed of its driving agent is constant **2** : any of a set of interchangeable gears for varying the speed ratio between two shafts (as on a screw-cutting lathe) — called also *change wheel*

change house *n* [prob. so called fr. its original use as a station where horses were changed] **1** *Scot* : a small inn or alehouse **2** : a locker building in which workers may wash and change their clothes — called also *dryhouse*

change key *n* : a key that operates only one lock of a master-keyed lock system

change·less \ləs\ *adj* : that does not change : UNCHANGING, CONSTANT — **change·less·ly** *adv* — **change·less·ness** *n* -ES

1change·ling \ˈchānjliŋ, -lēŋ\ *n* -s [1*change* + *-ling*] **1** *archaic* : one that wavers : one marked by fickleness or inconstancy; *esp* : TRAITOR, TURNCOAT **2 a** *obs* : a fraudulent substitute surreptitiously left in place of a valued object or personage **b** (1) : a child left in place of another child carried away surreptitiously in early infancy (as a lowborn substitute for one of noble birth) (2) *in folk tradition* : a deformed or weak-witted offspring of fairies or elves substituted by them surreptitiously for a comely human child — called also *elf child* **3** *archaic* : IMBECILE **4** : COLOR CHANGELING

2changeling \"\ *adj* **1** *archaic* : WAVERING, INCONSTANT **2** : markedly altered from an original or native condition ⟨his return to his family in Bombay . . ., half a stranger in dress and speech, wholly ~ in his un-Indian attitudes —John Woodburn⟩

changemaker \ˈ=,==\ *n* [2*change* (money) + *maker*] : a device that mechanically supplies change in coins of desired denominations upon the operation of the proper levers or keys

change·ment \-mənt\ *n* -s [MF, fr. *changier* to change + *-ment* — more at CHANGE] *archaic* : CHANGE 1, 2, 3

change·ment de pied \shäⁿzhmäⁿtpyā\ *n, pl* **changements de pied** \"\ [F, lit., change of foot] *ballet dancing* : a jump starting and ending with the feet crossed but with their positions interchanged

change note *n* [2*change* (money)] : a note of irregular issue in a low denomination serviceable as small change locally and redeemable in regular notes of larger denominations

change-of-day line *n* : DATELINE 2

change of edge : a skating figure or maneuver in which the skater shifts from one edge of the blade to the other — compare SERPENTINE

change off *vi* **1** : to alternate with another at performing an act **2** : to alternate between two different acts or instruments or between an action and a rest period

change of heart : a full reversal in position or attitude

change of life **1** : CLIMACTERIUM **2** : MENOPAUSE

change of pace **1** : an interruption of continuity by a sudden and usu. temporary shift to a sharply different manner of action (as for relief from monotony) ⟨he found the work tedious, so . . . for a *change of pace*, he joined the army —John Kobler⟩ **2** : a slow pitch in baseball that is thrown for deception with the same motion as a fast ball — called also *change-up*

change of voice : the gradual change in quality and pitch of voice occurring in boys about the age of puberty

change over *vt* : to convert to a different purpose or system or from use of one method or technique to another ⟨*change over* a plant to production of jet engines⟩ ~ *vi* : to make a transfer, abrupt transition, or conversion ⟨the industry *changed over* from steam to electricity⟩

change·over \ˈ=,==\ *n* -s [*change over*] **1** : the action of changing over ⟨the point of ~ from low to high pressure⟩ **2** : an instance of changing over: **a** : a shift from one operation, one set of equipment or facilities, or one production model to another **b** : a conversion to a different system, program, or method **c** : a change to a different group of personnel **3** : a transition from one set of economic or social conditions or cultural standards or ideals to another **4** : the changing from one projector to another between reels during the continuous screening of a motion picture or program of motion pictures

change pocket *n* [2*change* (money)] : a small pocket often within a larger pocket (as in a woman's purse or a man's jacket) for holding small change

chang·er \ˈchānjə(r)\ *n* -s [ME *changere*, alter. (*influenced by* ME *-ere* -er) of *changeour*, fr. MF *changeor* money changer, fr. *changier* to change + *-eor* -or] : one that changes: as **a** : one that changes or alters the form of something **b** : one that exchanges one thing for another; *esp* : RECORD CHANGER **c** *obs* : MONEY CHANGER **d** : one that wavers; *esp* : one inconstant in his views

change ringer *n* : one skilled at change ringing

change ringing *n* : the art or practice of ringing a set of tuned bells in continually varying order in such a way as to avoid (1) shifting the place of any one bell in the striking order by more than one step at each change and (2) repeating any order before completing the whole series — used in strict terminology of the ringing of hung tower bells by a team with one man assigned to each bell; called also *peal ringing;* see PEAL

PLAIN HUNTING | GRANDSIRE WITH BOB | TREBLE BOB | GRANDSIRE | GRANDSIRE WITH SINGLE

change ringing: diagram showing the order in which the bells (indicated by numbers) are struck in successive changes, beginning in rounds (at R), each horizontal row of dots representing a change

changeroom \ˈ=,=\ *n* : a room suitable for changing one's clothes

changes *pres 3d sing of* CHANGE, *pl of* CHANGE

change three *n* : a three-lobed fancy skating figure consisting of a right forward outside-to-inside change of edge with an inside three, a left outside-to-inside change of edge followed by an inside back three

change-up \ˈ=,=\ *n* -s : CHANGE OF PACE 2 ⟨a fast ball that moves, a fine slider and a good *change-up* —Arthur & Milton Richman⟩

change wheel *n* : CHANGE GEAR 2

changing *pres part of* CHANGE

changing bag *n* : a lighttight bag with sleeves to fit the arms in which procedures such as loading film holders may be carried out without a darkroom

changing box *n* : a holder for a number of sheet films or plates that can be attached to a camera and permits exposure in turn

changing note *or* **changing tone** *n* **1** : an accented passing note or tone in old strict musical counterpoint **2** : a usu. unaccented nonharmonic note or tone that resolves to its neighboring chord tone after touching an intervening tone typically a third distant : CAMBIATA — compare ESCAPE NOTE

chan·go \ˈchäŋ(ˌ)gō, -aŋ-\ *n, pl* **chango** *or* **changos** *usu cap* [Sp, of AmerInd origin] **1 a** : an extinct people of the north Chilean coast **b** : a member of such people **2** : the language of the Chango people

chan·go·an \-ˌgōən\ *n* -s *usu cap* [Sp *chango* (of AmerInd origin) + E *-an*] : a language family consisting of Chango

changs *pl of* CHANG

chang·sha \ˈchäŋˈshä\ *adj, usu cap* [fr. *Changsha*, China] : of or from the city of Changsha, China : of the kind or style prevalent in Changsha

ch'ang shan \ˈchäŋˈshän\ *n* -s [prob. fr. Chin] : a shrub (*Dichroa febrifuga*) of the family Saxifragaceae found in China, northeastern India, Java, and the Philippines, with opposite serrate leaves, paniculate blue flowers and blue fruits, and roots that have long been used by the Chinese in the manufacture of a home remedy for malaria

chan·i·dae \ˈkanəˌdē\ *n pl, cap* [NL, fr. *Chanos*, type genus (fr. Gk *chanos* mouth) + NL *-idae*] : a family of rather large brilliant silvery toothless fishes related to the herrings and including among recent forms only a milkfish (*Chanos chanos*)

ch'an·ism \ˈchäˌnizəm\ *n* -s *usu cap* [2*ch'an* + *-ism*] : Ch'an Buddhism

ch'an·ist \-ˌnəst\ *n* -s *usu cap* [2*ch'an* + *-ist*] : an adherent of the Ch'an school of Buddhism

1chank \ˈchaŋk, -ȯ-,-ä-\ *vb* -ED/-ING/-S [prob. alter of 1*champ*] *dial* : chew noisily : CHAMP

2chank \ˈchaŋk\ *also* **chank shell** *n* -s [Skt *śaṅkha* — more at CONCH] : any of a family (Xancidae) of tropical heavy-shelled pear-shaped gastropod mollusks; *esp* : a species (*Xancus pyrum*) commonly appearing in Hindu religious pictures and writings

chank·ings \ˈchaŋkənz, -ōŋ-,-äŋ-, -kiŋz\ *n pl* [pl. of *chanking*, gerund of 1*chank*] *dial* : scraps or rejected parts of fruit or nuts (as chewed pieces or parings)

1chan·nel \ˈchanᵊl\ *n* -s [ME *chanel*, fr. OF, fr. L *canalis* pipe, channel — more at CANAL] **1 a** : the hollow bed where a natural body or stream of water runs or may run **b** : the deeper part of a moving body of water (as a river, harbor, or strait) where the main current flows or which affords the best passage **c** : a strait or narrow sea between two close land masses ⟨the English *Channel*⟩ ⟨the Mozambique *Channel*⟩ **d** : a means or instrumentality aiding communication or expression or commercial exchange ⟨alongside the familiar press, radio, and film media . . . other ~s have multiplied —E.D.Canham⟩ **e channels** *pl* : a fixed, accustomed, or official course of communication or transmission of information or of commercial interchange ⟨submitting material to the Defense Department without going through prescribed . . . Army ~s —*N.Y.Times*⟩ **f** : a person through whom information is transmitted ⟨he . . . appears to have been one of Beckford's ~s for communication with Courtenay —*Times Lit. Supp.*⟩ **g** : a way, course, or direction of thought or action ⟨the accident which directed my curiosity originally into this ~ —Charles Lamb⟩; *specif* : a restricted path of movement (as of traffic directed between islands at an intersection) **h** : RIVER 4 **i** : a band of frequencies of sufficient width for a single radio or television communication being as little as a few cycles per second wide for telegraphy or as great as several megacycles wide for television **j** : the mechanism providing a single path in multiple-path systems for simultaneously and separately recording or transmitting sounds from more than one source; *also* : the complete system from microphone to recorder in single-path systems **2 a** : an esp. tubular enclosed passage : CONDUIT, PIPE, DUCT ⟨the poison ~ in a snake's fangs⟩ **b** : any of the chambers holding identical matrices in a circulating-matrix typesetting machine **3** : a long gutter, groove, or furrow: as **a** : a street or road gutter **b** : CANAL 4 **c** : a flute in a column **d** : a groove cut along the line where rock is to be split **e** : a slanting groove cut around the edge of an outsole of a shoe on the grain surface for embedding stitches; *also* : one of two parallel grooves cut around the edge of an insole on the flesh surface forming a ridge to which the welt is sewed **f** : the track for the rope in a tackle block **g** : a metal beam or strip having a U-shaped section **syn** see MEAN

2channel \"\ *vb* **channeled** *or* **channelled**; **channeled** *or* **channelled**; **channeling** *or* **channelling**; **channels** *vt* **1 a** : to form, cut, or wear a channel in ⟨spring freshets may ~ the fields⟩ ⟨the river ~*ed* a new course⟩ **b** : to incise with a series of parallel flutes : GROOVE ⟨~ a chair leg⟩ **c** : to lower (an automobile body) by rebuilding with channels which fit around the frame rails — compare 1CHOP *vt* 4 **2** : to traverse by or as if by channels ⟨moors ~*ed* by pastoral valleys⟩ **3 a** : to send or convey through or as if through a channel ⟨~ materials and labor into housing⟩; *specif* : to direct through or into a fixed or official course **b** : to direct (feelings or human drives) into particular channels of behavior or action ⟨~ the aggressive impulses of adolescents into sports activity⟩ **4 :** to confine in or as if in a channel ⟨troops *~ed* in a narrow road with blocks at either end⟩ **5 :** to shape or stamp (as a metal strip) into a form having a U-shaped section ~ *vi* **1 :** to move in or as if in a channel ⟨the molten metal *~s* into a belt of troughs⟩ **2 :** to have a channel cut in ⟨gear lubricants may congeal and ~ in cold weather⟩

³channel \"\ *n* -s [alter. of *chainwale*] **:** one of the flat ledges of heavy plank or metal to which the chain plates are fastened and which are bolted edgewise to the outside of a ship, serving to increase the spread of the shrouds and carry them clear of the bulwarks

⁴channel \"\ *adj* [¹*channel*] **:** CHANNELED ⟨~ molding⟩

channel-back *adj* **:** having deep vertical channels in the back-rest — used of an upholstered chair

channel bass \-ˌbas, -aa(ə)s,-ais\ *n* **:** a large coppery drum (*Sciaenops ocellatus*) with a black spot at the base of the tail that is an outstanding game fish of the Atlantic coast of No. and So. America and is used as food when young — called also *red drum*

channelbill \'==,=\ *or* **channelbill cuckoo** *n* [so called fr. its grooved bill] **:** a large Australian cuckoo (*Scythrops novaehollandiae*)

channel black *n* [*channel* (*iron*)] **:** a fine carbon black obtained as soot by impingement of small natural-gas flames on a metal surface (as a channel iron) — called also *gas black*

channel-back chair

channel bone *n, now dial Eng* **:** CLAVICLE

channel cat *or* **channel catfish** *n* **:** any of several large catfishes (esp. of the genus *Ictalurus*) of deep fresh waters of interior No. America that are important food fishes of the Mississippi drainage and the Gulf states as **a :** a spotted cat (*I. lacustris punctatus*) **b :** BLUE CAT

channeled wrack *n* **:** a brown alga (*Pelvetia canaliculata*) every part of which is grooved on one side

chan·nel·er *or* **chan·nel·ler** \'chanᵊlə(r)\ *n* -s **:** one that cuts channels or grooves: as **a :** one who hand-feeds insoles or outsoles of shoes into a channeling machine **b :** one who operates a channeling machine in a mine or quarry

channel fever *n* [prob. fr. English *Channel*, strait between southern England & northern France] **:** an unusual excitement or restlessness common among a ship's crew when the ship nears port after a voyage

channel goose *n* **:** the common gannet

channeling *or* **channelling** *n* -s **1 :** a channel or a system of channels **:** GROOVING, FLUTING **2 :** channeled work (as a grooved architectural member)

channel iron *n* **:** ¹CHANNEL 3g

chan·nel·i·za·tion \ˌchanᵊlə'zāshən, -ˌī'z-\ *n* -s **1 :** the act or process of channeling **2 :** CHANNELING 1

chan·nel·ize \'chanᵊlˌīz\ *vb* -ED/-ING/-S **:** CHANNEL

channelized intersection *n* **:** a road intersection where raised or colored islands have been installed to direct vehicles or pedestrians into fixed channels

channel of distribution : the course taken by the title to goods from the point of origin or production to the point of consumption by an industrial or commercial user or by the ultimate consumer including all agencies that facilitate the transfer of title (as brokers) as well as those who actually take title to the goods (as wholesalers and retailers)

channel piloting *n* **:** piloting by nonmathematical methods (as by buoys, beacons, or landmarks) near shoal waters

channel pin *n* **:** a tapered metal plug with one or two grooves used to fasten one or two bond wires (as to a railroad rail)

channels *pl of* CHANNEL, *pres 3d sing of* CHANNEL

channel section *n* **:** a part of a structure composed of a channel iron — compare CHANNEL 3g

channel stone *also* **channel stane** *n* **1** *Scot* **:** CURLING STONE **2** *Scot* **:** CURLING

channelure *var of* CANNELURE

channelwale *n* [³*channel* + *wale*] **:** one of several strakes worked between the upper and lower deck ports in 2-decked ships and between the upper and middle deck ports in 3-decked ships to strengthen the topside

channelway \'==,=\ *n* **:** CHANNEL: as **a :** a crack, intergranular space, or other opening in rocks through which fluids or gases may pass **b :** a tunnel or other opening in a glacier through which water may flow

channel wing *n* **:** an airplane wing having an engine with a rear propeller mounted in a downward-curved semicylindrical section near the fuselage

chan·ner \'chanə(r)\ *vi* -ED/-ING/-S [ME *channeren*, prob. of imit. origin] *dial Brit* **:** to scold complainingly **:** MUTTER, GRUMBLE

cha·no·yu \ˌchänō'yü\ *n* -s [Jap, fr. *cha* tea (fr. Chin *ch'a²*) + *no* of + *yu* hot water — more at TEA] **:** a Japanese ceremony consisting of the serving and taking of tea in accordance with an elaborate ritual

chan·son \shäⁿsōⁿ\ *n, pl* **chansons** \-ōⁿ(z)\ [F, fr. L *cantion-, cantio* — more at CANZONE] **:** a lyric intended for singing **:** SONG; *specif* **:** a music-hall or cabaret song or recitative often French or in the French manner

chan·son de geste \-d(ə)zhest\ *n, pl* **chansons de geste** \", -ōⁿzdəzh-\ [F, lit., song of heroic deeds] **:** any of several Old French epic poems of the 11th to the 13th centuries about real or legendary events or exploits written orig. in assonant verse usu. of 10 or 12 syllables

chan·son·nette \ˌshäⁿsən'et; -än(t)sən-, -an(-\ *n* -s [F, fr. *chanson* + *-ette*] **:** a little song

chan·son·nier \ˌshäⁿsən'yā\ *n* -s [F, fr. *chanson*] **1 :** a writer or singer of chansons; *esp* **:** a cabaret singer **2 :** a collection of songs or of verses for singing

chanst \'chan(t)st\ *n* [by alter.] *dial* **:** CHANCE

¹chant \'chant, -aa(ə)-,-ai-,-à-\ *or archaic* **chaunt** \-ä-,-ȯ-,-à-\ *vb* -ED/-ING/-S [ME *chanten*, fr. MF *chanter*, fr. L *cantare*, fr. *cantus*, past part. of *canere*] *vi* **1 :** to make melodic sounds with the voice **:** SING, WARBLE, INTONE; *esp* **:** to sing a chant or something resembling a chant **2 :** to utter a statement in a monotonous tone esp. repetitively **:** recite monotonously or with insistent repetition ~ *vt* **1 :** to utter as in chanting **:** SING, WARBLE, INTONE **:** recite monotonously ⟨singers *. . . ~ed* some of the Psalms —K.S.Latourette⟩ ⟨the auctioneer *. . . ~ing* his peculiar singsong jargon —*Amer. Guide Series: Mo.*⟩ **2 :** to celebrate or praise in song or chant ⟨*~ing* the virtues of patriotism⟩ ⟨*~ing* one's love⟩

²chant \"\ *n* -s [F, fr. L *cantus*, fr. *cantus*, past part. of *canere* to sing; akin to OE *hana* rooster, OHG *hano*, ON *hani*, Goth *hana*, Gk *kanachē* ringing sound, and prob. to Russ *kanya*, a bird of prey with a harsh voice] **1 :** SONG, SINGING ⟨with ~ of tuneful birds resounding loud —John Milton⟩ **2 a :** a hymnlike repetitive melody used in liturgical singing (as of psalms, canticles, or anthems) to which the successive nonmetrical verses are fitted by assigning as many syllables to each tone as required ⟨neither the magnificence of the church . . . nor the harmony of the ~ form the substance of religion —Valentine Ughet & Eleanor Davis⟩ **b :** a singing or speaking in monotone often with strongly marked rhythmic stresses and usu. repetitively ⟨the rhythmical ~ of an auctioneer⟩ **c :** a composition serving for or designed for such singing or speaking **d :** WAY 19 **3 :** the act, practice, or art of performing liturgical chants **4 :** a statement of opinion that has been frequently repeated ⟨the consumer's ~ for lower prices⟩

chant·a·ble \-əbəl\ *adj* **:** capable of being chanted **:** lending itself easily to chanting ⟨a clearly ~ rhyme⟩

chan·tage \shäⁿtäzh\ *n* -s [F, fr. *chanter* to yield to extortion, be compliant, lit., to sing + *-age*] **:** BLACKMAIL, EXTORTION

chan·tant \shäⁿtäⁿ\ *adj* [F, fr. pres. part. of *chanter* to sing] **:** of a melodious and singing style **:** TUNEFUL

chantecler *var of* CHANTICLEER

²chan·te·cler \ˌchantə'kli(ə)r, -aan-,-ain-, -le(ə)r,-liə,-leə *also* 'sh-\ *n, usu cap* [CanF, fr. F *Chantecler* Chanticleer — more at CHANTICLEER] **:** a breed of robust general-purpose fowls of Canadian origin with small comb and wattles and white or partridge plumage

chant·er \'chantə(r), -aan-,-ain-,-àn-\ *n* -s [ME *chantour*, fr. OF *chanteor*, fr. L *cantator*, fr. *cantatus* (past part of *cantare* to sing) + *-or* — more at CHANT] **1 :** one that chants: **a :** CHORISTER **b :** CANTOR **2 :** the chief singer in a chantry **3 :** the reed pipe of a bagpipe with finger holes on which the melody is played **4** *obs slang* **:** a deceitful horse dealer

¹chan·te·relle *also* **chan·ta·relle** \ˌshantə'rel, -än-\ *n* -s [F, fr. NL *cantharella*, dim. of L *cantharus* drinking vessel — more at CANTHARUS] **:** a widely distributed edible mushroom (*Cantharellus cibarius*) that is rich yellow in color and has a pleasant apricotlike aroma

²chan·te·relle *also* **chan·ta·relle** \"\ *or* **chan·ta·rel·la** \ˌ==relə\ *n* -s [F *chanterelle*, fr. *chanter* to sing — more at CHANT] **:** the highest string of various stringed musical instruments (as the violin or banjo)

chant·er·ship \'===ˌship\ *n* -s [*chanter* (chief singer) + *-ship*] **:** the office of chanter (sense 2)

chan·teur \(')shäⁿ'tər, -tœ\ *n* -s [F, fr. *chanter* to sing + *-eur* -or — more at CHANT] **:** SINGER; *esp* **:** a singer of ballads

chan·teuse \(')shäⁿ¦tə(r)z, -än¦-, -tǝz, -tüz; (')shan¦tüz\ *n, pl* **chan·teuses** \-ə(r)z(əz),-ǝz(əz),-üzəz\ [F, fem. of *chanteur*] **:** a female singer; *esp* **:** a woman who sings in concert halls or nightclubs

chan·tey *or* **chan·ty** \'shantē, -aan-,-ain-,-ån-, -ti *also* 'ch-\ *also* **shan·tey** *or* **shan·ty** \'sh-\ *n, pl* **chanteys** *or* **chanties** [modif. of F *chanter* to sing] **:** a song orig. sung by sailors in rhythm with their work (as when heaving at a capstan)

chan·tey·man *or* **shan·ty·man** *also* **shan·tey·man** \-mən\ *n, pl* **chanteymen** *or* **shantymen 1 :** one who sings the verses of chanteys and thereby sets the time and rhythm for them and for the work they accompany **2 :** one noted for singing of chanteys often with improvisations

chan·ti·cleer \ˌchantə'kli(ə)r, -aan-,-ain-, -iə *also* ¦sh-\ *also* **chan·te·cler** \", -le(ə)r,-leə\ *n* -s [ME *Chantecleer*, rooster appearing as a character in verse narratives, fr. OF *Chantecler*, rooster in the *Roman de Renart* (Reynard the Fox), fr. *chanter* to sing + *cler* clear — more at CLEAR] **:** ¹COCK 1

chan·tier \shäⁿtyā\ *n, pl* **chantiers** \-ā(z)\ [CanF — more at SHANTY] *in southern Quebec* **:** a hut esp. in a lumber camp; *also* **:** a lumber camp

¹chan·til·ly \(')shan¦tilē *also* (')shän-; *F* shäⁿtēyē\ *adj, usu cap* [F (in *crème à la Chantilly* cream in the Chantilly manner), fr. *Chantilly*, France] **1** *of cream* **:** whipped and usu. sweetened and flavored with vanilla ⟨crème *Chantilly*⟩ **2** *of foods* **:** prepared or garnished with whipped cream ⟨*Chantilly* potatoes⟩

²chantilly \"\ *or* **chantilly lace** *n* -ES *usu cap C* [*Chantilly* fr. F, short for *dentelle de Chantilly*; *Chantilly lace*, trans. of F *dentelle de Chantilly*, fr. *Chantilly*, France, where it was first made] **:** a delicate sometimes white but usu. black silk or linen bobbin-type lace made by hand or machine and having a 6= sided mesh ground and a scrolled and floral design outlined in cordonnet

³chantilly \"\ *n* -ES *usu cap* [F, fr. *Chantilly*, France, where it was produced] **:** an 18th century soft-paste porcelain

chanting *adj* [fr. pres. part. of ¹*chant*] **:** SINGSONG — **chant·ing·ly** *adv*

chanting falcon *or* **chanting goshawk** *n* **:** any of several African hawks (genus *Melierax*) noted for their whistling song

chantment *n* -s [ME *chantement*, short for *enchantement* enchantment] *archaic* **:** ENCHANTMENT, INCANTATION

chant roy·al \shäⁿrwä¦yäl\ *n, pl* **chants roy·aux** \shäⁿrwä¦yō\ [F, lit., royal song] **:** an elaboration of the ballade that was favored for serious poetry in France in the late middle ages

chan·try \'chan·trē, -àn-, -ri\ *n* -ES [ME *chanterie*, fr. MF, singing, fr. *chanter* to sing — more at CHANT] **1 :** an endowment or foundation for the chanting of masses and offering of prayers commonly for the founder **2 :** a chapel, altar, or part of a church endowed by a chantry

chantry priest *n* [ME *chanterie prest*, fr. *chanterie* chantry + *prest* priest] **:** the incumbent of a chantry endowment

chants *pres 3d sing of* CHANT, *pl of* CHANT

chanukah *also* **chanukkah** *usu cap, var of* HANUKKAH

cha·obor·i·dae \ˌkāə'bȯrəˌdē, -är-\ *n pl, cap* [NL, fr. *Chaoborus*, type genus (fr. LGk *chaoun* to destroy utterly — fr. Gk *chaos* space, abyss — + NL *-borus* — fr. Gk *bora* food, meat) + *-idae* — more at VORACIOUS] **:** a family of gnats related to and often included as a subfamily of Culicidae but distinguished by the short mouth parts, nonbiting habit, and absence of scales on the wing veins and with larvae that are aquatic and predaceous on other insect larvae (as those of mosquitoes) — **cha·ob·o·rine** \kā'äbəˌrīn\ *n* -s

¹cha·os \'kāˌäs *sometimes* -āəs *or* -āˌōs\ *n* -ES [L, fr. Gk — more at GUM] **1** *obs* **:** CHASM, GULF, ABYSS **2 a** *sometimes cap* **:** a state of things in which chance is supreme **:** nature that is subject to no law or that is not necessarily uniform; *esp* **:** the confused unorganized state of primordial matter before the creation of distinct and orderly forms — contrasted with *cosmos* **b :** a state of utter confusion completely wanting in order, sequence, organization, or predictable operation ⟨a process calculated to reduce the orderly life of our complicated societies to ~ —Aldous Huxley⟩ ⟨the ~ of a subjectivity that lacks objective control —John Dewey⟩ **c :** a confused mass or agglomerate of matters or heterogeneous items that are hard to distinguish, isolate, or interpret ⟨a work where nothing's just or fit, one glaring ~ and wild heap of wit —Alexander Pope⟩ **syn** see CONFUSION

²chaos \"\ *n, cap* [NL, fr. L] **:** a genus of large amoebas variously delimited and sometimes regarded as equivalent to *Amoeba* or to *Pelomyxa*

cha·ot·ic \kā'äd·ik, -ätik, -ēk, *attrib sometimes* '=¸==\ *adj* [fr. *chaos*, after such pairs as Gk *eros* love: E *erotic*] **1 :** of or belonging to chaos **2 :** in a state of or marked by chaos **:** completely confused or disordered ⟨objects . . . piled up in a ~profusion —David Sylvester⟩ ⟨a ~ battle ground —Marion Wilhelm⟩ ⟨a ~ mind⟩ — **cha·ot·i·cal·ly** \-ək(ə)lē, -ēk-, -li\ *adv* — **cha·ot·ic·ness** \-iknəs, -ēk-\ *n* -ES

¹chap \'chap\ *vb* **chapped; chapped; chapping; chaps** [prob. fr. ME *chappen*, *chapien*, fr. OE *cēapian* — more at CHEAP] **1** *dial Eng* **:** BUY, BARTER **2** *Scot* **:** to fix upon **:** CHOOSE

²chap \"\ *n* -s [short for *chapman*] **1** *now dial Eng* **:** BUYER, CUSTOMER, CHAPMAN **2 :** MAN, BOY, FELLOW ⟨a rare plum for a ~ of 25 —F.B.Vickers⟩ ⟨the newspaper *~s* —Erle Stanley Gardner⟩ **3** *South & Midland* **:** CHILD, BABY

³chap \"\ *vb* **chapped; chapped; chapping; chaps** [ME *chappen*; akin to MD *cappen* to cut down, G dial. (southern Alsatian) *kchapfe* to chop up; all prob. fr. a prehistoric E-D-G word borrowed fr. (assumed) VL *cappare* to castrate, cut, chop (whence ML *cappare* to cut), fr. (assumed) VL *cappo* capon, fr. L *capo* — more at CAPON] *vt* **1** *Scot* **:** to break into small pieces **:** CHOP, POUND **2 a :** to cause to open in slits or chinks **:** SPLIT, CRACK **b :** to cause the skin of (as the face) to crack or become rough **3** *chiefly Scot* **:** STRIKE ⟨~ the hour⟩ **:** BEAT ~ *vi* **1 :** to crack or open in slits ⟨the hands or lips ~⟩ **2** *chiefly Scot* **:** STRIKE, KNOCK, RAP

⁴chap \"\ *n* -s [ME, fr. *chappen* to chop, become cracked] **1 :** a crack in or a sore roughening of the skin from exposure to wind or cold **2** *Scot* **:** BLOW, RAP, KNOCK, STROKE

⁵chap \'chäp, -ap\ *n* -s [³*chap*] **1** *usu pl* **a :** one of the jaws or the fleshy covering of a jaw ⟨the animal's *~s* were smeared with blood⟩ **b :** the forepart of the face ⟨a dog hairless around the *~s*⟩ ⟨puckered a little about the *~s* —Christopher Morley⟩ — called also *chop* **2 :** one of the jaws or cheeks of a vise (as a vise)

chap *abbr* **1** chaplain **2** chapter

chap and lie *n, pl* **chap and lies** [Sc *chap* to strike] **:** the bowling of a bowl or a curling stone so that it hits another bowl or stone and remains in or near its place

chapaneca *or* **chapanecas** *var of* CHIAPANECAS

cha·pa·ra·jos *or* **chap·a·re·jos** \ˌshapə'rā(ˌ)ōs, -ˌəs *sometimes* ˌch-\ *n pl* [modif. (prob. influenced by Sp *aparejo* equipment, gear) of MexSp *chaparreras*, fr. *chaparro*] **:** CHAPS

chap·ar·ral *also* **chap·pa·ral** \ˌshapə'ral, -el *sometimes* ˌch-\ *n* -s [Sp, fr. *chaparro* dwarf evergreen oak, fr. Basque *txapar*, dim. of *saphar* thicket] **1 :** a thicket of dwarf evergreen oaks **2 :** a dense impenetrable thicket of stiff or thorny shrubs or dwarf trees **3 :** a community comprising shrubby plants widely distributed in southern California that are esp. adapted to dry sunny summers and moist winters

chaparral bird *or* **chaparral cock** *n* **:** ROAD RUNNER; *esp* **:** the male roadrunner

chaparral broom *n* **:** COYOTE BRUSH

chaparral pea *n* **:** a thorny California shrub (*Pickeringia montana*) of the family Leguminosae having showy rose-purple flowers and forming dense thickets in tracts of chaparral

chap·ar·re·ras *or* **chap·a·re·ras** \ˌshapə'rerəs *sometimes* ˌch-\ *n pl* [MexSp *chaparreras*, fr. *chaparro*] **:** CHAPS

cha·par·ro \shə'pä(ˌ)rō, ch-\ *n* -s [AmerSp, fr. Sp, dwarf evergreen oak] **1 :** a Mexican oak (*Quercus reticulata*) with close-grained hard brown wood **2** *or* **chaparro prieto :** a Mexican acacia (*Acacia amentacea*) with sweet-scented yellow flowers **3 :** a tropical American tree (*Curatella americana*) of the family Dilleniaceae distinguished by very rough leaves that are widely used for polishing and scouring — called also *sandpaper tree* **4 :** any of several trees of the genus *Byrsonima* most of which have edible fruits and bark useful for tanning

cha·pa·ti *or* **cha·pat·ti** *n, pl* **chapati** *or* **chapaties** *or* **chapatti** *or* **chapatties** \chə'päd·ē, -pa-\ [Hindi *capati*, fr. Skt *carpaṭī* thin cake, fr. *carpaṭa* flat] **:** a pancake-shaped unleavened bread that is common in northern India and is made of wheat flour and baked on a griddle

chap·book \'chap,bu̇k\ *n* [*chapman* + *book*] **1 :** a small book or pamphlet of a kind formerly sold by chapmen containing popular tales, treatises, ballads, or nursery rhymes **2 :** a small book or pamphlet resembling a chapbook

chape \'chāp, -ap\ *n* -s [ME, fr. MF, cape, cover, chape of a scabbard, fr. LL *cappa* head covering, cloak — more at CAP] **1 a** *obs* **:** SCABBARD, SHEATH **b :** the metal mounting or trimming of a scabbard or sheath at its upper end that bears the ring or hook for attaching it to the belt **c :** the metal trimming that covers the point of a scabbard or sheath **2 :** the tip of a fox's brush **3 :** the metal piece at the back of a buckle that fastens it to a strap **4 :** the outer case of a foundry mold

cha·peau \(')sha¦pō\ *n, pl* **chapeaus** \-ōz\ *or* **cha·peaux** \-ō(z)\ [MF, fr. OF *chapel* hat — more at CHAPLET] **1 :** CAP OF MAINTENANCE 3 **2 :** HAT

chapeau bras \(ˌ)=¦=ˈbrä\ *n, pl* **cha·peaux bras** \-ō(z)'b-\ [F *chapeau* hat + *bras* arm, fr. L *brachium* — more at BRACE] **:** a bicorne or a modified tricorne that is often folded and carried under the arm as part of ceremonial, diplomatic, or naval dress

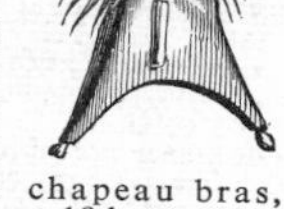

chapeau bras, 18th century

chapeau chi·nois \(ˌ)=¦=ˌshēn'wä\ *n, pl* **cha·peaux chinois** \-ō,sh-, -ōz(h)sh-\ [F, lit., Chinese hat] **:** PAVILLON CHINOIS

¹chap·el \'chapəl\ *n* -s [ME, fr. OF *chapele*, fr. ML *cappella* chapel, short cloak, dim. of LL *cappa* cloak; fr. the preservation of the cloak of St. Martin of Tours as a sacred relic in an oratory specially built for that purpose — more at CAP] **1 a :** a small or subordinate place of worship; *esp* **:** a Christian sanctuary other than a parish or cathedral church **b :** a church subordinate to and dependent on the principal parish church to which it is a supplement of some kind **2 :** a private place of worship: **a :** a building or portion of a building or institution (as a palace, hospital, prison, college) set apart for private devotions and often also for private religious services **b :** a room or recess in a church that often contains an altar and is separately dedicated and that is designed esp. for meditation and prayer but is sometimes used also for small religious services **3 a :** a choir of singers belonging to a chapel (as of a prince) **b :** the choir or the orchestra attached to the court of a prince or nobleman **4 a :** a chapel service or assembly esp. at an educational institution and often only semireligious **b :** attendance at chapel services ⟨~ is required of all students⟩ **5 a** *obs* **:** a printing office **b :** an association or meeting of the workmen (as the compositors) in a printing office for dealing with matters or questions affecting their interests **6 :** a place of worship used by members of a religious denomination or faith other than that of the established church ⟨Anglican churches and nonconformist *~s* of England⟩ **7 a :** FUNERAL HOME **b :** a room or section of rooms in a funeral home where funeral services are conducted **c :** a place in a cemetery for holding funeral services in inclement weather

²chapel \"\ *vt* **chapeled** *or* **chapelled; chapeled** *or* **chapelled; chapeling** *or* **chapelling** \-p(ə)liŋ\ **chapels :** to cause (a ship taken aback in a light breeze) to recover the original tack by the use of the helm alone without bracing the yards

³chapel \"\ *adj, chiefly Brit* **:** of or belonging to a Protestant nonconformist church ⟨~ I was born and . . . bred —Angela Thirkell⟩

cha·pel-de-fer \(ˌ)shaˌpeldə'fe(ə)r\ *n, pl* **chapels-de-fer** \-l(z)d-\ [OF *chapel de fer*, lit., hat of iron] **:** an iron or steel skullcap that was worn with a coif of mail in medieval armor

chap·el·man \'chapəlmən\ *n, pl* **chapelmen :** a clergyman or official of a chapel

chapelmaster \'==,==\ *n* [trans. of F *maître de chapelle* or G *kapellmeister*] **:** CHOIRMASTER

chapel of ease : a chapel or dependent church built for the accommodation of an increasing parish

chapel royal *n, pl* **chapels royal 1 :** a chapel officially connected with the court of a Christian sovereign or attached to a royal palace **2** *usu cap C&R* **:** a Church of England establishment that consists usu. of dean, subdean, canons, chaplains, and choir, some of whom attend the king, and is located with his court

chap·el·ry \'chapəlrē\ *n* -ES **1 a :** the territorial district assigned to a chapel or having its own chapel **b :** a chapel with its precinct and appurtenances **2** *obs* **:** the congregation of a nonconformist chapel

¹chap·er·on *or* **chap·er·one** \'shapəˌrōn\ *n* -s [ME, fr. MF, fr. *chape* cape — more at CHAPE] **1** *chaperon* **:** a round stuffed covering for the head with folds of cloth falling from the crown that was esp. popular in the 15th century **2** [F, lit., hood] **a :** a person (as a matron) who accompanies one or more young unmarried women in public or in mixed company for propriety and esp. formerly as a protector **b :** an older person who accompanies young people esp. in attendance at a dance, party, or other social gathering to ensure proper behavior ⟨their English teacher who accompanied them as ~ —Christopher Morley⟩ **c :** one delegated to ensure proper behavior ⟨in his guarded cell, was allowed to see no visitors . . . without a Navy ~ present —Drew Pearson⟩

²chaperon *or* **chaperone** \"\ *vb* **chaperoned; chaperoned; chaperoning; chaperons** *or* **chaperones** *vt* **1 :** to attend upon **:** ESCORT, GUIDE ⟨~ a sightseer around the park⟩ ⟨personally *~ing* a confidential communication to the president's desk⟩ **2 a :** to act as chaperon to or for ⟨~ a college dance⟩ ⟨~ a group of young ladies on tour⟩ **b :** to take care of **:** SUPERVISE ⟨a job *~ing* cattle to So. Africa —J.T.Winterich⟩ ⟨a . . . salesgirl . . . should ~ the cart . . . and be responsible for restocking it daily —*Lingerie Merchandising*⟩ ~ *vi* **:** to act as a chaperon ⟨part of the woman's duty was to ~ at all sorority dances⟩

chaperon 1

chap·er·on·age \'==,=nij, ,=='==\ *n* -s [²*chaperon* + *-age*] **:** the act or the practice of chaperoning **:** attendance or supervision by or as if by a chaperon ⟨strict ~ of girls⟩ ⟨wise in their ~ of the camera —John Mason Brown⟩

chap·er·on·less \-ləs\ *adj* **:** having no chaperon

chapes *pl of* CHAPE

chap·fall·en \'chap,- *also* -ä-\ *or* **chop·fall·en** \'chäp,-\ *adj* [⁵*chap* or ⁴*chop* + *fallen*] **1 :** having the lower jaw hanging loosely ⟨a tired and ~ hound⟩ **2 :** DEJECTED, DEPRESSED ⟨sallied forth . . . with an air quite desolate and ~ —Washington Irving⟩

cha·pin \chə'pēn\ *n* -s [Sp *chapin*, lit., chopine — more at CHOPINE] **:** BOXFISH; *esp* **:** one of a common species (*Lactophrys triqueter*) of the eastern coast of No. America

chap·i·ter \'chapəd·ə(r)\ *n* -s [ME *chapiter*, *chapitre* — more at CHAPTER] **:** the capital of a column

chap·lain \'chaplən\ *n* -s [ME *chapeleyn*, fr. OF *chapelain*, fr. ML *cappellanus* chaplain, secretary of a king or noble, custodian of sacred relics, fr. *cappella* chapel, short cloak — more at CHAPEL] **1 a :** a clergyman appointed to officiate in a chapel **b :** a Church of England clergyman without a title or benefice in the place where he officiates who performs religious services in a chapel, cathedral, or collegiate church **2 :** a clergyman officially attached to the army or navy, to some public institution, or to a family or court **3 :** any person chosen to conduct religious exercises (as for a society)

chap·lain·cy \-sē, -i\ *n* -ES **:** the office, position, or station of a chaplain

chaplain in ordinary : one of the 36 honorary chaplains to the king of England

chap·lain·ry \-rē, -i\ *obs var of* CHAPLAINCY

chap·less \'chăpləs, -ap-\ *adj* [⁵*chap* + *-less*] **:** having no lower jaw ⟨a ~ skull⟩

chap·let \'chaplət, *usu* -əd+V\ *n* -s [ME *chapelet*, fr. MF, fr. OF, dim. of *chapel* garland, hat, fr. ML *cappellus* head covering, fr. LL *cappa* head covering, cloak — more at CAP] **1 a :** a garland or wreath to be worn on the head **b :** a heraldic bearing consisting of a garland of leaves or of leaves and flowers; *specif* **:** a heraldic garland of leaves with four roses placed at equal distances around the circle **2 a :** a string of beads; *esp* **:** a part of a rosary or usu. 55 beads used in praying by Roman Catholics **b :** the prayers recited over such a string of beads **c :** something resembling a string of beads ⟨the most northerly of the ~ of large lakes —*Chambers's Encyc.*⟩ **3 :** a small molding (as an astragal or baguette) carved with small decorative forms (as beads, pearls, or olives) **4 :** any of various metal devices for holding a core or section of a foundry mold in place

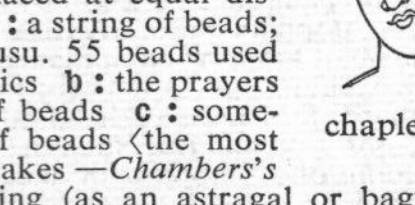
chaplet 1a

chap·let·ed \'chapləd·əd\ *adj* **:** provided with or having a chaplet

chap·lin·esque \,chaplə'nesk\ *adj, usu cap* [Charles S. *Chaplin* *b*1889 Eng.-born comedian + E *-esque*] **:** resembling or suggesting the largely pantomime comedy of the motion-picture comedian Charles Chaplin, esp. its central comedy figure, a pathetic ineffectual good-hearted tramp with torn baggy pants, long-worn shoes, cane and bowler hat, an odd jerky walk, and pretensions to gentility ⟨*Chaplinesque* comedy⟩ ⟨waddling with all their *Chaplinesque* might —Russell Owen⟩

chap·man \'chapmən\ *n, pl* **chapmen** [ME, fr. OE *cēapman* (akin to OHG *koufman*, ON *kaupmathr*), fr. *cēap* trade + *man* — more at CHEAP] **1** *archaic* **:** MERCHANT, TRADER **2** *Brit* **:** an itinerant dealer **:** PEDDLER, HAWKER **3** *archaic* **:** PURCHASER, CUSTOMER

chapman horse *n* [so called fr. its former popularity among chapmen] **:** CLEVELAND BAY

chap·man·ite \'chapmə,nīt\ *n* -s [Edward *Chapman* †1904 Eng. mineralogist + E *-ite*] **:** a mineral $Fe_5Sb_2Si_5O_{20}.2H_2O$ consisting of a silicate of iron and antimony

chap·man's zebra \-mən(z)'zē-\ *n, usu cap C* [after James *Chapman* †1872 Eng. traveler in Africa] **:** a variety (*Equus burchelli chapmanni*) of the Burchell's zebra distinguished by distinct shadow striping on the body and largely restricted to northern Bechuanaland and western Matabeleland — compare GRANT'S ZEBRA

cha·pon \(')sha¦pōⁿ\ *n* -s [F, lit., capon, fr. L *capon-, capo* — more at CAPON] **:** a piece of bread rubbed with garlic and placed in a salad for flavor

cha·po·te \chə'pōd·ē\ *n* -s [MexSp, alter. of Sp *zapote* sapodilla — more at SAPODILLA] **:** MEXICAN PERSIMMON

chapparal *var of* CHAPARRAL

chappati *var of* CHAPATI

chap·paul \chə'pȯl\ *n* -s [origin unknown] **:** SQUAWFISH

chappe *var of* SCHAPPE

¹**chapped** \'chapt\ *also* **chopped** \-ä-\ *adj* [ME *chapped*, fr. past part. of *chappen* to chap — more at CHAP (to split)] **1 :** CRACKED, FISSURED, ROUGHENED ⟨~ hands⟩ **2** *Scot* **:** CHOPPED, MASHED

²**chapped** \'chăpt, -apt\ *also* **chopped** \-äpt\ *adj* [⁵*chap* or ⁴*chop* + *-ed*] **:** having a jaw — used in combination with a qualifying adjective ⟨a sour long-*chapped* face⟩

chap·pie *also* **chap·py** \'chapē, -pi\ *n, pl* **chappies** [²*chap* + *-ie*] **:** FELLOW, CHAP ⟨that other ~ had come back from Africa with money —Donn Byrne⟩

chap·pin \'chapən, -äp-\ *var of* CHOPIN

chapping *pres part of* CHAP

chap·pow \chə'pau̇\ *n* -s [Per *chapū* pillage or *chāpaul* raid] *India* **:** RAID, FORAY

chap·py \'chapē\ *adj* ER/-EST [⁴*chap* + *-y*] **:** CHAPPED

cha·pras·si *also* **cha·pra·si** \chə'präsē\ *n* -s [Hindi *caprāsī*, *caprāsī*, fr. *caprās*, *caprās* badge] *India* **:** an official messenger **:** FUNCTIONARY, OVERSEER, SERVANT, PORTER, BEARER

¹**chaps** *pl of* CHAP, *pres 3d sing of* CHAP

²**chaps** \'shaps *sometimes* 'ch-\ *n pl* [modif. of MexSp *chaparreras* — more at CHAPARAJOS] **:** leather leggings resembling trousers without a seat and often with fringed and decorated extensions in the width of the outer part of the leg that are worn over regular pants as a leg protection esp. by western ranch hands for riding through brush

chaps

chapt *archaic var of* CHAPPED

chap·tal·i·za·tion \,==lə'zāshən, -,lī'z-\ *n* -s **:** the act or process of chaptalizing

chap·tal·ize \'shaptə,līz\ *vt* -ED/ -ING/ -S [F *chaptaliser*, fr. Jean-Antoine *Chaptal* †1832 Fr. chemist + F *-iser* -ize] **:** to normalize the composition of a wine before fermentation by adding a neutralizer if the must is too acid or by adding sugar if there is not enough to produce the desired alcohol

chap·ter \'chaptə(r)\ *n* -s [ME *chapitre* division of a book, meeting of canons, body of canons, fr. OF, fr. LL *capitulum* division of a book & ML *capitulum* meeting place of canons (where the meetings were frequently opened by the reading of a chapter from the Scriptures), fr. L, small head, dim. of *capit-, caput* head — more at HEAD] **1 a :** a main division of a book or treatise usu. beginning on a new page **b :** a significant portion of anything conceived as adaptable to presentation in such divisions ⟨begin a new ~ in one's life⟩ ⟨with his death a ~ in the development of the north . . . was closed —Harold Griffin⟩ **2 :** a regular meeting or assembly for business or conference of the canons of a cathedral or collegiate church or of canonesses, monks, or members of a religious or nonreligious order **3 a :** the body of canons of a cathedral or collegiate church who are presided over by a dean **b :** an organized esp. local branch or unit of a society or fraternity **4 :** one of the hour numerals on a clock or watch dial **5 :** a short passage of scripture between the last psalm and the hymn in lauds and the little hours

¹**chapter and verse** *n, pl* **chapters and verses** [so called fr. the tradition of citing biblical sources by chapter and verse number] **1 :** the exact reference or source of information or justification for what one has said or written ⟨he claims, and gives *chapter and verse* for it, that he was an accurate and skillful rhymer —*Modern Language Notes*⟩ **2 :** full precise information or detail ⟨giving *chapter and verse* for what was already known in general terms —*Newsweek*⟩ ⟨impressed her with the far-reaching program and gave her *chapter and verse* to prove its value —*N.Y. Herald Tribune Bk. Rev.*⟩

²**chapter and verse** *adv* **1 :** with precise exactness ⟨repeat *chapter and verse* the ideas Croly had advanced —C.B.Forcey⟩ **2 :** in full precise detail ⟨explain slowly, *chapter and verse*, what we were to do⟩

chapter head *n* **:** printed matter (as the chapter number or title, quotations, illustrations, or decorative letters) preceding the text at the beginning of a chapter

chapter house *n* [ME *chapitre hous*, fr. *chapitre* chapter + *hous* house] **1 :** a building, room, or suite of rooms where a chapter meets or transacts its business **2 :** a meeting place or residence of a local chapter of a college fraternity or sorority

chapter of accidents : the succession of unforeseen events ⟨make no plans but leave things to the *chapter of accidents*⟩

chap·trel \'chaptrəl\ *n* -s [irreg. fr. *chapiter* + *-el*] **:** ³IMPOST

chap·wom·an \'chap,-\ *n, pl* **chapwomen** [¹*chap* + *woman*] **:** a female peddler or hawker

¹**char** *var of* CHARE

²**char** *or* **charr** \'chär, -å(r\ *n, pl* **char** *or* **chars** *or* **charr** *or* **charrs** [origin unknown] **:** a trout of the genus *Salvelinus*

³**char** \"\ *vb* **charred; charred; charring; chars** [back-formation fr. *charcoal*] *vt* **1 :** to convert to charcoal or carbon usu. by exposing to heat ⟨heat ~*s* wood and paper⟩ **2 :** to burn partly, usu. on the outside, with a blackened carbonized effect ⟨the beams badly *charred* and unsafe⟩ ~ *vi* **:** to burn to charcoal **:** BURN ⟨sugar ~*s* at 400°C⟩ **syn** see BURN

⁴**char** \"\ *n* -s **:** a charred substance or charred remains **:** CHARCOAL; *esp* **:** animal or vegetable charcoal used in decolorizing the sugar in sugar manufacturing

⁵**char** \'chär, -å(r\ *vi* **charred** *or* **chared; chared** *or* **charred; charing** *or* **charring; chars** [partly fr. *chare, char* (to do or complete), partly back-formation fr. *charwoman*] **:** to work as a charwoman or at the tasks often assigned to a charwoman

⁶**char** \'chär, -å(r\ *n* -s [short for *charwoman*] **1** *Brit* **:** a woman who does domestic cleaning or the cleaning of public buildings or offices for a living, often by the day **:** CHARWOMAN ⟨the domestic staff . . . reduced to an occasional ~ —Agnes M. Miall⟩ **2 :** the work of routine housecleaning or the cleaning of public buildings or offices as a livelihood ⟨~ employees —*U.S. Post Office Manual*⟩

⁷**char** \"\ *n* -s [Hindi *cā*, fr. Chin (Pek) *ch'a²*] *slang Brit* **:** TEA

char *abbr* **1** character; characteristic **2** charity **3** charter

chara \'ka(a)rə\ *n* [NL, fr. L, a plant] **1** *cap* **:** a genus (the type of the family Characeae) of plants common in freshwater lakes of limestone districts and usu. having the central internodal cells of the stem, often encrusted with calcareous deposits, sheathed by smaller cells — see NITELLA **2** -s **:** any plant of the genus *Chara*

char·a·banc *or* **char-à-banc** \'sharə,baŋ, -bäⁿ\ *n, pl* **charabancs** *or* **char-à-bancs** \-aŋz,-äⁿz\ [modif. of F *char à bancs*, lit., wagon with benches] *Brit* **:** a horse-drawn vehicle or a motor coach usu. open and orig. having several rows of seats extending across its width and facing forward; *specif* **:** a sight-seeing motor coach

cha·ra·ce·ae \kə'rāsē,ē\ *n pl, cap* [NL, fr. *Chara*, type genus + *-aceae*] **:** a family of aquatic green algae (order Charales) comprising the stoneworts, resembling the horsetails in general appearance, and having jointed stems with whorls of slender branchlike leaves at the joints — see CHARA, NITELLA — **cha·ra·ceous** \-shəs\ *adj*

cha·rac·i·dae \kə'rasə,dē\ *n pl, cap* [NL, fr. *Charac-*, *Charax*, type genus (fr. Gk *charak-, charax* pointed stake, or a fish, prob. the sea bream) + *-idae*] **:** a large family of freshwater fishes of Africa and tropical America typically having a deep scaly body and strong jaws but exhibiting many lines of specialization and with related forms commonly constituting a division of the Cyprinoidea — see CARIBE

¹**char·a·cin** \'karəsən\ *n* -s [ISV *charac* (fr. NL *Characeae*) + *-in*] **:** a white substance with a moldy odor found in members of the genus *Chara* and some other fatty algae

²**characin** \"\ *also* **cha·rac·i·nid** \kə'rasənəd\ *n* -s [NL *Characinidae*] **:** a fish of the family Characidae often kept in tropical aquariums for varied form and bright colors

char·a·cin·i·dae \,karə'sinə,dē\ [NL, fr. *Characinus*, type genus (fr. Gk *charak-, charax* pointed stake, or a fish, prob. the sea bream) + *-idae*; akin to Gk *charassein* to sharpen] *syn of* CHARACIDAE

char·act \'ka,rakt, kə'r-\ *n* -s [ME *charecte* mark, prob. alter. (influenced by L *character* mark, sign) of *carecte* — more at CARACT] **:** CHARACTER 1g

¹**char·ac·ter** \'karəktə(r), -rēk- *also* 'ker-\ *n* -s [alter. (influenced by L *character*) of earlier *caracter*, fr. ME, fr. MF *caractère*, fr. L *character* mark, sign, distinctive quality, fr. Gk *charaktēr*, fr. *charassein* to sharpen, cut into furrows, engrave; akin to Lith *žerti* to scratch, scrape] **1 :** a distinctive differentiating mark: **a :** a conventionalized graphic device, token, or symbol typically single or simple in form esp. impressed or engraved as an indication of ownership or origin or capable of being impressed or engraved **b :** a device indicating a special characteristic or relationship ⟨the ~ of the fish is often used to indicate early Christians⟩ **c :** a graphic symbol (as a hieroglyph, ideograph, alphabet letter, punctuation mark, or shorthand mark) used as a unit in writing or printing (a typewriter keyboard with special ~*s*) ⟨mathematical ~*s*⟩ **d :** a conventionalized figure, representation, or expression ⟨a medieval ~ of Christ⟩ **e characters** *pl, obs* **:** SHORTHAND **f** *Roman Catholicism* **:** an indelible mark impressed on the soul by the sacraments of baptism, confirmation, and holy orders by which the recipient is empowered to produce or receive something sacred **g :** a cabalistic, magical, or astrological emblem ⟨charms, images, ~*s* stamped of sundry metals —Robert Burton⟩ **h :** a particular set of letters or other symbols used in writing **:** ALPHABET **2 :** CHARACTERISTIC: as **a** (1) **:** one of the essentials of structure, form, materials, or function that together make up and usu. distinguish the individual **:** any feature used to separate distinguishable things (as organisms) into categories (2) **:** the detectable expression of the action of a gene or group of genes — see UNIT CHARACTER (3) **:** the aggregate of distinctive qualities characteristic of a breed, strain, or type **b :** the complex of accustomed mental and moral characteristics and habitual ethical traits marking a person, group, or nation or serving to individualize it ⟨it depended wholly on the governors' individual ~*s* whether their terms of office were equitable or oppressive —John Buchan⟩ ⟨to comprehend the full ~ of these United States —Ruth Suckow⟩ **c :** main or essential nature esp. as strongly marked and serving to distinguish **:** individual composite of salient traits, consequential characteristics, features giving distinctive tone ⟨each town came to have a ~ of its own —Sherwood Anderson⟩ ⟨the president had taken those measures which gave to Union war policy its controlling ~ —*Dict. of Amer. History*⟩ **3 a :** WRITING, INSCRIPTION, PRINTING; *also* **:** what is represented in such writing, inscription, or printing **b :** style of writing or printing esp. in physical qualities ⟨you know the ~ to be your brother's —Shak.⟩ **c :** a private mode of communication in writing **:** CIPHER **4** *obs* **:** APPEARANCE **:** outward and visible quality or trait **5 :** a piece of printer's type that produces a character **6 :** POSITION, RANK, CAPACITY, STATUS ⟨in the ~ of a slave⟩ ⟨his ~ as a town official⟩ **7 a** *archaic* **:** a description, delineation, or detailed account of the qualities or peculiarities — now used of a person, but formerly of a thing ⟨give the police a ~ of the thief⟩ **b** [trans. of Gk *charaktēr*] **:** a descriptive often satiric analysis usu. in the form of a short literary sketch of a human virtue or vice as embodied in a representative human being, of a general type of human character (as a busybody, an old man, a country bumpkin), or of a quality of a particular place or thing — most frequently applied to the form as it developed in 17th century English and French literature **c :** a written statement as to the behavior, habits, and competence of an employee given by an employer **8 a :** a person regarded as characterized by or exemplifying distinctive or notable traits **:** PERSONAGE, PERSONALITY ⟨Caesar is a great historical ~⟩ ⟨the Toronto financier . . . an almost fabulous ~ in Canadian mining circles —J.D.Hillaby⟩ **b :** personality as represented or realized in fiction or drama ⟨a play weak in ~ but strong in plot⟩; *also* **:** a given representation or realization of this kind ⟨the main ~ in the novel⟩ **c :** the personality or part which an actor recreates **d :** characterization esp. in fiction or drama ⟨a novelist good in both ~ and setting⟩ **e :** a unique, extraordinary, or eccentric person ⟨the cheery, cheeky, undefeatable ~ — the cockney —*London Calling*⟩; *esp* **:** a dramatic role calling for the representation of such a person **f** *slang* **:** PERSON, INDIVIDUAL, MAN ⟨an underworld ~⟩ ⟨romantic ~*s* will often camp out on the site —Jacquetta & Christopher Hawkes⟩ **9 :** reputation esp. when good ⟨his association with evil companions detracted from his ~⟩ **10 :** a composite of good moral qualities typically of moral excellence and firmness blended with resolution, self-discipline, high ethics, force, and judgment ⟨that stiffening of the moral fiber which we call ~ —F.A.Swinnerton⟩ ⟨his eldest brother . . . had not ~ enough to reproach me —John Galsworthy⟩ **11 :** the crimp of wool fiber esp. with respect to its evenness **12** *of a dog* **:** style of action or deportment in field trial

syn SYMBOL, SIGN, MARK, NOTE: CHARACTER is likely to suggest a simple form or shape, sometimes the individual forms or devices that constitute signs or symbols. CHARACTER is likely to be used in reference to familiar conventionalized patterns. ⟨*characters* include letters of the alphabet, digits, simple musical notes, and so on⟩ SYMBOL, sometimes interchangeable with CHARACTER, is likely to stress the fact that the device in question means or stands for something ⟨a *symbol* is a sign, figure, or physical object the meaning of which is established by convention —Kurt Seligmann⟩ ⟨in the expression *Cu*, the *C* and the *u* are *characters*; *Cu* is the *symbol* for copper⟩ SIGN may be used to designate something less arbitrary and conventional than CHARACTER, something that hints by its form at what is meant, as arrows as direction markers ⟨*symbols* and *signs*, then, may be seen to differ in this wise: signs are proxy for the objects they represent; symbols are "vehicles for the conception of objects" —W.V.O'Connor⟩ MARK may be close to CHARACTER in suggesting simplicity; it usu. indicates something that is arbitrarily and conventionally adopted ⟨consignee *mark* — a symbol placed on packages for export, generally consisting of a square, triangle, diamond, circle, cross, etc., with designated letters . . . for the purpose of identification —*Marine Corps Manual*⟩ NOTE, except in reference to musical notation or perhaps to punctuation marks, is now uncommon as a synonym for CHARACTER. In various subjects use of these words is determined more by convention than by consideration of exact meanings and shades of connotation. **syn** see in addition DISPOSITION, QUALITY, TYPE

— **in character 1 :** in accord with a person's normal or usual qualities or traits **2 :** befitting a role or character type — **out of character 1 :** not in accord with a person's normal or usual qualities or traits ⟨his rude behavior was quite *out of character*; he was generally meticulously well-bred⟩ **2 :** unbefitting a role or character type ⟨the protagonist's curtain speech in act II was so *out of character* it was omitted after the first performance⟩

²**character** \"\ *vt* -ED/-ING/-S **1 :** ENGRAVE, INSCRIBE, WRITE **2 a** *archaic* **:** REPRESENT, PORTRAY **b :** CHARACTERIZE

³**character** \"\ *adj* **1 :** portraying or adept at portraying a usu. subordinate dramatic role whose distinctive mental or moral qualities are of first dramatic interest; *esp* **:** portraying an unusual or eccentric personality often markedly different (as in age) from the player ⟨a ~ actor⟩ ⟨a ~ actress⟩ **2 :** calling for the qualities of a character actor ⟨a ~ part⟩ ⟨~ acting⟩

character assassination *n* **:** the slandering of another person (as a public figure) with the intention of destroying public trust in him

character dance *n* **1 :** a mimetic dance esp. in ballet representing a character **2 :** a characteristic national dance

char·ac·ter·ful \-fəl\ *adj* **1 :** markedly expressive of character⟨the ~ high-cheekboned face of a Tataric Abraham Lincoln —James Cerruti⟩ **2 :** marked by character ⟨~ as the fluent grace of Sterne's prose —*Times Lit. Supp.*⟩

character-gradient \'===,==\ *n* **:** CLINE

¹**char·ac·ter·is·tic** \¦karəktə¦ristik, -rēk-, -tēk *also* ¦ker-\ *adj* [Gk *charaktēristikos*, fr. *charaktēr* + *-istikos* -istic] **:** belonging to or esp. typical or distinctive of the character or essential nature of ⟨the gaiety ~ of children on a holiday⟩ ⟨the white cliffs ~ of the coast at Dover⟩ ⟨a poetic style ~ of the epic⟩ ⟨folklore is ~ only of the group which creates it —Abram Kardiner⟩

syn CHARACTERISTIC, INDIVIDUAL, PECULIAR, and DISTINCTIVE all describe special or identifying qualities or traits. CHARACTERISTIC often stresses the typical nature of the qualities mentioned but is likely also to indicate that they distinguish the item described ⟨the dispersed settlement, large plantations, loose government, and individualism *characteristic* of the South, as compact village communities were *characteristic* of New England —S.E.Morison & H.S.Commager⟩ ⟨having nothing in them that is *characteristic*, or that discriminates them from the letters of any other young man —William Cowper⟩ INDIVIDUAL stresses distinguishing or identifying qualities ⟨the *individual* idiosyncrasies of each member of the great family —Sherwood Anderson⟩ ⟨his letters to her . . . are a simple, perfectly *individual*, daily record of a great passion —Arthur Symons⟩ PECULIAR, sometimes interchangeable with INDIVIDUAL, may stress the uncommon and may have a wider application and less force ⟨in these aspects or parts of his work we pretend to find what is *individual*, what is the *peculiar* essence of the man —T.S.Eliot⟩ ⟨the product of a force which was not *peculiar* to England but was operative in England and in France simultaneously —A.J.Toynbee⟩ ⟨habits both universal among mankind and *peculiar* to individuals —F.H. Allport⟩ DISTINCTIVE, less individualizing than PECULIAR or INDIVIDUAL indicates uncommon distinguishing characteristics, often praiseworthy ones ⟨it is rather the exquisite craftsmanship of France . . . that has given to free verse . . . its most *distinctive* qualities —J.L.Lowes⟩ ⟨lacks *distinctive* personal traits —M.R.Cohen⟩

²**characteristic** \"\ *n* -s **1 :** a trait, quality, or property or a group of them distinguishing an individual, group, or type **:** that which characterizes or is characteristic ⟨the Welsh ~*s* are indelibly stamped —Wilfrid Goatman⟩ ⟨the usual ~*s* of matter — mass, rigidity, etc. —A.S.Eddington⟩ ⟨reptilian ~*s*⟩ **2** *physics* **a :** any of the variables pertaining to the normal performance of a device (as the grid voltage, plate current, or tube resistance of a vacuum tube or the voltage and watt rating of a lamp) **b :** CHARACTERISTIC CURVE **3 :** the integral part of a common logarithm, being for a number greater than unity one less than the number of digits to the left of the decimal point, and for a number less than unity negative and numerically one more than the number of zeros between the decimal point and the first digit

char·ac·ter·is·ti·cal·ly \-ək(ə)lē, -ēk-, -li\ *adv* **:** in a characteristic manner

characteristic curve *n* **:** the graphic curve or the graph picturing it that shows the relation between two variables ⟨a *characteristic curve* plotting the variations of grid potential and plate current in the normal operation of a vacuum tube⟩ ⟨the patient's fever chart showed the *characteristic curve* for the disease⟩: **a :** the curve indicating the variation of density in a developed photographic image that results from the increase of exposure expressed logarithmically — called also *H and D curve, sensitometric curve* **b :** a curve showing the relationship between frequency and recording intensity or frequency and reproducing intensity in sound recording

characteristic function *n* **:** EIGENFUNCTION

characteristic impedance *n* **:** the impedance of a uniform alternating-current transmission line of indefinite length (as a long telephone cable) measured at the input end where the voltage is applied

char·ac·ter·is·tic·ness *n* -ES **:** the quality or state of being characteristic

characteristic radiation *n* **:** radiation in the form of light or X rays of wavelengths peculiar to the substance emitting or absorbing it

characteristic temperature *n* **:** DEBYE TEMPERATURE

characteristic x rays *n pl, usu cap X* **:** X rays of definite wavelengths characteristic of a pure substance and emitted by it under proper excitation

char·ac·ter·iz·a·ble \'karəktə,rīzəbəl, -rēk- *also* 'ker-\ *adj* **:** capable of being characterized

char·ac·ter·i·za·tion \,==tərə'zāshən, -,rī'z-\ *n* -s [ML *characterizatus* (past part. of *characterizare*) + E *-ion*] **:** the act, process, or result of characterizing; *esp* **:** the representation of human character or personality (as in fiction or drama)

char·ac·ter·ize \'===,rīz\ *vb* -ED/-ING/-S *see -ize in Explan Notes* [ML *characterizare* to write, print, fr. Gk *charaktērizein* to engrave, inscribe, fr. *charaktēr* character + *-izein* -ize] *vt* **1** *obs* **:** ³EXPRESS 1 **2 :** to describe the essential character or quality of **:** DELINEATE ⟨a ~ friend in a few words⟩ ⟨~ an action as childish⟩ **3 :** to be a distinguishing characteristic of **:** DISTINGUISH ⟨metaphor ~*s* the language of poetry —R.M. Weaver⟩ ~ *vi* **:** to portray, delineate, or represent character (as in a work of art) ⟨a writer excellent at *characterizing*⟩

char·ac·ter·less \'==tə(r)ləs\ *adj* **:** lacking character

character loan *n* **:** an unsecured loan made by a bank or loan company because of the known integrity of the borrower

character neurosis *n* **:** a personality disturbance in which character traits are thought to be the functional equivalent of neurotic symptoms

character note *n* **:** SHAPE NOTE

char·ac·ter·o·log·i·cal \¦==tərə¦läjəkəl\ *also* **char·ac·ter·o·log·ic** \-jik\ *adj* **:** of, relating to, or based on character or characterology

char·ac·ter·ol·o·gist \ˌ===ˈräləjəst\ *n* -s : a specialist in characterology

char·ac·ter·ol·o·gy \-jē\ *n* -ES [ISV [1]*character* + *-o-* + *-logy;* orig. formed as G *charakterologie*] : the study of character including its development and its differences in different individuals

character piece *n* [trans. of G *charakterstück*] : a short musical composition esp. for piano conveying a single mood or impression — compare PROGRAM MUSIC

characters *pl of* CHARACTER, *pres 3d sing of* CHARACTER

character sketch *n* : a sketch devoted to an analysis or representation of a character esp. of peculiar, eccentric, or strongly marked individuality or to a description stressing the character of a place

character study *n* **1** : analysis or portrayal in literature of the traits of character of an individual **2 a** : a brief narrative or sketch devoted primarily to character study **b** : a realistic portrait in one of the plastic arts or in photography typically of an anonymous sitter whose face or figure reveals strong personality or character traits

character witness *n* : one that gives evidence concerning the reputation, conduct, and moral nature of a party to a legal action

char·ac·tery \ˈkarəkt(ə)rē, kəˈrak-\ *also* **char·ac·try** \ˈkarəktrē\ *n* -ES [[1]*character* + *-y*] : characters or symbols esp. unusual used in the expression of thought

cha·rade \shəˈrād, *US sometimes & Brit usu* -äd *or* -ȧd\ *n* -s [F, fr. Prov *charrado* chat, fr. *charra* to chatter, of imit. origin] **1 a** : a word represented in riddling verse or by picture, tableau, or dramatic action (as *intrusion* represented by depiction of *inn, true,* and *shun*) **b charades** *pl but sing or pl in constr* : a game in which a group is divided into two sides each alternately devising charades to be guessed by the other **2** : something resembling or felt to resemble a charade: as **a** : an almost transparent pretense **b** : a symbolic action ⟨sleepwalkers acting out some fantastic Freudian ~ of their own illusions —J.R.Ullman⟩

cha·rad·rii \kəˈradrēˌī\ *n pl, cap* [NL, fr. pl. of *Charadrius,* type genus] : the suborder of Charadriiformes comprising the shorebirds

char·a·dri·i·dae \ˌkarəˈdrīəˌdē\ *n pl, cap* [NL, fr. *Charadrius,* type genus + *-idae*] : the family of Charadrii consisting of the plovers, turnstones, and surfbirds and sometimes the related snipes, sandpipers, and woodcocks (family Scolopacidae) — **char·a·drine** \ˈkarəˌdrīn\ *adj* — **cha·rad·ri·oid** \kəˈradrēˌȯid\ *adj or n*

cha·rad·ri·i·form \kəˈradrēəˌfȯrm\ *adj* [NL *Charadriiformes*] : of or relating to Charadriiformes or to Charadrii

cha·rad·ri·i·for·mes \kəˌradrēəˈfȯrˌmēz\ *n pl, cap* [NL, fr. *Charadrius,* type genus + *-iformes*] : an order of birds including the shorebirds, auks, gulls, and related forms

cha·rad·ri·us \kəˈradrēəs\ *n, cap* [NL, fr. LL, a bird, perh. the thick-knee, fr. Gk *charadrios,* fr. *charadra* ravine; akin to Gk *charassein* to sharpen, cut into furrows — more at CHARACTER] : a genus (the type of the family Charadriidae) of plovers comprising small or medium-sized birds (as the piping plover) but sometimes (as formerly) including also the golden plovers

cha·ra·les \kəˈrā(ˌ)lēz\ *n pl, cap* [NL, fr. *Chara* + *-ales*] : an order of algae (division Chorophyta) containing the single family Characeae — see CHAROPHYTA

cha·ran·go \chəˈraŋ(ˌ)gō\ *n* -s [Sp, alter. of *charanga* out-of-tune orchestra, military music made by wind instruments, of imit. origin] : a small guitar of Spanish America with a body typically made of an animal shell

[1]charas *pl of* CHARA

[2]cha·ras \ˈchärəs\ *or* **chur·rus** *also* **chur·us** \ˈchərəs\ *n* -ES [Hindi *caras*] : a narcotic and intoxicating resin that exudes esp. from the flower heads of hemp — compare CANNABIN; *also* : a smoking mixture containing this resin

char·bon \ˈshärbən, -ˌbän, *F* shȧrbōⁿ\ *n* -s [F, lit., ember, charcoal (trans. of Gk *anthrax* charcoal, ember, carbuncle, malignant pustule), fr. L *carbon-, carbo* ember, charcoal — more at HEARTH] : ANTHRAX 2

char·bray \ˈshär(ˌ)brā\ *n, usu cap* [irreg. fr. *Charolais* + *Brahman* (zebu)] : a type or breed of beef cattle developed in the southern U.S. by intercrossing animals of the Charolais breed with Brahmans

char·co \ˈchär(ˌ)kō\ *n* -s [Sp] *Southwest* : a usu. small natural depression in which water collects : WATER HOLE

char·coal \ˈchärˌkōl, -ȧˌk-\ *n* -s [ME *charcole,* perh. fr. MF *charbon* charcoal + ME *cole* coal — more at CHARBON, COAL] **1** : a dark-colored or black porous form of carbon made from vegetable or animal substances (as from wood by charring in a kiln or retort from which air is excluded) and used for fuel and in various mechanical, artistic, and chemical processes **2 a** : a piece or pencil of fine charcoal used as a drawing implement **b** : a charcoal drawing **3** : a dark purplish gray that is bluer and duller than slate, pigeon, taupe gray, or dusk (sense 3b)

charcoal black *n* : a black pigment consisting of a charred substance (as wood charcoal or bone black)

charcoal burner *n* : a person whose work is making charcoal

charcoal burning *n* : the making of charcoal

charcoal gray *n* **1** : a nearly neutral slightly greenish black **2** : PELICAN 4

charcoal iron *n* : iron made in a furnace burning charcoal

charcoal pencil *n* : a strip or cylinder of artist's charcoal in a slender wooden casing

charcoal plate *n* **1** : tin plate made from charcoal iron **2** : tin plate having the heaviest coating and highest polish

charcoal powder *n* **1** : powdered charcoal **2** : GUNPOWDER 1a

charcoal rot *n* : a disease of plants that is common in the southern U.S. and destructive to sweet and white potatoes and to corn and is caused by a fungus (*Macrophomina phaseoli*) which attacks the lower stem and roots destroying much of the tissues and forming myriads of tiny black sclerotia on what remains

char·cot joint \(ˈ)shärˈkō-\ *n, usu cap C* [after J. M. *Charcot* †1893 Fr. neurologist] : a destructive condition affecting one or more joints, occurring in diseases of the spinal cord, and ultimately resulting in a flail joint

char·cu·te·rie \(ˌ)shärˌküd·əˈrē, =ˈ==(ˌ)=\ *n* -s [F, fr. MF *chaircuiterie,* fr. *chaircuitier*] **1** : a French pork butcher's shop **2 a** : a delicatessen in France specializing in dressed meats and meat dishes (as cold cuts and sausages) **b** : the cold cuts and meat dishes sold in such a shop; *also* : a single item of such meats

char·cu·tier \(ˌ)shärˌküd·ēˈā, =ˈ==ˌ=\ *n* -s [F, fr. MF *chaircuitier,* fr. *chair cuite* cooked meat, fr. *chair* meat, flesh (fr. L *carn-, caro*) + *cuite,* fem. of *cuit,* past part. of *cuire* to cook, fr. L *coquere* — more at CARNAL, COOK] **1** : a pork butcher **2** : one that prepares or sells charcuterie (sense 2b)

chard \ˈchärd, -ȧd\ *n* -s [modif. (prob. influenced by F *chardon* thistle) of F *carde* edible leafstalk of the cardoon or the artichoke, fr. MF, cardoon with edible leafstalks, fr. OProv *cardo,* fr. L *carduus* thistle, artichoke; akin to MLG *harst* rake, L *carrere* to card, Skt *kaṣati* he scratches] : a beet (*Beta vulgaris cicla*) producing large yellowish green leaves with thick succulent stalks and often cooked as a potherb — called also *seakale beet, Swiss chard*

char·don·nay \ˈshärdᵊnˈā\ *n* -s *usu cap* [F] : a dry white table wine of Chablis type — called also *Pinot Chardonnay*

[1]chare \ˈcha(a)(ə)r, -e(ə)r, -a(a)ə, -eə\ *or* **char** \chär, chȧ(r\ *n* -s [ME *cherre, char* turn, time, piece of work, fr. OE *cierr, cyrr;* akin to OE *cierran* to turn, ON *kjarr* underbrush, Gk *gerron* wicker shield, wicker body of a cart; basic meaning: turn, bend, twist] **1** : an occasional piece of work : an odd job or task esp. of housework : CHORE **2** *dial Eng* : a narrow lane, alley, or street

[2]chare \"\ *or* **char** \"\ *vt* **chared** *or* **charred; chared** *or* **charred; charing** *or* **charring; chares** *or* **chars** [ME *charren, charen* to turn, fr. OE *cierran*] *archaic* : to finish off (as a job)

chared *past of* CHAR *or of* CHARE

charet *n* -s [ME *charrette,* fr. MF, cart] *obs* : a wheeled vehicle : CART, CHARIOT

[1]cha·rette *or* **char·rette** \shəˈret\ *n* -s [F *charrette* cart (used to transport drawings), fr. OF, cart, fr. *char* wheeled vehicle + *-ette* — more at CHARIOT] : the intense final effort made by architectural students to complete their solutions to a given architectural problem in an allotted time or the period in which such an effort is made

[2]charette *or* **charrette** \"\ *vi* **charetted** *or* **charretted; charetted** *or* **charretted; charetting** *or* **charretting; charettes** *or* **charrettes** : to exert oneself in a charette

[1]charge \ˈchärj, ˈchȧj\ *vb* -ED/-ING/-S [ME *chargen,* fr. OF *chargier,* fr. LL *carricare,* fr. L *carrus* wheeled vehicle — more at CAR] *vt* **1 a** *archaic* (1) : to put a load on or in ⟨horses *charged* with heavy burdens⟩ (2) : to place as a load ⟨directing the servants . . . to ~ the Saratoga trunk upon the dickey —R.L.Stevenson⟩ **b** (1) *obs* : to place too heavy a burden on : OVERLOAD (2) : to weigh down with a heavy burden (as of guilt, sickness, or expense) ⟨his spirit was *charged* with sorrow⟩ (3) : EMPHASIZE, EXAGGERATE; *esp* : to render more striking (a detail in a work of art) ⟨~ a line by reinforcing with black⟩ **c** (1) : to place a charge (as of materials to be treated or consumed) in ⟨~ the magazine with three rounds⟩ : load or fill to capacity or up to the required amount ⟨~ a blast furnace with ore⟩ (2) : to impart an electric charge to (3) : to restore the active materials in (a storage battery) by the passage of a direct current through in the opposite direction to that of discharge (4) : to load (a charge) into something ⟨granulated cork is *charged* into suitable molds and heat is applied —G.B.Cooke⟩ (5) : to fill or load (as a brush or pen) with pigment or ink (6) : to fill (as a fire hose) with water under pressure (7) : EMBED ⟨~ abrasive grains in a metal disk for grinding⟩ **d** (1) : to assume as a heraldic bearing ⟨he ~s three roses or⟩ (2) : to place a heraldic bearing on ⟨he ~s his shield with three roses or⟩ **e** (1) : to fill full : furnish fully ⟨a brain *charged* with fancies⟩; *esp* : to fill with a particular mood, tone, or spirit ⟨~s the air with its cosmopolitan sense of freedom —Harry Levin⟩ (2) : to cause to be mixed or saturated : IMPREGNATE ⟨warehouses ~*ing* the air with odors of spice and coffee⟩ **2 a** : to impose a particular duty or task on ⟨board chairman specifically *charged* with leading the board —G.B.Hurff⟩ : entrust with a responsibility, duty, or task : entrust with the care, custody, or management ⟨one brigade . . . is *charged* with a section of land the season through —A.R. Williams⟩ — used with *with* **b** : to command or exhort with authority ⟨Badoglio was *charged* by the king to form a new cabinet —Sir Winston Churchill⟩ : urge earnestly ⟨I ~ thee be not thou more grieved than I am —Shak.⟩ **c** *of a judge* : to give a charge to (a jury) **3 a** : to bring an accusation against : call to account : BLAME ⟨*charged* him as the instigator of the disorder⟩ **b** : to make an assertion against esp. by ascribing guilt or blame for an offense or wrong : ACCUSE — used with *with* ⟨reluctant to ~ a dead man with an offense from which he could not clear himself —Edith Wharton⟩ **c** : to place the blame or guilt for (a fault or wrongdoing) — now usu. used with *to* ⟨he *charged* the fiasco to overconfidence⟩ **d** : to assert as an accusation ⟨*charged* that the . . . line would tend to become a monopoly —*Current Biog.*⟩ **4 a** : to bring (a weapon) to a position suited for attack : LEVEL ⟨~ a lance⟩ **b** : to drive upon, rush against, or bear down upon rapidly and violently ⟨~ an enemy position⟩ ⟨the car *charged* the bank and broke through the fence⟩ **5 a** (1) : to impose a pecuniary burden on ⟨~ his estate with any debts incurred⟩ (2) : to impose or record as a pecuniary obligation ⟨~ debts to an estate⟩ **b** (1) : to fix or ask (a sum) as a fee or payment ⟨~ $10 for his services⟩ (2) : to ask payment of (a person) ⟨~ a client for expenses⟩ — often used with a double object ⟨~ a student $50 for meals⟩ **c** (1) : to record (an item) as an expense, debt, obligation, or liability — usu. used with *to* or *against* ⟨~ a purchase to a customer⟩ ⟨~ a library book to a borrower⟩ ⟨~ a mistake against a person⟩ (2) : to record a debt, obligation, or liability against ⟨~ your account with the goods ordered⟩ ⟨~ a person with a book borrowed from a library⟩ ⟨~ a fielder with an error⟩ (3) : to enter on the debit side of an account ⟨~ a sum against income for depreciation⟩ ⟨~ rent and phone bill to administration⟩ ~ *vi* **1** : to drive or rush violently forward typically in attack ⟨the cavalry *charged* to the flank⟩ ⟨came *charging* through the door, wearing a baseball mitt on one hand —Jean Stafford⟩ **2** : to ask or set a price ⟨~ high for goods⟩ : ask payment ⟨he doesn't ~ at all for it⟩ **3** *of a judge* : to give a charge to the jury **4** *of a dog* : to lie down with head on forepaws **syn** see ACCUSE, ASCRIBE, BURDEN, COMMAND, RUSH — **charge to capital** : to debit a capital asset account ⟨additions and betterments should be *charged to capital* and not to expense⟩ — **charge to revenue** : to debit an expense account

[2]charge \"\ *n* -s [ME, fr. OF, fr. *chargier,* v.] **1 a** *obs* : a material load or weight **b** : a figure borne on a heraldic field : BEARING **c** : a plaster or ointment used on a domestic animal **d** (1) : the quantity of explosive used in a single discharge ⟨a cartridge with a powder ~ of 70 grains⟩ ⟨an artillery shell with an explosive bursting ~⟩ ⟨a ~ of dynamite under the stump⟩ (2) : the powder and shot in a cartridge **e** : the quantity of material to be used or consumed that is loaded at one time into an apparatus or that a mechanism is intended to receive in any single operation ⟨the ~ of chemicals in a fire extinguisher⟩ ⟨the ~ of mixed fuel and air in the cylinder of a gas engine⟩ ⟨the ~ of coal placed in a coal-gas retort⟩ **f** (1) : ELECTRIC CHARGE (2) : the quantity of electricity that a storage battery is capable of yielding expressed usu. in ampere-hours (3) : the process of charging a storage battery **g** (1) : a store or accumulation of force (as emotion, excitement, or affective power) ⟨poetry with an emotional ~, deeply felt and communicated to the reader⟩ : impelling esp. emotional force : DRIVE ⟨a man with a high emotional ~⟩ (2) : CATHEXIS 2 (3) *slang* : a strong feeling of amusement, pleasure, or excitement : KICK ⟨the children got a big ~ out of the clown⟩ **h** : the abrasive powder or grains in the surface of a lap used for grinding, polishing, or sawing **2** *obs* : CONSEQUENCE, IMPORTANCE ⟨this army of such mass and ~ —Shak.⟩ **3 a** : something that one is obligated for : a duty or task laid upon one : OBLIGATION ⟨to maintain this readiness . . . is . . . a first ~ upon our military effort —Sir Winston Churchill⟩ **b** : control of the acts, workings, or disposition of something : MANAGEMENT, SUPERVISION ⟨he assumed full ~ of the business⟩ : CARE, CUSTODY ⟨remained under his uncle's ~ during his minority⟩ **c** : the parish, church, district, or congregations regularly served by a clergyman **d** : a person or thing committed or entrusted to the care, custody, management, or support of another ⟨nursemaids sunning their ~s by the sea —D.G.Gerahty⟩ ⟨he entered the poorhouse, becoming a county ~⟩ **4 a** : INSTRUCTION, COMMAND, ORDER, INJUNCTION ⟨he gave them ~ about the queen to guard and foster her forevermore —Alfred Tennyson⟩ **b** : a formal address containing instruction or exhortation: as (1) : an official address of instruction by a senior church official to his clergy or upon the ordination of a minister (2) : an instruction given by the court to the jury for the purpose of governing their action in coming to or making their decision; *specif* : the statement made by the judge to the jury at the close of a trial of the principles of law that the latter are bound to apply to the facts as proved in deciding upon their verdict **5 a** : expenditure or incurred expense ⟨living at the ~ of his brother⟩: as (1) : payment of costs : money paid out (2) : a pecuniary liability (as rents or taxes) against property, a person, or an organization ⟨~s upon the estate⟩ ⟨smoking has become . . . a fixed ~ on the expenditures of every family —Morris Fishbein⟩ — often used in pl. **b** : the price demanded for a thing or service ⟨a 10-cent admission ~⟩ — often used in pl. ⟨reverse the ~s for a telephone call⟩ **c** : a debit to an account ⟨a ~ to expense account⟩ : an entry in an account of what is due from one party to another ⟨a ~ to a customer's account⟩ : something that is debited ⟨the purchase was a ~⟩ **d** : the record of a loan (as of a book from a library) **6 a** : an accusation of a wrong or offense : ALLEGATION, INDICTMENT ⟨arrested on the ~ of bribery⟩ **b** : a statement of complaint or hostile criticism ⟨the ~ that earned incomes are based upon no principle of equity⟩ **7 a** *of a weapon* : a position of readiness for attack ⟨pikes held in ~⟩ **b** (1) : a violent and impetuous rush toward or upon some person or object ⟨the lion's ~ carried him past the antelope⟩; *specif* : an attack with the intent of closing with an enemy ⟨a tank ~⟩ — compare [1]ASSAULT 2 (2) : the signal for attack ⟨the bugle sounds the ~⟩ **c** : a lunge used chiefly in gymnastics in which the trunk and stationary leg form a straight line — **in charge 1** : having the control or custody of something ⟨the assistant manager was placed *in charge* of the shop⟩ **2** *or* **in the charge** *or* **in one's charge** : into or under the control or custody ⟨given these pills *in charge* of Mrs. Sylk —Gabrielle Long⟩ ⟨the papers were *in the charge* of the custodian of documents⟩ **3** : under supervision ⟨the boy was taken *in charge* by his grandmother⟩ **4** *Brit* : into the hands of the police to be charged with violation of the law ⟨caught the thief and gave him *in charge*⟩

[3]char·gé \(ˈ)shärˈzhā *also* (ˈ)chärˈjā; -ȧˈ-\ *n* -s [by shortening] : CHARGÉ D'AFFAIRES

charge·able \ˈchärjəbəl, ˈchȧj-\ *adj* [ME, weighty, important, burdensome, fr. [1]*charge* (load) + *-able*] **1** *obs* : involving burdensome expense : EXPENSIVE, COSTLY **2 a** [[1]*charge* + *-able*] : liable to be charged: as (1) : liable to be accused or held responsible ⟨a man ~ for assault⟩ (2) : capable of being charged to a particular account or as an expense or liability ⟨~ to printing expense⟩ ⟨debts ~ on the estate⟩ **b** [[2]*charge* (person committed to care of the parish) + *-able*] : qualified to be made a charge on the county or parish — **charge·able·ness** *n* -ES

charge account *n* [[2]*charge* (debit)] **1** : a customer's account with a creditor (as a merchant) to which the purchase of goods is charged **2** : ACCOUNT RECEIVABLE

charge-a-plate \ˈchärjəˌplāt, -ȧj-\ *or* **charge plate** *n* [fr. *Charga-plate,* a trademark] : an embossed plate (as of metal) used to identify a customer having a charge account

charge-back \ˈ=ˌ=\ *n* -s : a debit to a depositor's account that offsets a previous credit that was not collected

charged *adj* [ME, loaded, fr. past part. of *chargen* to charge] **1** : showing or possessing strong emotion or vigorous purpose ⟨attacking the author in an emotionally ~ review⟩ : tensely expectant : INTENSE ⟨the ~ atmosphere of the room⟩ **2** : capable of arousing violence, emotion, or strong opinion ⟨a highly ~ political theme⟩

char·gé d'af·faires \(ˈ)shärˌzhādəˈfa(a)(ə)r, -ȧˌzh-, -zhā(ˌ)daˈ-, -fe(ə)r, -a(a)ə, -eə *also* (ˈ)chärˌjˈā- *or* -ȧˌj- *or* -rz *or* -əz\ *n, pl* **chargés d'affaires** \-zhā(z)(ˌ)d-, -jāz(ˌ)d-\ [F, lit., one charged with affairs] **1** : a lower-ranking member of the diplomatic corps who directs diplomatic affairs during the absence of the ambassador or minister **2** : a diplomatic representative inferior in rank to an ambassador or minister accredited by the government of one country to the minister of foreign affairs of another

charge down *vt* : to stop with one's body (a football kicked by an opponent, as in rugby)

charged water *n* : SODA WATER 2a

charge·ful *adj, obs* : COSTLY

chargehand \ˈ=ˌ=\ *n* [[2]charge (supervision)] *Brit* : FOREMAN, SUBFOREMAN : STRAW BOSS

charge·less \ˈ=ləs\ *adj* : being without a charge

charge·man \ˈ=mən, -ˌman\ *n, pl* **chargemen** [[2]*charge* (supervision) + *man*] **1** : one placed in charge; *esp* : a workman placed in charge of other workmen **2** : one that tends the devulcanizer that removes the fabric content and partially restores the original properties of scrap rubber **3** : BLASTER a **4** : BATTERYMAN 1

charge off *vt* : to reduce (the value at which an asset has been carried on the books) by an amount representing a loss, partial or complete ⟨*charge off* obsolete inventory⟩

charge-off \ˈ=ˌ=\ *n* -s [*charge off*] **1** : the reduction of the value at which an asset has been carried on the books ⟨bad debt *charge-offs*⟩ **2** : the amount by which an account is reduced by charging off decline in value

charge of quarters [[2]*charge* (supervision)] : a noncommissioned officer designated usu. for a 24-hour period to maintain order and handle administrative matters esp. after duty hours in the area of his unit — abbr. *CQ*

charge plate *var of* CHARGE-A-PLATE

[1]char·ger \ˈchärjər, -ȧjə\ *n* -s [ME *chargeour;* akin to ME *chargen* to charge — more at CHARGE] *archaic* : a large flat dish or platter for carrying meat

[2]charg·er \"\ *n* -s [ME *chargere* one that charges, fr. *chargen* to charge + *-ere* -er] **1** : a device for charging: as **a** : an appliance for holding or inserting a charge of powder or shot in a gun **b** : a cartridge clip **c** : a device for charging storage batteries — called also *battery charger* **2** : a horse suitable for cavalry use : a mount for battle or parade **3 a** : a workman who charges materials (as ore) into a receptacle or operating unit (as a furnace) for processing **b** : BATTERYMAN 1 **c** : a workman who applies decorative pastes to jewelry or who prepares the parts for soldering

[1]charges *pres 3d sing of* CHARGE, *pl of* CHARGE

[2]chargés *pl of* CHARGÉ

charges forward *n pl* : charges connected with the collection of a draft and paid by the drawee — contrasted with *charges here*

charge sheet *n* **1** : a memorandum of the names of those to be tried in police and magistrates' courts with a summary statement of the charge against each **2** : a statement of charges against one brought for trial before a court-martial

charges here *n pl* : charges connected with the collection of a draft that are paid by the drawer — contrasted with *charges forward*

charge sister *n* [[2]*charge* (supervision)] *Brit* : a trained nurse who has charge of a ward in an infirmary or hospital

charging *pres part of* CHARGE

charging order *n, Brit* : an order of court making a judgment debt a charge upon the stocks or funds of the debtor

charier *comparative of* CHARY

chariest *superlative of* CHARY

char·i·ly \ˈcha(a)rəlē, ˈcher-, -li\ *adv* [*chary* + *-ly*] : in a chary manner : CAREFULLY, CAUTIOUSLY, FRUGALLY

char·i·ness \-rēnəs, -rin-\ *n* -ES [*chary* + *-ness*] **1** : the quality or state of being chary : CAUTION, HEEDFULNESS, SPARINGNESS, FRUGALITY **2** : carefully preserved state : INTEGRITY

charing *pres part of* CHAR *or of* CHARE

cha·ri-nile \ˈshärēˈnīl, -īəl\ *n, usu cap C&N* [fr. *Chari* + *Nile,* rivers in Africa] : a family of African languages of which the Nilotic, Nubian, Kunama, and Central Sudanic groups are branches — called also *Macrosudanic*

[1]char·i·ot \ˈcharēət *also* -er-; *often* -əd·+V\ *n* -s [ME, fr. MF, fr. OF, fr. *char* wheeled vehicle, fr. L *carrus* — more at CAR] **1** : a vehicle (as a cart or wagon) for transporting goods **2** : a vehicle for conveying persons esp. in state (as a triumphal car or a coach of state) **3** : a 2-wheeled vehicle usu. drawn by two horses and used in ancient warfare and also in processions and races **4** : a light 4-wheeled carriage having a coach box and back seats only

ancient Greek chariot (biga)

[2]chariot \"\ *vb* -ED/-ING/-S *vt* : to convey or carry in or as if in a chariot ⟨they . . . were ~*ed* swiftly up that thronging noble street —Thomas Wolfe⟩ ~ *vi* : to drive, ride, or go in or as if in a chariot

char·i·ot·ed \-əd·əd, -ətəd\ *adj* : furnished with a chariot

char·i·o·tee \ˈ==əˈtē\ *n* -s [irreg. fr. [1]*chariot*] : a light covered 4-wheeled pleasure carriage with two seats

[1]char·i·o·teer \ˈ===ˈti(ə)r, -iə\ *n* -s [alter. (influenced by E *-eer*) of earlier *charioter,* fr. ME *charietere,* modif. (prob. influenced by MF *chariot*) of MF *charretier,* fr. OF, fr. *charrette* cart — more at CHARETTE] : one that drives a chariot

[2]charioteer \"\ *vb* -ED/-ING/-S *vi* : to act as charioteer : drive a chariot or other vehicle ~ *vt* **1** : DRIVE ⟨~ a vehicle⟩ **2** : to drive (a person) in a vehicle

char·i·ot·ry \ˈ==ətrē\ *n* -ES : the part of a military force that fights from chariots ⟨the Egyptian ~⟩

cha·ris·ma \kəˈrizmə\ *or* **char·ism** \ˈkaˌrizəm\ *n, pl* **cha·ris·ma·ta** \kəˈrizməd·ə\ *or* **char·isms** [Gk *charisma* favor, gift, fr. *charizesthai* to favor, fr. *charis* grace; akin to Gk *chairein* to rejoice — more at YEARN] **1** : a spiritual gift or talent regarded as divinely granted to a person as a token of grace and favor and exemplified in early Christianity by the power of healing, gift of tongues, or prophesying **2** : supernatural power or virtue attributed esp. to a person or office regarded as set apart from the ordinary by reason of a special relationship to that which is considered of ultimate value and as endowed with the capacity of eliciting enthusiastic popular support in the leadership, symbolic unification, or direction of human affairs ⟨proletarian movements have found means . . . of transferring the charm of the ~ from the person of the leader to the movement as a whole —Werner Cohn⟩

char·is·mat·ic \¦karəz¦mad·ik\ *adj* [Gk *charismat-*, *charisma* + E *-ic*] **1 :** constituting or resulting from charisma ⟨~ gifts⟩ **2 :** exhibiting or based on charisma ⟨~ sects⟩ **:** possessing charisma ⟨~ leaders⟩

cha·ris·ti·cary \kəˈristəˌkerē\ *n* -ES [perh. fr. MGk *charistikarios*, fr. Gk *charistikos* bounteous (fr. *charizesthai* to favor, give freely) + MGk *-arios* -ary, fr. L *-arius*] **:** a medieval Greek official who received the revenue from a monastery or benefice

char·i·ta·ble \ˈcharəd·əbəl, -rətəb- *also* -er-\ *adj* [ME, fr. MF, fr. OF, fr. *charité* charity + *-ité* -ity — more at CHARITY] **1 :** exhibiting the virtue of Christian love **:** full of love and goodwill for others **:** BENEVOLENT, KINDLY **2 a :** practicing or showing charity **:** generous in assistance to the poor ⟨a man ~ to all in need⟩ **b :** of, for, or relating to charity ⟨~ gifts⟩ **:** having the quality of charity ⟨a ~ impulse⟩ ⟨money spent for ~ purposes⟩ **:** administering charity ⟨~ institutions⟩ **3 :** liberal in judging others **:** inclined to look on the best side and to avoid harsh judgment ⟨it is more ~ to suspend judgment —Ellen Glasgow⟩ **:** arising from or dictated by kindness ⟨a ~ interpretation of his actions⟩ — **char·i·ta·ble·ness** \-bəlnəs\ *n* -ES — **char·i·ta·bly** \-əblē, -li\ *adv*

charitable trust *n* **:** a trust set up for the benefit of the public usu. setting out a definite charitable purpose for an undetermined number of beneficiaries

char·i·tar·i·an \¦=ˌ=ˈterēən\ *n* -S [*charity* + *-arian* (as in *humanitarian*)] **:** a charitable person **:** one that aids or supports charitable enterprises

char·i·ty \ˈcharəd·ē, -ətē, -i *also* -er-\ *n* -ES *often attrib* [ME *charite*, fr. OF *charité*, fr. LL *caritat-*, *caritas* Christian love, fr. L, costliness, high regard, love, fr. *carus* dear, costly, loved + *-itat-*, *-itas* -ity; akin to OIr *caraim* I love, Skt *kāma* love, desire] **1 :** Christian love: **a :** the virtue or act of loving God with a love which transcends that for creatures and of loving others for the sake of God **b :** divine love for man **:** love in its perfection **c :** the act of loving or the disposition to love all men as brothers because they are sons of God **:** love of fellow men **2 a :** the kindly and sympathetic disposition to aid the needy or suffering **:** liberality to the poor, to benevolent institutions, or to worthy causes ⟨the ~ of the neighbors was exhausted and there was no more food in the house —Vicki Baum⟩ **b:** an act or series of acts of aid to the needy ⟨performed many *charities* among her neighbors⟩ **c :** whatever is given to the needy or suffering for their relief **:** ALMS ⟨give her a ~⟩ **d :** an organization or institution engaged in the free assistance of the poor, the suffering, or the distressed ⟨a list of deserving *charities*⟩ **e :** public provision for the care or relief of the needy ⟨too proud to accept ~⟩ **f :** the recipient of charitable assistance ⟨he is one of my father's *charities*⟩ **3 a** (1) **:** love or affection for others **:** a disposition to good will, kindliness, and sympathy ⟨no one minded him laughing at them when they saw the endless ~ of his eyes —Mary Webb⟩ (2) **:** an act or instance of good will or affection **b :** an eleemosynary gift **:** a gift (as by grant or devise) of real or personal property to the use of the public or any portion of it as distinct from specific individuals for any beneficial or salutary purpose **c :** an institution (as a hospital, library, or school) founded by a gift and intended for the use of the public **4 :** a disposition to liberal lenient tolerant judgment and toward minimizing shortcomings and putting the best possible construction on the characteristics or actions of others ⟨a kindly critic liked for his ~ and moderation⟩ **5 :** a refreshment dispensed between meals in a monastery **6 :** JACOB'S LADDER 1a **7 :** CHARITY STAMP **syn** see MERCY

charity school *n* **:** a school for poor children that is supported by charitable bequests or contributions

charity stamp *n* **1 :** a semipostal stamp the surcharge on which goes for some charity **2 :** a charity seal

¹cha·ri·va·ri \ˌshivəˈrē, ˈ==ˌ=, *Brit* ˌshärəˈväri *or* ˌshär-\ *or* **chiv·a·ree** *or* **chiv·a·ri** \ˌshivəˈrē, ˈ==ˌ=\ *n* -S [F *charivari*, fr. LL *caribaria* headache, fr. Gk *karēbaria*, fr. *karē*, *kara* head + *-baria* heaviness (fr. *barys* heavy) — more at CEREBRAL, GRIEVE] **1 :** SHIVAREE 1 **2 a :** a confusion of noises **b :** MEDLEY, HODGEPODGE

²charivari \ˌshivəˈrē, ˈ==ˌ=\ *vb* **charivaried; charivaried; charivariing; charivaries :** SHIVAREE

¹chark \ˈchärk\ *vt* -ED/-ING/-S [back-formation fr. obs. *chark-coal*, alter. of *charcoal*] **:** to burn to charcoal or coke **:** CHAR

²chark \"\ *n* -S *now dial Eng* **:** charred wood or coal **:** CHARCOAL, COKE, CINDER

char·ka *or* **char·kha** \ˈchərkə, -är-\ *n* -S [Hindi *carkha*, fr. Per *charkha*, *charkh* wheel, fr. MPer *chark*; akin to Av *chaxra-* wheel, Skt *cakra* — more at WHEEL] **:** a domestic spinning wheel used in India chiefly for cotton

charlady \ˈ=ˌ==\ *n* [¹*chare* + *lady*] *Brit* **:** CHARWOMAN

char·la·tan \ˈshärlətən, -ətᵊn, -äl- *sometimes* ˈch-\ *n* -S [It *ciarlatano*, alter. (influenced by It *ciarlare* to chatter, of imit. origin) of *cerretano*, lit., inhabitant of Cerreto, fr. *Cerreto*, village near Spoleto, Italy + It *-ano* -an] **1** *archaic* **:** a barker of dubious remedies ⟨~*s* at a county fair⟩ **2 a :** a pretender to medical knowledge **:** QUACK ⟨~*s* killing their patients by empiric procedures⟩ **b :** one making esp. noisy or showy pretenses to knowledge or ability **:** FRAUD ⟨replaced by the ~*s* and the rogues — by those without learning, without scruples, or both —Asher Moore⟩

char·la·tan·ic \¦==¦tanik, -ēk\ *or* **char·la·tan·i·cal** \-ēkəl, -ēk-\ *adj* **:** of or like a charlatan **:** marked by or given to pretension and quackery

char·la·tan·ish \ˈ== tə(ˌ)nish, -tᵊn(ˌ)i-\ *adj* **:** CHARLATANIC

char·la·tan·ism \ˈ== təˌnizəm, -tᵊnˌi-\ *n* -S **:** CHARLATANRY ⟨the dross of fraud and ~ —Lewis Mumford⟩

char·la·tan·ry \ˈ===rē, -ri\ *also* **char·la·tan·ery** *like first, or* ˈ==ˌtan(ə)rē *or* -ri *or* ˌ==ˈ=(=)=\ *or* **char·la·tan·e·rie** *like second, or* ˌ==ˌtan(ə)ˈrē\ *n* -ES **1 :** the practice of a charlatan **:** QUACKERY, IMPOSTURE ⟨a man given to absurd freaks of intellectual ~ —P.E.More⟩ **2 :** an act or instance of charlatanry

charles's law \ˈchärlzəz-, -äl-\ *n, usu cap C* [after Jacques A.C. *Charles* †1823 Fr. physicist, its formulator] **:** a statement in physics: the volume of a given mass of gas at a constant pressure varies directly as its absolute temperature — called also *Gay-Lussac's law*

¹charles·ton \ˈchärlztən, -äl-, -lst-\ *adj, usu cap* [fr. *Charleston*, S.C. & *Charleston*, W.Va.] **1 :** of or from Charleston, S.C. **:** of the kind or style prevalent in Charleston, S.C. ⟨a *Charleston* custom⟩ **2 :** of or from Charleston, the capital of West Virginia ⟨a *Charleston* resident⟩ **:** of the kind or style prevalent in Charleston, W.Va.

²charleston \"\ *n* -S *usu cap* [fr. *Charleston*, S.C.] **:** a ballroom dance in which the knees are twisted in and out and the heels are swung sharply outward on each step

³charleston \"\ *vi* -ED/-ING/-S *often cap* **:** to dance the Charleston

charles·to·ni·an \chärlzˈtōnēən, -äl-, -lˈst-, -nyən\ *n* -S *cap* [*Charleston*, S.C. *or Charleston*, W.Va. + E *-ian*] **:** a native or resident of Charleston, esp. Charleston, S. C., or Charleston, W.Va.

char·ley *or* **char·lie** \ˈchärlē, -älē, -li\ *n* -S *often cap* [dim. of *Charles*, proper name] **1** [perh. after *Charles* I †1649 king of England, who in 1640 improved the watchman system in London] *slang* **:** NIGHT WATCHMAN **2** [after *Charles* I, who wore such a beard] **:** a short pointed beard **3 :** a usu. black-faced or toothbrush-mustached clown whose forte is lugubrious pathos **4** [perh. after *Charlie* Chan, fictional Chin. detective created by Earl Derr Biggers †1933 Am. novelist] **:** an Oriental person

charley horse *n, sometimes cap C* [fr. *Charley* (the name) + *horse*; perh. fr. the occurrence of Charley as a typical name for old lame horses kept for family use] **1 :** pain and stiffness resulting from a bruise usu. of a thigh muscle followed by hardening of the bruised tissue **2 :** muscular strain or soreness esp. in a leg

charley no·ble *or* **charlie noble** \¦==ˈnōbəl\ *n, usu cap C&N* [prob. fr. the name *Charlie Noble*] **:** the galley smoke pipe

charley pitcher *n, usu cap C* [*Charley* + *pitcher* (vender)] *slang Brit* **:** a vagrant sharper

char·lie \ˈchärlē, -älē, -li\ *usu cap* [fr. the name *Charlie*] — a communications code word for the letter *c*

charlie mc·car·thy \¦==məˈkär¦thē, -kȧ\, ¦thi *also* ¦d·ē *or* ¦tē *or* -i\ *n, pl* **charlie mccarthys** *usu cap 1st C&M&3dC* [after *Charlie McCarthy*, ventriloquist's dummy made famous by Edgar Bergen *b*1903 Am. ventriloquist & comedian] **:** one under the complete domination of another often while enjoying apparent independence **:** STOOGE, YES-MAN, DUMMY ⟨uses him as a *Charlie McCarthy* to prove that even a schoolboy can see through the fallacious arithmetic of the opposition —Elmer Davis⟩

char·lier shoe \ˈshärlēˌā-, -lˌyā-\ *n, often cap C* [prob. fr. the name *Charlier*] **:** a narrow light horseshoe without a toe clip that is nailed in a groove made in the lower edge of the wall of a horse's hoof

char·lock \ˈchärˌläk, -ˌlək\ *or* **chad·lock** \ˈchad-\ *n* -S [ME *cherlok*, *carlok*, fr. OE *cerlic*] **:** any of several yellow-flowered weeds of the family Cruciferae; *specif* **:** a wild mustard (*Brassica kaber*) that is often troublesome in grainfields

¹char·lotte \ˈshärlət, ˈshäl-, *usu* -əd·+V\ *n* -S [F, prob. fr. the name *Charlotte*] **:** a dessert made by lining a dish with strips of bread, cake, or ladyfingers and filling it with fruit, whipped cream, custard, or other filling

²charlotte \"\ *adj, usu cap* [fr. *Charlotte*, N.C.] **:** of or from the city of Charlotte, N.C. ⟨a *Charlotte* suburb⟩ **:** of the kind or style prevalent in Charlotte

charlotte russe \¦=lət·ˈrüs\ *n, pl* **charlotte russ·es** \-səz\ [F, lit., Russian charlotte] **:** a charlotte made with sponge cake or ladyfingers and a whipped-cream or custard-gelatin filling

char·lotte·town \ˈ=lətˌtau̇n\ *adj, usu cap* [fr. *Charlottetown*, Prince Edward Island, Canada] **:** of or from Charlottetown, the capital of Prince Edward Island, Canada **:** of the kind or style prevalent in Charlottetown

charl·ton white \ˈchärltᵊn-, -tən-\ *n, often cap C* [prob. fr. the name *Charlton*] **:** LITHOPONE

¹charm \ˈchärm, -ȧm\ *n* -S *often attrib* [ME *charme*, fr. OF, fr. L *carmen* song, incantation, fr. *canere* to sing — more at CHANT] **1 a :** the chanting or reciting of a verse supposed to have magic or occult power **:** INCANTATION **b :** an action, process, or thing (as a word, phrase, or verse) believed to have such power **:** a magic spell **2 :** something worn about the person to ward off evil or ensure good fortune **:** AMULET **3 a :** a trait that fascinates, allures, or delights **:** a combination of entirely attractive and delightful traits ⟨a new and even greater ~ — the fascination of the unknown and mysterious —W.H.Hudson⟩ ⟨one of the great ~*s* of Lawrence . . . was that he could never be bored —Aldous Huxley⟩ **b :** an alluring physical attribute — used in pl. ⟨a dancer revealing her ~*s*⟩ **c :** compelling attractiveness and appeal dispelling any possible reserved or antagonistic feeling ⟨Alan, whose educated ~ had enabled him to marry an heiress —John Galsworthy⟩ ⟨an island of great ~, with its pleasing Mediterranean climate, its forest-clad mountains, its vineyards —Charles Woolley⟩ **4 :** a small ornament worn usu. on a bracelet or chain; *esp* **:** a metal miniature replica so worn ⟨a ~ bracelet⟩ — **like a charm :** as if by magic **:** most successfully and effectively ⟨a machine working *like a charm*⟩

²charm \"\ *vb* -ED/-ING/-S [ME *charmen*, fr. OF *charmer*, fr. LL *carminare* to enchant, sing, make verses, fr. L *carmin-*, *carmen* song, incantation] *vt* **1 :** to influence or control by or as if by charms: **a :** to subdue, dominate, change, or hold under a spell by magic power or power like magic in its supposed effectiveness **b :** to summon or sway by an attraction magical or otherwise compelling ⟨only his daughter had the power of ~*ing* this black brooding from his mind —Charles Dickens⟩ **c :** to please, soothe, or delight by compelling attraction ⟨what had ~*ed* her in it would still ~ her, even though . . . against her will —Edith Wharton⟩ **d :** to check, assuage, or calm as if by magic ⟨~ his rage with soft answers⟩ ⟨~ his grief⟩ **2 :** to endow with supernatural powers by means of charms; *esp* **:** to protect by spells, charms, or supernatural influences ⟨Milo brought an action against him for violence, but Clodius was ~*ed* even against forms of law —J.A.Froude⟩ **3** *obs* **:** to conjure or exhort (a person) typically with a special appeal ⟨~ a woman, by her husband's love, to speak⟩ **4 :** to summon, guide, control, or inveigle (an animal) typically by charms, music, or blandishment ⟨an early Norwich Pied Piper used a violin to ~ rattlesnakes —*Amer. Guide Series: Conn.*⟩ ⟨you can still ~ a bird off a tree —Philip Barry⟩ ~ *vi* **1 :** to use enchantments and spells **:** practice magic and enchantment ⟨no fairy takes, nor witch hath power to ~ —Shak.⟩ **2 :** to have the effect of a charm **:** PLEASE, DELIGHT, FASCINATE ⟨a philosophy that ~*s* by its completeness —H.O.Taylor⟩ **syn** see ATTRACT

³charm \"\ *n* -S [prob. by folk etymology fr. ¹*chirm*] **1** *now dial Eng* **:** a blended or confused noise (as of voices or bird songs) **:** CHIRM **2** *of finches* **:** FLOCK

⁴charm *vt* -ED/-ING/-S *obs* **:** to make music upon **:** PLAY, TUNE

char·man \ˈchärmən, -ˌman\ *n, pl* **charmen** [¹*chare* + *man*] **:** a man who does janitor's odd jobs

char·mat process \(ˈ)shär¦mä-\ *n, usu cap C* [after Eugene *Charmat* *fl*1907, its inventor] **:** a process for producing champagne in which the second fermentation takes place in a large glass-lined tank instead of in the bottle

charmed *adj* **:** extremely pleased or gratified **:** ENTRANCED ⟨how ~ I was with these new acquaintances —L.P.Smith⟩ — **charmed·ly** \ˈchärm(ə)dlē, -äm-, -li\ *adv*

charmed circle *n* **:** a group or coterie marked by severe exclusiveness ⟨only if they amassed very vast riches did they . . . find their way into the *charmed circle* of gentility —J.H. Plumb⟩

charmed life *n* **:** a life protected as if by magic charms **:** a life unusually unaffected by dangers and difficulties

charm·er \ˈchärmər, -ȧm-\ *n* -S [ME *charmere*, fr. *charmen* to charm + *-ere* -er] **:** one that charms: **a :** ENCHANTER, MAGICIAN **b :** one that pleases, intrigues, fascinates, or overcomes hostile, harsh, or dubious feeling; *esp* **:** an attractive woman

Char·meuse \(ˈ)shär¦m(y)üz, -¦ȧm-, -müs; ˈär¦mə(r)z, -ä¦məz\ *trademark* — used for a fine semilustrous crepe in satin weave

charm·ful \ˈchärmfəl, -ȧm-\ *adj* **:** employing charms **:** concerned with magic

charming *adj, sometimes* -ER/-EST [ME, fr. pres. part. of *charmen* to charm] **1 :** employing magic ⟨~ spells⟩ **2** *obs* **:** MELODIOUS, HARMONIOUS ⟨~ pipes⟩ **3 :** fascinating and delighting **:** extremely pleasing **:** marked by compelling attraction or appeal ⟨~ tapestries of rose and green —Elinor Wylie⟩ ⟨endowed with ~ manners, . . . he fascinated all whom he met —V.L.Parrington⟩ — **charm·ing·ly** *adv* — **charm·ing·ness** *n* -ES

charm·less \-mləs\ *adj* **:** lacking charm

charm school *n* **:** a school in which social graces are taught

charmstone \ˈ=ˌ=\ *n* **:** a smoothed stone often pointed at both ends and used as a ceremonial object by Indian shamans

char·ne·co \shärˈnā(ˌ)kü, -kō\ *n* -ES [prob. fr. *Charneco*, Portugal] **:** a sweet wine popular in Elizabethan and Jacobean England

¹char·nel \ˈchärnᵊl, -ȧn-\ *n* -S [ME, fr. MF, fr. ML *carnale*, fr. LL, neut. of *carnalis* fleshly — more at CARNAL] **1** *obs* **:** CEMETERY **2 a** *or* **charnel house :** a building, chamber, or other area in which bodies or bones are deposited **b :** a mortuary chapel

²charnel \"\ *adj* **1 :** constituting a charnel **2 :** gruesomely indicative or suggestive of death **:** SEPULCHRAL, GHASTLY ⟨a chest filled full of dead men's bones. A ~ smell came from them —Hope Muntz⟩ ⟨devices to which the ~ superstition of the monks has given rise —E.A.Poe⟩

³charnel *n* -S [ME, fr. MF *chernel*, fr. L *cardinalis* of a hinge — more at CARDINAL] *obs* **:** a hinge esp. of a helmet

char·nock·ite \ˈchärnəˌkīt\ *n* -S [Job *Charnock* †1693 Eng. founder of Calcutta + E *-ite*; fr. the fact that his tombstone is made of this rock] **1 :** any of a series of rocks ranging from granite to norite and pyroxenite all containing hypersthene **2 :** hypersthene-granite

cha·ro·lais *or* **cha·rol·lais** \¦sharə¦lā\ *n, usu cap* [F (*boeuf*) *charolais*, *charollais*, fr. *Charolais*, *Charollais*, district in France] **:** a breed of large white cattle developed in France for draft purposes but now kept chiefly as a beef breed and important for crossbreeding — see CHARBRAY

cha·roles cattle *or* **cha·rolles cattle** \shəˈrōl-, -ōl-\ *n, often cap 1st C* [fr. *Charoles*, *Charolles*, town in the Charolais district] **:** cattle of the Charolais breed

char·on's staircase \ˈka(a)rənz-, ˈkär-, -ˌränz-\ *n, usu cap C* [after *Charon*, ferryman of the dead in Hades, fr. L, fr. Gk *Charōn*; trans. of Gk *Charōnioi klimates*; fr. the steps' supposedly leading to the underworld] **:** a flight of steps from the middle of the stage to the orchestra of an early Greek theater

char·o·phy·ce·ae \ˌkarəˈfīsēˌē, -fis-\ *n pl, cap* [NL, fr. *Chara* + *-o-* + *-phyceae*] **:** a class of green algae (division Chlorophyta) coextensive with the order Charales

cha·roph·y·ta \kəˈräfəd·ə\ *n pl, cap* [NL fr. *Chara* + *-o-* + *-phyta*] *in some classifications* **:** a group of plants equivalent to the order Charales and variously treated as a division, subdivision, or often as a class of the green algae — **char·o·phyte** \ˈkarəˌfīt\ *n* -S

charoseth *or* **charoset** *or* **charoses** *var of* HAROSETH

char·pie \(ˈ)shär¦pē, ˈshärpē\ *n* -S [F, fr. MF, fr. fem. of *charpi*, past part. of *charpir* to card, ravel out, modif. of L *carpere* to pluck — more at HARVEST] **:** LINT; *esp* **:** scraped lint

¹charpit \ˈ=ˌ=\ *n* [³*char* + *pit*] **:** a pit in which wood is charred; *esp* **:** a pit between tree roots for burning out stumps

²charpit \"\ *vt* **charpitted; charpitted; charpitting; charpits :** to burn or burn out with a charpit ⟨*charpitting* stumps⟩

char·poy \ˈchärˌpȯi\ *also* **char·pai** \-ˌpī\ *n* -S [Hindi *cārpāī*, fr. Per *chārpāī*, lit., four-footed, fr. *chahār*, *chār* four (fr. MPer) + *pāī* foot, fr. MPer; akin to Av *chathwārō* four, Skt *catvāra* and to Av *pad-*, *pād-* foot, Skt *pādā* — more at FOUR, FOOT] **:** a bed consisting of a frame strung with tapes or light rope used esp. in India

char·py machine \ˈshär(ˌ)pē-\ *n, usu cap C* [after A. G. A. *Charpy* *b*1865 Fr. engineer] **:** a machine for measuring the breaking strength of materials under impact

charpy test *n, usu cap C* **:** a test made with a Charpy machine

char·qui *also* **char·que** \ˈchärkē, ˈsh-\ *n* -S [Sp, fr. Quechua *ch'arki* dried meat] **:** jerked meat; *esp* **:** jerked beef

charr *var of* CHAR

charred *past of* CHAR *or of* CHARE

char·rer \ˈchärər, -ȧrə\ *n* -S [³*char* + *-er*] **:** one that chars the interiors of barrels in which whiskey is to be aged

charrette *var of* CHARETTE

charring *pres part of* CHAR *or of* CHARE

char·ro \ˈchä(ˌ)rō\ *n* -S [MexSp, fr. Sp, rude, coarse, rustic, of poor taste, fr. Basque *txar* bad, defective, weak] **:** a Mexican horseman or cowboy typically dressed in an elaborately decorated outfit of close-fitting pants, jacket or serape, and sombrero

char·ro·nia \kəˈrōnēə\ *n, cap* [NL] **:** a genus of mammals consisting of the yellow-throated marten

char·rua \chəˈrüə\ *n, pl* **charrua** *or* **charruas** *usu cap* [Sp *charrúa*; of AmerInd origin] **1 a :** an extinct Indian people of Uruguay and adjacent parts of Argentina and Brazil **b :** a member of such people **2 :** the language of the Charrua people

char·ry \ˈchärē\ *adj, usu* -ER/-EST [⁴*char* + *-y*] **1 :** forming or constituting charcoal **2 :** suggestive of charring or charcoal

chars *pres 3d sing of* CHAR, *pl of* CHAR

¹chart \ˈchärt, -ȧt, *usu* -d·+V\ *n* -S [MF *charte* map, charter, fr. L *charta* document, piece of papyrus — more at CARD] **1 a** *obs* **:** MAP **b :** an outline map for conveying information about something other than the purely geographic ⟨a ~ of temperature variations⟩ ⟨a ~ showing military maneuvers⟩ ⟨a ~ of the town lots⟩ **c :** a hydrographic map **:** a map on which is projected a portion of water and usu. adjacent or included land intended esp. for use by navigators ⟨the U. S. Coast Survey ~*s*⟩ ⟨the British Admiralty ~*s*⟩ **d :** a small-scale representation of an area of the earth's surface, its culture and relief, and various aeronautical aids intended for use in air navigation **2** *archaic* **:** CHARTER, GRANT, DEED **3** *archaic* **:** CARD, PLAYING CARD **4 :** a form designed to record or provide information quickly and simply esp. about something fluctuating or changing **:** TABLE, GRAPH, DIAGRAM ⟨a ~ of rainfall for the past year⟩ ⟨a ~ of price changes⟩ ⟨a clinical ~ for a hospital patient⟩ **5 :** a summary of a racehorse's form

²chart \"\ *vt* -ED/-ING/-S **1 :** to make a map or chart of **:** record or indicate by map, chart, outline, or graph **:** DELINEATE ⟨the 1728 expedition that ~*ed* the dividing line between the two colonies —*Amer. Guide Series: N. C.*⟩ ⟨above the boiling cloud cap of a hurricane, an Air Force plane ~*s* the size of the disturbance —*N. Y. Times Mag.*⟩ **2 :** to lay out a plan for typically in orderly outline **:** PLAN, PROJECT ⟨we have ~*ed* the course to a stable world peace —H.S.Truman⟩ ⟨Churchill and Roosevelt met to ~ strategy —*N. Y. Times Mag.*⟩

char·ta \ˈkärd·ə\ *n, pl* **char·tae** \-ˌrˌtē\ [NL, fr. L, leaf of paper, writing, letter] **1 :** a strip of paper impregnated or coated with a medicinal substance and used for external application **2 :** a paper folded to contain a medicinal powder

char·ta·ceous \(ˈ)kär¦tāshəs\ *adj* [LL *chartaceus*, fr. L *charta* + *-aceus* -aceous] **:** resembling paper **:** made of paper ⟨a ~ plant tissue⟩

¹char·ter \ˈchär¦d·ər, -ä¦d·ə, ¦tə(r)\ *n* -S [ME *chartre*, fr. OF, fr. L *chartula* little paper, dim. of *charta*] **1 :** a written evidence, instrument, or contract executed in due form between man and man **:** DEED, CONVEYANCE **2 a :** an instrument in writing from the sovereign power of a state or country granting or guaranteeing rights, franchises, or privileges **b :** an instrument in writing creating and defining the franchises of a city, university, company, or other public or private corporation **c :** CONSTITUTION ⟨the *Charter* of the United Nations⟩ **3 :** an instrument in writing from the constituted authorities of an order or society creating a lodge, branch, or local unit and defining its powers **4 :** a special privilege, immunity, or exemption that is usu. publicly conceded or generally understood ⟨a ~ to speak freely⟩ **5** *or* **charter party :** a mercantile lease of a ship **:** a specific contract by which the owners of a ship let the entire ship or some principal part of it to another person to be used by him in transportation for his own account either under their charge or under his charge

²charter \"\ *vt* **chartered; chartered; chartering** \-d·əriŋ, -tər- *also* -ärˌtriŋ *or* -ȧ·tr-\ **charters** [ME *charteren*, fr. *charter*, n.] **1 :** to grant or issue a charter to: **a :** to establish or call into being by charter **:** acknowledge the existence of by charter ⟨a state university ~*ed* in 1825⟩ **b :** to endow with certain rights or functions by charter **:** assign a given status to by charter **:** FRANCHISE ⟨an organization ~*ed* to undertake the work⟩ **c :** to convey by charter ⟨Lyndon was ~*ed* in 1780 to Jonathan Arnold —*Amer. Guide Series: Vt.*⟩ **d** *Brit* **:** to certify or authorize (a person) as qualified ⟨a ~*ed* mechanical engineer⟩ **2 :** to grant special privilege or license to ⟨~*ed* libertines of imperial Rome⟩ **3 :** to hire, rent, or lease (as a ship, airplane, or bus) esp. for exclusive use

charter chest *n* **:** a chest used esp. in Scotland as a repository for family papers and documents (as charters or deeds) ⟨from the private *charter chest* the next step was to the public records of the kingdom —A.R.Wagner⟩

charter colony *n, often cap 1st C* **:** one of the three British colonies in America (Massachusetts, Connecticut, and Rhode Island) governed by royal charter without direct interference from the crown — compare PROPRIETARY COLONY, ROYAL COLONY

chartered accountant *n, Brit* **:** a member of an institute of chartered or accredited accountants — compare CERTIFIED PUBLIC ACCOUNTANT

chartered company *n, Brit* **:** a corporation created by charter

char·ter·er \-d·ərə(r), -tər-\ *n* -S **:** one that charters; *esp* **:** one that charters a ship

charter hand *n* **:** COURT HAND

char·ter·house \ˈ=ˌ=ˌ=\ *n* [by folk etymology fr. MF *chartrouse*, irreg. (prob. influenced by *chartre* prison, fr. L *carcer*) fr. *Chartosse* (now Saint-Pierre-de-*Chartreuse*), locality near Grenoble, France, the site of the first Carthusian monastery — more at CANCEL] **:** a Carthusian monastery

char·ter·ite \-əˌrīt\ *n* -S **:** an advocate or supporter of a charter

charter member *n* **:** an original member of a society or corporation; *esp* **:** one named in a charter

charter party *n* [by folk etymology fr. ML *charta partita*, lit., divided charter, one part being given to each of the contractors] **:** CHARTER 5

charter school *n, usu cap C* [fr. *Charter* (*Society*), Irish educational organization founded 1733] **:** any of the schools established in Ireland in the 18th century to furnish Protestant education for the Roman Catholic poor

chart house *n* : a compartment on or near the bridge of a ship where charts and other navigational equipment are kept and used — called also *chart room*

charting *pres part of* CHART

char·tism \'chär|d·,izəm, -ä|, |,ti-\ *n* -s *usu cap* [*charter* + *-ism*] : the principles and practices of a body of 19th century English political reformers advocating better social and industrial conditions for the working classes

1char·tist \|d·əst,|tə-\ *n* -s *usu cap* [*charter* + *-ist*] : an advocate of Chartism

2chartist \"\ *n* -s [1*chart* + *-ist*] **1** : CARTOGRAPHER **2** : one that studies, interprets, and makes predictions as to stock-market action from charts and graphic records

chart·less \-tləs\ *adj* : UNCHARTED ⟨a ~ sea⟩

chart of accounts : a list of account names arranged systematically and usu. coded numerically or alphabetically or both to form the general framework of the accounting system of a specific business and to establish a scheme of account classification

chart·og·ra·pher \chärd·'ägrəfər, -r'tä-; kär'tä-\ *or* **chart·og·ra·phist** \-fəst\ *n* -s [by alter.] : CARTOGRAPHER

chart·ol·o·gy \chärd·'äləjē, -r'tä-; kär'tä-\ *n* -ES [1*chart* + *-o-* + *-logy*] : CARTOGRAPHY

chart·om·e·ter \-ämәd·ər, -ətər\ *n* -s [1*chart* + *-o-* + *-meter*] : an instrument for measuring distances on charts or maps

char·toph·y·lax \kär'täpfə,laks\ *n* -ES [LGk, fr. Gk *charto-* (fr. *chartēs* paper) + Gk *phylax* guard — more at CARD] : a chancellor of a bishop or diocese of the Eastern Orthodox Church who serves as an archivist and has certain administrative and judicial duties

char·treuse \(')shär¦trüz, -ä¦t-, -üs, *sometimes esp in senses 1 & 3* -är¦trə(r)z *or* -ä¦trəz\ *n* -s [F, fr. La Grande *Chartreuse*, chief monastery of the Carthusian order near Grenoble, France, where it was made — more at CHARTERHOUSE] **1** *sometimes cap* : a liqueur usu. green or yellow in color flavored with orange peel, hyssop, peppermint, and other ingredients **2** [so called fr. the color of chartreuse liqueurs] **a** : a variable color averaging a brilliant yellow green — see CHARTREUSE GREEN **b** : a strong greenish yellow — see CHARTREUSE YELLOW **3** [F, fr. La Grande *Chartreuse* monastery] **a** : several vegetables arranged and cooked in a mold **b** : a mold of two or more foods with meat or fish in the center

chartreuse green *n* : a dark greenish yellow that is redder, less strong, and very slightly lighter than average olive yellow

chartreuse tint *n* : a pale yellow green that is yellower, lighter, and slightly stronger than smoke gray, lighter than oyster gray, and yellower, less strong, and much lighter than average Nile

chartreuse yellow *n* **1** : a variable color averaging a strong greenish yellow that is duller than bright chartreuse yellow **2** : a light to moderate greenish yellow that is greener and slightly stronger than primrose yellow or canary

chartreux *n, pl* **chartreux** *usu cap* [F, back-formation fr. *chartreuse* monastery, fr. MF *chartrouse* — more at CHARTERHOUSE] *obs* : CARTHUSIAN

chart room *n* : CHART HOUSE

charts *pl of* CHART, *pres 3d sing of* CHART

char·tu·la \'kärchələ\ *n, pl* **char·tu·lae** \-,lē\ [L, little paper —more at CHARTER] : a folded paper containing a single dose of a medicinal powder

1char·tu·lary \'kärchə,lerē\ *n* -ES [ML *chartularium* case for storing papers, fr. L *chartula* little paper + *-arium* -ary] : CARTULARY

2chartulary \"\ *n* -ES [LL *chartularius*, fr. L *chartula* + *-arius* -ary] : a keeper of archives

charwoman \'≈,≈≈\ *n, pl* **charwomen** [1*chare* + *woman*] **1** *Brit* : a woman hired to char **2** : a cleaning woman usu. in a large building

chary \'cha(a)rē, -er-, -är-, -ri\ *adj, often* -ER/-EST [ME *charry*, *chary* sorrowful, dear, fr. OE *cearig* sorrowful, fr. *cearu* sorrow; akin to OHG *charag* sorrowful — more at CARE] **1** *archaic* : PRECIOUS, TREASURED, DEAR **2** : marked by discreet caution: **a** : hesitant and vigilant about dangers and risks : unwilling to proceed without much consideration ⟨a ~ investor⟩ ⟨the hunter was ~⟩ ⟨yet let us be ~ of casting the first stone —J.L.Lowes⟩ **b** : FASTIDIOUS ⟨~ about the food he eats⟩ **c** : DIFFIDENT, RESERVED ⟨the *chariest* maid is prodigal enough if she unmask her beauty to the moon —Shak.⟩ **d** : sparing and reluctant in granting, accepting, or expending : tending to withhold, preserve, or guard ⟨a busy man ~ of his time⟩ ⟨I wanted my father's good opinion because he was ~ of his compliments and shy in his affection —W.A.White⟩ **syn** see CAUTIOUS

cha·ryb·dis \kə'ribdəs\ *n* -ES *usu cap* [fr. *Charybdis* (now *Galofalo*), whirlpool off the northeastern extremity of Sicily, fr. L, fr. Gk] : a destructive peril — usu. used as the alternative to *Scylla* ⟨between the Scylla of national parochialism and the *Charybdis* of complete exoticism —Bernard Smith⟩

chas·a·ble *or* **chase·a·ble** \'chāsəbəl\ *adj* [ME *chaceable*, fr. *chacen*, *chasen* to chase + *-able*] : suitable for being chased : fit for hunting

1chase \'chās\ *vb* -ED/-ING/-s [ME *chacen*, *chasen*, fr. MF *chasser*, fr. OF *chacier*, fr. (assumed) VL *captiare*, fr. L *captare* to seize, strive after — more at CATCH] *vt* **1 a** : to follow usu. rapidly and intently in order to or as if to trail or overtake, seize, molest, or do violence to : PURSUE ⟨some police *chasing* a criminal in a taxi⟩ ⟨a dog *chasing* a rabbit⟩ ⟨the pirates *chased* the treasure galleon⟩ ⟨children *chasing* each other in play⟩ ⟨waves *chased* each other up the beach⟩ **b** : HUNT ⟨rose to ~ the deer at five —Alfred Tennyson⟩ **c** : to follow or attend upon usu. persistently and hopefully with the intention of attracting, alluring, or persuading into companionship or intimacy ⟨a bobby-soxer *chasing* boys⟩ ⟨a middle-aged man *chasing* women half his age⟩ **d** : to follow (as an ambulance) to the scene of an accident in order to solicit business **e** : to follow up (a strong drink) with a chaser **2** *obs* : PERSECUTE, HARASS **3** : to move usu. rapidly in the direction of in order to observe, obtain, or find out about ⟨children *chasing* a fire⟩ ⟨library attendants *chasing* books called for by readers⟩ ⟨salesmen *chasing* new orders⟩ — sometimes used with *down* ⟨detectives *chased* down all possible clues to the murder⟩ **4 a** : to cause to depart or flee esp. by the use of or threat of violence or other harassment : DRIVE, EXPEL, DISPEL ⟨love hath *chased* sleep from my enthralled eyes —Shak.⟩ ⟨I'll ~ the whole rebel army all the way to South Carolina —Kenneth Roberts⟩ ⟨~ cattle out of a wheat field⟩ **b** *slang* : to take (oneself) off ⟨go ~ yourself; you're too small to play with us⟩ **c** *baseball* : to cause the removal of (as a pitcher by a batting rally) or oust from a game ~ *vi* **1** : to chase an animal, person, or thing — usu. used with *after* ⟨the children of Israel returned from *chasing* after the Philistines —1 Sam 17: 53 (AV)⟩ ⟨*chasing* after material possessions⟩ ⟨a girl who ~s after boys⟩ **2** : RUSH, HASTEN ⟨*chasing* all over town looking for a place to stay⟩ **syn** see FOLLOW

2chase *also* **chace** \"\ *n* -s [ME *chace*, *chase*, fr. OF *chace*, fr. *chacier*, v.] **1 a** : the act of pursuing for the purpose of seizing, capturing, molesting, doing violence, or killing : PURSUIT **b** : the searching out and pursuit of wild animals for the purpose of killing them as an occupation or sport — used with *the*; see HUNTING **c** : the act of pursuing for the purpose of putting to flight : ROUT **d** : a usu. earnest or frenzied seeking after something greatly desired ⟨this mad ~ of fame —John Dryden⟩ ⟨the excitements of the intellectual ~ —R.W. Southern⟩ **2** : something pursued (as a hunted animal or a ship) : QUARRY **3 a** *Eng law* : a liberty or franchise to hunt within certain limits of land not necessarily owned by the one having the liberty or of keeping beasts of chase therein **b** *in England* : a tract of unenclosed land used as a game preserve usu. distinguished from a forest in being smaller, having fewer law-enforcement officers, and being sometimes private property — compare FOREST, PARK, WARREN **4** : a stroke in court tennis similar to a placement in lawn tennis which requires that the players replay the point; *also* : the point so replayed **5** *dial* : a lane between fields on a farm **6** *obs* : the chase guns of a ship; *also* : the part of a ship in which the chase ports are **7** : the length of yarn in one traverse of the winding faller in winding the cop in cotton spinning **8** [by shortening] : STEEPLECHASE **9** : a sequence of a melodrama or now usu. of a motion picture representing the pursuit of one character by others

3chase \"\ *vt* -ED/-ING/-s [ME *chasen*, modif. of MF *enchasser* to set (as a jewel) — more at ENCHASE] **1 a** : to ornament (a metal, esp. silver, surface) by indenting with a hammer and tools without a cutting edge **b** : to make (as a decoration) by such indentation **c** : to set esp. with gems **2** : to cut (a thread) with a chaser

4chase \"\ *n* -s [F *chas* eye of a needle, space between beams, compartment of a house, fr. OF, fr. LL *capsus* enclosed space in a house, nave of a church, bladder, fr. L, cage, part of a wagon, alter. of *capsa* box — more at CASE] **1 a** *obs* : the furrow on a crossbow in which the arrow lies **b** *obs* : the bore of a cannon **c** : the part of a cannon from the trunnions or part where trunnions would be if the piece had them to the mouth or the swell of the muzzle — see CANNON illustration **2 a** : a groove or channel for something to lie in or pass through: as **a** : TRENCH **b** : a channel in the inner face of a masonry wall of a building to provide space for pipes, ducts, or wiring **c** : a groove cut lengthwise for the reception of a part to make a joint **3** : a kind of joint in ship building by which an overlap joint is changed to a flush joint by means of a gradually deepening rabbet (as at the ends of clinker-built boats)

5chase \"\ *vt* : GROOVE, INDENT

6chase \"\ *n* -s [prob. fr. F *châsse* frame — more at CHASSE] **1 a** : a rectangular steel or iron frame into which letterpress matter is locked for printing or plating — compare FORM **b** : any of certain analogous devices (as for holding work in photocomposing and duplicating machines or for holding carton-cutting dies) **2** : typeset matter before it is placed in a chase

chaseable *var of* CHASABLE

chase around *vi* : to rush from one diversion to another esp. with one of the opposite sex — often used to imply illicit sexual relations

chased *past of* CHASE

chase doll \'chās-\ *n, usu cap C* [after Martha J. *Chase* *fl*1880, its inventor] : a dummy used for teaching purposes in hospitals maintaining training schools for nurses

chase gun \'chās\ *or* **chase piece** *n* : a cannon at the bow or stern of an armed ship used in pursuit

chase literature *n* : literature in which suspense is created by a chase of one person or group by another

chase mortise *n* [4*chase*] : a mortise one or both ends of which slope from the bottom to the surface to permit the insertion of the tenon when the clearance outside is limited

chase mortise

chase port *n* [*chase* (*gun*)] : a porthole from which a chase gun is fired

1chas·er \'chāsə(r)\ *n* -s [ME *chasur*, fr. OF *chaceour*, fr. *chacier* to chase + *-eour* -or — more at CHASE] **1** : one that chases: as **a** : HUNTER **b** : SUBMARINE CHASER **c** : PHILANDERER **d** : a piece of music played or an inferior vaudeville act or motion picture presented to induce an audience to leave **e** *slang* : a prison guard **2** : CHASE GUN ⟨a bow ~⟩ ⟨a stern ~⟩ **3 a** : one that follows logs out of the forest in order to signal the yarder engineer to stop them if they become fouled — called also *frogger* **b** : one that unhooks the cable used to drag logs from the forest to the yard and readies the equipment to be sent back **4 a** : a drink or occas. food taken after a drink of strong alcoholic content **b** : something (as a literary work or portion of a literary work) that is of a light or mollifying nature in comparison with that which it follows or accompanies **5** [by shortening] : STEEPLECHASER

2chaser \"\ *n* -s [3*chase* + *-er*] : one that ornaments by chasing: as **a** : a skilled worker who produces raised designs on silver or similar metals **b** : a skilled worker who cuts the design and finishes the shaping of molds used to cast jewelry articles

3chaser \"\ *n* -s [5*chase* + *-er*] **1 a** : a threading tool either many-toothed or having a single cutting edge shaped for cutting or finishing external or internal screw threads of specified pitch and standard usu. on work revolving in a lathe **b** : one of the cutting bits in a composite die or tap **2** : a grinding machine used in ore dressing and made with a revolving pan or base and fixed rollers **3** : a lathe operator whose specialty is cutting screw threads

chaser stone *n* [2*chaser*] : a flat circular stone set on edge and rolled on a stone pavement to pulverize minerals

chases *pres 3d sing of* CHASE

chasid *n, pl* **chasidim** *usu cap, var of* HASID

1chasing *n* -s [by shortening] : STEEPLECHASING

2chasing *n* -s [fr. gerund of 3*chase*] **1 a** : the act or art of ornamenting by chasing **b** : the design produced by chasing or the work chased **2** : the process of finishing the surface of castings by polishing and removing small imperfections **3** : a calendered finish for improving the luster and appearance of fabrics (as cotton or linen)

chasm \'kazəm\ *n* -s [L *chasma*, fr. Gk; akin to L *hiare* to gape, yawn — more at YAWN] **1 a** : a deep opening (as in the earth) : a narrow deep steep-walled valley, gorge, or canyon : a yawning abyss : a deep gap impassable by ordinary means ⟨the brink of a precipice, of a ~ in the earth over two hundred feet deep, the sides sheer cliffs —Willa Cather⟩ **b** : CLEFT, FISSURE, RAVINE **c** : BLANK, OMISSION, HIATUS ⟨if I leave anywhere a ~ in my narrative, tell me —Sheridan Le Fanu⟩ **2** : a marked esp. irreconcilable division, separation, or difference ⟨our only way of closing the ~ between the magnificent richness of human potentiality and the paltriness of human achievement —Paul Pickrel⟩; *esp* : one due to a marked opposition of attitude, opinion, belief, or loyalty ⟨trade between the two countries had attained a considerable volume despite the . . . political ~ between them —*Collier's Yr. Bk.*⟩ ⟨the rifts that seemed to cleave soldier from civilian, in habit and state of mind, tempting the former to make the ~ permanent —Dixon Wecter⟩

chasma *n* -s [L] **1** *obs* : a gaping or yawning esp. of the earth or sea **2** *obs* : a large rent or fissure in the earth **3** *obs* : a wide gap or breach

chas·mal \'kazməl\ *adj* : resembling a chasm

chasmed \-zmd\ *adj* : having chasms

chas·mic \-zmik\ *adj* : resembling a chasm (as in grandeur or proportions)

chas·mo·gam·ic \¦kazmə¦gamik\ *also* **chas·mog·a·mous** \(')kaz'mägəməs\ *adj* : characterized by chasmogamy

chas·mog·a·my \kaz'mägəmē\ *n* -ES [ISV *chasm-* (fr. Gk *chasma* opening) + *-o-* + *-gamy*] : the opening of the perianth at maturity for the purpose of fertilization (as in most flowers) — compare CLEISTOGAMY

chas·mo·phyte \'kazmə,fīt\ *n* -s [ISV *chasm-* + *-o-* + *-phyte*; prob. orig. formed as G *chasmophyt*] : a plant that grows in the crevices of rocks

chasmy \'kaz(ə)mē\ *adj* **1** : abounding with chasms **2** : CHASMIC

1chasse \'shäs\ *n* -s [F *châsse*, fr. OF *chasse*, fr. L *capsa* box, case — more at CASE] : a reliquary or shrine of a saint

2chas·sé \(')sha¦sā\ *vi* **chasséd; chasséd; chasséing; chassés** [F, n.] **1** : to make the dance movement called *chassé* **2** : SASHAY

3chas·sé \"\ *n* -s [F, fr. past part. of *chasser* to chase, fr. OF *chacier* — more at CHASE] **1** : a dance step in which a slide on one foot is followed closely by a slide on the other foot in a rhythm resembling that of the galop **2** : a chassé step in figure skating

4chasse \'shas, -ä-\ *n* -s [F] : a liqueur taken after coffee

chasse-ca·fé \¦≈(,)ka¦fā\ *n* -s [F, lit., coffee-chaser, fr. *chasser* to chase + *café* coffee, fr. Turk *kahve* — more at COFFEE] *archaic* : 4CHASSE

chas·sé-croi·sé \sha¦säkr(ə)wä¦zā\ *n, pl* **chassé-croisés** [F, lit., crossed chassé, fr. *chassé* the dance + *croisé*, past part. of *croiser* to cross, fr. OF, fr. *crois* cross, fr. L *cruc-*, *crux* — more at CROSS] : a movement in a quadrille or country-dance in which partners exchange places by means of a chassé

chasse-ma·rée \¦shasmə¦rā\ *n* -s [F, lit., tide-chaser, fr. *chasser* to chase + *marée* tide, fr. OF, fr. *mer* sea, fr. L *mare* — more at MERE] : a French coasting lugger

chasse·pot \'sha,spō\ *n* -s [F, fr. Antoine A. *Chassepot* †1905 Fr. inventor who designed it] : a bolt-action rifle firing a paper cartridge having in its base a percussion cap exploded by a firing pin

chas·seur \sha'sər, +V -ər·\ *n* -s [F, fr. OF *chaceour* — more at CHASER] **1** : HUNTER, HUNTSMAN **2** : one of a body of light cavalry or infantry trained for rapid maneuvering **3 a** : an attendant upon persons of rank or wealth who wears a plume and sword **b** : an employee in a continental European hotel having any of various duties (as those of a bellboy or doorman)

chas·sez \(')sha¦sā\ *n, pl* **chassez·es** \sha'sā(zə)z\ [by alter.] : 3CHASSÉ

chassid *n, pl* **chassidim** *usu cap, var of* HASID

chas·si·gnite \'shasən,yīt, sha'sēn-\ *n* -s [G *chassignit*, fr. *Chassigny*, eastern France + G *-it* -ite] : an achondritic meteorite of olivine and chromite

chas·sis \'chasē, 'sh-, -aasē, -si *sometimes* -səs\ *n, pl* **chassis** \-a(a)sēz, -iz\ *also* **chassises** \-a(a)səsəz\ [F *châssis*, fr. OF *chassiz*, fr. (assumed) VL *capsicium*, fr. L *capsa* box, case — more at CASE] **1** *obs* : a wooden frame fitted or to be fitted with a sheet of paper, linen, or glass : a sash esp. of a window **2 a** : the frame upon which is mounted the body (as of an automobile or airplane), the working parts (as of a radio or other electronic device), the barrel and other recoiling parts (of a cannon), or the roof, walls, floors, and facing (as of a building) **b** : the frame and working parts as opposed to the body (as of an automobile) or cabinet (as of a radio or television set) **c** *slang, of a woman* : FIGURE 8b **3** : a calibrated frame used by a sculptor in making an enlarged or reduced copy of his plaster model

chas·ta·cos·ta \,shastə'kóstə\ *n, pl* **chastacosta** *or* **chastacostas** *usu cap* [Chastacosta *Shista-Kwûsta*] **1 a** : an Athapaskan people in the Illinois and Rogue river valleys, Oregon **b** : a member of such people **2** : the language of the Chastacosta people

chaste \'chāst\ *adj, usu* -ER/-EST [ME, fr. OF, fr. L *castus* pure, chaste — more at CASTE] **1 a** : abstaining from sexual intercourse that is reprobated by religion or condemned by morality ⟨~ behavior⟩ **b** : abstaining from such intercourse and in addition from any willful acts or thoughts that are likely to lead to its occurrence **2 a** : abstaining from all sexual relations ⟨Galahad's ~ life⟩ **b** : CLEAN, PURE, STAINLESS ⟨~ stars —Shak.⟩ **c** : free from lewdness, obscenity, indecency, suggestiveness, or offensiveness : MODEST, DECENT ⟨his conversation is ~ —Ernest Dimnet⟩ **d** : free of connection or association with anything crass, sordid, impure, or debasing ⟨the ~ and abstracted intellect of the scholar —Elinor Wylie⟩ **3 a** *archaic* : RESTRAINED, SUBDUED ⟨her tastes were, however, too feminine and ~ ever to render her eccentric —E.G.Bulwer-Lytton⟩ **b** : lacking that which provides sensual pleasure : severely simple : AUSTERE, ASCETIC, PLAIN ⟨a ~ meal⟩ **c** : decorous and somewhat severe in design or expression : free of anything meretricious, florid, or tawdry : REFINED, SIMPLE ⟨a ~ border of conventionalized flowers⟩

syn PURE, MODEST, DECENT: CHASTE stresses absence of immorality or sexuality in acts or behavior and sometimes even in thoughts or suggestions, and connotes a complete avoidance of anything meretricious ⟨all virtuous persons who hear this song whose lives are *chaste* and placid —Elinor Wylie⟩ ⟨she . . . withdrew to the *chaste* darkness of her own room where she knelt before a plaster virgin —Louis Bromfield⟩ PURE indicates avoidance of immoral action and lustful thoughts and desires ⟨it may have been that . . . he had never known any woman, that he had been *pure* as a saint —Louis Bromfield⟩ ⟨as down she knelt for heaven's grace and boon . . . she seem'd a splendid angel . . . so *pure* a thing, so free from mortal taint —John Keats⟩ MODEST stresses avoidance of anything brazen, bold, wanton, or suggestive in behavior, speech, or appearance ⟨she had previously made a respectful virginlike curtsey to the gentleman, and her *modest* eyes gazed so perseveringly on the carpet that it was a wonder how she should have found an opportunity to see him —W.M.Thackeray⟩ ⟨to suggest that it [the infidelity of Antony] had been largely Octavia's own fault in dressing in so *modest* a way and behaving with such decorum —Robert Graves⟩ DECENT indicates accord with conventions of what is seemly or proper in behavior or language ⟨sex must be treated from the first as natural, delightful, and *decent* —Bertrand Russell⟩ ⟨after only a *decent* period of mourning, Mr. Murdock married Marie Antoinette O'Daniel —W.A.White⟩ ⟨filthy beyond all powers of *decent* expression —Leslie Stephen⟩

chas·tek paralysis \'cha,stek-\ *n, usu cap C* [after J.S. *Chastek* *fl*1932 Am. fox rancher] : a fatal paralysis of ranch-raised foxes and minks fed raw freshwater fish that is due to inactivation of thiamine by an enzyme (thiaminase) present in fish

chaste·ly \'chās(t)lē, -li\ *adv* [ME, fr. *chaste* + *-ly*] : in a chaste manner

chas·ten \'chāsən\ *vt* **chastened; chastened; chastening** \-s(ə)niŋ\ **chastens** [alter. of obs. E *chaste* chasten, fr. ME *chasten*, *chastien*, fr. OF *chastier*, fr. L *castigare* to punish, fr. *castus* pure + *-igare* (fr. *agere* to lead, drive) — more at CHASTE, ACT] **1 a** : to subject to pain, suffering, deprivation, or misfortune in order to correct, strengthen, or perfect in character, in mental or spiritual qualities, or in conduct : DISCIPLINE ⟨whom the Lord loveth he ~*eth* —Heb 12:6(AV)⟩ **b** : to act upon or affect in any way so as to correct, strengthen, or perfect (as in character, conduct, or mental or spiritual qualities) **2 a** : to make (a work of art or literature, an artistic or literary style, or some natural object regarded with respect to its aesthetic qualities) more decorous, restrained, or refined : remove floridity, excessive exuberance or luxuriance, or irregularity from : CORRECT, PURIFY **b** : to increase the purity or refinement of (the mind or mental faculties) ⟨~ and enlarge the mind —A.H.Layard⟩ ⟨the once common practice of making children commit passages to memory had a ~*ing* effect on the general ear and literary conscience —George Sampson⟩ **c** : to keep from being excessive or overintense : RESTRAIN, TEMPER ⟨his air of ~*ed* triumph —Dorothy Sayers⟩ **d** : to cause to be more humble, modest, restrained, or cautious : SUBDUE **syn** see PUNISH

chas·ten·er \-s(ə)nə(r)\ *n* -s : one that chastens

chaste·ness \-s(t)nəs\ *n* -ES : the state or quality of being chaste

chas·ten·ing·ly *adv* : in a chastening manner

chas·ten·ment \'chāsənmənt\ *n* -s : the action of chastening

chaster *comparative of* CHASTE

chastest *superlative of* CHASTE

chaste tree \'≈,≈\ *n* [trans. of L *agnus castus*, by folk etymology (influence of L *agnus* lamb) fr. Gk *agnos* (associated with chastity rites because of influence of *hagnos* chaste, sacred)] : AGNUS CASTUS

chas·tise \(')cha¦stīz, -aas-\ *vt* -ED/-ING/-s [ME *chastisen*, alter. of *chastien* — more at CHASTEN] **1** : to inflict pain or suffering on for punishment or reformation ⟨~ children by spanking⟩ **2 a** *now dial* : REPROVE, REBUKE, SCOLD **b** : to censure severely in denunciation or in an attempt to correct or improve : CASTIGATE ⟨the world of moral and intellectual weaklings that she felt herself appointed to ~ —Tennessee Williams⟩ **3** *archaic* : CHASTEN 2 **syn** see PUNISH

chas·tise·ment \cha'stīzmənt *also* 'cha,stīz- *or* 'chastəz-; -aas-\ *n* -s [ME, fr. *chastisen* + *-ment*] : the action, an act, or the means of chastising; *esp* : PUNISHMENT

chas·tis·er \(')≈¦stīzə(r)\ *n* -s [alter. of ME *chastysowre*, fr. *chastisen* + *-owre* -or] : one that chastises

chas·ti·ty \'chastəd·ē, -aas-, -ətē, -i\ *n* -ES [ME *chastete*, *chastitie*, fr. OF *chasteté*, fr. L *castitat-*, *castitas*, fr. *castus* pure + *-itat-*, *-itas* -ity — more at CHASTE] **1** : the quality or state of being chaste: as **a** : abstention from sexual intercourse that is reprobated by religion or condemned by morality **b** : abstention from all sexual intercourse **c** : freedom from immorality and lewdness in act and intention : purity in act and will : DECENCY, MODESTY **d** : decorousness in design or expression often tending toward the severe : freedom from meretricious ornament, floridity, or tawdriness **2** : the obligation of lifelong celibacy and continence assumed in some monastic vows **3** : ethical integrity

chastity belt *n* : a belt device esp. of earlier times designed to prevent sexual intercourse on the part of the woman wearing it

chas·tush·ka \cha'stùshkə\ *n* -s [Russ, fr. *chasty* often, fr. ORuss *častŭ*; akin to OSlav *čęstŭ* often, Lith *kimštas* stuffed] : a rhymed folk verse usu. of four lines traditional in form but often having political or topical content

chas·u·ble \'chazəbəl, -asə-, -azhə- *sometimes* -azyə- *or* -asyə- *or* -äz(y)ə-\ *n* -s [F, fr. OF, fr. LL *casubla* hooded garment, prob. alter. of LL *casula* cloak, fr. L, dim. of *casa* small house, hut — more at CASA] **:** an outer ecclesiastical vestment in the form of a wide sleeveless cloak or mantle that slips over the wearer's head but remains open at the sides, the color of which varies with either the season or the occasion, worn by the celebrant at eucharistic services in the Roman Catholic and Eastern Orthodox churches and some churches of the Anglican Communion

chasubles: Gothic (left) and fiddleback (right)

¹chat \'chat, *usu* -ad·+V\ *n* -s [ME *chatte* catkin, fr. MF, lit., female cat, fr. OF *chat* cat, fr. LL *cattus*; prob. fr. its resemblance to a cat's tail — more at CAT] **1 a :** the inflorescence or seed of various plants (as an ament or a samara) **b** *now dial* **:** STROBILE, CONE **2** *dial Eng* **:** a twig or little branch suitable for kindling **3** *Brit* **:** a small inferior potato **4 :** TAILING 2c — often used in pl.

²chat \"\ *vb* **chatted; chatted; chatting; chats** [ME *chatten*, short for *chatteren* to chatter] *vi* **1 :** CHATTER, PRATTLE **2 :** to talk in a light and familiar manner **:** converse without ceremony or stiffness ⟨~ about trifles⟩ ~ *vt* **1** *obs* **:** CHATTER, PRATTLE **2** *dial Brit* **:** to talk to; *esp* **:** to address in a tentative manner **:** APPROACH

³chat \"\ *n* -s **1 :** idle unimportant talk **:** PRATTLE, CHATTER **2 a :** light familiar talk ⟨a magazine devoted to ~ about the arts⟩; *esp* **:** CONVERSATION ⟨kept up a continual ~ with the lady —Michael McLaverty⟩ **b :** an instance of such talk ⟨a TV ~ broadcast at intervals⟩ ⟨a long ~ between old friends⟩ **3** [imit.] **:** any of several songbirds: as **a :** a bird of the genus *Saxicola* (as the stonechat and whinchat of Europe) **b :** a bird of an Australian genus *Epthianura* (family Turdidae) **c :** a bird of an American genus *Icteria* (family Parulidae) — see YELLOW-BREASTED CHAT

châ·teau \(')sha¦tō *sometimes* -ä¦- *or* -á¦-\ *n, pl* **châteaus** \-ōz\ *or* **châ·teaux** \-ō(z)\ [F, fr. OF *chastel*, fr. L *castellum* — more at CASTLE] **1 :** a feudal castle or fortress in France **2 :** a large country house **:** MANSION **3 :** a French vineyard estate esp. in the Bordeaux wine region — often used prepositively in compounds naming such estates and their wines (as *Château-Haut-Brion*, the name of a vineyard in the Graves district in the Gironde and the red wine produced from its grapes) — compare CLOS, CÔTE

château bottled *adj* **:** ESTATE BOTTLED

cha·teau·bri·and \,sha,tōbrē'äⁿ\ *n* -s *often cap* [after François René, vicomte de *Chateaubriand* †1848 Fr. writer and statesman] **1 :** a steak in which a pocket is cut and stuffed with shallots, chives, cayenne, and salt **2 :** a thick tenderloin steak

châ·teau d'eau \,sha,tō'dō\ *n, pl* **château d'eaus** \-dōz\ *or* **cha·teaux d'eau** \-tō(z)'dō\ [F, lit., castle of water] **:** a fountain terminating an aqueduct and having an architectural background

chateau gray *n* **:** FROST GRAY

châ·teau·neuf-du-pape \shätōnœfdüpäp\ *n* -s *usu cap C&P* [fr. *Châteauneuf-du-Pape*, commune near Avignon, France] **:** a usu. red wine produced in the Rhone valley north of Avignon

chateau potatoes *n pl* **:** potato balls parboiled briefly and then braised in butter

cha·te·lain \'shad·ᵊl,än, ,≈≈'≈\ *n* -s [MF *châtelain*, fr. L *castellanus* occupant of a castle — more at CASTELLAN] **:** CASTELLAN

cha·te·laine \"\ *n* -s [F *châtelaine*, fem. of *châtelain*] **1 a :** the wife of a castellan **:** the mistress of a château **b :** the mistress of the household, esp. of a large establishment **2 :** an ornamental chain, pin, or clasp usu. worn at a woman's waist to which trinkets, keys, a purse, or other articles are attached

cha·te·let \'shad·ᵊl,ā, ,≈≈'≈\ *n* -s [F *châtelet*, fr. OF *chastelet*, dim. of *chastel* castle] **:** a small castle — more at CHÂTEAU] **:** CASTELLANY

chat·el·lany \'shad·ᵊl,anē, -,änē,-,ənē, sha'telənē\ *n* -ES [F *châtellenie*, fr. OF *chastelenie*] **:** CASTELLANY

châ·tel·per·ro·ni·an \¦sha,telpə¦rōnēən\ *adj, usu cap* [fr. *Châtelperron*, Allier dept., France + E *-ian*] **:** of or relating to the first phase of the Aurignacian epoch characterized by a special flint-chipping technique and a blade tool with one straight sharp edge and one curved over to the point and blunted

chat·e·nay pink \'shatᵊn,ā-\ *n, often cap C* [so called fr. Mme. Abel *Chatenay*, a variety of rose] **:** a light to moderate yellowish pink that is stronger and much redder than seashell pink

chat·ham·ite \'chad·ə,mīt\ *n* -s [*Chatham*, Conn., its locality + E *-ite*] **:** a mineral consisting of a variety of chloanthite containing much iron

cha·ti·no \chə'tē(,)nō\ *n, pl* **chatino** *or* **chatinos** *usu cap* [Sp, of AmerInd origin] **1 a :** an Indian people of Oaxaca state, Mexico **b :** a member of such people **2 :** a Zapotecan language of the Chatino people

cha·ton \(')sha¦tōⁿ\ *n, pl* **chatons** \-ōⁿ(z)\ [F, fr. OF *chastun*, of Gmc origin; akin to OHG *kasto* container, MD *kaste* barn, OE *bēocere* beekeeper, OHG *kar* vessel, ON *ker*, Goth *kas*] **1 :** the head of a ring in which a stone is set or on which a device is engraved **2 :** the stone set in a chaton **3** *or* **chaton foil :** a coating (as a foil or lacquer) applied to the back of a cheap gemstone to give it greater brilliancy

cha·tot \(')sha¦tō\ *n, pl* **chatot** *or* **chatots** *usu cap* [F, fr. Choctaw *Chahta* Choctaw] **1 :** an extinct Muskogean people of Florida west of the Apalachicola river **2 :** a member of the Chatot people

cha·toy·ance \shə'tȯiən(t)s, ,sha·,twä'yäⁿs\ *or* **cha·toy·an·cy** \shə'tȯiənsē\ *n, pl* **chatoyances** *or* **chatoyancies :** the quality or state of being chatoyant ⟨the blue *chatoyancy* of moonstone — G.P.Merrill & W.F.Foshag⟩

¹cha·toy·ant \shə'tȯiənt, ¦sha·,twä¦yäⁿ\ *adj* [F, fr. pres. part. of *chatoyer* to shine like a cat's eyes, fr. *chat* cat, fr. LL *cattus* — more at CAT] **:** having a changeable luster or color esp. marked by an undulating narrow band of white light ⟨a dress of ~ silk⟩ ⟨a cat's eye ~ in the dark⟩ ⟨an unusual ~ aquamarine —*Jour. of Gemmology*⟩

²chatoyant \"\ *n* -s **:** a chatoyant gem

chats *pres 3d sing of* CHAT, *pl of* CHAT

chat·ta \'chad·ə, -äd·ə\ *n* -s [Hindi *chātā*, fr. Skt *chattraka*] *India* **:** UMBRELLA

chattak *or* **chattack** *var of* CHITTAK

chat·ta·noo·ga \¦chad·ə¦nügə, -atᵊn¦ü-,-atə¦nü-\ *adj, usu cap* [fr. *Chattanooga*, Tenn.] **:** of or from the city of Chattanooga, Tenn. ⟨*Chattanooga* physicians⟩ **:** of the kind or style prevalent in Chattanooga

chat·ta·noo·gan \,≈≈'≈gən\ *n* -s *cap* [*Chattanooga*, Tenn. + E *-an*] **:** a native or resident of Chattanooga, Tenn.

chatted *past of* CHAT

chat·tel \'chad·ᵊl, -atᵊl\ *n* -s [ME *chatel* goods, property, fr. OF, fr. ML *capitale* — more at CATTLE] **1 :** an item of tangible movable or immovable property except real estate, freehold, and things which are parts of a freehold, and that movable property which is by its nature considered to be essential to such an estate **2 :** SLAVE, BONDSMAN

chattel corporeal *n, pl* **chattels corporeal :** a chattel having a physical body visible and tangible and of substantial value as distinguished from an incorporeal chattel (as a chose in action)

chattel interest *n* **:** a legal interest in land less than a freehold estate

chat·tel·ism \-,izəm\ *n* -s **1 :** the state or quality of being a chattel **2 :** the treatment of things or esp. persons as chattels

chat·tel·i·za·tion \,≈≈,ə'zāshən, -,ī'z-\ *n* -s **:** the act of chattelizing a person or thing

chat·tel·ize \'≈≈,īz\ *vt* -ED/-ING/-S **:** to make a chattel of

chattel mortgage *n* **:** a mortgage of chattel property as opposed to estate

chattel personal *n, pl* **chattels personal :** a movable chattel (as goods, plate, or money) — distinguished from *chattel real*

chattel real *n, pl* **chattels real :** a chattel consisting of a right in land that is less than a freehold (as a lease or a growing crop) — distinguished from *chattel personal*

¹chat·ter \'chad·ə(r), -atə-\ *vb* -ED/-ING/-S [ME *chatteren*, of imit. origin] *vi* **1 a :** to utter rapidly succeeding sounds somewhat like language but inarticulate and indistinct — orig. used of birds ⟨~*ing* like a flock of blackbirds —Ellen Glasgow⟩ ⟨squirrels and chipmunks came to ~ and play about them —Sherwood Anderson⟩ ⟨the leaves began to ~ —George Meredith⟩ ⟨a tiny stream that ~*s* and twists through dells and dingles —*Amer. Guide Series: Conn.*⟩ **b** *of a pickup cartridge* **:** to produce unwanted sound acoustically **2 :** to talk idly, carelessly, incessantly, or with undue rapidity **:** JABBER ⟨men who followed the sea were always ~*ing* about the ease and security of life in the country —L.C.Douglas⟩ ⟨all through the rest of the meal I ~*ed* of the cottage —Adrian Bell⟩ ⟨men who are silent are set against men who ~ —*Times Lit. Supp.*⟩ **3 a :** to make the sound of or as if of rapidly repeated noisy contacts (as of the teeth of one who is extremely cold or frightened) ⟨master's teeth ~*ed* with horror —Donn Byrne⟩ ⟨~ like castanets in a Spanish dance⟩ ⟨skis will ~ in a turn if they are edged too much —*Operations in Snow & Extreme Cold* (U.S. War Dept.)⟩ ⟨machine guns ~*ing* —Philip Wylie⟩ **b** *of a cutting tool* **:** to vibrate rapidly in the action of cutting so as to form ridges or nicks ⟨the plane ~*ed* along the edge of the plank⟩ **c :** to operate or perform with any irregularity that causes rapid intermittent noise or vibration ⟨the motor ~*ed* in reverse⟩ ~ *vt* **1 :** to utter or speak rapidly, idly, or indistinctly ⟨English is ~*ed* here —Claudia Cassidy⟩ ⟨the woman ~*ed* her silly tale⟩ **2** *dial Eng* **:** TEAR, SHATTER **3** *of a cutting tool* **:** to cut unevenly because of vibration ⟨variation in the thickness of an oil film produces ~*ed* work —*New Departure Handbook*⟩

²chatter \"\ *n* -s [ME *chatere*, fr. *chatteren*, v.] **1 :** the action or sound of chattering ⟨the ~ of magpies⟩ ⟨the ~ of rivet guns⟩ ⟨the ~ of the plane along the wood⟩ ⟨the ~ of the worn clutch trying to take hold⟩ **2 :** idle talk **:** PRATTLE ⟨my ~ was as gay and sprightly as a bird song —R.P.Warren⟩ ⟨the ~ of small voices around him —M.W.Fishwick⟩

chatterbox \'≈≈,≈\ *n* **:** one who talks incessantly and idly **:** a habitual chatterer

chatterbox tree *n* [so called fr. the clatter made by its dry pods] **:** LEBBEK

chat·ter·er \-ərə(r)\ *n* -s **1 :** one that chatters **2 :** any of various passerine birds, esp. the waxwings and members of the Cotingidae

chat·ter·ing·ly *adv* **:** in a chattering manner

chatter mark *n* **1 :** a fine undulation or ripple formed on the surface of work by a chattering tool **2 :** one of a series of short curved cracks on a glaciated rock surface roughly transverse to the glacial striae

chatter water *n, Brit* **:** weak tea

chat·ti·ly \'chad·ᵊlē, -atl, ¦əlē, -lē, -li\ *adv* **:** in a chatty manner ⟨writes ~ of his pet canaries —R.K.Buehrle⟩

chat·ti·ness \-d·ēnəs, -tē-, -in-\ *n* **:** the quality or state of being chatty

chatting *pres part of* CHAT

chat·ting·ly *adv* **:** in a chatting manner

¹chat·ty \'chad·ē, -atē, -i\ *adj, often* -ER/-EST **1 :** given to chat **:** informal, friendly, and talkative ⟨a ~ woman⟩ **2 :** being or resembling chat ⟨a ~ letter⟩ ⟨a ~ magazine article⟩

²chat·ty \"\ *also* **chat·ti** \"\ *n, pl* **chatties** *also* **chattis** [Tamil-Malayalam *caṭṭi*] **:** an earthenware water jar used in India

¹chau·ce·ri·an \(')chȯ¦sirēən, -ēr-\ *adj, usu cap* [Geoffrey *Chaucer* †1400 Eng. poet + E *-ian*] **:** of, relating to, befitting, or resembling the English medieval writer Geoffrey Chaucer or his writings

²chaucerian \"\ *n, usu cap* **1 :** an imitator of Chaucer; *esp* **:** one of a group of Scottish imitators of the 15th century **2 :** an admirer of Chaucer's writings **3 :** a scholar or teacher specializing in the study or the teaching of Chaucer

chau·cer·ism \'chȯsə,rizəm\ *n, usu cap* [*Chaucer* + E *-ism*] **:** a word, expression, or quality of style characteristic of or imitative of the writings of Chaucer ⟨Spenser's ~*s*⟩

chaud-froid \(')shō¦frwä, -ōfrə¦wä\ *n* -s [F, lit., hot-cold, fr. *chaud* hot (fr. L *calidus*) + *froid* cold, fr. L *frigidus* — more at CALDRON, FRIGID] **1 :** a jellied sauce (as a white or brown sauce fortified with gelatin) used as a garnish esp. for meat or fish **2 :** food (as meat or fish) covered with a chaudfroid sauce usu. molded into shapes after cooking, and served cold

chaud-medley *or* **chaud-melle** *or* **chaud-mella** *n* -s [*chaud-medley*, *chaud-mella*, alter. of *chaud-melle*; *chaud-melle* fr. ME *chaudmellee*, *chawdmelle*, fr. MF *chaude mellee*, lit., hot fight] **1** *Scots law* **:** an affray in the heat of passion **2** *Scots law* **:** the wounding or killing of a person in a chaud-medley without premeditation

chau·dron \(')shō¦drōⁿ\ *n* -s [F, kettle, fr. OF *chauderon*, dim. of *chaudiere*, fr. LL *caldaria* — more at CALDRON] **:** ANTIQUE RED

chauf·fer \'chȯfə(r)\ *n* -s [alter. (prob. influenced by F *chauffer* to heat, warm, fr. OF *chaufer*) of ²*chafer* — more at CHAFE] **:** a portable stove usu. with a grate at the bottom and an open top

¹chauf·feur \'shōfə(r); (')shō¦fər, +V -¦fər·; (')shō¦fə, +V -¦fər *also* -¦fər\ *n* -s [F, lit., stoker, fr. *chauffer* to heat, warm + *-eur* -er] **1 :** one that is employed to operate a motor vehicle for the transportation of persons or property **2 :** one that transports (as persons) by operating a motor vehicle ⟨to be ~ for a group of friends who could not drive⟩

²chauffeur \"\ *vb* **chauffeured; chauffeured; chauffeuring** \-¦f(ə)riŋ, -fər·iŋ *also* -¦fəriŋ\ **chauffeurs** *vi* **:** to do the work of a chauffeur ⟨~ for a livelihood⟩ ~ *vt* **1 :** to transport in the manner of a chauffeur ⟨has time to garden, ~ the kids to school, and sleep —Bernard Kalb⟩ ⟨at twelve I ~*ed* him around the country—C.A.Lindbergh b. 1902⟩ **2 a :** to operate (as an automobile) as chauffeur ⟨~ a sporty town car for a crippled relative⟩ ⟨~*ing* a plane for a millionaire candy magnate —*Newsweek*⟩ **b :** to operate (a motor vehicle) by means of a chauffeur ⟨two company cars, both ~*ed* —Pearl Buck⟩

¹chauf·feuse \(')shō¦fə(r)z, -¦fəz\ *n* -s [F, fr. *chauffer* to heat, warm] **:** a low-seated French fireside chair

²chauffeuse \"\ *n* -s [F, fem. of *chauffeur*] **:** a female chauffeur

chau·ki·dar \¦chaùkē¦där\ *var of* CHOKIDAR

chau·li·o·don·ti·dae \kȯ,līə'däntə,dē, ,kȯlēō'd-\ *n pl, cap* [NL, fr. *Chauliodont-*, *Chauliodus*, type genus (fr. Gk *chauliodont-*, *chauliodous* with projecting teeth, fr. *chauli-* — irreg. fr. *chaunos* wide open, loose, foolish, fr. the stem of *chaos* space, abyss, gen. *chaous* — + *-odont-*, *-odous*, fr. *odont-*, *odōn* tooth) + *-idae* — more at GUM, TOOTH] **:** a widely distributed family (order Isospondyli) of large-headed long-bodied deep-sea fishes with large mouths and greatly enlarged fangs

chaul·moo·gra *also* **chaul·mu·gra** \chȯl'mügrə\ *or* **chaul·mau·gra** \-mȯ-\ *n* -s [Beng *cāulmugrā*, *cālmugrā*, fr. *cāul*, *cāl* rice + *mugrā* bowstring hemp (*Sansevieria zeylanica*)] **:** any of several East Indian trees of the family Flacourtiaceae that yield chaulmoogra oil: **a :** a large-fruited tree (*Taraktogenos kurzii*) **b :** any of several trees of the genus *Hydnocarpus* (esp. *H. anthelminticus* and *H. wightiana*)

chaulmoogra oil *n* **:** any of several fixed oils or fats similar in physical and chemical properties that are expressed from seeds of certain trees of the family Flacourtiaceae and used esp. formerly in the treatment of leprosy and skin diseases: **a :** an oily or soft fat from seeds of any chaulmoogra tree composed chiefly of glycerides of chaulmoogric, hydnocarpic, and gorlic acids **b :** GORLI OIL

chaul·moo·grate \-grət, -,grāt\ *n* -s [*chaulmoogric* + *-ate*] **:** a salt or ester of chaulmoogric acid

chaul·moo·gric acid \(')chȯl¦mügrik-\ *n* **:** a crystalline unsaturated acid $C_5H_7(CH_2)_{12}COOH$ found as an ester in chaulmoogra oil and hydnocarpus oil; 13-(2-cyclopenten-1-yl)-tridecanoic acid

chau·mer \'chämər, -ȯm-\ *Scot var of* CHAMBER

chaunt *archaic var of* CHANT

chaunter *archaic var of* CHANTER

chauntry *obs var of* CHANTRY

chauri *var of* CHOWRIE

chaus \'kaùs, 'ch-\ *n, pl* **chaus** [origin unknown] **:** an Old World wildcat, possibly the Kaffir cat

chaus·sée \(')shō¦sā\ *n* -s [F, fr. ML *calciata* paved road — more at CAUSEY] **:** a paved road **:** CAUSEWAY, HIGHWAY

chausses \'shōs\ *n pl* [F, pl. of *chausse*, fr. ML *calcea*, fr. L *calceus* shoe, fr. *calc-*, *calx* heel — more at CALCANEUM] **1 :** a medieval tight-fitting garment worn by men to cover the legs and feet and sometimes the body below the waist **2 :** the early medieval armor of linked mail that fitted like chausses

chaus·sure \shō'sü(ə)r\ *n* -s [ME *chauceore*, *chaucer*, fr. MF *chaussure*, fr. *chausser* to put on footwear, fr. L *calceare*, fr. *calceus* shoe] **1 :** FOOTGEAR **2 chaussures** *pl* **:** SHOES

chau·tau·qua \shə'tȯkwə\ *n* -s *sometimes cap* [fr. *Chautauqua* lake, western New York, where it was founded] **1 a :** a stationary or traveling institution that flourished in the late 19th and early 20th centuries providing popular education usu. combined with entertainment in the form of lectures, concerts, or dramatic performances often presented outdoors or in a tent ⟨~ is no more, its place taken by the radio everywhere —Lancaster Pollard⟩ **b :** a particular instance of meetings belonging to this institution as held in any one place or a single traveling unit of such lectures or concerts ⟨lecture circuits usually suggest canvas-topped ~*s* —*Infantry Jour.*⟩ **2 :** any institution or series of popular presentations similar to a chautauqua in purpose or organization ⟨in six states, ~ courses were held at various times throughout the states in four to twelve centers —*Jour. Amer. Med. Assoc.*⟩

chautauqua muskellunge *n, usu cap C* [fr. *Chautauqua* Lake, N. Y.] **:** a muskellunge of a variety (*Esox masquinongy ohiensis*) distinguished by dark crossbars and paucity of spots and found chiefly in the Ohio and St. Lawrence river drainages

chau·tau·quan \-wən\ *adj, usu cap* [in sense 1, fr. *chautauqua* + *-an*; in sense 2, fr. *Chautauqua* lake + E *-an*] **1 :** *sometimes cap* **:** of or relating to a chautauqua or chautauquas **2 :** of or relating to a subdivision of the No. American Devonian — see GEOLOGIC TIME table

chauve-sou·ris \,shōvsü'rē\ *n, pl* **chauve-sou·rises** \-'rēz\ [F, fr. OF *chauve soriz*, fr. ML *calva sorex*, fr. L *calva* bald (fem. of *calvus*) + *sorex* shrew — more at CALVARIUM, SOREX] **:** ³BAT 1

chau·vin·ism \'shōvə,nizəm\ *n* -s [F *chauvinisme*, fr. *chauvin* warmonger (after *Chauvin*, a very patriotic soldier in *La Cocarde tricolore*, play written 1831 by Charles T. and Jean Hippolyte Cogniard, after Nicolas *Chauvin fl* 1815 legendary French soldier very devoted to Napoleon) + *-isme* -ism] **1 :** excessive esp. blind patriotism — compare JINGOISM **2 :** undue esp. invidious attachment or partiality for a group or place to which one belongs or has belonged ⟨professional ~*s* —Wilbur Zelinsky⟩ ⟨the passionate ~ of a child away from home —John Woodburn⟩

¹chau·vin·ist \-,nəst\ *n* -s **:** one who practices chauvinism

²chauvinist \"\ *or* **chau·vin·is·tic** \¦shōvə¦nistik, -ēk\ *adj* **:** marked by chauvinism — **chau·vin·is·ti·cal·ly** \-tək(ə)lē, -ēk-, -li\ *adv*

cha·van·te \shə'vantē\ *n, pl* **chavante** *or* **chavantes** *usu cap* [Pg, of AmerInd origin] **1 :** OTI **2 a :** an Indian people of Mato Grosso state, Brazil **b :** a member of such people **3 a :** a Gesan people of Goiaz state, Brazil **b :** a member of such people — **cha·van·te·an** \-ēan\ *adj, usu cap*

chav·el \'chavəl\ *vb* -ED/-ING/-S [ME *chavlen*, *chaulen*, fr. *chavel*, *chauel* jaw — more at JOWL] *now dial Eng* **:** NIBBLE, GNAW

chav·en·der \'chavəndə(r)\ *n* -s [ME *chevender*, irreg. fr. *cheveyne* chevin] **:** CHUB 1

cha·ver \'kävər\ *n, pl* **chave·rim** \kä'värim\ *var of* HAVER

chav·i·be·tol \,chavə'bē,tōl, -ōl\ *n* -s [ISV *chavi-* (fr. NL *chavica* — prob. modif. of Skt *cavika*, a pepper (*Piper chaba*) — genus name of *Chavica betle*, syn. of *Piper betle*) + *bet-* (fr. NL *betle*, prob. fr. Pg) + *-ol* (fr. L *oleum* oil); prob. orig. formed in G — more at BETEL, OIL] **:** an oily phenol $C_3H_5C_6H_3(OCH_3)OH$ found in the essential oil from the leaves of the betel pepper; 5-allyl-guaiacol

chav·i·cine \'chavə,sēn, -sən\ *n* -s [ISV *chavic-* (fr. NL *Chavica*) + *-ine*] **:** an alkaloid $C_{17}H_{19}NO_3$, isomeric with piperine obtained from black pepper as a pungent greenish resinous substance

chav·i·col \-,kōl, -ōl\ *n* -s [ISV *chavic-* (fr. NL *Chavica*) + *-ol* (fr. L *oleum*); prob. orig. formed as G *chavikol*] **:** a colorless oily phenol $C_3H_5C_6H_4OH$ found esp. in the oil from the leaves of the betel pepper and in bay oil; *para*-allyl-phenol

cha·vin \chə'vēn\ *adj, usu cap* [fr. *Chavín* or *Chavín* de Huantar, town in central Peru, its type station] **:** of or relating to a Peruvian culture of the 1st to the 6th centuries A.D. characterized by a platform type of stone building with masonry in alternating thick and thin courses, sculpture of human, animal, and monster heads in the round and outlines on slabs, and monochrome pottery decorated in relief or by incision with feline or geometric designs

cha·vish \'chāvish\ *n* -ES [prob. imit.] *dial Eng* **:** CHATTERING, PRATTLING

¹chaw \'chȯ\ *vb* **chawed; chawed; chawing** \-ȯ(·)iŋ\ **chaws** [alter. of ¹*chew*] *vt* **1** *now dial* **:** to grind with the teeth **:** CHEW **2** *now dial* **:** mull over **:** PONDER **3** *dial* **:** VEX, EMBARRASS ~ *vi, now dial* **:** CHEW

²chaw \"\ *n* -s *now dial* **:** a chew esp. of tobacco

³chaw *n* -s [alter. (influenced by ²*chaw*) of ¹*jaw*] *obs* **:** JAW — usu. used in pl.

cha·wa·sha \chə'wȯshə -'wä-\ *n, pl* **chawasha** *or* **chawashas** *usu cap* **1 :** a Chitimachan people of Louisiana at the mouth of the Mississippi **2 :** a member of the Chawasha people

chawbacon \'≈,≈≈\ *n* -s [¹*chaw* + *bacon*] **:** RUSTIC, BUMPKIN, HICK, YOKEL

¹chawbuck *n* [Hindi *cābuk*, fr. Per *chābuk*] *archaic, chiefly India* **:** a large whip

²chawbuck *vt, archaic, chiefly India* **:** to flog with a chawbuck

chaw·dron \'chȯdrən\ *n* -s [ME *chaudoun*, *chaudern*, fr. MF *chaudun* tripe, fr. ML *calduna* intestine, prob. fr. L *calidus* warm — more at CALDRON] *archaic* **:** the entrails of an animal used as a food

chawl \'chȯl\ *n* -s [Hindi *cāl* thatched roof] **:** a large tenement house esp. in the factory cities of India

chawn \'chȯn\ *n* -s [prob. irreg. fr. obs. *chine*, v., to crack, fr. ME *chinen*, fr. OE *cinan* — more at CAUL] *now dial Eng* **:** GAP, CLEFT

chawng *var of* CHUANG

chawstick \'≈,≈\ *n* -s [²*chaw* + *stick*] **:** a woody vine (*Gouania lupuloides*) of the buckthorn family the twigs of which are chewed as a stomachic — called also *chewstick*

¹chay \'chī\ *or* **chaya** \'chī(y)ə\ *also* **choy** \'chȯi\ *or* **choya** \'chȯi(y)ə\ *n* -s [Tamil-Malayalam *cāya-vēr*, perh. fr. Skt *chāyā* color, shadow — more at SCENE] **:** the root of an East Indian herb (*Oldenlandia umbellata*) that yields a red dye

²chay \'shā\ *n* -s [back-formation fr. *chaise*, taken as pl.] **:** CHAISE

chayaroot \'≈≈,≈\ *also* **choyroot** \'≈,≈\ *n* -s [*chaya*, *choy* + *root*] **:** ¹CHAY

chayma *usu cap, var of* CHAIMA

cha·yo·te \chī'yōd·ē, chī'ō-\ *n* -s [Sp, fr. Nahuatl *chayotli*] **1 :** the rounded or pear-shaped fruit of a West Indian annual vine (*Sechium edule*) of the cucumber family that is widely cultivated as a vegetable **2 :** the plant bearing the chayote

chazan *or* **chazzan** *n, pl* **chazanim** *or* **chazzanim** *var of* HAZAN

chazanuth *or* **chazanut** *or* **chazzanuth** *or* **chazzanut** *var of* HAZANUTH

chazar *usu cap, var of* KHAZAR

CHB *abbr* center halfback

chd *abbr* **1** chaldron **2** chord

che *pron* [alter. of ʼch, fr. ME *ich* — more at I] *obs dial Eng* **:** I

ChE *abbr or n* -s chemical engineer

¹cheap *vt* -ED/-ING/-S [ME *chepen*, fr. OE *cēapian* to buy; akin to OHG *koufōn*, ON *kaupa*, Goth *kaupōn*] **1** *obs* **:** to ask the price of **:** PRICE **2** *obs* **:** to bargain or bid for

²cheap \'chēp\ *n* -s [ME *chep*, fr. OE *cēap* trade, purchase, sale; akin to OHG *kouf* trade, *koufo* merchant, ON *kaup* bargain, Goth *kaupōn* to trade; all fr. a prehistoric Gmc word stem borrowed fr. L *caupo* tradesman, innkeeper; perh. akin to Gk *kapēlos* tradesman, innkeeper] *obs Brit* **:** BARGAIN — now used only in the phrase *on the cheap* — **on the cheap** *adv* **:** at minimum expense **:** CHEAPLY ⟨called the "Penny Crowning" because it was done *on the cheap* —H.V.Morton⟩

³cheap \"\ *adj* -ER/-EST [²*cheap* (in such phrases as *at good cheap* at a bargain)] **1 a :** of small cost **:** inexpensive esp. as compared with the going price or the real value ⟨living is ~*er*

during the summer than in winter⟩ — formerly used with *good* or *great* ⟨food is good ~ in a time of plenty⟩ **b :** charging a comparatively low price ⟨the ~*er* stores⟩ **c :** dealing in low-priced goods ⟨the ~ stores along the waterfront⟩ **d :** depreciated in value (as by currency inflation) ⟨~ dollars⟩ **2 :** costing little labor or effort or involving little trouble to obtain **:** easily obtained or attained ⟨a ~ victory⟩ ⟨~ kisses⟩ — formerly used with *good* or *great* ⟨compliments are good ~⟩ **3 a :** of inferior quality **:** of small intrinsic worth **:** SHODDY, TAWDRY, MERETRICIOUS ⟨the ~ novel does not itself turn back to reality —Bernard De Voto⟩ ⟨nothing is ~ about this volume but its price —S.L.Faison⟩ ⟨~ publicity⟩ **b :** worthy of scorn or rejection **:** unredeemed by any fine or lofty qualities **:** CONTEMPTIBLE ⟨a ~ and nasty life —G.B.Shaw⟩ ⟨a ~ and vulgar remark⟩ ⟨he feels pretty ~⟩ **4 a :** yielding small satisfaction ⟨~ entertainment⟩ **b :** paying or able to pay less than given amounts ⟨a ~*er* class of customers⟩ **5** *of money* **:** obtainable at a low rate of interest **6** *Brit* **:** specially reduced in price ⟨a ~ day ticket to Manchester —S.P.B.Mais⟩ **syn** see CONTEMPTIBLE — **cheap of** *Scot* **:** getting no more than one's deserts **:** well deserving of

[4]cheap \"\ *adv* **:** CHEAPLY ⟨bought the article ~⟩

cheap·en \'chēpən\ *vb* **cheapened**; **cheapened**; **cheapening** \-p(ə)niŋ\ **cheapens** [[1, 2, or 3]*cheap* + *-en*] *vt* **1 a :** to ask the price of **b :** to bid or bargain for **2 :** to make cheap: as **a :** to lessen the price or the value of ⟨a glutted market ~*s* the goods in all categories⟩ **b :** to lower in general esteem **c :** to make tawdry, vulgar, or inferior in some moral sense ⟨how a group of human beings can be ~*ed* by the constant waterdrop of shabbiness . . . during the depression —Henry Hewes⟩ **~** *vi* **:** to become cheap ⟨food ~*s* in summer⟩

cheap·ie \'chēpē\ *n* -s [[3]*cheap* + *-ie*] **:** something that costs relatively little in money or effort to produce; *esp* **:** an inexpensive motion picture

[1]cheap-jack \'=,jak\ *also* **cheap-john** \'=,jän\ *n* -s *sometimes cap J* [[3]*cheap* + *Jack* or *John* (the names) — more at JACK, JOHN] **1 :** a hawker or peddler **:** HUCKSTER; *esp* **:** a hawker who bargains over his goods ⟨*cheap-jacks* have mingled with showmen, especially on fairgrounds, since the 18th century —Eric Partridge⟩ **2 :** a dealer in cheap often inferior or worthless merchandise ⟨so many *cheap-jacks* with their bottled, spiritual cure-alls —G.S.Fraser⟩

[2]cheap-jack \"\ *also* **cheap-john** \"\ *adj, sometimes cap J* **:** of, relating to, or befitting a cheap-jack: as **a :** often inferior, cheap, or worthless ⟨*cheap-jack* wares⟩ ⟨*cheap-jack* dramaturgy⟩ **b :** opportunistic esp. unscrupulously or in dealing in inferior goods ⟨the *cheap-jack* speculators . . . destroying the beauty of London —Robert Lutyens⟩

cheap·ly \-lē,-li\ *adv* [[3]*cheap* + *-ly*] **:** in a cheap manner: as **a :** INEXPENSIVELY ⟨borrow as ~ as possible⟩ ⟨if their products are ~ and well produced —Brian Inglis⟩ **b :** VULGARLY ⟨rather ~ dressed⟩ **c :** with little expenditure of effort or time ⟨if we seek peace ~ or meanly —A.E.Stevenson †1965⟩

cheap·ness \-nəs\ *n* -ES **:** the quality or state of being cheap

cheap·skate \'=,=\ *n* [[3]*cheap* + *skate* (miserly person)] **:** a miserly or ungenerous person; *esp* **:** one who tries to avoid his share of costs ⟨if we were courageous enough to demur at the price we were made to feel in no uncertain terms that we were *cheapskates* —Frances W. Browin⟩

chear *archaic var of* CHEER

[1]cheat \'chēt, *usu* -ēd·+V\ *n* -s [earlier *cheat* forfeited property, booty, fr. ME *chet* escheat, short for *achet*, alter. of *eschet* — more at ESCHEAT] **1 a :** the act or action of cheating or fraudulently deceiving **:** DECEPTION, FRAUD ⟨his financial activity turned out to be a great ~⟩ **b :** a means of cheating, misleading, tricking, or deluding one putting credence in seeming honesty or genuineness **:** whatever invites disappointment ⟨the elaborate ~ that the positivistic movement has perpetrated upon the human spirit —Allen Tate⟩ **c :** an act or instance of cheating ⟨tax ~*s* being discovered⟩ **d :** one that cheats esp. habitually **:** PRETENDER, DECEIVER, SHARPER ⟨if I passed myself off . . . as a gentleman, I should deserve to be exposed as a ~ —G.B.Shaw⟩ **2** *archaic* **:** THING, ARTICLE — usu. used with a distinguishing modifier ⟨a smelling ~ is a nose⟩ ⟨a nubbing ~ is the gallows⟩ **3** [prob. so called fr. its resemblance to grain among which it grows] **a :** the common chess (*Bromus secalinus*) **b :** DOWNY BROME **c :** BEARDED DARNEL **4** *law* **:** the obtaining of property from another by an intentional active distortion of the truth; *esp* **:** the common-law offense later enlarged by statute consisting in defrauding numbers of people by means of deceitful or illegal symbols or tokens but not so as to constitute a felony — compare [1]FRAUD 1 **syn** see IMPOSTURE

[2]cheat \"\ *vb* -ED/-ING/-S [earlier *cheat* to confiscate, fr. ME *cheten* to escheat, short for *acheten*, alter. of *escheten* — more at ESCHEAT] *vt* **1 :** to deprive of something valuable by the use of deceit or fraud **:** DEFRAUD, SWINDLE ⟨~ a man out of his savings⟩ ⟨suspicious . . . lest she should be ~*ed* out of the salary she had come resolved to demand —G.B.Shaw⟩ **2 :** to condition, influence, or lead by or as if by deceit, trick, or artifice ⟨~*ed* into cordial admiration by the splendor of the verses —Thomas De Quincey⟩ **3 :** to defeat in an expectation or purpose by or as if by deceit and trickery **:** DISAPPOINT, FOIL ⟨by God's mercy Ludendorff was ~*ed* of the Channel Ports —S.L.A.Marshall⟩ ⟨then I ~*ed* my despair. I said that you were safe —Maurice Baring⟩ **4** *archaic* **:** to obtain by fraud or trickery **~** *vi* **1 a :** to practice fraud or trickery **b :** to violate rules dishonestly (as at cards) **2 :** to be sexually unfaithful ⟨the divorce suit alleged that he had been ~*ing* on his wife⟩

syn SWINDLE, DEFRAUD, COZEN, OVERREACH: CHEAT is a general term indicating dishonest and deceitful trickery and is likely to imply censure, blame, or contempt ⟨Jane Orange . . . was not liked. She was called stingy and it was said that she and her husband had *cheated* every one with whom they had dealings —Sherwood Anderson⟩ SWINDLE implies gross and large-scale cheating for gain by means of imposture or mean abuse of confidence ⟨the despised Chinese, who were cuffed and maltreated and *swindled* by the Californians —Van Wyck Brooks⟩ ⟨Barnum knew the American public loved to be gulled . . . His genius consisted in knowing how to *swindle* them —W.L.Phelps⟩ DEFRAUD, a more legalistic word, indicates taking away from or withholding from another his rights or possessions by calculated perversion of truth, chicanery, or coercive pressure ⟨she ever claimed more than she could receive; they, as constantly, called themselves robbed and *defrauded* —Hilaire Belloc⟩ COZEN implies artful or tricky persuading, wheedling, bamboozling, or chiseling in deluding or obtaining ⟨I fought . . . to save my niche . . . Old Gandolf *cozened* me, despite my call —Robert Browning⟩ ⟨the Popular Front — that famous opportunity for men of good will to be *cozened* by the Communists —C.G.Poore⟩ OVERREACH indicates outwitting, as in dealing or bargaining, or cheating, by crafty dishonesty ⟨the suspicion that most of the talk they [the deaf] cannot hear consists in plottings and schemings to *overreach* or get around them —J.G.Cozzens⟩

[3]cheat *n* -s [ME *chet*] *obs* **:** wheat bread inferior to manchet

cheat·er \'chēd·ə(r), -ētə-\ *n* -s [ME *chetour*, modif. of AF *eschetour* — more at ESCHEATOR] **1** *obs* **:** ESCHEATOR **2 :** one that cheats **3 cheaters** *pl, slang* **:** SPECTACLES ⟨through heavy horn-rimmed ~*s* —*Time*⟩ **4 cheaters** *pl, slang* **:** FALSIES

cheat·ery \'chēd·ərē, -ētə-\ *or* **cheat·ry** \'chētrē\ *n* -ES **:** CHEATING, SWINDLING

cheatgrass \'=,=\ *n* **:** DOWNY BROME

cheat·ing·ly *adv* **:** in a cheating manner

cheats *pl of* CHEAT, *pres 3d sing of* CHEAT

cheat shot *n* **:** a motion-picture camera shot in which a part of the action necessary for filming a scene is suppressed in the finished picture in order to create or sustain a desired illusion

che·bac·co boat \shə'ba(,)kō-, -akə-\ *n* [fr. *Chebacco*, former parish of Ipswich, Mass., (now in the town of Essex), where it originated] **:** a narrow-sterned boat formerly much used in Newfoundland fisheries

[1]che·bec \shə'bek\ *or* **che·beck** \"\ *n* -s [F *chebec, chébec* — more at XEBEC] **:** XEBEC

[2]che·bec \chē'bek, chə-\ *n* -s [imit.] **:** LEAST FLYCATCHER

ché·be·ro \'chebə,rō, 'chā-\ *n, pl* **chébero** *or* **chéberos** *usu cap* [Sp, of AmerInd origin] **1 a :** a Cahuapana people of northern Peru **b :** a member of such people **2 :** the language of the Chébero people

che·bog \'ch ,bäg, -ȯg, ='=\ *n* -s [prob. fr. Natick *chippeog*, lit., they are separated or dead; fr. its use as manure by the Indians] **:** MENHADEN

che·bule \kə'b(y)ül\ *n* -s [F *chébule*, fr. Pashto *halīla-ī-kābulī* myrobalan from Kabul, fr. *Kabul*, city in Afghanistan] **:** the dried astringent fruit of an East Indian tree (*Terminalia chebula*)

cheb·u·lin·ic acid \¦kebyə¦linik-\ *n* [ISV *chebulinic* (fr. NL *chebula*, specific epithet of *Terminalia chebula* — fr. F *chébule* — + ISV *-in* + *-ic*) + *acid*; orig. formed as G *chebulinsäure*] **:** a crystalline tannin $C_{41}H_{32}O_{27}$ found in dried fruits of an East Indian tree (*Terminalia chebula*)

chechako *or* **chechaqua** *var of* CHEECHAKO

che·che·het \¦chāchə¦het, -ech-\ *n, pl* **chechehet** *or* **chechehets** *usu cap* [Sp *chechehet, chechaet*, of AmerInd origin] **1 a :** an extinct people of central Argentina **b :** a member of such people **2 :** the language of the Chechehet people constituting a linguistic family — called also *Het*

che·chem \chə'chem\ *n* -s [prob. native name in the West Indies] **:** a tree (*Metopium brownii*) of British Honduras, Cuba, and Santo Domingo yielding a dark wood used in cabinet and furniture making and for interior finishes

che·chen \chə'chen\ *n, pl* **chechen** *or* **chechens** *usu cap* [modif. of Russ *chechenets*, prob. fr. *chechenit' sya* to talk mincingly, of imit. origin] **1 a :** a Japhetic people living north of Dagestan, U.S.S.R. **b :** a member of such people **2 :** the North Caucasic language of the Chechen people

che·chia \(')shāsh¦yä\ *n* -s [F *chéchia*, fr. Maghribi *shāshiya*, fr. *Shāsh*, town in Persia where it was manufactured in medieval times] **:** a cylindrical brimless cap of Arab origin often having a tassel on the crown

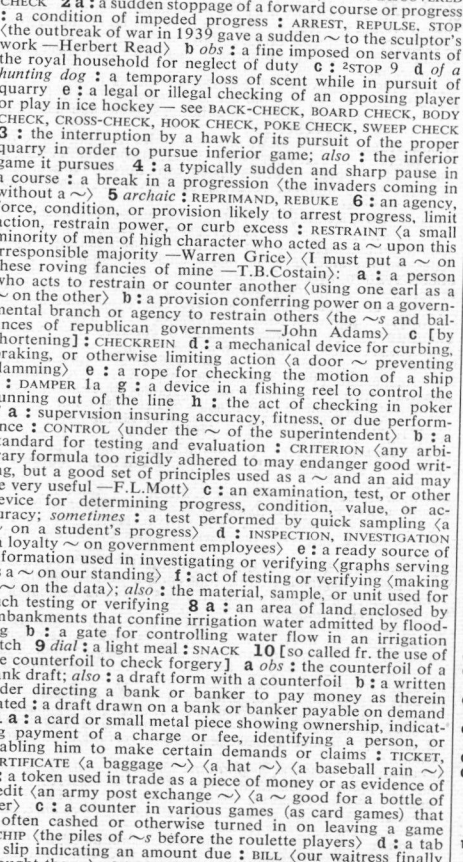

chechia

[1]check \'chek\ *interj* [ME *chek*, interj. & n.] — used to warn a chess opponent that his king is attacked

[2]check \"\ *n* -s [ME *chek* check at chess, attack, quarrel, reproof, fr. OF *eschec, eschac* check at chess, repulse, fr. Ar *shāh* check at chess, fr. Per, lit., king; akin to Av *xshayeti* he rules, has power, Skt *kṣayati* he possesses, rules, Gk *ktasthai* to acquire] **1 :** exposure of a chess king to an opponent's piece in such a way that if it were not the king and not immediately protected (as by interposing another piece) it could be captured on the next move ⟨with his king in ~⟩ ⟨relieving the ~⟩ — see DISCOVERED CHECK **2 a :** a sudden stoppage of a forward course or progress **:** a condition of impeded progress **:** ARREST, REPULSE, STOP ⟨the outbreak of war in 1939 gave a sudden ~ to the sculptor's work —Herbert Read⟩ **b** *obs* **:** a fine imposed on servants of the royal household for neglect of duty **c :** [2]STOP 9 **d** *of a hunting dog* **:** a temporary loss of scent while in pursuit of quarry **e :** a legal or illegal checking of an opposing player or play in ice hockey — see BACK-CHECK, BOARD CHECK, BODY CHECK, CROSS-CHECK, HOOK CHECK, POKE CHECK, SWEEP CHECK **3 :** the interruption by a hawk of its pursuit of the proper quarry in order to pursue inferior game; *also* **:** the inferior game it pursues **4 :** a typically sudden and sharp pause in a course **:** a break in a progression ⟨the invaders coming in without a ~⟩ **5** *archaic* **:** REPRIMAND, REBUKE **6 :** an agency, force, condition, or provision likely to arrest progress, limit action, restrain power, or curb excess **:** RESTRAINT ⟨a small minority of men of high character who acted as a ~ upon this irresponsible majority —Warren Grice⟩ ⟨I must put a ~ on these roving fancies of mine —T.B.Costain⟩: **a :** a person who acts to restrain or counter another ⟨using one earl as a ~ on the other⟩ **b :** a provision conferring power on a governmental branch or agency to restrain others ⟨the ~*s* and balances of republican governments —John Adams⟩ **c** [by shortening] **:** CHECKREIN **d :** a mechanical device for curbing, braking, or otherwise limiting action ⟨a door ~ preventing slamming⟩ **e :** a rope for checking the motion of a ship **f :** DAMPER 1a **g :** a device in a fishing reel to control the running out of the line **h :** the act of checking in poker **7 a :** supervision insuring accuracy, fitness, or due performance **:** CONTROL ⟨under the ~ of the superintendent⟩ **b :** a standard for testing and evaluation **:** CRITERION ⟨any arbitrary formula too rigidly adhered to may endanger good writing, but a good set of principles used as a ~ and an aid may be very useful —F.L.Mott⟩ **c :** an examination, test, or other device for determining progress, condition, value, or accuracy; *sometimes* **:** a test performed by quick sampling ⟨a ~ on a student's progress⟩ **d :** INSPECTION, INVESTIGATION ⟨a loyalty ~ on government employees⟩ **e :** a ready source of information used in investigating or verifying ⟨graphs serving as a ~ on our standing⟩ **f :** act of testing or verifying ⟨making a ~ on the data⟩; *also* **:** the material, sample, or unit used for such testing or verifying **8 a :** an area of land enclosed by embankments that confine irrigation water admitted by flooding **b :** a gate for controlling water flow in an irrigation ditch **9** *dial* **:** a light meal **:** SNACK **10** [so called fr. the use of the counterfoil to check forgery] **a** *obs* **:** the counterfoil of a bank draft; *also* **:** a draft form with a counterfoil **b :** a written order directing a bank or banker to pay money as therein stated **:** a draft drawn on a bank or banker payable on demand **11 a :** a card or small metal piece showing ownership, indicating payment of a charge or fee, identifying a person, or enabling him to make certain demands or claims **:** TICKET, CERTIFICATE ⟨a baggage ~⟩ ⟨a hat ~⟩ ⟨a baseball rain ~⟩ **b :** a token used in trade as a piece of money or as evidence of credit ⟨an army post exchange ~⟩ ⟨a ~ good for a bottle of beer⟩ **c :** a counter in various games (as card games) that is often cashed or otherwise turned in on leaving a game **:** CHIP ⟨the piles of ~*s* before the roulette players⟩ **d :** a tab or slip indicating an amount due **:** BILL ⟨our waitress finally brought the ~⟩ **e :** CHECKROOM ⟨there's a hat ~ in the hotel lobby⟩ **12** [ME *chek*, short for *cheker* checker (chessboard)] **a :** a pattern in squares **:** a design that resembles a checkerboard **b :** a fabric woven or printed with such a design **c :** a square in such a design **d :** a square made by vertical and horizontal lines to facilitate planned planting ⟨planting the trees in ~*s*⟩ **13 :** a mark typically √ placed beside an item to show its having been noted, examined, or verified **14 a :** CRACK, CHINK, BREAK: (1) **:** a lengthwise separation in wood that usu. extends across the annual growth rings and commonly results from stresses set up during seasoning — compare SHAKE (2) **:** an almost imperceptible crack in steel caused by uneven quenching in hardening (3) **:** a short shallow crack in a paint, varnish, or lacquer film occurring as a result of age and disintegration of film **b** *pl* **checks** *also* **chex** \-ks\ **:** a poultry egg with a minuscule break in the shell due to improper sealing but with unbroken membrane — contrasted with *crack* (sense 13) **15 :** a rabbet-shaped cutting **:** RABBET, REBATE — **in check :** in restraint **:** in a situation precluding free activity or development **:** under control ⟨Lee held the left of the Union army *in check* —G.J. Fiebeger⟩

[3]check \"\ *vb* -ED/-ING/-S [ME *cheken*, fr. MF *eschequier* to play chess, put in check, defeat, fr. *eschecs* chess or *eschec* check] *vt* **1 :** to place (a chess king) in check — see CHECKMATE **2 :** CHECKROW **3** *now chiefly dial* **:** REBUKE, REPRIMAND **4 a** *archaic* **:** to penalize, fine, or mulct by withholding wages ⟨~ a delinquent servant⟩ **b :** GARNISHEE, MULCT ⟨~ a delinquent's salary⟩ **5 a :** to bring to a sudden stop and halt the course, progress, or action of often abruptly, forcefully, and certainly ⟨the army of the Huns under Attila had been ~*ed* and turned back at Châlons —Tom Wintringham⟩ ⟨he . . . went on pacing . . . but suddenly he ~*ed* himself, stood still for a moment —Joseph Conrad⟩ **b :** to block the progress of (an opposing hockey player or a hockey play) by a check **6 a :** to restrain or abate the course, action, or force of **:** cause to act more slowly with less force or effect **:** have the power or ability to restrain or control ⟨the Parliament Act of 1911, which made our House of Lords less able to thwart or ~ the purposes of the House of Commons —Ernest Barker⟩ **b :** to slack or ease off and then belay again (as a purchase or rope) **:** STOPPER ⟨~ a cable when it's running out⟩ **7 a** *obs* **:** DRIVE ⟨~ thy fiery steeds —Shak.⟩ **b :** to hold in restraint **:** CONTROL **:** act as a check, curb, or counter to ⟨~ for a time the inward sweeping waves of melancholy —Louis Bromfield⟩ **8 a :** to compare with source of information (as an original, another version, a record, or body of data) **:** VERIFY ⟨we ~*ed* our information by looking up meteorological records —V.G. Heiser⟩ ⟨numerous scholars do not ~ quotations, references, or bibliographies —E.S.McCartney⟩ — often used with *with* or *against* **b :** to inspect and ascertain the condition of esp. in order to determine that the condition is satisfactory **:** find out about **:** investigate and ensure accuracy, authenticity, reliability, safety, or satisfactory performance of ⟨the applicant must be ~*ed*, much as a bank ~*s* the credit rating of a would-be borrower —Craig Thompson⟩ ⟨incoming fishing boats were ~*ed* for radiation —*Time*⟩ ⟨I ~*ed* the ship out, testing the engine at full power —B.T.Guyton⟩ **c :** to note or mark often with a check as examined, verified, present, satisfactory, finished, or in order ⟨~ an inventory list⟩ — often used with *off* ⟨~ off the names of men reporting⟩ **9 a :** to consign for shipment typically as a service extended to the holder of a passenger ticket ⟨~ the trunk at the station⟩ **b :** to ship or accept for shipment under such a consignment arrangement ⟨the agent ~*ed* our baggage through⟩ **10 a** [ME *cheken*, fr. *chek* (square)] **:** to mark into squares **:** mark with a pattern of crossing lines **:** CHECKER ⟨~ the cloth⟩ **b :** to mark (ground) to facilitate planting in squares ⟨~ the field with a marker⟩ **11** [[2]*check* (token)] **a :** to leave in safekeeping typically with receipt of a check or token indicating ownership ⟨~ your hat and coat at the theater⟩ **b :** to accept for safekeeping under such an arrangement ⟨working in a nightclub ~*ing* hats⟩ **12** [[2]check (crack)] **:** to make checks or chinks in **:** cause to crack ⟨the sun ~*s* timber⟩ **13** [[2]*check* (draft)] **:** to use checks to withdraw or pay over (money held in a bank) — usu. used with *out* ⟨~ out over a thousand dollars⟩ **~** *vi* **1** *obs* **:** to come into jarring conflict **:** CLASH ⟨heat ~*ing* against cold⟩ **2** *falconry* **:** to turn when in pursuit of proper game and fly after inferior game — used with *at* **3** *obs* **:** to take offense **:** become offended **4 a** *of a dog* **:** to stop in a chase esp. when scent is lost **b :** to halt suddenly **:** pause in one's procedure often through caution, uncertainty, or fear **:** STOP ⟨she ~*ed* for a moment in the dance and missed a step —Monica Ewer⟩ ⟨the train ~*ed* with a jolt —B.A.Williams⟩ **5 :** to prevent or hinder (as by a pad, cup, or ring) the escape of gas in a gun **6 a :** to investigate and make sure about conditions or circumstances **:** obtain confirmation or substantiation ⟨~*ing* on her passengers' safety belts —E.K.Gann⟩ ⟨he ~*ed* to be sure the *Savo's* deck was ready —J.A.Michener⟩ **b :** to correspond often detail for detail **:** AGREE, CONCUR, TALLY ⟨the description ~*s* with the photograph⟩ **7 :** to draw a check (as upon a bank or banker) **8** *poker* **a :** to bet one chip of lowest value in games in which one must bet or drop in each turn **b :** to announce one's intention of postponing his right to bet with privilege of betting later in games in which this is permitted **9 :** CRACK, SPLIT: **a :** to crack open (as of wood in drying or as biscuits in cooling) **b :** to develop small cracks (as of varnish or eggs) **10 a :** to check off or tally items in a list or group esp. of prices **b :** to place a check beside items in tallying, listing, or otherwise accounting for them **syn** see ARREST, RESTRAIN — **check into :** to check in at ⟨*check into* a hotel⟩ — **check on :** to examine or inspect to discover the condition of **:** find the facts about

[4]check \"\ *adj* [in sense 1, fr. [2]*check* (square); in sense 2 & 3, fr. [2&3]*check*] **1 :** marked with checks **:** showing a check pattern **:** CHECKED, CHECKERED **2 :** serving to check, stop, baffle, or regulate ⟨a ~ valve⟩ **3 :** serving as a control **:** affording a likely means of verifying, correcting, codifying, or measuring ⟨~ areas in soils research projects⟩

[5]check \"\ *interj* [[2]*check* (mark)] — used to express assent or agreement

check·a·ble \'chekəbəl\ *adj* **1 :** capable of being checked ⟨a ~ statement⟩ **2 :** suitable for being checked on a passenger ticket ⟨~ baggage⟩

check·age \-ij\ *n* -s **1 :** act of checking **2 :** items or amount checked

checkback \'=,=\ *n* -s **:** a check on or verification of something already completed, once figured, or presumably accounted for; *esp* **:** a check of this kind that goes over the matter in reverse order

check beam *n* **:** a radio beam for use of pilots in checking exact position preparatory to landing airplanes

check binding *n* [[2]*check* (draft); fr. its use in commercial checkbooks] **:** a simple and inexpensive style of bookbinding featuring paper-covered board sides with edges trimmed flush

checkbite \'=,=\ *n* -s [[3]*check* + *bite*; fr. its function of checking or testing] **1 a :** an act of biting into a sheet of wax or other material to record the relation between the opposing surfaces of upper and lower teeth **b :** the record obtained **2 :** wax or other material for checkbites

check block *n* **:** a delaying block in football

checkbook \'=,=\ *n* -s **1 :** a book containing items by which other items are checked or verified (as a book with a bank's record of checks issued to customers) **2 :** a book containing blank checks on a bank

checkbook money *n* **:** demand bank deposits subject to check

check certifier *n* **:** a machine used in banking that certifies checks by printing on them a form of endorsement

check collar *n* [[3]*check*] **:** a collar that chokes when pulled upon and that is used in breaking horses or training dogs

check dam *n* **:** an often improvised barrier in a channel to retard the flow of water esp. for controlling soil erosion

check damper *n* **:** DAMPER 1a

checked *adj* [fr. past part. of [3]*check*] **1 :** consisting of, provided with, or subject to a check or checks **:** CHECKERED **2** *phonetics* **a** *of a syllable* **:** ended by a consonant **b** *of a vowel* **:** standing in such a syllable — opposed to *free* **syn** see VARIEGATED

[1]check·er \'chekə(r)\ *n* -s *often attrib* [ME *cheker*, fr. OF *eschequier* chessboard, fr. *eschec* check in the game of chess + *-ier* -er — more at CHECK] **1** *archaic* **:** CHESSBOARD **2** *obs* **:** TREASURY, EXCHEQUER **3 :** a square, other rectangle, mark, or spot resembling checkerboard markings ⟨an aerial view of the country showing ~*s* of green and brown⟩ **4** [so called fr. the checkered appearance of the fruit] **:** the fruit of the service tree **5 a :** a European service tree (*Sorbus domestica*) **b :** a wild service tree (*S. torminalis*) **6** *also* **checkerman** [back-formation fr. *checkers*] **:** one of a set of disks used in the game of checkers **7 checkers** *pl* **:** CHECKERWORK 3 **8** *slang* **:** the fit thing **:** the most appropriate condition — used with *the*

[2]checker \"\ *vt* **checkered**; **checkered**; **checkering** \-k(ə)riŋ\ **checkers** [ME *chekeren*, fr. *cheker* chessboard — more at CHECKER] **1 a :** to variegate with different colors or shades typically with a small square or diamond pattern throughout ⟨his face ~*ed* by the shadow of the grating —William Faulkner⟩ **b :** to vary with differing or contrasting elements or situations (as alternating prosperity and hardship) ⟨life's ~*ed* scene of joy and sorrow —Sir Walter Scott⟩ ⟨pride ~*ed* by many painful feelings —T.B.Macaulay⟩ **2 a :** to mark into different colored squares, diamonds, or more or less rectangular figures ⟨farm lands that are ~*ed* with dense tracts of timber —*Amer. Guide Series: Mich.*⟩ **b :** to mark into squares irrespective of color; *esp* **:** to lay out (land) in checks or squares before planting **c :** to intersperse in a fashion suggestive of squares on a chessboard ⟨~ veteran units in the ranks of an inexperienced army⟩ **3 :** to ornament with a pattern of diamond-shaped projections by intersecting grooves ⟨a ~*ed* rifle stock⟩

[3]checker \"\ *n* -s [[3]*check* + *-er*] **:** one that checks: as **a :** one that marks, counts, or tallies ⟨a freight ~ in a shipping house⟩ **b :** one that examines materials or products for completeness and conformity to standards, checks data or articles against records for verification, or observes and records the presence or condition of things for purposes of comparison and administration **c :** one that checks articles of personal property for the patrons of an establishment **d :** one that totals purchases and usu. accepts payment (as in a supermarket) **:** CASHIER

checkerbelly \'==,==\ *or* **checkerbreast** *n, in California* **:** WHITE-FRONTED GOOSE

checkerberry \'==,==\ *n* [*checker* (wild service tree) + *berry*] **1 :** any of several reddish berries: as **a :** the spicy red berry-like fruit of a wintergreen (*Gaultheria procumbens*) **b :** PARTRIDGEBERRY 2 **2 :** a plant producing checkerberries

checkerbloom \'==,=\ *n* [prob. fr. [1]*checker* + *bloom*] **:** a perennial purple-flowered mallow (*Sidalcea malvaeflora*) that occurs wild in the western U.S. and is also cultivated

1checkerboard \R -kə(r),b-, –R -kə,b-\ *n* [*1checker* + *board*] **1 :** a board used in checkers, chess, and other games with a typical pattern of 64 squares in 2 alternating colors arranged in 8 rows of 8 squares each **2 :** a pattern or arrangement like a checkerboard ⟨a ~ of cultivated fields, pasture lands and wooded tracts —*Amer. Guide Series: Texas*⟩

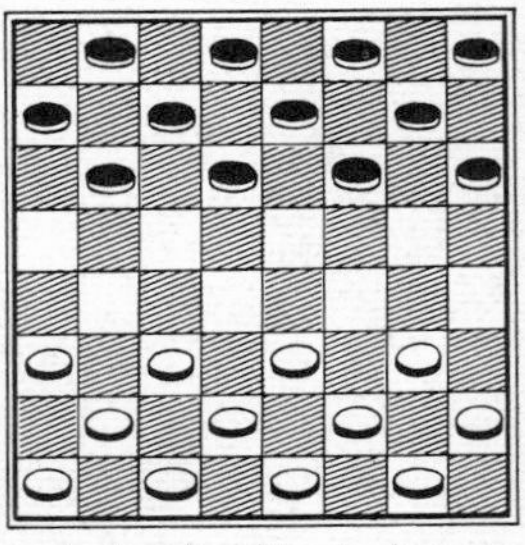
checkerboard with checkers arranged as at the beginning of a game

2checkerboard \"\ *vt* -ED/-ING/-S **:** to arrange, mark, line, or split up into a checkerboard pattern ⟨with fields and forests ~*ed* around —*Amer. Guide Series: Ark.*⟩; *specif* **:** to purchase or lease (scattered parcels of land) in acquiring oil rights in a given area ⟨the company's holdings are ~*ed* over the prospective oil territory⟩

checker–brick \ˈ=,=\ *n* **:** CHECKERWORK 3; *also* **:** the material composing it or an individual brick in it

checkered *adj, sometimes* -ER/-EST **1 :** marked by alternating squares of different colors, shades, or materials in checkerboard fashion **:** showing a pattern of alternating rectangles differing in color or shade ⟨hills ~ with pastures among small forests —Sinclair Lewis⟩ **2 :** marked by alternation, contrast, vicissitude, or diversity esp. of fortune ⟨a man with a ~ business career, but who survived all storms —George Santayana⟩ **3 :** provided with checkerwork **syn** see VARIEGATED

checkered adder *n* **:** MILK SNAKE

checkered lily *or* **checkered daffodil** *n* **:** a plant of the genus *Fritillaria; esp* **:** GUINEA-HEN FLOWER

checkering *pres part of* CHECKER

check·er·ist \ˈchekərəst\ *n* -S **:** a checker player or enthusiast

check·er·man \-mən\ *n, pl* **checkermen :** 1CHECKER 6

checker roll *n* [ME *chekerrolle*, fr. *cheker* + *rolle* — more at CHECKER, ROLL] *obs* **:** a list of persons (as of those to be paid from the royal exchequer)

check·ers \ˈchekə(r)z\ *n pl but sing in constr* [pl. of 1*checker* (chessboard)] **:** a game played on a checkerboard by two players each having 12 men that move diagonally forward one square at a time or backward as well if crowned, the object being to capture or block all the opponent's men

checkerspot \ˈ=,=\ *or* **checkerspot butterfly** *n* **:** CHALCEDON

checker–up \ˈ==ˈ=\ *n* -S [3*checker* + *up*] **:** one that checks up

checkerwise \ˈ=,=\ *adv* **:** in the form or pattern of a checkerboard **:** in alternating squares

checkerwork \ˈ=,=\ *n* **1 :** work with a checkered pattern **:** work marked by checks **:** checkered design ⟨a ~ of light and shadow⟩ **2 :** sequence of changing fortune **:** VICISSITUDE ⟨the ~ of our lives⟩ **3 :** a structure of firebrick (as in a regenerative furnace) built so that the bricks alternate with open spaces permitting the passage of gases which give heat to or receive heat from the firebrick

check·hook \ˈche,ku̇k, -ek,hu̇k\ *n* [3*check*] **:** a hook on the saddle of a harness over which a checkrein is looped

check in *vi* **:** to register esp. at a hotel **:** show or report one's presence or arrival by satisfying requisite forms ⟨*check in* at a convention⟩ ⟨*check in* for a certain flight⟩ **~** *vt* **:** to make a record of **:** REGISTER ⟨records were *checked in* and verified⟩

check–in \ˈ=,=\ *n* -S [*check in*] **:** an act, instance, or occasion of checking in

checking *pres part of* CHECK

checking account *n* **:** an account in a bank against which the depositor can draw checks without giving notice or presenting a passbook — distinguished from *savings account*

check key *n* [4*check;* fr. its function of hindering entry] *Brit* **:** LATCHKEY

checkle *vi* -ED/-ING/-S [prob. imit.] *obs* **:** to laugh violently or hysterically

check·less \ˈchekləs\ *adj* **:** being without a check

check ligament *n* [4*check*] **:** either of a pair of strong fibrous bands passing upward and outward from the upper part of the odontoid process to the inner side of the corresponding occipital condyle and limiting the rotation of the head

checkline \ˈ=,=\ *n* [4*check* + *line*] **:** a hawser made fast on a dock and checked on a ship's bitts and used when coming alongside a wharf for taking off way or snubbing toward the wharf

checklist \ˈ=,=\ *n* [4*check* + *list*] **:** a list intended for ready checking and reference **:** INVENTORY, CATALOG; *often* **:** a complete list ⟨a ~ of voters' names⟩ ⟨a ~ of editions of an author⟩ ⟨a ~ of reptiles of the island⟩

check lock *n* [4*check*] **:** a small lock for checking or securing a large lock (as by closing its keyhole)

check mark *n* [4*check*] **:** a mark indicating that a thing has been checked, noted, examined, or approved

1check·mate \ˈchek,māt\ *interj* [ME *chekmate*, fr. MF *eschec mat*, fr. Ar *shāh māt*, fr. Per, lit., the king is left unable to escape, fr. *shāh* king + *māt* left, perplexed, fr. *māndan* to remain, fr. MPer, fr. OPer *man-*; akin to Av *man-* to remain — more at CHECK, MANSION] — used in chess to tell an opponent that his king has been checkmated

2checkmate \", *usu* -ād+V\ *vt* -ED/-ING/-S [ME *chekmaten*, fr. *chekmate*, n.] **1 :** to arrest, check, thwart, or counter completely ⟨for several centuries Britain *checkmated* the rise of rival powers on the continent of Europe by a balance-of-power policy —H.W.Baldwin⟩ **2 :** to check (a chess opponent's king) so that escape from or capture of the attacking piece is impossible

3checkmate \"\ *n* -S [ME *chekmate*, fr. *chekmate*, interj.] **1 a :** the act of checkmating **b :** the situation of a checkmated king — called also *mate* **2 :** a complete check **:** an utter defeat **:** effective thwarting or countering ⟨to give ~ to an old adversary⟩

check nut *n* [4*check*] **:** LOCK NUT

check off *vt* **1 :** to check or mark as noted **:** tick off **:** note item by item **2 :** to eliminate from further consideration ⟨robbery was *checked off* as a motive⟩ **3 :** to handle by the checkoff ⟨*check off* each miner's dues⟩

checkoff \ˈ=,=\ *n, often attrib* [*check off*] **:** an authorized withholding of union dues, fees, fines, and assessments from the wages of union members and a turning of such withheld money over to the union

check out *vi* **1 :** to satisfy requisite forms in departing ⟨*check out* of a hotel⟩ ⟨*check out* of an office⟩ **2** *slang* **:** DIE ⟨really *checked out* the hard way —Charles Burgess⟩ **3 :** to become substantiated or verified **:** ACCORD ⟨his story *checked out* with the facts⟩ **4 :** to satisfy requirements **:** pass a competency test **:** QUALIFY ⟨the trainee *checked out* all right on his first flight⟩ **~** *vt* **1 :** to satisfy all requirements in taking away (as in borrowing a library book or withdrawing money from a bank account) ⟨he *checked out* two books from the library⟩ ⟨would deposit sufficient cash in the bank to cover the premium, and then *check it out* —Mary R. Rinehart⟩ **2 :** to submit to examination **:** verify, substantiate, or gain approval for ⟨an electronics man assigned to *check out* carefully the new plane's radio and radar system⟩ ⟨all . . . testimony which could be *checked out* has turned out to be correct —Arthur Schlesinger b.1917⟩ ⟨*checked out* his ideas with an expert⟩ **3 :** to itemize and reckon up the total cost of and receive payment for (outgoing merchandise or services) esp. in a self-service store ⟨*checking out* groceries in a supermarket⟩ ⟨employed in *checking out* cleaned suits in a dry-cleaning establishment⟩

check–out \ˈ=,=\ *n* -S [*check out*] **1 a :** the completion of the usu. fixed procedure or requirements (as the paying of one's bill) in relinquishing or vacating a hotel room **b :** the time at which a hotel guest must relinquish his room or be charged for retaining it ⟨*check-out* is at 12 noon⟩ **2 a :** a satisfactory performance in a competency test **b :** itemization and receiving of amounts due ⟨taking care of *check-outs* in the supermarket⟩ ⟨a *check-out* counter in a self-service department store⟩

check over *vt* **:** EXAMINE, INVESTIGATE

check–over \ˈ=,=\ *n* -S [*check over*] **:** EXAMINATION, INSPECTION, INVESTIGATION

check paper *n* [2*check*] **:** a paper treated with chemicals that make alteration in writing very difficult

check passer *n* [2*check* (draft)] **:** one that passes worthless checks

check pinochle *n* [2*check*] **:** partnership pinochle in which, after the play of each hand, settlement is made in chips for each particular scoring feature (as melds and bids that are fulfilled)

checkpoint \ˈ=,=\ *n* [4*check* + *point*] **1 :** a point at which vehicular traffic is halted for examination, inspection, or clearance ⟨allowing Allied traffic to move through Russian ~*s* —*N.Y.Times*⟩ **2 :** a geographical feature used by a flier to determine his location ⟨he glanced at the terrain below, looking for a ~ —Walt Sheldon⟩

check protector *n* [2*check* (draft)] **:** CHECKWRITER

check rail *n* [4*check* + *rail;* prob. fr. its hindering the entrance of rain or snow] **:** MEETING RAIL

check rate *n* [2*check* (draft)] **:** the rate at which sight drafts payable in foreign currency are bought and sold **:** the basic quotation of foreign exchanges at a particular time

1checkrein \ˈ=,=\ *n* [4*check* + *rein*] **1 a :** a short rein looped over the checkhook to hold a horse's head up or back — called also *bearing rein;* see HARNESS illustration **b :** a branch rein connecting the driving rein of one horse of a span or pair with the bit of the other horse **2 :** measures calculated to check or govern **:** CONTROL ⟨he held a tight administrative ~ upon expenditures —*Current Biog.*⟩ ⟨new import controls and other ~*s* seem to have worked . . . overseas trade into at least a temporarily favorable balance —*Newsweek*⟩

2checkrein \"\ *vt* **:** hold in check **:** CONTROL ⟨civilian authority ~*ing* the military⟩

checkroll \ˈ=,=\ *n* [ME *chekrolle*, prob. alter. of *chekerrolle* — more at CHECKER ROLL] **1** *archaic* **:** CHECKER ROLL **2** *obs* **:** a list of household servants **3 :** MUSTER ROLL, CHECKLIST

check roller *n* [2*check* (crack)] **:** a tool used in graining for imitating the cracks of weathered wood

checkroom \ˈ=,=\ *n* [3*check* (to deposit)] **:** a room at which baggage, parcels, clothing, or other personal articles are checked

1checkrow \ˈ=,=\ *n* [2*check* (square) + *row*] **:** one of a series of rows (as of corn) dividing land into squares to permit cultivation both between and across the rows

2checkrow \"\ *vt* **:** to plant or set in checkrows

check·row·er \-ō(ə)r\ *n* **:** a device in a corn-planting machine for dropping the seed so that the hills will lie in checkrows

checks *pres 3d sing of* CHECK, *pl of* CHECK

check sheet *n* **:** a form prepared to facilitate ready checking off or marking

check side *n* [2*check*] *Brit* **:** REVERSE ENGLISH 1

checkstones \ˈ=,=\ *n pl but usu sing in constr* [perh. fr. *check* (short for *checker*)] *Brit* **:** a children's game like jackstones usu. played with pebbles

check stopper *n* [4*check*] **:** one of a series of light cables that are fastened to a heavier cable (as an anchor cable) and are designed to check a ship's speed esp. during launching by holding for a moment before breaking as the heavier main cable runs out

checkstrap \ˈ=,=\ *n* [4*check*] **:** a strap designed to check, control, or secure: as **a :** a helmet fastening consisting of a strap passing under the chin **b :** a leather or composition strap for checking the motion of the picker stick in a loom

check system *n* [2*check*] **:** irrigation of checks

check up *vb* **:** EXAMINE, INSPECT, TEST, INVESTIGATE ⟨the police became suspicious and *checked up*⟩ ⟨*check up* some doubtful points⟩ — often used with *on* ⟨*check up* on his alibi⟩

checkup \ˈ=,=\ *n* -S [*check up*] **:** act of checking up **:** EXAMINATION, INSPECTION, VERIFICATION ⟨a ~ is made of the physical condition of every child —*School & Society*⟩; *esp* **:** a general physical examination ⟨went to the hospital every year for a ~⟩

checkup man *n* **:** an editor who examines illustration layouts to detect and remedy inaccuracies of detail or color

check valve *n* [4*check*] **:** a valve that permits flow in one direction but prevents a return flow

check viewer *n* [4*check*] **:** one that inspects leased portions of mines to see that all agreements and safety precautions are observed

check washer *n* [4*check*] **:** LOCK WASHER

check weave *n* [2*check* (pattern)] **:** a simple weave in basketry or rushwork in which one cane strip or rush is woven alternately under and over the parallel canes or rushes at right angles to it

checkweigher \ˈ=,==\ *or* **checkweighman** \ˈ=,==\ *n* [4*check* + *weigher* or *weighman*] **:** one that checks weight; *specif* **:** one employed by miners or unions to check weighing of coal or ore by a company weighmaster

checkwork \ˈ=,=\ *n* [2*check* (pattern) + *work*] **:** CHECKERWORK

checkwriter \ˈ=,==\ *n* [2*check* (draft)] **:** a device (as a machine) that imprints figures or amounts on the faces of bank checks or drafts in such a way (as by perforation or embossing) as to prevent fraud by alteration or erasure

checky *also* **chequ·ey** *or* **chequy** \ˈchekē\ *adj, usu* -ER/-EST [modif. of MF *eschequé*, past part. of *eschequer* to mark with checks, fr. *eschec* check — more at CHECK] **1 :** CHECKERED **2** *heraldry* **:** divided into usu. equilateral rectangles of alternate tinctures

1ched·dar \ˈchedə(r)\ *or* **cheddar cheese** *n* -S *often cap Cheddar* [fr. *Cheddar*, England, where it was first made] **:** a hard pressed cheese of smooth texture widely made esp. in America as standard factory cheese — called also *American cheddar, American cheese, store cheese*

2cheddar \"\ *vt* -ED/-ING/-S **:** to pile and repile (slices of curd) so as to expel any remaining free whey in cheddar-making

cheddar pink *n, usu cap C* [fr. *Cheddar*, England] **:** a European pink (*Dianthus gratianopolitanus*) with pale rose-colored flowers

chedd·ite \ˈshed,īt, ch-\ *n* -S [*Chedde*, town in Haute-Savoie, France, where it was first made + E *-ite*] **:** a blasting explosive consisting essentially of a mixture of a chlorate or perchlorate (as of potassium) with an aromatic nitro compound (as nitronaphthalene) and usu. a fatty substance (as castor oil)

cheder *also* **chedar** *n, pl* **chadarim** *also* **cheders** *or* **chedars** *var of* HEDER

chee·cha \ˈchēchə\ *n* -S [native name in Ceylon] **:** a small Ceylonese lizard (*Hemidactylus frenatus*) of the family Gekkonidae found about houses

chee·cha·ko *or* **chee·cha·co** *or* **che·cha·ko** \chēˈchä(,)kō\ *or* **che·cha·qua** \-ˈäkə\ *n* -S [Chinook Jargon *chee chahco*, fr. Chinook *t'shi* new + Nootka *chako* to come] **:** a tenderfoot in Alaska or the Pacific northwest

chee–chee \ˈchē(,)chē\ *n* -S [prob. fr. Hindi *chī-chī* fie!, lit., dirt] **:** a Eurasian half-caste — usu. taken to be offensive

1cheek \ˈchēk\ *n* -S [ME *cheke* jawbone, cheek, fr. OE *cēace;* akin to OFris *zīāke* jawbone, MLG *kāke*, OE *acēocian* to suffocate, strangle, and perh. to OE *cēowan* to chew — more at CHEW] **1 a :** the fleshy wall or side of the mouth in man and mammals **:** the side of the face below the eye and above and to the side of the mouth **b :** the lateral aspect of the head of a lower vertebrate or an invertebrate (as an insect) **:** GENA **c :** the portion of a hide corresponding to the cheek of the animal — see HIDE illustration **d :** the lateral part of the cephalic shield of a trilobite **2 :** a lateral side of any mass, structure, or opening: as **a :** either of the side posts of a door or gate **b :** a sidepiece around the eye of the head of a pike, hammer, or pick by which it is secured to the staff or handle **c :** a sidepiece on a mast, supporting a crosstree **d :** one of two laterally paired parts of a mechanism or structure ⟨the ~*s* of a vise⟩ ⟨the ~ of a mortise⟩ ⟨the ~ of a pulley block⟩ **e :** a wall of a mineral vein **f :** one of the vertical side faces of a dormer window **g :** a middle part of a foundry flask **3 a** *of a bridle* **:** CHEEK STRAP **b** *of a bit* **:** CHEEKPIECE **4 :** the shoulder of an artificial fly — see FLY illustration **5 :** BUTTOCK 1 **6 :** insolent boldness and flaunted self-assurance in speech or action **:** IMPUDENCE ⟨he has plenty of ~⟩ **syn** see TEMERITY — **cheek by jowl :** with cheeks close together **:** in close proximity or intimate relationship ⟨people who live *cheek by jowl* and breathe the same air —Virginia Woolf⟩

2cheek \"\ *vt* -ED/-ING/-S **1** *obs* **:** to form a side to **2 :** to place in or against the cheek **3 a :** to speak impudently or saucily to **b :** TEASE

cheekbone \ˈ=,=\ *n* **:** the prominence below the eye that is formed by the zygomatic bone; *also* **:** ZYGOMATIC BONE

cheek·er \-kə(r)\ *n* -S [1*cheek* + *-er*] **:** a slaughterhouse worker who cuts loosened meat from hog heads and sometimes also removes tongue and brain

cheek·i·ly \-əlē, -li\ *adv* **:** IMPUDENTLY, BOLDLY

cheek·i·ness \-kēnəs, -in-\ *n* -ES **:** insolence or impudence of speech or behavior

cheek knee *n* **:** one of the knees worked horizontally above and below the hawseholes in the angle of the bow and cutwater of a ship

cheek·less \ˈchēkləs\ *adj* **:** having no cheek

cheekpiece \ˈ=,=\ *n* **:** a piece or part forming, crossing, or covering a cheek: as **a** (1) *of a bridle* **:** CHEEK STRAP (2) *of a bit* **:** either of the sidepieces at the ends of the mouthpiece **b :** the portion of the stock of certain firearms that is specially constructed to offer a convenient rest for the firer's cheek

cheek pouch *n* **:** a saclike dilatation of the cheeks of certain monkeys and rodents used for holding food

cheek strap *n* **:** either of those straps of a bridle that pass down the sides of the horse's head connecting the crownpiece with the bit or noseband — called also *cheekpiece;* see BRIDLE illustration

cheek tooth *n* **:** 1MOLAR

cheeky \ˈchēkē, -i\ *adj* -ER/-EST **1 :** having or showing cheek **:** BRAZENFACED, IMPUDENT **2 :** having well-developed cheeks — used esp. of a bulldog

chee·ny *or* **chee·ney** \ˈchēni, -āni\ *dial Brit var of* 1CHINA 1

1cheep \ˈchēp\ *vb* -ED/-ING/-S [imit.] *vi* **1 :** to utter faint shrill sounds esp. of a young bird **:** CHIRP, PEEP **:** SQUEAK ⟨a mouse ~*ed*⟩ **2 :** to make a small sound **:** utter a word — often used with negative ⟨he didn't even ~⟩ **~** *vt* **:** CHIRP

2cheep \"\ *n* -S **1 :** a feeble shrill sound (as by a young bird or mouse) **:** CHIRP, PEEP, SQUEAK **2 :** HINT, WORD, SOUND — usu. used with negative ⟨not a ~ out of him⟩

cheep·er \-pə(r)\ *n* -S **:** one that cheeps: as **a :** a young partridge, grouse, or quail **b** *in England* **:** MEADOW PIPIT

cheepy \-pē\ *adj* -ER/-EST **:** inclined to cheep

1cheer \ˈchi(ə)r, -iə\ *n* -S [ME *chere* face, welcome, cheer, fr. OF *chiere, chere* face, perh. fr. LL *cara* head, fr. Gk *kara* head, face — more at CEREBRAL] **1 a** *obs* **:** FACE **b** *archaic* **:** facial expression ⟨meek and mild of ~ —Edmund Spenser⟩ **2 :** state of mind or heart **:** FEELING, SPIRIT ⟨be of good ~ —Mt 9:2(AV)⟩ **3 :** lightness of mind and feeling **:** GAIETY ⟨the wives of the officers came to the camp, and these brave women gave of their ~ to its dreary life —H.E.Scudder⟩ **4 :** hospitable entertainment **:** WELCOME **5 :** something that is provided for entertainment esp. at table **:** food and drink prepared for a feast **:** FARE ⟨the fewer the better ~⟩ **6 :** something that gladdens ⟨words of ~⟩ **7 a :** a shout or acclamation expressing enthusiasm, applause, favor, encouragement ⟨~*s* from the audience⟩ **b :** a set form of words for this purpose ⟨the college ~⟩

2cheer \"\ *vb* -ED/-ING/-S [ME *cheren*, fr. *chere*, n.] *vt* **1 a :** to give new hope to **:** lift from discouragement, dejection, or sadness to a more happy state **:** SOLACE, COMFORT ⟨and through all Europe ~ desponding men with new-born hope —William Wordsworth⟩ **b :** to instill with gladness **:** make glad or cause to be happy with or as if with gaiety or festivity ⟨a fandango usually ~*ed* the weary legislators . . . after strenuous hours of deliberation —*Amer. Guide Series: Calif.*⟩ **2** *obs* **:** to supply with good cheer **:** FEAST **3 :** COMFORT, INSPIRIT, INVIGORATE ⟨food ~*s*⟩ ⟨cups that ~ but not inebriate —William Cowper⟩ **4 :** to instill with courage, good spirits, and optimism and to inspire to continue or persevere by or as if by cheers, applause, commendation, aid ⟨~ the survivors of the attack⟩ — often used with *on* ⟨~ on the team⟩ **5 :** to salute or applaud with shouts ⟨the contest winner was ~*ed* as she came in sight⟩ **~** *vi* **1** *obs* **:** to be mentally or emotionally disposed ⟨how *cheer'st* thou, Jessica —Shak.⟩ **2 :** to grow or be cheerful **:** make merry **:** become glad or joyous **:** REJOICE **:** take or pluck up courage — used now only with *up*, often imperatively **3 :** to utter a shout of applause or triumph ⟨what is there to ~ about⟩ **syn** see ENCOURAGE

3cheer \"\ *dial var of* CHAIR

4cheer \"\ *or* **cheer pheasant** *n* -S [Garhwali *chīr*, perh. of imit. origin] **:** a buff or grayish pheasant (*Catreus wallichi*) of the lower Himalayan mountains distinguished by a bare red eye patch and a long narrow dark-barred tail

cheer·er \ˈchirə(r)\ *n* -S *dial Brit* **:** a cheering drink or cup (as of spirits)

cheer·ful \ˈchirfəl, -iəf-\ *adj, sometimes* **cheerfuller** \-f(ə)lə(r)\ *sometimes* **cheerfullest** \-f(ə)ləst\ [ME *cherefull*, fr. *chere* + *-full -ful*] **1 :** marked by cheer or by spontaneous good spirits arising from a carefree sanguine attitude and a hearty bright lively disposition ⟨the incessant warble of the red-eyed vireo, ~ . . . as the merry whistle of a schoolboy —John Burroughs⟩ **2 :** conducive to cheer **:** likely to brighten, encourage, and dispel gloom or worry ⟨her flat was always . . . ~, gay with flowers, and the chintzes in the drawing room were bright and pretty —W.S.Maugham⟩ **syn** see GLAD

cheer·ful·ize \-fə,līz\ *vt* -ED/-ING/-S **:** to render cheerful

cheer·ful·ly \-f(ə)lē, -li\ *adv* **:** in a cheerful manner **:** GLADLY

cheer·ful·ness \-fəlnəs\ *n* -ES **:** the quality or state of being cheerful

cheer·i·ly \ˈchirəlē, -li\ *adv* **:** in a cheery manner **:** CHEERFULLY

cheer·i·ness \-rēnəs, -rin-\ *n* -ES **:** the quality or state of being cheery

cheer·ing·ly *adv* **:** in a cheering manner

cheering section *n* **:** a section of a grandstand reserved for rooters for one of the contending teams; *also* **:** rooters esp. when led by a cheerleader ⟨the *cheering section* went wild⟩

cheer·io \ˌchi(ə)rīˈō\ *also* **cheero** \ˈchi(ə)(,)rō\ *interj* [*cheery*, 1*cheer* + *-o*] *chiefly Brit* — usu. used as a farewell, sometimes as a greeting or a toast

cheerleader \ˈ=,==\ *n* **:** one that calls for and directs organized cheering (as at a football game) — **cheerleading** \ˈ=,==\ *n*

cheer·less \ˈchirləs, -iəl\ *adj* **:** lacking anything cheering, comforting, gladdening, or heartening **:** BLEAK, DISPIRITING ⟨there was something ~ and stiff about the room which had always seemed so friendly —W.S.Maugham⟩ **syn** see DISMAL

cheer·less·ly \-slē, -li\ *adv* **:** in a cheerless manner **:** DISMALLY

cheer·less·ness \-snəs\ *n* -ES **:** the quality or state of being cheerless

1cheer·ly \-irlē,-iəlē\ *adj, archaic* **:** GAY, CHEERFUL

2cheerly \"\ *adv* **1 :** with a will **:** CHEERILY, HEARTILY — now used chiefly as a cry of encouragement among sailors **2 :** CHEERFULLY

cheer pine *var of* CHIR PINE

cheers \-i(ə)rz,-iəz\ *interj* [fr. pl. of 1*cheer*] *chiefly Brit* — used as a toast

cheery \ˈchirē, -ri\ *adj* -ER/-EST **:** causing or suggesting lightness of spirits **:** lively in voice, manner, or appearance **:** GAY, UNTROUBLED ⟨his heart belied the ~ flippancy of his tone —Donn Byrne⟩

1cheese \ˈchēz\ *n* -S *often attrib* [ME *chese*, fr. OE *cēse;* akin to OHG & OS *kāsi;* all fr. a prehistoric WGmc word borrowed fr. L *caseus;* akin to OSlav *kvasŭ* sour dough, OE *hwatherian* to foam, ON *hvethnir* milker, Goth *hwatho* foam, Skt *kvathati* he boils] **1 a :** curd that has been separated from whey, consolidated by molding for soft cheese or subjected to pressure for hard cheese, and ripened for use as a food **b :** a cake of this food typically in the shape of a wheel or of a flat cylinder **c :** CHEDDAR **2 :** something shaped like a cheese: as **a :** a mass of pomace in a cider press **b :** a package in which yarn is commonly wound **c :** a batch of raw fiber stock as it leaves the dyeing kettle **d :** SKITTLE BALL **e :** a compressed mass of tobacco to be cut up by machine into smoking or chewing tobacco **3 :** something like cheese in texture (as soft wood or paraffin wax saturated with oil) or odor — often used as a generalized term of disapproval ⟨surveys, generally speaking, are the ~ —*Atlantic Bull.*⟩ ⟨a lawyer simply has to convince the poor ~*s* on the jury —Sinclair Lewis⟩ **4 :** DWARF MALLOW; *also* **:** the flat fruits of the dwarf mallow or of the cheeseflower — usu. used in pl.

2cheese \"\ *vt* -ED/-ING/-S **1 :** to form (a rope end) into a tight neat coil — usu. used with *down* **2 :** to wind (yarn) onto a cheese **:** SPOOL

3cheese \"\ *vt* -ED/-ING/-S [origin unknown] *slang* **:** to leave off **:** STOP — **cheese it 1** *slang* **:** look out **:** be quiet **:** STOP **2** *slang* **:** get out **:** get away **:** VAMOOSE

⁴cheese \"\ *n* -s [perh. fr. Urdu *chīz* thing, fr. Per] **1** *slang* **:** something first-rate ⟨this car is certainly the ~⟩ **2** *slang* **:** someone important **:** BOSS ⟨he is a big ~ in the company⟩
cheese bolt *n* [¹*cheese* + *bolt;* fr. the round flat head] **:** a cheese-head bolt
cheesebox \ˈ=,=\ *n* **1 :** a box or case (as a low cylinder) for holding a cheese **2 :** something shaped like a cylindrical cheesebox (as a gun turret, a tank, or a building)
cheese·burg·er \-,bərgə(r), -bəgə(r), -bəigə(r)\ *n* -s [¹*cheese* + *hamburger*] **:** a hamburger with a slice of toasted cheese
cheesecake \ˈ=,=\ *n* **1 :** a dessert made by baking a mixture of cottage cheese, eggs, and sugar or a filling of similar texture in a pastry shell or a mold lined with sweet crumbs **2 a :** photography or photographs (as in advertisements or publicity) featuring the natural curves of shapely female legs, thighs, or trunk, usu. scantily clothed — called also *leg art* **b :** something resembling such cheesecake
cheese cement *n* **:** a kind of casein glue made from cheese or milk curd and used for mending earthenware
cheesecloth \ˈ=,=\ *n* -s **:** a very lightweight unsized cotton fabric loosely woven in plain weave and used orig. in cheese-making and now also for surgical gauze, costumes, curtains, and wrapping for food — compare TOBACCO CLOTH
cheese color *n* **:** ANNATTO 1a
cheese cutter *n* **:** a slicing implement whose cutting edge is a wire stretched on a frame furnished with one or two handles
cheesed off *adj* [prob. fr. past. part. of ³*cheese*] *slang chiefly Brit* **:** extremely discontented **:** very indignant
cheese dream *n* **:** a toasted or sautéed cheese sandwich
cheese–eater \ˈ=,==\ *n, slang* **:** INFORMER, STOOL PIGEON, RAT
cheeseflower \ˈ=,==\ *n* [so called fr. the shape of the fruit] **:** the common tall mallow (*Malva sylvestris*) adventive from Europe in the U.S., Canada, and Mexico
cheese fly *n* **:** a black two-winged fly (*Piophila casei*) that is the adult of the cheese skipper
cheese food *n* **:** cheese (as cheddar) finely ground and mixed with seasoning and other ingredients (as cream, milk solids, preservative agents)
cheese–head \ˈ=,=\ *or* **cheese–headed** \ˈ=ˈ==\ *adj, of a screw or bolt* **:** having a raised cylindrical head
cheese hoop *n* **:** a broad usu. wood hoop or cylinder in which the curd is pressed in making cheese
cheese knife *n* **1 :** a large spatula used to break down the curd in making cheese **2 :** a knife with a curved blade for cutting cheese **3 :** CHEESE CUTTER
cheese·lip \ˈchēz,lip, -ləp\ *or* **cheese·lep** \-,lep, -,ləp\ *n* -s [ME *cheslypp, cheslep,* fr. OE *cēselybb,* fr. *cēse* cheese + *lybb* medicinal herb, poison, magic; akin to OHG *luppi* sap, poison, magic, ON *lyf* medicinal herb, poison, magic, Goth *lubjaleisei* magic, OIr *luib* herb, OE *lēaf* leaf — more at LEAF] **1** *dial Brit* **:** RENNET **2** *dial Brit* **:** the dried stomach of a calf
cheese mite *n* **:** a minute whitish mite (*Acarus siro*) infesting cheese or dried meat and sometimes causing grocer's itch
cheese·par·er \ˈ=,==\ *n* **:** a parsimonious person **:** SKINFLINT
¹cheese·par·ing \ˈ=,==\ *n* -s **1 :** something saved or valued only by a parsimonious or very needy person **:** a worthless bit **:** an insignificant quantity **2 :** miserly or petty economizing ⟨administrative ~ that could not have plugged up more than a pinhole in France's leaking economy —Ray Alan⟩
²cheeseparing \"\ *adj* **:** given to or marked by mean economies and picayune frugality **syn** see STINGY
cheese pitch *n* **:** asphalt in a mass whose surface has dried and formed a skin
cheese press *n* **:** an appliance for pressing cheese curd in a mold or hoop
cheese rennet *n* [so called fr. its use as a milk coagulant] **:** YELLOW BEDSTRAW
chees·ery \ˈchēz(ə)rē, -ri\ *n* -ES **:** an establishment in which cheese is made
cheeses *pl of* CHEESE, *pres 3d sing of* CHEESE
cheese scoop *n* **:** a pointed spoonlike table implement for scooping out cheese
cheese skipper *or* **cheese hopper** *or* **cheese maggot** *n* **:** the cheese fly larva that lives in cheese, ham, and smoked beef and that can jump several inches
cheese spread *n* **:** a cheese food soft enough to spread
cheese–starter \ˈ=,==\ *n* **:** a culture of lactic acid-producing bacteria used in the preliminary fermentation of milk for cheese production
cheese straw *or* **cheese stick** *n* **:** a narrow strip of puff paste sprinkled with grated cheese before baking
cheese vat *also* **cheese tub** *n* **:** a round vat in which the curd is formed and cut or broken in cheese making
cheese week *n, usu cap C&W, Eastern Church* **:** the week from Monday through Sunday preceding the first day of Lent during which period cheese and eggs may be eaten for the last time before Easter
cheesewood \ˈ=,=\ *n* [so called fr. its yellowish white appearance] **:** either of two Australasian timber trees (*Pittosporum bicolor* and *P. undulatum*) — called also *bonewood* **2 :** the hard yellowish wood of either of the cheesewoods
chees·i·ness \ˈchēzēnəs, -zin-\ *n* -ES **:** the quality or state of being cheesy
cheesing *pres part of* CHEESE
¹cheesy *also* **chees·ey** \-zē, -zi\ *adj* **cheesier; cheesiest** [ME *chesy,* fr. *chese* + *-y*] **1 a :** resembling or suggesting cheese esp. in consistency or odor **b** *slang* **:** SHABBY, CHEAP ⟨a ~ comedy⟩ **2 :** CASEOUS
²cheesy \"\ *adj* -ER/-EST [⁴*cheese* + *-y*] *slang* **:** STYLISH, FIRST-RATE
chee·tah *or* **chee·ta** *also* **che·tah** *or* **chi·ta** \ˈchēd·ə, -ētə\ *n* -s [Hindi *cītā,* fr. Skt *citrakāya* tiger, panther, fr. *citra* variegated, bright, speckled + *kāya* body; akin to Skt *cinoti* he gathers, heaps up — more at -HOOD, POET] **:** a long-legged swift-moving somewhat doglike African and formerly Asiatic cat (*Acinonyx jubatus*) about the size of a small leopard that has a tawny pelt spotted with dark brown or black and blunt nonretractile claws and is often tamed and trained to run down antelopes and other game
cheetal *or* **cheetul** *var of* CHITAL
cheewink *var of* CHEWINK
chef \ˈshef\ *n* -s [F, chief, head — more at CHIEF] **1 :** a chief or head person — now used only in French phrases **2** [F, short for *chef de cuisine* head of the kitchen] **a :** a man skilled in food preparation who has charge of the kitchen and kitchen personnel in a large establishment (as a hotel or restaurant), planning menus, ordering foodstuffs, directing and assisting cooks, preparing special dishes **b :** COOK
chef de ca·bi·net \ˌshefdə,kabēˈnā\ *n, pl* **chefs de cabinet** \-f(s)d-\ [F, lit., office head] **:** the chief secretary of a French minister or prefect
chef d'é·cole \ˌshefdāˈkȯl, -ōl\ *n, pl* **chefs d'école** \-f(s)d-\ [F] **:** a leader of a school (as of painters, musicians, writers)
chef de cui·sine \ˌshefdəkwēˈzēn\ *n, pl* **chefs de cuisine** \-f(s)d-\ [F, lit., kitchen head] **:** CHEF 2
chef d'oeu·vre \shāˈdə(r)v(rᵊ), -dəv-, -vrə, (ˈ)shef'd-, *F* shedœvr(ᵊ) *or* -v(rə)\ *n, pl* **chefs d'oeuvre** \"\ [F, lit., leading work] **:** a masterpiece esp. in art or literature
cheffonier *var of* CHIFFONIER
che·foo \ˈjōˈfü\ *adj, usu cap* [fr. *Chefoo,* China] **:** of or from the city of Chefoo, China **:** of the kind or style prevalent in Chefoo
chegoe *or* **chegre** *var of* CHIGOE
che·ha·lis \chəˈhālə̇s\ *n, pl* **chehalis** *or* **chehalises** *usu cap* [fr. *Chehalis,* one of their villages on Grays Harbor, Wash., fr. *Chehalis,* lit., sand] **1 a :** a Salishan people of the Chehalis river valley and Grays Harbor, Washington **b :** a member of such people **2 :** the language of the Chehalis people
cheil- *or* **cheilo-** — see CHIL-
chei·lan·thes \kīˈlan(,)thēz\ *n, cap* [NL, fr. *chil-* + *-anthes*] **:** a widely distributed genus of ferns (family Polypodiaceae) having indusia with whitish reflexed margins — see LIP FERN — **chei·lan·thoid** \-,thȯid\ *adj*
cheil·ec·tro·pi·on *also* **chil·ec·tro·pi·on** \ˌkīˌlekˈtrōpē,än, -ēən\ *n* -s [NL, fr. *chil-* + *ectropion*] **:** an abnormal turning outward of one or both lips
-chei·lia \ˈkīlēə\ *also* **-chi·lia** \"\, ˈkil-\ *n comb form* -s [NL, fr. Gk *-cheilēs* having (such) lips (fr. *cheilos* lip) + NL *-ia* — more at CHIL-] **:** lip formation (of a specified type) ⟨macro-cheilia⟩

chei·li·on \ˈkīlē,än, -ēən\ *n* -s [NL, fr. *chil-* + Gk *-ion* (dim. suffix)] **:** the lateralmost point at the angle of the lips
chei·li·tis *or* **chi·li·tis** \kīˈlīd·ə̇s\ *n* [NL, fr. *chil-* + *-itis*] **:** inflammation of the lip
chei·lo·dac·tyl·i·dae \ˌkī(,)lō,dakˈtilə,dē\ *n pl, cap* [NL, fr. *Cheilodactylus,* type genus (fr. *chil-* + Gk *daktylos* finger) + *-idae* — more at DACTYL] **:** a family of marine percoid fishes resembling members of the family Serranidae and widely distributed in the southern Pacific — see MORWONG
chei·lo·plas·ty \ˈkīlō,plastē\ *n* [*chil-* + *-plasty*] **:** plastic surgery to repair lip defects
chei·los·chi·sis \kīˈläskəsə̇s\ *n, pl* **cheiloschi·ses** \-,sēz\ [NL, fr. *chil-* + *-schisis*] **:** HARELIP
chei·lo·sis \kīˈlōsə̇s\ *n, pl* **cheilo·ses** \-ō,sēz\ [NL, fr. *chil-* + *-osis*] **:** an abnormal condition of the lips characterized by scaling of the surface and fissuring in the corners of the mouth
chei·lo·spi·ru·ra \ˌkī(,)lō,spīˈrùrə\ [NL, fr. *chil-* + *Spirura* genus of nematode worms, fr. *spir-* + *-ura*] *syn of* ACUARIA
chei·lo·sto·ma·ta \ˌkīlōˈstōməd·ə\ *n pl, cap* [NL, fr. *chil-* + *-stomata*] **:** a large order of bryozoans (class Gymnolaemata) having the colony erect or encrusting, the zooecia more or less tubular, and the aperture closed by a chitinous operculum when the polypide is retracted
chei·lo·stom·a·tous *or* **chi·lo·stom·a·tous** \ˌ==ˈstäməd·əs, -ōm-\ *adj* [NL *Cheilostomata* + E *-ous*] **:** of or relating to the Cheilostomata
cheir- *or* **cheiro-** — see CHIR-
chei·ran·thus \kīˈran(t)thəs\ *n, cap* [NL, fr. *cheir-* (fr. Ar *khīrī* wallflower) + *-anthus*] **:** a genus of perennial herbs (family Cruciferae) including the true wallflower
-cheiria — see -CHIRA
chei·ro·ga·le·us \ˌkīrōˈgālēəs\ *n* [NL, fr. *chir-* + Gk *galeē, galē* weasel — more at GALEA] **1** *cap* **:** a genus of small arboreal Malagasy lemurs **2** -ES **:** a lemur of the genus *Cheirogaleus* **3** -ES **:** MOUSE LEMUR
chei·ro·glos·sa \ˌ==ˈgläsə, -ōsə\ *n, cap* [NL, fr. *chir-* + *-glossa*] **:** a small genus of epiphytic ferns (family Ophioglossaceae) having palmately divided fronds bearing pendent spikes near their bases
chei·ro·lin \ˈ==lə̇n\ *n* -s [ISV *cheir-* (fr. NL *Cheiranthus* genus of herbs, fr. Gk *chir-* + *-anthus*) + *-ol* + *-in;* orig. formed in G] **:** a colorless crystalline sulfone $CH_3SO_2(CH_2)_3$-NCS occurring as a glucoside in seeds of a wallflower (*Cheiranthus cheiri*) and in those of plants of the genus *Erysimum*
cheiromancy *var of* CHIROMANCY
chei·ro·mys \ˈkīrō,mis\ [NL, fr. *chir-* + *-mys*] *syn of* DAUBENTONIA
cheironomy *var of* CHIRONOMY
chei·ro·pom·pho·lyx \ˌkīrōˈpämfə,liks\ *n* -ES [NL, fr. *chir-* + *pompholyx*] **:** a skin disease characterized by itching vesicles or blebs occurring in groups on the hands or feet
cheiropterophilous *var of* CHIROPTEROPHILOUS
chei·ros·tro·bus \kīˈrästrəbəs\ *n, cap* [NL, fr. *chir-* + L *strobus* labdanum] **:** a form genus of sphenopsid fossil plants based on only the strobilus which consists of numerous crowded verticils of sporophylls, each sporophyll being divided in two planes
che·ka \ˈchā(,)kä\ *n* -s [Russ, fr. *che* + *ka,* names of initial letters of *Chrezvychainaya Kommissiya* extraordinary commission] **:** secret police (as in a Communist-dominated country) having virtually unrestrained power over life and death
che·khov·i·an \ˈche,kōfēən, -äf-, ==ˈ==; cheˈkōvē-\ *adj, usu cap* [Anton Pavlovich *Chekhov* †1904 Russ. writer + E *-ian*] **:** suggestive of the characterization or atmosphere (as of frustration and introspective complexity) in the plays and short stories of the Russian writer Chekhov ⟨a worrier of *Chekhovian* proportions —Herbert Mitgang⟩
che·kist \ˈchākəst\ *n* -s [Russ, fr. *cheka* + *-ist*] **:** a member of a cheka
chek·ker \ˈchekə(r)\ *n* -s [origin unknown] **:** a stringed keyboard instrument of the 14th and 15th centuries
chel- *or* **cheli-** *comb form* [NL, fr. ¹*chela*] **:** claw ⟨chelicera⟩
¹che·la \ˈkēlə\ *n, pl* **che·lae** \-(,)lē\ [NL, modif. of obs. E *chely,* fr. Gk *chēlē* claw] **1 :** the pincerlike organ or claw borne by certain of the limbs of Crustacea and Arachnida **2 :** a somewhat curved sponge spicule with recurved processes at each end

chela of a lobster

²che·la \ˈchā(,)lä\ *n* -s [Hindi *celā,* fr. Skt *ceṭa, ceṭaka* servant, slave; akin to Pali *ceṭo* servant, boy, Prakrit *ceḍa, cilla* boy] **:** a disciple (as of a mahatma) **:** a follower (as of an occult philosopher or esoteric philosophy)
chel·a·mela \ˌcheləˈmelə\ *n, pl* **chelamela** *or* **chelamelas** *usu cap* [Kalapooia] **1 :** a Kalapooian people in western Oregon **2 :** a member of the Chelamela people
¹che·late \ˈkē,lāt\ *adj* [NL ¹*chela* + E *-ate*] **1 :** like or having chelae **2** [Gk *chēlē* hoof, claw + E *-ate*] **a :** relating to, producing, or characterized by a cyclic structure usu. containing five or six atoms in a ring in which a central metallic ion (as bivalent copper or bivalent or trivalent iron) is held in a coordination complex by one or more groups (as citrate or ethylenediamine) each of which can attach itself to the central ion by at least two bonds ⟨a ~ ring⟩ ⟨chlorophyll and hemoglobin are ~ compounds⟩ **b :** relating to or characterized by a cyclic structure (as of the ring formed by salicylaldehyde) resulting from the formation of a hydrogen bond
²chelate \"\ *vb* -ED/-ING/-S *vt* **:** to combine with (a metal) so as to form a chelate ring or rings — compare SEQUESTER ~ *vi* **:** to react so as to form a chelate ring or rings
³chelate \"\ *n* -s **:** a compound formed by chelation **:** a chelate compound
che·la·tion \kēˈlāshən\ *n* -s [²*chelate* + *-ion*] **:** the process of chelating or the quality or state of being chelated ⟨~ of trace metals in nutrient solutions⟩
chel·e·ryth·rine \ˌkelərˈi,thrēn, kəˈlerə,-, -,thrən\ *n* -s [ISV *chelerythr-* (fr. Gk *chelidonion* celandine + *erythros* red) + *-ine;* orig. formed as G *chelerythrin* — more at CELANDINE, RED] **:** a colorless crystalline poisonous alkaloid $C_{21}H_{19}NO_5$ obtained from celandine and other papaveraceous plants and forming yellow salts with a violet fluorescence
che·lic·era \kəˈlisərə\ *also* **chel·i·cer** \ˈkeləsər\ *or* **chel·i·cere** \-,si(ə)r\ *n, pl* **chelicer·ae** \-sə,rē\ *also* **chelicers** \-sərz\ *or* **cheliceres** \-,si(ə)rz\ [*chelicera,* NL, modif. of F *chélicère,* fr. *chél-* chel- + *-cère* (fr. Gk *keras* horn); *chelicer, chelicere* fr. F *chélicère* — more at CEREBRAL] **:** one of the anterior pair of appendages of an arachnid prob. derived from antennae, distinguished in scorpions by being short, chelate, and lacking a poison gland, in spiders by terminating in a sharp-pointed tip near which a venom duct opens, and in ticks by being modified into piercing and attachment organs — **che·li·cer·al** \kəˈlisərəl\ *adj*
che·lic·er·ata \kə,lisəˈrād·ə, -ād·ə\ *n pl, cap* [NL, fr. *chelicera* + *-ata*] *in some classifications* **:** a subphylum or superclass of Arthropoda comprising forms having chelicerate appendages and lacking antennae and including the king crabs and eurypterids, spiders, scorpions, and sea spiders — compare ARACHNIDA, MEROSTOMATA, PYCNOGONIDA
che·lic·er·ate \kəˈlisə,rāt, -,rə̇t\ *adj* [NL *chelicera* + E *-ate*] **1 :** provided with chelicerae **2 :** having the form of a chelicera
chel·i·dam·ic acid \ˌkeləˈdamik-\ *n* [ISV *chelidonic* + *ammonia* + *-ic*] **:** a crystalline acid $C_7H_5NO_5$ prepared from chelidonic acid and ammonia; 4-pyridone-2,6-dicarboxylic acid
chel·i·don·ic acid \ˌkeləˈdänik-\ *n* [ISV *chelidonic* (fr. Gk *chelidonion* celandine + ISV *-ic*) + acid; orig. formed as G *chelidonsäure*] **:** a crystalline acid $C_7H_4O_6$ occurring combined in celandine sap and in white hellebore roots; 4-pyrone-2,6-dicarboxylic acid
chel·i·do·nine \ˌkeləˈdō,nēn, keˈlidᵊn,ēn\ *n* -s [ISV *chelidon-* (fr. Gk *chelidonion* celandine) + *-ine;* orig. formed as F *chélidonine*] **:** a crystalline alkaloid $C_{20}H_{19}NO_5$ found in celandine and other papaveraceous plants
chel·i·do·ni·um \ˌkeləˈdōnēəm\ *n, cap* [NL, fr. Gk *chelidonion* celandine, fr. *chelidonion,* neut. of *chelidonios* of the swallow — more at CELANDINE] **:** a genus of herbs of the family Papaveraceae characterized by brittle stems, yellowish acrid juice, pinnately divided leaves, and small yellow flowers in pedunculate umbels — see CELANDINE

chel·i·fer \ˈkeləfə(r)\ *n, cap* [NL, fr. *chel-* + *-fer*] **:** the genus of the common book scorpion (order Pseudoscorpiones)
chel·i·fer·id·ea \ˌkeləfəˈridēə\ [NL, fr. *Chelifer* + *-idea*] *syn of* PSEUDOSCORPIONES
che·lif·er·ous \kəˈlifərəs\ *adj* [*chel-* + *-ferous*] **:** bearing a chela or chelae
che·li·form \ˈkēlə,fȯrm, ˈke-\ *adj* [*chel-* + *-form*] **:** having a movable joint or finger closing against the adjacent segment so as to form a forcepslike organ — used esp. of a crab's claw
che·lin·ga \chəˈliŋgə\ *or* **che·lin·go** \-(,)gō\ *n* -s [Tamil *calaṅku,* perh. fr. Skt *jalaṅga* water-going, fr. *jalaṁ* (nom. & acc. of *jala* water) + *-ga* (akin to *gam* to go, come) — more at COME] **:** a boat of light draft pointed at both ends and used on the Coromandel coast
che·li·ped \ˈkēlə,ped, ˈke-\ *n* -s [*chel-* + *-ped*] **:** one of the pair of legs that bears the large chelae in decapod crustaceans
chel·le·an *or* **chel·li·an** \ˈshelēən\ *adj, usu cap* [F *chelléen,* fr. *Chelles,* France + F *-éen* -ean] **1 :** of or relating to Chelles, France **2 :** ABBEVILLIAN
chel·o·di·na \ˌkeləˈdīnə\ *n, cap* [NL, prob. fr. *chelo-* (fr. Gk *chelys* tortoise) + *-dina* (fr. Gk *deinos* terrible) — more at CHELYS, DIRE] **:** a genus of freshwater turtles of Australia including the long-necked turtle — **chel·o·dine** \ˈkelə,dīn, -,dən\ *adj or n*
cheloid *var of* KELOID
¹che·lo·ne \keˈlōnē\ *n* [NL, fr. Gk *chelōnē* tortoise] **1** *cap* **:** a small genus of perennial herbs (family Scrophulariaceae) of the eastern U.S. having serrate leaves and large white or purple flowers in nearly sessile spikes **2** -s **:** any plant of the genus *Chelone* — called also *turtlehead*
²chelone \"\ [NL, fr. Gk *chelōnē*] *syn of* ²CHELONIA
chel·o·ne·thi \ˌkeləˈnē,thī\ *also* **chel·o·neth·i·da** \-ˈnethədə\ *or* **chel·o·ne·thid·ea** \-lōnəˈthidēə\ [*Chelonethi* fr. NL, fr. *chel-* + *-nethi* (fr. Gk *nēthein* to spin); *Chelonethida, Chelonethidea* fr. NL, fr. *chel-* + Gk *nēthein* + NL *-ida, -idea;* akin to Gk *nēn* to spin — more at NEEDLE] *syn of* PSEUDOSCORPIONES
chel·o·ne·thid \ˌkeləˈnēthə̇d, -eth-\ *n* -s [NL *Chelonethida, Chelonethidea*] **:** PSEUDOSCORPION
¹che·lo·nia \keˈlōnēə, -nyə\ [NL, fr. Gk *chelōnē* + NL *-ia*] *syn of* TESTUDINATA
²chelonia \"\ *n, cap* [NL, fr. Gk *chelōnē* + NL *-ia*] **:** the genus of Cheloniidae comprising the green turtles
¹che·lo·ni·an \-nēən, -nyən\ *adj* [NL ²*Chelonia* + E *-an*] **:** resembling, having the characteristics of, or being a tortoise or turtle
²chelonian \"\ *n* -s **:** TORTOISE, TURTLE
chel·o·nib·ia \ˌkeləˈnibēə\ *n, cap* [NL, fr. *cheloni-* (fr. Gk *chelōnē* tortoise) + *-bia*] **:** a widely distributed genus of turtle barnacles
che·lon·i·dae \kəˈlänə,dē\ [NL, fr. ²*Chelonia,* type genus + *-idae*] *syn of* CHELONIIDAE
che·lo·ni·id \kəˈlōnēə̇d\ *also* **chel·o·nid** \ˈkelə,nid, kəˈlōnə̇d\ *n* -s [NL *Cheloniidae, Chelonidae*] **:** one of the Cheloniidae
chel·o·ni·i·dae \ˌkeləˈnīə,dē\ *n pl, cap* [NL, fr. ²*Chelonia,* type genus + *-idae*] **:** a family of large marine turtles including the commercially important green turtle and hawksbill
che·lo·nus \kəˈlōnəs\ *n, cap* [NL, fr. Gk *chelōnos* turtle; fr. the shape of the abdomen] **:** a genus of small ichneumon flies (family Braconidae) parasitic on various lepidopterous larvae and introduced in many regions in attempts at biological control of plant-eating larvae
¹chelp \ˈchelp\ *vi* -ED/-ING/-S [prob. of imit. origin] **1** *dial Eng* **:** CHIRP **2** *dial Eng* **:** to talk pertly
²chelp \"\ *n* -s **1** *dial Eng* **:** the chirp of a young bird **2** *dial Eng* **:** pert talk
chel·sea china \ˈchelsē-\ *n, usu cap 1st C* [fr. *Chelsea,* England, where it was made] **:** soft-paste porcelain made from about 1745 until 1770
chelsea–der·by ware \-ˈdärbē-, -ˈdər-\ *n, usu cap C&D* [fr. *Chelsea* and *Derby,* England] **:** soft paste porcelain made at Chelsea or Derby from the taking over of the Chelsea works by Derby in 1770 to their closing in 1784
chel·ten·ham \ˈchelt(ᵊ)nəm\ *n* -s *usu cap* [fr. *Cheltenham,* town in Gloucestershire, England] **:** a large family of printing types orig. designed by Bertram G. Goodhue in 1900
che·lu·ra \kəˈlùrə\ *n, cap* [NL, fr. *chel-* + *-ura*] **:** a genus of marine amphipod Crustacea that bore into and sometimes destroy timber
che·lus \ˈkēləs, ˈke-\ *n, cap* [NL, irreg. fr. Gk *chelys* tortoise] **:** a genus of turtles including solely the matamata
che·lya·binsk \chelˈyäbənsk\ *adj, usu cap* [fr. *Chelyabinsk,* U.S.S.R.] **:** of or from the city of Chelyabinsk, U.S.S.R. **:** of the kind or style prevalent in Chelyabinsk
che·lyd·i·dae \kəˈlidə,dē\ *n pl, cap* [NL, fr. *Chelyd-* (irreg. fr. *Chelys,* type genus) + *-idae*] **:** a family of side-necked freshwater turtles inhabiting So. America and Australasia
chel·y·dra \ˈkelədrə\ *n, cap* [NL, modif. of Gk *chelydros* amphibious serpent, tortoise] **:** the type genus of Chelydridae comprising the common snapping turtles — **chel·y·droid** \-,drȯid\ *adj*
che·lyd·ri·dae \kəˈlidrə,dē\ *n pl* [NL, fr. *Chelydra,* type genus + *-idae*] **:** a family of large powerful freshwater turtles of No. America and Central America including the snapping turtles (sense 1) and the alligator turtle
che·lys \ˈkēləs, ˈke-\ [NL, fr. Gk, tortoise; akin to OSlav *želŭvĭ* tortoise] *syn of* CHELUS
chem- *or* **chemo-** *or* **chemico-** *also* **chemi-** *or* **chemio-** *comb form* [*chem-* & *chemo-* fr. NL, fr. LGk *chēmeia* alchemy; *chemico-* fr. *chemical; chemi-* & *chemio-* prob. fr. Dan *kemi-,* fr. *kemi* chemistry, fr. LGk *chēmeia* — more at ALCHEMY] **1 :** chemical **:** chemistry ⟨*chemosmosis*⟩ ⟨*chemotaxis*⟩ **2 :** chemically ⟨*chemisorb*⟩ ⟨*chemiotropic*⟩ **:** chemical and ⟨*chemicophysical*⟩
chem·a·ku·an \ˌchemaˈküən\ *or* **chim·a·ku·an** \ˌchim-\ *n, pl* **chemakuan** *or* **chemakuans** *or* **chimakuan** *or* **chimakuans** *usu cap* [*Chemakum* + *-an*] **:** a language stock of the Mosan phylum in Washington comprising Chemakum and Quileute
chem·a·kum \ˈchemakəm\ *or* **chim·a·kum** \ˈchim-\ *n, pl* **chemakum** *or* **chemakums** *or* **chimakum** *or* **chimakums** *usu cap* **1 a :** a Salishan people of northwestern Washington **b :** a member of such people **2 :** a Chemakuan language of the Chemakum people
che·ma·wi·nite \chəˈmäwə,nīt\ *n* -s [*Chemahawin, Chemayin,* the Indian name of a Hudson Bay post near which it was found + E *-ite*] **:** a fossil resin similar to amber
chem·e·hue·vi \ˌcheməˈwāvē\ *n, pl* **chemehuevi** *or* **chemehuevis** *usu cap* [Sp, fr. Yuma] **1 a :** a Shoshonean people resident in ancient times in the Mojave desert and later in the Colorado river valley, California **b :** a member of such people **2 :** the language of the Chemehuevi people
chem·i·at·ric \ˌkemēˈa·trik\ *adj* [NL *chemiatria* iatrochemistry (fr. *chem-* + *-iatria* -iatry) + E *-ic*] **:** IATROCHEMICAL
¹chem·ic \ˈkemik, -ēk\ *adj* [alter. (influenced by LGk *chēmeia* alchemy) of earlier *chimic,* fr. NL *chimicus* alchemist, fr. ML *alchimicus,* fr. *alchimia, alchymia* alchemy + L *-icus* -ic — more at ALCHEMY] **1** *archaic* **:** of or relating to alchemy **2 :** of or relating to chemistry **:** CHEMICAL
²chemic *also* **chem·ick** \"\ *n* -s **1** *obs* **a :** ALCHEMIST **b :** CHEMIST **2** *textile manuf* **a** *usu chemick, archaic* **:** a bleaching powder or a solution of bleaching powder or of calcium hypochlorite **b :** a dilute solution of sodium hypochlorite
³chemic *var of* CHEMICK
¹chem·i·cal \ˈkemə̇kəl, -ēk-\ *adj* [alter. of earlier *chimical,* fr. *chimic* (earlier form of *chemic*) + *-al*] **1 a** *obs* **:** ALCHEMICAL **b** *archaic* **:** of or relating to Paracelsian medicine specif. as it opposes Galenic medicine **2 :** relating to applications of chemistry: as **a :** acting or operated by chemical means ⟨a ~ extinguisher⟩ **b :** treated with or performed by the aid of chemicals ⟨~ development in photography⟩ **c :** produced by chemical means or synthesized from chemicals ⟨~ fiber⟩ ⟨~ rubber⟩ **d :** suitable for use in or used for operations in chemistry ⟨a ~ laboratory⟩ ⟨a ~ plant⟩ **3 :** having reference to or relating to the science of chemistry: as **a :** occupied with chemistry ⟨a ~ researcher⟩ ⟨a ~ journal⟩ ⟨~ nomenclature⟩ **b :** dealing with chemistry ⟨a ~ journal⟩ ⟨~ nomenclature⟩ **c :** characterized by the phenomena of chemistry ⟨~ changes⟩ ⟨~ forces⟩ **4 :** of or relating to rocks (as gypsum, salt, and most limestones) that are deposited from solution

[2]**chemical** \"\ *n* -s [alter. of earlier *chimical*, fr. *chimical*, adj.] **:** a substance (as an acid, alkali, salt, synthetic organic compound) obtained by a chemical process, prepared for use in chemical manufacture, or used for producing a chemical effect — see FINE CHEMICAL, HEAVY CHEMICAL

[3]**chemical** \"\ *vt* -ED/-ING/-S **:** CHEMICALIZE

chemical balance *n* **:** a balance used in chemical work; *esp* **:** an analytical balance

chemical cellulose *n* **:** CELLULOSE 2e

chemical closet *n* **:** CHEMICAL TOILET

chemical cotton *n* **:** a pure form of cellulose obtained from cotton linters by treatment with dilute sodium hydroxide solution

chemical engineer *n* **:** a specialist in chemical engineering

chemical engineering *n* **:** a branch of engineering that deals with the development and application of manufacturing processes in which materials undergo changes in properties and that deals esp. with the design and operation of plants and equipment to perform such work

chemical focus *n* **:** ACTINIC FOCUS

chem·i·cal·i·za·tion \ˌkeməkələ'zāshən, -mēk-, -ˌlī'z-\ *n* -s **:** the act or process of chemicalizing ⟨~ of agriculture⟩

chem·i·cal·ize \'==ˌlīz\ *vt* -ED/-ING/-S [[2]*chemical* + *-ize*] **:** to treat with chemicals **:** use chemicals extensively in

chemical kinetics *or* **chemical dynamics** *n* **:** REACTION KINETICS

chemical lead *n* **:** lead of sufficient purity for use in tanks, pipes, and other apparatus in chemical manufacture; *specif* **:** lead of this character made from the ores of southeastern Missouri

chem·i·cal·ly \'kemək(ə)lē, -mēk-, -li\ *adv* **1 :** by a chemical process or processes ⟨vitamin A can be estimated biologically, optically, or ~ —*Science*⟩ **2 :** according to chemical principles or from the chemist's standpoint ⟨a ~ impossible formula⟩

chemically pure *adj* **:** free from all impurities detectable by chemical analysis — used in commerce rather indefinitely of chemicals of a relatively high degree of purity

chemical mediation theory *n* **:** a theory in physiology: nervous transmission is due to the release of specific substances (as acetylcholine) at nerve endings and synapses — compare NEUROHUMORAL THEORY

chemical microscopy *n* **:** microscopy for the purpose of chemical identification and also recognition of physical structures and phases — compare MICROANALYSIS

chemical pneumonia *n* **:** an acute generalized inflammation of the lungs occurring in warfare and industry and caused by the inhalation of irritating gases or soluble dusts

chemical porcelain *n* **:** a porcelain that has low expansibility and acid-resisting glaze and is used in chemical laboratories and plants

chemical property *n* **:** a property of a substance relating to its chemical reactivity (as the explosive property of nitroglycerin)

chemical pulp *n* **:** pulp from chemically digested wood used chiefly for making paper and rayon and acetate fibers — compare GROUNDWOOD

chemicals *pl of* CHEMICAL, *pres 3d sing of* CHEMICAL

chemical sense *n* **:** a nervous mechanism for the physiological reception of and response to chemical stimulation; *specif* **:** the central nervous process (as in smelling and tasting) initiated by excitation of special receptors sensitive to chemical substances in solution — see COMMON CHEMICAL SENSE; compare CHEMORECEPTOR

chemical telegraph *n* **:** a telegraphic apparatus by which a message is recorded on a moving slip of paper moistened with a solution having a chemical composition that is altered on the passage of current through a stylus

chemical telephone *n* **:** a telephone operating by chemical or electrolytic action

chemical toilet *n* **:** a toilet rendering waste matter innocuous by chemical decomposition and employed where running water is not available — called also *chemical closet*

chemical warfare *n* **:** warfare in which incendiary mixtures, smokes, or irritant, burning, or asphyxiating gases are used for tactical purposes

chemical wood *n* **1 :** the wood of any of various trees used as a chemical raw material (as for the production of acetic acid, wood alcohol, or acetone by carbonization) **2 :** CHEMICAL PULP

chemic blue *n* **:** INDIGO CARMINE 2

chemic green *n* **:** BREMEN BLUE 1

[1]**chemick** *var of* CHEMIC

[2]**chem·ick** *also* **chem·ic** \'kemik, -mēk\ *vt* **chemicked; chemicked; chemicking; chemicks :** to treat (textile materials) with chemic

chemico- — see CHEM-

chemics *pl of* CHEMIC

chem·i·graph \'kemə̇ˌgraf\ *n* -s [ISV *chem-* + *-graph*; orig. formed in G] **:** an engraving made by chemigraphy

che·mig·ra·phy \ke'migrəfē\ *n* -ES [ISV *chem-* + *-graphy*; orig. formed as G *chemigraphie*] **:** a process of etching on metal (as zinc) in which photography is not used

chemi·ground·wood pulp \'kemē'=ˌ=-\ *n* [*chem-* + *groundwood*] **:** wood pulp produced by treating wood chemically before it is ground up

chemi·luminescence \ˌkemē+\ *n* -s [ISV *chem-* + *luminescence*; prob. orig. formed as G *chemilumineszenz*] **:** luminescence due to chemical reaction; *esp* **:** luminescence due to the formation of new compounds (as the oxidation of phosphorus vapor or of luciferin in fireflies) — **chemiluminescent** \"+\ *adj*

che·min de fer \shə'mandə'fe(ə)r\ *n, pl* **chemins de fer** [F, lit., railroad] **:** a card game in which any number of players may participate in betting against the dealer, in which the dealer and one other player each receive two cards and may draw one additional card, the winning hand being the one totaling closest to 9, 19, or 29, and in which aces count one each, face cards 10 each, and other cards their numerical value — compare BACCARAT

chemio- — see CHEM-

chemi·photic \ˌkemē+ˈ-\ *adj* [*chem-* + *photic*] **:** relating to a change of chemical energy to light — contrasted with *photochemical*

che·mise \shə'mēz\ *n* -s [ME, fr. OF, shirt, fr. LL *camisa, camisia* shirt, thin dress, prob. of Gmc origin; akin to OE *hemethe* shirt, OS *hemithi*, OHG *hemidi*, OE *hama* cover, skin — more at HAME] **1** *archaic* **:** a shirtlike outer garment or undergarment usu. with long sleeves and of linen and formerly worn by both men and women **2 :** a woman's one-piece undergarment consisting usu. of panties and straight-hanging vest with straps **3 :** a loose straight-hanging dress sometimes belted

chem·i·sette \ˌshemē'zet, -mə'-\ *n* -s [F, dim. of *chemise*] **:** a woman's vestlike outergarment or undergarment; *esp* **:** one (as of lace) used as a fill-in for the open front of a dress

chem·ism \'keˌmizəm\ *n* -s [modif. (influenced by E *chemistry*) of F *chimisme*, fr. *chimie* chemistry (fr. ML *chimia*, fr. *alchimia* alchemy) + *-isme* -ism — more at ALCHEMY] **1 :** chemical activity or affinity **2 :** chemical property or relationship

chem·i·sorb \'kemēˌsȯrb, -məˌ-\ *or* **chem·o·sorb** \-mōˌ-\ *vt* [*chem-* + *sorb*] **:** to take up and hold by chemisorption

chem·i·sorp·tion *also* **chem·o·sorp·tion** \ˌ==ˈsȯrpshən\ *n* -s [*chem-* + *sorption*] **:** adsorption, esp. when irreversible, by means of chemical forces in contrast with physical forces ⟨~ of gaseous nitrogen on iron catalysts⟩

chem·ist \'keməst\ *n* -s [alter. (influenced by LGk *chēmeia* alchemy) of earlier *chimist, chymist*, fr. NL *chimista, chymista*, short for ML *alchimista* — more at ALCHEMIST] **1 a** *obs* **:** ALCHEMIST **b :** one trained in or engaged in chemistry **2** *Brit* **:** DRUGGIST

chem·is·try \-trē, -i\ *n* -ES [alter. (influenced by LGk *chēmeia* alchemy) of earlier *chimistry, chymistry*, fr. *chimist, chymist* + *-ry*] **1 a** *obs* **:** ALCHEMY **b** *obs* **:** IATROCHEMISTRY **c :** a science that deals with the composition, structure, and properties of substances and of the transformations that they undergo — see INORGANIC CHEMISTRY, ORGANIC CHEMISTRY **2 a :** the composition and chemical properties of a substance ⟨the ~ of iron⟩ **b :** chemical processes and phenomena (as of an organism) ⟨blood ~⟩ ⟨the ~ of fungi⟩ **3 a :** peculiar makeup ⟨the ~ of modern diplomacy⟩ **b :** AGITATION, UNREST ⟨there was a ~ in his blood stirring him on to write —E.A.Weeks⟩ **c :** an often inexplicable or intangible function or process ⟨struggle against the *chemistries* . . . of desire and self-love —Bruce Marshall⟩

chemist's shop *n, Brit* **:** DRUGSTORE

chem·my \'shemē\ *n* -ES [by shortening & alter.] **:** CHEMIN DE FER

chem·nitz \'kemˌnits, -ˌnə̇-\ *adj, usu cap* [fr. *Chemnitz*, Germany] **:** of or from the city of Chemnitz, Germany **:** of the kind or style prevalent in Chemnitz

che·mo- *in pronunciations below*, ˈ== = ˈkēmō *or* -mə *or sometimes* ˈke-\ — see CHEM-

chemo·autotroph \ˌ==+\ *n* -s [*chem-* + *autotroph*] **:** an organism having a chemoautotrophic method of nutrition

chemo·autotrophic \ˈ==+\ *adj* [*chem-* + *autotrophic*] **:** autotrophic and oxidizing some inorganic compound as a source of available energy ⟨a number of bacteria and a few protozoans are ~⟩ — compare PHOTOAUTOTROPHIC — **chemoautotrophically** *adv* — **chemo·au·to·trophy** \+ˈȯd·əˌträfē, -ōfē, ˌȯˈtä·trəfē\ *n* -ES

chemo·differentiation \ˈ==+\ *n* -s [*chem-* + *differentiation*] **:** differentiation at the molecular level assumed to precede morphological differentiation in embryogenesis

che·mo·gen·ic \ˈ==+ˈjenik\ *or* **che·mog·e·nous** \ke'mäjənəs\ *adj* [*chem-* + *-genic, -genous*] **:** arising in or resulting from chemical action ⟨~ humus⟩

chemo·kinesis \ˈ==*at* CHEMO- +\ *n, pl* **chemokineses** [NL, fr. *chem-* + *-kinesis*] **:** increased activity of free-moving organisms produced by a chemical agency — **chemo·kinetic** \+(ˌ)=ˈ==\ *adj*

chemo·organotrophic \ˈ==+\ *adj* [*chem-* + *organotrophic*] **:** requiring an organic source of carbon and metabolic energy — compare AUTOTROPHIC

chemo·prophylactic \ˈ==+\ *adj* [*chem-* + *prophylactic*] **:** of or relating to chemoprophylaxis

chemo·prophylaxis \ˈ==+\ *n, pl* **chemoprophylaxes** [*chem-* + *prophylaxis*] **:** the prevention of infectious disease by the use of chemical agents

chemo·reception \ˈ==+\ *n* -s [ISV *chem-* + *reception*] **:** the physiological reception of chemical stimuli — compare CHEMICAL SENSE — **chemo·receptive** \+=ˈ=\ *adj* — **chemo·receptivity** \ˈ==+\ *n* -ES

chemo·receptor \ˈ==+\ *n* -s [ISV *chem-* + *receptor*] **:** any sense organ responding to chemical stimuli (as a taste or smell receptor or one of the carotid body receptors that react to changes in the chemical composition of the blood)

[1]**chemo·reflex** \ˌ==+\ *n* -ES [*chem-* + *reflex*] **:** a physiological reflex initiated by a chemical stimulus or in a chemoreceptor

[2]**chemo·reflex** \ˈ==+ˈ-\ *adj* **:** of, relating to, or dependent on a chemoreflex

chemo·resistance \ˌ==+\ *n* -s [*chem-* + *resistance*] **:** the quality or state of being chemoresistant

chemo·resistant \ˈ==+=ˈ=\ *adj* [*chem-* + *resistant*] **:** resistant to the action of a (particular) chemical — used esp. of certain insects

chemo·sensitive \ˈ==+ˈ-\ *adj* [*chem-* + *sensitive*] **:** susceptible to the action of a (particular) chemical — used esp. of strains of bacteria) — **chemo·sensitivity** \ˈ==+\ *n* -ES

che·mo·sis \kə̇'mōsə̇s\ *n, pl* **che·mo·ses** \-ōˌsēz\ [NL, fr. Gk *chēmōsis* swelling of the cornea resembling a cockleshell, fr. *chēmē* cockle + *-ōsis* -osis — more at CHAMA] **:** swelling of the conjunctival tissue around the cornea

chem·osmosis \ˈkēm, ˈkem+\ *n, pl* **chemosmoses** [NL, fr. *chem-* + *osmosis*] **:** chemical action taking place through an intervening membrane — **chem·osmotic** \"+\ *adj*

chemosorption *var of* CHEMISORPTION

che·mo·stat \'== *at* CHEMO- +ˌstat\ *n* -s [*chem-* + *-stat* (as in *thermostat*)] **:** a device in which bacteria are kept uniformly suspended in a culture medium constantly renewed and maintained chemically unaltered by a continuous flow of new medium through it and which is used esp. in quantitative studies of mutation rates

chemo·synthesis \ˌ==+\ *n* [ISV *chem-* + *synthesis*; orig. formed as G *chemosynthese*] **:** synthesis of organic compounds by energy derived from chemical reactions (as in certain autotrophic bacteria) — opposed to *photosynthesis* — **chemo·synthetic** \ˈ==+(ˌ)=ˈ==\ *adj*

chemosynthetic bacteria *n pl* **:** bacteria that obtain energy required for metabolic processes from exothermic oxidation of inorganic or simple organic compounds without the aid of light

chemo·tactic \ˈ==+ˈ-\ *adj* [ISV *chem-* + *-tactic*; prob. orig. formed as G *chemotaktisch*] **1 :** involving chemotaxis ⟨~ response⟩ **2 :** exhibiting chemotaxis ⟨slime molds ~ to dextrose⟩ — **chemotactically** *adv*

che·mo·tax·is \ˌ==+'taksə̇s\ *also* **che·mo·taxy** \'==+ˌtaksē\ *n, pl* **chemotax·es** \-'takˌsēz\ *also* **chemotax·ies** \-ˌtakˌsēz\ [*chemotaxis*, NL, fr. *chem-* + *-taxis*; *chemotaxy*, ISV *chem-* + *-taxy*] **:** orientation or movement of cells or organisms in relation to chemical agents — compare TAXIS 2

chemo·therapeusis \ˈ==+\ *n* [NL, fr. *chem-* + *therapeusis*] **:** CHEMOTHERAPY

che·mo·ther·a·peu·tant \ˈ==+ˌtherə'pyüt³nt\ *n* -s [*chemotherapeutic* + *-ant*] **:** a chemotherapeutic agent

[1]**chemo·therapeutic** \ˈ==+\ *or* **chemo·therapeutical** \ˈ==+\ *adj* [*chem-* + *therapeutic, therapeutical*] **:** of or belonging to chemotherapy — **chemotherapeutically** *adv*

[2]**chemotherapeutic** \"\ *or* **chemotherapeutical** \"\ *n* -s **:** an agent used in chemotherapy

chemotherapeutic index *n* **:** the ratio of the maximum tolerated dose of a chemical agent used in chemotherapy to its minimum effective dose

chemo·therapeutics \'== *at* CHEMO- +\ *n pl but sing or pl in constr* **:** CHEMOTHERAPY

chemo·therapist \ˈ==+\ *n* **:** a specialist in chemotherapy

chemo·therapy \ˌ== *at* CHEMO- +\ *n* [ISV *chem-* + *-therapy*; orig. formed as G *chemotherapie*; *chemotherapeutics*, fr. *chem-* + *therapeutics*; *chemotherapeusis*, NL, fr. *chem-* + *therapeusis*] **:** the prevention or treatment of esp. infectious disease in man, animals, or plants by the use of chemical agents

che·mot·ic \kə̇'mäd·ik\ *adj* [fr. NL *chemosis*, after such pairs as NL *sclerosis*: E *sclerotic*] **:** marked by or belonging to chemosis

chemo·trophic \ˈ== *at* CHEMO- +\ *adj* [*chem-* + *-trophic*] **:** CHEMOAUTOTROPHIC

chemo·tropic \ˈ==+\ *adj* [ISV *chem-* + *-tropic*] **:** involving or exhibiting chemotropism — **chemotropically** *adv*

che·mot·ro·pism \ke'mä·trəˌpizəm, kə̇'-\ *n* -s [ISV *chem-* + *-tropism*; orig. formed as G *chemotropismus*] **:** orientation of cells or organisms in relation to chemical stimuli — compare TROPISM

che·mur·gic \(ˈ)ke'mərjik, kə̇'m-\ *adj* **:** relating to or produced by chemurgy — **che·mur·gi·cal·ly** \-jə̇k(ə)lē\ *adv*

chem·ur·gist \'ke(ˌ)mərjə̇st; ke'm-, kə̇'m-\ *n* -s **:** a specialist in chemurgy

chem·ur·gy \'ke(ˌ)mərjē *sometimes* ke'm- *or* kə̇'m-\ *n* -ES [*chem-* + *-urgy*] **:** a branch of applied chemistry that deals with industrial utilization of organic raw materials esp. from farm products (as in the use of soybean oil for paints and varnishes and of southern pine for paper pulp)

chen \'ken\ *n, cap* [NL, fr. Gk *chēn* goose — more at GOOSE] **:** a genus (or subgenus of *Anser*) of geese having the adult plumage chiefly white — see SNOW GOOSE

chen- *or* **cheno-** *comb form* [Gk *chēn-, chēno-*, fr. *chēn*] **:** goose ⟨*Chenopodium*⟩

che·na \'chānə, -(ˌ)nä\ *n* -s [Hindi *cenā*, fr. Skt *cīna, cīnaka, cīnaka*] **:** an area of virgin or secondary timberland in a tropical region cleared and cultivated for only a few years and then abandoned

chenango *var of* SHENANGO

chenar *var of* CHINAR

chen·chu \'chen(ˌ)chü\ *n, pl* **chenchu** *or* **chenchus** *usu cap* [native name in India] **1 :** a primitive people of Hyderabad in central India most of whom have been influenced by the Telugu population but some of whom cling to a food-gathering economy and represent, racially and culturally, survivals of ancient India **2 :** a member of the Chenchu people

che·neau \shā'nō\ *n* -s [F *chéneau*, fr. L *canalis* canal, channel — more at CANAL] **:** a cresting above a cornice or at the ends of eaves

che·net \shə'nā\ *n, pl* **chenets** \-'nā(z)\ [F, fr. OF, prob. dim. of *chien* dog, fr. L *canis*; fr. the dog heads frequently ornamenting them — more at HOUND] **:** ANDIRON

chen·e·vix·ite \ˈshenəˌvikˌsīt\ *n* -s [F, fr. Richard *Chenevix* †1830 Irish chemist and mineralogist + F *-ite*] **:** a mineral $Cu_2Fe_2(AsO_4)_2(OH)_4.H_2O(?)$ consisting of a hydrous copper iron arsenate occurring in greenish masses

chen·fish \'chenˌ-\ *n* [origin unknown] **:** KINGFISH 1a (2)

cheng *var of* SHENG

chen·gal \'cheŋgəl\ *n* -s [Malay *chĕngal*] **1 :** the hard heavy durable wood of a large Malayan tree (*Balanocarpus heimii*) **2 :** the tree that produces chengal and from which a damar is obtained **3 :** the wood of a tree (*Balanocarpus maximus*) related to the chengal

cheng·tu \'chəŋˈdü, 'cheŋˈtü\ *adj, usu cap* [fr. *Chengtu*, China] **:** of or from the city of Chengtu, China **:** of the kind or style prevalent in Chengtu

ch'eng-tzu-yai \ˈcheŋ(t)ˌsü'yī\ *adj, usu cap* [prob. fr. a place name in China] **:** of or relating to a late Neolithic culture of China from Shantung southward and inland of about 1000 B.C. characterized by black pottery

che·nier *or* **chê·nière** \'shinərē, -ri\ *n* -s [AmerF (La.) *chênière*, fr. F *chêne* oak] **:** a wooded ridge or sandy hummock in a swampy region — compare SHINNERY

che·nille \shə'nēl, *esp before pause or consonant* -ēəl\ *n* -s [F, lit., caterpillar (so called fr. the appearance of the cord), fr. L *canicula*, dim. of *canis* dog; fr. its hairy appearance — more at HOUND] **1 a :** a wool, cotton, silk, or rayon yarn with pile protruding all around made by weaving a cloth with warp threads about soft filling threads and cutting it into narrow strips that are used esp. for tufting and fringes **b :** a pile-face fabric made with a filling of this yarn and commonly used for curtains, bedspreads, and rugs **c :** an imitation of this yarn or fabric **2** *also* **chenille plant :** an East Indian herb (*Acalypha hispida*) having long pendent spikes of crimson flowers resembling pieces of chenille

chenille axminster *n, usu cap A* **:** AXMINSTER

chenille carpet *or* **chenille rug** *n* **:** a carpet or rug with a chenille weft

chenille weed *n* **:** a common red alga (*Dasya elegans*) of the family Rhodomelaceae of the U.S. Atlantic coast

cheno- — see CHEN-

che·no·de·oxy·cho·lic acid \ˈkē(ˌ)nōˌdēˌäksēˈkōlik-, ˈke-, -äl-\ *or* **che·no·des·oxy·cho·lic acid** \-ˌdeˌzäkse\ *n* [ISV *chenodesoxycholic* or *chenodeoxycholic* (fr. *chen-* + *desoxy-*, *deoxy-* + *cholic*) + *acid*; orig. formed as G *chenodesoxycholsäure*] **:** a bile acid $C_{23}H_{37}(OH)_2COOH$ found in the bile of man, goose, hen, and ox; 3,7-dihydroxy-cholanic acid

che·no·pod \'kēnəˌpäd, 'ke-\ *n* -s [NL *Chenopodiaceae*] **:** a plant of the family Chenopodiaceae

che·no·po·di·a·ce·ae \ˌ==ˌpōdē'āsēˌē\ *n pl, cap* [NL, fr. *Chenopodium*, type genus + *-aceae*] **:** a family of plants (order Caryophyllales) distinguished by small inconspicuous apetalous greenish flowers and utricular fruit — see GOOSEFOOT

che·no·po·di·a·ceous \ˈ==ˌ==ˈāshəs\ *adj* **:** of or relating to the family Chenopodiaceae

che·no·po·di·a·les \-ˈā(ˌ)lēz\ [NL, fr. *Chenopodium* + *-ales*] *syn of* CARYOPHYLLALES

che·no·po·di·um \-'pōdēəm\ *n, cap* [NL, fr. *chen-* + *-podium*] **:** a large genus (the type of the family Chenopodiaceae) of glabrous or mealy herbs having a 4-parted or 5-parted calyx, including the goosefoots, and occurring in temperate regions of the world — see LAMB'S-QUARTERS, WORMSEED

chenopodium oil *n* **:** a colorless or pale yellow toxic essential oil of unpleasant odor and taste obtained from Mexican tea plants and formerly used as an anthelmintic

che·o·plastic \ˈkēə+ˈ-\ *adj* **:** of, relating to, or used in cheoplasty

che·o·plas·ty \'==ˌplastē\ *n* -ES [*cheo-* (fr. Gk *chein* to pour) + *-plasty* — more at FOUND] **:** a process of molding artificial teeth by the use of low-fusing metals or alloys

che·pen·a·fa \chə'penəˌfō\ *n, pl* **chepenafa** *or* **chepenafas** *usu cap* [Calapooya *Chep-en-a-pho*] **1 :** a Kalapooian people near present Corvallis, Oregon **2 :** a member of the Chepenafa people

cheque \'chek\ *chiefly Brit var of* [2]CHECK 10

che·queen *or* **che·quin** \chə'kēn\ *n* -s [alter. of earlier *chikino*, modif. of It *zecchino* — more at SEQUIN] **:** SEQUIN 1

che·quer \'chekə(r)\ *chiefly Brit var of* CHECKER

che·quered \'chekə(r)d\ *chiefly Brit var of* CHECKERED

chequ·ey *or* **chequy** \'cheki\ *var of* CHECKY

che·raw \chē'rō, 'ˌ=\ *n, pl* **cheraw** *or* **cheraws** *usu cap* [alter. of earlier *Saraw*, prob. modif. of Cherokee *Suala*] **1 :** a people of the Carolinas tentatively assigned to the Siouan language family **2 :** a member of the Cheraw people

cherem *var of* HEREM

cher·e·mis *or* **cher·e·miss** \ˈcherəˈmis, -mēs\ *n, pl* **cheremis** *or* **cheremises** *or* **cheremiss** *or* **cheremisses** *usu cap* [Russ *Cheremis*, fr. ORuss *Čermisy*, prob. fr. Chuvash *Šarmis*] **1 :** one of a Finnish people of eastern Russia that are farmers and forest dwellers in the Mari and Bashkir republics of the U.S.S.R. — called also *Mari* **2 :** the Finno-Ugric language of the Cheremis people — see URALIC LANGUAGES table

[1]**cher·e·mis·si·an** \ˈcherəˈmisēən\ *adj, usu cap* [*Cheremis* + *-ian*] **:** of or relating to the Cheremis

[2]**cheremissian** *n* -s *usu cap* **:** CHEREMIS

cherenkov radiation *usu cap C, var of* CERENKOV RADIATION

cher·e·thim \'kerəˌthim\ *or* **cher·e·thims** \-mz\ *n pl, cap* [Heb *Kĕrēthīm*, pl. of *Kĕrēthī*] **:** CHERETHITES

cher·e·thite \-ˌthīt\ *n* -s *cap* [Heb *Kĕrēthī* + E *-ite*] **:** a member of a group of the ancient Philistines from which the bodyguard of Israel's King David was recruited

cher·i·moya \ˌcherə'mȯiə\ *also* **cher·i·moy·er** \-ə(r)\ *or* **chir·i·moya** \ˌchir-\ *n* -s [Sp *chirimoya*, prob. fr. Quechua *chirimúya, chirimóya*] **:** a small widely cultivated tropical American tree (*Annona cherimola*) with 3-petaled yellowish brown flowers and round, oblong, or heart-shaped fruit with pitted rind that somewhat resembles the custard apple

cher·ish \'cherish, -ēsh, *esp in pres part* -ash\ *vt* -ED/-ING/-ES [ME *cherisshen*, fr. MF *cheriss-*, stem of *cherir* to cherish, fr. OF, fr. *chier* dear, fr. L *carus* — more at CHARITY] **1 a :** to hold dear **:** feel or show fond affection for ⟨he admired them . . . ~*ed* and protected them like pets —Edmund Wilson⟩ **b :** to keep or guard with care and affection ⟨a birthright of freedom to be ~*ed* and fought for⟩ ⟨to ~ an illusion⟩ ⟨to love and to ~, till death us do part —*Bk. of Com. Prayer*⟩ **c :** to care for, tend, cultivate, or nurture usu. with care, affection, or love ⟨sought to ~ whatever of these forms could be made to work —John Buchan⟩ ⟨the seeds of love⟩ **d** *archaic* **:** PAT, FONDLE **2** *obs* **:** ENTERTAIN **3** *archaic* **:** WARM **4 a :** to have at heart **:** think of fondly or reverentially ⟨Socrates would have men ~ preciously this fraction of knowledge —Irving Babbitt⟩ **b :** to contemplate, imagine, or recall fondly with joy or pleasure ⟨she only ~*es* her illness as an instrument of power —Scott Fitzgerald⟩ **c :** to entertain or harbor in one's mind deeply and resolutely, often tacitly and often pleasurably ⟨a large school of thought ~*es* a curious animus against what it calls intellectualism —W.R.Inge⟩ ⟨few of us who do not ~ a feeling of self-complacency —Jane Austen⟩

syn see APPRECIATE, NURSE

cher·ish·ing·ly *adv* **:** in a cherishing manner

cher·kess \chə(r)'kes\ *n, pl* **cherkess** *or* **cherkesses** *usu cap* [Russ *Cherkes*] **:** CIRCASSIAN

cher maî·tre \sher'mātr(ᵊ), -t(rə)\ *n* [F, lit., dear master] **:** a person regarded as a master or model in his art or profession — often used as a form of address to such a person

cher·mes \['kər(ˌ)mēz\ [NL, fr. Ar *qirmiz* kermes — more at CRIMSON] *syn of* ADELGES, PSYLLA

cher·mi·dae \'kərməˌdē\ [NL, fr. *Chermes*, type genus + *-idae*] *syn of* PSYLLIDAE

cher·na \'chernə, -(ˌ)nä\ *n* -s [Sp, fr. LL *acernia*, prob. fr. LGk *acherna*] **1 :** any of several groupers (sense 1) **2 :** PRIESTFISH **3 :** [3]GAR c

cher·ne·vi·ye tatar \chə(r)'nāvē(y)ə-\ *n, usu cap C&T* [Russ *chernevïye*, nom. pl. of *cherny* black] **:** a member of a Tatar subdivision of the Altai mountains

cher·nov·tsy \cher'nȯftsē, chər-\ *adj, usu cap* [fr. *Chernovtsy*, Ukraine, U.S.S.R.] **:** of or from the city of Chernovtsy, Ukraine, U.S.S.R. **:** of the kind or style prevalent in Chernovtsy

cher·no·zem \ˈchernəˌzȯm\ *n* -s [Russ, lit., black earth, fr. *cherno-* (fr. *cherny* black) + *-zem* earth (fr. ORuss *zem* earth); akin to Lith *kérszas* black and white spotted, Skt *kr̥ṣṇa* black, and to OSlav *zemlja* earth, L *humus* — more at HUMBLE] **:** a dark-colored zonal soil with a deep and rich humus horizon found in temperate to cool subhumid climates (as in the grasslands of central European Russia and central No. America)

cherogril *n* -s [LL *choerogryllus*, fr. Gk *choirogryllos*, fr. *choiros* young pig + *gryllos* young pig; akin to Gk *gryzein* to grunt — more at CHAEROPUS, GRUNT] *obs* **:** HYRAX

cher·o·kee \ˈcherə(ˌ)kē, ˌ==ˈ=\ *n, pl* **cherokee** *or* **cherokees** [prob. fr. Creek *tciloki* people of a different speech] **1** *usu cap* **a :** an Iroquoian people orig. of the Appalachian mountains of Tennessee and No. Carolina, later spreading as far south as Alabama and Georgia and as far west as Texas and Oklahoma **b :** a member of such people **2** *usu cap* **:** the language of the Cherokee people **3 :** TILE RED 2

cherokee rose *n, usu cap C* **:** a Chinese climbing rose (*Rosa laevigata*) with a fragrant white blossom

che·roon·jie nut \chəˈrünjē-\ *n* [Hindi *cirañjī*] **:** the seed of a medium-sized East Indian tree (*Buchanania latifolia*) of the family Anacardiaceae used in the unripe state as an ingredient of curry

che·root \shəˈrüt, chə-\ *n* -s [Tamil *curuṭṭu*, lit., roll, fr. *curuḷ* to become coiled, rolled, curled] **:** a cigar cut off square at both ends

¹cher·ry \ˈcherē, -ri\ *n* -ES [ME *chery*, modif. of ONF *cherise* (taken as a plural), fr. LL *ceresia*, fr. L *cerasus* cherry tree, cherry, fr. Gk *kerasos* cherry tree — more at CORNEL] **1 a :** any of numerous trees and shrubs of the genus *Prunus* that have pale yellow to deep red or blackish smooth-skinned nearly globular rather small fruits which are drupes enclosing a smooth seed and that include various improved forms cultivated for their fruits or for their ornamental flowers — see JAPANESE FLOWERING CHERRY, SOUR CHERRY, SWEET CHERRY; compare PEACH, PLUM **b :** the fruit of the cherry **c :** the reddish brown wood of any of the larger cherry trees (as the sweet cherry or the American black cherry) much used in cabinetmaking **2 :** BARBADOS CHERRY **3 :** COFFEE CHERRY **4 :** a variable color averaging a moderate red that is yellower, lighter, and stronger than cerise, claret (sense 3a), Turkey red, or average strawberry (sense 2a) and bluer, lighter, and stronger than catsup **5** *slang* **a :** ²HYMEN **b :** VIRGINITY **6 :** a milling cutter used to make small circular or spherical cavities (as in bullet molds) **7 :** the knocking down of only the front pin or pins in trying for a spare in bowling

²cherry \"\ *adj* **1 :** of or resembling a cherry: as **a :** of the color cherry ⟨~ cheeks⟩ **b :** made of cherry wood ⟨a ~ table⟩ **2** *slang* **:** ¹VIRGINAL 2

³cherry \"\ *vt* -ED/-ING/-ES **:** to mill with a cherry

cherry aphid *n* **:** a large dark aphid (*Myzus cerasi*) infesting the cherry tree and making the leaves crumple and roll

cherry apple *n* **:** SIBERIAN CRAB

cherry birch *n* **:** SWEET BIRCH

cherry blossom *n* **:** a moderate red that is bluer and paler than cerise, claret (sense 3a), Turkey red, or average strawberry (sense 2a) and deeper than carnation red

cherry bomb *n* [so called fr. its cherrylike shape & color] **:** a powerful globular red firecracker detonated by lighting a relatively long fuse

cherry bounce *n* **1** *Brit* **:** CHERRY BRANDY 1 **2 :** an often homemade American cherry-flavored liqueur concocted from rum or whiskey and sometimes cider

cherry brandy *n* **1 :** a liqueur made from brandy flavored with cherries and sweetened with sugar **2 :** a brandy distilled from fermented cherry juice

cherry casebearer *n* **:** a casebearer (*Coleophora pruniella*) closely related to and similar in habits to the pistol casebearer but chiefly attacking wild and cultivated cherries

cherry coal *n* [so called fr. its size] **:** a soft noncaking coal that burns readily

cherry crab *n* **:** SIBERIAN CRAB

cherry currant *n* **:** a variety of the red currant having a very large berry

cherry fruit fly *n* **:** a small brown fly (*Rhagoletis cingulata*) of the family Trypetidae whose larva lives in the fruit of the cherry

cherry fruit sawfly *n* **:** an American sawfly (*Hoplocampa cookei*) whose larva feeds on the cherry and plum

cherry fruitworm *n* **:** the larva of a small mottled gray moth (*Grapholitha packardi*) that feeds in the fruits of cherries and blueberries

cherry gum *n* **:** CHERRY-TREE GUM

cherry holly *n* **:** ISLAY

cherry laurel *n* **1 :** a European evergreen shrub (*Prunus laurocerasus*) common in cultivation — called also *laurel* **2 :** an evergreen shrub (*Prunus caroliniana*) of the southern U.S. — called also *laurel cherry*

cherry leaf beetle *n* **:** a small red beetle (*Pyrrhalta cavicollis*) that attacks the leaves of cherry and peach trees

cherry leaf spot *n* **:** a disease of the cherry caused by a fungus (*Higginsia hyemalis*) that produces localized dead spots on the foliage, fruit, and pedicels, a general chlorosis often occurring and the dead spots on the leaves often dropping out — called also *yellow leaf;* compare SHOT HOLE 3a

cherrylike \ˈ==ˌ=\ *adj* **:** resembling or like a cherry

cherry liqueur *n* **:** a liqueur whose base is grape brandy or neutral spirits and whose flavor derives from wild black cherries

cherry maggot *n* **:** the larva of the cherry fruit fly

cherry mahogany *n* **:** MAKORE

cherry mildew *n* **:** a powdery mildew (*Podosphaera oxycanthae*) esp. destructive of the cherry

cherry orange *n* **1 :** KUMQUAT **2 :** a shrub of the genus *Citropsis*

cherry pepper *n* **1 :** a hot pepper (*Capsicum frutescens cerasiforme*) with small rounded extremely pungent fruits **2 :** the fruit of the cherry pepper

cherry picker *n* **:** any of various small traveling cranes; *esp* **:** one suitable for holding a passenger at the end of the boom

cherry pie *n* **1** *chiefly Brit* **:** GARDEN HELIOTROPE 2 **2 :** HAIRY WILLOW HERB

cherry pink *n* **:** BLOSSOM PINK

cherry pit *n* **1 :** CHERRYSTONE **2 :** an old game consisting of throwing cherrystones into a small hole in the ground

cherry plum *n* **1 :** an Asiatic plum (*Prunus cerasifera*) used extensively in Europe as a stock on which to bud domestic varieties — called also *myrobalan* **2 :** EUROPEAN BIRD CHERRY

cherry red *n* **:** a variable color averaging a strong red that is yellower and lighter than geranium red, redder and yellower and paler than Goya, and yellower and darker than geranium (sense 3a) — compare CHERRY

cherry rose *n* **:** a deep pink that is bluer and stronger than average coral (sense 3b) and bluer and deeper than fiesta or begonia

cherry scab *n* **:** PEACH SCAB

cherry scale *n* **:** FORBES SCALE

cherry slug *n* **:** PEAR SLUG

cherrystone \ˈ==ˌ=\ *n* **1 :** the stone or endocarp of the cherry **2 :** something of little or no value ⟨I wouldn't give a ~ for his opinion⟩ **3 :** a small quahog ⟨a ~ clam⟩

cherry tomato *n* **1 :** any of several tomatoes bearing bunches of small fruits that resemble cherries: as **a :** a thin-leaved tomato (*Lycopersicon esculentum cerasiforme*) with globular to oblong red or yellow fruits **b :** CURRANT TOMATO **2 :** GROUND-CHERRY **3 :** the fruit of a cherry tomato

cherry-tree gum *n* **:** a gum that resembles gum arabic and is formed as an exudation from various trees of the genus *Prunus*

cherry wine *n* **:** a deep red

cher·so·nese \ˈkərsəˌnēz, -ēs\ *n* -s [L *chersonesus*, fr. Gk *chersonēsos*, fr. *chersos* dry land + *nēsos* island; akin to L *horrēre* to bristle, and to L *nare* to swim — more at HORROR, NATANT] **:** PENINSULA ⟨Thracian ~⟩

cher·syd·ri·dae \(ˌ)kərˈsidrəˌdē\ [NL, fr. *Chersydrus*, type genus (fr. Gk *chersydros* amphibious snake, fr. *chersos* dry land + *hydros* water snake) + *-idae*; akin to Gk *hydōr* water — more at WATER] *syn of* ACROCHORDIDAE

chert \ˈchərt, ˈchat\ *n* -s [origin unknown] **:** an impure flintlike rock essentially of cryptocrystalline quartz or fibrous chalcedony and usu. dark in color

chert·y \ˈchərd·ē, ˈchad·ē\ *adj, usu* -ER/-EST **1 :** like chert **2 :** containing chert **:** FLINTY

cher·ub \ˈcherəb\ *also* **cher·u·bim** \-r(y)əˌbim *also* -ēm *sometimes* ˈker- *or* ˌ==ˈ=\ *or* **cher·u·bin** \-n,-ēn\ *n, pl* **cherubs** *or* **cherubim** *also* **cherubims** *or* **cherubins** [Heb *kĕrūbh*] **1 :** a biblical figure frequently represented as a composite being with large wings, a human head, and an animal body and regarded as a guardian of a sacred place and as a servant of God **2 a :** one of an order of angels ordinarily symbolizing divine wisdom or justice and variously placed in the heavenly hierarchies usu. below the seraphim — see CELESTIAL HIERARCHY **b** *cherubin* **:** a beautiful or beloved woman ⟨thou young and rose-lipped *cherubin* —Shak.⟩ **3** *pl cherubs* **a** *in painting or sculpture* **:** a beautiful child, generally winged **:** CUPID **b** *in painting* **:** a child's head with wings **c :** an innocent-looking esp. chubby and rosy child **d :** an adult resembling or suggesting an innocent-looking, chubby, or rosy child **4 :** a moderate yellowish pink that is yellower and paler than coral pink, yellower and less strong than peach pink, and redder and slightly paler than average peach

che·ru·bic \chəˈrübik, che-, -bēk *sometimes* -ˈrəb- *or* ˈcherə(ˌ)bik\ *adj* [*cherub* + *-ic*] **:** of, resembling, or befitting a cherub ⟨a ~ face⟩ ⟨a ~ smile⟩

cherup *archaic var of* CHIRRUP

cher·vil \ˈchərvəl\ *n* -s [ME *chervell, cherville*, fr. OE *cerfelle, cerfille;* akin to OHG *kervila, kervola;* both fr. a prehistoric WGmc word borrowed fr. (assumed) VL *cerfolia*, fr. L *caerefolium*, part trans. of Gk *chairephyllon*, fr. *chairein* to take pleasure in + *phyllon* leaf — more at YEARN, BLADE] **1 :** an aromatic annual Old World herb (*Anthriscus cerefolium*) that is cultivated for its finely divided often curled leaves which are used esp. in soups and salads — called also *beaked parsley* **2 :** any of several plants that are related to chervil — usu. used with a qualifying term ⟨wild ~⟩ ⟨cow ~⟩

cher·vo·nets *or* **cher·vo·netz** \chərˈvȯnəts\ *n, pl* **cher·von·tsi** *or* **chervon·tzi** \-ntsē\ [Russ *chervonets*, alter. of ORuss *červonyi*, fr. OPol *czerwony* golden, purple] **1 :** the gold 10-ruble coin of Soviet Russia authorized by decree 1922 and struck 1923 **2 :** a unit of value equivalent to one gold chervonets designated by law of 1924 as the basic monetary unit but never such in practice **3 :** a currency note representing one chervonets

ches·a·peake bay retriever \ˈchesəˌpēk-, *rapid* -eˌspēk-\ *or* **chesapeake bay dog** *also* **chesapeake** *n, usu cap C&B* [fr. *Chesapeake Bay*, inlet of the Atlantic ocean in Virginia and Maryland] **:** a large powerful sporting dog that was developed in Maryland apparently by crossing Newfoundlands with native retrievers, is broad-headed and deep-chested with a short muscular neck, and has a coat, short but very dense and slightly waved on the back, varying from straw-colored to dark brown

chesapeake canoe *n, usu cap 1st C* **:** a fishing and working craft of Chesapeake Bay, from 20 feet to 40 feet long, rigged with one or two masts and leg-of-mutton sails spread by means of sprits, and sometimes with a jib of peculiar shape, orig. built from a single log and later from three, five, or seven logs bolted together — compare BUGEYE

¹chesh·ire \ˈcheshə(r) *also* -ˌshi(ə)r *or* -ˌshiə\ *adj, usu cap* [fr. *Cheshire* (Chester), county of England] **:** of or from the county of Chester, England **:** of the kind or style prevalent in the county of Chester

²cheshire \"\ *n* -s *usu cap* **:** an American breed of medium-sized white swine

cheshire cat *n, usu cap 1st C* **:** a fictitious cat with a broad grin

cheshire cheese *n, usu cap 1st C* **:** a cheese similar to cheddar and made chiefly in Cheshire, England

cheshvan *usu cap, var of* HESHVAN

chesnut *archaic var of* CHESTNUT 1

¹chess \ˈches\ *n* -ES [ME *ches*, fr. OF *esches*, acc. pl. of *eschec* check at chess — more at CHECK] **:** a game of ancient origin for two played on a chessboard in which each player moves his chessmen according to fixed types of movements for each across the board in such a way as to try to checkmate the opponent's king

²chess \"\ *n* -ES [ME *ches* tier, modif. of MF *chasse* frame, mounting — more at CHASSE] **1** *now dial Eng* **a :** TIER, LAYER **b :** ⁴ROW **2** *pl* **chess** *or* **chesses :** one of the boards placed transversely on the balk of a pontoon bridge to form the flooring

³chess \"\ *n* -ES [origin unknown] **:** a weedy annual bromegrass (*Bromus secalinus*) native to Europe but widely distributed as a weed esp. in grain and sometimes popularly believed to be a degenerate wheat; *broadly* **:** any of several weedy bromegrasses

chessboard \ˈ=ˌ=\ *n* **1 :** a checkerboard used in the game of chess **2 :** the scene of any contest like chess in requiring subtle scheming and cautious manipulation ⟨the political ~⟩

ches·sel \ˈchesəl\ *n* -s [prob. fr. ¹*cheese* + *well*] **:** CHEESE VAT

ches·set \ˈchesət\ *n* -s [by alter.] *Scot* **:** CHEESE VAT

chess·man \ˈchesˌman, -ˌmən, -ˌmaa(ə)n\ *n, pl* **chessmen** [by folk etymology fr. earlier *chesse meyne*, fr. *chesse* chess + *meyne* company, fr. MF *meyné, mesniée* company, servants, fr. L *mansio* house — more at MANSION] **:** one of 32 men used in chess with each player having a set of 16 consisting of 8 pieces and 8 pawns

chessboard with chessmen arranged as at the beginning of a game

chessom *adj* [*chess-* (perh. alter. of *cheese*) + *-som* (alter. of *-some*)] *obs, of soil* **:** loose, friable, and free from stones

chess pie *also* **chess cake** \ˈches-\ *n* [prob. alter. of *cheese pie, cheese cake*] **:** a dessert consisting essentially of a filling made of eggs, butter, and sugar and baked in individual tart shells of rich pastry

chess rook *n, heraldry* **:** a representation of the rook in chess in a shape now obsolete

chess·tree \ˈchesˌtrē\ *n* [perh. by folk etymology fr. F *châssis* framework — more at CHASSIS] **:** a piece of wood with a sheave or sheaves formerly bolted in the topsides of a ship and through which a tack or sheet was rove

chess rook

ches·sy cat \ˈchesē-\ *sometimes cap 1st C, slang var of* CHESHIRE CAT

ches·sy·lite \ˈshesəˌlīt\ *or* **ches·sy copper** \ˈshesē-, sheˈsē-\ *n* -s *usu cap 1st C* [*Chessy*, France, one of its localities + E *-lite*] **:** AZURITE

chessylite blue *n* **:** AZURITE BLUE

¹chest \ˈchest\ *n* -s [ME, fr. OE *cest, cist* chest, box, basket, coffin; akin to OFris *kiste* box, chest, OHG & ON *kista;* all fr. a prehistoric NGmc-WGmc word borrowed fr. L *cista* box, basket, fr. Gk *kistē* basket, hamper; perh. akin to OIr *cess, ciss* basket] **1 :** any of various containers for storage: as **a :** a box usu. with a hinged lid esp. for the safekeeping of valuables or the storing of tools or belongings ⟨a tool ~⟩ ⟨a jewel ~⟩ ⟨a ~ lock⟩ **b :** a cupboard esp. for the storing of medicines or first-aid supplies ⟨a medicine ~⟩ **c :** a reusable storage or shipping container generally made or fitted for a special commodity or group of items **d :** CHEST OF DRAWERS **e :** a storage tank for pulp during processing in papermaking **2** *now dial* **:** COFFIN **3 a :** the place for the keeping of the money of a public institution **:** TREASURY, COFFER **b :** a fund of money esp. in or from such a chest — see COMMUNITY CHEST **4 :** the part of the body enclosed by the ribs and breastbone **:** THORAX — see DOG illustration **5 :** the seat of the emotions **6 :** the breast of an arrow

²chest \"\ *vt* -ED/-ING/-S [ME *chesten* to put into a coffin, fr. *chest*, n.] *now dial Brit* **:** to place in a coffin

chest beating *n* **:** the striking of overly dramatic attitudes esp. in personal confession of errors ⟨the ritualistic *chest beating* of self-criticism⟩

chest·ed \ˈchestəd\ *adj, of an arrow* **:** thickest at the breast, tapering toward the point and usu. also toward the nock

¹ches·ter \ˈchestə(r)\ *adj, usu cap* [fr. *Chester*, England] **1 :** of or from the county borough of Chester, England **:** of the kind or style prevalent in the county borough of Chester **2 :** CHESHIRE

²chester \"\ *n, usu cap* **:** CHESHIRE CHEESE

ches·ter·field \ˈchestə(r)ˌfēld\ *n* -s *sometimes cap* [after a 19th cent. Earl of *Chesterfield*] **1 :** a semifitted overcoat of dark plain woolen fabrics made in single-breasted or double-breasted style with a velvet collar, flap pockets, a fly-front closure, and no belt, orig. for men's wear, and adapted for women **2 a :** a style of davenport usu. having upright armrests at both ends **b** *Brit* **:** DAVENPORT, SOFA

ches·ter·field·i·an \ˌ==ˈ=dēən\ *adj, usu cap* [Philip Dormer Stanhope, fourth Earl of *Chesterfield* †1773 Eng. statesman & man of letters + E *-ian*] **:** of, relating to, or befitting the writings or the attitudes of Chesterfield, distinguished for his elegant manners and for his *Letters* to his son in which he expounded his principles of conduct said to reflect sharply the pragmatic morality of the age

chesterfield suite *n, sometimes cap C, Brit* **:** a matching suite of davenport and easy chairs

ches·te·ri·an \(ˈ)cheˈstirēən\ *adj, usu cap* [*Chester*, Ill. + E *-ian*] **:** of or relating to a division of the Mississippian geologic period — see GEOLOGIC TIME table

chester white *n, usu cap C&W* [fr. *Chester* county, Pa., where it originated] **:** a breed of large white swine of the lard type

chest founder *n* **:** a hollow appearance of the chest and a stiff gait, suggesting a painful chest, sometimes seen in older horses and dogs, esp. those lacking exercise or suffering from strain or injury of the shoulder area

chestier *comparative of* CHESTY

chestiest *superlative of* CHESTY

chest·i·ly \ˈchestəlē, -li\ *adv* **:** in a chesty manner

chest·i·ness \-tēnəs, -tin-\ *n* -ES **:** the quality or state of being chesty ⟨with the ~ of a town bully⟩

¹chest·nut \ˈches(ˌ)nət, *usu* -əd-+V\ *n* -s [earlier *chesten nut*, fr. ME *chesten, chesteine, chasteine*, fr. MF *chastaigne*, fr. L *castanea*, fr. Gk *kastanea, kastanon*] **1 a :** the sweet edible nut produced by any shrub or tree of the genus *Castanea* **b :** any plant bearing this nut: (1) **:** a European tree (*C. sativa*) (2) **:** a closely related American tree (*C. dentata*) — see JAPANESE CHESTNUT **c :** the light coarse-grained wood of this tree **d :** any of numerous trees having edible nuts: as (1) **:** CAPE CHESTNUT (2) **:** MORETON BAY CHESTNUT — usu. used with an attributive modifier **2 a :** a color like or close to that of a chestnut **b :** a grayish brown that is slightly redder than coconut and redder and slightly darker than new cocoa — called also *brown bay, brownstone;* compare CHESTNUT BROWN **3 :** HORSE CHESTNUT 1 **4 :** an animal of a chestnut color; *specif* **:** a horse having a body color of any shade of pure or reddish brown with mane, tail, and points of the same or a lighter shade — compare ²BAY 1; see ¹SORREL 1a **5 :** one of the small round or oval horny callosities on the inner sides of the forelegs and hind legs of the horse and on the forelegs of asses and zebras **6 a :** an old usu. stale joke or story ⟨a comedy act trying to get by with nothing but ~s⟩ **b :** something repeated (as a generalization, a musical piece, or a play) or hashed over (as a philosophic problem or concept) very frequently esp. to the point of staleness ⟨Thursday's philharmonic program . . . contained a couple of . . . old ~s that could have been lent interest only by brilliant performances —Winthrop Sargeant⟩ ⟨then tackle the age-old ~s — so traditionally chewed over that they have capitalized names: the Problem of Being, the Problem of Evil —Susanne K. Langer⟩ **7** *Puerto Rico* **:** BREADFRUIT 1, 2

²chestnut \"\ *adj* **:** of, relating to, or like chestnut or a chestnut; *esp* **:** of the color chestnut

chestnut-backed chickadee *n* **:** a brown-backed chickadee (*Penthestes rufescens*) of the western U.S.

chestnut bean *n* **:** CHICK-PEA

chestnut blight *or* **chestnut-bark disease** *or* **chestnut canker** *n* **:** a destructive disease of the American chestnut caused by a fungus (*Endothia parasitica*) and attacking the bark and cambium to produce sunken or swollen cankers that ultimately girdle and kill the affected part

chestnut borer *n* **:** an insect that bores in the wood of the chestnut tree; *specif* **:** a small blue-black yellow-striped beetle (*Agrilus bilineatus*) having a flattened larva that bores in various deciduous trees — called also *two-lined chestnut borer*

chestnut-breasted finch *n* **:** a small Australian finch (*Donacola castaneothorax*) that is ashy brown above shading into rich chestnut on the back and wings with lighter chestnut breast and tail and white underparts and is often kept in aviaries though something of a pest in its native habitat, feeding on various seed crops

chestnut brown *n* **:** a moderate brown that is yellower and duller than toast brown, yellower, less strong, and slightly lighter than bay, redder and lighter than coffee, and yellower and slightly duller than auburn — compare CHESTNUT 2b

chestnut coal *n* **:** anthracite coal of medium size — see ANTHRACITE table

chestnut-collared longspur *n* **:** a longspur (*Calcarius ornatus*) of the central prairies of the U.S.

chestnut-eared finch *n* **:** ZEBRA FINCH

chestnut extract *n* **:** an extract of chestnut wood esp. from the European chestnut or American chestnut oak that is used chiefly in tanning heavy leathers (as sole and belting leathers)

chestnut oak *n* **:** an oak having leaves resembling those of the chestnut: as **a :** DURMAST **b :** CHINQUAPIN OAK **c :** a large oak (*Quercus montana*) of eastern No. America having oblong leaves with rounded teeth that are shiny yellow-green above and paler beneath and large acorns

chestnut rail *n* **:** a fence with rails made of chestnut wood

chestnut-sided warbler *n* **:** a common warbler (*Dendroica pensylvanica*) of eastern No. America

chestnut soil *n* **:** any of an agriculturally important group of zonal soils typically having a dark-brown surface horizon that grades downward into a lighter zone and then into a horizon of lime accumulation and being characteristic of certain cool semiarid grasslands and steppes (as in the northern U.S. prairie states)

chest·nut·ty \ˈches(ˌ)nəd·ē, -ətē, -i\ *adj* **1 :** tinged with or resembling the color chestnut **2 :** of or like a chestnut

chestnut weevil *n* **:** either of two brownish weevils (*Curculio auriger* and *C. proboscideus*) that lay eggs in the nut of the chestnut tree, the larvae feeding in and destroying the fruit

chest of drawers : a piece of case furniture designed almost solely to contain drawers

chest of viols : a set of matching viols of different sizes (as treble, tenor, gamba)

chest-on-chest *n* -s **:** a double chest of drawers, the lower section with short feet and the upper slightly smaller than the lower

chest-on-frame *n* -s **:** a chest of drawers raised on a frame with legs **:** HIGHBOY

chest pulse *n* **:** a sudden expiratory movement of the chest muscles or the impulse of breath so produced

chest register *n* **:** the lower register of the voice

chests *pl of* CHEST, *pres 3d sing of* CHEST

chest server *n* **:** a chest of drawers that serves also as a sideboard

chest shot *n* **:** a two-handed basketball set shot from chest height

chest thumping *n* **:** conduct or expression marked by pompous or arrogant self-assertion

chest tone *n* **:** a tone in the chest register

chest weight *n* **:** a weight (as one of a pair of weights) raised by a cord-and-pulley device for exercising and developing the muscles of the chest, back, and arms

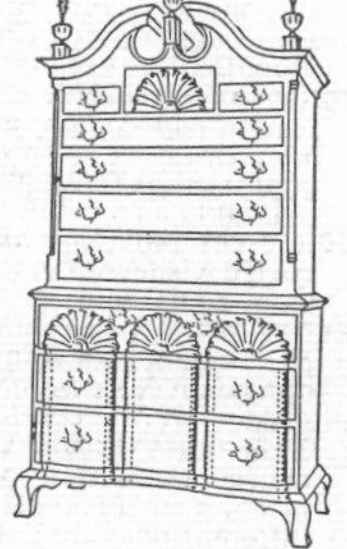

chest-on-chest

chesty \'chestē, -ti\ *adj* -ER/-EST **1 :** marked by a large or well-developed chest **2** *slang* **:** arrogantly or pridefully self-assertive ⟨~ as a peacock —Milton Mezzrow & Bernard Wolfe⟩ **3 :** marked by chest tones — used of a singer or his tone quality

chesvan *usu cap, var of* HESHVAN

chetah *var of* CHEETAH

chet·co \'chet,kō\ *n, pl* **chetco** *or* **chetcos** *usu cap* [Chetco *Cheti,* lit., close to the mouth of the stream] **1 :** an Athapaskan people in the Chetco river valley of Oregon **2 :** a member of the Chetco people

cheth *var of* HETH

chet·nik \(')chet¦nēk, -ik\ *n* -S *usu cap* [Serb *četnik,* fr. *četa* band, troop; perh. akin to L *caterva* band, troop, IrGael *cethern* troop, battalion] **:** a member of a Pan-Serbian movement or home-defense band for resistance to oppressors by guerrilla tactics

chetopod *var of* CHAETOPOD

chet·ty *or* **chet·tie** \'ched·ē\ *n, pl* **chet·tis** *or* **chetties** \-d·ēz\ *or* **chetty·ars** \-d·ē,ärz\ *often cap* [Tamil-Malayalam *ceṭṭi,* fr. Skt *śreṣṭhin*] **:** a member of a caste of Tamil moneylenders or merchants in southern India, Ceylon, Burma, Malaya, Fiji, and So. Africa

chet·ty·ar \'ched·ē,är\ *adj, often cap* **:** of or relating to the Chettyars

chet·vert \'chetvə(r)t\ *n* -S [Russ *chetvert',* lit., quarter, fr. *chetverty* fourth; akin to Skt *catur* four — more at FOUR] **:** a Russian unit of capacity equal to about 5.96 bushels

chev *abbr* **1** chevalier **2** chevron

che·vage \'chēvij\ *or* **chiv·age** \'chiv-\ *n* -S [ME *chyvage,* fr. MF *chevage,* fr. OF, fr. *chief* head + *-age* — more at CHIEF] **:** a capitation tax or tribute formerly paid to a lord or a superior

chevaine *var of* CHEVIN

che·val-de-frise \shə'valdə¦frēz\ *also* **che·vaux-de-frise** \-¦vōd-\ *n, pl* **chevaux-de-frise** \-¦vōd-\ [F, lit., horse or horses from Friesland; fr. its being first used there] **1 :** a piece of timber or an iron barrel from which iron-pointed spikes, spears, or pointed poles project five or six feet long, used in warfare to defend a passage, stop a breach, or impede cavalry — usu. used in pl. **2 :** a protecting line of sharp points (as of spikes or nails) set firmly into the top of a fence or wall — usu. used in pl.

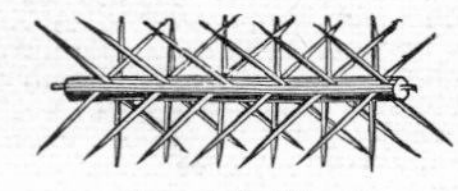
cheval-de-frise 1

chevaleresque *var of* CHIVALRESQUE

che·va·let \shə'va(,)lā, shevə¦lā\ *n* -S [F, dim. of *cheval* horse, fr. L *caballus* — more at CAVALCADE] **:** the bridge of a stringed musical instrument

che·val glass \shə'val-\ *n* [F *cheval,* lit., horse; fr. the resemblance of the frame to a horse] **:** a full-length mirror in a frame by which it may be moved or tilted

cheval glass

cheva·lier \shevə¦li(ə)r, -liə *or* (*esp in senses other than 1a & 3*) shə'val,yā *or* -ăl- *or* -āl- *or* ==\ *n* -S [ME *chevaler,* fr. MF *chevalier,* fr. LL *caballarius* horseman — more at CAVALIER] **1 a** *archaic* **:** HORSEMAN; *esp* **:** CAVALIER 3 **b** (1) **:** a member of certain orders of knighthood (2) **:** a member of the lowest rank of a French order of merit ⟨the coveted ribbon of the ~ of the Legion of Honor —W.H.Downes⟩ **2 a :** a member of the lowest rank of French nobility **b :** a cadet of the French nobility **3 :** a chivalrous man

cheva·lier crab \¦shevə¦li(ə)r-, -liə-\ *n* [so called fr. its rapid pace] **:** a swift-running seacoast crab (genus *Ocypode*)

chev·a·line \'shevə,lēn\ *adj* [MF, fem. of *chevalin,* fr. OProv *cavalin,* fr. L *caballinus,* fr. *caballus* horse + *-inus* -ine — more at CAVALCADE] **:** of or relating to horses

che·vee \shə'vā\ *n* -S [F *chevée,* fr. fem. of *chevé,* past part. of *chever* to hollow out, fr. L *cavare,* fr. *cavus* hollow — more at CAVE] **:** a flat gemstone with a smooth depression — compare CUVETTE

cheve·lure \¦shevə¦lü(ə)r, shəv'l-\ *n* -S [F, lit., head of hair, wig, fr. L *capillatura,* fr. *capillus* hair] **1 :** hair of the head **:** head of hair **2 :** a nebulous envelope (as around the nucleus of a comet or of a nebulous star) **:** COMA

chev·er·el \'shev(ə)rəl\ *or* **chev·er·il** \-əl\ *n* -S [ME *chevrelle,* fr. MF *chevrele* kid, dim. of *chèvre, chievre,* fr. L *capra* she-goat, fem. of *capr-, caper* goat — more at CAPRIOLE] **:** soft elastic leather made of kidskin **:** KID LEATHER

cheveron *var of* CHEVRON

cheveronel *var of* CHEVRONEL

cheveronny *var of* CHEVRONY

chev·e·saile \'shevə,sāl\ *n* -S [ME, fr. MF *chevesçaille* opening for the head in a garment, fr. OF, fr. *chevesce* head opening, fr. (assumed) VL *capitia,* pl. (taken as sing.) of L *capitium* opening for the head] **:** the ornamented collar of a medieval garment

che·vet \shə'vā\ *n* -S [F, alter. of OF *chevez,* fr. L *capitium* head covering, opening for the head, fr. *caput* head — more at HEAD] **:** the apsidal eastern termination of a church choir typically having a surrounding ambulatory that opens onto a number of radiating apses or chapels — used esp. of French Gothic architecture

che·ville \shə'vē\ *n* -S [F, lit., peg, fr. L *clavicula,* dim. of *clavis* key — more at CLAVICLE] **1 :** a redundant word or phrase used to fill out a sentence or verse **2 :** a peg of a stringed musical instrument

chev·in \'chevən\ *also* **che·vaine** *or* **che·vesne** \shə'vān\ *or* **chiv·en** \'chivən\ *n* -S [ME *chevin, cheveyne,* fr. MF *chevenne, chevesne,* fr. (assumed) VL *capitin-, capito,* fr. LL *capiton-, capito,* fr. L, large-headed one, fr. *caput* head] **:** the chub of Europe

chev·i·ot \'shevēət, *Brit usu & US sometimes* 'ch-\ *n* [fr. the Cheviot hills, England and Scotland] **1** *usu cap* **:** a breed of very hardy hornless medium-wooled meat-type sheep originating in the Cheviot hills **2** -S *sometimes cap* **a :** a fabric of Cheviot wool **b :** a heavy rough napped suiting and coating having a plain or twill weave and made of coarse wool or worsted often mixed with mungo **c** -S *broadly* **:** any of several fabrics resembling this suiting; *esp* **:** a sturdy soft-finished cotton shirting of a plain or twill weave **3** -S **:** a lightweight paper decorated to simulate the weave of cheviot fabric and used for covering and ornamenting boxes

chev·i·sance \'shevəsən(t)s, -zən-\ *n* -S [ME *chevisaunce* achievement, resource, supply, booty (whence by misunderstanding the meaning "enterprise"), fr. MF *chevisance,* fr. OF, fr. *chevir* to come to an end, perform, fr. *chief* head — more at CHIEF] **1** *archaic* **:** UNDERTAKING, ENTERPRISE; *esp* **:** chivalrous enterprise or prowess **:** CHIVALRY **2 :** an unlawful transaction or contract; *esp* **:** a transaction intended to evade the statutes against usury

chev·kin·ite \'chefkə,nīt, -evk-\ *n* -S [G *tschewkinit,* fr. Konstantin V. Chevkin (*Tschewkin*) †1875 Russ. general and chief of Dept. of Mines of Russia + G *-it* -ite] **:** a mineral approximately $(Fe,Ca)(Ce,La)_2(Si,Ti)_2O_8$ consisting of silicotitanate of iron, calcium, and rare-earth elements

chev·on \'shevən\ *n* -S [F *chèvre* goat (fr. L *capra* she-goat, fem. of *capr-, caper* goat) + E *mutton,* fr. ME *motoun,* fr. OF *moton* ram — more at CAPRIOLE, MUTTON] **:** the flesh of the goat used as food ⟨to many inhabitants of the tropics ~ is as palatable as mutton⟩

chev·ret \shəv'rā\ *also* **chè·vre** \'shevr(ᵊ), -v(rə)\ *or* **chev·ro·tin** \'shevrə,tan\ *n* -S [F, fr. *chèvre* goat] **:** a cheese made from goats' milk

chev·rette \shəv'ret\ *n* -S [F, kid, dim. of *chèvre* goat] **:** a thin goatskin

¹chev·ron \'shevrən\ *n* -S [ME, fr. MF, fr. (assumed) VL *caprion-, caprio,* fr. L *capra*] **1** *or* **chev·er·on** \-v(ə)rən\ *heraldry* **:** a charge consisting of two diagonal stripes meeting at an angle, the point up unless a different position is specified **2 :** a chevron-shaped figure, pattern, or object; *esp* **:** an ornamental unit of this shape often used (as in a chevron molding) as one of a number of attached identical units forming a continuous zigzag **3 :** a sleeve badge awarded or worn usu. as an indication of rank or of a completed term of service or used esp. formerly in the armed services as an indication that one has been wounded, usu. consisting of one or more V-shaped stripes sometimes with arcs, bars, and other devices, and distinctive in detail in the various organizations that employ them — compare ¹BAR 4d — **in chevron** *of a pair of heraldic charges* **:** one bendwise and the other bendwise sinister with the upper ends approaching or touching each other in the midline of the field ⟨on a chevron azure two swords *in chevron* proper⟩

chevron 1

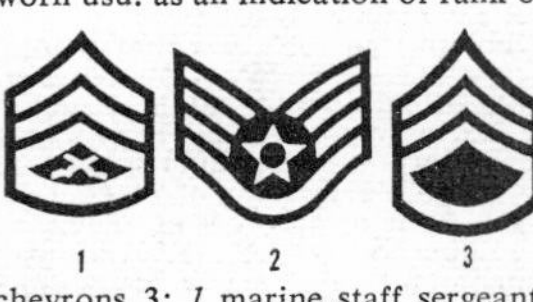

chevrons 3: *1* marine staff sergeant; *2* air force staff sergeant; *3* army staff sergeant

²chevron \"\ *n* -S [perh. fr. MF, kid, dim. of *chèvre* goat; fr. their being orig. made of kidskin — more at CHEVEREL] *archaic* **:** GLOVE

chevron bone *n* [¹*chevron*] **:** HEMAL ARCH b(2)

chev·ron·el \¦shevrə¦nel\ *or* **chev·er·on·el** \-v(ə)rə-\ *n* -S [¹*chevron* + *-el*] *heraldry* **:** a narrow chevron

chevron molding *n* [¹*chevron*] **:** a molding ornamented with chevrons (as in Norman architecture) **:** a zigzag molding

chevron rattler [¹*chevron* + *rattler;* fr. its markings] *n* **:** TIMBER RATTLESNAKE

chev·ron·wise \'shevrən,wīz\ *also* **chev·ron·ways** \-,wāz\ *adv* **:** in chevron

chev·rony *or* **chev·ron·ny** \'shevrənē\ *or* **chev·er·on·ny** \-v(ə)rə-\ *adj* [F *chevronné,* past part. of *chevronner* to adorn with chevrons, fr. *chevron,* n.] *heraldry* **:** divided into chevrons

chev·ro·tain \'shevrə,tān\ *also* **chev·ro·tin** \-,tan\ *n* -S [F, dim. of *chevrot* kid, fawn, fr. MF, dim. of *chèvre* goat — more at CHEVEREL] **:** any of several very small hornless deerlike ruminant mammals of tropical Asia, the Malay archipelago, and West Africa superficially resembling the musk deer, the male having short tusks, and being among the smallest known ruminants, standing only about a foot high — called also *mouse deer;* see WATER CHEVROTAIN

chevy *var of* CHIVY

¹chew \'chü\ *vb* -ED/-ING/-S [ME *chewen,* fr. OE *cēowan* to chew, gnaw, eat; akin to OHG *kiuwan* to chew, ON *tyggva* to chew, OSlav *žĭvati*] *vt* **1 a :** to crush or grind (as food) in the mouth by continued action of the teeth with the help of the tongue and other masticatory organs usu. in preparation for swallowing **:** MASTICATE **b :** to injure, destroy, or consume as if by chewing ⟨logs ~*ed* up for paper⟩ ⟨a weather-*chewed* white flag —Ivan Innerst⟩ **2 :** to utter indistinctly **:** MUMBLE **3** *slang* **:** UPBRAID, REPRIMAND ⟨not going to ~ him just because he cuts out now and then —J.G.Cozzens⟩ ~ *vi* **:** to chew something; *specif* **:** to chew tobacco — **chew the rag** *or* **chew the fat** *slang* **:** to make friendly familiar conversation **:** CHAT ⟨sitting in an old chair in front of the warehouse on the St. Paul levee . . . *chewing the rag* with anybody who came up the river —Meridel Le Sueur⟩ — **chew the scenery :** to act a stage or screen part with undue or inappropriate violence **:** OVERACT

²chew \"\ *n* -S **1 :** the act of chewing **2 a :** something that is chewed **:** a portion (as of tobacco) suitable for chewing **:** QUID, CUD **b :** a piece of chewy candy ⟨a molasses ~⟩

che·wa *also* **ce·wa** \'chā(,)wä\ *n, pl* **chewa** *or* **chewas** *also* **cewa** *or* **cewas** *usu cap* **1 :** a Bantu-speaking agricultural people of Nyasaland **2 :** a member of the Chewa people

chew·er \'chüə(r), -ü(ə)r,-üə\ *n* -S **:** one that chews; *esp* **:** one that chews tobacco habitually

chew·et \'chüət\ *n* -S [MF *chouette* owl, chough, of imit. origin] **1 :** CHOUGH **2 :** CHATTERER

chewing gum *n* **:** a preparation of chicle sometimes mixed with other plastic insoluble substances, sweetened and flavored for chewing

chew·ings fescue \'chüiŋz, -ùi-\ *n, often cap C* [after Charles *Chewings* †1937 Australian scientist] **:** a perennial pasture and turf grass (*Festuca rubra commutata*) closely related to red fescue but producing a closer firmer sod and tolerating partial shade

chewing the cud *n* **:** RUMINATION

chewing tobacco *n* **:** tobacco, usu. in the form of a plug, that contains a large percentage of flavoring material

che·wink *also* **chee·wink** \chə'wiŋk, chē-\ *n* -S [imit.] **:** the common towhee (*Pipilo erythrophthalmus*) of eastern No. America

chew out *vt, slang* **:** to bawl out **:** REPRIMAND, UPBRAID ⟨some niggling Quartermaster lieutenant *chewed* them *out* because they were a few hundred cases short —A.J.Leibling⟩ ⟨watched him *chew out* an umpire —*Time*⟩

chew over *vt* **:** to meditate on **:** think about reflectively ⟨likes to *chew over* some of the basic problems of our lives —Lewis Mumford⟩ ⟨have in the last decades *chewed over* Plato and Bacon and Freud —J.M.Barzun⟩

chewstick \'=,=\ *n* -S **1** *tropical America* **:** BOARWOOD 1 **2 :** CHAWSTICK

chewy \'chüē, -ùl, ¦i\ *adj* -ER/-EST **:** requiring chewing — used esp. of candy

chex *pl of* ²CHECK 14b

¹chey·enne \(')shī¦an, -aa(ə)n *also* -en\ *n, pl* **cheyenne** *or* **cheyennes** *usu cap* [CanF, fr. Dakota *Shaiyena,* fr. *shaia* to speak strangely, unintelligibly, fr. *sha* red + *ya* to speak] **1 a :** an Indian people of the western plains ranging between the Arkansas and Missouri rivers **b :** a member of such people **2 :** an Algonquian language of the Cheyenne people

²cheyenne \"\ *adj, usu cap* [fr. *Cheyenne,* Wyoming] **:** of or from Cheyenne, the capital of Wyoming ⟨a *Cheyenne* street⟩ **:** of the kind or style prevalent in Cheyenne

¹chey·le·tid \kī'lēd·əd, -le-\ *adj* [NL *Cheyletidae*] **:** of or relating to the Cheyletidae

²cheyletid \"\ *n* -S **:** one of the Cheyletidae

chey·let·i·dae \-'led·ə,dē\ *n pl, cap* [NL, fr. *Cheyletus,* type genus + *-idae*] **:** a small family of minute chiefly ectoparasitic mites distinguished by a pair of immense palpi attached to an anterior beak that are usu. ultimately beneficial because of feeding on debris and other ectoparasites of their bird or mammal hosts

chey·le·tus \-'lēd·əs\ *n* [NL, irreg. fr. Gk *chēlē* claw — more at CHELA] **1** *cap* **:** the type genus of Cheyletidae comprising certain free-living predatory mites that feed chiefly on grain mites **2** *pl* **cheyletus :** a mite of the genus *Cheyletus*

cheyne-stokes respiration *or* **cheyne-stokes breathing** \'chān(ē)'stōks-\ *n, usu cap C&S* [after John *Cheyne* †1836 Scottish physician who first described it, and William *Stokes* †1878 Irish physician who also noted it] **:** cyclic breathing marked by a gradual increase in the rapidity of the respirations followed by a gradual decrease and total cessation for from 5 to 50 seconds observed in cardiac and cerebral and related conditions

chey·ney \'chānē\ *n* -S [prob. fr. Per *chīnī* Chinese] **:** a woolen fabric in use during the 17th and 18th centuries

chez \(¦)shā\ *prep* [F, fr. L *casae* at home, locative of *casa* house — more at CASA] **:** at or in the home or business place of ⟨hair dressed ~ Pierre⟩ **:** WITH — used with a French personal pronoun ⟨will you dine ~ nous⟩ or a proper name ⟨a British politician lunched ~ Hitler —John Gunther⟩

chf *abbr* chief

chg *abbr* **1** change **2** charge

chgd *abbr* **1** changed **2** charged

chha·tri \'chə·trē\ *n* -S [Hindi *chatrī*] *India* **1 :** a funerary monument **:** a chapel built over a tomb **2 :** a resthouse for visitors to a temple or other sacred site

chhat·tis·garh·i \,chəd·ēs'gärē\ *n, usu cap* [Hindi *Chattīsgaṛhī,* fr. *Chattīsgaṛh,* district in India] **:** a dialect of Hindi spoken by the peoples of Madhya Pradesh and Orissa in northeast India

chi \'kī\ *n* -S [Gk] **:** the 22d letter of the Greek alphabet — symbol X or χ; see ALPHABET table

chia \'chēə\ *n* -S [Sp *chía,* fr. Nahuatl *chia, chian,* fr. Maya *chihâan* strong, strengthening] **1 :** any of several plants of the genus *Salvia* of Mexico and the southwestern U.S. (*Salvia columbariae, S. hispanica, S. tiliaefolia,* and *S. chia*) from the seeds of which the natives prepare a beverage **2 :** a beverage prepared from chia seeds **3** *also* **chia oil :** an edible oil made from chia seeds

chi·ack \'chīək\ *vt* -ED/-ING/-S [prob. alter. of *cheek*] *Austral* **:** to jeer at **:** RAZZ ⟨the spectators continued to ~ him⟩

chiam *usu cap, var of* CHAM

¹chi·an \'kīən\ *adj, usu cap* [*Chios,* island in the Aegean sea (fr. Gk) + E *-an*] **:** of, relating to, or characteristic of Chios (modern Khíos), island in the Aegean sea

²chian \"\ *n* -S *cap* **:** a native or inhabitant of Chios

chi·an·ti \kē'äntē, -'än-, *Ital* 'kyän-\ *n* -S *usu cap* [It, fr. the *Chianti* mt. area, Italy, where it was first made] **:** a still dry usu. red table wine often bottled in squat green wicker-covered bottles and orig. produced in the Chianti mountain region of Italy but now also elsewhere (as in California)

chian turpentine *n, usu cap C* **:** TURPENTINE 1a

chia·pa·nec \chē'äpə,nek\ *or* **cha·pa·nec** \'chäp-\ *n, pl* **chiapanec** *or* **chiapanecs** *or* **chapanec** *or* **chapanecs** *usu cap* [Sp *chiapaneca, chapaneca,* of AmerInd origin] **1 a :** a Chorotegan people of western Chiapas, Mexico **b :** a member of such people **2 :** the language of the Chiapanec people

chia·pa·nec·an \chē¦äpə¦nekən\ *n, usu cap* **:** CHOROTEGAN

chia·pa·ne·cas \chē,äpə'näkəs\ *or* **cha·pa·ne·cas** \-kəs\ *also* **cha·pa·ne·ca** \,chäpə'näkə\ *n, pl* **chiapanecas** *or* **chapanecas** [Sp, fem. pl. (*chiapanecas*) or sing. (*chiapaneca*) of *chiapaneco* of Chiapas, fr. *Chiapas,* state of Mexico] **:** a mestizo girls' dance from the Mexican state of Chiapas with hops, waltz steps, and hand clapping

chia·ro·scu·rist \,kyärə'sk(y)ürəst, kē,är-, -ar-, -rō'sk-, -ürə-\ *n* -S [*chiaroscuro* + *-ist*] **:** an artist in chiaroscuro

chia·ro·scu·ro \-ür(,)ō, -ü(,)rō\ *also* **chia·ro·oscu·ro** \-rō'ōs-,-rōə's-\ *n* -S *often attrib* [It, fr. *chiaro* light (fr. L *clarus*) + *oscuro* dark, fr. L *obscurus* — more at CLEAR, OBSCURE] **1 :** pictorial representation in terms of light and shade without regard for or use of colors in the objects depicted ⟨a sketch in ~⟩; *specif* **:** drawing or painting in black and white **2 a :** the arrangement or treatment of the light and dark parts in a pictorial work of art **b :** interplay, variety, or contrast of dissimilar qualities (as of mood, style, character, or spirit) thought of as lightness and darkness ⟨Mynheer had little ~ in his composition; he was prone to call a spade a spade — Norman Douglas⟩ **3 a :** a 16th century woodcut technique in which forms are defined in terms of light and shade through the use of several blocks one of which is used to print deep, sometimes black, shadows and the others moderated shades of a single color **b :** a print produced by this technique **4 :** the use of marked light and shade contrasts for decorative or dramatic effect in painting ⟨the great power of high light and deep shadow that we today call ~ —*Christian Science Monitor*⟩ — compare SFUMATO, TENEBROSO **5 :** interplay of light and shadow on or as if on a surface ⟨a spotlight revealing a ~ of ridges and craters on a mountainside⟩ **6 :** the quality of being veiled or partly in shadow

chi·asm \'kī,azəm\ *n* -S [in sense 1, fr. NL *chiasma;* in sense 2, fr. NL *chiasmus*] **1 :** CHIASMA **2 :** CHIASMUS

chi·as·ma \kī'azmə\ *n, pl* **chiasma·ta** \-məd·ə\ *or* **chiasmas** [NL, fr. Gk, crosspiece of wood, cross bandage, fr. *chiazein* to mark with a chi, fr. *chi* (X)] **1** *anat* **:** a decussation or intersection ⟨the optic ~⟩ **2** *biol* **:** a fusion and exchange of segments of chromatids occurring between members of a bivalent during diplotene **:** the source of genetic crossovers — **chi·as·mal** \(')kī¦azməl\ *adj* — **chi·as·mat·ic** \¦kīaz¦mad·ik, -¦az-\ *adj* — **chi·as·mic** \(')kī¦azmik\ *adj*

chi·as·ma·type \kī'azmə,tīp-\ *adj* [back-formation fr. *chiasmatypy*] **:** of or relating to chiasmatypy

chiasmatype theory *n* **:** a theory in biology: genetic crossing over and chiasma formation are causally related — compare CHIASMATYPY

chi·as·ma·typy \-,tīpē\ *n* -ES [ISV *chiasma-* (fr. NL *chiasma*) + *-typy;* orig. formed as F *chiasmatypie*] **:** the spiral twisting of homologous chromosomes during zygotene that results in intimate association of chromatids with chiasma formation and provides the mechanism for crossing over

chi·as·mo·don \kī'azmə,dän\ *n, cap* [NL, fr. Gk *chiasma* + NL *-odon*] **:** a genus of deep-sea percoid fishes — see BLACK SWALLOWER — **chi·as·mo·don·tid** \¦=¦==¦=təd\ *n or adj*

chi·as·mus \kī'azməs\ *n, pl* **chias·mi** \-,mī\ [NL, fr. Gk *chiasmos,* fr. *chiazein* to mark with a chi] **:** the inversion of the order of syntactical elements in the second of two juxtaposed and syntactically parallel phrases or clauses (as *a superman in physique but in intellect a fool*); *also* **:** an instance of this — **chi·as·tic** \(')kī¦astik\ *adj*

chiasto- *comb form* [G, fr. Gk *chiastos*] **:** marked with or characterized by a cross **:** crossed at right angles ⟨*chiasto*basidium⟩

chi·as·to·basidial \kī¦astō+\ *adj* [*chiasto-* + *basidial*] **:** having the nuclear spindles of the basidia at right angles to the longitudinal axis — compare STICHOBASIDIAL — **chi·as·to·basidium** \"+\ *n*

chi·as·to·lite \kī'astə,līt\ *n* -S [G *chiastolith,* fr. *chiasto-* + *-lith* -lite] **:** a mineral consisting of a variety of andalusite whose crystals have a tessellated appearance in cross section due to the arrangement of impurities — called also *macle*

chiaus \'chaùs(h)\ *n* -ES [Turk *çavuş* sergeant, doorkeeper, messenger, fr. *çav* voice, news] **1 :** a Turkish messenger or sergeant **2 :** CHEAT, SWINDLER

chi·a·vet·ta \kyə'ved·ə, kyä'-\ *n, pl* **chiavet·te** \-ed·ē\ [It, dim. of *chiave* key, clef, fr. L *clavis* key — more at CLAVICLE] **:** a clef (as one of the C clefs) formerly used to shift temporarily the pitch range of a staff carrying a voice part and so avoid the use of ledger lines

chi·ba \'chēbə\ *adj, usu cap* [fr. *Chiba,* Japan] **:** of or from the city of Chiba, Japan **:** of the kind or style prevalent in Chiba

chib·cha \'chibchə\ *n, pl* **chibcha** *or* **chibchas** *usu cap* [Sp, of AmerInd origin] **1 a :** a people of central Colombia constituting one of the peoples of the Chibchan language family — called also *Muisca* **b :** a member of such people **2 :** the extinct language of the Chibcha people

chib·chan \-chən\ *adj, usu cap* **1 :** of or relating to a language stock of Colombia and Central America including Andaki, Barbacoa, Bribri, Cabecar, Cágaba, Chibcha, Coiba, Colima, Cueva, Cuna, Guatuso, Guaymi Guetar, Ica, Paez, Rama, San Blas, Tulamanca, and Valiente **2 :** of or relating to the peoples speaking Chibchan languages

chi·bi·gou·a·zou \,shēbē,gü'ä(,)zü\ *n* -S [Pg, fr. Guarani] **:** a brightly marked ocelot (*Felis pardalis chibigouazou*) of the Mato Grosso

chib·ol \'chibəl\ *dial Brit var of* CIBOL

chi·bouk *or* **chi·bouque** \chə'bük, -ük\ *n* -S [F *chibouque,* fr. Turk *çıbuk, çubuk*] **:** a Turkish tobacco pipe having a clay or meerschaum bowl and a long stem with a mouthpiece often of amber

¹chic \'shēk *also* -ik\ *n* -S [F, perh. fr. G *schick* fitness, order, skill, fr. LG, fr. *schicken* to put into order, fr. MLG; akin to MHG *schicken* to prepare, arrange, send] **1 :** artistic cleverness and dexterity esp. in painting **2 :** easy elegance and sophistication of dress or manner **:** STYLE, SWANK, CHARM **3 :** VOGUE, FASHION, MODISHNESS ⟨the ~ of the latest hats⟩

²chic \"\ *adj* [F, fr. *chic,* n.] **1 :** cleverly stylish **:** having chic **2 :** in vogue **:** currently fashionable **:** MODISH

¹chica *var of* CHICHA

²chi·ca \'chēkə\ *n* -S [AmerSp] **:** CARAJURA 2

chicadee *var of* CHICKADEE

¹chi·ca·go \shə'kä(,)gō, -'kò(- *sometimes* -'kā(- *or* -gə — *natives of the city prob most often use* ò *in the second syllable*\ *adj, usu cap* [fr. *Chicago,* Ill.] **:** of or from the city of Chicago, Ill. **:** of the kind or style prevalent in Chicago

²chicago \"\ *n* -S *usu cap* [fr. *Chicago,* Ill.] **1 :** a method of playing contract bridge in sets of four deals rather than rubbers **2 :** MICHIGAN

chicago acid *n, usu cap C* **:** a crystalline acid $NH_2C_{10}H_4(OH)(SO_3H)_2$ used as an intermediate in making azo dyes; 8-amino-1-naphthol-5,7-disulfonic acid

chi·ca·go·an \-,gəwən\ *n* -S *cap* [*Chicago* + E *-an*] **:** a native or inhabitant of Chicago

chicago blue *n, usu cap C & often cap B* **:** any of several direct dyes — see DYE table I (under *Direct Blue 1, 4,* and *22*)

chicago piano *n, usu cap C, slang* **:** POM-POM

chicago pool *n, usu cap C* **:** rotation pool in which at the start of play the object balls are placed around the table at the diamonds in numerical order

chicago style *n, usu cap C* **:** a widely used method of butchering animal carcasses

chi·ca·lo·te \ˌchikə'lōd·ē\ *n* -s [Sp, fr. Nahuatl *chicalotl*] **:** a white-flowered prickly poppy (*Argemone platyceras*) of Mexico and the southwestern U.S.

¹**chi·cane** \shə'kān, chə-\ *vb* -ED/-ING/-s [F *chicaner*, fr. MF, to quibble, prevent justice] *vi* **:** to use chicanery **:** employ shifts, subterfuges, or artifices ⟨a wretch he had taught to lie and ~ —George Meredith⟩ ~ *vt* **:** to cavil at **:** quibble over; *also* **:** TRICK, CHEAT, DUPE ⟨he *chicaned* the widow out of her property⟩

²**chicane** \"\ *n* -s [F, fr. MF, fr. *chicaner*] **1 a :** deception usu. by legalistic subterfuge **:** CHICANERY ⟨the lawyer is exclusively occupied with the details of predatory fraud, either in achieving or checkmating ~ —Thorstein Veblen⟩ **b :** an instance of chicane **:** SUBTERFUGE, QUIBBLE **2 :** an obstacle esp. on a racecourse **3 :** the absence of any trumps in a hand of cards just dealt, in some forms of bridge formerly scoring as simple honors **syn** see DECEPTION

³**chicane** \"\ *adj* [²*chicane*] **1 :** having no trumps — used of a player or his hand of cards **2** *slang* **:** having no money **:** BROKE

chi·can·er \-nə(r)\ *n* -s [earlier *chicaneur*, fr. F, fr. MF, fr. *chicaner* + -*eur* -or] **:** one that uses chicanery

chi·ca·nery \-n(ə)rē, -i\ *n* -ES [F *chicanerie*, fr. MF, fr. *chicaner* + -*erie* -ery] **1 :** deception by artful subterfuge, sophistry, pettifogging, misrepresentation, conniving, or similar artifice ⟨the administrative ~ of governments —*New Republic*⟩ **2 :** a piece of sharp practice (as at law) **:** TRICK — usu. used in pl. **syn** see DECEPTION

chic·a·ric \'chikəˌrik, ˌ==ˈ=\ *n* -s [imit.] **:** TURNSTONE

chiccory *var of* CHICORY

chich \'chich\ *n* -ES [ME *chiche*, fr. MF, fr. L *cicer*; akin to Arm *siseṙn* chick-pea] **:** CHICK-PEA

chi·cha \'chēchə\ *or* **chi·ca** \-ēkə\ *n* -s [Sp, prob. fr. Cuna *chichah* (*co-pah*), lit., corn drink] **:** a So. American and Central American beer made chiefly from fermented maize

chi·char·ro \chē'chä(ˌ)rō\ *n* -s [Sp] **:** BIG-EYED SCAD

chiches *pl of* CHICH

¹**chi·chi** \'chē(ˌ)chē, 'shē(ˌ)shē *sometimes* shē'shē\ *adj* [F] **1 :** elaborately or conspicuously ornamented or ornamental **:** FRILLY, SHOWY **2 :** limited in appeal to a small artistic or intellectual cult **:** ARTY, PRECIOUS, AFFECTED **3 :** placing excessive emphasis on fashion or elegance **:** CHIC

²**chichi** \"\ *n* -s **:** something that is chichi **:** ORNAMENTATION, FRILLINESS, SHOW, AFFECTATION

ch'i-chia \'chē'jä\ *adj, usu cap 1st C* [prob. fr. a place name in China] **:** of or relating to the earliest Neolithic stage in China characterized by a distinctive painted pottery

chi·chi·mec \'chēchəˌmek\ *or* **chi·chi·me·ca** \ˌ==ˈmākə\ *or* **chi·chi·me·co** \-'mā(ˌ)kō\ *n, pl* **chichimec** *or* **chichimecs** *or* **chichimeca** *or* **chichimecas** *or* **chichimeco** *or* **chichimecos** *usu cap* [Sp *chichimeca*, fr. Nahuatl *chichimecatl*] **1 a :** any one of the Nahuatlan peoples in Mexico before the rise of the Aztec empire **b :** a warlike people of northern Mexico **c :** a member of any such people **2 :** the language of the Chichimec people — **chi·chi·mecan** \ˌ==ˈmākən, -mek-\ *adj, usu cap*

chi·chi·pa·te \ˌchichə'päd·ē\ *n* -s [AmerSp, fr. Nahuatl *chichipatli*, lit., bitter medicine, fr. *chichic* bitter + *patli* medicine] **:** a tropical American timber tree (*Sweetia panamensis*) of the family Leguminosae

chi·chi·pe \chə'chēpē\ *n* -s [MexSp *chichipe*, *chichibe*] **:** a tall treelike Mexican cactus (*Lemaireocereus chichipe*) with edible red fruits

chi·chi·tu·na \ˌchēchə'tünə\ *n* -s [MexSp] **:** the fruit of the chichipe

¹**chick** \'chik\ *n* -s [ME *chike*, *chiken* — more at CHICKEN] **1 a :** CHICKEN; *esp* **:** one newly hatched or still downy **b :** the young of any bird **2 :** CHILD — often used as a term of endearment **3** *slang* **:** a young woman

²**chick** \"\ *vi* -ED/-ING/-s [ME *chicken*, *chykkyn*, perh. of imit. origin; fr. the cracking of seeds when they germinate] *dial Eng* **:** SPROUT

³**chick** \"\ *n* -s [Hindi *ciq*, fr. Per *chiq*] **:** a screen used in India and southeast Asia esp. for a doorway and constructed of bamboo slips loosely bound by vertical strings and often painted

⁴**chick** \"\ *n* -s [short for earlier *chickeen*, *chickino*, fr. It *zecchino* — more at SEQUIN] *India* **:** a sequin formerly current at the ports of India at the value of four rupees

chick·a·bid·dy \'chikəˌbidē, -di\ *n* -ES [¹*chick* + connective -*a*- + *biddy*] **1 :** CHICKEN — a child's term **2 :** CHILD — a term of endearment

chick·a·dee *also* **chic·a·dee** \'chikə(ˌ)dē, -ˌdi\ *n* -s [imit.] **:** any of several crestless American titmice (genus *Penthestes* or *Parus*) usu. having the crown of the head sharply demarked and darker than the body plumage — see ACADIAN CHICKADEE, BLACK-CAPPED CHICKADEE

chick·a·mau·ga \ˌchikə'mȯgə\ *n, pl* **chickamauga** *or* **chickamaugas** *usu cap* **1 :** a Cherokee people living near the present location of Chattanooga, Tenn. **2 :** a member of the Chickamauga people

chick·a·ree \'chikəˌrē\ *n* -s [imit.] **:** the American red squirrel or certain related squirrels

chick·a·saw \'chikəˌsȯ *also* -kˌsȯ\ *n, pl* **chickasaw** *or* **chickasaws** *usu cap* **1 a :** a Muskogean people of northern Mississippi and Alabama **b :** a member of such people **2 :** a dialect of Choctaw spoken by the Chickasaw

chickasaw plum *n, usu cap C* **:** a native American shrub or small tree (*Prunus angustifolia*) that has red or yellowish cherrylike fruit and has given rise to several cultivated varieties in the southern U.S.

chick bronchitis *n* [¹*chick*] **:** INFECTIOUS BRONCHITIS 1

chick disease *n* [¹*chick*] **:** a virus infection of young chicks that is of uncertain relationship to the avian leukosis complex and is characterized by focal lesions in liver and heart muscle

chickee *var of* CHIKEE

chick·ell \'chikəl\ *n* -s [imit.] *Brit* **:** WHEATEAR

¹**chick·en** \'chikən *sometimes* -kᵊŋ *esp when another word, as "coop" or "pie", follows without pause*\ *n* -s [ME *chiken*, fr. OE *cicen*, *cycen* young chicken; akin to MHG *kuchen* young chicken, ON *kjūklingr* gosling, OE *cocc* cock — more at COCK] **1 a :** the common domestic fowl (*Gallus gallus*); *also*, *now Brit* **:** the young of this bird when less than one year old **b :** the flesh esp. of the young of such fowl used as food **2 :** the young of any of various esp. gallinaceous birds whose young run about soon after hatching **3** *slang* **:** a young person, esp. a woman **:** ¹CHICK 3 **4 :** COWARD, SISSY **5** *slang* **:** a young woman of easy familiarity **6** *slang* **:** the details of duty or discipline considered unnecessary or an imposition **:** petty detail rigorously emphasized

²**chicken** \"\ *adj* [prob. short for *chickenhearted* or *chicken-livered*] **1** *slang* **:** CHICKENHEARTED, COWARDLY **2** *slang* **:** insistent on petty or irksome esp. military discipline

³**chicken** \"\ *vi* **chickened; chickened; chickening** \-k(ə)niŋ\ **chickens** *slang* **:** to lose one's nerve **:** show cowardice **:** DESERT — often used with *out* ⟨~*ed* out on an earlier plan to march into a package store wearing a mask —*Springfield (Mass.) Union*⟩

chickenberry \'==ˌ==\ *n* **1 :** WINTERGREEN 2a **2 :** PARTRIDGEBERRY

chicken body louse *n* **:** a common yellowish biting louse (*Menacanthus stramineus*) of poultry

chicken breast *n* **:** PIGEON BREAST — **chicken-breasted** *adj*

chicken bug *n* **:** ADOBE BUG

chicken cac·cia·to·re \-ˌkächə'tōrē, -ˌkach-\ *n* **:** chicken fried in olive oil, seasoned with herbs, and simmered in tomato and white wine liquor

chicken cholera *n* **:** FOWL CHOLERA

chicken colonel *n* [so called fr. the eagle worn on the shoulders] *slang* **:** a colonel as distinguished from a lieutenant colonel

chicken corn *n* **:** an annual nonsaccharine sorghum (*Sorghum vulgare drummondii*) that is often a troublesome weed in the southern U.S.

chicken feed *n, slang* **:** a trifling or contemptible sum (as in profit or wages) **:** SMALL CHANGE

chicken-fighters \'==ˌ==\ *also* **chicken-fights** *n pl* [so called fr. a children's game in which each of two participants tries to decapitate the other's flower by pulling on the stem of his own, one spurred petal (likened to a cock's spur) of which is interlocked with that of his adversary's flower] **:** the flowers of several violets (as *Viola cucullata*) one petal of which is spurred

chicken flu *n* **:** INFECTIOUS LARYNGOTRACHEITIS

chicken grape *n* **:** a stout tall-growing grape (*Vitis vulpina*) of the eastern and central U.S. with small shining black fruits that sweeten with the first frosts —called also *frost grape*

chicken gumbo *n* **:** a gumbo made with chicken

chicken halibut *n* **:** a young halibut

chicken hawk *n* **:** any of various hawks that sometimes prey or are reputed to prey on chickens: as **a :** SHARP-SHINNED HAWK **b :** COOPER'S HAWK

chickenhearted \ˌ==ˈ==\ *adj* **1 :** TIMID, COWARDLY **2 :** lacking in necessary sternness **:** SOFT-HEARTED — **chickenheartedly** \ˌ==ˈ===\ *adv*

chicken-livered \ˌ==ˈ==\ *adj* **:** FAINTHEARTED, COWARDLY

chicken lobster *n* **:** a young lobster

chicken mite *n* **:** a small mite (*Dermanyssus gallinae*) infesting poultry esp. in warm regions

chicken pepper *n* **:** a common small-flowered buttercup (*Ranunculus abortivus*) of the eastern U.S.

chicken pest *n* **:** FOWL PEST 1

chicken pox *n* **1 :** an acute contagious disease principally of children and not commonly dangerous caused by a virus and characterized by low-grade fever and other symptoms and blisterlike vesicles **2 :** FOWL POX

chicken pull *n* **:** a contest in horsemanship in which the rider tries at full gallop to snatch up a half-buried chicken

chickens *pl of* CHICKEN, *pres 3d sing of* CHICKEN

chicken septicemia *n* **:** hemorrhagic septicemia of poultry

chicken skin *n* [so called fr. the pin-point marks resembling chicken skin] **:** a fine thin vellum used in covering fans

chicken's-meat \'==ˌ=\ *n, dial Eng* **:** CHICKWEED

chicken snake *n* **1 :** any of a number of large harmless No. American colubrid snakes (genus *Elaphe*) — called also *rat snake* **2 :** the tropical rat snake (*Spilotes pullatus*), a large colubrid closely related to the indigo snake

chicken's-toes \'==ˌ=\ *n pl but sing or pl in constr* [so called fr. the shape of its roots] **:** a coralroot (*Corallorhiza odontorhiza*)

chicken terrapin *or* **chicken tortoise** *or* **chicken turtle** *n* **1 :** a small or medium-sized edible aquatic turtle (*Deirochelys reticularia*) of the southern Atlantic states having a long snakelike neck and an elongated carapace marked with a network of yellow lines **2 :** the young of the green turtle

chicken tick *n* **:** an argasid tick (*Argas persicus* syn. *miniatus*) attacking fowls in the warmer parts of the world and transmitting the fowl spirochetosis organism (*Spirochaeta gallinae*)

chickenweed \'==ˌ=\ *n* [ME *chikenwede*, fr. *chiken* chicken + *wede* weed] **:** CHICKWEED

chicken wire *n* [so called fr. its use in fencing chicken pens] **:** a light galvanized wire netting of hexagonal mesh

chick·ery \'chik(ə)rē\ *n* -ES [¹*chick* + -*ery*] **:** a poultry hatchery

chicking *pres part of* CHICK

chick·ling \'chikliŋ\ *or* **chickling vetch** *n* -s [by folk etymology (prob. influence of ¹*chick*) fr. earlier *chichling*, fr. *chich* + -*ling*] **:** the grass pea (*Lathyrus sativus*) of Europe cultivated for seeds and forage

chick-pea \'=ˌ=\ *n* [by folk etymology (prob. influence of ¹*chick*) fr. earlier *chich-pea*, fr. *chich* + *pea*] **1 :** an Asiatic herb (*Cicer arietinum*) now widespread in the western hemisphere that bears short pods with one or two seeds somewhat resembling peas in flavor **2 :** the seed of the chick-pea constituting an important article of diet esp. in southern Europe and in India — called also *chestnut bean*, *chich*, *dwarf pea*, *garbanzo*, *garavance* and in India *gram* or *Bengal gram*

chicks *pl of* CHICK, *pres 3d sing of* CHICK

chickweed \'=ˌ=\ *n* -s [alter. of *chickenweed*] **1 :** any of various low-growing small-leaved weedy plants of the family Caryophyllaceae (as members of the genera *Arenaria*, *Cerastium*, and *Stellaria*) several of which are relished by birds or used as potherbs **2 :** any of various plants of families other than Caryophyllaceae that resemble chickweeds — usu. used in combination ⟨red ~⟩; compare CARPETWEED

chickweed phlox *n* **:** a diffuse herb (*Phlox stellaria*) found in rocky places in the U.S. and having small linear leaves and bluish white flowers

chickweed wintergreen *n* **:** an American starflower (*Trientalis americana*) or its Eurasian relative (*T. europaea*)

chi·cle \'chikəl *sometimes* 'chēkəl *or* 'chiklē\ *n* -s [Sp, fr. Nahuatl *chictli*, *tzictli*] **1 :** a gum reported to contain both rubber and gutta-percha obtained as pinkish to reddish brown pieces from the latex of the sapodilla largely from Yucatan and Central America and used as the chief ingredient of chewing gum **2 :** any of several gums derived from tropical So. American trees of the families Moraceae and Apocynaceae

chicle bleeder *n* **:** CHICLERO

chi·cle·ro \chi'kler(ˌ)ō\ *n* -s [AmerSp, fr. Sp *chicle* + -*ero* -er] **:** a gatherer of chicle

chiclero ulcer *n* **:** leishmaniasis of the mouth, nose, and throat

¹**chi·co** \'chē(ˌ)kō\ *n* -s [MexSp (*juego*) *chico*, lit., small game, fr. Sp *juego* game + *chico* small, baby talk modif. of L *ciccum* pomegranate core, integument, trifle, fr. Gk *kikkos*] **:** the game played in the composite card game frog when the bid is won by the player naming as trumps any suit but hearts, the widow being set aside but belonging finally to the bidder — compare ²GRAND 4a (2)

²**chico** \"\ *n* -s [modif. of Sp *chicalote* — more at CHICALOTE] **:** the common greasewood (*Sarcobatus vermiculatus*) of the western U.S.

³**chico** \"\ *n* -s [in sense 1, fr. AmerSp, short for Sp *chicozapote*, fr. Nahuatl *xicatzapotl*, fr. *xicotl* juice + *tzapotl* sapote; in sense 2, PhilSp, fr. AmerSp] **1** *Philippines* **:** SAPODILLA 2 **2** *Philippines* **:** MARMALADE TREE

chico mamey *n* [PhilSp, fr. AmerSp *chico* sapodilla, marmalade tree + Sp *mamey* mammee — more at CHICO, MAMMEE] *Philippines* **:** the fruit of the marmalade tree; *also* **:** MARMALADE TREE

chi·co·mu·cel·tec \ˌchēkō'müsəlˌtek\ *n, pl* **chicomuceltec** *or* **chicomuceltecs** *usu cap* [Sp *Chicomuceltecа*, of AmerInd origin] **1 a :** an Indian people of southern Chiapas, Mexico **b :** a member of such people **2 :** a Mayan language of the Chicomuceltec people

chic·o·ry *also* **chic·co·ry** *or* **chick·o·ry** \'chik(ə)rē, -ri\ *n* -ES [alter. (influenced by F *chicorée*) of ME *cicoree*, fr. MF *chicorée*, *cichorée*, fr. L *cichoreum*, *cichorium*, fr. Gk *kichora*, *kichoreia*] **1 a :** a thick-rooted usu. blue-flowered perennial herb (*Cichorium intybus*) that is native to Europe but widely grown for its young leaves which are used as salad greens and for its roots and that in many areas (as in parts of Australia and the U.S.) has escaped to become a serious weed pest — called also *witloof*; see ENDIVE **2 :** the dried ground roasted root of chicory used to flavor or adulterate coffee **3** *or* **chicory blue :** a light bluish gray that is greener and deeper than sky gray — called also *succory blue*

chicory family *n* **:** CICHORIACEAE

chi·cot \shē'kō\ *n* -s [AmerF, fr. F, stub, stump] **:** KENTUCKY COFFEE TREE

chi·co·te \chē'kōd·ē\ *n* -s [AmerSp, fr. Sp, end of a rope, piece of rope, perh. fr. MF *chicot* stump] *West* **:** a long whip that has a wooden handle and is used by cowboys

chi·co·za·po·te \ˌchēkōzə'pōd·ē, ōsə-\ *n* -s [Sp, fr. Nahuatl *xicotzapotl*, fr. *xico* bee + *tzapotl* sapote] **:** SAPODILLA

chics *pl of* CHIC

chi-dan *usu cap C, var of* KHITAN

chide \'chīd\ *vb* **chid** \'chid\ *or* **chid·ed** \'chīdəd\ *or archaic* **chode** \'chōd\ **chid** \'chid\ *or* **chid·den** \'chidᵊn\ *or* **chided; chid·ing** \'chīdiŋ\ **chides** [ME *chiden*, fr. OE *cīdan* to quarrel, chide, fr. *cīd* strife] *vi* **1 :** to speak out in angry or displeased rebuke **:** CONTEND, BRAWL, WRANGLE **:** clamor stridently ⟨the people did ~ with Moses —Exod 17:2 (AV)⟩ **2 :** to make an uproar or clamor (as of a tempest or the sea) suggesting violent anger ⟨the *chiding* flood —Shak.⟩ **3 :** to express disapproval in correcting or appealing for change and improvement ⟨*chiding* against the king for his blind infatuation⟩ ~ *vt* **1 :** to voice disapproval to (for some shortcoming) now often mildly and charitably as a parent, mentor, or friendly critic in the interests of amendment or improvement **:** SCOLD ⟨*chiding* the child for his inattention⟩ ⟨*chiding* the maid for her carelessness⟩ **2 :** to seem to scold, complain against, rebuke, or threaten with strident or brawling sound ⟨the sea that ~*s* the banks of England —Shak.⟩ **syn** see REPROVE

chiding *n* -s [ME, fr. OE *cīding*, fr. *cīdan* + -*ing*] **1** *archaic* **:** CONTENTION, QUARRELING **2 :** REPROOF, REBUKE

chid·ing·ly *adv* **:** in a chiding manner

chi·dra \'chēdrə\ *n* -s [AmerSp] **:** JIPIJAPA

¹**chief** \'chēf\ *n, pl* **chiefs** \'chēfs *sometimes* -ēvz\ [ME *chief*, *chef*, fr. OF *chief*, *chef*, fr. L *caput* head — more at HEAD] **1 a** *obs* **:** the top or uppermost part **:** HEAD **b** *heraldry* (1) **:** the upper part of the field — compare ESCUTCHEON 1 (2) **:** a horizontal band at the top of the field **2 a :** the head or leader of any body of men **:** a commander (as of an army) or a headman (as of a tribe, clan, or family) **b :** the directing head of a political party, government bureau or department, or office organization ⟨~ of mission⟩; *also* **:** one's superior in such a body **c :** an officer in charge of any of certain branches or departments of the service — used in titles ⟨*Chief* of Staff⟩ ⟨*Chief* of Ordnance⟩ **d :** a chief officer of a department of government ⟨*Chief* of Police⟩ ⟨Fire *Chief*⟩ **e :** CHIEF PETTY OFFICER **3 :** the principal part **:** the most valuable portion ⟨this London where the ~ of his life must pass —John Galsworthy⟩ — **in chief 1** *feudal law* **a :** of tenure or holding directly from the lord paramount, that is, in England, the king, to whom the tenure service is rendered personally **b :** by perpetual ground rent or fee-duty as distinguished from the limited lease **2** *heraldry* **:** borne on the part of the field that would be occupied by a chief **3 :** in the chief position or place — often used in titles ⟨Commander-*in-Chief*⟩

chief 1b (2)

²**chief** \"\ *adj* -ER/-EST [ME *chef*, *chief*, fr. *chef*, *chief*, n.] **1 :** accorded highest rank, office, or rating ⟨~ executive⟩ **:** superior in authority, power, or influence ⟨~ prelate of our church, archbishop, first in council —Alfred Tennyson⟩ **2 :** marked by greatest importance, significance, influence **:** SALIENT **:** subordinating other persons, things, items of the same kind or class ⟨his ~ fame rests on his important volumes —A.V.W.Jackson⟩ **3** *now chiefly Scot* **:** INTIMATE, FRIENDLY, CLOSE ⟨a whisperer separates ~ friends —Prov 16:28 (RSV)⟩

syn PRINCIPAL, MAIN, LEADING, FOREMOST, CAPITAL all indicate first in importance and are often interchangeable. CHIEF may stress the fact of the existence of subordinate matters ⟨so many young people of today have lost sight of the fact that duty, not pleasure, is the *chief* aim of living —Ellen Glasgow⟩ ⟨one of the performances I remember extremely vividly, because the *chief* turn consisted of four performing elephants —Osbert Sitwell⟩ PRINCIPAL is likely to indicate greatest importance or power and influence, with other matters as minor ⟨after summing all the rest, religion ruling in the breast, a *principal* ingredient —William Cowper⟩ ⟨the central point of interest, unforgotten, absorbing, *principal* —Matthew Arnold⟩ ⟨the country of the Shilluk is almost entirely in grass, hence the *principal* wealth of the people consists in their flocks and herds —J.G.Frazer⟩ MAIN stresses greater size, power, or importance ⟨the *main* line express services tended to further this concentration, and the feeder lines and cross country services ran down, died out, or were deliberately extirpated —Lewis Mumford⟩ ⟨the literary critic . . . will yet find, like the historian, his *main* subject-matter in the past —L.P.Smith⟩ LEADING stresses precedence or coming before others in a series, sequence, or progression ⟨if John of Gaunt was fallen from his old power he was still the *leading* noble in the realm —J.R.Green⟩ ⟨Massachusetts furnished one of the *leading* defenders of the disturbing views of Darwin in the person of Asa Gray Fisher, professor of botany at Harvard —*Amer. Guide Series: Mass.*⟩ FOREMOST is often the equivalent of LEADING but may more strongly suggest the notion of a course, race, chase, or contest ⟨within a year the Bulletin had outstripped all other papers in the city, winning recognition as the *foremost* champion of the people's right —*Amer. Guide Series: Calif.*⟩ ⟨the clock has been the *foremost* machine in modern technics: and at each period it has remained in the lead: it marks a perfection toward which other machines aspire —Lewis Mumford⟩ CAPITAL stresses the idea of major significance or importance ⟨the *capital* as well as the trivial sins —Henry Miller⟩

³**chief** \"\ *adv* [²*chief*] *archaic* **:** CHIEFLY, PRINCIPALLY

chief cell *n* **1 :** one of the cells that line the lumen of the fundic glands of the stomach: **a :** a small cell with granular cytoplasm that secretes pepsin **b :** a larger cell with hyaline cytoplasm and a mucoid secretion — compare PARIETAL CELL **2 :** one of the secretory cells of the parathyroid glands

chief·dom \-dəm\ *n* -s **1 :** the position or office of chief **:** LEADERSHIP **2 :** a region or a people ruled by a chief

chief·ery \'chēf(ə)rē\ *or* **chief·ry** \-frē\ *n* -ES [¹*chief* + -*ery*, -*ry*] **1 :** CHIEFTAINCY — used mostly of Celtic institutions **2 :** dues, tribute, or rent belonging to a chief

chief·ess \'chēfəs\ *n* -ES [¹*chief* + -*ess*] **:** a female chief — used esp. in Polynesia

chief hare *n* **:** LITTLE CHIEF HARE

chief justice *n* **:** the justice who is the official head of a judicial body (as the head of one of the supreme courts of the various states or of the Supreme Court of the U.S.) — **chief-justiceship** \ˈ==ˌ==ˌ=\ *n*

chief·less \'chēfləs\ *adj* **:** being without a chief

¹**chief·ly** \'chēflē, -li\ *adv* [ME *chefly*, *chiefly*, fr. *chef*, *chief*, adj. + -*ly*] **1 :** most importantly **:** above all **:** PRINCIPALLY, PREEMINENTLY, ESPECIALLY **2 :** for the most part **:** MOSTLY, MAINLY

²**chiefly** \"\ *adj* [¹*chief* + -*ly*] **:** relating or belonging to a chief

chief master sergeant *n* **:** an air force noncommissioned officer rating just above a senior master sergeant

chief master sergeant of the air force : a noncommissioned officer of the highest enlisted rank in the air force — see RANK table

chief of state : the formal head of a national state as distinguished from the head of the government

chief petty officer *n* **:** a petty officer ranking just below senior chief petty officer and just above petty officer first class

chief point *n* **1 :** MIDDLE CHIEF POINT **2 :** DEXTER CHIEF POINT

chiefs *pl of* CHIEF

chief·tain \'chēftən *also* -tin *sometimes* -ˌtān\ *n* -s [ME *cheftaine*, *chieftaine*, fr. MF *chevetain*, alter. (influenced by MF *chev-*, fr. ML *capi-*, fr. L *caput* head) of OF *chastain*, fr. LL *capitaneus* commander, fr. *capitaneus*, adj., outstanding, fr. L *caput* — more at HEAD] **1 :** CHIEF, RULER **2** *archaic* **:** the leader of a troop or army **:** CAPTAIN **3 :** the leader or headman of a band (as of robbers) or gang (as of thieves) **4 a :** the head of a branch of a Scottish clan; *also* **:** the chief of a Scottish clan **b :** a chief ruling a primitive tribe or people

chief·tain·cy \-tənsē, -tin-, -si\ *n* -ES **1 :** the rank, dignity, office, or rule of a chieftain **2 :** a subdivision of the land in early England ruled over by a chieftain **3 :** CHIEFDOM

chief·tain·ess \-nəs\ *n* -ES **:** a female chieftain

chief·tain·ry \-nrē\ *n* -ES **1 :** the office or territory of a chieftain **2 :** a collective body of chieftains

chief·tain·ship \-nˌship\ *n* -s **:** CHIEFTAINCY

chief·tess \'chēftəs\ *n* -ES [contr. of *chieftainess*] **:** CHIEFESS

chief warrant officer *n* **:** a senior warrant officer in the armed forces

chiel \'chē(ə)l\ *or* **chield** \-l(d)\ *n* -s [ME *cheld*, var. of *child* —more at CHILD] *chiefly Scot* **:** FELLOW, LAD, CHILD

ch'ien lung \chē'en'lüŋ\ *adj, usu cap C&L* [after *Ch'ien Lung* (Kien Lung) †1799 Chinese emperor, fourth of the Ch'ing dynasty] **:** of, relating to, or having the characteristics of Chinese ceramic art or Chinese porcelain wares of the latter half of the 18th century

chieve \'chēv\ *vi* -ED/-ING/-s [ME *cheven*, *chieven* to reach an end, succeed, thrive, fr. OF *chevir* to reach an end, finish, satisfy, come to terms, fr. *chief*, *chef* end, extremity, head — more at CHIEF] *now dial Eng* **:** THRIVE, PROSPER

chiff·chaff \'chifˌchaf\ *n* -s [imit.] **:** a small grayish European warbler (*Phylloscopus collybita*) related to the common willow warbler

chif·fer *also* **chif·fre** \'shifə(r)\ *n* -s [F *chiffre*, fr. It *cifra* figure, fr. ML, zero — more at CIPHER] **:** FIGURE, NUMBER; *specif* **:** a figure in a music score indicating the harmony (as in a figured bass)

[1]**chif·fon** \shi'fän, 'shif,än *sometimes* -ōn\ *n* -s [F, lit., rag, fr. *chiffe* old rag, alter. (influenced by *chiffre* thing of no value, zero) of MF *chipe*, fr. ME *chip* — more at CHIP] **1 :** any of various ornamental additions to a woman's dress (as a knot of ribbons) **2 :** a sheer plain-weave very lightweight clothing fabric made of hard-twisted single yarns of wool, silk, cotton, rayon, or nylon and usu. given a dull soft finish

[2]**chiffon** \"\ *adj* **1 :** like the fabric chiffon in sheerness or softness ⟨~ taffeta⟩ **2** *of pie, cake, or pudding* **:** having a light delicate texture achieved usu. by adding whipped egg whites or whipped gelatin ⟨lemon ~ pie⟩

chif·fo·nade \,shifə'näd, -ād\ *n* -s [F *chiffonnade*, fr. *chiffon* + *-ade*; fr. the shredded vegetables, resembling rags] **:** shredded or finely cut vegetables used in soup or salad dressing

chif·fo·nier *also* **chif·fon·nier** \¦shifə¦ni(ə)r, -iə\ *or* **chef·fo·nier** \¦shef-\ *n* -s [F *chiffonnier*, fr. *chiffon* + *-ier* -er] **1 :** an ornamental cabinet with drawers or shelves; *specif* **:** a high and narrow chest of drawers **2 :** RAGPICKER

chif·fo·robe \'shifə,rōb\ *n* -s [*chiffo*nier + ward*robe*] **:** a combination of wardrobe and chest of drawers

chig·e·tai \'chigə,tī\ *or* **dzeg·ge·tai** \'jeg-\ *n* -s [Mongolian *tchikhitei*, lit., long-eared, fr. *tchikhi* ear] **:** a wild ass of Mongolia being prob. a variety of the kiang

chig·ger \'chigə(r) *also* 'ji-\ *also* **chig·ga** \-gə\ *n* -s [of African origin; akin to Wolof *jiga* insect, Yoruba *ji'ga³* jigger] **1** [influenced in meaning by *chigoe*] **:** CHIGOE 1 **2 :** one of many 6-legged larval mites (family Trombiculidae) that attach themselves to various vertebrates including man to suck blood causing intense itching and local irritation and in some instances serving as vectors of scrub typhus or other infectious diseases — called also *chigoe, harvest mite, jigger, red bug*

chiffonier

chi·gnon \'shēn,yän, ≈'≈ *also* -ōn\ *n* -s [F, alter. (influenced by MF *tignon* chignon, fr. *tigne, teigne* moth, scurf, fr. L *tinea* moth) of MF *chaignon* chain, collar, nape of the neck, fr. (assumed) VL *catenion-, catenio*, fr. L *catena* chain — more at CHAIN] **:** a smooth knot, twist, or arrangement of hair, either natural or artificial that is worn at the back of the head esp. at the nape of the neck

chig·oe \'chig(,)ō, -gə *also* 'chē-\ *also* **che·goe** \'chē-\ *or* **che·gre** \'chēgə(r)\ *n* -s [of Cariban origin; akin to Galibi *chico* chigoe] **1** *also* **chigoe flea :** a flea (*Tunga penetrans*) which is common in the West Indies and So. America and has been introduced into other tropical regions and of which the fertile female burrows under the skin of the foot or other exposed part of the body of man and animals causing great discomfort — called also *chigger* **2** [influenced in meaning by *chigger*] **:** CHIGGER 2

chignon

chi·hua·hua \chə'wä(,)wä, shə-, -'wä(,)wə, - wə\ *n* -s *usu cap* [MexSp, fr. *Chihuahua*, state and city in Mexico] **:** a very small round-headed large-eared short-coated dog (average weight two to six pounds) reputed to antedate Aztec civilization

chihuahua pine *n, usu cap C* [fr. *Chihuahua* state, its locality] **:** a coniferous tree (*Pinus leiophylla chihuahuana*) forming extensive forests chiefly in Mexico and yielding soft durable wood

chi·ka·ra \chə'kärə\ *n* -s [Hindi *cikārā*, fr. Skt *chikkāra*, a kind of antelope, prob. of Dravidian origin; akin to Kannada *cigari, cigare* black antelope] **1** *or* **chin·ka·ra** \chiŋ'-, -in'-\ **:** the common gazelle (*Gazella benettii*) of India **2 :** FOUR-HORNED ANTELOPE

chi·kee \chə'kē; 'chikē, 'chē-\ *or* **chic·kee** \chə'kē, 'chikē\ *n* -s [prob. fr. Creek] **:** a stilt house of the Seminole Indians that is built open on all sides and thatched usu. with palmetto leaves

chil \'chēl\ *n* -s [Panjabi *cīl* pine; akin to Hindi *cīr* pine] **:** CHIR PINE

chil- *or* **chilo-** *also* **cheil-** *or* **cheilo-** *comb form* [NL, fr. Gk *cheil-, cheilo-*, fr. *cheilos* — more at GILL] **:** lip ⟨*Chilopsis*⟩ ⟨*Chilomastix*⟩

chi·la·ca·yo·te *or* **chi·li·co·jo·te** \,chiləkə'yōd·ē\ *n* -s [AmerSp, fr. Nahuatl *tzilakayútli*, perh. fr. *tzilak* smooth + *ayútli* gourd] **1 :** any of several gourds of Mexico and the southwestern U.S. (as *Echinocystis fabacea, E. marah, Cucurbita ficifolia*, and *C. foetidissima*) or their fruits **2 :** the pulp of a chilacayote fruit

chi·lar·i·um \kī'la(a)rēəm\ *n, pl* **chilar·ia** \-ēə\ [NL, fr. *chil-* + *-arium*] **:** one of a pair of anatomical processes between the bases of the last (fourth) pair of walking legs in the king crab

chil·blain \'chil,blān\ *n* -s [[3]*chill* + *blain*] **:** a redness and swelling of toes, fingers, nose, or ears or sometimes cheeks in cold weather accompanied by itching and burning and sometimes followed by cracking of skin and ulceration and believed to be based on a constitutional instability of the local circulation

chilcat *usu cap, var of* CHILKAT

chil·co·tin \chil'kōt·ᵊn\ *n, pl* **chilcotin** *or* **chilcotins** *usu cap* [fr. *Chilcotin* river, British Columbia, Canada] **1 a :** an Athapaskan people in the Chilcotin river valley, British Columbia **b :** a member of such people **2 :** the language of the Chilcotin people

[1]**child** \'chīld, *esp before pause or consonant* -īəld\ *n, pl* **chil·dren** \'childrən, -dərn *also* -dən *sometimes* -ūl-\ [ME, fr. OE *cild*; akin to OSw *kulder* all the children of the same marriage, litter, Goth *kilthei* womb, *inkiltho* pregnant, Skt *jaṭhara* belly, L *galla* gallnut — more at GALL] **1 a :** an unborn or recently born human being **:** FETUS, INFANT, BABY **b** *now dial* **:** a female infant **2 a :** a young person of either sex esp. between infancy and youth ⟨a play for both *children* and adults⟩ ⟨a ~ bride⟩ ⟨these ~ authors —Louis Auchincloss⟩ **b :** one who exhibits the characteristics of a very young person (as innocence or lack of restraint) ⟨she would stay what she was — a placid grownup ~ until she died —Ida A.R.Wylie⟩ ⟨I am a ~ in most matters of practical business —O.W.Holmes †1935⟩ **c :** a person who has not yet come of age — compare AGE 1d(2), AGE OF CONSENT, AGE OF DISCRETION **3** *usu* **childe** \'chī(ə)ld\, *usu cap, archaic* **:** a child or youth wellborn or of noble birth — usu. used as a title esp. in early English ballads and romances ⟨*Childe* Harold⟩ ⟨*Childe* Roland⟩ **4 a :** a son or a daughter **:** a male or female descendant in the first degree **:** the immediate progeny of human parents **b :** an adopted child **c :** any specified direct descendant (as a grandchild) — used esp. in wills **5 :** DESCENDANT **:** a member of the tribe or clan — usu. used in pl. ⟨the *children* of Israel⟩ **6 a :** one who in character or practices shows strong signs of the relationship to or the influence of another (as a disciple of a teacher) ⟨a ~ of God⟩ **b :** one who has been strongly conditioned by a place, a type of action or occupation, or a state of affairs ⟨a ~ of New York⟩ ⟨a ~ of toil⟩ ⟨a ~ of the depression⟩ **7 :** something in a relationship suggesting that of child to parent: as **a :** PRODUCT, RESULT ⟨technical development, the *children* of British brains and ingenuity —Roy Lewis & Angus Maude⟩ ⟨barbed wire . . . is truly a ~ of the plains —W.P.Webb⟩ ⟨Holland is the ~ of its rivers and of the sea —S.L.A.Marshall⟩ **b :** DEPENDENT, SUBSIDIARY ⟨another ~ of both competing outfits was marketing their products in the Middle East and Africa —E.O.Hauser⟩ — **this child** *dial* **:** I, ME — **with child 1 :** PREGNANT ⟨she is *with child*⟩ **2** *obs* **:** EAGER, IMPATIENT

[2]**child** *vb* -ED/-ING/-S [ME *childen*, fr. *child*, n.] *obs* **:** to bear young **:** give birth

[1]**childbearing** \'≈,≈≈\ *n* -s [ME *childbering*, fr. *child* + *bering*, fr. gerund of *beren* to bear — more at BEAR] **:** the act of producing or bringing forth children **:** PARTURITION

[2]**childbearing** \"\ *adj* **:** of, relating to, or suitable for childbearing ⟨the ~ period of life⟩ ⟨women of ~ age⟩

childbed \'≈,≈\ *n* [ME, fr. *child* + *bed*] **:** the condition of a woman in childbirth **:** PARTURITION, LYING-IN ⟨women in ~⟩ ⟨visiting her the first week after her ~ —Samuel Putnam⟩

childbed fever *n* **:** PUERPERAL FEVER

childbirth \'≈,≈\ *n* -s **:** the act of bringing forth a child or offspring **:** LABOR, PARTURITION, TRAVAIL

child-centered \'≈¦≈≈\ *adj* **:** designed to develop the individual and social qualities of a student rather than provide a generalized information or training by way of prescribed subject matter — used of elementary or secondary education or schools ⟨a *child-centered* curriculum⟩ ⟨today, the school is more and more *child-centered* —Kimball Young⟩

childcrowing \'≈,≈≈\ *n* **:** the loud crowing sound made by an infant or child with spasmodic croup

childe *var of* [1]CHILD 3

chil·der \'childə(r)\ *chiefly dial pl of* CHILD

child guidance *n* **1 :** the clinical study and treatment of the personality and behavior problems of esp. maladjusted and delinquent children by a staff of specialists usu. comprising a physician or psychiatrist, a clinical psychologist, and a psychiatric social worker **2 :** the field of study or practice of child guidance or the movement devoted to it

child·hood \'chīld,hůd\ *n* -s [ME *childhod*, fr. OE *cildhād*, fr. *cild* child + *-hād* -hood] **1 :** the period of being a child ⟨a happy ~ but an adulthood fraught with troubles⟩ **2 :** the quality or state of being a child ⟨the ignorance and infirmities of ~ stand in need of restraint and correction — John Locke⟩ ⟨reach manhood without having experienced ~⟩ ⟨experience the bonds of ~ and parental love⟩ **3 :** CHILDREN ⟨a toy designed to appeal to ~⟩ **4 :** the early period in the development of something ⟨there was a ~ of religion as there was a ~ of science —*Times Lit. Supp.*⟩ ⟨industrial hygiene in America had an uneasy ~ —Victor Robinson⟩

child·ing \'chīldiŋ\ *adj* [ME, fr. pres. part. of [2]*child*] **1 :** bearing children or young **:** PREGNANT, PARTURIENT **2 :** PRODUCTIVE, FRUITFUL **3** *of flowers* **:** producing younger or smaller blossoms around an older blossom

childing pink *n* **:** an annual pink (*Dianthus prolifer*) naturalized from Europe with small flowers in terminal bracted heads

child·ish \'chīldish, -ēsh\ *adj* [ME *childishe*, fr. OE *cildisc*, fr. *cild* child + *-isc* -ish] **1 :** of, relating to, befitting, or resembling a child ⟨a ~ simplicity⟩ ⟨I fell sick with some ~ complaint —Corra Harris⟩ ⟨a ~ face⟩ **2 :** marked by immaturity or simplemindedness **:** PUERILE, PETTY ⟨a ~ and spiteful remark⟩ — **child·ish·ly** *adv* — **child·ish·ness** *n* -ES

child labor *n* **:** the employment of a child in a business or industry esp. in violation of state or federal statutes prohibiting the employment of children under a specified age

child·less \'chī(ə)l(d)ləs\ *adj* **:** having no offspring ⟨till he dies ~; and the family will die out with him —J.C.Powys⟩ — **child·less·ness** *n* -ES

[1]**childlike** \'≈,≈\ *adj* [[1]*child* + *-like*] **:** of, relating to, or having the characteristics of a child or childhood; *esp* **:** marked by innocence, trust, frankness, and ingenuousness

[2]**childlike** \"\ *adv* **:** in the manner of a child — **child·like·ness** *n* -ES

child·ly \'chī(ə)l(d)lē\ *adj* -ER/-EST [ME, fr. OE *cildlīc*, fr. *cild* child + *-līc* -ly] **:** CHILDLIKE, CHILDISH 1

childminder \'≈,≈≈\ *n* -s *Brit* **:** BABY-SITTER

child psychiatry *n* **:** psychiatry applied to the treatment of children — compare CHILD PSYCHOLOGY

child psychology *n* **:** the study of the psychological characteristics of infants and children and the application of general psychological principles to infancy and childhood

children *pl of* CHILD

chil·dren·ite \'childrə,nīt\ *n* -s [John George *Children* †1852 Eng. scientist + E *-ite*] **:** a mineral $(Fe,Mn)Al(PO_4)(OH)_2 \cdot 2H_2O$ consisting of a hydrous basic iron aluminum phosphate in translucent pale yellowish to dark brown orthorhombic crystals (hardness 4.5–5, sp. gr. 3.18–3.24)

children of Israel : the Jewish people

children of light [trans. of Gk *huioi ton phōtos*] **1 :** Christians as having received the divine light or being enlightened by it — in allusion to Luke 16: 8 (RSV) **2 :** a name assumed by the early Quakers

children's-bane \'≈≈,≈\ *n* **:** a water hemlock (*Cicuta maculata*)

children's court *n* **:** JUVENILE COURT

children's day *n, usu cap C&D* **:** a special day (usu. the second Sunday in June) observed throughout the world by Protestant churches with exercises for children

childs *pres 3d sing of* CHILD

child's play *n* **1 :** extremely simple work **:** an extremely simple task ⟨nor will it be exactly *child's play* . . . to dispose of 197 ships —*N.Y.Times*⟩ **2 :** an act of small importance ⟨his injury was *child's play* compared with the damage he inflicted⟩

child welfare *n* **:** social work centered upon the welfare of children (as upon improvement in health and home conditions) and upon vocational training

[1]**chile** *var of* CHILI

[2]**chile** \'chilē, -li\ *adj, usu cap* [fr. *Chile*, country in So. America] **:** of or from Chile **:** of the kind or style prevalent in Chile **:** CHILEAN

[1]**chil·ean** *or* **chil·ian** \'chilēən *also* -lyən\ *adj, usu cap* [*Chile*, country in So. America + E *-an* or *-ian*] **1 :** of, relating to, or characteristic of Chile **2 :** of, relating to, or being the subregion of the Neotropical biogeographic region that includes temperate So. America

[2]**chilean** \"\ *n* -s *cap* **:** a native or inhabitant of Chile

chilean bellflower *n, usu cap C* **1 :** CHILE-BELLS **2 :** a prostrate perennial herb (*Nolana atriplicifolia*) of southwestern So. America that is sometimes cultivated for its large bell-shaped flowers which are usu. blue with a yellow and white throat

chilean guava *n, usu cap C* **:** a Chilean shrub (*Myrtus ugni*) bearing an edible berry with a pleasant flavor

chilean jasmine *n, usu cap C* **:** a showy woody vine (*Mandevilla laxa*) of the family Apocynaceae used as an ornamental and having axillary or terminal racemes of white or blush flowers each of which may be two inches across

chilean laurel *n, usu cap C* **:** PERUVIAN NUTMEG

chilean nitrate *n, usu cap C* **:** sodium nitrate from Chile

chilean nut *n, usu cap C* **:** a Chilean shrub (*Guevina heterophylla*) of the family Proteaceae; *also* **:** its coral-red fruit containing an edible seed like the hazelnut — called also *Chile hazel*

chilean strawberry *n, usu cap C* **:** a New World strawberry (*Fragaria chiloensis*) from a variety of which (*F. chiloensis ananassa*) many of the common cultivated strawberries originated — called also *beach strawberry*

chile-bells \'chilē-\ *n pl but sing or pl in constr, usu cap C* **:** a showy Chilean twining vine (*Lapageria rosea*) that is related to the smilax, has leathery alternate leaves, and produces deep rosy red trumpet-shaped blossoms followed by oval edible yellowish fruits

chile bonito *also* **chilean bonito** *n, usu cap C* **:** a common bonito (*Sarda chiliensis*) of the Pacific coast of the Americas being metallic blue above and silvery below with dark oily flesh that cans esp. well — compare ATLANTIC BONITO

chilectropion *var of* CHEILECTROPION

chile hazel *n, usu cap C* **:** CHILEAN NUT

chile mill *or* **chilean mill** *n, usu cap C* **:** a machine for crushing substances (as ore) by means of heavy rollers moving in a circle

chile nettle *n, usu cap C* **:** a plant of the family Loasaceae

[1]**chi·le·no** \chə'lā(,)nō, -ān(,)yō\ *n* -s *cap* [Sp, adj. & n., fr. *Chile*] **:** a native or inhabitant of Chile

[2]**chileno** \"\ *n* -s *often cap* [MexSp, fr. Sp, adj., of Chile] **:** a severe curb bit with the curb strap replaced by a metal ring

chile pine *or* **chilean pine** *n, usu cap C* **:** MONKEY PUZZLE

chile saltpeter *also* **chile niter** *n, usu cap C* **:** sodium nitrate esp. occurring naturally (as in caliche)

chili *or* **chile** *or* **chil·li** \'chilē, -li\ *n, pl* **chilies** *or* **chiles** *or* **chillies** [Sp *chile*, fr. Nahuatl *chilli*] **1 a :** HOT PEPPER 1; *esp* **:** LONG PEPPER 2b **b** *usu* **chilli**, *chiefly Brit* **:** a pepper whether hot or sweet **2 :** HOT PEPPER 2 **3 a :** a thick sauce made principally of meat and chilies **b :** CHILI CON CARNE **4 :** a moderate reddish orange that is yellower and duller than flamingo and duller and very slightly yellower than crab apple **5 :** a hot dry southerly wind in Tunisia

-chilia — see -CHEILIA

chil·i·ad \'kilē,ad\ *n* -s [LL *chiliad-, chilias*, fr. Gk *chilias*, fr. *chilioi* thousand; akin to Skt *sahasra* thousand, and perh. L *mille* — more at MILE] **1 :** a group of 1000 ⟨a ~ of errors⟩ ⟨~*s* of years⟩ **2 :** a period of 1000 years **:** MILLENNIUM

chil·i·ad·al \¦≈≈¦ad'l\ *also* **chil·i·ad·ic** \-dik\ *adj* **:** of or relating to a chiliad

chilian *usu cap, var of* CHILEAN

chil·i·arch \'kilē,ärk\ *n* -s [Gk *chiliarchēs, chiliarchos*, fr. *chilioi* thousand + *-archēs, -archos* -arch] **:** the commander of a thousand men in ancient Greece

chil·i·asm \-azəm\ *n* -s [NL *chiliasmus*, fr. LL *chiliastes* chiliast (after such pairs as Gk *enthousiastēs* enthusiast: *enthousiasmos* enthusiasm), fr. (*assumed*) Gk *chiliastēs*, fr. *chilioi* thousand] **:** the theological doctrine that Christ will come to earth in a visible form and set up a theocratic kingdom over all the world and thus usher in the millennium

chil·i·ast \-,ast\ *n* -s [LL *chiliastes*] **:** one that believes in chiliasm **:** MILLENARIAN

chil·i·as·tic \¦≈≈¦astik\ *adj* **:** MILLENARIAN — **chil·i·as·ti·cal·ly** \-tək(ə)lē\ *adv*

chilicojote *var of* CHILACAYOTE

chili con car·ne \¦chilē¦kän'kärnē, -li|, |kən-, -'kän-, -ni\ *n* [Sp *chile con carne* chili with meat] **:** a highly spiced stew of chopped or ground beef and minced chilies or chili powder and usu. served with beans

chil·i·co·the \,chilə'kōthē\ *n* -s [modif. of MexSp *chilicote*] **:** a Californian herbaceous vine (*Echinocystis macrocarpa*) of the family Cucurbitaceae having ball-like prickly fruit

chi·lid·i·al \kī'lidēəl\ *adj* [NL *chilidium* + E *-al*] **:** of or relating to a chilidium

chi·lid·i·um \-ēəm\ *n* -s [NL, fr. *chil-* + *-idium*] **:** the convex plate that covers the cardinal process of the dorsal valve of certain brachiopods

chil·i·pep·per \'chilē¦pepə(r)\ *n* [so called fr. its color] **:** a common rockfish (*Sebastodes goodei*), brick-red above and pink below, that is a well-known market fish of the California coast

chili pepper *n* [*chili* + *pepper*] **:** CHILI

chili powder *n* **:** a condiment made of chilies ground to a powder

chili sauce *n* **:** a condiment sauce consisting of pureed tomatoes, seasonings, and spices orig. made with chilies but now usu. prepared with red and green sweet peppers

chilitis *var of* CHEILITIS

chili vinegar *n* **:** PEPPER SAUCE

chil·kat *or* **chil·cat** \'chil,kat\ *n, pl* **chilkat** *or* **chilkats** *or* **chilcat** *or* **chilcats** *usu cap* [prob. fr. Tlingit *tcil-xāt*, lit., storehouses for salmon] **1 :** a Tlingit people of southeastern Alaska **2 :** a member of the Chilkat people

[1]**chill** \'chil\ *vb* -ED/-ING/-S [ME *chillen, chilen*, fr. *chile, chele* cold (n.), frost, fr. OE *cele, ciele*; akin to OE *ceald, cald* cold (adj.) — more at COLD] *vi* **1 a :** to grow or become cold or chill often rapidly ⟨as the hot mixture ~*s*, it begins to thicken⟩ **b :** to shiver or quake with cold or as if with cold ⟨wake up in the morning alternately sweating and ~*ing* in an emotional seizure —R.E.McGill⟩ **2 :** to become taken with a chill (sense 1a) **:** have a chill **3** *of a metal* **:** to become surface-hardened by sudden cooling while solidifying ~ *vt* **1 a :** to make cold or chilly ⟨the cold wind from the north ~*ed* the day⟩ ⟨the water ~*ed* the swimmer to the marrow⟩ **b :** to treat (as a food or beverage) by cooling ⟨~ the wine before serving⟩ **c :** to refrigerate (as food) without freezing **2 :** to affect as if with cold **:** CHECK ⟨was forced to ~ his enthusiasm⟩ **:** DAMPEN, DEPRESS, DISCOURAGE, DISPIRIT ⟨rain ~*ed* the glittering pageant —Bill Sumner⟩ **3 :** to cool (metal) suddenly at the surface so as to effect a change in solidification that often increases the hardness **4 :** to produce a dull or clouded appearance upon (a varnished surface) by cold **:** [3]BLOOM *vt* 2 **5** *dial Eng* **:** to take the chill off (a liquid)

[2]**chill** \"\ *adj, usu* -ER/-EST **1 a :** moderately but unpleasantly cold ⟨a ~ night⟩ **b :** COLD, RAW ⟨a ~ wind⟩ **2 :** affected by a penetrating cold **:** benumbed or shivering with cold **:** CHILLED ⟨~ travelers⟩ **3 :** cool in manner or feeling **:** lacking warmth **:** DISTANT, FORMAL, UNFRIENDLY ⟨a ~ reception⟩ **4 :** DISCOURAGING, DEPRESSING, DISPIRITING ⟨~ penury —Thomas Gray⟩

[3]**chill** \"\ *n* -s [[1]*chill*] **1 a :** a sensation of cold attended with shivering or convulsive shaking of the body due to a disturbance of the temperature-regulating mechanism of the body resulting from exposure to cold, from infection accompanied by fever, or from a reaction to adverse nervous stimuli ⟨nervous ~⟩ **b :** a disagreeable sensation of coldness ⟨feel a ~ in both hands and feet⟩ ⟨she felt the ~ of fear —E.T.Thurston⟩ **c** *chiefly Brit* **:** a usu. respiratory illness resulting esp. from exposure to cold or damp ⟨he caught a ~ from sitting in a draft⟩ ⟨take a ~⟩ **2 a :** a degree of cold that would induce shivering in a lightly dressed person ⟨an autumn ~ in the air⟩ **b :** a cold atmospheric condition ⟨the ~ of the night⟩ **3 :** a check to enthusiasm or warmth of feeling **:** an atmosphere of discouragement **:** a depressing influence or effect upon the feelings or spirit ⟨a ~ spread over the group at the sad news⟩ ⟨a ~ in his attitude toward opponents⟩ **4 a :** a metal mold or portion of a mold serving to cool rapidly and often to harden the surface of molten metal brought in contact with it **b :** the hardened part of a casting (as the tread of a car wheel) **5 :** a jointed steel bar that actuates the platen in some hand printing presses

[4]**chill** \,chəl\ [contr. of ME *ich wille* I will] *now dial* **:** I will

chil·la·gite \'chilə,gīt\ *n* -s [*Chillagoe*, Queensland, Australia, + E *-ite*] **:** a mineral consisting of a tungstic wulfenite

chill-cast \'≈¦≈\ *adj, of a metal or alloy* **:** cast with a chill (sense 4a) — **chill casting** *n*

chilled iron *n* **:** chilled cast iron — compare CAST IRON

chilled shot *n* **:** lead shot that has an antimony content of 3 to 6 percent

chill·er \'chilə(r)\ *n* -s [[1]*chill* + *-er*] **1 :** an eerie or frightening story of murder, violence, or the supernatural **2 :** a refrigerator compartment for chilling foods **3 :** an apparatus used in petroleum refineries to remove wax from paraffin distillates by chilling **4 :** a coolerman in a meat-packing establishment

chilli *var of* CHILI

chill·i·ly \'chiləlē, -li\ *adv* **:** CHILLY

chill·i·ness \'chilēnəs, -in-\ *n* -ES [[1]*chilly* + *-ness*] **:** the quality or state of being chilly

chillingly *adv* **:** in a chilling manner

chill mold *n* **:** CHILL 4a

chill·ness \-lnəs\ *n* -ES **:** CHILLINESS

chill plow *or* **chilled plow** *n* **:** a plow having the share and moldboard of chilled semisteel or cast iron

chillproof \'≈¦≈\ *vt* [[3]*chill* + *proof*] **:** to treat (beer) so as to prevent the development of turbidity on exposure to cold — **chillproofing** \'≈¦≈≈\ *n*

chillroom \'≈,≈\ *n* [[1]*chill* + *room*] **:** a room for refrigeration usu. at temperatures above freezing

chills and fever *n* **:** MALARIA 2

chill·some \'chilsəm\ *adj* **:** CHILLY, COLD ⟨a ~ November⟩

chil·lum \'chiləm\ *n* -s [Hindi *cilam*, fr. Per *chilam*] **:** the part of a hookah containing the tobacco or the charge of tobacco used in it ⟨it was the bitterest ~ I ever smoked —W.M.Thackeray⟩

chil·lum·chee \-,chē\ *n* -s [Hindi *cilamcī*, fr. Per *chilamchī*] *India* **:** a metal wash basin

[1]**chilly** \'chilē, -li\ *adj, usu* -ER/-EST [[2]*chill* + *-y*] **1 a :** noticeably cold **:** cold enough to chill **:** CHILLING ⟨~ weather⟩ ⟨a ~ drink⟩ **b :** CHILL 1 ⟨a ~ wind, cold, damp, and miserable⟩ **2 :** unpleasantly affected by cold ⟨in the thin coat the boy was manifestly ~⟩ **3 :** having a tendency to chill: as **a :** lacking humanly warm qualities, esp. warmth of feeling ⟨a . . . model of . . . ~ virtues —John Buchan⟩ ⟨a female figure in marble — a ~ but ideal medium for depicting abstract virtues —C.W. Cunnington⟩ ⟨a ~ personality⟩ ⟨a ~ laugh⟩ **b :** UNFRIENDLY ⟨a ~ reception⟩ **c :** coldly critical ⟨a calm and ~ mind —G.N. Shuster⟩ **4 :** having a tendency to arouse fear or apprehension ⟨a giggling, degenerate handyman . . . a ~ thing to watch —Wolcott Gibbs⟩ ⟨this study of a mind for which reality has . . . ceased to exist is a nice ~ piece of work —*New Yorker*⟩

[2]**chil·ly** \'chil(l)ē, -l(l)i\ *adv* **:** in a chilly manner ⟨the whole landscape of Asia to which I had hitherto been so ~ indifferent —Edmond Taylor⟩

chill zone *n* **:** a border zone in intrusive igneous rocks that are fine-grained because of rapid cooling

chi·lo \'kī(,)lō\ *n, cap* [NL, fr. L *Chilo*, a nickname, lit., having large lips, prob. modif. of Gk *cheilos* lip] **:** a genus of small slender dull colored nocturnal moths (family Pyralididae) the larvae of which are borers in cereals and other grasses

chilo- — see CHIL-

chi·lo·don \'kīlə,dän\ *n* [NL, fr. *chil-* + *-odon*] *syn of* CHILODONELLA

chi·lo·do·nel·la \,kīlədə'nelə\ *n, cap* [NL, fr. *Chilodon* + *-ella*] **:** a large genus of freshwater or brackish water holotrichous ciliates that are ovoid and dorsoventrally flattened and that include a number of ectoparasites some of which are destructive pests of the skin and gills of cyprinoid fishes

chi·log·nath \'kīlăg,nath\ *n* -s [NL *Chilognatha*] **:** one of the Chilognatha

¹chi·log·na·tha \kī'lägnəthə\ *n pl, cap* [NL, fr. *chil-* + *-gnatha*] **:** a subclass of Diplopoda that includes the typical millipedes with chitinous exoskeleton reinforced with calcareous deposits — compare PSELAPHOGNATHA — **chi·log·na·than** \(')≠;≠≠thən\ *adj or n* — **chi·log·na·thous** \(')≠;≠≠thəs\ *adj*

²chilognatha \"\ [NL, fr. *chil-* + *-gnatha*] *syn of* DIPLOPODA

chi·lo·mas·tix \,kīlō'mastiks\ *n, cap* [NL, fr. *chil-* + *-mastix*] **:** a genus (often made the type of the family Chilomastigidae) of small pear-shaped 4-flagellated protozoans (order Polymastigina) commensal in the intestines of various vertebrates including man

chi·lom·o·nad \kī'lämə,nad\ *n* -s [NL *Chilomonad-, Chilomonas*] **:** a flagellate of the genus *Chilomonas*

chi·lom·o·nas \kī'lämənəs\ *n, cap* [NL, fr. *chil-* + *-monas*] **:** genus of small colorless freshwater plantlike flagellates (family Cryptomonadidae) with two anterior flagella and without pyrenoids that have been much used in biological research

chi·lop·la·cus \kī'läpləkəs\ *n, cap* [NL, fr. *chil-* + *-placus* (fr. Gk *plak-, plax* anything flat and broad) — more at PLEASE] **:** a genus of usu. saprophagous soil-dwelling nematode worms (family Cephalobidae) sometimes associated with root blindness of seedling plants and with failure of cuttings to root

chi·lo·pod \'kīlə,päd\ *n* -s [NL *Chilopoda*] **:** one of the Chilopoda **:** CENTIPEDE

chi·lop·o·da \kī'läpədə\ *n pl, cap* [NL, fr. *chil-* + *-poda*; fr. their foot jaws] **:** a class of arthropods comprising the centipedes — **chi·lop·o·dan** \(')≠;≠≠dən,-dᵊn\ *adj or n* — **chi·lop·o·dous** \-dəs\ *adj*

chi·los·to·ma \kī'lästəmə\ *or* **chi·lo·sto·ma·ta** \,kīlə'stōmədə\ [NL, fr. *chil-* + *-stoma, -stomata*] *syn of* CHEILOSTOMATA

chilostomatous *var of* CHEILOSTOMATOUS

chi·lo·stome \'kīlə,stōm\ *n* -s [NL *Chilostoma*] **:** a bryozoan of the suborder Cheilostomata

chil·te \'chiltē\ *n* -s [MexSp] **:** a bushlike Mexican tree (*Jatropha tepiquensis*) of the spurge family yielding a latex and also a chicle used as a chewing-gum base

chil·tern \'chiltə(r)n\ *adj, usu cap* [fr. *Chiltern* hills, range of chalk hills in south-central England] **:** of, relating to, or being chalky, sandy, gravelly, and loamy soils of England that are naturally dry and lie in dry situations

chil·u·la \'chilələ,lä\ *n, pl* **chilula** *or* **chilulas** *usu cap* [modif. of Yurok *Tsulu-la*, lit., people of the Bald hills] **1 a :** an Athapaskan people of northwestern California **b :** a member of such people **2 :** a dialect of Hupa spoken by the Chilula people

chil·ver \'chilvə(r)\ *n* -s [fr. (assumed) ME, fr. OE *cilforlamb*; akin to OHG *kilbur, kilburra* ewe lamb, OE *cealf* calf — more at CALF] *now dial Eng* **:** a ewe lamb

¹chimaera *var of* CHIMERA

²chi·mae·ra \kī'mirə, -mē- *also* kə-\ *n* [NL, fr. L] **1** *cap* **:** a widely distributed genus (type of the family Chimaeridae) of marine elasmobranch fishes that sometimes includes all holocephalans with a blunt snout and a prolonged or threadlike tail but is now usu. restricted to forms having also a true anal fin **2** -s **:** any fish of the family Chimaeridae

chi·mae·rae \-ir(,)ē, -ē(,)rē\ *n pl, cap* [NL, fr. pl. of *Chimaera*] **:** an order of marine elasmobranch fishes comprising the chimaeras and extinct related forms and being coextensive with the subclass Holocephali — see CHIMAERIDAE

chi·mae·ri·dae \-mirə,dē, -mer-\ *n pl, cap* [NL, fr. *Chimaera*, type genus + *-idae*] **:** a family of Holocephali that includes the chimaeras and with extinct related forms constitutes the order Chimaerae

¹chi·mae·roid \-mir,ȯid, -mē,rȯid\ *adj* [NL *chimaera* + E *-oid*] **:** of, relating to, or like a chimaera

²chimaeroid \"\ *n* -s **:** a fish of the subclass Holocephali

chi·mae·roi·dei \,kīmə'rȯidē,ī\ [NL, fr. *Chimaera* + *-oidei*] *syn of* CHIMAERAE

chimakuan *usu cap, var of* CHEMAKUAN

chimakum *usu cap, var of* CHEMAKUM

chi·man \chə'män\ *n, pl* **chima·nes** \-ä(')näs\ [AmerSp *chimán*, fr. Mam] **:** a shaman-priest of the Mam Indians whose function is to mediate between man and the supernatural through prayers, soothsaying, and divination

chi·maph·i·la \kī'mafələ\ *n, cap* [NL, fr. Gk *cheima* winter + NL *-phila*; akin to Gk *cheimōn* winter — more at HIBERNATE] **:** a small genus of herbs (family Pyrolaceae) having long creeping subterranean shoots, thick shining leaves, and white or pinkish flowers in terminal clusters — see PIPSISSEWA

chim·a·ri·kan \,chimə'rēkən\ *n* -s *usu cap* [*Chimariko* + *-an*] **:** a language family of the Hokan stock in California comprising the Chimariko language

chim·a·ri·ko \-(,)kō\ *n, pl* **chimariko** *or* **chimarikos** *usu cap* [modif. of Chimariko *Djimaliko*, fr. *djimar* man] **1 a :** an extinct Indian people of the Trinity river valley, California **b :** a member of such people **2 :** a Chimarikan language of the Chimariko people

chim·ar·rog·a·le \,kimə'rägə(,)lē\ *n* [NL, fr. *chimarro-* (fr. Gk *cheimarrhos* torrent, fr. *cheimarrhos*, adj., winter-flowing, fr. *cheima* winter + *-rhos*, fr. *rhein* to flow) + Gk *galē* weasel; akin to Skt *giri, girikā* mouse — more at HIBERNATE, STREAM] **1** *cap* **:** a genus of Asiatic water shrews **2** -s **:** any shrew of the genus *Chimarrogale*

chim·bly \'chim(b)lē, -li\ *dial var of* CHIMNEY

¹chime \'chīm\ *n* -s [ME *chime, chimbe* cymbal, fr. OF *chimbe, cymbe*, fr. L *cymbalum* — more at CYMBAL] **1 :** a mechanical or electrical apparatus for chiming a bell or set of bells ⟨wind a clock ~⟩; *specif* **:** an electrically operated chime used in place of a doorbell **2 a :** a set of bells tuned in a scale and capable of playing melody but not properly harmony — compare CARILLON **b :** one of a set of objects giving a bell-like sound when struck — usu. used in pl. ⟨stone ~s⟩ ⟨gong ~s⟩ ⟨organ ~s⟩ **c :** BELL 6a **3 a :** the sound of a set of bells — usu. used in pl. ⟨we have heard the ~s at midnight —Shak.⟩ **b :** a musical sound resembling or suggesting that of bells **c :** a sequence of musical or harmonious sounds **4 :** order and proportion **:** ACCORD, HARMONY ⟨nature's ~⟩ ⟨each keeping ~ with the other⟩

chime 2b

²chime \"\ *vb* -ED/-ING/-S [ME *chimen, chimben* to resound when struck, to produce a ringing sound, fr. *chime, chimbe* cymbal] *vi* **1 a :** to make a musical esp. harmonious sound (as of a bell) ⟨the bells in the bell tower *chimed* throughout the day⟩ ⟨words ~ and ring in her ears —Virginia Woolf⟩ ⟨some could harmonize . . . and some could barely carry a tune, but they all *chimed* together —Marcia Davenport⟩ **b :** to make the sounds of a chime ⟨the doorbell *chimed* twice⟩ **2 :** to be or act in harmonious accord ⟨the music and the mood *chimed* well together⟩ — usu. used with *with* ⟨the swan singing before death . . . ~s so perfectly with Yeats's conception of pride —D.A.Stauffer⟩ **3 :** to call by means of bells or chimes ⟨churches and chapels that ~ to services all day —J.P. O'Donnell⟩ ~ *vt* **1 a :** to strike (as a bell or set of bells) so as to produce a musical sound or a chime ⟨a device to ~ bells for morning service⟩; *specif* **:** to sound (a bell) by striking from the outside or by swinging only a bell clapper or by describing only a small arc in sounding — distinguished from *ring* and *peal* **b :** to cause to sound or chime esp. harmoniously in this way ⟨he ~s one note against another —Virginia Woolf⟩ **2 :** to produce by chiming **:** give forth (as sound or music) in chimes ⟨a church bell tower *chiming* hymns⟩ **3 :** to indicate (an hour of the day) by chiming ⟨a clock *chiming* midnight⟩ **4 :** to call or bring to a place or condition by chiming ⟨bells *chiming* a congregation to church⟩ ⟨the soft sounds of the distant city *chimed* her to sleep⟩ **5 :** to utter repetitively or mechanically **:** DIN 2 ⟨~ the same phrases over and over⟩ ⟨~ a foolish slogan into our ears⟩

³chime \'chīm\ *or* **chine** \'chīn\ *also* **chimb** \'chīm\ *n* -s [ME *chimbe*, fr. OE *cimb-* (in *cimbstān* base of a pillar); akin to MD *kimme* edge of a cask, MLG, outer edge, horizon, OE *camb* comb — more at COMB] **1 a :** the portion of the staves of a cask that extend from the croze to the rim **b :** the rim of a cask or of any casklike container **2 :** the chamfer on the rim of a cask or on a single cask stave

⁴chime \"\ *vt* -ED/-ING/-S **:** to chamfer the ends of the staves to form the chime of (a cask)

chime clock *n* [¹*chime*] **:** a clock that indicates the half and quarter hours by playing short melodies on bells or gongs in addition to striking the hours

chime in *vb* [²*chime*] *vi* **1 a :** to join in (as in singing) ⟨the audience *chimed in* on the chorus⟩ ⟨the shrill of grasshoppers *chiming in* with the monotonous hum of the auctioneer's voice —Ellen Glasgow⟩ **b :** to join in in expression of unanimity or agreement ⟨dealers denounced the stricter installment regulations . . . and certain labor unions *chimed in* for fear of a drop in employment —John Harriman⟩ **2 :** to be consistent or harmonious — used with *with* ⟨asserted that deep feeling *chimed in* with Christian morals and religion —Roy Pascal⟩ ⟨the artist's illustrations *chime in* perfectly with the text —*Book Production*⟩ **3 :** to break into the conversation or discussion to express oneself ⟨critics *chiming in* every few minutes⟩ ~ *vt* **:** to remark while chiming in ⟨"but he was busy," *chimed in* Miss Parton —Dorothy Sayers⟩

chime maul *n* [³*chime*] **:** a hammer or mallet designed esp. for driving head hoops on casks

chi·me·ra *or* **chi·mae·ra** \kī'mirə, -mē- *also* kə-\ *n* -s [L *chimaera*, fr. Gk *chimaira* chimera, she-goat; akin to ON *gymbr* yearling ewe, L *bimus* two years (winters) old, *hiems* winter — more at HIBERNATE] **1 a** *usu cap* **:** a she-monster in Greek mythology represented as vomiting flames and usu. as having a lion's head, goat's body, and dragon's or serpent's tail or a lion's body and head together with a goat's head rising from the back — compare GRYLLUS **b :** a similar imaginary monster; *specif* **:** a grotesque animal form in painting or sculpture compounded from parts of different real or imaginary animals **c :** a horrible or frightening manifestation **d :** an often fantastic combination of incongruous parts, esp. a fabrication **2 :** an illusion or fabrication of the mind or fancy ⟨that unintelligible ~—substance —Frank Thilly⟩; *esp* **:** a utopian or unrealizable dream or aim ⟨concluded that the democratic hope of rational policy . . . was a ~ —C.B. Forcey⟩ ⟨universal justice and equality . . . were ~s one could chase for generations and never capture —Victor Canning⟩ **3 :** an individual, organ, or part consisting of tissues of diverse genetic constitution occurring esp. in plants and most frequently at a graft union, the tissues from both stock and cion retaining their distinctness in the chimera — see MERICLINAL, PERICLINAL, SECTORIAL

¹chi·mere \shə'mi(ə)r, chə-, -miə\ *also* **chim·er** \'chimə(r), 'sh-\ *n* -s [ME *chimmer, chemer*, prob. fr. ML *chimera*] **:** a loose sleeveless robe often with balloon sleeves of lawn attached worn by some bishops of the Anglican communion

²chi·mere \kī'mi(ə)r, kə-, -iə\ *n* -s [ME, fr. MF, fr. L *chimaera*] **:** CHIMERA

chi·mer·i·cal \kī'merəkəl, -rēk- *also* kə- *or* -mir-\ *or* **chi·mer·ic** \-rik, -ēk\ *or* **chi·me·ral** \-mirəl, -mē-\ *adj* [*chimera* + *-ic, -ical* or *-al*] **1 :** being, relating to, or like a chimera; *esp* **:** unreal and existing only as the product of wild unrestrained imagination ⟨his Utopia is not a ~ commonwealth but a practicable improvement on what already exists —Douglas Bush⟩ **2 :** inclined to or indicative of unrestrained imagination **:** UNREALISTIC ⟨~ to demand that a government . . . should exercise the art of governing purely for its own sake —George Santayana⟩ **3** *usu chimeral or chimeric* **:** of, relating to, or being a chimera ⟨a *chimeric* tetraploid⟩ ⟨the *chimeral* nature of some ornamental plants⟩ **syn** see IMAGINARY

chimesmaster \'≠,≠\ *n* **:** the chief performer on a chime of bells, esp. tower bells

chim·ic *or* **chim·ick** \'kimik\ *archaic var of* CHEMIC

chi·mi·la \chə'mēlə\ *n, pl* **chimila** *or* **chimilas** *usu cap* [Sp, of AmerInd origin] **1 a :** an Indian people of Colombia classified by some Americanists as Chibchan and by others as Arawakan **b :** a member of such people **2 :** the language of the Chimila people

chiming bell *n* [so called fr. its bell-shaped flowers] **:** a plant of the genus *Mertensia*

chim·ist \'kiməst\ *archaic var of* CHEMIST

chim·la \'chim(,)lä\ *or* **chim·ley** \-,lē\ *dial var of* CHIMNEY

chimley lug *n, chiefly Scot* **:** CHIMNEY CORNER

chimley neuck *or* **chimley nuik** \-;nyük\ *n* [Sc *neuck, nuick*, var. of *nook*] *Scot* **:** CHIMNEY CORNER

chimmesyan *usu cap, var of* TSIMSHIAN

¹chim·ney \'chimnē, -ni\ *n* -s *often attrib* [ME, fr. MF *cheminée*, fr. LL *caminata*, fr. L *caminus* furnace, fireplace, fr. Gk *kaminos*; akin to Gk *kamara* vault — more at CHAMBER] **1** *dial* **:** FIREPLACE, HEARTH — compare CHIMNEY CORNER **2 a :** a vertical structure incorporated into a building and enclosing a flue or flues that carry off smoke or other undesirable fumes or gases; *esp* **:** the part of such a structure extending above a roof — compare CHIMNEY BREAST **b :** a pipelike more or less vertical natural vent or opening in the earth: (1) **:** the conduit of a volcano (2) **:** a passage or shaft in the roof or floor of a cave (3) **:** a moulin of small diameter **c :** a columnar geological erosion feature that is smaller than a stack on a wave-cut platform **3** *Brit* **:** the smokestack of a locomotive **4 a :** a tube usu. of glass and usu. shaped placed around a flame (as of a lamp) to serve as a shield and to create a draft and promote combustion **b :** a glass shield made to resemble or resembling such a tube and enclosing an electric light **5 :** a steep and very narrow cleft or gully in the face of a cliff or mountain **6 :** a small tube through the top of a stopped metal pipe of an organ permitting air to escape to sharpen the pitch **7 :** a vertical or steeply inclined shoot of roughly columnar shape in a body of ore

chimney 4a

²chimney \"\ *vt* -ED/-ING/-S **:** to climb (a chimney) in mountaineering by the use of body pressure against the sides

chimney back *n* **:** the back or the backing of a fireplace

chimney bar *n* **:** a bar to support the masonry above a fireplace

chimney bellflower *n* **:** CHIMNEY PLANT

chimney block *n* **:** a concrete block made to form a continuous round flue when a number of such blocks are placed in position one on top of another

chimney breast *n* **1 :** the projection of a chimney from a wall into a room **2 :** an ornamental casing (as paneling) that surrounds or covers a chimney breast over and around a fireplace opening **:** CHIMNEYPIECE

chimney cap *n* **:** a cap or cover for a chimney; *specif* **:** a device fitted to the top of a chimney to improve the draft by presenting an exit aperture to leeward

chimney cloth *n* **:** a valance hung around the mantel of a fireplace for decoration or to impede smoke

chimney-corner \'≠≠,≠≠\ *adj* **:** such as might be devised by one sitting idly in a chimney corner ⟨a *chimney-corner* legend⟩ ⟨*chimney-corner* law⟩ ⟨*chimney-corner* philosophy⟩

chimney corner *n* **1 a :** the area to the side of a large open fireplace **b :** FIRESIDE **2 :** the settle or bench often formerly occupying the chimney corner

chimney flute *n* [prob. trans. of F *flûte à cheminé*] **:** ROHRFLÖTE

chimney glass *n* **:** a mirror placed over a chimney piece

chimneyhead \'≠≠,≠\ *n* **:** the upper end of a chimney

chimney hood *n* **:** an ornamental or protective covering over a chimneyhead

chimney hook *n* **:** a hook attached to the inside, back, or side walls of a fireplace for holding pots and kettles over a fire or one esp. in the side wall for holding implements (as fire tongs)

chim·ney·less \'≠≠ləs\ *adj* **:** lacking a chimney

chimney money *n* **:** HEARTH MONEY

chimneypiece \'≠≠,≠\ *n* **1** *obs* **:** a picture or piece of tapestry hung as an ornament over a fireplace **2 a :** an ornamental construction above and around a fireplace opening embracing the mantel and the ornament or casing of the chimney breast **b :** MANTEL 2

chimney pink *n* **:** SOAPWORT

chimney plant *n* [so called fr. its use as a fireplace ornament] **:** a bellflower (*Campanula pyramidalis*) of southeastern Europe cultivated in gardens

chimney pot *n* **:** a cylindrical or prismoidal pipe of earthenware or metal placed at the top of a chimney to increase the draft and carry off the smoke

chimney red *n* **:** a moderate to deep red that is yellower than cadmium purple or burnt carmine

chimney rock *n* **1 :** a column of rock rising above its surroundings or isolated on the face of a slope **2 :** a porous phosphate rock that hardens on exposure to the air and is used esp. in construction of chimneys

chimney shelf *n, dial* **:** a mantel shelf

chimney stack *n* **1 :** a number of flues embodied in one chimney; *esp* **:** the part of a multiple-flue chimney rising above a roof **2 :** a chimney shaft containing only one flue

chimney stalk *Brit var of* CHIMNEY STACK

chimney swallow *n* **1 :** CHIMNEY SWIFT **2 :** the European barn swallow

chimney sweep *or* **chimney sweeper** *n* **1 :** one whose occupation is the removal of soot by means of scraper, brushes, or vacuum cleaner from the flues of a chimney and from pipes connecting with a furnace **2** *dial* **:** CHIMNEY SWIFT

chimney swift *n* **:** a small sooty-gray American swift (*Chaetura pelagica*) commonly called a swallow and noted for its habit of attaching its nest inside of a chimney

chimney tax *n* **:** HEARTH MONEY

chimney throat *n* **:** a part of a chimney immediately above the fireplace where the walls of the flue are gathered or brought close together to increase the draft

chimney top *n* **1 :** the upper part of a chimney: **a :** the part of a chimney extending above a roof **b :** CHIMNEY POT **2 :** CHIMNEY 6

chi·mo·nan·thus \,kīmə'nan(t)thəs\ *n* [NL, fr. Gk *cheimōn* winter + NL *-anthus* — more at HIBERNATE] **1** *cap* **:** a genus of evergreen or deciduous Asiatic shrubs (family Calycanthaceae) often included in the genus *Calycanthus* but having scaly buds and yellow flowers with five or six stamens **2** -s **:** any plant of the genus *Chimonanthus*; *esp* **:** JAPAN ALLSPICE

chi·mo·pelagic \;kīmō+\ *adj* [*chim-* (fr. Gk. *cheima*, *cheimōn* winter) + *-o-* + *pelagic*] **:** being or belonging to marine organisms living in the depths of the sea except in winter when they rise to the surface

chimp \'chimp, 'sh-\ *n* -s [by shortening] **:** CHIMPANZEE

chim·pan·zee \,chim,pan,zē, shim-; chim'panzē, shim-, -zi; -paan-; *also* chim'pənˌzē *or* ;shimpən-*sometimes* '≠(,)≠,zē *or* '≠(,)≠,zi *or* (*prob by dissimilation of nasals*) chə'panzē *or* shə- *or* -zi\ *n* -s [Kongo dial. *chimpenzi, kimpenzi*] **:** an anthropoid ape (*Pan troglodytes* syn. *Anthropopithecus troglodytes* or *Simia satyrus*) of the equatorial forests of Africa that rarely stands erect, habitually uses its arms in walking, rests on the knuckles, and that is smaller and more arboreal in habit than the gorilla, less fierce, being easily tamed when taken young, and having a rounder head with large ears

chimpanzee

chim·pan·zoid \'chim,pan,zȯid, 'shim-; chim'p-,shim'p-; -aan-; 'chimpən-, 'shimpən-\ *adj* [ISV *chimpanzee* + *-oid*] **:** belonging to or resembling a chimpanzee

¹chi·mu \chē'mü\ *n, pl* **chimu** *or* **chimus** *usu cap* [Sp *chimú*, of AmerInd origin] **1 a :** an extinct Yuncan people of the northwest coast of Peru **b :** a member of such people **2 :** the language of the Chimu people — compare YUNCA

²chimu \"\ *adj, usu cap* **:** of or relating to a pre-Inca Peruvian culture characterized by the construction of large cities and by white and red pottery portrait vases and metalworking

chi·myl alcohol \'kīməl-\ *n* [NL *Chimaera* + E *-yl*] **:** a crystalline alcohol $C_{16}H_{33}OCH_2CH(OH)CH_2OH$ obtained esp. from shark-liver oil and other fish-liver oils and from the yellow marrow of cattle bones; glycerol α-cetyl ether

¹chin \'chin\ *n* -s *often attrib* [ME, fr. OE *cinn*; akin to OHG *kinni* chin, ON *kinn* cheek, Goth *kinnus*, L *gena*, Gk *genys* jaw, cheek, Skt *hanu* jaw] **1 :** the lower portion of the face lying below the lower lip and including the prominence of the lower jaw and the overlying soft tissues **2 :** the surface lying beneath the lower jaw or between the branches of the jaw — used chiefly of lower vertebrates in which a mental prominence is lacking from the jawbone **3 :** a casual or random conversation **:** CHAT ⟨get together for a ~ —C.G.Norris⟩ — **chin up :** courage or spirits high — used chiefly in the expression *keep your chin up*

²chin \"\ *vb* **chinned; chinned; chinning; chins** *vt* **1 :** to bring to or hold with the chin ⟨the weary fiddler *chinning* his violin —Christopher Morley⟩ **2 a :** to raise oneself on (as a horizontal bar) while hanging by the hands from a position in which the arms are fully extended to a position in which the chin is level with or above the support ⟨he *chinned* the bar 12 times⟩ **b :** to raise (oneself) in this manner ⟨looked up at the top of the doorway, and . . . it was in his mind to leap up and seize it and ~ himself on it —Kenneth Roberts⟩ **3 :** to talk to esp. volubly or boldly **:** chatter to ~ *vi* **:** to talk esp. idly or casually **:** CHATTER ⟨the janitor can come in and ~ with me any time he wants —W.H.Whyte⟩

³chin \"\ *n, pl* **chin** *or* **chins** *usu cap* [Burmese, lit., hill-man] **1 a :** a people in Burma differing from the Burmese in shorter stature and darker skin that inhabit the Chin hills and the Arakan Yoma in the southern part of the India-Burma frontier **b :** a member of such people **2 :** the language of the Chin people similar to the Naga language and including numerous dialects

⁴chin \"\ *n* -s *usu cap* [by shortening] **:** CHINCHILLA 5

chin- *or* **chino-** *comb form* [alter. (influenced by G *chin-, chino-*, fr. *China* quinine) of *quin-, quino-*] **:** quinine ⟨*chinotoxine*⟩ ⟨*chinol*⟩

¹chi·na \'chīnə\ *n* -s [modif. (influenced by *China*, the country) of Per *chīnī* (Chinese) porcelain] **1 a :** PORCELAIN 1a; *also* **:** vitreous porcelain wares (as dishes, vases, ornaments) for domestic use as distinguished from industrial whitewares **b :** earthenware or porcelain tableware ⟨set the table with the good ~⟩ **c :** CROCKERY **2 a** [by shortening] **:** CHINAROOT **b** [fr. *China*, the country] **:** SWEET ORANGE

²china \"\ *adj* [fr. *China*, country in Asia] **1** *usu cap* **:** of, from, or native to China ⟨a *China* pig⟩ ⟨a *China* pheasant⟩ **:** produced in or of a kind or type prevalent or orig. produced in China ⟨*China* silk⟩ **:** CHINESE **2** [¹*china*] **a :** made of china **b :** resembling porcelain (as in hardness or finish) ⟨a woman with a set ~ face⟩; *also* **:** of the opaque blue characteristic of certain chinas ⟨a *china*-eyed dog⟩

³chi·na \'kēnə\ *n* -s [modif. of Sp *quina*, perh. fr. Quechua *kina*] **:** CINCHONA

⁴chi·na \'chīnə\ *n* -s [perh. short for *china plate*, rhyming slang for *mate*] *slang Brit* **:** COMPANION, PAL ⟨swapping yarns with my two old ~s⟩

chi·na ale \'chīnə-\ *n* **:** ale flavored with chinaroot

china aster *n, usu cap C* **:** an annual aster (*Callistephus chinensis*) which is native to rocky uplands of northern China and from which have been developed under cultivation numerous varieties differing in flower and petal form and occurring in white and shades of blue, red, or purple

chinaball \'==,=\ *n* : CHINABERRY 2
china bean *n, usu cap C* : COWPEA
china bedbug *n, usu cap C* : CONENOSE
chinaberry \'==,==\ *n* -ES **1** : a soapberry (*Sapindus saponaria*) of the southern U. S. and Mexico **2** *also* **chinaberry tree** : a small rapid-growing Asiatic tree (*Melia azedarach*) that has large twice-compound leaves and fragrant purplish flowers in open clusters, the latter followed by smooth yellow berries, and that is naturalized in the southern U. S. where it is widely planted as a shade or ornamental tree **3** : the fruit of the chinaberry
china blue *n, often cap C* : a grayish to moderate blue — called also *Nikko*
china brier *n, usu cap C* [so called fr. its similarity to *chinaroot*] : a bullbrier (*Smilax bona-nox*) with scurfy stem bases
china cantharides *n pl but sing or pl in constr, usu cap 1st C* : cantharides obtained from bruchid beetles of the genus *Mylabris* and chiefly produced in eastern Asia
china cinnamon *n, usu cap 1st C* : CASSIA BARK
china clay *n* [1*china*] : KAOLIN; *esp* : English plastic kaolin
china clay rock *n, sometimes cap 1st C* [1*china*] : CHINA STONE
china closet *also* **china cabinet** *n* [1*china*] : a cupboard or cabinet for the storage and often display of household crockery or china
chinacrin *also* **chinacrine** *var of* QUINACRINE
china eye *n* : WALLEYE 1a
china fir *n, usu cap C* : an Asiatic tree (*Cunninghamia lanceolata*) with brownish outer bark that scales off in irregular plates exposing the reddish inner bark and having sharply pointed leaves
chinafish \'==,=\ *n, often cap* **1** : SNAKEHEAD 3 **2** : any of several rockfishes (genus *Sebastodes*) of the Pacific coast of No. America
chi·na·fy \'chīnə,fī\ *vt* -ED/-ING/-ES *often cap* [*China* (country) + E *-fy*; fr. the political impotence of China in 1915, when it was coined] : to reduce (as a country) to a state of passivity and helplessness
chi·na·graph pencil \'chīnə,graf-\ *n* [1*china* + *-graph*] : a pencil for marking on porcelain or other hard glazed surfaces that do not take lead or wax pencil marks satisfactorily
china grass *n, usu cap C* **1** : the stiff dried hand-cleaned but not completely degummed fiber of ramie — called also *bon* **2** : RAMIE 1
china hat *n, usu cap C&H* [by folk etymology fr. Kwakiutl *Xāexaes*] : one of the five Indian peoples comprising the Heiltsuk group
china ink *n, usu cap C* : INDIA INK
china jute *n, usu cap C* : CHINGMA
1**chi·na·man** \'chīnəmən\ *n, pl* **chinamen** [1*china* + *man*] *archaic* : a dealer in or manufacturer of porcelain
2**chinaman** \"\ *n, pl* **chinamen** [*China* (the country) + E *man*] **1** *cap* : a native of China : CHINESE — often taken to be offensive **2** *usu* **china man** *usu cap C* : PEKING MAN
chi·na·man's chance *n, usu cap 1st C, slang* : the slightest or barest chance — usu. used in negative constructions ⟨he hasn't a *Chinaman's chance* of winning⟩
china mark \'chīnə-\ *n, usu cap C* [origin unknown] : any of various moths commonly placed in the family Pyraustidae whose larvae live in floating cases and feed on water plants
china mink *n, usu cap C* : JAPANESE MINK 2
chi·nam·pa \chə'nampə, -ām-\ *n* -S [MexSp, fr. Nahuatl, fr. *chinamitl* reed or twig mat + *pa* on] : a Mexican artificial meadow or garden reclaimed from a lake or pond by piling soil dredged from the bottom onto a mat of twigs and planting thereon
chi·nan·tec \'chinən,tek\ *n, pl* **chinantec** *or* **chinantecs** *usu cap* [Sp *chinanteca*, of AmerInd origin] **1** : an Indian people of the state of Oaxaca, Mexico **2** : a member of the Chinantec people
chi·nan·tec·an \,==ˈtākən, -ekən\ *n* -S *usu cap* : the language of the Chinantec people constituting a Mexican Indian language family
china orange *n, usu cap C* : CALAMONDIN
chi·naphthol \kē, ki+'-\ *n* -S [ISV, blend of *chin-* and *naphthol*; orig. formed in G] : a bitter yellow powder formerly used as an intestinal antiseptic — called also *quinaphthol*
china pink *n, usu cap C* : a biennial or short-lived perennial pink (*Dianthus chinensis*) often grown as an annual and having little or no basal branching, stiff stems, and usu. whitish or rosy lilac flowers often with a purplish eye — called also *rainbow pink*; see JAPANESE PINK
chi·na po·bla·na \,chēnəpə'blänə\ *n, sometimes cap C&P* [MexSp, lit., bold and attractive mestizo woman of Puebla] : a colorful Mexican costume consisting of an embroidered white blouse and a red and green skirt with sequins
china press *n* [1*china*] : CHINA CLOSET
chi·nar *also* **chinar tree** *or* **che·nar** \chə'när\ *n* -S [Hindi *cinār*, *canār*, fr. Per *chanār*] : ORIENTAL PLANE
china rooster *n, usu cap C, dial* : a ring-necked pheasant cock
chinaroot \'==,=\ *n* [perh. trans. of Pg *raiz de China*] : the rootstock of an East Indian climbing shrub (*Smilax china*)
china rose *n, usu cap C* **1 a** : a shrubby Chinese rose (*Rosa chinensis* — called also *Bengal rose* **b** : any of numerous garden roses derived from this rose having single or double flowers of white, pink, or red and tending to be recurrent blooming **2** : a large showy-flowered Asiatic shrub (*Hibiscus rosa-sinensis*)
chi·nar·ra \chə'närə\ *n, pl* **chinarra** *or* **chinarras** *usu cap* [Sp, of AmerInd origin] **1** : an Indian people comprising a major subdivision of the Concho group **2** : a member of the Chinarra people
chinas *pl of* CHINA
china shot *n, usu cap C* : INDIAN SHOT
china silk *n, usu cap C* : a lightweight silk made in China; *broadly* : any of various soft thin silks in plain weave with irregular threads
china stone *n* [1*china*] : a partly decomposed granite (as Cornish stone) frequently used as a flux to produce vitrification and translucency or mixed with silica and lime to form a glaze in the manufacture of porcelain
china tea *n, usu cap C* : a tea prepared from a small-leaved dwarf variety (*Camellia sinensis bohea*) of the tea plant grown chiefly in southern China
chinatown \'==,=\ *n, usu cap* : the Chinese quarter of a city
china tree *n, usu cap C* **1** : CHINABERRY 1, 2 **2** : GOLDENRAIN TREE
chinaware \'==,=\ *n* [1*china*] : CHINA 1
china wax *n, usu cap C* : CHINESE WAX
china wood oil *n, usu cap C* : TUNG OIL 1
chinbeak molding \'=,=-\ *n* [1*chin* + *beak*] : a molding consisting of a convex followed below by a concave profile with or without a fillet below or between
chinbone \'=¦=\ *n* [ME, fr. OE *cinbān*, fr. *cin* chin + *bān* bone] : MANDIBLE; *esp* : the median anterior part of the human mandible
chincapin *var of* CHINQUAPIN
chin·cha \'chēn(,)chä\ *n, pl* **chincha** *or* **chinchas** *usu cap* [Sp, of AmerInd origin] : a subdivision of the Yunca
chin·chai·su·yu \,chēn,chī'sü(,)yü\ *or* **chin·cha·su·yu** \-,chə's-\ *n, pl* **chinchaisuyu** *or* **chinchaisuyus** *or* **chinchasuyu** *or* **chinchasuyus** *usu cap* [Quechua *chinchaysúyu*] **1** : the peoples of a territorial division of the Inca empire occupying most of central and northern Peru and Ecuador and their present-day descendants **2** : the dialects of Quechua spoken by the Chinchaisuyu peoples
chin·cha·yo·te \,chinchə'yōd·ē\ *n* -S [MexSp, fr. Nahuatl *tzinchayotli*, fr. *tzintli* rear or bottom part + *chayotli* chayote] : CHAYOTE
chinch bug *also* **chinch** \'chinch\ *or* **chintz** \-n(t)s\ *n* -ES [Sp *chinche*, fr. L *cimic-*, *cimex*; akin to Lith *šemas* blue-gray, Skt *śyāma* black, dark, OE *hār* gray, old — more at HOAR] **1** : a small bug (*Blissus leucopterus*) of the family Lygaeidae that is black and white in color when adult and very destructive to grass, wheat, corn, and other grains esp. in the central U.S. during dry seasons **2** *chinch or sometimes chintz* : BEDBUG
chin·che·rin·chee \,chinchə'rinchē\ *or* **chin·che·rich·ee** \-richē\ *or* **chin·ke·rich·ee** *also* **chin·ke·rin·chee** \,chiŋkə-\ *n, pl* **chincherinchees** *or* **chincherinchees** *or* **chincherichee** *or* **chincherichees** *or* **chinkerichee** *or* **chinkerichees** *also* **chinkerinchee** *or* **chinkerinchees** [origin unknown] : a southern African perennial bulbous herb (*Ornithogalum thyrsoides*) with long-lasting spikes of starry white blossoms that are shipped in quantity to Europe and America for use as winter cut flowers — called also *star-of-Bethlehem*
chin·chil·la \chin'chilə\ *n* [Sp, prob. fr. Aimara or Quechua] **1** -S : a small rodent (*Chinchilla laniger*) the size of a large squirrel having very soft fur of a pearly gray color and native to the mountains of Peru and Chile but now extensively bred in captivity **2** -S : the fur of the chinchilla **3** *cap* [NL, fr. Sp] : a genus (the type of the family Chinchillidae) of hystricomorph rodents comprising the chinchillas **4** -S : a heavy twilled woolen coating with double cloth construction and with deep napping that is rubbed into curled tufts and nubs **5** -S *often cap* : a domestic rabbit of a breed distinguished by dense soft fur each hair of which is banded with slate blue, pearl gray, and white and tipped with black **6** -S *often cap* : a domestic long-haired cat having green eyes and a pale silver coat sometimes tipped with black **7** : genetic lack of ability to produce yellow pigment occurring as a member of a polygenic series of variants in mammalian coat color, dominant to albinism and Himalayan but recessive to wild type, and resulting in a silvery coat suggesting that of the chinchilla

chinchilla

chinchilla rat *n* : ABROCOME
chin·chil·li·dae \,=ˈ=lə,dē\ *n pl, cap* [NL, fr. *Chinchilla*, type genus + *-idae*] : a family of small bushy-tailed burrowing hystricomorph rodents of the uplands of So. America that includes the chinchillas, the vizcachas, and extinct related forms
chin·chil·lon *or* **chin·chil·lone** \¦chinchə¦lōn, -chə¦yōn\ *n* -S [Sp *chinchillón*, aug. of *chinchilla*] : VIZCACHA
1**chin-chin** \'chin,chin\ *interj* [Chin (Pek) *ch'ing*3, *ch'ing*3 *-ch'ing*3, an expression of courtesy] — used to express greeting or farewell
2**chin-chin** \"\ *vi* **chin-chinned; chin-chinned; chin=chinning; chin-chins** **1** : to make a request ceremoniously : converse politely **2** : to talk esp. casually or at random
3**chin-chin** \"\ *n* -S **1** : ceremonious talk : SALUTATION **2** : casual or trivial talk : CHATTER ⟨idle *chin-chin* to pass a hot afternoon⟩
chinchona *or* **chincona** *var of* CINCHONA
chin·chow \'jin¦jō\ *adj, usu cap* [fr. *Chinchow*, Manchuria] : of or from the city of Chinchow, Manchuria : of the kind or style prevalent in Chinchow
chinch·weed \'chinch,wēd\ *n* [prob. fr. *chinch* + *weed*; fr. its unpleasant odor] : a slender or wiry glandular-dotted strongly-scented herb (*Pectis papposa*) of the family Compositae having narrow opposite leaves and flower heads with yellow rays
chinchy \'chinchē\ *adj* -ER/-EST [ME, fr. *chinche* miser, miserly (fr. OF *chinche*, *chiche*, fr. — assumed — VL *ciccus*, fr. L *ciccum* trifle) + ME *-y* — more at CHICO] *chiefly South & Midland* : STINGY
chinc·ing iron \'chin(t)siŋ-\ *n* [fr. pres. part. of *chince*, *chinse* to caulk, prob. var. of *chink*] : a tool used by coopers to insert cooper's flag between the head and staves of a barrel after the head is in place
chin·cough \'chin,kȯf, -äf\ *n* [by folk etymology fr. 5*chink* + *cough*] *dial Brit* : WHOOPING COUGH
chin·di *also* **chin·dee** \'chindē\ *n* -S [Navaho *chindi*] : a Navaho evil spirit of the dead
1**chine** \'chīn\ *n* -S [ME *chin*, *chine* crack, fissure, chasm, fr. OE *cine*, *cinu*; akin to OE *cīnan* to gape, yawn, crack, OHG *kīnan*, *chīnan* to sprout, split open, Sw *kina* to sprout, Goth *keinan*, OHG *kīmo*, *chīmo* sprout, *kīl* wedge, OE *cīth* sprout, shoot, and perh. to Arm *cil*, *ciul*, *cel* stem, Latvian *ziêt* to bloom; basic meaning: to sprout, split apart] *dial Eng* : a narrow and deep ravine or gorge
2**chine** \"\ *n* -S [ME *chyne*, fr. MF *eschine*, of Gmc origin; akin to OHG *scina* needle, shinbone — more at SHIN] **1 a** *archaic* : the back or spine of an animal or man **b** : a piece of the backbone of an animal carcass with the adjoining parts cut for cooking : a saddle or a portion of it — see COW illustration **2** : RIDGE, CREST ⟨walking carefully along the ~*s* of the rocks⟩ **3 a** : the thick part of the waterway of a ship projecting above the deck and hollowed on the inboard edge to form a watercourse **b** : the intersection of the bottom and the sides of a flat or V-bottomed boat; *also* : a longitudinal member lying along the bilge at this point
3**chine** \"\ *vt* -ED/ -ING/ -S **1** : to cut through the backbone of: **a** : to split (as a carcass) through the length of the backbone **b** : to cut up (as a salmon or other fish) **2** : to break the back of
4**chine** *var of* CHIME
5**chi·né** \shə'nā, shē-\ *adj* [F, past part. of *chiner* to dye threads of a fabric in different colors so as to produce a figure, fr. *Chine* China] *of a fabric* : having a mottled pattern of a supposed Chinese fashion produced by printing, dyeing, or painting the stretched warp, sometimes the warp or weft threads, before weaving
6**chiné** \"\ *n* -S : a fabric with a chiné design
chi·nee \chī'nē *also* '=,=\ *n, usu cap* [back-formation fr. *Chinese*, pl.] *substand* : CHINESE
chine hoop *n* [4*chine*] : the hoop round each end of a cask
chi·ne·la *also* **chi·ne·le** \chə'nālə\ *n* -S [Sp *chinela*, alter. of *chanela*, prob. fr. It dial. *cianella*, var. of *pianella*, fr. *piano* flat (fr. L *planus*) + *-ella* fem. dim. suffix — more at FLOOR] : SLIPPER; *esp* : a flat slipper with no heel worn by Philippine women
1**chi·nese** \(')chī¦nēz, -ēs\ *adj, usu cap* [*China* + E *-ese*] **1 a** : of, relating to, or characteristic of China **b** : of, relating to, or characteristic of the Chinese **2** : of, relating to, or characteristic of a Chinese language or of the Chinese branch of the Sino-Tibetan language family
2**chinese** \"\ *n, cap* **1** *pl* **chinese** : a native or inhabitant of China or one of his descendants **2** -S : a group of related languages mutually unintelligible in their spoken form but sharing a single system of writing in which the visual symbols directly represent words regardless of the sounds involved used by the people of China and constituting a branch of the Sino-Tibetan language family; *specif* : MANDARIN — see AMOY, CANTONESE, FOOCHOW, HAKKA, PEKINGESE, SWATOW, WU
chinese air plant *n, usu cap C* : a red-flowered epiphytic orchid (*Renanthera coccinea*) of Indochina
chinese alligator *n, usu cap C* : a small alligator (*Alligator sinensis*) of the Yangtze valley distinguished from the American alligator by its completely unwebbed fingers
chinese angelica *n, usu cap C* : an Asiatic shrub (*Aralia chinensis*) resembling Hercules'-club but less prickly and with a long inflorescence
chinese anise *n, usu cap C* : an evergreen tree (*Illicium verum*) of southern China — see BADIAN
chinese arborvitae *n, usu cap C* : an Asiatic evergreen tree (*Thuja orientalis*) widely planted for ornament
chinese artichoke *n, usu cap C* : a hardy perennial (*Stachys sieboldii*) native to China and Japan that is cultivated for its crisp edible tubers eaten either raw or cooked — called also *chorogi, crosnes, Japanese artichoke, knotroot*
chinese azalea *n, usu cap C* : a deciduous shrub (*Rhododendron molle*) having leaves two to six inches long and golden yellow clustered flowers up to two inches across
chinese banana *n, usu cap C* : DWARF BANANA
chinese bean oil *n, usu cap C* : SOYBEAN OIL
chinese bellflower *n, usu cap C* : any of several plants of the genus *Platycodon*; *specif* : BALLOONFLOWER
chinese bezique *n, usu cap C* : SIX-PACK BEZIQUE
chinese bladdernut *n, usu cap C* : GOLDENRAIN TREE
chinese blister fly *or* **chinese blistering fly** *or* **chinese blistering beetle** *n, usu cap C* : a beetle (genus *Mylabris*) that yields China cantharides
chinese block *n, usu cap C* : CHINESE TEMPLE BLOCK
chinese blue *n, usu cap C* **1** : any of various blue pigments: as **a** : an iron blue esp. having a relatively greenish tint **b** : a mixture of ultramarine or of cobalt blue with white lead **2** : PRUSSIAN BLUE 2
chinese boxes *n pl, usu cap C* : a set of graduated boxes each fitting into the one next larger
chinese bridge *n, usu cap C* **1** : CHINESE WHIST **2** : a variety of whist in which the object is to win not tricks but scoring cards, the ace and ten counting 10 each and the five counting 5
chinese bush cherry *n, usu cap 1st C* : a flowering almond (*Prunus japonica*)
chinese cabbage *n, usu cap 1st C* : either of two Asiatic brassicas (*Brassica pekinensis* and *B. chinensis*) somewhat resembling cabbage and widely used as greens, the first forming an elongated compact head of broad light green leaves, the second a loose chardlike head of dark green leaves — called also respectively *pe-tsai* and *pakchoi* and together *celery cabbage, lettuce cabbage*
chinese checkers *n pl but sing or pl in constr, usu cap 1st C* : a game for from two to six people played on a pitted board the object being for each player in turn to transfer a set of marbles from a home point to the opposite point of a 6-pointed star by a series of moves similar to those in checkers
chinese chestnut *n, usu cap 1st C* : an Asiatic chestnut (*Castanea mollissima*) of importance chiefly for its resistance to chestnut blight
chinese chippendale *n, usu cap both Cs* : Chippendale furniture employing chiefly straight lines, bamboo turnings, and as surface decoration fluting and fretwork in a variety of lattice patterns
chinese cinnamon *n, usu cap 1st C* : the bark of a Chinese tree (*Cinnamomum cassia*) generally considered less agreeable in flavor or fragrance than Ceylon and Saigon cinnamon — called also *cassia bark*
chinese cinnamon oil *n, usu cap 1st C* : CASSIA OIL
chinese civet *n, usu cap 1st C* : a civet cat (*Viverra zibetha ashtoni*) of southern China
chinese copy *n, usu cap 1st C* : an exact imitation or duplicate made without discrimination reproducing defects as well as desired qualities
chinese cork tree *n, usu cap 1st C* : an eastern Asiatic tree (*Phellodendron amurense*) that has light-gray corky bark and is cultivated as an ornamental and shade tree
chinese crescent *n, usu cap 1st C* : PAVILLON CHINOIS
chinese crested dog *n, usu cap 1st C* : a small now nearly extinct dog of a breed native to northern Tibet and China and distinguished by slender greyhoundlike build, naked body, and head crest and tail brush of long usu. white hairs
chinese date *n, usu cap C* **1** : a tree (*Ziziphus jujuba*) with leaves used in China as food for the tussah silkworm **2** : the edible plumlike fruit of the Chinese date — called also *jujube*
chinese dogskin *n, usu cap C* : MANCHURIAN DOG
chinese drum *n, usu cap C* : a small gaily decorated drum with two thick heads used chiefly in dance orchestras
chinese elm *n, usu cap C* **1** : a small rapid-growing tree or shrub (*Ulmus parvifolia*) that is native to eastern Asia, has shining coriaceous leaves, and is used widely for shelterbelts and hedges **2** : SIBERIAN ELM
chinese evergreen *n, usu cap C* : an erect or semiclimbing herb (*Aglaonema modestum*) often kept as a house plant for its green or variegated drought-resisting leaves — called also *Japanese leaf*
chinese export porcelain *n, usu cap C* : LOWESTOFT WARE 2
chinese fan palm *n, usu cap C* : a fan palm (*Livistona chinensis*) of China growing up to six feet in height and sold as a pot or tub plant in cultivation under the name of *Latania borbonica*
chinese fiddle *n, usu cap C* : a Chinese or central Asian bowed lute having two strings and no fingerboard
chinese fir *n, usu cap C* : an ornamental east Asian evergreen tree (*Cunninghamia lanceolata*) with narrow flat leaves close-set along the spreading branches
chinese fleecevine \,=,=ˈ=,=\ *n, usu cap C* : SILVER-LACE VINE
chinese forget-me-not *n, usu cap C* : any of several plants of the genus *Cynoglossum*; *esp* : a biennial herb (*C. amabile*) grown for its usu. bright blue flowers
chinese gall *n, usu cap C* : a gall very rich in tannin produced by insects on an Asian sumac (*Rhus semialata*)
chinese gelatin *n, usu cap C* : AGAR 1a
chinese ginger *n, usu cap C* : GALINGALE 1b(1)
chinese gong *n, usu cap C* : GONG 1
chinese goose *n, usu cap C* **1** : a very large wild goose (*Anser cygnoides* syn. *Cygnopsis cygnoides*) of northeastern Asia that interbreeds freely with the grayleg and is probably an ancestor of various eastern domesticated geese **2** : a brown or white goose of a breed that originated in China probably from the Chinese goose and is distinguished by upright carriage, large knob at the base of the bill, and small size
chinese gooseberry *n, usu cap C* : a vigorous chiefly subtropical twining vine (*Actinidia chinensis*) the brownish hairy fruit of which is eaten fresh or in preserves esp. in New Zealand
chinese green *n, usu cap C* : LOKAO
chinese hat plant *n, usu cap C* [so called fr. its large spreading calyx] : a straggling evergreen Himalayan shrub (*Holmskioldia sanguinea*) of the family Verbenaceae sometimes cultivated in the southern U.S.
chinese hibiscus *n, usu cap C* : CHINA ROSE 2
chinese holly *n, usu cap C* : a dense rounded evergreen shrub (*Ilex cornuta*) native to China, widely used as an ornamental, and distinguished by its quadrangular oblong leaves each usu. with three strong spines at its dilated apex
chinese homer *n, usu cap C, slang* : a cheap home run; *specif* : a fly ball that is barely over a barrier or into stands that are unusually close to home plate
chinese horn *n, usu cap C* : an oboe with a flaring end
chinese ink *n, usu cap C* : INDIA INK
chinese insect wax *n, usu cap C* : CHINESE WAX
chinese isinglass *n, usu cap C* : AGAR 1a
chinese jujube *n, usu cap C* : any of several large-fruited jujubes developed in China from the common jujube (*Ziziphus jujuba*) and cultivated in warm regions (as California)
chinese jute *n, usu cap C* : CHINGMA
chinese lacquer *n, usu cap C* : LACQUER 1b
chinese lake *n, often cap C* : CARMINE 2
chinese lantern *n, usu cap C* **1** : a collapsible lantern of thin colored paper mostly for ceremonial or decorative use **2** : CHINESE LANTERN PLANT; *also* : one of the brilliant inflated calyxes of the Chinese lantern plant
chinese lantern plant *n, usu cap C* : a perennial Old World ground-cherry (*Physalis alkekengi*) that is widely cultivated for its showy inflated leafy calyxes that are brilliant orange-red when mature and are often used for decoration — called also *winter cherry*
chinese layering *n, usu cap C* : MARCOTTAGE
chinese lemon *n, usu cap C* : CITRON 1a, 1b
chinese lilac *n, usu cap C* : a hybrid lilac produced by crossing Persian lilac and common lilac and having broader leaves and much longer flower clusters than the Persian parent
chinese lily *n, usu cap C* : CHINESE SACRED LILY
chinese liver fluke *n, usu cap C* : a common and destructive Asian liver fluke (*Clonorchis sinensis*) that invades the human liver
chinese matrimony vine *n, usu cap C* : a strongly growing vinelike shrub (*Lycium chinense*) having purplish flowers and red berries
chinese millet *n, usu cap C* **1** : the common sorghum (*Sorghum vulgare*) **2** *Austral* : MILLET 1a **3** : a foxtail (*Setaria faberii*)
chinese money plant *n, usu cap C* : HONESTY 3
chinese musk *n, usu cap C* : MUSK 1
chinese mustard *n, usu cap C* : INDIAN MUSTARD; *also* : any of several Asiatic brassicas sometimes used as potherbs
chinese nut *n, usu cap C* : LITCHI 1
chinese olive *n, usu cap C* : JAVA ALMOND
chinese orange *n, usu cap C* **1** : a kumquat (*Fortunella japonica*) having globular fruit **2** : a vivid yellowish pink to strong reddish orange that is very slightly redder than capucine red — called also *Japanese yellow*
chinese parasol tree *also* **chinese parasol** *n, usu cap C* : an Asiatic tree (*Firmiana simplex*) of the family Sterculiaceae now widely planted as an ornamental in warmer parts of the U.S. having large maplelike leaves and greenish white flowers in clusters

chinese pavilion *n, usu cap C* [trans. of F *pavillon chinois*] **:** PAVILLON CHINOIS
chinese pear *n, usu cap C* **:** SAND PEAR 2a
chinese pea tree *n, usu cap C* **:** a bushy shrub (*Caragana sinica*) with angular branches, stipules that become stiff thorns, and solitary reddish yellow flowers
chinese peel *n, usu cap C* **:** rattan interwoven with grasses ⟨*Chinese peel* furniture⟩
chinese pheasant *n, usu cap C* **:** RING-NECKED PHEASANT
chinese preserving melon *n, usu cap C* **:** WAX GOURD
chinese primrose *n, usu cap C* **:** a cultivated Asiatic primrose (*Primula sinensis*); *sometimes* **:** any of several related cultivated Asiatic primroses
chinese pusley *also* **chinese pussley** *n, usu cap C* **:** SEASIDE HELIOTROPE
chinese puzzle *n, usu cap C* **1 :** an intricate or ingenious puzzle such as those made by the Chinese — see TANGRAM **2 :** something intricate and obscure ⟨the rules of taxonomy are a *Chinese puzzle* to the novice⟩
chinese quince *n, usu cap C* **:** a half-evergreen medium-sized tree (*Chaenomeles sinensis*) resembling dwarf Japanese quince but with solitary pink flowers
chinese red *n, usu cap C* **1 :** any of various red pigments: as **a :** a basic lead chromate (as chrome red) **b :** VERMILION 1a **c :** an iron red **2 a :** VERMILION 2b **b :** INDIAN RED 2b **c :** a deep reddish orange that is slightly yellower and stronger than average tomato
chinese rhubarb *n, usu cap C* **:** a rhubarb (*Rheum officinale*) from whose thick caudex medicinal rhubarb is obtained
chinese rose *n, usu cap C* **:** CHINA ROSE 2
chinese rose beetle *n, usu cap C* **:** a common leaf-eating beetle (*Adoretus sinicus*) of southeast Asia accidentally introduced into Hawaii where it is a serious pest on many cultivated plants
chinese rouge *n, often cap C* [*³rouge*] **:** CARTHAMUS RED
chi·nes·ery \chī'nēz(ə)rē\ *n* -ES *usu cap* [modif. of F *chinoiserie*] **:** CHINOISERIE
chinese sacred lily *n, usu cap C* **:** a narcissus (*Narcissus tazetta orientalis*) that constitutes a variety of yellow polyanthus narcissus
chinese scale *n, usu cap C* **:** SAN JOSE SCALE
chinese scholartree *n, usu cap C* **:** JAPANESE PAGODA TREE
chinese silk plant *n, usu cap C* **:** RAMIE 1
chinese snowball *n, usu cap C* **:** a shrub (*Viburnum macrocephalum sterile*) that is a cultivated variety of a Chinese shrub with ball-like white flowers
chinese squill *n, usu cap C* **:** an herb (*Scilla scilloides*) native to China having elongated racemes of pink flowers
chinese stick *n, usu cap C* **:** a black pigment in stick form used to make India ink
chinese sumac *n, usu cap C* **:** TREE OF HEAVEN
chinese tallow *or* **chinese vegetable tallow** *n, usu cap C* **:** a hard white fat obtained from the surface of the seeds of the Chinese tallow tree and used for making candles and soap
chinese tallow tree *n, usu cap C* **:** an Asiatic tree (*Sapium sebiferum* or *Stillingia sebifera*) that yields a hard wood used for engraving and from its seeds a drying oil and vegetable tallow — called also *stillingia*; see CHINESE TALLOW
chinese temple block *n, usu cap C* **:** a hollow slotted wooden box struck with a drumstick or hammer adapted by jazz bands from the wooden fish used by Buddhist priests — called also *clog box, tap box*
chinese tree wax *n, usu cap C* **:** CHINESE WAX
chinese trumpet creeper *or* **chinese trumpet vine** *n, usu cap 1st C* **:** a deciduous vine (*Campsis grandiflora*) having orange or scarlet flowers shorter and broader than those of the common trumpet creeper
chinese vampire *n, usu cap C* **:** an Asiatic big-eared bat (*Lyroderma lyra sinensis*) that is not a true vampire but an insectivorous bat
chinese varnish tree *n, usu cap C* **:** CANDLENUT 2
chinese vermilion *n, usu cap C* **1 :** VERMILION 1a **2 :** a vivid red that is yellower, lighter, and slightly stronger than apple red, yellower, lighter, and stronger than carmine or scarlet, and yellower and lighter than madder crimson — called also *Harrison red, signal red*
chinese violet *n, often cap C* **:** a moderate purple that is redder and paler than heliotrope (sense 4a), bluer and lighter than average amethyst, and paler than manganese violet
chinese wall *n, usu cap C & sometimes cap W* [fr. the *Chinese Wall*, a defensive wall built in the 3d cent. B.C. & extending 1500 miles between China and Mongolia] **:** a strong barrier; *esp* **:** a serious obstacle to free intercourse or understanding (as between individuals or nations) ⟨go backwards towards an old *Chinese wall* policy of isolation —F.D.Roosevelt⟩
chinese watermelon *n, usu cap C* **:** WAX GOURD
chinese wax *n, usu cap C* **:** a white or yellowish white crystalline wax resembling spermaceti but harder, more friable, and higher melting that is deposited on certain trees by a scale (*Ceroplastes ceriferus*) common in China and India or a related scale (*Ericerus pela*) of China and Japan and is used chiefly for making candles, polishing materials, and sizes for paper — called also *Chinese insect wax, insect wax*
chinese whist *n, usu cap C* **:** a card game for two, three, or four players resembling whist except that six of each player's cards are dealt face down on the table and a like number of cards face up upon them, the lower cards being revealed only as the cards above them are removed in the course of the play
chinese white *n, usu cap C* **:** ZINC WHITE; *esp* **:** a dense form of it
chinese windlass *n, usu cap C* **:** DIFFERENTIAL WINDLASS
chinese wistaria *n, usu cap C* **:** a wistaria (*Wisteria chinensis*) with nearly glabrous mature leaves, blue-violet flowers, and velvety pubescent pods
chinese witch hazel *n, usu cap C* **:** either of two plants of the family Hamamelidaceae that are native to China: **a :** a white-flowered evergreen shrub or small tree (*Loropetalum chinense*) **b :** a large deciduous shrub (*Hamamelis mollis*) having large fragrant yellow flowers
chinese wood oil *n, usu cap C* **:** TUNG OIL 1
chinese yam *n, usu cap C* **:** CINNAMON VINE
chinese yellow *n, usu cap C* **1 :** either of two pigments: **a :** KING'S YELLOW **b :** YELLOW OCHER 1 **2 a :** YELLOW OCHER 2 **b :** LEMON YELLOW 1b
chinfest \'=,=\ *n* [*¹chin* + *fest*] *slang* **:** an instance of talking together or conferring esp. informally **:** DISCUSSION, GAB
chin fly *n* [so called fr. its laying its eggs about the mouth of the horse] **:** THROAT BOTFLY
¹ch'ing \'chiŋ\ *n, often cap* [Chin (Pek) *ch'ing* azure] **:** a vivid blue that is redder and duller than Cleopatra and greener and duller than ultramarine
²ching \'jiŋ\ *n* -S [Chin (Pek) *ching¹* classic (book), the classics] **:** a Chinese authoritative or canonical book; *specif* **:** a Chinese scripture
ching·ma \'chiŋ'mä\ *n* -S [Chin (Pek) *ch'ing³ma²*] **:** the bast fiber of Indian mallow used for cordage — called also *China jute, Chinese jute*
ch'ing ming \'chiŋ'miŋ\ *n, usu cap C&M* [Chin (Pek) *ch'ing¹ ming²*, lit., clear and bright] **:** a spring festival in China when graves are put in order and special offerings are made to the dead
ching·paw \'chiŋ,pȯ\ *n, pl* **chingpaw** *or* **chingpaws** *usu cap* **1 :** a Tibeto-Burman ethnic group inhabiting upper Burma and the north Burma-Chinese frontier region, esp. the Irrawaddy drainage above Myitkyina known as "the Triangle" and the Hukawng valley — called also *Singpho;* see KACHIN **2 :** a member of the Chingpaw
chin·hsien \'jinshē¦en\ *adj, usu cap* [fr. *Chinhsien* (Chinchow), China] **:** CHINCHOW
chinidine *var of* QUINIDINE
chi·nin \chə'nēn\ *n* -S [MexSp *chinin*, fr. Nahuatl *xinene*] **:** COYO
chining *pres part of* CHINE
chi·ni·o·fon \kə'nīə,fän\ *n* -S [*chin-* + *iodine* + *sulfonic*] **:** a yellow powder composed of a sulfonic acid $C_9H_4NI(OH)SO_3H$ derived from quinoline, the sodium salt of this acid, and sodium bicarbonate and used in the treatment of amebiasis
chi·ni·pa \chə'nēpə\ *n, pl* **chinipa** *or* **chinipas** *usu cap* [Sp, of AmerInd origin] **1 :** a Taracahitian people in Chihuahua state, Mexico **2 :** a member of the Chinipa people
¹chink \'chiŋk\ *n* -S [prob. alter. of ME *chin, chine* crack, fissure, chasm] **1 a :** an opening, space, break, or hole typically of greater length than breadth (as between planks in a wall) **:** CRACK, CREVICE, CRANNY, INTERSTICE **b :** a means of evasion or escape **:** LOOPHOLE **:** a weak spot (as in a plan or system) ⟨he was indicted but his lawyers found a ~ in the law⟩ **2 :** something used to fill a chink; *specif* **:** a strip of wood used to close the crevice between adjoining logs in a log cabin **3 :** a beam of light of similar form to or perceived through a chink **4** *or* **chink shell :** any of several gastropod mollusks: **a :** KEYHOLE LIMPET **b :** any of a family (Lacunidae) of conical thin-shelled marine snails having a slit on the columella opposite the aperture **syn** see CRACK
²chink \"\ *vb* -ED/-ING/-S *vi, obs* **:** to open in cracks **:** CRACK ~ *vt* **1** *obs* **:** to cause to open in cracks **:** CRACK **2 :** to fill the chinks of (as by caulking) **:** stop up ⟨~ and daub a log cabin⟩
³chink \"\ *n* -S [imit.] **1 :** a short sharp sound (as of metal or small sonorous bodies struck with a slight tap) **2 a chinks** *pl, obs* **:** pieces of money **:** COINS **b** *slang* **:** COIN, MONEY, CASH
⁴chink \"\ *vb* -ED/-ING/-S *vi* **:** to make a slight sharp metallic sound (as of coins or glasses in collision) **:** strike or strike together with a chink ⟨the sound . . . of ~*ing* china —Nancy Hale⟩ ~ *vt* **:** to cause (as coins) to make a chink
⁵chink \"\ *vi* -ED/-ING/-S [perh. fr. (assumed) ME *chinken;* akin to ME *kinken* to gasp convulsively, OE *cincung* hearty laughter, obs. D *kincken* to pant, MHG *kīchen* to breathe heavily, prob. of imit. origin] *dial Eng* **:** to catch one's breath **:** gasp convulsively
⁶chink \"\ *n* -S [imit.] **1 :** CHAFFINCH **2 :** REED BUNTING
⁷chink \"\ *n* -S *often cap* [alter. (prob. influenced by *chink* small cleft) of *Chinese;* fr. their slant eyes] **:** CHINESE — usu. taken to be offensive
chinkapin *var of* CHINQUAPIN
chinkara *var of* CHIKARA
chink·er \'chiŋkə(r)\ *n* -S [*²chink* + *-er*] **1 :** something that fills or can be used to fill chinks **2 chinkers** *pl, slang* **:** pieces of money **:** COIN 5
chinkerichee *also* **chinkerinchee** *var of* CHINCHERINCHEE
chin·kiang \'jinjē¦äŋ\ *adj, usu cap* [fr. *Chinkiang*, China] **:** of or from the city of Chinkiang, China **:** of the kind or style prevalent in Chinkiang
chinking *n* -S [*¹chink* + *-ing*] **:** material (as mud or chips) to fill chinks
chin·kle \'chiŋkəl\ *vb* -ED/-ING/-S [freq. of *⁴chink*] **:** CHINK JINGLE
chinks \'chiŋks\ *n* [origin unknown] **:** WINTERGREEN 2a
chink shell *n* **:** ¹CHINK 4
chinky \'chiŋkē, -i\ *adj* -ER/-EST [*¹chink* + *-y*] **:** having chinks **:** full of chinks
chin·less \'chinləs\ *adj* **:** lacking a chin **:** having a receding chin
chin music *n, slang* **:** idle talk **:** CHATTER, GABBLE
chinned \'chind\ *adj* [*¹chin* + *-ed*] **:** having a chin of a specified kind ⟨weak-*chinned*⟩
chinning *pres part of* CHIN
¹chi·no \'chē(,)nō\ *n* -S [AmerSp, masc. of *china* Indian woman, woman of mixed blood, fr. Quichua & Aymara, female animal, servant — more at CHINA] **:** a Spanish-American of mixed blood; *esp* **:** one with one quarter Indian and three quarters Negro blood
²chino \"\ *n* -S [modif. of AmerSp *china*, short for Sp *naranja china* Chinese orange] **:** SWEET ORANGE
³chino \" *sometimes* 'shē-\ *n* -S [AmerSp] **1 :** a usu. khaki-colored cotton twill of the type used for military uniforms **2 :** an article of clothing made of chino — usu. used in pl.
¹chi·no- \¦chī(,)nō\ *comb form, usu cap* [*China*] **:** Chinese and ⟨*Chino*-Japanese⟩ — compare SINO-
²chino- — see CHIN-
chi·noi·se·rie \,shēn,wäz(ə)'rē, shēn'wäzərē\ *n* -S *sometimes cap* [F, fr. *chinois* Chinese (fr. *Chine* China) + *-erie* -ery] **1 a :** a style in art (as in decoration) reflecting or felt to reflect Chinese artistic esp. decorative qualities or motifs (as in costume, furniture, objects of virtu, or architecture); *esp* **:** such a style akin to the rococo in decorative intricacy popular in 18th century Europe — compare CHINESE CHIPPENDALE **b :** an art object or instance of decoration in this style **2 :** conduct felt to suggest the Chinese
chinoline *var of* QUINOLINE
chinone *var of* QUINONE
chi·nook \shə'nu̇k *sometimes* chə- *or* -ük\ *n, pl* **chinook** *or* **chinooks** [Chehalis *Tsinúk*] **1** *usu cap* **a :** an Indian people of the north shore of the Columbia river at its mouth **b :** a member of such people **2** *usu cap* **:** a Chinookan language of the Chinook and other nearby peoples — see LOWER CHINOOK, UPPER CHINOOK **3 a :** a warm moist southwest wind of the Pacific coastal region of No. America from Oregon northward **b :** a warm dry foehnlike wind that descends the eastern slopes of the Rocky mountains
¹chi·nook·an \-ən\ *adj, usu cap* **:** of or relating to Chinook or a Chinookan
²chinookan \"\ *or* **chinook** *n* -S *usu cap* **:** a language family of the Penutian stock in Washington and Oregon comprising Lower Chinook and Upper Chinook
chinook jargon *also* **chinook** *n, usu cap C&J* **:** a pidgin language based on Lower Chinook and other Indian languages, French, and English and at one time used as a lingua franca in the northwestern U.S. and on the Pacific coast of Canada and Alaska — called also *Jargon, Oregon Jargon*
chinook licorice *n, usu cap C* **:** a silky blue-flowered American herb (*Lupinus littoralis*) found in the Pacific coastal dunes
chinook salmon *also* **chinook** *n* -S *usu cap C* **:** KING SALMON
chi·not·to \kē'nōd·(,)ō\ *or* **chinotto orange** *n, pl* **chinot·ti** \-d·ē\ [origin unknown] **:** SOUR ORANGE; *esp* **:** a broad-leafed variety of the sour orange tree
chinovic acid *var of* QUINOVIC ACID
chinovin *var of* QUINOVIN
chi·nov·nik \chə'nōvnik\ *n* -S [Russ, fr. *chinovny* having rank (fr. *chin* rank + *-ovny*, adj. suffix) + *-ik* (nominal suffix); akin to Russ *chinit'* to do, OSlav *činiti* to arrange — more at POET] **:** a minor official in czarist Russia
chinovose *var of* QUINOVOSE
chinpiece \'=,=\ *n* **:** a piece (as of armor) to fit around and usu. protect the chin
chin·qua·pin *also* **chin·ca·pin** *or* **chin·ka·pin** \'chiŋkə,pin, -kē-\ *n* -S [alter. of earlier *chincomen*, of Algonquian origin; akin to *chechinkamin* chestnut (in some Algonquian language of Virginia); perh. akin to Delaware *chinqua* large, great and to Delaware *mihn* berry, Natick *min* berry, nut] **1 a :** any of several trees (genus *Castanea*); *esp* **:** a dwarf chestnut (*C. pumila*) of the U. S. **b :** the sweet edible nut of this tree usu. solitary in the bur **2 :** CHINQUAPIN OAK **3 a :** any of several trees of a genus (*Castanopsis*) closely related to *Castanea; esp* **:** a tree (*Castanopsis chrysophylla*) of California and Oregon **b :** the nut of any of these trees **4 :** WATER CHINQUAPIN **5** *or* **chinquapin perch :** WHITE CRAPPIE
chinquapin oak *n* **:** either of two No. American chestnut oaks: **a :** a medium to large oak (*Quercus muhlenbergii*) of the eastern U.S. that yields a strong durable timber — called also *yellow oak* **b :** a small shrubby oak (*Q. prinoides*) of the same area that has a sweet edible acorn and often forms dense thickets — called also *dwarf chinquapin oak, scrub oak, yellow chestnut oak*
chin rest *n* **:** a device for the top of a violin or viola to enable a player to hold the instrument more firmly under his chin
chins *pres 3d sing of* CHIN, *pl of* CHIN
chinse *or* **chintze** \'chin(t)s\ *vb* -ED/-ING/-S [alter. of E dial. *chinch* to fill up cracks, perh. var. of *²chink*] **:** to calk in a makeshift or temporary fashion
chin shield *n* **:** one of certain paired elongate scales below the lower labials on the chin in some reptiles
chin stay *n* **:** a stay or supporting band passing under the chin
chin strap *n* **1 :** a strap worn under or in front of the chin esp. as a means of holding a hat on the head **2 :** a strap connecting the throatlatch and noseband of a halter or bridle
¹chintz \'chin(t)s\ *n* -ES *often attrib* [earlier *chints*, pl. (taken as sing.) of earlier *chint*, fr. Hindi *chīṭ*] **1 :** a printed calico from India **2 :** a firm usu. glazed cotton fabric of plain weave commonly with colorful printed designs generally in not less than five colors used for clothing and for interior decoration
²chintz *var of* CHINCH BUG
¹chintzy \'chin(t)sē, -si\ *adj, usu* -ER/-EST [*¹chintz* + *-y*] **1 :** decorated with or like chintz **2 :** GAUDY, CHEAP ⟨gave him a ~ toy⟩
²chintzy \"\ *var of* CHINCHY
¹chin-up *also* **chins-up** \'=,=\ *adj* **:** COURAGEOUS ⟨the *chin-up* British spirit⟩
²chin-up \"\ *n* -S [*chin up* to chin oneself] **:** the act of chinning oneself ⟨doing a dozen *chin-ups* each morning⟩
chin-wag \'=,=\ *n or vi, slang* **:** GOSSIP
chi·nyan·ja \chə'nyanjə\ *n, usu cap* **:** NYANJA
chi·o·coc·ca \,kīə'käkə\ *n, cap* [NL, fr. *chion-* + *-cocca* (fr. L *coccum* berry, fr. Gk *kokkos* kermes berry, seed)] **:** a small genus of tropical American shrubs (family Rubiaceae) having white or yellowish flowers and a white 2-seeded berry and usu. having roots with purgative properties — see CAHINCA ROOT
chi·og·e·nes \kī'äjə,nēz\ *n, cap* [NL, fr. *chion-* + Gk *-genēs* born — more at -GEN] *in some classifications* **:** a genus of creeping evergreens containing solely the creeping snowberry that is commonly placed in *Gaultheria*
chi·o·lite \'kīə,līt\ *n* -S [G *chiolith*, fr. *chion-* + *-lith* -lite] **:** a mineral $Na_5Al_3F_{14}$ resembling cryolite in color and composition
chion- *or* **chiono-** *also* **chio-** *comb form* [*chion-, chiono-* fr. NL, fr. Gk, fr. *chiōn* snow; *chio-* fr. G & NL, fr. Gk *chiōn;* akin to Gk *cheimōn* winter — more at HIBERNATE] **:** snow ⟨*chion*anthus⟩ ⟨*chio*lite⟩ ⟨*chiono*doxa⟩
chi·on·ablep·sia \,kī,än +\ *n* -S [NL, fr. *chion-* + *ablepsia*] **:** SNOW BLINDNESS
chi·o·nan·thus \,kīə'nan(t)thəs\ *n, cap* [NL, fr. *chion-* + *-anthus*] **:** a genus of low trees or shrubs (family Oleaceae) having drooping panicles of fragrant flowers with narrow petals — see FRINGE TREE
chi·o·nas·pis \-'naspəs\ *n, cap* [NL, fr. *chion-* + *-aspis*] **:** a genus of scales with elongate often white scales — see SCURFY SCALE
chi·o·ne \'kīə,nē\ *n, cap* [NL, fr. *Chione*, a mythological character shot by Diana, fr. L] **:** a genus of rock cockles (family Veneridae)
chi·o·nid·i·dae \,kīə'nidə,dē\ *n pl, cap* [NL, fr. *Chionid-, Chionis*, type genus (irreg. fr. Gk *chiōn* snow) + *-idae*] **:** a family of birds (order Charadriiformes) containing a single genus (*Chionis*) consisting of the sheathbills
chi·o·no·doxa \,kīənō'däksə, kī,änə'd-\ *n* [NL, fr. *chion-* + Gk *doxa* glory; akin to Gk *dokein* to seem good — more at DECENT] **1** *cap* **:** a genus of small bulbous herbs of the family Liliaceae having narrow leaves and the perianth segments united below — see GLORY-OF-THE-SNOW **2** -S **:** any plant of the genus *Chionodoxa*
chiot *usu cap, var of* SCIOT
¹chip \'chip\ *n* -S [ME; prob. akin to OE *-cippian* to cut] **1 a :** a small usu. somewhat thin and flat piece of wood, stone, or other material separated by a quick blow (as with a cutting or striking instrument) or by natural flaking **:** FRAGMENT, FLAKE **b (1) :** a small thin slice of food ⟨orange ~*s*⟩ ⟨just a ~ more⟩; *esp* **:** a thin crisp bit of cooked food **(2) :** a piece of potato french fried **c :** palm leaf, straw, or wood split into thin pieces for making women's hats ⟨~ bonnet⟩ **d (1) :** a metal often continuous fragment or curl cut during machining from material being machined **(2) :** the thread of material cut from a blank during the process of disc recording **e (1) :** a small piece from a crystal **(2) :** a piece of usu. uncut diamond weighing less than three fourths of a carat ⟨wearing a diamond ~ ring —Betty Smith⟩ **f** *chiefly Brit* **(1)** *or* **chip basket :** a ventilated container (as for fruit) made of thin sheets of split wood commonly overlapped at the bottom and secured at the upper edge by a band of similar wood **(2) :** the contents of such a container ⟨strawberries at two shillings a ~⟩ **g (1) :** CHIPBOARD **(2) :** logged wood for use in pulp manufacture **h chips** *pl* **:** soap in flakes or granules **i :** one of the thin slices or shreds into which beets are cut in sugar making — called also *cossette* **j :** a small piece of bark (as of cinchona or cinnamon) **2 a (1) :** something valueless or trivial ⟨I don't care a ~ for his views⟩ **(2) :** something small of its kind **:** BIT ⟨a ~ of a lad⟩ **b :** something dried up, withered, or flavorless ⟨meat roasted to a ~⟩ **3 :** something having the distinctive qualities of that from which it is derived or taken — used chiefly of persons with reference to resemblance of son to father ⟨Jack's exactly like his father, he's a real ~ off the old block⟩ **4 :** the triangular piece of wood attached to the end of a log line **5 :** a coin or a unit (as a small disk) equivalent to a coin in value: **a :** one of the counters used as a token for money in poker and other games of chance and usu. of a distinctive color to indicate its relative value **:** CHECK 11c **b :** a playing counter in such games as tiddledywinks **c chips** *pl, slang* **:** MONEY — used esp. in the phrase *in the chips* **d** *slang Brit* **:** any of various coins (as a shilling, rupee, or sovereign) **e chips** *pl* **:** something that is hazarded on some issue or the interest that one holds in some venture ⟨the industrialists that had their *chips* on Hitler⟩ **6 :** a piece of dried dung — used usu. in combination ⟨a cow ~⟩ ⟨buffalo ~*s*⟩ **7 :** a flaw in a surface remaining after a chip has been removed ⟨a cup with a ~ in its rim⟩ **8 :** CHIP SHOT **9 :** BEACH 3 — **chip on one's shoulder** [so called fr. the allusion to a chip of wood placed on the shoulder to be knocked off as a challenge to fight] **:** a challenging or bellicose attitude **:** readiness to take offense
²chip \"\ *vb* **chipped; chipped; chipping; chips** [ME *chippen*, fr. OE *-cippian* (as in *forcippian* to cut off); akin to obs. G *kipfen* to cut the point off, MLG *kēp* notch, ON *keipr* oarlock] *vt* **1** *obs* **:** to cut the crust from (bread) **2** *now dial Eng* **:** to fissure the surface of **:** CRACK, CHAP **3 a :** to cut or hew with or as if with an ax, chisel, or other edged tool **:** CHOP, HACK **b :** to cut or break (a small piece) from something ⟨~ a piece off the rock⟩ **:** cut or break a fragment from ⟨~ my best platter⟩ ⟨with the egg tooth the young bird ~*s* the shell⟩ **c :** to shape (a material or an object) by cutting or breaking away a little at a time ⟨~ flint to a point⟩ ⟨~ an arrowhead out of flint⟩ **d :** to cut or break up into fragments ⟨~ ice⟩ **:** reduce to chips (as wood for pulping) **e :** to decorate (as silver or enamel) by cutting chips from or chasing **4 :** to cut a piece or pieces of bark from (a tree) esp. in tapping for turpentine **5** *Austral* **:** HOE, HARROW **6** *slang Brit* **:** CHAFF, BANTER, TAUNT ~ *vi* **1** *obs* **:** to break into bud, shoot, or blossom **:** GERMINATE **2 :** to break or fly off in small pieces ⟨fine porcelain often ~*s* less readily than softer ware⟩ **3 a :** to bet one chip or a minimum amount in a poker game **:** CHECK *vi* 8a **b :** to play a chip (as in stops) when unable to play a card **4 :** to play a chip shot **5** *of an egg* **:** PIP 2b
³chip \"\ *vb* **chipped; chipped; chipping; chips** [perh. fr. *²chip*] *vt, dial Eng* **:** to trip or throw in wrestling ~ *vi* **1** *dial Eng* **:** to trip along nimbly **2** *dial Eng* **:** QUARREL — often used with *out*
⁴chip \"\ *n* -S **:** a trick or special attack for throwing a wrestling opponent
⁵chip \"\ *vi* **chipped; chipped; chipping; chips** [imit.] **:** ¹CHEEP
⁶chip \"\ *n* -S **:** ²CHEEP
chip away *vt* [*²chip*] **:** to remove, take away, or withdraw gradually ⟨night restores the magnificence that man has *chipped away* —Brooks Atkinson⟩ ~ *vi* **:** to chip away something — often used with *at* ⟨men who *chip away* at the American way of life⟩
chip ax *n* [*²chip*] **:** a small ax for chipping timber or stone into shape
chi·paya \chə'pīə\ *n, pl* **chipaya** *or* **chipayas** *usu cap* [Sp, of AmerInd origin] **1 a :** a people of Bolivia **b :** a member of such people **2 :** the language of the Chipaya people
chip basket *n* **:** CHIP 1 f (1)
chip bird *n* [*⁶chip*] **:** CHIPPING SPARROW
chip-blower \'=,==\ *n* **:** a dental instrument typically consisting of a rubber bulb with a long metal tube and used to blow drilling debris from a tooth cavity that is being prepared for filling
chipboard \'=,=\ *n* [*chip* "kind of paper stock" (fr. *¹chip*) + *board*] **:** a paperboard made from waste paper — called also *chip*
chip breaker *n* **:** a shoulder in a machine tool made by grinding a groove parallel to the cutting edge or by attaching a plate to the top to form a wall against which the chip produced in turning or other machining will be broken up

chip budding *n* **:** budding that is effected by the insertion of a bud on a chip of bark and wood into a mortise cut in the stock and that is used esp. for budding small grapevines

chip cap *n* **:** a plate fitted to the upper side of the cutting iron of a carpenter's plane and shaped to give the iron rigidity and break up the shavings

chip carving *n* **1 a :** hand carving of soft wood by cutting chips with a knife or other instrument usu. in simple geometric designs **b :** the decoration wrought by such carving **2 :** a surface decoration imitating chip carving

chip·e·wy·an *or* **chip·pe·wai·an** *or* **chip·pe·wy·an** \ˌchipə-ˈwīən\ *n, pl* **chipewyan** *or* **chipewyans** *or* **chippewaian** *or* **chippewaians** *or* **chippewyan** *or* **chippewyans** *usu cap* [Cree *Chipwayanawok*, lit., pointed skins, fr. *chipwa* pointed + *weyanaw* skin + *-ok* (suffix denoting pl.): fr. their pointed skin shirts or parkas] **1 a :** an Athapaskan people closely related to the Slave and Yellowknife people and living north of the Churchill river between the Great Slave lake and the Slave and Athabaska rivers on the west and Hudson Bay on the east **b :** a member of such people **2 :** the language of the Chipewyan people

chip hat palm *n* **:** a medium-sized fan palm (*Thrinax microcarpa*) of southern Florida and the Bahamas the leaves of which are used in making hats and baskets

chip in *vb* [²*chip*] *vi* **1 :** to put up a chip or chips as one's stake at cards **2 :** to contribute money or assistance to an enterprise ⟨all our people *chipped in* generously⟩ **3 :** to interject a comment into a conversation **:** INTERPOSE ~ *vt* **:** CONTRIBUTE ⟨*chip in* my time⟩ ⟨each of us *chipped* 10 dollars *in* to help pay for the damage⟩

chip log *n* **:** the common log consisting of a chip and log line

chip·man \ˈchipmən, -ˌman\ *n, pl* **chipmen** [*chip* + *man*] **1 :** a worker who cleans up metal chips and shavings from machining processes — called also *scrapman* **2 :** a worker who removes the flavor-giving wooden chips from beer-fermenting tanks and washes them for reuse

chip·muck \ˈchip,mək\ [by alter.] *now dial var of* CHIPMUNK

chip·munk *also* **chip·monk** \ˈchip,məŋk\ *n* -s [alter. (prob. influenced by *chipping squirrel*) of earlier *chitmunk*, of Algonquian origin; akin to Ojibwa *atchitamō* squirrel] **1 :** any of numerous small striped American squirrels (genera *Tamias* and *Eutamias*) that are semiterrestrial in habits and intermediate between the typical tree squirrels and the true ground squirrels — called also *ground squirrel, striped squirrel* **2 :** any of various other squirrels of similar habits or appearance (as the mantled ground squirrel)

chip·o·la·ta \ˌchipəˈläd·ə\ *n* -s [F, fr. It *cipollata*, fr. fem. of *cipollato* with onions, fr. *cipolla* onion (fr. LL *cepulla*, dim. of L *cepa, caepa* onion) + *-ato* -ate] **:** a small spicy sausage used chiefly as a garnish or hors d'oeuvre; *also* **:** a dish (as a ragout) of which such sausages are an ingredient

chip·pa·ble \ˈchipəbəl\ *adj* [²*chip* + *-able*] **:** capable of being chipped

chip·page \ˈchipij\ *n* -s [²*chip* + *-age*] **:** wood lost in felling trees with an ax

chipped *adj* [fr. past part. of ²*chip*] *of glass* **:** having a fernlike design resulting from fine chipping induced by coating the clear glass surface with glue and allowing it to dry

chipped beef \-p(t)ˈb-\ *also* **chip beef** *n* **:** smoked dried beef sliced thin

¹**chip·pen·dale** \ˈchipən,dāl *sometimes* -pᵊm,d-\ *adj, usu cap* [after Thomas *Chippendale* †1779 English cabinetmaker] **:** of, relating to, or closely imitating a style of furniture originating in late 18th century England that in its earlier forms closely resembled the Queen Anne style but in its more typical form is characterized by a graceful outline but often ornate rococo ornamentation, its chairs, in which the style is esp. typified, usu. distinguished by a seat wider at the front than back, by relatively sharp corners, and by a back usu. widened toward the top with carvings at the corners — see CHINESE CHIPPENDALE, FRENCH CHIPPENDALE, GOTHIC CHIPPENDALE

Chippendale chair

²**chippendale** \"\ *n* -s *usu cap* **1 :** an article of Chippendale furniture **2** [so called fr. its similarity to the color of Chippendale furniture] **:** a dark grayish brown that is stronger, slightly darker, and very slightly redder than average chocolate brown and deeper and very slightly yellower than African brown — called also *Afghan*

¹**chip·per** \ˈchipə(r)\ *n* -s [²*chip* + *-er*] **:** one that chips: as **a :** a tool, device, or machine used for removing unwanted material or surface roughness by chipping (as in finishing castings or forgings or cleaning painted metal); *specif* **:** a narrow blade with diametrically opposite and broad cutting points to be fitted between two circular saw blades in a dado head and designed to cut out the wood between the grooves cut by the circular blades **b :** a machine for reducing something (as pulpwood) to chips **c :** a workman who dresses, cleans, or finishes something by chipping or grinding ⟨ore ~⟩ ⟨pottery ~⟩ ⟨tire ~⟩ **:** an operator of a chipper **d :** a worker who chips trees for turpentine

²**chipper** \"\ *vi* -ED/-ING/-S [⁵*chip* + *-er*] **1** *of a bird* **:** CHIRP, TWITTER **2** *of a person* **:** CHATTER, BABBLE — see CHIPPER UP

³**chipper** *adj* [perh. var. of *kipper*] **:** being in high spirits **:** CHEERFUL, GAY, SPRIGHTLY ⟨looked ~, like a man who has been diverted by his own wit — Frances G. Patton⟩ **:** TRIM, TRIG ⟨a ~ man with a bandbox look⟩ **:** being in good health **:** being in a state of physical well-being **:** VIGOROUS ⟨as ~ as when I had last seen him, ten years before —James Thurber⟩

chipper up *vb* [³*chipper*] *vt* **:** to cause to be or become cheerful ~ *vi* **:** to cheer up

chip·pe·wa \ˈchipə,wȯ, -,wä, -,wā, -wə *also* -p(,)w-\ *n, pl* **chippewa** *or* **chippewas** *usu cap* **:** OJIBWA

chippewaian *or* **chippewyan** *var of* CHIPEWYAN

chipping *n* -s [fr. gerund of ²*chip*] **1 a :** the action of a chipper (as in dressing or shaping an object of iron, timber, or stone) **b :** the breaking off in small pieces (as of the edges of pottery or glassware) **2 :** a small piece separated in the process of chipping **:** CHIP, FRAGMENT **3 a :** the process of making chipped glass **b :** the decorative effect wrought by this process

chipping chisel *n* [fr. pres. part. of ²*chip*] **:** COLD CHISEL

chipping hammer *n* [fr. pres. part. of ²*chip*] **:** a pneumatically operated chisel

chipping sparrow *n* [fr. pres. part. of ⁵*chip*] **:** a small sparrow (*Spizella passerina*) that is one of the most familiar No. American birds, often building its nest sometimes lined with horsehair in the immediate vicinity of dwellings and having a weak monotonous trilling song — called also *chippy*

chipping squirrel *n* [fr. pres. part. of ⁵*chip*] **:** CHIPMUNK

chip potato *n* **:** FRENCH FRY

chip–proof \ˈ=ˌ=\ *adj* **:** not subject to chipping ⟨a *chip-proof* enamel finish⟩

¹**chip·py** \ˈchipē, -pi\ *adj* -ER/-EST [¹*chip* + *-y*] **1 :** like a chip esp. in dryness **2** *slang* **:** UNWELL; *specif* **:** suffering from a hangover

²**chippy** *or* **chip·pie** \"\ *n, pl* **chippies** [⁵*chip* + *-y, -ie*] **1 :** CHIPPING SPARROW **2** *slang* **:** a boldly flirtatious or sexually promiscuous woman; *sometimes* **:** PROSTITUTE **3** [by shortening and alter.] **:** CHIPMUNK **4 :** a narrow-gage railroad car

chipre *var of* CHYPRE

chips \ˈchips\ *n pl but sing in constr* [prob. fr. pl. of ¹*chip*] *slang* **:** a ship's carpenter

chip shop \ˈ=,=\ *n, Brit* **:** a fish-and-chip shop

chip shot *n* **:** a short usu. low approach shot in golf that lofts the ball to the green and allows it to roll — called also *pitch-and-run shot;* compare PITCH SHOT

chipyard \ˈ=,=\ *n* [¹*chip* + *yard*] **:** an area or enclosure where wood is cut up for fuel

chi·que·ro \chəˈker(,)ō\ *n* -s [Sp, fr. Ar dial. (Spain) *shirkair*] **:** TORIL

chi·qui·chi·qui palm \ˌchēkēˈchēkē-\ *n* [Sp *chiquichique*, fr. Tupi] **:** either of two So. American palms (*Leopoldinia piassaba* and *Attalea funifera*) yielding piassava fiber

chi·qui·to \chəˈkēd·(,)ō\ *n, pl* **chiquito** *or* **chiquitos** *usu cap* [Sp, dim. of *chico* little — more at CHICO] **1 a :** a people of southeastern Bolivia **b :** a member of such people **2 :** the language of the Chiquito people

chi·qui·to·an \-ēd·əwən\ *n, pl* **chiquitoan** *or* **chiquitoans** *usu cap* **:** a language family comprising Chiquito and including Manasi, Pinoki and Pinyoca

chir *var of* CHIR PINE

chir- *or* **chiro-** *also* **cheir-** *or* **cheiro-** *comb form* [L *chir-, chiro-*, fr. Gk *cheir-, cheiro-*, fr. *cheir;* akin to Alb *dore* hand, Hitt *kesar*, Toch A *tsar*] **:** hand ⟨*chiragra*⟩ ⟨*chiromancy*⟩ ⟨*cheirology*⟩

chi·rag·ra \kīˈragrə\ *n* -s [L, fr. Gk *cheiragra*, fr. *cheir-* chir- + *-agra*] **:** pain in the hand

chi·rap·sia \kīˈrapsēə\ *n* -s [NL, fr. Gk *cheirapsia* rough handling, fr. *cheir-* chir + *-apsia* (fr. *hapsis* contact, touching, fr. *haptein* to touch) — more at APSIS] **:** friction with the hand **:** MASSAGE

chi·ra·ta \chəˈräd·ə\ *also* **chi·ret·ta** \-red·ə\ *n* -s [Hindi *cirāitā*, fr. Skt *cirātikta, ciratikta*, perh. fr. *cira* long-lasting (perh. akin to Skt *cinoti* he gathers, heaps up) + *tikta* sharp, pungent; akin to Skt *tejate* it is sharp — more at POET, STICK] **:** the dried tissues of a green gentian (*Swertia chirata*) of northern India that has been used as a bitter tonic

chi–rho \ˈkēˈrō, ˈkī-\ *n* -s *usu cap C & R* [*chi* + *rho*, names of the 1st two letters of Gk *Christos* Christ] **:** a Christian monogram and symbol formed of the first two letters, *chi* (X) and *rho* (P), of the Greek word for *Christ* — called also *chrismon, christogram;* compare LABARUM

-chi·ria \ˈkīrēə, ˈkir-\ *or* **-chei·ria** \ˈkīr-\ *n comb form* -s [NL, fr. Gk *-cheiria*, fr. *cheir* hand — more at CHIR-] **:** -handedness ⟨*allochiria*⟩ ⟨*macrochiria*⟩

chir·i·ca·hua \ˌchirəˈkäwə\ *n, pl* **chiricahua** *or* **chiricahuas** *usu cap* [modif. of Sp *chiricahue*, fr. Apache, lit., great mountain; fr. their former residence around the Chiricahua mountains in southeastern Arizona] **1 a :** an American Indian people constituting a subdivision of the Gileños **b :** a member of such people **2 :** the language of the Chiricahua people

chir·i·gua·no \ˌchirəˈgwä(,)nō\ *n, pl* **chiriguano** *or* **chiriguanos** *usu cap* [Sp, of AmerInd origin] **1 a :** a Guaranian people inhabiting the slopes of the Bolivian cordillera and including the Guarayú, Pauserna, and Sirionó **b :** a member of the Chiriguano people **2 :** the language of the Chiriguano people

chi·ri·mia \ˌchirəˈmēə\ *or* **chi·ri·mi·lla** \-ē(y)ə\ *n* -s [Sp *chirimia, chirimilla*, modif. (influenced by *charamela*, a wind instrument) of MF *chalemie* — more at SHAWM] **:** a high-pitched oboe of Spain and Spanish America, esp. of the more remote areas of these countries

chirimoya *var of* CHERIMOYA

chi·ri·no \chəˈrē(,)nō\ *n, pl* **chirino** *or* **chirinos** *usu cap* [Sp, of AmerInd origin] **1 a :** an extinct people of western Ecuador **b :** a member of such people **2 :** the language of the Chirino people

¹**chi·ri·pa** \ˌchirəˈpä\ *n* -s [AmerSp *chiripá*, fr. Quechua *chiripak*, lit., for the cold, fr. *chiri* cold + *-pak* for] **:** a man's woolen garment rectangular in shape, usu. tucked in at the belt and wrapped in various ways around the hips and thighs, and worn by gauchos and Indians in southern So. America

²**chi·ri·pá** \"\ *n, pl* **chiripá** *or* **chiripás** *usu cap* [Sp & Pg, of AmerInd origin] **:** a significant subdivision of the Cayuá people of Brazil and Paraguay

chi·ri·qui \ˌchirəˈkē\ *also* **chi·ri·qui·an** \-ēən\ *adj, usu cap* [fr. *Chiriquí*, province of Panama] **:** of or relating to a prehistoric culture of western Panama noted for its pottery on which a design is produced by removing areas of a surface layer of pigment so that the original color of the pottery shows through

chi·ri·vi·ta \ˌchirəˈvēd·ə\ *n* -s [Sp *chiribita*] **:** the black angelfish or a related form

¹**chirk** \ˈchərk, -ōk\ *vb* -ED/-ING/-S [ME *chirken, charken*, fr. OE *cearcian* to creak, gnash — more at CRACK] *vi* **1 :** to make a shrill creaking, squeaking, or chirping noise (as of a door, a mouse, or a bird) ⟨the birds ceased from cheeping and ~*ing* —Gwyn Jones⟩ **2** *archaic* **:** to chirp like a bird **:** CHIRRUP **3 :** to become cheerful **:** CHEER — usu. used with *up* ~ *vt* **:** to make cheerful **:** CHEER — usu. used with *up*

²**chirk** \"\ *adj* -ER/-EST [prob. fr.¹*chirk*] *dial* **:** in good spirits **:** LIVELY, CHEERFUL

¹**chirl** \ˈchir(ə)l, -ər(-ə)l\ *n* -s [imit.] **1** *Scot* **:** CHIRP, WARBLE **2** *Scot* **:** a low melancholy sound

²**chirl** \"\ *vi* -ED/-ING/-S **1** *Scot* **:** CHIRP, SING, WARBLE **2** *Scot* **:** to emit a low melancholy sound

¹**chirm** \ˈchərm, ˈchi(ə)rm\ *n* -s [ME, fr. OE *cirm;* akin to OIr *gairm* cry, shout, OE *cearu* anxiety, sorrow — more at CARE] *dial* **:** NOISE, DIN; *esp* **:** confused noise, clamor, or hum (as of voices or insects)

²**chirm** \"\ *vi* -ED/-ING/-S [ME *chirmen*, fr. OE *cirman*, fr. *cirm*] **1** *dial* **:** to make a chirm **:** CHIRP **2** *dial* **:** CROON

chi·ro \ˈchē(,)rō\ *n* -s [origin unknown] **:** TENPOUNDER

chiro- — see CHIR-

chi·ro·cen·trus \ˌkīrōˈsen·trəs\ *n, cap* [NL, fr. *chir-* + *-centrus* (fr. L *centrum* center) — more at CENTER] **:** a genus of clupeoid fishes comprising the wolf herrings

chi·rog·a·le \kīˈrägəlē\ [F *chéirogale*, fr. NL *cheirogaleus*] *syn of* CHEIROGALEUS 1

chi·rog·no·mist \kīˈrägnəməst\ *n* -s **:** PALMIST

chi·rog·no·my \-mē\ *n* -ES [modif. (influenced by *-gnomy*) of F *chirognomonie*, fr. *chir-* + *-gnomonie*, fr. Gk *-gnōmonia* judging (as in *physiognōmonia* physiognomy) — more at -GNOMY] **:** PALMISTRY

chi·ro·graph \ˈkīrə,graf\ *n* -s [MF *chirographe*, fr. L *chirographum* autograph, that which is written with one's own hand, fr. neut. of Gk *cheirographos* written with the hand, fr. *cheir-* chir- + *-graphos* -graph] **1 :** any of various legal instruments formally written or signed: as **a :** an indenture formerly made in duplicate on one sheet, the sheet or parchment being divided and often the word *chirographum* written in where the division was made **b :** the indenture of a fine of lands; *also* **:** one of the counterparts of such an indenture **c :** an obligation (as a bond or note) given in one's own handwriting **2 :** an apostolic letter in the handwriting and with the signature of the pope

chi·rog·ra·phary \kīˈrägrə,ferē, ˌkīrəˈgrafərē\ *adj* [LL *chirographarius*, fr. L *chirographum* chirograph + L *-arius* -ary] *of a legal entity* **:** created or evidenced by means of a chirograph ⟨a ~ debt⟩ ⟨a ~ creditor⟩

chi·rog·ra·pher \kīˈrägrəfə(r)\ *n* -s [alter. (influenced by LL *chirographarius*) of earlier *cirographer*, fr. AF or ML; AF *cirografer* fr. ML *chirographarius*, fr. LL, signed, of handwriting, fr. *chirographus* + *-arius* -er] **:** one who studies or practices chirography

chi·ro·graph·ic \ˌkīrəˈgrafik\ *or* **chi·ro·graph·i·cal** \-əkəl\ *adj* [*chirograph* + *-ic, -ical*] **:** of, relating to, or in handwriting

chi·rog·ra·phy \kīˈrägrəfē\ *n* -ES [*chirograph* + *-y*] **1 :** HANDWRITING, PENMANSHIP ⟨a document in the ~ of the late governor⟩ **2 :** CALLIGRAPHY 1 ⟨skilled in ~⟩

chi·ro·man·cer \ˈkīrə,man(t)sə(r)\ *also* **chi·ro·man·cist** \-səst\ *n* -s [*chiromancy* + *-er* or *-ist*] **:** one who practices chiromancy

chi·ro·man·cy *also* **chei·ro·man·cy** \-sē\ *n* -ES [prob. fr. MF *chiromancie, cyromancie*, fr. ML *chiromantia*, fr. (assumed) MGk *cheiromanteia* (after Gk *cheiromantis* chiromancer), fr. Gk *cheir-* chir- + *manteia* divination — more at -MANCY] **:** divination by examination of the hand **:** PALMISTRY

chi·ro·man·tic \ˌkīrəˈmantik\ *or* **chi·ro·man·ti·cal** \-əkəl\ *adj* [MF *chiromantique*, fr. ML *chiromantia* chiromancy + MF *-ique* -ic] **:** of or relating to chiromancy or chiromancers

chi·ro·meg·a·ly \ˌkīrəˈmegəlē\ *n* -ES [ISV *chir-* + *-megaly*] **:** abnormal increase in the size of the hands

chi·ro·mys \ˈkīrə,mis\ [NL, fr. *chir-* + *-mys*] *syn of* DAUBENTONIA

chi·ro·nec·tes \ˌkīrəˈnek,tēz\ *n, cap* [NL, fr. *chir-* + *-nectes*] **:** a genus of tropical American marsupial mammals consisting of the yapok

chi·ro·nom·ic *or* **chei·ro·nom·ic** \ˌkīrəˈnämik\ *adj* [*chironomy* + *-ic*] **:** related to or based upon chironomy — used of musical notation, esp. neumes

¹**chi·ron·o·mid** \kīˈränəməd\ *adj* [NL *Chironomidae*] **:** of or relating to the Chironomidae

²**chironomid** \"\ *n* -s **:** an insect of the family Chironomidae

chi·ro·nom·i·dae \ˌkīrəˈnämə,dē\ *n pl, cap* [NL, fr. *Chironomus*, type genus + *-idae*] **:** a family of minute long-legged nematocerous two-winged flies that is now usu. restricted to forms without piercing mouthparts but formerly also including the biting midges and related forms

chi·ron·o·mus \kīˈränəməs\ *n, cap* [NL, fr. LGk *cheironomos* one who gestures with the hands, fr. Gk *cheir-* chir- + *-nomos* manager (fr. *nemein* to manage)] **:** the type genus of Chironomidae

chi·ron·o·my *or* **chei·ron·o·my** \kīˈränəmē\ *n* -ES [L *chironomia*, fr. Gk *cheironomia*, fr. *cheir-* chir- + *-nomia* management, fr. *nemein* to distribute, manage — more at NIMBLE] **:** a method of directing the singing of Gregorian chant by hand gestures indicating the rise and fall of the melody

chi·ro·patagium \ˌkīrə+\ *n, pl* **chiropatagia** [NL, fr. *chir-* + *patagium*] **:** the wing membrane between the fingers in bats

chi·ro·plast \ˈkīrə,plast\ *n* -s [*chir-* + *-plast*] **:** a mechanical device for teaching hand position at the piano

chi·ro·plasty \-ē\ *n* -ES [*chir-* + *-plasty*] **:** plastic surgery of the hand

chi·ro·po·di·al \ˌkīrəˈpōdēəl\ *adj* [*chiropody* + *-al*] **:** of or relating to chiropody

chi·rop·o·dist \kəˈräpədəst *also* ÷ shəˈr- *sometimes* kīˈr-\ *n* -s [*chir-* + *-pod* + *-ist*] **:** one who practices chiropody — called also *podiatrist*

chi·rop·o·dous \kīˈräpədəs\ *adj* [*chiropod-* (fr. obs. NL *Cheiropoda*, former name for mammals with handlike feet, fr. *cheir-* chir- + *-poda*) + *-ous*] **:** having the feet modified for grasping and climbing

chi·rop·o·dy \kəˈräpədē *also* ÷ shəˈr- *sometimes* kīˈr-\ *n* -ES [*chiropodist* + *-y*] **:** the care and treatment of the human foot in health and disease — called also *podiatry*

chi·ro·prac·tic \ˈkīrə,praktik, ˌ==ˈ==\ *n* -s [*chir-* + Gk *praktikos* effective, practical — more at PRACTICAL] **:** a system of healing based upon the theory that disease results from a lack of normal nerve function and employing treatment by scientific manipulation and specific adjustment of body structures (as the spinal column) and utilizing physical therapy when necessary

chi·ro·prac·tor \ˈ==,=tə(r)\ *n* -s [*chiropractic* + *-or*] **:** a practitioner of chiropractic

chi·ro·prax·is \ˈ==,praksəs, ˌ==ˈ==\ *n, pl* **chiroprax·es** \-sēz\ [NL, fr. *chir-* + *-praxis*] **:** CHIROPRACTIC

chi·rop·sal·mus \ˌkī,räpˈsalməs\ *n, cap* [NL, fr. *chir-* + Gk *psalmos* twitching, plucking, string music, psalm, fr. *psallein* to pluck, twitch — more at PSALM] **:** a genus of Cubomedusae comprising the fire medusae

chi·rop·ter \ˈkī,räptə(r), =ˈ==\ *n* -s [NL *Chiroptera*] **:** ³BAT 1

chi·rop·tera \=ˈ=tərə\ *n pl, cap* [NL, fr. *chir-* + *-ptera*] **:** an order of eutherian mammals modified for true flight comprising the recent and extinct bats, all believed to have differentiated from an ancestral insectivore line during the early Eocene — **chi·rop·ter·an** \(ˈ)=ˈ==rən\ *adj or n* — **chi·rop·ter·ous** \(ˈ)=ˈ==rəs\ *adj*

chi·rop·ter·ite \=ˈ==,rīt\ *n* -s [NL *Chiroptera* + E *-ite*] **:** guano formed by bats in prehistoric times

chi·rop·ter·oph·i·lous \(ˈ)kī,räptəˈräfələs\ *adj* [NL *Chiroptera* + E *-o-* + *-philous*] **:** pollinated by bats

chi·rop·te·ryg·i·um \ˌkī,räptəˈrijēəm\ *n* -s [NL, fr. *chir-* + *pterygium*] **:** the typical jointed and fingered limb of a vertebrate animal conceived of as having developed from a finlike appendage — compare ICHTHYOPTERYGIUM

chi·ros·o·phy \kīˈräsəfē\ *n* -ES [*chir-* + *-sophy*] **:** CHIROMANCY

chi·ro·spasm \ˈkīrə+,-\ *n* [*chir-* + *spasm*] **:** WRITER'S CRAMP

chi·ro·tes \kīˈrōd·ēz\ *n, cap* [NL, irreg. fr. Gk *cheir* hand — more at CHIR-] **:** a genus of wormlike burrowing lizards related to *Amphisbaena* having small forelimbs but no hind limbs

chi·ro·the·sia \ˌkīrōˈthēzh(ē)ə\ *n* -s [LGk *cheirothesia*, fr. Gk *cheir-* chir- + *-thesia* (fr. *thesis* setting, placing, fr. *tithenai* to set, place) — more at DO] **:** imposition of hands as in the ecclesiastical rites of confirmation and ordination

chi·rot·o·ny \kīˈrätᵊnē\ *n* -ES [Gk *cheirotonia*, fr. *cheir-* chir- + *-tonia* (fr. *tonos* stretching, tension) — more at TONE] **:** the extension of hands in bestowing a blessing in an ecclesiastical rite

¹**chirp** \ˈchərp, -ōp\ *vb* -ED/-ING/-S [imit.] *vi* **1 :** to make a usu. repetitive short sharp sound (as of small birds or crickets) **:** CHIRRUP ⟨grasshoppers ~*ing* and birds singing —G.B.Shaw⟩ **2 :** to make a sound imitating or resembling the chirping of a bird esp. in speaking ⟨someone turned on the water down the hall and all the second floor faucets ~*ed* at once —Nelson Algren⟩ ~ *vt* **:** to say or utter with a sound of chirping ⟨wait until the boldest ~s: "It was tonight, dear, wasn't it?" —Archibald MacLeish⟩

²**chirp** \"\ *n* -s **1 :** a short sharp note natural to some birds or insects (as crickets) **:** CHIRRUP **2 :** a sound imitating or resembling a chirp

chirp·i·ly \-pəlē, -li\ *adv* **:** in a chirpy manner

chir pine *or* **chir** *also* **cheer pine** \ˈchi(ə)r\ *n* [Hindi *cīr* pine] **:** an East Indian resinous timber pine (*Pinus roxburghii*) the wood of which is used as a substitute for northern pine or fir

chirp·i·ness \ˈchərpēnəs, -ōp-, -pin-\ *n* -ES **:** the quality or state of being chirpy

chirping *adj* **1 :** noisily lively as from high spirits ⟨a ~ and merry companion⟩ **2 :** CHEERING, ENLIVENING ⟨a ~ drink⟩ — **chirp·ing·ly** *adv*

chirpy \ˈchərpē, -ōp-, -pi\ *adj* -ER/-EST **1 a :** given to chirping ⟨as ~ as a sparrow —Ruth Park⟩ **b :** resembling or suggesting chirping **:** marked by a quality similar to that of chirping ⟨the average coloratura's ~ twitter —Irving Kolodin⟩ ⟨~ little voices⟩ **2 :** cheerfully lively **:** CHEERFUL ⟨a ~ indifference to reality —*Times Lit. Supp.*⟩

¹**chirr** \ˈchər, +V -ər-; ˈchə, +V -ər- *also* -ōr\ *n* -s [imit.] **1 :** the short esp. vibrant or trilled and repetitive sound characteristic of certain insects (as grasshoppers and cicadas) and some birds and animals and often suggesting the rubbing together of two rough surfaces **2 :** a sound like a chirr

²**chirr** \"\ *vi* -ED/-ING/-S **:** to make a chirr ⟨the ~*ing* of a squirrel —Archie Binns⟩ ⟨the crickets never ~*ed* so blithely —Rex Ingamells⟩ ⟨the endless ~*ing* of their bills against the rice grains —Archibald Rutledge⟩

¹**chir·rup** \ˈchər·əp, ˈchirəp\ *vb* -ED/-ING/-S [imit.] *vi* **1 :** CHIRP **2 :** to make a sound like a chirrup esp. by sucking in air through compressed lips (as in urging on a horse) ⟨~ to a pony⟩ ⟨the bullets ~*ed* by in the soft buzzing sound of insects on the wing —Norman Mailer⟩ ~ *vt* **:** to utter by chirruping

²**chirrup** \"\ *n* -s **:** the act or the sound of chirruping ⟨the house sparrow's metallic ~ —*British Birds in Colour*⟩ ⟨the sudden ~ of police whistles —Dan Wickenden⟩

chir·rupy \-ē,-i\ *adj* **1 :** CHEERFUL, LIVELY, CHIRPY ⟨standing, gay and ~ before the footlights, eyes twinkling from audience to fellow actors in enjoyment —*Fortnight*⟩ **2 :** CHATTY ⟨a ~ chronicle of how Hollywood romped and played —Gordon Kahn⟩

chirs *pres 3d sing of* CHIR, *pl of* CHIR

chiru \ˈchir(,)ü\ *n* -s [prob. native name in Tibet] **:** a pinkish-fawn goat antelope (*Pantholops hodgsoni*) of the Tibetan plateau the male being distinguished by a laterally swollen muzzle and very long nearly straight horns

chirurgeon *n* -s [alter. (influenced by L *chirurgia* surgery) of ME *cirurgian*, fr. OF *cirurgien*, fr. *cirurgie* surgery + *-ien* -ian] *archaic* **:** SURGEON

chirurgery *n* -ES [alter. (influenced by L *chirurgia* surgery) of earlier *cyrurgery*, fr. ME *syrurgery*, fr. OF *cirurgerie* — more at SURGERY] *archaic* **:** SURGERY

-chi·rur·gia \ˌkīˈrərjēə, -ˈrəj-,-ˈrəij-\ *n comb form* -s [NL, fr. L *chirurgia*] **:** surgery **:** cutting ⟨enterochirurgia⟩ ⟨pneumochirurgia⟩

chirurgic *or* **chirurgical** *adj* [*chirurgic*, fr. F or L; F *chirurgique* fr. L *chirurgicus*, fr. *chirurgia* + *-icus* -ic; *chirurgical*, alter. of earlier *cyrurgical*, fr. MF or ML; MF *cirurgical* fr. ML *cirurgicalis, chirurgicalis*, fr. L *chirurgicus* + *-alis* -al] *archaic* **:** of, concerned with, or treating of surgery **:** SURGICAL

chis *pl of* CHI

¹**chis·el** \ˈchizəl\ *n* -s [obs. *chisel, chesil* gravel, fr. ME, fr. OE *cisel, ceosel;* akin to OHG *kisil* pebble, OPruss *sixdo* sand, Lith *žiezdrà* gravel, grain] *dial Eng* **:** BRAN **:** coarse flour

²chisel \"\ *n* -s [ME, fr. ONF, prob. alter. of *chisoir* gold-

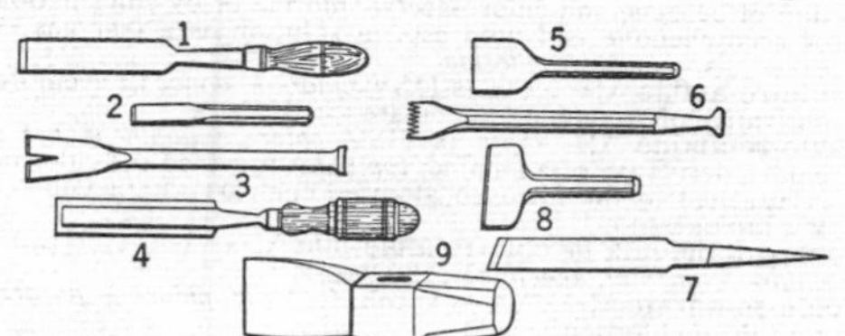

chisels: *1* socket paring chisel, *2* cold chisel, *3* box chisel, *4* beveled firmer chisel, *5* floor chisel, *6* stonecutter's tooth chisel, *7* turning chisel, *8* bricklayer's chisel, *9* blacksmith's chisel

smith's chisel, fr. (assumed) VL *caesorium* cutting instrument, fr. L *caesus* (past part. of *caedere* to cut) + *-orium* -ory — more at CONCISE] **1 :** a tool consisting of a metal bar with a sharpened edge at one end used for working on the surface of various materials by chipping, carving, turning, or other cutting action and often driven by a mallet **2 a :** a strong heavy tractor-drawn tillage tool with curved points used for deep stirring without turning the soil

³chisel \"\ *vb* **chiseled** *or* **chiselled; chiseled** *or* **chiselled; chiseling** *or* **chiselling** \-z(ə)liŋ\ **chisels** *vt* **1 :** to cut, pare, gouge, engrave, or shape with or as if with a chisel — often used with *out* ⟨~ a block of marble into a statue⟩ **2 a :** to cut close (as in a bargain) **:** CHEAT **b :** to employ shrewd sometimes unfair practices on (as a person) to obtain one's end; *also* **:** to obtain by such practices **3 :** to stir (soil) with a chisel ~ *vi* **1 :** to work with a chisel ⟨the actual cutter merely ~*ed* within the outlines of a preliminary drawing —F.W. Goudy⟩ **2 a :** to employ shrewd sometimes unfair practices to obtain an end ⟨~ for good marks in a college course⟩ **b :** to thrust oneself **:** INTRUDE — used with *in* or *in on* ⟨trying to ~ in on the beer racket —Polly Adler⟩

chiseled *or* **chiselled** *adj* **1 :** cut, shaped, or wrought with a chisel **2 :** appearing as if chiseled **:** CLEAR-CUT, CARVEN ⟨~ phrases⟩ ⟨a ~ face⟩ **3 :** shaped like a chisel ⟨a ~ crowbar⟩

chis·el·er *or* **chis·el·ler** \'chiz(ə)lə(r)\ *n* -s **1 :** one that chisels **:** CHEAT; petty crook **:** GOUGER **2** *Irish* **:** CHILD

chis·el·ly \-lē\ *adj* [obs. E *chisel* gravel + *-y* — more at CHISEL (bran)] **1** *dial Eng* **:** GRAVELLY, GRITTY **2** *dial* **:** UNPLEASANT, DISAGREEABLE

chiselmouth \'=,=\ *n* -s **:** a cyprinoid fish (*Acrocheilus alutaceus*) of the Columbia river having a large straight-edged horny plate in each jaw

chisel tooth *n* **:** a tooth shaped like a chisel; *esp* **:** one of the incisor teeth of a rodent

chisel-tooth saw *n* **:** a circular wood saw having inserted teeth with chisel-shaped cutting edges

chish·ti \'chishtē\ *n, usu cap* [after Mu'īn al-Din Muhammad *Chishti*, saint of India †1236, its founder] **:** a Sufi brotherhood centered in India

chislev *usu cap, var of* KISLEV

chi-square \'kī,-\ *n* **:** the sum of the quotients obtained by dividing the square of the difference between the observed and theoretical values of a quantity by the theoretical value

chis·set \'chizət\ *var of* CHESSET

chist \'chist\ *dial var of* CHEST

chis·te·ra \chi'sterə\ *n* -s [Sp, fr. Basque *xistera* basket, chistera, fr. L *cistella*, dim. of *cista* box, chest, basket — more at CHEST] **:** a wicker scoop used by a jai alai player

chist·ka \'chis(t)kə\ *n* -s [Russ, lit., cleaning, cleansing, fr. *chistit'* to clean, fr. *chisty* clean, fr. ORuss *čistŭ*; akin to L *scindere* to split — more at SHED] **:** a political purge

¹chit \'chit, *usu* -id·+V\ *n* -s [ME *chitte* kitten, cub, perh. alter. (influenced by such pairs as *church: kirk*) of *kit*, short for *kitling*] **1** *obs* **:** the offspring of an animal (as a cub or whelp) **:** KIT **2 a :** CHILD **b :** a person likened to a child; *esp* **:** a pert or forward young woman ⟨has no use for young ~s of girls —Christopher Isherwood⟩

²chit \"\ *n* -s [prob. alter. of ME *chithe* sprout, fr. OE *cīth*; akin to OS *kīth* bud, young shoot, OHG *-kīdi* shoot — more at CHINE] **1 chits** *pl, obs* **:** rice of second or third grade **2 :** SHOOT, SPROUT

³chit \"\ *vb* **chitted; chitted; chitting; chits** *vi, dial Eng* **:** GERMINATE, SPROUT ⟨after a period of about 48 hours, the grain begins to ~ —Norman Wymer⟩ ~ *vt* **:** to remove chits from (as potatoes)

⁴chit \"\ *n* -s [short for *chitty* fr. Hindi *ciṭṭhī*] **1 :** a short letter or note **:** a written message **:** MEMORANDUM ⟨a ~ written by the president specifically to be read to them —*Time*⟩; *esp* **:** a certificate of recommendation (as one given to a servant) **2 a :** a signed voucher or memorandum of a small debt (as for food or drinks) ⟨seldom carries money; signing a ~ is so much easier —Nancy B. Shea⟩ **b :** CHECK, DRAFT, ORDER, BILL, RECEIPT ⟨put in a ~ for ninety cents' fare —McKenzie Porter⟩ ⟨23 percent of your bill is added automatically to the ~ as the tip —Tad Szulc⟩; *broadly* **:** a small slip of paper with writing on it

¹chita *var of* CHEETAH

²chi·ta \chə'tä\ *adj, usu cap* [fr. *Chita*, U.S.S.R.] **:** of or from the city of Chita, U.S.S.R. **:** of the kind or style prevalent in Chita

chi·tal *also* **chee·tal** *or* **chee·tul** \'chēd·ᵊl\ *n, pl* **chital** *also* **cheetal** *or* **cheetul** [Hindi *cītal*, fr. Skt *citrala* variegated, fr. *citra* spotted, bright — more at -HOOD] **:** AXIS DEER

chi-tan *usu cap C, var of* KHITAN

chi·tar·ri·no \,kēd·ə'rē(,)nō\ *n, pl* **chitarri·ni** \-(,)nē\ [It, dim. of *chitarra*, fr. Gk *kithara* lyre] **:** a small guitar

chi·tar·ro·ne \,kēd·ə'rō(,)nā\ *n, pl* **chitarro·ni** \-(,)nē\ [It, aug. of *chitarra*] **:** a bass or a contrabass of the lute family

¹chit·chat \'chit,chat, *usu* -ad·+V\ *n* [redupl. of *chat*] **:** familiar or trifling talk or conversation **:** SMALL TALK, GOSSIP ⟨the ~ between contestant and quizmaster —*Time*⟩

²chitchat \"\ *vi* **:** to make chitchat **:** indulge in small talk **:** GOSSIP ⟨a girl can't get along anymore just by *chitchatting* on the dance floor —Louis Auchincloss⟩ ⟨*chitchatted*, swopping experiences —Rose Thurburn⟩

chit·chat·ty \-ad·ē\ *adj, usu* -ER/-EST **:** given to or full of chitchat

chit·i·ma·cha \,chid·ə'mäshə\ *n, pl* **chitimacha** *or* **chitimachas** *usu cap* [perh. Choctaw *Chutimasha*, lit., they have cooking pots, fr. *chúti* cooking pot + *másha* they possess] **1 a :** an Indian people of the Mississippi delta **b :** a member of such people **2 :** the language of the Chitimacha people

¹chit·i·ma·chan \;==;=shən\ *adj, usu cap* **:** of or relating to the Chitimacha or their language

²chitimachan \"\ *n, pl* **chitimachan** *or* **chitimachans** *usu cap* [¹*Chitimachan*] **:** a language family of the Gulf phylum in Louisiana comprising the Chitimacha language

chi·tin \'kītᵊn\ *n* -s [F *chitine*, fr. Gk *chitōn* chiton, tunic + F *-ine* -in] **:** a white or colorless amorphous horny substance that forms part of the hard outer integument of insects, crustaceans, and some other invertebrates and occurs also in fungi, being a polysaccharide structurally similar to cellulose except that the repeating unit is derived from acetylglucosamine instead of glucose

chi·tin·i·za·tion \,kītᵊnə'zāshən\ *n* -s [*chitin* + *-ization*] **:** the process of becoming chitinous **:** the state of being chitinous

chi·tin·ized \'kītᵊn,īzd\ *adj* [*chitin* + *-ized*] **:** filled in with chitin esp. with a hardening effect ⟨elytra strongly ~⟩

chi·tin·og·e·nous \,kītᵊn¦äjənəs\ *adj* [*chitin* + *-o-* + *-genous*] **:** producing chitin ⟨~ hypodermal cells of arthropods⟩

chi·tin·oid \'kītᵊn,ȯid\ *adj* [*chitin* + *-oid*] **:** resembling chitin esp. in physical properties

chi·tin·o·phosphatic \¦kītᵊn,ō+\ *adj* [*chitin* + *-o-* + *phosphatic*] *of certain marine shells* **:** made up of chitin and calcium phosphates — used chiefly of inarticulate brachiopods

chi·tin·ous \'kītᵊnəs\ *adj* [*chitin* + *-ous*] **:** of or like chitin

chitlings *or* **chitlins** *var of* CHITTERLINGS

chit·munk \'chit,məŋk\ *dial var of* CHIPMUNK

chi·to melon \'kē,tō-\ *n* [NL *chito*, specific epithet of *Cucumis chito*] **:** MANGO MELON

chi·ton \'kītᵊn, -,tän\ *n* [NL, fr. Gk *chitōn* tunic, of Sem origin; akin to Heb *kuttōneth* coat, Syr *kettānā* linen, Assyr-Bab *kitū*, *kitinnu* linen] **1** *cap* **:** a large genus (the type of the family Chitonidae) of mollusks of the order Polyplacophora (class Amphineura) having the girdle covered with imbricating scales, no eyes, and gills extending the length of the foot **2** -s **:** a mollusk of the order Polyplacophora **3** -s [Gk *chitōn*] **:** the basic garment of ancient Greece worn usu. knee-length by men and full-length by women and made in two styles: **a :** an oblong of usu. wool cloth with a wide turndown at the top to form a double waist, folded in half about the body, pinned once on each shoulder with a fibula, and girdled at the waist in the Doric style **b :** a garment usu. of wool or linen differing from the Doric in being fuller and more elaborate and in having sewn sides and sleeves formed by a series of pins along the upper fold in the later Ionic style

Doric chiton

chi·to·sa·mine \kī'tōsə,mēn, -,mən\ *n* -s [ISV *chitin* + *-ose* + *-amine*; orig. formed as G *chitosamin*] **:** glucosamine esp. as obtained from chitin by hydrolysis

chi·to·san \'kīdə,san\ *n* -s [ISV *chit-* (fr. *chitin*) + *-ose* + *-an*] **:** a substance formed from chitin by partial deacetylation with alkali

chi·tose \'kī,tōs *also* -ōz\ *n* -s [*chitin* + *-ose*] **:** a nonfermentable sugar formed from glucosamine by the action of nitrous acid

chi·tra \'chi·trə\ *n, pl* **chitra** [Hindi *citra* spotted, fr. Skt, spotted, bright — more at -HOOD] **:** AXIS DEER

chi·tra·li \chi'trälē\ *n, pl* **chitrali** *also* **chitralis** *usu cap* [fr. *Chitral*, state in Pakistan] **1 a :** a people living on the slopes of the Hindu Kush, Afghanistan **b :** a member of such people **2 :** the language of the Chitrali people

chits *pl of* CHIT, *pres 3d sing of* CHIT

chit·ta·gong \'chid·ə,gäŋ, -ȯŋ\ *adj, usu cap* [fr. *Chittagong*, Pakistan] **:** of or from the city of Chittagong, Pakistan **:** of the kind or style prevalent in Chittagong

chittagong wood *n, usu cap C* [fr. *Chittagong*, division of East Bengal, Pakistan] **:** the wood of either of two Indian trees (*Chukrasia tabularis* and *Toona ciliata*) of the family Meliaceae used for its mahoganylike qualities in cabinetwork

chit·tak *or* **chit·tack** *or* **chat·tak** *or* **chat·tack** \chə'täk\ *n* -s [Bengali *chaṭāk*] **:** an Indian unit of weight equal to 1/16 seer or 900 grains

chit·tam bark *also* **chit·tem bark** *or* **chit·tim bark** \'chid-əm-\ *n* [perh. of Muskogean origin; akin to Choctaw *shitimmi* puff, swell] **:** the bark of the cascara buckthorn

chittamwood *or* **chittimwood** \'==,=\ *n* **1 :** SMOKE TREE 1b **2 :** CASCARA BUCKTHORN **3 :** BUCKTHORN 2; *esp* **:** FALSE BUCKTHORN

chitted *past of* CHIT

¹chit·ter \'chid·ə(r)\ *vi* -ED/-ING/-S [ME *chiteren*, prob. of imit. origin] **1 :** to twitter like a bird **:** CHIRP **:** chatter like a squirrel **2** *dial Brit* **:** to shiver or chatter esp. with cold

²chitter \"\ *n* -s **:** the act or sound of chittering **:** TWITTER

chit·ter-chat·ter \'chid·ə(r),chad·ə(r)\ *n* -s [redupl. (prob. influenced by *chit-chat*) of ²*chatter*] **1 :** light and lively discussion **2 :** trivial, nonsensical, or incessant talk

chit·ter·lings \'chitlənz *sometimes* -id·ə|lənz *or* -id·|ᵊliŋz *or* -id·ə(r)liŋz *or* -it| *or* -itliŋz\ *or* **chit·lings** \'chitlənz *sometimes* -liŋz\ *or* **chit·lins** \'chitlənz\ *n pl* [ME *chitirling*; prob. akin to MHG *kutel* tripe, OE *cwith* womb, OHG *quiti* vulva, ON *kviðr* belly, Goth *qiþus* womb, L *botulus* intestine, sausage, Skt *guda* intestine, Gk *gyros* round — more at COWER] **:** the intestines of hogs esp. prepared as food

chitting *pres part of* CHIT

chiurm *n* -s [F & It; F *chiourme* fr. It *ciurma*, fr. L *celeusma*, command given by head oarsman so that rowers can keep in time, fr. Gk *keleusma*, *keleuma* command, command given to rowers, fr. *keleuein* to command, incite; akin to Gk *kellein* to land a ship, drive on — more at HOLD] *obs* **:** a gang of galley slaves

¹chiv \'chiv, 'sh-\ *var of* ²,³CHIVE

²chiv \"\ *n* -s [perh. short for E dial. *Chivy Chase*, *Chevy Chase* chase, pursuit, noise, confusion (used in rhyming slang to mean "face") — more at CHIVY] *slang Austral* **:** FACE

chivage *var of* CHEVAGE

chiv·al·resque \¦shivəl¦resk, shə¦valə¦resk\ *or* **che·va·le·resque** \shə¦valə¦resk, F shəvålresk\ *adj* [*chivalry* + *-esque* (after F *chevaleresque*, after It *cavalleresco*)] **1 :** of, relating to, or befitting chivalry ⟨~ knights⟩ ⟨~ manners⟩ **2 :** having the spirit or manners of chivalry ⟨a ~ romance⟩ ⟨a ~ gentleman⟩

chi·val·ric \shə'valrik, -ēk *sometimes* 'shivəl(,)rik\ *adj* [*chivalry* + *-ic*] **:** relating to chivalry **:** CHIVALROUS

chivalric rite *n, usu cap C & often cap R* **:** the ceremonial observed by the Knights Templar body of Freemasons

chiv·al·rous \'shivəlrəs *sometimes* shə'val-\ *adj* [ME, fr. MF *chevalereus*, fr. *chevalier* knight + *-eus* -ous — more at CHEVALIER] **1 :** characteristic of or like a knight of feudal times esp. in valor **:** VALIANT, WARLIKE ⟨in brave pursuit of ~ emprise —Edmund Spenser⟩ **2 :** relating to, according with, or suggestive of the system of chivalry and knight-errantry obtaining in the age of chivalry in the later medieval period ⟨the austere inspection of . . . these battlemented city walls and these dark churches could not have been more ~ —George Santayana⟩ **3 a :** characteristic of or relating to the ideal knight of feudal and Renaissance times according to modern romantic tradition **b :** marked by honor, fairness, generosity, and kindliness esp. to foes, the weak and lowly, and the vanquished according to knightly tradition ⟨Robert E. Lee, the great Southern general, ~, gentle —S.V.Benét⟩ **c :** marked by especial courtesy and high-minded disinterested consideration to women ⟨a broken heart made an irresistible appeal to a ~ mind —Ellen Glasgow⟩ **4 :** of or relating to a knight **:** KNIGHTLY ⟨~ rank⟩ **syn** see CIVIL

chivalrously *adv* **:** in a chivalrous manner

chiv·al·rous·ness \-nəs\ *n* -ES **:** quality of being chivalrous **:** COURTESY

chiv·al·ry \'shivəlrē, -ri\ *n* -ES [ME *chivalrie*, fr. OF *chevalerie*, fr. *chevalier* knight + *-ie* -y] **1 a :** mounted men at arms **:** heavy cavalry of the middle ages; *also* **:** a medieval army whose strength was in its mounted men **b :** cavalry of ancient times **2** *archaic* **a :** the rank, position, or characteristics of a feudal knight; *esp* **:** martial valor **b :** a gallant deed **:** EXPLOIT **c :** knightly skill **:** dexterity in arms ⟨the glory of our Troy this day doth lie on his fair worth and single ~ —Shak.⟩ **3 :** a body of knights or illustrious mounted soldiers **:** gallant and distinguished warriors or brave gentlemen ⟨Belgium's capital had gathered then her beauty and her ~ —Lord Byron⟩ **4 :** the dignity or system of knighthood **:** the spirit, usages, or manners of knighthood **:** the practice of knight-errantry ⟨but Lancelot on him urged all the devisings of their ~ —Alfred Tennyson⟩ **5 :** the qualifications or character of the ideal knight of the age of chivalry according to the romantic traditions (as honor, protective kindness to the weak, generosity to foes, and gallantry) **:** CHIVALROUSNESS ⟨~ demanded of him that he be conspicuous through his gallant, courteous, and generous behavior —H.W.Van Loon⟩ **6 :** the slaveholding class of southern society before the Civil War

chivaree *or* **chivari** *var of* CHARIVARI

¹chive \'chīv *sometimes* 'sh-\ *n* -s [ME *chyve*, fr. ONF *chive*, fr. L *cepa*, *cepe* onion] **1 :** a perennial plant (*Allium schoenoprasum*) related to the onion and having slender rushlike leaves that are used for seasoning (as in soups and omelets) — usu. used in pl. **2** *archaic* **:** BULBIL 1a; *esp* **:** a clove of garlic

²chive \'chiv, 'sh-, -īv\ *n* -s [perh. fr Romany *chiv* blade] *slang* **:** KNIFE — compare SHIV

³chive \"\ *vt* -ED/-ING/-S *slang* **:** KNIFE

chiven *var of* CHEVIN

¹chivey *var of* CHIVY

²chiv·ey \'shivē\ *n* -s [prob. fr. Natick *chippe*, lit., it is separated or dead; fr. its use as manure by the Indians] **:** MENOMINEE WHITEFISH

chiv·i·a·tite \,chivē'ä,tīt\ *n* -s [G *chiviatit*, fr. *Chiviato*, Peru, its locality + G *-it* -ite] **:** a mineral $Pb_2Bi_6S_{11}$ consisting of a lead bismuth sulfide in lead-gray foliated masses

¹chivy \'chivē, -vi\ *or* **chevy** \" *sometimes* -ev-\ *n* -ES [prob. short for E dial. *Chevy Chase* chase, pursuit, noise, confusion, fr. the name of a ballad describing the Battle of Otterburn (1388), prob. alter. of *Cheviot Chase*, fr. *Cheviot* hills, range of hills in northern England and Scotland, near which the battle took place] **1** *Brit* **a :** ²HUNT 1, ²CHASE 1 **b :** ¹FLIGHT **2** *Brit* **:** PRISONER'S BASE

²chivy \"\ *or* **chevy** \"\ *or* **chiv·vy** *also* **chiv·ey** \-iv-\ *vt* -ED/-ING/-ES **1 :** CHASE, PURSUE **2 a :** to harass, annoy, or tease esp. with persistence and by petty vexations and often for a specific purpose **:** HARRY ⟨he drove his staff hard but never nagged or *chivied* his writers —*Time*⟩ ⟨the skua *chivies* the herring gull and makes it surrender the booty —J.A.Thomson⟩ **b :** to acquire, attain, direct, or manipulate by persistent petty maneuvering ⟨*chivying* the polo ball with small strokes —George Orwell⟩ ⟨~ an olive out of a bottle⟩ **syn** see BAIT

chi·were \chə'werē\ *n, pl* **chiwere** *usu cap* [Chiwere *Che-waerae*, lit., belonging to this place] **:** a Siouan language of the Iowa, Missouri, and Oto peoples

chi·zo \'chē(,)zō, -sō\ *n, pl* **chizo** *or* **chizos** *usu cap* [Sp, of AmerInd origin] **1 :** a people constituting a major subdivision of the Concho **2 :** a member of the Chizo people

chk *abbr* check

chka·lov \chə'kälə|f, -,lȯ|f, |v\ *adj, usu cap* [fr. *Chkalov*, U.S.S.R.] **:** of or from the city of Chkalov, U.S.S.R. **:** of the kind or style prevalent in Chkalov

chka·lov·ite \chə'kälə,vīt\ *n* -s [Russ *chkalovit*, fr. *Chkalov*, city of Chkalov region, U.S.S.R. + Russ *-it* -ite] **:** a mineral $Na_2BeSi_2O_6$ that consists of a rare silicate of sodium and beryllium

chlad·ni figures \'klädnē-, -ad-\ *n pl, usu cap C* [trans. of G *Chladnische figuren*, after Ernst F. *Chladni* †1827 Ger. physicist] **:** SONOROUS FIGURES

chlad·nite \'klad,nīt\ *n* -s [Ernst F. *Chladni* + E *-ite*] **1 :** meteoritic material composed of enstatite **2 :** pure enstatite

chlamyd- *or* **chlamydo-** *comb form* [NL, fr. Gk *chlamyd-*, *chlamys*] **:** mantle ⟨*chlamydo*spore⟩ ⟨*Chlamydo*zoa⟩

chlam·y·date \'klamə,dāt, -,dət\ *adj* [L *chlamydatus* dressed in a chlamys, fr. *chlamyd-*, *chlamys* + *-atus* -ate] **:** having a mantle ⟨a ~ mollusk⟩

chla·myd·e·ous \klə'midēəs\ *adj* [prob. back-formation fr. *achlamydeous*, *archichlamydeous*, *metachlamydeous*, *monochlamydeous*] **1 :** relating to the floral envelope of a plant — used chiefly in combinations ⟨*archichlamydeous*⟩ ⟨*metachlamydeous*⟩ **2 :** having a perianth — opposed to *achlamydeous*

chla·myd·ia \klə'midēə\ *n, cap* [NL, fr. Gk *chlamyd-*, *chlamys* mantle + NL *-ia*] **:** the type genus of Chlamydiaceae comprising coccoid to spherical gram-negative intracellular parasites and including the causative agent of trachoma

chla·myd·i·a·ce·ae \klə¦midē'āsē,ē\ *n pl, cap* [NL, fr. *Chlamydia*, type genus (fr. Gk *chlamyd-*, *chlamys* mantle + NL *-ia*) + *-aceae*] **:** a family of rickettsiae that are obligate parasites in the cells of warm-blooded vertebrates, that esp. attack the conjunctiva, and that include the causative agents of trachoma and of lymphogranuloma inguinale

chlam·y·do·bac·te·ri·a·ce·ae \¦klamə,dō(,)bak,tirē'āsē,ē\ *n pl, cap* [NL, fr. *chlamyd-* + *bacterium* + *-aceae*] **:** a family (order Chlamydobacteriales) of free-floating filamentous algalike bacteria that contain no sulfur granules and occur chiefly in stagnant water

chlam·y·do·bac·te·ri·a·les \-'ā(,)lēz\ *n pl, cap* [NL, fr. *Chlamydobacteriaceae*, typical family + *-ales*] **:** an order of chiefly free-living aquatic filamentous bacteria that are commonly ensheathed by an organic matrix which may contain oxides of iron or manganese, that produce no endospores but reproduce by conidia or flagellated swarm spores, and that may exhibit gliding motility like that of certain blue-green algae

chlam·y·do·bac·te·ri·um \-'tirēəm\ *n, pl* **chlamydobacteria** \-rēə\ [NL, fr. *chlamyd-* + *bacterium*] **:** a higher bacterium of the family Chlamydobacteriaceae or the order Chlamydobacteriales

chlam·y·do·mon·a·da·ce·ae \-,mänə'dāsē,ē\ *n pl, cap* [NL, fr. *Chlamydomonad-*, *Chlamydomonas*, type genus + *-aceae*] **:** a family of green algae (order Volvocales) that in botanical classifications includes *Chlamydomonas* and related algae some of which are colored red by hematochrome

chlam·y·dom·o·nas \,klamə'dämənəs\ *n, cap* [NL, fr. *chlamyd-* + *-monas*] **:** a genus of solitary biflagellated plantlike flagellates or algae common in fresh water and damp soil and sometimes multiplying so freely as to be a pest about filtration plants — see CHLAMYDOMONADACEAE

chlam·y·do·sau·rus \,klamədō'sȯrəs\ *n, cap* [NL, fr. *chlamyd-* + *-saurus*] **:** a genus of reptiles containing the frilled lizard of Australia

chlam·y·do·sel·a·chus \-'seləkəs\ *n, cap* [NL, fr. *chlamyd-* + *Selachus* (syn. of *Cetorhinus*), fr. Gk *selachos* cartilaginous fish — more at SELACHII] **:** a genus (coextensive with the family Chlamydoselachidae) comprising sharks with diplospondylic vertebrae, including the frilled shark and certain extinct related forms, and being placed with the Hexanchidae in the suborder Notidanoidea or isolated in a separate suborder

chla·myd·o·spore \klə'midə,spō(ə)r\ *n* -s [ISV *chlamyd-* + *spore*; prob. orig. formed in F] **:** a thick-walled spore: as **a :** a unicellular resting spore in certain fungi usu. borne terminally on a hypha and rich in stored reserves — called also *gemma*; compare AKINETE **b :** the usu. black or dark brown zygote of a smut — see USTILAGINALES **c :** a bacterial cell transformed into a resting spore by accumulation of reserves and thickening of the cell wall — compare ENDOSPORE — **chlamyd·o·spor·ic** \=¦==¦spȯrik\ *adj*

chlam·y·do·zo·a·ce·ae \,klamə,dōzō'āsē,ē\ *n pl, cap* [NL, fr. *Chlamydozoon*, type genus + *-aceae*] *syn of* CHLAMYDIACEAE

¹chlam·y·do·zo·on \,===='zō,än\ *n* [NL, fr. *chlamyd-* + *-zoon*] *syn of* CHLAMYDIA

²chlamydozoon *n, pl* **chlamydo·zoa** \-'zōə\ **1 :** INCLUSION BODY **2 :** any of certain microorganisms related to the typical rickettsias; *esp* **:** an organism of the family Chlamydiaceae

chlam·y·phore \'klamə,fō(ə)r\ *also* **chla·myd·o·phore** \klə'midə,f-\ *n* -s [*chlamyphorus*, fr. NL *chlamyphorus*, fr. Gk *chlamys* mantle + L *-phorus* -phore; *chlamydophore* fr. NL *chlamydophorus*, fr. *chlamyd-* + L *-phorus*] **:** PICHICIAGO

chla·myph·o·rus \klə'mifərəs\ *n, cap* [NL, fr. *chlamy-* (fr. L *chlamys* mantle) + *-phorus*] **:** a genus of So. American armadillos comprising the pichiciago and related forms

chlam·ys \'klaməs, -ām-\ *n, pl* **chla·mys·es** \-məsəz\ *or* **chlam·y·des** \'klamə,dēz\ [L, fr. Gk] **:** a short oblong mantle fastened with a fibula usu. at the right shoulder or in front and worn chiefly by young men of ancient Greece

chlamys

chleuh \shə'lü, 'shlü\ *n, pl* **chleuh** *or* **chleuhs** *usu cap* **:** SHILHA

chlo·an·thite \klō'an,thīt\ *n* -s [G *chloanthit*, fr. Gk *chloanthēs* budding, pale (fr. *chloos* light green color + *-anthēs* blooming, flowered) + G *-it* -ite; fr. its frequent green coating — more at GLOW, -ANTHES] **:** a mineral $NiAs_{2-3}$ consisting of nickel arsenide isomorphous with skutterudite, smaltite, and nickel-skutterudite and being white or grayish with metallic luster and usu. massive

chlo·as·ma \klō'azmə\ *n, pl* **chloasma·ta** \-məd·ə\ [NL, fr. LGk, greenness, fr. Gk *chloazein* to be green, fr. *chloos* light green color] **:** a skin discoloration marked by yellowish brown pigmented patches or spots — called also *liver spots*

chlor \'klō(ə)r, -ō(ə)r\ *n* -s [Gk *chlōros*] **:** a hue between yellow and green; *specif* **:** yellowish green

chlor- *or* **chloro-** *comb form* [NL, fr. Gk, fr. *chlōros* greenish yellow — more at YELLOW] **1 :** green ⟨*chloro*phyll⟩ ⟨*chloro*phane⟩ **2 :** yellowish green **:** pale green **:** anemic ⟨*chlor*osis⟩ **3 a :** chlorine ⟨*chlor*hydrate⟩ ⟨*chloro*form⟩ **b** *now usu* *chloro-* **:** containing chlorine in place of hydrogen — in names of organic compounds ⟨*chloro*aniline⟩ **c** *now usu chloro-* **:** containing chlorine regarded as replacing hydroxyl or oxygen or as coordinated to a central atom — in names of inorganic acids and salts ⟨*chloro*auric acid⟩ ⟨*chloro*chromate⟩ **d :** containing chlorine as chloride sometimes replacing another element or group — in names of minerals and salts occurring as minerals ⟨*chloro*sulfate⟩

chloracetic acid *var of* CHLOROACETIC ACID

chloracetophenone *var of* CHLOROACETOPHENONE

chlor·ac·ne \(ˈ)klōrˌaknē\ *n* -S [*chlor-* + *acne*] **:** an eruption on the skin resembling acne and resulting from exposure to chlorine or its compounds — compare HYPERKERATOSIS

chloraemia *var of* CHLOREMIA

chlor·a·go·cyte \ˈklōrəgəˌsīt\ *n* -S [*chloragogen* + *-cyte*] **:** a chloragogen cell

chlor·a·go·gen \ˌklōrəˈgōjən, -ōgən\ *or* **chlor·a·gogue** \ˈklōrəˌgäg\ *adj* [*chloragogen*, fr. *chlor-* + Gk *agōgos* leading (fr. *agein* to lead) + E *-en; chloragogue*, fr. *chlor-* + Gk *agōgos* — more at AGENT] **:** of, relating to, or being certain cells that line the outer surface of the alimentary tract in earthworms and other annelids and are believed to function in excretion and waste storage

chlo·ral \ˈklōrəl, -ōr-, -ˌral\ *n* -S [F, fr. *chlor-* + *al*cool alcohol] **1 :** a colorless oily aldehyde CCl_3CHO having a pungent odor, obtained by the action of chlorine on ethyl alcohol, and used in making DDT and chloral hydrate; trichloro-acetaldehyde **2 :** CHLORAL HYDRATE

chlo·ral·formamide \ˌ≈≈+\ *n* [ISV *chloral* + *formamide*] **:** a colorless crystalline compound $C_3H_4Cl_3NO_2$ of chloral and formamide used as a hypnotic

chloral hydrate *n* **:** a bitter colorless crystalline compound $CCl_3CH(OH)_2$ formed by treating chloral with water and used usu. by oral administration for producing sleep

chlo·ral·ide \ˈklōrəˌlīd, -ləd\ *n* -S [ISV *chloral* + *-ide; orig.* formed as G *chloralid*] **1 :** a white crystalline cyclic compound $C_5H_2Cl_6O_3$ formed by heating chloral with trichloro-lactic acid **2 :** a compound formed by the condensation of chloral with an alpha-hydroxy acid

chlo·ral·o·sane \ˌklōrəˈlōˌsān\ *also* **chlo·ral·o·san** \-ˌsan\ *n* -S [*chloralose* + *-ane*] **:** CHLORALOSE

chlo·ra·lose \ˈklōrəˌlōs *also* -ōz\ *n* -S [ISV *chloral* + *-ose; orig.* formed in F] **1 :** a bitter crystalline compound $C_8H_{11}Cl_3O_6$ formed by heating chloral with dextrose and used as a hypnotic **2 :** a condensation product of chloral with a sugar similar to chloralose

chlo·ra·losed \-ōst,-ōzd\ *adj* **:** treated with chloralose

¹chlor·al·um \klōrˈaləm\ *n* [ISV *chlor-* + *alum*inum] **:** aluminum chloride in the form of yellowish white to colorless deliquescent crystals or powder of the hydrate $AlCl_3.6H_2O$ or its aqueous solution used esp. in salting out glycerin lyes in soapmaking, in carbonizing wool, and as a disinfectant, deodorant, and astringent

²chlo·ra·lum \ˈklōrələm, klōrˈal-\ *n* [NL, fr. ISV *chloral* + NL *-um*] **:** CHLORAL

chlor·alu·mi·nite \ˌklōrəˈlüməˌnīt\ *n* [ISV *chlor-* + *aluminite;* orig. formed as It *cloralluminite*] **:** a mineral $AlCl_3.6H_2O$ consisting of hydrous aluminum chloride

chlor·am·ide \klōrˈaˌmīd, -məd, ˈklōrə,-\ *n* -S [*chlor-* + *amide*] **1 :** an organic amide in which chlorine has replaced hydrogen attached to the nitrogen atom (as in chloramine-T); an *N*-chloroamide — called also *chloramine* **2 :** the chloramine NH_2Cl

chlor·am·ine \klōrˈaˌmēn, -mən, ˈklōrəˌmēn\ *n* -S [ISV *chlor-* + *ammonia* + *-ine*] **1 :** any of three compounds formed by the reaction of dilute hypochlorous acid with ammonia; *esp* **:** a colorless oily bactericidal compound NH_2Cl having an ammoniacal odor and being formed in one process of water purification by the interaction of ammonia, chlorine, and water — compare DICHLORAMINE 1, NITROGEN TRICHLORIDE **2 :** any of various organic compounds containing nitrogen and chlorine, esp. having the chlorine attached to the nitrogen atom (as in the groups —NHCl and —NCl_2): as **a :** CHLOROAMINE 1 **b :** any of various chloramides (sense 1); *esp* **:** CHLORAMINE-T **c :** CHLORIMIDE

chloramine–B *n* **:** a white crystalline compound $C_6H_5SO_2NClNa.2H_2O$ used as an antiseptic **:** sodium benzene-sulfonchloramide

chloramine–T *n* **:** a white or faintly yellow crystalline compound $CH_3C_6H_4SO_2NClNa.3H_2O$ used as an antiseptic (as in treating wounds) **:** sodium *para*-toluene-sulfonchloramide — called also *chloramine;* compare DICHLORAMINE-T

chlor·am·phen·i·col \ˌklōrˌamˈfenəˌkōl, -ōl\ *n* -S [*chlor-* + *am*ide + *phen-* + *nitr-* + *glycol*] **:** a colorless crystalline antibiotic $C_{11}H_{12}Cl_2N_2O_5$ isolated from cultures of a soil microorganism (*Streptomyces venezuelae*) and also prepared synthetically (as from *p*-nitro-acetophenone) that is effective against certain diseases caused by bacteria, rickettsiae, or viruses

chlor·ane·mia *or* **chlor·anae·mia** \ˌklōr+\ *n* -S [NL, fr. *chlor-* + *anemia, anaemia*] **:** CHLOROSIS — **chlor·anemic** \"+\ *adj*

chlor·an·il \klōrˈanᵊl, ˈklōrəˌnil\ *n* -S [G, fr. *chlor-* + *anilin* aniline] **:** a bright yellow crystalline compound $C_6Cl_4O_2$ made usu. by chlorination and oxidation of phenol or aniline and used chiefly in dye manufacture and as a seed disinfectant; tetrachloro-quinone

chlo·ran·tha·ce·ae \ˌklōrˌanˈthāsēˌē\ *n pl, cap* [NL, fr. *Chloranthus*, type genus + *-aceae*] **:** a small family of tropical herbs, shrubs, or trees (order Piperales) distinguished by opposite stipulate leaves and united petiole bases — **chlo·ran·tha·ceous** \ˌ≈ˌ≈ˈ≈shəs\ *adj*

chlo·ran·thy \ˈklōrˌan(t)thē\ *n* -ES [F *chloranthie*, fr. *chlor-* + Gk *anthos* flower + F *-ie* -y — more at ANTHOLOGY] **:** reversion of normally colored floral leaves to green foliage leaves

chlor·apatite \(ˈ)klōr+\ *n* -S [ISV *chlor-* + *apatite*] **:** a common apatite containing chlorine: as **a :** apatite in which chlorine predominates over fluorine, hydroxyl, and carbonate **b :** calcium phosphate chloride $Ca_5Cl(PO_4)_3$

chlor·argyrite \(ˈ)klōr\ *n* -S [ISV *chlor-* + *argyr-* + *-ite;* orig. formed as G *chlorargyrit*] **:** CERARGYRITE

chlor·ar·sen \klōrˈärsᵊn\ *n* -S [*chlor-* + *arsen* (alter. of *arsine*)] **:** the hydrochloride of dichlorophenarsine

chlor·as·tro·lite \klōrˈastrəˌlīt\ *n* -S [*chlor-* + *astr-* + *-lite*] **:** a mineral like prehnite that occurs as green pebbles of a stellate structure and is found near Lake Superior

chlo·rate \ˈklōrˌāt, -lō,r-, -ˌrət\ *n* -S [*chlor-* + *-ate*] **:** a salt (as the potassium or the sodium salt) of chloric acid

chlorate of potash **:** POTASSIUM CHLORATE

chlorauric acid *var of* CHLOROAURIC ACID

chlor·az·ide \klōrˈaˌzīd, -zəd, ˈklōrə-\ *n* -S [ISV *chlor-* + *azide;* prob. orig. formed as G *chlorazid*] **:** a colorless highly explosive gas ClN_3 made by the reaction of sodium azide with sodium hypochlorite; chlorine azide

chlo·ra·zol black E \ˈklōrəˌzōl-, -ōl-\ *n, usu cap C & often cap B* [*chlor-* + *az-* + *-ol*] **:** DIRECT DEEP BLACK EW

chlorbenzene *var of* CHLOROBENZENE

chlorbutanol *var of* CHLOROBUTANOL

chlor·bu·tol \ˈklōrbyəˌtōl, -ōl\ *n* -S [by contr.] **:** CHLOROBUTANOL

chlor·co·sane \ˈklōrkōˌsān\ *n* -S [*chlor-* + *-cosane* (as in tetra*cosane*)] **:** a yellow oily liquid consisting of chlorinated paraffins and used chiefly as a solvent for dichloramine-T

chlor·cy·cli·zine \(ˈ)klōrˈsīkləˌzēn, -zən\ *n* -S [*chlor-* + *cycl-* + *i-* + piper*azine*] **:** a cyclic antihistaminic agent $C_{18}H_{21}ClN_2$, administered as the hydrochloride; 1-(*p*-chloro≈benzhydryl)-4-methyl-piperazine

chlor·dane \ˈklōrˌdān\ *or* **chlor·dan** \-ˌdan\ *n* -S [*chlor-* + *indane, indan*] **:** a viscous usu. amber-colored volatile liquid insecticide $C_{10}H_6Cl_8$ consisting of a highly chlorinated compound derived from indan or of a mixture of this compound with related compounds

chlore \ˈklō(ə)r\ *vt* -ED/-ING/-S [short for ²*chlorine*] **:** to treat with a dilute solution of bleaching powder **:** CHLORINATE

chlo·rel·la \kləˈrelə\ *n* [NL, fr. *chlor-* + *-ella*] **1** *cap* **:** a genus (the type of the family Chlorellaceae) of nonmotile unicellular green algae (order Chlorococcales) potentially important as a cheap source of high grade protein and B-complex vitamins **2** -S **:** any alga of the genus *Chlorella* — **chlo·rel·la·ceous** \ˌklōrəˈlāshəs\ *adj*

chlor·e·mia *or* **chlor·ae·mia** \klōrˈēmēə\ *n* -S [NL, fr. *chlor-* + *-emia, -aemia*] **1 :** CHLOROSIS **2 :** excess of chlorides in the blood

chlor·en·chy·ma \klōrˈeŋkəmə\ *n* -S [NL, fr. *chlor-* (fr. ISV *chlorophyll*) + *-enchyma*] **:** chlorophyll-containing tissue — **chlor·en·chym·a·tous** \ˌklōrˌenˈkimədəs, -eŋ-\ *adj* — **chlo·ren·chy·mous** \(ˈ)klōrˈeŋkəməs\ *adj*

Chlo·re·tone \ˈklōrəˌtōn\ *trademark* — used for chlorobutanol (sense 2)

chlorguanide *var of* CHLOROGUANIDE

chlorhydrin *var of* CHLOROHYDRIN

chlo·ric acid \ˈklōrik-, -ōr-, -rēk-\ *n* [*chlor-* + *-ic*] **:** a strong acid $HClO_3$ like nitric acid in oxidizing properties but far less stable that is obtained from its salts (as sodium chlorate) as a colorless aqueous solution

chlo·ride \ˈklōˌrīd, -ō,r-, -ˌrəd\ *n* -S [G *chlorid*, fr. *chlor* chlorine (fr. Gk *chlōros* greenish yellow) + *-id* -ide — more at YELLOW] **1 :** a compound of chlorine with another element or radical **:** a salt or ester of hydrochloric acid ⟨sodium ∼⟩ ⟨ethyl ∼⟩ **2 :** chloride paper or a photographic print made on it

chlo·ri·del·la \ˌklōrəˈdelə\ [NL, fr. L *Chlorid-, Chloris* the goddess Flora (fr. Gk *Chlōrid-, Chlōris*, a feminine name) + NL *-ella*] *syn of* SQUILLA

chlo·ri·del·li·dae \-ləˌdē\ [NL, fr. *Chloridella*, type genus + *-idae*] *syn of* SQUILLIDAE

chloride of lime **:** BLEACHING POWDER

chloride paper *n* **:** paper coated with silver chloride and used in photography chiefly for contact printing

chlo·rid·er \ˈklōrˌīdə(r)\ *n* -S **:** one that mines on a small scale for ore (as silver) in the form of a chloride

chloride shift *n* **:** the passage of chloride ions from the plasma into the red blood cells when carbon dioxide enters the plasma from the tissues and their return to the plasma when the carbon dioxide is discharged in the lungs, a major factor both in maintenance of blood pH and in transport of carbon dioxide

chlo·ri·dize \ˈklōrəˌdīz\ *also* **chlo·ri·date** \ˈ≈≈ˌdāt, *usu* -ād+V\ *vt* -ED/-ING/-S **:** to treat with chlorine or with a chloride; *esp* **:** to convert (the metal of an ore) into chloride

chlor·im·ide \klōrˈiˌmīd, -məd\ *n* -S [*chlor-* + *imide*] **1 :** an organic imide in which chlorine has replaced the hydrogen attached to the nitrogen atom (as in succinchlorimide); an *N*-chloro-imide — called also *chloramine* **2 :** DICHLORAMINE 1

chlo·rin \ˈklōrən, -ōr-\ *also* **chlo·rine** \", -ōˌrēn, -ōˌrēn\ *n* -S [*chlorophyll* + *-in, -ine*] **:** any of several derivatives of chlorophyll obtained by hydrolysis, removal of the magnesium, sometimes with replacement by another metal (as copper), and opening of the carbocyclic ring — see CHLOROPHYLLIN 2

¹chlo·rin·ate \ˈ≈rəˌnāt, *usu* -ād+V\ *also* **chlo·rin·ize** \-ˌnīz\ *vt* -ED/-ING/-S [²*chlorine* + *-ate* or *-ize*] **:** to treat or cause to combine with chlorine or a compound of chlorine: as **a :** to treat (paper pulp) with chlorine for the purpose of bleaching **b :** to apply chlorine or a hypochlorite to (water, sewage, or wastes) esp. for purposes of disinfection, oxidation of organic matter, or retardation of putrefaction **c :** to treat (wool) with a solution usu. of a hypochlorite and acid for the purpose of increasing resistance to shrinking **d :** CHLORIDIZE **e :** to introduce chlorine into (a compound); *specif* **:** to cause substitution of chlorine for hydrogen in (an organic compound)

²chlo·rin·ate \ˈ≈rəˌnāt, -ˌnət, *usu* -d+V\ *n* -S **:** a chlorinated product

chlorinated camphene *n* **:** TOXAPHENE

chlo·rin·at·ed lime *n* **:** BLEACHING POWDER

chlorinated paraffin *also* **chlorinated paraffin wax** *n* **:** any of various pale yellow viscous liquids or resinous solids obtained by treating molten paraffin wax with chlorine and used chiefly as plasticizers, as additives for lubricants, and as weatherproofing and flameproofing agents for textiles

chlorinated rubber *n* **:** an odorless tasteless nonflammable white powder that is resistant to many chemicals, is usu. obtained by treating a solution of rubber (as in carbon tetrachloride) with chlorine, and is used chiefly in coatings, inks, and adhesives

chlo·rin·a·tion \ˌklōrəˈnāshən, -ōr-\ *n* -S **:** the act or process of chlorinating

chlo·rin·a·tor \ˈ≈≈ˌnād·ə(r), -atə\ *n* -S **:** an apparatus (as a cylindrical tank) for chlorinating

¹chlo·rine \ˈklōˌrēn, -ō,r-, -ˌrən\ *adj* **:** of the color grass green

²chlorine \"\ *n* -S [*chlor-* + *-ine*] **:** a common nonmetallic univalent and polyvalent element belonging to the halogens that is best known as a heavy greenish yellow irritating toxic gas of disagreeable odor, is usu. made by electrolysis of aqueous solutions of sodium chloride, and is used chiefly as a powerful bleaching, oxidizing, and disinfecting agent in water purification and in making numerous products (as bleaching powder, chlorinated solvents, military gases, insecticides, herbicides, and synthetic resins and plastics) — symbol *Cl;* see ELEMENT table

chlorine demand *n* **:** the greatest amount of chlorine that added to water is completely utilized in the process of sterilizing the water

chlorine dioxide *also* **chlorine peroxide** *n* **:** a heavy reddish yellow odorous explosive gas ClO_2 made by the action of chlorine on sodium chlorite and used chiefly in bleaching (as of paper pulp, flour, starch, and soap) and in water purification

chlorine water *n* **:** a yellowish aqueous solution of chlorine used for bleaching

chlo·rin·i·ty \klōˈrinəd·ē, -ōˈr-\ *n* -ES [¹*chlorine* + *-ity*] **:** the quality or degree of being chlorinous

chlo·rin·ol·y·sis \ˈ≈ˈnäləsəs\ *n, pl* **chlorinoly·ses** \-əˌsēz\ [NL, fr. ISV *chlorine* + NL *-o-* + *-lysis*] **:** a chemical reaction analogous to hydrolysis in which chlorine plays a role similar to that of water

chlo·rin·ous \ˈklōrənəs, -ōr-\ *adj* **:** of, relating to, or like chlorine ⟨∼ tastes in water⟩

chloriodide [*chlor-* + *iodide*] *var of* CHLOROIODIDE

chlo·ri·on \ˈklōrēˌän, -ēən\ *n, cap* [NL, fr. Gk *chlōriōn*, a kind of yellow bird, fr. *chlōros* greenish yellow — more at YELLOW] **:** a genus of digger wasps (family Sphecidae)

chlo·ris \ˈklōrəs\ *n, cap* [NL, fr. L, the goddess Flora, fr. Gk *Chlōris*, a feminine name] **:** a genus of grasses with spikelets in two rows along one side of the rachis and with the spikes being arranged digitately — see FINGER GRASS

¹chlo·rite \ˈklōˌrīt, -ō,rīt\ *n* -S [G *chlorit*, fr. L *chloritis*, a kind of green stone, fr. Gk *chlōritis*, fr. *chlōros* greenish yellow] **:** any of a group of monoclinic minerals of extensive occurrence that are essentially hydrous silicates of aluminum, ferrous iron, and magnesium, include clinochlore, penninite, prochlorite, and corundophilite, are associated with and resemble the micas, and are usu. green in color — **chlo·rit·ic** \klōˈrid·ik, -ōˈr-\ *adj*

²chlorite \"\ *n* -S [prob. fr. F, fr. *chlor-* + *-ite*] **:** a salt of chlorous acid

chlo·rit·i·za·tion \ˌklōrˌīd·əˈzāshən, -rətəˈz-\ *n* -S **:** production of or conversion into chlorite

chlo·ri·tize \ˈklōrəˌtīz\ *vt* -ED/-ING/-S [¹˒²*chlorite* + *-ize*] **1 :** to introduce chlorite in **2 :** to alter into mineral chlorite

chlo·ri·toid \ˈ≈rəˌtȯid\ *n* -S [G, fr. *chlorit* chlorite (mineral) + *-oid*] **:** a mineral $(Mg,Fe)AlSiAlO_5(OH)_2$ consisting of a silicate of aluminum and ferrous iron with magnesium occurring usu. in dull green to gray or grayish black masses of brittle folia and related to the brittle micas (as clintonite)

chlor·man·ga·no·ka·lite \klōrˈmaŋgəˌnōˈkaˌlīt\ *n* -S [*chlor-* + *mangan-* + *kalium* + *-ite*] **:** a rare chloride of potassium and manganese found in blocks of rock ejected from Vesuvius in 1906

chlo·ro \ˈklōr(ˌ)ō, -ō(ˌ)rō\ *adj* [*chlor-*] **:** containing chlorine — used esp. of organic compounds; compare CHLOR- 3

chloro- *in pronunciations below,* ˌ≈≈ = ˌklōrō *or* ˌklōrō *or* -rə\ — see CHLOR-

chlo·ro·acetate \ˌ≈≈+\ *n* -S [ISV *chlor-* + *acetate*] **:** a salt or ester of chloroacetic acid

chlo·ro·ace·tic acid \ˌ≈≈+ . . . -\ *also* **chlor·ace·tic acid** \ˌklōr, -ōr+ . . . -\ *n* [ISV *chlor-* + *acetic*] **:** a crystalline acid $ClCH_2COOH$ obtained by direct chlorination of acetic acid and used in organic synthesis — called also *monochloroacetic acid;* compare DICHLOROACETIC ACID, TRICHLOROACETIC ACID

chlo·ro·acetophenone \ˌ≈≈+\ *or* **chlor·acetophenone** \(ˌ)klōr, -ōr+\ *n* -S [*chlor-* + *acetophenone*] **:** a chlorine derivative of acetophenone; *specif* **:** the alpha derivative $C_6H_5COCH_2Cl$ obtained as irritating white crystals by reaction of benzene and chloro-acetyl chloride or by chlorination of acetophenone and used esp. in solution as a tear gas — called also *phenacyl chloride*

chlo·ro·amide \ˌ≈≈+\ *n* -S [ISV *chlor-* + *amide*] **:** a chloro derivative of an amide — compare CHLORAMIDE

chlo·ro·amine \ˌ≈≈+\ *n* -S [ISV *chlor-* + *amine*] **1 :** a chloro derivative of an amine; *esp* **:** one in which the chlorine is attached to the nitrogen atom — compare CHLORAMINE 2 **2 :** CHLORAMINE 1

chlo·ro·ane·mia *or* **chlo·ro·anae·mia** \ˌ≈≈+\ *n* -S [NL, fr. *chlor-* + *anemia, anaemia*] **:** CHLOROSIS 1

chlo·ro·aurate \ˌ≈≈+\ *n* -S [prob. fr. F, fr. *chlor-* + *aurate*] **:** a salt of chloroauric acid

chlo·ro·auric acid \ˌ≈≈+ . . . -\ *also* **chlor·auric acid** \(ˈ)klōr, -ōr+ . . . -\ *n* [ISV *chlor-* + *auric*] **:** an acid $HAuCl_4$ formed when gold is dissolved in aqua regia and obtainable as long yellow deliquescent crystals

chlo·ro·az·o·din \ˌ≈≈ˈazōdᵊn\ *n* -S [blend of *chloro-formamidine* and *az-*] **:** a yellow crystalline compound $C_2H_4Cl_2N_6$ used in solution as a surgical antiseptic; α,α'-azo-bis-(chloro≈formamidine)

chlo·ro·bacteriaceae \ˌ≈≈+\ *n pl, cap* [NL, fr. *Chlorobacterium*, type genus + *-aceae*] **:** a family of eubacteria (suborder Rhodobacteriinae) comprising the green sulfur bacteria and distinguished by a photosynthetic pigment related to but distinct from both the chlorophyll of higher plants and the bacterio-chlorophyll of the purple sulfur bacteria

chlo·ro·bacterium \ˌ≈≈+\ *n, cap* [NL, fr. *chlor-* + *bacterium*] **:** the type genus of Chlorobacteriaceae comprising green sulfur bacteria that live symbiotically with various protozoans

chlo·ro·benzene \ˌ≈≈+\ *also* **chlor·benzene** \(ˈ)klōr, -ōr+\ *n* -S [ISV *chlor-* + *benzene*] **:** a colorless flammable volatile toxic liquid C_6H_5Cl with an almondlike odor made usu. by direct chlorination of benzene and used in organic synthesis and as a solvent — called also *monochlorobenzene;* compare DICHLOROBENZENE

chlo·ro·bromide *also* **chlo·ro·bromid** \ˌ≈≈+\ *n* -S [*chlor-* + *bromide, bromid*] **1 :** a compound of chlorine and bromine with an element or radical **2 :** chlorobromide paper or a photographic print made on it

chlo·ro·butanol \ˌ≈≈+\ *also* **chlor·butanol** \(ˈ)klōr, -ōr+\ *n* -S [*chlor-* + *butanol*] **1 :** a monochloro derivative of 1- or 2-butanol **2 :** a white crystalline alcohol $CCl_3C(CH_3)_2OH$ with a camphorlike odor and taste that is made by the reaction of acetone and chloroform in the presence of alkali and is used as a local anesthetic, sedative, and preservative (as for hypodermic solutions); β,β,β-trichloro-*tert*-butyl alcohol — called also *chlorbutol*

chlo·ro·calcite \ˌ≈≈+\ *n* -S [ISV *chlor-* + *calcite;* orig. formed in It] **:** HYDROPHILITE

chlo·ro·carbonate \ˌ≈≈+\ *n* -S [ISV *chlor-* + *carbonate*] **:** CHLOROFORMATE

chlo·ro·carbonic acid \ˌ≈≈+ . . . -\ *n* [*chlor-* + *carbonic*] **1** *obs* **:** PHOSGENE **2 :** CHLOROFORMIC ACID

chlo·roch·ro·us \klōˈräkrəwəs\ *adj* [*chlor-* + *-chrous* (alter. of *-chroous*)] **:** of a hue approximating green

chlo·ro·chy·tri·um \ˌ≈≈ *at* CHLORO- + ˈkītrēəm, ˈki-\ *n, cap* [NL, fr. *chlor-* + *-chytrium* (fr. Gk *chytrion* cup, dim. of *chytra* earthen pot)] **:** a genus of unicellular green algae (family Endosphaeraceae) living within the tissues of red algae, mosses, and certain aquatic flowering plants (as the duckweed)

chlo·ro·coc·ca·les \ˌ≈≈(ˌ)käˈkā(ˌ)lēz\ *n pl, cap* [NL, fr. *Chlorococcum* + *-ales*] **:** an order of unicellular green algae (class Chlorophyceae) distinguished from other similar forms in not dividing vegetatively but reproducing only by spores

chlo·ro·coc·cine \ˌ≈≈ˈkäkˌsīn, -ēn\ *adj* [NL *Chlorococcum* + E *ine*] **:** lacking motility except in reproductive cells and having no capacity for vegetative division ⟨∼ algae⟩

chlo·ro·coc·cum \ˌ≈≈ˈkäkəm\ *n, cap* [NL, fr. *chlor-* + *-coccum* (fr. L *coccum* berry, fr. Gk *kokkos* kermes, grain, seed)] **:** a genus (the type of the family Chlorococcaceae) of unicellular green algae (order Chlorococcales) occurring singly or in a layer on soil or damp rock, reproducing only by spores, and varying greatly in size of the vegetative cells — compare PROTOCOCCUS

chlo·ro·cresol \ˌ≈≈+\ *n* -S [*chlor-* + *cresol*] **:** any of several chlorine derivatives of the cresols; *esp* **:** the para derivative $Cl(CH_3)C_6H_3OH$ obtained as colorless crystals by chlorination of *meta*-cresol and used as an antiseptic and preservative (as for glue and leather)

chlo·ro·cru·o·rin \ˌ≈≈ˈkrüərən\ *n* -S [*chlor-* + *cruorin* (old name for hemoglobin), fr. L *cruor* blood) + E *-in* — more at RAW] **:** a green iron-containing respiratory pigment related chemically to hemoglobin and found in the blood of certain marine polychaete worms

chlo·ro·dyne \ˈ≈≈ˌdīn\ *n* -S [fr. *Chlorodyne*, a trademark] **:** a preparation of varying composition containing numerous narcotic and sedative drugs

chlo·ro·ethane \ˌ≈≈+\ *n* [*chlor-* + *ethane*] **:** ETHYL CHLORIDE

chlo·ro·ethyl \ˌ≈≈+\ *n* -S [ISV *chlor-* + *ethyl*] **:** a chloro derivative of ethyl; *esp* **:** the beta or 2-derivative $ClCH_2CH_2$—

¹chlo·ro·form \ˈklōrəˌfȯrm, -lōr-\ *n* -S [F *chloroforme*, fr. *chlor-* + *-forme* (fr. *formyle* formyl); fr. its having been regarded as a trichloride of this radical] **:** a colorless volatile heavy toxic liquid $CHCl_3$ of ethereal odor and sweetish taste made usu. by chlorination and oxidation of acetone or by chlorination of methane or methyl chloride and used chiefly as a solvent and esp. formerly as a general anesthetic or as a carminative and anodyne; trichloro-methane

²chloroform \"\ *vt* -ED/-ING/-S **:** to treat with chloroform or to place under its influence esp. so as to produce insensibility or anesthesia; *also* **:** to kill with chloroform

chlo·ro·form·ate \ˌ≈≈ˈfȯrmāt, -ˌmāt\ *n* -S [ISV ¹*chloroform* + *-ate*] **:** a salt or ester of chloroformic acid — called also *chlorocarbonate*

chlo·ro·for·mic acid \ˌ≈≈ˈfȯrmik-\ *n* [ISV *chloroform* + *-ic*] **:** an acid $ClCOOH$ best known in the form of its esters — called also *chlorocarbonic acid*

chloroformic ester *n* **:** an ester (as ethyl chloroformate $ClCOOC_2H_5$) of chloroformic acid made by reaction of phosgene on an alcohol or phenol and used in organic synthesis (as of esters of carbonic acid)

chlo·ro·form·ize \ˈ≈≈ˌfȯrˌmīz\ *vt* -ED/-ING/-S [¹*chloroform* + *-ize*] *immunol* **:** to treat with chloroform (esp. a living antigen for purposes of attenuation)

chlo·ro·for·myl \ˈ≈≈ˌfȯrməl\ *n* -S [*chloroformic* + *-yl*] **:** the univalent radical $ClCO$– of chloroformic acid

chlo·ro·gen·ic acid \ˌ≈≈ˈjenik-\ *n* [ISV *chlor-* + *-genic;* orig. formed as F *chlorogénique*] **:** a crystalline acid $C_{16}H_{17}O_7COOH$ occurring in coffee beans as the potassium caffeine salt, in potatoes, and in other plant products and yielding caffeic acid and quinic acid on hydrolysis

chlo·ro·gen·in \ˌ≈≈+ˈjenən\ *n* -S [ISV *chloro-* (fr. NL *chlorogalum pomeridianum*) + *-genin*] **:** a steroidal sapogenin $C_{27}H_{44}O_4$ obtained from a soap plant (*Chlorogalum pomeridianum*)

chlo·rog·e·nine \klōˈräjəˌnēn, -nən\ *n* -S [ISV *chlor-* + *-genine*] **:** ALSTONINE

chlo·ro·go·gen *or* **chlo·ro·gogue** *adj* [by alter.] **:** CHLORAGOGEN

chlo·ro·gua·nide \ˌ≈≈+ˈgwäˌnīd, -nəd\ *or* **chlor·gua·nide** \(ˈ)klōr, -ōr+\ *n* -S [*chlor-* + *biguanide*] **:** an antimalarial drug $C_{11}H_{16}N_5Cl$ derived from biguanide and administered as the bitter crystalline hydrochloride

chlo·ro·hy·drin \ˌ≈≈+ˈhīdrən\ *also* **chlor·hy·drin** \ˌklōr, -ōr+\ *n* -S [ISV *chlor-* + *-hydrin*] **:** any of a class of organic compounds derived from glycols or polyhydroxy alcohols (as glycerol) by substitution of chlorine for part of the hydroxyl groups: as **a :** either of the two syrupy liquid mono-chlorohydrins of glycerol distinguished as alpha-chlorohydrin $CH_2ClCHOHCH_2OH$ and beta-chlorohydrin $CH_2OHCHClCH_2OH$ and used chiefly in organic synthesis and as solvents **b :** ETHYLENE CHLOROHYDRIN

chlo·ro·hydrocarbon \ˌ≈≈+\ *n* -S [*chlor-* + *hydrocarbon*] **:** a chlorine derivative of a hydrocarbon

chlo·ro·io·dide \ˌ≈≈+\ *also* **chlor·io·dide** \(ˈ)klōr, -ōr+\ *n* -S [*chlor-* + *iodide*] **:** a compound of chlorine and iodine with an element or radical — called also *iodochloride*

chlo·ro·leucite \ˈ⁼⁼+\ *n* -s [ISV *chlor-* + *leucite;* orig. formed in F] : CHLOROPLAST

chlo·ro·leukaemia *or* **chlo·ro·leukemia** \ˈ⁼⁼+\ *n* -s [NL, fr. *chlor-* + *leukemia, leukaemia*] : CHLOROMA

chlo·ro·ma \klə'rōmə\ *n, pl* **chloromas** \-məz\ *or* **chloro·ma·ta** \-məd·ə\ [NL, fr. *chlor-* + *-oma*] : leukemia originating in the bone marrow and marked by the formation of tumorlike growths of myeloid tissue beneath the periosteum of flat bones (as the skull, ribs, or pelvis) — **chlo·rom·a·tous** \-'rämәd·əs, -ōm-\ *adj*

chlo·ro·magnesite \ˈ⁼⁼+\ *n* -s [ISV *chlor-* + *magnesite;* orig. formed as It *cloromagnesite*] : a mineral $MgCl_2$ found on Vesuvius and consisting of a deliquescent anhydrous chloride of magnesium

chlo·ro·melanite \ˈ⁼⁼+\ *n* -s [ISV *chlor-* + *melan-* + *-ite;* orig. formed as F *chloromélanite*] : a dark green or nearly black variety of jadeite

chlo·rom·e·ter \klō'rämәd·ə(r)\ *n* -s [F *chloromètre,* fr. *chlor-* + *-mètre* -meter] : a device for measuring chlorine

chlo·ro·methane \ˈ⁼⁼ *at* CHLORO- +\ *n* -s [ISV *chlor-* + *methane*] : METHYL CHLORIDE

chlo·ro·methyl \ˈ⁼⁼+\ *n* -s [*chlor-* + *methyl*] : the univalent radical $ClCH_2$— formed by removal of one hydrogen atom from methyl chloride

chlo·ro·methylation \ˈ⁼⁼+\ *n* -s [*chlor-* + *methylation*] : the introduction of a chloromethyl group into a compound usu. by use of formaldehyde and hydrogen chloride

chlo·rom·e·try \klō'rämə·trē\ *n* -ES [prob. fr. F *chlorométrie,* fr. *chlor-* + *-métrie* -metry] : the measurement of chlorine: as **a** : the determination of available chlorine (as in bleaching powder) **b** : analysis by the use or liberation of chlorine similar to iodometry

chlo·ro·monadina \ˈ⁼⁼ *at* CHLORO- +\ *n pl, cap* [NL, fr. *chlor-* + *Monadina*] : a small order of biflagellate plantlike flagellates distinguished from the euglenoids by production of oily reserve products

Chlo·ro·my·ce·tin \ˌ⁼⁼+ˌmī'sēt°n\ *trademark* — used for chloramphenicol

chlor·opal \(ˈ)klōr¦ōpəl, -lō¦rō-\ *n* -s [G, fr. *chlor-* + *opal*] : a yellowish green or greenish yellow clay mineral consisting of hydrous silicate of iron and aluminum and occurring in compact masses or earthy forms resembling opal

chlo·ro·pal·la·date \ˌ⁼⁼ *at* CHLORO- + 'palə,dāt\ *n* -s [*chlor-* + *palladium* + *-ate*] : a salt analogous to a chloroplatinate containing the anion $PdCl_6^{--}$

chlo·ro·phane \ˈ⁼⁼,fān\ *n* -s [F, fr. *chlor-* + *-phane*] : a variety of fluorite that when heated emits a beautiful green light

chlo·ro·phenol \ˈ⁼⁼+\ *also* **chlor·phenol** \(ˈ)klōr, -ōr+\ *n* -s [ISV *chlor-* + *phenol*] **1** : any of three monochloro derivatives ClC_6H_4OH of phenol distinguished as *ortho*-chlorophenol, *meta*-chlorophenol, and *para*-chlorophenol and used chiefly as dye intermediates **2** : a chlorine derivative of a phenol — compare PENTACHLOROPHENOL

chlorophenol red *also* **chlorphenol red** *n* : a dye $C_{19}H_{12}Cl_2O_5S$ used as an acid-base indicator; dichloro-phenolsulfonephthalein

chlo·ro·phen·o·thane \ˌ⁼⁼+'fenə,thān\ *n* -s [*dichloro*⁼ *diphenyl-trichloro-ethane*] : DDT

chlo·ro·phoe·ni·cite \ˌ⁼⁼+'fēnə,sīt\ *n* -s [*chlor-* + *phoenic-* (fr. Gk *phoinik-, phoinix* purple) + *-ite;* fr. its colors by daylight and by artificial light — more at PHOENICIAN] : a mineral $(Mn,Zn)_5AsO_4(OH_7)$ consisting of a basic arsenate of manganese and zinc and occurring in monoclinic crystals

chlo·roph·o·ra \klō'räfərə\ *n, cap* [NL, fr. *chlor-* + *-phora*] : a small genus of tropical timber trees (family Moraceae) with rather hard heavy wood — see FUSTIC, IROKO

chlo·ro·phy·ce·ae \ˌ⁼⁼ *at* CHLORO- + 'fīsē,ē, 'fis-\ *n pl, cap* [NL, fr. *chlor-* + *-phyceae*] : a class of algae (division Chlorophyta) distinguished chiefly by having a clear green color, their chlorophyll being masked or altered little or not at all by other pigments — **chlo·ro·phy·cean** \ˈ⁼¦fīshən, -¦fish-\ *adj*

chlo·ro·phyll *also* **chlo·ro·phyl** \'klōrə,fil, -ōr-, -,fəl *sometimes* -ăr-\ *n* -s [F *chlorophylle,* fr. *chlor-* + *-phylle* -phyll] **1 a** : the green coloring material of plants that is essential to photosynthesis, occurs usu. in discrete bodies and only in the presence of light and where iron is available in the living cell, and is extractable as a mixture of chlorophyll a and chlorophyll b together with various amounts of other pigments (as carotene and xanthophyll) — see CHLOROPLAST **b** : any of several oil-soluble pigments making up this green coloring matter: as (1) : an ester $C_{55}H_{72}MgN_4O_5$ obtained as a blue-black powder that is a magnesium-containing porphyrin derivative related structurally to heme and that yields phytol and methanol on hydrolysis — called also *chlorophyll a* (2) : an ester $C_{55}H_{70}MgN_4O_6$ obtained as a dark green powder and very closely related structurally to chlorophyll a — called also *chlorophyll b* **2** : a dark green waxy substance obtained by extraction of green plants (as nettles or alfalfa) that contains chlorophyll or chlorophyll derivatives and often other plant constituents and is used esp. as a coloring agent or for its claimed deodorant properties

chlo·ro·phyl·la·ceous \ˈ⁼⁼,fi¦lāshəs, -,fə¦-\ *adj* : consisting of or containing chlorophyll : CHLOROPHYLLOSE

chlo·ro·phyl·lase \ˈ⁼⁼fə,lās, -āz, ,⁼⁼'fi,l-\ *n* -s [ISV *chlorophyll* + *-ase;* orig. formed in G] : an enzyme present in leaves that hydrolyzes chlorophyll to chlorophyllides and phytol

chlo·ro·phyl·lide \ˈ⁼⁼fə,līd, ,⁼⁼'fi,l-\ *n* -s [ISV *chlorophyll* + *-ide;* orig. formed as G *chlorophyllid*] : any of the pigments obtained from chlorophyll by removal of the phytyl radical

chlo·ro·phyl·lin \ˈ⁼⁼,filən, ,⁼⁼'⁼\ *n* -s [*chlorophyll* + *-in*] **1** : any of several water-soluble pigments derived from chlorophyll by hydrolysis with alkali with replacement of both the methyl and phytyl radicals by hydrogen or a metal **2** : any of various derivatives of chlorophyll (as copper chlorins) used as breath and body deodorants

chlo·ro·phyl·lite \ˈ⁼⁼fə,līt, ,⁼⁼'fi,l-\ *n* -s [*chlor-* + *-phyll* + *-ite*] : a mineral consisting of a green foliated alteration product of cordierite

chlo·ro·phyl·lose \ˈ⁼⁼fə,lōs, ¦⁼⁼¦fi,lōs\ *also* **chlo·ro·phyl·lous** \¦⁼⁼¦filəs\ *adj* : relating to, being, or containing chlorophyll

chlo·roph·y·ta \klō'räfәd·ə\ *n pl, cap* [NL, fr. *chlor-* + *-phyta*] : a division or other category of lower plants including the true green algae and the stoneworts

chlo·ro·phyte \ˈ⁼⁼ *at* CHLORO-+,fīt\ *n* -s [*chlor-* + *-phyte*] : a green-pigmented flagellate

chlo·ro·pia \klō'rōpēə\ *n* -s [NL, fr. *chlor-* + *-opia*] : CHLOROPSIA

chlo·ro·pic·rin \ˌ⁼⁼ *at* CHLORO- + 'pikrən\ *also* **chlor·pic·rin** \klōr, -ōr+\ *n* -s [G *chlorpikrin,* fr. *chlor-* + *-pikrin* -picrin] : a heavy colorless liquid CCl_3NO_2 that has a sweetish odor, causes tears and vomiting, is now usu. made by reaction of nitromethane and a hypochlorite, and is used chiefly as a soil fumigant: trichloro-nitromethane — called also *nitrochloroform*

¹chlo·ro·pid \ˈ⁼⁼+,pid\ *adj* [NL *Chloropidae*] : of or relating to the Chloropidae

²chloropid \"\ *n* -s : an insect of the family Chloropidae : FRIT FLY

chlo·rop·i·dae \klō'räpə,dē\ *n pl, cap* [NL, fr. *Chlorops,* type genus (fr. *chlor-* + *-ops*) + *-idae*] : a family of small nearly hairless acalyptrate flies with broad heads and short antennae comprising the frit flies some of which have larvae that are borers in various cereals and other grasses, others being irritating though nonbiting pests about the eyes of man and various animals and sometimes implicated in the transmission of diseases (as yaws)

chlo·ro·plast \ˈ⁼⁼ *at* CHLORO-+,plast\ *n* -s [ISV *chlor-* + *-plast;* orig. formed in G] : a plastid containing chlorophyll being the seat of photosynthesis and starch formation, in higher plants having commonly the form of a minute flattened granule, and in algae occurring in varied sizes and shapes that are often diagnostic for particular forms

chlo·ro·platinate \ˌ⁼⁼+\ *n* -s [*chlor-* + *platinate*] : a salt of chloroplatinic acid

chlo·ro·platinic acid \¦⁼⁼+ . . . -\ *n* [*chlor-* + *platinic*] : an acid H_2PtCl_6 obtained usu. as red-brown deliquescent crystals of the hexahydrate by the action of aqua regia on metallic platinum and used chiefly in analysis — called also *platinic chloride*

chlo·ro·plat·i·nite \ˌ⁼⁼+'plat°n,īt\ *n* -s [*chlor-* + *platinum* + *-ite*] : a salt of chloroplatinous acid

chlo·ro·platinous acid \¦⁼⁼+ . . . -\ *n* [*chlor-* + *platinous*] : an acid H_2PtCl_4 formed in solution by dissolving platinous chloride in aqueous hydrochloric acid

chlo·ro·prene \ˈ⁼⁼,prēn\ *n* -s [*chlor-* + *isoprene*] : a colorless liquid $CH_2{=}CClCH{=}CH_2$ made from acetylene and hydrochloric acid and used esp. in making neoprene by polymerization; 2-chloro-butadiene

chlo·ro·procaine \¦⁼⁼+\ *n* -s [*chlor-* + *procaine*] : a local anesthetic $C_{13}H_{19}ClN_2O_2$ used chiefly in the form of a salt (as the white powdery hydrochloride)

chlo·rop·sia \klō'räpsēə\ *n* -s [NL, fr. *chlor-* + *-opsia*] : a visual defect in which all visible objects appear green

chlo·rop·sis \-psəs\ *n* [NL, fr. *chlor-* + *-opsis*] **1** *cap* : a genus of passerine birds comprising the green bulbuls and included in the family Pycnotidae or placed with a few related forms in a separate family Aegithinidae **2** *pl* **chloropsis** : GREEN BULBUL

chlo·ro·quine \ˈ⁼⁼ *at* CHLORO- + ·,kwīn, -ēn\ *also* **chlo·ro·quin** \-·,kwin\ *n* -s [*chlor-* + *-quine, -quin* (fr. *quinoline*)] : an antimalarial drug $C_{18}H_{26}ClN_3$ derived from quinoline that is administered as the bitter crystalline diphosphate

chlo·ro·silane \ˈ⁼⁼+\ *n* -s [*chlor-* + *silane*] **1** : a gas SiH_3Cl derived from monosilane — called also *monochlorosilane* **2** : a chlorine derivative of a silane; *esp* : a derivative [as dimethyl-dichloro-silane $(CH_3)_2SiCl_2$] of an organic silane used in making silicones — called also *organochlorosilane*

chlo·ro·sis \klə'rōsəs\ *n, pl* **chloro·ses** \-ō,sēz\ [NL, fr. *chlor-* + *-osis*] **1** : an iron-deficiency anemia in young girls characterized by a greenish color of the skin, weakness, and menstrual disturbances — called also GREENSICKNESS **2** *plant pathol* : a diseased condition in chlorophyll-bearing plants manifested as yellowing or blanching of the normally green parts due to causes other than the absence of light (as attacks of parasites or mineral deficiencies) — compare ETIOLATE — **chlo·rot·ic** \-'räd·ik\ *adj* — **chlo·rot·i·cal·ly** \-ək(ə)lē\ *adv*

chlo·ro·spinel \ˌ⁼⁼ *at* CHLORO- +\ *n* -s [ISV *chlor-* + *spinel;* orig. formed as G *chlorospinell*] : a grass-green spinel

chlo·ro·sulfonate \¦⁼⁼+\ *n* -s [*chlor-* + *sulfonate*] : a salt or ester of chlorosulfonic acid

chlo·ro·sulfonic acid \¦⁼⁼+ . . . -\ *also* **chlor·sulfonic acid** \¦klōr, -ōr+\ *n* [*chlor-* + *sulfonic*] : a colorless fuming corrosive liquid $ClSO_3H$ made usu. by reaction of gaseous hydrogen chloride with sulfur trioxide and used chiefly in organic synthesis (as of sulfa drugs, saccharin, and sulfonic acids)

chlo·ro·then \ˈ⁼⁼+,then\ *n* -s [*chlor-* + *thenyl*] : an antihistaminic agent $C_{14}H_{19}Cl_2N_3S$ usu. administered in the form of its crystalline mono-citrate

chlo·ro·thi·o·nite \ˌ⁼⁼+'thīə,nīt\ *n* -s [ISV *chlor-* + *thion-* + *-ite*] : a mineral $K_2Cu(SO_4)Cl_2$ consisting of potassium copper sulfate chloride found on Vesuvius

chlo·ro·thymol \¦⁼⁼+\ *n* -s [ISV *chlor-* + *thymol*] : any of several chlorine derivatives of thymol; *esp* : the para derivative $Cl(CH_3)(C_3H_7)C_6H_2OH$ obtained as colorless crystals with a pungent taste and used as a germicide (as in mouthwashes)

chlorotic streak *n* : a systemic disease of sugar cane caused by a virus and characterized by striking yellow or whitish streaks on the leaves

chlo·rous acid \'klōrəs-\ *n* [F *chloreux,* fr. *chlor-* + *-eux* -ous] : a strongly oxidizing acid $HClO_2$ known only in solution and in the form of its salts (as sodium chlorite)

chlo·rox·i·phite \klō'räksə,fīt\ *n* -s [*chlor-* + Gk *xiphos* sword + E *-ite;* fr. the bladed crystals] : a mineral $Pb_3CuO_2(OH)_2Cl_2$(?) consisting of a basic chloride of lead and copper found in the Mendip hills of England

chlo·ro·xylenol \ˌ⁼⁼ *at* CHLORO- +\ *n* -s [*chlor-* + *xylenol*] : any of several chlorine derivatives of the xylenols; *esp* : the para derivative $Cl(CH_3)_2C_6H_2OH$ obtained as colorless crystals by chlorination of 3,5-xylenol and used as an antiseptic and germicide

chlo·ro·zincate \¦⁼⁼+\ *n* -s [*chlor-* + *zincate*] : a compound with zinc chloride; *specif* : one containing the anion $ZnCl_4^{--}$

chlorphenol *var of* CHLOROPHENOL

chlorphenol red *var of* CHLOROPHENOL RED

chlorpicrin *var of* CHLOROPICRIN

chlor·prom·a·zine \klōr'prämə,zēn, -ōr-, -,zən\ *n* -s [*chlor-* + *promethazine*] : a gray-white crystalline compound $C_{17}H_{19}ClN_2S$ derived from phenothiazine and administered as the hydrochloride in the treatment esp. of vomiting and of anxiety states and mental disorders

chlors *pl of* CHLOR

chlor·tetracycline \¦klōr, -ōr+\ *n* -s [*chlor-* + *tetracycline*] : a yellow crystalline antibiotic $C_{22}H_{23}ClN_2O_8$ produced by one strain of a soil actinomycete (*Streptomyces aureofaciens*), administered usu. in the form of its hydrochloride in the treatment of certain bacterial, rickettsial, and viral diseases and added in crude form to animal feeds for stimulating growth

chm *abbr* **1** chairman **2** checkmate

chmn *or* **chn** *abbr* chairman

cho \'chō\ *n, pl* **cho** [Jap *chō*] : a Japanese unit of land measure equal to about 2½ acres

choak *obs var of* CHOKE

choan- *or* **choano-** *comb form* [NL, fr. Gk *choanē* funnel, fr. *chein* to pour — more at FOUND] : funnel : funnel-shaped opening or part ⟨*choanate*⟩ ⟨*choanocyte*⟩

cho·a·na \'kōənə\ *n, pl* **choa·nae** \-,nē\ [NL, fr. Gk *choanē* funnel] **1** *anat* : a funnellike opening; *esp* : either of the posterior nares **2** : a collarlike contractile protoplasmic cup or rim surrounding the flagellum of certain flagellates and the endoderm cells of sponges

¹cho·a·nate \-,nāt\ *adj* [*choan-* + *-ate*] : having a choana; *specif* : having internal nares — compare CHOANICHTHYES

²choanate \"\ *n* -s : a choanate fish : one of the Choanichthyes

cho·a·neph·o·ra \,kōə'nefərə\ *n, cap* [NL, fr. Gk *choanē* funnel + *-phora*] : a genus of fungi typifying the family Choanephoraceae

cho·a·neph·o·ra·ce·ae \-,nefə'rāsē,ē\ *n pl, cap* [NL, fr. *Choanephora,* type genus + *-aceae*] : a family of fungi (order Mucorales) with both sporangiophores and conidiophores swollen at their tips and with naked zygospores

cho·a·nich·thy·es \,kōə'nikthē,ēz\ *n pl, cap* [NL, fr. *choan-* + Gk *ichthyes,* pl. of *ichthys* fish — more at ICHTHUS] : a subclass of Teleostomi comprising fishes with internal nares that were dominant life-forms in the Devonian but are now nearly extinct and including the Crossopterygii and the aberrant Dipnoi — compare LATIMERIA — **cho·a·nich·thys** \-thəs\ *n, pl* **choa·nichthys**

cho·a·no·cy·tal \¦kōə(,)nō¦sīd·°l, kō¦anə¦s-\ *adj* : of or relating to a choanocyte

cho·a·no·cyte \'kōə(,)nō,sīt, kō'anə,s-\ *n* -s [ISV *choan-* + *-cyte*] : one of the choanate and flagellate endodermal cells lining the cavity of a sponge

cho·a·no·flagellata \¦kōə(,)nō+\ *n pl, cap* [NL, fr. *choan-* + *Flagellata*] *in some classifications* : an order or other major division of Mastigophora comprising the choanoflagellates — compare LISSOFLAGELLATA

cho·a·no·flagellate \"+\ *n* -s [NL *Choanoflagellata*] : any of numerous small solitary or colonial aquatic flagellates constituting three families (Phalansteriidae, Codosigidae, and Bicosoecidae) of the order Protomonadina and distinguished from all other flagellates by possession of a contractile protoplasmic collar about the single anterior flagellum — compare CHOANOCYTE

cho·a·no·fla·gel·li·da \"+flə'jeləd·ə\ [NL, fr. *choan-* + *flagellum* + *-ida*] *syn of* CHOANOFLAGELLATA

cho·a·no·fla·gel·li·dae \-,dē\ *n pl, cap* [NL, fr. *choan-* + *flagellum* + *-idae*] *in some esp former classifications* : a family comprising the choanoflagellates — invalid because it lacks a type

cho·a·noph·o·rous \¦kōə¦näf(ə)rəs\ *adj* [*choan-* + *-phorous*] : CHOANATE

cho·a·no·som·al \¦kōə(,)nō¦sōməl, kō¦anə¦s-\ *adj* : of or relating to a choanosome

cho·a·no·some \'kōə(,)nō,sōm, kō'anə,s-\ *n* -s [*choan-* + *-some*] : the inner layer containing the choanocytes of a sponge

cho·a·no·tae·nia \,kōə(,)nō'tēnēə\ *n, cap* [NL, fr. *choan-* + *Taenia*] : a genus of taenioid tapeworms including a number of intestinal parasites of birds that utilize various insects as intermediate hosts

cho·ate \'kōət, 'kō,āt\ *adj* [fr. *inchoate,* after such pairs as E *invisible: visible*] : COMPLETE

chob·dar \'chōb,där\ *n* -s [Hindi *cobdār,* fr. Per *chōbdār, chūbdār,* fr. *chōb, chūb* staff, wood (fr. MPer *chōp* wood) + *-dār* having] *India* : USHER, ATTENDANT

cho·bie \'chōbē\ *n* -s [origin unknown] : TRIPLETAIL

cho·ca·lho \shü'kal(,)yü\ *n* -s [Pg, cowbell, rattle, fr. (assumed) VL *cloccaculum,* fr. ML *clocca* bell — more at CLOCK] : a Brazilian rattle commonly consisting of a gourd with its dried seeds inside or a metal sphere with pellets and used as a rhythm instrument

cho·chem \'ḳōḳəm\ *n, pl* **cha·cha·mim** \ḳäḳä'mēm\ *or* **cha·cho·mim** \ḳä'ḳōmim\ *var of* HAKAM

¹cho·cho \'chō(,)chō\ *or* **cho·ko** \-(,)kō\ *n* -s [AmerSp] : CHAYOTE

²cho·cho \'chō(,)chō\ *n, pl* **chocho** *or* **chochos** *usu cap* [Sp, of AmerInd origin] **1 a** : a Popolocan people of northern Oaxaca, Mexico **b** : a member of such people **2 a** : a Popolocan people of southern Puebla, Mexico — called also *Popoloca* **b** : a member of such people **3** : the language of a Chocho people

¹chock \'chäk\ *n* -s [origin unknown] **1** *also* **chuck** \'chək\ : a wedge or block (as of wood or metal) for steadying a body (as a cask or boat) and holding it motionless, or for filling in an unwanted space, or for blocking the movement of a wheel (as of a vehicle) **2** *Brit* : ⁸COG 2 **3** : a heavy metal casting fitted usu. at the sides of the upper deck and at the bow and stern of a ship and having two short horn-shaped arms curving inward between which ropes or hawsers may pass for mooring or towing — compare ¹CLEAT 1b

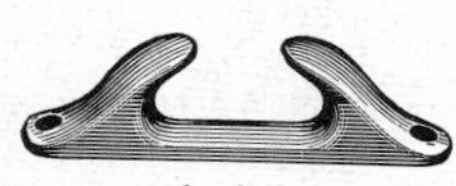
chock 3

²chock \"\ *vb* -ED/-ING/-S *vt* **1** : to provide, fit, stop, or make fast with or as if with chocks — often used with *off* **2** : to raise or support with chocks **3** : CHOKE ⟨caves and inlets ~*ed* up with cinders — Norman Douglas⟩ ~ *vi* : to fit closely — used with *in* or *into*

³chock \"\ *or* **chuck** \'chək\ *adv* : as close as possible ⟨~ aft⟩ ⟨~ up against the wall⟩ : as nearly or as completely as possible ⟨a wagon ~ full of chunks of wood⟩ — usu. used with another adverb or an adjective

⁴chock \"\ *n* -s [imit.] : a sharp somewhat hollow sound (as of wooden blocks striking together) ⟨the loud ~ of croquet balls⟩

¹chock·a·block \¦chäkə¦bläk\ *adj* [¹*chock* + ¹*a-* + *block;* fr. the position of a tackle when hoisting has reached its limit, with both blocks touching] **1** : brought close together ⟨the two blocks of a tackle in hoisting or hauling are ~⟩ : fully hoisted : hauled tight **2** : very full : CROWDED, CRAMMED ⟨exhibition floors were ~ with racing and sports cars —*New Yorker*⟩

²chockablock \"\ *adv* : in a crowded or overflowing manner ⟨lilies living ~⟩

chock·er·man \'chäkə(r)mən\ *n, pl* **chockermen** [by alter.] : CHOKERMAN

chock-full *or* **chock·ful** \'chək¦fu̇l, 'chäk-\ *or* **chuck-full** \'chək-\ *also* **choke-full** \'chōk-\ *adj* [ME *chokkefulle, chekefull,* prob. fr. *choken, cheken* to choke + *full*] : full to the extreme limit : CRAMMED ⟨the hotels were *chock-full*⟩ — compare ³CHOCK

chockstone \'⁼,⁼\ *n* -s [¹*chock* + *stone*] : a mass of rock wedged in a mountain chimney

¹cho·co \chə'kō\ *n, pl* **choco** *or* **chocos** *usu cap* [Sp *chocó, chocoa, chocoe,* of AmerInd origin] **1 a** : a people of northwestern Colombia and Panama **b** : a member of such people **2** : the language of the Choco people, prob. Cariban

²choco \'chä(,)kō, 'chō-\ *n* -s [short for *chocolate soldier;* prob. fr. the new uniforms worn by recruits] *Austral* : a militiaman or a conscript in World War II

¹choc·o·late \'chäklət, 'chòk- *also* -kəl-\ *n* -s [Sp, fr. Nahuatl *xocoatl,* perh. fr. *xococ* sour, bitter + *atl* water, drink] **1** : a food obtained by grinding roasted cacao beans that have been freed from germ and shell — sometimes called *plain chocolate, bitter chocolate, cooking chocolate;* see CACAO, COCOA **2** : a beverage made by cooking a portion of chocolate in water or milk **3** : a small candy with a center (as of fondant, nougat, or nut) and a coating of chocolate — distinguished from *bonbon* **4** : a variable color averaging a brownish gray that is deeper and slightly redder than taupe, redder and darker than mouse gray, and redder and deeper than castor **5** : a warm light brown approximating the color of fresh milk chocolate and occurring as a variant coat color in certain mammals (as the Siamese cat or the mink) **6** *also* **chocolate root** : WATER AVENS

²chocolate \"\ *adj* **1** : composed of chocolate : flavored or coated with chocolate **2** : of the color chocolate

chocolate-box \'⁼(⁼)⁼,⁼\ *adj, of a painting* : superficially pretty or sentimental ⟨his fiancée wanted him to paint her, and always in a *chocolate-box* pose —L.S.Gannett⟩

chocolate brown *n* : a variable color averaging a dark grayish brown that is very slightly yellower and duller than African brown and redder than cordovan (sense 3a) — compare CHOCOLATE 4

chocolate cream *n* : a chocolate with a creamy fondant center

chocolate flower *n* : a wild geranium (*Geranium maculatum*)

chocolate house *n* : a public house or room serving chocolate

chocolate maroon *n* : OLD ROSELEAF

chocolate moth *n* : ALMOND MOTH

chocolate prune *n* : a prune dried to the color of chocolate

chocolate soldier *n* **1** : a soldier that does not fight **2** : ²CHOCO

chocolate spot *n* : a disease of beans and other legumes caused by fungi of the genus *Botrytis* and characterized by brown spotting of leaves and stems and withering of shoots

chocolate tree *n* : a cacao (*Theobroma cacao*)

choc·o·laty \-ləd·ē, -ətē, -i\ *adj* : made of or like chocolate

choc·taw \'chäk,tò\ *n, pl* **choctaw** *or* **choctaws** *usu cap* [Choctaw *Chahta*] **1 a** : a Muskogean people of Mississippi, Alabama, and Louisiana **b** : a member of such people **2 a** : the language of the Choctaw and Chickasaw people **b** : strange or incomprehensible language : JARGON, GIBBERISH **3** *sometimes cap, in fancy skating* : a stroke forward on either edge of either skate followed by a stroke backward on the opposite edge of the other skate

choctaw beer *n, usu cap C* : a bootleg beer made in the southwestern U.S. during national prohibition

chode [ME, alter. (influenced by *rode,* past of *riden* to ride) of *chidde,* past of *chiden* to chide] *archaic past of* CHIDE

choe·ro·pus \'kirəpəs\ *syn of* CHAEROPUS

-choe·rus \'kirəs, 'kēr-\ *n comb form* [NL, fr. Gk *choiros* pig; akin to L *horrēre* to bristle — more at HORROR] : pig : piglike animal — in generic names in zoology ⟨*Hydrochoerus*⟩

chof·fer \'chäfər\ *n* -s [alter. of ME *chaufour* — more at CHAFER] *Scot* : a portable heater or chafing dish

cho·ga \'chōgə\ *n* -s [Sindhi, of Altaic origin; akin to Turk *çuha* cloth] : a long-sleeved long-skirted cloak for men worn mainly in India and Pakistan

chog·set \'chägsət, -gzət\ *n* -s [of Algonquian origin; akin to Pequot *cachauxet* cunner, Natick *chohchohkesit* striped, spotted] : CUNNER b

¹choice \'chòis\ *n* -s [ME *chois,* fr. OF, fr. *choisir* to choose, of Gmc origin; akin to Goth *kausjan* to examine, test, *kiusan* to choose — more at CHOOSE] **1** : the act of choosing; *typically* : the voluntary and purposive or deliberate action of picking, singling out, or selecting from two or more that which is favored or superior : the decision reached by such action ⟨the ~ made by the voters⟩ ⟨Lincoln's ~ of Grant as general⟩ **2 a** : the right, privilege, opportunity, or faculty of freely choosing, picking out, or deciding : freedom to pick or decide : OPTION ⟨a captive has little ~⟩ **b** : situation demanding choosing or justifying consideration of alternatives ⟨there is no ~ between right and wrong⟩ **3 a** : a person, thing, part, way, or characteristic chosen, singled out, or favored typically as best or most likely, fit, or advantageous ⟨New York was the delegates' first ~ as capital⟩ **b** : an example, part, or instance worthy of being chosen as excellent or best : PRIME, PICK, FLOWER, CREAM, ELITE ⟨of the cavalry the king's own was the ~⟩ **c** : a person or thing available, fit, or likely to be picked out or designated ⟨several ~s for the nomination⟩ **4 :** a sufficient or ample number or variety for wide or free selection ⟨more ~ of fruits at the larger market⟩ **5 :** care and judgment in choosing **:** DISCRIMINATION ⟨pick words with ~⟩ **6 :** a dilemma involving a decision between alternatives; *also* **:** the one way, person, or thing to be preferred to another ⟨death or exile was the ~⟩

syn PREFERENCE, SELECTION, ELECTION, OPTION, ALTERNATIVE: CHOICE may suggest freedom in picking out, valuing, or deciding ⟨the oracle has no *choice;* it must produce an answer —W.D.Howells⟩ Specifically it may suggest individual modifications in obvious or logical criteria ⟨the *choice* of a cook not for her culinary skill but for her ability to make pretty dishes —Herbert Spencer⟩ PREFERENCE may heighten notions of personal bias, predilection, or individuality of judgment; it is less likely to suggest a single act of picking, choosing, or deciding ⟨a sterilization of the self, an elimination . . . of the human bias and *preference* —Lewis Mumford⟩ ⟨his *preferences* betray him more than his aversions —J.E.E.Acton-Dalburg⟩ SELECTION may suggest careful or wise judgment and discrimination in picking out from a sizable number ⟨when schools attempted, at least, to cultivate discrimination and to furnish the material on which *selection* can be founded —C.H.Grandgent⟩ ELECTION may refer to a definitive or formal choosing after deliberation and to choosing for some explicit role, duty, or function ⟨the solemnity with which religious and ideological groups claim *election* for special destinies beyond the grave or upon peculiar peaks of history —Cecil Sprigge⟩ In nontechnical uses in today's English OPTION is likely to suggest genuine conferred or guaranteed liberty to choose deliberately ⟨it was the privilege of the English parent to choose whether his children should be instructed or not . . . the Education Act of 1870 abolished this *option* —George Sampson⟩ ALTERNATIVE stresses the idea that things not chosen must necessarily be rejected and vice versa ⟨the necessary *alternative* was to deny it altogether —O.W.Holmes †1935⟩ Although objected to, it is quite common in situations involving more than two choices ⟨our three *alternatives* —T.E.Lawrence⟩ ⟨no third *alternative* —Walter Moberly⟩ ⟨other *alternatives* existed —Sidney Hook⟩ **—by choice** *or* **for choice :** by preference ⟨Austrian by birth and French *by choice* —A.E.Wier⟩ ⟨in the evening sat *for choice* without a light —H.W.Glover⟩; *also* **:** most usually ⟨hired outlaws *for choice* to skin and drive and cook for him on the buffalo range —W.S.Campbell⟩ **— of choice :** to be chosen first **:** PREFERRED, RECOMMENDED — used esp. of drugs and treatments

2choice \"\ *adj* -ER/-EST [ME *chois,* fr. *chois,* n.] **1 :** worthy of being chosen above others **:** of highest quality **:** without blemish, demerit, or disadvantage **:** FINE, SELECT ⟨Monseigneur . . . sat down alone to his sumptuous and ~ supper —Charles Dickens⟩ ⟨accepting *choicest* candidates⟩ ⟨stamps in ~ condition⟩ **2 :** well-chosen **:** selected by keen intuition or by care and deliberation **:** most appropriate ⟨sinister stories of Paris landlords . . . told . . . with singularly ~ words —F.M.Ford⟩ **3 a :** FASTIDIOUS, DISCRIMINATING ⟨~ of his food⟩ **b :** CAREFUL, FOND ⟨uncommon ~ over her daughters —*West Somerset Word Bk.*⟩ **4 a** *of meat and other products* **:** of highest or next highest quality **b** *of beef* **:** of a grade between prime and good

syn EXQUISITE, ELEGANT, RARE, RECHERCHÉ, DAINTY, DELICATE: CHOICE indicates preeminence or superiority and may or may not connote the idea of being selected ⟨as from the beds and borders of a garden *choice* flowers are gathered —William Wordsworth⟩ ⟨when education in America began, it was intended for the fit and designed to produce a *choice* type —C.H. Grandgent⟩ EXQUISITE implies near perfection, esp. in craftsmanship, and may also imply an especial appeal to the discriminating ⟨selected for their beauty . . . and beautified with the numerous Indian cosmetics, these girls were of the most *exquisite* loveliness —C.B.Nordhoff & J.N.Hall⟩ ⟨an *exquisite* skill of eye and hand which gave them their unique success in that artistic craftsmanship —C.W.Eliot⟩ ELEGANT applies to a refined luxury or richness restrained by good taste ⟨they [the Cavaliers] had more both of profound and of polite learning than the Puritans. Their tempers were more engaging . . . their tastes more *elegant* —T.B.Macaulay⟩ ⟨his trousers were extremely *elegant,* a light cloth, black and white check, hung on his legs —George Moore⟩ RARE, in this sense, may apply to any uncommon excellence ⟨the *rarest* cordials old monks ever schemed to coax from pulpy grapes —Amy Lowell⟩ ⟨nowhere else do we find such *rare* and costly marbles —H.T. Buckle⟩ RECHERCHÉ may apply to a studied opulent elegance ⟨the sangfroid, grace, abandon, and *recherché* nonchalance with which Charles Yates ushers ladies and gentlemen to their seats in the opera house —O.Henry⟩ DAINTY may apply to the graceful and fragile; it usually applies to what pleases the fastidious ⟨the touch is so light, the fancy so *dainty,* and the conceit so delicate that the poem remains immortally fresh and young —J.W.Draper⟩ ⟨this *dainty* and somewhat supercilious guest has been brought to the supper by a young Roman —Agnes Repplier⟩ DELICATE, in this sense, suggests subtlety and fineness and either sensuous or intellectual appeal ⟨the *delicate* fan tracery and crenellated molding of the screen —Dorothy Sayers⟩ ⟨not, however, an effervescing wine, although its *delicate* piquancy produced a somewhat similar effect —Nathaniel Hawthorne⟩ ⟨the exquisite transparency and *delicate* finish of her work —P.E.More⟩

choice–drawn *adj, obs* **:** chosen with care **:** PICKED

choice·less \-ləs\ *adj* **:** offering or permitting no choice **:** unable to choose

choice·ly \-lē, -li\ *adv* [ME *choisly,* fr. *chois,* adj. + *-ly*] **:** in a choice manner: **a :** with care in choosing **:** CAREFULLY, DISCRIMINATINGLY **b :** in a preferable or excellent manner **:** DAINTILY, EXQUISITELY

choice·ness \-nəs\ *n* -ES **:** the quality or state of being choice

choicy \'chȯisē, -si\ *adj, usu* -ER/-EST [¹*choice* + *-y*] *slang* **:** FASTIDIOUS, CHOOSY

1choil \'chȯi(ə)l\ *n* -S [origin unknown] **:** the angle in a pocketknife blade at the junction of the wedge-shaped cutting part with the tang or the corresponding part of any knife

2choil \"\ *vt* -ED/-ING/-S **:** to form a choil on (a knife blade)

1choir *also* **quire** \'kwī(ə)r, -īə\ *n* -S [ME *quer,* fr. OF *cuer,* fr. ML *chorus* body of singers in church, place for singers in church, fr. L, chorus, choral dance — more at CHORUS] **1 :** an organized company of singers esp. in church service **:** a choral society **:** a chorus or a subdivision of a chorus **2 :** a group of instruments of the same class (as in an orchestra) ⟨the woodwind ~⟩ **3 :** an organized assemblage **:** a band of persons **:** a group or rank of things ⟨Illilouette Fall, one of the most beautiful of all the Yosemite ~ —John Muir †1914⟩ **4 :** an order or division of angels **5 :** a company of dancers or of dancers and singers **6 :** the part of a church appropriated to the singers: **a :** such a part separated from the nave on the one hand and the sanctuary on the other **b** *of a large church* **:** the entire section in which the choir (sense a) is situated **7 :** CHOIR ORGAN **8 :** a group organized for ensemble speaking — compare CHORAL SPEAKING

2choir *also* **quire** \"\ *vb* -ED/-ING/-S **:** to sing or sound in chorus or concert ⟨what company, in masks, can ~ it with the naked wind —Wallace Stevens⟩

3choir \"\ *adj* [¹*choir*] **:** specially appointed to community recitation or singing of the divine office — distinguished from *lay* ⟨~ monks⟩ ⟨~ nuns⟩

choir aisle *n* **:** an aisle flanking the choir of a church

choirboy \'⸗,⸗\ *n* **:** a boy member of a church choir — called also *chorister*

choir loft *n* **:** a gallery appropriated to a choir

choir manual *n* **:** the manual of a choir organ

choirmaster \'⸗,⸗⸗\ *n* **:** the director of a choir (as in a church)

choi·ro·pot·a·mus \,kīrō'pädəməs\ *syn of* KOIROPOTAMUS

choir organ *n* **:** a division of a pipe organ designed for accompanying singing

choir rail *n* **:** a rail enclosing the choir of a church

choir school *n* **:** a school for the general education of choirboys maintained by a cathedral or large church esp. of the Anglican Communion

choir screen *n* **1 :** a screen (as of ornamental woodwork or wrought iron) enclosing the choir (sense 6a) **2 :** the part of a choir screen that closes the western end of the choir and separates it from the crossing or the nave

choir stall *n* **:** a seat in the choir of a church enclosed wholly or partly at the back and sides and often canopied and elaborately carved

choir wall *n* **:** a wall enclosing the choir (sense 6a) often built in between the columns surrounding the choir

choirwise \'⸗,⸗\ *adv* [¹*choir* + *-wise*] **:** by choirs **:** ANTIPHONALLY

1choke \'chōk\ *vb* -ED/-ING/-S [ME *cheken, choken,* alter. of *acheken, achoken,* fr. OE *acēocian* to suffocate, strangle — more at CHEEK] *vt* **1 :** to make normal breathing difficult or impossible for (a person or animal) (1) by compressing the throat with strong external pressure ⟨an unwary guard *choked* to death by a murderous prisoner⟩, (2) by obstructing or clogging the windpipe ⟨a fish bone *choking* a kitten⟩, (3) by poisoning (as with gas) or otherwise adulterating air being breathed ⟨gas fumes were *choking* the rescue squad⟩, or (4) through nervous agitation ⟨rage *choked* him as he tried to speak⟩ **2 :** to check, suppress, or repress expression or delivery of (as an utterance) ⟨a cloture rule designed to ~ off discussion⟩ ⟨trying to ~ down my laughter⟩ **:** suppress or check manifestation of (as an emotion) ⟨~ down his rage⟩; *also* **:** to check or suppress utterance by (as a speaker) **:** shut up **:** SILENCE ⟨the moderator could not ~ her off⟩ ⟨fear of . . . punishment may often ~ those who would otherwise speak out —Zechariah Chafee⟩ — often used with *off, back, down* **3 a :** to check or stop the growth, development, activity, or vitality of with or as if with forceful constriction ⟨antagonism to an environment whose complications are *choking* his life —C.D.Lewis⟩ **b :** to check or obstruct flow, motion, progress, or other activity through (as a pipe) by clogging, congesting, crowding, filling densely, or sometimes external constriction ⟨the drifting ice which *choked* the bay —R.E.Byrd⟩ ⟨the channels are nearly *choked* with weeds and reeds —C.S. Forester⟩ ⟨the hallway . . . was *choked* with rubbish —Liam O'Flaherty⟩ **c :** to fill completely or chock-full **:** PACK, GLUT, JAM ⟨windows were *choked* with the merchandise of a summer sale —William McFee⟩ **4 :** to make a choke in (as a cartridge or the barrel of a shotgun) **5 :** to check or stop the motion or action of (as a cable, rudder, or machine) by clogging or jamming **6 :** to enrich the fuel mixture of (a motor) by partially shutting off the air intake of the carburetor **7** *sports* **:** to grip (a bat, club, racket, or stick) some distance from the end of the handle **:** shorten one's grip on (a bat or other implement) in order to alter the effective length — often used with *up* ⟨the power hitter seldom ~s up his bat very much⟩ ~ *vi* **1 :** to suffer from interference with breathing typically by having the windpipe obstructed or irritated with resulting throat spasms ⟨we *choked* in the dust of the desert —T.B.Costain⟩ ⟨he *choked* on a fish bone⟩ **2 :** to become obstructed, stopped, or checked by or as if by constriction or obstruction ⟨the words *choked* in his throat —Sir Walter Scott⟩ **3 :** to shorten one's grip on the handle of a bat or similar implement **syn** see SUFFOCATE

2choke \"\ *n* -S **1 a :** the act of choking **:** SUFFOCATION **:** partial or complete obstruction that prevents the passage of air through the throat to the lungs **b chokes** *pl* **:** caisson disease when marked by suffocation — used with *the* **2 :** an obstruction to passage or flow: **a :** a valve for choking a gasoline engine **b :** a constriction in an outlet (as of a gas or oil well) to limit the flow **c :** REACTOR 3 **3 a :** a narrowing of the bore immediately before the muzzle of a shotgun that serves to concentrate the shot pellets as they leave the muzzle of the gun **b :** an attachment that allows variation of muzzle constriction of a shotgun **4 :** the filamentous or scaly center of an artichoke head **5 :** an interference with the development of the inflorescence of certain grasses caused by growth of the cattail fungus while the flowers are still in the leaf sheath **6** *in judo* **:** an application of pressure on the jugular vein

3choke \"\ *adj* [¹*choke*] *sports* **:** shortening the effective length of (a bat, racket, or club) ⟨a ~ grip⟩ **:** using a shortening grip ⟨a ~ hitter⟩

4choke \"\ *n* -S [ME, perh. fr. ON *kjālki* jawbone; akin to *kjölr* keel — more at KEEL] *chiefly Scot* **:** JAW, CHEEK, NECK — usu. used in pl.

chokeberry \'⸗,⸗⸗\ *n* [so called fr. the bitter taste] **1 :** the small berrylike astringent fruit of any plant of the genus *Aronia* **2 :** a plant of the genus *Aronia*

1chokebore \'⸗,⸗\ *n* [²*choke* + *bore*] **1 :** ²CHOKE 3 **2 :** a shotgun with a choke

2chokebore \"\ *vt* -ED/-ING/-S **:** to provide with a choke

3chokebore \"\ *adj, of a dog* **:** having a keen accurate nose

chokecherry \'⸗,⸗⸗\ *n* [so called fr. the bitter taste] **1 a :** a common cherry (*Prunus virginiana*) of eastern No. America **b :** a cherry (*P. demissa*) of the western U.S. **c :** BLACK CHERRY 2 **2 :** the astringent fruit of any chokecherry

choke coil *n* **:** REACTOR 3

choke collar *n* **:** a collar that may be tightened as a noose used esp. in training and controlling powerful or fractious dogs

choked *past of* CHOKE

chokedamp \'⸗,⸗\ *n* **:** BLACKDAMP

choked disk \chōkt-\ *n* **:** swelling and protrusion of the optic disk caused by edema and occurring in various diseases, esp. brain tumor — called also *papilledema*

choke–full *var of* CHOCK-FULL

choke pear *n* **1 a :** a pear with an astringent taste **b :** CHOKEBERRY **2** *obs* **:** a sarcasm by which one is put to silence **:** something that cannot be answered

choke point *n* **1 :** THROAT 2f(3) **2 :** BOTTLENECK

1chok·er \'chōkə(r)\ *n* -S [¹*choke* + *-er*] **1 :** one that chokes **2 :** something worn closely about the throat or neck: as **a :** a wide neckcloth; *esp* **:** STOCK **b :** a formal white necktie **c :** a very high usu. stiffened collar **d :** a short necklace or jeweled collar **e :** a narrow fur piece for women **3 :** a noose of wire rope for hauling a log

2choker \"\ *adj* **:** worn closely about the throat or neck ⟨~ beads⟩

chok·ered \'chōkə(r)d\ *adj* **:** wearing a choker

chok·er·man \'chōkə(r)mən\ *n,* pl **chokermen :** one who puts chokers around logs and gets them ready for hauling — called also *choker setter*

chokes *pres 3d sing of* CHOKE, *pl of* CHOKE

chokestrap \'⸗,⸗\ *n* [alter. of *checkstrap*] **:** a checkstrap on a horse's harness

choke up *vi* **1 :** to become or feel constricted in the throat (as from a strong emotion) ⟨rising to answer their tribute he *choked up* and could not utter a word⟩ **2** *of an athlete or performer* **:** to become hampered by nervousness or overeagerness (as in competition)

1cho·key \'chōkē\ *n* -S [Hindi *caukī,* dim. of *cauk* market place, fr. Skt *catuṣka* consisting of four, quadrangular, fr. *catur* four — more at FOUR] **1** *India* **:** a station or post esp. for collection of customs or for palanquin bearers or police **2** *slang Brit* **:** JAIL, LOCKUP

2chokey *var of* CHOKY

cho·ki·dar \,chōkē'dār\ *n* -S [Hindi *caukīdār,* fr. *caukī* police station, guard's post + *-dār* possessing — more at CHOKEY] *India* **:** WATCHMAN; *esp* **:** a private watchman (as at a gate)

choking *adj* [fr. pres. part. of ¹*choke*] **:** producing the feeling of strangulation ⟨a ~ cloud of dust⟩ **2 :** indistinct in utterance —used esp. of the voice of a person affected with strong emotion — **chok·ing·ly** *adv*

choking coil *n* **:** REACTOR

chokmah *usu cap, var of* HOKHMAH

choko *var of* CHOCHO

cho·kra \'chōkrə\ *n* -S [Hindi *chokrā*] *India* **:** a boy employed as a servant

chok·we \'chäkwē\ *n, pl* **chokwe** *or* **chokwes** *usu cap* [Chokwe] **1 a :** a scattered people of the southern Congo and northern Angola noted for the religious masks that they produce **b :** a member of such people **2 :** a Bantu language of the Chokwe people closely related to or perhaps a dialect of Lwena

choky *or* **chok·ey** \'chōkē. -ki\ *adj* **chokier; chokiest** [¹*choke* + *-y*] **1 :** tending to choke or suffocate **:** having power to choke ⟨the air was ~ with wood smoke⟩ **2 :** inclined or having a tendency to choke — used esp. of one moved by strong emotion

chol \'chōl\ *n, pl* **chol** \"\ *or* **cho·les** \-ō,lās\ *usu cap* [Sp, of AmerInd origin] **1 a :** an Indian people of northern Chiapas, Mexico **b :** a member of such people **2 :** a Mayan language of the Chol people

chol- *or* **chole-** *or* **cholo-** *comb form* [Gk *chol-, cholē-, cholo-,* fr. *cholē, cholos* — more at GALL] **:** bile **:** gall ⟨*chol*ane⟩ ⟨*chole*lith⟩ ⟨*cholo*genetic⟩

cho·la \'chōlə, -,lä\ *n* -S [AmerSp, fem. of *cholo*] **:** a woman of mixed Spanish and Indian ancestry

cholaemia *var of* CHOLEMIA

chol·a·gog·ic \¦kälə¦gäjik, -ōl-\ *adj* **:** being a cholagogue **:** inducing a flow of bile

chol·a·gogue \'kälə,gäg, -ōl-\ *n* -S [F, fr. Gk *cholagōgos,* leading off bile, fr. *chol-* + *-agōgos* -agogue] **:** an agent that promotes an increased flow of bile — compare CHOLERESIS

cho·lam \'chōləm\ *n* -S [Tamil *cōlam*] *India* **:** GRAIN SORGHUM

cho·lane \'kō,lān\ *n* -S [*chol-* + *-ane*] **:** a crystalline steroid hydrocarbon $C_{24}H_{42}$ from which the bile acids are derived

chol·angiogram \kō'l+an . . .\ *n* -S [ISV *chol-* + *angiogram*] **:** a roentgenogram of the bile ducts made after the ingestion or injection of a radiopaque substance

chol·an·gi·o·graph·ic \kō¦lanjēə¦grafik\ *adj* [ISV *cholangiography* + *-ic*] **:** of or relating to cholangiography

chol·an·gi·og·ra·phy \⸗,⸗⸗'ägrəfē\ *n* -ES [ISV *chol-* + *angiography*] **:** roentgenographic visualization of the bile ducts after ingestion or injection of a radiopaque substance

chol·an·gi·ole \kō'lanjē,ōl\ *n* -S [NL *cholangiola*] **:** a bile canaliculus

chol·an·gi·o·lit·ic \⸗¦⸗⸗,ə¦lid·ik\ *adj* [NL *cholangiolitis* + E *-ic*] **:** relating to or involving cholangiolitis ⟨~ cirrhosis⟩

chol·an·gi·o·li·tis \⸗,⸗⸗⸗'līd·əs\ *n, pl* **cholangiolit·i·des** \-'lid·ə,dēz\ [NL, fr. *cholangiola* bile canaliculus (fr. *chol-* + *angi-* + L *-ola* -ole) + *-itis*] **:** inflammation of bile capillaries

chol·an·gi·o·ma \kō,lanjē'ōmə\ *n, pl* **cholangiomas** \-məz\ *also* **cholangioma·ta** \-məd·ə\ [NL, fr. *chol-* + *angioma*] **:** carcinoma of a bile duct

chol·an·gi·tis \,kō,lan'jīd·əs\ *n, pl* **cholangit·i·des** \-'jid·ə,dēz\ [NL, fr. *chol-* + *angitis*] **:** inflammation of one or more bile ducts

cho·lan·ic acid \(')kō¦lanik-\ *n* [ISV *chol-* + *-an-* + *-ic*] **:** a colorless crystalline acid $C_{23}H_{39}COOH$ some of whose hydroxy and keto derivatives constitute the bile acids

chol·an·threne \kō'lan,thrēn\ *n* -S [*chol-* + *-anthrene*] **:** a pale yellow crystalline pentacyclic carcinogenic hydrocarbon $C_{20}H_{14}$ that can be made from deoxycholic acid; 7,8-ethylene-benz[a]anthracene — compare METHYLCHOLANTHRENE

cho·late \'kō,lāt\ *n* -S [*chol-* + *-ate*] **:** a salt or ester of cholic acid

chole- — see CHOL-

c–hole \'⸗,⸗\ *n, usu cap C* [so called fr. its shape] **:** the sound hole in the body of viols and guitars

cho·le·ate \'kōlē,āt\ *n* -S [prob. fr. G *choleat,* fr. *chol-* + *-at* -ate] **:** a salt or ester of choleic acid

cho·le·cal·cif·er·ol \,kōlə,kal'sifə,rȯl, ,käl-, -rōl\ *n* -S [ISV *chol-* + *calci-* + *-fer* + *-ol*] **:** VITAMIN D_3

cho·le·cyst \'kōlə,sist, 'käl-\ *also* **cho·le·cys·tis** \,⸗⸗'sistəs\ *n, pl* **cholecysts** [NL *cholecystis,* fr. *chol-* + *-cystis*] **:** GALLBLADDER — **cho·le·cys·tic** \¦⸗⸗¦⸗tik\ *adj*

cho·le·cys·tec·to·my \,⸗⸗,si'stektəmē\ *n* -ES [ISV *cholecyst* + *-ectomy*] **:** surgical excision of the gallbladder

cho·le·cys·ti·tis \-'stīd·əs\ *n, pl* **cholecystit·i·des** \-'stid·ə,dēz\ [NL, fr. *cholecystis* + *-itis*] **:** inflammation of the gallbladder

cho·le·cys·to·gram \-'sistə,gram\ *n* -S [*cholecyst* + *-o-* + *-gram*] **:** a roentgenogram of the gallbladder made after ingestion or injection of a radiopaque substance

cho·le·cys·to·graph·ic \⸗⸗⸗¦⸗⸗¦grafik\ *adj* [ISV *cholecystography* + *-ic*] **:** of or relating to cholecystography

cho·le·cys·tog·ra·phy \,⸗⸗,⸗'stägrəfē\ *n* -ES [ISV *cholecyst* + *-o-* + *-graphy*] **:** the roentgenographic visualization of the gallbladder after ingestion or injection of a radiopaque substance

cho·le·cys·to·ki·nin \,⸗⸗,sistə'kīnən\ *n* -S [*cholecyst* + *-o-* + Gk *kinein* to move + E *-in*] **:** a hormone produced in the mucosa of the upper intestine that stimulates contraction of the gallbladder

cho·le·cys·tos·to·my \,⸗⸗,si'stästəmē\ *n* -ES [ISV *chol-* + *cystostomy* "operation into the bladder", fr. *cyst-* + *-stomy*] **:** surgical incision of the gallbladder usu. to effect drainage

cho·le·doch \'kōlə,däk, 'käl-\ *or* **cho·le·doch·al** \¦⸗⸗¦däkəl, kə'ledəkəl\ *adj* [*choledoch* fr. NL *choledochus,* fr. Gk *cholēdochos,* fr. *cholē* bile + *dochos* containing; *choledochal* fr. *choledoch* + *-al;* akin to Gk *dechesthai* to receive, *dokein* to seem good — more at GALL, DECENT] **:** conveying bile ⟨the ~ duct is the common bile duct⟩

cho·led·o·cho·li·thi·a·sis \kə¦ledə(,)kōlə'thīəsəs\ *n* [NL, fr. *choledochus* + *-o-* + *lithiasis*] **:** a condition marked by presence of calculi in the gallbladder and common bile duct

cho·led·o·chos·to·my \⸗,⸗⸗'kästəmē; ,kōlə,dä'k-, ,kälə-\ *n* -ES [*choledoch-* + *-o-* + *-stomy*] **:** surgical incision of the common bile duct usu. to effect drainage

cho·led·o·chus \kə'ledəkəs\ *n, pl* **choledo·chi** \-,kī, -,kē\ [NL, short for *ductus choledochus* choledoch duct] **:** the common bile duct

cho·le·glo·bin \¦kōlə¦glōbən, ¦käl-\ *n* -S [*chol-* + *globin*] **:** a green pigment that occurs in bile, is a combination of globin and a ferric salt of biliverdin, and is formed by breakdown of hemoglobin

cho·le·ic \kə'lēik, kō-\ *adj* [ISV *chol-* + *-ic*] **:** of, relating to, or derived from bile

choleic acid *n* **:** DEOXYCHOLIC ACID; *also* **:** a molecular compound of this acid (as with a fatty acid or a hydrocarbon)

cho·le·lith \'kōlə,lith, 'käl-\ *n* -S [ISV *chol-* + *-lith*] **:** GALLSTONE

cho·le·li·thi·a·sis \,kōləlә'thīəsəs, ,kä-\ *n* [NL, fr. *chol-* + *lithiasis*] **1 :** the production of gallstones ⟨stasis and inflammation usu. precede ~⟩ **2 :** an abnormal state characterized by the presence of gallstones ⟨the obese are particularly subject to ~⟩

cho·le·mia *or* **cho·lae·mia** \kō'lēmēə\ *n* -S [NL, fr. *chol-* + *-emia, -aemia*] **:** the presence of excess bile in the blood usu. indicative of liver disease — **cho·lem·ic** \-mik\ *adj*

cho·lent \'chȯlənt, 'chəl- *also* 'sh-\ *n* -S [Yiddish *tsholnt, tshont, shalet, shalent*] **:** a Jewish Sabbath-day dish of slow-baked meat and vegetables

cho·le·poi·e·sis \,kōlə,pȯi'ēsəs, ,käl-\ *n, pl* **cholepoie·ses** \-ē,sēz\ [NL, fr. *chol-* + Gk *poiēsis* creation, manufacture, fr. *poiein* to make — more at POET] **:** production of bile — compare CHOLERESIS — **cho·le·poi·et·ic** \¦⸗⸗,⸗⸗¦ed·ik\ *adj*

chol·er \'kälə(r), 'kōl-\ *n* -S [ME *coler,* fr. MF *colere,* fr. L *cholera* bilious disease, fr. Gk, fr. *cholē* bile; akin to IrGael *galar* disease — more at GALL] **1 a** *archaic* **:** YELLOW BILE **b** *obs* **:** BILE 1a **2** *obs* **:** BILIOUSNESS **3 :** IRASCIBILITY **:** ready disposition to anger and irritation ⟨my ~ rising at the virulence of her invective —Ellery Sedgwick⟩

chol·era \'kälərə *also* -lrə\ *n* -S *often attrib* [ME *colera* bile, fr. ML, fr. L *cholera* bilious disease] **:** any of several diseases of man and domestic animals usu. marked by severe gastrointestinal symptoms: as **a :** ASIATIC CHOLERA **b :** FOWL CHOLERA **c :** HOG CHOLERA

cholera belt *n* **:** a flannel or wool band or cincture around the waist

chol·er·a·ic \¦kälə¦rāik\ *also* **chol·er·ic** \'kälərik; kə'lerik, kä'-, -rēk\ *adj* [*cholera* + *-ic*] **:** relating to, resulting from, or resembling cholera

cholera in·fan·tum \-in'fantəm\ *n* [NL, lit., cholera of infants] **:** an acute noncontagious intestinal disturbance of infants formerly common in congested areas of high humidity and temperature but now rare

cholera mor·bus \-'mȯrbəs, -ō(ə)b-\ *n* [NL, lit., the disease cholera] **:** a gastrointestinal disturbance characterized by griping, diarrhea, and sometimes vomiting and usu. resulting from overeating or from contaminated foods

cholera vib·rio \-'vibrē,ō\ *n* [NL] **:** the bacterium (*Vibrio comma*) that causes Asiatic cholera

cho·le·re·sis \,kōlə'rēsəs, ,käl-\ *n, pl* **choleres** \-ē,sēz\ [NL, fr. *chol-* + *-resis* (modif. — influenced by such words as *diuresis* — of Gk *rhysis* flowing) — more at STREAM] **:** the flow of bile from the liver esp. when increased above a previous or normal level — compare CHOLAGOGUE, CHOLEPOIESIS

1cho·le·ret·ic \¦⸗⸗¦red·ik\ *adj* [fr. NL *choleresis,* after such pairs as NL *diuresis:* E *diuretic*] **:** of or relating to choleresis

²cho·le·ret·ic \¦==¦red·ik\ *n* -s **:** an agent that induces choleresis

¹chol·er·ic \'kälərik; kə'lerik, kä'-, -rēk; *sometimes* 'kōlərik\ *adj* [ME *colerik*, fr. MF *colerique*, fr. L *cholericus* bilious, fr. Gk *cholerikos*, fr. *cholera* + *-ikos* -ic] **1** *obs* **:** having yellow bile as the predominating bodily humor; *also* **:** having the bodily conformation and temperament thought to be characteristic of such predominance **2 a :** easily moved to anger **:** HOT-TEMPERED, IRASCIBLE ⟨where melancholic men abandon effort, men of the ~ type take to kicking and smashing —H.G.Wells⟩ ⟨a ~ disposition⟩ **b :** ANGRY, IRATE, WRATHFUL ⟨a ~ outburst⟩ **syn** see IRASCIBLE

²choleric *var of* CHOLERAIC

chol·er·i·cal·ly \-lərəklē, -li; -lerək(ə)l-, -rēk-\ *or* **cho·ler·ly** \-rəklē, -rēk-, -li\ *adv* **:** in a choleric manner

cho·ler·ic·ness *n* -ES **:** the quality or state of being choleric

chol·er·i·form \'käl(ə)rə,fȯrm\ *adj* [ISV *cholera* + *-iform*; prob. orig. formed as F *choleriforme*] **:** resembling cholera

chol·er·oid \'kälə,rȯid\ *adj* [*cholera* + *-oid*] **:** like cholera

choles *pl of* CHOL

cho·les·tane \kə'le,stān\ *n* -s [*cholesterol* + *-ane*] **:** a crystalline saturated steroid hydrocarbon $C_{27}H_{48}$ obtained from cholesterol by reduction

cho·les·ta·nol \-,stə,nōl, -ōl\ *n* -s [ISV *cholestane* + *-ol*; orig. formed in G] **:** a monohydroxy alcohol $C_{27}H_{47}OH$ derived from cholestane

cho·les·te·a·to·ma \kə,lestēə'tōmə, ,kōlə,stē-, ,kälə,-\ *n*, *pl* **cholesteatomas** \-məz\ *or* **cholesteatoma·ta** \-məd·ə\ [NL, fr. *chol-* + *steatoma*] **1 :** an epidermoid cyst usu. in the brain arising from aberrant embryonic rests and appearing as a compact shiny flaky mass — called also *pearly tumor* **2 :** a tumor usu. growing in a confined space (as the middle ear or mastoid) and frequently constituting a sequel to chronic otitis media

cho·les·tene \kə'le,stēn\ *n* -s [ISV *cholesterol* + *-ene*] **:** any of several crystalline hydrocarbons $C_{27}H_{46}$ differing from cholestane by having one double bond in the molecule, 5= cholestene being the parent hydrocarbon of cholesterol

cho·les·ter·ic \kə'lestərik; ¦kōlə¦ster-, ¦käl-\ *adj* [F *cholestérique*, fr. *cholestér*ine cholesterin + *-ique* -ic] **:** of, relating to, or resembling cholesterol or its derivatives

cho·les·ter·in \kə'lestərən\ *n* -s [F *cholestérine*, fr. *chol-* + *stérine*, fr. Gk *stereos* solid + F *-ine* -in — more at STARE] **:** CHOLESTEROL

cho·les·ter·ol \-,rōl, -,rȯl\ *n* -s [ISV *cholesterin* + *-ol*] **:** a fat-soluble crystalline steroid alcohol $C_{27}H_{45}OH$ that occurs as an essential constituent of animal cells and body fluids, is important in physiological processes, has been implicated experimentally as a factor in arteriosclerosis, is synthesized in the body esp. in the liver and adrenal cortex, is usu. extracted from beef spinal cord and wool grease, and is used in the synthesis of vitamin D_3 and steroid hormones (as testosterone) and in the making of ointments and lotions — compare STRUCTURAL FORMULA

cholesterol

cho·les·ter·ol·emia *also* **cho·les·ter·ol·ae·mia** \kə,lestə(,)rō'lēmēə, -(,)rō'-\ *or* **cho·les·ter·emia** *or* **cho·les·ter·ae·mia** \kə,lestə'rēmēə\ *n* -s [NL, fr. ISV *cholesterol* + NL *-emia*, *-aemia*] **:** the presence of cholesterol in the blood

cho·les·ter·o·sis \kə,lestə'rōsəs\ *n*, *pl* **cholestero·ses** \-,ō,sēz\ [NL, fr. ISV *cholesterol* + NL *-osis*] **:** abnormal deposition of cholesterol (as in blood vessels or gallbladder)

cho·les·ter·yl \kə'lestərəl, -,rēl\ *n* -s [ISV *cholesterin* + *-yl*] **:** the radical $C_{27}H_{45}$ formed by removal of the hydroxyl group from cholesterol

chol hamoed *sometimes cap, var of* HOL HAMOED

cho·li \'chōlē\ *n* -s [Hindi *colī*, fr. Skt *cola*, *coda*, prob. of Dravidian origin; akin to Tamil *coli* bark, Malayalam *toli*] **:** a short-sleeved bodice with a very low neckline worn esp. in India

cho·li·amb \'kōlē,am(b)\ *or* **cho·li·am·bus** \,kōlē'ambəs\ *n*, *pl* **choliambs** \-,amz\ *or* **choliam·bi** \-'am,bī, -(,)bē\ [LL *choliambus*, fr. Gk *choliambos*, fr. *chōlos* lame + *iambos* iamb] **:** a quantitative iambic trimeter verse of six feet having a spondee or trochee in the last foot — called also *scazon*

cho·li·am·bic \¦kōlē¦ambik\ *adj* [LL *choliambus* choliamb + E *-ic*] **:** of or belonging to a choliamb **:** consisting of choliambic lines

cho·lic acid \'kōlik-, -äl-\ *n* [Gk *cholikos*, fr. *chol-* + *-ikos* -ic] **:** a crystalline bile acid $C_{23}H_{36}(OH)_3COOH$ obtained by hydrolysis of taurocholic or glycocholic acid; 3,7,12-trihydroxy-cholanic acid

cho·line \'kō,lēn, 'kä-\ *n* -s [ISV *chol-* + *-ine*, *-in*; orig. formed as G *cholin*] **:** a crystalline or syrupy liquid base $(CH_3)_3N(CH_2CH_2OH)OH$ that is widely distributed among animal and plant products, in which it is combined in lecithins, that can be made synthetically, that constitutes a vitamin of the B complex and is essential to the metabolism of fat esp. in the liver, and that is used in the form of its salts in the treatment of certain liver disorders and in the feeding of animals, esp. poultry; (β-hydroxyethyl)-trimethyl-ammonium hydroxide — compare ACETYLCHOLINE

cho·lin·er·gic \¦kōlə¦nərjik, -äl-\ *adj* [ISV acetyl*choline* + *erg-* (fr. Gk *ergon* work) + *-ic* — more at WORK] **1** *of autonomic nerve fibers* **a :** liberating acetylcholine **b :** activated by acetylcholine — compare ADRENERGIC **2 :** resembling acetylcholine or simulating its physiologic action **3 :** involving or induced by the physiologic action of acetylcholine

cho·lin·es·ter·ase \,kōlə'nestə,rās, -äl-, -āz\ *also* **choline esterase** *n* -s [*choline* + *esterase*] **:** any of several enzymes that hydrolyze choline esters (as acetylcholine) and possibly certain other esters, occur esp. in nervous tissue and the blood, and apparently play a part with acetylcholine in the transmission of the nervous impulse — compare CHOLINERGIC; see ANTICHOLINESTERASE

chol·la \'chȯiə; 'chōyə, -(,)yä\ *n* -s [MexSp, fr. Sp. head, perh. fr. OF dial. *cholle* ball, of Gmc origin; akin to MHG *kiule* club, *kūle* ball, ON *kūla* knob, ball, OE *cēol* ship — more at KEEL] **:** any of several arborescent very spiny cacti of the southwestern U.S. and Mexico esp. of the genus *Opuntia* (as *O. cholla*)

chol·ler \'chälə(r)\ *n* -s [fr. (assumed) ME, fr. OE *ceolor* throat; akin to OHG *kelur* throat, OE *ceole* — more at KEEL] *dial Brit* **:** the flesh on the lower jaw esp. when fat and hanging **:** DOUBLE CHIN

cho·lo \'chō(,)lō\ *n* -s [AmerSp] **1** *sometimes cap* **:** a Spanish-American Indian; *esp* **:** an acculturated Quechuan of Peru and Bolivia **2 :** a person of mixed Spanish and Indian blood **:** MESTIZO **3** *Southwest* **:** a lower-class Mexican or person of Mexican ancestry — often used disparagingly

cholo- — see CHOL-

cho·loe·pus \kō'lēpəs\ *n*, *cap* [NL, irreg. fr. LGk *chōlopous* lame-footed, fr. Gk *chōlos* lame + *pous* foot — more at FOOT] **:** the genus consisting of the two-toed sloth

¹cho·lón \chə'lōn\ *also* **cho·lo·na** \-nə\ *n*, *pl* **cholón** \-ōn\ *or* **cholo·nes** \-ō,nās\ *also* **cholonas** \-ōnəz\ *usu cap* [Sp, of AmerInd origin] **:** a language family of central Peru consisting of two dialects — **cho·lo·nan** \-ōnən\ *adj*, *usu cap*

²cho·lon \'chō,län, 'chə¦lən\ *adj*, *usu cap* [fr. *Cholon*, So. Vietnam] **:** of or from the city of Cholon, So. Vietnam **:** of the kind or style prevalent in Cholon

chol·uria \kōl'yu̇rēə, käl'ü-, kä-,kə-\ *n* -s [NL, fr. *chol-* + *-uria*] **:** presence of bile in urine

chomer *var of* HOMER

chometz *var of* HAMETZ

chomp \'chämp\ *dial var of* ¹CHAMP

¹chon \'chōn\ *n*, *pl* **chon** [Korean] **1 :** a Korean subsidiary unit of value equal to 1/100 won or 1/100 hwan **2 :** a coin representing one chon

²chon \"\ *n*, *pl* **chon** *or* **chons** *usu cap* [Sp *chona*, of AmerInd origin] **1 :** a language family of southern Argentina and Tierra del Fuego comprising the languages spoken by the Tehuelche and the Ona people **2 a :** a people speaking a Chonan language **b :** a member of any such people — **chonan** \'chōnən\ *adj*, *usu cap*

chondr- *or* **chondri-** *or* **chondro-** *comb form* [NL, fr. Gk *chondr-*, *chondro-*, fr. *chondros* grain, cartilage — more at GRIND] **1 :** cartilage **:** cartilaginous and ⟨chondrectomy⟩ ⟨chondrify⟩ ⟨*chondro*-osseous⟩ ⟨chondrocele⟩ **2 :** grain ⟨chondrite⟩

chon·dral \'kändrəl\ *adj* [*chondr-* + *-al*] **:** of or relating to cartilage or a cartilage

chon·dre \'kändə(r)\ *n* -s [Gk *chondros* grain, cartilage] **:** CHONDRULE

chondri *pl of* CHONDRUS

¹chondri- — see CHONDR-

²chondri- *or* **chondrio-** *comb form* [G, fr. Gk *chondrion* small grain, dim. of *chondros*] **:** grain **:** granular ⟨*chondrio*some⟩ ⟨*chondrio*somal⟩ ⟨*chondrio*cont⟩ ⟨*chondri*ome⟩

chon·dric \'kändrik\ *adj* [*chondr-* + *-ic*] **:** CHONDRAL, CARTILAGINOUS

chon·drich·thi·an \kän'drikthēən\ *n* -s [NL *Chondrichthyes* + E *-ian*] **:** a member of the class Chondrichthyes **:** an elasmobranch fish

chon·drich·thy·es \-thē,ēz\ *n pl*, *cap* [NL, fr. *chondr-* + Gk *ichthyes*, pl. of *ichthys* fish — more at ICHTHUS] **:** a class comprising cartilaginous fishes with well-developed jaws and including the sharks, skates, and rays, chimaeras, and extinct related forms — *compare* AGNATHA, CYCLOSTOMI, PLACODERMI

chon·dri·fi·ca·tion \,kändrəfə'kāshən\ *n* -s [*chondr-* + *-fication*] **:** formation of or conversion into cartilage

chon·dri·fy \'kändrə,fī\ *vb* -ED/-ING/-ES [*chondr-* + *-ify*] *vt* **:** to convert into cartilage ~ *vi* **:** to become converted into cartilage

chon·dril·la \kän'drilə\ *n*, *cap* [NL, fr. L *chondrille*, fr. Gk *chondrilē*] **:** a genus of Old World herbs (family Compositae) having large basal mostly pinnatifid leaves, small stem leaves, and few-flowered heads with spinulose achenes — see GUM SUCCORY

chon·drin \'kändrən\ *n* -s [*chondr-* + *-in*; orig. formed in G] **:** a horny substance obtainable from cartilage and similar to and often associated with gelatin — compare CHONDROMUCOID

chon·drio·cont \'kändrēō,känt\ *n* -s [ISV *chondri-* + *-cont* (fr. Gk *kontos* pole); orig. formed as G *chondriokont* — more at -KONT] **:** a rod-shaped or fibrillar chondriosome

chon·drio·gene \-,jēn\ *n* -s [ISV *chondri-* + *-gene*] **:** a hypothetical cytoplasmic determiner responsible for maintaining the continuity of mitochondria

chon·drio·kinesis \¦kändrē(,)ō+\ *n*, *pl* **chondriokineses** [NL, fr. *chondri-* + *kinesis*] **:** division of the chondriome

chon·dri·ome \'kändrē,ōm\ *also* **chon·dri·o·ma** \,==ˈōmə\ *n* -s [ISV *chondri-* + *-ome*; orig. formed as G *chondriom*] **:** the chondriosomes of a cell regarded as a functional unit

chon·drio·mere \'kändrēō,mi(ə)r\ *n* -s [ISV *chondri-* + *-mere*; orig. formed as G *chondriomer*] **:** the chondriosomal portion of a sperm cell

chon·drio·mite \-,mīt\ *n* -s [ISV *chondri-* + Gk *mitos* thread; orig. formed as G *chondriomit* — more at DIMITY] **:** a chain of granular chondriosomes; *also* **:** one such chondriosome

chon·drio·som·al \¦kändrēō¦sōməl\ *adj* **:** of or relating to chondriosomes or the chondriome

chon·drio·some \'===,sōm\ *n* -s [ISV *chondri-* + *-some*; orig. formed as G *chondriosom*] *biol* **:** any of a class of minute granular, rodlike, or threadlike apparently self-perpetuating lipoprotein complexes in the cytoplasm of most cells that are thought to function in cellular metabolism and secretion **:** MITOCHONDRION

chon·drio·sphere \-,sfi(ə)r\ *n* -s [ISV *chondri-* + *sphere*; orig. formed as G *chondriosphäre*] **:** a large or aggregated spherical chondriosome

chon·drite \'kän,drīt\ *n* -s [ISV *chondr-* + *-ite*; orig. formed as G *chondrit*] **:** a meteoric stone characterized by the presence of chondrules

chon·drit·ic \(')kän¦drid·ik\ *adj*, *of minerals* **:** relating to or having the granular structure characteristic of chondrites **:** GRANULAR

chondro- *in pronunciations below*, ¦== = ¦kändrō *or* -rə\ — see CHONDR-

chon·dro·blast \'==,blast\ *n* -s [ISV *chondr-* + *-blast*] **:** a cell that produces cartilage — **chon·dro·blas·tic** \¦==¦blastik\ *adj*

chon·dro·clast \'==,klast\ *n* -s [ISV *chondr-* + *-clast*] **:** a cell that absorbs cartilage — compare OSTEOCLAST

chon·dro·coc·cus \,==ˈkäkəs\ *n*, *cap* [NL, fr. *chondr-* + *-coccus*] **:** a genus of chiefly soil-inhabiting and dung-inhabiting myxobacteria including a species (*C. columnaris*) highly pathogenic to fishes — see COLUMNARIS

chon·dro·costal \¦==+\ *adj* [ISV *chondr-* + *costal*] **:** of or relating to the costal cartilages and the ribs

chon·dro·cranium \¦==+\ *n*, *pl* **chondrocrania** [*chondr-* + *cranium*] **:** the cartilaginous cranium; *also* **:** the part of the adult skull derived therefrom — compare OSTEOCRANIUM

chon·dro·cyte \'==,sīt\ *n* -s [*chondr-* + *-cyte*] **:** a cartilage cell

chon·dro·dite *also* **con·dro·dite** \'==,dīt\ *n* -s [Sw *kondrodit*, fr. Gk *chondrōdēs* granular (fr. *chondros* grain) + *-it* -ite — more at CHONDR-] **:** a mineral $(Mg,Fe)_5SiO_4(OH,F)$ consisting of basic silicate of magnesium and sometimes iron belonging to the humite group and found in certain metamorphic rocks

chon·dro·dit·ic \¦==¦did·ik\ *adj*, *of minerals* **:** characterized by the presence of chondrodite ⟨a ~ limestone⟩

chon·dro·dys·pla·sia \¦==dəˈsplāzh(ē)ə\ *n* -s [NL, fr. *chondr-* + *dys-* + *-plasia*] **:** a hereditary skeletal disorder characterized by the formation of exostoses at the epiphyses and resulting in arrested development and deformity — called also DYSCHONDROPLASIA

chon·dro·dystrophia \¦==+\ *n* -s [NL, fr. *chondr-* + *dystrophia*] **:** ACHONDROPLASIA

chon·dro·dystrophic \¦==+\ *adj* [ISV *chondrodystrophy* + *-ic*] **:** characterized by chondrodystrophy

chon·dro·dystrophy \¦==+\ *n* -ES [ISV *chondr-* + *dystrophy*] **:** ACHONDROPLASIA

chon·dro·ganoidei \¦==+\ [NL, fr. *chondr-* + *Ganoidei*] *syn of* CHONDROSTEI

chon·dro·genesis \¦==+\ *n*, *pl* **chondrogeneses** [ISV *chondr-* + *genesis*] **:** the development of cartilage — **chon·dro·genetic** \"+\ *adj*

chon·dro·gen·ic \¦==¦jenik\ *or* **chon·drog·e·nous** \(')kän¦dräjənəs\ *adj* [*chondr-* + *-genic*, *-genous*] **:** CHONDROGENETIC

chon·drog·e·ny \kän'dräjənē\ *n* -ES [*chondr-* + *-geny*] **:** CHONDROGENESIS

chon·dro·glos·sus \,== *at* CHONDRO- + 'gläsəs\ *n*, *pl* **chondroglossi** \-ä,sī, -(,)sē\ [NL, fr. *chondr-* + *-glossus* (fr. Gk *glōssa* tongue) — more at GLOSS] **:** a muscle arising from the lesser cornu of the hyoid bone and blending with the intrinsic muscles of the tongue

chon·droid \'kän,drȯid\ *adj* [*chondr-* + *-oid*] **:** resembling cartilage

chon·dro·it·ic acid \¦kändrə¦wid·ik-\ *n* [ISV *chondroitic* (fr. *chondr-* + *-itic*) + *acid*; orig. formed as G *chondroitsäure*] **:** CHONDROITINSULFURIC ACID

chon·dro·i·tin \kän'drōətən\ *n* -s [ISV *chondroitic* + *-in*; orig. formed in G] **:** a gummy nitrogenous polysaccharide acid occurring as chondroitinsulfuric acid

chon·dro·i·tin·sulfuric acid \"+. . .\ *n* [*chondroitin* + *sulfuric*] **:** a white amorphous acid found esp. in cartilage that is a derivative of glucuronic acid and chondrosamine and constitutes the polysaccharide portion of one class of mucoproteins

chon·drol·o·gy \kän'dräləjē\ *n* -ES [F *chondrologie*, fr. *chondr-* + *-logie* -logy] **:** the branch of anatomy that treats of cartilages

chon·dro·ma \kän'drōmə\ *n*, *pl* **chondromas** \-məz\ *also* **chondroma·ta** \-məd·ə\ [NL, fr. *chondr-* + *-oma*] **:** a benign tumor containing the structural elements of cartilage — compare CHONDROSARCOMA — **chon·drom·a·tous** \(')kän¦drämәd·əs, -ōm-\ *adj*

chon·dro·mucoid \¦== *at* CHONDRO- +\ *n* -s [ISV *chondr-* + *mucoid*; orig. formed as G *chondromukoid*] **:** a white amorphous substance obtainable from the matrix of cartilage and consisting of a protein that resembles gelatin and is combined with chondroitinsulfuric acid — compare CHONDRIN

chon·dro·my·ces \,==+'mī,sēz\ *n*, *cap* [NL, fr. *chondr-* + *-myces*] **:** a genus of saprophytic myxobacteria (family Polyangiaceae) occurring in soil or on decaying organic matter

chon·dro·pha·ryn·ge·us \¦==+fə'rinjēəs, *or* ,farən¦jēəs\ *n*, *pl* **chondropharyn·gei** \-ē,ī\ [NL, fr. *chondr-* + *pharyngeus* pharyngeal (fr. *pharynx*)] **:** the muscle arising from the lesser cornu of the hyoid bone and forming part of the middle constrictor of the pharynx

chon·droph·o·ra \kän'dräfərə\ *n pl*, *cap* [NL, fr. *chondr-* + *-phora*] *in some classifications* **:** a suborder of Decapoda comprising the squids

chon·dro·phore \'== *at* CHONDRO-+,fō(ə)r\ *n* -s [*chondr-* + *-phore*] **:** a cavity or process that supports the internal hinge cartilage of the shell of a bivalve mollusk

chon·dro·phyte \'==,fīt\ *n* -s [ISV *chondr-* + *-phyte*] **:** an outgrowth or spur of cartilage

chon·dro·plast \'==,plast\ *n* -s [*chondr-* + *-plast*] **:** CHONDROBLAST

chon·dro·protein \¦==+\ *n* -s [ISV *chondr-* + *protein*] **1 :** any of various glycoproteins (as chondromucoid) that yield on hydrolysis chondroitinsulfuric acid and a protein **2 :** any glycoprotein whose carbohydrate radical is combined with sulfuric acid — not used systematically

chon·drop·te·ryg·ii \,kän,dräptə'rijē,ī\ *n pl*, *cap* [NL, fr. *chondr-* + *-pterygii*] *in former classifications* **:** a group of fishes including the elasmobranchs, sturgeons, and lampreys

chon·dro·sa·mine \kän'drōsə,mēn, -,mən\ *n* -s [ISV *chondr-* + *osamine*] **:** an amino sugar $H(CHOH)_4CH(NH_2)CHO$ obtained from chondroitinsulfuric acid and related compounds; 2-deoxy-2-amino-D-galactose

chon·dro·sarcoma \¦== *at* CHONDRO- +\ *n*, *pl* **chondrosarcomas** *also* **chondrosarcomata** [NL, fr. *chondr-* + *sarcoma*] **:** a sarcoma containing cartilage cells rarely arising as a primary neoplasm but more frequently developing as a secondary growth by malignant degeneration of a chondroma

chon·dro·septum \¦==+\ *n* -s [NL, fr. *chondr-* + *septum*] **:** the part of the nasal septum formed of cartilage

chon·dro·sin \'kändrəsən\ *n* -s [G, fr. Gk *chondros* grain, cartilage + G *-in* — more at GRIND] **:** a gummy nitrogenous monobasic acid with strong reducing power obtained by hydrolysis of chondroitin

chon·dro·sis \kän'drōsəs\ *n*, *pl* **chondro·ses** \-ō,sēz\ [NL, fr. *chondr-* + *-osis*] **:** CHONDROGENESIS

chon·dro·skeleton \¦==+\ *n* -s [*chondr-* + *skeleton*] **1 :** a cartilaginous skeleton **2 a :** the cartilaginous parts of a skeleton **b :** the parts of a bony skeleton that originated in cartilage

¹chon·dros·te·an \(')kän¦drästēən\ *adj* [NL *Chondrostei* + E *-an*] **1 :** having a cartilaginous skeleton **2 :** of or relating to the Chondrostei

²chondrostean \"\ *n* -s **:** one of the Chondrostei

chon·dros·tei \kän'drästē,ī\ *n pl*, *cap* [NL, fr. *chondr-* + *-ostei* (pl. of *-osteus*)] **:** an order of Teleostomi comprising fishes having a largely cartilaginous skeleton and skin that is scaleless or bears bony bucklers and including the sturgeons, paddlefishes, and extinct related fishes — compare GLANIOSTOMI, SELACHOSTOMI

chon·dro·sternal \¦== *at* CHONDRO- +\ *adj* [*chondr-* + *sternal*] **:** of or relating to the costal cartilages and sternum

chon·dro·xiphoid \¦==+\ *adj* [*chondr-* + *xiphoid*] **:** connecting a costal cartilage and the xiphoid process

chon·drule \'kän,drül\ *n* -s [NL *chondrus* (mineral) + E *-ule*] **:** a rounded granule of cosmic origin usu. consisting of enstatite or chrysolite and occurring embedded more or less abundantly in the mass of many meteoric stones and sometimes free in marine sediments

chon·drus \'kändrəs\ *n* [NL, fr. Gk *chondros* grain, cartilage] **1** *pl* **chon·dri** \-,drī\ **:** CHONDRULE **2** *cap* **:** a small genus of red algae (family Gigartinaceae) having rather coarse branching fronds **3** *pl* **chondri :** IRISH MOSS 1a

chong·jin \'chōŋ¦jin\ *adj*, *usu cap* [fr. *Chongjin*, Korea] **:** of or from the city of Chongjin, Korea **:** of the kind or style prevalent in Chongjin

chon·ju \'jōn¦jü\ *adj*, *usu cap* [fr. *Chonju*, Korea] **:** of or from the city of Chonju, Korea **:** of the kind or style prevalent in Chonju

chonk \'chōŋk\ *vt* -ED/-ING/-S [alter. of *chomp*] *dial* **:** to chew energetically **:** CHAMP

cho·no \'chō(,)nō\ *n*, *pl* **chono** *or* **chonos** *usu cap* [Sp, of AmerInd origin] **1 :** an extinct Indian people that formerly inhabited the Chonos archipelago and the adjacent coast of Chile **2 :** a member of the Chono people — **cho·no·an** \'chōnəwən\ *adj or n*, *usu cap*

cho·no·lith \'kōnə,lith, -än-\ *n* -s [Gk *chōnē* mold, crucible (fr. *chein* to pour) + E *-o-* + *-lith* — more at FOUND] **:** an intrusive igneous rock mass of wholly irregular form

cho·no·trich \-,trik\ *n* -s [NL *Chonotricha*] **:** one of the Chonotricha

cho·not·ri·cha \kō'nä·trəkə\ *n pl*, *cap* [NL, fr. *chono-* (irreg. fr. Gk *chonnos* copper cup) + *-tricha*] **:** a small order of euciliate protozoans that are commensal on the surface of aquatic invertebrates, have a more or less vasiform body with reduced ciliation and complex terminal peristome, and reproduce by budding and in some cases by conjugation — **cho·not·ri·chous** \-kəs\ *adj*

chon·ta \'chäntə, -ōn-\ *n* -s [AmerSp, fr. Quechua *chunta* palm tree] **1 :** any of several palms with hard durable wood used in making implements and weapons: as **a :** any of various tropical American palms of the genera *Guilielma* and *Astrocaryum* — compare TUCUM **b :** a palm (*Juania australis*) of the southern Pacific **2** *also* **chontawood** \-,=\ **:** the wood of a chonta

chon·tal \chōn·'täl\ *n*, *pl* **chontal** \"\ *or* **chonta·les** \-ä,lās\ *usu cap* [Sp, fr. Nahuatl *chontalli* stranger] **1 a :** an Indian people of the state of Tabasco, Mexico **b :** a member of such people **2 :** a Mayan language of the Chontal people **3 :** TEQUISTLATEC

chon·ta·qui·ro \,chäntə'kē(,)rō, -ōn-\ *n* -s *usu cap* [Sp *chontaquiro*, *chontapiro*, of AmerInd origin] **:** PIRO

choo·choo \'chü,chü\ *n* -s [imit.] **:** LOCOMOTIVE, TRAIN

chook \'chu̇k, -ük\ *n* -s [imit.] *chiefly Austral* **:** CHICKEN

chookchie *usu cap*, *var of* CHUKCHI

chook·ie \'chu̇ki, -üki\ *n* -s [*chook* + *-ie*] *slang Brit* **:** a child or young person; *specif* **:** SWEETHEART

choop \'chüp\ *n* -s [prob. of Scand origin; akin to Icel (dial.) *kjupa* hip of the rose, Icel *hjupa*, OE *hēope* — more at HIP] *dial Brit* **:** the hip of the wild rose

¹choose \'chüz\ *vb* **chose** \'chōz\ **cho·sen** \'chōzᵊn\ *or obs* **chose**; **choosing**; **chooses** [ME *chesen*, *chosen*, *chusen*, fr. OE *cēosan*; akin to OHG *kiosan* to choose, ON *kjōsa*, Goth *kiusan* to choose, test, L *gustare* to taste, enjoy, Gk *geuesthai* to taste, Skt *juṣate* he enjoys, tastes, loves] *vt* **1 a :** to select (as one thing over another) esp. with free will and by exercise of judgment ⟨~ the lesser of two evils⟩ **b :** to decide upon esp. by vote **:** ELECT ⟨the town twice *chose* him as mayor⟩ **2 a :** to consider or assume as fitting, proper, or advantageous esp. from personal preference ⟨for recreation he ~*s* tennis and swimming⟩ **b :** to be inclined to (as by arbitrary decision or personal preference) — often used with the infinitive ⟨I do not ~ to enter into particulars —Tobias Smollett⟩ **3** *now dial* **:** to wish to have **:** WANT ⟨the landlady now returned to know if we did not ~ a more genteel apartment —Oliver Goldsmith⟩ ~ *vi* **1 :** to make a selection ⟨he may ~ as best he can⟩ **2** *archaic* **:** to do as one pleases ⟨if you will not have me, ~ —Shak.⟩ **3 :** to take an alternative — used only after *can* in the negative ⟨they go because they cannot ~⟩ and often followed by *but* plus infinitive ⟨he can't ~ but to listen⟩ **4 :** to see fit **:** have the inclination ⟨you can take them all if you ~⟩

²choose \"\ *n* -s [ME *chose*, alter. (influenced by *chosen* to choose) of *chois* choice] **1** *obs* **:** SELECTION **2** *dial* **:** turn to choose **:** CHOICE

choos·er \-zə(r)\ *n* -s [ME *cheser*, fr. *chesen* to choose + *-er*] **1 :** one that chooses **2** *archaic* **:** VOTER, ELECTOR

choose up *vt* **:** to form (sides) for a game esp. by having opposing captains choose their players ~ *vi* **:** to form sides for a game ⟨let's *choose up* and play ball⟩

choosy *or* **choos·ey** \'chüzē, -zi\ *adj* **choos·i·er; choos·i·est** [¹*choose* + *-y*] **:** fastidiously selective **:** PARTICULAR ⟨~ with food⟩ **:** hesitant or reluctant esp. in accepting or receiving ⟨pretty ~ about making new friends⟩ **:** difficult to satisfy ⟨~ customers⟩

¹chop \'chäp\ *vb* **chopped; chopped; chopping; chops** [ME *choppen*, var. of *chappen* — more at CHAP (to split)] *vt* **1 a :** to cut into or esp. through with or as if with a heavy implement (as an ax or cleaver) usu. by a forceful slanting blow ⟨~ off a length of rope⟩ or by a series of such blows ⟨~ down a tree⟩ **b :** to mince, dice, or cut into small pieces ⟨*chopped* vegetables⟩ — often used with *up* ⟨~ the meat up⟩ **2 :** to work at or labor over with a heavy cleaving or hewing implement ⟨~ wood⟩; *specif* **:** to weed and thin out (young cotton) usu. with a hoe **3 a** *obs* **:** to thrust quickly and forcibly **:** STICK, DART **b :** to hit or strike (as a ball in tennis, baseball, or cricket) esp. with a short quick downward glancing blow — compare DRIVE 10 **4 :** to cut metal from the corner posts of (an automobile) to lower the body profile ⟨~ a top⟩ ⟨~ a sedan⟩ **:** cut metal from (part of an automobile) to reduce weight ⟨~ a flywheel⟩ — compare ²CHANNEL 1c **5 a :** to reduce the power, influence, or extent of — usu. used with *down* **b :** to retard or close (an airplane throttle) with a sudden motion **:** diminish or shut off the flow of fuel to (an airplane engine) ~ *vi* **1 :** to strike with or as if with a heavy implement (as an ax or cleaver) using a forceful slanting blow or a series of such blows ⟨he was *chopping* at an old stump⟩ **2** *archaic* **:** to go, come, or make some movement suddenly or violently **:** SWOOP, POUNCE ⟨the hawk ~*s* upon its prey⟩ **:** intervene or interpose **:** INTERRUPT — used with *in* or *into* ⟨~ into a conversation⟩ **3** *now dial* **:** to break open in fissures **:** CHAP **4 :** to strike something (as a ball in tennis, baseball, or cricket or an opponent in boxing) with a chopping blow **5** *of a hound* **:** to bay in chops **syn** see CUT

²chop \"\ *n* -s [ME *choppe*, fr. *choppen*, v.] **1 a :** a forceful often slanting blow made with or as if with a heavy implement (as an ax or cleaver) **:** a cutting stroke **:** SWIPE ⟨the prowler took a ~ at the dog with his stick⟩ **b :** a sharp downward blow (as in boxing) or stroke (as in baseball and tennis) **2** *archaic* **:** a crack or cleft (esp. on the lips and hands, on stone, or in the crust of dry earth **3 :** a small slice or cut of meat often including a part of a rib and usu. served individually — see LAMB illustration **4 :** a cut or indentation made by or as if by a cleaving or hewing stroke ⟨a hoe ~⟩ ⟨we left ~*s* in every tenth tree to mark the trail⟩ **5 :** material that has been chopped up: as **a :** ground or chopped feed usu. of one or more cereal grains or by-products — often used in pl. ⟨milo ~*s*⟩ ⟨corn ~*s*⟩ **b :** crushed unbolted particles of grain that are the product of an initial break in milling (as in the milling of flour) **c chops** *pl* **:** slices of apple that are usu. of inferior grade (as culls) and are dried by evaporation **6 a :** a short abrupt motion (as of waves) **:** CHOPPINESS **b :** a stretch of choppy sea; *esp* **:** one caused by a current or tide opposed in direction to the wind or to another current **7 :** the sharp clipped bay of a hound **8 :** ¹CHERRY 7

³chop \"\ *vb* **chopped; chopped; chopping; chops** [ME *choppen*, var. of *chappen* — more at CHAP (to barter)] *vt* **1** *dial Eng* **:** TRADE, SWAP ⟨~ horses⟩ **2** *obs* **:** to bandy back and forth **:** EXCHANGE ~ *vi* **1** *obs* **:** to make an exchange **:** BARTER **2** *obs* **:** to bandy words **:** answer back **3 a :** to change direction ⟨the wind *chopped* round to the north⟩ **b :** veer or change with or as if with the wind ⟨the next day he *chopped* about and accepted the plan he had previously rejected⟩ — **chop logic :** to make unnecessary distinctions or dispute with an affected use of logical terms

⁴chop \"\ *n* -s [var. of ⁵*chap*] **1 :** JAW — now used only in the pl. ⟨his ~*s* fell in astonishment⟩ **2 chops** *pl* **a :** MOUTH ⟨he never opens his ~*s* unless someone speaks to him⟩ **b :** the fleshy covering of the jaws **:** the jowls or chaps ⟨the fox left the henyard licking his ~*s*⟩ — sometimes sing. of the flews of a dog ⟨a bulldog with a fine ~⟩ **3 chops** *pl* **:** the passage into something (as the straits leading to a large body of water, the entrance to a valley, the muzzle of a cannon) **4 a :** ⁵CHAP 2 **b :** either of a pair of metal jaws that grip the end of the pendulum suspension spring in a pendulum clock **5 chops** *pl*, *slang* **:** EMBOUCHURE, LIP ⟨the trumpet player had no ~*s* after a bout with pneumonia⟩

⁵chop \"\ *vt* **chopped; chopped; chopping; chops 1** *obs* **:** to seize with the jaws and eat **:** SNAP **2** *Brit* **:** to come upon and kill (prey) esp. without chase ⟨the hounds *chopped* the fox in its covert⟩

⁶chop \"\ *n* -s [Hindi *chāp* stamp, brand] **1** *in the India and China trade* **a :** a seal or its impression **:** an official stamp **b :** a license rendered valid by a seal **:** PERMIT, CLEARANCE — see GRAND CHOP **2 a :** a mark used on goods or coins in the China trade to indicate nature or quality **b :** a particular kind, brand, or lot of goods bearing the same chop **c :** quality, class, or grade ⟨first-*chop* tea⟩ ⟨an author of the first ~⟩

⁷chop \"\ *vt* **chopped; chopped; chopping; chops 1** *in the China trade* **:** to attest the legality of ⟨~ passengers⟩ ⟨~ a ship's papers⟩ **2 :** to stamp (a coin) with a seal or indentation usu. as evidence of legality — used esp. of coins often of non-Oriental origin circulated in China ⟨a *chopped* dollar⟩

⁸chop \"\ *n* -s [prob. native word in W. Africa] *slang Brit* **:** FOOD — used chiefly in African colonial areas

cho·pa \'chōpə, -äpə\ *n* -s [Sp, fr. Pg *choupa*, fr. L *clupea*, a fish] **:** any of several rudderfishes (family Kyphosidae)

¹chop and change *vi* [ME *choppen and chaungen* to barter, fr. *choppen* to chop (barter) + *and* + *chaungen* to change, exchange] **1** *archaic* **:** to buy and sell **2 :** to change esp. pointlessly or capriciously ⟨a book which, however fashions may *chop and change*, must hold its place among the great English novels —Virginia Woolf⟩

²chop and change *n*, *pl* **chops and changes :** CHANGE, FLUCTUATION, VICISSITUDE ⟨the *chops and changes* of a political career⟩

cho·part's joint \(')shō¦pärz-\ *n*, *usu cap C* [after François *Chopart* †1795 French surgeon] **:** a tarsal joint comprising the talonavicular and calcaneocuboid articulations

chop box *n* [⁸*chop*] **:** a box used in Africa (as on a safari) to transport food

chop–cherry *n* [⁵*chop*] *obs* **:** a game of trying to catch a suspended cherry between the teeth

chop–chop \'chäp¦chäp\ *adv* [pidgin E, fr. a Chin dial. word akin to Cant *kap⁴kap⁴*] **:** QUICKLY, PROMPTLY

chop·dar \'chōp,där\ *var of* CHOBDAR

chop dollar *n* [⁶*chop*] **:** a chopped dollar — see ⁷CHOP 2

chopfallen *var of* CHAPFALLEN

chop hill *n* [prob. fr. ¹*chop*] *in Nebraska* **:** SAND HILL

chop·house \'chäp,haus, -ä,paůs\ *n* [²*chop* (cut of meat)] **:** RESTAURANT

cho·pi *or* **cho·pe** \'chōpē\ *n*, *pl* **chopi** *or* **chopis** *or* **chope** *or* **chopes** *usu cap* **1 a :** a Bantu-speaking people of northern Mozambique on the borders of Tanganyika **b :** a member of such people **2 :** a Bantu language of the Chopi people

chop·in \'chäpən\ *n* -s [ME, fr. MF *chopine*, a liquid measure, fr. MLG *scōpe*, *scōpen* scoop, ladle or MD *schoepe* scoop — more at SCOOP] **:** an old Scottish unit of liquid capacity equal to half a Scottish pint or about an English quart

cho·pine \chō'pēn, 'chäpən\ *n* -s [MF *chapin*, fr. OSp *chapín*, prob. of imit. origin] **:** a woman's shoe of the 16th and 17th centuries having a high often stiltlike sole designed to increase stature and protect the feet from mud and dirt — compare ¹PATTEN 1

¹chop·log·ic \'⸗,⸗⸗\ *n* [³*chop*] **1 :** involved and often specious argumentation **2** *obs* **:** an absurdly argumentative person

²choplogic \"\ *also* **choplogical** \'⸗,⸗⸗⸗\ *adj* **:** given to complex often erroneous and absurd argumentation ⟨a ~ speech⟩

chop mark *n* [⁶*chop*] **:** an indentation or stamp made (as by a Chinese banking or business firm) on a coin to attest weight, silver content, or legality — see ⁶CHOP 2a — **chop–marked** *adj*

¹chopped *past of* CHOP

²chopped *var of* CHAPPED

¹chop·per \'chäpə(r)\ *n* -s [¹*chop* + *-er*] **1 a :** a person who cuts something (as wood) off, up, or into segments (as with an ax or knife); *specif* **:** a logger that fells and lops trees **b :** a person who chops or cuts into segments with a machine-driven implement (as a slaughterhouse worker who operates a meat-chopping machine or a worker who operates a machine that cuts fur from pelts) **2 :** an implement (as an ax or knife) or mechanical device worked by machine or by hand and designed to chop or cut into segments: as **a :** a tool for thinning out plants in drills **b** (1) **:** any domestic or commercial tool that chops food (2) **choppers** *pl*, *slang* **:** TEETH **c** *or* **chopper tool :** a stone tool with a handhold end rounded or unfinished and a lower end chipped to an edge which in the early Paleolithic of Asia takes the place of the biface hand ax of Europe **3 :** a meat animal not esp. suitable for sale in fresh butcher's cuts — used of an overweight or aged hog in Australia and New Zealand or an aged ewe in poor to moderate flesh in the U.S. **4 :** a device that interrupts an electric current, a beam of light, or other radiation at short regular intervals **5 :** a canary having a song with loud trills, each component note being distinct — distinguished from *roller* **6 :** a gangster armed with a machine gun; *also* **:** a gangster's machine gun **7** *slang* **:** HELICOPTER

²chopper \"\ *n* -s [Hindi *chappar* sloping thatch, thatched roof, shed, hut, tester of a bed, fr. Skt *chattvara* house] **:** a thatched roof

chopper cot \-,kät\ *n* [Hindi *chappar-khāṭ*, fr. *chappar* tester of a bed + *khāṭ* bedstead — more at COT] *India* **:** a bedstead having curtains

chop·pi·ness \'chäpēnəs, -pin-\ *n* -ES **:** the quality or state of being choppy

¹chopping *adj* [fr. pres. part. of ¹*chop*] **1 :** characterized by fits and starts **:** JERKY ⟨a ~ manner of speaking⟩ **2 a** (1) **:** having a tumbling dashing movement ⟨a ~ tide⟩ (2) **:** breaking in short abrupt waves ⟨a ~ sea⟩ **b :** shifting or changing suddenly ⟨a ~ wind⟩ **3** *archaic* **:** large and vigorous **:** STRAPPING

²chopping *n* -s [fr. gerund of ¹*chop*] **:** an area where trees are being felled or have been felled

chopping block *n* **:** a wooden block on which material (as meat, wood, or vegetables) is cut, split, or diced

chopping knife *n* **:** a knife often with a crescent-shaped blade for chopping or mincing (as meat or vegetables)

¹chop·py \'chäpē, -pi\ *adj* -ER/-EST [²*chop* (crack) + *-y*] **:** ¹CHAPPED 1 ⟨her ~ finger laying upon her skinny lips —Shak.⟩

²choppy \"\ *adj* -ER/-EST [²*chop* (of waves) + *-y*] *of the wind* **:** repeatedly veering about **:** CHANGEABLE, VARIABLE

³choppy \"\ *adj* -ER/-EST [¹*chop* + *-y*] **1 :** somewhat chopping ⟨a ~ sea⟩ ⟨a ~ lake⟩ **2 a :** interrupted by ups and downs ⟨~ countryside⟩ **b :** abrupt in transition **:** JERKY ⟨a ~ style⟩ **c :** marked by poorly integrated components **:** DISCONNECTED ⟨a ~ novel⟩

chops *pl of* CHOP, *pres 3d sing of* CHOP

¹chop·stick \'⸗,⸗\ *n* [perh. fr. ¹*chop* + *stick*] **:** the crosspiece (as of wire or whalebone) from which the hooks hang on a deep-sea fishing line

²chopstick \"\ *n* [pidgin E, fr. *chop* fast (fr. a Chin dial. word akin to Cant *kap*) + E *stick*; trans. of Chin (Cant) *faai tsz*] **:** one of a pair of slender sticks held between the thumb and fingers of one hand and used chiefly in Oriental countries to lift food to the mouth

chop·sticks \'⸗,⸗\ *n pl but sing in constr* [perh. fr. pl. of ²*chopstick*; fr. the manner of playing with straight fingers] **:** music played in a mechanical or expressionless way; *esp* **:** a simple old fast waltz for four hands played in a manner stressing its mechanical rhythmic and harmonic qualities

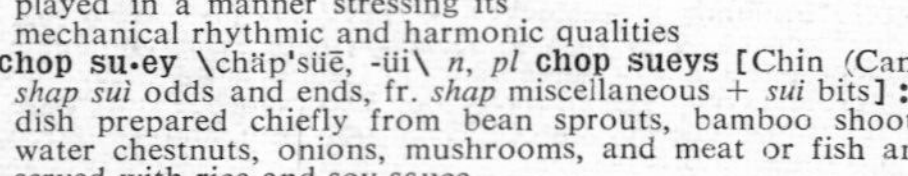
chopsticks

chop su·ey \chäp'süē, -üi\ *n*, *pl* **chop sueys** [Chin (Cant) *shap sui* odds and ends, fr. *shap* miscellaneous + *sui* bits] **:** a dish prepared chiefly from bean sprouts, bamboo shoots, water chestnuts, onions, mushrooms, and meat or fish and served with rice and soy sauce

chop·tank \'chäp,taŋk\ *n*, *pl* **choptank** *or* **choptanks** *usu cap* [perh. fr. *Choptank* river, Maryland, where they settled] **1 :** an Algonquian people once resident on the Choptank river in Maryland — compare NANTICOKE **2 :** a member of the Choptank people

cho·pun·nish \chō'pənish\ *n*, *pl* **chopunnish** *or* **chopunnishes** *usu cap* [perh. modif. of Nez Percé *Tsútpēli*] **:** NEZ PERCÉ

chor- *or* **choro-** *comb form* [L, fr. Gk *chōr-*, *chōro-*, fr. *chōros* place, clear space; akin to Gk *chēros* left, bereaved — more at HEIR] **:** place **:** land ⟨*chor*episcopus⟩ ⟨*choro*logy⟩

cho·rag·ic \kə'rajik\ *adj* [Gk *chorēgikos*, *chorēgikos*, fr. *choragos*, *chorēgos*] **:** of or relating to a choragus; *esp* **:** honoring a successful choragus ⟨a ~ monument⟩

cho·ra·gus \kə'rāgəs\ *or* **cho·re·gus** \-rē-\ *also* **cho·ra·gos** -rä,gäs, -gəs\ *n*, *pl* **cho·ra·gi** \-,jī, -,gī\ *or* **choraguses** \-,gəsəz\ *or* **chore·gi** \-,jī, -,gī\ *or* **choreguses** \-,gəsəz\ *also* **chora·goi** \-,gȯi\ [L & Gk; L *choragus*, fr. Gk *choragos*, *chorēgos*, fr. *choros* chorus + *-agos*, *-ēgos* (fr. *agein* to lead) — more at CHORUS, AGENT] **1 :** the leader of a chorus or choir; *broadly* **:** the leader of any group or movement ⟨the ~ of the Victorian poets⟩ **2 a :** a leader of a dramatic chorus in ancient Greece — called also at later periods *coryphaeus* **b :** an Athenian who provided a dramatic chorus at his own expense

¹cho·ral \'kōrəl, -ȯr- *sometimes* -är-\ *adj* [F or ML; F *choral*, fr. ML *choralis*, fr. L *chorus* + *-alis* -al — more at CHORUS] **1 a :** of or belonging to a choir or chorus **:** performed by a chorus or in chorus **b :** accompanied with song ⟨a ~ dance⟩ **2 :** sung or intended for singing by a chorus ⟨a ~ arrangement⟩ ⟨~ counterpoint⟩ **:** containing a chorus ⟨Beethoven's ~ symphony⟩ — **cho·ral·ism** \-rə,lizəm\ *n* -s — **cho·ral·ist** \-rələst\ *n* -s — **cho·ral·ly** \-rəlē, -li\ *adv*

²choral *var of* CHORALE

choral bass *n* [¹*choral*] **:** a flue pedal stop in a pipe organ usu. of 4-foot pitch and prominently voiced to sustain the melodic line in a choral prelude

cho·ral·celo \'⸗⸗'che(,)lō\ *n* -s [¹*choral* + *-celo* (alter. of *cello*)] **:** a keyboard instrument like the piano but with electromagnets vibrating the strings and producing an organlike effect with string quality

cho·rale *also* **cho·ral** \kə'ral, kō-,kō-; kə'räl, kō-,kō-, -rȧl\ *n* -s *often attrib* [G *choral*, short for *choralgesang*, part trans. of ML *cantus choralis*, lit., choral song, fr. L *cantus* song + ML *choralis* choral] **1 a :** a hymn or psalm sung by choir or congregation or both to a traditional or composed melody in a church service; *also* **:** a hymn tune or sacred melody or a harmonization of a traditional melody ⟨a Bach ~⟩ **b :** a group formed to sing such music **:** CHORUS, CHOIR **2 :** something resembling a chorale; *esp* **:** a song in high praise ⟨the singing of paeans and *chorals* —P.L.Dunbar⟩ ⟨the novel, a passionate ~ on the themes of sin and salvation —*Time*⟩

chorale prelude *n* **1 :** an improvisatory organ prelude to the congregational singing of the hymn in the Protestant churches of 17th and 18th century Germany **2 :** a composition, usu. for organ, based upon a chorale or hymn tune

choral service *n* **:** a church service in which a part or all of the liturgy is intoned and sung by clergy, choir, and congregation

choral speaking *n* **:** ensemble speaking by a group often using various voice combinations and contrasts to bring out the meaning or tonal beauty of a passage of poetry or prose

¹cho·ras·mi·an \kə'razmēən\ *adj*, *usu cap* [*Chorasmia*, province of ancient Persia + E *-an*] **:** of or relating to Chorasmia

²chorasmian \"\ *n* -s *usu cap* **:** a native or inhabitant of ancient Chorasmia

chor bishop \'kō(ə)r-\ *n* [part trans. of LL *chorepiscopus* — more at CHOREPISCOPUS] **:** CHOREPISCOPUS

¹chord \'kō(ə)rd, -ȯ(ə)d\ *n* -s [alter. (influenced by ³*chord*) of *cord*, fr. ME, short for *accord*] **:** a combination of two or more tones sounded together, esp. tones that blend harmoniously because of the simple ratios of their pitch frequencies; *specif* **:** COMMON CHORD

²chord \"\ *vb* -ED/-ING/-S *vi* **1 :** to harmonize together **:** ACCORD ⟨this tone ~*s* with that⟩; *also* **:** to sound together in harmony **2 :** to play chords on a stringed instrument usu. as an accompaniment ⟨when she played something . . . , Mother ~*ed* for her on the piano —Frances Judge⟩ ~ *vt* **1 :** to make chords on (a musical instrument) by stopping the strings **2 :** to furnish (a melody) with chords **:** HARMONIZE

³chord \"\ *n* -s [alter. (influenced by L *chorda*) of ¹*cord*] **1 :** CORD 3a **2 a :** a straight line joining two points on a curve; *specif* **:** the segment of a secant between the two points of its intersection with a curve **b** *of an arch* **:** ²SPAN 3b **3 a** *obs* **:** CORD 1a **b** *archaic* **:** a string of a musical instrument **c :** a particular emotional or intellectual response ⟨the story struck a popular ~⟩ **:** a particular disposition or orientation of mind or spirit ⟨surrealism . . . touched old ~*s* of native, creative eccentricity —*Saturday Rev.*⟩ **4 :** either of the two outside members of a truss connected and braced by the web members **5 :** an arbitrary datum line from which the ordinates and position angles of an airfoil are measured; *esp* **:** the straight line joining the leading and trailing edges

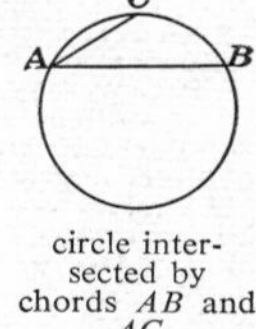

circle intersected by chords *AB* and *AC*

chord- *or* **chordo-** *comb form* [NL, fr. Gk *chordē* gut, string — more at YARN] **:** an anatomical cord: as **a :** vocal cord ⟨*chord*itis⟩ **b :** spinal cord ⟨*chordo*tomy⟩ **c :** notochord ⟨*Chord*ata⟩

¹-chord \,kȯrd, -ȯ(ə)d\ *n comb form* -s [partly fr. ME *-corde* (in *monacorde* monochord), fr. MF, fr. LL *-chordon*, fr. Gk, fr. *-chordos* stringed, fr. *chordē* string; partly fr. ML *-chordium* (in *clavichordium* clavichord), fr. L *chorda* string, fr. Gk *chordē*] **1 :** musical instrument having (such or so many) strings ⟨lyri*chord*⟩ **2 :** musical scale or interval (of a specified extent) ⟨hexa*chord*⟩

²-chord \"\ *adj comb form* [LL *-chordus*, fr. Gk *-chordos*] **:** having (so many) strings ⟨septi*chord*⟩

chor·da \'kȯrdə\ *n* [NL, fr. L — more at CORD] **1** *cap* **:** a genus of brown algae typifying the family Chordaceae and having usu. hollow blackish fronds **2** *pl* **chor·dae** \-,dē\ **:** CORD 3a; *specif* **:** NOTOCHORD

chor·da·ce·ae \kȯr'dāsē,ē\ *n pl*, *cap* [NL, fr. *Chorda*, type genus + *-aceae*] **:** a family of brown algae (order Laminariales) having slender cordlike fronds

chor·da·centrum \¦kȯrdə+\ *n* [NL, fr. *chorda* (anat.) + *centrum*] **:** a centrum of a vertebra formed by segmentation of the cartilaginous or calcified sheath of the notochord (as in elasmobranchs) — compare ARCOCENTRUM

¹chord·al \'kȯrdᵊl, -ȯ(ə)d-\ *adj* [¹*chord* + *-al*] **1 :** of, relating to, or resembling a chord ⟨~ assonance is important in modern music⟩ ⟨the ~ howling of a storm —Paul Hindemith⟩ **2 :** relating to music characterized more by vertical harmony than by linear contrapuntal motion

²chordal \"\ *adj* [³*chord* + *-al*] **:** of or relating to an anatomical cord (as the notochord or spinal cord) — used chiefly in combination ⟨peri*chordal*⟩ — **chord·al·ly** \-dᵊlē, -i\ *adv*

chordal pitch *n* **:** CHORD PITCH

chordal thickness *n* **:** the tangential thickness of a circular-gear tooth measured along a chord of the pitch circle

chor·da·mesoderm \¦kȯrdə+\ *or* **chor·do·mesoderm** \-dō+\ *n* -s [NL *chorda* or E *chord-* + *mesoderm*] **:** the portion of the embryonic mesoderm that forms notochord and related structures and serves as an inductor of ectodermic neural structures — **chor·da·mesodermal** *or* **chor·do·mesodermal** \"+\ *adj*

chor·dar·i·a·les \(,)kȯr,darē'ā(,)lēz\ *n pl*, *cap* [NL, fr. *Chordaria* genus of algae (fr. *chord-* + *-aria*) + *-ales*] **:** an order of brown algae (class Heterogeneratae) having a branched filamentous sporophyte that is not markedly compacted with a pseudoparenchymatous mass

chor·da·ta \kȯr'dād·ə, -ädə\ *n pl*, *cap* [NL, fr. L *chorda* cord + NL *-ata* — more at CORD] **:** a phylum or subkingdom comprising animals having at least at some stage of development a more or less well-developed notochord, dorsally situated central nervous system, and gill clefts in the walls of the pharynx and including the vertebrates, lancelets, tunicates, and usu. the hemichordates

¹chor·date \'kȯrdāt, -dət\ *adj* [NL *chorda* + E *-ate*] **1 :** having a notochord **2** [NL *Chordata*] **:** of or relating to the Chordata

²chordate \"\ *n* -s **:** a chordate animal

chorda ten·din·ea \-,ten'dinēə\ *n*, *pl* **chordae tendine·ae** \-nē,ē\ [NL, lit., tendinous cord] **:** any of the delicate tendinous cords that are attached to the edges of the auriculoventricular valves of the heart and to the papillary muscles and serve to prevent the valves from being pushed into the auricle during the ventricular contraction

chord·ed \'kȯrdəd, -ȯ(ə)d-\ *adj* **:** having or combined in chords

chor·dee \kȯr,dē, -,dā, ⸗'⸗\ *n* -s [F *cordée*, fem. of *cordé* corded (in *chaude-pisse cordée* corded gonorrhea), fr. *corde* cord — more at CORD] **:** painful erection of the penis often with a downward curvature, common as a lesion of gonorrhea

chor·dei·les \kȯr'dī(,)lēz\ *n*, *cap* [NL, irreg. fr. Gk *chordē* string of a lyre or harp + *deilē* afternoon, evening; fr. its cry at twilight — more at YARN] **:** a genus of nocturnal birds (family Caprimulgidae) consisting of the nighthawks

chording *pres part of* CHORD

chor·di·tis \kȯr'dīd·əs\ *n* -ES [NL, fr. *chord-* + *-itis*] **:** inflammation of a cord or cords (as the vocal or spermatic cords)

chordo- — see CHORD-

chor·doid \'kȯr,dȯid\ *adj* [*chord-* + *-oid*] **:** like a chorda ⟨a ~ notochord⟩

chor·do·mesoblast \kȯr(,)dō +\ *also* **chor·da·mesoblast** \-,də+\ *n* -s [ISV *chord-* or *chorda-* (fr. NL *chorda*) + *mesoblast*] **:** CHORDAMESODERM — **chor·do·mesoblastic** \"+\ *adj*

chor·do·nia \kȯr'dōnēə\ *n pl*, *cap* [NL, fr. *chordon*- (irreg. fr. L *chorda*) + *-ia*] **:** the Chordata exclusive of the hemichordates

chor·do·phone \'kȯrdə,fōn\ *n* -s [ISV *chord-* + *-phone*] **:** a member of the class of musical instruments having strings and including for classifying purposes the zithers, lutes, lyres, and harps — **chor·do·phon·ic** \¦⸗⸗¦fänik\ *adj*

chor·do·plasm \'kȯrdə,plazəm\ *n* -s [*chord-* + *-plasm*] **:** the portion of a mosaic egg that consists of potential notochord

chor·dot·o·my *or* **cor·dot·o·my** \kȯr'däd·əmē\ *n* -ES [ISV *chord-* + *-tomy*] **:** the surgical division of certain areas of the spinal cord for relief of severe intractable pain

chor·do·tonal \¦kȯrdə +\ *adj* [ISV *chord-* + *tonal*; orig. formed in G] **:** relating to or being certain sensory organs found in various parts of the bodies of insects and believed to be receptors of auditory or other vibrational stimuli

chord pitch *or* **chordal pitch** *n* [¹*chord*] **:** distance between corresponding points of consecutive gear teeth measured in a straight line

chords *pl of* CHORD, *pres 3d sing of* CHORD

-chords *pl of* -CHORD

chordwise \'⸗,⸗\ *adj* **:** directed, moving, or placed along the chord of an airfoil section — compare SPANWISE

¹chore \'chō(ə)r, -ȯ(ə)r, -ōə, -ȯ(ə)\ *n* -s [alter. of *chare*, *char* — more at CHARE] **1 chores** *pl* **:** recurrent tasks performed at more or less regular intervals in the operation or maintenance of a farm, home, or business; *specif* **:** the morning and evening care of the livestock on a farm **2 a :** a usu. routine or accustomed small task or odd job **3 :** a task or duty; *esp* **:** one that is dull, difficult, or disagreeable ⟨make the job more exciting and less of a ~⟩ ⟨to get across its lanes of skidding traffic is a perilous ~ —Truman Capote⟩ **syn** see TASK

²chore \"\ *vb* -ED/-ING/-S *vi* **:** to do chores ~ *vt* **:** to win, work, or gain by doing odd jobs ⟨he *chored* his way through college⟩

chore- — see CHOREO-

-chore \,kō(ə)r, -ȯ(ə)r,-ōə,-ȯ(ə)\ *n comb form* -s [Gk *chōrein* to withdraw, advance, go, spread; akin to Gk *chēros* left, bereaved — more at HEIR] **:** plant distributed by a (specified) means or agency ⟨zoo*chore*⟩ — **-cho·rous** \¦kōrəs, -ȯr-\ *adj comb form* — **-cho·ry** \,kōrē, -ȯr-, -ri\ *n comb form* -ES

cho·rea \kə'rēə\ *n* -s [NL, fr. L, dance, fr. Gk *choreia*, fr. *choros* — more at CHORUS] **:** any of various nervous disorders of infectious or organic origin in man and dogs having as common features involuntary uncontrollable purposeless movements of body and face and marked incoordination of limbs — see CANINE CHOREA, HUNTINGTON'S CHOREA, SYDENHAM'S

CHOREA — **cho·re·al** \-ēəl\ *adj* — **cho·re·at·ic** \¦kōrē¦ad·ik\ *adj* — **cho·re·ic** \kə'rēik\ *adj*

chore boy *n* **1 :** one who does chores; *esp* **:** a man who does the domestic maintenance tasks and helps the cook in a lumber camp **2 :** a person who assumes responsibility for onerous detail in any situation

cho·ree \'kōr,ē, kə'rē\ *n* -s [F *chorée,* fr. L *choreus,* fr. Gk *choreios,* adj., of a dance, of a chorus, fr. *choros* dancing area, dance, chorus — more at CHORUS] **:** CHOREUS — **cho·re·ic** \kə'rēik\ *adj*

choregus *var of* CHORAGUS

cho·re·i·form \kə'rēə,fȯrm\ *adj* [ISV *chorea* (fr. NL) + *-iform*] **:** resembling chorea ⟨~ convulsions⟩

chore·man \'chōrmən, -ȯr-, -,man\ *n, pl* **choremen :** a worker who performs any of numerous menial jobs in a factory or camp (as a leather factory or a logging, mining, or construction camp) — compare BULL COOK

choreo- *also* **chore-** *or* **chorio-** *comb form* [choreo-, chore-, fr. F *choréo-, choré-,* fr. Gk *choreia* dance, fr. *choros* dance, place for dancing; *chorio-,* alter. of *choreo-* — more at CHORUS] **:** dance ⟨*choreo*mania⟩ ⟨*choreo*graphy⟩

cho·reo·ath·e·toid \¦kōrē(,)ō¦athə,tȯid\ *or* **cho·reo·ath·e·tot·ic** \-¦athə¦täd·ik\ *adj* [*choreoathetoid* fr. NL *choreoathetosis* + E *-oid; choreoathetotic* fr. NL *choreoathetosis,* after such pairs as NL *sclerosis:* E *sclerotic*] **:** resembling choreoathetosis

cho·reo·ath·e·to·sis \-,athə'tōsəs\ *n* [NL, fr. *chorea* + *-o-* + *athetosis*] **:** a nervous disturbance marked by the involuntary purposeless and uncontrollable movements characteristic of chorea and athetosis

cho·reo·drama \¦kōrē(,)ō +\ *n* -s [*choreo-* + *drama*] **:** a dance drama for large groups

cho·re·o·graph \'kōrēə,graf, -ȯr-, -rēō,-, -raa(ə)f,-raif,-räf, *Brit often & US sometimes* 'kär-\ *vb* -ED/-ING/-S [back-formation fr. *choreography*] *vt* **:** to undertake or compose the choreography of (as a ballet or a poem) ⟨has ~*ed* a lively string of . . . musicals —R.L.Taylor⟩ ~ *vi* **:** to serve as choreographer **:** engage in choreography

cho·re·og·ra·pher \,==¦ägrəfə(r)\ *n* -s **:** one engaging in the composing and often the teaching of choreography

cho·re·o·graph·ic \¦==¦grafik, -ō¦-, -fēk\ *also* **cho·re·o·graph·i·cal** \-fəkəl, -ēk-\ *adj* **:** of, belonging to, or concerned with choreography — **cho·re·o·graph·i·cal·ly** \-fək(ə)lē, -ēk-, -li\ *adv*

cho·re·og·ra·phy \,==¦ägrəfē, -fi\ *or* **cho·reg·ra·phy** \kə'reg-\ *n* -ES [F *chorégraphie,* fr. *choré-* choreo- + *-graphie* -graphy] **1 :** the art of representing dancing by signs as music is represented by notes **2 :** DANCING; *esp* **:** stage dancing as distinguished from social or ballroom dancing **3 :** the composition and arrangement of dance movements and patterns (as for a ballet) created usu. to accompany a particular piece of music or to develop a theme or a pantomime; *also* **:** a composition created by this art

cho·re·oid \'kōrē,ȯid\ *adj* [NL *chorea* + E *-oid*] **:** CHOREIFORM

chor·episcopal \¦kȯr+\ *adj* **:** of, performed by, or relating to a chorepiscopus

chor·epis·co·pus \,kȯrə'piskəpəs\ *n, pl* **chorepisco·pi** \-,pī, -pē\ *or* **chorepiscopuses** [LL, fr. LGk *chōrepiskopos,* fr. Gk *chōr-* chor- + *episkopos* overseer, bishop — more at BISHOP] **:** a bishop who is appointed by a diocesan bishop to assist him in the exercise of his episcopal jurisdiction in a rural district

chores *pl of* CHORE, *pres 3d sing of* CHORE

cho·re·us \kə'rēəs\ *n, pl* **cho·rei** \-ē,ī\ [L, fr. Gk *choreios,* lit., of a chorus, fr. *choros* chorus — more at CHORUS] **:** a trochee in classical prosody — used at first esp. of the trochee when resolved into the tribrach

cho·reu·tic \kə'rüd·ik\ *adj* [Gk *choreutikos,* fr. *choreutēs* choral dancer, fr. *choreuein* to dance, fr. *choros*] **:** of or belonging to a chorus

[1]**chori-** *or* **chorio-** *comb form* [NL, fr. Gk *chorio-,* fr. *chorion*] **1 :** chorion **:** chorionic ⟨*chorio*carcinoma⟩ ⟨*chori*oma⟩ **2 :** choroid **:** choroid and ⟨*chorio*cele⟩ ⟨*chorio*retinal⟩

[2]**chori-** *comb form* [NL, fr. Gk *chōri, chōris* apart; akin to Gk *chēros* left, bereaved — more at HEIR] **:** separated **:** distinct ⟨*chori*petalous⟩

cho·ri·al \'kōrēəl\ *adj* [ISV [1]*chori-* + *-al*] **:** of or relating to a chorion **:** CHORIONIC

cho·ri·amb \'kōrē,am(b)\ *n, pl* **choriambs** \-mz\ [LL *choriambus,* fr. Gk *choriambos,* fr. *choreios* choreus + *iambos* iambus] **:** CHORIAMBUS

cho·ri·am·bic \¦kōrē¦ambik\ *adj* [LL *choriambicus,* fr. Gk *choriambikos,* fr. *choriambos* + *-ikos* -ic] **:** of, relating to, consisting of, or containing choriambuses

cho·ri·am·bus \,kōrē'ambəs\ *n, pl* **choriambuses** \-bəsəz\ *or* **choriam·bi** \-,bī\ [LL] **:** a foot of four syllables in classical prosody in which the cadence of the trochee is followed by that of the iambus (–◡◡–) the corresponding pattern of cadence in accentual prosody (ó o o ó) consisting of the combination of trochee and iambus in succession

cho·ric \'kōrik, -ȯr-, -ēk *also* -är-\ *adj* [LL *choricus,* fr. Gk *chorikos,* fr. *choros* chorus] **:** of, relating to, or in the style of a chorus ⟨a ~ Greek tragedy⟩ or sometimes of a choir

choric speaking *n* **:** CHORAL SPEAKING

-chories *pl of* -CHORY

cho·rine \'kōr,ēn, 'kȯ,rēn\ *n* -s [*chorus* + *-ine*] **:** CHORUS GIRL

choring *pres part of* CHORE

[1]**chorio-** — see CHOREO-

[2]**chorio-** — see [1]CHORI-

cho·rio·allantoic \¦kōrē,ō+\ *also* **cho·rio·allantoid** \"+\ *adj* [NL *chorioallantois* + E *-ic* or *-oid*] **:** of, relating to, or produced by chorioallantois

cho·rio·allantois \"+\ *n* -ES [NL, fr. [1]*chori-* + *allantois*] **:** a very vascular fetal membrane composed of the more or less fused chorion and adjacent wall of the allantois, that of the developing hen's egg being used as a living culture medium for a number of viruses pathogenic to man or animals and for certain tissues — called also *chorioallantoic membrane*

cho·rio·carcinoma \"+\ *n* [NL, fr. [1]*chori-* + *carcinoma*] **:** a malignant tumor derived from chorionic tissue arising spontaneously in the testis, in the ovary following pregnancy, or extragenitally in the mediastinum — called also *chorioepithelioma*

cho·rio·epithelioma \"+\ *n* [NL, fr. [1]*chori-* + *epithelioma*] **:** CHORIOCARCINOMA — **cho·rio·epitheliomatous** \"+\ *adj*

chorioid *or* **chorioidal** *var of* CHOROID

cho·ri·oi·dea \,kōrē'ȯidēə\ *n* -s [NL, alter. of *choroides* — more at CHOROID] **:** CHOROID

chorioiditis *var of* CHOROIDITIS

cho·ri·o·ma \,kōrē'ōmə\ *n, pl* **choriomas** \-məz\ *also* **chorioma·ta** \-məd·ə\ [NL, fr. [1]*chori-* + *-oma*] **:** a tumor formed of chorionic tissue (as a choriocarcinoma)

cho·rio·meningitis \¦kōrē(,)ō+\ *n* [NL, fr. [1]*chori-* + *meningitis*] **:** cerebral meningitis; *specif* **:** LYMPHOCYTIC CHORIOMENINGITIS

cho·ri·on \'kōrē,än, -ȯr-, -ēən\ *n* -s [NL, fr. Gk] **1 :** the highly vascular outer embryonic membrane of higher vertebrates (reptiles, birds, and mammals) that in the more advanced placental mammals is associated with the allantois in the formation of the placenta and is commonly separable into (1) a villous part that enters into the placenta and (2) a smooth part that does not — called also respectively (1) *chorion frondosum* and (2) *chorion laeve;* see AMNION **2 :** any of various envelopes (not homologous with the chorion of mammals) of the eggs of different animals; *esp* **:** a membrane of the eggs of many insects secreted by the follicular cells surrounding the egg in the ovary — **cho·ri·on·ic** \¦==¦änik\ *adj*

cho·ri·on·epithelioma \"+\ *n* [NL, fr. *chorion* + *epithelioma*] **:** CHORIOCARCINOMA

cho·ri·op·tes \,kōrē'äp,tēz\ *n, cap* [NL, prob. fr. Gk *chorion* chorion, leather (hence taken here to mean animal skin) + NL *-optes* (as in *Sarcoptes*)] **:** a genus of small parasitic mites infesting domestic animals and causing certain forms of mange — **cho·ri·op·tic** \¦==¦tik\ *adj*

chorioptic mange *n* [NL *Chorioptes* + E *-ic*] **:** mange caused by mites (genus *Chorioptes*) that usu. attack only the surface of the skin esp. about the feet and lower legs or in cattle at the base of the tail — compare DEMODECTIC MANGE, SARCOPTIC MANGE

cho·rio·retinitis \¦kōrē(,)ō +\ *also* **cho·roido·retinitis** \kə¦rȯi(,)dō +\ *n* [NL, fr. [1]*chori-* or *choroido-* (fr. *choroides*) + *retinitis*] **:** inflammation of the retina and choroid coat of the eye

cho·ri·pet·a·lae \,kōrə'ped·ᵊl,ē\ *n pl, cap* [NL, fr. [2]*chori-* + *-petalae*] *in some classifications* **:** a group of Archichlamydeae comprising plants with the floral corolla divided into distinct petals — compare APETALAE, METACHLAMYDEAE

cho·ri·petalous \¦kōrə+\ *adj* [[2]*chori-* + *-petalous*] **1 :** POLYPETALOUS **2** [NL *Choripetalae* + E *-ous*] **:** belonging to the Choripetalae

cho·ri·sis \'kōrəsəs\ *n, pl* **chori·ses** \-ə,sēz\ [LGk *chōrisis* separation, fr. Gk *chōrizein* to separate, fr. *chōris* apart — more at CHORI-] **:** the separation of a leaf or floral organ into two or more parts by division during development — called also *collateral chorisis* when the parts are side by side and *parallel chorisis* or *median chorisis* when they are one in front of another

cho·rist \'kōrəst\ *n* -s [F or ML; F *choriste* fr. ML *chorista,* fr. L *chorus* + *-ista* -ist — more at CHORUS] *archaic* **:** a member of a chorus or choir

chorist- *or* **choristo-** *comb form* [NL, fr. Gk *chōristos* separable] **:** separated **:** misplaced ⟨*choristo*blastoma⟩ ⟨*chorist*oma⟩

cho·ris·tate \kə'ristāt, -,stāt\ *adj* [Gk *chōristos* separable, separate (fr. *chōrizein* to separate) + E *-ate*] **:** exhibiting chorisis

cho·ris·ter \'kȯrəstə(r), 'kōr-,'kär-\ *n* -s [ME *querister,* fr. AF *cueristre, cueriste,* fr. ML *chorista*] **1 :** one of a choir or chorus of singers; *specif* **:** CHOIRBOY **2** *obs* **:** SINGER **3 :** the singer in a church choir who leads the singing and in the absence of instrumental accompaniment sets the pitch and tempo

cho·ri·zo *also* **cho·ri·so** \chə'rē(,)zō, -sō\ *n* -s [Sp *chorizo*] **:** pork sausage highly seasoned with cayenne pepper, pimientos, and garlic

c-horizon \'sē=¦==\ *n, usu cap C* **:** the layer of a soil profile lying beneath the B-horizon and consisting essentially of more or less weathered rock of the kind that has contributed the major mineral part of the A-horizon and B-horizon

cho·ro \'shōr(,)ü\ *n* -s [Pg *chôro,* lit., weeping, fr. *chorar* to weep, fr. L *plorare* to cry out, to bewail, prob. of imit. origin] **1 :** a Brazilian dance band; *also* **:** a piece played by such a band **2 :** a musical piece in the style of or suggesting Brazilian folk music

choro- — see CHOR-

cho·ro·gi \'chōrō,gē\ *n* -s [Jap] **:** CHINESE ARTICHOKE

cho·rog·ra·pher \kə'rägrəfə(r)\ *n* -s [*chorography* + *-er*] **:** a specialist in chorography

cho·ro·graph·ic \¦kōrə¦grafik\ *also* **cho·ro·graph·i·cal** \-fəkəl\ *adj* **:** of, relating to, or employing the methods of chorography — **cho·ro·graph·i·cal·ly** \-fək(ə)lē\ *adv*

cho·rog·ra·phy \kə'rägrəfē\ *n* -ES [L *chorographia,* fr. Gk *chōrographia,* fr. *chōr-* chor- + *-graphia* -graphy] **1 :** the art of describing or mapping a particular region or district esp. one larger than that considered by topography but smaller than that by geography **2 :** a description, map, or chart of a particular region or district; *also* **:** the physical conformation and features of such an area

[1]**cho·roid** \'kōr,ȯid, 'kȯ,rȯid\ *or* **cho·ri·oid** \'kōrē,ȯid, -ȯr-\ *n* -s [NL *choroides,* fr. Gk *choroeidēs,* MS var. of *chorioeidēs,* fr. *chori-* [1]chori- + *-oeidēs* -oid] **:** the choroid coat of the eye — see EYE illustration

[2]**choroid** \"\ *or* **cho·roi·dal** \kə'rȯidᵊl\ *also* **cho·ri·oid** \'kōrē,ȯid, -ȯr-\ *or* **cho·ri·oi·dal** \¦==¦ȯidᵊl\ *adj* **1 :** resembling a chorion esp. in being of highly vascular membranous structure — see CHOROID COAT, CHOROID PLEXUS **2** *usu choroidal* **:** of or relating to a choroid part ⟨~ arteries⟩

choroid coat *also* **choroid membrane** *n* **:** a vascular membrane containing large branched pigment cells that lies between the retina and the sclerotic coat of the vertebrate eye

cho·roid·itis \,kōr,ȯi'dīd·əs\ *or* **cho·ri·oid·itis** \,kōrē,ȯi'd-\ *n* -ES [NL, fr. *choroides* or *chorioidea* + *-itis*] **:** inflammation of the choroid coat of the eye

choroidoretinitis *var of* CHORIORETINITIS

choroid plexus *n* **:** a highly vascular portion of the pia mater that projects into the ventricles of the brain and is thought to secrete the cerebrospinal fluid

cho·ro·log·ic \¦kōrə¦läjik\ *or* **cho·ro·log·i·cal** \-jəkəl\ *adj* **:** of or relating to chorology — **cho·ro·log·i·cal·ly** \-jək(ə)lē\ *adv*

cho·rol·o·gy \kə'räləjē\ *n* -ES [ISV *chor-* + *-logy;* orig. formed as G *chorologie*] **:** biogeography esp. as concerned with the migrations and areas of distribution of organisms

cho·ro·te·ga \,chōrə'tāgə\ *n, pl* **chorotega** *or* **chorotegas** *usu cap* [Sp, of AmerInd origin] **1 a :** a people of Honduras, Nicaragua, and Costa Rica **b :** a member of such people **2 :** the language of the Chorotega people

cho·ro·te·gan \¦==¦gən\ *n, pl* **chorotegan** *or* **chorotegans** *usu cap* **:** a language family of Mexico and Central America, including the languages of the Chiapanecs, Chorotegas, Mangues, and Orotiñas

cho·ro·ti \chə'rōd·ē\ *n, pl* **choroti** *or* **chorotis** *usu cap* [Sp *choroti, choroté,* of AmerInd origin] **1 a :** a Matacan people of northwestern Paraguay and southeastern Bolivia **b :** a member of such people **2 :** the language of the Choroti people

-chorous — see -CHORE

chor·ten \'chȯr,ten\ *n* -s [Tibetan *chörten,* alter. of *mchod rten,* fr. *mchod* offering + *rten* holder] **:** a Lamaist shrine or monument

chor·ti \'chȯrd·ē\ *n, pl* **chorti** *or* **chortis** *usu cap* [Sp, of AmerInd origin] **1 a :** an Indian people of eastern Guatemala and western Honduras **b :** a member of such people **2 :** a Mayan language of the Chorti people

[1]**chor·tle** \'chȯrd·ᵊl, -ȯ(ə)|, |tᵊl\ *vb* **chortled; chortled; chortling** \|d·liŋ, |t(ᵊ)l-\ **chortles** [blend of [1]*chuckle* and *snort*] *vi* **1 :** to sing or chant exultantly ⟨he *chortled* in his joy —Lewis Carroll⟩ **2 :** to utter a chuckling laugh or a sound like a chortle **:** speak with a chuckling laugh ⟨~ over the team's defeat⟩ **3** *of a motor vehicle* **:** to progress noisily ⟨flivvers *chortling* up the avenue⟩ **4 :** to express usu. somewhat contemptuous amusement ~ *vt* **:** to express effervescently or with a chortling intonation ⟨~ one's joy⟩

[2]**chortle** \"\ *n* -s **:** a sound expressive of pleasure or exultation; *also* **:** an act or instance of chortling

chor·toi·ce·tes \,kȯr,tȯi'sēd·ēz, ,kȯrd·ə's-\ *n, cap* [NL, fr. Gk *chortos* pasturage, grass, enclosure + *oikētēs* dweller, fr. *oikos* house — more at YARD, VICINITY] **:** a genus of grasshoppers including a very destructive Australian migratory plague grasshopper (*C. terminifera*)

[1]**cho·rus** \'kōrəs, -ȯr-\ *n* -ES [L, ring dance, dance accompanied with singing, group of dancers and singers, fr. Gk *choros;* prob. akin to Lith *žaras* course, way] **1 a :** a company of singers and dancers acting as a unit and in the developed Athenian drama acting as participants in or commenters on the action; *also* **:** a similar company in later plays imitating or adapted from Greek models **b :** a character in the Elizabethan drama who speaks the prologue and epilogue and comments on the action **c :** an organized company of singers who sing in concert **:** CHOIR; *specif* **:** a body of singers who sing choral parts (as in opera) — distinguished from *soloist* **d :** a company of singers who join a soloist in singing a refrain **e :** a group of dancers and usu. singers supporting the featured players in a musical comedy or revue **2 :** something suitable for or intended for performance by a choral group: as **a :** a part of a song or hymn recurring at intervals (as the refrain at the end of stanzas) **b :** the part of a drama sung or spoken by the chorus, typically consisting in Greek drama of a series of odes for antiphonal singing interspersed between the scenes of the play **c :** a composition usu. of two or more parts in harmony intended to be sung by a number of voices in concert ⟨a double ~ of eight parts⟩ **d :** the main or characteristic part of a popular song as distinguished from the introductory verse **3 :** something performed by or as if by a choral group: as **a :** the simultaneous singing or song of a number of persons **b :** the simultaneous utterance (as of speech, laughter, or cries) by a number of persons or animals ⟨the ~ of dogs in the chase⟩: *also* **:** sounds so uttered ⟨the insects . . . raising a ~ from the woods and grasses —D.C.Peattie⟩ **c :** any utterance that follows immediately upon another or that comes as a response to another, suggesting the refrain to a song ⟨their laughter was a ~ to his stories⟩ **d :** a unanimous utterance by the members of a group, giving the impression of a chorus ⟨the ~ of critical praise⟩ ⟨a ~ of boos⟩ — **in chorus** *adv* **:** in unison **:** by all giving utterance simultaneously

[2]**chorus** \"\ *vb* **chorused** *also* **chorussed; chorused** *also* **chorussed; chorusing** *also* **chorussing; choruses** *also* **chorusses** *vi* **:** to sing or make utterance in chorus ~ *vt* **1 :** to furnish with a chorus **2 :** to sing (a song) in chorus **3 :** to utter (as a greeting) together or simultaneously **:** ECHO ⟨they ~*ed* their agreement with his views⟩

chorus boy *or* **chorus man** *n* **:** a usu. young man who sings or dances in the chorus of a theatrical production (as a musical comedy or revue)

chorus girl *n* **:** a usu. young woman who sings or dances in the chorus of a theatrical production (as a musical comedy or revue)

chorus master *n* **:** the director of a chorus; *specif* **:** one who directs and rehearses the singing chorus of an opera company

chorus reed *n* **:** a heavy reed pipe-organ stop of brass-wind quality and of 16-foot, 8-foot, or 4-foot pitch and usu. one of a group

chor·wat \kȯr'vät\ *n* -s *usu cap* [Russ *Khorvat*] **:** CROAT

-chory — see -CHORE

cho·rzow \'kō(,)zhüf, 'k-\ *adj, usu cap* [fr. *Chorzów,* Poland] **:** of or from the city of Chorzow, Poland **:** of the kind or style prevalent in Chorzow

[1]**chose** *past or obs past part of* CHOOSE

[2]**chose** \'shōz\ *n* -s [F, fr. L *causa* cause, reason — more at CAUSE] **:** a piece of personal property **:** THING — see CHOSE IN ACTION

chose in action [[2]*chose*] **1 :** any right to a personal as opposed to a real thing that is not in one's possession or actual enjoyment but is recoverable by suit at law; *esp* **:** any right to an act or forbearance (as in case of debts, stocks, shares, and negotiable instruments or claim of reparation for a tort) **2 :** the thing (as a bond or note) that is the subject of chose in action — compare CHOSE IN POSSESSION

chose in possession [[2]*chose*] **:** a thing in one's actual possession — compare CHOSE IN ACTION

chose ju·gée \shōz·zhüzhā\ *n* [F] **:** a matter that has been settled **:** RES JUDICATA

chose local \(')shōz'lōkəl\ *n, pl* **choses local** \-z(əz)'-\ [[2]*chose*] **:** a thing annexed to a place (as a house) as distinguished from something movable — distinguished from *chose transitory*

[1]**cho·sen** \'chōzᵊn\ *adj* [ME, fr. past part. of *chesen, chosen* to choose — more at CHOOSE] **1 :** selected or marked for favor or to receive special privilege ⟨privileges granted to a ~ few⟩ **2 :** selected by God **:** ELECT

[2]**chosen** \"\ *n, pl* **chosen :** one who is the object of choice or of divine favor **:** an elect person ⟨this prophet, the ~ of the Most High⟩ ⟨the ~ are freed of all sin⟩

cho·sen·ese \¦chō,se¦nēz, chō¦s-, -ēs\ *adj or n, usu cap* [*Chosen,* former official name for Korea (fr. Jap *Chōsen*) + E *-ese*] **:** KOREAN

chosen freeholder *n* **:** one of a board of county officers in New Jersey having charge of county finances and similar to county commissioners or county supervisors in other states

chosen instrument *n* **:** a person or agency favored by an individual, group, or government in furtherance of the latter's own interests; *specif* **:** a commercial airline sponsored or subsidized by its national government for foreign transport esp. in a given part of the world

chosen people *n, often cap C&P* **:** a people that is considered or that considers itself to be chosen esp. by God as his people and specially consecrated to holy purposes: *specif* **:** ISRAELITES

chose transitory *n, pl* **choses transitory** [[2]*chose*] *law:* MOVABLE

cho·ta \'chōd·ə, -ō(,)tä\ *adj* [Hindi *choṭā*] *India* **:** LITTLE

chota haz·ri \-'häzrē\ *n* [Hindi *choṭā hāzirī* small breakfast] *India* **:** a light meal eaten very early in the morning

cho·ta·peg \'chōd·ə,peg\ *n* -s [Hindi *choṭā* small + E *peg*] *India* **:** a half-sized drink esp. of whiskey or whiskey and soda

chott *or* **shott** \'shät\ *n* -s [F & Ar; F *chott,* fr. Ar *shaṭṭ*] **:** a shallow saline lake of northern Africa; *also* **:** the dried bed of such a lake

chou \'shü\ *n, pl* **choux** *in sense* 1 -üz, *in other senses* -ü\ [F, lit., cabbage, fr. L *caulis* stalk — more at HOLE] **1 :** a soft cabbage-shaped ornament or rosette of fabric used in women's wear (as a knot of ribbons on a dress or a crushed crown on a hat) **2 :** CABBAGE 1 **3 :** DARLING — used as a term of endearment

chou·an \'shü,än, =¦=, *F* shwäⁿ\ *n, pl* **chouans** \-änz,-äⁿ\ *usu cap* [after Jean *Chouan* (nickname of Jean *Cottereau* †1794 Fr. revolutionary, one of the leaders), fr. F dial. *chouan* owl, alter. of MF *javan,* fr. LL *cavannus,* of Celt origin; akin to W *cwan* owl, Bret *kaouenn*] **:** one of the royalist insurgents in western France during and after the French revolution

chou·croute \shü·krüt\ *n* -s [F, by folk etymology (influence of *chou* cabbage), fr. G *sauerkraut* — more at SAUERKRAUT] **1 :** SAUERKRAUT **2** *or* **choucroute gar·nie** \-gärnē\ **:** sauerkraut cooked and served with meat

chou·ette \shü'et, 'shwet\ *n* -s [F, fr. *faire la chouette* to play a lone hand at cards, lit., to act like a barn owl, fr. *chouette* barn owl, alter. of OF *çuete,* of imit. origin] **:** a method of scoring by which more than two persons can participate in a two-handed game (as backgammon), one player accepting the bets of all other players on the result of a game between himself and one other active player — see *in the box* at [2]BOX, CAPTAIN 1p

chough \'chəf\ *n* -s [ME *chough, choge, chowe;* prob. akin to OE *cēo, cīo* jackdaw, jay, chough, MD *cauwe* rook, OHG *kāa, kā* jackdaw, jay, Toch A *kāk* he called, Skt *gāyati* he sings] **1 :** a bird of the Old World genus *Pyrrhocorax* (family Corvidae) of small or medium size with red legs and glossy black plumage — see ALPINE CHOUGH, CORNISH CHOUGH **2 :** any of various related or similar birds (as a jackdaw)

chou·kou·tien \¦jō,kō¦tyen\ *or* **chou·kou·tien·ian** \-nēən\ *adj, usu cap* [fr. *Choukoutien,* town near Peking, China, its type station] **:** of or relating to a middle Pleistocene culture of China characterized by rude chopper tools produced from cores or large flakes

choul·try \'chaul·trē\ *n* -ES [modif. of Tamil-Malayalam *cāvaṭi*] **1** *India* **:** INN, CARAVANSARY **2** *India* **:** a pillared hall or colonnade of a temple

chou·moel·lier \shə'mälyə(r)\ *n* -s [F, lit., marrow cabbage] **:** a hybrid of cabbage, kohlrabi, and kale that is used for forage and feed esp. in New Zealand and Australia — called also *marrow cabbage*

chounse *also* **chounce** \'chaun(t)s\ *vt* -ED/-ING/-S [prob. alter. of *jounce*] *South & Midland* **:** SHAKE, BOUNCE; *esp* **:** to freshen (as a pillow or tick) by shaking

choup \'chüp\ *var of* CHOOP

chou·pique *also* **chou·pic** \'shü,pik\ *n* -s [AmerF (La.) *choupique,* fr. Choctaw *shupik*] **:** BOWFIN

[1]**chouse** *also* **chowse** \'chaüs\ *n* -s [Turk *çavuş* sergeant, doorkeeper, messenger, fr. *çav* voice, news] **1** *obs* **:** CHIAUS **2** *obs* **:** one easily cheated **:** GULL, DUPE **3 :** TRICK, SHAM, IMPOSITION

[2]**chouse** \"\ *vt* -ED/-ING/-S **:** CHEAT, TRICK, DEFRAUD ⟨~ him out of his money⟩

[3]**chouse** \"\ *vt* -ED/-ING/-S [origin unknown] *West* **:** to drive or herd (as livestock) roughly; *also* **:** to chase, harass, or stir up (livestock, esp. cattle)

choux *pl of* CHOU

[1]**chow** \'chaü\ *n* -s [perh. fr. Chin (Pek) *chiao*³ meat dumpling] **1** *slang* **:** FOOD, VICTUALS; *also* **:** a meal or mealtime **2** *often cap, Austral* **:** CHINESE 1 — often used disparagingly

[2]**chow** \"\ *vi* -ED/-ING/-S **:** EAT

Chow \'chaü\ *trademark* — used for a mixed balanced animal ration

[3]**chow** *var of* CHOW CHOW

[1]**chow-chow** \'chaü,chaü\ *adj* [pidgin E] **:** consisting of several kinds mingled together **:** ASSORTED, MIXED, MISCELLANEOUS

[2]**chowchow** \"\ *n* -s [pidgin E] **:** something mixed or commingled: **a** (1) **:** a Chinese preserve or confection of ginger, fruits, and peels in heavy syrup (2) **:** a spicy relish of chopped mixed pickles in mustard sauce **b :** HODGEPODGE, MISCELLANY

[3]**chowchow** \"\ *n* -s [prob. imit.] **:** YELLOW-BILLED CUCKOO

chow chow \"\ *or* **chow** *n* -s *often cap both Cs* [fr. a Chin dial. word akin to Cant *kaú* dog] **:** a heavy-coated blocky powerfully built dog that is believed to have originated in north China and that has a broad flat head and short broad muzzle set off by a very full ruff of long hair usu. somewhat lighter than the rest of the coat, which may be of any clear solid color, and a distinctive blue-black tongue and black-lined mouth

1chow·der \'chaudə(r)\ *n* -s [F *chaudière* kettle, pot, its contents, fr. LL *caldaria* — more at CALDRON] **1 :** a thick soup or stew of seafood (as clams or white-fleshed sea fishes) usu. made with milk and containing salt pork or bacon, onions, and potatoes and sometimes other vegetables **2 :** any of various thickened soups more or less resembling chowders — used often in combination ⟨corn ~⟩

2chowder \"\ *vt* **chowdered; chowdered; chowdering** \-d(ə)riŋ\ **chowders :** to make a chowder of

chow·der·head \'chaudə(r),hed\ *n* [alter. of *jolter-head*] **:** DOLT, BLOCKHEAD — **chow·der·head·ed** \-¦hedəd\ *adj*

chowhound \'=,=\ *n, slang* **:** one excessively fond of food **:** GLUTTON, GOURMAND

chowk \'chauk\ *n* -s [Hindi *cauk* — more at CHOKEY] *India* **:** MARKETPLACE, BAZAAR; *also* **:** a main street

chow·ki·dar \¦chaukē¦där\ *var of* CHOKIDAR

chow line *n* **:** a queue waiting to be served food (as in a military mess)

chow mein \(')chau'mān\ *n, pl* **chow meins** [Chin (Pek) *ch'ao³ mien⁴*, fr. *ch'ao³* to fry + *mien⁴* flour, dough, vermicelli] **1 :** fried noodles **2 :** a thick stew of shredded or finely diced meat, mushrooms, vegetables, and seasonings that is served with fried noodles

chow·rie *also* **cau·ri** *or* **chau·ri** \'chaurē\ *n* -s [Hindi *caūrī*, fr. Skt *camara* yak, yak tail employed as whisk] **:** a whisk to keep off flies that is used in the East esp. as a mark of rank

chowse *var of* CHOUSE

choy *or* **choya** *var of* CHAY

choyroot *var of* CHAYAROOT

chp *abbr* championship

chq *abbr* cheque

chrem·a·tis·tic \¦kremə¦tistik, -ēm-\ *adj* [Gk *chrēmatistikos* of business or moneymaking, fr. *chrēmatistēs* businessman (fr. *chrēmatizein* to deal, transact business, make money — fr. *chrēmat-, chrēma* thing, possession, fr. *chrēsthai* to need, use — + *-istēs* -ist) + *-ikos* -ic] **:** of, relating to, or occupied in the gaining of wealth

chrem·a·tis·tics \,==¦=stiks\ *n pl but sing in constr, also* **chrem·a·tis·tic** \-stik,\ [F *chrématistique*, fr. Gk *chrēmatistikē*, fr. fem. of *chrēmatistikos*] **:** the study of wealth or a particular theory of wealth as measured in money

chrem·sel \'kremzəl, 'kr-\ *also* **chrim·sel** \-rim-\ *n, pl* **chrems·lach** \-emzlək, -,läk, -k\ [Yiddish *chremzel*] **:** a flat fried cake made with matzoth meal and filled usu. with prunes

chre·sard \'krē,särd\ *n* -s [Gk *chrēsis* use + *ardein* to water; akin to Gk *chreō* need — more at CHRESTOMATHY, ARDELLA] **:** the soil water available for plant growth — compare ECHARD, HOLARD

chres·to·math·ic \¦krestə¦mathik\ *adj* [*chrestomath-* (fr. F, G, or Gk; F *chrestomathie*, fr. G, fr. Gk *chrēstomatheia*) + *-ic*] **:** belonging to or devoted to useful knowledge or learning

chres·tom·a·thy \kre'stäməthē, -thi\ *n* -ES [NL *chrestomathia*, fr. Gk *chrēstomatheia*, fr. *chrēstos* useful (fr. *chrēsthai* to need, use) + *-matheia* (fr. *mathein, manthanein* to learn); akin to Gk *chreō* need, necessity, OIr *gair* short, Skt *hrasva* short, small; basic meaning: small, scarce — more at MATHEMATICAL] **1 a :** a selection of passages from various authors compiled as an aid to learning a language **2 :** a volume of selected passages or stories of an author

1chrism \'krizəm\ *n* -s [ME *crisme*, fr. OE *crisma*, fr. LL *chrisma*, fr. Gk, ointment, fr. *chriein* to anoint; akin to OE *grēot* sand — more at GRIT] **1 a :** consecrated oil that is generally mixed with balm or balm and spices and used by some liturgical churches in the administration of certain sacraments (as baptism, confirmation, or ordination) and sometimes in other ceremonies (as the consecration of churches or altars) **b :** OINTMENT, UNGUENT **2 a :** a sacramental anointing **:** UNCTION **b** *usu cap* **:** a sacrament of the Eastern Orthodox Church corresponding to confirmation in the Western Church

2chrism *vt* -ED/-ING/-S *obs* **:** to anoint with chrism

chris·ma \'krizmə\ *n, pl* **chrisma·ta** \-mədə,-mətə\ [alter. of *chrismon*] **:** CHRISMON

1chris·mal \'krizməl\ *adj* [ML *chrismalis*, fr. LL *chrisma*] **:** of or relating to chrism

2chrismal \"\ *n* -s [ML *chrismale*, fr. LL *chrisma* chrism] **:** a vessel or flask for holding the chrism

chris·ma·tion \kriz'māshən\ *n* -s *usu cap* [ML *chrismation-, chrismatio*, fr. LL *chrismare* to chrism] **:** a confirmatory sacrament of the Eastern Orthodox Church in which a baptized member is anointed with chrism and which corresponds to confirmation in the West

1chris·ma·to·ry \'krizmə,tōrē\ *n* -ES [ME *crismatorie*, fr. ML *chrismatorium*, fr. LL *chrismat-, chrisma* chrism + L *-orium* -ory] **1 :** a cruet or vessel or a place in which the chrism is kept **2 :** sacramental anointment **:** UNCTION

2chrismatory \"\ *adj* **:** of or relating to sacramental unction

chris·mon \'kriz,män\ *n, pl* **chris·ma** \-mə, -,mä\ [ML, fr. *chris-* (fr. L *Christus* Christ) + *-mon* (fr. LL *monogramma* monogram)] **:** CHI-RHO

chris·om *also* **chrys·om** *or* **chrys·ome** \'krizəm\ *n* -s [ME *crisom*, alter of *crisme* — more at CHRISM] **1 :** CHRISM **2** [ME *crisom*, short for *crisom cloth*] **:** a white cloth, robe, or mantle put upon a person at baptism as a symbol of innocence **3** [by shortening] **:** CHRISOM CHILD

chrisom child *n* **1 :** an innocent child **:** INFANT **2 :** a child that dies in its first month

Christ \'krīst\ *n* -s [after Jesus *Christ* †*ab* A.D.29, fr. ME *Crist*, fr. OE, fr. L *Christus*, fr. Gk *Christos*, lit., anointed (fr. *chriein* to anoint), trans. of Heb *māshīaḥ* anointed, Messiah — more at CHRISM, MESSIAH] **1** *cap* **:** one who is accepted as the Messiah ⟨this Jesus, whom I proclaim to you, is the *Christ* — Acts 17:3 (RSV)⟩ **2** *usu cap* **a :** one who in his outlook or activities resembles Jesus ⟨the legend of Thunupa, the Andean *Christ*, who was stoned to death and abandoned on a drifting raft for preaching virtue and goodness —F.D. de Medina⟩ **b :** an ideal and perfect type of humanity **3** *cap, Christian Science* **:** the ideal truth that comes as a divine manifestation of God to destroy incarnate error

1chris·ta·del·phi·an \,kristə'delfēən\ *n* -s *usu cap* [*Christ* + Gk *adelphos* brother + E *-ian* — more at ADELPHOUS] **:** one of a premillennial religious sect that was founded in the U. S. about 1850 and that rejects the doctrine of the Trinity in favor of a Unitarian and Adventist theology

2christadelphian \¦==¦===\ *adj, usu cap* **:** of or relating to Christadelphians ⟨*Christadelphian* doctrine⟩

chris·ta·del·phi·an·ism \,==¦===,nizəm\ *n* -s *cap* **:** the beliefs and practices of Christadelphians

christ·church \'krīs(t),chərch\ *adj, usu cap* [fr. *Christchurch*, New Zealand] **:** of or from the city of Christchurch, New Zealand **:** of the kind or style prevalent in Christchurch

christ·cross \'kri,skrȯs *also* -äs\ *n* [ME *Crist cross*, fr. *Crist* Christ + *cross*] **:** the mark of the cross formerly put before the alphabet or as the sign of 12 o'clock on a dial **:** a crosslike mark or figure esp. when used as a signature by one unable to write

christ·cross-row \¦=,=¦rō\ *n* [so called fr. the figure of a cross heading it in old hornbooks] **:** ALPHABET

1christen *adj or n, cap* [ME *cristen*, fr. OE] *obs* **:** CHRISTIAN

2chris·ten \'kris°n\ *vb* **christened; christened; christening** \-s(°)niŋ\ **christens** [ME *cristnen, cristen*, fr. OE *cristnian*, fr. *cristen* Christian, fr. L *christianus*] *vt* **1** *obs* **:** CHRISTIANIZE **2 a :** to receive or initiate into a Christian church by the rite of baptism **:** BAPTIZE **b :** to name at baptism **3** *obs* **:** to stand sponsor to (a child) at baptism **4 :** to name or dedicate in naming (as a ship) by a ceremony suggestive of baptism **5 :** to give a name to **:** NAME, DENOMINATE ⟨the latter hill they ~*ed* Mount Joy —*Amer. Guide Series: Pa.*⟩ **6 :** to use for the first time esp. with a sense of the formality of the occasion ⟨~ a new car by taking a Sunday drive⟩ ~ *vi* **:** to administer baptism

chris·ten·die \¦kris°n¦dē\ *n, cap* [alter. (prob. influenced by *christendom*) of ME *cristentie*, fr. OF *crestienté* — more at CHRISTIANITY] *Scot* **:** CHRISTENDOM

chris·ten·dom \'kris°ndəm\ *n* -s [ME *cristendom*, fr. OE *cristendōm*, fr. *cristen* Christian + *-dōm* -dom] **1 a** *often cap, obs* **:** CHRISTIANITY 3 **b** *usu cap* **:** CHRISTIANITY 1,2 ⟨across the first thousand years of *Christendom* the principal church was the Roman Catholic Church —F.S.Mead⟩ **2** *usu cap* **:** the portion of the world in which Christianity prevails or which is governed principally under Christian institutions

chris·ten·ing \'kris(°)niŋ\ *n* -s [ME *cristening*, fr. gerund of *cristnen*] **1 :** the ceremony of baptizing and officially naming a child often including following festivities **2 :** the esp. official or ceremonial naming of something ⟨the colorful ~ of an aircraft carrier⟩

christ·er \'krīstə(r)\ *n* -s *cap* [*Christ* + *-er*] **1** *slang* **:** one thought to associate himself too prominently or overpiously with the Christian church or its principles (as with the stricter forms) or with organizations or activity dedicated to spreading such principles **2** *slang* **:** one who is overly pious or prudish

christ·hood \'krīst,hu̇d, 'krīst,hu̇d\ *n* -s *usu cap* [ME *Cristhod*, fr *Crist* + *-hod* -hood] **:** the quality or state of being a Christ

1chris·tian \'kris(h)chən, *Brit often & US sometimes* -styən *or* -stēən; *in sense 1b sometimes* 'krī- *by nonmembers of these groups*\ *n* -s *usu cap* [L *christianus*, adj. or n., fr. Gk *christianos*, fr. *Christos* Christ] **1 a :** one who believes or professes or is assumed to believe in Jesus Christ and the truth as taught by him **:** an adherent of Christianity **:** one who has accepted the Christian religious and moral principles of life **:** one who has faith in and has pledged allegiance to God thought of as revealed in Christ **:** one whose life is conformed to the doctrines of Christ ⟨in Antioch the disciples were for the first time called *Christians* —Acts 11:26 (RSV)⟩ **b :** a member of a church or group professing Christian doctrine or belief: as (1) **:** a member of the Disciples of Christ (2) **:** a member of one of the Churches of Christ, a body of churches dedicated to the restoring of New Testament Christianity and the promotion of Christian unity by dispensing with creeds and sectarian names and relying on the Bible as the sole rule of faith and practice (3) **:** a member of the Christian Church that united with Congregationalists in 1931 to form the Congregational Christian Churches (4) **:** one of the Plymouth Brethren **2** *now chiefly dial* **:** a human being as distinguished from a lower animal ⟨my dog bears malice just like a *Christian*⟩ **3 :** one born in a Christian country or of Christian parents who has not definitely adhered to an opposing system

2christian \"\ *adj, usu cap* [alter. (influenced by L *christianus*) of earlier *cristen*, fr. ME — more at CHRISTEN] **1 :** professing or belonging to Christianity ⟨a *Christian* people⟩ ⟨a *Christian* country⟩ **2 a :** of or relating to Jesus Christ ⟨*Christian* religion⟩ **b :** of or based on Christianity **:** according to Christian principles ⟨*Christian* art⟩ ⟨a *Christian* burial⟩ **c :** of or relating to a Christian or Christians ⟨one drop of *Christian* blood —Shak.⟩ **d :** representing Christianity ⟨his most *Christian* majesty, the king⟩ **3 a :** characteristic of Christian people **:** following Christ's precepts and example **b** *now chiefly dial* **:** human as distinguished from brutish **c :** DECENT, CIVILIZED ⟨act in a *Christian* fashion⟩ **4** *obs* **:** relating to the church **:** ECCLESIASTICAL — used chiefly in the phrase *court Christian* or *Christian court* **5** *of a door* **:** having the panels so placed that the design of a Latin cross is formed, formerly as a deterrent to evil spirits

christian brethren *n, cap C&B* **:** PLYMOUTH BRETHREN

christian brother *n, usu cap C&B* **:** BROTHER OF THE CHRISTIAN SCHOOLS

chris·tian d'or \¦krist,yän¦dȯ(ə)r, -stē,än-\ *n, pl* **christian d'ors** \-rz\ [F, fr. *Christian* VII †1808 king of Denmark and duke of Holstein, under whom it was struck + *d'or* of gold (as in *louis d'or*)] **:** a Danish gold coin of the 19th century

christian era *n, usu cap C* **:** the era used in Christian countries for numbering the years since the birth of Christ, its first year corresponding with the Roman year 754, Christ's birth having been placed by Dionysius Exiguus († *ab* 540), who first used this era, at December 25 in Roman year 753

christian existentialism *n, usu cap C* **:** a form of existentialism stressing subjective aspects of the human person considered as a creature of God; *esp* **:** such a theory emphasizing (1) the natural desire of the creature to seek his creator (as in the philosophers and thinkers Augustine, Pascal, Nikolai Berdyaev, and Gabriel Marcel) or (2) the distance between guilty man and omnipotent God (as in Kierkegaard and the dialectical or crisis theology of Karl Barth and Emil Brunner) — called also respectively (1) *Catholic existentialism* (2) *Protestant existentialism*

chris·ti·an·ia \,kris(h)chē'anēə, -stē- *also* -än-\ *or* **christy** *or* **chris·tie** \'kristē\ *also* **chris·ti·ana** \,kris(h)chē'anə, -stē- *also* -änə\ *n, pl* **christianias** *or* **christies** *also* **christianas** *often cap* [*christiania* fr. *Christiania* (now Oslo), Norway; *christy, christie, christiana*, by shortening and alter. fr. *Christiania*] **:** a skiing turn used for altering the direction of hill descent usu. from one diagonally transverse direction to the other or for checking or stopping and executed usu. at relatively high speed largely by shifting the body weight forward and skidding into a turn with parallel skis — see STEM CHRISTIANIA

chris·tian·ism \'kris(h)chə,nizəm *sometimes* -styə,n- *or* -stēə,n-\ *n* -s *cap* [MF *christianisme*, fr. LL *christianismus*, fr. Gk *christianismos*, fr. *christianos* Christian + *-ismos* -ism — more at CHRISTIAN] **:** the religious system, tenets, or practices of Christians

chris·ti·an·i·ty \,kris(h)chē'anəd·ē, -nətē, -i *also* ,kristē'a- *or* kris(h)'cha- *sometimes* krist'ya-\ *n* -ES [ME *cristiente, cristiantee*, fr. MF *crestienté*, fr. LL *christianitat-, christianitas*, fr. L *christianus* Christian + *-itat-, -itas* -ity — more at CHRISTIAN] **1** *usu cap* **:** the whole body of Christian believers **:** CHRISTENDOM **2** *cap* **:** the religion of Christians **:** the religion stemming from the life, teachings, and death of Jesus Christ **:** the religion that believes in God as the Father Almighty who as a just and merciful creator and sustainer of the universe works redemptively through the Holy Spirit for men's salvation and that affirms Jesus Christ as Lord and Savior who proclaimed to man the gospel of salvation **:** the religion that recognizes the New Testament as its book of sacred scripture **3** *usu cap* **:** the quality or state of being a Christian **:** Christian character or spirit **:** practical conformity of one's inward and outward life to the spirit of the Christian religion

chris·tian·iza·tion \,kris(h)chənə'zāshən, -,nī'z- *sometimes* -styə- *or* -stēə-\ *n* -s *usu cap* **:** the act or process of christianizing or being christianized

chris·tian·ize \'=(=)=,nīz\ *vb* -ED/-ING/-S *often cap* [¹*christian* + *-ize*] *vt* **1 :** to make Christian **:** convert to Christianity **2 :** to imbue with or deeply affect by Christian principles ~ *vi* **:** to adopt the character or beliefs of a Christian **:** become Christian

chris·tian·iz·er \-zə(r)\ *n* -s *often cap* **:** one that christianizes

chris·tian·ly *adj, usu cap* **:** belonging to or befitting a Christian **:** Christian in spirit **:** GENTLE, GENEROUS, CHARITABLE ⟨moderate and *Christianly* of attitude⟩ ⟨a *Christianly* greeting⟩

christian name *n, often cap C* **:** the name given at birth or christening as distinct from the family name **:** FIRST NAME, FORENAME

chris·tian·ness \-n(n)əs\ *n* -ES *usu cap* **:** the state or the quality of being Christian

christian reformed *adj, usu cap C&R* **:** of or relating to the Christian Reformed Church formed in the Netherlands in 1834 by dissenters from the Netherlands Reformed Church or to the Christian Reformed Church formed in the U.S. in 1857 by dissenters from the Reformed Church in America

christian science *n, cap C&S* **:** a religion discovered by Mary Baker Eddy in 1866 that was organized under the official name of the Church of Christ, Scientist, that derives its teachings from the Scriptures as understood by its adherents, and that includes a practice of spiritual healing based upon the teaching that cause and effect are mental and that sin, sickness, and death will be destroyed by a full understanding of the divine principle of Jesus's teaching and healing

christian scientist *n, usu cap C&S* **:** a believer in Christian Science **:** one who practices the teachings of Christian Science

christian year *n, usu cap C* **1 :** a year of the Christian era **:** a Gregorian year **2 :** the year as it is observed by Christian churches marked by various festivals or commemorations at special seasons and on special days — called also *church year*

christ·less \'krīstləs\ *adj, usu cap* **:** without faith in the teachings of Christ **:** UNCHRISTIAN

christ·like \'krīst,līk\ *adj, usu cap* **1 :** like or like that of Christ in character, spirit, or action ⟨dedicated men leading *Christlike* lives⟩ **2 :** in accord with the teaching and example of Christ ⟨in behalf of virtue, holiness, brotherly love, and whatsoever else is *Christlike* and Godlike —W.F.Tillett⟩

christ·ly \-lē,-li\ *adj, usu cap* **:** like Christ or like that of Christ in spirit ⟨*Christly* self-denial—*Emporia (Kans.) Gaz.*⟩ ⟨*Christly* activities⟩ — sometimes used as a generalized term of disparagement ⟨a *Christly* mess⟩

1christ·mas \'krisməs\ *n* -ES *cap* [ME *Cristemasse, Cristes mæsse*, fr. OE *Cristes mæsse*, fr. *Cristes* (gen. of *Crist* Christ) + *mæsse* mass — more at CHRIST, MASS] **1 :** an annual church festival kept on December 25 or by the Armenians on January 6 in memory of the birth of Christ, celebrated generally by a particular church service, special gifts, and greetings, and observed in most Christian communities as a legal holiday **2 :** the Christmas season **:** CHRISTMASTIDE **3** *dial Eng* **:** evergreens used for decorations at Christmas

2christmas \"\ *vi* -ED/-ING/-ES *cap* **:** to celebrate Christmas ⟨an evening of *Christmasing*⟩

christmas begonia *n, usu cap C* **:** any of various bulbous begonias usu. considered as of a single species (*Begonia cheimantha*) but derived chiefly from an Asiatic form (*B. socotrana*) either directly as sports or by hybridization with a southern African form (*B. dregei*) or other species

christmas bell *n, usu cap C* **1 :** any of several plants of the genus *Blandfordia* — usu. used in pl. **2 :** the flower of the Christmas-bell plant

christmasberry \'==,==\ *n, usu cap* **:** the fruit of the toyon; *also* **:** the shrub itself

christmas bush *n, usu cap C* **:** an Australian tree (*Ceratopetalum gummiferum*) of the family Cunoniaceae often used in Christmas decorations — called also *Christmas tree*

christmas cactus *n, usu cap 1st C* **:** CRAB CACTUS

christmas card *n, usu cap 1st C* **:** an ornamental card with a greeting sent at Christmas

christmas club *n, usu cap 1st C* **:** a savings account in which regular usu. weekly deposits are made throughout the year to provide money for Christmas shopping in December

christmas disease *n, usu cap C* [after Stephen *Christmas*, 20th cent. English boy who was first patient found with the disease] **:** a hereditary sex-linked hemorrhagic disease involving absence of a coagulation factor in the blood and failure of the clotting mechanism — compare HEMOPHILIA

christmas fern *n, usu cap C* **:** a No. American evergreen fern (*Polystichum acrostichoides*) used for decoration in winter and having the fertile terminal pinnae much smaller than the sterile ones

christmas flower *n, usu cap C* **1 :** CHRISTMAS ROSE **2 :** AMERICAN HELLEBORE **3 :** a poinsettia (*Euphorbia pulcherrima*) of Mexico

christmas gift \'==', *with exclamatory intonation*\ *interj, usu cap C, South & Midland* — used as a Christmas greeting and sometimes esp. formerly as part of a custom requiring that the first person to speak the greeting to another on Christmas morning be given a gift by the other

christmas green *n, usu cap C* **:** GROUND PINE 2

christmas holly *n, usu cap C* **:** any of several shrubs or trees of the genus *Ilex*: as **a :** ENGLISH HOLLY **b :** AMERICAN HOLLY

christmas pepper *n, usu cap C* **:** an annual pepper (*Capsicum frutescens*) grown for its ornamental round or cone-shaped red or purple fruits

christmas pie *n, usu cap C, chiefly Brit* **:** MINCE PIE

christmas rose *n, usu cap C* **:** a European herb (*Helleborus niger*) having white or purplish roselike flowers produced in winter

christmas stocking *n, usu cap C* **:** a stocking or sometimes a pillowcase customarily hung up usu. on the mantel of a fireplace by children on Christmas eve to hold Christmas presents

christmastide \'==,=\ *n, usu cap* [¹*Christmas* + *tide* (time)] **:** the festival season from Christmas eve till after New Year's or esp. in England till Epiphany

christmastime \'==,=\ *n, usu cap* **:** CHRISTMASTIDE

christmas tree *n, usu cap C* [trans. of G *weihnachtsbaum* or *Christbaum*] **1 :** a usu. small evergreen tree customarily decorated at Christmas with ornaments and lights and often when in the home with Christmas presents around the base **2 a :** CHRISTMAS BUSH **b** *NewZeal* **:** POHUTUKAWA **c :** any of several evergreen trees of the north temperate zone esp. of the genera *Abies* and *Picea* **3** *dial* **:** a Christmas gathering or celebration **4 :** an oil-well control manifold consisting of an assembly of fittings (as valves, clamps, anchors, and connections) placed on the casinghead of a flowing well to control its production **5** *slang* **:** a submarine control-room panel of red and green lights that flash on and off to indicate valve conditions

christ·masy *or* **christ·mas·sy** \'krisməsē, -si\ *adj, usu cap* **:** befitting Christmas or the Christmas season; *esp* **:** colorful, cheerful, or festive in a way usu. associated with the celebration of Christmas or with the bustle of preparing for it ⟨a *Christmasy* glitter⟩

chris·to- *comb form, cap* [LGk, fr. Gk *Christos*] **:** Christ ⟨*Christo*centric⟩ ⟨*Christo*latry⟩ ⟨*Christo*cracy⟩

chris·to·cen·trism \,kristə'sen,trizəm\ *n* -s *usu cap* [*Christo-* + *centr-* + *-ism*] **:** the placing of Christ at the center of one's thought, action, or theological system

chris·to·gram \'==,gram\ *n* -s *usu cap* [*Christo-* + *-gram*] **:** a graphic symbol of Christ; *esp* **:** CHI-RHO

Christogram

chris·to·log·i·cal \¦==¦läjəkəl\ *adj, often cap* **:** of or belonging to Christology

chris·tol·o·gy \kri'stäləjē\ *n* -ES *usu cap* [*Christo-* + *-logy*] **1 :** the theological interpretation of the person and work of Christ often expressed doctrinally **2 :** the branch of theology that deals with the person and work of Christ

christom child *n* [by alter.] *obs* **:** CHRISOM CHILD

chris·toph·a·ny \kri'stäfənē\ *n* -ES *usu cap* [*Christo-* + *-phany*] **:** an appearance of Christ after resurrection esp. as recorded in the Gospels

chris·to·phine \'kristə,fēn\ *n* -s [AmerF, prob. fr. *Christophe* Christopher + F *-ine*] **:** CHAYOTE

christs *pl of* CHRIST

christ's-thorn \'krīs(t)+, -īs(t)s+\ *n, pl* **christ's-thorns** *usu cap C* **:** any of several prickly or thorny shrubs of Palestine (esp. the shrub *Paliurus spina-christi* or the jujube *Ziziphus jujuba*)

christ within *n, usu cap C&W* **:** INNER LIGHT

christy *often cap, var of* CHRISTIANIA

-chroia \'krȯiə *also* -ȯiyə\ *n comb form* -s [NL, fr. Gk, fr. *-chroos* -chroous + *-ia*] **:** coloration ⟨dys*chroia*⟩ **:** discoloration ⟨cyano*chroia*⟩

-chro·ic \¦krōik\ *adj comb form* [Gk *-chroos* -chroous + ISV *-ic*] **:** -CHROOUS ⟨erythro*chroic*⟩

chrom- *or* **chromo-** *comb form* [F, fr. Gk *chrōma* color] **1 :** chromium⟨*chrom*ammine⟩ ⟨*chromo*arsenate⟩ **2 a :** color **:** colored ⟨*chrom*idrosis⟩ ⟨*chromo*meter⟩ **b :** pigment **:** pigmented ⟨*chromo*cyte⟩ ⟨*chromo*gen⟩

chro·ma \'krōmə\ *n* -s [Gk *chrōma* color — more at CHROMATIC] **1 :** SATURATION 4a **2 :** the color dimension on the Munsell scales that correlates most closely with saturation — see the Color Charts explanation at COLOR **syn** see COLOR

chro·ma·ble \'krōməbəl\ *adj* [*chrom-* + *-able*] **:** capable of combining with chromium or a chromium compound — used of a mordant ⟨~ dyes⟩

chro·ma·dor·i·da \,krōmə'dȯrədə\ *n pl, cap* [NL, fr. *Chromadora*, genus of nematode worms (fr. Gk *chrōma* color + *dora* skin) + *-ida*; akin to Gk *derein* to skin, flay — more at CHROMATIC, TEAR] **:** an order of Aphasmidia comprising free-living or occas. commensal nematode worms having the esophagus divisible into three regions and the amphids spiral, vesicular, or circular — compare ENOPLIDA

chro·maf·fin \krō'mafən, 'krōmə-\ *also* **chro·maf·fine** \-(,)fēn, -¦fən\ *adj* [ISV *chrom-* + L *affinis* associated with, related by marriage; prob. orig. formed in G — more at AFFINITY] **:** staining deeply with chromium salts ⟨~ tissue⟩; *specif* **:** indicating, relating to, or made up of certain pigmented cells derived from the sympathetic ganglia and capable of secreting adrenaline and forming in higher vertebrates the medulla of the suprarenal glands and the paraganglia — **chro·maf·fin·ic** \¦krōmə¦finik, -,ma¦-\ *adj*

chromaffin body *n* **:** PARAGANGLION
chrom·am·mine \krō'ma,mēn,-,mən; ¦krōmə¦mēn\ *n* -s [ISV *chrom-* + *ammine;* orig. formed as F *chromamine*] **:** an ammine of chromium
chro·man \'krō,man\ *n* -s [ISV *chrom-* (color) + *-an*] **:** a bicyclic heterocyclic compound $C_9H_{10}O$ that is the parent nucleus of the tocopherols; dihydro-benzo-pyran
chro·ma·phil \'krōmə,fil\ *adj* [Gk *chrōma* color + E *-phil*] **:** CHROMAFFIN
chro·ma·scope \'==,skōp\ *n* -s [Gk *chrōma* color + E *-scope*] **:** an instrument for testing the optical effects of color
-chro·ma·sia \krō'māzh(ē)ə\ *n comb form* -s [NL, fr. Gk *chrōmat-, chrōma* color + NL *-ia*] **1 :** color ⟨*achromasia*⟩ **2 :** stainability **:** colorability ⟨*polychromasia*⟩
chromat- *or* **chromato-** *comb form* [Gk *chrōmat-, chrōma* color] **1 :** color ⟨*chromatology*⟩ **:** colored ⟨*chromatopsia*⟩ **2 :** chromatin ⟨*chromatolysis*⟩
[1]**chro·mate** \'krō,māt, -mət\ *n* -s [F, fr. *chrom-* + *-ate*] **:** a salt or ester of chromic acid
[2]**chro·mate** \-,māt\ *vt* -ED/-ING/-S **:** to treat or impregnate with a chromate or dichromate esp. with potassium dichromate
chromate method *n* **:** the metachrome method in dyeing
[1]**chro·mat·ic** \krō'mad·|ik, krə-, -at|, |ēk, *attrib also* 'krō,m-\ *adj* [Gk *chrōmatikos*, fr. *chrōmat-, chrōma* skin, color, modification of diatonic music consisting of the use of tones altered in pitch; akin to Gk *chrōs* skin, color, OE *grēot* sand; basic meaning: to rub, grind — more at GRIT] **1 a :** having to do with color **:** with respect to color phenomena **b :** evoking, resulting from, or associated with color sensations **c :** full of color **:** highly colored **2 a :** having or manifesting chroma **b :** exhibiting hues or embracing the hues **c :** with respect to hue or saturation **3 a** *of a Greek tetrachord* **:** comprising successive steps of 1½, ½, and ½ — distinguished from *diatonic* and *enharmonic* **b :** of, relating to, or giving all the tones of the chromatic scale ⟨a ~ harmonica⟩ ⟨~ intervals⟩ **c** *of harmony* **:** characterized by frequent use of tones foreign to the basic mode or key of the piece containing the harmony **4** *biol* **a :** capable of being colored by staining agents **b :** of, like, or relating to chromatin **5** *of language or prose* **:** of, relating to, or having colorful connotations or evocative power ⟨the full ~ and diatonic possibilities of the prose medium —G.M.Hopkins⟩ ⟨~ words —F.R.Leavis⟩ **6 :** executed in fine usu. colorful detail ⟨~ coverage of the Dark Continent —*Newsweek*⟩ ⟨a masterpiece of ~ mendacity —J.J.Ingalls⟩ — **chro·mat·i·cal·ly** \-ək(ə)lē, -ēk-, -li\ *adv*
[2]**chromatic** \"\ *n* -s [F *chromatique*, fr. *chromatique*, adj., fr. Gk *chrōmatikos*] **:** [2]ACCIDENTAL 3
chromatic aberration *n* **:** aberration caused by the different refrangibilities of the colored rays of the spectrum
chromatic alteration *n* **:** the raising or lowering of a musical tone by a half step
chromatic chord *n* **:** a chord having tones foreign to a given key or mode
chromatic figure *n* **:** the mitotic or meiotic chromosomes — compare ACHROMATIC FIGURE
chromatic interval *n* **:** a normal musical scale interval raised or lowered by a half step
chro·mat·i·cism \=¦=ə,sizəm\ *n* -s **1 :** the quality or state of being chromatic **2 a :** the act or action of chromaticizing **:** the use of chromatic notes or tones ⟨excessive ~ means excessive increase in harmonic tension —Mosco Carner⟩ — contrasted with *diatonicism* **b :** an instance of this use
chro·ma·tic·i·ty \,krōmə'tisəd·ē, -ətē, -i\ *n* -ES **1 :** the quality or state of being chromatic **2 :** the quality of color characterized by its dominant or complementary wavelength and purity taken together
chromaticity coordinate *n* **:** the ratio of the amount of one primary color to the total amount of all three necessary to reproduce a given color
chromaticity diagram *n* **:** a triangular graph on which points for all chromaticity coordinates may be systematically plotted, the apexes of the triangle representing the primary colors — called also *color triangle, Maxwell triangle*
chro·mat·i·ci·za·tion \krō,mad·əsə'zāshən, krə-, -atə-, -,sī'z-\ *n* -s **:** CHROMATICISM 2
chro·mat·i·cize \=¦=ə,sīz\ *vb* -ED/-ING/-S *vi* **:** to use in chords and progressions notes that are foreign to a given tonality **:** use the tones of the chromatic scale ~ *vt* **:** to make chromatic in harmonic structure
chro·mat·ic·ness \-iknəs, -ēk-\ *n* -ES **:** the quality of color characterized by its hue and saturation taken together
chro·mat·ics \-ks\ *n pl but sing in constr* **1 :** the part of optics that deals with the properties of colors **2 :** the branch of colorimetry that deals with hue and saturation
chromatic scale *n* **:** any musical sequence of half steps **:** all the notes, in series, possible to a keyboard or wind instrument with fixed tempered intervals
chromatic sign *n* **:** [2]ACCIDENTAL
chromatic vision *n* **1 :** normal color vision in which the colors of the spectrum are distinguished and evaluated — opposed to *color blindness* **2 :** CHROMATOPSIA
chro·ma·tid \'krōmətəd\ *n* -s [ISV *chromat-* + *-id*] **:** one of the paired complex constituent strands of a chromosome — compare CHROMONEMA — **chro·mat·i·dal** \krō'mad·əd°l, ¦krōmə¦tīd°l\ *adj*
chro·ma·tin \'krōmətən, -məd·ən\ *n* -s [ISV *chromat-* + *-in;* orig. formed in G] **1 a** (1) **:** the part of a cell nucleus that stains intensely with basic dyes and is usu. divisible into more stainable basichromatin and less stainable oxychromatin and linin — not used technically (2) **:** a cytoplasmic constituent that because of similar staining reactions is considered identical with nuclear chromatin — not used technically **b :** an ampholytic complex of highly polymerized deoxyribose nucleic acid with basic proteins of protamine or histone type that exhibits differential staining of various parts of the complex at different periods in the nuclear cycle prob. due to fluctuation in the degree of polymerization, that is regarded as the physical carrier of genes, and that is typically manifest in chromomeres which in mitosis form chromosomes **2 :** KARYOTIN — **chro·ma·tin·ic** \¦==¦tinik\ *adj*
chromatin diminution *n* **:** elimination of parts of the chromosomes from prospective soma during early cleavage
chro·ma·tism \'krōmə,tizəm\ *n* -s [Gk *chrōmatismos* coloring, fr. *chrōmatizein* to color, fr. *chrōmat-, chrōma* color] **1 :** COLORING 1c; *esp* **:** abnormal pigmentation **2 :** CHROMATIC ABERRATION **3 :** CHROMESTHESIA
chro·ma·tist \-məd·əst\ *n* -s **:** a specialist in chromatics — compare COLORIST
chro·ma·ti·um \krō'māshēəm\ *n, cap* [NL, fr. *chromat-* + *-ium*] **:** a genus of purple sulfur bacteria (family Thiorhodaceae) that are ovoid to bean-shaped or rod-shaped, motile by polar flagella, reddish from a mixture of bacteriochlorophyll and carotenoid pigments, and widely distributed in fresh or salt water, some having been reported also from soil
chro·ma·tize \'krōmə,tīz\ *vt* -ED/-ING/-S [*chromat-* + *-ize*] **:** CHROMATE
chromato- *in pronunciations below,* =¦== = krō¦mad·ə *or* krə- *or* -atə, ¦=== = ¦krōmad·¦ə *or* -ət¦ *or* ¦ō\ — see CHROMAT-
chro·mato·cyte \=¦==, '===+,sīt\ *n* -s [ISV *chromat-* + *-cyte*] **:** a unicellular chromatophore **:** a pigment cell
chro·mato·gram \-,gram\ *n* -s [*chromat-* + *-gram*] **:** the series of separate zones on an adsorbent medium into which the different substances in a mixture are separated by chromatography
[1]**chro·mato·graph** \-,graf\ *n* -s [*chromat-* + *-graph*] *archaic* **:** a colored print
[2]**chromatograph** \"\ *vt* -ED/-ING/-S **1 :** to make a chromatic representation or reproduction of **2 :** to separate into components by chromatography
chro·mato·graph·ic \=¦==, ¦===+¦grafik\ *adj* **:** of or relating to chromatography — **chro·mato·graph·i·cal·ly** \-fək(ə)lē\ *adv*
chro·ma·tog·ra·phy \,krōmə'tägrəfē\ *n* -ES [*chromat-* + *-graphy*] **:** a process of separating gases, liquids, or solids in a mixture or solution by adsorption (as selective adsorption on clay, silica gel, or alumina or on paper) as the mixture flows over the adsorbent medium, often in a column, each substance finally appearing in the medium at a different level or band that is often colored and then being recoverable (as by washing out with pure solvent)
chro·ma·toid \'krōmə,tȯid\ *adj* [ISV *chromat-* + *-oid;* orig. formed in G] **:** resembling chromatin esp. in affinity for stains
chro·ma·tol·y·sis \,krōmə'täləsəs\ *n, pl* **chromatoly·ses** \-ə,sēz\ [NL, fr. *chromat-* + *-lysis*] **:** the dissolution and breaking up of chromophil material (as Nissl bodies or chromatin) of a cell — **chro·mato·lyt·ic** \=¦==, ¦=== *at* CHROMATO- +¦lid·ik\ *adj*
chro·ma·tom·e·ter \,krōmə'täməd·ə(r)\ *n* -s [F *chromatomètre*, fr. *chromat-* + *-mètre* -meter] **1 :** a color diagram or chart so arranged as to serve as a scale of colors **2 :** an instrument for measuring color perception **3 :** CHROMOMETER
chro·ma·tone process \'krōmə,tōn-\ *n* [Gk *chrōma* color + E *tone*] **:** a photographic color process in which three colored images are formed separately by toning, stripped from their special paper, and superimposed in register
chromatophil *or* **chromatophile** *var of* CHROMOPHIL
chro·mato·phil·ia \=¦==, ,=== *at* CHROMATO-+'filēə\ *also* **chro·moph·i·ly** \krō'mäfəlē\ *n, pl* **chromatophilias** *also* **chromophilies** [NL *chromatophilia*, fr. *chromat-* + *-philia*] **:** the quality or state of being chromophil
chro·ma·toph·o·ral \¦krōmə¦täf(ə)rəl, krō¦mad·ə¦fōrəl\ *adj* **:** of or belonging to a chromatophore
chro·mato·phore \=¦==, '=== *at* CHROMATO-+,fō(ə)r\ *n* -s [ISV *chromat-* + *-phore*] **1 :** a pigment-bearing cell; *esp* **:** one of those cells in the integument of various animals capable of changing the apparent pigmentation of the skin by expanding or contracting **2 :** a chromoplast or chloroplast — **chro·mato·phor·ic** \=¦==, ¦===+¦fōrik\ *or* **chro·ma·toph·o·rous** \¦krōmə¦täf(ə)rəs\ *adj*
chro·mato·plasm \=¦==, '=== *at* CHROMATO- + ,plazəm\ *also* **chro·mo·plasm** \'krōmə,p-\ *n* -s [ISV *chromat-* or *chrom-* + *-plasm;* orig. formed as G *chromatoplasma*] **:** the peripheral protoplasm of a blue-green alga containing chlorophyll and accessory pigments together with stored substances
chro·ma·top·sia \,krōmə'täpsēə\ *n* -s [NL, fr. *chromat-* + *-opsia*] **:** a disturbance of vision which is sometimes caused by drugs and in which colorless objects appear colored
chro·mato·scope \=¦==, '=== *at* CHROMATO- + ,skōp\ *n* -s [ISV *chromat-* + *-scope;* prob. orig. formed in F] **:** an instrument for the mixing of color stimuli by means of light beams
chro·ma·to·sis \,krōmə'tōsəs\ *n, pl* **chromato·ses** \-ō,sēz\ [NL, fr. *chromat-* + *-osis*] **:** PIGMENTATION; *specif* **:** deposit of pigment in a normally unpigmented area or excessive pigmentation in a normally pigmented site
chro·ma·trope \'krōmə-,trōp\ *n* -s [ISV *chroma-* (fr. Gk *chrōma* color) + *-trope* — more at CHROMATIC] **:** CHROMOTROPE
chro·ma·type \-mə,tīp\ *n* -s [Gk *chrōma* + E *type*] **1 a :** a photograph made upon paper sensitized with potassium bichromate and a metallic sulfate (as copper sulfate) **2 :** the process of making a chromatype — compare CARBON PROCESS
[1]**chrome** \'krōm\ *n* -s [F, fr. Gk *chrōma* color, fr. the beautiful colors of its compounds — more at CHROMATIC] **1 :** CHROMIUM **2 :** CHROME YELLOW **3 :** CHROME LEATHER
[2]**chrome** \"\ *vb* -ED/-ING/-S *vt* **1 :** to treat with a compound of chromium: **a** *in dyeing* **:** to treat with a solution of a dichromate (as sodium dichromate) or complex chromium chromate **b :** to subject to chrome tanning **2 :** to give chroma to ⟨~ a neutral background⟩ **3 :** to surface (as an electrotype) with chromium ~ *vi* **:** to acquire or to increase in chroma
-chrome \(,)krōm\ *n comb form or adj comb form* [ML *-chromat-, chroma* colored thing, fr. Gk *chrōmat-, chrōma* color] **1 :** colored thing **:** colored ⟨*monochrome*⟩ **2 :** coloring matter ⟨*endochrome*⟩
chrome alum *n* **:** an alum in which chromium is the trivalent metal; *esp* **:** potassium chromium sulfate $KCr(SO_4)_2.12H_2O$ obtained as dark purple crystals by treating potassium dichromate with sulfur dioxide and used in tanning, as a mordant, and as a hardening agent for gelatin in photography
chrome black *n* **:** a black produced by dyeing with logwood after chroming
chrome brick *n* **:** a refractory brick manufactured substantially or entirely of chrome ore
chrome cake *n* **:** sodium sulfate containing some chromium, obtained as a by-product in the manufacture of sodium dichromate, and used in the paper industry
chrome dye *n* **:** any of a class of mordant acid dyes applied usu. to wool with a chromium compound as the mordant — see DYE table I (under *Mordant*)
chrome green *n* **1 a** *Brit* (1) **:** a chromic oxide either anhydrous or hydrated (2) **:** any of several similar green pigments consisting essentially of some chromic salt (as the phosphate) — compare CHROME OXIDE GREEN **b :** any of various brilliant green pigments essentially mixtures of chrome yellow and iron blue, often with barite or clay, used as oil colors, in printing inks, and in textile printing — called also *Brunswick green* **2 :** any of several mordant acid dyes **3 a :** any of several yellowish greens that are mixtures of characteristic colors of iron blue and chrome yellow including three with varying amounts of white pigment: (1) **:** DEEP CHROME GREEN (2) **:** MEDIUM CHROME GREEN (3) **:** LIGHT CHROME GREEN **b :** VIRIDIAN 2 **c :** the color of chromic oxide
chrome iron *or* **chrome iron ore** *n* **:** CHROMITE 1
chrome leather *n* **:** chrome-tanned leather used largely in the manufacture of shoe uppers
chrome leather fast black S *n, usu cap C&L&F&B* **:** a direct dye — see DYE table I (under *Direct Black 41*)
chrome lemon *or* **chrome citron** *n* **:** a light yellow that is greener, lighter, and stronger than average maize, greener and slightly paler than jasmine, and lighter and stronger than popcorn
chrome liquor *n* **:** a solution of a chromium compound that is used in chrome tanning
chrome-mordant \'=¦=\ *adj* **:** relating to a method of dyeing esp. wool by applying a chromium mordant before the dye
chrome orange *n* **1 :** any of several pigments varying from reddish yellow to deep orange and consisting essentially of varying proportions of normal and basic lead chromates that are usu. prepared similarly to chrome yellows **2 :** any of several mordant acid dyes **3 :** a vivid reddish orange that is yellower, less strong, and much lighter than international orange and duller and slightly yellower than golden poppy — called also *orange chrome yellow*
chrome oxide green *n* **:** chromic oxide used as a pigment — compare CHROME GREEN 1a
chrome primrose *n* **:** a light to brilliant yellow
chrome red *n* **1 :** any of several pigments consisting essentially of basic lead chromate **2 :** any of several mordant acid dyes **3 :** vermilion or a color resembling it
chrome re·tan \-'rē,tan\ *n* **:** a leather produced by a combination of chrome tanning and vegetable tanning and usu. used for boots and heavy shoes
chrome scarlet *n* **:** a moderate to strong reddish orange — called also *deep chrome orange, midnight sun, russet orange*
chrome sole *n* **:** a heavy greenish gray leather tanned with chromium salts and used for making soles of boots and shoes
chrome spinel *n* **:** PICOTITE
chrom·esthesia \¦krōm+\ *n* -s [NL, fr. *chrom-* + *esthesia*] **:** synesthesia in which color is seen in response to nonchromatic stimuli (as words or numbers) — called also *color hearing*
chrome tan *vt* **:** to tan (an animal skin) by impregnating with chromium salts — **chrome-tanned** *adj* — **chrome tanning** *n*
chrome tannage *n* **:** the process or the product of chrome tanning
chrome vermilion *n* **:** a variety of chrome red
chrome yellow *n* **1 :** any of several bright pigments with good hiding power that vary from light greenish yellow to reddish medium yellow, consist essentially of normal lead chromate now usu. without extenders (as barite or clay) but often contain other lead compounds (as lead sulfate) for the lighter shades, and are prepared by precipitation from solutions of a lead salt (as lead nitrate) and sodium chromate or dichromate **2 :** any of several mordant acid dyes **3 a :** DEEP CHROME YELLOW **b :** LIGHT CHROME YELLOW
chrome yellow orange *n* **:** DEEP CHROME YELLOW
chro·mia \'krōmēə\ *n* -s [NL, fr. *chromium* + *-a*] **:** CHROMIC OXIDE
-chro·mia \¦krōmēə\ *n comb form* -s [NL, fr. LGk *-chrōmia*, fr. Gk *-chrōmos* colored (fr. *chrōma* color) + *-ia* — more at CHROMATIC] **:** state of pigmentation ⟨*anisochromia*⟩
chro·mic \'krōmik, -mēk\ *adj* [F *chromique*, fr. *chrome* + *-ique* -ic] **1 :** of, relating to, or derived from chromium — used esp. of compounds in which this element is trivalent and of the acid in which it is hexavalent; compare CHROMOUS **2 :** subjected to chrome tanning
chromic acid *n* **1 :** an acid H_2CrO_4 analogous to sulfuric acid but known only in solution and esp. in the form of its salts (as lead chromate) most of which are yellow and are toxic causing ulcers on the skin or mucous membranes **2 :** CHROMIC ANHYDRIDE — used chiefly commercially
chromic anhydride *n* **:** a brilliant red crystalline substance essentially CrO_3 that is made from sodium dichromate and sulfuric acid and that is used esp. in chromium plating and as an oxidizing agent — called also *chromium trioxide, chromic acid*
chromic hydroxide *n* **:** a substance obtained as a gray-green gelatinous precipitate or bluish amorphous powder by reaction of a chromic salt with alkali that is usu. assigned the formula $Cr(OH)_3$ but is better considered a hydrated chromic oxide $Cr_2O_3.xH_2O$ — compare GUIGNET'S GREEN
chromic iron *n* **:** CHROMITE 1
chro·mi·cize \'krōmə,sīz\ *vt* -ED/-ING/-S [*chromic* + *-ize*] **:** to treat (catgut) with a compound of chromium
chromic oxide *n* **:** an oxide Cr_2O_3 obtained as a green powder by thermal decomposition of most chromium compounds or by reduction of sodium dichromate or sodium chromate and used as the very permanent pigment chrome oxide green, as a coloring agent for glass and ceramic ware, and as a catalyst — compare CHROMIC HYDROXIDE
chro·mi·dae \'krōmə,dē\ [NL, fr. *Chromis* + *-idae*] *syn of* CICHLIDAE
chro·mide \'krō,mīd\ *n* -s [NL *Chromides*] **:** any of several small brightly colored African fishes (family Cichlidae); *esp* **:** a brilliant orange or yellow fish (*Etroplus maculatus*) that is spotted with red, has a large black spot on either side, and is frequently kept in the tropical aquarium — called also *orange chromide*

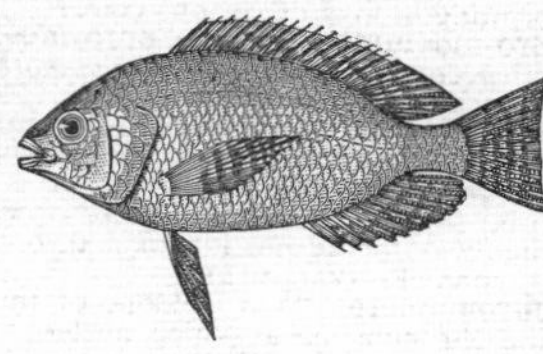
chromide

chro·mi·des \'krōmə-,dēz, -'räm-\ *n pl, cap* [NL, irreg. fr. *Chromis*, genus of fishes, fr. L *chromis*, a sea fish, fr. Gk; perh. akin to Gk *chremizein* to neigh — more at GRIM] *in some classifications* **:** an order of spiny-finned fishes comprising the percoid families Cichlidae and Pomacentridae and sometimes related forms
chro·mid·i·al \krō'midēəl\ *adj* [NL *chromidium* + E *-al*] **:** of or relating to chromidia
chro·mid·i·um \krō'midēəm\ *n, pl* **chromid·ia** \-ēə\ [NL, fr. *chrom-* + *-idium*] **:** a chromatin or chromatinlike granule in the cytoplasm of a cell; *esp* **:** one of nuclear origin
chro·mi·dro·sis \,krōmə'drōsəs\ *also* **chrom·hi·dro·sis** \-m(h)ə-\ *n, pl* **chromidro·ses** *or* **chromhidro·ses** \-ō,sēz\ [NL, fr. *chrom-* + *-idrosis*] **:** secretion of colored sweat
-chromies *pl of* -CHROMY
chro·mif·er·ous \(')krō¦mif(ə)rəs\ *adj* [ISV *chrom-* + *-i-* + *-ferous;* prob. orig. formed as F *chromifère*] *of a mineral* **:** containing chromium
chro·mi·nance \'krōmənən(t)s\ *n* -s [*chrom-* + luminance] *color television* **:** the difference determined by quantitative measurements between a color and a chosen reference color of the same luminous intensity, the reference color having a specified color quality **:** the quality of a color without reference to brightness
chroming *pres part of* CHROME
chro·mi·ole \'krōmē,ōl\ *n* -s [*chrom-* + *-i-* + *-ole*] **1 :** a hypothetical subdivision of a chromomere **2 :** CHROMIDIUM
chro·mite \-,mīt\ *n* -s [in sense 1, fr. G *chromit*, fr. *chrom-* + *-it* -ite; in sense 2, *chrom-* + *-ite*] **1 :** a mineral of the spinel group consisting of an oxide of iron and chromium $FeCr_2O_4$, occurring massive, and valuable as a source of chromium and refractories **2 :** a compound of chromic oxide and a metal oxide (as sodium chromite $Na_2Cr_2O_4$)
chromite series *n* **:** a series of isomorphous minerals in the spinel group consisting of magnesiochromite and chromite
chro·mi·tite \-mə,tīt\ *n* -s [ISV *chromite* + *-ite;* orig. formed as G *chromitit*] **:** a rock composed chiefly of the mineral chromite
chro·mi·um \'krōmēəm, *esp Brit* -myəm\ *n* -s [NL, fr. F *chrome* + NL *-ium* — more at CHROME] **:** a blue-white multivalent metallic element hard and brittle as usu. prepared and resistant to corrosion that is found only in combination and principally in the mineral chromite from which it is separated by the aluminothermic, silicothermic, or electrolytic process and that is used chiefly in alloys (as ferrochromium for use in chromium steel or as nickel-chromium electrical resistance alloys) and in electroplating (as for automobile bumpers and trim and for cutting tools) — symbol *Cr;* see ELEMENT table
chromium green *n* **1 :** CHROME GREEN 1 **2 a :** CHROME GREEN 3a **b :** a moderate yellow green that is greener and deeper than average moss green and yellower and duller than average pea green or apple green (sense 1)
chromium oxide *n* **:** an oxide of chromium; *specif* **:** CHROMIC OXIDE
chromium oxide green *n* **:** CHROME OXIDE GREEN
chromium sesquioxide *n* **:** CHROMIC OXIDE
chromium trioxide *n* **:** CHROMIC ANHYDRIDE
chromium yellow *n* **:** CHROME YELLOW
chro·mize \'krō,mīz\ *vt* -ED/-ING/-S [*chrom-* + *-ize*] **:** to treat (a metal, esp. steel) with chromium or a chromium compound to form a protective surface alloy
chro·mo \'krō(,)mō\ *n* -s [short for *chromolithograph*] **1 :** CHROMOLITHOGRAPH **2 :** an often badly executed or garish picture printed in colors
chromo- *in pronunciations below,* ¦== = ¦krōmə *or* -mō\ — see CHROM-
chro·mo·bacterium \¦==+\ *n* [NL, fr. *chrom-* + *bacterium*] **1** *cap* **:** a genus of aerobic gram-negative saprophytic soil and water bacteria (family Rhizobiaceae) producing a violet pigment **2** *pl* **chromobacteria :** a bacterium of the genus *Chromobacterium*
chro·mo·blast \'==+,blast\ *n* -s [ISV *chrom-* + *-blast*] **:** an anatomical cell that develops into a pigment cell
chro·mo·blastomycosis \¦==+\ *n, pl* **chromoblastomycoses** [NL *chrom-* + *blastomycosis*] **:** a skin disease that is caused by any of several pigmented fungi esp. of the genera *Hormodendrium* or *Phialophora* and is marked by the formation of warty colored nodules usu. on the legs
chro·mo·center *also* **chro·mo·centre** \'==+,-\ *n* -s [ISV *chrom-* + *center, centre;* orig. formed as It *cromocentro*] **:** a densely staining nuclear body associated with the chromatin of certain cells — **chro·mo·centric** \¦==+\ *adj*
chro·mo·citronine R *n, usu cap* [*chrom-* + *citron* + *-ine*] **:** a mordant dye — see DYE table I (under *Mordant Yellow 26*)
chro·mo·collograph \¦==+\ *n* -s [*chrom-* + *collograph*, a kind of duplicating machine, fr. *coll-* + *-graph*] **:** CHROMOCOLLOTYPE — **chro·mo·collographic** \"+\ *adj* — **chromocollography** \"+\ *n* -ES
chro·mo·collotype \¦==+\ *n* -s [*chrom-* + *collotype*] **:** collotype in two or more colors — **chro·mo·collotypy** \"+\ *n* -ES
chro·mo·cyte \'==+,sīt\ *n* -s [ISV *chrom-* + *-cyte*] **:** a pigmented anatomical cell — called also *color cell*
chro·mo·gen \'==+,jen, -,jən\ *n* -s [ISV *chrom-* + *-gen*] **1** *biochem* **:** a precursor (as urobilinogen) of a pigment (as urobilin) **2 :** a compound containing a chromophore that is not itself a dye but is capable of becoming one on introduction of an auxochromic group into the molecule **3 :** a pigment-producing microorganism ⟨many bacteria are ~s⟩
chromogene \'==+,-\ *n* -s [ISV *chrom-* + *gene*] **:** GENE — used to distinguish the nuclear gene from the cytogene in an otherwise ambiguous context
chro·mo·genesis \¦==+\ *n* [NL, fr. *chrom-* + *genesis*] **:** color production (as by the metabolic activities of microorganisms, esp. bacteria and fungi)
[1]**chro·mo·gen·ic** \¦krōmə¦jenik\ *adj* [*chromogen* + *-ic*] **:** of or relating to a chromogen

²chromogenic \"\ *also* **chro·mo·ge·net·ic** \-jə¦ned·ik\ *or* **chro·mog·e·nous** \krō'mäjənəs\ *adj* [*chrom-* + *-genic, -genetic, -genous*] **:** producing color ⟨~ bacteria⟩

³chromogenic \¦krōmə¦jenik\ *adj* [*chromogene* + *-ic*] **:** of, relating to, or involving the action of chromogenes ⟨~ inheritance⟩ ⟨~ bacteria⟩

chro·mo·gram \'==+,gram\ *n* -s [*chrom-* + *-gram*] **1 :** a stereoscopic pair of positive images used in some processes of color photography **2 :** KROMOGRAM

chro·mo·graph \'==+,graf\ *n* -s [ISV *chrom-* + *-graph*] **1 :** CHROMOLITHOGRAPH **2 :** a compact device for making quick semiquantitative tests for one or more chemical elements — **chro·mo·graph·ic** \¦==¦grafik\ *adj*

chro·mo·iso·mer \¦==+\ *n* -s [*chrom-* + *isomer*] **:** a compound that is chromoisomeric with another or others

chro·mo·iso·mer·ic \¦==+\ *adj* **:** of, relating to, or exhibiting chromoisomerism

chro·mo·isom·er·ism \¦==+\ *n* -s **:** isomerism in which the isomers are of different colors — used esp. of cases in which the isomers are tautomeric

chro·mo·lipoid \¦==+\ *n* -s [*chrom-* + *lipoid*] **:** LIPOCHROME

chro·mo·lith \'==+,lith\ *n* -s [by shortening] **:** CHROMOLITHOGRAPH — **chro·mo·lith·ic** \¦==¦lithik\ *adj*

¹**chro·mo·lithograph** \¦==+\ *n* -s [back-formation fr. *chromolithography*] **:** a picture printed by chromolithography

²**chromolithograph** \"\ *vt* **:** to print or reproduce by chromolithography

chro·mo·lithographic \¦==+\ *adj* **:** of or relating to chromolithography

chro·mo·lithography \¦==+\ *n* -ES [F *chromolithographie*, fr. *chrom-* + *lithographie* lithography] **:** lithography adapted to printing in inks of various colors

chro·mo–luminarism *or* **chro·mo–luminism** \¦==+\ *n* -s *often cap C&L* [*chrom-* + *luminarism* or *luminism*] **:** NEO-IMPRESSIONISM

chro·mo–luminarist *or* **chro·mo–luminist** \¦==+\ *n* -s *often cap C&L* [*chrom-* + *luminarist* or *luminist*] **:** NEO-IMPRESSIONIST

¹**chro·mo·mere** \'==+,mi(ə)r\ *n* -s [ISV *chrom-* + *-mere*; orig. formed as F *chromomère* or G *chromomer*] *anat* **:** the highly refractile portion of a thrombocyte or blood platelet — compare HYALOMERE

²**chromomere** \"\ *n* -s **:** one of the visible enlargements of the chromonema at which nucleoproteins appear to be concentrated, by some held to be the physical seat of the genes and by others considered optical artifacts due to the coiled state of the chromonema — compare CHROMOSOME — **chro·mo·mer·ic** \¦==+¦merik, -mir-\ *adj*

chro·mom·e·ter \krō'mämәd·ә(r), krә-\ *n* -s [*chrom-* + *-meter*] **:** an apparatus for comparing the color of a substance (as a refined ore) with a standard esp. to determine the degree of purity or percentage of a constituent **:** COLORIMETER

chro·mone \'krō,mōn\ *n* -s [ISV *chrom-* + *-one*] **:** a colorless crystalline cyclic ketone $C_9H_6O_2$; 1,4-benzo-pyrone; *also* **:** a derivative (as flavone) of this ketone

chro·mo·ne·ma \,== *at* CHROMO- + 'nēmә\ *n, pl* **chromone·ma·ta** \-mәd·ә\ [NL, fr. *chrom-* + *-nema*] *biol* **:** the coiled threadlike core of a chromatid commonly regarded as the actual carrier of the genes **:** GENE-STRING — **chro·mo·ne·mal** \¦==¦nēmәl\ *or* **chro·mo·ne·mat·ic** \-nә¦mad·ik, -nē-\ *or* **chro·mo·ne·mic** \-¦nēmik\ *adj*

chromo paper *n* **:** a coated paper suitable for color printing

chro·mop·a·rous \(')krō¦mäpәrәs\ *adj* [*chrom-* + *-parous*] *bacteriol* **:** excreting pigment either soluble or insoluble in water — compare PARACHROMOPHOROUS

chro·mo·pexy \'== *at* CHROMO- + ,peksē\ *n* -ES [ISV *chrom-* + *-pexy*] **:** the capacity of certain living cells to take up and store dyes

¹**chro·mo·phil** \'==+,fil\ *or* **chro·mato·phil** \='==, '=== *at* CHROMATO- +\ *also* **chro·mo·phile** \"+,fīl\ *or* **chro·mato·phile** \='==, '=== *at* CHROMATO- +\ *or* **chro·mo·phil·ic** \¦==+¦filik\ *adj* [ISV *chrom-* or *chromat-* + *-phil, -phile, -philic*] **1** *biol* **:** staining readily **2 :** CHROMAFFIN

²**chromophil** \"\ *or* **chromophile** \"\ *or* **chro·mato·phil** *or* **chro·mato·phile** \(')=¦==, '=== *at* CHROMATO- + ,-\ *n* -s **:** a chromophil cell or substance

chromophily *var of* CHROMATOPHILIA

¹**chro·mo·phobe** \'== *at* CHROMO- + ,fōb\ *or* **chro·mo·pho·bic** \¦==¦fōbik *also* -äb-\ *adj* [ISV *chrom-* + *-phobe, -phobic*] *biol* **:** not readily absorbing stains **:** difficult to stain — **chro·mo·pho·by** \'==,fōbē, krō'mäfәbē\ *n* -ES

²**chromophobe** \"\ *n* -s **:** a chromophobe cell esp. in the pituitary body

chro·mo·phore \'==+,fō(ә)r\ *n* -s [ISV *chrom-* + *-phore*; orig. formed as G *chromophor*] **:** a functional group (as nitroso, nitro, azo, or the conjugated unsaturated grouping of quinone) that gives rise to color in a molecule and that with the assistance of an auxochrome (as a hydroxyl or amino group) produces a dye

chro·mo·phor·ic \¦==¦fōrik\ *adj* **:** color-bearing; *esp* **:** relating to a chromophore ⟨~ groups⟩ ⟨~ function⟩

chro·moph·o·rous \(')krō¦mäf(ә)rәs\ *adj* [*chrom-* + *-phorous*] *bacteriol* **:** containing pigment as an integral part of the protoplasm

chro·mo·phyll \'== *at* CHROMO- + ,fil\ *n* -s [ISV *chrom-* + *-phyll*] **:** a plant pigment (as chlorophyll)

chromoplasm *var of* CHROMATOPLASM

chro·mo·plast \'==+,plast\ *n* -s [ISV *chrom-* + *-plast*; orig. formed as G *chromoplastid*] **1 :** a colored plastid usu. not including chloroplasts **2 :** a chromatin nucleolus

chro·mo·plas·tid \¦==¦plastәd\ *n* -s [ISV *chrom-* + *-plastid*; orig. formed as G *chromoplastid*] **:** CHROMOPLAST 1

chro·mo·protein \¦==+\ *n* -s [*chrom-* + *protein*] **:** any of a class of compounds (as hemoglobin) of a protein with a metal-containing pigment (as heme) or with a carotenoid

chro·mo·scope \'==+,skōp\ *n* -s [ISV *chrom-* + *-scope*] **:** an optical instrument for combining colored images so as to produce a picture in natural colors — **chro·mo·scop·ic** \¦==¦skäpik\ *adj* — **chro·mos·co·py** \krō'mäskәpē\ *n* -ES

chro·mo·som·al \¦krōmә¦sōmәl\ *adj* **:** of or relating to chromosomes ⟨the geographic distribution of ~ prime types —*New York Times*⟩ — **chro·mo·som·al·ly** \-mәlē\ *adv*

chromosomal vesicle *n* **:** KARYOMERE

chro·mo·some \'krōmә,sōm\ *n* -s [ISV *chrom-* + *-some*; orig. formed as G *chromosom*] **:** one of the more or less rodlike chromatin-containing basophilic bodies constituting the genome and chiefly detectable in the mitotic or meiotic nucleus that are regarded as the seat of the genes, consist of one or more intimately associated chromatids functioning as a unit, and are relatively constant in number in the cells of any one kind of plant or animal — see SEX — **chro·mo·so·mic** \¦==¦sōmik\ *adj*

chromosome complement *n* **1 :** the entire group of chromosomes in a nucleus **2 :** the chromosomes received from one parent without regard to ploidy

chromosome number *n* **:** the number of chromosomes characteristic of a particular kind of plant or animal

chromosome set *n* **:** a group of chromosomes in a polyploid nucleus presumably constituting a haploid component derived from some diploid ancestor **:** GENOME

chro·mo·so·min \¦krōmә¦sōmәn\ *n* -s [*chromosome* + *-in*] **:** an acid protein rich in tryptophan isolated from fish sperm and regarded by some as a major component of the chromosomes

chro·mo·som·ol·o·gy \,==(,)sō'mälәjē\ *n* -ES [*chromosome* + *-o-* + *-logy*] **:** the branch of cytology devoted to study of the chromosomes

chro·mo·sphere \'==+,-\ *n* -s [*chrom-* + *sphere*] **:** the lower part of the atmosphere of the sun thousands of miles thick and composed predominantly of hydrogen gas that is responsible for its rosy color; *also* **:** a similar portion of the atmosphere of any star — **chro·mo·spheric** \¦==+\ *adj*

chro·mo·therapy \¦==+\ *n* -ES [*chrom-* + *therapy*] **:** treatment of disease by colored lights

chro·mo·trich·i·al \¦==+¦trikēәl\ *adj* [NL *chromotrichia* hair pigmentation (fr. *chrom-* + *-trichia*) + E *-al*] **:** concerned with or modifying hair color

chro·mo·trope \'==+,trōp\ *also* **chro·mo·trop** \-äp\ *n* -s *often cap* [ISV *chrom-* + *-trope*; orig. formed as G *chromotrop*] **:** any of several acid dyes — see DYE table I (under *Acid Red 29, Acid Violet 6* and *13*)

chro·mo·trop·ic \¦==+¦träpik\ *adj* **:** relating to or causing chromotropism

chromotropic acid *also* **chromotrope acid** *n* [ISV *chromotropic, chromotrope* (fr. *chrom-* + *-tropic, -trope*) + *acid*; orig. formed as G *chromotropsäure*] **:** a colorless crystalline acid $C_{10}H_4(OH)_2(SO_3H)_2$ used as a dye intermediate and as an analytical reagent

chro·mot·ro·pism \krō'mä·trә,pizәm\ *also* **chro·mot·ro·py** \-,pē\ *n, pl* **chromotropisms** *also* **chromotropies** **1 :** change of color esp. of certain salts known in differently colored modifications — compare CHROMOISOMERISM **2 :** the orientation of living organisms in relation to color stimuli — compare TROPISM

chro·mo·type \'== *at* CHROMO- + ,tīp\ *n* -s [*chrom-* + *type*] **:** a sheet printed in colors by any process (as chromolithography)

chro·mo·typ·ic \¦==¦tipik\ *adj* **:** CHROMOTYPOGRAPHIC

chro·mo·typographic \¦==+\ *adj* **:** used in or produced by chromotypography

chro·mo·typography \¦==+\ *n* [F or G *chromotypographie*, fr. *chrom-* + *typographie* typography] **:** the art or the process of printing in chromatic colors

chro·mo·typy \'==+,tīpē\ *n* -ES [ISV *chrom-* + *-typy*] CHROMOTYPOGRAPHY

chro·mous \'krōmәs\ *adj* [¹*chrome* + *-ous*] **:** of, relating to, or derived from chromium — used esp. of chemical compounds in which this element is bivalent; compare CHROMIC

chro·mo·xylograph \¦== *at* CHROMO- + \ *n* -s [*chrom-* + *xylograph*] **:** a print made by chromoxylography

chro·mo·xylography \¦==+\ *n* -ES [*chrom-* + *xylography*] **:** the art or process of printing in colors from wooden blocks

¹**-chro·my** \,krōmē\ *n comb form* -ES [Gk *chrōma* color + ISV *-y*; prob. orig. formed as G *-chromie* — more at CHROMATIC] **:** painting **:** coloring ⟨litho*chromy*⟩ ⟨stereo*chromy*⟩

²**-chromy** \"\ *n comb form* -ES [NL *-chromia*] **:** -CHROMIA

chro·myl \'krōmәl, -,mēl\ *n* -s [ISV *chrom-* + *-yl*] **:** the bivalent radical CrO_2 analogous to sulfuryl

chromyl chloride *n* **:** a red fuming toxic liquid compound CrO_2Cl_2 obtained by distilling a chromate or dichromate with a soluble chloride and concentrated sulfuric acid

chron- *or* **chrono-** *comb form* [Gk, fr. *chronos*] **:** time ⟨*chron*axie⟩ ⟨*chrono*gram⟩

chron *abbr* **1** chronicle **2** chronological; chronology

chro·nal \'krōnᵊl\ *adj* [*chron-* + *-al*] **:** of or relating to time

chron·anagram \(')krän+\ *n* -s [NL *chronanagramma*, fr. *chron-* + *anagramma* anagram — more at ANAGRAM] **:** an anagram of a chronogram

chro·nax·ie \'krō,naksē, 'krä-, ='==\ *also* **chro·nax·ia** \='=sēә\ *or* **chro·naxy** \'=,=sē, ='==\ *n* -s [F *chronaxie*, fr. *chron-* + Gk *axia* value, fr. *axios* worthy, weighing as much as — more at AXIOM] *physiol* **:** the minimum time required for excitation of an excitable structure (as a nerve cell) by a constant electric current of twice the threshold voltage — compare RHEOBASE

chro·nax·im·e·ter \,krō,nak'simәd·ә(r), ,krä-\ *n* [*chronaxie* + *-meter*] **:** a device for measuring chronaxie

chro·nax·i·met·ric \(¦)krō¦naksә¦me·trik, (¦)krä¦-\ *adj* [ISV *chronaxie* + *metric*] **:** of or relating to measurement of the duration of chronaxie — **chro·nax·i·me·tri·cal·ly** \(¦)=¦sә-¦me·trәk(ә)lē\ *adv*

chro·nax·im·e·try \,krō,nak'simә·trē, ,krä-\ *n* -ES [ISV, fr. *chronaxie* + *-metry*] **:** the measurement of chronaxie

¹**chron·ic** \'kränik, -nēk\ *adj* [F *chronique*, fr. L *chronicus*, fr. Gk *chronikos* of time, fr. *chronos* time + *-ikos* -ic] **1 a :** marked by long duration, by frequent recurrence over a long time, and often by slowly progressing seriousness **:** not acute ⟨~ indigestion⟩ ⟨her hallucinations became ~⟩ **b :** suffering from a disease or ailment of long duration or frequent recurrence ⟨~ arthritic⟩ ⟨~ sufferers from asthma⟩ **2 a :** marked by long continuation or frequent recurrence **:** always present or encountered **:** long-lasting **:** unending; *esp* **:** constantly vexing, weakening, or troubling ⟨war between states and civil war within a nation — the ~ state of affairs when Hobbes lived —John Dewey⟩ ⟨the ~ financial predicament of American colleges and universities — *Nation*⟩ **b :** given to steady or frequently repeated behaving or acting **:** given to being habitually **:** HABITUAL, ACCUSTOMED ⟨the ~ amateur of causes — always eager, always profoundly convinced . . . never quite expert — James Gray⟩ ⟨a ~ grumbler⟩ ⟨a ~ joiner⟩ **3** *of a pathologic process* **:** characterized by a slow progressive course of indefinite duration — used esp. of degenerative invasive diseases, some infections, psychoses, inflammations, and the carrier state ⟨~ heart disease⟩ ⟨~ arthritis⟩ ⟨~ tuberculosis⟩ ⟨~ carrier⟩ — compare ACUTE 5a (2) **4** *slang Brit* **:** INTENSE, SEVERE, DISAGREEABLE ⟨she started howling and carrying on . . . something ~ —Richard Llewellyn⟩ **syn** see INVETERATE

²**chronic** \"\ *n* -s **:** one that suffers from a chronic disease

chron·i·cal \'kränәkәl, -nēk-\ *adj* [F *chronique* + E *-al*] **:** CHRONIC ⟨~ dysentery⟩

chronic alcoholism *n* **:** a symptom or disease that involves complex psychologic factors characterized by compulsive drinking or the inability to stop drinking once started and that results if long continued in neurologic, psychiatric, and nutritional disturbances — compare ACUTE ALCOHOLISM

chron·i·cal·ly \'kränәk(ә)lē, -nēk-, -li\ *adv* **:** in a chronic manner **:** CONTINUALLY, REPEATEDLY

chro·nic·i·ty \krä'nisәd·ē\ *n* -ES [¹*chronic* + *-ity*] **:** the quality or state of being chronic ⟨~ of a disease⟩

¹**chron·i·cle** \'kränәkәl, -nēk-\ *n* -s [ME *cronicle*, fr. AF, alter. (prob. influenced by such words as OF *article*) of OF *chronique*, fr. L *chronica*, fr. Gk *chronika*, fr. neut. pl. of *chronikos*, adj.] **:** an esp. historical account of facts or events that are arranged in order of time and usu. continuous and detailed but without analysis or interpretation; *broadly* **:** HISTORY, NARRATIVE

²**chronicle** \"\ *vt* **chronicled; chronicled; chronicling** \-k(ә)liŋ\ **chronicles** [ME *croniclen*, fr. *cronicle*, n.] **1 :** to record or present in or as if in a chronicle ⟨the greater French novelists from Stendhal to Proust ~ the rise, the regime, and the decay of the upper bourgeoisie in France —T.S.Eliot⟩ **2 :** LIST, DESCRIBE ⟨it is impossible to ~ all the splendors and humbler delights to be found in these volumes —*Times Lit. Supp.*⟩

chronicle drama *n* **:** CHRONICLE PLAY; *collectively* **:** CHRONICLE PLAYS

chronicle play *or* **chronicle history** *n* **:** a play with a theme from history consisting usu. of rather loosely connected episodes chronologically arranged

chron·i·cler \-k(ә)lә(r)\ *n* -s [ME *cronicler*, fr. *croniclen* + *-er*] **:** a writer or compiler of a chronicle ⟨a historian without philosophy is but a ~ —John Mason Brown⟩ ⟨disillusioned ~ of social disintegration —Carlos Baker⟩ ⟨successful ~ of the upper middle class —Taliaferro Boatwright⟩

chro·nique scan·da·leuse \,krōnēkskäⁿdälœ̄z\ *n, pl* **chroniques scandaleuses** \"\ [F, lit., scandalous story] **:** a history, biography, or report that stresses scandalous details

chron·ist \'kränәst\ *n* -s [*chron-* + *-ist*] **1 :** CHRONOLOGIST **2 :** CHRONICLER

chrono- *in pronunciations below*, ¦== = ¦kränә *or* ¦krōnә *or* -nō\ — see CHRON-

chrono·cinematography \¦==+\ *n* -ES [blend of *chronography* and *cinematography*] **:** chronography (sense 2) by means of motion-picture photography

chrono·cline \'==+,-\ *n* -s [*chron-* + *cline*] **:** a cline manifested by successive changes in the members of a natural group (as a species) in successive fossiliferous strata

chrono·ge·neous \¦==+¦jēnyәs, -nēәs\ *adj* [*chron-* + *-geneous* (as in *homogeneous*)] *psychol* **:** appearing at a given chronological age — compare PHASOGENEOUS

chrono·genesis \,==+\ *n, pl* **chronogeneses** [NL, fr. *chron-* + *-genesis*] *biol* **:** the history of the development of a group of organisms

chrono·genetic \¦==+\ *adj* [*chron-* + *-genetic*] **:** of or relating to chronogenesis

chron·o·gram \'==+,gram\ *n* -s [*chron-* + *-gram*] **1 :** an inscription, sentence, or phrase in which certain numeral letters usu. made specially conspicuous express a particular date or epoch on being added together (as in the motto of a medal struck by Gustavus Adolphus in 1632 — ChrIstVs DVX; ergo trIVMphVs — the capitals of which, added as numerals, make 1632) **2 :** the record made by a chronograph

chron·o·gram·mat·ic \¦==+grә¦mad·ik\ *or* **chron·o·gram·mat·i·cal** \-d·әkәl\ *adj* [fr. *chronogram*, after such pairs as E *anagram: anagrammatic, anagrammatical*] **:** containing or bearing a chronogram — **chron·o·gram·mat·i·cal·ly** \-d·әk(ә)lē\ *adv*

chron·o·gram·ma·tist \,==+'gramәd·әst\ *n* -s [fr. *chronogram*, after such pairs as E *anagram: anagrammatist*] **:** a writer or maker of chronograms

chron·o·gram·mic \¦==+¦gramik\ *adj* [*chronogram* + *-ic*] **:** CHRONOGRAMMATIC

¹**chron·o·graph** \'==+,graf\ *n* -s [*chron-* + *-graph*] **:** an instrument for measuring and recording time: **a :** an instrument consisting of a recording apparatus (as a stylus and revolving drum) connected with a clock or chronometer and used for recording the precise clock time of astronomical and other occurrences **b :** a watch having in addition to conventional hour, minute, and second hands a center sweep-second hand that can be stopped, started, or reset to zero and that indicates intervals of time as small as ⅕ second **c :** an instrument used for measuring the time of flight of projectiles — **chron·o·graph·ic** \¦==¦grafik\ *adj* — **chron·o·graph·i·cal·ly** \-fәk(ә)lē\ *adv*

²**chronograph** \"\ *vt* -ED/-ING/-S **:** to measure (velocity) by means of a chronograph (sense c)

chro·nog·ra·pher \krә'nägrәfә(r)\ *n* -s [*chron-* + *-grapher*] *obs* **:** CHRONOLOGIST, CHRONICLER

chro·nog·ra·phy \-fē\ *n* -ES [MF *chronographie*, fr. Gk *chronographia*, fr. *chron-* + *-graphia* -graphy] **1** *obs* **:** a record of past time **:** HISTORY **2 :** the measurement by graphic methods of intervals of time (as in studying the successive phases of a rapid and complex motion) **:** the use of the chronograph

chrono·iso·ther·mal \¦== *at* CHRONO- +\ *adj* [*chron-* + *isothermal*] *meteorol* **:** relating to a diagram exhibiting the course of the mean monthly temperature of a place for each hour of the day

chro·nol·o·ger \krә'nälәjә(r)\ *n* -s [NL *chronologia* + E *-er*] **:** CHRONOLOGIST

chron·o·log·ic \¦krän³l¦äjik, -ōn-, -jēk\ *adj* **:** of or relating to chronology **:** CHRONOLOGICAL ⟨the first principle of ~ reconstruction —Edward Sapir⟩

chron·o·log·i·cal \-jәkәl, -ēk-\ *adj* **:** relating to or dealing with chronology **:** arranged in order of time ⟨~ tables⟩ **:** reckoned in units of time ⟨~ age⟩ — **chron·o·log·i·cal·ly** \-jәk(ә)lē, -ēk-, -li\ *adv*

chro·nol·o·gist \krә'nälәjәst\ *n* -s [F *chronologiste*, fr. NL *chronologista*, fr. *chronologia* + *-ista* -ist] **:** a person who investigates dates and records of events **:** one expert in chronology

chro·nol·o·gize \-,jīz\ *vt* -ED/-ING/-S [*chronology* + *-ize*] **:** to arrange chronologically **:** establish the order in time of (as events, documents)

chro·nol·o·gy \krә'nälәjē, krō-, krä-\ *n* -ES [NL *chronologia*, fr. *chron-* + *-logia* -logy] **1 :** the science that treats of measuring or computing time by regular divisions or periods and that assigns to events or transactions their proper dates **2 :** a chronological table or list **3 :** an arrangement (as of data, events) in the order of time of occurrence or appearance **:** chronological relation ⟨his ~ of the facts is confused⟩; *specif* **:** the classification of archaeological sites or prehistoric periods of culture according to their time relationship by stratigraphy, typology, or actual dating

chron·o·man·cy \'== *at* CHRONO- + ,man(t)sē\ *n* -ES [*chron-* + *-mancy*] **:** divination to determine the favorable time for action formerly practiced esp. in China

chron·o·man·tic \¦==+¦mantik\ *adj* [fr. *chronomancy*, after such pairs as E *necromancy: necromantic*] **:** of or relating to chronomancy

chro·nom·e·ter \krә'nämәd·ә(r), krō-,krä-, -әtә(r)\ *n* -s [*chron-* + *-meter*] **:** an instrument for measuring time: **a :** a portable timepiece usu. having a detent escapement and compensation balance and beating half seconds for keeping time where great accuracy is essential (as in determining longitude at sea) — called also *box chronometer, marine chronometer* **b :** a watch of great esp. officially certified accuracy **c** *obs* **:** METRONOME

chron·o·met·ric \¦== *at* CHRONO- + ¦me·trik\ *or* **chron·o·met·ri·cal** \-trәkәl, -ēk-\ *adj* [*chron-* + *-metric*] **:** relating to a chronometer or chronometry **:** measured by a chronometer — **chron·o·met·ri·cal·ly** \-trәk(ә)lē, -ēk-, -li\ *adv*

chro·nom·e·try \krә'nämә·trē, krō-,krä-\ *n* -ES [*chron-* + *-metry*] **:** the science of measuring time **:** the measuring of time by periods or divisions (as by a chronometer or chronograph)

chro·non·o·my \-'nänәmē\ *n* -ES [*chron-* + *-nomy*] **:** method of reckoning and measuring time

chron·o·pher \'== *at* CHRONO- + fә(r)\ *n* -s [*chron-* + *-pher*] **:** an instrument signaling the correct time to distant points by electricity

chrono·photograph \¦== +\ *n* -s [*chron-* + *photograph*; part trans. of F *chronophotographie*] **:** one of a set or a set of photographs of a moving object taken to record and exhibit successive phases of the motion — **chrono·photographic** \" +\ *adj* — **chrono·photography** \" +\ *n* -ES

chron·o·scope \'== + ,skōp\ *n* -s [*chron-* + *-scope*] **:** an instrument for the precise measurement of small time intervals (as by means of a falling rod, released pendulum, or an electronic device) — **chron·o·scop·ic** \¦==¦skäpik\ *adj* — **chron·o·scop·i·cal·ly** \-pәk(ә)lē\ *adv*

chro·nos·co·py \krә'näskәpē\ *n* -ES [F *chronoscopie*, fr. *chron-* + *-scopie* scopy] **:** the study of very brief intervals of time by means of a chronoscope

chrono·se·mic \¦== *at* CHRONO- + ¦sēmik\ *adj* [*chron-* + Gk *sēma* sign + E *-ic* — more at SEMANTICS] **:** employing intervals of time with a fixed significance (as in a system of signaling) by exposing visual objects or sounding audible signals for selected intervals of time

chrono·thermal \¦== *at* CHRONO- +\ *adj* [*chron-* + *thermal*] **:** relating to both time and temperature ⟨~ equation⟩

chrono·thermometer \¦== +\ *n* [*chron-* + *thermometer*] **:** a timepiece so constructed as to exaggerate the effect of changes of temperature upon its rate and used to indicate mean temperature

chron·o·tron \'== + ·,trän\ *n* -s [*chron-* + *-tron*] **:** a device for measuring very small intervals of time by observing on an indicator the distance between electric pulses

chron·o·trop·ic \¦== + ¦träpik\ *adj* [*chron-* + *-tropic*] **:** influencing the rate esp. of the heartbeat — used esp. of the inhibitory and accelerator cardiac nerves and of certain drugs

chro·not·ro·pism \krә'nä·trә,pizәm\ *n* -s [*chron-* + *-tropism*] **:** interference with the rate of the heartbeat

-chro·nous \krәnәs\ *adj comb form* [Gk *-chronos*, fr. *chronos* time] **:** of (such) a time or period ⟨homeo*chronous*⟩ ⟨iso*chronous*⟩

chro·o·coc·ca·ce·ae \,krōә,kä'kāsē,ē\ *n pl, cap* [NL, fr. *Chroococcus*, type genus + *-aceae*] **:** a family of usu. colonial, ensheathed marine or freshwater blue-green algae that reproduce by colonial fragmentation and simple cell division and are usu. isolated in a distinct order — see GLOEOCAPSA — **chro·o·coc·ca·ceous** *adj* \¦==,=¦kāshәs\ — **chro·o·coc·coid** \¦==¦kä,kōid\ *adj*

chro·o·coc·ca·les \,krōә,kä'kā(,)lēz\ *n pl, cap* [NL, fr. *Chroococcus* + *-ales*] **:** an order of Myxophyceae coextensive with the family Chroococcaceae

chro·o·coc·cus \¦krōә¦käkәs\ *n, cap* [NL, fr. Gk *chrōs* color + NL *-o-* + *-coccus*] **:** the type genus of Chroococcaceae

-chro·ous \krәwәs\ *adj comb form* [Gk *-chroos*, fr. *chrōs* skin, color — more at CHROMATIC] **:** -colored ⟨iso*chroous*⟩

chrot·ta \'kräd·ә\ *n* -s [LL *crotta, chrotta*, of Celt origin; akin to W *crwth* fiddle, MIr *crott* harp — more at CROWD] **1 :** CRWTH **2 :** a small medieval harp

chrs *abbr* chambers

chrys- *or* **chryso-** *comb form* [Gk, fr. *chrysos* gold — more at CHRYSALIS] **:** gold **:** golden **:** yellow ⟨*chrys*amine⟩ ⟨*chryso*phyll⟩

chrys·al *also* **crys·al** \'krisәl\ *n* -s [origin unknown] **:** a transverse line of crushed fibers in the belly of an archery bow beginning as a pinch — called also *fret*

¹**chrys·a·lid** \'krisәlәd\ *n* -s [L *chrysallid-, chrysallis*] **:** CHRYSALIS

²**chrysalid** \"\ *adj* **:** relating to or like a chrysalis — **chrys·al·i·dal** \krә'salәdᵊl\ *adj* — **chrys·a·lid·i·an** \¦krisә¦lidēәn\ *adj*

chrys·a·lis \ˈkrisələs\ *n, pl* **chry·sal·i·des** \krəˈsalə,dēz\ *or* **chrysalises** \ˈkrisələsəz\ [L *chrysallis* gold-colored pupa of butterflies, fr. Gk, fr. *chrysos* gold, of Sem origin; akin to Heb *ḥārūṣ* gold, Assyr-Bab *khurāṣu*] **1 :** the pupa of insects (as of butterflies) that pass the pupal stage in a quiescent and helpless condition without taking food, being enclosed in a more or less firm integument; *also* **:** the enclosing integument or case of a pupa **2 :** a protecting covering **:** a sheltered state or stage of being or growth

chrysalis 1

chrys·a·loid \ˈkrisə,lȯid\ *adj* [*chrysalis* + *-oid*] **:** like a chrysalis

chrys·amine G \ˈkrisə,mēn-\ *n, usu cap C* [ISV *chrys-* + *amine*] **:** a direct dye — see DYE table I (under *Direct Yellow 1*)

chrys·amphora \krəs + \ [NL, fr. *chrys-* + *amphora*] *syn of* DARLINGTONIA

chrys·aniline \krəs + \ *n* -s [ISV *chrys-* + *aniline;* orig. formed as G *chrysanilin*] **:** a yellow crystalline base $C_{19}H_{15}N_3$ obtained as a by-product in the manufacture of fuchsine — see PHOSPHINE

chrys·anisic acid \ˌkris + . . . -\ *n* [ISV *chrys-* + *anisic;* orig. formed as F *chrysanisique*] **:** a golden yellow crystalline acid $C_6H_2(NO_2)_2(NH_2)CO_2H$ obtained indirectly from anisic acid and used in preparing some dyes

chry·san·the·min \krəˈsan(t)thəmən *also* kriˈz-\ *n* -s [ISV *chrysanthem-* (fr. NL *Chrysanthemum*) + *-in;* orig. formed in G] **:** an anthocyanin pigment $C_{21}H_{20}O_{11}$ obtained from a chrysanthemum (*Chrysanthemum indicum*) and other plants; the 3-glucoside of cyanidin

chry·san·the·mum \krəˈsan(t)thəməm, -aan- *also* kriˈz-\ *n* [L, fr. Gk *chrysanthemon,* fr. *chrys-* + *anthemon* flower, fr. *anthos* — more at ANTHOLOGY] **1** -s **a :** CORN MARIGOLD **b :** any of various cultivated plants of the genus *Chrysanthemum; also* **:** one of the large double flower heads **2** [NL, fr. L] **a** *cap* **:** a large genus of perennial herbs (family Compositae) that are widely distributed in the Old World, include many plants derived chiefly from two species (*C. morrifolium* and *C. indicum*) which are prob. Asiatic though known only in cultivation and cultivated for their showy often very double and brightly colored flower heads, others that are pernicious weeds, and still others that are of economic importance as sources of medicinals and insecticides — see MARGUERITE, PYRETHRUM **b** -s **:** any plant or flower of the genus *Chrysanthemum* **3** -s **:** a chrysanthemum flower in a conventionalized form with 16 complete rays used as the chief badge of the Japanese imperial family — called also *kikumon;* compare MON **4** -s **:** a dark to deep red that is yellower and slightly lighter than garnet red — called also *Turkish-crescent red*

chrysanthemum 3

chrysanthemum-dicarboxylic acid *n* **:** an acid $C_{10}H_{14}O_4$ derived from chrysanthemumic acid that occurs in the form of esters in pyrethrum flowers — compare PYRETHRIN

chrysanthemum dog *n* **:** TIBETAN TERRIER

chrysanthemum eelworm *or* **chrysanthemum leaf nematode** *n* **:** a plant-parasitic nematode worm (*Aphelenchoides ritzema-bosi*) of the family Aphelenchidae that damages the leaves and buds of chrysanthemums

chrysanthemum gall midge *or* **chrysanthemum midge** *also* **chrysanthemum gall fly** *n* **:** a small orange fly (*Diarthronomyia chrysanthemi*) forming galls on the flowers and leaves of chrysanthemums esp. in greenhouses

chry·san·the·mum·ic acid \(ˌ)=ˌ==ˌməmik-\ *n* [NL *Chrysanthemum* + E *-ic*] **:** an acid $C_9H_{15}COOH$ that occurs in the form of esters in pyrethrum flowers — called also *chrysanthemummonocarboxylic acid;* compare PYRETHRIN

chrysanthemum rust *n* **:** a rust of chrysanthemums caused by a fungus (*Puccinia chrysanthemi*)

chrys·a·ro·bin \ˌkrisəˈrōbən\ *n* -s [*chrys-* + *araroba* (Goa powder) + *-in*] **1 :** a brownish to orange-yellow powder that is a mixture of neutral principles obtained from Goa powder and is used in the treatment of skin diseases **2 :** a yellow crystalline compound $C_{15}H_{12}O_3$

chrys·a·zin \ˈkrisəzən\ *n* -s [ISV *chrysammic* + *alizarin*] **:** an orange or reddish brown compound $C_{14}H_6O_2(OH)_2$ used as a dye intermediate; 1,8-dihydroxy-anthraquinone

chrys·elephantine \(ˌ)kris + \ *adj* [Gk *chryselephantinos,* fr. *chrys-* + *elephantinos* made of ivory, fr. *elephant-, elephas* ivory, elephant] **:** composed of or adorned with gold and ivory ⟨she might have been ~ — made, that is, like some old Greek statues, out of ivory and gold —G.K.Chesterton⟩

chrys·e·mys \ˈkrisəməs\ *n, cap* [NL, fr. *chrys-* + *Emys*] **:** a genus of small brightly marked American freshwater turtles or terrapins — see PAINTED TURTLE

chry·sene \ˈkrī,sēn\ *n* -s [F *chrysène,* fr. *chrys-* + *-ène* -ene] **:** a white crystalline hydrocarbon $C_{18}H_{12}$ with violet fluorescence obtained from coal-tar fractions and from petroleum by cracking and prepared from indene by catalytic dehydrogenation; 1,2-benzo-phenanthrene

chrys·i·del·la \ˌkrisəˈdelə\ *n, cap* [NL, fr. Gk *chrysid-, chrysis* vessel of gold (fr. *chrysos* gold) + NL *-ella* — more at CHRYSALIS] **:** a genus of symbiotic plantlike flagellates (order Cryptomonadina) with yellow chromatophores that are often considered algae and are the zooxanthellae of the protoplasm of certain higher protozoans (as many radiolarians)

chry·sid·i·dae \krəˈsidə,dē, krīˈ-\ *n pl, cap* [NL, fr. *Chrysid-, Chrysis,* type genus + *-idae*] **:** a family comprising brilliantly colored wasps of medium size with a shining metallic luster and with a few related forms commonly constituting a superfamily of the hymenopterous suborder Clistogastra — see CUCKOO WASP

chry·sin \ˈkrīsᵊn\ *n* -s [ISV *chrys-* + *-in;* orig. formed in G] **:** a yellow crystalline flavone pigment $C_{15}H_{10}O_4$ found esp. in the buds of species of poplar; 5,7-dihydroxy-flavone

chry·sis \ˈkrīsəs, -ris-\ *n, cap* [NL, fr. Gk *chrysid-, chrysis* vessel of gold, fr. *chrysos* gold — more at CHRYSALIS] **:** the type genus of Chrysididae

chryso- *—in pronunciations below,* ˈ== = ˈkrisə *or* -sō\ — see CHRYS-

chrys·o·bal·a·nus \ˌ== + ˈbalənəs\ *n, cap* [NL, fr. *chrys-* + L *balanus* acorn, fr. Gk *balanos* — more at GLAND] **:** a small genus of tropical shrubs or trees (family Rosaceae) having a pulpy drupe with a ridged stone — see COCO PLUM

chryso·beryl \ˈ== + ,-\ *n* [L *chrysoberyllus,* fr. Gk *chrysobēryllos,* fr. *chrys-* + *bēryllos* beryl] **1** *obs* **:** beryl that has a yellow tinge **2** [G *krisoberil, chrysoberyll,* fr. L *chrysoberyllus*] **:** a hard mineral $BeAl_2O_4$ usu. yellow or pale green consisting of beryllium aluminum oxide with a small amount of iron and occurring in tabular orthorhombic crystals that when transparent are used as gems — see ALEXANDRITE, CAT'S-EYE

chryso·bull \ˈ== + ,bu̇l\ *n* [ML *chrysobulium,* MGk *chrysoboullon,* fr. ML & MGk *chrys-* + ML *-bulium,* MGk *-boullon* (respectively alter. & modif. of ML *bulla* seal, bull) — more at BULL] **1 :** a pendent seal made of gold — compare BULLA 2 **2 :** a document issued under a chrysobull

chrys·o·cap·sa·les \ˌ==,kapˈsā(,)lēz\ *n pl, cap* [NL, fr. *Chrysocapsa,* type genus (fr. *chrys-* + L *capsa* box) + *-ales* — more at CASE] **:** an order of yellow-green algae (class Chrysophyceae) having nonmotile vegetative cells in palmelloid colonies within a gelatinous matrix

chryso·car·pous \ˌ== + ˈkärpəs\ *adj* [L *chrysocarpus,* fr. Gk *chrysokarpos,* fr. *chrys-* + *-karpos* -carpous] **:** having or bearing yellow fruits

chrys·o·chlore \ˌ== + ,klō(ə)r\ *n* -s [NL *Chrysochloris*] **:** a mole of the genus *Chrysochloris*

chrys·o·chlo·ris \ˌ== ˈklōrəs\ *n, cap* [NL, fr. *chrys-* + *-chloris* (modif. of Gk *chlōros* greenish yellow) — more at YELLOW] **:** a genus (the type of the family Chrysochloridae) of African golden moles

chrys·o·chlo·rous \ˌ== + ˈklōrəs\ *adj* [*chrys-* + Gk *chlōros* greenish yellow] **:** of the color golden green

chrys·o·col·la \ˌ== + ˈkälə\ *n* -s [L, fr. Gk *chrysokolla,* fr. *chrys-* + *kolla* glue — more at PROTOCOL] **1 :** a mineral $CuSiO_3.2H_2O$ consisting of a hydrous silicate of copper occurring massive and of a blue to green color **2 :** MALACHITE GREEN

chryso·er·i·ol \ˌ== + ˈerē,ōl, -,ōl\ *n* -s [*chrys-* + NL *Eriodictyon* + E *-ol*] **:** a yellow crystalline flavone pigment $C_{16}H_{12}O_6$ found in the leaves of yerba santa

chrys·o·gen \ˈ== + ,jen, -jən\ *n* -s [ISV *chrys-* + *-gen;* orig. formed in G] **:** NAPHTHACENE

chrys·o·graph \ˈ== + ,graf\ *vt* [Gk *chrysographia* writing with gold letters, fr. *chrys-* + *-graphia* -graphy] **:** to write in letters of gold

chry·sog·ra·phy \krəˈsägrəfē\ *n* -ES [Gk *chrysographia*] **:** writing executed in gold letters

chry·so·idine \krəˈsōədən, -,dēn\ *n* -s [ISV *chrysoid-* (fr. Gk *chrysoeidēs* like gold, fr. *chrys-* + *-oeidēs* -oid) + *-ine;* orig. formed as G *chrysoidin*] **1 :** a yellow crystalline base $C_6H_5N{=}NC_6H_3(NH_2)_2$ made from diazotized aniline and meta-phenylenediamine — see DYE table I (under *Solvent Orange 3*) **2** *usu cap* **a :** the reddish brown crystalline monohydrochloride of chrysoidine base used chiefly for dyeing leather and paper and as a biological stain — called also *Chrysoidine G, Chrysoidine Y;* see DYE table I (under *Basic Orange 2*) **b :** any of certain other basic azo dyes — see DYE table I (under *Basic Orange 1*)

chry·sol·i·na \krəˈsälənə\ *n, cap* [NL, modif. of Gk *chrysolinon* gold thread, fr. *chrys-* + *linon* cord, thread, flax — more at LINEN] **:** a genus of small leaf-eating beetles (family Chrysomelidae) that have been extensively used in biological control of Klamath weed and other species of *Hypericum*

chrys·o·lite \ˈ== *at* CHRYSO- + ,līt\ *n* -s [ME *crisolite,* fr. OF *crisolite,* fr. L *chrysolithos,* fr. Gk *chrysolithos,* fr. *chrys-* + *-lithos* -lite] **1 :** any of several yellow or greenish gems (as chrysoberyl) — not now used technically **2 :** OLIVINE; *specif* **:** olivine in which the ratio of magnesium to total magnesium plus iron is between 0.90 and 0.70 — **chrys·o·lit·ic** \ˌ==ˈlid·ik\ *adj*

chrysolite green *n* **:** a moderate yellow green that is lighter, stronger, and slightly yellower than average moss green, yellower and lighter than average pea green, and yellower, lighter, and slightly stronger than spinach green

chry·sol·o·phus \krəˈsäləfəs\ *n, cap* [NL, fr. Gk *chrysolophos* golden crested, fr. *chrys-* + *lophos* nape, crest] **:** the genus consisting of the golden pheasant and Lady Amherst's pheasant

chrysom *or* **chrysome** *var of* CHRISOM

¹chrys·o·mel·id \ˌ== *at* CHRYSO- + ˈmeləd, -ēl-\ *adj* [NL *Chrysomelidae*] **:** of or relating to the Chrysomelidae

²chrysomelid \"\ *n* -s **:** one of the Chrysomelidae

chrys·o·mel·i·dae \ˌ== + ˈmelə,dē\ *n pl, cap* [NL, fr. *Chrysomela,* type genus (modif. of Gk *chrysomēlon* quince, fr. *chrys-* + *mēlon* apple, tree-fruit, influenced in meaning by Gk *chrysomēlolonthion* little golden cockchafer, fr. *chrys-* + *mēlolonthē* cockchafer + dim. suff. *-ion*) + *-idae*] **:** a large family of small usu. oval or rounded and often smooth, shining and brightly colored beetles comprising the leaf beetles having small heads, short antennae, and inconspicuous mouthparts and feeding on leaves both as larvae and adults, some (as the cucumber beetles and the Colorado potato beetle) being serious pests of cultivated plants

¹chry·som·o·nad \krəˈsämə,nad\ *also* **chrys·o·mon·a·dine** \ˌkrisōˌmänəˌdīn\ *adj* [NL *Chrysomonad-, Chrysomonas* & *Chrysomonadina*] **:** of or relating to the Chrysomonadina

²chrysomonad \"\ *also* **chrysomonadine** \"\ *n* -s **:** a flagellate of the order Chrysomonadina

chrys·o·mon·a·da·les \ˌkrisō,mänəˈdā(,)lēz\ *n pl, cap* [NL, fr. *Chrysomonad-, Chrysomonas,* genus of algae (fr. *chrys-* + *-monas*) + *-ales*] **:** the Chrysomonadina regarded as an order of yellow-green algae

chrys·o·mo·nad·i·da \-məˈnadədə\ [NL, fr. *Chrysomonad-, Chrysomonas* + *-ida*] *syn of* CHRYSOMONADINA

chrys·o·mon·a·di·na \-,mänəˈdīnə, -ēnə\ *n pl, cap* [NL, fr. *Chrysomonad-, Chrysomonas* + *-ina*] **:** an order of minute plastic often ameboid plantlike flagellates usu. with yellow or brown chromatophores, solitary or forming palmella colonies, and commonly producing calcareous or siliceous skeletons that is treated by botanists as an order of the class Chrysophyceae — see COCCOLITHOPHORIDAE, SILICOFLAGELLATA

chrys·o·mya \ˌ==ˈmīə\ *n, cap* [NL, fr. *chrys-* + *-mya*] **:** the genus of blowflies including the Old World screwworms

¹chrys·o·my·ia \-ˈmī(y)ə\ [NL, fr. *chrys-* + *-myia*] *syn of* CHRYSOMYA

²chrysomyia \"\ [NL, fr. *chrys-* + *-myia*] *syn of* CALLITROGA

chrys·opal \kriˈsōpəl\ *n* [F *chrysopale,* fr. *chrys-* + *opale* opal] **1 :** CHRYSOBERYL **2 :** opalescent chrysolite

chrys·o·phan·ic acid \ˌ== *at* CHRYSO- + ˈfanik\ *n* [*chrysophanic* ISV *chrysophan-* (fr. Gk *chrysophanēs* shining like gold, fr. *chrys-* + *-phanēs* shining) + *-ic* — more at -PHANE] **:** a yellow crystalline phenol $C_{15}H_{10}O_4$ obtained from rhubarb, senna leaves, and chrysarobin; 1, 8-dihydroxy-3-methylanthraquinone

chry·soph·a·nol \krəˈsäfə,nōl, -ōl\ *n* -s [ISV *chrysophanic* + *-ol*] **:** CHRYSOPHANIC ACID

chry·soph·e·nine \krəˈsäfə,nēn, -nən\ *n* -s *often cap* [ISV *chrys-* + *phenine*] **:** a direct disazo stilbene dye that dyes cotton and viscose rayon yellow — called also *Chrysophenine G;* see DYE table I (under *Direct Yellow 12*)

chry·soph·i·list \krəˈsäfələst\ *or* **chry·soph·i·lite** \-ə,līt\ *n* -s [LGk *chrysophilos* gold-loving (fr. Gk *chrys-* + *-philos* -phile) + E *-ist* or *-ite*] **:** a lover of gold

chrys·o·phlyc·tis \ˌ== *at* CHRYSO- + ˈfliktəs\ [NL, fr. *chrys-* + Gk *phlyktis* blister; akin to L *fluere* to flow — more at FLUID] *syn of* SYNCHYTRIUM

chrys·o·phy·ce·ae \ˌ== + ˈfīsē,ē\ *n pl, cap* [NL, fr. *chrys-* + *-phyceae*] **:** a class of the yellow-green algae (division Chrysophyta) having cells solitary or in colonies of definite form, with few yellow or golden brown chromatophores in each cell, reserves occurring as fats and leucosin but not as starch, and motile cells when present having the flagella at their anterior end and more or less equal in length

chrys·o·phyll \ˈ== + ,fil\ *n* -s [*chrys-* + *-phyll*] **:** a yellow coloring matter in plants that is prob. a decomposition product of chlorophyll — compare XANTHOPHYLL

chrys·o·phyl·lum \ˌ== + ˈfiləm\ *n, cap* [NL, fr. *chrys-* + *-phyllum*] **:** a large genus of tropical American trees (family Sapotaceae) having the leaves oblong and silky golden beneath and the flowers small and clustered chiefly in the leaf axils

chry·soph·y·ta \krəˈsäfəd·ə\ *n pl, cap* [NL, fr. *chrys-* + *-phyta*] **:** a division or other category of lower plants that comprises algae with pigments localized in yellowish green to golden brown chromatophores and usu. with a cell wall made up of overlapping halves and that includes the classes Xanthophyceae, Chrysophyceae, and Bacillariophyceae

¹chry·so·pid \krəˈsōpəd\ *adj* [NL *Chrysopidae*] **:** of or relating to the Chrysopidae

²chrysopid \"\ *n* -s **:** a chrysopid fly **:** GOLDENEYE, STINK FLY

chry·so·pi·dae \krəˈsōpə,dē\ *n pl, cap* [NL, fr. *Chrysopa,* type genus (fr. *chrys-* + *-opa,* fr. Gk *ōp-, ōps* face) + *-idae*] **:** a family of pale green golden-eyed unpleasant-smelling lacewing flies having carnivorous larvae called aphis lions

chrys·o·prase \ˈkrisə,prāz\ *n* -s [alter. (influenced by F *chrysoprase*) of ME *crisopace,* fr. OF *crisopace, crisoprasse,* fr. L *chrysoprasus,* fr. Gk *chrysoprasos,* fr. *chrys-* + *prasos* (fr. *prason* leek) — more at PRASINE] **1 :** an apple-green variety of chalcedony valued as a gem **2** *or* **chrysoprase green :** a brilliant to light green that is very slightly darker than seafoam

chrysoprasus *n, pl* **chrysoprasi** [L] *obs* **:** CHRYSOPRASE

chrys·ops \ˈkri,säps\ *n, cap* [NL, fr. Gk *chrysōps* gold-colored, fr. *chrys-* + *ōps* eye, face — more at OPTIC] **:** a large widely distributed genus of small horseflies (family Tabanidae) of which the American forms commonly known as *deerflies* are pests of man and beast and in certain areas transmit tularemia while those of Africa called *mango flies* are vectors of the eye worm (*Loa loa*)

chry·sop·sis \krəˈsäpsəs\ *n, cap* [NL, fr. *chrys-* + *-opsis*] **:** a genus of No. American chiefly perennial woolly, hairy, or glutinous herbs (family Compositae) having large often corymbose heads — see GOLDEN ASTER

chrys·o·sphae·ra·les \ˌ== *at* CHRYSO- + sfəˈrā(,)lēz\ *n pl, cap* [NL, fr. *Chrysosphaera* genus of algae (fr. *chrys-* + *-sphaera*) + *-ales*] **:** an order of yellow-green unicellular or nonfilamentous colonial algae (class Chrysophyceae) having the cell content not transformed directly into a zoospore or other motile form

chrys·o·sple·ni·um \ˌ== + ˈsplēnēəm\ *n, cap* [NL, fr. *chrys-* + L *splenium* spleenwort (fr. Gk *splēnion,* fr. *splēn* spleen)] **:** a small genus of widely distributed semiaquatic herbs (family Saxifragaceae) having minute greenish yellow apetalous flowers

chrys·o·tham·nus \ˌ== + ˈthamnəs\ *n, cap* [NL, fr. *chrys-* + Gk *thamnos* shrub — more at THAMN-] **:** a genus of low branching shrubs (family Compositae) of the alkali plains of western No. America comprising some of the rayless goldenrods and characterized by linear entire leaves and clusters of golden yellow flowers

chryso·therapy \ˌ== + \ *n* -ES [ISV *chrys-* + *therapy*] **:** treatment (as of arthritis) by injection of gold salts

chrys·o·thrix \ˈ== + ,thriks\ [NL, fr. *chrys-* + *-thrix*] *syn of* SAIMIRI

chrys·o·tile \ˈ== + ,tīl\ *n* -s [G *chrysotil,* fr. *chrys-* + Gk *tilos* anything plucked (as hair or fiber), fr. *tillein* to pluck] **:** a fibrous silky serpentine $Mg_3Si_2O_5(OH)_4$ constituting one kind of asbestos

chrys·o·tri·cha·les \ˌ== + trəˈkā(,)lēz\ *n pl, cap* [NL, fr. *Chrysotrich-, Chrysothrix,* + *-ales*] **:** an order of yellow-green algae (class Chrysophyceae) distinguished by their branching filamentous form

chrys·to·crene \ˈkristə-,krēn\ *n* -s [*chrysto-* (prob. irreg. fr. *crystal*) + Gk *krēnē* spring, well] **:** a mass of loose rock fragments remarkably similar to a glacier **:** ROCK GLACIER

cht *abbr* **1** chemist **2** chest

chthon·ic \ˈthänik\ *or* **chtho·ni·an** \ˈthōnēən\ *adj* [*chthonic* fr. Gk *chthon-, chthōn* earth + E *-ic; chthonian* fr. Gk *chthonios* in or under the earth (fr. *chthon-, chthōn*) + E *-an* — more at HUMBLE] *of a divinity or a spirit* **:** dwelling or reigning in the underworld **:** INFERNAL ⟨Pluto was the ~ counterpart of Zeus⟩ **:** relating to infernal deities or spirits **:** GHOSTLY ⟨~ worship⟩

chtr *abbr* charter

CHU *abbr* centigrade heat unit

chuana *usu cap, var of* TSWANA

chuang \ˈjwäŋ\ *or* **chawng** \ˈjȯŋ\ *n, pl* **chuang** *or* **chuangs** *or* **chawng** *or* **chawngs** *usu cap* **:** any of a large number of tribal peoples of southern China under a variety of names but all having cultural and linguistic affiliation with the Thai or Siamese

chub \ˈchəb\ *n, pl* **chub** *or* **chubs** [ME *chubbe*] **1 :** a common European freshwater cyprinoid fish (*Leuciscus cephalus*) little valued as food — called also *chevin* **2 a :** any of various cyprinoid fishes (as the fallfish, horned dace, golden shiner, squawfish, hornyhead) **b :** any of several marine species (as the tautog, Bermuda chub or related forms, spot, pinfish) **c :** LARGEMOUTH BLACK BASS **d** *in the Great Lakes region* **:** LAKE HERRING **e :** CHUB SUCKER

chu·ba \ˈchübə\ *n* -s [origin unknown] **:** a game adapted in America from mancala using a board with 4 rows of 11 holes each

chu·bas·co \chüˈbä,skō\ *n* -s [Sp, fr. Pg *chuvasco,* fr. *chuva* rain, fr. L *pluvia,* fr. *pluere* to rain — more at FLOW] **:** a severe squall of rain and wind esp. along the west coast of Central America

chub·bi·ly \ˈchəbəlē, -li\ *adv* **:** in the manner of one who is chubby

chub·bi·ness \ˈchəbēnəs, -in-\ *n* -ES **:** the quality or state of being chubby **:** PLUMPNESS

chub·by \ˈchəbē, -bi\ *adj* -ER/-EST [*chub* + *-y*] **:** short, thick, and well-rounded **:** CHUNKY, PLUMP ⟨a ~ cigar⟩ ⟨a ~ boat⟩ **:** marked wholesomely by ample flesh **:** well-fed and not lean or wiry ⟨of middle height . . . stocky though not ~ —W. A.White⟩ ⟨a ~ little boy⟩ **syn** see FAT

chub mackerel *n* **:** a small mackerel (*Pneumatophorus grex*) found in most warm seas — called also *tinker mackerel*

chub sucker *n* **:** either of two common suckers (*Erimyzon sucetta* and *E. oblongus*) of stout build widely distributed in the eastern and central U. S.

chucalho *var of* CHOCALHO

chu·cho \ˈchü,chō\ *n* -s [Sp, perh. fr. *chucho* dog, owl, of imit. origin] **:** EAGLE RAY

¹chuck \ˈchək\ *vb* -ED/-ING/-S [ME *chukken,* of imit. origin] *vi* **1 a** *of a hen* **:** to make a clucking noise **b :** to make a noise suggesting the chucking of a hen **2** *obs* **:** CHUCKLE **:** laugh inwardly **~** *vt* **1 :** to call (as chickens) by clucking **2 :** to urge (a horse) forward by a chuck or palatal cluck

²chuck \"\ *n* -s [ME *chuk,* fr. *chukken,* v.] **1 :** DEAR — used as a term of endearment ⟨sweet ~⟩ **2** *dial Brit* **:** FOWL, CHICKEN

³chuck \"\ *vt* -ED/-ING/-S [origin unknown] **1 :** to give a pat or caress to under the chin orig. to make the mouth close ⟨~*ed* the barmaid under the chin —Washington Irving⟩ **2 a** (1) **:** to toss or jerk out of the hand **:** throw with a short action of the arm and usu. in an easy or careless manner (2) **:** to throw (a baseball) to a batter or fielder **b :** to throw away **:** DISCARD ⟨he had ~*ed* his old suit⟩ **c :** DISMISS, EJECT, OUST — used esp. with *out* ⟨~*ed* out of office⟩ **3 :** to throw up **:** give up **:** have done with — often used with *up* ⟨~ up a job⟩ **4 :** to clear (the ground) of obstructions with horses or machinery in logging — **chuck it :** QUIT, YIELD

⁴chuck \"\ *n* -s **1 :** a pat or nudge under the chin **2 :** TOSS, JERK; *esp* **:** a toss or short cast (as of a stone) from the hand **3 :** CHUCK-FARTHING **4** *slang Brit* **:** DISMISSAL ⟨to get the ~⟩

⁵chuck \"\ *n* -s [prob. var. of *chock*] **1** *now dial* **:** a log or lump **:** CHUNK **2 a :** a portion of a side of dressed beef including most of the neck, the parts about the shoulder blade, and those about the first three ribs ⟨a ~ roast⟩ — see BEEF illustration **b :** a similar cut from a carcass of dressed veal or lamb **3** *chiefly West* **:** FOOD, GRUB **4 :** a tapered piece of wood used in founding to stiffen the bars of a flask or connect them with parts below the joint **5 a :** an attachment for holding a workpiece or tool in a machine (as a drill press or lathe) usu. by means of adjustable jaws or setscrews — see COLLET CHUCK, DRILL CHUCK, INDEPENDENT CHUCK, MAGNETIC CHUCK, UNIVERSAL CHUCK **b :** a hydrant carried on fire apparatus for attaching to a chuck hydrant

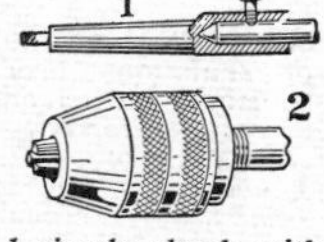

1 simple chuck with setscrew; *2* drill chuck

⁶chuck \"\ *vt* -ED/-ING/-S **:** to place in a chuck **:** hold by means of a chuck

⁷chuck \"\ *var of* CHOCK

⁸chuck \"\ *n* -s [by shortening] **:** WOODCHUCK

⁹chuck \ˈchu̇k, ˈchək\ *n* -s [alter. (prob. influenced by ³*chuck*) of ²*check* (checkstone)] *dial Brit* **:** CHECKSTONE

¹⁰chuck \ˈchək\ *n* -s [Chinook Jargon, water, river, stream, sea, prob. fr. Nootka *chauk*] *Northwest* **:** INLET, HARBOR ⟨salmon caught right in front of the ~ entrance⟩ ⟨a sizable stream . . . met the salt ~ —N.C.McDonald⟩

chuck–a–luck \ˈchəkə,lək\ *also* **chuck-luck** \ˈ=,=\ *n* [prob. fr. ³*chuck* (throw) + connective *-a-* + *luck*] **:** a banking game played with three dice, the players betting that a certain number will appear on one or more of the dice, that the sum of the three dice will make a certain number, or that all three dice will turn up alike — called also *birdcage;* compare RAFFLE

chuckawalla *var of* CHUCKWALLA

chuckchee *usu cap, var of* CHUKCHI

chucked *past of* CHUCK

¹chuck·er \ˈchəkə(r)\ *n* -s [³*chuck* (throw) + *-er*] **:** one that chucks: as **a :** BOUNCER **b :** a baseball pitcher

²chucker \"\ *var of* CHUKKER

³chucker \"\ *n* -s [⁶*chuck* + *-er*] **1 :** one that chucks **2 :** an operator of a crozing machine that cuts, grooves, and trims ends of staves in a headless barrel while it is held in chucks — called also *crozer*

chucker-out \ˈ=ˈ=\ *n, pl* **chuckers-out** [¹*chucker*] *Brit* **:** BOUNCER

chuck-farthing \ˈ=,=\ *n* [³*chuck*] **:** an old game in which the player who pitched coins nearest to a mark tossed all the coins at a hole and won those that went into it — called also *pitch-farthing;* compare PITCH-PENNY

chuck-full *var of* CHOCK-FULL

chuckhole \ˈ=,=\ *n* [³*chuck* + *hole*] **:** a hole, depression, or rut in a road **:** MUDHOLE ⟨washouts and the biggest ~*s* were filled up —Bernard De Voto⟩

chuck hydrant *n* [⁵*chuck*] **:** a fire hydrant having a cover set flush with the pavement and to which a chuck can be attached — called also *flush hydrant*

¹chuck·ie \ˈchəkē, -ki\ *n* -s [²*chuck* (chicken) + -*ie*] *Scot* **:** ²CHUCK 2

²chuckie \"\ *or* **chuckie stane** \-ˌstān\ *n* -s [⁹*chuck* + -*ie*] *Scot* **:** a small pebble (as one used in checkstones)

chuck·ing·ly \ˈchəkiŋlē, -li\ *adv* [fr. pres. part. of ²*chuck* + -*ly*] **:** CHUCKLINGLY

chucking reamer *n* [fr. pres. part. of ⁶*chuck*] **:** a reamer (as a twist drill) held in a chuck and usu. being stationary while the workpiece revolves

¹chuck·le \ˈchəkəl\ **chuckled; chuckled; chuckling** \-k(ə)liŋ\ **chuckles** *vi* -ED/-ING/-S [prob. freq. of ¹*chuck*] **1 :** to laugh convulsively (as with marked heaving of the shoulders) ⟨this breezy approach . . . soon had the reader racing along, *chuckling* —J.M.Chase⟩ **2 :** to laugh inwardly or quietly ⟨hummed snatches of some vagrant melody and *chuckled* at some private joke —Harold Sinclair⟩ **3 :** to make a continuous gentle sound resembling suppressed mirth (as of a wobbling millstone or a brook over stones) ⟨sometimes there were sunny rips where the clear bright water *chuckled* over gravel —B.A.Williams⟩

²chuckle \"\ *n* -s **:** a quiet hardly audible laugh (as of satisfaction, appreciation of humor, exultation, or derision) **:** CHUCKLING ⟨the gladsome ~ of the announcer as he archly nears the commercial —Bergen Evans⟩ ⟨a photographer gets a picture that gives a ~ to thousands of perspiring readers —F.L.Mott⟩

³chuckle *adj* [perh. irreg. fr. ⁵*chuck*] *obs* **:** CLUMSY, STUPID

chucklehead \ˈ≈≈ˌ≈\ *n* -s [³*chuckle* + *head*] **1 :** BLOCKHEAD, DOLT ⟨a ~ advertising his stupidity to thousands of TV viewers⟩ **2 :** a rockfish (*Sebastodes chlorostictus*) of the California coast **3** *or* **chucklehead cat :** BLUE CAT

chuck·le·head·ed \ˌ≈≈ˈ≈≈\ *adj* **:** BLOCKHEADED, STUPID ⟨a ~ play cost them the game⟩

chuck·ler \ˈchəklə(r)\ *n* -s [Tamil-Malayalam *cakkiliyar*, honorific pl. of *cakkiliyan*] *India* **:** a worker in leather **:** COBBLER

chuck line *n* [⁵*chuck* (food)] *West* **:** ranch houses visited for free meals — usu. used in the phrase *ride the chuck line* with reference to an unemployed cowboy

chuck·ling·ly \ˈchək(ə)liŋlē, -li\ *adv* [fr. pres. part. of ¹*chuckle* + -*ly*] **:** with a chuckle

chuck–luck *var of* CHUCK-A-LUCK

chuck plate *n* [⁵*chuck*] **1 :** a plate on which a chuck is fastened and which is arranged for attaching to a lathe spindle (as by a screw thread) **2 :** a lathe faceplate

chuckram *or* **chuckrum** *var of* CHAKRAM

chuck ring *n* [⁵*chuck*] **:** one of a pair of heavy steel rings that form a chuck for holding a keg when turning grooves in the ends of staves

¹chucks *pres 3d sing of* CHUCK, *pl of* CHUCK

²chucks \ˈchu̇ks, ˈchəks\ *n pl but sing or pl in constr* [pl. of ⁹*chuck*] *dial Brit* **:** CHECKSTONES

chuck wagon *n* [⁵*chuck* (food)] **:** a wagon that is equipped with a stove and provisions for cooking (as on a ranch or in a lumber camp)

chuck·wal·la \ˈchəkˌwälə\ *or* **chuck·a·wal·la** \ˈchəkə-\ *n* -s [modif. of MexSp *chacahuala*, fr. Cahuilla *tcáxxwal*] **:** a large harmless herbivorous iguanid lizard (*Sauromalus ater*) of the desert regions of the southwestern U.S. sometimes eaten by the Indians

chuck–will's–widow \ˈchəkˌwilz,≈≈\ *n, pl* **chuck–will's–widows** [so called fr. its note] **:** a goatsucker (*Caprimulgus carolinensis*) of the southern U.S. resembling but larger than the whippoorwill

chucky \ˈchəkē, -ki\ *n* -ES [²*chuck* + -*y*] *dial Brit* **:** ²CHUCK

chu·cu·na·que \ˌchükü'näˌkwā\ *n, pl* **chucunaque** *or* **chucunaques** *usu cap* [Sp, of AmerInd origin] **1 :** a Cunan people of the Mulatas islands, Panama **2 :** a member of the Chucunaque people

chud \ˈchu̇d\ [alter. of ME *ich wolde* I would] *dial Eng* **:** I would

chuddar *or* **chudder** *var of* CHADOR

Chud·ic \ˈchüdik\ *adj, usu cap* [Russ *Chud'* Chud, Finn (perh. of Gmc origin; akin to Goth *thiuda* people) + E -*ic* — more at DUTCH] **:** constituting or belonging to the West Finnic languages

chue·ta \ˈchwād-ə\ *n* -s [Sp, fr. Catal *juéuet*, dim. of *jueu* Jew, fr. L *Judaeus* — more at JEW] **1** *in the Balearic islands* **:** a descendant of a Christianized Jew **2** [AmerSp, fr. Sp] *in Puerto Rico* **:** a descendant of the Majorcan Jews

chu·fa \ˈchüfə\ *n* -s [Sp, fr. OSp, tidbit, trifle, joke, fr. *chufar* to joke, alter. (influenced by *trufar* to fib) of *chuflar* to ridicule, whistle, fr. (assumed) VL *sufilare* to whistle, alter. of L *sibilare* — more at SIBILANT] **:** a European sedge (*Cyperus esculentus*) with small edible nutlike tubers — called also *earth almond, ground almond, rush nut*

¹chuff \ˈchəf\ *n* -s [ME *chuffe, choffe*] **1 :** BOOR, CHURL ⟨coarse country ~s⟩ **2 :** MISER

²chuff \ˈchəf, -üf\ *adj* -ER/-EST *dial* **:** SURLY, SULLEN

³chuff \"\ *adj* -ER/-EST [perh. fr. ¹*chuff*] **1** *dial Brit* **:** FAT, CHUBBY, SWOLLEN **2** *dial Eng* **:** PROUD, ELATED, SATISFIED

⁴chuff \ˈchəf\ *n* -s [origin unknown] **:** a brick cracked by rain during burning

⁵chuff \"\ *n* -s [imit.] **:** a sound made by or suggestive of noisy exhaust or exhalation; *typically* **:** the sound of a steam engine ⟨the engine giving off quiet ~s like a giant breathing —Helen Eustis⟩

⁶chuff \"\ *vi* -ED/-ING/-S **:** to make chuffs **:** emit noisy exhaust or exhalations **:** proceed or operate with chuffs ⟨the ~*ing* and snorting of switch engines —Paul Gallico⟩ ⟨the ferryboat ~*ed* across the wide river —Walter Havighurst⟩

¹chuffy \ˈchəfē, -üfē, -fi\ *adj* -ER/-EST [perh. fr. ³*chuff* + -*y*] **1** *now dial, of a person* **:** short and stout **:** FAT, CHUBBY **2** *of swine* **:** short-coupled and fat ⟨a new boar . . . with heftier ham, but not so ~ —*Breeder's Gazette*⟩ — opposed to *rangy*

²chuffy \"\ *adj* -ER/-EST [¹*chuff* + -*y*] *now dial Eng* **:** CHUFF, SURLY

¹chug \ˈchəg\ *also* **chug–chug** \ˈ≈ˌ≈\ *n* -s [imit.] **:** a sound made by or suggestive of the muffled firing of an engine; *typically* **:** one of a series of dull explosive sounds made by a laboring engine

²chug \"\ *vi* **chugged; chugged; chugging; chugs 1 :** to make chugs **:** make the intermittent explosive sound of a firing motor ⟨*chugging* overladen old cars —Russell Lord⟩ **2 :** to proceed or operate with or as if with chugs **:** travel in a vehicle or ship that chugs ⟨with 75 pounds of steam from her wood-fired boiler she puffed and *chugged* —Tom Marvel⟩ ⟨over these highways the farmers *chugged* to market —*Amer. Guide Series: Wash.*⟩

chug·ger \ˈchəgə(r)\ *n* -s [E dial *chug* to pull, jerk + -*er*] **:** a surface casting plug used in angling

chug·hole \ˈchəgˌhōl\ *dial var of* CHUCKHOLE

chug step *n* **:** a forward push on one foot in dancing

chuh·ra \ˈchürə\ *n, pl* **chuhra** *or* **chuhras** [Hindi *cūhṛā*] **:** a member of a lower caste of India now usu. engaged in agriculture

chuj \ˈchü(k̠), -üē\ *n, pl* **chuj** \"\ *or* **chu·jes** \ˈchüˌkās\ *usu cap* [Sp, of AmerInd origin] **1 a :** an Indian people of northwestern Guatemala **b :** a member of such people **2 :** a Mayan language of the Chuj people

chu·kar *or* **chukar partridge** \chə'kär\ *also* **chu·kor** \-ōr, -ȯr\ *n, pl* **chukar** *or* **chukars** [Hindi *cakor*, fr. Skt *cakora*, prob. of imit. origin] **:** an Indian rock partridge (*Alectoris graeca chukar*) that is gray with black and white bars on the sides and with red bill and legs and that has been introduced into dry parts of the western U.S. where it is rapidly becoming established and is highly esteemed as a game bird; *broadly* **:** any rock partridge

chuk·chi *or* **chuk·chee** *also* **chook·chie** \ˈchu̇kˌchē\ *n, pl* **chukchi** *or* **chukchis** *or* **chukchee** *or* **chukchees** *also* **chookchie** *or* **chookchies** *usu cap* [Russ *Chukcha*] **1 a :** a Siberian Americanoid people allied to the Kamchadal and Koryak and inhabiting the Chukchi peninsula **b :** a member of such people **2 :** the Luorawetlan language of the Chukchi people frequently cited for its extreme differentiation in pronunciation between men and women

¹chukka *var of* CHUKKER

²chuk·ka \ˈchəkə\ *or* **chukka boot** *n* -s [¹*chukka*; fr. a similar boot's being worn by polo players] **:** a short leather boot usu. ankle-length and having two pairs of eyelets — compare JODHPUR

chukka boot

chuk·ker *or* **chuk·kar** \ˈchəkə(r)\ *n* -s [Hindi *cakkar, cakar*, fr. Skt *cakra* wheel, circle — more at WHEEL] **1** *India* **:** a circular course **:** WHEEL, CIRCLE **2** *or* **chuk·ka** \ˈchəkə\ *or* **chuck·er** \ˈchəkə(r)\ **:** a playing period of a polo game

chukker brown *n* **:** MUMMY BROWN 2b

chul·ha *also* **chu·la** \ˈchülə\ *n* -s [Hindi *cūlhā, cūlā*, fr. Skt *culli* fireplace, hearth, prob. of Dravidian origin; akin to Tamil *cuḷḷai, cūḷai* hearth] *India* **:** a small earthen or brick stove

chu·llo \ˈchüˌlyō\ *n* -s [AmerSp] **:** a knitted wool cap with ear flaps worn in Peru

chull·pa *or* **chul·pa** \ˈchülpə\ *n* -s [AmerSp *chulpa*, fr. Aymara *chullpa*] **:** a stone tower or tomb erected by the pre-Incan inhabitants of Peru and Bolivia

chu·lo \ˈchü(ˌ)lō\ *n* -s [Sp, fr. OSp, boy, fr. OIt *ciullo*, short for *fanciullo*, dim. of *fante*, fr. L *infant-, infans* young child — more at INFANT] **:** a matador's assistant in the ring

chul·tun \ˈchülˌtün\ *n, pl* **chultu·nes** \chül'tüˌnās\ [Maya] **:** a circular or bottle-shaped stone cistern constructed by the Mayas of Yucatan

chu·ly·ma tatar \chü'limə-\ *n, usu cap C&T* [fr. *Chulym*, river in Siberia, their locality] **1 :** a people inhabiting the Tomsk and Yeniseisk areas of Siberia **2 :** a member of the Chulyma Tatar people

¹chum \ˈchəm\ *n* -s [perh. by shortening & alter. fr. *chamber fellow*] **1** *archaic* **:** ROOMMATE **2 :** an habitual intimate companion **:** a close friend ⟨a boyhood ~ of his⟩

²chum \"\ *vb* **chummed; chummed; chumming; chums** *vi* **1 :** to share quarters **:** room together ⟨the two bedrooms to each study favored the pleasant custom of *chumming* —George Santayana⟩ **2 a :** to be a chum **:** be on terms of intimate friendship — usu. used with *with* ⟨he soon *chummed* with du Maurier and me in several languages and became one of our set —Felix Moscheles⟩ **b :** to show affable friendliness **:** form close friendship — usu. used with *up* ⟨two husbands might ~ up and slip out for a light ale —Elizabeth Taylor⟩ ~ *vt* **:** to place in the same quarters with another — usu. used with *on* ⟨the college *chummed* him on a student from Duluth⟩

³chum \"\ *n* -s [origin unknown] **1 :** chopped fish, vegetable matter, or small live fishes thrown overboard to draw fish to a fishing boat **2 a :** refuse or scrap fish (as in a fish cannery) **b :** the pulp left after expressing oil from menhaden

⁴chum \"\ *vb* **chummed; chummed; chumming; chums** *vi* **:** to attract fish with chum ~ *vt* **:** to attract by chumming ⟨*chumming* the fish with cut-up shrimp⟩

⁵chum \"\ *n* -s [perh. fr. Chinook Jargon *tsum, tzum* spots, writing, fr. Chinook] **:** a dog salmon (*Oncorhynchus keta*)

⁶chum \"\ *n* -s [perh. alter. of ¹*chump*] **:** a cradle used in ceramics for turning a form

⁷chum \ˈchüm, ˈchəm\ *n* -s [Russ, of Finnic origin; akin to Zyrian *t'śom* tent, hut, Votyak *tšum*] **:** a tepeelike shelter esp. of skins, turf, or fibers used as a summer dwelling by the Samoyeds, Buryats, Tungus, and other peoples of northern Eurasia — compare YURT

chu·mash \ˈchüˌmash\ *n, pl* **chumash** *or* **chumashes** *usu cap* **1 a :** an Indian people of southwestern California **b :** a member of such people **2 :** the Chumashan language of the Chumash people **3 :** CHUMASHAN

chu·mash·an \(ˈ)chü¦mashən\ *n* -s *usu cap* [*Chumash* + E -*an*] **:** a language family of the Hokan stock comprising only the Chumash language

chum·ble \ˈchəmbəl\ *vb* **chumbled; chumbled; chumbling** \-b(ə)liŋ\ **chumbles** [prob. freq. of ²*chump*] **:** GNAW, CHEW ⟨clashing jaws of moth *chumbling* holes in cloth —Robert Graves⟩

chum·mage \ˈchəmij\ *n* -s [²*chum* + -*age*] **:** the quartering of persons together in the same room ⟨~ of various collegians together⟩

chum·mer \ˈchəmə(r)\ *n* -s [⁴*chum* + -*er*] **:** one that scatters chum in fishing

chum·mery \ˈchəm(ə)rē, -ri\ *n* -ES [¹*chum* + -*ery*] *India* **:** the living quarters of chums ⟨a ~ he shared with another bachelor —John Masters⟩

chum·mi·ly \ˈchəməlē, -li\ *adv* [³*chummy* + -*ly*] **:** in a chummy manner

chum·mi·ness \-ēnəs\ *n* -ES [³*chummy* + -*ness*] **:** the quality or state of being chummy

¹chum·my \ˈchəmē, -mi\ *n* -ES [perh. alter. of *chimney*] *slang Brit* **:** CHIMNEY SWEEP **:** a boy helper to a chimney sweep

²chummy \"\ *n* -ES [¹*chum* + -*y*] **:** ¹CHUM

³chummy \"\ *adj* -ER/-EST [¹*chum* + -*y*] **:** marked by or affording easy familiarity, companionability, and shared interests **:** intimately sociable ⟨the secretary is on ~ terms with a host of congressmen —Philip Hamburger⟩ ⟨a ~ little cocktail lounge⟩ **syn** see FAMILIAR

¹chump \ˈchəmp\ *n* -s [perh. blend of ¹*chunk* and *lump*] **1 :** a short thick heavy piece of wood **2** *slang chiefly Brit* **:** HEAD **3 a :** stupid lout **:** BLOCKHEAD, FOOL **b :** GULL, DUPE; *specif* **:** intended victim — **off one's chump** *slang chiefly Brit* **:** out of one's mind **:** CRAZY

²chump \"\ *vb* -ED/-ING/-S [alter. of ¹*champ*] **:** MUNCH, CHAMP

chum·pa \ˈchəmpə\ *n* -s [perh. fr. Choctaw *chumpa* purchase] *West* **:** a faggot of pine kindling

chump chop *n* [¹*chump*] *Brit* **:** a mutton chop from the thick end of a loin

chumpy \ˈchəmpē, -pi\ *adj* -ER/-EST [¹*chump* + -*y*] *dial* **:** THICK, THICKSET

chums *pl of* CHUM, *pres 3d sing of* CHUM

chum salmon *n* [⁵*chum*] **:** DOG SALMON

chün \ˈjün, ˈjüen\ *adj, usu cap* [fr. *Chün* Chon (Fangcheng), Honan province, China, where it was made] **:** of or relating to a type of Chinese pottery produced in a great variety of colors at Fangcheng, Honan province, during the Sung period

chu·nam \chü'nam\ *n* -s [Tamil *cuṇṇam*, fr. Skt *cūrṇa* powder, flour, fr. *carvati* he grinds, chews; perh. akin to Slovak *čren* jaw, cheekbone, Latvian *ceruoklis* molar] **1** *India* **:** lime used esp. with betel leaf in making pan **2 :** a cement or plaster used in India that is usu. highly polished and decorated with paintings

chun·cho \ˈchünˌchō\ *n, pl* **chuncho** *or* **chunchos** *usu cap* [Sp, fr. Quechua *ch'unchu* uncivilized Indian of the eastern forests] **:** a member of any jungle people of So. America

chun·ga \ˈchəŋgə\ *n* -s [alter. of AmerSp *chuña*] **:** a cariama (*Chunga burmeisteri*) of northern Argentina that is smaller and darker than the crested cariama, has a shorter crest, and frequents more wooded terrain

chung·chia \ˈju̇ŋ'jyä\ *n pl, usu cap* **:** the Tai-related valley-dwelling people numbering over a million and inhabiting the plateau province of Kweichow in southern China

chung·king \ˈchu̇ŋ'kiŋ, -u̇ŋ'ch-\ *adj, usu cap* [fr. *Chungking*, China] **:** of or from the city of Chungking, China **:** of the kind or style prevalent in Chungking

¹chunk \ˈchəŋk\ *n* -s [perh. alter. of ⁵*chuck*] **1 a** *dial* **:** LOG, STUMP **:** a heavy piece of wood, esp. of firewood; *sometimes* **:** a piece of firewood made by splitting a log in quarters **b :** a piece of burning wood ⟨get a ~ from a neighbor's fire⟩ **c :** a short thick piece often crudely or roughly formed **:** LUMP ⟨a ~ of meat⟩ ⟨a sizzling summer day holds few finer refreshments than a great ~ of cold watermelon —Jane Nickerson⟩ **2 :** a sizable amount **:** a noteworthy quantity **:** a large portion ⟨six months is a ~ out of any man's life —Upton Sinclair⟩ **3 a :** a strong thickset horse usu. smaller than a typical draft horse **b :** a fair-sized or large person — often used with *of* ⟨her father was a fine ~ of a man⟩ **:** a sturdy or thickset person **:** a stocky or chubby child

²chunk \"\ *vt* -ED/-ING/-S [prob. fr. ¹*chunk*] **1** *chiefly South* **:** THROW ⟨~ sticks at grazing cows⟩ ⟨~*ed* three more stones into the water —Dan Wickenden⟩; *also* **:** throw things at **:** PELT **2** *dial* **:** to build or revive (a fire) by throwing on fuel or by raking or stirring — sometimes used with *up* **3 :** to remove chunks from (a skid road) — usu. used with *out*

³chunk \"\ *vt* -ED/-ING/-S [perh. by alter.] **:** ²CHINK 2

⁴chunk \"\ *vi* -ED/-ING/-S [imit.] **:** to make a dull plunging or explosive sound **:** proceed while making dull plunging sounds

⁵chunk \"\ *n* -s **:** a dull plunging or explosive sound

⁶chunk \"\ *n* -s [by shortening] **:** CHUNKEY

chunk·ed \ˈchəŋkəd\ *adj* [¹*chunk* + -*ed*] **1 :** CHUNKY **2** *Southwest* **:** IMPUDENT

chunk·ey *or* **chunky** \ˈchəŋkē\ *n, pl* **chunkeys** *or* **chunkies** [perh. modif. of Catawba *Chenco*] **:** a Muskogean Indian game in which players try to throw or slide a pole so that a crook at one end curves around a disk

chunk honey *n* [¹*chunk*] **:** mixed extracted and comb honey

chunk·i·ly \ˈchəŋkəlē, -li\ *adv* [¹*chunky* + -*ly*] **:** in a chunky manner ⟨another man — brown-suited, ~ built, with a square face and rather heavy features —R.M.Coates⟩

chunk·i·ness \ˈchəŋkēnəs\ *n* -ES **:** the quality or state of being chunky

¹chunky \ˈchəŋkē, -ki\ *adj* -ER/-EST [¹*chunk* + -*y*] **:** short and thick or broad; *esp* **:** having or characterized by a stout robust solid body ⟨short, ~ . . . far removed from the elegant, willowy statesmen —Mollie Panter-Downes⟩ ⟨a ~ topcoat —*New Yorker*⟩ **syn** see STOCKY

²chunky *var of* CHUNKEY

chu·ño \chü'nyō\ *also* **chu·ñu** \-ˌnyü\ *n* -s [AmerSp, fr. Quechua *ch'uñu*] **:** potatoes processed by successive freezing, thawing, and dehydrating prepared and eaten esp. by the native peoples of the Andes

chun·ter \ˈchəntə(r), -ünt-\ *or* **chun·ner** \ˈchənə(r), -ün-\ *vi* -ED/-ING/-S [prob. of imit. origin] **1** *dial Brit, of a person* **:** to talk in a low inarticulate way **:** MUTTER; *also* **:** COMPLAIN, GRUMBLE **2** *dial Brit, of an animal* **:** to emit typical outcries

chu·nu·pí \ˌchünü'pē\ *n, pl* **chunupí** *or* **chunupis** *usu cap* [Sp, of AmerInd origin] **1 :** a people of the Vilela group **2 :** a member of the Chunupí

chu·pat·ti \chə'päd·ē, -pa-\ *var of* CHAPATI

chu·pon \chü'pōn\ *n* -s [AmerSp *chupón*] **1 a :** a tropical American timber tree (*Bumelia obtusifolia*) with yellowish brown very hard heavy wood **b :** a So. American timber tree (*Gustavia yaracuyensis*) of the family Lecythidaceae with dark black-streaked wood **2 :** a sucker of the chocolate tree

chuppah *also* **chupah** *n, pl* **chuppoth** *or* **chuppot** *also* **chuppahs** *var of* HUPPAH

chu·pras·si \chə'präsē\ *var of* CHAPRASSI

chu·ra·pa \chə'räpə\ *n, pl* **churapa** *or* **churapas** *usu cap* [Sp, of AmerInd origin] **1 :** an Indian people of the Chiquitoan group now found in or near Buenavista, Bolivia **2 :** a member of such people

¹church \ˈchərch, -ə̄ch,-əich\ *n* -ES [ME *chirche*, fr. OE *cirice*; akin to OS *kirika*, OHG *kirihha*; all fr. a prehistoric WGmc word borrowed fr. (assumed) Goth *kyriko* (whence OSlav *crŭky*), fr. LGk *kyrikon*, alter. of *kyriakon*, short for *kyriakon dōma* the Lord's house, fr. Gk *kyriakon* (neut. of *kyriakos* of the lord or master, fr. *kyrios* lord, master, fr. *kyros* power) + *dōma* house; akin to W *cawr* giant, Skt *śūra* strong, L *cavus* hollow — more at CAVE] **1 :** a building set apart for public esp. Christian worship ⟨visit the ~*es* of a city⟩: as **a :** the principal house of a parish **b :** a house of worship in Great Britain for members of the established or formerly established church as distinguished from those of nonconformists and Roman Catholics — compare CHAPEL 6 **2 :** a place of worship of any religion ⟨a Muslim ~⟩ **3 :** church service **:** divine worship or religious service in a church **:** the church building with the service going on in it ⟨go to ~⟩ ⟨attend ~⟩ **4** *often cap* **a :** the organization of Christianity or of an association of Christians; *esp* **:** an historical institution composed of believing Christians **b :** the clergy or officers of such an organization **c :** a body of Christian believers holding the same creed, observing the same rites, and acknowledging the same ecclesiastical authority regarded either as the only true representative of or as a separate branch of the church universal and often confined to territorial or historical limits **:** DENOMINATION ⟨the Presbyterian *Church*⟩ **d :** the total body of Christians regarded as a spiritual society **e :** a formally organized body of Christian believers worshiping together **:** a local Christian congregation ⟨they had appointed elders for them in every ~ — Acts 14:23 (RSV)⟩ **f :** ecclesiastical power, authority, or government **5 :** the clerical profession ⟨to go into the ~⟩ ⟨the youngest son was destined for the ~⟩ **6 :** a body of worshipers **:** a religious society or organization: as **a :** the congregation or company of God's worshipers under the old dispensation or in Old Testament times, the analogue and precursor of the Christian church **b :** a society, school, or the like resembling the Christian church (as in having a set of opinions held in common) ⟨the Jewish ~⟩ **syn** see RELIGION

²church \"\ *vt* -ED/-ING/-ES [ME *chirchen*, fr. *chirche*, n.] **1 :** to bring or conduct to church to receive one of its rites **2** *in some high liturgical churches* **:** to perform the rite of blessing (a woman) after childbirth —see CHURCHING **3** *Midland* **:** to discipline by church action

³church \"\ *adj* [¹ *church*] **1 :** of or relating to a church ⟨~ work⟩ ⟨~ government⟩ **2 :** composed of or conducted by members of a church ⟨~ socials⟩ **3** *chiefly Brit* **:** of or relating to the established or formerly established church ⟨we were ~ not chapel —E.L.Thomas⟩

church–ale \ˈ≈ˌ≈\ *n* [ME *chirche ale*, fr. *chirche* church + *ale* (festival)] **:** a festival formerly held in English country parishes at which ale was sold to raise money for church expenses and relief of the poor

church assembly *n, usu cap C&A* **:** the Church of England body for the governance of the church consisting of a house of clergy and a house of laity which since 1919 have together had the power to pass measures relating to the church for submission to Parliament for approval or rejection

church bell *n* **1 :** a large metal bell; *esp* **:** one cast in traditional shape and producing a true bell tone **2 :** an instrument (as an organ stop) imitating the sound of church bells — usu. used in pl; compare CATHEDRAL CHIMES

church book *n* **:** any of several books used in or by a church (as a service book, a record of church proceedings, or a parish register of births, marriages, and deaths)

church concerto *n* **:** CONCERTO 1

church congress *n, usu cap both Cs* **:** a semiofficial annual conference of the clergy and laity of the Church of England

church council *n* **:** a lay group appointed in certain Lutheran churches to assume responsibility with and assist the pastor in spiritual guidance and in such practical matters as the handling of church property and the collection and distribution of money for benevolences

church father *n, sometimes cap C&F* **:** FATHER 4

churchgoer \ˈ≈ˌ≈≈\ *n* -s **:** one who attends church; *esp* **:** one who attends habitually or zealously

¹churchgoing \ˈ≈ˌ≈≈\ *n* -s **:** church attendance esp. when habitual

²churchgoing \ˌ≈ˈ≈≈\ *adj* **:** attending church esp. habitually

church hand *n* **:** TEXT HAND

church house *n* [ME *chirche hous*, fr. *chirche* church + *hous* house] **1 :** a house belonging to a church (as a rectory or a parish house) **2** *South & Midland* **:** CHURCH, MEETINGHOUSE

church·i·an·i·ty \ˌchərchē'anəd·ē, -ə̄ch-,-əich-, -ətē, -i\ *also* **church·an·i·ty** \ˌ≈'chan-\ *n* -ES [¹*church* + -*ianity*, -*anity* (as in *Christianity*)] **:** the usu. excessive or sectarian attachment to the practices and interests of a particular church

churchier *comparative of* CHURCHY

churchiest *superlative of* CHURCHY

church·i·fied \ˈchərchəˌfīd, -ə̄ch-,-əich-\ *adj* [fr. past part. of *churchify*, fr. ¹*church* + -*ify*] **:** brought into accord or sympathy with church principles or forms

church·ill·i·an *also* **church·ill·e·an** \chər'chilēən\ *adj, usu cap* [Sir Winston *Churchill* b1874 Brit. statesman and author + E -*ian*, -*ean*] **:** relating to or suggestive of Sir Winston Churchill

church·ing \ˈchərchiŋ, -ə̄ch-,-əich-\ *n* -s [fr. gerund of ²*church*] **:** the administration or reception of a rite of the church; *specif* **:** a ceremony in some high liturgical churches by which after childbirth women are received in the church with prayers, blessings, and thanksgiving

church invisible *n* **:** the entire company of those on earth and in afterlife who whether members of the church visible or not belong to the faithful for whom it is believed God has destined salvation

church·ism \'chər,chizəm, -ə,ch-,-əi,ch-\ *n* -s [¹church + -ism] **:** strong adherence to church practices or beliefs, esp. sectarian practices or beliefs

¹church·ite \-,chīt, *usu* -īd.+V\ *n* -s [¹church + -ite] **:** a church supporter or advocate

²churchite \"\ *n* -s [Arthur H. *Church* †1915 Eng. chemist + E *-ite*] **:** a mineral (Ce,Ca) $(PO_4).2H_2O$ consisting of a hydrous cerium calcium phosphate occurring in thin drusy crusts of small light gray to pink crystals (sp. gr. 3.1)

church·less \-ləs\ *adj* [¹church + -less] **:** having no church **:** not affiliated or connected with a church

church·ly \-lē, -li\ *adj, sometimes* -ER/-EST [¹church + -ly] **1 :** of or relating to a church **:** suitable to or suggestive of a church ⟨~ custom⟩ ⟨~ truth⟩ **2 :** adhering to a church **:** inclined to religion ⟨~ people⟩

churchman \'=mən\ *n, pl* **churchmen 1 :** ECCLESIASTIC, CLERGYMAN, PRIEST **2 :** an adherent or member of a church

church·man·ly \-lē\ *adj* **:** ECCLESIASTICAL

church·man·ship \'==,ship\ *n* -s **:** the attitude, belief, or practice of a churchman

church militant *n, often cap C&M* [trans. of ML *ecclesia militans*] **:** the Christian church on earth regarded as engaged in a constant warfare against its enemies, the powers of evil — distinguished from *church triumphant*

church mode *n* **:** ECCLESIASTICAL MODE

church papist *n* **:** a Roman Catholic who was a conformist to the Church of England in England in the 17th century

church pennant *n* **:** a pennant flown on a ship during church service, in the U.S. Navy being white with a blue Latin cross and flown above the ensign

church rate *n* **:** a rate upon the lands and houses in a parish in England or Ireland assessed on the occupiers for the maintenance of the church and its services compulsory by law until 1868 but now payable voluntarily or fixed at the request of the annual vestry meeting

church register *n* **:** a parish register of baptisms, marriages, and deaths

church school *n* **1 a :** a school providing a general education but supported by a particular church in contrast to one supported by the public authority or a nondenominational private school **b** *Brit* **:** a school providing a general education but in which denominational religious teaching is also given and where certain rights are vested in a board of managers composed of church people with the incumbent of the parish as chairman **2 :** an organization of moral and religious officers, teachers, and pupils for purposes of moral and religious education under the supervision of a local church

church·scot \'chərch,skät, -ēch-,-əich-\ *or* **church·shot** \-,shät\ *n* -s [alter. & part trans. of OE *ciricsceat*, fr. *cirice* church + *sceatt* payment, treasure; akin to OHG *scaz* money, ON *skattr*, Goth *skatts*, L *scatere* to bubble up, Gk *skatamizein* to jump, Lith *skasti*] **:** a tribute formerly collected by the clergy for their support or as a due prob. orig. in the form of a portion of grain

church slavic *or* **church slavonic** *n, cap C&S* **:** OLD CHURCH SLAVONIC

church suffering *n, often cap C&S, Roman Catholicism* **:** the souls in purgatory

church triumphant *n, often cap C&T* **:** members of the church who have died and are regarded as enjoying eternal happiness through union with God — compare CHURCH MILITANT, CHURCH SUFFERING

church visible *n* **:** the whole body of actually professed Christians on earth — distinguished from *church invisible*

church·ward·en \'chərch¦wȯrdᵊn, -ēch-, -əich-, -ō(ə)d-\ *n* [ME *chirche wardein*] **1 :** a lay honorary parish official in the Church of England whose duties include the protection of the church building and property, the making and executing of various parochial regulations, and criticism though not control with respect to divine worship **2 :** a church officer in the Protestant Episcopal Church whose duties though they vary in the different dioceses now relate chiefly to the oversight and management of the temporal affairs of the parish (as the care of the parish property and the raising of money) **3** *Brit* **:** a long-stemmed clay pipe

churchway \'=,=\ *n* **:** the way leading to a church

churchwoman \'=,==\ *n, pl* **churchwomen :** a woman who is a member of a church

church work *n* **:** work in behalf of a church esp. in furtherance of its purpose (as in charity, visitation of the sick, or support of the church's world mission)

churchy \'chərchē, -ēch-, -əich-, -chi\ *adj, usu* -ER/-EST **:** of or suggesting a church; *esp* **:** marked by strict conformity or zealous adherence to the forms or beliefs of a church

churchyard \'=,=\ *n* [ME *chircheyerd*] **:** a yard which belongs to a church and which is often used as a burial ground

churchyard beetle *n* **:** a large dull black European beetle (*Blaps mortisaga*)

church year *n, usu cap C* **:** CHRISTIAN YEAR

chu·rel \chü'rāl\ *n* -s [Hindi *curail*] *India* **:** GOBLIN; *specif* **:** the ghost of a woman who has died while pregnant that haunts lonely places

chu·rin·ga \chü'riŋgə\ *also* **tju·run·ga** \tyü'rəŋgə\ *or* **tju·rin·ga** \-'riŋgə\ *n, pl* **churingas** *or* **churinga** [native name in Australia] **:** an object of wood or stone that is considered sacred by various aboriginal tribes of Central Australia and that is often elliptical in shape, bears incised designs, is believed to represent either the spiritual double of a living native or the embodiment of the spirit of a totemic ancestor, and is generally regarded as secret; *sometimes* **:** the quality of sacredness — compare BULL-ROARER

churl \'chərl, -əl, -əil\ *n* -s [ME *cherl, churl*, fr. OE *ceorl* man, husband, freeman of the lowest rank; akin to OHG *karal* man, husband, ON *karl*, Gk *gerōn* old man, *gēras* old age — more at CORN] **1 a** *obs* **:** a male person **:** MAN, HUSBAND **b :** VILLEIN, SERF, BONDMAN **2** *in early England* **:** a man without rank **:** a man in the lowest rank of freemen below the earl and thane **:** YEOMAN 2a **3 :** RUSTIC, COUNTRYMAN, PEASANT ⟨not framed for village ~s, but for high dames and mighty earls —Sir Walter Scott⟩ **4 a :** a person (as a rustic) who is ungracious, mean, ill-bred, and rude ⟨the boy might well believe this ~ was lying —George Meredith⟩ **b :** a stingy, grasping, and morose person ⟨when a few words can rescue misery . . . I hate a man who can be a ~ of them —Tobias Smollett⟩ **syn** see BOOR

churl·ish \-lish, -lēsh\ *adj* [ME *churlish, cherlish*, fr. OE *ceorlisc, cierlisc*, fr. *ceorl* + *-isc* -ish] **1 :** of or like a churl **:** having the position or rank of a churl **:** RUSTIC, VULGAR, MEAN **2 :** characteristic of or befitting a churl **:** BASE, RUDE, ILL-BRED **:** lacking refinement or higher feelings **3 :** difficult to work with or deal with **:** UNMANAGEABLE, UNYIELDING, INTRACTABLE ⟨~ soil⟩ ⟨~ intractable minerals⟩ — **churl·ish·ly** *adv* — **churl·ish·ness** *n* -ES

churly \-lē,-li\ *adj* [*churl* + *-y*] **:** CHURLISH

churm \'chərm, -əm\ *chiefly Scot var of* CHIRM

¹churn \'chərn, -ən, -əin\ *n* -s [ME *chyrne, cherne*, fr. OE *cyrin, cyrn*; akin to MHG *kern* churn, G dial. *kern* cream, ON *kjarni* churn, OE *cyrnel* kernel, dim. of *corn* grain; fr. the granular appearance of cream as it turns to butter — more at CORN] **1 :** a vessel in which milk or cream is stirred, beaten, or otherwise agitated (as by a plunging or revolving dasher or by shaking) in order to separate the oily globules from the other parts and thus to obtain butter **2 :** an agitated state (as of water) **:** CHURNING ⟨the ground is a ~ of straw and mud —John Galsworthy⟩ **3** *Brit* **:** a large metal can for conveying milk

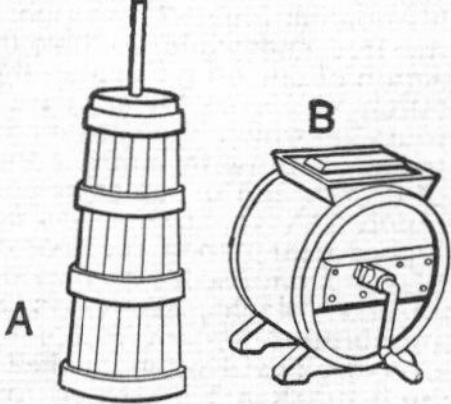

churns: *A* with plunging dasher, *B* cylinder churn

²churn \"\ *vb* -ED/-ING/-S [ME *chyrnen*, fr. *chyrne*] *vt* **1 :** to stir, beat, or agitate (milk or cream) in a churn in order to make butter **:** make (butter) by churning **2 a :** to stir or agitate violently, heavily, or continuously **b :** to make (as foam) by thus doing **3 :** to produce by vigorous or continuous mental activity ⟨whose head was ~*ing* ideas for social change —*Saturday Rev.*⟩ ~ *vi* **1 :** to work a churn (as in making butter) **2 a :** to produce or be in violent or continuous agitation ⟨the steamer's screw ~*s*⟩ **b :** to proceed by means of rotating members (as wheels or propellers) ⟨the tug ~*s* down the bay⟩ ⟨the car veered into a snowdrift and ~*ed* to a halt⟩

churn·a·bil·i·ty \-nə'biləd·ē, -ətē, -i\ *n* -ES **1** *of milk or cream* **:** ease of churning **2 :** completeness of formation of butter in churning

churn barrel *adj, of an animal* **:** having the trunk or body deep and capacious with well-sprung ribs

churn-butted \'=,==\ *adj, of a tree* **:** SWELL-BUTTED

churn drill *n* **:** a piece of drilling equipment in which the drill is raised by a rope or cable and allowed to drop, pulverizing the rock with successive blows

churning *n* -s [fr. gerund of ²*churn*] **:** the making of a batch of butter; *also* **:** the quantity of butter made at one operation

churnmilk \'=,=\ *n, chiefly dial* **:** BUTTERMILK

churn supper *n* **:** a feast at the end of the hay harvest

churn up *vt* **:** to dig into (as a driveway) with spinning wheels

chu·ro·ya \chü'rōyə\ *n, pl* **churoya** *or* **churoyas** *usu cap* [Sp *churoy*, of AmerInd origin] **1 a :** a Guahiban people of eastern Colombia **b :** a member of such people **2 :** the language of the Churoya people

chu·ro·yan \-yən\ *adj, usu cap* **:** relating or belonging to a branch of Guahiban formerly considered a distinct stock

¹churr \'chər, +V -ər-; 'chə̄, +V -ər- *also* -ər\ *vi* -ED/-ING/-S [imit.] **:** to make a churr

²churr \"\ *n* -s **:** a vibrant or whirring noise such as that made by some insects (as the cockchafer) or by some birds (as the nightjar or the partridge)

chur·ras·co \chü'räˌskō\ *n* -s [AmerSp] **:** beef broiled on a spit over an open fire or grilled under an oven flame

chur·ri·gue·resque \ˌchürēgə¦resk\ *adj* [Sp *churrigueresco*, fr. José *Churriguera* †1723 Spanish architect + Sp *-esco* -esque] **1 :** relating or belonging to a Spanish baroque architectural style characterized by elaborate surface decoration **2 :** of or relating to the Latin-American adaptation of Spanish churrigueresque forms esp. as executed by native craftsmen

chur·ro \'chü,rō\ *n* -s [Sp, coarse, coarse-wooled, coarse-wooled sheep; akin to Sp *churre* thick grease, Pg *churro, surro* dirty, unprocessed (of wool), miserable, lowly; all prob. of Iberian origin; akin to Basque *txur* miserly, economical] **:** a hardy coarse-wooled sheep originating in northwest Spain but surviving chiefly in Mexico and among the Navahos of the southwestern U.S.

churr-owl \'=,=\ *n, dial Eng* **:** the European nightjar

¹chur·rus \'chərəs\ *n* -ES [Hindi *caras*] **:** a device used in India for drawing water from deep wells that consists of a leather bag hung on a rope running over a pulley and drawn by oxen

²churrus *also* **churus** *var of* CHARAS

chuse *archaic var of* CHOOSE

chut *a t sound formed by suction rather than pressure, or* cht, *or* sht *with prolonged* sh; *often read as* 'chət\ *interj* [F, of imit. origin] — used to express impatience

¹chute *also* **shute** \'shüt, *usu* -üd.+V\ *n* -s [F, fr. OF, fem. of *chu*, past part. of *cheoir* to fall, fr. L *cadere* — more at CHANCE] **1 a :** FALL 3b **b :** a quick descent (as in a river), steep channel, or narrow sloping passage by which water falls to a lower level **:** RAPID **2 :** an artificial or natural inclined plane, sloping channel, or partially or completely covered passage (as a trough, framework) down or through which substances or bodies (as water, coal, ore, grain, or logs) may pass or slide usu. to a lower level **:** FLUME, SLIDE **3 a :** a narrow high-walled passageway or similar device for holding or restraining animals (as cattle for branding or dehorning) **b :** a straight extension of the home stretch of a race track **:** an extension of the straightaway portion of an oval running track **c :** ORE SHOOT **4** [by shortening] **:** PARACHUTE

²chute \"\ *vb* -ED/-ING/-S *vt* **:** to convey by a chute ~ *vi* **1 :** to go in or as if in a chute **2 :** to utilize a chute (as by passing ore down it) — **chute the chutes :** to go down a chute, esp. a steep slide made for amusement

chute man *n* **:** one who tends chutes esp. by receiving and disposing of loads from or into them: as **a :** a worker in a metal mine who loads mine cars underground **b :** a coal miner who tends chutes from tipple to railroad cars **c :** a millworker who receives sacks of flour, meal, or feed and readies them for storage **d :** a collector of soiled laundry in an institution

chute-the-chute *or* **chute-the-chutes** \'=='=\ *n* **1 :** a slide (as in an amusement park) often ending in a pool of water **2 :** ROLLER COASTER

chut·ing board \'shüd·iŋ-, -ütiŋ-\ *n* [by alter.] **:** SHOOTING BOARD

chut·ist \'shüd·əst, -ütəst\ *n* -s [by shortening] **:** PARACHUTIST

chut·ney \'chətnē, -ni\ *n* -s [Hindi *caṭnī*, fr. *caṭnā* to be licked, tasted, fr. *cāṭnā* to lick, taste, fr. Prakrit *caṭṭei* he licks] **:** a condiment that has the consistency of jam and is made of acid fruits with added raisins, dates, and onions and seasoned to taste with spices and vinegar ⟨apple ~⟩

chu·vash \'chü,väsh, chü'väsh\ *n, pl* **chuvash·es** \-əz\ *or* **chuvash** *or* **chu·va·shi** \chü'väshē\ *usu cap* [Russ, fr. Chuvash *Tšəvaš*; akin to Turk *yavaş* gentle, mild, docile] **1 a :** a people related to Mordvin and Cheremis inhabiting the Chuvash Republic of eastern Russia **b :** a member of such people **2 :** the Turkish dialect spoken by the Chuvash people

chuz·wi \'chəz,wē\ *n, pl* **chuzwi** *or* **chuzwis** [of African origin; akin to Umbundu *ochisovo, ochisema* waterbuck] **:** an iron-gray or blackish gray medium-sized waterbuck (*Kobus crawshayi*) of central Africa

chwdn *abbr* churchwarden

chy *abbr* chimney

chyack \'chīək\ *var of* CHIACK

chyl- *or* **chyli-** *or* **chylo-** *comb form* [F or NL, fr. Gk *chyl-, chylo-*, fr. *chylos*] **1 :** chyle ⟨*chyl*uria⟩ ⟨*chyli*form⟩ ⟨*chylo*cyst⟩ **2 :** juice ⟨*chylo*cauly⟩

chy·la·ceous \(')kī¦lāshəs\ *adj* [*chyl-* + *-aceous*] **:** possessed of the properties of chyle **:** consisting of chyle

chyle \'kīl, *esp bef pause or cons* -īəl\ *n* -s [earlier *chylus*, fr. LL, fr. Gk *chylos* juice, chyle, fr. *chein* to pour — more at FOUND] **:** lymph that is milky in appearance due to the presence of emulsified fats, that is characteristically present in the lacteals, and that is most apparent during intestinal absorption of ingested fats which pass to the blood and tissues largely by way of the lacteals and the thoracic duct

-chy·lia \'kīlēə\ *n comb form* -s [NL, fr. Gk, fr. *chyl-* + *-ia*] **:** condition of having (such) chyle ⟨*achylia*⟩

chy·li·fac·tion \ˌkīlə¦fakshən, ¦kil-\ *n* -s [by alter.] **:** CHYLIFICATION

chy·li·fac·tive \-tiv\ *or* **chy·li·fac·to·ry** \-t(ə)rē, -ri\ *or* **chy·lif·ic** \(')kī¦lifik\ *or* **chy·lif·i·ca·to·ry** \(')=¦=fəkə,tōrē, -ōr-, =¦=¦kād·ərē\ *adj* [*chylifactive* fr. *chyl-* + *-factive*; *chylifactory* fr. *chyl-* + *-factory* (fr. L *factus* — past part. of *facere* to do — + E *-ory*); *chylific* fr. NL *chylificus*, fr. *chyl-* + L *-ficus* -fic; *chylificatory* alter. (influenced by *chylification*) of *chylifactory* — more at DO] **:** producing or converting into chyle **:** having the power to form chyle

chy·lif·er·ous \(')kī¦lif(ə)rəs\ *adj* [*chyl-* + *-ferous*] **:** transmitting or conveying chyle ⟨~ vessels⟩

chy·li·fi·ca·tion \ˌkīləfə'kāshən, ˌkil-\ *n* -s [NL *chylification-, chylificatio*, fr. *chyl-* + *-fication-, -ficatio* -fication] **:** the formation of chyle

chy·li·form \'kīlə,fȯrm\ *adj* [ISV *chyl-* + *-form*] **:** resembling chyle

chy·li·fy \-,fī\ *vb* -ED/-ING/-ES [F *chylifier*, fr. *chyl-* + *-fier* -fy] *vt* **:** to make chyle of ~ *vi* **:** to become converted into chyle

chy·lo·cau·lous \¦kīlə¦kȯləs\ *adj* [G *chylocaul* chylocaulous (fr. *chyl-* + Gk. *kaulos* stem) + E *-ous* — more at HOLE] **:** having fleshy or succulent stems — used of cacti and similar plants — **chy·lo·cau·ly** \-lē, -li\ *n* -ES

chy·lo·cyst \'kīlə,sist\ *n* -s [*chyl-* + *-cyst*] **:** CISTERNA CHYLI

chy·loid \'kī,lȯid\ *adj* [*chyl-* + *-oid*] **:** CHYLIFORM

chy·lo·mi·cron \ˌkīlə'mī,krän, -'mi,k-\ *n* [*chyl-* + Gk *mikron* (neut. of *mikros* small) — more at MICR-] **:** a microscopic particle of fat common in the blood during the digestion and assimilation of ingested fat

chy·lo·phyl·lous \¦==¦filəs\ *adj* [*chyl-* + *-phyllous*] **:** having fleshy or succulent leaves ⟨~ desert plants⟩ — **chy·lo·phylly** \'==,filē, -li\ *n* -ES

chy·lo·poi·e·sis \¦==pȯi'ēsəs\ *n, pl* **chylopoie·ses** \-,sēz\ [NL, fr. *chyl-* + *-poiesis*] **:** CHYLIFICATION — **chy·lo·poi·et·ic** \-¦ed·ik\ *or* **chy·lo·po·et·ic** \-pō¦ed·-\ *adj*

chy·lo·sis \kī'lōsəs\ *n, pl* **chylo·ses** \-,sēz\ [NL, fr. Gk *chylōsis*, fr. *chyl-* + *-ōsis* -osis] **:** CHYLIFICATION

chy·lous \'kīləs\ *adj* [prob. fr. F *chyleux*, fr. MF, fr. *chyl-* + *-eux* -ous] **:** consisting of or like chyle ⟨~ ascites⟩

chy·lu·ria \kī'lürēə, kīl'yü-\ *n* -s [NL, fr. *chyl-* + *-uria*] **:** the presence of chyle in the urine as a result of organic disease (as of the kidney) or of mechanical lymphatic esp. parasitic obstruction

chy·mase \'kī,mās, -āz\ *n* -s [*chyme* + *-ase*] **:** RENNIN

chyme \'kīm\ *n* -s [NL *chymus*, fr. LL, chyle, fr. Gk *chymos* juice, fr. *chein* to pour — more at FOUND] **:** the semifluid mass of partly digested food resulting from the action of the gastric juice and expelled by the stomach into the duodenum

chymic *obs var of* CHEMIC

chy·mif·er·ous \(')kī¦mif(ə)rəs\ *adj* [ISV *chyme* + *-i-* + *-ferous*; prob. orig. formed as F *chymifère*] **:** bearing or containing chyme

chy·mi·fi·ca·tion \ˌkīməfə'kāshən, ˌkim-\ *n* -s [*chyme* + *-i-* + *-fication*] **:** the conversion of food into chyme by the digestive action of gastric juice

chy·mi·fy \'kīmə,fī\ *vt* -ED/-ING/-ES [*chyme* + *-ify*] **:** to convert into chyme

chymist *archaic var of* CHEMIST

chy·mo·plasm \'kīmə,plazəm\ *n* -s [*chyme* + *-o-* + *plasm*] **:** a portion of a mosaic egg consisting of potential mesenchyme

chy·mo·sin \'kīməsən\ *n* -s [F *chymosine*, fr. *chyme* (fr. NL *chymus*) + *-ose* + *-ine* -in] **:** RENNIN

chy·mo·trypsin \ˌkīmə +\ *n* -s [*chyme* + *-o-* + *trypsin*] **:** a crystalline proteinase known in several forms that occurs in the pancreas as chymotrypsinogen and differs from crystalline trypsin in its ability to clot milk

chy·mo·trypsinogen \ˌkīmə +\ *n* -s [ISV *chyme* + *-o-* + *trypsinogen*] **:** a precursor of a chymotrypsin prepared in crystalline form usu. from the pancreas of cattle or hogs and converted by trypsin into a chymotrypsin

chy·mous \'kīməs\ *adj* **:** of or relating to chyme

chy·pre *also* **chi·pre** \'shēprᵊ\ *n* -s [F *Chypre* Cyprus] **:** a nonalcoholic perfume containing oils and resins

chy·tra \'kī·trə, 'ki-·\ *n, pl* **chy·trae** \-(,)trē\ *or* **chy·trai** \-,trī\ [Gk, fr. *chein* to pour — more at FOUND] **:** a usu. earthenware cooking pot of ancient Greece

chy·trid \-,trəd\ *n* -s [NL *Chytridiales*] **:** one of the Chytridiales

chy·trid·i·a·ce·ae \kī-,tridē'āsē,ē, kə- -\ *n pl, cap* [NL, fr. *Chytridium*, type genus (fr. Gk *chytra* + NL *-idium*) + *-aceae*] **:** a family of aquatic fungi (order Chytridiales) having a monocentric thallus

chy·trid·i·a·ceous \(')=¦==¦āshəs\ *adj* [NL *Chytridiaceae* + E *-ous*] **:** of, resembling, or relating to the Chytridiales

chy·tri·di·a·les \=,=='ā(,)lēz\ *n pl, cap* [NL, fr. *Chytridium* + *-ales*] **:** an order of simple aquatic fungi (subclass Oomycetes) that have little or no mycelium, that have zoospores with single flagella posterior or lacking, and that are mostly saprophytic except for several which are parasitic on higher plants, animals, or freshwater fungi

chy·trid·i·o·sis \kə,tridē'ōsəs\ *also* **chy·trid·i·ose** \=¦==,ōs\ *n, pl* **chy·trid·i·o·ses** \=,==ō,sēz\ [*chytridiosis*, NL, fr. *Chytridium* + *-osis*; *chytridiose* fr. NL *Chytridium* + E *-ose*] **:** a disease caused by a chytrid

CI *abbr* **1** cast iron **2** cephalic index **3** certificate of insurance **4** chief inspector **5** color index **6** consular invoice **7** cost and insurance **8** counterintelligence

Ci·ba·cron \'sēbə,krän\ *trademark* — used for any of several fiber-reactive dyes; see DYE table I

¹ci·bar·i·al \sə'ba(a)rēəl\ *adj* [L *cibarius* of food (fr. *cibus* food, fodder, perh. of Gk origin; akin to dial. Gk *kibba* fodder bag) + E *-al*] **:** relating to food

²cibarial \"\ *adj* [NL *cibarium* + E *-al*] **1 :** relating to the cibarium **2 :** CIBARIAN

ci·bar·i·an \-ēən\ *adj* [NL *cibarium* + E *-an*] **:** of or relating to the mouthparts of an insect — used chiefly in the phrase *cibarian system of classification*

ci·bar·i·um \-ēəm\ *n, pl* **cibaria** \-ēə\ [NL, fr. L *cibus* food + *-arium*] **:** the space anterior to the true mouth cavity in which the food of an insect is chewed

cibation *n* -s [ME *cibacioun*, fr. LL *cibation-, cibatio* feeding, meal, fr. L *cibatus* (past part. of *cibare* to feed, fr. *cibus* food) + *-ion-, -io* -ion] *obs* **:** the process of feeding the alchemical crucible with fresh material during the course of an operation

cib·e·cue \'sibə,kyü\ *n, pl* **cibecue** *or* **cibecues** *usu cap* **1 :** an Apache people belonging to the San Carlos subdivision **2 :** a member of the Cibecue people

cib·ol *also* **cib·oul** *or* **cib·oule** \'sibəl\ *n* -s [F *ciboule*, fr. Prov *cebula*, fr. LL *cepulla*, dim. of L *cepa, cepe* onion] **1 :** WELSH ONION **2 :** SHALLOT 1a

cibolan *n or adj, usu cap* [Sp *Cíbola*, land of the Zuñis in New Mexico and Arizona (fr. Zuñi *šiwona*) + E *-an*] *obs* **:** ZUÑI

cib·o·le·ro \ˌsibə'le,rō\ *n* -s [MexSp, fr. Sp *cibolo* buffalo (fr. *Cíbola*) + *-ero* -er (fr. L *-arius*)] *Southwest* **:** a buffalo hunter

ci·bo·ney *also* **si·bo·ney** \ˌsēbə'nā, -bō-\ *n, pl* **ciboney** \"\ *or* **cibo·neys** \-z\ *or* **cibone·yes** \-'nā,yās\ *usu cap* [Sp, perh. fr. Arawak *siba-eyeri*, fr. *siba* rock + *eyeri* man] **1 a :** an aboriginal people of Cuba closely related to or a division of the Arawaks **b :** a member of the Ciboney people — compare TAINO **2 :** the Arawakan language of the Ciboney people

ci·bo·ri·um \sə'bōrēəm, -ȯr-\ *n, pl* **ci·bo·ria** \-ēə\ *or* **cibo·riums** [ML, fr. L, cup, fr. Gk *kibōrion* seed vessel of the Indian lotus, cup made of or shaped like this seed vessel] **1 :** a usu. covered goblet-shaped ecclesiastical vessel holding the consecrated eucharistic bread **:** PYX **2** *archit* **:** BALDACHIN; *specif* **:** a freestanding vaulted canopy supported by four columns (as that over the high altar in some churches)

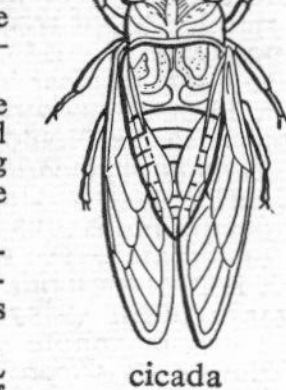
ciborium

ci·bo·ti·um \sə'bōd·ēəm\ *n, cap* [NL, fr. Gk *kibōtion*, dim. of *kibōtos* box, chest] **:** a genus of ornamental tree ferns (family Cyatheaceae) with coarse gracefully drooping fronds bluish green on the under side and with 2-valved indusia (as the Scythian lamb)

CIC *abbr* commander in chief

cic·ad \'sikəd, -,kad, 'sī,kad\ *n* -s [L *cicada*] **:** CICADA

ci·ca·da \sə'kādə, -ädə, -ādə *also* sī- *sometimes* 'sikədə\ *n* [NL, fr. L] **1** *cap* **:** a genus (the type of the family Cicadidae) of homopterous insects with a stout body, wide blunt head, and large transparent wings **2** *pl* **cicadas** *also* **cica·dae** \-(,)dē\ **:** any insect of the family Cicadidae (order Hemiptera) — called also *harvest fly, locust*

cicada

cicada bird *n* **:** a common cuckoo shrike (*Edolisoma tenuirostre*) of Australia and islands of the southwestern Pacific having the male largely bluish gray and the female olive brown

cicada killer *n* **:** a large black or rusty yellow-marked American digger wasp (*Sphecius speciosus*) that provisions its nests with cicadas

cic·a·del·la \ˌsikə'delə\ *n, cap* [NL, fr. L *cicada* + NL *-ella*] **:** the type genus of Cicadellidae

cic·a·del·lid \-ə̇d\ *n* -s [NL *Cicadellidae*] **:** a leafhopper of the family Tettigellidae; *broadly* **:** LEAFHOPPER

cic·a·del·li·dae \-ə,de'\ *n pl, cap* [NL, fr. *Cicadella*, type genus + *-idae*] *in some esp formerly classifications* **:** a large family of leafhoppers: **a :** very large family comprising all the leafhoppers and certain related insects **b :** a family more or less exactly coextensive with Tettigellidae

ci·cad·i·dae \sə'kadə,dē\ *n pl, cap* [NL, fr. *Cicada*, type genus + *-idae*] **:** a family of large insects comprising the cicadas and with the spittle insects, treehoppers, and leafhoppers commonly constituting a superfamily of Homoptera

ci·ca·la \sə'kälə\ *n* -s [It, fr. ML, alter. of L *cicada*] **1 :** CICADA **2 :** GRASSHOPPER

cic·a·trice \'sikə·trəs, -,trēs\ *n* -s [ME, fr. MF, fr. L *cicatric-, cicatrix*] **:** CICATRIX

cicatrices *pl of* CICATRIX

cic·a·tri·cial \,sikə'trishəl\ *adj* [*cicatrice* + *-ial*] **:** relating to or having the character of a cicatrix ⟨~ tissue⟩

cic·a·tri·cle \'sikə·,trikəl\ *n* -s [L *cicatricula* small scar, dim. of *cicatric-, cicatrix*] **1 :** CICATRIX 2b **2 :** BLASTODISC

ci·cat·ri·cose \sə'ka·trə,kōs, 'sikə·trə-\ *adj* [L *cicatricosus*, fr. *cicatric-, cicatrix* + *-osus* -ose] *bot* **:** marked with or as if with scars

cic·a·tri·sive \,sikə'trīsiv\ *adj* [irreg. fr. *cicatrize* (after such words as *incisive, decisive*)] **:** CICATRIZANT

cic·a·trix \'sikə·,triks *also* sə'kā·triks\ *n, pl* **cic·a·tri·ces** \,sikə·'trī(,)sēz, sə'kā·trə,sēz\ *also* **cic·a·trix·es** \'sikə·,triksəz *also* sə'kā·triksəz\ [L, scar] **1 :** a scar resulting from cicatrization of a flesh wound **2 :** a scarlike mark esp. when caused by the previous attachment of a part or organ: as **a :** the impression on the inside of a bivalve shell caused by the insertion of the adductor muscle **b** (1) **:** the permanent mark left on the stem after the fall of a leaf or bract (2) **:** the hilum of a seed

cic·a·tri·zant \,sikə·'trīzᵊnt\ *adj* [F *cicatrisant*, pres. part. of *cicatriser* to scar, fr. ML *cicatrizare*, fr. L *cicatric-, cicatrix*] **:** promoting the healing of a wound or the formation of a cicatrix

cic·a·tri·za·tion \,sikə·trə'zāshən, -ə·,trī'z-\ *n* -s [MF *cicatrisation*, fr. *cicatriser* + *-ation*] **:** the formation of a scar at the site of a healing wound by replacement of the fibroblasts of the granulation tissue by collagenous fibrous tissue followed by overgrowth of epithelium from the margin of the wound, contraction of fibrous tissue, and reduction of blood supply

cic·a·trize \'sikə·,trīz\ *vb* -ED/-ING/-S [MF or ML; MF *cicatriser*, fr. ML *cicatrizare*, fr. L *cicatrix* + ML *-izare* -ize] *vt* **1 :** to induce the formation of a scar in (a wound) **:** heal by cicatrization **2 :** SCAR ~ *vi* **:** to heal by forming a scar

cic·a·trose \-,trōs\ *adj* [by contr.] **:** CICATRICOSE

cic·e·ly \'sisᵊlē, -lī\ *n* -ES [by folk etymology (influence of proper name *Cicely*) fr. *seseli*] **:** any of several herbs of the family Umbelliferae (as of the genus *Myrrhis* or *Osmorhiza*) — see SWEET CICELY

ci·cer \'sīsə(r)\ *n* [ME *cycer*, fr. L *cicer*; akin to Gk *krios* chick-pea, LGk (Maced. dial.) *kikerros*, a kind of pea (prob. *Lathyrus ochrus*), Arm *sisern* chick-pea] **1** -S *obs* **:** CHICK-PEA **2** *cap* [NL, fr. L, chick-pea] **:** a genus of Asiatic herbs (family Leguminosae) having odd-pinnate leaves of several small dentate leaflets and solitary white or pink-tinged flowers

cic·e·ro·nage \'sisə'rōnij, ,chichə-, ,chēchə-\ *n* -S **:** the act or office of a cicerone **:** GUIDANCE

¹cic·e·ro·ne \,sisə'rōnē, ,chichə-, ,chēchə-, -ni\ *n, pl* **cicero·ni** \-(,)nē, ,ni\ *or* **cicerones** [It, after *Cicerone* Cicero; fr. the talkativeness of guides] **1 :** a guide who conducts sightseers to places or objects of interest (as a museum or a monument) **2 :** GUIDE, MENTOR

²cic·e·rone \"\ *vt* **ciceroned; ciceroned; cicero·ne·ing** \-'rōnēiŋ\ *or* **cice·ron·ing** \-'rōniŋ\ **cicerones :** to act as cicerone to **:** show the sights to

¹cic·e·ro·nian \,sisə'rōnēən, -ōnyən\ *adj, usu cap* [L *Ciceronianus*, after Marcus Tullius *Cicero* †43 B.C. Roman orator] **:** of or relating to Cicero; *specif* **:** resembling Cicero esp. in the rhythm and cadence of his periodic sentences, the balance of antitheses, or any more general oratorical or literary qualities ⟨*Ciceronian* eloquence⟩

²ciceronian \"\ *n* -S *usu cap* **:** one that admires or imitates the style of Cicero (as in purity and elegance of diction)

cic·e·ro·nian·ism \,==='nēə,nizəm, -nyə,-\ *n* -S *usu cap* **:** imitation of or resemblance to the oratorical or literary style of Cicero esp. as practiced or produced by the Ciceronians of the early Renaissance; *also* **:** any use of language characteristic of Cicero's writings

cic·e·ro·nian·ist \-,nəst\ *n* -S *usu cap* **:** one characterized by Ciceronianism

cic·e·ro·nism \,sisə'rō,nizəm, ,chichə-, ,chēchə-\ *n* -S **:** the practice or office of guiding

cich·la·so·ma \,siklə'sōmə\ *n, cap* [NL, fr. Gk *kichlē*, a wrasse + NL *-soma*] **:** a genus of small cichlid fishes including several brightly marked African species popular in the tropical aquarium

¹cich·lid \'sikləd\ *adj* [NL *Cichlidae*] **:** of or relating to the family Cichlidae **:** characteristic of a fish of this family

²cichlid \"\ *n* -S **:** a fish of the family Cichlidae

cich·li·dae \'siklə,dē\ *n pl, cap* [NL, fr. *Cichla*, type genus (fr. Gk *kichlē* thrush, also, a kind of wrasse) + *-idae*; akin to Gk *chelidōn* swallow — more at CELANDINE] **:** a large family of chiefly tropical freshwater percoid fishes similar in many respects to the American sunfishes, some (as the bolti) being important food fishes while a number of small forms are favored for the tropical aquarium

ci·cho·ri·a·ce·ae \sə,kōrē'āsē,ē, -ōr-\ *n pl, cap* [NL, fr. *Cichorium*, type genus + *-aceae*] *in some classifications* **:** a family of herbs or shrubs comprising all the composites (as chicories) that have milky juice and flower heads made up of only ligulate flowers — see COMPOSITAE — **ci·cho·ri·a·ceous** \=,==='āshəs\ *adj*

ci·cho·ri·um \sə'kōrēəm, -ōr-\ *n, cap* [NL, fr. L — more at CHICORY] **:** a genus of deep-rooted biennial or perennial herbs (family Compositae) having flowers bright blue or occas. pink or white all ligulate and with flower heads solitary or in twos or threes — see CHICORY, ENDIVE

cic·in·del·i·dae \,sisən'delə,dē\ *n pl, cap* [NL, fr. *Cicindela*, type genus (fr. L, glowworm) + *-idae*; akin to L *candēre* to shine — more at CANDID] **:** a family of active free-flying usu. bright colored diurnal predaceous beetles comprising the tiger beetles

ci·cis·be·ism \,chēchəz'bā,izəm\ *n* -S [It *cicisbeismo*, fr. *cicisbeo* + *-ismo* -ism] **:** the social institution of the cicisbeo

ci·cis·beo \-'bā(,)ō\ *n, pl* **cicis·bei** \-ā,ē\ [It] **:** the recognized gallant of a married woman in Italy esp. in the 18th century **:** CAVALIER SERVENTE

ci·co·nia \sə'kōnēə\ *n, cap* [NL, fr. L, stork; prob. akin to L *canere* to sing — more at CHANT] **:** the type genus of Ciconiidae including the common stork of Europe

ci·co·ni·idae \,sikə'nīə,dē\ *n pl, cap* [NL, fr. *Ciconia*, type genus + *-idae*] **:** a family of birds comprising the storks and jabirus and with the ibises, spoonbills, and a few related forms constituting a suborder of the order Ciconiiformes

ci·co·ni·ifor·mes \sə,kōnēə'fōr,mēz\ *n pl, cap* [NL, fr. *Ciconia* + *-iformes*] **:** an order of chiefly tropical fish-eating wading birds including the herons, storks, spoonbills, flamingos, and related forms all relatively large and usu. with long legs and bills, upright carriage, and excepting the flamingos unwebbed feet

cic·o·nine \'sikə,nīn, -,nən\ *adj* [L *ciconia* + E *-ine*] **:** of, relating to, or resembling the storks

cicurate *vt* -ED/-ING/-S [L *cicuratus*, past part. of *cicurare* to tame, fr. *cicur* tame; akin to Skt *śakura* tame] *obs* **:** to make mild or innocuous **:** TAME

ci·cu·ta \sə'kyüd·ə\ *n* [NL, fr. L, poison hemlock (prob. *Conium maculatum*)] **1** *cap* **:** a small genus of perennial herbs (family Umbelliferae) having tuberous usu. fascicled deadly poisonous roots and the leaves twice or thrice pinnate or ternate — see POISON HEMLOCK, WATER HEMLOCK **2** -S [L] **:** POISON HEMLOCK 1

cic·u·toxin \,sikyə+\ *n* [ISV *cicu-* (fr. NL *Cicuta*) + *toxin*] **:** an amorphous poisonous principle $C_{19}H_{26}O_3$ in plants of the genus *Cicuta*

CID *abbr* criminal investigation department; criminal investigation detachment; criminal investigation division

-cidal \,sīdᵊl\ *adj comb form* [LL *-cidalis*, fr. L *-cida* + *-alis* -al — more at -CIDE] **1 :** killing **:** having power to kill ⟨filari*cidal*⟩ **2 :** cutting ⟨loculi*cidal*⟩

cid·a·rid \'sidərəd\ *n* -S [NL *Cidaridae*] **:** a sea urchin of the family Cidaridae

ci·dar·i·dae \sə'darə,dē\ *n pl, cap* [NL, fr. *Cidaris*, type genus + *-idae*] **:** a family of sea urchins including all recent members of the order Cidaroida and comprising a number of forms that are widely distributed in warm seas

cid·a·ris \'sidərəs\ *n* **1** *pl* **cida·res** \-,rēz\ [L, fr. Gk *kidaris*, prob. of Sem origin; akin to Heb *kether* crown] **:** the royal tiara of the ancient Persian kings **2** *cap* [NL, fr. L] **:** the type genus of Cidaridae

cid·a·roi·da \,sidə'rȯidə\ *n pl, cap* [NL, fr. *Cidaris* + *-oida*] **:** the oldest surviving order of sea urchins containing the most primitive of living forms, all lacking peristomial gills and sphaeridia but having an apically located anus — see CIDARIDAE

-cide \,sīd\ *n comb form* -S [MF, fr. L *-cida*, fr. *caedere* to kill — more at CONCISE] **1 :** killer ⟨frat*ricide*⟩ ⟨insecti*cide*⟩ **2** [MF, fr. L *-cidium*, fr. *caedere*] **:** killing ⟨homi*cide*⟩ ⟨sui*cide*⟩

ci·der \'sīdə(r)\ *n* -S [ME *sidre, sider, cidre*, fr. OF *sidre*, fr. LL *sicera* strong drink, fr. LGk *sikera*, of Sem origin; akin to Heb *shēkhār* strong drink] **1 :** the expressed juice of apples or sometimes other fruits used as a beverage or for making other products (as applejack, vinegar, and apple butter) — called also *sweet cider* **2** *Brit* **:** fermented apple juice often made sparkling by carbonation or fermentation in a sealed container

cider apple *n* **1 :** an apple grown esp. because it produces a superior cider **2 :** an apple below marketable grade for eating or storage but suitable for making cider

cider gum *or* **cider tree** *n* **:** an Australian tree (*Eucalyptus gunnii*) from the sap of which a ciderlike beverage is made

ci·der·kin \'sīdə(r)kən\ *n* -S [*cider* + *-kin*] **:** weak cider made by steeping the refuse pomace from cider making

cider royal *also* **cider oil** *n* **:** concentrated cider with honey

cider vinegar *n* **:** vinegar made from fermented cider

cider wine *n, dial Eng* **:** hard cider sugared and spiced

ci·dery \'sīdərē, -ri\ *adj* **:** smelling or tasting of or like cider or rotting apples

¹ci-de·vant \sēdᵊväⁿ\ *adj* [F, lit., hitherto, formerly] **:** FORMER, LATE, EX- ⟨*ci-devant* governor⟩

²ci-devant \"\ *n* -S **1 :** one that had been a noble before titles were abolished during the French Revolution **2 :** a person or thing of the past **3 :** one retired or no longer having power or influence **:** HAS-BEEN

¹ciel *obs var of* CEIL

²ciel \'sel, 'syel\ *n* -S [F, sky, fr. L *caelum* — more at -HOOD] **:** a pale or light blue like that of the clear sky

cieling *obs var of* CEILING

cié·na·ga *or* **cie·ne·ga** \'syänəgə, 'syen- 'sin-, -,gä\ *n* -S [Sp *ciénaga*, fr. *cieno* mud, slime, fr. L *caenum* dirt, filth — more at OBSCENE] *Southwest* **:** SWAMP, MARSH; *esp* **:** one formed by hillside springs

-cies *pl of* -CY

CIF *abbr* cost, insurance, and freight

CIFC *abbr* cost, insurance, freight, and charges; cost, insurance, freight, and commission

CIFE *abbr* cost, insurance, freight, and exchange

CIFI *abbr* cost, insurance, freight, and interest

cig \'sig\ *n* -S [by shortening] *slang* **:** CIGARETTE

ci·ga·la \sə'gälə\ *or* **ci·gale** \-'gäl\ *n* -S [F & Prov; F *cigale*, fr. Prov *cigala*, fr. ML *cicala*, alter. of L *cicada*] **:** CICADA

ci·gar *also* **se·gar** \sə'gär, -gȧ(r *sometimes* 'si,g-, *chiefly substand* 'sē,g-\ *n* -S [Sp *cigarro*, perh. of Mayan origin; akin to Maya *sīc* tobacco, cigar, pipe, *sicar* to perfume, smoke] **:** a tubular roll of tobacco designed for smoking usu. consisting of a core bound together by a leaf with the whole being encased in another leaf of smooth and even texture — see BINDER, FILLER, WRAPPER

cigar-box cedar \='=,=-\ *n* **:** SPANISH CEDAR

cigar casebearer *n* **:** a larval moth (*Coleophora serratella*) that is enclosed in a brown cigar-shaped case and that feeds on apple-tree and other fruit-tree foliage

cig·a·resque \,sigə'resk; sə,gä'resk, -gȧ-\ *adj* **:** featured by a cigar

cig·a·rette *also* **cig·a·ret** \,sigə'ret, '==,=, *usu* -ed·+V\ *n* -S [F *cigarette*, dim. of *cigare* cigar, fr. Sp *cigarro*] **1 a :** a tube of finely cut tobacco enclosed in paper, designed for smoking, and usu. narrower and shorter than a cigar **b :** a similar tube for smoking filled wholly or partly with some substance other than tobacco **2 :** ANTIQUE BROWN

cigarette beetle *n* **:** a small brown beetle (*Lasioderma serricorne*) of the family Anobiidae often very destructive to stored tobacco products, other vegetable materials, and animal materials

cigarette drain *n* **:** a cigarette-shaped gauze wick enclosed in rubber dam tissue or rubber tubing for draining wounds

cigarette girl *n* **:** a girl who walks about a dining room or nightclub selling cigarettes

cigarette paper *n* **:** a thin strong tissue paper that burns evenly and is of the proper porosity to control the burning of the tobacco it surrounds

cigarfish \='=,=\ *n* [so called fr. its shape] **:** ROUND SCAD; *also* **:** the related mackerel scad (*Decapterus macarellus*)

cigar flower *also* **cigar plant** *n* [so called fr. the shape of the flower] **:** a tender spreading perennial (*Cuphea ignea*) used as a pot plant and having solitary bright-red tubular flowers with a dark ring at the end and a white mouth

cig·a·ril·lo \,sigə'ril,ō\ *also* **cig·a·ri·to** \-'rēd·,ō\ *n* -S [Sp *cigarrillo, cigarrito*, dim. of *cigarro* cigar] **1 :** a very small cigar **2 :** a cigarette wrapped in tobacco rather than paper

ci·gar·less *pronunc at* CIGAR +ləs\ *adj* **:** lacking a cigar

ci·gar·ro \sə'gär,ō\ *n* -S [Sp] **:** CIGAR, CIGARILLO

cigar spot *n* **:** frogeye of tobacco

cigar store *n* **:** a shop selling tobacco products and related items

cigar-store indian \='=,=-\ *n, usu cap I* **:** a wooden effigy of an American Indian at a cigar-store door

cigar tree *n* [so called fr. the shape of the pods] **:** WESTERN CATALPA

ci·gua \'sēgwə\ *n* -S [Sp *cigua, sigua*, fr. Taino] **:** a lancewood (*Ocotea coriacea*)

ci·gua·te·ra \,sēgwə'terə\ *n* -S [AmerSp, prob. fr. *cigua* sea snail, fr. Taino] **:** poisoning caused by eating fish or mollusks with flesh toxic to man

cilery *or* **cillery** *n* -ES [alter. of earlier *celure* bed canopy, bed hangings, tapestry, fr. ME *celure, sillour, siller*, fr. OF *celeure* ceiling, canopy, fr. ML *celatura* canopy, carved ceiling, fr. L *caelatura* carving, fr. *caelare* to carve — more at CEIL] *obs* **:** the carved ornamentation of the capital of a column

cili- *or* **cilii-** *or* **cilio-** *comb form* [NL, fr. *cilia*] **1 :** ciliary body ⟨*cili*otomy⟩ **:** ciliary body and ⟨*cilio*retinal⟩ **2 :** cilia ⟨*cili*ferous⟩ ⟨*cilii*form⟩ ⟨*cilio*grade⟩

cilia [NL, pl. of *cilium*, fr. L, eyelid, prob. back-formation fr. *supercilium* eyebrow — more at SUPERCILIOUS] *pl of* CILIUM

cil·i·ary \'silē,erē, -i\ *adj* [F *ciliaire*, or L *cilia* + E *-ary*; F *ciliaire* fr. L *cilia* + F *-aire* -ary — more at CILIA] **1 :** of or relating to cilia **2** *of ocular structures* **:** of, relating to, or being the ciliary body ⟨a ~ arteriole⟩ ⟨the ~ zonule⟩

ciliary body *n* **:** an annular structure on the inner surface of the anterior wall of the eyeball composed largely of the ciliary muscle and bearing the ciliary processes

ciliary flame *n* **:** a tuft of cilia functioning in excretion (as in the nephrostomes of annelids or the flame cells of flatworms)

ciliary ganglion *n* **:** a small autonomic ganglion on the nasociliary branch of the ophthalmic nerve receiving preganglionic fibers from the oculomotor nerve and sending postganglionic fibers to the ciliary muscle and to the circular muscle of the iris

ciliary muscle *n* **:** an annular muscle composed of nonstriated fibers situated in the ciliary body and serving as the chief agent in accommodation — see EYE illustration

ciliary process *n* **:** any one of the vascular folds on the inner surface of the ciliary body that give attachment to the suspensory ligament of the lens

cil·i·a·ta \,silē'ād·ə\ *n pl, cap* [NL, fr. *cilium* + *-ata* — more at CILIA] **:** a large class (commonly divided into the subclasses Protociliata and Euciliata) of chiefly free-living and holozoic protozoans distinguished by possession of cilia or cirri throughout the vegetative stages of the life cycle and usu. having nuclei of two kinds

¹cil·i·ate \'silēət, -,āt, *usu* -d·+V\ *or* **cil·i·at·ed** \'==,ād·əd\ *adj* [*ciliate* fr. NL *ciliatus*, fr. *cilium* + L *-atus* -ate; *ciliated* fr. NL *ciliatus* + E *-ed*] **:** provided with cilia ⟨a ~ leaf⟩ ⟨~ infusorians⟩ — **cil·i·ate·ly** *adv*

²ciliate \"\ *n* -S **:** a protozoan of the subphylum Ciliophora

cil·i·a·tion \,=='āshən\ *n* -S **:** the state or degree of being ciliate **:** the cilia of a part

cil·ice \'siləs\ *n* -S [F, fr. L *cilicium*, fr. *Cilicius* Cilician, fr. *Cilicia*, ancient region in Asia Minor] **1 :** HAIRCLOTH **2 :** a hair shirt or undergarment

¹ci·li·cian \sə'lishən\ *adj, usu cap* [*Cilicia*, ancient region in Asia Minor (fr. L) + E *-an*] **1 :** of, relating to, or characteristic of Cilicia, an ancient country and region in southeast Asia Minor **2 :** of, relating to, or characteristic of Cilicians

²cilician \"\ *n* -S *cap* **:** a native or inhabitant of ancient Cilicia

cilii- *or* **cilio-** — see CILI-

cil·io·flag·el·la·ta \,silēō,flajə'lād·ə\ [NL, fr. *cili-* + *Flagellata*] *syn of* DINOFLAGELLATA

cil·io·late \'silēə,lāt, -,lət\ *adj* [NL *ciliolum* + E *-ate*] **:** minutely ciliate

ci·li·o·lum \sə'līələm\ *n, pl* **cilio·la** \-lə\ [NL, dim. of *cilium*] **:** a minute or secondary cilium

¹cil·i·oph·o·ra \,silē'äf(ə)rə\ *n pl, cap* [NL, fr. *cili-* + *-phora*] **:** a subphylum of Protozoa including those protozoans that possess cilia during some phase of the life cycle and usu. have nuclei of two kinds and comprising the classes Ciliata and Suctoria — compare PLASMODROMA — **cil·i·oph·o·ran** \,=='äf(ə)rən\ *adj or n*

²ciliophora \"\ [NL, fr. *cili-* + *-phora*] *syn of* CILIATA

cil·i·um \'silēəm\ *n, pl* **cil·ia** \-ēə\ *also* **ciliums** [NL, fr. L, eyelid — more at CILIA] **1 :** EYELASH **2 :** a minute hairlike process often forming a fringe (as between the teeth of the moss peristome or on the margins of many leaves) **3 :** a hairlike process found on many cells that is capable of vibratory or lashing movement and that serves in free-swimming unicellular organisms and in some small multicellular forms as an organ of locomotion or in the higher animal as a producer of a current of fluid (as in the human external nares, trachea, and bronchi where ciliated cells beating constantly toward the nose assist in removal of mucus and dust particles) **4 :** a barbicel of a feather

cill *var of* SILL

cillery *var of* CILERY

¹cima *var of* CYMA

²ci·ma \'chēmə\ *n* -S [It, top, summit, mountain peak, fr. L *cyma* young sprout of a cabbage, the tip of the stalk — more at CYME] **:** a mountain peak or dome

cim·ar·ron *also* **cim·ma·ron** \'simə,rän, -,rōn, ,=='=; '==,rən\ *or* **cim·a·roon** \,=='rün\ *n, pl* **cimarrons** \-nz\ *or* **cimarrones** \,=='rō(,)nēz, -(,)nās\ *sometimes cap* [AmerSp *cimarrón* — more at MAROON] **1 a :** a fugitive slave **:** a descendant of an escaped slave **:** MAROON ⟨the ~s of the West Indies and Central America⟩ **b :** a feral animal **2** *West* **:** BIGHORN

cim·ba·lom *also* **cym·ba·lom** \'simbələm\ *or* **cymbalon** \-lən\ *or* **cem·ba·lon** \'sem-\ *n* -S [Hung *cimbalom*, fr. It *cembalo* dulcimer, cymbal, fr. L *cymbalum* cymbal — more at CYMBAL] **:** a Hungarian gypsy dulcimer

cimbia *n* -S [It, fr. ML *cymbia* arch, vault, fr. LL, canopy, fr. L *cymbium* small cup, fr. Gk *kymbion*, dim. of *kymbē* cup, boat — more at CYMBA] *obs* **:** a fillet or band around the shaft of a column

cimblin *var of* CYMLING

cim·bo·rio \sim'bōrē,ō\ *n* -S [Sp, fr. ML *ciborium* — more at CIBORIUM] *in Spanish architecture* **:** a raised structure like a dome or a cupola; *specif* **:** a lantern usu. octagonal in plan built over the crossing of a Gothic cathedral

cim·bri \'sim,brī, 'kim(,)brē\ *n pl, usu cap* [L] **:** a prob. Celtic or Teutonic people that invaded Italy and were destroyed by the Romans in 101 B.C. — **cim·bri·an** \-,brēən\ *adj or n, usu cap* — **cim·bric** \-,brik\ *adj, usu cap*

ci·me·lia \sə'mēlēə, -lyə\ *n pl* [ML, fr. Gk *keimēlia*, pl. of *keimēlion*; akin to Gk *keisthai* to lie — more at CEMETERY] **:** TREASURES: **a :** HEIRLOOMS **b :** church treasures

cimeter *var of* SCIMITAR

ci·mex \'sī,meks\ *n* [L — more at CHINCH] **1** *pl* **cim·i·ces** \'simə,sēz\ **:** BEDBUG **2** *cap* [NL, fr. L] **:** the type genus of Cimicidae comprising the common bedbug and a few related insects

ci·mi·cid \'sīməsəd, 'sim-, -,sid\ *n* -S [NL *Cimicidae*] **:** a bug of the family Cimicidae

ci·mic·i·dae \sī'misə,dē, sə'-\ *n pl, cap* [NL, fr. *Cimic-, Cimex*, type genus + *-idae*] **:** a small family of flat-bodied wingless bloodsucking bugs (order Hemiptera) including the bedbug and certain pests of birds and bats

cim·i·cif·u·ga \,simə'sifyəgə\ *n, cap* [NL, fr. *Cimic-, Cimex* + *-i-* + *-fuga* -fuge] **:** a small genus of perennial herbs (family Ranunculaceae) having two or three ternately divided serrate leaves and white flowers in long rodlike racemes — see BUGBANE

cim·i·cif·u·gin \-jən\ *n* -S [NL *cimicifuga* + E *-in*] **:** an eclectic resinoid prepared from the bugbane (*Cimicifuga racemosa*) and used as a nerve tonic and antispasmodic

ci·mi·coid \'sīmə,kȯid, 'sim-\ *adj* [prob. fr. F *cimicoïde*, fr. L *cimic-, cimex* bug + F *-oïde* -oid] **:** of or resembling the Cimicidae

cim·i·nite \'chimə,nīt, 'sim-\ *n* -S [Monti *Cimini* (Ciminian hills), Italy, its locality + E *-ite*] **:** an extrusive rock intermediate between trachyte and andesite that is marked by the presence of olivine

cimmaron *var of* CIMARRON

¹cim·me·ri·an \sə'mirēən, -mēr-\ *adj, usu cap* [L *Cimmerii*, a mythical people (fr. Gk *Kimmerioi*) + E *-an*] **1 :** of or suggestive of the Cimmerians **2 :** suggestive of the fabled home of the Cimmerians **:** marked by intensity of darkness or gloom **:** STYGIAN ⟨in ~ gloom, darker than starless midnight — a darkness that could be felt —Norman Douglas⟩

²cimmerian \"\ *n* -S, *usu cap* **1 :** one of a mythical people described by Homer as dwelling in a remote realm of mist and gloom **2 :** one of a nomadic people of antiquity dwelling about the Crimea who overran Asia Minor about 635 B.C. and were succeeded in southern Russia by the Sarmatians and Scythians

cim·o·lite \'simə,līt, sə'mō,l-\ *n* -S [G *zimolit*, fr. *Cimolus*, island in the Aegean sea + G *-it* -ite] **:** a mineral $2Al_2O_3.9SiO_2.6H_2O$ consisting of a hydrous aluminum silicate occurring in soft white to reddish claylike masses

cin- — see KIN-

C in C *abbr* commander in chief

¹cinch \'sinch\ *n* -ES [Sp *cincha*, fr. L *cingula* girdle, girth, fr. *cingere* to gird — more at CINCTURE] **1 :** a strong girth often of braided horsehair or canvas for a pack or saddle **2 :** a tight clinched hold or grasp ⟨a ~ on what was going on⟩ **3 a :** a thing accomplished with great ease **:** a thing obtained or condition attained to very easily ⟨the country's flatness makes cycling a ~ —Israel Shenker⟩ **b :** a certainty as indicated **:** a person or thing sure to do as predicted — often used with an infinitive or dependent clause ⟨not only political naturals but surefire ~s to make newspaper headlines —Andy Logan⟩ ⟨it's a ~ that the Blues will win⟩

²cinch \"\ *vb* -ED/-ING/-ES *vt* **1 a :** to put a cinch or girth on ⟨~ a horse⟩ **:** GIRTH **b :** to bind closely **:** fasten tightly or snugly with or as if with a belt ⟨~ his arms fast⟩ ⟨a waistline ~*ed* with a belt⟩ **c :** to get a sure hold on **:** place (one) in a tight situation, in difficulties, or at a disadvantage ⟨these grafters ~*ing* honest businessmen⟩ **d :** to secure firmly **:** TIGHTEN — used with *up* or *on* ⟨~ up your belt⟩ **2 :** to make utterly certain **:** GUARANTEE, ASSURE ⟨his speed ~*ed* the victory for his team⟩ ⟨this speech by the candidate has ~*ed* his nomination⟩ **3 :** to tighten (a roll of film) by pulling on the free end while holding the spool ~ *vi* **:** to perform the action of cinching **:** tighten the cinch — often used with *up*

³cinch \"\ *n* -ES [*¹cinch*] **:** a variety of the card game of all fours in which the players bid for the privilege of naming trump, a draw to improve the hand is permitted, and the five of trumps and of the same-colored suit have special values

⁴cinch \"\ *vt* -ED/-ING/-ES *in the game of cinch* **:** to play a higher trump than the five on (a trick) so that a following player cannot score by playing a five

cin·cha \'sinchə, 'sēn-\ *n* -S [Sp — more at CINCH] **:** ¹CINCH 1

cinchbinder \'=,==\ *n* **:** a horse that balks, rears, or falls over backward when cinched too tight

cinch mark *n* **:** a scratch formed on the emulsion by friction between adjacent layers of a photographic film during cinching

cin·cho·caine \'siŋkə,kān, 'sin-\ *n* -S [NL *Cinchona* + E *-caine* (as in *cocaine*)] **:** DIBUCAINE

cin·cho·loi·pon \,siŋkə'lȯi,pän, ,sin-\ *n* -S [ISV *cinchon*ine + Gk *loipon*, *loipos* remainder, fr. *leipein* to leave — more at LOAN] **:** a yellow crystalline acid $C_5H_9N(C_2H_5)CH_2COOH$ obtained esp. by oxidation of cinchonine

cin·cho·me·ron·ic acid \¦══mə¦ränik-\ *n* [ISV *cinchomeronic* (fr. *cinchonine* + *mer-* + *-onic*) + *acid*; orig. formed as G *cinchomeronsäure*] **:** a colorless crystalline acid $C_5H_3N(COOH)_2$ made by oxidizing cinchonine, quinine, or isoquinoline; 3,4-pyridine-dicarboxylic acid

cin·cho·na \siŋˈkōnə, sin- *also* -nˈchō-\ *n* [NL, after Doña Francisca Henríquez de Ribera, countess of *Chinchón* †1641 vicereine of Peru, who was said to have introduced it to Europe] **1** *cap* **:** a large genus of trees (family Rubiaceae) being native to the Andean region of northeastern So. America and now extensively cultivated both there and in Indonesia and having panicled flowers with a salver-shaped corolla and an ovary crowned with a fleshy disk **2** *also* **chin·cho·na** \chinˈch-\ *or* **chin·co·na** \chinˈk-\ -s **:** a tree of the genus *Cinchona* **3** *or* **cinchona bark** *also* **chinchona** *or* **chincona** -s **:** the dried bark of any of several trees of the genus *Cinchona* (esp. *C. ledgeriana* and *C. succirubra* or their hybrids) containing alkaloids (as quinine, cinchonine, quinidine, and cinchonidine) and being used esp. formerly as a specific in malaria, an antipyretic in other fevers, and a tonic and stomachic — called also *Jesuits' bark, Peruvian bark*

cin·chon·a·mine \-ˈkänə,mēn, -kōn-, -,mən\ *n* -s [ISV *cinchon-* (fr. NL *Cinchona*) + *amine*; orig. formed in F] **:** a white crystalline alkaloid $C_{19}H_{24}N_2O$ obtained from certain So. American shrubs (genus *Remijia*) that has been used as a substitute for and is more toxic than quinine

[1]**cin·chon·ic** \(ˈ)siŋ¦känik, (ˈ)sin¦-\ *adj* [NL *Cinchona* + E *-ic*] **:** belonging to or obtained from cinchona

[2]**cinchonic** \"\ *n* -s **:** a constituent or preparation of cinchona used in medicine

cin·chon·i·cine \siŋˈkänə,sēn, sinˈk-, -kōn-, -,sən\ *n* -s [ISV *cinchonic* + *-ine*; orig. formed in F] **:** CINCHOTOXINE

cin·chon·i·dine \-,dēn, -,dən\ *n* -s [ISV *cinchon-* (fr. NL *Cinchona*) + *-idine*; orig. formed in F] **:** a bitter crystalline levorotatory alkaloid $C_{19}H_{22}N_2O$ stereoisomeric with cinchonine that is found in cinchona bark and used like quinine

cin·cho·nine \ˈ═kə,nēn, -,nən\ *n* -s [F, fr. NL *cinchona* + F *-ine*] **:** a bitter white crystalline dextrorotatory alkaloid $C_{19}H_{22}N_2O$ stereoisomeric with cinchonidine that is found in cinchona bark and cuprea bark and used like quinine

cin·cho·nin·ic acid \¦══¦ninik-\ *n* [ISV *cinchonine* + *-ic*; orig. formed as G *cinchoninsäure*] **:** a white crystalline acid C_9H_6NCOOH made by reaction of isatin and a pyruvic salt or by oxidation of cinchonine; 4-quinoline-carboxylic acid

cin·cho·nism \ˈsiŋkə,nizəm, ˈsin-\ *n* -s [ISV *cinchon-* (fr. NL *Cinchona*) + *-ism*] **:** a condition either produced by excessive or long-continued use of or activated by sensitivity to cinchona or its alkaloids (as quinine) and marked by temporary deafness, ringing in the ears, headache, dizziness, and rash

cin·cho·nize \-,nīz\ *vt* -ED/-ING/-S [NL *Cinchona* + E *-ize*] **:** to treat (as a malarial patient) with cinchona or its alkaloids (as quinine) **:** produce intensive cinchonism in

cin·cho·nol·o·gy \,siŋkəˈnäləjē, sin-, -ji\ *n* -ES [NL *Cinchona* + E *-logy*] **:** a branch of pharmacology dealing with cinchona and its derivatives

cin·cho·phen \ˈ══,fen, -,fən\ *n* -s [*cinchoninic* + *phenyl*] **:** a bitter white crystalline compound $C_9H_5N(C_6H_5)COOH$ made synthetically and used for treating gout and rheumatism but damaging to the liver; 2-phenyl-cinchoninic acid

cin·cho·tine \-,tēn, -,tən\ *n* -s [F, irreg. fr. NL *Cinchona* + F *-ine*] **:** a crystalline alkaloid $C_{19}H_{24}N_2O$ in cinchona bark — called also *hydrocinchonine*

cin·cho·tox·ine \,siŋ-, ,sin- +\ *n* -s [ISV *cincho-* (fr. NL *Cinchona*) + *toxine*] **:** a crystalline alkaloid $C_{19}H_{22}N_2O$ obtained from cinchonine or cinchonidine by heating — called also *cinchonicine*

cinch ring *n* [[1]*cinch*] **:** a metal ring terminating a cinch and used to make it fast to a saddle

[1]**cin·cin·nati** \¦sin(t)sə¦nad·ē, -at|, |i, |ə\ *adj*, *usu cap* [fr. *Cincinnati*, Ohio] **:** of or from the city of Cincinnati, Ohio **:** of the kind or style prevalent in Cincinnati

[2]**cincinnati** \"\ *n*, *usu cap* [fr. *Cincinnati*, Ohio] **:** a wild-card poker game

[1]**cin·cin·nat·i·an** \|ēən\ *n* -s *cap* [*Cincinnati*, Ohio + E *-an*] **:** a native or resident of Cincinnati, Ohio

[2]**cincinnatian** \"\ *adj*, *usu cap* **1 :** CINCINNATI **2** [so called fr. the succession of formations found in the region of Cincinnati] **:** of or relating to a division of the American Ordovician — see GEOLOGIC TIME table

cin·clus \ˈsiŋkləs\ *n*, *cap* [NL, fr. Gk *kinklos*, a kind of bird] **:** the genus consisting of the water ouzels sometimes placed in the Turdidae or isolated in a separate family

cinct \ˈsiŋ(k)t\ *adj* [ME *cincte*, fr. L *cinctus*] **:** ENGIRDLED

[1]**cinc·ture** \ˈsiŋ(k)chə(r), -)shə(r)\ *n* -s [L *cinctura* girdle, fr. *cinctus*, past part. of *cingere* to gird; akin to Gk *kakala* walls, Skt *kāñci* girdle, Lith *kinkyti* to harness a horse] **1 :** GIRDING, ENCOMPASSING, ENCLOSURE **:** act of encircling ⟨an island in the ~ of the sea⟩ **2 :** GIRDLE, BELT ⟨a robe gathered with a ~⟩ **3 :** the fillet, list, or band next to the apophyge at the extremity of the shaft of a column

[2]**cincture** \"\ *vt* **cinctured**; **cinctured**; **cincturing** \-chəriŋ, -sh(ə)riŋ\ **cinctures :** to girdle with or as if with a cincture **:** GIRD, ENCIRCLE ⟨a valley *cinctured* with mountains⟩ ⟨her hair *cinctured* with a band⟩

[1]**cin·der** \ˈsində(r)\ *n* -s *often attrib* [ME *cinder*, alter. (influenced by F *cendre* ash) of *sinder*, fr. OE; akin to OHG *sintar* dross, slag, ON *sindr*, OSlav *sędra* stalactite] **1 a :** the slag from a metal furnace **:** DROSS, SCORIA **b :** a scale thrown off in forging metal **2 cinders** *pl* **a :** ASHES **:** the incombustible residue of something burnt; *esp* **:** small fragments of clinker left by burning soft coal **b** *obs* **:** the residue of a human body following cremation or decomposition **3 a :** a partly burned combustible in which fire is extinct or which no longer gives off flame — often distinguished from *ash* and *ashes* **b :** a hot coal without flame **:** EMBER **c :** a piece of partly burned coal capable of further burning without flame **4 :** one of the small commonly vesicular fragments of lava that are projected from an erupting volcano, are about ¼ to 1½ inches in diameter, and are coarser than volcanic ash and smaller than volcanic bombs — compare LAPILLUS, SCORIA **5** *or* **cinder gray :** a purplish gray that is redder and lighter than crane, slightly less strong than dove gray, lighter than granite, and redder than zinc — called also *crystal gray, silverwing* **6 cinders** *pl* **:** a cinder running track **:** an outdoor track ⟨faster in indoor races than on ~*s*⟩

[2]**cinder** \"\ *vt* **cindered**; **cindered**; **cindering** \-d(ə)riŋ\ **cinders** [ME *scindern*, fr. *cinder, sinder*, n.] **1** *archaic* **:** to burn or reduce to cinders **2 :** to sprinkle with cinders

cinder block *n* **1 :** a block closing the front of a blast furnace and containing the cinder notch **2 :** a hollow rectangular unit made of cinder concrete and used in walls, partitions, and foundations of buildings

cinder concrete *n* **:** portland-cement concrete in which clean well-burned coal cinders are used as coarse aggregate

cinder cone *n* **:** a conical hill formed by the accumulation of volcanic debris around a vent

cinder dick *n*, *slang* **:** a railroad policeman or special agent

cin·der·el·la \,sindəˈrelə, *attrib* ¦══¦══\ *n* -s *often cap* [after *Cinderella*, heroine of a fairy tale who is mistreated by her stepmother but elevated to happiness and affluence through the intervention of her fairy godmother] **:** a person, place, or thing likened to Cinderella of the fairy tale: **a :** one suffering neglect usu. undeservedly in a lowly despised position ⟨bats are the ~*s* of the mammal world⟩ **b :** one suddenly lifted often fortuitously from obscurity and neglect to honor and significance ⟨uranium is a ~ among the world's metals⟩

cinderella dance *n*, *usu cap C* [so called fr. the episode in the Cinderella fairy tale in which Cinderella's fine raiment and equipage, metamorphosed by her fairy godmother from baser materials to enable her to attend a royal ball, are converted to their original state at the stroke of midnight] *Brit* **:** a dancing party that is to end at midnight

cin·der·man \ˈ══,man, -,maa(ə)n,-,mən\ *n*, *pl* **cindermen 1 :** a worker who removes ashes or slag **2** [*cinder* (track) + *man*] **:** FOOT RACER

cinder notch *also* **cinder tap** *n* **:** the opening in a blast furnace through which molten slag flows out

cin·der·ous \ˈsind(ə)rəs\ *adj* **:** composed of or suggestive of cinders **:** CINDERY

cinder path *n* **:** a path or running track surfaced with cinders

cinder pig *n* **:** pig iron made from a mixture of mill cinder with ore or crude metal

cinder track *n* **:** a running track surfaced with hard-packed cinders

cin·dery \ˈsind(ə)rē, -ri\ *adj* **1 :** like a cinder **2 :** composed of or full of cinders **:** sprinkled or begrimed with cinders

cine *also* **ciné** \ˈsinē, -nā\ *n* -s [partly short for *cinema*, partly fr. F *ciné*, short for *cinématographe*] **1 :** MOTION PICTURE **2** [Sp, It & F; Sp & It *cine*, fr. F *ciné*] **:** a motion-picture theater

cine- *comb form* [*cinema*] **:** motion picture ⟨*cine*camera⟩ ⟨*cine*film⟩ ⟨*cine*-X ray⟩

cin·e·ast *also* **cin·é·aste** \ˈsinē,ast, -nā-, -əst\ *n* -s [F *cinéaste* scenario writer, movie fan, fr. *ciné* + *-aste* (as in *enthusiaste* enthusiast)] **:** a devotee of motion pictures

cin·e·dance \ˈsinə,═\ *n* [*cine-* + *dance*] **:** a dance composition or performance esp. devised for motion-picture photography

cin·e·fluorogram \¦sinə+\ *n* [*cine-* + *fluorogram*] **:** a motion picture produced by cinefluorography

cin·e·fluorographic \"+\ *adj* **:** of, used in, or relating to cinefluorography

cin·e·fluorography \"+\ *n* [*cine-* + *fluorography*] **:** the process of making motion pictures of images of objects by means of X rays with the aid of a fluorescent screen (as for revealing the motions of organs in the body or the movement of inanimate objects) — compare CINERADIOGRAPHY

cin·e·ma \ˈsinəmə *sometimes* -,mä\ *n* -s [short for *cinematograph*] **1** *chiefly Brit* **a :** MOTION PICTURE **b :** a motion-picture showing **c :** a motion-picture theater **2 a :** the art or technique of making motion pictures — usu. used with *the* **b :** the production and distribution of motion pictures or the industry devoted to their production and distribution — usu. used with *the* **c :** motion pictures exhibited as a medium of communication and entertainment — usu. used with *the* **3 :** material or method of a specified suitability for motion-picture production ⟨this story is good ~⟩

cinemagoer \ˈ═══,══\ *n* -s **:** one that attends motion pictures with frequency

cin·e·mat·ic \¦sinə¦mad·ik, -atik, -ēk\ *adj* [*cinema*tograph + *-ic*] **1 :** played, narrated, or otherwise presented for photographing with a motion-picture camera and projection on a screen or suited or adapted for such reproduction ⟨a ~ fantasy on a musical theme⟩ ⟨his first ~ appearance⟩ ⟨the most ~ Shakespeare yet brought to the screen —Arthur Knight⟩ **2 a :** peculiar to the art and technique of making motion pictures ⟨replacing period background with fast ~ action⟩ ⟨all his films therefore lacked a ~ continuity —Lewis Jacobs⟩ ⟨tension between the dramatic and ~ principles cannot always be avoided —E.R.Bentley⟩ **b :** having essential technical and aesthetic qualities of motion-picture art (as episodic composition, sustained movement, pictorial brilliance, suspense, the spotlighting of dramatic moments) **3 :** using methods or devices or obtaining effects suggestive of motion-picture technique ⟨some stream of consciousness fiction is notably ~⟩ ⟨gave stilted and generally ~ performances in the leading roles —Wolcott Gibbs⟩ **4 :** relating to the production or showing of motion pictures ⟨has had a great deal of ~ training and experience⟩ ⟨the ~ fortunes of a novel or stage play⟩

cin·e·mat·i·cal·ly \-ək(ə)lē, -li\ *adv* **1 :** in or for cinematic production **2 :** from the point of view of cinematic art or technique **3 :** according to cinematic principles

[1]**cinematics** *var of* KINEMATICS

[2]**cin·e·mat·ics** \,sinəˈmad·iks, -atiks\ *n pl but usu sing in constr* **:** the art or technique of cinematic presentation

cin·e·mat·i·za·tion \¦sinəmad·əˈzāshən, -,mad··, -īˈz-\ *n* -s **1 :** the making of a motion picture from a narrative or dramatic work **2 :** an adaptation for presenting as a motion picture

cin·e·mat·ize \ˈsinəmə,tīz, -ə,tīz\ *vt* -ED/-ING/-S [*cinema* + *-tize* (as in *dramatize*)] **:** to make a motion picture of (as a novel or stage play) **:** adapt for motion pictures

[1]**cin·e·mat·o·graph** \,sinəˈmad·ə,graf, -atə-, -aa(ə)f,-äf\ *n* -s [F *cinématographe*, fr. Gk *kinemat-, kinēma* movement (fr. *kinein* to move) + *-o-* + *-graphe* -graph; akin to Gk *kiein* to go — more at CITE] **1** *now chiefly Brit* **:** a motion-picture camera, projector, theater, or show **2** *now chiefly Brit* **:** the art and techniques of producing motion pictures — often used with *the*

[2]**cinematograph** \"\ *vt* -ED/-ING/-S *now chiefly Brit* **:** to photograph with a motion-picture camera

cin·e·ma·tog·ra·pher \,══məˈtägrəfə(r)\ *n* -s **1 :** a motion-picture cameraman **2 :** a motion-picture projectionist

cin·e·mat·o·graph·ic \¦══,mad·ə¦grafik, -atə-, -aaf-,-äf-, -ēk\ *also* **cin·e·mat·o·graph·i·cal** \-fəkəl\ *adj* [*cinematography* + *-ic, -ical*] **1 a :** peculiar to, used in, or connected with cinematography **b :** skilled in cinematography **2 :** filmed for or reproduced by means of motion-picture projection **3 a :** conveyed or evoked by motion pictures **b :** having qualities in common with cinematography; *specif* **:** using devices suggestive of motion-picture technique — **cin·e·mat·o·graph·i·cal·ly** \-fək(ə)lē, -li\ *adv*

cin·e·ma·tog·ra·phist \,══məˈtägrəfəst\ *n* -s *Brit* **:** CINEMATOGRAPHER

cin·e·ma·tog·ra·phy \-fē,-fi\ *n* -ES **:** the art or science of motion-picture photography

cinema van *n*, *Brit* **:** CINEMOBILE

cin·e·ma·za·tion \,sinəməˈzāshən\ *n* -s [*cinema* + *-zation* (as in *dramatization*)] **:** CINEMATIZATION

cin·e·micrograph \¦sinə+\ *n* [*cine-* + *micrograph*] **:** a motion picture produced by cinemicrography

cin·e·micrography \¦══+\ *n* [*cine-* + *micrography*] **:** CINEPHOTOMICROGRAPHY

cin·e·mize \ˈsinə,mīz\ *vt* -ED/-ING/-S [*cinema* + *-ize*] **:** CINEMATIZE

cin·e·mo·bile \ˈsinəmə¦bēl, ,══ˈmō,bēl, *esp bef pause or cons* -ēəl\ *n* -s [*cine-* + *automobile*] **:** a truck or trailer that carries the film and equipment necessary for showing outdoor movies

ci·ne·mo·graph \səˈnēmə,graf, ˈsinəmə-\ *n* -s [Gk *kinēma* movement + E *-graph* — more at CINEMATOGRAPH] **:** an instrument for registering velocity (as of the wind)

cin·e·ole \ˈsinē,ōl\ *also* **cin·e·ol** \-,ōl, -ōl\ *n* -s [ISV *cine-* (fr. NL *cina* — in *oleum cinae* wormseed oil, *semen cinae* Levant wormseed) + *-ole, -ol*; orig. formed as G *cyneol*] **:** a syrupy liquid $C_{10}H_{18}O$ of camphorlike odor found in many essential oils (as Levant wormseed, eucalyptus, and cajeput) and used esp. as an expectorant — called also *1,8-cineole, eucalyptole*

cin·e·photomicrograph \¦sinə+\ *n* [*cine-* + *photomicrograph*] **:** a motion picture made by cinephotomicrography

cin·e·photomicrography \"+\ *n* [*cine-* + *photomicrography*] **:** photomicrography in which the product is a motion picture

cin·e·plas·tic \¦sinə¦plastik\ *adj* [ISV *cineplasty* + *-ic*] **:** of, relating to, or used in cineplasty

cin·e·plasty \ˈ══,tē\ *n* -ES [ISV *cine-* (var. of *kine-*) + *-plasty*] **1 :** surgical fitting of a lever to a muscle in an amputation stump to facilitate the operation of an artificial hand **2 :** surgical isolation of a loop of muscle of chest or arm, covering it with skin, and attaching to it a prosthetic device to be operated by contraction of the muscle in the loop

cin·e·ra·ceous \¦sinə¦rāshəs\ *adj* [L *cineraceus*, fr. *ciner-, cinis* ashes + *-aceus* -aceous — more at INCINERATE] **:** CINEREOUS

cin·e·radiography \¦sinə+\ *n* [*cine-* + *radiography*] **:** the process of making radiographs of moving objects in sufficiently rapid sequence so that the radiographs or copies made from them may be projected as motion pictures — compare CINEFLUOROGRAPHY

cin·e·rar·ia \,sinəˈra(a)rēə\ *n* -s [NL, fr. fem. of L *cinerarius* of ashes, fr. *ciner-, cinis* ashes + *-arius* -ary; fr. the ash-colored down on the leaves] **:** any of several pot plants derived from a perennial herb (*Senecio cruentus*) of the Canary islands and having heart-shaped leaves and large clusters of flower heads with white, red, blue, or purple rays

cin·e·rar·i·um \-ēəm\ *n*, *pl* **cinerar·ia** \-ēə\ [L, fr. *ciner-, cinis* + *-arium*] **:** a place to receive the ashes of the cremated dead

cin·er·ary \ˈsinə,rerē\ *adj* [L *cinerarius*] **:** containing or used for ashes esp. of the cremated dead

cin·e·ra·tor \ˈsinə,rād·ə(r), -ātə(r)\ *n* -s [*cineration* + *-or*] **:** a crematory furnace

ci·ne·rea \səˈnirēə\ *n* -s [NL, fr. fem. of L *cinereus*] **:** the gray matter of nerve tissue

ci·ne·re·al \-ēəl\ *adj* [L *cinereus* ash-colored + E *-al*] **:** CINEREOUS

ci·ne·re·ous \-ēəs\ *adj* [L *cinereus*, fr. *ciner-, cinis* ashes + *-eus* -eous — more at INCINERATE] **1 a :** ASHEN 2 **b :** gray tinged or shaded with black — used esp. in technical descriptions in biology **2 :** like ashes esp. in inert and powdery quality **:** consisting of ash

cinereous vulture *n* **:** a large vulture (*Aegypius monachus*) that has entirely dark brown plumage and that is found from southern Europe and northern Africa east to northern India and China

cin·er·in \ˈsinərən\ *n* -s [L *ciner-, cinis* ashes + E *-in*] **:** either of two oily liquid esters $C_{20}H_{28}O_3$ and $C_{21}H_{28}O_5$ of cinerolone having high insecticidal properties and occurring in pyrethrum flowers and distinguished by the numerals I and II

cin·er·i·tious \¦sinə¦rishəs\ *adj* [L *cineritius, cinericius*, fr. *ciner-, cinis* ashes] *archaic* **:** CINEREOUS

cin·e·roentgenography \¦sinə+\ *n* [*cine-* + *roentgenography*] **:** CINERADIOGRAPHY

cin·er·ol·one \ˈsinə(,)rō,lōn, -,rə-\ *n* -s [*cinerin* + *-ol* + *-one*] **:** an oily keto alcohol $C_{10}H_{14}O_2$ derived from cyclopentene and obtained by hydrolysis of the cinerins — compare PYRETHROLONE

cin·er·ous \ˈsinərəs\ *n* -ES [L *ciner-*, cinis ashes + E *-ous*] **:** a light bluish gray to light gray that is redder and darker than skimmed-milk white and very slightly redder than glaucous gray

cines *pl of* CINE

-cinesia — see -KINESIA

cinesis *var of* KINESIS

cinet- *or* **cineto-** — see KINET-

cingalese *also* **cinghalese** *usu cap*, *var of* SINHALESE

cin·gle \ˈsiŋgəl\ *n* -s [ME *syngle, sengle*, fr. MF & L; MF *cengle*, fr. L *cingula*, fr. *cingere* to gird — more at CINCTURE] *archaic* **:** GIRTH, BELT

cin·gu·lar \ˈsiŋgyələ(r)\ *adj* [L *cingulum*, *cingula* girdle + E *-ar*] **:** ANNULAR

cin·gu·la·ta \,siŋgyəˈlād·ə, -ād·ə\ *n pl*, *cap* [NL, fr. L *cingulum*, *cingula* girdle + NL *-ata*] *in some classifications* **:** a major division of Edentata comprising armadillos and extinct related forms

cin·gu·late \ˈsiŋgyələt, -,lāt, *usu* -d·+V\ *adj* [NL *cingulatus*, fr. L *cingulum, cingula* girdle + *-atus* -ate] **:** having a girdle esp. of transverse bands or markings

cin·gu·lum \ˈsiŋgyələm\ *n*, *pl* **cingu·la** \-lə\ [NL, fr. L, girdle, fr. *cingere* to gird — more at CINCTURE] **1 :** a ridge about the base of the crown of a tooth **2 :** the clitellum of an annelid **3 :** a tract of association fibers running chiefly in the substance of and connecting the callosal and hippocampal convolutions of the brain **4 :** a band of color or raised spiral line (as on certain gastropod shells) **5 :** the outer zone of cilia on the disk of certain rotifers **6 :** the girdle of a diatom

cin·na·bar \ˈsinə,bär, -ā(r\ *n* -s [ME *cynoper, cynabare*, fr. MF & L; MF *cenobre*, fr. L *cinnabaris*, fr. Gk *kinnabari*, of non-IE origin; akin to Ar *zinjafr* cinnabar] **1 :** a mineral HgS consisting of mercuric sulfide occurring in brilliant red crystals or in red or brownish masses and being the only important ore of mercury **2 :** artificial red mercuric sulfide used principally as a pigment **:** VERMILION 1a **3** *or* **cinnabar moth :** a European moth (*Tyria jacobeae*) having grayish black fore wings marked with red, hind wings clear reddish pink, and larvae that feed on the leaves of ragwort of which attempted biological control brought about its introduction into several areas in the U.S.

cinnabar green *n* **1 :** a mixture of Prussian blue and chrome yellow **2 :** the color of the cinnabar-green mixture **:** DEEP CHROME GREEN

cin·na·bar·ine \ˈsinəbə,rēn, -,rən\ *also* **cin·na·bar·ic** \¦══¦barik\ *adj* [*cinnabar* + *-ine* or *-ic*] **:** like, relating to, consisting of, or containing cinnabar ⟨~ sand⟩

cinnabar red *n* **:** GOYA

cinnam- *or* **cinnamo-** *comb form* [F, fr. L *cinnamum*] **1 :** cinnamon ⟨*cinnamo*dendron⟩ **2 :** cinnamic acid ⟨*cinnamoyl*⟩

cin·na·mal \ˈsinə,mal, ,══ˈ═\ *n* -s [prob. short for *cinnamaldehyde*] **:** the bivalent radical $C_6H_5CH{:}CHCH<$ derived from cinnamaldehyde by removal of the oxygen atom

cin·na·mal·de·hyde \,sinəˈmaldə,hīd\ *n* -s [ISV *cinnam-* + *aldehyde*] **:** an aromatic oily aldehyde $C_6H_5CH{:}CHCHO$ occurring as the chief constituent of cinnamon-bark oil and cassia oil and used as a flavor

cin·na·mate \ˈsinə,māt, siˈnamət, *usu* -d·+V\ *n* -s [F, fr. *cinnam-* + *-ate*] **:** a salt or ester of cinnamic acid

cin·nam·e·in \səˈnamēən\ *n* -s [ISV *cinnam-* + *-ein*; orig. formed as F *cinnaméine*] **:** benzyl cinnamate or a mixture of this ester with other esters

cin·na·mene \ˈsinə,mēn\ *n* -s [ISV *cinnam-* + *-ene*; orig. formed as G *zinnamen*] **:** STYRENE

cin·nam·e·nyl \səˈnamə,nil, -ēl\ *n* -s [*cinnamene* + *-yl*] **:** STYRYL

cin·nam·ic acid \səˈnamik- *also* ˈsinəmik-\ *n* [F *cinnamique*, fr. *cinnam-* + *-ique* -ic] **:** a white crystalline odorless acid $C_6H_5CH{:}CHCOOH$ found esp. in cinnamon oil and storax and made synthetically for preparing esters for perfumes

cinnamic alcohol *n* **:** CINNAMYL ALCOHOL

cinnamic aldehyde *n* **:** CINNAMALDEHYDE

cin·na·mo·den·dron \,sinəməˈdendrən\ *n*, *cap* [NL, fr. *cinnam-* + *-dendron*] **:** a small genus of tropical American shrubs or small trees (order Parietales) having pungent aromatic bark resembling canella bark

cin·na·mo·mum \,sinəˈmōməm\ *n*, *cap* [NL, fr. L, cinnamon (the tree and the bark)] **:** a large genus of Asiatic and Australian aromatic trees and shrubs of the family Lauraceae having mostly opposite leaves with three to five prominent longitudinal veins and small flowers in panicles — see CAMPHOR TREE, CHINESE CINNAMON, CINNAMON

cin·na·mon \ˈsinəmən\ *n* -s *often attrib* [ME *cynamone, cynamum*, fr. MF & L; MF *cinnamome*, fr. L *cinnamomum, cinnamon, cinnamum*, fr. Gk *kinnamōmon, kinnamon*, of non-IE origin; akin to Heb *qinnāmōn* cinnamon] **1 a :** the highly aromatic bark of any of several trees of the genus *Cinnamomum* yielding cinnamaldehyde and other aromatic products in the form of cinnamon oil — see CEYLON CINNAMON, CHINESE CINNAMON, SAIGON CINNAMON **b :** a culinary spice prepared from cinnamon either by powdering or by drying in small rolls **2 :** a tree that yields cinnamon **3 :** a light yellowish brown that is redder and stronger than khaki, deeper and slightly redder than walnut brown, and redder and deeper than fallow or manila

cinnamon apple *n* **:** SWEETSOP

cinnamon bark *n* **1 :** CANELLA BARK **2 :** CINNAMON 1a

cinnamon–bark oil \ˈ═══,═-\ *n* **:** a light-yellow essential oil obtained from the bark of Ceylon cinnamon and used in medicine, flavoring, and perfumery — called also *cinnamon oil*

cinnamon bat *n* **:** a tropical American cave bat (genus *Mormoops*) often living in great flocks

cinnamon bear *n* **:** a dark chestnut color phase of the American black bear

cinnamon brown *n* **:** a moderate yellowish brown that is duller and slightly redder than maple sugar, lighter and redder than bronze, and slightly redder and slightly less strong than Bismarck brown

cin·na·moned \ˈsinəmənd\ *adj* **:** spiced with cinnamon

cinnamon fern *n* **:** a large No. American fern (*Osmunda cinnamomea*) having woolly rich cinnamon-colored spore-bearing fronds shorter than and produced separately from the green foliage fronds

cinnamon flower *n* **:** CASSIA BUD

cinnamon honeysuckle *n* **:** SWAMP AZALEA

cin·na·mon·ic \¦sinə¦mänik\ *adj* **:** of or like cinnamon

cinnamon–leaf oil \ˈ═══,═-\ *n* **:** a pale yellow essential oil obtained from the leaves of Ceylon cinnamon and used chiefly as a source of eugenol

cinnamon oak *n* **:** BLUEJACK 2

cinnamon oil *n* **:** an oil obtained from a tree or shrub of the genus *Cinnamomum:* as **a :** CINNAMON-BARK OIL **b :** CASSIA OIL

cinnamon rose *n* **:** a Eurasian rose (*Rosa cinnamomea*) with slender stems and solitary fragrant flowers

cinnamon sedge *n* **:** SWEET FLAG
cinnamon stone *n* **:** ESSONITE
cinnamon teal *n* **:** a small wild duck (*Anas cyanoptera*) of western No. America much resembling the blue-winged teal in appearance and habits but having the male more markedly brownish red about the head and body
cinnamon vine *n* **:** a hardy Chinese vine (*Dioscorea batatas*) cultivated as an ornamental climber for its glossy heart-shaped leaves and in the tropics for its edible tubers — called also *Chinese yam*
cinnamon water *n* **:** a saturated solution of cinnamon oil in distilled water used as a vehicle for certain drugs
cinnamonwood \'==,=\ *n* **:** SASSAFRAS 1b
cin·na·mony \'sinəmənē, -ni\ *adj* **:** like or like that of cinnamon **:** due to cinnamon ⟨a warm ~ fragrance⟩
cin·nam·o·yl \sə'namə,wil, -ēl\ *or* **cin·na·myl** \-məl; 'sinə,mil, -el\ *n* -s [ISV *cinnam-* + *-yl*] **:** the acid radical $C_6H_5CH{=}CHCO{-}$ of cinnamic acid
cin·na·myl \sə'naməl; 'sinə,mil, -ēl\ *n* -s [F *cinnamyle*, fr. *cinnam-* + *-yle* -yl] **:** the univalent radical $C_6H_5CH{=}CHCH_2{-}$
cinnamyl alcohol *n* **:** a crystalline alcohol $C_6H_5CH{=}CHCH_2OH$ of hyacinth odor occurring as an ester in liquid storax and balsam of Peru and used in synthetic perfumes — called also *cinnamic alcohol*
cin·na·myl·i·dene \,sinə'milə,dēn\ *n* -s [ISV *cinnamyl* + *-id* + *-ene*] **:** CINNAMAL
cin·no·line \'sinə,lēn, -,lən\ *n* -s [G *cinnolin*, alter. of *chinolin* quinoline, fr. *chin-* + *-ol* + *-in*] **:** a poisonous crystalline base $C_8H_6N_2$; 1,2-benzo-diazine
cino- — see KIN-
cin·o·bufagin \,sinə, ,sīnə+\ *n* [*cino-* (prob. fr. NL *Bufo chinensis*, species of toad from which senso is produced) + *bufagin*] **:** a bufagin $C_{26}H_{34}O_6$ obtained from senso
cin·o·ster·ni·dae \,sinə'stərnə,dē, ,sī-\ *syn of* KINOSTERNIDAE
cin·o·ster·non \-,nän\ *syn of* KINOSTERNON
cinq–cents \saⁿsäⁿ\ *n pl but sing in constr* [F, lit., five hundred, fr. *cinq* five (fr. L *quinque*) + *cents*, pl. of *cent* hundred, fr. L *centum* — more at FIVE, HUNDRED] **:** a card game like bézique but played with one 32-card pack
cin·quain \siŋ'kān, '=,=\ *n* -s [F, fr. *cinq* + *-ain* (as in *quatrain*)] **:** a five-line stanza; *specif* **:** the five-line verse form that is analogous to the Japanese tanka and that has two syllables in its first and last lines, four, six, and eight in the intervening three lines, and generally iambic cadence
cinque \'siŋk, 'saŋk\ *n* -s [ME *cink*, fr. MF *cinq*, fr. L *quinque* — more at FIVE] **1 :** FIVE; *esp* **:** the number five in dice or cards **2 cinques** *pl* **:** change ringing on 11 bells that are treated as 5 pairs, the tenor bell added after each change
cin·que·cen·tist \,chiŋkwə'chentəst, ,cheŋkwā-\ *n, pl* **cin·quecentists** \-əs(t)s\ *or* **cinquecentis·ti** \-(,)chen'ti(,)stē\ [It *cinquecentista*, fr. *cinquecento* + *-ista* -ist] **1 :** an Italian of the cinquecento; *usu* **:** a poet or artist of this period **2 :** a student of the art or literature of the cinquecento
cin·que·cen·to \-'chen(,)tō\ *n* -s *sometimes cap* [It, lit., five hundred (abbr. of fifteen hundred), fr. *cinque* five (fr. L *quinque*) + *cento* hundred, fr. L *centum* — more at FIVE, HUNDRED] **:** the 16th century; *specif* **:** the 16th century period in Italian literature and art
cin·que·dea \,chiŋkwə'dēə, -dāə\ *n* -s [It, fr. *cinque* five (fr. L *quinque*) + It dial. *dea* fingers; akin to It *dita*, pl. of *dito* finger, fr. L *digitus* — more at FIVE, TOE] **:** a heavy broad-bladed medieval dagger
cinque·foil \'siŋk,fȯil, 'saŋ-, *dial* 'siŋkē,f-\ *also* **cinq·foil** \-ŋk,f-\ *n* -s [ME *sink foil*, fr. MF *cincfoille*, fr. L *quinquefolium* (trans. of Gk *pentaphyllon*), fr. *quinque* five + *folium* leaf — more at FIVE, BLADE] **1 :** a plant of the genus *Potentilla* **2 :** a figure enclosed by five joined foils; *specif* **:** a 5-lobed foliation in Gothic tracery **3 :** a conventionalized heraldic flower showing five lobelike petals

cinquefoil 2

cinque·foiled \-ld\ *adj* **:** made like a cinquefoil **:** made with a cinquefoil or cinquefoils
cinque·pace \'siŋk(ə),pās\ *or* **cinque·pas** \-,pas, saⁿk(ə)pä\ *n, pl* **cinquepaces** \-āsəz\ *or* **cinquepas** \-,pas,-pä\ [alter. of earlier *cinquepas*, fr. MF *cinq pas*, fr. *cinq* five + *pas* dance step, pace — more at CINQUE, PACE] **:** a 16th century dance with steps regulated by the number five prob. related to the galliard
cion *var of* SCION
cion- *or* **ciono-** *comb form* [NL, fr. Gk *kion-*, *kiono-*, fr. *kion-*, *kiōn* pillar, uvula] **1 :** uvula ⟨*cionitis*⟩ ⟨*cionotomy*⟩ **2 :** pillar ⟨*cionocranial*⟩
ci·o·na \'sīənə\ *n, cap* [NL, fr. Gk *kion-*, *kiōn* pillar; akin to Arm *siun* pillar] **:** a genus (coextensive with the family Cionidae) comprising relatively large simple ascidians and including a single cosmopolitan species (*C. intestinalis*) — **ci·o·nid** \'sīənəd, -,nid\ *adj or n*
ci·o·no·cranial \,sīənō+\-\ *or* **ci·o·no·cranian** \"+\ *adj* [*cion-* + *cranial*] **:** having a rodlike epipterygoid bone in the skull — used of some lizards
¹cioppino *obs var of* CHOPINE
²ciop·pi·no \chə'pē(,)nō\ *n* -s [It] **:** a dish of fish and shellfish cooked in tomato sauce and usu. seasoned with wine, spices, and herbs
¹ci·pher \'sīfə(r)\ *n* -s *often attrib* [ME, fr. MF *cifre*, fr. ML *cifra* zero, fr. Ar *ṣifr* empty, cipher, zero] **1 :** the symbol 0 denoting the absence of all magnitude or quantity **:** NAUGHT, ZERO — see NUMBER table **2 a :** a method of transforming a text in order to conceal its meaning (1) by systematically replacing the letters of the plaintext by substitutes in the same sequence either singly or in pairs or other polygraphs (as by writing 1 for A, 2 for B, etc., or F for A, S for B, etc., or QL for AB, etc.) or (2) by systematically rearranging the plaintext letters into another sequence (as by writing them normally in a rectangle and then copying them off from the columns taken in an arbitrary succession) — called also respectively (1) *substitution cipher* and (2) *transposition cipher;* compare CODE 3 **b :** a prescription for a cipher system **:** a key or memorandum that enables decipherment **c :** a message in cipher **:** a text in secret writing **3 :** an arabic numeral **:** NUMBER, FIGURE **4 a** *obs* **:** a symbolic character (as a letter, hieroglyph, or astrological sign) **b :** a combination of symbolic letters; *esp* **:** the interwoven initials of a name **:** DEVICE, MONOGRAM ⟨an engraver's ~⟩ **c :** a sign in Karl Jaspers' existentialism serving to mediate between the existent and the transcendent **5 :** one that has no weight, worth, or influence **:** NONENTITY ⟨doomed to die as a ~ in some vast statistical operation in which our teeth would be counted . . . but our death itself would be unknown — Norman Mailer⟩ **6 :** the sounding of an organ pipe caused by a mechanical defect

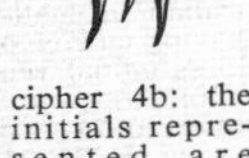

cipher 4b: the initials represented are Noah Webster's

²cipher \"\ *vb* **ciphered; ciphered; ciphering** \-f(ə)riŋ\ **ciphers** *vi* **1 :** to use figures in a mathematical process **:** do sums in arithmetic **:** FIGURE **2 :** to produce a cipher — used of an organ pipe ~ *vt* **1 a** *archaic* **:** to express (as thoughts or words) by written or graven characters **b** *obs* **:** to show forth **:** make plain by visible evidence **:** PORTRAY **c :** ENCIPHER **d** *obs* **:** DECIPHER **2** *in shipbuilding* **:** BEVEL, CHAMFER **3 a :** to compute in figures **:** calculate or figure arithmetically — sometimes used with *out* ⟨a sum ~*ed* out⟩ **b** *dial* **:** to figure out as if by calculation **:** solve by pondering
cipher clerk *n* **:** a person who routinely encrypts and decrypts messages — called also *code clerk*
cipher component *or* **cipher sequence** *n* **:** the sequence of a substitution alphabet that identifies the ciphertext letters — compare ALPHABET 1j
cipher disk *or* **cipher wheel** *n* **:** a device for enciphering and deciphering in substitution cipher consisting of two movable concentric disks with the letters of the alphabet written around the margin of each
ci·pher·dom \-fə(r)dəm\ *n* -s **:** the state of being a nonentity
ci·pher·er \-fərə(r)\ *n* -s **:** one that ciphers **:** one skilled in the use of cipher
cipher machine *n* **:** an enciphering and deciphering instrument **:** CRYPTOGRAPH; *esp* **:** one that telegraphs or prints its output — see CONVERTER e (1)
cipher square *n* **:** VIGENÈRE TABLEAU
ciphertext \'==,=\ *n* **:** the cipher form of a text or of its elements ⟨this message looks like ~⟩ ⟨in the Playfair scheme no ~ J is possible⟩ — compare PLAINTEXT; ³C 4
ci·po \sē'pō\ *n* -s [Sp *cipó*, *sipó*, *isipó*, fr. Guarani *icipó*] **:** LIANA
cipo·lin \'sipələn, ˌsēpə'laⁿ\ *or* **ci·pol·li·no** \,chēpə'lē(,)nō\ *n* -s [F & It; F *cipolin*, fr. It *cipollino*, dim. of *cipolla* onion, fr. LL *cepulla*, dim. of L *cepa*, *cepe* onion] **:** a light-colored Roman marble containing layers of micaceous minerals and abundant silicates
ci·pol·let·ti weir \ˌchēpə'led·ē-\ *n, usu cap C* [after Cesare *Cipolletti*, 20th cent. Ital. engineer] **:** a weir that is trapezoidal in shape with the sides inclining outward from the base
cippi *pl of* CIPPUS
cip·pus \'sipəs\ *n, pl* **cip·pi** \-,pī\ [L — more at CEPE] **:** a small low pillar usu. inscribed and used in ancient Rome and Greece as a gravestone or landmark
cir *or* **circ** *abbr* **1** circa **2** circle; circular **3** circuit **4** circulation **5** circumference
¹cir·ca \'sərkə, 'kir(,)kä\ *prep* [L, fr. *circum* round about — more at CIRCUM-] **:** ABOUT, AROUND — often used with numerals ⟨~ 1740⟩ — abbr. *ca, c*
²circa \"\ *n* -s **:** APPROXIMATION ⟨a ~ of reasonable probability —George Saintsbury⟩
cir·caea \(,)sər'sēə\ *n, cap* [NL, fr. L, fem. of *Circaeus* of Circe — more at CIRCEAN] **:** a genus of low perennial herbs (family Onagraceae) with whitish to roseate flowers in racemes and an indehiscent fruit covered with bristly hooked hairs that are widely distributed in cool and temperate regions of the northern hemisphere and that comprise the enchanter's nightshades
circ·aetus \(,)sər'kēəd·əs\ *n, cap* [NL, fr. Gk *kirkos* hawk + NL *-aëtus*; akin to L *crocire* to croak (as of a raven), Skt *krkara*, a kind of partridge, OE *hringan* to ring — more at RING] **:** a genus of large Old World hawks intermediate in characters between the eagles and the harriers
circar *often cap, var of* SIRCAR
¹cir·cas·sian \(,)sər'kashən, sə'-,sš'-, -aash-,-aish-\ *n* -s *cap* [*Circassia*, region in Russia (fr. NL or ML, alter. of Russ *Cherkes* Circassian + L *-ia*) + E *-an*] **1 :** a member of a group of peoples of the Caucasus of Caucasian race but not of Indo-European speech noted for their physical beauty and being tall with oval face, brown eyes, and chestnut hair **2 :** the North Caucasic language of the Circassian peoples
²circassian \'==\ *adj, usu cap* **:** of, relating to, or characteristic of Circassia or the Circassians
circassian seed *n, usu cap C* **:** the seed of a red sandalwood tree (*Adenanthera pavonina*) used for ornament in the Orient
circassian walnut *n, usu cap C* **1 :** the light-brown but irregularly black-veined wood of the English walnut much used for veneer and cabinetwork **2 :** ENGLISH WALNUT
circe *abbr* circumstance
cir·ce·an \'sərsēən, ,sər's-\ *adj, usu cap* [L *circaeus* (fr. *Circe*, sorceress deity who transformed men into beasts, fr. Gk *Kirkē*) + E *-an*] **1 :** relating to or resembling Circe **2 :** having the quality of a fascinating sorceress **:** dangerously or fatally attractive or misleading **:** LULLING
cir·cen·sian \(,)sər'senchən\ *adj, sometimes cap* [L *circensis* of the circus (fr. *circus*) + E *-an* — more at CIRCUS] **:** of or relating to the Circus in ancient Rome
cir·ci·nate \'sərsⁿn,āt\ *adj* [L *circinatus*, past part. of *circinare* to make round, fr. *circinus* pair of compasses, fr. *circus* circle] **:** rounded in outline: as **a :** characterized by or having the form of a flat coil of which the apex is the center ⟨the retracted tongue of a butterfly forms a ~ coil⟩ — used esp. of arrangements of plant parts in vernation and of developing fern fronds ⟨~ bracken fronds unfolding⟩; see SCORPIOID **b** *med, of lesions* **:** having a sharply circumscribed and somewhat circular margin — **cir·ci·nate·ly** *adv*
circingle *var of* SURCINGLE
cir·ci·ter \'sərsəd·ər, 'kirkə,te(ə)r\ *prep* [L] **:** ABOUT
¹cir·cle \'sərkəl, -ək-,-əik-\ *n* -s [alter. (influenced by L *circulus*) of ME *cercle*, fr. OF, fr. L *circulus*, dim. of *circus* ring, fr. or akin to Gk *kirkos*, *krikos* ring; perh. akin to Lith *kreīvas* crooked, Russ *kriv'*, Gk *korōnē* ring — more at CROWN] **1 a :** a bright ring (as around the moon) **:** HALO **b :** a closed plane curve every point of which is equidistant from a fixed point within the curve **:** CIRCUMFERENCE, RING — see DIAMETER, RADIUS **c :** the plane surface bounded by such a curve — see AREA table, PI 2a **2 a** *obs* **:** the sphere in which a celestial body was thought to revolve **b :** the orbit of revolution of such a sphere **c :** the period of revolution through the orbit of such a sphere **3 :** something having the shape of a closed curve or a section of one; as: **a :** RING, CIRCLET **b :** CROWN, DIADEM **c :** an instrument of astronomical observation the graduated limb of which consists of an entire circle **d :** a balcony or tier of seats in a theater or opera house **e :** a group of people (as dancers) or things (as stones, campfires) forming a ring **f :** a circle of latitude or longitude **g :** a small circular park or garden **h :** ROTARY **4 :** something having the shape of an area enclosed by a circle: as **a :** a circus ring **b :** a round plate or sheet ⟨cutting cloth into ~*s*⟩ **5 a** *obs* **:** a region thought of as bounded by a circle ⟨in the ~ of this forest —Shak.⟩ **b :** an area of action or influence **:** REALM — compare SPHERE **6 a :** a series ending at its starting point **:** CYCLE, ROUND ⟨the ~ of 24 hours⟩ ⟨the wheel has come full ~⟩ **b** *logic* **:** fallacious reasoning in which something that ostensibly is being proved or demonstrated is taken for granted or covertly assumed esp. in the premises ⟨arguments in a ~ are instances of begging the question⟩ **7 a :** things grouped in or as if in a system of coordinate members ⟨a ~ of sciences⟩ **b :** a group of people thought of as held together by a common point of interest ⟨theatrical ~*s*⟩ **:** an exclusive group **:** COTERIE, CLIQUE, ELITE ⟨the gossip of court ~*s*⟩ ⟨the charmed ~ of 20-game winners⟩ **c :** a chapter or local group of any of various societies **8 : a :** any one territorial or administrative division or district: **a :** any one of the 10 territorial divisions of Germany under the Holy Roman Empire **b :** KREIS **c :** a district in India for the issue of government paper currency **9** *bookbinding* **:** ROLL **10 :** a circular course or path of movement; *specif* **:** the operation of rounding up cattle ⟨he would . . . take the lead for the morning's ~ —Will James⟩

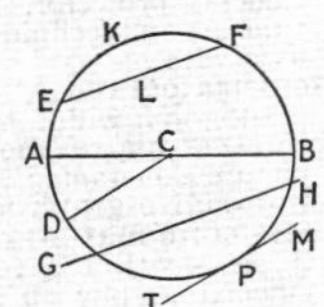

circle: *AB* diameter; *C* center; *CD*, *CA*, *CB* radii; *EKF* arc on chord *EF*; *ACD* (area) sector; *GH* secant; *TPM* tangent at point *P*; *EKFBPDAE* circumference

²circle \"\ *vb* **circled; circled; circling** \-k(ə)liŋ\ **circles** [ME *cerclen*, fr. *cercle*, n.] *vt* **1 :** to enclose in or as if in a circle **:** form a circle or oval around ⟨the gridiron was *circled* with a cinder track⟩; *specif* **:** to draw a circle around for special attention (as for correction or deletion) ⟨~ the misspelled words⟩ **2 a :** to move or revolve around **:** travel around or traverse so as to describe a circle, arc, or curved figure ⟨fast planes *circling* the earth⟩ **b :** to cause to move in a circle **c :** to proceed in an arc or curve around (as for avoiding or eluding) ⟨the ship *circled* the cape⟩ ⟨~ an opposing end in football⟩ **3 :** to form into a circle **:** make circular ~ *vi* **1 a :** to move around or proceed in or as if in a circle or circles ⟨~ around over a landing strip⟩; *sometimes* **:** to meander or proceed aimlessly ⟨grass-mounds where water *circled*, running from scoops and cups to curves and brook streams —George Meredith⟩ ⟨winding and *circling*, at last it reaches a conclusion from some point unforeseen —H.O. Taylor⟩ **b :** CIRCULATE **c :** to turn in a usu. wide loop esp. in reversing one's course — often used with *back* ⟨~ back toward home⟩ **2 :** to form, describe, or extend in a circle ⟨the lighthouse sent out its slow steady *circling* beam —R.O. Bowen⟩ **syn** see SURROUND, TURN
circle brick *n* **:** an arc-shaped brick used in making arches or other curved forms
circle dance *n* **:** a dance in which the dancers join hands and move in a circular direction; *esp* **:** a dance in which women form a circle and move clockwise, men form a circle around them and move counterclockwise, the man and woman opposite one another when the music stops becoming partners for the next dance
circle eight *n, figure skating* **:** a figure comprised of two tangent circles, the first usu. skated on the right foot, the second on the left foot
circle graph *n* **:** PIE CHART
circle of ap·ol·lo·nius \-,apə'lōnyəs, -nēəs\ *usu cap A* [after *Apollonius* of Perga, 3d cent. B.C. Greek mathematician] **:** a circle that is the locus of points the ratio of whose distances from two given fixed points is constant
circle of confusion : the indistinct circular patch formed by a lens representing the out-of-focus image of a single object point — called also *blur circle;* compare CIRCLE OF LEAST CONFUSION
circle of curvature : the osculating circle of a curve
circle of fifths : keys or tonalities ordered by ascending (for sharp keys) or descending (for flat keys) intervals of a fifth
circle of latitude 1 : a great circle perpendicular to the plane of the ecliptic **2 :** a meridian of the terrestrial sphere along which latitude is measured; *sometimes* **:** PARALLEL OF LATITUDE
circle of least confusion *physics* **:** the minimum cross section of a symmetrical bundle of rays that have no common focus because of spherical aberration
circle of position *navigation* **:** a circle on the earth whose center is the point directly under a celestial body and whose radius is the zenith distance of the celestial body, the observer's location being somewhere on this circle — compare SUMNER LINE
circle of wil·lis \-'wiləs\ *usu cap W* [after Thomas *Willis* †1675 Eng. anatomist who described it] **:** a complete ring of arteries formed by the anastomosing branches of the carotid and basilar arteries at the base of the brain
circle rider *n* **:** one of a group of cowpunchers who cover a range in search of cattle by riding from outlying points to a central meeting place
circle shear *n* **:** a machine that cuts circular disks by rotating the sheet stock between cutting wheels
cir·clet \'sərklət, -ək-,-əik-\ *n* -s [ME *serclett* ornamental band, fr. MF *cerclet*, dim. of *cercle*] **1 a :** a little circle; *esp* **:** an ornament for the person having the form of a circle **b :** something that encircles (as a ring, a bracelet, or a headband) **c :** a circular or oval ring about the central medallion of a badge of an order of knighthood or a baronet's badge usu. inscribed with the motto of the order; *also* **:** a representation of this ring placed about the escutcheon in the coat of arms of a knight or baronet **2 :** a small horseshoe-shaped tubelet of steel driven into the top lift of a shoe heel to lessen wear
circle turn *n* **:** a turn in ballroom dancing in which the feet of the couple trace a circle
circ·line \'sər,klīn\ *n* -s [prob. blend of *circle* and *line*] **:** a fluorescent lamp in the form of a ring
circling *pres part of* CIRCLE
circling disease *n* [so called fr. the typical circling ambulations of affected animals] **:** listerellosis of sheep or cattle
cir·co·var·i·an \ˌsərk+\ *adj* [*circ-* (irreg. fr. *circum-*) + *ovarian*] **:** around the ovary
circs \səks\ *n pl* [by shortening] *chiefly Brit* **:** CIRCUMSTANCES ⟨I hope to see you again in better ~⟩
¹cir·cuit \'sərkət, -ək-,-əik-, *usu* -kəd·+V\ *n* -s *often attrib* [ME, fr. MF *circuite*, fr. L *circuitus*, fr. past part. of *circuire*, *circumire* to go around, fr. *circum-* + *ire* to go — more at ISSUE] **1 a :** a usu. more or less circular line encompassing an area **:** CIRCUMFERENCE ⟨a swamp about 10 miles in ~⟩ **b :** the course around the four bases in baseball ⟨he hit for the ~⟩ **2 :** the act of moving around typically in an orbit or a circular course **:** a circular route **:** a course around a periphery **:** REVOLUTION ⟨the periodic ~ of the earth around the sun⟩ ⟨the sightseeing newcomer makes the ~ of the state —*Amer. Guide Series: Fla.*⟩ **3 a :** a roundabout way **:** a circuitous or indirect course ⟨describing a ~ rather than a straight course⟩ **b** *obs* **:** roundabout speech **:** CIRCUMLOCUTION **4 :** space enclosed within a circumference or periphery **:** AREA, SCOPE ⟨the ~ of the duke's lands⟩ **5 a :** an appointed or accustomed course from place to place in following a calling ⟨the old "mail rider", who was just returning on his ~ of twenty-six miles —Ellen Glasgow⟩ **b :** the route of a traveling judge or preacher around a district or territory assigned to him ⟨lawyers rode the ~*s* like the backwoods preachers of the day —*Amer. Guide Series: Tenn.*⟩ **c :** a judicial district legally established ⟨the state shall be divided into thirteen circuits —*W.Va.Constitution*⟩; *also* **:** the judges and lawyers making a circuit **d :** a group of church congregations ministered to or under the supervision of one pastor (as in the Methodist Church) **6 a :** the complete path of an electric current including any displacement current **b :** a specified portion of a circuit ⟨external ~⟩ ⟨generator ~⟩ **c :** the region through which the magnetic flux from any source extends esp. when largely confined within a ferromagnetic body (as a magnet) **7 a :** ASSOCIATION, CONFERENCE, LEAGUE ⟨baseball ~⟩ ⟨football ~⟩ **b :** a series of harness races held at associated tracks according to a more or less permanent schedule **c :** a group of motion-picture theaters owned by one company **d :** a number of associated theaters at which productions are presented in turn **e :** an association, ring, or coterie sharing common interests or similar practices and gathering or performing at various places at different times ⟨the nightclub ~⟩ ⟨the small college ~⟩ **8 a :** an assemblage of electronic elements **:** HOOKUP **b :** a system for two-way communication between two places (as by telegraph, telephone, or radio) **9 :** a closed path followed by a fluid in a mechanical system ⟨hydraulic ~⟩ ⟨oil ~⟩
²circuit \"\ *vb* -ED/-ING/-S *vt* **:** to make a circuit about ⟨an automobile route ~*ing* the Back Bay section of Portland —*Amer. Guide Series: Maine*⟩ **:** go or move in a circuit about ~ *vi* **:** to go or move over a circuit ⟨while five of my brethren are ~*ing* about the state —O.W.Holmes †1935⟩
cir·cuit·al \-kəd·ᵊl\ *adj* **:** concerning a circuit **:** resembling a circuit
circuital field *n* **:** a vector field having the nature of a circuit ⟨the *circuital field* of a magnet⟩
circuit binding *n* **:** DIVINITY CIRCUIT BINDING
circuit breaker *n* **:** a switch that automatically interrupts an electric circuit under an infrequent abnormal condition (as overload)
circuit court *n* **:** a court that sits at two or more places within one judicial district: as **a :** an English court authorized by commission from the crown that is held in one of the seven circuits of the kingdom by a judge designated by the lord chancellor to hold assizes to try civil and criminal cases **b :** any of several courts in the U.S.: as (1) **:** a court of original common-law jurisdiction sitting with a jury (2) **:** an intermediate appellate court (3) **:** a court with both original and appellate jurisdiction (4) **:** a court having equity or probate jurisdiction or both (5) **:** any of the U.S. courts of appeal — not used technically (6) **:** a former court of original jurisdiction existing in each of the seven judicial circuits of the U.S. and its territories until abolished by law in 1912
circuit edges *n pl* **:** the projecting flaps in a divinity circuit binding
cir·cu·i·teer \ˌsərkə'ti(ə)r\ *vi* -ED/-ING/-S *archaic* **:** to travel in a circuit
circuit element *n* **1 :** a part of an electric circuit or network (as a generator, switch, lamp, or vacuum tube) **2 :** one of the three quantitative attributes (resistance, inductance, capacitance) characteristic of an electric circuit
cir·cuit·er \'=kəd·ər\ *also* **cir·cui·teer** \'=kə'ti(ə)r\ *n* -s **:** one that makes or travels a circuit (as the judge of an English circuit court)
cir·cu·i·tion \ˌsərkyə'wishən\ *n* -s [L *circuition-*, *circuitio*, fr. *circuitus* (past part. of *circuire* to go around) + *-ion-*, *-io* -ion — more at CIRCUIT] **1** *archaic* **:** the act of circuiting **2** *archaic* **:** a circuitous mode of reasoning or arguing **:** CIRCUMLOCUTION
circuit judge *n* **:** a judge who holds a circuit court
cir·cuit·or \'sərkəd·ər\ *n* -s [L, fr. *circuitus* (past part. of *circuire*) + *-or*] *archaic* **:** one that makes a circuit
cir·cu·i·tous \ˌsər-'kyüəd·əs, (')sə:'-,(')səi'-, ˌsə(r)'k-, -ətəs\ *adj* [ML *circuitosus*, fr. L *circuitus* circuit + *-osus* -ous —

more at CIRCUIT] **1 :** being a circular or winding course **:** INDIRECT, ROUNDABOUT ⟨two lines possible — the one direct by sea, the other ~ through Gaul —A.T.Mahan⟩ ⟨in one ~ mile through the business district it [the San Antonio river] ends up less than eight hundred yards from where it started —Green Peyton⟩ **2 :** marked by roundabout, indirect, or devious procedure ⟨~ actions⟩ **:** not forthright, direct, or to the point ⟨~ in speech⟩ — **cir·cu·i·tous·ly** *adv* — **cir·cu·i·tous·ness** *n* -ES

circuit rider *n* **:** a typically Methodist preacher assigned to a circuit esp. on the frontier

cir·cuit·ry \ˈsərkətrē, -ə̄k-,-əik-, -tri\ *n* -ES **1 :** the detailed plan of an electric circuit or network (as of a radio or television receiver) **2 :** the components of an electric circuit or network (as tubes and resistors)

circuits *pl of* CIRCUIT, *pres 3d sing of* CIRCUIT

circuit steward *n* **:** a church official of certain Methodist bodies charged with ushering and advising the minister and church board concerning the temporal interests of the circuit

cir·cu·i·ty \ˌsər·ˈkyüəd·ē, ˌsər'k-\ *n* -ES [irreg. fr. *circuit*] **:** roundabout circuitous procedure **:** INDIRECTION **:** lack of straightforwardness ⟨mired so deeply in its own complicated ~ of words —C.O.Gregory⟩

circuity of action : an unnecessarily long course of proceedings

cir·cu·lant \ˈsərkyələnt, -ə̄k-,¦-əik-\ *n* -S [L *circulant-, circulans,* pres. part. of *circulare* to make round — more at CIRCULATE] **:** a mathematical determinant in which each row is derived from the preceding by cyclic permutation, each constituent being pushed into the next column and the last into the first so that constituents of the principal diagonal are all the same

1cir·cu·lar \ˈsərkyələr; ˈsə̄kyələ(r, ˈsəik-\ *adj* [alter. (influenced by LL *circularis*) of earlier *circuler,* fr. ME, fr. MF *circuler, circulier,* fr. LL *circularis,* fr. L *circulus* circle — more at CIRCLE] **1 a :** having the exact or approximate form or outline of a circle **:** ROUND ⟨a ~ orbit⟩ ⟨a ~ cavity⟩ ⟨a ~ area⟩ **b :** made in round shape or tubular form **:** so made as to form a circle when spread flat ⟨a ~ cape⟩ **2 :** marked by motion in a circle ⟨a ~ dance⟩ **:** describing a circle or spiral ⟨a ~ staircase⟩ **:** going in a circle **:** operating with a circular arrangement ⟨a ~ machine for knitting⟩ **3 :** relating to the circle or its properties ⟨a ~ arc⟩ **4** *obs* **:** PERFECT, COMPLETE **5 :** CIRCUITOUS, INDIRECT ⟨a ~ treatment of the problem⟩ **6 :** marked by or similar to reasoning or arguing in a circle ⟨paucity of evidence tends to make the arguments ~ —*Times Lit. Supp.*⟩ **7 :** marked by or moving in a cycle of repetition **8 :** intended for circulation either widely or within a particular group ⟨a subcommittee drafted a ~ letter to all the disaffected groups⟩ — **cir·cu·lar·ly** *adv* — **cir·cu·lar·ness** *n* -ES

2circular \"\ *n* -S **1 :** an announcement, advertisement, or directive typically in the form of a printed leaflet intended to be sent to many persons or otherwise distributed widely ⟨the first government ~ relative to the medical examination of aviators —H.G.Armstrong⟩ ⟨a ~ to be sent to the police of the areas in which the twenty-nine men lived —F.W.Crofts⟩ **2** *also* **circular cloak :** a long full often fur-lined cape popular in the 19th century

circular canal *n* **:** a canal running around the circumference of the bell of a jellyfish

circular canon *n* **1 :** a musical canon in which the subject leads back to its own beginning so that it may be endlessly repeated — called also *perpetual canon* **2 :** a canon in which the repetitions modulate through a succession of fifths

circular error *n* **:** the error in a timepiece resulting from variations in extent of the arc described by a pendulum

circular flow *n* **:** the continuing and recurrent transfers of money and goods among producers and consumers

circular function *n* **:** TRIGONOMETRIC FUNCTION

circular insanity *or* **circular psychosis** *n* **:** manic-depressive psychosis specif. involving the alternation of manic and depressive states

cir·cu·lar·i·ty \ˌsərkyəˈlarəd·ē, -ə̄k-,-əik-, -ətē, -i *also* -ler-\ *n* -ES [ML *circularitas,* fr. LL *circularis* circular + L *-itas* -ity — more at CIRCULAR] **:** the quality or state of being circular esp. in thought or expression

cir·cu·lar·i·za·tion \ˌsərkyələrəˈzāshən, -ə̄k-, -əik-, -ˌrīˈz-\ *n* -S **:** the act of circularizing

cir·cu·lar·ize \ˈsərkyələˌrīz, -ə̄k-,-əik-\ *vt* -ED/-ING/-S *see -ize in Explan Notes* **1 a :** to send circulars to **:** ply with circulars ⟨all the retail outlets were *circularized* well ahead of time⟩ **b :** to send questionnaires to **:** poll by questioning **:** ascertain the knowledge or beliefs of (a number of persons) ⟨farmers, who were recently *circularized* on the subject, indicated that they wanted 200,000 additional tractors —D.C.McKay⟩ **2 :** to announce or advertise by circular or circulars **:** PUBLICIZE ⟨took the unusual step of seeing that this opinion was *circularized* throughout the United States —C.B.Swisher⟩

circular-knit \¦==¦=¦=\ *adj* **:** knitted in tubular form by machine and usu. later shaped or cut ⟨*circular-knit* sweaters and seamless hosiery⟩ — contrasted with *flat-knit*

circular knitting machine *n* **:** a machine with needles and yarn feeds arranged in a circle for knitting fabrics, hosiery, sweaters, and underwear

circular level *n* **:** BOX LEVEL

circular measure *n* **:** the measure of an angle in radians

circular mil *n* **:** a unit of area used esp. for the cross section of wire equal to the area of a circle having a diameter of one mil and equivalent to 0.000000785 square inch

circular note n **:** LETTER OF CREDIT

circular pitch *n* **:** the distance between corresponding points of consecutive gear teeth measured along the pitch circle

circular plane *n* **:** a woodworking plane with flexible face adjustable for planing convex or concave surfaces — called also *compass plane*

circular reaction *or* **circular response** *n, psychol* **:** a chain reflex in which the final response acts as stimulus for the initial response

circular saw *n* **:** a saw in the form of a thin steel disk with teeth on its periphery that revolves upon a spindle

circular sinus *n* **:** a circular venous channel at the base of the brain formed by the intercavernous sinuses

circular tale *n* **:** a factitious jocular narrative indefinitely repeated in which the last element leads to repetition of the first

circular tour *n, Brit* **:** ROUND TRIP

circular vamp *n* **:** a shoe vamp that covers the forepart of the foot and extends to the shank

circular velocity *n* **:** VELOCITY OF CIRCULATION

cir·cu·late \ˈsərkyəˌlāt, ˈsə̄k-,ˈsəik-, *usu* -ād.+V\ *vb* -ED/-ING/-S [L *circulatus,* past part. of *circulari, circulare* to go around in a circle, make round, fr. *circulus* circle — more at CIRCLE] *vi* **1** *of a vital fluid* **:** to flow or become propelled naturally (as of blood, lymph, or sap) **2 :** to move in a circle, circuit, or orbit **:** move along a course having curves or bends; *esp* **:** to move around and return to the same point ⟨steam *circulating* through the pipes⟩ ⟨the wine decanter *circulated* around the table⟩ **3 :** to move, pass, or go around freely from person to person or from place to place: **a :** to move or flow without obstruction ⟨air *circulating* through the boards being seasoned⟩ **b :** to spread widely **:** become widespread **:** become known or familiar to many ⟨the news made its way up to Airlie and *circulated* through the village —William Black⟩ ⟨the obscene tales that *circulated* so widely in the Italian Renaissance —R.A.Hall b. 1911⟩ **c :** to go from person to person or group to group greeting, chatting, and talking ⟨our host and hostess *circulated* diligently from guest to guest —Nora Waln⟩ ⟨no one can ~ among members of Congress without hearing frequent and sharp criticism —Harold Zink⟩ **d :** to come into the hands of readers; *often* **:** to become sold or distributed ⟨the satire, *circulating* in manuscript copies, had a great local vogue —E.V.Lucas⟩ ⟨these magazines ~ mostly

circular saws

in rural areas⟩ ~ *vt* **1** *chem, obs* **:** to subject to continuous redistillation in a closed vessel **2 :** to cause to move in a circle or circuit **:** REVOLVE, ROTATE ⟨fans ~ the air through the pipes⟩ **3 :** to cause to pass from person to person and usu. to become widely known **:** DISSEMINATE ⟨this evidence of weakening enemy morale was instantly *circulated* to our own people —D.D.Eisenhower⟩ **syn** see SPREAD

circulating assets *n pl* **:** CURRENT ASSETS

circulating capital *n* **:** capital consumed in the process of production (as fuel, power, and raw materials) — contrasted with *fixed capital*

circulating decimal *n* **:** REPEATING DECIMAL

circulating fan *n* **:** a motor-driven fan used to maintain air circulation (as in a building, automobile, or air-conditioning system)

circulating library *n* **1 :** RENTAL LIBRARY **2 :** a collection of books rotated among a group of institutions (as small public libraries or schools)

circulating medium *n* **:** a medium of exchange (as coin, bank notes, or government notes) that passes from hand to hand without endorsement

cir·cu·la·tion \ˌsərkyəˈlāshən, -ə̄k-,-əik-\ *n* -S [MF or L; MF, fr. L *circulation-, circulatio,* fr. *circulatus* + *-ion-, -io* -ion] **1 :** movement or passage in a circuit or other curving or bending course typically with return to a starting point ⟨~ of air through the building⟩ ⟨~ of water in the lake⟩ **2 :** the orderly movement of liquid or dissolved matter through a living body: **a :** the movement of blood through the vessels of the body that is induced by the pumping action of the heart and serves to distribute nutrients and oxygen to and remove waste products from all parts of the body; in man, other mammals, and birds being double, the blood making two distinct circuits and the arterial and venous blood being completely separated by capillary networks; in amphibians and reptiles the circuits being imperfect with some mixing of blood in the single ventricle; and in fishes, a single circuit occurring, the blood passing over the gills and thence to the tissues and back to the heart — see PULMONARY CIRCULATION, SYSTEMIC CIRCULATION **b :** analogous movement of fluid through defined channels and tissue spaces in the bodies of various invertebrates **c :** the flow of sap in a plant **3** *obs* **:** continuous repetition of actions in a set order ⟨a daily ~ of sorrow —Daniel Defoe⟩ **4 :** the act of circulating or being circulated **:** passage or transmission from person to person or place to place: **a :** popular dissemination **:** DISTRIBUTION **:** widespread transmission ⟨the book had wide ~ and its first publication was followed by many successive editions —J.T.Howard⟩ ⟨the report which was in general ~ within five minutes after his entrance —Jane Austen⟩ **b :** passage of money or other means of exchange from person to person throughout a group or society ⟨calling in gold coins in ~⟩ **:** money so circulated **:** CURRENCY ⟨the ~ was again so worn and clipped that the sixth recoinage followed —John Craig⟩ **5 a :** the average number of copies of a publication sold or less frequently distributed over a given period ⟨a country paper with little more than five hundred ~ —W.A.White⟩ **b :** the number of persons exposed to an advertisement or sales message by the use of a certain advertising medium; *esp* **:** potential audience with available receiving sets ⟨the ~ of a radio program⟩ ⟨increasing TV ~⟩ **6 a :** the elements of communication within a building (as foyers, halls, corridors, stairways, and elevators) **b :** unhindered passage or motion about an area ⟨this arrangement of doors permits easy ~⟩ ⟨a parking garage with free ~ of cars⟩ **7 :** the line integral of a vector field around a closed curve **8 a :** the lending of books or other library materials for outside use **b :** the total number of items taken by borrowers from a library **c :** a single borrowing of a library book ⟨a strong binding good for 100 ~s⟩ **9 :** free active social life with different persons or groups ⟨getting back into ~ after her divorce⟩

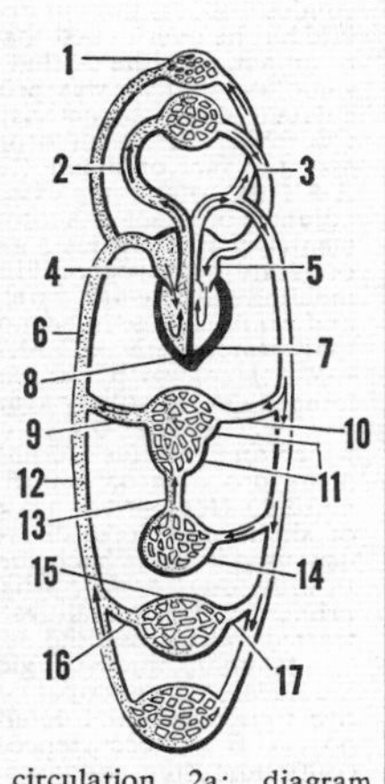

circulation 2a: diagram showing course of circulation in the mammal. Heavier shading represents unoxygenated blood; arrows indicate direction of flow. *1* capillaries of head, *2* pulmonary arteries, *3* pulmonary veins, *4* right auricle, *5* left auricle, *6, 12* postcaval veins, *7* left ventricle, *8* right ventricle, *9* hepatic vein, *10* hepatic artery, *11* capillaries of the liver, *13* portal vein, *14* capillaries of digestive tract, *15* capillaries of kidney, *16* renal veins, *17* renal arteries

cir·cu·la·tive \ˈ==ˌlād·iv, -ˌlət, ¦tiv\ *adj* [L *circulatus* (past part. of *circulari*) + E *-ive*] **:** marked by circulation **:** CIRCULATING **:** promoting circulation

cir·cu·la·tor \-ˌlād·ə(r), -ātə-\ *n* -S [L, peddler, mountebank, fr. *circulatus* (past part. of *circulari* to go around) + *-or* — more at CIRCULATE] **:** one that circulates: **a** *obs* **:** MOUNTEBANK, QUACK **b :** GOSSIP, SCANDALMONGER **c :** a machine for circulating fluids or heating by convection **d :** a worker in a copper refinery who maintains circulation in electrolysis tanks and removes copper incrustations

1cir·cu·la·to·ry \-ləˌtōrē, -ōr-, -ri\ *n* -ES [NL *circulatorium,* fr. L *circulatus* + *-orium* -ory] *chem, obs* **:** a vessel (as a pelican) in which to circulate liquids

2circulatory \"\ *adj* [prob. fr. NL *circulatorius,* fr. L *circulatus* + *-orius* -ory — more at CIRCULATE] **1 :** of or relating to circulation (as of the blood, air, or traffic) **:** causing or concerned in circulation **2** *chem, obs* **:** of or relating to the process of circulating liquids

circulatory system *n* **:** the system of blood, blood vessels, lymphatics, and heart concerned with the circulation of the blood and lymph

cir·cu·lin \ˈsərkyələn\ *n* -S [NL *circulans* (specific epithet of NL *Bacillus circulans*) + E *-in*] **:** an antibiotic consisting of a mixture of polypeptides related to polymyxin that is obtained from a soil bacterium (*Bacillus circulans*) and is active esp. against gram-negative bacteria (as colon bacilli)

cir·cu·lus \-ləs\ *n, pl* **circu·li** \-ˌlī\ [NL, fr. L, circle — more at CIRCLE] **:** one of the usu. concentric ridges on a fish scale each representing an increment of growth

circulus in de·fin·i·en·do \-ˌindəˌfinēˈen(ˌ)dō\ *n* [NL, circle in definition] *logic* **:** a vicious circle in definition

circulus in pro·ban·do \-prōˈban(ˌ)dō\ *n* [NL] *logic* **:** a circle in proof — compare CIRCLE 6b

cir·cum \ˈsərkəm, ˈkirkəm\ *prep* [L] **:** AROUND, ABOUT, SURROUNDING

circum- *in pronunciations below,* ¦== = ¦sərkəm *or* -ə̄k- *or* -əik-\ *prefix* [OF or L; OF, fr. L, fr. *circum* round about, fr. *circus* circle — more at CIRCLE] **1** *adverbially* **:** around **:** about **:** on all sides ⟨*circum*rotate⟩ ⟨*circum*gyration⟩ **2** *prepositionally* **:** around **:** surrounding ⟨*circum*basal⟩ ⟨*circum*corneal⟩ ⟨*circum*lunar⟩ **:** revolving around ⟨*circum*solar⟩ **3 :** circumscribed ⟨*circum*polygon⟩

cir·cum·ambages \¦==+\ *n pl* [*circum-* + *ambages,* pl. of *ambage*] **:** instances of indirectness or deviousness in speaking or writing **:** CIRCUMLOCUTIONS — **cir·cum·ambagious** \¦==+\ *adj*

cir·cum·ambience *or* **cir·cum·ambiency** \¦==+\ *n, pl* **circumambiences** *or* **circumambiencies :** the quality or state of being circumambient

cir·cum·ambient \¦==+\ *adj* [LL *circumambient-, circumambiens,* pres. part. of *circumambire* to surround in a circle, fr. L *circum-* + *ambire* to go around — more at AMBIENT] **1 :** going around **:** ENCIRCLING ⟨~ black lines that are intended . . . to reveal the construction of the picture —Clive Bell⟩ **2 :** SURROUNDING, ENCOMPASSING **:** being on all sides ⟨the ~ air⟩ ⟨the ~ Unknown —C.D.Lewis⟩

cir·cum·ambulate \¦==+\ *vb* -ED/-ING/-S [L *circum ambulatus,* past part. of *circum ambulare* to walk around, fr. *circum* + *ambulare* — more at CIRCUM-, AMBLE] *vi* **1 :** to walk or go around; *esp* **:** to walk or go around an object of worship or reverence or in a ritual circular course ⟨one ~s with the object of worship as well as one's physical as well as spiritual focus —S.W.Nakamura⟩ **2 :** to wander about at leisure without definite purpose or as a result of indirection ~ *vt* **:** to walk around esp. ritualistically ⟨she might have gone and *circumambulated* the Yeobrights' premises at Blooms-End —Thomas Hardy⟩ ⟨the stupa which the worshipers *circumambulated* —W.N.Brown⟩ — **cir·cum·ambulation** \"+\ *n* -S — **cir·cum·ambulator** \"+\ *n* -S

cir·cum·ambulatory \¦==+\ *adj* [L *circum ambulatus* + E *-ory*] **1 :** CIRCUMAMBULATING ⟨the ~ scholar⟩ **2 :** designed for esp. ritualistic circumambulation ⟨the ~ passage made of lime concrete —H.D.Sankalia⟩

cir·cum·bend·i·bus \ˌ==+ˈbendəbəs\ *n* -ES [L *circum* round about + E *bend* + L *-ibus,* abl. pl. ending — more at CIRCUM] **:** an indirect or roundabout course esp. in writing or speaking **:** CIRCUMLOCUTION

cir·cum·boreal \¦==+\ *adj* [*circum-* + *boreal*] **:** throughout the boreal regions

cir·cum·cel·lion \ˌ==+ˈselyən\ *n* -S *usu cap* [LL *circumcellion-, circumcellio,* fr. L *circum-* + LL *-cellion-, -cellio* (fr. L *cella* cell) — more at CELL] **:** one of a group of the Donatists composed of runaway slaves, ruined peasants, and the non-Roman population of northern Africa who combining social with ecclesiastical revolt and courting martyrdom were suppressed by the government

cir·cum·center \¦==+\ *n* [*circum-* + *center*] **:** the center of the circle circumscribing a triangle or a regular polygon of more than three sides

cir·cum·circle \¦==+\ *n* [*circum-* + *circle*] **:** a circumscribed circle

cir·cum·cise \ˈ==+ˌsīz\ *vt* -ED/-ING/-S [ME *circumcisen,* fr. L *circumcisus,* past part. of *circumcidere* to cut around, circumcise, fr. *circum-* + *caedere* to cut — more at CONCISE] **1 a :** to cut off the prepuce of (a male) or the clitoris of (a female) **b :** to cut around, off, or away — now used only in medicine **2 :** to purify spiritually ⟨~ therefore the foreskin of your heart, and be no longer stubborn —Deut 10:16 (RSV)⟩

cir·cum·cis·er *or* **cir·cum·ci·sor** \-zə(r)\ *n* -S **:** one that circumcises

cir·cum·ci·sion \ˌ==+ˈsizhən\ *n* -S [ME *circumcisioun,* fr. OF *circumcision, circoncision,* fr. LL *circumcision-, circumcisio,* fr. L *circumcisus* + *-ion-, -io* -ion] **1 :** the act of circumcising or being circumcised: **a :** the cutting off of the prepuce of males being practiced as a religious rite by Jews and Muslims and as a sanitary measure in modern surgery **b :** the cutting off of prepuce and clitoris being practiced as religious rites or as a practical or punitive measure by some primitive peoples **2 :** spiritual purification **3** *usu cap* **:** a feast commemorating the circumcision of Jesus held on January 1 in the Roman Catholic, Eastern, and Anglican churches

cir·cum·cres·cence \¦==+¦kresᵊn(t)s\ *n* -S [*circum-* + obs. E *crescence* "growth", fr. L *crescentia,* fr. *crescere* to grow — more at CRESCENT] **:** a growing around or over **:** EPIBOLY — **cir·cum·cres·cent** \-ᵊnt\ *adj*

cir·cum·denudation \¦==+\ *n* -S [*circum-* + *denudation*] **:** denudation or erosion around an object leaving it isolated

cir·cum·duce \¦==+¦dyüs\ *vt* -ED/-ING/-S [LL *circumducere* to annul, cancel, fr. L, to lead around, fr. *circum-* + *ducere* to lead — more at TOW] *Scots law* **:** to set a limit to or declare to be at an end by a judicial decision

cir·cum·duct \¦==+¦dəkt\ *vt* -ED/-ING/-S [L *circumductus,* past part. of *circumducere* to lead around, fr. *circum-* + *ducere* to lead — more at CIRCUM-, TOW] **1 :** to turn about an axis **:** REVOLVE, ROTATE; *esp* **:** to move (as a leg) so that the distal end describes a circle with the proximal end remaining fixed **2 a** *law* **:** to put a limit or end to **b** *civil law* **:** ABROGATE, ANNUL ⟨~ a law or citation⟩

cir·cum·duc·tion \ˌ==+ˈdəkshən\ *n* -S [L *circumduction-, circumductio,* fr. *circumductus* + *-ion-, -io* -ion] **:** the act or action of circumducting; *specif* **:** TERMINATION, ABROGATION, CANCELLATION

cir·cum·ero·sion \¦==+\ *n* -S [*circum-* + *erosion*] **:** CIRCUMDENUDATION

circumesophageal ring \¦==+ . . .-\ *n* [*circum* + *esophageal*] **:** ESOPHAGEAL RING

cir·cum·e·ter \ˌsərˈkəməd·ər\ *n* -S [blend of *circum-* and *-meter*] **:** a device for measuring the circumference of a fruit

cir·cum·fer·ence \sərˈkəm(p)fərn(t)s, -f(ə)rən(t)s, *-R & often R* səˈk-\ *n* -S [ME, fr. MF *circumference, circonference,* fr. L *circumferentia,* fr. *circumferre* to carry around, fr. *circum-* + *ferre* to carry — more at BEAR] **1 :** the line that bounds a circular plane surface or the length of this line equal to π times the diameter **:** PERIMETER; *broadly* **:** PERIPHERY, CIRCUIT **2 a :** the surface or outer limits of a sphere or rounded body **:** the measure of the perimeter of a great circle or sphere ⟨from the center to the ~ of the spheroid⟩ **b :** LIMITS, BOUNDS ⟨within the ~ of a grain of sand⟩ ⟨that mysterious intellectual magnetism that enlarges the ~ of his ego —J.C.Powys⟩

cir·cum·fer·en·tial \sə(r)ˌkəm(p)fəˈrenchəl; ˌsər,=ˈ=ˈ==, ˌsə̄,-, ˌsəi,-\ *adj* [L *circumferentia* circumference + E *-al*] **:** of or relating to the circumference esp. of a town or city: as **a :** ENCIRCLING ⟨~ seam welding —*Industrial Equipment News*⟩ ⟨a ~ highway around a city —*U.S. Code*⟩ **b :** PERIPHERAL, SKIRTING ⟨bypass or ~ roads to enable through traffic to keep out of cities —*New Internat'l Yr. Bk.*⟩ ⟨parkways and ~ drives —*Amer. Builder*⟩ ⟨these efforts . . . are nevertheless peripheral, ~, apart from the curricular body of knowledge which is central to any educational institution —K.I. Brown⟩ — **cir·cum·fer·en·tial·ly** \-ch(ə)lē, -li\ *adv*

cir·cum·fer·en·tor \sə(r)ˈkəm(p)fəˌrentə(r)\ *n* -S [L *circumferentia* circumference + E *-or*] **1 :** a surveyor's compass with diametral projecting arms each carrying a vertical slit sight **2 :** a graduated wheel formerly used to measure tires

1cir·cum·flex \ˈsərkəmˌfleks, ˈsə̄k-,ˈsəik-\ *vt* -ED/-ING/-ES [L *circumflexus,* past part. of *circumflectere* to bend around, mark with a circumflex, fr. *circum-* + *flectere* to bend] **:** to mark with a circumflex

2circumflex \"\ *adj* [L *circumflexus;* in ref. to accent, approximate trans. of Gk *perispōmenos,* pres. middle part. of *perispan* to draw off, divert, fr. *peri-* + *span* to draw — more at SPAN] **1 a :** characterized by the pitch, quantity, or quality indicated by a circumflex (sense 1); *esp* **:** first rising and then falling in pitch ⟨a ~ intonation⟩ ⟨the long *o* of Greek *dōron* "gift" is spoken with a ~ accent⟩ **b :** being a circumflex (sense 1) ⟨the *a* of French *bâtir* "to build" is written with a ~ accent⟩ **c :** marked with a circumflex (sense 1) ⟨~ *e*⟩ **2** *of nerves and blood vessels* **:** bending around

3circumflex *n* -ES **1** *or* **circumflex accent :** a mark ˆ, ˆ, or ˜ orig. used in Greek over long vowels to indicate a rising-falling tone and thence in other languages to mark length, contraction, or a falling-rising tone and in still others and in phonetic notation to indicate a particular vowel quality — see ACCENT 5; compare TILDE **2 :** a rising-falling or falling-rising intonation of a vocalic or syllable

circumflex artery *n* **:** any of several paired curving arteries as: **a :** either of two branches of the deep femoral artery, an external supplying the front of the thigh and an internal the adductor muscles and adjacent parts **b :** either of two branches of the axillary artery that wind around the neck of the humerus **c :** either circumflex iliac artery **d :** a branch of the subscapular artery supplying the muscles of the shoulder

circumflex iliac artery *n* **:** either of two arteries arching anteriorly near Poupart's ligament: **a :** an artery lying internal to the iliac crest and arising from the external iliac artery **b :** a more superficially located artery that is a branch of the femoral artery

circumflex nerve *n* **:** AXILLARY NERVE

cir·cum·flu·ent \(ˌ)sərˌkəmfləwənt\ *also* **cir·cum·flu·ous** \-wəs\ *adj* [*circumfluent* fr. L *circumfluent-, circumfluens,* pres. part. of *circumfluere* to flow around, surround, fr. *circum-* + *fluere* to flow; *circumfluous* fr. L *circumfluus,* fr. *circum-* + *-fluus* (fr. *fluere*) — more at FLUENT] **:** flowing round or surrounding in the manner of a fluid ⟨the earth and its ~ air⟩

cir·cum·fo·ra·ne·ous \ˌsərkəmfəˈrānēəs, sərˌk-\ *adj* [L *circumforaneus*, fr. *circum-* + *-foraneus* (fr. *forum* market place) — more at FORUM] **:** going about from market to market **:** wandering from place to place ⟨a ∼ jester⟩

cir·cum·fuse \ˌ⁼⁼ *at* CIRCUM- + ˈfyüz\ *vt* -ED/-ING/-S [L *circumfusus*, past part. of *circumfundere* to pour around, fr. *circum-* + *fundere* to pour — more at FOUND] **1 :** to spread or diffuse round ⟨his army, *circumfused* on either wing —John Milton⟩ **2 :** to surround, envelop, or bathe esp. by a pouring or diffusing around ⟨education and civilization are gradually *circumfusing* the earth —L.M.Winters⟩ ⟨a face all *circumfused* with light —Ben Jonson⟩

cir·cum·fu·sion \ˌ⁼⁼+ˈfyüzhən\ *n* -S [LL *circumfusion-*, *circumfusio*, fr. L *circumfusus* + *-ion-*, *-io* -ion] **:** the act of circumfusing or state of being circumfused ⟨the ∼ of the smoke⟩ ⟨the ∼ of the island by fog⟩

cir·cum·gyration \ˌ⁼⁼+\ *n* -S [LL *circumgyratus* (past part. of *circumgyrare* to turn around, fr. L *circum-* + *gyrare* to turn) + E *-ion* — more at GYRATE] **1 :** GYRATION **2 :** movement in a circular course ⟨Aristotle's view that all the heavenly bodies . . . move in circular orbits in which each ∼ is an exact repetition of every one that has preceded it —A.J.Toynbee⟩

cir·cum·horizontal arc \ˌ⁼⁼+ . . -\ *n* **:** a colored halo of 90° extent or less that is red on the upper side, parallel to the horizon and 46° or a little more below the sun, and produced by the refraction of light across 90° angles at the undersides of ice crystals in suspension in the air

cir·cum·in·ces·sion *also* **cir·cum·in·ses·sion** \ˌ⁼⁼+in-ˈseshən\ *n* -S [ML *circumincession-*, *circumincessio* (fr. L *circum-* + ML *incessio*, fr. L *incessus*, past part. of *incedere* to go along, fr. *in* + *cedere* to go), trans. of MGk *perichōrēsis*, fr. Gk *perichōrein* to go around, rotate, fr. *peri-* + *chōrein* to go, withdraw (akin to *chēros* left, bereaved) — more at IN-, CEDE, HEIR] **:** the theological doctrine of the reciprocal existence in each other of the three persons of the Trinity

cir·cum·ja·cen·cies \ˌ⁼⁼+ˈjāsᵊnsēz\ *n pl* **:** adjacent parts **:** areas that surround **:** SURROUNDINGS ⟨the ∼ of the school⟩

cir·cum·ja·cent \ˌ⁼⁼+ˈjāsᵊnt\ *adj* [L *circumjacent-*, *circumjacens*, pres. part. of *circumjacēre*, fr. *circum-* + *jacēre* to lie — more at CIRCUM-, GIST] **:** lying adjacent on all sides **:** SURROUNDING ⟨the ∼ hills —John Buchan⟩ ⟨the whole ∼ region of which it is the capital —George Borrow⟩

cir·cum·len·tal \ˌ⁼⁼+ˈlentᵊl\ *adj* [*circum-* + NL *lent-*, *lens* lens (fr. L, lentil) + E *-al* — more at LENS] **:** encircling a lens

cir·cum·lo·cu·tion \ˌ⁼⁼+lōˈkyüshən\ *n* -S [L *circumlocution-*, *circumlocutio* (fr. *circum-* + *locutio* speaking, speech, fr. *locutus*, past part. of *loqui* to speak), trans. of Gk *periphrasis* — more at PERIPHRASIS] **1 a :** the use of an unnecessarily large number of words to express an idea **:** indirect or roundabout expression ⟨the gift of the pamphleteer, who cuts through academic ∼ —Vera M. Dean⟩ **b :** evasion in speech ⟨a preference for ∼ rather than forthrightness⟩ **2 :** an instance of circumlocution — **cir·cum·lo·cu·tion·al** \ˌ⁼⁼⁼ˈ⁼shənᵊl, -shnəl\ *or* **cir·cum·lo·cu·tion·ary** \-shəˌnerē, -ri\ *adj*

cir·cum·lo·cu·tion·ist \ˌ⁼⁼⁼ˈ⁼sh(ə)nəst\ *n* -S **:** one who uses circumlocution

cir·cum·lo·cu·tious \ˌ⁼⁼⁼ˈ⁼shəs\ *adj* [*circumlocution* + *-ous*] **:** CIRCUMLOCUTORY

cir·cum·loc·u·to·ry \ˌ⁼⁼ˈläkyəˌtōrē, -ȯr-, -ri\ *adj* [*circumlocution* + *-ory*] **:** marked by or exhibiting circumlocution ⟨∼ detail —Dorothy Sayers⟩ ⟨∼ remarks⟩

cir·cum·lunar \ˌ⁼⁼+\ *adj* [*circum-* + *lunar*] **:** revolving about or surrounding the moon

cir·cum·meridian \ˌ⁼⁼+\ *adj* [*circum-* + *meridian*] **:** at or in relation to the meridian — used of a celestial body or the observation of it

cir·cum·mure \ˌ⁼⁼+ˈmyů(ə)r\ *vt* -ED/-ING/-S [*circum-* + *mure*] **:** to encompass with a wall

cir·cum·navigable \ˌ⁼⁼+\ *adj* [*circumnavigate* + *-able*] **:** capable of being circumnavigated

cir·cum·navigate \ˌ⁼⁼+\ *vt* -ED/-ING/-S [L *circumnavigatus*, past part. of *circumnavigare* to sail around, fr. *circum-* + *navigare* to sail — more at CIRCUM-, NAVIGATE] **1 :** to go or travel completely around (as the earth) esp. by water ⟨∼ the globe in a small craft⟩ **2 :** to go around as opposed to going through (as a congested area) **:** SKIRT, BYPASS ⟨roads . . . which neatly ∼ industrial areas —Joseph Wechsberg⟩ ⟨Magellan had *circumnavigated* South America in 1520 —L.A.Brown⟩

cir·cum·navigation \ˌ⁼⁼+\ *n* -S **:** the act or process of circumnavigating an object (as the earth) ⟨when Malacca Henry arrived . . . he had been around the world although Magellan's men had not yet finished their ∼ —R.P.Ludlum⟩

cir·cum·navigator \ˌ⁼⁼+\ *n* -S **:** one that circumnavigates an object (as the earth) ⟨disputed that Magellan was the first ∼⟩

cir·cum·navigato·ry \ˌ⁼⁼+\ *adj* **:** consisting of circumnavigation ⟨Magellan's ∼ voyage⟩

cir·cum·neutral \ˌ⁼⁼+\ *adj* [*circum-* + *neutral*] *of soil* **:** nearly neutral **:** having a pH between 6.5 and 7.5

cir·cum·nutate \ˌ⁼⁼+\ *vi* -ED/-ING/-S [*circum-* + *nutate*] **:** to grow in a way characteristic of circumnutation

cir·cum·nutation \ˌ⁼⁼+\ *n* -S [*circum-* + *nutation* (influenced by G *rotierende nutation*, lit., revolving nutation)] **:** a movement of the growing portions of a plant to form spirals, irregular curves, or ellipses — compare NUTATION

cir·cum·oral \ˌ⁼⁼+\ *adj* [*circum-* + *oral*] **:** surrounding the mouth

cir·cum·polar \ˌ⁼⁼+\ *adj* [*circum-* + *polar*] **1** *of a celestial body* **:** remaining above the horizon during the entire 360 degrees of daily travel **2 :** surrounding, lying near, or found in the vicinity of a terrestrial pole

cir·cum·position \ˌ⁼⁼+\ *n* -S [LL *circumposition-*, *circumpositio*, fr. L *circumpositus*, past part. of *circumponere* to place around (fr. *circum-* + *ponere* to place) + *-ion-*, *-io* — more at CIRCUM-, POSITION] **:** AIR LAYERING

cir·cum·radius \ˌ⁼⁼+\ *n* [*circum-* + *radius*] **:** the radius of a circumscribed circle

cir·cum·scissile \ˌ⁼⁼+\ *adj* [L *circumscissus* (past part. of *circumscindere* to tear or cleave around, fr. *circum-* + *scindere* to cleave) + E *-ile* — more at SHED] *bot* **:** dehiscing by a transverse fissure around the circumference — compare LOCULICIDAL, PYXIDIUM; see FRUIT illustration

cir·cum·scrib·a·ble \ˌsərkəmˌzˈskrībəbəl, ˈsək-, ˈsəik-, -mˈsk-\ *adj* **:** capable of being circumscribed

cir·cum·scribe \ˈ⁼kəmzˌkrīb, -mˌsk-, ˌ⁼⁼ˈ⁼\ *vt* -ED/-ING/-S [L *circumscribere*, fr. *circum-* + *scribere* to write, draw — more at SCRIBE] **1 a :** to draw a line around **:** encompass with or as if with a line ⟨∼ a word on a page⟩ ⟨a voyage that ∼s the world⟩ **b :** to surround by or as if by a boundary **:** BOUND ⟨that the American nation was not to be *circumscribed* by narrow isthmuses and gulf streams —*Encyc. Americana*⟩ **2 :** to set limits or bounds to: as **a :** to constrict the range or activity of ⟨∼ a heart patient's activity⟩ ⟨a London physician whose round of practice remained among the poor and was *circumscribed* by poverty —H.V.Gregory⟩ **b :** to define, mark off, or demarcate carefully ⟨rulership by the best and wisest under well-considered laws, *circumscribed* by a written constitution —V.L.Parrington⟩ **3 :** to draw or be drawn around (a geometrical figure) so as to touch at as many points as possible ⟨a curve *circumscribing* a polygon⟩ — compare INSCRIBE 4 **syn** see LIMIT

cir·cum·scrip·tion \ˌ⁼kəmˈkripshən, -mˈsk-\ *n* -S [L *circumscription-*, *circumscriptio*, fr. *circumscriptus* (past part. of *circumscribere*) + *-ion-*, *-io* -ion] **1 :** the quality or state of being circumscribed: as **a** *obs* **:** the property of having limitation in space as opposed to omnipresence or infiniteness **b** *obs* **:** CONFINEMENT **2 :** something that circumscribes or encloses: **a :** LIMIT, BOUNDARY **b :** RESTRICTION ⟨rigid ∼ of tradition⟩ **c :** an esp. clearly defined outline ⟨the oval ∼ of the man's head⟩ **3 :** the act or action of circumscribing: as **a :** DELIMITATION, DEFINITION ⟨an idea that does not lend itself easily to ∼⟩ **b :** LIMITATION ⟨the ∼ of a patient's movements during convalescence⟩ **4 :** a circumscribed area or district ⟨a ∼ controlled by a given political group⟩

cir·cum·spect \ˈ⁼kəmˌzpekt, -mˌsp-, ˌ⁼⁼ˈ⁼\ *adj* [ME, fr. MF or L; MF *circonspect*, fr. L *circumspectus*, past part. of *circumspicere* to look around, be cautious, fr. *circum-* + *specere* to look — more at CIRCUM-, SPY] **:** marked by caution and earnest attention to all significant circumstances and possible consequences of action (as action to be undertaken) and usu. by prudence and discretion ⟨a ∼ investor⟩ ⟨a ∼ action⟩ ⟨the wicked are always alert and ∼ —George Meredith⟩ **syn** see CAUTIOUS

cir·cum·spec·tion \ˌ⁼kəmzˈpekshən, -mˈsp-\ *n* -S [ME *circumspeccioun*, fr. MF or L; MF *circonspection*, fr. L *circumspection-*, *circumspectio*, fr. *circumspectus* + *-ion-*, *-io* -ion] **:** the quality or state of being circumspect ⟨I was followed or watched by one or other of the Indians, so that great ∼ was needed —W.H.Hudson †1922⟩

cir·cum·spec·tive \ˌ⁼⁼ˈ⁼tiv\ *adj* [*circumspection* + *-ive*] **:** CIRCUMSPECT

cir·cum·spect·ly *adv* [ME, fr. *circumspect* + *-ly*] **:** in a circumspect manner

cir·cum·spect·ness *n* -ES **:** CIRCUMSPECTION

cir·cum·stance \ˈsərkəmzˌtan(t)s, ˈsək-, ˈsəik-, -mˌst-, -taa(ə)n-, -tain- *Brit usu & US also* -ˌtən- *or* -ˌstən-; *sometimes* -ˌtàn- *or* -ˌstàn-\ *n* -S [ME, fr. MF, fr. L *circumstantia*, fr. *circumstant-*, *circumstans*, pres. part. of *circumstare* to stand around, fr. *circum-* + *stare* to stand — more at STAND] **1 a :** a specific part, phase, or attribute of the surroundings or background of an event, fact, or thing or of the prevailing conditions in which it exists or takes place **:** a condition, fact, or event accompanying, conditioning, or determining another **:** an adjunct or concomitant that is present or logically likely to be present ⟨it was late but he overlooked that ∼⟩ ⟨the time, place, and other ∼s of an action⟩ ⟨the ∼ that the man was happy raised the presumption that he was prosperous enough⟩ ⟨every ∼ of calculated and characteristic . . . treachery —Sir Winston Churchill⟩ **b :** a subordinate detail **:** an adventitious nonessential fact or detail ⟨the gist of the matter, not the ∼s⟩ **2 a :** the total complex of essential attributes and attendant adjuncts of a fact or action **:** the sum of essential and environmental characteristics **:** arrangement, situation, composition, or nature of an event or thing — usu. used in singular without the indefinite article and rarely with the definite article ⟨constant and rapid change in economic ∼, social custom, and intellectual atmosphere —G.M.Trevelyan⟩ ⟨the fell clutch of ∼ —W.E.Henley⟩ **b :** OCCURRENCE, EVENTUALITY ⟨the unofficial minority voted solidly against a government measure — a rare ∼ —W.T.Stace⟩ **c :** an evidential condition on the basis of which an event (as a crime) may be inferred or an accusation made probable or improbable ⟨the ∼s of the case indicate murder⟩ ⟨the ∼s tell against the accused⟩ **d :** surroundings or situation as regards wealth, property, assured income — usu. used in pl. ⟨a bachelor in easy ∼s with a large inheritance to draw on⟩ **e** *obs* **:** a likely appurtenance **:** a characteristic property **3 :** formalities and ritualistic display esp. as contrasted with essential procedure **:** attendant ceremonial ⟨pride, pomp, and ∼ of glorious war —Shak.⟩ ⟨with appropriate ducal and episcopal ∼ —Francis Hackett⟩ **4** *in a narrative* **:** circumstantial detail ⟨stress ∼ rather than action in a novel⟩ **5 :** an occurrence or fact viewed as a detail in a larger continuum ⟨the conqueror weeping for new worlds or the like ∼s in history —Joseph Addison⟩ **6 :** CHANCE, FATE ⟨a training in self-reliance, endurance, and indifference to ∼ —*Geog. Rev.*⟩ ⟨a mere victim of ∼ —Fritz Stern⟩ **syn** see OCCURRENCE — **in the circumstances** *or* **under the circumstances :** as matters stand **:** things being the way they are ⟨we had no means of transportation to the picnic so *in the circumstances* we stayed home⟩ — **not a circumstance to** *slang* **:** insignificant by comparison with ⟨a squall is *not a circumstance to* a hurricane wind⟩ — **under no circumstances :** under no conditions ⟨*under no circumstances* were they to go unattended⟩

cir·cum·stanced \-n(t)st\ *adj* **:** being or placed in a particular condition or in certain circumstances esp. in regard to property or income ⟨comfortably ∼ and for the first time in her life commanding ready money —Thomas Hardy⟩ ⟨those more happily ∼ in their birth —Reginald Hargreaves⟩

¹**cir·cum·stan·tial** \ˌ⁼kəmzˈtanchəl, -mˈst-, -aan-, -ain-\ *adj* [L *circumstantia* circumstance + E *-al*] **1 :** belonging to, consisting in, influenced by, or dependent on circumstances ⟨a historical novel . . . full of ∼ life —Jean Garrigue⟩ ⟨∼ developments not covered in the main plan⟩ ⟨a purely ∼ outcome to the play⟩ **2 :** pertinent but not essential to **:** ACCOMPANYING, INCIDENTAL, ADVENTITIOUS ⟨a hard life, stripped of every ∼ grace —Isabel Paterson⟩ ⟨the forces which thrust him down are ∼ rather than inevitable —C.C.Walcutt⟩ **3 :** marked strongly by attention to small incidents and details, esp. attendant circumstances or conditions ⟨his ∼ accounts of his adventures —Richard Griffith⟩ **4 :** marked by ceremony and pomp ⟨the ∼ splendor of the coronation⟩

syn MINUTE, PARTICULAR, PARTICULARIZED, DETAILED, ITEMIZED: CIRCUMSTANTIAL may suggest precise or detailed treatment (as that of an acute eyewitness) of circumstances and secondary incidents and items ⟨I solemnly declare that I am at this time in the possession of my right mind — that my memory is exact and *circumstantial* —Charles Dickens⟩ ⟨the story of the rattlesnake chasing the squirrel was too *circumstantial* to have been invented —Constance M. Rourke⟩ MINUTE suggests searching, close attention even the smallest details ⟨she was interested in the little details and writes with *minute* care about the change of fashion —Gamaliel Bradford⟩ ⟨Plato, the foe of the mechanical, in the Laws . . . provides for the state a perfect jumble of *minute* regulations —John Buchan⟩ PARTICULAR implies a zealous care about and attention to details ⟨I should have been more *particular* in my account of Miss Unwin if I had had materials for a minute description —William Cowper⟩ PARTICULARIZED, that is, treated or presented with full particulars, has pretty much superseded PARTICULAR in reference to accounts, descriptions, and so on ⟨a most concrete, *particularized*, earthy series of small diurnal recognitions —J.C. Powys⟩ DETAILED simply indicates treatment with a wealth of detail and lacks any special connotation ⟨his [Ruskin's] *detailed* criticisms of architecture and painting —Bliss Perry⟩ ITEMIZED, mostly commercial in use and suggestion, indicates a specific and separate listing or inclusion of each item, as each charge, cost, or deduction ⟨an *itemized* bill from the hotel⟩ ⟨an *itemized* list of stock losses accompanying the tax return⟩

²**circumstantial** \"\ *n* -S **:** an attendant circumstance **:** DETAIL; *esp* **:** something incidental to the main subject — usu. used in pl. ⟨the main point of an argument and the ∼s⟩ ⟨the essence and the ∼s of a religion⟩

circumstantial evidence *n* **:** evidence that tends to prove a fact in issue by proving other events or circumstances which according to the common experience of mankind are usu. or always attended by the fact in issue and that therefore affords a basis for a reasonable inference by the jury or court of the occurrence of the fact in issue

cir·cum·stan·ti·al·i·ty \ˌ⁼kəmzˌtancheˈaləd-ē, -mˌst-, -aan-, -ain-, -əte, -i\ *n* -ES **1 :** the quality or state of being circumstantial **:** particularity or minuteness of real or plausible detail ⟨a legend arose of such ∼ that the wise historian would hesitate to attack it —W.S.Maugham⟩ **2 :** a circumstantial matter **:** DETAIL ⟨the *circumstantialities* of the event⟩

cir·cum·stan·tial·ly \ˌ⁼⁼ˈ⁼chəlē, -li\ *adv* **:** in a circumstantial manner: as **a :** in respect to circumstances ⟨an account that was ∼ accurate though incomplete⟩ **b :** not essentially **:** ACCIDENTALLY ⟨a mere acquaintance only ∼ related to the victim⟩ **c :** in detail **:** MINUTELY ⟨sit down, and compose herself, and tell him ∼ what had been done —George Meredith⟩ **d :** according to or by means of circumstantial evidence ⟨finally convicted not by eyewitnesses but ∼⟩

cir·cum·stan·tial·ness *n* -ES **:** CIRCUMSTANTIALITY

¹**cir·cum·stan·ti·ate** \ˌ⁼⁼ˈ⁼chēˌāt, *usu* -ād+V\ *vt* -ED/-ING/-S [L *circumstantia* circumstance + E *-ate*] **:** to provide the circumstantial evidence or support for ⟨∼ a theory⟩ ⟨∼ a claim⟩ — **cir·cum·stan·ti·a·tion** \ˌ⁼⁼ˌ⁼⁼ˈāshən\ *n* -S

²**cir·cum·stan·ti·ate** \ˌ⁼⁼ˈ⁼⁼ət, -ˌāt\ *adj* [L *circumstantia* + E *-ate*] *archaic* **:** CIRCUMSTANTIATED

cir·cum·tropical \ˌ⁼⁼ *at* CIRCUM- + \ *adj* [*circum-* + *tropical*] **:** surrounding or distributed throughout the tropics — compare TROPICOPOLITAN

¹**cir·cum·val·late** \ˌ⁼⁼+ˈvaˌlāt, -ˌlət\ *adj* [L *circumvallatus*] **1 :** surrounded or enclosed by or as if by a rampart **2** *anat* **:** surrounded by a ridge or elevation

²**cir·cum·val·late** \ˌ⁼⁼ˈ⁼ˌlāt\ *vt* -ED/-ING/-S [L *circumvallatus*, past part. of *circumvallare* to surround with a wall, fr. *circum-* + *vallare* to surround with a wall, fr. *vallum* rampart — more at CIRCUM-, WALL] **:** to surround or enclose with or as if with a rampart ⟨ramparts . . . ∼ more than an obscure village —D.C. Peattie⟩ ⟨a fir copse . . . *circumvallated* by a stout wire fence —Rose Macaulay⟩

circumvallate papilla *n* **:** any of approximately 12 large papillae each surrounded with a marginal sulcus and richly supplied with taste buds chiefly responsive to bitter flavors and arranged in a V-shaped row near the back of the tongue — called also *vallate papilla*

cir·cum·val·la·tion \ˌ⁼⁼ˌvaˈlāshən\ *n* -S [L *circumvallatus* + E *-ion*] **1 :** the act of circumvallating **2 :** something that circumvallates; *esp* **:** ramparts or entrenchments around a besieged place or a besieging army

cir·cum·vene \ˌ⁼⁼ˈvēn\ *vt* -ED/-ING/-S [F *circonvenir*, fr. L *circumvenire* to surround, afflict, cheat] **:** CIRCUMVENT

cir·cum·vent \ˌsərkəmˈvent, ˈsək-, ˈsəik-\ *vt* -ED/-ING/-S [L *circumventus*, past part. of *circumvenire* to surround, afflict, cheat, fr. *circum-* + *venire* to come — more at COME] **1 a :** to surround and cut off the escape of **:** hem in and capture ⟨∼*ed* by the enemy, he had to yield⟩ **b :** ENCIRCLE **:** form a circling boundary around ⟨little islands ∼*ed* by a river⟩ **c :** to encompass with evils, difficulties, or enemies ⟨the melodrama's heroine ∼*ed* with perils⟩ **d :** to go around **:** make a full circuit around or bypass without going through ⟨a lake allows an average father, walking slowly, to ∼ it in an afternoon —W.H.Auden⟩ ⟨an alternative path, ∼*ing* Kentucky through the states to its north —*New Republic*⟩ **2 :** to overcome or avoid the intent, effect, or force of **:** anticipate and escape, check, or defeat by ingenuity or stratagem **:** make inoperative or nullify the purpose or power of esp. by craft or scheme ⟨∼*ing* his enemies by craft and driving them out . . . by force —P.N.Ure⟩ ⟨rules which they ∼ or openly violate —Jerome Frank⟩ **syn** see FRUSTRATE

cir·cum·ven·tion \ˌ⁼⁼ˈvenchən\ *n* -S [LL *circumvention-*, *circumventio*, fr. L *circumventus* + *-ion-*, *-io* -ion] **:** the act or action, instance, or means of circumventing ⟨the ∼ of the law⟩ ⟨the ∼ of an enemy's clever plan⟩

cir·cum·vo·lute \(ˌ)sərˈkəmvəˌlüt, ˈsərkəmvōˌlüt\ *vb* -ED/-ING/-S [L *circumvolutus*, past part. of *circumvolvere* to revolve, roll around, fr. *circum-* + *volvere* to roll — more at VOLUBLE] *vi* **:** to wind or turn in volutions esp. in an inward spiral (as of a snail shell or the capital scroll of an Ionic column) ∼ *vt* **:** to encircle or entangle with something twisted or wound around

cir·cum·vo·lu·tion \(ˌ)sərˌkəmvəˈlüshən, ˌsərkəmvōˈlüshən\ *n* -S [ME *circumvolucioun*, fr. ML *circumvolution-*, *circumvolutio*, fr. L *circumvolutus* + *-ion-*, *-io* -ion] **1 a :** a turning or winding around a center or axis **:** ROTATION, GYRATION **b :** a single revolution or rotation **2 a :** a folding or twisting of one thing about another **b :** a winding in an inward spiral (as in the scroll of an Ionic capital) **c :** a single turn of such a folding or winding ⟨the ∼ of a boa constrictor⟩ ⟨the ∼s of a snail's shell⟩

circumvolve *vt* -ED/-ING/-S [L *circumvolvere*] *obs* **:** to wind, wrap, or bend round **:** SURROUND, ENVELOP

cir·cum·zenithal arc \ˌ⁼⁼ *at* CIRCUM- + . . . -\ *n* [ISV *circum-* + *zenithal*; orig. formed as F *circumzénithal*] **:** a bright rainbow-colored circular halo arc about the zenith as center convex to the sun and about 46 degrees above it

¹**cir·cus** \ˈsərkəs, ˈsək-, ˈsəik-\ *n* -ES *often attrib* [L, circle, ring, circus (sense 1) — more at CIRCLE] **1 a :** a large oblong or circular structure similar to an amphitheater and enclosed by tiers of seats on three or all four sides and used for athletic contests, exhibitions of horsemanship or in ancient times chariot racing and public esp. gladiatorial spectacles — compare HIPPODROME, STADIUM **b :** a spectacle presented in such an area or structure **c** (1) **:** a spectacular public entertainment given usu. in a large tent and made up of acts of physical skill (as horsemanship) and daring (as gymnastic and aerial acrobatics) and acts with trained wild animals (as lions, tigers, and elephants) interspersed with showing off elaborate and colorful costumes and trappings and with informally interjected comedy by clowns and often accompanied by menageries and sideshows held in separate tents featuring biological freaks, trick acts (as sword swallowing and fire eating), and rather crude girly shows (2) **:** the physical plant, livestock, and personnel of such a circus ⟨the ∼ moved out of winter quarters in its special train⟩ **d :** an activity suggesting a circus ⟨loudspeakers, parades, jazz records, rallies . . . made a ∼ of the noon hour —*New Republic*⟩ **e** *slang* **:** an esp. lively or diverting entertainment ⟨so funny it was a ∼⟩ ⟨men in boats are having a ∼ with mackerel, yellowtails, barracuda, and dolphin —*Ford Times*⟩ **2 a** *obs* **:** CIRCLE, RING **b** *Brit* **:** an esp. circular area at an intersection of streets — often used in proper names ⟨Piccadilly *Circus*⟩ **c :** CIRQUE 3 **3 :** FLYING CIRCUS

²**circus** \"\ *n*, *cap* [NL, fr. Gk *kirkos* hawk — more at CIRCAETUS] **:** a genus of hawks comprising the harriers — see MARSH HAWK

³**circus** \"\ *vi* -ED/-ING/-ES [back-formation fr. *circus movement*] **:** to exhibit circus movements after an injury

circus catch *n* **:** a catch (as in baseball) requiring an extraordinary or spectacular effort

circus duck *n* [so called fr. its plumage] **:** HARLEQUIN DUCK

circus makeup *n* **:** an extreme variegated makeup of a newspaper page featuring a profusion of sizes and kinds of attention-catching headlines, cuts, and boxes in unbalanced array

circus movement *n* [L *circus* (circle)] **1 :** involuntary circling in one direction due to injury to the central nervous system, esp. to the cerebellum or the semicircular canals — compare NYSTAGMUS **2 :** movement of a wave of excitation through excitable tissue in such a manner that it makes and repeats more or less indefinitely a complete circuit back to the point of origin, considered to be a possible cause of auricular fibrillation in man

cir·cusy \-kəsē\ *adj* **:** befitting or suggesting a circus esp. in having spectacular qualities (as highly colored or ornate ornamentation)

ci·ré *also* **ci·re** \səˈrā\ *n* -S [F, fr. past part. of *cirer* to wax, fr. *cire*, n., wax, fr. L *cera* — more at CEREUS] **1 :** a brilliant highly glazed finish for fabrics usu. achieved by applying wax to the fabric and subjecting it to hot calendering **2 :** a fabric with a ciré finish — **ci·réd** \səˈrād\ *adj*

cire per·due \ˈsir,perˈd(y)ü, F sēerperdüe\ *n* [F (*moulage à*) *cire perdue*, lit., lost wax casting] **:** a process used in metal casting that consists of making a wax model (as of a statuette), coating it with a refractory (as clay) to form a mold, heating until the wax melts and runs out of small holes left in the mold, and then pouring metal into the space left vacant

cir·io \ˈsirēˌō\ *n* -S [AmerSp, fr. Sp, thick candle, fr. L *cereus* waxen, fr. *cera* wax] **:** a Mexican candlewood (*Fouquieria columnaris*) having tall columnar stems

cirl bunting \ˈsər(-ə)l-\ *n* [NL *cirlus* (specific epithet of *Emberiza cirlus*), fr. It *cirlo*, of imit. origin] **:** a small European finch (*Emberiza cirlus*) brightly marked with yellow, olive, and black

cir·o·grille \ˈsirəˌgril\ *n* -S [ME, fr. LL *choerogryllos*, fr. LGk *choirogryllos*, fr. Gk *choiros* pig, young pig + *gryllos* young pig; akin to Gk *gryzein* to grunt — more at -CHOERUS, GRUNT] **:** SYRIAN HYRAX

ci·ro·lana \ˌsirəˈlanə, -lä-, -lā-\ *n*, *cap* [NL, coined *ab*1818 by William E. Leach †1836 Brit. naturalist] **:** a widely distributed genus (the type of the family Cirolanidae) of small more or less ovate gregarious marine isopods with setose palps and maxillipeds that are sometimes pests at bathing beaches because of their vicious biting

cirque \ˈsərk\ *n* -S [F, fr. L *circus* — more at CIRCUS] **1 :** CIRCUS 1a **2 :** CIRCLE, CIRCLET — used chiefly in poetry **3 :** a deep steep-walled basin high on a mountain usu. shaped like half a bowl and often containing a small lake, caused esp. by glacial erosion, and usu. forming the blunt head of a valley

cirr- *or* **cirri-** *or* **cirro-** *also* **cirrhi-** *or* **cirrho-** *comb form* [L *cirrus* curl] **1 :** cirrus of a plant or animal ⟨*cirriferous*⟩ ⟨*cirrigrade*⟩ **2 :** cirrus cloud ⟨*cirrostratus*⟩

cir·ral \ˈsirəl\ *adj* [ISV *cirr-* + *-al*] **:** of or relating to a cirrus

cir·rate \ˈsiˌrāt, -ˌrət\ *adj* [L *cirratus* having ringlets, fr. *cirrus* curl + *-atus* -ate] **1 :** bearing a cirrus **2 :** curled like a cirrus — used esp. of a leaf tipped with a tendril

cir·rat·u·lid \səˈrachələd\ *adj* [NL *Cirratulidae* family of marine worms, fr. *Cirratulus*, type genus + *-idae*] **:** of or relating to the genus *Cirratulus* or family Cirratulidae

cir·rat·u·lus \-ləs\ *n, cap* [NL, fr. L *cirratus* + *-ulus*] **:** a genus (the type of the family Cirratulidae) of marine burrowing polychaete worms

cir·rhit·i·dae \sə'rid·ə,dē\ *n pl, cap* [NL, fr. *Cirrhitus*, type genus (irreg. fr. L *cirritus* having filaments, fr. *cirrus* curl) + *-idae*] **:** a family of small brilliantly colored percoid fishes of the tropical Indian and Pacific oceans esp. abundant about coral reefs

cirrhose *var of* CIRROSE

cir·rhosed \sə'rōst, 'si,r-\ *adj* [NL *cirrhosis* + E *-ed*] **:** affected with cirrhosis

cir·rho·sis \sə'rōsəs\ *n, pl* **cirrho·ses** \-ō,sēz\ [NL, fr. Gk *kirrhos* orange-colored + NL *-osis;* fr. the yellowish appearance which the diseased liver often presents when cut] **1 :** a chronic progressive disease of the liver that is characterized by an excessive formation of connective tissue followed by hardening and contraction and that results from unknown cause or from toxemia, nutritional deficiency, or parasites **2 :** a condition of other organs than the liver resembling cirrhosis — now used chiefly in veterinary medicine

1**cir·rhot·ic** \sə'räd·ik\ *adj* [ISV *cirrhotic*, fr. NL *cirrhosis*, after such pairs as NL *neurosis*: ISV *neurotic*] **:** of, relating to, caused by, or affected with cirrhosis ⟨~ degeneration⟩ ⟨a ~ liver⟩

2**cirrhotic** \"\ *n* -s **:** an individual affected with cirrhosis

cir·rhous \'sirəs\ *adj* [alter. of *cirrous*] **:** CIRROSE

cirrhus *var of* CIRRUS

cirri *pl of* CIRRUS

cirri- — see CIRR-

cir·ri·form \'sirə,fȯrm\ *adj* [*cirr-* + *-form*] **:** having the form of a cirrus **:** slender and prolonged and usu. curved — used of processes ⟨a mollusk having a foot with a ~ tip⟩

cir·rip·e·da \sə'ripədə\ *syn of* CIRRIPEDIA

1**cir·ri·pede** \'sirə,pēd\ *or* **cir·ri·ped** \-,ped\ *adj* [NL *Cirripedia*] **:** of or relating to the Cirripedia

2**cirripede** \"\ *or* **cirriped** \"\ *n* -s **:** one of the Cirripedia

cir·ri·pe·dia \,sirə'pēdēə\ *n pl, cap* [NL, fr. *cirr-* + *-pedia* footed ones (fr. L *ped-*, *pes* foot) — more at FOOT] **:** a subclass of Crustacea comprising the barnacles, goose barnacles, and a few highly modified parasitic related forms, all being free-swimming in the larval stages but permanently attached or parasitic as adults — **cir·ri·pe·di·al** \¦==¦=dēəl\ *adj*

cirro- — see CIRR-

cir·ro·cumular *or* **cir·ro·cumulative** *or* **cir·ro·cumulous** \¦si(,)rō +\ *adj* [NL *cirrocumulus* + E *-ar* or *-ative* or *-ous*] **:** of, relating to, or consisting of cirrocumulus

cir·ro·cumulus \¦si(,)rō+\ *n, pl* **cirrocumuli** [NL, fr. *cirr-* + *cumulus*] **:** a cloud form of small white rounded masses at a high altitude usu. in lines and regular groupings forming a mackerel sky and often preceding a change in the weather esp. from calm to windy — see CLOUD illustration

cir·ro·lite \'sirə,līt\ *n* -s [ISV *cirro-* (fr. Gk *kirrhos* orange-colored) + *-lite;* orig. formed as Sw *kirrolit*] **:** a mineral consisting of pale yellow alkaline calcium aluminum phosphate

cir·ro·nebula \¦si(,)rō +\ *n, pl* **cirronebulae** *or* **cirronebulas** [NL, fr. *cirr-* + *nebula*] **:** a thin cirrus veil without structure

cir·rop·o·dous \sə'räpədəs\ *adj* [*cirr-* + *-podous*] **:** CIRRIPEDE

cir·rose *or* **cir·rhose** \'si,rōs\ *adj* [NL *cirrosus*, fr. *cirr-* + L *-osus* -ose] **:** CIRRATE

cir·ros·to·mi \sə'rästə,mī\ *n pl, cap* [NL, fr. *cirr-* + *-stomi*] **:** the order comprising the lancelets — compare AMPHIOXUS

cir·ro·stra·tive \¦si(,)rō¦strād·iv\ *or* **cir·ro·stra·tous** \-ād·əs\ *adj* [NL *cirrostratus* + E *-ive* or *-ous*] **:** having the character of cirrostratus

cir·ro·stratus \¦si(,)rō+\ *n, pl* **cirrostrati** [NL, fr. *cirr-* + *stratus*] **:** a fairly uniform layer of high whitish stratus darker than the white cirrus

cir·rous \'sirəs\ *adj* [L *cirrus* curl + E *-ous*] **1 :** CIRRATE **2 :** resembling cirrus clouds

cir·ro·ve·lum \¦si(,)rō'vēləm\ *n, pl* **cirro·ve·la** \-lə\ [NL, fr. *cirr-* + L *velum* veil] **:** cirrus in sheet form veiling the whole sky **:** a continuous cirrostratus

cir·rus *also* **cir·rhus** \'sirəs\ *n, pl* **cir·ri** \-,rī\ [NL, fr. L *cirrus* curl, ringlet, bird's crest] **1 :** a curllike tuft **:** TENDRIL **2 :** any of various slender usu. flexible appendages of animals: as **a :** any of the curved many-jointed arms of barnacles **b :** any of the filaments growing from the stalk and sometimes from the aboral surface of crinoids **c :** any of the tactile barbels about the mouth of many fishes **d :** any of certain tufts of hair on the legs or antennae of many insects **e :** a fused limblike group of cilia on certain protozoans **f :** the male copulatory organ of various invertebrate animals (as certain worms and mollusks) **3 :** a white filmy variety of cloud usu. formed in the highest cloud region at altitudes of 20,000 to 40,000 feet and normally consisting of minute ice crystals — see CLOUD illustration

cirs- *or* **cirso-** *comb form* [MF, fr. Gk *kirs-*, *kirso-*, fr. *kirsos*] **:** swollen vein **:** varix ⟨*cirs*oid⟩ ⟨*cirso*tomy⟩

cir·si·um \'sərs(h)ēəm\ *n, cap* [NL, fr. Gk *kirsion*, a thistle, prob. fr. *kirsos* swollen vein; fr. the use of the thistle in antiquity in the treatment of swollen veins] **:** a widely distributed genus of prickly herbs (family Compositae) having the bristles of the pappus plumose — compare CARDUUS; see BULL THISTLE

cir·soid \'sər,sȯid\ *adj* [*cirs-* + *-oid*] **:** resembling a dilated tortuous vein

ciru·e·la \,sirə'wālə\ *n* -s [AmerSp, fr. Sp, plum, fr. L *cereola* (*pruna*) wax-colored plums, fr. *cereolus* wax-colored, fr. *cereus* waxen, fr. *cera* wax — more at CEREUS] **:** the plumlike fruit of any of several tropical American trees belonging to the genus *Spondias* — compare HOG PLUM, OTAHEITE APPLE

cis \'sis\ *adj* [L, on this side] **:** having or characterized by certain atoms or groups on the same side of the molecule ⟨~ fusion of two steroid rings⟩ — opposed to *trans*

cis- *prefix* [L, fr. *cis* — more at HE] **1 :** on this side **:** on the nearer side — often joined to second element with a hyphen ⟨*cis*alpine⟩ ⟨*cis*-Alleghany⟩; compare TRANS-, ULTRA- **2 :** nearer in time **:** since ⟨*cis*atomic⟩ **3** *usu ital* **:** cis ⟨*cis*-dichloroethylene⟩ — opposed to *trans-;* see CIS-TRANS ISOMERISM

1**cis·alpine** \sis+\ *adj* [L *cisalpinus*, fr. *cis-* + *Alpinus* of the Alps, Alpine] **1 a :** of, relating to, or situated on this side of the Alps **b :** situated on the southern side of the Alps **:** nearer Rome ⟨~ Gaul⟩ **c :** situated on the northern side of the Alps **:** nearer France — opposed to *transalpine* **2 :** holding a doctrine of limited papal power **:** GALLICAN

2**cisalpine** \"\ *n* -s *usu cap* [L *cisalpinus*] **:** 2GALLICAN

cis·andine \sis +\ *adj* [*cis-* + *Andine* (after Sp *cisandino*] **:** situated on this or the nearer side of the Andes mountains ⟨~ forests⟩

cis·co \'si(,)skō\ *n* -ES [short for CanF *ciscoette* — more at SISCOWET] **:** any of various whitefishes of the genus *Leucichthys* which are important food fishes of the Great Lakes region (esp. *L. artedi*) — see LAKE HERRING

ci·seaux \sē'zō\ *n pl but usu sing in constr* [F, lit., scissors, fr. OF, pl. of *cisel* chisel, scissors, alter. of (assumed) OF *cisoir* goldsmith's chisel, fr. (assumed) VL *caesorium* cutting instrument — more at CHISEL] **:** a ballet jump in which the legs are opened to a wide second position in the air

ci·se·lé \¦sēzə¦lā, (')sēz¦lā\ *adj* [F, fr. past part. of *ciseler* to chisel, shear velvet, fr. OF, to chisel, fr. *cisel* chisel] **:** having a chased or chiseled appearance ⟨velvet ~⟩

cis·gangetic \¦sis +\ *adj* [*cis-* + *Gangetic*] **:** situated on this esp. the western side of the Ganges river

cis·jurane \sis +\ *adj* [F *cisjuran*, fr. ML *cisjuranus*, fr. L *cis-* + ML *Juranus* Jurane] **:** situated on this esp. the western side of the Jura mountains

cis·lei·than \(')si¦slīthən\ *adj* [modif. of G *zisleithanisch*, fr. *zis-* cis- + *Leitha*, river in eastern Austria + G *-anisch* (fr. L *-anus* -ane + G *-isch* -ish)] **:** situated on this esp. the western or Austrian side of the Leitha river

cis·mon·tane \(')si¦smän·,tān\ *adj* [F or L; F *cismontain*, fr. L *cismontanus*, fr. *cis-* + *montanus* mountainous, fr. *mont-*, *mons* mountain — more at MOUNT] **1 :** CISALPINE — compare TRAMONTANE, ULTRAMONTANE **2 :** situated on the nearer side of any mountains ⟨~ California⟩

cis·pa·dane \¦sispə¦dān, (')si¦spā,dān\ *adj* [F *cispadan*, fr. *cis-* + *padane*, fr. L *padanus* of the Po, fr. *Padus* Po, river in Italy] **:** situated on this esp. the Roman side of the Po river

cis·pon·tine \(')si¦spän·,tīn\ *adj* [*cis-* + L *pont-*, *pons* bridge + E *-ine* — more at FIND] **:** situated on this or the nearer side of the bridge

cis·rhe·nane \¦sisrə¦nān; sis'rē,nān, -re,n-\ *adj* [L *cisrhenanus*, fr. *cis-* + *rhenanus* of the Rhine, fr. *Rhenus* Rhine] **:** situated on this or the nearer side of the Rhine river

cis·sa \'sisə\ *n* -s [NL (old syn. of *Kitta*), fr. Gk *kissa*, *kitta* jay] **:** any of several green or blue magpies (genus *Kitta*) of southeast Asia

cis·sam·pe·los \si'sampə,läs\ *n, cap* [NL, fr. Gk *kissos* ivy + *ampelos* vine] **:** a genus of tropical woody vines (family Menispermaceae) having alternate simple leaves and dioecious mostly tetramerous flowers — see FALSE PAREIRA, VELVETLEAF

cis·sie *or* **cis·sy** \'sisi\ *Brit var of* SISSY

cis·sing \'sisiŋ\ *n* -s [origin unknown] **:** the gathering of a wet film (as of varnish) into drops or streaks leaving parts of the surface bare or imperfectly covered

cis·soid \'si,sȯid\ *n* -s [LGk *kissoeidēs*, fr. Gk, like ivy, fr. *kissos* ivy + *-oeidēs* -oid] **:** a plane curve with two branches meeting at a cusp at one end of a diameter of a fixed circle, each point of the cissoid being obtained by going from the cusp along any chord to its intersection when extended with the tangent diametrically opposite the cusp and then returning along the extended chord a distance equal to the length of the chord — **cis·soi·dal** \(')si¦sȯidᵊl\ *adj*

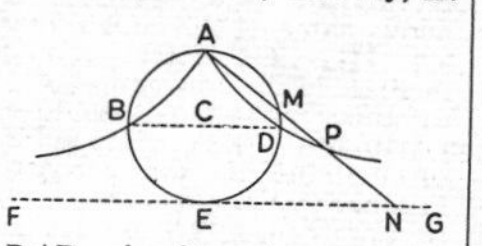

BAP cissoid; *A* cusp located on generating circle *ABEDM;* *AMPN* secant; *FENG* tangent; *AMP* = *MPN*

cis·sus \'sisəs\ *n* [NL, fr. Gk *kissos* ivy] **1** *cap* **:** a large genus of widely distributed chiefly tropical woody vines (family Vitaceae) related to the grape but differing esp. in having tetramerous flowers with expanding separate petals and largely persistent foliage and often fleshy or somewhat succulent leaves **2** *pl* **cissus :** any plant of the genus *Cissus* — see MARINE IVY

1**cist** \'sist, 'kist\ *also* **kist** \'k-\ *n* -s [W *cist* chest, fr. L *cista* — more at CHEST] **1 :** a Neolithic grave lined with stone slabs **2 :** a roofed storage pit often lined with stones found in the southwestern U.S. in Basket Maker sites

2**cist** \'sist\ *or* **cis·ta** \'sistə, 'ki-\ *n, pl* **cists** \'sis(t)s\ *or* **cis·tae** \'si,stē, 'ki,stī\ [L cista] **:** a receptacle orig. made of wicker for carrying sacred utensils in procession in ancient Rome

cis·ta·ce·ae \si'stāsē,ē\ *n pl, cap* [NL, fr. *Cistus*, type genus + *-aceae*] **:** a family of shrubs or somewhat woody herbs (order Parietales) with simple entire leaves and a capsular fruit — **cis·ta·ceous** \(')si¦stāshəs\ *adj*

1**cis·ter·cian** \(')si¦stərshən, -ēsh-,-əish-\ *adj, usu cap* [ML *Cistercium* (now *Cîteaux*) site of the abbey near Dijon, France + E *-an*] **:** of or relating to Cistercians or Cistercianism

2**cistercian** \"\ *n* -s *usu cap* **:** a member of an austere order founded on the Benedictine rule as adapted by Robert de Molesme at Cîteaux, France, in 1098, the order being now divided into a group that follows a mitigated rule and a group that follows a more strictly interpreted rule — compare TRAPPIST

cistercian of the common observance *usu cap both Cs&2dO* **:** a Cistercian who follows the mitigated rule

cistercian of the strict observance *usu cap C&S&2dO* **:** a Cistercian who follows the more strictly interpreted rule

cis·ter·cian·ism \-,nizəm\ *n* -s *usu cap* **:** the state, system, or practices of Cistercians

cis·tern \'sistə(r)n\ *n* -s [ME, fr. OF *cisterne*, fr. L *cisterna*, fr. *cista* box, chest — more at CHEST] **1 :** an artificial reservoir or tank for holding or storing water or other liquids; *specif* **:** an often underground tank for storing rainwater collected from a roof **2 a** *obs* **:** LAVER **b** *obs* **:** a large vessel for use (as in cooling wine) at the dining table **3 :** a natural reservoir **:** a hollow place containing water **4 :** a fluid-containing sac or cavity in an organism

cis·ter·na \si'stərnə\ *n, pl* **cister·nae** \-,nē\ [NL, fr. L, cistern] **:** CISTERN 4: as **a :** CISTERNA MAGNA **b :** CISTERNA CHYLI

cisterna chy·li \-'kī,lī\ *n, pl* **cisternae chyli** [NL, lit., cistern of the chyle] **:** a dilated lymph channel usu. opposite the 1st and 2d lumbar vertebrae and marking the beginning of the thoracic duct

cis·ter·nal \(')si¦stərnᵊl\ *adj* [ISV *cistern-* (fr. NL *cisterna*) + *-al*] **:** of or relating to a cisterna, esp. the cisterna magna ⟨~ puncture⟩ — **cis·ter·nal·ly** \-ᵊlē, -ᵊli\ *adv*

cisterna mag·na \-'magnə\ *n, pl* **cisternae mag·nae** \-,nē\ [NL, lit., large cistern] **:** a large subarachnoid space between the caudal part of the cerebellum and the medulla oblongata

cistern of pec·quet \-pə'kā\ *usu cap P* [after Jean *Pecquet* †1674 French physician and anatomist] **:** CISTERNA CHYLI

cist grave *n* [1*cist*] **:** CIST 1

cis·to·phor·ic \¦sistə¦fȯrik\ *adj* **:** relating to a cistophorus

cis·toph·o·rus \si'stäfərəs\ *n, pl* **cistopho·ri** \-,rī\ [L, fr. Gk *kistophoros*, fr. *kisto-* (fr. *kistē* basket) + *-phoros* -phorous — more at CHEST] **:** any of certain silver coins of the 2d and 1st centuries B.C. chiefly of Pergamum bearing the picture of the sacred basket that was carried in the worship of Dionysus

cis–trans \'si¦stran(t)s, -nz\ *adj* [*cis-* + *trans-*] **:** relating to, exhibiting, or being a particular type of stereoisomerism — see CIS-TRANS ISOMERISM

cis–trans isomerism *n* **:** geometric isomerism in unsaturated compounds or cyclic compounds depending usu. on the presence in the molecule of a pair of substituted groups (as unsymmetrically substituted methylene groups) so that the isomers have comparable substituents on either the same or opposite sides of the molecule: as **a :** stereoisomerism in compounds (as maleic and fumaric acids) containing one or more carbon-to-carbon double bonds **b :** SYN-ANTI ISOMERISM **c :** stereoisomerism in various cyclic compounds (as disubstituted cyclohexanes) which in many cases may also exhibit optical isomerism

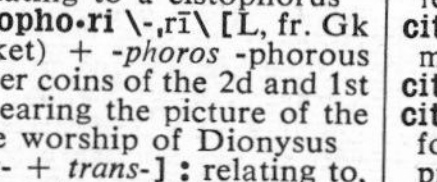

R-C-X ‖ R-C-X	R-C-X ‖ X-C-R
cis form	trans form

cis·tu·do \si'st(y)ü(,)dō\ [NL, fr. L *cista* box + *-udo* (as in *testudo* tortoise) — more at CHEST, TESTUDO] *syn of* TERRAPENE

cis·tus \'sistəs\ *n* [NL, fr. Gk *kistos*, *kisthos* rockrose] **1** *cap* **:** a genus (the type of the family Cistaceae) of shrubs or woody herbs widely distributed in the Mediterranean region and the Orient and distinguished by opposite leaves and capsular fruits with 5 or 10 valves — see ROCKROSE **2** -ES **:** any plant of the genus *Cistus* **:** ROCKROSE

cit \'sit\ *n* -s [short for *citizen*] **1 :** an inhabitant of a city **:** TOWNSMAN, TRADESMAN, SHOPKEEPER **2** *slang* **a :** one not in the armed forces **b cits** *pl* **:** civilian clothes as opposed to military uniform **:** CIVVIES

cit *abbr* **1** citation; cited **2** citizen **3** citrate

cit·a·del \'sid·ədᵊl, -itə-, -,del\ *n* -s [MF *citadelle*, fr. OIt *cittadella*, dim. of *cittade* city, fr. L *civitat-*, *civitas* — more at CITY] **1 :** a fortress that commands a city both for control and defense; *broadly* **:** a strong fortress **:** STRONGHOLD **2** *archaic* **:** the protected central structure in heavily armored ships of war that contains the engines, boilers, magazines and in and upon which the broadside battery is mounted **3 :** a mission hall of the Salvation Army

cital *n* -s [by shortening] *obs* **:** RECITAL

ci·ta·tion \sī'tāshən\ *n* -s [ME *citacioun* summoning, fr. OF *citation*, fr. L *citation-*, *citatio*, fr. *citatus* (past part. of *citare* to put in movement, summon) + *-ion-*, *-io* -ion] **1 a :** an official summons giving notice to a person to appear (as before a tribunal of justice) ⟨the congressional committee issued several contempt ~*s*⟩; *broadly* **:** SUMMONS **b :** the paper embodying such a summons ⟨gave a certified copy of the ~⟩ **2 a :** the act of citing verbatim the spoken, written, or printed words of another **b :** the act of citing a previously settled case or a recognized legal authority as support for a point of view or course of action; *also* **:** the formal caption by which such a case is designated in citation **c :** a quoted word or passage **3 :** ENUMERATION, MENTION: as **a :** a formal statement of the justifying merits or achievements of a person receiving an academic honor (as an honorary degree) **b :** specific mention in military orders or dispatches; *often* **:** a written narrative statement of an act or of meritorious performance of duty for which a military decoration is awarded **c :** a formal commendation (as by an organization) for action adjudged meritorious

citation form *n* **:** HYPOSTASIS 7b

ci·ta·tor \sī'tād·ə(r), '=,==\ *n* -s **:** one that cites; *specif* **:** a record or indexed list of legal decisions and cases ⟨there is a ~ for statutes and for cases —*Brit. Book News*⟩

ci·ta·to·ry \'sīd·ə,tōrē\ *adj* [ML *citatorius*, fr. L *citatus* + *-orius* -ory] **:** relating to citing or summoning **:** being or constituting a citation or summons ⟨letters ~⟩ ⟨a body with ~ powers⟩

cite \'sīt, *usu* -īd·+V\ *vt* -ED/-ING/-S [MF *citer* to cite, summon, fr. L *citare* to put in motion, summon, fr. *citus* quick, fr. past part. of *cire*, *ciēre* to put in motion, excite — more at HIGHT] **1 a :** to call upon officially or authoritatively to appear before a court **:** SUMMON **b** *obs* **:** to summon to some action **:** AROUSE, EXCITE ⟨~ the young desires —William Shenstone⟩ **2 :** to quote by way of evidence, authority, proof ⟨a list of Biblical phrases *cited* in a recent volume —J.L.Lowes⟩ **3 a :** to bring to mind **:** RECALL ⟨*citing* praise⟩ ⟨~ his virtuous life⟩ **:** refer to **:** KNOW ⟨these irregulars, *cited* as the duke's scouts⟩ **b :** to name formally, typically in commendation or praise ⟨*cited* by the trustees for his work in public health⟩ **c :** to name in a citation **4 :** to bring forward, mention, call to another's attention esp. as an example, proof, or precedent ⟨one could ~ other examples without number —B.N.Cardozo⟩ **5** [Sp *citar*, fr. L *citare*] *of a bullfighter* **:** to challenge or provoke (a bull) esp. by a movement of the cape

syn ADVANCE, ADDUCE, ALLEGE: CITE indicates bringing forward as relevant, cogent, and specific in an argument, inquiry, or discussion ⟨many works also have been the product of extensive consultation . . ., Child's *English and Scottish Ballads*, to *cite* . . . one of the very great monuments —F.N.Robinson⟩ ⟨Columbus had also some objective evidence to *cite* —G.C. Sellery⟩ ADVANCE stresses the notion of bringing forward for or as if for consideration, discussion, analysis without implications about its validity ⟨once or twice psychoanalysts have *advanced* that idea to me as a theoretical possibility —Bernard De Voto⟩ ⟨the story may well be regarded as untrue, as it was not *advanced* until six centuries after Amr's death —*Encyc. Americana*⟩ ADDUCE is close to CITE in its suggestions about bringing forth as evidence; it may lack some of the specific suggestion of the latter ⟨the old arguments from miracle and prophecy are now seldom *adduced* —W.R.Inge⟩ ⟨numerous examples to the contrary might be *adduced* from the history of the Catholic church or of the socialist movement —M.R. Cohen⟩ ALLEGE may indicate bringing forward and stating or affirming without proving ⟨younger scholars nevertheless can *allege* a very strong point on their side and win at least a debater's victory —Howard M. Jones⟩ ALLEGE may stress doubt about an assertion and convey a warning and a disclaimer of responsibility for the truth of whatever is under discussion ⟨the presence, real or *alleged*, of some hostile group —John Dewey⟩ **syn** see in addition QUOTE

ci·tel·lus \sī'teləs\ *n, cap* [NL, prob. modif. of G *ziesel* suslik, fr. MHG *zisel*, *zisemūs*, fr. OHG *zisimūs*, *sisimūs*, of Slavic origin; akin to Pol *susel*, Russ *suslik* — more at SUSLIK] **:** a genus of rodents (family Sciuridae) consisting of the typical ground squirrels

cith·a·ra \'sithərə, 'ki-; ki'thärə\ *n* -s [L — more at ZITHER] **1 :** an ancient Greek musical instrument of the lyre class having a wooden sounding board **2 :** an early medieval instrument prob. resembling the harp

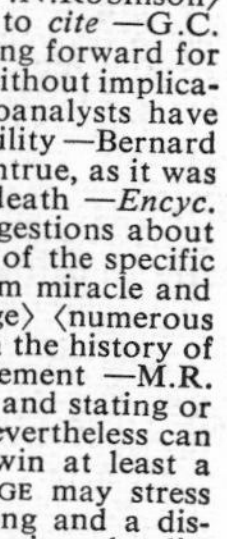

cithara 1

cith·a·rex·y·lum \,sithə'reksələm\ *n, cap* [NL, fr. *cithare-* (irreg. fr. L *cithara*) + *-xylum*] **:** a genus of tropical American trees and shrubs (family Verbenaceae) often cultivated for their small panicled flowers and berrylike drupes seated in the persistent calyx

cith·a·rist \'sithərəst, 'ki-; ki'thärəst\ *also* **cith·a·ris·ta** \,sithə'ristə, ,ki-\ *n* -s [*citharist* fr. ME, fr. MF *cithariste*, fr. L *citharista*, fr. Gk *kitharistēs*, fr. *kithara* cithara + *-istēs* -ist; *citharista* fr. L] **:** a player on the cithara

cith·a·roe·dic \¦sithə¦rēdik, ¦ki-\ *adj* [L *citharoedicus*, fr. Gk *kitharōidikos*, fr. *kitharōidos* singer who accompanies himself on the cithara, fr. *kithara* cithara + *aoidos* singer, fr. *aeidein* to sing — more at ODE] **:** of or relating to a cithara or citharist

cith·er \'siṯẖə(r), -th-\ *n* -s [F *cithare*, fr. L *cithara*, fr. Gk *kithara*] **:** CITTERN

cith·e·ro·nia \,sithə'rōnyə\ *n, cap* [NL, fr. *Citheron*, *Cithaeron*, mountain in Boeotia (fr. L, fr. Gk *Kithairōn*) + NL *-ia*] **:** a genus (the type of the family Citheroniidae) including the regal moth and certain other large moths

cith·e·ro·ni·idae \,sithərō'nīə,dē\ *n pl, cap* [NL, fr. *Citheronia*, type genus + *-idae*] **:** a family of large No. American moths lacking a frenulum, having small maxillary and labial palpi, and having larvae commonly armed with hairs and spines that feed on the leaves of deciduous trees

cit·ied \'sid·|ēd, -it|, |id\ *adj* [*city* + *-ed*] **1 :** resembling or made into a city **2 :** containing or occupied by a city

cities *pl of* CITY

cit·i·fi·ca·tion \,sid·əfə'kāshən, -itəf-\ *n* -s **:** growth or transformation into the status or character of a city **:** the action or process of becoming citified

cit·i·fied \-,fīd\ *adj* **:** marked by the manners and general behavior of a city dweller **:** accustomed to city life — usu. used disparagingly

cit·i·fy \-,fī\ *vt* -ED/-ING/-ES [*city* + *-fy*] **1 :** to make citylike **:** cause to become urban ⟨the wooded glens gone, the stream bank straightened and *citified*⟩ **2 :** to stamp with or conform to city ways, manners, and customs

ci·tig·ra·dae \sə'tigrə,dē\ *n pl, cap* [NL, fr. *citi-* (fr. L *citus* swift) + *-gradae* (nom. pl. fem. of *-gradus* -grade) — more at CITE] *in former classifications* **:** a group comprising running spiders that chase their prey and including the wolf spiders and related forms — **cit·i·grade** \'sid·ə,grād\ *adj or n*

citing *pres part of* CITE

cit·i·zen \'sid·əzən, -itə- *also* -əsən\ *n* -s [ME *citizein*, fr. AF *citezein*, alter. of OF *citeien*, fr. *cité* city + *-ien* -ian — more at CITY] **1 a :** an inhabitant of a city or town; *esp* **:** one that is entitled to the civic rights and privileges of a freeman **b :** a townsman as contrasted with a rustic ⟨both ~*s* and peasants⟩ **2 a :** a member of a state **:** one who is claimed as a member of a state **b :** a native or naturalized person of either sex who owes allegiance to a government and is entitled to reciprocal protection from it and to enjoyment of the rights of citizenship ⟨all persons born or naturalized in the U.S., and subject to the jurisdiction thereof, are ~*s* of the U.S. and of the state wherein they reside —*U.S. Constitution*⟩ — compare ALIEN, SUBJECT **3 :** a resident in or member of a community or institution (as a school) — compare INHABITANT **4 :** a civilian as opposed to a soldier, policeman, or other specialized servant or functionary of the state **:** a commoner without the interests or affiliations of any special group ⟨not only by professionals but also by parents and ~*s* —J.B.Conant⟩

syn SUBJECT, NATIONAL: CITIZEN may indicate being a member of a sovereign state, esp. one showing democratic forms and usages, owing it allegiance, and, usu., sharing in individual political rights. SUBJECT may imply a state of subjection to a person, as a monarch, without much sense of membership in a political community or sharing in political rights ⟨the line of distinction between the citizen and the *subject*, the free and the subjugated races —R.B.Taney⟩ It may on the other hand simply indicate membership in a political community with a personal sovereign to whom allegiance is owed ⟨*subjects* of Saxon Aella —William Wordsworth⟩ NATIONAL, a more general word, may apply to anyone owing permanent allegiance to a nation and usu. indicates one belonging to a broad category that includes both people who are legally citizens or subjects and also people who have not attained such legal status ⟨Polish *nationals* in this country⟩

cit·i·zen·ess \-nəs\ *n* -ES **:** a female citizen

cit·i·zen·ly \-nlē, -li\ *adj* **:** belonging to or characteristic of a citizen

cit·i·zen·ry \-nrē, -ri\ *n* -ES **:** citizens often as distinguished from soldiery or sometimes from the official or intellectual class

cit·i·zen·ship \-n,ship\ *n* -s **1 :** the status of being a citizen

2 a : membership in a community **b :** the quality of an individual's adjustment, responsibility, or contribution to his community **:** social conduct ⟨a pupil's ~ in his school⟩

citizens' ticket *n* **:** a nonpartisan ticket esp. of reform candidates for local or municipal offices

ci·tole \sə'tōl, 'si,tōl\ *or* **ci·to·la** \sə'tōlə\ *n* -s [ME *citole*, fr. MF, prob. fr. L *cithara*, fr. Gk *kithara*] **:** a small flat-backed lute of late medieval times

ci·tol·er \sə'tōlə(r), 'si,t-\ *n* -s **:** one that plays the citole

citr- *or* **citri-** *or* **citro-** *comb form* [NL, fr. *Citrus*] **1 :** citrus ⟨*citropsis*⟩ ⟨*citriculture*⟩ **2 a :** citric acid ⟨*citramide*⟩ **b :** citrate ⟨*citrochloride*⟩

citra- *prefix* [ML, fr. L *citra* — more at HE] **:** cis- ⟨*citramontane*⟩ — opposed to *ultra-*

cit·ra·con·ate \,si·trə'kä,nāt, sə·'trakə,n-\ *n* -s [ISV *citraconic* + *-ate*] **:** a salt or ester of citraconic acid

cit·ra·con·ic acid \¦si·trə¦känik-\ *n* [ISV *citr-* + *aconic*; prob. orig. formed as F *citraconique*] **:** a white crystalline deliquescent dicarboxylic acid $CH_3C(COOH){=}CHCOOH$ obtained by distillation of citric acid; methyl-maleic acid

cit·ral \'si·,tral\ *n* -s [ISV *citr-* + *-al*] **:** an unsaturated liquid aldehyde $C_9H_{15}CHO$ that has a strong lemon and verbena odor, is found in many essential oils (as lemon oil and citronella oil), is used in flavoring and perfumery and in synthesizing the ionones, and consists of a mixture of two stereoisomeric forms (1) the form obtained by the oxidation of geraniol and (2) the form obtained by the oxidation of nerol — called also respectively (1) *citral a, geranial* (2) *citral b, neral*

cit·range \'si·trənj\ *n* -s [*citr-* + *orange*] **:** a citrus fruit resulting from a cross between the sweet orange and the trifoliate orange and having a more acid flavor and a more pronounced aroma than the orange

ci·tran·ge·din \sə'tranjədən\ *n* -s [*citrange* + calamon*din*] **:** a citrus fruit resulting from a cross between the citrange and the calamondin and having fruit suggestive in flavor of the lime

cit·range·quat \'si·trənj,kwät\ *n* -s [*citrange* + kum*quat*] **:** a citrus fruit resulting from a cross between the citrange and the kumquat and having small acid limelike fruits

¹cit·rate \'si,trāt, 'sī,trāt, 'si·trət\ *n* -s [ISV *citr-* + *-ate*] **:** a salt or ester of citric acid

²cit·rate \-·,trāt\ *vt* -ED/-ING/-S **:** to treat with a citrate esp. of sodium or potassium ⟨to ~ blood to prevent coagulation⟩

citrated caffeine *n* **:** a mixture of caffeine and citric acid — called also *caffeine citrate*

cit·re·an \'si·trēən\ *adj* [L *citreus* citreous + E *-an*] **:** CITRINE

cit·rene \'si·,trēn\ *n* -s [ISV *citr-* + *-ene*] **:** dextrorotatory limonene

cit·re·ous \'si·trēəs\ *adj* [L *citreus*, fr. *citrus* citron tree] **:** of the color citron yellow

cit·ric acid \'si·trik-, -ēk\ *n* [*citric* ISV *citr-* + *-ic*] **:** a colorless crystalline or white powdery tricarboxylic acid $HOOCCH_2C(OH)COOHCH_2COOH$ that has a pleasant acid taste, occurs widely in plants (as citrus fruits), is extracted from lemon and lime juices or obtained by fermentation of sugars, and is used as a flavoring agent in foods, carbonated beverages, and pharmaceuticals

citric acid cycle *n* **:** KREBS CYCLE

ci·tric·o·la scale \sə·'trikələ-\ *also* **citricola** *n* -s [NL, fr. *citr-* + *-cola*] **:** a scale (*Coccus pseudomagnoliarum*) believed to be native to Japan but injurious to citrus fruit trees in California

cit·ri·culture \'si·trə+,-\ *n* -s [*citr-* + *-culture*] **:** the cultivation of citrus fruits (as oranges, lemons, and grapefruit)

cit·ri·culturist \¦si·trə+\ *n* -s **:** a pomologist who specializes in the cultivation of citrus fruits

cit·rin \'si·trən\ *n* -s [ISV *citr-* + *-in*; orig. formed in G] **:** a crystalline water-soluble flavonoid concentrate that was orig. prepared from lemons and considered to be a source of vitamin P and to consist of hesperidin and eriodictyol glycoside and that is now used as a source of bioflavonoids

cit·ri·na·tion \,si·trə'nāshən\ *n* -s [ME *citrinacioun*, fr. ML *citrination-, citrinatio*, fr. *citrinus* + L *-ation-, -atio* -ation] *obs* **:** an alchemical operation in which a base metal was made more yellow and therefore thought to have been brought nearer to gold

¹cit·rine \'si·,trēn *sometimes* -īn\ *adj* [ME, fr. MF *citrin*, fr. ML *citrinus*, fr. L *citrus* citron tree + *-inus* -ine] **1 :** resembling a citron or lemon **2 :** of the color citrine

²citrine \"\ *n* -s **1 :** a light olive color that is redder and deeper than grape green, redder and paler than old moss green, and redder and duller than average willow green — called also *rhubarb* **2 :** a semiprecious yellow stone resembling topaz but actually black quartz changed in color by heating

citrine ointment *n* **:** a yellow ointment of mercuric nitrate and lard used as an antiparasitic

ci·tri·nin \sə·'trīnən\ *n* -s [NL *citrinum* (specific epithet of *Penicillium citrinum*) + E *-in*] **:** a toxic antibiotic $C_{13}H_{14}O_5$ that is produced by certain molds (esp. *Penicillium citrinum*) and is bactericidal towards some gram-positive bacteria

cit·ri·nous \'si·trənəs\ *adj* [ML *citrinus* — more at CITRINE] **:** CITRINE

citro- — see CITR-

cit·ro·my·ces \,si·trō'mī(,)sēz\ *n, cap* [NL, fr. *citr-* + *-myces*] *in some classifications* **:** a genus of molds comprising those species of the genus *Penicillium* as usu. understood that are monoverticillate and that change sugar into citric acid

cit·ron \'si·trən\ *n* -s [ME, fr. MF, fr. OProv, modif. of L *citrus* citron tree, sandarac tree (*Tetraclinis articulata*); akin to Gk *kedros* cedar — more at CEDAR] **1 a :** a citrus fruit that resembles the lemon in appearance and structure but is larger and without a terminal nipple **b :** a small shrubby citrus tree (*Citrus medica*) that produces citrons **c** *also* **citron melon :** any of various melons derived from a variety (*Citrullus vulgaris citroides*) of the watermelon having the hard fruit often mottled and with white flesh **2 :** the preserved rind of the citron used in cakes, breads, and puddings **3 a :** a grayish greenish yellow **b :** a light yellow

cit·ro·nel·la \,si·trə'nelə, *attrib* ¦==¦==\ *n* -s [NL, fr. F *citronnelle* lemon balm, Barbados water (a cordial), fr. *citron*] **1 :** CITRONELLA OIL **2** *also* **citronella grass :** a fragrant grass (*Cymbopogon nardus*) of southern Asia **3 :** HORSE BALM 1

cit·ro·nel·lal \,==ˈ=,lal, -,lal\ *n* -s [ISV *citronell-* (fr. NL *citronella*) + *-al*] **:** an unsaturated liquid aldehyde $C_9H_{17}CHO$ that has a lemonlike odor, is found in two optically active forms in many essential oils (as Java citronella oil), is formed by oxidation of citronellol, and is used in perfumery and organic synthesis

citronella oil *n* **:** a yellowish essential oil with lemonlike odor obtained from either of two grasses and used esp. as an insect repellent: **a :** an oil from citronella grass containing chiefly geraniol **b :** an oil from a related grass (*Cymbopogon winterianus*) containing citronellal, citronellol, and geraniol — called also *Java citronella oil*

cit·ro·nelle \¦si·trə¦nel\ *n* -s [*citron* + *-elle* (fr. F, dim. suffix, fr. L *-ella*)] *Austral* **:** ROUGH LEMON

cit·ro·nel·lol \,si·trə'ne,lōl, -ōl\ *n* -s [ISV *citronell-* (fr. NL *citronella*) + *-ol*] **:** an unsaturated liquid alcohol $C_{10}H_{19}OH$ that has a roselike odor, is found in two optically active forms in many essential oils (as geranium and rose oils), and is used in perfumery and for soaps; 3,7-dimethyl-6-octen-1-ol; *esp* **:** the dextrorotatory form found in Java citronella oil and a gland secretion of the alligator and prepared by reduction of citronellal — see RHODINOL

citron gray *n* **:** a variable color averaging a light grayish olive that is greener and lighter than Quaker gray, greener and paler than hemp, and greener and lighter than twine

citron green *n* **:** a grayish to moderate greenish yellow that is greener and lighter than russet green

citronwood \'==,=\ *n* **1 :** the wood of the citron tree **2 :** the wood of the sandarac tree used in cabinetwork

citron yellow *n* **1 :** a variable color averaging a moderate greenish yellow that is redder, stronger, and slightly lighter than linden green and redder, lighter, and stronger than Javel green or oil yellow **2 :** ZINC YELLOW

ci·troph·i·lus mealybug *also* **ci·troph·i·lous mealybug** \sə·'träfələs-\ *n* [*citrophilus* fr. NL, fr. *citr-* + *-philus*; *citrophilous* alter. (influenced by *-philous*) of *citrophilus*] **:** a mealybug (*Pseudococcus fragilis*) esp. destructive to citrus

ci·trop·sis \sə·'träpsəs\ *n, cap* [NL, fr. *citr-* + *-opsis*] **:** a small genus of spiny evergreen African shrubs or trees (family Rutaceae) differing from the closely related *Citrus* in having compound leaves — see CHERRY ORANGE

ci·trop·ten \sə'träptən\ *also* **ci·trop·tene** \-,tēn\ *n* -s [ISV *citr-* + stear*opten*, stear*optene*] **:** a colorless crystalline compound $C_{11}H_{10}O_4$ found in some essential oils (as lime and lemon oils); 5,7-dimethoxy-coumarin — called also *limettin*

cit·rous \'si·trəs\ *adj* [in sense 1, fr. NL *Citrus*; in sense 2, fr. *citrus* + *-ous*] **1 :** of or relating to the genus *Citrus* ⟨a hardier strain of ~ trees⟩ **2 :** of, relating to, devoted to the production of, or affecting plants or fruit of the genus *Citrus* ⟨a ~ disease⟩ ⟨an important ~ area⟩

ci·trov·o·rum factor \sə·'trävərəm-\ *n* [NL *citrovorum* (specific epithet of *Leuconostoc citrovorum*), fr. *citr-* + *-vorum* (neut. sing. of L *-vorus* -vorous)] **:** FOLINIC ACID

ci·trul·lin \sə·'trələn\ *n* -s [NL *Citrullus* (genus name of *Citrullus colocynthis*) + E *-in*] **:** a purgative yellow resinous preparation of the colocynth

ci·trul·line \-,lēn, -lən\ *n* -s [ISV *citrull-* (fr. NL *Citrullus*, genus name of *Citrullus vulgaris*) + *-ine*] **:** a crystalline amino acid $H_2NCONH(CH_2)_3CH(NH_2)COOH$ formed as an intermediate in the conversion of ornithine to arginine in the living organism; α-amino-δ-ureido-valeric acid

ci·trul·lus \-ləs\ *n, cap* [NL, fr. ML *citrullus, citrolus*, a kind of cucumber, fr. (assumed) OIt dial. *citrulo* (It. *cetriolo*), fr. (assumed) VL *citriolum*, fr. LL *citrium*, a kind of cucumber, fr. L, citron, fr. *citrus*] **:** a genus of African plants (family Cucurbitaceae) having pinnatifid leaves, small sepals, solitary staminate flowers, a corolla 5-parted to the base, and fleshy succulent fruits and including the widely cultivated watermelon and the colocynth

cit·rus \'si·trəs\ *n, often attrib* [NL, fr. L, citron tree — more at CITRON] **1** *cap* **:** a genus of often thorny trees and shrubs (family Rutaceae) having alternate unifoliolate leaves with a winged petiole, tetramerous flowers with many stamens, and large baccate fruits with pulpy endocarp and firm exocarp, including the orange, lemon, lime, and related fruits, and being native to tropical Asia but now widely cultivated for their fruits — compare CITRANGE, KUMQUAT, MANDARIN, SHADDOCK, TANGELO **2** *pl* **citruses** *or* **citrus :** any plant or fruit of the genus *Citrus* **3 :** SULPHUR YELLOW 2

citrus anthracnose *n* **:** a disease of various citrus plants (as orange, lemon, and grapefruit) caused by a fungus (*Colletotrichum gloeosporioides*) and characterized by twig blight of mature tips, leaf spots, and fruit stains, spots, or rots — compare TEARSTAIN

citrus blackfly *n* **:** an insect (*Aleurocanthus woglumi*) of the family Aleyrodidae that is destructive to citrus, coffee, and other plants

citrus blast *n* **:** a disease of citrus trees caused by a bacterium (*Pseudomonas syringae*) and characterized by a drying out and browning of leaves and twigs and a black pitting of the fruit

citrus bud mite *n* **:** a widely distributed eriophyid mite (*Aceria sheldoni*) feeding on new growth and flower buds of citrus and esp. destructive to the lemon in California

citrus butterfly *n, Austral* **:** either of two swallowtail butterflies (*Papilio aegeus* and *P. anactus*) the larvae of which feed on the foliage of citrus trees

citrus canker *n* **:** a destructive disease of citrus fruits caused by a bacterium (*Xanthomonas citri*) producing lesions on the leaves, twigs, and fruits

citrus fruit *n* **:** any of several edible fruits (as the orange, lemon, and grapefruit) produced by plants of *Citrus* and related genera

citrus gall wasp *n* **:** a chalcid fly (*Eurytoma fellis*) producing twig galls on citrus in Australia

citrus mealybug *n* **:** a widely distributed mealybug (*Planococcus citri*) feeding on a wide variety of cultivated plants but esp. destructive to citrus

citrus molasses *n* **:** molasses made from citrus fruit wastes and commonly fed to livestock

citrus nematode *n* **:** a microscopic roundworm (*Tylenchulus semipenetrans*) that infests the roots of citrus trees causing malnutrition and dwarfing

citrus red mite *or* **citrus red spider** *n* **:** a comparatively large mite (*Panonychus citri*) resembling the European red mite and being a destructive pest of citrus, feeding on the foliage and turning the leaves speckled or silvery by extracting the chlorophyll

citrus rust mite *n* **:** a rust mite (*Phyllocoptruta oleivorus*) that is esp. destructive to growing fruits, causing a russeting of oranges and a silvering of lemons by its feeding

citrus scab *n* **:** a disease of citrus plants caused by an imperfect fungus (*Elsinoë fawcettii*) producing scablike or warty lesions on trees, leaves, and fruits

citrus thrips *n* **:** a small yellow thrips (*Scirtothrips citri*) that is a major pest of citrus, esp. the orange, in the southwestern U.S.

citrus whitefly *n* **:** a widely distributed whitefly (*Dialeurodes citri*) having a scalelike larva that is a destructive pest of citrus

ci·tryl·i·dene \sə'trilə,dēn\ *n* -s [*citral* + *-ylidene*] **:** the bivalent radical $C_9H_{15}CH{<}$ formed by removal of the oxygen atom from citral

cits *pl of* CIT

cit·tern \'sid·ə(r)n\ *or* **cith·ern** \-ithə(r)n, -th-\ *or* **cith·ren** \-ithrən\ *n* -s [blend of *cither* and *gittern*] **:** a guitar with a pear-shaped flat-backed body and wire strings popular esp. in Renaissance England

cittern

citternhead *n, obs* **:** BLOCKHEAD, DUNCE

cit·to·tae·nia \,sid·ə'tēnēə\ *n, cap* [NL] **:** a genus of taenioid tapeworms parasitic in rodents

city \'sid·ē, -itē, -i\ *n* -ES *often attrib* [ME *citie*, fr. OF *cité*, fr. L *civitat-, civitas*, fr. *civis* citizen + *-itat-, -itas* -ity — more at HOME] **1** *archaic* **:** an inhabited place **:** HAMLET, VILLAGE **2 a :** a large or important incorporated town or borough in Great Britain holding a royal charter and usu. being the seat of an episcopacy — a title bearing traditional and honorary significance but not specific legal significance **b :** a populous place **:** a place larger than a village or town **:** a large, prominent, or important center of population ⟨the *cities* of the ancient world⟩; *specif* **:** a relatively permanent and highly organized center having a population with varied skills, lacking self-sufficiency in the production of food, and usu. depending primarily on manufacture and commerce to satisfy the wants of its inhabitants ⟨the ~ offers real cultural advantages⟩ **c :** CITY-STATE **d :** a municipal corporation in the U.S. occupying a definite area and subject to the state from which it derives its powers and for which it exists as an area of local government governed under a legal charter by a mayor and council, by a commission, or by a city manager and council and being usu. more populous than a town, borough, or village — see COMMISSION PLAN, COUNCIL-MANAGER PLAN **e :** a Canadian municipality of the highest class varying in character in the different provinces **f :** an administrative area centering in a municipality and set up under the protection of an international body (as the League of Nations) chiefly for the purpose of insuring freedom of trade and communication — see FREE CITY c **3 :** the inhabitants or citizens of a city **4 :** an aggregation of dwellings or other structures that is of such size or importance as to suggest a city ⟨a trailer ~ of construction workers⟩ ⟨Radio *City*⟩

city central *n* **:** an organization made up of locals of several labor unions within a city

city chicken *n* **:** pieces of boneless veal on skewers cooked by braising

city council *n* **:** the legislative body of a city

city crop *n* **:** the part of the annual crop of cotton, statistically considered, that has been rebaled and that consists of samples, sweepings, and pickings from damaged bales

city desk *n* **:** a department or section of a newspaper editorial office where local news is edited

city edition *n* **:** an edition of a usu. metropolitan newspaper that is designed for sale within the city and that is later than and distinguished from a suburban edition or mail edition — called also *home edition*

city editor *n* **1** *often cap C* [fr. (The) *City*, the financial section of London, England] *Brit* **:** the editor of financial and commercial news on a newspaper **2 :** a newspaper editor with varying functions but usu. in charge of local news and staff assignments

city father *n* **:** a member of the governing body of a city (as an alderman or councilman)

city hall *n* **1 :** the chief municipal building of a city **2 :** a municipal government **:** city officialdom or bureaucracy

city·ite \'==,īt\ *n* -s **:** a resident of a city

city·less \-ləs\ *adj* **:** lacking a city

city manager *n* **:** an official employed by an elected council to direct the administration of a city government — see COUNCIL-MANAGER PLAN

city-manager plan *n* **:** COUNCIL-MANAGER PLAN

city·ness *n* -ES **:** the quality or state of being citified

city of god *cap C&G* [trans. of LL *Civitas Dei*, an ideal heavenly city described by Saint Augustine (*Aurelius Augustinus*) †430 early Christian church father in his work *De Civitate Dei* (*The City of God*)] **:** NEW JERUSALEM **:** PARADISE, HEAVEN

city of refuge : a city in ancient Israel appointed as a place of asylum for unintentional murderers

city plan *n* **:** an organized arrangement or laying out (as of the streets, parks, and business sections) of a city with a view to general convenience, attractiveness of appearance, and the encouragement of healthier living

city planner *n* **:** one that makes city plans; *esp* **:** a professional who participates in such activity

city room *n* **1 a :** the room or department where local news is handled in a newspaper editorial office **b :** the personnel of such a room or department **2 :** a newspaper editorial room

city·scape \'==,skāp\ *n* -s [*city* + *-scape*] **1 :** a pictorial representation of a city **2 :** a city viewed as a scene or picture ⟨the skyscrapers which now bedizen the American ~ —*Amer. Mercury*⟩ **3 :** a pictorial composition of urban elements

city slicker *n* **:** SLICKER 3; *broadly* **:** someone regarded as sophisticated or effete

city-state \'==¦=\ *n* [trans. of Gk *polis* & L *civitas*] **:** a state (as in classical antiquity) in which the sovereignty is vested in the free citizens of an independent city and extends over the territories under its direct control — compare FREE CITY a

city·ward \'==wə(r)d\ *or* **city·wards** \-wə(r)dz\ *adj (or adv)* [ME *cite-ward*, fr. *cite, citie* city + *-ward* — more at CITY] **:** to or toward the city ⟨~ migration⟩ ⟨hastening ~⟩

ciu·dad juá·rez *or* **ciudad juarez** \syü'dädʰhwä(,)rās, -'thäthʰh-\ *adj, usu cap C&J* [fr. *Ciudad Juárez*, Mexico] **:** of or from Ciudad Juárez, Mexico **:** of the kind or style prevalent in Ciudad Juárez

ciudad tru·ji·llo \-trü'hi(,)lō, -'hē(,)yō\ *adj, usu cap C&T* [fr. *Ciudad Trujillo*, former name of Santo Domingo, Dominican Republic] **:** of or from Ciudad Trujillo, Dominican Republic **:** of the kind or style prevalent in Ciudad Trujillo

civ *abbr* civil; civilian

cive \'sīv\ *n* -s [ME, fr. MF, chives, onion, fr. L *cepa, cepe* onion] **:** ¹CHIVE 1

¹ci·vet \'sivət\ *n* -s [MF *civette*, fr. It *zibetto*, fr. Ar. *zabād* civet perfume] **1 :** CIVET CAT **2 :** a substance found in a pouch near the sexual organs of the true civet cats that is of the consistency of butter or honey, clear yellowish or brownish in color, with a strong musky odor, used in perfume, and chemically a complex mixture chiefly of fats and volatile oils **3 :** the fur of a civet or of a little spotted skunk

²ci·vet \sēvā\ *n* -s [F, alter. of OF *civé* hare or venison stew cooked in onion-flavored wine sauce, fr. *cive* onion, chives] **:** a highly seasoned stew of game

civ·et bean \'sivət-\ *n* [prob. by folk etymology fr. *Sieva bean*] **:** SIEVA BEAN

civet cat *n* **1 a :** any of various carnivorous mammals of the family Viverridae; *esp* **:** a brownish gray black-marked African animal (*Civettictis civetta*) two to three feet long that produces most of the civet of commerce — compare BUSH CAT 2, PALM CIVET, VIVERRA **b :** the cacomistle or any other animal of the genus *Bassariscus* **c :** LITTLE SPOTTED SKUNK **2 :** the fur of a civet cat

civ·e·tone \'sivə,tōn\ *n* -s [ISV *civet* + *-one*; prob. orig. formed as G *zibeton*] **:** a crystalline ketone $C_{17}H_{30}O$ that constitutes the characteristic odorous constituent of civet and that is used in perfumes, the odor becoming sweet on dilution

ci·vet·ta \sə'ved·ə\ *n* -s [NL, fr. *Civetta*, old genus including the civet, fr. F *civette* civet] **:** CIVET 2

ci·vette green \sə'vet-\ *n* [F *civette* civet] **:** a dark yellowish green that is yellower and paler than average hunter green or holly green (sense 1) and yellower, lighter, and stronger than deep chrome green

civ·ic \'sivik, -ēk\ *adj* [L *civicus*, fr. *civis* citizen — more at CITY] **1 :** inherent in or owing or accruing to the individual citizen **:** attendant on citizenship ⟨pledged by treaty to observe ~ liberties⟩ ⟨giving dissidents full ~ rights⟩ — used less commonly than *civil* in this sense **2 :** forming a component of or connected with the functioning, integration, and development of a civilized community (as a town or city) involving the common public activities and interests of the body of citizens ⟨the mayor urged low-cost housing as a prime ~ project⟩ ⟨~ pride⟩ ⟨~ opera⟩ ⟨this suburb is growing gradually with deepening ~ consciousness⟩ **3 :** concerned with or contributory to general welfare and the betterment of life for the citizenry of a community or enhancement of its facilities; *esp* **:** devoted to improving health, education, safety, recreation, and morale of the general public through nonpolitical means ⟨giving generously to various ~ clubs and causes⟩ ⟨lacking ~ initiative⟩ ⟨architectural congruity calls for ~ imagination⟩ ⟨a real sense of ~ and social responsibilities⟩ **4 :** essential to or obligatory on citizens in connection with the administration of laws and regulations **:** relating to government ⟨public office as a ~ duty⟩

civ·i·cal·ly \-vək(ə)lē, -ēk-, -li\ *adv* **1 :** with respect to or regard for civic demands and activities ⟨~ aroused about housing conditions⟩ **2 :** into one civic unit

civic center *n* **:** a section of a city or town usu. near the center where administration buildings, courts, libraries, galleries, and other public buildings are grouped

civic crown *also* **civic wreath** *n* [trans. of L *corona civica*] **1 :** a crown or garland of oak leaves and acorns bestowed by the Romans for saving the life of a citizen in battle **2 :** a representation of a civic crown esp. in architecture or heraldry

civ·i·cism \'sivə,sizəm\ *n* -s [*civic* + *-ism*] **:** devotion to civic interests and causes **:** CIVIC-MINDEDNESS

civ·i·cize \-,sīz\ *vt* -ED/-ING/-S **:** to infuse with civic consciousness

civic-minded \¦==¦==\ *adj* **:** disposed to look after civic needs and interests — **civ·ic-mind·ed·ness** *n* -ES

civ·ics \'siviks, -ēks\ *n pl but usu sing in constr* **:** study of the workings of the national and local government esp. as the subject of a secondary school course suited as training for citizenship

civic university *n* **:** one of the modern universities in Great Britain founded since the early 19th century orig. designed for the education of middle-class youth and therefore usu. nonresidential and situated in a large city

civie *var of* CIVVY

civ·il \'sivəl, *esp Brit sometimes* -(,)vil\ *adj* [ME, fr. MF, fr. L *civilis*, fr. *civis* citizen — more at CITY] **1 a :** relating to, growing out of, or involving the relations of citizens one with another or with the body politic or organized state or its divisions and departments ⟨~ institutions⟩ ⟨interested in ~ affairs⟩ ⟨a contribution to ~ philosophy⟩ **b :** concerned with or pertinent to internal affairs of a state or its citizenry in contrast to external affairs ⟨~ strife between two political groups⟩ ⟨~ embargo⟩ **2 a :** composed of or shared by individuals living and participating in a community ⟨the oldest form of ~ society were the early city-states of oriental antiquity —H.E.Barnes⟩ **b :** given to or marked by group activity or organization ⟨man is a ~ creature⟩ **3 :** concerning, befitting, or applying to the collective citizenry or the individual citizen ⟨a ~ duty⟩ ⟨the individual's ~ right of free speech⟩ — see CIVIL LIBERTY, CIVIL RIGHTS **4 a :** living in or exhibiting a condition of social advancement marked by organization and stability of community life or government **:** not uncivilized or primitive ⟨tribal anarchy giving way to ~ order⟩ **b :** marked by public order **:** quiet and peaceable in behavior ⟨areas still ~ in the turbulent country⟩ **c :** educated, cultured, or sophisticated **:** not rustic and unlettered ⟨a ~ philosophy⟩ ⟨~ jests⟩ **5 a :** based on or skilled in the Roman civil law ⟨a ~ doctor —Shak.⟩ **b :** relating to private rights and to legal proceedings in connection with them : relating to rights and remedies sought by action or suit distinct from criminal proceedings — distinguished from *criminal* and *political* ⟨a ~ liability⟩ ⟨~ jurisdiction⟩ ⟨a ~ suit⟩ ⟨a ~ remedy⟩; see CIVIL LAW **c** : as defined by law : having to do with legal rights or status ⟨~ disabilities⟩ — compare NATURAL 5; see CIVIL DEATH **6 a** *sometimes* -ER/-EST : adequate in courtesy and politeness : marked by satisfactory adherence to social usage and sufficient but not noteworthy consideration for others : MANNERLY ⟨even if he didn't like them he should have been ~ —W.S.Maugham⟩ ⟨it was all he could do to be ~ to her —Mary Austin⟩ ⟨I asked a ~ question, and I expect a ~ answer —D.H.Lawrence⟩ **b** *sometimes* -ER/-EST : showing goodwill, humaneness, or clemency : not savage or fierce ⟨the *civilest* and most friendly people that we met with —Daniel Defoe⟩ **c** *obs* : SOBER, STAID : not showy or audacious : QUIET **d** : seemly in aspect : compatible with human sensibilities : PRESENTABLE, SHIPSHAPE **e** *dial, of weather* : not inclement : FAVORABLE **7** *of time* : based on the mean sun and legally recognized for use by the general public in ordinary affairs — distinguished from *sidereal* ⟨the ~ calendar⟩ ⟨a ~ day begins at mean midnight⟩ **8 a** : belonging or relating to the general public, the pursuits, experiences, ways, and interests of the citizenry, or to civic or temporal affairs as distinguished from military, naval, ecclesiastical, or like specialized membership or affairs : CIVILIAN ⟨new educational techniques, learned in the war just ended, should be put into ~ use —Henry Wallace⟩ ⟨the old conflict between the ~ and the sacerdotal powers —Edward Clodd⟩ **b** : representing or serving the general public in the sphere of political rule or administration; *esp* : belonging to or sanctioned by an executive department of a nation, state, or municipality ⟨officials of a ~ board⟩ ⟨prohibiting a member of Congress from being appointed to any ~ office⟩ ⟨rates and hours set by ~ regulations⟩ **9** *obs* : virtuous by nature but not regenerate : moral as distinguished from religious ⟨~ righteousness⟩

syn POLITE, COURTEOUS, COURTLY, GALLANT, CHIVALROUS: CIVIL now implies adequate consideration of others and forbearance from rudeness or unpleasantness ⟨remember, then, that to be *civil* . . . is the only way to be beloved and well received in company, that to be ill-bred . . . is intolerable —Earl of Chesterfield⟩ ⟨I mean to return his visit tomorrow. It will be only *civil* in return for his politeness, to ask to see him —Sheridan Le Fanu⟩ POLITE may imply cold, formal, perfunctory deference to etiquette ⟨let's be *polite*, but act as though she didn't exist —Sherwood Anderson⟩ Often it differs from CIVIL in suggesting somewhat warmer or more sincere consideration of others ⟨the bishop seldom questioned Jacinto about his thoughts or beliefs. He didn't think it *polite* —Willa Cather⟩ ⟨under ordinary circumstances he would have tried to be *polite*. As it was, he could hardly bring himself to give them a *civil* word of welcome —Norman Douglas⟩ COURTEOUS may suggest a certain polish and delicacy of action; it may connote either mere formal deference, however perfect, to custom, or a genuine sincere consideration and regard ⟨the baronet peeped at his grandson with the *courteous* indifference of one who merely wishes to compliment that mother of anybody's child —George Meredith⟩ ⟨M. Laval owns a fine old historical painting in Chateldon, and he was *courteous* enough to permit me to view it —Upton Sinclair⟩ COURTLY suggests the stately or ceremonious ⟨Pitt Crawley treated her to a profound *courtly* bow, such as he had used to H. H. the Duchess of Pumpernickel, when he was attaché at that court —W.M. Thackeray⟩ GALLANT and CHIVALROUS, in this sense, indicate esp. courtesy and attention to women, the former often suggesting either the spirited and dashing or the elaborate and over-attentive ⟨the qualities . . . of surface chivalry and *gallant* attentiveness in her brilliant American friend had for a moment seemed to reveal a lack in me —Havelock Ellis⟩ CHIVALROUS in this sense often connotes high-mindedness and disinterested attention ⟨ladies were supposed to be without sexual desire . . . gracious beings they were, without a sordid thought, according to the *chivalrous* notions of the time —W.E.Woodward⟩ ⟨she had fainted from weakness, and he had felt strangely *chivalrous* and paternal —Ellen Glasgow⟩

civil affairs *n pl* : affairs and operations of the civil population of a territory that are supervised and directed by a friendly occupying power

civil airway *n* : an airway designated by the national civil aeronautic authority as suitable for interstate or foreign air commerce

civil architecture *n* : ARCHITECTURE 1

civil authority clause *n* : a clause in fire and similar insurance policies excluding loss caused by order of civil authorities unless destruction is for the purpose of checking the progress of the hazard insured against

civil bond *n, Brit* : a security issued by a sovereign or quasi-sovereign state and usu. not secured by collateral

civil contempt *n* : willful disobedience to a lawful order or decree entered as a civil remedy for the benefit of a party to a lawsuit

civil corporation *n* : a corporation organized for business purposes — contrasted with *eleemosynary corporation*

civil day *n* : a day adopted for time reckoning in civil affairs; *usu* : the mean solar day of 24 hours beginning at mean midnight

civil death *n* : a change of status of a person equivalent in its legal consequences to natural death : deprivation of rights and privileges as a citizen or a member of society

civil defense *n* : protective measures and emergency relief activities conducted by civilians under civilian authority for minimizing civilian casualties and property damage and for maintaining vital facilities and services in case of hostile attack or natural disaster

civil disobedience *n* : refusal to obey the demands or commands of the government esp. as a nonviolent collective means of forcing concessions from the government — see NONCOOPERATION

civil district *n* : a district formed for administrative purposes; *specif* : a minor political division of a county in certain states

civil embargo *n* : a government's embargo on the movement of ships under its own registry — compare HOSTILE EMBARGO

civil engineer *n* : an engineer whose training or occupation is in civil engineering —abbr. *C.E.*

civil engineering *n* : a branch of engineering concerned primarily with public works (as land surveying, the building of highways, bridges, waterways, or harbors, or the provision of artificial water supply, sewage disposal, irrigation) but also embracing private enterprises (as railroad and airport building, private building construction, farm drainage)

¹ci·vil·ian \sə'vilyən\ *n* -s [ME, fr. *civile* civil law (fr. L, short for *jus civile*) + *-ian*] **1 a** : one who practices or has made a special study of the Roman or modern civil law esp. as distinguished from the canon law and the English common law **b** : one esp. skilled in or devoted to the law affecting civil rights and remedies **2** : an employee in the former imperial civil service of India **3 a** : a resident of a country who is not on active duty in one of the armed services **b** : a resident not an active member of a police or fire-fighting force organized with ranks like military ranks **4 civilians** *pl* : CIVVIES

²civilian \"\ *adj* **1 a** : made up of civilians ⟨the ~ population⟩ **b** : belonging to or issuing from the aggregate body of civilians ⟨~ customers⟩ ⟨~ demands⟩ : peculiar to civilians ⟨~ habits of mind⟩ **c** : having the status of a civilian ⟨a ~ pilot⟩ **2 a** : operated or controlled by civilians ⟨~ industry⟩ : possessed by or vested in civilians ⟨~ authority⟩ **b** : undergone or sustained by civilians ⟨~ sacrifices⟩ **3 a** : intended or allotted for use or consumption by civilians ⟨~ goods⟩ **b** : suitable for civilians

ci·vil·ian·ism \-,nizəm\ *n* -s : dominance of civilian interests and their implementation over military force

ci·vil·ian·i·za·tion \-,==nə'zāshən, -,nī'z-\ *n* -s : the action of civilianizing

ci·vil·ian·ize \='==,nīz\ *vt* -ED/-ING/-s *see -ize in Explan Notes* : to convert from military to civilian status or control

civil imprisonment *n* : imprisonment by civil process

civ·i·lise *Brit var of* CIVILIZE

civ·i·list \'sivələst\ *n* -s [ML *civilista*, fr. L *civile* civil law + *-ista* -ist] *archaic* : CIVILIAN 1

ci·vil·i·té \sə'vilə(,)tā, ==='=\ *n* -s [F, lit., civility] : an early French cursive hand; *also* : a type styled therefrom

ci·vi·li·ter mor·tu·us \sə¦viləter'mȯrchəwəs, kə¦vilə,ter-'mȯrd-əwəs\ *adj* [NL] : civilly dead

ci·vil·i·ty \sə'viləd-ē, -ətē, -i\ *n* -ES [ME *civylite*, fr. MF *civilité*, fr. L *civilitat-, civilitas*, fr. *civilis* + *-itat-, -itas* -ity] **1 a** *obs* : deference or allegiance to the social order befitting a citizen **b** *obs* : civil government or polity **c** : solidarity of civil rights and obligations and civil justice in the civil order ⟨our great traditions of ~, the liberties western man has won for himself after centuries of struggle —Walter Lippmann⟩ **2** : the state of being civilized : CIVILIZATION 3 ⟨I have heard ladies say that the measure of a people's ~ is the position it accords to women —Clive Bell⟩ **3** *archaic* : training in the humanities **4 a** : civil conduct; *esp* : bare observance of the forms of accepted social behavior or adequate perfunctory politeness **b** *obs* : decent behavior or treatment : PROPRIETY **c** : an act or expression conforming to conventional patterns of social behavior

civ·i·liz·a·ble \'sivə,līzəbəl\ *adj* [F *civilisable*, fr. *civiliser* to civilize + *-able*] : capable of being civilized

civ·i·li·za·tion *or* **civ·i·li·sa·tion** \,sivələ'zāshən, sivə,lī'zāshən, *Brit often & US sometimes* -vi-\ *n* -s [*civilize* + *-ation*, prob. influenced in meaning by F *civilisation*] **1** *obs* : the act of making a criminal process civil **2 a** : an ideal state of human culture characterized by complete absence of barbarism and nonrational behavior, optimum utilization of physical, cultural, spiritual, and human resources, and perfect adjustment of the individual within the social framework ⟨true ~ is an ideal to be striven for⟩ **b** : a particular state or stage of human advance toward civilization: as (1) : the culture characteristic of a particular time or place ⟨medieval ~⟩ ⟨the impact of European ~ on primitive peoples⟩; *sometimes* : a widely diffused long-lived culture often with subcultures ⟨the Aegean ~ was a confluence of many Bronze Age cultures⟩ (2) : the stage of cultural development at which writing and the keeping of written records is attained; *also* : the stage marked by urbanization, advanced techniques (as of agriculture and industry), expanded population, and complex social organization ⟨modern ~ with its helpless dependence on technology⟩ **3** : the process of becoming civilized : progressive development of arts, sciences, statescraft, and human aspirations and spirituality ⟨~ is a slow process marked by many failures and setbacks⟩ **4** : the act of civilizing; *esp* : the forcing of a particular cultural pattern on a population to which it is foreign ⟨much of the nation's strength was wasted on the bloody ~ of unwilling peoples⟩ **5** : the whole of the advances of human culture and aspirations beyond the purely animal level ⟨~ is the descriptive inventory of all the modifications brought about in . . . the normal life of man in society —Pierre Lecomte du Noüy⟩ ⟨the first man to chip a stone into a better tool took a great step forward in ~⟩ **6** : conformity to conventional patterns of behavior or expression : refinement of thought, manners, or taste **7 a** : the parts of the earth characterized by a relatively high level of cultural and technological development ⟨made his way across the lands of two hostile tribes to reach ~⟩ **b** : a situation of urban comfort : city life ⟨we enjoy our country weekends but it's good to get back to ~ and hot running water⟩

civ·i·li·za·tion·al \¦==(,)='zāshənᵊl, -shnəl\ *adj* : dealing with or relating to civilization — **civ·i·li·za·tion·al·ly** \-shənᵊlē, -shnəlē, -i\ *adv*

civ·i·liz·a·to·ry \¦==¦līzə,tōrē\ *adj* [*civilization* + *-ory*] : tending to advance civilization : CIVILIZING

civ·i·lize \'sivə,līz, *Brit often & US sometimes* -vi-\ *vb* -ED/-ING/-s *see -ize in Explan Notes* [F *civiliser*, fr. *civil* + *-iser* -ize] *vt* **1** : to give a civil character to: **a** : to cause (as a people) to develop out of a primitive state through establishment of a system of social custom and political organization : instruct in the rules and standards of a civil order **b** : to bring (a people) to a technically advanced and rationally ordered stage of development of knowledge, polity, and international relations **2** : to raise up to a rationally and aesthetically refined and humanely oriented level of adjustment to the collective relations of mankind: **a** : to instruct in the sophisticated attitudes, polished elegance, and polite observances of elite society and good breeding : train in urbanity **b** : to instruct in or bring into line with the standards of self-control, uprightness, and impartial consideration of common needs and aspirations of humankind that are essential to social harmony and security of human freedoms : SOCIALIZE 2 **c** : to bring to recognition of or to accord with cultivated and refined aesthetic standards of classic literature and the fine arts **3** *obs* : to bring under civil authority **4** *obs* : to declare or treat as socially permissible or acceptable ~ *vi* **1** : to acquire the customs and amenities of a civil community **2** *dial* : to array or tidy oneself according to the standard of seemliness acceptable in a community

civilized *adj* **1** : advanced in social culture : characterized by progress esp. in statecraft and in the arts and sciences ⟨the essential characteristic of a highly ~ society is . . . that it is appreciative —Clive Bell⟩ **2** : of or relating to peoples or nations in a state of civilization ⟨must not be supposed that there is any essential stability in a ~ way of life —Bertrand Russell⟩ **3 a** : characterized by politeness, refinement, or good breeding ⟨had become a ~ chivalrous Christian knight —Charles Kingsley⟩ **b** : characterized by sophistication or urbanity ⟨he is humorous, ironic, and penetrating in a dispassionate ~ way —Marvin Lowenthal⟩ — **civ·i·lized·ness** \'==,līzədnəs, -z(d)n-\ *n* -ES

civ·i·liz·ee \¦==¦līz¦ē\ *n* -s : a civilized person

civ·i·liz·er \'==,līzə(r)\ *n* -s : one that civilizes

civil law *n, sometimes cap C&L* [ME *lawe civile*, trans. of L *jus civile*] **1** *Roman law* **a** : the local law of a state or of Rome—distinguished from *jus gentium* and *jus naturae* **b** : the strict law as distinguished from the praetorian law established by edicts **2** : Roman law as applied in the middle ages and set forth chiefly in the Justinian Code **3 a** : the body of private law that has developed from the Roman law in the states where the legal system is still substantially Roman but has been influenced by Germanic, ecclesiastical, and purely modern institutions — compare COMMON LAW **b** : the law of private rights — distinguished from *criminal law*

civil libertarian *n* : one who upholds the principles of civil liberty; *esp* : one who defends civil liberties against invasion

civil liberty *n* : freedom from arbitrary governmental interference (as with the right of free speech) specif. by denial of governmental power and in the U.S. esp. as guaranteed by the Bill of Rights — usu. used in pl.

civil list *n* **1** *British Commonwealth* : a list of sums appropriated annually to pay members of the civil government (as judges, ambassadors, secretaries) and civil servants — obs. in U.S. **2** : a list of sums appropriated by a parliament to pay expenses of the sovereign and his household

civ·il·ly \'sivəl(l)ē, -ivi-, -)i\ *adv* **1** : with just ordinary cool or perfunctory politeness **2 a** : in connection with civil rights and liabilities or civil affairs **b** : in civil relations ⟨a ~ united Europe⟩ **3** : in accordance with civil law or obligation

civilly dead *adj* : dead in the eyes of the law

civil marriage *n* : a marriage solemnized before a civil magistrate as distinguished from one before a clergyman

civil process *n* : a writ or order of court in a civil action; *esp* : a writ for arrest in a civil proceeding

civil rights *n pl* **1** : those rights the enjoyment of which does not involve participation in the establishment, support, or management of the government; *specif* : the rights secured to citizens of the U.S. by the 13th and 14th amendments to the constitution and certain acts passed by Congress April 9, 1866, May 31, 1870, and March 1, 1875, abolishing the civil incidents of involuntary servitude **2** : rights that guarantee to all citizens equal opportunities (as for employment, schooling, housing, or voting) regardless of race, religion, sex, or national origin

civils *n pl, obs* : civil affairs

civil servant *n* **1** : a member of a civil service **2** : a member of the administrative staff of an international agency

civil service *n* **1 a** : the branch of the service of the East India Company conducted by covenanted servants not belonging to the army or navy **b** : the whole public administrative service of a government including all branches except the armed services **c** : the whole body of public servants employed by a government other than those in the armed services **2** : government service in which appointments and status are determined by merit or examination rather than by political patronage

civil-spoken \¦==¦==\ *adj* : given to speaking courteously

civil time *n* : clock time reckoned in mean solar hours, minutes, and seconds and commonly divided into 12-hour periods beginning alternately at midnight and noon of each civil day — see STANDARD TIME

civil twilight *n* : the period after sunset or before sunrise ending or beginning when the sun is about 6 degrees below the horizon and during which on clear days there is enough light for ordinary outdoor occupations

civil war *n* : a war between different sections or parties of the same country or nation

civ·ism \'si,vizəm\ *n* -s [F *civisme*, fr. L *civis* citizen + F *-isme* -ism — more at HOME] : the virtues and sentiments of a good citizen — used orig. of devotion to the cause of the French revolution of 1789

ci·vi·tas \'kēwē,täs\ *n, pl* **civita·tes** \,kēwē'tä,täs\ [L — more at CITY] : a body of people constituting a politically organized community : STATE; *esp* : CITY-STATE

civitas dei \-'dā,ē\ *n, usu cap C&D* [LL — more at CITY OF GOD] : CITY OF GOD

civ·vy *also* **civ·ie** \'sivē, -vi\ *n, pl* **civvies** *also* **civies** [by shortening and alter. fr. *civilian*] **1** *civvies pl* : civilian clothes as distinguished from military or naval uniform **2** : CIVILIAN

civvy street *n, Brit* : civilian life

cixi·id \'siksēəd\ *n* -s [NL *Cixiidae*] : an insect of the family Cixiidae

cixi·idae \sik'sīə,dē\ *n pl, cap* [NL, fr. *Cixius*, type genus (fr. LGk *kixios* cicada) + *-idae*] : a family of small elongated somewhat depressed insects (suborder Homoptera) related to the lantern flies

CJ *abbr* chief judge; chief justice

ck *abbr* **1** cake **2** cask **3** chalk **4** check **5** cook **6** countersink

CKD *abbr* completely knocked down

ckw *abbr* clockwise

cl *abbr* **1** centiliter **2** claim; claiming **3** class; classification **4** classical **5** clause **6** clearance **7** clergyman **8** clerk **9** close; closure **10** cloth **11** clove **12** clutch **13** coil

CL *abbr* **1** carload; carload lot **2** cash letter **3** center line **4** civil law **5** common law **6** connecting line

Cl *symbol* chlorine

¹clab·ber \'klabə(r) *sometimes* -läb-\ *also* **clabbered milk** *or* **clabber milk** *n* -s [short for *bonnyclabber*] *now chiefly dial* : sour milk that has thickened or curdled

²clabber \"\ *vb* **clabbered; clabbered; clabbering** \-b(ə)riŋ\ **clabbers** *chiefly Midland* : CURDLE, LOPPER

³clab·ber \'klabə(r), -läb-,-läb-\ *n* -s [ScGael & IrGael *clābar*] *dial Brit* : MUD, MIRE

⁴clab·ber \'kläbə(r), 'klab-\ *n* -s [by shortening & alter. fr. *klaberjass*] : klaberjass or a similar card game derived from it

clabber cheese *n* [¹*clabber*] *dial* : COTTAGE CHEESE

cla·chan \'klakən\ *n* -s [ME, fr. ScGael, hamlet, stepping-stones, prob. fr. *clach* stone; akin to OIr *cloch* stone] *Scot & Irish* : HAMLET

¹clack \'klak\ *vb* -ED/-ING/-s [ME *clacken*, of imit. origin] *vi* **1** : to utter words or sounds rapidly and continually : let the tongue run on : CHATTER ⟨just get her started and she'll ~ all day —J.C.Lincoln⟩ **2** : to make a sharp abrupt noise ⟨the whiplash ~*ed*, the jog-trot sharpened —Edmund Blunden⟩ or succession of such noises ⟨teletypes ~*ed* in all police stations —*Time*⟩ : CLATTER ⟨she ~*ed* up the aisle and entered a front pew —Bruce Marshall⟩ **3** *of fowl* : CACKLE, CLUCK ⟨hen voices ~*ing* —Edith Sitwell⟩ ~ *vt* **1** : to cause to make a sharp noise : make clatter ⟨grasshoppers . . . ~*ing* their desiccate wings —William Goyen⟩ **2** : to produce with a cracking or clapping sound; *specif* : BLAB, BABBLE ⟨all sorts of rumors were ~*ed* about⟩

²clack \"\ *n* -s [ME *clakke*, fr. *clacken*, v.] **1** : loud confused noise (as of many voices) : loud continual, importunate, or foolish talk : CHATTER, PRATTLE ⟨nothing but a farrago of the ~ of nurses —Laurence Sterne⟩ **2** *archaic* : an object (as a rattle or clack valve) that produces clapping or cracking noises usu. in regular rapid sequence **3** : a sharp abrupt noise or succession of such noises often produced by the striking together of objects ⟨dull ~*s* of plates and cups —Elizabeth M. Roberts⟩ **4 a** : a gossiping tongue ⟨her ~ was going all day —Mark Twain⟩ **b** : one having such a tongue ⟨that old ~⟩

clack·a·mas *or* **clak·a·mas** \'klakəməs\ *n, pl* **clackamas** *or* **clakamas** *usu cap* [modif. of Clackamas *Guithlákimas*] **1 a** : an Indian people of the Clackamas river valley of northwestern Oregon **b** : a member of such people **2** : a dialect of Upper Chinook

clack·dish \'klak,dish\ *n* [so called fr. the sound made by the lid] : CLAPDISH

clack·er \'klakə(r)\ *n* -s : one that clacks: as **a** *dial Brit* : a gossiping tongue **b** *dial Brit* : a rattle to frighten away birds

clack·et \'klakət\ *vb* [MF *claqueter*, fr. *claquet* clapper of a mill, fr. *claque* slap, clatter, of imit. origin] *dial* : CLACK

clack goose \'klak-\ *var of* CLAIK GOOSE

clack·man·nan·shire \(')klak¦manən,shi(ə)r, -,shər\ *or* **clack·man·nan** \(')=¦==\ *adj, usu cap* [fr. *Clackmannanshire* or *Clackmannan* county, Scotland] : of or from the county of Clackmannan, Scotland : of the kind or style prevalent in Clackmannan

clack valve *n* : a valve usu. hinged at one edge that permits flow of fluid in one direction only and that closes with a clacking sound — called also *clapper valve*

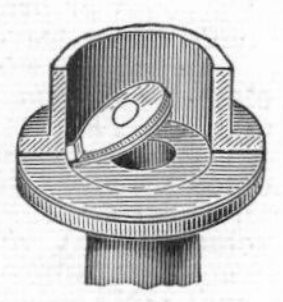

clack valve (open)

cla·co \'klä(,)kō\ *n* -s [MexSp, alter. of Sp *tlaco*] : TLACO

clac·to·ni·an \(')klak¦tōnēən, -nyən\ *adj, usu cap* [*Clacton*-on-Sea, England, where the flaking tools were first found + E *-ian*] : of or relating to a lower Paleolithic culture of England characterized by a peculiar method of flaking stone that resulted in flakes having a half cone at the point where the hammerstone struck

¹clad \'klad, -aa(ə)d\ [ME *clad, cladde*, fr. OE *clǣthde*, past of *clǣthan* to clothe, fr. *clāth* garment, cloth — more at CLOTH] *past of* CLOTHE

²clad \"\ *adj* [ME *cladd*, fr. OE *geclǣthd*, past part. of *clǣthan* to clothe] **1 a** : CLOTHED ⟨well-*clad* children⟩ **b** : DECKED, ADORNED ⟨ivy-*clad* buildings⟩ **2 a** : SHEATHED, COVERED ⟨an armor-*clad* car⟩ **b** *of a metal* : overlaid on one or both sides with a metal coating of a different composition to promote electrical conductivity or corrosion resistance or to impart other special properties ⟨copper-*clad* steel⟩ ⟨~ coins⟩

³clad \"\ *vt* **clad; clad; cladding; clads** [ME *claden*, fr. *cladd*, adj] **1** : CLOTHE ⟨*cladding* himself with the ornaments belonging to his degree —Edward Dacres⟩ **2** : SHEATHE, FACE ⟨the long wall . . . ~ in vertical boarding of walnut —Michael Rosenauer⟩; *specif* : to cover (a metal) with another metal by bonding

clad- *or* **clado-** *comb form* [NL, fr. Gk *klad-, klado-*, fr. *klados* — more at GLADIATOR] : slip : sprout ⟨*cladanthous*⟩ ⟨*cladophyll*⟩

cla·dan·thous \klə'dan(t)thəs\ *adj* [*clad-* + *-anthous*] : PLEUROCARPOUS

clad·au·toi·cous \¦kladə¦tȯikəs, -a,dȯ¦t-\ *adj* [*clad-* + *autoicous*] *of mosses* : having the male sexual organ on a special branch

clad·ding \'kladiŋ, -aad-, -ēŋ\ *n* -s [fr. gerund of *clad*] : something that covers or overlays; *specif* : metal coating bonded to a metal core by heat and pressure or by casting — compare ²CLAD 2b

cladi *pl of* CLADUS

cla·dis·tia \klə'distēə\ *n pl, cap* [NL, fr. *clad-* + *-istia* (fr. Gk *histia*, pl. of *histion* web, cloth, sail, fr. *histanai* to make stand, stand) — more at STAND] : an order of Teleostomi comprising primitive bony freshwater African fishes that have scales, head skeleton, and pectoral arch which resemble those of the extinct Archistia and that include the bichir and the reedfish — compare POLYPTERUS

clad·o·car·pous \ˈkladəˌkärpəs\ *adj* [*clad-* + *-carpous*] : PLEUROCARPOUS

cla·doc·era \kləˈdäsərə\ *n pl, cap* [NL, fr. *clad-* + *-cera*] : an order of minute chiefly freshwater branchiopod crustaceans comprising the water fleas

1**cla·doc·er·an** \-rən\ *or* **cla·doc·er·ous** \-rəs\ *adj* [NL *Cladocera* + E *-an* or *-ous*] : of or relating to the Cladocera

2**cladoceran** \ˈ"\ *n* -s : a crustacean of the order Cladocera

clad·o·chyt·ri·a·ce·ae \ˌkladō,ki·trēˈāsēˌē\ *n pl, cap* [NL, fr. *Cladochytrium*, type genus (fr. *clad-* + Gk *chytrion*, dim. of *chytris, chytra* pot) + NL *-aceae*] : a family of fungi (order Chytridiales) characterized by uniflagellate zoospores and a rhizomycelial plant body with frequent enlargements into spindle bodies, several species esp. in the type genus *Cladochytrium* being parasitic in algae, aquatic seed plants, and some plants of economic importance (as alfalfa, corn, beets)

clad·o·chyt·ri·a·ceous \ˌ==ˌ=əˌ=ˈāshəs\ *adj* [NL *Cladochytriaceae* + E *-ous*] : of or relating to the Cladochytriaceae

clad·ode \ˈklaˌdōd\ *n* -s [NL *cladodium*, fr. LGk *kladōdēs* having many sprouts (fr. Gk *klad-* clad- + *-ōdēs* -odes) + NL *-ium*] : CLADOPHYLL — **cla·do·di·al** \kləˈdōdēəl, (ˈ)klaˌd-\ *adj*

clad·o·dus \ˈkladədəs\ *n, cap* [NL, fr. *clad-* + *-odus*] *in some classifications* : a genus of primitive Carboniferous sharks supposedly distinguished by teeth with a tall central cusp, a broad base, and one or more pairs of lateral tubercles, a character now known to have occurred widely in early elasmobranchs

cla·do·nia \kləˈdōnyə, -nēə\ *n, cap* [NL, fr. LGk *kladon-*, *kladōn* sprout (fr. Gk *klados*) + NL *-ia* — more at CLAD-] : a genus (the type of the family Cladoniaceae) of lichens characterized by its crustose plant body and capitate fruiting bodies borne on simple or branched podetia — see REINDEER MOSS

cla·do·ni·a·ceous \kləˌdōnēˈāshəs\ *adj* [NL *Cladonia* + *-aceous*] : CLADONIOID

cla·do·ni·oid \kləˈdōnēˌȯid\ *adj* [NL *Cladonia* + E *-oid*] : of or relating to the genus *Cladonia*

cla·doph·o·ra \kləˈdäfərə\ *n, cap* [NL, fr. *clad-* + *-phora*] : a genus (the type of the family Cladophoraceae of the order Cladophorales) of branched filamentous septate green algae usu. firmly attached and with the branches arising from the upper end of the cells each of which has a reticulate chloroplast and several nuclei, the genus also being placed sometimes in the order Siphonocladales and sometimes in Ulotrichales

cla·doph·o·ra·ceous \kləˌdäfəˈrāshəs\ *adj* [NL *Cladophora* + E *-aceous*] : of or relating to the genus *Cladophora* or family Cladophoraceae

cla·doph·o·ra·les \kləˌdäfəˈrā(ˌ)lēz\ *n pl, cap* [NL, fr. *Cladophora* + *-ales*] : an order of green algae (class Chlorophyceae) having a simple or branching thallus and containing a single family — see CLADOPHORA

clad·o·phyll \ˈkladəˌfil\ *also* **clad·o·phyl·lum** \ˌkladəˈfiləm\ *n, pl* **clado·phylls** \-ˌfilz\ *also* **cladophyl·la** \-ˈfilə\ [NL *cladophyllum*, fr. *clad-* + *-phyllum*] : a branch assuming the form of and closely resembling an ordinary foliage leaf and borne in the axil of a true leaf, often bearing leaves or flowers on its margins (as in butcher's-broom) — called also *cladode*; see PHYLLOCLADE

clad·op·to·sis \ˌklaˌdäpˈtōsəs\ *n, pl* **cladopto·ses** \-ōˌsēz\ [NL, fr. *clad-* + *ptosis*] : an annual dropping of twigs or branches instead of leaves in plants of various genera (as *Thuja* and *Taxodium*)

cla·dose \ˈklaˌdōs, -lāˌd-\ *adj* [*clad-* + *-ose*] : BRANCHED, RAMOSE

clad·o·sel·a·che \ˌkladōˈselə(ˌ)kē\ *n, cap* [NL, fr. *clad-* + *-selache* (fr. Gk *selachos* fish with cartilaginous skeleton) — more at SELACHII] : a genus (the type of the family Cladoselachidae) comprising the most primitive known sharklike fishes, restricted to the upper Devonian and with a few other extinct forms constituting the subclass Pleuropterygii — **cladoselachian** \ˌkladōsəˈlākēən\ *adj or n*

clad·o·se·la·chea \ˌkladōsəˈlākēə\ *also* **clad·o·se·la·chii** \-kēˌī\ *or* **clad·o·se·la·chi·for·mes** \ˌkladōsəˌlākəˈfȯrˌmēz\ *or* **clad·o·sel·a·choi·dea** \ˌkladōˌseləˈkȯidēə\ [NL, fr. *Cladoselache*] *syn of* PLEUROPTERYGII

clad·o·spo·ri·um \ˌkladəˈspōrēəm\ *n, cap* [NL, fr. *clad-* + *-sporium*] : a form genus of imperfect fungi (family Dematiaceae) having conidia borne on branched conidiophores and the conidia with usu. one or in age two or three septa and including some economically important plant parasites

1**clad·o·thrix** \ˈkladəˌthriks\ [NL, fr. *clad-* + *-thrix*] *syn of* ACTINOMYCES

2**cladothrix** \ˈ"\ [NL, fr. *clad-* + *-thrix*] *syn of* SPHAEROTILUS

-cla·dous \ˌkladəs\ *adj comb form* [NL *-cladus*, fr. Gk *-klados*, fr. *klados* sprout, twig — more at GLADIATOR] : branched ⟨acantho*cladous*⟩

cla·dox·y·la·ce·ae \kləˌdäksəˈlāsēˌē\ *n pl, cap* [NL, fr. *Cladoxylon*, type genus + *-aceae*] : a family of fossil plants that is coextensive with the genus *Cladoxylon* and is placed in the order Psilophytales or Cladoxylales

cla·dox·y·la·les \-ˈā(ˌ)lēz\ *n pl, cap* [NL, fr. *Cladoxylon* + *-ales*] *in some classifications* : an order of fossil plants (class Filicineae) coextensive with the family Cladoxylaceae

cla·dox·y·lon \kləˈdäksəˌlän\ *n, cap* [NL, fr. *clad-* + *-xylon*] : a genus (the type of the family Cladoxylaceae) of Devonian to mid-Carboniferous fossil plants having dichotomously branched stems and leaves, each forking of the fertile segments bearing a single sporangium

cla·dras·tis \kləˈdrastəs\ *n, cap* [NL, irreg. fr. *clad-* + Gk *thraustos* brittle (fr. *thrauein* to shatter) — more at DREARY] : a genus of ornamental trees (family Leguminosae) having odd-pinnate leaves and white flowers borne in showy panicles — see YELLOWWOOD 1a

clads *pres 3d sing of* CLAD

cla·dus \ˈklādəs, -lad-\ *n, pl* **cla·di** \-ˌdī\ [NL, fr. Gk *klados* sprout] : a branch of a ramose spicule

claes \ˈklāz\ *n pl* [ME (northern dial.) *clais, claithes, clathes*, fr. OE *clāthas* — more at CLOTHES] *chiefly Scot* : CLOTHES

1**clag** \ˈklag\ *vb* **clagged; clagged; clagging; clags** [ME *claggen*, prob. of Scand origin; akin to Dan *klægge* sticky mud, ON *kleggi* horsefly; akin to OE *clǣg* clay — more at CLAY] *vt* **1** *dial Brit* : to bedaub usu. with a sticky substance (as mud or dirt) **2** *dial Brit* : CLOG, CLOT **3** *dial Brit* : to cause to adhere ~ *vi, dial Brit* : ADHERE, STICK

2**clag** \ˈ"\ *n* -s *dial Brit* : a clot or lump esp. of dirt or snow

clag·gum \ˈklagəm\ *n* -s [prob. fr. 1*clag* + *-um* (as in *medium*)] *dial Brit* : a gummy sweetmeat; *esp* : taffy made with molasses or treacle

clag·gy \ˈklagi, -aigi\ *adj* -ER/-EST [2*clag* + *-y*] **1** *dial* : STICKY, GUMMY **2** *dial* : MUDDY

claik \ˈklāk\ *Scot var of* CLACK

claik goose \ˈ"-\ *n, Scot* : BARNACLE GOOSE

1**claim** \ˈklām\ *vb* -ED/-ING/-S [ME *claimen*, fr. *claim-*, pres. ind. sing. stem of OF *clamer*, fr. L *clamare* to cry out, call; akin to L *calare* to call, summon — more at LOW] *vt* **1** *obs* : NAME, ANNOUNCE, PROCLAIM **2 a** : to demand recognition of (as a title, distinction, possession, or power) esp. as a right ⟨the papal-imperial partnership which ~*ed* universal rule over all Christendom —W.K.Ferguson⟩; *also* : to have as a property or quality ⟨each rhyme in the verse ~*s* four lines⟩ ⟨the small child ~*s* the family red hair⟩ **b** : to call for : REQUIRE ⟨public health must ~ everyone's attention⟩ : demand esp. as a consequence ⟨the plague ~*ed* thousands of lives⟩ **3 a** (1) : to demand delivery or possession of by or as if by right ⟨he went to ~ their bags at the station⟩ (2) : BUY ⟨~*ed* a fine horse after the race⟩ **b** : to recognize the fact of or assert often proudly the right to a close or special relationship with (as by reason of birth, residence, common circumstances, or special affinity) ⟨Paris can ~ many significant writers and artists⟩ ⟨the city can ~ the highest accident rate in 10 years⟩ **4** : to assert esp. with conviction and in the face of possible contradiction or doubt : MAINTAIN ⟨~*ed* he saw a ghost⟩ ⟨some people ~ to see beauty in a puddle —Andrew Buchanan⟩ ~ *vi, obs* : to assert or establish a right or privilege **syn** see DEMAND

2**claim** \ˈ"\ *n* -s [ME *claim, claime*, fr. OF *claim*, fr. *clamer*] **1 a** (1) : an authoritative or challenging request : DEMAND ⟨the present age makes great ~*s* upon us —Matthew Arnold⟩ (2) : a demand of a right or supposed right ⟨Holland withdrew her ~ to the annexation of German territory⟩ (3) : a calling on another for something due or supposed to be due ⟨the speaker laid no ~ on the intelligence of his audience⟩ **b** : a demand for compensation, benefits, or payment (as one made in conformity with provisions of the Social Security Act or of a workmen's compensation law, one made under an insurance policy upon the happening of the contingency against which it is issued, or one made against a transportation line because of loss occasioned by carrier negligence or overcharge); *also* : the amount or payment of such a demand **2** : a privilege to something : RIGHT ⟨his ~ to be called Europe's leading spokesman⟩ ⟨a ~ to fame⟩ ⟨liberty itself became . . . a principle of anarchy rather than a body of ~*s* to be read in the context of the social process —H.J.Laski⟩; *specif* : a title to any debt, privilege, or other thing in the possession of another ⟨an applicant has a special ~ on . . . funds listed —*Official Register of Harvard Univ.*⟩ **3** : an assertion, statement, or implication (as of value, effectiveness, qualification, eligibility) often made or likely to be suspected of being made without adequate justification ⟨his ~*s* to sound scholarship⟩ ⟨appraising the authenticity of some dealer's ~ —Edith Diehl⟩; *specif* : the formal assertion of novelty and patentability with specification of particulars made by an applicant for a patent **4** : an assertion of title made (as by a settler, lumberman, prospector) on a tract of land (as one in the public domain) and evidenced by staking or otherwise marking as required by law; *also* : the tract of land for which such an assertion is made

claim adjuster *n* : ADJUSTER 2

claim agent *or* **claim man** *n* **1** : one who investigates and adjusts claims for shortage, damage, loss, or overcharge on shipments of goods **2** : one who acts as agent in transactions with holders of property on which pipelines are to be laid or oil or gas wells drilled and who investigates and adjusts their claims

claim·ant \ˈklāmənt\ *n* -s [1*claim* + *-ant*] : one that asserts a right or title ⟨the ~ to an estate⟩

claim·er \ˈklāmə(r)\ *n* -s [ME, fr. *claimen* + *-er*] **1** : one that claims : CLAIMANT **2 a** : CLAIMING RACE **b** : a horse entered in a claiming race : PLATER

claiming race *n* : a horse race before which each owner pledges to sell a horse he enters at a given price and after which must sell it if so requested usu. by someone who has entered a horse in a race at the same meeting

claim·less \ˈklāmləs\ *adj* : being without a claim

claim shanty *n* : a cabin built hastily on a land claim to legalize possession of the land

claims·man \ˈklāmzmən\ *n, pl* **claimsmen** [*claims* (pl. of 2*claim*) + *man*] : ADJUSTER 2

clair-audience \kla(a)r, kler +\ *n* [*clair-* (as in *clairvoyance*) + *audience* (act of hearing)] : the act or the power of hearing something not present to the ear but regarded as having objective reality

clair·audient \(ˈ)=+\ *adj* : of, relating to, or having clairaudience — **clair·au·di·ent·ly** *adv*

clair de lune \ˌkla(a)rdᵊlˈün, -ler-\ *n, pl* **clair de lunes** [F, lit., moonlight] **1** : a pale blue or green-blue glaze used on porcelain; *also* : porcelain of this color **2** : a bluish gray that is greener and paler than average dusk (sense 3a), lighter than Medici blue, and stronger than puritan gray

claire \ˈkla(a)(ə)r, -le(ə)r\ *n* -s [F, fr. fem. of *clair*, adj.] : a small enclosed pond for growing or observing the growth of oysters

clair-obscure *also* **clare-obscure** \ˌkla(a)r, -ler-+\ *n* [F *clair-obscur* — more at CLEAR-OBSCURE] : CHIAROSCURO

clai·ron \klärōⁿ\ *n* -s [F — more at CLARION] : CLARION 3

clairschach *var of* CLARSACH

clair·sentience \kla(a)r, -ler+\ *n* -s [*clair-* (as in *clairvoyance*) + *sentience*] : perception of what is not normally perceptible

clair·sentient \(ˈ)=+\ *adj* : having clairsentience

clair·voy·ance \kla(a)rˈvȯiən(t)s, klerˈv-, kla(a)əˈv-, kleəˈv- *also* -ȯiyə-\ *also* **clair·voy·an·cy** \-nsē, -si\ *n, pl* **clairvoyanc·es** *also* **clairvoyan·cies** [F *clairvoyance*, fr. *clairvoyant*] **1** : the act or power professed by certain persons of discerning objects hidden from sight or at a great distance **2** : ability to perceive matters beyond the range of ordinary perception : PENETRATION, DISCERNMENT, CLEAR-SIGHTEDNESS

1**clair·voy·ant** \(ˈ)=ˈ=(y)ənt\ *adj* [F, adj. & n., fr. *clair* clear (fr. L *clarus*) + *voyant*, pres. part. of *voir* to see, fr. L *vidēre* — more at CLEAR, VIEW] **1** : able to perceive matters beyond the range of ordinary perception : CLEAR-SIGHTED, DISCERNING ⟨if the poet is not ~ he is nothing —C.D.Lewis⟩ **2** : of or relating to clairvoyance ⟨the ~ revelations of a medium⟩ — **clair·voy·ant·ly** *adv*

2**clairvoyant** \ˈ"\ *n* -s [F] : one held to possess the power of clairvoyance

clair·voy·ante \-nt\ *n* -s [F, fem. of *clairvoyant*] : a female clairvoyant

clai·sen flask \ˈklāsᵊn-, ˈklīzᵊn-\ *n, usu cap C* [after Ludwig *Claisen* b1851 Ger. chemist] : a distilling flask with a branched neck esp. designed for vacuum distillation — see DISTILLING FLASK illustration

clakamas *usu cap, var of* CLACKAMAS

clal·lam \ˈklaləm\ *n, pl* **clallam** *or* **clallams** *usu cap* [Clallam, lit., strong people] **1 a** : a Salishan people of the south shore of the straits of Juan de Fuca, Washington **b** : a member of such people **2** : the language of the Clallam people

1**clam** \ˈklam, -aa(ə)m\ *n* -s [ME, fr. OE *clamm* bond, fetter; akin to OHG *klamma* constriction, ON *klām* obscene language, L *glomus* ball, Gk *glamōn* blear-eyed, L *galla* gall on a plant — more at GALL] : a viselike or pincerlike device designed to hold or constrict something : CLAMP: as **a** : a tight ligature used in bloodless castration of domestic animals **b** : a comblike frame used for holding feathers for clothing decoration

2**clam** \ˈ"\ *vt* **clammed; clammed; clamming; clams** *dial Brit* : to grasp with the hand : GROPE, CLUTCH

3**clam** \ˈ"\ *vb* **clammed; clammed; clamming; clams** [ME *clammen*, alter. of *clemen* to smear, fr. OE *clǣman* — more at CLOAM] *vt, dial Eng* : to daub, smear, or clog esp. with glutinous or viscous matter; *specif* : to plug up (a kiln) with wet clay ~ *vi, dial Eng* : to become clammy : STICK, ADHERE

4**clam** \ˈ"\ *adj* [ME; akin to *clammen*, v.] **1** *dial chiefly Brit* : STICKY, ADHESIVE **2** *dial chiefly Brit* : damp and cold

5**clam** \ˈ"\ *n* -s *often attrib* [1*clam* (clamp); fr. the clamping action of the shells] **1 a** : any of a number of bivalve mollusks; *esp* : any of various equivalved edible marine mollusks that live wholly or partially buried in sand or mud — see BUTTER CLAM, QUAHOG, RAZOR CLAM, SOFT-SHELL CLAM **b** : a freshwater mussel **c** : the flesh of a clam used as food — usu. used in pl. **2** : a stolid or closemouthed person **3** : CLAMSHELL 2

clam: *1* siphon, *2* incurrent orifice, *3* excurrent orifice, *4* mantle, *5* shell, *6* foot

6**clam** \ˈ"\ *vb* **clammed; clammed; clamming; clams** *vi* : to gather clams esp. by digging ~ *vt* : to harvest clams from ⟨these beds are *clammed* mostly by summer people⟩

7**clam** \ˈ"\ *var of* 1CLEM

cla·mant \ˈklāmənt, -lam-\ *adj* [L *clamant-, clamans*, pres. part. of *clamare* to call — more at CLAIM] **1** : crying out : CLAMOROUS, LOUD ⟨a world distracted everywhere by ~ national creeds —*Times Lit. Supp.*⟩ **2** : demanding notice : PRESSING, URGENT ⟨~ need⟩ — **cla·mant·ly** *adv*

clam·a·roo \ˌklaməˈrü\ *n* -s [irreg. fr. 5*clam*] : CLAMBAKE 2a

clam·a·to·res \ˌklaməˈtōr(ˌ)ēz\ *n pl, cap* [NL, fr. L, pl. of *clamator* bawler, fr. *clamatus*, past part. of *clamare* + *-or*] *in some classifications* : a suborder or superfamily of Passeriformes nearly coextensive with the modern suborder Tyranni

clam·a·to·ri·al \ˌklaməˈtōrēəl\ *adj* [NL *Clamatores* + E *-ial*] : of or relating to the Clamatores

clambake \ˈ=ˌ=\ *n* [5*clam* + *bake*] **1 a** : a social gathering where food is prepared and eaten outdoors; *specif* : a seashore outing where clams and fish are baked (as on heated rocks covered by seaweed) **b** *slang* : an often noisy and pretentious social entertainment esp. attended by a great many people ⟨seldom attend the fancier ~*s* in which Washington abounds —*N.Y. Times*⟩; *esp* : a political rally ⟨the party faithful gathered . . . for the great New York ~ —*Time*⟩ **2** *slang* **a** : a radio or television program or rehearsal that is confused, badly organized, or full of mistakes **b** : JAM SESSION; *esp* : one that is disorganized or unsuccessful

1**clam·ber** \ˈklam(b)ə(r), -aamb-\ *vb* **clambered; clambered; clambering** \-m(b)(ə)riŋ\ **clambers** [ME *clambren*; akin to MHG *klamben* to fit together tightly, ON *klembra* to clamber, OE *climban* to climb — more at CLIMB] *vi* : to move (as up, around, through, or under something) by or as if by catching hold with the hands and feet : CRAWL, STRUGGLE, CLIMB ⟨~ into a tank⟩ ⟨~ out of an overcoat⟩ ⟨~ to emotional heights⟩ ⟨construction workers ~*ed* down from their scaffolding —Robert Shaplen⟩ ~ *vt* : to scramble up : CLIMB ⟨hodmen, ~*ing* a ladder —Washington Irving⟩

2**clamber** \ˈ"\ *n* -s : the act or action of clambering

clam·ber·er \-m(b)ərə(r)\ *n* -s : one that clambers; *esp* : a clambering plant

clam catcher *n, usu cap both Cs* [5*clam*] : NEW JERSEYITE — used as a nickname

1**clame** \ˈklām\ *var of* 3CLAM

2**clame** \ˈ"\ *var of* CLEAM

clam·e·hew·it \ˌklaməˈh(y)üət\ *n* -s [origin unknown] *Scot* : BLOW, DRUBBING

clamflat \ˈ=ˌ=\ *n* [5*clam* + *flat*] : a flat often muddy tidal area where clams are abundant

clam·jam·fry *or* **clam·jam·fery** \klamˈjamfri\ *n, pl* **clamjamfrys** *or* **clamjamfries** *or* **clamjamfreys** [perh. fr. obs. *clam* base, mean + Sc *jamph* to sneer, scoff + E *-ry*] **1** *chiefly Scot* : RABBLE, MOB **2** *chiefly Scot* : ODDS AND ENDS, RUBBISH

clammed *past of* CLAM

1**clam·mer** \ˈklamə(r), -aam-\ *n* -s [6*clam* + *-er*] : one that digs, dredges, tongs, or rakes for clams

2**clammer** \ˈ"\ *n* -s [2*clam* + *-er*] : 4CLAMPER

clam·mer·some \ˈklamə(r)səm\ *var of* CLAMOURSOME

clam·mi·ly \-məlē, -li\ *adv* : in a clammy manner

clam·mi·ness \-mēnəs, -min-\ *n* -ES : the quality or state of being clammy

clamming *n* -s [fr. gerund of 6*clam*] : the harvesting of clams ⟨the ~ industry⟩

clammish *adj* [4*clam* + *-ish*] *obs* : CLAMMY

clam·my \ˈklamē, -mi\ *adj* -ER/-EST [ME, prob. fr. *clammen*, *clemen* to stick + *-y* — more at CLAM] **1 a** (1) : moist and sticky ⟨~ flesh⟩ ⟨a plant with a ~ stem⟩ (2) : drearily sticky and wet ⟨a ~ and intensely cold mist —Charles Dickens⟩ **b** (1) : damp and cold ⟨~ air⟩ : suffused or covered with a cool sticky dampness ⟨a ~ uniform⟩ (2) : unpleasantly sticky and cold ⟨the ~ moisture of the Burma night —Ed Cunningham⟩ **2 a** (1) : lacking normal human warmth ⟨~ statistics⟩ ⟨the ~ atmosphere of an institution⟩ (2) : unnaturally or perversely cold : OFFISH ⟨that American captain was a bit on the ~ side —Bennett Cerf⟩ **b** : unpleasantly or uncomfortably sickly, furtive, or aberrant : UNNATURAL ⟨a rather ~ sense of humor⟩ ⟨~ fear that once held the country in its grip —H.H.Martin⟩

clammy azalea *also* **clammy honeysuckle** *n* : SWAMP AZALEA

clammy cherry *n* : a tall West Indian tree (*Cordia collococca*) with soft wood and cherrylike fruit

clammy chickweed *n* **1** : MOUSE-EAR CHICKWEED **2** : a fleshy-leaved stitchwort (*Stellaria crassifolia*) of the western U.S.

clammy cuphea *n* : WAXWEED

clammy everlasting *n* : an aromatic silvery herb (*Gnaphalium macounii*) of Canada and the U.S.

clammy locust *n* : a small rough-barked locust (*Robinia viscosa*) native to the southeastern U.S. and cultivated elsewhere and having glandular twigs and racemes of pale pink flowers

clammy sage *n* : 2CLARY

clammyweed \ˈ=ˌ=ˌ=\ *n* : any of several plants of the genus *Polanisia*; *esp* : a strong-scented herb (*P. graveolens*) having glandular-pubescent foliage and being common in the western U.S.

1**clam·or** \ˈklamə(r)\ *n* -s *see -or in Explan Notes* [ME, fr. MF *clamur, clamour*, fr. L *clamor*, fr. *clamare* to cry out — more at CLAIM] **1 a** : the loud and continued uproar of many human voices : HUBBUB, RUMPUS ⟨the ~ of children at play⟩ **b** : a loud continued and usu. confused noise (as of animals, birds, musical instruments, or a storm) : TUMULT, DIN ⟨finches and flickers . . . gave out a dissonant and reedy ~ —Jean Stafford⟩ ⟨the even ~ of a waterfall⟩ **2** : a loud and insistent expression (as of dissatisfaction, support, indignation) : popular outcry ⟨~ against exorbitant taxes⟩ ⟨~ for home rule⟩

2**clamor** \ˈ"\ *vb* **clamored; clamored; clamoring** \-m(ə)riŋ\ **clamors** *see -or in Explan Notes, vi* **1** : to make a din : utter loud, mixed, and confused outcries or sounds ⟨a ~*ing* group whose voices were like the squalling of gulls —Kenneth Roberts⟩ **2** : to appeal, demand, or protest by sustained noisy outcry ⟨threatening him with impeachment . . . and ~*ing* for the suppression of his command —J.A.Froude⟩ ⟨he can borrow no more, and his debtors are ~*ing* —Gertrude Atherton⟩ ~ *vt* **1** : to utter or proclaim insistently and noisily ⟨~*ed* their piteous prayer incessantly —H.W.Longfellow⟩ **2** : to reduce to a certain condition or to effect a certain objective from by means of clamor **syn** see ROAR

3**clamor** *vt* -ED/-ING/-S *see -or in Explan Notes* [prob. fr. 2*clam* + *-or*] *obs* : to put an end to the noise of : SILENCE ⟨~ your tongues, and not a word more —Shak.⟩

clam·or·ous \ˈklam(ə)rəs\ *adj* [1*clamor* + *-ous*] **1 a** : marked by din or outcry ⟨the ~ streets⟩ : NOISY, TUMULTUOUS ⟨our theater has to be brassier, more ~ and more audacious —Brooks Atkinson⟩ **b** : RESONANT, VIBRANT ⟨iron is strong and heavy, ~ when struck —D.C.Peattie⟩ ⟨tales . . . ~ with the surge of Antarctic seas —Clifton Fadiman⟩ **2 a** : crying out ⟨we'll be ~ for something to do —Jack London⟩ : IMPORTUNATE, PRESSING ⟨~ demands⟩ ⟨hounded by ~ bill collectors⟩ **b** : DEMONSTRATIVE, EFFUSIVE ⟨the death penalty will seem . . . an anachronism . . . mocking . . . our ~ professions of the sanctity of life —B.N.Cardozo⟩ **syn** see VOCIFEROUS

clam·or·ous·ly *adv* : in a clamorous manner

clam·or·ous·ness *n* -ES : the quality or state of being clamorous

clam·our·some \ˈklamə(r)səm\ *adj* [*clamour, clammer* (vars. of 1*clamor*) + *-some*] *dial chiefly Brit* : CLAMOROUS

1**clamp** \ˈklamp, -aa(ə)mp, -aimp\ *n* -s [ME, prob. fr. (assumed) MD *klampe* (whence D *klamp*); akin to OHG *klampfer* clamp, ON *kleppr* lump, OE *clamm* bond, fetter — more at CLAM] **1 a** : a device (as a band or brace) designed to bind or constrict or to press two or more parts together so as to hold them firmly in their relative position **b** : any of various instruments or appliances having parts brought together (as by a screw) for holding or compressing something: as (1) : an instrument used to hold, compress, or crush vessels and hollow organs and to aid in surgical excision of parts (2) : one of a pair of false jaws **2** *obs* : CLAM, MOLLUSK **3** *also* **clamp strake** : a structural member of a ship running inside the frames from the stempost to the transom or sternpost and fastened to the frames and deck beams or shelf and serving to increase longitudinal stiffness of the hull — see SHIP illustration **4 a** : STOP, OBSTACLE ⟨a ~ on debate⟩ **b** : HOLD, GRIP ⟨takes a firm ~ on the reader's imagination —Martin Levin⟩

2**clamp** \ˈ"\ *vt* -ED/-ING/-S **1 a** : to fasten or press with or as if with a clamp ⟨~ two boards together⟩ ⟨a pipe ~*ed* between his teeth⟩ **b** : to grasp firmly : HOLD ⟨the ground was ~*ed* by winter —A.J.Cronin⟩ **2** : to force or impress authoritatively — often used with *on* or *upon* ⟨~*ed* a censorship on the news of his defeat —*Nation*⟩ ⟨controls were ~*ed* on bank lending —E.L.Dale⟩

3**clamp** \ˈ"\ *n* -s [prob. fr. D *klamp* heap; akin to OE *clympre* lump of metal — more at CLUMP] : a compact pile or heaped-up mass of materials: as **a** : a number of bricks piled up in a particular form for burning **b** *Brit* : a heap of produce covered over usu. with straw or earth to prevent freezing

4**clamp** \ˈ"\ *vt* -ED/-ING/-S *Brit* : to heap or stack (as bricks or root crops) in a clamp

5**clamp** \ˈ"\ *n* -s [imit.] : 1CLUMP 4

6**clamp** \ˈ"\ *vi* -ED/-ING/-S : 2CLUMP 1

clamp connection *or* **clamp cell** *also* **clamp** *n* : a bulgelike hyphal outgrowth in many basidiomycetous fungi that is formed at cell division over the cross wall between the two daughter cells and provides a connection through which one of the involved nuclei may pass in order to maintain the binucleate state of the resulting cells — called also *buckle*

clamp down *vb* [*²clamp*] *vt* **1 :** to clean (the deck of a boat) by spraying with water and swabbing down **2 :** to impose (as a curfew, blackout, censorship) esp. in a sudden, arbitrary, or violent manner ⟨the police *clamped down* a deadline after which all slot machines were to disappear⟩ ~ *vi* **:** to become suddenly or violently repressive, dire, or dictatorial ⟨a military adventurer took over control of a free people and then *clamped down* —*New Yorker*⟩ — usu. used with *on* ⟨the government was *clamping down* on Moslem activities —*N.Y. Times*⟩

clampdown \'=,=\ *n* -s [*clamp down*] **:** the act or action of making regulations and restrictions more stringent or infractions thereof liable to greater punishment **:** CRACKDOWN ⟨a ~ on charge accounts, bank loans, and other inflationary influences —*Time*⟩

¹clamp·er \'klampə(r)\ *vt* -ED/-ING/-S [freq. of *²clamp*] *now chiefly Scot* **:** to patch together esp. clumsily or hastily ⟨I can ~ up the story —J.G.Lockhart⟩

²clamper \"\ *n* -s *now chiefly Scot* **:** a patched-together argument or charge ⟨his defense was a mere ~⟩

³clamp·er \'klampə(r), -laam-\ *n* -s [*²clamp* + *-er*] **:** CREEPER 5a

⁴clamper \"\ *n* -s [*¹clamp* + *-er*] **:** a skilled workman who operates a special rotary press that transfers an engraved design from one small steel roller to another in raised form so that it can later be impressed in a large copper roller for printing cloth — called also *clammer*

clamping *pres part of* CLAMP

clamping circuit *n* **:** a device that maintains at a constant value the positive or the negative extreme of voltage in an alternating-current circuit

clamps *pl of* CLAMP, *pres 3d sing of* CLAMP

clamp screw *or* **clamping screw** *n* **:** a screw used to hold some part tightly in place by forcing it against an immovable part (as one used to secure a drill or other tool in a simple chuck) — compare SETSCREW

clamp strake *n* **:** CLAMP 3

clams *pl of* CLAM, *pres 3d sing of* CLAM

clamshell \'=,=\ *n* [*⁵clam* + *shell*] **1 :** the shell of a clam **2 :** an object or esp. a piece of equipment or apparatus resembling or having a part that resembles a clam or the valves of a clam (as in mechanical operation): as **a :** a bucket or grapple (as on a crane, dredge, or shovel) having two hinged jaws — called also *grab bucket* **b :** either of a pair of doors in the nose or tail of an airplane that open outward and away from each other when loading or unloading ⟨~ cargo doors⟩

clam up *vi* [*⁵clam*] *slang* **:** to become silent ⟨the people on the porches all *clammed up* and watched him go by —R.O. Bowen⟩; *esp* **:** to refuse further talk or divulging of information ⟨news sources suddenly seemed to be *clamming up* all over town —*Newsweek*⟩

clam worm *n* [*⁵clam*] **:** any of several large burrowing polychaete worms often used as bait and usu. of the genus *Nereis*

¹clan \'klan, -aa(ə)n\ *n* -s [ME, fr. ScGael *clann* offspring, clan, akin to OIr *cland* plant, offspring, fr. L *planta* sprout, cutting — more at PLANT] **1 :** a social unit smaller than a tribe and larger than the family and claiming descent from a common ancestor: **a :** a Celtic group esp. in the Scottish Highlands comprising a number of households the heads of which claim descent from a common ancestor, bear a common surname, and acknowledge the preeminence of a chief who bears a distinctive title — compare SEPT, TARTAN **b :** an exogamous tribal division that traces descent in either the male or the female line from a common real, totemic, or mythological ancestor, that has a common name and often a common territory, and that constitutes the chief political, religious, and social unit of tribal society — used by some ethnologists of such a tribal division tracing descent in the female line only; compare GENS, MOIETY, PHRATRY **2 :** a group united by a common trait, qualification, or program and often appearing self-interested, overexclusive, or narrow ⟨a whole ~ of cousins, aunts, uncles, and in-laws⟩ ⟨a ~ of poets⟩ **3 a :** a collection of animals, plants, or inanimate things **b :** a minute ecological community being typically a climax formation covering an area of a few square yards and having a single dominant species

²clan \"\ *vi* **clanned; clanned; clanning; clans :** to unite in or as if in a clan **:** form a clique **:** GATHER — used esp. with *together* ⟨the whole family used to ~ together at Christmas⟩

clancular *adj* [L *clancularius*, fr. *clanculum* secretly, fr. *clam*] *obs* **:** secret and often underhanded **:** CLANDESTINE ⟨the ~ whispering of temptation⟩ — **clancularly** *adv, obs*

clan·des·tine \klan'destən, klaan-\ *adj* [MF or L; MF *clandestin*, fr. L *clandestinus*, fr. (assumed) L *clamde* secretly (fr. L *clam* secretly) + L *-stinus* (as in *intestinus* internal); akin to L *celare* to hide — more at HELL, INTESTINE] **:** marked by, held in, or conducted with secrecy and concealment **:** not openly avowed or generally known **:** given to wary concealment ⟨a ~ love affair⟩ ⟨to elude the vigilance of church and state . . . a number of Tolstoy's pamphlets were printed by a ~ press —*New Republic*⟩ **syn** see SECRET

clandestine evolution *n* **:** evolutionary change affecting only developmental stages of an organism and not readily detectable in the mature organism or phylogenetically effective

clan·des·tine·ly *adv* **:** in a clandestine manner

clan·des·tine·ness \-ən(n)əs\ *n* -ES **:** the quality or state of being clandestine

clan·des·tin·i·ty \,kla(a)n,de'stinəd·ē\ *n* -ES [perh. fr. F *clandestinité*, fr. *clandestin* + *-ité* -ity] **:** the quality or state of being secret esp. in political or social activities normally overt, manifest, or apparent

¹clang \'klaŋ, -aiŋ\ *now dial past of* CLING

²clang \"\ *vb* -ED/-ING/-S [L *clangere* to sound (as of a trumpet), scream (as an eagle); akin to Gk *klazein* to scream, bark, roar, Lith *klagėti* to cackle, cluck, and OE *hlōwan* to moo — more at LOW] *vi* **1 a :** to make a loud resounding sound like that of a trumpet or esp. like pieces of metal struck together ⟨~*ing* anvils⟩ ⟨every steeple . . . began to ~ joyfully —Dorothy C. Fisher⟩ **b :** to proceed or function in such a way as to produce a loud resounding noise ⟨a cable car ~*ed* up the hill —J.B.Clayton⟩ ⟨the convoy . . . ~*ed* over cobblestones —Earle Birney⟩ **2** *of a bird* **:** to produce a harsh cry or scream ⟨wedges of ~*ing* geese —*Nature Mag.*⟩ ⟨a stream of ducks flowed ~*ing* by —Eileen Duggan⟩ ~ *vt* **:** to produce a resonant noise with or on **:** RING ⟨~ a bell⟩ ⟨the gates of the elevator are ~*ed* in his face —Rebecca West⟩

³clang \"\ *n* -s **:** a loud resounding sound or noise like that made by a trumpet or esp. by metal objects struck together **:** RING ⟨the ~ of a gong⟩ ⟨the ~ and bang of a boiler factory —*Lamp*⟩; *specif* **:** the resonant cry of a bird (as a crane or goose)

clang association *n* **:** association through the sound and not the meaning of words (as in psychological word-association tests)

¹clang·or \'klaŋə(r), -aiŋ- *sometimes* -ŋgə-\ *n* -s *see -or in Explan Notes* [L, noise, sound, clang, fr. *clangere* to clang — more at CLANG] **:** a loud deeply resounding sound like that made by a trumpet or esp. by metal objects struck together ⟨the ~ of hammers⟩ or a loud medley of such sound ⟨the ~ of battle⟩

²clangor \"\ *vi* **clangored; clangored; clangoring** \-ŋ(ə)riŋ *sometimes* -ŋg(ə)r-\ **clangors** *see -or in Explan Notes* **:** to make a clanging noise ⟨the long train . . . ~*ed* through the night —J.W.Vandercook⟩

clang·or·ous \-ŋərəs *sometimes* -ŋgə-\ *adj* **:** noisy and resounding ⟨~ locomotive works —C.V.Hancock⟩ **:** filled with usu. confused noise ⟨jammed streets and ~ air —R.H.Rovere⟩ — **clang·or·ous·ly** *adv*

clang tint *n* [part trans. of G *klangfarbe*, fr. *klang* noise, sound (fr. OHG *klanc*) + *farbe* color] **:** the quality of a complex sound **:** TIMBRE

clan·gu·la \'klaŋgyələ\ *n, cap* [NL, fr. Gk *klangē* scream + NL *-ula*; akin to L *clangere* to scream — more at CLANG] **:** a genus containing such ducks as the old-squaw and formerly also the goldeneye

clan·jam·frey \klan'j-\ *var of* CLAMJAMFRY

¹clank \'klaŋk, -aiŋk\ *vb* -ED/-ING/-S [prob. imit.] *vi* **1 :** to make a sharp abrupt ringing sound like a piece of heavy metal striking a hard surface ⟨the prison gate ~*ed* shut⟩ or series of such sounds ⟨the steam radiators . . . ~*ed* and spewed —Robert Hazel⟩ **2 :** to proceed or function with a sharp abrupt ringing sound or series of such sounds ⟨armored cars ~*ed* through the streets⟩ ~ *vt* **1 :** to put or set with a sharp abrupt ringing sound or series of such sounds ⟨~ a pail down⟩ **2 :** to cause to make a sharp abrupt ringing sound or series of such sounds ⟨~ chains⟩

²clank \"\ *n* -s **:** a sharp abrupt ringing sound like a piece of heavy metal striking a hard surface ⟨the hammer fell with a ~⟩

clank·ety-clank \;kla(i)ŋkəd·ē;kla(i)ŋk\ *n* [redupl. of *²clank*] **:** sharp successive often metallic and ringing noises ⟨the *clankety-clank* of a windlass hoisting anchor⟩

clank·ing·ly *adv* **:** in a clanking manner

clan·less \'klanləs, -aa(ə)n-\ *adj* **:** being without a clan

clanned *past of* CLAN

clanning *pres part of* CLAN

clan·nish \'klanish, -aan-, -nēsh\ *adj* **1** *archaic* **:** of or relating to a clan ⟨~ ceremonies⟩ **2 :** characteristic or suggestive of clan psychology or organization ⟨~ loyalty⟩; *specif* **:** tending to associate only with others of like origins, sympathies, and prejudices ⟨~ immigrants⟩ ⟨~ party members⟩ — **clan·nish·ness** *n* -ES

clans *pl of* CLAN, *pres 3d sing of* CLAN

clan·ship \-n,ship\ *n* -s **1 a :** the clan system ⟨the ~ of the Highlands⟩ **b :** the state of belonging to a clan ⟨to reckon ~ by matrilineal descent⟩ **2 :** a tendency to stick together **:** clannish spirit ⟨the ~ of mountain climbers⟩

clans·man \'klanzmən, -laanz-\ *n, pl* **clansmen :** one belonging to a clan or clanlike group

clan·wil·liam cedar \(')klan;wilyəm-\ *n, usu cap 1st C* [fr. *Clanwilliam*, town in western Cape Province, Union of South Africa] **:** a southern African evergreen tree (*Callitris arborea*) yielding timber and gum

cla·o·sau·rus \,klāə'sórəs\ *n, cap* [NL, fr. *clao-* (fr. Gk *klan* to break off, as shoots of a vine) + *-saurus* — more at GLADIATOR] **:** a genus of dinosaurs (suborder Ornithopoda) from the Upper Cretaceous of No. America — compare IGUANODON

¹clap \'klap\ *vb* **clapped** *also* **clapt; clapped** *also* **clapt; clapping; claps** [ME *clappen, cleppen*, fr. OE *clappian, clæppan* to clap, beat, throb; akin to OHG *klaphōn* to beat, ON *klappa*, L *glēba* clod — more at CLIP] *vt* **1 a :** to strike together (as two flat hard surfaces) so as to produce a sharp percussive noise or series of such noises ⟨*clapped* his head on a rafter⟩ ⟨~ shut a book⟩ ⟨~ a stick along a picket fence⟩ **b** *of a bird* **:** to beat (the wings) so as to strike each other, the sides, or the air noisily **2 a :** to beat (one's hands usu. flat or slightly cupped palm against palm) together repeatedly so as to produce a series of sharp percussive noises ⟨the children *clapped* hands as they danced⟩ often as a sign of pleasure or approval ⟨the curtain went up and everyone *clapped* hands⟩ **b :** to show pleasure at or approval of (as a performer or performance) by making such noises esp. with one's hands **:** APPLAUD ⟨they *clapped* the speaker⟩ **3 a** (1) **:** to strike with the flat of the hand and often as a gesture of friendship or encouragement ⟨*clapped* his friend on the back⟩ (2) *dial Brit* **:** to pat endearingly **:** STROKE, CARESS **b** (1) *obs* **:** to strike (hands) with someone as a sign of closing a bargain (2) *obs* **:** PLEDGE ⟨ere I could make thee open thy white hand and ~ thyself my love —Shak.⟩ **4 :** to strike (as bread dough or laundry) with a flat surface esp. to smooth or flatten **5 a :** to place, put, or set esp. with haste or energy ⟨*clapped* a piece of candy into his mouth⟩ ⟨~ him into jail⟩ ⟨~ eyes on a person⟩ ⟨~ an awning up⟩ **b :** to put on and fasten securely ⟨~ a muzzle on a dog⟩ **6 :** to make, contrive, or provide in a hasty or botched-up manner — used with *together* or *up* ⟨they *clapped* the house together⟩ ⟨~ up a conspiracy⟩ **7 :** to lay or apply (as a legal action or writ) — often used with *on* or *upon* ⟨~ an attachment on a person's house⟩ ~ *vi* **1 :** to produce a percussive or explosive noise or series of such noises ⟨the loose shutters *clapped* against the house⟩ ⟨the thunder *clapped* against the valley walls⟩ **2 :** to close noisily **:** SLAM ⟨the windows *clapped* shut⟩ ⟨the doors *clapped to*⟩ **3 :** to talk noisily **:** chatter on **:** PRATE ⟨her tongue could ~ until midnight⟩ **4 :** to begin, move, or act briskly or energetically ⟨~ into a song⟩ ⟨his hand *clapped* over my mouth⟩; *specif* **:** to rush precipitously **:** throw oneself **:** POUNCE ⟨he *clapped* out the door after the thief⟩ **5 :** to produce a series of sharp percussive noises by clapping the hands esp. as a sign of pleasure or approval ⟨the curtain rose and the audience *clapped*⟩ **6** *dial Brit* **:** to sit down abruptly ⟨~ down in a chair⟩ **:** crouch suddenly

²clap \"\ *n* -s [ME *clappe, cleppe*, prob. fr. ME *clappen, cleppen*, v.] **1 :** a device (as the clapper of a mill) that makes a clapping noise **2** *obs* **:** the human tongue **3** *obs* **:** a sudden stroke or turn of fortune, esp. ill fortune **4 :** a loud percussive or explosive noise: as **a** *obs* **:** the report of a gun ⟨the ~ of a musket⟩ **b :** a sudden crash of thunder **5 a :** a sudden sometimes resounding blow or stroke ⟨the guard gave him a ~ in the ribs with his stick⟩ or series of such blows or strokes ⟨the flock rose with a great ~ of wings⟩ **b :** a blow (as with the flat of the hand) given as a gesture of encouragement or friendship ⟨he gave his pal a ~ on the back⟩ **6 :** the lower part of the beak of a hawk **7 :** the noise made by clapping the hands ⟨the ~ and cry of children at play⟩ or esp. by clapping one's hands as a token of pleasure or approval ⟨the audience gave him a good ~⟩ — **at a clap :** at once **:** TOGETHER — **in a clap :** in a moment **:** IMMEDIATELY

³clap \"\ *n* -s [MF *clapoir* bubo, prob. fr. *clapoire, clapier* rabbit warren, house of prostitution, fr. OProv *clapier* rabbit warren, heap of stones] **1 :** GONORRHEA — often used with *the* **2 a :** a swelling in the legs of horses caused by a disease **b :** the disease producing such a swelling **3 :** bovine mastitis

⁴clap \"\ *vt* **clapped; clapped; clapping; claps :** to infect with gonorrhea — sometimes used with *up*

¹clap·board \'klabə(r)d; 'kla,bōrd, 'klap,bōrd, -ōrd,-ōəd, -ò(ə)d\ *n* -s [part trans. of D *klaphout* stave wood, fr. MD *clapholt*, prob. fr. *clappen* to clap, hit + *holt* wood; akin to OE *clæppan* to throb and to OE *holt* wood — more at CLAP, HOLT] **1** *archaic* **:** a size of board esp. of split oak used for making staves and wainscoting **2 :** a narrow board that is usu. thicker at one edge than the other and is used for weatherboarding outside walls ⟨a ~ house⟩ **3 :** material for clapboards; *collectively* **:** CLAPBOARDS

²clapboard \"\ *vt* -ED/-ING/-S **:** to cover (as an outside wall) with clapboards ⟨the house was ~*ed* and then painted white⟩

clap·bread \'klap,bred\ *n* [*¹clap* + *bread*] *dial Eng* **:** oatmeal cake clapped or patted out thin and baked

clapdish \'=,=\ *n* [*²clap* "lid" + *dish*] **:** a wooden dish once carried by alms seekers having a lid that could be clapped to attract attention and also, if carried by a leper, to warn of approach

cla·pey·ron equation \'klapā,rōn-, -rän-\ *or* **clapeyron's equation** *n, usu cap C* [after B.P.E. *Clapeyron* †1864 Fr. physicist] **:** an equation relating to change of phase in a pure substance (as vaporization of a liquid) that gives the rate of change with temperature of the pressure at equilibrium between the phases in terms of the heat of transition and the volumes of the phases before and after the transition — compare CLAUSIUS-CLAPEYRON EQUATION

clap-in-clap-out \'=='=\ *n* -s **:** a parlor game in which a player who has been sent from the room returns and tries to guess which of the other players has chosen him for a partner, the other players clapping when his guess is right

clapmatch *var of* KLAPMATCH

clapnest \'=,=\ *n* [*¹clap* + *nest*] **:** a net or other enclosure designed to be dropped over a nest or pool for the capture of ground-nesting or water birds

clapnet \'=,=\ *n* [*¹clap* + *net*] **:** a net made to close or clap together suddenly for capturing birds

clapped *past of* CLAP

¹clap·per \'klapə(r)\ *n* -s [ME *clapper, clepper*, fr. *clappen, cleppen* to clap + *-er*] **1 a** (1) **:** a mendicant's noisemaking device (as the lid of a clapdish or a leper's rattle) (2) **:** a wooden rattle used in some Christian churches instead of a bell on the last three days of Holy Week **b** *Brit* **:** a rattle used to frighten away birds **c** (1) **:** a noisemaker having a metal plate and two balls on flexible wires attached to a stick (2) **:** one of a pair of flat sticks held between the fingers and clapped usu. rhythmically **:** KNACKER — usu. used in pl. **2 a** (1) **:** the tongue of a bell — see BELL illustration (2) *slang* **:** the tongue of a talkative person **b :** the piece of wood or metal that strikes a mill hopper so as to cause the grain to pass down **:** CLAP **3 :** a piece of board with a handle for dressing and flattening newly molded bricks

clapper 1a(2)

²clapper \"\ *vt* **clappered; clappered; clappering** \-p(ə)riŋ\ **clappers :** to ring (a bell) by moving the clapper

clapper boards *n pl* **:** a pair of boards hinged at one end and banged together in front of a motion-picture camera before or after a take to facilitate synchronization of sound and picture prints

clapper box *n* **:** a hinged part on the toolhead of a reciprocating machine (as a planer or shaper) that permits the tool to clear the workpiece on the return stroke

clapper boy *n* **:** a member of a motion-picture camera crew who works the clapper boards and holds the slate up to be photographed

clapperclaw \'=,=,=\ *vt* [perh. fr. *¹clapper* + *claw* (v.)] **1** *now dial chiefly Eng* **:** to thrash or abuse clumsily by or as if by striking with the hand and clawing with the nails **2** *dial Eng* **:** to abuse with scolding **:** REVILE

clap·per·dud·geon \'klapə(r),dəjən\ *n* -s [perh. fr. *¹clapper* + *dudgeon* (dagger)] **:** BEGGAR

clapper rail *n* [*¹clapper* + *rail*] **:** any of several large long-billed New World rails; *specif* **:** a dull-plumaged form (*Rallus longirostris*) common on salt marshes of the Atlantic coast of the U.S. — see CALIFORNIA CLAPPER RAIL

clapper valve *n* **:** CLACK VALVE

clapping *pres part of* CLAP

claps *pres 3d sing of* CLAP, *pl of* CLAP

clapstick \'=,=\ *n* **:** CLAPPER BOARDS — often used in pl.

clapt *past of* CLAP

¹claptrap \'=,=\ *n* [*¹clap* + *trap*] **:** literature or other expression that attempts to convince or gain applause, credit, or recognition by the use of cheap, empty, or meretricious means **:** pretentious nonsense **:** TRASH ⟨speeches full of ~⟩ ⟨~ selling as science fiction⟩

²claptrap \"\ *adj* **:** characterized by or suggestive of claptrap esp. in showiness of a cheap nature, spiritual emptiness, or poor technique ⟨~ eloquence⟩ ⟨~ sentiment⟩ ⟨a ~ plot⟩

clap up *vt* **:** to imprison hastily ⟨they *clapped* the smugglers *up* without trial⟩

clapwort \'=,=\ *n* -s [*³clap* + *wort*] **:** SQUAWROOT a

claque \'klak\ *n* -s [F, fr. *claquer* to applaud, fr. *claque* clap; of imit. origin] **1 :** an opera hat with a collapsible crown **:** CRUSH HAT **2 a :** a group hired to applaud at a performance (as an opera, play, recital) in order to promote its success or the success of a performer ⟨the ~ gave her three curtain calls⟩ **b :** a group of often demonstrative or self-seeking supporters or adherents ⟨surrounded by a ~ of fair-weather friends⟩

cla·queur \kla'kər(·)\ *also* **claqu·er** \'klakər\ *n* -s [F *claqueur*, fr. *claquer* + *-eur* -or] **:** a member of a claque

clar *abbr* clarinet

clar·a·bel·la *or* **clar·i·bel·la** \,klarə'belə\ *n* -s [L *clara* (fem. of *clarus* clear) + *bella*, fem. of *bellus* beautiful — more at CLEAR, BEAUTY] **:** an 8-foot organ stop with open wooden pipes — called also *claribel flute*

clar·ain \'kla(a),rān\ *n* -s [F, fr. L *clarus* bright + F *-ain* (as in *fusain, durain*) — more at CLEAR] **:** one of the materials composing the lustrous layers present in some coals — compare DURAIN, FUSAIN, VITRAIN

¹clare \'kla(ə)r, -le(ə)r\ *adj, usu cap* [fr. County *Clare*, Ireland] **:** of or from County Clare, Ireland **:** of the kind or style prevalent in County Clare

²clare *n* -s *usu cap* **:** POOR CLARE

clar·ence \'klarən(t)s\ *n* -s [after the duke of *Clarence*, later William IV of England (†1837)] **:** a closed 4-wheeled carriage with seats for four inside and a seat for the driver outside — called also *growler*

clarence

clar·en·ceux king of arms *also* **clarenceux** *or* **clar·en·cieux king of arms** *or* **clarencieux** \'klarən,sü(·)\ *n, pl* **clarenceux kings of arms** \-,sü-\ *also* **clarenceux** \-,sü(z)\ *or* **clar·encieux kings of arms** \-,sü-\ *or* **clarencieux** \-,sü(z)\ *usu cap C&K&A* [trans. of AF *Roy d'Armes de Clarenceux*, fr. *Clarenceux*, English dukedom, fr. *Clare*, Suffolk, England] **:** an English king of arms having jurisdiction south of the river Trent — compare COLLEGE OF ARMS, GARTER KING OF ARMS, NORROY AND ULSTER KING OF ARMS, NORROY KING OF ARMS

clare-obscure *var of* CLAIR-OBSCURE

clar·et \'klarət *also* -ler- *sometimes* -(,)rā\ *n* -s [ME, fr. MF (*vin*) *claret* clear wine, fr. *vin* wine + *claret* clear, fr. *cler* clear — more at CLEAR] **1 a :** a dry red table wine from the Bordeaux wine district of France **b :** any dry red table wine — often used with a term designating origin ⟨California ~⟩ ⟨New Zealand ~⟩ **2** *slang* **:** BLOOD **3 a** *or* **claret red** *or* **claret brown :** a moderate red that is slightly lighter than cerise, lighter than Harvard crimson (sense 1), very slightly bluer and paler than average strawberry (sense 2a), bluer and lighter than Turkey red, and bluer and stronger than pepper red — called also *Bordeaux* **b** *of textiles* **:** a dark purplish red that is redder and duller than pansy purple

¹cla·re·tian \klə'rēshən, kla(a)'r-\ *adj, usu cap* [Anthony *Claret* (Antonio María *Claret* y Clara) †1870 Spanish priest who founded the order + E *-ian*] **:** of or relating to the Claretians

²claretian \"\ *n* -s *usu cap* **:** a member of the Congregation of the Missionary Sons of the Immaculate Heart of Mary founded in Vich, Spain, in 1849

claret wine *n* [part trans. of MF *vin claret* — more at CLARET] **:** a variable color averaging a dark red that is yellower and slightly duller than average wine, yellower and duller than cranberry, and yellower and less strong than average garnet

clar·ety \'klarəd·ē\ *adj* [*claret* + *-y*] **:** having a color resembling or suggesting the color of claret wine ⟨a *clarety*-complexioned, opinionated country gentleman —P.H.Newby⟩

cla·i·as \kla(a)rēəs\ *n, cap* [NL, modif. of Gk *Klarios*, an epithet of Apollo, lit., of Klaros, fr. *Klaros* city of ancient Greece near Colophon] **:** a genus of large eellike freshwater catfishes of Africa and southern Asia that survive the dry season buried deep in the mud

clar·i·bel flute \'klarə,bel-\ *n* [by alter.] **:** CLARABELLA

clar·i·fi·a·ble \-,fīəbəl — *see* CLARIFY\ *adj* **:** capable of being clarified

cla·rif·i·cant \klə'rifəkənt\ *n* -s [LL *clarificant-, clarificans*, pres. part. of *clarificare*] **:** a clarifying substance **:** CLARIFIER

clar·i·fi·ca·tion \,klarəfə'kāshən *also* ,kler-\ *n* -s [F or LL; F, fr. LL *clarification-, clarificatio* glorification, fr. *clarificatus* (past part. of *clarificare*) + L *-ion-, -io* -ion] **:** the act or process of clarifying

clar·i·fi·er \'=,=,fī(ə)r, -īə\ *n* -s **:** one that clarifies: as **a :** one that filters a substance (as paint, varnish, or wine) to remove impurities **b :** one that purifies oleo stock by straining and skimming it while it is heated in a tank **c :** one that changes the filters that strain cellulose solution before it is spun into rayon yarn or made into transparent wrapping material — called also *filterer*

clar·i·fy \'klarə,fī *also* 'kler-\ *vb* -ED/-ING/-ES [ME *clarifien*, fr. MF *clarifier*, fr. LL *clarificare*, fr. L *clarus* clear + *-i-* + *-ficare* -fy — more at CLEAR] *vt* **1 a** *archaic* **:** to make clear and bright by lightening the darkness and obscurity of ⟨the sun *clarifies* the earth⟩ **b :** to clear (the air or atmosphere) of clouds or fog **c** *obs* **:** GLORIFY, TRANSFIGURE **2 :** to make (a liquid or something liquefied) clear, pure, or pellucid **:** free from unwanted solid matter ⟨~ coffee with eggshells⟩ ⟨~ syrup⟩ ⟨~ sewage⟩ **3 a :** to free (the mind or understanding) of confusion, doubt, or uncertainty ⟨the conference did help to harmonize, as well as ~, the thinking of the leaders of the republics on a number of controversial questions —*Atlantic*⟩ ⟨the cold night air *clarified* his muddled brain⟩ ⟨hoped a long rest would ~ his mind⟩ **b :** to explain clearly **:** make understandable **:** REVEAL, INTERPRET ⟨~ a process by the use of diagrams⟩ **4 :** to make less complex or less ambiguous **:** put in order **:** DEFINE ⟨~ one's life⟩ ⟨~ an issue⟩ ~ *vi* **:** to grow or become clear ⟨waiting for the present muddled diplomatic situation to ~ —*Newsweek*⟩

cla·rin \klə'rēn\ *n* -s [Sp *clarín* trumpet, prob. modif. of F *clairon, claron*] **:** a very long trumpetlike wind instrument used by the aborigines in Mexico

cla·ri·na \klə'rēnə\ *n* -s [G, alter. of It *clarino* trumpet] **:** a wind instrument combining the qualities of oboe and clarinet invented by Heckel in 1891

clar·i·net \ˌklarəˈnet *also* -ler- *sometimes* ˈ==ˌnət; *usu* -d·+V\ *also* **clar·i·o·net** \ˈ=rēəˈne-\ *n* -s [F *clarinette,* prob. fr. It *clarinetto,* dim. of *clarino* trumpet] **1 :** a single-reed wood-wind instrument; *specif* **:** an orchestral and band instrument having a cylindrical tube with moderately flaring end, a chromatic-scale compass of about 3½ octaves upward from about D below middle C, and a strong flexible violinlike tone **2 :** a usu. 8-foot reed organ stop with a clarinetlike tone

clarinet 1

clar·i·net·ist *or* **clar·i·net·tist** \ˌ==ˈned·əst, -etəst\ *n* -s [G *klarinettist,* fr. *klarinette* clarinet (fr. F *clarinette*) + *-ist*] **:** a performer on the clarinet

¹**cla·ri·no** \klə'rē(ˌ)nō\ *n, pl* **clari·ni** \-(ˌ)nē\ *or* **clarinos** [It, trumpet, prob. fr. Sp *clarín*] **1 :** CLARION **2 a :** the trumpet as played in the 17th century in its high range without valves — compare OVERBLOW **b :** the first trumpet part — called also *clarin trumpet* **3 :** the middle register of the clarinet — called also *clarion*

²**clarino** \"\ *n* -s [modif. of Sp *clarín,* lit., trumpet] **:** SOLITAIRE 5b — used esp. of aviary or cage birds kept for their song

¹**clar·i·on** \'klarēən *also* 'kler-\ *n* -s [ME *clarioun,* fr. MF &ML; MF *clairon, claron,* fr. ML *clarion-, clario,* fr. L *clarus*] **1 :** a medieval trumpet; *specif* **:** one capable of melody as distinguished from a field or military trumpet **2 :** the sound of a clarion or a similar sound **3 :** a 4-foot reed organ stop of trumpetlike quality **4 :** CLARINO 3 **5 :** a heraldic bearing somewhat resembling a panpipe and understood to represent an organ — called also *organ rest, rest*

clarion 5

²**clarion** \"\ *vb* -ED/-ING/-s *vi* **:** to give out a clarion sound **:** blow the clarion ~ *vt* **:** to proclaim with or as if with a clarion

³**clarion** \"\ *adj* **:** CLEAR; *esp* **:** brilliantly clear ⟨the clean ~ sky —R.M.Coates⟩

clar·i·ty \'klarəd·ē, -ətē, -i *also* 'kler-\ *n* -ES [ME *clarte, clarite,* fr. MF & L; MF *clarté,* fr. L *claritat-, claritas,* fr. *clarus* + *-itat-, -itas* -ity] **1** *obs* **:** BRILLIANCY, BRIGHTNESS, SPLENDOR, GLORY **2 a :** CLEARNESS ⟨the ~ of the atmosphere⟩ ⟨the ~ of the wine⟩ **:** PELLUCIDNESS **:** distinctness of shape, outline, or sound ⟨the ~ of the drawing⟩ ⟨a great ~ of speech⟩ ⟨~ of tone⟩ **:** degree of flawlessness ⟨the ~ of the diamond⟩ **b :** directness, orderliness, and precision of thought or expression ⟨he relied more on a forceful ~ to convince his readers than on the brilliant and exciting ambiguities of propagandist eloquence —Aldous Huxley⟩

clark \'klärk, -äk\ *now dial var of* CLERK

clark cell *or* **clark standard cell** \"-\ *n, usu cap 1st C* [after Josiah L. *Clark* †1898 Eng. engineer] **:** a voltaic cell in early use as a standard of electromotive force having zinc amalgam and mercury as electrodes and zinc sulfate as electrolyte with an electromotive force at 15° C of 1.4328 volts

clarke·ite \'klär,kīt\ *n* -s [Frank W. *Clarke* †1931 Am. chemist + E *-ite*] **:** a rare dark brown radioactive mineral whose chief constituent is uranium oxide (sp. gr. 6.39)

clarke's column *or* **clarke's nucleus** \'klärks-\ *n, usu cap 1st C* [after Jacob A. L. *Clarke* †1880 Eng. physician] **:** NUCLEUS DORSALIS

clarke's gazelle *n, usu cap C* [perh. after George S. *Clarke,* Baron Sydenham †1933 colonial administrator in Egypt and Sudan] **:** DIBATAG

clarke's spheroid *n, usu cap C* [after Alexander R. *Clarke* †1914 Eng. geodesist] **:** an ideal oblate spheroid generally recognized as representing the figure of the earth at average sea level

clark·ia \'klärkēə\ *n* [NL, fr. William *Clark* †1838 Am. explorer + NL *-ia*] **1** *cap* **:** a small genus of showy annual herbs (family Onagraceae) of the Pacific slope of No. America having petals with a distinct claw and fruit capsulate **2** -s **:** any plant of the genus *Clarkia*

clark nutcracker *or* **clark's nutcracker** *also* **clark's crow** \'klärk(s)-\ *n, usu cap C* [after William *Clark* †1838 Am. explorer] **:** a grayish white bird (*Nucifraga columbiana*) of the family Corvidae of western No. America with black-and-white wings and tail

cla·ro \'klä(ˌ)rō\ *n* -ES [Sp, fr. L *clarus*] **:** a light-colored generally mild cigar

cla·ro·ne \klə'rōnē, -ō(ˌ)nā\ *n, pl* **claro·ni** \-(ˌ)nē\ [It, fr. F *claron, clairon* — more at CLARION] **1 :** BASS CLARINET **2 :** BASSET HORN

clar·sach *or* **clar·seach** *or* **clar·seth** *or* **clar·sech** *or* **clar·sheeh** *or* **clair·schach** \'kla(ə)r,s(h)ak, -är-,-er-,-ār-,-ōi(ə)r-, -ˌs(h)ək\ *n, pl* **clar·saich** \"\ [alter. (influenced by ScGael *clàrsach* & IrGael *cláirseach*) of ME *clareschaw,* modif. of ScGael *clàrsach;* akin to MIr *cláirseach* harp] **:** the ancient small harp of Ireland and Scotland

clarsach or Irish harp of the early 13th century

¹**clart** \'klärt, -ät\ *n* -s [akin to ME *biclarten* to soil] **1** *dial Brit* **:** a clot or daub of mud or other sticky substance **2** *dial Brit* **:** MUD, MIRE — often used in pl. **3** *dial Brit* **:** SLOVEN

²**clart** \"\ *vt* -ED/-ING/-s *dial Brit* **:** to daub or smear esp. with mud or dirt

clarty \-tī\ *adj* -ER/-EST *dial* **:** bedaubed with sticky dirt **:** DIRTY, MUDDY; *also* **:** STICKY, GOOEY

¹**clary** \'kla(a)rē\ *n* -ES [ME *clare, clarrie,* fr. OF *claré,* fr. *clar, cler* clear — more at CLEAR] **:** a beverage consisting of a mixture of wine, honey, and spices strained till clear

²**clary** \"\ *also* **clary sage** *n* -ES [ME *clare, clarie,* fr. MF *sclaree,* fr. ML *sclareia, scarleia*] **:** any of several aromatic herbs of the genus *Salvia* (esp. *S. sclarea*) of southern Europe cultivated esp. in England as a potherb and widely as an ornamental

³**clary** \"\ *n* -ES [by alter. and shortening] *slang* **:** CLARINET

-clase \ˌklās, -āz\ *n comb form* -s [F, fr. Gk *klasis* breaking, fr. *klan* to break — more at GLADIATOR] **:** a mineral having a (specified) kind of cleavage ⟨clino*clase*⟩ ⟨plagio*clase*⟩

¹**clash** \'klash, -aa(ə)sh,-aish\ *vb* -ED/-ING/-ES [imit.] *vi* **1 a :** to make a jarring resounding metallic noise by or as if by striking or ringing ⟨the bells of St. Paul's ~*ed* out —Rose Macaulay⟩ ⟨gears ~*ed* loudly as the truck moved on⟩ **b :** to meet and hit together violently usu. with a metallic noise ⟨the swords ~*ed* together⟩ ⟨the empty oil drums ~*ed* as the truck sped along⟩ **2 :** to meet in opposition, controversy, or variance **:** CONFLICT: **a :** to fight or engage in conflict esp. in sharp skirmish or rough brawl — often used with *with* ⟨the settlers often ~*ed* with the Indians⟩ **b :** to compete sharply **:** be completely and sharply in disagreement, incompatibility, discord, or inconsistency ⟨American and British interests ~*ed* in the fur-producing areas⟩ ⟨colors that ~ badly⟩ ⟨political expediency and the law of morality frequently ~ —V.L.Parrington⟩ **3** *chiefly Scot* **:** GOSSIP ~ *vt* **1 :** to strike together **:** hit, thrust, dash, or hurl against sharply and forcefully typically with a loud ringing noise ⟨dark and passionate shapes . . . ~ their weapons —Norman Douglas⟩ ⟨when two males [wildebeest] are engaged in single combat, they rush together, ~*ing* their horns —James Stevenson-Hamilton⟩ **2** *now dial Brit* **:** DASH, SLAM **syn** see BUMP

²**clash** \"\ *n* -ES **1 :** a loud harsh esp. metallic jangling sound or series of sounds produced esp. by striking or grinding together **:** a noisy collision ⟨the ~ of swords⟩ ⟨a ~ of cymbals⟩ ⟨the ~ of gears⟩ **2 a :** a meeting in conflict or opposition **:** a sharp affray **:** BRAWL, SKIRMISH ⟨the ~*es* of minutemen and British at Lexington and Concord⟩ **b :** a situation sharply marked by disagreement, incompatibility, discord, rivalry, or opposition **:** a sharp usu. jarring or unpleasant contrast ⟨the tragedy of politics is not the ~ of right and wrong but the ~ of one right with another —H.J.Laski⟩ ⟨buildings marked by a ~ of architectural styles⟩ **3** *dial Brit* **:** a quantity or mass esp. of mud or water **4** *dial* **:** NEWS, GOSSIP, SCANDAL — often used in pl. **syn** see IMPACT

clash·ing·ly *adv* **:** in a clashing manner

clashy \-shī\ *adj* -ER/-EST *dial Eng* **:** WET, SHOWERY

-cla·sia \'klāzh(ē)ə\ *n comb form* -s [NL, fr. Gk. *klasis* breaking (fr. *klan* to break) + NL *-ia* — more at GLADIATOR] **:** breaking ⟨arthro*clasia*⟩ **:** breaking up ⟨hemo*clasia*⟩

-cla·sis \kləsəs\ *n comb form, pl* **-cla·ses** \kləˌsēz\ [NL, fr. Gk *klasis*] **:** -CLASIA ⟨dia*clasis*⟩

-cla·site \'klāˌsīt, ˌklə-, -zīt, *usu* -īd· + V\ *n comb form* -s [ISV *-clase* + *-ite;* orig. formed as G *-klasit*] **:** -CLASE

clas·mat·o·cyte \klaz'mad·əˌsīt\ *n* -s [ISV *clasmat-* (fr. Gk *klasmat-, klasma* fragment, fr. *klan* to break) + *-o-* + *-cyte* — more at GLADIATOR] **:** HISTIOCYTE — **clas·mat·o·cyt·ic** \(ˈ)=ˈ==ˈsid·ik\ *adj*

clas·ma·to·sis \ˌklazmə'tōsəs\ *n, pl* **clasmato·ses** \-ōˌsēz\ [NL, fr. Gk *klasmat-, klasma* fragment + NL *-osis*] *biol* **:** fragmentation esp. of cells

¹**clasp** \'klasp, -aa(ə)sp,-aisp,-äsp\ *n* -s [ME *claspe, clapse;* perh. akin to OE *clyppan* to embrace — more at CLIP] **1 a :** a releasable catch for holding together two or more objects (as necktie and shirt) or complementary parts of something (as of a book, necklace, or handbag) **b :** a device designed to encircle a tooth to hold a denture in place **c** *mil* **:** a bar of metal attached across the suspension ribbon of a service medal and inscribed with the name of (1) an action or (2) a country or area — called also respectively *battle clasp, service clasp* **2 a** *obs* **:** TENDRIL **b** *of an insect* **:** TENACULUM 2 **3 :** a holding or enveloping with or as if with the arms or hands **:** EMBRACE, GRIP ⟨the hearty ~ of his hand⟩ ⟨the iron ~ of never-ending cold—Walter O'Meara⟩

²**clasp** \"\ *vb* **clasped** *or archaic* **claspt; clasped** *or archaic* **claspt; clasping; clasps** [ME *claspen, clapsen,* fr. *claspe, clapse,* n.] *vt* **1 a :** to fasten or shut together with or as if with a clasp ⟨a robe ~*ed* with a brooch⟩ **b :** to furnish with a clasp ⟨a ~*ed* binding of a book⟩ **2 :** to surround and hold **:** hold (as a large object) against the body ⟨~*ing* a bulging briefcase⟩ **:** entwine about **:** cling to ⟨~*ing* ivy⟩ **3 a :** to enclose and hold or press with the arms **:** EMBRACE, ENWRAP **b :** to encircle within joined hands usu. with interlocked fingers ⟨her hands ~*ed* round one knee —George Meredith⟩ **4 :** to press (the hands) together esp. with interlocked fingers (as in prayer, grief, supplication, or anxiety) ⟨~*ing* her hands tightly in her lap⟩ **5 :** to seize or hold (another's hand) firmly (as in greeting, show of affection, congratulation, or encouragement) **:** grasp cherishingly or protectively ⟨~*ing* her baby to her bosom⟩ **6 :** to engage in a clasp **:** WRAP — used with *around, round,* or *over* ⟨~*ed* his enormous fingers tight around the chair arm —Kenneth Roberts⟩ ~ *vi* **1 :** CLING, EMBRACE **2** *of lower animals* **:** MATE, COPULATE

clasp·er \-pə(r)\ *n* -s **:** any of various structures modified to assist in copulation (as the gonapophyses of many male insects); *specif* **:** one of a pair of male copulatory organs on the anterior of the pelvic fins of sharks, rays, and chimaeroids

clasping *adj* [fr. pres. part. of ²*clasp*] *of a leaf or petiole* **:** partly or wholly surrounding the stem — compare PERFOLIATE

clasp knife *n* **:** a large pocketknife the blade or blades of which fold or shut into the handle **:** JACKKNIFE; *esp* **:** a large one-bladed folding knife having a catch to hold the blade open rigidly

clasp lock *n* **:** a self-locking spring lock

clasp nail *n* **:** CUT NAIL

clasp nut *n* **:** a split nut arranged so that it grips its mating screw when closed

¹**class** \'klas, -aa(ə)s,-ais,-äs\ *n* -ES *often attrib* [F *classe,* fr. L *classis* class, men called to arms, fleet; akin to L *calare* to call, summon — more at LOW] **1 a :** one group of a usu. society-wide grouping of people according to social status, political or economic similarities, or interests or ways of life in common ⟨the ruling ~⟩ ⟨the upper and lower ~*es*⟩ ⟨the professional ~⟩ ⟨these occupational classes are admittedly not internally homogeneous in respect to such ~ criteria as "income", "prestige" or "social equality" —Louis Schneider⟩ ⟨*class*-conscious behavior⟩ — see CASTE **b :** social rank; *esp* **:** high social rank ⟨a feeling of ~⟩ **c :** an economic or social rank above that of the proletariat ⟨the ~*es* as opposed to the masses⟩ — usu. used in pl. **d :** high quality or outstanding ability **:** METTLE ⟨the actors were adequate but without real ~⟩ **e** *slang* **:** elegance in appearance or outward behavior **:** OSTENTATION — usu. used to express naïve admiration ⟨this hotel certainly has ~⟩ or ironic appraisal; see CLASSY **2 a :** a course of instruction esp. considered apart from other courses ⟨education can no longer be separated into courses or ~*es* in half a dozen main subjects⟩ **b :** a body of students meeting regularly to study the same subject under the guidance of an instructor, to listen to lectures, or to engage in guided discussions or in recitations ⟨a Spanish ~⟩ ⟨a Bible ~⟩ **c :** the period during which such a body meets or the meeting itself **d** *at Brit universities* **:** the final rating achieved by a student reading for Honours ⟨a First-*Class* Honours degree⟩ — distinguished from *pass* **e :** a body of alumni who have graduated or of students who expect to graduate in the same year from the same institution **:** a body of students having similar academic standing ⟨donated by the ~ of 1925⟩ **f :** a church group consisting of approximately 12 members under the direction of a class leader formed for religious study and instruction in early Methodism and continued in some Methodist bodies today **3 a :** a group, set, or kind marked by common attributes or a common attribute ⟨any ~ or description of persons —R.B. Taney⟩ ⟨such contraptions are symbolic of a whole ~ of labor-saving devices —F.L.Allen⟩; *esp* **:** a major category in biological taxonomy ranking above the order, in modern taxonomy falling below the phylum or division and in the Linnaean system being the highest category ⟨the ~ Musci includes all the mosses⟩ **b :** a group, division, distinction, or rating based on quality, degree of competence, or condition ⟨a ~ of travel accommodation⟩ ⟨a ~ A movie⟩ ⟨a ~ B tuberculosis patient⟩ **c :** one of the genders usu. not associated with sex and often greatly exceeding three in number into which nouns are divided in the Bantu languages and some others

syn CATEGORY, GENUS, SPECIES, DENOMINATION, GENRE, PREDICAMENT: these words are herein discussed only in their general, nonspecialized use, and the following comments may be inapplicable to such studies as philosophy and the sciences. CLASS is a very general term for a group including all individuals with a common characteristic ⟨as soon as we employ a name to connote attributes, the things which happen to possess those attributes are constituted ipso facto a *class* —J.S.Mill⟩ CLASS sometimes suggests a value judgment as a basis of classification ⟨Hickey is the first *class* of English memoirists —*Times Lit. Supp.*⟩ ⟨the *class* of nominal Christians for whom there might be a chance —R.M.Lovett⟩ CATEGORY may be interchangeable with CLASS but is sometimes more precise in suggesting classification or grouping on the basis of a certain readily perceived criterion or on a predication, often an explicit one ⟨we cannot approach a work of art with our laws and *categories.* We have to comprehend the artist's own values —Havelock Ellis⟩ ⟨none of the writings of the fathers of the English Church belongs to the *category* of speculative philosophy —T.S.Eliot⟩ GENUS and SPECIES, scientific in their suggestion, may differ in that the first may imply a larger, less specific group, the latter a smaller, more specific one ⟨English society, in other words, is . . . a *species* of a larger cultural *genus* —Morris Watnick⟩ ⟨the word "infringement" is almost never used to describe acts of the *genus,* unfair competition. It is applied only to the *species,* namely trademark misuse —Beverly W. Pattishall⟩ DENOMINATION usu. indicates that the group under consideration has been or may be named explicitly and clearly; it is common in religious use ⟨Methodist, Presbyterian, and other *denominations*⟩ and use with a series of closely related units ⟨*denominations* of currency⟩ GENRE refers to a specific, named type; its use is mainly restricted to literature and art ⟨some of his prose poems, a *genre* . . . which he invented —*Saturday Rev.*⟩ ⟨the larger literary types or *genres,* such as the drama or novel —Max Lerner & Edwin Mims⟩ PREDICAMENT is a rather uncommon synonym for CATEGORY, esp. in situations showing a close Aristotelian connection.

²**class** \"\ *vt* -ED/-ING/-ES **1 :** to divide or distribute into classes **:** CLASSIFY ⟨~ wool by grade and staple⟩ **2 :** to place in a class — often used with *with* or *among* ⟨~*ed* as one of the world's greatest men⟩

class a \(ˈ)=ˈā\ *adj, cap A* **:** FIRST-CLASS

class-angle \ˈ=ˌ==\ *vt* **:** to present or treat (as a news story) in such a way as to point up or emphasize class interests or social conflict

class cleavage *n* **:** the occurrence of a linguistic form in more than one form class (as *one* in "one hat", "if one only knew", "the other one")

class-conscious \ˈ=ˌ==\ *adj* **:** actively aware of one's position or of one's responsibilities or privileges as a member of a particular social or economic class or of one's identity of interest or common status with others of the same class usu. as against other such classes; *esp* **:** actively aware in this way of one's membership in the proletariat — **class consciousness** *n*

class day *n* **:** a day of the commencement season in American universities, colleges, and schools on which the senior class holds exercises usu. consisting of the reading of a class history and poem, or the delivery of a class oration, and other similar observances

classed *past of* CLASS

classed catalog *n* [²*class*] **:** CLASSIFIED CATALOG

class·er \ˈ=ə(r)\ *n* -s **:** one that classifies (as wool, cotton, or tobacco) — called also *grader*

classes *pl of* CLASS *or of* CLASSIS, *pres 3d sing of* CLASS

¹**clas·sic** \'klasik, -aas-, -ēk\ *adj* [F or L; F *classique,* fr. L *classicus* of the classes of the Roman people, of the first class, of the first rank, fr. *classis* class — more at CLASS] **1 a :** of the highest quality or rank **:** having recognized and permanent value **:** of enduring interest and appeal — used esp. of literature, art, and music ⟨his achievement as a writer was that out of his knowledge of common speech he forged a ~ prose⟩ ⟨a ~ quartet for strings⟩ **b :** forming part of the permanent cultural achievement of mankind **:** felt to be among the great works esp. literary and artistic of mankind ⟨the annals of the Jews and the Scots have become a ~ heritage⟩ ⟨the really ~ products of the human imagination endure for all time⟩ **c :** characterized by simple tailored lines correct for a variety of places and occasions and basically in fashion year after year — used of wearing apparel **2 :** ²CLASSICAL 2 **3 a :** ²CLASSICAL 3a, 3b(5), 3c **b** *usu cap* (1) **:** of or belonging to the Hohokam culture of the period A.D. 1150–1400 characterized by polished red pottery, houses having solid walls and contiguous rooms, and artifacts for use rather than ornament (2) **:** of or relating to the culture of the Old Empire period of the Maya **c** *of a postage stamp* **:** obsolete and scarce and having special significance in postal or philatelic history; *esp* **:** dating from mid-19th century when postage stamps first came into use **4 a :** historically memorable ⟨their execution became a ~ national tragedy⟩ **b :** noted because of special literary or historical associations ⟨the ~ districts of London⟩ **c :** well known as customary or traditional ⟨Paris, the ~ refuge of expatriates⟩ **5 :** particularly definitive, reliable, or authoritative — used generally of reference works and scholarly studies ⟨a ~ study of the American Indian⟩ **6 a :** standard or recognized esp. because of great frequency or consistency of occurrence ⟨~ symptoms of pneumonia⟩ ⟨a ~ appeal to patriotism⟩ **b :** typical or regarded as typical **:** ideally illustrative ⟨a ~ instance of guilt by association⟩ ⟨he had the ~ eccentricities of the absent-minded professor⟩ **7 a :** particularly appropriate or effective (to a given end) ⟨his appointment was a ~ answer to many problems⟩ **b :** basic and often traditional to an art or skill ⟨he demonstrated the five ~ passes in bullfighting⟩

²**classic** \"\ *n* -s **1 a :** a work of literature of ancient Greece and Rome **b :** the body of such writings ⟨study of the ~*s* is no longer required for a college degree⟩ — usu. used in pl. and with *the* **c** *archaic* **:** a student of the literature of Greece and Rome **2 a :** a work that is classic ⟨his manual of botany has become a ~ among scientists⟩ **b :** a work esp. of literature, art, or music meriting the highest respect ⟨a ~ of operettas⟩ **c :** the author of any such work ⟨he had already become a ~ many years before his death⟩ **3 :** something regarded as perfect of its kind or fitting to serve as a model ⟨his march through the wilderness of Maine has been regarded as a ~ of perseverance⟩ **4 :** a traditional contest or race having special significance and honorific value ⟨the racing ~ at Churchill Downs⟩ **5 :** a classic article of clothing **6 :** a classic postage stamp

clas·si·cal \-sə̇kəl, -sēk-\ *adj* [NL *classis* + E *-ical*] **:** of or relating to a classis esp. in the Reformed Church or to the system of polity of which it is a part

²**classical** \"\ *adj* [L *classicus* + E *-al*] **1 :** ¹CLASSIC 1a, 1b **2 a :** of or relating to the ancient Greek and Roman world, esp. to its literature, art, architecture, or ideals ⟨the strong influence of ~ civilization upon the western world⟩ **b :** having order, balance, restraint or other qualities felt to derive from or suggest those characteristic of the literature, art, architecture, or ideals of ancient Greece and Rome ⟨a ~ serenity of mood⟩ ⟨a ~ integration of artistic elements⟩ **:** conforming to the models of or the rules derived from or felt to be derived from the Greek and Roman classics; *esp* **:** NEOCLASSIC — compare ROMANTIC **c :** specializing in or devoted to the literature or the languages of ancient Greece and Rome ⟨a ~ scholar⟩ **d :** of or relating to places inhabited by the Greeks and Romans or rendered famous by their deeds, art, or writings ⟨a trip to the ~ islands of the Aegean⟩ **e** (1) **:** appealing to critical interest or developed musical taste or conforming to an established and elaborated form of the art (as the fugue, suite, or sonata) — compare ROMANTIC (2) **:** relating to a musical composition characterized by classicism or to a composer of such music (3) **:** relating to art music or all music other than popular music or music for entertainment **3 a :** regarded as of first historical significance — used of a coherent and authoritative theory, method, or body of ideas commonly after new developments or general change of view have made it less authoritative **b :** of or relating to a form or system felt to be of first significance before modern times: as (1) **:** based on formerly generally accepted concepts in physics, esp. the mechanics of Newton and the electromagnetic theories of Maxwell **:** not involving relativity, wave mechanics, or quantum theory (2) **:** of or relating to the evolutionist school of anthropologists (3) **:** of or relating to the economics doctrines that were developed largely in England by Adam Smith, David Ricardo, T. R. Malthus, and J. S. Mill prior to 1848 and that constituted the first unified explanation of the capitalist system (4) **:** relating to the theory of penal reform mainly associated with the Italian jurist Beccaria (1738–?1794) and notable for its emphasis on deterrence and punishment proportional to the grievousness of the criminal act (5) **:** of, relating to, or felt to suggest traditional ballet (as in formality or grace of movement) **c :** of any form or system felt to be the authentic, authoritative, or time-tested one in comparison with later modified or more radical forms deriving from it ⟨the ~ goals of socialism⟩ ⟨a ~ folk dance⟩ ⟨a ~ golf swing⟩ **d :** ¹CLASSIC 5 ⟨a ~ study of juvenile delinquency⟩ **4 :** ¹CLASSIC 4 **5 :** ¹CLASSIC 6 ⟨the ~ symptoms of alcoholism⟩ **6 :** ¹CLASSIC 7 ⟨the ~ cure for malaria⟩ **7** *of language* **:** conforming to a pattern of usage sanctioned by a body of literature rather than by everyday speech ⟨~ Arabic⟩ **8 :** concerned with or giving instruction in the humanities, the fine arts, and the broad aspects of science ⟨a ~ high school⟩ ⟨a ~ curriculum⟩

classical humanism *n* **:** HUMANISM 1

clas·si·cal·ism \-ˌlizəm\ *n* -s **:** CLASSICISM

clas·si·cal·ist \-ˌləst\ *n* -s **:** CLASSICIST

clas·si·cal·i·ty \ˌ=sə'kaləd·ē, -ətē, -i\ *n* -ES **1 :** the quality or state of being classic (as in literary or artistic style); *also* **:** classical scholarship **2 :** a piece or example of classicality **:** a classical feature

clas·si·cal·ize \ˈ=səkəˌlīz, -sē-\ *vb* -ED/-ING/-s **:** to imitate or cause to imitate Greek or Roman antiquity **:** CLASSICIZE ⟨the names of many towns in New York state were *classicized*⟩

clas·si·cal·ly \-ək(ə)lē, -ēk-, -li\ *adv* **1 :** in a classic or classical manner: as **a :** according to the manner or style of classical authors **b :** in or by the study of the classics **2 :** in a traditionally accepted or prescribed manner **:** TYPICALLY ⟨the experiment as ~ performed⟩

classical suite *n* : a form of instrumental composition prevalent in the 18th century consisting strictly of the allemande, courante, saraband, and gigue often with the interpolation of gavotte, bourrée, minuet, musette, and passepied

clas·si·cism \'⸗sə,sizəm\ *n* -s [¹*classic* + *-ism*] **1 a** : the principles or the style of classical literature, art, or architecture **b** : classical scholarship **2** : an ancient Greek or Roman word or expression esp. in an English context; *also* : a word or expression closely akin to the ancient Greek or Roman form **3** : adherence to or practice of the virtues thought to be characteristic of classical art, literature, and in modern times music or to be universally and enduringly valid (as formal elegance and correctness, simplicity, dignity, restraint, order, proportion) — often opposed to *romanticism*; compare HELLENISM

clas·si·cist \-ˌsəst\ *n* -s [¹*classic* + *-ist*] **1** : an advocate or follower of classical style, rules, or models — often opposed to *romanticist* **2** : one learned in the classics : a classical scholar **3** : an advocate of the school study of the classics

clas·si·cis·tic \ˌ⸗⸗'sistik\ *adj* : adhering to or influenced by classical models or precepts ⟨~ architecture⟩ ⟨~ drama⟩

clas·si·cize \'⸗⸗,sīz\ *vb* -ED/-ING/-S [¹*classic* + *-ize*] *vt* : to make classic or classical ~ *vi* : to follow or affect classic style or form

classico- *comb form* [F, fr. *classique* — more at CLASSIC] **1** : classical : classical and ⟨*classico*-Lombardic⟩ **2** : the classics ⟨*classico*latry⟩

classic pitch *also* **classical pitch** *n* : a tuning standard in use during the latter half of the 18th century of 415 to 429 vibrations per second for A above middle C

classic revival *or* **classical revival** *n, usu cap C&R* : an artistic style inspired by or imitative of classical modes of expression — used esp. of works of art of the 15th and the 19th centuries

classics *pl of* CLASSIC

classier *comparative of* CLASSY

classiest *superlative of* CLASSY

clas·si·fi·a·ble \'klasə,fīəbəl, -laas-\ *adj* : capable of being classified or discriminated

clas·si·fi·ca·tion \ˌ⸗əfə'kāshən, *rap.* -sf-\ *n* -s [prob. fr. F, fr. *classe* class + *-i-* + *-fication*] **1** : the act or a method of classifying : the act or a method of distributing into groups, classes, or families : an assigning to a proper class : SORTING: as **a** : the systematic arrangement or method of arrangement of animals and plants in groups or categories according to a definite plan or in a definite sequence either as in earlier practice by assuming static morphological relationships among the various groups and so producing typically broadly inclusive categories or as in modern practice by recognizing the dynamic evolutionary quality of biologic relationship and with the aid of physiology, ecology, and cytogenetics in analyzing underlying relations producing an ever-increasing subdivision of categories into groups expressive of natural relationships : TAXONOMY — compare CLASS, DIVISION, FAMILY, GENUS, ORDER, PHYLUM, SPECIES; LUMPER, SPLITTER **b** : a system for the arrangement of books or other library material according to subject or form — see DECIMAL CLASSIFICATION, EXPANSIVE CLASSIFICATION, LIBRARY OF CONGRESS CLASSIFICATION, UNIVERSAL DECIMAL CLASSIFICATION **c** : the classifying of ships by a classification society **d** : the arrangement of positions in public service or in an occupational catalog into classes on the basis of duties and qualification requirements **e** : a systematic assignment of prisoners in a penal institution to a program of prison treatment appropriate to their individual needs after study and examination by a staff of specialists — compare INDIVIDUALIZATION **f** : the classifying of esp. documentary information into groupings (in the U.S. usu. designated top secret, secret, and confidential) according to the stringency of the measures to be taken to prevent its falling into the hands of an enemy or potential enemy **g** : the grouping of articles of freight or express into classes for rate-making purposes **2** : the result of classifying : a system of classes or groups or a systematic division of a series of related phenomena; *also* : one of such classes : CATEGORY, RATING **3** : a publication containing for the purpose of tariff assessment a list of articles, the classes to which they are assigned, and the rules and regulations governing the application of class rates

clas·si·fi·ca·tion·ist \-sh(ə)nəst\ *n* -s : one skilled in or primarily interested in classification

classification number *n* : CLASS NUMBER

classification rating *n* : the class to which an article is assigned in the process of making or determining a class rate for freight or express charges

classification society *n* : a society for the promulgation of rules for the construction of vessels, the supervision of such construction, the classification of vessels according to merit, and the publication of a register listing them and classifying their essential features

classification track *n* : any track of a group of railroad tracks in a freight yard used in the separation of cars esp. according to destination or contents and their arrangement in preparation for train movement

classification yard *n* : a railroad yard consisting of classification tracks

clas·si·fi·ca·to·ri·ly \ˌklasəfəkə'tōrəlē, kla'sif-, *esp Brit* 'klasifi,kātərəli\ *adv* : in a manner that accords with the terminology of a classificatory system

clas·si·fi·ca·to·ry \'klasəfəkə,tōrē, kla'sif-, *esp Brit* 'klasifi,kātəri\ *adj* [fr. *classify*, after such pairs as E *justify: justificatory*] **1** : relating to or involving classification : tending or designed to classify : TAXONOMIC **2** *ethnol* **a** : characterized by a small number of kinship terms grouping in one kinship name class not only lineal relatives but also collateral relatives and even individuals having only a remote genetic relationship or none — compare DESCRIPTIVE **b** : included in a name class in a system of this kind

classified *adj* [fr. past part. of *classify*] **1 a** : consisting of classes **b** : divided into classes or placed in a class **2** : forbidden to be disclosed outside a specified ring of secrecy for reasons of national security; *specif* : having a particular security classification

classified advertisement *n* : a single advertisement in a classified advertising section (as of a newspaper) — usu. called *classified ad*

classified advertising *n* : advertisements grouped by subject usu. appearing under categorical headings in a section of a publication given over to such advertisements and consisting chiefly of descriptive listings in text type

classified catalog *n* : a catalog having entries arranged according to subject or class — compare DICTIONARY CATALOG

classified station *n* : a postal station occupying government quarters and operated by government employees — compare CONTRACT STATION

clas·si·fi·er \'klasə,fī(ə)r, -laas-, -īə\ *n* -s [*classify* + ²*-er*] **1** : one that classifies or sorts; *specif* : a machine or device for separating the constituents of a material (as ore, coal, sand) according to relative sizes and densities thus facilitating concentration and treatment **2** : a word or morpheme used with nouns designating countable or measurable objects or with numerals and often indicating a class to which the object designated by the noun is assignable on the basis of shape or function (as Japanese *hon* in *empitsu ni hon* "two pencils", literally, "pencil two cylindrical-object", or Chinese *pen³* in *san¹ pen³ shu¹* "three books", literally, "three origin book") **3** : RADICAL 2c, ²DETERMINATIVE 2

clas·si·fy \-,fī\ *vt* -ED/-ING/-ES [¹*class* + *-ify*] **1** : to group or segregate in classes that have systematic relations usu. founded on common properties or characters : SORT **2** : to put into a class, classification, or category : RATE; *specif* : to assign (as a document) to one of the graded categories of matter restricted for national security

class interval *n, statistics* : an interval setting bounds to a class of a frequency distribution

clas·sis \'klasəs\ *n, pl* **clas·ses** \-a,sēz\ [NL, fr. L, class — more at CLASS] **1** : an ecclesiastical governing body of a district in certain churches of presbyterian polity (as Dutch and German Reformed churches in Europe and America) consisting of the ministers and representative elders of the district **2** : the ecclesiastical district governed by a classis and corresponding to a presbytery

class·less \'klasləs, 'klaa-,'klai-,'klȧ-\ *adj* **1** *of a society* : free from distinctions of social class **2** *of a person* : belonging to no particular social class

class lottery *n* : DUTCH LOTTERY

class mark *n, statistics* : a value represented by the mid-value of a class interval

classmate \'⸗,⸗\ *n* [¹*class* + *mate*] : one belonging to the same class (with another) at school or college

class meaning *n, linguistics* : the meaning common to all forms belonging to the same form class ⟨the words *cars, departures,* and *ideas* as members of the form class of plurals have the *class meaning* "more than one"⟩

class number *or* **class letter** *n* : a number or letter (from a classification scheme) assigned to a book or other library material to show its location on the library shelf

class publication *n* : a publication other than a trade journal designed for a group of readers with a common interest

class rate *n* : the transportation charge applicable to ratings of articles listed in class tariffs of common carriers and distinguished from commodity rates

classroom \'⸗,⸗\ *n, often attrib* : a place for conducting formal instruction of students by a teacher in a school or college

class struggle *or* **class war** *or* **class warfare** *n* : opposition of and contention between social or economic classes; *esp* : such a struggle between or felt to exist between the proletariat and the capitalist classes

class suit *or* **class action** *n, law* : a suit or action by one or more persons for their own benefit and considered to be ultimately for the benefit of all persons who are for the purposes of the suit considered to be in the same class or group (as the taxpayers of a city)

class tariff *n* : a printed schedule of charges and related rules applicable to classes of articles transported by common carrier

classwork \'⸗,⸗\ *n* : the part of a student's work that is done in class : the combined work of a class and teacher ⟨the book would be suitable for ~⟩ ⟨student responsibility is even more important in homeroom activities than it is in ~⟩ — often used in contrast with *homework* or *nonacademic student activity*

classy \'klasē, -aas-, -ais-, -ȧs-, -si\ *adj* -ER/-EST [¹*class* + *-y*] **1** *slang* : of superior type : notably excellent : HIGH-CLASS ⟨~ fielding⟩ ⟨a ~ suburb⟩ **2** *slang* : ostentatiously elegant : SLICK, STYLISH ⟨a ~ dresser⟩

¹-clast \,klast, -aa(ə)st,-aist\ *n comb form* -s [ML *-clastes*, fr. MGk *-klastēs*, fr. Gk *klan* to break — more at GLADIATOR] **1** : one that breaks or destroys ⟨icono*clast*⟩ ⟨biblio*clast*⟩ **2** [G *-klast*, fr. ML *-clastes*] : something that breaks or destroys; *esp* : a tool for breaking ⟨cranio*clast*⟩

²-clast \"\ *n comb form* -s [back-formation fr. ²*-clastic*] : rock composed of fragmental material (of a specified type) ⟨pyro*clast*⟩ ⟨cata*clast*⟩

clas·tic \'klastik, -aas-,-ais-\ *adj* [ISV *clast-* (fr. Gk *klastos* broken, fr. *klan* to break) + *-ic*; orig. formed as G *klastisch* — more at GLADIATOR] **1** : capable of being taken apart — used of anatomical models made of detachable pieces **2** : of, belonging to, or being a rock (as a conglomerate or a sandstone) made up of fragments of preexisting rocks

¹-clastic \ˌ⸗⸗\ *adj comb form* [¹*-clast* + *-ic*] **1 a** : breaking, destroying ⟨icono*clastic*⟩ ⟨mytho*clastic*⟩ **b** : disintegrating ⟨proteo*clastic*⟩ **2** [Gk *klastos* broken (fr. *klan* to break) + E *-ic*] : curved ⟨anti*clastic*⟩

²-clastic \ˌ⸗⸗\ *n comb form* -s : breaker : destroyer ⟨dendro*clastic*⟩ ⟨pan*clastic*⟩

³-clastic \ˌ⸗⸗\ *adj comb form* [ISV *-clast* (fr. Gk *klastos* broken) + *-ic*; orig. formed as G *-klastisch*] : composed of fragmental material (of a specified type) — used in names of rocks ⟨crypto*clastic*⟩ ⟨pyro*clastic*⟩

¹clat \'klat\ *n* -s [perh. var. of ¹*clot*] *dial Brit* : a clot or clod (as of dirt or dung); *also* : a dirty condition : MESS

²clat \"\ *vt* **clatted**; **clatted**; **clatting**; **clats** *dial Brit* : DIRTY, BEDAUB

³clat \"\ *n* -s [short for ²*clatter*] *dial chiefly Eng* : CHATTER, GOSSIP

⁴clat \"\ *vi* **clatted**; **clatted**; **clatting**; **clats** *dial Eng* : CHATTER, GOSSIP, PRATE

clatch \'klach\ *n* -ES [prob. alter. of ¹*clat*] **1** : a clod (as of mud) : DAUB, MESS **2** *Scot* : a sluttish or slipshod woman

clatchy \-chē,-chi\ *adj, Scot* : MUDDY

clath·ra·ce·ae \kla'thrāsē,ē\ *n pl, cap* [NL, fr. *Clathrus*, type genus (fr. L *Clathri* lattice) + *-aceae*] : a family of fleshy fungi (order Phallales) typified by the genus *Clathrus* and distinguished from the true stinkhorns (family Phallaceae) by having the spore-bearing region enclosed or between the arms of the latticed receptacle — **clathraceous** \(')⸗;⸗shəs\ *adj*

clath·rar·ia \kla'thra(a)rēə\ *n, cap* [NL, fr. L *clathri* lattice + NL *-aria*] : a genus of fossil cycadlike plants known only from their tree trunks with clathrate markings — **clath·rar·i·an** \(')⸗;⸗rēən\ *adj*

clath·rate \'kla,thrāt, -,thrət\ *adj* [L *clathratus*, past part. of *clathrare* to furnish with lattice, fr. *clathri* lattice, fr. Gk *klēthra*, pl. of *klēthron, kleithron* bar, fr. *kleiein* to shut — more at CLOSE] **1** *biol* : shaped like a lattice : CANCELLATE **2** : relating to a type of solid molecular compound in which one component (as argon or heptane) is trapped in cavities of cagelike crystals of another component (as hydroquinone or urea)

clath·ri·na \kla'thrīnə, -ēnə\ *n, cap* [NL, fr. L *clathri* lattice + NL *-ina*] : a genus (the type of the family Clathrinidae) of primitive ascon sponges

clath·ro·cys·tis \,klathrō'sistəs\ [NL, fr. *clathro-* (fr. L *clathri* lattice) + *-cystis*] *syn of* POLYCYSTIS

clath·roid \'kla,thrȯid\ *adj* [L *clathri* lattice + E *-oid*] : CLATHRATE

clath·rose \-,thrōs\ *adj* [L *clathri* lattice + E *-ose* — more at CLATHRATE] : marked with latticelike furrows

clath·ru·late \-,thrə,lāt\ *adj* [NL *clathruli* (dim. of L *clathri* lattice) + E *-ate*] : minutely clathrate

clats·ka·nie \'klatskə,nī\ *n, pl* **clatskanie** *or* **clatskanies** *usu cap* **1** : an Athapaskan people of the Chehalis and Clatskanie river valleys, Oregon **2** : a member of the Clatskanie people

clat·sop \'klatsəp\ *n, pl* **clatsop** *or* **clatsops** *usu cap* [modif. of Upper Chinook *tlaak'eelak*, lit., dried salmon] **1 a** : an Indian people of northwestern Oregon **b** : a member of such people **2** : a dialect of Lower Chinook

¹clat·ter \'klad·ə(r), -atə-\ *vb* -ED/-ING/-S [ME *clatren*, fr. (assumed) OE *clatrian*; akin to OE *clatrung* clattering, MD *clāteren* to rattle, Norw *klatra* to beat; of imit. origin] *vi* **1** : to make a loud rattling sound by striking hard bodies together : RATTLE **2** : to move or go rapidly and noisily ⟨~*ing* over the cobblestones⟩ **3 a** : CHATTER, PRATTLE **b** *Scot* : TATTLE, GOSSIP ~ *vt* : to cause to clatter : make a rattling noise with ⟨~*ing* the dishes on the tray⟩

²clatter \"\ *n* -s [ME, noisy talk, fr. *clatren*, v.] **1** : a loud rattling noise esp. when made by the collision of hard bodies : a series of sharp clashes ⟨the ~ of pots and pans⟩ ⟨~ of a typewriter⟩ **2** : COMMOTION, DISTURBANCE ⟨the midday ~ of the business district⟩ **3 a** : rapid, noisy, or idle talk : BABBLE, CHATTER, GABBLE **b** *Scot* : a piece of gossip : TATTLE, RUMOR

clat·ter·ing·ly *adv* [fr. pres. part. of ¹*clatter* + *-ly*] : with clattering

clat·tery \-ərē,-əri\ *adj* [²*clatter* + *-y*] : marked by clatter : CLATTERING, NOISY

clat·ty \'klad·ē\ *adj* [¹*clat* + *-y*] *dial* : DIRTY, SLOVENLY, CLUTTERED

clau·ber \'klȯbər\ *Scot var of* CLABBER

claude lor·raine glass \ˌklȯdlə'rān-, -ōd-, -lȯ'r-\ *or* **claude glass** \'⸗-\ *n, usu cap C&L* [*Claude Lorraine* (earlier E spelling of *Lorrain*) pseudonym of Claude Gellée †1682 Fr. landscape painter; fr. the similarity of the effects it gives to those of a picture by him] : a convex hand mirror of dark or colored glass that reflects an image of diminished size and subdued color

claude process \'klōd-, -ōd-\ *n, usu cap C* [after Georges *Claude b*1870 French chemist and physicist] : a synthetic ammonia process characterized by higher operating pressures than other processes and by the use of a train of converters

clau·de·tite \'klōdə,tīt\ *n* -s [F *claudétite*, fr. F. *Claudet*, 19th cent. Fr. chemist, its discoverer + F *-ite*] : a mineral consisting of a native arsenic trioxide As_2O_3 crystallizing in the monoclinic system — compare ARSENOLITE

clau·di·an \'klȯdēən\ *adj, usu cap* [L *Claudius*, a Roman gens name + E *-an*] : of or relating to any of several celebrated Romans of the name of Claudius or the gentes, one patrician and the other plebeian, to which they belonged; *esp* : of, belonging to, or characteristic of the emperors who belonged to the patrician gens (Tiberius, Caligula, Claudius, and Nero) or their time

clau·di·ca·tion \ˌklȯdə'kāshən\ *n* -s [L *claudication-, claudicatio* (fr. *claudicatus*, past part. of *claudicare* to limp, fr. *claudus* lame) + *-ion-, -io* -ion; akin to L *claudere* to close — more at CLOSE] **1** *med* : LAMENESS, LIMPING **2** : INTERMITTENT CLAUDICATION

¹claught *or* **claucht** *past of* CLEEK

²claught *or* **claucht** \'klȯkt\ *n* -s [¹*claught, claucht*] *Scot* : CLUTCH, GRASP, HANDFUL

claus·al \'klȯzəl\ *adj* [¹*clause* + *-al*] : relating to or of the nature of a clause or clauses

clause \'klȯz\ *n* -s [ME, fr. OF, clause, fr. ML *clausa* close (of a rhetorical period), fr. L, fem. of *clausus*, past part. of *claudere* to close, shut — more at CLOSE] **1** : a short sentence : a distinct section of a discourse or writing; *specif* : a distinct article, stipulation, or proviso in a formal document ⟨the attestation ~ to a will⟩ **2 a** : a group of words containing a finite verb but not constituting a whole sentence either because it functions as a noun (as in "I don't know *how he got there*"), adjective (as in "the account *that he gave was true*"), or adverb (as in "he stopped *when he saw the signal*") in the larger sentence to which it is subordinate or because it contains or is modified by one or more clauses subordinate to it (as in "*I don't know* how he got there") or because it is joined to another clause of equal rank with itself (as the two clauses in "*he stopped the car* and *they got out*") **b** : a group of words containing a nonfinite verb and functioning in its sentence somewhat like a subordinate clause (as in "he saw *the man leave*" and in "*his tire fixed*, the man drove off") — compare PHRASE

clau·se·witz \'klau̇zə,vits\ *n* -ES *usu cap* [after Karl von *Clausewitz* †1831 Prussian army officer and expert on military science] : an expert on military strategy

clau·sil·ia \klȯ'zilēə, -'si-\ *n, cap* [NL, irreg. fr. L *clausus* closed] : the type genus of Clausiliidae comprising a large number of Old World land snails

clau·si·li·i·dae \ˌklȯzə'līə,dē, -ōsə-\ *n pl, cap* [NL, fr. *Clausilia*, type genus + *-idae*] : a family of terrestrial pulmonate snails having a fusiform sinistral spiral shell in which a rodlike clausilium functions as an operculum

clau·sil·i·um \klȯ'zilēəm, -si-\ *n, pl* **clausil·ia** \-lēə\ [NL, irreg. fr. L *clausus* closed + NL *-ium*] : the rodlike closure of the aperture of a mollusk of the family Clausiliidae

clau·si·us–clapeyron equation \ˌklȯzēəs-'klapā,rōn-, -,rän-\ *n, usu cap both Cs* [after Rudolf J. E. *Clausius* †1888 German mathematical physicist and B. P. E. *Clapeyron* †1864 French engineer] : the Clapeyron equation as modified for liquid⸗vapor phases by assuming that the vapor is an ideal gas and that the volume of the liquid phase is negligible in comparison with the volume of the vapor

clausius cycle \'⸗⸗⸗-\ *n, usu cap 1st C* [after Rudolf J. E. *Clausius* †1888 Ger. physicist] : RANKINE CYCLE

claus process \'klau̇s,-\ *n, usu cap C* [after C. F. *Claus fl*1885 Eng. chemist who helped develop it] : a process for converting hydrogen sulfide to elemental sulfur by oxidation with air

claus·thal·ite \'klau̇stə,līt\ *n* -s [F *clausthalie* clausthalite (fr. *Clausthal*, Germany, its locality + F *-ie*) + E *-ite*] : a mineral consisting of lead selenide PbSe and resembling galena in appearance (sp. gr. 7.6–8.8)

claustra *pl of* CLAUSTRUM

claus·tral \'klȯstrəl\ *adj* [ME, fr. ML *claustralis*, fr. LL, of a fortress, fr. L *claustrum* bar, bolt, barricade — more at CLOISTER] : of or belonging to a cloister : like or savoring of the cloister : CLOISTRAL

claustral prior *n* : the coadjutor of an abbot ranking next to him in a monastery

claus·tra·tion \klȯ'strāshən\ *n* -s [prob. fr. F, fr. ML *claustrum* monastery + F *-ation* — more at CLOISTER] : the act of confining in or as if in a cloister

claus·tro·phobe \'klȯstrə,fōb *sometimes* 'klau̇s-\ *n* -s [back⸗formation fr. *claustrophobia*] : one having claustrophobia

claus·tro·pho·bia \ˌ⸗⸗'fōbēə\ *n* -s [NL, fr. *claustro-* (fr. L *claustrum* bar, bolt) + *-phobia*] : abnormal dread of being in closed or narrow spaces — contrasted with *agoraphobia*

claus·tro·pho·bic \ˌ⸗⸗'fōbik, -ēk *also* -äb-\ *or* **claus·tro·pho·bi·ac** \-'fōbē,ak\ *adj* **1** : suffering from or inclined to claustrophobia **2** : inducing or suggesting claustrophobia ⟨the ~ confines of the urban detective novel —*Times Lit. Supp.*⟩

claus·trum \'klȯstrəm, 'klau̇s-\ *n, pl* **claus·tra** \-rə\ [NL, fr. L, bar] : a thin lamina of gray matter in each cerebral hemisphere between the lenticular nucleus and the island of Reil

clau·su·la \'klȯzhələ\ *n, pl* **clausu·lae** \-,lē\ [ML, fr. L, end, close of a rhetorical period, fr. *clausus*, past part. of *claudere* to close — more at CLOSE] **1** : a rhythmic close or terminal cadence esp. in ancient and medieval Latin prose rhythm — see CURSUS **2** *in medieval music* : an ornamented cadence or close **3** : a composition in descant style developed from a melismatic phrase of plainsong — **clau·su·lar** \-lə(r)\ *adj*

clausure *n* -s [ME, fr. L *clausura* — more at CLOSURE] *obs* : CLOSURE

¹claut \'klät, -ōt\ *vb* -ED/-ING/-S [origin unknown] *chiefly Scot* : SCRATCH, TEAR; *also* : SCRAPE, RAKE

²claut \"\ *n* -s **1** *Scot* : GRASP, CLUTCH **2** *Scot* : HANDFUL, LUMP, CHUNK **3** *Scot* : RAKE

cla·va \'klāvə, -ävə\ *n, pl* **cla·vae** \-ā,vē,-ä,vī\ [NL, fr. L, club — more at CLAVI-] : a clublike structure: as **a** : the club⸗shaped end of certain insect antennae **b** : the fruiting body of certain fungi **c** : a slight bulbous enlargement that forms part of the wall of the 4th ventricle of the brain and is the seat of a nucleus contributing axons to the lemniscus

clav·a·cin \'klavəsən, 'klä-\ *n* -s [*clava-* (fr. NL *clavatus*, specific epithet of *Aspergillus clavatus*, a species of fungus) + *-cin* (as in *actinomycin, streptothricin*)] : a colorless crystalline very toxic antibiotic $C_7H_6O_4$ produced by several molds (as *Aspergillus clavatus* and *Penicillium patulum*) — called also *clavatin, claviformin, patulin*

cla·val \'klāvəl, 'klä-\ *adj* [NL *clava* + E *-al*] *anat* : of or relating to the clava

cla·var·ia \klə'va(a)rēə\ *n, cap* [NL, fr. L *clava* club + NL *-aria*] : a genus (the type of the family Clavariaceae) of fleshy mostly saprophytic and edible fungi having the hymenium over the surface of simple or branched club-shaped or corallike sporophores

cla·var·i·a·ce·ae \⸗,⸗⸗'āsē,ē\ *n pl, cap* [NL, fr. *Clavaria*, type genus + *-aceae*] : a family of fleshy fungi (order Polyporales) having the characters of the genus *Clavaria* — **cla·var·i·a·ceous** \⸗;⸗⸗;āshəs\ *adj*

cla·vate \'klā,vāt\ *also* **cla·vat·ed** \-vād·əd\ *adj* [NL *clavatus*, fr. L *clava* club + *-atus* -ate, -ated; akin to L *claudere* to close — more at CLOSE] *biol* : gradually thickening near the distal end : shaped like a club — see ANTENNA illustration — **cla·vate·ly** *adv*

clav·a·tin \'klavətən, 'klä-\ *n* -s [*clavat-* (fr. NL *clavatus*, specific epithet of *Aspergillus clavatus*, a species of fungus) + *-in*] : CLAVACIN

cla·va·tion \klā'vāshən\ *n* -s : the condition of being clavate

¹clave [ME, var. of *clove*, past of *cleven* to cleave (split) and of *clevede*, past of *clevien* to cleave (stick)] *past of* ¹CLEAVE, *archaic past of* ²CLEAVE

²cla·ve \'klä(,)vā\ *n* -s [AmerSp, fr. Sp, keystone, clef, fr. L *clavis* key — more at CLAVICLE] : one of a pair of small cylindrical wooden sticks used as percussion instruments by being struck together while held in cupped hands (as in accompaniment to the rumba) — usu. used in pl.

clav·e·cin \'klavəsən\ *n* -s [F, short for MF *clavycimbale*, fr. ML *clavicymbalum* — more at CLAVICYMBAL] : HARPSICHORD

clav·e·cin·ist \-nəst\ *n* -s : a performer on the clavecin

clav·el \'klavəl\ *n* -s [MF *clavel* keystone of an arch, fr. L *clavis* key — more at CLAVICLE] *now dial Eng* : the lintel over a fireplace : MANTEL

clav·e·li·za·tion \ˌklavələ'zāshən\ *n* -s [F *clavelisation*, fr. *claveliser* to clavelize (inoculate with sheep virus) (fr. *clavelée* sheep pox, fr. MF, fr. *clavel*, fr. LL *clavellus* nail-shaped pustule, dim. of L *clavus* nail) + *-ation* — more at CLAVUS] **:** inoculation with virus from sheep pox **:** OVINATION

clav·el·lat·ed \ˈklavə,lād·əd\ *adj* [ML *clavellatus* (fr. *clavellus* nail — fr. LL, small sore resembling the head of a nail, dim. of L *clavus* nail — + L *-atus* -ate) + E *-ed* — prob. fr. the nail-studded appearance of the surface of clavellated ashes — more at CLAVUS] *old chem* **:** made of the dried and burned lees or dregs of wine or vegetable matter ⟨~ ashes⟩

¹cla·ver \ˈklāvə(r), -av-\ *vb* -ED/-ING/-S [ME *claveren;* akin to D *klaveren* to clamber, Dan *klavre*, OE *clifian* to cling — more at CLEAVE] *dial Eng* **:** CLAMBER

²clav·er \ˈklavə(r), -āv-\ *n* -S [ME — more at CLOVER] *dial Brit* **:** CLOVER

³cla·ver \ˈklāvər\ *vi* -ED/-ING/-S [prob. of Celtic origin; akin to ScGael *clabaire* babbler, IrGael *claibéir* chatter, W *clebar, clebran* to chatter, prate] *chiefly Scot* **:** PRATE, GOSSIP

⁴claver \ˈ"\ *n* -S *chiefly Scot* **:** idle talk **:** CHATTER, GOSSIP — usu. used in pl.

cla·ver grass \ˈklāvə(r)-\ *n* [by alter.] **:** CLEAVERS

claves *pl of* CLAVE *or of* CLAVIS

clavi *pl of* CLAVUS

¹clavi- *or* **clavo-** *comb form* [ML *clavi-*, fr. L, fr. *clavis* key — more at CLAVICLE] **1 :** key **:** keyboard ⟨*clavichord*⟩ ⟨*clavilux*⟩ **2** [NL *clavi-, clavo-*, fr. L *clavi-*] **:** clavicle **:** clavicular **:** clavicular and ⟨*clavipectoral*⟩ ⟨*clavodeltoid*⟩

²clavi- *comb form* [NL, fr. L, fr. *clava;* perh. akin to L *clavis*] **:** club ⟨*Clavicornia*⟩ ⟨*claviform*⟩

cla·vi·al *var of* CLAVIOL

clav·i·a·ture \ˈklavēə,chu̇(ə)r, -āv-\ *n* -S [G *klaviatur*, fr. L *clavis* key — more at CLAVICLE] **1 :** the keyboard of a piano or organ **2 :** a system of fingering a keyboard instrument

clavi·cembalo \,klavə +\ *n, pl* **clavicembali** [It, fr. ML *clavicymbalum* — more at CLAVICYMBAL] **:** HARPSICHORD

clav·i·ceps \ˈklavə,seps\ *n, cap* [NL, fr. ²*clavi-* + L *-ceps* headed (fr. L *caput* head) — more at HEAD] **:** a genus of ascomycetous fungi (family Hypocreaceae) parasitic upon the ovaries of various grasses and forming characteristic sclerotia from which arise the ascus-bearing stromatal heads

clav·i·chord \ˈklavə,kȯrd, -ō(ə)d\ *n* -S [ML *clavichordium*, fr. *clavi-* ¹clavi- + *-chordium* -chord] **:** an early keyboard instrument smaller and much weaker in tone than the piano, having strings pressed by tangents attached directly to the key ends, the pitch produced by any one string being determined by the point at which it was divided by the tangent — compare MONOCHORD

clav·i·chord·ist \-dəst\ *n* -S **:** a performer on the clavichord

clav·i·cle \ˈklavəkəl, -vēk-\ *n* -S [F *clavicule*, fr. NL *clavicula*, fr. L, dim. of *clavis* key; akin to L *claudere* to close — more at CLOSE] **:** a bone of the vertebrate shoulder girdle typically serving to link the scapula and sternum: **a :** a bone in man situated just above the first rib on either side of the neck and having the form of a narrow elongated S — called also *collarbone* **b :** a corresponding but rudimentary bone in some of the ungulates and carnivores **c :** one of the two bones fused into the wishbone of a bird **d :** a large crescent-shaped bone under the pectoral fin of many teleost fishes

clav·i·cor \ˈklavə,kȯ(ə)r\ *n* -S [F, fr. *clavi-* + *cor* horn, trumpet, fr. L *cornu* horn — more at HORN] **:** BASS HORN 2

clav·i·corn \-ȯrn\ *adj* [ISV ²*clavi-* + *-corn*] **:** having club-shaped antennae

clav·i·cor·nia \,==ˈkȯrnēə\ *n pl, cap* [NL, fr. ²*clavi-* + *-cornia* (neut. pl. of L *-cornis* -corn)] *in some classifications* **:** a superfamily or other group of beetles having the antennae usu. club-shaped or capitate

cla·vic·u·la \kləˈvikyələ, kla-\ *n, pl* **clavicu·lae** \-,lē, -,lī\ [NL, fr. L, small key — more at CLAVICLE] **:** CLAVICLE

cla·vic·u·lar \-lə(r)\ *adj* [prob. fr. F *claviculaire*, fr. *clavicule* clavicle + *-aire* -ar — more at CLAVICLE] **:** of or relating to the clavicle

cla·vic·u·lar·i·um \klə,vikyəˈla(a)rēəm, kla-\ *n, pl* **clavicu·lar·ia** \-rēə\ [NL, fr. *clavicula* clavicle + *-arium*] **:** the epiplastron of turtles regarded as representing the clavicle

cla·vic·u·late \=ˈ==,lət, -,lāt\ *adj* [NL *clavicula* clavicle + E *-ate* — more at CLAVICLE] *anat* **:** having clavicles

claviculo- *comb form* [NL *clavicula* clavicle] **:** clavicular and ⟨*claviculohumeral*⟩

clavi·cylinder \ˈklavə +\ *n* -S [G *klavizylinder*, fr. *klavi-* ¹clavi- + *zylinder* cylinder, fr. L *cylindrus* — more at CYLINDER] **:** a keyboard instrument producing its tones by the friction of metal rods against a set of glass cylinders

clavi·cymbal \ˈ"+\ *n* -S [ME *clavysymbal*, fr. MF *clavycimbale*, fr. ML *clavicymbalum*, fr. *clavi-* ¹clavi- + L *cymbalum* cymbal] **:** an early Italian harpsichord

clavi·cy·the·ri·um \,klavə,sīˈthirēəm\ *n, pl* **clavicythe·ria** \-rēə\ [NL, fr. *clavi-* ¹clavi- + *-cytherium, -citerium* (fr. L *cithara*) — more at ZITHER] **:** an early upright spinet

cla·vier \kləˈvi(ə)r, kla-, -iə; ˈklavēə(r), -av-; *sometimes* klävyā\ *n* -S [F, fr. OF, key bearer, fr. L *clavis* key + OF *-ier* -er] **1 :** the keyboard of a musical instrument ⟨the ~ of a carillon⟩ **2** [G *klavier*, fr. F *clavier*] **:** one of the family of stringed instruments having a keyboard **3 :** a dummy keyboard for practice

cla·vier·ist \-ˈvirəst, -ˈvēərəst\ *n* -S **:** a performer on the clavier

cla·vier·is·tic \klə,viˈristik; ˈklavēə¦r-, -av-\ *adj* [prob. fr. G *klavieristisch* suitable for a piano, fr. *klavier* piano + *-istisch* -istic] **:** suited to or suggesting a keyboard stringed instrument

clav·i·form \ˈklavə,fȯrm\ *adj* [L *clava* club + E *-iform*] **:** shaped like a club

clav·i·for·min \,klavəˈfȯrmən\ *n* -S [NL *claviforme* (specific epithet of *Penicillium claviforme*, a species of fungus) + E *-in*] **:** CLAVACIN

clav·i·ger \ˈklavəjə(r)\ *n* -S [L, fr. *clavi-* ¹clavi- + *-ger* bearing, bearer — more at -GEROUS] **:** one that keeps the key or keys **:** CUSTODIAN, WARDEN

clav·i·lux \-və,ləks\ *n* -ES [¹*clavi-* + L *lux* light — more at LIGHT] **:** an instrument for throwing upon a screen varying patterns of light and color that permit combinations analogous to the successive phrases and themes of music — called also *color organ*

clav·i·ol *or* **clav·i·ole** \ˈklavē,ōl, -āv-\ *or* **cla·vi·al** \ˈklāvēəl\ *n* -S [blend of ¹*clavi-* and *viol, viole*] **:** a viollike instrument played from a keyboard by means of a rotary bow — compare SOSTINENTE PIANOFORTE

clavi·pectoral \ˈklavə +\ *adj* [ISV *clavi-* + *pectoral;* orig. formed in F] **:** relating to the clavicle and pectoral muscles

cla·vis \ˈklāvəs, -āv-\ *n, pl* **cla·ves** \-,vēz\ *or* **clavises** [L — more at CLAVICLE] **:** a key or glossary serving as an aid to interpretation

clavo- — see ¹CLAVI-

clav·o·la \ˈklavələ\ *n, pl* **clavo·lae** \-,lē, -,lī\ [NL, fr. L, dim. of *clava* club — more at CLAVI-] **:** CLAVA a

cla·vus \ˈklāvəs, -āv-\ *n, pl* **cla·vi** \-ā,vī, -ä,vē\ [L, lit., nail; akin to L *claudere* to shut — more at CLOSE] **1 :** ³CORN 1 **2 :** a vertical stripe or band of purple on a tunic worn broad by early Roman senators and narrow by the equites as a mark of rank **3** [NL, fr. L] *zool* **:** any of various rounded or fingerlike parts or processes: as **a :** the pointed anal area of the hemelytron of a bug **b :** the club of an insect's antenna

clavy \ˈklavi\ *var of* CLAVEL

¹claw \ˈklȯ\ *n* -S *often attrib* [ME *clawe*, fr. OE *clawu*, alter. of *clēa*, gen. dat. acc. *clawe;* akin to OHG *klāwa, chlōa* claw, ON *klō*, OE *cliewen* sphere, ball, ball of yarn — more at CLEW] **1 :** a sharp nail on the toe of an animal esp. when such a nail is slender and curved (as that of a bird or cat); *also* **:** either lateral half of the hoof of a cloven-footed mammal — see COCK illustration **2 :** any of various similar sharp curved processes esp. if at the end of a limb (as those on the legs of insects); *sometimes* **:** the limb if it ends in such a process **3 :** one of the pincerlike organs terminating certain limbs of some arthropods (as the lobsters and scorpions) **4 :** something shaped like or grasping in a way felt to suggest an animal's claw: as **a :** the curved and forked end of a hammer or nail puller **b :** the slender projecting part of a jewelry setting that holds a stone **c :** the slender prolonged basal portion of certain petals (as in the pink) — compare BLADE 1c(2) **d :** a pronged grasp at the end of a derrick hoist **e :** a gardening tool for loosening soil **f :** a part of the intermittent mechanism of a motion-picture camera, printer, or projector that engages the perforations of and moves the film **5 :** a wound from or as if from a claw

²claw \ˈ"\ *vb* -ED/-ING/-S [ME *clawen*, fr. OE *clawan, clawian;* akin to MD *klouwen*, OHG *klāwēn;* denominative fr. the root of E ¹*claw*] *vt* **1 :** to pull, tear, scratch, scrape, seize, clutch, or dig with or as if with claws or nails **2** *chiefly Scot* **:** to scratch softly esp. in order to relieve itching or uneasiness **3 :** to force forward or upward as if with claws ⟨~*ed* his way to the top of the mountain⟩ or at the expense of others ⟨~ his way to the top of his profession⟩ **4 :** to attack spitefully, treacherously, or unexpectedly (as with a veiled insult) ⟨an actress ~*ing* her rival⟩ ~ *vi* **1 :** to scrape, scratch, dig, or pull with a claw or with the hand as a claw **2 :** to grope or clutch in desperation or panic ⟨~*ing* for the door handle⟩ **3** *of a boat* **:** to work to windward (as from a lee shore)

claw-and-ball foot *n* **:** a foot on a piece of furniture shaped like a bird's or animal's claw grasping a ball — see FOOT illustration

clawback \ˈ=,=\ *n* -S [²*claw* (scratch softly) + *back*] *now dial* **:** FLATTERER, SYCOPHANT

claw bar *n* **:** a ripping bar or crowbar with a forked claw for drawing spikes (as from railroad ties)

claw chisel *n* **:** a stonecutter's toothed chisel

claw clutch *n* **:** a mechanical clutch in which jaws or claws interlock when pushed together — called also *positive clutch*

clawed *adj* [¹*claw* + *-ed*] **:** furnished with or having claws — used chiefly in compounds ⟨bare-clawed⟩ ⟨sharp-clawed⟩

clawed frog *or* **clawed toad** *n* **:** a frog (*Xenopus laevis*) of southern Africa that is much used in pregnancy tests — see XENOPUS

claw foot *n* **1 :** a foot that is or that resembles or is felt to resemble a claw; *specif* **:** a foot on a piece of furniture in the shape of a claw ⟨a *claw-foot* chair⟩ **2 :** a deformity of the foot characterized by an exaggerated curvature of the longitudinal arch — **claw-footed** \ˈ=¦==\ *adj*

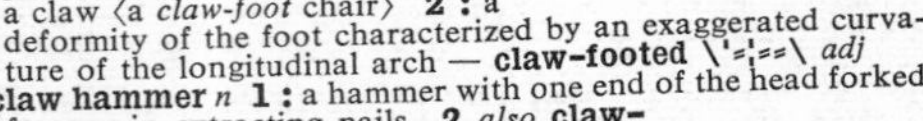

simple claw clutch

claw hammer *n* **1 :** a hammer with one end of the head forked for use in extracting nails **2** *also* **claw-hammer coat :** TAILCOAT

claw hand *n* **:** a deformity of the hand characterized by extreme extension of the wrist and first phalanges and extreme flexion of the other phalanges

claw hammer

claw hatchet *n* **:** a hatchet with one end of the head forked for nail pulling — see HATCHET illustration

clawk \ˈklȯk\ *vt* -ED/-ING/-S [alter. (prob. influenced by *claw*) of ME *cloke, cluke*] *dial Eng* **:** CLAW, SCRATCH; *also* **:** SNATCH

claw·less \ˈklȯləs\ *adj* **:** having no claw **:** having the claws reduced or rudimentary

clawless otter *n* **1 :** a small southern Asiatic otter (*Amblyonyx cinerea*) with claws weakly developed **2 :** a large easily domesticated otter (*Aonyx capensis*) of western and southern Africa with the claws reduced or wanting

claw nut *n* **:** CLASP NUT

claw off *vi, of a boat* **:** to beat to windward to prevent going aground on a lee shore

claws *pl of* CLAW, *pres 3d sing of* CLAW

claw–tailed \ˈ=¦=\ *adj* **:** having a tail resembling a claw

claw toe *n* **:** HAMMERTOE

claw tool *n* **:** a fireman's implement for forcible entry or demolition consisting of a bar or pole with a hook at one end and a 2-pronged claw at the other

clax·on \ˈklaksən\ *n* -S [alter. of *Klaxon*] **:** a Klaxon horn

¹clay \ˈklā\ *n* -S [ME, fr. OE *clǣg;* akin to OS *klei* clay, MD *clei*, OHG *klīwa* bran, LL *glut-, glus* glue, MGk *glia*, Lith *glitùs* slippery and prob. to L *galla* gall on a plant — more at GALL] **1 a :** a widely distributed colloidal lusterless earthy substance, plastic when moist but permanently hard when fired, that is composed primarily of decomposed igneous and metamorphic rocks rich in the mineral feldspar in the form of crystalline grains less than .002 mm in diameter, whose essential constituents are kaolinite and other hydrous aluminous minerals and fine particles, and that is used widely in the manufacture of such articles as porcelain, building blocks, sewer pipe, tile, and earthenware or in its raw form in paper manufacture, filtration, and oil refining **b :** CLAY SOIL **c :** earth esp. when moist **2 a :** a claylike substance; *esp* **:** one used by a potter or sculptor **b :** the mortal human body as distinguished from an immortal spirit animating it **c :** the human character regarded as serving the purpose of a divine creator ⟨aspirants to be noble ~ plastic under the Almighty effort —R.W.Emerson⟩ **d :** NATURE 3, ABILITY, ENDOWMENT ⟨common ~⟩ ⟨the stupid feeling of employers that they are of a different ~ —O.W. Holmes †1935⟩ **3 a :** PIPE CLAY **b :** a clay tobacco pipe **4 :** CLAY PIGEON **5 :** a moderate to strong yellowish brown that is lighter than tobacco brown and slightly yellower and lighter than Aztec

²clay \ˈ"\ *vt* -ED/-ING/-S **:** to treat with clay: as **a :** to cover, daub, plaster, or dress with clay — often used with *up* ⟨~ up an auto body model⟩ **b :** to apply clay to (soil) **:** mix clay into **c :** to filter through clay

³clay \ˈ"\ *var of* CLEE

claybank \ˈ=,=\ *n* **1 :** a brownish orange that is yellower and paler than leather or spice and yellower and lighter than gold pheasant **2 :** a horse of yellowish color produced by a mixture of sorrel and dun coloration

clayboard *n* **:** SCRATCHBOARD

claybrained \ˈ=¦=\ *adj* [¹*clay* + *brained*] **:** STUPID, DULL

clay burning *n* **:** the burning or roasting of clay esp. in Great Britain for use in improving the soil

clay-colored sparrow \ˈ=,==-\ *n* **:** a small sparrow (*Spizella pallida*) of the dry interior of western No. America that resembles the chipping sparrow but has a buffy-brown rump

clay court *n* **:** a tennis court with a clay or dirt surface ⟨*clay-court* championship⟩ — compare GRASS COURT, HARD COURT

clay·den effect \ˈklādᵊn-\ *n, usu cap C* [after Arthur W. *Clayden* †1944 Eng. meteorologist] **:** partial desensitization of the emulsion layer of a photographic material by an initial high-intensity exposure of very short duration so that a later exposure of lower intensity and longer duration produces less effect than expected from the combined exposures, sometimes resulting in reversal of an image — compare DARK LIGHTNING

clay digger *n* **:** a spade held in the hands but power-driven (as by compressed air) and used to dig hard soil or soft rock

clay drab *n* **:** a moderate yellowish brown to light olive brown that is duller than Isabella and very slightly redder than medal bronze

clayen *adj* [ME, fr. *clay* + *-en*] *obs* **:** made of clay **:** EARTHENWARE

clay·ey \ˈklāē, -āi\ *adj* [ME *claiy*, fr. ¹*clay* + *-y*] **1 :** consisting of or characterized by the presence of clay **:** abounding in or being clay **:** like clay **2 :** covered, daubed, or soiled with clay **3 :** resembling that of clay ⟨a ~ color⟩

clay fever *n* [prob. so called fr. its being contracted under muddy conditions] *of a horse* **:** GREASE HEEL

clay·i·ness *also* **clay·ey·ness** \-āēnəs, -āin-\ *n* -ES [*clayey* + *-ness*] **:** clayey state or quality **:** STICKINESS

clay ironstone *n* **:** siderite ore occurring admixed with clayey rock material

clay·ish \-āish, -āēsh\ *adj* [¹*clay* + *-ish*] **:** like clay or containing particles of it ⟨~ soil⟩ **:** somewhat clayey (as in color)

clay loam *n* **:** a loam consisting of from 20 to 30 percent clay, from 20 to 50 percent silt, and from 20 to 50 percent sand

clay·man \ˈklāmən, -,man\ *n, pl* **claymen :** one that works with or digs clay; *specif* **:** one that mixes clay, water, and dispersing agents for use in papermaking

clay marl *n* **:** a whitish smooth chalky clay **:** a marl in which clay largely predominates

clay mill *n* **:** PUG MILL

clay mineral *n* **:** one of a group of hydrous silicates of aluminum and sometimes other metals (as magnesium and iron) formed chiefly in weathering processes, found in clays, soils, shales and other rocks, and characterized by small particle size and ability to adsorb substantial amounts of water, other molecules, and ions on the surface of the particles

clay·more \ˈklā,mō(ə)r, =ˈ=\ *n* -S [ScGael *claidheamh mōr*, lit., great sword] **1 :** a large 2-edged occas. 2-handed sword used formerly by the Scottish Highlanders **2 :** a basket-hilted often one-edged broadsword first used in the 16th century by the Scottish Highlanders

clay·o·quot \ˈklāə,kwät\ *n, pl* **clayoquot** *or* **clayoquots** *usu cap* **1 :** a subdivision of the Nootka people of western Vancouver Island, British Columbia **2 :** a member of the Clayoquot people

claypan \ˈ=,=\ *n* -S [¹*clay* + *pan*] **1 :** hardpan consisting mainly of clay **2** *Austral* **:** a shallow silted depression in which water collects after rain

clay pigeon *n* **:** a saucer-shaped target composed of baked clay and pitch or similar substances and thrown from a trap in skeet and trapshooting

clay pigeon

clay press *n* **:** a filter press used for expressing excess water from slip in pottery making

clays *pl of* CLAY, *pres 3d sing of* CLAY

clay slip *n* **:** a slurry of clay and water used in casting ware as an engobe and with certain clays (as Albany slip) as a high-fire glaze

clay soil *n* **:** a soil that contains a high percentage of fine particles and colloidal substance and becomes sticky when wet

clay stone *n* **1 :** a calcareous concretion formed in a bed of clay **2 :** a dull earthy feldspathic rock containing clay

clay·ton fern \ˈklātᵊn-\ *n, usu cap C* [after John *Clayton* †1773 Am. botanist] **:** INTERRUPTED FERN

clayton gas *n, usu cap C* [after T. A. *Clayton*, Eng. chemist] **:** a gaseous mixture used on ships for exterminating vermin

clay·to·nia \klāˈtōnēə\ *n* [NL, fr. John *Clayton* + NL *-ia*] **1** *cap* **:** a genus of mainly No. American succulent herbs (family Portulacaceae) having cormlike or thickened roots and a single pair of leaves **2** -S **:** any plant of the genus *Claytonia*

clay·ver-grass \ˈklāvə(r),=\ *n* [alter. of *claver grass*] **:** CLEAVERS

clayware \ˈ=,=\ *n* [¹*clay* + *ware*] **:** an article made of fired clay; *collectively* **:** such articles (as crockery or bricks)

clayweed \ˈ=,=\ *n* [¹*clay* + *weed*] **:** COLTSFOOT a

cld *abbr* **1** called **2** canceled **3** cleared **4** cloud **5** colored **6** cooled

CLD *abbr* cost laid down

-cle \kəl\ *n suffix* -S [ME, fr. OF, fr. L *-culus, -cula, -culum*] **:** little one ⟨denticle⟩ ⟨corpuscle⟩ ⟨funicle⟩ — **-cu·lar** \kyələ(r)\ *adj suffix*

clea \ˈklē\ *var of* CLEE

clead \ˈklēd\ *vt* -ED/-ING/-S [ME *clethen, cleden*, fr. ON or OE; ON *klætha*, fr. OE *clǣthan*, fr. *clāth* garment, cloth — more at CLOTH] *dial Brit* **:** CLOTHE

clead·ing \ˈklēdiŋ\ *n* -S [ME *clething, cleding*, fr. the gerund of *clethen, cleden* to clothe] **1** *chiefly Scot* **:** CLOTHING, ATTIRE **2 :** a lining or covering of boards, planks, battens, or nonconducting material (as for lining a ship's cabin or a mine shaft or for insulating a boiler or engine cylinder) **:** LAGGING

cleam \ˈklēm, -ām\ *vb* -ED/-ING/-S [ME *clemen* — more at CLAM] **1** *dial Eng* **:** SMEAR, DAUB, SPREAD **2** *dial Eng* **:** ADHERE, STICK

¹clean \ˈklēn\ *adj* -ER/-EST [ME *clene*, fr. OE *clǣne* pure, clear; akin to OS *klēni* delicate, dainty, fine, OHG *kleini*, Gk *glainoi* ornaments, Arm *calr* laughter; basic meaning: bright, gay] **1 a :** free from matter that adulterates, contaminates, or pollutes ⟨add ~ mercury to the solution⟩ **b :** free from admixture with whatever diminishes the distinctive quality or essential character ⟨the ~ thrill of one's first flight⟩ ⟨the ~ satisfaction that comes from the stern performance of duty — F.D.Roosevelt⟩ **c** *of a precious stone* **:** having no interior flaws visible to the unaided eye **d** *of stock* **:** free of slow-moving goods or inventory **2 a :** free from or freed of dirt, filth, refuse, or remains ⟨wearing ~ linen⟩ ⟨requested a ~ plate⟩ **:** free from any putrefying or infecting agent ⟨fowl reared on ~ litter⟩ **b :** free from disease, often from a specified disease ⟨a pullorum-*clean* flock⟩ ⟨keep installations ~ of TB infection⟩ **c :** accustomed to keep free of dirt and foulness ⟨raccoons are ~*er* than other cage animals⟩ **d** *of a domestic animal* **:** that has never been bred **e** *of a ship* **:** having the bottom free from fouling accumulation **f** (1) **:** free from smudges or anything that tends to obscure ⟨a ~ set of fingerprints⟩ (2) *of copy* **:** easy to read with corrections clearly and neatly made (3) *of typesetting or a proof* **:** relatively free from error — opposed to *dirty* (4) *of a proof* **:** pulled from type in which errors detected on a previous proof have been corrected for sending to the author — compare FOUL **g** *of a deer or antlers, Brit* **:** having shed the velvet **h :** freeing or freed of weeds and other harmful growth and rubbish and of growth that hinders tillage ⟨the pros and cons of ~ culture between fruit trees⟩ ⟨~ farming is detrimental to wild life⟩ **3 a :** free from moral taint or corruption or sinister connections of any kind **:** GUILTLESS ⟨police confirmed he had had a ~ record for two years⟩ ⟨~ candidates are needed for ~ government⟩ **b :** free from looseness in sex relations **:** free from offensive treatment of sexual subjects and from the use of obscenity **c :** observing the rules **:** SPORTSMANLIKE, FAIR ⟨a ~ fighter⟩ ⟨~ rivalry⟩ **d** *slang* **:** free from involvement in a matter under police investigation **e** *slang* **:** carrying no concealed weapons **4 :** ceremonially or spiritually pure ⟨. . . and took of every ~ animal . . . and offered burnt offerings on the altar —Gen 8:20 (RSV)⟩ ⟨and all who are ~ may eat flesh —Lev 7:19 (RSV)⟩ **5 a :** so decisive, complete, or thoroughgoing as to leave no remainder, loose ends, or uncertainty ⟨a ~ sweep in the challenge round⟩ ⟨making a ~ break with his past⟩ **:** OUTRIGHT, UNRESERVED, INCONTESTABLE ⟨a ~ beat for his paper⟩ ⟨a ~ miss with a torpedo⟩ **b :** precisely, deftly, or unerringly directed or executed esp. without a trace of strain or awkwardness **:** FAULTLESS ⟨every hunter, if he is a real sportsman, wants quick, ~ kills —R.R.Camp⟩ ⟨~ sword work required of a matador⟩ ⟨some ~ ballet technique⟩ **:** showing no deficiency or deviation from a high standard of skill ⟨a steeplechaser must be a ~ jumper⟩ **c** *sports* **:** swiftly, skillfully, and decisively executed **:** free from error or misjudgment ⟨a ~ double play⟩ or played or scored with a decided margin of success or safety ⟨a ~ single over second base⟩ ⟨a ~ backhand shot⟩ **6 a :** free from obstruction or encumbrance ⟨and I envy the ~ straight sweep of your mind —H.J.Laski⟩ **b** *of cash* **:** in hand subject to no deduction or further liability **c** (1) *of a bond* **:** free from any endorsement or marks (2) *of a bill of lading or ship's receipt* **:** free from any statement about damage or poor condition of goods or containers (3) *of a draft or bill of exchange* **:** free from attached documents **7 a :** having simplicity, definiteness, articulateness, and usu. gracefulness of form ⟨architecture with ~ almost forbiddingly austere lines⟩; *specif* **:** constructed on fine sharp lines ⟨a ship with a ~ body slips through the water with little or no disturbance⟩ **b** *in the arts* **:** marked by straightforward presentation or concise composition **:** free from nonessential elements or affectation ⟨a ~, spare, expressive prose style⟩; *specif* **:** precise and flawless in execution or reproduction ⟨efforts to obtain a ~ bass in orchestral recordings⟩ **c :** free from unevenness or irregularity of outline or partition ⟨this saw leaves a ~ edge⟩ ⟨a sharp blow causing a ~ break⟩ **d** *archaic, of a party ticket* **:** STRAIGHT **e** *of a horse's leg* **:** free from curbs or bunches below the hock **f** *of an airplane* **:** well streamlined and free from external protuberances or projections that give rise to increased aerodynamic drag **g** *radio & television* **:** sharply defined and unwavering **:** free from distortion and interference ⟨a speaker providing ~ output⟩ **8 a :** empty esp. of what might be expected to be carried or stocked ⟨the whaling ship returned with a ~ hold⟩ **b** *slang* **:** cleaned out of one's money **:** without funds **9 a :** having a distinctive, unmixed, and fresh quality to the senses ⟨the ~ scent of pine⟩ ⟨a ~ yellow⟩ **b :** marked by no failure or deficiency ⟨a ~ record of victories⟩ **10** *of an atom bomb or hydrogen bomb* **:** having little or no fallout

²clean \ˈ"\ *adv, sometimes* -ER/-EST [ME *clene*, fr. OE *clǣne* clearly, purely, fr. *clǣne*, adj.] **1 a :** in such a manner as to keep or leave free of dirt or refuse ⟨a new broom sweeps ~⟩ **:** without distortion or error ⟨played the difficult piano accompaniment very ~⟩ **b :** in a manner free from cheating or unsportsmanlike conduct ⟨play the game ~⟩ ⟨he doesn't fight ~⟩ **c** *archaic* **:** PRECISELY, UNERRINGLY ⟨the arrow flew ~ to the center of the target⟩ **2 :** without qualification **:** THOROUGHLY, ENTIRELY, COMPLETELY ⟨an area burned over ~⟩

⟨gone ~ out of his head⟩ ⟨thrown ~ off balance⟩ ⟨my own view is ~ contrary —F.R.Leavis⟩ : all the way ⟨a bullet ~ through the chest⟩ ⟨~ back to colonial times⟩ : far or remotely ⟨living ~ out in the sticks⟩

³clean \"\ *vb* -ED/-ING/-S [ME *clenen*, fr. *clene* clean] *vt* **1** : to make clean or free of dirt or any foreign or offensive matter: as **a** : to wash with water and soap or with any aqueous liquid medium **b** : to bathe, brush, or treat with an acid, alkaline, or organic agent, rub with an oil or cream, or sponge or swab with a disinfectant for removing undesired matter ⟨~ a wound⟩ **c** : to wipe or polish esp. with a solvent for removing grime ⟨~ the domestic silver⟩ **d** : to free of dirt, refuse, or litter and set in order — often used with *up* ⟨~ up the attic⟩ **e** : DRY-CLEAN **2 a** : to rid (land) of weeds and rubbish by cultivation — often used with *up* **b** : to scrape (a ship's bottom) free of accretions of barnacles and fouling matter **c** : to brush, scrape, or blow clean of dirt or other accumulation — often used with *out* ⟨~ one's shoes before entering⟩ ⟨specimens from an archaeological excavation need expert *~ing*⟩ ⟨~ out a drain⟩ **d** (1) : to brush (the teeth) with a cleanser, esp. a dentifrice (2) : to perform dental prophylaxis on (the teeth) **e** : to blast with grit for removing undesired accumulations ⟨~ a brick wall of layers of paint⟩ **f** : to free (a surface) of what adheres, covers, or obstructs (as by brushing, wiping, or scraping) — often used with *off* ⟨~ off a slate⟩ ⟨~ flues⟩ ⟨earning pocket money by *~ing* sidewalks⟩ ⟨hard to ~ a windshield of a coating of sleet⟩ **g** : to remove cancellation marks from (a stamp) so as to give an appearance of being unused **3 a** : to remove the outer shell, husk, hull, or hairy appendages from ⟨rough rice is *~ed* before milling⟩ **b** : to free (as by screening) of dirt, chaff, stray weed seeds, and other foreign matter ⟨~ grain coming from the thresher⟩ **c** : to gin (cotton) **4 a** : to remove the entrails from : GUT, DRESS ⟨~ fish, fowl, or game⟩ **b** : to strip bare or to empty of contents ⟨the lumberjacks quickly *~ed* the platter⟩ ⟨the tree was *~ed* of fruit by hurricane winds⟩ ⟨a play that *~ed* the board of the opponent's checkers⟩ **c** *slang* : to defeat decisively in a contest or competition — sometimes used with *up* ⟨we took on their best bridge players and *~ed* them⟩ **d** *slang* : to deprive wholly of money or possessions in a gambling game, by robbery, or through skulduggery or stock-market speculation — often used with *out* ⟨they started *~ing* him . . . bit by bit they were taking everything he had, his banks, his factories —Louis Bromfield⟩ ⟨a few disastrous plunges and he found himself *~ed* out⟩ **e** : to exhaust or strip clean ⟨carp may ~ a pond of indigenous fish⟩ : PRUNE ⟨~ a roster of inactive members⟩ **f** *baseball* : to empty (the bases) by enabling all base runners to score **~** *vi* : to undergo or perform a process of cleaning : become clean — often used with *up* — **clean house** : to eradicate by stern vigorous thoroughgoing measures whatever is obstructive, thwarting, or degrading ⟨the industry is full of troublemakers and must *clean house*⟩ ⟨in departments where graft was rife the new mayor began to *clean house*⟩

⁴clean \"\ *n* -S : an act of cleaning dirt esp. from the surface of something ⟨give footwear a daily ~ with polish⟩

clean·a·bil·i·ty \ˌklēnəˈbiləd·ē\ *n* -ES : the property of being cleanable or accessible to cleaning

clean·a·ble \ˌklēnəbəl\ *adj* : capable of being cleaned

clean and jerk *n* : a lift in weight lifting in which the weight is momentarily raised from the floor, held at shoulder height, and then jerked overhead — compare PRESS, SNATCH

clean bill *n* **1** : a legislative resolution introduced by a committee incorporating provisions of an original bill and embodying amendments adopted by the committee **2** : CLEAN BILL OF HEALTH 2

clean bill of health 1 : a bill of health certifying absence of infectious disease **2** : an unqualified finding or certification of the moral or political soundness of ⟨dismissing charges of racketeering, the committee gave the organization a *clean bill of health*⟩

clean bill of lading : a bill of lading free from statements about damage or poor condition of goods or containers

clean-boled \ˈ=ˌbōld\ *adj* : having a bole free or trimmed of branches

clean-bowled \ˈ=ˌ=\ *adj, cricket* : bowled by a ball that does not touch the bat or any part of the batsman's person

clean-built \ˈ=ˌ=\ *adj* : of trim shapely build

clean-cut \ˈ=ˌ=\ *adj* **1** : having a clean and distinct outline as if evenly and precisely cut along the border : seen in high relief as if chiseled, sculptured, or shaped in a mold ⟨the skyline stands out *clean-cut* —G.R.Stewart⟩ ⟨he had *clean-cut* features and piercing eyes⟩ ⟨the *clean-cut* youthful figure leaning over her friend —Ellen Glasgow⟩ **2 a** : accomplished or attained through precision so as to give clear demarcation or distinctness of effect or result ⟨the habit of *clean-cut* articulation⟩ **b** : explicit and unmistakable in intent and distinct in detail ⟨the difficulties that have beset investigators in getting *clean-cut* answers —J.B.Conant⟩ **c** : narrowly limiting or limited in range : quite definite ⟨his responsibility in the matter is *clean-cut*⟩ **3** : presented concisely and vividly by avoidance of vagueness, oversubtlety, or diverting embellishment and a minimum of shading and transition ⟨detectives have made a *clean-cut* case⟩ ⟨one of the *cleanest-cut* of all his stories⟩ **4** : wholesome and uncontaminated : wholly up to standard in sterling qualities ⟨a *clean-cut* and well-bred young man⟩

clean cutting *n* : CLEAR-CUTTING

clean dollar *n, in the China trade* : a dollar that has not been chopped

cleaned *past of* CLEAN

¹cleaner *comparative of* CLEAN

²clean·er \ˈklēnə(r)\ *n* -S **1** : one whose work is cleaning: as **a** : one employed to do cleaning esp. of the interiors of buildings or transportation vehicles **b** : a worker who cleans materials, equipment, or working areas either for the sake of neatness or as part of a manufacturing process **c** : a worker who cleans spots from such materials as fabrics or tinware by washing, scraping, or any means suitable to the material **d** : one whose business is the dry cleaning of garments, rugs, upholstery, or other articles not normally washed **e** : a worker who examines completed garments for defects, cuts off loose threads, cleans soiled spots, and folds or hangs the garments — called also *clipper, folder* **f** : a worker who cleans radio condenser terminals and moistureproofs them with chemicals **2** : a preparation for cleaning, cleaning off, or cleaning out something; *specif* : a liquid preparation for household use in removing dirt and spots from clothing or furnishings **3** : an implement or machine for cleaning: as **a** : a currier's 2-handled knife **b** : a contrivance for cleaning a steam boiler **c** : a molder's tool having a long flat blade with a turned-up end **d** : a machine for cleaning the air of dirt or other foreign matter **e** : VACUUM CLEANER **4** : a flotation machine used in mining that re-treats concentrates and produces a clean finished product (as coal) — **to the cleaners** *adv, slang* : to or through an experience of being deprived of all one's money (as in a game of chance or a confidence game) ⟨some sharpies took him *to the cleaners*⟩

cleaner tooth *n* : a special tooth on a circular saw for cleaning out the kerf

cleaner-up \ˈ==ˌ=\ *n, pl* **cleaners-up** : one that cleans up refuse or cleans the surface of some product

cleanest *superlative of* CLEAN

clean fallow *n* : uncropped land kept free of weeds and other growth by frequent cultivation

clean-fingered \ˈ=ˌ==\ *adj* **1** : SCRUPULOUS **2** : DEFT

cleanhanded \ˈ=ˌ==\ *adj* : innocent of wrongdoing

clean hands *n* **1** : freedom from guilt, esp. from dishonesty in money matters or elections **2** : the condition of being free from wrongdoing, misconduct, or deceit as a prerequisite of application for relief in a court of equity

clean-hewn \ˈ=ˌ=\ *adj* : CLEAN-CUT 1

¹cleaning *pres part of* CLEAN

²cleaning *n* -S **1** *Brit* : CLEANSING 2 — usu. used in pl. **2 cleanings** *pl* : things collected by cleaning **3** *slang* : a decisive defeat ⟨gave the visiting team a ~⟩; *also* : a total loss of resources in a business venture or in speculation or gambling ⟨got a good ~ on the stock market⟩ **4** : a thinning of a young stand (as of trees) **5** : a large profit or gain : KILLING ⟨makes his little ~ and then leaves us all flat —George Abbott & J.C.Holm⟩

cleaning crop *n, Brit* : any crop (as turnips or potatoes) adapted to cultivation and suitable for cleaning weedy land

cleaning hinge *n* : a sliding hinge for a window sash that permits the sash to swing to such a position that the outside of the glass may be cleaned from within the room

cleaning mark *n* : an indelible identification mark applied to an article in a cleaning establishment

cleaning shoe *n* : a threshing-machine mechanism that consists of sieves and a fan and that separates the clean grain from the dirt and refuse

cleaning tissue *n* : CLEANSING TISSUE

cleaning woman *n* : a woman who hires herself out for housecleaning

clean-legged \ˈ=ˌleg(ə)d\ *adj* **1** *of poultry* : having legs free from feathers **2** : having legs free from a feathery fringe or tuft of hair — used esp. of a horse or dog

clean·li·ly \ˈklenlәlē, -əli\ *adv* **1** : in a cleanly or neat manner **2** : in a clean-cut manner : accurately and smoothly : so as to fit or blend neatly **3** : CHASTELY, INNOCENTLY ⟨I, too, might have lived ~ —J.B.Cabell⟩

clean-limbed \ˈ=ˌlimd\ *adj* : with well-proportioned or shapely limbs or parts likened to limbs : TRIM ⟨*clean-limbed* youths⟩ ⟨the *clean-limbed* racers tacked and put about gracefully⟩

clean·li·ness \ˈklenlēnəs, -lin-\ *n* -ES [ME *clenlynesse*, fr. *clenly* cleanly + *-nesse* -ness] : the quality or state of being cleanly: **a** : freedom from superficial foulness or imperfections (as dust, grease, incrustation, mechanical burrs) **b** : the condition or habit of being clean; *specif* : diligence in keeping clean in person and dress ⟨~ is indeed next to godliness —John Wesley⟩ **c** : unalloyed or unblemished quality or purity ⟨Huxley's effort to introduce fresh air and intellectual ~ into the Augean stables of official science —M.R.Cohen⟩; *specif* : freedom from moral frailty or impurity of motive ⟨as he spoke of the ~ of Washington's soul —Van Wyck Brooks⟩

clean-living \ˈ=ˌ==\ *adj* : leading a life free from immorality

¹cleanly \ˈklenlē, -li\ *adj, often* -ER/-EST [ME *clenly*, fr. OE *clǣnlic* pure, fr. *clǣne* pure + *-lic* -ly — more at CLEAN] **1** *obs* : clean morally or ceremonially ⟨the *cleanlier* in his office for his new-washed surplice —John Milton⟩ **2** : free from dirt or litter **3 a** : careful to keep clean ⟨~ in their persons and habitations —Meriwether Lewis⟩ ⟨the badger is a most ~ animal⟩ **b** : habitually kept clean **c** : chaste and refined in quality ⟨turn the jargon into ~ English⟩ **4** *obs* : cleverly devised or deftly executed ⟨~ knavery —Edmund Spenser⟩ **5** *archaic* : conducive to cleanness

²cleanly \ˈklēnlē, -li\ *adv* [ME *clenly*, fr. OE *clǣnlīce* purely, fr. *clǣne* pure + *-līce* -ly] : in a clean manner

clean-mouthed \ˈ=ˌ=\ *adj* : given to propriety of speech

clean·ness \ˈklēnnəs\ *n* -ES : the state or condition of being clean

clean out *vt* [³*clean* + *out*] **1** : to strip or exhaust of all contents, supplies, or resources ⟨the redecorating job *cleaned out* the club treasury⟩ **2 a** : to eliminate, dismiss, or expel (as from a group or organization) ⟨intent on *cleaning out* inefficient personnel in the department⟩ ⟨*cleaned out* both open foes and lukewarm friends in the old cabinet⟩ **b** : to rout out or exterminate the occupants of ⟨*clean out* an enemy machine-gun nest⟩ **3** : to exhaust the stock of ⟨tourists *cleaned out* the shops⟩ ⟨heavy rains *cleaned* us *out* of boots⟩

cleanout \ˈ=ˌ=\ *n* -S **1** : the act of cleaning out ⟨a ~ of his predecessor's assistants⟩ **2** : an opening that is usu. covered by a cap, plate, or door and is provided for cleaning out an enclosure (as a furnace dome, chimney, or plumbing trap)

clean-run \ˈ=ˌ=\ *adj* **1** *of a salmon* : having the bright color and healthy plumpness characteristic of a recent arrival in fresh water for spawning **2** *Brit* : redolent of health and fresh vitality

cleans *pres 3d sing of* CLEAN, *pl of* CLEAN

cleans·a·ble \ˈklenzəbəl\ *adj* : capable of being cleansed

cleanse \ˈklenz\ *vb* -ED/-ING/-S [ME *clensen*, fr. OE *clǣnsian* to purify, fr. *clǣne* pure] *vt* **1 a** : to release, deliver, or absolve from sin or guilt : rid of any moral blemish ⟨a group of sinners reveal their wickedness and are *cleansed* and redeemed —A.M. Sullivan⟩ ⟨seeking for that which shall ~ me —George Meredith⟩; *also* : FREE, ABSOLVE ⟨our hearts *cleansed* of all evil⟩ **b** : to rid one of (moral or spiritual taint) as if by washing — sometimes used with *away* ⟨mysterious means of purification by which they proposed to ~ away the defilements of the soul —W.R.Inge⟩ **c** : to free or purge of what is spurious, degrading, or vitiating ⟨a city *cleansed* of graft, gangsterism, and prostitution⟩; *also* : to eradicate as spurious, degrading, or vitiating — used with *from* ⟨all feeling of pity had been *cleansed* from him⟩ **d** : to free or rid of any undesirable feature or condition ⟨a smile *cleansing* his face of all severities —R.P.Warren⟩; *esp* : to purge (a political party or other organization) of disruptive or dissident elements ⟨found it necessary to ~ party ranks⟩ **2 a** : to wash, brush, or scrub with water or a detergent solution ⟨a floor covering that is easily *cleansed*⟩; *also* : to wipe clean (as with oil or cosmetic cream) **b** : to wipe free of surface accumulation (as with absorbent waste or tissues) **c** : to free of extraneous or undesired matter; *esp* : to rid (air) of foul or noxious gases **d** *archaic* : to cause to recover from disease or injury to health : HEAL ⟨raise the dead, ~ lepers —Mt 10:8(RSV)⟩ ⟨and immediately his leprosy was *cleansed* —Mt 8:3(RSV)⟩ **e** *Brit* : to sweep and clean (streets) of refuse and snow : SCAVENGE **f** : to wash or flush out or dislodge ⟨~ nematodes from the intestines of sheep⟩ ⟨~ dirt from a wound⟩ **3** : to make ceremonially clean : free from pollution or purify in a religious sense ⟨*cleansed* through baptism⟩ ⟨*cleansed* from the effects of a ritual oath⟩ **~** *vi* : to undergo a cleansing process : become clean ⟨utensils that ~ easily⟩

cleans·er \ˈklenzə(r)\ *n* -S [*cleanse* + *-er*] **1** : one whose work is cleansing something: **a** *Brit* : STREET CLEANER **b** : DRY CLEANER **2 a** : a preparation including a solvent or other cleaning agent for cleansing the skin, the teeth, or glass surfaces **b** : a powdered cleaning agent for scouring the dampened surface of kitchen utensils, sinks, or flooring material

clean-shaven \ˈ=ˌ==\ *adj* : having the hair shaved from cheeks, lips, chin, and throat

¹cleans·ing \ˈklenziŋ, -zēŋ\ *n* -S [ME *clensing*, fr. gerund of *clensen* to cleanse] **1** : the action or an act of cleansing; *esp* : moral or spiritual purification **2** : the afterbirth and sometimes also the fetal membranes of a domesticated mammal — usu. used in pl.

²cleansing \"\ *adj* [ME *clensing*, fr. pres. part. of *clensen* to cleanse] : serving to dispel (as shams or illusions) ⟨a mordant . . . wit which is at once ~ and devastating —H.G. Laski⟩ or to relieve (as emotional tension) ⟨how often during my life have I turned back and back to the ~ comfort of technique —Agnes de Mille⟩

cleansing tissue *n* : a square piece of soft absorbent tissue paper for use chiefly in wiping skin cream, cosmetics, or moisture from the face or hands

cleanskin \ˈ=ˌ=\ *n, Austral* : an unbranded animal — compare MAVERICK

clean-till \ˈ=ˌ=\ *vt* : to cultivate by stripping the soil clean of weeds and other harmful growth — compare CLEAN 2a

clean-timbered \ˈ=ˌ==\ *adj, obs* : CLEAN-LIMBED

clean up *vt* **1** : to make in clear profit : NET ⟨by selling when prices rose he *cleaned up* a small fortune⟩ **2** *archaic* : to catch and collect (grains of valuable mineral) from an accumulation in a sluice or stamping mill **3 a** : to strip or empty of the whole of the contents or supply ⟨taught to *clean up* his plate⟩ **b** : to extinguish or eliminate remaining enemy resistance from ⟨marines sent to *clean up* the atoll⟩ **c** : to sweep clean (as of political corruption or organized vice) ⟨a reform administration pledged to *clean up* the city⟩ : root out as a social evil ⟨helped the district attorney *clean up* the rackets⟩ : rid of debasing or harmful features or elements ⟨demand for *cleaning up* the movies⟩ **4 a** : to free from a state of ruin or disorder : rid of accumulated debris ⟨a section *cleaned up* of bomb damage⟩ **b** : to make final disposal of : SETTLE ⟨*clean up* pending cases⟩ ⟨*clean up* past-due bills⟩ **c** : to free from defects of performance : eliminate any remaining faults from ⟨*clean up* the stage business in early rehearsals⟩ **~** *vi* **1** : to wash up, change or arrange one's clothes, and tidy oneself ⟨*clean up* for dinner⟩ **2** : to make a spectacular or sensational profit in a business enterprise or a killing in speculation or gambling **3** *slang* : to inflict a severe thrashing or decisive defeat — used with *on* ⟨a chance to *clean up* on his critics⟩ **4** : to make a sweep of wins ⟨to *clean up* in a series of yacht races⟩

cleanup \ˈ=ˌ=\ *n* -S [*clean up*] **1 a** : a selling off of remaining stock **b** : the disposal of final details or making of final trials or a tidying up of litter (as when completing an undertaking) **c** : removal of residual gas from an incandescent lamp or vacuum tube due to the action of the getter, the absorption of gas by the anodes, or the driving of gas molecules into the electrodes **d** : the fourth position in the batting order of a baseball team **2 a** : a periodical cleaning up in a gold or silver mill or placer mine or dredge; *also* : the material thus collected **b** : an extraordinarily large return or profit on a shrewdly or opportunely timed sale; *specif* : KILLING **3 a** : a cleaning up or stamping out (as of vice, crime, or other undesirable conditions); *also* : a clearing out or purging (as of gangsters or other undesirable elements) **b** : a cleaning out or liquidation of remaining enemy resistance ⟨the ~ of enemy machine-gun nests⟩ **c** *slang* : a decisive defeat of a competitor

clean-up fund *n* : a personal fund usu. provided by life insurance to pay debts and final expenses incident to death

¹clear \ˈkli(ə)r, -iə\ *adj* -ER/-EST [ME *clere*, fr. OF *cler*, fr. L *clarus* clear, bright, loud, distinct, renowned; akin to L *calare* to call — more at LOW] **1 a** (1) : shining brightly : GLEAMING, LUSTROUS ⟨bonfires ~ and bright —Shak.⟩ (2) : entirely light : UNDIMMED, UNDARKENED, BRIGHT ⟨it is almost ~ dawn —Shak.⟩ **b** (1) : having the sky free from clouds ⟨watching the stars on ~ nights⟩ : having the air free from mist, haze, or dust ⟨on a ~ day one could see for miles⟩ (2) *meteorol* : relating to the sky when it is less than one-tenth covered with clouds (3) : unclouded or serene as if undisturbed by doubt, uncertainty, or guilt ⟨eyes so straight and ~ that everybody loved him —Stark Young⟩ **c** : giving free passage to light or to the sight : easily seen through : not cloudy, turbid, or opaque ⟨fish seen swimming through water ~ as air⟩ ⟨~ glass⟩ **d** (1) *of the skin or complexion* : good in texture and color and without blemish or discoloration (2) *of an animal coat* : of uniform shade throughout : UNSPOTTED — sometimes opposed to *ticked* **e** : having no color, smoke, or suspended matter to impede the passage of light : TRANSLUCENT ⟨~ varnish⟩ ⟨~ soup⟩ ⟨a candle burning with a ~ flame⟩ **f** *of color* : without admixture of other color : PURE ⟨~ reds and blues⟩ **2 a** : easily or distinctly heard : distinct and audible in detail ⟨her speech was ~ and easy to understand⟩ : having purity of tone : free from roughness or harshness ⟨you could hear ~ laughter like a waterfall —Edith Sitwell⟩ **b** *of an l sound* : formed with the tip of the tongue on the teethridge and the rest of the tongue in a position similar to that of a front vowel — compare DARK **3 a** : easily understood : without obscurity or ambiguity ⟨a ~ description of his point of view⟩ : thoroughly understood or comprehended ⟨the consequences of his act were not ~ at the time⟩ ⟨make it ~ that there will be no discussion⟩ : easy to perceive or determine with certainty ⟨it is ~ that you were wrong⟩ : sharply distinguished : readily recognized : UNMISTAKABLE ⟨a ~ instance of favoritism⟩ **b** : easily visible or distinguishable without blurring or becoming obscure : sharp and distinct in outline ⟨though the gloom had increased . . . the white surface of the road remained almost as ~ as ever —Thomas Hardy⟩ : readily seen : in plain sight ⟨~ identification of the product on the label⟩ **4 a** : having no doubt, uncertainty, or confusion of mind : straight-thinking ⟨a complex problem requiring a ~ brain⟩ : having a sure understanding or a confident certainty ⟨we are not ~ about what we are going to do⟩ : without misconception, error, or vagueness ⟨a *~er* understanding of the issue⟩ **b** : undistorted or unweakened in perception or vision ⟨~ sight⟩ ⟨~ eyes⟩ **5** : free from obstruction, burden, limitation, defect, or other restricting features: as **a** : free from guile, guilt, or stain : UNSULLIED, INNOCENT ⟨in action faithful, and in honor ~ —Alexander Pope⟩ ⟨a ~ conscience⟩ **b** : free from pecuniary liabilities, charges, or deductions ⟨a good income ~ for life⟩ ⟨a ~ profit of 6 percent⟩ **c** : free from qualification or limitation : UNQUESTIONED, ABSOLUTE ⟨a ~ victory over his opponent⟩ ⟨that wall is a ~ 20 feet high⟩ **d** : free from anything that impedes movement or action ⟨a road ~ for traffic⟩ ⟨a field ~ of trees⟩; *also* : indicating freedom from obstruction ⟨a ~ signal on a railroad⟩ **e** : freed or emptied of burden, contents, or cargo ⟨a ship is ~ after unloading⟩ **f** (1) *of tree boles or timbers* : free of knots, branches, or other projections (2) *of lumber* : free of defect or blemish **g** : free from contact : out of the way ⟨~ of the hose⟩; *esp* : free from contact or association with anything that encumbers, impedes, entangles, or obscures ⟨the moon was ~ of the trees⟩ ⟨~ of the storm area⟩ ⟨~ of trouble⟩ **h** *of a measurement of space or time* : without deduction or diminution : FULL ⟨a ~ 15 yards from side to side⟩ — compare CLEAR DAYS **i** (1) : having nothing within or upon : empty of content : free of occupancy ⟨walls ~ of ornament⟩ ⟨a mind ~ of all such notions⟩ (2) *of a fabric* : having a finished surface free of nap, fuzz, or loose fibers (3) *of an egg* : INFERTILE **j** : NORMAL; *specif* : free from abnormal sounds — used esp. in auscultation of the chest or lungs **k** : having won no hearts or other penalty card in tricks in the game of hearts

syn TRANSPARENT, TRANSLUCENT, LUCID, PELLUCID, DIAPHANOUS, LIMPID: CLEAR stresses absence of clouding or other obscuring of vision ⟨the launch moved slowly through water *clear* as air —C.B.Nordhoff & J.N.Hall⟩ TRANSPARENT stresses complete absence of obstruction to vision ⟨guavas, with the shadows of their crimson pulp flushing through a *transparent* skin —Herman Melville⟩ TRANSLUCENT applies to that which permits passage of light but bars clear and complete vision ⟨*translucent* amber that cages flies —Elinor Wylie⟩ ⟨poured out a goblet full of the *translucent* crimson liquid —Joseph Hergesheimer⟩ LUCID, a rather romantic and literary word, may suggest luminous transparency ⟨changed . . . their hue (like clouds of sunset) into *lucid* amber —William Wordsworth⟩ PELLUCID intensifies the idea of CLEAR ⟨a *pellucid* plain of waters, azure with the noontide day —P.B.Shelley⟩ DIAPHANOUS suggests a gossamer translucency, a virtual transparency ⟨in her flowery loveliness, she looked *diaphanous*, ethereal —Maurice Hewlett⟩ LIMPID usu. suggests soft clearness ⟨the eyes are of that soft, *limpid*, turquoise blue so often sung by the poets —Wilkie Collins⟩ ⟨in the light of the dawn, growing more *limpid* rather than brighter —Joseph Conrad⟩ Applied to intangibles in more figurative senses, CLEAR stresses freedom from obscurity or possibility of misunderstanding ⟨making our age one of bewildered groping where our ancestors walked in the *clear* daylight of unquestioning certainty —Bertrand Russell⟩ ⟨experience in India had made it abundantly *clear* that the government of a great empire required special training and disinterested selection —Felix Frankfurter⟩ TRANSPARENT implies either commendable utter clarity or obvious, easily perceived deception ⟨*transparent* and disprovable untruths . . . and histories far-fetched a million miles —Elinor Wylie⟩ LUCID, more common in this use, suggests especial clearness, sometimes of order and arrangement ⟨he thought little of recasting a chapter in order to obtain a more *lucid* arrangement —G.O.Trevelyan⟩ PELLUCID and LIMPID stress simple complete clarity ⟨[Goldsmith's] *pellucid* simplicity —Frederic Harrison⟩ ⟨utter simplicity, *limpid* clearness . . . these are the salient qualities of the diction of the men who wrote the Bible —J.L.Lowes⟩

syn LUCID, PERSPICUOUS: CLEAR and LUCID have been dealt with in the preceding synonymy. PERSPICUOUS may stress the clearness and understandability of the general style of a passage ⟨the ode is not wholly *perspicuous*. Wordsworth himself seems to have thought it difficult —Lionel Trilling⟩ **syn** see in addition EVIDENT

²clear \"\ *adv* -ER/-EST [ME *clere*, fr. *clere*, adj.] : in a clear manner: as **a** : without confusion or obscurity : DISTINCTLY ⟨now ~ I understand —John Milton⟩ **b** : with clear voice or sound ⟨to cry loud and ~⟩ **c** : all the way : for the entire distance, extent, or time ⟨beyond the fence was open country ~ to the skyline —Hartley Howard⟩ : WHOLLY, ENTIRELY ⟨I was sore ~ through at myself —W.A.White⟩

³clear \"\ *vb* -ED/-ING/-S [ME *cleren*, fr. *clere*, adj.] *vt* **1 a** (1) : to make clear, transparent, or translucent : free from darkening elements, turbidness, muddiness, clouds, or cloudiness ⟨~ the river water by filtering⟩ (2) : to free (sugar crystals) from mother liquor by spraying with water or steam (3) : to free or almost free (the emulsion of a photographic film or plate) from silver halide during fixing so that unexposed parts are transparent (4) : to render (a specimen for microscopic examination) transparent by the use of an agent (as an essential oil) that modifies the refractive index **b** (1) *obs* : to remove guilt or the stain of sin from : make pure : wash away (as a sin) : ABSOLVE (2) : to free from imputation of guilt or from accusation or blame : JUSTIFY, VINDICATE ⟨to take the stand, tell the truth, and ~ his name —S.H.Adams⟩ ⟨his accusers never gave him an opportunity to ~ himself⟩ — often used with *of* or *from* before the thing imputed ⟨he is ~ of all suspicion of duplicity⟩ (3) : to certify (as by investigation of one's personal history and background) as loyal to the national interest and safely to be trusted with secret information or employed in responsible work ⟨~ a man for top-secret military work⟩ **c** (1) : to make clear mentally : give clear understanding to : ENLIGHTEN ⟨~ my mind about the new arrangement⟩ (2) : to make intelligible : free from obscurity or ambiguity : EXPLAIN ⟨many knotty points there are which all discuss but few can ~ —Matthew Prior⟩ **d** : to make (the eyes or sight) clear or keen (as by strengthening or cleaning) **e** *obs* : to prove the truth of : DEMONSTRATE **2 a** : to remove from (as a space) all that occupies or encumbers or that impedes or restricts use, passage, or action ⟨~*ed* his calendar in order to give full time to the problem⟩ ⟨~ a room upstairs for the guest⟩ ⟨~ two downtown blocks for the new civic center⟩ ⟨~ the way for the landing forces⟩ ⟨~ an acre of woodland with a bulldozer⟩ **b** : to free, rid, or empty (as an area or object) of accumulated, intruding, or encumbering things ⟨~ your mind of foolish fancies⟩ ⟨~ land of trees and brush⟩ ⟨~ a ship of her cargo⟩ ⟨~ an equation of fractions⟩ **c** : to remove (something that occupies, intrudes, obstructs, or encumbers) from an area or place ⟨spend a week ~*ing* timber⟩ ⟨~ snow from the walk⟩ ⟨~ the plates and serve dessert⟩ — often used with *away, off, out* **d** : to establish one's remaining cards in (a specified suit) by forcing the opponents to play all their cards or all their remaining cards in that suit ⟨he ~*ed* the spade suit in two leads⟩ ⟨the ace ~*ed* the trump suit⟩ **e** : to clear for action **f** : to de-energize (an electric circuit) manually or by means of an automatic circuit-interrupting device **g** (1) : to make (the voice) free from harshness or huskiness (2) : to rid (the throat) of phlegm or of something that makes the voice indistinct or husky (3) : to make a rasping noise in (the throat) as if clearing phlegm used often as a nonlinguistic sound and esp. to call attention to something said or done **h** : to exhaust the available market supply of (a commodity) by purchase or sale ⟨buyers ~*ed* the day's cattle run at steady rates⟩ : dispose of the supply on hand of (a commodity) often by special sale ⟨unsold stock was ~*ed* at a loss⟩ **i** : to move (as a hockey puck or soccer ball) out of the defensive zone **j** : to classify and distribute, transmit, or dispatch (as messages, mail, or freight) to the intended destination ⟨that post office ~*s* 300 pieces of mail an hour⟩ ⟨~*ed* messages for the state police over his shortwave set —Mary H. Vorse⟩ **k** : to remove accumulated totals, stored information, or previously made settings from (a business or calculating machine) : replace stored information by zero in (a computing machine) **3** : to make clear or free from obligation, esp. from pecuniary liability: as **a** : SETTLE, PAY, DISCHARGE ⟨~ an account⟩ ⟨money sent to ~ our debts⟩ : make free from debt or pecuniary encumbrance ⟨money paid to ~ his estate⟩ **b** (1) : to free (a ship or shipment) for passage by payment of customs duties or harbor fees : pass through (customs) by conforming to regulations ⟨the baggage ~*ed* customs⟩ (2) : to leave (a port) after conforming to customs and port regulations ⟨the ship ~*ed* New York harbor⟩ **c** : to gain without deduction : earn as a net profit ⟨~ a good profit on the sale⟩ ⟨~ $1500 a year on the investment⟩ **d** : to pass (as a check) through a clearinghouse; *sometimes* : to get the cash for (a check) — compare CLEARING 3 **4 a** : to free (as from contact or entanglement) : DISENTANGLE ⟨~ a hawser⟩ ⟨~ a fishing line⟩ **b** : to leap over ⟨the horse ~*ed* the fence in a bound⟩ or pass by or over ⟨~*ing* the ridge, we saw below us a great valley⟩ : go over or by without touching, colliding, or getting entangled ⟨the planes barely ~*ed* the tops of the trees⟩ **c** : to pass free of, out of, or away from ⟨the tax bill ~*ed* the legislature a week ago⟩ **5 a** : to submit (something proposed or intended) to an authority for review and approval before placing in effect ⟨important appointments are first ~*ed* with the committee⟩; *also* : to review and approve (as a proposal) : give approval to : AUTHORIZE ⟨the chairman ~*ed* the article for publication⟩ **b** : to obtain official permission to use (as a song) in broadcasting **c** : to authorize (an aircraft) to proceed under specified traffic conditions ⟨~*ed* the plane for landing⟩ ~ *vi* **1** : to become clear, bright, or transparent: as **a** : to become free of clouds, mist, fog, or rain : become fair — often used with *up* or *off* ⟨it ~*ed* up quickly after the rain⟩ **b** : to become transparent, translucent, or free of sediment or turbidity ⟨the muddy water ~*s*⟩ **c** : to become free of care, doubt, uncertainty, disorder, or of anything that puzzles or troubles the mind or obscures or confuses the situation ⟨his face ~*ed* as he heard my explanation⟩ ⟨with the improvement in sales the business prospect ~*s*⟩ **2 a** *obs* : to adjust differences : pay claims : make a settlement — used with *with* **b** : to conform to the customs and other port regulations by payment of duties and fees so as to obtain permission to leave port ⟨the ship ~*ed* yesterday and is ready to leave⟩; *also* : to leave port with clearance papers ⟨ships ~*ed* from Boston with cargoes for the west⟩ **c** : to pass for clearing or collection through a clearinghouse or through another bank (as of a check) — see CLEARING 3a **3 a** : to go away : DISAPPEAR, VANISH ⟨these symptoms should ~ gradually⟩ ⟨the crowds ~*ed* rapidly, leaving the streets deserted⟩ — often used with *away, up, off* **b** *of a commodity* : to become sold out ⟨hogs ~*ed* at steady rates⟩ **c** : to remove the dishes, food, and other remains of a meal (as from a table or a room) ⟨you are to ~ after every meal⟩ **d** : to move a puck or ball away from the goal area ⟨the goalie ~*ed* to an open teammate⟩ **4 a** : to go to an authority (as for scrutiny, review, or approval) before becoming effective ⟨all tax bills must ~ through our committee⟩ **b** : to pass through or undergo handling by a single authority or office usu. with the purpose of achieving efficiency or consistency of handling ⟨outgoing letters ~ through this office where they are checked against our files⟩ **syn** see RID — **clear for action** : to clear a ship's decks and fighting spaces of unnecessary encumbrances and fire hazards and make ready in all respects for battle — **clear hawse** : to untwist anchor cables when a ship that is riding to two anchors has fouled her cables by shifting with the tide — **clear one's skirts** : to clear oneself of accusation of guilt or one's character of a stigma — **clear the air** *also* **clear the atmosphere** : to remove elements of hostility, tension, confusion, or uncertainty from the mood or temper of the time : remove the confusions or ambiguities from a conception or a problem ⟨the government announcement *cleared the air* of speculation and suspicion⟩ — **clear the decks 1** : to clear for action **2** : to remove all impediments to or make everything ready for a particular course of action or series of developments ⟨*clearing the decks* so that we can now set about attacking the real problems —*Times Lit. Supp.*⟩ — **clear the land** *of a ship* : to gain such a distance from shore as to have sea room — **clear the way** : to make preparations for : get everything out of the way in order to be ready for new developments or a new course of action ⟨*clear the way* for the entertainment of the visitor⟩

⁴**clear** \"\ *n* -S [¹*clear*] **1** [trans. of It *chiaro*] **clears** *pl* : the parts of a painting shown in a state of illumination as opposed to those in shadow **2 clears** *pl* : a less refined flour consisting of the bolted portion of the meal recovered in the manufacture of patent flour and graded in several grades according to the quality resulting from further milling **3** : a board or piece of lumber free from defects **4** : an infertile hatching egg **5** : a bird or animal having clear plumage or coat **6** : a deep shot over the opponent's head in badminton **7** : plain or unencrypted language ⟨a message sent in ~⟩ : PLAINTEXT ⟨~ alphabet⟩ — **in the clear** *adv (or adj)* **1** : in inside measurement ⟨corridors three feet *in the clear*⟩ **2** : free of restriction, obstruction, obligation, or anything that restricts or impedes action ⟨the airplane had just passed through a squall and was *in the clear*⟩ **3** : free of guilt or not subject to suspicion or imputation of guilt ⟨as for the charge of cowardice, he was now *in the clear*⟩ **4** : in plaintext : not in code or cipher ⟨a message sent *in the clear*⟩

clear·age \ˈklirij\ *n* -S : the act of clearing : CLEARANCE

clear·ance \ˈklirən(t)s\ *n* -S **1** : the act of making clear of whatever may obstruct, occupy, encumber, or hinder: as **a** : the removal of buildings from an area (as a city slum) in order to permit new construction **b** (1) : the act or an instance of clearing a ship at the customhouse (2) *or* **clearance papers** : the papers showing that a ship has cleared **c** : the offsetting of checks and other claims among banks through a clearinghouse, the Federal Reserve banks, or other agencies **d** : approval or certification as clear of objection, prohibition, suspicion, or guilt ⟨security ~ of those with access to secret atomic information —J.G.Palfrey⟩ ⟨given ~ by the FBI⟩ : permission to proceed without objection, check, or reservation ⟨you have to have the general's personal ~ —J.G.Cozzens⟩ **e** : the sale usu. at reduced prices of stock (as excess inventory) which it is desired to move from the store ⟨a January ~ of men's suits⟩ **f** : authorization for an airplane to proceed under specified traffic conditions **2** : the distance by which one object clears another or the clear space between them ⟨a car with a road ~ of 7⅛ inches⟩ ⟨a bridge with a 100 foot ~ above water⟩: as **a** (1) : the distance between the piston and the cylinder head at the end of a stroke in an engine (2) : the total volume (as of steam) remaining in the cylinder and ports at the end of the exhaust or compression stroke; *also* : the line or area on an indicator diagram noting this distance or volume **b** : the space between adjacent structural members or their component parts to allow for inaccuracies in cutting and to permit them to be placed in a structure **c** : the distance by which the top of a gear tooth clears the bottom of the space between two teeth on the mating gear **d** : the margin of space between the structures along a railroad track (as poles, buildings, or tunnel walls) and the periphery of the largest locomotive or car that will pass over that track **e** *or* **clearance angle** : the angle between the face of a cutting tool and the work **f** : the interval stipulated in the lease of a motion picture that must elapse after the film's exhibition in a first-run theater before it can be leased to other theaters within a specified surrounding area **g** : a quantitative measure of renal efficiency in the transfer of any solute from the blood to the urine, being determined as the volume of blood that would be freed of a specified constituent by removal of a quantity equal to the measured renal excretion of that constituent during one minute — called also *renal clearance* **3** : a space or area that has been cleared of that which formerly occupied it (as trees or brush) ⟨a ~ in the forest⟩ ⟨~*s*, the Highland equivalent of enclosures, in which the . . . peasants were treated . . . as mere squatters —Russell Kirk⟩ **4** : a permission-to-work order to a line crew after a power line has been de-energized for the crew's safety **5** : a part of a foundry mold or core beveled off to prevent contact of friable surfaces when closing the mold **syn** see ROOM

clearance fit *n* : a fit (as of mechanical parts) in which there is clearance

clearance lamp *n* : one of the usu. colored lamps on the left and right of the front and rear of a truck that indicate the extreme sides of the vehicle

clearance loan *n* : DAY LOAN

clear and present danger *n* : such danger as satisfies a court that the invasion of freedom of speech and press by legislation is justified by the gravity and degree of probability of a substantial evil (as overthrow of the government) that the legislature in the exercise of its lawful powers is seeking to prevent

clear away *vt* **1** : to remove or dispose of (something that obstructs, impedes, or inconveniences) ⟨the recent adjudication *cleared away* all obstacles to the bond issue⟩ **2** : to free from entanglement or obstruction so as to make ready for use ⟨*clear away* an anchor ready to let go⟩ ~ *vi* : to remove from a table or a room the dishes, food, and other remains of a meal

clear belly *n* : a square bacon slab without pigmentation (as from the mammary gland)

clear board *n* : a signal to an approaching railroad train that the block ahead is clear

¹**clear·cole** \ˈklir,kōl\ *n* -S [part trans. of F *claire colle*, fr. *claire* clear + *colle* glue, fr. (assumed) VL *colla*, fr. Gk *kolla* — more at PROTOCOL] : a priming of size mixed with whiting or white lead used esp. in house painting; *also* : a size upon which gold leaf is applied in gilding

²**clearcole** \"\ *vt* -ED/-ING/-S : to coat or paint with clearcole

¹**clear-cut** \ˈ=ˌ=\ *adj* **1** : having a sharp clear outline with regular distinct lines : not obscure, hazy, softened, or shadowed ⟨a *clear-cut* pattern⟩ ⟨a cold and *clear-cut* face . . . perfectly beautiful —Alfred Tennyson⟩ **2 a** : showing distinct lucid analysis, plan, or presentation : having unmistakable clarity and definiteness : not vague, ambiguous, or confused ⟨the Hoosier novels, simple in plot, *clear-cut* in characterization, concise and lucid in language —Carl Van Doren⟩ **b** : marked by certainty, definiteness, unmistakableness : beyond reservation or doubt ⟨a *clear-cut* victory⟩ ⟨the decision of the court was *clear-cut* and final⟩ ⟨the announcement may be *clear-cut* or again it may be somewhat equivocal⟩ **syn** see INCISIVE

²**clear-cut** \"\ *vt* : to remove all timber from (an area) : cut all the trees in (a stand of timber)

clear-cutting \ˈ=ˌ==\ *n* : removal of all timber from an area; *also* : the area so treated

clear days *n pl* : days reckoned from one day to another with exclusion of both the first and the last day ⟨from Sunday to Sunday there are six *clear days*⟩

cleared *past of* CLEAR

clearedness *n* -ES : the quality or state of being cleared

¹**clear·er** \ˈklirə(r)\ *comparative of* CLEAR

²**clearer** \"\ *n* -S **1** : a person or worker who clears: as **a** : a worker who clears goods of faults or working places of debris and objects not in use **b** : one who bleaches extract-tanned hides by brushing with weak acid solution **c** : PROPERTY MAN **2** : an instrument, device, apparatus, or agent that clears esp. as part of a manufacturing process: as **a** : CLEARING AGENT **b** : a reservoir into which the brine is conveyed in the manufacture of salt **c** (1) : one of the small rapidly revolving rollers in a carding machine the teeth of which catch the material from the worker rollers (2) : a contrivance (as a roller or flat board covered with flannel or as an endless flannel band) in a drawing, roving, or spinning frame to collect the fly from the rollers (3) : a device in a ring spinner consisting of an upward projecting piece of metal that catches the fly on the traveler and removes it

clearest *superlative of* CLEAR

clear-eyed \ˈ=ˌ=\ *adj* **1** : having clear eyes : seeing clearly **2** : perceiving, thinking, or analyzing clearly : not subject to self-deception or misinterpretation of facts or evidence

clear-fell \ˈ=ˌ=\ *vt* : CLEAR-CUT

clear fork \ˈ=ˌ=\ *adj, usu cap C&F* [fr. *Clear Fork* river, Texas, near which the artifacts were discovered] : ABILENE

clear-hawse pendant \ˈ=ˌ=-\ *n* : a heavy chain having a pelican hook and tailed with a hemp hawser or wire rope used in mooring and clearing hawse

clearheaded \ˈ=ˌ==\ *adj* : having a clear understanding : quick of perception : not confused in mind : not subject to misinterpretation of fact — **clear·head·ed·ly** \ˈ=ˌ===\ *adv*

clear ice *n* : a transparent ice coating or glaze

clear in *vi* : to obtain permission to discharge cargo by conforming to customs or port regulations

clearing *n* -S [ME *clering*, fr. gerund of *cleren* to clear] **1** : the act or process of making or becoming clear **2** : a tract of land cleared of wood and brush (as for cultivation) **3 a** : a method adopted by banks and bankers for making an exchange of checks and bills held by each against the others in which checks deposited in the banks of a particular area are set off against each other with cash settlement only of the balances due after the clearing **b** : a similar method adopted by railroads and by buyers and sellers of merchandise for adjusting their accounts with each other; *also* : the machinery or procedure established under this method **c clearings** *pl* : the gross amount of balances so adjusted **4 a** : NATURAL PRUNING **b** : the cutting of all mature trees at one time **5** : the collection, classification, and distribution of information or other matter requiring wide distribution ⟨an agency for the ~ of reconstruction projects and plans⟩ ⟨a ~ center for management ideas⟩

clearing agent *n* : any substance used to clear a specimen or preparation for microscopic examination

clearing agreement *n* : an agreement between nations as to the method of settlement of commercial accounts that is usu. designed to avoid transfer of foreign exchange; *specif* : an agreement between two countries designed to force a balance of trade between them with exports being offset by imports and the use of cash remittances minimized

clearing bath *n* : a solution for bathing photographic negatives or prints to remove stains, unwanted or foreign deposits, or oxidizing substances

clearinghouse \ˈ==ˌ=\ *n* **1** : an institution or establishment for carrying on the business of clearing **2** : an agency for collection, classification, and distribution esp. of information or other matter or items requiring wide distribution ⟨functioning as a ~, the committee farms out for special study the questions that must be settled —*Newsweek*⟩ ⟨a ~ for information on management problems⟩

clearinghouse agent *n* : a clearinghouse member bank that clears checks for nonmember banks

clearinghouse stock *n* : a security in which transactions may be settled through the stock exchange's clearing department

clearing nut *n* : the seed of an East Indian tree (*Strychnos potatorum*) that is used in the Orient for clearing muddy water

clearing shower *n* : the final and usu. heaviest shower of a storm; *specif* : a line-squall shower of a cyclone

clearing station *n* : a medical installation in a combat area where casualties are received from collecting stations, given additional treatment, classified, and if necessary evacuated

clear lake gnat \ˌ=ˈ=ˌ=\ *n, usu cap C&L* [fr. *Clear Lake*, Calif.] : a minute nonbiting fly (*Chaoborus asticopus*) that is a major pest about Clear Lake, Calif., where it swarms in great numbers — compare CHAOBORIDAE

clear lead *n* : FAIRLEAD

clear length *n* : the part of a tree trunk that is clear of branches or of branches of a specified size

clear·ly \ˈkli(ə)rlē, -ələ̄, -li\ *adv* **1** : in a clear manner ⟨that which is ~ and distinctly conceived as the truth —C.W.Hendel⟩ **2** *of something asserted or observed* : without doubt or question ⟨~ we are in a transitional stage —Vera M.Dean⟩ ⟨its dominance was ~ waning —Louise Pound⟩

clear·ness \ˈkli(ə)rnəs, -iən-\ *n* -ES **1** : the quality or state of being clear : freedom from confusion or obstruction : DISTINCTNESS **2** : precise unambiguous transmission of meaning in writing or speaking : LUCIDITY, CLARITY

clear obscure *n* [trans. of F or It; F *clair-obscur*, fr. It *chiaroscuro* — more at CHIAROSCURO] : CHIAROSCURO

clear off *vt* : to get rid of or dispose of (troublesome, burdensome, or encumbering things); *specif* : to pay off (a debt or other financial obligation) ~ *vi* : to go or run away : leave esp. in a hurry ⟨*clear off* as fast as you can⟩

clear out *vi* **1** : to go through the procedure of clearing from a port **2** : to go or run away often suddenly or secretly : DECAMP, DESERT : get or move out ~ *vt* : to drive out or away usu. forcibly ⟨*cleared* the Persians *out* of Europe⟩

clear plate *n* : the layer of fat on top of the butt of a pork shoulder

clears *pres 3d sing of* CLEAR, *pl of* CLEAR

clearsach *var of* CLARSACH

clear-sighted \ˈ=ˌ==\ *adj* : having clear vision, discernment, or judgment — **clear-sight·ed·ly** \ˈ=ˌ===\ *adv* — **clear-sight·ed·ness** \ˈ=ˌ===\ *n* -ES

clearskin \ˈ=ˌ=\ *n* [¹*clear* + *skin*] *Austral* : CLEANSKIN

clear-starch \ˈ=ˌ=\ *vi* : to stiffen fabrics with clear translucent starch ~ *vt* : to starch (clothes) with a clear starch

clearstory *var of* CLERESTORY

clear tare *n* : a tare established by weighing all of the packages of a shipment

clear up *vt* **1** : to explain or make clear ⟨*cleared up* the doubtful points in his story⟩ : SOLVE ⟨*clearing up* the mystery⟩ **2** : to remove, dispose of, or set right (a source of trouble or dissatisfaction) ⟨arbitrators *cleared up* the controversy⟩ : bring or restore to a normal, ordered, or acceptable condition ⟨*clear up* the disturbed condition of the market⟩ ⟨*clear* the rubbish *up*⟩

clear-up \ˈ=ˌ=\ *n* -S [*clear up*] : a clearing up or settlement (as of accounts)

clearweed \ˈ=ˌ=\ *n* [so called fr. the translucence of the leaves and stems] : RICHWEED 1

clearwing \ˈ=ˌ=\ *n* : a moth having the wings largely devoid of scales and transparent: as **a** : a moth of the family Aegeriidae **b** : any of various hawkmoths (as the bumblebee hawkmoth)

clear-winged grasshopper \ˈ=ˌ=-\ *n* : a widely distributed and very destructive No. American grasshopper (*Camnula pellucida*) distinguished by its small size and colorless nearly transparent hindwings

clearwing moth \ˈ=ˌ=-\ *n* : a clearwing (family Aegeriidae)

¹**cleat** \ˈklēt, *usu* -ēd· + V\ *n* -S [ME *cleete, clete* wedge, fr. (assumed) OE *clēat;* akin to MHG *klōz* lump — more at CLOUT] **1 a** : a wedge-shaped piece of wood or other material fastened to or projecting from something and serving as a support or check **b** : a wooden or metal fitting usu. with two projecting horns around which a rope may be made fast (as by belaying it) **2** : a strip of wood, iron, or other material fastened across something to give strength, hold in position, or furnish a grip: as **a** : a projecting strip or cone usu. of leather, rubber, or metal fastened to or built into the sole or heel of a shoe to increase traction or provide a firm grip; *also* : a plate of metal on the heel or sole of a shoe for minimizing wear **b** : a similar projection on any surface demanding traction (as on a tractor tread or a machine belt) **c** : an often porcelain support with grooves or channels for electric wiring — see INSULATOR illustration **d** (1) : a strip usu. of wood but sometimes of metal or paperboard used to align and hold several boards (as in a barrelhead or box) or to connect adjacent panels or sides of a box (2) : BATTEN 2b(3) (3) : a piece of metal attached to a can or drum to secure a handle or a cover **3** : a system of joints along which coal breaks when mined; *also* : a single joint of cleavage

cleat 1b

²**cleat** \"\ *vt* -ED/-ING/-S **1** : to secure to or by a cleat **2** : to provide or strengthen with a cleat

cleat·er \-ə(r)\ *n* -S : one that saws out cleats or attaches cleats (as to shipping cases)

cleating *n* -S [fr. gerund of *cleat*] : CLEAT 3

cleats \ˈklēts\ *n pl* [origin unknown] : COLTSFOOT a

cleav·a·bil·i·ty \ˌklēvəˈbiləd·ē, -ətē, -i\ *n* -ES : the degree of ease with which a material can be split

cleav·a·ble \ˈklēvəbəl\ *adj* [²*cleave* + *-able*] : capable of being cleaved or divided

cleav·age \ˈklēvij, -ēj\ *n* -S *often attrib* [²*cleave* + *-age*] **1 a** : the quality possessed by many crystallized substances of splitting readily in one or more definite directions and yielding surfaces always parallel to actual or possible crystal faces ⟨~ planes⟩; *also* : the direction of the dividing plane — compare PARTING **b** : the structure possessed by some rocks by virtue of which they break more readily and more persistently in one direction or in certain directions than in others —compare SCHIST, SLATE **2** : the action of cleaving or splitting : the state of being cleft : DIVISION; *specif* : a division into distinct and often opposed or hostile groups ⟨a sharp ~ of fundamental interests that kept farmers and wage earners separate —F.L.Paxson⟩ **3** : a fragment (as of a diamond) obtained by splitting **4** : cell division: **a** : the series of mitotic divisions of the egg that results in the formation of the blastomeres and changes the single-celled zygote into a multicellular embryo : SEGMENTATION — see DETERMINATE CLEAVAGE, INDETERMINATE CLEAVAGE; DISCOIDAL CLEAVAGE, SUPERFICIAL CLEAVAGE; HOLOBLASTIC, MEROBLASTIC **b** : any division belonging to this series **c** : a process of cell formation in which the whole mass of cytoplasm is segmented progressively into small usu. uninucleate portions leaving no epiplasm (as in spore formation in certain fungi, esp. Phycomycetes) — compare FREE CELL FORMATION **5** : the splitting of a molecule into simpler molecules ⟨hydrolytic ~⟩ **6** : the depression between a woman's breasts esp. when made visible by the wearing of low-cut dresses

cleavage cavity *n* : BLASTOCOEL

cleavage cell *n* : BLASTOMERE

cleavage crystal *n* **:** a crystal fragment having a regular form because bounded by cleavage faces

cleavage nucleus *n* **:** the zygote nucleus formed by the fusion of male and female pronuclei

¹cleave \ˈklēv\ *vi* **cleaved** \-vd\ *also* **clave** \ˈklāv\ *or* **clove** \ˈklōv\ **cleaved; cleaving; cleaves** [ME *clevien, clivien,* fr. OE *clifian, cleofian;* akin to OHG *kleben* to stick, ON *klīfa* to clamber, cling to, Serb *glîb* filth, OE *clæg* clay — more at CLAY] **1 :** to adhere firmly and closely as though evenly and securely glued ⟨the rain continued . . . their uniforms *cleaved* uncomfortably to their bodies —Norman Mailer⟩ ⟨the homespun shirt . . . was sodden and *clove* coldly to her shivering body —Florette Henri⟩ **2 :** to adhere firmly, loyally, or unwaveringly ⟨the creed . . . embodied doctrines to which the believer must ~ —Frank Thilly⟩ ⟨insisted that his students ~ to the facts⟩ ⟨a man . . . shall ~ unto his wife —Gen 2:24 (AV)⟩ **syn** see ADHERE

²cleave \"\ *vb* **cleaved** \-vd\ *also* **cleft** \ˈkleft\ *or* **clove** \ˈklōv\ *or archaic* **clave** \ˈklāv\ **cleaved** *also* **cleft** *or* **clo·ven** \ˈklōvən\ **cleaving; cleaves** [ME *cleven, cleoven,* fr. OE *clēofan;* akin to OHG *klioban* to split, ON *kljūfa,* L *glubere* to peel, Gk *glyphein* to carve or hollow out, and perh. to OPruss *gleuptene* smoothing board of a plow] *vt* **1 a :** to divide into two parts by a cutting blow **:** SPLIT ⟨the final blow *cleaving* the archbishop's skull —E.V.Lucas⟩ **:** pass swiftly through (as water or air) as if by cutting ⟨our bow . . . *cleaving* . . . the surface of the deep blue water —Ernest Beaglehole⟩ **b :** to divide into distinct parts or portions esp. into groups having divergent or opposing views or interests **c :** to cause to undergo cleavage **2 a :** to sever or separate by cutting or splitting off **b :** to separate (as a person) from the group or (a part) from the whole ⟨rifts that seemed to ~ soldier from civilian in habit and state of mind —Dixon Wecter⟩ **3 :** to penetrate, pierce, or drive a way through ⟨her slim body . . . *clove* the water like a straight gold sword —Elinor Wylie⟩ **:** force (a passage) as if by cutting or hewing ⟨~ one's way through thick underbrush⟩ ~ *vi* **1 :** to split open or apart esp. along the grain ⟨pine fir wood ~*s* easily⟩ **2 :** to penetrate, pierce, or pass through something usu. swiftly as if by cutting or hewing ⟨a ship *cleaving* through the water⟩ ⟨his acumen *clove* clean to the heart of a piece of writing —D.G.Mandelbaum⟩ **3 :** to undergo cleavage **syn** see TEAR

³cleave \"\ *n* -S [IrGael *cliabh,* fr. MIr *cliab*] *Irish* **:** BASKET

cleave·land·ite *or* **cleve·land·ite** \ˈklēvlən,dīt\ *n* -S [Parker *Cleaveland* †1858 Am. mineralogist + E *-ite*] **:** a white lamellar variety of albite

cleav·er \ˈklēvə(r)\ *n* -S [ME *clever,* fr. *cleven* to split + *-er*] **1 :** one that cleaves: as **a :** a tool for cutting animal bodies into joints or pieces (as in butchering) **b :** one who prepares gems by cleaving off imperfect pieces **2 :** a prehistoric ax-like stone implement having a sharp somewhat straight cutting edge at one end

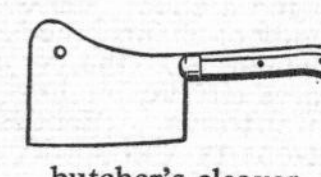

butcher's cleaver

cleav·ers \-(r)z\ *also* **cliv·ers** \ˈklivə(r)z\ *n pl but usu sing in constr* [ME *clivre,* alter. of OE *clife* cleavers, burdock; akin to OHG *chliba,* OE *clifian* to stick — more at CLEAVE] **:** any of several plants of the genus *Galium* (esp. *G. aparine*) having the stems beset with curved prickles — called also *catchweed, goose grass*

cleav·er·wort \ˈklēvə(r) + ,\ *n* [*cleavers* + *wort*] **:** CLEAVERS

cleav·ing·ly *adv* **:** in a cleaving manner

cle·chée *also* **cle·ché** \klāˈshā, kleˈ-, ˈkleshē\ *or* **clechy** \ˈkleshē\ *adj* [F *cléché,* fr. (assumed) VL *clavicatus,* fr. L *clavis* key — more at CLAVICLE] *of a heraldic cross* **:** voided and having each extremity shaped like the handle of a medieval key — compare URDÉE; see CROSS illustration

cleck \ˈklek\ *vb* -ED/-ING/-S [ME *clekken,* fr. ON *klekja;* perh. akin to OE *clyccan* to clutch — more at CLUTCH] *chiefly Scot* **:** HATCH

clee \ˈklē\ *n* -S [ME *clee, cleu, clea,* fr. OE *clēa* — more at CLAW] *now dial Eng* **:** CLAW

cleed \ˈklēd\ *var of* CLEAD

¹cleek \ˈklēk\ *vb* **claught** \ˈklȯkt\ *or* **cleeked** \ˈklēkt\ *or* **claucht** \ˈklȯkt\ **cleeked; cleeking; cleeks** [ME (northern dial.) *cleken;* prob. akin to OE *clyccan* to clutch — more at CLUTCH] *vt* **1** *chiefly Scot* **:** to seize or clutch **:** SNATCH, PLUCK **2** *chiefly Scot* **:** to catch or draw out **:** HOOK ~ *vi, chiefly Scot* **:** to link arms **:** go arm in arm

²cleek \"\ *n* -S [ME (northern dial.) *cleke* hook, act of clutching, fr. *cleken,* v.] **1** *chiefly Scot* **a :** a large hook or crook (as for a pot over a fire) **b :** FISHHOOK **2 :** either of two golf clubs: **a :** a narrow-bladed driving iron formerly in use for short drives **b :** a number four wood

cleeve \ˈklēv\ *var of* CLEVE

clef \ˈklef\ *n* -S [F, key, a key in music, fr. L *clavis* key — more at CLAVICLE] **:** a character placed at the beginning of the musical staff to determine the position of the notes

G, or Treble, Clef · Soprano Clef · Alto Clef · Tenor Clef · F, or Bass, Clef · C Clef

¹cleft \ˈkleft\ *n* -S [alter. of ME *clift,* fr. OE *geclyft;* akin to OS *kluht* tongs, OHG *kluft* gap, tongs, ON *Kluftir,* a place name, OE *clēofan* to split — more at CLEAVE] **1 a :** a space or opening made by or as if by splitting **:** SPLIT, CLEAVAGE, INDENTATION ⟨a spring bubbling out of a ~ in the rock⟩ **b :** an abrupt defile, chasm, or cut ⟨a ~ in the mountains⟩ **c :** a usu. V-shaped indented formation **:** a hollow between ridges or protuberances ⟨the anal ~ of the human body⟩ **d :** the hollow space between the two branches of the frog or the frog and bars or between the bulbs of the heel of a horse's hoof **e :** a crack on the bend of the pastern of a horse **f :** a wide, deep, or insurmountable division (as of belief or opinion) ⟨a ~ opened between sacred and profane science, which has not yet been closed —W.R.Inge⟩ **2 :** a piece or part separated by or as if by cleaving **:** DIVISION; *specif* **:** a division of the cleft foot of an animal **syn** see CRACK

²cleft \"\ *adj* [ME, fr. the past part. of *cleven* to cleave (split)] **1 :** split or divided for a part of the depth or length **:** formed with a partial division ⟨his nose ends in a puggy knob, ~ at the tip —N.M.Clark⟩ **2** *of a leaf* **:** divided about halfway to the midrib often with narrow lobes or sinuses — compare DIVIDED, PARTED — **in a cleft stick :** in an inextricable position **:** in a dilemma **:** in a fix ⟨I never saw his equal to put a fellow *in a cleft stick* —Charles Lever⟩

cleft·ed \ˈkleftəd\ *adj* **:** having clefts **:** FISSURED, CLEFT

cleft-footed \ˈ=ˌ=\ *adj* **:** having a cloven foot

cleft graft *n* **:** a plant graft made by cutting the stock squarely across, splitting the cut end, and inserting one or two scions in the split so that the cambiums of stock and scion are in contact — see GRAFT illustration

cleft lip *n* **:** HARELIP

cleft palate *n* **:** congenital partial or complete fissure of the roof of the mouth often associated with harelip

cleftstone \ˈ=,=\ *n* [²*cleft* + *stone*] **:** FLAGSTONE

cleft weld *n* **:** a weld made by upsetting the ends of the work by cutting a V-shaped opening in the end of one piece, by forming the end of the other piece to fit the first, and by joining the pieces by welding

cleg *or* **clegg** \ˈkleg\ *n* -S [ME, fr. ON *kleggi;* akin to Norw *klegg* burr, OE *clæg* clay — more at CLAY] *Brit* **:** a horsefly or gadfly

cleid- *or* **cleido-** *comb form* [NL, fr. Gk *kleid-, kleido-,* fr. *kleid-, kleis* key; akin to L *clavis* key — more at CLAVICLE] **1 a :** clavicle **:** clavicular ⟨*cleidagra*⟩ **b :** clavicular and ⟨*cleidoscapular*⟩ **2 :** key ⟨*cleidomancy*⟩

clei·do·ic \(ˈ)klīˈdōik\ *adj* [Gk *kleidoun* to fasten, lock in (fr. *kleid-, kleis* key, bolt) + E *-ic*] *of an egg* **:** cut off or isolated from free exchange with the environment by reason of a more or less impervious shell ⟨the eggs of birds are ~⟩

cleik \ˈklēk\ *var of* CLEEK

-clei·sis *or* **-cli·sis** \ˈklīsəs\ *n comb form, pl* **-clei·ses** *or* **-cli·ses** \-ī,sēz\ [NL, fr. Gk *kleisis,* kleisis, fr. *kleiein* to close — more at CLOSE] **:** closure **:** occlusion ⟨arthro*cleisis*⟩ ⟨entero*clisis*⟩

cleist- *or* **cleisto-** *also* **clist-** *or* **clisto-** *comb form* [G *kleist-, kleisto-,* fr. Gk *kleistos;* akin to Gk *kleis* key] **:** closed ⟨*cleistocarp*⟩ ⟨*cleistogamy*⟩

cleis·to·carp \ˈklīstə,kärp\ *also* **clis·to·carp** \", ˈklis-\ *n* -S [*cleist-* + *-carp*] **:** CLEISTOTHECIUM

cleis·to·car·pous *also* **clis·to·car·pous** \ˌ=ˈkärpəs\ *adj* [*cleist-* + *-carpous*] **1** *of mosses* **:** having the capsule opening irregularly without an operculum **2** *of fungi* **:** having or forming cleistothecia

cleis·to·gam·ic *also* **clis·to·gam·ic** \-ˈgamik\ *adj* [ISV *cleist-* + *-gamic*] **:** CLEISTOGAMOUS — **cleis·to·gam·i·cal·ly** \-mək(ə)lē\ *adv*

cleis·tog·a·mous \(ˈ)klīˈstägəməs\ *also* **clis·tog·a·mous** \", (ˈ)kliˈs-\ *adj* [*cleist-* + *-gamous*] **:** exhibiting or relating to cleistogamy — **cleis·tog·a·mous·ly** *adv*

cleis·tog·a·my *also* **clis·tog·a·my** \=ˈ==mē\ *n* -ES [ISV *cleist-* + *-gamy;* orig. formed as G *kleist gamismus*] **:** the production (as in violets and pansies) of small inconspicuous nonopening self-pollinating flowers additional to and often bearing more seeds than the showier type — compare CHASMOGAMY

cleis·to·gene \ˈklīstə,jēn\ *also* **clis·to·gene** \", ˈklis-\ *n* -S [*cleist-* + *-gene*] **1 :** a plant producing cleistogamous flowers **2 :** a cleistogamous flower

cleis·tog·e·nous \(ˈ)klīˈstäjənəs\ *adj* [*cleist-* + *-genous*] **:** bearing cleistogamous flowers

cleis·to·the·ci·um \,klīstəˈthēs(h)ēəm\ *n, pl* **cleistothe·cia** \-ēə\ [NL, fr. *cleist-* + *-thecium*] **:** a closed spore-bearing structure in ascomycetous fungi (as the Aspergillaceae and Erysiphaceae) from which the asci and spores are released only by decay or disintegration — called also *cleistocarp*

clei·thral \ˈklīthrəl\ *adj* [Gk *kleithra* lattice + E *-al* — more at CLATHRATE] *of a temple* **:** having a roofed central space — opposed to *hypaethral*

clei·thrum \-rəm\ *n, pl* **clei·thra** \-rə\ [NL, fr. Gk *kleithron*] **:** a bone external to and beside the clavicle in the pectoral arch of some fishes, stegocephalians, and primitive reptiles

¹clem \ˈklem\ *vb* **clemmed; clemmed; clemming; clems** [ME *clemmen* to pinch — more at CLAM] *vt, dial Eng* **:** to cause to suffer from hunger, thirst, or cold **:** STARVE ~ *vi, dial Eng* **:** to suffer from hunger, thirst, or cold

²clem \"\ *n* -S [origin unknown] *slang* **:** a fight or brawl esp. between circus or carnival workers and the local townsfolk

clem·a·tis \ˈklemə\|d·əs, \|təs; kləˈma-, -ˈmā-,-ˈmä-,-ˈmȧ-\ *n* [NL, fr. L, periwinkle, fr. Gk *klēmatis* brushwood, clematis, fr. *klēmat-, klēma* twig; akin to Gk *klan* to break — more at GLADIATOR] **1** *cap* **:** a genus of opposite-leaved slightly woody vines or erect herbs (family Ranunculaceae) having elongate plumose styles — see TRAVELER'S-JOY, VIRGIN'S BOWER **2** *pl* **clematises** *or* **clematis :** a plant of the genus *Clematis* or of the related genera *Atragene* and *Viorna* **3** *pl* **clematises :** a strong violet that is redder and paler than pansy, redder, stronger, and slightly lighter than royal purple (sense 2), and redder than lobelia

clem·en·cy \ˈklemənsē, -si\ *n* -ES [L *clementia,* fr. *clement-, clemens* mild, calm + *-ia* -y] **1 a :** disposition to be clement, mild, and compassionate and to moderate possible severity of judgment and punishment ⟨show ~ to first offenders⟩ **b :** an act or instance of leniency **2 :** mildness and moderateness esp. of weather **syn** see MERCY

clem·ent \ˈklemənt\ *adj* [ME, fr. L *clement-, clemens;* prob. akin to Gk *klinein* to lean — more at LEAN] **1 a :** characterized by mercy and humaneness in the exercise of power to judge or punish ⟨a master as intelligent, as cultivated, and as ~ as Caesar —R.P.Oliver⟩ **b :** giving the impression or creating an effect of mildness, gentleness, or tenderness ⟨a bright and ~ star shining through the powdery bloom of the dusk —Ellen Glasgow⟩ **2** *of weather* **:** MILD ⟨birds that . . . seek the ~ South —Edna S. V. Millay⟩ **syn** see FORBEARING

¹clem·en·tine \ˈklemən,tēn, -tīn\ *adj, usu cap* [ML & NL *clementinus,* fr. L, ML, & NL *Clement-, Clemens* Clement (the name) + L *-inus* -ine] **:** of or relating to Clement: **a** [after *Clement* I (Clemens Romanus) †*ab* A.D. 100 bishop of Rome] **:** relating to the homilies and liturgies falsely attributed to Clement I, bishop of Rome **b** [after Pope *Clement* V (Bertrand de Got) †1314 Fr. prelate] **:** relating to the compilations of canon law made by Pope Clement V **c** [after Pope *Clement* VIII (Ippolito Aldobrandini) †1605 Ital. prelate] **:** relating to the revised edition of the Vulgate issued under the direction of Pope Clement VIII

²clementine \"\ *n* -S *usu cap* **:** a follower of any of various leaders named Clement (as Clement of Alexandria or Clement VII of Avignon)

clem·ent·ly *adv* **:** in a clement manner

clem·men·sen reduction \ˈklemənsən-\ *n, usu cap C* [after Erik *Clemmensen* †1941 Dan. chemist] **:** the reduction of a ketone or aldehyde directly to a hydrocarbon by the action of amalgamated zinc and hydrochloric acid

clem·mys \ˈkleməs\ *n, cap* [NL, fr. Gk *klemmys* tortoise] **:** a genus of nearly cosmopolitan semiaquatic turtles (family Testudinidae) that includes the No. American wood tortoise and spotted turtle

¹clench \ˈklench\ *vb* -ED/-ING/-ES [ME *clenchen,* fr. OE *-clencan* (in *beclencan* to hold fast); akin to OHG *klenken* to tie, MHG *klank* snare, OE *clingan* to cling — more at CLING] *vt* **1 :** CLINCH *vt* **1 2 :** to hold fast by or as if by grasping tightly **:** CLUTCH ⟨he ~*ed* the arms of his chair⟩ **3 a :** to set or strain (as the jaws) closely or tightly together ⟨~*ed* his teeth⟩ **:** close tightly ⟨~*ed* his fists⟩ **b :** to strain tight or tense (as the body or mind) under or as if under the stress of emotion ⟨you are always ~*ed* against her —D.H.Lawrence⟩ **4 :** CLINCH *vt* **3 5 :** CLINCH *vt* **4** ~ *vi* **1 :** CLINCH *vi* **2 2 :** to set together or close tightly **:** strain tight or tense ⟨her hands ~*ed* in her pockets⟩ ⟨your stomach ~*es* and unclenches —Alvah Bessie⟩

²clench \"\ *n* -ES **1 a :** the end of a nail or other fastening that is turned back in clinching it **b :** a strong fitting (as on the deck of a ship) designed to provide anchorage for cables or shackles under heavy strain **2** *archaic* **:** a play on words **:** PUN **3 :** the action of clenching

clench-built \ˈ=ˌ=\ *adj* **:** CLINKER-BUILT

cle·oid \ˈklē,ȯid\ *n* -S [Gk *kleis* key, catch, hook + E *-oid* — more at CLOSE] **:** an excavator with a claw-shaped working point used in dentistry

cle·o·me \klēˈōmē\ *n* [NL] **1** *cap* **:** a large genus of herbs or low shrubs (family Capparidaceae) having showy flowers with clawed petals and an elongate-linear stalked pod — see SPIDER FLOWER **2** -S **:** any plant of the genus *Cleome*

cle·o·nus \klēˈōnəs\ *n, cap* [NL, fr. L *Cleon,* a proper name (fr. Gk *Kleōn*) + NL *-us*] **:** a genus of Old World weevils (family Curculionidae) including one (*Cleonus punctiventris*) that is a destructive pest of sugar beet, the adults feeding on the leaves and the larvae on the roots

cle·o·pat·ra \,klēəˈpa·trə *also* -pä- *or* -pā- *or* -pȧ-\ *n* -S *often cap* [prob. after *Cleopatra* VII (or VI) †30 B.C. queen of Egypt] **:** a vivid blue that is greener, lighter, and stronger than Ch'ing and greener than ultramarine

clepe \ˈklēp\ *vt* **cleped** \-ēpt,-ept\ **cleped** \"\ *or* **ycleped** \iˈklēpt, ēˈk-, -ept\ *or* **yclept** \-ˈept\ **clep·ing** \-ēpiŋ\ **clepes** \-ēps\ [ME *clepen,* fr. OE *clipian, cleopian* to speak, cry out, call; akin to OFris *kleppa, klippa* to ring, knock, MLG *kleperen* to clatter and perh. to OE *clæppan* to clap — more at CLAP] *archaic* **:** to call by the name of **:** NAME, CALL ⟨they ~ us drunkards —Shak.⟩ ⟨a loose lady *yclept* Julie —Will Cuppy⟩

clepht *var of* KLEPHT

clep·si·ne \klepˈsīnē\ [NL] *syn of* GLOSSIPHONIA

clep·sy·dra \ˈklepsədrə\ *n, pl* **clepsydras** \-rəz\ *or* **clepsy·drae** \-,drē\ [L, fr. Gk *klepsydra,* fr. *kleps-* (fr. *kleptein* to steal) + *-ydra* (fr. *hydōr* water) — more at KLEPT-, WATER] **:** WATER CLOCK

clep·to·biosis \ˌkleptō+\ *n, pl* **cleptobioses** [NL, fr. *clepto-* (fr. Gk *klepto-* theft, fr. *kleptein* to steal) + *-biosis*] **:** a mutual relation in which members of one species (as of ants) habitually steal food from another — see LESTOBIOSIS — **clep·to·biotic** \"+\ *adj*

cleptomania *var of* KLEPTOMANIA

clere·storied \ˈklir, -iə+\ *adj* **:** having a clerestory ⟨~ roof⟩

clere·story *or* **clear·story** \ˈklir, -iə+,-\ *n* -ES [ME, fr. *clere* clear + *story*] **1 :** an outside wall of a room or building (as a church) carried above an adjoining roof and pierced with windows which admit light to the interior **2 :** interior space on the level of the clerestory in a room or building **:** GALLERY **3 :** a raised section of a railroad car roof having windows or openings for ventilation on the sides

building exterior showing clerestory, *1*

clergical *adj, obs* **:** of or belonging to the clergy

cler·gy \ˈklərjē, -ōj-, -əij-, -ji\ *n* -ES [ME *clergie,* fr. OF, fr. *clerg-* (alter. — influenced by *clergié* body of ecclesiastics — of *clerc* clergyman) + *-ie* -y — more at CLERK] **1 :** LEARNING, KNOWLEDGE — used chiefly in the proverb *an ounce of mother wit is worth a pound of clergy* **2 :** the body of men and women duly ordained to the service of God in the Christian church **:** the body of ordained ministers **:** clergymen and clergywomen **3 :** a body of religious officials or functionaries prepared and authorized to conduct religious services and attend to other religious duties ⟨the Taoist ~⟩ ⟨the Jewish ~⟩ **4 :** BENEFIT OF CLERGY 1

cler·gy·able *also* **cler·gi·a·ble** \-jēəbəl\ *adj* **:** entitled to or admitting the benefit of clergy ⟨a ~ felony⟩

cler·gy·man \-jəmən, -jē\ *n, pl* **clergymen 1 :** a member of the clergy **:** an ordained minister **:** a man regularly authorized to preach the gospel and administer its ordinances **:** one in holy orders **2** *Brit* **:** a minister of the Church of England

clergyman's sore throat *n* **:** chronic inflammation of the pharynx often occurring in persons who habitually overstrain or misuse the voice (as in public speaking)

cler·gy·woman \-jə, -jē+,-\ *n, pl* **clergywomen 1** *archaic* **:** a woman member of a religious order **:** NUN **2 :** a woman who is an ordained minister **3** *archaic* **:** a clergyman's wife or female relative esp. when officiously meddlesome

¹cler·ic \ˈklerik, -rēk\ *n* -S [LL *clericus,* adj. & n. — more at CLERK] **1 :** CLERGYMAN **2 :** one who has received the ecclesiastical tonsure **:** CLERK

²cleric \"\ *adj* [LL *clericus*] **:** CLERICAL

¹cler·i·cal \-rəkəl, -ēk-\ *adj* [LL *clericalis,* fr. *clericus*] **1 :** of, belonging to, or characteristic of the clergy, a clergyman, or a cleric ⟨~ vows⟩ **2 :** of, suitable to, or belonging to a clerk in an office or business ⟨~ occupations such as bookkeeping⟩ **:** being or consisting of an office clerk or clerks ⟨~ staff⟩ **3 :** governed by or supporting the principles of clericalism ⟨a ~ party⟩ — **cler·i·cal·ly** \-rək(ə)lē, -ēk-, -li\ *adv*

²clerical \"\ *n* -S **1 :** a clergyman or cleric **2 :** one who believes in or supports clericalism **:** a member of a clerical party ⟨the ~*s* proposed compulsory religious education in the public schools⟩ **3 clericals** *pl* **:** clerical garments **4 :** one who does clerical work in an office or business ⟨permanent jobs as secretaries, ~*s,* typists —*N.Y. Times*⟩

clerical collar *n* **:** a narrow stiffly upright white collar buttoned at the back of the neck and worn by various clergymen — called also *reversed collar*

clerical error *n* **:** an error made in copying or writing

cler·i·cal·ism \-,lizəm\ *n* -S **1 :** a policy that attempts to maintain or augment the temporal power (as the political power) of a church or religious hierarchy **2 a :** a policy favoring the maintenance or increase of power over religious matters by an ecclesiastical hierarchy or clergy **b :** dogmatic and authoritarian control of religious matters by clergy

cler·i·cal·ist \-,ləst\ *n* -S **:** one who favors the increase of ecclesiastical power and influence

cler·i·cal·i·ty \,klerəˈkaləd·ē\ *n* -ES **:** clerical quality, state, or characteristic

cler·i·cal·ize \ˈklerəkə,līz, -rēk-\ *vt* -ED/-ING/-S [F *cléricaliser,* fr. *clérical* + *-iser* -ize] **:** to cause to become clerical or be influenced by clericalism

clerical technician *n* **:** one who studies the clerical and statistical procedures of business establishments for the purpose of improving the methods used

cler·i·ca·ture \ˈklerəkə,chù(ə)r\ *n* -S [F *cléricature,* fr. ML *clericatura,* fr. *clericatus* (past part. of *clericare* to make a cleric, fr. LL *clericus*) + L *-ura* -ure] **:** clerical position or function

cle·ri·ci solution \kləˈrēchē-\ *n, usu cap C* [fr. the name *Clerici*] **:** a water solution of thallium malonate and thallium formate used as a liquid of high specific gravity to separate mixtures of solids into their components

clerico- *comb form* [LL *clericus* priest] **:** clerical (sense 1) **:** clerical and ⟨*clerico*political⟩ ⟨*clerico*fascist⟩

cler·id \ˈklerəd\ *n* -S [NL *Cleridae*] **:** a beetle of the family Cleridae

cler·i·dae \ˈklerə,dē\ *n pl, cap* [NL, fr. *Clerus,* type genus (fr. Gk *klēros,* a kind of beetle, prob. of the genus *Clerus*) + *-idae*] **:** a family of beetles related to the soldier beetles and fireflies and usu. of bright checkered colors or metallic luster and predaceous on other insects

cler·i·hew \ˈklerə,hyü\ *n* -S [after Edmund *Clerihew* Bentley †1956 Eng. writer of detective fiction, its originator] **:** a light verse quatrain in lines usu. of varying length, rhyming *aabb,* and making a statement usu. concerning a person whose name typically supplies the initial rhyme

cler·i·sy \ˈklerəsē\ *n* -ES [G *klerisei* clergy (often used contemptuously), fr. ML *clericia,* fr. LL *clericus* priest] **:** the well-educated or learned class **:** the academic class **:** INTELLIGENTSIA ⟨the ~ of a nation . . . whether poets or philosophers or scholars —S.T.Coleridge⟩

¹clerk \ˈklərk, -ōk,-əik, *Brit usu* ˈklȧk\ *n* -S [ME, fr. OF *clerc* & OE *clerc, cleric,* both fr. LL *clericus,* fr. Gk *klērikos,* fr. Gk *klēros* lot, allotment, clergy + *-ikos* -ic; akin to Gk *klan* to break — more at GLADIATOR] **1 :** a clergyman or cleric: as **a :** an ordained minister of the Church of England ⟨a ~ in holy orders⟩ **b** *Roman Catholicism* (1) **:** one who has received the ecclesiastical tonsure (2) **:** a person who under canon law enjoys benefit of clergy (as a monk or nun) **2** *archaic* **a :** a person who can read or read and write **b :** a learned person **:** SCHOLAR, MAN OF LETTERS **3 a :** an employee or official responsible (as to a corporation or a government agency) for correspondence, the keeping of records and accounts, and the management of routine affairs and vested with certain specified powers or authority (as to issue writs or other processes as ordered by a court) **:** SECRETARY ⟨~ of a court⟩ ⟨town ~⟩ ⟨~ of the society⟩ **b** (1) **:** one employed (as in a business office) to keep records or accounts or to perform more or less routine office tasks ⟨tally ~⟩ ⟨filing ~⟩ (2) **:** one in charge of records and accounts on a steamboat **:** purser of a steamboat **c** (1) **:** a postal employee who works at the sales and service windows in a post office and esp. in a small post office sometimes performs operations connected with the sorting of mail (2) **:** one who sorts mail in a railway post office **d :** a hotel employee usu. stationed at the desk who serves the hotel and its guests esp. by assigning rooms and performing small services (as giving guests their mail and holding their keys when they are out of the hotel) **4 :** a layman who performs some ecclesiastical office: **a :** a Church of England minister regarded in civil law as a layman whose office is to assist the clergy, lead the responses, and teach in schools — called also *parish clerk* **b :** a layman or laywoman in the Protestant Episcopal Church serving as the scribe of the vestry and sometimes also of the parish or parish meeting **c :** a chief official appointed to serve at a regularly organized meeting of the Society of Friends **5 :** a salesperson in a store **:** one who shows and sells articles of merchandise in a store ⟨a grocery ~⟩ **6 :** one who holds a clerkship (sense 3)

²clerk \"\ *vb* -ED/-ING/-S *vi* **:** to act or work as a clerk ⟨~*ing* in the feed store at six dollars a week —Elmer Davis⟩ ~ *vt, chiefly Scot* **:** WRITE, COMPOSE

clerk·ess \-kəs\ *n* -ES *chiefly Scot* **:** a female clerk

clerk·ish \-kish\ *adj* **1 :** CLERICAL **2 a :** suggesting a clerk or the work of a clerk **b :** overprecise or particular of detail

clerk·less \-ləs\ *adj* **:** having no clerk

1clerk·ly \-lē\ *adv* [ME, fr. *clerk* + *-ly*] **:** in a clerkly manner; *esp* **:** LEARNEDLY

2clerkly \"\ *adj* -ER/-EST [*clerk* + *-ly*] **:** of, relating to, suitable to, or characteristic of a clerk: as **a :** belonging to or befitting the clergy ⟨~ privilege⟩ ⟨the Wife of Bath's ~ husband —G.G.Coulton⟩ **b** *archaic* **:** LEARNED, SCHOLARLY **c :** showing skill in penmanship ⟨to write a ~ hand⟩ **d :** quiet or studious in conduct **:** precise or modest in appearance ⟨a timid ~ fellow⟩ **e :** of or in the capacity of a clerk ⟨~ career⟩

clerk of the course : an official who acts as executive secretary to the board of judges of races or track athletics

clerk of the scales : an official who weighs jockeys and their gear before and after a horse race

clerk regular *n* [trans. of ML *canonicus regularis*] **:** a religious combining monastic life with the ministry of a diocesan priest

clerk·ship \-ˌship\ *n* -S **1 :** the office or business of a clerk **:** a position as a clerk **2** *archaic* **:** LEARNING, SCHOLARSHIP **3 :** the part of the undergraduate medical curriculum during which the student under supervision serves as a clerk performing routine clinical work for stated periods in a hospital that is affiliated with a medical school

clerk vicar *n* **:** a layman in the Church of England who is employed in a cathedral to take those parts of the liturgy not reserved to the clergy — called also *lay vicar, secular vicar*

cler·mont-fer·rand \ˌklermōⁿfeˈräⁿ\ *adj, usu cap C&F* [fr. *Clermont-Ferrand*, France] **:** of or from the city of Clermont-Ferrand, France **:** of the kind or style prevalent in Clermont-Ferrand

cle·ro·den·dron \ˌklirəˈdendrən, ˌkler-\ *n, cap* [NL, fr. *clero-* (fr. Gk *klēros* lot) + *-dendron* — more at CLERK] **:** a genus of chiefly Old World tropical sometimes climbing shrubs and trees (family Verbenaceae) that are often cultivated esp. in greenhouses and have opposite simple leaves, irregular flowers in headlike clusters, and a drupelike fruit enclosed in the calyx

cle·ro·den·drum \-drəm\ *syn of* CLERODENDRON

cle·ro·man·cy \ˈ==ˌman(t)sē\ *n* -ES [MF or ML; MF *cleromancie*, fr. ML *cleromantia*, fr. *clero-* + *-mantia* -mancy] **:** divination by means of casting lots

cle·ruch \ˈkliˌrük, -lēˌr-, -ˌrək\ *n* -S [Gk *klērouchos*, fr. *klēro-* (fr. *klēros* lot, allotment) + *-ochos* holder (fr. *echein* to have, hold) — more at SCHEME] **:** a citizen of ancient Greece who received an allotment of land in a conquered country and usu. migrated to it without loss of his citizenship — **cle·ru·chi·al** \klə'rükēəl\ *or* **cle·ru·chic** \-kik\ *adj*

cle·ru·chy \ˈkliˌrükē, -lēˌr-, -ˌrəkē\ *n* -ES [Gk *klērouchia*, fr. *klērouchos*] **:** a body or settlement of cleruchs

cle·rus \ˈklirəs\ *n, cap* [NL, fr. Gk *klēros*, a beetle (*Clerus apiarius*)] **:** the type genus of the family Cleridae

cless \ˈkles\ *Scot var of* CLASS

cletch \ˈklech\ *n* -ES [alter. (perh. influenced by *3clutch*) of *cleck*] **1** *dial Eng* **:** HATCHING, CLUTCH, BROOD **2** *dial Eng* **:** a brood of persons **:** FAMILY

cle·thra \ˈklēthrə, -eth-\ *n, cap* [NL, fr. Gk *klēthra* alder; akin to G (Tirolese dial.) *lutter* green alder (*Alnus viridis*)] **:** a genus (coextensive with the family Clethraceae) of deciduous shrubs or trees with stellate pubescence and capsular fruits of three locules — see SWEET PEPPER BUSH, WHITE ALDER

cle·thra·ce·ae \klə'thrāsēˌē, kle-\ *n pl, cap* [NL, fr. *Clethra*, type genus + *-aceae*] **:** a family of dicotyledonous plants (order Ericales) coextensive with the genus *Clethra*

cleth·ri·on·o·mys \ˌklethrēˈänəməs\ *n, cap* [NL, fr. *clethriono-* (modif. of Gk *kleithrion*, dim. of *kleithron* entrance of the windpipe, fr. *kleiein* to close) + *-mys* — more at CLOSE] **:** a genus of rodents consisting of the red-backed mice

cleuch *or* **cleugh** \ˈklük\ *n* -S [ME (Sc), fr. (assumed) OE *clōh* —more at CLOUGH] *chiefly Scot* **:** CLOUGH

cleuk \ˈkl(y)ük\ *n* -S [ME (northern dial.) *cluk, cluke, cloke*; akin to ME *cleken* to catch or snatch — more at CLEEK] *chiefly Scot* **:** CLAW, HAND **:** GRASP, CLUTCH ⟨he has her in his ~s⟩

cleve \ˈklēv\ *n* -S [ME *cleve, cleove*, fr. OE *clif*, nom. & acc. pl. *cleofu* — more at CLIFF] **1** *dial Eng* **:** CLIFF **2** *dial Eng* **:** steep sloping ground **:** BRAE

cleve·ite \ˈklēˌvīt, ˈklāvəˌīt\ *n* -S [Sw *cleveit*, fr. P. T. *Cleve* †1905 Swed. chemist + Sw *-it* -ite] **:** URANINITE

cleve·land \ˈklēvlənd\ *adj, usu cap* [fr. *Cleveland*, Ohio] **:** of or from the city of Cleveland, Ohio ⟨a *Cleveland* terminal⟩ **:** of the kind or style prevalent in Cleveland

cleveland bay *n, usu cap C & often cap B* [fr. *Cleveland*, district in Yorkshire, England, where it was developed] **:** a horse of a breed developed for light draft and carriage use, being uniformly bay in color with black points and legs and of good conformation and strong constitution

cleve·land·er \-ləndə(r)\ *n* -S *cap* [*Cleveland*, Ohio + E *-er*] **:** a native or resident of Cleveland, esp. Cleveland, Ohio

clevelandite *var of* CLEAVELANDITE

1clev·er \ˈklevə(r)\ *adj* -ER/-EST [ME *cliver*, prob. of Scand origin; akin to Dan dial. *kløver* clever, skillful, alert, ON *kljūfa* to split, pierce — more at CLEAVE] **1 :** showing deftness, skill, or adroitness in using the hands or in other bodily movements **:** NIMBLE ⟨~ with the gloves⟩ **2 :** having mental quickness, intelligence, resourcefulness in improvising often accompanied by craft, wit, or physical dexterity ⟨you are a ~ man, . . . you reason well, and your wit is bold —Bram Stoker⟩ ⟨through the porcelain . . . a ~ artisan had thrust a rivet —Elinor Wylie⟩; *often* **:** intelligent, quick, ingenious, and resourceful but lacking in depth, soundness, wisdom, or morality ⟨too ~ to be sound —Van Wyck Brooks⟩ ⟨an exercise in ~ film-making without ever striking fire as a film —Arthur Knight⟩ **3 :** characterized by the display of wit or ingenuity ⟨a ~ poem⟩ ⟨his judgments were wise rather than ~ —James Hilton⟩ ⟨applauded his ~ sparkling speech⟩ **4** *now dial* **a :** in good health ⟨wasn't looking too ~ —Thomas Wood †1950⟩ **b :** well-shaped **:** CLEAN-LIMBED — used esp. of an animal ⟨a right ~ horse⟩ **c :** well-made **:** carefully constructed ⟨a ~ spade⟩ **5** *now chiefly dial* **:** convenient or easy to use or handle ⟨a sweet craft, trim, staunch, and ~ to handle —S.H. Adams⟩ **:** SATISFACTORY, PLEASING ⟨~ land for farming⟩ — a generalized expression of approval **6** *dial* **:** GOOD-NATURED, OBLIGING, AMIABLE, HOSPITABLE ⟨good ~ man —Elizabeth M. Roberts⟩

syn ADROIT, CUNNING, INGENIOUS: although CLEVER still occas. retains its old meaning of physical dexterity, agility, and deftness, it usu. indicates mental alertness and resourcefulness ⟨curiously *clever* at all kinds of things . . . a sort of impromptu conjuring, making fifteen matches set fire to each other like a regular firework —G.K.Chesterton⟩ ⟨"who invented the story — you or her?" "He did, monsieur. He was very *clever*. He thought of everything" —Dorothy Sayers⟩ ⟨Austin was not *clever* like Adrian: he seldom divined other people's ideas and always went the direct road to his object —George Meredith⟩ ADROIT suggests shrewd and wily or alert and agile expedients ⟨the cool prudence, the sensitive selfishness, the quick perception of what is possible, which distinguish the *adroit* politician —J.R.Green⟩ ⟨'tis said he could shave himself with the axe — so all *adroit* . . . does he work and play at once —Robert Browning⟩ CUNNING may apply to high creative skill or low guileful craft ⟨he knew how . . . to construct a plot, he was *cunning* in his manipulation of stage effects —T.S.Eliot⟩ ⟨it is, of course, possible that a *cunning* man might change the tire of his bicycle in order to leave unfamiliar tracks —A. Conan Doyle⟩ INGENIOUS suggests brilliant or notable inventiveness and resourcefulness ⟨the batteries being kept recharged by an *ingenious* device —Dorothy Sayers⟩ ⟨the *ingenious* Yankee, quick to adapt himself everywhere, easily extricating himself from situations —Matthew Josephson⟩ **syn** see in addition INTELLIGENT

2clever \"\ *adv* **1** *now dial* **:** very well **:** EXCELLENTLY ⟨treated him real ~ —Willa Cather⟩ **2** *dial Brit* **:** DIRECTLY, STRAIGHT ⟨you must go ~ through the city⟩ ⟨the dog jumped ~ over the hedge⟩

clev·er·al·i·ty \ˌklevə'ralətī\ *n* -ES [*1clever* + *-ality* (as in *comicality*)] *chiefly Scot* **:** CLEVERNESS

clev·er·ish \ˈklev(ə)rish\ *adj* **:** somewhat clever — **clev·er·ish·ly** *adv*

clev·er·ly *adv* **1 :** in a clever manner **2** *dial* **:** FULLY, COMPLETELY ⟨as soon as he was ~ out of hearing —T.C.Haliburton⟩ **:** ENTIRELY, QUITE ⟨the boy wasn't ~ grown⟩ **3** *dial* **:** SATISFACTORILY, CONVENIENTLY

clev·er·ness \-və(r)nəs\ *n* -ES **:** the quality of being clever; *esp* **:** ADROITNESS

cle·ve's acid \ˈklāvəz-, ˈklēvz-\ *n, usu cap C* [after P.T. *Cleve* — more at CLEVEITE] **:** either of two colorless crystalline isomeric monosulfonic acids $NH_2C_{10}H_6SO_3H$ derived from alpha-naphthylamine and used as intermediates in making azo dyes; *also* **:** a mixture of these acids

clev·is \ˈklevəs\ *n* -ES [earlier *clevi* (akin to Sc *clivvie, clevie* cleft branch, cleft instrument), prob. of Scand origin; akin to ON *klofi* cleft stick, groove for a door, *kljūfa* to split — more at CLEAVE] **1 :** a fitting for attaching or suspending parts (as a cable to another structural member of a bridge or a hanger for supporting pipe) that consists usu. of a U-shaped piece of metal with the ends drilled to receive a pin or bolt **2 :** any of various connections in which one part is fitted between the forked ends of another and fastened by means of a bolt or pin passing through the forked ends

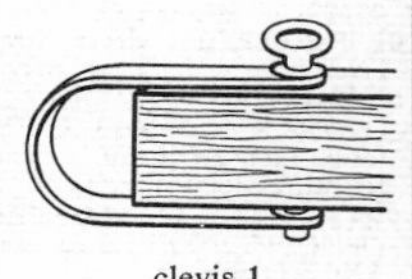

clevis 1

clevy \ˈklevē, -vi\ *n* -ES [back-formation fr. *clevis*, taken as pl.] **:** CLEVIS

1clew *or* **clue** \ˈklü\ *n* -S [ME *clewe*, fr. OE *cliewen*; akin to OHG *kliuwa* ball, ON *klō* claw, Gk *ginglymos* hinge, Skt *glau* round lump — more at GALL] **1 :** a ball of thread, yarn, or cord **2 a :** the information or key that guides through an intricate procedure or a maze of difficulties ⟨provide a ~ through the complex negotiations⟩ **b :** the thread of narrative (as in a story) or of thought or argument **c** *usu clue* **:** a piece of evidence tending to lead one toward the solution of a problem **:** an indication that properly interpreted may lead to full understanding of something or to the discovery of something unknown or hidden ⟨the flight of birds might furnish a valuable *clue* to the problem of blind flying —H.G.Armstrong⟩ ⟨possess a rough *clue* as to what the conversation has previously been about —Paul Dehn⟩ **3 a :** a lower corner of a square sail or the after lower corner of a fore-and-aft sail — see SAIL illustration **b clews** *pl* **:** a combination of lines or nettles by which a hammock is suspended

2clew *or* **clue** \"\ *vt* **clewed** *or* **clued**; **clewed** *or* **clued**; **clewing** *or* **clueing** *or* **cluing**; **clews** *or* **clues** **1 :** to roll into a ball **2** *usu clue* **a :** to provide with a clue (as to something hidden or unknown) ⟨nothing to ~ us to what happened⟩ **b** *slang* **:** to give reliable information to ⟨~ me on how it works⟩ **3 a :** to haul (a sail) by means of the clew garnets or clew lines up to a yard or mast — used with *up* **b :** to force (a yard) down by hauling on the clew lines — used with *down*

clew garnet *n* **:** one of the ropes by which the clews of the courses of square-rigged ships are hauled up to lower yards

clew jigger *n* **:** a small tackle used instead of clew lines to trice up the clew of a sail

clew line *n* **:** a rope by which a clew of an upper square sail is hauled up to its yard — see SAIL illustration

clg *abbr* ceiling

CLI *abbr* cost-of-living index

cli·an·thus \klī'an(t)thəs\ *n* [NL, fr. *cli-* (irreg. fr. Gk *kleos* glory) + *-anthus*; akin to Gk *klytos* famous — more at LOUD] **1** *cap* **:** a genus of Australasian semiprostrate shrubs or vines (family Leguminosae) with compound leaves and pealike red flowers in drooping racemes **2** -ES **:** any plant of the genus *Clianthus* (esp. *C. dampieri*) — see GLORY PEA

1cli·ché \klē'shā, ˈ=ˌ=, kli'shā\ *n* -S [F, fr. past part. of *clicher* to stereotype, of imit. origin; fr. the noise of the die striking the metal] **1 :** a stereotype or electrotype; *esp* **:** a single stamp of which a number are joined to form a plate for printing a whole sheet of stamps at once **2 a :** a trite or stereotyped phrase or expression; *also* **:** the idea expressed by it **b :** a hackneyed theme, plot, or situation in fiction or drama **:** an overworked idea or its expression in music or one of the other arts ⟨such photographic ~s as indicating change of seasons by the transition from snow to fruit in the orchards —John McCarten⟩

2cliché \"\ *adj* **:** HACKNEYED ⟨those desperate perceptions of our life which . . . have become so obvious and ~ that they seem to close for us the possibility of thought and imagination —Lionel Trilling⟩

cli·chéd \-ād\ *adj* **1 :** marked by or abounding in clichés ⟨the ~ pattern of her mind —Russell Thacher⟩ **2 :** CLICHÉ ⟨the somewhat ~ phrase, *horrified fascination* —Neville Braybrooke⟩

1click \ˈklik\ *vb* -ED/-ING/-S *vt* **1 a :** to strike or move with a click **:** cause to click ⟨~ his heels together⟩ ⟨~*ed* down the lid of the card file —Emelie Glenn⟩ **b :** to produce with clicks — usu. used with *out* ⟨~ out a rhythm on castanets⟩ ⟨~ out a message on a typewriter⟩ **2 :** to cut out (as parts of a shoe upper) by using a small knife or by operating a die-cutting machine ~ *vi* **1 a :** to make a click ⟨the latch ~*ed* as the door closed⟩ ⟨billiard balls ~*ed* in the next room⟩ **b :** to move with a click ⟨hearing her heels ~ across the kitchen tiles —Leslie Ford⟩ ⟨the camera adjustment lever ~*ed* into position⟩ **2 a :** to fit or agree exactly ⟨personal opinions have their value particularly when they ~ with experimental results —W.C. Allee⟩ **b :** to fit together **:** hit it off ⟨the thought of Dornford and Dinny and whether they would ~ —John Galsworthy⟩ ⟨explores the nature of the diversity of human beings and their compulsions, what makes them ~ as mates —David Tilden⟩ ⟨we were sitting on the . . . big town bridge trying to ~ with a few girls —Walter Macken⟩ **c :** to function or operate efficiently, smoothly, and successfully esp. in or as one of a team ⟨the platoon's teamwork was still ~*ing* —Mack Morriss⟩ **d :** SUCCEED; *esp* **:** to make a hit ⟨the selling aid that ~s . . . for any promotional effort —*Retailing Daily*⟩ ⟨a movie that ~s⟩ ⟨a bit player who finally ~*ed* in a first-rate Broadway play⟩ **3 :** FORGE *vi* 3 **4 :** to emphasize a musical beat by suddenly quickening the baton's motion toward the end of its stroke

2click \"\ *n* -S [prob. of imit. origin] **1 a :** a slight sharp noise (as that made by the cocking of a pistol or the latching of a door) ⟨the ~ of billiard balls⟩ **b** (1) **:** a sound that in some languages is a speech sound made by enclosing air between two stop articulations of the tongue, enlarging the enclosure to rarefy the air, and suddenly opening the enclosure **:** a velaric suction stop (2) *usu cap* **:** a language family of Africa including Khoisan, Sandawe, and Hatsa characterized by extensive employment of clicks **c :** the audible movement from one graduation to another in the rear sight of a firearm; *also* **:** such a graduation in a sight **2 :** a part (as a ratchet catch or lock tumbler) to control the movement of a mechanism or the movable part of a device: as **a :** DETENT **b :** a pawl esp. of small size **3** *dial Eng* **:** a sharp unexpected blow or rap **4** *of a horse* **:** the act of forging **5 :** a sudden flick of a conductor's baton marking an emphatic musical beat

3click \"\ *vb* -ED/-ING/-S [alter. of *1cleek*] *dial Brit* **:** CLUTCH, SEIZE, SNATCH

click beetle *n* [*2click*] **:** an adult beetle of the family Elateridae — called also *skipjack, snapping beetle*; compare WIREWORM

1click-clack \ˈkliˌklak\ *n* [reduplic. of *2click*] **:** a succession of clicks or of alternating clicks and clacks ⟨the *click-clack* of the pendulum of the old grandfather clock⟩

2click-clack \"\ *vi* **:** to make a click-clack sound (as in walking) ⟨*click-clacked* out of the room⟩

click·er \ˈklikə(r)\ *n* -S [*1click* + *-er*] **1 :** a horse that forges **2** *Brit* **:** PULLER-IN **3 :** one that operates a die-cutting machine which cuts small shapes from materials (as cloth, paper, cardboard, or leather) **4** *chiefly Brit* **:** the chargehand of a companionship or comparable group of compositors

1click·et \ˈklikət\ *n* -S [ME *cliket*, fr. MF *cliquet*, fr. *cliquer* — more at CLICK] *now dial Eng* **:** LATCH, LATCHKEY

2clicket \"\ *vi* -ED/-ING/-S [origin unknown] **:** to be in heat **:** COPULATE — used chiefly of the fox or hare

click·ety-clack \ˌklikəd·ēˈklak\ *or* **click·ety-click** \-klik\ *n* [alter. of *1click-clack*] **:** a rhythmic usu. fast click-clack ⟨the *clickety-clack* of the wheels along the railroad track⟩ ⟨the *clickety-click* of typewriters⟩

click hook *n* [*3click*] *dial Eng* **:** a large barbed hook for catching or landing fish

click·less \ˈkliklәs\ *adj* **:** lacking a click

click off *vt* **1 :** to click out ⟨*click off* a message on the typewriter⟩ **2 :** to record usu. with clicks ⟨the speedometer *clicked off* the miles⟩ **3 :** to list or enumerate unhesitatingly or with unerring precision ⟨*clicked off* his facts and figures without a slip —E.P.Snow⟩

click stop *n* **:** a diaphragm setting device on a camera or enlarger for selecting desired apertures by means of a series of audible clicks

cli·das·tes \klī'da(ˌ)stēz\ *n, cap* [NL, prob. irreg. fr. Gk *kleid-, kleis* key; akin to L *claudere* to shut — more at CLOSE] **:** a genus of large extinct No. American Cretaceous fish-eating marine lizards in many respects resembling the recent monitors — compare MOSASAURUS, VARANIDAE

cli·ent \ˈklīənt\ *n* -S [ME, fr. MF & L; MF *client*, fr. L *client-, cliens* client, dependent, lit., one who has someone to lean on; akin to ON *hlīta* to be satisfied with, L *clinare* to lean — more at LEAN] **1 :** a person under the protection of another **:** VASSAL, DEPENDENT ⟨an impecunious ~ and favored dinner companion of Lorenzo the Magnificent and his court —G.C. Sellery⟩ ⟨a first-rate power, able to defend her political ~s in central and eastern Europe —W.W.Kulski⟩; *esp* **:** a dependent (as a freed slave or one of the plebs) in ancient Rome who was obliged to perform certain services in return for the protection he received from his patrician patron **2 a :** a person who engages the professional advice or services of another ⟨results . . . discouraging to the ~ as well as the veterinarian —O.V. Brumley⟩ ⟨professional relationship of architect and ~⟩; *specif* **:** a person who consults or engages the services of a legal advisor **b :** PATRON, CUSTOMER ⟨hotel ~s⟩ ⟨the single ~ examining the secondhand books on the stand outside the paper shop —Kay Boyle⟩ **c :** a person served by or utilizing the services of a social agency or a public institution ⟨one set of laws for ~s of social agencies and another for the rest of our citizens —J.E.Rinck⟩ ⟨relief and old-age ~s —*N. Y. State Legislative Committee on Problems of the Aging*⟩ ⟨was spreading for the benefit of new ~s —F.L.Paxson⟩

cli·ent·age \-tij\ *n* -S **1 :** a body of clients **:** CLIENTELE ⟨the ~ of a Roman nobleman⟩ ⟨one of those little shops . . . where they sell such smart things so cheaply to a ~ of minor actresses and cocottes —Aldous Huxley⟩ **2 :** the relationship of a client to a patron or benefactor ⟨the specific tie which bound the herdsmen to their leader was in the nature of ~ —Kalervo Oberg⟩

cli·en·tal \(ˈ)klī'entᵊl, ˈklīən-\ *adj* **:** of or relating to a client ⟨I sat down in the ~ chair —Charles Dickens⟩

cli·en·tele \ˌklīən·ˈtel, -lēən- *also* -lēˌän-\ *n* -S [F *clientèle*, fr. L *clientela*, fr. *client-, cliens*] **1** *archaic* **:** the quality or state of being a client (sense 1) **:** the institution of clientship **2 :** a body of clients ⟨the ~ of an advertising agency⟩ ⟨the theater's regular ~⟩ ⟨the ~ of our colleges —R.W.Livingstone⟩ ⟨a large city hospital ~ —*Jour. Amer. Med. Assoc.*⟩

cli·ent·less \ˈklīəntləs\ *adj* **:** having no clients

cli·ent·ry \ˈklīəntrē\ *n* -ES *archaic* **:** CLIENTELE

clies *pl of* CLY

1cliff \ˈklif\ *n* -S [ME *clif*, fr. OE; akin to OS *klif*, OHG *klep*, ON *klif*, OE *clīfan, clifian* to adhere to — more at CLEAVE] **1 :** a very steep, perpendicular, or overhanging face of rock, earth, or glacial ice of considerable height **:** PRECIPICE — see FAULT-LINE SCARP, FAULT SCARP, SCARP; compare ESCARPMENT **2** *Brit* **:** a steep slope or hill **:** CLEVE

2cliff \"\ *vb* -ED/-ING/-S **:** to erode so as to form a cliff ⟨the shores of both mainland and continental islands are ~*ed* and drowned —*Jour. of Geol.*⟩ ⟨postglacial ~*ing* —F.P.Shepard⟩

cliff brake *n* **:** a fern of the genus *Pellaea* (esp. *P. atropurpurea*) growing usu. on cliffs and walls

cliff dweller *n* **1** *often cap C&D* **a :** one of the people of the Anasazi culture of the American southwest who erected their dwellings on rock ledges or in the recesses of canyon walls and cliffs **b :** a member of any cliff-dwelling people **2 :** a person who lives in a large usu. metropolitan apartment building ⟨the *cliff dwellers* of Chicago —M.D.Geismar⟩ — **cliff dwelling** *n*

cliffed \-ft\ *adj* **:** consisting of or marked by the presence of a cliff ⟨a ~ shoreline⟩ ⟨a commanding scarp . . . , ~ at the top —P.E.James⟩

cliff-green \ˈ=ˌ=\ *n* **:** MOUNTAIN LOVER

cliff-hang \ˈ=ˌ=\ *vi* **:** to end an installment of a cliff-hanger with a suspenseful usu. melodramatic unresolved conflict designed to entice the audience to read or view the succeeding installment to discover the resolution of the conflict ⟨to forbid *cliff-hanging* in children's radio serials⟩

cliff-hanger \ˈ=ˌ==\ *n* **1 :** an adventure serial or melodrama; *esp* **:** one presented in installments each of which ends in suspense ⟨*cliff-hangers* on radio⟩ **2 :** a contest whose outcome is in doubt up to the very end ⟨the election was a *cliff-hanger*⟩

cliff·less \ˈklifləs\ *adj* **:** lacking cliffs

cliff rose *n* **1:** a thrift (*Armeria maritima*) **2 :** a small evergreen shrub (*Cowania stansburiana*) of the family Rosaceae common on the desert ranges of the southern U.S. and Mexico, useful as a browse plant, and characterized by briliant golden-yellow flowers followed by clusters of achenes with long feathery tails — called also *quinine bush*

cliffside \ˈ=ˌ=\ *n* **:** the steep side of a cliff or of any abrupt natural incline of considerable size ⟨picking his way up the dangerous ~⟩ ⟨~ caves⟩

cliff swallow *n* **:** any of a number of chiefly No. American swallows (genus *Petrochelidon*) that build their bottlelike nests of mud against cliffs or under eaves — called also *eaves swallow*

cliffy \-fē\ *adj* -ER/-EST **:** characterized by or abounding in cliffs **:** STEEP, CRAGGY ⟨a ~ shoreline⟩

1clift \ˈklift\ *archaic or dial var of* CLEFT

2clift \"\ *n* -S [ME, alter. (influenced by *clift* cleft) of *clif* cliff — more at CLIFF, CLEFT] *now chiefly dial* **:** CLIFF

clif·ton·ite \ˈkliftəˌnīt\ *n* -S [Robert B. *Clifton* †1921 Eng. physicist + E *-ite*] **:** carbon found in minute cubic crystals in meteoric iron

clifty \ˈkliftē\ *adj* [*2clift* + *-y*] **:** CLIFFY

clim *dial past of* CLIMB

cli·ma·ci·um \klī'mās(h)ēəm\ *n, cap* [NL, fr. Gk *klimak-, klimax* ladder + NL *-ium* — more at CLIMAX] **:** a small genus (the type of the family Climaciaceae) of treelike branching true mosses — compare BRYALES; see TREE MOSS

climacter *n* -S [L, fr. Gk *klimaktēr*, lit., rung of a ladder, fr. *klimak-, klimax* ladder] *obs* **:** a climacteric period

cli·mac·te·ri·al \ˌklīˌmakˈtirēəl\ *adj* [NL *climacterium* + E *-al*] **:** relating to or involving the climacterium

1cli·mac·ter·ic \(ˈ)klī'maktərik *also* ˌklīˌmakˈterik\ *also* **cli·mac·ter·i·cal** \ˌ==ˈterəkəl\ *adj* [*climacteric* fr. L *climactericus*, fr. Gk *klimaktērikos*, fr. *klimaktēr*; *climacterical* fr. L *climactericus* + E *-al*] **1 :** constituting or relating to a climacteric (as a climacterium) **2 :** CRITICAL, CRUCIAL, CLIMACTIC

2climacteric \"\ *n* -S **1 a :** a major turning point or critical stage in a person's life ⟨the first ~ of his maturity —W.H. Gardner⟩; *also* **:** a decisive or critical period or stage in any course, career, or developmental process ⟨the Middle Ages advanced to their ~ —H.O.Taylor⟩ **b :** MENOPAUSE; *also* **:** a corresponding phenomenon of reduced sexual activity and competence in the male **2 :** an individual passing through a climacteric (as a climacterium) **3 :** the maximum to which the respiratory rate of fruit rises just prior to full ripening and from which it falls during senescence

cli·mac·te·ri·um \ˌ=ˌ=ˈtirēəm\ *n, pl* **climacte·ria** \-ēə\ [NL, fr. L *climacter* climacteric + NL *-ium*] **:** the bodily and psychic involutionary changes accompanying the transition from middle life to old age; *specif* **:** menopause and the bodily and mental changes that accompany it

cli·mac·tic \(ˈ)klī'maktik, -tēk *sometimes* klə'm-\ *also* **cli·mac·ti·cal** \-təkəl, -ēk-\ *adj* [fr. *climax*, after such pairs as E *syntax: syntactic, syntactical*] **:** of, being, or relating to a climax **:** forming or involving a climax ⟨a year of great decisions and ~ events ending in triumph —*Saturday Rev.*⟩ ⟨the ~ stunt of a time of marvelous stunts —John Lardner⟩ ⟨a story, witty and ~⟩ ⟨the ~ assault of outraged creditors . . . upon the beleaguered man —Arthur Knight⟩ — **cli·mac·ti·cal·ly** \-tək(ə)lē, -ēk-, -li\ *adv*

climagraph *var of* CLIMOGRAPH

1cli·mate \ˈklīmət, *usu* -d·+V\ *n* -S [ME *climat*, fr. MF *climat*, fr. LL *climat-, clima*, fr. Gk *klimat-, klima* inclination, the supposed slope of the earth toward the pole, region, clime, fr.

klinein to slope, incline — more at LEAN] **1** *in ancient and old geography* **a :** any of seven astrological belts or zones of the earth each presided over by a planet **b :** any of the 30 zones (24 between the equator and either polar circle) into which the surface of the earth was divided according to the successive increase of half an hour in the length of the longest day within successive zones **2 :** a region of the earth esp. considered with reference to its climatic conditions **:** CLIME ⟨his physician advised moving to another ~⟩ **3 a :** the average course or condition of the weather at a particular place over a period of many years as exhibited in absolute extremes, means, and frequencies of given departures from these means, of temperature, wind velocity, precipitation, and other weather elements **b :** the prevailing set of conditions (as of temperature, humidity, or freshness of atmosphere) in any place ⟨the ~ maintained inside our houses —E.L.Ullman⟩ ⟨the ~ in the vault has to be carefully controlled —Joseph Wechsberg⟩ **4 :** the prevailing temper, outlook, set of attitudes, or environmental conditions (as in regard to a particular activity or concern) characterizing a group or period **:** MILIEU ⟨a financial ~ favorable to the nation's economic health —*Economist*⟩ ⟨a petty and bickering office ~⟩ ⟨the 19th century ~ of opinion⟩ ⟨a ~ of fear⟩

²climate *vi* -ED/-ING/-S *obs* **:** to dwell or visit for a period in a particular climate or region

cli·mat·ic \(ˈ)klīˈmad·ik, -atik, -ēk *sometimes* klə'm-\ *also* **cli·mat·i·cal** \-əkəl, -ēk-\ *or* **cli·mat·al** \ˈklīmədᵊl, -mətᵊl\ *adj* **1 :** of or relating to a climate ⟨a ~ position more or less similar to that . . . of the Gulf Coast of Texas —P.E.James⟩ ⟨~ variations⟩ ⟨sensitive to the ~ changes of feeling —V.S. Pritchett⟩ **2** *of ecological formations* **:** resulting from climatic differences ⟨forests that had reverted to the ~ type⟩ — opposed to *edaphic* — **cli·mat·i·cal·ly** \(ˈ)klīˈmad·ək(ə)lē, -atək-, -ēk-, -li *sometimes* klə'm-\ *adv*

climatic climax *n* **1 :** CLIMAX 4 **2 :** the ecological climax of those possible in a particular climatic area whose stability is directly due to the influence of climate — compare EDAPHIC CLIMAX

cli·ma·ti·us \klīˈmāsh(ē)əs\ *n, cap* [NL, fr. Gk *klimat-, klima* slope — more at CLIMATE] **:** a genus of small Devonian acanthodian fishes (family Diplacanthidae) — see DIPLACANTHUS

cli·ma·tize \ˈklīmə,tīz\ *vb* -ED/-ING/-S [by shortening] **:** ACCLIMATIZE

climatograph *var of* CLIMOGRAPH

cli·ma·tog·ra·pher \,klīməˈtägrəfə(r)\ *n* -S **:** a specialist in climatography

cli·ma·to·graph·i·cal \ˌklīmədəˌgrafəkəl, (ˈ)klīˌmad-\ *adj* **:** of or relating to climatography

cli·ma·tog·ra·phy \,klīməˈtägrəfē\ *n* -ES [ISV *climat-* (fr. LL *climat-, clima* climate) + *-o-* + *-graphy*] **:** the description or study of climates

cli·ma·to·log·i·cal \ˌklīmədᵊlˈäjəkəl, (ˈ)klīˌmad-\ *also* **cli·ma·to·log·ic** \-jik\ *adj* **:** relating to climatology

cli·ma·tol·o·gist \,klīməˈtäləjəst\ *n* -S **:** a specialist in climatology

cli·ma·tol·o·gy \-jē,-ji\ *n* -ES [¹*climate* + *-o-* + *-logy*] **:** the science that deals with climates and investigates their phenomena and causes

cli·ma·tom·e·ter \-ˈtäməd·ə(r)\ *n* -S [¹*climate* + *-o-* + *-meter*] **:** an instrument for measuring the sensible temperature of the atmosphere

cli·ma·to·physiological \ˌklīmə,tō+\ *adj* [¹*climate* + *-o-* + *physiological*] **:** of, relating to, or caused by interaction of climatic and physiologic factors

cli·ma·to·therapy \ˌklīməd·ō+\ *n* [ISV *climat-* (fr. LL *climat-, clima* climate) + *-o-* + *therapy*] **:** treatment of disease by means of residence in a suitable climate

cli·ma·ture \ˈklīmə,chu̇(ə)r\ *n* -S [*climate* + *-ure* (as in *temperature*)] **1** *obs* **:** REGION **2 :** climatic conditions **:** CLIMATE

cli·ma·type \ˈklīmə,tīp\ *n* [LL *clima* climate + E *type* — more at CLIMATE] **:** a climatic ecotype ⟨in grasses . . . there are definite ~*s* which each characterize a particular climatic zone —Julian Huxley⟩

¹cli·max \ˈklī,maks\ *n* -ES [L, fr. Gk *klimax* ladder, fr. *klinein* to lean — more at LEAN] **1 :** a figure of speech in which a number of phrases or sentences are arranged in ascending order of rhetorical forcefulness **2 a :** the last and highest member of a rhetorical climax **b :** the highest point or one of a number of high points (as of significance, intensity, or achievements) in anything conceived as growing, developing, or unfolding ⟨this group of brilliant paintings marks the ~ of the artist's career⟩ ⟨the revolutionary upsurge reached its ~ in bitter street fighting⟩ **c :** the point of highest dramatic tension or a major turning point in the action of a play, story, or other literary composition **d :** ORGASM **e :** CLIMACTERIUM, MENOPAUSE **f :** the focus or center of interest in an artistic (as architectural) composition **3 :** the peak or point of maximum development of a cultural tradition in a given area and period of time **4 :** the relatively stable stage or community attained by an available population of organisms in a given environment, often constituting the culminating development in a natural succession or being one of the transitory stable states through which many populations pass before attaining such culminating development — see CLIMATIC CLIMAX, DISCLIMAX, EDAPHIC CLIMAX, POSTCLIMAX, PRECLIMAX, SUBCLIMAX

²climax \"\ *vb* -ED/-ING/-ES *vi* **:** to come or ascend to a climax ⟨that decade which ~*ed* in 1912 was a time of tremendous change in our national life —W.A.White⟩ ⟨~*ing* in the hair-raising death of Rasputin —*Publisher's Weekly*⟩ ~ *vt* **:** to bring to a climax **:** provide a culminating event for ⟨he ~*ed* his school career . . . by winning the Barbados Scholarship —Gordon Bell⟩ ⟨scenic interest . . . is ~*ed* in the Goat Rocks Primitive Area —*Amer. Guide Series: Wash.*⟩ ⟨~*ing* bitter hardship, an epidemic took 156 of the 600 settlers —*Amer. Guide Series: Texas*⟩

climax basket *n* [*climax* "kind of plum", prob. fr. ¹*climax*] **:** a small oblong veneer basket with rounded ends, a solid-wood bottom, usu. a veneer or wire handle across the midpoint, and sometimes a cover

climax basket

¹climb \ˈklīm\ *vb* **climbed** \-md\ *or dial* **clim** \ˈklim\ *or now dial* **clomb** \ˈklōm\ *or chiefly Midland* **clum** \ˈkləm\ **climbed** *or dial* **clim** *or now dial* **clomb** *or chiefly Midland* **clum; climbing; climbs** [ME *climben*, fr. OE *climban*; akin to OHG *klimban*, ON *klembra* to clamber, OE *clamm* bond, fetter — more at CLAM] *vi* **1 a** (1) **:** to rise or go upward with gradual or continuous motion ⟨watching the smoke ~⟩ (2) **:** to gain altitude ⟨the airplane ~*ed* suddenly⟩ **b :** to increase gradually ⟨stock-market prices ~*ing* a little each day⟩ **c :** to slope upward **:** form an upward or rising grade **:** serve as way or means of going up or higher ⟨the road ~*s* steadily until . . . you are high up on the mountain —Norman Cousins⟩ ⟨a staircase, which ~*ed*, steep and slender, to the upper story —Ellen Glasgow⟩ **d :** to become situated on a rising grade ⟨pleasant middle-class houses ~*ing* up the hill —R.M.Lovett⟩ **2 a :** to go upwards, rise, or raise oneself esp. by grasping or clutching with the hands ⟨~*ed* up a steep hill⟩ ⟨~ aboard a car⟩ ⟨~*ed* upon her father's knee⟩ **b** *of a plant* **:** to ascend in growth by twining about or scrambling over a support or by the attachment thereto of tendrils or aerial roots **3 :** to rise or seek to rise in dignity, rank, or eminence **:** come to rate more highly or occupy a higher state ⟨from this humble beginning he ~*ed* to a position at the very top —J.M.England⟩ **4 :** to go about or down usu. by grasping, clinging, or holding with the hands to facilitate progress or ensure safety ⟨~ down a ladder⟩ ⟨~*ing* around in a haymow⟩ ⟨~ out on a limb⟩ **5 :** to get into or out of clothing or an article of dress typically with some haste or effort ⟨the firemen ~*ed* into their clothes⟩ ⟨the diver ~*ed* out of his heavy suit⟩ ~ *vt* **1 a :** to go or proceed upwards upon or along, to the top of, or over **:** get to the top of or go over typically with some effort ⟨~ a hill⟩ ⟨energy spent ~*ing* stairs⟩ ⟨the car ~*ed* the long hill⟩ **b :** to reach by climbing ⟨~ the summit of a hill⟩ **2 :** to draw or pull oneself up, over, or to the top of by using hands and feet ⟨~ a ladder⟩ ⟨children ~*ing* the tree⟩ **3 :** to ascend through or to the higher parts of ⟨the sun ~*ing* the eastern sky⟩ **4 :** to grow up or creep up to the top of typically by twisting, twining, or cleaving ⟨ivy ~*ing* the western wall⟩ **5 :** to occupy or be situated on the ascending slope of ⟨the battlemented town . . . ~*s* a high hill crowned by the cathedral —Ellery Sedgwick⟩ **6 :** to cause (an aircraft) to climb **syn** see ASCEND

²climb \"\ *n* -S **1 :** a place (as a steep incline) where climbing is necessary to progress; *esp* **:** a trail up a mountain designed or mapped out for mountain climbers ⟨the approach to the Westmore mountain ~ —*Amer. Guide Series: Vt.*⟩ ⟨the commandos . . . began to rename many of the ~*s* —R.W.Clark⟩ **2 :** the act or an instance of climbing **:** ascent by climbing ⟨the slow ~ up the steep hills —E.H.Collis⟩ ⟨farm prices showed an upward ~⟩ ⟨an airplane with a rapid rate of ~⟩ ⟨its program includes several mountain ~*s* —*Bull. of Bates Coll.*⟩

climb·able \ˈklīməbəl\ *adj* **:** capable of being climbed ⟨some thought the mountain was not ~⟩

climb down *vi* **:** to retreat from a position previously taken ⟨after taking a bold stand on foreign policy, the ambassador *climbed down* at the first sign of opposition⟩

climb–down \ˈ=,=\ *n* -S **:** the act or an instance of climbing down ⟨a last minute *climb-down* by the government⟩

climb·er \ˈklīmə(r)\ *n* -S [ME, fr. *climben* + *-er*] **1 :** one that climbs: as **a :** one that cuts limbs and tops from tall trees chosen for use as spar trees — called also *topper* **b :** RIGGER **c :** HIGH RIGGER **d :** one that climbs about scaffolding to assist in construction work **e :** SOCIAL CLIMBER **f :** a vine or twining plant that readily grows up a support (as a trellis) or over other plants **2 :** a device to assist one in climbing esp. up steep places: as **a :** CLIMBING IRON **b :** a strip of material (as sealskin or mohair) attachable to the running surface of a ski to prevent sliding backward while going uphill — called also *creeper* **3 :** JUNGLE GYM

climbing bindweed *or* **climbing buckwheat** *n* **:** BLACK BINDWEED 1

climbing–boy \ˈ=,=\ *n* **:** a small child formerly employed by a chimney sweep to ascend and clean flues

climbing cutworm *n* **:** any of various cutworms that feed on the foliage of trees and other plants

climbing false buckwheat *n* **:** a slender twining annual (*Polygonum scandens*) characterized esp. by thin scarious brown or rosy wings on the mature fruiting calyx

climbing fern *n* **:** any of several ferns of the genus *Lygodium*; *esp* **:** a delicate No. American fern (*L. palmatum*) having a twining stem, palmately lobed sterile fronds, and sporiferous fronds that are much forked, form a terminal panicle, and are highly valued for decoration — called also *creeping fern*

climbing fig *n* **:** CREEPING FIG

climbing fumitory *n* **:** an herbaceous vine (*Adlumia fungosa*) having feathery leaves and white or pinkish flowers

climbing hardfern *n* **:** a high-climbing New Zealand fern (*Lomaria filiformis*) of the family Polypodiaceae with upper pinnae that are often two feet long

climbing hempweed *also* **climbing boneset** *n* **:** a plant of the genus *Mikania*; *esp* **:** an herb (*M. scandens*) that climbs up trees

climbing hydrangea *n* **1 :** a climbing vine (*Schizophragma hydrangeoides*) of the family Saxifragaceae having flowers with only one style, the sterile marginal flowers in each cluster having only one sepal **2 :** any of certain climbing plants of the related genus *Hydrangea* (esp. *H. petiolaris*)

climbing iron *n* **:** any of various steel frameworks with spikes attached that may be affixed to one's boots for climbing trees, poles, or snow-covered mountains — see CRAMPON 2; compare CREEPER 5

climbing lily *n* **:** GLORIOSA 2

climbing maidenhair *n* **:** a climbing fern (*Lygodium scandens*) — compare NITO

climbing milkweed *n* **:** SAND VINE

climbing nightshade *n* **:** BITTERSWEET 2a

climbing onion *n* **:** a much-branched leafless twining southern African herb (*Bowiea volubilis*) of the family Liliaceae sometimes cultivated as an ornamental for its bright green stems that arise from large aboveground bulbs

climbing perch *n* **:** a small perchlike Indian fish (*Anabas scandens*) that has part of the gill apparatus modified into leaflike expansions for the breathing of air, often travels overland by means of its spiny projecting fin rays, and is said to climb trees

climbing rope *n* **:** a rope used in mountain climbing

climbing rose *n* **:** any of numerous rather strong-growing garden roses that produce long flexible canes by which they cling to and scramble over any available support — see RAMBLER 2

climbing sumac *n* **:** POISON IVY 1

climbing tea rose *n* **:** any of certain climbing garden roses derived from the tea rose

climb milling *n* **:** milling in which the cutting motion of the tool is in the same direction as the feeding direction of the work — called also *down milling*; compare UPCUT

climbs *pres 3d sing of* CLIMB, *pl of* CLIMB

clime \ˈklīm\ *n* -S [L *clima* — more at CLIMATE] **:** CLIMATE

cli·mo·graph \ˈklīmə,graf\ *also* **cli·mat·o·graph** \klīˈmad·ə-\ *or* **cli·ma·graph** \ˈklīmə,graf\ *n* -S [*climo-* or *climato-* (fr. *climate*) + *-graph*] **:** a graphic representation of the relation of two climatic elements (as temperature and humidity) plotted at monthly intervals throughout the year — **cli·mo·graph·ic** \ˌklīməˈgrafik\ *adj* — **cli·mo·graph·i·cal·ly** \-fək(ə)lē\ *adv*

clin- *or* **clino-** *comb form* [NL, fr. Gk *klin-, klino-*, fr. *klinē* couch; akin to Gk *klinein* to lean — more at LEAN] **1 :** bed ⟨*clinium*⟩ ⟨*clinoid*⟩ **2 :** lean **:** slant ⟨*clinochlore*⟩ ⟨*clinometer*⟩ **3 :** decline ⟨*clinology*⟩ **4** *clino-, mineralogy* **:** monoclinic

clin *abbr* clinical

clin·al \ˈklīnᵊl\ *adj* [*cline* + *-al*] **:** of or relating to a cline — **cli·nal·ly** \-nᵊlē\ *adv*

-cli·nal \ˌklīnᵊl\ *adj comb form or n comb form* [ISV *-clin-* (fr. Gk *-klinēs* leaning, fr. *klinein* to lean) + *-al*] **1 :** sloping **:** slope ⟨*centroclinal*⟩ **2 :** ²-CLINOUS ⟨*matroclinal*⟩

cli·na·men \klīˈnāmən\ *n, pl* **clinam·i·na** \-ˈnamənə\ [L, fr. *clinare* to bend — more at LEAN] **:** TURN, BIAS, TWIST

cli·nan·dri·um \klīˈnandrēəm\ *n, pl* **clinan·dria** \-ēə\ [NL, fr. *clin-* + *andr-* + *-ium*] **:** a cavity or area in which the anther is situated on the column in flowers of the Orchidaceae

¹clinch \ˈklinch\ *vb* -ED/-ING/-ES [prob. alter. of ¹*clench*] *vt* **1 a :** to turn over or flatten the protruding pointed end of (a driven nail) in order to secure; *also* **:** to treat (a screw, bolt, or rivet) in a similar way **b :** to fasten by means of a nail, bolt, or similar article treated in this way ⟨~ two planks together⟩ **c :** to fasten firmly in a manner resembling this way or as if in this way ⟨this new method takes regular flat stitching wire . . . then drives and ~*es* the stitch⟩ ⟨~*ed* their hold⟩ **2 :** CLENCH 2 ⟨he spoke between his ~*ed* teeth —W.F.Davis⟩ **3 a :** to settle or make final, irrefutable, definite, or beyond dispute ⟨~ an argument⟩ ⟨~ a sale⟩ ⟨the rain ~*ed* the matter — we would have to stay indoors⟩ ⟨~ a bargain⟩ ⟨the many laboratory tests which finally ~*ed* his suspicions —*Brit. Book News*⟩ **b :** to secure or gain conclusively or beyond question **:** WIN ⟨~ a basketball title⟩ ⟨~ the governorship⟩ **4 :** to fasten (as a rope) by means of a clinch ~ *vi* **1 a :** to grasp and struggle at close quarters (as in wrestling) **b :** to hold an opponent (as in boxing) at close quarters (as by the arms or around the waist) with one or both arms so that no blows or only blows at short range can be exchanged ⟨after a furious trading of punches, the fighters ~*ed*⟩ **c** *slang* **:** to embrace esp. passionately ⟨lovers about to ~ —Bernard Hollowood⟩ **2 :** to hold fast or firmly — usu. used of a nail, bolt, or rivet that has been clinched ⟨if the floor is cement, clout nails will ~ automatically —Herbert Philippi⟩

²clinch \"\ *n* -ES **1 a :** a slip noose consisting of a small loop made with seizings in the end of a line around its own standing part — compare INSIDE CLINCH, OUTSIDE CLINCH **b :** the part of the rope fastened with this type of noose **2 a :** a fastening by means of a clinched nail, rivet, or bolt (as a rivet or bolt with the protruding end flattened down over a ring put around it for the purpose); *also* **:** the clinched part of a nail, bolt, or rivet **b :** a device that grips or fastens securely **:** CLAMP **3** *archaic* **:** a pun or play on words **4 :** the act or an instance of clinching (as an argument, case, sale, or title) **5 a :** a scuffle involving clinching between two persons **b :** the act or fact of clinching in boxing **c** *slang* **:** a passionate embrace

clinch 1a: *A* simple clinch with two seizings, *B* inside clinch, *C* outside clinch, *D* double clinch

³clinch \"\ *or* **clinch·er** \-chə(r)\ *adj* [*clinch* fr. ²*clinch* (fastening); *clincher* fr. *clincher*, n., "fastener"] **:** LAP-JOINTED, LAPSTRAKE

clinch bolt *or* **clink bolt** *n* **:** RIVET

clinch–built \ˈ=,=\ *or* **clincher-built** \ˈ==,=\ *adj* **:** CLINKER-BUILT

clinch·er \ˈklinchə(r)\ *n* -S **:** one that clinches: as **a :** a decisive fact, argument, act, or remark ⟨the expense was the ~ that persuaded us to give up the enterprise⟩ **b :** a machine in commercial canning for positioning a lid loosely on the can prior to sealing it **c** *or* **clincher tire :** an automobile tire with flanged beads fitting into the wheel rim

clinching iron *n* **:** a tool for clinching nails

clinch·ing·ly *adv* **:** in a clinching manner

clinch joint *n* [³*clinch*] **:** LAP JOINT

clinch knot *n* **:** a knot used to tie a fishing leader or spinning line to a hook or fly and made by passing the end through the eye of the hook and twisting it around the standing part several times before pushing it back through the loop that holds the hook or fly

clinch nail *n* **:** a nail made of soft metal or so cut that the pointed end may be bent over easily for clinching

clinch nut *n* **:** a nut intended to be riveted into position in sheet metal

cline \ˈklīn\ *n* -S [Gk *klinein* to lean] **:** a graded series of characters (as morphological or physiological differences) exhibited by a species or other group of related organisms usu. along a line of environmental or geographic transition — see STEP-CLINE

-cline \,klīn\ *n comb form* -S [back-formation fr. *-clinal*] **1 :** slope ⟨anti*cline*⟩ **2 :** gradient **:** layer ⟨thermo*cline*⟩

cli·ner \ˈklīnə(r)\ *n* -S [origin unknown] *slang Austral* **:** GIRL

¹cling \ˈkliŋ\ *vb* **clung** \ˈkləŋ\ *also now dial* **clang** \ˈklaŋ, -aiŋ\ **clung; clinging; clings** [ME *clingen*, fr. OE *clingan*; akin to OHG *klunga* tangled ball of thread, ON *klungr* hip, haw, MIr *glacc* hand, Gk *gelgis* head of garlic, Skt *gṛñja* kind of garlic, L *galla* gallnut — more at GALL] *vi* **1 a :** to hold to each other cohesively and firmly **:** resist forces or influences acting to separate or disperse — often used with *together* ⟨the fused particles ~ together⟩ ⟨all our vessels *clung* together, as if for company —Kenneth Roberts⟩ **b :** to hold or hold on tightly or tenaciously (as with the hands or feet) and to resist pressure to separate or dislodge ⟨the sailors were obliged to ~, to prevent being washed away —Frederick Marryat⟩ **:** to adhere closely and firmly as if glued ⟨their soaked garments ~*ing* to the curves of their figures —J.C.Powys⟩ **c :** to become situated as if holding firmly and resisting pressure to dislodge or separate ⟨a bluff to which hotels and residences ~⟩ ⟨parched plants ~*ing* to the drought-stricken soil⟩ **2** *now dial Brit* **:** to become emaciated **:** SHRINK, SHRIVEL, WITHER **3 a :** to have a strong emotional attachment or dependence ⟨weak-willed and purposeless he *clung* to all who offered the least sign of sympathy⟩ **b** (1) **:** to have or continue to have strong emotional or intellectual loyalty or stubborn attachment or belief ⟨~*ing* pathetically to his worn-out creeds and dogmas⟩ ⟨*clung* to the hope that her son had survived⟩ (2) **:** to continue on a course of action or policy as if resisting efforts to interrupt or distract ⟨*clung* resolutely to his work —J.A.Froude⟩ (3) **:** to hold on tenaciously as if resisting dispossession ⟨~*ing* grimly to his few wretched acres⟩ **c :** to remain or linger as if resisting complete dissipation or dispersal ⟨the odor of mignonette still *clung* to the room⟩ **:** remain habitually or continuously associated ⟨the nickname *clung* to him throughout his life⟩ **d :** to become retained and survive as a practice or belief ⟨this habit of saving . . . would ~ to her for the rest of her life —Ellen Glasgow⟩ ~ *vt* **1** *now dial Eng* **:** to stick (objects) together **:** cause to adhere **2** *obs* **:** to cause (as one's fingers) to hold tightly **syn** see ADHERE

²cling \"\ *n* -S **1 :** the act or an instance of clinging **:** ADHERENCE **2 :** CLINGSTONE

³cling \"\ *n* -S [prob. alter. of ²*clink*] **:** a sharp high metallic ringing sound ⟨the ~ of the coin as it fell on the stone floor⟩ ⟨the ~ of the busy till —John Prebble⟩

⁴cling \"\ *vi* -ED/-ING/-S **:** to make a cling ⟨the coin ~*ed* as it hit the stone floor⟩

cling–clang \ˈ=,=\ *n* -S [³*cling* + *clang*] **:** a repeated metallic ringing sound (as of a bell) ⟨the buoys toll a slow *cling-clang* —D.C.Peattie⟩

clingfish \ˈ=,=\ *n* [¹*cling* + *fish*] **:** any of various fishes (as of the order Xenopterygii) having a sucker on the underside of the body by which they cling to objects (as stones)

cling·i·ness \ˈkliŋēnəs\ *n* -ES **:** the quality of being clingy ⟨the ~ of certain types of dress material⟩

cling·ing·ly *adv* **:** in a clinging manner

cling·ing·ness *n* -ES **:** CLINGINESS

cling·stone \ˈkliŋ,stōn, -ŋ,st-\ *n* -S [¹*cling* + *stone*] **:** a fruit (as a peach or plum) in which the flesh adheres strongly to the pit — compare FREESTONE

clingy \ˈkliŋē, -ŋi\ *adj, often* -ER/-EST [¹*cling* + *-y*] **:** having the quality of clinging ⟨a soft and ~ dress⟩

-clinia *pl of* -CLINIUM

clin·ic \ˈklinik, -nēk\ *n* -S [F *clinique*, fr. Gk *klinikē* medical practice at the sickbed, fr. *klinikos* physician who attends bedridden patients, fr. *klinikos*, adj., of a bed, fr. *klinē* bed, fr. *klinein* to lean, recline — more at LEAN] **1 a :** a session or class of medical instruction in a hospital held at the bedside of patients serving as case studies **b :** a group of selected patients presented with discussion before doctors (as at a convention) for purposes of instruction **2 :** a class, session, or group meeting devoted to the presentation, analysis, and treatment or solution of actual cases and concrete problems in some special field or discipline ⟨writing ~*s* for feeble students were established here and there —H.L.Creek⟩ ⟨holding ~*s* with businessmen on their troubles —W.B.Barnes⟩ ⟨a monthly fashion ~ —*Time*⟩ **3 a :** an institution connected with a hospital or medical school where diagnosis and treatment are made available to outpatients **b :** a form of group practice in which several physicians (as specialists) work in cooperative association

-clin·ic \ˈ==\ *adj comb form* [ISV *-clin-* (fr. Gk *-klinēs* leaning, bending, fr. *klinein* to lean) + *-ic*] **1 :** inclining **:** dipping ⟨iso*clinic*⟩ **2 :** having (a certain number of) oblique intersections of the axes ⟨mono*clinic*⟩ ⟨tri*clinic*⟩ **3 :** ²-CLINOUS ⟨matro*clinic*⟩

clin·i·cal \ˈklinəkəl, -nēk-\ *adj* [*clinic* + *-al*] **1 :** of, relating to, or conducted in or as if in a clinic (as a medical clinic): as **a :** involving or depending on direct observation of the living patient ⟨~ diagnosis⟩ ⟨~ examination⟩ **b :** observable by clinical inspection ⟨~ tuberculosis⟩ **c :** based on clinical observation ⟨~ picture⟩ ⟨~ treatment⟩ **d :** applying objective or standardized methods (as interviews and personality or intelligence tests) to the description, evaluation, and modification of human behavior ⟨~ psychology⟩ **2 a** *of a sacrament* **:** administered on a sickbed or deathbed ⟨~ baptism⟩ **b** *of a religious convert or conversion* **:** made on a sickbed or deathbed **3 :** analytical, detached, or coolly dispassionate (as in attitude, judgment, or description) ⟨the direct and unabashed appeal to the emotions . . . has been . . . diminished in favor of studied impersonality, a ~ detachment —Louis Untermeyer⟩ ⟨writes with intensity, insight, and a ~ sense of scrutiny —Catherine M. Brown⟩ ⟨a largely ~ analysis of the whole "loyalty program" —W.S.White⟩

clin·i·cal·ly \-nək(ə)lē, -nēk-, -li\ *adv* **:** in a clinical manner ⟨classical literature also was subjected to ~ detailed examination —Gilbert Highet⟩ ⟨~portrayed —W.J.Schultz⟩

clinical clerk *n* **:** one who holds a clerkship (sense 3)

clinical thermometer *n* **:** a self-registering thermometer for determining the temperature of a human or animal body

cli·ni·cian \kləˈnishən\ *n* -S [F *clinicien*, fr. *clinique* clinic + *-ien* -ian] **:** one who directs, is closely allied with, or works in or through a clinic or with clinical methods; *esp* : one qualified or engaged in the clinical practice of medicine, psychiatry, or psychology as distinguished from one specializing in laboratory or research techniques in the same fields

clinico- *comb form* [*clinical*] : clinical : clinical and ⟨*clinico*pathology⟩

clin·i·co·pathologic *also* **clin·i·co·pathological** \ˌklinə̇ˌkō+\ *adj* [*clinico-* + *pathologic, pathological*] : involving both clinical and pathologic factors, aspects, or approaches ⟨~ analysis⟩

clin·i·dae \ˈklinəˌdē\ *n pl, cap* [NL, fr. *Clinus*, type genus + *-idae*] : a family of viviparous blennies widely distributed in the intertidal zone of temperate and tropical seas and esp. abundant in California and southern Africa

-clinies *pl of* -CLINY

-cli·nism \ˈklīˌnizəm\ *n comb form* -s [ISV *-clin-* (fr. NL *-clinus*) + *-ism*] : the state of having the androecium and gynoecium in a (single or different) flower or (two separate) flowers ⟨di*clinism*⟩

-clin·i·um \ˈklinēəm\ *n comb form, pl* **-clinia** [NL, fr. Gk *klinion*, dim. of *klinē* couch — more at CLIN-] *bot* : receptacle ⟨antho*clinium*⟩

[1]clink \ˈkliŋk\ *vb* -ED/-ING/-S [ME *clinken*, prob. fr. MD, of imit. origin] *vi* **1 a** : to give out a slight sharp short metallic sound ⟨the coin ~*ed* as it hit the floor⟩ ⟨swished the highball gently around in his glass so that the ice ~*ed* —Leslie Charteris⟩ **b** : to move or act so that such a sound is given out (as by the heels) ⟨a man in hobnailed boots ~*ed* in at the door⟩ **2** *of words or verses, archaic* : RHYME, JINGLE **3** *dial Brit* : to move or throw oneself quickly and abruptly — usu. used with *down* ⟨~*ed* down beside her on the sofa⟩ or *off* ⟨~*ed* off . . . and jumped safe over hedge —Thomas Hardy⟩ ~ *vt* **1** : to cause to clink : strike together so as to produce a clinking sound ⟨~*ed* the coins in his purse —T.B.Costain⟩ **2** *archaic* : to make (words or lines) rhyme or jingle **3** *dial Brit* : to strike or beat sharply : SLAP

[2]clink \"\ *n* -s [ME, fr. *clinken*, v.] **1 a** : a clinking sound ⟨the ~ of glasses⟩ ⟨the ~ of coins⟩ **b** *chiefly Scot* : MONEY, CASH, COIN **2** : RHYME, ASSONANCE, JINGLE **3** : the sharp note of certain birds (as the stonechat) **4 a** *dial Brit* : a quick sharp blow : RAP **b** *dial* : INSTANT, MOMENT ⟨in a ~⟩

[3]clink \"\ *vt* -ED/-ING/-S [ME *clinken*, perh. fr. OE *-clencan* (in *beclencan* to hold fast) — more at CLENCH] *chiefly Scot* : to clinch esp. with nails or rivets

[4]clink \"\ *n* -s [fr. *Clink*, a prison in Southwark, borough of London, England, prob. fr. *Clink*, a part of the Manor of Southwark] *slang* : JAIL, PRISON : prison cell : GUARDHOUSE ⟨put in the ~ for petty thievery⟩ ⟨safeguards the reputation of the arresting policeman by riding with him when he takes the girl to the county ~ —G.S.Perry⟩

clink bolt *var of* CLINCH BOLT

clink–clank \ˈ=ˌ=\ *n* [*[2]clink* + *clank*] : a usu. repeated noise made up of generally alternating clinks and clanks

[1]clink·er \ˈkliŋkə(r)\ *n* -s [earlier *klincard*, fr. obs. D *klinkaard* (now *klinker*), fr. *klinken* to clink, fr. MD *clinken*; fr. its resonance when struck — more at CLINK] **1** : DUTCH CLINKER **2 a** *or* **clinker brick** : a brick that has been overburned in the kiln **b** : a quantity of bricks of this kind **c** : stony matter vitrified or fused together (as that formed in a furnace from impurities in the coal or that ejected from a volcano) : SLAG; *also* : a lump of such matter — see CEMENT CLINKER **3** : a scale of iron oxide formed in forging

[2]clinker \"\ *vb* **clinkered; clinkered; clinkering** \-k(ə)riŋ\ **clinkers** *vt* **1** : to cause to form clinker ⟨a piece of ~*ed* coke⟩ **2** : to clear out the clinkers from ⟨fires were not ~*ed* as frequently as desirable —*Amer. Gas Jour.*⟩ ~ *vi* : to turn to clinker under heat

[3]clinker \"\ *n* -s [*[3]clink* + *-er*] : CLINCH

[4]clinker \"\ *n* -s [*[1]clink* + *-er*] **1** : a shoemaker's nail usu. driven into the shoe sole as a protective stud **2** *Brit* : one that is first-rate or of extraordinary quality ⟨a good dog — a real well-bred ~⟩ **3** *slang* : a wrong note or a badly sounded note played or sung by a performer ⟨a couple of ~*s* and Sol would know that he was no clarinet player —Harold Sinclair⟩ **4** *slang* **a** : a serious mistake or error or notably inferior performance (as in music, drama, or sports) : BONER ⟨dropping the ball, a ~ that cost his team the game⟩ **b** : one that is regarded as a notable failure or of poor quality ⟨the play turned out to be a ~ —*Springfield (Mass.) Daily News*⟩

clinker beech *n* [*[1]clinker*; fr. the color of the wood] : RED BIRCH 3

clinker boat *n* [*[3]clinker*] : a clinker-built boat

clinker–built \ˈ==ˌ=\ *adj* [*[3]clinker*] : having the external planks (as on a boat) or plates (as on a boiler) lap-jointed : LAPSTRAKE — compare CARVEL-BUILT

clinkered *adj* [*[4]clinker* + *-ed*] : studded with nails (as clinkers) ⟨a climber, noisy in ~ boots —Wilfred Noyce⟩

clink·er·er \ˈkliŋkərə(r)\ *n* -s [*[2]clinker* + *-er*] : one whose occupation is the removing of clinkers from furnaces or gas generators

clink·ery \-k(ə)rē, -ri\ *adj* [*[1]clinker* + *-y*] : consisting of or resembling clinkers ⟨the surfaces of volcanic lavas show the . . . smooth, ropy, and ~ structures —E.B.Branson & W.A. Tarr⟩

clink·ety–clank \ˌkliŋkədˈēˌklaŋk, -aiŋk\ *n* [*clinkety* (alter. of *[2]clink*) + *clank*] : a repeated usu. rhythmic clanking sound ⟨the *clinkety-clank* of a loose chain on an automobile wheel⟩

clink·ety–clink \-ˈkliŋk\ *n* [*clinkety* + *[2]clink*] : a repeated usu. rhythmic clinking sound ⟨the *clinkety-clink* of coins in his pocket as he walked⟩ — compare CLINKETY-CLANK

clink·ing \ˈkliŋkiŋ\ *adv* [prob. fr. pres. part. of *[1]clink*] *slang* : VERY, EXTREMELY ⟨it's going to be a ~ fine day —John Buchan⟩

clinks *pres 3d sing of* CLINK, *pl of* CLINK

clink shell *n* [*[1]clink*] : JINGLE SHELL

clinkstone \ˈ=ˌ=\ *n* -s [*[1]clink* + *stone*] : PHONOLITE

clin·kum clan·kum \ˌkliŋkəmˈklaŋkəm, -laiŋkəm\ *n* [alter. of *clink-clank*] : a rhythmic clink-clank

clino- — see CLIN-

cli·no·axis \ˈklīnō+\ *n, pl* **clinoaxes** [*clin-* + *axis*] : the diagonal or lateral axis that makes an oblique angle with the vertical axis in the monoclinic system of crystallography

cli·no·chlore \ˈklīnəˌklō(ə)r\ *or* **cli·no·chlorite** \ˌ==ˈklōrˌīt\ *n* -s [*clin-* + Gk *chlōros* pale green or E *chlorite* — more at YELLOW] : a mineral $(Mg,Fe,Al)_3(Si,Al)_2O_5(OH)_4$, of the chlorite group consisting of magnesium aluminum silicate usu. containing iron, and occurring in monoclinic pseudohexagonal crystals, in folia or scales, or massive and commonly of a green color — called also *ripidolite*

cli·no·clase \ˈklīnəˌklās, -āz\ *or* **cli·no·cla·site** \ˌklīnəˈklāˌsīt, klīˈnäkləˌ-\ *n* -s [*clinoclase* fr. G *klinoklas*, fr. *klin-* clin- + *-klas* -clase; *clinoclasite* fr. G *klinoklas* + E *-ite*] : a mineral $Cu_3(AsO_4)_2.3Cu(OH)_2$ consisting of basic copper arsenate and being dark green and translucent in prismatic crystals or massive

[1]cli·no·diagonal \ˈklī(ˌ)nō+\ *n* -s [*clin-* + *diagonal*] : CLINOAXIS

[2]clinodiagonal \"\ *adj* [ISV *clin-* + *diagonal*] : being or belonging to a clinoaxis

cli·no·do·mat·ic \ˌklīnə(ˌ)dōˈmad·ik\ *adj* [*clinodome* + *-atic* (as in *prismatic*)] : being or belonging to a clinodome

cli·no·dome \ˈklīnəˌdōm\ *n* -s [ISV *clin-* + *dome*] : a dome in which the planes are parallel to the inclined axis in a monoclinic crystal — compare BRACHYDOME, MACRODOME, ORTHODOME

cli·no·enstatite \ˌ=(ˌ)=+\ *n* -s [ISV *clin-* + *enstatite*; orig. formed as G *klinoenstatit*] : a monoclinic magnesium-iron pyroxene with magnesium substantially in excess of iron; *specif* : the magnesium silicate $MgSiO_3$

cli·no·ferrosilite \ˌklī(ˌ)nō +\ *n* [*clin-* + *ferrosilite*] : a mineral $FeSiO_3$ consisting of iron silicate in the monoclinic form — compare FERROSILITE, ORTHOFERROSILITE

cli·no·graph \ˈklīnəˌgraf\ *n* -s [*clin-* + *-graph*] **1** : an instrument for ascertaining the deviation from the vertical of a borehole, well, or shaft **2** : a drawing instrument having two straight edges united by a hinge and capable of being set at any desired angle

cli·no·graph·ic \ˌ==ˈgrafik\ *adj* [*clin-* + *-graphic*] : representing by so locating the object with reference to the plane of projection that no face will be projected as a line — used of a system of oblique projection that is used esp. for representing crystals

cli·no·he·dral \ˌklīnōˈhēdrəl\ *adj* [*clin-* + *-hedral*] : of or relating to a rare class of crystals of the monoclinic system having a plane but not an axis of symmetry

cli·no·he·drite \-ˈhēˌdrīt\ *also* **cli·no·edrite** \-ōˈēˌ-\ *n* -s [ISV *clin-* + Gk *hedra* seat, base + ISV *-ite*; orig. formed as G *klinoëdrit* — more at SIT] : a calcium zinc silicate $CaZnSiO_3(OH)_2$ occurring in the form of colorless, white, or purplish monoclinic crystals (hardness 5.5, sp. gr. 3.33)

cli·no·humite \ˈklīnō+\ *n* [ISV *clin-* + *humite*] : a mineral $Mg_9Si_4O_{16}(F,OH)_2$ of the humite group crystallizing in the monoclinic system

cli·no·hypersthene \ˈklīnō +\ *n* [ISV *clin* + *hypersthene*; orig. formed as G *klinohypersthen*] : a monoclinic magnesium-iron pyroxene $(Mg,Fe)_2Si_2O_6$ common in certain basaltic rocks

cli·noid process \ˈklīˌnȯid-\ *n* [NL *clinoides*, fr. *clin-* + *-oides* -oid] : any of certain processes of the sphenoid bone

cli·no·lim·ni·on \ˌklīnəˈlimnēˌän\ *n, pl* **clinolim·nia** \-nēə\ [NL, fr. *clin-* + *-limnion*] : the upper layers of a hypolimnion in which the rate of warming falls off exponentially with depth — compare BATHYLIMNION

cli·nom·e·ter \klīˈnämədə(r), klə̇-\ *n* -s [*clin-* + *-meter*] : any of various instruments (as the short telescope, bubble tube, and graduated vertical arc used by surveyors) for measuring or indicating angles of slope, elevation, or inclination (as the dip of geological beds or strata, the slope of an embankment or cutting, or the angle of elevation of a gun) — compare ABNEY LEVEL — **cli·nom·e·try** \-ə·trē\ *n* -ES

clinometer: *1* clamp nut, *2* cross hairs, *3* eyepiece, *4* quadrant, *5* index

cli·no·metric \ˌ==+\ *also* **cli·no·metrical** \ˌ==+\ *adj* : of, relating to, or ascertained by a clinometer

cli·no·pinacoid \ˌklīnə+\ *n* -s [ISV *clin-* + *pinacoid*] : a pinacoid whose planes are parallel to the inclined and vertical axes in a monoclinic crystal

cli·no·po·di·um \ˌklīnəˈpōdēəm\ [NL, fr. *clin-* + *-podium*] *syn of* SATUREIA

cli·no·stat \ˈklīnəˌstat\ *n* -s [ISV *clin-* + *-stat*; orig. formed as G *klinostat*] : an apparatus consisting of a slowly revolving disk usu. regulated by clockwork by means of which the action of external agents (as light and gravity) on the movements of growing plants mounted on the disk may be modified or eliminated by the change of direction

cli·nos·to·mum \klīˈnästəməm\ *n* [NL, fr. *clin-* + *-stomum*] **1** *cap* : a genus of digenetic trematodes occurring as adults in the mouth and esophagus of fish-eating birds and as metacercaria encysting in the muscles of various fishes and other aquatic vertebrates **2** *pl* **clinostoma** \-mə\ : any worm of the genus *Clinostomum*; *esp* : YELLOW GRUB

cli·no·ungemachite \ˌklīˌnō+\ *n* -s [*clin-* + *ungemachite*] : a rare mineral consisting of a sulfate of iron and alkalis and prob. dimorphous with ungemachite

[1]-cli·nous \ˈklīnəs\ *adj comb form* [ISV *-clin-* (fr. NL *-clinus*, fr. Gk *klinē* couch — more at CLIN-) : having the androecium and gynoecium in a (single or different) flower or (two separate) flowers ⟨di*clinous*⟩ ⟨hetero*clinous*⟩ ⟨mono*clinous*⟩

[2]-clinous \"\ *adj comb form* [ISV *-clin-* (fr. Gk *-klinēs* leaning, bending, fr. *klinein* to lean) + *-ous* — more at LEAN] : inherited from : having characteristics inherited from ⟨matro*clinous*⟩ ⟨patro*clinous*⟩

cli·no·zoisite \ˈklīnə+\ *n* -s [ISV *clin-* + *zoisite*; orig. formed as G *klinozoisit*] : a monoclinic mineral $Ca_2Al_3Si_3O_{12}(OH)$ consisting of a basic silicate of calcium and aluminum — compare ZOISITE

[1]clin·quant \ˈkliŋkənt\ *adj* [MF, glittering, making a clinking sound, fr. pres. part. of *clinquer*, of imit. origin] : glittering esp. with gold decoration : SPANGLED : showily ornate

[2]clinquant \"\ *n* -s [F, short for *or clinquant*, gold in leaf or thin plates, lit., glittering or clinking gold] **1** : imitation gold leaf : TINSEL, DUTCH METAL **2** : something with a false and showy glitter

clint \ˈklint\ *n* -s [ME, perh. fr. MLG *klint* cliff, crag; akin to OSw *klinter* mountain top, ON *klettr* cliff, crag, L *galla* gallnut — more at GALL] **1** *chiefly Scot* : a hard or flinty rock : a rocky cliff : a projecting rock or ledge **2** *dial Eng* : a crevice or gully in limestone rocks

clin·to·nia \klinˈtōnēə\ *n* [NL, fr. DeWitt *Clinton* †1828 Am. statesman + NL *-ia*] **1** *cap* : a genus of perennial herbs (family Liliaceae) having yellow or white flowers on a naked stalk in early summer with the stalk sheathed below by the bases of two to four oblong or ovate leaves **2** -s : any plant of the genus *Clintonia* — called also *Clinton's lily*

clin·ton·ite \ˈklintᵊnˌīt\ *n* -s [DeWitt *Clinton* + E *-ite*] **1** : SEYBERTITE **2** : a group of micas that contain calcium instead of potassium — see BRITTLE MICA

-cli·ny \ˌklīnē, -ni\ *n comb form* -ES [ISV *[2]-clinous* + *-y*] : fact or condition of having characteristics inherited from ⟨matro*cliny*⟩

clio \ˈklī(ˌ)ō\ *n, cap* [NL, fr. *Clio*, one of the Muses, also, a sea nymph, fr. L, fr. Gk *Kleiō*, one of the Muses, fr. *kleiein* to make famous; akin to Gk *klytos* famous — more at LOUD] : a genus of pteropod mollusks having an external symmetrical shell

cli·o·na \klīˈōnə\ *n, cap* [NL, irreg. fr. *Clio*, the Muse] : a genus (the type of the family Clionidae) of boring sponges

cli·o·ne \-ˌnē\ *n, cap* [NL, irreg. fr. *Clio*] : a genus (the type of the family Clionidae) of naked pelagic pteropod mollusks that are abundant in the Arctic ocean and that constitute a large part of the food of the Greenland whale

[1]cli·on·i·dae \klīˈänəˌdē, -ˈīˈōn-\ *n pl, cap* [NL, fr. *Cliona*, type genus + *-idae*] : a family (order Hadromerina) of small sponges with monaxon spicules that bore in shells and soft limestone rocks — see CLIONA

[2]clionidae \"\ *n pl, cap* [NL, fr. *Clione*, type genus + *-idae*] : a family of naked pteropod mollusks comprising forms intermediate in many characters between typical pteropods and nudibranchs

[1]clip \ˈklip\ *vb* **clipped; clipped; clipping; clips** [ME *clippen*, fr. OE *clyppan*; akin to OHG *klāftra* fathom, ON *klafi* yoke, L *galla* gall on a tree, *gleba* clod, *globus* globe, Lith. *globti* to embrace — more at GALL] *vt* **1 a** *now dial Brit* : EMBRACE, HUG **b** : to encircle closely : ENCOMPASS ⟨a belt *clipped* her waist⟩ **2 a** : to hold in a tight grip : CLUTCH **b** : to clasp or fasten with a clip **3** *football* : to block (an opposing player other than the ball carrier) illegally by hitting with the body from behind ~ *vi, football* : to block an opponent from behind

[2]clip \"\ *n* -s [ME *clipp*, fr. *clippen* to clip (embrace)] : any of a number of devices which grip, clasp, or hook or with which one grips, clasps, or hooks: as **a** : GRAPPLING IRON **b** : an encircling often metal strap for connecting parts (as the metal strap of a whiffletree) **c** : the upward projection at the extreme front or at the side of a horseshoe over the margin of the hoof **d** : a holder or container (as for letters, bills, or music) consisting wholly or partly of a metal spring clamp **e** : a device to hold cartridges for charging the magazines of some rifles; *also* : a magazine from which ammunition is fed into the chamber of a firearm **f** : a device for confining the bottom of a trouser leg used esp. when riding a bicycle without a chain guard **g** : a device used to arrest bleeding from vessels or tissues during operations **h** : a wire resembling and applied like a staple and used to hold together wound margins or tissues or structures separated or opened during operations **i** : a metal device to connect up angle and T irons to rolled beams without drilling or bolting **j** : a clamplike wire or cable terminal for temporary electrical connections **k** : a piece of jewelry (as a pin or an earring) that is held in position by a spring clip

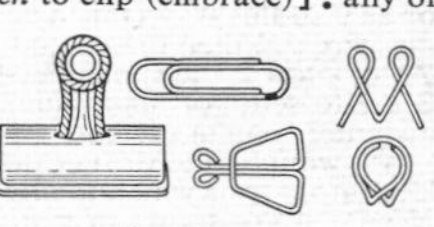
clips for paper

[3]clip \"\ *vb* **clipped; clipped** *also* **clipt; clipping; clips** [ME *clippen*, fr. ON *klippa*] *vt* **1 a** : to cut or cut off with or as if with shears ⟨~ a string in two⟩ ⟨~ the wool of a sheep⟩ ⟨~ her hair close⟩ ⟨~ an hour off traveling time⟩ **b** : to cut off the margins, ends, or a small portion of : PARE, TRIM ⟨~ rosebushes⟩ ⟨~ a coin⟩ ⟨~ a bird's wings⟩ : cut or snip off a part of the hair or surface growth of : SHEAR ⟨~ a sheep⟩ : MOW ⟨~ a lawn⟩ **c** (1) : EXCISE ⟨~*ed* imperfect passages from the recording⟩ (2) : to cut items out of (as a newspaper) ⟨*clipped* a week's papers⟩ : cut out of esp. a publication **d** *of a radio or television circuit* : REJECT ⟨~*ing* the instantaneous signals above or below a predetermined amplitude or frequency⟩ **2 a** : CURTAIL, DIMINISH ⟨~*ing* his power or authority⟩ ⟨worked to ~ the senator's influence⟩ **b** : to abbreviate (as a word or a customary sequence of sounds) in speech or writing in some way (as *ad* for *advertisement*, \ˈnesəsri\ for \ˈnesəˌseri\) ⟨the *clipped* "n'kyou" of the bus conductors and the ticket collectors —Richard Joseph⟩ ⟨*clipped* dialogue —D.M.Friedenberg⟩ ⟨to most unsophisticated users of the language "a short circuit" has nothing to do with either "short" or "circuit" (except insofar as the phrase itself has been *clipped* to "a short") —D.L.Bolinger⟩ **c** : REDUCE ⟨appliance stores . . . were *clipping* prices for people with ready cash —*Newsweek*⟩ ⟨the company *clipped* his wages two dollars a week⟩ **3** *slang* : to hit esp. with a short sharp blow ⟨*clipped* him with a left hook —Ernest Hemingway⟩ ⟨both got *clipped* by drunk drivers —*Pasadena (Calif.) Independent*⟩ **4** : to take money from unfairly or dishonestly esp. by charging exorbitant prices or by deception ⟨the nightclub *clipped* the diner for $23⟩ ⟨~ a patient by excessive charges for surgery⟩ **5** : to touch or go very close to esp. in moving past ⟨the bearings should just ~ the shaft —John Southward⟩ ⟨~ the edge of the cliff as closely as possible —F.W.Booth⟩ ~ *vi* **1** : to clip something ⟨remove a portion of it by *clipping*⟩ ⟨the record was made by a good deal of *clipping*⟩ **2 a** *archaic* : to move the wings swiftly : fly swiftly ⟨some falcon . . . ~*s* it down the wind —John Dryden⟩ **b** : to travel or pass rapidly ⟨a rock *clipped* through the air —Max Steele⟩ ⟨the half hour *clipped* along with pace and movement —Goodman Ace⟩ — **clip one's wings** : to place an effectual check on the ambitions or efforts of : make powerless : RESTRAIN

[4]clip \"\ *n* -s **1 a clips** *pl, Scot* : SHEARS **b** : a 2-bladed instrument for cutting esp. the nails ⟨a wire ~⟩ **2** : something that is clipped: as **a** : a clipping esp. from a newspaper **b** : the product of a single shearing (as of sheep) **c** : a season's crop of wool of a sheep, a flock, or a region **d** : a section of filmed material (as a stock shot or a portion of a newsreel); *esp* : a fragment of film deleted during the editing of a motion picture **3** : an act of clipping : CUTTING, SHEARING **4 a** : a sharp blow esp. with the fist ⟨hit someone a ~ on the jaw⟩ **5** : a rapid gait or pace ⟨the train was snaking along at a brisk ~ —Robert Shaplen⟩ **6** : TIME : a single instance or occasion ⟨he charged $10 a ~⟩ — often used in the phrase *at a clip* ⟨to train 1000 workers at a ~⟩

clipboard \ˈ=ˌ=\ *n* [*[2]clip* + *board*] : a small portable rectangle of wood or other stiff backing material to one end of which is attached a spring clip for holding sheets of paper or a writing tablet securely

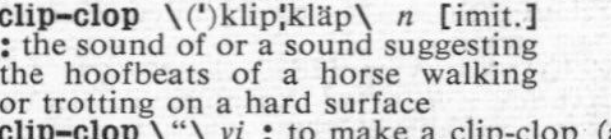
clipboard

clip bond *n* [*[3]clip*] : a masonry wall bond formed by clipping off the inner corners of face bricks and used to unite diagonal bond with a face composed entirely of stretchers — see PLUMB BOND

[1]clip–clop \(ˈ)klipˈkläp\ *n* [imit.] : the sound of or a sound suggesting the hoofbeats of a horse walking or trotting on a hard surface

[2]clip–clop \"\ *vi* : to make a clip-clop (as in walking) ⟨*clip-clopping* in slippers across the floor —Elizabeth Bowen⟩

clipfish *var of* KLIPFISH

clip hook *n* : SISTER HOOK

clip joint *n* [*[3]clip*] *slang* **1** : a place of public entertainment (as a café or nightclub) that makes a practice of defrauding patrons (as by gross overcharging) **2** : a business establishment regarded as making a practice of overcharging

clip man *n* [*[4]clip*] : a clerk who keeps track of the sales on the tobacco auction floor and prepares a seller's bill covering each lot sold

clip off *vt* [*[3]clip*] : to make (as a fast run) or cover rapidly (as a distance) ⟨some of the fastest runs *clipped off* on the Ohio river —Frederick Way⟩ ⟨his long legs *clipped off* the distance⟩

clip on *vi* [*[1]clip*] : to fasten on or be capable of being fastened by an attached clip ⟨the medal has no pin but merely *clips on* to the coat lapel⟩

clip–on \ˈ=ˌ=\ *adj* : that clips on ⟨a *clip-on* bow tie⟩ ⟨*clip-on* earrings⟩

clipped *adj* [fr. past part. of *[3]clip*] : characterized by more fortis articulation, more frequent syncope, and often more rapid tempo than the usual speech in another dialect or language (as southern British speech in comparison with most U.S. speech, the former often having for example a full stop \t\ instead of a flap \d·\ for the *t* of *city*, a vigorously flapped consonantal sound instead of the more laxly articulated vocalic or vowellike sound for the *r* of *very*, an \i\ instead of the laxer \ə\ for the *e* of *naked*, and \ˌtri\ instead of unsyncopated \ˌterē\ for the *-tery* of *cemetery*) ⟨a ~ crackling elliptical French —Dorothy C. Fisher⟩

clipped gable *n* [*[3]clip*] : JERKIN-HEAD

[1]clip·per \ˈklipə(r)\ *n* -s [ME *clippere*, fr. *clippen* to clip (cut) + *-ere* -er] **1** : one that clips esp. as a livelihood: as **a** : one that clips coins **b** : one that shears sheep **c** : any of various workers who cut fur from pelts, ravelings from cloth, or threads from garments or inspect stitching and other details of garments **d** : a worker who puts brooms into a machine that clips the rough ends to the desired length **2 a** : an instrument or tool for clipping esp. hair, fingernails, or toenails — usu. used in pl. ⟨the barber's ~*s* hummed⟩ **b** : an electronic circuit or part of one esp. in radio or television that clips certain instantaneous signals **3** : one that moves, runs, or scuds along swiftly: as **a** : a fast horse **b** *or* **clipper ship** : a fast sailing ship; *esp* : a full-rigged ship of a type developed by American builders about 1840 characterized by long slender lines, an overhanging bow, tall raking masts, and a large sail area **4 a** : a shorn sheep **5** : HELLGRAMITE

animal clipper

[2]clipper \"\ *n* -s [*[1]clip* + *-er*] : one that grasps or clips on: as **a** : a mining worker who attaches receptacles to or detaches them from haulage ropes **b clippers** *pl* : SISTER HOOKS

[3]clipper \"\ *adj* [*[1]clipper* (ship)] : CLIPPER-BUILT ⟨~ schooner⟩ ⟨~ packet⟩

clipper bow *n* [*[3]clipper*] : an overhanging ship's bow with a concave profile

clipper–built \ˈ==ˌ=\ *adj* [*[3]clipper*] : built like a clipper esp. on slender fast lines

clipper man *n* [*[3]clip* + *-er*] **1** : one who feeds sheet steel from which a pipe is to be made into a machine that tapers and cups the end **2** : one who operates a power shear to cut veneer to size and to cut out imperfections

clip·pe·ty–clop \ˌklipədˈēˈkläp\ *n* -s [imit.] : a rhythmic usu. repeated sound resembling a clip-clop but having one or two more beats in its basic rhythm ⟨the *clippety-clop* of the horse and hansom cab going by⟩

clip·pie \ˈklipē, -pi\ *n* -s [*[3]clip* "to punch a hole" + *-ie*] *slang Brit* : a woman conductor and ticket-taker on a bus

clipping *n* -s [fr. gerund of *[3]clip*] : something that is clipped off or out of something : a piece severed or removed by clipping — often used in pl. ⟨the barber swept up the hair ~*s*⟩; *esp* : an item clipped from a publication ⟨a newspaper ~⟩

clipping bureau *or* **clipping service** *n* : an organization or business that supplies to order clippings on any given subject cut from publications

clip·ping·ly *adv* : in a clipping manner

clips *pl of* CLIP, *pres 3d sing of* CLIP

clipsheet \ˈ=ˌ=\ *n* [*[3]clip* + *sheet*; fr. their being printed on one side for convenience in cutting] **:** a sheet of newspaper material (as news items, features, interviews, fillers, or cartoons) issued by a publisher, publicity bureau, or other organization and usu. printed on only one side of the sheet to facilitate clipping and reprinting by newspapers and periodicals

clipt *past part of* CLIP

clique \ˈklēk, ˈklik\ *n* -s [F, perh. fr. MF, latch, fr. *cliquer* to click; fr. the secrecy involved in some such groups] **:** a narrow exclusive circle or group of persons; *esp* **:** one held together by a presumed identity of interests, views, or purposes ⟨a number of ~*s* developed within the union leadership⟩ ⟨the court ~⟩ ⟨~*s* within the student body⟩

clique·less \-ləs\ *adj* **:** lacking a clique

cli·quey *also* **cli·quy** \ˈklēkē, ˈklikē, -ki\ *adj, often* **cli·qui·er**; *usu* **cli·qui·est :** CLIQUISH 1

cli·quish *also* **clique·ish** \ˈklēkish, ˈklik-, -kēsh\ *adj* **1 :** tending toward narrow exclusiveness or to form a clique ⟨~ attitudes developed among children coming from the fashionable west side⟩ ⟨newly arrived immigrants tend to be ~ for a while⟩ **2 :** marked by a tendency to divide into cliques ⟨ballet companies by reputation are . . . ~ —Al Hine⟩

cli·quism \ˈklēˌkizəm, ˈkliˌk-\ *n* -s **:** the tendency to form cliques **:** a cliquish spirit

cli·se·ral \ˈklīsərəl\ *adj* **:** of, relating to, or typical of a clisere

cli·sere \ˈklīˌsi(ə)r\ *n* [*climate* + *sere* (cycle)] **:** the succession of ecological communities that results from climatic changes; *esp* **:** one preceding the reestablishment of a stable state following an intense climatic change (as the advance or recession of a major glaciation)

clish·ma·cla·ver \ˌklishməˈklāvər, ˌklēsh-\ *n* -s [Sc *clish* to gossip (of imit. origin) + connective *-ma-* + *claver*] *chiefly Scot* **:** idle talk **:** GOSSIP

-clisis — see -CLEISIS

clist- *or* **clisto-** — see CLEIST-

clistocarp *var of* CLEISTOCARP

clistogamy *var of* CLEISTOGAMY

clis·to·gas·tra \ˌklīstəˈgastrə, ˌklis-\ *n pl, cap* [NL, fr. *cleist-* + *-gastra* (fr. Gk *gastr-, gastēr* belly)] **:** a suborder of Hymenoptera including the ants, typical wasps, and bees, all having a legless grub as larva and a constricted second abdominal segment that forms a narrow waist or petiole — compare CHALASTROGASTRA

clistogene *var of* CLEISTOGENE

clit \ˈklit\ *adj* [perh. fr. ME *clyht,* past part. of *clicchen*] *dial Eng* **:** HEAVY, DOUGHY, CAKED, STICKY

clitch \ˈklich\ *vb* -ED/-ING/-ES [ME *clicchen, clycchen,* fr. OE *clyccan* — more at CLUTCH] *vt* **1** *dial Eng* **:** to grasp tightly **:** CLUTCH **2** *dial Eng* **:** to cause to adhere **:** stick together ~ *vi, dial Eng* **:** to stick together **:** ADHERE

cli·tel·la·ta \ˌklīd·ᵊlˈäd·ə, -ˈlād·ə\ *n pl, cap* [NL, fr. *clitellum* + *-ata*] *in certain classifications* **:** a major division of annelid worms comprising the Oligochaeta and Hirudinea

cli·tel·late \kləˈtelət,(ˌ)klīˌt-\ *adj* [NL *clitellum* + E *-ate*] **:** having a clitellum

cli·tel·lum \kləˈteləm, klī-\ *n, pl* **clitel·la** \-elə\ [NL, modif. of L *clitellae* packsaddle; akin to Gk *klinein* to lean — more at LEAN] **:** a thickened glandular section of the body wall of certain annelid worms that functions as an accessory reproductive organ secreting a viscid material that forms the cocoon in which the eggs are deposited

clit·ic \ˈklid·ik\ *n or adj* [back-formation fr. *enclitic* & *proclitic*] **:** ENCLITIC, PROCLITIC

clit·i·on \ˈklid·ēˌän\ *n, pl* **clit·ia** \-ēə\ [NL, fr. Gk *klitos* slope; akin to Gk *klinein* to lean] **:** the median point of the anterior margin of the clivus

cli·tocy·be \klīˈtäsəˌbē\ *n, cap* [NL, fr. *clito-* (fr. Gk *klitos* slope) + MGk *kybē* head; perh. akin to Gk *kyphos* bent, humpbacked — more at CYPHELLA] **:** a genus of white-spored agarics (family Agaricaceae) with flat or funnel-shaped pileus and elastic stem — see JACK-O'-LANTERN

clit·o·ral \ˈkli|d·ərəl, ˈklī|, |tərəl\ *or* **clit·o·ric** \ˈkli|d·ərik, ˈklī|, |tərik\ *adj* [NL *clitoris* + E *-al* or *-ic*] **:** of or relating to the clitoris

cli·to·ria \klīˈtōrēə, -tȯr-, kləˈ-\ *n, cap* [NL, fr. *clitoris* + *-ia;* — fr. the appearance of the flower] **:** a genus of herbs or woody vines (family Leguminosae) having pinnate leaves and large axillary flowers often in short racemes — see BUTTERFLY PEA

clitorid- *or* **clitorido-** *comb form* [NL, fr. *clitorid-, clitoris*] **:** clitoris ⟨*clitorid*auxe⟩ ⟨*clitorido*tomy⟩

cli·to·rid·e·an \ˌklidəˈridēən, ˌklīd-\ *adj* [*clitorid-* + *-ean*] **:** CLITORAL

clit·o·ri·dec·to·my \ˌklid·ərəˈdektəmē, ˌklīd·-\ *n* -ES [*clitorid-* + *-ectomy*] **:** excision of the clitoris **:** female circumcision

clit·o·ris \ˈkli|d·ərəs, ˈklī|, |tərəs, kləˈtōrəs, -ˈtȯr-\ *n* -ES [NL, fr. Gk *kleitoris*] **:** a small organ at the anterior or ventral part of the vulva homologous to the penis in the male

[1]clit·ter \ˈklid·ə(r)\ *vi* -ED/-ING/-S [prob. alter. of *clatter*] **:** to make a frictional or rattling sound **:** stridulate esp. softly ⟨a cicada ~*ing*⟩ ⟨her breath made in her throat a little ~*ing* sound —F.M.Ford⟩

[2]clitter \ˈklitə(r)\ *n* -s *dial Eng* **:** a mass of loose stones ⟨tumbled ~*s* of granite⟩

cliv \ˈkliv\ *Scot var of* CLOOF

clivers *var of* CLEAVERS

cli·via \ˈklīvēə, -iv-\ *n, cap* [NL, fr. Lady Charlotte *Clive* †1866 duchess of Northumberland + NL *-ia*] **:** a small genus of fleshy southern African herbs (family Amaryllidaceae) having distichous leaves and large funnel-shaped flowers — see KAFIR LILY

cli·vis \ˈklīvəs, ˈklēv-\ *n* -ES [ML] **:** a neume denoting two notes or tones with the first higher in pitch than the second

cli·vus \ˈklīvəs\ *n, pl* **cli·vi** \-ˌvī\ [NL, fr. L, hill; akin to Gk *klinein* to lean — more at LEAN] **:** the smooth sloping surface on the upper posterior part of the body of the sphenoid bone supporting the pons

clk *abbr* **1** clerk **2** clock

clkg *abbr* calking

clmg *abbr* claiming

clo·a·ca \klōˈākə\ *n, pl* **cloa·cae** \-ˈā(ˌ)sē\ [L; akin to Gk *klyzein* to wash — more at CLYSTER] **1 :** [3]SEWER 2 **2** [NL, fr. L] **a :** the common chamber into which the intestinal, urinary, and generative canals discharge in birds, reptiles, amphibians, and many fishes **b :** a chamber or passage having similar functions in invertebrates

clo·a·cal \klōˈākəl\ *adj* [L *cloacalis,* fr. *cloaca* + *-alis* -al] **1 :** constituting or carried by a cloaca **2 :** having a cloaca **3 :** concerned with or replete with obscenity or out-and-out indecency ⟨a writer with a ~ obsession⟩

cloacal gland *n* **:** any of several glands located in the cloaca of lower vertebrates: as **a :** one of the glands producing foul-smelling defensive secretions in certain snakes **b :** one of several glands believed to have hedonic function in many caudate amphibians

clo·ac·a·line \klōˈakəlᵊn, -ˈāk-, -ˌlīn\ *adj* [*cloacal* + *-ine*] **:** CLOACAL

cloacal membrane *n, anat* **:** a plate of fused ectoderm and endoderm closing the fetal anus in the vertebrate embryo

cloaca max·i·ma \-maksəmə\ *n, pl* **cloacae maxi·mae** \-ˌmē\ [L, largest sewer, fr. the main drain of ancient Rome] **:** a general repository of filth

clo·a·ci·nal \ˌklōəˈsīnᵊl\ *adj* [*cloaca* + *-ine* + *-al*] **:** CLOACAL

clo·a·ci·tis \ˌ==ˈsīd·əs\ *n* -ES [NL, fr. *cloaca* + *-itis*] **:** a venereal disease of the common fowl occurring as an ulcerative inflammation of the vent and cloaca and having no known etiology but apparently transmitted by copulation — called also *vent gleet*

[1]cloak \ˈklōk\ *n* -s [ME *cloke,* fr. ONF *cloque* cloak, bell, fr. ML *clocca* bell; fr. the bell-like shape — more at CLOCK] **1 :** a loose outer garment (as a cape or an overcoat) **2 :** something resembling or suggesting an outer garment: as **a :** a distinctive character or role ⟨laying aside the ~ of military commander⟩ ⟨a ~ of martyrdom had no appeal for the rebel leader⟩ **b :** an encompassing veil serving to exclude interruption or interference ⟨a ~ of secrecy around ships' movements —Hamilton Basso⟩ ⟨draped himself in a ~ of heavy thoughtfulness —Hamilton Basso⟩ **c :** a deceptive pretense or disguise to screen an unpalatable fact, devious action, or ulterior design ⟨use by the unscrupulous of watchwords of western democracy as a ~⟩ ⟨onslaughts of a populace using liberty as a ~ for an attack upon order and stability —John Dewey⟩

[2]cloak \"\ *vt* -ED/-ING/-S **1 :** to cover with or as if with a cloak ⟨the inside of the church was ~*ed* with black drapes⟩ ⟨hills ~*ed* with heather⟩ **2 a :** HIDE, DISGUISE, SCREEN ⟨preparations ~*ed* in secrecy⟩ ⟨~*ed* by diplomatic immunity⟩ ⟨the attack upon Germany appeared to ~ an assault upon China —F.L.Paxson⟩ **b :** to clothe in a given often false or misleading form or appearance ⟨the stories . . . perhaps ~ in symbolic form an old quarrel —Catharine McClellan⟩ ⟨self-assurance ~*ed* by a quiet, repressed, and rather deadly manner —W.A. White⟩ **syn** see DISGUISE

cloak-and-dagger \ˌ===ˈ==\ *adj* **1 a :** dealing in intrigue and action of a romantic and melodramatic kind usu. with characters in a colorful historical setting and involving espionage, duels, pursuit, and rescue **b :** resembling or suggesting such intrigue or action **2 :** concerned with espionage; *specif* **:** engaged in or connected with undercover activities of secret agents of a national intelligence or counterintelligence service behind enemy lines

cloak-and-sword \ˌ===ˈ=\ *adj* [trans. of Sp. (*comedia de*) *capa y espada* cloak-and-sword comedy] **:** dealing in fictional or semifictional romance and adventure of the nobility in a period when swordplay and colorful elaborate dress were common

cloak-and-sworder \ˌ===ˈ==\ *n* -s **:** a cloak-and-sword novel or drama

cloak fern *n* **:** a fern of the genus *Notholaena*

cloaking *n* -s **:** material of which cloaks are made

cloak·less \ˈklōkləs\ *adj* **:** lacking a cloak

cloak·let \ˈklōklət\ *n* -s **:** a little cloak

cloakroom \ˈ=ˌ=\ *n* **1 :** a room in which outdoor wraps may be placed during one's stay **2 :** an anteroom of a legislative chamber where members may keep their wraps, rest, and confer with colleagues **3 :** a room or cubicle where garments, parcels, and luggage may be checked for temporary safekeeping (as in a theater, cabaret, or hotel) **:** CHECKROOM **4** *Brit* **:** a room with lavatory and toilet

cloam \ˈklōm\ *n* -s [ME *clome,* fr. OE *clām;* akin to OE *clǣman* to smear, daub, MD *clēm* mud, OE *clǣg* clay — more at CLAY] *dial Eng* **:** EARTHENWARE, CROCKERY

cloam·en \ˈklōmən\ *adj* [*cloam* + *-en*] *dial Eng* **:** of earthenware **:** EARTHEN

[1]clob \ˈkläb\ *dial Eng var of* [4]COB

[2]clob \"\ *n* -s [by shortening & alter.] **:** KLABERJASS

[1]clob·ber \ˈkläbə(r)\ *n* -s [prob. alter. of *clothes*] **1** *slang Brit* **:** wearing apparel ⟨dressed in his bathing ~⟩ **2** *slang Brit* **:** GEAR ⟨loaded himself with a lot of ~⟩

[2]clobber \"\ *vt* **clobbered; clobbered; clobbering** \-b(ə)riŋ\ **clobbers** *slang Brit* **:** DRESS, TOG — often used with *up*

[3]clobber \"\ *chiefly dial var of* [1]CLABBER

[4]clobber \"\ *chiefly Midland var of* [2]CLABBER

[5]clobber \"\ *n* -s [by alter. and shortening] **:** KLABERJASS

[6]clobber \"\ *vt* **clobbered; clobbered; clobbering** \-b(ə)riŋ\ **clobbers** [obs. *clobber* to patch, fr. obs. *clobber* paste to fill cracks, fr. ScGael *clàbar* mud] **:** to load (already decorated porcelain) with added overglaze enameling

[7]clobber \"\ *vb* **clobbered; clobbered; clobbering** \-b(ə)riŋ\ **clobbers** [origin unknown] *vt* **1 a** *slang* **:** to pound mercilessly **:** beat up **:** knock out **:** knock down **b :** to strike with crushing force **2** *slang* **:** to defeat overwhelmingly **:** SMEAR **3 :** to hit and demolish or severely damage (the target) ~ *vi* **:** to crash in an aircraft **:** make a crash landing

clob·ber·er \ˈkläbərə(r)\ *n* -s [obs. *clobber* to patch + *-er*] *Brit* **:** a repairer of clothes and shoes

[1]clo·chard \ˈklōshə(r)d, klōˈshär\ *n* -s [by alter.] **:** CLOCHER

[2]clochard \"\ *n* -s [F, fr. *clocher* to limp (fr. — assumed — VL *cloppicare,* fr. LL *cloppus* lame) + *-ard*] **:** TRAMP, BUM, HOBO ⟨a ~*'s* views on Parisian life⟩

cloche \ˈklōsh, ˈkläsh, ˈklȯsh\ *n* -s [F, lit., bell, fr. ML *clocca*] **1 :** a translucent cover for a young plant or shoot often used to force plants in the early part of the growing season **2 :** a woman's small helmetlike hat usu. with deep rounded crown and very narrow brim **3 :** BELL 6a **4 :** BELL 5g

clo·cher \ˈklōshə(r), klōˈshā\ *n* -s [ME, fr. MF, fr. *cloche*] **:** BELL TOWER

clo·chette \klōˈshet, klō-\ *n* -s [F, dim. of *cloche*] **:** a small bell-shaped ornament

[1]clock \ˈkläk\ *n* -s *often attrib* [ME *clok,* fr. MD *clocke* clock, bell, fr. ONF or ML; ONF *cloque* bell, fr. ML *clocca,* of Celt origin; akin to MIr *clocc* bell, W *cloch;* akin to OE *hliehhan* to laugh — more at LAUGH] **1 a :** a device other than a watch for indicating or measuring time chiefly consisting of a train of wheels actuated by various devices (as falling weights, a tensed spring, changes in temperature, or electrical impulses), regulated through an escapement in various ways (as by a pendulum, dripping water, a synchronized electrical motor, or the vibrations of atoms), and indicating time most commonly by means of hands moving on a dial often with accompanying bells made to strike at regular intervals (as once each hour) — see ELECTRIC CLOCK, PROGRAM CLOCK, SIDEREAL CLOCK, TURRET CLOCK, WATCHMAN'S CLOCK, WATER CLOCK; compare CHRONOMETER, HOUR GLASS, WATCH **b** *obs* **:** WATCH; *esp* **:** one that strikes **c :** the downy fruiting head of the common dandelion **d :** a form of solitaire in which packets of cards are laid out in a circle to resemble the dial of a clock **2** *obs* **a :** a stroke of a clock sounding the hour **b :** the hour indicated by strokes of a clock **3 :** a registering device with a dial and indicator attached to a mechanism to measure or gauge its functioning or to record its output ⟨a pick ~ on a loom⟩ ⟨a hank ~ on a roving frame⟩; *specif* **a :** TAXIMETER **b :** SPEEDOMETER **4 :** TIME CLOCK ⟨punched the ~ at 8:45⟩ **5 :** an inflexible time schedule or timing plan ⟨uranium and thorium are also wasting assets, but to a much slower ~ —Stuart Chase⟩ ⟨he threw the whole weight of his genius into an effort to stop the ~ of history —J.T.Farrell⟩ **6** *slang Brit* **:** the human face — **around the clock 1 :** continuously for 24 hours **:** day and night without cessation **2 :** without relaxation and heedless of time — **hold the clock on :** to time (as a racer in a workout) with a stopwatch — **turn back the clock :** to revert to a condition existing well in the past — usu. with an implication of surrendering progress or improvement ⟨would not such a "Balkanization of the United States" be a clear *turning back of the clock* —E.N.Griswold⟩

[2]clock \"\ *vb* -ED/-ING/-S *vt* **1 a :** to time (a person or a performance) with a stopwatch or by an electric timing device ⟨~*ed* his practice quarter mile at 48 seconds⟩ **b :** to be timed at ⟨other Americans had ~*ed* 8:55.7 in the two-mile⟩ **c :** to register (time, distance, rate, velocity, or number) on a mechanical recording device ⟨wind velocities were ~*ed* at 80 miles per hour⟩ ⟨~*ed* an average of 4000 visitors a day⟩ **d :** to determine the timing of ⟨a station ~*ed* to broadcast one minute in each hour⟩ **2 :** to sound (a bell) either by pulling the clapper or by striking with a hammer from outside and without swinging ~ *vi* **:** to register on a time sheet or time clock **:** PUNCH — used with *in, out, on, off* ⟨it would be too late to load after the driver ~*s* in at eight⟩ ⟨a workshop where workers are required to ~ on and off⟩

[3]clock \"\ *vb* -ED/-ING/-S [ME *clokken,* fr. OE *cloccian* to cluck; like MD *klucke* brood hen, OHG *cloccōn* to beat, ON *klaka* to gossip, L *glocire* to cluck, Gk *klōzein,* Lith *klukšėti* of imit. origin] *vi, now dial Brit* **1 :** CALL, CLUCK — used esp. of a hen **2 :** SET, BROOD ~ *vt, now dial Brit* **:** SET, INCUBATE

[4]clock \"\ *n* -s [prob. fr. [1]*clock* (bell); fr. its original shape] **:** an ornamental figure or figured work on the ankle or side of a stocking or sock

[5]clock \"\ *vt* -ED/-ING/-S **:** to ornament with figured work

[6]clock \"\ *n* -s [prob. of Scand. origin; akin to Sw dial. *klocka* beetle] **:** BEETLE

clockbird \ˈ=ˌ=\ *n, Austral* [[1]*clock* + *bird;* fr. its calling regularly at dawn and dusk] **:** KOOKABURRA

clock calm *n, archaic* **:** a dead calm

clock card *n* **:** a card on which the periods an employee has worked are recorded by a time clock

[1]clock·er \ˈkläkə(r)\ *n* -s [[2]*clock* + *-er*] **1 :** one that times racehorses during workouts and records information that will be useful in grouping and handicapping the horses **2 :** one that times a race or measures a flow (as of traffic) **3 :** a worker who measures lens blanks for conformance to specified dimensions, verifies their focal strength, and inspects and sorts them — called also *neutralizer, sizer*

[2]clocker \"\ *n* -s [[5]*clock* + *-er*] **:** one that embroiders clocks on stockings

clockface \ˈ=ˌ=\ *n* **:** the dial face of a clock

clockface method *n* **:** a method of target designation and marking by reference to a known description point conceived as the center of a clockface, the targets being pointed out as on the hour radii of the imaginary dial

clock golf *n* **:** a lawn game that is played and scored like golf but confined to putting and that uses a single cup placed eccentrically within a circle of 12 tee positions

clock hour *n* **:** a full sixty minutes ⟨the certificate required a minimum of forty *clock hours* of instruction which could not be satisfied by forty class hours of only fifty minutes each⟩

clocking *n* -s [fr. gerund of [2]*clock*] **:** the time used to traverse a measured course (as in a race) ⟨a near world record ~ for the mile⟩

clock·less \ˈkläkləs\ *adj* **:** lacking a clock

clock·like \ˈ=ˌlīk\ *adj* **:** unusually regular, undeviating, and precise ⟨do his job with ~ efficiency⟩

clockmaker \ˈ=ˌ==\ *n* [ME *clokmaker,* fr. *clok* clock + *maker*] **:** one that makes or repairs clocks

clock plant *n* **:** TELEGRAPH PLANT

clock stamp *n* **:** a combination clock and dating stamp for stamping the exact time

clockstar \ˈ=ˌ=\ *n* **:** a star of accurately known right ascension used to ascertain the correction of an astronomical clock

clock·ster \ˈklākstə(r)\ *n* -s **:** HOROLOGER

clock vine *n* **:** a plant of the genus *Thunbergia* (esp. *T. alata*)

clock watch *n* **:** a watch that strikes the hours consecutively

clock watcher *n* **:** a worker having the habit of overfrequently consulting a timepiece

[1]clock·wise \ˈkläkˌwīz\ *adv* **:** in the direction in which the hands of a clock rotate as viewed from in front, circularly from horizontal left, up or away, down or approaching, to horizontal right **:** with the sun — opposed to *counterclockwise*

[2]clockwise \"\ *adj* **:** moving or directed clockwise **:** RIGHT-HANDED, DEXTROROTATORY, POSITIVE

clockwork \ˈ=ˌ=\ *n* **1 :** machinery composed of or containing a train of wheels of small size; *esp* **:** a mechanism of delicate construction that operates with unfailing regularity and minute accuracy (as in a meter) **2 :** a timing device similar to the works of a clock and operated usu. by a spring esp. for actuating a signal, a set of motions in a toy, or a bomb **3 :** something that by its effects seems to perform in response to clockwork or to be controlled by clockwork ⟨Emil Ludwig adapted psychoanalytic methods in exposing the psychical ~ of his subjects —Siegfried Mandel⟩ ⟨like a waxen lady with ~ breathing —Elizabeth Bowen⟩

[1]clod \ˈkläd\ *n* -s [ME *clodde,* alter. of *clot, clotte* — more at CLOT] **1** *obs* **:** CLOT **2 a :** a lump or mass esp. of earth, turf, or clay **b :** SOIL, GROUND, EARTH; *also* **:** a spot of earth or turf **c :** something as unfeeling or as insensitive as a clod of earth **:** one that is gross and stupid **:** DOLT ⟨remind oneself that the lifeless ~ he is writing about is the author of some . . . most important novels —J.W.Aldridge⟩ **3 :** a part of the shoulder of a beef or of the neck piece near the shoulder **4 :** soft shale esp. over a coal seam

[2]clod \"\ *vb* **clodded; clodded; clodding; clods** [ME *clodden,* fr. *clodde,* n.] *vt* **1 a :** to throw clods of earth at ⟨caught Henry on the outside stairs and *clodded* him vivaciously —Dixon Wecter⟩ **b :** to drive by pelting with clods ⟨came a turtle, and I *clodded* it back into the water —W.A.White⟩ **2** *dial Brit* **:** to throw violently **:** HURL ~ *vi* **:** to form into clods

clod·di·ness \ˈklädēnəs\ *n* -ES **:** the quality or state of being cloddy

clodding press *n* [*clodding* (pres. part. of *clod* to make clods of) + *press*] **:** a press used for squeezing the oil from meal made from flax and other seeds

clod·dish \ˈklädish\ *adj* **1 :** heavy and spiritless ⟨our thoughts ~ from unending toil⟩ **2 :** stolid and boorish ⟨set apart from the ~ world about them by their heightened capacity for feeling —Mark Schorer⟩

clod·dy \ˈklädē\ *adj, sometimes* -ER/-EST [[1]*clod* + *-y*] **1 :** consisting of clods **:** full of clods **:** like a clod **2 :** of low stature and heavily set — used of an animal, esp. a dog

clod·hop·per \ˈkläd,häpə(r)\ *n* -s **1 a :** a rustic (as a plowman) typically clumsy, heavy-footed, uncouth, and uninformed esp. of urbane ways ⟨~*s* . . . that never handled a sword —Mark Twain⟩ **b :** a clumsy heavy-footed cloddish person **:** DOLT **2 :** a large heavy shoe **syn** see BOOR

clod·hop·per·ish \-p(ə)rish\ *adj* **:** LOUTISH

clod·hop·ping \-piŋ\ *adj* **1 :** suitable for or serving a farm laborer **2 :** BOORISH ⟨Mr. Lewis . . . with this ~ blaring potwalloper —Ezra Pound⟩

clodknocker \ˈ=ˌ==\ *n* **:** CLODHOPPER

clod·let \ˈklädlət\ *n* -s **:** a small clod

clod·ly \ˈklädlē\ *adv* [[1]*clod* (dolt) + *-ly*] **:** clumsily and insensibly

clod·pate \ˈkläd,pāt\ *n* -s [[1]*clod* (lump) + *pate*] **:** BLOCKHEAD 2

clod·pat·ed \ˈ=ˌpād·əd\ *adj* **:** THICKHEADED

clodpoll \ˈ=ˌ=\ *also* **clodpole** \ˈ=ˌ=\ *n* -s [[1]*clod* (lump) + *poll* (head) or *pole,* alter. of *poll*] **:** CLODPATE

clod smasher *or* **clod crusher** *n* **:** [1]FLOAT 5d(1)

cloff \ˈkläf\ *n* -s [perh. alter. of [3]*clove*] **:** an allowance of two pounds in every three hundredweight formerly given on certain goods to cover small losses in retailing

[1]clog \ˈkläg *also* -ȯg\ *n* -s [ME *clogge*] **1** *dial Brit* **:** a short thick piece of wood (as of a tree trunk or root) **:** LOG **2 a :** a weight attached to a man or an animal to hinder motion **b :** something that shackles, restricts, or impedes motion or desired freedom of action **:** ENCUMBRANCE 2 ⟨there are two inconsistent passions, which . . . are commonly ~*s* upon each other . . . ambition and avarice —Earl of Chesterfield⟩ **3 :** a heavy shoe, sandal, or overshoe having a thick typically wooden sole — compare CHOPINE, GETA, PATTEN, PLATFORM, SABOT **4 :** CLOG ALMANAC **5 :** CLOG DANCE

[2]clog \"\ *vb* **clogged; clogged; clogging; clogs** [ME *cloggen* to fasten a clog to, to fetter, fr. *clogge,* n.] *vt* **1 :** ENCUMBER: **a :** to impede the motion of (as with a chain or a burden) ⟨mustangs are tamed by being *clogged* until they have run themselves footsore⟩ ⟨her sides were *clogged* with the lazy weed that spawns in the Eastern seas —Rudyard Kipling⟩ **b :** to halt or retard operation, progress, or growth of ⟨restraints that have been *clogging* the market —T.W.Arnold⟩ ⟨all common ambitions, rank, possessions, power, the things which ~ man's feet —John Buchan⟩ **2 a :** to obstruct so as to hinder motion in or through **:** fill beyond capacity (as a limited space or narrow thoroughfare) ⟨for . . . years drovers *clogged* the turnpikes with herds —*Amer. Guide Series: N.Y.*⟩ ⟨the telephone lines were *clogged* —F.L.Allen⟩ ⟨the jury system has undergone serious criticism in recent years, due in part to the *clogging* of the courts —C.B.Swisher⟩ **b :** to fill or block up the hollows, interior, interstices, or working parts of with an adhesive accumulation ⟨excessive ink ~*s* the type⟩ ⟨valves *clogged* with carbon⟩ **3 a :** to fill (as the mind or the senses) so as to impair function ⟨fear ~*s* the mind —Jawaharlal Nehru⟩ **b :** to overload (as a work of art) with irrelevant matter so as to obscure the essence ⟨a great deal of . . . philosophizing ~*s* such movement as the book has —Elizabeth Janeway⟩ **4 a :** to put clogs on **b :** to make into clogs **:** put wooden soles on (as on shoes) ~ *vi* **1 :** to become clogged **:** become filled with extraneous matter ⟨the heater *clogged* with dust, preventing proper circulation⟩ **2 :** to coalesce or unite in a mass **:** come together ⟨they meant to run him until his blood *clogged* on his heart as his brush with mud —John Masefield⟩ **3 a :** to dance a clog dance ⟨began to ~ on the brick fireplace —Scott Fitzgerald⟩ **b :** to walk heavily **:** walk wearing or as if wearing clogs ⟨he grabbed a towel and *clogged* out to take a shower —Thomas Gallagher⟩ **syn** see HAMPER

clog almanac *n* **:** a calendar formerly used in England made by cutting notches and figures on the four edges of a square block of hard wood

clog box *n* **:** CHINESE TEMPLE BLOCK

clog dance *n* **:** a dance in which the performer wears clogs and beats out a clattering rhythm upon the floor — **clog dancer** *n* — **clog dancing** *n*

clog·gage \ˈklägij *also* -ȯg-\ *n* -s **:** condition of being clogged

clog·ger \'klägə(r) *also* -ôg-\ *n* -s [¹*clog* (shoe) + *-er*] **1** *dial Eng* **:** CLOGMAKER **2 :** CLOG DANCER

clog·gy \'klägē *also* -ôgē\ *adj, sometimes* -ER/-EST **1 :** like a clog **:** characterized by clogs or lumps **2 :** clogging or having power to clog **:** STICKY

clogwheel \'⸗,⸗\ *n, dial Eng* **:** a cartwheel of solid wood fixed firmly on its axle

clogwood \'⸗,⸗\ *n* **:** wood (as the wood of the yamanai) used for making clogs

clog·wyn \'klōg(,)wēn, -äg-, -(,)win\ *n* -s [W *clogwyn, clog;* akin to OIr *cloch* stone — more at CLACHAN] **:** PRECIPICE, CLIFF

cloi·son \'klȯiz°n, *F* klwȧzōⁿ\ *n* -s [F, partition, fr. (assumed) VL *clausion-, clausio,* fr. L *clausus,* past part. of *claudere* to close — more at CLOSE] **:** one of the wire fillets or metal dividing strips used in cloisonné

¹**cloi·son·né** \¦klȯiz°n¦ā, *F* klwȧzȯnā\ *adj* [F, fr. past part. of *cloisonner,* to partition, fr. *cloison*] **:** consisting of, used in, or forming cloisonné

²**cloisonné** \"\ *n* -s **:** a multicolored decoration made of enamels poured into the divided areas in a design outlined with bent wire fillets or metal strips secured to a usu. metal ground — compare CHAMPLEVÉ

¹**clois·ter** \'klȯistə(r)\ *n* -s [ME *cloistre,* fr. OF, alter. (influenced by *cloison* partition) of *clostre,* fr. ML *claustrum* room in a monastery, fr. L, bar, bolt, enclosure, fr. *clausus,* past part. of *claudere* to close — more at CLOSE] **1** *obs* **:** an enclosed space (as in a ring of stones or within a seed or nut) **2 :** a monastic establishment **:** a monastery or convent; *also* **:** monastic life **3 a :** a covered passage or ambulatory on the side of a court usu. having one side walled and the other an open arcade or colonnade and typically connecting different buildings of a group or running round an open court esp. of a monastery or college **b :** a covered walk, passageway, or arcade (as along a street) **4 :** the status of being cloistered ⟨he ordered the ~ of the new monastery to become effective —*Springfield (Mass.) Daily News*⟩

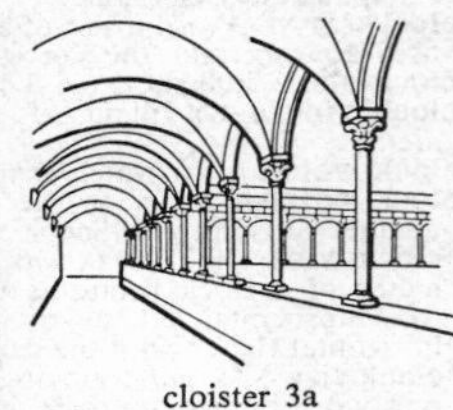
cloister 3a

²**cloister** \"\ *vt* **cloistered; cloistered; cloistering** \-t(ə)riŋ\ **cloisters 1 :** to confine in or as if in a cloister **:** seclude from the world **:** IMMURE ⟨a physicist who ~*s* himself in his laboratory⟩ **2 :** to surround with a cloister **:** make a cloister of ⟨a small hill-*cloistered* college town⟩

cloistered *adj* **1 :** living or remaining in seclusion and aloof from normal social participation or secular concerns or from public notice or public affairs ⟨he is not a ~ intellectual —Clifton Daniel⟩ ⟨men with burning causes are generally more eloquent than ~ dons —Heywood Broun⟩ **2 :** narrowly restricted or insulated in outlook and interests **:** preoccupied and detached ⟨the phenomenon of a college professor leaving his ~ life to enter a political fight⟩ ⟨the ~ thinking of certain isolationists⟩ **3 a :** sheltered or providing shelter from contact with common life and relations with the outer world **:** intent on its own affairs to the exclusion of external affairs ⟨you might have expected such a man to end his days in the ~ academic world of books and blackboards —Philip Pollack⟩ **b :** such as is provided by the isolation of a cloister ⟨to recapture the ~ serenity in his work which he had grown to love —Marcia Davenport⟩ **c :** cultivated or conducted in the privacy of seclusion sheltered from outside interference and the bustle of mundane life ⟨a fugitive and ~ poetry that never at any time heard the chimes at midnight —J.L.Lowes⟩

cloistered arch *or* **cloistered vault** *n* **:** CLOISTER VAULT

cloistered heart *n* **:** CLOSED GENTIAN

clois·ter·er \'klȯistərə(r)\ *n* -s [ME *cloistrer,* fr. MF *cloistrier,* fr. *cloistre* + *-ier* -er] **:** one belonging to or living in a cloister **:** RECLUSE

cloister garth *n* **:** an open court surrounded by cloisters esp. in a group of buildings of a monastery or college

clois·ter·less \'klȯistə(r)ləs\ *adj* **:** lacking a cloister

clois·ter·ly \'klȯistə(r)lē\ *adj* **:** proper to a cloister **:** CLOISTRAL

cloister vault *n* **:** a cupolalike vault on a square or polygonal base with diminishing courses to the top and of similar horizontal section throughout and in shape like a pyramid or frustum of a pyramid with sides curved convexly outward

clois·tral \'klȯistrəl\ *also* **clois·ter·al** \-t(ə)rəl\ *adj* **1 :** belonging to a cloister or suggestive of a cloister or the austerity of a cloister **2 :** such as is characteristic of cloistered recluses or scholars **3 :** closely limited in outlook as if isolated in a cloister

cloistress *n* -ES *obs* **:** NUN

¹**cloit** \'klȯit\ *vi* [origin unknown] *Scot* **:** to fall down heavily

²**cloit** \"\ *n* -s *Scot* **:** a heavy fall

cloke *archaic var of* CLOAK

cloky *var of* CLOQUE

¹**clomb** [*clomb,* past, fr. ME, alter. of *clamb,* fr. OE, past of *climban* to climb; *clomb,* past part., fr. ME, alter. of *clomben, clumben,* fr. OE *clumben,* past part. of *climban* — more at CLIMB] *now dial past of* CLIMB

²**clomb** *var of* CLOMB

¹**clomp** \'klämp\ *vi* -ED/-ING/-S [by alter.] **:** ²CLUMP *vi* 1

²**clomp** \"\ *n* -s [by alter.] **:** ¹CLUMP 4

clo·nal \'klōn°l\ *adj* [*clone* + *-al*] **:** of, relating to, or occurring in or as a clone — **clo·nal·ly** \-nəlē\ *adv*

clone \'klōn\ *also* **clon** \'klōn, -än\ *n* -s [Gk *klōn* twig, slip; akin to Gk *klan* to break — more at GLADIATOR] *biol* **:** the aggregate of the asexually produced progeny of an individual whether natural (as the products of repeated fission of a protozoan) or otherwise (as in the propagation of a particular plant by budding or by cuttings through many vegetative generations)

clo·nic \'klōnik, 'klän-\ *adj* [NL *clonus* + E *-ic*] **:** exhibiting, relating to, or involving clonus ⟨~ contraction⟩ ⟨~ spasm⟩ — **clo·nic·i·ty** \klō'nisəd·ē, klä'-\ *n* -ES

clo·nism \'klō,nizəm, 'klä,-\ *n* -s [NL *clonismus,* fr. *clonus* + L *-ismus* -ism] **:** the condition of being affected with clonus

¹**clonk** \'klōŋk, 'kläŋk\ *vb* -ED/-ING/-S [alter. of ¹*clank*] *vi* **:** to make a dull echoless thumping sound as if from impact of a hard object on a hard but hollow surface ~ *vt* **:** to produce a clonk or clonks on

²**clonk** \"\ *n* -s **:** a clonking sound

clo·nor·chi·a·sis \,klōnȯr'kīəsəs\ *also* **clo·nor·chi·o·sis** \klō,nȯrkī'ōsəs\ *n, pl* **clonorchia·ses** \-'kīə,sēz\ *also* **clonorchio·ses** \-kī'ō,sēz\ [NL, fr. *Clonorchis,* type genus + *-iasis*] **:** infestation with or disease caused by an oriental liver fluke (*Clonorchis sinensis*) that invades the bile ducts of the liver and when present in numbers causes severe systemic reactions including edema, liver enlargement, and diarrhea

clo·nor·chis \klō'nȯrkəs\ *n, cap* [NL, fr. Gk *klōn* twig + *orchis* testis — more at ORCHIS] **:** a genus of trematode worms (family Opisthorchiidae) containing the Chinese liver fluke (*C. sinensis*), having a complex life cycle involving a mollusk and a fish as intermediate hosts, and constituting a serious parasite of man in eastern and southeastern Asia with human infection resulting from consumption of raw infected fish

clo·no·thrix \'klōnō,thriks\ *n, cap* [NL, fr. *clono-* (fr. Gk *klōn* twig) + *-thrix*] **:** a genus of chlamydobacteria that have organic sheaths encrusted with iron or manganese, that reproduce by spherical conidia borne in chains, and that are known chiefly from waterworks and pipes

clo·nus \'klōnəs\ *n* -ES [NL, fr. Gk *klonos* turmoil; akin to L *celer* swift — more at CELERITY] **:** a series of alternating contractions and partial relaxations of a muscle that in certain nervous diseases occurs in the form of convulsive spasms involving complex groups of muscles and is believed to result from alteration of the normal pattern of motor neuron discharge — compare TONUS

cloof \'klüf\ *n* -s [prob. of Scand origin; akin to ON *klauf* cleft, cloven hoof, *klof* cleft, *kljūfa* to split — more at CLEAVE] *dial Brit* **:** HOOF

¹**clook** \'klük\ *var of* CLEUK

²**clook** \"\ *n* -s [PaG *gluck,* fr. MHG *kluck,* of imit. origin] *Midland* **:** ²CLUCK 2

¹**cloop** \'klüp\ *n* -s [imit.] **:** the sound made when a cork is forcibly drawn from a bottle

²**cloop** \"\ *vi* **:** to make a cloop

cloot \'klüt\ *n* -s [prob. of Scand origin; akin to ON *klō* claw — more at CLAW] **1** *chiefly Scot* **:** a cloven hoof **2** *usu cap, chiefly Scot* **:** DEVIL — usu. used in pl.

cloot·ie \'klütē, -i\ *n* -s *usu cap* [dim. of *cloot*] *chiefly Scot* **:** DEVIL

¹**clop** \'kläp\ *n* -s [imit.] **:** a sound made by or as if by a hoof or wooden shoe against pavement

²**clop** \"\ *vi* **clopped; clopped; clopping; clops :** to make or move with a succession of clops ⟨a milkman's horse *clopping* down an empty city street —M.D.Geismer⟩ ⟨*clopped* over to the bar in her wooden-soled sandals —Dawn Powell⟩

¹**clop-clop** \'⸗¦⸗\ *n* -s [redupl. of ¹*clop*] **:** a sound of rhythmically repeated clops

²**clop-clop** \"\ *vi* **:** to move with a clop-clop

clop·py \'kläpē, -pi\ *adj* **:** marked by the sound of successive clops

clo·que \klō'kā, '⸗(,)⸗\ *also* **clo·ky** \'klōkē\ *n, pl* **cloques** *also* **clokies** *often attrib* [F *cloqué,* fr. *cloqué,* adj., with an embossed design, fr. past part. of *cloquer* to become blistered, fr. F dial. *cloque* bell, blister, fr. ML *clocca* bell — more at CLOCK] **1 :** a fabric with an embossed design **2 :** a fabric esp. of piqué with small woven figures

clos \'klō\ *n, pl* **clos** \"\ [F, fr. OF, enclosure — more at ³CLOSE] **:** a French vineyard; *esp* **:** one enclosed by a wall — often used prepositively in a compound naming such a vineyard or its wine (as *Clos-Vougeot,* a vineyard in the Côte-d'Or, or the red Burgundy produced from its grapes); compare CHÂTEAU 3, CÔTE

clos·a·ble *or* **close·a·ble** \'klōzəbəl\ *adj* **:** capable of being closed

¹**close** \'klōz\ *vb* -ED/-ING/-S [ME *closen,* fr. OF *clos-,* stem of *clore,* fr. L *claudere* — more at ⁴CLOSE] *vt* **1 a :** to move (some part, esp. some hinged or sliding part) so as to bar passage through something ⟨~ the gate of the plant⟩ ⟨keep this valve *closed*⟩ **b** (1) **:** to block or shut off (a channel, path, or area) against entry or passage ⟨~ a street for snow removal⟩ ⟨~ a range to settlers⟩ (2) **:** to stop or deny access to or prohibit use of ⟨~ a firing area during target practice⟩ ⟨an attempt to ~ the mails to communist propaganda periodicals⟩ (3) *linguistics* **:** to make (a morphological or syntactic construction) incapable of having an additional constituent of a particular kind (as an adjective or a derivational suffix) ⟨the addition of *all* before *these young men* ~*s* the construction⟩ ⟨the addition of *-s* to *normalize* ~*s* the construction⟩ **c** (1) **:** to block or refuse admission to the inside, interior, or contents of ⟨keep the drawer *closed*⟩ ⟨continued drought caused the governor to ~ the woods⟩ ⟨volumes kept on *closed* shelves⟩ ⟨a seal used in Charlemagne's time to ~ letters and wills⟩ (2) **:** to exclude outside blood from (a herd, strain, or breed) **d :** to block out **:** SCREEN, EXCLUDE ⟨~ a view⟩ **:** form a boundary to ⟨a church ~*s* the vista⟩ **e :** to make or keep inaccessible, imperceptive, or inscrutable ⟨even a neutral cannot be asked to ~ his mind or his conscience —F.D.Roosevelt⟩ ⟨magazines *closed* to inexperienced writers⟩ **f** (1) **:** to suspend or stop the services, sessions, or operations of ⟨snow and high wind *closed* the airport⟩ ⟨~ school because of an outbreak of polio⟩ ⟨a theater *closed* for repairs⟩ (2) **:** to force to discontinue or end a business enterprise ⟨a manufacturer *closed* by his creditors⟩ (3) **:** to exclude the public from ⟨health authorities *closed* the swimming pools⟩ **2 a** *archaic* **:** ENCLOSE, ENCOMPASS, CONTAIN ⟨leaving the whole establishment to her, *closing* only himself in invisible bonds —F.M.Ford⟩ **b :** to arrange (the strands of a wire rope) spirally around a center **3 a :** to bring to an end or period **:** shut off or preclude further continuation of ⟨the Peace of Westphalia . . . which *closed* the Thirty Years' War —Stringfellow Barr⟩ ⟨he *closed* his military career with an idealized concept —Jeannette P. Nichols⟩ ⟨he *closed* his business and moved away⟩ **b :** to serve as last, final, or ultimate in (a series, sequence, or development) ⟨Madame Defarge being first . . . Mr. Lorry *closing* the little procession —Charles Dickens⟩ ⟨the . . . duet which ~*s* the first act —*Saturday Rev.*⟩ **c :** to conclude discussion or negotiation about **:** terminate or bring to agreement, decision, or settlement ⟨questions that have been *closed* for centuries suddenly yawn wide open —G.B. Shaw⟩ ⟨~ a deal or bargain⟩ ⟨~ a real estate transfer of title⟩ **d :** to render (an account) no longer current **4 a :** to bring or bind together the parts or edges of ⟨a *closed* fist⟩ ⟨cut the sides and back to fit and ~ them with a slide fastener⟩ ⟨after amputation ~ the stump for good scar line⟩ ⟨in no hurry to ~ the wound⟩ ⟨*closing* the break in the metal bar by welding⟩ **b :** to fill up (as a hole or opening) with something serving as a sealer, filler, or stopper ⟨first ~ the cracks with plaster of paris⟩ ⟨~ a grave⟩ **c :** to fill (a gap) so as to attain full continuity or smooth integration ⟨help them to ~ their dollar gap⟩ ⟨efforts to ~ the sharp division within the alliance⟩ ⟨tax loopholes that should be *closed*⟩ **d :** to complete by way of circling or enveloping or by making circumferentially or circuitously continuous ⟨the centripetal force constraining the planets to move in *closed* orbits —S.F.Mason⟩ ⟨to connect electric conductors so as to ~ a circuit⟩ **e :** to stitch together parts forming the upper of (a shoe) **f :** to reduce to nil ⟨milers fast *closing* the distance to the tape⟩ ⟨the ferry *closed* the last few feet of water between it and the ship⟩ **5** *of a ship* **:** to come close to ⟨the minesweeper *closed* the island under cover of darkness⟩ **6 :** to convert (granular soap) into a homogeneous pasty form (as by adding water and boiling) **7 :** to alter (a stance in golf or baseball batting) so that the left foot is closer to the line of play than the right ~ *vi* **1 :** to close itself or become closed: **a :** to contract, fold, swing, or slide so as to leave no opening ⟨a camera shutter adjusted to ~ after $\frac{1}{50}$ second⟩ ⟨the jackknife *closed* on my finger⟩; *also* **:** to admit of being closed ⟨this valve won't ~⟩ **b :** to cease operation ⟨forced the mine to ~⟩ **:** discontinue institutional activities ⟨banks and schools ~ for the holiday⟩ — often used with *down, up* **c :** to suspend business or end the business day ⟨this store ~*s* at 5 p.m.⟩ — often used with *down, up; also* **:** to remain closed ⟨barbershops ~ Mondays⟩ **d :** to end a theatrical run or tour ⟨the play *closed* after two weeks⟩ **e :** to cease to be passable for boats because of an ice cover ⟨the river has the appearance of *closing* for the winter⟩ **2 a :** to come near or approach close ⟨radar showed a plane *closing* fast⟩ ⟨a ship fast *closing* with the land⟩ **b** *of a racehorse* **:** to lessen the gap with the lead horse or horses esp. near the finish of a race ⟨*closing* fast in the home stretch⟩ **c :** to engage in a struggle at close quarters **:** GRAPPLE ⟨forbidding terrain prevented our *closing* with the enemy⟩ **3 a :** to join together **:** MEET, UNITE ⟨the jaws of the vise imperceptibly *closing*⟩; *also* **:** to tighten in a grasping or crushing motion ⟨a hand *closed* on my collar⟩ ⟨sullen anger *closed* down on the community⟩ **b :** to become filled in ⟨find themselves in a tight place when the gaps begin to ~ —W.R.Inge⟩; *also* **:** DIMINISH ⟨the distance between us rapidly *closed*⟩ **c :** to draw together, join, or gather so as to cover, conceal, or confine something ⟨clouds soon ~ over the sun⟩ ⟨just as the sea *closed* over the sinking ship⟩ **d :** to form or approach in a tight or diminishing circle ⟨his comrades *closed* around him protectively⟩ **e :** to tighten fingers or jaws in a grasping motion — used often with *on* ⟨seeing a rope dangling I *closed* on it⟩ ⟨the clamshell bucket *closed* on a load of dirt⟩ ⟨the idea faded before I could ~ on it⟩ **f** *dancing* **:** to draw the free foot up to and into contact with the supporting foot **4 :** to enter into or complete an agreement **:** make a contract ⟨before I can ~ with a new employer⟩ **5 a :** to come to an end or period **:** cease from further continuation ⟨his diplomatic career *closed* with this incident⟩ ⟨the services *closed* with a short prayer⟩ **b :** to bring one's discourse or a debate to a conclusion ⟨I ~ with this warning⟩ ⟨the senior debater of each team is to ~⟩ **c :** to make an announcement or play in certain card games that ends some phase of the game; *esp* **:** to turn the trump card face down in a game of sixty-six in order to stop the draw from the stock and compel players to follow suit **6** *civil engin* **:** to give a closed figure when plotted ⟨this survey of the tract fails to ~⟩ — see ERROR OF CLOSURE **7 a :** to become priced in the last recorded sale of the trading day in an exchange ⟨to compensate for stock opened at 126, *closed* at 128⟩ ⟨hogs *closed* strong⟩ **b :** to show an overall price average at the end of a trading period ⟨the market managed to ~ slightly lower⟩

syn END, CONCLUDE, FINISH, TERMINATE, COMPLETE: all of these words, along with CLOSE, are near in meaning and often interchangeable. CLOSE may suggest that the matter in question is no longer open to further continuation ⟨the case is now *closed* and needs no further discussion⟩ ⟨these discoveries *closed* his career in the church⟩ END may more strongly connote finality; likely to contrast with *begin,* it may imply a certain progress, sequence, or development ⟨difficulties in determining when the medieval period *ends*⟩ ⟨the book *ends* on a happier note⟩ CONCLUDE may be more formal in suggestion ⟨the meeting *concluded* with a vote of thanks to the hostess⟩ FINISH may suggest full execution or resolution of the last steps or stages of a continued action or process ⟨the War of the Confederacy over but not *finished* —Elizabeth M. Roberts⟩ ⟨at three o'clock his business was *finished* and he was ready to return —Sherwood Anderson⟩ TERMINATE may suggest a definite term or limit involved, an attaining definitively to that term, with or without completing or fulfilling ⟨the old arrangement with the company, now *terminated*⟩ ⟨the interim appointments having *terminated*⟩ COMPLETE may indicate an ending marked by fulfilling, perfecting, leaving nothing undone ⟨he did not *complete* the picture until three years later⟩ Words of this series are often close synonyms, and any one of this set may be substituted for CLOSE in a sentence like "singing the Alma Mater *closes* the services".

—close its doors 1 : to bar entrance or refuse admission ⟨keeping *its doors closed* to immigrants⟩ **2 :** to cease operation **:** go out of business ⟨a school forced by economic considerations to *close its doors*⟩ **— close one's eyes to :** to deliberately ignore **:** decline to acknowledge **— close ranks :** to unite in a militant attitude and submerge differences esp. to meet a challenge **— close the books 1 a :** to cease accepting subscriptions to a new security offering because orders have been received in excess of the amount offered **b :** to intermit the use of certain books of account or record of a corporation or business concern (as prior to the payment of a dividend) **2** *accounting* **:** to transfer periodically after adjustment to the proprietorship accounts the balances of the income and expense accounts **— close the door :** to take a determined and uncompromising obstructive position ⟨an action that *closes the door* on any amicable settlement⟩

²**close** \"\ *n* -s [ME *clos,* fr. *closen* to close — more at ¹CLOSE] **1 a :** a coming or bringing of something to a conclusion or end ⟨the things that a busy life and its premature ~ left him no time to give —D.M.Davin⟩ ⟨at the ~ of hostilities⟩ **b :** a conclusion or end in time or existence **:** CESSATION ⟨as the decade drew to a ~⟩ ⟨bring the chapter to a ~⟩ ⟨after the ~ of the war⟩ **c :** a final stage, outcome, or finish ⟨conduct the negotiations to a satisfactory ~⟩ **d :** the concluding passage (as of a speech or play) **e :** COMPLIMENTARY CLOSE **2 :** the conclusion of a musical strain or period **:** CADENCE **3** *archaic* **:** a bringing together **:** MEETING, JOINING ⟨attested by the holy ~ of lips —Shak.⟩ **4** *archaic* **:** a hostile encounter ⟨unwounded from the dreadful ~ —Sir Walter Scott⟩ **5 :** the closing price on a stock or a commodity or the closing prices on an exchange or over-the-counter market **6** *dancing* **:** the movement of a free foot towards and into contact with the supporting foot, with or without transfer of weight

³**close** \'klōs\ *sometimes* -ōz\ *n* -s [ME *clos,* fr. OF *clos,* fr. L *clausum* enclosure, fr. neut. of *clausus,* past part. of *claudere*] **1 :** ENCLOSURE: **a** *dial Brit* **:** an enclosed field esp. near a farmhouse **:** FARMYARD **b** *Brit* **:** the precinct of a cathedral or abbey; *esp* **:** an enclosed space close to a cathedral bordered by the archdeanery, deanery, and residences (as of the canons) **c** *Brit* **:** a walled enclosure (as a paddock or school playground) **d** *Brit* **:** an open space (as a quadrangle) that is partially or wholly closed in by a group of dwellings **2** *chiefly Brit* **a :** a narrow passage or entry leading from a street to a court and the houses within or to the common stairway of tenements **b :** a road closed at one end **3 a :** a parcel of land in which a person has an interest involving at least a right of present possession whether enclosed or not, an ideal boundary being there in legal fiction **b :** the interest itself entitling the owner to an action of trespass for breach of the close

⁴**close** \'klōs\ *adj* -ER/-EST [ME *clos,* fr. MF *clos,* fr. L *clausus,* past part. of *claudere* to close; akin to Gk *kleid-, kleis* key, bolt, *kleiein* to close, OIr *clō* nail, OSlav *ključiti* to close, MLG *slūten* to close, OHG *sliozan,* OFris *slūta*] **1 a :** having no openings **:** CLOSED ⟨a ~ hatch⟩ ⟨drove off in a ~ carriage⟩ **b** *heraldry* (1) **:** with wings folded to the body — used of a bird (2) **:** with the visor down — used of a helmet **2** *archaic* **:** closed in or around by or as if by walls or hills ⟨~ streets of the old city⟩ **3 a :** confined or confining strictly **:** narrowly restricting or restricted ⟨a ~ prisoner⟩ ⟨~ quarters⟩ ⟨five days of ~ arrest⟩ ⟨so ~ was her hold upon his arm that he feared to detach himself lest he should hurt her —Charles Dickens⟩ ⟨to escape from a ~, systematic, cultivated life into an open and relatively barbarous existence —Lewis Mumford⟩ **b** (1) *of a vowel* **:** ¹HIGH 1a(6) (2) **:** formed with the tongue in a higher position than for another vowel — used of one of two vowels constituting a pair because similar in articulation or identical in orthography ⟨Italian has a ~ and an open *e*⟩ (3) *of lip rounding* **:** EXTREME **c :** restricted (as in membership, prerogatives, admission to competition) to a privileged class ⟨a ~ scholarship⟩ **d :** CLOSED 3g ⟨the ~ season for hunting deer⟩ **e :** *of a chess game* **:** characterized by a restricted development of pieces behind the pawns **4 a :** out of the way of observation **:** SECLUDED, SECRET ⟨the bandits kept ~ during the day⟩ **b :** marked by a disposition to secrecy, taciturnity, or extreme discreetness about divulging information ⟨she could tell us something if she would . . . but she was as ~ as wax —A. Conan Doyle⟩ **5 :** maintained or achieved by virtue of unrelaxing scrutiny, acute discernment, and exacting minuteness **:** STRICT, RIGOROUS ⟨keeping a ~ watch on expenditures⟩ ⟨~ control over the credit structure⟩ ⟨keeping records in ~ accord with facts⟩ ⟨nothing short of a ~ critical analysis will do⟩ ⟨a prisoner in ~ custody⟩ **6 :** causing a sensation of being slightly smothered or stifled **:** SULTRY, STUFFY ⟨it seemed from the dreadfully ~ atmosphere that no window had been opened in it for weeks past —Anthony Trollope⟩ ⟨I lolled on the couch and breathed its ~ smell of cloth in hot weather —Edmund Wilson⟩ **7 :** reluctant to part with money or possessions **:** stingy or cautious about expenditures ⟨a ~ buyer and a good marketer —W.A.White⟩ **8 :** marked by an arrangement leaving little space between items or units ⟨~ texture⟩ ⟨~ grain in wood⟩: **a :** having individuals pressed, arranged, or arrayed quite near each other ⟨in so ~ and murderous a conflict the valor of no single individual could decide the day —J.L.Motley⟩ ⟨flying in ~ formation⟩ **b :** having characters written or inscribed with a minimum of space between ⟨she was handicapped by her almost illegible ~ handwriting⟩ **c** *of type* **:** set with minimum spacing between words or lines **d** *of a library classification* **:** having relatively small subdivisions — compare BROAD **e** *of an animal's coat* **:** sleek and smooth with the hairs more or less parallel and close to the body **:** not loose or fluffy ⟨a *close*-coated dog is better for working briery uplands⟩ **9 a :** fitting quite tightly or exactly with very little looseness, play, or ease ⟨a ~ gown⟩ ⟨a bathing suit skintight and ~⟩ **b :** very short or near to the ground, skin, or other surface ⟨the fall mowing of the grass was too ~⟩ ⟨the barber gave him a ~ shave⟩ **c :** accurately matching or blending without interval or gap **:** PRECISE ⟨a concession that brought him into ~ harmony with his colleagues⟩ ⟨unable to escape the force of ~ reasoning⟩ **d** *of a tolerance* **:** MINUTE **10 :** marked by being near, by nearness of any sort, or by adjacency, proximity, approach, or approximation in space ⟨as ~ together as bungalows in a suburban town —*Amer. Guide Series: Calif.*⟩ ⟨St. Louis is *closer* to Chicago than it is to Detroit⟩ ⟨an . . . ibis, strikingly colorful at ~ range —*Amer. Guide Series: Fla.*⟩ or in time ⟨these dates come ~ to the Christmas holidays⟩ or in kind ⟨a strong intense smell ~ to that of burning garbage —Norman Mailer⟩ ⟨Spanish is ~ to French and Italian⟩ or in feeling ⟨Whittier was ~ in spirit to the Rhode Island Quakers —*Amer. Guide Series: R.I.*⟩ ⟨farmers in overalls . . . proclaim again how ~ to the soil is Minneapolis —*Amer. Guide Series: Minn.*⟩ or in effect ⟨*crude* and *vulgar* are ~ synonyms⟩ ⟨the banker has got to be ~ to the property he is financing —*Encyc. Americana*⟩ or in degree ⟨a speed ~ to that of sound⟩ ⟨a salary ~ to the presi-

dent's⟩ or in action ⟨his reply left her ~ to tears⟩ or in relationship ⟨first cousins are ~ relatives⟩ **11 a :** marked by, given to, or enjoying strong liking or regard, mutual ready confidence, general accord, or constant association ⟨you loved your mother and your sister, all the ~ circle that was bound to you by blood and habit —Mary Austin⟩ ⟨too ~ to Theodore Roosevelt ever to receive the confidence of Woodrow Wilson —F.L.Paxson⟩ **b :** marked by or given to compatibility or conformity of interests, aims, pursuits, preferences, or by cordiality, accord, coperation, or alliance ⟨the ~ ties that bind them together⟩ ⟨~ relations between Norway and Sweden⟩ **12 a :** marked by careful or searching attention to details and their relationships or by consideration of or familiarity with details ⟨many of the 18th century policemen of usage were not ~ students of the language —Charlton Laird⟩ ⟨a ~ study⟩ ⟨~ knowledge of French⟩ ⟨~ questioning about his activities⟩ ⟨a ~ observer of weather conditions⟩ **b :** marked by fidelity in details esp. to an original ⟨a ~ copy of an old master⟩ ⟨a ~ analogy between their customs and ours⟩ **c :** marked by terse economical expression of details ⟨his exact, ~, sober classical style —Edmund Wilson⟩ **13 a :** decided by a narrow margin or a slight edge **:** long undecided because almost evenly balanced **:** marked by or showing opposed tendencies nearly even ⟨a ~ baseball game ending with a score of 10–9⟩ ⟨the base runner was safe at second on a ~ play⟩ ⟨the ~ election of 1916⟩ ⟨Minnesota was ~, with twelve votes whose disposition must await final count —F.L.Paxson⟩ ⟨a ~ race won by a nose⟩ **b :** taking a favorable turn only by a very small margin (as just barely in time or missing disaster by a hair) ⟨looking at the vanishing train, he breathed "that was ~"⟩ **c :** having given the winning candidate only a slight majority (as less than 60 percent) in a two-party vote ⟨a congressman from a ~ district⟩ ⟨dividing the seats in the legislature into sure and ~ seats⟩ **14** *Eng law* **:** CLOSED, SEALED — used esp. of writs or letters directed to particular persons for particular purposes and therefore not left open; opposed to *patent* **15** *finance* **:** difficult to obtain ⟨money is ~⟩ **16 :** CLOSED 1j **17 a** *of punctuation* **:** characterized by liberal use of punctuation marks, esp. commas **b** *of the punctuation of a letter* **:** characterized by the use of a comma at the end of each line of the heading and inside address except the last and after the complimentary close and of a period at the end of the last line of the heading and the inside address and after the signature — opposed to *open*

syn DENSE, COMPACT, THICK: indicating a tight massing together with little intervening empty space, these words may be interchangeable in many contexts. CLOSE typically suggests a pressing together of things separable or often separated ⟨*close* stitching⟩ ⟨*close* formations⟩ ⟨between the *close* moss violet-inwoven —P.B.Shelley⟩ ⟨a *close* impervious soil —*Amer. Guide Series: N. C.*⟩ In literary criticism it may indicate effective compression into few words ⟨a relief to turn back to the austere, *close* language of Everyman, the simplicity of the mysteries —T.S.Eliot⟩ DENSE describes an aggregation of particles or component units set very near each other and making penetration or perception difficult ⟨the *dense* trees of the avenue rendered the road dark as a tunnel —Thomas Hardy⟩ ⟨surrounded by a throng so *dense* that I could scarcely breathe —C.B.Nordhoff & J.N.Hall⟩ ⟨Proust's book is a gigantic *dense* mesh of complicated relations —Edmund Wilson⟩ COMPACT may suggest a consolidation within a circumscribed area or space making for order, firmness, efficiency, or strength ⟨the village has ceased to be a *compact* unit and it is no longer easy to find its center —*Times Lit. Supp.*⟩ ⟨below the ordinary height . . . he was all *compact* and under his swart, tattooed skin the muscles worked like steel rods —Herman Melville⟩ THICK may suggest a concentrated abundance ⟨chestnuts near, that hung in masses *thick* —Alfred Tennyson⟩ ⟨what the dry weather doesn't spoil, the tobacco worms will. They were *thick* as hops —Ellen Glasgow⟩ ⟨sometimes the isle was *thick* with savages . . . sometimes full of dangerous animals —R.L. Stevenson⟩ **syn** see in addition FAMILIAR, SILENT, STINGY — **close to home :** within one's strong personal interests so that one is affected esp. strongly ⟨the audience felt that the speaker's remarks were pretty *close to home*⟩ ⟨if . . . this book might not be too *close to home* for the average teen-age boy to appreciate —L.T.Bulman⟩

⁵close \"\ *adv* -ER/-EST [ME *clos*, fr. *clos*, adj.] **1 a :** in proximity of space or time ⟨in fog stick ~ to the white guideline⟩ ⟨strangers draw ~ and ask each other two questions —E.W. Smith⟩ ⟨its nucleons draw *closer* to one another —G.W.Gray b.1886⟩ ⟨~ to my cheek⟩ ⟨~ under the roof⟩ ⟨building a school ~ by⟩ ⟨overlooking the tasks lying ~ at hand⟩ ⟨it is only ~ up that the impact of his power-charged personality makes itself felt —R.C.Doty⟩ ⟨having their babies *closer* together⟩ — often used in combination ⟨*close*-set⟩ **b :** in proximity of approach ⟨anxious to come *closer* to the truth of life⟩ ⟨as for solving the problem, we haven't come ~⟩ **2** *archaic* **:** SECRETLY, COVERTLY ⟨His Royal Highness must lie very ~ here till tomorrow evening —John Buchan⟩ **3 :** in a close state **:** TIGHTLY ⟨there is not a door, nor a window, that shuts ~ —Tobias Smollett⟩ **4 :** in a close manner ⟨on looking *closer*, it struck me that Hamlet often does one thing instead of another —Karl Polanyi⟩ **5 :** in close likeness or conformity ⟨sticking ~ to the classic models⟩ **6 :** in a close or intimate association ⟨the cause that touches me *closest*⟩ ⟨there is something in the heart of street dogs that draws them ~ to men —William Saroyan⟩ ⟨it is up to the illustrator to get as ~ as he can to the spirit of the text —Mervyn Peake⟩ — **close to the wind** *of a ship* **:** with the head directed as nearly to the point from which the wind blows as it is possible to sail

closeable *var of* CLOSABLE

close-at-hand \ˈklōs·ə·ˈ\ *adj* **:** approaching in the immediate future **:** lying in the immediate vicinity

close attack \ˈklōs-\ *n* **:** the three forward attacking positions on a lacrosse team

close bolt \ˈklōs-\ *n* **:** a wall or layer composed of bricks laid close together in brickmaking (as for the casing of a clamp)

close bolting \ˈ≈-\ *n* **1 :** the stacking of bricks without leaving any spaces between them **2 :** the bricks stacked in a close bolt

close borough \ˈ≈-\ *n, Brit* **:** a borough with a restricted electorate and self-perpetuating council

close breeding \ˈ≈-\ *n* **:** breeding from closely related individuals — used esp. of relationships less close than in inbreeding

close-by \ˈ≈ˈ≈\ *adj* **:** being close at hand **:** ADJACENT

close call \ˈ≈-\ *n* **:** a narrow escape

close chair \ˈklōz-, ˈklōs-\ *n, Brit* [¹*close*] **:** a closestool equipped with the back and arms of a chair

close communion \ˈklōs-\ *or* **closed communion** \-ōzd-\ *n* **:** Communion in the Lord's Supper restricted to the baptized members belonging to the same denomination or the same church — opposed to *open communion* — **close communionist** *n*

close corporation \ˈklōs-\ *n* **1 :** a self-perpetuating body each part of which fills its own vacancies **2 :** a corporation whose stock is held by a few persons who are often those active in the management **3 :** a small tightly exclusive group cool to outsiders

close-coupled \ˈ≈ˈ≈≈\ *adj* **1** *of an animal* **:** short in loins and back **2** *of an automobile* **:** having the space between front and rear seats restricted **3 :** directly united — used of a closed and an open electrical circuit in combination

close coupling \ˈ≈-\ *n* **:** a coupling of two electrical circuits such that any change of current in one produces a relatively large change in the other

close-cropped \ˈ≈ˈ≈\ *adj* **1 :** clipped short **2 :** having the hair clipped short

¹closecross \ˈ≈,≈\ *n* **1 :** a cross between individuals of related strains **2 :** the progeny of a closecross

²closecross \"\ *vt* -ED/-ING/-ES [¹*closecross*] **:** to breed (animals) from closely related individuals, esp. members of related strains within a breed

closed \ˈklōzd\ *adj* [ME, past part. of *closen* to close] **1 a** *of a vehicle* **:** having a permanently enclosed body with stationary back, side panels, and top **b :** structurally enclosed or closed in ⟨a ~ porch⟩ ⟨a ~ freight car⟩ ⟨a ~ stairway⟩ **c :** covered over ⟨bake in a ~ dish⟩ **d :** blocked up or blocked in ⟨~ valleys⟩ **e :** barring or barred to traffic ⟨illegally entering a ~ port⟩ ⟨a ~ street⟩ **f** *phonetics* **:** CHECKED **g :** kept secret ⟨a ~ file on suspects⟩ ⟨the ~ ballot⟩ **h** *of the face of an animal* **:** covered esp. with wool or hair **i** (1) **:** covered by unbroken skin ⟨~ fracture⟩ (2) **:** not discharging pathogenic organisms to the outside ⟨a case of ~ tuberculosis⟩ — compare OPEN **j :** not free **:** COVERED — used of a tone in music, specif. a tone of the upper register; opposed to *open* **2 a** (1) **:** forming a self-contained unit admitting of no additions ⟨a ~ collection of documents⟩ ⟨organisms are not self-sufficient ~ systems —Weston La Barre⟩ (2) **:** *of habitats or communities* **:** so completely stocked as to offer no opportunity for additional kinds of organisms to enter and establish themselves ⟨a ~ association⟩ **b :** lacking boundaries and having no point or element that has an infinite coordinate — used of lines, surfaces, and extents of any number of dimensions ⟨the ~ circumference of a circle⟩ **c :** existing with few external relations ⟨treating atomic physics as a ~ subject⟩; *specif* **:** having only limited foreign trade and approaching economic self-sufficiency ⟨a ~ economy⟩ **d** (1) *of a flock or herd* **:** bred from a single strain (2) *of a stud book* **:** permitting solely the registration of animals of which both sire and dam are registered therein — compare OPEN **e** *of a racetrack* **:** having the same starting and finishing point **f :** characterized by continuous return and reuse of the working medium — used esp. of water in a heating system or of air in a cooling system **g :** established in an invariable pattern ⟨a ~ program⟩ **h** (1) *dancing* **:** placing the free foot up to and in contact with the supporting foot (2) *ballroom dancing* **:** facing each other with the man's right arm around the woman's waist, the woman's left hand on the man's right shoulder, and their free hands joined **3 a :** rigidly excluding outside influence **:** having minimum contact ⟨to any but the most ~ of minds —R.E.McGill⟩ **b :** excluding participation of outsiders and witnesses **:** conducted in strict secrecy ⟨taking part in ~ international conferences⟩ **c :** confined to a few **:** restricted to selective membership ⟨a ~ hospital staff⟩ ⟨a ~ circle of believers⟩ **d :** intolerant of the influx of new members and ideas and approaching a state of social immobility and self-containment with respect to customs and traditions ⟨a ~ society⟩ ⟨a ~ class system⟩ **e :** not accessible to other nations ⟨unlimited sovereignty implies the policy of the ~ sky⟩ **f** *sports* **:** restricted to entrants of a specified kind or class ⟨a women's ~ golf tournament⟩ ⟨a ~ event for amateurs only⟩ — contrasted with *open* **g :** restricted with respect to the time or place for taking game **:** CLOSE ⟨woods ~ to hunters⟩ ⟨a ~ season for trout⟩ **4 :** having no cambium in the bundle, all meristematic tissue having been differentiated into xylem and phloem — used of certain vascular bundles; compare OPEN **5** *logic, of an expression* **:** containing variables all of which are bound — contrasted with *open* **6** *of the punctuation of a letter* **:** ⁴CLOSE 17b **7 :** COMPLETED — used of a canasta meld containing seven or more cards esp. when it has been turned facedown

closed account *n* **1 :** an account whose total debit and total credit entries are equal and show no balance **2 :** an activity that has definitely ended

closed bank note *n* **:** BROKEN BANK NOTE

closed bolt *n* **:** a bookbinding in which the edge folds of the sections are left uncut

closed book *n* **:** something beyond comprehension ⟨railway operation is a *closed book* for many people —O.S.Nock⟩ **:** something that resists clarification ⟨a modern age in which the law is a *closed book* —B.N.Cardozo⟩

closed chain *n* **:** ¹RING 22 — opposed to *open chain*

closed circuit *n* **:** a circuit whose path carries completely around a course or through a cycle without break in continuity: **a :** an electric circuit made up of a continuous endless conductor or series of conductors with electrically conducting connections **b :** a television installation in which picture and sound are not broadcast but transmitted over a closed channel to a limited number of interconnected receivers ⟨*closed-circuit* television⟩

closed-circuit cell \ˈ≈ˈ≈≈-\ *n* **:** a voltaic cell that is used where the duty is continuous and that does not polarize when furnishing current

closed-circuit winding \"-\ *n* **:** a mesh winding

closed corporation *n* **:** CLOSE CORPORATION ⟨many boroughs had previously been *closed corporations* in which aldermen co-opted whom they pleased to fill vacancies —W.H.Wickwar⟩ ⟨snobbish to the core and its society is still a *closed corporation* —J.E.Jennings⟩

closed couplet *n* **:** a rhymed couplet in which the sense is relatively complete or independent

closed-door \ˈ≈ˈ≈\ *adj* **:** done or carried on in a closed session barring public and press ⟨a *closed-door* session of the investigating committee⟩

close defense \ˈklōs-\ *n* **:** the three defending positions closest to the goalie on a lacrosse team

closed-end \ˈklōzd+\ *adj* **1 :** having a fixed capitalization of shares that are traded on the open market instead of being redeemed daily by the company at the demand of the holders ⟨a *closed-end* investment company⟩ — opposed to *open-end* **2 :** issued to the full amount authorized or substantially the full amount ⟨a *closed-end* bond issue⟩

closed fold *n* **1 :** ISOCLINAL FOLD **2 :** a quaquaversal flexure around which a structure-contour line will close upon itself

closed form *n, crystallog* **:** a form whose faces enclose a space (as an octahedron)

closed gate *n* **:** a slalom obstacle consisting of two poles set one directly below the other in line with the vertical descent of the ski slope — compare OPEN GATE

closed gentian *n* **:** any of several fall-blooming No. American plants of the genus *Gentiana* (esp. *G. andrewsii* and *G. clausa*) having tubular usu. blue flowers that open little or not at all

closed hand *n* **:** the declarer's hand in bridge

closed issue *n* **:** an issue, question, or problem on which a decision has been reached and announced

closed-minded \ˈ≈ˈ≈≈\ *adj* **:** obstinately resistant to argument or to unfamiliar or unwelcome ideas

closed mortgage *n* **:** a mortgage under which no or virtually no additional bonds can be sold under the indenture — contrasted with *open-end mortgage*

close down \ˈklōz-\ *vi* **1 :** to settle or appear close around so as to block any outward view ⟨fog presently *closed down*⟩ **2 :** to put a stern curb (as on an illegal operation by raids and arrests) ⟨a campaign to *close down* on slot machines⟩

closedown \ˈ≈,≈\ *n* -S [*close down*] **1 :** a closing down (as of night) **2 :** a stoppage of operations **3** *Brit* **:** a signing off of a radiobroadcasting station

closed pair *n, physics* **:** a pair of bodies in which the relative motion is completely constrained

closed planer *n* **:** a planer having the crossrail supported by housings on each of the two sides

closed poker *n* **:** a game of poker in which all cards are dealt facedown and are not legally exposed until the showdown

closed pouch *n* **:** a mail pouch transported in a baggage car or by trolley line or truck and not opened for distribution en route as is done in a railway post office

closed primary *n* **:** a primary at which members of only one political party vote — compare OPEN PRIMARY

closed reduction *n, med* **:** the reduction of a displaced part (as a fractured bone) by manipulation without incision

closed rule *n* **:** a parliamentary rule barring amendments from the floor

closed sea *n* **:** MARE CLAUSUM

closed shop *n* **:** an establishment in which the employer by agreement hires and retains in employment only union members in good standing except that by some agreements when union members are unavailable the employer may hire nonunion workers provided they apply for union membership or obtain work permits before beginning work — compare MAINTENANCE OF MEMBERSHIP, OPEN SHOP, UNION SHOP

closed stance *n* **:** a preparatory position (as in baseball batting or golf) in which the left foot of a right-handed person is closer to the line of play than the right foot — contrasted with *open stance*

closed string *n* **:** CLOSE STRING

closed union *n* **:** a labor union that limits its size to guard against an oversupply of available workers

close fertilization \ˈklōs-\ *n* **:** fertilization in seed plants of the ovules of a flower by pollen from the same flower

close-fertilize \(ˈ)≈ˈ≈≈,≈\ *vt* **:** to subject to close fertilization

close-fights \ˈ≈,≈\ *n pl* **:** barriers with loopholes formerly erected on the deck of a ship to shelter men in a close engagement with boarders — called also *close quarters*

closefisted \ˈ≈ˈ≈≈\ *adj* **:** not openhanded or liberal **:** TIGHT-FISTED, CLOSE ⟨~ deacons objecting to expenses⟩ **syn** see STINGY

close-fitting \ˈ≈ˈ≈\ *adj* **:** fitting snugly to the body or limbs

close girl \ˈklōs-, ˈklōz-\ *n* **:** JOINER 1b

closegirt \ˈklōs+\ *adj* **:** fitting or fitted snugly round the waist

close-grained \ˈ≈ˈ≈\ *also* **close-grain** \ˈ≈ˈ≈\ *adj* **1 :** having fine and closely arranged fibers, crystals, or particles **:** having a closely compacted smooth texture; *specif, of wood* **:** having narrow annual rings or small wood elements or both **2 :** careful and precise as to order and articulation ⟨a book of fairly *close-grained* reasoning —N.M.Lawrence⟩

closehanded \ˈ≈ˈ≈≈\ *adj, archaic* **:** CLOSEFISTED

close harmony \ˈklōs-\ *n* **1** *in traditional harmony* **:** the arrangement or distribution of the notes or tones of a chord so that the three upper parts lie within an octave — compare OPEN HARMONY **2 :** BARBERSHOP 2

close-hauled \ˈ≈ˈ≈\ *adj, of a sailing ship* **:** having the yards braced up sharp and sheets aft if square-rigged or having the boom hauled in close to the center line if fore-and-aft rigged and sailing as nearly against the wind as the ship will go

close helm *or* **close helmet** \ˈklōz-\ *n* **:** ARMET

close-herd \ˈklōs+\ *vt* [⁵*close*] *West* **:** to herd (cattle) in a close group

close in \ˈklōz-\ *vb* [¹*close*] *vi* **1 :** to gather in close all around with an oppressing or isolating effect ⟨the suffocating heaviness of New York's summer had already *closed in* —Marcia Davenport⟩ ⟨a brief bloom of fortune . . . before adversity *closed in* —Dixon Wecter⟩ ⟨despair *closed in* on her⟩ **2 :** to approach from various directions to close quarters esp. for an attack, raid, or arrest ⟨military intelligence agents *closed in* on him⟩ **3 :** to grow dark; *often* **:** to grow dark early — used of the day or the evening ⟨the short November day was already *closing in* —Ellen Glasgow⟩ **~** *vt* **1 :** to encircle closely and isolate **2 :** to enshroud to such an extent as to preclude approach or egress ⟨scouts report target *closed in*⟩ ⟨the airport is *closed in*⟩ **3 :** to shut off the flow of (an oil well)

close-in \ˈklōs+\ *adj* [⁵*close*] **1 :** near to a central part esp. of a city ⟨need for a *close-in* landing field⟩ **2 :** operating or delivered from close quarters ⟨*close-in* bombardment⟩

close juncture \"-\ *or* **close internal juncture** *n* **:** a juncture between two consecutive sounds in speech of the kind found in a simplex word (as between \t\ and \r\ in the pronunciation of *trait* or *nitrate* or between \ī\ and \n\ in the pronunciation of *mine* or *minus* — compare OPEN JUNCTURE, TERMINAL JUNCTURE

close-knit \ˈ≈ˈ≈\ *adj* **1 :** bound together by intimate social or cultural ties or closely bound by economical or political ties ⟨the immigrants had left their *close-knit* little villages —Oscar Handlin⟩ **2 :** having the elements firmly and logically joined together ⟨the argument is *close-knit*⟩

close-lipped \ˈ≈ˈ≈\ *adj* **:** TIGHT-LIPPED ⟨*close-lipped* and silent about the misadventure⟩ **syn** see SILENT

close·ly \ˈklōslē, -li\ *adv sometimes* -ER/-EST [⁴*close* + -*ly*] **:** in a close position, state, manner, or relation: **a :** with close attention or scrutiny ⟨now listen ~⟩ ⟨ability to read ~⟩ **b** *obs* **:** SECRETLY, COVERTLY **c :** in close proximity ⟨a ~ built-up area⟩ ⟨~ held to his desk⟩ ⟨~ printed⟩ **d :** in a close state **:** TIGHTLY **:** in the hands of a few ⟨~ held private companies⟩ ⟨~ knit into the Soviet orbit⟩ **e :** in close conformity to a model ⟨~ resembling our housefly⟩ ⟨a coating most ~ matching the cover⟩ **f :** in close relation **:** INTIMATELY ⟨incidents in the book are quite ~ connected⟩ ⟨the two had worked ~ during the war⟩ ⟨made friends quickly but not ~⟩ **g :** ACCURATELY, MINUTELY ⟨indicating fairly ~ the true conditions⟩ ⟨questioned ~ and at length⟩ **h :** STRICTLY ⟨a ~ reasoned argument⟩ ⟨~ controlled sources of supply⟩

closemouthed \ˈklōs+\ *adj* **:** marked by customary caution against disclosing much information in speaking ⟨a ~ private secretary⟩ **syn** see SILENT

clos·en \ˈklōsᵊn\ *vb* **closened; closened; closening** \ˈklōs(ᵊ)niŋ\ **closens** [⁴*close* + -*en*] *vt* **:** to make close **~** *vi* **:** to become close or more close ⟨the ~*ing* bonds between two countries⟩

close·ness \ˈklōsnəs\ *n* -ES [ME, fr. ⁴*close* + -*ness*] **:** the quality or state of being close

close off \ˈklōz-\ *vt* **1 :** to isolate or keep in seclusion **2 :** to stop the flow of

close on \ˈklōs-\ *or* **close onto** *prep* [⁵*close*] **1 :** within a very short time or distance of ⟨*close on* fifty years ago⟩ ⟨for *close on* five miles⟩ **:** within a very small number, amount, or quantity of ⟨housing *close on* a million volumes⟩ **:** just short of ⟨a deficit *close on* four billion dollars⟩ **2 :** closely approaching ⟨respect *close on* veneration⟩

close order \"-\ *n* **:** an arrangement of troops for formations, drill, or marching according to an exact scheme prescribing fixed distances and intervals — distinguished from *extended order*

close out \ˈklōz-\ *vt* **1 a :** EXCLUDE **b :** PRECLUDE ⟨*close out* his chances⟩ **2 a :** to dispose of a whole stock of by sale often at a concession **b :** to make final disposal of (a business) **c :** SELL ⟨*closed out* his share of the business⟩ **d :** to put (an account) in order for disposal or transfer **3 a :** to bring to a rapid or abrupt conclusion **:** TERMINATE **b :** to withdraw from operation **:** dismantle and discontinue **~** *vi* **1 :** to sell out a business **2 :** to buy or sell securities or commodities in order to terminate an account (as when margin is exhausted)

close-out \ˈklō,zau̇t\ *n* -S [*close out*] **1 :** a closing out; *specif* **:** a clearing out by a sale usu. at reduced price of the whole remaining stock whether of a closing business or of a particular discontinued item **2 :** an article offered or bought at a closeout

close position \ˈklōs-\ *n* **:** CLOSE HARMONY 1

close price \"-\ *n* **:** a price in a stock exchange showing slight variation between bid and asked prices or between successive transactions

close-price \ˈ≈,≈\ *vi* [*close price*] **:** to limit prices so as to allow only a slight margin of profit esp. through government negotiation with manufacturers when competition is not effective

close-quarter \ˈ≈ˈ≈≈\ *or* **close-quartered** \ˈ≈ˈ≈≈\ *adj* **:** done or used at close quarters or in a narrowly restricted space

close quarters \klōs-\ *n pl* **1 :** CLOSE-FIGHTS **2 a :** immediate contact or close range ⟨fighting at *close quarters* with gun butts and fists⟩ **b :** an attitude of intently searching scrutiny ⟨coming to *close quarters* with a theory⟩

¹closer *comparative of* CLOSE

²clos·er \ˈklōzə(r)\ *n* -S [¹*close* + -*er*] **1 :** one that closes by hand or by machine: as **a :** a lid closer **b :** one that operates a sewing machine for joining the parts of a shoe upper esp. at the back seam or for stitching lining parts **c :** a sewing-machine operator who sews the seams of garments, gloves, and mattresses **2 :** something that closes: **a** *masonry* (1) **:** the last stone in a horizontal course if smaller than the others or a piece of brick finishing a course (2) **:** a piece of brick inserted in each alternate course to enable a bond to be formed by preventing two headers from exactly superimposing on a stretcher **b :** a device for closing something (as a door) **c :** an act, number, or play that brings a program to a close

close reach \ˈklōs-\ *n* **:** a reach sailed by a ship with the wind well forward of the beam but not as close-hauled as possible

close reading \"-\ *n* **:** detailed and careful analysis of a written work; *also* **:** the product of such analysis

close reef \ˈklōs-, ˈklōz-\ *n* **:** the last ordinary reef that can be put in a sail — compare BALANCE REEF

close-reef \ˈ≈ˈ≈\ *vt* [*close reef*] **:** to reduce the area of (a sail) as much as possible

close-reefed \ˈ≈ˈ≈\ *adj* **:** having all the reefs taken in — used of a sail

close-rounded \ˈklōs+\ *adj, of a vowel sound* **:** made with great rounding of the lips ⟨the vowel in "boot" is *close-rounded*⟩

closes *pres 3d sing of* CLOSE, *pl of* CLOSE

close score \ˈklōs-\ *n* **:** a musical score in which two or more parts are put on the same staff — compare OPEN SCORE

close shake \"-\ *n* **:** BEBUNG

close shave \"-\ *n* **:** a narrow escape

close shot \"-\ *n* : a motion-picture shot made with the camera near the person or object but far enough away to include some of the background

closest *superlative of* CLOSE

close·stool \'klōz, 'klōs + ,-\ *n* [ME *close stol*, fr. *closen* to close + *stol* stool] : a stool or chair holding a chamber pot — compare COMMODE

close stretto \'klōs-\ *n* : a stretto in which the answer follows very closely after the subject

close string \'klōs-\ *n* : a string of a stair having its upper edge straight and usu. parallel with the lower edge so that the outer ends of the steps are entirely enclosed

close support \"-\ *n* : close-in fire or bombing delivered by a ground unit or by an air unit to assist another unit

¹clos·et \'kläzət *also* -lōz-; *usu* -əd·+V\ *n* -s [ME, fr. MF, dim. of *clos* enclosure — more at CLOSE] **1** : an apartment or small room for retirement or privacy : as **a** : a monarch's, statesman's, or official's private chamber for counsel or devotions ⟨that diplomacy at critical stages is something for the ~ and not a mass meeting —C.G.Bowers⟩ **b** *chiefly Midland* : PRIVY **2** : a cabinet or recess for china, household utensils, or clothing : CUPBOARD **3** : a place of retreat or privacy ⟨~ of the heart⟩ **4** : a diminutive of the bar in heraldry of one half its width **5** : the bowl of a water closet

²closet \"\ *adj* **1** : closely private ⟨a ~ utterance⟩ ⟨~ vows⟩ **2** *archaic* : suited to a closet ⟨~ prayer⟩ **3 a** : theoretical as opposed to practical ⟨a ~ politician⟩ **b** : working in or fitted for use or enjoyment only in the closet as the place of seclusion, study, or speculation ⟨the danger of intellectual anemia which threatens all ~ philosophers —M.R.Cohen⟩ ⟨the universe refutes our ~ rationalizations —W.L.Sullivan⟩

³closet \"\ *vt* -ED/-ING/-S **1** : to shut up in or as if in a closet ⟨he ~*ed* himself in a phone booth⟩ **2** : to take into a closet for a secret interview ⟨the inspector was ~*ed* with the district attorney⟩

close tail \'klōs-\ *n* : a tailing by a detective close on the heels of his subject; *also* : the detective doing this

closet drama *n* : drama suited primarily for reading rather than production; *also* : a play of this type

closeted *adj* : ²CLOSET 3b

close time \'klōs-\ *n, chiefly Brit* : a closed season

close-tongued \'=;=\ *adj* : CLOSEMOUTHED

close-up \'klō,səp\ *adj* [*close up*, adv.] : detailed and intimate from or as if from a point of vantage in close proximity

close-up \"\ *n* -s [*close up*, adv.] **1 a** : a motion picture taken very near an object or person to emphasize detail strongly or accentuate mood **b** : a photograph taken at close range **c** : photographic presentation produced with camera and object in close proximity ⟨television is mostly in *close-up*⟩ **2 a** : a close or intimate view or examination of anything **b** : a voice amplified to give the effect of issuing from close proximity **c** : a theatrical scene in which action is focused on the facial expression and emotional tension of certain characters **d** : a compact intimate biography ⟨it affords unique *close-ups* of key actors in political melodrama being played in Europe⟩

close up \-ōz-\ *vb* [¹*close*] *vt* **1** : to bring to a complete conclusion or settlement **2** : to restrain by legal measures from further business operations **3** *printing* **a** : to remove or reduce the spacing material between (units of set type matter) **b** : to assemble (type matter set in separate takes) ~ *vi* **1** : to converge in close array **2** : to discontinue business operations **3** : to retreat into complete silence : become uncommunicative —**close up shop** \"-\ **1** : to shut up shop **2** : to cease all activities

close with \'klōz-\ *vt* **1** : to approach close to **2** : to engage in hostile encounter at close quarters **3** : to ratify an agreement with

closh \'kläsh\ *n* -ES [origin unknown] : a post on a whaling ship fitted with hooks for hanging blubber to be sliced

¹clos·ing \'klōziŋ, -zēŋ\ *n* -s [ME, fr. gerund of *closen* to close] **1 a** : the concluding portion of a speech or debate : PERORATION **b** : a complimentary close of a letter **2 a** : a closable gap in an article of wear or luggage; *specif* : the section of an article that opens and closes for convenience of use (as a placket in a garment or the fastening of a bag)

²closing \"\ *adj* [fr. pres. part. of ¹*close*] : constituting the last stage or the final portion or item ⟨the ~ years of the century⟩ ⟨the ~ campaign of the revolution⟩

closing entry *n* : any one of a series of journal entries necessary to close the books of a business

closing error *n* : ERROR OF CLOSURE

closing layer *n, bot* : one of the layers of small compact cells that subdivide the complementary cells

closing line *n, math* : the line vector that is necessary to complete the polygon representing a vector sum and thus to render the sum zero (as in obtaining the equilibrant of a set of forces); *esp* : the closing side of a plane traverse

closing machine *n* : a machine that sews a lock stitch with two threads in heavy material

closing membrane *n* : PIT MEMBRANE

closing price *n* : the final price quoted for a bond, stock, or commodity on a stock exchange or produce exchange for a given day

clos·ish \'klōsish\ *adj* [⁴*close* + *-ish*] : rather close

clost \'klōst\ *dial var of* CLOSE

clos·te·ri·um \klä'stirēəm\ *n, cap* [NL, fr. Gk *klōstēr* spindle + NL *-ium*] : a genus of crescent-shaped desmids

clos·trid·i·al \(')klä¦stridēəl\ *or* **clos·trid·i·an** \-ēən\ *adj* [NL *clostridium* + E *-al* or *-an*] : of, relating to, produced by, or resembling a clostridium

clos·trid·i·um \=¦=ēəm\ *n* [NL, fr. *clostr-* (fr. Gk *klōstēr* spindle) + *-idium*] **1** *cap* : a genus of anaerobic or microaerophilic saprophytic rod-shaped or spindle-shaped bacteria (family Bacillaceae) that are nearly cosmopolitan in soil, animal intestines, and dung, that are distinguished from members of the genus *Bacillus* by the swollen drumstick shape assumed during spore formation, by the absence of aerobic growth, and by lack of the enzyme catalase, that are very active biochemically comprising numerous fermenters of carbohydrates with vigorous production of acid and gas, many nitrogen fixers, and others which rapidly putrefy proteins, and that include forms of considerable importance to man in certain industrial fermentations (as *C. butyricum* or *C. acetobutylicum*) or as pathogens of himself, his domestic animals, or his cultivated plants — compare BLACKLEG, BOTULISM, GAS GANGRENE, LIMBERNECK, TETANUS **2** *pl* **clostrid·ia** \-ēə\ **a** : any bacterium of the genus *Clostridium* **b** : a spindle-shaped or ovoid bacterial cell; *esp* : one swollen at the center by an endospore

¹clo·sure \'klōzhə(r)\ *n* -s [ME, fr. MF, fr. L *clausura*, fr. *clausus* (past part. of *claudere* to close) + *-ura* -ure — more at CLOSE] **1 a** *archaic* : means of enclosing ⟨formed a ~ around a plot of land⟩ **b** *obs* : FORT **c** *obs* : encircling bounds ⟨within the guilty ~ of thy walls —Shak.⟩ **d** *obs* : a space enclosed **e** *civil engin* : a giving of a closed figure when plotted — compare CLOSE *vi* 6 **2 a** *obs* : the action of confining or condition of being confined in an enclosing place **b** : the absence of social mobility in a social group : social self-containment of a group **3 a** : a bringing to a point of completion **b** *cricket* : an act or right of declaring an innings closed **c** *linguistics* : a closed construction — compare CLOSE *vt* 1b (3) **4 a** : an act of closing up or condition of being closed up ⟨~ of the eyelids⟩ ⟨the captain checked the ship's ~ for the pending attack⟩ **b** : a filling up of a space to seal or render impervious ⟨be sure the container has a tight ~ to keep it free from contamination⟩ **c** : a drawing together of edges or parts to form a united integument ⟨wound ~ by suture immediately after laceration⟩ **d** *phonetics* (1) : the extent to which an articulation blocks the passage of air (2) : the outer and the inner closure in a consonant articulation **5 a** : a means of filling a space or gap esp. by sealing it or of closing an opening (as in a garment or luggage): as (1) : FASTENER, CLOSING ⟨styled with fly-front ~⟩ ⟨pocket with zipper ~⟩ ⟨~ buttons for tubular furniture⟩ (2) : CLOSER 2 (3) : a cap, lid, or other form of stopper on or in a container esp. for sealing it **b** : the part of a container where the final seal is made **6** *archaic* : a coming to an agreement ⟨a precipitate ~ with this gentleman's proposals —Jane Austen⟩ **7** [trans. of F *clôture* — more at CLOTURE] : CLOTURE **8 a** : the vertical distance between the highest point in a quaquaversal flexure or doubly plunging anticline and the lowest structure-contour line that closes around it **b** *Brit* : a fold of a close-textured rock over a layer of porous rock to form a trap **9** : a bringing of some activity to a stop ⟨a ~ on smoking in the woods during a dry spell⟩ : cessation of operation ⟨~ of foreign-owned industries⟩ **10** : a closing with a particular destination on the part of a ship **11** *psychol* : the perception of incomplete figures or situations as though complete by ignoring the missing parts or by compensating for them by projection based on past experience

²closure \"\ *vt* **closured; closured; closuring** \-zh(ə)riŋ\ **closures** : CLOTURE ⟨debate was *closured* so the bill could be put to an almost immediate vote⟩

¹clot \'klät, *usu* -äd·+V\ *n* -s [ME, fr. OE *clott* lump, mass; akin to MHG *kloz* lumpy mass, ball, *klōz* lump, ball — more at CLOUT] **1 a** : a portion of a substance cleaving together in a thick nondescript mass (as of clay or gum) ⟨dodging ~*s* of dirt from the horse's hoofs⟩ **b** *archaic* : a hard lump : CLOD **2 a** : a roundish viscous lump formed by coagulation of a portion of liquid or by melting : a sizable blob or gob ⟨~*s* of cream forming in the churn⟩ **b** : a semisolid coagulum produced by entrapment of formed elements of the blood in a meshwork of precipitated fibrin filaments **c** : something seen esp. from some distance as an amorphous patch (as of color or light) or group ⟨coloring the ridges with ~*s* of shadow —H.L.Davis⟩ ⟨a small ~ of officials at the door⟩ **d** : an intangible knot resulting from a congealing and separating out from some moving stream ⟨public opinion is beginning to congeal in two ~*s*⟩ **3** *dial Eng* : BLOCKHEAD 2 **4** : a closely grouped or intertwined or interweaving assemblage of living beings : CLUSTER, CLUMP ⟨~*s* of black ducks migrating south⟩ ⟨the Filipinos lived and worked in ~*s* of five or six —John Steinbeck⟩ ⟨almost a hundred marines, soldiers, and sailors drawn up into a ~ in the street —E.L.Burdick⟩

²clot \"\ *vb* **clotted; clotted; clotting; clots** *vi* **1** : to form into a clot ⟨*clotting* masses of hydrocarbon molecules⟩ ⟨spectators *clotted* around the more closely contested field events⟩ ⟨when darkness seeped across the hill and *clotted* in the valley below us —H.D.Skidmore⟩ **2** : to undergo a sequence of complex chemical and physical reactions that results in conversion of fluid blood into a coagulum and that in vertebrates prob. involves the following course: shedding of blood, release of thromboplastin from blood platelets and injured tissues, inactivation of heparin by thromboplastin permitting calcium ions of the plasma to convert prothrombin to thrombin, interaction of thrombin with fibrinogen to form an insoluble fibrin network in which blood cells and plasma are trapped, and contraction of the network to squeeze out excess fluid : COAGULATE ~ *vt* **1** : to gather, press, or stick together in a clot ⟨perspiration *clotted* his hair⟩ ⟨the milk was *clotted* by the addition of a coagulant before it was used⟩ **2** : to fill, strew, or overspread with clots ⟨streets *clotted* with traffic⟩ ⟨a mud-*clotted* pony⟩ ⟨an elder grew leaning forward, its branches *clotted* with waxen blossom —Elizabeth Bowen⟩ ⟨fruit and flower paintings that *clotted* the walls —Truman Capote⟩ **3** : to cause to form into a clot or clump that halts, obstructs, or stagnates ⟨each night *clotted* the intership phones with "alerts", warnings, and alarms —John Mason Brown⟩ ⟨the meaning is often *clotted* by metaphor —Edmund Wilson⟩ ⟨a people whose new, raw culture was not yet *clotted* with inhibition —R.L.Taylor⟩

clot·bur \'klät +,-\ *n* [*clote* + *bur*] : BURDOCK

clote \'klōt\ *n* -s [ME, fr. OE *clāte* burr, burdock; akin to L *glut-, glus* glue, Lith *gliēti* to grease — more at CLAY] *dial Eng* : any of several plants related to the burdocks (as the cleavers, the butterbur, the coltsfoot, and the SPATTERDOCK)

¹cloth \'klȯth *also* -läth\ *n, pl* **cloths** \-thz,-ths\ *often attrib* [ME, fr. OE *clāth*; akin to OFris *klāth*, MD *cleet*, MHG *kleit*, OE *clīthan* to adhere to, Lith *glitùs* slippery — more at CLAY] **1 a** : something made by weaving, felting, knitting, knotting, bonding, or crocheting natural or synthetic fibers and filaments and used in variations of texture, finish, weight, width for clothing, upholstery, rugs, and industrial purposes or treated so that it will serve a special purpose (as made semirigid for bookbinding) **b** : a similar material (as of plastic, wire, or glass) **2 a** : a piece of cloth of varying length esp. as taken from a loom, as measured in a bolt, or as required for a garment **b** : a particular kind of cloth ⟨velvet is a ~ with a pile face⟩ ⟨cotton is the commonest woven ~⟩ **c** : a piece of cloth adapted by size, texture, or finish for a particular purpose — often used in combination ⟨dustcloth⟩ ⟨facecloth⟩ **d** : TABLECLOTH **e** *obs* : a piece of fabric of a standard quantity or length **f** (1) : canvas made into a sail (2) : one of the breadths of canvas sewed together to make a sail **g** *archaic* : canvas for a painting **h** *theater* : a painted cloth drop **3 a** *obs* : wearing apparel : CLOTHING **b** *archaic* : LIVERY **c** : a piece of cloth worn as a garment **4 a** : distinctive dress esp. of any profession or calling ⟨how any naval officer who respected his profession or calling could go fishing on equal terms with enlisted men —Fletcher Pratt⟩ **b** : the dress of the clergy or the clerical profession; *also* : CLERGY

²cloth *vt, obs* : to make into cloth

cloth beam *n* : the cylinder of a loom on which cloth is rolled as it is woven — called also FORE BEAM

clothbound \'=;=\ *adj, of a book* : bound in full cloth with stiff boards

clothe \'klōth\ *vb* **clothed** *or* **clad** \'klad, -aa(ə)d\ **clothed** *or* **clad; clothing; clothes** \'klō(th)z\ [ME *clothen*, fr. OE *clāthian*, fr. *clāth* garment, cloth — more at CLOTH] *vt* **1 a** : to put garments on : cover with clothes **b** : to provide with clothes ⟨trying to feed and ~ a family⟩ **c** *obs* : to hang or spread cloth over ⟨they *clothed* the royal bed with purple⟩ **d** : to fit out ⟨horses heavily *clothed* with armor⟩ ⟨natives *clothed* in ritual beads⟩ ⟨gold and diamonds to ~ their harlots⟩ **e** : to invest with the habit of a religious or the robes of a dignitary ⟨to attend the *clothing* of two lay sisters⟩ **f** : RIG ⟨~ a ship⟩ ⟨~ a mast⟩ **g** : to cover (carding equipment) with card clothing **h** : to cover (a sieve in milling equipment) with silk or woven wire **i** : to house in an intimate protective sheath suggestive of a garment ⟨a simple coffin to ~ the body of their friend —D.V.Steere⟩ ⟨*clothed* in its complicated shell⟩ **2 a** : to serve as a blanket overspreading the surface of esp. as adding or emphasizing some visual effect ⟨dense coniferous forests ~ the high bordering ridges —C.D.Forde⟩ ⟨foothills *clothed* in magnificent jungle⟩ **b** : to cover or overspread the integument or exterior of ⟨their bodies and wings densely *clothed* with hair⟩ ⟨scales ~ its whole body⟩ ⟨apple trees *clothed* in blossoms⟩ **3** : to express, convey, or enhance by suitably significant language : COUCH ⟨treaties *clothed* in stately phraseology⟩ ⟨the sweep of its ideas and the something akin to perfection of form in which they are *clothed* —H.J.Laski⟩ **4 a** : to envelop, finish out, or flesh out ⟨the roof and sides of the cavern begin to ~ themselves with that quivering violet sheen —Norman Douglas⟩ ⟨to ~ the dry bones of the law⟩ **b** : to wrap or cloak esp. in a way to provide delusion or borrow prestige ⟨by no whit lessened his agitation, which he sought to ~ with a semblance of debonair indifference —Osbert Sitwell⟩ ⟨~ themselves in Bismarck's conception of a nation standing between East and West —M.W.Straight⟩ **c** : PRESENT, REPRESENT, PORTRAY ⟨*clothing* its message in allegory⟩ ⟨meticulously *clothing* the period with authenticity⟩ : to present or represent through an illustrative or interpretive medium ⟨her innate tact, *clothed* in tender warmth and naturalness —Marcia Davenport⟩ **5** : to endow esp. with power or a quality ⟨an act *clothing* Indians with U. S. citizenship⟩ ⟨~ a commission with power to fix utility rates⟩ ~ *vi, archaic* : to clothe oneself

clothes \'klō(th)z\ *n pl, often attrib* [ME, fr. OE *clāthas*, pl. of *clāth* cloth, article of clothing — more at CLOTH] **1** : CLOTHING 1a **2** : BEDCLOTHES **3** : all the cloth articles of personal and household use that can be washed ⟨I always wash ~ on Mondays⟩ **4 a** : distinctive style : GUISE ⟨old theories in contemporary verbal ~⟩ **b** : CHARACTER, ROLE ⟨stepping into the ~ of the departed leader⟩

clothes basket *n* : a deep open usu. oval-shaped basket for carrying clothes and household linen to and from the place of laundering or drying : HAMPER

clothes closet *n* : a small room for hanging clothes

clothes hanger *n* : COAT HANGER

clothes·horse \'=,=\ *n* **1** : a frame on which to hang clothes or household linen (as for airing or drying) **2 a** : one whose marked or often sole claim to attention is in undue variety or conspicuous fashionableness of dress **b** : one overly concerned with appearing fashionable in dress esp. by conspicuously frequent changes

clotheshorse

clothesline \'=,=\ *n* : a line (as a length of cord or wire) stretched over some distance for hanging and drying clothes

clothes louse *n* : BODY LOUSE

clothes maid *or* **clothes maiden** *n, dial Brit* : CLOTHESHORSE 1

clothes moth *n* : any of several small yellowish or buff-colored tineid moths whose larvae eat organic matter (as woolen goods, furs, or feathers) — see CASEMAKING CLOTHES MOTH, WEBBING CLOTHES MOTH

clothes-peg \'=,=\ *n, Brit* : CLOTHESPIN

clothes·pin \'=,=\ *n* : a forked piece of wood or plastic or a small spring clamp used for fastening clothes on a line

clothespin graft *n* : a piece of bone shaped like a clothespin and used as a bone graft in spine fusion operations to bridge several vertebrae

clothespins

clothes·pole \'=,=\ *n* : a pole forked at the top for propping up a clothesline

clothes·press \'=,=\ *n* **1** : a receptacle for clothes: as **a** : a tall piece of furniture having a compartment in which clothes may be hung **b** : a piece of case furniture with sliding trays to hold clothes **2** *North & Midland* : CLOTHES CLOSET

clothes screen *n* : CLOTHESHORSE 1

clothes stick *n* : a staff or bat with forked tip for turning and handling clothes being boiled or rinsed

clothes stop *n* : cotton line used for fastening washed clothes to a line or for tying up rolled clothes in bags or lockers

clothes tree *n* : an upright postlike stand with hooks or pegs around the top on which to hang clothes — called also *costumer, hall tree, hatstand, hat tree*

clothesyard \'=,=\ *n* : a section of a yard of a dwelling used for hanging clothes to dry or air

cloth hall *n* [trans. of F *halle aux draps*] : a building serving as a medieval exchange for the cloth merchants

cloth house *n* : a flat-topped shelter of loosely woven cloth used to protect growing plants (as tobacco) from insects, fungus pests, heavy rain, and wind and to reduce light intensity and evaporation and hence induce greater stem length and larger blooms or a thinner or higher quality of leaf

cloth·ier \'klōthyə(r), -thēə-\ *n* -s [ME, alter. of earlier *clother*, fr. ¹*cloth* + *-er*] **1** *obs* : a maker of cloth **2** *archaic* : a fuller of cloth **3 a** : a retailer of cloth and often also a tailor **b** : a retailer of men's clothes **4** : one that covers with cloth the steel drawing rollers of textile machines

cloth·ier's-brush \'=,=,=\ *n, pl* **clothier's-brushes** : WILD TEASEL

cloth·i·fy \'klōthə,fī\ *vt* -ED/-ING/-ES [¹*cloth* + *-ify*] *archaic* : CLOTHE

clothes tree

cloth·ing \'klōthiŋ, -ēŋ *but see sense 5*\ *n* -s [ME, fr. gerund of *clothen* to clothe] **1 a** : covering for the human body or garments in general : all the garments and accessories worn by a person at any one time **b** *obs* : LIVERY **c** : the equipment (as blankets, hoods, or bandages) used to cover and protect a domestic animal (as a horse) **d** : characteristic exterior properties and aspects, style, and atmosphere in which something intangible is discerned ⟨the moral ~ of legislation⟩ **2** : CLEADING 2 **3 a** : SAILS **b** : the bowsprit rigging **4** : CLOTHING WOOL **5** \'klōth- *also* 'klāth-\ : CARD CLOTHING **6** : the felts and wires of papermaking machines

clothing wool \'klōthiŋ-, -ēŋ-\ *n* **1** : short staple wool usu. under 1¾ inches in length and suitable only for carding and woolen goods — called also *carding wool* **2** : wool used in apparel fabrics as distinguished from wool used in carpets

cloth measure *n* : a unit or system of units for measuring cloth; *specif* : a system of ells, quarters, and nails

cloth of gold : a fabric woven wholly or partly of gold thread esp. for ceremonial use

cloth-of-gold cone \;=;=;=-\ *n* : TEXTILE CONE

cloth of silver : a cloth wholly or partly of silver thread

cloth of state : a rich cloth forming a canopy and background to a throne or chair of state

cloth oil *n* : WOOL OIL 1

cloth plate *n* : the metal plate in a sewing machine through which the needle passes and on which the work rests

cloth red B *n, usu cap C&R* : an acid dye — see DYE table I (under *Acid Red 115*)

cloths *pl of* CLOTH

cloth scarlet G *n, usu cap C&S* : an acid dye — see DYE table I (under *Acid Red 151*)

cloth wheel *n* : a polishing wheel consisting of built-up layers of cloth charged with an abrasive or polishing material

clothworker \'=,=\ *n* : a textile worker or manufacturer

clothy \'klōthē *also* -äthē\ *adj* : resembling cloth

cloth yard *n* : a yard esp. for measuring cloth; *specif* : a unit of 37 inches equal to the Scotch ell and used also as a length for arrows ⟨*cloth yard* shafts used by English archers at Crécy⟩

clot molder *n, Brit* : a molder's assistant who works clots of clay and rough-shapes them into bricks

clot·poll \'klät,pōl\ *n* [by alter.] : CLODPOLL

clot retraction time *n* : the time required for the fibrin of a fresh blood clot to contract and squeeze out excess serum

clots *pl of* CLOT, *pres 3d sing of* CLOT

clot·ta·ble \'kläd·əbəl, -lätə-\ *adj* : capable of being clotted

clotted *adj* [fr. past part. of ²*clot*] **1** : choked with thickened masses or compact assemblages suggestive of gobbets : CLUTTERED, CLOGGED ⟨roads ~ with trucks and tanks⟩ **2** *Brit* : UNQUALIFIED, SHEER ⟨~ nonsense⟩ — **clot·ted·ness** *n* -ES

clotted cream *n* : DEVONSHIRE CREAM

clot·ter \'klätə(r)\ *vi* [ME *cloteren*, fr. ¹*clot* + *-eren* (freq. suffix)] *now dial Brit* : CLOT, COAGULATE

clotting *pres part of* CLOT

clot·ty \'kläd·ē, -lätē\ *adj* : clotted or inclined to clot

¹clo·ture \'klōchə(r)\ *n* -s [F *clôture*, alter. (influenced by such words as *fermeture* closing, *ouverture* opening) of OF *closure* — more at CLOSURE] : the closing or limitation of debate in a legislative body by calling for a vote or by other authorized methods — compare GUILLOTINE, KANGAROO CLOSURE

²cloture \"\ *vt* -ED/-ING/-S : to end debate of by cloture

clotweed \'=,=\ *n* [*clote* + *weed*] : COCKLEBUR 1

clou \'klü\ *n* -s [F, lit., nail, fr. L *clavus* — more at CLAVUS] : the point of chief interest or attraction

¹cloud \'klau̇d\ *n* -s *often attrib* [ME, rock, hill, cloud, fr. OE *clūd*; akin to Gk *gloutos* buttock, Slovenian *glûta* bump, Skt *glau* round lump — more at GALL] **1 a** : a visible assemblage of particles of water or ice in the form of fog, mist, or haze formed by the condensation of vapor in the air and suspended in the air generally at a considerable height — see CIRRUS, CUMULUS, NIMBUS, STRATUS **b** : the material of which such a mass is composed **c** : a light filmy, puffy, or billowy mass seeming to float in the air ⟨a clipper ship under a

clouds, 1a: *1* cirrus, *2* cirrostratus, *3* cirrocumulus, *4* altostratus, *5* altocumulus, *6* stratocumulus, *7* nimbostratus, *8* cumulus, *9* cumulonimbus, *10* stratus

~ of sail⟩ ⟨a girl with a lustrous ~ of long golden hair⟩ **2 a :** a usu. visible assemblage of minute particles of a substance suspended in the surrounding air or in a gas ⟨enveloped in a ~ of steam⟩ ⟨when the wind drops, the sand ~ disappears with it —R.A.Bagnold⟩ ⟨the mushroom ~ arising from an atomic blast⟩ ⟨the flower smell came up in a heavy invisible ~ from the bed —Paul Bowles⟩ **b :** one of the aggregations of obscuring matter in space that reveal themselves as dark areas against the background of more distant bright objects or by stationary lines in stellar spectra ⟨fine yellow dust forming the ~s of the morning star⟩ **c :** a group of microscopic waves or electrically charged particles ⟨a ~ of electrons exists in the space surrounding the cathode —A.V. Eastman⟩ **3 a :** a flying swarm (as of birds, insects, or airplanes) **b :** a great crowd or multitude ⟨a host of individual geniuses and a ~ of admirable painters notwithstanding —Clive Bell⟩ ⟨in a mystifying ~ of words⟩ **4 a :** something that has a dark, lowering, or threatening aspect ⟨the ~s of World War II began to loom over the horizon⟩ **b :** something that temporarily overshadows or depresses ⟨occasionally a ~ darkens my reflections —P.E.More⟩ **5 a :** something that obscures or disrupts ⟨tried to veil his testimony in a ~ of sanctity —L.P.Stryker⟩ **b :** something that impairs, detracts, subjects to suspicion or controversy **:** BLEMISH ⟨justice demands removal of the ~ on the title to this land⟩ ⟨a ~ rests over the transaction⟩ ⟨emerging from under the ~ of international disapprobation⟩ **6 a :** a dark or opaque vein or spot on a lighter or transparent material (as in marble) **b :** a similar spot of any shade or color against a different ground ⟨precipitated as a reddish ~ in the bottle⟩; *specif* **:** a patch of color marking ⟨a blackish ~ on the mare's forehead⟩ **7 :** a large lightweight loosely knitted head scarf — **in the clouds :** given over to or in a state of impractical fancy; *specif* **:** rapt in abstruse cogitation, nebulous theorizing, or aesthetic transport — **under a cloud 1 :** in disfavor or disgrace **2 :** subject to a stigma or to suspicion as not fully cleared of a damaging charge **3 :** suffering repression or derangement

[2]**cloud** \"\ *vb* -ED/-ING/-S *vi* **1 a :** to grow cloudy **:** become overcast — usu. used with *over* or *up* ⟨~ over before a rain⟩ **b** *of a transparent surface* **:** to become overspread or obscured with spots or streaks ⟨a windshield often ~s in winter with condensation of the breath⟩ **2 a** *of facial features* **:** to become troubled, apprehensive, or distressed in appearance ⟨his eyes ~ed with indignation⟩ **b :** to become blurry, dubious, or ominous ⟨the outlook . . . ~ed abruptly —Michael Clark⟩ **3 :** to billow up in the form of a cloud ~ *vt* **1 a :** to envelop or hide with a cloud or as if by a cloud ⟨the mountain peak was ~ed all day⟩ ⟨the smog ~ed our view⟩ **b :** to make opaque (as a mirror or window) esp. by condensation of moisture ⟨the steam from the shower ~ed the windows⟩ **c :** to darken or make murky esp. with smoke or mist ⟨smoke ~ed the sky and the atmosphere of the hillside⟩ **d :** to darken or overshadow with a dispirited or dispiriting cast (as of perplexity, gloom, shame) ⟨with a distressing melancholy ~ing her features⟩ **2 :** to make unclear **:** OBSCURE, CONFUSE: **a :** to make uncertain or disputable (as a title or an issue) ⟨both the title and the legal right are ~ed by the loss⟩ ⟨~ the issue of fault and blame⟩ **b :** to make indistinct or difficult to discern or clarify ⟨language which will not ~ the nature of the problem⟩ **c :** to make (the mind or the reasoning) confused or illogical ⟨a religiosity which ~ed their minds⟩ **d :** to make torpid ⟨a disease characterized by a ~ing of consciousness⟩ **3 a :** TAINT, SULLY ⟨a ~ed reputation⟩ ⟨a ~ed character⟩ ⟨the slightly dishonest deed ~ed his good name all his life⟩ ⟨no misunderstanding ever ~ed their friendship —John Buchan⟩ **b :** to impair or distort the sound state or purity of ⟨letting his feelings ~ his sense of justice⟩ **c :** to cast gloom over or put a blighting influence on — usu. implying a certain persistence of the cause ⟨the latter part of his life was ~ed by disillusionment⟩ ⟨discouragements ~ the life of every man at some time⟩ **d :** to impoverish of spirit or morale ⟨his future was ~ed by poor eyesight⟩ **4 :** to mark with or darken in patches or spots ⟨the hot water ~ed the surface of the table⟩ ⟨the wind ~ed the lake⟩ **syn** see OBSCURE

cloud·age \'klau̇dij\ *n* -s [[1]*cloud* + *-age*] **:** a mass of clouds

cloud band *n* **:** a sinuous stylization of a cloud used as a motif in Chinese art and esp. in Persian and other oriental rugs

cloud banner *n* **:** BANNER CLOUD

cloudberry \'=— *see* BERRY\ *n* -ES [[1]*cloud* + *berry*; prob. fr. its shape] **1 :** a creeping herbaceous raspberry (*Rubus chamaemorus*) of north temperate regions bearing large white flowers and edible fruit — called also *dwarf mulberry* **2 :** the reddish amber-colored fruit of the cloudberry

cloud blower *n* **:** a straight clay pipe used by Pueblo Indians for sending symbolic puffs of smoke in different directions during rites

cloud blue *n* **:** a very pale blue that is less strong and slightly redder and lighter than baby blue (sense 1) and greener and paler than pastel blue (sense 2)

cloud-built \'=,=\ *adj* **:** UNSUBSTANTIAL, IMAGINARY

cloudburst \'=,=\ *n* -s **1 :** a sudden copious rainfall as if a whole cloud had been precipitated at once **2 :** DELUGE 2 **3 :** pseudopregnancy of the goat

cloudcap \'=,=\ *n* **:** CAP CLOUD

cloud-capped \'=,=\ *adj* **:** having clouds about the top or peaks **:** reaching to the clouds

cloud chamber *n* **:** a closed vessel containing air saturated with water vapor in which ionizing particles (as electrons or protons) passing through the vessel simultaneously with the sudden expansion and resultant cooling of the vapor leave visible white tracks of droplets condensed on the ions created by the particles, these tracks usu. being photographed — called also *expansion chamber*

cloud-cuckoo-land \'=,=,=,=\ *n, sometimes cap C&C&L* [trans. of Gk *nephelokokkygia*] **:** a whimsically conceived realm of utopian fantasy

cloud drift *n* **1 :** a mass of drifting clouds **2 :** a method of distributing by airplane a powdered insecticide that drifts slowly like a cloud over the area under treatment

cloud·ed \'klau̇dəd\ *adj* **1 :** of variegated material **:** MOTTLED **2 :** obscure or obscured in form or expression **:** BLURRED ⟨sometimes one understood clearly and sometimes the meaning was ~ —H.G.Wells⟩ **3 :** mentally confused **:** DISORDERED **4** *of title to land* **:** having some defect that constitutes a cloud on title **5 :** QUESTIONABLE 4

clouded leopard *n* **:** a medium-sized arboreal cat (*Felis nebulosa*) of southeastern Asia and the East Indies that is mottled and striped with black on a brownish gray ground

clouded sulphur *n* **:** a medium-sized yellow butterfly (*Colias philodice*) with black-bordered wings that is common in most of the U.S. and has a larva that feeds on several economic leguminous plants — compare ALFALFA CATERPILLAR

clouded tiger *n* **:** CLOUDED LEOPARD

clouded ware *n* **:** glazed ware dabbed with spots colored by metallic oxides

cloud forest *n* **:** a dense forest esp. on coastal slopes in the rainy regions of low latitudes that is almost constantly under clouds and differing from tropical rain forest mainly in being cooler and more humid

cloud funnel *n* **:** the funnel-shaped pendent cloud of a tornado

cloud grass *n* **:** a Spanish grass (*Agrostis nebulosa*) with a light feathery panicle cultivated for dried bouquets

cloud gray *n* **:** ZINC 2

cloud·i·ly \'klau̇dᵊlē, -dəlē\ *adv* **:** in a cloudy or clouded manner **:** INDISTINCTLY, OBSCURELY

cloud·i·ness \-dēnəs, -din-\ *n* -ES **:** cloudy or clouded condition or appearance; *esp* **:** the amount of cloud formation covering the sky — usu. expressed in tenths or eighths

cloud·ing \-diŋ\ *n* -s **1 :** a cloudy marking or appearance **:** fogginess esp. of shadows in an X ray **2 :** dull blurry and usu. mottled coloration

clouding of consciousness : mental confusion with impaired awareness of the environment

cloud·land \'klau̇d,land, -lənd\ *n* **1 :** a region in the upper atmosphere occupied by clouds **2 :** the realm of visionary hypothesis or uncertain speculation **3 :** the realm of poetic imagination

cloud·less \'klau̇dləs\ *adj* **:** free from any cloud ⟨one of the most ~ loves in life, this for books —Mary Stolz⟩

cloud·less·ly *adv* **:** in a cloudless manner

cloud·less·ness *n* -ES **:** the quality or state of being cloudless

cloudless sulphur *n* **:** a widely distributed New World butterfly (*Phoebis sennae*) resembling the clouded sulphur but lacking the broad black margin on the wings and being a strong migrant with a larva that is a pest on senna

cloud·let \'klau̇dlət\ *n* -s [[1]*cloud* + *-let*] **:** a small cloud

cloud·ling \-dliŋ\ *n* -s [[1]*cloud* + *-ling*] **:** a little cloud

cloud meter *n* **:** an instrument for measuring rates of collection of atmospheric water and ice by means of a porous plug through which the moisture is drawn and then measured to give an indication of liquid water content

cloud on title : a defect in the owner's title to a piece of land arising from a written instrument, a judgment, or an order of court purporting to create an interest in or lien upon the land and therefore impairing the marketability of the owner's title though it may be shown to be invalid by evidence

cloud pink *n* **:** a grayish yellowish pink that is redder and slightly stronger than iris mauve

cloud point *n* **:** the temperature at which a liquid (as a petroleum oil) begins to cloud (as from the separation of wax on cooling)

cloud rack *n* **:** [1]RACK 2a

cloud rat *n* [so called fr. their mountain habitation] **:** any of several large long-haired mountain-dwelling rats of two Philippine genera (*Crateromys* and *Phloeomys*) that may attain a length of 30 inches nearly half of which is made up by the bushy hairy tail — called also *bushy-tailed rat*

cloud ring *n* **:** a ring of clouds; *specif* **:** the nearly permanent belt of clouds along the equator

clouds *pl of* CLOUD, *pres 3d sing of* CLOUD

cloud·scape \'klau̇d,skāp\ *n* -s [[1]*cloud* + *-scape*] **:** a view or pictorial representation of a cloud formation

cloud street *n* **:** a group of cumulus clouds arranged in rows

cloud track *n* **:** a slender train of minute water droplets left in the path of an ionizing particle that passes through saturated vapor in a cloud chamber

cloud·ward \'klau̇dwə(r)d\ *or* **cloud·wards** \-dz\ *adv* **1 :** toward the clouds **2 :** upward in aspiration or achievement esp. to lofty heights

cloudy \'klau̇dē, -di\ *adj* -ER/-EST [ME, fr. OE *clūdig* rocky, fr. *clūd* rock, hill — more at CLOUD] **1 :** made or consisting of cloud ⟨the mountain with its ~ veil⟩ **:** like cloud in appearance ⟨~ smoke⟩ **2 :** darkened (as in mood or spirit) by gloom, anxiety, ill temper, or other emotion ⟨a ~ mood⟩ ⟨a ~ eye⟩ **3 :** overcast with clouds ⟨a ~ sky⟩ ⟨~ moon⟩ **:** having the sky overcast ⟨~ morning⟩ ⟨~ day⟩; *specif, in meteorology* **:** with clouds obscuring six tenths to nine tenths of the sky **4 :** obscure in meaning **:** hard to perceive, understand, or comprehend ⟨gropes among ~ issues toward a feeble conclusion —H.T.Moore⟩ **:** uncertain as to fact or outcome ⟨a ~ future⟩ **:** vague or inexact in thought or meaning **:** HAZY ⟨his ~ obsessions and obstinacies —F.M.Ford⟩ **5 :** dimmed or dulled or made obscure as if by clouds **:** lacking clearness, brightness, or luster ⟨a ~ diamond⟩ ⟨a ~ mirror⟩ ⟨the violins had a rather ~ tone⟩ **6 :** like cloud in being light or floating in a light, airy, or translucent mass ⟨dream faces, pale, with ~ hair —G.W. Russell⟩ **7 :** having irregular light and dark areas or markings **:** uneven in color or texture **8 :** having visible material in suspension **:** MURKY ⟨a ~ liquid⟩

cloudy amber *n* **:** GOLDEN GREEN

cloudy swelling *n* **:** a form of degeneration in the tissues of various organs (as the liver, the kidneys, or the heart) marked by swelling and a cloudy appearance of the cells from a deposition in them of granules of protein nature

cloudy-winged whitefly \'=,=,=-\ *n* **:** a common whitefly (*Dialeurodes citrifolii*) important in Florida as a destructive sap-sucking pest of citrus

cloué *also* **clou·ée** \(')klü;ā\ *adj* [F, past part. of *clouer* to nail, fr. *clou* nail — more at CLOU] *heraldry* **:** emblazoned with nailheads ⟨a trellis gules ~ argent⟩

clough \'kləf *also* 'klau̇\ *n* -s [ME *clough, cloge, clou,* fr. (assumed) OE *clōh;* akin to OHG *Clāhuelde,* a place name, *klingo, klinga* ravine, mountain brook and perh. to OE *clingan* to cling — more at CLING] **:** a cleft in a hill **:** a narrow valley **:** RAVINE

[1]**clour** \'klü(ə)r\ *n* -s [origin unknown] *chiefly Scot* **:** a bump on the head made by a blow; *also* **:** the blow itself

[2]**clour** \"\ *vt* -ED/-ING/-S *chiefly Scot* **:** BATTER, THUMP

clous *pl of* CLOU

[1]**clout** \'klau̇t, *usu* -d.+V\ *n* -s [ME, fr. OE *clūt;* akin to MHG *klōz* lump, ON *klūtr* kerchief, Russ *gluda* lump, L *galla* gall on a plant — more at GALL] **1 a** *now dial Brit* **:** a patch esp. of cloth or leather **:** a shred or rag esp. of cloth **b :** CLOTH; *esp* **:** a cloth for household use (as a towel or cover) **c :** an article of clothing (as for infants); *specif* **:** DIAPER **2 a :** an iron plate on an axletree or other wood to keep it from wearing **b :** CLOUT NAIL **3 :** a blow esp. with the fist ⟨gave him a ~ on his old head —Arnold Bennett⟩ **:** a hit esp. in baseball ⟨a long ~ over the fence⟩ **4 a :** the mark shot at in archery; *specif* **:** a white cloth placed on a stake or stretched on a hoop or frame used as a target in distance shooting — see CLOUT SHOOTING **b :** a hit in the clout

[2]**clout** \"\ *vt* -ED/-ING/-S [ME *clouten,* fr. *clout* patch — more at CLOUT] **1 a :** to mend with a patch **:** PATCH **b :** to stud with nails **:** protect (as shoe soles) by studding with nails **c :** to protect (an axletree) with a clout **d :** to cover with or as if with a cloth **2 :** to strike forcefully esp. with the hand or fist ⟨the troublesome boy whose mother has just ~ed his head —G.B.Shaw⟩ **:** hit (as a ball) with force ⟨~ the ball into the bleachers⟩ **3** *slang* **:** STEAL **syn** see STRIKE

[1]**clout·ed** \'klau̇dəd\ *adj* [ME, fr. past part. of *clouten*] **:** protected or patched with clouts **:** PATCHED ⟨dark wool dresses and ~ boots —Anne Green⟩

[2]**clouted** \"\ *adj* [obs. *clout* curds (fr. ME) + *-ed;* akin to ME *clott* lump — more at CLOT] *dial Brit* **:** CLOTTED — used esp. of cream

clouterly *adj* [obs. *clouter* cobbler, botcher (fr. ME, fr. *clouten* + *-er*) + *-ly*] *archaic* **:** CLUMSY, AWKWARD

clout nail *n* **:** a nail having a large flat head used for fastening clouts to axletrees, studding timber, or fastening down sheet metal

clout-shoe *n* [[1]*clout* (iron plate) + *shoe*] *obs* **:** a wearer of clouted shoes **:** RUSTIC

clout shooting *n* [[1]*clout* (white cloth)] **:** archery shooting in contest in which rounds of arrows are shot from long range at a very large circular target marked on the ground

[1]**clove** \'klōv\ *n* -s [ME, fr. OE *clufu;* akin to OS *clufloc* garlic, OHG *chlobilouh,* ON *klofi* cleft, OE *clēofan* to split — more at CLEAVE] **:** one of the small bulbs developed in the axils of the scales of a large bulb (as in garlic)

[2]**clove** *past of* CLEAVE

[3]**clove** \"\ *n* -s [modif. (influenced by L *clavus*) of AF *clou,* lit., nail, fr. L *clavus* — more at CLAVUS] **:** any of various old English units of weight (as for wool, cheese); *esp* **:** one equal to eight pounds

[4]**clove** \"\ *n* -s [alter. (prob. influenced by [1]*clove*) of ME *clowe, cloue,* fr. OF *clou (de girofle),* lit., nail of clove, fr. L *clavus* nail] **1 a :** the pungent fragrant aromatic reddish brown dried flower bud of a tropical tree **b :** a spice consisting of whole or ground cloves — usu. used in pl.; see CLOVE OIL **2 :** a moderate-sized very symmetrical red-flowered tropical evergreen tree (*Eugenia caryophyllata* or *Syzygium aromaticum*) of the family Myrtaceae that is probably native to the Moluccas but is now widely cultivated in the tropics (as Zanzibar and Madagascar) for its flower buds which are the source of cloves **3 :** SHERRY 2

[5]**clove** \"\ *n* -s [D *klove, kloof;* akin to OE *clēofan* to split — more at CLEAVE] **:** CLEFT, GAP, RAVINE — used chiefly in place names

clove brown *n* [[4]*clove*] **1 :** a dark yellowish brown **2 :** a brownish gray that is yellower and lighter than average chocolate and yellower and deeper than taupe (sense 1) — called also *eagle*

clove carnation *n* [[4]*clove*] **:** CLOVE PINK 1

clove cassia *n* [[4]*clove*] **:** the bark of a Brazilian tree (*Dicypellium caryophyllatum*) used for mixing with other spices

clove cinnamon *n* [[4]*clove*] **:** CLOVE CASSIA

clove currant *n* [[4]*clove*] **1 :** BUFFALO CURRANT 1 **2 :** GOLDEN CURRANT 1

clove gillyflower *n* [[4]*clove*] **:** CLOVE PINK 1

clove hitch *n* [*clove* (var. of *cloven*) + *hitch*] **:** a knot used to secure a rope temporarily to an object (as a post or spar) and consisting of a turn around the object, over the standing part, around the object again, and under the last turn

clove hitch

clove hook *n* [*clove* (var. of *cloven*)] **:** SISTER HOOK

[1]**cloven** *past part of* [2]CLEAVE

[2]**cloven** *adj* [ME, fr. OE *clofen,* past part. of *clēofan* to split — more at CLEAVE] **:** divided or split esp. to a certain depth

clo·vene \'klō,vēn, =ˈ=\ *n* -s [[4]*clove* + *-ene*] **:** a liquid sesquiterpene $C_{15}H_{24}$ obtained from caryophyllene

clo·ven foot *or* **cloven hoof** \'klōvən-\ *n* **1 :** a foot (as of an ox or sheep) that is divided or cleft into two or more parts esp. at its distal extremity — compare SOLID HOOF **2** [fr. the traditional representation of Satan as cloven-footed] **:** the sign of devilish character ⟨show the *cloven hoof*⟩ — **cloven-footed** \';=';=\ *or* **cloven-hoofed** \';=';=\ *adj*

clove nutmeg *n* [[4]*clove*] **1 :** a tree (*Ravensara aromatica*) of Madagascar resembling a nutmeg and having small leathery leaves **2 :** the nutmeglike fruit of this tree

clove oil *n* [[4]*clove*] **:** a colorless to pale yellow essential oil obtained from cloves and used in medicine as a flavor and perfume and as a source of eugenol

clove pepper *n* [[4]*clove*] **:** ALLSPICE 1

clove pink *n* [[4]*clove*] **1 :** a pink (*Dianthus caryophyllus*) or any of several varieties developed therefrom having a rich clovelike fragrance — see CARNATION **2 :** a dark red that is yellower, less strong, and slightly darker than cranberry, lighter, stronger, and slightly yellower than average garnet, and bluer, lighter, and stronger than average wine

clo·ver \'klōvə(r)\ *n* -s [ME *claver, clovere,* fr. OE *clāfre, clǣfre;* akin to MLG *klēver* clover, MD *clāver,* OHG *klēo,* and perh. to OE *clīfian* to stick to — more at CLEAVE] **1 :** an herb of the genus *Trifolium* characterized by trifoliolate leaves and flowers in dense heads — see ALSIKE CLOVER, CRIMSON CLOVER, RED CLOVER, WHITE CLOVER **2 :** any of several plants of the family Leguminosae (as sweet clover, bush clover, prairie clover, or spotted clover) — **in clover** *or* **in the clover :** in prosperity or in pleasant circumstances ⟨the farmers were *in clover,* and it was about time —F.L.Allen⟩

clover-and-alfalfa disease \'=,=,=,=-\ *n* **:** CLOVER DISEASE 1

clover aphid *n* **:** a common aphid (*Nearctaphis bakeri*) chiefly of western and northwestern U.S. that in early spring feeds on apple and later on clover to which it is often very destructive

clover broom *n* **:** INDIGO BROOM

clover broomrape *n* **:** a European broomrape (*Orobanche minor*) parasitic on clover roots

clover butterfly *n* **:** SULPHUR

clover casebearer *n* **:** a casebearer moth (*Coleophora spissicomis*) the larvae of which feed on the developing seeds of clover esp. in New Zealand

clover club *also* **clover club cocktail** *n* [fr. *Clover Club,* name of a legal and literary club of Philadelphia] **:** a cocktail consisting of gin, white of egg, and lemon or lime juice flavored with grenadine and sweetened

clover disease *also* **clover sickness** *n* **1 :** an acute photosensitization of white or light-skinned animals feeding on certain clovers and other leguminous plants characterized by swelling and inflammation esp. of the skin of the face and the mucous membranes of the mouth **2 :** SWEET CLOVER DISEASE

clover dodder *n* **:** a common dodder (*Cuscuta epithymum*) that infests clover

clover fern *n* **:** a water fern of the genus *Marsilea* distinguished by four cloverlike leaflets

clover hay worm *n* **:** the larva of a small moth (*Hypsopygia costalis*) of the family Pyralididae that is often destructive to clover hay

clover head caterpillar *n* **:** a larval moth (*Grapholitha interstinctana*) that feeds on the flower heads or foliage of various clovers

[1]**cloverleaf** \'=,=\ *adj* **:** resembling a clover leaf in shape ⟨a ~ roll⟩

[2]**cloverleaf** \"\ *n, often attrib* **:** something resembling a clover leaf in shape; *specif* **:** a road plan passing one highway over another and routing turning traffic onto connecting roadways which branch only to the right and lead around in a circle to enter the other highway from the right and thus merging traffic without left-hand turns or direct crossings

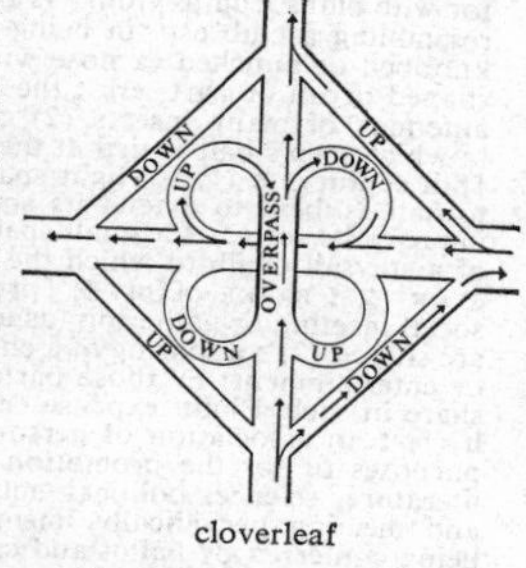

cloverleaf

clover leafhopper *n* **:** a widely distributed leafhopper (*Aceratagallia sanguinolenta*) feeding chiefly on clovers and related plants but sometimes a vector of certain virus diseases of potatoes

clover leaf midge \'=,=,=-\ *n* **:** a small two-winged fly (*Dasyneura trifolii*) whose larvae develop on the leaves of clover and fold together the halves of the leaflets

clover leaf weevil *n* **:** a small brownish or blackish widely distributed weevil (*Hypera punctata*) native to Europe and sometimes highly destructive both as adult and larva to clovers and other leguminous plants

cloverlike \'=,=\ *adj* **:** resembling clover

clover mite *n* **:** a small reddish mite (*Bryobia praetiosa*) that is seriously destructive to legumes, wheat, fruits, and other crops and often a pest in houses into which it may enter in great numbers esp. in the spring of the year — called also *brown mite, house mite*

clove·root \'klōv+,-\ *n* [[4]*clove* + *root;* fr. its odor] **:** HERB BENNET

clover pink *n* **:** a dark purplish pink that is bluer than Persian lilac and bluer and stronger than rhodonite pink

clover root borer *n* **:** a small brown weevil (*Hylastinus obscurus*) of the family Scolytidae that bores in clover roots

clover root curculio *n* **:** a small dark broad-snouted weevil (*Sitona hispidula* or a closely related species) that feeds on clovers, alfalfa, and other legumes, the larva on the root surface, scoring and girdling the roots, and the adult on the leaves

clover rootworm *n* **:** GRAPE COLASPIS

clover rot *or* **clover wilt** *n* **:** a disease of clover plants caused by a fungus (*Sclerotinia trifoliorum*)

clover rust *n* **1 :** a disease of clovers caused by fungi of the genus *Uromyces* and characterized by rusty brown pustules **2 :** any of the fungi causing clover rust

clover seed chalcid *n* **:** a tiny dark chalcid fly (*Bruchophagus platyptera*) the larva of which feeds on the developing seeds of clovers and alfalfa and is in certain areas a major factor restricting production of clover seed

clover seed midge \'=,=,=-\ *n* **:** a small two-winged fly (*Dasyneura leguminicola*) that infests the heads of red and white clover destroying the flower and is in certain areas a chief factor limiting clover-seed production

clover seed weevil *n* **:** a tiny grayish brown weevil (*Miccotrogus picirostris*) the larva of which feeds on developing seeds of various clovers

clover-sick \'=,=\ *adj, of soil* **:** incapable of yielding profitable crops of clover because of the presence of an organism capable of causing disease — **clover sickness** *n*

clover weevil *n* **:** a small European weevil (*Apion apricans* or related species) that feeds on clover

clo·very \'klōv(ə)rē\ *adj* **:** like clover or abounding in clover

cloves *pl of* CLOVE

clove-strip \'=,=\ *n* **:** a primrose willow (*Jussiaea diffusa*) of eastern No. America

clove tree *n* [[4]*clove*] **:** [4]CLOVE 2

clovewort \'=,=\ *n* -s [fr. (assumed) ME, fr. OE *clufwyrt,* fr. *clufu* clove + *wyrt* -wort] **1** *dial chiefly Eng* **:** a crowfoot (*Ranunculus acris*) **2** *obs* **:** HERB BENNET

clow \'klau̇\ *n* -s [alter. of ME *clowse* (taken as pl.), fr. OE clūs, clūse bar, bolt, enclosure, fr. ML *clusa* enclosure, fr. L, fem. of *clusus, clausus,* past part. of *claudere* to close — more at CLOSE] **1 :** an outfall sluice for water from a tidal river after it has deposited its sediment on flooded land **2 :** a floodgate esp. for a lock or water mill

clowd·er \ˈklaủdə(r)\ *n* -s [prob. var. of ²*clutter*] **:** a group of cats

¹clown \ˈklaủn\ *n* -s [perh. fr. MF *coulon* settler, fr. L *colonus* colonist, farmer — more at COLONY] **1 :** a husbandman or farmer **:** COUNTRYMAN, RUSTIC **2 :** a man of coarse nature and manners **:** a rude, ill-bred person **:** BOOR ⟨thou art mated with a ~ and the grossness of his nature will have weight to drag thee down —Alfred Tennyson⟩ **3 a :** a fool, jester, or comedian in a play or other entertainment; *specif* **:** a comedy performer in a circus grotesquely made up and dressed **b :** one who frequently or habitually plays the buffoon or engages in comedy **:** JOKER ⟨practical jokes by the office ~⟩ **4 :** a dancer who performs ridiculous or satirical dances usu. in disguise and often for magical or ritualistic purposes **syn** see BOOR

²clown \"\ *vb* -ED/-ING/-S *vi* **:** to act as a clown **:** play the clown **:** jest ridiculously ~ *vt* **:** to jest at or ridicule grotesquely **:** act out or perform in burlesque or farcical manner ⟨the actor ~*ed* his part splendidly⟩

clown·age \ˈklaủnij\ *n* -s **:** the behavior or function of a clown

clown·ery \ˈklaủnərē\ *n* -ES **:** clownish behavior or an instance of clownishness **:** BUFFOONERY

clown fish *n* **:** a small brilliantly colored barb (*Barbus everetti*) of southeastern Asia and Borneo that is often kept in the tropical aquarium

clownheal \ˈ=,=\ *n* -s [*clown* (countryman) + *heal;* fr. its use in rustic remedies] **:** a hedge nettle (*Stachys palustris*)

clown·ish \ˈklaủnish, -ēsh\ *adj* **:** of or resembling a clown **:** having the characteristics of a clown **syn** see BOORISH

clownishly *adv* **:** in a clownish manner

clown·ish·ness \-nəs\ *n* -ES **:** clownish quality **:** RUDENESS, BUFFOONERY

clown's allheal *n* **:** CLOWNHEAL

cloy \ˈklȯi\ *vb* -ED/-ING/-S [short for *accloy*] *vt* **1** *obs* **:** to prick (a horse) with a nail in shoeing **2** *obs* **:** to fill or choke up **:** stop up **:** CLOG **3 :** to surfeit or make weary with an excess usu. of something orig. pleasing ⟨Cordelia has been ~*ed* by her sisters' excessive protestations of affection —Rebecca West⟩ ~ *vi* **:** to cause surfeit **:** be or become insipid or distasteful usu. through an excess of an orig. pleasurable quality (as sweetness) ⟨persons and places had begun to ~ —*Time*⟩ ⟨few pleasures sooner ~ than reading what the reviewers say —A.T.Quiller-Couch⟩ **syn** see SATIATE

cloyed·ness \ˈklȯidnəs\ *n* -ES **:** the state of being cloyed

cloy·ing \ˈklȯi·iŋ\ *adj* **:** having an excess of a quality (as sweetness or sentimentality) to the point of arousing distaste or disgust ⟨a sweet but not ~ manner —W.A.White⟩ ⟨sentiment more real and less ~ —Katherine G. Jackson⟩ — **cloy·ing·ly** *adv* — **cloy·ing·ness** *n* -ES

cloy·less \ˈklȯiləs\ *adj* **:** that does not cloy

cloy·some \ˈklȯisəm\ *adj* **:** tending to cloy **:** CLOYING

clr *abbr* **1** clear; clearance **2** color

clt *abbr* **1** claimant **2** collateral

CLU *abbr* certified life underwriter; chartered life underwriter

¹club \ˈkləb\ *n* -s [ME *clubbe,* fr. ON *klubba;* akin to OHG *kolbo* club, OE *clympre* lump of metal, *clamm* bond, fetter — more at CLAM] **1 a** (1) **:** a heavy staff esp. of wood usu. tapering and sometimes having an attached head of stone or metal wielded with the hand as a striking weapon ⟨struck down by a blow from his great ~⟩ — see BOOMERANG, MACE, POGAMOGGAN (2) **:** something (as a threat, an argument, or a concept) used as a weapon of attack or intimidation ⟨his threat of resignation becomes a . . . ~ to beat a dissenting majority into line —M.R.Cohen⟩ **b :** a stick or bat used to hit a ball with in any of various games (as golf and hockey) **c** (1) **:** a playing card, in a pack of playing cards, of the suit having a figure like the trefoil or clover leaf represented by the symbol ♣ (2) **:** the figure on such a card (3) **clubs** *pl* **:** the suit of cards having such figure (4) **:** an odd trick won or contracted for with clubs trumps ⟨four ~s bid and made⟩ **d :** something resembling a club esp. in being tapered, short and thick, or knobbed or bunched ⟨a nose with a red ~⟩: as (1) **:** a club-shaped organ or part; *esp* **:** the enlarged terminal part of the antennae of many insects (2) **:** a club-shaped tail or knot in which men's hair is tied at the back, fashionable in the late 18th century **e** (1) **:** a light spar to which the foot of a gaff topsail is bent to extend its spread beyond the gaff and to improve its set (2) **:** a small spar at the after part of the foot of a staysail or jib to which the sheet is attached **f :** INDIAN CLUB **g :** BRAKE CLUB **2** [prob. fr. ²*club*] **a** *obs* (1) **:** a social meeting or gathering (as at a tavern) at which expenses are shared (2) **:** a sharing of a charge or expense (as for a meal or entertainment) by those partaking; *also* **:** one individual's share in such a joint expense ⟨my ~ came to three shillings⟩ **b** (1) **:** an association of persons for social and recreational purposes or for the promotion of some common object (as literature, science, political activity) usu. jointly supported and meeting periodically, membership in social clubs usu. being conferred by ballot and carrying the privilege of use of the club property (2) *obs* **:** a periodical meeting of a society (3) **:** the building, rooms, or other property owned by a club ⟨the dock at the yacht ~⟩ **:** the meeting place of a club ⟨a livery stable . . . served also as a ~ for the male population —Agnes S. Turnbull⟩ **c** *obs* **:** a set or group of persons having common opinions or aims ⟨to bear up under the . . . condemnation of his own ~ —John Locke⟩ **d :** an association of persons participating in a plan by which they agree to make regular payments (as into a savings account) or regular purchases in order to secure some advantage (as price reduction) ⟨book ~⟩ ⟨savings ~⟩ **e :** a commercial establishment serving food and liquor and often featuring music, dancing, or other entertainment **:** NIGHTCLUB ⟨singing at a ~ in Miami —Mary Deasy⟩ **f :** an amateur or professional athletic organization devoted to a particular sport; *also* **:** the team representing such an organization ⟨a major league baseball ~⟩ ⟨a boxing ~⟩

²club \"\ *vb* **clubbed; clubbed; clubbing; clubs** *vt* **1 a :** to beat or strike with or as if with a club ⟨*clubbed* him with the butt of a riding crop⟩ **b :** to gather or combine into a clublike mass or body ⟨~ the hair⟩ **c :** to hold like a club ⟨*clubbed* his newspaper⟩; *esp* **:** to turn (as a musket or rifle) butt uppermost so as to use as a club **2 :** to unite or combine for a common cause or goal ⟨*clubbed* their small means together —Thomas Carlyle⟩ **:** contribute to a common stock, supply, or fund ⟨each ~s his penny toward the purchase⟩ **3** *chiefly Brit* **:** to throw (a body of troops) into confusion ⟨~ a battalion⟩ ~ *vi* **1 :** to come together to form a club or mass **2 :** to combine for the promotion of some common object or joint action ⟨~ together and work out a plan —Julian Huxley⟩ **3 :** to pay an equal or proportionate share of a common charge or expense **:** pay for something by contribution ⟨the owl, the raven, and the bat, *clubbed* for a feather to his hat —Jonathan Swift⟩ **4 :** to drift in a current with an anchor down to ensure control — usu. used with *down*

³club \"\ *adj* **1 :** of or relating to a club **2 :** consisting of foods in a fixed combination offered on a menu at a set price ⟨~ breakfast⟩ ⟨~ luncheon⟩

club·ba·ble *also* **club·a·ble** \ˈkləbəbəl\ *adj* [¹*club* + *-able*] **:** inclined to club together with others **:** SOCIABLE, COMPANIONABLE ⟨a ~ man⟩

club bag *n* **:** a rectangular usu. leather traveling bag that tapers to a purselike opening at the top and that is often zippered

clubbed \ˈkləbd\ *adj* [ME, fr. ¹*club* + *-ed*] **:** shaped like a club: as **a** *of a finger* **:** having a bulbous enlargement of the tip with convex overhanging nail **b** *of a foot* **:** exhibiting the deformity clubfoot **c :** thickened to clublike form at the top — used of the tall letters of Carolingian minuscule writing **d :** affected with the disease clubroot ⟨~ cabbages⟩

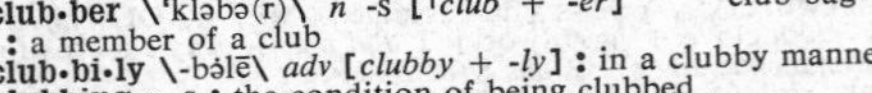

club bag

club·ber \ˈkləbə(r)\ *n* -s [¹*club* + *-er*] **:** a member of a club

club·bi·ly \-bəlē\ *adv* [*clubby* + *-ly*] **:** in a clubby manner

clubbing *n* -s **:** the condition of being clubbed

club·bish \-bish,-bēsh\ *adj* [¹*club* + *-ish*] **:** disposed to club together ⟨a ~ set⟩

club·bist \-bəst\ *n* -s [F *clubiste,* fr. *club* (fr. E) + *-iste* -ist] **:** an advocate of the principles of a political club (as French revolutionary clubs)

club·by \-bē,-bi\ *adj* -ER/-EST [¹*club* + *-y*] **:** characteristic of a club or club members: as **a :** displaying or offering informality, cordiality, or friendliness esp. to other members of the same set or social group **:** SOCIABLE ⟨we got rather ~ —Raymond Chandler⟩ **b :** open only to qualified or approved persons **:** SELECT ⟨the legitimate theater . . . is an uncommonly ~ field of enterprise —E.J.Kahn⟩

club car *n* **:** LOUNGE CAR

club chair *n* **:** a deep low thickly upholstered easy chair often with rather low back and heavy sides and arms

club cheese *n* **:** a process cheese made by grinding cheddar and other cheeses usu. with added condiments and seasonings

club convention *n* [¹*club* (suit)] **:** a system of bidding in contract bridge employing an artificial bid of one club to show a strong hand with 3½ or more quick tricks and an artificial response of one diamond to show a hand with less than 2 quick tricks

club coupe *n* **:** an automobile resembling a coupe in having only two doors but with a full-width rear seat accessible by tilting the front-seat backs forward

club dance *n* [¹*club* (weapon)] **:** a group dance by men armed with clubs and similar to stick and sword dances

clubfoot \ˈ=,=\ *n* [¹*club* + *foot*] **1** *pl* **clubfeet a :** a congenital deformity of the foot in which the forepart of the foot is twisted into one of several directions — called also *talipes* **b :** a foot with such a deformity **2** *pl* **clubfoots :** CLUBROOT — **club-footed** *adj*

club foot *n* [¹*club*] **:** a rounded foot on a flat base on a furniture leg — compare DUTCH FOOT; see FOOT illustration

clubfoot moss *n* **:** CLUB MOSS

club fungus *n* **:** a fungus of the family Clavariaceae

clubhand \ˈ=,=\ *n* [¹*club* + *hand*] **1 :** a congenital deformity in which the hand is short and distorted **2 :** a hand with such a deformity

clubhaul \ˈ=,=\ *vt* [¹*club* (spar) + *haul*] **:** to put (a ship) on the other tack when in danger of going into irons by dropping the lee anchor as the vessel's head comes to the wind and hauling on a hawser from the lee quarter to the anchor until the vessel pays off on the other tack

clubhouse \ˈ=,=\ *n* [¹*club* (association) + *house*] **1 :** a house occupied by a club or commonly used for club activities **2 :** a section of a racetrack pavilion reserved for special ticket holders **3 :** dressing or locker rooms used by an athletic team (as a baseball team) **4 :** a communal dwelling for the unmarried men of certain primitive tribes

club·i·on·i·dae \ˌkləbēˈänəˌdē\ *n pl, cap* [NL, fr. *Clubiona,* type genus (irreg. fr. Gk *kleos* glory + *bioun* to live) + *-idae;* akin to Gk *klytos* famous, Gk *bios* life — more at LOUD, QUICK] **:** a family of terrestrial tube-weaving spiders lacking cribellum, calamistrum, and colulus

clubland \ˈ=lənd, -ˌland\ *n* [¹*club* (association) + *land*] **:** the region or realm of clubs, esp. social clubs

club link *n* **:** a specially formed link which with two or three other links is permanently shackled to the ring of the anchor and by which the anchor is secured to the chain

club·man \ˈ=mən-,-ˌman,-ˌmaa(ə)n\ *n, pl* **clubmen** [¹*club* (association) + *man*] **:** a man given to club life; *esp* **:** a usu. wealthy man belonging to one or more exclusive clubs

club·mo·bile \ˈkləbmōˌbēl\ *n* -s [¹*club* (association) + auto*mobile*] **:** a trailer equipped like a clubroom for serving hot coffee, doughnuts, candy, cigarettes, and supplying recreational equipment to troops or workers

club link

club mold *n* [prob. so called fr. the swollen apex of the conidiophore] **:** a fungus of the genus *Aspergillus*

club moss *n* [trans. of NL *muscus clavatus*] **:** a plant of the order Lycopodiales esp. of the genus *Lycopodium* or the closely related *Selaginella* in some species of which the sporangia are borne in club-shaped strobiles

club-moss family \ˈ=-,=\ *n* **:** LYCOPODIACEAE

club palm *n* [¹*club*] **:** a plant of the genus *Cordyline*

clubroom \ˈ=,=\ *n* **:** a room designed for or as if for the use of a club

clubroot \ˈ=,=\ *n* -s [¹*club* + *root*] **:** a common disease of cabbages and related plants caused by a slime mold (*Plasmodiophora brassicae*) producing swellings or distortions of the root followed often by decline in vigor or by death

club rush *n* [¹*club* (weapon) + *rush*] **1 :** a cattail (*Typha latifolia*) **2 :** a sedge of the genus *Scirpus* **:** BULRUSH

clubs *pl of* CLUB, *pres 3d sing of* CLUB

club sandwich *n* **:** a sandwich usu. of three slices of toast with chicken or turkey, lettuce, tomato, bacon or ham, and mayonnaise

club-shaped \ˈ=,=\ *adj* **:** cylindrical and enlarging gradually toward the end

club shell *n* **:** a mollusk of the genus *Cerithium* **:** HORN SHELL

club skate *n* [prob. short for *New York Club skate,* after a New York skating organization of the 1860s] **:** a skate made to fasten to the shoe by means of clamps or screws

club soda *n* **:** SODA WATER 2a

club sofa *n* **:** a sofa of the same style as a club chair

clubstart \ˈklu̇bˌstärt, ˈkləb-, -ˌstȧt\ *n* -s [¹*club* + *start* (tail)] *dial Eng* **:** STOAT

club steak *n* **:** a small steak cut from the end of the short loin and containing no part of the tenderloin — see BEEF illustration

club·ster \ˈklu̇bstə(r)\ *n* -s [alter. of *clubstart*] *dial Eng* **:** STOAT

club stripe *n* **:** an arrangement of stripes of two or more colors on an article of dress (as a scarf or blazer) orig. representing the colors of a particular club and worn by a club member — compare CLUB TIE

club tie *n* **1 :** a necktie worn by members of a club and bearing the club's colors, usu. in stripes, or the club emblem — compare CLUB STRIPE **2 :** a silk necktie having diagonal stripes of two or more colors

club tooth *n* [¹*club*] **:** a club-shaped tooth used in lever escapement wheels in timepieces designed esp. to retain oil

clubweed \ˈ=,=\ *n* [¹*club* + *weed*] **:** a knapweed (*Centaurea nigra*)

club wheat *n* [¹*club*] **:** a wheat (*Triticum compactum*) or any of its varieties used either as spring wheat or winter wheat and having short thick compact club-shaped spikes and grain that does not shatter and that may be harvested long after it is ripe

clubwoman \ˈ=,==\ *n, pl* **clubwomen :** a woman belonging to a club or active in club and other social or community affairs

clubwood \ˈ=,=\ *n* [¹*club* + *wood*] **1 :** the wood of any species of *Casuarina* **2 :** WAMARA

¹cluck \ˈklək\ *vb* -ED/-ING/-S [imit.] *vi* **1 :** to make the noise of a brooding hen or a similar sound **2 :** to make a clicking sound with the tongue often expressive of alarm, distress, or concern; *also* **:** to express interest or concern ⟨critics ~*ed* over the new developments⟩ ~ *vt* **1 :** to call together, urge, or impel as a hen does her chicks ⟨his mother ~*ed* them hastily to their feet —T.H.Jones⟩ **2 :** to express usu. with interest or concern ⟨~*ed* his approval of the victory⟩ **3 :** to move (the tongue) in such a way as to produce clucks ⟨the driver ~*ed* his tongue and the horse started forward at a sharp trot⟩

²cluck \"\ *n* -s **1 :** the characteristic sound made by a hen esp. in calling her chicks; *also* **:** a sound resembling this **2** *also* **cluck hen :** a broody fowl **3** *slang* **:** a stupid or naive person

clue *var of* CLEW

cluif \ˈklüf\ *Scot var of* CLOOF

cluj \ˈklüzh\ *adj, usu cap* [fr. *Cluj,* Romania] **:** of or from the city of Cluj, Romania **:** of the kind or style prevalent in Cluj

clum *chiefly Midland past of* CLIMB

clum·ber spaniel \ˈkləmbə(r)-\ *n, often cap C&S* [fr. *Clumber,* estate in Nottinghamshire, Eng.] **:** a large spaniel of a breed brought to England from France about 1720 that is massive, heavy-set, and somewhat slow-moving but an expert game finder and very steady and reliable and has a dense silky coat of moderate length lemon and white or orange and white in color, the color preferably being restricted to the head

¹clump \ˈkləmp\ *n* -s [prob. fr. LG *klump;* akin to OE *clympre* lump of metal, OE *clamm* bond, fetter — more at CLAM] **1 :** a group of things clustered together ⟨a ~ of bushes⟩ ⟨people standing around in little ~s⟩ ⟨a ~ of buildings along the road⟩ **2 :** a compact mass **:** a closely compact group or lump ⟨a ~ of roots⟩ ⟨a ~ of dates⟩ **3 :** an aggregation or mass of particles (as of bacteria or blood cells) — compare AGGLUTINATION **4 :** a heavy tramping sound **5 clumps** *pl* **:** a team game in which two players, one from each side, are sent out to agree upon some object, then upon their return each is surrounded by the members of the opposing team who try to guess the chosen object by asking questions to which the answers may be only "Yes," "No," or "I don't know" **6** *Brit* **:** a less-than-type-high slug used as spacing material

²clump \"\ *vb* -ED/-ING/-S *vi* **1 :** to tread clumsily and noisily **2 :** to cluster together in clumps **:** form clumps ⟨the molecules tended to ~⟩ ~ *vt* **1 :** to arrange or cluster in a clump ⟨ships are ~*ed* in the harbor like sitting ducks —*Newsweek*⟩ **:** cause to form clumps ⟨the serum ~s the bacteria⟩ **2 :** to strike heavily **3 :** to group together indiscriminately **:** LUMP ⟨~*ing* the various classes under one heading⟩

clump block *n* **:** a short thick strongly made block with a thick metal sheave having a large opening

clump foot *n* **:** CLUBFOOT 1

clump-head grass \ˈ=,=-\ *n* **:** WOOL GRASS 1

clumproot \ˈ=,=\ *n* **:** CLUBROOT

clumpy \ˈkləmpē\ *adj* -ER/-EST [¹*clump* + *-y*] **:** composed of clumps **:** abounding in clumps **:** growing in clumps

clum·si·ly \ˈkləmzəlē, -li\ *adv* **:** in a clumsy manner

clum·si·ness \ˈkləmzēnəs, -zən-\ *n* -ES **:** the quality of being clumsy

clum·sy \ˈkləmzē, -zi\ *adj* -ER/-EST [prob. fr. obs. E *clumse* benumbed with cold + E *-y;* of Scand origin (like ME *clumsen* to become stiff); akin to Icel *klumsa* lock-jawed, Sw dial. *klumsen* benumbed; akin to OE *clamm* bandage, bond, fetter — more at CLAM] **1 a :** lacking dexterity, skill, nimbleness, or grace (as in the use of the body or limbs or the performance of an action) **:** stiff or awkward in motion ⟨he was a ~ dissector because of his injury —H.G.Wells⟩ **b :** lacking intellectual skill or adroitness, grace or elegance (as in handling words or ideas) **:** lacking tact or subtlety ⟨a ~ joke⟩ ⟨~ diplomacy⟩ **2 :** heavy and unwieldy **:** awkwardly or poorly made ⟨roads were very bad, wagons very slow and ~ —Tom Wintringham⟩ **:** inconvenient, inefficient, or ineffective in use ⟨~ as it was . . . the Aztec picture writing seems to have been adequate —W.H.Prescott⟩ **syn** see AWKWARD

clunch \ˈklənch, ˈklün-\ *n* -ES [origin unknown] **1** *dial Eng* **:** indurated clay **2** *dial Eng* **:** a soft limestone

¹clung *past of* CLING

²clung \ˈkləŋ\ *adj* [ME *clung, clungen,* fr. OE *clungen,* past part. of *clingan* to shrivel, adhere — more at CLING] **1** *dial Brit* **:** collapsed from emptiness **:** SHRUNKEN, SHRIVELED **:** STARVING **2** *dial Eng* **:** stiff and clinging ⟨~ clay⟩

¹clu·ni·ac \ˈklünēˌak\ *adj, usu cap* [ML *Cluniacus,* fr. Abbey of *Cluny,* Cluny, France + L *-acus,* adj. suffix, fr. Gk *-akos*] **:** of or relating to the Cluniacs

²cluniac \"\ *n* -s *usu cap* **:** a monk of a reformed Benedictine congregation established in 910 at Cluny, France

¹clunk \ˈkləŋk\ *n* -s [imit.] **1** *chiefly Scot* **:** a sound such as is made when a cork is suddenly drawn or when liquid flows intermittently from a bottle **2 :** a blow or the sound of a blow **:** THUMP **3 :** a dull or stupid person

²clunk \"\ *vb* -ED/-ING/-S *vi* **1 :** to make a clunk, esp. a dull thumping or bumping **2 :** to hit something with a clunk ⟨the gun . . . ~*ed* on the floor —Mickey Spillane⟩ ~ *vt* **1** *dial Eng* **:** to swallow with audible effort **2 :** to strike or hit with a clunk

clunk·er \-kə(r)\ *n* -s [prob. fr. ²*clunk* + *-er*] *slang* **:** a dilapidated rattling old machine; *esp* **:** JALOPY

clun·ter \ˈkləntə(r)\ *vi* -ED/-ING/-S [origin unknown] *dial Eng* **:** to make a clumping or clattering noise

clu·ny lace \ˈklünē-, =ˈ=-\ *n, usu cap C* [fr. the Abbey of *Cluny,* Cluny, France, where it was used by the monks] **:** a fairly sturdy bobbin lace for clothing and interior decoration made by hand or machine of linen or cotton thread and characterized by wheat or wheel designs on a coarse mesh

clu·pan·o·don·ic acid \(ˌ)klüˌpanəˈdänik-, ¦klüpə(ˌ)nō¦-\ *n* [ISV *clupanodon-* (fr. NL *Clupanodon* genus name of the small Japanese fish *Clupanodon melanosticta,* fr. L *clupea,* a small fish + Gk *anodōn* toothless, fr. *an-* an- + *odōn* tooth) + *-ic* — more at TOOTH] **:** a highly unsaturated acid $C_{21}H_{33}COOH$ obtained as a light yellow oil from fish, liver, and blubber oils

clu·pea \ˈklüpēə\ *n, cap* [NL, fr. L, a small river fish] **:** the type genus of Clupeidae comprising the typical herrings

¹clu·pe·id \ˈklüpēəd, -ˌid\ *adj* [NL *Clupeidae*] **:** of or relating to the Clupeidae

²clupeid \"\ *n* -s **:** a fish of the family Clupeidae

clu·pe·i·dae \klüˈpēəˌdē\ *n pl, cap* [NL, fr. *Clupea,* type genus + *-idae*] **:** a large family of soft-finned teleost fishes (order Isospondyli) including the herrings, sardines, shads, menhaden, and related forms all having a narrow compressed body and forked tail

clu·pe·ine \ˈklüpēˌēn, -ˌən\ *also* **clu·pe·in** \-ēən\ *n* -s [ISV *clup-* (fr. NL *Clupea*) + *-ine, -in*] **:** a protamine contained in the spermatozoa of the herring

¹clu·pe·oid \-pēˌȯid\ *adj* [NL *Clupeoidea*] **:** of or relating to or like the herrings or the Clupeoidea

²clupeoid \"\ *n* -s **:** a clupeoid fish

clu·pe·oi·dea \ˌklüpēˈȯidēə\ *n pl, cap* [NL, fr. *Clupea* + *-oidea*] **:** a large suborder (order Isospondyli) comprising the herrings and related fishes

clu·pe·oi·dei \-dēˌī\ *syn of* CLUPEOIDEA

cluse \ˈklüz\ *n* -s [F, fr. MF (dial.), fr. ML *clusa,* fr. L, fem. of *clusus, clausus,* past part. of *claudere* to close — more at CLOSE] **:** a narrow gorge cutting transversely through an otherwise continuous ridge

clu·sia \ˈklüzh(ē)ə\ *n* [NL, fr. Charles de Lécluse (Carolus *Clusius*) †1609 Fr. botanist + NL *-ia*] **1** *cap* **:** a large genus of tropical American aromatic trees or shrubs (family Guttiferae) having opposite coriaceous leaves and large white, yellow, or pink flowers **2** -s **:** any tree of the genus *Clusia* — see WAXFLOWER, WILD FIG

clu·si·a·ce·ae \ˌklüz(h)ēˈāsēˌē\ [NL, fr. *Clusia,* type genus + *-aceae*] *syn of* GUTTIFERAE

¹clus·ter \ˈkləstə(r)\ *n* -s [ME *cluster, clustre,* fr. OE *clyster, cluster;* akin to LG *kluster* cluster, OE *clott* lump, mass — more at CLOT] **1 :** a number of things of the same kind (as fruit or flowers) growing closely together **:** BUNCH ⟨a flower ~⟩ ⟨a ~ of coral animals⟩ **2 :** a number of similar things grouped together in association or in physical proximity ⟨a ~ of houses⟩ ⟨little ~s of settlers scattered along the coast⟩: as **a :** a number of honeybees clinging together in a solid mass **b :** an aggregation of stars, galaxies, or supergalaxies that appear close together in the sky and seem to have common properties (as distance and motion) — see GLOBULAR CLUSTER, MOVING CLUSTER **c :** two or more electric lamps grouped together on a single fixture **d :** the group of four cups that connect the teats of a cow to a milking machine **3 :** a number of similar things considered as a group because of their relation to each other or their simultaneity of occurrence or for convenience in treatment or discussion ⟨tone ~s which are known as blue —Rudi Blesh⟩ ⟨the great ~ of inventions of the last quarter of the 19th century —Bruce Bliven b.1889⟩ ⟨a ~ of characteristics⟩ **4 :** two or more consecutive consonants or vowels in a segment of speech ⟨the consonant sounds for the italics in "*winch sprocket*" are a ~⟩

²cluster \"\ *vb* **clustered; clustered; clustering** \-t(ə)riŋ\ **clusters** [ME *clusteren,* fr. *cluster,* n.] *vt* **1 :** to collect into a cluster or clusters **:** gather into a bunch ⟨~ ten or a dozen of these together, with several smaller sheds and tents —Walt Whitman⟩ **2 :** to furnish or cover with clusters ⟨the bridge was ~*ed* with men and officers —Herman Wouk⟩ ~ *vi* **:** to grow in clusters or assemble in groups **:** collect, gather, or unite in a cluster or clusters ⟨men ~ around the stove⟩ ⟨legends have already ~*ed* about his name⟩

cluster bean *n* **:** GUAR

clusterberry \ˈ==- — *see* BERRY\ *n* **:** MOUNTAIN CRANBERRY

cluster clover *also* **clustered clover** *n* **:** an annual clover (*Trifolium glomeratum*) having globular purplish heads native to Europe but now grown elsewhere esp. in No. America and Australasia as a hay and forage plant

cluster cup *n* : AECIUM
cluster–cup stage \'==,=-\ *n* : the aecial stage of a rust fungus
clustered *adj* [ME, fr. ¹*cluster* + *-ed*] **1** : formed or located in clusters — compare SOLITARY 5a **2** : composed or apparently composed of several similar elements clustered together ⟨a ~ pier⟩ ⟨a ~ column⟩
clustered bluet *n* : a weed (*Oldenlandia uniflora*) having buttonlike clusters of tiny flowers
clustered poppy mallow *n* : a perennial herb (*Callirhoë triangulata*) of the prairie regions of the U.S. with purple flowers in panicled clusters
cluster fig *n* : an East Indian fig (*Ficus glomerata*) often planted as a shade tree having tapering leaves, small clusters of red fruit, and astringent bark — called also *country fig*
cluster flower *n* : a plant of the genus *Cestrum*
cluster fly *n* : a large dark-brown fly (*Pollenia rudis*) related to the bluebottles and often gathering in large clusters in attics and other sheltered places during cool autumn weather
cluster gear *n* : a set of gears of different sizes mounted as a unit on the same shaft — called also *gear cluster*

clustered pier

clus·ter·ing·ly *adv* : in a clustering manner
cluster pepper *n* **1** : a hot pepper (*Capsicum frutescens fasciculatum*) with slender elongated bright red and extremely pungent fruits borne erect in clusters **2** : the fruit of a cluster pepper
cluster piles *n pl* : piles driven in a close bundle and usu. lashed together with chains or steel bands
cluster pine *also* **cluster fir** *n* [so called fr. its cones] : a pyramidal pine (*Pinus pinaster*) of the Mediterranean region with reflexed bud scales and needles in pairs
clusters *pl of* CLUSTER, *pres 3d sing of* CLUSTER
cluster variable *n* : a short-period variable star of Cepheid characteristics and a period of light fluctuations not longer than a day orig. found in globular clusters but abundant elsewhere in the Milky Way galaxy — called also *cluster-type Cepheid*
cluster wheat *n* : CLUB WHEAT
¹**clutch** \'kləch\ *vb* -ED/-ING/-ES [ME *clucchen*, fr. OE *clyccan*; akin to OFris *kletsie* spear, Sw *klyka* fork, crotch, MHG *klok* spot, ON *klakkr* lump, MIr *glacc* hand — more at CLING] *vt* **1 a** : to seize, grip, or hold with the hand or claws usu. strongly, tightly, or suddenly ⟨sleeps . . . with his musket . . . ~*ed* tightly —S.V.Benét⟩ ⟨~*ed* his arm fiercely⟩ **b** : to hold or try to retain control or possession of : SEIZE ⟨~ power⟩ **2** *obs* : to close tightly : CLENCH ⟨~*ing* hands⟩ ~ *vi* **1** : to seek to hold or retain possession ⟨~*ed* at her son's devotion —Andrea Parke⟩ : take immediate advantage or make immediate use (as of an idea or an opportunity) — often used with *at* ⟨~ at remedies that her calmer self would have put by —H.O.Taylor⟩ **2** : GRASP, HOLD ⟨roots that ~ deeply into the earth⟩ **3** : to operate a clutch (sense 3) **syn** see TAKE
²**clutch** \"\ *adj* **1** *of a woman's coat* : lacking fasteners and suitable for holding closed with the hand or arm **2** *of a woman's handbag* : lacking handles and of a size and shape suitable for clasping in the hand
³**clutch** \"\ *n* -ES [ME *cloche, clowche*, alter. (influenced by ME *clucchen* to clutch) of *cloke, cluke*; akin to OE *clyccan* to clutch] **1 a** : the claws or a hand in the act of grasping or seizing firmly ⟨a rabbit in the ~ of a hawk⟩ **b** : control, power, or possession esp. of a rapacious or cruel person or an unrelenting force ⟨in the dry, womanless ~ of the army —Irwin Shaw⟩ ⟨the fell ~ of circumstance —W.E.Henley⟩ — often used in pl. ⟨in the ~*es* of a desperate infatuation —Delmore Schwartz⟩ **c** : the act of grasping, holding, or restraining : GRASP, GRIP ⟨the gravitational ~ of the earth —*N.Y. Times*⟩ **2** : a device for gripping an object, as at the end of a chain or tackle **3 a** : a coupling used to connect and disconnect a driving and a driven part of a mechanism esp. one that permits the former part to engage the latter gradually and without shock — see BAND CLUTCH, CENTRIFUGAL CLUTCH, CONE CLUTCH, DISK CLUTCH, FRICTION CLUTCH, MAGNETIC CLUTCH, MAGNETIC FLUID CLUTCH **b** : a lever operating such a clutch **4** : a tight or critical situation (as when the outcome of a game is at stake) : PINCH ⟨a batter able to come through with a hit in the ~⟩ ⟨a good ~ hitter⟩
⁴**clutch** \"\ *n* -ES [alter. of *cletch*] **1 a** : a nest of eggs or a brood of chicks **b** : a group of offspring produced at a birth **2** : the eggs laid by a bird at regular consecutive intervals without intervening longer pauses **3** : GROUP, BUNCH ⟨a whole ~ of people trooped in together —Mollie Panter-Downes⟩
clutch·man \'=mən, -,man\ *n, pl* **clutchmen** [³*clutch* + *man*] : one who operates a clutch; *specif* : one operating a clutch on a beet-slicing machine — called also *cutterman*
cluth·er \'klu̇thə(r), -əth-\ *n* -S [var. of ²*clutter*] *dial Brit* : a large quantity : CLUSTER, BUNCH
¹**clut·ter** \'klədə(r), -ətə-\ *vb* -ED/-ING/-S [alter. of earlier *clotter*, fr. ME *clotteren* to clot, fr. *clot* + *-eren* (freq. suffix) — more at CLOT] *vt* **1** *dial* : to crowd together in disorder **2** : to fill or cover with things in disorder or scattered at random or with things that impede movement or action or reduce effectiveness ⟨a ~*ed* room⟩ ⟨an author . . . may ~ his explanations with digressive evidence that delays the reader —G.W.Sherburn⟩ — often used with *up* ⟨the roads of France ~*ed* up with refugees —Henri Peyre⟩ ~ *vi* **1** *now chiefly dial* **a** : to run together in knots or confused crowds : run in disorder **b** : to make a confused noise : BUSTLE **2** *archaic* : to speak confusedly or inarticulately : jumble words
²**clutter** \"\ *n* -S **1 a** : a crowded or confused mass or collection ⟨a ~ of shops and tenements⟩ : a mass of disorderly or distracting objects or details ⟨pure and noble design, unspoiled by ~ or ornament —E.K.Brown⟩ ⟨steaming . . . seaward among a ~ of sister ships—K.M.Dodson⟩ **b** : LITTER, DISORDER ⟨photographs . . . propped up amid a ~ of china ornaments —Hamilton Basso⟩ ⟨pushing aside the ~ on the table —Harriet LaBarre⟩ **c** : the visual indication on a radar screen of interference or echo from objects other than the target tending to obscure target indication — compare SEA RETURN **2** *now dial* : turmoil or confusion of movement or activity : DISTURBANCE, HUBBUB : confused noise ⟨ladies who were apt to make the greatest ~ upon such occasions—Jonathan Swift⟩ **syn** see CONFUSION
clut·ter·er \-ərə(r)\ *n* -S : one whose speech is defective by reason of cluttering
cluttering *n* -S : a speech defect in which phonetic units are dropped, condensed, or otherwise distorted as a result of overly rapid agitated utterance
¹**cly** \'klī\ *vt* [perh. fr. LG *kleien* to scratch, fr. MLG; akin to Flem *klauwen* to scratch, steal, G *klauen*, OHG *klāwa* claw — more at CLAW] *slang* : SEIZE, STEAL
²**cly** \"\ *n* -ES [perh. fr. ¹*cly*] *slang* : POCKET, PURSE
clydes·dale \'klīdz,dāl\ *n* -S *usu cap* [fr. *Clydesdale*, valley in Scotland where it originated] : a heavy draft horse of a breed orig. from Clydesdale, Scotland, distinguished by a dark brown or black coat, white blaze and stockings, and heavy feathering about the fetlock
clydesdale terrier *n, usu cap C* [fr. *Clydesdale*, valley in Scotland where it originated] : a small terrier of a breed resulting from selective breeding of the Skye terrier and distinguished by tiny erect ears, a long and silky coat, and short legs
clyde·side \'klīd,sīd\ *adj, usu cap* [*Clyde*, river in Scotland + E *side*] : of or relating to the region along the Clyde in Scotland; *esp* : having to do with shipbuilding, the chief industry of this region
clyde·sider \-də(r)\ *n* -S *cap* : a native or resident of the region along the Clyde in Scotland
cly·er \'klī(ə)r\ *n* -S [D *klier* gland, scrofula, fr. MD *cliere*; akin to Fris *klīr* gland] **1** : a tuberculous lymph gland in cattle **2** **clyers** *pl* : tuberculosis of the bovine lymphatic system
cly·me·nel·la \,klīmə'nelə, ,klim-\ *n, cap* [NL, fr. L *Clymene*, an Oceanid (fr. L, fr. Gk *Klymenē*) + NL *-ella*] : a genus of polychaete worms common in shallow waters of the northern Atlantic coasts — see BAMBOO WORM
¹**clym·e·nid** \'klimənəd, -,nid\ *adj* [NL *Clymenidae*] : of or relating to the Clymenidae
²**clymenid** \"\ *n* -S : a clymenid ammonoid
cly·men·i·dae \klī'menə,dē, klə'-\ *n pl, cap* [NL, fr. *Clymenia*, type genus (fr. *Clymene* + NL *-ia*) + *-idae*] : a family of extinct Devonian ammonoids having the siphuncle at the dorsal margin of the whorls
clype \'klīp\ *vi* -ED/-ING/-S [alter. of earlier *cleip*, fr. ME *clepien* to call — more at CLEPE] *Scot* : to tell secrets : TATTLE
clyp·e·al \'klipēəl\ *adj* [NL *clypeus* + E *-al*] : of or relating to a clypeus
clyp·e·as·ter \,klipē'astə(r)\ *n, cap* [NL, fr. L *clypeus* round shield + NL *-aster*] : a widely distributed genus (the type of the family Clypeastridae) of large burrowing cake urchins
clyp·e·as·trid·ea \,=pēə'stridēə\ [NL, fr. *Clypeastr-*, *Clypeaster* + *-idea*] *syn of* CLYPEASTRINA
clyp·e·as·tri·na \-ə'strīnə, -rēnə\ *n pl, cap* [NL, fr. *Clypeaster* + *-ina*] : a suborder of sea urchins (order Exocycloida) comprising a large number of flattened more or less discoidal sea urchins (as the cake urchins and sand dollars) — compare SPATANGINA
¹**clyp·e·as·troid** \,==';a,strȯid\ *adj* [NL *Clypeastroida*] : of or relating to the Clypeastrina
²**clypeastroid** \"\ *n* -S : one of the Clypeastrina : CAKE URCHIN
clyp·e·as·troi·da \,==ə'strȯidə\ *or* **clyp·e·as·troi·dea** \-ēə\ [NL *Clypeastroida*, alter. of *Clypeastroidea*, fr. *Clypeaster* + *-oidea*] *syn of* CLYPEASTRINA
clyp·e·ate \'klipēət, -ē,āt, *usu* -d· + V\ *or* **clyp·e·at·ed** \-,ād·əd\ *or* **clyp·e·i·form** \-pēə,fȯrm\ *adj* [*clypeate* fr. L *clypeus* round shield + E *-ate*; *clypeated* fr. L *clypeus* + E *-ate* + *-ed*; *clypeiform* fr. L *clypeus* + E *-iform*] **1** *biol* : shaped like a round buckler or shield : SCUTATE **2** *biol* : furnished with a clypeus or with a shieldlike plate or process
clyp·e·ole \-,ōl\ *also* **cly·pe·o·la** \klə'pēələ\ *n, pl* **clypeoles** \-lz\ *or* **clypeo·lae** \-ə,lē\ [NL *clypeola*, fr. L *clypeus* round shield + *-ola* -ole] : one of the shield-shaped sporophylls composing the fertile spike in members of the genus *Equisetum*
clyp·e·us \'klipēəs\ *n, pl* **clyp·ei** \-ē,ī\ [NL, fr. L *clipeus, clupeus, clypeus* round shield] **1** : a plate or shield on the anterior median aspect of an insect's head that commonly consists of two fused sclerites and bears the labrum on its anterior margin **2** *bot* : a black disklike tissue formed about the mouth of the perithecia in certain ascomycetes **3** : the area on the front of a spider's head bounded by the eyes and the first pair of appendages
cly·sis \'klīsəs\ *n, pl* **cly·ses** \-,sēz\ [NL, fr. Gk *klysis*, fr. *klyzein* to wash] : the introduction of large amounts of fluid into the body usu. by parenteral injection to replace that lost (as from hemorrhage or in dysentery or burns), to provide nutrients, or to maintain blood pressure — see HYPODERMOCLYSIS, PHLEBOCLYSIS, PROCTOCLYSIS
clys·ma \'klizmə\ *n, pl* **clysma·ta** \-məd·ə\ [NL, fr. Gk *klysma*, fr. *klyzein*] : ENEMA
clys·ter \'klistə(r)\ *n* -S [ME, fr. MF or L; MF *clistere*, fr. L *clyster*, fr. Gk *klystēr*, fr. *klyzein* to wash out; akin to OE *hlūtor* clean, pure, OHG *hlūtar*, ON *hlēr* sea, Goth *hluts* pure, clean, L *cluere* to purge, W *clir* clear, clean, Lith *šlúoti* to sweep] : ENEMA
clys·sus \'klisəs\ *n, pl* **clys·si** \-,sī\ [NL] : a quintessence or efficacious principle
clyte \'klīt\ *var of* CLOIT
cm *abbr* **1** centimeter **2** cumulative
CM *abbr* **1** *often not cap* [L *causa mortis*] by reason of death **2** center matched **3** certificated master; certificated mistress **4** circular measure **5** *often not cap* circular mil **6** common meter **7** corresponding member **8** countermark; countermarked **9** courtmartial
Cm *symbol* curium
c major *n, usu cap C* : the major musical key having neither sharps nor flats in its signature
cmd *abbr* command
CMD *abbr* common meter double
cmdg *abbr* commanding
cmdr *abbr* commander
cmdre *abbr* commodore
c melody *n, usu cap C* : a tenor saxophone in C instead of the usual B flat
c minor *n, usu cap C* : the minor musical key having a signature of three flats
c–mitosis \'sē+\ *n* [colchicine + *mitosis*] : an artificially induced abortive nuclear division in which the chromosome number is doubled (as that caused by exposure of cells to colchicine)
c–mitotic \" +\ *adj* : of, like, or inducing c-mitosis
cml *abbr* commercial
cn *abbr* **1** canon **2** consolidated
CN *abbr* **1** case of need **2** circular note **3** compass north **4** consignment note **5** cover note **6** credit note
-cne·mia \(k)'nēmēə\ *n comb form* [NL, fr. F *-cnémie*, fr. Gk *knēmē* shin + F *-ie* -y] : -shinnedness ⟨platy*cnemia*⟩
cne·mi·al \'nēmēəl\ *adj* [Gk *knēmē* shin + E *-ial*] : relating to the shin or shinbone
-cne·mic \(k)'nēmik\ *adj comb form* [ISV *-cnem-* (fr. Gk *knēmē* shin) + *-ic*; prob. orig. formed as F *-cnémique*] : -shinned ⟨platy*cnemic*⟩
cne·mi·do·cop·tes \,nēmə(,)dō'käp,tēz\ [NL, alter. of *knemidokoptes*, fr. Gk *knēmid-, knēmis* greave (fr. *knēmē* shin) + MGk *koptēs* cutter, fr. Gk *koptein* to cut — more at CAPON] *syn of* KNEMIDOKOPTES
cne·mi·doph·o·rus \,nēmə'däfərəs\ *n, cap* [NL, fr. Gk *knēmidophoros* wearing greaves, fr. *knēmid-, knēmis* greave + *-phoros* -phorous] : a genus of American lizards of the family Teiidae — see RACE RUNNER
cne·mis \'nēməs\ *n, pl* **cnem·i·des** \'nemə,dēz\ [NL, fr. Gk *knēmis* greave, fr. *knēmē* shin] : SHIN, TIBIA
-cne·mus \(k)'nēməs\ *n comb form* [NL, modif. of Gk. *knēmē* shin] : -legged one — in generic names of animals ⟨Octa*cnemus*⟩
cne·o·rum \nē'ōrəm, -ȯr-\ *n, cap* [NL, fr. Gk *kneōron*, a plant, prob. spurge flax (*Daphne gnidium*); prob. akin to Goth *hnasqus* soft, Skt *kiknasa* grits, and L *cinis* ashes — more at INCINERATE] : a small genus (constituting a family Cneoraceae of the order Geraniales) of low evergreen shrubs of the Mediterranean region having oblong or spatulate coriaceous leaves and small axillary cymose or solitary flowers
cni·cus \'nīkəs\ *n, cap* [NL, fr. L *cnicus, cnecus* safflower, fr. Gk *knēkos* safflower, thistle, yellow — more at HONEY] : a genus of European herbs of the family Compositae — see BLESSED THISTLE
cnid- *or* **cnido-** *comb form* [NL, fr. *cnida*] : cnida ⟨*cnido*sac⟩ ⟨*cnido*glandular⟩ ⟨*Cnid*aria⟩
cni·da \'nīdə\ *n, pl* **cni·dae** \-(,)dē\ [NL, fr. Gk *knidē* nettle, sea nettle; akin to L *nidor* smell of roasting meat — more at NIDOR] : NEMATOCYST
cni·dar·ia \nī'da(a)rēə\ [NL, fr. *cnid-* + *-aria*] *syn of* COELENTERATA — used esp. to distinguish the narrow from the more inclusive scope of Coelenterata
¹**cni·dar·i·an** \(')=;rēən\ *adj* [NL *Cnidaria* + E *-an*] : of or relating to a cnida or the Cnidaria
²**cnidarian** \"\ *n* -S : one of the Cnidaria
cni·do·blast \'nīdə,blast\ *n* -S [ISV *cnid-* + *-blast*; orig. formed in G] : a cell that develops a nematocyst or develops into a nematocyst
cni·do·cell \-,sel\ *n* -S [*cnid-* + *cell*] : NEMATOCYST
cni·do·cil \-,sil\ *n* -S [ISV *cnid-* + NL *cilium* hairlike process — more at CILIA] : a minute process of a nematocyst that when touched is believed to cause the projection of the stinging thread
cni·do·cyst \-,sist\ *n* -S [ISV *cnid-* + *-cyst*] : NEMATOCYST
cni·do·phore \-,fō(ə)r\ *n* -S [*cnid-* + *-phore*] : a structure bearing nematocysts — **cni·doph·o·rous** \(')nī'däfərəs\ *adj*
cni·do·pod \-,päd\ *n* -S [*cnid-* + *-pod*] : the stalklike base of a nematocyst
cni·do·sco·lus \,==';skōləs\ *n, cap* [NL, fr. *cnido-* (fr. Gk *knidē* nettle) + Gk *skōlos* thorn, pointed stake; akin to Gk *skallein* to hoe — more at CNIDA, SHELL] : a genus of stinging perennial herbaceous or shrubby plants (family Euphorbiaceae) characterized by alternate mostly long-petioled palmately veined and often lobed or divided leaves and stipules armed with stinging bristles
cni·do·spo·rid·ia \-spə'ridēə\ *n pl, cap* [NL, fr. *cnid-* + *-sporidia*] : a subclass of Sporozoa comprising protozoans that have complex spores with polar capsules and coiled polar filaments and are single-host parasites of lower vertebrates and invertebrates — see ACTINOMYXIDIA, MICROSPORIDIA, MYXOSPORIDIA — **cni·do·spo·rid·i·an** \;===;ridēən\ *adj or n*
cnossian *usu cap, var of* KNOSSIAN
c–note \'sē + ,-\ *n* -S *usu cap C, slang* : a 100-dollar bill
cnr *abbr* corner
CNS *abbr* central nervous system
co- *prefix* [ME, fr. L, fr. *com-*; akin to OE *ge-*, perfective, associative, and collective prefix, OHG *gi-, ga-*, Goth *ga-*, OIr *com-, con-* with, together, Alb *kë-*, Gk *koinos* common] **1** : with : together : joint : jointly : shared : mutual : mutually ⟨*co*exist⟩ ⟨*co*inheritance⟩ ⟨*co*sustain⟩ ⟨*co*operate⟩ **2** : in or to the same degree ⟨*co*extensive⟩ ⟨*co*eval⟩ **3 a** : fellow : partner ⟨*co*author⟩ ⟨*co*-worker⟩ **b** : having a usu. lesser share in duty or responsibility : alternate : deputy ⟨*co*chairman⟩ ⟨*co*pilot⟩ **4 a** : operating together or reciprocally ⟨*co*term⟩ **b** : of the complement of an angle ⟨*co*sine⟩ ⟨*co*declination⟩
co *abbr* **1** colon **2** company **3** container **4** coral **5** county
CO \'sē'ō\ *abbr or n* -S **1** commanding officer **2** conscientious objector
CO *abbr* **1** *often not cap* care of — usu. separated by a virgule **2** carried over **3** cash order **4** certificate of origin **5** colonial office **6** commissioner for oaths **7** communications officer **8** cut out
Co *symbol* cobalt
¹**co·acer·vate** \kō'asər,vāt, ,kōə'sər,-\ *vt* -ED/-ING/-S [L *coacervatus*] : to heap up : gather together in a heap or group : COLLECT; *esp* : to cause to form a coacervate
²**co·acer·vate** \,kōə'sərvət, (')kō;asər,vāt\ *adj* [L *coacervatus*, past part. of *coacervare* to heap up, fr. *co-* + *acervare* (fr. *acervus* heap); perh. akin to L *acus* chaff — more at EAR] **1** : piled up : collected into a crowd **2** : growing in dense clusters
³**coacervate** \"\ *n* -S : an aggregate of colloidal droplets (as of two hydrophilic sols or of a sol and ions of opposite charge) held together by electrostatic attractive forces
co·acer·va·tion \(,)kō,asə(r)'vāshən\ *n* -S : the process of becoming a coacervate : mutual precipitation : AGGREGATION, COAGULATION ⟨~ of gelatin and gum arabic⟩
¹**coach** \'kōch\ *n* -ES *often attrib* [ME *coche*, fr. MF, fr. G *kutsche*, prob. fr. Hung *kocsi* (*szekér*) wagon from Kocs, fr. *Kocs*, village in Hungary] **1 a** : a large usu. closed 4-wheeled carriage having doors in the sides and generally a front and a back seat inside and an elevated seat in front for the driver **b** *Brit* : a railway passenger or mail car **c** : a railroad passenger car with reclining or nonreclining seats that is intended primarily for day travel **d** : BABY CARRIAGE **e** : a closed 2-door single-compartment automobile with permanent back panel and top and in front two separate seats which may be turned down and in the rear a full-width cross seat **f** : MOTOR COACH **g** : HOUSE TRAILER **h** : an automobile body esp. of a closed model **i** : a class of passenger air transportation at a lower fare than first class **2** : a cabin on the afterpart of the quarterdeck of a man-of-war usu. occupied by the captain **3 a** [so called fr. the tutor's being regarded as a means for conveying the student through his examinations] : a private tutor who assists students esp. in preparing for examination **b** : one who instructs or trains a performer or a team of performers (as in debating or in musical or dramatic performance); *specif* : one who instructs players in the fundamentals of a competitive sport and directs team strategy ⟨fencing ~⟩ ⟨football ~⟩ — compare MANAGER, TRAINER **c** : a manual with a condensed body of information on a subject to be committed to memory **d** : a member of a team at bat in baseball who is posted near first or third base to direct base runners and signal to batters **4** *Austral* : a decoy bullock used to catch wild cattle **5** : SPONSOR 4b

coach 1a

²**coach** \"\ *vb* -ED/-ING/-ES *vt* **1** *archaic* : to transport in, place in, or provide with a coach **2 a** : to train intensively by detailed instruction, frequent demonstration, and repeated practice (as for an examination, a dramatic performance, or a public appearance) ⟨~ pupils⟩ ⟨there never was a witness so obviously ~*ed*⟩ **b** : to act as coach to (an athletic team or performer) **c** : to direct the movements of (a base runner) **d** : to give instructions, directions, or prompting to (one performing or attempting something) ⟨two escort vessels, the first maintaining sound contact . . . while it ~*ed* the second . . . by signals —J.P.Baxter b.1893⟩ ~ *vi* **1** : to go in a coach ⟨he ~*ed* to that licentious city —S.H.Adams⟩ **2 a** : to instruct as a coach : receive instruction from a coach **b** : to direct the movements of a base runner **syn** see TEACH
coach–and–four \;=;=ˈs\ *n* -S : a coach with four horses
coach box *n* : the driver's seat on a coach
coachbuilding \'=,=\ *n, Brit* : the design and manufacture of automobile bodies
coach dog *n* [so called fr. its formerly being used to run in attendance on a coach] : DALMATIAN
coach·ee \kō'chē *often and in sense 2 usu* '=(,)=\ *n* -S **1** : an American carriage shaped like a coach but longer and open in front **2** : COACHMAN
coach·er \'kōchə(r)\ *n* -S [In sense 1, fr. MF *cocher*, fr. *coche*; in sense 2, fr. ¹*coach* + *-er*; in sense 3, fr. ²*coach* + *-er*] **1** *obs* : COACHMAN **2** : COACH HORSE **3** : one that coaches; *specif* : COACH 3d
coach horn *n* : a long straight tapering copper horn with slight flare — compare POST HORN
coach horse *n* : a horse used or adapted for drawing a coach, being typically heavier and of more compact build than a road horse and exhibiting good style and action
coach house *n* : an outbuilding for a coach or carriage
coaching *n* -S **1 a** : traveling by coach **b** : pleasure driving in a coach (as in a tallyho) **2 a** : the profession or occupation of a coach **b** : instruction given esp. in private by or as if by a coach ⟨she learned reading under the ~ of her mother⟩
coaching house *n* : an inn serving coach travelers
coaching traffic *n* [¹*coach* (railroad car) + *-ing*] *Brit* : railroad passenger traffic
¹**coach·man** \'=mən\ *n, pl* **coachmen** [¹*coach* + *man*] **1** : a man whose business is to drive a coach or carriage **2** *angling* : an artificial fly with white wings, peacock herl body, brown hackle, and gold tag
²**coachman** \"\ *adj, of women's clothing* : imitative of the double-breasted coat with fitted waist and wide lapels formerly worn by coachmen
coach roof *n, chiefly Brit* : the roof of the cabin on a small boat
coach screw *n* : LAG SCREW
coachwhip \'=,=\ *n* **1** : a whip usu. provided with a long lash and used in driving a coach **2** : OCOTILLO 1 **3** : COACHWHIP SNAKE **4** : LONG PENNANT
coachwhip bird *n* : a babblerlike Australian passerine bird of the genus *Psophodes*; *esp* : a bird (*P. olivaceus*) having a note resembling the crack of a whip
coachwhip snake *n* : a long slender active colubrid snake (*Coluber*, syn. *Masticophis*, *flagellum*) of the southern U.S. of which the scale pattern resembles a braided whip
coachwood \'=,=\ *n* [so called fr. its use in coachbuilding] **1** : either of two Australian trees of the family Cunoniaceae: **a** : a medium-sized tree (*Ceratopetalum apetalum*) with grayish bark and dry hard fruits surrounded by winglike calyx lobes — called also *leatherjacket* **b** : a medium-sized to large tree (*Schizomeria ovata*) with a succulent egg-shaped fruit — called also *white cherry* **2** : the heavy tough fine-grained wood of the coachwood (sense 1a) pinkish in color but darkening on exposure and used chiefly for veneers and in cabinetwork — called also *scented satinwood*
coachwork \'=,=\ *n* : the design, building, and finishing of automobile bodies
¹**coachy** \'kōchē, -chi\ *n* -ES [alter. of *coachee*] : COACHMAN
²**coachy** \"\ *adj* [¹*coach* (*horse*) + *-y*] : like a coach horse esp. in configuration
¹**co·act** \kō'akt\ *vt* -ED/-ING/-S [ME *coacten*, fr. L *coactus*, past part. of *cogere* to compel — more at COGENT] : FORCE, COMPEL, DRIVE, CONTROL

[2]**coact** \(ˈ)kō +\ *vi* -ED/-ING/-S [*co-* + *act* (verb)] **:** to act or work together

co·act·ee \ˌkō,akˈtē, kōˌakˈtē\ *n* -S [[2]*coact* + *-ee*] **:** an organism that passively participates in coaction (as a food species in a food chain)

[1]**co·ac·tion** \kōˈakshən\ *n* -S [ME *coaccioun*, fr. MF *coaction*, fr. L *coaction-, coactio* collection, fr. *coactus* (past part. of *cogere* to collect, compel) + *-ion-, -io* -ion — more at COGENT] **:** force or compulsion in restraining or impelling **:** CONTROL

[2]**coaction** \(ˈ)kō +\ *n* [*co-* + *action*] **1 :** action taken together **:** joint action **:** an acting together **2 :** the relation or interaction that exists between individuals or kinds of organisms (as species) in an ecological community and typically takes the form of cooperation, disoperation, or competition — compare REACTION

[1]**co·ac·tive** \(ˈ)kōˈaktiv\ *adj* [[1]*coact* + *-ive*] **:** serving to compel or constrain **:** of compulsory nature **:** RESTRICTIVE ⟨any ~ power of the civil kind —William Warburton⟩ — **co·ac·tive·ly** *adv* — **co·ac·tiv·i·ty** \ˌkōakˈtivəd·ē\ *n* -ES

[2]**co·active** \(ˈ)kō +\ *adj* [*co-* + *active*] **:** acting in concurrence or together — **co·actively** \" +\ *adv* — **co·activity** \" +\ *n*

co·ac·tor \ˌkōˌakˈtō(r); kōˌakˈtō(r), ≈ˈ≈tə(r)\ *n* [*co-* + *actor*] **:** an organism that participates in ecological coaction; *esp* **:** one (as a predator) that actively initiates coaction with another — compare COACTEE

co·adaptation \ˌkō +\ *n* [*co-* + *adaptation*] **:** mutual adaptation (as of a flower and the insect that pollinates it)

coade stone \ˈkōd-\ *n, usu cap C* [after Eleanor *Coade*, 19th cent. Brit. manufacturer] **:** a very durable artificial stone made in London from 1760 to about 1840 apparently from ground stone and clay

co·adjacent \ˌkō +\ *adj* [*co-* + *adjacent*] **:** mutually adjacent; *specif* **:** contiguous in thought

co·adjust \ˌkō + \ *vt* [*co-* + *adjust*] **:** to adjust by mutual adaptation — **co·adjustment** \" + \ *n* -S

[1]**co·adjutant** \(ˈ)kō +\ *adj* [*co-* + *adjutant*] **:** mutually assisting

[2]**coadjutant** \"\ *n* -S **:** ASSISTANT, HELPER

co·ad·jute \ˌkōəˈjüt\ *vb* -ED/-ING/-S [back-formation fr. *coadjutor*] *vi* **:** COOPERATE ~ *vt* **:** to cooperate with

co·ad·ju·tor \ˌkōəˈjüd·ə(r), -ütə(r) *also* kōˈajəd·ə(r) *or* -ətə(r)\ *n* -S [ME *coadjutour*, fr. MF *coadjuteur*, fr. L *coadjutor*, fr. *co-* + *adjutor*, fr. *adjutare* to help — more at AID] **1 :** one who works together with another usu. in a somewhat subordinate position **:** fellow worker **:** ASSISTANT **2** *or* **coadjutor bishop :** BISHOP COADJUTOR

co·ad·ju·tor·ship \-ˌship\ *n* -S **:** the office of a coadjutor

co·ad·ju·tress \ˌkōəˈjütrə̇s *also* kōˈajətrə̇s\ *n* -ES [*coadjutor* + *-ess*] **:** COADJUTRIX

co·ad·ju·trix \-ˌtriks\ *n, pl* **coadjutri·ces** \kōˌajəˈtrīˌsēz\ [NL, fem. of *coadjutor* — more at -TRIX] **:** a female coadjutor

co·adjuvancy \(ˈ)kō+\ *n* -ES [*co-* + *adjuvancy*] **:** COOPERATION

co·adsorbent \ˌkō+\ *n* [*co-* + *adsorbent*] **:** an agent that increases the effectiveness of an adsorbent

[1]**co·ad·u·nate** \kōˈajəˌnāt\ *vt* -ED/-ING/-S [LL *coadunatus*, past part. of *coadunare*, fr. L *co-* + LL *adunare*, fr. L *ad-* + LL *unare*, fr. L *unus* one — more at ONE] **:** to unite into one **:** COMBINE

[2]**coadunate** \(ˈ)≈ˈ≈≈nə̇t, -ˌnāt\ *adj* [L *coadunatus*] **:** grown together and confluent **:** UNITED

co·ad·u·na·tion \≈ˌ≈≈ˈnāshən\ *n* -S [LL *coadunation-, coadunatio*, fr. *coadunatus* + *-ion-, -io* -ion] **:** the union (as of dissimilar substances) in one body or mass

co·ad·u·na·tive \(ˈ)≈ˈ≈≈ˌnād·iv, -ātiv\ *adj* [L *coadunatus* + E *-ive*] **:** concerning, producing, or tending to produce coadunation — **co·ad·u·na·tive·ly** *adv*

coaetaneous *var of* COETANEOUS

co·a·gel \ˈkōəˌjel\ *n* -S [blend of *coagulate* and *gel*] **:** a gelatinous precipitate (as of aluminum hydroxide) formed by coagulation of a sol — compare GEL

co·agency \(ˈ)kō+\ *n* [*co-* + *agency*] **:** combined or joint agency

co·agent \"+\ *n* [*co-* + *agent*] **:** a person, force, cause, or other agency working together with another

co·ag·ment \ˌkōagˈment\ *vt* -ED/-ING/-S [L *coagmentare*, fr. *coagmentum* act of joining together, joint, fr. *cogere* to drive together — more at COGENT] **:** to join together (as parts into a whole) **:** UNITE

coagmentate *vt* -ED/-ING/-S [L *coagmentatus*, past part. of *coagmentare*] *obs* **:** COAGMENT — **coagmentation** *n* -S *obs*

coagula *pl of* COAGULUM

co·ag·u·la·bil·i·ty \≈ˌ≈≈≈ˈbiləd·ē, -ətē, -i\ *n* -ES **:** the quality or state of being coagulable

co·ag·u·la·ble \kōˈagyələbəl\ *adj* [F, fr. *coaguler* to coagulate (fr. L *coagulare*) + *-able*] **:** capable of being coagulated

co·ag·u·lant \kōˈagyələnt\ *n* -S [L *coagulant-, coagulans*, pres. part. of *coagulare*] **:** something that produces coagulation

co·ag·u·lase \-ˌlās\ *n* -S [ISV *coagulate* + *-ase*] **:** any of several enzymes that cause coagulation (as of blood) ⟨the antigenic ~s of some staphylococci⟩

[1]**co·ag·u·late** \kōˈagyələt, -ˌlāt, *usu* -d.+V\ *adj* [ME *coagulat*, fr. L *coagulatus*] **:** COAGULATED

[2]**co·ag·u·late** \-ˌlāt, *usu* -d.+V\ *vb* -ED/-ING/-S [L *coagulatus*, past part. of *coagulare* to curdle, fr. *coagulum* curdling agent, rennet, fr. *cogere* to drive together — more at COGENT] *vt* **1 :** to cause or bring about the coagulation of **:** CURDLE, CLOT ⟨~ the blood⟩ ⟨rennet ~s milk⟩ **2 :** to gather together or form into a mass or a group ⟨~ all these many programs into one general program⟩ ⟨smaller particles can be *coagulated* into lumps of matter⟩ ~ *vi* **1 :** to undergo coagulation **2 :** to gather together into a mass or group ⟨industry has *coagulated* in dense masses along the railroad lines —W.D. Teague⟩ **:** take form or shape ⟨vague uneasy feelings *coagulated* into a desire for action⟩

[3]**co·ag·u·late** \-lət, -ˌlāt, *usu* -d.+V\ *n* -S [[1]*coagulate*] **:** COAGULUM 2

co·ag·u·la·tion \≈ˌ≈≈ˈlāshən\ *n* -S [F or L; F *coagulation*, fr. L *coagulation-, coagulatio*, fr. *coagulatus* + *-ion-, -io* -ion] **1 a :** the process of becoming viscous, jellylike, or solid or of uniting into a coherent mass; *esp* **:** the change from a liquid to a thickened curdlike state not by evaporation but by chemical reaction ⟨the spontaneous ~ of freshly drawn blood⟩ ⟨the ~ of egg albumen by heat⟩ **b :** the process by which such change of state takes place consisting of the alteration of a soluble substance, usu. protein, into an insoluble form or of the flocculation or separation of colloidal or suspended matter **2 :** a substance or body formed by coagulation **:** COAGULUM 2

coagulation time *n* **:** the time required by shed blood to clot, being a measure of the normality of the blood

co·ag·u·la·tive \≈ˈ≈≈ˌlād·iv, -ātiv\ *adj* [*coagulate* + *-ive*] *obs* **:** having the power to cause coagulation or the property of coagulating

co·ag·u·la·tor \≈ˈ≈≈ˌlād·ə(r), -ātə(r)\ *n* -S [*coagulate* + *-or*] **:** an agent that causes coagulation — **co·ag·u·la·to·ry** \-ləˌtōrē, -ˌtòrē\ *adj*

co·ag·u·lin \kōˈagyələ̇n\ *n* -S [*coagulate* + *-in*] **1 :** PRECIPITIN **2 a :** a hypothetical tissue constituent able to induce conversion of fibrinogen to fibrin in the absence of prothrombin or thrombin **b :** THROMBOPLASTIN

co·ag·u·lom·e·ter \kōˌagyəˈlämə̇d·ə(r), -ətə(r)\ *n* -S [*coagulate* + *-o-* + *-meter*] **:** an apparatus for measuring the time required for a sample of fluid (as blood) to coagulate

co·ag·u·lum \kōˈagyələm\ *n, pl* **coagu·la** \-lə\ [L — more at COAGULATE] **1** *obs* **:** COAGULANT **2 :** a coagulated mass or substance **:** CLOT, CURD — called also *coagulate*

co·a·huil·tec \ˌkōəˈwēlˌtek\ *n, pl* **coahuiltec** *or* **coahuiltecs** *usu cap* [Sp *coahuilteca*, fr. *Coahuila* state in Mexico + Sp *-teca* (as in *azteca* Aztec)] **1a :** an Indian people of northeastern Mexico and Texas **b :** a member of such people **2 :** a Coahuiltecan language of the Coahuiltec people

co·a·huil·tec·an \ˌkōəˈwēlˈtekən\ *n, pl* **coahuiltecan** *or* **coahuiltecans** *usu cap* **:** a presumed language family of possible Hokan relationship of northeastern Mexico and southern Texas including Coahuiltec, Comecrudo, Cotoname, and Tamaulipec

co·ai·ta \kwīˈtä\ *n* -S [obs. Pg *coaitá* (now *coatá*), fr. Tupi *coaitá, coatá*] **:** any of various spider monkeys (esp. *Ateles paniscus*)

[1]**coak** *obs var of* COKE

[2]**coak** \ˈkōk\ *n* -S [prob. fr. (assumed) ONF *coque* notch, fr. L *coccum* excrescence on a tree, berry of the scarlet oak (whence OF *coche* notch), fr. Gk *kokkos* berry of the scarlet oak, core of fruit] **1 a :** a projecting tenon connecting the face of a scarfed timber with the similarly scarfed face of another timber — compare SCARF JOINT **b :** a dowel of hard wood or metal let into timbers to unite them or keep them from slipping — compare COG **2 :** a metallic bushing or strengthening piece in the center of a wooden block sheave

[3]**coak** \"\ *vt* -ED/-ING/-S **:** to unite by a coak

coak·um \ˈkōkəm\ *n* -S [origin unknown] **:** POKEWEED

[1]**coal** \ˈkōl\ *n* -S *often attrib* [ME *cole*, fr. OE *col*; akin to OHG & ON *kol* coal of fire, IrGael *gual* coal, Arm *krak* glowing coals] **1 a :** a piece of carbon or charred wood or other combustible substance glowing without flame **:** a hot ember ⟨food cooked on the ~s⟩ ⟨burned by a ~ from the grate⟩ ⟨heated by a bed of hot ~s⟩ **b :** a piece of charred wood or other combustible substance more or less completely consumed **:** CINDER **2 :** CHARCOAL 1 **3 a :** a black or brownish black solid combustible mineral substance formed by the partial decomposition of vegetable matter without free access of air and under the influence of moisture and in many cases increased pressure and temperature, the substance being widely used as a natural fuel and containing carbon, hydrogen, oxygen, nitrogen, and sulfur as well as inorganic constituents that are left behind as ash after burning — see ANTHRACITE, BITUMINOUS COAL, COKE, LIGNITE; compare PEAT **b coals** *pl, Brit* **:** pieces or a quantity of the fuel broken up for burning ⟨a ton of ~s⟩ **c :** a particular kind or size of coal ⟨a good stove ~⟩

[2]**coal** \"\ *vb* -ED/-ING/-S *vt* **1 :** to convert to charcoal by burning **:** CHAR ⟨~ a cord of wood in one day⟩ **2 :** to supply with coal for fuel ⟨~ a steamer⟩ ~ *vi* **:** to take in coal ⟨the steamer ~*ed* as soon as she reached port⟩

coala *var of* KOALA

coal ball *n* **:** a nodule found in coal usu. composed of calcite or silica and carbonaceous matter and having fragmentary or microscopic plant remains

coal black *n* **:** a very dark black

coal blacking *n* **:** iron founders' blacking made from ground coal

coal brass *or* **coal blende** *n* **:** pyrite found with coal

coal·brook·dale \ˈkōlˌbrukˌdāl\ *n* -S *usu cap* [after *Coalbrookdale*, Shropshire, England] **:** COALPORT

coal bucket *n, chiefly Midland* **:** COAL SCUTTLE

coal cutter *n* **:** a hand-manipulated but power-driven machine that is used to detach coal from the vein usu. by sawing or drilling

coal·er \ˈkōlə(r)\ *n* -S [[1]*coal* + *-er*] **:** something (as a railroad or ship) wholly or chiefly employed in transporting or supplying coal

co·a·lesce \ˌkōəˈles\ *vb* -ED/-ING/-S [L *coalescere*, fr. *co-* + *alescere* to grow — more at OLD] *vi* **1 :** to grow together ⟨the edges of a wound ~⟩ **:** unite by growth into one body ⟨the outer suburbs of the two neighboring cities have now almost *coalesced*⟩ **2 a :** to unite or join together into one body or product **:** become integrated into a whole ⟨the tables . . . have . . . *coalesced* and . . . the customers who came in by twos and fours and sixes have become one big party —*N.Y. Times*⟩ **b :** to unite for a common end **:** join forces **:** agree in principle or effect ⟨all the divergent forces of the insurrection had *coalesced* for the final thrust —Paul Willen⟩ ⟨these two political parties often ~ on a candidate⟩ ~ *vt* **:** to cause to unite **:** bring together to form a unit or a single body ⟨~*s* moralities hardly ever found together —Randall Jarrell⟩ **syn** see MIX

co·a·les·cence \-ˈlesᵊn(t)s\ *n* -S [L *coalescere* + E *-ence*] **:** a growing together or union in one body, form, or group **:** COMBINATION ⟨~ of coal dust, gas, or small particles in interstellar space —A.E.Benfield⟩ ⟨~ of two similar theories into one great system⟩

coalescency *n* -ES *obs* **:** COALESCENCE

[1]**co·a·les·cent** \ˌkōəˈlesᵊnt\ *adj* [L *coalescent-, coalescens*, pres. part. of *coalescere*] **:** growing together **:** COHERING, COALESCING

[2]**coalescent** \"\ *n* -S **:** one that coalesces

coalfield \ˈ≈,≈\ *n* [[1]*coal* + *field*] **1 :** a region in which deposits of coal occur ⟨the rich ~s of the U.S.⟩ **2 :** the coal mines of a region — often used in pl. ⟨industrial peace in the ~s⟩

coalfish \ˈ≈,≈\ *n* [so called fr. its color] **:** any of several blackish or dark-backed fishes: as **a :** POLLACK **b :** COBIA **c :** SABLEFISH

coal gas *n* **:** gas made from coal: as **a :** the mixture of gases thrown off by burning coal (as in the furnace of a house) **b :** the gas consisting chiefly of hydrogen and methane made by carbonizing bituminous coal in retorts and used for heating and lighting — see COKE-OVEN GAS

coal hod *n, chiefly Northeast* **:** COAL SCUTTLE

coalhole \ˈ≈,≈\ *n* **1 :** a hole for coal (as a trap or opening in a sidewalk leading to a coal bin) **2** *Brit* **:** a compartment for storing coal

coal house *n* **:** a building (as a shed) or an enclosed place (as a bin) for storage of coal

coalier *comparative of* COALY

coalies *pl of* COALY

coaliest *superlative of* COALY

coal·i·fi·ca·tion \ˌkōləfə̇ˈkāshən\ *n* -S **:** the process in which vegetable matter becomes converted into coal of increasingly higher rank with anthracite as the final product

coal·i·fy \ˈkōləˌfī\ *vb* -ED/-ING/-ES [*coal* + *-ify*] **:** to change into coal by the process of coalification

coaling *pres part of* COAL

coaling station *n* [fr. pres. part. of [2]*coal*] **:** a port at which vessels may coal

Coal·ite \ˈkōˌlīt\ *trademark* — used for a smokeless fuel made by heating bituminous coal in a retort until much of the volatile matter has been given off

co·a·li·tion \ˌkōəˈlishən\ *n* -S *often attrib* [MF, fr. L *coalitus* + *-ion-, -io* -ion] **1 a :** the act of coalescing **:** the union of things separate into a single body or group ⟨~ of water vapor into raindrops⟩ **b :** a group or body formed by the coalescing of orig. distinct elements **:** COMBINATION ⟨they formed a ~ with the theater owners⟩ **2** *in government or politics* **:** a temporary alliance of distinct parties, persons, or states for joint action or to achieve a common purpose ⟨the party could keep control only by ~ with two smaller parties⟩ ⟨the parties of the right formed a ~ against the Communists⟩ ⟨a ~ of free nations⟩

co·a·li·tion·al \-shənᵊl, -shnəl\ *adj* **:** of or concerning coalition

co·a·li·tion·ist \-sh(ə)nə̇st\ *or* **co·a·li·tion·er** \-shənə(r)\ *n* -S **:** one who joins, aids, or favors a coalition

coal·less \ˈkōlləs\ *adj* **:** lacking coal

coal measures *n pl* **:** beds of coal with the associated rocks varying in thickness from a few feet to several thousand feet and consisting of shales, sandstones, limestones, and conglomerates with interstratified beds of coal and occas. of iron ore

coal·mouse \ˈkōlˌmau̇s\ *n, pl* **coal·mice** \-ˌmīs\ [by folk etymology fr. ME *colmose*, fr. OE *colmāse*, fr. *col* coal + *māse* titmouse; fr. its dark color — more at COAL, TITMOUSE] **:** COAL TIT

coal oil *n* **1 :** petroleum or a refined oil prepared from it **2** *chiefly Midland & South* **:** KEROSINE

coal-oil brush \ˈ≈,≈-\ *n* **:** a low spreading horsebrush (*Tetradymia glabrata*) chiefly of the Intermountain region and a leading cause of bighead

coal passer *n* **:** one that brings coal from a ship's bunkers to furnaces and removes ashes

coal pipe *n* **:** a very thin and irregular seam of coal

coalpit \ˈ≈,≈\ *n* [ME *colpit*, fr. OE *colpytt*, fr. *col* coal + *pytt* pit — more at COAL, PIT] **1** *dial* **:** a place where charcoal is made **2 :** a pit where coal is dug **:** a coal mine

coal plant *n* **:** one of the impressions or fossilized remains of plants found in the coal measures

coal pocket *n* **:** a plant equipped for the storage and loading of coal esp. for retail distribution

coal·port \ˈkōlˌpōrt, -ˌpȯrt\ *n* -S *usu cap* [fr. *Coalport*, near Shrewsbury, England, where it was produced] **:** a soft paste porcelain and later bone china ware produced both in table wares and in elaborate ornamental pieces often in the manner of Meissen or Sèvres

coalrake \ˈ≈,≈\ *n* [ME (northern dial.) *colrake*, fr. *cole* coal + *rake*] **:** a pronged instrument for stirring ashes or coals in an oven or furnace

coal road *n* **:** a railroad concerned primarily with the transportation of coal

coals *pl of* COAL, *pres 3d sing of* COAL

coal scuttle *n* **:** a metal pail for holding and carrying coal typically having a bail and a sloping lip for ease in pouring

coal-scuttle bonnet \ˈ≈,≈≈-\ *n* **:** a woman's bonnet with flat back and stiff projecting brim somewhat resembling a coal scuttle

coal scuttle

coal seam *n* **:** a bed of coal usu. thick enough to be mined with profit

coal tar *n* **:** tar obtained by the destructive distillation of bituminous coal usu. in coke ovens or retorts and consisting of numerous constituents (as benzene, xylenes, naphthalene, pyridine, quinoline, phenol, cresols, light oil, creosote) that may be obtained by distillation

coal-tar dye \ˈ≈,≈-\ *n* **:** a dye made from a coal-tar derivative; *broadly* **:** any synthetic organic dye — compare ANILINE DYE

co·alternate \(ˈ)kō, ˈkō+\ *adj* [*co-* + *alternate*] *logic* **:** related so as to express alternatives which taken together exhaust the possibilities — used of propositions and judgments — **co·alternation** \(ˈ)kō+\ *n* — **co·alternative** \ˌkō+\ *adj*

coal tit *or* **cole·tit** \ˈkōlˌtit\ *n* [*coal, cole* + *tit*] **:** a small European tit (*Parus ater*) greenish gray with black cap and white patch on the neck

co·altitude \(ˈ)kō+\ *n* [*co-* + *altitude*] **:** the complement of the altitude **:** the zenith distance

coal-whipper \ˈ≈,≈≈\ *n, Brit* **:** one (as a laborer or a machine) that raises coal out of the hold of a ship

[1]**coaly** \ˈkōlē, -li\ *adj* -ER/-EST [[1]*coal* + *-y*] **:** covered or impregnated with coal **:** containing or resembling coal ⟨~ shale⟩

[2]**coaly** \"\ *n* -ES [[1]*coal* + *-y*] **:** a coal heaver

coam·ing \ˈkōmiŋ\ *n* -S [prob. fr. *coam-* (alter. of [1]*comb*) + *-ing*] **1 a :** the raised frame of wood or steel around a hatchway, skylight, or other opening in the deck of a ship to prevent water from running below — sometimes used in pl. **b :** the raised frame along the sides of the cockpit of a boat **c :** the lower strake of plating on a deckhouse or casing **2 :** a raised frame around a floor or roof opening or esp. a scuttle to keep water from running in — sometimes used in pl.

co·an \ˈkōən\ *adj, usu cap* [Cos, (now *Kos*), an island of the Dodecanese in the Aegean sea + E *-an*] **:** of or relating to the island of Kos

co·appear \ˌkō+\ *vi* [*co-* + *appear*] **:** to appear together or at the same time — **co·appearance** \"+\ *n*

co·apt \kōˈapt\ *vt* -ED/-ING/-S [LL *coaptare* (past part. *coaptatus*), fr. L *co-* + *aptare*, fr. *aptus* fit — more at APT] **1 :** to fit or join to each other **2 :** to close or fasten together **:** cause to adhere ⟨the margins of the wound were then closely ~*ed* with sutures —*Biol. Abstracts*⟩

co·ap·ta·tion \ˌkōapˈtāshən\ *n* -S [LL *coaptation-, coaptatio*, fr. *coaptatus* + *-ion-, -io* -ion] **:** the adaptation or adjustment of parts to each other **:** the joining or fitting together (as of the ends of a broken bone or the edges of a wound)

co·a·ra·tion \ˌkōəˈrāshən\ *n* -S [*co-* + obs. *aration* tilling of the soil, fr. L *aration-, aratio*, fr. *aratus* (past part. of *arare* to plow) + *-ion-, -io* -ion — more at EAR] **:** cooperative tilling of the soil as practiced by early village communities

co·arb \ˈkōˌärb\ *n* -S [IrGael *comharba* successor, fr. OIr *comarbe* heir, fr. *com-* with, together + *orbe* inheritance; akin to Gk *orphanos* orphan — more at CO-, ORPHAN] *in the early Irish and Scottish churches* **:** the incumbent of an abbey or bishopric as successor to the patron saint or founder

co·arct \kōˈärkt, -ākt\ *vt* -ED/-ING/-S [ME *coarten, coharten*, fr. L *coarctare, coartare* — more at COARCTATE] **1 a** *obs* **:** to press or draw together **b :** to cause (the aorta) to become narrow or (the heart) to constrict **2 :** to restrict the action of **:** CONFINE, RESTRAIN

co·arc·tate \(ˈ)kōˈärkˌtāt, -ˌtə̇t\ *adj* [L *coarctatus*, past part. of *coarctare, coartare* to press together, contract, fr. *co-* + *artare*, fr. *artus* narrow, confined; akin to L *artus* joint — more at ARTICLE] *biol* **:** pressed together **:** closely connected; *specif* **:** enclosed in a rigid case formed from the last larval skin — used of insect pupae

co·arc·ta·tion \ˌ≈≈ˈtāshən\ *n* -S [L *coarctation-, coarctatio*, fr. *coarctatus* + *-ion-, -io* -ion] **1** *obs* **:** confinement to a narrow space **:** COMPRESSION, RESTRICTION **2 :** a stricture or narrowing (as of a vessel or canal, esp. the aorta)

coarse \ˈkō(ə)rs, -ó(ə)rs, -ōəs, -ó(ə)s\ *adj* -ER/-EST [ME *cors, corse* common, fr. *cors, corse*, n., customary sequence of events — more at COURSE] **1 :** of ordinary or inferior quality or value **:** COMMON, BASE ⟨of what ~ metal ye are molded —Shak.⟩ **2 a :** composed of relatively large parts or particles ⟨~ sand⟩ **:** loose or rough in texture ⟨~ skin⟩ ⟨the Southern textile industry developed first in . . . ~ goods; the North went in for medium and fine grade yarns —*Amer. Guide Series: R.I.*⟩ **b :** of crude, unskilled, or careless workmanship or design **:** roughly or crudely formed **:** without delicacy or grace of feature ⟨~ imitations, completely lacking in the original delicacy⟩ ⟨a ~ heavy face, loose-featured, red and sensual —Thomas Wolfe⟩ **c** *of paper* **:** of a grade suitable for wrapping or industrial use **d :** adjusted, set, or designed for heavy, fast, or less delicate work ⟨a ~ saw with large teeth⟩ ⟨a high-speed milling cutter with ~ pitch⟩ **e :** not precise or detailed with respect to adjustment, classification, discrimination **:** roughly approximate ⟨to fill in the details of the rather ~ picture obtained by the earlier studies⟩ ⟨one dial for ~ adjustment, one for fine⟩ **f** *med, of a tremor* **:** of wide excursion ⟨a ~ tremor of the extremities⟩ **3 a :** crude or unrefined in taste, manners, or sensibilities **:** without cultivation of taste, politeness or civility of manner, or delicacy of feeling ⟨many of the muckraking novels . . . were simple parables of the ~ businessman and the sensitive intellectual —Bernard De Voto⟩ **b :** crude and indelicate of language or idea esp. with violation of social taboos on language **:** OBSCENE, PROFANE **4 a** *dial, of the weather* **:** ROUGH, STORMY **b** *dial Brit, of persons or circumstances* **:** BRUTAL, HARSH **5 :** harsh, raucous, or rough in tone **:** not melodious or mellow ⟨the ~ jangling of ordinary bells —G.B.Shaw⟩ — used also of certain sounds heard in auscultation in pathological states of the chest ⟨~ rales⟩

syn VULGAR, GROSS, OBSCENE, RIBALD: COARSE suggests unrefined crudeness, indelicacy, or robust roughness ⟨he was forever making eyes at me — a *coarse*, puffy-faced, red≈moustached young man, with his hair plastered down on each side of his forehead. I thought he was perfectly hateful . . . —A. Conan Doyle⟩ ⟨the landlady who had tyrannized over her when ill-humoured and unpaid, or when pleased had treated her with a *coarse* familiarity scarcely less odious —W.M.Thackeray⟩ In this sense, VULGAR, a stronger term, describes what offends good taste or decency and may suggest boorishness ⟨his passion for physical luxury nakedly revealed itself as simply the *vulgar* longing of the idle rich for conspicuous waste —Granville Hicks⟩ ⟨her father is a . . . *vulgar* person, mean in his ideals and obtuse in his manners —John Erskine †1951⟩ ⟨it was, in fact, the mouth that gave his face its sensual, sly, and ugly look, for a loose and *vulgar* smile seemed constantly to hover about its thick coarse edges —Thomas Wolfe⟩ GROSS stresses crude animal inclinations and lack of refinement ⟨merely *gross*, a scatological rather than a pornographic impropriety —Aldous Huxley⟩ ⟨Clif Clawson, at forty, was *gross*. His face was sweaty, and puffy with pale flesh; his voice was raw; he fancied checked Norfolk jackets, tight across his swollen shoulders and his beefy hips —Sinclair Lewis⟩ ⟨a spirituelle amoureuse, she is repelled by the *gross* or the voluptuary —S.N.Behrman⟩ OBSCENE is the strongest of this group in stressing impropriety, indecency, or nastiness ⟨it was, of course, easy to pick out a line here and there . . . which was frank to indecency, yet certainly not *obscene* —H.S. Canby⟩ ⟨his innate belief that human flesh is in some way *obscene*. In the old days artists . . . had painted decently and had draped their figures —Ellen Glasgow⟩ ⟨there are depths beneath depths in what happened last night — obscure fetid chambers of the human soul. Black hatreds, unnatural desires, hideous impulses, *obscene* ambitions are at the bottom of it —W.H.Wright⟩ RIBALD suggests rough merriment or crude humor at the irreverent, scurrilous, or vulgar ⟨they had their backs to him, shaking with the loose laughter which punctuates a *ribald* description —Mary Austin⟩ ⟨a *ribald* folksong about fleas in straw —J.L.Lowes⟩

coarse aggregate *n* **:** the portion of the aggregate used in concrete that is larger than about 3/16 inch

coarse fish *n* **1 :** ROUGH FISH **2** *chiefly Brit* **:** a freshwater fish not belonging to the family Salmonidae

coarse fodder *n* **:** a feeding stuff containing a relatively large percentage of crude fiber or water (as grass, hay, corn fodder, mangel-wurzels) — called also *roughage*

coarse–grained \ˈ=ˌ=\ *adj* **1 :** of a coarse grain or texture; *esp, of wood* **:** having wide annual rings, large wood elements, or both **2 :** lacking in culture **:** CRUDE, UNREFINED

coarsely *adv* **:** in a coarse manner

coars·en \ˈkōrsᵊn, -ȯr-,-ōəs-,-ó(ə)s-\ *vb* **coarsened; coarsening** \-sᵊniŋ, -sniŋ\ **coarsens** [*coarse* + *-en*] *vt* **:** to make coarse ~ *vi* **:** to become coarse

coarse·ness *n* -ES **:** the quality or state of being coarse

coarser *comparative of* COARSE

coarsest *superlative of* COARSE

coarse stuff *n* **:** the mixture of plastering materials consisting of lime, sand, and hair used in the scratch and brown coats

coarse wool *or* **coarse–wooled sheep** *n* **:** a sheep having long strong coarse-fibered wool esp. suitable for carpet weaving (as those of various large mutton breeds of English origin)

co·articulation \ˌkō+\ *n* -s [*co-* + *articulation*] *phonetics* **:** action or position of such part of an articulator as is not directly participating in an articulation

¹coast \ˈkōst\ *n* -s [ME *cost*, fr. MF *coste*, fr. L *costa* rib, side; akin to OSlav *kostĭ* bone] **1** *obs* **a :** a region or area esp. of the earth ⟨through all the ~*s* of dark destruction —John Milton⟩ **b :** the border or frontier of a country **:** the land near a border **c :** a point of the compass **:** DIRECTION **2 a :** the seashore or land near it **:** sea margin **:** SEABOARD **:** the land immediately abutting the sea ⟨they saw across the water the English ~⟩ **b :** the littoral or coastal region **:** that area of a country regarded as near the coast, sometimes including the whole of the coastal plain ⟨a plant native to the Pacific ~⟩ **c** *dial* **:** the border or bank of any body of water **d** *often cap* **:** the Pacific coast of the U.S. **3 :** a hill or slope suited to coasting (as on a sled); *also* **:** a slide or run down a slope on a coasting vehicle — **coast is clear :** no enemies or obstacles in sight

²coast \ˈ"\ *vb* -ED/-ING/-S [ME *costen*, fr. *cost*, n.] *vt* **1 a** *obs* **:** to move along or past the side of **:** SKIRT ⟨~*ing* the wall of Heaven —John Milton⟩ **b** *obs* **:** to move along in company with or at the side of **c :** to sail along the shore of **:** follow the coastline of ⟨the entire shoreline of the Gulf of Mexico had been ~*ed* —Bernard DeVoto⟩ **2** *obs* **a :** BORDER, ADJOIN **b :** to go throughout **:** traverse all parts of (a country) **3** *obs* **:** to locate with reference to or to mark with the points of the compass **4 :** to cause to go or move without continual application of propulsive power (as by momentum or gravity) ⟨~ a car down the hill⟩ ~ *vi* **1** *obs* **a :** to come near or approximate (as in nature or time) **b :** to draw near or approach **2 a** *archaic* **:** to travel on land along a coast or along or past the side of something **b** *obs* **:** to make a tour **:** travel around ⟨~ up and down the country —Henry Blount⟩ **c :** to sail along the shore **:** sail from port to port along the coast ⟨~*ing* steadily southward along the margin of the lake —C.S. Forester⟩ **3 a :** to slide, run, or glide down hill by the force of gravity (as on a sled or a bicycle) **b :** to move along without further application of propulsive power (as by momentum or by gravity) ⟨to ~ from Earth to the moon . . . we must achieve a velocity of 25,000 mph —A.C.Clarke⟩ **c :** to proceed without further application of effort **:** drift easily along without special effort or concern ⟨the country . . . seems in a mood to ~ along —*U.S.News & World Report*⟩

coast·al \ˈkōstᵊl\ *adj* [¹*coast* + *-al*] **:** of or relating to a coast **:** located on or near a coast ⟨~ marshes⟩ ⟨~ traffic⟩ **:** bordering on a coast ⟨the Atlantic ~ plain⟩ ⟨~ waters⟩ — **coast·al·ly** \-tᵊlē, -li\ *adv*

coastal erysipelas *n* **:** ONCHOCERCIASIS

coastal fever *n* **:** EAST COAST FEVER

coastal plain *n* **:** a plain extending inland from a seashore commonly the result of geologically recent emergence of the land

coastal staggers *n pl but sing in constr* **:** an ataxia of uncertain origin affecting Australian horses possibly as a result of ingestion of toxic plant matter or of a trace-element deficiency

coast artillery *n* **:** artillery esp. organized and equipped to defend a coastline

coast disease *n* **:** a disease of Australian sheep caused by deficiency of dietary copper and cobalt and marked by general debility and severe hypochromic anemia — compare ¹PINE 3

coast·er \ˈkōstə(r)\ *n* -s **1 :** one that coasts: as **a :** a person engaged in coastal traffic or commerce **b :** a vessel employed in sailing along a coast or engaged in the coasting trade; *specif, in statute law* **:** a vessel carrying to a port a cargo taken in at another port of the same country **2 a :** a resident of a seacoast **b :** one of the longhorn cattle of Texas esp. of the coastal region **c** (1) **:** a very large brook trout found along the northern shores of Lake Superior and Lake Michigan (2) **:** RAINBOW TROUT **3 a :** a round tray usu. of silver and often on wheels that is used for circulating a decanter after a meal **b :** a shallow container or a plate or mat to protect a surface (as a table from moisture from drinking vessels) **c** [²*coast* + *-er*] **:** a small vehicle (as a sled or wagon) on or in which a child may coast **d :** ROLLER COASTER

coaster brake *n* **:** a brake in the hub of the rear wheel of a bicycle that is applied by back pressure on the pedals and released by moving the pedals forward

coaster wagon *n* **:** a child's toy wagon often used for coasting

coast fever *n* **:** EAST COAST FEVER

coast gorilla *n* **:** a gorilla found in southeastern Nigeria usu. regarded as forming a subspecies (*Gorilla gorilla gorilla*) — compare MOUNTAIN GORILLA

coast guard *n* -s **1** *Brit* **:** a body of men orig. employed along the coast to prevent smuggling and later established as a naval reserve **2 :** a military or naval force employed in guarding a coast or responsible for the safety, order, and effective operation of maritime traffic in neighboring waters **3 :** a member of a coast guard

coast guard cutter *n* **:** CUTTER 5c

coastguardsman \ˈ=ˌ=mən\ *or* **coastguardman** \ˈ=ˌ=mən\ *n, pl* **coastguardsmen** *or* **coastguardmen :** a member of a coast guard

coast·ing \ˈkōstiŋ\ *n* -s **:** configuration of a coast **:** COASTLINE

coasting trade *n* **:** trade along a coast esp. as regulated by the laws of a particular country

coastland \ˈ=ˌ=\ *n* **:** land bordering the sea **:** a section of seacoast

coast lily *n* **:** a lily (*Lilium maritimum*) of the Pacific coast of the U.S. having orange flowers

coastline \ˈ=ˌ=\ *n* **1 a :** the line that forms the boundary between the land and the water esp. of a sea or ocean **b :** a broad zone of land and water extending indefinitely both landward and seaward from a shoreline **2 :** the general configuration of the land along a coast

coast live oak *n* **:** a highly variable evergreen oak (*Quercus agrifolia*) of the coastal zone of western No. America from Puget Sound to Lower California with rather small thick usu. spiny-toothed leaves that are dark green above but paler and somewhat shining below — called also *California live oak*

coast pilot *n* **1 :** one who pilots coasting vessels **2 :** an official publication giving a description of a particular section of coast and usu. sailing directions for coastal navigation

coast rat *n* **:** a southern African rodent (*Bathyergus maritimus*) that is about the size of a rat and is noted for its extensive burrows

coast redwood *n* **:** REDWOOD 3a

coast rhododendron *n* **:** a medium-sized rhododendron (*Rhododendron californicum*) of the Pacific coast of No. America with large rosy brown-spotted flowers

coasts *pl of* COAST, *pres 3d sing of* COAST

coastwaiter \ˈ=ˌ==\ *n, Brit* **:** a landwaiter over coastal shipping

¹coast·ward \ˈkōstwə(r)d\ *or* **coastwards** \-dz\ *adv* **:** toward the coast

²coastward \ˈ"\ *adj* **:** situated near or directed toward the coast

coast·ways \-ˌwāz\ *archaic var of* COASTWISE

¹coast·wise \-ˌwīz\ *adv* **:** by way of the coast **:** along the coast

²coastwise \ˈ"\ *adj* **:** moving along the coast **:** carried on by water between places on a coast ⟨~ business⟩ **:** engaged in commerce between places on a coast **:** COASTAL ⟨~ shipping⟩

¹coat \ˈkōt, *usu* -d·+V\ *n* -s *often attrib* [ME *cote*, fr. OF *cote*, *cotte*, of Gmc origin; akin to OHG *kozza*, *kozzo* coarse mantle, OS *kot* woolen coat, and prob. to G dial. *chūz* disheveled hair, *chūder*, *kauder* oakum; perh. akin to Gk *beudos* feminine attire] **1 a :** an outer garment (as a raincoat) usu. with long sleeves, a collar, and a single-breasted or double-breasted front opening made of fabric, fur, or plastic and varying in length and style according to fashion and use **b** (1) *now dial* **:** PETTICOAT, SKIRT — usu. used in pl. (2) *South* **:** DRESS 3 **c** *archaic* **:** habit or clothing indicating the order, class, profession, or office **:** CLOTH, PROFESSION ⟨men of his ~ should be minding their prayers —Jonathan Swift⟩ **d :** something resembling a coat in covering ⟨a ~ of tan⟩ or pervading ⟨a thick ~ of gloom enveloped the prairies —J.H.Gray⟩ or serving as an article of dress ⟨if malice and vanity wear the ~ of philanthropy —R.W.Emerson⟩ **2 :** COAT OF ARMS **3 :** the external growth on animals like a garment (as of fur, skin, wool, or feathers) ⟨the horses' ~*s* were sleek⟩ **4 :** a layer of any substance covering another: as **a :** a cover or lining esp. of an animal organ **:** MEMBRANE **:** HUSK, BARK ⟨the ~ of the eyeball⟩ ⟨the ~*s* of an onion⟩ **b :** a layer of a protective or ornamental substance (as paint or plaster) laid on in a single application ⟨three ~*s* of paint on the wall⟩ **5** *obs* **:** COAT MONEY **6** *obs* **:** FACE CARD **7** *naut* **:** a piece of tarred or painted canvas to keep out water fastened about the mast, bowsprit, or pumps where they pass through the deck or about the rudder casing

²coat \ˈ"\ *vt* -ED/-ING/-S [ME *coten*, fr. *cote*, n.] **1 :** to cover or dress with a coat or outer garment **2 :** to cover or spread with a finishing, protecting, or enclosing layer of any substance ⟨~ a surface with paraffin⟩ ⟨frost ~*s* the window⟩ ⟨~ glass with silver to make a mirror⟩

coat armor *n* [alter. of *cote-armour*] **1** *obs* **:** COAT OF ARMS 1 **2** *obs* **:** COAT OF ARMS 2a **3 :** COATS OF ARMS 2b **:** armorial ensigns

coat arms *n* [modif. of MF *cote d'armes*] *archaic* **:** COAT ARMOR 3

coat card *n* [so called fr. the coated figure drawn on the card] **:** FACE CARD

coatdress \ˈ=ˌ=\ *n* **:** a dress made on coat lines usu. with a front buttoning from neckline to hemline

coatdress

coated *adj* **:** covered with or dressed in a coat: as **a** *of paper or paper board* **:** faced with a surface coating (as of china clay and an adhesive) and made smooth by calendering ⟨~ paper is specially suitable for halftone printing⟩ **b** *of the tongue* **:** covered with a yellowish white deposit of desquamated cells, bacteria, and debris usu. as an accompaniment of digestive disorder **c** *of cloth* **:** covered or impregnated with a durable chemical or rubber compound (as of oilcloth) **d** *of an optical lens* **:** covered with a thin coating of a substance to reduce reflection and increase light transmission

coated ginger *n* **:** BLACK GINGER

coated rice *n* **:** rice coated with glucose and talc to give it a pearly luster

coat·ee \ˌkōˈtē\ *n* -s [¹*coat* + *-ee*] **:** a short coat; *esp* **:** a close-fitting coat with short skirts or tails

coat·er \ˈkōd·ə(r), -ōtə-\ *n* -s **:** one that coats surfaces: as **a :** a workman or a machine that applies a coating to materials in manufacture (as the chemical emulsion on photographic paper) **b :** a workman or a machine that forms or finishes material in sheets by dispersing a liquid film of the material usu. onto a drying surface

coat flower *n* [perh. trans. of L *tunica;* fr. the shape of its bracts] **:** a tufted spreading perennial garden herb (*Tunica saxifraga*) of the family Caryophyllaceae with very slender hairlike stems, narrow leaves, and small pink or pale purple flowers

coat hanger *n* **:** a slender arched device (as of wood, metal, or plastic) which is shaped typically somewhat like a person's shoulders, over which a coat or dress may be hung, and which is usu. fitted with a crossbar for hanging trousers or a skirt

co·a·ti \kəˈwäd·ē\ *n* -s [Pg *coati*, fr. Tupi *coati*, *cuati*] **:** a mammal of tropical America of the genus *Nasua* that is related to the raccoon but with a longer body and tail and a long flexible snout

co·a·ti·mun·di *or* **co·a·ti·mon·di** \=ˌ==ˈmənˌdē\ *n* -s [Tupi] **:** COATI

coating *n* -s **1 :** a layer of any substance used as cover, protection, decoration, or finish ⟨porcelain enamel is widely used as a ~⟩ ⟨~*s* applied for ceramic glazes⟩ ⟨a thin ~ of soil over the ore⟩ **:** COAT, COVERING ⟨a protective ~ of cynicism⟩ **2 :** cloth for coats ⟨new woolen ~*s*⟩

coat·less \ˈkōtləs\ *adj* **:** having or wearing no coat

coat money *n* **:** money to provide coats for men in British military service esp. as exacted by Charles I — used esp. in the phrase *coat and conduct money*

coat of arms [tr. of F *cotte d'armes*] **1 :** a tabard or surcoat embroidered with armorial bearings **2 a :** a heraldic achievement **b :** any emblem or group of emblems whether or not inclusive of an escutcheon of arms that is regarded as having a symbolic function equivalent or comparable to that of a heraldic achievement ⟨the *coats of arms* of all the sovereign nations⟩

coat of mail : a defensive garment of metal scales or chain mail **:** HAUBERK — compare CHAIN MAIL

coat-of-mail shell \ˌ==ˈ=ˌ=\ *n* **:** CHITON

coat·rack \ˈkōt·+ˌ-\ *n* **:** a stand or rack fitted with pegs, hooks, or hangers and used for the temporary storage of outdoor garments (as coats, cloaks, or rain gear)

coatroom \ˈ"+ˌ-\ *n* **:** CLOAKROOM

coats *pl of* COAT, *pres 3d sing of* COAT

coattail \ˈkō(t)+ˌ-\ *n* -s **1 :** the rear flap of a man's coat **2 coattails** *pl* **:** the skirts of a dress coat, cutaway, or frock coat — **on one's coattails :** in a state of dependence on another for assistance ⟨a lazy man still riding *on his* father's *coattails*⟩ **:** with the help of another; *esp* **:** with the benefit of another's political prestige ⟨congressmen riding into office *on the coattails* of a popular president⟩

coattailed \ˈ"+ˌ-\ *adj* **:** having or wearing coattails

coat-tree \ˈ"+ˌ-\ *n* **:** a coatrack with a vertical shaft from the upper part of which pegs or hooks diverge like branches

¹co·author \(ˈ)kō+\ *n* [*co-* + *author*] **:** one who collaborates with another in the production of a literary or dramatic work, a document, or other composition ⟨two ~*s* of many books and plays⟩ ⟨~*s* of the new tax bill⟩

²coauthor \ˈ"\ *vt* **:** to be coauthor of ⟨the two ~*ed* a charter⟩

¹coax \ˈkōks\ *vb* -ED/-ING/-ES [earlier *cokes*, fr. *cokes*, n.] *vt* **1** *obs* **:** to make a fool of **:** DUPE **2** *obs* **:** FONDLE, PET caressing, or flattering **:** treat lovingly **3 :** to influence or persuade by gentle urging, caressing, or flattering **:** WHEEDLE ⟨some sisters would have ~*ed* him for a little sugar —George Meredith⟩ ⟨tried to ~ her into arranging her nursery elsewhere —Mary S. Broome⟩ **4 :** to draw, gain, or persuade forth (a desired object from its possessor or its place) by means of gentle urging or flattery or by persistent effort ⟨~*s* bits of raw meat from the cook —Edita Morris⟩ ⟨how many isolated facts can be ~*ed* out of an overstuffed memory by the offer of a washing machine —J.M. Barzun⟩ **5 :** to manipulate with great perseverance and usu. with considerable effort toward a desired state or activity ⟨~ a fire to burn⟩ ⟨~ a cold engine to start⟩ ~ *vi* **:** to persuade or influence a person by gentle urging or flattery

²coax \ˈ"\ *n* -ES **:** a coaxing speech or act

³co·ax \ˈkōˌaks\ *n* -ES [by shortening] **:** COAXIAL CABLE

co·ax·al \(ˈ)kō+\ *adj* [*co-* + *axal*] **:** COAXIAL: as **a** *of circles* **:** having collinear centers and the same radical axis **b** *of triangles* **:** having the intersections of corresponding sides on a straight line called the axis of the triangles

co·ax·a·tion \ˌkōakˈsāshən\ *n* -s [L *coaxatus* (past part. of *coaxare* to croak, prob. fr. Gk *koax* noise made by a frog, of imit. origin) + E *-ion*] **:** a croaking esp. of frogs

co·axial \(ˈ)kō+\ *adj* [*co-* + *axial*] **1 :** having coincident axes ⟨~ ellipses⟩ ⟨~ cylinders⟩ **2 :** referred to the same set of coordinate axes **3 :** mounted on concentric shafts — used esp. of airplane propellers or rotors driven independently and in different directions — **co·axially** \ˈ"+\

coaxial cable *also* **coaxial** *n* **:** a cable consisting of a tube of conducting material surrounding a central conductor held in place by insulators with the whole assembly being covered with insulation and used to transmit telegraph, telephone, and television signals of high frequency — called also *concentric cable*

coaxial speaker *n* **:** a loudspeaker in which the high-frequency reproducer is mounted at the center of and on the same axis as the low frequency reproducer (as a high-frequency horn mounted in a paper cone speaker)

¹cob \ˈkäb\ *vt* **cobbed; cobbed; cobbing; cobs** [ME *cobben* to fight, give blows; akin to Icel *kubba* to chop, Norw *kubbe* log, ME *cobbe* big man, leader — more at ³COB] **1 :** STRIKE, THUMP: as **a** *archaic* **:** to beat on the buttocks (as with a flat stick) **b** *dial Eng* **:** THRESH ⟨~ grain⟩ **2** *dial Eng* **:** to toss effortlessly or carelessly **3 :** to break (ore) into small pieces preliminary to sorting; *esp* **:** to break off waste or low-grade material from (lumps of ore) with hand hammers **4 :** SURPASS, EXCEL, BEAT, OUTDO

²cob \ˈ"\ *or* **cobb** \ˈ"\ *n* -s **:** a blow or a beating esp. upon the buttocks

³cob \ˈ"\ *n* -s [ME *cobbe;* akin to ON *kobbi* seal (the animal), OE *cot* den, cottage — more at COT] **1** *now dial Eng* **:** an eminent person **:** LEADER, TOPMAN **2 :** a male swan — compare ⁵PEN **3** *dial Eng* **:** a lump or piece (as of coal or stone) or a rounded heap or mass: as **a :** COBNUT **b :** a nut used in the game of cobnut or conker **c cobs** *pl* **:** TESTES **d :** a small stack of grain or hay **e :** a small loaf of bread **4** *obs* **:** the head of a herring **5 a :** a piece of eight or a Spanish-American dollar — used in Ireland and the British colonies during the period when Spanish-American gold and silver coins were irregularly shaped and crudely struck **b :** any crude, irregularly shaped coin of early Spanish-American issue ⟨a ~ dollar⟩ ⟨~ money⟩ ⟨~ gold⟩ **6 a :** CORNCOB 1 **b** *chiefly Africa* **:** an ear of Indian corn **7 :** a short-legged stocky horse; *esp* **:** one having an artificially high stylish action **8** *Brit* **:** the seed head of clover **9 :** a string of crystals of sugar of milk usu. cylindrical in shape — compare LACTOSE

⁴cob \ˈ"\ *n* -s [prob. fr. ³*cob* (lump)] *Brit* **:** a mixture that consists of unburned clay usu. with straw as a binder and is used for constructing walls of small buildings ⟨windows set in ~ walls three foot thick —Clemence Dane⟩

⁵cob \ˈ"\ *or* **cobb** \ˈ"\ *n* -s [prob. fr. D *kobbe*, *kob* sea gull, fr. MD *cobbe* crested bird or animal; akin to Fris *kobbe* sea gull and prob. to Icel *kobbi* seal — more at ³COB] **:** SEA GULL; *esp* **:** GREAT BLACK-BACKED GULL

⁶cob \ˈ"\ *or* **cobb** \ˈ"\ *n* -s [origin unknown] *dial Eng* **:** a wicker basket

⁷cob \ˈ"\ *n* -s [modif. of NL *Kobus*] **:** a waterbuck of the genus *Kobus*

co·baea \kōˈbēə, kəˈ-\ *n, cap* [NL, irreg. fr. Bernabé *Cobo* †1657 Span. naturalist] **:** a small genus of woody tendril-climbing tropical American vines (family Polemoniaceae) with pinnate leaves and large bell-shaped purple or white flowers — see CATHEDRAL BELLS

co·bal·a·min \kōˈbȯləˌmēn, kəˈ-; ˌkō(ˌ)bȯˈlamən, -ˌbaˈl-\ *n* -s [*cobalt* + *-amin* (as in *vitamin*)] **:** a member of the vitamin B_{12} group; *broadly* **:** the vitamin B_{12} group

co·balt \ˈkōˌbȯlt *also* -bält *or chiefly Brit* kəˈbȯlt\ *n* -s [G *kobalt*, alter. (influenced by NL *cobaltum*, modif. of G *kobold*) of G *kobold* cobalt, kobold, fr. MHG *kobolt* kobold, fr. *kobe* hut, cage + *-olt* (prob. akin to OHG *holdo* spirit, fr. *hold* gracious); fr. its appearance in silver ore where it was believed to have been placed by silver-stealing goblins; akin to OE *cofa* den and to OHG *hald* inclined — more at COVE, HEEL] **1 :** a hard magnetic silver-white bivalent and trivalent metallic element belonging to the same family as iron and nickel, occurring usu. with nickel or copper either native in nickel-iron alloys (as in meteors) or combined in minerals from which it is isolated chiefly as a by-product, being essential as a trace element in animal and plant nutrition, and being used to produce magnetic alloys and hard alloys resistant to abrasion, corrosion, and high temperatures — symbol *Co;* see COBALT 60, ELEMENT table **2 :** the azure of the cloudless sky

cobaltammine \ˌ=ˌ=ˈ=, ˌ=ˌ=+\ *n* -s [ISV *cobalt* + *ammine;* prob. orig. formed as G *kobaltammin*] **:** any of numerous ammines of cobalt

cobalt bloom *n* **:** ERYTHRITE 2

cobalt blue *n* **1 a :** a permanent greenish blue pigment consisting essentially of cobalt oxide and alumina — called also *cobalt ultramarine, King's blue* **b :** POWDER BLUE **2 :** a strong greenish blue that is bluer and deeper than grotto, greener, lighter, and stronger than average cerulean blue (sense 1a), and bluer, lighter, and stronger than indigo carmine — called also *cobalt ultramarine, Hungary blue, Leithner's blue, Leyden blue, Olympic blue, Thenard's blue, Venetian blue*

cobalt bronze *n* **:** a violet colored cobalt double salt of bronze-like luster; cobalt ammonium phosphate

cobalt chloride *n* **:** a chloride of cobalt; *usu* **:** the dichloride $CoCl_2$ crystallizing ordinarily with six molecules of water, being dark red when hydrated, blue when dehydrated, and used in solution as a secret ink

cobalt fluoride *n* **:** either of two fluorides of cobalt: **a :** the difluoride CoF_2 obtained as a rose colored granular powder — called also *cobaltous fluoride* **b :** the trifluoride CoF_3 obtained as a brown crystalline material and used as a carrier of fluorine in the preparation of fluorocarbons — called also *cobaltic fluoride*

cobalt glance *n* **:** COBALTITE

cobalt glass *n* **:** SMALT 2

cobalt green *n* **1 :** a permanent green pigment consisting essentially of cobalt and zinc oxides — called also *zinc green* **2 :** a moderate yellowish green that is greener and stronger than tarragon and yellower and deeper than malachite green or verdigris — called also *Rinnemann's green, Saxony green, smalt green, zinc green*

co·bal·ti- *comb form* [*cobalt*] **:** trivalent cobalt **:** cobaltic ⟨*cobaltinitrite*⟩

co·bal·tic \(ˈ)kōˈbȯltik, kəˈb-, -ēk\ *adj* [ISV *cobalt* + *-ic*] **:** of, relating to, or containing cobalt — used esp. of compounds in which this element is trivalent; compare COBALTOUS

cobaltic fluoride *n* **:** COBALT FLUORIDE b

co·bal·ti·cyanic acid \kōˌbȯltə+-\ *n* [ISV *cobalti-* + *cyanic*] **:** a stable complex colorless crystalline acid $H_3Co(CN)_6.xH_2O$

co·bal·ti·cyanide \kōˌbȯltə+\ *n* [ISV *cobalti-* + *cyanide*] **:** a salt of cobalticyanic acid

co·balt·if·er·ous \ˌkō(ˌ)bȯlˈtif(ə)rəs\ *adj* [*cobalti-* + *-ferous*] **:** containing cobalt ⟨~ ores⟩

co·bal·ti·nitrite \ˌkō(ˌ)bȯltə+\ *n* -s [*cobalti-* + *nitrite*] **:** any of a series of complex salts of cobalt having the general formula $M_3Co(NO_2)_6$ — see POTASSIUM COBALTINITRITE

co·bal·tite \kəˈbȯlˌtīt, kōˈ-, ˈkōˌ-\ *or* **co·balt·ine** \ˈkōˌbȯlˌtēn, -tən\ *n* -s [*cobaltite*, alter. of *cobaltine; cobaltine*, fr. F, fr. *cobalt* + *-ine*] **:** a mineral consisting of a grayish to silver-white cobalt sulfarsenide CoAsS used in the manufacture of smalt and occurring massive and in isometric crystals related to those of pyrite

co·balt·ized *or* **co·balt·ised** \ˈkōˌbȯlˌtīzd\ *adj, of fertilizers* **:** treated with a compound of cobalt (as cobalt sulfate)

co·bal·to- *comb form* [*cobalt*] **:** bivalent cobalt **:** cobaltous ⟨*cobaltocyanic*⟩

co·bal·to·calcite \kəˌbȯl(ˌ)tō+\ *n* -s [*cobalto-* + *calcite*] **:** a mineral consisting of carbonate of cobalt $CoCO_3$ isomorphous with calcite

co·bal·tom·e·nite \ˌkōˌbȯlˈtäməˌnīt\ *n* -s [ISV *cobalto-* + Gk *mēnē* moon + ISV *-ite;* orig. formed in F] **:** a mineral consisting of cobalt selenium oxide of uncertain composition, possibly hydrous

co·bal·tous \(ˈ)kōˈbȯltəs\ *adj* [*cobalt* + *-ous*] **:** of, relating to, or containing cobalt — used esp. of cobalt compounds in which this element is bivalent; compare COBALTIC

cobaltous chloride *n* **:** the cobalt chloride $CoCl_2$

cobaltous fluoride *n* : COBALT FLUORIDE a

cobaltous sulfate *n* : the cobalt sulfate $CoSO_4$

cobalt oxide *n* : an oxide of cobalt: as **a** : the monoxide CoO obtained usu. as a grayish powder — called also *cobaltous oxide* **b** : a gray to blue-black powder containing cobalt monoxide and higher oxides (as tricobalt tetroxide Co_3O_4) and used chiefly in coloring glass and ceramic ware blue

cobalt pyrites *n* : LINNAEITE

cobalt red *n* : a moderate purplish red that is bluer and deeper than average rose or violine pink and bluer and lighter than magenta rose

cobalt 60 \-'sikstē\ *n* : a heavy radioactive isotope of cobalt having the mass number 60 produced in nuclear reactors and used as a source of gamma rays esp. in place of radium (as in the treatment of cancer and in radiography) — called also *radiocobalt*; symbol Co^{60} or ^{60}Co

cobalt sulfate *n* : a sulfate of cobalt; *usu* : the salt $CoSO_4$ crystallizing in pale red monoclinic prisms containing seven molecules of water and occurring native as bieberite

cobalt ultramarine *n* : COBALT BLUE 1a, 2

cobalt violet *n* **1** : any of several purple pigments containing a compound of cobalt (as cobalt phosphate) **2** : a moderate purple that is redder and duller than heliotrope (sense 4a), redder, lighter, and stronger than average amethyst, redder and less strong than manganese violet, redder and deeper than average lilac (sense 3a), and redder and stronger than mignon — called also *thistle*

cobalt vitriol *n* : the cobalt sulfate $CoSO_4$

cobalt yellow *n* **1** : a bright yellow pigment consisting essentially of potassium cobaltinitrite — called also *aureolin* **2** : a strong to brilliant yellow — called also *aureolin*

cobang *var of* KOBAN

cobb *var of* COB

cobbed *past of* COB

[1]**cob·ber** \'käbə(r)\ *n* -s [[1]*cob* + *-er*] : a worker who breaks asbestos fibers away from asbestos-bearing rock or chips waste rock from lumps of ore

[2]**cobber** \"\ *n* -s [origin unknown] *Austral* : a close friend and companion ⟨staunchest ~ a man could have —Rex Ingamells⟩

cob·bing *pres part of* COB

[1]**cob·ble** \'käbəl\ *vt* **cobbled; cobbled; cobbling** \-b(ə)liŋ\ **cobbles** [ME *coblen*, perh. back-formation fr. *cobelere* cobbler] **1** *Brit* : to mend, patch, or repair coarsely or roughly ⟨any holes he would ~ with sack-needle and string —Adrian Bell⟩ **2 a** : MEND, REPAIR **b** : MAKE ⟨*cobbled* shoes⟩ **3** : to make or put together roughly, clumsily or hastily often in a temporary or improvised fashion — often used with *up*

[2]**cobble** \"\ *n* -s : a cobbled place : a coarse mending

[3]**cobble** \"\ *n* -s [back-formation fr. *cobblestone*] **1 a** : a naturally rounded stone larger than a pebble and smaller than a boulder often arbitrarily limited by geologists to a size ranging from 64 to 256 millimeters in diameter **b** : such a stone used in paving a street or in other construction **2 cobbles** *pl, also* **cobble coal** *chiefly Brit* : lump coal about the size of small cobblestones **3** : a ball or piece of waste iron or steel

[4]**cobble** \"\ *vt* : to pave with cobblestones

[5]**cobble** \"\ *n* -s [perh. fr. [3]*cobble*] *Northeast* : a rounded hill usu. of moderate elevation

[6]**cobble** \"\ *n* -s [perh. fr. [3]*cob* (swan) + *-le* (dim. suffix)] : a common loon (*Gavia immer*); *also* : RED-THROATED LOON

cobbled *adj* [fr. past part. of [4]*cobble*] : paved or covered with cobblestones

cobble gravel *n* [[3]*cobble*] : gravel containing rounded fragments of rock usu. ranging in size between 64 and 256 millimeters in diameter

cob·bler \'käblə(r)\ *n* -s [ME *cobelere*] **1** : a repairer or maker of shoes and often of other leather goods **2** *archaic* : one that does clumsy or coarse work : BOTCHER **3** : a tall drink that consists usu. of wine, rum, or whiskey and sugar and is served esp. in a goblet filled with shaved ice and garnished with a sprig of mint or slice of lemon or orange ⟨claret ~⟩ ⟨whiskey ~⟩ **4** : a deep-dish fruit pie without a bottom crust and with a thick biscuit top crust **5 a** : a spiny Australian catfish (*Cnidoglanis macrocephalus*) **b** : THREADFISH 1 **c** : a long-spined European sea scorpion (*Cottus bubalis*) **d** : a scaleless So. Australian scorpaenid fish (*Gymnopistes marmoratus*) related to and greatly resembling the fortescue **e** : POMPANO 1 **6** *chiefly Austral* : a sheep left to the last at shearing time; *also* : a sheep difficult to handle

cobblerfish \'==,=\ *n* **1** [so called fr. the fancied resemblance of their rays to a cobbler's strings] : THREADFISH 1 **2** : POMPANO 1

cobbler's-awl \'käblə(r)z + ,-\ *n, pl* **cobbler's-awls 1** : AVOCET **2** *Austral* : a spinebill (*Acanthorhynchus tenuirostris*)

cobbler's bench *n* : a low 4-legged bench formerly used by cobblers that has a seat at one end, compartments for tools and supplies, and a working area; *also* : an occasional table suggesting a cobbler's bench

cobbler's peg *n* [prob. fr. the appearance of the pappi] : either of two chiefly Australian weedy composite herbs (*Erigeron linifolius* and *Bidens pilosa*) — often used in pl. but sing. or pl. in constr.

cobblestone \'==,=\ *n* [ME, fr. *cobble-* (prob. fr. [3]*cob* (lump) + *-le*) + *stone*] : [3]COBBLE 1b

cob·bly \'käb(ə)lē, -li\ *adj* [[3]*cobble* + *-y*] : containing cobbles : STONY, ROUGH, LUMPY

cob·bra \'käbrə\ *n* -s [native name in New So. Wales] *Austral* : HEAD, SKULL

cobb's disease \'käbz-\ *n, usu cap C* [after Nathan A. *Cobb* †1932 Am. biologist] : a disease of sugarcane caused by a bacterium (*Xanthomonas vascularum*) and characterized by a slime in the vascular bundles accompanied by dwarfing, streaking of leaves, and decay — called also *sugarcane gummosis*

cob·by \'käbē, -bi\ *adj* -ER/-EST [[3]*cob* + *-y*] **1** *dial Eng* **a** : HEARTY, LIVELY **b** : HEADSTRONG **2** : like a cob horse in shape : having a deep strong short-coupled body and relatively short sturdy legs ⟨a ~ cat⟩ : STOCKY ⟨~ in build⟩

cob cactus *n* [[3]*cob* (corncob); fr. its shape] : STRAWBERRY CACTUS

cob coal *n* [[3]*cob* (lump)] : coal in rounded lumps from the size of an egg to that of a football

cob·den·ism \'käbdə,nizəm\ *n* -s *usu cap* [Richard *Cobden* †1865 Eng. statesman and economist + E *-ism*] : the political and economic doctrines of Richard Cobden, 19th century English statesman and economist whose national policy was for peace, for withdrawal from the European competition for balance of power, and for free trade

cob·den·ite \-,nīt\ *n* -s *usu cap* [Richard *Cobden* †1865 + E *-ite*] : an adherent of Cobdenism

co·be·go \kə'bē(,)gō\ *n* -s [modif. of Malay *kubong*] : FLYING LEMUR

co·belligerency \¦kō+\ *n* -ES [*co-* + *belligerency*] : the state of being a cobelligerent

[1]**co·belligerent** \¦kō+\ *n* -s [*co-* + *belligerent*] : a country fighting together with another power against a common enemy often without a formal alliance — usu. distinguished from *ally*

[2]**cobelligerent** \"\ *adj* : having the status of or fighting as a cobelligerent

cobhouse \'=,=\ *n* [[3]*cob* (corncob) + *house*] **1** : a toy house of corncobs or sticks laid in parallel pairs piled on one another each at right angles to the preceding pair **2** : a flimsy unstable structure or arrangement ⟨a ~ of lies ready to fall⟩

co·bia \'kōbēə\ *also* **ca·bio** \'kābē(,)ō\ *n* -s [origin unknown] : a large percoid fish (*Rachycentron canadum*) cream to brown above fading to white below with one or more longitudinal dark stripes along the sides that is widely distributed in warm seas and regarded as an outstanding food and game fish

cob·iron \'kä,bī(ə)rn, -īən\ *n* -s [ME *cobiren*, fr. [3]*cob* (lump) + *iren* iron; fr. the knobs on the ends] **1** : an iron for supporting a spit **2** : ANDIRON

co·bit·i·dae \kō'bidə,dē\ *n pl, cap* [NL, fr. *Cobitis*, type genus (fr. Gk *kōbitis* like the gudgeon, fr. *kōbios* gudgeon) + *-idae*] : a family of slender Old World cyprinoid fishes having long barbels at the mouth and living at the bottom of flowing waters where they feed on small invertebrates

co·ble \'kōbəl, 'käb-\ *n* -s [ME, prob. of Celt origin; akin to W *ceubal* ferryboat, skiff, OBret *caubal*; perh. akin to L *cavus* hollow — more at CAVE] **1** *Scot* : a short flat-bottomed boat **2** : a flat-floored fishing boat with a drop rudder extending below the keel, bilge keels beneath the stern, and a dipping lugsail on a raking mast that is used chiefly in the North sea

co·blenz·ian \(')kō¦blen(t)sēən, -nzē-\ *adj, usu cap* [*Koblenz, Coblenz*, city in western Germany + E *-an*] : of or relating to a division of the European Devonian — see GEOLOGIC TIME table

cob·less \'käbləs\ *adj* : being without a cob

cob meal *n* [[3]*cob* (corncob)] : corn meal in which the cob is also ground

cob-nosed \'=,=\ *adj* [[3]*cob* (lump)] : having a large and bulbous nose

cobnut \'=,=\ *n* -s [[3]*cob* (lump) + *nut*] **1 a** : a filbertlike fruit yielded by a variety (*Corylus avellana grandis*) of the hazel much grown in Europe **b** : a plant bearing this fruit **2 a** : a game in which a player pitches a nut at a pile of nuts and wins any that he knocks down **b** : a game played with nuts tied on a string in which one tries to strike and break his opponent's with one of his own

co·bo·la \kə'bōlə\ *n* -s [AmerSp] : a Central American tree of the genus *Podocarpus*

co·boss \'kō, 'kə(m) + ,-\ *v imper* [alter. of *come, Boss*] — a call to cows

cob pipe *n* [[3]*cob* (corncob)] : CORNCOB PIPE

[1]**co·bra** \'kōbrə\ *n* -s [Pg *cobra* (*de capello*), lit., hooded snake, fr. L *colubra*, fem. of *coluber* snake — more at COLUBER] **1** : any of several very venomous Asiatic and African elapid snakes of the genus *Naja* that, when excited, expand the skin of the neck into a broad hood by movement of the anterior ribs — see INDIAN COBRA, KING COBRA **2** : either of two African snakes that spit their venom from a distance: **a** : BLACK-NECKED COBRA **b** : RINGHALS **3** : MAMBA

cobra (*Naja naja*)

[2]**cobra** \"\ *n* -s *Austral* : SHIPWORM

cobra de ca·pel·lo \-dēkə'pe(,)lō\ *n, pl* **cobras de capello** [Pg] : INDIAN COBRA

cobra plant *n* : CALIFORNIA PITCHER PLANT

co·bri·form \'kōbrə,fȯrm\ *adj* [*cobra* + *-iform*] : like or related to the cobras

cob rot *n* [[3]*cob* (corncob)] : a disease of corn due to a fungus (*Nigrospora sphaerica*) of the family Dematiaceae that causes yellowish basal rot and shredding of the ear

cobs *pl of* COB, *pres 3d sing of* COB

co·bus \'kōbəs\ *syn of* KOBUS

[1]**cob·web** \'käb,web\ *n* [alter. of ME *coppeweb*, fr. *coppe* spider (fr. OE *ātorcoppe*) + *web*; akin to MD *coppe* spider, Dan *edderkop*, Sw dial. *etterkoppa* and prob. to OE *copp* top — more at COP] **1 a** : the network spread by a spider to catch its prey **b** : a single thread spun by a spider; *also* : tangles of such thread with adherent dirt and dust that have accumulated ⟨the windows dark with ~⟩ ⟨festooned with grimy ~*s*⟩ **c** : a thread or web spun by an insect larva **2** : a slight or flimsy texture ⟨a ~ of fine-spun casuistry is dissipated in a breath —B.N.Cardozo⟩ **3 cobwebs** *pl* : a clogging or obscuring accumulation esp. as a result of disuse, neglect, or stagnation ⟨the magazine . . . helped to sweep away the aesthetic ~*s* of half a century —H.L.Mencken⟩ : confusion or disorder esp. of the mind ⟨~*s* go out of my mind as I write —H.J.Laski⟩ **4** : a snare of insidious meshes ⟨~*s* of law and politics⟩

[2]**cobweb** \"\ *vt* **cobwebbed; cobwebbed; cobwebbing; cobwebs 1** : to obscure (as a mind or a subject) by confusion or stagnation ⟨the drunk whose mind is *cobwebbed* and confused —Lucius Garvin⟩ **2** : to cover with a network resembling cobwebs ⟨*cobwebbed* with ropes —Osbert Sitwell⟩

cobwebbed *adj* : covered or filled with cobwebs

cobweb bird *also* **cobweb** *n* [so called fr. its use of cobwebs in its nest] *dial Eng* : SPOTTED FLYCATCHER

cob·web·by \-,webē\ *adj* -ER/-EST **1** : covered with cobwebs **2** : resembling, suggesting, or having the character of cobwebs ⟨Corot painted thousands of such ~ canvases —*Time*⟩ **3** : MUSTY, STAGNANT, COBWEBBED ⟨~ brain⟩

cobweb disease *n* : a disease of cultivated mushrooms caused by a fungus (*Dactylium dendroides*) that produces a white or pink-tinted coating of mycelium over the fruiting bodies

cobweb houseleek *n* : a low European herb (*Sempervivum arachnoideum*) having bright red flowers and a basal rosette of small succulent leaves connected by cobwebby strands

cobweb theorem *n* : a theorem in economics: in some cases successive adjustments of supply and demand amplify rather than diminish price fluctuations

cobwork \'=,=\ *n* [prob. fr. *cob* (*house*) log cabin (formerly, mud hut; fr. [4]*cob*) + *work*] : construction or a structure of elements (as logs) laid horizontally with the ends joined at the corners

[1]**co·ca** \'kōkə\ *n* -s [Sp, fr. Quechua *kúka*] **1** : any of several So. American shrubs of the genus *Erythroxylon*; *esp* : a shrub (*E. coca*) with leaves resembling tea leaves that are chewed with alkali by natives of the Andean uplands to impart endurance **2** : the dried leaves of either of two cocas both containing several alkaloids of which cocaine is the most important: **a** : those of the coca (*Erythroxylon coca*) — called also *Bolivian coca, Huanuco coca* **b** : those of the related plant (*E. novagranatense*) — called also *Peruvian coca, Truxillo coca*

[2]**coca** \"\ *usu cap* — a communications code word for the letter *c*

co·caine \kō'kān, kə'-, 'kō,k- *sometimes* 'kōkə,ēn *or* -k(ə)in\ *n* -s [ISV *coca* + *-ine*; orig. formed as G *kokain*] **1** : a bitter crystalline alkaloid $C_{17}H_{21}NO_4$ obtained from coca leaves and synthesized from ecgonine that has first a stimulating then a narcotic effect if taken internally, in large doses produces intoxication like that from hemp, and acts as a local anesthetic and mydriatic; methyl-benzoyl-ecgonine **2** : any of several alkaloids found in coca that are derived from ecgonine

cocaine family *n* : ERYTHROXYLACEAE

cocaine plant *n* : COCA 1

co·cain·ism \kō'kā(ə),nizəm, kə'k-; 'kō,kā(ə),n-, -,kə,n-\ *n* -s [ISV *cocaine* + *-ism*] : addiction to cocaine

co·cain·i·za·tion \¦kō,kā(ə)nə¦zāshən, kə¦k-, -nī¦-\ *n* -s : the act of cocainizing or the state of being cocainized

co·cain·ize \kō'kā(ə),nīz, kə'k-, 'kō,k-\ *vt* -ED/-ING/-S [*cocaine* + *-ize*] : to treat or anesthetize with cocaine

co·ca·ma \kō'kämə, kə'-\ *n, pl* **cocama** *or* **cocamas** *usu cap* [Sp, of AmerInd origin] **1 a** : a group of Tupian peoples of Peru including the Omagua **b** : a member of such peoples **2** : the language of the Cocama

co·carboxylase \(')kō + \ *n* -s [*co-* + *carboxylase*] : a coenzyme $C_{12}H_{19}ClN_4O_7P_2S{\cdot}H_2O$ that is the pyrophosphate of thiamine, functions in conjunction with various carboxylases, and is physiologically important esp. in the decarboxylation of pyruvic acid

co·carcinogen \(')kō +\ *n* -s [*co-* + *carcinogen*] : an agent that acts synergistically with one or more carcinogens to produce a cancer — **co·carcinogenic** \¦kō +\ *adj*

co·carde \kō'kärd, kə'-, -kȧd\ *n* -s [F — more at COCKADE] **1** : a distinguishing mark worn usu. on the hat to indicate esp. military status : COCKADE; *also* : a similar distinguishing mark on an airplane **2** : an ornament often of pleated ribbon for a woman's hat

cocardes 2

co·cash \kō'kash\ *n* -ES [of Algonquian origin; akin to Natick *kōshki* it is rough] **1** : a No. American herb (*Aster puniceus*) having red or purple flower heads in terminal clusters **2** : HORSEWEED 1

cocashweed \'=,=\ *n* : GOLDEN RAGWORT

cocc- *or* **cocci-** *or* **cocco-** *comb form* [NL, fr. *coccus* & L *coccum* kermes berry, both fr. Gk *kokkos* grain, seed, kermes berry] : grain : seed : berry : coccus ⟨*cocc*oid⟩ ⟨*cocci*form⟩ ⟨*cocco*bacillus⟩

coc·ca·ce·ae \kə'kāsē,ē, kä'-\ *n pl, cap* [NL, fr. *cocc-* + *-aceae*] *in some classifications* : a family of bacteria comprising those more or less spherical in shape now rarely regarded as a natural assemblage — compare BACILLACEAE, BACTERIACEAE — **coc·ca·ceous** \-'kāshəs\ *adj*

coc·ca·gee \,käkə'jē\ *n* -s [IrGael *cac a' ghéidh* goose dung; fr. its color] **1** : a cider apple formerly popular in England **2** : cider made from the coccagee

coc·cal \'käkəl\ *adj* [NL *coccus* + E *-al*] : of or relating to a coccus

coc·ce·ian \käk'sēyən\ *n* -s *usu cap* [Johannes *Cocceius* (Koch) †1669 Ger. theologian + E *-an*] : an adherent of Cocceianism

coc·ce·ian·ism \-,nizəm\ *n* -s *usu cap* [Johannes *Cocceius* (Koch) †1669 + E *-an* + *-ism*] : the theological belief that the whole history of the Christian church is foreshadowed in the Old Testament

coc·ce·rin \'käksərən\ *n* -s [*cocceryl* + *-in*] : a wax $C_{92}H_{182}O_6$ found in cochineal

cocci *pl of* COCCUS

-cocci *pl of* -COCCUS

coc·cid \'käksəd, -,sid\ *n* -s [NL *Coccidae*] : a scale or mealybug : any member of the superfamily Coccoidea

coc·ci·dae \'käksə,dē\ *n pl, cap* [NL, fr. *Coccus*, type genus + *-idae*] : an important family of homopterous insects mostly of small size, sometimes including all the scales, mealybugs, and related forms but now often restricted to the soft and tortoise scales

coccidi- *or* **coccidio-** *comb form* [*coccidium*] : Coccidia ⟨*coccidi*ocide⟩ ⟨*coccidio*stasis⟩

[1]**coc·cid·ia** \käk'sidēə\ *pl of* COCCIDIUM

[2]**coccidia** \"\ *n pl, cap* [NL, fr. pl. of [1]*Coccidium*] : a large order of schizogonous telosporidian protozoans, typically parasites of the digestive epithelium of vertebrates and higher invertebrates and including several forms of great economic importance — see EIMERIA — **coc·cid·i·al** \(')käk¦sidēəl\ *adj* — **coc·cid·i·an** \-dēən\ *adj or n*

coc·ci·di·ida \,käksə'dīədə\ *or* **coc·cid·i·id·ea** \käk,sidē'idēə\ [NL, fr. [1]*Coccidium* + *-ida* or *-idea*] *syn of* COCCIDIA

coc·cid·i·oi·dal \(')käk¦sidē¦ȯidᵊl\ *adj* [NL *Coccidioides* + E *-al*] : belonging to, like, or caused by fungi of the genus *Coccidioides*

coccidioidal granuloma *n* : COCCIDIOIDOMYCOSIS — now used chiefly of the generalized form or stage characterized by formation of nodular lesions throughout the body

coc·cid·i·oi·des \käk,sidē'ȯi,dēz\ *n, cap* [NL, fr. *coccidi-* + *-oides* -oid] *in some classifications* : a genus of parasitic zygomycetous fungi usu. included in Blastomycetes but of doubtful taxonomic position, having septate mycelium and endospores — see COCCIDIOIDOMYCOSIS

coc·cid·i·oi·din \(')=¦=dē¦ȯidᵊn, -ȯi(,)din\ *n* -s [NL *Coccidioides* (genus name of *Coccidioides immitis*) + E *-in*] : an antigen prepared from asparagine-synthetic cultures of a fungus (*Coccidioides immitis*) and used to detect skin sensitivity to and, by inference, infection with this organism

coc·cid·i·oi·do·mycosis \käk,sidē,ȯidō, -ȯidə + \ *also* **coc·cid·io·mycosis** \(')käk¦sidē(,)ō, -sidēə + \ *n* [NL, fr. *Coccidioides* (genus name of *Coccidioides immitis*) + *mycosis*] : an infective disease of man and various wild and domestic animals caused by a fungus (*Coccidioides immitis*) usu. inhaled as spores and marked by fever and localized pulmonary symptoms but sometimes becoming generalized with granulomatous nodular lesions in various parts of the body

coc·cid·io·mor·pha \(')käk¦sidē(,)ō¦mȯrfə, -sidēə¦-\ *n pl, cap* [NL, fr. *coccidi-* + *-morpha*] *in some classifications* : a subdivision of Sporozoa comprising the schizogonous forms (orders Coccidia and Haemosporidia) and being equivalent to Telosporidia with the gregarines omitted

coc·cid·io·sis \(')käk¦sidē¦ōsəs\ *n, pl* **coccidio·ses** \-,sēz\ [NL, fr. *coccidi-* + *-osis*] : infestation with or disease caused by coccidia — compare EIMERIA, ISOSPORA

coc·cid·io·stat \(')käk¦sidēō,stat, -dēə,-\ *n* -s [*coccidi-* + *-stat*] : an agent that serves to retard the life cycle or reduce the population of a pathogenic coccidium to the point that disease is minimized and immunity is developed by the host

coc·cid·io·stat·ic \(')=¦=¦==¦stad·ik\ *adj* [*coccidi-* + *-o-* + Gk *statikos* causing to stand — more at STATIC] : inhibiting the growth and development of coccidia

[1]**coc·cid·i·um** \käk'sidēəm\ [NL, fr. *cocc-* + *-idium*] *syn of* EIMERIA

[2]**coccidium** \"\ *n, pl* **coccid·ia** \-dēə\ : a protozoan of the order Coccidia

coc·ci·dol·o·gy \,käksə'däləjē\ *n* -ES [NL *Coccidae* + E *-o-* + *-logy*] : the branch of zoology that treats of the scales, mealybugs, and other members of the superfamily Coccoidea

coc·ci·doph·a·gous \¦==¦däfəgəs\ *adj* [*coccid* + *-o-* + *-phagous*] : feeding on scales ⟨~ ladybugs⟩ — compare VEDALIA

coc·ci·nel·la \,käksə'nelə\ *n, cap* [NL, fr. L *coccinus* scarlet-colored (fr. Gk *kokkinos*, fr. *kokkos* kermes berry) + *-ella*] : a cosmopolitan genus of small beetles that is the type of the family Coccinellidae and includes a number of typical ladybugs

[1]**coc·ci·nel·lid** \¦==¦=ləd\ *adj* [NL *Coccinellidae*] : of or relating to the Coccinellidae

[2]**coccinellid** \"\ *n* -s : a beetle of the family Coccinellidae : LADYBUG

coc·ci·nel·li·dae \-'nelə,dē\ *n pl, cap* [NL, fr. *Coccinella*, type genus + *-idae*] : a family of small usu. hemispherical beetles that are known as ladybugs and that have larvae which are mostly beneficial predators of aphids and other small insects — compare MEXICAN BEAN BEETLE

coccineous *adj* [L *coccineus*, var. of *coccinus*] *obs* : SCARLET

coc·cin·ic acid \(')käk¦sinik-\ *n* [F *coccinique*, fr. *coccine* carmine (fr. L *coccinus* scarlet, fr. Gk *kokkinos*, fr. *kokkos* grain, seed) + *-ique* -ic] : any of three isomeric crystalline diacids $C_6H_2(OH)(CH_3)(COOH)_2$ distinguished as alpha, beta, and gamma with the alpha acid being obtained by oxidizing cochineal

coc·ci·nite \'käksə,nīt\ *n* -s [G *kokzinit*, fr. L *coccinus* scarlet + G *-it* -ite] : a native mercury iodide HgI_2 found esp. at Broken Hill, New So. Wales, and in Mexico

cocco- — see COCC-

coc·co·bacillary \¦kä(,)kō, ¦käkə +\ *adj* [NL *coccobacillus* + E *-ary*] : of, relating to, or being a coccobacillus

coc·co·bacilliform \" +\ *adj* [NL *coccobacillus* + E *-iform*] : resembling a coccobacillus — used esp. of certain small bacillary organisms recovered chiefly from respiratory infections of poultry and regarded as related to the pleuropneumonia group

[1]**coc·co·bacillus** \" +\ *n* [NL, fr. *cocc-* + *bacillus*] : a very short coccuslike bacillus esp. of the genus *Pasteurella*

[2]**coccobacillus** [NL, fr. *cocc-* + *bacillus*] *syn of* PASTEURELLA

coc·co·gen·ic \¦käkō¦jenik, -kə¦j-\ *or* **coc·ci·gen·ic** \¦käksə¦-\ *adj* [*cocc-* + *-genic*] : caused by a coccus

[1]**coc·coid** \'kä,kȯid\ *or* **coc·coi·dal** \(')kä¦kȯidᵊl\ *adj* [*cocc-* + *-oid, -oidal*] : belonging to or resembling a coccus : GLOBOSE — compare -COCCUS 2

[2]**coccoid** \"\ *n* -s : a coccoid cell or body

coc·coi·dea \kä'kȯidēə\ *n pl, cap* [NL, fr. *cocc-* + *-oidea*] : a superfamily of Hemiptera including scales and mealybugs and being equivalent to Coccidae in the broadest sense

coc·co·lite \'käkə,līt\ *n* -s [F, fr. *cocc-* + *-lite*] : a granular variety of pyroxene of various colors

coc·co·lith \-,lith\ *n* -s [*cocc-* + *-lith*] : a minute calcareous body found in chalk and deep-sea ooze and constituting the skeletal remains of a coccolithophore — **coc·co·lith·ic** \¦==¦lithik\ *adj*

coc·co·lith·o·phore \,käkō'lithə,fō(ə)r, ,käkə'-\ *n* -s [NL *Coccolithophora*] : any of numerous minute mostly marine planktonic biflagellated organisms with brown chromatophores and complex calcareous, less commonly siliceous, shells that are sometimes considered to constitute the family Coccolithophoridae of the order Chrysomonadina — **coc·co·li·thoph·o·rid** \¦==lə¦thäfərəd, -,rid\ *adj or n*

coc·co·lith·o·phor·i·dae \,==,lithə'fȯrə,dē\ *n pl, cap* [NL, fr. *Coccolithophora*, type genus (fr. E *coccolith* + NL *-o-* + *-phora*) + *-idae*] : a family of minute marine chrysomonad flagellates having a skeleton of calcareous plates — see COCCOLITHOPHORE

coc·col·o·ba \kə'käləbə\ *n, cap* [NL, alter. of *Coccolobis*, fr. *cocc-* + *-lobis* (fr. Gk *lobos* lobe, capsule, pod) — more at SLEEP] : a genus of tropical and subtropical American evergreen trees, shrubs, and woody vines (family Polygonaceae) having greenish flowers in axillary spikes or racemes — see SEA GRAPE

coc·col·o·bis \-bəs\ [NL, fr. L, a kind of Spanish grape] *syn of* COCCOLOBA

coc·co·my·ces \ˌkäkōˈmīˌsēz, ˌkäkəˈ-\ *n, cap* [NL, fr. *cocc-* + *-myces*] **:** a genus of ascomycetous fungi (family Phacidiaceae) with filiform 1-celled, 2-celled, or many-celled ascospores and with conidial stages that are often referred to the form genus *Cylindrosporium*

coc·co·sphere \ˈkäkō, ˈkäkə + ˌ-\ *n* -S [*cocc-* + *-sphere*] **:** a coccolithophore or its skeleton

coc·cos·te·an \kəˈkästēən\ *n* -S [NL *Coccosteus* + E *-an*] **:** a fish of the genus *Coccosteus* or family Coccosteidae

coc·co·ste·i·dae \ˌkäkōˈstēəˌdē, ˌkäkəˈ-\ *n pl, cap* [NL, fr. *Coccosteus*, type genus + *-idae*] **:** a family (subclass Arthrodira) of armored extinct fishes — see COCCOSTEUS

coc·cos·te·us \kəˈkästēəs\ *n, cap* [NL, fr. *cocc-* + *-osteus*] **:** a genus of Devonian fishes having broad armored plates about the head and being the type of the family Coccosteidae

coc·co·thraus·tes \ˌkäkōˈthrȯˌstēz, ˌkäkəˈ-\ *n, cap* [NL, fr. *cocc-* + Gk *thraustēs* crusher (fr. *thrauein* to shatter) — more at DREARY] **:** a genus of large finches comprising the hawfinches and in some classifications the evening grosbeaks — **coc·co·thraus·tine** \ˌ≈≈ˈ≈ˌstīn, -ˌstən\ *adj*

coc·co·thri·nax \-ˈthrīˌnaks\ *n, cap* [NL, fr. *cocc-* + *Thrinax*] **:** a small genus of West Indian and Floridian fan palms having short unarmed trunks and small white flowers in dense sheathed clusters

coc·cous \ˈkäkəs\ *adj* [NL *coccus* + E *-ous*] **:** composed of cocci **:** COCCOID

coc·cu·lin \ˈkäkyələn\ *n* -S [ISV *coccul-* (fr. NL *cocculus*, specific epithet of *Anamirta cocculus*) + *-in*; orig. formed as G *kokkulin*] **:** PICROTOXIN

¹coc·cu·lus \-ləs\ *n, cap* [NL, lit., small berry, fr. *cocc-* + *-ulus*] **:** a small genus of slender woody vines (family Menispermaceae) with alternate leaves, paniculate flowers, and drupaceous fruits — see CAROLINA MOONSEED

²cocculus \"\ *or* **cocculus in·di·cus** \-indəkəs\ *n, pl* **cocculus** [NL *cocculus indicus*, fr. *cocculus* small berry + L *indicus* of India — more at INDIC] **:** the very poisonous bean-shaped berry of a woody vine (*Anamirta cocculus*) of the East Indies that yields picrotoxin and is used locally to stupefy fishes and in an ointment to control vermin

coc·cus \ˈkäkəs\ *n* [NL, fr. Gk *kokkos* grain, seed, kermes berry] **1** *pl* **coc·ci** \ˈkäˌkī, -ˌkē, -äkˌsī, -äksē\ **:** MERICARP **2** *pl* **cocci :** a spherical bacterium **3** *cap* **:** the type genus of Coccidae formerly including most scales, lac insects, and cochineal insects but now restricted to certain typical scales **4** *pl* **cocci :** COCHINEAL 1

-coccus \ˌkäkəs\ *n comb form, pl* **-cocci** \ˌkäˌkī, ˌkäkē, ˌkäkˌsī, ˌkäksē\ [NL, fr. Gk *kokkos*] **1 :** plant having berries, seeds, or cocci (of a specified type) — usu. in generic names ⟨Oxycoccus⟩ ⟨Pterococcus⟩ **2 :** berry-shaped organism — esp. in generic names of algae and bacteria ⟨Proto*coccus*⟩ ⟨Micro*coccus*⟩ ⟨Strepto*coccus*⟩ ⟨Staphylo*coccus*⟩

coc·cy·dyn·ia \ˌkäksəˈdinēə\ *n* -S [NL, by shortening] **:** COCCYGODYNIA

coccyg- *or* **coccygo-** *comb form* [NL, fr. *coccyg-*, *coccyx*] **:** coccyx ⟨*coccyg*ectomy⟩ ⟨*coccygo*tomy⟩

coc·cyg·e·al \(ˈ)käkˈsijēəl\ *adj* [ML *coccygeus* of the coccyx (fr. *coccyg-*, *coccyx*) + E *-al*] **:** of or relating to the coccyx

coccygeal ganglion *n* **:** a small ganglion anterior to the coccyx at the caudal junction of the two gangliated cords of the sympathetic nervous system

coccygeal gland *n* **1** *also* **coccygeal body :** a small mass of vascular tissue situated near the tip of the coccyx **2 :** the oil gland near the base of the tail of a bird

coc·cy·gec·to·my \ˌkäksəˈjektəmē\ *n* -ES [*coccyg-* + *-ectomy*] **:** the surgical removal of the coccyx

coccygeo- *comb form* [NL, fr. *coccygeus*] **:** coccygeal and ⟨*coccygeo*anal⟩ ⟨*coccygeo*mesenteric⟩

coc·cyg·e·us \käkˈsijēəs\ *n, pl* **coccyg·ei** \-jēˌī\ [NL, fr. *coccyg-*, *coccyx*] **:** a muscle arising from the ischium and sacrospinous ligament and inserted into the coccyx and sacrum

coc·cy·go·dyn·ia \ˌkäksə(ˌ)gōˈdinēə\ *n* -S [NL, fr. *coccyg-* + *-odynia*] **:** pain in the coccyx and adjacent regions

coc·cyx \ˈkäksiks\ *n, pl* **coccy·ges** \ˈkäksəˌjēz, käkˈsī(ˌ)j-\ *also* **coccyxes** \ˈkäksiksəz\ [NL (L, cuckoo), fr. Gk *kokkyx* cuckoo, coccyx; fr. its resemblance to a cuckoo's beak — more at CUCKOO] **1 :** the end of the vertebral column beyond the sacrum in man and certain other primates comprising usu. four small vertebrae that are more or less completely fused in the adult and represent a vestigial tail **2 :** a bone in vertebrates (as birds) corresponding to the primate coccyx; *sometimes* **:** UROSTYLE

coc·cy·zus \käkˈsīzəs\ *n, cap* [NL, irreg. fr. Gk *kokkyx* cuckoo] **:** a genus of American arboreal cuckoos

coch *abbr* COCHLEARE

co·cha·both \kōˈchäbət\ *n, pl* **cochaboth** *or* **cochaboths** *usu cap* **1 :** MACÁ **2 :** a division of the Macá language family

co·chairman \(ˈ)kō+\ *n, pl* **cochairmen** [*co-* + *chairman*] **:** joint chairman, vice-chairman, or assistant chairman

co·chal \kōˈchäl\ *n* -S [MexSp] **:** the edible fruit of a tall cactus (*Myrtillocactus cochal*) of Lower California; *also* **:** the plant producing this fruit

co·che \kō(ˌ)chā\ *n* -S *usu cap* [Sp] **:** a language family of Colombia and Ecuador comprising Sebundoy, Quillacinga, and Patoco — called also *Mocoa*

co·cher \kōˈshā, kōshā\ *n* -S [F, fr. *coche* cab — more at COACH] **:** CABDRIVER

co·chief \(ˈ)kō+\ *n* [*co-* + *chief*] **:** joint chief, alternate chief, or vice-chief

co·chil sa·po·ta \kōˈchēlsəˈpōd·ə\ *n* [Sp *cochilzapote*, fr. Nahuatl *cochiztzapotl*, fr. *cochitl* sleep + *tzapotl* sapote; fr. the belief that eating the fruit would put one to sleep] **1 :** a large Mexican tree (*Casimiroa edulis*) with fruit about the size of a large apple and resembling the peach in flavor **2 :** the fruit of the cochil sapota

co·chi·mi \kōchəˈmē\ *n, pl* **cochimi** *or* **cochimis** *usu cap* [Sp *cochimi*, of AmerInd origin] **1 a :** an Indian people of central Lower California, Mexico **b :** a member of such people **2 :** a Yuman language of the Cochimi people

co·chin \ˈkōchən, ˈkäch-\ *n* -S [fr. *Cochin* China, a region of Vietnam] **1** *or* **cochin china** *often Cochin & usu Cochin China* **:** a large domestic fowl of an Asian breed having soft thick plumage of white, black, buff, or partridge, small wings and tail, and densely feathered legs and feet **2 :** ARGUS BROWN

coch·i·neal \ˌkächəˌnēl, ˌ≈≈ˈ≈ *sometimes* -ōch-, *esp bef pause or cons* -nēəl\ *n* -S [MF & Sp; MF *cochenille*, fr. OSp *cochinilla* cochineal, wood louse] **1 a :** a red dyestuff consisting of the dried bodies of females of the cochineal insect that is obtained in various grades (as silver cochineal and black cochineal, according to whether dry heat or boiling water is used to kill the insects) and that was formerly used as a mordant wool dye and food color and is now used as a biological stain and as an indicator — see CARMINE, CARMINIC ACID; DYE table I (under *Natural Red 4*) **b :** a synthetic product resembling cochineal — see DYE table I (under *Acid Red 18*) **2 :** CASTILIAN RED **3** [by shortening] **:** COCHINEAL INSECT

cochineal fig *or* **cochineal cactus** *or* **cochineal plant** *n* **:** a cactus (*Nopalea cochinellifera*) of Central and So. America that is widely cultivated as food for the cochineal insect

cochineal insect *n* **1 :** a small bright red insect (*Dactylopius coccus*) that is related to and resembles the mealybug in appearance and habits, feeds on cactus (esp. of the genera *Nopalea* and *Opuntia*), and has long been a source of red dyes **2 :** any of certain other insects closely related to the cochineal insect and us. of similar coloring

cochin ginger *n, usu cap C* [fr. *Cochin* China, where it is produced] **:** WHITE GINGER

cochin kino *n, usu cap C* [fr. *Cochin*, India] **:** a commercial variety of kino

cochin oil *n, often cap C* [fr. *Cochin*, India] **:** a fine grade of coconut oil

co·chise \(ˈ)kōˈchēs, -ēz\ *adj, usu cap* [fr. *Cochise* county, Arizona] **:** of or belonging to a prehistoric culture of southeastern Arizona and adjacent New Mexico characterized by an abundance of flat milling slabs and lack of defensive weapons in the first stage and evidences of change from a seed-gathering to an agricultural economy in the later stages

co·chi·ti \ˌkōchəˈtē, ˈ≈≈ˌ≈\ *n, pl* **cochiti** *or* **cochitis** *usu cap* **1 a :** a subdivision of the Keresan-speaking Indian people of New Mexico **b :** a member of such people **2 :** the language of the Cochiti

cochl *abbr* cochleare

coch·lea \ˈkäklēə\ *n, pl* **coch·le·ae** \-ēˌē, -lēˌī\ *or* **coch·le·as** \-ēəz\ [NL, fr. L, snail, snail shell, Archimedean screw, spiral stairway, fr. Gk *kochlias*, fr. *kochlos* land snail (also, a kind of shellfish with a spiral shell); akin to Gk *konchē* mussel, cockle — more at CONCH] **:** a division of the labyrinth of the ear wanting or rudimentary in the lower vertebrates but well developed in birds and mammals and in all the latter except the monotremes coiled into the form of a snail shell, in man consisting of a spiral canal in the petrous part of the temporal bone in which lies a smaller membranous spiral passage that communicates with the sacculus at the base of the spiral, ends blindly near its apex, and contains the organ of Corti — see EAR illustration

¹coch·le·ar \-ēə(r)\ *adj* [NL *cochlea* + E *-ar*] **:** of or belonging to the cochlea

²cochlear \"\ *n* -S [L *cochlear*, *cochleare* spoon] **:** the spoon used in the Eastern Church in serving the consecrated wine sometimes with a particle of the Host

coch·le·are \ˌkäklēˈa(a)rē, -ˈärē\ *n* -S [L, spoon with pointed handle for eating snails from the shell, spoonful, fr. *cochlea* snail — more at COCHLEA] **:** SPOONFUL — used in medical prescriptions; abbr. *cochl*

coch·le·ar·ia \-ˈa(a)rēə, -ärēə\ *n, cap* [NL, fr. L *cochleare* spoon + NL *-ia*; fr. the shape of the leaves] **:** a genus of fleshy maritime herbs (family Cruciferae) with thick leaves and globose seed pods — see SCURVY GRASS

coch·le·ar·i·form \ˌ≈≈ˈa(a)rəˌfȯrm\ *adj* [ISV *cochlear* (fr. L *cochlear* spoon) + *-iform*] **:** shaped like a spoon

cochleariform process *n* **:** the thin plate of bone between the eustachian tube and the canal for the muscle that adjusts the tension of the tympanic membrane

coch·le·a·ri·idae \ˌkäklēəˈrīəˌdē\ *n pl, cap* [NL, fr. *Cochlearius*, type genus (fr. L *cochleare*) + *-idae*] **:** a family of neotropical wading birds (order Ciconiiformes) comprising the boat-billed herons

cochlear nerve *n* **:** the branch of the auditory nerve supplying the cochlea and subserving the sense of hearing

cochlear nucleus *n* **:** the nucleus of the cochlear nerve in the floor of the fourth ventricle of the brain

coch·le·ate \ˈkäklēət, -lēˌāt\ *or* **coch·le·at·ed** \-lēˌād·əd\ *adj* [L *cochleatus* spiral, fr. *cochlea* snail + *-atus* -ate — more at COCHLEA] **:** having the form of a snail shell

coch·le·i·form \(ˈ)käkˈlēəˌfȯrm\ *adj* [ISV *cochlea* (fr. L) + *-iform*] **:** COCHLEATE

¹coch·li·di·idae \ˌkäkləˈdīəˌdē\ [NL, fr. *Cochlidium*, type genus (fr. Gk *kochlidion*, dim. of *kochlos* land snail) + *-idae*] *syn of* EUCLEIDAE

²cochlidiidae \"\ [NL, fr. *Cochlidium*, type genus + *-idae*] *syn of* EUCLEIDAE

coch·lio·dont \ˈkäklēəˌdänt\ *n* -S [NL *Cochliodontidae*] **:** a fish of the family Cochliodontidae

coch·lio·don·ti·dae \ˌ≈≈≈ˈdäntəˌdē\ *n pl, cap* [NL, fr. *Cochliodont-*, *Cochliodus*, type genus (fr. *cochli-*, fr. Gk *kochlos*, a kind of shellfish + NL *-odus*) + *-idae* — more at COCHLEA] **:** a family of Carboniferous and Permian tectospondylic elasmobranch fishes having the few teeth broad and arched

¹coch·lio·my·ia \ˌ≈≈≈ˈmīyə\ [NL, fr. Gk *kochlios* anything spiral, screw + NL *-myia*] *syn of* CALLITROGA

²cochliomyia \"\ *n, cap* [NL, fr. Gk *kochlios* anything spiral, screw + NL *-myia*] *in some classifications* **:** a genus of two-winged flies comprising the secondary screwworm

coch·lo·so·ma \ˌkäkləˈsōmə\ *n, cap* [NL, fr. Gk *kochlos* shellfish with a spiral shell + NL *-soma*; akin to Gk *konchē* mussel — more at CONCH] **:** a genus of endocommensal flagellated protozoans known from the intestines of various vertebrates and possibly implicated in diarrheal conditions of young turkeys

coch·lo·sper·mum \-ˈspərməm\ *n, cap* [NL, fr. *cochlo-* (fr. Gk *kochlos*, a kind of shellfish with a spiral shell) + *-spermum*; fr. the coiled embryo — more at COCHLEA] **:** a genus (typifying the family Cochlospermaceae of the order Parietales) of trees native to tropical America and Africa and having palmate leaves and seeds covered with a silky down — see STERCULIA GUM

co·cil·lana \ˌkōsəˈlanə, -ˈlänə *also* -ˈlänə\ *n* -S [prob. fr. AmerSp] **:** the dried bark of a So. American tree (*Guarea rusbyi*) used as an expectorant

co·cin·er·ite \ˌkōsəˈneˌrīt\ *n* -S [*Cocinera*, mine at Ramos, San Luis Potosi, Mexico, where it was found + E *-ite*] **:** a rare mineral consisting of sulfide of copper and silver Cu_4AgS

co·ci·ne·ro \-ˈne(ˌ)rō, -ˈnā-\ *n* -S [Sp, fr. L *coquinarius*, fr. *coquina* kitchen + *-arius* -ary] *Southwest* **:** COOK

¹cock \ˈkäk\ *n* -S [ME *cok*, fr. OE *cocc*; prob. akin to obs. D *cocke* cock, ON *kokr*; all of imit. origin] **1 a :** the adult male of the domestic fowl (*Gallus gallus*) — distinguished from *cockerel* **b :** the male of birds other than the domestic fowl, esp. of other gallinaceous birds **c :** WOODCOCK — usu. used without regard to sex **d** *archaic* **:** the crowing of a cock; *also* **:** COCKCROW **1 e :** a representation of a cock; *specif* **:** WEATHERCOCK **2 :** a faucet, tap, valve, or similar device for starting, stopping, or regulating the flow of a liquid ⟨a ball ~⟩ ⟨a sill ~⟩ ⟨an automobile radiator ~⟩; *sometimes* **:** the amount of opening permitted by or as if by a cock ⟨a faucet turned on full ~⟩ **3 a :** one occupying a position of success and control **:** VICTOR; *often* **:** one dominating some field or leading some circle usu. through determined aggressive individual effort **b :** a person of pluck and spirit and often a certain swagger or arrogance ⟨all the young ~*s* dashing in new uniforms⟩ — often esp. formerly used as a term of intimate address ⟨you're sure doing fine, old ~⟩ **4 a** *in older firearms* **:** the hammer in the lock of a firearm **b :** the cocked position of the hammer ⟨a gun at half ~⟩ **5 a :** PENIS — usu. considered vulgar **b** *chiefly South & Midland* **:** the female pudenda — usu. considered vulgar **6 a :** GNOMON 1a **b :** an overhanging bracket containing a bearing for a watch or clock arbor or a wheel bridge supported at one end only **7** [perh. short for *cock-and-bull story*] *slang Brit* **:** NONSENSE, POPPYCOCK ⟨"you were talking some awful ~ about righteousness," the brigadier said —Bruce Marshall⟩ — **cock of the walk :** one that dominates a group or situation esp. overbearingly

cock 1a: diagram of a male fowl showing parts: *1* maintail, *2* sickles, *3* saddle, *4* back, *5* cape, *6* ear lobe, *7* ear, *8* eye, *9* blade, *10* points, *11* base, *12* comb, *13* beak, *14* wattles, *15* hackle, *16* wing bow, *17* breast, *18* wing bar, *19* secondaries, *20* primaries or flight feathers, *21* hock, *22* claw, *23* spur, *24* shank, *25* fluff, *26* saddle feathers, *27* tail coverts, *28* lesser sickles

²cock \"\ *adj* **1 :** MALE — used of birds and sometimes of other animals ⟨~ lobster⟩ **2** *slang* **:** CHIEF, LEADING, TOP ⟨a ~ swordsman⟩ ⟨a ~ wencher⟩ ⟨his house having been ~ house at football for three years running —Joyce Cary⟩

³cock \"\ *vb* -ED/-ING/-S [ME *cocken*, fr. ¹*cok* cock, male fowl] *vi* **1 :** to act big, arrogant, or menacing **:** STRUT, SWAGGER ⟨did a lot of bragging and ~*ing* after winning the game⟩ **2 :** to turn, tip, or stick up ⟨the show horse's abbreviated tail ~*ing* almost straight up⟩ ⟨green or poorly seasoned deck lumber can warp and cause ~*ing* of the shingle tabs —*Amer. Builder*⟩ ⟨a common failing with two-wheeled traps was ~*ing*, a tendency to tip up when in use so that the shafts pointed upwards and the tailboard down —Hugh McCausland⟩ **3 :** to position the hammer of a firearm for firing ~ *vt* **1 a** *obs* **:** to put (the match) into the cock of a matchlock gun **b :** to draw the hammer of (a firearm) fully back and set it for firing; *also* **:** to set (the trigger) for firing **c :** to draw or bend back (as the arm, the wrist, or by extension something held in the hand) in preparation to throw or hit ⟨a boxer with his fist ~*ed*⟩ ⟨a forward passer ~*ing* his arm to throw⟩ ⟨a ballplayer at the plate with his bat ~*ed*⟩ ⟨~ the wrists at the top of the backswing in golf⟩ **d :** to set a trip mechanism (as a camera shutter) for tripping **2 a :** to set erect esp. with a certain jaunty conspicuousness ⟨a peafowl ~*ed* its tail feathers⟩ ⟨a dog with one ear ~*ed*⟩ **b :** to turn, tip, or tilt usu. to one side esp. alertly, jauntily, or defiantly ⟨the engine was ~*ed* over at an angle of 60 degrees from the vertical —Eugene Jaderquist⟩ ⟨a hat ~*ed* over his right ear⟩ ⟨an eye incessantly ~*ed* on the main chance —R.L.Cook⟩ **c :** to lift and place high (as the feet) ⟨leaning back and ~*ing* his feet up on his desk —James Jones⟩ **3 :** to turn up (as the brim of a hat) **4** *of a cricket batsman* **:** to hit or deflect (a bowled ball) in the air unintentionally and usu. rather weakly — used with *up* ⟨~ up an easy catch⟩ — **cock a snook** *or* **cock snooks** *also* **cock a snoot :** to thumb the nose ⟨an unmannerly upstart *cocking snooks* at venerable men —Adrian Bell⟩ ⟨in the Highlands where they traditionally *cock a snoot* at rationing laws —John Calder⟩

⁴cock \"\ *n* -S **:** TILT, SLANT ⟨the ~ of his hat⟩ ⟨~ of the head⟩

⁵cock \"\ *n* -S [ME *cok*, alter. (influenced by *cok* cock, male fowl) of *God*] *obs* **:** GOD — used in oaths often in the possessive form which is sometimes spelled *cox* ⟨by *Cock!*⟩ ⟨by *Cock's* soul!⟩ ⟨by *Coxbones!*⟩

⁶cock \"\ *n* -S [ME *cok*, of Scand origin; akin to Dan *kok* pile; akin to OHG *coccho* pile, Lith *guga* pommel of a saddle, OE *cot* den, cottage — more at COT] **:** a small pile esp. of hay, dung, or turf

⁷cock \"\ *vt* -ED/-ING/-S **:** to put (as hay) into cocks

⁸cock \"\ *n* -S [ME *cok*, fr. OF *coque*, *coche*, fr. ML *caudica*, fr. L *caudic-*, *caudex* trunk of a tree — more at CODE] *obs* **:** COCKBOAT

⁹cock \"\ *vt* -ED/-ING/-S [prob. fr. (assumed) ONF *coquer* to notch, fr. (assumed) ONF, *coque*, n., notch — more at COAK] **:** to secure by a cog **:** ⁷COG

¹cock·ade \käˈkād\ *n* -S [modif. of F *cocarde*, fr. the fem. of *cocard* vain, proud, fr. *coq* cock (of imit. origin) + *-ard*] **:** a rosette or knot of ribbons or leather or any similar ornament worn usu. on the hat as a badge of office, of party allegiance, or of livery service or as a decoration

²cockade \"\ *adj, of an ore* **:** like a comb **:** having a profile like that of a cock's comb ⟨~ ore⟩ ⟨~ structure⟩

cock·ad·ed \-ˈkādəd\ *adj* **1 :** wearing a cockade ⟨~ guards patrolling the presidential palace —Claudia Cassidy⟩ **2 :** decorated with a cockade ⟨plumed helmets and ~ top hats —James Laver⟩

¹cock-a-doo·dle-doo \ˌkäkəˌdüdᵊlˈdü\ *n* -S [imit.] **:** ³CROW

²cock-a-doodle-doo \"\ *also* **cock-a-doodle** \ˌ≈≈ˈ≈≈\ *vi* -ED/-ING/-S **1 :** ²CROW 1 ⟨a rooster *cock-a-doodle-dooing* at dawn⟩ **2 :** ²CROW 3 ⟨all the papers were *cock-a-doodle-dooing* over the wonderful performance —*Sydney (Australia) Bulletin*⟩

cock-a-hoop \ˌkäkəˈhüp, -hu̇p\ *adj* [perh. fr. ¹*cock* (male fowl) + ³*a* + *hoop* (measure of grain); fr. the phrase *to set the cock a hoop*, to live extravagantly, lit., to put the cock on the (full) measure of grain] **1 a :** elated and exulting esp. with abandon **:** triumphantly boastful ⟨exaggeratedly *cock-a-hoop* and strutting deportment —R.H.Rovere⟩ ⟨*cock-a-hoop* with success⟩ **b :** in buoyant spirits **:** LIVELY ⟨the cat . . . just went off into the bush and probably ate something, for he came back in a few days quite *cock-a-hoop* and as ready to eat snakes as ever —R.A.W.Hughes⟩ **2 :** AWRY, COCKEYED ⟨porch askew, chimneys all *cock-a-hoop* —Kenneth Roberts⟩ ⟨knock an argument *cock-a-hoop*⟩

cock·aigne *also* **cock·ayne** \käˈkān, kəˈ-\ *n* -S *usu cap* [ME *cokaygne*, fr. MF (*pais de*) *cocaigne* land of plenty] **1 :** an imaginary land of extreme luxury and ease where physical comforts and pleasures are always immediately at hand **2 :** any actual place resembling or suggesting such an imaginary land

cock·al \ˈkäkəl\ *n* -S [origin unknown] **1** *obs* **:** the knucklebone esp. of a sheep **2 :** a game played with knucklebones **:** DIBS

cock ale *n* [¹*cock* (male fowl)] *obs* **:** ale fermented with fruits, spices, and the jelly or mincemeat of a boiled cock

cock-a-leek·ie *or* **cock·ie-leek·ie** *or* **cock·y-leek·ie** *or* **cock·y·leeky** \ˌkäkəˈlēkē\ *n, pl* **cock-a-leekies** *or* **cockie-leekies** *or* **cockyleekies** [alter. of *cockieleekie*, fr. *cockie* (dim. of ¹*cock*) + *leekie*, dim. of *leek*] **:** a soup made of chicken boiled with leeks

cock·a·lo·rum \ˌkäkəˈlōrəm, -lȯr-\ *n* -S [prob. modif. (influenced by the L gen. pl. ending *-orum*) of obs. Flem *kockeloeren* to crow, of imit. origin; akin to OE *cocc* cock — more at COCK] **1 :** a strutting little fellow **:** a small boastful or self-important person **2 :** the game of leapfrog **3 :** boasting talk **:** BRAGGARTISM ⟨the crowing ~ of the pioneer —D.G.Hoffman⟩

cock·a·ma·roo \ˌkäkəməˈrü\ *n* -S [origin unknown] **:** RUSSIAN BAGATELLE

cock-and-bull story \ˌ≈≈ˈ≈-\ *n* [perh. so called fr. the legendary sexual prowess of cocks and bulls] **:** a fabricated tale passed off as true esp. in self-glorification ⟨*cock-and-bull stories* about the big jobs he had held⟩

cock-and-hen \ˌ≈≈ˈ≈\ *adj* **:** including both men and women ⟨a *cock-and-hen* party⟩

cock·an·dy \käˈkandē\ *n* -ES [perh. fr. ¹*cock* + *Andy*, the name] *Scot* **:** PUFFIN

cock·a·pert \ˈkäkəˌpərt\ *adj* [prob. fr. ¹*cock* + *apert* (bold)] *archaic* **:** IMPUDENT

cock·a·rouse *or* **cock·e·rouse** \ˈkäkəˌrau̇s\ *n* -S [of Algonquian origin; akin to *caucauasu* elder (in some Algonquian language of Virginia) — more at CAUCUS] **:** a person of consequence among the American colonists

cock·a·tiel *also* **cock·a·teel** \ˌkäkəˈtē(ə)l\ *n* -S [modif. (influenced by ¹*cock*) of D *kaketielje*, prob. fr. Pg *cacatilha*, dim. of *cacatua* cockatoo, fr. Malay *kakatua*] **:** a small crested Australian parrot (*Nymphicus hollandicus*) that is gray with a yellow head — called also *cockatoo parrot*

cock·a·too \ˈkäkəˌtü, ˌ≈≈ˈ≈\ *n* -S [modif. (influenced by ¹*cock*) of D *kaketoe*, fr. Malay *kakatua*, *kakak-tua*, fr. *kakak* elder sibling + *tua* old] **1 :** any of numerous large noisy chiefly Australasian parrots esp. of the genus *Kakatoe* that are often kept as cage birds, many (as the pink cockatoo) having large erectile crests and most (as the sulphur-crested cockatoo) having basically white plumage more or less tinged or marked with red, orange, or yellow — see GREAT BLACK COCKATOO **2 :** ³COCKY 1 **3** *slang Austral* **:** a lookout or sentinel (as one that warns criminals of approaching police) **4 :** a light yellow that is greener, less strong, and slightly lighter than average maize and greener, less strong, and very slightly darker than jasmine

pink cockatoo

cockatoo bush *n* **:** BLUEBERRY

cockatoo fence *n, Austral* **:** a rough fence of logs and saplings

cockatoo-parrot \ˌ≈≈ˈ≈ˌ≈≈\ *n* **:** COCKATIEL

cock·a·touche *or* **cock·a·tush** \ˈkäkəˌtüsh, -təsh\ *n, pl* **cockatouches** *or* **cockatushes** [origin unknown] **:** a small freshwater fish (*Triglopsis thompsonii*) of the family Cottidae living in deep waters of the Great Lakes and Canadian arctic streams

cock·a·trice \ˈkäkəˌtrəs, -ˌtris, *chiefly Brit* -rīs\ *n* -S [ME *cocatrice*, fr. MF *cocatris* ichneumon, crocodile, cockatrice, fr. ML *cocatric-*, *cocatrix* ichneumon, perh. alter. (influenced by L *cocodrilus*, *crocodilus* crocodile) of LL *calcatric-*, *calcatrix* trampler, fr. L *calcare* to tread, fr *calc-*, *calx* heel — more at CALK] **1 :** a legendary serpent with deadly glance said to be hatched by a reptile from a cock's egg on a dunghill and often conceived of and represented esp. in heraldry as having the head, wings, and legs of a cock and the tail of a serpent — compare BASILISK **2 :** an extremely offensive esp. pernicious person **3** *obs* **:** PROSTITUTE

cockatrice

cock·a·wee \ˈkäkə,wē\ *n* -s [imit.] : OLD-SQUAW

cock-a-whoop \¦käkə¦(h)wüp\ *adj* [by alter.] : COCK-A-HOOP 1 ⟨a *cock-a-whoop* speech . . . about the government's success in the housing program —*Economist*⟩

cockayne *usu cap, var of* COCKAIGNE

cock bead *n* [³*cock* (stick up)] : a bead in carpentry or joinery so molded or applied as to project beyond a surface — compare ASTRAGAL, QUIRK BEAD; see BEAD illustration

cock-beaded \ˈ≈¦≈≈\ *adj* : decorated with a cock bead or cock beads

cock·bell \ˈkäk,bel\ *n* [ME *cokbelle* small bell, perh. fr. *cok* male fowl + *belle* bell] *dial Eng* : ICICLE

cock·bill \ˈkäk,bil\ *vt* -ED/-ING/-S [back-formation fr. *acockbill*] **1** : to tilt or set acockbill **2** : to suspend (an anchor) by the ring stopper esp. before dropping

cockbird \ˈ≈,≈\ *n* [¹*cock* + *bird*] : a male bird

cock·boat \ˈkäk,bōt\ *n* [ME *cokbote*, fr. *cok* cockboat + *bote* boat — more at COCK] : a small boat; *esp* : one used as a tender to a larger boat

cock-brained \ˈ≈¦≈\ *adj* [¹*cock*] : FOOLISH, SCATTERBRAINED

cockchafer \ˈ≈,≈≈\ *n* -s [¹*cock* + *chafer*; perh. fr. its size] : a large European scarablike beetle (*Melolontha melolontha*) that is destructive to vegetation, the larva feeding on roots, the adult on the foliage; *also* : any of various related beetles of similar habits formerly constituting a subfamily of Scarabeidae but now often made a separate family, Melolonthidae (as the pasture cockchafers or the New World rose chafer) — compare JUNE BEETLE; see GRASS-GRUB

cockcrow \ˈ≈,≈\ *n* [ME *cokcrowe*, fr. *cok* rooster + *crowe* crow (crowing)] **1** : DAWN ⟨arise each morning at ~ to be ready for the sunrise⟩ **2** : any utterance or other kind of expression suggesting the triumphant crowing of a cock ⟨bawled a triumphant ~ to the rising sun —I.L.Idriess⟩

cockcrowing \ˈ≈,≈≈\ *n* -s [ME *cokcrowing*, fr. *cok* cock + *crowing*, fr. gerund of *crowen* to crow] : COCKCROW

cocked *adj* [fr. past part. of ³*cock*] *of dice* : resting unevenly after a throw so that it is difficult to tell which face is up

cocked ankle *n* : an ankle (as of a horse) in which the relative position of the pastern to the cannon is changed, the former becoming too upright and causing a partial dislocation of the joint — used chiefly in pl.; called also *knuckling*

cocked hat *n* **1 a** : a hat with brim turned up at three places to give a three-cornered appearance — called also *tricorne* **b** : a hat with brim turned up on two sides to give a two-cornered shape and worn either front to back or sideways — called also *bicorne* **2** : a bowling game in which only the three corner pins are set up

cocked hat, 18th century

¹**cock·er** \ˈkäkə(r)\ *n* -s [ME *coker* quiver, boot, fr. OE *cocer* quiver; akin to OHG *kohhari* quiver] **1** *archery* : a ground quiver **2** *now dial Eng* : a half boot or legging

²**cocker** \"\ *vt* **cockered; cockered; cockering** \-k(ə)riŋ\ **cockers** [ME *cokeren*, prob. fr. *cok* male fowl + *-eren* (freq. suffix) — more at COCK] **1** : INDULGE, PAMPER ⟨~ a child⟩ ⟨~ oneself too much⟩ ⟨~ foolishness⟩ **2** : to nurture or foster indulgently or encouragingly — used with *up* ⟨be cared for and ~*ed* up in an illness by good friends⟩

³**cocker** \"\ *n* -s [¹*cock* + *-er*] : one that keeps or handles fighting cocks

⁴**cocker** \"\ *n* -s [¹*cocking* (woodcock hunting) + *-er*; fr. their having been used to flush woodcocks & similar game] : COCKER SPANIEL

cock·er·el \ˈkäk(ə)rəl\ *n* -s [ME *cokerelle*, fr. OF dial. *kokerel*, dim. of OF *coc* cock, fr. LL *coccus*, of imit. origin like OE *cocc* cock — more at COCK] : a young male domestic fowl; *esp* : one less than a year old — compare COCK

cock·er·meg \ˈkäkə(r),meg\ *n* -s [E dial. *cocker* prop, support (fr. ³*cock* — to set erect, turn or tip — + *-er*) + *Meg*, nickname for *Margaret* (as in *roaring Meg*, a cannon)] : a set of props used for the temporary support of a coal face in an upwardly inclined mine working

cock·er·nony *or* **cock·er·non·nie** \ˈkäkərˈnänē\ *n, pl* **cock·erno·nies** *or* **cockernon·nies** [origin unknown] *Scot* : the gathering of a young woman's hair under the snood or fillet

cocker spaniel *n* [⁴*cocker*] : a small spaniel of a breed believed to have originated in Spain that is of medium length with fairly short legs, long low-set ears, a square muzzle, and a flat or slightly waved silky coat which is usu. red, black, buff, or parti-colored and that is bred particularly for work in heavy cover

¹**cock·et** \ˈkäkət\ *n* -s [ME *cocquet*, fr. AF *cokkette* or ML *coketa, coketum* customhouse seal] **1 a** : a seal formerly used by the English or Scottish king's customhouse **b** : any one of certain other seals formerly used to seal permits **2** : a certified document given to a shipper as a warrant that his goods have been duly entered and have paid duty

²**cocket** \"\ *n* -s [ME *cocket, coket*] *obs* : fine wheaten leavened bread

³**cocket** \"\ *adj* [MF *coquet* coquettish — more at COQUETTE] *now dial Eng* **1** : PERT, SAUCY **2** : LIVELY, BRISK, MERRY

cocket center *or* **cocket centering** *n* [obs. E *cocket* to mortise, join, fr. It *cocchetta*, dim. of *cocca* notch, knot, prob. fr. L *coccum* excrescence on a tree, berry of the scarlet oak — more at COAK] : an arch center or centering in which the horizontal tie beam is replaced by bracing that allows headway above the springers to permit passage through while building

¹**cockeye** \ˈ≈,≈\ *n* [³*cock* + *eye*] **1** : a squinting eye : STRABISMUS **2** : COCKEYE PILOT

²**cockeye** \"\ *n* [¹*cock* + *eye*] **1** : the loop at the end of a trace by which it is attached to the carriage or to the singletree **2** : the socket in the underside of a millstone balance rind and resting on the cockhead

cockeye bob *also* **cockeyed bob** *n* [prob. modif. of native name in Australia] *Austral* : a sudden violent storm ⟨a *cockeye bob* roared out of the north and tore the front veranda off —Xavier Herbert⟩

cock-eyed \ˈkä,kīd\ *adj* **1** : having a cockeye or cockeyes **2 a** : turned, slanted, or twisted off the proper line : ASKEW, AWRY ⟨his hat is always a little ~⟩ ⟨after the house settled, most of the door frames were ~⟩ ⟨knock a lamp ~⟩ **b** : slightly crazy : CONFUSED, WRONG, INCOMPREHENSIBLE : TOPSY-TURVY ⟨in this ~ realm of matter where temperatures are close to absolute zero, tough steel turns brittle, rubber loses its elasticity, and a kind of liquid helium runs straight up —*Springfield (Mass.) Union*⟩ ⟨a ~, willful quite unjustified inference from something said —J.M.Barzun⟩ ⟨a ~ scheme⟩ **c** : DRUNK ⟨gets wonderfully ~ in the neighborhood bar —Jane Cobb⟩

cockeye pilot *n* : BEAU GREGORY

cockeyes \ˈ≈,≈\ *n pl* [prob. fr. pl. of ¹*cockeye*] *in craps* : a throw of three

cock feather *n* [prob. fr. ³*cock*] : the feather of an arrow that is at right angles to the nock — compare HEN FEATHER

cock-feathered \ˈ≈¦≈≈\ *adj* [¹*cock*] : having plumage of the pattern characteristic of a cock bird — distinguished from *hen-feathered*

¹**cockfight** \ˈ≈,≈\ *n* [¹*cock* + *fight*] **1** : a match or contest of gamecocks usu. heeled with metal gaffs and set at each other in a cockpit **2** : a boy's game in which the contestants, trussed into a squatting position or maintaining an awkward position on one leg, try to knock one another off balance

²**cockfight** \"\ *vi* : to engage in a cockfight ⟨~ with knees and hands tied together⟩

cockfight chair *n* [so called fr. its use for viewing sports] : READING CHAIR

cockfighting \ˈ≈,≈≈\ *n* -s : the sport of matching gamecocks in a cockfight; *also* : the patronizing of such matches esp. for the purpose of betting on the outcome ⟨addicted to card playing, ~, and drinking —H.E.Starr⟩

cockhead \ˈ≈,≈\ *n* [¹*cock* + *head*] : the rounded or pointed top of a grinding-mill spindle forming a support for the stone

¹**cockhorse** \ˈ≈¦≈\ *n* [perh. fr. ²*cock* + *horse*] **1** : something (as an adult's knee, a broomstick, or a hobbyhorse) on which a child may sit astride and pretend to ride as if on a horse ⟨ride a ~⟩ **2** : an extra horse led behind a coach to be hitched before the regular team to assist in passing over steep or difficult terrain

²**cockhorse** \"\ *adv* : ASTRIDE, ALOFT ⟨ride ~ on a broomstick⟩ ⟨emaciated beasts that were lame and blindfolded and padded, but ridden ~ —J.H.Allen⟩

cockie *var of* COCKY

cockieleekie *var of* COCK-A-LEEKIE

cockier *comparative of* COCKY

cockies *pl of* COCKY

cockiest *superlative of* COCKY

cock·i·ly \ˈkäkəlē, -li\ *adv* [²*cocky* + *-ly*] : in a cocky manner

cock·i·ness \ˈkäkēnəs\ *n* -ES [²*cocky* + *-ness*] : the quality or state of being cocky ⟨self-confidence, variously called ~ and courage —N.M.Clark⟩

¹**cocking** *n* -s [ME *cokking* fighting, fr. gerund of *cocken* to fight — more at COCK] **1** : COCKFIGHTING **2** [¹*cock* (woodcock) + *-ing*] : woodcock shooting

²**cocking** *adj* [fr. pres. part. of ³*cock*] *obs* : STRUTTING, COCKY

³**cocking** *n* -s [fr. gerund of ⁶*cock*] : COGGING

cocking cart *n* [¹*cocking* (woodcock shooting)] : a short-bodied high 2-wheeled sporting cart used for tandem driving and having a seat for a groom behind the box

cocking dog *n* [¹*cocking* (woodcock shooting)] : COCKER SPANIEL

cocking main *n* [¹*cocking* (cockfighting)] : ³MAIN 3

cocklaird \ˈ≈,≈\ *n* [¹*cock* + *laird*] *Scot* : one who owns and cultivates a small plot

¹**cock·le** \ˈkäkəl, ˈkək-\ *n* -s [ME *cockel, cockle*, fr. OE *coccel*] **1 a** : BEARDED DARNEL **b** : CORN COCKLE **c** : any of several other plants growing in grainfields (as the cowherb, corn poppy, or cocklebur) **2** : a small gall resembling a seed of the corn cockle that is produced on wheat by a nematode worm (*Anguina tritici*)

²**cockle** \ˈkäkəl\ *n* -s [ME *cokille*, fr. MF *coquille* shell, modif. (influenced by *coque* shell, fr. L *coccum* excrescence on a tree) of L *conchylia*, pl. of *conchylium*, fr. Gk *konchylion*, fr. *konchē* shell — more at COAK, CONCH] **1 a** : a bivalve mollusk of the family Cardiidae characterized by a shell that has convex radially ribbed valves and prominent umbones and is somewhat heart-shaped as seen from one end; *esp* : a common edible European bivalve (*Cardium edule*) **b** : any of many small or medium bivalves more or less resembling members of the Cardiidae — used usu. with a qualifying word ⟨beaked ~s⟩ ⟨false ~s⟩ **2** : COCKLESHELL **3** : a confection inscribed with a motto **4 cockles** *pl* : COCKLES OF THE HEART

³**cockle** \"\ *n* -s [MF *coquille*] **1** : PUCKER, WRINKLE, BULGE, RIPPLE ⟨a ~ in glass⟩ ⟨~s in paper⟩ **2** : a warty outgrowth constituting a defect on sheepskins

⁴**cockle** \"\ *vb* **cockled; cockled; cockling** \-k(ə)liŋ\ **cockles** [MF *coquiller*, fr. *coquille*, n.] *vi* **1** : to contract, pucker, or bulge so as to produce cockles esp. (of fabrics or paper) after wetting or (of fabrics) because of the uneven tension of the yarn during weaving ⟨vellum leaves ~ badly with atmospheric changes —*All the King's Horses*⟩ **2** : RIPPLE ⟨the *cockling* waves along the shore⟩ ~ *vt* : to cause to cockle ⟨the humidity of the room *cockled* the documents⟩

⁵**cockle** \"\ *adj* [prob. fr. ²*cockle* (shell)] *Scot* : WHIMSICAL, QUEER — used in compounds ⟨*cockle*-headed⟩

⁶**cockle** \"\ *n* -s [modif. (influenced by ²*cockle*) of D *kachel* (obs. D also *kaeckel*), short for *kacheloven*, fr. MHG, earthen oven, fr. *kachel* earthen pot (fr. OHG *chachala*, fr. — assumed — VL *caculus, cacculus*, alter. of LL *cacabulus, caccabulus*, dim. of *cacabus, caccabus* cooking pot, fr. Gk *kakkabos*, perh. fr. a Sem word akin to Assyr *kukubu* a vessel) + *oven*, fr. OHG *ovan* — more at OVEN] **1** : any of various stoves or heaters now largely disused: as **a** : COCKLE OAST **b** : COCKLE STOVE **2 a** : the fire chamber of an air stove or certain furnaces **b** : the dome of a heating furnace

⁷**cockle** \"\ *vi* **cockled; cockled; cockling** \-k(ə)liŋ\ **cockles** [perh. fr. ²*cockle* ("boat")] *dial Brit* : WOBBLE

cock·le·bur *or* **cock·le·burr** \ˈkäkəl, ˈkəkəl + ,-\ *n* -s [¹*cockle* + *bur*] **1** : a plant of the genus *Xanthium* **2** : the prickly fruit of a cocklebur that readily attaches itself to any passing object by means of the stiff hooked spines with which it is clothed

cockle button *n* [¹*cockle*] : BURDOCK 1

cockled *adj* **1** [²*cockle* + *-ed*] : having a shell **2** [fr. past part. of ⁴*cockle*] : WRINKLED, PUCKERED, CURLED

cockle hat *n* [²*cockle* (shell)] : a hat bearing a cockleshell as the badge of a pilgrim esp. to the shrine of St. James of Compostela in Spain

cockleloft \ˈ≈≈,≈\ *n* [by alter.] : COCK LOFT

cockle oast *n* [⁶*cockle*] : a hop-drying kiln

cock·ler \ˈkäk(ə)lə(r)\ *n* -s **1** : one that gathers and sells cockles **2** : a cockler's boat

cockleshell \ˈ≈≈,≈\ *n* [ME *cokille shelle*, fr. *cokille* cockle + *shelle* shell] **1 a** : the shell or one of the shell valves of a cockle **b** : any shell suggesting this (as a scallop shell) **2** : something resembling a cockleshell ⟨the ~s of fair hair —Roger Senhouse⟩; *specif* : a light usu. flimsy boat

cockleshell

cockles of the heart [perh. fr. ²*cockle*, with influence of NL *cochlea* ventricle, fr. L, snail, snail shell — more at COCHLEA] : the center or core of one's sentient being — usu. used in the phrase *to warm the cockles of the heart*

cockle stove *n* [⁶*cockle*] : a large heating stove in which the air currents are conducted around the fire chamber before passing into the apartments to be warmed

cocklight \ˈ≈,≈\ *n* [*cock* + *light*] *dial Eng* : twilight at cockcrow or roosting time

cockling *pres part of* COCKLE

cock·loche \ˈkä,klōch\ *n* -s [origin unknown] : a silly or contemptible fellow

cockloft \ˈ≈,≈\ *n* [prob. fr. ¹*cock*; fr. the use of attics as roosting places for fowls] **1** : a small garret; *esp* : one immediately under the ridgepole of a roof and accessible by ladder **2** *slang* : the cupola of a railroad caboose

cock·ly \ˈkak(ə)lē, -li\ *adj* [³*cockle* + *-y*] : marked by or abounding in cockles ⟨a ~ fabric⟩

¹**cock·ney** \ˈkäknē, -ni\ *n* -s [ME *cokenay, cokeney* misshapen egg, spoiled child, effeminate person, lit., cocks' egg, fr. *coken* (gen. pl. of *cok* cock) + *ey, ay* egg, fr. OE *æg* — more at COCK, EGG] **1** *obs* **a** : a spoiled child **b** : an effeminate man : MILKSOP **c** : a townsman as opposed to a sturdy manly countryman — used disparagingly to suggest effeminacy **d** : a squeamish or affected woman **2** *often cap* **a** : someone born within the range of sound of the bells of Bow Church, London : a native or a long-established resident of London **b** : the dialect of London or of the East End of London **3** : a young Australian snapper — **cock·ney·ish** \-nē(,)ish\ *adj*

²**cockney** \"\ *adj, sometimes cap* : of, relating to, or resembling a cockney

cock·ney·fy *or* **cock·ni·fy** \ˈkäknə,fī\ *vt* -ED/-ING/-ES [²*cockney* + *-fy, -ify*] : to make cockney or what may be regarded as cockney in quality or characteristics; *esp* : to make vulgar or showy

cock·ney·ism \-nē,izəm\ *n* -s [¹*cockney* + *-ism*] **1 a** : cockney manners, speech, or attitudes **b** : the writing or the qualities of the writing esp. the poetry of the 19th century English writers John Keats, Percy B. Shelley, William Hazlitt, and Leigh Hunt — used disparagingly by some contemporaries, esp. the Scottish critic John Lockhart **2** : a feature of cockney dialect ⟨~s found in London records⟩

cock of the rock [so called fr. the location of its nest] : a bird (*Rupicola rupicola*) of the family Cotingidae of northern So. America the male being chiefly orange in color with a high disklike crest; *sometimes* : a related bird (*R. peruviana*) of the Andean forests

cock of the wood 1 : PILEATED WOODPECKER **2** : CAPERCAILLIE

cockpaddle \ˈ≈,≈≈\ *n* [¹*cock* + *paddle*; prob. fr. the resemblance of its dorsal ridge to a cock's comb] *Scot* : LUMPFISH

cock penny *n* [¹*cock*] : a payment formerly made at Shrovetide to masters of certain schools in northern England and orig. spent for cockfighting or cockthrowing

cockpit \ˈ≈,≈\ *n* [¹*cock* + *pit*] **1 a** : a pit or enclosure for cockfights **b** : any place noted for esp. bloody, violent, or long-continued conflict ⟨Italy . . . was wearied by the long years when she had been the ~ of Europe —John Buchan⟩ ⟨its capital city . . . is a ~ of East-West intrigue —W.M.Healy⟩ **2** *obs* : the pit of a theater **3 a** : an apartment of an old sailing warship usu. on the after part of the orlop deck below the waterline used as quarters for junior officers and for treatment of the wounded in an engagement **b** : an open space aft of a decked area from which a yacht or other small vessel is steered **c** : a space in the fuselage of an airplane for the seating of the pilot or the pilot and passengers or in large passenger planes the pilot and crew **d** : any space (as in a sports car) resembling such a place in an airplane ⟨a racing driver hunched over in the ~ of his car⟩

cock·roach \ˈkä,krōch\ *n* [by folk etymology fr. Sp *cucaracha* cockroach, scolopendra, irreg. fr. *cuca* caterpillar, moth] : an insect of the order Blattaria a few of which are troublesome pests esp. in warm countries, being generally flat and with the head directed downward and covered dorsally by the pronotum, having long many-jointed antennae, sometimes having long wings and flying freely but often having wings short and of little use or, esp. in the female, absent, and being chiefly nocturnal, hiding in dark, moist places during the daytime — see AMERICAN COCKROACH, AUSTRALIAN COCKROACH, GERMAN COCKROACH, GIANT COCKROACH, ORIENTAL COCKROACH

cockroach

cock robin *n* [²*cock*] **1** : the male of the robin, esp. of the European robin **2** : HOODED MERGANSER

cocks *pl of* COCK, *pres 3d sing of* COCK

cocks·comb \ˈkäks + ,-\ *n* [ME *cokkes comb*, fr. *cokkes* (gen. of *cok* cock) + *comb*] **1** : a cock's comb **2** : something resembling or suggesting a cockscomb: as **a** : COXCOMB 1a **b** : a garden plant of the genus *Celosia* cultivated for its showy usu. red, purplish, or yellow inflorescence **3** : COXCOMB 1b, 2

cockscomb oyster *n* : a very large tropical edible oyster (*Pycnodonta hyotis* or *Ostrea cristi-galli*) having the margins of both valves strongly scalloped

cockscomb pyrites *n* : a crestlike variety of marcasite

cockscomb 2b

cock's egg *n* [¹*cock* (male fowl); fr. its small size] : a small usu. yolkless egg — see COCKATRICE

cock's-eggs \ˈ≈,≈\ *n, pl* **cock's-eggs 1** : the egg-shaped white or yellow fruit of a weedy herbaceous vine (*Salpichroa rhomboidea*) of the family Solanaceae of Argentina **2** : the plant bearing cock's-eggs

cocks·foot \ˈkäks+,-\ *n, pl* **cocksfoots** [so called fr. the shape of its spikes] : ORCHARD GRASS

cock·shut \ˈkäk,shət, -shət\ *n* -s [¹*cock* + *shut*; fr. the time poultry are shut in to rest] *now dial Eng* : evening twilight

cockshy \ˈ≈,≈\ *n* -ES [¹*cock* + *shy* (throw)] **1 a** : a throw at an object set up or taken as a mark **b** : a mark or target so set up or taken **c** : any object or person taken as a butt (as of constant or persistent criticism or ridicule) ⟨another of his favorite *cockshies* . . . was Respectability —*Manchester Guardian Weekly*⟩ ⟨our public men . . . in moments of annoyance . . . are our first *cockshies* —John Buchan⟩ **2 a** *chiefly Brit* : an arrangement or construction of usu. balanced coconuts or other objects set up (as at a fair) to be thrown at with sticks or balls **b** : a booth (as at a fair) in which a cockshy is set up

cock snapper *n* [¹*cock* + *snapper* (fish)] : a young Australian snapper

cock sparrow *n* [²*cock*] : a cocky little man

cockspur \ˈ≈,≈\ *n* [¹*cock* + *spur*] **1** : a cock's spur **2 a** : COCKSPUR THORN **b** : a small West Indian tree (*Pisonia aculeata*) **c** *in Honduras* : any of several spiny trees of the genus *Acacia* **d** : a bur grass (*Cenchrus echinatus*) **e** : an annual European weed (*Centaurea melitensis*) naturalized in No. and So. America **f** : ORCHARD GRASS **3** : SPUR 5e

cockspur flower *n* : any of several tropical plants of the genus *Plectranthus* (family Labiatae)

cockspur grass *n* : a grass of the genus *Echinochloa*; *esp* : BARNYARD GRASS

cockspur thorn *or* **cockspur hawthorn** *n* : a hawthorn (*Crataegus crus-galli*) having long straight thorns

cock-stride \ˈ≈,≈\ *n* [¹*cock*] : a short distance ⟨not far from Brisbane — that is, only a matter of six hundred miles, a *cock-stride* in Australia —*Manchester Guardian Weekly*⟩

¹**cocksure** \ˈ≈¦≈\ *adj* [prob. fr. ¹*cock* + *sure*] **1** *obs* **a** : quite safe **b** : of certain outcome **c** : sure of doing, receiving, or acting as indicated **2 a** : marked by certainty and conviction with no doubt or reservation : perfectly sure ⟨not being ~ of my position, [I] have often lacked the passionate conviction —W.A.White⟩ **b** : given to or marked by overconfidence, presumptuousness, lack of thoroughness, or cockiness ⟨how cautious and profound a thinker he was — how very far from being that arrogant and ~ materialist —Aldous Huxley⟩ **syn** see SURE

²**cocksure** \"\ *adv* : with complete security or certainty

cock·sure·ly *adv* [¹*cocksure* + *-ly*] : in a cocksure manner ⟨answer a question a bit too ~⟩

cock·surety \ˈkäk + \ *n* : the state of being cocksure

cockswain *var of* COXSWAIN

cocksy \ˈkäksē, -si\ *adj var of* COXY

¹**cocktail** \ˈ≈,≈\ *n* [¹*cock* + *tail*] **1 a** : a horse with its tail docked **b** : a horse (as a race horse) not of pure breed **c** : a person passing for a gentleman but underbred **2** : a form of cirrus cloud suggesting the tail of a cock

²**cocktail** \"\ *n* [prob. fr. ¹*cock* + *tail*] **1 a** : a short iced drink containing a strong alcoholic base (as rum, whiskey, or gin) or occas. wine with the admixture either by stirring or shaking of flavoring and sometimes coloring ingredients (as fruit juice, egg, bitters, liqueur, or sugar) and often garnished (as with a sprig of mint or slice of lemon) **b** : something resembling or suggesting such a drink esp. as being a mixture of notably diverse elements ⟨fog and smoke in equal parts — a city ~ familiar to all —*New Yorker*⟩ ⟨a musical ~⟩ **2** : an appetizer (as tomato juice, fruit in a syrup, or shrimp in a sauce of catsup, chili sauce, tabasco, and other seasoning) served as a first course at a meal

³**cocktail** \"\ *adj* **1** : of, belonging to, or set aside for a cocktail ⟨a ~ cherry⟩ ⟨the ~ hour⟩ **2** *of women's clothing* : designed for semiformal wear ⟨a ~ dress⟩ ⟨a series of ~ hats in white felt —*Women's Wear Daily*⟩

⁴**cocktail** \"\ *vb* -ED/-ING/-S *vt* : to entertain by a cocktail party esp. as a guest of honor ⟨finds himself ~*ed*, partied, and dined like the year's most eligible bachelor —Ray Josephs⟩ ~ *vi* : to drink cocktails

cocktail cabinet *n, Brit* : LIQUOR CABINET

cock-tailed \ˈ≈¦≈\ *adj* [¹*cock*] *of an animal* : with the tail or hinder part of the body cocked up; *esp, of a horse* : docked and nicked in the tail so that the stump sticks up

cocktail glass *n* : a bell-shaped drinking glass usu. having a foot and stem and holding about three ounces

cocktail hour *n* : the hour when cocktails are customarily served usu. just before dinner or between four and six in the afternoon

cocktail lounge *n* : a public room in a hotel, club, or restaurant where cocktails and other drinks are served

cocktail party *n* : an informal or semiformal party or gathering, usu. for conversation and during the cocktail hour, at which drinks, esp. alcoholic drinks, are a major item

cocktail ring *n* : DINNER RING

cocktail table *n* : COFFEE TABLE

cock-throttled \ˈ≈¦thrät°ld\ *or* **cock-throppled** \-¦thräp°ld\ *adj* [¹*cock*] *of a horse* : having a long neck with the head carried high like that of a fowl

cockthrowing \ˈ≈,≈≈\ *n* [¹*cock* + *throwing*] : an old sport of throwing sticks at a cock tied to a stake popular esp. at Shrovetide

¹cockup \ˈ=,=\ *n* -s [³*cock* + *up*] **1 :** a hat or cap turned up in front **2** [²*cockup*] **:** a cockup letter or character in printing **3 :** BEGTI

²cockup \"\ *adj* [³*cock* + *up*] **1 :** markedly taller than the text capitals but aligning with them at the bottom — used of an ornamental initial **2 :** SUPERIOR 5

cock up *vt* [³*cock*] *Brit* **:** to cheer up **:** INSPIRIT ⟨disencourage any attempt to *cock* them *up* with any kind of comfort —Sean O'Casey⟩

cock–up splint \ˈ=,=-\ *n* [*cock up*] **:** a splint designed to immobilize the hand in the position of function (dorsal extension) during healing (as of a fracture)

¹cocky \ˈkäkē, -ki\ *n* -ES [¹*cock* (fowl) + -*y*] **:** a little cock —used formerly as a term of endearment

²cocky \"\ *adj* -ER/-EST [¹*cock* + -*y*] **1 :** PERT, ARROGANT ⟨like a ~ little bird, waxed, ruffling, wonderfully insolent, he would stand his ground —Mollie Panter-Downes⟩ ⟨lean on the news, but ~, caustic, brilliantly written —W.A.Swanberg⟩ **2 :** JAUNTY

³cocky *or* **cock·ie** \ˈkäkē, -ki\ *n, pl* **cockies** [by shortening & alter. fr. *cockatoo*] **1** *chiefly Austral* **:** a farmer who farms on a small scale **2 a :** COCKATOO 1 **b :** COCKATIEL

⁴cocky \ˈkäkē, -ki\ *adj* [¹*cock* + -*y*] **:** of, belonging to, or proper to a cock ⟨customary to speak of the plumage of adult birds as either ~ or henny —L.V.Domm⟩

cockyleekie *or* **cockyleeky** *var of* COCK-A-LEEKIE

cocky·ol·ly bird *or* **cocky·oly bird** \ˌkäkēˈälē,-\ *n* [baby-talk, perh. fr. ¹*cock* + *yellow*] **:** any small bird — used as a pet name

cocky's joy \ˈkäkēz-, -kiz-\ *n* [³*cocky*] *slang Austral* **:** TREACLE

co·clé \(ˈ)kōˌklā\ *adj, usu cap* [fr. *Coclé*, province of Panama] **:** of or relating to the prehistoric culture of central Panama

¹co·co *also* **co·coa** \ˈkō(ˌ)kō\ *n* -s [Sp & Pg; Sp *coco*, fr. Pg *côco*, lit., bogeyman, prob. baby-talk redupl. of (assumed) *co!* boo!; fr. the resemblance of a coconut to a grotesque head] **1 a :** COCONUT PALM **b :** COCONUT 1 **2** *slang* **:** COCONUT 2 **3 a :** NUT GRASS 1 **b :** TARO **c :** YAUTIA **d :** an Argentine timber tree (*Zanthoxylon coco*) with a green light wood **e :** SAPUCAIA

²coco *also* **cocoa** \"\ *adj* **:** made from the fibrous husk of the coconut ⟨~ matting⟩

co·coa \"\ *n* -s [modif. (influenced by ¹*coco*) of Sp *cacao* — more at CACAO] **1 :** CACAO 2 **2 a :** chocolate (sense 1) deprived of a portion of its fat and pulverized **b :** a beverage prepared by cooking the resulting powder with water or milk **3 :** a moderate brown that is stronger and slightly redder and lighter than bay, redder and stronger than chestnut brown, and redder and deeper than average cocoa brown

cocoa bean *n* **:** CACAO 1

cocoa brown *n* **:** a variable color averaging a moderate brown that is paler and slightly yellower than bay, redder and slightly lighter than chestnut brown, and yellower and paler than cocoa

cocoa butter *or* **cacao butter** *n* **:** a yellowish or white brittle but low-melting fat with a chocolatelike odor and taste obtained from cacao beans and used in the manufacture of chocolate candy, cosmetics, and pharmaceutical preparations — called also *theobroma oil*

cocoanut *var of* COCONUT

cocoa palm *var of* COCONUT PALM

cocoa plant *n* **1 :** the cacao tree **2 :** COCA 1

cocoa plum *var of* COCO PLUM

cocoa powder *n* **1 :** BROWN POWDER **2 :** COCOA 2a

cocoa red *n* **:** the brown-red coloring matter of cocoa and chocolate formed by oxidation of tannin in the cacao bean

cocoa sedge *n* **:** NUT GRASS 1

cocoas *pl of* COCOA

cocoa shells *n pl* **:** the husks of cacao beans used as a stock feed or fertilizer or in the preparation of a beverage

cocoawood *var of* COCOWOOD

co·co·bo·lo \ˌkōkəˈbō(ˌ)lō\ *also* **co·co·bo·la** \-lə\ *n* -s [Sp, fr. Arawak *kakabali*] **:** any of several valuable tropical American timber trees of the genus *Dalbergia* (esp. *D. retusa*)

co·co–de–mer \ˌkō(ˌ)kōdəˈma(a)(ə)r\ *n* -s *sometimes cap* [F] **:** SEA COCONUT 1b

co·co·dette \ˌkōkəˈdet\ *n* -s [F, alter. of *cocodète*, fem. of *cocodès* fop, dandy, fr. *coq* cock — more at COCK] **:** a French prostitute esp. in fashionable society

coco grass *or* **cocoa grass** *n* [¹*coco*, *cocoa;* prob. fr. the appearance of the fruit] **:** NUT GRASS

co·com \kōˈkōm\ *n, pl* **cocom** *or* **cocoms** *usu cap* [Sp, of AmerInd origin] **1 :** a ruling Mayan people that dominated Yucatán until the war of 1201 along with the Itza and then became the sole overlords of the peninsula from 1201 to the revolution of 1485 **2 :** a member of the Cocom people — compare ITZA

co·co·mat \ˈkō(ˌ)kōˌmat\ *n* -s [*coconut mat*] **1 :** a matting made of coconut fiber **2 :** a doormat having a stiff bristly pile made of coconut fiber

co·co·na \kəˈkōnə\ *n* -s [AmerSp] **:** the tart applelike fruit of a shrubby plant (*Solanum hyporhodium*) of the upper Amazon

¹co·conscious \(ˈ)kō+\ *adj* [*co-* + *conscious*] **1 :** experiencing or aware of the same things **2 :** of or belonging to the coconscious

²coconscious \"\ *or* **co·consciousness** *n* -ES **:** mental processes outside the main stream of consciousness but sometimes available to it **:** secondary consciousness

co·conspirator \ˌkō+\ *n* -s [*co-* + *conspirator*] **:** CONSPIRATOR

co·co·nu·can \ˌkōkəˈnükən\ *adj, usu cap* **1 :** of, relating to, or characteristic of the Coconuco peoples **2 :** of, relating to, or characteristic of the Coconuco language

co·co·nu·co \ˌ=ˈ=(ˌ)kō\ *also* **coconu·ca** \-kə\ *n, pl* **coconuco** *or* **coconucos** *also* **coconuca** *or* **coconucas** *usu cap* [Sp, of AmerInd origin] **1 a :** a group of Chibchan peoples of the department of Cauca, Colombia **b :** a member of any people in this group **2 :** the language of the Coconuco people constituting a language family of Chibchan stock

¹co·co·nut *also* **co·coa·nut** \ˈkōkə(ˌ)nət\ *n* [¹*coco*, *cocoa* + *nut*] **1 :** the fruit of the coconut palm that is a drupe consisting of an outer fibrous husk that yields coir and a large nut containing the thick edible meat and, in the fresh fruit, a clear fluid called coconut milk — see COCONUT PALM, COIR, COPRA **2** *also* **co·co** \ˈkō(ˌ)kō\ *slang* **:** HEAD; *esp* **:** the human head ⟨hit on the ~ with a hockey stick⟩ **3 :** a hollow shell often half a coconut shell used to make the sound of hoofbeats esp. in an orchestra **4 :** a grayish brown that is slightly redder and darker than new cocoa and slightly yellower than chestnut — called also *Ascot tan, brown stone, Kermanshah, warm sepia*

²coconut *also* **cocoanut** \"\ *adj* **:** made from or involving as an element any of the various products of the coconut palm (as the fiber or the fruit or its meat) ⟨~ matting⟩ ⟨~ baskets⟩ ⟨a ~ cake⟩

coconut brown *n* **:** a moderate brown that is yellower and slightly deeper than toast brown, yellower, lighter, and stronger than bay or auburn, and lighter, stronger, and slightly redder than chestnut brown — called also *burnt almond*

coconut bud rot *n* **:** a disease of the coconut palm caused by a fungus (*Phytophthora palmivora*) that destroys the terminal bud and adjacent leaves finally killing the tree

coconut cake *n* **:** a palatable oil cake obtained as a residue in the production of coconut oil and used esp. in animal feeds — called also *copra cake*

coconut crab *n* **:** PURSE CRAB

coconut cream *n* **:** the white liquid obtained from the compressed meat of fresh coconuts and constituting the principal sauce and flavoring of the Pacific islands

coconut meal *n* **:** ground coconut cake — called also *copra meal*

coconut mealybug *n* **:** a short-tailed mealybug (*Nipaecoccus nipae*) that is destructive to coconut, avocado, fig, and other fruiting plants

coconut milk *or* **coconut water** *n* **:** the clear liquid within the fruit of the fresh coconut

coconut oil *n* **:** a nearly colorless fatty oil or white semisolid fat, lathering readily in water, extracted from fresh coconuts or from copra, and used chiefly in making soap, in foods, and as a raw material for the production of fatty acids and of lauryl alcohol and related alcohols by reduction

coconut palm *or* **coconut tree** *or* **coco palm** *or* **cocoa palm** *n* **:** a tall pinnate-leaved palm (*Cocos nucifera*) found throughout the tropics but believed to have originated in tropical America and bearing a large edible fruit and leaves that are used in thatching or are split for use in weaving (as hats, baskets, and matting) — see COCONUT 1

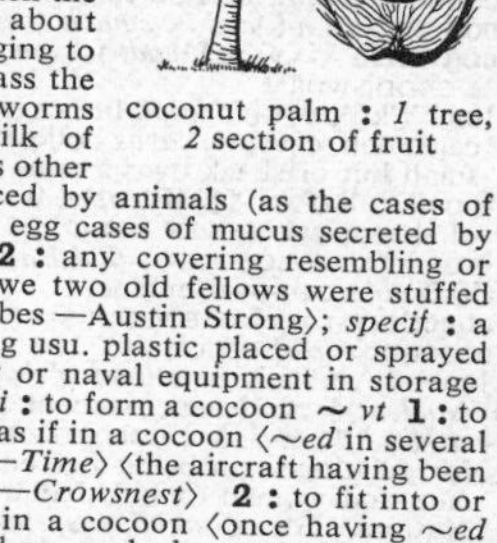

coconut palm **:** *1* tree, *2* section of fruit

coconut shy *n, chiefly Brit* **:** a cockshy with coconuts as the targets

¹co·coon \kəˈkün *also* kuˈk- *or sometimes esp Brit* käˈk-\ *n* -s [F *cocon*, fr. Prov *coucoun* cocoon, eggshell, fr. *coco* shell, fr. L *coccum* excrescence on a tree — more at COAK] **1 a :** the envelope often composed largely of silk which the larvae of many insects form about themselves previous to changing to a pupa and in which they pass the pupa stage, those of silkworms being the source of the silk of commerce **b :** any of various other protective coverings produced by animals (as the cases of silk made by spiders or the egg cases of mucus secreted by leeches and earthworms) **2 :** any covering resembling or suggesting a cocoon ⟨soon we two old fellows were stuffed into a tight ~ of buffalo robes —Austin Strong⟩; *specif* **:** a long-term protective covering usu. plastic placed or sprayed over a gun or other military or naval equipment in storage

²cocoon \"\ *vb* -ED/-ING/-S *vi* **:** to form a cocoon ~ *vt* **1 :** to wrap or envelop esp. tightly as if in a cocoon ⟨~*ed* in several layers of shawls and scarves —*Time*⟩ ⟨the aircraft having been ~*ed* at the U.S. Navy base —*Crowsnest*⟩ **2 :** to fit into or enclose in esp. snugly as if in a cocoon ⟨once having ~*ed* myself in Quongdong, I could never pluck up enough courage to go forth —Rex Ingamells⟩ ⟨a sense of . . . being in a steel box packed against another steel box, inhumanly ~*ed*, came over her —William Sansom⟩

co·coon·ery \-n(ə)rē\ *n* -ES [¹*cocoon* + -*ery*] **:** a place for raising silkworms

co·co·pa *or* **co·co·pah** \ˌkōkəˌpä\ *n, pl* **cocopa** *or* **cocopas** *or* **cocopah** *or* **cocopahs** *usu cap* [Sp *cocopa*, of AmerInd origin] **1 a :** a Yuman people living around the mouth of the Colorado river **b :** a member of such people **2 :** a Yuman language of the Cocopa and Halyikwamai peoples

coco palm *var of* COCONUT PALM

co·co·pan \ˈkō(ˌ)kōˌpan, ˈkōkə,-\ *n* -s [prob. by folk etymology fr. Afrik *koekpan*, lit., cake pan, fr. *koek* cake (fr. MD *coeke*, *couke*) + *pan*, fr. MD *panne;* akin to OHG *kuocho* cake and to OHG *pfanna* pan — more at CAKE, PAN] *Africa* **:** a mining tipcart

coco plum *also* **cocoa plum** *n* [*coco* by folk etymology fr. Sp *icaco*, *hicaco* — more at ICACO] **1 :** a small spreading tree (*Chrysobalanus icaco*) of tropical America **2 :** the plum-shaped fruit of the coco plum tree varying from nearly white to almost black and used for preserves

co·co·ra \kəˈkōrə, -ȯrə\ *n, pl* **cocora** *or* **cocoras** *usu cap* [Sp, of AmerInd origin] **1 :** a Chibchan people of the Río Cocora valley in southeastern Nicaragua **2 :** a member of the Cocora people

co·co·ri·co \ˌkōkəˈrē(ˌ)kō, kəˌkōrēˈkō\ *n* -s [F, of imit. origin] **:** a small game bird (*Ortalis ruficauda*) of Trinidad

co·cos \ˈkōˌkäs\ *n, cap* [NL, fr. Pg *côco* — more at COCO] **:** a genus of pinnate-leaved palms of which all except possibly the coconut palm are natives of tropical So. America and all are characterized by a large fruit with thick fibrous pericarp enclosing a bony nut — see COCONUT

coco sedge *n* [¹*coco;* prob. fr. the appearance of the fruit] **:** NUT GRASS 1

cocoswood *var of* COCUSWOOD

co·cotte \kōˈkät, kəˈk-\ *n* -s [F, fr. (baby-talk) *cocotte* hen, of imit. origin] **1 :** PROSTITUTE **2** [F, alter. of *cocasse*, a kind of pot, alter. of *coquemar*, a kind of pot, fr. L *cucuma* cooking pot] **:** a small shallow individual baking dish usu. with one or two handles

cocowood *also* **cocoawood** \ˈ=(ˌ)=ˌ=\ *n* [¹*coco*, *cocoa* + *wood*] **1 :** the hard dark brown wood of an East Indian tree (*Aporosa dioica*) of the family Euphorbiaceae — called also *kokra wood* **2 :** a wood somewhat similar to cocowood from a West Indian tree (*Inga vera*) **3 :** PORCUPINE WOOD

cocoyam \ˈ=(ˌ)=ˌ=\ *n* -s [*cocoa* + *yam;* fr. its being planted in cocoa groves] **:** EDDO

coc·o·zel·le \ˌkäkəˈzelē\ *n* -s [prob. fr. an It dial. word akin to It *cocuzza* squash, fr. ML *cocutia*] **:** a smooth cylindrical dark green summer squash usu. with lighter green to yellow stripes or mottlings and firm white to greenish flesh growing over a foot in length and four to five inches thick but usu. used when half that size — called also *Italian vegetable marrow;* compare ZUCCHINI

coct *vt* -ED/-ING/-S [L *coctus*, past part. of *coquere* to cook, boil — more at COOK] *obs* **:** BOIL

coc·tile \ˈkäktəl, -ˌtīl\ *adj* [L *coctilis*, fr. *coctus*, past part. of *coquere* to cook, bake + -*ilis* -ile] **:** made by baking or exposing to heat (as a brick)

coc·tion \ˈkäkshən\ *n* -s [L *coction-*, *coctio* cooking, digestion, fr. *coctus* + -*ion-*, -*io* -ion] **1** *archaic* **:** the act or process of attaining a more perfect, more mature, or more desirable condition either through natural processes or by the intervention of foreign agents (as heat); *specif* **:** digestion of food **2** *archaic* **:** suppuration conceived of esp. by humoralists as a stage in the normal process of wound healing or as a phase in the development of any disease

cocto *usu cap, var of* COTO

cocto- *comb form* [L *coctus*, past part. of *coquere* to cook] **:** boiled **:** modified by heat ⟨*cocto*antigen⟩ ⟨*cocto*protein⟩ **:** at boiling point ⟨*cocto*stable⟩

cocum *var of* KOKUM BUTTER

co·current \(ˈ)kō+\ *adj* [*co-* + *current*] **:** involving flow of materials in the same direction ⟨acetic acid separated from chloroform by ~ extraction with water⟩

co·curricular \ˌkō+\ *adj* [*co-* + *curricular*] **:** outside of but usu. complementing the regular curriculum — usu. contrasted with *extracurricular*

co·cus·wood *also* **co·cos·wood** \ˈkōkəs + ˌ-\ *n* [NL *Cocos* + E *wood*] **:** the wood of the granadilla tree used for making clarinets and other musical instruments

¹cod \ˈkäd\ *n* -s [ME, fr. OE *codd;* akin to ON *koddi* pillow, testicle, OHG *kutti* herd, Hitt *ku-u-tar* nape of the neck, upper arm, L *guttur* throat — more at COT] **1** *obs* **:** a small bag esp. for perfume **2** *now dial Eng* **:** HUSK, POD — compare PEASECOD **3 a :** SCROTUM **b cods** *pl, dial* **:** TESTES **4** *or* **cod end :** the closed saclike terminal part of a trawl (sense 1) in which fish are trapped **5** *now dial* **:** a bag-shaped area of water or land; *esp* **:** the inmost recess of a bay, marsh, or meadow

²cod \"\ *n* -s [ME, fr. ON *koddi*] *chiefly Scot* **:** a pillow or cushion

³cod \"\ *n, pl* **cod** *also* **cods** [ME] **1 a :** a soft-finned fish

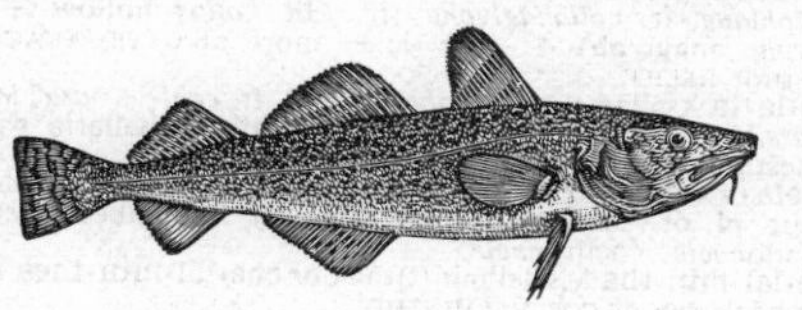
cod 1a

(*Gadus morrhua*) of the colder parts of the North Atlantic, being one of the leading food fishes of the world, living near the bottom of comparatively shallow water and averaging 10 to 35 pounds though occas. attaining very large size, and being taken, chiefly with hand lines or trawl lines, mainly from certain restricted areas, as off the Norwegian and New England coasts and on the Banks of Newfoundland, where the fishes congregate at certain seasons in waters of 20 to 40 fathoms' depth **b :** any fish of the family Gadidae; *esp* **:** a member of a Pacific species (*Gadus macrocephalus*) that is closely related to the cod of the Atlantic but less common and of less commercial importance **2 :** any of a number of spiny-finned fishes (esp. of the groups Percoidea and Scleroparei) more or less resembling members of the Gadidae — often used with a qualifying word; see BLUE COD, LINGCOD, RED COD, ROCK COD, TOMCOD

⁴cod \"\ *vb* **codded; codded; codding; cods** [origin unknown] *dial* **:** TEASE, HOAX, BANTER, KID

⁵cod \"\ *n* -s *dial* **:** HOAX

cod *abbr* codex

COD *abbr* cash on delivery; collect on delivery

co·da \ˈkōdə\ *n* -s [It, lit., tail, fr. L *coda*, *cauda* — more at COWARD] **1 a :** a final or concluding musical section that is formally distinct from the main structure of a composition or movement (as a fugue or rondo) **b :** a concluding portion of a literary or dramatic work; *usu* **:** a portion or scene that rounds off or integrates preceding themes or ideas ⟨a generalized discussion falling into two divisions . . . a third part entitled "dedication" forming a sort of ~ for the whole —Howard M. Jones⟩ **c :** anything that serves to round out, conclude, or summarize yet has an interest of its own ⟨the penetration of the ionosphere . . . in making radar contact with the moon, is a magnificent ~ to the invalidation of all that once insulated and protected human life —J.H.Spigelman⟩ **d :** the finale of a classical ballet; *also* **:** the third part of a pas de deux in which the male and female dancers dance together after completion of their respective variations **2 :** a tail (sense 16) added to a stanza (as a sonnet)

coda mark *or* **coda sign** *n* **:** a character consisting of a circle superimposed on a cross used in music to mark a part to be omitted in a repeated section and to direct the performer to skip from the sign to the coda

co·da·mine \ˈkōdəˌmēn, -mən\ *n* -s [ISV *codeine* + *amine;* orig. formed as G *kodamin*] **:** a crystalline alkaloid $C_{20}H_{25}NO_4$ found in the aqueous extract of opium

codbait \ˈ=,=\ *n* [¹*cod* + *bait*] **:** CADDISWORM

codbank \ˈ=,=\ *n* [³*cod* + *bank*] **:** a submarine bank frequented by cod

codd *abbr* codices

codding *adj* [prob. fr. *cod* (scrotum) + -*ing*] *obs* **:** LECHEROUS

cod·ding·ton lens \ˈkädiŋtən-\ *n, usu cap C* [after Henry *Coddington* †1845 Eng. mathematician] **:** a hand magnifier consisting of a lens made from a glass sphere around which a deep equatorial groove acting as a diaphragm has been cut

¹cod·dle \ˈkäd°l\ *vt* **coddled; coddled; coddling** \-d(°)liŋ\ **coddles** [perh. alter. of ¹*caudle*] **1 :** to cook (as eggs) in liquid slowly and gently just below the boiling point **2 :** to treat with extreme usu. excessive care **:** PAMPER

²coddle \"\ *n* -s **:** a coddled or self-indulged person

¹code \ˈkōd\ *n* -s [ME, fr. MF *code*, fr. L *codex*, *caudex* trunk of a tree, split block of wood, tablet of wood covered with wax on which the ancients wrote, book, a writing; akin to L *cudere* to beat — more at HEW] **1** *law* **a** *in ancient times* **:** any written collection of laws **b** *in more modern times* **:** a systematic complete written collection of law arranged logically with index and table of contents and covering fully one or more subjects of law ⟨The Internal Revenue *Code*⟩ **c** *in the jurisdictions following the common law* **:** a written compilation periodically amended of the existing statutes of general and permanent importance, sometimes expressly repealing all prior laws inconsistent with the compilation, sometimes being only a restatement of the existing statutes and only prima-facie evidence of the true laws passed by the legislature ⟨The *Code* of Laws of the U.S.⟩ **d :** a written revision of all existing statutory laws of permanent and general importance eliminating clerical errors and obsolete portions and occas. including amendments and new provisions **e** *in the jurisdictions following the most advanced theory of the civil law* **:** a written complete logical systematic statement of the entire law in effect in the jurisdiction with complete index and table of contents and repealing all prior laws ⟨the Napoleonic *Code*⟩ **2 :** any of various systems or collections of principles, rules, or regulations that do not constitute a legal code: as **a :** any set of traditional rules of conduct that are considered morally binding upon the individual as a member of a particular group, a resident of a particular place, or a participant in a particular activity ⟨the ~ of a gentleman⟩ ⟨the ~ of the West⟩ ⟨the ~ of organized crime⟩; *broadly* **:** customary socially acceptable behavior (as of an individual or group) ⟨a complex fashion ~ also requires that women have more clothes than men —*Time*⟩ **b :** a set of rules for or standards of professional practices or behavior set up by an organized group (as an association of manufacturers) and usu. reinforced by certain police and punitive powers of the group against nonconforming members ⟨the medical association may close the hospitals to physicians who transgress its ethical ~⟩; *often* **:** a formal statement of such a set of rules or standards ⟨the International *Code* of Botanical Nomenclature⟩ **c :** a set of rules of procedure and standards of materials designed to secure uniformity and protect the public interest in such matters as building construction and public health established usu. by a public agency and commonly having the force of law in a particular jurisdiction ⟨a building ~⟩ ⟨changes in the sanitary ~⟩ **3 :** any system of symbols for meaningful communication: **a :** a system of standardized signals for mechanically conveying information (as by telegraph, heliograph, flags, drums, or smoke) between points separated by a finite distance **b :** a system of symbols designed primarily to restrict comprehension (as of a message) to particular individuals: (1) **:** a system in which arbitrary meanings are assigned to letters, numbers, words, or other symbols and often used to procure brevity or system as well as secrecy ⟨each case history written up in a simple ~⟩; *specif* **:** a complete cryptographic system employing code groups of standard lengths (as 3742 or XEQSJ) each group representing a plaintext segment of any convenient length (as a sentence, phrase, word, or affix, or a letter of the alphabet for spelling out words otherwise unprovided for) and normally embodied in a code book — see AGENT CODE, BOOK CODE, CODE BOOK; PERMUTATION TABLE (2) **:** a record of such a system **:** CODE BOOK (3) **:** CIPHER 2 — not used technically **c :** language conceived as a stock of signals from which the speaker or writer chooses certain ones with which to convey his message **d :** any system of symbols for introducing information and instructions into an automatic computer or tabulating machine; *also* **:** a recording of such symbols (as by punching cards or magnetizing spots on magnetic tape) **4 a :** a word or other symbol used in a code system instead of a plaintext term ⟨"hocus" was the ~ for the city editor⟩ **b :** a group of numbers indicating the order, position, and form of the wards required on a key to draw the bolt of a particular lock **c :** a symbol used to identify something that lacks a specific name ⟨several of the new fibers, esp. ~s 500, 610, and 687, look promising⟩

²code \"\ *vt* -ED/-ING/-S **1 :** to put in or into the form or symbols of a code ⟨~ a system of laws⟩ ⟨~ a message for transmission by shortwave radio⟩ **2 :** to classify or categorize by a code esp. to facilitate tabulation ⟨*coded* the information⟩ ⟨*coding* . . . words into numbers so that answers to questions may be punched on tabulating cards and tabulated by machine —J.H. Platten⟩ ⟨personnel who ~ diseases and operations according to standard nomenclature —*Jour. Amer. Med. Assoc.*⟩ ⟨nearly 800 other treated patients have been *coded* and analyzed — P.H.Wilcox⟩

code book *n* **:** a list of code groups and their meanings arranged as a dictionary

co·decarboxylase \ˌkō+\ *n* [*co-* + *decarboxylase*] **:** the coenzyme $C_8H_{10}NO_6P$ of various amino acid decarboxylases and transaminases; pyridoxal phosphate

code clerk *n* **:** CIPHER CLERK

co·declination \(ˈ)kō+\ *n* [*co-* + *declination*] **:** the complement of the declination

code duello *n, pl* **codes duello** *or* **code duellos** [*code* + *duello;* after such terms as *Code Napoléon*] **:** the rules of etiquette governing duels

co·defendant \ˌkō+\ *n* **:** a joint defendant

code flag *n* **:** one of the flags patterned for maximum visibility that are used to exchange messages between ships at sea, the distinctive pattern of each flag symbolizing a particular letter, word, or phrase

code group *n, cryptology* **:** the significant unit of code text usu. a group of letters or numerals (as XEQSJ)

co·dehydrogenase I \ˈ¦kō+ . . . ˈwən\ *n* [*co-* + *dehydrogenase*] **:** DIPHOSPHOPYRIDINE NUCLEOTIDE

codehydrogenase II \" + . . . ˈtü\ *n* **:** TRIPHOSPHOPYRIDINE NUCLEOTIDE

co·deine \ˈkō(,)dēn, -ˌdēən, -dē,ēn\ *n* -s [F *codéine*, fr. Gk *kōdeia* poppyhead (fr. *kōos* cavity) + F *-ine* -ine; akin to Gk *koilos* hollow — more at CAVE] **:** a crystalline alkaloid $C_{18}H_{21}NO_3.H_2O$ associated in opium with morphine, usu. made from morphine, and similar to the latter but feebler in its action; morphine methyl ether

code·less \ˈkōdləs\ *adj* **:** lacking a code **:** not regulated by a code

co·den \ˈkōdᵊn\ *n, pl* **coden** [irreg. fr. ¹*code*] **:** a code classification assigned to a document or other library item consisting typically of four capital letters followed by two hyphenated groups of arabic numerals

code name *n* **:** a word made to serve as a code designation disguising single items in otherwise intelligible discourse

cod end *n* [¹*cod*] **:** COD 4

code pennant *n* **:** an answering pennant used in the International Signal Code when hoisted under the ensign to denote a signal taken from the International Code

code pleading *n, law* **:** pleading done in accordance with the rules set forth in a code

cod·er \ˈkōdə(r)\ *n* -s **1 :** one that codes: as **a :** a device for putting information into a form (as on the perforated tape fed into an automatic telegraph keyer) that facilitates its transmission in code over a communication circuit **b :** one that translates information or instructions into the code of an automatic computer **2 :** any of a number of esp. electronic devices that translate one set of impulses into another set often of a different kind: as **a :** a device to change or modulate an electric current (as on a track) so that it will operate corresponding controls on a car or other apparatus **b :** a telephone relay device by which a given set of signals (as a dialed telephone number) actuates a selective set of electronic processes **c :** an electronic device by which a number of single-pole single-throw switches can actuate a number of parallel, overlapping, or interrelated circuits **d :** an electronic device used in airplanes for sending coded identification signals **e :** a unit in a radar receiver that translates a simple impulse from a receiver into several impulses

codes *pl of* CODE, *pres 3d sing of* CODE

co·determination \ˌ¦kō+\ *n* [*co-* + *determination*] **:** the participation of labor with management in the determination of business policy; *specif* **:** the legally required participation of labor representatives in the ultimate decision-making body (as a board of directors) of large West German industrial corporations

co·det·ta \kōˈded·ə, -etə\ *n* -s [It, dim. of *coda* tail — more at CODA] **1 :** a short coda **2 :** a musical passage connecting the parts of a movement or the entries in a fugue

code wheel *n* **:** CIPHER DISK

code word *n* **1 :** CODE NAME **2 :** CODE GROUP

co·dex \ˈkō(,)deks\ *n, pl* **co·di·ces** \ˈkōdə,sēz, -ˈäd-\ [L — more at CODE] **1** *obs* **:** CODE 1, 2 **2 :** a usu. ancient book or unbound sheets in manuscript esp. of Scripture, Greek and Latin classics, or ancient mythological or historical annals — distinguished from *scroll* **3 :** a collection of drug formulas ⟨a ~ similar to the British Pharmaceutical Codex⟩

codex re·scrip·tus \-rēˈskriptəs, -rē·\ *n* [NL, lit., rewritten codex] **:** PALIMPSEST 2

cod family *or* **codfish family** *n* [³*cod*] **:** GADIDAE

codfish \ˈ≈,≈\ *n* [³*cod* + *fish*] **1 :** ³COD **2 :** the flesh of the cod used as food esp. when cured or salted

codfish aristocracy *n* **1 :** the social aristocracy of the Massachusetts families enriched from the trade in codfish **2 :** an esp. parvenu aristocracy based on commercial success

codg·er \ˈkäjə(r)\ *n* -s [prob. var. of *cadger*] **:** FELLOW, CHAP — usu. used of the aged as an affectionate or mildly derogatory term ⟨a nice old ~⟩ ⟨pompous old ~ —Claud Cockburn⟩

codhead \ˈ≈,≈\ *n* [³*cod* + *head*; fr. the shape of the flowers] **:** TURTLEHEAD

co·di·a·ce·ae \ˌkōdēˈāsē,ē\ *n pl, cap* [NL, fr. *Codium*, type genus + *-aceae*] **:** a family of marine coenocytic green algae (order Siphonales) — **co·di·a·ceous** \¦≈≈¦≈shəs\ *adj*

co·di·ae·um \ˌ≈≈ˈēəm\ *n, cap* [NL, prob. fr. Malay *kodiho*] **:** a small genus of Indo-Malayan trees and shrubs of the family Euphorbiaceae having thick leathery highly colored often variegated leaves — see CROTON 2

co·di·a·les \-ˈā(,)lēz\ [NL, fr. *Codium* + *-ales*] *syn of* SIPHONALES

cod·i·cal \ˈkädəkəl\ *adj* [L *codic-, codex* + E *-al*] **:** of or relating to a codex or code

codices *pl of* CODEX

cod·i·cil \ˈkädəsəl\ *n* -s [MF *codicille*, fr. L *codicillus*, dim. of *codic-, codex* book — more at CODE] **1 a :** a legal instrument made subsequently to a will and modifying it in some respects, executed in the same manner as the will itself and forming a part of it, superseding it so far as inconsistent with it **b** *Roman law* **:** an informal will that could not institute an heir but could set forth instructions binding upon the heirs and could give legacies, that was initially free from specific requirements (as the appointment of executors) and made orally or in writing often before a public official, but that was later required to be witnessed by five citizens if oral or signed if in writing **c :** a provision, as of a document, made subsequently to and appended to the original **d :** APPENDIX, SUPPLEMENT **2 a** *obs* **:** a writing tablet **b** *archaic* **:** ³LETTER 2

cod·i·cil·lary \¦≈≈¦siləré, -ri\ *adj* [F *codicillaire*, fr. *codicille* codicil + *-aire* -ary] **:** of, being, or belonging to a codicil

cod·i·fi·ca·tion \ˌkädəfəˈkāshən, -ōd-\ *n* -s **:** the act of codifying or being codified

cod·i·fy \ˈkädə,fī, ˈkōd-\ *vt* -ED/-ING/-ES [¹*code* (body of laws) + *-ify*] **1 :** to reduce to a code (as laws) **2 a :** SYSTEMATIZE **:** arrange in systematic or comprehensible order **b :** to make an appropriate part of a system or classification **:** CLASSIFY

co·di·mer \(ˈ)kō¦dīmə(r)\ *n* -s [*co-* + *dimer*] **:** a copolymer formed from two dissimilar molecules (as two olefins); *specif, in petroleum refining* **:** the mixture of hydrocarbons formed by the copolymerization of the butylenes which on hydrogenation yields a mixture of octanes used as a blending agent in aviation gasoline

coding *pres part of* CODE

co·directional \ˌ¦kō +\ *adj* [*co-* + *directional*] **:** coinciding in direction

co·di·um \ˈkōdēəm\ *n, cap* [NL, fr. Gk *kōidion* fleece, dim. of *kōas*; fr. the fleecy thallus; perh. akin to L *cutis* skin — more at HIDE] **:** a genus (the type of the family Codiaceae) of green algae having a tubular thallus made up of interwoven threads that often end in club-shaped cells and often branching or forming spherical or cushion-shaped masses

codl *abbr* codicil

cod line *n* [³*cod*] **:** an 18-thread line used esp. in cod fishing

¹**cod·ling** \ˈkädliŋ\ *n, pl* **codlings** *also* **codling** [ME, fr. ³*cod* + *-ling*] **1 :** a young cod **2 :** ¹HAKE 2

²**codling** \" *or* **codlin** \-lən\ *n* -s [alter. of ME *querdlyng*] **:** a small immature or inferior apple used chiefly for cooking; *also* **:** any of several elongated greenish English cooking apples — compare COSTARD, PIPPIN

³**codling** \-liŋ\ *n* -s [origin unknown] **:** a balk sawed in lengths to be cleft into staves

codling moth *or* **codlin moth** *n* [²*codling*] **:** a small moth (*Carpocapsa*, or *Cydia, pomonella*) having a larva that lives in apples, pears, quinces, and English walnuts, often doing great damage, leaves the fruit to hibernate, and pupates in the spring

cod·lins and cream \-lənz-\ *n* [alter. of ²*codling*; fr. the smell of the leaves and flowers when crushed] *dial Eng* **:** FIREWEED b

cod-liver meal *n* [³*cod*] **:** the ground residue of the cod liver after the extraction of the oil

cod-liver oil *n* **:** a pale yellow fatty oil obtained from the liver of the cod and related fishes and used in medicine chiefly as a source of vitamins A and D in conditions due to abnormal calcium and phosphorus metabolism (as rickets, infantile tetany, osteomalacia) — see COD OIL

cod·man \ˈkädmən\ *n, pl* **codmen** [³*cod* + *man* (vessel)] **:** a ship used in fishing for cod

cod net *n* [¹*cod*] **:** a net with a cod (sense 4)

cod oil *n* [³*cod*] **:** a dark-colored inferior cod-liver oil used in leather manufacture

co·dominance \(ˈ)kō +\ *n* -s **:** the quality or state of being codominant

¹**co·dominant** \" +\ *adj* [*co-* + *dominant*] **1** *of trees* **:** forming part of the main canopy of a forest — compare DOMINANT **2** *of kinds of organisms* **:** sharing in the controlling influence of a biotic community **:** present in equal and highest frequency with some other kind of organism ⟨a forest in which spruce and fir are ~⟩

²**codominant** \"\ *n* -s **:** a codominant individual or kind of organism; *esp* **:** a codominant plant

codpiece \ˈ≈,≈\ *n* [ME *kodpese*, fr. *kod, cod* (testis) + *pese, pece* piece] **1 :** an often ornamented flap or bag concealing an opening in the front of men's breeches esp. in the 15th and 16th centuries **2** *obs* **:** PENIS

cods *pl of* COD, *pres 3d sing of* COD

cod smack *n* [³*cod* + *smack* (vessel)] **:** CODMAN

codworm \ˈ≈,≈\ *n* [¹*cod*; fr. the case or tube in which it lives] **:** CADDISWORM

¹**coe** \ˈkō\ *n* -s [D *kooi*, lit., cage, fr. MD *cōie, coie*, fr. L *cavea* cage, den, cave, fr. *cavus* hollow — more at CAVE] *dial Eng* **:** a small hut or shack over a mine shaft

²**coe** \", ˈkō\ *n* -s [ME *cothe*, fr. OE *cothu*] *dial Eng* **:** a disease of sheep; *usu* **:** LIVER ROT

³**coe** \"\ *vt* -ED/-ING/-S *dial Eng* **:** to infest with coe

COE *abbr* cab-over-engine

coecilian *var of* CAECILIAN

coecum *var of* CECUM

¹**co-ed** \ˈkō¦ed *sometimes* ≈ˈ≈\ *n* -s [short for *coeducational* (*student*)] **:** a female student in a coeducational institution

²**co-ed** \"\ *adj* **1 :** COEDUCATIONAL ⟨*co-ed* schools⟩ **2 :** of, for, relating to, or being a co-ed ⟨*co-ed* hairdos⟩ **3 :** for both men and women ⟨a bill that would make the Army and Air National Guard *co-ed* —*Springfield (Mass.) Union*⟩

co·editor \(ˈ)kō+\ *n* [*co-* + *editor*] **:** one who collaborates with another in editing a newspaper, magazine, or book

co·educate \(ˈ)kō+\ *vt* [back-formation fr. *coeducation*] **1 :** to subject to coeducation **2 :** to train (the different senses) to coordinated reaction

co·education \(¦)kō+\ *n* -s [*co-* + *education*] **:** the education of students of both sexes at the same institution, esp. a college or university — **co·educational** \" +\ *adj* — **co·educationally** \" +\ *adv*

¹**co·efficient** \ˌkō+\ *adj* [*co-* + *efficient*] **:** acting together to produce an effect — **co·efficiently** \" +\ *adv*

²**coefficient** \"\ *n* -s [NL *coefficient-, coefficiens*, fr. L *co-* + *efficient-, efficiens* — more at EFFICIENT] **1 :** something that unites in action to produce an effect **:** a joint agent **2 :** any of the factors (as constants) of a product considered in relation to another factor (as a variable) ⟨in $6x$, bx, $x(a+b)$, $3xyz$ the ~s of x are respectively 6, b, $(a+b)$, $3yz$⟩ **3 a :** a number that serves as a measure of some property (as of a substance or body) or characteristic (as of a device or process) and that is commonly used as a factor in computations ⟨the ~ of expansion of a metal⟩ ⟨the absorption ~ of a medium for light⟩ ⟨the coupling ~ of a transformer⟩ **b :** MEASURE, DEGREE ⟨a ~ of culture that greatly surpassed the cultural mean —V.V.Nabokov⟩ ⟨~s of feeling —C.I.Glicksberg⟩

coefficient of absorption : ABSORPTION COEFFICIENT

coefficient of compressibility : the decrease in volume per unit volume (as of a gas) produced by a unit change in pressure

coefficient of contingency : a measure of association between statistical variables which have quantitative categories of unequal magnitude or at least one of which can be classified only qualitatively

coefficient of contraction *physics* **:** the ratio of the cross-sectional area of the first vena contracta to the area of the discharge aperture

coefficient of correlation : CORRELATION COEFFICIENT

coefficient of discharge : the ratio of the actual discharge to the ideal discharge, assuming unit coefficients of contraction and velocity, equal to the product of these coefficients

coefficient of elasticity : MODULUS OF ELASTICITY

coefficient of expansion : the ratio of the increase of length, area, or volume of a body per degree rise in temperature to its length, area, or volume, respectively, at some specified temperature, commonly 0°C, the pressure being kept constant — called also *expansivity*

coefficient of friction : the ratio of the tangential force that is needed to start or to maintain uniform relative motion between two contacting surfaces to the perpendicular force holding them in contact, the ratio usu. being larger for starting than for moving friction

coefficient of inbreeding *or* **coefficient of relation :** a measure of the degree of inbreeding of an individual expressed as the percentage homozygous in that individual of characters heterozygous in the general population of its kind

coefficient of kinematic viscosity : the ratio of the coefficient of viscosity to the density of a fluid — compare ²STOKE

coefficient of leakage : the ratio of total magnetic flux to useful flux

coefficient of racial likeness : a measure of the resemblance between two races as determined by a comparison of measurements taken on two or more series of skulls

coefficient of resistance : the ratio of the loss of head to the remaining head of a fluid discharging through an orifice or over a weir

coefficient of restitution : the ratio of the relative velocity of two elastic bodies after rebounding to velocity before impact

coefficient of variation *or* **coefficient of variability :** the ratio of the measure of variability, usu. the standard deviation, to an average, usu. the arithmetical mean, about which the variation occurs

coefficient of velocity : the ratio of the actual velocity to the theoretical velocity of a fluid jet

coefficient of viscosity : the ratio of the tangential frictional force per unit area to the velocity gradient perpendicular to the direction of flow of a liquid **:** the ratio of the shearing stress in a moving fluid to the time rate of shearing strain

coehorn *var of* COHORN

coeing *pres part of* COE

coel- *or* **coelo-** *also* **cel-** *or* **celo-** *comb form* [NL, fr. Gk *koil-, koilo-*, fr. *koilos* hollow — more at CAVE] **:** hollow **:** cavity ⟨*coel*odont⟩ ⟨*coelo*zoic⟩

¹**coe·la·canth** \ˈsēlə,kanth\ *or* **coe·la·can·thid** \¦≈≈¦kan(t)thəd\ *adj* [NL *Coelacanthidae*] **:** of or belonging to the family Coelacanthidae

²**coelacanth** \"\ *also* **coelacanthid** \"\ *n* -s **:** a fish or fossil of the family Coelacanthidae

coe·la·can·thi·dae \ˌsēləˈkan(t)thə,dē\ *n pl, cap* [NL, fr. *Coelacanthus*, type genus (fr. *coel-* + *-acanthus*) + *-idae*] **:** a family of crossopterygian fishes usu. regarded as coextensive with the order Actinistia — compare LATIMERIA — **coe·la·can·thine** \¦≈≈¦kan,thīn, -an(t)thən\ *adj* — **coe·la·can·thoid** \-an,thȯid\ *adj or n* — **coelacanthous** \-an(t)_thəs\ *adj*

coe·la·can·thi·ni \-thə,nī\ [NL, fr. *coel-* + *acanth-* + *-ini*] *syn of* ACTINISTIA

coe·lan·a·glyph·ic relief \(ˈ)sē¦lanə¦glifik-\ *n* [F *coilanaglyphique*, fr. *coilanaglyphe* (fr. Gk *koilos* hollow + *anaglyphe* anaglyph) + *-ique* -ic — more at CAVE, ANAGLYPH] **:** SUNK RELIEF

coe·la·ta \səˈlād·ə, sē-\ *n pl, cap* [NL, fr. *coel-* + *-ata*] *in some classifications* **:** a group comprising all Turbellaria with an intestine — distinguished from *Acoela*

-coele *or* **-coel** *also* **-cele** *n comb form* -s [prob. fr. NL *-coela*, fr. neut. pl. of *-coelus* -coelous)] **:** cavity **:** chamber **:** ventricle ⟨endo*coele*⟩ ⟨neuro*coele*⟩

coe·lel·min·tha \ˌsēlelˈmin(t)thə\ *or* **coe·lel·min·thes** \-min(,)thēz\ *syn of* COELHELMINTHES

coe·len·tera \səˈlentərə, sē-\ [NL, by shortening] *syn of* COELENTERATA

coe·len·ter·a·ta \sə,lentəˈrād·ə, sē-\ *n pl, cap* [NL, fr. *coel-* + Gk *enteron* intestine + NL *-ata* — more at INTER-] **:** a phylum or other major division of more or less radially symmetrical invertebrate animals lacking a true body cavity and including hydroids, jellyfishes, sea anemones, corals, and formerly sponges and ctenophores — see ANTHOZOA, HYDROZOA, SCYPHOZOA — **coe·len·ter·ate** \(ˈ)sē¦lentə,rāt, sə¦-\ *adj or n* — **coe·len·ter·ic** \¦sē¦terik\ *adj*

coe·len·ter·on *or* **ce·len·ter·on** \≈ˈlentə,rän\ *n, pl* **coelentera** *or* **ce·len·tera** \-_rə\ [NL, fr. *coel-* + Gk *enteron* intestine] **:** the internal cavity of a coelenterate

coelestine *var of* CELESTINE

coel·hel·minth \(ˈ)sēl¦helmin(t)th\ *n* -s [NL *Coelhelminthes*] **:** one of the Coelhelminthes

coel·hel·min·thes \¦sēl+\ *n pl, cap* [NL, fr. *coel-* + *Helminthes*] *in some classifications* **:** a major division of Metazoa including diverse coelomate vermiform invertebrate animals — **coel·hel·min·thic** \" +\ *adj*

coeli- *or* **coelio-** *also* **celi-** *or* **celio-** *comb form* [Gk *koili-, koilio-*, fr. *koilia* cavity of the body, belly] **:** belly **:** abdomen ⟨*coeli*algia⟩ ⟨*coelio*scopy⟩

coe·lia \ˈsēlēə\ *n, pl* **coeli·ae** \-ē,ē,-ē,ī\ [NL, fr. Gk *koilia*] **:** a bodily cavity esp. of the brain

¹**coe·li·ac** *or* **ce·li·ac** \ˈsēlē,ak\ *adj* [L *coeliacus*, fr. Gk *koiliakos*, fr. *koilia* cavity, belly, fr. *koilos* hollow — more at CAVE] **:** of, located in, or belonging to the cavity of the abdomen

²**coeliac** *n* -s **:** a coeliac part (as an artery or nerve)

coeliac artery *or* **coeliac axis** *n* **:** a short thick artery arising from the aorta just below the diaphragm and dividing almost immediately into the gastric, hepatic, and splenic branches

coeliac ganglion *n* **:** either of a pair of collateral sympathetic ganglia, the largest of the autonomic system, lying one on each side of the coeliac artery near the suprarenal gland

coeliac plexus *n* **:** SOLAR PLEXUS

coe·lic·o·list \səˈlikələst, sē-\ *n* -s *usu cap* [L *coelicola, caelicola* heaven-worshiper (fr. *coelum, caelum* heaven, sky + *colere* to worship, cultivate, dwell) + E *-ist* — more at -HOOD, WHEEL] **:** one of an obscure heretical sect of the 4th and 5th centuries combining Jewish and Christian doctrines

coe·lin \ˈsēlən\ *or* **coe·line** \-,lēn,-ˌlən\ *n* -s [ISV *coel-* (fr. L *coelum, caelum* sky) + *-in* or *-ine*] **:** CERULEAN BLUE 1b

coelo- — see COEL-

coe·lo·blast \ˈsēlə,blast, -lō-\ *n* -s [*coel-* + *-blast*; trans. of G *darmdrüsenblatt*] **:** HYPOBLAST

coe·lo·blas·tic \¦≈≈¦blastik\ *adj* **:** of, relating to, or derived from the hypoblast

coe·lo·blastula \,≈≈ +\ *n* [NL, fr. *coel-* + *blastula*] **:** a hollow blastula — compare BLASTOCOEL

coe·lo·coc·cus \ˈ≈≈,käkəs\ *n, cap* [NL, fr. *coel-* + *-coccus*] **:** a small genus of Polynesian pinnate-leaved palms — see APPLENUT

coe·lo·gastrula \,≈≈ + \ *n* [NL, fr. *coel-* + *gastrula*] **:** a typical gastrula derived from a coeloblastula

coe·log·y·ne \səˈläjə(,)nē, sē-\ *n* [NL, fr. *coel-* + Gk *gynē* woman; fr. the hollow stigma — more at QUEEN] **1** *cap* **:** a large genus of tropical Asiatic epiphytic orchids having mostly yellow or white flowers with membranaceous perianth **2** -s **:** a plant of the genus *Coelogyne*

coe·lo·lep·id \ˈsēlə,lepəd, -lō,-\ *n* -s [NL *Coelolepida*] **:** an ostracoderm of the order Coelolepida

coe·lo·lep·i·da \,≈≈ˈlepədə\ *n pl, cap* [NL, fr. *Coelolepid-, Coelolepis*, genus of ostracoderms (fr. *coel-* + *-lepis*) + *-ida*] *in some classifications* **:** an order of very small scaly Silurian and Lower Devonian ostracoderms

coe·lom \ˈsēləm\ *also* **coe·lome** \-,lōm,-ləm\ *or* **ce·lom** \-ləm\ *n, pl* **coeloms** \-mz\ *or* **coe·lo·ma·ta** \sēˈlōmədə, -ˈläm-\ [G *zölom, coelom*, fr. Gk *koilōma* cavity, fr. *koilos* hollow — more at CAVE] **:** the body cavity or perivisceral cavity of metazoans above the lower worms usu. being lined by a distinct epithelium and where well developed forming a large space between the alimentary viscera and the body walls — compare HEMOCOEL, HEMOCOELOM, PSEUDOCOEL

coe·lo·ma·ta \səˈlōməd·ə, sē-, -ˈäm-\ *n pl, cap* [NL, fr. *coeloma* coelom (fr. Gk *koilōma* cavity) + *-ata*] *in some classifications* **:** a group including all Metazoa except sponges and coelenterates

¹**coe·lo·mate** \ˈsēlə,māt, sēˈlōmət\ *or* **coe·lom·a·tous** \(ˈ)sē¦läməd·əs, -ōm-\ *adj* **:** having a coelom

²**coelomate** \"\ *n* -s [NL *Coelomata*] **:** a coelomate animal **:** one of the Coelomata

¹**coe·lo·mat·ic** \¦sēlə¦mad·ik, -lō-\ *adj* **:** COELOMIC

²**coelomatic** \"\ *n* -s [NL *Coelomata* + E *-ic*] **:** COELOMATE

coe·lo·mesoblast \,sēlō, -lə +\ *n* [*coel-* + *mesoblast*] **:** MESOTHELIUM

coe·lom·ic *or* **ce·lom·ic** \səˈlämik,(ˈ)sē¦-\ *adj* [ISV *coelom, celom* + *-ic*] **:** of, relating to, or found in the coelom

coe·lo·mo·coe·la \,sēlōməˈsēlə, -ləm- sə,lō-\ *n pl* [NL, fr. *coelom* + *-o-* + *-coela* (neut. pl. fr. *-coelus*)] *syn of* COELOMATA

coe·lo·mo·cyte \ˈsē(,)lōmə,sīt, -lə-, səˈlō-\ *n* -s [*coelom* + *-o-* + *-cyte*] **:** a cell free in the coelom esp. of an invertebrate animal — compare AMOEBOCYTE, ELEOCYTE

coe·lo·mo·duct \-,dəkt\ *n* [*coelom* + *-o-* + *duct*] **:** an excretory and genital duct that is typical of certain invertebrates (as annelid worms) and has a wide and usu. ciliated lumen opening into the coelom by a broad funnel and terminating externally by a small pore in the body wall

coe·lo·mo·my·ces \,sē(,)lōməˈmī,sēz, -lə-, sə,lō-\ *n, cap* [NL, fr. ISV *coelom* + NL *-o-* + *-myces*] **:** a genus (coextensive with the family Coelomomycetaceae of the order Blastocladiales) of water molds that have naked mycelium without rhizoids and that live as parasites on insects (as mosquitoes)

coe·lo·mo·stome \ˈsē(,)lōmə,stōm, -lə-, səˈlō-\ *n* -s [*coelom* + *-o-* + *-stome*] **:** the coelomic opening of a coelomoduct

coe·lo·my·ar·i·an \¦≈(,)≈mī¦a(a)rēən\ *adj* [*coel-* + *my-* + *-arian*] *of nematode muscle cells* **:** having the myofibrils extending centrally in the periphery of the cell and partially enclosing the sarcoplasm — compare PLATYMYARIAN

coe·lo·phy·sis \səˈläfəzəs, -lăf-, -səs\ *n, cap* [NL, fr. *coel-* + Gk *physis* nature, appearance — more at PHYSIC] **:** a genus of small primitive carnivorous saurischian dinosaurs (suborder Theropoda) of the Upper Triassic of No. America

coe·lo·pi·dae \səˈlōpə,dē, sē-\ *n pl, cap* [NL, fr. *Coelopa*, type genus (fr. *coel-* + *-opa*, fr. Gk *ōp-, ōps* face, eye) + *-idae*] — more at EYE] **:** a small family of acalyptrate muscoid flies that have flattened bodies and frequent seashores — see KELP FLY

coe·lo·planula \,sēlə, -lō +\ *n* [NL, fr. *coel-* + *planula*] *zool* **:** a hollow planula with a wall of two layers

coe·lo·stat \ˈsēlə,stat\ *n* -s [ISV *coelo-* (fr. ML *caelum* sky, heaven, fr. L *caelum* heaven) + *-stat*] **:** an instrument consisting of an adjustable plane mirror clock-driven on an axis parallel to the axis of the earth and a second fixed mirror that act together to send light from a celestial body in a fixed direction — compare HELIOSTAT

-coelous *adj comb form* [NL *-coelus*, fr. Gk *-koilos* hollow, concave, fr. *koilos* — more at CAVE] **1 :** cavitied ⟨dendro*coelous*⟩ **2 :** concave ⟨pro*coelous*⟩ ⟨opistho*coelous*⟩

coe·lo·zoic \¦sēlə¦zōik, -lō-\ *adj* [*coel-* + *-zoic*] **:** inhabiting a cavity of an animal's body

coe·lur·o·saur \səˈlůrə,sȯ(ə)r, sē-\ *also* **coe·lur·o·sau·ri·an** \≈¦≈≈¦sȯrēən\ *n* -s [NL *Coelurosauria*] **:** a dinosaur of the subdivision Coelurosauria

coe·lur·o·sau·ria \≈,≈≈ˈsȯrēə\ *n pl, cap* [NL, fr. *coel-* + *ur-* + *-sauria*] **:** a subdivision of Theropoda (order Saurischia) comprising a number of small primitive generalized bipedal dinosaurs of the Upper Triassic, Jurassic, and Cretaceous

co·emp·tio \kōˈempshē,ō, -emptē-\ *n* -s [L] *Roman law* **:** a ceremony symbolizing the sale of a woman to a man and bringing the woman under the manus of the man usu. (1) as a plebeian marriage but sometimes (2) as a device of the woman to displace her guardian — called also respectively (1) *coemptio matrimoni causa*, (2) *coemptio fiduciae causa*

co·emp·tion \kōˈempshən\ *n* -s [L *coemption-, coemptio* coemption, coemptio, fr. *coemptus*, past part. of *coemere* to buy up (fr. *co-* + *emere* to buy) + *-ion-, -io* -ion — more at REDEEM] *obs* **:** purchase of all supplies of a commodity in the market esp. to gain a monopoly — **co·emp·tive** \(ˈ)kō¦emptiv, -ēv\ *adj*

coen- *or* **coeno-** *also* **cen-** *or* **ceno-** *or* **caen-** *or* **caeno-** *comb form* [NL, fr. Gk *koin-, koino-*, fr. *koinos* — more at CO-] **:** common **:** general ⟨*coeno*blast⟩ ⟨*coen*esthesia⟩

coe·na·gri·idae \,sēnəˈgrīə,dē, ,sen-\ *n pl, cap* [NL, fr. *Coenagria*, type genus (fr. *coen-* + *-agria*, fr. Gk *agrios* wild) + *-idae*] **:** a large cosmopolitan family of damselflies

coe·na·gri·on·i·dae \-,grī'änə,dē\ [NL] *syn of* COENAGRIIDAE
co·en·di·dae \kō'endə,dē\ [NL, fr. *Coendou*, type genus + *-idae*] *syn of* ERETHIZONTIDAE
co·en·dou \kō'en(,)dü\ *n* [NL, fr. Tupi *coendu*] **1** *cap* **:** a genus (family Erethizontidae) comprising the prehensile-tailed porcupines of Central and So. America **2** -s **:** a member of the genus *Coendou*
coe·nen·chy·ma \sə'neŋkəmə, sē-\ *n, pl* **coenen·chym·a·ta** \,sēneŋ'kimədə\ [NL, fr. *coen-* + *-enchyma*] **:** COENENCHYME
coe·nen·chy·mal \sə'neŋkəməl, 'sē;-\ *or* **coe·nen·chym·a·tous** \'sēneŋ'kimədəs\ *adj* [*coenenchymal* fr. *coenenchyme* + *-al; coenenchymatous* fr. NL *coenenchymat-, coenenchyma* + E *-ous*] **:** of, relating to, or being coenenchyme
coe·nen·chyme \sə'neŋ,kīm, sē-\ *or* **coe·nen·chym** \-,kəm\ *n* -s [NL *coenenchyma*] **:** the complex mesogloea uniting the polyps of a compound anthozoan
coe·nes·the·sia \,sēnes'thēzh(ē)ə, ,sen-\ *or* **coe·nes·the·sis** \-thēsəs\ *or* **ce·nes·the·sia** \-thēzh(ē)ə\ *n, pl* **coenesthe·sias** \-əz\ *or* **coenesthe·ses** \-ē,sēz\ *or* **cenesthesias** \-əz\ [NL, fr. *coen-* + *esthesia, esthesis*] **:** the totality of sensations arising from bodily organs through which one perceives his own body
coe·nes·thet·ic \¦==¦thed·ik\ *adj* **:** of or relating to coenesthesia
coe·no·bi·ar *or* **ce·no·bi·ar** \sə'nōbēə(r), (')sē¦-\ *adj* [NL *coenobium, cenobium* + E *-ar*] **:** of or relating to a coenobium
coe·no·bi·oid \-,ȯid\ *adj* [NL *coenobium* + E *-oid*] **:** like a coenobium
coenobite *var of* CENOBITE
coe·no·bi·um *or* **ce·no·bi·um** \sə'nōbēəm, sē-\ *n, pl* **coeno·bia** *or* **ceno·bia** \-ēə\ [LL *coenobium* — more at CENOBY] **1 :** CENOBY **2** *also* **coe·nobe** *or* **ce·nobe** \'sē(,)nōb, 'se(,)-\ -s [NL, fr. LL] **:** a usu. spherical colony of unicellular organisms surrounded by a common investment; *esp* **:** a colony having a definite number and specific arrangement of cells
coe·no·blast \'sēnə,blast, -en-, -nō-\ *n* -s [ISV *coen-* + *-blast*; orig. formed as G *zönoblastem*] **:** MESENDODERM — **coe·no·blas·tic** \¦==¦ik\ *adj*
coenoby *var of* CENOBY
coe·no·car·pic \¦==¦kärpik\ *also* **coe·no·car·pous** \-pəs\ *adj* [*coen-* + *-carp* + *-ic* or *-ous*] **:** SYNCARPOUS — **coe·no·car·py** \'==,pē\ *n* -ES
coe·no·cen·trum \,==¦sen·trəm\ *n, pl* **coenocen·tra** \-trə\ [NL, fr. *coen-* + L *centrum* center] **:** a dense deep-staining cytoplasmic structure in the egg cells of certain fungi
coe·no·cyte \'==,sīt\ *n* -s [ISV *coen-* + *-cyte*] **1 a :** a multinucleate mass of protoplasm resulting from repeated nuclear division unaccompanied by cell fission **b :** an organism (as certain algae) consisting of such a structure — compare PLASMODIUM **2 :** SYNCYTIUM 1 — **coe·no·cyt·ic** \¦==¦sid·ik, -itik\ *adj*
coe·noe·ci·um \sə'nēs(h)ēəm, sē-\ *n, pl* **coenoe·cia** \-ēə\ [NL, fr. *coen-* + Gk *oikion* house (fr. *oikos*) — more at VICINITY] **:** the common often chitinous or calcareous investment of a bryozoan colony
coe·no·gamete \¦sēnə, -enə, -nō+\ *n* [*coen-* + *gamete*] *bot* **:** a multinucleate gamete
coenogenesis *var of* CENOGENESIS
coenogonous *var of* CENOGONOUS
coe·no·les·tes \,==¦le(,)stēz\ *syn of* CAENOLESTES
coe·nop·ter·i·da·les \sə,näp,terə'dā(,)lēz, ,se-\ *n pl, cap* [NL, fr. *coen-* + Gk *pterid-, pteris* fern + NL *-ales* — more at PTERIS] **:** an order of extinct Devonian and Carboniferous ferns that is usu. considered as part of or coextensive with the subclass Primofilices and that has both simple and pinnate leaves with the latter having pinnae at an angle to the plane of the leaf blade
coe·no·sarc \'sēnə,särk, -en-, -nō-\ *n* -s [*coen-* + Gk *sark-, sarx* flesh — more at SARCASM] **1 :** the hollow living tube consisting of hydrocaulus and stolons that connects the zooids of a hydroid colony **2 :** COENENCHYME
coenospecies *var of* CENOSPECIES
coe·nos·te·um \sə'nästēəm, sē-\ *n, pl* **coenos·tea** \-ēə\ [NL, fr. *coen-* + Gk *osteon* bone — more at OSSEOUS] **:** the calcareous skeleton of a compound coral or a bryozoan colony
coe·no·the·ca·lia \,sēnəthə'kālēə, -en- -nō-\ *n pl, cap* [NL, fr. *coen-* + *thec-* + *-alia*] **:** an order of massive calcareous corals including solely the blue corals of the Indo-Pacific
coe·no·type \'==,tīp\ *n* [*coen-* + *type*] *biol* **:** an organism having the type of structure fundamental to a group — **coe·no·typ·ic** \¦==¦tipik\ *adj*
coe·no·zygote \,==+\ *n* [*coen-* + *zygote*] **:** the product of fusion of two coenogametes
coe·nu·ro·sis \,sēnyə'rōsəs, -en-\ *or* **coe·nu·ri·a·sis** \-'rīəsəs\ *n, pl* **coenuro·ses** \-ō,sēz\ *or* **coenuria·ses** \-ə,sēz\ [NL *coenurus* + *-osis* or *-iasis*] **:** infestation with or disease caused by coenuri (as gid of sheep)
coe·nu·rus \sə'n(y)ürəs, sē-\ *n, pl* **coenu·ri** \-,rī,-(,)rē\ [NL, fr. *coen-* + *-urus*] **:** a complex tapeworm larva growing interstitially in vertebrate tissues and consisting of a large fluid-filled sac from the inner wall of which numerous scolices develop — see GID, MULTICEPS; compare CYSTICERCOID, CYSTICERCUS, HYDATID
co·enzyme \(')kō+\ *n* [*co-* + *enzyme*] **:** any thermostable nonprotein compound (as cocarboxylase) that forms the active portion of an enzyme system after combination with an apoenzyme — compare PROSTHETIC
coenzyme A \-'ā\ *n* **:** a coenzyme $C_{21}H_{36}N_7O_{16}P_3S$ occurring in all living cells that is essential to the metabolism of carbohydrates, fats, and some amino acids and in the form of its acetyl or other acyl derivatives promotes biological acetylations or other acylations and that is a nucleotide consisting of a pyrophosphoric ester of both adenylic acid and pantetheine — called also *CoA*
coenzyme I \-'wən\ *n* **:** DIPHOSPHOPYRIDINE NUCLEOTIDE
coenzyme R *n* **:** BIOTIN
coenzyme II \-'tü\ *n* **:** TRIPHOSPHOPYRIDINE NUCLEOTIDE
co·equal \(')kō+\ *adj* [ME, fr. *co-* + *equal*] **:** equal with one another (as in rank, power, age, or extent) ⟨a confederacy of ~ sovereign states —S.E.Morison & H.S.Commager⟩ — **co·equality** \¦kō+\ *n* -ES — **coequally** \(')kō+\ *adv*
co·erce \kō'ərs, -'əs,-'əis\ *vt* -ED/-ING/-S [L *coercēre*, fr. *co-* + *arcēre* to shut up, enclose — more at ARK] **1 :** to restrain, control, or dominate, nullifying individual will or desire (as by force, power, violence, or intimidation) ⟨religion has in the past tried to ~ the irreligious, by garish promises and terrifying threats —W.R.Inge⟩ **2 :** to compel to an act or choice by force, threat, or other pressure ⟨a person might no longer be *coerced* into an agreement not to join a union —*Amer. Guide Series: Mass.*⟩ **3 :** to effect, bring about, establish, or enforce by force, threat, or other pressure ⟨struggles to ~ uniformity of sentiment —Felix Frankfurter⟩ **syn** see FORCE
co·erc·i·ble \-səbəl\ *adj* [*coerce* + *-ible*] **1 :** capable of being coerced **2 :** COMPRESSIBLE; *specif* **:** condensable to a liquid state
co·er·cion \-'ərzhən, -'ə|,-'əi|, |shən\ *n* -s [ME *cohercion*, fr. MF, fr. L *coertion-, coertio* (also *coerction-, coerctio*), alter. of *coercitio*, fr. *coercitus*, past part. of *coercēre* + *-ion-, -io* -ion] **1 a :** the act of coercing **:** use of physical or moral force to compel to act or assent ⟨some form of ~, overt or covert, which encroaches upon the natural freedom of individuals —John Dewey⟩ **b :** a power or force that coerces ⟨the submissive way of one long accustomed to obey under ~ —Charles Dickens⟩ **2 :** the application of sanctions or force by a government usu. accompanied by the suppression of constitutional liberties in order to compel dissenters to conform ⟨~ acts⟩ **3 :** physical force tending to constrict or compress ⟨the ~ of the ice around the ship's bows⟩ **syn** see FORCE
co·er·cive \|siv,|sēv\ *adj* [*coerce* + *-ive*] **:** serving or intended to coerce **:** being or exerting coercion ⟨self-created will rather than ~ force —Adrienne Koch⟩ ⟨~ measures for compelling a restitution —C.G.Bowers⟩ ⟨authority is directional instead of ~ —Theodore Bienenstok⟩ — **co·er·cive·ly** *adv*
coercive force *also* **coercive field** *n* **:** the opposing magnetic intensity that must be applied to a magnetized substance to reduce the residual magnetic induction in the material to zero — compare COERCIVITY
co·er·civ·i·ty \,kō,ər'sivəd·ē\ *n* -ES [*coercive* + *-ity*] **:** the property of a material determined by the value of the coercive force when the material has been magnetized to saturation
coe·reb·i·dae \sə'rebə,dē\ *n pl, cap* [NL, fr. *Coereba*, type genus (fr. Tupi *guira coereba*, a bird) + *-idae*] **:** a family of songbirds comprising the honeycreepers
coe·ru·le·in *also* **ce·ru·le·in** \sə'rülēən\ *n* -s *often cap* [ISV *coerul-, cerul-* (fr. L *coeruleus, caeruleus* cerulean) + *-in*] **:** a xanthene dye $C_{20}H_{10}O_6$ that is obtained by heating gallein with concentrated sulfuric acid and that dyes mordanted cotton, silk, and wool green
coe·ru·le·o·lac·tite \sə,rülē(,)ō'lak,tīt\ *n* -s [*coeruleo-* (fr. L *coeruleus, caeruleus* cerulean) + *-lactite*, fr. L *lact-, lac* milk + E *-ite* — more at CERULEAN, GALAXY] **:** a mineral consisting of an aluminum phosphate $Al_3(PO_4)_2(OH)_3.4H_2O$ of a milk-white to sky-blue color
coerulignol *var of* CERULIGNOL
coerulignone *var of* CERULIGNONE
coes *pl of* COE, *pres 3d sing of* COE
co·essential \¦kō+\ *adj* [ME, fr. *co-* + *essential*] **:** being of one essence ⟨a prophet who considers himself as ~ with God⟩ — **co·essentially** \"+\ *adv*
co·e·ta·ne·i·ty \,kōəd·ə'nēəd·ē\ *n* -ES [L *coaetaneus* of the same age (fr. *co-* + *aetas* age) + E *-ity* — more at AGE] **:** the quality or state of being coetaneous
co·e·ta·ne·ous *or* **co·ae·ta·ne·ous** \¦kōə¦tānēəs\ *adj* [L *coaetaneus*, fr. *co-* + *-aetaneus* (fr. *aetas* age) — more at AGE] **:** COEVAL ⟨to far surpass her peers, the ~ dames —Robert Browning⟩ **syn** see CONTEMPORARY
coeteris paribus *var of* CETERIS PARIBUS
co·eternal \¦kō+\ *adj* [ME, fr. *co-* + *eternal*] **:** equally or jointly eternal ⟨the three Persons of the Trinity are believed ~⟩ — **co·eternally** \"+\ *adv* — **co·eternity** \"+\ *n* -ES
coeur à la crème \,kər-,älə-'krem\ *n* [F, lit., heart with cream] **:** a dessert of cream cheese molded in small heart shapes served with cream and fine preserves
coeur d'a·lene \,kərdᵊl'ān\ *n, pl* **coeur d'alene** *or* **coeur d'alenes** *usu cap C&A* [F *cœur d'alêne*, lit., awl-heart; fr. a tribal chief's characterization of the size of a trader's heart] **1 a :** a Salishan people of northern Idaho — called also *Skitswish* **b :** a member of such people **2 :** a language of the Coeur d'Alene people
[1]co·e·val \(')kō¦ēvəl\ *adj* [L *coaevus* of the same age (fr. *co-* + *aevum* age) + E *-al* — more at AGE] **:** of the same or equal age or antiquity **:** originating or occurring in and often lasting through the same era or epoch ⟨the theory requires that these ~ stars should be nearly the same in mass and brightness —A.S.Eddington⟩ ⟨California, too, has its ranches, many of them of Mexican genesis and ~ with those of Texas —P.A. Rollins⟩ **syn** see CONTEMPORARY
[2]coeval *n* -s **:** one of the same age **:** CONTEMPORARY ⟨the American actor seems "younger" than his ~s abroad —H.E. Clurman⟩ ⟨he spoke and wrote to children as a ~ —John Buchan⟩
co·e·val·i·ty \,kōē'valəd·ē\ *n* -ES **:** the quality or state of being coeval
co·exist \¦kō+\ *vi* [*co-* + *exist*] **1 :** to exist together or at the same time ⟨its educational and manufacturing interests ~ without friction —*Amer. Guide Series: Mich.*⟩ **2 :** to live in peace with each other esp. as a matter of policy — used esp. of countries with seemingly incompatible policies — **co·existence** \"+\ *n* -s
[1]co·existent \"+\ *adj* [*coexist* + *-ent*] **:** existing at the same time or in conjunction with **:** COEXISTING
[2]coexistent \"+\ *n* -s **:** something that coexists **:** CONCOMITANT
co·extended \¦kō+\ *adj* **:** COEXTENSIVE
co·extension \"+\ *n* [*co-* + *extension*] **:** the quality or state of coextending or being coextensive
co·extensive \"+\ *adj* [*co-* + *extensive*] **:** having the same scope or boundaries **:** occupying the same space or period of time — **co·extensively** \"+\ *adv*
co·factor \(')kō+\ *n* [*co-* + *factor*] **1 :** a factor occurring in multiplication with another factor or factors; *specif* **:** the determinant multiplier of any constituent of a determinant in expansion of the determinant **2 :** a substance (as coenzyme) that acts with another substance to bring about certain effects
co·fán \kō'fän\ *n, pl* **cofán** *usu cap* [Sp, of AmerInd origin] **1 a :** a nearly or wholly extinct people of western Ecuador **b :** a member of this people **2 :** the language of the Cofán people sometimes considered to constitute a language family
C of B *abbr* confirmation of balance
C of C *abbr* chamber of commerce
[1]co·feature \(')kō+\ *n* [*co-* + *feature*] **:** a feature (as in an entertainment) accompanying but usu. presumed subordinate in interest to a main attraction
[2]cofeature \"\ *vt* [*co-* + *feature*] **1 :** to give equal prominence to esp. in an entertainment **:** feature equally **2 :** to present as a cofeature
co·ferment \(')kō+\ *n* [*co-* + *ferment*] **:** COENZYME
coff \'kăf\ *vt* **coft** \-ft\ **coft; coffing; coffs** [back-formation fr. *coft* (past tense and past part.), fr. ME (Sc), fr. MD *coft, cocht* bought, past tense of *copen* to buy — more at COPE] *Scot* **:** BUY
cof·fea \'kȯfēə\ *n, cap* [NL, fr. obs. Sw *coffe, coffé* (now *kaffe*), fr. obs. G or E; obs. G *coffée, coffee* (now *kaffee*) fr. E *coffee*] **:** a genus of small trees and shrubs of the family Rubiaceae native to the tropical Old World (as Africa) having white fragrant flowers borne in clusters at the base of the shining evergreen leaves, and including several species (esp. *C. arabica, C. liberica,* and *C. robusta*) that are widely grown in tropical and subtropical uplands for their cherrylike fruits which contain seeds from which coffee is prepared
cof·fee \'kȯfē, -fi *also* 'käf-\ *n* -s *often attrib* [It & Turk; It *caffè*, fr. Turk *kahve* coffee, café, fr. Ar *qahwah* wine, coffee] **1 a :** a drink made by infusion or decoction from the roasted and ground or pounded seeds of plants of the genus *Coffea* **b :** a cup of coffee ⟨the waitress brought two ~s⟩ **c :** any social occasion at which coffee is served esp. for informal entertaining or during a rest period of a workday — see COFFEE BREAK **2 :** the edible green or roasted seeds obtained from the fruit of various plants of the genus *Coffea* — compare COFFEE CHERRY **3 :** a plant of the genus *Coffea* **4 :** a drink or substance used as a substitute for coffee — usu. used with an identifying modifier ⟨barley ~⟩ ⟨acorn ~⟩ **5 :** a moderate brown that is yellower and duller than bay, auburn, or toast brown, darker and slightly yellower than chestnut brown, and yellower, less strong, and slightly lighter than tobacco **6 :** seeds of the Kentucky coffee tree

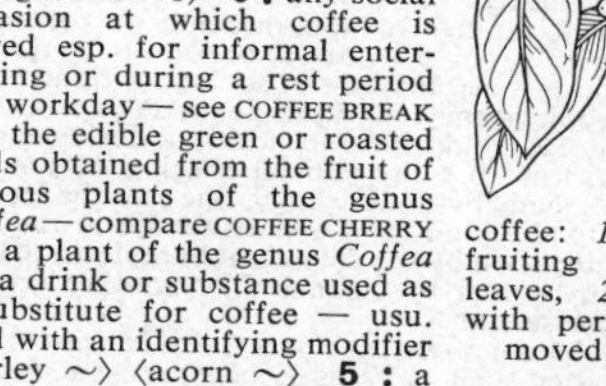

coffee: *1* flowering and fruiting branch with leaves, *2* fruit, *3* fruit with pericarp partly removed to show seeds

coffee-and \¦==¦and\ *n* [by shortening] *slang* **:** coffee and doughnuts
coffee bean *n* **:** the seed of any plant of the genus *Coffea* or of the Kentucky coffee tree
coffee-bean weevil *n* **:** a small stocky dark brown weevil (*Araecerus fasciculatus*) prob. native to India but now nearly cosmopolitan in warm regions where it feeds and breeds in a great variety of products (as dried fruits, coffee beans, grains, or cornstalks)
coffeeberry \'==,==\ *n* **1 :** any of several California shrubs with fruits suggesting coffee cherries: **a** (1) **:** CASCARA BUCKTHORN (2) **:** CALIFORNIA COFFEE 2 **b :** a chaparral shrub (*Ceanothus divaricatus*) **c :** JOJOBA **2 :** SOYBEAN **3 :** either of two shrubs (genus *Coprosma*) related to coffee: **a :** a New Zealand shrub (*C. lucida*) **b :** a Tasmanian shrub (*C. hirtella*) **4 :** the fruit of a coffeeberry
coffee berry *n* **:** COFFEE CHERRY
coffee bread *n* **:** COFFEE CAKE
coffee break *n* **:** a short rest period (as in the mid-morning or mid-afternoon) during which coffee or other refreshment is often consumed
coffeebush \'==,=\ *n* **:** any of several coffeeberries
coffee cake *n* **1 a :** a breakfast bread of yeast dough enriched with eggs, butter, and sugar, baked in a sheet topped with streusel or with added fruit and spices shaped into any of various forms (as rings, braids, rolls, or pinwheels), and glazed with melted sugar after baking **b :** a similar bread leavened with baking powder **2 :** a dark fruited raised bread
coffee cherry *n* **:** the fruit of any plant of the genus *Coffea* being cherrylike in shape, color, and size and containing two seeds enclosed by pulp and an outer skin — compare COFFEE BEAN
coffee cocktail *n* [prob. so called fr. the color] **:** a cocktail consisting of equal parts of port wine and brandy into which are shaken sweetening and an egg
coffee cooler *n, obs slang* **:** a petty crook or opportunist
coffee cream *n* **:** cream that is legally required to contain at least 18 percent but less than 30 percent of butterfat — compare WHIPPING CREAM
coffee disease *n* **:** LEAF DISEASE
coffee fern *n* **:** a Californian evergreen fern (*Pellaea andromedaefolia*)
coffee-ground vomit \'==,=-\ *n* **:** BLACK VOMIT
coffee hour *n* **1 :** a usu. fixed occasion of informal meeting and chatting at which coffee and other refreshment is served **2 :** COFFEE BREAK
[1]coffeehouse \'==,=\ *n* **1 :** a place where coffee and other refreshments are sold often (as in 17th and 18th century England) resembling a club and being a center for the dissemination of news and for informal discussion (as of politics or literature) **2 :** CAFÉ
[2]coffeehouse \"\ *vi* -ED/-ING/-S [[1]*coffeehouse*] **:** to make aimless conversation
coffee klatch *or* **coffee klatsch** \-,klach, -ä-\ *n* [G *kaffeeklatsch*, fr. *kaffee* coffee + *klatsch* gossip] **:** a meeting, often over coffee, for informal conversation
coffeeleaf \'==,=\ *n* **:** SHINLEAF
coffee maker *n* **:** any of various utensils in which coffee is brewed
coffee mill *n* **:** a small mill for grinding coffee beans
coffee nib *n* **:** COFFEE BEAN
coffee nut *n* **1 :** KENTUCKY COFFEE TREE **2 :** the fruit of the Kentucky coffee tree
coffee party *n* **:** a social occasion usu. in the afternoon and often with a guest of honor at which coffee and other light refreshment are served
coffee pea *n* [so called fr. the use of its seeds as a substitute for coffee] **:** CHICKPEA
coffee plant *n* **1 :** COFFEE 3 **2 :** SOYBEAN **3 :** an evening primrose (*Oenothera biennis*)

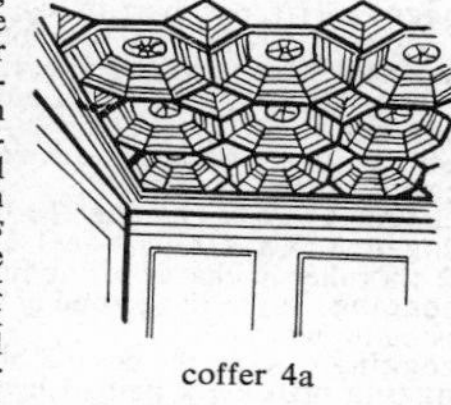
coffee mill

coffeepot \'==,=\ *n* **1 a :** a covered pot with a spout and handle in which coffee is prepared **b :** a utensil from which coffee is served ⟨a silver ~⟩ **2 :** a small lunchroom; *esp* **:** one that stays open all night
coffee ring *n* **:** a coffee cake in the shape of a ring that is plain or fruited and often glazed with melted sugar
coffee roll *n* **:** coffee cake or similar sweet raised bread shaped into rolls with or without raisins, nuts, and spices and sometimes glazed with melted sugar
coffee royal *n* **:** a drink of black coffee and a liquor (as brandy or rum) often sweetened with sugar
coffee sack *n, Midland* **:** a large burlap sack
coffee senna *n* **:** a tropical weed (*Cassia occidentalis*) having rank-scented foliage and seeds that have been used as an adulterant for coffee — called also *mogdad coffee, negro coffee*
coffee service *n* **:** a usu. sterling silver or silverplate service consisting of coffeepot, sugar bowl, creamer, and tray — compare TEA SERVICE
coffee set *n* **1 :** COFFEE SERVICE **2 :** a set of porcelain or pottery for the serving of coffee consisting typically of coffeepot, cream pitcher, and sugar bowl together with a number of matching cups and saucers
coffee shell *n* **:** any of several small ear snails (genus *Melampus*) chiefly of tropical seas
coffee shop *n* **:** a small restaurant that is either independent or attached to a hotel and where light refreshments or regular meals are served
coffee spoon *n* **:** a small spoon for use with after-dinner coffee cups — see SPOON illustration
coffee table *n* **:** any low table customarily placed in front of a sofa; *esp* **:** such a table used to accommodate a coffee or other service while serving
coffee tree *n* **1 :** COFFEE 3 **2 :** KENTUCKY COFFEE TREE **3 :** CASCARA BUCKTHORN
coffeeweed \'==,=\ *n* **1** [so called fr. its use as a substitute for coffee] **:** CHICORY **2 a :** either of two herbs (*Cassia marylandica* and *C. tora*) having seeds that resemble coffee beans **b :** COFFEE SENNA **3 :** CURLED DOCK
coffee wit *n, obs* **:** a coffeehouse wit
coffeewood \'==,=\ *n* [so called fr. its color] **1 :** GRANADILLA WOOD **2 :** wood from coffee (sense 3)
[1]cof·fer \'kȯfə(r), 'käf-\ *n* -s [ME *coffre*, fr. OF *cofre, coffre*, fr. L *cophinus* basket, fr. Gk *kophinos*] **1 :** CHEST, CASKET, BOX; *esp* **:** a strongbox for the safe storage of money or other valuables **2 :** TREASURY, EXCHEQUER, FUNDS — usu. used in pl. ⟨captives . . . whose ransoms did the general ~s fill —Shak.⟩ ⟨working children contribute to the household ~s —D.G.Bettison⟩ **3 a :** the chamber of a canal lock **b :** CAISSON **c :** FLOATING DOCK **d :** COFFERDAM **4 a :** a recessed panel usu. forming with other panels a continuous pattern in a vault, ceiling, or soffit **b :** a space (as in a wall or pier) filled with concrete, rubble, or other materials

coffer 4a

[2]coffer \"\ *vt* **coffered; coffered; coffering** \-f(ə)riŋ\ **coffers** [ME *cofren*, fr. *cofer*, n.] **1 :** to put into, store, or hoard up in a coffer; *broadly* **:** to keep securely **:** treasure up **:** HOARD **2 :** to form (as a ceiling) with recessed panels; *sometimes* **:** to recess (as a panel) **3 :** to secure (as a mining shaft) from leaking by ramming clay behind the masonry or timbering
cofferdam \'==,=\ *n* [[1]*coffer* + *dam*] **1 a :** a temporary watertight enclosure (as of piles packed with clay or of metal plates) from which the water is pumped to expose the bottom of a body of water and permit construction (as of foundations or piers) **b :** a watertight structure for making repairs below the waterline of a ship **2 a :** a compartment formerly provided near the waterline of a man-of-war and filled with cellulose which would swell on contact with water and plug a hole **b :** the space between two closely located bulkheads in a ship
cof·fer·er \'==ə(r)\ *n* -s [MF *coffrier*, fr. *coffre* + *-ier* -er] *archaic* **:** TREASURER; *esp* **:** a former officer of the British royal household subordinate to the controller
cofferfish \'==,=\ *n* [so called fr. its boxlike body] **:** BOXFISH
cof·fer·ing \'kȯf(ə)riŋ, 'käf-\ *n* -s [[1]*coffer* + *-ing*] **:** a system or structure of coffers ⟨carved and gilded ceiling ~⟩
[1]cof·fin \'kȯfən *also* 'käf-\ *n* -s [ME, basket, receptacle, fr. MF *cofin*, fr. L *cophinus* — more at COFFER] **1** *obs* **a :** BASKET, CHEST, CASE **b :** a casing, crust, or mold of pastry (as for a pie); *also* **:** a pie dish **c :** BIER **2 :** a box or chest for a corpse to be buried in formerly often of a hexagonal or wedge shape, wider at the head than at the foot — compare CASKET **3** *archaic* **:** a paper cornucopia (as for groceries or filtration) **4 :** the horny body forming the hoof of a horse's foot **5** *printing* **a :** the bed or carriage of a handpress **b :** a wooden frame enclosing an imposing stone
[2]coffin \"\ *vt* -ED/-ING/-S **:** to enclose in or as if in a coffin
coffin bone *n* **:** the foot bone enclosed within the hoof of the horse and other equines
coffin corner *n* **:** one of the corners formed by a goal line and a sideline on a football field into which a punt is often aimed so that it may go out of bounds close to the defenders' goal line
coffing *pres part of* COFF
coffin joint *n* **:** the joint next above the coffin bone
cof·fin·less \'kȯfənləs *also* 'käf-\ *adj* **:** lacking a coffin
coffin nail *n* [so called fr. the presumed pernicious effects of smoking, each cigarette being likened to a nail driven into one's coffin] *slang* **:** CIGARETTE

coffin ship *n* **:** an unseaworthy ship
coffin stool *n* **:** JOINT STOOL
coffin text *n* **:** any of many inscriptions on coffins of the Middle Kingdom in Egypt consisting usu. of charms or prayers and forming a stage between the Pyramid Texts and the Book of the Dead
cof·fle \'kȯfəl, -äf-\ *n* -S [Ar *qāfilah* caravan] **:** a gang of men or a train of animals fastened together; *esp* **:** a group of slaves chained together (as when traveling)
cof·fre *like* ¹COFFER\ *n* -S [ME — more at COFFER] **:** COFFER 1
cof·fret \'kȯfrət, 'käf-\ *n* -S [F, dim. of *coffre* coffer — more at COFFER] **:** a small coffer
coffs *pres 3d sing of* COFF
C of M *abbr* certificate of merit
co·fra·dia \,kōfrə'dēə, -rä'-\ *n* -S [Sp *cofradía*, fr. *cofrade* member of a confraternity (fr. OSp *confrade*, fr. *con-* — fr. L *com-* — + *frade* brother, monk, priest, fr. L *fratr-*, *frater*) + *-ia* (fr. L *-ia*) — more at BROTHER] **:** a group or organization of Roman Catholic laymen in Mexico and Central America responsible for the material care of religious images, pilgrimages, and ceremonies
C of S *abbr* **1** chief of section **2** chief of staff
coft *past of* COFF
co·function \'kō+,==\ *n* [*co-* + *function*] **:** the corresponding trigonometric function of the complement of an angle ⟨the ~ of the tangent is the cotangent⟩
¹cog \'käg *also* 'kȯg\ *n* -S [ME *cogge*, of Scand origin; akin to Norw *kug* cog, Sw *kugge*; akin to OE *cycgel* cudgel — more at CUDGEL] **1 :** a tooth on the rim of a wheel **:** a gear tooth **2 :** one that functions as a necessary but subordinate part of a larger process, organization, or system ⟨the jobber is an important ~ in the scheme of distribution —*Marketing Toys*⟩ ⟨the Malayan tiger . . . constitutes an important and necessary ~ in the natural balance wheel of Malaya —R.R.Camp⟩
²cog \"\ *vt* **cogged; cogged; cogging; cogs** [ME *coggen*, fr. *cogge*, n.] **:** to furnish with a cog
³cog \"\ *n* -S [ME *cogge*, fr. MD *cogghe*, fr. MF *coque* — more at COCK] **:** any of several boats: **a :** a broadly built ship with bluff prow and stern used prior to the 16th century chiefly for freighting and transport **b** *obs* **:** a British riverboat **c** *also* **cogboat** \'=,=\ **:** COCKBOAT
⁴cog \"\ *n* -S [origin unknown] *obs* **:** an act of trickery or deception esp. at dice **:** TRICK, DECEPTION, FALSEHOOD; *sometimes* **:** something (as a piece of money) used as bait for dupes **:** COME-ON
⁵cog \"\ *vb* **cogged; cogged; cogging; cogs** *vi* **1** *obs* **:** to use any of certain tricks in throwing dice **2** *obs* **:** DECEIVE, CHEAT **3** *obs* **:** to use venal flattery **:** FAWN ~ *vt* **1 :** to direct the fall of (dice) fraudulently **2** *obs* **:** ENTICE **:** get by flattery or cajolery **:** WHEEDLE
⁶cog \'käg, 'kōg\ *n* -S [origin unknown] *chiefly Scot* **:** a wooden vessel varying as to size and usu. having a handle formed by an extension of one or two of the staves
⁷cog \'käg *also* 'kȯg\ *vb* **cogged; cogged; cogging; cogs** [prob. alter. (influenced by ¹*cog*) of ⁹*cock*] **:** to connect (as timbers or joists) by means of tenons
⁸cog \"\ *n* -S **1 :** a tenon on the face or side of a beam or timber received into a mortise in another beam to secure the two together: as **a :** the tabular projection at the end of a scarfed timber **:** COAK **b :** a tenon (as a dovetail) in a beam or joist resting in a notch in the bearing surface of another so that the two are flush (as in the corner joints of wall plates) **c :** a tongue in the upper surface of a beam to fit into a notch in the lower surface of a beam crossing it **2** *Brit* **:** a pillar or column consisting of blocks of wood or stone set vertically upon each other or of timbers set crosswise two by two upon each other to support the roof of a mine — called also *chock*
⁹cog \"\ *vt* **cogged; cogged; cogging; cogs** [E dial. *cog* to beat] **:** to consolidate (iron or steel) by hammering or rolling; *sometimes* **:** to rough (iron or steel) to shape by rolling — see COGGING MILL
cog *abbr* cognate
cog and round *n* [¹*cog*] **:** a device common in clocks consisting of a cogwheel working into the trundles of a lantern pinion
co·gen·cy \'kōjənsē, -si\ *also* **co·gence** \-n(t)s\ *n, pl* **cogencies** *also* **cogenc·es :** the quality or state of being cogent
cogener *var of* CONGENER
co·gent \'kōjənt\ *adj* [L *cogent-*, *cogens*, pres. part. of *cogere* to drive together, collect, compel, fr. *co-* + *agere* to drive — more at AGENT] **1 :** having the power of compelling or constraining ⟨the ~ forces of nature⟩ **2 a :** appealing forcibly to the mind or reason **:** CONVINCING ⟨a ~ argument⟩ ⟨a ~ description⟩ ⟨criticism that shows his argumentative style at its most ~ —Edmund Wilson⟩ **b :** forcefully concise, pertinent, and often timely **:** to the point **:** APPOSITE ⟨the most searching and ~ analysis of economic trends —*Economist*⟩ ⟨the 14th chapter of St. Luke's Gospel, which says some ~ things about the futility of aspiration —C.B.Marshall⟩ ⟨be able to write ~ and expert briefs —*Current Biog.*⟩ **syn** see VALID
cogently *adv* **:** in a cogent manner
cogged *adj* [fr. past part. of ²*cog*] **1 :** provided with a cog or cogs ⟨~ rim of a wheel⟩ ⟨a ~ timber dressed to join firmly with a mortised member⟩ **2 :** operated by means of cogged wheels ⟨a ~ railway running up a mountain⟩
¹cog·ger \-gə(r)\ *n* -S [⁵*cog* + *-er*] *archaic* **:** a cheat or deceiver esp. at dice **:** SHARPER; *sometimes* **:** a false fawning person **:** SYCOPHANT, FLATTERER
²cogger \"\ *n* -S [by alter.] **:** ¹COCKER 2
³cogger \"\ *n* -S [⁸*cog* + *-er*] **1** *Brit* **:** one that erects mine cogs **2 :** a roller in charge of the first set of rolls in a steelworks
¹cogging *n* -S [fr. the gerund of ²*cog*] **:** COGS ⟨the ~ of the wheel is badly worn⟩
²cogging *n* -S [fr. the gerund of ⁷*cog*] **:** a cogged joint
cogging mill *n* **:** a pair of heavy rolls through which heated steel ingots are passed
¹cog·gle \'kägəl\ *vi* -ED/-ING/-S [perh. alter. of ⁷*cockle*] *dial Brit* **:** WOBBLE, TOTTER
²coggle \"\ *vt* -ED/-ING/-S [perh. alter. of ¹*cobble*] *dial* **:** to repair roughly **:** COBBLE — usu. used with *up*
³coggle \"\ *n* -S [perh. fr. ¹*cog* + *-le*] **:** a ceramics tool that consists mainly of a wheel or disk and is used to make indentations or grooves in the outer edges of plates
cog·gly \'käglē, -li\ *adj* [¹*coggle* + *-y*] *dial chiefly Brit* **:** UNSTEADY, WOBBLY
co·gi·da \kō'hēthə\ *n* -S [Sp, fr. fem of *cogido*, past part. of *coger* to receive, seize, get, fr. L *colligere* to bind together — more at COLLECT] **:** a tossing of a bullfighter by a bull
cog·ie \'kägi, 'kōgi\ *n* -S [⁶*cog* + *-ie*] *Scot* **:** ⁶COG
cog·i·ta·ble \'käjəd·əbəl, -ətəb-\ *adj* [L *cogitabilis*, fr. *cogitare* to think + *-bilis* -able] **:** capable of being brought before the mind as a thought or idea **:** THINKABLE ⟨the practical steps to achieve the maximum utilization of heat become more ~ —*Times Rev. of Industry*⟩
cog·i·ta·bund \-,bənd\ *adj* [L *cogitabundus*, fr. *cogitare*] *archaic* **:** given to deep thought **:** having the appearance of being in deep meditation **:** PENSIVE
cog·i·tate \'käjə,tāt, *usu* -ād.+V\ *vb* -ED/-ING/-S [L *cogitatus*, past part. of *cogitare* to think, think about, fr. *co-* + *agitare* to drive, agitate, turn over in the mind — more at AGITATE] *vt* **:** to ponder on or meditate upon usu. with intentness and objectivity ⟨*cogitating* what they should do⟩ ⟨*cogitating* how to answer⟩; *sometimes* **:** PLAN, PLOT ⟨he sat and *cogitated* the trick he would play on his big brother⟩ ~ *vi* **:** to ponder, meditate, or think deeply, intently, or objectively ⟨~ on his previous mistakes⟩ ⟨the three of us were silent, *cogitating* —Kenneth Roberts⟩ **syn** see THINK
cog·i·ta·tion \,käjə'tāshən\ *n* -S [ME *cogitacioun*, fr. OF or L; OF *cogitation*, fr. L *cogitation-*, *cogitatio*, fr. *cogitatus* + *-ion-*, *-io* -ion] **1 a :** the act of cogitating **:** REFLECTION, MEDITATION ⟨agree to a plan after considerable ~⟩ **b :** the capacity to think or reflect ⟨some people think animals not capable of ~⟩ **2 a :** THOUGHT ⟨agreeable ~*s*⟩ ⟨present her ~*s* in the form of a treatise⟩ **b** *obs* **:** PLAN, PURPOSE ⟨evil ~*s* and nefarious designs⟩ **c** *obs* **:** CONCEPTION, IDEA ⟨he dislikes other people's ~*s* of God⟩
cog·i·ta·tive \'käjə,tād·iv, -,təl, \tiv, -ēv\ *adj* [MF or ML; MF *cogitatif*, fr. ML *cogitativus*, fr. L *cogitatus* + *-ivus* -ive] **1 a :** of or relating to cogitation ⟨the ~ faculty⟩ **b :** possessing the faculty or power of thinking or meditating ⟨man is a ~ being⟩ **2 :** marked by or given to cogitation ⟨eyes . . . hardly ~ in their gaze —Anne D. Sedgwick⟩ ⟨the mere ~ pagans of the twenties —Wylie Sypher⟩
co·gi·to \'kōgə,tō, 'käjə-\ *n* -S [L, I think (as in NL *cogito ergo sum* I think, therefore I am), 1st pers. sing. pres. ind. of *cogitare*] **1 :** the philosophic principle that one's existence is demonstrated by the fact that one thinks **2 :** the intellectual processes of the self or ego
cog·man *n, pl* **cogmen** \'=mən\ [⁸*cog* + *man*] **:** ³COGGER
co·gnac \'kōn,yak *also* 'kän- *or* 'kȯn-\ *n* -S [F, fr. *Cognac*, Charente department, France, where it is made] **1** *usu cap* **:** a brandy from the departments of Charente and Charente-Maritime, France, distilled from white wine **2 :** BRANDY; *esp.* **:** a French brandy — not used technically **3 :** a moderate brown that is yellower, lighter, and stronger than bay or auburn and lighter, stronger, and slightly yellower than chestnut brown
¹cog·nate \'käg,nāt, *usu* -ād.+V\ *adj* [L *cognatus*, fr. *co-* + *gnatus*, *natus*, past part. of *nasci* to be born; akin to L *gignere* to beget — more at KIN] **1 a :** related by blood **:** kindred by birth ⟨~ families⟩ ⟨a family ~ with another⟩ ⟨a boy ~ to several royal families⟩ **b :** related on the mother's side — used in some legal systems **2 a** *of a language* **:** related by descent from the same recorded or assumed ancestral language ⟨Spanish and French are ~ languages⟩ — often used with *with*, sometimes with *to* ⟨English is ~ to German⟩ **b** *of a word or morpheme* **:** related by descent from the same root or affixal element in a recorded or assumed ancestral language ⟨English *eat* and German *essen* are ~⟩ ⟨Latin *-us* and Old Norse *-r* are ~⟩ or by the processes of derivation or composition within a single language ⟨English *boyish* and *boyhood* are ~⟩ — often used with *with*, sometimes with *to* ⟨English *foot* is ~ with Greek *pous*⟩ **c** *of a word* **:** related in a manner that involves borrowing rather than descent from or as well as descent from an ancestral language ⟨English *tobacco* and French *tabac* are ~⟩ — often used with *with*, sometimes with *to* ⟨German *panzer* is ~ with English *paunch*⟩ **d** *of a substantive* **:** related usu. in derivation but sometimes only in meaning to the verb of which it is the object (as *song* in "she sang the song"; *race* in "he ran the race") ⟨~ object⟩ ⟨~ accusative⟩ **3 :** related, akin, or similar esp. in having the same or common or similar nature, elements, qualities, or origin ⟨illustrated books and ~ reference materials —*Current Biog.*⟩ ⟨you know exactly how a man looks and behaves and, with ~ clarity, something of what he feels and thinks —Thomas Dozier⟩ ⟨action engendered in regard to drugs may spill over into the ~ problem of the alcoholic —*New Republic*⟩ **4 a :** closely related logically through certain specifiable factors; *esp, of propositions* **:** having the same subject or predicate **b :** belonging to volcanic fragments in solidified lava which are part of the same extrusion **c :** HOMORGANIC — **cog·nate·ly** *adv*
²cog·nate \"\ *n* -S [L *cognatus*, fr. *cognatus*, adj.] **:** one that is cognate with another: as **a :** a person related to another on the mother's side — compare AGNATE **b :** a cognate word or morpheme
cognate inclusion *n* **:** AUTOLITH
cog·nat·ic \käg'nad·ik\ *adj* [F *cognatique*, fr. *cognat* cognate (fr. L *cognatus*) + *-ique* -ic] **:** of or relating to cognates or to the maternal line
cog·na·tion \käg'nāshən\ *n* -S [ME *cognacioun*, fr. L *cognation-*, *cognatio*, fr. *cognatus* cognate + *-ion-*, *-io* -ion] **:** cognate relationship esp. by blood
cog·na·tus \-'nād·əs\ *n, pl* **cogna·ti** \-d·,ī, -ē\ [L — more at COGNATE] **:** a relative by blood esp. on the mother's side — usu. used in pl.
cog·ni·tion \käg'nishən\ *n* -S [ME *cognicioun*, fr. L *cognition-*, *cognitio*, fr. *cognitus* (past part. of *cognoscere* to become acquainted with, know, fr. *co-* + *gnoscere*, *noscere*) + *-ion-*, *-io* -ion — more at KNOW] **1 a :** the act or process of knowing in the broadest sense; *specif* **:** an intellectual process by which knowledge is gained about perceptions or ideas — distinguished from *affection* and *conation* **b :** a product of this act, process, faculty, or capacity **:** KNOWLEDGE, PERCEPTION **2** *Scots law* **:** the act or process of cognoscing **:** adjudication of rights
cog·ni·tion·al \-shən°l,-shnəl\ *adj* **:** being, belonging to, or based on cognition
cog·ni·tive \'kägnəd·iv, -ətiv\ *adj* [*cognition* + *-ive*] **1 :** of, relating to, being, or involving cognition ⟨the ~ elements of perception —C.H.Hamburg⟩ ⟨~ experiences as opposed to emotional⟩ ⟨the ~ content of a sentence⟩ **2 :** based on or capable of being reduced to empirical factual knowledge ⟨to debate whether normative statements can be ~⟩ — **cog·ni·tive·ly** *adv*
cog·ni·tiv·ism \-,vizəm\ *n* -S **:** the ethical theory of a cognitivist
cog·ni·tiv·ist \-,vəst\ *n* -S **:** an ethicist who holds that genuine ethical judgments are cognitive or empirically confirmable; *usu* **:** UTILITARIAN, PRAGMATIST
cog·ni·za·ble *or* **cog·ni·sa·ble** \'kägnəzəbəl, (')käg'nīz- *sometimes* 'känəz- *esp in sense 2*\ *adj* [*cognizance* + *-able*] **1 :** capable of being known ⟨~ events⟩ **2 :** competent as a subject of judicial investigation **:** capable of being judicially heard and determined — **cog·ni·za·bly** \-blē, -i\ *adv*
cog·ni·zance *or* **cog·ni·sance** \'kägnəzən(t)s *sometimes* 'känə- *esp in sense 3*\ *n* -S [alter. (influenced by *cognition*) of ME *conisaunce*, fr. OF *conoissance*, fr. *conoistre* to know, fr. L *cognoscere* — more at COGNITION] **1 :** a distinguishing mark or emblem (as a heraldic bearing, crest, or cockade); *specif* **:** the badge worn by an armed knight and his followers **2 a** *obs* **:** knowledge or understanding in general **b :** SURVEILLANCE, CONTROL ⟨the engineering department also has ~ over all engineering compartments —A.A.Ageton⟩ ⟨reserves them to his own jurisdiction unless he chooses to give ~ of them to anyone as a mark of unusual honor —F.W. Stenton⟩ **c :** particular knowledge **:** conscious recognition **:** APPREHENSION, PERCEPTION ⟨the officer's power to arrest without a warrant depends upon his own sensory ~ that a crime has been committed —Paul Wilson⟩ ⟨seemed to have no ~ of the crime⟩ **d :** range of apprehension or perception ⟨beyond the children's ~⟩ **e :** NOTICE, OBSERVANCE ⟨nothing could happen, among a certain class of society, without the ~ of some philanthropic agency —Arnold Bennett⟩ ⟨to take ~ of a fault⟩ **3 a :** the right and power to hear and decide controversies **:** JURISDICTION **b :** the judicial hearing of a matter **4 a :** an admission made by one levying a fine that the lands in question belong to the plaintiff **:** a plea admitting the facts alleged **b :** a justification by the defendant in replevin that the goods were taken by him by command of another lawfully entitled to their possession
cog·ni·zant \'kägnəzənt *sometimes* 'känə- *esp in sense b*\ *adj* [fr. *cognizance*, after such pairs as E *abundance: abundant*] **:** having cognizance: **a :** AWARE, CONSCIOUS ⟨~ of the facts⟩ ⟨~ of the fascinated gaze I bent upon him —Jack London⟩ **b :** having the surveillance, responsibility, or jurisdiction ⟨legislative proposals have been introduced in the Congress and referred to the ~ congressional committees —*U.S. Code*⟩ **syn** see AWARE
cognize \(')käg'nīz\ *vt* -ED/-ING/-S *see -ize in Explan Notes* [back-formation (influence of *recognize*) fr. *cognizance*] **:** KNOW, PERCEIVE **:** have cognizance of esp. in any philosophically fundamental or ultimate sense ⟨to doubt whether we ~ anything as it really is⟩
cog·no·men \käg'nōmən\ *n, pl* **cognomens** \-ənz\ *or* **cog·nom·i·na** \-nämənə, -nōm-\ [L, fr. *co-* + *-gnomen*, alter. (influenced by *gnoscere* to know) of *nomen* name — more at NAME, KNOW] **1 :** SURNAME ⟨having the ~ Smith⟩; *esp* **:** the third of the usual three names of a person among the ancient Romans — compare PRAENOMEN, NOMEN; see AGNOMEN **2 :** NAME; *esp* **:** a distinguishing nickname or epithet ⟨who gained, and richly earned, the ~ of Tom-Tom —G.W.Johnson⟩
cog·nom·i·nal \(')käg'nämən°l, -nōm-\ *adj* [L *cognomin-*, *cognomen* + E *-al*] **:** of, relating to, or being a cognomen
cog·nom·i·na·tion \(,)=,==='nāshən\ *n* -S [L *cognomination-*, *cognominatio*, fr. *cognominatus* + *-ion-*, *-io* -ion] **:** COGNOMEN
cog·nosce \(')käg'näs\ *vt* -ED/-ING/-S [L *cognoscere* to become acquainted with — more at COGNITION] *Scots law* **:** to determine judicially esp. with respect to insanity
cog·nos·cent \(')=¦=°nt\ *adj* [L *cognoscent-*, *cognoscens*, pres. part. of *cognoscere*] *archaic* **:** COGNIZANT
co·gno·scen·te \,kānyō'shentē, ,kägnə'-\ *n, pl* **cognoscen·ti** \-tē\ [obs. It (now *conoscente*), fr. *cognoscente*, adj., wise, having good judgment, fr. L *cognoscent-*, *cognoscens*, pres. part. of *cognoscere* to know] **:** a person having or claiming expert knowledge in one or more realms of the fine arts or of fashion **:** CONNOISSEUR ⟨art dealers, collectors, and other *cognoscenti* —Janet Flanner⟩
¹cog·nos·ci·ble \(')käg¦näsəbəl\ *adj* [LL *cognoscibilis*, fr. L *cognoscere* + *-ibilis* -ible] **:** COGNIZABLE, KNOWABLE
²cognoscible \"\ *n* -S **:** a cognizable thing
cog·nos·ci·tive \-səd·iv\ *adj* [L *cognoscere* to know + E *-itive*] **:** having the power of knowing ⟨~ abilities⟩
cog·no·vit note \(')käg¦nōvət-\ *n* [L *cognovit*, lit., he has acknowledged] **1 :** a note authorizing an attorney to confess judgment **2 a :** a note indicating that its maker acknowledges a debt **b** *in some jurisdictions* **:** PROMISSORY NOTE
co·gon \kō'gōn\ *also* **co·gon·grass** \(')=¦=,=\ *or* **ko·gon** \=¦=\ *n* -S [Sp *cogón*, fr. Tag, Bisayan, Bikol *kugon*] **:** any of several grasses of the genus *Imperata*; *esp* **:** either of two coarse tall grasses (*I. cylindrica koenigii* and *I. exaltata*) used in the Philippines and adjacent lands for thatching — called also *alang-alang*
co·go·nal \,kōgə'näl, -gō'-, '==,=\ *n, pl* **cogona·les** \-(,)lās\ [Sp, fr. *cogón*] *Philippines* **:** an area overgrown with cogon
cograil \'=,=\ *n* [¹*cog* + *rail*] **:** a cogged rail — called also *rack rail*
cog railway *also* **cog railroad** *n* **:** a steep mountain railroad that has in the middle or on the side of its track a cograil that engages a cogwheel on the locomotive to ensure traction
cogroad \'=,=\ *n* [¹*cog* + *road*] **:** COG RAILWAY
cogs *pl of* COG, *pres 3d sing of* COG
cogs·well chair *also* **cogswell chair** \'kägz,wel-, -,wəl-\ *or* **cox·well chair** \'käk,swel-, -,swəl-\ *n, often cap 1st C* [fr. the name *Cogswell*] **:** an upholstered easy chair with inclined back, seat cushion, thin open arms, and often cabriole front legs
cogs·wel·lia \käg'zwelēə\ *n* [NL, fr. Joseph G. *Cogswell* †1871 Am. librarian + NL *-ia*] *syn of* LOMATIUM
cogue \'kōg\ *n* -S *chiefly Scot* **:** ⁶COG
cogway \'=,=\ *n* [by contr.] **:** COG RAILWAY
cogwheel \'=,=\ *n* [ME *cogwhele*, fr. *cogge* cog + *whele* wheel] **:** a wheel with cogs or teeth
cogwheel ore *n* **:** BOURNONITE
cogwood \'=,=\ *n* [¹*cog* + *wood*] **:** the hard tough wood of a West Indian tree (*Zizyphus chloroxylon*)

cogwheel

co·hab \'kō,hab, ='=\ *n* -S [short for *cohabitant*] *slang* **:** one living in illegal cohabitation; *esp* **:** a polygamous Mormon
co·hab·it \kō'habət, *usu* -əd·+V\ *vb* -ED/-ING/-S [LL *cohabitare*, fr. L *co-* + *habitare* to inhabit, dwell, fr. *habitus*, past part. of *habēre* to have — more at HABIT] *vi* **1 :** to live together as husband and wife usu. without a legal marriage having been performed **2 a :** to live together or in company ⟨buffaloes ~*ing* with crossbred cows —*Biol. Abstracts*⟩ **b :** to be intimately together or in company ⟨two strains in his philosophy . . . ~ in each of his major works —Justus Buchler⟩ ~ *vt* **:** to live together in ⟨two closely related species of freshwater cottids . . . ~ the Arrow lakes in British Columbia —*Copeia*⟩ — **co·hab·i·tant** \-bəd·ənt, -bətə- *also* -bət°nt\ *n* -S
co·hab·i·ta·tion \(,)kō,habə'tāshən\ *n* -S [ME *cohabitacioun*, fr. LL *cohabitation-*, *cohabitatio*, fr. *cohabitatus* (past part. of *cohabitare*) + *-ion-*, *-io* -ion] **1 :** act or state of cohabiting esp. as or as if husband and wife **2 :** COITUS
co·hee \'kō,hē\ *or* **coo·hee** \'kü,-\ *n* -S *cap* [origin unknown] **:** an inhabitant of western Pennsylvania or western Virginia
co·heir \(')kō+\ *n* [*co-* + *heir*] **:** a joint heir
co·heiress \(')kō+\ *n* [*co-* + *heiress*] **:** a joint heiress
co·hen *or* **ko·hen** \'kō(h)ən\ *n, pl* **co·ha·nim** \-nəm, ,kō(h)ə'nēm\ *also* **cohens** *usu cap* [Heb *kōhēn* priest] **:** a member of one of the families or clans descended from the high priest Aaron having certain hereditary religious privileges and responsibilities
co·hen·ite \'kōə,nīt\ *n* -S [G *cohenit*, fr. Emil *Cohen* †1905 Ger. mineralogist + G *-it* -ite] **:** a tin-white crystalline mineral $(Fe,Ni,Co)_3C$ consisting of a carbide of iron, nickel, and cobalt and occurring in some meteorites
co·here \kō'hi(ə)r, -iə\ *vb* -ED/-ING/-S [L *cohaerēre*, fr. *co-* + *haerēre* to stick, cling — more at HESITATE] *vi* **1 a :** to hold together firmly, solidly, stickily, with resistance to separation (as of ingredients in a conglomeration or similar particles in a mass) ⟨particles of wet sand ~⟩ ⟨the two sticky surfaces ~⟩; *often* **:** STICK, ADHERE — usu. used of a substance stuck to a similar substance **b** *bot* **:** to display cohesion **2 a :** to consist of or become marked by parts, ingredients, or elements which cohere ⟨despite the addition of a bonding agent the mass would not ~⟩ **b** (1) *of a group or community* **:** to become harmoniously united by common interests or sense of social membership or by emotional ties and esp. with the cooperative playing down of any individual differences or disagreements ⟨torn by personal animosities, the town did not ~ in any of its endeavors⟩ (2) *of an individual* **:** to be a cooperative part of a group or community united in this way ⟨the necessity that he shall conform, that he shall ~ —T.S.Eliot⟩ **c :** to have unambiguous connectedness and logical or aesthetic interrelation of parts **:** fit together naturally and consistently with suitable order, proportion, and similarity of tone without jar or wrench ⟨did not the whole composition ~, were its unity broken, it would be not one picture —Irwin Edman⟩ **d :** to become fittingly connected or unified by certain principles, relationships, or themes esp. in the study or presentation of one purpose or idea ⟨pure arithmetic ~*s* with its basal elements given in whole numbers —Samuel Alexander⟩ **3 :** to be consistent **:** SUIT, FIT ⟨the account ~*s*⟩ ⟨the adornments ~ with the base design⟩ ~ *vt* **:** to make (parts or components) fit or stick together in a suitable or orderly way ⟨amends, ~*s*, and sharpens our map —*Times Lit. Supp.*⟩ **syn** see ADHERE
co·her·ence \kō'hirən(t)s *also* -her- *or* -hēr-\ *n* -S [MF & L; MF *cohérence*, fr. L *cohaerentia*, fr. *cohaerent-*, *cohaerens* (pres. part. of *cohaerēre*) + *-ia*] **1 :** the quality or state of cohering: as **a :** systematic or methodical connectedness or interrelatedness esp. when governed by logical principles **:** CONSISTENCY, CONGRUITY **b :** integration of social and cultural elements based on a consistent pattern of values and a congruous set of ideological principles **2** *obs* **:** mutual understanding **:** fellow feeling
coherence theory *n* **:** the theory that the ultimate criterion of truth is the coherence of all its separate parts with one another and with experience — contrasted with *correspondence theory*
co·her·en·cy \-nsē, -i\ *n* -ES [L *cohaerentia*] **:** COHERENCE
co·her·ent \-nt\ *adj* [MF or L; MF *cohérent*, fr. L *cohaerent-*, *cohaerens*] **1 :** having the quality of cohering ⟨two ~ substances⟩ ⟨the felting of the individual fibers into a ~ sheet requires the use of a bonding agent —A.C.Morrison⟩ ⟨a ~ plan⟩ ⟨a ~ speech⟩ ⟨a place and time ~ with a plan of action⟩; *specif, bot* **:** displaying cohesion — compare ADNATE 1 **2 :** logically consistent and ordered ⟨a ~ way of explaining⟩ ⟨a ~ thinker⟩ **3 :** having such phase relationships as to permit interference — used of two or more wave trains or of scattered or reflected photons or particles (as electrons and neutrons) — **co·her·ent·ly** *adv*
co·her·er \-hirə(r)\ *n* -S [so called fr. the assumption that the current caused the loosely connected points to cohere] **:** a radio detector in which an imperfectly conducting contact between pieces of metal or other conductors loosely resting against each other is materially improved in conductance by the passage of high-frequency current
co·he·sion \kō'hēzhən\ *n* -S [fr. *cohere*, after such pairs as E *adhere: adhesion*] **1 :** the act, quality, or state of cohering (as tangibly or morally) **:** a sticking together ⟨the ~ of two substances⟩ ⟨the ~ of the tribal group —D'Arcy McNickle⟩ ⟨the ~ of the free nations —Dean Acheson⟩ ⟨cultural ~⟩ **2 :** union between similar plant parts or organs (as between petals of a flower) — compare ADHESION **3 :** molecular attraction by which the particles of a body are united throughout the mass whether like or unlike — distinguished from *adhesion*
co·he·sive \-hēsiv, -sēv *also* -hēz-\ *adj* [*cohesion* + *-ive*] **1 :** COHERING ⟨a beautifully ~ whole —Arthur Knight⟩ ⟨a ~ family unit⟩ **2 :** causing to cohere **:** producing cohesion ⟨~ forces⟩ — **co·he·sive·ly** *adv* — **co·he·sive·ness** *n* -ES
co·hib·it \kō'hibət\ *vt* -ED/-ING/-S [L *cohibitus*, past part. of

cohibēre, fr. *co-* + *habēre* to have, hold — more at HABIT] *archaic* : RESTRAIN, RESTRICT

co·hi·tre \kō'hē·(,)trā\ *n* -s [Sp *cojitre*] : a dayflower (*Commelina longicaulis*) troublesome as a weed esp. in Puerto Rico

cohn·heim's area \'kōn,hīmz-\ *n, usu cap C* [trans. of G *Cohnheimsche felder*, after Julius F. *Cohnheim* †1884 Ger. pathologist] : one of the polygonal areas seen in transverse sections of a striated muscle fiber representing a bundle of cut ends of fibrils surrounded by sarcoplasm

co·ho *or* **co·hoe** \'kō(,)hō\ *or* **coho salmon** *or* **cohoe salmon** *n* -s [origin unknown] : SILVER SALMON

co·ho·ba \kō'hōbə\ *n* -s [AmerSp *cohoba, cojoba*, of Arawakan origin; akin to Taino *cohoba* tobacco, cohoba] : a narcotic snuff made from the seeds of a tropical American tree (*Piptadenia peregrina*)

co·ho·bate \'kōə,bāt, -ō(h)ō,-, kə'hō,-\ *vt* -ED/-ING/-S [NL *cohobatus*, past part. of *cohobare*, perh. fr. Ar *ka'aba* to repeat an action, double a number] : to redistill formerly esp. by pouring a distillate back upon the matter from which it was distilled but now usu. by subjecting a distillate to a new act of distillation — **co·ho·ba·tion** \,==ˈbāshən\ *n* -s

cohol *var of* KOHL

co·ho·ni·na \,kō(h)ə'nēnə\ *adj, usu cap* [fr. the name *Cohonina*] : of or relating to a prehistoric Indian culture which flourished in northwestern Arizona from the 8th to the 11th centuries

co·horn \'kō,hȯrn\ *also* **coe·horn** \'kōō,-, 'kō,-\ *n* -s [fr. earlier *Coehorn mortar*, part trans. of D *Coe-hoorn-mortier*, after Baron Menno van *Coehoorn* †1704 Dutch engineer, its inventor] : a small bronze mortar that was mounted on a wooden block with handles and used for throwing light shells

co·hort \'kō,hȯ(ə)rt, -ō(ə)t, *usu* -d.+V\ *n* -s [MF & L; MF *cohorte*, fr. L *cohort-, cohors* enclosure, cohort — more at COURT] **1 a** : one of ten divisions of an ancient Roman legion comprising at first 300 but later 500 to 600 soldiers **b** : a similar subdivision in some organizations of Roman cavalry or auxiliary troops **c** : a group of warriors or soldiers **d** : COMPANY, BAND, GROUP ⟨a loyal ~ of adherents —S.N.Behrman⟩ **e** : a group of individuals or vital statistics about them having a statistical factor in common in a demographic study (as year of birth) ⟨data that tells what happened to a ~ of patients admitted in a specific year —*Diagnostic & Statistical Manual*⟩ ⟨a ~ of 100,000 females starting life together⟩ **2** : a taxonomic category of somewhat indefinite rank: **a** *bot* : a category nearly equivalent to and now generally replaced by the modern order **b** *zool* : SUBORDER **3 a** : COMPANION, ACCOMPLICE ⟨he and three alleged housebreaking ~s were arraigned on attempted burglary charges —*Springfield (Mass.) Republican*⟩ **b** : FOLLOWER, SUPPORTER ⟨a congressman accompanied by a group of loyal ~s⟩

co·hor·ta·tion \,kō,hȯ(r)'tāshən\ *n* -s [L *cohortation-, cohortatio*, fr. *cohortatus*, past part. of *cohortari* to exhort (fr. *co-* + *hortari* to urge) + *-ion-, -io* -ion — more at YEARN] : EXHORTATION

¹co·hor·ta·tive \kō'hȯ(r)d·əd·iv\ *n* -s [ISV *cohortat-* (fr. L *cohortatus*) + *-ive*; prob. orig. formed as G *kohortativ*] : a set of verb forms expressing exhortation; *also* : a form belonging to such a set

²cohortative \(')=;===\ *adj* : belonging to or constituting a set of verb forms expressing exhortation

co·hosh \'kō,häsh, =', kə'häsh\ *n* -ES [of Algonquian origin; akin to Natick *kôshki* it is rough] : any of several American medicinal plants: as **a** : a bugbane (*Cimicifuga racemosa*) **b** : BLUE COHOSH **c** : WHITE BANEBERRY **d** : RED BANEBERRY

cohow *or* **cohowe** *var of* CAHOW

co·hune \kō'hün\ *or* **cohune palm** \(')=;=-\ *n* -s [AmerSp, fr. Mosquito *óchuñ, uchún*] : a commercially important Central and So. American pinnate-leaved palm (*Orbignya cohune*) valued esp. for the oil and the hard ivory-nutlike shell of its fruit

cohune oil *also* **cohune-nut oil** *or* **cohune fat** *n* : a yellowish semisolid fat obtained from cohune fruits and used in cooking and in soapmaking

coi·ba \'kȯivə\ *n, pl* **coiba** *or* **coibas** *usu cap* [Sp, of AmerInd origin] **1 a** : a Cunan people of southwestern Panama **b** : a member of such people **2** : the Chibchan language of the Coiba people

co·identity \¦kō+\ *n* [*co-* + *identity*] : identity between two or more things

¹coif *also* **coiffe** \'kȯif, *in sense 4 usu* 'kwäf *or* -af *or* -aa(ə)f *or* -äf\ *n* -s [ME *coyfe*, fr. MF *coife, coiffe*, fr. LL *cofea, cofia*] **1** : a cap covering the sides of the head like a small hood, having various shapes and sizes, and worn at various periods of history by men and women ⟨a nun's ~⟩ **2** : a defensive usu. iron or steel skullcap formerly worn by soldiers (as under the hood of mail); *also* : a hood of mail **3** : a white cap formerly worn by lawyers in England, esp. serjeants-at-law; *also* : the order or rank of a serjeant-at-law **4** : COIFFURE **5** : a small close-fitting woman's hat worn on the crown or the back of the head

²coif *also* **coiffe** \'kȯif, *in sense 3 usu* 'kwäf *or* -af *or* -aa(ə)f *or* -äf\ *vt* **coiffed** *or* **coifed; coiffed** *or* **coifed; coiffing** *or* **coifing; coifs** [MF *coiffer*, fr. *coiffe*, n.] **1** : to cover or dress with or as if with a coif **2** : to invest with a coif **3** : to arrange (hair) by combing, brushing or curling

coif·feur \kwä'fər, kwa-,kwá-, +V -ər-; -'fə, +V -ər- *also* -ər\ *n* -s [F, fr. *coiffer* + *-eur* -er] : a male hairdresser

coif·feuse \kwä'fə(r)z, kwa'-kwá'-, -'fōz\ *n* -s [F, fem. of *coiffeur*] : a female hairdresser

¹coif·fure \kwä'fyù(ə)r, kwa'-,kwá'-, -ùə, 'ə,=(=), *F* kwäfüer\ *n* -s [F, fr. *coiffer* + *-ure*] : a manner of arranging or styling the hair : HEADDRESS

²coiffure \"\ *vt* -ED/-ING/-S : ²COIF 3

¹coign *var of* QUOIN

²coign \'kȯin\ *n* -s [earlier spelling of ¹*coin*] : a projecting corner; *specif* : a corner of a crystal formed by the intersection of three or more faces at a point

coign of vantage : a position advantageous for action or observation ⟨from the *coign of vantage* which the present age affords . . . we will . . . retell the history of Christianity —K.S.Latourette⟩

coigny *var of* COYNYE

coi·gue \kȯi'gā, '=,=\ *or* **coi·hue** \kȯi'wā, '=,=\ *n* -s [Sp *coigüé, coihué*, fr. Araucan *coyhue*] : a Chilean evergreen tree (*Nothofagus dombeyi*) the leafy boughs of which are used for thatching

¹coil \'kȯil, *esp before pause or consonant* -ȯiəl\ *n* -s [origin unknown] **1** : noisy disturbance : TUMULT, TURMOIL **2 a** : a troublesome activity or disturbance esp. over a trifling matter : a great ado : FUSS ⟨here's a ~ raised, a pother and for what —Robert Browning⟩ **b** : worldly activities, affairs, or troubles ⟨in that sleep of death . . . when we have shuffled off this mortal ~ —Shak.⟩

²coil \"\ *vb* -ED/-ING/-S [MF *coillir* to collect, gather together — more at CULL] *vt* **1** : to wind (something long and pliable, as a rope) into rings laid within or on top of one another or wound spirally about an object ⟨~ down loose rope when it is not in use⟩ ⟨the snake ~*ed* itself about its victim⟩ ⟨she ~*ed* her hair at the back of her head⟩ **2** : to encircle and hold with or as if with coils **3** : to roll or twist (as oneself) into a shape resembling a coil ⟨she ~*ed* herself upon the bed with a book⟩ ~ *vi* : to move in a circular, spiral, or winding course ⟨under the image on the water the water ~*s* and goes —R.P.Warren⟩ : form a coil : lie in coils : WIND **syn** see WIND

³coil \"\ *n* -s **1 a** : a series of loops or a spiral (as of a flexible strand or sheet) ⟨her hair hung in neat ~*s*⟩ : an arrangement of something in a spiral or in concentric rings ⟨large ~*s* of sheet metal⟩ **b** : a single loop or part of such a coil ⟨the town nearly enclosed by a ~ of the river⟩ **2** : a helix or spiral of insulated wire wound on a spool or other structure usu. for electromagnetic effect or for providing resistance **3** : a series of connected pipes in rows, layers, or windings (as in steam-heating or water-heating apparatus) **4** : a roll of postage stamps for use in a stamp machine or other type of stamps dispenser; *also* : a stamp from such a roll **5 a** : the action of coiling, winding up, or tensing (as of a spring) ⟨the better ~ in the legs, the greater spring for lift —H.O. Crisler⟩ **b coils** *pl* : something resembling a coil or a coiling (as of rope) in that it binds, restricts, or entangles ⟨wrestled with the ~*s* of convention —Clive Bell⟩

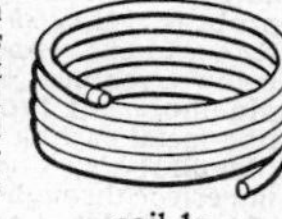
coil 1a

⁴coil \"\ *n* -s [origin unknown] *dial* : HAYCOCK

⁵coil \"\ *vt* -ED/-ING/-S : COCK ⟨~*ing* hay⟩

coil antenna *n* [³*coil*] : a radio antenna of one or more complete turns of wire or other conductor functioning as an inductance rather than as a capacitor — compare LOOP ANTENNA

coiled *adj* [fr. past part. of ²*coil*] **1** : under tension : straining to be released ⟨an impression of ~ power⟩ **2** *of a basket* : of a close weave, circular in form and made by coiling the fiber

coil·er \'kȯilə(r)\ *n* -s [²*coil* + *-er*] **1** : an apparatus used in spinning cotton and other fibers that coils the sliver by feeding it through a tube attached to an annular revolving plate into oppositely revolving cans **2** : one that makes coils (as by winding wire to form springs)

coiling *n* -s [fr. gerund of ²*coil*] : the construction of coil pottery

coil pottery *or* **coiled pottery** *n* [³*coil*] : a pottery common among American Indians made by building up sides of pots with successive rolls of clay

coil spring *n* [³*coil*] : a flat-spiral, volute, or helical spring

coil waste *n* [³*coil*] : postage stamps intended orig. to be coils but constituting remnants sold as sheet stamps

coim·ba·tore \¦kȯimbə¦tō(ə)r, -tȯ(ə)r\ *adj, usu cap* [fr. *Coimbatore*, India] : of or from the city of Coimbatore, India : of the kind or style prevalent in Coimbatore

co·implicant \(')kō+\ *adj* [*co-* + *implicant*] *logic* : mutually implying : EQUIVALENT 2b

¹coin \'kȯin\ *n* -s [ME *coyne*, fr. MF *coing, coin* wedge, stamp, corner, fr. L *cuneus* wedge; perh. akin to L *culex* gnat — more at CULEX] **1** *archaic* **a** : CORNER, CORNERSTONE, QUOIN **b** : a wedge used for blocking, securing, or tightening **c** : a small corner cupboard esp. of the 18th century **2** : the stamped device or impress on coined money **3** : a piece of metal or rarely of some other material (as leather or porcelain) certified by a mark or marks upon it as being of a definite intrinsic or exchange value and issued by governmental authority for use as money; *collectively* : such pieces — see MINOR COIN, STANDARD COIN, SUBSIDIARY COIN, TOKEN, TOKEN COIN **4** : something accepted as having value or validity ⟨perhaps wisecracks . . . are respectable literary ~ in the U.S. —*Times Lit. Supp.*⟩ : something given or offered in an exchange ⟨too much softened . . . to answer his obstinacy in like ~ —J.C.Powys⟩; *specif* : a unit (as an expression or idea) of intellectual or social exchange ⟨they exchanged a few small ~*s* of country talk —Mollie Panter-Downes⟩ **5** *slang* : MONEY ⟨I'm in it for the ~ —Sinclair Lewis⟩

²coin \"\ *vt* -ED/-ING/-S [ME *coynen*, fr. MF *coignier*, fr. *coin, coing*, n.] **1 a** : to make (a coin) by stamping the design onto the planchet ⟨~ pennies⟩ : convert (metal) into coins ⟨~ silver⟩ **b** : to make (a coin) by any process or series of processes : MINT, STRIKE ⟨~ dimes⟩ : manufacture or issue (money) in the form of coins **c** : to shape (a piece of metal) in a mold or die by applying great pressure **2** : to make up or invent (something false or spurious) ⟨~ smile and fair words⟩ **3** : CREATE, INVENT ⟨adept at repartee and forever ~*ing* epigrams⟩ ⟨~ a phrase⟩ **4** : to make money out of ⟨~ your brains⟩ : convert into something valuable ⟨~ his talent into verses⟩ **5** : to make or earn (money) rapidly and in large quantity ⟨~*ed* a small fortune . . . in the real estate boom —Irving Dilliard⟩

coin·age \'kȯinij, -ēj\ *n* -s [ME, fr. MF *coignaige*, fr. *coin, coing* + *-age*] **1 a** : the act or process of coining (as money) : the manufacture of coins **b** : the official stamping of tin blocks of standard weight **c** : the fabricating or inventing esp. of new words ⟨a word of recent ~⟩ **2** : something that has been coined: as **a** : COINS **b** : a quantity of coins produced at one time from a particular metal or by a particular mint : a series of coins minted under a particular ruler, government, or dynasty or in a particular country or city ⟨the Jubilee ~ of 1887⟩ **c** : something that is made up or invented ⟨this is the very ~ of your brain —Shak.⟩; *specif* : a coined word ⟨*chortle* is a ~ of Lewis Carroll's⟩ **d** : something that passes current (as in the language of a group) or is of recognized worth ⟨the term has become common ~⟩

coinage ratio *n* : RATIO 2c

coin box *n* : a locked receptacle to store the coins inserted in a coin-operated device (as in a pay phone)

coin changer *n* : a key-operated machine which from a store of coins drops into a coin tray a required number of coins in required denominations (as in making quick change for paper money)

co·in·cide \,kōən'sīd, '=,=\ *vi* -ED/-ING/-S [ML *coincidere*, fr. L *co-* + *incidere* to fall on, fr. *in* + *cadere* to fall — more at CHANCE] **1 a** : to occupy the same place in space ⟨the base of the triangle ~*s* with one side of the square⟩ **b** : to occur at the same time or occupy the same period of time ⟨the fall of Granada *coincided* with the discovery of America⟩ **c** : to occupy exactly corresponding or equivalent positions on a scale or in a series ⟨100° centigrade ~*s* with 212° Fahrenheit⟩ **2** : to be identical or correspond in nature, character, or function : be in harmony ⟨our sentiments *coincided* in every particular —Jane Austen⟩ ⟨engaged in a work which *coincided* with his own inclinations —H.W.H.Knott⟩ **3** : to be in accord or agreement : CONCUR ⟨she *coincided* with his views on most subjects⟩ **syn** see AGREE

co·in·ci·dence \kō'in(t)sədən(t)s\ *n* -s [F *coïncidence*, fr. MF *coincidance*, fr. *coincider* + *-ance*] **1** : the occupation of the same position in space ⟨the ~ of a point in space with another point⟩, in time ⟨~ of two events⟩, or in a series or on a scale ⟨~ of the readings on two thermometers⟩ : the coming together or simultaneous occurrence or existence of things or events ⟨the ~ of the last note of the violin with the sound of the bell⟩ **2** : correspondence or agreement in nature, character, or detail ⟨a perfect ~ between truth and goodness —Robert South⟩ **3** : an instance of coinciding or corresponding ⟨the ~*s* between the Arabic and the Sanskrit versions —F.M.Müller⟩ **4** : the concurrence of events or circumstances appropriate to one another or having significance in relation to one another but between which there is no apparent causal connection ⟨the ~ that Mr. Baines should have died while there was a show of mourning goods in his establishment —Arnold Bennett⟩ **5** *biol* : the ratio between the observed number of double crossovers and the number predicted on a random basis — compare INTERFERENCE **6** : the simultaneous indication by two or more counting tubes of the passage presumably of the same ionizing particle through both or all of them (as in a cosmic-ray telescope) — compare ANTICOINCIDENCE

coincidence method *n* : a precise method of comparing the frequencies of two periodic phenomena (as the ticking of two clocks) by observing the interval between their successive coincidences, the interval being the least common multiple of the periods compared

co·in·ci·den·cy \-dənsē, -si\ *n* -ES [F *coïncidence* + E *-y*] *archaic* : COINCIDENCE

¹co·in·ci·dent \(')kō¦insədənt, -,dent\ *adj* [F *coïncident*, fr. MF, fr. *coincider* + *-ent*] : marked by or showing coincidence: **a** : occurring or operating at the same time : CONCOMITANT, ATTENDING ⟨hand weaves and their ~ expense —*New Yorker*⟩ **b** : occupying the same space : having the same position, direction, or setting ⟨the culture areas . . . would be essentially ~ with language areas —Harry Hoijer⟩ **c** : having accordant characteristics or nature : HARMONIOUS ⟨they had a sincere affection for each other and ~ opinions on the proper conduct of life —A.T.Quiller-Couch⟩ **syn** see CONTEMPORARY

²coincident \"\ *n* -s *archaic* : a coincident thing or event

co·in·ci·den·tal \(')=;==¦dent°l\ *adj* [²*coincident* + *-al*] : being or resulting from a coincidence ⟨similarity between the two texts is too consistent to be ~⟩ : characterized by coincidence : occurring or existing at the same time ⟨rebellion in Burma was ~ with . . . insurrection in Malaya —W.B. Hamilton⟩ — **co·in·ci·den·tal·ly** \-t(ə)lē, -li\ *adv*

co·in·ci·dent·ly \(')kō¦insə¦dentlē, -sədəntlē, -li\ *adv* : COINCIDENTALLY

co·indicate \(')kō+\ *vt* [*co-* + *indicate*] : to provide conjoint indications of — **co·indication** \¦kō+\ *n*

coin dot *n* : a pattern (as on a fabric) resembling a polka dot but usu. with large dots

coin·er \'kȯinə(r)\ *n* -s [ME *coyner*, fr. *coynen* + *-er*] : one that coins: as **a** : a maker of coins **b** : one that performs the stamping operation in the manufacture of a coin **c** *chiefly Brit* : one that makes coins illegally : COUNTERFEITER **d** : an inventor or fabricator esp. of new words or expressions

co·infinite \(')kō+\ *adj* [*co-* + *infinite*] : equally infinite : conjointly infinite

coin gold *n* : gold of the fineness legalized for coins (as .900 fine in the U. S., .9166 or 11/12 fine in Great Britain)

co·inhabit \¦kō+\ *vi* [*co-* + *inhabit*] : to dwell together — **co·inhabitant** \¦kō+\ *n*

coining *n* -s [fr. gerund of ²*coin*] **1** : the stamping or manufacture of coins **2** *chiefly Brit* : the counterfeiting or illegal manufacture of coin

coining die *n* : one of a set of dies between which a piece of metal is squeezed in or as if in coining money

coin lesion *n* : a round well-circumscribed nodule in a lung that is seen in the roentgenogram as a shadow the size and shape of a coin

coin lock *n* : a lock released by the insertion of a coin; *also* : a lock operated by inserting a coin which releases the key

coin machine *n* : SLOT MACHINE

coin note *n* : a currency note bearing a statement that redemption will be made in coin; *specif* : any one of two series of U.S. treasury notes, the first issued 1863–65, the second 1890–91

coin of the realm : the legal money of a country

coins *pl of* COIN, *pres 3d sing of* COIN

coin seal \'=,=\ *n* : a metal seal with a design on both face and back

coin silver *n* : silver of the fineness legalized for coins (as .900 fine in the U. S., .500 fine for Great Britain since 1920)

co·instantaneity \¦kō+\ *n* -ES [*coinstantaneous* + *-ity*] : the quality or state of being coinstantaneous

co·instantaneous \(')kō+\ *adj* [*co-* + *instantaneous*] : happening at the same instant — **co·instantaneously** \(')kō+\ *adv*

co·insurance \¦kō+\ *n* [*co-* + *insurance*] **1** : joint assumption of risk with another or others (as the sharing of a risk jointly by two or more underwriters) **2** : a system of insurance (as fire insurance) in which the insured is obligated to maintain coverage on a risk at a stipulated percentage of its total value or in the event of loss suffer a penalty in proportion to the deficiency

co·insure \¦kō+\ *vb* [*co-* + *insure*] *vi* : to insure a property jointly or upon the basis of coinsurance ~ *vt* : to insure (a property) jointly or with another or others

co·insurer \¦kō+\ *n* [*co-* + *insurer*] : one that assumes liability as an insurer jointly with another : one subject to penalty under a coinsurance clause

coin·tise \kwan'tēz\ *n* -s [ME (also, wisdom, skill), fr. OF, fr. *cointe* wise, skillful, elegantly dressed — more at QUAINT] : a fanciful or symbolical article of apparel; *esp* : a scarf worn on a lady's headdress or as a token of favor on a knight's helmet

Coin·treau \kwaⁿ·trō\ *trademark* — used for a sweet colorless orange-flavored liqueur

coin weight *n* : a weight (sense 3b) used in assaying coins

coir \'kȯi(ə)r, -ȯiə\ *n* -s [Tamil *kayiṟu* rope] : a stiff coarse fiber from the outer husk of the coconut

cois·trel \'kȯistrəl\ *n* -s [MF *coustillier* soldier carrying a short sword, squire of a knight, fr. *coustille* short sword (alter. of *coustele* knife, fr. L *cultellus*) + *-ier* -er — more at CUTLASS] **1** *archaic* : a groom employed to care for a knight's horses **2** *archaic* : a mean fellow : VARLET

co·i·tal \'kōəd·°l, -ət°l\ *adj* [L *coitus* + E *-al*] : of or relating to coitus

coital exanthema *n* : a highly contagious virus disease of horses and cattle transmitted chiefly by copulation and marked by the formation of vesicles and pustules on the mucous membranes of the genital tract, the viruses in horses and in cattle being commonly considered distinct

co·i·tion \kō'ishən\ *n* -s [L *coition-, coitio*, fr. *coitus* (past part. of *coire* to come together, fr. *co-* + *ire* to go) + *-ion-, -io* -ion — more at ISSUE] **1** *obs* : a coming together or meeting : conjunction esp. of planets **2** *obs* : mutual attraction esp. of iron and a magnet **3** [LL, fr. L] : COITUS — **co·i·tion·al** \-shən°l, -shnəl\ *adj*

co·i·tus \'kōəd·əs, -ōtəs\ *n* -ES [L, fr. *coitus*, past part. of *coire*] : the act of conveying the male semen to the female reproductive tract involving insertion of the penis in the vaginal orifice followed by ejaculation — compare ORGASM

coitus in·ter·rup·tus \-,intə'rəptəs\ *also* **coitus re·ser·va·tus** \-,rezər'vād·əs\ *n, pl* **coitus interrup·ti** \-,tī,-(,)tē\ *also* **coitus reserva·ti** \-d·,ī,-d·(,)ē\ [NL, interrupted coitus] : coitus which is purposely interrupted in order to prevent ejaculation of semen into the vagina

co·ix \'kōəks\ *n* [NL, fr. Gk *koix* doom palm] **1** *cap* : a small genus of coarse Asiatic monoecious grasses having the pistillate flowers and seeds enclosed in a shining capsulelike involucre **2** -ES : any plant of the genus *Coix*; *esp* : JOB'S-TEARS

co·jo·nes \kə'hō,nās\ *n pl* [Sp, pl. of *cojón* testis, fr. (assumed) VL *coleon-, coleo* — more at CULLION] **1** : TESTES **2** : COURAGE, GUTS

co·juror \(')kō+\ *n* [*co-* + *juror*] : COMPURGATOR

¹coke \'kōk\ *n* -s [ME *coke, colke*; akin to Sw *kälk* pith, Gk *gelgis* bulb of garlic, Skt *gr̥ñjana* garlic, L *galla* gall on a plant — more at GALL] **1** *dial Eng* : the core esp. of a fruit **2 a** : the infusible cellular coherent residue from carbonized coal that consists mainly of carbon, is hard, porous, and gray with a submetallic luster, and is used as a fuel (as in blast furnaces and domestic furnaces) **b** : a similar residue from various other carbonized substances (as petroleum, shale oil, or copal) **c** : a piece of coke ⟨put a ~ on the fire⟩

²coke \"\ *vb* -ED/-ING/-S *vt* : to change into coke ⟨a uniform controlled heat makes it impossible to ~ or char the material⟩ ~ *vi* : to become coky ⟨the *coking* of petroleum oils on distillation —R.F.Goldstein⟩

³coke \"\ *n* -s [by alter. and shortening] *slang* : COCAINE

Coke \"\ *trademark* — used for a cola drink

coke breeze *n* : fine coke separated by screening from the larger sizes before or after crushing

coked *adj* [³*coke* + *-ed*] *slang* : stimulated by an addicting drug (as cocaine) — often used with *up* ⟨a *coked*-up gunman⟩

coke dust *n* : powdered coke

coke iron *n* : iron made in a furnace using coke as fuel

coke oven *n* : an oven made usu. of refractory brick and blocks and used for carbonization (as of coal) for the production of coke — see BEEHIVE OVEN, BY-PRODUCT OVEN

coke-oven gas \'=,==\ *n* : a gas that is similar in composition to coal gas and that is obtained in the carbonization of coal esp. at high temperatures for the production of coke

coke plate *or* **coke tin** *n* **1** : tin plate made from coke iron **2** : tin plate having lighter coating than charcoal plate

co·ker \'kōkə(r)\ *n* -s [alter. of *coco*] : COCO — used in the port of London to avoid confusion with *cocoa*

co·ker·nut \'kōkə(r),nət\ *n* [alter. of *coconut*] **1** : COCONUT 1 **2** : the edible seed of the coquito palm (*Jubaea spectabilis*) of Chile enclosed in a fruit like a small coconut

cok·ery \'kōk(ə)rē\ *n* -ES [¹*coke* + *-ery*] : a plant for making coke

cokes *n* [orig. unknown] *obs* : SIMPLETON, GULL

¹cok·ie *also* **cok·ey** \'kōkē\ *n* -s [³*coke* + *-ie, -y*] *slang* : a cocaine addict

²cokie *also* **cokey** \"\ *adj, slang* : addicted to cocaine

coking coal *n* [fr. pres. part. of ²*coke*] : a bituminous coal suitable for making into coke

coky \'kōkē\ *adj* -ER/-EST [¹*coke* + *-y*] : resembling coke (as in physical properties)

col \'käl\ *n* -s [F, fr. MF, neck, fr. L *collum* — more at COLLAR] **1 a** : a high pass in a mountain range generally across a watershed **b** : a saddlelike depression in the crest of a ridge **2** : a neck of low pressure between two anticyclones

¹col- — see COM-

²col- *or* **coli-** *or* **colo-** *comb form* [NL, fr. L *colon*] **1** : large intestine ⟨*colitis*⟩ ⟨*colostomy*⟩ **2** : colon bacillus ⟨*coliform*⟩

³col *abbr* **1** *often cap* colonel **2** colonial; colony **3** colophon **4** color; colored **5** column **6** counsel

²col *or* **coll** *abbr* **1** collated **2** collateral **3** colleague **4** collect; collected; collective; collector **5** college; collegiate **6** colloquial; colloquialism

COL *abbr* cost of living

¹cola *pl of* COLON

²co·la \ˈkōlə\ *n* [of African origin; akin to Temne *k'ola* kola nut, Mandingo *kolo*] **1** *cap* **:** a large genus of African trees (family Sterculiaceae) having capsular fruits containing large seeds **2** -s **a** *or* **ko·la** **:** \"\ a tonic extract derived from the kola nut **b** [fr. *Coca-Cola*, a trademark] **:** a carbonated soft drink flavored with extract from coca leaves, kola nut, sugar, caramel, and acid and aromatic substances

³co·la \ˈkōlə\ *n* -s [Sp, lit., tail, fr. L *coda, cauda*] **:** LINE, QUEUE ⟨a ~ of ticket holders⟩

-co·la \kələ, kōlə\ *n comb form* -s [NL, fr. L — more at -COLOUS] **:** inhabitant ⟨Arenicola, Rupicola⟩

co·la·ci·a·les \kə,lāsēˈā(,)lēz\ *n pl, cap* [NL, fr. *Colacium* (fr. Gk *kolak-, kolax* parasite, flatterer + NL *-ium*) + *-ales;* perh. akin to Gk *kelein* to beguile — more at CALUMNY] **:** an order of algae (class Euglenophyceae) comprising those forms that have immobile cells with an encapsulating wall and that develop amorphous or dendroid colonies with sometimes temporary naked flagellate stages, the members of some of its genera (as *Colacium*) occurring on rotifers, copepods, and other minute aquatic animals

col·a·co·bi·o·sis \,kälə,kōbīˈōsəs, -bē-\ *n, pl* **colacobio·ses** \-,sēz\ [NL, fr. Gk *kolak-, kolax* parasite + NL *-o-* + *-biosis*] *zool* **:** permanent social parasitism (as that between certain species of ants)

co·la·mine \,kōlə¦mēn, kōˈlamən\ *n* -s [ISV alcohol + *amine*] **:** ethanolamine esp. as a component of certain phosphatides (as cephalin)

col·an·der \ˈkələndə(r), ˈkäl-\ *also* **cul·len·der** \ˈkəl-\ *n* -s [ME *colyndore*, prob. modif. of OProv *colador*, fr. ML *colatorium*, fr. L *colatus*, past part of *colare* to filter, strain, sieve, fr. *colum* sieve — more at HEDGE] **:** a bowl-shaped usu. metal utensil having perforations permitting use as a strainer

colander

co·lane \kəˈlān\ *n* -s [origin unknown] **:** EMU APPLE

cola nut *var of* KOLA NUT

colarian *usu cap, var of* KOLARIAN

co·la·scio·ne \,kōlə¦shōnē, -nā\ *n, pl* **colascio·nes** \-,nēz\ [It] **:** an Italian long-necked lute of the 16th and 17th centuries

cola seed *n* **:** KOLA NUT

co·la·tion \kəˈlāshən\ *n* -s [L *colatus* + E *-ion*] **:** removal of solids from a liquid by straining esp. through filter paper

co·latitude \(ˈ)kō+\ *n* [*co-* + *latitude*] **:** the complement of the latitude

cola tree *var of* KOLA TREE

col·a·ture \ˈkäləchə(r)\ *n* -s [LL *colatura*, fr. L *colatus* (past part. of *colare* to strain) + *-ura* -ure] **:** STRAINING

col bas·so \kōlˈbä(,)sō\ *adv* [It] **:** with the bass — used as a direction in music to play the same part as the bass

col·ber·teen *or* **col·ber·tine** \ˈkälbə(r),tēn, ˈkōl-\ *n* -s [after Jean B. *Colbert* †1683 Fr. statesman + E *-een* or *-ine*] **:** a lace with a coarse network of open square mesh

col·bert·ism \ˈkälbə(r),tizəm, ˈkōl-, kōlˈba(a),rizəm\ *n* -s *usu cap* [Jean B. *Colbert* + E *-ism*] **:** the mercantilistic policies and practices of Colbert

col·by \ˈkōlbē\ *also* **colby cheese** *n* -ES *sometimes Colby* [prob. fr. the name *Colby*] **:** a porous soft moist mild cheese

col·can·non \kəlˈkanən, ˈkäl,k-\ *n* -s [IrGael *cāl ceannan*, lit., white-headed cabbage, fr. *cāl* cabbage, kale (fr. OIr, fr. L *caulis*) + *ceannan* white-headed, bald, fr. *ceann* head (fr. OIr *cend, cenn*) + *fionn* white, fr. OIr *find* — more at COLE, ARPENT, FINNOCK] **:** potatoes and cabbage or other greens boiled and mashed together

col·cha \ˈkōlchə\ *n* -s [Sp, bedspread, quilt, fr. OSp, bed, couch, fr. OF *colche, couche* — more at COUCH] **:** a wool-embroidered coverlet of Mexican origin

col·ches·tri·an \(ˈ)kōl¦chestrēən\ *n* -s *cap* [*Colchester*, Essex, England + E *-ian*] **:** a native or resident of Colchester

¹col·chi·an \ˈkälkēən\ *adj, usu cap* [L *Colchis* (fr. Gk *Kolchis*) + E *-an*] **1 :** of, relating to, or characteristic of Colchis, an ancient region in Asia **2 :** of, relating to, or characteristic of Colchians

²colchian \"\ *n* -s *usu cap* **:** a native or inhabitant of Colchis

col·chi·ce·ine \kälˈchisēən, -ˈkis-; ¦kälchə¦sēən, -lkə¦-\ *n* -s [ISV, fr. *colchicine*] **:** a crystalline compound $C_{21}H_{23}NO_6$ of which colchicine is the methyl ether

col·chi·cine \ˈkälchə,sēn, ˈkälkə-, -sən\ *n* -s [G *kolchizin*, fr. NL *Colchicum* + G *-in* -ine] **:** a poisonous yellow crystalline alkaloid $C_{22}H_{25}NO_6$ extracted from the seed and corm of the meadow saffron that on application to mitotic cells induces polyploidy, an effect used experimentally and commercially to create new plant varieties, and that is used medicinally in the treatment of acute attacks of gout

col·chi·cin·ize \ˈ==sə,nīz\ *vt* -ED/-ING/-s **:** to treat with colchicine in order to induce c-mitosis ⟨*colchicinized* root-tips — *Biol. Abstracts*⟩

col·chi·cum \ˈkälchəkəm, -älkə-\ *n* [NL, fr. L, a kind of plant with a poisonous root, fr. Gk *kolchikon*, fr. *kolchikos* Colchian, fr. *Kolchis* Colchis] **1** *cap* **:** a genus of chiefly fall-blooming Old World cormous herbs (family Liliaceae) having crocuslike flowers with a very long perianth tube and six stamens — see MEADOW SAFFRON; compare CROCUS **2** -s **:** a plant, bulb, or flower of the genus *Colchicum* **3** *or* **colchicum root** -s **:** the dried corm or dried ripe seeds of autumn crocus that contain the alkaloid colchicine and possess an emetic, diuretic, and cathartic action used chiefly for gout and rheumatism

col·co·thar \ˈkälkəthə(r)\ *n* -s [ML, fr. MF or OSp; MF *colcotar*, fr. OSp *cólcotar* (now *colcótar*), fr. Ar dial. *qulquṭār*, prob. modif. of Gk *chalkanthos* — more at CHALCANTHITE] **1 :** a reddish brown iron oxide left as a residue when ferrous sulfate is highly heated and used formerly in polishing glass and as a pigment **2 :** a moderate reddish brown that is yellower and deeper than roan, yellower, stronger, and slightly darker than mahogany, and yellower, less strong, and slightly darker than oxblood — called also *angel red, Coromandel, English red, Mars red, Prussian red, Tuscany*

¹cold \ˈkōld\ *adj* -ER/-EST [ME, fr. OE *cald, ceald;* akin to OHG *kalt* cold, ON *kaldr*, Goth *kalds*, L *gelu* frost, *gelare* to freeze, congeal] **1 a :** having a temperature notably below an accustomed norm, often notably below that of the human body or below that compatible with human comfort **:** notably lacking in warmth **:** having a low temperature ⟨quite ~ weather⟩ ⟨it was ~ yesterday⟩ ⟨the rain was very ~ now, almost frigid, and they shuddered —Norman Mailer⟩ ⟨a ~ and drafty hallway⟩ ⟨~ arctic seas⟩ ⟨have trouble starting with a ~ motor⟩ — distinguished from *cool* **b :** likely to lose heat quickly **:** likely to feel cool ⟨a ~ metallic substance⟩ **c :** receptive to the sensation of coldness **:** stimulated by cold ⟨a ~ spot is the typical ~ receptor in higher vertebrates⟩ **2 a :** naturally without heat — used in ancient and medieval sciences to describe one of the qualities of the four elements **b** *of a sign of the zodiac* **:** having a cold complexion **3 a :** marked by lack of warm feeling **:** without ardor, zeal, or sympathy **:** DISTANT ⟨he's a pretty ~ one —Ernest Hemingway⟩ ⟨the ~, correct, regular, narrow poetry of Pope —A.L.Kroeber⟩ ⟨this novel leaves the reader ~⟩ **b :** free from emotion or passion, esp. sexual passion **:** FRIGID, INHIBITED ⟨one of the ~ kisses that he disliked so much —Archibald Marshall⟩ **c :** lacking cordiality, heartiness, friendliness, or affability **:** UNFRIENDLY ⟨forbiddingly reserved **:** ALOOF, CHILLING ⟨his ~, mean, selfish policy toward those whom he liked to segregate and hate as his enemies —W.A.White⟩ ⟨the court becomes a ~ place for the self-exiled queen —H.O.Taylor⟩ **d :** lacking feeling **:** EMOTIONLESS, DETACHED, INDIFFERENT, APATHETIC, COLD-BLOODED ⟨the ~ neutrality of an impartial judge —Edmund Burke⟩ ⟨~, sullen, unreliable, brusque, unconventional, grasping, a man of iron will —C.L.Jones⟩ **e :** feeling or showing no interest, excitement, or sympathy **:** UNENTHUSIASTIC ⟨the discouragement of playing to a ~ audience⟩ ⟨the mawkish appeal left him ~⟩ ⟨to his astonishment, he finds the people of his village ~ to this noble and time-honored sentiment — Arthur Knight⟩ **f :** marked by deliberate intent or plan **:** not shaped or influenced by passion or strong feeling **:** activated or executed deliberately ⟨a ~ calculated punishing punch in the mouth —John Steinbeck⟩ ⟨that a goodly part of the illegal drug supply is grown and processed in China; that it is spread with ~ deliberation to other countries —Meyer Berger⟩ **g :** unemotionally calculated or calculating **:** marked by analysis and calculation uninfluenced by warmer feelings **:** UNFEELING ⟨how ~ economic considerations and calculations prevail in all matters of international importance —H.W.Van Loon⟩ ⟨the ~ argument and unhurried process of trial in the courts of law —W.C.Dickinson⟩ **4 a :** previously cooked but served or eaten cold ⟨a ~ collation⟩ ⟨~ boiled ham⟩ **b :** not hot enough **:** heated insufficiently or permitted to cool ⟨the soup was ~⟩ **c :** not heated ⟨stored in a ~ cellar⟩ **d :** made cold **:** COOLED, ICED ⟨~ soft drinks⟩ **e :** unheated while being worked ⟨drive rivets ~⟩ ⟨a *cold*-bent iron pipe⟩ ⟨*cold*-forged steel⟩ **5 a :** inducing discouragement **:** DEPRESSING, CHEERLESS, DISPIRITING, GLOOMY ⟨a ~ correctness in the way he put his bicycle in its place that made her heart sink —D.H. Lawrence⟩ ⟨the ~ respectability of a Pharisee's dining room —W.L.Sullivan⟩ **b :** producing a sensation of cold **:** CHILLING ⟨I hold a key in my hand and it is ~ —Muriel Rukeyser⟩ ⟨~ blank walls⟩ **c** *of a color* **:** COOL; *esp* **:** having a cool hue and low value **6 a :** DEAD ⟨lay ~ in his coffin —Margaret A. Barnes⟩ **b :** unconscious typically from a blow or shock or from complete intoxication **:** INSENSIBLE ⟨knocked out ~⟩ ⟨pass out ~⟩ **c :** completely at one's mercy **:** without hope of escape **:** DEFENSELESS ⟨you're as good as found guilty because they never crack down unless they have you ~ —Polly Adler⟩ **d :** marked by complete knowledge or errorless familiarity **:** CERTAIN, SURE ⟨the actors had their lines ~ a week before the opening night⟩ **e** *slang* **:** sure to be fulfilled — used of a contract in a card game **7 a** *of a soil* **:** retentive of moisture, often compact and clayey, and responding only slowly to atmospheric temperature changes **b** *of a manure* **:** decaying slowly with little evolution of heat ⟨~ pig manure⟩ **8 :** feeling cold **:** made uncomfortable by cold — usu. used postpositively ⟨the children came back in when they were ~⟩ **9** *obs, of foods* **:** BLAND, MILD **:** not strong, hot, or pungent ⟨~ plants⟩ **10 :** lacking power to influence, incite, animate, inspire, impassion, or affect in other ways ⟨the Roman copy is almost inevitably ~*er*, less alive, less emotional, and (above all) less expressive than the Greek —Hunter Mead⟩ ⟨a ~ traffic of minds and ideas and, for all the melodrama, not a clash of living people —J.R.Newman⟩**: a :** FAINT **:** not strong; *usu* **:** old and being obscured ⟨dogs trying to follow the ~ scent⟩ **:** retaining only faint scents, traces, or clues ⟨the trail had become ~⟩ **b :** STALE, UNINTERESTING; *often* **:** having undergone loss of timeliness ⟨the story is now too ~ to be newsworthy⟩ **c :** old and showing lack of power to communicate ⟨a stenographer trying to transcribe ~ notes⟩ **d :** not illegal or involved in a crime **:** not suspect ⟨trading the hot car for a ~ one⟩ **e :** allowing little or no possibility of contact with radioactivity — used esp. of area in a plant or laboratory; opposed to *hot* **11 :** presented or regarded in a straightforward, blunt, or matter-of-fact way **:** not influenced or relieved by emotional presentation or persuasive appeal **:** IMPERSONAL ⟨competing on a basis of sheer ~ efficiency —T.W.Arnold⟩ ⟨the ~ facts of the case⟩ ⟨presenting ~ statistics⟩ **12 a :** far from finding, discovering, or solving **b :** marked by poor or unlucky performance ⟨an erratic bowler, sometimes hot, sometimes ~⟩ ⟨hot and ~ periods even fall . . . upon writers —C.B.Davis⟩ **c :** not in operation **:** IDLE ⟨a ~ munitions plant in peace times⟩ **d** *slang, of dice* **:** not producing many passes or results that win for the shooter **13 a :** marked by lack of preparation, rehearsal, preliminary performance, preliminary exercise or operation, introduction, or knowledge and familiarity ⟨instead of opening ~ in New York, all the productions have had a week of preliminary performing in Hartford —Brooks Atkinson⟩ ⟨they came here ~, years ago, not knowing many people —J.P.Marquand⟩ ⟨a substitute entering the game ~⟩ **b** *in radio & television* **:** without music or embellishments ⟨a program that comes on ~⟩ ⟨~ drama⟩ ⟨the salesman had to approach the prospective customer ~⟩ ⟨~ selling⟩ **14 :** certain to be as indicated **:** ASSURED ⟨a ~ five thousand dollars⟩ **15 :** lacking in thoroughbred blood ⟨a ~ cross⟩ **16 :** designed for use in cutting cold metal **17 :** living in or characteristic of a cold environment ⟨the ~ fauna of glacial epochs⟩ **18 a :** intense and barely controlled ⟨a ~ fury⟩ ⟨a ~ irritation⟩ **b :** checked short of sustained overt violence (as military action) but marked by deep antagonism and conducted with all available economic, political, or social means ⟨a ~ pogrom⟩ ⟨~ revolution⟩ **19 a :** intended for use without being heated ⟨a ~ glue⟩ **b :** using or produced by cold type ⟨~ composition⟩ — **in cold blood** *adv* **:** with premeditation **:** DELIBERATELY — used of an action generally avoided or condemned ⟨kill a man *in cold blood*⟩

²cold \"\ *n* -s [ME, fr. OE *cald*, fr. *cald*, adj. — more at COLD] **1 a :** a condition of low temperature **:** COLDNESS ⟨the ~ was intense⟩ **b :** cold weather **2 :** bodily sensation produced by loss or lack of heat **:** CHILL ⟨they groan with pain and shudder with the ~ —S.T.Coleridge⟩ **3 :** a respiratory infection: **a** *in man* **:** COMMON COLD ⟨to catch ~⟩ ⟨he has a ~⟩ **b** *in domestic animals* **:** CORYZA b **4 :** chill discouragement **:** a feeling of blended fear, crushing disappointment, shock, depression, or despair — **in the cold :** without heating — **out in the cold :** NEGLECTED, IGNORED **:** left unconsidered **:** deprived of benefits given others ⟨the plan helps engineers and firemen but leaves brakemen *out in the cold*⟩

³cold \"\ *vb* -ED/-ING/-s [ME *colden*, fr. (assumed) OE *caldian, cealdian*, fr. *cald* cold — more at COLD] *vi* **:** to become cold ⟨the nights were ~*ing* —Maristan Chapman⟩ ~ *vt* **:** to make cold ⟨~ his blood with the thought of dying —John Masefield⟩

⁴cold \"\ *adv* -ER/-EST [¹*cold*] **1 :** with utter finality **:** in a completely unmitigated way **:** TOTALLY, ABSOLUTELY ⟨he was stopped ~⟩ ⟨be turned down ~⟩ ⟨know the answers ~⟩ **2 :** while cold or without the application of heat — used esp. of metalworking processes ⟨*cold*-hammer a bar of iron⟩ ⟨*cold*-roll steel⟩ ⟨*cold*-swage metal parts⟩

cold abscess *n* **:** a chronic often tuberculous abscess of slow formation and with little evidence of inflammation

cold agglutination *n* **:** AUTOAGGLUTINATION

cold agglutinin *also* **cold hemagglutinin** *n* **:** any of certain agglutinins present in some bloods (as those of many patients with primary atypical pneumonia) that at low temperatures agglutinate compatible as well as incompatible erythrocytes, including the patient's own

coldbar \ˈ=,=\ *adj* [²*cold* + *bar*] **:** providing protection against extreme cold — used of a suit or uniform, esp. military

coldblood \ˈ=,=\ *n* -s [back-formation fr. *cold-blooded*] **:** an animal that is cold-blooded (senses 2, 3)

cold-blooded \ˈ=¦==\ *adj* **1 a :** marked by absence of warm feelings **:** without consideration, compunction, or clemency **:** UNFEELING, CALLOUS, HARDENED, CRUEL ⟨of *cold-blooded* expediency and sometimes of unscrupulous self-interest — Douglas Bush⟩ ⟨*cold-blooded* executions of innocent people — Sir Winston Churchill⟩ **b :** MATTER-OF-FACT, EMOTIONLESS ⟨the literary evidence must be tested by sidelights from *cold-blooded* documents —G.G.Coulton⟩ **2 :** having cold blood; *specif* **:** having a body temperature not internally regulated but approximating that of the environment ⟨*cold-blooded* amphibians and reptiles⟩ **:** POIKILOTHERMIC, HETEROTHERMIC **3** *or* **coldblood a** *of horses* **:** not possessing Arab or Thoroughbred ancestry — used esp. of members of the heavy draft breeds **b** *of horses and other livestock* **:** of mixed or inferior breeding **:** MONGREL **4 :** noticeably sensitive to cold ⟨too *cold-blooded* to enjoy skating⟩ — **cold-blood·ed·ly** *adv* — **cold-blood·ed·ness** *n* -ES

cold cash *n* **:** cash viewed as readily fluid or expendable, indicative of real value, or assured as gain or income ⟨enough *cold cash* to close the purchase⟩

cold cathode *n* **:** a cathode in an electron tube or fluorescent lamp that is unheated and that emits electrons when bombarded by ions or subjected to light, infrared, or ultraviolet rays ⟨*cold-cathode* tube⟩

cold cellar *n, Northeast* **:** a room or section of a cellar where root crops may be stored over winter at temperatures slightly above freezing

cold chisel *n* **:** a chisel made of tool steel of a strength, shape, and temper suitable for chipping or cutting cold metal — see CHISEL illustration

coldcock \ˈ=,=\ *vt* [perh. fr. ¹*cold* + *cock* (penis)] **:** to knock unconscious

cold comfort *n* **:** scant consolation **:** quite limited sympathy or encouragement

cold cream *n* **:** a soothing and cleansing ointmentlike usu. white cosmetic consisting typically of a perfumed emulsion of a bland vegetable oil or heavy mineral oil and other ingredients

cold cure *n* **:** the vulcanization esp. of thin rubber products by treatment at ordinary temperatures with a solution or vapors of a sulfur compound, usu. sulfur monochloride

cold-cut \ˈ=,=\ *adj* [⁴*cold*] *of a varnish or lacquer* **:** manufactured by dissolving one ingredient in another without the application of heat

cold cuts *n pl* **:** sliced assorted cold meats and cheeses — compare DUTCH LUNCH

cold deck *n* **1 :** a stacked pack of playing cards; *esp* **:** one prepared for surreptitious substitution for the pack in play **2 :** a pile of logs assembled when cut and left for later transportation to a mill — compare HOT DECK

cold-deck \ˈ=,=\ *vt* [*cold deck*] **:** CHEAT, DEFRAUD, SWINDLE

cold-draw \ˈ=,=\ *vt* **1 :** to draw (as metal or nylon) while cold or without the application of heat **2 :** to cold-press (vegetable oil) — **cold-drawing** \ˈ=,==\ *n* -s

cold emission *n* **:** FIELD EMISSION

cold enamel *n* **:** a solution of bichromated shellac or other colloid that does not require heating or burning in and is used as a sensitizer in photoengraving — called also *cold top*

¹colder *comparative of* COLD

²col·der \ˈkäldə(r), ˈkōd-\ *n* -s [origin unknown] *dial Eng* **:** refuse from threshing **:** HUSK

coldest *superlative of* COLD

cold feet *n pl* **:** apprehension, misgiving, doubt, or fear strong enough to prevent a planned course of action ⟨wanted to complain to the boss but at the last minute got *cold feet*⟩

cold fish *n* **:** a cold aloof emotionless person ⟨a *cold fish*, reserved and calculating —Polly Adler⟩

cold flour *n, dial* **:** sugared pulverized corn

cold flow *n* **1 :** the viscous flow of a solid at ordinary temperatures **2 :** the distortion of a solid under sustained pressure esp. with an accompanying inability to return to its original dimensions when the pressure is removed

cold-flow \ˈ=¦=\ *vi* [*cold flow*] **:** to exhibit cold flow

cold frame *n* **:** an outdoor shallow rectangular frame of boards or concrete with a usu. glass cover to protect small plants from wind and low temperature esp. early in the growing season — compare HOTBED

cold front *n* **:** an advancing edge of a cold air mass that is displacing warm air in its path often recognized by a wind shift and drop in air temperature as it passes — see FRONT illustration

cold hands *n pl* **:** poker in which each player is dealt five cards face up and the highest hand wins without betting or draw

cold-head \ˈ=,=\ *vt* **:** to upset a head on a rod or wire without heating the metal (as in forming bolts, screws, and rivets)

coldhearted \ˈ=¦==\ *adj* **:** marked by lack of sympathy, interest, normal sensitivity, kindliness, or mercy ⟨a ~ judge⟩ ⟨a ~ refusal⟩ — **cold·heart·ed·ly** *adv* — **cold·heart·ed·ness** *n* -ES

cold house *n* **:** a greenhouse (as for grapes) maintained at a low temperature

cold·ish \ˈkōldish, -dēsh\ *adj* **:** somewhat cold ⟨~ weather⟩

cold-jaw \ˈ=,=\ *vi, West* **:** to become hard-mouthed ⟨when a horse *cold-jaws* on you and wants to run, let him go till he runs down his mainspring —R.F.Adams⟩

cold-jawed \ˈ=¦=\ *adj, West* **:** HARDMOUTHED

cold light *n* **1 :** light emitted by any body whose temperature is below that of incandescence — compare LUMINESCENCE **2 :** visible light from whatever source unaccompanied by appreciable amounts of infrared and having therefore little heating effect

coldly *adv* [ME, fr. ¹*cold* + *-ly*] **:** in a cold manner ⟨he answered ~⟩ ⟨staying ~ aloof⟩

cold meat *n, slang* **:** CORPSES, CORPSE

cold-meat fork \ˈ=¦=-\ *n* **:** a large serving fork with flat pointed tines

cold nail *n* **:** a cut nail

cold·ness *n* -ES [ME, fr. ¹*cold* + *-ness*] **:** the quality or state of being cold

cold pack *n* **:** a sheet or blanket wrung out of cold water, wrapped around the patient's body, and covered with dry blankets

cold-pack \ˈ=,=\ *vt* **:** to can or tin by the cold-pack method ⟨*cold-pack* peaches⟩

cold-pack method \ˈ=¦=-\ *n* **1 :** a method of canning fruits or vegetables that consists of (1) scalding or blanching, (2) packing immediately into hot containers and covering or sealing, (3) processing or sterilizing in a hot-water bath or pressure cooker, and (4) sealing or resealing at once while contents are still hot — called also *raw-pack method* **2 :** FROZEN-PACK

cold patch *n* **1 :** a mixture of crushed stone and bituminous binder that may be used cold for mending pavement **2 :** a rubber patch cemented without vulcanizing to a pneumatic-tire tube

cold-patch *vt* [*cold patch*] **:** to repair with a cold patch

cold peace *n* **:** an unstable peace among nations formerly engaged in a cold war

cold pig *n, slang Brit* **:** a wetting with cold water to awaken one

cold pit *n* **:** an excavation with walls that is usu. covered with glass and is used for rooting potted bulbs and resting half-hardy plants

cold plague *n, archaic* **:** a severe ague

cold pole *n* **:** POLE OF COLD

cold-press \ˈ=,=\ *vt* **:** to subject to pressure or to express without heating ⟨*cold-press* metal⟩ ⟨*cold-press* petroleum oil for separation of wax by filtration⟩

cold pressor test *n* **:** the response of a person's blood pressure to immersion of one hand in ice water for one minute, an excessive rise or slow return to normal being considered an indication of susceptibility to the development of hypertension

cold process *n* **:** a soapmaking process in which melted fats are treated with lye without further heating

cold prophet *var of* COLEPROPHET

cold-roll \ˈ=,=\ *vt* **:** to roll (metal) without applying heat

cold room *n* **:** a room in which a low temperature is maintained (as for refrigeration)

cold rubber *n* **:** a synthetic rubber of the GR-S type that is made at a relatively low temperature (as 41°F) and is characterized by a lowered viscosity and usu. by increased resistance to wear (as in tire treads)

colds *pl of* COLD, *pres 3d sing of* COLD

cold saw *n* **1 :** a saw (as a circular saw) for cutting cold metal — distinguished from *hot saw* **2 :** a soft-steel or iron disk operated at such an angular velocity, corresponding to a velocity of a point on its periphery of about 15,000 feet per minute, that it grinds off metal by friction — compare FUSING DISK

cold seeds *n pl* [²*cold*] **:** the seeds of various cucurbitaceous fruits (as the melon or cucumber) sometimes used as emollients

cold set *n* **:** a chisel ground to a flat edge and used in metalworking esp. for flattening seams

cold-set \ˈ=,=\ *adj* [⁴*cold*] **:** used in a method of printing in which ink is kept fluid by heat until it contacts the cold paper when it quickly solidifies ⟨*cold-set* ink⟩; *also* **:** using or done by this method ⟨the *cold-set* process⟩ ⟨*cold-set* printing⟩

cold shape *n* **:** a blancmange pudding that is molded and chilled

cold-short \ˈ=¦=\ *adj* [by folk etymology fr. Sw *kallskör*, fr. *kall* cold (fr. ON *kaldr*) + *skör* brittle, fr. OSw *skör, skyr*, prob. fr. MLG *schör;* akin to MLG *schoren* to break, OHG *sceran* to cut — more at COLD, SHEAR] *of metal* **:** brittle when below a red heat — compare HOT-SHORT

cold shot *n* **1 :** round shotlike particles formed by a cold shut in a metal casting **2 :** COLD SHUT 1

cold-shot \ˈ=¦=\ *adj* [⁴*cold*] **:** chilled by the mold in casting or imperfect through such chilling — used of a foundry casting

cold shoulder *n* **:** intentionally cold or unsympathetic treatment **:** scornful neglect **:** deliberate coldness ⟨hurt at getting the *cold shoulder* from an old friend⟩

cold-shoulder \ˈ=¦==\ *vt* [*cold shoulder*] **:** to give the cold shoulder to ⟨insulted in the streets, *cold-shouldered* by his friends —Bertrand Russell⟩

cold-shut \'ˌ=ˌ=\ *adj* [⁴*cold*] **:** closed while too cold to become thoroughly welded — used of a forging; compare COLD SHUT 2

cold shut *n* [*cold-shut*] **1 :** the freezing of the surface of liquid metal during the pouring of an ingot or casting due to interrupted or improper pouring; *also* **:** an imperfection thus caused **2 :** the imperfect weld caused in a forging by the inadequate heat of one surface under working or by an oxide film **3 :** a split ring or link used to mend or fasten chains

cold·slaw \'kōl(d),slȯ\ *n* -s [by folk etymology fr. D *koolsla,* fr. *kool* cabbage + *sla* salad, fr. *salade,* fr. F; akin to OE *cāl* cabbage — more at COLE, SALAD] **:** COLESLAW

cold-smoke \'ˌ=ˌ=\ *vt* [⁴*cold*] **:** to smoke (as ham) at a temperature between 70 and 90 degrees F

cold soldering *n* **:** soldering in which two pieces are joined without heat (as by means of a copper amalgam)

cold sore *n* [²*cold*] **:** the group of blisters appearing about or within the mouth in herpes simplex

cold steel *n* **:** a steel weapon (as a sword or bayonet)

cold stoking *n* **:** the operation in glass manufacturing of reducing the glass to the proper degree of viscosity for being worked

cold storage *n* **1 :** storage esp. of food in a place kept cold often by refrigeration for preservative purposes ⟨meats in *cold storage*⟩ — compare DRY STORAGE **2 :** a condition of being held or continued without being acted on **:** ABEYANCE ⟨the second world war effectively put the question into *cold storage* —Leo Marquard⟩

cold-storage training \'ˌ=ˌ==-\ *n* **:** the training of workers for positions usu. of relatively high levels in advance of need

cold store *n* [short for *cold storage*] **:** a building for cold storage

cold-store \'ˌ=ˌ=\ *vt* [back-formation fr. *cold storage*] **:** to place or hold in cold storage ⟨the excess eggs are *cold-stored*⟩

cold sweat *n* [¹*cold*] **:** perspiration accompanied by feelings of chill or cold and usu. induced or accompanied by dread, fear, or shock ⟨the blush of embarrassment or the *cold sweat* of fear —*Jour. Amer. Med. Assoc.*⟩

cold-sweat \'ˌ=ˌ=\ *vt* [⁴*cold*] **:** to sweat (as hides) in cold water

cold test *n* **:** a test of oils (as lubricating oils) to determine the temperature at which a cooled sample begins to deposit solid material or becomes too viscous to flow; *also* **:** the temperature so determined

cold top *n* **:** COLD ENAMEL

cold-trail \'ˌ=ˌ=\ *vb* **:** to follow on a cold trail ⟨a dog *cold-trailing* more than a mile⟩

cold trailing *n* **:** a method of controlling smoldering forest fires by feeling the edge of a burning area with the hand and digging out or trenching round burning spots

cold turkey *n* **1 :** unrelieved blunt matter-of-fact statement or procedure **:** statement with irrevocable finality ⟨I'm talking *cold turkey* to you . . . I think it wise if your relationship has ended —J.B.Clayton⟩ **2 :** a sure victim **:** one facing certain defeat, punishment, or destruction ⟨a *cold turkey* for the enemy⟩ **3 :** abrupt complete cessation without medication of the use of drugs by a drug addict ⟨trying the *cold-turkey* cure⟩ **4 :** a cold aloof person ⟨the head nurse was a *cold turkey*⟩

cold type *n* **:** a method of printing (as from photocomposition or photoreproduction of typewriting) that does not involve the use of cast or cut letterpress type

cold war *n* **1 :** conflict between two nations or groups of nations by means of power politics, economic pressures, spy activities, or hostile propaganda and often sabotage and exclusion of opposing nationals but without engagement by arms **2 :** conflict short of violence esp. between power groups (as labor and management)

cold water *n* **:** deprecation (as of a plan or an expectation) as being ill-advised, unwarranted, or worthless **:** DISCOURAGEMENT, DISPARAGEMENT ⟨throw *cold water* on our hopes⟩ ⟨pour *cold water* on a scheme⟩

cold-water \'ˌ=ˌ==\ *adj* [*cold water*] **1 :** of or relating to temperance groups **:** preferring cold water to alcoholic beverages **2 a :** provided only with running cold water **b :** not having all modern plumbing or heating facilities ⟨a *cold-water* flat⟩

cold-wa·ter paint *n* **:** a paint consisting of a pigment held in suspension by a binder dissolved in cold water

¹**cold wave** *n* **:** a sudden large drop in temperature; *broadly* **:** a period of unusually cold weather

²**cold wave** *n* **:** a machineless permanent wave set by a chemical preparation usu. containing a salt of thioglycolic acid

cold-weld \'ˌ=ˌ=\ *vt* [⁴*cold*] **:** to weld (metal) cold by pressure without the application of heat

cold-work \'ˌ=ˌ=\ *vt* [*cold work*] **:** to work (metal) without using heat

¹**cole** \'kōl\ *n* -s [ME, fr. OE *cāl, cawel,* fr. L *caulis* stalk of a plant, cabbage — more at HOLE] **1 :** a plant of the genus *Brassica; esp* **:** RAPE **2** *Brit* **:** SEA KALE

²**cole** *obs var of* COAL

-cole \ˌkōl\ *adj comb form* [by alter. (influenced by F *-cole*)] **:** -COLOUS ⟨saxicole⟩

cole- *or* **coleo-** *comb form* [NL, fr. Gk *koleo-,* fr. *koleon*] **:** sheath **:** covering ⟨coleitis⟩ ⟨*Coleoptera*⟩ ⟨coleorhiza⟩

co·lec·ti·vo \ˌkōlek'tē(ˌ)vō\ *n* -s [AmerSp, fr. Sp, adj., collective, fr. L *collectivus* — more at COLLECTIVE] **:** a small bus, a station wagon, or a limousine serving as a public conveyance

col·ec·to·my \kə'lektəmē, kō-, -mi\ *n* -ES [ISV *col-* + *-ectomy*] **:** excision of a portion or all of the colon

co·legatee \ˌkō +\ *n* [*co-* + *legatee*] **:** a joint legatee

co·le·gio \kə'lāhē,ō, -hyō\ *n* -s [Sp, fr. ML *collegium* college — more at COLLEGE] **:** SECONDARY SCHOOL

cole·man·ite \'kōlmə,nīt\ *n* -s [William T. *Coleman* †1893 owner of mine where mineral was discovered + E *-ite*] **:** a mineral $Ca_2B_6O_{11}.5H_2O$ consisting of a hydrous calcium borate occurring in brilliant colorless or white massive monoclinic crystals

co·le·o·chae·ta·ce·ae \ˌkōlē,ōkē'tāsē,ē, ˌkäl-\ *n pl, cap* [NL, fr. *Coleochaete,* type genus + *-aceae*] **:** a family of green algae (order Ulotrichales) having the features of *Coleochaete* — **co·le·o·chae·ta·ceous** \ˌ==ˌ==ˌ=ˈtāshəs\ *adj*

co·le·o·chae·te \-'kēd,ē\ *n, cap* [NL, fr. *cole-* + Gk *chaitē* hair — more at CHAETA] **:** a genus (the type of the family Coleochaetaceae) of aquatic epiphytic green algae having cells solitary or in branching filaments that in some members form cushionlike masses

co·le·on·yx \ˌ==ˈänəks\ *n, cap* [NL, fr. *cole-* + *-onyx*] **:** a genus of lizards comprising the ground geckos of the western U.S.

co·le·oph·o·ra \-'äf(ə)rə\ *n, cap* [NL, fr. *cole-* + *-phora*] **:** a genus (the type of the family Coleophoridae) of small moths comprising the casebearer moths — **co·le·oph·o·rid** \-rəd, -,rid\ *adj or n*

co·le·op·te·ra \-'äptərə\ *n pl, cap* [NL, fr. Gk *koleoptera,* neut. pl. of *koleopteros* sheath-winged, fr. *koleo-* cole- + *-pteros* -pterous] **:** the largest order of insects comprising the beetles and weevils and sometimes the Strepsiptera, being distinguished by an anterior pair of wings that are usu. hard and rigid, are never used for flight, and serve as a protective covering for the delicate membranous flight wings and the upper surface of the abdomen, having usu. a heavily armored body and strong mouthparts that are always of the chewing type, typically producing larvae that are grubs and pass into an inactive pupal stage with a pupa in which the appendages are not cemented to the body and which is rarely enclosed in a cocoon, varying in size from tropical goliath beetles several inches in length to minute forms that pass their lives within the spore tubes of polypore fungi, and including numerous destructive pests of economic plants and of stored products as well as others (as the ladybugs or the fireflies) that are of economic or aesthetic value to man

co·le·op·ter·ist \-rəst\ *n* -s [NL *Coleoptera* + E *-ist*] **:** a specialist in the Coleoptera

¹**co·le·op·ter·oid** \ˌkōlē'äptə,rȯid, ˌkäl-\ *adj* [ISV *coleopter-* (fr. NL *Coleoptera*) + *-oid*] **:** like the Coleoptera **:** like a beetle

²**coleopteroid** \"\ *n* -s **:** a coleopteroid insect

co·le·op·ter·o·log·i·cal \ˌ==ˌ==ˌ=rə'läjəkəl\ *adj* **:** of or relating to coleopterology

co·le·op·ter·ol·o·gy \ˌ==ˌ=ˈrälәjē\ *n* -ES [ISV *coleopter-* (fr. NL *Coleoptera*) + *-o-* + *-logy*] **:** a branch of zoology that deals with the Coleoptera

co·le·op·te·ron \ˌ==ˈäptə,rän, -,rən\ *n, pl* **coleop·te·ra** \-tərə\ [NL, sing. of *Coleoptera*] **:** one of the Coleoptera **:** BEETLE

co·le·op·te·rous \ˌ==ˌäptərəs\ *adj* [NL *Coleoptera* + E *-ous*] **1 :** of or relating to the beetles **2** *of an insect* **:** SHEATH-WINGED

co·le·op·ti·lar \-ˌäptələ(r)\ *adj* **:** of or relating to a coleoptile

co·le·op·tile \ˌkōlē'äptəl, ˌkäl-\ *also* **co·le·op·ti·lum** \-tələm\ *n, pl* **coleop·tiles** \-təlz\ *also* **coleopti·la** \-tələ\ [NL *coleoptilum,* fr. *cole-* + *-ptilum* (fr. Gk *ptilon* down) — more at PTIL-] **:** the first leaf of a monocotyledon forming a protective sheath about the plumule

co·le·o·rhi·za \-lēə'rīzə\ *n, pl* **coleorhi·zae** \-(ˌ)zē\ [NL, fr. *cole-* + *-rhiza*] **:** the sheath investing the hypocotyl in some plants through which the roots burst

co·le·o·spo·ri·um \-lēə'spōrēəm, -spȯr-\ *n, cap* [NL, fr. *cole-* + *-sporium*] **:** a genus of rusts (family Melampsoraceae) having the teliospores united in a single-layered or double-layered waxy cushion

coleprophet *n* [obs. *cole* trick, deceiver, cheat (fr. ME) + *prophet*] *obs* **:** DIVINER, SOOTHSAYER

¹**cole·ridg·e·an** *also* **cole·ridg·i·an** \ˌkōl'rijēən\ *adj, usu cap* [Samuel Taylor *Coleridge* †1834 Eng. poet and critic + E *-an, -ian*] **:** of, relating to, or suggestive of Coleridge or his writings ⟨critical treatment along *Coleridgean* lines⟩

²**coleridgean** *also* **coleridgian** \"\ *n* -s *usu cap* **:** an admirer or follower of Coleridge

cole·seed \'kōl,sēd\ *n* [trans. of D *koolzaad*] **:** the seed of the rape; *also* **:** ²RAPE 2

cole·slaw \'kōl,slȯ\ *n* -s [alter. (influenced by D *kool* cabbage) of *coldslaw*] **:** a salad made of raw sliced or chopped cabbage

co·le·ta \kə'lād·ə\ *n* -s [Sp, dim. of *cola* tail — more at COLA] **:** the pigtail worn by a bullfighter

coletit *var of* COAL TIT

co·le·us \'kōlēəs\ *n* [NL, fr. Gk *koleos, koleon* sheath; fr. the manner in which the stamens are united] **1** *cap* **:** a large genus of herbs (family Labiatae) having showy and often highly variegated leaves and spicate blue flowers **2** -ES **:** a plant of the genus *Coleus* (esp of *C. blumei* and its garden varieties)

colewort \'ˌ=ˌ=\ *n* [ME, fr. *cole* + *wort*] **1 :** COLE 1 **2 :** a cabbage in which the leaves do not form a compact head **3 :** a young cabbage

co·li \'kō,lī\ *adj* [L, of the colon, gen. of *colon*] **:** of or relating to bacteria normally inhabiting the intestine or colon, esp. to species of the genus *Escherichia* (as *E. coli*)

coli- — see COL-

co·li-aerogenes \ˌkōlē +\ *adj* [NL, fr. ²*col-* + *aerogenes,* any of several bacterial species, fr. *aer-* + *-genes*] **:** of, relating to, or being bacteria of the genera *Escherichia* and *Aerobacter*

co·li·as \'kōlē,as\ *n, cap* [NL, fr. Gk *Kōlias,* Attic goddess] **:** a large cosmopolitan genus of butterflies (family Pieridae) which have primarily yellow or orange wings and whose larvae feed mostly on legumes but sometimes on willows or blueberries — see ALFALFA BUTTERFLY, CLOUDED SULPHUR

co·li·bacillary \ˌkōlə +\ *adj* [ISV ²*col-* + *bacillary*] **:** of, relating to, or caused by the colon bacillus

co·li·bacillosis \ˌkōlə +\ *n, pl* **colibacilloses** [NL, fr. ²*col-* + *bacill-* + *-osis*] **:** infection with or disease caused by colon bacilli (esp. *Escherichia coli*)

coli bacillus *also* **coli** *n* **:** COLON BACILLUS

¹**col·ic** \'kälik, -ēk\ *n* -s [ME *colike,* fr. MF *colique,* fr. L *colicus* sick with the colic, fr. Gk *kōlikos,* fr. *kōlon* (alter. of *kolon* colon) + *-ikos* -ic; fr. being seated in or near the colon — more at COLON] **:** a paroxysm of acute abdominal pain in man or animals localized in a hollow organ or tube and caused by spasm, obstruction, or twisting ⟨biliary ~⟩ ⟨ureteral ~⟩

²**colic** \"\ *adj* **:** of or relating to colic **:** COLICKY

³**co·lic** \'kōlik, -äl-, -ēk\ *adj* [²*col-* + *-ic*] **:** of or relating to the colon

col·i·cal \'käləkəl\ *adj* [¹*colic* + *-al*] **1 :** likely to have colic **2 :** relating to or resembling colic

colic artery *n* [³*colic*] **:** any of three arteries supplying the large intestine, the right and middle colic arteries being branches of the superior mesenteric and serving the ascending and transverse colon and the left colic artery deriving from the inferior mesenteric and supplying the descending colon — called also respectively *colica dextra, colica media,* and *colica sinistra*

co·liche·marde \ˌkō(ˌ)lēsh'märd\ *n* -s [F *colismarde, colichemarde,* after Otto Wilhelm, Count von *Königsmark* †1688 Ger. soldier and statesman, its inventor] **:** a long sword with a large forte narrowing abruptly into a slender foible

col·i·cin *or* **col·i·cine** \'käləsən, -,sēn\ *n* -s [NL *coli* (specific epithet of *Escherichia coli,* a bacterium that produces it) + E connective *-c-* + *-in, -ine*] **:** any of certain antibacterial substances produced by some strains of intestinal bacteria and considered to have possible affinity with the coliphages

col·ick·er \'käləkə(r)\ *n* -s [¹*colic* + *-er*] **:** a horse esp. subject to colic

col·icky \-kē, -ki\ *adj* [¹*colic* + *-y*] **1 :** relating to or resembling colic **:** attended by colic ⟨~ disorders⟩ **2 :** suffering from colic ⟨a ~ child⟩ **3 :** causing colic ⟨~ foods⟩

coli count *n* **:** a test of freedom of water from fecal contamination based on determining the number of colon bacteria in a specified volume

colicroot \'ˌ=ˌ=\ *n* [¹*colic* + *root*] **1 :** any of certain plants having roots reputed to cure colic; *esp* **:** either of two bitter herbs (*Aletris farinosa* and *A. aurea*) — called also *crow corn* **2 a :** the dried rhizome and roots of the colicroot (*Aletris farinosa*) **b :** the rhizome of a wild yam (*Dioscorea paniculata*) **:** DIOSCOREA 2

colicweed \'ˌ==ˌ=\ *n* [¹*colic* + *weed*] **:** SQUIRREL CORN

colicwort \'ˌ==ˌ=\ *n* [¹*colic* + *wort*] **:** a colicroot (*Aletris farinosa*)

colies *pl of* COLY

¹**col·i·form** \'kälə,fȯrm, 'kōl-\ *adj* [²*col-* + *-form*] **:** relating to, resembling, or being the colon bacillus

²**coliform** \"\ *n* -s [by shortening] **:** a coliform bacillus

coliform index *or* **coli index** *n* **:** an index of the purity of water based on a coli count

co·li·idae \kə'līə,dē\ *n pl, cap* [NL, fr. *Colius,* type genus + *-idae*] **:** a family of birds comprising the colies

co·li·ifor·mes \ˌ==ˌ='fȯr,mēz\ *n pl, cap* [NL, fr. *Colius* + *-iformes*] **:** an order of birds comprising the colies

¹**co·li·ma** \kə'lēmə\ *n* -s [MexSp] **:** a prickly tropical American shrub or small tree (*Zanthoxylum fagara*) — called also *wild lime*

²**colima** \"\ *n, pl* **colima** *or* **colimas** *usu cap* [Sp, of AmerInd origin] **1 a :** a Chibchan people of southern Colombia **b :** a member of such people **2 :** a language of the Colima people

col·in \'kälən; kə'lin, -lēn\ *n* -s [Sp *colín,* modif. of Nahuatl *çolin*] **:** the bobwhite or any of several related New World game birds

-co·line \kə,līn, -,lən\ *adj comb form* [NL *-colinae,* fr. *-cola* + *-inae*] **:** -COLOUS ⟨fluvicoline⟩

co·lin·e·ar \(ˈ)kō'linēə(r)\ *adj* [by alter.] **:** COLLINEAR

co·lingual \(ˈ)kō +\ *n* -s [*co-* + *lingual*] **:** one speaking the same native language as another ⟨a poet who has done so much to set the taste of his ~s as has Shakespeare —Allan Gilbert⟩

co·li·nus \kə'līnəs\ *n, cap* [NL, fr. Sp *colín*] **:** the genus of birds (family Phasianidae) consisting of the bobwhites

col·i·phage \'kälə,fāj\ *n* -s [²*col-* + *-phage*] **:** a bacteriophage active against the colon bacillus

col·i·se·um \ˌkälə'sēəm\ *n* -s [ML *Colisseum, Colyseus,* modif. of L *colosseum,* neut. of *colosseus* colossal, fr. *colossus*] **:** a large building designed to hold many spectators or activities calling for a good deal of room (as a basketball game or horse show) **:** a large assembly hall **:** STADIUM

coliseum ivy *n* **:** KENILWORTH IVY

co·lit·ic \kə'lid·ik, -itik, -ēk\ *adj* [NL *colitis* + E *-ic*] **:** belonging to or affected with colitis ⟨~ pain⟩ ⟨~ patient⟩

co·li·tis \kə'līd·əs, -ītəs\ *n* -ES [NL, fr. ²*col-* + *-itis*] **:** inflammation of the colon — see MUCOUS COLITIS, ULCERATIVE COLITIS

co·li·us \'kōlēəs\ *n, cap* [NL, fr. Gk *kolios* green woodpecker] **:** a genus of birds comprising the colies

colk \'kōk\ *n* -s [ScGael *colc*] *dial Eng* **:** EIDER DUCK

¹**coll** \'käl, 'kal\ *vt* -ED/-ING/-S [ME *collen,* fr. OF *coler,* fr. *col* neck, fr. L *collum* — more at COLLAR] *dial* **:** EMBRACE, HUG

²**coll** \'käl, 'kōl\ *vt* -ED/-ING/-S [perh. fr. ON *kollr* rounded point, head; akin to MLG *kol, kolle* head, top of a plant, OE *cēol* ship — more at KEEL] *chiefly Scot* **:** CLIP, POLL

coll- *or* **collo-** *comb form* [NL, fr. Gk. *koll-, kollo-,* fr. *kolla* — more at PROTOCOL] **1 :** glue ⟨collenchyma⟩ ⟨*Collocalia*⟩ **2 :** colloid ⟨collochemistry⟩

-coll \ˌkäl\ *n comb form* -s [ME *-col* (in *sarcocol*), fr. L *-colla* fr. Gk *-kolla,* fr. *kolla*] **:** glue ⟨glycocoll⟩ ⟨pyrocoll⟩

coll *abbr* — see COL

¹**colla** *pl of* COLLUM

²**col·la** \'kōlyə\ *n* -s [Sp] *Philippines* **:** a period of rainy windy weather from the southwest

col·la·bent \(ˈ)kō'lābənt, kə'l-\ *adj* [L *collabent-, collabens,* pres. part. of *collabi* to collapse — more at COLLAPSE] **:** sunken or falling in **:** collapsing in the middle

col·labo \kə'la(ˌ)bō\ *n* -s [short for *collaborator*] **:** one who collaborates with an enemy

col·lab·o·rate \kə'labə,rāt, *usu* -ād· + V\ *vi* -ED/-ING/-S [LL *collaboratus,* past part. of *collaborare* to labor together, fr. L *com-* + *laborare* to labor] **1 :** to work jointly esp. with one or a limited number of others in a project involving composition or research to be jointly accredited ⟨Beaumont and Fletcher *collaborated* in writing plays⟩ ⟨Sullivan *collaborated* with Gilbert to produce operettas⟩ **2 :** to cooperate with or assist usu. willingly an enemy of one's country (as an invading or occupying force) ⟨Frenchmen who *collaborated* with the Nazis⟩ **3 :** to cooperate usu. willingly with an agency or instrumentality with which one is not immediately connected often in some political or economic effort ⟨attempts of the West to win Russia⟩ ⟨the two universities ~ on library services⟩

col·lab·o·ra·teur \ˌ==ˌ=rə'tər, + V -ər-; -tə̄, + V -ər- *also* -ər\ *n* -s [F, fr. ML *collaborator*] **:** COLLABORATOR

col·lab·o·ra·tion \kə,labə'rāshən\ *n* -s [F, fr. L *collaboratus* (past part. of *collaborare*) + F *-ion*] **1 :** the act of collaborating or a situation marked by collaborating ⟨either in ~ or independently⟩ ⟨the machinery of international ~ —Vera M. Dean⟩; *esp* **:** collaborating with an enemy or an opposed group rather than struggling or resisting ⟨a Norwegian accused of ~⟩ ⟨the ~ of less militant unionists⟩ **2 :** a product of collaboration ⟨this play is a ~⟩

col·lab·o·ra·tion·ism \-shə,nizəm\ *n* -s **:** the theory or practice of collaboration **:** advocacy of collaboration

¹**col·lab·o·ra·tion·ist** \-ˌnəst\ *n* -s [*collaboration* + *-ist*] **:** one that advocates or practices collaboration with an enemy (usu. an invader or part of an occupying force) or with some other group opposed or antagonistic to his own ⟨punishment for ~s after the liberation⟩

²**collaborationist** \"\ *adj* **:** of or relating to a collaborationist ⟨the ~ tricks by which the success of the occupation was assured —Ann F. Wolfe⟩

col·lab·o·ra·tive \kə'labə,rād·iv, -ātiv; -lab(ə)rəd·iv, -ətiv\ *adj* **:** marked or produced by collaboration ⟨a ~ research project⟩ — **col·lab·o·ra·tive·ly** *adv*

col·lab·o·ra·tor \kə'labə,rādə(r), -ātə\ *n* -s [F *collaborateur,* fr. ML *collaborator,* fr. L *collaboratus* + *-or*] **:** one that collaborates esp. in some composition or research ⟨they were ~s on this book⟩ or with an enemy or opposed group ⟨purging ~s from the newly established government⟩

col·la des·tra \ˌkōlə'destrə\ *adv (or adj)* [It] **:** with the right hand — used as a direction in music

col·lage \kə'läzh\ *n* -s [F, gluing, pasting, fr. *coller* to glue (fr. *colle* glue, fr. — assumed — VL *colla,* fr. Gk *kolla*) + *-age* — more at PROTOCOL] **1 :** an artistic composition of fragments of printed matter and other materials pasted on a picture surface: as **a :** a cubist composition in which pieces of paper, string, and textile are used to represent planes and textures **b :** a surrealist pictorial composition in which figures from engravings, photographs, and printed illustrations are shown in an incongruous environment **2 :** the art of making collages **3 :** PHOTOMONTAGE **4 :** an assembly of diverse fragments ⟨a ballet program giving the impression of incompetent ~⟩ ⟨a witty ~ of quotations⟩

col·la·gen *also* **col·lo·gen** \'käləjən, -,jen\ *n* -s [ISV *colla-* (fr. Gk *kolla* glue) or *coll-* + *-gen* — more at PROTOCOL] **:** an insoluble fibrous protein that occurs in vertebrates as the chief constituent of the fibrils of connective tissue (as in skin and tendons) and of the organic substance of the bones and that is characterized by swelling in water solutions, by conversion to gelatin and glue on prolonged heating with water, and by conversion to leather on tanning — compare ELASTIN — **col·la·gen·ic** \ˌ==ˈjenik\ *adj* — **col·lag·e·nous** \kə'lajənəs, (ˈ)kä'l-\ *adj*

col·la·gen·ase \-jə,nās, -nāz\ *n* -s [ISV *collagen* + *-ase*] **:** any of a group of proteolytic enzymes that decompose collagen and gelatin and have been found in some bacteria of the genus *Clostridium* and in a few insect larvae

collagen disease *n* **:** any of various diseases or abnormal states marked by changes in connective tissue presumably involving destruction of collagen (as rheumatoid arthritis, rheumatic fever, or scleroderma)

col·la·gen·o·sis \ˌ==jə'nōsəs\ *n, pl* **collageno·ses** \-,sēz\ [NL, fr. ISV *collagen* + NL *-osis*] **:** COLLAGEN DISEASE

col·lag·ist \kə'läzhəst\ *n* -s **:** one who makes collages; *specif* **:** an artist who works in collage

col·la par·te \ˌkōlə'pär(ˌ)tā\ *adv (or adj)* [It, with the part] **:** with the solo part in tempo and phrasing — used as a direction in musical accompaniment

¹**col·lapse** \kə'laps\ *vb* -ED/-ING/-S [L *collapsus,* past part. of *collabi* to collapse, fr. *com-* + *labi* to fall, slide — more at SLEEP] *vi* **1 :** to break down completely **:** fall apart in confused disorganization **:** crumble into insignificance or nothingness **:** DISINTEGRATE ⟨his case had *collapsed* in a mass of legal wreckage —Erle Stanley Gardner⟩ ⟨a flimsy banking enterprise which *collapsed* —R.A.Billington⟩ **2 :** to fall or shrink together abruptly and completely **:** fall into a jumbled or flattened mass through the force of external pressure **:** fall in ⟨the sides of a limp empty boat ~⟩ ⟨our interest ~s like a pricked balloon —G.M.Trevelyan⟩ ⟨a blood vessel that *collapsed*⟩ **3 :** to cave in, fall in, or give away **:** undergo ruin or destruction by or as if by falling down **:** become dispersed ⟨its passage ripped away the crown of the arch and immediately the whole bridge *collapsed* —O.S.Nock⟩ ⟨a magnetic field *collapsing*⟩ **4 :** to suddenly lose force, significance, effectiveness, or worth ⟨all his annoyance *collapsed* in a heap —Hamilton Basso⟩ ⟨*collapsing* currencies of unstable countries⟩ **5 :** to break down in vital energy, stamina, or self-control through exhaustion or disease **:** lose ability to perform accustomed activities **:** fall helpless or unconscious ⟨a fireman *collapsing* from the fumes⟩ ⟨several oarsmen *collapsing* after the hard race⟩ ⟨*collapsed* into tears⟩ **6 :** to fold down into a more compact shape **:** close together ⟨a *collapsing* opera hat⟩ ⟨a telescope that ~s⟩ ~ *vt* **:** to cause to collapse ⟨~ the movement⟩ ⟨*collapsing* an infected lung⟩ ⟨the explosion *collapsed* several buildings⟩ ⟨~ an opera hat⟩

²**collapse** \"\ *n* -s **1 a :** a breakdown in vital energy, strength, or stamina **:** complete sudden enervation **:** sudden loss of accustomed abilities ⟨the daughter's mental ~ through mounting frustration —Leslie Rees⟩ **b :** a state of extreme prostration and physical depression resulting from circulatory failure, great loss of body fluids, or heart disease and occurring terminally in diseases such as cholera, typhoid fever, pneumonia — compare SHOCK **c :** an airless state of a lung in whole or in part of spontaneous origin or induced surgically — see ATELECTASIS **d :** an abnormal falling together of the walls of an organ, ⟨~ of blood vessels⟩ **2 :** the action of collapsing **:** the act or action of drawing together or permitting or causing a falling together ⟨the cutting of many tent ropes, the ~ of the canvas —Rudyard Kipling⟩ **3 a :** BREAKDOWN **:** sudden failure **:** DISINTEGRATION, RUIN, DESTRUCTION ⟨the speedy disruption and eventual ~ of our entire society —Lewis Mumford⟩ ⟨the panic . . . with its attendant ~ of grandiose dreams —*Amer. Guide Series: Minn.*⟩ **b :** sudden loss of force, value, effect, or significance ⟨the ~ of respect for ancient law and custom —L.S.B.Leakey⟩ ⟨to save the pound sterling from ~ —Leon Halden⟩ **4 :** a defect in wood due to abnormal and irregular shrinkage and resulting in a wrinkled or corrugated appearance of the surface and sometimes also an internal honeycombing **5 :** the sum of postbreeding regressive changes in the testes of a seasonal breeding male animal

collapse breccia *n* **:** a breccia formed by the collapse of rock overlying an opening

collapse therapy *n* **:** a surgical procedure that collapses a lung and is now used almost solely in the treatment of tuberculosis to rest an infected lung by immobilization

col·laps·i·ble *also* **col·laps·a·ble** \kə'lapsəbəl\ *adj* **:** capable of collapsing or being collapsed ⟨a ~ boat⟩ ⟨a false bag, ~ so that it may be concealed —Valentine Williams⟩

collapsible corporation *n* **:** a corporation that plans to liquidate or whose shares are to be sold to others before sale of goods produced so as to turn what should be taxable income into a capital gain for shareholders

col·lap·sion \kə'lapshən\ *n* -s [LL *collapsion-, collapsio,* fr. L *collapsus* + *-ion-, -io*] *archaic* **:** COLLAPSE

¹**col·lar** \'kälə(r)\ *n* -s *often attrib* [ME *coller, coler,* fr. OF *coler, colier* necklace, collar, fr. L *collare,* fr. *collum* neck; akin to OE *heals* neck, OHG, ON, & Goth *hals* neck, OE *hwēol* wheel — more at WHEEL] **1 :** a band, strip, or chain worn or placed around the neck: as **a** *obs* **:** neck armor **:** a hauberk neckpiece **b :** an attached or separate band that varies in shape and size and serves to finish or decorate the neckline of a garment or costume — see RUFF, SHAWL COLLAR, WING COLLAR **c :** a short necklace **:** an ornamental band or chain **d :** a band placed around the neck of a dog, cat, or other animal to lead, restrain, identify, or adorn **e :** a part of the harness of draft animals fitted over the shoulders and taking the strain when a load is being drawn **f :** a band often of iron placed around a prisoner's or slave's neck to confine or identify **g :** an ornament or badge (as a necklace) used as an insignia of an order of knighthood **h :** an indication of control **:** a token that another is subservient to one ⟨an independent refusing to wear any man's ~⟩ **i :** a bandage, brace, cast, or other protecting or supporting device worn around the neck **2 :** an encircling band, strap, or ring to check, guide, guard, or adorn: as **a :** an eye in the bight or end of a stay or shroud to go over the masthead **b :** a strap or grommet to secure a heart or deadeye **c :** a filler plate or shape fitted around a structural shape (as an angle or beam) passing through a bulkhead or deck **d :** a ring or round flange upon, around, or against an object chiefly to restrain motion within given limits, to hold something in place, or to cover an opening (as on a shaft to prevent endwise motion or around a pipe where it enters a wall) **e** (1) **:** a curb around the mouth of a mine shaft **:** the immediate vicinity of the mouth of a shaft (2) **:** the rock surrounding the mouth of a drill hole **f :** a piece of leather, fur, or fabric stitched around the top of a shoe or boot upper usu. for ornament — compare CUFF; see SHOE illustration **g :** a ring on a coining press confining a planchet while it is being struck and impressing a milling or edge lettering **h :** a narrow molding near the top or bottom of the leg of a piece of furniture **3 a** *Brit* **:** a piece of meat or fish rolled or coiled and tied close **b** *zool* **:** any of various structures or markings likened to a collar: as (1) **:** a band of specially colored feathers about a bird's neck (2) **:** the prothorax of an insect esp. when lengthened, narrowed, or specially modified (3) **:** the choana of a choanocyte or a choanate flagellate **c** (1) **:** RING, CINCTURE (2) **:** a necking in certain orders (as the classic Tuscan) (3) **:** COLLAR BEAM **d** (1) **:** ¹COLLET 3 (2) **:** the annulus of a mushroom (3) **:** a ringlike mass of tissue around the base of the ovule in ginkgo **e :** an abrupt increase in the thickness of the rim of a pottery vessel or a change of direction in the vessel wall that serves to set off a band near the top **f :** the layer of foam on top of a glass of beer **g :** a band of rocks encircling rocks of another kind or of different structure ⟨a ~ of sedimentary rock⟩ **4 :** an act of collaring **:** ARREST, CAPTURE

collars 2d on a shaft

²**collar** \"\ *vb* -ED/-ING/-S *vt* **1 a :** to seize by the collar or neck **:** obtain a hold on the neck of ⟨a wrestler ~*ing* an opponent⟩ **b :** CAPTURE, TACKLE, NAB ⟨to dart among the crowd and ~ the delinquent —Sheridan Le Fanu⟩ **c :** to attain to forceful possession of **:** GRASP, GRAB ⟨the circle broke up, each ~*ing* his own jug —Thomas Hughes⟩ **d :** lay hold of **:** PREEMPT, CORNER **:** come to possess or control **:** STEAL ⟨~ his partner's share of the profits⟩ **e :** to stop or corner and detain in unwilling conversation ⟨~ the guest of honor⟩ **f :** to draw up to and pass ⟨the favorite ~*ed* the tiring longshot in the stretch⟩ **2 a :** to put a collar on **:** adorn with a collar ⟨~ a coat⟩ **:** form a collar around **b :** to fasten a collar on (an animal) **3 :** to roll up and tie (meat or fish) for cooking; *specif* **:** to roll up and fit into a mold and cook with herbs and spices ⟨~*ed* eels⟩ ~ *vi* **:** to wind around a roll instead of moving straight through — used of a steel bar in a rolling mill

collarband \'==,=\ *n* **:** NECKBAND

collar beam *n* **:** a tie beam connecting the rafters at a level considerably above the wall plate in a roof truss

collar bearing *n* **:** a thrust bearing having a suitably formed face or faces that resist the axial pressure of one or more collars on a rotating shaft

collar blight *n* **:** pear and apple blight affecting the trunk base

collarbone \'==,=\ *n* [ME (Sc) *collar bane,* fr. *colar* collar (fr. ME *coler*) + *bane* bone, fr. OE *bān*] **:** CLAVICLE

collar button *n* **:** a button-sized stud consisting of a disk joined by a shank to a smaller disk, knob, or hinged flap and used for buttoning a collar to a shirt

collar cell *n* **:** CHOANOCYTE

coll' ar·co \(')kō¦lär(,)kō\ *adv (or adj)* [It] **:** with the bow — used as a direction following a pizzicato passage in a musical score for strings

col·lard \'kälə(r)d\ *n* -s [alter. of *colewort*] **:** KALE ⟨spinach and ~ greens⟩ — usu. used in pl. when applied to the food ⟨potatoes and ~*s* for supper⟩

col·lared \'kälə(r)d\ *adj* [ME *colleryd, colered,* fr. *coller, coler* collar + *-yd, -ed* -ed] **1 :** wearing, having, or depicted with a collar ⟨~ executives⟩ **2 :** having a marking or part that resembles a collar ⟨a ~ jug⟩ ⟨a crimson-*collared* bird⟩

collared dove *n* **:** RINGDOVE 2

collared lemming *n* **:** a stout-bodied murine rodent (*Dicrostonyx hudsonius*) of arctic America that is white-pelted in winter and more or less brown in summer

collared lizard *n* **:** a brightly colored iguanid lizard (*Crotaphytus collaris*) of the south-central U.S. and Mexico — called also *mountain boomer, ring-necked lizard*

collared monad *or* **collared flagellate** *n* **:** CHOANOFLAGELLATE

collared peccary *n* **:** a peccary (*Tayassu angulatus*) about three feet long and marked with an indistinct white collar

col·lar·et *or* **col·lar·ette** \,kälə'ret, '==,=\ *n* -s [F *collerette,* dim. of *collier* collar — more at COLLAR] **1 a :** usu. small or tight collar **2 :** NECKLACE **:** jewelry worn on or near a collar

collarette dahlia *n* **:** any of various dahlias having flower heads with one row of true ray florets and with shorter rays forming a collarlike fringe around the disk

col·lar·less \'kälə(r)ləs\ *adj* **:** lacking a collar

collar nut *n* **:** a screw-thread nut and collar

collar of SS \-'es'es\ **:** a heraldic collar with the letter S continually repeated that was orig. a badge of adherents of the house of Lancaster and is now part of certain official costumes — called also *SS collar*

collar roof *n* **:** a roof using collar beams

collar rot *or* **collar girdle** *n* **:** any of various plant diseases in which the lesion is localized at or about the collet between stem and root

collars *pl of* COLLAR, *pres 3d sing of* COLLAR

collar tie *n* **:** a board used to prevent the roof framing from spreading or sagging

collar-to-collar \¦===¦==\ *adj* **:** PORTAL-TO-PORTAL

collar work *n* **:** hard work (as that causing a horse to strain against a collar)

collas *pl of* COLLA

col·la si·nis·tra \¦kōlasə'nistrə\ *adv (or adj)* [It] **:** with the left hand — used as a direction in keyboard music

col·late \kə'lāt, kä-; 'kä,lāt, 'kō-, *usu* -ād·+V\ *vb* -ED/-ING/-S [partly fr. L *collatus,* used as past part. of *conferre* to bring together, partly back-formation fr. *collation*] *vt* **1** *obs* **:** CONFER, BESTOW, GRANT **2 a :** to bring together for close comparison **:** compare critically with careful attention to particulars and minute points **:** verify fidelity of to an original **b :** to collect, compare carefully in order to verify, and often to integrate or arrange into informative or significant order ⟨the data gathered by the local study groups are being *collated* for publication —*Saturday Rev.*⟩ **c :** ¹GATHER 2d **d** *printing* **:** to assemble in final order (as matter set in more than one typeface or by more than one typesetter) **3 :** to admit and institute (a cleric) to a benefice — compare COLLATION 4a **4 a :** to examine (a set of gathered sheets or a book) to verify the order and number of signatures, pages, plates, or maps **b :** to arrange or assemble (paper, sheets, or forms) according to an orderly system ⟨*collating* the pages of the report⟩ **5** *civil law* **:** to bring into an estate for equal division ~ *vi* **1 :** to appoint a cleric to a benefice **2** *civil law* **:** to bring goods into an estate for division **syn** see COMPARE

¹**col·lat·er·al** \kə'lad·ərəl, -latərəl, -la·trəl\ *adj* [ME, prob. fr. MF, fr. ML *collateralis,* fr. L *com-* + *lateralis* lateral] **1 a :** accompanying as a secondary fact, activity, or agency but usu. extrinsic to a main consideration **:** similar but subordinate **:** CONCOMITANT, SUBSIDIARY ⟨wrong on the main question and on all the ~ questions springing out of it —T.B.Macaulay⟩ ⟨digress into ~ matters⟩ **b :** INDIRECT ⟨no direct objection, but several ~ ones⟩ **c :** serving to support or reinforce **:** ANCILLARY ⟨sometimes literature will provide the historian of art with a pretty piece of ~ evidence —Clive Bell⟩ **2 :** belonging to the same ancestral stock but not in a direct line of descent ⟨brothers, cousins, uncles, and nephews are ~ kinsmen⟩ — distinguished from *lineal;* compare CONSANGUINITY **3 :** placed or regarded as side by side **:** parallel, coordinate, or corresponding in position, order, time, or significance ⟨~ mountain ranges⟩ ⟨~ states like Athens and Sparta⟩ **4 a :** being or belonging to an obligation or security attached to another to secure its performance ⟨a ~ assurance to a deed⟩ ⟨~ funds⟩ **b :** secured or guaranteed by additional security, esp. by personal as opposed to real property ⟨a ~ loan secured by stocks and bonds deposited with the lender⟩ ⟨a ~ loan from a finance company on one's promissory note⟩ **5** *bot, of a vascular bundle* **:** having phloem only external to the xylem — compare BICOLLATERAL 2

²**collateral** \"\ *n* -s **1 :** one that is collateral: as **a :** a collateral relative ⟨a greedy ~ who inherited the estate —J.G. Lockhart⟩ **b :** COLLATERAL SUBJECT **2 :** something used as collateral security **3 a :** a branch esp. of a blood vessel, nerve, or the axon of a nerve cell **b :** a bodily part that is lateral in position (as a ligament) **4** *chiefly NewEng* **a :** a miscellaneous clutter of personal belongings ⟨got your ~ packed⟩ **b :** odds and ends of trash **:** RUBBISH ⟨a woodshed full of ~⟩

collateral circulation *n* **:** circulation of blood established through enlargement of minor vessels and anastomosis of vessels with those of adjacent parts when a major vein or artery is functionally impaired (as by obstruction); *also* **:** the modified vessels through which such circulation occurs

collateral fact *n, law* **:** a fact that has no direct relation to or immediate bearing on the cause or matter in question

collateral fissure *n* **:** a fissure of the tentorial surface of the cerebrum lying below and external to the calcarine fissure and causing an elevation on the floor of the lateral ventricle between the hippocampi

collateral fraud *n* **:** EXTRINSIC FRAUD

collateral ganglion *n* **:** any of several autonomic ganglia not in the sympathetic chain (as the coeliac ganglion)

collateral issue *n* **:** an issue taken upon a matter aside from the general issue or the merits of a law case

col·lat·er·al·i·ty \kə,lad·ə'ralədē, -latə'r-, -ralətē, -i\ *n* -ES **1 :** the quality or state of being collateral **2 :** use in kinship classification of terms for collateral relatives distinct from those for lineal relatives of the same generation

col·lat·er·al·ize \kə'lad·ərə,līz, -latər-, -la·trə,l-\ *vt* -ED/-ING/-S **1 :** to make secure (as a loan) by pledge of collateral ⟨loans *collateralized* by government securities —*Mag. of Wall Street*⟩ **2 :** to use as collateral for a loan

col·lat·er·al·ly \kə'lad·ərəlē, -latər-, -la·trə-, -li\ *adv* [ME, fr. ¹*collateral* + *-ly*] **1 :** side by side **2 :** in an auxiliary or subordinate manner **:** INDIRECTLY **3 :** in collateral relation **:** not lineally

collateral power *n* **:** a power granted to one who has no interest or estate in the property to which the power relates (as a power of sale granted to an executor who is not a legatee or devisee) — called also *naked power, power in gross;* distinguished from *power coupled with an interest*

collateral reading *n* **:** required or recommended reading to supplement school or college class assignments

collateral subject *n* **:** a subject complementary to a student's major field of concentration

collateral trust bond *n* **:** a bond secured by negotiable securities deposited with a trustee

collates *pres 3d sing of* COLLATE

collating *pres part of* COLLATE

collating mark *n* **:** a black mark differently positioned on the outside fold of each different signature in bookbinding to aid in collating

col·la·tio bo·no·rum \kə'läsh(ē)ōbə'nōrəm, -ȯr-\ *n, pl* **col·la·tio·nes bonorum** \=,=shē'ō,nēz-\ *or* **collatio bonorums** [LL] *civil law* **:** collation of goods

¹**col·la·tion** \kə'lāshən, kä-, kō-\ *n* -s [ME *collacioun* bringing together, comparison, fr. L *collation-, collatio,* fr. *collatus* (used as past part. of *conferre* to bring together) (fr. *com-* + *latus*) + *-ion-, -io* -ion — more at TOLERATE] **1** [ME, fr. LL, fr. L bringing together] **a :** a reading from or conference upon some edifying book at a gathering of the members of a monastery at close of day **b** *obs* **:** an often informal conference **2** [ME, fr. ML, fr. LL, conference] **a :** the refreshment taken at a monastic collation **b :** a light meal allowed on fast days in place of lunch or supper **c :** a light meal or other refreshment at an unusual hour served in connection with a ceremony or meeting ⟨a ~ after the church services⟩ **3 a :** the act of bringing together for comparing **:** a usu. close, detailed, and careful comparison **:** comparative scrutiny **:** ordered arrangement made by comparison **b :** comparison of manuscripts or editions of a text to determine the original or the condition or authenticity of a particular copy; *also* **:** the conclusions drawn and recorded from such comparison **c :** the act of collating a book or set of sheets; *also* **:** the bibliographical description of a book expressed in a formula in which information about size, signatures, and pagination is represented by symbols **d :** the verification of a telegraphic message by repetition **4 a :** the bestowal of a living or other preferment upon a clergyman; *specif* **:** the bestowal of a living in the Church of England where the bishop is the patron **b :** the right of bestowing such a living **5 :** the act of an heir or legatee under civil or Scots law in giving back to his ancestor's or testator's estate the property received from him during the ancestor's or testator's lifetime in order to bring about an equal distribution of property among those entitled **:** the return of advancements to an estate **:** HOTCHPOT **syn** see COMPARISON

²**collation** *vb* -ED/-ING/-S *vt, obs* **:** COLLATE ~ *vi, obs* **:** to eat a collation

col·la·tion·al \-'lāshən°l, -shnəl\ *adj* **:** of or relating to a collation

collation in·ter hae·re·des \-'intərhe'rē,dēz\ *n* [part trans. of NL *collatio inter haeredes* collation among heirs] *Scots law* **:** collation by an heir to heritable property who is also entitled to share in the movable property to prevent unfair diminution in the shares of those taking the movable property

collation in·ter li·be·ros \-'libə,rōs, -lē-\ *n* [part trans. of NL *collatio inter liberos* collation among the children (descendants)] *Scots law* **:** collation by one entitled to legitim in order to preserve equality among all entitled to legitim

col·la·tive \kə'lād·iv, (')kä¦l-, (')kō¦l-, -ātiv\ *adj* [L *collativus* brought together, fr. *collatus* + *-ivus* -ive] **1 :** having the quality or power of conferring **2 :** passing, held, or conferred by collation (sense 4a) **3 :** marked by collation or systematic comparison ⟨a ~ act or function⟩

col·la·tor \-lād·ə(r), -ātə-\ *n* -s [L, fr. *collatus* + *-or*] **:** one that collates or makes a collation: as **a :** a punched-card machine that matches, selects, and files identical cards of two sets fed into the machine **b :** a machine that gathers or gathers and glues printed sheets from separate groupings

col·la vo·ce \'kōlə¦vō(,)chā\ *adv (or adj)* [It, with the voice] **:** COLLA PARTE

¹**col·league** \'kä,lēg *sometimes* 'kō,lēg *or* kä'lēg *or* kə'lēg\ *n* -s [MF *collègue,* fr. L *collega* one chosen at the same time with another partner in office, fr. *com-* + *-lega* (fr. *legare* to choose or send as deputy) — more at LEGATE] **:** an associate or coworker typically in a profession or a civil or ecclesiastical office and often of similar rank or state ⟨the professor and his ~*s*⟩

²**colleague** *vb* -ED/-ING/-S [MF *colliguer, colleguer* to unite, ally, fr. L *colligare* to bind together — more at COLLIGATE] *vt, obs* **:** become allied with **:** JOIN, UNITE ~ *vi* **:** to enter into an alliance **:** COOPERATE, CONSPIRE ⟨*colleaguing* with a score of petty kings —Alfred Tennyson⟩

³**col·league** \kä'lēg\ *Scot var of* COLLOGUE

¹**col·lect** \'kälikt, -(,)lekt\ *n* -s [ME *collecte,* fr. OF, fr. ML *collecta* (short for *oratorio ad collectam* prayer upon assembly), fr. LL, assembly, fr. L, collection, assemblage, fr. fem. of *collectus,* past part. of *colligere* to bind together, fr. *com-* + *-ligere* (fr. *legere* to gather) — more at LEGEND] **1** *often cap* **:** a short prayer used in the opening part of Western church services that is usu. general in nature and that varies in Roman Catholic and Anglican usage with the day **2** [ME *collecte,* fr. L *collecta*] *archaic* **:** COLLECTION, GATHERING **3** [prob. fr. ²*collect*] *dial* **:** a place where water collects **:** SINKHOLE

²**col·lect** \kə'lekt\ *vb* -ED/-ING/-S [ME, adj., collected, fr. L *collectus*] *vt* **1 a :** to bring together into a band, group, assortment, or mass **:** GATHER ⟨~ an army⟩ ⟨~ all the available chairs⟩ ⟨~*ing* facts about immigration⟩ **b :** to receive, gather, or exact from a number of persons or other sources ⟨the Congress shall have power to lay and ~ taxes on incomes, from whatever source derived —*U.S. Constitution*⟩ **c :** to serve as a point of attraction or focus for (a crowd or accumulation) ⟨a positive genius for ~*ing* impossible people —Ngaio Marsh⟩ **2 :** INFER, DEDUCE, CONCLUDE ⟨he ~*s* our destination from the way in which things appear to have gone in the past 150 years —*Times Lit. Supp.*⟩ ⟨I ~ thou art to be my fatal enemy —John Milton⟩ **3 :** to regain control of **:** gather or summon up **:** overcome distraction of ⟨they were excited and unsteady and . . . required time to ~ themselves —J.A.Froude⟩ ⟨~ his thoughts, before setting to work, in a quiet room —Laurence Binyon⟩ **4 :** to bring together esp. in accordance with a principle of selection or an informative or profitable end **:** come to own as a collection or part of a collection **:** include as part of one's experience ⟨a volume of 122 ballads . . . which he had ~*ed* in the mountains —*Amer. Guide Series: N.C.*⟩ ⟨having spent some months in successfully ~*ing* and arranging my materials —Mary W. Shelley⟩ ⟨in the matter of ~*ing* books — I mean owning them —J.C.Powys⟩ ⟨I tried to ~ lakes —O.S.J. Gogarty⟩ **5 a :** to bring (a saddle horse) into a state of collection by use of the aids **b** *of a horse* **:** to bring (himself) into a state of collection — compare EXTEND **6 a :** to claim and receive in payment or fair recompense ⟨unable to ~ his wife's retirement benefits⟩ ⟨~*ing* social security payments⟩ **b :** to present as due and receive payment for ⟨~ a bill⟩ **c :** to call for **:** pick up **:** take or bring with one **:** ESCORT ⟨waited only long enough to ~ a letter of introduction —Harvey Graham⟩ ⟨~ his girl and bring her in to the cinema —F.T.B.Macartney⟩ **7 :** to unite (two or more lines of fire hose) to form a more powerful jet of water ~ *vi* **1 :** to come together in a band or group **:** form into or as if into a crowd ⟨crowds of folk used to ~ on the beach to see the fun —Norman Douglas⟩ **2 :** form a layer, heap, or mass **:** ACCUMULATE ⟨dust ~*s* on the furniture⟩ ⟨junk will ~ in the attic⟩ **3 a :** to collect matter or objects ⟨the botanists were out ~*ing* in full force⟩ **b :** to receive payment, remuneration, or other return — often used with *on* ⟨~*ing* on his insurance⟩ **syn** see GATHER

³**collect** \"\ *adv (or adj)* **:** to be paid for by the receiver ⟨send the package ~⟩ ⟨a ~ telephone call⟩

col·lec·ta·nea \,kä(,)lek'tānēə\ *n pl* [L, neut. pl. of *collectaneus* collected, fr. *collectus,* past part. of *colligere* to collect] **:** collected writings **:** literary items forming a collection ⟨its past development, as partly revealed by present ~ —S.P. Bayard⟩

col·lec·tar·i·um \-'ta(a)rēəm\ *n, pl* **collectariums** \-ēəmz\ *or* **collectar·ia** \-ēə\ [ML, fr. *collecta* collect + L *-arium*] **:** a service book containing collects

collected *adj* **1 :** gathered together ⟨the ~ works of Scott⟩ **2 :** freed from agitation, excitement, or distraction **:** possessed of calmness and composure often through concentrated effort ⟨such an intellect . . . cannot be at a loss, cannot but be patient, ~, majestically calm —J.H.Newman⟩ **3** *of a gait* **:** performed or performable by a horse from a state of collection ⟨~ gaits include the trot, canter, and rack⟩ **syn** see COOL

collected edition *n* **:** a uniform usu. complete edition of an author's work

col·lect·ed·ly *adv* **1 :** all together **:** in an assembled or collected state **:** COLLECTIVELY **2 :** with coolness and composure **:** in a collected way

col·lect·ed·ness *n* -ES **:** the quality or state of being collected

collect for the day \'kälikt, -(,)lekt\ **:** a collect appropriate for a particular day of the church year

col·lect·i·bil·i·ty *or* **col·lect·a·bil·i·ty** \kə,lektə'biləd·ē, -'lətē, -i\ *n* -ES **:** the quality or state of being collectible or readily exchangeable for money ⟨the ~ of the debt⟩

col·lect·i·ble *or* **col·lect·a·ble** \kə'lektəbəl\ *adj* **1 :** suitable for a collection **:** fit for being collected ⟨~ specimens⟩ **2 :** due for present payment **:** capable of being collected **:** exchangeable for cash **:** PAYABLE ⟨a ~ bill⟩ ⟨a ~ account⟩

collecting cell *n* **:** one of the spongy parenchyma cells having dilated ends and underlying the palisade cells of leaves and reputedly conveying the products of photosynthesis from the palisade cells to the vascular system of the plant

collecting station *n* **:** a medical installation in a forward combat area where casualties are received from aid stations, treated, classified, and either returned to duty or prepared for evacuation to a clearing station in the rear

collecting tubule *n* **:** the nonsecretory part of a nephron by which urine passes to the calyx of the kidney

col·lec·tion \kə'lekshən\ *n* -s *often attrib* [ME *collectioun,* fr. MF *collection,* fr. L *collection-, collectio,* fr. *collectus* (past part. of *colligere* to bind together) + *-ion-, -io* -ion — more at COLLECT] **1 :** the act of collecting (as taxes by a tax collector); *specif* **:** the securing of payment of a check, bond coupon, or other credit instrument by presentation to the payer for cash **2 :** a number of objects or persons or a quantity of a substance that has been collected or has collected often according to some unifying principle or orderly arrangement: as **a :** an assembly of objects or specimens for the purposes of education, research, or interest ⟨the magnificent ~ of trees —Edmund Wilson⟩ **b :** AGGREGATION, GROUP, NUMBER ⟨a ~ of buffalo-hide huts —*Amer. Guide Series: Texas*⟩ ⟨a ~ of different personalities —Warwick Braithwaite⟩ **c :** apparel that is displayed for sale in a particular season (as by a particular designer) **3** *obs* **:** DEDUCTION, INFERENCE, INTERPRETATION ⟨wrong ~*s* have been hitherto made out of those words by modern divines —John Milton⟩ **4 a :** an attaining to composure **:** a becoming collected **:** a bringing under control ⟨some time was required for the ~ of her faculties⟩ **b :** a standard pose of a well-handled saddle horse in which it is brought well up to the bit and flexion of the body predominates with jaw relaxed, head arched at the poll, and hocks tucked under the body so that the center of gravity is shifted toward the rear quarters; *also* **:** the act of bringing a horse into a state of collection **5 collections** *pl* **:** a term examination at some English colleges **6 :** ³AGGREGATE 5

collection at source : STOPPAGE AT SOURCE

collection line *n* **:** HOUSE DRAIN

collection plate *n* **:** ¹PLATE 3e(1)

collection station *n* **:** COLLECTING STATION

¹**col·lec·tive** \kə'lektiv, -ēv *also* -əv\ *adj* [MF or L; MF *collectif,* fr. L *collectivus,* fr. *collectus* + *-ivus* -ive] **1 a** *of a word or term* **:** indicating a number of persons or things considered as constituting one group or aggregate ⟨*family* and *flock* are ~ words⟩ **b** *of a noun or pronoun* **:** singular in form but sometimes or always plural in construction ⟨*family* in "the family were proud" is a ~ word⟩ **2 a :** formed by collecting **:** gathered into a mass, sum, or body **:** AGGREGATED **b** *of fruit* **:** MULTIPLE **3 :** by, characteristic of, or relating to a group of individuals, esp. a public group such as a social class or a whole society ⟨~ interests of the society⟩ **4 :** originating in, authorized by, or composed of a group (as a governing

group) ⟨~ leadership⟩ **5 :** involving or characterized by the united action or cooperative endeavors of all members of an aggregation or group as distinct from that of individuals ⟨~ work⟩ **6 :** marked by simultaneity, uniformity, or similarity (as of a response to a stimulus) among all the members of a group (as a whole society) ⟨~ feeling⟩ ⟨the ~ opinion of all Americans —F.D.Roosevelt⟩ **7 :** collectivized or characterized by collectivism **8 a :** having the same general characteristics as the group and thus tending to lack any individual personal traits **:** DEPERSONALIZED ⟨~ man⟩ **:** TYPICAL, REPRESENTATIVE ⟨the ~ New Yorker⟩ **b :** shared or assumed by all members of the group ⟨the ~ responsibility of the cabinet⟩ ⟨the ~ guilt of all party members⟩ **9 :** comprising a number of imperfectly differentiated entities — used esp. of a species made up of several imperfectly separable types

²**collective** \"\ *n* -s **1 :** a collective word or term **2 :** a collective body **:** GROUP ⟨a social ~⟩ **3 :** a cooperative unit or organization; *specif* **:** COLLECTIVE FARM

collective action *n* **:** united action by an association (as of nations against an aggressor)

collective agreement *n* **:** an agreement between an employer and a union usu. reached through collective bargaining and establishing wage rates, hours of labor, and working conditions

collective bargaining *n* **:** negotiation for the settlement of the terms of a collective agreement between an employer or group of employers on one side and a union or number of unions on the other; *broadly* **:** any union-management negotiation

collective behavior *n* **:** the mass behavior of a group whether animal or human (as mob action) **:** the unified action of an assembly of persons whether organized or not; *also* **:** the like or similar response of the members of a society to a given stimulus or suggestion

collective biography *n* **:** a volume containing biographies of a number of people

collective farm *n* **:** a farm (as in a communist country) formed from many small holdings collected into a single unit for joint operation under governmental supervision

col·lect·ive·ly \-tə̇vlē, -li\ *adv* [¹*collective* + *-ly*] **:** in a collective sense or manner **:** in a mass or body **:** in a collected state **:** in the aggregate **:** by collective acts

collective mark *n* **:** a trademark or a service mark of a group (as a cooperative or other association)

col·lect·ive·ness *n* -ES **:** the quality or state of being collective

collective psychology *n* **:** SOCIAL PSYCHOLOGY

collective representation *n* **:** a symbol that articulates and embodies the collective beliefs, sentiments, and values of a social group

collective security *n* **1 :** a policy by an association of nations to maintain international peace through a league or confederation that would oppose by united action violations of the peace by an aggressor **2 :** security of all members of an association of nations from aggression by collective action

collective unconscious *n* **:** the psychical inheritance of racial experience functionally potential in each individual — called also *racial unconscious*

col·lec·tiv·ism \kə'lektə̇,vizəm\ *n* -s [F *collectivisme*, fr. *collectif* collective + *-isme* -ism] **1 a :** a politico-economic system characterized by collective control esp. over production and distribution of goods and services in contrast to free enterprise ⟨forces that have led to individualism have in the last fifty years been successfully opposed by the forces of ~ —M.R.Cohen⟩ **b :** extreme control of the economic, political, and social life of its subjects by an authoritarian state (as under communism or fascism) **c :** a doctrine or system that makes the group or the state actively responsible for the social and economic welfare of its members **2 :** a social theory or doctrine that emphasizes the importance of the collective (as the society or state) in contrast to the individual and that tends to analyze society in terms of collective behavior — see HOLISM **3 :** ²COLLECTIVE 2, 3

¹**col·lec·tiv·ist** \-və̇st\ *n* -s [F *collectiviste*, fr. *collectivisme* + *-iste* -ist] **1 :** an advocate or adherent of collectivism **2 :** a member of a collective or collectivity

syn SOCIALIST, COMMUNIST: COLLECTIVIST is likely to apply to a person approving or desiring greater control or outright ownership of major industries and resources by the state, presumably in the interests of a degree of economic equality among the whole people, this control or ownership to be achieved gradually and without violence but with some restriction on individual action. SOCIALIST is a close synonym for COLLECTIVIST in this sense, but is likely to evoke more of an emotional reaction than COLLECTIVIST. COMMUNIST is likely to suggest one desiring more rigid and far-reaching control, often control achieved by force. The words SOCIALIST and COMMUNIST are naturally affected in their connotations by whatever particular Socialist or Communist Party or Socialism or Communism happens to be prominent in world affairs at the moment. In matters historical or philosophical, the two words, esp. the latter, may be used without praise or stigma to refer to persons favoring or accepting conditions in which the wishes and activities of the individual are checked and guided by the interests of the group, as in Plato's ideal republic, in ancient Sparta, in some of the earliest Christian communities

²**collectivist** \"\ *also* **col·lec·tiv·is·tic** \=¦==¦vistik, -ēk\ *adj* **1 :** favoring collectivism **:** based on the principles of collectivism **2 :** relating to or having the characteristics of collectivism

col·lec·tiv·i·ty \,kä(,)lek'tivəd·ē, -,lə̇k-, -vətē, -i\ *n* -ES **1 :** the quality or state of being collective **2 a :** collective sum **:** totality esp. of persons in social organization **:** AGGREGATE ⟨great *collectivities* that bury, if they do not destroy, individuality —Robert Lindner⟩ **b :** a group of persons acting in concert or considered as a single unit (as a state, corporation, or class) **3 :** the processes or results of collectivism

col·lec·ti·vi·za·tion \kə,lektə̇və̇'zāshən, -,vī'-\ *n* -s **:** the action or process of collectivizing **:** the state of being collectivized

col·lec·tiv·ize \kə'lektə̇,vīz\ *vt* -ED/-ING/-S *see -ize in Explan Notes* **1 :** to organize according to the principles of collectivism ⟨institute a *collectivized* society⟩ **:** influence by or as if by a collective process or method with decrease of individualism **2 :** to bring into a system of or under the control of collective farms ⟨~ the land⟩ **3 :** to make collective **:** consider as collective ⟨the *collectivized* emotions of the people⟩

collect on delivery *adj (or adv)* **:** to be paid for in cash at the time of delivery to the buyer — abbr. *COD*

col·lec·tor \kə'lektə(r)\ *n* -s [ME *colector, collectour*, fr. MF & ML; MF *collecteur*, fr. ML *collector* one who collects, fr. L *collectus* (past part. of *colligere* to bring together) + *-or* — more at COLLECT] **1 :** an official who collects funds or moneys: as **a :** an officer commissioned to collect and receive revenues **b** *Brit* **:** one that collects parish alms **c :** the administrative head of a district in some provinces of British India **d :** one authorized to collect debts and accounts due: as (1) **:** a clerk or agent who by telephone, correspondence, or personal visits attempts to collect delinquent accounts and sometimes cuts off service or repossesses merchandise if payment is not made (2) **:** one that makes collection at regular intervals of installment payments or insurance premiums **e :** a messenger who acts as a bank's agent in presenting checks, drafts, and money orders to local banks for payment or acceptance **f :** one that collects money from coin boxes of public and private pay telephones and computes and pays a percentage refund to subscribers when cash exceeds the maximum guarantee **2 :** one that makes a collection ⟨a stamp ~⟩ ⟨a ~ of first editions⟩ **3 :** an object or device that collects ⟨the statuette was a fine dust ~⟩ ⟨a ~ lowered overboard to gather plankton specimens⟩ **4 a :** a conductor maintaining contact between moving and stationary parts of an electric circuit (as one of the tinsel brushes on an induction machine or the third-rail shoe of an electric-railway car) **b :** a device (as an electrode) that collects moving electrons **c :** the output terminal of a transistor **5** *in the flotation process of ore dressing* **:** a chemical used to increase the floating capacity of a mineral

col·lec·to·rate \=ˈ=tərə̇t\ *n* -s **:** COLLECTORSHIP 1

collector ring *n* **1 :** one or more continuous conducting rings in a dynamo or motor from which the brushes take or to which they deliver current **2 :** the ring-shaped exhaust manifold of a radial airplane engine

col·lec·tor·ship \=ˈ==,ship\ *n* -s **1 :** the jurisdiction, residence, office, or staff of a collector **2 :** the practice of one that collects

collector's item *n* **:** an item whose rarity or perfection makes it esp. worth collecting

collects *pl of* COLLECT, *pres 3d sing of* COLLECT

colled *past of* COLL

col·leen \'kä,lēn; kə'-, kä'-\ *n* -s [IrGael *cailīn*, dim. of *caile*, prob. fr. L *paelex* concubine — more at PERI] **1** *Irish* **:** a young girl **2 :** an Irish girl

col·lege \'kälij, -ēj\ *n* -s *often attrib* [ME, fr. MF, fr. L *collegium* society, fr. *collega* colleague — more at COLLEAGUE] **1 :** a body of clergy living in common on a foundation **2 :** a building or a number of buildings used in connection with some specific educational or religious purpose: as **a :** the precinct of an English cathedral **b :** a dormitory for students **3** [ME, fr. ML *collegium*, fr. L, society] **a :** a self-governing constituent body of a university offering living quarters and instruction, sometimes limited, but not granting degrees ⟨Balliol and Magdalen *Colleges* at Oxford⟩ **b :** UNIVERSITY ⟨Edinburgh *College*⟩ **c :** preparatory or high school ⟨Eton *College*⟩ ⟨Girard *College*⟩ **d :** an independent institution of higher learning offering a course of general studies and usu. preprofessional training leading to a bachelor's degree **e :** a part of a university offering a specialized group of courses ⟨this university has a ~ of dentistry⟩ ⟨the ~ of engineering at the university⟩ **f :** an institution offering instruction usu. in a professional, vocational, or technical field ⟨teachers ~⟩ ⟨business ~⟩ ⟨army war ~⟩ ⟨barber ~⟩ ⟨~ of embalming⟩ **4 a :** COMPANY, ASSEMBLAGE, COTERIE, CLUB ⟨a ~ of courtesans⟩ ⟨some dusty ~ of pedants⟩ **b :** a meeting or reunion of companions or associates ⟨a ~ of Collegiants⟩ **5 :** an organized body, guild, society, or group of persons engaged in a common pursuit, having common interests or a common duty or role and sometimes a charter or special rights and privileges ⟨a ~ of cardinals serving as papal councillors and electors⟩ ⟨a ~ of craftsmen⟩ ⟨a ~ of witches was entrusted with the duty of annually choosing a beautiful girl to be the bride of the water-god —J.G.Frazer⟩; *specif* **:** COLLEGE OF ARMS **6 a :** a collection of persons treated in law in one or more respects as a unit **b :** a body of electors — see ELECTORAL COLLEGE **7** *slang* **:** PRISON, REFORMATORY **8 :** a course of study or of lectures ⟨taking three ~s a year⟩ **9 :** a charitable foundation in England providing residence and care **:** ASYLUM, HOSPITAL **10 :** the faculty, students, or administrative body of a college ⟨the ~ stood behind any move to improve education⟩ ⟨the ~ was at the football game in force⟩

college boards *n pl, sometimes cap C&B* **:** a set of examinations given by a college entrance examination board and required by some colleges of all candidates for admission and by others of all those whose academic records are below a certain standard

college–bred \'==¦=\ *adj* **:** educated in a college ⟨forgotten who of their gownsmen was *college-bred* —R.W.Emerson⟩

college ice *n, NewEng* **:** SUNDAE

college of arms *or* **college of heralds 1** *usu cap C&A* **a :** a corporation in England dependent upon the crown and consisting of three kings of arms, six heralds, and four pursuivants under the earl marshal's headship who have retained from the middle ages certain of the ceremonial duties of heralds but whose principal responsibility in modern times is the designing, grant, and registration of armorial bearings **b :** the building occupied by this corporation **2 :** an officially incorporated body of officers of arms of any nation

college-preparatory \¦kälij+\ *adj* **:** of or relating to a school or course of studies designed to qualify students for admission to a college — compare COMMERCIAL, GENERAL

col·leg·er \'käləjə(r)\ *n* -s **1 :** a student at Eton College who lives on the original foundation — compare OPPIDAN 3 **2 :** a college student

college scrip *n* **:** scrip issued to facilitate the establishment of colleges

college spirit *n* **:** demonstrative enthusiastic zeal for one's college esp. in matters athletic

college try *n* **:** a zealous all-out uninhibited effort for complete success without expedient compromise ⟨an outfielder making the old *college try* for a low liner⟩

college widow *n* **:** a young woman in a college town who dates students of successive college classes

collegia *pl of* COLLEGIUM

col·le·gi·al \kə'lējēəl, -jəl\ *adj* [MF or L; MF *collegial*, fr. L *collegialis*, fr. *collegium* society — more at COLLEGE] **1 :** of or relating to a college or university **:** COLLEGIATE **2 :** of or relating to a collegium or group of colleagues

col·le·gi·al·ism \-,lizəm\ *n* -s [G *kollegialismus*, fr. *kollegial* (fr. L *collegialis*) + *-ismus* -ism] **:** a theory of church polity that defines the church as a society of voluntary members independent of the state, self-governing, and with authority vested in the members

col·le·gi·al·i·ty \kə,lējē'aləd·ē, -ətē\ *n* -ES [F *collégial* of a colleague (fr. MF, fr. L *collegialis*) + E *-ity*] **:** the relationship of colleagues; *specif* **:** adherence to collegialism ⟨the impediment of ~, under which in old days one tribune could nullify the work of another —John Buchan⟩

collegial system *n* **:** COLLEGIALISM

col·le·gian \kə'lēj(ē)ən\ *n* -s [ME, fr. ML *collegianus*, fr. *collegium* + *-anus* -an] **:** a member of a college **:** a college student or recent college graduate

col·le·gian·er \-ə(r)\ *n* -s *Scot* **:** a student at a university **:** COLLEGIAN

col·le·gi·ant \-jēənt, -jənt\ *n* -s *usu cap* [D, fr. NL *collegium* congregation (fr. L, society) + D *-ant* (fr. L *-ant-, ans* -ant — more at COLLEGE] **:** a member of an Arminian sect started in 1619 by Jan, Adrian, and Gilbert van der Kodde and forming congregations in Holland

¹**col·le·giate** \-j(ē)ə̇t, *usu* -d·+V\ *adj* [ML *collegiatus*, fr. ML *collegium* + L *-atus* -ate — more at COLLEGE] **1 :** of or relating to a collegiate church ⟨a ~ pastor⟩ ⟨a ~ charge⟩ ⟨monasteries and other ~ bodies such as the cathedral churches —R.W. Southern⟩ **2 :** of, relating to, or comprising a college or colleges: **a :** having college rank or standards ⟨a ~ education⟩ **b :** resembling that of a college ⟨~ architecture⟩ ⟨~ living⟩ **c** *of a university* **:** composed of several autonomous colleges **3 :** marked by power or authority vested equally in each of a number of colleagues **:** COLLEGIAL ⟨abolished the ~ executive and restored full powers to the presidency —M.I. Vanger⟩ **4 a :** characteristic of college students (as in appearance, attitude, or behavior) ⟨~ clothes⟩ ⟨~ humor⟩ **b :** designed for the use or relevant to the life of college students often on the nonacademic side ⟨~ athletics⟩ — **col·le·giate·ly** *adv* — **col·le·giate·ness** *n* -ES

²**col·le·gi·ate** \-jē,āt, *usu* -d·+V\ *vt* -ED/-ING/-S **:** to constitute or organize as a college or as a collegiate church

³**col·le·giate** \-j(ē)ə̇t, *usu* -d·+V\ *n* -s **1 :** COLLEGIAN **2 :** a British or Canadian secondary school

collegiate church *n* **1 :** a church that although not a cathedral or bishop's church has a college or chapter of canons and, in the Church of England, a dean (as Westminster Abbey or St. George's Chapel at Windsor) **2 :** a Presbyterian church that regularly has two or more ministers of equal rank **3 :** a church or an association of churches in the U.S. possessing common revenues administered under the joint pastorate of several ministers

collegiate gothic *n, usu cap G* **:** the style of Gothic architecture exemplified in English college buildings (as at Oxford)

col·le·gi·enne \kə,lējē'en\ *n* -s [fr. *collegian*, after such pairs as E *comedian*: *comedienne*] **:** a female college student — used esp. in fashion advertisements

col·le·gi·um \kə'lējēəm, -jəm\ *n, pl* **colle·gia** \-jēə, -jə\ *or* **collegi·ums** \-mz\ [L — more at COLLEGE] **1 a :** COLLEGE 5 **b** *Roman & civil law* **:** an association of individuals of the same class or rank formed to promote their common interest in some business pursuit or enterprise **2** [modif. (influenced by L *collegium*) of Russ *kollegya*, fr. L *collegium*] **:** an executive body with each member having approximately equal power and authority; *specif, often cap* **:** a board or committee responsible for the work of a commissariat or a nationalized industry under a soviet system of government

col legno \kō'lān(,)yō\ *adv* [It] **:** with the wood — used as a direction in music to players of bowed instruments to use the wood and not the hair of the bow in playing

col·lem·bo·la \kə'lembələ\ *n pl, cap* [NL, fr. *coll-* + *-embola* (fr. Gk *embolos, embolon* peg, wedge); fr. their collophore — more at EMBOL-] **:** an order of small primitively wingless arthropods that are related to or sometimes classed among the true insects, are characterized by possession of a median collophore, not more than 6 abdominal segments, 3 pairs of legs, and usu. a forked caudal furcula, are found esp. in soil rich in organic debris or on the surface of snow or water, and comprise the springtails — **col·lem·bo·lan** \-lən\ *adj or n* — **col·lem·bo·lous** \-ləs\ *adj*

col·len·chy·ma \kə'leŋkəmə\ *n, pl* **col·len·chym·a·ta** \,kälən'kimәd·ə\ [NL, fr. *coll-* + *-enchyma*] **1 :** a tissue that is found chiefly in the outer parts of young stems, petioles, and leaf midribs, consists of elongated living cells with rectangular, oblique, or tapering ends and walls variously thickened esp. in the angles, and provides temporary support and elasticity prior to differentiation of the vascular elements — compare SCLERENCHYMA **2 :** COLLENCHYME

col·len·chym·a·tous \¦kälən¦kimәd·әs\ *adj* [NL *collenchymat-, collenchyma* + E *-ous*] **1 :** of, relating to, or resembling collenchyma **2 :** of or relating to collenchyme — **col·len·chym·a·tous·ly** *adv*

col·len·chyme \'kälən,kīm\ *n* -s [NL *collenchyma*] **:** a loose mesenchyme containing few cells and much gelatinous material that occupies the space between the ectoderm and endoderm of the body wall of many lower invertebrates (as sponges)

col·len·cyte \'kälən,sīt\ *n* -s [*collen*chyme + *-cyte*] **:** one of the branched cells of collenchyme

col·lery \'kälərē\ *n, pl* **collery** *or* **colleries** *usu cap* [prob. modif. of Tamil *kaḷḷar* thieves, fr. *kaḷ* to steal] **1 :** a Dravidian people of southern India **2 :** a member of the Collery people

col·les's fracture \'käləsə̇z-,'kä,lēzəz-\ *n, usu cap C* [after Abraham *Colles* †1843 Irish surgeon] **:** a fracture of the lower end of the radius with backward displacement of the lower fragment and radial deviation of the hand at the wrist that produces a characteristic deformity

¹**col·let** \'kälə̇t, *usu* -d·+V\ *n* -s [MF, dim. of *col* collar, neck, fr. L *collum* neck — more at COLLAR] **1 :** a metal band, collar, ferrule, or flange: **a :** a small collar pierced to receive the inner end of a balance spring and fixed friction-tight on the balance staff of a watch or chronometer **b** (1) **:** a casing or socket for holding a drill or other tool **:** COLLET CHUCK (2) **:** a bushing that keeps stuffing-box packing in place (3) **:** a ring forming part of or secured to a spindle or arbor **c :** a circle or flange in a ring or other piece of jewelry in which a precious stone is set **2 :** a nonmetallic insert that interrupts the conduction of heat through a metal teapot handle **3 :** the often hypothetical although sometimes physically identifiable boundary between the stem and root of a plant — called also *collar* **4** [modif. (influenced by *collet*) of F *culet* — more at CULET] **:** CULET 1

²**collet** \"\ *vt* -ED/-ING/-S **:** to furnish or surround with a collet

collet chuck *n* **:** a chuck consisting of a collet that grips the workpiece (as a bar of metal to be shaped)

¹**col·le·ter** \kə'lēd·ə(r)\ *n* -s [G *kolleter*, irreg. fr. Gk *kollan* to glue, fr. *kolla* glue — more at PROTOCOL] **:** one of the mucilage-secreting hairs that clothe many plant surfaces esp. on various winter buds (as those of the horse chestnut)

²**col·let·er** \'kälə̇d·ə(r)\ *n* -s [*collet* + *-er*] **:** a worker who attaches the inner coil of a watch hairspring to a collet for assembly to the balance wheel

col·le·te·ri·al gland \¦kälə¦tirēəl-\ *n* [*colleterial* fr. *colleterium* + *-al*] **:** COLLETERIUM

col·le·te·ri·um \-rēəm\ *n, pl* **collete·ria** \-rēə\ [NL, irreg. fr. Gk *kollan* to glue] **:** a gland in female insects that secretes a cement by which the eggs are glued together

col·le·tia \kə'lēsh(ē)ə, -lēd·ēə\ *n, cap* [NL, fr. Philibert *Collet* †1718 Fr. jurisconsult and botanist + NL *-ia*] **:** a small genus of spiny So. American shrubs (family Rhamnaceae) often quite leafless and with small white or yellow flowers — see ANCHOR PLANT

col·let·in \'kälət°n, -,tin\ *n* -s [F, fr. *collet*] **:** plate armor for neck and shoulders

col·le·tot·ri·chum \,kälə'tä·trəkəm\ *n, cap* [NL, fr. *colleto-* (fr. Gk *kollētos* glued, fr. *kollan* to glue) + *-trichum* (fr. Gk *trich-, thrix* hairs) — more at TRICH-] **:** large and widely distributed form genus of imperfect fungi (family Melanconiaceae) having the conidia borne in erumpent acervuli surrounded by setae — compare ANTHRACNOSE

colletside \'==,=\ *n* -s [¹*collet* + *side*] **:** PAVILION 4

col·ley \'kälē, -li\ *var of* ⁴COLLY

col·li·bert \'kälə,bərt\ *n* -s [F, fr. ML *collibertus*, fr. L, fellow freedman, fr. *com-* + *libertus* one made free, fr. *liber* free — more at LIBERAL] **:** a peasant tenant next superior to the serfs

col·li·cle \'käləkəl\ *n* -s [NL *colliculus*] **:** COLLICULUS; *specif* **:** VERUMONTANUM — **col·lic·u·lar** \kə'likyələ(r)\ *adj*

col·lic·u·late \kə'likyələt, ,lāt\ *adj* [L *colliculus* (dim. of *collis* hill) + E *-ate* — more at HILL] *zool* **:** having small elevations

col·lic·u·lus \-yələs\ *n, pl* **collicu·li** \-,lī, -lē\ [NL, fr. L] *anat* **:** PROMINENCE; *specif* **:** any of the four prominences constituting the corpora quadrigemina — see INFERIOR COLLICULUS, SUPERIOR COLLICULUS

col·lide \kə'līd\ *vb* -ED/-ING/-S [L *collidere*, fr. *com-* + *laedere* to injure] *vt, archaic* **:** to strike against ~ *vi* **1 a :** to become impelled into violent contact ⟨waves *colliding* with the rocks⟩ **b :** to strike or dash together in collision typically by accident with a degree of force and shock and with solid rather than glancing or sideswiping impact ⟨the car and truck *collided*⟩ ⟨the car *collided* with the truck⟩ **2 :** to meet in sharp direct opposition **:** be sharply, forcefully, and directly at variance, in discord, disagreement, or conflict ⟨liberty, equality, fraternity . . . these three ideas *collided* with the vested interests of decaying monarchy and feudal privilege —Stringfellow Barr⟩ **syn** see BUMP

col·li·dine \'kälə,dēn, -,dən\ *n* -s [ISV *coll-* + *-idine*] **:** any of a number of organic bases $C_8H_{11}N$ that are the trimethyl, methyl-ethyl, and propyl homologues of pyridine, that are in general pungent oily poisonous liquids, and are obtained chiefly as by-products in the coking process or are synthesized: as **a :** the liquid symmetrical trimethyl homolog made by reaction of acetone and ammonia and used as a solvent in chromatography — called also *s-collidine, 2,4,6-collidine, 2,4,6-trimethylpyridine* **b :** METHYLETHYLPYRIDINE

col·lie \'kälē, -li\ *n* -s [prob. fr. ²*colly*] **1 :** a dog of a breed developed in Scotland and used for generations in herding sheep, standing 20 to 24 inches at the shoulder, weighing 50 to 60 pounds, having a long pointed muzzle with little or no stop, and occurring in two varieties, the long-haired with profuse coat, very full ruff and feathering, and plumy tail, and the less common short-haired with somewhat harsh close coat **2 :** OLIVE WOOD

collied *adj* [fr. past part. of ¹*colly*] *now chiefly dial Brit* **:** blackened as if by colly **:** SOOTY

¹**col·lier** \'kälyə(r), *chiefly Brit* -lēə(r)\ *n* -s [ME *colier*, fr. *col* coal + *-ier* — more at COAL] **1 :** one that produces charcoal by burning wood in a beehive kiln **2 a** *obs* **:** a charcoal or coal dealer **b :** a coal miner **3 :** a ship employed in transporting coal **4 a :** BEAN APHID **b** *dial Eng* **:** a swift (*Apus apus*) **c :** WILSON'S PLOVER

²**collier** *comparative of* COLLY

col·liery \'kälyərē, -ri\ *n* -ES [*collier* + *-y*] **:** a coal mine and the buildings connected with it

collies *pres 3d sing of* COLLY, *pl of* COLLY

col·lie·shang·ie \'kälē,shaŋē\ *n* -s [perh. fr. *collie* (cur) + *shang* kind of meal (perh. fr. ScGael *seang* thin, hungry-looking) + *-ie*; akin to OIr *seng* thin, OE *swancor* pliable, MHG *swanger* swaying, ON *svangr* thin, hungry, OE *swingan* to beat, flog — more at SWING] *Scot* **:** SQUABBLE, BRAWL, UPROAR

colliest *superlative of* COLLY

col·li·gate \'kälə,gāt, *usu* -ād·+V\ *vt* -ED/-ING/-S [L *colligatus*, past part. of *colligare*, fr. *com-* + *ligare* to tie — more at LIGATURE] **1 :** to bind, unite, or group together often according to a subsuming principle ⟨*colligating* a number of instances⟩ **2 :** to bring together (isolated facts) inductively to organize under one conception or elicit a general principle

col·li·ga·tion \,==ˈgāshən\ *n* -s [L *colligation-, colligatio*, fr. *colligatus* + *-ion-, -io* -ion] **1 :** CONNECTION, CONJUNCTION

2 : the act or process of colligating ⟨the truth emerges spontaneously and directly from a sufficiently thorough ~ of particular instances —*Times Lit. Supp.*⟩

col·li·ga·tive \ˈkälə,gād·iv, kəˈligəd·-\ *adj* [ISV *colligat-* (fr. L *colligatus*) + *-ive;* orig. formed as G *kolligativ*] **:** depending on or varying according to the number of particles (as molecules, atoms, and ions) and not on or according to nature ⟨gaseous pressure is a ~ property⟩

col·li·mate \ˈkälə,māt, *usu* -ād.+V\ *vt* -ED/-ING/-S [NL *collimatus*, past part. of *collimare*, var. reading in some editions for L *collineare*] **1 a :** to render parallel to a certain line or direction **b :** to render parallel (as rays of light) **2 :** to adjust the line of sight of (a transit or level) to proper position relative to the other parts **3 :** to set the fiducial marks of (a surveying camera) so that they define the principal point (as in photogrammetry)

collimating lens *n* **:** a lens used for producing parallel rays of light

col·li·ma·tion \,==ˈmāshən\ *n* -s [NL *collimatus* + E *-ion*] **1 :** the act of collimating **2 :** the state of being collimated

col·li·ma·tor \ˈ==,mād·ə(r)\ *n* -s **1 :** a device for producing a beam of parallel rays of light or other radiation or for forming an infinitely distant virtual image that can be viewed without parallax usu. consisting of a tube having an objective lens at the end toward the observer and a slit or cross hairs in the objective focal plane at the other end — see SPECTROMETER illustration **2 :** a device for obtaining a beam of molecules, atoms, or nuclear particles of limited cross section and moving in parallel lines

col·lin·ear \kəˈlinēə(r), (ˈ)kō¦l-, (ˈ)kä¦l-\ *adj* [ISV *com-* + *linear*] **1 :** lying in the same straight line **2 :** having a straight line in common ⟨~ intersecting planes⟩ — **col·lin·ear·ly** *adv*

col·lin·ea·tion \=,==ˈāshən\ *n* -s [NL *collineation-, collineatio*, fr. L *collineatus* (past part. of *collineare* to direct in a straight line, fr. *com-* + *lineare* to make straight, fr. *linea* line) + *-ion-, -io* -ion — more at LINE] **:** a mathematical transformation in which collinear elements (as points or lines) are transferred as corresponding elements to another plane or space

colling *n* -s [fr. pres. part. of ¹*coll*] *now dial Eng* **:** EMBRACING, PETTING

col·lin·gual \kəˈliŋgwəl, (ˈ)kō¦l-, (ˈ)kä¦l-\ *adj* [*com-* + *lingual*] **:** using the same language

¹col·lins \ˈkälənz\ *n* -ES *sometimes cap* [prob. fr. the name *Collins*] **:** a tall drink that is served iced in a large tumbler and that has a gin, whiskey, rum, brandy, or vodka base to which are added sugar, carbonated water, and lemon or lime juice

²collins \"\ *n* -ES [after William *Collins*, character in *Pride and Prejudice* (1813), by Jane Austen †1817 Eng. novelist] *Brit* **:** a bread-and-butter letter

col·lin·sia \kəˈlinzēə, -sēə\ *n* [NL, fr. Zaccheus *Collins* †1831 Am. botanist + NL *-ia*] **1** *cap* **:** a genus of U.S. biennial or annual herbs (family Scrophulariaceae) with irregular whorled flowers **2** -s **:** any plant of the genus *Collinsia*

col·lins·ite \ˈkälən,zīt\ *n* -s [William H. *Collins* †1937 Can. geologist + E *-ite*] **:** a mineral consisting of a hydrous phosphate of calcium, magnesium, and iron $Ca_2(Mg,Fe)(PO_4)_2 \cdot 2H_2O$ occurring in concentric layers in phosphorite nodules

col·lin·so·nia \,kälənˈsōnēə\ *n* [NL, fr. Peter *Collinson* †1768 Eng. naturalist + NL *-ia*] **1** *cap* **:** a genus of aromatic herbs (family Labiatae) with large ovate leaves and terminal spikes of yellow flowers — see HORSE BALM **2** -s **:** any plant of the genus *Collinsonia*

colliquate *vt* -ED/-ING/-S [NL *colliquatus*, past part. of *colliquare*, fr. L *com-* + *liquare* to melt; akin to *liquor* liquid — more at LIQUID] *obs* **:** MELT

col·li·qua·tion \,kälə'kwāzhən, -āsh-\ *n* -s [F, fr. MF, fr. NL *colliquatus* + MF *-ion*] **1** *obs* **:** the action or process of melting, liquefying, or fusing **2** *med* **:** the breakdown and liquefaction of tissue

col·liq·ua·tive \ˈkälə,kwād·iv, kəˈlikwəd·iv\ *adj* [F *colliquatif*, fr. MF, fr. NL *colliquatus* + MF *-if* -ive] **:** causing colliquation

col·li·sion \kəˈlizhən\ *n* -s *often attrib* [ME, fr. L *collision-, collisio*, fr. *collisus* (past part. of *collidere* to collide) + *-ion-, -io* -ion] **1 :** the action or an instance of colliding, violent encounter, or forceful striking together typically by accident and so as to harm or impede ⟨a ~ between the two ships⟩ ⟨the ~ of the car with the trolley⟩ **2 :** a clashing meeting **:** a coming together of things opposed or diverse **:** ENCOUNTER **: a :** a meeting in sharp direct opposition **:** DISAGREEMENT ⟨when the English expansion had at length come into ~ with the borders of the French forest preserve —*Encyc. Americana*⟩ **b :** an unpleasant discordant juxtaposition of sounds ⟨the ~ of difficult consonant clusters in some words⟩ **c :** an encounter or impingement marked by activity or consequence; *sometimes* **:** a noteworthy accidental juxtaposition ⟨the fruits that spring from an intercourse and ~ with other minds from other mental regions —Van Wyck Brooks⟩ ⟨the unexpected ~ of incidents —Thomas Hardy⟩ **d :** an encounter between particles (as atoms or molecules) resulting in exchange or transformation of energy **syn** see IMPACT

col·li·sion·al \-zhənᵊl, -zhnəl\ *adj* **:** marked by or ensuing from a collision

collision bulkhead *n* **:** the first watertight bulkhead in the forward part of a ship designed to keep out water in the event of a collision

collision clause *n* **:** a policy provision that the insurer agrees to assume the legal liability of an insured shipowner to owners of another vessel and its cargo for loss resulting from collision with the insured ship

collision course *n* **:** a course (as of a ship, plane, or antiaircraft shell) that will result in a collision if continued unaltered

collision insurance *n* **:** insurance provided for a motor-vehicle owner against damage to the motor vehicle due to collision with another object

collision mat *n* **:** a large canvas or heavy rope mat used to close a hole made in a ship's side (as by a collision or explosion)

collo- — see COLL-

col·lo·blast \ˈkälə,blast\ *n* -s (*coll-* + *-blast*) **:** ADHESIVE CELL

col·lo·cal \kəˈlōkəl, (ˈ)kō¦l-\ *adj* [*com-* + *local*] **:** present in or belonging to the same place with another

col·lo·ca·lia \,käləˈkālēə\ *n, cap* [NL, fr. *coll-* + Gk *kalia* nest — more at HALL] **:** a genus of small chiefly cave-nesting swifts (family Apodidae) which produce the edible bird's nests

col·lo·cate \ˈkälə,kāt, *usu* -ād.+V\ *vt* -ED/-ING/-S [L *collocatus*, past part. of *collocare*, fr. *com-* + *locare* to place, fr. *locus* place — more at STALL] **:** to set or arrange in a place or position; *esp* **:** to set side by side

col·lo·ca·tion \,==ˈkāshən\ *n* -s [L *collocation-, collocatio*, fr. *collocatus* + *-ion-, -io* -ion] **:** the act or result of placing or arranging esp. with something else ⟨outcome of accidental ~s of atoms —Bertrand Russell⟩; *often* **:** a noticeable arrangement or conjoining of words or other linguistic elements ⟨the ~ of these two names — that of an elderly French marquise and of an English actor —L.P.Smith⟩

col·lo·ca·tive \ˈ==,kād·iv\ *adj* [*collocate* + *-ive*] **:** of, relating to, or similar to collocation **:** tending to collocate

col·lo·chore \ˈkälə,kō(ə)r\ *n* -s [*coll-* + Gk *chōros* place — more at CHOR-] **:** a specialized segment of certain chromosomes that functions like a chiasma in bivalent formation and is thought to be lacking in genes and comparable to a centromere

col·loc·u·tor \kəˈläkyəd·ə(r), kōˈ- ˈkälə,kyüd·ə(r)\ *n* -s [It & LL; It *collocutore*, fr. LL *collocutor*, fr. L *collocutus* (past part. of *colloqui* to converse, fr. *com-* + *loqui* to speak) + *-or*] **:** a person to or with whom one speaks

collodio- *comb form* [*collodion*] **:** collodion ⟨*collodiotype*⟩

col·lo·di·on \kəˈlōdēən\ *n* -s *often attrib* [modif. of NL *collodium*, fr. Gk *kollōdēs* glutinous (fr. *kolla* glue + *-eidēs* -oid) + NL *-ium* — more at COLL-] **:** a viscous solution of pyroxylin in a mixture of alcohol and ether or sometimes in some other solvent (as acetone) used chiefly as a coating for wounds and for photographic films and plates and as a membrane (as for dialysis)

collodion cotton *n* **:** PYROXYLIN 1

col·lo·di·on·ize \-dēə,nīz\ *vt* -ED/-ING/-S [*collodion* + *-ize*] **:** to treat with collodion

collodion process *n* **:** a photographic process in which collodion is used as a vehicle for sensitive salts; *specif* **:** an early process in which the negative is prepared by coating a glass plate with collodion containing iodide, exposing in a camera while wet, developing with pyrogallol or acidified ferrous sulfate, and fixing in a cyanide solution or hypo

col·lo·di·um \kəˈlōdēəm\ *n* -s [NL — more at COLLODION] **:** COLLODION

col·lo·form \ˈkälə,fȯrm\ *adj* [*coll-* + *-form*] **:** having the form or shape of a colloidal deposit **:** botryoidal, mammillary, and usu. internally banded concentrically

collogen *var of* COLLAGEN

col·logue \kəˈlōg\ *vi* -ED/-ING/-S [origin unknown] **1** *obs* **:** to employ flattery **:** speak cajolingly ⟨fawn on and ~ with some leader⟩ **2** *obs* **:** to feign assent or adherence **3** *dial* **:** INTRIGUE, CONSPIRE ⟨that villain . . . had been in the works *colloguing* with one of the men —Charles Reade⟩ **4 :** to talk privately **:** CONFER ⟨he *collogued* long of nights with the head-priest —Rudyard Kipling⟩

¹col·loid \ˈkä,lȯid\ *adj* [*coll-* + *-oid*] **:** COLLOIDAL

²colloid \"\ *n* -s [ISV *coll-* + *-oid;* prob. orig. formed as F *colloïde*] **1 a :** a substance (as gelatin, albumin, or starch) that, when apparently dissolved in water or other liquid, diffuses not at all or very slowly through a membrane and shows other special properties (as lack of pronounced effect on the freezing point or vapor pressure of the liquid); *also* **:** any substance (as an aggregate of atoms or molecules), whether a gas, liquid, or solid, in a fine state of subdivision with particles too small to be visible in an ordinary optical microscope that is dispersed in a continuous gaseous, liquid, or solid medium and does not settle or settles very slowly (as the liquid droplets in fog, solid particles in smoke, bubbles in foam, or gold particles in ruby glass) **b :** matter consisting of a colloid and the medium in which it is dispersed **:** DISPERSE SYSTEM — compare AEROSOL, CRYSTALLOID, EMULSION, GEL, MICELLE, SOIL COLLOID, SOL, SUSPENSION **2 :** a gelatinous or mucinous substance found in colloid degeneration and colloid carcinoma **3 :** a gelatinous substance in the vesicles in the thyroid gland and occas. in the interstices between the secreting cells that is thought to be the stored secretion

³colloid \", kəˈlȯid\ *vt* -ED/-ING/-S **:** to convert (cellulose nitrate in smokeless powder) into a colloidal state (as by treating with a mixture of ether and alcohol)

col·loi·dal \kəˈlȯidᵊl, (ˈ)kä¦l-\ *adj* [²*colloid* + *-al*] **:** of, relating to, or having the properties of a colloid ⟨~ state⟩ ⟨~ graphite⟩ — **col·loi·dal·i·ty** \,käl,ȯiˈdaləd·ē, ˈ==,===, -ətē, -i\ *n* -ES — **col·loi·dal·ly** \kəˈlȯidᵊlē, (ˈ)kä¦l-, -i\ *adv*

colloidal fuel *n* **:** a stabilized suspension of a solid fuel (as powdered coal) in an oil (as fuel oil)

colloidal gold test *n* **:** GOLD SOL TEST

colloid carcinoma *or* **colloid cancer** *n* **:** carcinoma characterized by excessive production of a colloidal or mucinous material

colloid chemistry *n* **1 :** the branch of chemistry that deals with colloids and colloidal phenomena **2 :** the branch of chemistry that deals with surfaces and large molecular particles

col·loid·er \kəˈlȯidə(r), ˈkä,lȯid-, ˈkä,l-\ *n* -s [³*colloid* + *-er*] **:** a mechanical device (as a filter) used to remove or coagulate colloidal matter in sewage or industrial wastes

col·loid·ize \-,dīz\ *vt* -ED/-ING/-S [²*colloid* + *-ize*] **:** to change into a colloid **:** COLLOID

colloid mill *n* **:** a machine utilizing shearing action for very fine grinding and dispersion esp. by breaking down the particles in an emulsion or paste to extremely fine dispersions of liquid or solid — compare HOMOGENIZER

col·loi·do·pexy \kəˈlȯidə,peksē, ˈkä,l-\ *n* -ES [ISV *colloid* + *-o-* + *-pexy;* orig. formed as F *colloïdopexie*] **:** the capacity of certain cells to ingest colloidal material

col·lo·mia \kəˈlōmēə\ *n* [NL, irreg. fr. Gk *kolla* glue; fr. the nature of the seed — more at PROTOCOL] **1** *cap* **:** a genus of herbs (family Polemoniaceae) found in western No. America with alternate leaves and terminal clusters of phloxlike flowers **2** -s **:** any plant or flower of the genus *Collomia*

¹col·lop \ˈkäləp\ *n* -s [ME *colope, colhoppe* egg fried on bacon] **1 :** a small piece or slice of meat; *sometimes* **:** a rasher of bacon **2 :** a fold of fat flesh **3 :** SLICE, PIECE, PORTION

²col·lop \ˈkäləp, ˈkōl-\ *also* **colp** \ˈkälp, ˈkōlp\ *n* -s [IrGael *colpa*, lit., full-grown horse or cow] **1 :** an Irish measure of quantity or quality of land based on the grazing requirements of an adult cow or horse (reckoned as an acre of good land) **2 a :** a cow or horse or a grazing equivalent in sheep **b :** the pasturage for one of these for a year

col·loped \ˈkäləpt\ *adj* [¹*collop* + *-ed*] **:** cut up into collops ⟨~ venison⟩

col·lo·phane \ˈkälə,fān\ *or* **col·loph·a·nite** \kəˈläfə,nīt, ˈkäləf-\ *n* -s [ISV *coll-* + *-phan* or *-phane* + *-ite;* orig. formed as G *kollophan*] **:** any of the massive cryptocrystalline varieties of apatite, often opaline or horny in appearance, used as a source of phosphate for fertilizers; *usu* **:** a hydroxylapatite containing carbonate

col·lo·phore \ˈkälə,fō(ə)r\ *n* -s [*coll-* + *-phore*] **:** a thick median tubular pouch usu. terminating in a bilobate vesicle and projecting from the ventral surface of the first abdominal segment of all members of the order Collembola

col·loque \kəˈlōk\ *vi* -ED/-ING/-S [L *colloqui* — more at COLLOQUY] **:** CONVERSE

colloquia [L] *pl of* COLLOQUIUM

¹col·lo·qui·al \kəˈlōkwēəl\ *adj* [*colloquy* + *-al*] **1 :** of or relating to conversation **:** expressed in conversation **:** CONVERSATIONAL **2 :** used in or characteristic of conversation, esp. familiar and informal conversation ⟨~ English⟩ ⟨a letter written in ~ style⟩ ⟨the great majority [of the common words of English are] at once literary and ~ —*Oxford English Dict.*⟩ **:** using or characterized by conversational style ⟨a ~ poet⟩

²colloquial \"\ *n* -s **:** colloquial style or diction **:** a colloquial language or dialect ⟨literary Chinese and the various ~s⟩

col·lo·qui·al·ism \-,lizəm\ *n* -s **1 a :** an expression considered more appropriate to familiar conversation than to formal speech or to formal writing ⟨slang words frequently rise to the rank of ~s —G.L.Kittredge⟩ **b :** an expression belonging to local or regional dialect — not used technically **2 :** informal or conversational style in language ⟨the appeal of Wordsworth's ~⟩

col·lo·qui·al·ist \-,ləst\ *n* -s **:** CONVERSATIONALIST

col·lo·qui·al·i·ty \kə,lōkwēˈaləd·ē, -ətē, -i\ *n* -ES **:** colloquial quality or style; *also* **:** an instance of this

col·lo·qui·al·ize \kəˈlōkwēə,līz\ *vb* -ED/-ING/-S **:** to write employing colloquialisms

col·lo·qui·al·ly \-əlē, -i\ *adv* **:** in a colloquial manner **:** with use of colloquial expressions **:** CONVERSATIONALLY

col·lo·qui·al·ness *n* -ES **:** the quality or state of being colloquial

col·lo·quist \ˈkäləkwəst\ *n* -s [*colloquy* + *-ist*] **:** COLLOCUTOR, TALKER

col·lo·qui·um \kəˈlōkwēəm\ *n, pl* **colloqui·ums** \-ēəmz\ *or* **collo·quia** \-ēə\ [L] **1** *obs* **:** CONVERSATION **2 :** the part of the plaintiff's pleading in an action for slander that avers that the defendant spoke the slanderous words concerning the plaintiff or the subject matter in question in a certain conversation **3 a :** discussion meeting **:** CONFERENCE; *specif* **:** a seminar that several lecturers take turns in leading **b :** a lecture prepared for such a seminar

col·lo·quize \ˈkälə,kwīz\ *vi* -ED/-ING/-S [L *colloquium* + E *-ize*] **:** to hold colloquy **:** CONVERSE

col·lo·quy \ˈkäləkwē, -wi\ *n* -ES [L *colloquium* conversation, fr. *colloqui* to converse, fr. *com-* + *loqui* to speak] **1 a :** CONVERSATION, DIALOGUE ⟨a ~ between two old Connecticut codgers gossiping —Dixon Wecter⟩ ⟨a ~ between senators⟩ **b :** high-level serious discussion **:** CONFERENCE ⟨the Sino-Soviet ~ for drafting new treaties —*Current Biog.*⟩ **2 :** an ecclesiastical court much like the presbytery of Presbyterian churches formerly existing in certain churches with a presbyterian polity (as the Reformed Church in France)

coll'ot·ta·va \(ˈ)kōlōˈtävə, -lə'-\ *adv (or adj)* [It, with the octave] **:** with the addition of the octave above or the octave below the note on the written score — used as a direction in music; abbr. *coll' 8*

col·lo·type \ˈkälə,tīp\ *n* -s [ISV *coll-* + *type*] **1 :** a photomechanical process for making prints directly from a hardened film of gelatin or other colloid, the sensitized film being exposed under a reversed negative, desensitized, and then soaked in glycerin and salt water to cause swelling in the parts that have not been exposed to light, the swelled parts becoming ink-repellent and the unswelled parts ink-receptive, thereby forming a printing surface that functions on the lithographic principle — called also *photogelatin process* **2 :** a print made by collotype

col·low \ˈkälō\ *dial Eng var of* COLLY

colls *pres 3d sing of* COLL

col·luc·ta·tion \,käləkˈtāshən\ *n* -s [L *colluctation-, colluctatio*, fr. *colluctatus* (past part. of *colluctari* to struggle, fr. *com-* + *luctari*) + *-ion-, -io* -ion — more at LOCK] **:** STRUGGLE

col·lude \kəˈlüd\ *vi* -ED/-ING/-S [L *colludere*, fr. *com-* + *ludere* to play, fr. *ludus* game — more at LUDICROUS] **:** to connive with another **:** CONSPIRE, PLOT

col·lum \ˈkäləm\ *n, pl* **col·la** \-lə\ [L, neck — more at COLLAR] **1** *anat* **:** a neck or necklike part or process **2 :** COLLET 3

col·lu·nar·i·um \,käləˈna(a)rēəm\ *n, pl* **collunar·ia** \-ēə\ [NL, fr. L *colluere* to wash out, rinse + *nares* nostrils, nose + NL *-ium* — more at COLLUVIES, NOSE] **:** a medicated solution for instillation into the nostrils as a wash or spray or as drops

col·lu·sion \kəˈlüzhən\ *n* -s [ME *colluciounn*, fr. MF *collusion*, fr. L *collusion-, collusio*, fr. *collusus* (past part. of *colludere*) + *-ion-, -io* -ion] **:** secret agreement **:** secret cooperation for a fraudulent or deceitful purpose ⟨acting in ~ with the enemy⟩: as **a :** a secret agreement between two or more persons to defraud a person of his rights often by the forms of law **b :** agreement between parties considered adversaries at the law (as in a divorce proceeding) **c :** a secret agreement considered illegal for any reason

col·lu·sive \-ˈlüs|iv, -lüz|, |ēv also |əv\ *adj* [*collusion* + *-ive*] **1 :** constituting, marked by, or done with collusion **:** FRAUDULENT ⟨~ agreement between pope and king —G.M.Trevelyan⟩ ⟨~ bidding arrangements by contractors ostensibly competing⟩ **2 :** given to or acting in collusion ⟨~ parties —Edmund Burke⟩ — **col·lu·sive·ly** *adv*

col·lu·so·ry \-|ərē\ *adj* [F *collusoire*, fr. *collusion* + *-oire* -ory] **:** COLLUSIVE

col·lu·to·ri·um \,käləˈtōrēəm, -tȯr-\ *n, pl* **colluto·ria** \-rēə\ [NL, fr. L *collutus* (past part. of *colluere*) + *-orium*] **:** MOUTHWASH

col·lu·vi·al \kəˈlüvēəl\ *adj* [*colluvies* + *-al*] **:** indicating, relating to, or marked by colluvium

col·lu·vi·a·tion \kə,lüvēˈāshən\ *n* -s [*colluvies* + *-ation*] **:** a process that produces colluvial deposits

col·lu·vi·es \kəˈlüvē,ēz\ *n, pl* **colluvies** [L, collection of washings, dregs, offscourings, fr. *colluere* to wash, fr. *com-* + *-luere* (fr. *lavere* to wash) — more at LYE] **:** COLLECTION, GATHERING: **a :** an accumulation of foulness **b :** HOTCHPOTCH, JUMBLE ⟨a ~ of low characters⟩

col·lu·vi·um \-vēəm\ *n, pl* **collu·via** \-vēə\ *or* **colluvi·ums** \-mz\ [ML, alter. of L *colluvies*] **:** a heterogeneous mass of rock detritus or soil material emplaced primarily by gravitational processes on or at the foot of slopes; *also* **:** alluvium emplaced at the foot of slopes by creek and slope wash

¹col·ly \ˈkälē, -li\ *vt* -ED/-ING/-ES [alter. (influenced by ²*colly*) of ME *colwen*, fr. (assumed) OE *colgian*, fr. *col* coal — more at COAL] *dial chiefly Brit* **:** to blacken with or as if with soot or smut

²colly \"\ *adj, often* -ER/-EST [earlier *colie*, fr. (assumed) ME *coly*, fr. ME *cole* coal + *-y*] *dial chiefly Brit* **:** grimed with or as if with coal dust or soot **:** BLACK

³colly \"\ *n* -ES *chiefly dial Brit* **:** SOOT, SMUT

⁴colly \"\ *n* -ES *dial Eng* **:** BLACKBIRD

col·ly·ba *or* **col·y·ba** \ˈkäləbə\ *n pl* [Gk *kollyba* sweet cakes, pl. of *kollybon*, prob. alter. of *kollybos* small coin] **:** small sweet cakes made of crushed wheat, raisins, nuts, almonds, and honey, and blessed and distributed on certain commemorative occasions in the Eastern Church

col·lyb·ia \kəˈlibēə\ *n, cap* [NL, fr. Gk *kollybos* small coin + NL *-ia*] **:** a genus of white-spored agarics (family Agaricaceae) lacking both volva and ring, having the thin fleshy cap incurved when young, and including some forms that are on tree roots

collyria *pl of* COLLYRIUM

col·lyr·i·clum \kəˈlirəkləm\ *n, cap* [NL, alter. of L *collyriolum* (prob. read as *collyriclum*), dim. of *collyrium*] **:** a genus of digenetic trematodes (family Troglotrematidae) including a form (*C. faba*) commonly encountered encysted in the skin of chickens, turkeys, and various wild birds exposed to marshy environment

col·ly·rid·i·an \,käləˈridēən\ *n* -s *usu cap* [ML *Collyridianus*, fr. LL *collyrida* thin cake of bread, fr. Gk *kollyrid-, kollyris*, dim. of *kollyra* roll of bread] **:** one of a heretical sect in the 4th and 5th centuries chiefly in Arabia that employed women as priestesses to offer sacrifices in the form of rolls of bread to the Virgin Mary

col·lyr·i·um \kəˈlirēəm\ *n, pl* **collyr·ia** \-rēə\ *or* **collyri·ums** \-mz\ [L, fr. Gk *kollyrion* eye salve, pessary, suppository, dim. of *kollyra* roll of bread] **:** an eye lotion **:** EYEWASH

col·ly·wob·bles \ˈkälē,wäbəlz\ *n pl but sing or pl in constr* [prob. by folk etymology (influence of *colic* and *wobble*) fr. NL *cholera morbus*] **:** a slight intestinal usu. diarrheal disturbance accompanied by abdominal cramps **:** BELLYACHE

col·mar \ˈkälmə(r)\ *n* -s *sometimes cap* [perh. fr. *Colmar*, France] **:** a fan in fashion in Queen Anne's reign

col·ma·tage \ˈkälməd·ij\ *n* -s [F, fr. *colmater* to impound silt-laden water (fr. *colmate* silt, fr. It *colmata*, fr. *colmare* to heap up, to build up by silt-laden water, fr. *colmo* top, summit, fr. L *culmin-, culmen*) + *-age* — more at HILL] *NewZeal* **:** the impounding of silt-laden water to build up low-lying areas

coln *abbr* column

colo *abbr* colophon

colo- — see ²COL-

colobi *pl of* COLOBUS

col·o·bin \ˈkäləbən\ *n* -s [F, fr. NL *Colobinae* (subfamily of apes), fr. *Colobus* type genus + *-inae*] **:** a monkey of the genus *Colobus*

co·lo·bi·um \kəˈlōbēəm\ *n, pl* **colo·bia** \-bēə\ [LL, fr. LGk *kolobion*, fr. Gk *kolobos* docked, curtailed — more at HALT] **:** a sleeveless or short-sleeved tunic used as an ecclesiastical vestment **:** a similar garment worn as a coronation robe

col·o·bo·ma \,käləˈbōmə\ *n, pl* **coloboma·ta** \-məd·ə\ [NL, fr. Gk *kolobōma* part taken away in mutilation, fr. *koloboun* to mutilate, fr. *kolobos* docked] **:** a fissure of the eye usu. of congenital origin — **col·o·bo·ma·tous** \¦==¦bōməd·əs\ *adj*

col·o·bus \ˈkäləbəs\ *n* [NL, fr. Gk *kolobos* docked, mutilated; fr. the rudimentary thumbs] **1** *cap* **:** a genus of slender long-tailed African monkeys sometimes made the type of a separate family but usu. included in the Cercopithecidae **2** *pl* **colobi** \-,bī, -,bē\ *or* -ES **:** GUEREZA

col·o·ca·sia \,käləˈkāzh(ē)ə\ *n, cap* [NL, fr. L, East Indian lotus, fr. Gk *kolokasia, kolokasion*, lit., root of the East Indian lotus] **:** a small genus of Asiatic and Polynesian tuberous-rooted aroids having the spadix terminated by a club-shaped or subulate appendage — see TARO

col·o·ceph·a·li \,käləˈsefə,lī\ *n pl, cap* [NL, fr. *colo-* (fr. Gk *kolos* docked, hornless) + *-cephali* (pl. of *-cephalus* -cephalous) — more at HALT] *in some classifications* **:** a suborder of Apodes consisting of the morays — **col·o·ceph·a·lous** \¦==¦sefələs\ *adj*

col·o·col·ic \¦kälə¦kälik, ¦kōl-\ *adj* [²*col-* + *colic*] **:** relating to two parts of the colon

col·o·cynth \ˈkälə,sinth\ *n* -s [L *colocynthis*, fr. Gk *kolokynthis*] **1** *or* **colocynth apple :** a Mediterranean and African herbaceous vine (*Citrullus colocynthis*) which is related to the watermelon and from which a powerful cathartic is prepared — called also *bitter apple, bitter cucumber, bitter gourd* **2 :** the spongy fruit of the colocynth

co·logarithm \(ˈ)kō+\ *n* -s [*co-* + *logarithm*] **:** the logarithm of the reciprocal

¹co·logne \kəˈlōn\ *adj, usu cap* [fr. *Cologne*, Germany] **:** of or from the city of Cologne, Germany **:** of the kind or style prevalent in Cologne

²cologne \"\ *n* -s [short for *Cologne water*, trans. of F *eau de Cologne*, fr. *Cologne*, Germany, where it was manufactured] **1** *also* **cologne water** *sometimes cap C* **:** a perfumed liquid composed of alcohol and certain aromatic oils chiefly derived from the citrus family and used as a toilet water — called also *eau de Cologne* **2 :** a cream or paste of cologne sometimes formed into a semisolid stick

cologne brown *n, usu cap C* [trans. of G *Kölner braun*, *Kölner erde*, fr. *Cologne* (*Köln*), Germany, where it was discov-

ered] **1** or **cologne earth :** VANDYKE BROWN 1b **2 :** VANDYKE BROWN 2
cologne plant *n* [²cologne] **:** COSTMARY
cologne spirit *or* **cologne spirits** *n, usu cap C* [²cologne] **:** ethyl alcohol in 95 percent concentration
cologne ware *n, usu cap C* **:** a glazed stoneware mottled with gray and brown and made into tankards and jugs esp. in the 16th and 17th centuries — called also *grès de Flandres*
cologne yellow *n* **1** *usu cap C* **:** a pigment composed essentially of chrome yellow containing lead chromate and lead sulfate **2** *often cap C* **:** LIGHT CHROME YELLOW
colomba *var of* CALUMBA
co·lom·bia \kə'ləmbēə, -'lōm-\ *adj, usu cap* [fr. *Colombia*, country in So. America] **:** of or from Colombia **:** of the kind or style prevalent in Colombia **:** COLOMBIAN
¹co·lom·bi·an \-bēən\ *adj, usu cap* [*Colombia*, country in So. America + E *-an*] **1 :** of, relating to, or characteristic of Colombia **2 :** of, relating to, or characteristic of Colombians
²colombian \"\ *n* -s *cap* **:** a native or resident of Colombia
colombian mahogany *n, usu cap C* **1 :** a tropical American timber tree (*Cariniana pyriformis*) **2 :** the wood of the Colombian mahogany often sold as true mahogany — called also *albarco*
colombin *var of* COLUMBIN
¹colombo *var of* CALUMBA
²co·lom·bo \kə'ləm(,)bō\ *adj, usu cap* [fr. *Colombo*, Ceylon] **1 :** of or from Colombo, the capital of Ceylon **:** of the kind or style prevalent in Colombo **2** [fr. the first conference's having taken place in Colombo] **:** of, concerning, or participated in by India, Pakistan, Burma, Ceylon, and Indonesia ⟨the *Colombo* plan⟩
co·lo·met·ric \¦kōlə¦me·trik, ¦käl-\ *adj* **:** of or relating to colometry — **co·lo·met·ric·al·ly** \-trək(ə)lē, -li\ *adv*
co·lom·e·trize \kə'lämə,trīz, 'kōləm-,'käləm-\ *vt* -ED/-ING/-S **:** to analyze or divide into cola **:** apply colometry to ⟨~ a manuscript or verse⟩
co·lom·e·try \kə'lämətrē, -ri\ *n* -ES [MGk *kōlometria*, fr. Gk *kōlo-* (fr. *kōlon* part of a strophe) + *-metria* -metry — more at COLON] **:** measurement or division (as of a manuscript or a rhythmic utterance) by cola
¹co·lon \'kōlən, -,län\ *n, pl* **colons** \-nz\ *or* **co·la** \-lə\ [L, large intestine, fr. Gk *kolon*; perh. akin to Lith *skilvis* belly, Arm *k'aird* guts] **1 :** the part of the large intestine that extends from the cecum to the rectum and in man is divided into an initial portion which passes up on the right side of the abdomen, a midportion which passes across to the left side, a descending portion which passes downward on the left side, and a terminal tortuous portion continuous with the rectum — called respectively (1) *ascending colon*, (2) *transverse colon*, (3) *descending colon*, (4) *sigmoid flexure* — see DIGESTION illustration **2 :** the second division of an insect's intestine
²colon \"\ *n, pl* **colons** *or* **cola** *see numbered senses* [L, part of a poem, fr. Gk *kōlon* limb, part of a strophe, clause of a sentence — more at CALK] **1** *pl* **cola a :** a rhythmical unit of an utterance: (1) *in Greek or Latin verse* **:** a system or series of from two to not more than six feet having a principal accent and forming part of a line (2) **:** a division of an utterance by sense or rhythm that is smaller and less independent than the sentence and larger and less dependent than the phrase — compare COMMA, PERIOD **b :** a unit that is used in measuring the length of manuscripts and that is equal to what was regarded as the average length of a colon **2** *pl* **colons a :** the punctuation mark **:** used before an explanation, example, definition, restatement, recapitulation, quotation, appositive, or list and esp. after or in place of such expressions as *namely*, *as follows* or sometimes between the clauses of a compound sentence esp. when no conjunction is used and when the clauses balance each other antithetically **b :** the sign **:** used between the parts of a numerical expression of time in hours and minutes (as in 1:15) or in hours, minutes, and seconds (as in 8:25:30), of a bibliographical reference (as in *Nation* 130:20), a ratio where it is usually read as "to" (as in 4:1 read "four to one"), or a proportion where it is usually read as "is to" or when doubled as "as" (as in 2:1::8:4 read "two is to one as eight is to four")
³co·lon \'kō,lān, kə'lōn\ *n* -s [L *colonus* colonist, farmer, inhabitant — more at COLONY] **:** a colonial farmer, planter, or plantation owner
⁴co·lon \kə'lōn, kō'l-\ *n, pl* **co·lo·nes** \-,nās\ *also* **colons** \-nz\ [Sp *colón*, after Cristóbal *Colón* Christopher Columbus — more at COLUMBIAN] **1 :** the basic monetary unit of Costa Rica and El Salvador — see MONEY table **2 :** a coin representing one colon **3 :** a Salvadoran note representing one colon
colon bacillus *n* [¹colon] **:** any of a number of bacilli esp. of the genera *Escherichia* and *Aerobacter* normally commensal in vertebrate intestines or living in soil and only occas. of pathogenic significance although one species (*E. coli*) may be implicated in urinary tract and biliary infections and in a variety of suppurative lesions esp. in the tropics and another (*A. aerogenes*) has been reported as a cause of cystitis
colon crayfish *n, often cap first C* [¹colon] **:** a common Central American crayfish (*Macrobrachium jamaicense*)
col·o·nel \'kərnᵊl, 'kōnᵊl\ *n* -s [alter. (influenced by MF or OIt; MF *colonel*, fr. OIt *colonnello*) of earlier *coronel*, fr. MF, modif. of OIt *colonnello* column of soldiers, colonel, dim. of *colonna* column, fr. L *columna* — more at COLUMN] **1 :** an army, marine, or air force officer ranking below a brigadier general and above a lieutenant colonel and entitled to the insignia of a silver eagle **2 :** a minor purely titular officer or official of a state or similar instrumentality esp. in southern or midland U.S. — used as an honorific title without much significance and without military rating; used sometimes of an auctioneer or drummer **3 :** a Salvation Army officer ranking above a lieutenant colonel and below a lieutenant commissioner
colonel blimp *n, cap C&B* [after *Colonel Blimp*, a cartoon character created by David Low *b*1891 British cartoonist] **:** an army officer or government official notoriously stuffy, pompous, short-sighted, and unobservant of or hostile to up-to-date procedures; *broadly* **:** an elderly pompous reactionary
col·o·nel·cy \-sē, -si\ *n* -ES **:** the office, rank, or commission of a colonel
colonel general *n, pl* **colonels general** *or* **colonel generals :** an officer in some foreign armies usu. equivalent to a U.S. full general
colonel-in-chief *n, pl* **colonels-in-chief** *or* **colonel-in-chiefs :** an honorary rank in some corps or regiments of foreign armies (as the British) usu. held by a member of a royal family or a distinguished military leader
co·longitude \(')kō+\ *n* -s [*co-* + *longitude*] **:** the complement of a longitude
coloni *pl of* COLONUS
¹co·lo·ni·al \kə'lōnyəl, -nēəl\ *adj* [F, fr. *colonie* colony (fr. OF) + *-al* — more at COLONY] **1 a :** of, for, or relating to a colony **:** having the characteristics or status of a colony ⟨~ possessions⟩ ⟨~ administration⟩ **b** *often cap* **:** of or relating to the 13 English colonies that first formed the United States of America: as (1) **:** made or prevailing in America during the colonial period ⟨a ~ spoon dated 1730⟩ ⟨~ architecture was a modification of English Georgian⟩ (2) **:** adapted from or reminiscent of an American colonial mode of design ⟨a ~ piano⟩ **c :** possessing colonies **:** composed of colonies ⟨Britain's ~ empire⟩ **d** (1) **:** of or relating to the period of A.D. 500–900 in southwestern U.S. characterized by Hohokam expansion (2) **:** of or relating to the period of Spanish overlordship in Mexico about 1535–1821 (3) **:** of or relating to the period about 1544–1824 in Peru characterized by a continuation of Spanish conquest and merging of native states **2** *biol* **:** forming, existing in, consisting of, or used by a colony ⟨a ~ organism (as *Volvox*)⟩ ⟨~ burrows⟩ — **co·lo·ni·al·ly** \-əlē, -li\ *adv* — **co·lo·ni·al·ness** *n* -ES
²colonial \"\ *n* -s **1 :** a member or inhabitant of a colony ⟨battles between Indians and the ~s⟩ ⟨British ~s in India⟩ **2 :** a low shoe with a broad flaring tongue and usu. a large buckle worn in the colonial days of America **3 a :** a product made for use in a colony; *specif* **:** a coin or stamp issued for use in a colony; *esp* **:** a coin of colonial America **b :** a security involving a colonial enterprise or development — usu. used in pl. **c :** a product showing colonial style
colonial bent *n* **:** RHODE ISLAND BENT
colonial blue *n* **:** a variable color averaging a moderate greenish blue that is bluer and paler than average peacock, greener and duller than Brittany, and bluer and duller than larkspur
colonial bouquet *n* **:** a small round bouquet with a paper backing showing
colonial buff *n* **:** BARIUM YELLOW 2
colonial dollar *n* **:** HOLEY DOLLAR
colonial furniture *n* **:** furniture made in the American colonies before the end of the Revolution and largely influenced by contemporary European styles (as the Queen Anne and Georgian) but having some indigenous features (as greater variety in woods and more extensive use of turnings)
colonial goose *n, Austral* **:** a boned leg of mutton stuffed with savory herbs
co·lo·ni·al·ism \kə'lōnēə,lizəm, -nyə,l-\ *n* -s **1 :** the quality or state of being colonial **2 :** a custom, idiom, idea, notion, or style characteristic of a colony **:** PROVINCIALISM **3 :** the aggregate of various economic, political, and social policies by which an imperial power maintains or extends its control over other areas or peoples **:** practice of or belief in acquiring and retaining colonies
¹co·lo·ni·al·ist \-ələst\ *n* -s [¹colonial + *-ist*] **:** an adherent or advocate of colonialism
²colonialist \"\ *adj* **:** marked by belief in or support or practice of colonialism
co·lo·ni·al·is·tic \kə¦lōnēə¦listik, -nyə¦l-\ *adj* **1 :** ²COLONIALIST **2 :** factitiously colonial in style or characteristics ⟨a building that is ~ rather than colonial⟩
co·lo·ni·al·i·za·tion \kə,lōnēələ'zāshən\ *n* -s **:** the act of colonializing or being colonialized; *esp* **:** subjugation by colonial policies ⟨outcries against ~ and economic imperialism —*Economist*⟩
co·lo·ni·al·ize \kə'lōnēə,līz, -nyə,l-\ *vt* -ED/-ING/-S [¹colonial + *-ize*] **:** to make colonial
colonial pine *n* **:** an Australian evergreen tree (*Araucaria cunninghamii*) that yields a soft timber
colonial rose *n* **:** a variable color averaging a dark pink that is less strong and slightly darker than wild rose and bluer and darker than dusty coral
colonial teak *n* **:** FLINDOSA
colonial yellow *n* **:** a moderate yellow that is greener, lighter, and stronger than brass, lighter and stronger than mustard yellow, and redder and lighter than quince yellow
co·lon·ic \(')kō¦länik, kə'l-\ *adj* [¹colon + *-ic*] *anat* **:** of or relating to the colon
col·o·nist \'kälənəst\ *n* -s [*colony* + *-ist*] **1 :** a member or inhabitant of a colony **2 :** one that colonizes or settles in a new country
col·o·ni·za·tion \,kälənə'zāshən, -,nī'z-\ *n* -s **1 :** the act of establishing colonies **:** the state of being colonized ⟨English ~ of America in the 17th century⟩ **2 a :** the placing of nonresidents in doubtful electoral districts and qualifying them to vote **b :** infiltration of zealous militants into a neutral, opposed, or uncertain group to alter its orientation ⟨left-wing ~ of the society⟩ **3 :** the resettlement chiefly in Africa of freed American Negro slaves by interested organizations **4 :** the spread and development of a species or other natural group in a new area
col·o·ni·za·tion·ist \-shənəst\ *n* -s **:** one that advocates resettling American Negroes in Africa
col·o·nize \'kälə,nīz\ *vb* -ED/-ING/-S *see -ize in Explan Notes* [*colony* + *-ize*] *vt* **1 a :** to establish a colony in or on **:** send out colonists to ⟨it may happen . . . that Venus may be *colonized* by the earth as America was once *colonized* by Europe —Waldemar Kaempffert⟩ **b :** to migrate to and settle in ⟨the French who *colonized* Canada⟩ **2 :** to send illegal or irregularly qualified voters into ⟨the machine was *colonizing* doubtful districts⟩ **3 :** to migrate to **:** come to live in as a new species ⟨forms which have been able to ~ cold regions —S.A. Cain⟩ **4 :** to infiltrate with usu. subversive militants for propaganda and strategy reasons ⟨the left-wingers *colonized* key industries with trusted party members⟩ **5 :** to isolate (as the feeble-minded) in supervised groups ⟨the chronic alcoholics, the psychopaths . . . some of these should be hospitalized and some *colonized* —L.N.Robinson⟩ ~ *vi* **1 :** to make or establish a colony **:** SETTLE ⟨~ in Africa⟩ **2** *of microorganisms* **:** to become established in a habitat (as a host or a wound) ⟨these bacteria in turn ~ in other parts of the body —R.A.Runnells⟩
col·o·niz·er \-zə(r)\ *n* -s **:** one that colonizes
col·on·nade \,kälə'nād, '==,=\ *n* -s [F, alter. of *collonate*, fr. It *colonnato*, fr. *colonna* column + *-ato* -ade — more at COLONEL] **1 :** a series or range of columns placed at regular intervals usu. with an architrave and sometimes with adjuncts (as pavement, stylobate, or roof) — see PERISTYLE, PORTICO **2 :** a row of trees, posts or other uprights suggestive of columns

colonnade 1

col·on·nad·ed \-ādəd\ *adj* **:** having a colonnade
col·on·nette \,kälə'net\ *n* -s [F, dim. of *colonne* column, fr. L *columna* — more at COLUMN] **:** a small column esp. in a group in a parapet, balustrade, or clustered column
colons *pl of* COLON
co·lo·nus \kə'lōnəs\ *n, pl* **colo·ni** \-,nī, -(,)nē\ [L] **:** a freeborn serf or tenant farmer in the later Roman Empire who could sometimes own property but who was bound to the land and obliged to pay a rent usu. in produce
col·o·ny \'kälənē, -ni *sometimes* 'käln-\ *n* -ES *often attrib* [ME *colonie*, fr. MF & L; MF *colonie*, fr. L *colonia*, fr. *colonus* colonist, farmer, inhabitant (fr. *colere* to cultivate, dwell) + *-ia* -y — more at WHEEL] **1 :** a body of people settled in a new territory, foreign and often distant, retaining ties with their motherland or parent state **:** a settlement in a new country **:** the territory inhabited by such a body or occupied by such a settlement **:** the body of descendants of settlers wholly or partially retaining their ideology and organization: **a :** a settlement made in hostile, newly conquered, or unstable country as a means of facilitating established occupation and governed by the parent state ⟨the Roman *colonies* in Gaul⟩ **b :** a settlement in a new territory enjoying a degree of autonomy or semiresponsible government without severing ties with the parent state and without attaining the more free status of a dominion — see CROWN COLONY; compare MANDATE, PROTECTORATE **c :** such a settlement including in its control autochthonous groups in any of a number of statuses **2 a :** a distinguishable localized population within a species (as a community of termites or bees) ⟨bird *colonies* on the islands and promontories —P.E.James⟩ **b :** a group of two or more kinds of organisms (as species or clones) usu. migrant into and developing in a barren area or the interstices of an existent ecological community; *often* **:** an incompletely developed community consisting of two or more kinds of organisms **c :** an assemblage of fossils apparently contained in rocks older than those in which they normally belong **3 a :** a circumscribed mass of microorganisms developed from a single cell or small cluster of cells, usu. growing in or upon a solid or semisolid medium — compare FAMILY **b :** the aggregation of zooids of a compound animal **c :** COENOBIUM **4 a :** a group of persons united by a common characteristic or interest living in a limited section surrounded by others not so united ⟨the American ~ in Paris⟩ ⟨New York City's Syrian ~⟩ ⟨an artist ~⟩ ⟨the film ~⟩; *also* **:** the section or quarter occupied by such a group **b :** a group of persons institutionalized away from others for some particular kind of care, treatment, correction, or punishment ⟨a leper ~⟩ ⟨a ~ for epileptics⟩ ⟨a penal ~⟩; *also* **:** the land or buildings occupied by such a group **c :** a cluster or somewhat discrete group (as of dwellings) usu. with common characteristics or functions ⟨a ~ of ranch houses⟩ ⟨crowded *colonies* of tiny shingled shacks —F.L.Allen⟩ **d :** a group of institution inmates quartered away from main buildings or centers ⟨the children's ~⟩ **e :** a nucleus of militants infiltrated into a group or organization ⟨a Communist ~ at the power plant⟩
colony house *n* **:** a small usu. somewhat isolated building used to accommodate a group of animals (as chickens or pigs) esp. when on range
col·o·pexy \'kälə,peksē\ *n* -ES [NL *colopexia*, fr. ²*col-* + *-pexia* -pexy] **:** the operation of suturing the sigmoid flexure to the abdominal wall
col·o·phene \'kälə,fēn, -,fän\ *n* -s [ISV *colophony* + *-ene*; orig. formed as F *colophène*] **:** an oily liquid that is a high-boiling component of the mixture obtained by treating turpentine (sense 2) with sulfuric acid
col·o·phon \'käləfən, -,fän\ *n* -s [L, fr. Gk *kolophōn* summit, finishing touch; prob. akin to L *collis* hill — more at HILL] **1 :** an inscription usu. placed at the end of a book or manuscript and usu. containing facts relative to its production (as the designer's, artist's, and printer's names and the type faces and paper used) **2 :** an identifying mark, emblem, or device used by a printer or a publisher sometimes on the title page, cover, shelfback, or jacket
col·o·pho·nite \'käləfə,nīt, kə'läf-\ *n* -s [G *kolophonit*, fr. *kolophonium* colophony + *-it* -ite] **:** a coarse garnet of the variety andradite
col·o·pho·ny \'kälə(,)fōnē, kə'läfə-\ *also* **col·o·pho·ni·um** \,kälə'fōnēəm\ *n, pl* **colophonies** *also* **colophoniums** [*colophony* fr. ME *colophonie*, fr. L *colophonia*, fr. Gk *kolophōnia*, fem. of *kolophōnios* colophonian, fr. *Kolophōn* Colophon, an Ionian city; *colophonium*, NL, alter. of L *colophonia*] **:** ROSIN
col·o·quin·ti·da \,kälə'kwintədə\ *n* -s [ML *coloquintida*, alter. of L *colocynthis* — more at COLOCYNTH] **:** COLOCYNTH
¹col·or \'kələ(r)\ *n* -s *see -or in Explan Notes* [ME *colour*, fr. OF *color*, *colour*, fr. L *color*; akin to L *celare* to conceal— more at HELL] **1 a :** any of manifold phenomena of light (as red, brown, pink, gray, green, blue, white) or of visual sensation or perception that enables one to differentiate objects even though the objects may appear otherwise identical (as in size, form, or texture) **b :** the aspect of the appearance of objects and light sources that may be described and specified in terms derivable wholly from one's perceptions most conveniently involving hue, lightness, and saturation for objects and hue, brightness, and saturation for light sources — used in this sense as the psychological basis for definitions of color in this dictionary **c :** the characteristic of light by means of which two areas of identical size and shape that are juxtaposed, structure-free, and steadily and uniformly illuminated may be distinguished by a human observer and which is commonly identified for spectral colors by dominant wavelength, luminance, and purity and for nonspectral colors (as purples) by complementary wavelength, luminance, and purity — used in this sense as the psychophysical basis for measuring color which in turn makes it possible to define the limits for each color definition used in this dictionary; see the Color Charts **d :** a hue as contrasted to black, white, or gray **e :** a hue or tint noticeable as different, not prevalent, unusual, unexpected **2 a :** an outward show often concealing an underlying true character **:** ASPECT, APPEARANCE, SEMBLANCE, GUISE ⟨related processes of thought, beliefs, and standards prevailed and imparted a spiritual ~ to the time —H.O.Taylor⟩ ⟨he suddenly, to give his conclusions the ~ of religion, slips in a false analogy —P.E.More⟩ **b :** a legal claim to or appearance of a right, authority, or office **c :** appearance or pretense offered as justification or extenuation **:** show of reason **:** PRETEXT ⟨she could have drawn from the Versailles treaty the ~ of legality for any action she chose —*Yale Rev.*⟩ **:** qualified justification **d :** appearance of validity or authenticity **:** PLAUSIBILITY ⟨lending ~ to this notion⟩ ⟨army officers spread the word that this ship had brought 800 troops, and to give ~ to the story, they ordered tents pitched —*Amer. Guide Series: Md.*⟩ **e :** CHARACTER, COMPLEXION, TONE, QUALITY, NATURE ⟨something was happening that changed the whole ~ of the political scene —H.L.Mencken⟩ ⟨England was up against a foe of its own weight and ~ —O.S.J.Gogarty⟩ **:** nature as regards genuineness ⟨see the ~ of one's money⟩ **3 :** complexion tint: **a :** the tint characteristic of good health and spirits or of at least a normal amount of outdoor activity ⟨to bring the ~ back to her pale cheeks⟩ ⟨the prisoners had lost ~ during their confinement⟩ **b :** the ruddy suffusion of or as if of a blush ⟨she had recovered some of her poise but her ~ showed beneath her makeup —Hartley Howard⟩ **4 a colors** *pl, archaic* **:** rhetorical ornaments of language **:** stylistic decorations; *esp* **:** figures of speech **b :** vividness or variety of emotional effects of language (as of sound and image) in prose or poetry ⟨that ~ and force of style which were later to make him outstanding —Arthur Krock⟩ **c :** LOCAL COLOR **5 a** (1) **:** a distinctively colored badge or device or distinctively colored clothing distinguishing one as a member of a particular group or organization, a follower or representative of a particular person or thing, or a partisan of a particular cause — usu. used in pl. ⟨wearing the college ~s⟩ ⟨a jockey riding under the ~s of a stable⟩ ⟨the ~s of the prince's household —Sir Walter Scott⟩ (2) **:** COGNIZANCE 1 — usu. used in pl. **b** *Brit* **:** an athlete or player awarded the right to a color in recognition of status as a team member **c colors** *pl* (1) **:** position with reference to a question or course of action **:** STAND, POINT OF VIEW ⟨we did not know how to act until our antagonist had clearly shown his ~s⟩ (2) **:** appearance or conduct in respect to its reflecting a person's character or nature ⟨showing himself finally in his true ~s⟩ **6 a** (1) **:** a color usu. used in armory excepting those classified as metals **:** a heraldic tincture that is not a metal or a fur (2) **colors** *pl* **:** LIVERY COLORS 2a **b :** a variegation of hues, tints, or shades or a basic hue marked with spots, patches, bands, or streaks of one or more shades ⟨of tabby ~⟩ **c :** a striking hue or combination of hues in foliage esp. other than or in combination or contrast with green **d** (1) **:** the use or combination of colors; *esp* **:** the use of color regarded as determining the total effect of a painting ⟨Titian is a master of ~⟩ (2) **:** an effect of a variety of colors produced with a monochrome medium (as an etching or engraving) (3) **:** two or more hues employed in a medium of presentation ⟨movies in ~⟩ ⟨~ printing⟩ ⟨~ television⟩ (4) **:** one hue of two or more used in a printing job **e :** the general overall shade or tone of ink on a page of printed matter **f :** contrast between what is printed, whatever its hue, and what it is printed on ⟨this print lacks ~; it is too gray⟩; *also* **:** ability of a typeface to achieve such contrast **g :** ink regardless of its hue ⟨the pressman calls out for ~ when he needs more ink —Howard Lockwood⟩ **7 a :** a flag, ensign, or pennant usu. symbolic (as of a country): as (1) **:** one carried by an army regiment — see KING'S COLOR, REGIMENTAL COLOR (2) **colors** *pl, in the British navy* **:** the ensign, jack, and pennant or distinguishing flag flown instead of the pennant **:** the ensign and jack (3) **colors** *pl* **:** a set of two or more flags that are customarily displayed together (as on parade) by any group or organized body or a group representing such an organization and that includes typically at least one civic flag (as the national, state, or municipal flag) and one organizational flag (4) **colors** *pl, usu cap* **:** the national flag **b :** the regiment or service distinguished by the color **c colors** *pl* **:** a navy or nautical salute to a flag when it is hoisted **d colors** *pl* **:** the armed forces of one's country — usu. used in the phrase *serve with the colors* **8 :** VITALITY, VIVIDNESS, INTEREST ⟨the play had a good deal of ~ to it⟩ ⟨the wonderful ~ of a foreign market place⟩ **9 :** something that is used to give color **:** coloring matter **:** PIGMENT, DYE ⟨oil ~s⟩ ⟨butter ~⟩ **10 a :** TIMBRE 1b **b :** the tonal quality of a voice or instrument or the effect produced by a combination of such qualities in the performance of music — called also *tone color* **11 a :** skin pigmentation other than white characteristic of race (as of the Negro race) ⟨a person of ~⟩ ⟨~ prejudices⟩ **b :** the members of a race or group with such pigmentation; *esp* **:** NEGROES **12 :** a small particle of gold in a gold miner's pan after most of the waste has been washed away **13 :** animating, striking, or vividly picturesque character **:** attendant features evoking interest or stimulating the imagination **:** striking quality commanding attention ⟨the ~ of the Mardi Gras⟩ ⟨a ballplayer with ~⟩; *specif* **:** such quality or character as a marked characteristic of a composition ⟨having all the ~ of a romantic tale⟩ ⟨add ~ to the event in recounting it⟩ **14 :** a coating mixture of pigment and adhesive, whether colored or not, used in papermaking **15 a :** all the red cards (hearts and diamonds) or all the black cards (spades and

Color samples arranged in a systematic order exhibit certain marked differences from each other. They may be arranged according to the characteristics of their appearance or according to variations in the spectral composition of the light reflected or transmitted by them. The hue variation in the normal solar spectrum is illustrated in A. The numbers on the bottom of the diagram refer to the length of the light waves that are associated with characteristically different parts of the spectrum, 400 millimicrons for the blue end of the spectrum to 700 millimicrons for the red end. Measurements of the spectral composition of light in wavelengths require instruments, but an analysis of colors by their appearance may be made in terms based wholly on perception.

As analyzed in terms of appearance, most colors have a *hue* that more or less resembles one of the hues in the spectrum illustrated in A or in the hue circle illustrated in B. The purple hues, while not found in the spectrum itself, show a resemblance to the blue and red ends and complete the hue circuit. Such colors are *chromatic* and differ characteristically from those illustrated in the black-to-white scale of C, which have no hue and hence are called *achromatic* or *neutral*.

If colors, either chromatic or achromatic, are arranged in further order, as in the black-to-white scale in C, some colors appear to be light, others dark, and still others are intermediate in *lightness*. Some light colors may be described as *very* light, some dark colors as *very* dark.

If a number of chromatic colors are selected to be constant in hue and lightness, as is the intention with the series of reds illustrated in C, some of these red colors stand out more vividly than others. Such a series may be arranged in an order of difference that increases from the grayest color to the most vivid. This difference is one of *saturation*.

These three attributes — hue, lightness, and saturation — may be thought of as dimensions of color which can be related in the three-dimensional form suggested in D (skeleton form) and E (solid form). In this color solid *hue* extends in a circular direction about the neutral axis, *lightness* extends in the vertical direction from black at the bottom through a series of grays to white at the top, and *saturation* extends in a radial direction horizontally from the central neutral axis at which the saturation is zero out to the strongest saturation, as far as this may extend from the central axis.

This dictionary defines color names by a method that depends upon this three-dimensional analysis of color. The method is one standardized, developed, and published by the Inter-Society Color Council and the National Bureau of Standards as the ISCC-NBS Method of Designating Colors and a Dictionary of Color Names (NBS Circular 553, National Bureau of Standards, Washington, 1955). The method is simple in principle. The terms *light*, *medium*, and *dark* designate decreasing degrees of lightness, and the adverb *very* extends the lightness scale to *very light* and *very dark*. The adjectives *grayish*, *moderate*, *strong*, and *vivid* designate increasing degrees of saturation. These and a series of hue names, used both as nouns and in adjective forms, are combined to form names for describing color in terms of its three perceptual attributes. Certain other adjectives cover combinations of lightness and saturation, as *brilliant* for "light, strong", *pale* for "light, grayish", and *deep* for "dark, strong".

There are 267 ISCC-NBS name blocks in the complete system and each defines a block in the color solid. This number is sufficient for naming colors from memory, but since it is estimated that man can distinguish several million surface colors, it necessarily follows that each name block contains a number of distinguishable colors. The important thing about this method that distinguishes it from all others is that the boundaries of each color term are specified. These boundaries are in terms of the numerical scales of hue, value, and chroma of the Munsell color notation, illustrated in B and C. (Under standard daylight conditions these scales correlate closely with the hue, lightness, and saturation scales of color perception: see footnote definitions [1] and [2] for Munsell and C.I.E. color systems.) Each ISCC-NBS color designation defines a block in the color solid bounded by vertical planes of constant hue, horizontal planes of constant value, and cylindrical surfaces of constant chroma.

The following table contains the hue names and abbrs. used in the ISCC-NBS system; Fig. 1 shows the scheme of hue modifiers, the "-ish" grays and the neutrals with their modifiers.

[1]MUNSELL COLOR SYSTEM : a system of specifying colors in terms of appearance on scales of hue, value, and chroma, exemplified first in 1915 by a collection of color chips (later, 1943, standardized and defined to the theoretical limits by tables and diagrams, July 1943 *Journal Opt. Soc. Amer.*, in terms of the internationally adopted C.I.E. color mixture system), these chips forming an atlas of charts that shows scales in which two of the three variables are constant, the hue scale containing five principal and five intermediate hues (to provide a color notation in the decimal system), the value scale containing ten steps from black to white, and the chroma scales showing 10 or more steps from the equivalent gray, all three scales intended to represent equal visual (not physical) intervals for a normal observer and daylight viewing with gray to white surroundings, so that under these conditions hue, value, and chroma of the color chips correlate closely with hue, lightness, and saturation of the color perception, though under other conditions the correlation for these chips is lost, and their hue value, and chroma designations become terms of psychophysical significance since they refer to their appearance only under these standard conditions.

[2]C.I.E. COLOR SYSTEM : a world-known and world-used color mixture system for specifying any color, recommended in 1931 by the International Commission on Illumination (Commission Internationale de l'Eclairage, C.I.E.) (1) by giving the amounts (tristimulus values) X, Y, Z of three primary colors required by a standard observer to match it, which are calculable from the spectral composition of the radiant energy leaving the color specimen or (2) by giving one of the tristimulus values Y, expressing the luminous value of the color, combined with two of the fractions: $X/(X+Y+Z)$, $Y/(X+Y+Z)$, $Z/(X+Y+Z)$, known as chromaticity coordinates x, y, z, respectively.

HUE NAMES AND ABBREVIATIONS

NAME	ABBREVIATION	NAME	ABBREVIATION
red	R	purple	P
reddish orange	rO	reddish purple	rP
orange	O	purplish red	pR
orange yellow	OY	purplish pink	pPk
yellow	Y	pink	Pk
greenish yellow	gY	yellowish pink	yPk
yellow green	YG	brownish pink	brPk
yellowish green	yG	brownish orange	brO
green	G	reddish brown	rBr
bluish green	bG	brown	Br
greenish blue	gB	yellowish brown	yBr
blue	B	olive brown	OlBr
purplish blue	pB	olive	Ol
violet	V	olive green	OlG

The color solid, extended to the pigment limits available today, is illustrated in the black and white diagrams E and F and in color in H and I. The drawing in F shows one quarter of the solid removed to demonstrate the relation of the interior sampling for color charts of constant hue, in which lightness (value) changes in a vertical direction and saturation (chroma) varies in a horizontal direction from the center to outside limits. The color illustrations H and I show the general appearance of the outside colors from two sides of the solid, 180° apart. One side (H) illustrates the progression from purplish blue through blues and greens to the yellows, and the other side (I) starts with the yellows and progresses through the yellowish reds to reds and purples, back to the purplish blues. Actually this color solid has no rigid boundary for saturation (except in terms of theoretical limits, which are not approached today in any except yellow pigments and dyes). To illustrate the relation of ISCC-NBS color names to the color solid, a diagram of the purple section is shown in G. (The outside limits would have to be expanded if colors were found saturated enough to extend beyond the surface indicated.) The name limits are set up in relation to Munsell value-chroma charts which represent vertical slices cut through the neutral center of the solid, as illustrated in F. Two diagrams illustrate how this is done: Figure 2 represents an uncomplicated name diagram in the Munsell 3P to 9P hue range, and Figure 3 represents a complicated diagram in the 5YR to 7YR hue range in which the pale colors are *yellowish pinks*, the light and strong yellow-reds are *oranges*, and the dark yellow-reds are *browns*.

This ISCC-NBS naming method does not provide for describing colors to a close tolerance, but it does provide a description that is understandable. For colorimetry, when it is important to distinguish to a very close tolerance among the thousands of colors that in the ISCC-NBS system might bear an identical designation, a numerical notation must be used, preferably one that is as internationally standardized as the C.I.E. colorimetric coordinate system or the Munsell system of notation, both of which are included in the group of standards adopted in 1951 by the American Standards Association to specify a method of measuring and specifying color (ASA-Z58.7.1,2,3).

Following is a list of the 267 color name pockets grouped by hue names. The relationships are as shown in Figure 1 for such modifiers as are used with each hue name. Color matches, within tolerances close enough if they are to be useful in illustrating these names, are not possible with usual conditions of color printing. The color illustrations on these pages have been limited therefore to those that would aid in developing the concepts involved in describing or naming colors. Color names are defined in this dictionary in terms of the 267 color name pockets of the ISCC-NBS system.

COLOR NAME POCKETS

pinks
1—vivid Pk
2—strong Pk
3—deep Pk
4—light Pk
5—moderate Pk
6—dark Pk
7—pale Pk
8—grayish Pk
9—pinkish white
10—pinkish gray

reds
11—vivid R
12—strong R
13—deep R
14—very deep R
15—moderate R
16—dark R
17—very dark R
18—light grayish R
19—grayish R
20—dark grayish R
21—blackish R
22—reddish gray
23—dark reddish gray
24—reddish black

yellowish pinks
25—vivid yPk
26—strong yPk
27—deep yPk
28—light yPk
29—moderate yPk
30—dark yPk
31—pale yPk
32—grayish yPk
33—brownish pink

reddish oranges
34—vivid rO
35—strong rO
36—deep rO
37—moderate rO
38—dark rO
39—grayish rO

reddish browns
40—strong rBr
41—deep rBr
42—light rBr
43—moderate rBr
44—dark rBr
45—light grayish rBr
46—grayish rBr
47—dark grayish rBr

oranges
48—vivid O
49—brilliant O
50—strong O
51—deep O
52—light O
53—moderate O
54—brownish orange

browns
55—strong Br
56—deep Br
57—light Br
58—moderate Br
59—dark Br
60—light grayish Br
61—grayish Br
62—dark grayish Br
63—light brownish gray
64—brownish gray
65—brownish black

orange yellows
66—vivid OY
67—brilliant OY
68—strong OY
69—deep OY
70—light OY
71—moderate OY
72—dark OY
73—pale OY

yellowish browns
74—strong yBr
75—deep yBr
76—light yBr
77—moderate yBr
78—dark yBr
79—light grayish yBr
80—grayish yBr
81—dark grayish yBr

yellows
82—vivid Y
83—brilliant Y
84—strong Y
85—deep Y
86—light Y
87—moderate Y
88—dark Y
89—pale Y
90—grayish Y
91—dark grayish Y
92—yellowish white
93—yellowish gray

olive browns
94—light OlBr
95—moderate OlBr
96—dark OlBr

greenish yellows
97—vivid gY
98—brilliant gY
99—strong gY
100—deep gY
101—light gY
102—moderate gY
103—dark gY
104—pale gY
105—grayish gY

olives
106—light Ol
107—moderate Ol
108—dark Ol
109—light grayish Ol
110—grayish Ol
111—dark grayish Ol
112—light Ol gray
113—Ol gray
114—Ol black

yellow greens
115—vivid YG
116—brilliant YG
117—strong YG
118—deep YG
119—light YG
120—moderate YG
121—pale YG
122—grayish YG

olive greens
123—strong OlG
124—deep OlG
125—moderate OlG
126—dark OlG
127—grayish OlG
128—dark grayish OlG

yellowish greens
129—vivid yG
130—brilliant yG
131—strong yG
132—deep yG
133—very deep yG
134—very light yG
135—light yG
136—moderate yG
137—dark yG
138—very dark yG

greens
139—vivid G
140—brilliant G
141—strong G
142—deep G
143—very light G
144—light G
145—moderate G
146—dark G
147—very dark G
148—very pale G
149—pale G
150—grayish G
151—dark grayish G
152—blackish G
153—greenish white
154—light greenish gray
155—greenish gray
156—dark greenish gray
157—greenish black

bluish greens
158—vivid bG
159—brilliant bG
160—strong bG
161—deep bG
162—very light bG
163—light bG
164—moderate bG
165—dark bG
166—very dark bG

greenish blues
167—vivid gB
168—brilliant gB
169—strong gB
170—deep gB
171—very light gB
172—light gB
173—moderate gB
174—dark gB
175—very dark gB

blues
176—vivid B
177—brilliant B
178—strong B
179—deep B
180—very light B
181—light B
182—moderate B
183—dark B
184—very pale B
185—pale B
186—grayish B
187—dark grayish B
188—blackish B
189—bluish white
190—light bluish gray
191—bluish gray
192—dark bluish gray
193—bluish black

purplish blues
194—vivid pB
195—brilliant pB
196—strong pB
197—deep pB
198—very light pB
199—light pB
200—moderate pB
201—dark pB
202—very pale pB
203—pale pB
204—grayish pB

violets
205—vivid V
206—brilliant V
207—strong V
208—deep V
209—very light V
210—light V
211—moderate V
212—dark V
213—very pale V
214—pale V
215—grayish V

purples
216—vivid P
217—brilliant P
218—strong P
219—deep P
220—very deep P
221—very light P
222—light P
223—moderate P
224—dark P
225—very dark P
226—very pale P
227—pale P
228—grayish P
229—dark grayish P
230—blackish P
231—purplish white
232—light purplish gray
233—purplish gray
234—dark purplish gray
235—purplish black

reddish purples
236—vivid rP
237—strong rP
238—deep rP
239—very deep rP
240—light rP
241—moderate rP
242—dark rP
243—very dark rP
244—pale rP
245—grayish rP

purplish pinks
246—brilliant pPk
247—strong pPk
248—deep pPk
249—light pPk
250—moderate pPk
251—dark pPk
252—pale pPk
253—grayish pPk

purplish reds
254—vivid pR
255—strong pR
256—deep pR
257—very deep pR
258—moderate pR
259—dark pR
260—very dark pR
261—light grayish pR
262—grayish pR

neutrals
263—white
264—light gray
265—medium gray
266—dark gray
267—black

FIGURE 1

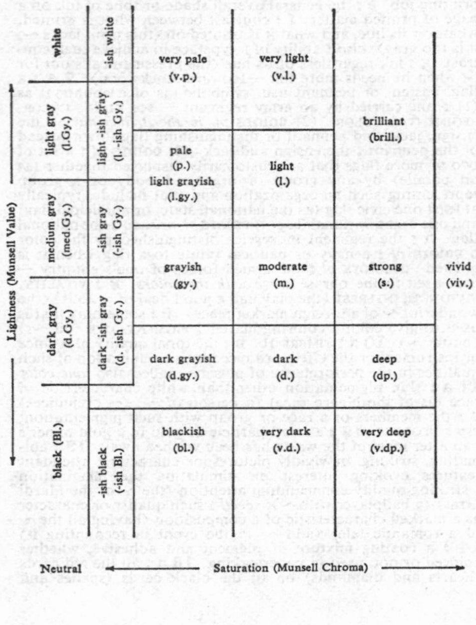

white
-ish white
very pale (v.p.)
very light (v.l.)
light gray (l.Gy.)
light -ish gray (l.-ish Gy.)
brilliant (brill.)
pale (p.)
light grayish (l.gy.)
light (l.)
medium gray (med.Gy.)
-ish gray (-ish Gy.)
grayish (gy.)
moderate (m.)
strong (s.)
vivid (viv.)
dark gray (d.Gy.)
dark -ish gray (d. -ish Gy.)
dark grayish (d.gy.)
dark (d.)
deep (dp.)
black (Bl.)
-ish black (-ish Bl.)
blackish (bl.)
very dark (v.d.)
very deep (v.dp.)
Lightness (Munsell Value)
Neutral
Saturation (Munsell Chroma)

FIGURE 2

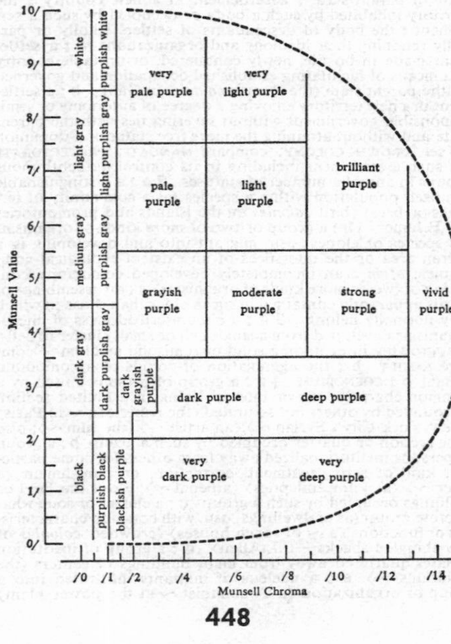

10/
9/
8/
7/
6/
5/
4/
3/
2/
1/
0/
Munsell Value
white
purplish white
very pale purple
very light purple
light gray
light purplish gray
pale purple
light purple
brilliant purple
medium gray
purplish gray
grayish purple
moderate purple
strong purple
vivid purple
dark gray
dark purplish gray
dark grayish purple
dark purple
deep purple
black
purplish black
blackish purple
very dark purple
very deep purple
/0
/1
/2
/4
/6
/8
/10
/12
/14
Munsell Chroma

FIGURE 3

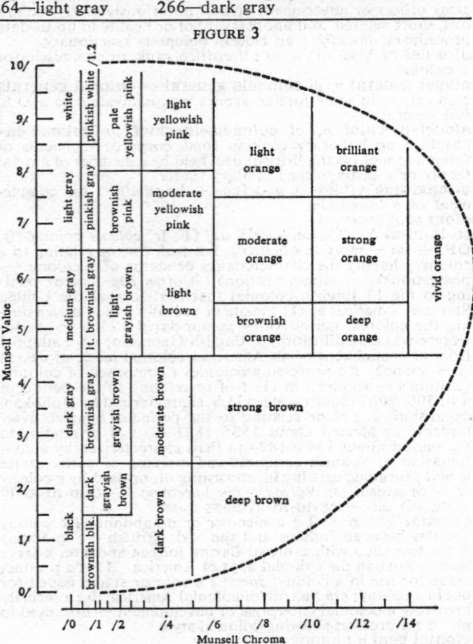

COLOR

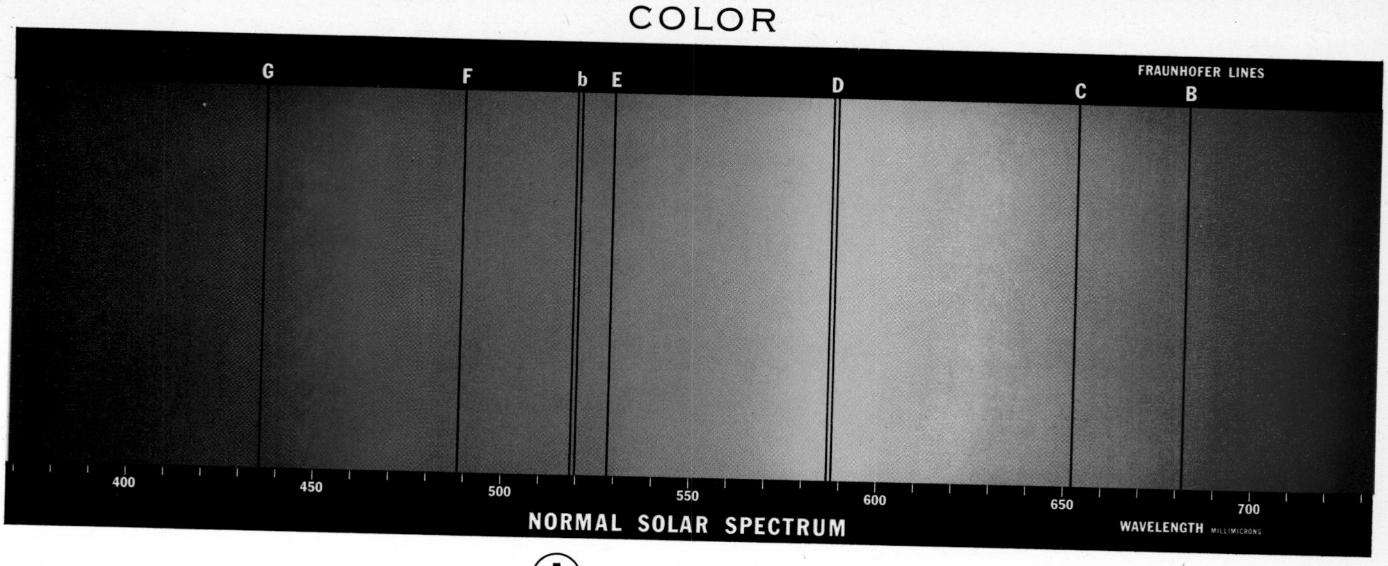

FRAUNHOFER LINES

G F b E D C B

400 450 500 550 600 650 700

NORMAL SOLAR SPECTRUM

WAVELENGTH MILLIMICRONS

(A)

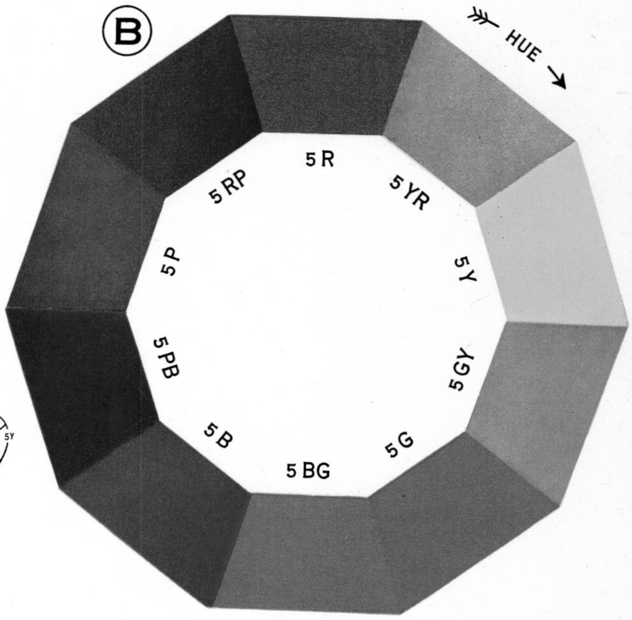

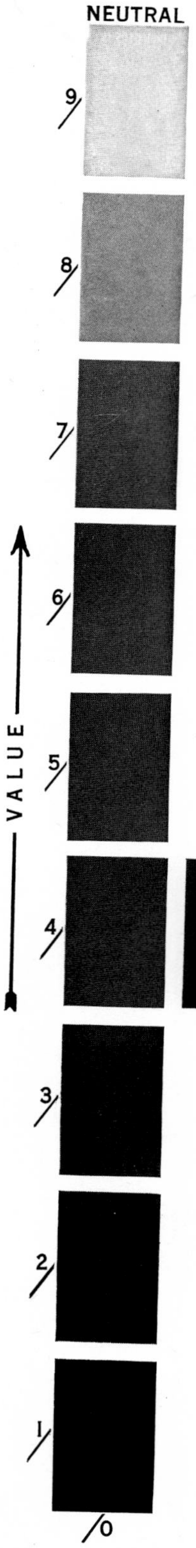

NEUTRAL

9/ 8/ 7/ 6/ 5/ 4/ 3/ 2/ 1/ /0

VALUE

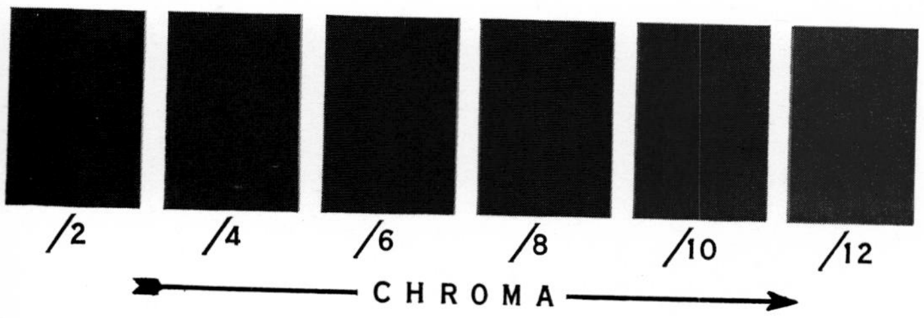

/2 /4 /6 /8 /10 /12

CHROMA

(C)

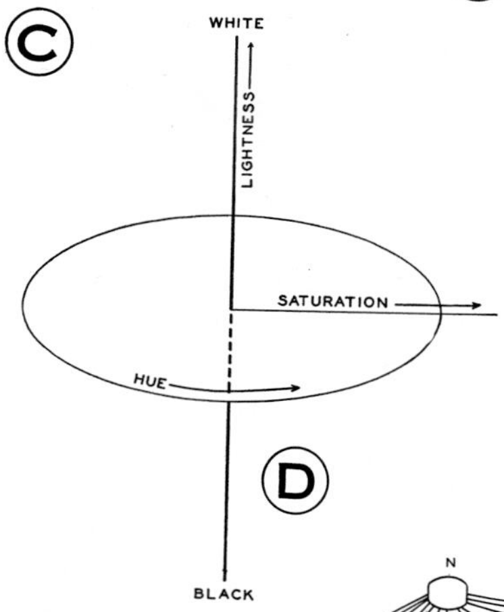

WHITE

LIGHTNESS

SATURATION

HUE

BLACK

(D)

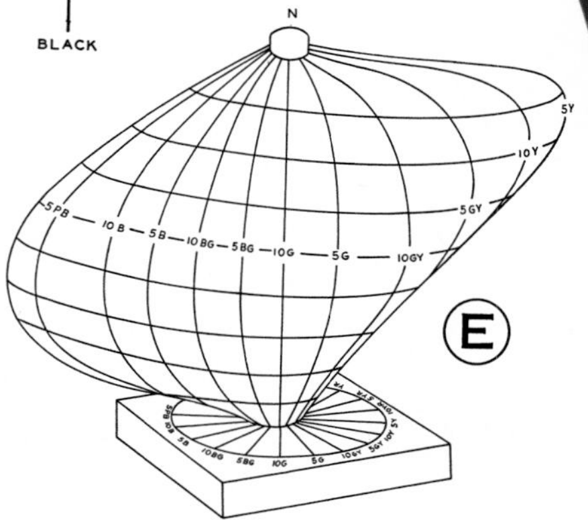

(B)

HUE

5 R 5 YR 5 Y 5 GY 5 G 5 BG 5 B 5 PB 5 P 5 RP

N

5Y 10Y 5GY 10GY 5G 10G 5BG 10BG 5B 10B 5PB

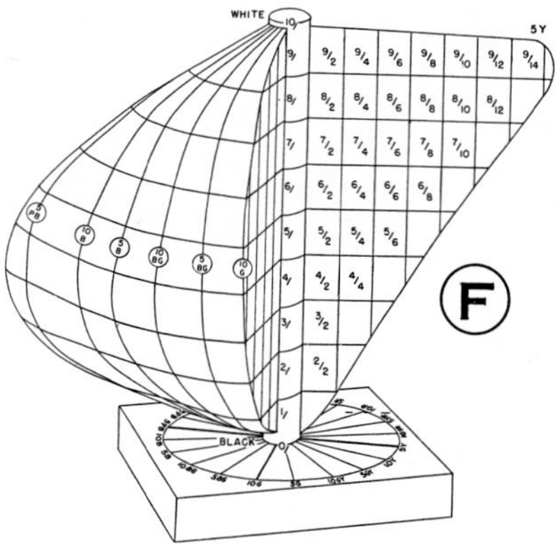

(E)

WHITE 5Y

BLACK

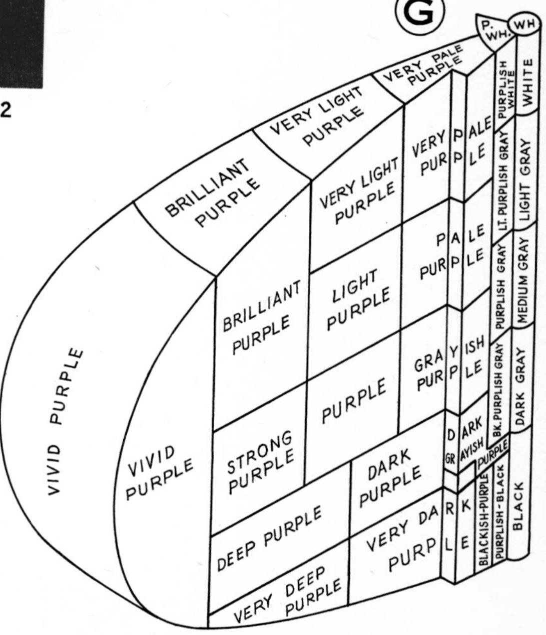

(F)

(G)

VIVID PURPLE

VIVID PURPLE

BRILLIANT PURPLE

VERY LIGHT PURPLE

VERY PALE PURPLE

P. WH.

WH

BRILLIANT PURPLE

VERY LIGHT PURPLE

VERY PURPLE

PALE

PURPLISH WHITE

WHITE

LIGHT PURPLE

PALE PURPLE

LT. PURPLISH GRAY

LIGHT GRAY

STRONG PURPLE

PURPLE

GRAYISH PURPLE

PURPLISH GRAY

MEDIUM GRAY

DEEP PURPLE

DARK PURPLE

DARK GRAYISH PURPLE

BK. PURPLISH GRAY

DARK GRAY

VERY DEEP PURPLE

VERY DARK PURPLE

BLACKISH PURPLE

PURPLISH-BLACK

BLACK

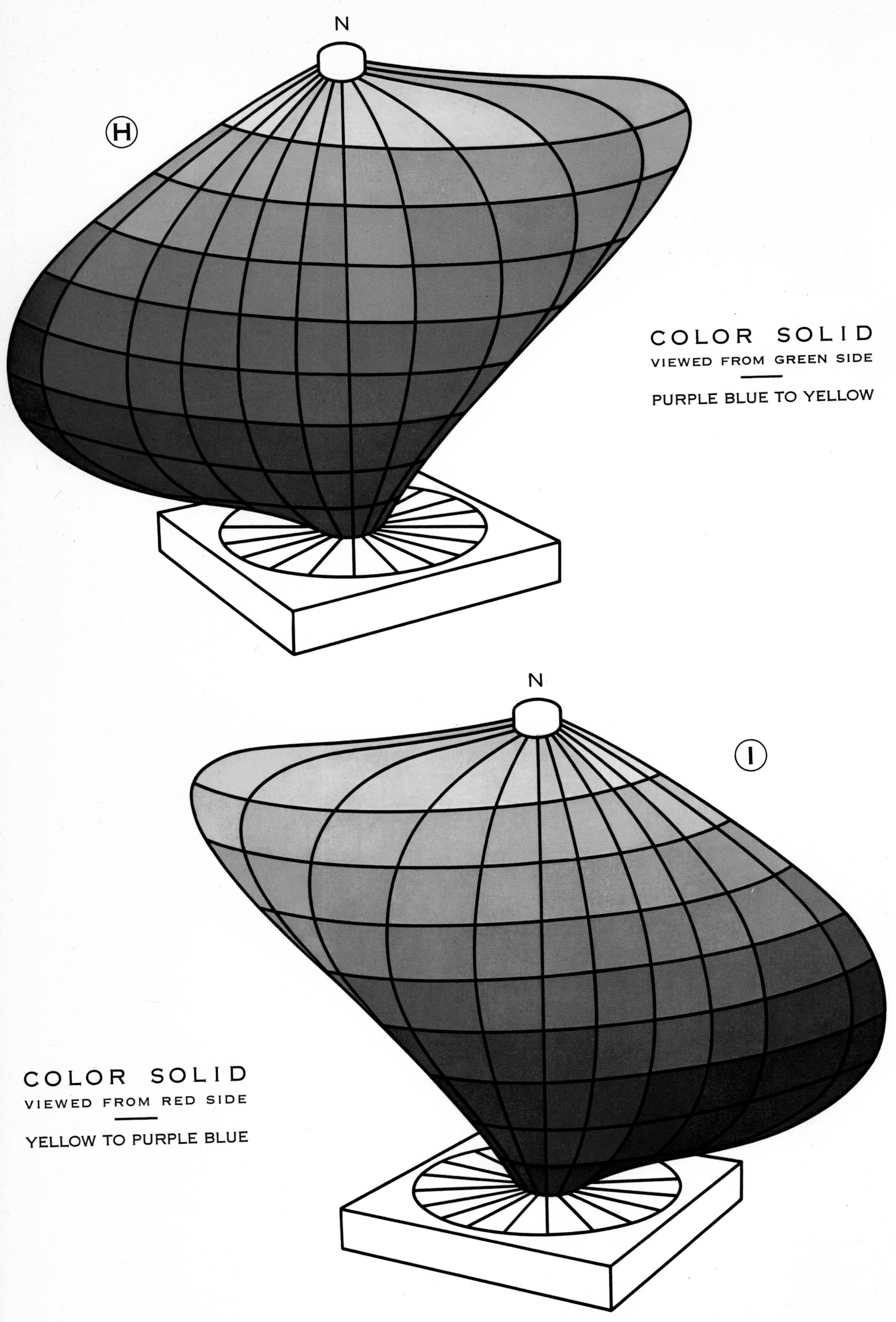

COLOR SOLID
VIEWED FROM GREEN SIDE

PURPLE BLUE TO YELLOW

COLOR SOLID
VIEWED FROM RED SIDE

YELLOW TO PURPLE BLUE

clubs) **b** : the other suit of the same color as the trump suit **c** : SUIT 7a(1) **d** : COULEUR 2b

syn CHROMA, HUE, SHADE, TINT, TINGE, TONE: COLOR is the generic and most general term in this set. CHROMA, usu. limited to scientific or technical writing, may stress the attributes of hue and saturation, as in bright red or dull green, in contrast to white, grays, or black, which do not possess these attributes. HUE may suggest that property by which colors of the spectrum are distinguished one from another and from corresponding grays ⟨all the gradational *hues* of the spectrum from red through yellow, green, blue, to violet —*Scientific Monthly*⟩ In less scientific use it indicates merely color or gradation or modification of color ⟨livid with the *hue* of death —Mary W. Shelley⟩ ⟨their shining green has changed to a less vivid *hue* —Lafcadio Hearn⟩ SHADE is usu. used to indicate a gradation of a color or hue according to lightness or brightness. It often but not always suggests a darker rather than lighter gradation. TINT indicates a gradation of a color or hue, usu. either a lighter gradation, one oriented toward white, or a gradation of a light color ⟨Father Latour had often remarked that this tree seemed especially designed in shape and color for the adobe village. The sprays of bloom which adorn it are merely another *shade* of the red earth walls, and its fibrous trunk is full of gold and lavender *tints* —Willa Cather⟩ TINGE suggests an interfusion or an overlay, stain, dappling, or freaking of one color over or into another general background color ⟨in ore it [copper] is red in color, but a freshly fractured surface of the pure metal has a pinkish or yellowish *tinge* —*New Yorker*⟩ In nontechnical writing COLOR, HUE, SHADE, and TINT are often interchangeable ⟨flowing . . . now over rocks of greenish *hue* and again over those of brownish *tint* —*Amer. Guide Series: N. H.*⟩ TONE, while often equivalent to COLOR, suggests more particularly hue or a modification of hue, as tint or shade ⟨from strand to cloud-capped peak, the *tone* was purple —William Beebe⟩ ⟨it [dun] was also very much used as a couplet to other terms, like brown, red, yellow, etc., to express dull, grayed *tones* of such colors —A.J.Maerz & M.R.Paul⟩

syn see in addition FLAG

— **under colors** *of a horse* : in an official race ⟨the colt . . . made his first appearance *under colors* at Hialeah —G.F.T. Ryall⟩ — **with flying colors** : eminently successful : VICTORIOUS, UNDEFEATED, IRREPROACHABLE

2**color** \"\ *vb* **colored; colored; coloring** \ˈkəl(ə)riŋ\ **colors** *see -or in Explan Notes* [ME *colouren*, fr. OF *colorer*, fr. L *colorare*, fr. *color*, n.] *vt* **1 a** : to give color to : imbue with color **b** : to change or alter the color of (as by dyeing, staining, or painting) : DYE, TINGE, TINT, SHADE, PAINT, STAIN **2** : to change or alter as if by dyeing or painting: as **a** : MISREPRESENT, DISGUISE, DISTORT, BIAS ⟨a highly ~*ed* version of the facts⟩ **b** : GLOSS, PALLIATE, EXCUSE ⟨~ a lie⟩ **3** *obs* : to misrepresent as one's own **4** : INFLUENCE, SHAPE, CONDITION, AFFECT ⟨the lives of most of us have been ~*ed* by politics —Christine Weston⟩ ⟨how much the contemplation of death has ~*ed* human thought —H.L.Mencken⟩ **5** : to imbue (as a piece of writing) with a subjective quality or cause to produce a particular emotional effect ⟨his writings were ~*ed* by his feelings⟩ **6** : to produce a fine finish on (a metal) by polishing with rouge or lime **7** : to modify the articulation or acoustic quality of (a speech sound) ⟨an r-*colored* vowel⟩ ~ *vi* : to take on or acquire a color: **a** : to take on the color of ripeness (as of grapes) **b** : BLUSH, FLUSH ⟨~*ed* as though she had said something very daring —Willard Robertson⟩

3**color** \"\ *adj* — *see -or in Explan Notes* [1*color*] : showing or dealing with or concerned with color: **a** : concerned with skin pigmentation : RACIST ⟨the ~ line⟩ **b** : capable of reproducing color : showing things in color ⟨~ photography⟩ : capable of producing more than one color at a single operation ⟨a two-*color* press⟩; *also* : used to print one color in a job printed in two or more colors ⟨a ~ cut⟩ ⟨a ~ border⟩

col·or·a·bil·i·ty \ˌkəl(ə)rəˈbiləd·ē, -ətē, -i\ *n* -ES : the quality of being colorable

col·or·a·ble \ˈkəl(ə)rəbəl\ *adj* [ME, fr. MF *colorable*, fr. *color* + *-able*] **1** : seemingly valid and genuine : having an appearance of truth, right, or justice : PLAUSIBLE ⟨any ~ pretext for refusing —Bertrand Russell⟩ **2** : FEIGNED, FACTITIOUS, COUNTERFEIT ⟨~ and false pretenses⟩ — **col·or·a·bly** \-blē, -bli\ *adv*

1**col·o·rad·an** \ˌkäləˈradᵊn, -rä-, -rȧ- *archaic* -rā-\ *or* **col·o·rad·o·an** \-dəwən\ *adj, usu cap* [*Colorado*, state of U.S. + E *-an*] **1** : of, relating to, or characteristic of the state of Colorado **2** : of, relating to, or characteristic of Coloradans

2**coloradan** \"\ *or* **coloradoan** \"\ *n* -S *cap* : a native or resident of the state of Colorado

1**col·o·rado** \-(ˌ)dō, -də\ *adj, usu cap* [fr. *Colorado*, state of U.S., fr. the *Colorado* river, fr. Sp, lit., red, reddish (past part. of *colorar* to color) fr. L *coloratus*, past part. of *colorare* to color — more at COLOR] **1** : of or from the state of Colorado ⟨the *Colorado* mountains⟩ : of the kind or style prevalent in Colorado : COLORADAN **2** : of or relating to a subdivision of the American Upper Cretaceous — see GEOLOGIC TIME table

2**colorado** \"\ *n, pl* **colorado** *or* **colorados** *usu cap* [Sp, lit., red, reddish] **1 a** : a Barbacoan people at the foot of the western Andes, Ecuador **b** : a member of such people **2** : the language of the Colorado people

3**colorado** \"\ *n* -ES [AmerSp, fr. Sp *colorado*, adj.] : a cigar of medium color and strength

colorado blue spruce *n, usu cap C* : COLORADO SPRUCE; *esp* : a pendulous-branched spruce (*Picea pungens kosteriana*) that is a variety of this tree

colorado bur *n, usu cap C* : BUFFALO BUR

colorado fir *n, usu cap C* : WHITE FIR 1a(1)

colorado grass *n, usu cap C* : TEXAS MILLET

col·o·rad·o·ite \-də,wīt\ *n* -S [*Colorado*, its locality + E *-ite*] : a grayish black mineral with metallic luster consisting of mercury telluride HgTe (sp. gr. 8.6)

colorado manroot *n, usu cap C* : MAN-OF-THE-EARTH

colorado potato beetle *or* **colorado beetle** *n, usu cap C* : a black-and-yellow striped beetle (*Leptinotarsa decemlineata*) orig. found in the eastern foothills of the Rocky mountains where it fed on the sandbur (*Solanum rostratum*) but now feeding in both the larval and adult stages on the leaves of the potato, often doing great damage, and spread into most potato-growing regions of the world

colorado ranger *n, usu cap C* [1*Colorado*] : a parti-colored horse of a breed developed in the western U.S. by interbreeding barbs with native stock ultimately of Spanish origin

colorado river hemp *n, usu cap C&R* : a tall-growing annual legume (*Sesbania exaltata*) of the southwestern U.S. that produces a strong tough bast fiber formerly used by the Indians for cordage and that is widely used as a green manure esp. on heavy moist soils — called also *sesbania*

colorado rubber plant *or* **colorado rubber weed** *n, usu cap C* : any of several herbs of the genus *Hymenoxys* (family Compositae) of the western U.S. that contain small quantities of rubber

colorado spruce *n, usu cap C* : a tall wide-spreading evergreen tree (*Picea pungens*) often planted for ornament — called also *blue spruce, Colorado blue spruce, silver spruce*

colorado steer hide *or* **colorado steer** *n, usu cap C* : a hide from a side-branded steer

colorado tick fever *n, usu cap C* : a mild noneruptive disease that is characterized by intermittent fever, short course, and long convalescence and that is caused by a virus transmitted by a wood tick (*Dermacentor andersoni*)

colorado white balsam *or* **colorado white fir** *n, usu cap C* : WHITE FIR 1a(1)

colorado wild potato *n, usu cap C* : an herb (*Solanum jamesii*) of Colorado and adjacent states with white flowers and small tubers

col·or·ant \ˈkəl(ə)rənt\ *n* -S [F, fr. pres. part. of *colorer* to color, fr. L *colorare* — more at COLOR] : a substance capable of or used for coloring a material : DYE, PIGMENT

col·or·a·tion \ˌkələˈrāshən\ *n* -S [F, fr. MF, fr. *colorer* to color + *-ation*] **1 a** : the state of being colored : COLORING 1c ⟨a rock with a strange and interesting ~⟩ ⟨the ~ of the skin from a bruise⟩ **b** : use or choice of colors (as by an artist) ⟨Millet's subdued ~⟩; *specif* : arrangement or combination of colors ⟨the brilliant ~ of a butterfly's wing⟩ **2 a** : characteristic quality : TIMBRE ⟨the newspapers . . . took on the former ~ of the magazines —L.B.Seltzer⟩ **b** : aspect suggesting an attitude : PERSUASION, ATTITUDE, INCLINATION ⟨the chameleon talent for taking on the intellectual ~ of whatever idea he happened to fasten onto —Budd Schulberg⟩ **3** : subtle variation of intensity or quality of tone ⟨a haunting ~ in the string passages of the concerto⟩ ⟨a certain odd ~ in his voice⟩

col·or·a·tion·al \¦⸗⸗¦rāsh(ə)nəl\ *adj* : of, relating to, or depending on coloration

col·or·a·tive \ˈkələ,rād·iv\ *adj* [*coloration* + *-ive*] **1** : that colors **2** : consisting of or depending upon coloration ⟨the ~ protection of certain animals⟩

col·or·a·tu·ra \ˌkələrəˈtu̇rə, ˌkäl-, ˌkōl-\ *n* -S *often attrib* [obs. It, lit., coloring, fr. LL, fr. L *coloratus* + *-ura* -ure] **1** : the florid ornamentation in vocal music (as runs, trills, arpeggios); *broadly* : music characterized by ornate figuration **2** : one that sings or has the ability to sing coloratura; *usu* : a soprano singer of coloratura

col·or·a·ture \ˈkələrəchə(r)\ *n* -S [G or It; G *koloratur*, fr. It *coloratura*] : COLORATURA

color balance *n* **1** : a distribution of colors (as in a painting) resulting in a feeling of fitness, satisfaction, and beauty **2** : the chromatic characteristics of the reproduction of gray tones in a color photograph

color–ball pool \ˈ⸗⸗,⸗-\ *n* : ENGLISH POOL

color bar *n* : a bar or barrier hindering or preventing colored persons from participating with whites in various activities and ranging in severity from social discrimination and conventional debarring from some occupations to a strict legally enforced exclusion from any skilled occupations (as in the Union of So. Africa)

color base *n* : DYE BASE

color–bearer \ˈ⸗⸗,⸗⸗\ *n* : one that carries a color or standard esp. in a military parade or drill

color–blind \ˈ⸗⸗,⸗\ *adj* **1 a** : afflicted with a congenital or acquired partial or total inability to distinguish one or more chromatic colors **b** : not noticing or considering : BLIND, INSENSITIVE, OBLIVIOUS ⟨laws *color-blind* to economic reality⟩ **2** *of a photographic film or emulsion* : sensitive only to blue, violet, and ultraviolet light

color blindness *n* : the state of being color-blind : inability or marked difficulty in distinguishing chromatic color — compare CHROMATIC VISION; DICHROMATISM, MONOCHROMATISM, TRICHROMATISM

colorbreed \ˈ⸗⸗,⸗\ *vt* : to breed selectively for the development of particular colors ⟨~*ing* canaries for red⟩

color camera *n* : a camera of special design for making color-separation negatives (as a beam-splitter camera or a one-shot camera)

1**colorcast** \ˈ⸗⸗,⸗\ *n* -S [*color* + *telecast*] : a television broadcast in color

2**colorcast** \"\ *vb* **colorcast** *also* **colorcasted; colorcast** *also* **colorcasted; colorcasting; colorcasts** : to broadcast in color over television

color cell *n* : CHROMOCYTE

color change *n* : a fraudulent or accidental change in the color of a particular postage stamp; *also* : an authorized change in a particular denomination of stamps

color changeling *n* : a postage stamp whose color has changed as a result of chemical action

color chart *n* : a systematic arrangement of colors or their representations with respect to either the attributes of the colors or the mixing relations of their stimuli

color chest *n* : a chest for signal flags (as on a ship)

color chip *n* : a small usu. paper sample representing a color

color cinematography *n* : cinematography that uses a color photography process

color circle *n* : an arrangement of hues in their natural spectrum order (red, orange, yellow, green, blue, violet plus the purples) about the circumference of a circle usu. with pairs of complementary hues represented on the opposite ends of diameters

color collotype *n* : collotype in more than one color; *often* : collotype in four or more colors

color company *n* : the company with which the colors are posted for military ceremonies and drills

color constancy *n* : tendency of the colors perceived as belonging to objects to remain invariable in spite of changes in amount and spectral quality of illumination

color cycle *n* **1** : COLOR CIRCLE **2** : recurrence of colors as they reach peak in fashion

color developer *n* : a developer in color photography that after becoming oxidized combines with a coupler to form a dye that is deposited along with the developed silver in the image, the silver image being then bleached to leave the colored image

color diagram *n* : a diagram showing relations between colors or facts of color mixture; *specif* : COLOR CHART

color dimension *n* : one in any set of three dimensions used for describing or measuring color — compare COLOR SOLID

1**col·ored** \ˈkələ(r)d\ *adj* [ME *coloured*, fr. past part. of *colouren* to color — more at COLOR] **1** : marked by color : having or showing usu. chromatic color ⟨white and ~ lights⟩ ⟨advertisements on ~ paper⟩; *sometimes* : having a color other than the accustomed or expected ⟨~ glass⟩ ⟨a green and a ~ leaf⟩ **2 a** : FEIGNED, PRETENDED ⟨a ~ ally⟩ **b** : glossed over : made to appear less extreme : PALLIATED ⟨his ~ crimes⟩ **c** : ADORNED, EMBELLISHED ⟨the ~ verse of Claudian —Arthur Symons⟩ : made colorful ⟨the pictures, ~ and racy, which Captain Nichols' vivid account offered —W.S.Maugham⟩ : EXAGGERATED, SLANTED, BIASED ⟨~ political news —F.L.Mott⟩ ⟨the prosecutor's well-*colored* evidence —Arthur Morrison⟩ **d** : ORIENTED, ALIGNED ⟨politically ~ labor unions⟩ **3** *sometimes cap* **a** : of some other race than the white; *often* : Negro or having some proportion of Negro blood **b** : of, for, or relating to colored persons ⟨a teacher in ~ schools⟩ **4** *sometimes cap* **a** : of mixed race ⟨the ~ people, as contrasted with the Negroes of St. Thomas⟩ **b** *Africa* : of or relating to the Cape Colored

2**colored** \"\ *n* -S *sometimes cap* **1** : colored people ⟨education of the ~⟩ **2** : a colored person ⟨a school for ~*s*⟩

colored corpuscle *n* : a red blood cell

colored vision *n* : CHROMATOPSIA

color emissivity *n* : monochromatic emissivity

col·or·er \ˈkəl(ə)rə(r)\ *n* -S : one that colors: as **a** : one that coats gold articles with zinc or gold to secure uniform color **b** : one that applies colored glaze to tiles using a bulb pen **c** : a worker who brushes coloring fluid over hides

colorfast \ˈ⸗⸗,⸗\ *adj* : having color that retains its original hue esp. without fading or running in washing, cleaning, wearing, or long exposure to light — **col·or·fast·ness** *n* -ES

color–feed \ˈ⸗⸗,⸗\ *vt* : to feed (as canaries) elements intended to enrich the color of plumage

color film *n* : a photographic film used for making color pictures

color filter *n* : a filter (as of glass, gelatin, or liquid) that absorbs light of certain wavelengths or colors selectively and is used for modifying the light that reaches a sensitized material esp. for increasing contrast, photographing through haze, or making color-separation negatives — called also *color screen, light filter*

col·or·ful \ˈkələ(r)fəl\ *adj* **1** : marked by much color or many colors esp. those that are bright or vivid ⟨the ~ scenery of the area⟩ : attractively colored **2** : compelling attention or interest : striking because of lively animation, diverting variety, compelling individual manner, distinctive procedure, or unusual content often exaggerated ⟨a ~ pageant⟩ ⟨a ~ athlete⟩ ⟨version . . . garnished with boasts of his own exploits, is a ~ . . . account —*Amer. Guide Series: Calif.*⟩ — **col·or·ful·ly** \-f(ə)lē, -li\ *adv* — **col·or·ful·ness** *n* -ES

col·or·gravure \¦kələ(r)+\ *n* -S : gravure printed in more than one color

color guard *n* : a guard of honor for the colors of an organization, in the armed forces consisting of four men of which two are senior noncommissioned officers who carry the colors — compare GUARD OF THE STANDARD

color hearing *n* : CHROMESTHESIA

colories *pl of* COLORY

col·or·if·ic \ˌkələˈrifik\ *adj* **1** : capable of communicating color **2** *archaic* : with respect to color **3** *archaic* : abounding in literary color

col·or·im·e·ter \ˌkələˈriməd·ə(r)\ *n* -S [ISV *color* + *-i-* + *-meter*] **1** : an instrument or device for determining and specifying colors by reference either to other colors or to complex stimuli not in general identical with the actual color stimulus and giving results not independent of abnormalities in the observer's color vision — distinguished from *spectrophotometer* and *spectroradiometer* **2** : an instrument for chemical analysis of liquids by comparison of the color of the given liquid with standard colors — compare COMPARATOR

col·or·i·met·ric \¦kələrə¦me·trik\ *or* **col·or·i·met·ri·cal** \-trəkəl\ *adj* : of or relating to colorimetry ⟨a ~ procedure⟩; *also* : determined or to be determined by the use of a colorimeter ⟨~ analysis⟩ — **col·or·i·met·ri·cal·ly** \-trək(ə)lē, -li\ *adv*

colorimetric photometer *n* : a photometer measuring light intensities for several spectral regions by means of filters successively interposed in the path of the light

colorimetric purity *n* : purity (sense 2a) found by evaluating the components in luminance terms

colorimetric quality *n* : CHROMATICNESS

col·or·i·met·rics \ˌkələrəˈme·triks\ *n pl but usu sing in constr* : COLORIMETRY

col·or·im·e·trist \ˌkələˈrimə·trəst\ *n* -S : a specialist in colorimetry

col·or·im·e·try \ˌkələˈrimə·trē, -tri\ *n* -ES [ISV *color* + *-i-* + *-metry*] **1** : the science and practice of determining and specifying colors — compare COLORIMETER **2** : quantitative chemical analysis by color comparison (as by a colorimeter)

col·or·in \ˈkələrən, ¦kələ¦rēn, ¦kōl-\ *n* -S [MexSp *colorín*, fr. Sp, linnet, bright color, fr. *color*, fr. L — more at COLOR] : a spiny Mexican tree (*Erythrina americana*) with showy red flowers and brilliant scarlet seeds

color index *n* **1 a** : the photographic magnitude of a star or other celestial body minus visual magnitude **b** : the difference between the magnitudes of a star or other celestial body as measured in two distinct wavelength regions of the spectrum and intended to indicate the object's color **2** : a figure representing the ratio of the amount of hemoglobin to the number of red cells in a given volume of blood and being a measure of the normality of the hemoglobin content of the individual cells

coloring *n* -S [ME *colouring*, fr. gerund of *colouren* to color — more at COLOR] **1 a** : the act of applying colorants : the application of color **b** : something that produces color or color effects ⟨pouring the ~ into the paint before mixing⟩ **c** (1) : the effect produced by applying or combining colors or shades ⟨a painting with startling ~⟩ (2) : natural color or a combination of natural colors ⟨the dun ~ of the mole⟩ ⟨the startling ~ of the peacock⟩ ⟨a sunset with vivid ~⟩ (3) : COMPLEXION 3a ⟨the ~ of a blonde⟩ **d** : the final stage in buffing a metallic surface wherein a high polish is imparted **2 a** : false semblance : SHOW, DISGUISE; *esp* : a pleasing masking of something bad ⟨lies under the ~ of truth⟩ **b** : a slanting or suggesting added extrinsically : ORIENTATION, SLANT, BIAS ⟨although given a Christian ~ here and there . . . this poetry is essentially heathen —*Encyc. Americana*⟩ **3 a** : COLOR 4b **b** : COLOR 13 **c** : the indirect disclosure of sympathies or point of view in writing or speaking **4 a** : TIMBRE, QUALITY **b** : COLORATURA, ORNAMENTATION

col·or·ism \ˈkələ,rizəm\ *n* -S : COLORATION, COLORING

col·or·ist \ˈkələrəst\ *n* -S [F *coloriste*, fr. *colorer* to color + *-iste* -ist — more at COLOR] **1** : one that colors: **a** : an artist, designer, or composer who excels in the use of color or to whom color is of prime importance **b** : one who duplicates the exact colors of customers' samples used in printing cloth to order **2 a** : a chemist who develops color formulas for plastics to match customer specifications **b** : one who advises about fashionable color shades and combinations **c** : one who colors photographs

col·or·is·tic \¦kələ¦ristik\ *adj* : relating to color or coloring ⟨~ truth in a landscape⟩ ⟨a concept formulated in ~ terms⟩ ⟨~ treatment of orchestral instruments⟩ — **col·or·is·ti·cal·ly** \-tək(ə)lē\ *adv*

color lake *n* : 4LAKE 1b

col·or·less \ˈkələ(r)ləs\ *adj* [ME *colourless*, fr. *colour* + *-less*] **1** : without color: **a** : transparent and not distinguished by any hue ⟨a ~ gas⟩ **b** : PALLID, BLANCHED ⟨a ~ sallow complexion⟩ **2** : without distinctive character: as **a** : lacking variety and contrast, energetic individuality, animating qualities such as spontaneity, or ability to command interest ⟨~ histories, so passionless and so lacking in distinctive mark or motive —Woodrow Wilson⟩ **b** : free from any manifestation of partial or peculiar feeling : NEUTRAL ⟨did not try to write a ~ story —W.A.White⟩ — **col·or·less·ly** *adv*

colorless corpuscle *n* : LEUKOCYTE

col·or·less·ness *n* -ES : the quality or state of having no color

color line *n* **1** : a line of stacked rifles on which the colors rest while troops are engaged in activities without arms **2** : the line of social demarcation that some people maintain between the white race and colored races (as between whites and Negroes); *also* : a similar line between groups of lighter and darker colored people

col·or·man \ˈkələ(r)mən, -,man\ *n, pl* **colormen 1** *Brit* : a dealer in colors and paints **2 a** : a workman who mixes dyes (as in leather manufacturing) **b** : one that plans, supervises, or carries out dyeing processes in manufacturing **3** : one that distributes identifying silks and numbers to jockeys **4** : one that obtains colored finishes in the electroplating of metal objects by the use of various plating solutions

color mixer *n* : an apparatus for color mixture; *esp* : a wheel provided with concentric colored disks slit along a radius and dovetailed so as to reveal differently colored sectors which when whirled rapidly blend into a circle of uniform color

color music *n* : the portrayal (as on a screen) of successive shades of color often in patterns and with rhythm similar to that of sounds in music; *also* : the artistic effect so produced — compare CLAVILUX

color of office : the pretense or appearance of official authority in one who being an officer in law or fact is without the authority claimed

color of title 1 : an apparent but invalid title based upon a written instrument or record; *also* : the instrument itself **2** : an apparent ownership claimed by adverse possession

color organ *n* : CLAVILUX

col·o·ro·to \ˌkələˈrōd·(ˌ)ō\ *n* -S [blend of *color* and *roto*] : rotogravure printed in more than one color

color party *n, Brit* : the color guard of a regiment

color phase *n* **1 a** : a genetic variant manifested by the occurrence of a skin or pelage color unlike the wild type of the animal group in which it appears and usu. produced by a number of different factors interacting in accord with Mendel's laws ⟨the silver *color phase* of the red fox⟩ **b** : an individual exhibiting or a pelt or skin that is the result of such a genetic variant ⟨these foxes are all *color phases*⟩ — compare MUTATION **2** : a seasonally variant pelage color ⟨the drab summer *color phase* of the ermine⟩

col·or·pho·bia \¦kələ(r)¦fōbēə\ *n* -S : hatred of Negroes

col·or·pho·to \ˈ⸗⸗,fōd·ō\ *n* : a photograph produced by color photography

color photography *n* : photographic production of pictures in nearly natural colors

col·or·plate \ˈkələ(r),plāt, *usu* -ād·+V\ *n* : any of a set of process color printing plates; *also* : a print made from a complete set of such plates

color point *n* : HONOR POINT

color print *n* : a print in two or more colors

color printing *n* : the making of color prints esp. in three or more colors

color quality *n* : CHROMA

color question *n* : the problem of race antagonisms and their elimination in human relations esp. as affecting whites and Negroes

color ratio *n* : the volumetric ratio of dark minerals to light in igneous rocks

colors *pl of* COLOR, *pres 3d sing of* COLOR

color salute *n* : a salute made by dipping the colors

color scheme *n* : a combination or arrangement of colors regarded as elements in a systematic conception ⟨the *color scheme* of a costume⟩ ⟨a room with a blue and green *color scheme*⟩

color screen *n* : COLOR FILTER

color–sensitize \¦⸗⸗¦⸗⸗,⸗\ *vt* : to make (a photographic material) sensitive to colors other than those to which the material is naturally sensitive

color separation n : the isolation on separate photographic negatives by the use of color filters of the parts of a picture or design that are to be printed in the given colors; also : any of these separate negatives
color sergeant n 1 : a sergeant in a color guard who carries one of the colors 2 : a Salvation Army soldier appointed as a flag bearer
color slab n : a tile of white china on which a palette of colors has been burned
color-slide \'=,=\ n : a color transparency for projection
color solid or **color space** n : three-dimensional space each point of which represents a color
color striker n : one that makes colorants
color temperature n : the temperature at which a blackbody emits radiant energy competent to evoke a color of the same hue and saturation as that evoked by radiant energy from a given source (as a lamp)
color tone n 1 : TONE 8 2 : the general effect of a pleasing color harmony
color top n : COLOR MIXER
color transparency n : a color photograph to be examined by transmitted light
color trial n : a proof of a stamp that was made for testing the use of a certain color subsequently rejected — called also *trial color proof*
color triangle n : CHROMATICITY DIAGRAM

color solid

col·or·type \'kələ(r),tīp\ n 1 : a color print produced by process plates; also : a process by which such prints are produced — compare COLOR SEPARATION 2 : a halftone print in three or more colors
color vision n : perception of and ability to distinguish colors
color wash n : a whitewash or a cold-water paint tinted with colored pigments
color weakness n : a partial inability to distinguish colors that is not so marked as in color blindness
color wheel n : a color mixer using a wheel of colored disks
¹**col·ory** \'kəl(ə)rē, -ri\ adj [¹color + -y] 1 : characterized by color : showing color : COLORFUL 2 : having a color indicating good quality ⟨~ coffee⟩
²**colory** \"\ n -ES : a colory product; specif : leaf tobacco with the lightest color of the type
color zone n, in some theories of vision : one of the three concentric areas of the retina as distinguished on the basis of their color sense, the outer zone giving practically only the grays, the intermediate zone adding yellow and blue, and the central zone adding red and green so that only the central zone is sensitive to all colors
co·loss or **co·losse** \kə'läs\ n, pl **colosses** [MF & L; MF colosse, fr. L colossus] archaic : COLOSSUS
co·los·sal \kə'läsəl\ adj [F, fr. L colossus + F -al — more at COLOSSUS] 1 : like or relating to a colossus : of very great size ⟨a ~ statue⟩ 2 : characterized by extremely great bulk, extent, force, strength, power, or effect, approaching or suggesting the stupendous or incredible ⟨the ~ speed of 15,000 miles a second —James Jeans⟩ ⟨their wars have now become so ~ that every woman's husband, father, son, brother, or sweetheart ... must go to the trenches —G.B.Shaw⟩ 3 : characterized by an exceptional or astonishing degree ⟨~ impudence⟩
syn see HUGE
col·os·sal·i·ty \,kälə'salədē\ n -ES : colossal nature or characteristics ⟨the ~ of the skyscraper⟩
co·los·sal·ly \kə'läs(ə)lē, -li\ adv : in a colossal manner
colossal order n : an architectural order extending in height beyond one interior story; esp : with the columns or pilasters reaching from the basement to nearly the top of the wall
col·os·se·um \,kälə'sēəm\ n -S [ML, fr. L colosseum, neut. of colosseus colossal, fr. colossus] : COLISEUM
co·los·si \kə'läsē, -,sī\ pl of COLOSSUS
¹**co·los·si·an** \kə'läsh(ē)ən, -äsēən, -äsyən\ adj, usu cap [Colossæ, ancient city in Phrygia, Asia Minor + E -ian] 1 : of, relating to, or characteristic of Colossae, an ancient city of Phrygia in Asia Minor where there was an early Christian church 2 : of, relating to, or characteristic of Colossians
²**colossian** \"\ n -S usu cap : a native or inhabitant of Colossae; esp : a member of its Christian church
colosso n, pl **colossos** or **colossoes** [It, fr. L colossus] obs : COLOSSUS
col·os·soch·e·lys \,kälə'säkələs\ n, cap [NL, fr. Gk kolosso- (fr. kolossos colossus) + chelys tortoise — more at CHELYS] : a genus of gigantic extinct Pliocene tortoises of India
co·los·sus \kə'läsəs\ n, pl **colossuses** \-səsəz\ or **colossi** \-,sī, -,sē\ [L, fr. Gk kolossos] 1 : a huge statue of greater than heroic size and proportions ⟨fronting the Amon temple four gigantic colossi were erected —D.A.Mackenzie⟩ 2 : one marked by great size, scope, strength, power, or effect and able to dwarf or dominate others : a : a nation vastly larger and more powerful than those near it ⟨Latin-American distrust and fear of the ~ to the north⟩ b : a huge and powerful industrial concern ⟨a ~ with eight plants, some 44,000 employees —Time⟩ c : one remarkably outstanding and preeminent over others ⟨such an artistic ~ as Michelangelo —Hunter Mead⟩
co·los·to·mize \kə'lästə,mīz\ vt -ED/-ING/-S : to perform a colostomy on
co·los·to·my \kə'lästəmē\ n -ES [ISV col- + -stomy] 1 : the surgical formation of an artificial anus by making an opening from the colon through the abdominal wall; also : the orifice so made 2 : a surgical joining of one part of the colon with another part of the intestine (as ileum)
colostomy bag or **colostomy pouch** n : a container kept constantly in position to receive feces discharged through a colostomy
colostomy belt n : a belt or girdle designed to hold a colostomy bag securely against a colostomy
co·los·tral \kə'lästrəl\ or **co·los·tric** \-rik\ or **co·los·trous** \-rəs\ adj [colostrum + -al or -ic or -ous] : of, relating to, or caused by colostrum
co·los·trum \kə'lästrəm\ n -S [L, beastings] : a specialized secretion of the mammary glands that is produced during the first few days after parturition, that differs from typical milk in its higher content of protein (as albumin and globulins) and antibodies, vitamins, and minerals and its lower content of sugars and fats, and that supplies essential immune bodies to the young animal and aids in the establishment of the intestinal function
colostrum corpuscle n : a cell in the colostrum supposed to be a degenerated cell of the mammary alveoli
co·lot·lan \,kōlōt'län\ n, pl **colotlan** or **colotlans** usu cap [Sp colotlán, of AmerInd origin] 1 : a Piman people in Jalisco, Mexico 2 : a member of the Colotlan people
co·lot·o·my \kə'läd·əmē\ n -ES [ISV ²col- + -tomy] : surgical incision of the colon — compare COLOSTOMY
colour \'kələ(r)\ chiefly Brit var of COLOR
-co·lous \k(ə)ləs\ adj comb form [L -cola inhabitant + E -ous; akin to L colere to cultivate, inhabit — more at WHEEL] : living or growing in or on ⟨arenicolous⟩ ⟨saxicolous⟩
colp var of COLLOP
colp- or **colpo-** comb form [NL, fr. Gk kolp-, kolpo-, fr. kolpos bosom, fold, vagina, womb — more at GULF] : vagina ⟨colpitis⟩ ⟨colposcope⟩
col·pate \'käl(,)pāt, -,pət\ adj [Gk kolpos + E -ate] of pollen grains : having longitudinal germinal furrows in the exine
col·peo \käl'pāō\ n -S [Sp culpeo, fr. Araucanian culpeu] : a So. American dog (Pseudalopex culpaeus) somewhat resembling a fox; also : any of various closely related dogs
col·pid·i·um \käl'pidēəm\ n [NL, fr. Gk kolpos bosom, fold, vagina, womb + NL -idium — more at GULF] 1 cap : a genus of small aquatic holotrichous ciliates that are much used in biological research 2 pl **colpidia** : a member of the genus Colpidium
col·pin·dach \'kōlpənd°k\ n -S [ME, prob. modif. of ScGael colpach] early Scots law : a yearling heifer
col·pi·tis \käl'pīd·əs\ n -ES [NL, fr. colp- + -itis] : VAGINITIS

col·po·clei·sis \,kälpō'klīsəs\ n, pl **colpoclei·ses** \-,sēz\ [NL, fr. colp- + -cleisis] : the suturing of posterior and anterior walls of the vagina to prevent uterine prolapse
col·po·da \käl'pōdə\ n, cap [NL, fr. Gk kolpōdēs embosomed, embayed, winding, fr. kolpos bosom, fold, vagina, womb + -ōdēs -ode — more at GULF] : a genus (the type of the family Colpodidae) of small flattened reniform holotrichous freshwater ciliates
col·po·di·dae \käl'pōdə,dē\ n pl, cap [NL, fr. Colpoda, type genus + -idae] : a large family of common and widely distributed chiefly aquatic free-living holotrichous ciliates
col·por·tage \'käl,pōrd-ij, -,pȯr-, kȯlpȯrtäzh\ n -S [F, fr. colporter (alter. of MF comporter) + -age] : a colporteur's work
col·por·teur \'käl,pōrd·ər, -,pȯr-, kȯlpȯrtœr\ also **col·por·ter** \'käl,pōrd·ər, -,pȯr-\ n -S [F colporteur, alter. (influenced by porter à col to carry on one's back, lit., neck) of MF comporteur (fr. comporter to hawk, peddle, carry, bring together) + -eur -or — more at COMPORT] : a peddler of books, esp. of bibles and religious books and tracts; also : a missionary or publicist for some usu. religious cause
-col·pos \,kälpəs, -,päs\ n comb form -ES also **-col·pus** \,kälpəs\ [NL, fr. Gk kolpos bosom, fold, vagina, womb — more at GULF] : vaginal disorder (of a specified type) ⟨hematocolpos⟩
col·po·scope \'kälpə,skōp\ n -S [ISV colp- + -scope] : an instrument designed to facilitate visual inspection of the vagina — **col·po·scop·i·cal** \,==skäpəkəl\ adj — **col·po·scop·i·cal·ly** \-pək(ə)lē, -li\ adv — **col·pos·co·py** \käl'päskəpē\ n -ES
col·po·stat \'kälpə,stat\ n -S [colp- + -stat] : a medical appliance or instrument (as a radium applicator) designed to facilitate vaginal treatment
col·pot·o·my \käl'päd·əmē\ n -ES [ISV colp- + -tomy] : surgical incision of the vagina
cols pl of COL
¹**colt** \'kōlt\ n -S [ME, fr. OE; akin to Sw (dial.) kult half-grown pig, ON kjolta lap, skirt, Skt gadi young bull, OE cild child — more at CHILD] 1 a : the young of the camel — obs. except in Scripture b : the young of the horse or any other equine (as a zebra or an ass) — not used technically c : a male horse or other equine that has not attained sexual maturity or been gelded d : a young male horse before the attainment of an arbitrarily designated age (as three, four, or five years) — used esp. of race horses 2 a : a young untried person : NOVICE, ROOKIE, TYRO; specif : a novice cricketer esp. when trying for a place on a team 3 : a short rope knotted or with something heavy attached to the end formerly used as an instrument of punishment in the navy ⟨the welts of a British ~ on my back —Kenneth Roberts⟩
²**colt** \"\ vt -ED/-ING/-S 1 obs : CHEAT, BEFOOL 2 : to beat or punish with a colt
colt distemper n : STRANGLES
col·ter also **coul·ter** \'kōltə(r)\ n -S [ME colter, fr. OE culter & OF coltre, both fr. L culter plowshare, knife; akin to OHG scala husk, ON skilja to separate, Goth skilja butcher, Gk skalis hoe, mattock, Lith skélti to split — more at SHELL] : a knife, sharp disc, or other cutting tool that is attached to the beam of a plow to cut the sward in advance of the plowshare and moldboard

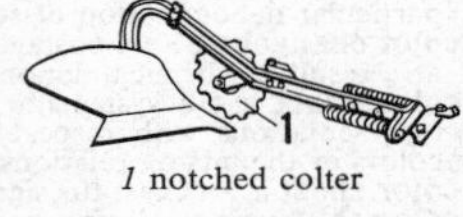

1 notched colter

colt evil or **colt ill** n 1 obs : inflammation or swelling of the sheath and vicinity in horses 2 a : navel ill of the foal b : STRANGLES
colt·ish \'kōltish, -tēsh\ adj 1 : UNDISCIPLINED: a obs : WANTON b : FRISKY, PLAYFUL, SPORTIVE ⟨~ antics of children⟩ 2 : of, relating to, or resembling a colt — **colt·ish·ly** adv
colt·pix·ie or **colt·pixy** \'kōlt,piksē\ n, pl **coltpixies** : a mischievous hobgoblin supposed to appear as a colt and mislead men or horses into bogs
colts·foot \'kōlts,fu̇t\ n, pl **coltsfoots** : any of various plants with large rounded leaves resembling the foot of a colt: a : a perennial herb (Tussilago farfara) native to Europe but now nearly cosmopolitan, having yellow heads of flowers appearing before the leaves and being used esp. formerly in pharmacy and as a flavoring agent b also **coltsfoot snakeroot** : WILD GINGER 2a c : GALAX 2 d : OCONEE BELLS e : a tropical American herb (Pothomorphe peltata) of the family Piperaceae with inconspicuous flowers in spikes f : SWEET COLTSFOOT
colt·skin \'=,=\ n : leather made of the skin of a colt
colt's-tail \'=,=\ n, pl **colt's-tails** 1 : HORSEWEED 1 2 : FIELD HORSETAIL
colt's tooth n 1 : youthful wantonness : concupiscent desire 2 : wolf tooth in horses
col·u·ber \'käləbə(r), -lyə-\ n [NL, fr. L coluber, colubra snake; perh. akin to Gk kolon limb — more at CALK] 1 cap : an extensive genus (the type of the family Colubridae) of nonpoisonous snakes 2 -S : any snake of the genus Coluber
¹**col·u·brid** \-brəd\ adj [NL Colubridae] : of or relating to Colubridae or to a snake of this family
²**colubrid** \"\ n -S : a snake of the family Colubridae
co·lu·bri·dae \kə'lübrə,dē\ n pl, cap [NL, fr. Colubr-, Coluber, type genus + -idae] 1 : a very large cosmopolitan family of nonvenomous terrestrial, arboreal, or sometimes aquatic snakes with aglyphous teeth in both jaws, imbricating scales, and reduced postfrontal bones 2 in some esp former classifications : a more inclusive family in which Colubridae is merged as a subfamily as are also the families Acrochordidae and Dasypeltidae of aglyphous snakes, Boigidae, Elachistodontidae, and Homalopsidae of venomous opisthoglyphous snakes, and sometimes Elapidae and Hydrophidae of venomous proteroglyphous snakes
co·lu·bri·form \-brə,fȯrm\ adj [ISV colubr- (fr. L colubr-, coluber) + -iform] : being or resembling a colubrine snake
col·u·bri·na \,käl(y)ə'brīnə, -brēnə\ n, cap [NL, fr. LL, a plant, fr. fem. of L colubrinus snakelike] : a genus of mostly tropical American shrubs or small trees (family Rhamnaceae) with small yellowish flowers and yellow or red fruits
col·u·bri·nae \-nē\ n pl, cap [NL, fr. Colubr-, Coluber, type genus + -inae] : a subfamily of Colubridae (sense 2) almost exactly coextensive with Colubridae (sense 1)
¹**col·u·brine** \'käl(y)ə,brīn, -,brən\ adj [L colubrinus, fr. colubra snake + -inus -ine — more at COLUBER] 1 : relating or similar to a snake ⟨his ~ nature⟩ 2 [NL Colubrinae] : of or relating to the subfamily Colubrinae
²**colubrine** \-,brēn, -,brən\ n -S [blend of NL Colubrina and E -ine] : either of two colorless crystalline alkaloids $C_{22}H_{24}N_2O_3$ occurring with strychnine and distinguished as alpha-colubrine and beta-colubrine
¹**col·u·broid** \'käl(y)ə,brȯid\ adj [ISV colubr- (fr. L coluber, colubra snake) + -oid — more at COLUBER] : COLUBRINE, COLUBRIFORM
²**colubroid** \"\ n -S : a snake of the family Colubridae
co·lu·go \kə'lügō\ n -S [prob. native name in Malaya] : FLYING LEMUR
col·u·lus \'käl(y)ələs\ n, pl **colu·li** \-,lī,-,lē\ [NL, dim. of L colus distaff; akin to L colere to cultivate, dwell — more at WHEEL] : an apparently vestigial organ consisting of a slender process between the bases of the anterior spinnerets of spiders lacking a cribellum
¹**columba** var of CALUMBA
²**co·lum·ba** \kə'ləmbə\ n, cap [NL, fr. L, dove, pigeon — more at COLUMBINE] : a large genus consisting of the typical pigeons and including the rock pigeon and band-tailed pigeon
col·um·ba·ceous \,käləm'bāshəs\ adj [L columba + E -aceous] : of or relating to pigeons
co·lum·bae \kə'ləmbē\ n pl, cap [NL, fr. L, pl. of columba] : a suborder of birds (order Columbiformes) consisting of the doves and pigeons and the extinct dodo and solitaire
co·lum·ba·mine \kə,ləmbə'mēn, =',==,=\ n -S [ISV, blend of ¹columba and amine] : an alkaloid $C_{20}H_{21}NO_5$ that occurs in calumba and is related in structure to berberine
co·lum·ban \kə'ləmbən\ adj, usu cap [St. Columba †597 Ir. missionary + E -an] : of, relating to, or founded by Saint Columba or his disciples

col·um·ba·ri·um \,käləm'ba(a)rēəm\ n, pl **columba·ria** \-rēə\ [L, lit., dovecote, fr. columba dove — more at COLUMBINE] 1 : a structure of vaults lined with recesses for cinerary urns ⟨a ~ containing glass-doored marble compartments for the ashes of cremated bodies —Amer. Guide Series: N.Y.City⟩ 2 : a recess in a columbarium
col·um·bary \'käləm,berē\ n -ES [L columbarium] : DOVECOTE, PIGEON HOUSE
co·lum·bate \kə'ləm(,)bāt, -,bət\ n -S [NL columbium + E -ate] : NIOBATE
col·um·batz fly \'käləm,bats-\ n, usu cap C [fr. Hung Kolumbács (Serbo-Croatian Golubac), town in Yugoslavia] : a black fly (Simulium columbatczense) of the Balkan region said to be sometimes present in such numbers as to be fatal to children or animals
col·um·bel·la \,käləm'belə\ n, cap [NL, fr. L columba dove + NL -ella; fr. the color of the shell — more at COLUMBINE] : a genus (the type of the family Columbellidae) of small marine gastropods having a thick fusiform shell and being abundant in tropical seas
col·um·bel·li·dae \,käləm'belə,dē\ n pl, cap [NL, fr. Columbella, type genus + -idae] : a family (order Pectinibranchia) of marine gastropods comprising the dove shells some of which were formerly used as ornaments or as money
¹**co·lum·bia** \kə'ləmbēə\ adj, usu cap [fr. Columbia, S.C.] : of or from Columbia, the capital of So. Carolina ⟨a Columbia resident⟩ : of the kind or style prevalent in Columbia : COLUMBIAN
²**columbia** \"\ n, pl **columbia** or **columbias** usu cap [fr. Columbia river, southwestern Canada & northwestern U.S., near which they dwelt] 1 a : a Salishan people of eastern Washington b : a member of such people 2 : a language of the Columbia and Wenatchee peoples — called also Sinkiuse
columbia black n, usu cap C, often cap B : any of several direct dyes — see DYE table I (under Direct Black 9 and 38)
columbia blue n, often cap C [prob. fr. NL Columbia United States] : a pale blue that is redder and deeper than average powder blue or Sistine and redder, stronger, and slightly darker than average cadet gray
co·lum·bi·ad \kə'ləmbē,ad\ n -S [F colombiade, fr. NL Columbia United States + F -ade -ad] 1 cap : any of certain epics recounting the beginning and growth of the U.S.; also : any epic with similar subject matter 2 : an obsolete heavy long-chambered muzzle-loading gun that is very thick behind the trunnions and designed for throwing shells and shot at high angles of elevation
¹**co·lum·bi·an** \kə'ləmbēən\ adj [NL Columbia United States (fr. Christopher Columbus †1506) + E -an] 1 usu cap : of or relating to America, the U. S., or Christopher Columbus 2 sometimes cap : having or indicating a color pattern characteristic of the plumage of certain varieties of poultry in which the head, body, and leg feathers are white and the tail, neck, and parts of the wing are black or black with white edging
²**columbian** \"\ n -S cap : AMERICAN; specif : a native of the U.S.
columbian ground squirrel n, usu cap C [Columbia river + E -an] : a mottled-gray burrowing squirrel (Citellus columbianus) with rusty-colored muzzle common in the Columbia river region of Washington
columbian pine n, usu cap C [Columbia river + E -an] : DOUGLAS FIR
columbian red n, often cap C [¹Columbian] : CASTILIAN BROWN
columbian spirit n, usu cap C [¹Columbian] : METHANOL — often used in pl.
columbia river salmon n, usu cap C&R [fr. Columbia river, southwestern Canada & northwestern U.S.] : KING SALMON
columbia river sucker n, usu cap C&R : a large sucker (Catostomus macrocheilus) of the Columbia river basin
columbia sheep n, usu cap C [fr. NL Columbia United States; fr. its being the first breed of sheep developed in America] : a large hardy open-faced utility sheep of an American breed developed by crossing Lincoln and Rambouillet and distinguished by a high yield of fine wool longer than that of the Rambouillet and by satisfactory mutton conformation
¹**co·lum·bic** \kə'ləmbik\ adj [¹columba + -ic] : relating to or derived from the calumba root
²**columbic** \"\ adj [NL columbium + E -ic] : NIOBIC
columbic acid n : NIOBIC ACID
co·lum·bi·dae \kə'ləmbə,dē\ n pl, cap [NL, fr. Columba, type genus + -idae] : a family of game birds comprising the doves and pigeons
col·um·bif·er·ous \,käləm'bif(ə)rəs\ adj [NL columbium + E -i- + -ferous] : containing columbium
co·lum·bi·for·mes \kə,ləmbə'fȯr,mēz\ n pl, cap [NL, fr. Columba + -iformes] : a cosmopolitan order of land birds with four unwebbed toes, short legs, small heads, and usu. little visible difference between the sexes that includes the sandgrouse and the pigeons and doves together with their extinct relatives, the dodo and solitaire
co·lum·bin or **co·lom·bin** \kə'ləmbən\ n -S [alter. of earlier calumbin, fr. calumba + -in] : a bitter crystalline constituent of calumba
¹**col·um·bine** \'käləm,bīn, -,bən\ n -S [ME, fr. ML columbina, fr. fem. of L columbinus dovelike, fr. columba dove + -inus -ine; fr. the fancied resemblance of the inverted bloom to a group of five doves; akin to Gk kolymbos, a bird (prob. a grebe), OHG holuntar elder tree, OSw hylle elder, Gk kelainos black, Skt kalanka spot, nest; basic meaning: spot] 1 : a plant of the genus Aquilegia: as a : a red-flowered plant (A. canadensis) of eastern No. America b : a blue-flowered plant (A. coerulea) of the Rocky mountains 2 or **columbine blue** : a moderate purplish blue to violet
²**columbine** \"\ adj [ME, fr. MF colombin, fr. L columbinus] : of, relating to, or similar to a dove ⟨a ~ form⟩ ⟨~ innocence⟩
³**columbine** \", -,bēn\ n -S usu cap [It Colombina, dim. of colomba dove, fr. L columba] : the pert and adroit young girl in English harlequinade and in the later commedia dell' arte, in the English harlequinade usu. being Pantaloon's daughter or ward in love with Harlequin
co·lum·bite \kə'ləm,bīt\ n -S [NL columbium + E -ite] : a black mineral that is essentially an iron columbate $(Fe,Mn)(Cb,Ta)_2O_6$ grading into tantalite and having a bright submetallic luster (hardness 6, sp. gr. 5.4–6.5)
co·lum·bi·um \kə'ləmbēəm\ n -S [NL, fr. Columbia United States + -ium — more at COLUMBIAN] : NIOBIUM — used chiefly in America esp. by metallurgists; symbol Cb
columbium pentoxide n : NIOBIUM PENTOXIDE
¹**columbo** var of CALUMBA
²**co·lum·bo** \kə'ləmbō\ n -S : AMERICAN COLUMBO
co·lum·boid \kə'ləm,bȯid\ adj [L columba dove + E -oid — more at COLUMBINE] : relating to or resembling pigeons
columbo wood n [¹Columbo] : an East Indian plant (Coscinium fenestratum) of the family Menispermaceae that possesses a bitter property and is medicinally like calumba
¹**co·lum·bus** \kə,ləmbəs\ adj, usu cap [fr. Columbus, Ohio] : of or from Columbus, the capital of Ohio ⟨our Columbus office⟩ : of the kind or style prevalent in Columbus
²**columbus** \"\ n -ES [after Christopher Columbus †1506 Ital. explorer, discoverer of America] : EXPLORER, DISCOVERER
columbus day n, usu cap C&D [after Christopher Columbus] : October 12, observed as a legal holiday in many states of the U.S. and in most of the countries of Latin America in celebration of the anniversary of the landing of Columbus in the Bahamas in 1492 — called also Discovery Day
columbus's crab or **columbus crab** n, cap 1st C [after Christopher Columbus] : GULFWEED CRAB
col·u·mel·la \,käl(y)ə'melə\ n, pl **columel·lae** \-lē, -,lī\ [NL, fr. L, small column, dim. of columna column — more at COLUMN] 1 : any of various anatomical parts likened to a column: as a or **columella cra·nii** \-'krānē,ī\ : the epipterygoid bone of the skull of many lizards b or **columella au·ris** \-'ȯrəs, -'au̇r-\ : the bony or partly cartilaginous rod, often with several distinct parts, connecting the tympanic membrane with the internal ear in birds and many reptiles and amphibians c : the bony central axis of the cochlea d : the central column or axis of a spiral univalve shell e : the central pillar in the calyx of many corals 2 a : the carpophore of various seed plants b : the axis of the capsule in mosses and in some of the liverworts (as those of the genus Anthoceros) consisting of sterile tissue c : the central sterile portion of the sporangium

in fungi of *Mucor* and related genera **d :** STALACE **3 :** a columnar thickening of the peripheral protoplasm of spirochetes

col·u·mel·lar \ˌ≈≈ˈmelə(r)\ *adj* [L *columellaris* pillar-shaped, fr. *columella* + *-aris* -ar] **:** of, relating to, or like a columella

columellar muscle *n* **:** a muscle that has its origin on the columella of a gastropod mollusk shell and serves to retract the animal into the shell

col·u·mel·late \ˌ≈≈ˈmelət, -me(ˌ)lāt\ *adj* [NL *columella* + E *-ate*] **:** possessing or forming a columella

col·u·mel·lia \ˌkäl(y)əˈmelēə\ *n, cap* [NL, fr. Lucius J.M. *Columella* 1st cent. A.D. Roman agricultural writer + NL *-ia*] **:** a small genus (coextensive with a family Columelliaceae of the order Polemoniales) of bitter evergreen shrubs of the northern Andes that have yellow cymose flowers with two stamens and capsular fruit enclosed by the calyx

col·u·mel·li·a·ceous \ˌ≈≈ˌmelēˈāshəs\ *adj* [NL *Columellia* + E *-aceous*] **:** of or relating to the genus *Columellia* or the family Columelliaceae

col·u·mel·li·form \ˌ≈≈ˈmeləˌfȯrm\ *adj* [NL *columella* + E *-iform*] **:** like a columella

col·umn \ˈkäləm, *sometimes* ÷ -lyəm\ *n* -s [ME *columne*, fr. MF *colomne*, fr. L *columna*, fr. *columen* top, summit; akin to L *collis* hill — more at HILL] **1 a :** a vertical arrangement of items printed or written on a page or otherwise inscribed **:** a vertical list ⟨with students' names in ∼*s*⟩ ⟨adding a ∼ of figures⟩ **b :** one of two or more vertical sections of a printed page or table that are separated by a rule or blank space **c :** an accumulation arranged vertically **:** STACK **d :** a special department or feature (as of humor, sports, literary reviewing, or gossip) in a newspaper or periodical under a permanent title and generally reflecting the writer's individual tastes and point of view **e :** a list of those showing, favoring, or approving something ⟨swinging the state into the Republican ∼⟩ **f :** a vertical array of positions in a punched card used in a business machine **2 :** a supporting pillar: as **a :** a pillar consisting of a shaft, a capital, and usu. a base, the shaft being of circular section except as it is fluted or channeled **b :** one of a building's vertical supporting members made of steel, cast iron, reinforced concrete, timber, or stone and often extending from the foundation through several floors, which it supports, to the roof **c :** a hollow steel cylinder with a jackscrew base usu. set up between the floor and roof of mining workings to serve as a mounting for rock drills, light hoists, and other equipment **3 :** a form, structure, or formation shaped like a column: as **a :** an upright mass **:** a somewhat cylindrical upright body ⟨the springs occasionally spouted ∼*s* of water far into the air —*Amer. Guide Series: Mich.*⟩ ⟨the metal ∼ of the water spout⟩ ⟨a ∼ of smoke from the burning ship⟩; *specif* **:** a cylindrical dripstone formation made by union of stalactite and stalagmite **b :** a tower or other cylindrical construction **c :** a mass of air conceived of as columnar in shape but not necessarily vertical ⟨a ∼ of air sweeping through the tunnel⟩ **d :** a vertical tube or tower through which gases or vapors are passed to purify them; *esp* **:** one used in connection with distillation equipment for effecting a fractionation of the vapors (as by the use of plates with bubble caps or of packing) **4 a :** a military, naval, or aeronautic formation in which elements (as soldiers, vehicles, ships, or planes) proceed one after another — contrasted with *line* **b :** an arrangement of elements moving or placed one after another **:** an active group likened to such a column ⟨a ∼ of strikers picketing the mill⟩ ⟨a ∼ of cars crossing the bridge⟩ — see FIFTH COLUMN **5 a :** the united monadelphous stamens in mallows **b :** the united androecium and gynoecium in orchids **c :** PROP, SUPPORT **d :** a decorative element made to resemble a pillar ⟨a cabinet with ∼*s* running up the length of each corner⟩ **6 :** any of various bodily parts or structures likened to a column or pillar: as **a :** the body of an actinian as distinguished from the base and disk **b :** the stalk of a crinoid **c :** a longitudinal subdivision of the spinal cord: as (1) **:** any of the principal longitudinal bundles of nerve fibers disposed as the anterior, the lateral, and the posterior divisions of white matter on each side and separated by the median fissures and spinal nerve roots — called also *funiculus* (2) **:** any of a number of smaller bundles of spinal nerve fibers **:** FASCICULUS ⟨the ∼ of Burdach⟩ (3) **:** any of the confluent longitudinal masses of nerve cells constituting the gray matter of each side — called also *gray column, gray horn;* see DORSAL COLUMN, LATERAL COLUMN, VENTRAL COLUMN **7 :** one of the vertical lines of a determinant or matrix in mathematics **8 :** the vertical or chronologic succession of geologic formations in a region

column 2a showing *1* base, *2* shaft, *3* capital

co·lum·na \kəˈləmnə\ *n, pl* **co·lum·nae** \-ˌnē, -ˌnī\ *also* **columnas** [L] **:** an anatomical structure that suggests a column in form — usu. used in combination

¹co·lum·nal \kəˈləmnəl\ *adj* [*column* + *-al*] **:** COLUMNAR

²columnal \"\ *n* -s **:** a columnar part or structure; *specif* **:** one of the vertical segments that make up the stem of a crinoid

co·lum·nar \kəˈləmnə(r)\ *adj* [LL *columnaris*, fr. L *columna* column + *-aris* -ar] **1 :** formed in columns **:** having the form of a column **:** like the shaft of a column ⟨∼ forms⟩ **2 :** of, relating to, or characterized by columns ⟨∼ construction⟩: as **a** *cryptology* **:** in columns **:** VERTICAL ⟨∼ writing⟩ **b :** by columns ⟨∼ transposition⟩ **3 :** of, derived from, or appearing in a newspaper column ⟨a popular ∼ character⟩

columnar epithelium *n* **:** epithelium consisting of or having the superficial layer composed of tall narrow somewhat cylindrical or prismatic cells and occurring in man chiefly in the digestive tract from the esophageal end of the stomach to the anus and in various glands and in parts of the kidneys — compare SQUAMOUS EPITHELIUM

col·um·nar·ia \ˌkäləmˈna(a)rēə\ *n, cap* [NL, fr. L *columna* column + NL *-aria*] **:** a genus of Silurian and Devonian compound tetracorals with small prismatic septate corallites

columnaris disease *also* **col·um·na·ris** \ˌkäləmˈna(a)rəs\ *n* -ES [NL *columnaris*, specific epithet of *Chondrococcus columnaris*, species causing the disease, fr. LL, columnar] **:** a highly fatal disease of fingerling trout and salmon esp. when concentrated in hatchery ponds that is caused by a myxobacterium (*Chondrococcus columnaris*)

co·lum·nar·ized \kəˈləmnəˌrīzd\ *adj* [*columnar* + *-ize* + *-ed*] **:** arranged in columns

co·lum·nar·ly *adv* **:** by means of a columnar transposition

columnar root *n* **:** PROP ROOT

columnar structure *n* **1 :** the structure of a mineral aggregate that is made up of nearly parallel slender columns and that is intermediate between an equant and acicular structure (as in some amphiboles) **2 :** a geologic structure common in basalts and other lavas that is characterized by the division of the rock into more or less regular often vertical prisms or columns which ordinarily have six but may have from three to eight sides and which may be nearly vertical or nearly horizontal

columnar transposition *n* **:** encipherment in which letters of the alphabet or of a message first written normally in the cells of a rectangle are copied out of it by reading down the columns in an agreed or keyed sequence to form a mixed alphabet or a ciphertext of the message — compare ROUTE TRANSPOSITION

column bone *n* **:** ²EPIPTERYGOID

column chart *n* **:** a chart representing comparative periods of fluctuation or the comparative size, length, value, or endurance of a group of things by means of juxtaposed proportional columns

co·lum·nea \kəˈləmnēə\ *n* [NL, after Fabio Colonna (Latinized as *Columna*) †*ab* 1640 It. scholar] **1** *cap* **:** a genus of tropical American evergreen herbs or subshrubs (family Gesneriaceae) that are often creeping or climbing, have thick opposite hairy leaves frequently unequal and somewhat toothed, produce axillary solitary or clustered yellow to scarlet flowers, and include several forms cultivated for their flowers and ornamental foliage **2** -s **:** any plant of the genus *Columnea*

col·umned \ˈkäləmd\ *adj* **:** having columns ⟨a ∼ portico⟩ **:** made in the form of or resembling a column ⟨trees with ∼ trunks⟩ **:** made up of columnar elements ⟨the ∼ foreshore⟩

co·lum·ni·a·tion \kəˌləmnēˈāshən\ *n* -s [modif. (influenced

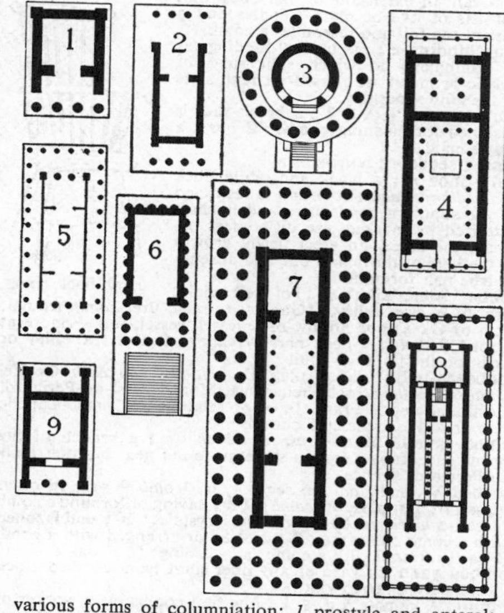

various forms of columniation: *1* prostyle and apteral; *2* amphiprostyle, amphistylar, and apteral; *3* monopteral; *4* and *5* peripteral; *6* pseudoperipteral; *7* dipteral; *8* pseudodipteral; *9* in antis

by E *intercolumniation*) of L *columnation-, columnatio*, fr. *columna* + *-ation-, -atio* -ation] **:** the employment or the arrangement of columns esp. free columns in a structure — see AMPHISTYLAR, APTERAL, DIPTERAL, DISTYLE, INTERCOLUMNIATION, MONOPTERAL, PERISTYLAR, PROSTYLE

co·lum·ni·form \kəˈləmnəˌfȯrm\ *adj* [L *columni-* (fr. *columna*) + E *-form*] **:** marked by column form **:** COLUMNAR

column inch *n* **:** a unit of measure for printed matter one column wide and one inch deep

col·um·nist \ˈkäləmnəst, -ləməst *sometimes* ÷ -lyəm-\ *n* -s **:** one that writes a newspaper column or conducts a radio or television program resembling such a column in its material and style ⟨a newspaper ∼⟩ ⟨a radio ∼⟩

column of ber·tin \bertaⁿ\ *usu cap B* [after Exupère-Joseph *Bertin* †1781 Fr. anatomist] **:** any of the masses of cortical tissue extending between the sides of the Malpighian pyramids of the kidney as far as the pelvis

column of lis·sau·er \ˈliˌsau̇ə(r)\ *cap L* [after Heinrich *Lissauer* †1891 Ger. neurologist] **:** LISSAUER'S TRACT

column of the fornix : either of the anterior pillars of the fornix

column of türck \ˈtœrk\ *usu cap T* [trans. of G *Türcksche Säule*, after Ludwig *Türck* †1868 Austrian physician] **:** the direct pyramidal tract in the spinal cord

column rule *n* **:** a rule usu. of exact column length used between columns of a page or table

columns *pl of* COLUMN

column still *n* **:** a still equipped with a column (sense 3 d)

co·lure \kəˈlu̇(ə)r, ˈkōˌl-\ *n* -s [LL *coluri*, pl., fr. Gk *kolouroi* colures, pl. of *kolouros* stump-tailed, fr. *kol-* (fr. *kolos* docked) + *-ouros* -urous; fr. the fact that in temperate latitudes a part is always below the horizon — more at HALT] **:** a great circle on the celestial sphere passing through the poles and the equinoxes or the solstices

co·lu·site \kəˈlüˌsīt\ *n* -s [*Colusa*, mining claim near Butte, Montana + E *-ite*] **:** a mineral consisting of a sulfide of copper and arsenic, tin, vanadium, iron, tellurium $Cu_3(As,Sn,V,Fe,Te)S_4$ occurring in tetrahedral crystals of bronze color

co·lu·tea \kəˈlüd·ēə\ *n, cap* [NL, fr. Gk *koloutea, koloitia*, a kind of tree or shrub (perh. a species of *Cytisus*)] **:** a small genus of Eurasian shrubs (family Leguminosae) with yellow flowers and a bladdery inflated fruit pod — see BLADDER SENNA

col·ville \ˈkälvəl\ *n, pl* **colville** *or* **colvilles** *usu cap* [fr. Fort *Colville*, old trading post near Kettle Falls, Wash.] **1 a :** a Salishan people of the Colville and Columbia river valleys, Washington **b :** a member of such people **2 :** a dialect of Okanagon, a Salishan language

colwort *obs var of* COLEWORT

co·ly \ˈkōlē\ *n* -ES [NL *colius*, prob. fr. Gk *kolios* green woodpecker] **:** any of a small group of fruit-eating African birds with long tails and soft somewhat hairy grayish brown plumage comprising the genus *Colius* (family Coliidae) and ranking as a distinct order (Coliiformes) — called also *mousebird*

colyba *var of* COLLYBA

co·lym·bi·dae \kəˈlimbəˌdē\ *n pl, cap* [NL, fr. *Colymbus*, type genus + *-idae*] **:** a family (coextensive with the order Colymbiformes) of aquatic birds that comprise the grebes and are closely related to the loons

co·lym·bi·form \kəˈlimbəˌfȯrm\ *adj* [NL *Colymbiformes*] **:** of, relating to, or like the Colymbiformes

co·lym·bi·for·mes \≈ˌ≈≈ˈfȯrˌmēz\ *n pl, cap* [NL, fr. *Colymbus* + *-iformes*] **:** a small cosmopolitan order of strong-flying water birds comprising the grebes that are distinguished from the related loons by their generally smaller size and their lack of webbed feet

co·lym·bus \kəˈlimbəs\ *n, cap* [NL, fr. Gk *kolymbos*, a kind of bird (prob. a grebe) — more at COLUMBINE] **:** the type genus of the family Colymbidae

co·lyt·ic \kəˈlid·ik\ *adj* [Gk *kōlytikos* hindering, preventive, fr. *kōlyein* to hinder] **1 :** INHIBITORY **2 :** ANTISEPTIC

col·yum \ˈkälyəm\ *n* -s [by alter.] **:** COLUMN 1d — **col·yum·ist** \-məst\ *n* -s

col·za \ˈkälzə, ˈkōl-\ *n* -s [F, fr. D *koolzaad*, fr. MD *coolsaet*, fr. *coole* cabbage + *saet* seed; akin to OHG *chōlo* cabbage and to OE *sǣd* seed — more at COLE, SEED] **1 :** any of several coles: as **a :** ²RAPE 2 **b :** any of several Asiatic coles resembling rape and producing seed that is used esp. in India as a source of oil **2 :** rapeseed esp. when used as a source of rape oil

colza oil *n* **:** rape oil esp. of a refined grade

com \ˈkäm\ *n* -s [by shortening] *slang Austral* **:** COMMUNIST

com- *or* **col-** *or* **con-** *or* **cor-** *in words having the stress pattern seen in "complain", "collect", "congratulation", "correct" ä rather than ə is sometimes the vowel in these prefixes, and ŋ rather than n is esp in Brit speech sometimes the second consonant in con- words before a syllable beginning with a g or k sound, as in "congratulate", "conclude"; the ä and ŋ variants have usu not been shown at individual entries*\ *prefix* [*com-* fr. ME, fr. OF, fr. L; *col-* fr. ME, fr. L, fr. *com-; con-* fr. ME, fr. OE (in *consolde* consound), fr. OF, fr. L, fr. *com-; cor-* fr. ME, fr. MF, fr. L, fr. *com-* — more at CO-] **:** with **:** together **:** jointly — usu. *com-* before *b* ⟨*com*burgess⟩ and *p* ⟨*com*panion⟩ or *m* ⟨*com*mingle⟩, *col-* before *l* ⟨*col*lingual⟩, *cor-* before *r* ⟨*cor*relation⟩ and *con-* before other sounds ⟨*con*cyclic⟩

¹com *abbr* **1** comedy; comic **2** comma

²com *or* **comm** *abbr* **1** command; commandant; commander; commanding **2** commemorative **3** commentary **4** commerce; commercial **5** commissary **6** commission; commissioned; commissioner **7** committee **8** commodore **9** common; commoner **10** commonwealth **11** communication **12** communist **13** community

¹co·ma \ˈkōmə\ *n* -s [NL, fr. Gk *kōma* deep sleep; perh. akin to MIr *cuma* sorrow, Gk *kamnein* to work, be weary, Skt *śamati* he works] **1 :** a state of profound unconsciousness caused by disease (as diabetes or uremia), injury, or poison **2 :** a state of mental or physical sluggishness **:** TORPOR ⟨lay in a ∼ of repletion⟩ ⟨they will rouse Western civilization from the ∼ of the Dark Ages —A.W.Griswold⟩

²coma \"\ *n, pl* **co·mae** \-ˌmē, -ˌmī\ [L, hair, fr. Gk *komē*] **1** *bot* **:** a tuft or bunch: as **a :** an assemblage of branches forming a leafy crown (as in many palms) **b :** a cluster of empty bracts terminating an inflorescence (as in the pineapple) **c :** a tuft of hairs on certain seeds (as of cotton or milkweed) **2 :** the head of a comet usu. containing a nucleus **3 :** a manifestation of spherical aberration in which the image of a point source not on the axis of a lens or mirror is a comet-shaped blur of light being produced by the varying magnification of the lens or mirror with varying distance from the axis **4** *Southwest* **:** SOUTHERN BUCKTHORN

-co·ma \-ˌkəmə\ *n comb form* [NL, fr. Gk *komē* hair] **:** haired one — in generic names ⟨*Abrocoma, Pycnocoma*⟩

co·ma·cine \ˈkōməˌchēn, -ˌsēn\ *n* -s [It *comacino*, fr. ML *comacinus, commacinus*, fr. LL *comacenus*, adj., of Como, irreg. fr. L *Comum* Como, city in Italy] **:** an early medieval Italian mason; *esp* **:** a member of a guild of medieval Italian masons supposedly persistent from classical times

comacine masters *n pl, usu cap C* **:** the Lombard master builders of the middle ages who influenced architecture of the period

co·magmatic \ˌkō+\ *adj* [*co-* + *magmatic*] *of igneous rocks* **:** having mineral or chemical peculiarities indicative of a closely similar magmatic source; *also* **:** indicating a region, district, or province in which such rocks occur

co·maker \(ˈ)kō+\ *n* -s [*co-* + *maker*] **:** one that participates in the preparation or formulation of something (as a treaty); *specif* **:** a person who formally accepts responsibility for the payment of a loan made to another if the latter fails to pay

¹co·mal \ˈkōməl\ *adj* [²*coma* + *-al*] *bot* **:** having or being a coma ⟨a ∼ tuft⟩

²co·mal \kōˈmäl\ *n, pl* **comals** \-lz\ *or* **coma·les** \-(ˌ)lās\ [AmerSp, fr. Nahuatl *comalli*] **1 :** a flat slab of sandstone used as a griddle **2 :** a griddle of earthenware or metal

coman *usu cap, var of* CUMAN

¹co·man·che \kəˈma(a)nchē\ *n, pl* **comanche** *or* **comanches** *usu cap* [Sp, of Shoshonean origin; perh. akin to Hopi *komanči* scalp lock, fr. *kópa* top of the head + *mánči* tied lock of hair] **1 a :** a Shoshonean people orig. in Wyoming and later ranging from Wyoming and Nebraska south into New Mexico and northwestern Texas **b :** a member of such people **2 :** the language of the Comanche people

²comanche \"\ *adj or n, usu cap* [fr. *Comanche*, town and county in Texas, locality of its type station] **:** COMANCHEAN

¹co·man·che·an \-chēən\ *adj, usu cap* [*Comanche*, Tex. + E *-an*] **1 :** of or relating to a period of the Mesozoic between the Jurassic and the Upper Cretaceous during which the great expansion of reptiles was the most striking feature of animal life and the appearance and spread of angiosperms the most notable fact connected with plant life **2 :** of, or relating to the system of rocks deposited during the Comanchean period ⟨∼ fossils⟩ — see GEOLOGIC TIME table

²comanchean \"\ *n* -s *usu cap* **:** the Comanchean period or system

co·man·che·ro \kəˌma(a)nˈche(ˌ)rō, ˌkō,-\ *n* -s *often cap* [MexSp, fr. Sp *comanche* + *-ero* -er] **:** a trader with the Indians of the southwest during the unsettled period of the 19th century

co·man·dan·cia \ˌkämənˈdanch(ē)ə; kōmänˈdänthyä *or* -dänsyä\ *n* -s [Sp, fr. *comandante*] **:** a province or district under military control; *also* **:** the headquarters of the commander of such a district

co·man·dan·te \ˌkämənˈdantē, kōmänˈdäntā\ *n* -s [Sp, fr. (assumed) VL *commandant-, commandans*, pres. part. of (assumed) VL *commandare* — more at COMMAND] **:** COMMANDANT

co·man·dra \kəˈmandrə\ *n, cap* [NL, fr. L *coma* hair + NL *-andra;* fr. the hairy calyx lobes that are attached to the anthers — more at COMA] **:** a small genus of chiefly No. American herbs (family Santalaceae) that are usu. partial parasites attaching to other plants by underground holdfasts and that have creeping stems, whitish flowers in terminal clusters, and a dry nut as fruit

co·man·ic acid \(ˈ)kōˌmanik-\ *n* [ISV, alter. of *comenic acid*] **:** a crystalline acid $C_5H_3O_2COOH$ obtained by partial decarboxylation of chelidonic acid; 1,4-pyrone-2-carboxylic acid

co·ma·ni·to \ˌkōməˈnēd·(ˌ)ō\ *n, pl* **comanito** *or* **comanitos** *usu cap* [Sp] **1 :** a Taracahitian people of Sinaloa, Mexico **2 :** a member of the Comanito people

co·mar·ca \kōˈmärkə\ *n* -s [Sp, fr. ML *commarca* boundary, confines, fr. *com-* + *marca* boundary, border territory, of Gmc origin; akin to OHG *marca* border, border region — more at MARK] **:** a territorial subdivision (as a district or circuit) of a state — used chiefly of administrative units of certain Latin-American nations

co·mart \kōˈmärt\ *n* [prob. misprint of *cov'nant*] **:** COVENANT — used in the 1605 quarto of Shakespeare's *Hamlet* I. i. 93, but in later versions often considered a misprint and emended to *covenant or compact*

comas *pl of* COMA

¹co·mate \(ˈ)kō+\ *n* [*co-* + *mate*] **:** COMPANION

²co·mate \ˈkōˌmāt\ *adj* [L *comatus*, fr. *coma* hair + *-atus* -ate — more at COMA] **:** covered with hair or filaments **:** HAIRY, SHAGGY

co·mat·ic \(ˈ)kōˈmad·ik\ *adj* [irreg. (influence of *comatose*) fr. ²*coma* (blur) + *-ic*] *of an optical image* **:** blurred as a result of coma

co·ma·tose \ˈkōməˌtōs, ˈkäm-\ *also* **co·ma·tous** \-mə|d·əs, -təs\ *adj* [F *comateux*, fr. Gk *kōmat-, kōma* deep sleep + F *-eux* -ose, -ous — more at COMA] **1 :** relating to, resembling, or affected with coma ⟨∼ breathing⟩ ⟨a ∼ state⟩ ⟨∼ patients⟩ **2 :** LETHARGIC, TORPID, DROWSY ⟨stout old men ∼ on the sunny porch⟩ **:** dull and inactive ⟨the market has been ∼ for several days⟩ ⟨Broadway was theatrically ∼ that summer⟩ **syn** see LETHARGIC

co·mat·u·la \kōˈmachələ\ *n, pl* **comatulae** \-ˌlē\ [NL, former generic name (now *Antedon*), fem. of LL *comatulus* having hair neatly curled, fr. L *comatus* hairy] **:** COMATULID

co·mat·u·lid \-ləd\ *n* -s [NL *Comatulidae*, former family name (now *Antedonidae*), fr. *Comatula*, type genus + *-idae*] **:** a free-swimming stalkless crinoid — called also *feather sta*

coma vigil *n* [¹*coma*] **:** a state of coma in which the patient lies unconscious but with the eyes open

¹comb \ˈkōm\ *n, pl* **combs** \-mz\ [ME, fr. OE *camb;* akin

combs 2: *1* single, *2* pea, *3* rose, *4* V-shaped, *5* strawberry

to OHG *kamb*, ON *kambr* comb, Gk *gomphos* tooth, peg, Skt *jambha* molar, fang] **1 a :** an instrument consisting of a thin strip (as of plastic, metal, or bone) with a row of teeth on one or both edges or sides that is used for adjusting, cleaning, or confining the hair or for adornment **b :** any of several toothed devices used in handling or ordering textile fibers: (1) **:** a toothed instrument for separating, ordering, and cleansing fibers (as of wool, flax, or hair); *also* **:** the machine of which it is the basic part (2) **:** the serrated vibratory device used to strip fiber from the doffer of a carding machine (3) **:** a reed of a loom and esp. of a hand loom **c :** a toothed instrument for currying hairy animals or cleansing and smoothing their coats **:** CURRYCOMB **d :** the collector of an electrostatic machine **e** (1) **:** a toothed instrument used to form patterns on a painted surface that typically resemble grained wood or marbled paper (2) **:** a pattern so formed **f :** a tool having teeth similar to those on a saw and used in finishing stone **2 :** the fleshy crest or caruncle on the head of the domestic fowl and certain other gallinaceous birds usu. best developed in the male — see PEA COMB, ROSE COMB, SINGLE COMB, STRAWBERRY COMB **3 :** something resembling or suggesting the comb of a cock: as **a :** the crest of a helmet; *esp* **:** the upright blade on a morion **b** *dial* **:** the crest or ridge of a mountain or hill **c :** the ridge of a roof **d :** a ridge or crest of hair **e :** the upper edge of the buttstock of a shoulder firearm against which the firer's cheek rests during firing **f :** the curling crest of a wave **g :** a hook on which bacon slabs are hung for smoking **4 :** a structure resembling a comb (sense 1a): as **a :** the pecten of a scorpion **b :** the pecten of a bird's eye **c :** one of the ciliated swimming plates of a ctenophore **d :** STRIGIL 2 **e :** CTENIDIUM 2 **5 a :** HONEYCOMB; *also* **:** one of the somewhat similar masses of cells built by social wasps **b :** an aggregate of crystals resembling a honeycomb that have grown outward from the walls of a vein or cavity so that their closely set points or ends project

²comb \"\ *vb* **combed** \-md\ **combed** \"\ **combing** \-miŋ\ **combs** \-mz\ [ME *comben*, fr. *comb*, n.] *vt* **1 :** to draw a comb through **:** disentangle with or as if with a comb: **a :** to lay straight **:** DRESS, ARRANGE ⟨~ one's hair⟩ **b :** to cleanse, disentangle, and collect together (animal or vegetable fibers) by the use of a comb preparatory to spinning so that only the longer fibers are collected, the short staple being combed away — compare ¹CARD 1 **c :** to dress or finish (stone) with a comb **2 :** THRASH, BEAT **3 a :** SCRAPE, RAKE **:** afflict as by raking ⟨the storm ~*ed* the whole state⟩ **b :** FLATTEN, ERODE ⟨huge waves ~*ing* down the dunes⟩ **c :** to shell systematically ⟨~*ing* the enemy's position with our guns⟩ **4 a :** to remove or eliminate with or as if with a comb ⟨~ out snarls⟩ ⟨~ out head lice⟩ ⟨~ subversives out of the organization⟩ **:** treat with or as if with a comb in order to remove anything undesirable — usu. used with *out* ⟨~ out a staff in search of dishonest persons⟩ **b :** SEPARATE, SORT ⟨~*ing* out of the tangle the right elements⟩ ⟨~ army recruits from industries⟩ **5 a :** to search or examine systematically and thoroughly omitting or ignoring no part or detail ⟨~ all the evidence⟩ ⟨~ the whole trial record for reasons for appeal⟩ ⟨~ the woodland for traces of the lost children⟩ ⟨police ~*ing* the city for the killer⟩ **b :** to seek out and collect from — used esp. of one that gathers flotsam cast up by the sea ⟨added to his income by ~*ing* the little beach beyond the point⟩ **6 :** to use in the manner of a comb ⟨~*ing* his fingers through his long red beard⟩ **~** *vi* **1** *of a wave or its crest* **:** to roll over **:** break into foam **2 :** to flow or come over like a combing wave **syn** see SEEK

³comb \ˈküm, ˈkōm\ *var of* COMBE

comb *abbr* **1** combination; combined; combining **2** combustion

com·bas·sou *also* **com·ba·sou** \kəmˈba(,)sü\ *n* -s [native name in southern Africa] **:** a small southern African seed-eating finch (*Hypochera funerea*) with white bill and red feet, the male bluish black and the female brownish, that is often kept as a cage or aviary bird

¹com·bat \kəmˈbat, ˈkäm,bat *sometimes* ˈkəm,bat *or* kämˈbat *or* ˈkəmbət; *Brit usu & US sometimes* ˈkämbət; *usu* -d·+V\ *vb* **combated** *or* **combatted; combated** *or* **combatted; combating** *or* **combatting; combats** [MF *combattre*, fr. (assumed) VL *combattere*, fr. L *com-* + *-battere* (fr. *battuere* to beat) — more at BAT] *vi* **:** STRUGGLE, CONTEND, FIGHT ⟨~ fiercely with an enemy⟩ ⟨nations ~ to make one submit —Lord Byron⟩ ⟨fiercely ~*ed* with death —Amy Lowell⟩ **~** *vt* **1 :** to fight with **:** BATTLE **2 :** to struggle against or oppose esp. by argument ⟨there was nobody to ~ that royal will —Edith Sitwell⟩ **:** work against **:** strive to reduce or eliminate ⟨~ malnutrition and disease⟩ ⟨~ inflation⟩ **syn** see ¹CONTEST

²com·bat \ˈkäm,bat *sometimes* ˈkəm-; *Brit usu & US sometimes* -,bət; *usu* -d·+V\ *n* -s *often attrib* [MF, fr. *combattre*, v.] **1 :** a fight, encounter, or contest between individuals or groups ⟨furious ~ of antlered stags⟩ **:** DUEL; *specif* **:** an engagement between contending armed forces esp. when of lesser extent than a battle **2 :** CONFLICT, STRUGGLE, CONTROVERSY ⟨~ between contenders for political office⟩ ⟨two years of almost continuous parliamentary ~ —F.L.Paxson⟩ ⟨a quiet man, he hated ~⟩ ⟨such strenuous ~*s* as the humanist-naturalist or the aesthetic-sociological controversies —F.B.Millett⟩ **3 :** actual fighting engagement of military forces as distinguished from other military duties or periods of active service without fighting **:** ACTION **syn** see ²CONTEST

¹com·bat·ant \kəmˈbatᵊnt, -adənt *sometimes* ˈkäm,ba-; *Brit usu & US also* ˈkämbətᵊnt *or* -bəd·ənt *or* -bətᵊnt; *Brit sometimes* ˈkəmbə-\ *n* -s [MF *combattant*, fr. *combattant*, adj.] **:** one that engages in combat

²combatant \"\ *adj* [MF *combattant*, fr. pres. part. of *combattre*] **:** contending or disposed to contend: as **a :** taking part in or prepared to take part in active fighting ⟨a ~ officer⟩ **b** *also* **com·bat·tant** \"\ *heraldry* **:** rampant and facing each other as if in combat — used of representations of two animals ⟨two lions ~⟩

combat boot *n* **:** a heavy laced leather boot esp. with a wide cuff buckled above the ankle

combat command *n* **:** a major tactical unit within an armored division consisting of a headquarters and headquarters company and a variable number of attached units (as of armor, infantry, and artillery)

combat fatigue *also* **combat exhaustion** *n* **:** a traumatic psychoneurotic reaction (as of the anxiety type) or an acute psychotic reaction occurring during wartime combat or under conditions causing stress similar to that of combat — called also *fatigue syndrome*

combat intelligence *n* **:** military intelligence for use in a combat area gathered by combat units in the field or furnished to them from other sources

com·bat·ive \kəmˈbad·iv, |tiv, -ēv *also* -əv, *Brit usu & US sometimes* ˈkämbə|, *esp Brit sometimes* ˈkəmbə|\ *adj* **:** disposed to combat **:** marked by belligerence **:** PUGNACIOUS **syn** see BELLIGERENT

combative accent *n* **:** a speech accent that does not coincide with metrical ictus in classical verse

com·bat·ive·ly \-əvlē, -li\ *adv* **:** in a combative manner **:** BELLIGERENTLY

com·bat·ive·ness \-ivnəs, -ēv-\ *n* -ES **:** the state or quality of being combative **:** PUGNACITY, BELLIGERENCE ⟨admitting that man's nature will never lose the ~, hostility, and animosity which are so large a part of it —Norman Angell⟩

com·ba·tiv·i·ty \,kämbəˈtivəd·ē, *esp Brit sometimes* ,kəm-\ *n* -ES **:** COMBATIVENESS

combat jacket *n* **:** BATTLE JACKET 1

combat load *vt* **:** to load (a ship) so that combat supplies and materiel may be more readily unloaded (as by amphibious assault troops) than noncombat supplies and materiel

combat orders *n pl* **:** orders containing instructions for operations in a military campaign (as letters of instruction, operation orders, and administrative orders)

combat practice *n* **:** an individual or small-unit tactical problem that must be solved under simulated combat conditions and that requires firing live ammunition at appropriate targets

combat team *n* **:** a tactical nonorganic grouping of military forces capable of maintaining independent operation with its own weapons and supplies, usu. combining infantry and artillery, air and tank forces or surface craft, aircraft, and submarines; *specif* **:** an infantry regiment or battalion reinforced by the attachment of artillery, engineers, or medical or other troops for a particular combat mission

combat unit *n* **:** a military unit whose organization, equipment, and training are designed to fit it to engage in combat

combat zone *n* **:** the forward part of a theater of military operations extending from the front line to the forward boundary of the communication zone

comb-back \ˈ=,=\ *adj, of a Windsor chair* **:** having above the arm rail an extension of the back that consists of five or more spindles and a curved top rail and resembles a comb

comb-back chair

comb binding *n* **:** mechanical binding (as of pamphlets) in which split rings of plastic or metal are passed through slots at the gutter margin

comb-brush \ˈ=,=\ *n* **1 :** a brush that is designed for cleaning combs **2** *obs* **:** a lady's maid

comb disease *n* **:** WHITECOMB

comb duck *n* **:** a black and white duck (*Sarkidiornis melanotos*) that is restricted to the southern hemisphere and is characterized by marked size differences between the sexes, an erect fleshy growth at the base of the male's bill, and absence of true pair formation

combe \ˈküm, ˈkōm\ *n* -s [of Celt origin; akin to W *cwm* valley, IrGael *cum* vessel, Bret *komm* trough; akin to Gk *kymbē* hollow of a vessel, vessel, cup — more at HUMP] **1** *Brit* **:** a deep narrow valley **2** *Brit* **:** a valley or basin on the flank of a hill

combe-ca·pelle \¦kōm(,)ka¦pel\ *adj, usu cap both Cs* [fr. *Combe-Capelle*, a rock shelter near Montferrand-du-Périgord, Dordogne dept., France] **:** of or relating to Combe-Capelle man or to the associated culture

combe-capelle man *n, usu cap both Cs* **:** a branch of the Brünn race known from a skeleton found near Montferrand-du-Périgord, France

combed \¦kōmd\ *adj* [in sense 1, fr. ¹*comb* + *-ed;* in other senses, fr. past part. of ²*comb*] **1 a :** having or forming a comb ⟨a tall-*combed* cock⟩ ⟨~ quartz crystals⟩ **b :** emblazoned with a comb **:** CRESTED **2 :** dressed or arranged with a comb **3 :** as if dressed with a comb ⟨a ~ ceiling⟩ ⟨a ~ oak dresser⟩

combed yarn *n* **:** yarn of any fiber spun from combed stock — compare CARDED YARN

comb·er \ˈkōmə(r)\ *n* -s **1 :** one that combs (as a worker or machine that combs wool or flax) **2 :** a long curling wave of the sea **3 :** cotton of a staple length and grade suitable for combing

comber board *n* **:** a perforated wooden frame in a loom through which the lower ends of the harness cords are passed to keep them separate

comber leather *n* **:** a heavily greased cattlehide leather used in combing machines in the textile industry

comb fern *n* **:** CURLY GRASS

combflower \ˈ=,=\ *n* **1 :** COMMON SUNFLOWER **2 :** PURPLE CONEFLOWER

comb-footed \ˈ=¦==\ *adj, of a spider* **:** having calamistra

comb foundation *n* **:** FOUNDATION 5g

comb grain *n* **:** grain in quarter-sawed lumber of plainly marked narrow nearly parallel stripes of darker and lighter color — **comb-grained** \ˈ=¦=\ *adj*

comb honey *n* **:** honey kept intact in the honeycomb

combier *comparative of* COMBY

combiest *superlative of* COMBY

com·bin·abil·i·ty \kəm,bīnəˈbiləd·ē, -ətē, -i\ *n* -ES **:** ability (as relative ability) to enter into combination

com·bin·able \kəmˈbīnəbəl\ *adj* **:** that can be combined

¹com·bi·nate \ˈkämbə,nāt\ *vt* -ED/-ING/-S [LL *combinatus*, past part. of *combinare*] **1 :** COMBINE **2 :** to form (the teeth of a self-distributing linotype matrix) so that the matrix will fall into its proper channel **3 :** to set up the combination of (a lock)

²combinate *adj* [LL *combinatus*] *obs* **:** COMBINED, BETROTHED

¹com·bi·na·tion \,kämbəˈnāshən\ *n* -s [MF, fr. LL *combination-, combinatio* union, fr. *combinatus* (past part. of *combinare* to combine) + L *-ion-, -io* -ion — more at COMBINE] **1 :** the result or product of combining **:** a union or aggregate made by combining one thing with another: as **a** (1) **:** a union or alliance of individuals, corporations, or states for some special purpose formerly often to achieve a result contrary to law or public welfare but now usu. to achieve a legitimate social, political, or economic end — see COMBINATION IN RESTRAINT OF TRADE (2) **:** a binomial taxonomic name formed by combining a specific epithet with a generic name (3) **:** two or more members of a team in competitive sports who perform esp. well together (4) **:** a small jazz band esp. when playing without elaborate arrangements; *also* **:** any dance band **b :** a series of events or results occurring in an ordered sequence: as (1) **:** a sequence of moves in chess so planned as to force the responses of the opponent and gain a decisive advantage often at the expense of an initial sacrifice (2) **:** a sequence of letters or numbers in a particular order chosen in setting a combination lock; *also* **:** the mechanism operating or moved by the sequence (3) **:** any one of the different sets into which a number of individuals (as letters) may be grouped without regard to the order of arrangement within the group — compare PERMUTATION 3b (4) **:** a sequence of synchronized blows delivered by a boxer in rapid succession **c :** a union of mechanical parts so arranged that they interact to produce a practical result — compare AGGREGATION **d :** any of various one-piece garments covering the upper and lower parts of the body; *esp* **:** UNION SUIT — usu. used in pl. **e :** an instrument designed to perform two or more tasks ⟨a radio-phonograph ~⟩; *specif* **:** a haulage tractor and one or more trailers that it draws **2 a :** the act or process of combining **:** the quality or state of being combined **b :** the act or process of uniting to form a chemical compound; *sometimes* **:** the compound so formed **3 :** a group of organ stops used in performance at one or more specific points; *also* **:** the tonal effect produced by such a group

²combination \¦==¦==\ *adj* **1 :** of, relating to, or exhibiting combination **:** used in combination **:** resulting from combination **2 :** serving more than one purpose ⟨a ~ saddle and harness horse⟩ ⟨a ~ bed-sitting room⟩ **3 a** *of a plied yarn* **:** made of single yarns of different fibers, size, or twist **b** *of a fabric* **:** made of combination yarns or of two different yarns

com·bi·na·tion·al \¦==¦nāshənᵊl, -shnəl\ *adj* **:** of or relating to combination **:** having the quality of combining

com·bi·na·tion·al·ism \,=ˈ=ˈnāshənᵊl,izəm, -shnə,li-\ *n* -s **:** the practice of combining varying intellectual elements esp. without sufficient attention to systematic integration

combination board *n, papermaking* **:** a board made on a cylinder machine in which one or both of the outer plies differ from the middle ply as to color or material

combination by volume **:** the action, process, or ratio by which gaseous elements and compounds unite in definite proportions by volume to form distinct compounds

combination by weight **:** the action, process, or ratio by which substances unite (in compounds) in proportions by weight, relatively fixed and exact — see LAW OF DEFINITE PROPORTIONS

combination chuck *n* **:** a chuck with jaws that may be moved simultaneously or independently

combination door *n* **:** an outer door with interchangeable panels, one screened for warm-weather use, the other glazed for cold-weather use

combination in restraint of trade **:** any monopoly or attempt at monopoly or any contract, combination, or conspiracy intended to restrain trade or commerce among the states or with the territories, the District of Columbia, or foreign nations, all such, excepting resale price-maintenance agreements permitted by fair-trade laws, being declared illegal by the antitrust laws of the U.S. — compare COMBINATION

combination last *n* **:** a shoe last in which there is a variation from the standard measurements, the heel or instep portion being narrower than normal

combination lock *n* **:** a lock whose mechanism is controlled by one or more movable dials or rings inscribed with letters or figures and that may only be opened after the dial has been so turned as to combine the characters in a certain order

combination package *n* **:** a package of fourth-class mail to the outside of which is affixed a letter or other piece of first-class mail matter — used in the U.S. postal system

combination piston *n* **:** a device that acts on a combination of organ stops and allows the combination to be thrown on or off with a single movement

combination plane *n* **:** a plane that has interchangeable cutters of various shapes and is usable for rabbeting, grooving, making moldings, and other special processes

combination plate *n* **:** a photoengraving plate produced by more than one process; *specif* **:** a photomechanical engraving in which the printing surface contains both line and halftone images

combination pliers *n pl but sing or pl in constr* **:** slip-joint pliers with a notched inner grip for holding and grasping round objects and cutting and bending wire

combination plow *n* **:** a moldboard plow with interchangeable bottom parts suitable for different soil conditions

combination rate *n* **:** a through rate formed by combining two or more rates

combination room *n* **:** a common room at Cambridge University

combination rubber *n* **:** sheet rubber with a linen web or webs through it used esp. to pack pipe joints

combination sale *n* **:** a sale coupling two products at a unit price slightly higher than the price of one

combination shot *n* **1 :** a pool shot in which a ball is pocketed by causing another object ball to strike it **2 :** an English billiards shot in which a player scores in two ways (as by cannoning and pocketing the red ball)

combination square *n* **:** a measuring tool consisting of a steel rule that slides through an adjustable protractor head or level or a center head which can be fixed at any point on the rule by a lock bolt and being usable as an inside or outside try square, a marking or depth gauge, level, miter square, plumb, and straightedge

combination stacker *n* **:** a combined buck rake and hay stacker

combination tone *also* **combination note** *n* **:** a subjective tone heard by many observers when two pure tones of widely different frequency are sounded together and thought to be due to the fact that the human ear does not in general give a linear response to sound waves — compare AURAL HARMONIC, DIFFERENCE TONE, SUMMATION TONE

combination wrench *n* **:** a wrench with one open end and one socket end

combination wrench

com·bi·na·tive \ˈkämbə,nā|d·iv, kəmˈbīnə|\ *adj* [*combination* + *-ive*] **:** tending or able to combine **:** marked by, relating to, or resulting from combination; *specif, of sound change* **:** dependent on phonetic environment ⟨the change of an orig. short vowel into a long vowel in the ancestors of English *field* is ~ because of the vowel's being followed by a liquid and a homorganic voiced stop⟩

com·bi·na·to·ri·al \kəm¦bīnə¦tōrēəl\ *adj* [*combinatory* + *-al*] **:** of or relating to combination or combinations **:** involving combination

combinatorial analysis *n* **:** the mathematical study of permutations and combinations of finite sets of objects

com·bi·na·to·ry \kəmˈbīnə,tōrē\ *adj* [*combination* + *-ory*] **:** COMBINATIVE, COMBINATORIAL

combinatory logic *n* **:** a branch of symbolic logic that deals esp. with the notion of substitution and the eliminability of variables in favor of special function symbols

¹com·bine \kəmˈbīn\ *vb* -ED/-ING/-S [ME *combynen*, fr. MF *combiner*, fr. LL *combinare*, fr. L *com-* + *bini* two by two — more at BINARY] *vt* **1 :** to bring into close relationship: **a :** to join in physical or chemical union (as two substances) ⟨~ toxin and living tissue to produce antitoxin⟩; *specif* **:** to cause to unite into a chemical compound ⟨*combining* hydrogen with sulfur⟩ **b :** to cause to unite or associate harmoniously (as in a joint action or into an organic whole) ⟨~ their efforts to a common end⟩ ⟨the growing town of South Bethlehem was . . . to be *combined* with the mother town —*Amer. Guide Series: Pa.*⟩ **2 :** to cause (as two or more things or ideas) to mix together **:** MINGLE, BLEND ⟨*combining* the language of the gutter with ideas of undoubted worth⟩ ⟨~ the sugar, flour, and butter⟩ **3 :** to possess or exhibit (as qualities or attributes) in combination ⟨one who ~*s* creative imagination with true scholarliness⟩ **~** *vi* **1 a :** to become one **:** COALESCE, INTEGRATE ⟨the two papers *combined* as the *Chronicle*⟩ **b :** to unite in definite proportions by weight to form a distinct chemical compound **2 :** to come together or join forces (as for a common purpose) **:** act together to accomplish an aim ⟨the foreign powers *combined* in a note reprimanding the aggressor's action⟩ ⟨~ to raise wages in an industry⟩ **syn** see JOIN, UNITE

²com·bine \ˈkäm,bīn\ *n* -s **1 :** an act or result of combining **2 :** a combination (as of persons) to effect some object; *sometimes* **:** one having a purpose that is illegal or against the public interest **3** *also* **combine harvester :** a harvesting machine that heads, threshes, and cleans grain while moving over the field **4 :** a passenger-train car divided into two or more parts for handling different classes of items (as passengers and baggage)

³combine \"\ *vb* -ED/-ING/-S *vt* **:** to harvest with a combine **~** *vi* **:** to combine a crop

com·bined \kəmˈbīnd\ *adj* **1 a :** formed by combination **:** joined together into one **:** UNITED **b :** formed into a chemical compound **2 :** performed by agents in combination **3 :** concerned with or consisting of a combination — used of previously or usu. separate items or considerations ⟨a ~ intelligence service —A.L.Funk⟩ **4 :** considered as a whole **:** added together ⟨mercenaries outnumbered all other troops ~⟩ ⟨his talents and looks ~ got him the job⟩ — **com·bined·ly** \-n(ə)dlē\ *adv* — **com·bined·ness** \-nədnəs, -n(d)nəs\ *n* -ES

combined carbon *n* **:** the portion of the carbon in iron and steel that is chemically united in the form of carbides — distinguished from *graphitic carbon*

combined experience table *n* **:** a mortality table based on the experience of 17 British companies that was used in the U.S. prior to 1901

combined method *n* **:** a method of teaching the deaf in which features of both the manual method and the oral method are used

combined operation *n* **1 :** a military operation in which several allies coordinate their armed forces to accomplish a single mission, effect a defense, or gain some other goal **2** *Brit* **:** an often amphibious operation requiring the coordinated efforts of two or more services — often used in pl

com·bine·ment \kəmˈbīnmənt\ *n* -s *archaic* **:** COMBINATION

com·bin·er \-nə(r)\ *n* -s **:** one that combines: as **a :** a machine that applies adhesive to the plies of paper or board and presses them together to produce laminated board **b :** one that arranges plastics sheets in desired combinations and finishes and cements them and presses them in a hydraulic press

com·bi·net \¦kämbə¦net\ *n* -s [*combination* + *-et*] **:** a handled lidded pail usu. of enameled metal combining the function of chamber pot and slop jar

combine type *n* **:** a class or variety of a crop adapted to harvesting with a combine

combing *n* -s *often attrib* **1 :** the action or process of using a comb or combs: as **a :** the straightening and ordering of wool or other fibers of long staple by a combing machine with elimination of shorter fibers **b :** a method of decorating pottery in the wet state by scratching with a comb **2 combings** *pl* **:** loose hair removed with a comb **3 :** COMBING WOOL **4 :** an action of combing or like combing esp. in thoroughness ⟨a skillful ~ of the salvage incidents . . . for the stories that bear retelling —Alfred Stanford⟩

combing machine *n* **:** a machine for combing wool, flax, cotton, or other fibers and separating the longer and more valuable fiber from the shorter — compare CARDING MACHINE

combing wool *n* **:** long-stapled strong-fibered wool suitable for combing and used esp. in the manufacture of worsteds

combining *pres part of* COMBINE

combining form *n* **:** a linguistic form that occurs only in compounds or derivatives and can be distinguished descriptively from an affix by its ability to occur as one immediate constituent of a form whose only other immediate constituent is an affix (as *cephal-* in *cephalic*) or by its being an allomorph of a morpheme that has another allomorph that may occur alone (as *electro-* representing *electric* in *electromagnet*, *resini-* representing *resin* in *resiniferous*, *forma-* representing *formaldehyde* in *formalith*, *para-* representing *parachute* in *paratrooper*) or can be distinguished historically from an affix by

the fact that it is borrowed from another language in which it is descriptively a word (as French *mal* giving English *mal-* in *malodorous*) or a combining form (as Greek *kako-*, combining form of *kakos*, giving English *caco-* in *cacography*)
combining weight *n* **:** EQUIVALENT 2a
com·bite \kämˈbēt\ *also* **coum·bite** \küm-\ *n* -s [AmerF (Haiti)] **:** an informal cooperative group of Haitians helping a neighbor in his work to the accompaniment of drumming and singing
comb jelly *n* **:** CTENOPHORE
com·ble \kōⁿbl(ᵊ), -b(lə)\ *n* -s [F, fr. L *cumulus* heap, summit; akin to L *cavus* hollow — more at CAVE] **:** culminating point **:** ACME
combmaker \ˈ=,==\ *n* -s **:** one who makes combs
comb marbling *n, papermaking* **:** marbling in patterns produced by use of the comb — called also *drawn edge*
comb–mouth bryozoan *n* **:** one of the Ctenostomata
com·bo \ˈkäm(,)bō\ *n* -s [*comb-* (fr. *combination*) + *-o*] **1** *slang* **:** COMBINATION; *esp* **:** COMBINATION 1a(4) **2** *Austral* **:** a white man living with an aboriginal woman
comb–out \ˈ=,=\ *n* -s [fr. *comb out,* v.] **:** an act of combing (as of an industry for workers fit for military service or of criminals from a district)
com·boy \ˈkäm,bȯi\ *n* -s [Sinhalese *kambāya,* perh. fr. *Cambay,* India, where it is produced] *Ceylon* **:** SARONG
comb perforation *n* **:** a stamp perforation made by a machine that punches at one stroke the vertical perforations between the stamps in a single row across a sheet and the horizontal perforations at the top of this row
comb piece \ˈ=,=\ *n* **:** the extension of the back characteristic of a comb-back Windsor chair
comb pottery *n* **:** a late neolithic pottery found in Baltic countries that is ornamented by combing
comb rat *n* [so called fr. the comblike bristles of the hind feet] **:** the gundi or a related rodent
com·bre·ta·ce·ae \,kämbrəˈtāsē,ē\ *n pl, cap* [NL, fr. *Combretum,* type genus + *-aceae*] **:** a family of tropical shrubs and trees (order Myrtales) with usu. entire often terminal leaves, mostly perfect flowers with 4 to 6 ovules, and a single-celled indehiscent fruit — **com·bre·ta·ceous** \;==;==shəs\ *adj*
com·bre·tum \kəmˈbrēd·əm\ *n* [NL, fr. L, a kind of plant; akin to ON *hvönn* wild angelica, Ir *cuinneog,* Lith *švendrai* cattail] **1** *cap* **:** the type genus of the family Combretaceae, comprising numerous tropical and subtropical small shrubs and trees typically with hard tough wood, bark rich in tannins, flowers with bell-shaped calyces in spikes or racemes, and winged one-seeded fruits **2** -s **:** a plant of the genus *Combretum*
comb ridge *n* **:** a jagged steep-sided mountain ridge with pinnacles and notches along its crest like a cockscomb **:** ARÊTE; *esp* **:** the sharp divide between opposing cirques in a vigorously glaciated mountain range
combs *pl of* COMB, *pres 3 sing of* COMB
comb scab *n* **:** WHITECOMB
comb shell *n* **:** PECTEN 2b
comb speedwell *n* **:** a prostrate Asiatic herb (*Veronica pectinata*) with often pectinate or divided leaves
comb–toothed shark \ˈ=,=-\ *n* **:** a shark of the family Hexanchidae: *esp* **:** a cow shark (*Hexanchus griseus*)
[1]**com·bu·rent** *also* **com·bu·rant** \kəmˈbyu̇rənt\ *adj* [L *comburent-, comburens,* pres. part. of *comburere* to burn up — more at COMBUSTION] **:** burning or supporting combustion — distinguished from *combustible*
[2]**comburent** *also* **comburant** \"\ *n* -s **:** a substance that burns or that aids combustion
com·burgess \(ˈ)käm+\ *n* -ES [*com-* + *burgess;* trans. of ML *comburgensis*] **1 :** a fellow burgess **2 :** a onetime magistrate elected in certain English boroughs and associated with the alderman
com·bu·rim·e·ter \,kämbyəˈrimәd·ə(r)\ *n* -s [ISV *combur-* (fr. L *comburere* to burn up) + *-i-* + *-meter* — more at COMBUSTION] **:** an apparatus for determining the proportion of air required for the ideal combustion of a gas — **com·bu·rim·e·try** \-mə·trē\ *n* -ES
com·bu·riv·o·rous \;kämbyə;rivərəs\ *adj* [L *comburere* to burn + E *-i-* + *-vorous*] **:** consuming by combustion ⟨the ~ power of a gas⟩ — compare COMBURENT
[1]**com·bust** \kəmˈbəst\ *adj* [ME, fr. MF, fr. L *combustus,* past part. of *comburere* to burn up — more at COMBUSTION] **1** *of a planet* **:** so near the sun as to be obscured or overpowered by its light **2** *obs* **:** BURNED, CONSUMED
[2]**combust** \"\ *vb* -ED/-ING/-S *vt* **:** BURN, CONSUME ⟨machines are delivering up to 25 percent of the fuel they ~ —D.C. Peattie⟩ ~ *vi* **1 :** to burn fuel ⟨the engine regularly ~*ed* — Andy Logan⟩ **2 :** BURN **:** become consumed — used chiefly of fuels
com·bus·ti·bil·i·ty \kəm,bəstəˈbiləd·ē, -ətē, -i\ *n* -ES [ME *combustebyllyte,* fr. MF *combustible* + ME *-ite* -ity] **:** the quality or state of being combustible
[1]**com·bus·ti·ble** \kəmˈbəstəbəl\ *adj* [MF, fr. *combustion* + *-ible*] **1 :** capable of undergoing combustion or of burning — used esp. of materials that catch fire and burn when subjected to fire; compare FLAMMABLE **2 a :** easily kindled or excited ⟨the concentrated ~ essence of sex —Claudia Cassidy⟩ **b :** QUICK, FIERY, IRASCIBLE — **com·bus·ti·bly** \-təblē, -li\ *adv*
[2]**combustible** \"\ *n* -s **:** a thing that is combustible
combustible shale *n* **:** TASMANITE
com·bus·tion \kəmˈbəschən\ *n* -s [ME, fr. MF or LL; MF, fr. LL *combustion-, combustio,* fr. L *combustus* (past part. of *comburere* to burn up, irreg. — influenced by *amburere* to burn up, fr. *ambi-* + *urere* — fr. *com-* + *urere* to burn) + *-ion-, -io* -ion — more at EMBER] **1 :** a process or instance of burning: as **a :** any chemical process accompanied by the evolution of light and heat, being typically a vigorous union of substances with oxygen; *sometimes* **:** slower oxidation (as in the animal body) **b** *in quantitative analysis* **:** the entire operation of burning a measured portion of a substance to be analyzed and collecting the products — see COMBUSTION METHOD **2 :** violent agitation **:** CONFUSION, TUMULT ⟨the wasteful, uncontrolled ~ of Nasser's early career —R.C.Doty⟩
combustion chamber *n* **:** a chamber within which combustion occurs: as **a :** the space in some boiler furnaces where the gases from the fire become more thoroughly mixed with air and burned **b :** the clearance space in the cylinder of an internal-combustion engine where the charge is compressed and ignited **c :** the part of a jet engine or gas turbine in which the propulsive power is developed by combustion of the injected fuel and the expansive force of the resulting gases
combustion engine *n* **:** an engine that derives its motive force from the energy of combustion — compare EXTERNAL-COMBUSTION ENGINE, INTERNAL-COMBUSTION ENGINE
combustion method *n* **:** a method for the quantitative determination of certain elements (as carbon, hydrogen, and nitrogen) in organic compounds by combustion
combustion spoon *n* **:** DEFLAGRATION SPOON
combustion starter *n* **:** CARTRIDGE STARTER
com·bus·tious \kəmˈbəschəs\ *adj, obs* **:** FLAMMABLE, COMBUSTIBLE **:** being in combustion **:** TURBULENT
com·bus·tive \-bəstiv, -tēv\ *adj* **:** tending or able to effect combustion **:** relating to or marked by combustion — **com·bus·tive·ly** \-tәvlē, -li\ *adv*
com·bus·tor \-stə(r)\ *n* -s [[2]*combust* + *-or*] **:** the combustion chamber of a gas turbine or a jet engine along with associated burners, igniters, and injection devices
comb wheat grass *n* [so called fr. the comblike arrangement of the spikelets] **:** a European grass (*Agropyron pectinatum*) introduced into New Zealand and Australia
comby \ˈkōmē\ *adj* -ER/-EST [[1]*comb* + *-y*] **:** resembling a comb in structure ⟨~ veins of quartz⟩ **:** HONEYCOMBED
comd *abbr* **1** command; commander; commanding **2** commissioned
comdg *abbr* commanding
comdr *abbr* commander
comdt *abbr* commandant
[1]**come** \ˈkəm; *often when a stressed syllable, esp an adverb or preposition syllable, follows without pause* ,kəm\ *vb* **came** \(ˈ)kām\ *or substand* **come** \(ˈ)kəm\ *or* **comed** \-md\ *or dial Brit* **cam** \ (ˈ)kam\ **come** *or substand* **comed** *or dial Brit* **cam; coming** \ˈkəmiŋ\ **comes** \(ˈ)kəmz\ *or archaic* **cometh** \ˈkəməth\ [ME *comen,* fr. OE *cuman;* akin to OHG *queman* to come, ON *koma,* Goth *qiman,* L *venire* to come, Gk *bainein* to walk, go, Skt *gamati* he goes] *vi* **1 a :** to move toward or away from something **:** pass from one point toward another nearer or more central **:** APPROACH ⟨do ~ to church today⟩ ⟨he *came* quietly into the room⟩ ⟨when will they ~⟩ — distinguished from and sometimes opposed to *go;* usu. used with a preposition (as *toward, on, before, behind*) or an adverb (as *away, down, forth, up*) when the point of departure or terminus is expressed ⟨~ toward me slowly⟩ ⟨the babe *came* forth from the womb⟩ **b :** to move toward or enter a scene of action or into a field of interest whether partly physical or wholly ideal — usu. used with an implication of purpose that may be expressed by an infinitive or participle or a coordinate verb introduced by *and* ⟨he *came* to see us⟩ ⟨a man *came* asking after wisdom⟩ ⟨~ and help us set the table⟩ or by a prepositional phrase ⟨they'll ~ to the rescue when they hear⟩ **c :** to approach or reach a particular station in an expressed or implied series ⟨day is *coming*⟩ ⟨now we ~ to the section on health⟩: (1) **:** to approach in kind or quality — usu. used with *near* ⟨this ~*s* near perfection⟩ ⟨the pure in heart ~ near to God⟩ (2) **:** to result in or progress — often used with *to* ⟨all our good planning *came* to naught⟩ (3) **:** to approach or reach a condition through or as if through change ⟨their fury *came* quickly to a boil⟩ **d** (1) **:** to advance toward maturity or a culminating state or stage — often used with *on* or *along* ⟨the gray filly is *coming* nicely⟩ ⟨that corn will ~ along better if it rains⟩ (2) **:** to advance in a particular manner ⟨~ running when I call⟩ ⟨the referee *came* between the clinching boxers⟩ (3) **:** to advance, rise, or improve in rank or condition — often used with *up* ⟨a general who had *come* up through the ranks⟩ ⟨the neighborhood, after declining for years, was *coming* up again⟩ **e :** FARE **:** come along ⟨how're you *coming* now?⟩ **f** (1) **:** to reach or extend ⟨trousers scarcely *coming* to his shoe tops⟩ (2) **:** to extend along or occupy a denoted or understood space or situation ⟨a path ~*s* through the valley⟩ ⟨at high tide water ~*s* over the lower end of the walk⟩ (3) **:** to reach through the intellect or emotions ⟨this ~*s* very near to me⟩ ⟨the arguments ~ home forcibly⟩ **2 a** (1) **:** to arrive at a particular place, end, result, or conclusion ⟨he *came* slowly to his senses⟩ ⟨she *came* tired to bed each night⟩ ⟨the spirit of true humility ~*s* to those who seek it diligently⟩ (2) **:** to attain by connected or related stages ⟨~ to an understanding⟩ (3) **:** AMOUNT ⟨taxes ~ to more than the property is worth⟩ (4) **:** to appear to the mind **:** become recalled to memory ⟨after much thought the answer *came* to him⟩ ⟨it *came* to her that this was where she first met him⟩ (5) **:** to return in time or space ⟨the good old days never ~ back⟩ **b** (1) *of an event or condition* **:** HAPPEN, BEFALL, OCCUR ⟨no harm will ~ to you⟩ ⟨everything ~*s* to him who waits⟩ (2) **:** to reach a particular state or condition or to happen as the result of chance or of some process or development ⟨~ untied⟩ ⟨how did you ~ to have such an idea⟩ ⟨the whole plan was *coming* clearer and clearer —Willa Cather⟩ — compare COME UPON (3) **:** to come to pass **:** take place — used with inverted subject and verb to express the particular time or occasion concerning which a statement is being made and often in the subjunctive mood with the notion of futurity ⟨*came* Christmas and we had a merry time⟩ ⟨the house burned a year ago ~ March⟩ ⟨~*s* the revolution we'll all live, or hang, high⟩ ⟨~ the end of the war when costs fall⟩ (4) **:** to become merited or owed — usu. used as a present participle ⟨all the credit that's *coming* to him⟩ ⟨I've another dollar *coming* to me⟩ **c** (1) **:** to be the product or result **:** ORIGINATE, ARISE, FOLLOW ⟨pepper ~*s* from a bush⟩ ⟨most wine ~*s* from grapes⟩ ⟨good crops ~ from good soil⟩ ⟨they ~ of sturdy yeoman stock⟩ ⟨do not evil that good may ~⟩ ⟨kind deeds ~ from a kind heart⟩ ⟨after joy ~*s* sadness⟩ ⟨his wealth ~*s* by inheritance⟩ (2) **:** to be or have been a native or resident — used with *from* ⟨he ~*s* from Toronto, Canada⟩ ⟨she has been here in the city 20 years but who would doubt that she ~*s* from the backwoods?⟩ **d :** to enter or assume a given condition, relation, use, or position ⟨at sundown the artillery *came* into action⟩ ⟨he *came* to the peerage in 1892⟩ **e :** to fall within a field of view, an indicated or implied scope, or a range of application ⟨his follies ~ to mind along with his kindnesses⟩ ⟨this ~*s* within the terms of the treaty⟩ ⟨Connecticut, Rhode Island, then ~*s* Massachusetts⟩ **f** (1) *of an utterance* **:** to become produced **:** issue forth ⟨a dry sob *came* from her constricted throat⟩ ⟨some of the noblest thoughts to ~ from this generation⟩ (2) **:** to take shape **:** assume a given or desired form **:** JELL ⟨in spite of her best efforts the picture would not ~⟩ (3) *of cheese or butter* **:** to be formed by adhesion of particles (4) *of a bow* **:** to bend too much in one place when drawn **g :** to be available ⟨this model ~*s* in several sizes⟩ **:** EXIST ⟨as good as they ~⟩ **h :** to experience orgasm **3 :** to fall to a person in a division of property or as an inheritance ⟨several thousand dollars *came* to him from his uncle⟩ **4 :** pay attention **:** HEED — used only in the imperative and often intensified by repetition to imply rebuke, impatience, or encouragement ⟨~, we must hurry⟩ ⟨~, ~, that's no way to speak to your mother⟩ **5 :** to become moved favorably **:** RELENT ⟨he will relent; he's *coming;* I perceive't —Shak.⟩ **6 :** to command or require a specified exertion or expenditure **:** be possible or be obtainable at a specified cost or by a specified effort ⟨it ~*s* hard for me to accept your views⟩ ⟨good clothes ~ high⟩ ⟨easy ~, easy go⟩ **7 :** RISE — used chiefly in the phrase *come to one's feet* **8 :** to appear to become **:** BECOME ⟨monsters ~ alive from a Goya picture —*New Republic*⟩ ⟨things will ~ clear if we are patient⟩ ~ *vt* **1 :** to approach or be near (an age) ⟨a pretty child *coming* eight years old⟩ **2 a :** to act or play the part of ⟨why should he ~ the dude like that⟩ **b :** PLAY ⟨~ a hand of cards⟩ **c** *Brit* **:** ATTAIN, DO ⟨he cannot ~ that⟩ — **come abroad** *archaic* **:** to appear in public **:** become public or known — **come a cropper 1 :** to fall headlong **2 :** to fail completely ⟨they'll *come a cropper* one of these days if they don't balance their budget⟩ — **come across 1 :** to occur or suggest itself to ⟨the possibility . . . *came across* her —Jane Austen⟩ **2 :** to meet, find, or encounter esp. unexpectedly or by chance ⟨I *came across* grandfather's diary in the attic⟩ ⟨perhaps we will *come across* your sister while we are shopping⟩ — **come again** *slang* **:** REPEAT; *also* **:** to speak further — **come alive :** to show signs of life or awareness ⟨Zack and George *came alive* then, ready to go into the hog business —F.P.Gipson⟩ **:** appear real ⟨careful lighting made the scene *come alive*⟩ — **come a long way :** to make progress **:** SUCCEED ⟨he's *come a long way* since he left the boat at Ellis Island⟩ — **come apart :** to disintegrate physically or mentally ⟨after a good showing in the early rounds the challenger *came apart* in the ninth⟩ — **come at :** to accomplish an understanding or mastery of **:** ATTAIN ⟨art is not something to be *come at* by dint of study —Clive Bell⟩ — **come away 1** *now dial Brit* **:** come with me **:** come along ⟨*come away, come away,* death —Shak.⟩ **2 :** to depart from something or someone expressed or implied **:** LEAVE ⟨*come away* from there before you get dirty⟩ **3 a :** to become detached **:** SEPARATE ⟨the rail *came away* in his hand⟩ **b** *chiefly Brit, of a plant* **:** to come up **:** GROW — **come between :** to cause to be estranged ⟨theirs was a happy home until her mother *came between* them⟩ — **come by 1** *chiefly Midland* **:** to call at **:** VISIT **2 :** to get possession of **:** ACQUIRE ⟨many older recordings are hard to *come by*⟩ ⟨benevolence and selflessness . . . are only indirectly *come by* —C.W.Berenda⟩; *sometimes* **:** to get by or as if by inheritance ⟨he *comes by* his temper naturally⟩ — **come clean** *slang* **:** to tell the whole story **:** CONFESS ⟨after he *comes clean,* I'll do the best for you that I can —Erle Stanley Gardner⟩ — **come close :** to be or arrive near **:** APPROXIMATE ⟨this day has *come close* to perfection⟩ ⟨his quotation *came close* to our bid⟩ — **come compass** *of a bow* **:** to bend in a true arc when drawn — **come forward 1 :** to present oneself (as for candidacy or to public notice) **:** VOLUNTEER **2 :** to attain note or success **:** ADVANCE ⟨light woolens have *come forward* to enjoy marked fashion prestige⟩ — **come home 1 :** to come close or press closely; *esp* **:** to touch the feelings, interest, or reason ⟨the ideal of equality would *come home* with special meaning to men bred up . . . on the frontier —V.L.Parrington⟩ **2 :** to give way under strain (as of an anchor in weighing) — **come home to roost :** to return by way of retribution — **come into :** to enter upon or into possession of **:** acquire esp. as an inheritance ⟨he will *come into* a fortune when his father dies⟩ — **come into case** or **come into order** *of tobacco* **:** to acquire such moisture content that the leaf is pliable and readily handled without breaking — **come into one's own :** to acquire something (as rights or a position) that rightfully belongs or is felt to belong to one; *sometimes* **:** to gain recognition ⟨natural gas has *come into its own* —Gardiner Symonds⟩ — **come into play :** to have an effect **:** play a part ⟨his early training in self-expression *came into play* in his new situation⟩ — **come it :** to succeed in doing something **:** attain one's purpose ⟨I meant to pay him last week but I couldn't *come it*⟩ — **come it over 1** *slang* **:** to lord it over **:** DOMINATE, BULLY **2** *slang* **:** DECEIVE, TRICK — **come it strong** *slang* **:** OVERDO, EXAGGERATE — contrasted with *draw it mild* — **come off :** to cease to utter (pretentious or foolish talk) — used chiefly in the phrase *come off it* ⟨*come off* it, you're being silly⟩ — **come on :** to encounter by or as if by chance **:** NEAR ⟨*came on* him in the dark⟩ — **come one's way** *also* **come one's ways :** to fall to one's lot — **come over 1 :** to play or practice (something) upon a person by way of deceiving or taking advantage of him ⟨don't *come* the old soldier *over* me⟩ **2 :** to take advantage of **:** OVERREACH, TRICK ⟨you'll not *come over* me with your innocent looks⟩ **3 :** to take possession of **:** OVERTAKE ⟨quiet *comes over* the market at twilight⟩ — often used of an emotion, idea, or state of mind ⟨what's *come over* you; you're acting so strangely⟩ — **come round :** to circumvent by trickery or flattery ⟨you can't *come round* me that way⟩ — **come through :** to endure successfully **:** SURVIVE ⟨they *came through* that hard winter in good health⟩ — **come to a head 1** *of a pustule or boil* **:** to become distended with pus **:** RIPEN **2** *of affairs* **:** to reach a crisis or a point at which some new course, trend, or decision is inevitable and immediately required — **come to anchor 1** *of a ship* **:** to drop anchor **2 :** to come to rest **:** settle down — **come to blows :** to carry a disagreement to the point of physical violence — **come to grief :** to encounter misfortune (as calamity, defeat, or ruin) esp. when deserved or in some degree the result of one's own actions ⟨were he less self-willed he would be less likely to *come to grief*⟩ — **come to grips 1 :** to engage wholeheartedly and thoroughly **:** get down to business ⟨they could come to terms if they *came* truly *to grips* instead of scolding at each other over a barrier of misunderstanding —Edward Sapir⟩ — often used with *with* ⟨last week the way was opened for the West to *come to grips* with Russia on the atom —*N.Y.Times*⟩ **2 :** to grapple or deal on the most fundamental level — usu. used with *with* ⟨they failed to *come to grips* with the underlying evils of the system⟩ — **come to hand 1 :** to be received ⟨your letter *came to hand* early yesterday morning⟩ ⟨larger quantities of potatoes *came to hand* and values declined somewhat — *Farmer's Weekly* (So. Africa)⟩ **2 :** to come to light **:** be found **:** APPEAR ⟨new evidence has *come to hand* on the authorship of Shakespeare's plays⟩ — **come to life 1 :** to regain consciousness; *also* **:** to exhibit vitality or animation ⟨the birds *coming to life* in song to salute the new day⟩ **2 :** to produce an effect of reality **:** be lifelike ⟨his wife truly *comes to life* in his portrayal⟩ — **come to light :** to come forth **:** be made manifest — **come to nature :** to become pasty and granular — used of iron at the conclusion of the puddling process — **come to nothing** *also* **come to naught :** to be fruitless **:** result in failure ⟨all their efforts *came to nothing*⟩ — **come to oneself :** to come to **:** regain self-control — **come to pass :** HAPPEN — used impersonally with *it* — **come to stay :** to become a fixture or permanency ⟨the automobile has *come to stay*⟩ — **come to terms :** to reach an agreement or a state of comprehension that permits agreement with or adjustment to something ⟨some adaptability is essential if one is to *come to terms* with modern life⟩; *also* **:** SUBMIT — usu. used with *with* — **come to that :** for that matter **:** so far as that goes ⟨*come to that,* you still owe for the car⟩ — **come to time :** to fulfill an obligation — **come true 1 :** to happen as desired or expected **:** attain reality ⟨like a dream *come true*⟩ **2 :** to reproduce the characters of the parent — **come up** *naut* **:** to slacken off gently **:** ease off ⟨*come up* a tackle⟩ — **come upon 1 :** to befall as if descending from above **:** ATTACK, AFFLICT, AFFECT ⟨doubt *came upon* her as she waited⟩ **2** *archaic* **:** to become dependent on esp. financially ⟨he had saved nothing and finally *came upon* the town⟩ **3 :** to meet with **:** chance upon **:** ENCOUNTER ⟨he *came upon* them suddenly at the bend of the path⟩ ⟨not until 1890 did an English missionary *come upon* the curiously carved inscription —Tom Marvel⟩
[2]**come** \ˈkōm, ˈku̇m\ *n* -s [ME; perh. akin to OHG & OS *kīmo* shoot, sprout, OE *cīnan* to gape, yawn, crack — more at CHINE] **:** the dried rootlets produced in malting grain — usu. used in pl.
come about *vi* **1 :** to come to pass **:** attain fulfillment **:** HAPPEN ⟨how did this accident *come about*⟩ **2 :** to change direction **:** come round ⟨the wind has *come about* into the north⟩ **3** *of a sailing craft* **:** TACK
come across *vi* **1 :** to supply or furnish something demanded or requested; *esp* **:** to pay over money **:** CONTRIBUTE — often used with *with* ⟨*come across* now, I've asked for it often enough⟩ ⟨the man *came across* with the price of a drink⟩ **2 :** to succeed in producing a desired effect ⟨he never *came across* as well on the stage as on radio⟩
come–all–ye *also* **come–all–you** \(,)kəˈmȯlyə, -yē\ *n, pl* **come–all–ye's** *also* **come–all–you's** [so called fr. the typical opening words] **:** a popular narrative ballad
come along *vi* **1 :** to move on in company ⟨she *came along* with us⟩ or toward one — often used imperatively and with an implication of impatience or irritation ⟨*come along* now, let's have no more dawdling⟩ **2 :** to make progress **:** get along **:** SUCCEED ⟨the paper was *coming along* nicely —S.H.Adams⟩ **3 :** APPEAR ⟨if another dealer *comes along* and offers a better price⟩
come–along \ˈ==,=\ *n* -s [*come along*] **1 :** a gripping device (as for pulling in or stretching wire) consisting of two jaws so attached to a ring that they are closed by pulling on the ring **2 :** any device, method, or hold used to compel an unwilling or resisting person or animal to come along in order to avoid physical discomfort (as a slip noose, a judo hold)
[1]**come–and–go** \;==ˈ=\ *n* -s **:** coming and going; *esp* **:** contraction and expansion
[2]**come–and–go** \"\ *adj* **:** APPROXIMATE, VARIABLE ⟨the *come-and-go* dimensions of a piece of glass⟩ ⟨a man of *come-and-go* honesty⟩
come around *vi* **:** to come round
come–at–able \(,)kəˈmad·əbəl, ˈkə;m-\ *adj* [*come at* + *-able*] **:** capable of being come at or attained **:** ACCESSIBLE
come back *vi* **1 :** to return to life or vitality ⟨of course vampires *come back*⟩ ⟨after lying in a coma for several months he slowly *came back*⟩ **2 :** to return to memory or the mind ⟨it all *comes back* to me now⟩ **3 :** REPLY, RETORT ⟨when questioned, he *came* right *back* with a vehement denial⟩ **4 :** to return to a former condition, state, or position from which one has declined or been deposed **:** stage a comeback ⟨no heavyweight champion has ever *come back*⟩ ⟨rigid closed season may be needed if the birds are to *come back*⟩
[1]**comeback** \ˈ=,=\ *n* -s [*come back*] **1 a :** an answer or retort usu. sharp or biting; *sometimes* **:** REPARTEE **b :** cause for complaint **c :** return of merchandise to a seller usu. because unsatisfactory in quality; *also* **:** the merchandise so returned **2 a** *Austral* **:** a sheep suitable for both wool and meat production that is obtained by breeding a half-breed sheep with one wool-type parent (as a Merino) and one meat-type parent (as a Leicester) to a sheep of one of the parent breeds **b :** the wool from such a sheep **3 :** the act or an instance of coming back esp. to a former state or condition **:** RECOVERY; *also* **:** one that comes back **4 :** any of several shrubs or vines with burs or prickles that catch in one's clothing and impede progress **5 :** money bet by a bookmaker to hedge a bet or to reduce the odds on a heavily backed entry (as in a horse race)
[2]**come·back** \,kəmˈbak\ *n* -s [imit.] *dial Eng* **:** GUINEA FOWL
come bet \ˈkəm,bet\ *n* **:** a bet on whether or not a crapshooter engaged in a series of rolls to settle bets previously made will pass from the point of view of treating his next cast as though it were his first
come–between \ˈ==,=\ *n* -s [*come between*] **:** one that comes between
come by *vi* **:** to pay a call ⟨next time you're over this way, *come by*⟩
come–by–chance \ˈ=bə,=\ *n* -s **:** one that comes by chance **:** BASTARD
co·me·chin·gón \,kōməchinˈgän\ *n* -s *usu cap* [Sp, of AmerInd

origin] : an extinct language of Argentina that is classed by some Americanists with Huarpean and by others with Calchaqui

co·me·cru·do \kōmə'krü(,)dō, -(,)thō\ *n, pl* **comecrudo** *or* **comecrudos** *usu cap* [Sp, fr. Sp. *comer* to eat, (fr. L *comedere* to eat up) + *crudo* raw, fr. L *crudus* — more at COMESTIBLE, RAW] **1 a :** an Indian people of northeastern Mexico **b :** a member of such people **2 :** a Coahuiltecan language of the Comecrudo people

comed *substand past of* COME

comeddle *vt* -ED/-ING/-S [*co-* + *meddle*] *obs* : COMMINGLE

co·me·dia \kə'mādēə, kō'māthyä\ *n* -S [Sp, fr. L *comoedia* — more at COMEDY] : a Spanish regular-verse drama or comedy : COMEDY

co·me·di·al \kə'mēdēəl\ *adj* [*comedy* + *-al*] : of or relating to comedy

co·me·di·an \kə'mēdēən\ *n* -S [MF *comédien*, fr. *comédie* comedy, + *-ien* -ian — more at COMEDY] **1 :** a writer of comedy **2 :** an actor who plays comedy; *sometimes* : any stage player **3 :** a comical or amusing individual — often used ironically ⟨you're quite the ~ aren't you⟩

co·me·dic \-mēdik, -med-\ *also* **co·me·di·cal** \-dəkəl\ *adj* [*comedic* fr. L *comoedicus*, fr. Gk *kōmōidikos*, fr. *kōmōidia* comedy + *-ikos* -ic; *comedical* fr. L *comoedicus* + E *-al*] : of, relating to, or having the attributes of comedy ⟨~ incantations⟩ ⟨a ~ hero⟩ : like or like that of comedy ⟨high, ~ raillery —F.A.Swinnerton⟩ — **co·me·di·cal·ly** \-dək(ə)lē\ *adv*

co·me·di·enne \kə'mēdē,en *sometimes* -mād; ⸗,⸗⸗'⸗\ *n* -S [F *comédienne*, fem. of *comédien*] : an actress who plays comedy

co·me·di·et·ta \kə,mēdē'edə, -mād-\ *n* -S [obs. It (now *commedietta*), dim. of obs. *comedia* (now *commedia*), fr. L *comoedia*] : a light farcical comedy

com·e·dist \'kämədəst\ *n* -S [*comedy* + *-ist*] : one who writes comedies

com·e·do \'kämə,dō\ *n, pl* **com·e·do·nes** \,kämə'dō(,)nēz\ [NL, fr. L, glutton, fr. *comedere* to eat, fr. *com-* + *edere* — more at EAT] : a collection of dead cells and oily secretion that plugs a hair follicle and duct of an oil gland and is usu. covered with a black dot — called also *blackhead;* compare MILIUM

com·e·do·carcinoma \;⸗⸗,⸗+\ *n* [NL, fr. *comedo* + *carcinoma*] : a breast cancer that arises in the larger ducts and is characterized by slow growth, late metastasis, and the accumulation of solid plugs of atypical and degenerating cells in the ducts

come down *vi* **1 :** to reduce itself : AMOUNT — used with *to* ⟨it *comes down* to this⟩ **2 :** to lose or fall esp. in estate or condition — used chiefly in the phrase *come down in the world* **3 a :** to place oneself in opposition esp. in speech or writing ⟨the judge *came down* hard on gambling⟩ **b :** to utter a reprimand : inflict punishment or punish — usu. used with *on* **4** *chiefly Brit* : to make payment or to make a gift of money ⟨old Mr. Pontifex then *came down* more handsomely than expected and settled £10,000 on his son —Samuel Butler †1902⟩ **5 :** to fall sick : become affected or infected — used with *with* ⟨they *came down* with measles⟩

comedown \'⸗,⸗\ *n* -S [*come down*] : a descent from rank or dignity or from a higher to a lower state or quality : a disappointment or humiliation : SETBACK

com·e·dy \'kämədē, -di\ *n* -ES [ME *comedye*, fr. MF *comedie*, fr. L *comoedia*, fr. Gk *kōmōidia*, fr. *kōmos* revel, village festival, festal procession, ode sung in this procession (fr. *kōmē* village) + *-ōidia* (fr. *aeidein* to sing) — more at HOME, ODE] **1 a :** a drama of light and amusing character and typically with a happy ending **b** *obs* : a mystery play or interlude with a happy ending **2 a :** any medieval narrative that ends happily; *esp* : one written in a vernacular language **b :** any literary composition written in a comic style or treating a theme suitable for comedy **3 :** the genre of dramatic literature that deals with the light or the amusing or with the serious and profound in a light, familiar, or satirical manner — compare TRAGEDY **4 :** matter suitable for treatment in comedy : a ludicrous, farcical, or amusing event or series of events ⟨a ~ of misunderstandings⟩ **5 :** the comic element (as in a play, story, or motion picture) ⟨the ~ was furnished by the parlormaid⟩

comedy ballet *n* : ballet with features of comedy, with stress on the dramatic element, and with an overture, recitatives, airs, and choruses

comedy drama *n* : serious drama with comedy interspersed

comedy of character : comedy in which the emphasis is on characterization rather than plot or lines — compare COMEDY OF SITUATION

comedy of intrigue : a comedy of situation in which complicated conspiracies and stratagems dominate the plot

comedy of manners : comedy that satirically portrays the manners and fashions of a particular class or set

comedy of situation : comedy in which the comic effect depends chiefly upon the involvement of the main characters in a predicament or ludicrous complex of circumstances — compare COMEDY OF CHARACTER

comedy relief *n* : a light tension-breaking interlude in a serious drama; *also* : any comparable interruption of a serious, distressing, or ponderous production or situation

come-hith·er \(,)kəm'hith̲ə(r), (,)kə'mi-\ *n* -S [fr. *come hither!*, a call to animals] **1 :** an enticing invitation **2** *chiefly Irish* : winning talk or ways : PERSUASION, BEGUILING ⟨she could put the *come-hither* on any man⟩

come in *vi* **1 :** to place (as in a race or competition) among those finishing ⟨*came in* second in the golf tournament⟩ **2 :** to accrue or come as gain or revenue ⟨we can afford it as long as the money keeps on *coming in* so freely⟩ **3 a :** to become of use ⟨gunpowder first *came in* in China⟩ **b :** to fit in : enter into or assume its place or course ⟨this *comes in* pat⟩ : take a part or perform a usu. useful service ⟨old newspapers . . . *come in* handy for lighting the fire —Victoria Sackville-West⟩ **c :** to make reply to a signal or call : come on to a communication channel : RETURN, REPLY — used esp. by communications units ⟨*come in*, San Francisco⟩ **4 :** to be the recipient — used with *for* ⟨the chancellor's policy has *come in* for increasing criticism —Douglas Stuart⟩ **5 a :** to take or perform one's part or function (as in a joint activity) ⟨that's where you *come in*⟩ **b :** to assume official duties or station ⟨if the Republicans *come in* next fall⟩ : take possession or command ⟨when his heirs *came in* they found the estate gutted⟩ **6 :** to attain maturity, fruitfulness, or production: **a** *of a crop* : to mature and produce a harvest; *also, of a seasonal food* : to be in season **b** *of a female mammal* (1) : to bring forth young : CALVE — used esp. of dairy cattle (2) : to be in heat **c** *of an oil well* : to begin to yield oil

comelily *adv* [ME *comlyly*, fr. *comly* + *-ly*] *obs* : in a suitable or comely manner : with propriety or dignity

come·li·ness \'kəmlēnəs, -lin- *sometimes* 'kōm- *or* 'käm-\ *n* -ES [ME *comlynesse*, fr. *comly* + *-nesse* -ness] : the condition of being comely esp. with respect to grace or beauty of external form

come·ling \'kəmliŋ\ *n* -S [ME *comling*, fr. *comen* to come + *-ling* — more at COME] *archaic* : one not native to the place where he is : NEWCOMER, IMMIGRANT

[1]**come·ly** \'kəmlē, -li *sometimes* 'kōm- *or* 'käm-\ *adj, usu* -ER/-EST [ME *comly*, alter. (influenced by *comen* to come) of OE *cȳmlic* lovely, glorious, fr. *cȳme* lovely, fine, glorious + *-lic* -ly; akin to OHG *kūmig* weak, powerless, ON *kȳmiligr* peculiar, ridiculous, OE *ciegan* to cry out, L *gavia* sea gull, Gk *goan* to lament, Skt *gavate* it sounds; basic meaning: crying out] **1 :** having a pleasing appearance : attractive through a measure of good looks, good proportions, pleasing coloration, neat or wholesome aspect : not homely or plain ⟨those dark-featured ~ womenfolk healthy and tall —Robert Browning⟩ **2 :** generally pleasant and attractive-looking : SEEMLY; *specif* : pleasurably conforming to notions of fitness, proportion, or decorum ⟨going in with him, they observed that all was neat and ~ —Willa Cather⟩ ⟨the best architect seeks to present . . . the *comeliest* possible fulfillment of certain practical requirements —C.E.Montague⟩ **syn** see BEAUTIFUL

[2]**comely** *adv* [ME *comly*, alter. (influenced by *comen* to come) of OE *cȳmlice*, fr. *cȳmlic*, adj.] *obs* : COMELILY

co·men·ic acid \('kō;menik-, -mēn-\ *n* [ISV *comenic* (anagram of *meconic*) + *acid*] : a yellow crystalline acid, $C_5H_3O_3COOH$ formed from meconic acid; 5-hydroxy-1,4-pyrone-2-carboxylic acid

come off *vi* **1 a :** to acquit oneself ⟨they *came off* well from the encounter⟩ **b :** to issue or emerge (as from a contest or situation whose outcome is uncertain) ⟨the American nation has not *come off* untouched —J.S.Dickey⟩ ⟨he *came off* well in the distribution of honors⟩ **c :** to give a satisfactory performance : acquit oneself ⟨the new player *came off* very well in the match⟩ **2 :** to prove satisfactory : SUCCEED ⟨the meeting of the prime ministers *came off* well⟩; *specif* : to produce a desired effect (as an illusion of reality) ⟨in spite of excellent lighting and scenery the production of his play did not quite *come off*⟩ **3 :** to take place : HAPPEN, OCCUR **4 :** to turn out to be ⟨the day *came off* fine⟩

come–off \'⸗,⸗\ *n* -S [*come off*] **1 :** a conclusion or finish **2 :** an evasion esp. of a duty : evasive statement : EXCUSE

come–of–will *or* **come–o'–will** \'⸗ə(v)¦⸗\ *n* -S *Scot* : one that comes uninvited and unexpected (as a volunteer plant)

come on *vi* **1 :** to begin by degrees — used esp. of natural phenomena ⟨it *came on* dark⟩ ⟨rain *came on* toward noon⟩ **2 :** to make progress esp. in growth or development : THRIVE, IMPROVE ⟨the corn is *coming on* splendidly⟩ ⟨he deserves credit for the way he has *come on* lately⟩ **3 a :** to enter or appear ⟨lights were beginning to *come on*⟩ **b :** to be brought forward (as a case in court) **4** *of a physical condition or disease* : to begin to affect one ⟨a cold may *come on* quite unexpectedly⟩ **5 :** PLEASE — used in cajoling or pleading ⟨*come on*, give me another apple⟩

come–on \'⸗,⸗\ *n* -S [*come on*] **1 :** an allurement or bait: as **a :** something designed to induce a person to become a victim of trickery ⟨let him win a few bets as a *come-on*⟩ **b :** a special inducement (as a premium or an article offered at less than cost) intended to attract customers to a store or other selling agency **2 :** the discard of a high card as a signal for one's partner to lead back a card of the same suit **3** *slang* : SWINDLER; *also* : a person victimized by a swindler : EASY MARK

come out *vi* **1 :** to pass to a place thought of as away from or remote from the center of affairs — often used of passage to a remote or unsettled area ⟨my father *came out* to New Zealand in the '60s⟩ **2 :** to come into view : EMERGE: as **a :** to become published **b :** to become public ⟨his shameful secret finally *came out*⟩ **c :** to make one's professional or social debut **d :** to break out — used of rashes **3 :** to come to an end : TERMINATE; *esp* : to turn out ⟨how did the story *come out*⟩ ⟨that cake *came out* splendidly⟩ **4 :** to extend or project ⟨the fireplace *came out* into the room⟩ **5 :** to allow something to appear or become known: as **a :** to declare oneself ⟨he *came out* strongly against the administration⟩ **b :** CONFESS — usu. used with *with* ⟨he *came out* shyly with his regrets⟩

come–out \'⸗,⸗\ *n* -S [*come out*] **1 :** a capacity for growth or development : EMERGENCE **2 :** a crapshooter's first roll of the dice after new bets are made and faded; *also* : the number cast

come–out·er \(,)kə'maud·ə(r)\ *n* -S [*come out* + *-er*] : one who withdraws from something established or settled (as a religious body or a community); *broadly* : one who seeks to replace an existent organization (as a political party) : a radical reformer

come over *vi* ['come] **1 a :** to change from one side (as of a controversy) to the other **b** *of a product of distillation* : to rise and pass over from the heated vessel to a collecting system ⟨when the temperature reaches 300°, some of the heavier fractions begin to *come over*⟩ **c :** to visit casually : drop in ⟨*come over* when you're through sweeping⟩ **2** *Brit* : to experience an indicated feeling or condition : BECOME ⟨the sky *came over* dark as a cloud passed before the moon⟩ ⟨she *came over* queer and gasped for breath⟩

come–o'–will *var of* COME-OF-WILL

co·me pri·ma \,kō(,)mā'prēmə\ *adv (or adj)* [It, lit., as at first] : in the same manner as the first time — used as a direction in music

com·er \'kəmə(r)\ *n* -S [ME, fr. *comen* to come + *-er*] **1 a :** one that comes; *esp* : one that comes voluntarily or offers or chooses to come (as to a contest) — used chiefly in the pl. and in the phrase *all comers* **b :** one newly arrived : ARRIVAL **2 :** one making rapid progress or showing promise esp. of future success or prominence

come round *vi* **1 a :** to recur in regular course **b :** MENSTRUATE **c :** to return to a former condition of body or mind; *esp* : to recover from an illness or faint **2 :** to change in direction or opinion ⟨the wind *came round* at dawn⟩ ⟨sooner or later he'll *come round* to our point of view⟩; *also* : to come about : TACK

[1]**comes** *pres 3d sing of* COME, *pl of* COMES

[2]**co·mes** \'kō,mēz, -mes\ *n, pl* **com·i·tes** \'kämə,tēz, -tās\ [L, lit., companion — more at COUNT] **1 :** a legal or military adviser to the Roman emperor; *broadly* : any prominent military or civil officer of the Roman empire **2** [ML, fr. L] **a :** a wellborn attendant on a king or chief in medieval Europe subject to the duty of military service **b** *comites, pl* : the persons making up the suite of an ambassador **3** [LL, fr. L] : a Roman Catholic service book containing a complete index and sometimes the text of all the liturgical lessons **4** [NL, fr. L] **a :** the answer in a fugue **b :** the consequent in a canon — compare DUX **5** [NL, fr. L] : VENA COMES

co·me so·pra \,kō(,)mā'sōprə\ *adv (or adj)* [It, lit., as above] : as previously — used as a direction in music

[1]**co·mes·ti·ble** \kə'mestəbəl\ *adj* [MF, fr. ML *comestibilis*, fr. L *comestus* (past part. of *comedere* to eat up, fr. *com-* + *edere* to eat) + *-ibilis* -ible — more at EAT] : suitable to be eaten : EATABLE, EDIBLE

[2]**comestible** \"\ *n* -S : something comestible : FOOD, DISH — usu. used in pl.

com·et \'kämət, *usu* -əd·+V\ *n* -S [ME *comete*, fr. OE *cometa*, fr. L *cometa, cometes*, fr. Gk *komētēs*, lit., long-haired, fr. *koman* to wear long hair, fr. *komē* hair] **1 :** a nebulous celestial body that consists of a fuzzy head usu. surrounding a bright nucleus, that often when in the part of its orbit near the sun develops a long tail which points away from the sun because of radiation pressure, that has an orbit varying in eccentricity between nearly round and parabolic, that has an inclination from zero to 180 degrees, and that has a period from three to thousands of years **2** [prob. trans. of F *comète;* fr. the picture of a comet on one of the cards] **a :** a card game that is a form of stops **b :** the nine of clubs or nine of diamonds when assigned special values in this game **3** *sometimes cap* : a goldfish of a fancy breed **4 :** one of a class of racing sloops similar to the star boat but smaller in size **5 :** one that rapidly attains high position but fails to retain it

co·metallic \;kō+\ *adj* [*co-* + *metallic*] *of a coin* : having a center piece made of different metal from the rest

com·e·tary \'kämə,terē, -ri\ *adj* [*comet* + *-ary*] : of or relating to a comet : like a comet (as in erratic course or transience) : coming from comets ⟨meteors of ~ origin⟩

comet aster *n* : any member of a race of garden asters of compact growth with large heads of flowers

cometh *archaic 3d sing of* COME

co·meth·er \kə'meth̲ə(r)\ *dial var of* COME-HITHER

come through *vi* **1** *chiefly South & Midland* : to experience a religious conversion esp. at a revival meeting **2 :** to do what is needed or expected : PROVIDE, GIVE, CONTRIBUTE ⟨he knew that he had to *come through*⟩ ⟨after some hesitation they *came through* with the price⟩ **3 :** to attain reality : MATERIALIZE, EMERGE ⟨his personality *comes through* in his writing⟩

co·met·ic \kə'med·ik, (')kä¦m-\ *also* **co·met·i·cal** \-d·əkəl\ *adj* [*comet* + *-ic, -ical*] : COMETARY

come to *vi* **1 :** to recover consciousness or vitality **2** *now dial* : to reach an agreement or accord : become pleasant : AGREE, YIELD **3 a :** to bring a ship's head nearer the wind : LUFF **b :** to anchor or stop in a certain point

comet seeker *also* **comet finder** *n* : a telescope of wide field used in searching the sky for comets

comet tail *n* : something suggesting the tail of a comet esp. in brightness or form

cometwise \'⸗⸗,⸗\ *adv* [*comet* + *-wise*] : in the manner of a comet ⟨a blade curving ~⟩

come up *vi* **1 :** to become mentioned : arise esp. in conversation **2** *Brit* : to enter a university **3 :** to reach something as if by pursuit : MEET — used with *with* **4** *of a sailing ship* : to come to a certain direction esp. as near as may be to the wind **5 :** to come before an authoritative person, group, or body for consideration or decision ⟨the housing bill *came up* for a vote⟩ ⟨several senators *coming up* for reelection⟩ **6 a :** to be equal : to compare in quality or worth — usu. used with *to* ⟨few great moments *come up* to expectation⟩ **b :** to draw near ⟨the old man *came up* and welcomed them⟩ **7 :** to start or move along faster — used in the imperative and for directing horses or other draft animals **8 :** to supply what is needed or desired — used with *with* ⟨they *came up* with a solution that cut down on losses from rust⟩ ⟨he *came up* with a check for the swimming pool⟩

come·up·pance *also* **come·up·ance** \(,)kə'məpən(t)s\ *n* -S [*come up* + *-ance*] : a deserved rebuke or penalty : DESERTS

comfier *comparative of* COMFY

comfiest *superlative of* COMFY

[1]**com·fit** \'kəm(p)fət, 'käm-\ *n* -S [ME *confit*, fr. MF, fr. past part. of *confire* to prepare, preserve, pickle, fr. L *conficere* to prepare, fr. *com-* + *-ficere* (fr. *facere* to make) — more at DO] : a confection consisting of a solid center (as a piece of fruit, a root, or a seed) that is coated and preserved by layers of sugar

[2]**com·fit** *vt, obs* : to make into a comfit : PRESERVE

com·fi·ture \-fə,chü(ə)r\ *n* -S [ME *confiture*, fr. MF, fr. *confit* + *-ure*] : a comfit or preserve

com·form·a·ble \kəm'fórməbəl\ *adj* [by alter.] : CONFORMABLE

[1]**com·fort** \'kəm(p)fə(r)t *sometimes esp by clergymen* -,fórt *or* -ó(ə)t; *usu* -d·+V\ *n* -S [ME *comfort, confort*, fr. OF *confort*, fr. *conforter*, v.] **1 :** strengthening aid: **a :** ASSISTANCE, SUCCOR, SUPPORT ⟨optimists, those who put their faith in humanity, believers in God . . . will find little ~ anywhere in Jeffers' work —*Time*⟩ ⟨give aid and ~ to the enemies of us all⟩ **b :** consolation in trouble or worry : SOLACE ⟨it is a ~ too to have a man tackle his job in the old-fashioned way —O.W. Holmes †1935⟩ ⟨to give ~ to a bereaved parent⟩ **2 a :** state or feeling of having relief, encouragement, or consolation ⟨merely getting to the end of the journey provided some ~⟩ ⟨the sedative gave some small ~ to the patient⟩ **b :** contented enjoyment in physical or mental well-being esp. in freedom from want, anxiety, pain, or trouble ⟨living a life of ease and ~⟩ **3 :** SATISFACTION, ENJOYMENT ⟨I do not find ~ in Greek poetry as I should —H.J.Laski⟩ ⟨having the ~ of a draw on my pipe —Mary Deasy⟩ **4 :** something that gives or brings comfort: **a :** a person or thing that brings aid, support, or satisfaction ⟨the son was the ~ of his parents' old age⟩ **b :** an appurtenance or condition furnishing mental or physical ease ⟨the ~*s* of home life⟩ ⟨bathrooms, water supplies, lighting, heating, and the whole array of domestic ~*s* —Henry Adams⟩ **5** *chiefly South & Midland* : COMFORTER 3b **syn** see REST

[2]**comfort** \"\ *vb* -ED/-ING/-S [ME *comforten, conforten*, fr. OF *conforter*, fr. LL *confortare* to strengthen greatly, fr. *com-* + L *fortis* strong — more at FORT] *vt* **1** *obs* : to make strong : STRENGTHEN, ENCOURAGE : make secure : INVIGORATE **2** *obs* : ASSIST, HELP : AID, ABET — once commonly used in law **3 a :** to impart strength and hope to : GLADDEN, CHEER **b :** to relieve esp. of mental distress : allay the grief or trouble of : CONSOLE, EASE **4 :** to make comfortable ⟨~*ed* his aching feet in a tub of hot water⟩ ~ *vi, obs* : to take comfort

syn CONSOLE, SOLACE: COMFORT, more intimate in its suggestions than CONSOLE or SOLACE, may connote relieving, soothing, and encouraging with cheer, hope, assurance extended with sympathetic kindness ⟨"This war will go on forever", she would whisper. "It cannot go on for ever", I would *comfort* her —H.G.Wells⟩ ⟨he put the letter away. Later it would *comfort* him, as she meant it to do. Later it might make him happy —Susan Ertz⟩ CONSOLE, less intimate in suggestion, may stress alleviating grief and disappointment rather than cheering and encouraging ⟨his father's letter gave him one of his many fits of melancholy over his own worthlessness, but the thought of the organ *consoled* him —Samuel Butler †1902⟩ ⟨if you really want to *console* me, teach me rather to forget what has happened —Oscar Wilde⟩ ⟨*consoled* herself with going to parties, spoiling her babies, and flirting with other people —Rose Macaulay⟩ SOLACE applies to any agency tending to relieve grief, pain, disappointment, chagrin, weariness, despondency ⟨his father's death left Ariosto at the head of a large family, for which he had to provide out of a scanty patrimony. He *solaced* his cares by classical studies, which made him a fair Latin poet —Richard Garnett⟩ ⟨though you rail against the bar and the imperfect medium of speech, you will be *solaced*, even in your chagrin, by a sense of injured innocence —B.N. Cardozo⟩ ⟨liberals are constantly tempted to depart from their difficult path and either embrace some simple panacea or else *solace* themselves with a rather too easy skepticism —M.R. Cohen⟩

[1]**com·fort·able** \'kəm(p)(f)təbəl, -m(p)fə(r)d·əb-, -m(p)fə(r)təb- *also* ÷ -m(p)fə(r)b- *or* ÷ -m(p)(f)tərb-\ *adj* [ME *comfortable, confortable*, fr. MF *confortable*, fr. *conforter* + *-able*] **1 :** affording solace, sustenance, delight : COMFORTING: **a :** CONSOLING : extending consolation : CHEERING, ENCOURAGING : dispelling worry ⟨her presence warmed the atmosphere . . . she herself was a most ~ little person —Willa Cather⟩ ⟨for God's sake speak ~ words —Shak.⟩ **b** *obs* : REFRESHING, SUSTAINING **c :** uplifting or delighting spiritually or mentally ⟨~ religious contemplation⟩ **2 :** enjoying or showing solace or good cheer ⟨sooner than she could have supposed it possible . . . her spirits became absolutely ~ —Jane Austen⟩ **3 a :** giving or promising physical ease, pleasurable feeling, ample convenience, or cheerful well-being : calculated to operate against unpleasant feelings, distress, oppression, difficulty, or want ⟨a ~ fit⟩ ⟨a ~ summer suit⟩ ⟨a more ~ automobile⟩ ⟨~ houses set in spacious grounds —*Amer. Guide Series: Pa.*⟩ ⟨a makeshift arrangement not altogether . . . ~ for either of us —Havelock Ellis⟩ **b :** conducive to mental or spiritual ease, relaxation, placidity : occasioning no challenging difficulty, disconcerting obscurity, or worrying uncertainty ⟨the home team had a ~ 7 to 1 lead in the eighth⟩ ⟨irregular war was . . . more exhausting than service in the ~ imitative obedience of an ordered army —T.E.Lawrence⟩ ⟨~ compromises —V.L. Parrington⟩ ⟨the world will probably keep on getting better and better, which is a very nice ~ thought —*Atlantic Monthly*⟩ **c :** assuring or affording an easy tranquillity about money or a convenient, pleasant, and secure way of living, although without great wealth ⟨retiring on a ~ income⟩ ⟨in ~ circumstances by reason of prize money —C.O.Paullin⟩ **4 :** enjoying or showing comfort and ease: **a :** at ease physically : RELAXED : in a restful situation : without urgent unsatisfied wants : free from pain, irritation, stricture, or other unpleasant feelings ⟨making himself ~ in an armchair⟩ ⟨treatment by which the person with hay fever may be made more ~ —Morris Fishbein⟩ **b :** at ease mentally or socially : free from vexation, worry, doubt, fear : PLACID, UNRUFFLED : not disturbed or perturbed ⟨~ in his allegiance to his king⟩ ⟨Lamb was ~ in his ignorance of what he did not choose to know —John Mason Brown⟩ **c :** in assured or easy circumstances esp. financially : not hard pressed or harried by exigency ⟨a ~, though by no means affluent family —*Times Lit. Supp.*⟩

syn COMFORTABLE, COZY, SNUG, EASY, RESTFUL, and REPOSEFUL describe that which makes for contented tranquil ease and enjoyment. COMFORTABLE stresses absence of matters vexatious, worrisome, irritating, or painful in any way ⟨"I fear I should not be happy in that company . . ." "Then I give in. Do whatever will be most *comfortable* to yourself" —Thomas Hardy⟩ ⟨"Thank God for colonels", thought Mrs. Miniver; "sweet creatures, so easily entertained, so biddably diverted from senseless controversy into *comfortable* monologue" —Jan Struther⟩ COZY suggests warmth, shelter, and ease, and hints tranquillity and friendliness ⟨Wimsey gratefully took in the *cozy* sitting room, with its little tables crowded with ornaments, its fire roaring behind a chaste canopy of velvet overmantel —Dorothy Sayers⟩ SNUG indicates secure and assured warmth and comfort usu. in compact quarters ⟨Lady D. will find us in rather a smaller house than we are accustomed to receive our friends in, but it's *snug* —W.M.Thackeray⟩ EASY implies absence of anything likely to cause physical, social, or mental discomfort ⟨there's a pleasant feel in being gently . . . pinioned fast to the *easy* armchair —Robert Browning⟩ RESTFUL, applicable to indoor and outdoor situations, and the less common REPOSEFUL apply to whatever induces rest or repose ⟨a *restful*, friendly room, fitted to the uses of gentle life, covered, when it must be covered, with beauty —Mary Austin⟩ ⟨I . . . drank in deep, calm gladness from the sweet, *restful* scene—the gray old church with its clustering ivy and its quaint carved wooden porch, the white lane winding down the hill between tall rows of elms —J.K.Jerome⟩ ⟨the secretary's office, which his wife endowed with ship's lamps, ship's bells, crossed naval swords, and a generally *reposeful* colonial decor —*Time*⟩ COMFORTABLE, COZY, SNUG, and EASY may all describe an assured financial position. In reference to persons, COMFORTABLE, COZY, and SNUG may indicate mere absence of discomfort or, more positively, a pleasant, relaxed, warm, contented feeling ⟨we found the doctor and Zeke making themselves *comfortable*. The latter was reclining on the ground, pipe in mouth —Herman Melville⟩ ⟨Mrs. Carewe, faced with impecunious widowhood, had successfully daydreamed herself right out of bleak reality into *cozy* semiinvalidism —Edna Ferber⟩ ⟨there must be no open windows or drafty cracks to disturb his *cozy* reflections —M.R.Cohen⟩ ⟨ere that the fisherfolk were all *snug* under thatch and sheltering wall, breathing the cabin's air of gold, safe from blue storm and nipping cold —G.W.Russell⟩ ⟨all the gypsies and showmen who had remained on the ground lay *snug* within their carts and tents —Thomas Hardy⟩

²**comfortable** \"\ *n* -s **1** *chiefly Brit* **:** a knitted wristlet **2** *chiefly Brit* **:** COMFORTER 3a **3** *chiefly North* **:** COMFORTER 3b

com·fort·able·ness *n* -ES **:** the condition of being comfortable

com·fort·ably \-blē,-bli\ *adv* [ME, fr. *comfortable* + *-ly*] **:** in a comfortable manner: as **a** *obs* **:** ENCOURAGINGLY, REASSURINGLY, COMFORTINGLY **b :** in comfort **:** in an adequate and comfortable manner ⟨they live plainly but ~⟩ **c :** COMPLACENTLY **:** with calm self-assurance

com·fort·er *R* 'kəm(p)fə(r)d·ər, -fə(r)tər, -*R* -fəd·ə(r,-fəta(r\ *n* -s [ME *comfortoure, confortoure,* fr. MF *conforteor,* fr. *conforter* + *-eor* -or] **1 :** one that gives comfort (as by aid, consolation, cheer) **2** *cap* **:** HOLY SPIRIT **3 a :** a long narrow usu. knitted neck scarf **b :** a warm bedcover **:** QUILT, PUFF **4** *chiefly Brit* **:** PACIFIER a

com·fort·ful \-fə(r)tfəl\ *adj* **:** abounding in comfort

comforting *adj* [ME, fr. pres. part. of *comforten* to comfort] **:** providing or intended to provide comfort **:** CONSOLING, CHEERING — **com·fort·ing·ly** *adv*

com·fort·iza·tion \,kəm(p)fə(r)d·ə'zāshən\ *n* -s **:** the act of rendering (an aircraft) more comfortable (as by adequate heating and pressure control)

com·fort·ize \'kəm(p)fə(r)d·,īz\ *vt* -ED/-ING/-S **:** to make comfortable **:** adapt to the needs of the user **:** ADJUST, FIT

com·fort·less \-(r)tləs\ *adj* [ME, fr. ¹*comfort* + *-less*] **1 :** without comfort **:** DREARY **:** lacking in comforts **2** *obs* **:** offering no comfort — **com·fort·less·ly** *adv* — **com·fort·less·ness** *n* -ES

com·for·tress \-(r)·trəs\ *n* -ES [ME *confortouresse,* fr. MF *conforteresse,* fem. of *conforteor*] **:** a female comforter

comfortroot \'==,=\ *n* -s *in Florida* **:** COONTIE

comforts *pl of* COMFORT, *pres 3d sing of* COMFORT

comfort station *also* **comfort room** *n* **:** a place where toilet and lavatory facilities are available to the public

com·frey *also* **cum·frey** \'kəm(p)frē\ *n* -s [ME *comfirie, confirie,* fr. OF *cumfirie, cunfirie,* fr. L *conferva* — more at CONFERVA] **1 :** a plant of the genus *Symphytum* **2 :** DAISY 1

com·fy \'kəm(p)fē, -fi\ *adj* -ER/-EST [by shortening & alter.] **:** COMFORTABLE

¹**com·ic** \'kämik, -mēk\ *adj* [L *comicus,* fr. Gk *kōmikos,* fr. *kōmos* festivity with music and dancing — more at COMEDY] **1 a :** dealing or dealt with in comedy as contrasted with tragedy ⟨a standard ~ theme⟩ **b :** composing or acting in comedies ⟨a ~ dramatist⟩ **c :** showing or conveying an attitude of thoughtful mirth or amused detached reflection rather than sorrow, pain, or resolution ⟨he alone in the book has a remarkable ~ sense. He can prick the bubble of any illusion —John Erskine †1951⟩ **2 :** calling forth laughter by intentional wit, humor, or burlesque or by unintentional exaggeration or inappropriateness **:** COMICAL ⟨it would have been ~ if she were making all this fuss for nothing —Joseph Conrad⟩ **3 :** presenting a series of humorous incidents or dramatic adventures in a sequence of pictures usu. accompanied by balloons giving conversation ⟨the ~ section of a newspaper⟩ **syn** see LAUGHABLE

²**comic** \"\ *n* -s **1 :** an actor of comic roles **:** COMEDIAN **2 a :** the element in art or nature that provokes mirth or humorous reflection ⟨to inquire into the essence of the ~⟩ **b :** the representation of the incongruous (as in character and in conduct or in aim and in method) as amusing; *sometimes* **:** the representation of human error and weakness as provocative of amusement **3 a :** a group of cartoons or drawings arranged in a narrative sequence — compare ¹COMIC 3 **b comics** *pl* **:** the portion of a publication (as a daily or Sunday newspaper) devoted to such groups **4 :** a motion picture presenting broad comedy or farce

com·i·cal \-məkəl, -mēk-\ *adj* [*comic* + *-al*] **1** *obs* **a :** belonging or relating to comedy rather than tragedy **b :** like comedy in its conclusion **:** HAPPY **c :** not elevated or dignified enough to call for serious treatment **:** MEAN, TRIVIAL **2 :** calling forth often intentionally mirth and easy spontaneous laughter **:** FUNNY, HUMOROUS ⟨dancing up to Bligh with such a ~ expression . . . that the tension was relieved —C.B. Nordhoff & J.N.Hall⟩ **3** *dial Eng* **a :** queer in the mind **:** ODD, CRACKED **b :** DISAGREEABLE, CAPRICIOUS, UNCERTAIN **c :** out of sorts **:** UNWELL **syn** see LAUGHABLE

com·i·cal·i·ty \,==‵kaləd·ē, -ətē, -i\ *n* -ES **:** comical quality; *also* **:** something comical

com·i·cal·ly \'kämək(ə)lē, -mēk-, -li\ *adv* **:** in a comical manner

com·i·cal·ness \-kəlnəs\ *n* -ES **:** COMICALITY

comic book *n* **:** a publication in pamphlet format containing one or more comics

comico- *comb form* [NL, fr. L *comicus* — more at COMIC] **:** comic **:** comic and ⟨*comico*tragedy⟩ ⟨*comico*didactic⟩

comic opera *n* [trans. of F *opéra comique*] **1 :** a musical dramatic work of an amusing nature with or without spoken dialogue **:** OPÉRA BOUFFE, OPERETTA **2 :** a farcical action or behavior on the stage or in life; *typically* **:** a false or absurd display of emotion or excitement

comic paper *n* **:** COMIC 3b

comic relief *n* **:** a relief of emotional or other tension resulting from a comic episode or item interposed in the midst of serious or tragic elements (as in a drama); *also* **:** something that causes such relief

comic spirit *n* **:** the spirit of comedy **:** the point of view of the comic **:** the attitude of one who represents or regards human complications as subjects for mirth

comic strip *n* **:** COMIC 3a

com·in·form·ist \'kämən,fȯrməst, -ō(ə)m-\ *n* -s *usu cap* [*Cominform,* an international communist organization formed in 1947 (fr. *Com*munist *Inform*ation Bureau) + E *-ist*] **:** a member of the Russian Cominform organized to spread communism throughout the world

¹**coming** *n* -s [ME, fr. the gerund of *comen* to come] **:** an act or instance of approaching **:** APPROACH, ARRIVAL, ADVENT, MANIFESTATION

²**coming** *adj* [ME, fr. the pres. part. of *comen* to come] **:** that comes or is about to come: as **a :** APPROACHING ⟨a fine black studhorse ~ four this spring⟩ **:** lying in the near future **:** NEXT ⟨the ~ week or year⟩ **b** *archaic* **:** ready to offer or meet advances **:** FORWARD **c :** DUE, DESERVED — compare HAVE IT COMING **d :** on the way to attain importance or distinction — **coming and going :** with no escape **:** with no way out ⟨his lies put him in a position where she had him *coming and going*⟩ **:** HELPLESS, DEFENSELESS

coming in *n, pl* **comings in 1** *obs* **:** ENTRY, ENTRANCEWAY **2 :** ENTRANCE, BEGINNING **3 :** INCOME, REVENUE — usu. used in pl.

co·mingle \kə, kä+\ *vt* -ED/-ING/-S [*co-* + *mingle*] **:** COMMINGLE

coming-of-age \'===‵=\ *n, pl* **comings-of-age :** the attainment of legal age; *broadly* **:** the reaching of maturity or the fullness of development ⟨the *coming-of-age* of jazz⟩

coming-on \'==‵=\ *adj* **:** YIELDING, COMPLIANT ⟨a more *coming-on* disposition —Shak.⟩

coming out *n, pl* **comings out :** ISSUANCE; *esp* **:** social debut

comings and goings *n pl* **:** AFFAIRS, DOINGS, ACTIVITIES

co·mi·no \kə'mē(,)nō\ *n* -s [Sp, fr. L *cuminum* — more at CUMIN] **:** CUMIN

co·mique \kō'mēk, kä'-,kə'-,kȯ'-\ *n* -s [F, fr. *comique,* adj., fr. L *comicus* — more at COMIC] **:** ²COMIC 1

comitadji *var of* KOMITADJI

com·i·tal \'kämad·ᵊl\ *adj* [ML *comitalis,* fr. *comit-, comes* count (fr. L, companion, overseer, official) + *-alis* -al — more at COMES] **:** of, belonging to, or befitting a count or earl

co·mi·tas gen·ti·um \'kōmə,täs'gentēəm, 'kämə,tas'jench(ē)əm\ *or* **comitas in·ter gen·tes** \-,sintər'gen·,täs, -nta(r)-'jen·,tēz\ *n* [NL] **:** COMITY OF NATIONS

co·mi·tat \'‚kōmə'tät\ *n* -s [G *komitat,* fr. L *comitatus* retinue] **:** an administrative division or county in Hungary

com·i·ta·ten·sian \'kämətə'tenchən\ *adj* [LL *comitatensis* (fr. L *comitatus*) + E *-ian*] **:** of, belonging to, or relating to a comitatus

¹**com·i·ta·tive** \'kämə,tād·iv, -təd-\ *adj* [L *comitatus* + E *-ive*] **:** expressing accompaniment ⟨~ case⟩

²**comitative** \"\ *n* -s *linguistics* **:** a comitative inflectional form or set of inflectional forms; *esp* **:** a comitative case

com·i·ta·tus \,kämə'tād·əs, -tād-\ *n* -ES [L, escort, retinue, imperial court, fr. *comit-, comes* companion + *-atus* -ate — more at COUNT] **1 :** a body of wellborn men attached to a king or chieftain by the duty of military service; *also* **:** the status of the body so attached **2** [ML, fr. L] **:** COUNTY — used chiefly in the phrase *posse comitatus*

comites *pl of* COMES

co·mi·tia *n, pl* **comitia** \kə'mish(ē)ə\ [L, pl. of *comitium* assembly, assembly place, fr. *com-* + *-itium* (fr. *itus,* past part. of *ire* to go) — more at ISSUE] **:** an assembly at which the ancient Roman people acted on matters submitted by authorized officials

co·mi·tial \-shəl\ *adj* [L *comitialis,* fr. *comitium* + *-alis* -al] **:** of or relating to the Roman comitia

com·i·tje *var of* KOMMETJE

comi·tragedy \'‚kämə, -mē+\ *n* -ES [alter. of *tragicomedy*] **:** tragedy with a comedy ending

com·i·ty \'kämad·ē, -ətē, -i\ *n* -ES [L *comitat-, comitas,* fr. *comis* courteous (fr. OL *cosmis,* fr. *com-* + *-smis* — akin to Skt *smayate* he smiles) + *-tat-, -tas* -ty — more at SMILE] **1 :** kindly courteous behavior **:** friendly civility **:** mutual consideration between or as if between equals ⟨management should constantly point up every group activity until it actually promotes ~ —W.A.Hamor⟩: as **a :** courteous and friendly agreement and interaction between nations **b :** the informal and nonmandatory courtesy sometimes referred to as a set of rules to which the courts of one sovereignty often defer in determining questions (as of jurisdiction or applicable precedent) where the laws or interests of another sovereignty are involved **c :** the custom among Protestant churches of the U.S. of avoiding direct or indirect proselytizing of one another's members **2 :** association esp. for common and mutually pleasing purposes ⟨the honorable ~ of scholars in Phi Beta Kappa —*Key Reporter*⟩ ⟨a Europe which pretends to have founded its ~ upon brotherhood —Weston La Barre⟩

comity of nations *or* **comity of states** [trans. of NL *comitas gentium*] **1** *law* **:** the comity nations give effect to within their own territory **2 :** the friendly code whereby nations get along together

coml *abbr* commercial

com·ly *or* **comlye** *obs var of* COMELY

comm *abbr* — see COM

com·ma \'kämə\ *n* -s [LL & L; LL, comma (punctuation mark, musical interval) fr. L, part of a sentence, fr. Gk *komma* stamp, coinage, clause, fr. *koptein* to cut off, stamp — more at CAPON] **1 a** *pl also* **com·ma·ta** \-məd·ə\ **:** a short phrase or word group smaller than a colon **:** a fragment of a few words or feet — used of Greek and Latin prosody or rhetoric **b** *obs* **:** a clause or short section of a treatise or argument **2 a :** a punctuation mark, used esp. as a mark of separation within the sentence generally indicating a slight pause and appearing either singly to separate two related but distinct terms or in a pair, one at each end of a word, phrase, or clause, which the enclosing commas set off as an entity at the same time emphasizing the coherence of the preceding and following terms **b commas** *pl* **:** QUOTATION MARKS — compare INVERTED COMMA **3 :** PAUSE, INTERVAL **4 a :** a pause or break in the phrasing of a melodic line **b :** a mark indicating a pause for taking breath **5 :** a minute interval or difference in the pitches of the same musical tone occasioned by different systems of tuning — compare DITONIC COMMA, SYNTONIC COMMA

comma bacillus *also* **comma** *n* **:** a bacterium (*Vibrio comma* syn. *Spirillum cholerae asiaticae*) that causes Asiatic cholera

comma butterfly *also* **comma** *n* **:** a common No. American anglewing butterfly (*Polygonia comma*) having a silvery comma-shaped mark on the underside of the hind wings and larvae that feed on elm, nettles, and hop; *sometimes* **:** any of several other butterflies of the genus *Polygonia*

comma di·ton·i·cum \-dī'tänəkəm\ *n, pl* **com·ma·ta di·ton·i·ca** \'kämad·ə,dī'tänəkə\ [NL] **:** DITONIC COMMA

commadore *obs var of* COMMODORE

comma fault *n* **:** the careless or unjustified use of a comma between coordinate main clauses not connected by a conjunction — called also *comma splice*

¹**com·mand** \kə'mand, -maa(ə)nd,-mȧnd\ *vb* -ED/-ING/-S [ME *comanden,* fr. OF *comander* to command, commend, fr. (assumed) VL *commandare,* alter. (influenced by L *mandare* to commit to one's charge, order) of L *commendare* to commend, command — more at COMMEND] *vt* **1 :** to direct authoritatively **:** ORDER, ENJOIN ⟨the doctrine of that church ~*ed* man to love God with his whole soul —Stringfellow Barr⟩ **2 :** to exercise a dominating influence over **:** have within one's authority, control, or power: as **a :** to rule over, dominate, control, or govern authoritatively, without question or opposition ⟨England . . . had long ~*ed* the European market for raw wool —G.M.Trevelyan⟩ ⟨those young boys who have inherited great fortunes which they own but cannot ~ —Van Wyck Brooks⟩ **b :** to have at one's immediate bidding or disposal ⟨the produce of other men's labor which it enables him to purchase or ~ —Adam Smith⟩ **c :** to be able readily to call forth, evoke, exact, or compel, typically by some right or due ⟨the courage can scarcely fail to ~ our admiration —Virginia Woolf⟩ ⟨a successful pugilist ~*s* far higher terms for giving tuition in boxing than a tutor at one of the universities —G.B.Shaw⟩ **d :** to face, front on, or overlook so as to afford full view of ⟨the wide and peaceful rural landscape ~*ed* by the cottage —Joseph Conrad⟩ **e :** to dominate by strategic position, by fire, or by observation ⟨Fort Amsterdam, whose four bastions . . . ~*ed* both the North and East rivers —*Amer. Guide Series: N.Y. City*⟩ ⟨this island, which ~*s* one of the principal passages from the Atlantic to the Caribbean sea —F.J.Haskin⟩ **f :** to constitute the passageway or chief passageway to ⟨the hallway ~*s* the entrances to all the upstairs rooms⟩ **g :** to have military or naval command of as senior officer **h :** to hold the controlling cards of (a suit) in a card game **3 :** to cause or direct to come or go **:** SUMMON, DISPATCH, SEND ⟨I will ~ my blessing upon you —Lev 25:21 (RSV)⟩ **4** *obs* **:** to order or request to be given ~ *vi* **1 :** to have or to exercise direct authority **:** GOVERN **2 :** to give an order or orders **3 :** to be commander ⟨the general will ~ in person at the western front⟩ **4 :** to dominate as if from an elevated position ⟨far and wide his eye ~*s* —John Milton⟩

syn CHARGE, ORDER, ENJOIN, DIRECT, INSTRUCT, BID: in the meaning of issuing commands or orders, these words are often interchangeable. COMMAND is used in situations in which great or high authority is involved officially or formally ⟨as sovereign lord he can *command* —S.T.Coleridge⟩ ⟨the chairman *commands* the undertaking —Estes Kefauver⟩ CHARGE suggests a formal or solemn order with connotations of duty and responsibility ⟨the Marine Hospital service was *charged* with the duty of recommending for rejection immigrants afflicted with loathsome or contagious diseases —V.G.Heiser⟩ ⟨Gustavus . . . considered himself *charged* by God with the defense of the true Lutheran faith —Stringfellow Barr⟩ ORDER may indicate a specific or routine command or direction from one having due authority or right ⟨many of the managing posts will be filled up by pig-headed people only because they happen to have the habit of *ordering* poor people about —G.B. Shaw⟩ ENJOIN suggests an order or direction given authoritatively and urgently but with some admonition, sententiousness, or solicitude ⟨I *enjoin* upon all citizens to cooperate with the government in its endeavor to restore greater respect for law and order —F.D.Roosevelt⟩ ⟨St. Peter admirably *enjoins* us to be ready always to give an answer to every man that asks us a reason for the faith that is in us —J.L.Lowes⟩ DIRECT may suggest either a routine or an esp. mandatory order often on specific points of procedure or activity ⟨why otherwise does it [the Constitution] *direct* the judges to take an oath to support it? —John Marshall⟩ ⟨it is hoped that President Eisenhower will *direct* Ambassador Lodge to propose such action —*Nation*⟩ INSTRUCT may suggest an authoritative order, perhaps a formal one, delivered with care about its being fully understood ⟨"Don't waste oil", Miss Hannah had been *instructed* long ago —Margaret Deland⟩ ⟨Marvin was *instructed* . . . to uproot nothing until it was proved to have no remedial property —Mary Austin⟩ BID is likely to sound archaic or literary; it may indicate either a mild or a peremptory command ⟨the . . . Curate doth *bid* the Man to put a Ring on the Woman's fourth finger —George Meredith⟩ ⟨he seized him by the collar and sternly *bade* him cease making a fool of himself —G.B.Shaw⟩

²**command** \"\ *n* -s [MF *comand, comande,* fr. *comander,* v.] **1 :** the act of commanding ⟨the troops shall march at ~⟩ **2 a :** an order given **:** MANDATE, COMMANDMENT **b :** a word or phrase esp. in a set form by which an order is given ⟨at the ~ "halt" all troops will stop immediately⟩ **3 a :** the ability to control or the faculty of controlling **:** MASTERY ⟨the teacher has given evidence of ~ in her classes⟩ ⟨lose ~ of one's temper⟩ **b :** the authority or right to command conferred by official position ⟨the captain is in ~ of the ship⟩ **c** (1) **:** the power to dominate, control, or overlook ⟨the fort has ~ of the valley⟩ (2) **:** scope of vision **:** PROSPECT ⟨the tower provided a wide ~ of neighboring hills⟩ **d :** facility in use (as of a language) ⟨a good ~ of French⟩ **4 :** a body of persons (as military troops), an area, or a particular unit, usu. military, under one in command ⟨a top-ranking officer in the Middle East ~⟩ ⟨police put all ~*s* on alert against possible disorders or vandalism —*Springfield (Mass.) Union*⟩ — compare AIR COMMAND **5 :** height above the ground or the level commanded by a fortification or a gun **6 a :** the possession of the highest card or cards of a suit in a card game **b :** the highest card remaining unplayed in any suit **7** *contract bridge* **:** DEMAND BID **syn** see POWER — **at command :** ready to be commanded **:** available for service

³**command** \"\ *adj* **:** presented (as a stage play) or completed (as a study) as a result of a compelling command or request or of great need ⟨a ~ performance of the play for the queen⟩ ⟨a ~ study for the air force of the psychological makeup of good fliers⟩

com·man·dant \'kämən,dant, -dȧnt,-daa(ə)nt,-dȧnt, ,==‵=\ *n* -s [F, fr. pres. part. of *commander,* fr. OF *comander*] **:** the commanding officer of a place or of a military group ⟨the ~ of a naval district⟩ ⟨the ~ of the U.S. Marine Corps⟩

command car *n* **:** an open armored motor vehicle intended for military staff and reconnaissance duties, usu. with radio, six forward speeds, and four-wheel drive

com·man·deer \'‚kämən'di(ə)r, -iə\ *vb* -ED/-ING/-S [Afrik *kommandeer,* fr. F *commander* to command, fr. OF *comander* — more at COMMAND] *vt* **1 a :** to compel to perform military service **b :** to seize for military purposes **2 :** to take arbitrary or forcible possession of ~ *vi* **:** to commandeer men or goods

com·mand·er \kə'mandə(r), -maan-,-man-\ *n* -s [ME *commander, comandour,* fr. OF *comandeor,* fr. *comander* + *-eor* -or] **1 :** one in an official position of command or control: as **a :** the chief officer in command of a military force or unit **b :** a naval executive officer in command of a ship, station, or installation **c :** a senior naval officer ranking just below a captain and above a lieutenant commander **d :** the administrator or chief officer of a commandery in a medieval religious military order **e :** the presiding officer of certain societies (as the Knights Templars) at the local, regional, or national level — used esp. in secret orders and veterans' organizations **f :** the ranking officer (as a lieutenant or captain) in charge of a division, a district, a precinct, or a squad in certain metropolitan police departments **g :** the officer in charge of a fire company in certain fire departments **2 :** a heavy beetle or wooden mallet **:** RAMMER **3 :** a member of one of the higher grades or divisions in certain honorary orders of knighthood (as the French Legion of Honor)

commander in chief *n, pl* **commanders in chief :** one who holds the supreme command of an armed force often including more than one service and sometimes more than one nation

com·mand·er·ship \-,ship\ *n* **:** the rank or title of commander

com·mand·ery *or* **com·mand·ry** \-d(ə)rē, -ri\ *n* -ES [MF *commanderie,* fr. ML *commendaria,* fr. *commenda* benefice (fr. *commendare* to commend) + *-aria* -ary — more at COMMEND] **1 :** the office or rank of a commander — now used only of orders of knighthood **2 a** (1) **:** a district or a manor with lands and tenements appertaining thereto under the control of a commander of a religious military order of knights **:** PRECEPTORY (2) **:** a pension or benefice attached to a commandership of an order of knighthood **b :** a conventual priory of a religious order **c :** the house of a medieval commandery **3 :** an assembly or lodge in certain secret orders (as the Knights Templars) **4 :** a district under the administration of a commander or governor

command-in-chief \=‵==‵=\ *vt* **commanded-in-chief; commanded-in-chief; commanding-in-chief; commands-in-chief** [back-formation fr. *commander in chief*] **:** to serve as commander in chief of ⟨he was authorized to *command-in-chief* all the local militia⟩

commanding *adj* [ME *comanding,* fr. pres. part. of *comanden* to command] **:** that commands or has the air of command ⟨he sought a ~ position in all he did⟩ ⟨a ~ view of the valley⟩ ⟨a ~ appearance⟩ — **com·mand·ing·ly** *adv* — **com·mand·ing·ness** *n* -ES

commanding officer *n* **:** an officer in command **:** COMMANDER; *esp* **:** a military officer below the rank of brigadier general who is in command of an organization or installation

com·man·di·taire \kə,mandə'ta(a)(ə)r\ *n* -s [F, fr. *commandite* + *-aire* -ary] *French law* **:** a silent partner in a commandite

com·man·dite \'‚kämən'dēt, kōⁿmäⁿ'dēt\ *n* -s [F, fr. It. *accomandita,* fr. fem. of *accomandito,* past part of *accomandare* to deposit in safe custody, fr. *ad-* + (assumed) VL *commandare* to commend, command — more at COMMAND] *civil law* **:** a form of partnership in which there are one or more silent partners who contribute funds but were liable orig. only for the capital invested and later only according to a registered scheme of liability

com·mand·ment \kə'man(d)mənt, -'maan-,-'mȧn-\ *n* -s [ME *comandement,* fr. OF *comandement,* fr. *comander* + *-ment*] **:** the act of commanding, power of command, or what is commanded; *specif* **:** one of the biblical ten commandments

commandment keeper *n, cap C&K* **:** one of a Negro Jewish religious sect of the Harlem section of New York City that practices orthodox Judaism and teaches that Negroes are true Hebrews whose ancestry is traceable back through the kings of Ethiopia to King Solomon — called also *Black Jew*

com·man·do \kə'man(,)dō, -maan-,-mȧn-\ *n, pl* **commandos** *or* **commandoes** [Afrik *kommando* unit of militia, fr. D *commando* command, fr. Sp *comando,* fr. *comandar* to command, fr. F *commander,* fr. OF *comander* — more at COMMAND] **1** *Africa* **a** (1) **:** a raid or expedition — used esp. in the phrase *on commando* (2) **:** militia service in the Boer army **b** (1) **:** a military unit or command of the Boers (2) **:** a member of a Boer military unit **2 a** (1) **:** a military unit of specially trained amphibious shock troops organized for hit-and-run raids into enemy territory for sabotage, destruction of stores and communications, obtaining information, and seizure of captives (2) **:** a member of a commando unit or other specialized raiders' organization — compare RANGER **b** (1) **:** any body of troops (as of frontier fighters or guerrillas) or of insurrectionists or saboteurs that is felt to resemble a commando unit on account of some similarity of function or tactics (as that of engagement in hit-and-run raids) (2) **:** a member of such a body **c :** a raid or attack of the type characteristic of commando units

com·man·do·man \-(,)dō,man,-,dōmən\ *n, pl* **commandomen :** a member of a commando unit

command paper *n* [so called fr. its being by command of the Crown] **:** a document published by the British government or a department at public expense

command pennant *n, in the U.S. Navy* **:** a swallow-tailed pennant flown by an officer below flag rank who is temporarily in command of a division or of a comparable or greater unit — see BROAD COMMAND PENNANT, BURGEE COMMAND PENNANT

command pilot *n* **:** a U.S. Air Force pilot who has had at least 3000 hours in the air and not less than 15 years flying service

command post *n* **:** a post established by the headquarters of a unit at which orders for the command are received and from which the commander of the unit exercises command

command post exercise *n* **:** a field exercise participated in by command, staff, and communication personnel only

com·man·dress \-ndrəs\ *n* -ES [*commander* + *-ess*] **:** a female commander

commands *pres 3d sing of* COMMAND, *pl of* COMMAND

command sergeant major *n* **:** a noncommissioned officer in the army ranking above a first sergeant — see RANK table

commas *pl of* COMMA

comma splice *n* **:** COMMA FAULT

com·ma syn·to·num \'kämə'sint³n|əm, -ntən-\ *n, pl* **comma·ta syn·to·na** \-ämədə's . . . |ə\ [LL] **:** SYNTONIC COMMA

commata *pl of* COMMA

com·mat·ic \kə'mad·ik, (')kä¦m-\ *adj* [LL *commat-, comma* musical comma + E *-ic*] **:** of or relating to a musical comma

comma tract *n* **:** a small tract medial to the lateral cervical and upper thoracic tract of the posterior white column of the spinal cord

com·mea·sur·able \kə'mezh(ə)rəbəl, -māzh-\ *adj* [*com-* + *measurable*] **:** COMMENSURATE

com·mea·sure \-zhə(r)\ *vt* -ED/-ING/-S [*com-* + *measure*] **:** to be commensurate with **:** EQUAL

com·me·dia \kə'mādēə, -med-\ *n* -S [It, fr. L *comoedia* — more at COMEDY] **1 :** COMEDY 2b **2** [by shortening] **:** COMMEDIA DELL'ARTE

commedia del·l'ar·te \-(,)de'lärd·ē\ *n, pl* **commedia dell'artes** *or* **commedias dell'arte** [It, lit., comedy of art] **:** Italian comedy as performed in the 16th to 18th centuries by companies of actors trained to improvise dialogue and business from a written plot built around standardized situations and certain stock characters — see ³COLUMBINE, PANTALOON

commedia eru·di·ta \-,erə'dēd·ə, -ärü'-\ *n, pl* **commedia eruditas** *or* **commedias eruditas** [It, lit., erudite comedy] **:** Italian comedy played from a written text — compare COMMEDIA DELL'ARTE

comme il faut \¦kə,mēl¦fō\ *adj* [F, lit., as it should be] **:** conforming to accepted social usage **:** PROPER ⟨it never can have been *comme il faut* . . . for a man of note to be constantly asking for money —T.B.Macaulay⟩ **syn** see DECOROUS

com·me·li·na \,kämə'līnə, -lēnə\ *n* [NL, after Kaspar *Commelin* †1731 Dutch botanist] **1** *cap* **:** a large widely distributed genus (the type of the family Commelinaceae) of herbs of branching or creeping habit with flowers having one petal smaller than the other two **2** -S **:** any plant of the genus *Commelina*

commelina blue *n* **:** a moderate blue that is redder and duller than average copen, redder and stronger than azurite blue, and redder and deeper than Dresden blue

com·me·li·na·ce·ae \,kämələ'nāsē,ē\ *n pl, cap* [NL, fr. *Commelina*, type genus + *-aceae*] **:** a large widely distributed family of herbaceous plants (order Xyridales) that have perfect flowers with a distinct calyx and corolla and upper leaves shaped like a spathe and that comprise the spiderworts — see COMMELINA, TRADESCANTIA — **com·me·li·na·ceous** \¦kämələ¦nāshəs\ *adj*

com·mem \kə'mem\ *n* -S [by shortening] **1** *slang Brit* **:** COMMEMORATION **2 :** a commemorative postage stamp

com·mem·o·ra·ble \kə'mem(ə)rəbəl\ *adj* [F *commémorable*, fr. L *commemorabilis*, fr. *commemorare* + *-abilis* -able] **:** worthy of being commemorated

com·mem·o·rate \kə'memə,rāt, *usu* -ād.+V\ *vt* -ED/-ING/-S [L *commemoratus*, past part. of *commemorare* to remind of, mention, fr. *com-* + *memorare*, fr. *memor* mindful — more at MEMORY] **1 :** to call to remembrance (as by speech, writing, or ceremony) **:** make mention of — now chiefly in ecclesiastical use **2 :** to mark by some ceremony or observation **:** CELEBRATE, OBSERVE ⟨~ a holiday⟩ ⟨~ an anniversary⟩ **3 :** to be a memorial of **:** preserve the remembrance of ⟨a tablet ~*s* his patriotic activities⟩ **syn** see KEEP

com·mem·o·ra·tion \kə,memə'rāshən\ *n* -S [ME *commemoracioun*, fr. L *commemoration-, commemoratio*, fr. *commemoratus* + *-ion-, -io* -ion] **1 :** the act of commemorating **2 :** something that commemorates (as a speech, statue, or ceremony); *specif* **:** a church service to commemorate a saint or sacred event — **com·mem·o·ra·tion·al** \kə¦memə¦rāshən³l, -shnəl\ *adj*

¹com·mem·o·ra·tive \kə'mem(ə)rəd·iv, -emə,rā|, |tiv, -ēv *also* -əv\ *adj* [F *commémoratif*, fr. MF, fr. *commémoration* (fr. L *commemoration-, commemoratio*) + *-if* -ive] **:** commemorating or intended as a commemoration ⟨a ~ speech in his honor⟩; *specif* **:** issued temporarily in commemoration of some notable event and bearing a design and inscription symbolizing that event ⟨a ~ stamp⟩ — **com·mem·o·ra·tive·ly** *adv*

²commemorative \"\ *n* -S **:** something commemorative; *specif* **:** a commemorative coin or postage stamp

com·mem·o·ra·tor \-emə,rād·ə(r), -āta-\ *n* -S [LL, fr. L *commemoratus* + *-or*] **:** one that commemorates

com·mem·o·ra·to·ry \-em(ə)rə,tōrē, -tȯr-, -ri\ *adj* [*commemorate* + *-ory*] **:** COMMEMORATIVE

com·mence \kə'men(t)s\ *vb* -ED/-ING/-S [ME *comencen*, fr. MF *comencer*, fr. (assumed) VL *cominitiare*, fr. L *com-* + LL *initiare* to begin, fr. L, to initiate — more at INITIATE] *vt* **1 :** to enter upon **:** BEGIN, START ⟨~ a literary career⟩ ⟨~ to buy securities⟩ ⟨they sat down and tried to ~ a conversation —George Meredith⟩ **2 :** to initiate formally by performing the first act of ⟨~ legal proceedings⟩ **~** *vi* **1 :** to have a beginning **:** BEGIN, START, ORIGINATE ⟨the program *commenced* with a prayer⟩ ⟨the debate will ~ on Tuesday⟩ **2 :** to begin to be **:** begin to act as **:** assume a role or function as **3** *chiefly Brit* **:** to take a degree at a university — usu. used with prepositional phrase indicating the faculty ⟨~ in arts⟩ or with a complement indicating the degree ⟨~ doctor⟩ **syn** see BEGIN

com·mence·ment \-mənt\ *n* -S [ME *commencement, comencement*, fr. OF *comencement*, fr. *comencer* + *-ment*] **1 :** the act, fact, or time of commencing (as of an era, season, career, or event) **2 a :** the ceremonies at which or the day when degrees or diplomas are conferred by an educational institution **b :** the period of festivities at this time **3 :** the part of a legal declaration that gives the parties and the capacities in which they sue or are sued and the necessary facts as to the summoning of the defendant and the form of action

com·mend \kə'mend\ *vb* -ED/-ING/-S [ME *commenden*, fr. L *commendare* to entrust, recommend, command, fr. *com-* + *-mendare* (fr. *mandare* to commit to one's charge, order) — more at MANDATE] *vt* **1 :** to commit, entrust, or give in charge for care or preservation ⟨Father, into thy hands I ~ my spirit —Lk 23:46 (AV)⟩ **2 a :** to recommend as worthy of confidence or regard **:** present as worthy of notice or favorable attention ⟨I ~ to you our sister Phoebe —Rom 16:1 (RSV)⟩ **b** *obs* **:** OFFER ⟨I ~ my duty to your lordship —Shak.⟩ **3 :** to mention with approbation **:** PRAISE ⟨they refer to what I am not in the habit of doing and they ~ me —S.M.Crothers⟩ **4** *archaic* **:** to mention with kindly remembrance and good will ⟨~ me to my son —William Robertson †1793⟩ **5** *obs* **:** to set off advantageously **:** GRACE, ADORN **6** *obs* **:** to bestow in commendam **7** *in the feudal system* **:** to commit or place as vassal under the protection of a lord — used of oneself or of land **~** *vi* **:** to commend or serve as a commendation of something — **commend me to :** give me by preference ⟨of all the homes I have been in *commend me to* my own home and fireside⟩

com·men·da \kə'mendə\ *n* -S [ML, back-formation fr. L *commendare* to entrust, command] **1 :** a form of trust in use in the middle ages in which goods are delivered to another for a particular enterprise (as for marketing abroad) **2 :** COMMENDAM **3 :** the insignia, title, rights, or stipend of membership in a medieval order of chivalry

com·mend·able \kə'mendəbəl, *archaic* ¦kämən¦dāb-\ *adj* [MF, fr. L *commendabilis*, fr. *commendare* + *-abilis* -able] *adj* **:** worthy of being commended **:** LAUDABLE — **com·mend·able·ness** *n* -ES

com·mend·ably \-dəblē, -li\ *adv* **:** in a commendable manner

com·men·dam \kə'men,dam\ *n* -S [ML, accus. of *commenda* trust (as used in the phrase *dare in commendam* to give in trust)] **1 a :** the custody or holding of a benefice by a cleric or a layman to whom it is given in charge often only until a proper incumbent is provided **b :** the enjoyment of the revenues from such a custody or holding **2 :** a benefice held in commendam

com·men·da·tion \kä,men'dāshən, -,mən-\ *n* -S [ME *commendacioun*, fr. MF *commendation*, fr. L *commendation-, commendatio*, fr. *commendatus* + *-ion-, -io* -ion] **1 a :** the act of commending **:** the expression of approval **b :** something that commends ⟨good nature is the most godlike ~ of man —John Dryden⟩; *specif* **:** an award (as to a military unit) for distinction in operations ⟨a meritorious unit ~⟩ **2** *archaic* **:** a message of affection or respect **:** COMPLIMENT, GREETING — usu. used in pl. **3 :** an office commending to God the souls of the dead or dying **4 :** the act of placing as a vassal under the protection of a lord **:** VASSALAGE **5 a :** the act of giving a benefice in commendam **b :** the state of a commendam

com·men·da·tor \'=(,)=,dād·ə(r)\ *n* -S [ML *commendator* commender, fr. L *commendatus* (past part. of *commendare* to entrust, recommend command) + *-or* — more at COMMEND] **1 :** one who holds a benefice in commendam **2 :** COMMENDATORE

com·men·da·to·re \kə,mendə'tōrē, (,)kä,m-\ *n* -S [It, fr. ML *commendator*] **:** a member of an Italian honorary order of chivalry who ranks next above an officer and next below a grand officer

¹com·men·da·to·ry \kə'mendə,tōrē, -tȯr-, -ri\ *adj* [LL *commendatorius*, fr. L *commendatus* (past part. of *commendare* to recommend) + *-orius* -ory — more at COMMEND] **1 :** of, relating to, or serving for commendation **2** [alter. of earlier *commendatary*, adj., fr. ML *commendatarius*, fr. L *commendatus* + *-arius* -ary] **:** holding or held in commendam

²commendatory *n* -ES **1** *obs* **:** COMMENDATION, EULOGY **2** *obs* **:** a knight commander of an order of chivalry **3** *obs* **:** COMMENDATOR 1 **4** *obs* **:** COMMANDERY 2a **5** *archaic* **:** COMMENDAM 1

commendatory letter *n* **:** a letter of commendation; *specif* **:** a letter of introduction testifying to an individual's good standing in a church and given by a bishop to a traveling member of his diocese or to a cleric transferring to another diocese

com·mend·ing·ly *adv* **:** in a commending manner

¹com·men·sal \kə'men(t)səl\ *adj* [ME, fr. ML *commensalis*, fr. L *com-* + LL *mensalis* of the table, fr. L *mensa* table + *-alis* -al — more at MENSA] **1 :** of or relating to those who habitually eat together ⟨~ pleasures⟩ **2** *biol* **:** living in a state of commensalism — **com·men·sal·ly** \-səlē\ *adv*

²commensal \"\ *n* -S [ME, fr. *commensal*, adj.] **1 :** one who eats at the same table with others **:** MESSMATE **2** *biol* **:** an organism living in a state of commensalism

com·men·sal·ism \-,lizəm\ *n* -S **1 :** the relation existing between two kinds of organisms in which one obtains food, protection, or other benefits from the other without damaging or benefiting it — compare PARASITISM, SYMBIOSIS **2 :** intimate association in a social group esp. at meals

com·men·sal·ist \-ləst\ *n* -S **:** COMMENSAL 1 — **com·men·sal·is·tic** \kə¦men(t)sə¦listik\ *adj*

com·men·sal·i·ty \,käm,en'saləd·ē\ *n* -ES **1 a :** the practice of eating together **b :** a social group that eats together **2 :** COMMENSALISM

com·men·su·ra·bil·i·ty \kə,men(t)s(ə)rə'biləd·ē *also* -mench(ə)-\ *n* -ES [MF *commensurabilité*, fr. *commensurable* + *-ité* -ity] **:** the quality or state of being commensurable

com·men·su·ra·ble \=ˈ=(=)rəbəl\ *adj* [MF or LL; MF *commensurable*, fr. LL *commensurabilis*, fr. L *com-* + LL *mensurabilis* measurable, fr. *mensurare* to measure, fr. L *mensura* measure — more at MEASURE] **1 :** having a common measure; *specif* **:** divisible by a common measure or unit an integral number of times ⟨10 and 25 are ~ since they have 5 as a common divisor⟩ **2 :** COMMENSURATE 2 ⟨the two punishments must be perfectly ~ —Jeremy Bentham⟩ — **com·men·su·ra·bly** \-blē\ *adv*

com·men·su·rate \kə'men(t)s(ə)rət *also* -mench(ə)-; *usu* -əd.+V\ *adj* [LL *commensuratus* equal, fr. L *com-* + LL *mensuratus*, past part. of *mensurare* to measure] **1 :** equal in measure or extent **:** COEXTENSIVE ⟨the life of Burleigh was ~ with one of the most important periods —T.B.Macaulay⟩ ⟨iron has defects almost ~ with its virtues —Lewis Mumford⟩ **2 :** corresponding in size, extent, amount, or degree **:** PROPORTIONATE ⟨an income ~ with his needs⟩ ⟨the child was started in a grade ~ with his mental ability —F.H.Allen⟩ **3** *archaic* **:** corresponding in nature **:** of the same sphere of phenomena **:** essentially interrelated **4 :** COMMENSURABLE 1 — **com·men·su·rate·ly** *adv* — **com·men·su·rate·ness** *n* -ES

com·men·su·ra·tion \kə,men(t)sə'rāshən *also* -menchə'-\ *n* -S [MF, fr. LL *commensuration-, commensuratio*, fr L *com-* + LL *mensuration-, mensuratio* act of measuring — more at MENSURATION] **1 :** the measuring of things in comparison with one another **2 :** the state of being proportionate ⟨fitness lies in a particular ~ . . . of one thing to another —Robert South⟩

¹com·ment \'kä,ment *sometimes* -,mənt\ *n* -S [ME, commentary, exposition, fr. LL *commentum* commentary, fr. L, invention, contrivance, fr. neut. of *commentus*, past part. of *comminisci* to invent, contrive, devise, fr. *com-* + *-minisci* (fr. the root of *ment-, mens* mind) — more at MIND] **1 :** an expository treatise **:** COMMENTARY **2 a :** a note or observation intended to explain, illustrate, or criticize the meaning of a writing **:** ANNOTATION ⟨~*s* upon the passage were printed in the margin⟩ **b :** the whole body of such matter ⟨two pages of ~ for every page of text⟩ **3 a :** an observation or remark expressing an opinion or attitude concerning what has been seen or heard or concerning the subject at hand ⟨she listens, and puts in from time to time some critical ~ —Rose Macaulay⟩ **b :** discussion, interpretation, or expression of opinion or attitude ⟨the paper also gave ~ on the news in signed editorials —Jacques Kayser⟩ **:** CRITICISM ⟨the brown tweeds, sir, . . . would have occasioned unfavorable ~ —T.S.Watt⟩ **4 :** a critical observation, interpretation, or expression of opinion conveyed by suggestion, implication, analogy, or other indirect means ⟨the painting is a ~ on the subject's character⟩ ⟨the film is an ironic ~ on the industrial age⟩

²comment \" *sometimes* kə'ment\ *vb* -ED/-ING/-S *vi* **:** to explain or interpret by comment **:** make or write comment **:** REMARK, OBSERVE ⟨neither could be induced . . . to ~ during general discussions —Victor Boesen⟩ ⟨~*ing* on the situation in the West⟩ **~** *vt* **1 :** to furnish (a written work) with comments **:** explain or interpret by comment **:** ANNOTATE ⟨translated and ~*ed* the Psalter —G.G.Coulton⟩ **2 :** to make a comment on **:** DISCUSS, CRITICIZE ⟨the discovery . . . is hardly ~*ed* by the press —*Nation*⟩

com·men·tary \'kämən,terē, -ri\ *n* -ES [L *commentarius, commentarium* notebook, commentary, fr. *commentari* to meditate upon (freq. of *comminisci* to invent, contrive, devise) + *-arius, -arium* -ary (n. suffix) — more at COMMENT] **1 a :** a treatise in explanation of some subject — usu. used in pl. ⟨Blackstone's *Commentaries*⟩ **b :** a record of a set of events usu. written by a participant and marked by less formality and elaborateness than a history — usu. used in pl. ⟨Caesar's *Commentaries on the Gallic War*⟩ **2 a :** a systematic series of explanations or interpretations of the text of a writing ⟨a ~ on Dante's *Divine Comedy*⟩ ⟨*commentaries* on the Scriptures⟩ **b :** COMMENT 2a **c :** a spoken description or series of comments accompanying a motion picture or other exhibition **3 a :** something that serves for illustration or explanation ⟨godly persons . . . whose lives might be a fitting ~ on their teaching —W.H.Prescott⟩ **:** a fact or piece of evidence that explains or illustrates a condition or characteristic ⟨the dark, airless apartments and sunless factories . . . are a sad ~ upon our civilization —H.A.Overstreet⟩ **b :** an observation or interpretation conveyed by suggestion, implication, analogy, or other indirect means ⟨both books are *commentaries* with tragic or ironic overtones on certain social groups⟩ ⟨a scene that is a gem of satiric ~ on the world of art —Rose Feld⟩ **4 :** the act of commenting

com·men·tate \'kämən,tāt, -,men-\ *vb* -ED/-ING/-S [back formation fr. *commentator*] *vt* **1 :** to write a commentary upon (as a text) **2 :** to deliver an oral commentary upon (as a fashion show or other exhibition) **~** *vi* **:** COMMENT; *specif* **:** to act as a commentator

com·men·ta·tion \,kämən'tāshən, -,men-\ *n* -S [MF or L; MF, commentary, fr. L *commentation-, commentatio* meditation, treatise, fr. *commentatus* (past part. of *commentari* to meditate upon) + *-ion-, -io* -ion] **1** *obs* **:** a commentary esp. on a text **2** *archaic* **:** the act of commenting **:** interpretation or expression of opinion

com·men·ta·tive \'kämən,tād·iv, kə'mentəd·-\ *adj* [¹*comment* + *-ative*] **:** of or concerning comment or commentary

com·men·ta·tor \'kämən,tād·ə(r), -āta- *also* -,men-\ *n* -S [LL, fr. L, deviser, contriver, fr. *commentatus* + *-or*] **:** one who comments or makes a commentary: as **a :** one who writes a commentary (as on a literary text) **:** ANNOTATOR **b :** one who reports and discusses current events or daily news esp. on radio or television usu. with interpretation and analysis — called also *news analyst* — **com·men·ta·to·ri·al** \¦kə,mentə¦tōrēəl, kä¦m-\ *adj*

com·men·ti·tious \¦kämən¦tishəs\ *adj* [L *commenticius, commentitius*, fr. *commentus* (past part. of *comminisci* to invent, contrive, devise) + *-icius, -itius* -itious — more at COMMENT] *archaic* **:** fictitious or imaginary **:** feigned or lying

¹com·merce \'kä(,)mərs, -,məs, -,mōs, -,mois\ *n* -S [MF, fr. L *commercium*, fr. *com-* + *merc-, merx* merchandise — more at MARKET] **1 a :** social intercourse **:** dealings between individuals or groups in society **:** interchange of ideas, opinions, or sentiments ⟨their ~ with the ancients appears to me to produce . . . a steadying . . . effect upon their judgment —Matthew Arnold⟩ **b :** dealings of any kind ⟨their conviction that art has no ~ with morality —C.J.Glicksberg⟩ **:** interrelationship, connection, or communication ⟨the ~ between our intellectual . . . interests and the nature of experience —Herbert Feigl & W.S.Sellars⟩ **2 a :** the exchange or buying and selling of commodities esp. on a large scale and involving transportation from place to place — compare TRADE, TRAFFIC **b commerces** *pl, obs* **:** commercial transactions **3 :** mental or spiritual intercourse or relationship **:** COMMUNION ⟨so hold I ~ with the dead —Alfred Tennyson⟩ **4** *obs* **:** an exchange (as of letters) ⟨a ~ of letters between friends⟩ **5 :** SEXUAL INTERCOURSE **6** *obs* **:** means of communication **:** PASSAGE **7 :** an old card game similar to whiskey poker in which each player in succession may exchange one of his three cards for another card until some one refuses, whereupon the best hand wins

²com·merce \", kə'mərs, kä'-, -'mōs,-'məis\ *vi* -ED/-ING/-S [MF *commercer*, fr. *commerce*, n.] **:** to hold personal intercourse or communication **:** COMMUNE — used with *with* ⟨less disposed to ~ with my kind —Cornelius Weygandt⟩

com·merce·less *pronunc at* ¹COMMERCE +ləs\ *adj* **:** lacking commerce

commercia *pl of* COMMERCIUM

com·mer·cia bel·li \kə¦mərsh(ē)ə'be,lī, -(,)lē; kə¦merkēə'be,lē\ *n pl* [NL, fr. L, pl. of *commercium belli* stipulation, treaty, lit., intercourse of war] **:** agreements between enemy states (as truces, capitulations, safe-conducts, and cartels)

¹com·mer·cial \kə'mərshəl, -mōsh-,-məish-\ *adj* [¹*commerce* + *-ial*] **1 :** of, in, or relating to commerce: as **a :** occupied with or engaged in commerce ⟨a ~ establishment⟩ ⟨the ~ world⟩ **b :** related to or dealing with commerce ⟨~ treaty⟩ **c :** used in or characteristic of commerce ⟨~ weights⟩ ⟨~ language⟩ ⟨~ ethics⟩ **d :** suitable to or adequate for commerce ⟨found oil in ~ quantities⟩ **e (1) :** of the kind or quality used in commerce **(2) :** of an average or inferior quality ⟨~ oxalic acid⟩ ⟨~ grade of beef⟩ — compare TECHNICAL **f :** produced or producible in large quantities for commerce ⟨relying on a balanced diet rather than ~ vitamin concentrates⟩ **2 a :** from the point of view of profit **:** having profit as the primary aim ⟨~ success⟩ ⟨~ failure⟩ ⟨~ aspect⟩ **b :** sacrificing artistic principles for qualities that bring financial success ⟨~ drama⟩ ⟨~ music⟩ **3** *of a school, a course, or a curriculum* **:** emphasizing skills and subjects considered useful in business occupations — compare BUSINESS EDUCATION, GENERAL **4 :** paid for by an advertiser — used esp. of a radio or television program

²commercial \"\ *n* -S **1** *Brit* **:** TRAVELING SALESMAN **2 a :** an advertisement broadcast during a sponsored radio or television program or between programs **b :** a radio or television program sponsored by an advertiser

commercial agency *n* **:** MERCANTILE AGENCY 2

commercial arbitration *n* **:** arbitration by which disputes arising out of business contracts or transactions may be settled out of court by a special tribunal

commercial art *n* **:** art applied to commercial purposes

commercial attaché *n* **:** an officer in the foreign commerce service of a country who is attached to an embassy or legation in those countries considered important for trade or business

commercial bank *n* **:** a bank including in its functions the acceptance of demand deposits subject to withdrawal by check

commercial blanket bond *n* **:** a fidelity bond or form of insurance issued to business firms that covers all losses due to theft by employees

commercial club *n* **:** CHAMBER OF COMMERCE

commercial code *n* **:** a code designed to achieve brevity or economy of words esp. in order to save telegraph tolls

commercial control *n* **:** insect pest control or crop disease control that is incomplete but adequate to prevent large losses

commercial credit *n* **:** credit granted by a bank to a business concern to finance commercial transaction

commercial credit company *n* **:** a finance company engaged in lending on or buying up accounts receivable or discounting installment contracts

commercial feed *n* **:** any mixed ration for animal feeding offered for sale on the open market

commercial fertilizer *n* **:** a manufactured chemical mixture prepared for use as fertilizer as distinguished from such natural substances as farm manures

commercial geography *n* **:** geography that deals with commodities according to their places of origin and their paths of transportation

commercial hotel *n* **:** a hotel for transients that caters esp. to salesmen (as by providing rooms for the display of samples)

com·mer·cial·ism \-,lizəm\ *n* -S **1 :** commercial spirit, institutions, or methods ⟨the vigor of the ~ of New England . . . led . . . to the conflict between Britain and the . . . colonies —W.A.Mackintosh⟩ **2 :** excessive emphasis on profit or financial success ⟨the new ~, the aim to "show results" that was undermining and vulgarizing education —Willa Cather⟩

com·mer·cial·ist \-,ləst\ *n* -S **:** one engaged in commerce or devoted to commercialism

com·mer·cial·is·tic \=¦=shə¦listik, -tēk\ *adj* **:** marked or motivated by a desire to accumulate wealth through business pursuits

com·mer·cial·i·ty \kə,mərshē'aləd·ē, ,kä,mər'shal-\ *n* -ES **:** commercial quality

com·mer·cial·i·za·tion \kə,mərsh(ə)lə'zāshən, -mōsh-, -məish-, -shə,lī'z-\ *n* -S **:** the act of commercializing or the state resulting from such action

com·mer·cial·ize \=ˈ=shə,līz\ *vt* -ED/-ING/-S **1 a :** to subject to the conditions of commerce **:** make into a form of trade ⟨agriculture . . . has been . . . *commercialized* and become a branch of trade —James Bryce⟩ **b :** to develop commerce in ⟨a highly *commercialized* country⟩ **:** organize for increased commercial efficiency or effectiveness ⟨*commercialized* vice⟩ **2 :** to cause (something having only a potential income-producing value) to be sold, manufactured, displayed, or utilized so as to yield income ⟨raise capital to ~ his invention⟩ ⟨only two of the five caves have been *commercialized*⟩ **3 :** to engage in, conduct, practice, or make use of for profit-seeking purposes as distinguished from participation, practice, or use for spiritual or recreational purposes or for other nonpecuniary satisfactions ⟨~ the celebration of Christmas⟩ ⟨bitterly opposed to *commercialized* Sunday sports⟩ **4 a :** to debase in quality, make more conventional and unoriginal, or employ for inferior purposes in the hope of securing a greater or more certain profit ⟨our somewhat *commercialized* theater —*Amer. Mercury*⟩ ⟨or he may give up poetry for some more popular form of literary entertainment — that is to say, he ~*s* his talent —Herbert Read⟩ **b :** to affect through commercialism so as to debase in quality or make more conventional and unoriginal ⟨our *commercialized* taste —S.H.Horton⟩

commercial law *n* **:** the legal rules or principles bearing esp. on commercial transactions and comprising matters of partnership, joint stock companies, agency, negotiable paper, contracts with carriers, insurance, sale, bottomry and respondentia, debt, guaranty, stoppage in transitu, lien, and bankruptcy

com·mer·cial·ly \-shəlē, -li\ *adv* **:** in a commercial manner

commercial paper *n* **1 :** short-term negotiable instruments (as bills of exchange, checks, and promissory notes) arising out of commercial transactions; *esp* **:** instruments constituting direct obligations of business firms that are sold through note brokers to banks, corporations, and other investors seeking liquid investments **2 commercial papers** *pl, in Universal Postal Union regulations* **:** pieces of mail matter in a classification comprising business papers and documents and including old correspondence, invoices, and bills of lading that have previously served their purpose and are not at the time of shipment being sent as current personal correspondence

commercial pilot *n* **:** a pilot who operates an airplane for transportation of mail, passengers, or freight or for other commercial purposes

commercial policy *n* **:** an accident or health and accident insurance policy sold to persons in such less hazardous occupations as clerical work, business administration, sales, and teaching

commercial room *n, Brit* **:** a public hotel room for use by traveling salesmen

commercials *pl of* COMMERCIAL

commercial traveler *n* **:** TRAVELING SALESMAN

commercial treaty *n* **:** a treaty that defines the conditions under which citizens of one country may do business in another and covers such matters as the right to hold property, mode of enforcing claims, and tariff privileges

commercial vehicle *n* **:** a vehicle that is designed for commercial use (as the transportation of cargo other than passengers)

commercing *pres part of* COMMERCE

com·mer·cium \kə'mərsh(ē)əm\ *n, pl* **commer·cia** \-(ē)ə\ [L — more at COMMERCE] *Roman law* **:** COMMERCE, TRAFFIC **:** commercial transaction **:** business intercourse; *also* **:** JUS COMMERCII

com·merge \kə'mərj, kä'-\ *vb* -ED/-ING/-S [*com-* + *merge*] **:** MERGE

com·mers *or* **kom·mers** *also* **com·merz** \kȯ'mers\ *n* -ES *often cap* [G *kommers*, fr. G dial. *kommers, kommersch* social intercourse, noisy social activity, fr. F *commerce* commerce — more at COMMERCE] **:** a social gathering of students in German universities

[1]**com·mie** *or* **com·my** \'kämē, -mi\ *also* **com·mon·ey** \-mənē, -ni\ *n, pl* **commies** *also* **commoneys** [*commie* & *commy* prob. by shortening & alter. fr. *common* (as in *common marble*); *commoney* fr. *common* + *-ey* (var. of *-y*] **:** a playing marble made of clay

[2]**com·mie** *also* **com·my** \'kämē, -mi\ *n, pl* **commies** *often cap* [by shortening and alter.] **:** COMMUNIST 3

com·mi·nate \'kämə,nāt\ *vb* -ED/-ING/-S [back-formation fr. *commination*] **:** to threaten with divine punishment

com·mi·na·tion \,kämə'nāshən\ *n* -S [ME *comminacioun*, fr. MF or L; MF *commination*, fr. L *commination-, comminatio*, fr. *comminatus* (past part. of *comminari* to threaten, fr. *com-* + *minari* to threaten) + *-ion-, -io* -ion — more at MOUNT] **1 a :** an instance or the action of announcing, warning of, or threatening punishment or vengeance, esp. divine punishment or vengeance **b :** DENUNCIATION **:** ANATHEMA ⟨those thunderous ~*s*, that jeering and abuse which make Milton's prose such lively reading —Aldous Huxley⟩ **2 :** a recital of God's anger and judgments against sinners read in the Church of England esp. after the litany on Ash Wednesday; *also* **:** the penitential office which contains this recital

com·mi·na·to·ry \'kämənə,tōrē, kə'min-, kə'mīn-\ *adj* [ML *comminatorius*, fr. L *comminatus* + *-orius* -ory] **1 :** conveying warning or threat of punishment or vengeance **2 :** DENUNCIATORY ⟨had nothing sensible and ~ to say against her —Rebecca West⟩

com·min·gle \kə'miŋgəl, kä'-\ *vb* -ED/-ING/-S [*com-* + *mingle*] *vi* **:** to mingle or mix together ⟨the *commingling* in him of earthiness and sophistication —Robert Pick⟩ ~ *vt* **1 :** to mix together ⟨savage ridicule, *commingled* with resentment —Jean Stafford⟩ **2 :** to combine (the funds or property of several individuals) into a common fund or stock (as for convenience of investment by a trust company) **syn** *see* MIX

com·min·gler \-g(ə)lə(r)\ *n* -S **:** a device for noiseless heating of water by steam in a vessel filled with a porous mass (as of pebbles)

[1]**com·mi·nute** \'kämə,n(y)üt\ *vt* -ED/-ING/-S [L *comminutus*, past part. of *comminuere*, fr. *com-* + *minuere* to lessen — more at MINOR] **:** to reduce to minute particles or fine powder **:** PULVERIZE, TRITURATE; *specif* **:** to break up, chop, or grind (as meat or cheese) into small particles

[2]**comminute** \"\ *adj* [L *comminutus*] **:** COMMINUTED

comminuted fracture *n* **:** a fracture in which the bone is splintered or crushed into numerous pieces

com·mi·nu·tion \,kämə'n(y)üshən\ *n* -S [L *comminutus* + E *-ion*] **1 :** the act or action of comminuting or the fact of being comminuted **:** TRITURATION, PULVERIZATION **2 :** gradual diminution by the removal of small particles at a time **:** wearing away **:** LESSENING ⟨natural and necessary ~ of our lives —Samuel Johnson⟩ **3 :** fracture (as of a bone) into a number of pieces

com·mi·nu·tor \-üd·ə(r)\ *n* -S [[1]*comminute* + *-or*] **:** a machine that cuts up solids in raw sewage in preparation for purifying treatment

com·miph·o·ra \kə'mifərə\ *n, cap* [NL, fr. Gk *kommi* gum + NL *-phora* — more at GUM] **:** a large genus of East Indian and African trees (family Burseraceae) yielding balsamic products (as the resins of *C. schimperi* of Abyssinia, *C. kataf* of Arabia, and others that are used as substitutes for myrrh) — see BALM OF GILEAD, MYRRH

com·mis \,kə'mē, kȯ'-\ *n, pl* **commis** \-ē(z)\ [F, fr. *commis* (past part. of *commettre* to commit, entrust), fr. L *commissus*, past part. of *committere* to connect, entrust — more at COMMIT] **:** DEPUTY, ASSISTANT, CLERK

com·mis·cu·um \kə'miskyəwəm\ *n, pl* **commis·cua** \-wə\ *also* **commiscuums** \-wəmz\ [NL, fr. L, neut. of *commiscuus* common, fr. *commiscere* to mix together — more at COMMIX] **:** a subdivision of a comparium comprising organisms that can interbreed to produce fertile hybrids and being usu. equivalent in scope to a taxonomic species

com·mis·er·a·ble \kə'miz(ə)rəbəl\ *adj* [*commiseration* + *-able*] **:** PITIABLE

[1]**com·mis·er·ate** \kə'mizə,rāt, *usu* -ād·+V\ *vb* -ED/-ING/-S [L *commiseratus*, past part. of *commiserari*, fr. *com-* + *miserari* to pity, fr. *miser* wretched] *vt* **:** to feel or express sorrow, pain, or compassion for **:** express pity for **:** PITY ⟨*commiserating* the state of her poor friend —Jane Austen⟩ ~ *vi* **:** CONDOLE, SYMPATHIZE — used with *with* ⟨set up an altar in the reception room, *commiserated* with the war criminals and their visiting relatives —*Time*⟩

[2]**com·mis·er·ate** \-z(ə)rət, *usu* -əd·+V\ *adj* [L *commiseratus*] **:** showing commiseration ⟨the first ~ touch of a smile —H.E. Bates⟩ — **com·mis·er·ate·ly** *adv*

com·mis·er·a·tion \kə,mizə'rāshən\ *n* -S [MF *commisération*, fr. L *commiseration-, commiseratio* part of an oration intended to excite compassion, fr. *commiseratus* + *-ion-, -io* -ion] **:** the act of commiserating **:** the feeling or showing of sorrow or the expression of condolence for the wants or distresses of another ⟨an adult who falls on the street is the object of . . . ~ —Agnes Repplier⟩ **syn** *see* SYMPATHY

com·mis·er·a·tive \kə'mizə,rā|d·iv, -z(ə)rə|, -tiv\ *adj* **:** given to commiseration **:** COMPASSIONATE ⟨made ~ clicking sounds with his tongue —Kenneth Roberts⟩

com·mis·sar \'kämə,sär, -sȧ(r, ,==\'=\ *n* -S [Russ *komissar*, fr. G *kommissar* commissary, fr. ML *commissarius* one to whom something is entrusted — more at COMMISSARY] **1 a :** a Communist party official assigned to a military unit or sometimes to a civilian group to teach party principles and policies and to ensure party loyalty — called also *political commissar* **b :** one resembling or held to resemble a political commissar esp. in attempting to control public opinion or its expression ⟨would-be ~*s* of culture —G.B.Oxnam⟩ **2 a :** a Soviet government official **b :** the head of a government department in the U.S.S.R. until 1946 ⟨*Commissar* of Justice⟩ ⟨*Commissar* for Foreign Affairs⟩ — called also *people's commissar*

com·mis·sar·i·at \,kämə'serēət *sometimes* -sa(a)r- *or* -ē,at; *in sense 3 also* -sär- *or* -sȧr-; *usu* -d·+V\ *n* -S [NL *commissariatus*, fr. ML *commissarius* + L *-atus* -ate] **1 a :** the organized system by which armies and military posts are supplied with food and daily necessaries **b :** the body of officers charged with such service **2 :** food supplies **:** one's stock of provisions **:** COMMISSARY **3** [Russ *komissariat*, fr. G *kommissariat*, fr. NL *commissariatus*] **:** a government department in the U.S.S.R. until 1946 — compare COLLEGIUM, COMMISSAR 2 **4 :** a board of commissioners **:** COMMISSION

com·mis·sar·i·ot \-rēət\ *n* -S [alter. of *commissariat*] **:** COMMISSARY COURT 2

com·mis·sary \'kämə,serē, -ri\ *n* -ES [ME *commissarie*, fr. ML *commissarius* one to whom something is entrusted, fr. L *commissus*, past part. of *committere* to entrust + *-arius* -ary — more at COMMIT] **1 a :** an officer in the Church of England with spiritual or ecclesiastical jurisdiction who represents a bishop in an esp. distant part of the diocese or who performs the bishop's duties in his absence **b :** a clergyman appointed by a bishop or other official in the Church of England as his deputy for certain specified purposes **2 :** one to whom some charge, duty, or office has been committed by a superior power; *esp* **:** one sent or delegated to execute a duty or an office as the representative of his superior **3 a :** a civilian official or military officer in charge of some special service or department ⟨~ of muster⟩ ⟨~ of Indian affairs⟩ ⟨~ of prisoners⟩; *esp* **:** one in charge of procuring or distributing food and other supplies for military forces **b :** a department or store supplying personal equipment and provisions (as on a military post or in a railroad, lumber, or mining camp) **c :** food supplies **:** one's stock of provisions **:** COMMISSARIAT **d :** a lunchroom or refectory esp. in a motion-picture studio **4 :** a superior French police official **5 :** a judge of a commissary court in Scotland **6 :** COMMISSAR ⟨ordinances of the Council of People's *Commissaries* —W.E.Walling⟩

commissary court *n* **1 :** the court of a bishop's commissary **2 a :** a former supreme probate and divorce court in Scotland absorbed by the Court of Sessions in 1863 **b :** a county or sheriff's court in Scotland that appoints and confirms executors of estates possessing personal property

commissary general *n, pl* **commissaries general 1 :** a supreme representative or deputy **2 :** the chief official or officer in charge of some special army service — compare COMMISSARY 3a

[1]**com·mis·sion** \kə'mishən\ *n* -S [ME *commissioun*, fr. MF *commission*, fr. L *commission-, commissio* act of bringing together, committing, fr. *commissus* + *-ion-, -io* -ion] **1 a :** a formal written warrant or authority granting certain powers or privileges and authorizing or commanding the performance of certain acts or duties ⟨whil'st our ~ from Rome is read, let silence be commanded —Shak.⟩ ⟨a ~ of jail delivery issued by the court⟩ ⟨a ~ to serve as notary public⟩ **b** *obs* **:** a warrant conferring authority to raise and command a body of troops **c :** a certificate conferring military or naval rank and authority on officers above a certain rank; *also* **:** the rank and command so conferred **d :** a document issued to a lay worker in the Salvation Army who undertakes certain duties **2 a :** an authorization or command to act in a prescribed manner or to perform prescribed acts or duties **:** INSTRUCTION, CHARGE ⟨the priest was a custodian of Christ's ~ to his apostles. "Whose sins you shall forgive, they are forgiven them" —M.W.Baldwin⟩ **b :** an order to perform a particular task or carry out a work ⟨provide a young painter with a profitable ~ for a portrait⟩ **3 a :** authority to act for, in behalf of, or in place of another ⟨had summoned all the clans which acknowledged his ~ —T.B.Macaulay⟩ **b :** a task or matter entrusted to one as agent for another ⟨executed a ~ for me while he was in Singapore⟩ **4 a :** a group of persons directed to perform some duty or execute some trust **:** a body of commissioners ⟨U.N. ~ to investigate differences between the two countries⟩ **b :** a government agency having administrative, legislative, or judicial powers ⟨regulatory powers exercised by the Federal Trade *Commission*⟩ **c :** a city council having legislative and executive functions — see COMMISSION PLAN **5 :** the act of committing, performing, or doing (as a crime, misdeed, or other offense) ⟨the ~ of an illegal act⟩ ⟨the sins of omission and ~⟩ **6 :** a fee paid to an agent or employee for transacting a piece of business or performing a service ⟨a broker receives a ~ on each share of stock bought for a customer⟩ ⟨a ~ of 50 cents for each car washed⟩; *esp* **:** a percentage of the money received in a sale or other transaction paid to the agent responsible for the business ⟨a ~ of 9 percent on each sale⟩ — see DEL CREDERE **7 :** the act of entrusting, committing, or giving authority ⟨the ~ of limited powers to the administrator⟩ — **in commission 1** *obs* **:** in the exercise of an authority or the performance of an authorized or delegated act ⟨the Moor himself . . . is *in* full *commission* here for Cyprus —Shak.⟩ **2** *or* **into commission** *of an office or public trust* **:** under the authority of a commission or commissioners (as during the abeyance of the incumbent) ⟨to usurp to itself the executive power of the king and in effect to put the kingship *into commission* —S.B.Chrimes⟩ **3** *of a ship* **:** equipped, manned, and under command in readiness for active service ⟨warships will remain *in commission* when not refitting⟩ **4 :** in use or service or in condition for service ⟨put the old car back *in commission* for a time⟩ — **on commission :** with commissions serving as partial or full remuneration for work or services performed ⟨selling bonds *on commission*⟩ — **out of commission 1 :** out of or retired from active service ⟨the ship was placed *out of commission* after the war⟩ **2 :** out of order **:** not in working order **:** not in use or operation ⟨the bicycle is *out of commission*⟩ ⟨the . . . strike . . . put Alaska's principal ship line *out of commission* —*N.Y. Times*⟩

[2]**commission** \"\ *vt* **commissioned; commissioned; commissioning** \-sh(ə)niŋ\ **commissions 1 :** to give a commission to or for: as **a :** to confer a formal commission on **:** furnish with a written commission ⟨officers will be ~*ed* upon graduation⟩ **b :** to endow with effective right or power **:** AUTHORIZE, EMPOWER ⟨judges are not ~*ed* to make and unmake rules at pleasure —B.N.Cardozo⟩ **c :** to appoint to a certain task, mission, function, or duty ⟨~*ed* to make out a deed of conveyance —Havelock Ellis⟩ **d :** to give an order to (a person) for a work (as an art work) ⟨~*ed* him to paint her portrait⟩ **:** order (as a work of art) made or performed ⟨~ a painting⟩ **2 :** to put in commission (as a ship) **syn** see AUTHORIZE

com·mis·sion·aire \kə¦mishə¦na(a)(ə)r\ *n* -S [F *commissionnaire*, fr. *commission* commission + *-aire* -ary — more at COMMISSION] **1 a** *chiefly Brit* **:** one (as a messenger or porter) entrusted with small commissions **b :** a member of an association of pensioned soldiers and sailors organized in London in 1859 for employment as doorkeepers, caretakers, or messengers **c** *chiefly Brit* **:** a uniformed attendant; *esp* **:** a doorman at a hotel or theater **2 :** a purchasing agent in the foreign market acting on commission for an importer

com·mis·sion·al \kə'mishənᵊl, -shnəl\ *adj* **:** of or relating to a commission

commissionate *vt* -ED/-ING/-S [[1]*commission* + *-ate*] *obs* **:** COMMISSION

commission day *n, Brit* **:** the opening day of the assizes when the judge's commission is read

commissioned officer *n* **:** an officer of the armed forces holding by virtue of a commission a rank of second lieutenant or ensign or above

com·mis·sion·er \kə'mish(ə)nə(r)\ *n* -S [ME, fr. *commissioun* + *-er*] **:** a person who has received a commission or has been delegated to perform some service or carry out some business: as **a :** a member of a commission **b :** the representative or agent of the sovereign power or governmental authority in a district, province, or other governmental unit often having both judicial and administrative powers ⟨he was appointed chief ~ of the colony⟩ **c :** the officer in charge of a department or bureau of the public service ⟨~ of patents⟩ ⟨a state ~ of education⟩ ⟨police ~⟩ **d :** one of the administrative officials of an unincorporated town in Scotland **e :** COUNTY COMMISSIONER **f :** the administrative head of an organized professional sport usu. having regulatory or judicial powers ⟨baseball ~⟩ **g :** a Salvation Army officer ranking above a colonel and below the general

commissioner-general \=¦=(=)=¦=(=)=\ *n, pl* **commissioners-general :** a chief commissioner

commissioners standard ordinary table *n, usu cap* C&S&O **:** a mortality table based on the experience of American life insurance companies during the 1930s and widely used by American companies for premium and reserve calculations for new policies

commission house *n* **1 :** a concern that sells goods for others on commission **2 :** a member firm on an exchange that executes orders to buy and sell listed securities or commodity future contracts

commissioning pennant *n, Brit* **:** COMMISSION PENNANT

commission merchant *n* **:** FACTOR 1a

commission of oyer and terminer : a commission authorizing an English judge (as a High Court judge on circuit) to hear and determine at the assizes all indicted cases of treason, felony, or misdemeanor committed in the county — called also *writ of oyer and terminer*

commission of the peace *English law* **:** a commission under the great seal constituting one or more persons justices of the peace

commission pennant *n* **:** a long pennant flown at the mainmast of a government ship which is in commission but not under the command of an officer entitled to a personal flag or pennant

commission plan *n* **:** a method of city government in which both the executive and legislative powers are held by a small elected commission, each commissioner being directly in charge of one or more municipal departments — compare COUNCIL-MANAGER PLAN

commissions *pl of* COMMISSION, *pres 3d sing of* COMMISSION

com·mis·sur·al \'kämə,shu̇rəl\ *adj* **:** of, relating to, or having the properties of a commissure

com·mis·sure \-u̇(ə)r\ *n* -S [ME, fr. MF or L; MF *commissure*, fr. L *commissura* a joining together, fr. *commissus*, past part. of *committere* to connect + *-ura* -ure — more at COMMIT] **1 :** JOINT, SEAM, CLOSURE **:** the place where two bodies or parts of one body meet and unite **:** INTERSTICE, CLEFT, JUNCTURE **2 :** the point or line of union between two parts (as the angles of the lips): **a :** the whole line along which the mandibles of a bird's bill close **b :** a connecting band of nerve tissue (as one connecting corresponding parts of the right and left halves of the brain or spinal cord) **c :** any of certain nerves that link ganglia in certain invertebrates **3 :** the plane of coherence of the two carpels or mericarps in fruits of the family Umbelliferae

com·mis·sur·ot·o·my \,kämə,shu̇'räd·əmē, -,shə'r-\ *n* -ES [ISV *commissure* + *-o-* + *-tomy*] **:** the operation of cutting through a band of muscle or nerve fibers; *specif* **:** the cutting through the mitral commissures to relieve mitral stenosis — compare FINGER FRACTURE, VALVULOTOMY

[1]**com·mit** \kə'mit, *usu* -id·+V\ *vb* **committed; committed; committing; commits** [ME *committen*, fr. L *committere* to connect, entrust, fr. *com-* + *mittere* to send — more at SMITE] *vt* **1 a :** to put into charge or keeping **:** give in trust **:** ENTRUST, CONSIGN ⟨~ all executive, legislative, and judicial powers to one man —A.T.Vanderbilt⟩ **b** (1) **:** to place in or send officially to confinement or other place of punishment ⟨~ a criminal to prison⟩ **:** sentence to punishment ⟨*committed* Anne Boleyn to a criminal death —Francis Hackett⟩ (2) **:** to consign legally to a mental institution ⟨a patient *committed* by the court to a state hospital⟩ **c :** to consign to a permanent form or to record for preservation (as by writing down or memorizing) ⟨turning the scenes . . . over in his mind . . . before he started *committing* his ideas to paper —Ernest Newman⟩ ⟨~ a poem to memory⟩ **d :** to put into a place for disposal or safekeeping ⟨~ the papers to the fire⟩ ⟨~ his body to the earth⟩ **e :** to refer (as a legislative bill) to a committee for consideration and report **2 :** DO, PERFORM ⟨convicted of *committing* crimes against the state⟩ ⟨~ suicide⟩ ⟨*committing* an even greater folly —O.S.Nock⟩ **3 a** *obs* **:** CONNECT, JOIN **b :** to bring (a force) into battle **:** assign to a military action ⟨should . . . Company C be unable to take the objectives, then Company A will be *committed* —*Infantry Jour.*⟩ **c :** to expose to risk or danger ⟨*committing* his letters to the dangers of censorship —Marcia Davenport⟩ **d** (1) **:** to obligate or bind to take some moral or intellectual position or course of action ⟨a resolution *committing* the party to build 300,000 houses a year —B.C.L.Keelan⟩ ⟨this belief in science, to which our forefathers then *committed* themselves —A.J.Toynbee⟩ (2) **:** to pledge to some particular course or use **:** contract or bind by obligation to a particular disposition ⟨the government has *committed* 135 million dollars worth of surplus commodities in foreign barter activity⟩ (3) **:** to express the opinion of **:** reveal the views of ⟨cautiously refusing to ~ himself on any controversial subject⟩ ~ *vi* **1** *obs* **:** to perform an act that is an offense (as illicit sexual intercourse) ⟨~ not with man's sworn spouse —Shak.⟩ **2 :** to consign a person to prison ⟨officers without power to ~⟩

syn ENTRUST, CONFIDE, CONSIGN, RELEGATE: COMMIT is the widest term; it may express merely the general idea of delivering into another's charge, or it may have the special sense of transfer to a superior power or to an agency for custody ⟨on landing in Boston in 1872, my father and I were able safely to *commit* our trunk to the expressman —George Santayana⟩ ⟨in some districts of Hungary women . . . run around the herd before they drive it out and *commit* it to the care of the herdsmen —J.G.Frazer⟩ ⟨into thy hands I *commit* my spirit —Ps 31:5 (RSV)⟩ ⟨the principal State institution for the mentally ill, caring for about 1,000 *committed* patients —*Amer. Guide Series: Del.*⟩ ENTRUST is to deliver with trust and confidence, with appeal to or security in another's good faith ⟨all he would do was to put the investigation into the hands of a detective, and *entrust* him with the business of collecting evidence —Rose Macaulay⟩ ⟨the governor is *entrusted* with broad executive powers —*Amer. Guide Series: N.H.*⟩ CONFIDE heightens suggestions of trust and good faith ⟨the right of naturalization was therefore, with one accord, surrendered by the States, and *confided* to the Federal Government —R.B.Taney⟩ ⟨our customers over there seem not to be able to *confide* their property to us fast enough —Charles Dickens⟩ CONSIGN implies a delivering or transferring with or as if with formality, certification, or finality ⟨the gaol to which he was *consigned* by the victorious Cavaliers —T.B.Macaulay⟩ ⟨the orthodox *consigned* the heretics and the heretics consigned the bishops to eternal flames —G.M.Trevelyan⟩ ⟨wrapping the ivory carefully in a handkerchief of fine white silk, he *consigned* it to his pocket —Elinor Wylie⟩ RELEGATE indicates consigning to a particular class, position, or sphere, often a secondary or less favored one ⟨within three years overland staging was *relegated* to a secondary place in frontier life by the coming of the railroad —R.A.Billington⟩ ⟨and it is not inherent in the astronomical category either, though it was for many years *relegated* there —E.M.Forster⟩ ⟨the stylistic and philosophical difficulty of Valéry's art would seem to *relegate* him to a very small circle of initiates —Wallace Fowlie⟩

[2]**com·mit** \'kämət\ *n* -S [alter. of *comet*] **:** the card game comet or another card game similar to and derived from it

com·mit·ment \kə'mitmənt\ *n* -S **1** *obs* **:** the act of doing or performing something **:** COMMISSION **2 a :** the act of committing to the charge, keeping, or trust: as (1) **:** the consignment or sentencing to confinement (as in a prison or mental hospital) (2) **:** the action of referring a matter to a legislative committee **b :** a warrant for imprisonment or confinement **:** MITTIMUS **3 a** (1) **:** the obligation or pledge to carry out some action or policy or to give support to some policy or person ⟨American military ~ to the Asian land mass —William Costello⟩ ⟨a ~ by the British to withdraw . . . from Egyptian territory —R.C. Doty⟩ (2) **:** an engagement by contract or purchase order to assume a financial obligation (as to accept goods at an agreed price, to pay for subscribed stock, or to make a mortgage loan upon the completion of a building) (3) **:** something that has been pledged ⟨their ~ to the alliance was 10 divisions⟩ **b** (1) **:** the state of being obligated or bound (as by intellectual conviction or emotional ties) ⟨~ to a given ideal is not equivalent to provincial intolerance toward other forms of excellence —Ernest Nagel⟩ **:** a state or declaration of adherence or association (as to a doctrine or ideal) (2) *philos* **:** a decisive moral choice that involves a person in a definite course of action

com·mit·ta·ble \kə'mid·əbəl, -itə-\ *adj* **:** capable of being committed **:** legally subject to being committed

com·mit·tal \-d·ᵊl,-tᵊl\ *n* -S *often attrib* **1 :** COMMITMENT ⟨~ of his wife . . . to the work house —J.C.Snaith⟩ ⟨enthusiastic

~ to the cause⟩ **2 :** the consignment of a body to the grave ⟨a public ~ service was conducted at the cemetery⟩

committed *past of* COMMIT

com·mit·tee *in sense 2* kə'mid·ē *or* -it| *or* |i, *in sense 1* ¦kä̈mə¦tē *or* kə,mid'ē *or* kə,mi¦tē\ *n* -s [ME, fr. *committen* to commit, entrust + *-ee* — more at COMMIT] **1 a** *archaic* **:** a person or one of a number of persons to whom some charge or trust is committed or some particular business is delegated **b :** a person to whom another person or his estate is legally given in charge **2 a :** a body of persons delegated to consider, investigate, or take action upon and usu. to report concerning some matter or business; *specif* **:** a body of members chosen by a legislative body to give special consideration to pending legislation or to other legislative matters **b :** COMMITTEE OF ONE **c :** a self-constituted organization for the promotion of some common object ⟨the Northwest Wildlife *Committee*⟩

com·mit·tee·man \kə'mid·ēmən, -it|, |im-, -,man, -maa(ə)n\ *n, pl* **committeemen 1 :** a member of a committee **2 a :** a party leader of a ward or precinct responsible for getting party members to vote and persuading other than party members to vote for his party's candidates or policies **b :** SHOP STEWARD

committee of correspondence : a body established by various towns or assemblies of the American colonies to exchange information with each other, mold public opinion, and take joint action against the British

committee of one : a person delegated to perform the duties of a committee

committee of selection *also* **committee on committees :** a legislative committee empowered to assign members to committee posts

committee of supply : a committee of the whole house in a British parliament for the purpose of considering and voting the ordinary state expenditure of the year

committee of the whole *or* **committee of the whole house :** the whole membership of a legislative house sitting as a committee and operating with its own chairman under informal and flexible rules for the purpose of considering a particular measure or some special business ⟨the house resolved itself into a *committee of the whole*⟩

com·mit·tee·wom·an \-,wu̇mən\ *n, pl* **committeewom·en** \-,wimən\ **1 :** a woman member of a committee **2 :** a woman doing the work of a committeeman esp. among women voters — compare COMMITTEEMAN 2

com·mix \kə'miks, kä'-\ *vb* [back-formation fr. earlier *commixt* mixed together, fr. ME *comyxt*, fr. L *commixtus*, past part. of *commiscēre* to mix together, fr. *com-* + *miscēre* to mix — more at MIX] **:** to mix or mingle together **:** BLEND

com·mix·tion \-schən\ *n* -s [ME, fr. LL *commixtion-, commixtio*, fr. L *commixtus* + *-ion-, -io* -ion] **1** *obs* **:** COMMIXTURE 1, 2 **2** *Roman, Scots, & civil law* **:** COMMIXTURE 3

com·mix·ture \-schə(r), 'kä,m-\ *n* -s [L *commixtura*, fr. *commixtus* + *-ura* -ure] **1 a :** the act or process of mixing or the state of being mixed **b :** the mass of things mixed **:** the result of mixing **:** COMPOUND, MIXTURE ⟨the Australian terrier is a ~ of several . . . breeds —Idris Davies⟩ **2 :** the act of putting a small piece of the Host into the consecrated wine, an old and widespread rite of uncertain origin **3** *common law* **:** the mingling of solid or liquid movables belonging to different owners — compare SPECIFICATION

commn *abbr* commission

commo *abbr* commodore

com·mo·da·ta·ry \,kä̈mə'dād·ə̇,rē\ *n* -ES [F *commodataire*, fr. *commodat* commodatum (fr. L *commodatum*) + *-aire* -ary] **:** the bailee in a commodatum

com·mo·date \'kämə,dāt\ *n* -s [L *commodatum* loan] **:** COMMODATUM

com·mo·da·tion \,kä̈mə'dāshən\ *n* -s [L *commodation-, commodatio*, fr. *commodatus* + *-ion-, -io* -ion] **:** the act of making a loan of commodatum

com·mo·da·tum \-ād·əm\ *n, pl* **commoda·ta** \-ād·ə\ [L, loan, fr. neut. of *commodatus*, past part. of *commodare* to make fit, give, lend, fr. *commodus* fit, convenient] **:** a loan of chattels to be returned without payment for their use — compare BAILMENT 2

¹commode *adj* [F] **1** *obs* **:** CONVENIENT, SUITABLE **2** *obs, of a woman* **:** free with her favors **:** COMPLIANT, ACCOMMODATING — **commodely** *adv, obs*

²com·mode \kə'mōd\ *n* -s [F, fr. *commode*, adj., convenient, fr. L *commodus*, fr. *com-* + *modus* measure, mode — more at METE] **1 :** a woman's cap made of lace, fine fabric, and ribbons over a high wire framework popular in the late 17th and early 18th centuries **2** *obs* **:** BAWD, PROCURESS **3 a :** a low chest of drawers or a cabinet on legs **b :** a movable sink or washstand with cupboard underneath **c :** a chair or similar framework holding a toilet utensil under an open seat; *also* **:** CHAMBER POT

commode 1

com·mo·di·ous \kə'mōdēəs\ *adj* [ME, fr. MF *commodieux*, fr. ML *commodiosus*, irreg. fr. L *commodum* convenience (fr. neut. of *commodus*) + *-osus* -ous] **1** *obs* **:** BENEFICIAL, USEFUL, ADVANTAGEOUS — often used with *to* or *for* **2** *archaic* **:** adapted to or suitable for use **:** SERVICEABLE — often used with *to* or *for* ⟨the cheapness of the conveyance made it equally ~ for dead fish and lively company —William Cowper⟩ **3 :** affording ample space and room **:** large or roomy and convenient esp. in permitting free motion **:** not narrow or confining ⟨the room . . . was of a ~, well-proportioned size —Jane Austen⟩ ⟨a ~ harbor for that city —*Amer. Guide Series: Del.*⟩ **syn** see AMPLE

com·mo·di·ous·ly *adv* [ME, fr. *commodious* + *-ly*] **:** in a commodious manner

com·mo·di·ous·ness *n* -ES **:** the quality or state of being commodious

com·mod·i·ty \kə'mäd·əd·ē, -ətē, -i, *rap.* -ädtē *or* -i\ *n* -ES [ME *commoditee*, fr. MF *commodité*, fr. L *commoditat-, commoditas* fitness, convenience, pleasantness, fr. *commodus* + *-itat-, -itas* -ity] **1** *obs* **a :** CONVENIENCE, USEFULNESS **b :** PROFIT, ADVANTAGE, EXPEDIENCY ⟨a good wit will make use of anything. I will turn diseases to ~ —Shak.⟩ **c :** something used or valued esp. when regarded as an article of commerce ⟨transformed from a rather fragile comedy into a durable ~ —John McCarten⟩ ⟨plenty of that ~ known as "temperament" —H.C.Schonberg⟩ **2 a :** an economic good; *esp* **:** a product of agriculture, mining or, sometimes manufacture as distinguished from services ⟨*commodities* such as meat, fats, and sugar —*Americana Annual*⟩ ⟨~ prices⟩ **b :** an article of commerce; *esp* **:** one delivered to a transportation company for shipment **3** *obs* **:** a parcel or quantity of goods **:** LOT ⟨I knew where a ~ of good names were to be bought —Shak.⟩

commodity dollar *n* **:** a unit of a proposed form of currency whose gold value is arbitrarily determined by and whose nominal gold content is periodically adjusted to an index number reflecting market prices of basic commodities — called also *compensated dollar*

commodity exchange *n* **:** an organized market where future delivery contracts for graded commodities (as grains, cotton, sugar, coffee, wool) are bought and sold

commodity paper *n* **:** a note or draft secured by a bill of lading or other document giving a lien upon or title to readily marketable nonperishable staples

commodity rate *n* **:** a common carrier rate distinguished from a class rate and applicable only to a specific commodity or group of related commodities carried between specific points or territories

commodity standard *n* **:** a monetary standard in which the medium of exchange consists of one or more economic goods ⟨the gold standard is one type of *commodity standard*⟩

commodity tariff *n* **:** a tariff containing only commodity rates and related rules for transportation on a common carrier

com·mo·do *var of* COMODO

com·mo·dore \'kämə,dō(ə)r, -dō(ə)r,-dōə,-dȯ(ə)\ *n* -s [prob. modif. of D *commandeur* commander, fr. F, fr. OF *comandeor*, fr. *comander* to command + *-eor* -or — more at COMMAND] **1 :** a naval officer usu. ranking next above a captain and below a rear admiral: **a :** a captain holding this rank temporarily while commanding a detached squadron or division of a fleet — used in the British navy **b** (1) **:** a captain in command of a squadron as senior officer — used in the U. S. Navy as a courtesy title prior to 1862 (2) **:** a naval officer commanding a squadron, division, ship of the first class, or naval station and having a rank corresponding to that of brigadier general in the army — used in the U.S. Navy 1862–99 and during World War II (3) **:** a naval captain with Civil War service receiving the rank upon retirement (4) **:** a naval officer of the rank of captain or below commanding a squadron, division, or other subdivision of a fleet esp. when consisting of small ships (as destroyers) — used only as a courtesy form of address **2 a :** the officer commanding a body of merchant ships sailing in company esp. in a convoy ⟨the convoy ~ . . . sees to the internal management of the convoy —J.P.Bishop⟩ **b :** the ranking captain of the fleet operated by a particular shipping company **3 :** the chief officer of a yacht club or boating association **4 :** AIR COMMODORE

¹com·mon \'kämən\ *adj, often* -ER/-EST [ME *commun, comon*, fr. OF *commun, comun*, fr. L *communis* — more at MEAN] **1 a :** of or relating to a community at large (as a family unit, social group, tribe, political organization, or alliance) **:** generally shared or participated in by individuals of a community **:** not limited to one person or special group ⟨we, the people of the U.S., in order to . . . provide for the ~ defense —*U.S. Constitution*⟩ ⟨a sense of ~ interest, a guild feeling in reaction against the extreme competitive individualism —J.M.Barzun⟩ **b :** known to the community; *esp* **:** notorious as an accustomed general vexation ⟨a ~ thief⟩ ⟨punished as a ~ scold⟩ ⟨maintaining a ~ nuisance⟩ **c :** belonging to or typical of all mankind **:** shared with all men ⟨our ~ humanity⟩ ⟨our ~ nature⟩ **2 a :** held, enjoyed, experienced, or participated in equally by a number of individuals **:** possessed or manifested by more than one individual ⟨a ~ attribute⟩ ⟨a ~ characteristic⟩ **:** calling forth, giving rise to as source, or sending out a number of different items **:** marked by the same relationship to a number of persons or things ⟨our ~ rights⟩ ⟨the sharp teeth ~ to all cats⟩ ⟨streets radiating out from a ~ center⟩ ⟨we will help our allies against our ~ enemy⟩ **b :** marked by or resulting from joint action of two or more parties **:** practiced or engaged in by two or more equally ⟨in the partnership of our ~ enterprise we must share in a unified plan —F.D.Roosevelt⟩ ⟨by ~ defense⟩ ⟨by ~ consent the partnership was dissolved⟩ **c :** open freely to the individual use of any member of a society or group ⟨"folk-land", the ~ property of the tribe —J.R.Green⟩ ⟨the front hall, ~ to all the tenants —Dorothy Sayers⟩ **d :** available for indiscriminate or promiscuous use ⟨a ~ woman⟩ ⟨the ~ cup⟩ **e :** belonging to or appointed for the common (sense 6) **f** *math* **:** belonging equally to two or more quantities **g** *anat* **:** formed of or dividing into two or more branches ⟨the ~ carotid artery⟩ ⟨~ iliac vessels⟩ **3 :** ceremonially or religiously unclean or unfit ⟨eating nothing ~ on the holy day⟩ **4 a :** occurring or appearing frequently esp. in the ordinary course of events **:** not unusual **:** known or referred to widely or generally because of frequent occurrence ⟨the ~ is that which is found in the experience of a number of persons —John Dewey⟩ ⟨the ~ judgment which sets tragedy above comedy as the greater art —Samuel Alexander⟩ **b** *archaic* **:** subject to or ensuing from widespread conversation **:** recognized or agreed on through copious discussion ⟨young Arthur's death is ~ in their mouths —Shak.⟩ **c** *chiefly Midland* **:** USUAL ⟨I'm as well as ~ —Ellen Glasgow⟩ **d :** VERNACULAR — used of plant and animal names ⟨cat is the ~ name for *Felis catus*⟩ **5 a :** of, relating to, or typical of the majority or to the many rather than the few **:** GENERAL, PREVALENT ⟨a sentiment ~, but not universal —W.G.Sumner⟩ ⟨this revelation has . . . passed into the ~ consciousness of the civilized world —W.R.Inge⟩ **b :** characterized by a lack of privilege or special status ⟨the ~ people⟩ ⟨was then forced to take on a job as a ~ laborer⟩ **6 a :** characteristic of a usual type or standard **:** representative of a type **:** quite usual and average **:** entirely ordinary and undistinguished esp. by anything superior ⟨the everyday man and woman, the ~ people —I.M.Price⟩ ⟨a ~ man, no holier than you and I —Thomas Hardy⟩ ⟨the great gods . . . were not exempt from the ~ lot. They too grew old and died —J.G.Frazer⟩ **b :** having no claim or showing no pretense to rank, position, polish, learning, or culture ⟨apart . . . from the ~ reader, there is an elite —A.L.Guérard⟩ **c :** satisfying accustomed criteria **:** attaining to an ordinary standard **:** ADEQUATE ⟨the ~ honesty to face it —W.R.Inge⟩ ⟨it was simply ~ courtesy to help him⟩ **d :** falling below ordinary standards **:** INFERIOR, MEAN, SECOND-RATE ⟨O hard is the bed . . . and ~ the blanket and cheap —A.E.Housman⟩ ⟨labor was scarce and ~ at that —*Amer. Guide Series: Del.*⟩ **e :** falling below accustomed standards of conduct **:** lacking polish, learning, or taste **:** marked by or suggestive of the lax, crass, tawdry, earthy, or crude ⟨a very ~ girl snubbed by the others⟩ ⟨as Harris said, in his ~ vulgar way, the city would have to lump it —J.K. Jerome⟩ **f** *of lumber* **:** of or relating to several grades that are inferior to finish lumber **:** DEFECTIVE, KNOTTY **7** *now chiefly dial* **:** easily approachable **:** UNRESERVED, INFORMAL ⟨he's such a nice ~ fellow⟩ **8 :** frequently met with and known better than types less often encountered ⟨~ salt⟩ ⟨the ~ fern⟩; *specif* **:** most frequent and best known of its kind in a particular region — used of plants and animals **9 a** *of gender* (1) **:** either masculine or feminine ⟨the gender of F *enfant* is ~⟩ (2) **:** characterizing words of which in an earlier stage of the language some were masculine and some feminine ⟨Danish has two genders, ~ and neuter⟩ **b** *of a substantive* **:** belonging to the common gender **c** *of a syllable* **:** either short or long ⟨in Greek prosody a syllable is ~ that has a short vowel followed by a stop and a liquid or nasal, as the first syllable of *teknon*⟩ **d** *of a grammatical case* **:** denoting relations by a single form that in a more highly inflected language might be denoted by two or more different case forms ⟨*moon*, as subject in "the moon is shining" and as object in "I see the moon", is in the ~ case⟩

syn ORDINARY, FAMILIAR, POPULAR, VULGAR: COMMON, ORDINARY, AND FAMILIAR all describe something that is very frequently or generally met with and hence is not at all strange or unusual. COMMON stresses lack of distinguishing or exceptional characteristics ⟨Norris quite definitely identified the romantic with that which is peculiar or special as opposed to the *common* —M.R.Cohen⟩ and may connote coarseness or lack of refinement ⟨weavers produced fine muslins, gauzes, calicoes, and the *common* cloths used by the poorer population —C.L.Jones⟩ ORDINARY applies to what is met with in the routine, regular, or accustomed order of events; it may connote lack of rareness or of superiority ⟨the business of the poet is not to find new emotions, but to use the *ordinary* ones —T.S.Eliot⟩ ⟨it is not an *ordinary* war. It is a revolution . . . which threatens all men everywhere —F.D.Roosevelt⟩ ⟨the mass of *ordinary* men, as definitely opposed to exceptional men —W.H.Mallock⟩ FAMILIAR applies to what is well known because encountered often and lacks any suggestion of the foreign or exotic ⟨the *familiar* arrangement of chairs and tables, always the same —Pearl Buck⟩ ⟨the curious impression . . . that she had seen everything and everybody before. Every face was *familiar* to her —Ellen Glasgow⟩ POPULAR indicates the common due to acceptance, sometimes enthusiastic, by the people, esp. commoners; it may imply a lack of qualities pleasing to the elite, upper classes, or learned groups ⟨the *popular* faith in the omnipotence of education —M.R.Cohen⟩ ⟨these brotherhoods were . . . thoroughly *popular*, drawing most of their support from the lower classes —W.R.Inge⟩ ⟨compromise its values by publishing work that could be described as merely cheap or *popular* —H.V.Gregory⟩ VULGAR is used only occas. to mean COMMON; it usu. suggests meanness, bad taste, crudeness, or crassness ⟨the now *vulgar* opinion that [Samuel] Johnson was more distinguished as a talker than as a writer —J.W.Krutch⟩ ⟨he never could have been *vulgar;* there is not in the whole range of English literature quite such a gentleman —George Saintsbury⟩ ⟨not for the *vulgar* gaze but for an aristocratic and urbane inspection⟩ **syn** see in addition RECIPROCAL, UNIVERSAL

²common \"\ *n* -s [ME *commun*, fr. *commun*, adj.] **1 a** *pl in constr, obs* **:** common people ⟨the ~s became agitated⟩ **b commons** *pl but sing or pl in constr* **:** COMMONALTY; *esp* **:** people lacking noble, knightly, or gentle rank ⟨the ~s were pleased⟩ **2 commons** *pl* **a** *sing or pl in constr* **:** provisions for a usu. ecclesiastical or collegiate community or company ⟨a modern university ~s⟩ **b** *sing in constr* **:** a common table **:** a dining hall **:** a building housing an institution's dining hall **c** *sing in constr* **:** RATIONS, FARE ⟨were eating an ample ~s⟩ ⟨shortening the ~s when our supply train was intercepted⟩ ⟨subsisting on short ~s⟩ **3 commons** *pl but sing or pl in constr* **a :** the political group or estate comprising the commoners **b** *sometimes cap* **:** parliamentary representatives of the commoners **c** *often cap* **:** a lower house of a parliament **4 :** the legal right that arises either from a grant or contract or from prescription or operation of a statute and that allows the taking of a profit in another's land in common with the owner or in common with other persons **5 a** *sometimes* **commons** *pl* **:** land used in common by people of a community esp. for pasture **b :** a stretch of land that is not enclosed or cultivated **:** WASTE, HEATH; *sometimes* **:** a vacant lot **c** *sometimes* **commons** *pl, chiefly NewEng* **:** a publicly owned typically grass-covered plot usu. in the center of a town or village **:** an open square **6** *sometimes cap* **a :** a religious service suitable for any of various festivals — compare PROPER **b :** the ordinary of the mass **c :** the part of a missal or breviary containing the common offices **7 :** COMMON STOCK **8 :** a common board or piece of lumber — **in common :** that is shared, experienced, or possessed together or equally **:** COMMONLY ⟨the two brothers own a bicycle *in common*⟩ ⟨the boss had much *in common* with his employees⟩ ⟨had a love of sports *in common*⟩ — **out of common** *or* **out of the common :** UNUSUAL, UNUSUALLY

³common *vi* -ED/-ING/-S [ME *communen*, fr. *commun*, adj.] **1** *obs* **:** PARTICIPATE, SHARE **2** *obs* **:** CONFER, TALK **3** *obs* **:** to exercise a right together

com·mon·able \'kämənəbəl\ *adj* [²*common* + *-able*] **1** *of an animal* **:** permitted to pasture on public commons **2** *of land* **:** held in common

common adjective *n* **:** a descriptive adjective that is not a proper adjective

com·mon·age \-nij\ *n* -s [²*common* + *-age*] **1 :** the right to pasture animals on another's land or on a common **2 :** COMMONALTY **3 :** common or community land **4 :** the condition of being held in common ⟨the ~ of the land⟩

com·mon·al·i·ty \,kämə'naləd·ē\ *n* -ES [ME *communalitie*, alter. (influenced by *-itie* -ity) of earlier *communalte, communaltie*] **1 :** possession with another of a certain attribute **:** COMMONNESS **2 :** FREQUENCY

com·mon·al·ty \'kämənəltē\ *n* -ES [ME *comonalte, communalte*, fr. OF *comunalté*, fr. *comunal* communal + *-té* -ty — more at COMMUNAL] **1** *or* **com·mon·al·i·ty** \,kämə'naləd·ē\ **:** common people without authority or rank **:** COMMONERS; *esp* **:** the political estate formed by the commons **2 :** body corporate **:** CORPORATION **3 :** the general group or body ⟨the ~ of scholars will welcome his research⟩ **4** *obs* **:** a self-governing commonwealth **:** DEMOCRACY

common appendant *n* **:** the right belonging by common law to the possession of arable land to pasture commonable beasts on another's land (as that of the owner of the manor of which the land possessed forms a part)

common appurtenant *n* **:** a common in the land of another not historically appurtenant to an estate but annexed to it by grant or by prescription from long enjoyment

common ash *n* **:** EUROPEAN ASH

common assumpsit *n* **:** a form of action employing the common counts that is used to recover liquidated damages on quasi contracts and was early extended to most cases where an action of debt would lie and later to nearly all cases where there is a money obligation not payable as damages — called also *general assumpsit, indebitatus assumpsit*

common assurance *n* **:** ASSURANCE 5

common at large : COMMON IN GROSS

common average *n* **:** PARTICULAR AVERAGE

common bail *n* **:** BAIL BELOW

common bar *n* **:** a bar in an action of trespass constituted by the defendant's pleading that the act complained of was on his own freehold

common barberry *n* **:** an upright shrub (*Berberis vulgaris*) that is widely naturalized in the U.S. from Europe, has gray branches, usu. forked prickles, bristle-toothed leaves, and juicy berries in elongate clusters, and is important as the alternate host of the fungus that causes stem rust of wheat — compare JAPANESE BARBERRY

common barrator *n* **:** one who practices barratry

common bile duct *n* **:** the duct formed by the union of the hepatic and cystic ducts and opening into the duodenum — see DIGESTION illustration

common bond *n* **:** AMERICAN BOND

common brick *n* **:** brick made from natural clay and having no special surface treatment; *also* **:** unselected kiln-run brick

common bronzewing *n* **:** an Australian bronzewing (*Phaps chalcoptera*) with a white forehead and chin, a brown back on which each feather is tipped with buff, a mauve breast, and brilliantly metallic bronze and green specula on the wing coverts

common buckthorn *n* **:** a common Eurasian shrub (*Rhamnus cathartica*) with oval leaves and black berries that sometimes are used as a laxative

common buckwheat *n* **:** an Asiatic buckwheat (*Fagopyrum esculentum*) that has short dense flower clusters and sharp-angled fruit and is now widespread esp. in cultivation — compare TARTARIAN BUCKWHEAT

common bundle *n* **:** a vascular bundle that passes from a stem into a leaf — compare CAULINE BUNDLE

common cardinal vein *n* **:** DUCT OF CUVIER

common carotid *also* **common carotid artery** *n* **:** the part of either carotid artery between its point of origin and its division into internal and external branches

common carrier *n* **1 :** one that undertakes for hire the carrying of goods, persons, or messages treating its whole clientele without individual preference or discrimination and being responsible for all losses and injuries except those in consequence of an act of God, of the enemies of the country, or of the owner of the property himself **2 :** a public utility or public service company **3** *in federal regulatory use* **:** a carrier offering its services to all comers for interstate transportation by railroad, motor vehicle, ship, aircraft, or pipeline — compare CONTRACT CARRIER

common chemical sense *n* **:** a chemical sense universally exhibited by body surfaces exposed to certain (as irritant) solutions or vapors that in vertebrates is mediated by both spinal and cranial nerves

common chickweed *n* **:** a Eurasian herb (*Stellaria media*) widely naturalized as a weed in No. America

common chord *n* **:** the major or minor triad

common coin *n* **:** something that is current through being commonly mentioned, discussed, accepted, or sanctioned ⟨his name became *common coin*⟩

common cold *n* **:** an acute contagious disease of the upper respiratory tract caused by a filterable virus and characterized by inflammation of the mucous membranes of the nose, throat, eyes, and eustachian tubes with watery then purulent discharge

common comfrey *n* **:** a European comfrey (*Symphytum officinale*) that is naturalized as a weed in No. America and has the upper part of the stem densely hispid

common cost *n* **:** expense chargeable in accounting to the business as a whole **:** cost assigned to several departments or operations

common council *n* **:** a legislative body or council of a municipal government — **common councilman** *n*

common count *n* **:** any of various technical counts in law that are of a general nature and are used in pleadings to prevent a failure of justice by reason of an inadvertent variance

common cracker *n* **:** BOSTON CRACKER

common curlew *n* **:** a large Old World curlew (*Numenius arquata*) with strong flight somewhat resembling that of a gull

common denominator *n* **1 :** a common multiple of the denominators of a number of fractions **2 a :** something that marks a group of things as alike or that characterizes a group or class **:** a trait or characteristic in common ⟨the essence of religious experience, the actual *common denominator* of the world's great religions —H.J.Muller⟩ ⟨diverse writings whose only *common denominator* was a supposed sophistication —J.D.Hart⟩ ⟨the *common denominator* in this collection of distraught . . . men and women is that they are all Americans who are dissatisfied with their lives —Harrison Smith⟩ **b :** something on which all in a group may agree ⟨trying to find a *common denominator* that would bring the opposing factions of the party together⟩ **c :** a strain, theme, quality, or trait persisting throughout a mass of material (as the writings of an author) ⟨the *common denominator*, the atmosphere and the whole tempo of a writer's work may be recorded by just one sentence —Paul Potts⟩

common difference *n* **:** the difference between two consecutive terms of an arithmetic progression

common disaster *n* **:** the simultaneous death of an insured and his beneficiary

common divisor *or* **common factor** *n* **:** a number, quantity, or expression that divides each of two or more numbers, quantities, or expressions without remainder

commoned *past of* COMMON

common entrance *n, sometimes cap C&E* **:** the general entrance examination required by British public schools

¹commoner *comparative of* COMMON

²com·mon·er \ˈkämənə(r)\ *n* -s [ME *communer*, fr. *commun*, adj., + *-er*] **1 :** one of the common people: as **a :** one not of the nobility; *sometimes* **:** one not of the titled nobility or of the peerage **b :** a person without special class distinction **2 :** one having a right of common **:** one having a right to common land **3** *obs* **:** a common prostitute **4 :** a student (as at Oxford University or Winchester) who pays for his own board instead of being dependent on a foundation — compare PENSIONER **5 a :** a member of the House of Commons **b** *usu cap* **:** a member of the Court of Common Council of the City of London

common era *n, usu cap C&E* **:** CHRISTIAN ERA

commonest *superlative of* COMMON

common establishment *n* **:** VULGAR ESTABLISHMENT

commoney *var of* COMMIE

common fig *n* **:** a fig not requiring caprification in order to set fruit — compare SMYRNA FIG

common fishery *n* **1 :** a fishery (sense 4) enjoyed by the public — compare COMMON OF PISCARY **2 :** a right to fish in another's waters with the owner or with others

common flute *n* **:** RECORDER

common form *n* **1** *Scholasticism* **:** a form belonging to a species **2 :** the form of probate of a will where the will is not contested and is proved by the executor's own oath **3 :** one of the forms of pleading used in the common-law actions (as assumpsit, covenant, debt, detinue, replevin, trespass on the case, and trover) in which the allegations were fixed in their general nature

common fraction *n* **:** a fraction in which both numerator and denominator are expressed

common garden *adj* **:** common or garden

common grace *n* **:** grace that relates to temporal concerns only — distinguished from *special grace*

common ground *n* **:** a basis of mutual interest or understanding in human relations ⟨she had no *common ground* with her iron-spirited Presbyterian father —*Times Lit. Supp.*⟩

common hazard *n* **:** a potential cause of fire common to all

common heliotrope *n* **:** GARDEN HELIOTROPE 2

commoning *n* -s [fr. gerund of ³*common*] **:** the exercise of common rights to land use

common in gross **:** a common not appendant or appurtenant to the ownership of any land but belonging to a person as an independent subject of property and requiring a deed for its transfer — called also *common at large*

common intendment *or* **common intent** *n* **:** customary or natural meaning as legally construed — compare INTENDMENT

common in the soil **:** the right to dig and take away a part of the soil or minerals of another's land — called also *common of digging*

com·mo·ni·tion \ˌkäməˈnishən\ *n* -s [L *commonition-*, *commonitio*, fr. *commonitus* (past part. of *commonēre* to remind, impress upon, fr. *com-* + *monēre* to remind, warn + *-ion-*, *-io* -ion — more at MIND] **:** ADMONITION

commonitory *adj* [LL *commonitorius*, fr. L *commonitus* + *-orius* -ory] *obs* **:** calling to mind

com·mon·i·za·tion \ˌkämənəˈzāshən, -ˌnīˈz-\ *n* -s **:** the formation or development of a common noun, a common adjective, or a verb from a proper noun (as *mercury, quixotic, to boycott*)

com·mon·ize \ˈkäməˌnīz\ *vt* -ED/-ING/-S [¹*common* + *-ize*] **:** to make common

common joist *n* **:** one of the ordinary floor beams to which flooring planks are secured

common juniper *n* **:** a small tree or sometimes a shrub (*Juniperus communis*) widespread in northern Europe, Asia, and No. America and the source of many cultivated junipers — see IRISH JUNIPER, SWEDISH JUNIPER

common jury *n* **:** a jury drawn in the ordinary manner for the trial of causes — distinguished from *special jury*

common labor *n* **:** UNSKILLED LABOR

common land *n* **:** ²COMMON 5a

common law *n* [ME *commune lawe*, trans. of L *jus commune*] **1 :** the system of unwritten law governing the rights and duties of persons that was developed in England in courts of superior jurisdiction having general application throughout the kingdom, that was declared in written opinions by the judges and based either on the general customs or on reason and fixed principles of justice but even in the absence of a precedent capable of being adapted to new situations or of being changed or modified in the light of different circumstances or needs, and that is distinguished both from the written statute laws enacted by the parliament and from other systems of law such as equity, ecclesiastical law, civil law, admiralty law, probate law, or the law merchant **2** *in U.S. state courts and statutes* **:** the common law as it existed in England at the time of the American Revolution or at some other time fixed by state statute with whatever modifications may have been made by the inclusion at that time of doctrines from other systems of law (as equity or civil law) together with such important English statutes of general application as were suitable to the needs and conditions of the state provided no such statute contravened any local statute **3 :** unwritten law as opposed to statute law **4 :** English common law unaffected by doctrines that originated in any system of law (as civil law) having a different tradition **5 :** law of general application throughout a political entity (as a state) as opposed to law having only a special or local application **6 :** the English common law as extended or modified by any doctrines taken from another system of law (as equity or civil law) or even by statutes whenever those doctrines or statutes may be judicially asserted to grant the remedies recognized under the English common law

common-law *adj* [*common law*] **:** of or belonging to a common-law marriage or similar relationship ⟨a *common-law* child⟩ **:** taking part in such an arrangement ⟨a *common-law* wife⟩

common-law estoppel *n* **:** an estoppel by record or by deed or an estoppel in pais whenever recognized in a court of common law (as distinguished from one of equity)

common-law lien *n* **:** a lien arising only in cases of possession of personal property usu. under a bailment (as a carrier's lien)

common-law marriage *n* **:** an agreement now not recognized in many jurisdictions as a legal marriage between a man and a woman to enter into the marriage relation without ecclesiastical or civil ceremony that in many jurisdictions must be followed by cohabitation to be legally valid and is provable by the writings, declarations, or conduct of the parties

common-law right *n* **:** a right that derives from common-law custom and usage

common-law trust *n* **:** MASSACHUSETTS TRUST

common lawyer *n* **:** a lawyer versed in common law

common learning *n* **:** any of certain skills, attitudes, and items of information that by some modern educators are held to be essential for all elementary and secondary pupils in handling life situations likely to arise outside the classroom

common ligament *n* **:** either of two strong fibrous bands, an anterior and a posterior, the latter within the spinal canal, that extend from the axis to the sacrum and are attached to and bind together the bodies of the vertebrae

common logarithm *n* **:** a logarithm whose base is 10

common loon *n* **:** a loon (*Gavia immer*) the size of a small goose having the back black spotted with white, the head and neck nearly all black, and the underparts white, being widely distributed in northern No. America and occurring less frequently in northern Europe and Asia

commonly *adv* [ME *communly*, fr. *commun* common + *-ly*] **1 :** as a general thing **:** often in the usual course of events **:** USUALLY, ORDINARILY **2 :** to a degree that is common

common mallow *n* **1 :** a procumbent biennial plant (*Malva neglecta*) with round-cordate leaves on long petioles and pale blue flowers in the axils **2** *Brit* **:** an erect plant (*Malva sylvestris*) related to the common mallow

common man *n* **:** the undistinguished commoner lacking class or rank distinction or special attributes

common measure *n* **1 :** COMMON TIME **2** *also* **common meter :** BALLAD METER

common mullein *n* **:** GREAT MULLEIN

common multiple *n* **:** a multiple of each of two or more numbers, quantities, or expressions

com·mon·ness \ˈkämən(n)əs\ *n* -ES **:** the quality or state of being common: as **a :** the quality of being possessed or shared by all mankind or by a group **:** jointness of possession or use; *also* **:** the quality of appealing to the general run of people ⟨although he came from the moneyed and landed aristocracy he preserved a certain ~ that made him a popular statesman and successful politician⟩ **b :** the possession of usual, standard, ordinary, or undistinguished qualities or character ⟨the ~ of the common man⟩; *also* **:** the quality of occurring or appearing frequently in the ordinary course of events ⟨they are the familiar folk one can come upon in any town, on any street, and in this book their ~ lends an extraordinary reality to the events that overtake them —Harrison Smith⟩ **c :** the marked display of lack of learning, refinement, or taste ⟨her father's ~ was what offended the daughter most, his habit of sitting in the parlor in his undershirt drinking beer⟩ **d :** INDISCRIMINATENESS, VULGARITY, PROMISCUOUSNESS ⟨behavior marked by the ~ of a prostitute⟩

common nightshade *n* **:** BLACK NIGHTSHADE

common noun *also* **common name** *n* **:** a noun that is used with limiting modifiers (as *a* or *an, some, every, my*) and that designates a being or thing of which more than one specimen exists ⟨in each of the phrases *no horse, such a crowd, some water, his courage, a Mozart*, the last word is a *common noun*⟩

common nuisance *n* **:** PUBLIC NUISANCE

common of digging **:** COMMON IN THE SOIL

common of estovers **:** the right to estovers

common of pasture **:** the right of pasturing animals on another's land

common of piscary *or* **common of fishery** **:** the right of fishing in waters belonging to another

common orange *n* **:** SWEET ORANGE

common or garden *adj* **:** frequently met with **:** ORDINARY ⟨a *common or garden* variety of nail⟩

common particular meter *or* **common particular measure** *n* **:** a variation of ballad meter in which the four-stress lines are doubled producing a stanza of six lines in tail-rhyme arrangement, the number of stresses in the lines being 4, 4, 3, 4, 4, 3

common pasturage *n, Scots law* **:** COMMON OF PASTURE

¹commonplace \ˈ==,= *sometimes* ¦==ˈ=\ *n* [trans. of L *locus communis* widely applicable argument or thesis, trans. of Gk *koinos topos*] **1 a** *obs* **:** a passage applicable to particular cases **:** THEME, TOPIC **:** the text of a discourse **b** *archaic* **:** a striking or esp. noticeable passage; *usu* **:** such a passage entered in a commonplace book **c** [by shortening] *obs* **:** COMMONPLACE BOOK **2 a :** an opinion, statement, or other expression lacking originality or freshness and often repeated and generally accepted **:** a stock comment or subject of remark **:** TRUISM, CLICHÉ ⟨a ~ in the study of human nature that men often turn against those who have raised them —Hilaire Belloc⟩ ⟨the superficial ~*s* which pass as axioms in our popular intellectual milieu —M.R.Cohen⟩ **b :** matter accepted as usual, ordinary, unworthy of notice, or trivial **:** the quality or state of commonness ⟨their originality has become our ~ —Virginia Woolf⟩ **c :** a thing commonly encountered **:** a common ordinary object or occurrence taken for granted and arousing no interest or curiosity ⟨to most of us railways are one of the ~*s* of life —O.S.Nock⟩

²commonplace \"\ *adj* **:** having nothing out of common **:** without originality, freshness, or interest **:** commonly encountered **:** ORDINARY, DULL, TRITE, STALE ⟨revolutionary in the seventies, but ~ by 1900 —F.L.Mott⟩ ⟨the lover whose imagination makes a goddess of some ~ young woman —C.E.Montague⟩ — **com·mon·place·ly** *adv* — **com·mon·place·ness** *n* -ES

³commonplace \"\ *vt* **:** to extract striking or memorable passages from (as for a commonplace book) esp. with arrangement of the passages under general heading ~ *vi* **:** to employ commonplaces in communication

commonplace book *n* [¹*commonplace*] **:** a book of literary passages, cogent quotations, occasional thoughts, or other memorabilia ⟨transcribing from an old manuscript volume into his *commonplace book* —J.G.Lockhart⟩

com·mon·plac·er \"+ə(r)\ *n* -S [¹*commonplace* + *-er*] **:** one that keeps a commonplace book

common pleas *n pl* [ME *common plees*, fr. AF *communs pletz*, trans. of ML *communia placita*] **1 a** *in English law* **:** those pleas or actions over which the crown did not claim exclusive jurisdiction **b :** civil actions between subjects — distinguished from *pleas of the crown* **2** *usu cap C&P* **:** COURT OF COMMON PLEAS

common prayer *n* **:** prayer in which a congregation unites

common privet *n* **:** PRIVET 1a(1)

common property *n* **1 :** land in which all members of the community hold equal rights **2 :** land or other property in which a person other than the owner holds certain rights in common with the owner — compare ESTOVERS **3 :** information generally known ⟨prevent the events of the evening from becoming *common property* —Hamilton Basso⟩

common pyrites *n* **:** PYRITE

common rafter *n* **:** one of the rafters to which the roofing is secured — see ROOF illustration

common rail *n* **:** a single fuel line that supplies oil under pressure to all the cylinders of a diesel engine **:** HEADER 3c

common ratio *n* **:** the ratio of each term of a geometrical progression to the term preceding it

common recovery *n* **:** a conveyance of real property through the medium of an action and judgment at law formerly widely used in England as a means of giving a tenant in tail an absolute power to dispose of his estate

common room *n* **1** *Brit* **:** a room available to all members of a residential community for relaxation and sociability ⟨the *common room* of an inn⟩ **2 a :** a room in a college reserved for the informal and exclusive use of the teaching staff — see SENIOR COMMON ROOM **b :** a room in a college reserved for the general use of students — see JUNIOR COMMON ROOM

commons *pl of* COMMON, *pres 3d sing of* COMMON

common school *n* **:** a free public school now usu. including primary and secondary grades; *sometimes* **:** a free public elementary school

common scold *n* **:** a woman who disturbs the public peace by noisy and quarrelsome or abusive behavior constituting a public nuisance

common seal *n* **:** a seal adopted and used by a corporation or similar body

common sense *n* [trans. of L or Gk; L *sensus communis*, trans. of Gk *koinē aisthēsis*] **1 :** a sense believed to unite the sensations of all senses in a general sensation or perception **2 :** good sound ordinary sense **:** good judgment or prudence in estimating or managing affairs esp. as free from emotional bias or intellectual subtlety or as not dependent on special or technical knowledge ⟨too absurdly metaphysical for the ears of prudent *common sense* —P.E.More⟩ **3 a** *among Cartesians* **:** something that is evident by the natural light of reason and hence common to all men **b** (1) **:** the intuitions that according to the school of Scottish philosophy are common to all mankind (2) **:** the capacity for such intuitions **c :** the unreflective opinions of ordinary men **:** the ideas and conceptions natural to a man untrained in technical philosophy — used esp. in epistemology **syn** see SENSE

commonsense \¦==¦=\ *adj* [*common sense*] **1 :** showing practical common sense ⟨canny ~ folk with a shrewd eye to interest —Charles Kingsley⟩ **2 :** perceptible by the ordinary senses **:** understood as commonly interpreted **:** CLEAR, PALPABLE ⟨a ~ object⟩ ⟨the ~ interpretation⟩

commonsense realism *n* **:** the philosophy of Thomas Reid and the Scottish school **:** NATURAL REALISM

common sensibility *n* **:** SENSUS COMMUNIS

com·mon·sen·si·ble \¦kämən¦sen(t)səbəl\ *adj* **:** marked by or conforming to common sense

com·mon·sen·si·cal \-en(t)səkəl\ *adj* **:** COMMONSENSIBLE ⟨countryfolk, unlearned and ~, were capable of solving problems that beset the more sophisticated —J.D.Hart⟩ — **com·mon·sen·si·cal·ly** \-k(ə)lē\ *adv*

common serjeant *n* **:** a judicial officer of the Corporation of London who is assistant to the recorder

common shell *n* **:** a gun shell having a comparatively large cavity filled with a bursting charge of high explosive intended to explode after passing through light protective armor

common shrew *n* **:** a widely distributed European shrew (*Sorex araneus*)

common sign *n* **:** one of the four zodiacal signs Gemini, Virgo, Sagittarius, and Pisces

common sorghum *n* **:** a strong erect annual grass (*Sorghum vulgare*) that is the source of many of the cultivated varieties of sorghum (as kafir and broomcorn)

common stock *n* **:** capital stock of a corporation having one or more classes of preferred stock that enjoy a preference in dividend distributions

common storage *n* **:** storage or a storage place that uses air at outside temperature for cooling; *specif* **:** a storage place esp. for fruits or vegetables that has openings just above ground level for admission of cool air and at the top for escape of warm air and other gases

common substitution *n* **:** SUBSTITUTION 1a(1)

common sunflower *n* **:** the annual sunflower (*Helianthus annuus*) often grown for silage and for its seeds which yield an edible oil and are used for stock feed — see SUNFLOWER illustration

common time *n* **:** duple or quadruple time; *esp* **:** four quarter notes per bar or its musical equivalent — called also *common measure*

common touch *n* **:** the trait or gift of appealing to or arousing the sympathetic interest of the generality of man esp. by having or giving the appearance of having basic qualities in common with them ⟨come a long way up the ladder of success without losing the *common touch* —Joseph Driscoll⟩ ⟨despite an excellent family and educational background, he has the *common touch* —Bill Wolf⟩

common traverse *n* **:** a legal traverse without the denial of inducement and amounting to a direct denial in common negative language

com·mon·ty \ˈkäməntē\ *n* -ES [ME *comunete, comountee*, fr. MF *comuneté* — more at COMMUNITY] **1 :** a right of ownership in land held in common by two or more persons and under certain servitudes; *also* **:** the land itself **2 :** COMMON OF PASTURE

common vetch *n* **:** a somewhat twining annual herb (*Vicia sativa*) that was introduced from Europe, that is grown esp. as a forage, silage, and green manure crop, and that often escapes to waste places and roadsides

com·mon·weal \ˈkämən,wēl, ¦==ˈ=\ *n* -S [ME *commun wele*, fr. *commun* common + *wele* weal] **1 :** the general welfare **2** *archaic* **:** COMMONWEALTH

com·mon·wealth \ˈkämən,welth, ¦==ˈ=\ *n* -S [ME *commen wealthe, commun* common + *wealthe, welthe* wealth (well-being)] **1 :** public welfare **:** wealth held in common **2 a :** a whole body of people united by common consent to form a nation, state, or politically organized community **b :** a state esp. conceived as a body politic founded on law and united by compact or by tacit agreement of the people for the common good **c :** a state in which the supreme power resides with the people and their representatives **:** REPUBLIC ⟨the ~ established in England under Oliver Cromwell⟩ **3 a :** a state of the U.S. ⟨~*s* joining the Union after the Civil War⟩ — used in the official designations of Kentucky, Massachusetts, Pennsylvania, and Virginia in preference to the word *state* **b :** a self-governing autonomous state; *usu* **:** a former colony that is associated by treaty or agreement in a loose political federation with a mother country or former colonial power ⟨*Commonwealth* of Australia⟩ **c :** an association of self-governing autonomous states united by a common allegiance to a mother country and forming by treaty or agreement a loose confederation having a somewhat common political and cultural background ⟨a ~ of nations⟩ ⟨the British *Commonwealth*⟩ **4 a :** a group of persons conceived of as united by common interests ⟨the ~ of artists or of literary men⟩ **b :** the range of interests uniting such a group ⟨the ~ of learning⟩

commonwealth's-man \-l(th)smən, -ˌsman\ *n, pl* **commonwealth's-men** **1** *obs* **:** a man in his relation to a commonwealth **2 a :** an adherent of a commonwealth (as the 17th century English Commonwealth) **b** *archaic* **:** REPUBLICAN 1

common year *n* **:** a calendar year not containing any intercalary period — see YEAR table

com·mo·ran·cy \ˈkämərənsē\ *n* -ES **:** ordinary residence or dwelling in a place **:** the habitation of a place

com·mo·rant \-rənt\ *adj* [L *commorant-, commorans*, pres. part. of *commorari* to sojourn, tarry, fr. *com-* + *morari* to delay, stay, remain — more at MORATORY] **:** having one's habitation **:** DWELLING ⟨a London man now ~ in Edinburgh⟩

com·mo·ri·ent \kəˈmōrēənt\ *n, pl* **commorients** \-ts\ *or* **commorien·tes** \kə,mōrēˈen·,tēz\ [L *commorient-, commoriens*, pres. part. of *commori* to die with, fr. *com-* + *mori* to die — more at MURDER] **:** one of two or a number of persons perishing at the same time by the same calamity

commos *var of* KOMMOS

com·mot \ˈkä,mät\ *or* **com·mote** \-mōt\ *n* -S [ME, fr. ML *commotum*, fr. MW *cymwd*] **:** an early Welsh territorial and administrative unit, two such units being normally equal to a cantred

com·mo·tion \kəˈmōshən\ *n* -S [ME *commocioun*, fr. MF *commotion*, fr. L *commotion-, commotio*, fr. *commotus* (past part. of *commovēre*) + *-ion-*, *-io* -ion] **1 :** a condition of civil unrest, public disorder, agitation, or insurrection ⟨18 years of ~ had made the majority of the people ready to buy repose at any price —T.B.Macaulay⟩ **2 :** continuous or recurrent motion ⟨the ~ of the steady gentle breeze⟩ ⟨the thermal ~ of the surface atoms —*Physical Rev.*⟩ **3 :** mental excitement, uncertainty, or confusion ⟨startled . . . into no ordinary state of ~ —Arnold Bennett⟩ **4 a :** violent or sharp disturbance **:** noisy, unruly, or tumultuous stir ⟨a gang of hooligans making a ~ in the street⟩ ⟨the children raising a ~ during recess⟩ **b :** noisy confusion **:** HUSTLE ⟨there was ~ all over the house at the return of the young heir —George Meredith⟩ **5** *med* **:** CONCUSSION, SHOCK

syn AGITATION, CONFUSION, TUMULT, TURMOIL, TURBULENCE, CONVULSION, UPHEAVAL: COMMOTION may suggest unusual, violent, or disturbing activity usu. accompanied by noise, uproar, hubbub, or activity bringing with it unrest ⟨wakened at midnight by a *commotion* in the street below⟩ ⟨trying to put out a drunk without distracting *commotion*⟩ ⟨agitators keeping up a *commotion* during the speech⟩ AGITATION may suggest a strong swirling, stirring, or seething, an emotional excitation similar to these physical actions, or a sustained effort to stir up excitement about some political or social issue ⟨the panting of the horses communicated a tremulous motion to the coach, as if it were in a state of *agitation* —Charles Dickens⟩ ⟨breathless with *agitation* —Jane Austen⟩ ⟨an anti-Catholic *agitation* that was marked by the destruction of churches —*Amer. Guide Series: N. Y.*⟩ CONFUSION describes a state in which things are mixed, poured, or heaped together in a jumble so that differentiation is hard, a mental condition marked by uncertainty, indecisiveness and doubt, or a social or political situation making for such a condition ⟨tremendous smokestacks rose out of a *confusion* of buildings —*New Yorker*⟩ ⟨if jostled they bowed profusely to the jostlers, and appeared overwhelmed with *confusion* —E.A.Poe⟩ TUMULT applies to commotion and agitation marked by uproar, din, or, more specif., the noise of a great mob in riot or to any similar noisy jarring inescapable confusion ⟨the *tumults* and disorders of the Great Rebellion —T.S.Eliot⟩ ⟨the whole knoll was suddenly in a *tumult* of movement; mounted officers clattered off —Kenneth Roberts⟩ TURMOIL indicates a state in which everything is in agitated disorder and pointless noisy activity, where nothing is at rest or in place ⟨the *turmoil* which attends departure from home —F.A.Swinnerton⟩ ⟨her life had been calm, regular, monotonous. And now it was thrown into an indescribable *turmoil* —Arnold Bennett⟩ ⟨the revolutionary *turmoil* in Mexico in 1913 —*Amer. Guide Series: Texas*⟩ TURBULENCE suggests swirling wild unruly disorder or a disposition to it ⟨scenes of public *turbulence* and crass overriding of parliamentary opinion —Cecil Sprigge⟩ ⟨the *turbulence* normal in a frontier community —R.A.Billington⟩ ⟨plenty of the *turbulence* of passion but none of the gravity of thoughtful emotion —A.T. Quiller-Couch⟩ CONVULSION indicates a violent, spasmodic, or sudden surging confused action — as in the earth's crust, the individual's mind, or the body politic ⟨flourishing cities were demolished by the earth's *convulsion* —Martin Gardner⟩ ⟨the *convulsions* of a soul storm-driven and unreconcilable spiritual conflicts —H.O.Taylor⟩ UPHEAVAL indicates a violent, very forceful thrusting out or up, heaving up, or overthrowing ⟨the vast social *convulsions* of a continent in travail are such a mystery to this type of mind that even the most catastrophic *upheavals* are attributed to mistakes made in our State Department —Reinhold Niebuhr⟩ ⟨new islands rising from the seas as a result of volcanic *upheavals*⟩

com·move \kə'müv, kä'-\ *vt* -ED/-ING/-S [ME *commoeven, commeven*, fr. MF *commuev-*, pres. stem of *commovoir*, fr. L *commovēre*, fr. *com-* + *movēre* to move — more at MOVE] **1** : to move violently : stir up : AGITATE **2** : stir to emotion : EXCITE, IMPASSION

commr *abbr* **1** commissioner **2** commoner

com·mu·na \kə'myünə\ *n, pl* **commu·nae** \-,nē, -,nī\ [ML — more at COMMUNE] : COMMUNE

com·mu·nal \kə'myün°l *also* 'kämyən- *sometimes esp in sense 1* (')kä¦myün-\ *adj* [F, fr. OF *comunal*, fr. LL *communalis*, fr. L *communis* of the community, common + *-alis* -al — more at COMMON] **1 a** : of or relating to a commune or a society characterized by communes ⟨~ electors⟩ ⟨~ organization⟩ **b** : belonging to or produced by the social environment of a primitive commune : characteristic of a simple social life ⟨~ poetry is typified by the ballad⟩ **2** : owned in common : participated in, shared, or used by a whole community : marked by sharing in common by members of a group ⟨a ~ settlement in which all wages, earnings and food were pooled —*Time*⟩ ⟨dipping each his bread into a ~ dish of stew —Paul Roche⟩ **3** : of or relating to rival communities, esp. the communities of India ⟨~ division⟩ ⟨the ~ problem⟩ : involving two or more communities competing (as for political advantage and patronage) ⟨~ strife⟩ — **com·mu·nal·ly** \-°lē, -°li\ *adv*

com·mu·nal·ism \-°l,izəm\ *n* -S **1** : a principle or system of organization in which the major social or political units of the society are communes or local self-governing communities **2** : belief in or practice of communal living **3** : a system or principle of communal organization in which rival minority groups are devoted to their own interests rather than to those of the whole society : strong loyalty and adherence to one's community and its values sometimes appearing in excess and with nationally divisive effects; *broadly* : ETHNOCENTRISM

com·mu·nal·ist \-°ləst\ *n* -S [F *communaliste*, fr. *communal* + *-iste* -ist] : an advocate of communalism

com·mu·nal·i·ty \,kämyə'naləd·ē\ *n* -ES **1** : communal state or character **2** : the sentiment of community solidarity : concordance or agreement in opinion or feeling throughout a group : group unity

com·mu·nal·i·za·tion \kə,myün°lə'zāshən, ,kämyən-, -°l,ī'z-\ *n* -S : act or process of making communal

com·mu·nal·ize \kə'myün°l,īz, 'kämyən-\ *vt* -ED/-ING/-S : to make communal; *specif* : to subject to the rights, methods, organization, or ownership of a community

communal marriage *n* : a hypothetical primitive promiscuity in which all the women of a social group belonged to all the men in common — called also *group marriage;* compare PUNALUA

communal ownership *n* : the ownership of land or other property by a community so that each member has a right to use the property or a portion of it

com·mu·nard \'kämyə,närd, ,==ˈ=\ *n* -S [F, fr. *commune* commune + *-ard* — more at COMMUNE] **1** : an adherent of the principles of communalism **2** *usu cap* : one who supported or participated in the Commune of Paris in 1871

¹com·mune \kə'myün, *archaic* 'kä,m-\ *vi* -ED/-ING/-S [ME *comunen, communen*, fr. OF *comuner* to put in common, share, fr. *comun* common — more at COMMON] **1** *archaic* : CONVERSE, CONFER **2** *archaic* : to associate together : have dealings **3** [ME *comunen* to administer Holy Communion, fr. MF *comunier* to administer or receive Communion, fr. LL *communicare* — more at COMMUNICATE] : to receive Communion : partake of the Eucharist **4 a** : to hold converse or intercommunication esp. with great mental or spiritual depth or intensity **b** : to attain to an earnest or deep feeling of unity, appreciation, and receptivity — used with *with* ⟨~ with nature⟩ ⟨~ with precious books, ancient and new, which bear the stamp of eternity —David Ben-Gurion⟩

²com·mune \'kä,myün\ *n* -S : COMMUNION, CONVERSATION ⟨in ~ with nature⟩

³com·mune \'kä,myün *also* kə'm- *or* kä'm-\ *n* -S [F, fr. ML *communa, commnia*, fr. L *communia*, neut. pl. of *communis* common — more at COMMON] **1** : a small administrative district (as one governed by a mayor and municipal council) usu. in a European country ⟨the provinces and ~s of Belgium⟩ — compare ARRONDISSEMENT **2** : a political or governmental body espousing revolutionary or communist principles **3 a** : COMMONALTY, COMMONS **b** : any of various bodies treated as a unit at law (as the peasantry sharing the common rights and property in a village community) **4 a** : a community in which the inhabitants have close personal ties of friendship and interest **b** : a small collective unit typically rural : a group practicing communal living

com·mu·ni·ca·bil·i·ty \kə,myünəkə'biləd·ē, -nēk-, -ətē, -i\ *n* -ES : the quality of being readily communicated or of having a message readily understood

com·mu·ni·ca·ble \=ˈ==kəbəl\ *adj* [MF, fr. LL *communicabilis*, fr. L *communicare* + *-abilis* -able] **1** : capable of being communicated: **a** : imparted without undue difficulty ⟨~ knowledge⟩ **b** : transmitted from one to another ⟨a ~ illness⟩ **2** : talkative, open, or frank rather than taciturn : given to communicating : COMMUNICATIVE — **com·mu·ni·ca·ble·ness** *n* -ES — **com·mu·ni·ca·bly** \-blē, -li\ *adv*

communicable disease *n* : an infectious disease transmissible from person to person, animal to animal, animal to man, or man to animal by direct contact with an affected individual or his discharges or by indirect means (as by a vector) — compare CONTAGIOUS DISEASE

¹com·mu·ni·cant \-kənt\ *n* -S [LL & L; LL *communicant-, communicans*, pres. part. of *communicare* to receive Holy Communion, fr. L, to share, impart, partake] **1** : one who partakes of the sacrament of the Lord's Supper or is entitled to partake of it : a church member; *broadly* : a member or adherent of a group **2** : one who communicates or imparts; *specif* : INFORMANT

²communicant \"\ *adj* [L *communicant-, communicans*] **1** : SHARING, PARTICIPATING **2** [LL *communicant-, communicans*, fr. L] : partaking in a church communion

com·mu·ni·cate \kə'myünə,kāt, *usu* -ād·+V\ *vb* -ED/-ING/-S [L *communicatus*, past part. of *communicare* to share, impart, partake, fr. *communis* common — more at MEAN] *vt* **1** *archaic* : partake of : use or enjoy in common : SHARE ⟨thousands that ~ our loss —Ben Jonson⟩ **2 a** : to make known : inform a person of : convey the knowledge or information of ⟨~ the news⟩ ⟨~ his secret to a friend⟩ **b** : IMPART, TRANSMIT ⟨~ his pleasure to us⟩ ⟨an odor *communicated* to one's fingers⟩ ⟨*communicating* the disease to others⟩ **c** : to make (itself) known — used of an intangible ⟨his tension *communicated* itself to his companion⟩ **3** [LL *communicatus*, fr. L] : to administer the Communion to (a person) ⟨the priest *communicating* him⟩ **4** *archaic* : to put (oneself) into close connection or relationship with — used with *to* **5** *archaic* : to give or deliver over (something material or tangible) : BESTOW ~ *vi* **1** [LL *communicatus*, fr. L] : to partake of the Lord's Supper : receive Communion ⟨Eastern Orthodox Christians ~ in both elements⟩ **2** *obs* : to have a common part : PARTICIPATE, SHARE **3** : to send information or messages sometimes back and forth : speak, gesticulate, or write to another to convey information : interchange thoughts ⟨they *communicated* with each other for years⟩ **4** : be connected : open into each other : afford unbroken passage : JOIN ⟨the two rooms ~⟩ ⟨the pantry ~s with the hall⟩ **5** *philos* : to have something logically in common : be further specifications of a common universal : be overlapping classifications or connotations **6** : to arouse or enlist the sympathetic interest or understanding — used with *with* ⟨old plays that . . . have long since lost their ability to ~ with an audience —Wolcott Gibbs⟩

com·mu·ni·ca·tee \kə'myünəkə¦tē, -nēk-\ *n* -S : one that receives a communication : one that is communicated with

communicating artery *n* : any of three arteries in the brain that complete the circle of Willis, one connecting the anterior cerebral arteries and two connecting the internal carotids with the posterior cerebrals

com·mu·ni·ca·tion \kə,myünə'kāshən\ *n* -S [ME *communicacioun*, fr. MF *communication*, fr. L *communication-, communicatio*, fr. *communicatus* (past part. of *communicare* to communicate) + *-ion-, -io*, -ion] **1** : the act or action of imparting or transmitting ⟨the ~ of the common cold⟩ ⟨the ~ of power to the machine⟩ **2 a** : facts or information communicated **b** : a letter, note, or other instance of written information ⟨he had not yet read the spy's ~⟩ **3 a** *obs* : CONVERSATION, TALK **b** *archaic* : personal dealings **c** *archaic* : SEXUAL INTERCOURSE **4** *archaic* : common participation **5 a** : access between persons or places : opportunity of communicating ⟨maintaining ~ between the regulars and guerrillas⟩ **b communications** *pl* : means of communicating: (1) : a system (as of telephones or telegraphs) for communicating information and orders (as in a naval service) (2) : a system of routes for moving troops, supplies, and vehicles in military operations (3) : the function in an industrial organization that transmits ideas, policies, and orders (4) *sometimes cap* : personnel engaged in communicating **c** : a medium through which information is carried ⟨channels of ~ in industry⟩ **6 a** : interchange of thoughts or opinions : a process by which meanings are exchanged between individuals through a common system of symbols (as language, signs, or gestures) **b** : close or intimate rapport that is sometimes intellectual and often affective **7** : a Masonic lodge meeting **8** *or* **communications** *pl but sing or pl in const* : an art that deals with expressing and exchanging ideas effectively in speech or writing or through the graphic or dramatic arts and that is taught as an integrated program at various levels of education in distinction to traditional separate courses in composition and speech

communication engineering *n* : engineering concerned with the sending and receiving of signals esp. by means of electrical or electroacoustic devices and electromagnetic waves

communications zone *n* : the part of a theater of military operations behind and contiguous to the combat zone

communication trench *n* : a connecting trench

com·mu·ni·ca·tive \kə'myünə,kād·iv, -nəkə|, -nēkə|, |tiv, -ēv *also* -əv\ *adj* [ME, fr. MF or ML; MF *communicatif*, fr. ML *communicativus*, fr. L *communicatus* (past part. of *communicare* to communicate) + *-ivus* -ive — more at COMMUNICATE] **1** : marked by the ability or tendency to communicate: **a** *obs* : capable of spreading or transmitting : DIFFUSIVE **b** *archaic* : disposed to give : GENEROUS, BENEFICENT **c** : ready to give information freely : free, unguarded, and open in conversation : TALKATIVE; *sometimes* : SOCIABLE, AFFABLE ⟨a ~ person and quickly told all she knew —W.M.Thackeray⟩ **2 a** *obs* : capable of being communicated : COMMUNICABLE **b** *obs* : commonly applicable **c** *archaic* : well adapted for use in communication **3** : of or relating to communication ⟨~ arts⟩ — **com·mu·ni·ca·tive·ly** *adv* — **com·mu·ni·ca·tive·ness** *n* -ES

com·mu·ni·ca·tor \-nə,kād·ə(r), -ātə-\ *n* -S [LL, fr. L *communicatus* + *-or*] : one that communicates; *sometimes* : a person who works with or on methods or devices used in communication or facilitating communication

com·mu·ni·ca·to·ry \-nəkə,tōrē, -nēk-, -tȯr-, -ri\ *adj* [ML *communicatorius*, fr. L *communicatus* + *-orius* -ory] : tending to communicate

communicatory letters *n pl* : letters of communication between ancient churches; *also* : letters of recommendation to the communion of distant churches

communing *pres part of* COMMUNE

com·mu·nion \kə'myünyən\ *n* -S [ME *comunioun*, fr. MF, LL, & L; MF *communion*, fr. LL *communion-, communio* union of Christians, Eucharist, fr. L, mutual participation, fr. *communis* common + *-ion-, -io* -ion — more at COMMON] **1** : an action or situation involving sharing: **a** : possession in common : joint ownership : the state of possessions thus held ⟨this ~ of goods —William Blackstone⟩ **b** : a function performed jointly : an interrelation in activity : an interdependent working together or cooperation ⟨~ of motion of a bird's wings⟩ **2** *usu cap* **a** : the Eucharist : the Lord's Supper **b** : a celebration of the Eucharist or the Lord's Supper either as a separate service or as a part of a larger service (as the mass in Roman Catholicism or the divine liturgy in Eastern Orthodoxy) **c** : the act of receiving the eucharistic elements **d** : the elements of the Eucharist ⟨take *Communion*⟩ **e** : the psalm or antiphon said or sung at Communion **3 a** : the fellowship of members of the same church **b** : general fellowship : a state marked by fellowship, sympathetic companionship, communication, and understanding : COMMUNICATION, CONVERSE, EXCHANGE ⟨the sentiment of ~ with others, of the breaking down of barriers —John Dewey⟩ **c** : intimate, sympathetic, reverential, or mystic interchange of ideas and feelings esp. dealing with matters innermost and spiritual in order to inspire, strengthen, or solace often as if between man and nature or the supernatural ⟨this ~ with the spirit of love at work in the universe —E.R.Bentley⟩ ⟨no sympathetic ~ between him and the solitude —Ellen Glasgow⟩ **d** : COMMUNICATION, DEALINGS ⟨having only limited ~ with the natives⟩ **4** : a group of religious persons bound together by essential agreement in religious consciousness; *esp* : a body of Christians having one common faith and discipline ⟨the Presbyterian ~⟩ ⟨the Roman Catholic ~⟩ **syn** see RELIGION

com·mu·nion·able \-nyənəbəl\ *adj* : open to or admissible to communion

com·mu·nion·al \-nyən°l\ *adj* : of or relating to communion

communion cloth *n* : ¹CORPORAL

communion cup *n* : a cup used for wine or grape juice in the Lord's Supper or Communion service; *specif* : either a small individual cup furnished each communicant or a single large cup from which all communicants sip

communion glass *n* : a small glass used as an individual communion cup

communion hymn *n* : a hymn sung in a Christian worship service immediately preceding the celebration of Holy Communion

com·mu·nion·ist \-nyənəst\ *n* -S **1** : one who holds a specified theory as to communion ⟨a strict ~⟩ ⟨a free ~⟩ **2** : COMMUNICANT

communion of saints [trans. of ML *communio sanctorum*] : the fellowship of all true Christian believers living and dead

communion rail *n* : the altar rail at which communicants receive Communion

communion sunday *n, usu cap C&S* : a Sunday on which Holy Communion is celebrated in Protestant churches

communion table *n* : the table used in the celebration of the Lord's Supper

com·mu·ni·qué \kə'myünə,kā, =,==ˈ=\ *n* -S [F, fr. past part. of *communiquer* to communicate, fr. L *communicare* — more at COMMUNICATE] : an official announcement; *typically* : a brief formal summation report

com·mu·nism \'kämyə,nizəm, *chiefly in substand speech* -mə,n-\ *n* -S [F *communisme*, fr. *commun* common + *-isme* -ism — more at COMMON] **1 a** : a theory advocating elimination of private ownership of property or capital **b** : a system or condition real or imagined in which goods are owned commonly rather than privately and are available as needed to each one in a unified group sometimes limited, sometimes inclusive, and often composed of members living and working together : a similar system preventing amassing of privately owned goods and assuring equalitarian returns to those working ⟨Plato's aristocratic ~⟩ ⟨the ~ of the early church groups⟩ ⟨the ~ obtaining among the early colonists⟩ **2** *often cap* [Russ & G; Russ *kommunizm*, fr. G *kommunismus*, fr. F *communisme*] **a** : a social and political doctrine or movement based upon revolutionary Marxian socialism that interprets history as a relentless class war eventually to result everywhere in the victory of the proletariat and the social ownership of the means of production with relative social and economic equality for all and ultimately to lead to a classless society **b** : BOLSHEVISM **c** : a totalitarian system of government in which the state as owner of the major industries and acting through the medium of a single authoritarian party controls in large measure the economic, social, and cultural life of the society **3** *often cap* : strong left-wing activity or inclination that is subversive or revolutionary **4** *biol* : COMMENSALISM

¹com·mu·nist \-myənəst, *chiefly in substand speech* -m(ə)n-\ *n* -S [F *communiste*, fr. *commun* + *-iste* -ist] **1 a** : one who believes in or adheres to a theory of communism or communal living ⟨the principle from which the ~s started was the Christian belief, widespread through the middle ages, that common possession was a more perfect way of life than private ownership —G.H.Sabine⟩ **b** : one who practices communism : one living in a society in which goods are owned in common ⟨more rigid sectarians living as ~s⟩ **2** : COMMUNARD **3** *usu cap* [Russ *kommunist*, fr. G, fr. F *communiste*] **a** : a member of a Communist party or movement; *esp* : an official member paying dues and carrying a party membership card — compare BOLSHEVIK **b** : one who consistently adheres to, supports, or aids a Communist government, party, or movement and opposes all others **c** : one who holds to notions or engages in activities conceived to be violently left-wing, subversive, or revolutionary — used rhetorically in political denigration ⟨it was a common habit of the East European dictatorships to denounce as *Communists* all who resolutely criticized social and political abuses —*Economist*⟩ ⟨their definition of a *Communist* is a man who wants reforms —Elmer Davis⟩ **syn** see COLLECTIVIST

²communist \"\ *adj* **1** : of or relating to communism : marked by communal living : adhering to or favoring communism ⟨a ~ community where possessions were commonly owned⟩ ⟨a ~ philosophy from ancient times⟩ **2** *usu cap* **a** : of or relating to a Communist party : composed of or participated in by Communists ⟨a *Communist* newspaper⟩ ⟨a *Communist* government⟩ ⟨a *Communist* plot⟩ **b** : advocating, aiding, or furthering Communism ⟨a *Communist* sympathizer⟩

com·mu·nis·tic \¦kämyə¦nistik, *chiefly in substand speech* -mə¦n-\ *adj* **1** : living in common : COMMUNIST, COMMUNAL : illustrating or favoring communal living and common ownership of wealth ⟨the ~ teachings of the old Fathers that all have an equal right to property —Frank Thilly⟩ ⟨the ~ sects, which require the renunciation of all personal property —W.L.Sperry⟩ **2** *sometimes cap* : of, relating to, or marked by communism : in accordance with, tending to, or influenced by communism ⟨had heard of ~ propaganda in the area⟩ **3** *of birds* : living or having their nests in common — **com·mu·nis·ti·cal·ly** \-tək(ə)lē, -tēk-, -li\ *adv*

¹com·mu·ni·tar·i·an \kə,myünə'terēən, -taar-, -tār-\ *n* -S [*community* + *-arian*; trans. of F *communautaire*] : an advocate of communitarianism : a member of a community practicing communitarianism

²communitarian \=¦==¦===\ *adj* : advocating, practicing, or based on communitarianism

com·mu·ni·tar·i·an·ism \=,=='==,nizəm\ *n* -S : a communal system of organization based on small cooperative communities practicing some communist principles

com·mu·ni·ty \kə'myünəd·ē, -ətē, -i\ *n* -ES [ME *comunete*, fr. MF *communité, comuneté*, fr. L *communitat-, communitas*, fr. *communis* common + *-itat-, -itas* -ity] **1** : a body of individuals organized into a unit or manifesting usu. with awareness some unifying trait: **a** : STATE, COMMONWEALTH **b** : the people living in a particular place or region and usu. linked by common interests; *broadly* : the region itself : any population cluster ⟨small, compact, homogeneous *communities* such as the Greek city-state or Elizabethan England —C.D.Lewis⟩ **c** : a monastic body or other unified religious group **d** : an interacting population of different kinds of individuals (as species) constituting a society or association or simply an aggregation of mutually related individuals in a given location ⟨a climax ~⟩ **e** : a group of people marked by a common characteristic but living within a larger society that does not share that characteristic ⟨the Chinese ~ in New York⟩ ⟨the artists' ~ downtown⟩ ⟨the Jewish ~ in London⟩; *esp* : such a group politically organized and recognized esp. as a separate voting group for election purposes ⟨Sikh and Muslim *communities* in India⟩ **f** : a group sharing a particular economic or social belief and living communally **g** : any group sharing interests or pursuits ⟨a ~ of scholars⟩ : a group linked by a common policy ⟨a tariff ~ of small nations⟩ **h** : a body of persons or nations united by historical consciousness or by common social, economic, and political interests ⟨the entire Christian ~⟩ ⟨the European coal and steel ~⟩ **2** : society at large : PUBLIC : people in general — used with the definite article ⟨the interests of the ~⟩ **3 a** : common or joint ownership, tenure, experience, or pertinence : COMMONNESS, SHARING, PARTICIPATION ⟨asserts that ~ of goods would be the ideal institution —G.L.Dickinson⟩ ⟨out of the atmosphere of controversy to the ~ of our love again —Mary Austin⟩ ⟨the essential ~ of interests shared by all branches of learning —G.W.Cottrell⟩ **b** : common character : fact of showing a trait or various traits in common : AGREEMENT, CONCORD, LIKENESS ⟨although there are varieties, the ~ of style is still more evident —O. Elfrida Saunders⟩ **c** : shared activity : social intercourse : FELLOWSHIP, COMMUNION; *esp* : social activity marked by a feeling of unity but also individual participation completely willing and not forced or coerced and without loss of individuality ⟨in order that there may be a ~, there must be conscious and purposive sharing —Ernest Barker⟩ **d** *obs* : frequent occurrence **e** : a social or societal state ⟨emerging from feral isolation into ~⟩ **4** : a civil-law partnership or society of property between husband and wife arising by virtue of the fact of marriage or by contract

community center *n* : a building or group of buildings constituting a focal point of educational and recreational activities and serving a whole community; *also* : a concentration of such activities

community chest *or* **community fund** *n* : a general fund accumulated from individual subscriptions to defray demands on a community's private charitable and welfare organizations

community church *n* : an interdenominational or nondenominational church for community use found in the U.S. and Canada

community college *n* : a college or junior college typically nonresidential serving a specific community often by fitting its curriculum to the community's needs

community house *n* **1** : a center consisting often of a single building for a community's social, cultural, recreational, and civic activities **2** : a large building providing separate quarters for families of common descent : PUEBLO

community organization *n* : social work concentrating upon the organized development of community social welfare through coordination of public and private agencies

community property *n* : property held jointly by husband and wife

community school *n* : a school that seeks to integrate children into the community by selected activities other than academic and at the same time serves as a community center for recreation and adult education

community singing *n* : unrehearsed mass singing of familiar songs by any assemblage or audience

community trust *n* : a fund acquired from bequests the income from which is to be used for the general betterment of the inhabitants of a community

community-wide \=¦===¦=\ *adj* : operative or effective throughout the whole community ⟨a *community-wide* service⟩

com·mu·ni·za·tion \,kämyənə'zāshən, -,nī'z- *sometimes* kə,myünə'z- — *see* COMMUNIZE\ *n* -S *often cap* [L *communis* common + E *-ization* — more at COMMON] : the act of communizing : state of being communized

com·mu·nize \'kämyə,nīz *sometimes in sense 1a* kə'myü,n-\ *vb* -ED/-ING/-S [back-formation fr. *communization*] **1 a** : to make common **b** : to make into state-owned property

2 *sometimes cap* **:** to subject to or bring into accord with Communist principles of organization

com·mut·able \kə'myüd·əbəl, -üt·ə-\ *adj* [L *commutabilis*, fr. *commutare* to exchange + *-abilis* -able — more at COMMUTE] **:** capable of being commuted or interchanged

com·mu·tate \'kämyə,tāt, *usu* -ād+V\ *vb* -ED/-ING/-S [back-formation fr. *commutation*] **1 :** to reverse the direction of (an electric current) by a change of connections **2 :** to reverse every other cycle of (an alternating current) so as to form a unidirectional current

commutating pole *n* **:** INTERPOLE

com·mu·ta·tion \,kämyə'tāshən\ *n* -S [ME, fr. MF, fr. L *commutation-, commutatio*, fr. *commutatus* (past part. of *commutare* to change) + *-ion-, -io* -ion — more at COMMUTE] **1 :** EXCHANGE, TRADE, BARTER ⟨the transatlantic ~ of experts —*Fortune*⟩ **2** *archaic* **:** CHANGE, ALTERATION **3 :** SUBSTITUTION, INTERCHANGE, REPLACEMENT **4 :** substitution in a charge, assessment, payment, or remuneration of one form, method, schedule, or amount for another **:** an arrangement effecting such substitution **:** money or other value involved ⟨~ by money payment in place of the exacted service⟩ ⟨a ~ whereby the remaining payments were lumped together⟩ ⟨officers living off the post receiving rental allowance ~⟩ **5 a :** change of a legal penalty or punishment to a lesser one ⟨~ of the death sentence to a long prison term⟩ **b :** substitution of one work for another in fulfilling a religious vow **6 :** act of commuting **:** travel back and forth between two points, esp. between home and work, repeated a certain number of times within a given interval **7 a :** reversal or transference of the connections between an armature coil and the external circuit in a direct-current dynamo or motor **b :** the partial overlapping of successive cycles of current from successive anodes in a polyphase rectifier

commutation ticket *n* **:** a transportation ticket for a fixed number of trips back and forth over the same route (as between a city and one of its suburbs) during a limited time (as a month) sold at a reduced rate because of the frequency and regularity of travel

com·mu·ta·tive \'kämyə,tād·iv, kə'myüd·əd·iv\ *adj* [ML *commutativus*, fr. L *commutatus* (past part. of *commutare* to exchange) + *-ivus* -ive — more at COMMUTE] **1 :** of or relating to commutation **:** effecting or showing commutation ⟨a ~ fine⟩ ⟨~ payment plans⟩ **2** *of a mathematical or logical operation* **:** consisting of a step or sequence of steps in which the final result is independent of the order of the elements or steps ⟨~ multiplication⟩ ⟨~ addition⟩

commutative algebra *n* **:** algebra in which the rule of multiplication is such that the product of *a* by *b* is the same as the product of *b* by *a*

commutative contract *n* **:** a civil-law contract in which each party gives and receives an equivalent

commutative justice *n* **:** justice bearing on the relations between individuals esp. in respect to the equitable exchange of goods and fulfillment of contractual obligations

commutative law *n* **:** a law applicable to certain mathematical operations: the order of the elements involved is immaterial

com·mu·ta·tor \'kämyə,tād·ə(r), -,tātə-\ *n* -S [*commutation* + *-or*] **1 :** a switch for reversing the direction of an electric current in a circuit by reversing connections **2 :** a series of bars or segments insulated from each other and so connected to armature coils of a dynamo that rotation of the armature will in conjunction with fixed brushes result in unidirectional current output in the case of a generator and in the reversal of the current into the coils in the case of a motor — see DYNAMO illustration

com·mute \kə'myüt, *usu* -üd+V\ *vb* -ED/-ING/-S [L *commutare* to change, exchange, fr. *com-* + *mutare* to change — more at MUTABLE] *vt* **1 a :** to place or give (a thing) in exchange for another **:** EXCHANGE, SUBSTITUTE, INTERCHANGE ⟨*commuting* foreign money to domestic⟩ ⟨*commuting* comfort for hardship⟩ **b :** CHANGE, ALTER ⟨*commuting* a base metal into gold⟩ **2 :** to convert (as a particular obligation, assessment, charge, or payment) into another often more convenient form **:** substitute one form of obligation or charge for (another) ⟨the tithe . . . was *commuted* to a rental to be paid in cash —K.S.Latourette⟩ ⟨~ the small debts into a lump sum due one person⟩ ⟨~ fringe benefits into cash⟩ **3 :** to exchange (a penalty) for another; *usu* **:** to revoke (a sentence) and impose something less severe ⟨~ the death sentence for a long prison term⟩ **4 :** COMMUTATE ⟨*commuting* an electric current⟩ ~ *vi* **1 :** to make up for something **:** serve as substitute for something **:** COMPENSATE ⟨*commuting* for her sins⟩ ⟨*commuting* with payments in place of labor⟩ **2 :** to pay or arrange to pay in gross instead of part by part **:** effect commutation of tithes or annuities **3 :** to travel by use of a commutation ticket esp. daily to and from a city and one's suburban residence **:** travel back and forth regularly or frequently ⟨*commuting* between London and New York⟩

commuted value *n* **:** the sum necessary to provide future payments as provided for in an annuity policy

com·mut·er \-üd·ə(r), -üta-\ *n* -S **:** one that commutes (as between suburban home and city work)

com·mutual \kə, (')kä+\ *adj* [*com-* + *mutual*] *archaic* **:** MUTUAL, RECIPROCAL ⟨long ~ friendship —Alexander Pope⟩

commy *often cap, var of* COMMIE

commy *abbr* commissary

com·ne·ni·an \(')käm¦nēnēən\ *adj, cap* [*Comnenus*, Byzantine noble family + E *-ian*] **:** of or belonging to a Byzantine dynasty of the 11th to the 15th centuries

co·mo·bo \kə'mō(,)bō\ *n, pl* **comobo** *or* **comobos** *usu cap* [Sp, of AmerInd origin] **1 a :** a Panoan people of central Peru **b :** a member of such people **2 :** the language of the Comobo people

co·mo·do *or* **com·mo·do** \'kōmə,dō, 'käm-\ *adv* [It *comodo* comfortable, convenient, fr. L *commodus* convenient, suitable — more at COMMODE] **:** in an easy or convenient tempo — a direction in music

co·moid \'kō,mȯid\ *adj* [*²coma* + *-oid*] **:** resembling a tress or tuft of hair

co·monomer \¦kō+\ *n* -S [*co-* + *monomer*] **:** one of the constituents of a copolymer

co·mo·quer \,kōmō'ker, kə'mōkər\ *n* -S [MexSp] **:** a card that can be combined in panguingue and other Mexican forms of rummy only with other cards of the same rank in the same or different suits (as three tens of spades or the tens of spades, hearts, and diamonds) — compare NONCOMOQUER

co·mose \'kō,mōs\ *adj* [L *comosus* hairy, fr. *coma* hair — more at COMA] **:** bearing a tuft of soft hairs ⟨~ seeds⟩

co·mous \'kōməs\ *adj* [L *comosus*] **:** HAIRY, COMOSE ⟨a ~ stalk⟩

co·mox \'kō,mäks\ *n, pl* **comox** *or* **comoxes** *usu cap* **1 a :** a Salishan people of eastern Vancouver Island and the opposite mainland of British Columbia **b :** a member of such people **2 :** the language of the Comox people

¹comp \'kämp\ *n* -S [by shortening] *slang* **:** COMPOSITOR

²comp \"\ *vb* -ED/-ING/-S *vi, slang* **:** to work as a compositor ~ *vt, slang* **:** COMPOSE *vt* 1c

comp *abbr* **1** companion **2** company **3** comparative; compare **4** compensation **5** compilation; compiled; compiler **6** complement **7** complete **8** composed; composer; composite; composition; compositor **9** compound; compounded **10** comprehensive **11** comprising **12** comptroller

¹com·pact \kəm'pakt, (')käm¦pakt\ *adj, sometimes* -ER/-EST [ME *compacte*, fr. L *compactus*, past part. of *compingere* to join, fr. *com-* + *pangere* to fasten — more at PACT] **1** *obs* **:** firmly put together, joined, or integrated **2 :** COMPOSED, MADE **:** predominately formed or filled **:** CHARACTERIZED — used with *of* ⟨a figure ~ of chivalry and faith⟩ ⟨Miss Austen's novels are ~ of delicate trivialities —Samuel Alexander⟩ **3 :** marked by an arrangement of parts or units closely pressed, packed, grouped, or knit together with very slight intervals or intervening space: as **a :** BRIEF, PITHY ⟨~ language⟩ ⟨a ~ style⟩ ⟨a ~ writer⟩ **:** not diffuse or verbose ⟨a ~ statement⟩ **b :** having the twigs or branches so close together as to form a dense often rounded mass ⟨~ evergreens⟩ **c** *of bone* **:** lacking in obvious interstices **:** DENSE, SOLID — compare CANCELLOUS **d :** DENSE 5 **4 a :** suggesting firmness, soundness, and a degree of strength **:** not gangling, weak, spare, or ill-formed in appearance **:** solid and without excess flesh ⟨he had a small, ~ body that looked full of life —D.H.Lawrence⟩ **b** *of an animal* **:** CLOSE-COUPLED **:** STOCKY, COBBY **5 :** marked by concentration in a limited area **:** homogeneous and located within a limited definite space without straggling or rambling over a wide area ⟨his long narrow strips did not lie next to one another in a ~ farm —G.M.Trevelyan⟩ ⟨downtown San Francisco, ~ and accessible —*Amer. Guide Series: Calif.*⟩ **syn** see CLOSE

²compact \"\ *vb* -ED/-ING/-S *vt* **1 a :** to knit or draw together (as into a unified or coherent whole) **:** COMBINE, CONSOLIDATE ⟨racial and religious similarities helped ~ the tribes into a great nation⟩ **b :** to press together (as parts, components, segments) **:** COMPRESS ⟨thousands of crates ~*ed* in a warehouse⟩ ⟨a great human document, ~*ing* the experience and reflection of a . . . unified life —M.R.Cohen⟩ **2 :** to make up (as by uniting, connecting, combining) **:** COMPOSE, CREATE ⟨a mob ~*ed* of all the more violent elements of the underworld⟩ ~ *vi* **:** to become compacted ⟨the old snow had ~*ed* into the hardness of ice⟩ **syn** see UNIFY

³compact \'käm,pakt\ *n* -S **1 a :** a compacted body, structure, or unit ⟨the ~ of business families forming the upper classes —Hugh MacLennan⟩ **b :** an object produced by the compression of metal powders **2 :** a small cosmetic case for the purse **3 :** a small automobile

⁴compact \"\ *vi* -ED/-ING/-S [MF *compacter*, fr. *compact* agreement, fr. L *compactum*] **:** to make a formal agreement

⁵compact \"\ *n* -S [L *compactum* agreement, fr. neut. of *compactus* past part. of *compacisci* to make an agreement, fr. *com-* + *pacisci* to agree, contract — more at PACT] **1** *obs* **:** CONSPIRACY, PLOT **2 :** an agreement, understanding, or covenant between two or more parties ⟨the matrimonial ~⟩ ⟨a ~ with the devil⟩ ⟨a five-nation ~ to control opium traffic⟩; *specif* **:** an interstate agreement entered into to handle a particular problem or task ⟨a Colorado River *Compact* . . . allocating rights to the waters of the Colorado among seven states —F.A.Ogg & P.O.Ray⟩ **3 :** SOCIAL CONTRACT ⟨a man not having the power of his own life cannot by ~ . . . enslave himself to anyone —John Locke⟩

com·pac·ta \kəm'paktə\ *n* -S [NL, fr. L, fem. of *compactus* (past part. of *compingere*)] **:** the part of a bone made up of compact bone (as the shaft wall of a long bone)

com·pact·ed·ly \kəm'paktədlē, -li\ *adv* **:** COMPACTLY

com·pact·ed·ness \-dnəs\ *n* -ES **:** COMPACTNESS

com·pac·tion \kəm'pakshən, käm-\ *n* -S [ME *compaccion*, fr. L *compaction-, compactio*, fr. *compactus* (past part. of *compingere* to join) + *-ion-, -io* -ion — more at COMPACT] **:** the act or action of compacting or being compacted ⟨the ~ of all this material into a single volume —*Natural History*⟩ ⟨a second evil of severe grazing . . . is ~ of the soil surface by trampling —*Conservation & Nevada*⟩

com·pact·ly *pronunc at* ¹COMPACT +lē *or* li\ *adv* **:** in a compact manner

com·pact·ness \"+nəs\ *n* -ES [¹*compact* + *-ness*] **:** the quality or state of being compact

com·pac·tor *or* **compacter** \kəm'paktə(r), (')käm¦p-\ *n* -S [²*compact* + *-or* or *-er*] **:** one that compacts; *specif* **:** a machine (as one having a roller or a vibrating tamper) for crushing or compacting material (as in preparing a seedbed or roadbed)

compacture *n* -S [MF or L; MF, fr. L *compactura*, fr. *compactus* (past part. of *compingere*) + *-ura* -ure] *obs* **:** close union or connection of parts **:** JOINING

com·pa·draz·go \,kōmpä'dräz(,)gō\ *n* -S [Sp, fr. *compadre*] **:** the reciprocal relationship or the social institution of such relationship existing between a godparent or godparents and the godchild and its parents in the Spanish-speaking world (as in So. America)

com·pa·dre \kəm'pädrē\ *n* -S [Sp, godfather, fr. ML *compater* — more at COMPEER] *chiefly Southwest* **:** a close friend **:** BUDDY

com·pa·ges \kəm'pā,jēz\ *or* **com·page** \'käm,pāj\ *n, pl* **com·pages** \kəm'pā,jēz, 'käm,pājəz\ [L *compages*; akin to L *compingere*] **:** a structure of many parts united into a functioning whole **:** a complex structure; *esp* **:** a large geographic region

com·pag·i·nate \kəm'pajə,nāt\ *vt* -ED/-ING/-S [LL *compaginatus*, past part. of *compaginare*, fr. L *compagin-, compago* connection; akin to L *compingere*] *archaic* **:** to join together

com·pag·i·na·tion \kəm,pajə'nāshən\ *n* -S [LL *compagination-, compaginatio*, fr. *compaginatus* + *-ion-, -io* -ion] *archaic* **:** union of parts **:** STRUCTURE

com·pa·ñe·ro \,kämpən'ye(,)rō\ *n* -S [Sp, fr. obs. Sp *compaña* company (fr. — assumed — VL *compania*, fr. LL *companio* companion) + *-ero* -er] *chiefly Southwest* **:** COMPANION, BUDDY

companiable *adj* [ME, fr. MF *compagnable*, fr. *compain* companion (fr. LL *companio*) + *-able*] *obs* **:** COMPANIONABLE

companied *past of* COMPANY

companies *pl of* COMPANY, *pres 3d sing of* COMPANY

¹com·pan·ion \kəm'panyən\ *n* -S *often attrib* [ME *compainoun*, fr. OF *compagnon*, fr. LL *companion-, companio* (prob. trans. of a Gmc word akin to Goth *gahlaiba* companion, fellow soldier, OHG *galeipo* companion), fr. L *com-* + *panis* bread, loaf, food — more at FOOD] **1 :** one that accompanies or is in the company of another **:** one much in the company of another **:** ASSOCIATE, COMRADE ⟨the ~*s* of one's youth⟩ ⟨armor and infighting are close ~*s* throughout warfare —Tom Wintringham⟩ ⟨the report and its ~ recommendations⟩ ⟨the captain and two ~ officers⟩ **2 a** *obs* **:** a partner or associate esp. in some legal or formal relationship (as a spouse or professional colleague) **b (1) :** a member of an order of knighthood or of chivalry ⟨a ~ of the Order of St. Michael and St. George⟩ — compare KNIGHT-COMPANION **(2) :** a member ranking below knight commander in orders having several grades or classes ⟨a ~ of the Bath⟩ **c :** a member of a companionship of compositors — not now in common use **3** *obs* **:** FELLOW, RASCAL **4 a :** one of a pair or set of things that match ⟨a ~ to the Gutenberg Bible is the Giant Bible of Mainz —Elizabeth E. Hamer⟩ ⟨a ~ sketch to the original drawing⟩ **b :** one employed to live with and to serve someone (as an elderly person or an invalid) **c** *usu cap* **:** one of Muhammad's closest associates; *specif* **:** a fellow emigrant from Mecca or one of the citizens of Medina who received and supported Muhammad following the hegira **d** *or* **companion star :** a celestial body attendant upon another but not necessarily associated with it in space (as the fainter component of a double-star system)

²companion \"\ *vb* -ED/-ING/-S *vt* **1** *obs* **:** to unite in fellowship **2 :** to attend or accompany in or as if in the manner of a companion ⟨nuns ~*ed* the pilgrims to the shrine⟩ ⟨a true humorist, whose humor is ~*ed* by compassion —B.R.Redman⟩ ~ *vi* **:** to keep company **:** chum with someone ⟨fellows he'd ~*ed* with long ago⟩

³companion \"\ *n* -S [by folk etymology fr. D *kampanje* poop deck, perh. fr. It *campagna* navigation on the open sea (in the phrase *camera della campagna* ship's storeroom), lit., open country, fr. LL *campania* level country — more at CAMPAIGN] **1 a :** a structure with frames and sashes formerly incorporated into the deck of a vessel to admit light to a cabin or lower deck **b :** a hood or other covering at the top of a companionway **2** [by shortening] **:** COMPANIONWAY

com·pan·ion·able \-yənəbəl\ *adj* **:** marked by, conducive to, or suggestive of friendly association or companionship **:** agreeable and pleasant through warm but unobtrusive affability ⟨greeted with a ~ wave of the hand⟩ **syn** see SOCIAL

com·pan·ion·able·ness *n* -ES **:** the quality or state of being companionable

com·pan·ion·ably \-blē, -li\ *adv* **:** in a companionable manner

com·pan·ion·age \-yənij\ *n* -S [¹*companion* + *-age*] **:** the companions of an order; also **:** a list of such companions

com·pan·ion·ate \-yənət\ *adj* **:** of, having to do with, or suggestive of a companion or companionship ⟨a ~ dog at one's heels⟩ ⟨a ~ union of words and music⟩; *specif* **:** harmoniously or suitably accompanying ⟨a skirt . . . with two or more ~ blouses —*Women's Wear Daily*⟩ ⟨old silver and ~ bone china⟩

companionate marriage *n* **1 :** a proposed form of marriage in which legalized birth control would be practiced, the divorce of childless couples by mutual consent would be permitted, and neither party would have any financial or economic claim on the other — compare TRIAL MARRIAGE **2 :** an informal association of a man and woman in a connubial relation that is usu. comparatively transitory and without legal status — compare COMMON-LAW MARRIAGE

companion cell *n* **:** one of the elongated parenchyma cells lying next to and supposedly associated physiologically with the sieve tube in many seed plants, developing with the sieve tube from the same mother cell, sometimes extending the full length of the sieve tube, and readily identified by its small size and denser protoplasm

companion crop *n* **:** a secondary crop planted to increase or hasten returns on a plot of land (as lettuce between tomatoes)

companion flange *n* **:** a pipe flange threaded internally to receive a pipe length and drilled so it may be bolted to another like flange; *sometimes* **:** a similar arrangement for coupling two parts of a shaft

companion ladder *n* [³*companion*] **:** COMPANIONWAY; *specif* **:** a companionway esp. on a naval vessel leading down from the quarterdeck to the officers' quarters

com·pan·ion·less \kəm'panyənləs\ *adj* **:** having no companion

companion piece *n* **:** one object that is associated with and has qualities in common with a related object usu. in the same class of objects; *esp* **:** a literary work that complements another work of the same author

companions *pl of* COMPANION, *pres 3d sing of* COMPANION

com·pan·ion·ship \-yən,ship\ *n* -S **1 :** the quality or state of being a companion **:** the fellowship existing among companions ⟨woman must no longer be barred from intellectual ~ with man —Robert Grant †1940⟩ ⟨secure in the ~ of family and friends⟩ **2 a :** a group of companions **b** *chiefly Brit* **:** a group of compositors working under a clicker — sometimes contracted to *ship*

companion star *n* **:** COMPANION 4d

companionway \ˌ=ˈ==,=\ *n* -S [³*companion* + *way*] **:** a ship's stairway running from one deck to another

¹com·pa·ny \'kəmp(ə)nē, -ni\ *n* -ES *often attrib* [ME *companie*, fr. OF *compagnie*, fr. *compain* companion (fr. LL *companio*) + *-ie* -y — more at COMPANION] **1 a :** the quality or state of being a companion or associate of another **:** association esp. on terms of intimacy **:** COMPANIONSHIP ⟨enjoy a person's ~⟩ ⟨with only her thoughts for ~ —Polly Adler⟩ ⟨in ~ with others⟩ **b :** persons affording companionship **:** ASSOCIATES ⟨know a person by the ~ he keeps⟩ **c :** visitors esp. to one's house **:** GUESTS ⟨invite ~ for dinner⟩ **2 a :** an assemblage or association of persons or things **:** BAND, RETINUE ⟨a great ~ of priests and monks⟩ ⟨a ~ of ships⟩ ⟨the ~ of sovereign nations⟩ ⟨the whole ~ of thinkers who have written philosophy —W.L. Sullivan⟩ **b :** a body of soldiers: as **(1) :** a tactical and administrative unit (as of infantry) consisting usu. of a headquarters and two or more platoons — compare BATTERY, TROOP **(2) :** a unit that is normally a fifth part of a battle group **c :** a band of musical or dramatic performers; *esp* **:** an organization of actors and singers producing dramatic or operatic compositions — compare STOCK COMPANY **d :** the officers and men of a ship — usu. used in the phrase *ship's company* **e :** a fire-fighting unit of men and apparatus often designed for a special duty ⟨hose ~⟩ ⟨ladder ~⟩ **f** *chiefly Brit* **:** a group or flock of widgeon **g :** a local congregation of Jehovah's Witnesses **h :** a unit of girl guides under the leadership of a captain **3 a :** a chartered commercial organization (as of merchant adventurers) or a trade guild during the medieval period **b :** an association of persons for carrying on a commercial or industrial enterprise or business (as a partnership or stock company) — see PRIVATE COMPANY **c :** those members of a partnership firm whose names do not appear in the firm name ⟨J. J. Smith and *Company*⟩ — sometimes used of the remaining members of a group represented by one or more named individuals ⟨Caesar, Napoleon, and ~⟩

²company \"\ *vb* -ED/-ING/-ES [ME *companien*, fr. MF *compagnier*, fr. OF, fr. *compain* companion (fr. LL *companio*) — more at COMPANION] *vt* **:** to accompany or go with **:** COMPANION ⟨may . . . fair winds ~ your safe return —John Masefield⟩ ~ *vi* **1 :** to keep company **:** associate on terms of intimacy ⟨those who *companied* with our Lord in the days of his flesh —J.C.Swaim⟩ **2** *obs* **:** COHABIT

company man *n* **:** a worker who is felt by his fellows to have the interests of the employer rather than those of the workers at heart; *sometimes* **:** an employee who is or is thought to be a spy upon his fellows — often used as a generalized term of abuse ⟨he's a *company man*, he'd sell his mother for a dime⟩

company officer *n* **:** a captain or lieutenant in the U.S. Army or Marine Corps

company punishment *n* **:** light punishment that may be imposed by a company commander without resort to a court-martial

company servant *n* **:** one who performs the function of a minister to a company of Jehovah's Witnesses

company store *n* **:** a retail store associated with and usu. owned and operated by an industrial company: **a :** a store usu. extending limited amounts of credit from which employees of a company may and are sometimes required to buy their groceries and other merchandise **b :** a store selling the product (as textiles) of a mill at retail — called also *mill outlet, mill store*

company town *n* **:** a community that is dependent on one firm for all or most of the necessary services or functions of town life (as employment, housing, stores, and government)

company union *n* **:** a labor union consisting of the employees of a single firm, having no affiliation with a larger outside union, and often felt to be dominated by the employer

com·pa·ra·bil·i·ty \,kämp(ə)rə'bilədē, -ətē, -i *sometimes* ÷kəm,par- *or* ÷kəm,per-\ *n* -ES **:** the quality or state of being comparable ⟨wrote a monograph on the ~ of related languages⟩ ⟨advocates of Virginia . . . pointed to its ~ in latitude with Palestine . . . encouraging the climatic similarities —R.H.Brown⟩

com·pa·ra·ble \'kämp(ə)rəbəl *sometimes* ÷kəm'par- *or* ÷kəm'per-\ *adj* [ME, fr. MF, fr. L *comparabilis*, fr. *comparare* + *-abilis* -able] **1 :** capable of being compared: **a :** having enough like characteristics or qualities to make comparison appropriate — usu. used with *with* ⟨differing from steel in some of the circumstances . . . but ~ with steel in respect of the necessity for a centralized control —Thorstein Veblen⟩ **b :** permitting or inviting comparison often in one or two salient points only — usu. used with *to* ⟨not too far below Jonson to be ~ to that master's work —T.S.Eliot⟩ ⟨hot cornbread baked with squash seeds — an Indian delicacy ~ to raisin bread —Willa Cather⟩ **2 :** suitable for matching, coordinating, or contrasting **:** EQUIVALENT, SIMILAR ⟨samples of subtlety . . . which made most of the ~ performances of the season sound clumsy —Irving Kolodin⟩ ⟨we have information about Arctic regions but lack ~ data for the Antarctic⟩ **syn** see LIKE

com·pa·ra·ble·ness *n* -ES **:** COMPARABILITY

com·pa·ra·bly \-blē, -li\ *adv* **:** in a comparable manner

comparascope *var of* COMPAROSCOPE

com·par·a·tist \kəm'parəd·əst\ *n* -S [F *comparatiste*, fr. L *comparatus* + F *-iste* -ist] **:** one that uses a comparative method in linguistics or literature

com·par·a·ti·val \kəm,parə¦tīvəl\ *adj* **:** of or belonging to the comparative degree

¹com·par·a·tive \kəm'parəd·iv, -rətiv *also* -per-\ *adj* [ME, fr. L *comparativus*, fr. *comparatus* (past part. of *comparare* to compare) + *-ivus* -ive] **1 :** belonging to or constituting the degree of comparison that is usu. expressed in English by placing *more* before an adjective (as *more natural*) or adverb (as *more clearly*) or by suffixing *-er* to it (*newer, sooner*) and that typically denotes increase in the quality, quantity, or relation expressed by the adjective or adverb ⟨the ~ degree⟩ ⟨the irregular ~ forms *elder* and *better*⟩ — compare COMPARISON 3; POSITIVE, SUPERLATIVE **2** *obs* **:** adept at making comparisons esp. of a scoffing or mocking nature **3 a :** considered as if with something or someone else held up to reveal contrast or likeness **:** seen as if in the light of something or someone implied or suggested **:** RELATIVE ⟨a ~ stranger⟩ ⟨in 1796 when ~ peace came to the frontier —*Amer. Guide Series: Pa.*⟩ **b :** approximating but not quite achieving (as a desired quality or state) **:** NEAR, APPROXIMATE ⟨~ comfort⟩ ⟨a position of mere ~ security⟩ **4 a :** making use of or capable of making use of a method whereby likenesses or dissimilarities are determined by simultaneous examination of two or more items ⟨the ~ viewpoint⟩ ⟨the study of blood types by ~ analysis⟩; *specif* **:** characterized by the comparison of things that have developed divergently from a common origin ⟨~

linguistics⟩ or of things that have developed convergently from different origins or of both ⟨~ anatomy⟩ — compare DESCRIPTIVE **b :** viewed or examined for the purpose of ascertaining or revealing likeness or dissimilarity ⟨the ~ morality of the sexes —Haldane Macfall⟩ **5** *obs* **:** COMPARABLE — **com·par·a·tive·ly** \-tə̇vlē, -li\ *adv* — **com·par·a·tive·ness** \-tivnə̇s\ *n* -ES

²**comparative** \"\ *n* -S [ME, fr. *comparative*, adj.] **1 :** one that compares with another esp. on equal footing **:** RIVAL; *specif* **:** one that makes witty or mocking comparisons **2 a :** the comparative degree in a language **b :** a comparative form of an adjective or adverb

comparative advantage *n* **:** the advantage enjoyed by a person or country in the cost ratio of one commodity to another in comparison with the ratio of costs of these same commodities elsewhere

comparative government *n* **:** the study and analysis of the general structure of governments throughout the world

comparative literature *n* **:** the study of the interrelationship of the literatures of two or more national cultures usu. of differing languages and esp. of the influences of one upon the other; *sometimes* **:** informal study of literary works in translation

comparative method *n* **:** a method of investigation (as of ethnologic phenomena and relations) based on comparison

comparative negligence *n* **:** the doctrine long the rule in admiralty and now adopted by statute for suits at law in a few states under which the negligence of the parties is weighed and the total damages divided up among them in proportion to the fault of each

comparative philosophy *n* **:** the study of philosophies from various cultures, nations, or epochs

comparative psychology *n* **1 :** the branch of psychology endeavoring to understand human behavior through the study of its similarities with and differences from infrahuman behavior **2 :** the study of the psychological similarities and differences between different races of humanity **:** FOLK PSYCHOLOGY

comparative religion *n* **:** comparative study of the origin, development, and interrelations of the religious systems of mankind — compare HISTORY OF RELIGIONS

comparative statement *n* **:** a business statement including two or more sets of figures arranged for comparison

com·par·a·tiv·ist \kəm'parəd·ə̇və̇st\ *n* -S [¹*comparative* + *-ist*] **:** COMPARATIST

com·par·a·tor \kəm'parəd·ə(r) *also* 'kämpə,rād·-\ *n* -S [F & L; F *comparateur*, fr. L *comparator* comparer, fr. *comparatus* (past part. of *comparare* to compare) + *-or*] **:** one that compares something to be measured with a standard measure: as **a** (1) **:** a device employing a micrometer screw or a vernier and a microscope in the precise measurement of short lengths (2) **:** any of various devices for the rapid inspection of mechanical parts to detect deviations from a standard piece **b :** an apparatus used for determining concentration of dissolved substances (as hydrogen ions) in solution by color comparison with known standards — compare COLORIMETER 2 **c :** an instrument, device, or set of charts (as for use in chemical analysis and medical diagnosis) for the determination and specification of colors by direct comparison with a standardized system of colors **d :** STEREOCOMPARATOR

¹**com·pare** \kəm'pa(a)(ə)r, -pe(ə)r, -pa(a)ə,-peə\ *vb* -ED/-ING/-S [ME *comparen*, fr. MF *comparer*, fr. L *comparare* to couple together, compare, fr. *compar* like, similar, fr. *com-* + *par* equal — more at PAIR] *vt* **1 :** to represent as similar (as for the purpose of illustration) **:** LIKEN ⟨~ a person's teeth to pearls⟩ — often used negatively in the passive infinitive of something inferior ⟨a drama not to be *compared* with any of Shakespeare's⟩ **2 a :** to examine the character or qualities of (as two or more persons or things) esp. for the purpose of discovering resemblances or differences ⟨~ today's medical costs with the mortality rates of 20 years ago⟩ **b :** to view in relation to something or someone else for the purpose of showing or establishing contrast or similarity — used in the past participle usu. preceded by *as* and followed by *to* or *with* ⟨Calcutta is the home of more than two million people *compared* to less than a million in Madras —*Science & Culture*⟩ ⟨the greater strength of steel as *compared* to cast iron⟩ **3 :** to inflect or modify (an adjective or adverb) according to the degrees of comparison **:** state the positive, comparative, and superlative forms of ~ *vi* **1 :** to bear being equated or likened ⟨his artistry does not ~ to his brother's⟩ ⟨can Dante ~ with Shakespeare and Milton⟩ **2 :** to assume or presume likeness or equality ⟨fools vainly striving to ~ with wise men⟩ **3 :** to make or draw comparisons ⟨if we now go to Italy at all, we go not to learn, but to ~ —Norman Douglas⟩ **4 :** to differ or stand out in some particular respect ⟨steel production this year ~*s* very poorly with the production of manufactured articles⟩ **5 :** to be equal or alike ⟨his performance at bat in 1951 ~*s* with his 1956 performance⟩ — often used in the negative in connection with something so different (as in superiority or inferiority) that anything being likened to it is as if impossible ⟨cannot ~ this year's crop with last year's⟩

syn COLLATE, CONTRAST: COMPARE indicates the placing together and examining of two things to discover resemblances and differences. It may but does not always concentrate on similarities rather than dissimilarities ⟨the discomforts of the road were light when *compared* to the discomforts of the sea, and the fatigue of the road was pleasurable when *compared* to the suffering and weariness entailed by a sea voyage —Agnes Repplier⟩ ⟨the army will have four armored, or tank, divisions, as *compared* to the single brigade, or less than half a division, available a year ago —H.W.Baldwin⟩ ⟨a hitherto unpublished letter by Hearn offers additional evidence of his independence of mind, his hostility toward the West as *compared* to the Orient, and his curiosity about his mother and her people —*Amer. Literature*⟩ COLLATE indicates painstaking minute orderly comparison, all small variations and differentiations being noted ⟨his books are for the most part built up around tables of statistics, carefully collected and *collated* and subjected to an unwearying critical scrutiny —*Times Lit. Supp.*⟩ CONTRAST always centers attention on differences between juxtaposed items ⟨with their large output of verse we may *contrast* the small amount of literary criticism that has been attempted by the younger poets —C.D.Lewis⟩ ⟨wind-swept dunes *contrast* with the otherwise rugged coastal scenery —*Amer. Guide Series: Maine*⟩

— **compare notes :** to exchange observations and views ⟨the two rival coaches got together after the game to *compare notes*⟩

²**compare** \"\ *n* -S **1 :** COMPARISON ⟨a ruffian in ~ to his comrades⟩ — used esp. in connection with something so superior it cannot be equaled by anything else ⟨her beauty was beyond ~⟩ ⟨a storm past ~ in violence⟩ **2** *obs* **:** illustration by comparison **:** SIMILE

³**compare** *n* -S [alter. (influenced by ¹*compare*) of *compeer*] **:** COMPEER

⁴**compare** *vt* -ED/-ING/-S [L *comparare* to prepare, acquire, buy, fr. *com-* + *parare* to prepare — more at PARE] *obs* **:** PROCURE, ACQUIRE

com·par·i·son \kəm'parəsən *also* -per-, *rap.* -rsən\ *n* -S [ME *comparisoun*, fr. MF *comparaison*, fr. L *comparation-*, *comparatio*, fr. *comparatus* (past part. of *comparare* to compare) + *-ion-*, *-io* -ion — more at COMPARE] **1 :** the act or action of comparing **:** LIKENING, EQUATING: as **a :** the representing of one thing or person as similar to or like another ⟨a ~ of man to a monkey⟩ — often used with *beyond*, *without*, or *out of all* in connection with something or someone so superior that likening to anything else is impossible ⟨wealth beyond ~⟩ ⟨out of all ~ the more beautiful of the two⟩ **b :** the placing together or juxtaposing of two or more items to ascertain, bring into relief, or establish their similarities and dissimilarities ⟨a ~ between American and British business procedures⟩ ⟨health record of rural areas . . . suffers by ~ with urban centers —*Commonweal*⟩ **2 :** identity (as of one feature or set of features with another) between two or more things or persons **:** SIMILARITY ⟨points of ~ between the two authors are many⟩ — used chiefly with a negative of something or someone decidedly inferior to another or of markedly unequal things or persons ⟨his technique bears no ~ with that of any other artist⟩ ⟨no ~ between the firepower of modern and 19th century armies⟩ **3 :** the modification (as by inflection) of an adjective or adverb to denote different levels of the quality, quantity, or relation expressed by the adjective or adverb — see ¹COMPARATIVE 1, POSITIVE, SUPERLATIVE **4** *obs* **:** a scoffing or mocking similitude

syn CONTRAST, ANTITHESIS, COLLATION, PARALLEL: COMPARISON is the most general term; in its broadest use it may imply no more than an impartial search for resemblances as well as differences ⟨there can be no *comparison* between the intelligence of native-born and foreign-born until differences due to language difficulties have been eliminated⟩ ⟨a *comparison* of many children from diverse backgrounds would yield an understanding of the common characteristics of childhood⟩ In a narrower use COMPARISON means likening ⟨a *comparison* to Sarah Bernhardt is flattering to any actress⟩ and in yet another use it implies a judgment ⟨parents should avoid *comparisons* between their children⟩ CONTRAST emphasizes difference intensified by physical nearness or by the association of the contrasting objects in an organic whole, a logical category, or an actual relationship ⟨the *contrast* the neat bright doctor . . . made with the coltish countryfolk —R.L.Stevenson⟩ ⟨Rembrandt achieves his greatest effect by the *contrast* of light and dark⟩ ⟨the *contrast* between democracy and fascism⟩ ⟨Electra's character given in a moment by the sharp *contrast* to her sister —Edith Hamilton⟩ ANTITHESIS implies comparison for the sake of revealing startling differences. But the objects of an antithesis always appear in pairs or sets of pairs; and antithesis suggests that the members of each pair are at opposite extremes or directly negate each other ⟨the century-old *antithesis* of heavenly justice and earthly fallibility, sin and innocence, Heaven and Hell, God and the Devil dominate Melville's mind —Charles Weir⟩ COLLATION denotes a close and far-going comparison, esp. a scrutiny of manuscripts, records, differing accounts or editions of a text, with the purpose of arriving at the most nearly complete, authentic, or true version of something said, written, or done ⟨this *collation* is relevant . . . to the question of Seneca's influence upon language —T.S.Eliot⟩ PARALLEL implies a similarity in growth, development, or action between people or events separated in time or place, background, or origin ⟨the controversy which raged as an earlier *parallel* to that which Darwin was to start later —W.E. Swinton⟩ ⟨the contribution of the Third Programme . . . is without *parallel* in the history of the art —Dyneley Hussey⟩

comparison lamp *n* **:** an incandescent lamp of constant and not necessarily known luminous intensity against which a working standard lamp and lamps to be tested are successively compared in a photometer

comparison microscope *n* **:** an apparatus consisting essentially of a pair of microscope objective lenses and tubes connected by prisms in such a way that images from both may be viewed side by side through a single ocular lens

comparison shopper *n* **:** a store employee who gathers information through actual visits and purchases about the quality, style, and price of merchandise in competitors' stores and about stock assortments, sales service, and customer response to special promotions

comparison slip *n* **:** EXCHANGE TICKET

comparison spectrum *n* **:** a line spectrum of accurately known wavelengths that is matched wavelength for wavelength with another spectrum for calibration of the latter

comparison star *n* **:** a star used as a reference in the measurement of another star's position, brightness, or other observable characteristic

com·par·i·um \kəm'pa(a)rēəm\ *n, pl* **compar·ia** \-ēə\ [NL, fr. L *comparare* to couple together, compare + NL *-ium* — more at COMPARE] **:** a group of organisms capable of direct or indirect interbreeding whether or not fertile hybrids result and being usu. equivalent in scope to a taxonomic genus

com·par·o·scope *also* **com·par·a·scope** \-parə,skōp\ *n* -S [¹*compare* + connective *-o-*, *-a-* + *-scope*] **:** an apparatus used for simultaneous microscopic study of two objects **:** COMPARISON MICROSCOPE

com·par·sa \kəm'pärsə\ *n* -S [AmerSp, fr. Sp, group of revelers costumed alike, entire group of supernumeraries in a play, supernumerary in a play, fr. It, supernumerary in a play, appearance, fr. fem. of *comparso*, past part. of *comparire* to appear, fr. L *comparēre*, fr. L *com-* + *parēre* to be visible — more at APPEAR] **1 :** a folk dance and song of Cuban Negro origin **2 :** a masked company of street dancers in Cuban carnival processions

com·part \kəm'pärt, -pät, *usu* -d·+V\ *vt* -ED/-ING/-S [It *compartire* to mark out into parts, share out, fr. LL *compartiri* to share out, fr. L *com-* + *partiri*, *partire* to share, fr. *part-*, *pars* part — more at PART] **:** to mark out into parts or subdivisions; *specif* **:** to lay out in parts according to a plan

com·par·ti·men·to \kəm,pärd·ə'men(,)tō\ *n, pl* **comparti·men·ti** \-n(,)tē\ [It] **:** an administrative district or region in Italy

com·par·ti·tion \,käm,pär'tishən, -mpər-\ *n* -S [ML *compartition-*, *compartitio* apportionment, fr. LL *compartitus* (past part. of *compartiri*) + L *-ion-* *-io* -ion] **:** distribution esp. of the parts of a design

¹**com·part·ment** \kəm'pärtmənt, -pät-\ *n* -S [MF *compartiment*, fr. It *compartimento*, fr. *compartire* + *-mento* -ment] **1 :** a subdivision of a plane surface: as **a :** a separate division of a structure or design (as a panel or coffer in a ceiling or a sculptured subdivision of a portal) **b** *obs* **:** COMPARTITION **2 :** a subdivision esp. of a series of abstractions, an integrated organization, or a body of knowledge **:** SECTION, PART ⟨the ~*s* of your mind⟩ **3 :** a subdivision of three-dimensional space: as **a :** a small chamber, receptacle, or container ⟨the seeds may be found in numerous ~*s* within the pod⟩ ⟨the ~*s* of a roulette wheel⟩ **b** (1) **:** a private room on a sleeping car that has toilet facilities and berths and is larger than a bedroom and smaller than a drawing room (2) *in Europe and elsewhere outside of the U.S.* **:** a private room on a railroad passenger car with or without berths and toilet facilities (3) *in Great Britain* **:** one of the subdivisions of a railroad passenger car having seats that face each other and opening into a side corridor or extending entirely across the car **c :** one of the sections into which the interior of a ship is divided by bulkheads **d** *mil* **:** an area bounded by such topographic features (as woods or ridges) that observation and direct fire into the area are limited — compare CORRIDOR

²**com·part·ment** \-t,ment, -tmənt\ *vt* -ED/-ING/-S **1 :** to break down (as into sections or segments) **:** divide up ⟨a ~*ed* box⟩ ⟨biology is ~*ed* into a host of special sciences —*Scientific American Reader*⟩ **2 :** to separate into mutually isolated units ⟨in the protected and ~*ed* society of Beacon Hill—John Mason Brown⟩ ⟨international treaties must be discussed as a whole; they may not be ~*ed* —H.M.Dorr & H.L.Bretton⟩

com·part·men·tal \kəm¦pärt¦mentᵊl, ¦käm,pärt-, -pät-\ *adj* **:** divided or tending to divide into separate or independent compartments ⟨a ~ organization⟩ ⟨~ seed pods⟩ — **compart·men·tal·ly** \-ᵊlē, -ᵊli\ *adv*

com·part·men·tal·i·za·tion \kəm¦pärt,mentᵊlə̇'zāshən, ¦käm,p-, -pät-, -ᵊl,ī'z-\ *n* -S **:** division esp. into units lacking normal interaction or cooperation ⟨the rigid ~ that has done so much to sterilize scientific knowledge by depriving scientific specialists of a broad social vision —T.S.Harding⟩

com·part·men·tal·ize \kəm,pärt'mentᵊl,īz, ,käm-, -pät-\ *vt* -ED/-ING/-S **:** to separate into compartments or categories in a manner tending to preclude interrelationships

com·part·men·ta·tion \kəm,pärtmən'tāshən, -pät-, -,men-\ *n* -S **:** division into separate sections or units ⟨elaborate ~ in submarines makes them difficult to sink⟩ ⟨~ and specialization go hand in hand with . . . the increasing complexities of civilization —V.D.Tate⟩

com·part·ment·ize \kəm'pärtmən,tīz, -pät-\ *vt* -ED/-ING/-S **:** COMPARTMENTALIZE

¹**com·pass** \'kəmpəs *also* 'käm-\ *vb* -ED/-ING/-ES [ME *compassen*, fr. OF *compasser* to measure, arrange, ponder, contrive, fr. (assumed) VL *compassare* to measure off by paces, fr. L *com-* + (assumed) VL *passare* to go, move, fr. L *passus* step, pace — more at PACE] *vt* **1 :** to devise or contrive often in a treacherous manner **:** PLOT **2 a :** to lie around **:** GIRDLE, ENCOMPASS ⟨island ~*ed* by the sea⟩ ⟨the Great Peace beyond all this turmoil and fret ~*ed* me around —L.P.Smith⟩ **b :** to move around **:** travel entirely around (as a circle or curved course) **:** ENCIRCLE ⟨Magellan's ship ~*ed* the earth⟩ **3 :** to hem in or enclose in or as if in a ring **:** SURROUND ⟨suddenly enemies ~*ed* him on all sides⟩ **4 a :** to bring about **:** ACHIEVE, ACCOMPLISH ⟨a writer . . . attempting a higher strain of elevation . . . than his powers can ~ —C.E.Montague⟩ **b :** to get at or within one's power **:** OBTAIN ⟨~ his freedom⟩ **5** *obs* **:** to bend into a circular form **:** CURVE **6** *obs* **:** to get around (someone) esp. for one's own advantage **7 :** GRASP ⟨~*ing* an idea⟩ **:** COMPREHEND ⟨could not ~ the smallest problems⟩ ~ *vi* **:** to assume a circular or curved form **:** CURVE, BEND ⟨a plank ~*ing* under pressure⟩ **syn** see REACH, SURROUND

²**compass** \"\ *n* -ES [ME *compas*, fr. MF, fr. *compasser* to go round, measure, divide] **1 a :** an often rounded or curved boundary limit **:** CIRCUMFERENCE ⟨within the ~ of the outer wall⟩ **b :** an enclosed or delimited space or area often circumscribed ⟨three passengers shut up in the narrow ~ of one lumbering old mail coach —Charles Dickens⟩ ⟨the narrow ~ of 21 pages —V.L.Parrington⟩ **c :** range or limit of perception, cognizance, knowledge, interest, concern, or treatment ⟨impossible within the ~ of this report to do justice to all the projects —J.B.Conant⟩ ⟨disposing of his property . . . within the ~ of the law —John Locke⟩ ⟨works . . . of such ~ and excellence as to supersede those of his predecessors —H.O.Taylor⟩

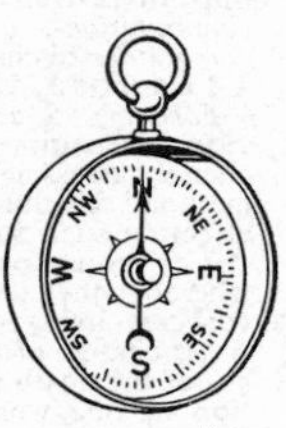

compass 4a

d : the range of pitch covered by a melody or lying within the capacity of a voice or instrument **e** *obs* **:** due bounds **:** limits imposed by moderation and good sense **2** *obs* **:** cunning ingenuity **3 a** *obs* **:** CIRCLE **b** *obs* **:** a ring, globe, or other object with circular outline **c :** a circular motion or course **:** a roundabout way ⟨finishing the ~ of his life⟩ ⟨hawks rising in ~*es* through the air⟩ ⟨a ~ of seven days' journey —2 Kings 3:9 (AV)⟩ **d** (1) **:** the curve of an arrow's flight (2) **:** the angle of elevation determining this curve **4 a :** a device for determining directions on the earth's surface by means of a magnetic needle or group of needles turning freely on a pivot and pointing to the magnetic north **b :** any of certain nonmagnetic devices that serve the same purpose as the magnetic compass (as the gyrocompass and the sky compass) — see GYROCOMPASS, MAGNETIC NEEDLE, MARINER'S COMPASS, SKY COMPASS, SURVEYOR'S COMPASS **c** *usu* **compasses** *pl* **:** an instrument for describing circles, transferring measurements, and similar operations consisting in its simple form of two pointed branches joined at the top by a pivot, one of the branches generally having a pen or pencil point — called also *pair of compasses* **syn** see RANGE

³**compass** \"\ *adj* **:** forming a curve **:** CURVED, CIRCULAR ⟨a ~ timber⟩

⁴**compass** *adv* [³*compass*] *obs* **:** in an arc **:** so as to form an arc or circle

com·pass·able \'kəmpəsəbəl *also* 'käm-\ *adj* **:** that may be compassed or attained ⟨a ~ distance⟩ ⟨materials easily ~⟩

compass bearing *n* **:** a bearing relative to north as indicated by a magnetic compass

compass brick *n* **:** curved or tapering brick for use in curved work (as in arches, shafts, and wells) — compare ARCH BRICK 1

compass calipers *n pl* **:** HERMAPHRODITE CALIPERS

compass card *n* **:** the circular card attached to the needles of a mariner's compass on which are marked the 32 points of the compass and the 360° of the circle

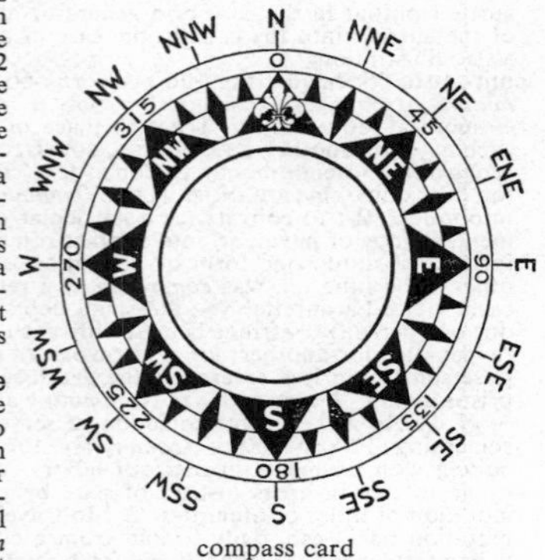

compass card

compass corrector *n* **:** a magnet or magnets or soft iron spheres or bars placed near a compass to neutralize the effect of the ship's magnetism

compass course *n* **:** the course with respect to true north in which a ship or an aircraft is intended to travel

compass dial *n* **:** a small pocket sundial fitted with a compass needle by which the gnomon may be adjusted to tell the hour of the day

compassed *past of* COMPASS

compass error *n* **:** the difference between compass heading and true heading expressed as the algebraic sum of variation and deviation

compasses *pres 3d sing of* COMPASS, *pl of* COMPASS

compass-headed \'==,==\ *adj* **:** having a semicircular head ⟨a *compass-headed* arch⟩

compass heading *n* **:** heading measured clockwise from north as indicated by the compass

compassing *adj* [ME, fr. pres. part. of *compassen* to compass] **1 :** ENCOMPASSING, INCLUSIVE ⟨~ knowledge⟩ **2 :** CURVED, BENT ⟨~ timbers⟩

¹**com·pas·sion** \kəm'pashən, -aash-,-aish-\ *n* -S [ME *compassioun*, fr. MF or LL; MF *compassion*, fr. LL *compassion-*, *compassio*, fr. *compassus* (past part. of *compati* to have compassion, fr. L *com-* + *pati* to bear, suffer) + *-ion-*, *-io* -ion — more at PATIENT] **:** deep feeling for and understanding of misery or suffering and the concomitant desire to promote its alleviation **:** spiritual consciousness of the personal tragedy of another or others and selfless tenderness directed toward it ⟨to have ~ on a person⟩ ⟨with ~ (so different from pity) she shows the sordid impact of this convict settlement on the lives of the natives —Sarah Campion⟩ **syn** see SYMPATHY

²**compassion** \"\ *vt* -ED/-ING/-S *archaic* **:** COMPASSIONATE

com·pas·sion·able \-sh(ə)nəbəl\ *adj* **1** *obs* **:** COMPASSIONATE **2** *archaic* **:** PITIABLE

¹**com·pas·sion·ate** \-sh(ə)nə̇t, *usu* -ə̇d·+V\ *adj* **1 :** marked by compassion, by a ready inclination to pity, sympathy, or tenderness **:** SYMPATHETIC ⟨not cold and blaming . . . but an older and wiser brother, very ~ —Sinclair Lewis⟩ ⟨there was a murmur of commiseration . . . the soft and ~ voices of women were conspicuous —Charles Dickens⟩ **2** *obs* **:** calling forth pity **:** PITIABLE **3 :** granted because of unusual distressing circumstances affecting an individual — used of leaves and other military privileges ⟨considered for a ~ discharge because of his domestic difficulties⟩ **syn** see TENDER

²**com·pas·sion·ate** \-shə,nāt, *usu* -ād·+V\ *vt* -ED/-ING/-S **:** to have compassion for **:** sympathize with **:** PITY ⟨even *compassionating* those who hold in bondage their fellowmen —John Quincy Adams⟩

com·pas·sion·ate·ly \-sh(ə)nə̇tlē, -li\ *adv* **:** in a compassionate manner

com·pas·sion·ate·ness *n* -ES **:** COMPASSION

com·pas·sion·less \-shənlə̇s\ *adj* **:** lacking compassion

com·pas·sive \kəm'pasiv\ *adj* [*compassion* + *-ive*] *archaic* **:** COMPASSIONATE

compass key *n* **:** a small screwdriver or pin wrench for tightening or loosening the joints of compasses

com·pass·less \'kəmpəslə̇s *also* 'käm-\ *adj* **:** lacking a compass

compass man *n* **:** one who accompanies a timber estimator in order to establish for him by use of a compass and other means the correct boundaries of the tract

compass plane *n* **:** CIRCULAR PLANE

compass plant *also* **compass flower** *n* **:** any of several plants whose leaves or branches are arranged on the axis so as to indicate the cardinal points of the compass: as **a :** a rosinweed (*Silphium laciniatum*) **b :** a prickly lettuce (*Lactuca scariola*) **c :** PRAIRIE BIRD'S-FOOT TREFOIL **d :** a low tufted white-woolly yellow-flowered composite herb (*Wyethia ovata*) of California

compass rafter *n* **:** a rafter that is cut to a curve and commonly used in an ornamented roof truss or in a gable framing

compass roof *n* **:** a timber roof in which each truss has its rafters, collar beams, and braces combined into an arched form

compass rose *n* **:** a circle graduated to degrees or quarter points and printed on a chart for reference (as of lines and courses) usu. showing both magnetic and true directions

compass saw *n* **:** a handsaw that has a thin tapering blade for cutting small circles, curves, or irregular edges

compass termite *n* **:** any of certain Australian termites that build flattened earthen nests which are shaped like steeples and have the broader faces always pointing east and west

compass window *n* **:** a bay or oriel window of semicircular plan

com·paternity \¦kämˌ+\ *n* -ES [ME *compaternite*, fr. ML *compaternitas*, fr. *compater*, after L *pater* father: LL *paternitas* paternity] **:** the spiritual relation between the godparents of a child; *also* **:** the spiritual relationship between godparents and the child's actual parents

com·pa·thy \'kämpəthē\ *n* -ES [*com-* + *-pathy*] **:** shared feeling (as of joy or sorrow)

com·pat·i·bil·i·ty \kəmˌpad·ə'bilədˌē, -atə-, -ətē, -i\ *n* -ES [F *compatibilité*, fr. *compatible* + *-ité* -ity] **1 :** the quality or state of being compatible **:** the capacity of two or more entities to combine or remain together without undesirable aftereffects **:** mutual tolerance **:** CONGRUITY ⟨the ~ of blood types⟩ ⟨~ between church and state⟩ **2 a :** the capability of cross-fertilizing freely — used chiefly of plants and plant parts **b :** the capability of components (as of an electronic system) to function together; *specif* **:** the ability of a color television transmission system to provide black-and-white service for monochrome receivers without special modification

com·pat·i·ble \kəm'pad·əbəl, -atə-\ *adj* [MF, fr. ML *compatibilis*, fr. LL *compati* to have compassion + L *-ibilis* -ible — more at COMPASSION] **1** *obs* **:** sharing in another's suffering **2 a :** capable of existing together without discord or disharmony — used usu. with *with* ⟨slavery, which nowadays . . . we no longer regard as ~ with high civilization —Havelock Ellis⟩ **b** *logic* **:** so related that both or all may hold or be true **:** NONCONTRADICTORY **c** (1) **:** capable of cross-fertilizing freely ⟨some plants are ~⟩ ⟨~ pollens⟩ (2) **:** uniting readily and usu. permanently — used of certain plant stocks and scions **d** *of drugs or medicines* **:** not incompatible **e :** having to do with a system in which color television broadcasts may be received in black and white on ordinary receivers without special modification **f :** capable of blending into a homogeneous mixture that neither separates nor is altered by chemical interaction of ingredients **syn** see CONSONANT

com·pat·i·ble·ness *n* -ES **:** COMPATIBILITY

com·pat·i·bly \-blē, -li\ *adv* **:** in a compatible manner

com·pat·ric \kəm'pa·trik, (')kämˌp-\ *adj* [*com-* + *-patric* (as in *sympatric*)] **:** SYMPATRIC

com·pa·tri·ot \kəm'pā·trēət, -ēˌät *also* käm-, *Brit usu* -pa·-; *usu* -d·+V\ *n* -S *often attrib* [F *compatriote*, fr. LL *compatriota*, fr. L *com-* + LL *patriota* fellow countryman — more at PATRIOT] **1 :** one of the same country **:** a fellow countryman ⟨our Southern ~*s*⟩ **2 :** COMPEER, COLLEAGUE

com·pa·tri·ot·ic \=ˌ=¦äd·ik\ *adj* [*compatriot* + *-ic*] **:** of or having to do with one's native land ⟨a ~ friend⟩ ⟨a ~ hymn⟩

compd *abbr* compound

compear *vi* -ED/-ING/-S [ME *compeiren*, *comperen*, fr. MF *comper-*, pres. indic. stem of *comparoir*, fr. L *comparēre*, fr. *com-* + *parēre* to be visible — more at APPEAR] *obs* **:** APPEAR; *specif, Scots law* **:** to appear in court personally or by attorney

com·pear·ance \kəm'pērən(t)s, -pār-\ *n* -S [ME *compeirance*, fr. *compeiren* + *-ance*] *Scots law* **:** formal appearance in court

comped *past of* COMP

¹com·peer \'kämˌpi(ə)r, kəm'p-,kəm'p-\ *n* -S [ME (influenced in meaning by ME *peer*), fr. *OF compere* godfather, comrade, fellow, fr. ML *compater* godfather, fr. L *com-* + *pater* father — more at FATHER, PEER] **1 :** an equal in rank, age, prowess **:** PEER ⟨Hitler as a strategist was not the ~ of Washington or Napoleon⟩; *specif* **:** COLLEAGUE ⟨the specialist and his ~*s* who examined the patient's heart⟩ **2 :** a close associate **:** COMPANION, COMRADE ⟨as a raw inductee he found himself no better off than any of his ~*s*⟩

²compeer *vt* -ED/-ING/-S *obs* **:** to be equal with **:** MATCH

com·pel \kəm'pel\ *vb* **compelled; compelled; compelling; compels** [ME *compellen*, fr. MF *compeller*, *compellir*, fr. L *compellere* to drive together, compel, urge, fr. *com-* + *pellere* to drive — more at FELT] *vt* **1 :** FORCE, DRIVE, IMPEL: as **a :** to force by physical necessity or evidential fact ⟨poverty *compelled* him to work⟩ — often used in the passive ⟨so lame that he was *compelled* to use a cane —*Amer. Guide Series: N.H.*⟩ ⟨*compelled* to confess that the project was a failure —R.P.Warren⟩ **b :** to urge irresistibly by moral or social pressure ⟨public opinion *compelled* President Lincoln to order McDowell to move forward —*Dict. of Amer. History*⟩ **:** force by authority, code, or custom **c :** to force by personal temperament or other subjective considerations ⟨*compelled*, as if by inner command, to listen —J.C.Powys⟩ ⟨his sense of order would ~ him to tidy up —Morley Callaghan⟩ **2 a :** to force or cause irresistibly **:** call upon, require, or command without possibility of withholding or denying ⟨Alexander . . . after the decisive victory at Legnano *compelled* Frederick's submission —*Encyc. Americana*⟩ **b :** to impel or force to appear, come, or go **:** summon peremptorily ⟨potent spells for *compelling* the Evil One —Charles Dickens⟩ ⟨wedging his tense arm imperatively under mine, Tom Buchanan *compelled* me from the room —Scott Fitzgerald⟩ **c** *archaic* **:** to cause to congregate **:** drive together **:** gather together irresistibly **3 a :** to domineer over so as to force compliance or submission **:** demand consideration or attention ⟨nobody will ~ you; you are perfectly free —Samuel Butler †1902⟩ **b :** to obtain (a response) by force, violence, or coercion ⟨~ assent at the point of a gun⟩ ~ *vi* **:** to employ force; *esp* **:** to exert an irresistible influence ⟨he had a presence that inspired and a voice that *compelled*⟩ **syn** see FORCE

com·pel·la·ble \-ləbəl\ *adj* **:** capable of being compelled

compellable witness *n* **:** a person that can claim no exemption from testifying in a legal proceeding

com·pel·la·tion \ˌkämpə'lāshən, -ˌpe'-\ *n* -S [L *compellation-*, *compellatio*, fr. *compellatus* (past part. of *compellare* to accost, fr. *com-* + *-pellare* as in *appellare* to address) + *-ion-*, *-io* -ion — more at APPEAL] **1 :** an act or action of addressing someone **2 :** the word or words used in addressing someone **3 :** APPELLATION 3

com·pel·lent \kəm'pelənt\ *adj* [L *compellent-*, *compellens*, pres. part. of *compellere*] **:** COMPELLING ⟨~ example of heroism⟩

compelling *adj* [fr. pres. part. of *compel*] **1 :** FORCING, IMPELLING, DRIVING ⟨~ circumstances⟩ ⟨~ ambition⟩ **2 :** demanding respect, honor, or admiration ⟨a ~ personality⟩ ⟨her singing was as ~ as her acting —*Time*⟩ **3 :** calling for examination, scrutiny, consideration, or thought ⟨new and ~ evidence⟩ **4 :** demanding and holding one's attention ⟨a ~ novel⟩ ⟨a ~ manner of speech⟩ **5 :** tending to convince or convert by or as if by forcefulness of evidence ⟨though his logic is often unconvincing, his documentation is always ~ —H.J.Muller⟩ — **com·pel·ling·ly** *adv*

com·pend \'kämˌpend\ *n* -S [ML *compendium*] **:** COMPENDIUM, EPITOME

com·pen·di·ary \kəm'pendēˌerē, käm-\ *adj* [L *compendiarius*, fr. *compendium* short cut + *-arius* -ary] **:** COMPENDIOUS: as **a :** BRIEF ⟨a ~ abridgment⟩ **b** *obs* **:** EXPEDITIOUS

com·pen·di·ous \-dēəs\ *adj* [ME, fr. L *compendiosus*, fr. *compendium* + *-osus* -ose] **1 :** marked by the brief expression of a comprehensive matter **:** like a compendium **:** resolving essentials into few words ⟨such looseness cannot be afforded in a short and ~ book —*Times Lit. Supp.*⟩ **2** *obs* **:** showing saving of time **:** EXPEDITIOUS, DIRECT **syn** see CONCISE

com·pen·di·ous·ly *adv* [ME, fr. *compendious* + *-ly*] **:** in a compendious manner

com·pen·di·um \kəm'pendēəm *sometimes* käm-\ *n, pl* **compendiums** \-ēəmz\ *or* **compen·dia** \-ēə\ [ML, fr. L, saving, gain, short cut, fr. *compendere* to weigh, fr. *com-* + *pendere* to weigh — more at PENDANT] **1 a :** a brief compilation or composition consisting of a reduction and condensation of the subject matter of a larger work **:** ABRIDGMENT, ABSTRACT ⟨a one-volume ~ of the multivolume original⟩ **b :** a work treating in brief form the important features of a whole field of knowledge or subject matter category ⟨a ~ of physics⟩ **c :** a list of a number of brief items **:** CATALOG, INVENTORY ⟨a ~ of all the fashionable faults likely to be found in a young . . . novelist —*Time*⟩ **2** *archaic* **:** SAVING, ECONOMY **3 :** a folder containing writing paper and envelopes

syn SYLLABUS, DIGEST, PANDECT, SURVEY, SKETCH, PRÉCIS, APERÇU: a COMPENDIUM gathers in brief, orderly, and intelligible form, sometimes outlined, the essential facts ⟨*A Treatise on Epidemic Cholera* which contained little original matter but was published as a *compendium* of the existing knowledge of this disease —W.R.Steiner⟩ A SYLLABUS, often presented with a series of headings, points, or propositions, gives concise statements affording a view of the whole and an indication of its significance ⟨no party program, no official *syllabus* of opinions, which we all have to defend —W.R.Inge⟩ A DIGEST presents a body of information gathered from many sources and arranged and classified for ready accessibility, often alphabetized and indexed; the word also indicates any condensed easy-to-read version ⟨the only hope of gaining such knowledge lies in a summarization and thorough *digest* of the huge body of county statistics already available —D.J.Bogue⟩ ⟨the *Current Digest of the Soviet Press*, now in its fifth year of uninterrupted weekly appearance, a seventy-thousand word a week *digest* of forty Russian newspapers and periodicals —Mortimer Graves⟩ A PANDECT is a systematic digest covering the whole of a monumental subject ⟨no printed body of modern social history, either by purpose or accident, contains a richer *pandect* of the efficient impulses of its age —Christopher Morley⟩ A SURVEY is a brief comprehensive presentation giving main outlines, often as a preliminary aid to later study of more detailed treatment ⟨the policy of the Board and its founder being to make first of all a thorough *survey* of the educational needs of the country —J.D.Greene⟩ ⟨an essay on the Renaissance, not a history of the Renaissance. It omits mention of many interesting details of that vast transformation in an effort to determine, through a broad *survey* of its more salient features, the fundamental nature of the movement —G.C.Sellery⟩ A SKETCH is a slight tentative preliminary presentation subject to much later change, emendation, and amplification ⟨to give anything but the most fragmentary *sketch* of the winter of '94 and '95 in Berlin is impossible —David Fairchild⟩ ⟨*The American Chancery Digest*, including state and federal equity decisions, with an introductory *sketch* of equity courts and their jurisdiction —V.L.Wilkinson⟩ A PRÉCIS is a concise clear-cut statement or restatement of main matters, often a report or a summary suggesting the style or tone of an original ⟨a carefully prepared critical text of Guido, with a short critical introduction, a full critical apparatus, and English *précis* printed concurrently —*Times Lit. Supp.*⟩ An APERÇU is a sketch giving a very quick, perhaps impressionistic compression of the whole, with all details omitted ⟨popular books which give an *aperçu* of recent research, in order to have some idea of the general scientific purpose served by particular facts and laws —Bertrand Russell⟩

com·penetrate \(')käm+\ *vt* -ED/-ING/-S [*com-* + *penetrate*] **:** to penetrate throughout **:** PERVADE

com·penetration \(¦)käm+\ *n* -S **:** pervasive penetration **:** mutual interfusion ⟨the ~ of two ideas⟩

com·pen·sa·bil·i·ty \kəmˌpen(t)sə'bilədˌē, (ˌ)käm-\ *n* -ES [*compensable* + *-ity*] **:** the capacity or fitness of something to be made up or made good ⟨the ~ of an unemployment claim⟩

com·pen·sa·ble \kəm'pen(t)səbəl, (')kämˌp-\ *adj* [F, fr. *compenser* to compensate + *-able* — more at COMPENSE] **:** that is to be or can be compensated ⟨hard work ~ by a sense of achievement⟩; *esp* **:** that can be compensated under the provisions of workmen's compensation laws ⟨~ injury⟩

compensables \-lz\ *n pl* **:** costs or losses entitling persons covered under social security to benefits

com·pen·sate \'kämpənˌsāt, -ˌpen-, *archaic* kəm'pen- *or* käm'-; *usu* -ād.+V\ *vb* -ED/-ING/-S [L *compensatus*, past part. of *compensare*, fr. *compensus*, past part. of *compendere* to weigh] *vt* **1 :** to be equivalent to (as in value or effect) **:** make up for **:** COUNTERBALANCE ⟨*compensating* evil with good⟩ ⟨her vanity, dearth of brains, and excessive sentimentality were *compensated* by her kindness —E.J.Simmons⟩ **2 :** to make proper payment to **:** requite suitably **:** REMUNERATE **:** RECOMPENSE ⟨~ a worker injured on his job⟩; *specif, civil law* **:** to extinguish or satisfy (as a claim) by compensation **3** *physics* **:** to provide with means of counteracting variation ⟨~ a magnetic needle⟩ **:** neutralize the effect of (variation or varying parts) **4 :** to alter gradient on (curved portions of railroad track) so that total resistance to movement equals that for tangent track ~ *vi* **:** to make amends **:** supply an equivalent — used with *for* ⟨~ for his feelings of loneliness by assertions of superiority —W.H.Auden⟩ **syn** see PAY

compensated *adj* [fr. past part. of *compensate*] *of an optically inactive chemical compound* **:** balanced with respect to asymmetric carbon atoms ⟨*meso*-tartaric acid is an internally ~ form⟩

compensated dollar *n* [*compensated* fr. past part. of *compensate*] **:** COMMODITY DOLLAR

compensating *adj* [fr. pres. part. of *compensate*] **:** serving or functioning as a compensation (as for some irregularity or flaw); *esp, of an auxiliary electrical or mechanical device* **:** correcting performance that has been adversely affected by some operating variant (as by friction in a watt-hour meter, pressure in a main cylinder, or variation in an electric circuit impedance) — **com·pen·sat·ing·ly** \¦=ˌ=ˌ==\ *adv*

compensating balance *n* **:** COMPENSATION BALANCE

compensating condenser *n* **:** BALANCING CONDENSER

compensating errors *n pl* **:** errors equal in amount but opposite in sense that cancel each other

compensating gear *n* **:** DIFFERENTIAL GEAR

compensating magnet *n* **:** COMPASS CORRECTOR

compensating winding *n* **:** a winding embedded in the pole faces of a commutating alternating-current or direct-current machine and connected in series with the armature, the magnetic field of the winding neutralizing the cross-magnetizing field of the armature

com·pen·sa·tion \ˌkämpən'sāshən, -ˌpen-\ *n* -S [ME *compensacioun*, fr. L *compensation-*, *compensatio* balancing of accounts, fr. *compensatus* (past part. of *compensare* to compensate) + *-ion-*, *-io* -ion] **1 :** the act or action of making up, making good, or counterbalancing **:** rendering equal **:** AMENDING: as **a** (1) **:** the counterbalancing of a defect in bodily structure or limitation in function of an organ by overgrowth of another or by increased function of unimpaired parts of the same organ ⟨cardiac ~⟩ — compare DECOMPENSATION (2) **:** a psychic mechanism or process whereby an individual compensates for a frustrated drive, inadequacy, or imperfection by substituting or stressing another drive, trait, or function **b :** adjustment of the phase retardation of one light ray with respect to that of another **c** *civil law* **:** extinction of the mutual debts of two persons that are reciprocally debtors and creditors (as in setoff) **d** *phonetics* **:** compensatory lengthening or compensatory doubling **2 :** something that constitutes an equivalent or recompense: as **a :** something that makes good a lack ⟨rewards which are no ~*s* for the abandoned gratifications —Abram Kardiner⟩ **b :** something that makes up for a loss ⟨~ will be made by Germany for all damage done to the civilian population of the Allies . . . by the aggression of Germany —J.M.Keynes⟩; *specif* **:** payment received by a worker or his dependents for claims under a workmen's compensation act or cash benefits received by eligible unemployed as provided for by legislation **c :** something that relieves, equalizes, or neutralizes (as pressure, stress, or stimuli) **:** means of alleviation ⟨nor did he use letter writing as a ~ for inner tensions —*Yale Rev.*⟩ ⟨for the men who are really up there, the war is a tough and dirty life, without immediate ~ —Walter Bernstein⟩ ⟨jazz began as the ~ music of a shackled race —*Esquire's Jazz Bk.*⟩ **d :** payment for value received or service rendered **:** REMUNERATION ⟨the ~ of U.S. government employees⟩ ⟨~ to the Indians for the land ceded by them consisted of livestock —D.E.Clark⟩ **e :** moral or spiritual reward or feeling or sense thereof ⟨however shoddy his life an artist knows the ~*s* of creation and achievement⟩ ⟨there are so many ~*s* that come from coaching small-time football —Bert LaBrucherie⟩ **f** *physics* **:** balance or counteraction of opposed forces

com·pen·sa·tion·al \¦=(ˌ)=¦=shənᵊl, -shnəl\ *adj* **:** of or relating to compensation

compensation balance *n* **:** a timepiece balance wheel so constructed (as of two metals of different expansivities) that variations of temperature produce such changes in its mean rim diameter as offset the changes produced in the hairspring

compensation guard *n* **:** a narrow strip of paper included at the binding margin of a book to compensate for the thickness of items mounted on pages

compensation insurance *n* **:** WORKMEN'S COMPENSATION INSURANCE

compensation neurosis *n* **:** a neurosis of work phobias manifested in physical symptoms that persist as long as unemployment compensation continues

compensation pendulum *n* **:** a clock pendulum so constructed as to remain of the same pendulum length by automatic compensation for the effect of changes of temperature

compensation point *n* **:** the light intensity at which the amount of carbon dioxide released in respiration equals the amount used in photosynthesis and the amount of oxygen used in respiration equals the amount released in photosynthesis, varying in different species of plants and in response to changes in temperature and other environmental factors

com·pen·sa·tive \'kämpənˌsād·iv, -ˌpen-; kəm'pen(t)səd·-, (')kämˌp-\ *adj* [*compensate* + *-ive*] **:** affording compensation **:** COMPENSATORY

com·pen·sa·tor \'kämpənˌsād·ə(r), -ˌpen-\ *n* -S [*compensate* + *-or*] **:** one that compensates: as **a :** AUTOTRANSFORMER **b :** BALANCER SET 1 **c :** COMPASS CORRECTOR **d :** a combination of quartz plates of wedge shape used to measure the phase difference between the two rectangular vibration components of elliptically polarized light **e :** a photographic device (as a star diaphragm or suitably graded neutral-density filter) for holding back the light in the middle of the field of a wide-angle lens to allow proper exposure at the corners **f :** a portion of a direction finder that automatically applies a correction to the direction indication and that commonly consists of a mechanical arrangement of cams **g :** a device fitted to the muzzle of a firearm that reduces recoil by directing part of the powder gases through a series of lateral vents — compare MUZZLE BRAKE **h :** an electrical equalizer designed to compensate for the recording characteristic of a record and usu. connected between a pickup and an amplifier

com·pen·sa·to·ry \kəm'pen(t)səˌtōrē, (')kämˌp-, -tȯr-, -ri\ *adj* [*compensate* + *-ory*] **:** serving as compensation **:** making amends **:** making up for loss ⟨a ~ enlargement of the heart⟩ ⟨to overcome this feeling of inferiority by developing such ~ mechanisms as intelligent aggression or shrewdness —Edward Sapir⟩: as **a :** designed to counteract extreme fluctuations in the business cycle esp. by governmental planning and adjustments in revenue programs and government expenditures ⟨theories of ~ fiscal policy⟩ ⟨a ~ economy⟩ **b :** maintaining the length of a syllable — used esp. of the lengthening of a vowel when a following consonant is lost (Latin *cānus*, earlier *căsnus*) or the doubling of a consonant when a preceding vowel becomes short (Latin *littera*, earlier *lītera*)

compensatory damages *n pl* **:** damages awarded to make good or compensate for an injury sustained — distinguished from *punitive damages*

compensatory interest *n, Roman Dutch law* **:** interest covering the creditor's direct loss from forgoing use of his money

compense *vb* -ED/-ING/-S [ME *compensen*, fr. MF *compenser*, fr. L *compensare* — more at COMPENSATE] *obs* **:** COMPENSATE

¹com·pere \'kämˌpa(a)ə, +V -a(a)(ə)r\ *n* -S [F *compère*, lit., godfather, fr. ML *compater* — more at COMPEER] *chiefly Brit* **:** the master of ceremonies of an entertainment (as a revue or radio program)

²compere \"\ *vb* -ED/-ING/-S *vt, chiefly Brit* **:** CONDUCT ⟨~ a radio program⟩ ~ *vi* **:** to act as a compere ⟨he spent six hours at their studios, rehearsing, editing, and *compering* —*advt*⟩

com·pesce \kəm'pes\ *vt* -ED/-ING/-S [ME *compessen*, fr. L *compescere*, fr. *com-* + *-pescere* (akin to L *parcere* to spare, abstain) — more at PARSIMONY] *archaic Scot* **:** to hold in check **:** RESTRAIN

com·pete \kəm'pēt, *usu* -ēd.+V\ *vi* -ED/-ING/-S [L *competere* to come together, agree, be suitable, belong, compete for, fr. *com-* + *petere* to go to, head for, seek — more at FEATHER] **1 :** to seek or strive for something (as a position, possession, reward) for which others are also contending **:** vie with another or others for or as if for a prize ⟨~ with top-notch performers⟩ ⟨a team that ~*s* against other teams⟩ ⟨~ for top honors⟩ ⟨the children *competed* with one another in seeing who could eat the most⟩ **2 a :** to stand comparison (as in fitness or value) ⟨the steam locomotive could no longer ~ with the diesel⟩ **b :** to come into rivalry esp. in economic value, usefulness, or efficiency ⟨rayon is steadily *competing* with wool in . . . fall and winter clothing —Desmond Reilly⟩

syn CONTEND, CONTEST: COMPETE may indicate simply the fact of struggle to win out over others, or to continue to exist despite the strength and efforts of others, or it may be used in reference to organized contests ⟨New Hampshire cannot *compete* with its neighboring State of Maine in raising potatoes —*Amer. Guide Series: N.H.*⟩ ⟨the dinosaurs were unable to *compete* successfully with the smaller mammals⟩ ⟨only at its best does the drama *compete* with the novel in finalities —Bernard De Voto⟩ ⟨the teams *competing* in the tournament⟩ CONTEND may suggest vigorous striving and struggling against an equal or stronger adversary ⟨a gray stone castle, for whose keep Bruces and Comyns and Macdowalls *contended* seven centuries ago —John Buchan⟩ ⟨two Greek schools of thought, the Stoic and the Epicurean, *contended* for the allegiance of Romans who aspired to philosophy —Benjamin Farrington⟩ ⟨the passions and hopes which he had excited had become too strong for him to *contend* against —J.A.Froude⟩ CONTEST is often a close synonym of COMPETE; typically, it may apply to a struggle that is limited, bounded, and definite in outcome, as a debate, race, match, fight, or battle ⟨New Orleans was . . . *contesting* with New York for first place among American ports —*Amer. Guide Series: Louisiana*⟩

com·pe·tence \'kämpəd·ən(t)s, -pətən- *also* -pətᵊn-\ *n* -S [MF *compétence*, fr. L *competentia* agreement, fr. *competent-*, *competens* (pres. part. of *competere*) + *-ia* -y] **1** *obs* **:** a sufficient supply **:** SUFFICIENCY **2 a :** property or means sufficient for the necessities and conveniences of life **:** sufficiency without excess ⟨his business acumen . . . provided his family with a comfortable ~ —Rex Ingamells⟩ ⟨those who . . . kept their shares . . . reaped ~*s* and small fortunes —Jack Alexander⟩ **b :** the condition of possessing or enjoying such sufficiency ⟨living in peace and ~⟩ **3 a :** the quality or state of being functionally adequate or of having sufficient knowledge, judgment, skill, or strength (as for a particular duty or in a particular respect) ⟨drugs that improve the ~ of a failing heart⟩ **:** range of ability or capability ⟨some ~ in the operation of a drill press⟩ ⟨a technicality beyond his ~ to master⟩; *specif* **:** legal authority, ability, or admissibility ⟨a matter within the ~ of a judge to adjudicate⟩ ⟨the committee has no actual ~ in criminal matters⟩ **b :** legitimacy or validity of a conclusion, logical process, point of view **:** ADEQUACY ⟨the schooled ~ of his observations⟩ **4 :** the ability of a stream to transport detritus as measured by the size of the largest particle, pebble, or boulder it can move forward — compare CAPACITY 1i **5 :** the capacity of living tissue to react; *specif* **:** the sum of the properties that permit a particular embryonic field to respond in a characteristic manner to the influence of an inductor — compare FIELD, INDUCTOR, POTENCY

com·pe·ten·cy \-nsē, -si\ *n* -ES [ML *competentia*, fr. L, agreement] **:** COMPETENCE

com·pe·tent \-nt\ *adj* [ME, suitable, appropriate, fr. MF & L; MF *compétent*, fr. L *competent-*, *competens*] **1 a :** possessed of or characterized by marked or sufficient aptitude, skill, strength, or knowledge **:** SATISFACTORY, ADEQUATE ⟨a ~ portraitist knows how to imply the profile in the full face —Aldous Huxley⟩ **b :** satisfactorily or moderately able **:** without marked weakness or demerit ⟨one way toward the ~ and salable, the other toward excellent and possibly unsalable —H.S.Canby⟩ **c :** possessed of knowledge, judgment, strength, or skill needed to perform an indicated action — followed by an infinitive phrase ⟨one of the finest raiders alive, and most ~ to judge my half-formed scheme —T.E.Lawrence⟩ **2 a** *archaic* **:** appropriate or suitable esp. to a certain social position or rank ⟨a moiety ~ was gaged by our king —Shak.⟩ **b :** proper for or rightly pertinent to **:** rightfully belonging to or exercised by ⟨if it be ~ for our government to segregate and impound one group of law-abiding innocent citizens —A.J.Nock⟩ **3** *geol, of a bed or stratum* **:** strong enough to transmit effectively the thrust when strata are folded by lateral compression and capable of sustaining the weight of overlying strata when arched into an anticline **4 :** legally qualified or capable: as **a :** authorized to act or possessed of jurisdiction ⟨a ~ court⟩ ⟨a ~ judge⟩ **b :** legally qualified in mental and physical makeup ⟨a ~ witness⟩ **c :** meeting legal requirements as to validity ⟨~ evidence⟩ **5** *biol* **:** exhibiting competence **:** FUNCTIONAL **syn** see ABLE, SUFFICIENT

com·pe·tent·ly *adv* [ME, fr. *competent* + *-ly*] **:** in a competent manner

competes *pres 3d sing of* COMPETE

competible *adj* [obs. *compete* to be suitable (fr. L *competere* to be suitable, compete for) + *-ible*] **1** *obs* **:** COMPATIBLE, SUITABLE, APPROPRIATE **2** *obs* **:** COMPETENT — used with *to* or *with*

competing *pres part. of* COMPETE

com·pe·ti·tion \ˌkämpəˈtishən\ *n* -s [LL *competition-, competitio*, fr. L *competitus* (past part. of *competere* to compete for) + *-ion-, -io* -ion — more at COMPETE] **1 :** the act or action of seeking to gain what another is seeking to gain at the same time and usu. under or as if under fair or equitable rules and circumstances **:** a common struggle for the same object esp. among individuals of relatively equal standing **:** RIVALRY ⟨to prevent the realization that cooperation, not ~, is the road to happiness —Bertrand Russell⟩ **2 :** a contest between rivals **:** a match or trial between contestants ⟨a ~ in essay writing⟩ ⟨a high-diving ~⟩ **3 :** RIVAL, COMPETITOR **4 a :** the effort of two or more parties to secure the custom of a third party by the offer of the most favorable terms **b :** a market condition in which a large number of independent buyers and sellers compete for identical commodities, deal freely with each other, and retain the right of entry and exit from the market **5 :** more or less active demand by two or more organisms or kinds of organisms at the same time for some environmental resource in excess of the supply available, typically resulting in ultimate elimination of the less effective organism from the particular ecologic niche

com·pe·ti·tion·er \-sh(ə)nə(r)\ *n* -s **:** one that competes (as to achieve an official position or entrance into a service)

com·pet·i·tive \kəmˈped·əd·|iv, -etət| *also* |əv\ *adj* [*competit-* (as in *competitor*) + *-ive*] **:** of or relating to competition: as **a :** characterized by, arising from, or designated to exhibit rivalry among two or more equally matched individuals or forces esp. for a particular goal, position, or reward ⟨~ sports⟩ ⟨~ spirit⟩ ⟨~ tactics⟩ ⟨~ examinations⟩ **b :** produced by, based on, resulting from, or capable of existing in rivalry of economic endeavor and without the presence of monopoly or collusion ⟨a ~ market⟩ ⟨~ bids⟩ ⟨~ prices⟩ ⟨chemical cotton prices are now ~ with wood pulp —*Wall Street Jour.*⟩ — **com·pet·i·tive·ly** *adv* — **com·pet·i·tive·ness** *n* -ES

competitive point *n* **:** a transportation point served by two or more independent lines

com·pet·i·tor \kəmˈped·əd·ə(r), -etətə(r) *also* -ed·əˌtȯ(ə)r *or* -etəˌtȯ(ə)r *or* -ˌtȯ(ə)r\ *n* -s [MF *compétiteur*, fr. L *competitor*, fr. *competitus* (past part. of *competere* to compete for) + *-or*] **1 a :** one that seeks what another seeks or claims what another claims **:** RIVAL; *esp* **:** one on equal footing with another rival or other rivals ⟨a ~ in an election⟩ ⟨a born ~⟩ ⟨a ~ nation⟩ **b :** an organism or kind of organism that lives in competition with another **2 :** one that is engaged in selling or buying goods or services in the same market as another **3** *obs* **:** ASSOCIATE, CONFEDERATE

com·pet·i·to·ry \-ed·əˌtōrē, -etə-,-\ *adj* [*competit-* (as in *competitor*) + *-ory*] **:** COMPETITIVE

com·pi·la·tion \ˌkämpəˈlāshən\ *n* -s [ME *compilacioun*, fr. MF & L; MF *compilation*, fr. L *compilation-, compilatio*, fr. *compilatus* (past part. of *compilare*) + *-ion-, -io* -ion] **1 :** the act or action of gathering together written material esp. from various sources ⟨the slow ~ of data⟩ **2 :** something that is a product of the putting together of two or more items: as **a :** a book or document composed of materials gathered from other books or documents ⟨"Italian Cooking" . . . is a businesslike ~ of Italian dishes —Mary Poore⟩ ⟨a ~ of the best bibliography in the field of agriculture or natural sciences —Helen T. Geer⟩ **b :** an accumulation of many things, elements, or influences **:** ACCRETION ⟨a ~ of detrital matter⟩ ⟨like most architecture erected since the Gothic age . . . a ~ rather than a design —Thomas Hardy⟩

com·pi·la·tor \ˈkämpəˌlād·ə(r), -ātə-\ *n* -s [ME *compilatour*, fr. LL *compilator* plunderer, plagiarist, fr. L *compilatus* + *-or*] **:** one that compiles **:** COMPILER

com·pi·la·to·ry \kəmˈpīləˌtōrē, -ˈpil-; ˈkämpələ-\ *adj* [*compilat-* (as in *compilator*) + *-ory*] **:** of, relating to, or being compilation ⟨a work ~ in nature and not truly original⟩ **:** of or relating to a compiler ⟨~ techniques⟩

com·pile \kəmˈpīl, *esp before pause or consonant* -īəl\ *vt* -ED/-ING/-S [ME *compilen*, fr. MF *compiler*, fr. L *compilare* to plunder, rob, fr. *com-* + *-pilare* (perh. akin to L *pila* pillar, pier) — more at PILE] **1 :** to collect and assemble (written material or items from various sources) into a document or volume or a series of documents or volumes ⟨~ authoritative books as well as numerous articles —W.M.Emery⟩ ⟨~ a weather map⟩ ⟨~ a statistical chart⟩ **2** *obs* **:** to compose as an original literary work ⟨~ sharp satires —Christopher Marlowe⟩ **3 a :** to put together ⟨"chlorophyll", a name *compiled* from the Greek words for "green-leaf" —W.E.Swinton⟩ **b :** to pile up ⟨~ a great majority of votes⟩ **:** LIST, ENUMERATE ⟨a whole literature on him that ~s defects as well as virtues⟩

compiled map *n* **:** a small-scale map developed from data not obtained from original surveys conducted in the field

com·pile·ment \-ī(ə)lmənt\ *n* -s *archaic* **:** COMPILATION

com·pil·er \-īlə(r)\ *n* -s [ME *compilour*, fr. MF *compileur*, fr. LL *compilator*] **:** one that compiles: as **a :** a person who assembles items of information for publication ⟨a ~ of maps⟩ ⟨a ~ of specialized bibliographies⟩ **b :** a person who develops mailing lists for advertisers or gathers and arranges information of a variety of types for use in publications (as catalogs and directories)

comping *pres part of* COMP

com·pi·tal \ˈkämpəd·ᵊl\ *adj* [L *compitalis* of crossroads, fr. *compitum* crossroads + *-alis* -al; akin to L *competere* to come together — more at COMPETE] **1** *of a leaf vein* **:** intersecting at a broad angle **2** *of a fern* **:** having the sori borne at the junction of two veins

com·pla·cence \kəmˈplāsᵊn(t)s\ *n* -s [ME, fr. ML *complacentia* satisfaction, good will, pleasure, fr. L *complacent-, complacens* + *-ia* -y] **1 :** calm or secure satisfaction with one's self or lot **:** SELF-SATISFACTION ⟨the general's bovine ~ at being after all a general⟩ **2** *obs* **a :** PLEASURE, SATISFACTION **b :** a source of gratification or joy **3** *obs* **:** disposition to give satisfaction: AFFABILITY, COMPLAISANCE

com·pla·cen·cy \-ᵊnsē, -si\ *n* -ES [ML *complacentia*] **1 a :** the quality or state of being satisfied **:** a calm sense of well-being and security ⟨any momentary ~ was generally sternly dispelled by the harsh criticism of the coach —A.C.Benson⟩; *esp* **:** satisfaction or self-satisfaction accompanied by unawareness of actual dangers or deficiencies ⟨a ~ doubtless engendered by railroading and banking —*Amer. Guide Series: Minn.*⟩ ⟨the immense ~ of our population about civil defense —Reinhold Niebuhr⟩ ⟨~ in the performance of her car⟩ **b :** SELF-SATISFACTION, VANITY ⟨his candor was . . . coated with ~ —John Woodburn⟩ **2** *archaic* **:** complaisance or an instance thereof **3** *obs* **:** passive acquiescence **4** *archaic* **:** PLEASURE, DELIGHT

com·pla·cent \-ᵊnt\ *adj* [L *complacent-, complacens* very pleasing, pres. part. of *complacēre* to please greatly, fr. *com-* + *placēre* to please — more at PLEASE] **1 a :** marked by sometimes unwarranted, uncritical, and irritating satisfaction and pleasure at one's own personality, accomplishments, or situation ⟨~ when they should have been self-critical —Allan Nevins & H.S.Commager⟩ ⟨the ~ ones, to those who love themselves much but not too well —M.R.Cohen⟩ **b :** marked by or as if by unruffled or blasé satisfaction about the security of one's position or by careless acceptance of events around one **:** disinclined to act, to change, or to guard ⟨the ~ case of obesity —Arnold Bennett⟩ ⟨in that ~ old world . . . youth did not easily feel the impact of national problems —John Buchan⟩ **2 a :** feeling or showing complaisance or desire to please ⟨the University of Colorado courteously released me from my contract, but the Garrett Biblical Institute was less ~ —R.M.Lovett⟩ **b :** marked by smooth even contented ease without notable activity, tension, or stress ⟨townfolk made a ~ living by trading with countryfolk —*Amer. Guide Series: Texas*⟩ **3** *of a tree or a forest* **:** marked by evenness and regularity in the growth of annual rings regardless of different conditions in different years — opposed to *sensitive*

syn SELF-COMPLACENT, SELF-SATISFIED, SMUG, PRIGGISH: COMPLACENT may imply a feeling of assured well-being and absence of worry or complaint ⟨the people who suffer most from their conscience are obviously the sensitive and high-minded, while self-approbation comes most easily to the *complacent* and fortune-favored Jack Horners —M.R.Cohen⟩ It may suggest a gloating superiority or a blameworthy lassitude and lack of drive ⟨his insufferable smile was more *complacent* than ever —A. Conan Doyle⟩ ⟨the chief occasion on which he aspired to rise above the level of *complacent* mediocrity —H.E.Nettles⟩ SELF-COMPLACENT and SELF-SATISFIED stress satisfaction at one's own personality or situation and may suggest ill-based pride, self-deception, depreciation of others, indolent or blind inactivity ⟨the strong, *self-complacent* Luther declares . . . that "God himself cannot do without wise men" —R.W.Emerson⟩ ⟨those flaunting childish family portraits, with their farce of sentiment and smiling lies, and innocence so self-conscious and *self-satisfied* —W.M. Thackeray⟩ ⟨Stroeve, eager for praise and naively *self-satisfied*, could never resist displaying his work —W.S.Maugham⟩ SMUG indicates accustomed feelings about oneself of superiority, rectitude, or utter security ⟨our *smug* conviction that somehow we are more virtuous than the rest of the world, and that everyone should realize it —Richard Watts⟩ ⟨a *smug* and arrogant look about him, as is often the case with men who have unexpectedly acquired great power or great wealth —Kenneth Roberts⟩ SMUG often suggests narrow provincialism. PRIGGISH may suggest finical adherence to one's ideas or notions, perhaps ill-based, and an odious self-righteousness ⟨there is something artificial and even *priggish* about Goethe's healthiness, as there is about Baudelaire's unhealthiness —T.S.Eliot⟩ ⟨that unpromising young man with high collar and pince-nez whose somewhat *priggish* air of superiority infuriated most of the Democrats —A.M.Schlesinger b.1917⟩

complacential *adj* [ML *complacentia* + E *-al*] *obs* **:** COMPLAISANT

com·pla·cent·ly \kəmˈplāsᵊntlē, -li\ *adv* **:** in a complacent manner

¹com·plain \kəmˈplān\ *vb* -ED/-ING/-S [ME *compleynen*, fr. MF *compleindre, complaindre* (3d pers. pl. pres. indic. *complaignent*), fr. (assumed) VL *complangere*, fr. L *com-* + *plangere* to beat, beat the breast, lament — more at PLAINT] *vi* **1** *obs* **:** to express sorrow with weeping and outcry **:** LAMENT **2 a :** to express discontent, dissatisfaction, protest, resentment, or regret usu. without recalcitrance or threat and as though expecting sympathy ⟨began to ~ of it and lament her being ill-used —Jane Austen⟩ ⟨his troubles were really little ones. He had nothing to ~ about —Lenard Kaufman⟩ **b** (1) *archaic* **:** to be ailing (2) **:** to speak of one's illness or symptoms **3 :** to make a formal accusation, charge, or complaint ⟨the French consulate and the English consulate had ~*ed* of him . . . charging him with being high-handed —Louis Bromfield⟩ **4 :** to groan, creak, or make an otherwise mournful sound as though protesting or lamenting ⟨the overloaded wagon ~*ing* at each turn⟩ **~** *vt* **1** *obs* **:** LAMENT **:** weep at **:** BEWAIL **2 :** to say or relate with dissatisfaction, protest, or regret as though expecting sympathy or redress ⟨Cotton Mather ~*ed*, "'Tis dreadful cold, my ink glass . . . is froze" —*Amer. Guide Series: Mass.*⟩ ⟨if we ~ that so vague a term fails to do justice —Edward Sapir⟩

syn REPINE, GRUMBLE, GROUSE, BEEF, GRIPE, CROAK, SQUAWK, BELLYACHE: COMPLAIN, which orig. meant lamenting or bewailing, is now a general term for uttering unhappiness or discontent; it may indicate that a sympathetic reaction is expected or feasible ⟨a voice *complaining* . . . a venomous and senile whimper —Jean Stafford⟩ ⟨he had heard Ed *complaining* of his lot in life and crying out for new times —Sherwood Anderson⟩ ⟨when the people *complain*, said Mirabeau, the people are always right —J.A.Froude⟩ REPINE, now always bookish or literary, may suggest querulous plaintiveness ⟨his old age may have been monotonous, but there was no *repining* about it —Brand Blanshard⟩ In contrast, the following words range from the echoic suggestion of GRUMBLE to the slang form BELLYACHE. GRUMBLE suggests discontented muttering, often from a personality hard to satisfy and given to ill-natured complaint ⟨the way people *grumble* about their rates and taxes —G.B.Shaw⟩ ⟨reluctant laughter and *grumbling* thanks —Kenneth Roberts⟩ GROUSE may be applied to sustained forceful grumbling at annoyances ⟨soldiers *grousing* about their food⟩ ⟨never once have I heard him *grouse* about how tough things are —*Saturday Rev.*⟩ BEEF may suggest angry or emphatic complaint ⟨the *beefing* and clamoring by certain groups for a change —*New Republic*⟩ ⟨a few who have drilled . . . *beef* about being kept in uniform —Dixon Wecter⟩ GRIPE may suggest continued strong grumbling or criticizing, as though motivated by being griped ⟨after two or three days in the Army, he *gripes* like a veteran at the brass, the shavetails, the chow —*Christian Science Monitor*⟩ CROAK, SQUAWK, and BELLYACHE may imply lack of sympathy with the complainer. CROAK may suggest pessimistic, doleful, dismal complaining, SQUAWK a loud raucous outcry, as of a fowl, perhaps ineffective, and BELLYACHE a peevish or disgruntled whining ⟨the little old lady in black . . . tells you how just last fall her husband died in Ohio, and damp mists her glasses; she blinks and *croaks* —R.P.Warren⟩ ⟨the first industries to be hit by the credit curbs have *squawked* —*Atlantic*⟩ ⟨*bellyaching* about rationing, curtailment of civilian goods, administrative confusion, and various other annoyances —*Harper's*⟩

²complain \"\ *n* -s [ME *compleyn*, fr. *compleynen*, v.] *archaic* **:** COMPLAINT

¹com·plain·ant \-nənt\ *adj* [ME *compleynant*, fr. MF *complaignant*, pres. part. of *complaindre*] **:** COMPLAINING

²complainant \"\ *n* -s [ME *compleynant*, fr. MF *complaignant*, fr. *complaignant*, adj.] **1 :** the party who makes the complaint in a legal action or proceeding; *esp* **:** the party filing the bill in equity pleading — compare PLAINTIFF **2** *archaic* **:** one that complains

com·plain·er \-ānə(r)\ *n* -s **:** one that complains ⟨a chronic ~⟩; *specif*, *Scot* **:** COMPLAINANT 1

com·plain·ing·ly *adv* **:** in a complaining manner

com·plain·ing·ness *n* -ES **:** DISCONTENT

com·plaint \kəmˈplānt\ *n* -s [ME *compleynte*, fr. MF *complainte*, fr. OF, fr. fem. of *complaint*, past part. of *complaindre*] **1 a** *obs* **:** a cry or loud utterance or series of utterances of pain, rage, or sorrow **:** grieved or sorrowful outcry **b :** a formerly popular poem that laments or protests unrequited love or tells of personal misfortune, misery, or injustice **c :** the act or action of expressing protest, censure, or resentment **:** expression of injustice ⟨a ~ about poor housing⟩ ⟨on ~ of neighbors action was taken⟩ **d :** formal allegation or charge against a party made or presented to the appropriate court or officer (as for a wrong done or a crime committed) and variously applied (as to the initial bill in proceedings in equity, the declaration in a common-law pleading, the statement of claim under the English practice acts, and the initial pleading under the code practice in various states of the U.S.) **2 a :** something that is the cause or subject of protest or grieved outcry ⟨lack of efficiency is the ~ of all who wish to better government⟩ **b :** an ailment or disease of the body ⟨given to taking all sorts of medicine for vague ~*s* —Morris Fishbein⟩

com·plaint·ive \-ntiv\ *adj* **:** prone to complain ⟨a ~ patient⟩

com·plai·sance \kəmˈplāsᵊn|(t)s *also* kəmˈplāzᵊn|(t)s *or* ˈkämpləˌzan|(t)s *or* -plə,z- *or* -ˌzaa(ə)n- *or* -ˌzän- *or* -ˌzän- *or* ,==\ *n* -s [F, fr. MF, fr. ML *complacentia* satisfaction, good will, pleasure — more at COMPLACENCE] **:** ready disposition to please (as by acceding to another's wishes) **:** pleasing ingratiating deportment ⟨with that ~ from which a stranger generally infers that he is welcome —William Cowper⟩

com·plai·sant \|t\ *adj* [F, fr. MF, pres. part. of *complaire* to acquiesce as a favor, gratify, fr. L *complacēre* to please greatly — more at COMPLACENT] **1 :** marked by an inclination to please or oblige or by courteous agreeability ⟨amid very ~ smiles and general encouragement —*Jane Austen*⟩ **2 :** marked by a willingness to please or serve others, to consent to their wishes, or to lend oneself compliantly to their purposes ⟨boss-ridden conventions turned him down for more ~ candidates —Allan Nevins & H.S.Commager⟩ **syn** see AMIABLE

com·plai·sant·ly *adv* **:** in a complaisant manner

com·pla·nate \ˈkämpləˌnāt\ *adj* [L *complanatus*, past part. of *complanare* to make even, make level, fr. *com-* + *-planare* (fr. *planus* level, flat) — more at FLOOR] **:** made level **:** in one plane ⟨~ leaves⟩ **:** FLATTENED

com·pla·na·tion \ˌkämpləˈnāshən\ *n* -s [L *complanare* + E *-ation*] **:** a leveling off **:** flattening out

compleat *archaic var of* COMPLETE

complect *vt* -ED/-ING/-S [L *complecti* — more at COMPLEX] *obs* **:** INTERTWINE, EMBRACE; *esp* **:** to plait together **:** INTERWEAVE

com·plect·ed \kəmˈplektəd\ *adj* [*complect-* (irreg. fr. *complexion*) + *-ed*] **:** COMPLEXIONED — usu. used in combination ⟨dark-*complected*⟩; not often in formal use

complection *var of* COMPLEXION

¹com·ple·ment \ˈkämpləmənt\ *n* -s [ME, fr. L *complementum*, fr. *complēre* to fill up, complete + *-mentum* -ment — more at COMPLETE] **1 :** something that fills up or completes: as **a :** something that fills out and makes perfect **:** a completing or consummating part, integral, or component **:** COMPLETION ⟨a European tour was then the necessary ~ of a gentle upbringing and a liberal education⟩ ⟨although Bergson often represented intuition as a ~ to reason, he as often separated and opposed them —H.J.Muller⟩ **b :** the quantity or number required to fill a thing or make it complete **:** full allowance ⟨a farm with a full ~ of stock⟩ ⟨a platoon with its normal ~ of weapons⟩ ⟨the usual ~ of office personnel⟩ **c :** the necessary and completing opposing item **:** one of two mutually completing parts **:** COUNTERPART ⟨he had found someone whose . . . masculinity was the very ~ of his own fragile graces —H.V.Gregory⟩ ⟨some kind of school was the ~ of each meetinghouse —*Amer. Guide Series: N. C.*⟩ **2** *obs* **a :** the act or action of fulfilling or making up **b :** the quality or state of being complete **3 a :** the amount of angle or arc by which a given angle or arc falls short of 90° **b :** ¹MINOR 4 **c :** the numerical amount that must be added to a number to give the least number containing one more digit ⟨the ~ of 4 is 6 and that of 45 is 55⟩ **4** *obs* **a :** something added for equipping or ornamentation esp. of the person **:** ACCESSORY **b :** a social quality or accomplishment **c :** a ceremonial or courteous observance that rounds off a service or action or the deportment of an individual **5 :** the whole force or personnel of a ship; *specif* **:** the entire force of officers and crew allowed to a naval vessel for wartime operations **6** *heraldry* **:** fullness of the moon **7 :** the interval in music required with a given interval to complete the octave **8 :** an added word by which a predication is made complete (as *president* in "they elected him president" or *white* in "he painted the house white") **9 :** a complementary color **10 :** the thermolabile substance in normal blood serum and plasma that in combination with antibodies causes the destruction of bacteria, foreign blood corpuscles, and other antigens **11** *logic* **:** the negate of a given class *a* or statement *p*

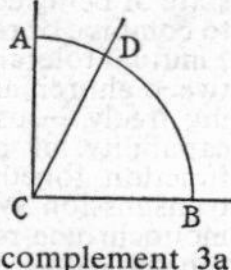

complement 3a: *ACB* right angle; *ACD* complement of *DCB* (and vice versa); *AD* complement of *DB* (and vice versa)

²com·ple·ment \-ˌment,-ˌmənt — *see* ²-MENT\ *vb* -ED/-ING/-S *vt* **1 :** to fill in or make up (what is lacking) **:** round off ⟨the museum is ~*ed* by a spacious garden —*Amer. Guide Series: Mich.*⟩ ⟨your chosen perfume ~*s* your personality —D.S.Lyle⟩ **2** *obs* **:** COMPLIMENT **~** *vi, obs* **:** COMPLIMENT

com·ple·men·tal \ˌkämpləˈmentᵊl\ *adj* **:** that has to do with a complement: as **a :** SUPPLEMENTAL, COMPLETING ⟨should the primary king or queen termite die, there are ~ ones to take their place —*Nature Mag.*⟩ **b** *obs* **:** ACCOMPLISHED **c** *obs* **:** CEREMONIOUS, COMPLIMENTARY

complemental air *n* **:** the quantity of air (about 3000 cubic centimeters) that can be inhaled in addition to one's tidal air

complementally *adv, obs* **:** in a ceremonious manner

complemental male *n* **:** a minute modified male barnacle that lives attached to certain hermaphroditic barnacles

com·ple·men·ta·ri·ness \ˌkämpləˈmentərēnəs, -en·trē-, -rin-\ *n* -ES **:** the quality or state of being complementary

com·ple·men·tar·i·ty \ˌkämplə(ˌ)menˈtarəd·ē, -ləmən-\ *n* -ES [*complementary* + *-ity*] **1 :** the interrelationship or the completion or perfection brought about by the interrelationship of one or more units supplementing, being dependent upon, or standing in polar position to another unit or other units ⟨the ~ of the sexes⟩ ⟨the ~ of nature and art⟩ **2 :** the complementary relationship of the electromagnetic wave and corpuscular theories in explaining the dual character of light and other quantized radiation **3 :** correspondence in reverse of part of one molecule to part of another; *esp* **:** the complementary arrangement of chemical groups and electric charges that enables a combining group of an antibody to combine with a specific determinant group of an antigen or hapten

¹com·ple·men·ta·ry \ˌkämpləˈmentərē, -n·trē, -ri\ *adj* [F *complémentaire*, fr. *complément* complement (fr. L *complementum*) + *-aire* -ary] **1 :** of, relating to, or suggestive of complementing, completing, or perfecting ⟨their economies are more ~ than competitive —William Petersen⟩ ⟨participation . . . as ~ to observation —Lewis Mumford⟩ **2 :** mutually dependent **:** supplementing and being supplemented in return ⟨farmer and townsman represent ~ interests —*Farmer's Weekly (So. Africa)*⟩ **3 :** being one of a pair of chromatic stimuli that produce an achromatic mixture when combined in suitable proportions ⟨a ~ color⟩ **4 :** serving as a grammatical complement ⟨a ~ infinitive⟩ **5 :** of or relating to sets of small bodies of igneous rock varying in composition that accompany large masses from which they were derived by differentiation ⟨aplites and other ~ dikes⟩ **6 :** related in relatively fixed proportions ⟨some pairs of commodities are ~ so that the consumer uses more of one the more he uses of the other —G.J. Stigler⟩ **7 :** of or relating to the negate of a given class or statement ⟨the ~ property to blue . . . is not blue —A.J.Ayer⟩ or to two classes or statements each of which is the negation of the other

²complementary \"\ *n* -ES **:** something that stands in a complementary relationship; *esp* **:** a complementary color

complementary afterimage *n* **:** a chromatic afterimage having a hue approximately the hue complementary to that of the sensation produced by the original stimulus — called also *negative afterimage*

complementary air *n* **:** COMPLEMENTAL AIR

complementary angles *n pl* **:** two angles whose sum is a right angle

complementary cell *n* **:** any of the loosely arranged cells in a lenticel — compare CLOSING LAYER

complementary distribution *n* **:** a distribution of a pair of speech sounds or a pair of linguistic forms such that the one is found only in environments where the other is not (as the unaspirated *t* of English *stone* and the aspirated *t* of English *tone* or English *your* occurring before a noun, *yours* in all other environments), esp. when used as a basic prerequisite for the classification of nonidentical sounds as allophones of the same phoneme or for the classification of nonidentical linguistic forms as allomorphs of the same morpheme

complementary function *n* **:** the general solution of the auxiliary equation of a linear differential equation

complementary gene *or* **complementary factor** *n* **:** one of two or more genes that when present together produce effects qualitatively distinct from the separate effect of any one of them

complementary male *n* **:** COMPLEMENTAL MALE

complementary pit *n* **:** a pit in one cell of many higher vascular plants complementary to another in an adjacent cell — compare PIT-PAIR

complementary wavelength *n* **:** wavelength of the portion of the visible spectrum required to produce achromatic color by additive mixture with a sample color — see COLOR 1c

com·ple·men·ta·tion \ˌkämpləmənˈtāshən, -lə(ˌ)men-\ *n* -s **1 :** the formation of neutral colors from complementaries **2 :** COMPLEMENTARY DISTRIBUTION **3** *logic* **:** the forming of a complement or negate specif. of a class

complemented *past of* COMPLEMENT

complement fixation *n* **:** the absorption of complement to the compound formed by the union of an antibody and the antigen for which it is specific occurring when complement is added to a mixture (in proper proportion) of such an antibody and antigen

complement-fixation test *n* **:** a test for the presence of a particular antibody made by addition of complement and an indicator system to a mixture of known antigen and a serum suspected to contain the specific antibody for this antigen and used esp. in the diagnosis of syphilis — see WASSERMANN TEST

complementing *pres part of* COMPLEMENT

complements *pl of* COMPLEMENT, *pres 3d sing of* COMPLEMENT

¹com·plete \kəm'plēt, *usu* -ēd.+V\ *adj, often* -ER/-EST [ME *complet,* fr. MF, fr. L *completus,* past part. of *complēre* to fill up, fr. *com-* + *plēre* to fill; akin to L *plenus* full — more at FULL] **1 a :** possessing all necessary parts, items, components, or elements **:** not lacking anything necessary **:** ENTIRE, PERFECT ⟨few households would regard breakfast ~ without a plate of porridge —L.D.Stamp⟩ ⟨this man . . . ~ with wings and four stripes on his uniform sleeve —E.K.Gann⟩ ⟨neither one of these publications gives the ~ poems of Smart —A.R.Benham⟩ **b :** having all four sets of floral organs — compare INCOMPLETE, MONOCLINOUS **c** (1) *of a subject or predicate* **:** including modifiers, complements, or objects if any ⟨in the sentence "the little boy hit the ball hard" *the little boy* is the ~ subject and *hit the ball hard* is the ~ predicate⟩ — compare SIMPLE (2) *of a verb* **:** filling out a predication without any object or complement ⟨*moved* in "the train moved" is a ~ verb⟩ **d** *of a diet or ration* **:** BALANCED **2 :** brought to an end or to a final or intended condition ⟨a ~ period of time⟩ ⟨a ~ act⟩ **:** CONCLUDED, COMPLETED ⟨five ~ days⟩ ⟨a ~ revolution⟩ **3** *of a person* **:** possessed of all necessary, usual, or typical qualities, habits, or accomplishments ⟨a ~ man⟩ ⟨a ~ gentleman⟩ ⟨a ~ Englishman⟩; *specif* **:** highly proficient (as in an art or skill) ⟨a ~ landscape artist⟩ ⟨a ~ horseman⟩ **4 :** fully realized **:** carried to the ultimate **:** THOROUGH, TOTAL ⟨in ~ sympathy with his views⟩ ⟨~ surrender⟩ ⟨his ~ inability to understand⟩

²complete \"\ *vt* -ED/-ING/-S **1 :** to bring to an end often into or as if into a finished or perfected state ⟨foolish to put his hand to a task which he could not ~ —John Buchan⟩; *specif* **:** to execute (a forward pass) successfully ⟨State *completed* 10 of 19 passes while Rutgers made good 4 of 10 —*N.Y. Times*⟩ **2 a :** to make whole, entire, or perfect **:** end after satisfying all demands or requirements ⟨art partly ~*s* what nature is herself sometimes unable to bring to perfection —Havelock Ellis⟩ **b :** to mark the end of **:** show attainment to the total or totality of ⟨small mammals, birds, and tropical fish . . . ~ the zoo exhibits —*Amer. Guide Series: N.Y.City*⟩ **c :** ACCOMPLISH, EXECUTE, FULFILL ⟨~ a contract⟩ ⟨a vow *completed*⟩ **d :** CONSUMMATE ⟨allowed the lovers to ~ their marriage —G.M.Trevelyan⟩ **syn** see CLOSE

com·plet·ed·ness *n* -ES **:** COMPLETENESS

complete fertilizer *n* **:** a fertilizer that contains the three primary plant nutrients (nitrogen, phosphoric acid, and potash)

complete integral *n* **:** a solution of a partial differential equation of the first order that contains as many arbitrary constants as there are independent variables

com·plete·ly *adv* **1 :** so as to be complete **:** FULLY ⟨a ~ furnished apartment⟩ **2 :** to a complete degree **:** ENTIRELY ⟨the horse rolled ~ over⟩ ⟨~ at fault⟩

com·plete·ment \-tmənt\ *n* -S **:** COMPLETION ⟨together we have all the elements of ~ —Betty Smith⟩

com·plete·ness \-tnəs\ *n* -ES **1 :** the quality or state of being complete **2** *of an axiomatized system of logic* **:** the state of being so constituted that a contradiction arises through the addition of any formula not previously deducible from the axioms of the system

complete pair *n* **:** CLOSED PAIR

complete primitive *n* **:** the complete integral regarded as the basis of the differential equation

complete quadrilateral *n* **:** a figure that is determined by four coplanar lines, and has four sides and three diagonal axes, each two of which cut the other harmonically in three centers of which one or even two may be at infinity

complete quadrilateral: *AB, BC, CD, DA* sides; *AC, BD, EF* axes

complete solution *n* **:** GENERAL SOLUTION

complete stop *n* **:** a set of organ pipes extending throughout the compass of the manual

com·ple·tion \kəm'plēshən\ *n* -S [L *completion-, completio* filling, fr. *completus* (past part. of *complēre* to complete) + *-ion-, -io* -ion — more at ¹COMPLETE] **1 :** the act or action of completing, becoming complete, or making complete ⟨his ~ of the late artist's unfinished masterpiece⟩; *specif* **:** a forward pass caught by the receiver ⟨out of 10 attempted passes, there were 5 ~*s*⟩ **2 :** the quality or state of being complete **:** FULFILLMENT ⟨his desires having reached ~⟩

completion test *n* **:** an intelligence test requiring that the one to be tested complete a whole (as a sentence or picture) from which certain parts have been omitted

com·ple·tive \kəm'plēd·iv\ *adj* [LL *completivus,* fr. L *completus* + *-ivus* -ive] **:** serving or tending to complete ⟨annotations ~ of the test⟩; *specif, of a verbal aspect* **:** expressing completion of an action — **com·ple·tive·ly** \-d·əvlē\ *adv*

¹com·ple·to·ry \-d·ərē\ *n* -ES [ME *completorie,* fr. LL *completorium,* fr. L *completus* + *-orium*] **:** COMPLINE

²completory \"\ *adj* [²*complete* + *-ory*] **:** COMPLETIVE

¹com·plex \(')kəm'pleks, kəm'p-\ *vt* -ED/-ING/-ES [L *complexus,* past part. of *complecti*] **1 :** to make complex or into a complex ⟨a ~*ing* problem⟩ **2 :** ²CHELATE

²complex \"\ *adj, sometimes* -ER/-EST [L *complexus,* past part. of *complecti* to entwine around, embrace, fr. *com-* + *plectere* to braid — more at PLY] **1 a :** composed of two or more separable or analyzable items, parts, constituents, or symbols **:** COMPOSITE — opposed to *simple* ⟨the ~ sign "2 × 5=10" —A.J.Ayer⟩ ⟨the sea is a ~ mixture of chemicals —W.H. Dowdeswell⟩ **b** (1) *of a word* **:** having a bound form as one or both of its immediate constituents ⟨*unmanly* is a ~ word⟩ — contrasted with *compound, simple* (2) *of a sentence* **:** consisting of a main clause and one or more subordinate clauses ⟨*make hay while the sun shines* is a ~ sentence⟩ — contrasted with *compound, simple* **2 a :** having many varied interrelated parts, patterns, or elements and consequently hard to understand fully ⟨a ~ camera with many attachments⟩ ⟨a ~ industrial process⟩ ⟨~ tissue⟩ **b :** marked by an involvement of many parts, aspects, details, notions, and necessitating earnest study or examination to understand or cope with ⟨an extremely ~ industrial and commercial enterprise far removed from the simplicities of farming —*Amer. Guide Series: Calif.*⟩ ⟨movements as vast and ~ as the migration of peoples —Lewis Mumford⟩ ⟨a ~ mass of diverse laws and customs, written and unwritten —H.O.Taylor⟩ **3 :** formed by union of simpler substances (as compounds or ions) — used of salts, ions, and other chemical combinations ⟨a ~ protein⟩

syn COMPLICATED, INTRICATE, KNOTTY, INVOLVED: COMPLEX stresses the fact of combining or folding together various parts and suggests that considerable study, knowledge, or experience is needed for comprehension or operation ⟨all legal definitions are highly *complex* —C.K.Ogden & I.A.Richards⟩ ⟨the *complex* details of naval, ground, and air activities —F.D.Roosevelt⟩ ⟨a *complex* apparatus of washers, scales, slicers, diffusion tanks, purifiers, filter presses, evaporators, vacuum pans, centrifugal machines, and driers —*Amer. Guide Series: Calif.*⟩ COMPLICATED may heighten notions of difficulty in understanding ⟨business so big and *complicated* that neither the propertied class nor the working class could understand it —G.B.Shaw⟩ INTRICATE suggests difficulty of understanding or appreciating quickly because of perplexing interconnecting, interweaving, or interacting of parts ⟨the economic situation is so complex, so *intricate* in the interdependence of delicately balanced factors —John Dewey⟩ ⟨complex in themselves, and *intricate* in their interaction —H.O.Taylor⟩ KNOTTY suggests so much perplexity, difficulty, or entanglement that solution or understanding is improbable ⟨many *knotty* problems . . . that it will require the combined resources of the linguist, the logician, the psychologist, and the critical philosopher to clear up for us —Edward Sapir⟩ ⟨your question . . . is a *knotty* one, and such as, had I the wisdom of Solomon, I should be puzzled to answer —William Cowper⟩ INVOLVED indicates an intertwining such that some parts return or seem to return upon themselves, as in certain difficult knots, making unraveling or understanding very hard ⟨public issues are so large and so *involved* that it is only a few who can hope to have any adequate comprehension of them —G.L.Dickinson⟩

³com·plex \'käm,pleks *also* 'ₛ'ₛ *sometimes* ₛ'ₛ\ *n* -ES [L *complexus* surrounding, embrace, fr. *complexus,* past part. of *complecti*] **1 :** an association of related things often in intricate combination: as **a :** a group of culture traits relating to a single activity (as hunting, maize growing, pottery making), process (as the use of flint, construction of megalithic monuments), or unit of culture (as Folsom, neo-Eskimo) **:** an aggregate of artifacts — called also *culture complex, trait-complex* **b** [G *komplex,* fr. L *complexus*] **:** a system of repressed or suppressed desires and memories that exerts a dominating influence upon the personality; *broadly* **:** exaggerated reaction (as of fear or sensitiveness) to some subject or situation ⟨she has always had a ~ about bugs⟩ **c :** a group of obviously related units (as of species) of which the degree and nature of the relationship is imperfectly known **d** (1) **:** a haploid chromosome set containing a specified set of genes arranged in a particular order (2) **:** a group of chromosomes that always pass together in meiosis to one daughter cell — compare GENOME **e :** a group of kinds of organisms (as clones, strains, or varieties) showing common adaptation of a particular kind, usu. to a specialized environment **2 :** a conjunction of varied contributing or interacting factors, elements, or qualities: as **a :** a complex substance (as a coordination compound, an ion containing several atoms, or an adsorption compound) ⟨molecular ~*es*⟩ ⟨enzyme-substrate ~⟩ — usu. distinguished from *mixture* **b :** an assemblage of different rocks having structural relations intricately involved ⟨the Archean ~⟩ **c :** a complex word — contrasted with *compound, simplex* **d :** the sum of factors (as symptoms and lesions) characteristic of a disease ⟨symptom ~⟩ ⟨primary tuberculous ~⟩ **syn** see SYSTEM

complexed *past of* COMPLEX

com·plexed·ness \kəm'pleksədnəs, -ks(t)nəs\ *n* -ES **:** COMPLEXITY

complexer *comparative of* COMPLEX

complexes *pres 3d sing of* COMPLEX, *pl of* COMPLEX

complexest *superlative of* COMPLEX

complex fraction *n* **:** a fraction having a fraction or mixed number in the numerator or denominator or in each — called also *compound fraction*

complex function *n* **:** a function of the complex variable

complex idea *n* **:** an idea formed by the mind out of simple ideas known by sensation and reflection

com·plex·i·fy \kăm'pleksə,fī, kəm-\ *vt* -ED/-ING/-ES **:** to make complex ⟨problems needlessly *complexified*⟩

complexing *pres part of* COMPLEX

complex integration *n* **:** the integration of a function of a complex variable along an open or closed curve in the plane of the complex variable

¹com·plex·ion *also* **com·plec·tion** \kəm'plekshən\ *n* -S [ME *complexioun* temperament, humor, combination of the humors, bodily constitution, fr. MF *complexion,* fr. ML *complexion-, complexio,* fr. L, combination, connection, complication, fr. *complexus* (past part of *complecti*) + *-ion-, -io* -ion] **1 a** *obs* **:** a humor (sense 1b(1)) or combination of humors **b** *in medieval physiology and natural philosophy* **:** the combination in a certain proportion of the hot, cold, moist, and dry qualities that determine the nature or quality of a body or plant **2 a** *obs* **:** bodily constitution or mental makeup ⟨if his ~ incline him to melancholy —John Milton⟩ **b :** a cast of mind **:** an individual complex of attitudes, inclinations, or ways of thinking or feeling ⟨being of more sensitive ~ of mind than myself they were made ill by the suspense —J.H.Newman⟩ **c :** a complex of attitudes, inclinations, orientations, or ways of thought ⟨all the armed partisan groups . . . of whatever political ~ immediately joined in the fighting —*Atlantic*⟩ **3 a :** the hue or appearance of the skin esp. of the face ⟨a fair ~⟩ **b :** the skin of the face ⟨creams for ~ cleaning⟩ **4 :** the appearance or impression of a person or thing ⟨weathering has changed the ~ of the town hall from bright newness to solid conformity with neighboring structures⟩ ⟨the warlike ~ of the news⟩ **5** [L *complexion-, complexio*] *archaic* **:** COMBINATION, AGGREGATE **syn** see DISPOSITION

²complexion \"\ *vt* -ED/-ING/-S [ME *complexiounen* to compose, fr. *complexioun,* n.] **:** to give a color or particular slant to **:** TINGE ⟨the early sun ~*ing* the mountains⟩ ⟨propaganda ~*ed* his views⟩

com·plex·ion·al \-shənᵊl,-shnəl\ *adj* [ME, fr. ML *complexionalis,* fr. *complexion-, complexio* + L *-alis* -al] **:** of or relating to physical constitution or mental temperament ⟨his ~ hue⟩ ⟨~ political views⟩ — **com·plex·ion·al·ly** \-ᵊlē,-əlē, -li\ *adv*

com·plex·ioned \kəm'plekshənd\ *adj* [ME *complexiouned* having a (specified) bodily constitution, fr. *complexioun* + *-ed*] **:** having a (specified) facial complexion — used chiefly in combination ⟨a dark-*complexioned* girl⟩ ⟨a muddy-*complexioned* man⟩

com·plex·ion·less \-nləs\ *adj* **:** lacking color **:** PALE

com·plex·i·ty \kăm'pleksəd·ē, kəm-, -ətē, -i\ *n* -ES **1 :** the quality or state of being complex **:** COMPOSITENESS, INTRICACY ⟨the ~ of modern society⟩ ⟨the ~ of an adding machine's mechanism⟩ **2 :** something complex **:** an intricacy or complication ⟨the political *complexities* of his office⟩

com·plex·ly \(')käm¦plekslē, kəm'-, -li\ *adv* **:** in a complex manner

complex mode *n* **:** a mode that according to the philosophy of the 17th century English philosopher John Locke results from the combination of simple ideas of several kinds (as beauty, gratitude) — contrasted with *simple mode;* compare ¹MODE 6

com·plex·ness \-snəs\ *n* -ES **:** COMPLEXITY

complex number *or* **complex quantity** *n* **:** a number or expression of the form $a+bi$, where a and b are real numbers and $i=\sqrt{-1}$

complex plane *n* **:** a plane whose points are identified by means of complex numbers

complex unit *n* **:** a complex number $a+ib$ whose absolute value $\sqrt{a^2+b^2}$ is 1

com·plex·us \kăm'pleksəs, kəm-\ *n, pl* **complexus** [L, surrounding, embrace — more at COMPLEX] **:** an interwoven complicated aggregate of parts **:** COMPLEX ⟨the entire cultural ~ —James Collins⟩ ⟨a baffling ~ of her own imaginings —John Farrelly⟩

complex variable *n* **:** a number or expression of the form $x+iy$ where $i=\sqrt{-1}$ and x and y are in general variables

com·pli·a·ble \kəm'plīəbəl\ *adj* [*comply* + *-able*] **1** *archaic* **:** disposed or apt to agree or yield **:** COMPLIANT **2** *obs* **:** that may be reconciled — **com·pli·a·bly** \-blē\ *adv*

com·pli·ance \kəm'plīən(t)s\ *n* -S [*comply* + *-ance*] **1** *obs* **a :** CIVILITY **b :** friendly or happy agreement **:** HARMONY, CONCORD ⟨~ between man and wife⟩ **2 a :** the act or action of yielding to pressure, demand, or coercion **:** CONFORMANCE ⟨the Counter Reformation was not a ~ with Reform but a defiance of it —H.R.Trevor-Roper⟩ **b :** inclination or readiness to yield to the demands of others often in a servile or spineless fashion ⟨worthy men may be rejected because of their very virtues and unworthy men selected because of their ~ —P.H.Douglas⟩ **3 :** the quality or state of yielding to bending under stresses within the elastic limit; *also* **:** the amount of displacement per unit of applied force **4 a :** conformity in fulfilling formal or official requirements ⟨a letter written in ~ with U.S. Army style⟩ ⟨the . . . provision was designed to tighten ~ with acreage allotments —*Wall Street Jour.*⟩ **b :** cooperation promoted by official or legal authority or conforming to official or legal norms ⟨cheerful, spontaneous cooperation and ~ to orders are results of proper discipline under a respected leader —A.A.Ageton⟩ ⟨an official oath of ~ with the statute —Florence Mishnun⟩ ⟨insure the ~ of all . . . nations —*U. N. Disarmament Commission Resolution*⟩

com·pli·an·cy \-nsē, -si\ *n* -ES [*comply* + *-ancy*] **:** COMPLIANCE

com·pli·ant \-nt\ *adj* [*comply* + *-ant*] **1 :** ready, disposed, or likely to yield (as to pressure or the wishes of another) **:** COMPLAISANT, SUBMISSIVE ⟨above all things ~ and anxious to suit his opinions to those whom he encounters —H.J.Laski⟩ **2** *obs* **:** PLIANT — **com·pli·ant·ly** *adv*

com·pli·ca·cy \'kämpləkəsē, -lēk-, -si\ *n* -ES [fr. *complicate,* adj., after such pairs as E *confederate: confederacy*] **1 :** the quality or state of being complicated ⟨the ~ of his subject matter⟩ **2 :** something that is complicated ⟨the ~ of a watch⟩

com·pli·cant \-kənt\ *adj* [L *complicant-, complicans,* pres. part. of *complicare* to fold together] **:** OVERLAPPING — used of the elytra of certain beetles

¹com·pli·cate \'kämplə,kāt, *usu* -ād.+V\ *vb* -ED/-ING/-S [L *complicatus*] *vt* **1** *obs* **a :** to unite intimately by or as if by intertwining **b :** to fold or twist up together into or as if into a confused or overly involved mass **2 :** to combine esp. in an involved or inextricable manner ⟨his ideals were somehow *complicated* with selfish interest⟩ **3** *obs* **:** to create esp. by joining two or more elements **:** COMPOUND **4 :** to make complex, involved, or difficult ⟨this ~*s* matters⟩ ⟨snobbery *complicated* their social contacts⟩ **5** *med* **:** INVOLVE; *esp* **:** to cause to be more complex or severe ⟨bacterial secondary invaders ~ many virus infections⟩ ~ *vi* **:** to become complicated ⟨the problems grew, multiplied, and *complicated* beyond all reason⟩

²com·pli·cate \-lәkәt, -lēk-, *usu* -kәd-+V\ *adj* [L *complicatus,* past part. of *complicare* to fold together, fr. *com-* + *plicare* to fold — more at PLY] **1 :** made up of intimately united parts **:** COMPLEX ⟨a machine ~ of handmade gears⟩ **2 :** DIFFICULT, INVOLVED ⟨a ~ problem⟩ **3 a :** CONDUPLICATE **b :** folded longitudinally one or more times — used of insects' wings

com·pli·cat·ed \-lə,kād·əd, -ātəd\ *adj* [fr. past part. of *complicate*] **1 :** marked by an interrelation of diverse and often numerous parts, elements, notions, phases, or influences difficult of analysis, solution, or understanding ⟨Virgil compares their ~ evolutions to the windings of the Cretan labyrinth —J.G.Frazer⟩ ⟨when life is so ~ as to lose all homogeneity and unity of purpose —Norman Douglas⟩ ⟨~ machinery⟩ **2 :** having many interconnected parts **:** not simple or easy to fabricate or comprehend ⟨the whole organization of modern industry is a ~ one, dependent upon a host of professionalized skills that link —Lewis Mumford⟩ **syn** see COMPLEX

com·pli·cat·ed·ly *adv* **:** in a complicated manner

com·pli·cat·ed·ness *n* -ES **:** COMPLICACY

com·pli·cate·ness *n* -ES **:** COMPLICACY

com·pli·ca·tion \,kämplə'kāshən\ *n* -S [LL *complication-, complicatio* fr. L *complicatus* + *-ion-, -io* -ion] **1** *obs* **:** a folding together **:** the quality or state of being folded together **2 a** *obs* **:** an intimate combining **:** the quality or state of being intimately combined **b** *psychol* **:** the combination of sense data (as from different senses) into a unitary impression **3 a :** a complicated relationship of parts ⟨because of its ~ no mechanic would touch the engine⟩ **b :** a making difficult, involved, or intricate ⟨his ~ of our plans by not showing up on time⟩ **c :** a complex or intricate feature or element ⟨the ~*s* of jet aircraft⟩ or one that makes complex or intricate ⟨omitted Canada because of the ~*s* of the bilingual culture of sections of that country —J.B.Conant⟩ **d :** a difficult factor or issue often appearing suddenly and unexpectedly and changing existing plans, methods, or attitudes ⟨another ~ . . . was the excess of imports over exports —*Collier's Yr. Bk.*⟩ ⟨~*s* arose on all sides⟩ **e :** a situation or a detail of a character entering into and complicating the main thread of a plot **4** [F, fr. ML *complication-, complicatio,* fr. LL] **:** a secondary disease or condition developing in the course of a primary disease either as a result of the primary disease or arising from independent causes

com·plice \'kämpləs, 'kəm-\ *n* -S [ME, fr. MF, fr. LL *complic-, complex* partner, confederate, fr. L *com-* + LL *-plic-, -plex* (akin to L *plicare* to fold)] *archaic* **:** an associate or accomplice esp. in crime

com·plic·i·ty \kəm'plisəd·ē, -ətē, -i\ *n* -ES [F *complicité,* fr. *complice* + *-ité* -ity] **:** association or participation in or as if in guilt ⟨two men acting in ~⟩ ⟨~ in election abuses —J.G. Randall⟩ ⟨mischievous ~ between brothers⟩

complied *past of* COMPLY

com·pli·er \kəm'plī(ə)r\ *n* -S [*comply* + *-er*] **1 :** one that complies **2** *obs* **:** CONFORMIST

complies *pres 3d sing of* COMPLY

¹com·pli·ment \'kämpləmənt\ *n* -S [F, fr. It *complimento,* fr. Sp *cumplimiento,* fr. *cumplir* to complete, accomplish, perform what is due, be courteous (fr. L *complēre* to fill up) + *-miento* -ment — more at COMPLETE] **1 a :** a formal expression (as by speech, gesture, or ceremony) of esteem, respect, affection, or admiration ⟨each candidate was introduced with the usual ~*s*⟩ ⟨a party given in ~ to the bride by her mother⟩ ⟨changed the name to Fort Knox, in ~ to the Secretary of War —T.R. Hay⟩; *specif* **:** a remark intended to praise or please ⟨paying his best girl all sorts of ~*s*⟩ **b :** formal recognition **:** respectful consideration ⟨he came only in ~ to the rank of his host⟩ ⟨it behooves us . . . to pay the craftsmen the ~ of making a study of their language —Kenneth Ullyett⟩ **2 compliments** *pl* **:** best wishes **:** REGARDS ⟨to send her ~*s* to a friend⟩ ⟨a free sample is enclosed with the ~*s* of the manufacturer⟩ **3** *now dial* **:** a complimentary gift **:** GRATUITY ⟨to make a ~ of a book⟩

²com·pli·ment \-,ment,-mənt — *see* ²-MENT\ *vb* -ED/-ING/-S [F *complimenter,* fr. *compliment,* n.] *vt* **1 a** *obs* **:** to greet ceremoniously or flatteringly **b :** to pay a compliment to ⟨~*ing* his friend on the steadfastness of his interest in science —Benjamin Farrington⟩ ⟨she was again ~*ed* at a bridal shower given in her home —*Springfield (Mass.) Union*⟩ **2 :** to present (a person) with a token of esteem, respect, affection, or admiration ⟨~*ed* with an honorary degree⟩ **3 :** CONGRATULATE ⟨~*ed* his men on their conduct⟩ ~ *vi* **:** to pay compliments (as to one another)

com·pli·men·tal \,kämplə¦mentᵊl\ *adj* **1 :** COMPLIMENTARY 1a ⟨his pleasing ~ remarks⟩ **2** *archaic* **:** prone to pay compliments — **com·pli·men·tal·ly** \-ᵊlē,-ᵊli\ *adv, obs*

com·pli·men·tar·i·ly \¦kämplə(,)men¦terəlē, -lemən-, -rəli; -¦men·trəl-, -ntərəl-\ *adv* **:** in a complimentary manner

com·pli·men·ta·ri·ness \,kämplə'mentərēnəs, -n·trē-, -rin-\ *n* -ES **:** the quality or state of being complimentary

com·pli·men·ta·ry \¦kämplə¦mentərē, -n·trē, -ri\ *adj* **1 a :** expressing regard or praise ⟨the book received ~ reviews —*Current Biog.*⟩ **:** of the nature of or containing a compliment ⟨references to his colleagues were ever ~⟩ **b :** given to or using compliments ⟨a person of a ~ nature⟩ **2 :** presented or given free esp. as a courtesy or favor ⟨a ~ ticket⟩ ⟨~ meals given all who donate over a certain sum⟩

complimentary close *or* **complimentary closing** *n* **:** the word or words that conventionally come immediately before the signature of a letter and express the sender's regard for the receiver (as *very truly yours, sincerely yours, cordially*)

com·pline \'kämplən, -,plīn\ *also* **com·plin** \-,plən\ *n* -S *often cap* [ME *compline, compelin, cumplie,* fr. OF *complie,* modif. (influenced by *complir* to accomplish, finish, fr. L *complēre* to fill up) of LL *completa,* fr. L, fem. of *completus* complete — more at COMPLETE] *Christian relig* **:** the seventh and last of the canonical hours **:** the last liturgical prayer of the day said after nightfall or just before retiring — called also *night song*

¹com·plot \'käm,plät\ *n* -S [MF *complot, complote* crowd, throng, plot] *archaic* **:** PLOT, CONSPIRACY

²com·plot \käm'plät, kəm-\ *vb* **complotted; complotted; complotting; complots** [MF *comploter,* fr. *complot,* n.] *archaic* **:** to plot together **:** CONSPIRE

complt *abbr* complainant

com·plu·ten·sian \,kämplü¦tenchən\ *adj, usu cap* [L *complutensis* (fr. *Complutum,* city in Spain — now *Alcalá de Henares*) + E *-ian*] **:** of or relating to the polyglot bible published in Alcalá de Henares, Spain, in 1513–17 and containing the Old Testament in Hebrew, the Targum of Onkelos on the Pentateuch, the Septuagint, the Vulgate, and the Greek New Testament ⟨the *Complutensian* Polyglot⟩

com·plu·vi·um \kəm'plüvēəm, (')käm¦p-\ *n, pl* **complu·via** \-ēə\ [L, fr. *compluere* to flow together, fr. *com-* + *pluere* to rain — more at FLOW] **:** a square opening in the roof of the ancient Roman atrium toward which the roof sloped and through which the rain fell into the impluvium

¹com·ply \kəm'plī\ *vb* -ED/-ING/-ES [It *complire,* fr. Sp *cumplir* to complete, accomplish, perform what is due, be courteous, fr. L *complēre* to fill up — more at COMPLETE] *vi* **1** *obs* **a :** to be ceremoniously courteous **:** execute all formalities **b :** to be complaisant, accommodating, or obsequious **c :** to suit or conform oneself (as to a situation) **2 :** to accord or assent : conform or adapt one's actions (as to another's wishes) ⟨she would not be able to refuse, since all her instinct at this moment was to ~ —Rebecca West⟩ — usu. used with *with* ⟨he usually *complies* with her wishes⟩ ⟨these regulations have been *complied* with⟩ ~ *vt* **1** *obs* : FULFILL, ACCOMPLISH **2** *obs* : to bring into accord or conformity **syn** see OBEY

²comply *vt* -ED/-ING/-ES [*com-* around (influenced by L *complecti* to embrace) + *ply* — more at COMPLEX] *obs* : ENFOLD, EMBRACE

¹com·po \'käm(,)pō\ *n* -s [short for *composition*] **1** : a mortar made of sand and cement **2** : a carver's mixture of resin, whiting, and glue used on walls and cornices **3** : a mixture of paper, fiber, and a binder that is molded to make ornamental details for furniture

²compo \"\ *n* -s [*comp-* (fr. *compensation*) + *-o*] *slang Austral* : worker's compensation for injuries received on the job

com·po·nen·cy \kəm'pōnənsē, 'käm,p-, käm'p-\ *n* -ES [*component* + *-cy*] : component quality

¹com·po·nent \kəm'pōnənt, 'käm,p-, käm'p-\ *n* -s [L *component-, componens*] **1** : a constituent part : INGREDIENT ⟨the various ~s of an electric motor⟩ ⟨the essential ~s of Kantian philosophy⟩ **2** *physics* : any one of the vector terms added to form a given vector sum or resultant **3** : an ingredient of a chemical system the concentration of which in the different phases is capable of independent variation ⟨copper and zinc are the ~s of brass⟩ — see PHASE RULE **4** : either of the sequences defining an alphabet in cryptography — see ALPHABET 1j **5** : the smallest unit of classification in the Midwestern system for American archaeology constituting a single complex of traits found in one site or level — see FOCUS; compare ASPECT, PATTERN, PHASE **syn** see ELEMENT

²component \"\ *adj* [L *component-, componens*, pres. part. of *componere* to put together — more at COMPOUND] : serving or helping to constitute : CONSTITUENT ⟨~ parts⟩ ⟨~ elements⟩ ⟨two ~ republics of the Union of Soviet Socialist Republics —Vera M. Dean⟩

com·po·nen·tial \¦kämpə¦nenchəl\ *also* **com·po·nen·tal** \-entᵊl\ *adj* : of or relating to a component : having components ⟨~ relations⟩ ⟨~ analysis⟩ ⟨~ structure⟩

com·po·ny \kəm'pōnē\ *also* **com·po·né** *or* **com·po·née** \kəm'pōnē, -(,)nā; ¦kämpə¦nā\ *adj* [MF *componé*, alter. (influenced by L *componere* to compose) of *coponné, couponné*, fr. *copon, coupon* piece — more at COUPON] **1** : composed of two alternate tinctures in a single row — used of a heraldic bearing **2** : divided into segments of alternate tinctures following the curve — used of a heraldic bearing having curved lines

¹com·port \kəm'pō(ə)rt, -ó(ə)rt, -ōət, -ó(ə)t; *usu* -d.+V\ *vb* -ED/-ING/-S [MF *comporter*, fr. L *comportare* to bring together, fr. *com-* + *portare* to carry — more at PORT] *vi* **1 a** *archaic* : BEAR, ENDURE **b** *obs* : BEHAVE, ACT **2** : AGREE, ACCORD, SUIT — used with *with* ⟨the emphasis on the beautiful . . . that ~s with the conventional conception of culture as a life of traditionally molded refinement —Edward Sapir⟩ ~ *vt* **1** *archaic* : to put up with : BEAR, TOLERATE **2** : CONDUCT, BEHAVE ⟨the probationer who ~s himself blamelessly remains obscure, while the one who reverts to crime is likely to hit the headlines —Telford Taylor⟩ **3** : carry or bring esp. together ⟨positivism . . . tried to make of philosophy . . . a technique of existence ~*ing* an inventory of behavior, a description of conduct —*Times Lit. Supp.*⟩ **syn** see BEHAVE

²comport *n* -s *obs* : BEHAVIOR, DEPORTMENT

³com·port \'käm,pō(ə)rt, -ó(ə)rt, -ōət, -ó(ə)t\ *n* -s [prob. by folk etymology fr. *compotier*] : a bowl-shaped dish with a stem and foot and sometimes with a cover for holding fruit or sweets : COMPOTE

com·port·a·ble \kəm'pōr|d·əbəl, -ó(r)|, -ōə|, |tə-\ *adj* **1** *obs* : ENDURABLE, TOLERABLE **2** : SUITABLE, CONSISTENT ⟨privileges ~ with our position as prisoners —C.B.Nordhoff & J.N. Hall⟩

comportance *n* -s *obs* : BEHAVIOR, COMPORT

com·port·ment \kəm'pōrtmənt, -ȯrt-,-ōət-,-ó(ə)t-\ *n* -s [MF *comportement*, fr. *comporter* + *-ment*] : manner of bearing: as **a** : DEPORTMENT, DEMEANOR ⟨the ~ of a gentleman⟩ **b comportments** *pl, obs* : CONDUCT, ACTIONS **c** : HABITS, BEHAVIOR ⟨the ~ of adult insects —*Biol. Abstracts*⟩

compos *pl of* COMPO

com·pose \kəm'pōz\ *vb* -ED/-ING/-S [MF *composer*, modif. (influenced by *poser* to put, place) of L *componere* to put together, arrange (perfect stem *compos-*), fr. *com-* + *ponere* to put, place — more at POSITION, POSE] *vt* **1 a** : to form by putting together two or more things, elements, or parts : put together : FASHION — now usu. in passive ⟨a well-*composed* body⟩ ⟨the assembly was *composed* of delegates from every state in the union⟩ **b** : to form the substance of : CONSTITUTE ⟨for the most part avarice and envy *composed* his personality⟩ — now used chiefly in passive ⟨a soup *composed* of many ingredients⟩ **c** (1) : to put (type) together piece by piece : SET (2) : to set the type for (a work to be printed); *also* : to prepare (a printing surface) by some analogous means (as by a keyboard typesetting machine, a photocomposing machine, or a typewriter) **2** : to create by mental or artistic labor : design and execute or put together (as by adapting forms of expression to ideas or to laws of harmony or proportion) : CREATE: as **a** : WRITE ⟨~ a book of poems⟩ : PRODUCE ⟨~ a ballad⟩ ⟨~ a history of English law⟩ **b** (1) : to formulate and write (a piece of music) ⟨*composed* a number of stirring marches⟩ (2) : to formulate music for ⟨*composed* several charming songs⟩ **3** : to treat, deal with, or act on so as to reduce (as points at issue) to an innocuous minimum ⟨~ disputes⟩ ⟨when labor and management cannot ~ their differences —H.S.Truman⟩ **4** : to arrange in a fitting, proper, or orderly way : free from an appearance of agitation or disturbance ⟨~ her clothing⟩ ⟨the two men had laid him on the bed and *composed* his limbs —Sheridan Le Fanu⟩ **5** : CALM, SETTLE, TRANQUILIZE ⟨~ a patient⟩ ⟨~ his passions⟩ : adjust (as oneself or one's feelings) esp. by suppressing or overcoming agitation and achieving calm ⟨life moves on . . . and one must ~ oneself to meet it —Rose Macaulay⟩ ~ *vi* **1** : to practice composition (as of literary, musical, or typographical work) : CREATE ⟨at the age of 10 he was *composing* at the piano⟩ **2** *obs* : to come to terms **syn** see CALM

com·posed \-zd\ *adj* [fr. past part. of *compose*] **1 a** *archaic* : formed of or made up of parts : COMPOSITE, COMPOUND **b** *obs* : put together well or artistically ⟨a ~ design⟩ **2** : free from indications of agitation or excitement : calm and self-possessed in reality or appearance ⟨cool, ~, mistress of herself and her destiny —Ellen Glasgow⟩ **syn** see COOL

com·pos·ed·ly \-zədlē, -li\ *adv* : in a composed manner

com·pos·ed·ness \-zədnəs, -z(d)n-\ *n* -ES : COMPOSURE

composed throughout *adj* [trans. of G *durchkomponiert*] : THROUGH-COMPOSED

com·pos·er \-zə(r)\ *n* -s : one that composes: as **a** : AUTHOR, WRITER ⟨the various ~s of the Old Testament⟩ **b** : a person who writes music ⟨a ~ of popular songs⟩ **c** : a person who settles, adjusts, or tranquilizes ⟨a determined ~ of differences —C.G.Bolte⟩

composing machine *n* : TYPESETTING MACHINE

composing room *n* : the department in a printing office where typesetting and related operations are performed

composing rule *n* : a thin strip of steel or brass usu. type-high and having an ear at each upper corner against which type is set in and removed from a composing stick

composing stick *n* : a shallow tray formerly of wood but now usu. of metal and having an adjustable slide that is held in one hand by a compositor as he sets type into it with the other hand; *also* : a device of comparable function (as for hand-setting matrices for a slug-casting machine or letters for photocomposition) — called also *stick*

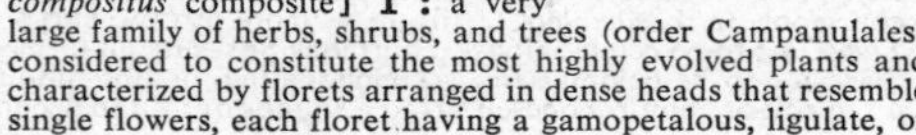

composing stick

composita *pl of* COMPOSITUM

com·pos·i·tae \kəm'päzə,tē, käm-, -tī\ *n pl, cap* [NL, fr. L, fem. pl. of *compositus* composite] **1** : a very large family of herbs, shrubs, and trees (order Campanulales) considered to constitute the most highly evolved plants and characterized by florets arranged in dense heads that resemble single flowers, each floret having a gamopetalous, ligulate, or tubular corolla and a calyx modified into a pappus (as in the dandelion, sunflower, aster, and ragweed) **2** *in some classifications* **a** : a superfamilial group that is coextensive with the family Compositae and is divided into the families Carduaceae, Cichoriaceae, and Ambrosiaceae **b** : CARDUACEAE

¹com·pos·ite \(')käm¦päzət, kəm'p-, *usu* -əd.+V; *Brit usu* 'kämpəz-\ *adj* [L *compositus*, past part. of *componere* to put together, fr. *com-* + *ponere* to put, place — more at POSITION] : made up of distinct parts : COMPOUNDED ⟨a ~ racial type⟩ ⟨~ material⟩ ⟨the knight was a ~ portrait of men whom Chaucer personally knew —J.L.Lowes⟩: **a** *usu cap* : belonging to or being a modification of the Corinthian order introduced in Roman imperial times by combining angular Ionic volutes with the acanthus-circled bell of the Corinthian **b** : belonging to, having the characteristics of, or being a member of the family Compositae ⟨a ~ inflorescence⟩ **c** *of a number or an algebraic expression* : made up of two or more integral or real rational prime factors (as $12=2\times2\times3$; $a^3-b^3=(a-b)(a^2+ab+b^2)$) — compare PRIME **d** *of a ship* : built with a metal framework and wooden keel, planking, and deck — **com·pos·ite·ly** *adv*

²composite \"\ *n* -s **1** : something that is made up of diverse elements: as **a** : COMPOUND 1a, 1b **b** : a fingerprint in which elements of varied types (as the arch, loop, and whorl) are combined **c** : a pictorial composition in which two or more images are combined or worked together; *specif* : a composition that fuses different images so that only selected parts of each are revealed in one harmonious formal relationship **d** *or* **composite can** : a container having a fiber body and one or more commonly both ends of metal **2** : a plant of the family Compositae

composite 2: section of a composite flower head, *1* disk floret, *2* ray flower, *3* bracts

³composite \"\ *vt* -ED/-ING/-S : to make composite or into something composite

composite cone *n* : a volcanic cone composed of intermingled masses or alternate layers of lava and fragmental material

composite dike *also* **composite sill** *n* : a dike or sill composed of two or more varieties of igneous rock presumably resulting from successive injections

composite engine *n* : COMPOUND ENGINE 2

com·pos·ite·ness *n* -ES : the quality or state of being composite

composite photograph *n* : a photograph made by combining several distinct photographs either made one over another on the same plate or made on one print from a number of negatives

composite print *n* **1** : a photographic print made from more than one negative **2** : a motion-picture print bearing both picture and sound-track images

composite sailing *n* : a combination of great circle and parallel sailing in navigation

com·po·si·tion \,kämpə'zishən\ *n* -s [ME *composicioun*, fr. MF *composition*, fr. L *composition-, compositio*, fr. *compositus* (past part. of *componere* to put together, fr. *com-* + *ponere* to put, place) + *-ion-, -io* -ion — more at POSITION] **1 a** : the act or action of composing : the formation of a whole esp. by different things being put together ⟨his ~ of long novels⟩ ⟨the slow ~ of a glacier⟩; *specif* : the ordering or arranging of something into proper proportion or relation ⟨force a ~ of overwrought thoughts⟩ **b** (1) : combination of words to form a compound (2) : combination of words, of combining forms, of a word and a combining form, of a word and an affix, or of a combining form and an affix to form a compound **c** : the construction of a literary work esp. with reference to its degree of success in meeting criteria of correctness, order, or proportion **d** *obs* : the reasoning from general principles or causes to particulars : synthetic reasoning **e** : the disposition of the parts of a work of art : FORM, PATTERN ⟨a triangular ~⟩ **f** *logic* (1) : the adjunction of two terms to form a compound term or the adjunction of two propositions or assertions to form a compound assertion (2) : the passage from a concept or assertion about individuals taken separately to a concept or assertion about the class which they compose — see FALLACY OF COMPOSITION **g** : the nature of a chemical compound or mixture as regards the kind and amounts of its constituents being usu. expressed for a chemical compound in numbers of atoms of each element in the molecule or in percentages of each element by weight **h** : the work of a compositor **i** : the kinds and relative numbers of different organisms that make up a population **2** : the manner in which something is composed or compounded: as **a** : the particular arrangement or combination of parts of a unit or whole ⟨the ~ of ingredients in a recipe⟩ ⟨the industrial ~ of a European country⟩ **b** : personal constitution (as of mind and body together) : general makeup ⟨a man with a touch of genius in his ~⟩ **c** : the particular mode or style in the combination of parts in a work of art that produces a harmonious whole ⟨a painting masterful in ~⟩ **d** *obs* : consistency esp. among the items of a report : CONGRUITY **e** : the combination of tones forming a compound organ stop **3** : mutual settlement or agreement: as **a** *archaic* : an agreement esp. between one person and another : SETTLEMENT **b** : an agreement or settlement whereby differences (as between factions) are resolved : TREATY, COMPROMISE ⟨the countries were joined by an ancient ~⟩ ⟨the ~ that was reached in Korea is not satisfactory to America, but it is far better than to continue the bloody, dreary sacrifice —D.D. Eisenhower⟩ **c** : the satisfaction of a wrong or injury by money payment or the money so paid **d** : the adjustment of a debt or avoidance of an obligation or liability by some form of compensation agreed upon between the parties or the sum of money agreed upon in the adjustment; *specif* : settlement of debts by agreement through partial payments of the sums due debtors to avoid bankruptcy **e** *Scots law* : the fine due a superior on the actual or implied entry of a singular successor **4 a** : an aggregate, mixture, mass, or body formed by combining two or more elements or ingredients ⟨a ~ of rubber and cork⟩ **b** : a material prepared from or composed of various ingredients and often taking the place of a more expensive or uncompounded material ⟨a facade made of ~ that looks like marble⟩ ⟨~ leather⟩ ⟨~ shingles⟩ **5** : an intellectual creation: as **a** : a piece of writing; *esp* : a written exercise done for a course in writing in school and usu. intended to show study and care in arrangement **b** : a written piece of music; *esp* : an original work of some magnitude and to whose formal structure appropriate attention has been given **c** : a work of art (as a drawing or painting) whose various elements are combined artistically **6** : the quality or state of being compound or composite ⟨the simplicity and absence of ~ in his arguments⟩ ⟨a point taken in ~ with other points⟩ **7** : a course in colleges and secondary schools designed to train students to write esp. exposition

com·po·si·tion·al \¦kämpə¦zishənᵊl, -shnəl\ *adj* : of or having to do with composition ⟨~ laws⟩ ⟨the ~ arrangement with horizontals, verticals, diagonals —E.M.Neumeyer⟩ — **com·po·si·tion·al·ly** \-ᵊlē,-əlē, -li\ *adv*

composition metal *n* : a cast copper alloy containing usu. more than 80 percent copper together with tin, lead, and zinc

composition of forces *physics* : the finding of a single force if such exists that shall be equal in effect to two or more given forces

composition roller *n* : a printer's inking roller consisting of a metal core covered with a flexible mixture of glue, molasses, and glycerin

com·pos·i·tive \kəm'päzəd·iv\ *adj* [LL *compositivus* suitable for uniting, fr. L *compositus* + *-ivus* -ive] : using or involving composition : SYNTHETIC

com·pos·i·tor \kəm'päzəd·ə(r), -z(ə)tə(r)\ *n* -s [ME *compositour* one that settles a disagreement, fr. MF *compositeur*, fr. ML *compositor*, fr. L, arranger, disposer, fr. *compositus* (past part. of *componere* to put together, fr. *com-* + *ponere* to put, place) + *-or* — more at POSITION] : one that composes; *specif* : one that sets, assembles, proofs, and generally prepares type and cuts for printing or plating for printing — **com·pos·i·to·ri·al** \kəm¦päzə¦tōrēəl\ *adj*

compositor's alley *n* : ALLEY 4b

com·pos·i·tum \kəm'päzətəm\ *n, pl* **compositums** \-təmz\ *or* **composi·ta** \-tə\ [LL, fr. L, agreement, fr. neut. of *compositus*] *archaic* : COMPOUND, COMPOSITION

com·pos men·tis \¦kämpə'smentəs\ *adj* [L, lit., having mastery of one's mind] : sane in mind : being of sound mind, memory, and understanding — usu. used predicatively ⟨he was judged *compos mentis*⟩; see NON COMPOS MENTIS

com·po·so·graph \kəm'pōzə,graf\ *n* -s [*compose* + *-o-* + *-graph*] : a synthetic photograph; *esp* : a photograph made up usu. of parts of other photographs and designed to show a scene that never existed

com·pos·si·bil·i·ty \(,)käm,päsə'biləd·ē, kəm-\ *n* -ES [ML *compossibilis* + E *-ity*] : ability or possibility of coexisting ⟨the real ~ of individuals —Grace De Laguna⟩

com·pos·si·ble \(')käm¦päsəbəl, kəm'p-\ *adj* [ML *compossibilis*, fr. L *com-* + *possibilis* possible] : able or possible to coexist with another ⟨a theory ~ with other theories⟩ ⟨contradictory but ~ statements⟩

¹com·post \'käm,pōst, *Brit usu* -päst\ *n* -s *often attrib* [ME, stew, compote, fr. MF *composte* compote, *compost* compost; MF *composte* fr. L *composita*, fem. of *compositus*; MF *compost* fr. L *compositus*] **1 a** : a mixture consisting usu. largely of decayed organic matter and used for fertilizing and conditioning land; *esp* : such a mixture produced by decomposition in a compost pile **b** : a complex potting soil that is usu. rich in organic matter **2** : MIXTURE, COMPOSITION, COMPOUND ⟨that strange ~ of contradictions, the Scottish character —John Buchan⟩ ⟨sheer melodrama, a ~ of sex and crime —Milton Rugoff⟩ ⟨a ~ of newspaper sensations and prejudice —T.S.Eliot⟩

²compost \"\ *vt* -ED/-ING/-S [ME *composten*, fr. MF *composter*, fr. *compost*, n.] **1** : to treat (as land) with compost : MANURE **2** : to cause (as plant debris) to be converted into compost usu. by mixing with suitable adjuncts and piling in a way that encourages decay and decomposition

compost pile *also* **compost heap** *n* : a stack of alternating layers of plant debris and soil with often an admixture of animal manure or chemical fertilizer arranged so as to encourage the rapid conversion of the constituents into compost

com·po·sure \kəm'pōzhə(r)\ *n* -s [*compose* + *-ure*] **1** *obs* : COMPOSITION **2** : calmness or repose esp. in frame of mind or in bearing or appearance : SELF-POSSESSION ⟨Hamlet's ~ in this last part of the play is of supreme beauty —Karl Polanyi⟩ ⟨gazing upon it all with a serene ~ in which one may detect a mild amusement —C.B.Tinker⟩ **syn** see EQUANIMITY

com·po·ta·tion \,kämpō'tāshən\ *n* -s [L *compotation-, compotatio* (trans. of Gk *symposion* drinking party), fr. *com-* + *potatio* potation] : a drinking or tippling together : CAROUSE

com·po·ta·tor \'kämpō,tād·ə(r)\ *n* -s [LL, fr. L *com-* + *potator* drinker, fr. *potatus*, past part. of *potare* to drink + *-or* — more at POTABLE] : one who drinks with another

com·pote *also* **com·pot** \'käm,pōt, *usu* -ōd.+V\ *n* -s [F *compote*, fr. OF *composte*] **1** : fruits cooked in syrup in such a way as to keep their form ⟨a ~ of pears⟩ **2 a** : a bowl-shaped dish of glass, porcelain, or metal usu. with a base and stem, and sometimes with a cover from which compotes, fruits, nuts, or sweets are served **b** : a small dish of similar form used for individual servings

com·po·tier \¦kämpō¦tyā\ *n* -s [F, fr. *compote* + *-ier* -er] : COMPOTE 2a

compote 2a

compotus *var of* COMPUTUS

¹com·pound \(')käm¦paund, kəm'p-\ *vb* -ED/-ING/-S [alter. of ME *compounen*, fr. MF *compon-*, stem of *compondre* to put together, arrange, fr. L *componere*, fr. *com-* + *ponere* to put, place — more at POSITION] *vt* **1** : to put together (as elements, ingredients, or parts) to form a whole : COMBINE, UNITE **2 a** : to form or make up (as a composite product) by combining different elements, ingredients, or parts ⟨~ a medicine⟩ ⟨a philosophy ~*ed* of affirmation, action, compassion, and universalism —Norman Cousins⟩ **b** *obs* : COMPOSE, CREATE ⟨~*ed* many hymns and psalms —Richard Montagu⟩ **3** : to settle amicably : adjust by agreement : discharge (an obligation) upon terms different from those which were stipulated, claimed, or demanded (as when a smaller sum is accepted than was asked) : COMPROMISE **4 a** : to increase by geometric progression or by an increment that itself increases ⟨interest is ~*ed* quarterly⟩ **b** : to cause to multiply at a faster and faster rate **c** : to add to : AUGMENT ⟨we ~*ed* our error in later policy —Robert Lekachman⟩ ⟨express roads and parkways . . . have ~*ed* . . . parking problems immensely —Hal Burton⟩ **5** : to forbear prosecution of (an offense) for a consideration ⟨~ a felony⟩ **6** : to wind the field magnets of (a dynamo) so as to make excitable by both a shunt and a series current **7** : to combine (as forces and velocities) into a single resultant ~ *vi* **1** : to unite into or as if into a compound ⟨his virtues and vices ~*ed* into a contradictory personality no one could understand⟩ **2** : to come to terms of agreement or payment : settle by a compromise : AGREE ⟨~ with the enemy for peace⟩ ⟨no attempt to ~ with God, to offer future good behavior in exchange for forgiveness —C.S.Forester⟩

²com·pound \(')käm¦paund *also* kəm'p-\ *adj* [ME *compouned*, fr. past part. of *compounen*] **1 a** : composed of or produced by the union of several elements, ingredients, parts, or things ⟨a ~ substance⟩ **b** : involving combination : COMPOSITE ⟨~ management⟩ **c** *logic* : consisting of several elements; *specif* : having more than one proposition **d** : having or consisting of two, three, or four groups of simple time units to the musical measure (6/8 and 9/8 are ~ rhythms) ⟨~ time⟩ **e** *bot* : composed of two or more similar parts forming a common whole ⟨a ~ ovary⟩ **f** : composed of several joined individuals or elements **2** *of an electrical machine* : compound-wound **3 a** *of a word* (1) : being a compound (sense 1a) — compare COMPLEX (2) : being a compound (sense 1b) **b** *of a sentence* : having more than one main clause ⟨*I told him to leave and he left* is a ~ sentence⟩ — compare COMPLEX **c** *of a tense* : formed by the use of an auxiliary verb ⟨*is going, are written, has seen, will arrive* are ~ tenses⟩ — opposed to *simple* **4** *of a fabric* : having one or more extra warps or wefts or both

³com·pound \'käm,paund\ *n* -s **1 a** : a word consisting of components that are words (as *rowboat, fireman, high school, devil-may-care, airtight, outrun, thereby, whereas, into*) — compare COMPLEX **b** : a word consisting of components that are words, are a word and a combining form (as *centimeter*), are a word and a noninflectional affix (as *builder, reenter*), are combining forms (as *biology*), or are a combining form and a noninflectional affix (as *cephalad, chlorate*) **c** *printing* : a hyphened term **2** : something (as a substance, idea, creation) that is formed by a union of elements, ingredients, or parts ⟨a poisonous ~⟩ ⟨a ~ of Christian mysticism and Greek philosophy⟩ ⟨a ~ of contradictions⟩: **a** : a chemically distinct substance formed by union of two or more ingredients (as elements) in definite proportion by weight and with definite structural arrangement ⟨water is a ~ of oxygen and hydrogen⟩ ⟨the benzene ring is characteristic of numerous complex organic ~s⟩ — see ADDITION COMPOUND, ADSORPTION COMPOUND **b** : a plastering base coat to which sand is added later on the job **c** : a compound engine or compound locomotive **d** : a system of gears on roving and spinning frames to keep yarn speed constant as bobbin circumference increases with the winding of added layers **e** : a mental process (as a blend or pattern) in which different components can be distinguished **3** : COMPOSITION ⟨the peculiar ~ of such material⟩

⁴compound \"\ *n* -s [by folk etymology (influence of ³*compound*) fr. Malay *kampung, kampong* group, gathering, cluster of buildings, village] **1 a** : a well-demarcated complex of European residences and commercial buildings (as warehouses and factories) esp. in the East Indies, India, and China **b** : an enclosure within which the laborers at So. African gold or diamond mines are confined **c** : a large fenced or walled-in area (as in a prison, detention camp, or cattle yard) **2** *Africa* : inferior beef

com·pound·able \(')käm¦paundəbəl, kəm'p-\ *adj* : capable of being compounded

compound animal *n* : an animal composed of a number of individuals each performing independently some or most of the vital functions yet organically connected so as to form a united colony of zooids ⟨most corals and bryozoans are *compound animals*⟩

compound attack *n* : a fencing attack combining two or more successive movements in order to deceive parries

compound benzoin tincture *n* : FRIAR'S BALSAM

compound-complex *adj, of a sentence* **:** having more than one main clause and at least one subordinate clause (as *he told me to leave and I left as soon as I could*)
compound curve *n* **:** a curve made up of two or more circular arcs of successively shorter or longer radii, joined tangentially without reversal of curvature, and used on some railroad tracks and highways as an easement curve to provide a less abrupt transition from tangent to full curve or vice versa

C, O_3, A, O_4, O_2, B, O_5, O_1

compound curve, *ACB:* successive centers, O_1, O_2, O_3, O_4, O_5

compound discount *n* **:** CHAIN DISCOUNT
compound duties *n pl* **:** a combination of specific and ad valorem customs duties on the same article
compounded *past of* COMPOUND
compound engine *n* **1 :** an engine (as a steam engine) in which the working fluid is expanded successively in two distinct phases so as to minimize losses (as from cylinder condensation) and so allow a high ratio of expansion to be used, the working fluid (as steam) after expanding in the high-pressure cylinder being exhausted into a low-pressure cylinder and then exhausted usu. into a condenser **2** *aeronautics* **:** a propulsive system consisting essentially of a reciprocating engine, a steady-flow gas turbine, and a compressor so arranged that (1) the exhaust from the reciprocating engine drives the turbine, the exhaust from the turbine being directed rearward for jet propulsion, (2) the turbine drives the compressor, the excess turbine power being delivered to the engine shaft through gearing, and (3) the net shaft power of the system is converted to propulsive power by means of a propeller
com·pound·er \(ˈ)käm¦paůndə(r), kəm'p-\ *n* -s **1** *obs* **:** one that compounds (as a debt, crime, or strife) by agreement or compromise **2 a :** one that compounds products (as drugs) from raw materials or ingredients **b :** one that mixes ingredients to produce specified qualities or quantities in the manufacture of a product; *specif* **:** a refinery worker who blends different grades of oils to meet customer or laboratory specifications **3** *usu cap* **:** a Jacobite favoring the restoration of James II on condition of a general amnesty and of guarantees for the security of the constitution
compound ether *n, archaic* **:** ESTER
compound eye *n* **:** an eye typical of the arthropods found esp. in insects and crustaceans and consisting essentially of a great number (sometimes thousands) of minute simple eyes closely crowded together but optically separated by dark pigment cells, arranged on a convex basal membrane, and covered externally by a chitinous cornea — see OMMATIDIUM; INSECT illustration
compound fold *n, geol* **:** a fold having minor folds imposed upon the main fold, the axes of all being approximately parallel
compound fraction *n* **:** COMPLEX FRACTION
compound fracture *n* **:** a bone fracture associated with lacerated soft tissues through which bone fragments usu. protrude
compound householder *n, Brit* **:** a householder whose taxes are included in his rent
compound infusion of senna : BLACK DRAFT
compounding *pres part of* COMPOUND
compound interest *n* **:** interest paid or computed on the combined sum of the original principal of a loan and interest accrued and payable at the end of each agreed period (as monthly, quarterly, semiannually, or annually) — compare ACCUMULATION FACTOR, SIMPLE INTEREST
compound-interest method *n* **:** a method of determining (as a provision for annual depreciation of an asset) a constant amount made up of an amount periodically set aside that with compound interest will equal the original cost plus interest on the declining investment in the asset — compare STRAIGHT-LINE METHOD
compound interval *n* **:** a musical interval greater than an octave — compare SIMPLE INTERVAL
compound jellyfish *n* **:** SIPHONOPHORE; *esp* **:** a siphonophore with more than one swimming bell
compound leaf *n* **:** a leaf in which the blade is divided to the midrib, forming two or more distinct blades or leaflets on a common axis, the leaflets themselves occas. being compound — compare PALMATE, PINNATE; SIMPLE LEAF
compound lens *n* **:** a lens made of simple lenses mounted on a common axis usu. in close juxtaposition and often cemented together — see ACHROMATIC LENS
compound lever *n* **:** a system (as in various testing machines and weighing scales) of two or more levers arranged to transmit motion or force by linking an arm of each lever to an arm of the next lever in the train
compound locomotive *n* **:** a steam locomotive having two or more cylinders in which the exhaust steam passes from one to another to do additional work before being released
compound magnet *n* **:** a set of magnets placed with like poles together so as to act as a single magnet
compound microscope *n* **:** a microscope consisting of an objective and an eyepiece mounted in a drawtube and focused by means of screw arrangements
compound middle lamella *n* **:** the middle lamella considered as comprising the intercellular cementing layer and the primary walls on both sides of it
compound nucleus *n* **:** an unstable nucleus formed by the coalescence of an atomic nucleus with a captured particle
compound number *n* **:** a number involving different denominations or more than one unit (as 2 ft. 5 in.)
compound ovary *n* **:** an ovary formed by the union of two or more carpels
compound pendulum *n* **:** PHYSICAL PENDULUM
compound perforation *n* **:** a stamp perforation having two perforation numbers, one for the top and bottom of the stamp and one for the sides
compound pier *n* **:** a clustered pier
compound pistil *n* **:** a pistil formed by the union of two or more carpels
compound raceme *n* **:** PANICLE
compound radical *n, archaic* **:** RADICAL 5c
compound ray *n* **:** AGGREGATE RAY
compound relative *n* **1 :** a relative pronoun, adjective, or adverb used without an antecedent (as *what* in "what he says is true", *where* in "this is where he was born") **2 :** a compound formed by adding *so, ever,* or *soever* to a relative pronoun (*whoso, whichever, whatsoever*)
compound rest *n* **:** a tool rest for a lathe having two slides, one mounted on the other
compounds *pres 3d sing of* COMPOUND, *pl of* COMPOUND
compound screw *n* **1 :** DIFFERENTIAL SCREW **2 :** a right-and-left screw
compound sieve plate *n, bot* **:** a sieve plate having the sieve areas in groups separated by a network or bar of cell-wall material
compound spirit of ether : an anodyne mixture of alcohol, ether, and a small quantity of ethereal oil — called also *Hoffmann's anodyne*
compound spirit of myrcia [*Myrcia* (genus of trees and shrubs); prob. fr. confusion between the bayberry (*Pimenta racemosa*) and a tree of the related genus *Myrcia*] **:** BAY RUM
compound stop *n* **:** an organ stop having more than one pipe or reed to each key
compound tincture of benzoin : FRIAR'S BALSAM
compound vault *n* **:** a vault of any form other than the simplest (as a groined vault, ribbed vault, or fan vault)
compound vein *n* **:** a lode composed of two or more nearly parallel veins
compound winding *n* **:** a combination of series winding and shunt winding on the field magnet of a direct-current machine
com·pra·dor \¦kämprə¦dō(ə)r\ *or* **com·pra·dore** \-dō(ə)r, -dȯ(ə)r\ *n* -s [Pg *comprador*, lit., buyer, fr. LL *comperator*, fr. (assumed) VL *comperatus* (past part. of assumed VL *comperare* to acquire, buy, fr. L *com-* + *-perare*, fr. *parare* to prepare) + L *-or* — more at PARE] **1 :** a Chinese agent, adviser, or factotum employed by a foreign establishment (as a consulate) in China to have charge of its Chinese employees or to act as an intermediary in business affairs **2 :** one held to be an agent of foreign domination or exploitation
com·pre·ca·tion \ˌkämprə'kāshən\ *n* -s [L *comprecation-, comprecatio*, fr. *comprecatus* (past part. of *comprecari* to pray to, fr. *com-* + *precari* to pray) + *-ion-, -io* -ion — more at PRAY] *archaic* **:** a praying together
com·preg \'käm,preg\ *n* -s [back-formation fr. *compregnate*] **:** wood impregnated with a resin and compressed under great heat before the resin sets and similar to impreg in its properties
com·preg·nate \käm'preg,nāt, kəm-\ *vt* -ED/-ING/-S [blend of *compress* + *impregnate*] **:** to compress with heat (thin sheets of wood impregnated with a solution of phenol and formaldehyde) into a dense hard homogeneous substance — compare COMPREG
com·pre·hend \¦kämprə¦hend, -rē¦-\ *vt* -ED/-ING/-S [ME *comprehenden*, fr. L *comprehendere*, fr. *com-* + *prehendere* to grasp, seize — more at PREHENSIBLE] **1 :** to see the nature, significance, or meaning of **:** grasp mentally **:** attain to the knowledge of ⟨~ where her duties lie⟩ ⟨stumbled through the brown book, not . . . ~*ing* what it meant —Rudyard Kipling⟩ **2 :** to contain or hold within a total scope, significance, or amount often as a part, item, concomitant, or factor **:** EMBRACE ⟨a magnificent view ~*ing* all the upper half of the floor of the valley —John Muir †1914⟩ ⟨for philosophy's scope ~*s* the truth of everything which man may understand —H.O.Taylor⟩ **3 :** to take in or include by construction or implication **:** COMPRISE, IMPLY ⟨and if there be any other commandment, it is briefly ~*ed* in this saying, namely, Thou shalt love thy neighbor as thyself —Rom 13:9 (AV)⟩ **4** *obs* **:** GRASP, SEIZE, ATTAIN **syn** see INCLUDE, UNDERSTAND
com·pre·hend·ible \-dəbəl\ *adj* **:** COMPREHENSIBLE
com·pre·hend·ing·ly *adv* **:** KNOWINGLY
com·pre·hen·si·bil·i·ty \ˌ==ˌhen(t)sə'biləd·ē, -ətē, -i\ *n* -ES **:** the quality or state of being comprehensible
com·pre·hen·si·ble \¦==¦hen(t)səbəl\ *adj* [L *comprehensibilis*, fr. *comprehensus* (past part. of *comprehendere*) + *-ibilis* -ible] **1** *archaic* **:** capable of being included, contained, or comprised ⟨God . . . is not or nor circumscribed —Thomas More⟩ **2 :** capable of being understood **:** INTELLIGIBLE, CONCEIVABLE ⟨an idea ~ to the average mind⟩ — **com·pre·hen·si·ble·ness** *n* -ES — **com·pre·hen·si·bly** \-blē, -li\ *adv*
com·pre·hen·sion \ˌ==ˈhenchən\ *n* -s [MF & L; MF *compréhension*, fr. L *comprehension-, comprehensio*, fr. *comprehensus* (past part. of *comprehendere*) + *-ion-, -io* -ion] **1 a :** the act or action of comprehending or comprising or the fact of being comprehended or comprised **:** INCLUSION ⟨the ~ of many items within a single book⟩ **b :** the faculty or capability of including **:** COMPREHENSIVENESS ⟨a concept whose ~ is so broad as to cover all other concepts⟩ **2 a :** the act or action of grasping (as an idea or process) with the intellect **:** UNDERSTANDING ⟨a real ~ of all difficulties⟩ **b :** the resultant of comprehending mentally **:** apperceptive knowledge or knowing ⟨he has not the slightest ~ of the subject⟩ **c :** the capacity or power of the mind for understanding fully ⟨some readers are dull of ~ —W.M.Thackeray⟩ **3** *obs* **:** SUMMARY, EPITOME **4** *obs* **:** a physical grasping (of something) **:** COMPRESSION **5** *logic* **:** the totality of attributes that make up the notion signified by a general term **:** the sum of the characteristics distinguishing a class **:** INTENSION, CONNOTATION **6 :** inclusion of nonconformists in the Church of England by widening the terms of communion (as by legal enactment during the 17th century)
[1]com·pre·hen·sive \¦==¦hen(t)siv, -sēv *also* -səv\ *adj* [LL *comprehensivus*, fr. L *comprehensus* + *-ivus* -ive] **1 a :** covering a matter under consideration completely or nearly completely **:** accounting for or comprehending all or virtually all pertinent considerations **:** INCLUSIVE ⟨a ~ question⟩ ⟨a ~ plan⟩ ⟨a ~ list⟩ ⟨a ~ index to rare coins⟩ ⟨a ~ whole⟩ **b** *of insurance* **:** covering all hazards of a given type with the exception of individual hazards specif. excluded ⟨a ~ insurance policy⟩ ⟨~ automobile liability⟩ ⟨~ coverage⟩ **2 :** having the power to understand or grasp **:** of wide mental grasp ⟨a ~ head for financial problems⟩ ⟨a ~ student of racial affairs⟩ ⟨a ~ knowledge of physics⟩ **3 a** *of a school* **:** CONSOLIDATED **b** *of a secondary school* **:** offering a full set of curricula (as college preparatory, commercial, and vocational courses together with extracurricular activities) ⟨a ~ high school⟩ **4** *logic* **:** relating to comprehension **:** CONNOTATIVE, INTENSIVE — **com·pre·hen·sive·ly** \-səvlē, -li\ *adv*
[2]comprehensive \"\ *n* -s **1 :** a finished or highly detailed layout (as of a proposed advertisement) intended to show how a printed version would appear **2** *or* **comprehensive examination :** an examination designed to test general mastery of a broad academic field (as one taken at the end of the sophomore college year to test a student's readiness to specialize or at the end of the senior college year to test a student's mastery of his field of concentration) — often used in pl.
com·pre·hen·sive·ness *n* -ES **:** the quality or state of being comprehensive
com·presence \(ˈ)käm+\ *n* [*com-* + *presence*] **:** the quality or state of being present together ⟨the ~ of diverse ideas in a single concept⟩
com·present \"+\ *adj* [*com-* + *present*] **:** present together **:** associated in the same complex or grouping **:** related as factors in the same process — used esp. of elements or factors in the same state of consciousness
[1]com·press \kəm'pres\ *vb* -ED/-ING/-ES [ME *compressen*, fr. LL *compressare*, fr. L *compressus*, past part. of *comprimere* to compress, fr. *com-* + *-primere* (fr. *premere* to press) — more at PRESS] *vt* **1 :** to reduce the volume, size, duration, density, or degree of concentration of by or as if by pressure: as **a :** to make (an opening or the inner capacity of) smaller **:** CONSTRICT, CLOSE ⟨~ a severed artery⟩ **b** (1) **:** to press together **:** SQUEEZE ⟨~ a bundle under one's arm⟩ ⟨his lips were . . . ~*ed* by thought —Thomas Hardy⟩ (2) *obs* **:** EMBRACE **c :** to make hard or solid ⟨the lint is then blown into the press and ~*ed* into bales —*Amer. Guide Series: Tenn.*⟩ **d :** REPRESS, RESTRAIN ⟨~ an angry mob⟩ ⟨the culprit . . . sat ~*ing* hysterics before him —George Meredith⟩ **e :** to reduce the volume of by pressure ⟨~ air⟩ **f :** CONDENSE ⟨~ much thought into few words⟩ ⟨the government . . . ~*ed* into less than five years . . . what might have otherwise taken a generation —F.L.Allen⟩ **g :** to make smaller in size ⟨when the bird drops it immediately squats and ~*es* its plumage —W.F.Brown b.1903⟩ ⟨the gunman ~*ed* his body against the shadowy wall⟩ **h :** to subject (a workman) to compression in an air lock ~ *vi* **:** to undergo compression ⟨if plates are mounted on wood blocks, these blocks may ~ a great deal under pressure —*Theory & Practice of Presswork*⟩ **syn** see CONTRACT
[2]com·press \'käm,pres\ *n* -ES [MF *compresse*, fr. *compresser* to compress, fr. LL *compressare*] **1 a :** a covering consisting usu. of a folded cloth that is applied and held firmly by the aid of a bandage over a wound dressing to prevent oozing **b :** a folded wet or dry cloth applied firmly to a part (as to allay inflammation) **2 :** a machine for compressing cotton bales as they come from the gin
com·pressed \kəm'prest *sometimes* 'käm,p-\ *adj* [ME, fr. past part. of *compressen*] **1 :** pressed together **:** COMPACTED **:** reduced in volume by pressure **:** CONDENSED **2 :** flattened as though subjected to compression: **a** *of plant parts* **:** flattened laterally — often used postpositively ⟨petioles ~⟩ **b** *of animals and animal parts* **:** narrow from side to side and correspondingly deep in a dorsoventral direction ⟨the flounders have strongly ~ bodies⟩ — compare DEPRESSED — **com·pressed·ly** \kəm'prestlē, -sədlē\ *adv*
compressed air *n* **:** air under pressure greater than that of the atmosphere — compare COMPRESS *vt* e
compressed-air illness *also* **compressed-air sickness** *or* **compressed-air disease** *n* **:** CAISSON DISEASE
compressed score *n* **:** SHORT SCORE
compressed tablet *n* **:** a pharmaceutical tablet formed by subjecting dry granular powders to sufficient pressure to make the particles cohere
compressed yeast *n* **:** a cake yeast made by filtering the cells from the liquid in which they are grown, subjecting them to heavy pressure, and mixing them with starch or flour
com·press·ibil·i·ty \kəm,presə'biləd·ē, -ətē, -i\ *n* -ES **1 :** capability of compression ⟨the ~ of a fluid⟩ **2** *also* **compressibility coefficient** *or* **compressibility modulus :** a number expressing the change in volume of a gas, liquid, or solid per unit pressure and being the reciprocal of the bulk modulus
compressibility burble *n* **:** a burble that occurs in the flow about an airplane at speeds approaching the speed of sound
compressibility coefficient *n* **:** COEFFICIENT OF COMPRESSIBILITY
compressibility effect *n* **:** any of the effects (as abrupt changes in control characteristics) that result from changes in the flow field about an airplane when the velocity at some point in the field reaches the local speed of sound and the air ceases to behave as an incompressible fluid
com·press·ible \kəm'presəbəl\ *adj* **:** capable of being compressed — **com·press·ible·ness** *n* -ES — **com·press·ibly** \-blē\ *adv*
com·press·ing·ly *adv* **:** in a compressing manner
com·pres·sion \kəm'preshən\ *n* -s *often attrib* [ME *compressioun*, fr. L *compression-, compressio*, fr. *compressus* (past part. of *comprimere* to compress) + *-ion-, -io* -ion] **1 :** the act or action of compressing: **a :** RESTRAINING, REPRESSING ⟨a stern ~ of all emotion⟩ **b :** CONDENSING, CONCENTRATING ⟨the poet's ~ of form and content⟩ **c** (1) **:** the process of compressing the working substance in a heat engine (as the fuel mixture in a cylinder of an internal-combustion engine prior to the explosion) (2) **:** COMPRESSION RATIO **d :** passage of larval stages within the egg whether due to accelerated development or to prolongation of the period preceding hatching **e :** subjection of a workman to compressed air in an air lock before he goes into a caisson to work **2 :** the quality or state of being compressed, pressed in, together, or upon or of being concentrated or condensed ⟨the ~ of tyranny⟩ ⟨a novel showing admirable ~ of phrase and idea⟩ **3 :** the result of being compressed: as **a :** INDENTATION, HOLLOW, DENT; *esp* **:** the effect of a compressive force upon a body part ⟨~ of an artery by forceps⟩ ⟨~ of the brain by the bones in a depressed fracture⟩ **b :** fossil plant remains that have been somewhat flattened by the vertical pressure of overlying strata **c** (1) **:** the shortening produced in a body by a longitudinal compressive force (as a load applied to a short column) (2) **:** this shortening per unit of length (3) **:** fractional decrease of volume due to pressure (4) **:** COMPRESSIVE STRESS **d :** the reduction of the volume range of an incoming radio signal whether purposely in order to counteract signal fading or distortion or because of some defect in the circuit
com·pres·sion·al \-shənᵊl, -shnəl\ *adj* **:** consisting of, having to do with, or producing compression ⟨a ~ force⟩
compressional wave *also* **compression wave** *n* **:** a longitudinal wave (as a sound wave) propagated by the elastic compression of the medium
compression cup *n* **:** an oil cup or grease cup in which the grease or oil is forced to the bearing surface by compression (as by screwing down the top)
compression dressing *n* **:** PRESSURE DRESSING
compression failure *n* **:** a collapse or buckling of wood fibers resulting from compression along the grain (as that caused by bending or strain)
compression faucet *n* **:** a faucet closed by a valve that is forced against its seat
compression ignition *n* **:** ignition in an internal-combustion engine in which the necessary high temperature is produced by compressing air in the cylinder before admission of the fuel (as in a diesel engine) ⟨*compression-ignition* engine⟩
compression member *n* **:** a structural member (as of a building or an airplane) that is subjected to compressive stresses
compression molding *n* **:** a molding process used esp. for plastics in which heat and pressure are brought to bear on the material in the mold
compression ratio *n* **:** the ratio of the maximum to the minimum volume of the space enclosed by the piston of an internal-combustion engine during a full stroke — called also *compression*
compression ring *n* **:** PISTON RING; *esp* **:** one placed nearest the working face of the piston
compression spring *n* **:** a spring usu. of coil type that is used to offer resistance to a force tending to compress the spring
compression stroke *n* **:** the stroke in the cycle of an internal-combustion engine in which the gases are compressed before firing
compression wood *n* **:** reaction wood formed on the lower sides of branches and leaning trunks and characterized by darker color, glassy appearance, relatively wide and eccentric annual rings, shorter vascular elements, and excessive and uneven shrinkage — compare TENSION WOOD
com·pres·sive \kəm'presiv\ *adj* [*compress* + *-ive*] **1 :** of or relating to compression **:** tending to compress ⟨a ~ force⟩ **2 :** characterized by dysphoria and exaggerated feelings of personal inadequacy — **com·pres·sive·ly** \-sāvlē\ *adv*
compressive strength *n* **:** the maximum compressive stress that under gradually applied load a given solid material will sustain without fracture — compare TENSILE STRENGTH
compressive stress *n* **:** the stress that results from the shortening in one dimension of an elastic body due to oppositely directed collinear forces tending to crush it
com·pres·som·e·ter \ˌkäm,pre'sämәd·ə(r), kəm'presə,mēd·ə(r)\ *n* -s [*compression* + *-o-* + *-meter*] **:** an instrument for measuring compression in an elastic solid
com·pres·sor \kəm'presə(r)\ *n* -s [L, fr. *compressus* (past part. of *comprimere* to compress) + *-or*] **:** one that compresses: as **a :** a muscle that compresses a part or parts **b :** a machine (as a pump or an engine part) that compresses air, fuel-air mixtures, or other gases — see JET ENGINE illustration **c** *naut* **:** a device for checking a line or cable **d :** a device that introduces intentional compression into a communications signal
com·pres·sure \kəm'preshə(r)\ *n* [¹*compress* + *-ure*] **:** COMPRESSION
com·priest \'käm,prēst\ *n* [*com-* + *priest*] **:** a fellow priest
com·pri·mar·io \ˌkämprə'ma(a)rē,ō, -mär-\ *n* -s [It, fr. *com-* (fr. L) + *primario* primary, principal, fr. L *primarius* principal — more at PRIMARY] **:** a singer or dancer esp. in an operatic organization who is ranked usu. just below the primary singers and dancers ⟨a ~ part⟩
comprisal *also* **comprizal** *n* -s [*comprise* + *-al*, n. suffix] *obs* **:** COMPENDIUM, EPITOME
com·prise *also* **com·prize** \kəm'prīz\ *vb* -ED/-ING/-S [ME *comprisen*, fr. MF *compris* (past part. of *comprendre* to comprehend), fr. L *comprehensus*, past part. of *comprehendere* — more at COMPREHEND] *vt* **1 :** to include esp. within a particular scope **:** sum up **:** COVER, CONTAIN ⟨a whole religion *comprised* within one book⟩ ⟨his program was *comprised* in the party slogan⟩ **2** *obs* **:** UNDERSTAND **3** *obs* **:** to lay hold of **:** SEIZE **4** *obs* **:** ENCLOSE, HOLD **5 a :** to consist of **:** be made up of ⟨the fortress ~*s* many miles of entrenchment and well-hidden artillery positions⟩ ⟨the thirty-five essays it ~*s* . . . are mostly reprinted from previous collections —Harry Levin⟩ **b :** to make up **:** CONSTITUTE ⟨the receipts . . . *comprised* the fifth-largest gate in boxing history —John Lardner⟩ ~ *vi* **:** to be made up **:** CONSIST — used with *of* ⟨the funds of the association shall ~ of members' subscriptions —*Education*⟩
com·pro·mis \¦kämprə¦mē\ *n* -ES [F, lit., compromise] **1 :** a formal agreement between nations submitting a dispute to arbitration and defining the terms of the submission, the powers of the tribunal to serve as arbitrator, and the procedure to be followed **2 :** an agreement in Roman civil law between private persons referring a dispute between them to a designated third person for decision
[1]com·pro·mise \'kämprə,mīz\ *n* -s [ME, fr. MF *compromis*, fr. L *compromissum*, fr. neut. of *compromissus*, past part. of *compromittere* to promise mutually to abide by the decision of an arbiter, fr. *com-* + *promittere* to promise — more at PROMISE] **1** *obs* **:** an agreement to refer matters in dispute to arbitrators **2 a** (1) *obs* **:** settlement of a dispute by means of an arbiter (2) **:** the delegation to one or more responsible persons of the right to elect — used esp. of papal elections **b :** a settlement by arbitration or by consent reached by mutual concessions **:** a reciprocal abatement of extreme demands or rights resulting in an agreement **:** COMPOSITION **3 :** a committal to something derogatory, hazardous, or objectionable **:** a prejudicial concession **:** SURRENDER ⟨a ~ of character⟩ **4 :** the result or embodiment of concession or adjustment

⟨hand down a ~⟩; *esp* **:** a thing intermediate between or blending qualities of two different things ⟨a ~ solution⟩
²compromise \"\ *vb* -ED/-ING/-S *vt* **1** *obs* **a** *of an arbiter* **:** to adjust or settle (a difference) between parties **b :** to bind by mutual agreement **2** *of factions* **:** to adjust or settle by partial mutual relinquishment of principles, position, or claims **:** settle by coming to terms ⟨husband and wife *compromised* their differences⟩ **3 a :** to put in jeopardy **:** endanger (as life, reputation, or dignity) by some act that cannot be recalled **:** expose to suspicion, discredit, or mischief ⟨~ one's conscience⟩ ⟨~ national security⟩ **b :** to cause (a person) embarrassment, humiliation, or shame by improper erotic advances or by allowing the suspicion of such to arise ⟨in those days a girl was *compromised* if she danced more than twice with the same man⟩ **c :** to reveal or expose to unauthorized persons and esp. to an enemy (the nature, details, or workings of classified matter or a classified device) ⟨capture of a number of unenciphered messages will ~ the cryptographic system⟩ ~ *vi* **1 :** to come to a settlement or agreement by mutual concession ⟨union and employer agreed to ~⟩ **2 :** to make a shameful or disreputable concession ⟨rather die than ~⟩ — often used with *with* ⟨gave up a lucrative editorial position . . . rather than ~ with his principles —H.L.Smith b.1906⟩
compromise formation *n* **:** a psychic product, symptom, symbol, or dream form that expresses simultaneously and partially satisfies both the unconscious impulse and the defense against it
compromise joint *n* **:** a step joint used for joining two rails of different sizes or shapes
com·pro·mis·sion \ˌkämprəˈmishən\ *n* -s [ME *compromissioun*, fr. ML *compromission-, compromissio*, fr. L *compromissus* (past part. of *compromittere*) + *-ion-, -io* -ion] **1 a :** delegation of a dispute to arbiters **b :** delegation of the right to elect to one or more persons **2 :** the act or action of jeopardizing (as one's moral or ethical principles)
compromit *vt* **compromitted; compromitted; compromitting; compromits** [ME *compromitten*, fr. L *compromittere*] *to promise mutually to abide by the decision of an arbiter* — more at COMPROMISE] *obs* **:** COMPROMISE
¹com·provincial \ˌ¦käm+\ *adj* [ML *comprovincialis*, fr. L *com-* + *provincialis* provincial] **:** of the same archiepiscopal province ⟨a ~ bishop⟩
²comprovincial \"\ *n* -s **:** one of the bishops of a particular archiepiscopal province ⟨a primate's control over his ~*s*⟩
comps *pl of* COMP, *pres 3d sing of* COMP
comp·si·lu·ra \ˌkämpsəˈlu̇rə\ *n, cap* [NL] **:** a genus of tachinid flies including one (*C. concinnata*) that is important in the biological control of several destructive phytophagous moths (as the gypsy, brown-tail, and satin moths)
comp·sog·na·thus \kämpˈsägnəthəs\ *n, cap* [NL, fr. Gk *kompso-* (fr. *kompsos* elegant) + NL *-gnathus* -gnathous; prob. akin to Lith *švankus* proper] **:** a genus of very small carnivorous saurischian dinosaurs (suborder Theropoda) from the Upper Jurassic of Bavaria with long hind limbs and three-toed feet much like those of a bird
comp·so·thlyp·i·dae \ˌkämpsəthˈlipəˌdē\ [NL, fr. *Compsothlypis*, genus of passerine birds + *-idae*] *syn of* PARULIDAE
¹compt \ˈkau̇nt, ˈkäm(p)t\ *archaic var of* COUNT
²compt *adj* [L *comptus*, past part. of *comere* to arrange, adorn, fr. *co-* + *emere* to buy (in preliterary Latin, to take) — more at REDEEM] *obs* **:** NEAT, SPRUCE, POLISHED
compt *abbr* **1** compartment **2** comptometer **3** comptroller
compt·er \ˈkau̇ntə(r), ˈkäm(p)t-\ *n* -s [alter. (influenced by F *compter* to calculate, count) of *counter* — more at COUNT] *archaic Brit* **:** a prison used esp. for debtors
comptible *adj* [alter. (influenced by *-ible*) of earlier *comptable*, alter. (influenced by MF *comptable* responsible) of *countable* — more at COUNTABLE (responsible)] **1** *obs* **:** RESPONSIBLE, ANSWERABLE **2** *obs* **:** SENSITIVE
comptie *var of* COONTIE
comp·ton effect \ˈkäm(p)tən-\ *also* **compton scattering** *n, usu cap C* [after Arthur H. *Compton* †1962 Am. physicist who first observed it] **:** the scattering of an X-ray or gamma-ray photon upon impact with an electron within an atom accompanied by transfer of a part of the photon's energy to the electron with consequent loss of frequency — compare COMPTON SHIFT
compton electron *n, usu cap C* **:** an electron ejected from an atom by the impact of incident radiation in the Compton effect
compton shift *n, usu cap C* **:** the increase in X-ray or gamma-ray wavelength resulting from the transfer of energy that accompanies the scattering of photons in the Compton effect
comp·trol·ler \kənˈtrōlə(r), ˈkäm(p)ˌt-, käm(p)ˈt-, ˈkän·ˌt-, känˈt-\ *n* -s [ME, alter. (influenced by MF *compte* account, count) of *conterroller* controller — more at CONTROLLER, COUNT] **1 :** a controller esp. of accounts or finances **2 :** a public officer whose duty it is to supervise accounts and determine the propriety of expenditures ⟨Army *Comptroller* in the office of the chief of staff at Washington —*Current Biog.*⟩
comptroller general *n, pl* **comptrollers general :** an officer in the U.S. federal government charged with the adjustment of all claims for or against the government and with the investigation of all matters related to the receipt, disbursement, and application of public funds
comptroller of the currency *usu cap both Cs* **:** an official of the Treasury Department of the U.S. government who exercises general control over all national banks and over the issue of federal reserve notes
comp·trol·ler·ship \-ˌship\ *n* -s **:** CONTROLLERSHIP
com·pul·sa·tive \kəmˈpəlsəd·iv\ *adj* [obs. *compulse* to compel (fr. ME *compulsen*, fr. L *compulsus*, past part. of *compellere*) + *-ative*] *obs* **:** COMPULSORY
com·pul·sa·to·ry \kəmˈpəlsəˌtōrē\ *adj* [obs. *compulse* + *-ate* + *-ory*] **:** COMPULSORY ⟨~ taxes⟩
com·pul·sion \kəmˈpəlshən\ *n* -s [ME *compulsioun*, fr. MF or LL; MF *compulsion*, fr. LL *compulsion-, compulsio*, fr. L *compulsus* (past part. of *compellere* to compel) + *-ion-, -io* -ion — more at COMPEL] **1 a :** an act of compelling **:** a driving by force, power, pressure, or necessity ⟨I do not assert that rational reform can wholly dispense with physical ~ —J.A.Hobson⟩ ⟨by ~ of the swirling currents —Mark Twain⟩ ⟨acting under ~, not on his own free will⟩ **b :** a force or agency that compels ⟨it is a shapeless book and it lacks the ~ of the best narrative —John Buchan⟩ **c :** a condition marked by compelling, by forced action or assent ⟨peonage is service to a private master at which a man is kept by bodily ~ against his will —O.W.Holmes †1935⟩ **2 :** an irresistible impulse to perform an irrational act the performance of which tends to disturb a neurotic doer but not a psychotic — compare OBSESSION **syn** see FORCE
compulsion neurosis *n* **:** OBSESSIVE-COMPULSIVE NEUROSIS
com·pul·si·tor \kəmˈpəlsəd·ər\ *n* -s [*compulsit-* (irreg. fr. *compulsatory*) + *-or*] *Scots law* **:** a compulsory agent or means (as a mandate)
¹com·pul·sive \kəmˈpəlsiv, -sēv *also* -səv\ *adj* [obs. *compulse* + *-ive*] **1 :** having power to compel ⟨admonishing the people in a strangely ~, resonant voice, to be orderly —L.C.Douglas⟩ **:** exercising or applying compulsion ⟨forced to adopt ~ measures to collect taxes⟩ **2** *archaic* **:** produced or caused by compulsion **:** FORCED **3 :** of, having to do with, caused by, or suggestive of psychological compulsion or obsession ⟨mechanical lovemaking, ~ drinking, and considerations of suicide —J.W.Aldridge⟩ — **com·pul·sive·ly** \-sävlē, -li\ *adv* — **com·pul·sive·ness** *n* -ES
²compulsive \"\ *n* -s **1 :** a compelling force ⟨cultural ~*s*⟩ **2 :** one who is subject to a psychological compulsion ⟨the excessive cleanliness of the ~, who is struggling against instinctual demands for dirt and disorder —G.S.Blum⟩
com·pul·so·ri·ly \-s(ə)rəlē, -li\ *adv* **:** in a compulsory manner ⟨candidates . . . must be ~ examined —Barbara Wootton⟩
com·pul·so·ri·ness \-rēnəs, -rin-\ *n* -ES **:** the quality or state of being compulsory
¹com·pul·so·ry \kəmˈpəls(ə)rē, -ri\ *adj* [ML *compulsorius* coercive, fr. L *compulsus* (past part. of *compellere*) + *-orius* -ory] **1 :** demanded, directed, or designated by authority **:** ENFORCED, MANDATORY ⟨~ retirement⟩ ⟨~ vaccination⟩ ⟨fees ~ for all applicants⟩ **2 :** having the power of compulsion **:** COERCIVE, COMPELLING ⟨~ measures⟩ **3 a** *of education* **:** requiring or insuring under law a minimum literary level and usu. promoted in the case of minors by attendance of an authorized school up to a specified age limit **b :** obligatory esp. for the fulfillment of degree or graduation requirements ⟨for science majors biology and astronomy are ~⟩
²compulsory \"\ *n* -ES [ML *compulsorium*, fr. neut. of *compulsorius*, adj.] *archaic* **:** a measure or means (as a legal injunction) compelling obedience
compulsory jurisdiction *n* **1 :** a jurisdiction existing by force of law over a person **2 :** a mandatory jurisdiction that a state has agreed to accept in certain prescribed matters
compulsory listing *n* **:** MULTIPLE LISTING
com·punc·tion \kəmˈpəŋ(k)shən\ *n* -s [ME *compunctioun*, fr. MF *componction*, fr. LL *compunction-, compunctio*, fr. L *compunctus* (past part. of *compungere* to prick hard, sting fr. *com-* + *pungere* to prick, sting) + *-ion-, -io* -ion — more at PUNGENT] **1 a :** anxiety of spirit arising from consciousness of sin **:** deep unease caused by knowledge of guilt ⟨~*s* of conscience⟩ **b :** normal human regret, pity, or anxiety **:** REMORSE ⟨he showed no ~ in planning devilish engines of military destruction —Havelock Ellis⟩ **c :** a twinge of uneasiness **:** SCRUPLE ⟨cheating without ~⟩ **2** *archaic* **:** compassionate sorrow **:** PITY **syn** see PENITENCE, SCRUPLE
com·punc·tion·less \-ləs\ *adj* **:** lacking compunction
com·punc·tious \-shəs\ *adj* [*compunction* + *-ous*] **1 :** arising from remorse or regret ⟨~ feelings⟩ **2 :** feeling remorse or regret ⟨deeply ~ for his outburst⟩ — **com·punc·tious·ly** *adv*
com·pur·ga·tion \ˌkäm(ˌ)pərˈgāshən\ *n* -s [LL *compurgation-, compurgatio*, fr. L *compurgatus* (past part. of *compurgare* to purify wholly, fr. *com-* + *purgare* to purify) + *-ion-, -io* -ion — more at PURGE] **:** vindication (as from a charge) or testimony or evidence that vindicates; *esp* **:** the clearing of a defendant or accused person by oaths of persons who swear to his veracity or innocence — often used of the mode of vindication of ecclesiastical courts or of the similar procedure in old Germanic courts; compare WAGER OF LAW
com·pur·ga·tor \ˈkäm(ˌ)pərˌgād·ər\ *n* -s [ML, fr. L *compurgatus* + *-or*] **:** one that defends or supports another ⟨spoke most kindly as my ~*s* —H.J.Laski⟩; *specif* **:** one that under oath vouches for the blameless character or conduct of an accused person attempting thereby to vindicate him
com·pur·ga·to·ri·al \kəm¦pərgə¦tōrēəl, käm¦p-, ¦käm,p-\ *adj* [*compurgatory* + *-al*] **:** COMPURGATORY
com·pur·ga·to·ry \kəmˈpərgəˌtōrē, (ˈ)käm¦p-\ *adj* [*compurgator* + *-ory*] **:** of or relating to a compurgator or compurgation
com·put·abil·i·ty \kəm,pyü¦d·əˈbiləd·ē, |təˈb-, -lətē, -i *also* ˌkämpyə\ *n* -ES **:** the quality or state of being computable
com·put·able \kəmˈpyü|d·əbəl, |təbəl *also* ˈkämpyə\ *adj* [L *computabilis*, fr. *computare* + *-abilis* -able] **:** capable of being computed — **com·put·ably** \-blē\ *adv*
com·pu·ta·tion \ˌkämpyəˈtāshən\ *n* -s [ME *computacion*, fr. L *computation-, computatio*, fr. *computatus* (past part. of *computare* to compute) + *-ion-, -io* -ion] **1 :** the act or action of computing **:** CALCULATION, RECKONING ⟨there had come many from the north — seven, by the squire's ~ —R.L.Stevenson⟩ **2 :** a way or system of reckoning ⟨conformity with Roman practice in regard to . . . the ~ of Easter —F.M.Stenton⟩ **3 :** the result of computation **:** amount computed
com·pu·ta·tion·al \ˌ¦kämpyə¦tāshənᵊl, -shnəl\ *adj* **:** having to do with computation ⟨~ errors⟩ ⟨~ aids⟩
com·pu·ta·tive \kəmˈpyüd·əd·iv *also* ˈkämpyəˌtād·iv\ *adj* [*compute* + *-ative*] **:** given to or employing computation
com·pu·ta·tor \ˈkämpyəˌtād·ə(r)\ *n* -s [L, fr. *computatus* + *-or*] **:** COMPUTER
¹com·pute \kəmˈpyüt, *usu* -üd·+V\ *n* -s [LL *computus*, fr. L *computare*] **:** COMPUTATION — used chiefly with *beyond* ⟨future wars will be complex beyond ~ —*U.S. Air Services*⟩
²compute \"\ *vb* -ED/-ING/-S [L *computare* — more at COUNT] *vt* **1 :** to determine or ascertain esp. by mathematical means **:** arrive at an answer to or sum for ⟨~ a bank balance⟩ ⟨~ the area of a field⟩ ⟨~ the diameter of the sun⟩ **2** *obs* **:** to make up (as a period of time) ~ *vi* **:** to make calculation **:** RECKON ⟨they ~ by weight in selling grain⟩ **syn** see CALCULATE
com·put·er *also* **com·pu·tor** \-üd·ə(r), -ütə-\ *n* -s **:** one that computes: as **a :** a calculator esp. designed for the solution of complex mathematical problems; *specif* **:** an automatic electronic machine for performing simple and complex calculations **b :** any of several devices for making rapid calculations in navigation or gunnery (as the computing of an air position or the range of fire of a gun) **c :** a person who calculates (as latitudes, longitudes, and areas) for map making from notes made by engineering survey parties
computing machine *n* **:** COMPUTER a
computing scale *n* **:** a weighing machine that indicates both weight and the proper selling price for that weight
com·put·ist \kəmˈpyüd·əst, -ütə-; ˈkämpyətə-\ *n* -s [alter. (influenced by *compute*) of earlier *compotist*, fr. ME *compotiste*, fr. MF, fr. ML *computista, compotista*, fr. LL *computus, compotus* + L *-ista* -ist] **:** one skilled in computing (as dates of the calendar, business accounts, astronomical problems)
com·pu·tus \ˈkämpyətəs\ *n* -ES [ML, fr. LL, computation] **1 :** a medieval set of tables for calculating astronomical events and movable dates in the calendar **2** *also* **com·po·tus** \-pət-\ [LL] **:** COMPUTATION, RECKONING
compy *abbr* company
com·quat *var of* KUMQUAT
comr *abbr* commissioner
¹com·rade \ˈkämˌrad, -ˌrəd, -ˌraa(ə)d, *Brit sometimes* ˈkəm- *or* -ˌrād\ *n* -s [MF *camarade* group of soldiers sleeping in one room, roommate, companion, fr. OSp *camarada*, fr. *cámara* room, fr. LL *camera* — more at CHAMBER] **1 a** *obs* **:** one that shares the same sleeping quarters as another **b :** one that shares the same fortunes or experiences as another **:** intimate friend **:** COMPANION ⟨an old ~ of fishing and hunting days⟩ — used as a form of address among members of the British Labor party and trade unions and among certain American organizations of a nonpolitical nature **c :** COMRADE-IN-ARMS ⟨his fallen ~*s*⟩ **2 a :** COMMUNIST ⟨the party had forbidden all ~*s* to go to court —Paul Hofmann⟩ — used as a form of address ⟨a speech by *Comrade* Jones⟩ **b :** a person with or suspected of communist or leftist tendencies
²comrade \"\ *vi* -ED/-ING/-S **:** to associate in comradeship ⟨the gentlemen *comraded* it with the yeomen —Adrian Bell⟩
comrade-in-arms \¦ₑ(ˌ)ₑₑ¦ₑ\ *n, pl* **comrades-in-arms :** a friend made in military service **:** a fellow soldier
com·rade·li·ness \ₑ(ˌ)ₑlēnəs, -lin-\ *n* -ES **:** CAMARADERIE
com·rade·ly \ₑ(ˌ)ₑlē, -li\ *adj* **:** of or like a comrade or partner **:** suitable to the relation of comrades ⟨a ~ handshake⟩
com·rade·ry \-drē, -ri\ *n* -ES [trans. of F *camaraderie*] **:** CAMARADERIE
com·rade·ship \-ˌship\ *n* **:** association as comrades ⟨could offer each other mutual aid and ~ —Oscar Handlin⟩
coms *pl of* COM
comsomol *usu cap, var of* KOMSOMOL
com·stock \ˈkämzˌtäk, -mˌst- *sometimes* ˈkəm-\ *also* **com·stock·er** \-kə(r)\ *n* -s [after Anthony *Comstock* †1915 Am. reformer] **:** a ludicrous prude esp. in matters relating to morality in art
com·stock·ery \-k(ə)rē, -ri\ *n* -ES **:** PRUDERY; *specif* **:** prudish concern in hunting down immorality esp. in books, papers, and pictures
comstock mealybug *or* **comstock's mealybug** *n, usu cap C* [after John H. *Comstock* †1931 Am. entomologist] **:** an Asiatic mealybug (*Pseudococcus comstocki*) introduced accidentally into No. America where it is a pest of various cultivated trees (as citrus and apples)
comte \kōⁿt\ *n* -s [F, fr. LL *comit-, comes* — more at COUNT] **:** ²COUNT
com·tesse \kōⁿˈtes\ *n* -s [F, fr. OF *comtesse, contesse*, fr. *comte, conte* + *-esse* -ess] **:** COUNTESS
comt·ian *also* **comt·ean** \ˈkäm(p)tēən, ˈkōnt-, ˈkōⁿt-\ *adj, usu cap* [Auguste *Comte* †1857 Fr. mathematician and philosopher + E *-ian* or *-an*] **:** of or relating to Auguste Comte or his writings or doctrines — compare POSITIVISM
comt·ism \-ˌtizəm\ *n* -s *often cap* [Auguste *Comte* + E *-ism*] **:** POSITIVISM 1a
comt·ist \-ˌtəst\ *adj or n* [Auguste *Comte* + E *-ist*] **:** POSITIVIST
co·mu·ni·dad \kō¦münə¦thä(th)\ *n, pl* **comunida·des** \ₑ,ₑₑ-ˈthä(ˌ)thās\ [Sp, *community*, fr. L *communitat-, communitas* — more at COMMUNITY] **:** a relatively independent Peruvian Indian community that developed out of the ayllu, constituted a collective social and economic unit, and also formed an intermediate administrative unit
¹con \ˈkän\ *vt* **conned; conned; conning; cons** [ME *connen*, alter. (influenced by *con*, 1st & 3d sing. pres. indic., fr. OE, var. of *can*) of *cunnen* — more at CAN] **1** *obs* **:** to have knowledge of **:** KNOW **2 a :** to study in order to know **:** regard or examine closely **:** PERUSE ⟨she had a complete set of "Standard Recitations" which she *conned* on Sundays —Willa Cather⟩ **b :** to commit to memory by vocal or mental repetition ⟨the orator had *conned* it by heart —S.H.Adams⟩ **c :** to reflect upon **:** PONDER ⟨the wise soldier will ~ himself, note his difference from the man he was —Christopher La Farge⟩ — **con thanks** \"-, ˈkən-\ *archaic* **:** to express gratitude **:** ACKNOWLEDGE
²con \"\ *var of* CONN
³con \"\ *adv* [ME, short for ¹*contra*] **:** on the negative side **:** in opposition — opposed to *pro* ⟨much was written pro and ~⟩
⁴con \"\ *n* -s **1 :** the arguments or evidence in opposition to a statement, proposition, or position **2 :** the negative position or one holding it **:** OPPOSITION — opposed to *pro* ⟨an appraisal of the pros and ~*s*⟩
⁵con \"\ *adj* **:** taking the opposing side **:** OPPOSITIONAL, NEGATIVE — opposed to *pro* ⟨pro and ~ arguments⟩
⁶con \"\ *prep* **:** in opposition to **:** on the negative side of **:** AGAINST — opposed to *pro* ⟨forces pro and ~ the issue⟩
⁷con \"\ *n* -s [prob. fr. F *cogner* to beat, fr. OF, fr. L *cuneus* wedge — more at COIN] *now dial Eng* **:** a rap with the knuckles
⁸con \"\ *adj* [by shortening] **:** ²CONFIDENCE
⁹con \"\ *vt* **conned; conned; conning; cons 1 :** to swindle esp. by the confidence game **:** DECEIVE, CHEAT ⟨she *conned* a victim out of his savings⟩ **2 :** to persuade or lure (a person) to the advantage of the persuader **:** TRICK, FOOL ⟨she *conned* her into buying an inferior product⟩ **3 :** CAJOLE, BLARNEY, SOFT-SOAP ⟨a mealymouthed football coach *conning* a boy with a broken knee into playing —A.J.Liebling⟩
¹⁰con \"\ *n* -s **:** fraudulent appropriation of money ⟨knew too much about ~ to fall for that one —Herbert Gold⟩
¹¹con \"\ *n* -s [by shortening] *slang* **:** CONVICT
¹²con \"\ *n* -s [by shortening] *slang* **:** CONDUCTOR 2c
¹³con \"\ *n* -s [short for *consumption*] *slang* **:** a destructive disease of the lungs: **a :** TUBERCULOSIS **b :** silicosis with superimposed tuberculous infection
¹con- — see COM-
²con- *or* **cono-** *comb form* [Gk *kōn-, kōno-*, fr. *kōnos* — more at HONE] **:** cone ⟨*conodont*⟩ ⟨*conoplain*⟩ ⟨*conoscope*⟩
con *abbr* **1** concerto **2** conclusion **3** conic **4** connecting; connection **5** consol; consolidated **6** [L *conjux*] consort **7** consul **8** continued **9** contra
con ab·ban·do·no \ˌkäˌnabənˈdō(ˌ)nō, ˌkō,-; ˌkōˌnäˌbän-\ *adv* [It, lit., with abandon] **:** UNRESTRAINEDLY **:** BRILLIANTLY — used as a direction in music
con·a·cas·te \ˌkänəˈkastē\ *n* -s [Sp *conacaste, guanacaste*, fr. Nahuatl *cuauhnacaztli*, lit., ear tree, fr. *cuahuitl* tree + *nacaztli* ear; fr. the shape of the fruit] **:** a tropical American timber tree (*Enterolobium cyclocarpum*) that has coiled ear-shaped fruits and produces a valuable wood
¹con·acre \ˈkäˌnākə(r)\ *n* -s [alter. of earlier *corn-acre*, lit., field of grain] *in a former Irish land system* **:** the subletting for a single season of small portions of a farm previously prepared for sowing or planting; *also* **:** a single parcel or tenancy so held
²conacre \"\ *vt* -ED/-ING/-S **:** to sublet (land) in conacre
con af·fet·to \ˌkänəˈfed·(ˌ)ō, ˌkōn-\ *adv* [It] **:** with feeling and tenderness — used as a direction in music
con agi·li·ta \-nə¦jilə¦tä\ *adv* [It *con agilità*, lit., with agility] **:** with liveliness — used as a direction in music
con agi·ta·zio·ne \ˌkäˌnajəˌtätsēˈōnē, ˌkō,-\ *adv* [It, lit., with agitation] **:** AGITATEDLY — used as a direction in music
con·a·kry *or* **kon·a·kri** *or* **kon·a·kry** \ˈkänəkrē\ *adj, usu cap* [fr. *Conakry, Konakri, Konakry*, seaport on Tombo Island, Guinea] **:** of or from Conakry, the capital of Guinea **:** of the kind or style prevalent in Conakry
co·nal \ˈkōnᵊl\ *adj* [NL *conus* (*arteriosus*) + E *-al*] **:** of or relating to the conus arteriosus
con·albumin \ˌ¦kän+\ *n* -s [*com-* + *albumin*] **:** a protein of the white of an egg that is obtained from the filtrate from the crystallization of ovalbumin and that combines with iron salts to form a red iron-protein complex
con al·cu·na li·cen·za \ˌkäˌnalˈkünəlēˈchen(t)(ˌ)sä, ˌkō,-, -(t)sə\ *adv* [It] **:** with some freedom — used as a direction in music
con amo·re \ˌkänəˈmōrē, ˌkōn-, -ōr(ˌ)ā\ *adv* [It] **1 :** with love or devotion **:** with zest or delight ⟨a translation made *con amore* from an obscure early writing⟩ **2 :** TENDERLY — used as a direction in music
con ani·ma \käˈnanəˌmä, kōˈnänē,-\ *or* **con ani·mo** \-mō\ *adv* [It, lit., with spirit] **:** SPIRITEDLY — used as a direction in music
co·nar·i·al \kōˈna(a)rēəl\ *adj* [NL *conarium* + E *-al*] **:** PINEAL
conarite *var of* CONNARITE
co·nar·i·um \kōˈna(a)rēəm\ *n, pl* **conar·ia** \-ēə\ [NL, fr. Gk *kōnarion*, lit., small cone, dim. of *kōnos* cone — more at HONE] **:** PINEAL BODY
co·na·tion \kōˈnāshən\ *n* -s [L *conation-, conatio* attempt, fr. *conatus* (past part. of *conari* to attempt) + *-ion-, -io* -ion — more at DEACON] **1 :** the conscious drive to perform apparently volitional acts with or without knowledge of the origin of the drive — distinguished from *affection* and *cognition* **2 :** an instinctually motivated biological striving that may appear in consciousness as volition or desire or in behavior as action tendencies — **co·na·tion·al** \-shənᵊl, -shnəl\ *adj*
¹co·na·tion·al \(ˈ)kō¦nashənᵊl, -naash-,-naish-, -shnəl\ *n* [*co-* + *national*] **:** a fellow national; *esp* **:** a fellow member of a minority national group in a state
²conational \"\ *adj* **:** of, relating to, or being a conational — **co·na·tion·al·ist** \"+əst\ *n*
¹co·na·tive \ˈkōnəd·iv, ˈkän-\ *adj* [*conation* + *-ive*] **1 :** having the characteristics of or involving conation ⟨literature and art appeal as much to the affective and ~ as to the merely cognitive side of man's being —Aldous Huxley⟩ **2 :** denoting an attempt to perform an action — used of verb forms or affixes in certain languages
²conative \"\ *n* -s **:** a conative verb form, set of verb forms, or affix
co·na·tus \kōˈnād·əs, -nād-\ *n, pl* **conatus** [NL, fr. L, effort, fr. *conatus*, past part. of *conari* to attempt — more at DEACON] **:** a natural tendency, impulse, or striving **:** CONATION — used in Spinozism with reference to the inclination of a thing to persist in its own being
con bra·vu·ra \ˌkänbrəˈv(y)u̇rə, ˌkōn-\ *adv* [It, lit., with boldness] **:** BOLDLY, BRILLIANTLY — used as a direction in music
con brio \känˈbrē(ˌ)ō, kōn-\ *adv* [It, lit., with vigor] **:** VIGOROUSLY, ENERGETICALLY ⟨a critic who voices his dislikes *con brio* —C.J.Rolo⟩ — often used as a direction in music
conc *abbr* **1** concentrated; concentration **2** concentric **3** concerning **4** concrete **5** [L *concilium*] council
con·cam·er·at·ed \(ˈ)kän¦kaməˌrād·əd, kənˈk-\ *adj* [L *concameratus* (past part. of *concamerare* to arch over, fr. *com-* + *camerare* to arch, fr. *camera* arch) + E *-ed* — more at CHAMBER] *archaic* **:** ARCHED, VAULTED
con·cam·er·a·tion \(ˌ)känˌkaməˈrāshən, kən-\ *n* -s [L *concameration-, concameratio*, fr. *concameratus* + *-ion-, -io* -ion] **1 :** a vaulted construction **:** a vaulted roof **:** a vaulted ceiling **2 :** VAULT 5
con·canavalin \ˌ¦kän+\ *n* -s [*com-* + *canavalin*] *biochem* **:** either of two crystalline globulins occurring with canavalin in the jack bean
¹con·cat·e·nate \(ˈ)kän¦kad·ənət, kənˈk-, -atən-,-atᵊn-, *usu* -əd·+V\ *adj* [ME *concatenat*, fr. LL *concatenatus*] **:** linked together
²con·cat·e·nate \känˈkad·əˌnāt, kən-, -atəˌnāt,-atᵊnˌāt, *usu* -ād·+V\ *vt* -ED/-ING/-S [LL *concatenatus*, past part. of *concatenare*, fr. L *com-* + *catenare* to chain, fr. *catena* chain — more at CHAIN] **:** to link together **:** unite in a series or chain ⟨the present work comprises five essays nicely *concatenated* —Richard Hocking⟩
con·cat·e·na·tion \(ˌ)känˌkad·əˈnāshən, kən-, -atəˈnā-, -atᵊnˈā-\ *n* -s [LL *concatenation-, concatenatio*, fr. *concatenatus* + *-ion-, -io* -ion] **1 a :** the act of concatenating **b :** the state of being concatenated **:** union in a linked series **2 :** a series of

links united : a series or order of things depending on each other as if linked together : CHAIN ⟨a complicated ~ of circumstances —Frederick Johnson⟩

con·cat·e·na·tor \kän'kad·ə,nād·ə(r), kən-, -atə,nā-,-atᵊn,ā-, -ātə-\ *n* -s : one that concatenates

con·caus·al \(')kän¦kȯzəl\ *adj* : operating as a concause

con·cause \'kän,kȯz\ *n* -s [ML *concausa*, fr. L *com-* + *causa* cause — more at CAUSE] : one of several causes acting together

[1]**con·cave** \'kän,kāv, *esp Brit sometimes* -äŋ,-\ *n* -s [MF, fr. *concave*, adj.] **1 a** : a hollow within a mass or in a surface ⟨Vulcan . . . splits the cliff and discloses a ~ fashioned by his art —E.K.Chambers⟩ **b** : a curved recess : a depression resembling a bowl **c** *obs* : the bore of a gun **2 a** : the inner face of a bowl-shaped structure **b** : the vault of the sky **3** *obs* : a concave lens or mirror **4** : a set of bars bearing teeth, rasps, or rubber facing curved partly around a rotating threshing cylinder as an aid in shelling grain or seeds in a thresher

[2]**concave** \(')=¦=\ *adj* [MF, fr. L *concavus*, fr. *com-* + *cavus* hollow — more at CAVE] **1** *obs* : having a hollow interior ⟨~ . . . as a worm-eaten nut —Shak.⟩ **2 a** : hollowed or rounded inward like the inside of a bowl **b** : having a shape that is thought of as curving inward — opposed to *convex* **3** : arched in : curving in — used of the side of a curve or surface on which neighboring normals to the curve or surface converge and on which lies the chord joining two neighboring points of the curve or surface; opposed to *convex* — **con·cave·ly** *adv* — **con·cave·ness** *n* -ES

[3]**concave** \"\ *vb* -ED/-ING/-S *vt* : to make concave ~ *vi* : to curve concavely

concave grating *n* : a reflection grating ruled on a concave mirror

concave polygon *n* : a polygon with one angle larger than a straight angle

con·cav·er \(')kän¦kāvə(r)\ *n* -s : one that shapes or forms a concave surface or edge

con·cav·i·ty \kän'kavəd·ē, -ətē, -i *sometimes* kən-\ *n* -ES [MF *concavité*, fr. LL *concavitat-*, *concavitas*, fr. L *concavus* + *-itat-* *-itas* -ity] **1 a** : a concave line or surface or the space included by it : a hollow esp. of a vault or a hemisphere **b** : a depression resembling a bowl **2** : CONCAVE 1 **3** : the quality or state of being concave

con·ca·vo–con·cave \kän¦kā(,)vō¦kän,kāv\ *adj* [*concavo-* (fr. L *concavus*) + E *concave*] : concave on both sides — used esp. of a lens

con·ca·vo–convex \kän¦kā(,)vō+\ *adj* [*concavo-* + *convex*] **1** : concave on one side and convex on the other **2** *of a lens* : having the concave side of greater curvature than the convex side

con·ceal \kən'sēl, *esp bef pause or cons* -ēəl\ *vt* -ED/-ING/-S [ME *concelen*, fr. MF *conceler*, fr. L *concelare*, fr. *com-* + *celare* to hide — more at HELL] **1** : to prevent disclosure or recognition of : avoid revelation of : refrain from revealing : withhold knowledge of : draw attention from : treat so as to be unnoticed ⟨confessing . . . things a woman ought to ~ —Thomas Hardy⟩ **2** : to place out of sight : withdraw from being observed : shield from vision or notice ⟨it grew so thickly as to ~ the roof —Richard Jefferies⟩
syn HIDE, BURY, SECRETE, CACHE, SCREEN, ENSCONCE: CONCEAL and HIDE are general terms often interchangeable. CONCEAL may be applied freely to persons and animals, objects, attributes, conditions, facts, or ideas ⟨Sophia had held the telegram *concealed* in her hand and its information *concealed* in her heart —Arnold Bennett⟩ ⟨Elizabeth was forced to *conceal* her lover from her father —Virginia Woolf⟩ ⟨politeness may *conceal* a legitimate wish that dare not put itself in bald speech —R.P.Blackmur⟩ CONCEAL may indicate any hiding or masking of any motive, from reprehensible secrecy to aesthetic improvement ⟨*conceal* a murder⟩ ⟨*conceal* a scar⟩ ⟨*concealing* a scratch on a piece of furniture⟩ ⟨*conceal* a bad odor⟩ It need not suggest covering. It often implies a certain design or artfulness. HIDE may differ from CONCEAL in suggesting less conscious intent and artfulness, and hence less effectiveness, but occas. more urgency ⟨*hidden* things that had never been concealed, that had merely been dropped away into forgotten corners and out-of-the-way places —Elizabeth M. Roberts⟩ ⟨with these consoling words he tried to *hide* from her the doubt that had entered his mind —Morley Callaghan⟩ It is less applicable than CONCEAL to senses other than sight. BURY suggests concealment in a low place by covering, esp. by heaping something amorphous ⟨loot *buried* under the ground⟩ or, in more figurative senses, it suggests relegation to obscurity ⟨I would myself be half *buried* in shadows and in darkness —Sherwood Anderson⟩ SECRETE is likely to have an increased suggestion of highly purposive, secretive, stealthy concealment ⟨she could scarcely . . . overcome the suspicion of there being many chambers *secreted* —Jane Austen⟩ ⟨and in mere sound *secretes* his inmost sense —Walter de la Mare⟩ CACHE suggests use of storage places affording security or protection as well as concealment, sometimes in the ground. SCREEN suggests protection or concealment from observation or danger by that which screens from a viewer's eyes ⟨*screened* himself under a bush and waited —Thomas Hardy⟩ ⟨the idea of a woman's appealing to her family to *screen* her husband's business dishonor —Edith Wharton⟩ ENSCONCE, in this sense, implies the security of concealment in a raised or walled area ⟨bounded into the vehicle and sat on a stool, *ensconced* from view —Thomas Hardy⟩ ⟨he *ensconced* the boy in a cubbyhole —Peggy Bacon⟩

con·ceal·able \-ēləbəl\ *adj* : capable of being concealed

concealed *adj*, *of a hand in canasta and certain forms of rummy* : fully matched and enabling one to go out without previously having melded

concealed asset *n* : a tangible or intangible asset that is not reflected on the balance sheet in accounting or finance or that is carried at nominal value (as stock of a subsidiary or a valuable patent)

concealed bed *n* : DISAPPEARING BED

concealed damage *n* **1** : damage to the contents of a package that is not apparent until the package is opened **2** : a seed rot of peanuts that is not visible until the seed is broken open and that is caused by invasion of the space between the seed halves by various fungi esp. of the genus *Diplodia*

con·cealed·ly \-ēlədlē, -ēl(d)lē, -li\ *adv* : in a concealed manner

concealed loss *n* : loss of goods from a container not apparent from the condition of the container

con·cealed·ness \-ēlədnəs, -ēl(d)n-\ *n*-ES : the quality or state of being concealed

concealed weapon *n* : a dangerous weapon so carried on the person as to be knowingly or willfully concealed from sight usu. in violation of statute

con·ceal·er \kən'sēlə(r)\ *n* -s : one that conceals

con·ceal·ment \-ē(ə)lmənt\ *n* -s [ME *concelement*, fr. MF, fr. *conceler* + *-ment*] **1 a** : the act or practice of concealing : the state of being concealed ⟨process . . . could not be served by reason of her absence from or ~ within the state —*Detroit Law Jour.*⟩ **b** : the practice or fact of concealing what ought to be revealed : improper secrecy ⟨his secrecy had the character of prudent reserve, not of cunning or ~ —George Bancroft⟩ **2** *obs* : out-of-the-way knowledge : secret information : MYSTERY **3 a** : a means of concealing : a hiding place **b concealments** *pl* : conditions or facilities for concealing

concealment cipher *n* : a method of hiding a message in a cover text (as the trellis cipher)

con·cede \kən'sēd\ *vb* -ED/-ING/-S [F or L; F *concéder*, fr. L *concedere*, fr. *com-* + *cedere* to go along, give way, yield — more at CEDE] *vt* **1** : to grant as a right or privilege : ALLOW, SURRENDER, PERMIT ⟨Britain *conceded* the independence of the colonies⟩ ⟨we cannot ~ an increase in wages now⟩ ⟨he is willing to ~ his share to his sister⟩ **2** : ADMIT, ACKNOWLEDGE ⟨the right of the state to tax is generally *conceded*⟩: **a** : to accept as true or accurate (as something discussed or debated) ⟨still less does he ~ that the British have any claim to the gratitude of the inhabitants —Michael Clark⟩ ⟨we have no choice but to ~ their figures⟩ **b** : to acknowledge grudgingly or hesitantly ⟨*conceded* that it might be a good idea⟩ ⟨they *conceded* that their decision had been unwise⟩ **c** : to acknowledge as won by an opponent without formal determination of the result ⟨South trumped the return and the opponents *conceded* the rest of the tricks⟩ ⟨the senator *conceded* the election shortly after midnight⟩ **d** : to acknowledge a person to have ⟨even his enemies ~ him courage⟩ ~ *vi* : to make concession : YIELD **syn** see GRANT

con·ced·ed·ly *adv* : INDISPUTABLY, ADMITTEDLY ⟨~ honest expressions of opinion —*Time*⟩ ⟨probably not more than one out of ten and ~ not more than one out of four . . . are actually rented —Charles Abrams⟩

[1]**con·ceit** \kən'sēt, *usu.* -ēd·+V\ *n* -s [ME *conceite*, fr. *conceiven* to conceive, after such pairs as ME *deceiven* to deceive: *deceite* deceit] **1 a** (1) : something that results from mental activity : THOUGHT, CONCEPT, CONCEPTION, IDEA (2) *obs* : mental activity : thinking or the capacity to think (3) : individual or personal opinion : JUDGMENT, VIEW **b** : high estimation : favorable opinion : ESTEEM, ADMIRATION; *esp* : excessive appreciation of one's own worth or virtue **2** [trans. of It *concetto* — more at CONCETTO] **a** : a whimsical or fancifully ingenious idea **b** : an elaborate, startling, extravagant, or strained metaphor **c** : the use or the presence of such conceits as an element of poetry **3** : a fancy article : attractive trifle; *esp* : an ingenious decorative item ⟨with new techniques of designing artificial flowers . . . some of the resulting ~*s* are quite fetching —*New Yorker*⟩ **4** *archaic* : capacity for imagination or fancifulness : active fancy **5** *obs* : a seizure of physical or mental illness
syn SELF-LOVE, EGOTISM, EGOISM, SELF-ESTEEM, AMOUR PROPRE: CONCEIT indicates a conviction or assumption of one's own superiority in one or more lines of achievement or a general overall highly favorable notion of oneself usu. accompanied by lack of evaluation and irritating offensiveness ⟨*conceit*, being a false estimate of one's abilities or an overestimate of those that are least important, is both a moral and an intellectual failing —C.W.H.Johnson⟩ ⟨Aristotle's "Poetics" was so hard that nobody could understand it and therefore he was fearful lest he should be thought guilty of presumption and *conceit* in trying to explain it at all —Irving Babbitt⟩ SELF-LOVE in nonphilosophic usages may suggest abnormal concentration on one's own wishes and considerations to the exclusion of others ⟨when I am led by *self-love* to keep my seat whilst ladies stand —James Ford⟩ ⟨but the proper meaning of *self-love* is regard to self in distinction from others or regard to some private interest —G.P.Fisher⟩ EGOTISM may indicate a tendency to attract attention to and center interest on oneself and one's achievements ⟨she had the simplest *egotism*, the most open desire to be thought first always —Virginia Woolf⟩ ⟨*egotism* resides more in a kind of proud isolation, in a species of contempt for the opinions and aims of others —A.C.Benson⟩ EGOISM implies a self-centered concentration on one's own desires and aspirations to the exclusion of interest in others ⟨it's not so much selfishness as a sort of—is *egoism* the word? When she wants to do a thing, she doesn't take into account the wants of others at all —B.A.Williams⟩ ⟨the essence of a self-reliant and autonomous culture is an unshakable *egoism*. It must not only regard itself as the peer of any other culture; it must regard itself as the superior of any other —H.L.Mencken⟩ SELF-ESTEEM may indicate either natural well-based commendable pride in self or more shaky and somewhat vain attempts at self-pride and self-adjustment ⟨I do some things very well; but my *self-esteem* is crushed by the multitude of things at which I am a hopeless duffer —G.B.Shaw⟩ ⟨Hollywood propping up the *self-esteem* of celluloid royalty —Gladys B. Stern⟩ AMOUR PROPRE indicates a pride in oneself, often commendable or pardonable but often delicate and susceptible to being wounded ⟨I should doubt the judgment of anyone who told me that the people of Egypt have no *amour propre* or that there does not exist in Egypt today a legitimate feeling of pride for the nation —*Manchester Guardian Weekly*⟩ ⟨our *amour propre* is concerned in believing the war in which we fought a righteous one and the victory in which we participated an unsullied one —*New Republic*⟩

[2]**conceit** \"\ *vb* -ED/-ING/-S *vt* **1** *obs* : to form a conception of : APPREHEND, UNDERSTAND ⟨our great need of him you have right well ~*ed* —Shak.⟩ **2** *now dial* : IMAGINE, SUPPOSE, THINK ⟨I did ~ a most delicious feast —George Herbert⟩ **3** : to fill with fancies **4** *now dial Brit* : to take a fancy to : LIKE **5** : to hold a favorable opinion of (oneself) : ESTEEM ⟨began to ~ himself already a poet —Robert Southey⟩ ~ *vi*, *now dial* : to form an idea : THINK

con·ceit·ed \-ēd·əd,-ētəd\ *adj* [[1]*conceit* + *-ed*] **1 a** *obs* (1) : endowed with intelligence or imagination : CLEVER (2) : disposed in opinion or attitude : MINDED; *esp* : favorably disposed or favorably minded — usu. used with *to* or *of* **b** : ingeniously contrived or designed: as (1) : having or exhibiting a literary style marked by conceits (2) : consisting of or constructed upon or around a conceit (3) : containing conceits **2** : entertaining an excessively or unjustifiably high opinion of oneself — **con·ceit·ed·ly** *adv* — **con·ceit·ed·ness** *n* -ES

conceitless *adj*, *obs* : lacking understanding or thought : IGNORANT

con·ceity \kən'sēd·ē, -sād·ē\ *adj* [[1]*conceit* + *-y*] **1** *chiefly dial* : CONCEITED, VAIN **2** *chiefly dial* : hard to please

con·ceiv·abil·i·ty \kən,sēvə'biləd·ē, -ətē, -i\ *n* -ES : the quality or state of being conceivable

con·ceiv·able \kən'sēvəbəl\ *adj* **1** : capable of being conceived, imagined, or understood **2** : logically possible — **con·ceiv·able·ness** *n* -ES

con·ceiv·ably \-blē, -li\ *adv* : in a conceivable manner : POSSIBLY

con·ceive \kən'sēv\ *vb* -ED/-ING/-S [ME *conceiven*, fr. OF *conceivre*, *conceveir*, fr. L *concipere* to take, receive, conceive, proclaim, fr. *com-* + *-cipere* (fr. *capere* to seize, take) — more at HEAVE] *vt* **1 a** *of a mammal, esp. a human being* (1) : to become pregnant with : be with (child or young) (2) : BEGET ⟨he *conceived* their child deliberately —Norman Mailer⟩ (3) *obs* : to make pregnant : IMPREGNATE (4) : to be engendered in the womb — used passively ⟨before he was *conceived* —Lk 2:21 (AV)⟩ **b** : to cause to begin : originate or start (something thought of as capable of subsequent growth and development) ⟨Texas was *conceived* in debt and nourished on depleted paper —R.A.Billington⟩ — usu. used figuratively **2 a** : to take into one's mind : be affected by ⟨I have *conceived* a profound prejudice against such methods⟩ **b** : to form in the mind (as a concept or idea) : evolve mentally (as a plan or stratagem) : form a conception of : IMAGINE, VISUALIZE, IMAGE ⟨a building badly *conceived* and carelessly constructed⟩ **3 a** *archaic* : to apprehend (something) by reason or imagination **b** : COMPREHEND ⟨~ the man⟩ : UNDERSTAND, GRASP **4** : to be of the opinion : THINK, SUPPOSE ⟨we cannot ~ that this course is expedient now⟩ **5** *archaic* : to give forth : EXHIBIT, PRODUCE **6** : to give expression to : COUCH, FRAME, PHRASE ~ *vi* **1** : to become pregnant **2** : to have a conception, idea, or opinion : THINK — usu. used with *of* **syn** see THINK

con·celebrant \kən, (')kän +\ *n* -s [L *concelebrant-*, *concelebrans*, pres. part. of *concelebrare*] : one of two or more members of the clergy celebrating the Eucharist or Mass together

con·celebrate \"+\ *vb* -ED/-ING/-S [L *concelebratus*, past part. of *concelebrare* to celebrate in great numbers, fr. *com-* + *celebrare* to celebrate — more at CELEBRATE] *vt* : to celebrate (as Mass) together ~ *vi* : to celebrate the Eucharist or Mass together

con·celebration \(¦)kän, kən +\ *n* -s : a celebration of the Eucharist or Mass in which two or more of the clergy unite in saying the words of the liturgy

con·cent \kən'sent\ *n* -s [L *concentus* harmony, fr. past part. of *concinere* to sing together, fr. *com-* + *-cinere* (fr. *canere* to sing) — more at CHANT] **1** *archaic* : a state of accordance : CONSISTENCY **2** *archaic* : concert of voices : concord of sounds

con·cen·ter \kən, (')kän-+\ *vb* -ED/-ING/-S [MF *concentrer*, fr. *com-* + *centre* center — more at CENTER] *vt* : to draw or direct to a common center : bring together at a focus or point (as lines, ideas, or emotions) : CONCENTRATE ~ *vi* : to come to one point : meet in, converge toward, or have a common center ⟨then begins to ~ the . . . nexus of . . . habits of reaction to experience —*Survey Graphic*⟩

con·cen·to \kən'chen(,)tō, -'sen-\ *n* -s [It, fr. L *concentus* harmony — more at CONCENT] : the simultaneous sounding of the tones of a chord — compare *arpeggio*

con·central \kən, (')kän+\ *adj* [*com-* + *central*] : CONCENTRIC — **con·centrally** \"+\ *adv*

[1]**con·cen·trate** \'kän(t)sən·,trāt *also* -än,sen-; *usu* -ād·+V\ *vb* -ED/-ING/-S [*com-* + L *centrum* center + E *-ate* (v. suffix) — more at CENTER] *vt* **1** : to bring or direct toward a common center or objective : FOCUS ⟨*concentrating* all their efforts on reaching shore⟩ : gather into one body, mass, or force ⟨there are times when power must be *concentrated* in a few able hands⟩ **2** : to render less dilute or diffuse: **a** (1) : to remove water from ⟨in making maple syrup one ~*s* the sap by boiling⟩ (2) : to separate dross from ⟨repeated *concentrating* of the ore is necessary⟩ (3) : to free from impurities ⟨copper may be *concentrated* electrolytically⟩ **b** : to express the essence of ⟨the message of the New Testament is *concentrated* in the Sermon on the Mount⟩ : render more condensed ⟨the essence of her sex was *concentrated* in her charming obstinacy⟩ ~ *vi* **1** : to draw toward or meet in a common center **2** : to settle closely : GATHER, COLLECT ⟨recent immigrants tend to ~ in port cities⟩ ⟨social and racial tensions ~ in industrial centers⟩ **3 a** : to bring all one's powers, faculties, or activities to bear (as upon a course of action, a thought, or an object) ⟨~ on a problem⟩ ⟨farmers are *concentrating* on wheat this year⟩ ⟨to be able to ~ on the same matter for a considerable time is essential to difficult achievement —Bertrand Russell⟩ **b** : MAJOR **syn** see UNIFY

[2]**concentrate** \"\ *adj* [*com-* + L *centrum* + E *-ate* (adj. suffix)] : CONCENTRATED

[3]**concentrate** \"\ *n* -s : something obtained by concentration : a concentration or concentrated substance: as **a** : the remainder of dressed ore that contains the mineral sought **b** : a feedstuff rich in digestible nutrients in comparison to its bulk (as grains, oil meals, or tankage) — opposed to *roughage* **c** : a food reduced in bulk by elimination of watery fluid ⟨orange juice ~⟩

concentrated *adj* **1** : rich in respect to a particular or essential element : STRONG, UNDILUTED ⟨~ sulfuric acid⟩ ⟨a narrow thread of ~ ore seaming the rocky canyon⟩ **2** : INTENSE ⟨her ~ passion held them at bay⟩ : INTENSIVE ⟨only through ~ study can he hope to qualify for the award⟩ — **con·cen·trat·ed·ly** *adv*

concentrated alum *n* : ALUMINUM SULFATE

concentrated feed *n* : any animal feed rich in concentrates and low in roughage

concentrated milk *n* : milk concentrated by removal of water; *esp* : PLAIN CONDENSED MILK

concentrate sprayer *n* : a power sprayer used to apply a highly concentrated pesticide in highly dispersed form usu. by delivering it into a strong air blast generated by fans or blowers — called also *low gallonage sprayer*, *mist concentrate sprayer*, *speed sprayer*

con·cen·tra·tion \,kän(t)sən·'trāshən *also* -än,sen-\ *n* -s [*com-* + L *centrum* + E *-ation*] **1** : the act or action of concentrating: as **a** : the bringing to a common center; *esp* : the assembling of troops in an area often as a prelude to military action **b** : a directing of the attention or of the mental faculties toward a single object **c** : an increasing of strength (as of a solute or a gas in a mixture) or a purifying (as of a mineral in ore) by partial or total removal of diluents, solvents, admixed gases, extraneous material, or waste (as by evaporation, diffusion, or selective flotation) **d** : the centering of a student's program of study in one department or field of learning in which he does work of advanced grade — compare DISTRIBUTION 1c **2** : a result of concentrating : a concentrated mass or thing: as **a** *pharmacy* : a crude active principle of a vegetable usu. in the form of a powder or resin **b** : a group of artillery shells fired on a particular area within a limited time — compare BARRAGE **3** *of a solution, mixture, or dispersion* : the relative content of a component (as dissolved or dispersed material) that may be expressed in percentage by weight or by volume, in parts per million, or in grams per liter : STRENGTH **4** : DENSITY 1 **5** : a card game for two or more players in which a pack of cards is laid out card by card face down and at random, the skill of the game consisting of remembering the position of such cards as are briefly turned up in play — called also *memory*

concentration camp *n* : a camp where persons (as prisoners of war, political prisoners, refugees, or foreign nationals) are detained or confined and sometimes subjected to physical and mental abuse and indignity

concentration point *n* : a place at which less than carload shipments on common carriers are assembled to be forwarded in carload lots

con·cen·tra·tive \'kän(t)sən,trād·iv *also* -än,sen-\ *adj* : serving or tending to concentrate : characterized by concentration

con·cen·tra·tor \-ād·ə(r)\ *n* -s : one that concentrates: as **a** : an apparatus by which something (as an ore or a solution) is concentrated; *sometimes* : an industrial plant specializing in concentration (as of ore) **b** : a worker who tends concentrating apparatus **c** : a student who concentrates (in a particular field of study)

[1]**con·cen·tric** \kən'sen·trik, (')kän¦s-, -rēk\ *also* **con·cen·tri·cal** \-rəkəl, -rēk-\ *adj* [ML *concentricus*, fr. L *com-* + *centrum* center + *-icus* -ic — more at CENTER] **1 a** : having a common center (as circles one within another) — opposed to *eccentric* **b** : having a common axis (as of two or more cones or moraines) : formed about the same axis : COAXIAL **2** *geol* : marked by the loosening and falling away of successive rounded or spherical shells ⟨~ weathering⟩ ⟨~ exfoliation⟩ — **con·cen·tri·cal·ly** \-rək(ə)lē, -rēk-, -li\ *adv*

[2]**concentric** \"\ *n* -s : something (as one of two concentric circles) that has a common center with something else

concentric bundle *n* : a plant vascular bundle in which (1) phloem surrounds xylem or (2) xylem surrounds phloem — called also respectively (1) *amphicribral bundle*, (2) *amphivasal bundle*

concentric cable *n* : COAXIAL CABLE

concentric corpuscle *n* : CORPUSCLE OF HASSALL

concentric groove *n* : the single continuous silent groove at the end of a disc recording, cut there to prevent the pickup from traveling further toward the center of the record

con·cen·tric·i·ty \,kän,sen·'trisəd·ē\ *n* -ES : the quality or state of being concentric

concents *pl of* CONCENT

con·cen·tus \kən'sentəs, kän-\ *n*, *pl* **concentus** [L, harmony — more at CONCENT] : the part of a church service (as that in which hymns or psalms are sung) that is sung by the whole choir — contrasted with *accentus*

con·cep·ci·ón *or* **con·cep·ci·on** \kən¦sepsē¦ōn, (¦)kän-, -ē¦än, -ē¦ȯn, kən'sepshən\ *adj*, *usu cap* [fr. *Concepción*, Chile] : of or from the city of Concepción, Chile : of the kind or style prevalent in Concepción

con·cept \'kän,sept\ *n* -s [LL *conceptus* thought, fr. L, collection, gathering, fetus, fr. *conceptus*, past part. of *concipere* to conceive — more at CONCEIVE] : something conceived in the mind : THOUGHT, IDEA, NOTION: as **a** *philos* : a general or abstract idea : a universal notion: (1) : the resultant of a generalizing mental operation : a generic mental image abstracted from percepts; *also* : a directly intuited object of thought (2) : a theoretical construct ⟨the ~ of the atom⟩ **b** *logic* (1) : an idea comprehending the essential attributes of a class or logical species : a universal term or expression or its meaning (2) : a propositional function, logical relation, or property **c** : an idea that includes all that is characteristically associated with or suggested by a term : CONCEPTION **syn** see IDEA

con·cep·ta·cle \kən'septəkəl\ *n* -s [F, fr. L *conceptaculum*, fr. *conceptus*, past part. of *concipere* to receive, conceive] **1** *obs* : a hollow vessel : RECEPTACLE **2** *bot* **a** *obs* : FOLLICLE **b** : an enclosing cavity just beneath the surface of the plant body that contains reproductive structures in members of the genus *Fucus* and certain other algae — **con·cep·tac·u·lar** \¦kän·sep-¦takyələ(r)\ *adj*

con·cep·tac·u·lum \,kän,sep'takyələm\ *n*, *pl* **conceptacu·la** \-lə\ [NL, fr. L] : CONCEPTACLE 2

con·cep·ti·ble \kən'septəbəl\ *adj* [ML *conceptibilis*, fr. L *conceptus* + *-ibilis* -ible] : CONCEIVABLE

con·cep·tion \kən'sepshən\ *n* -s [ME *concepcioun*, fr. OF *conception*, fr. L *conception-*, *conceptio*, fr. *conceptus* (past part. of *concipere* to conceive, receive) + *-ion-*, *-io* -ion — more at CONCEIVE] **1 a** : act of becoming pregnant : formation of a viable zygote ⟨fertilization results in the ~ of a new entity capable of developing into a being like its parent⟩ : state of being conceived; *also* : that which is conceived : EMBRYO, FETUS **b** *archaic* : BEGINNING **2** : the capacity, function, or process of forming ideas or abstractions or of grasping the meaning of symbols representing such ideas or abstractions ⟨the essential character of ~ is that in it the universal is thought of as such —G.F.Stout⟩ **3 :** an idea or general notion **:** CONCEPT: **a :** a product of abstract or reflective thinking (as an interpretation or design) **:** an ideal scheme or plan of action ⟨his ~ was on the grand scale but he lacked skill and determination needed to make it real⟩ **b :** the abstract, intellectual, or universal element in cognition as distinguished from the apprehension of concrete particulars in sense perception **c** *obs* **:** CONCEIT **4 :** the originating of something (as an idea or plan) in the mind **syn** see IDEA

con·cep·tion·al \-shənᵊl, -shnəl\ *adj* **:** of, relating to, or being a conception ⟨a plan abstruse and ~⟩

conception control *n* **:** CONTRACEPTION

con·cep·tion·ist \-sh(ə)nəst\ *n* -s **1 :** CONCEPTUALIST **2** *cap* [*(Immaculate) Conception* + *-ist*] *Roman Catholicism* **:** a member of any of the various orders or congregations dedicated to and named in honor of the Immaculate Conception

con·cept·ism \kän,sep,tizəm\ *n* -s [Sp *conceptismo*, fr. *concepto* concept, conceit, ingenious expression (fr. LL *conceptus* thought — influenced in meaning by It *concetto*) + *-ismo* -ism — more at CONCEPT] **:** an obscurely allusive style characterized by ambiguous metaphors and puns that was developed chiefly by Spanish mystics of the 17th century

con·cep·tive \kən'septiv\ *adj* [LL *conceptivus*, fr. L, formally proclaimed, fr. *conceptus* (past part. of *concipere* to conceive, proclaim formally) + *-ivus* -ive — more at CONCEIVE] **:** capable of or relating to conceiving — **con·cep·tive·ly** \-tə̇vlē\ *adv*

con·cep·tu·al \kən'sepchə(wə)l, (ˈ)kän¦s-, -psh-\ *adj* [ML *conceptualis*, fr. LL *conceptus* thought + L *-alis* -al — more at CONCEPT] **:** of or relating to concepts ⟨the schizophrenic shows a loss in the ability to abstract or do ~ thinking —Louise Heathers⟩ — **con·cep·tu·al·ly** \-)lē, -li\ *adv*

con·cep·tu·al·ism \-,lizəm\ *n* -s [F *conceptualisme*, fr. ML *conceptualis* + F *-isme* -ism] *philos* **:** a theory that is intermediate between nominalism and realism and holds that universals exist in the mind as subjects of discourse or as predicates which may be properly affirmed of reality

con·cep·tu·al·ist \-ˌləst\ *n* -s **:** an advocate of conceptualism

con·cep·tu·al·is·tic \kən¦sepchə(wə)¦listik, (ˌ)kän-, -psh-\ *adj* **1 :** typical of or involving conceptualism **2 :** employing or based on concepts

con·cep·tu·al·i·za·tion \kən,sepchə(wə)lə'zāshən, (,)kän-, -psh-, -,lī'z-\ *n* -s **:** the act or process of conceptualizing ⟨~ of field data is an essential prelude to formulation of a working hypothesis⟩

con·cep·tu·al·ize \ˌ≠'≠≠(≠),līz\ *vt* -ED/-ING/-S *see -ize in Explan Notes* **:** to form a concept of; *esp* **:** to interpret conceptually ⟨primitive peoples tend to ~ both groups and relations in terms of personalities⟩

con·cep·tus \kən'septəs, kän-\ *n, pl* **conceptus·es** \-təsəz\ *also* **concep·ti** \-,tī\ [L — more at CONCEPT] **:** a product of conception **:** CONCEPT, FETUS

1con·cern \kən'sərn, -sən,-səin\ *vb* -ED/-ING/-S [ME *concernen*, fr. MF & ML; MF *concerner*, fr. ML *concernere*, fr. LL, to mix or mingle together, fr. L *com-* + *cernere* to separate, sift — more at SHEAR] *vt* **1 a :** to relate or refer to **:** be about ⟨this story ~s the beginnings of the modern age⟩ **b :** to bear on ⟨another rather serious drawback associated with nucellar seedlings ~*ed* the fact that they were . . . slower in developing flower parts —*Farmer's Weekly (So. Africa)*⟩ **2 :** to have an influence on **:** AFFECT, INVOLVE ⟨racial unrest ~s us all⟩; *also* **:** to be the business or affair of **:** matter to ⟨quarrels between husband and wife ~ the whole family⟩ **3 :** to be a care, trouble, or distress to ⟨his failing health ~s me⟩ **4 :** ENGAGE, OCCUPY, INTEREST ⟨he ~s himself with trivia⟩ ~ *vi, obs* **:** to be of importance **:** MATTER

2concern \"\ *n* -s **1 a :** a connecting relation **:** an active or real part (as of interest or sharing) ⟨he has no ~ in the matter⟩ ⟨their ~ was chiefly to protect their sister's interests⟩ **b :** something that relates or belongs to one **:** BUSINESS, AFFAIR — often used in pl. ⟨let them mind their own ~s⟩ **2 :** matter for consideration **:** OCCUPATION, INTEREST ⟨a problem likely to be a major ~ of the new administration⟩ ⟨describing his ~s with satisfaction⟩ **3 a :** marked interest or regard usu. arising through a personal tie or relationship to the matter under consideration ⟨interest . . . ran . . . all the way from a determination to make war down to no ~ whatsoever —H.S.Canby⟩ **b :** an uneasy state of blended interest, regard, uncertainty and apprehension about a present condition or future development — usu. used without *a* or *the* ⟨an adult who falls on the street is the object of ~ and commiseration —Agnes Repplier⟩ **4 :** an organization or establishment for business or manufacture **:** a firm and its business ⟨a banking ~⟩ **5 :** CONTRIVANCE, GADGET, CONTRAPTION **6** *in Quaker terminology* **:** a strong conviction based on religious insight **syn** see CARE

concernancy *n* -ES [1*concern* + *-ancy*] *obs* **:** CONCERNMENT

concerned *adj* **1 a :** INTERESTED, SOLICITOUS ⟨greatly ~ not to disappoint a small child's expectations⟩ ⟨we are not ~ to decide which one of the different schools of social theory is correct —John Dewey⟩ **b :** TROUBLED, DISTURBED, BOTHERED, ANXIOUS ⟨a hard man not greatly ~ that his acts lead to misery and indigence for others⟩ ⟨reason . . . to be ~ by the confusions surrounding the old categories of American political thought —August Heckscher⟩ **2 a :** interestedly engaged **:** INVOLVED ⟨a business enterprise in which three men were ~⟩ ⟨too many people are ~ with the bare mechanics of life⟩ ⟨~ with books and music⟩ **b :** culpably involved **:** IMPLICATED ⟨intrigues that important men were ~ in⟩ ⟨everyone ~ in the bribery case has been identified⟩ **3** *dial Eng* **:** INTOXICATED — used esp. in the phrase *concerned in liquor* or *concerned with liquor* — **con·cern·ed·ly** \-nədlē, -li\ *adv* — **con·cerned·ness** \-nədnəs, -n(d)nəs\ *n* -ES

con·cern·ful \-nfəl\ *adj* **:** of concern ⟨an eyesight for ~ reality —Paul Goodman⟩

1con·cern·ing \-niŋ, -nēŋ\ *prep* [ME, fr. pres. part. of *concernen* to concern] **:** relating to **:** REGARDING, RESPECTING, ABOUT ⟨information ~ drug addiction⟩ ⟨skepticism ~ the effectiveness of controls and subsidies⟩

2concerning \"\ *n* -s [fr. gerund of 1*concern*] *obs* **:** an affair that concerns one **:** CONCERN

3concerning \"\ *adj* [fr. pres. part. of *concern*] *archaic* **:** giving concern **:** IMPORTANT — **con·cern·ing·ly** *adv, archaic* — **con·cern·ing·ness** *n* -ES *archaic*

con·cern·ment \-nmənt\ *n* -s [*concern* + *-ment*] **1 :** something in which one is concerned or interested **:** CONCERN, BUSINESS ⟨occupied strictly with his own ~s⟩ **2 :** RELATION, BEARING, IMPORTANCE, MOMENT, CONSEQUENCE ⟨a matter of general ~⟩ **3** *archaic* **:** INVOLVEMENT, PARTICIPATION **4 :** special interest **:** SOLICITUDE, ANXIETY

concerns *pres 3d sing of* CONCERN, *pl of* CONCERN

1con·cert \kən'sərt, -sōt, -səit *also* (ˈ)kän¦s-; *usu* -d·+V\ *vb* -ED/-ING/-S [MF *concerter*, fr. OIt *concertare*, fr. LL, to collaborate, fr. L, to contend, dispute, debate, fr. *com-* + *certare* to strive, fr. *certus* determined, decided — more at CERTAIN] *vt* **1 :** to plan together **:** settle or adjust by conference, agreement, or consultation ⟨the states involved ~*ed* their differences⟩ **2 :** to make a plan for **:** DEVISE, ARRANGE ⟨representatives . . . met . . . to ~ measures for a united offensive —A.C.Flick⟩ ~ *vi* **:** to act in harmony or conjunction **:** form combined plans — usu. used with *with* ⟨he refused to consult his partners or to ~ with them —*New Republic*⟩

2con·cert \'kän(t)sə(r)t, -n,sərt, -,sōt, -,səit, *usu* -d·+V\ *n* -s [F, fr. It *concerto*, fr. *concertare*] **1 a :** agreement in a design or plan **:** union formed by mutual communication of opinions and views **:** accordance in a scheme **b :** a concerted action ⟨the sacrifice was hailed with a ~ of praise⟩ **2 a :** musical accordance or harmony **:** CONCORD **b** *obs* **:** CONCERTO 1 **c :** a group of musicians performing concerted music **d :** a group (as of individuals or nations) acting in harmony **3 a :** a musical performance of some length by several voices or instruments or both — distinguished from *recital* **b :** a public entertainment (as of music or dancing) made up of a number of short compositions or episodes not joined in an integrated whole — compare BALLET, OPERA, VAUDEVILLE — **in concert :** TOGETHER ⟨our enemies working *in concert* could easily cause our downfall⟩ ⟨he acted *in concert* with the others⟩

3concert \"\ *adj* **:** adapted to or capable of performance in concerts ⟨~ hall⟩ ⟨~ pianist⟩

1con·cer·tante \,kän(t)sə(r)'täntē, ,känchə-, -tän·,tā; ¦kän(t)sə(r)¦tänt\ *also* **con·cer·ta·to** \,kän(t)sə(r)'täd·(,)ō, -nchə-\ *n* -s [*concertante* fr. It, n. & adj., fr. pres. part. of *concertare* to form or perform a concert, fr. *concerto* concert; *concertato* fr. It, n. & adj., fr. past part. of *concertare*] **1 :** a 17th or 18th century musical composition for orchestra with parts for solo instruments or for several solo instruments without orchestra — compare CONCERTO GROSSO **2 :** CONCERTINO 1

2concertante \"\ *also* **concertato** \"\ *adj* [It] **:** displaying or affording opportunity to display brilliancy in a solo part in an instrumental composition ⟨a ~ passage for violin⟩

concert band *n* **:** a band that is made capable of playing symphonic music by the addition of instruments (as the string bass and harp) not adapted to marching — called also *symphony band*

concert border *n* **:** FIRST BORDER

concert dance *n* **:** ballet characterized by seriousness and a minimum of theatrical effects

con·cert·ed \kən'sə≠≠ *also* (ˈ)kän¦-\ *adj* **1 a :** mutually contrived or planned **:** agreed on ⟨carefully ~ signals⟩ **b :** performed in unison **:** done together ⟨a ~ sigh that should have been heard in Australia —Bill Alcine⟩ **2 :** arranged in parts for several voices, musical instruments, or dancers (as a trio, string ensemble, or ballet)

con·cert·ed·ly *adv* **:** in concert

concert étude *n* **:** a particularly brilliant instrumental composition evolved from a single technical motive

concertgoer \'≠(,)≠,≠≠\ *n* -s **:** one that attends concerts esp. habitually

concert grand *n* **:** a grand piano of the largest size and adapted in volume, timbre, and brilliancy of tone to concert use

concerti *pl of* CONCERTO

1con·cer·ti·na \,kän(t)sə(r)'tēnə\ *n* -s [2*concert* + *-ina*] **1 :** a musical instrument resembling the accordion and differing from it chiefly in being hexagonal in shape, in having finger buttons for keys, and in having melody keys on both ends **2** *or* **concertina wire :** an entanglement of coiled usu. barbed wire that can be pushed together into a compact mass for transporting and extended for use as an obstacle

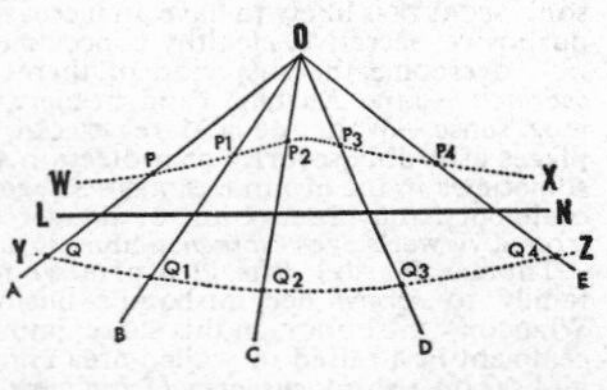
concertina 1

2concertina \"\ *vb* -ED/-ING/-S *vi* **:** to fold up like the bellows of a concertina **:** WRINKLE ⟨her stockings ~*ed* about her ankles⟩ ~ *vt* **:** to cause to fold up like the bellows of a concertina **:** crush together ⟨he dropped to a seat ~*ing* the preacher's hat beneath him⟩

3concertina \"\ *adj* **:** like or suggesting a concertina **:** ACCORDION ⟨a ~ chin⟩; *specif* **:** being or employing a hinged usu. folding mechanism to make enlargement possible ⟨a ~ card table⟩ ⟨a table with ~ extension⟩ ⟨a ~ gate⟩

concerting *pres part of* CONCERT

con·cer·ti·no \,känchər'tē(,)nō, -,cher-\ *n* -s [It, dim. of *concerto* concert, concerto — more at CONCERT] **1 :** the solo instruments in a concerto grosso — distinguished from *ripieno* and *tutti* **2 :** a short concerto typically in free form

con·cert·ize \'kän(t)sə(r),tīz, -ə(r)d·,īz\ *vi* -ED/-ING/-S [2*concert* + *-ize*] **:** to perform in concerts or recitals esp. professionally ⟨only 20 years old, yet he has been *concertizing* . . . for about a half a dozen years —*Consumer Reports*⟩

concertmaster \'≠≠ *also* '≠,≠ *pronunc at* 2CONCERT +,-\ *or* **con·cert·meis·ter** \+,mīstə(r); *G* kȯn·'tsert-,mīstər\ *n* [*concertmaster* trans. of G *konzertmeister; concertmeister* fr. G *konzertmeister*, fr. *konzert* concert (fr. It *concerto*) + *meister* master, fr. OHG *meistar*, fr. L *magister* — more at CONCERT, MASTER] **:** the leader of the first violins in an orchestra and by custom the subleader of the orchestra

concertmistress *pronunc at* 2CONCERT +,-\ *n* **:** a female concertmaster

con·cer·to \kən'cherl·d·(,)ō, -eəl, |(,)tō *sometimes* -chər| *or* -chəl| *or* -chəi|\ *n, pl* **concer·ti** \|d·(,)ē, |(,)tē, |d·,i, |,ti\ *or* **concertos** [It — more at CONCERT] **1 :** a composition characteristic of the 16th and 17th centuries for one or more solo voices or instruments with organ or orchestral accompaniment — called also *church concerto* **2 :** CONCERTO GROSSO **3 :** a virtuoso piece for solo instrument or voice and orchestra that is usu. in symphonic form with three contrasting movements, the themes stated alternately by soloist and orchestra, and that is characterized by a bravura solo cadenza

concerto flute *n* **:** FLAUTO TRAVERSO 2

concerto gros·so \≠¦≠≠'grō(,)sō *also* -rō-\ *n, pl* **concerti gros·si** \-(,)sē, -,si\ [It, lit., big concerto] **:** an orchestral composition of the Baroque period with a small group of solo instruments contrasting with the full orchestra

concert overture *n* **:** an orchestral composition that resembles an operatic overture in form or character and is intended for concert performance

concert pitch *n* **1 a :** PHILHARMONIC PITCH **b** INTERNATIONAL PITCH 2 **2 :** an unusually high state or degree of fitness, training, or tension (as in preparation for a concert or athletic contest) ⟨an intensive bit of work done at *concert pitch* —Ngaio Marsh⟩ ⟨a man with energy enough to bring up my plays to *concert pitch* —G.B.Shaw⟩ ⟨it's not easy to keep a filly at *concert pitch* from May to November —G.F.T.Ryall⟩

concerts *pres 3d sing of* CONCERT, *pl of* CONCERT

con·cert·stück *pronunc at* 2CONCERT +,shtik; *G* kȯn·'tsert-,shtek\ *n* -s [G *konzertstück*, fr. *konzert* + *stück* piece, fr. OHG *stucki* — more at STOCK] **:** CONCERTINO 2

con·ces·si·ble \kən'sesəbəl\ *adj* [*concession* + *-ible*] **:** capable of being conceded

con·ces·sion \kən'seshən\ *n* -s [F or L; F *concession*, fr. L *concession-, concessio*, fr. *concessus* (past part. of *concedere* to concede) + *-ion-, -io* -ion — more at CONCEDE] **1 a :** an act or instance of conceding or yielding esp. to an implied or expressed pressure, claim, demand, or request ⟨at my age I'll make no ~ to style⟩ ⟨the union will seek further ~s before accepting a long-term contract⟩ **b :** the admitting of a point claimed in argument; *esp* **:** the voluntary yielding of a disputable contention **2 :** something granted or conceded **:** a thing yielded **:** ACKNOWLEDGMENT, ADMISSION **:** BOON, GRANT: as **a :** a grant of land or other property esp. from a government in return for services rendered or proposed or for a particular use; *specif* **:** a tract granted to a foreign power in a Chinese treaty port or other trading center and permitted rights of extraterritoriality and local self-government **b :** a usu. exclusive right to undertake and profit by a specified activity ⟨a ~ to build a canal⟩ ⟨conflicting ~s in the oil fields⟩ **c :** a lease of premises or a portion of premises for a particular purpose, esp. for some purpose supplementary to another activity (as the storing of wraps of patrons of a theater) or for providing entertainment; *often* **:** the premises covered by such a concession or the activities for which it is granted ⟨it was reported that some of the ~s at the fair were not honest⟩ **d :** a reduction in price from the current price of a commodity — called also *price concession*

con·ces·sion·aire *also* **con·ces·sion·naire** \kən¦seshə¦na(a)(ə)r, -ne(ə)r,-na(a)ə,-neə\ *n* -s [F *concessionnaire*, fr. *concession* + *-aire* -ary] **:** a person or firm that is the beneficiary of a concession: as **a :** one that owns or operates a stand or booth to sell refreshments or opportunities for entertainment to patrons of a recreational center (as a beach, park, or fair) **b :** one that holds the right to sell a particular type of product or service in a given location **c :** one that provides food service in a factory, school, or other establishment

con·ces·sion·al \kən'seshənᵊl, -shnəl\ *adj* **:** of or relating to concession

1con·ces·sion·ary \-shə,nerē, -ri\ *adj* [*concession* + *-ary*] **:** of or relating to a concession

2concessionary \"\ *n* -ES [by alter.] **:** CONCESSIONAIRE

con·ces·sion·er \-sh(ə)nə(r)\ *n* -s [by alter.] **:** CONCESSIONAIRE

con·ces·sive \-'sesiv, -esēv *also* -esəv\ *adj* [LL *concessivus*, fr. L *concessus* (past part. of *concedere* to concede) + *-ivus* -ive — more at CONCEDE] **1 :** making for concession **:** being a concession **2 :** denoting concession ⟨the ~ conjunction *though*⟩ ⟨a ~ clause introduced by *although*⟩ — **con·ces·sive·ly** \-sə̇vlē, -li\ *adv*

con·cet·tism \kən'ched·,izəm\ *n* -s [It *concettismo*, fr. *concetto* + *-ismo* -ism] **:** employment of or liking for concetti

con·cet·to \kən'ched·(,)ō\ *n, pl* **concet·ti** \-d·'(,)ē\ [It, fr. LL *conceptus* thought — more at CONCEPT] **:** a conceit esp. in literary style ⟨a work full of orotund phrases and pompous *concetti*⟩

conch \'käŋk, 'känch *also* 'kȯŋk— -ŋk *is usual near waters where the conch occurs and hence in sense 3*\ *n, pl* **conchs** \-ŋks\ *or* **conch·es** \-nchəz\ [L *concha*, fr. Gk *konchē*; akin to Skt *śaṅkha* conch] **1 a** (1) **:** any of various large spiral-shelled marine gastropod mollusks; *esp* **:** any member of the genera *Strombus* and *Cassis* of the south Atlantic coast of No. America and the West Indies — see HORSE CONCH, KING CONCH, QUEEN CONCH (2) **:** the shell of a conch often used for cutting cameos and formerly made into horns (3) **:** the animal body of a conch as distinguished from its inanimate shelly parts; *esp* **:** the body as an article of food ⟨fried ~ is a tasty dish⟩ **b :** something resembling a conch (as a shell-shaped ornament) or made from a conch (as a horn) **2 :** the portion of the shell of a tetrabranch cephalopod mollusk that is developed after the embryonic shell **3** *often cap* **a :** a resident native of the Bahamas **b :** any of various persons resident in the Florida keys and nearby parts of the mainland; *esp* **:** one of Bahaman ancestry — often used disparagingly; compare CRACKER 5 **4 :** CONCHA 2b(1) **5 :** BRACKET 3c

conch

conch- *or* **concho-** *comb form* [Gk *konch-, koncho-*, fr. *konchē*] **1 :** shell ⟨*conch*iolin⟩ **2 :** concha ⟨*conch*itis⟩ ⟨*concho*tome⟩

1con·cha \'käŋkə *also* 'kȯŋ-\ *n, pl* **con·chae** \-ŋ,kē, -ŋ,kī\ [in sense 1, fr. It *conca*, fr. LL *concha* apse, fr. L, conch, shell-shaped object or cavity; in sense 2, fr. L] **1 a :** the plain semidome of an apse; *sometimes* **:** APSE **b :** the plain surface of a pendentive **2 :** something suggesting or shaped like a shell: as **a :** a shell-shaped vessel **b** (1) **:** the largest and deepest concavity of the external ear (2) **:** any of the turbinated bones esp. in man — **con·chal** \-ŋkəl\ *adj*

2con·cha \'känchə\ *also* **con·cho** \-n(,)chō\ *n* -s [AmerSp *concha*, fr. Sp, shell, fr. LL *conchula*, dim. of L *concha*] *West* **:** a metal usu. shell-shaped and silver disk that is used as decoration on clothing and harness

con·chate \'käŋ,kāt *also* 'kȯŋ-\ *adj* [*conch-* + *-ate*] **1 :** CONCHED **2 :** CONCHIFORM

1conche \'känch\ *n* -s [F, fr. F dial., trough, fr. OF, shell, fr. L *concha* — more at CONCH] **:** a machine in which chocolate is worked in the preparation of fine grades

2conche \"\ *vt* -ED/-ING/-S **:** to work (chocolate) in a conche

conched \'käŋ(k)t, 'käncht, 'kȯŋ(k)t — *see* CONCH\ *adj* [*conch* + *-ed*] **:** having a conch

conch·er \'känchə(r)\ *n* -s [*conche* + *-er*] **:** a tender of a conche

conch hat *n* [*conch* (native of the Bahamas)] **:** a wide-brimmed hat of plaited palmetto leaf worn in the Bahamas

con·chie *also* **con·chy** *or* **con·shy** \'känchē, -chi\ *n, pl* **conchies** [by shortening and alter.] *slang* **:** CONSCIENTIOUS OBJECTOR

con·chif·er·ous \(ˈ)käŋ¦kif(ə)rəs, (ˈ)kän¦chi-, (ˈ)kȯŋ¦ki-— *see* CONCH\ *adj* [ISV *conch-* + *-i-* + *-ferous*] **:** producing or having shells

con·chi·form \'käŋkə,fȯrm, 'känchə-,'kȯŋkə- — *see* CONCH\ *adj* [ISV *conch* + *-iform*] **:** shaped like one half of a bivalve shell **:** shell-shaped

con·chi·o·lin *also* **con·chy·o·lin** \käŋ'kīələn *also* kȯŋ-\ *n* -s [*conchiolin* fr. *conch-* + *-i-* + *-ol* + *-in*; *conchyolin* alter. of *conchiolin*] **:** a scleroprotein forming the organic basis of mollusk shells (as mother-of-pearl) — see NACRE 2

con·chit·ic \(ˈ)käŋ¦kid·ik *also* (ˈ)kȯŋ-\ *adj* [Gk *konchitēs* shelly (fr. *konch-* conch- + *-itēs* -ite) + E *-ic*] *of certain rocks* **:** composed of shells **:** containing many shells

1concho *var of* CONCHA

2con·cho \'kän(,)chō\ *n, pl* **concho** *or* **conchos** *usu cap* [Sp] **1 :** a group of Taracahitian peoples of the state of Chihuahua, Mexico, comprising two major subdivisions, the Chinarra and Chizo, and 29 minor groups **2 :** a member of the Concho peoples

concho- — see CONCH-

con·cho grass \'kän(,)chō-\ *n* [prob. fr. the *Concho* river, Texas] **:** TEXAS MILLET

con·choid \'käŋ,kȯid, 'kän,- *also* 'kȯŋ,-\ *n* -s [Gk *konchoeidēs*, lit., conchlike, fr. *konch-* conch- + *-oeidēs* -oid] **1 a :** plane curve determined as the collection of pairs of points located on converging rays crossing a fixed line or curve from which each point of the pair is equidistant, measured along a ray **2 :** BULB OF PERCUSSION

conchoid: *AO, BO, CO, DO, EO* rays converging at *O; LN* fixed line; *P, P¹, P², P³, P⁴* points equidistant from *LN; Q, Q¹, Q², Q³, Q⁴* points equidistant from *LN; WX, YZ* branches of conchoid

con·choi·dal \(ˈ)≠¦kȯidᵊl\ *adj* [Gk *konchoeidēs* conchoid + E *-al*] **1 :** of, relating to, or having the form or characteristics of a conchoid ⟨a ~ mechanism⟩ **2** *mineralogy* **:** having elevations or depressions shaped somewhat like the inside surface of a bivalve shell — used esp. of a surface produced by fracture — **con·choi·dal·ly** \-dᵊlē\ *adv*

con·cho·log·i·cal \¦käŋkə¦läjəkəl *also* ¦kȯŋ-\ *adj* **:** of or relating to conchology — **con·cho·log·i·cal·ly** \-jək(ə)lē\ *adv*

con·chol·o·gist \käŋ'käləjəst *also* kȯŋ-\ *n* -s **:** one specializing in conchology

con·chol·o·gize \-,jīz\ *vi* -ED/-ING/-S [*conchology* + *-ize*] **:** to collect and study mollusk shells esp. as a hobby or avocation ⟨*conchologizing* among some new discoveries⟩

con·chol·o·gy \-jē\ *n* -ES [*conch-* + *-logy*] **1 :** the branch of zoology that deals with shells — now usu. distinguished from *malacology* **2 :** a treatise on shells

con·chos·tra·ca \-ŋ'kästrəkə *also* -'kȯs-\ *n pl, cap* [NL, fr. *conch-* + *-ostraca*] **:** a small order of freshwater crustaceans (subclass Branchiopoda) entirely enclosed in a bivalve carapace — **con·chos·tra·can** \-rəkən\ *n* -s

conchs *pl of* CONCH

con·chu·cu \kən'chü(,)kü\ *n, pl* **conchucu** *or* **conchucus** *usu cap* [Sp, of AmerInd origin] **1 :** a division of the Chinchaisuyu people of Peru **2 :** a member of the Conchucu people

con·chu·e·la \,känchə'wālə\ *n* -s [MexSp, fr. Sp, small shell, dim. of *concha* shell — more at CONCHA] **:** a flat bright green bug (*Chlorochroa ligata*) that damages wheat, potatoes, and garden crops in the western U. S.

conchy *var of* CONCHIE

con·chyl·i·at·ed \käŋ'kilē,ād·əd, kən-\ *adj* [NL *conchylium* + E *-ate* + *-ed*] *of a dye* **:** derived from mollusks

con·chyl·i·um \-lēəm\ *n, pl* **conchyl·ia** \-ēə\ [NL, fr. L, shellfish, fr. Gk *konchylion* mollusk, shell, fr. *konchē* conch — more at CONCH] **:** the shell of a mollusk

conchyolin *var of* CONCHIOLIN

con·cierge \(ˈ)kōⁿ¦syerzh\ *n, pl* **con·cierges** \-zh(əz)\ [F, fr. OF *cumcerges*, fr. (assumed) VL *conservius*, for L *conservus* fellow slave, fr. *com-* + *servus* slave — more at SERVE] **1** *archaic* **:** one in charge of a property **:** a custodian or warden esp. of a castle or prison **2 :** an attendant at the entrance of a building **:** DOORKEEPER; *esp* **:** a resident attendant in a French building who oversees ingress and egress, handles mail, and performs various functions of a janitor or porter ⟨the harassment of a ~ during the tourist season⟩

con·cier·ge·rie \kōⁿ'syerzhərē\ *n* -s [F, fr. *concierge* + *-erie* -ery] **:** the lodging or office of a concierge

con·cil·i·a·ble \kən'silēəbəl, -lyə-\ *adj* [L *conciliare* to bring together + E *-able* — more at CONCILIATE] **:** capable of being conciliated or reconciled

con·cil·i·a·bule \-lē,byül\ *n* -s [F, fr. MF, fr. LL *conciliabulum*, fr. L, place of assembly, fr. *concilium* assembly, council] **:** a clandestine meeting esp. of conspirators or rebels against constituted authority in church or state

con·cil·i·ar \kən'silēər, -ē,är\ *adj* [L *concilium* council + E *-ar* — more at COUNCIL] **1 :** of, relating to, or issued by a council **2 :** of, based on, or relating to conciliarism — **con·cil·i·ar·ly** *adv*

con·cil·i·a·rism \-ēə,rizəm\ *n* -s **:** the theory of church government that places final ecclesiastical authority in representative church councils instead of in a papacy

con·cil·i·a·rist \-,rəst\ *n* -s **:** an advocate of conciliarism ⟨15th century ~*s* opened the first great modern debate of constitutionalism against absolutism⟩

con·cil·i·ar·i·ty \kən,silē'arəd·ē\ *n* -ES **:** the principle of government found in Eastern Orthodox churches that places final authority in representative councils — compare SOBORNOST

con·cil·i·ate \kən'silē,āt *usu* -ād·+V\ *vb* -ED/-ING/-S [L *conciliatus*, past part. of *conciliare* to bring together, unite, gain, fr. *concilium* assembly, council — more at COUNCIL] *vt* **1 :** to gain (as goodwill or favor) by pleasing acts **2** *obs* **:** ACQUIRE, WIN, GET **3 :** to make compatible **:** cause to be in accord ⟨it is hard to ~ the views of labor and management on this point⟩ **4 :** to win over from a state of hostility or distrust **:** gain the goodwill or favor of **:** MOLLIFY, PROPITIATE, APPEASE ⟨he *conciliated* her mother with shy signs of good blood and breeding⟩ ~ *vi* **:** to become or try to become friendly **:** make friends **syn** see PACIFY

conciliating *adj* **:** CONCILIATORY — **con·cil·i·at·ing·ly** *adv*

con·cil·i·a·tion \kən,silē'āshən\ *n* -s *often attrib* [L *conciliation-, conciliatio*, fr. *conciliatus* + *-ion-, -io* -ion] **1 a :** the act or process of conciliating **:** the effort to establish harmony and goodwill **b :** the intervention in a dispute by an outsider who seeks to achieve agreement between the disputing parties; *specif* **:** the mediation of a labor dispute by a third party, governmental or private, having no power to compel settlement of the dispute but relying only on persuasion and suggestion **2 :** the state of being conciliated **:** the manifesting of goodwill and cooperation ⟨a period of ~ between church and state⟩

con·cil·i·a·tion·ism \-shə,nizəm\ *n* -s **:** belief in or resort to conciliation; *esp* **:** use of a policy of conciliation esp. as contrasted with firmer measures ⟨those favoring open war violently opposed the ~ of their leaders⟩

con·cil·i·a·tion·ist \-sh(ə)nəst\ *n* -s **:** one who advocates conciliation

con·cil·i·a·tive \kən'silē,ād·iv; -lēəd· -,-lyəd· -\ *adj* **:** CONCILIATORY

con·cil·i·a·tor \-ē,ād·ə(r), -ātə-\ *n* -s [L, fr. *conciliatus* + *-or*] **:** one who conciliates **:** PEACEMAKER; *specif* **:** one employed by a labor union to negotiate disputes between the union and management — called also *arbitrator*

con·cil·ia·to·ri·ly \kən¦silyə¦tōrəlē, -lēə-, ÷ -lə-, -tȯr-, -li\ *adv* **:** in a conciliatory way

con·cil·ia·to·ri·ness \='=(=)=¦tōrēnəs, -,tȯr-, -ri-\ *n* -ES **:** the quality or state of being conciliatory

con·cil·ia·to·ry \kən'silyə,tōrē, -lēə-, ÷ -lə-, -tȯr-, -ri\ *adj* **:** tending to conciliate **:** PACIFIC, MOLLIFYING, PROPITIATING

con·cil·i·um \kən'silēəm\ *n*, *pl* **concil·ia** \-ēə\ [L — more at COUNCIL] **:** COUNCIL

¹con·cin·nate \kən'sinət\ *adj* [L *concinnatus*] *of speech or writing* **:** put together with neat propriety **:** of elegant style

²con·cin·nate \'kän(t)sə,nāt\ *vt* -ED/-ING/-S [L *concinnatus*, past part. of *concinnare*, fr. *com-* + *-cinnare* (fr. *cinnus*, a kind of mixed drink)] **:** to place fitly together **:** arrange in good order **:** ADJUST, TRIM

con·cin·ni·ty \kən'sinəd·ē\ *n* -ES [L *concinnitas*, fr. *concinnus* skillfully put together (back-formation fr. *concinnare*) + *-itas* -ity] **1 :** harmony or fitness in the adaptation of parts to a whole or to each other; *often* **:** studied elegance of design or arrangement — used esp. of literary style **2 :** an instance of concinnity

con·cin·nous \-nəs\ *adj* [L *concinnus*] **:** characterized by concinnity **:** NEAT, ELEGANT

concion *n* -s [L *contion-, contio*, fr. *co-* + *vention-, ventio* coming, fr. *ventus* (past part. of *venire* to come) + *-ion-, -io* -ion — more at COME] **1** *obs* **:** ASSEMBLY **2** *obs* **:** a public oration — **concional** *adj*, *obs*

concionate *vi* -ED/-ING/-S [L *contionatus*, past part. of *contionari*, fr. *contio* assembly, oration] *obs* **:** HARANGUE, PREACH — **concionatory** *adj*, *obs*

con·cip·i·ent \kən'sipēənt\ *adj* [L *concipient-, concipiens*, pres. part. of *concipere* to conceive — more at CONCEIVE] **:** CONCEPTIVE, CONCEIVING

con·cise \kən'sīs\ *adj*, *sometimes* -ER/-EST [L *concisus*, past part. of *concidere* to cut up, fr. *com-* + *-cidere* (fr. *caedere* to cut, hew, strike, kill); akin to MHG *heie* mallet, club, Arm *xait'* to prick] **1 :** marked by brevity in expression or by compact statement without elaboration or superfluous detail **2 :** accomplished in little time **:** brief and curtailed **:** cut short ⟨the effect is a ~ panorama of the city's character —*Amer. Guide Series: Texas*⟩

syn TERSE, SUCCINCT, LACONIC, SUMMARY, PITHY, COMPENDIOUS: CONCISE indicates the cutting out of all superfluities and avoidance of elaboration ⟨Carruthers took a telegram from his pocket . . . It was short and *concise:* "The old man is dead" —A. Conan Doyle⟩ ⟨he [Gladstone] asked whether he should be . . . *concise*, and Peel told him to be long and diffuse —*Times Lit. Supp.*⟩ TERSE may imply finish and pointedness in addition to brevity ⟨as a lecturer his command of *terse* English enabled him to give a maximum of instruction with a minimum of words —J.M.Phalen⟩ ⟨*terse* headlines are another part of the Tribune's campaign to save newsprint —*New Yorker*⟩ SUCCINCT implies extreme compactness and compression ⟨a book must have a title and today it must have a *succinct* title; therefore this book appears as *Richelieu* —Hilaire Belloc⟩ LACONIC indicates shortness to the point of seeming brusque, unconcerned, or mysterious ⟨again he paused longer, and raised his eyebrows still more. "It is sold, sir," was again his *laconic* reply —Bram Stoker⟩ ⟨the *laconic* announcement was made . . . that the sentences of death had been carried out —*Manchester Guardian Weekly*⟩ SUMMARY suggests the treatment of main points with no elaboration or additional explanation; it may apply to treatments and actions done with much promptness or even brusqueness ⟨a presentation as *summary* as is compatible with an adequate statement of the available information —*Internat'l Labor Office Recent Publications*⟩ ⟨a *summary* redress . . . was . . . provided by the crown in a royal proclamation —J.R.Green⟩ ⟨she seemed surprised, and offended . . . and waved us out of the house. *Summary* as the dismissal was, court etiquet no doubt required our compliance —Herman Melville⟩ PITHY suggests a wealth of forcible or telling material briefly presented ⟨a brief, *pithy*, and, as it then appeared to him, unanswerable argument against the immortality of the human soul —Nathaniel Hawthorne⟩ COMPENDIOUS applies to treatments at once full and comprehensive and brief and concise ⟨it would reduce all the feet and combinations of feet to *compendious* and intelligible formulas —R.W.Chapman⟩

con·cise·ly *adv* **:** in a concise manner

con·cise·ness *n* -ES **:** the quality or state of being concise

con·ci·sion \kən'sizhən\ *n* -s [ME *concisioun*, fr. L *concision-, concisio*, fr. *concisus* + *-ion-, -io* -ion] **1** *archaic* **a :** a cutting up or off **:** MUTILATION; *esp* **:** circumcision regarded purely as mutilation **b :** a rending esp. of the church **:** DIVISION, SCHISM **2 :** the quality or state of being concise — used esp. of literary style

con·ci·ta·tion \,kän(t)sə'tāshən\ *n* -s [L *concitation-, concitatio*, fr. *concitatus* (past part. of *concitare* to stir up, rouse, fr. *com-* + *citare* to set in motion) + *-ion-, -io* -ion — more at CITE] **:** the act of stirring up, exciting, or agitating

con·ci·ta·to \,känchə'täd·(,)ō\ *adv (or adj)* [It, lit., stirred up, fr. past part. of *concitare* to stir up, excite, fr. L] **:** in an excited or agitated style — used as a direction in music

concl *abbr* conclusion

con·cla·mant \(')kän¦klāmənt, -lam-\ *adj* [L *conclamant-, conclamans*, pres. part. of *conclamare*] **:** crying out together ⟨the ~ voices of common sense and decency⟩

con·cla·ma·tion \,känklə'māshən, -äŋk-\ *n* -s [L *conclamation-, conclamatio*, fr. *conclamatus* (past part. of *conclamare* to cry out together, fr. *com-* + *clamare* to cry out) + *-ion-, -io* -ion — more at CLAIM] **:** an outcry of many together **:** SHOUT

con·clave \'kän,klāv, *esp Brit sometimes* -äŋ,-\ *n* -s [ME, fr. MF or ML; MF, fr. ML, fr. L, room or apartment that can be locked up, fr. *com-* + *clavis* key — more at CLAVICLE] **1** *obs* **:** a private chamber **:** CLOSET **2 a :** a private meeting **:** a closed or secret assembly; *esp* **:** a meeting of Roman Catholic cardinals secluded continuously in a set of apartments while engaged in choosing a pope **b :** a meeting esp. of a group with shared or specialized interests (as a fraternal society) **:** CONFERENCE, CONVENTION, GATHERING **3 a :** the body of cardinals esp. when considered in respect to their electoral function **b :** any authoritative group exercising wide discretionary powers ⟨secret party ~*s* that pick the candidates behind the scenes⟩

con·clav·ist \-vəst\ *n* -s [It *conclavista*, fr. *conclave* (fr. ML) + *-ista* -ist] **:** an individual (as an ecclesiastical secretary or a lay servant) who attends a cardinal in a conclave ⟨cardinals who are ill or infirm may have two ~*s* —Arnaldo Cortesi⟩

con·clud·able *also* **con·clud·ible** \kən'klüdəbəl\ *adj* **:** capable of being inferred or concluded

con·clude \kən'klüd\ *vb* -ED/-ING/-S [ME *concluden*, fr. L *concludere*, fr. *com-* + *-cludere* (fr. *claudere* to shut) — more at CLOSE] *vt* **1 :** to shut up or off **:** ENCLOSE, CONFINE, CONSTRAIN: **a** *archaic* **:** to overcome in argument **:** CONVINCE, CONFUTE **b** *obs* **:** to bar from a course of action **:** PRECLUDE **c** *archaic* **:** to sum up **:** INCLUDE, COMPREHEND **d :** to constrain to a course of action **:** BIND, OBLIGE — now chiefly in legal use **2 :** to reach a final determination or judgment about **:** make a decision about **:** JUDGE, DECIDE — now usu. followed by a clause as object ⟨he *concluded* that he would wait⟩ **3 a :** to bring to an end **:** TERMINATE ⟨they often ~ their meetings with song⟩ ⟨*concluded* his speech with an appeal for unity⟩ **b :** COMPLETE ⟨unable to ~ any sales —*Farmer's Weekly (So. Africa)*⟩ **4 :** to reach an agreement on **:** bring into effect **:** EFFECT ⟨*concluded* an economic agreement⟩ ⟨having *concluded* the bargain they went their separate ways⟩ **5 :** to reach (as an end) by reasoning **:** infer esp. from premises ⟨no one should ~ another's evil deed from surface signs⟩ ~ *vi* **1 :** to come to a decision **:** reach a final judgment or agreement ⟨we *concluded* to wait for fair weather⟩ **2 :** to come to a close ⟨the meeting will probably ~ without any solution of this problem⟩ **:** END **3** *obs* **:** to be conclusive **syn** see CLOSE, INFER

concludent *adj* [L *concludent-, concludens*, pres. part. of *concludere*] *obs* **:** bringing to a close **:** DECISIVE

concluding *adj* **1** *obs* **:** CONCLUSIVE **2 :** FINAL **syn** see LAST

concluding line *n* **:** a line running down the middle of a rope ladder and made fast to each step

con·clud·ing·ly *adv* **:** in a concluding manner

con·clu·sion \kən'klüzhən\ *n* -s [ME *conclusioun*, fr. MF *conclusion*, fr. L *conclusion-, conclusio*, fr. *conclusus* (past part. of *concludere*) + *-ion-, -io* -ion] **1 a :** a reasoned judgment or an expression of one **:** INFERENCE ⟨haphazard thoughts occupy the place of rational ~*s* —Herbert Spencer⟩ **b** *logic* **:** the necessary consequence of two or more related propositions taken as premises; *esp* **:** the inferred proposition of a syllogism or other form of argument **2** *obs* **:** PURPOSE, AIM **3 :** the last part of anything **:** CLOSE, TERMINATION, END ⟨at the ~ of the contest⟩: as **a :** a final decision or settlement **:** RESULT, OUTCOME ⟨17th century attempts to solve the longitude problem came to no practical ~ —S.F.Mason⟩ **b conclusions** *pl* **:** trial of strength or skill — usu. in the phrase *try conclusions with* **c :** a final summing up (as of a discourse or writing) **d :** the final decision in a law case **e** *Scots law* **:** the final clause of a summons revealing the purpose of an action; *also* **:** the action itself **f :** the final speech of counsel to the court or the jury in a law case **g :** the final part of a pleading in law expressing willingness to offer proof or to submit the case to the court or the jury **4** *obs* **a :** PROPOSITION, PROBLEM, RIDDLE **b :** EXPERIMENT **5 :** ESTOPPEL **6 :** an act or instance of concluding: as **a :** SETTLEMENT **:** arrangement esp. of an armistice **b** *obs* **:** the drawing of an inference **7 :** the main clause of a conditional sentence — contrasted with *condition* **8 :** a pleader's allegation not sufficient in law because the basic facts warranting the statement are not set forth in the pleading — **in conclusion 1 :** FINALLY **2 :** in short

con·clu·sion·al \-zhən^əl,-zhnəl\ *adj* [ME, fr. *conclusioun* + *-al*] **:** of, relating to, or constituting a conclusion — **con·clu·sion·al·ly** \-^əlē, -əlē, -li\ *adv*

conclusion of fact *law* **:** a fact inferred to exist from other facts actually proved by evidence

conclusion of law : the court's statement of the law applicable to a case in view of certain facts found to be true or assumed by the jury to be true **:** the final judgment or decree which the law requires in view of the facts found or the verdict brought in

con·clu·sive \kən'klüs¦iv, ¦ēv *also* -üz| *or* |əv\ *adj* [LL *conclusivus*, fr. L *conclusus* + *-ivus* -ive] **:** belonging to a close or termination: as **a :** forming an end or termination **b :** putting an end to debate or question esp. by reason of irrefutability **:** involving a conclusion or decision **:** DECISIVE, FINAL ⟨~ evidence⟩ ⟨a ~ presumption⟩

syn DECISIVE, DETERMINATIVE, DEFINITIVE: applied most frequently to evidence or reasoning, CONCLUSIVE means so irrefutable as to end all uncertainty or question ⟨a very persuasive if not a *conclusive* argument —John Marshall⟩ ⟨the wisdom of the new rule was so manifest that it was accepted as a *conclusive* precedent —Frederick Pollock⟩ ⟨the evidence in the two poems which makes it *conclusive* that one is derived from the other —Amy Lowell⟩ Applied to events or influences, DECISIVE indicates that which settles controversy or ends uncertainty ⟨my words had been *decisive*. At least they had put an end to the discussion —Jack London⟩ ⟨he acted that brief period as commander-in-chief, but took no *decisive* steps towards settling the various problems confronting him —Stanley Pargellis⟩ DETERMINATIVE applies to decisions, causes, or influences serving to establish a fixed character or definite goal ⟨an appeal covering similar merchandise is pending . . . which will be *determinative* of this issue —*U.S. Treasury Decisions*⟩ DEFINITIVE, opposed to *tentative* or *provisional*, applies to something final, something obviating further dispute, investigation, or doubt ⟨it is not my purpose to try to offer any *definitive* answers to the questions involved . . . Publishing is now in a very problematical state —J.T.Farrell⟩ ⟨he is ineffably happy over the triumph of his principles and the *definitive* acceptance of his political philosophy —C.G.Bowers⟩

con·clu·sive·ly \|əvlē, -li\ *adv* **:** in a conclusive manner

con·clu·sive·ness \|ivnəs, |ēv- *also* |əv-\ *n* -ES **:** the quality or state of being conclusive

con·coct \kən'käkt, (')kän¦k-\ *vt* -ED/-ING/-S [L *concoctus*, past part. of *concoquere* to boil together, digest, mature, fr. *com-* + *coquere* to cook — more at COOK] **1** *obs* **:** to convert into nourishment by the organs of nutrition **:** DIGEST **2** *obs* **:** to prepare, perfect, or refine chemically by the action of heat **3** *archaic* **:** MATURE ⟨~ fruits⟩ **:** RIPEN ⟨~ a boil⟩ **4 a :** to prepare from crude materials (as food) **:** invent or prepare by combining different ingredients ⟨cleverly ~*ing* delicacies to tempt a flagging appetite⟩ **b :** to put together **:** COMPOSE, DEVISE, FABRICATE — usu. used disparagingly of the agent, the product, or both ⟨continued to ~ and publicize their unsavory views⟩ ⟨they ~*ed* an alibi for the missing man⟩ **syn** see CONTRIVE

con·coct·er *also* **con·coc·tor** \-tə(r)\ *n* -s **:** one that concocts **:** MAKER, FABRICATOR; *also* **:** one that aids in concoction

con·coc·tion \kən'käkshən, kän'k-, 'käŋ,k-\ *n* -s [L *concoction-, concoctio*, fr. *concoctus* + *-ion-, -io* -ion] **1** *obs* **:** digestion and assimilation of food **2** *obs* **:** a process of ripening or maturation **3 :** something that is concocted (as a food or scheme); *also* **:** something that suggests origin by concoction (as by mingling of diverse elements) **4 a :** the act of preparing (as a made dish or a remedy) by combining different ingredients **b :** an act of composing, fabricating, or making up (as a story or scheme)

con·coc·tive \-ktiv\ *adj* [*concoction* + *-ive*] **:** of or relating to concoction

con·col·or·ous \(')kän¦kələrəs, kən'k-\ *also* **con·col·or·ate** \-rət\ *or* **con·col·or** \'kän,kələ(r)\ *adj* [*concolorous*, fr. *concolor* fr. L *concolor* + E *-ous or -ate; concolor* fr. L, fr. *com-* + *color*] **1 :** of the same color as a specified article — used esp. to describe one part of an insect by comparison with another ⟨thorax ~ with abdomen⟩ **2 :** of uniform color

con·com·i·tance \kən'kämədən|(t)s, kän'k-, -mətən| *also* -mət^ən|\ *also* **con·com·i·tan·cy** \|sē,|si\ *n* -s [ML *concomitantia*, fr. L *concomitant-, concomitans* + *-ia* -y] **1 :** a state of accompanying **:** ACCOMPANIMENT; *esp* **:** regular and precise conjunction implying correlative variation of the concomitants **2 :** the doctrine in Roman Catholicism of the existence of both the body and blood of Christ in each element of the Eucharist so that both are received by communicating in one kind only **3 :** an instance of being concomitant **:** a concomitant thing or act ⟨the ~*s* of a marriage ceremony⟩

¹con·com·i·tant \kən'kämədənt, (')kän¦k-, -mətənt *also* -mət^ənt\ *adj* [L *concomitant-, concomitans*, pres. part. of *concomitari* to accompany, fr. *com-* + *comitari*, fr. *comit-, comes* companion — more at COUNT] **:** accompanying or attending esp. in a subordinate or incidental way **:** occurring along with or at the same time as and with or without causal relationship ⟨the scholastic belief that man is a child of God and . . . the ~ belief that all men are brothers —Hardin Craig⟩ **syn** see CONTEMPORARY

²concomitant \"\ *n* -s **1 :** something that accompanies or is collaterally connected with another **:** ACCOMPANIMENT ⟨tuberculosis, hookworm, and infant mortality — the pathological ~*s* of pauperism —Oscar Handlin⟩ **2** *archaic* **:** ASSOCIATE, COMPANION

con·com·i·tant·ly *adv* **:** in a concomitant manner

¹con·cord \'käŋ,kȯrd, -än,-, -ō(ə)d\ *n* -s [ME, fr. OF *concorde*, fr. L *concordia*, fr. *concord-, concors* of the same mind, agreeing, fr. *com-* + *cord-, cor* heart — more at HEART] **1 a :** a state of agreement **:** harmony esp. between persons **b :** an agreeable harmonious combination of tones simultaneously heard; *specif* **:** a chord satisfying in harmonic effect and not requiring resolution — contrasted with *discord* **2 :** agreement by stipulation, compact, or covenant **:** TREATY; *esp* **:** one establishing or reestablishing peaceful and amicable relationships between peoples or nations **3 :** AGREEMENT 4

²con·cord \kən'kȯ(ə)rd, -ō(ə)d\ *vi* -ED/-ING/-S [ME *concorden*, fr. MF *concorder*, fr. L *concordare*, fr. *concord-, concors*] **:** to act together **:** HARMONIZE, AGREE

³con·cord \'käŋkə(r)d\ *adj*, *usu cap* [fr. *Concord*, N.H.] **1 :** of or from Concord, the capital of New Hampshire ⟨*Concord* industries⟩ **:** of the kind or style prevalent in Concord **2** *of horse-drawn vehicles* **:** made in a variety of models originated in Concord and used widely throughout the U.S. in the 19th century ⟨*Concord* wagons⟩

⁴concord \"\ *n* -s *usu cap* [by shortening] **:** CONCORD COACH

con·cor·dance \kən'kȯrd^ən(t)s, kän-, -ō(ə)d-\ *n* -s [ME *concordaunce*, fr. MF *concordance*, fr. ML *concordantia*, fr. L *concordant-, concordans* + *-ia* -y] **1 :** an alphabetical verbal index showing the places in the text of a book or in the works of an author where each principal word may be found often with its immediate context; *also* **:** a similar index showing subjects **2 :** CONCORD, AGREEMENT

con·cor·dan·cy \-^ənsē, -si\ *n* -ES [ML *concordantia*] **:** AGREEMENT

con·cor·dant \kən'kȯrd^ənt, (')kän¦k-, -ō(ə)d-\ *adj* [ME *concordaunt*, fr. MF *concordant*, fr. L *concordant-, concordans*, pres. part. of *concordare*] **1 :** AGREEING, CORRESPONDENT, HARMONIOUS, CONSONANT ⟨results ~ with the experimental data⟩ ⟨expressed views ~ with his background and training⟩ **2** *geol* **:** manifesting conformity or parallelism of bedding or structure — used of strata **3** *of twins* **:** similar in respect to one or more particular characters — compare DISCORDANT — **con·cor·dant·ly** *adv*

con·cor·dan·tial \¦käŋ,kȯ(r)¦danchəl, ¦käŋ,-\ *adj* [ML *concordantia* + E *-al*] **:** of or relating to a concordance **:** like a concordance (as in completeness of detail)

con·cor·dat \kən'kȯr|,dat, -ōə|, |,dət, +V *usu* -ad· *or* -əd·\ *n* -s [F, fr. ML *concordatum*, fr. L, neut. of *concordatus*, past part. of *concordare*] **1 a :** a compact between a national government and a religious group establishing terms of agreement concerning matters of mutual interest **b :** a formal agreement between two religious groups establishing the bases of union or common action ⟨a proposed ~ to unite Episcopalian and Presbyterian churches⟩ **2 :** a compact, covenant, or agreement concerning something

con·cor·da·to·ry \kən'kȯrdə,tōrē, kän'-\ *adj* [*concordat* + *-ory*] **:** of, relating to, or established or maintained by means of a concordat

con·cord buggy \'käŋkə(r)d-\ *n*, *usu cap C* [fr. *Concord*, N.H., where it was first made] **:** a buggy having a body with side-spring suspension

Concord buggy

concord coach \"-\ *n*, *usu cap 1st C* [fr. *Concord*, N.H., where it was first made] **:** a large closed horse-drawn coach having the body swung on thorough braces, a driver's seat outside in front, and a covered baggage compartment at the rear

con·cor·di·al \(')käŋ¦kȯ(r)dēəl, -än¦-\ *adj* [LL *concordialis*, fr. L *concordia* harmony + *-alis* -al — more at CONCORD] **:** of or belonging to grammatical agreement

concords *pl of* CONCORD, *pres 3d sing of* CONCORD

¹con·corporate \(')kän, kən+\ *adj* [ME *concorporat*, fr. L *concorporatus*, past part. of *concorporare* to unite in one body, fr. *com-* + *corporare* to make into a body — more at CORPORATE] *archaic* **:** united in one body

²con·corporate \(')kän, kən+\ *vb* -ED/-ING/-S [L *concorporatus*] *vt*, *archaic* **:** to unite (diverse elements) into a single unit **:** make part of a whole ~ *vi*, *obs* **:** to coalesce into one mass or body

con·cours \kōⁿ'kü(ə)r\ *n*, *pl* **concours** \-r(z)\ [F, fr. MF, concourse] **:** a public competition **:** CONTEST

con·cours d'é·lé·gance \-r,dālā'gäⁿs\ *n* [F *concours d'élégance*, lit., contest of elegance] **:** a show or contest of vehicles or equipages in which the contestants are judged chiefly on excellence of appearance and turnout rather than roadworthiness

con·course \'kän,kōrs, -,kȯrs, -ōəs,-ȯ(ə)s *also* -äŋ,-\ *n* -s [ME *concurs, concours*, fr. MF & L; MF *concours*, fr. L *concursus*, fr. past part. of *concurrere* to run together — more at CONCUR] **1 :** an act or action of flocking, moving, or flowing together (as of persons or streams) **:** an approaching and merging **2 a :** a meeting produced by voluntary or spontaneous moving and coming together at one place **:** CONFLUENCE, GATHERING, MEETING, CROWD, THRONG **b** *obs* **:** an encounter of hostile forces **c :** CONJUNCTION 5 **3 :** a place or point of meeting: as **a :** an open space where several roads or paths meet **b :** an open space or hall where crowds may gather esp. by chance coming together (as in a large railroad terminal) **4** *law* **a :** the arising of two or more actions that are founded upon the same state of facts and may be pursued simultaneously or consecutively **b** *Scots law* **:** the arising of a criminal and a civil action on the same grounds **5** *archaic* **:** COOPERATION

con·cre·ate \¦känkrē¦āt, ='=,=\ *vt* -ED/-ING/-S [LL *concreatus*, past part. of *concreare*, fr. L *com-* + *creare* to create — more at CREATE] *archaic* **:** to create together — **con·cre·a·tion** \,känkrē'āshən\ *n* -s

concredit *vt* -ED/-ING/-S [L *concreditus*, past part. of *concredere*, fr. *com-* + *credere* to entrust, believe — more at CREED] *obs* **:** COMMIT, ENTRUST

con·cremation \(¦)kän+\ *n* -s [LL *concremation-, concrematio*, fr. L *concrematus* (past part. of *concremare* to burn up, fr. *com-* + *cremare* to burn) + *-ion-, -io* -ion — more at CREMATE] **:** BURNING, CREMATION; *specif* **:** SUTTEE

con·cre·ment \'käŋkrəmənt, -änk-\ *n* -s [L *concrementum*, fr. *concrescere*] **:** CONCRETION 3a

con·cresce \kən'kres, (')kän¦k-\ *vi* -ED/-ING/-S [L *concrescere* — more at CONCRETE] **:** to grow together **:** COALESCE

con·cres·cence \-s^ən(t)s\ *n* -s [L *concrescentia*, fr. *concrescent-, concrescens* (pres. part. of *concrescere*) + *-ia* -y] **1 a :** coalescence esp. of particles **b :** increase by the addition of particles — compare ASSIMILATION, INTUSSUSCEPTION 2 **2** *biol* **:** a growing together **:** a union or coalescence of parts originally separate; *specif* **:** convergence and fusion of the lateral lips of the blastopore to form the primordium of an embryo

con·cres·cent \-sᵊnt\ *adj* [back-formation fr. *concrescence*] **:** exhibiting concrescence **:** grown or growing together ⟨a flower with ~ petals⟩

concreta *pl of* CONCRETUM

¹con·crete \(ˈ)kän¦krēt *sometimes* (ˈ)kän¦k- *or* (*except sense 4*) kənˈk-; *in sense 4* ˈ‚ *also* (ˈ)ˈ‚; *usu* -ēd·+V\ *adj* [ME *concret*, fr. L *concretus*, past part. of *concrescere* to grow together, fr. *com-* + *crescere* to grow — more at CRESCENT] **1 :** united in growth: **a** *archaic* **:** compounded of different ingredients **:** COMPOSITE **b :** formed by coalition of separate particles into one mass **:** united in a solid form **2 a :** naming a thing or class of things — opposed to *abstract* ⟨the word *poem* is ~, *poetry* is abstract⟩ **b** *of a unit or number* **:** associated with or applied to particular objects or magnitudes ⟨three men, to give a ~ figure⟩ — opposed to *abstract* **3 a :** characterized by immediate experience of realities whether physical things, sensations, or emotions **:** belonging to or standing for actual things or events **:** not abstract or ideal **:** SPECIFIC, PARTICULAR ⟨a rainbow is ~ color⟩ ⟨they presented ~ proposals for improvement⟩ **b :** REAL, ACTUAL, TANGIBLE ⟨his suspicions had nothing very ~ to go on⟩ ⟨~ proof of the man's guilt⟩ **4 :** relating to or made of concrete

²con·crete *in sense 1* (ˈ)kän¦k- *sometimes* (ˈ)kän¦k- *or* kənˈk-; *in other senses* ˈkän¦k- *also* (ˈ)kän¦ˈk- *sometimes* -äŋ¦\ *n* -s **1 :** a concrete form or object; *also* **:** something that is concrete — used with *the* **2 :** a compound or mass formed by concretion, spontaneous union, or coalescence of separate particles of matter in one body ⟨a ~ of combustible materials⟩ **3 a :** a hard strong building material made by mixing a cementing material (commonly portland cement) and a mineral aggregate (as washed sand and gravel or broken rock) with sufficient water to cause the cement to set and bind used in the construction of bridges, buildings, dams, pavements, tunnels, and smaller products — compare CINDER CONCRETE, CYCLOPEAN CONCRETE **b :** a surface (as a path or roadway) paved with such artificial stone ⟨since the road was a through-way motorists were asked not to park on the ~⟩ **4 :** crude sugar obtained in compact masses by boiling down cane juice or maple sap **5 :** a waxy essence esp. of flowers prepared by extraction (as with petroleum ether) and removal of the solvent by vacuum distillation and used in perfumery ⟨~ of rose⟩ — compare ABSOLUTE 3 — **in the concrete :** in concrete manifestations, features, or detail **:** in particulars — opposed to *in the abstract*

³con·crete *in vt sense 3 and vi sense 2* ˈkän¦‚k- *also* (ˈ)kän¦ˈk- *sometimes* -äŋ¦; *in other senses* (ˈ)kän¦k- *sometimes* (ˈ)kän¦k- *or* kənˈk-\ *vb* -ED/-ING/-S *vt* **1 a :** to form into a solid mass (as by cooling, evaporation, coagulation, or cementation) **:** SOLIDIFY, CONGEAL **b :** COMBINE, BLEND, FUSE, UNITE ⟨art *concreted* with nature to produce a gracious whole⟩ **2 :** to make actual or real **:** cause to take on the qualities of reality **:** make concrete ⟨the basic *concreting* relation is a symmetrical relation of togetherness —Nelson Goodman⟩ **3 :** to cover with, form of, line with, or set or embed in concrete ~ *vi* **1** *of separate particles* **:** to unite or coalesce into a mass **:** SOLIDIFY, HARDEN, CONGEAL, COAGULATE **2 :** to pour or apply concrete

concrete block *n* **:** a hollow building unit of concrete — called also *cement block*

con·crete·ly *adv* **:** in a concrete manner

concrete masonry *n* **:** block, brick, or tile building units of molded concrete laid by masons in a wall

concrete mixer *n* **:** a machine for mixing the materials of which concrete is made — called also *cement mixer*

concrete nail *n* **:** a nail usu. of hardened steel for use in masonry

con·crete·ness *n* -ES **:** the quality or state of being concrete

concrete paint *n* **:** a paint especially adapted to use on concrete because of its resistance to the free lime in concrete

con·cret·er *or* **con·cre·tor** \-ēd·ə(r), -ētə-\ *n* -s **1 :** one that concretes; *specif* **:** one who builds or works with concrete **2 :** *usu concretor* **:** an apparatus for boiling down crude sugar solutions

concrete saw *n* **:** a saw used to cut grooves in the surface of green concrete pavement slabs to control cracking

concrete universal *n* **1 :** a universal whose connotation is so particularized that it denotes one concrete reality esp. an organized unity as distinguished from a universal that denotes any one of a class — used by Hegelians to contrast terms such as *man, book, church* with those that denote a totality, as *mankind, literature, the church* **2 :** something denoted by a concrete universal

concreting *n* -s **:** the operation involving the mixing, handling, placing, finishing, and curing of concrete

con·cre·tion \kän'krēshən, kən-\ *n* -s [L *concretion-, concretio*, fr. *concretus* (past part. of *concrescere* to grow together) + *-ion-, -io* -ion — more at CONCRETE] **1 a :** the act or process of making or becoming solid, substantial, or real ⟨unity must be achieved in deliance of the unique and particularistic forces of historical ~ —Reinhold Niebuhr⟩ ⟨when it falls back upon the accepted ~ of traditional knowledge —G.K.Anderson⟩ **b :** the action of growing together or being formed into a whole ⟨the ~ of ideas into a working hypothesis⟩ **2 :** the state of being concrete or concreted ⟨the ~ of the mass increases through the years⟩ **3 :** something that is or is made concrete ⟨the language of an art is a ~ of its symbols —*Dance Observer*⟩ **:** a concrete mass **:** a solid body formed by concreting particles: as **a :** a hard usu. inorganic mass (as a bezoar or tophus) formed in a natural body cavity or in the tissues **b :** a mass of mineral matter that is found generally in rock of a composition different from its own and that is produced by deposition from aqueous solution in the rock

con·cre·tion·ary \-shə‚nerē\ *adj* **:** relating to or formed by concretion or aggregation **:** producing or containing concretions

con·cret·ism \(ˈ)kän¦krēd·‚izəm, -ē‚tiz- *sometimes* -äŋ¦k- *or* kənˈk-\ *n* -s [¹*concrete* + *-ism*] **:** the representation of abstract things as concrete

concretive *adj* [³*concrete* + *-ive*] *obs* **:** promoting or tending toward concretion

con·cret·i·za·tion \(‚)kän‚krēd·ə'zāshən *sometimes* -äŋ‚k- *or* kən‚k-\ *n* -s **:** the act of concretizing or the state of being concrete ⟨~ of ideas⟩

con·cret·ize \(ˈ)kän¦krēd‚īz *sometimes* -äŋ¦k- *or* kənˈk-\ *vb* -ED/-ING/-S [¹*concrete* + *-ize*] *vt* **:** to make concrete, specific, or definite ⟨an agent *concretizing* abstractions—Alexis Carrel⟩ ~ *vi* **:** to become concrete ⟨the mental representation . . . ~s externally —Heinrich Zimmer⟩

con·cre·tum \kän'krēd·əm *sometimes* -äŋ'- *or* kən'-\ *n, pl* **concre·ta** \-d·ə\ [NL, fr. neut. of L *concretus* concrete — more at CONCRETE] **:** something that is concrete, particular, or directly given — contrasted with *abstractum*

con·cu·bi·nage \kän'kyübənij, kən-\ *n* -s [ME, fr. MF, fr. *concubine* + *-age*] **1 a :** cohabitation of persons not legally married; *esp* **:** a continued association between a man and a woman for such purpose, being under certain primitive systems a socially acceptable relation the offspring of which are neither bastards nor heirs of the male partner **b** *Roman law* **:** the permanent cohabitation of a man and woman that was not recognized in addition to a formal marriage and that was commonly considered an inferior form of marriage the offspring of which were entitled to support but did not come under the potestas of the father but might under the laws of Justinian be legitimated by a subsequent formal marriage **2 :** the state of being or having a concubine **3 :** a state of mental subserviency or bondage

concubinal *adj* [LL *concubinalis*, fr. L *concubina* + *-alis* -al] *obs* **:** CONCUBINARY

¹con·cu·bi·nary \kän'kyübə‚nerē, kən- *also* **con·cu·bi·nar·i·an** \¦kän‚kyübə¦na(a)rēən, kən¦k-\ *adj* [*concubinary* fr. ML *concubinarius*, fr. L *concubina* concubine + *-arius* -ary; *concubinarian* fr. *concubinary* + *-ian*] **:** relating to, living in, or sprung from concubinage

²concubinary \"\ *n* -ES **:** one living in concubinage

con·cu·bi·nate \kän'kyübənət, kən-, -‚nāt\ *n* -s [L *concubinatus*, fr. *concubina* concubine + *-atus* -ate] **:** CONCUBINAGE

¹con·cu·bine \ˈkäŋkyə‚bīn, -änk-\ *n* -s [ME, fr. OF, fr. L *concubina*, fr. *com-* + *-cubina* (fr. *cubare* to lie down) — more at HIP] **1 a :** a woman living in a socially recognized state of concubinage ⟨Hagar and Keturah were the ~s of Abraham⟩ **b :** a woman who cohabits with a man without being his wife **:** MISTRESS **2 :** a man living in a state of concubinage to another man or a woman

²concubine \"\ *vt* -ED/-ING/-S **1** *obs* **:** to make a concubine of **2 :** to provide with a concubine

conculcate *vt* -ED/-ING/-S [L *conculcatus*, past part. of *conculcare*, fr. *com-* + *calcare* to trample, fr. *calc-, calx* heel — more at CALK] *obs* **:** to tread or trample underfoot

con·cu·pis·cence \kän'kyüpəsən(t)s, kən'k- *also* ‚känkyü'pisᵊn-\ *n* -s [ME, fr. MF, fr. LL *concupiscentia*, fr. L *concupiscent-, concupiscens* + *-ia* -y] **:** strong or ardent desire: **a :** a longing of the soul for what will give it delight or for what is agreeable esp. to the senses — used chiefly by Scholastic philosophers **b :** sexual desire **:** LUST **syn** see DESIRE

con·cu·pis·cent \-nt\ *adj* [L *concupiscent-, concupiscens*, pres. part. of *concupiscere* to desire ardently, fr. *com-* + *-cupiscere* (fr. *cupere* to desire) — more at COVET] **:** LUSTFUL

con·cu·pis·cent·ly *adv* **:** with concupiscence

con·cu·pis·ci·ble \-səbəl\ *adj* [ME, fr. MF or LL; MF, fr. LL *concupiscibilis*, fr. L *concupiscere* + *-ibilis* -ible] **1 :** motivated by a desire for good under the aspect of the agreeable esp. the sensuously agreeable — used chiefly by Scholastic philosophers of the appetite and the passions; opposed to *irascible* **2 :** moved by concupiscence ⟨his ~ intemperate lust —Shak.⟩ **3** *archaic* **:** that merits desire **:** suitable to be longed for or lusted after **:** greatly desirable

con·cur \kən'kər, kän-, +V -ər·; -ˈkə̄, +V -ˈkər· *also* -ˈkə̄r\ *vi* **concurred; concurred; concurring; concurs** [ME *concurren*, fr. L *concurrere*, fr. *com-* + *currere* to run — more at CURRENT] **1** *obs* **:** to come or flow together esp. with force or violence **:** reach a common point or situation **:** CONVERGE, MEET **2 :** to happen together **:** COINCIDE ⟨leisure and opportunity do not always ~⟩ **3 :** to act together to a common end or to produce a single effect ⟨rival political parties ~ in this action⟩ ⟨physical and moral causes had *concurred* to prevent civilization from spreading to that region —T.B.Macaulay⟩ **4** *archaic* **:** to correspond esp. in quality or character ⟨this ~s directly with the letter —Shak.⟩ **5 a :** APPROVE — usu. followed by *in* ⟨do you ~ in his statement —J.G.Cozzens⟩ **b :** AGREE ⟨~ with an opinion⟩ **6 :** to join with other claimants in asserting claim against the estate of an insolvent **7 :** to fall on successive days so that celebration of one begins before that of the other ends — used esp. of Christian festivals; compare OCCUR **syn** see AGREE, UNITE

con·cur·rence \kən'kər·ən(t)s, kän'k-, -ˈkə·rə- *also* 'kän‚k-\ *also* **con·cur·ren·cy** \-ənsē, -si\ *n, pl* **concurrences** *also* **concurrencies** [ML *concurrentia*, fr. L *concurrent-, concurrens* + *-ia* -y] **1 a :** agreement or union in action **:** combination of power or influence **:** COOPERATION ⟨~ in doing good⟩ **b :** a meeting of minds **:** agreement in opinion **:** union in design; *also* **:** CONSENT **2 :** competition or rivalry **3 :** the act of concurring **:** a meeting or coming together **:** UNION, CONJUNCTION, COINCIDENCE, CONCOURSE **4** *law* **:** a coincidence of equal powers ⟨a ~ of jurisdiction in two different courts⟩ **5 :** the concurring of Christian festivals

¹con·cur·rent \kən'kər·ənt, (ˈ)kän¦k-, -kə·rə-\ *adj* [ME *concurrant*, fr. MF & L; MF *concurrent*, fr. L *concurrent-, concurrens*, pres. part. of *concurrere*] **1 a :** converging, meeting, intersecting, running together at a point ⟨in both heads the brow ridges are absent, and the eyebrows ~ —C.S.Coon⟩; *specif, math* **:** meeting in a point **b :** running parallel ⟨~ lines of force⟩ **2 :** occurring, arising, or operating at the same time often in relationship, conjunction, association, or cooperation ⟨the power of taxation in the general and state governments is acknowledged to be ~ —John Marshall⟩ ⟨the Germans launched a well-prepared full-scale invasion of southern Norway with the ~ occupation of Trondheim and Narvik —*Times Lit. Supp.*⟩ **3 a :** acting in conjunction **:** marked by accord, agreement, harmony, or similarity in effect or tendency ⟨the ~ testimony of all visitors to the spot⟩ **b :** *of insurance policies* **:** insuring the same property to the same extent or under identical clauses **4** *law* **:** joint and equal in authority **:** taking cognizance of or having authority over the same subject matters **:** operating on the same objects ⟨~ jurisdiction of courts⟩; *also* **:** operating simultaneously ⟨sentenced to serve three ~ life terms⟩ **syn** see CONTEMPORARY

²concurrent \"\ *n* -s **1 :** one that concurs **:** a joint or contributory cause ⟨to all affairs of importance there are three necessary ~s . . . time, industry, and faculties —Henry More⟩ **2** *archaic* **:** RIVAL, OPPONENT

con·cur·rent·ly *adv* **:** in a concurrent manner

concurrent majority *n* **:** a political majority created out of divergent interest groups and temporarily united by general agreement esp. in protecting a minority right

concurrent power *n* **:** a political power exercised independently in the same field of legislation by both federal and state governments

concurrent resolution *n* **:** a resolution passed by both branches of a legislative body; *esp* **:** such a resolution passed by the U.S. Congress expressing the general attitude or intention of Congress but not having the force of law or requiring the signature of the president — compare JOINT RESOLUTION

concurring *pres part of* CONCUR

con·cur·ring·ly *adv* **:** in a concurring manner

concurs *pres 3d sing of* CONCUR

con·cur·sion \kän'kərzhən, kən'-, -rshən\ *n* -s [L *concursion-, concursio*, fr. *concursus* (past part. of *concurrere* to run together) + *-ion-, -io* -ion — more at CONCUR] **:** the act of running together **:** CONCOURSE

con·cur·so \kən'kər(‚)sō, kän'-, -ˈkůr-\ *n* -s [Sp, fr. L *concursus* running together, concourse] *civil law* **:** a proceeding by which all creditors may equally establish their respective rights in a single fund

con·cur·sus \-ˈkərsəs\ *n, pl* **concursus** [ML, fr. L, concourse — more at CONCOURSE] *Christian relig* **:** the influx of divine causation upon secondary causes; *esp* **:** the doctrine that before the fall man was preserved from sin by the aid of God

con·cuss \kən'kəs\ *vt* -ED/-ING/-ES [L *concussus*, past part. of *concutere*] **1 :** SHAKE, AGITATE, JAR; *often* **:** to affect with concussion — usu. used as a participle ⟨suffered a ~*ing* blow⟩ ⟨unconscious Charlie who was clearly ~*ed* —C.S.Forester⟩ **2 :** to force or influence by intimidation **:** COERCE

con·cus·sion \kən'kəshən\ *n* -s [MF or L; MF, fr. L *concussion-, concussio*, fr. *concussus* (past part. of *concutere* to shake violently, fr. *com-* + *-cutere*, fr. *quatere* to shake) + *-ion-, -io* -ion — more at QUASH] **1 a :** JOLTING, SHAKING, AGITATING **b :** a smart or hard knock, blow, or collision; *also* **:** the shock of such a blow **:** a stunning, damaging, or shattering effect from such a blow ⟨wood, which responds to ~ with living vibration —Willa Cather⟩ ⟨it is the constant ~ of the cream in the churn which causes the butterfat to gather —*Westralian Farmers Co-op. Gazette*⟩ **2** *civil law, obs* **:** a forcing by threats **3 :** a jarring injury of the brain resulting in disturbance of cerebral function and sometimes marked by permanent damage; *also* **:** the condition of having been so injured **4 :** an inflammatory condition of the feet of horses caused by repeated violent contacts with hard roads **syn** see IMPACT

concussion bellows *n* **:** a small spring-controlled auxiliary bellows for an organ for compensating slight variations in wind pressure

concussion grenade *n* **:** a grenade that relies for its effect on the blast of its detonation rather than the fragmentation of its case and is often designed to stun rather than kill

con·cus·sive \kən'kəsiv\ *adj* [*concussion* + *-ive*] **:** having the power of or being by nature shaking, agitating, or jarring

con·cyclic \(ˈ)kän, kən+\ *adj* [*con-* + *cyclic*] **1 :** lying on one and the same circle — used of a system of points **2 :** cut in circles by the same parallel planes — used of certain systems of quadrics — **con·cyclically** \"\ *adv*

cond \ˈkänd\ *or* **cund** \ˈkənd\ *vt* -ED/-ING/-S [ME *conden* to conduct, alter. of *condien*, fr. MF *conduire*, fr. L *conducere* — more at CONDUCE] **:** CONN

cond *abbr* **1** condensed; condenser **2** condition; conditional **3** conduct; conducted; conductor

con·da·lia \kän'dālyə\ *n, cap* [NL, fr. Antonio *Condal*, 18th cent. Span. explorer + NL *-ia*] **:** a genus of spiny tropical American shrubs or trees (family Rhamnaceae) with small alternate leathery mostly 3-ribbed leaves and small apetalous flowers in sessile umbels

con·demn \kən'dem\ *vt* -ED/-ING/-S [ME *condempnen*, fr. OF *condemner, condempner*, fr. L *condemnare*, fr. *com-* + *-demnare* (fr. *damnare* to condemn) — more at DAMN] **1 :** to pronounce as ill-advised, reprehensible, wrong, or evil typically after definitive judgment and without reservation or mitigation ⟨no conceivable human action which custom has not at one time justified and at another ~*ed* —J.W.Krutch⟩ ⟨~ poetry equally with sex as something at best flippant and at worst immoral —C.D.Lewis⟩ **2 :** to declare the guilt of **:** make manifest the faults of **:** attest to the guilt of ⟨his words ~ him⟩ **3 a :** to pronounce a judicial sentence against **:** sentence to punishment or to suffering or loss **:** DOOM — often used with *to* ⟨driven out from bliss, ~*ed* in this abhorred deep to utter woe —John Milton⟩ **b :** to force, compel, or limit to an action or state ⟨the logic of his being a scientist ~s him to abstraction⟩ **4 :** to consign to perdition **:** DAMN — often used imperatively as a mild oath **5** *archaic* **:** to pronounce or find guilty **:** CONVICT — used with *of* ⟨till forging Nature be *condemn'd* of treason —Shak.⟩ **6 :** to adjudge or pronounce to be unfit for use or service **:** adjudge or pronounce to be forfeited ⟨jurisdiction to ~ the ship and her cargo⟩ **7 :** to block up (as a door) **:** close permanently **8 :** to pronounce to be taken for public use under the right of eminent domain **syn** see CRITICIZE

con·demna·ble \-m(n)əbəl\ *adj* **:** liable to be condemned **:** REPREHENSIBLE, BLAMABLE — **con·demna·bly** \-blē, -li\ *adv*

con·dem·na·tion \‚kän‚dem'nāshən, -‚dəm-\ *n* -s [ME *condempnacioun*, fr. L *condemnation-, condemnatio*, fr. *condemnatus* (past part. of *condemnare* to condemn) + *-ion-, -io* -ion] **1 :** the act of pronouncing to be wrong or morally culpable **:** CENSURE, BLAME, REPROBATION ⟨the Quakers, in their uncompromising ~ of war —W.R.Inge⟩ **2 :** the act of judicially condemning (as land for public uses) or adjudging unfit for use or forfeited (as a food product) **3 :** the state of being condemned ⟨the hopeless hour of ~ —Washington Irving⟩ **4 :** the ground or reason of condemning ⟨his conduct was sufficient ~⟩ **5** *Roman law* **:** one of the four principal parts of a formula by a praetor to a judex giving him authority to determine the facts of a lawsuit and specific instructions as to what disposition to make of the case if either the plaintiff's claims or the defendant's defenses were found to be true

con·dem·na·to·ry \kən'demnə‚tōrē, -tȯrē, -ri\ *adj* [*condemnation* + *-ory*] **:** containing or imposing condemnation or censure **:** CONDEMNING ⟨a ~ sentence⟩ ⟨a ~ decree⟩

condemned *adj* **1 :** pronounced to be wrong, guilty, worthless, or forfeited **:** sentenced to punishment, destruction, or confiscation **2 :** used for condemned persons or things ⟨the ~ cell⟩

con·demn·er *or* **con·demn·or** \kən'demə(r)\ *n* -s **:** one that condemns

condemning *adj* **:** CONDEMNATORY — **con·demn·ing·ly** *adv*

con·dens·able *also* **con·dens·ible** \kən'den(t)səbəl\ *adj* **:** capable of being condensed

con·den·sa·ry \-s(ə)rē, -ri\ *n* -ES [by alter.] **:** CONDENSERY

con·den·sate \kən'den‚sāt; 'kändən-, -‚den-\ *n* -s [L *condensatus*, past part.] **:** a product of condensation; *esp* **:** a liquid obtained by condensation of a gas or vapor ⟨steam ~⟩

con·den·sa·tion \‚kän‚den'sāshən, -‚dən-\ *n* -s [LL *condensation-, condensatio*, fr. L *condensatus* (past part. of *condensare*) + *-ion-, -io* -ion — more at CONDENSE] **1 a :** the act or process of condensing **b :** the state of being condensed or compressed **c :** a product of condensing **:** a condensed mass **2 a :** reduction of written or spoken expression to more compact form ⟨a prolix lecture greatly in need of ~⟩ **b :** conciseness or compactness of expression ⟨a literary style marked by great ~⟩ **c :** abridgment and usu. compression of a literary work ⟨a staff employed in the ~ of magazine articles⟩ **d :** the work produced by such condensation ⟨a ~ of a popular novel⟩ **3 :** a chemical reaction involving union between atoms (as of carbon in organic compounds) in the same or different molecules often with elimination of a simple molecule (as of water, alcohol, ammonia, or hydrogen chloride) to form a new compound of greater complexity and frequently greater molecular weight ⟨~ of oxygen to ozone⟩ ⟨~ of acetone with benzaldehyde⟩ — compare POLYMERIZATION **4 a :** transition of a substance from the vapor to the liquid phase (as steam to water) **b :** a state or region of maximum pressure and density in a medium traversed by compression waves (as sound waves) — compare RAREFACTION **5** *psychol* **:** representation of several apparently discrete ideas by a single symbol esp. in dreams

con·den·sa·tion·al \¦‚(‚)¦‚shənᵊl, -shnəl\ *adj* **:** of or relating to condensation ⟨~ energy⟩

condensation nucleus *n* **:** a small particle (as of dust) upon which water vapor condenses in the atmosphere

condensation polymerization *n* **:** polymerization in which a single molecule is eliminated — distinguished from *addition polymerization*

condensation pump *n* **:** DIFFUSION PUMP

condensation trail *n* **:** CONTRAIL

con·den·sa·tive \kən'den(t)səd·iv\ *adj* [*condensation* + *-ive*] **:** exhibiting, inducing, or tending to condensation

¹con·dense \kən'den(t)s\ *vb* -ED/-ING/-S [ME *condensen*, fr. MF *condenser*, fr. L *condensare*, fr. *com-* + *densare* to make thick or dense, fr. *densus* thick, dense — more at DENSE] *vt* **1 a :** to make more dense or compact **:** compress or concentrate into a smaller compass or volume ⟨the Senate *condensed* the five-year plan into three years —F.L. Paxson⟩ **b :** to reduce (sentences, paragraphs, or larger literary units) to compact form **:** ABRIDGE, COMPRESS ⟨~ a literary work⟩ **2 :** to subject (as atoms) to condensation ~ *vi* **1 a :** to become denser, more compact, or more intense **:** CONTRACT ⟨his anger did not evaporate in words but *condensed* and sank deeper —George Meredith⟩ **b :** to reduce what one says or writes to a concise form **2** *of a chemical substance* **:** to undergo condensation **syn** see CONTRACT

²condense *adj* [L *condensus*, back-formation fr. *condensare*] *obs* **:** CONDENSED, DENSE

condensed *adj* **1 :** reduced to a dense or denser form; *specif* **:** reduced from gaseous to liquid state **2 a :** concentrated esp. by evaporation or distillation **:** THICKENED, COMPACT **b :** CURT 1a **3** *of a letter or typeface* **:** having a face that is narrower than that of a typeface not so characterized — often used postpositively ⟨Futura Medium ~⟩ ⟨News Gothic Extra ~⟩; compare EXPANDED, EXTENDED

con·densed·ly \-en(t)sədlē, -en(t)(t)lē\ *adv* **:** in a condensed manner

condensed milk *n* **:** evaporated milk with sugar added

con·densed·ness \-en(t)sədnəs, -en(t)s(t)nəs\ *n* -ES **:** the quality or state of being condensed

condensed system *n* **:** a physical or chemical system in which there is no gaseous phase

con·dens·er \-sə(r)\ *n* -s **1 :** a person that condenses: as **a :** one that prepares short versions of literary material ⟨a ~ who prepared juvenile versions of many classic tales⟩ **b :** an operator of a condensing machine or device **2 :** a machine, instrument, or device that condenses: as **a :** COMPRESSOR b **b :** CAPACITOR **c :** a lens or mirror usu. of short focal length used to concentrate light upon an object **d :** a device that doffs the web from the carding machine and separates and condenses it into slivers or rovings **e :** an apparatus in which steam or water vapor is condensed to water esp. for the purpose of reducing the back pressure in a steam engine or steam turbine, which renders it possible to obtain a greater amount of useful work per pound of steam used **f** (1) **:** any of various pieces of apparatus for condensing gases or vapors to a liquid or solid state (as a tube surrounded by cold water in a still) — see STILL illustration (2) **:** a body that accepts heat rejected (as in a refrigerating system or a heat engine)

condenser antenna *n* **:** an antenna that consists of a lower conductor constituting a ground or a counterpoise and an upper conductor forming an aerial

condenser microphone *n* **:** a microphone in which the sound waves cause a variation in capacitance, the vibrating diaphragm acting as one plate of a condenser

condenser paper *n* **:** a very thin paper free from electrically conducting particles that is used as an insulator in electrical condensers

con·den·sery \-s(ə)rē, -ri\ *n* -ES [¹*condense* + *-ery*] **:** a plant where milk is concentrated by evaporating some of its water

condensible *var of* CONDENSABLE

condensing engine *n* **:** a steam engine in which the steam after exhausting from the cylinder is condensed in a separate condenser

condensing lens *n* **:** CONDENSER 2 c

con·den·sive load \kən'den(t)siv-\ *n* **:** a reactive load in which the current leads the voltage — called also *leading load*

con·de·scend \ˌkändə'send, -dē-\ *vb* -ED/-ING/-S [ME *condescenden*, fr. MF *condescendre*, fr. LL *condescendere*, fr. L *com-* + *descendere* to descend — more at DESCEND] *vi* **1** *obs* **:** to go or come down **:** DESCEND **2 :** to stoop or bend to action or speech less formal or dignified than is customary in one's social rank or importance **:** come down to the level of one socially inferior **:** UNBEND ⟨why, if he so dislikes and despises these people, does he ~ to mix with them —F.A. Swinnerton⟩ **3 :** to assume an air of superiority (as to one inferior or less fortunate) **:** act patronizingly ⟨well-fed tourists on their ~*ing* way through less happy lands⟩ — often used in irony ⟨if you will ~ to talk to a simple girl in intelligible terms —T.L.Peacock⟩ **4** *obs* **:** ACQUIESCE, CONSENT **5** *now chiefly Scot* **:** to make a settlement or specification — usu. used with *on* or *upon* ⟨the declaration was made to ~ upon particulars⟩ ~ *vt, obs* **:** to agree upon **:** settle upon **:** CONCEDE

con·de·scend·ence \ˌ≈≈'≈dən(t)s\ *n* -s [F *condescendance*, fr. *condescendant*, pres. part. of *condescendre*] **1 :** CONDESCENSION, COMPLIANCE, CONCESSION **2** *Scots law* **:** the pleading of the pursuer in a criminal action in which the facts material to the action are set forth

condescendency *n* -ES [modif. of F *condescendance* + E *-y*] *obs* **:** CONDESCENSION

con·de·scend·ent \-dənt\ *n* -s **:** one that condescends

condescending *adj* **:** showing or prompted by condescension

condescendingly *adv* **:** in a condescending manner

con·de·scend·ing·ness *n* -ES **:** CONDESCENSION

con·de·scen·sion \ˌkändə'senchən, -dē-\ *n* -s [LL *condescension-, condescensio*, fr. *condescensus* (past part. of *condescendere*) + L *-ion-, -io* -ion — more at CONDESCEND] **1 :** an act or instance of condescending: **a :** voluntary descent from one's rank or dignity in relations with an inferior **:** affability or informality toward inferiors **b :** disdain veiled by obvious indulgence or patience **2** *obs* **:** CONCESSION, ACQUIESCENCE

con·dic·tio \kən'dikshē,ō, -ktē,ō\ *n, pl* **condicti·o·nes** \kən,dikshē'ō(,)nēz, -ktē'ō,nās\ [L, fr. *condictus* (past part. of *condicere* to make a formal claim, fr. *com-* + *dicere* to say) + *-io* -ion — more at DICTION] *Roman law* **:** a formal claim for a thing **:** an action against a person orig. for a certain sum of money but later also for specific things and still later also for damages of uncertain extent; *also, under Justinian* **:** any claim for restitution or to prevent unjust enrichment

condictio ex le·ge \-ō,ek'slē,jē, -lā,gā\ *n* [LL, lit., formal claim according to law] *Roman law* **:** an action to enforce a statutory right or duty for which no specific remedy was provided

condictio fur·ti·va \-,ō,fər'tīvə, -fůr'tēvə\ *n* [NL, fr. L *condictio rei furtivae* formal claim for a stolen thing] *Roman law* **:** an action in quasi contract for the recovery of a specific stolen thing from the thief or his heirs or recovery of its value if it is not available — called also *condictio ex causa furtiva, condictio rei furtivae*

condictio in·de·bi·ti \-ōin'debə,tī, -,tē\ *n* [L, lit., formal claim for something not owed] *Roman law* **:** an action in quasi contract to recover money paid under a mistake usu. of fact rather than law

con·dic·tion \kən'dikshən\ *n* -s [L *condiction-, condictio*] **:** CONDICTIO — **con·dic·tious** \-shəs\ *adj*

condictio tri·ti·ca·ria \-,trid·ə'ka(a)rēə, -kär-\ *n* [NL, fr. LL *condictio triticiaria* formal claim relating to wheat] *Roman law* **:** an action for recovery of the same quality and quantity of fungible property (as wheat) previously loaned by plaintiff to defendant

con·did·dle \kən'didᵊl\ *vt* -ED/-ING/-S [prob. fr. *com-* + *diddle*] *dial Brit* **:** to make away with secretly **:** STEAL, WASTE

con·dign \kən'dīn, (')kän¦d-\ *adj* [ME *condigne*, fr MF, fr. L *condignus* very worthy, fr. *com-* + *dignus* worthy — more at DECENT] **1** *obs* **a :** of equal worth or dignity **b :** WORTHY **2 :** entirely in accordance with what is deserved or merited **:** neither exceeding nor falling below one's deserts — used only of punishments since the end of the 17th century ⟨when an adequate system for control of atomic energy . . . has been agreed upon . . . and ~ punishments set up for violations of the rules —B.M.Baruch⟩ **syn** see DUE

con·dig·ni·ty \kən'dignəd·ē, kän-\ *n* -ES [ML *condignitas*, fr. L *condignus* very worthy + *-itas* -ity] **1** *obs* **:** MERIT, WORTHINESS **2 :** merit described in scholastic theology as earned in distinction from that which is given **:** merit acquired by works performed in a state of grace — distinguished from *congruity*

con·dign·ly *adv* [ME *condignely*, fr. *condigne* + *-ly*] **:** in a condign manner **:** APPROPRIATELY, FITTINGLY — archaic except as applied to the action of punishing or meting out retribution ⟨~ sentenced to 10 years in jail⟩

con·di·ment \'kändəmənt\ *n* -s [ME, fr. MF, fr. L *condimentum*, fr. *condire* to pickle, season + *-mentum* -ment — more at CONDITE] **:** something usu. pungent, acid, salty, or spicy added to or served with food to enhance its flavor or to give added flavor **:** SEASONING: **a :** an appetizing and usu. pungent substance of natural origin (as pepper, vinegar, or mustard) **b :** any of various complex compositions having similar qualities (as curry or chili powder, pickles, or catsup) — **con·di·men·tal** \ˌkändə¦mentᵊl\ *adj*

condiment set *n* **:** a matched group of containers usu. with tray or rack, including containers for pepper, salt, and mustard and often stoppered cruets for oil and vinegar

con·disciple \ˌkän+\ *n* -s [L *condiscipulus*, fr. *com-* + *discipulus* disciple — more at DISCIPLE] **:** a fellow disciple or student **:** SCHOOLFELLOW

condite *vt* -ED/-ING/-S [ME *conditen*, fr. L *conditus*, past part. of *condire*, fr. *condere* to found, build, compose, store up, fr. *com-* + *-dere* to put — more at DO] **1** *obs* **:** PICKLE, PRESERVE **2** *obs* **:** EMBALM

¹con·di·tion \kən'dishən\ *n* -s [ME *condicioun*, fr. MF *condicion*, fr. L *condition-, conditio*, alter. of *condicion-, condicio* agreement, compact, condition, fr. *com-* + *-dicion-, -dicio* (fr. *dicere* to say, determine, proclaim) — more at DICTION] **1 a :** something established or agreed upon as a requisite to the doing or taking effect of something else **:** STIPULATION, PROVISION ⟨many are apt to believe remission of sins but they believe it without the ~ of repentance —Jeremy Taylor⟩ **b** *obs* **:** an agreement determining one or more such prerequisites **:** COVENANT ⟨such sum or sums as are expressed in the ~ —Shak.⟩ **2 :** something that exists as an occasion of something else **:** a circumstance that is essential to the appearance or occurrence of something else **:** PREREQUISITE: as **a** (1) **:** the antecedent of a hypothetical proposition (2) **:** the subordinate clause of a conditional sentence — contrasted with *conclusion* (3) **:** a proposition having a relation to the validity of another such that (1) validity of the first is sufficient evidence that the second is valid or (2) the second can only be valid if the first is also valid — called also respectively (1) *sufficient condition*, (2) *necessary condition* **b :** a provision in a contract, conveyance, grant, or will providing that the beginning, vesting, rescission, or a modification of an estate or interest in property or of a personal obligation must depend upon an uncertain event which may or may not exist or happen; *also* **:** the event itself **c :** a grade usu. designated by the letter E, given at many colleges and universities for work that does not meet the minimum standard required for passing but is not rated an absolute failure, and intended to serve notice on the student that he has a chance to raise his standing to passing level by doing additional work or passing a special examination **d :** a meld in the game panguingue for which a player immediately receives payment from other players **3 a :** something that limits or modifies the existence or character of something else **:** a restriction or qualification ⟨presence of oxygen is a ~ of animal life⟩ **b conditions** *pl* **:** attendant circumstances **:** existing state of affairs ⟨living ~*s*⟩ ⟨playing ~*s*⟩ **c :** something needing remedy **:** OBSTACLE **:** DEFECT, EVIL **:** unfavorable circumstance ⟨trains were late because of ~*s* west of the city⟩ **4 :** a mode or state of being ⟨matter in a gaseous ~⟩: **a :** social estate **:** RANK, POSITION ⟨all sorts and ~*s* of men —*Bk. of Common Prayer*⟩ **b** *obs* **:** state with reference to mental or moral nature, temperament, character, or disposition **c :** proper or good condition (as for work or sports competition) **:** the state of being fit **:** SHAPE ⟨the crew is out of ~⟩ ⟨getting in ~ for the big game⟩ **d** *of a domestic animal* **:** fat or the state of being fat **:** FINISH **e :** the physical status of the body as a whole ⟨good ~⟩ ⟨poor ~⟩ or of one of its parts — usu. used to indicate abnormality ⟨a serious heart ~⟩ ⟨a disturbed mental ~⟩ **f :** the financial position or state of a person or company **5 a** *obs* **:** QUALITY, ATTRIBUTE, TRAIT ⟨here is the catalog of her ~*s* —Shak.⟩ **b conditions** *pl, archaic* **:** personal nature **:** MANNERS, WAYS ⟨a woman of the most excellent ~*s* —Sir Walter Scott⟩ **6 :** LUPULIN

syn STIPULATION, TERM, PROVISION, PROVISO, RESERVATION, STRING: CONDITION indicates a requisite action, circumstance, or quality on which rests the validity or effectiveness of an agreement, a plan, promise, attribution ⟨to have some job in sight for the boy as a *condition* of his release at the end of his term —R.M.Lovett⟩ ⟨just had to keep writing — writing was a profession, a way of life, a *condition* of his survival —Sherwood Anderson⟩ ⟨respect for human life is undoubtedly, as we are never tired of preaching to some of our own communities, the first *condition* of civilization —W.C.Brownell⟩ STIPULATION may suggest formal, explicit, definite statement binding a party to a contract or agreement to a specified course ⟨the estate deeded the house to Clatsop County in 1936 with the *stipulation* that it be used for philanthropic purposes —*Amer. Guide Series: Oregon*⟩ ⟨a *stipulation* is a statement of conditions that are agreed to in the conduct of some affair —Felix Kaufmann⟩ TERM, used in the plural in this sense, indicates conditions offered or agreed to in a contract, deal, or agreement ⟨the *terms* of the lease are not harsh —C.E.Montague⟩ ⟨under the *terms* of the peace treaty, Bulgaria's armed forces are limited —*Americana Annual*⟩ ⟨to allow reunification on *terms* that meant alliance with the West —F.H.Hartmann⟩ PROVISION in this sense may specif. designate a written formal statement of a condition, directive, or right ⟨the admission of Arkansas with a *provision* in its constitution forbidding the abolition of slavery without the consent of the slaveowners —L.B.Evans⟩ ⟨Murray warned that even if the union were granted its wage increase, the dispute would not be settled until a union shop *provision* was inserted in the new contract —Mary K. Hammond⟩ ⟨this assumes that the framers of a law or constitution can foresee all possible future contingencies and make definite *provisions* for meeting them so that the judge can be merely a logical automaton —M.R.Cohen⟩ PROVISO is likely to indicate a definite binding stipulation ⟨passionate feeling is desirable, provided it is not destructive; intellect is desirable, with the same *proviso* —Bertrand Russell⟩ ⟨Field's company accepted with the *proviso* that it had the right to reject the job as substandard —James Dugan⟩ RESERVATION indicates a qualification or modification of the terms of an agreement or statement, often one to cover contingencies ⟨a blanket financial *reservation* was added that "any future claims and demands of the Allies and the United States of America remain unaffected". The armistice was for one month and was renewed from time to time until peace was signed —B.E.Schmitt⟩ STRING implies a reserving proviso, sometimes one unnoticed or unexpected and quite likely to modify drastically or annul agreements ⟨it is one thing to get a child to admit that he has money, and quite another to get him to part with it. For he will point out that the money was given to him without *strings* or conditions and that in strict commutative justice he may do what he likes with it —J.D.Sheridan⟩ **syn** see in addition STATE

— on condition that *or* **upon condition that :** with the provision that **:** IF

²condition \"\ *vb* **conditioned; conditioned; conditioning** \-sh(ə)niŋ\ **conditions** *vi* **1** *archaic* **:** to make conditions **:** set terms **:** STIPULATE **2 :** to attain proper or fit condition (as of beer in aging) **3 :** to limit and make definite an object of thought ~ *vt* **1 :** to agree by stipulating **:** CONTRACT — followed by an object clause or phrase ⟨~ that they marry⟩ ⟨~ to obey⟩ **2 :** to invest with, limit by, or subject to conditions **:** burden with a condition **:** make conditional ⟨freedom is ~*ed* by our opportunities⟩ ⟨his tenure was ~*ed* on good behavior⟩ **:** restrict or determine as a condition: as **a** *logic* **:** to limit or restrict in thought or conception **b** *law* **:** to charge with a condition **3 :** to put into proper or the desired condition: as **a :** to moisten (wheat) before grinding **b :** to trim (meat) of excess fat and other unsalable portions **c :** to restore the desired amount of moisture to (as fiber, yarn, or paper that has become dry during processing) **d** (1) **:** to purify and humidify (air) (2) **:** AIR-CONDITION **e :** to bring (as an athlete or a team) through a course of training to a state of fitness for contest **f :** FATTEN ⟨~ livestock⟩ **4 :** to test (textile fibers) for foreign inclusions (as of moisture or oil) **5 :** to require (a student) to pass a new examination or show a certain degree of proficiency in a specified study as a condition of remaining in a class or institution **6 a :** to adapt, modify, or mold (as by example, teaching, or training) to the basic patterns and standards of behavior existing in an environing culture ⟨traditional beliefs ~*ing* a child's attitude⟩ **b :** to modify (as an experimental organism) in such a way that an act or response previously associated with a given stimulus or class of stimuli becomes associated with a formerly unrelated stimulus or class of stimuli **syn** see PREPARE

¹con·di·tion·al \-shənᵊl,-shnəl\ *adj* [ME *condicionel*, fr. MF, fr. LL *condicionalis*, fr. *condicion-, condicio* + *-alis* -al] **1 :** containing, implying, subject to, or depending on a condition ⟨~ diplomatic recognition⟩ ⟨a ~ promise⟩ **:** not absolute **:** not certain **:** not full or unreserved ⟨~ loyalty⟩ — often used with *on* or *upon* ⟨my visit is ~ on his plans⟩ **2 :** expressing a condition or supposition **:** of or belonging to the expression of a condition **:** introducing, containing, or implying a supposition ⟨the ~ conjunctions *if, unless,* and *though*⟩ ⟨the ~ phrases *provided that* and *supposing that*⟩ ⟨the ~ clause *if he speaks*⟩ ⟨the ~ sentence *if he speaks you must listen*⟩ **3** *math* **:** stating the conditions ⟨~ equations⟩ **4** *of a reflex* **:** CONDITIONED

²conditional \"\ *n* -s **1 a :** a conditional word, clause, or verb form; *specif* **:** a verb form in the conditional mood **b :** the conditional mood **2 :** IMPLICATION 2b

conditional baptism *n* **:** Christian baptism administered when there is doubt whether a person was ever baptized or whether a former baptism is valid

conditional complex *n* **:** a conditional sentence

conditional fee *n, law* **:** any fee limited upon a condition; *specif* **:** FEE SIMPLE CONDITIONAL

con·di·tion·al·ism \-,lizəm\ *n* -s **:** the doctrine that divine grace and immortality are conditional — **con·di·tion·al·ist** \-,ləst\ *n* -s

con·di·tion·al·i·ty \kən,dishə'naləd·ē, -ətē, -i\ *n* -ES **:** the quality or state of being conditional

con·di·tion·al·ly \kən'dishənᵊlē, -shnəlē, -li\ *adv* [ME *condicionely*, fr. *condicionel* conditional + *-ly*] **:** in a conditional manner **:** subject to a condition **:** not absolutely ⟨~ canceled nine tenths of the obligations still surviving —S.F.Bemis⟩

conditional receipt *n* **:** BINDING RECEIPT

conditional sale *n* **:** a sale in which the vesting of title in the purchaser notwithstanding delivery to him is made to depend upon the due performance of conditions (as payment in full) made a part of the terms of sale — compare HIRE PURCHASE

conditionate *vt* -ED/-ING/-S [ML *conditionatus*, past part. of *conditionare*, fr. L *condition-, conditio* condition — more at CONDITION] *obs* **:** CONDITION **:** make conditional

conditioned *adj* [ME *condicioned*, fr. *condicioun* condition + *-ed*] **1 :** subjected to a condition ⟨a ~ student⟩: as **a** *of changes or variations of speech sounds* **:** occurring in a particular environment and predictable in terms of other sounds in the environment ⟨the ~ sound change of Proto-Germanic *k* to English *ch* before *e* or *i*⟩ **b :** brought into a fit condition ⟨a well-*conditioned* steer⟩ **c** *of cut flowers* **:** stored at just above freezing temperature in moistureproof but gas-permeable containers to enhance marketability and keeping qualities **2 :** determined or established by a condition or by conditioning ⟨a ~ reflex⟩

con·di·tion·er \kən'dish(ə)nə(r)\ *n* -s **:** one that conditions: as **a :** a worker who conditions a product (as yarns) **b :** a substance added to a material or a product to improve its physical state ⟨soil ~⟩ ⟨dough ~⟩ **c :** a trainer (as of athletes or show animals) **d :** an apparatus for air-conditioning

conditioning *pres part of* CONDITION

condition powder *n* **:** a veterinary nostrum supposed to improve the general health and well-being of an animal

condition precedent *n* **:** a condition whose fulfillment must precede the vesting of an estate, the taking effect of a contract, or the accruing of a right

conditions *pl of* CONDITION, *pres 3d sing of* CONDITION

condition subsequent *n* **:** a condition whose fulfillment invalidates or modifies an estate, right, or contract previously vested or in effect (as when a horse is bought on condition that he prove sound)

con·di·tio sine qua non \kən'dishē,ō, -did·ē,ō +\ *n* [L] **:** an indispensable condition

con·division \ˌkän +\ *n* -s [*com-* + *division*] *logic* **:** reciprocal or coordinate division or one of its resulting divisions

con·do·la·to·ry \kən'dōlə,tōrē\ *adj* [*condole* + *-atory* (as in *consolatory*)] **:** expressing or conveying condolence

con·dole \kən'dōl\ *vb* -ED/-ING/-S [LL *condolere*, fr. L *com-* + *dolēre* to feel pain, grieve; akin to L *dolare* to hew, Gk *daidalos* ingeniously formed, Skt *dālayati* he splits, causes to burst; basic meaning: to split, carve] *vi* **1** *obs* **:** to sorrow much **:** GRIEVE **2 :** to express sympathetic sorrow **:** grieve in sympathy — usu. used with *with* ⟨~ with her distress of mind —W.S. Gilbert⟩ ⟨we ~ with you in your misfortune⟩ ~ *vt, archaic* **:** to lament or grieve over **:** express one's sympathetic sorrow at (another's misfortune) ⟨came . . . to ~ the death of the late king —John Evelyn⟩; *often* **:** to express formal regrets over

con·do·lence \kən'dōlən(t)s, 'kändəl-\ *n* -s [MF, fr. *condoloir* to condole (fr. L *condolēre*) + *-ence*] **1** *obs* **:** sympathetic sorrow **2 a :** expression of sympathy with another in sorrow or grief ⟨a letter of ~⟩ **b condolences** *pl* **:** a formal avowal of such sympathy ⟨the bereaved parents received more than a hundred ~*s*⟩ **syn** see SYMPATHY

con·do·lent \-lənt\ *adj* [LL *condolent-, condolens*, pres. part. of *condolēre*] **:** feeling or expressing condolence

con·dol·ing \kən'dōliŋ, -lēŋ\ *adj* **:** CONDOLENT — **con·dol·ing·ly** *adv*

con·dom \'kändəm *also* 'kän-; ÷ 'kəndrəm\ *n* -s [after Dr. *Condom* or Conton, 18th cent. Eng. physician, its reputed inventor] **:** a very thin sheath commonly of rubber placed over the penis (as to prevent conception or venereal infection during coitus)

con·dom·i·nate \(')kän¦dämənət, kən'd-\ *adj* [NL *condominium* + E *-ate*] **:** enjoying or relating to joint rule

con·do·min·i·um \ˌkändə'minēəm\ *n* -s [NL, fr. L *com-* + *dominium*] **:** joint dominion or sovereignty: **a** *Roman law* **:** common ownership by two or more persons holding undivided fractional shares in the same property and having the right to alienate their shares resembling tenancy in common in Anglo-American law rather than joint tenancy with its rights of survivorship **b :** joint sovereignty or rule by two or more states over a colony or politically dependent territory ⟨the former Anglo-Egyptian ~ over Sudan⟩; *also* **:** the territory so ruled **c** (1) **:** individual ownership of a unit in a multi-unit structure (as an apartment building) (2) **:** a unit so owned (3) **:** a building containing condominiums

con·don·able \kən'dōnəbəl\ *adj* [*condone* + *-able*] **:** EXCUSABLE, FORGIVABLE

con·don·ance \-ōnən(t)s\ *n* -s [*condone* + *-ance*] **:** CONDONATION

con·do·na·tion \ˌkändō'nāshən, -də'-\ *n* -s [NL *condonation-, condonatio*, fr. L, giving away, fr. *condonatus* (past part. of *condonare*) + *-ion-, -io* -ion] **1 :** pardon of an offense **:** voluntary overlooking or implied forgiveness of an offense by treating the offender as if it had not been committed **2** *law* **:** expressed or implied forgiveness by a husband or a wife of a breach of marital duty (as adultery) by the other with an implied condition that the offense shall not be repeated

con·done \kən'dōn\ *vt* -ED/-ING/-S [L *condonare* to give, remit, forgive, fr. *com-* + *donare* to donate — more at DONATE] **:** to pardon or forgive (an offense or fault) **:** permit the continuance of (as vice, gambling) **:** cause or justify the condonation of **syn** see EXCUSE

con·done·ment \-nmənt\ *n* -s **:** cancellation in certain card games of a penalty normally due for a misplay or other irregularity if the next opponent makes a play before the irregularity is noticed or sometimes at the option of opposing players

con·dor \'kändə(r), -,dō(ə)r, -,dō(ə); *in sense 2* " *or* 'kōn-,dō(ə)r, -,dōə\ *n* -s [Sp *cóndor*, fr. Quechua *kúntur*] **1 :** a very large American vulture (*Vultur gryphus*) found in elevated parts of the Andes, having the head and neck bare and the plumage dull black with a downy white neck ruff and white patches on the wings, and being one of the largest and most powerful of flying birds though feeding preferably on carrion — see CALIFORNIA CONDOR **2** *pl* **condors** \-rz\ *or* **condo·res** \kən'dōr,ās, kōn'-\ **:** a coin bearing the picture of a condor: **a :** a gold coin formerly issued in Ecuador worth 25 sucres; *also* **:** a corresponding unit of value ⟨a 2-*condor* gold coin was issued⟩ **b :** a Chilean coin, orig. of gold, of silver in 1948 and later of copper and nickel, worth 10 pesos; *also* **:** a corresponding unit of value **c :** a 19th century Colombian gold coin worth 10 pesos; *also* **:** a unit of value equivalent to 10 pesos **3 :** TIFFIN 2

condor 1

con·dot·tiere \ˌkändə'tye(,)rā, -kän-,kōn-, -dō't-, kōndōtē'e(,)rā\ *also* **con·dot·tiero** \-(,)rō\ *n, pl* **condottieri** \-(,)rē\ [It *condottiere*, fr. *condotta* act of hiring, troop of mercenaries (fr. fem. of *condotto* — past part. of *condurre* to conduct, hire—, fr. L *conductus*, past part. of *conducere*) + *-iere* -er] **1 :** a leader of a band of mercenary professional soldiers common in Europe from the 14th to the 16th centuries **2 :** a member of the band of a condottiere; *broadly* **:** a professional mercenary soldier **:** FREE LANCE

condr *abbr* conductor

condrodite *var of* CHONDRODITE

con·duce \kən'd(y)üs\ *vb* -ED/-ING/-S [ME *conducen*, fr. L *conducere* to bring together, conduce, hire, fr. *com-* + *ducere* to lead — more at TOW] *vt* **1** *obs* **:** CONDUCT, GUIDE, BRING **2** *obs* **:** to bring about **:** EFFECT ~ *vi* **:** to lead or tend esp. with reference to a desirable result **:** CONTRIBUTE — used with *to* or *toward* ⟨the qualities that ~ to worldly success⟩

con·duce·ment \-smənt\ *n* -s **:** the act of conducing

conducible *adj* [L *conducibilis*, fr. *conducere* + *-ibilis* -ible] *obs* **:** CONDUCIVE, BENEFICIAL

con·du·cive \-siv, -ēv *also* -əv\ *adj* **:** of conducing nature or quality **:** tending to promote ⟨a dry season is ~ to forest fires⟩

con·du·cive·ness *n* -ES **:** the quality or state of being conducive

¹con·duct \'kän(,)dəkt\ *n* -s [alter. (influenced by L *conductus*) of earlier *conduit, condit*, fr. ME, fr. OF *conduit, conduite* action of leading, commanding, guiding, escorting, fr. ML *conductus* (masc.), *conducta* (fem.), past part. of *conducere* to escort, safeguard on the road, fr. L, to bring together — more at CONDUCE] **1 a** *obs* **:** a company of attendants or guards to guide and protect (as a traveler or caravan) on a journey **b** *obs* **:** a document granting permission to pass in safety **:** a formal permission to pass over, through, or to a particular place **:** SAFE-CONDUCT **c** *archaic* **:** GUIDE, LEADER **2 a :** the act, manner, or process of carrying out (as a task) or carrying forward (as a business, government, or war) **:** MANAGEMENT, DIRECTION ⟨the ~ of the examination should take less than an hour⟩ ⟨the ~ of foreign affairs⟩ **b :** a manner of arrangement or treatment (as of parts in a painting) **:** RENDITION ⟨~ of details⟩ **3 a** *obs* **:** leadership (as of an army) **b** *obs* **:** capability in leadership or management **:** aptitude in command **:** ADDRESS **c :** a mode or standard of personal behavior esp. as based on moral principles — sometimes distinguished from *behavior*

⟨animals . . . do not rise from behavior to ~ —J.S.Clarke⟩ **d** : behavior in a particular situation or relation or on a specified occasion ⟨~ unbecoming to a gentleman⟩ ⟨his disgusting ~ at the party⟩ **4** : the act or process of leading or guiding : GUIDANCE ⟨moving at random under the ~ of chance⟩ ⟨known for his editorial ~ of the local newspaper⟩

²**con·duct** \kən'dəkt\ *vb* -ED/-ING/-S [alter. (influenced by L *conductus*) of earlier *conduit, condit,* fr. ME *conduiten, conditen,* fr. *conduit, condit,* n. — more at CONDUCT] *vt* **1** : to bring by or as if by leading : LEAD, GUIDE, ESCORT ⟨I made a bridge to a rock whence I can reach the other side, so I shall ~ the lambs that way —Rachel Henning⟩ ⟨I never should have ~*ed* this chronicle to the stage it has now reached —F.M.Ford⟩ **2 a** : to lead as a commander ⟨~ a siege⟩ **b** : to have the direction of : RUN, MANAGE, DIRECT ⟨~ a scientific experiment⟩ ⟨~ a daily newspaper column⟩ ⟨~ a small business enterprise⟩ **c** : TREAT, HANDLE, EXECUTE ⟨~ a detail in a painting⟩ ⟨~ an episode in a poem⟩ **d** : to direct as leader the performance or execution of (as a musical work or a group of musicians) **3 a** : to convey in or as if in a channel ⟨phrases which once started on ~ us . . . along a well-worn channel to an inevitable end —J.L.Lowes⟩ **b** : to act as a medium for conveying (as heat or electricity) : TRANSMIT **4** : to behave or comport (oneself) : ACQUIT ~ *vi* **1** *of a road or passage* : to show the way : LEAD **2 a** : to act as leader or director ⟨one could always count on a superb performance from the orchestra when Charles ~*ed*⟩ **b** : to transmit or have the quality of transmitting light, heat, sound, or electricity

syn MANAGE, CONTROL, DIRECT: CONDUCT may imply a leader's supervision, his responsible guidance in a course which he determines ⟨the men who actually *conduct* and order the industry of the country —G.B.Shaw⟩ ⟨Douglas *conducted* conferences and studies which led to a reorganization of the Stock Exchange —*Current Biog.*⟩ ⟨missionaries of the Holy Family *conduct* a training school and home for students and missionaries —*Amer. Guide Series: Texas*⟩ MANAGE may imply handling or maneuvering, or guiding along a desired course or to a desired result; it often indicates a general overseeing, with authority to handle details, cope with problems, and make routine decisions ⟨my young wife who could *manage* a horse better than most men could —Rex Ingamells⟩ ⟨our purpose is to *manage* the government's finances so as to help and not hinder each family in balancing its own budget —D.D.Eisenhower⟩ ⟨now do you leave this affair in my hands. Only tell me which woman it is and I will *manage* the affair —Pearl Buck⟩ ⟨the delight she would take in *managing* a real house, not in any sense as its drudge, but magnificently as its mistress —Floyd Dell⟩ ⟨*manage* a silk mill⟩ ⟨*manage* a baseball team⟩ CONTROL stresses notions of authoritative guiding and, when necessary, checking deviation, excess, or error; it may imply complete subordination or subjection to authoritative or autocratic power ⟨"Come, come, Byron", said the master, *controlling* him with a broad, strong hand; "none of your nonsense, sir." —G.B.Shaw⟩ ⟨it was apparently regarded as impossible to root out bad desires; all we could do was to *control* them —Bertrand Russell⟩ ⟨pirates at one time practically *controlled* the coasts of Florida —*Amer. Guide Series: Fla.*⟩ DIRECT may imply constant guiding, regulating, and administering of activities in the interests of smooth operation ⟨*directing* a research program⟩ ⟨*directing* a manufacturing company⟩ ⟨*directing* Red Cross activities⟩ ⟨a physicist is not interfering with Nature, any more than an architect is interfering with Nature when he *directs* the building of a house —K.K.Darrow⟩ **syn** see in addition BEHAVE

con·duc·ta \kən'dúktə\ *n* -S [Sp, fr. ML *conducta,* fem. of *conductus,* past part. of *conducere* to escort, safeguard on the road — more at CONDUCT] *Southwest* : a guarded pack train or caravan; *esp* : one carrying bullion prior to the establishment of modern transport

con·duct·ance \kən'dəktən(t)s\ *n* -S **1** : the act of conducting : TRANSMISSION, CONVEYANCE **2 a** : capacity or fitness for conducting ⟨neural ~⟩ **b** : conducting power : measure of the readiness with which a given conductor allows an electric current to flow through it : the reciprocal of resistance measured by a unit *mho* that is the reciprocal of the ohm

conducting transportation *n* : an accounting heading designed to cover those items of expense that arise in the daily service of trains and terminals as distinct from repairs or capital charges

con·duc·tio \kən'dəkshē(,)ō\ *n, pl* **conduc·ti·o·nes** \kən-dəkshē'ō(,)nēz\ [L] : HIRING — compare LOCATIO CONDUCTIO

con·duc·tion \kən'dəkshən\ *n* -S [MF, conducting, hiring, fr. L *conduction-, conductio* bringing together, hiring, fr. *conductus* (past part. of *conducere* to bring together, hire) + *-ion-, -io* -ion — more at CONDUCE] **1** *archaic* : CONDUCT, MANAGEMENT, SKILL **2** : the act of conveying (as water through a pipe) **3** : the transfer of soluble foods, water, and other substances from one part of a plant to another — called also *translocation* **4** : HIRING **5 a** : transfer of heat through matter by communication of kinetic energy from particle to particle rather than by a flow of heated material — compare CONVECTION **b** : the maintenance of an electric current through metals by a general movement of conduction electrons, through electrolytes by a movement of both positive and negative ions, or through gases by the passage of cathode rays, ionized molecules, or anode rays **6** : the transmission of excitation through living tissue esp. in a nerve ⟨~ of impulses to the brain⟩

conduction anesthesia *n* : BLOCK ANESTHESIA

conduction current *n* : a movement of electricity in an electric conductor — compare DISPLACEMENT CURRENT

conductitious *adj* [L *conducticius, conductitius* hired, fr. *conductus* (past part. of *conducere* to hire) + *-icius, -itius* -itious] *obs* : HIRED; *also* : open to or kept for hire

con·duc·tive \kən'dəktiv, -tēv *also* -təv\ *adj* : having the quality or power of conducting : possessing conductivity : relating to or concerned with conduction (as of electricity) — **con·duc·tive·ly** \-tə̇vlē, -li\ *adv*

con·duc·tiv·i·ty \,kän,dək'tivəd·ē, -ətē, -i\ *n* -ES : the quality or power of conducting or transmitting (as heat or electricity): as **a** *physics* : the reciprocal of resistivity — compare THERMAL CONDUCTIVITY **b** : the quality of living matter responsible for the transmission of and progressive reaction to stimuli within the living system — compare IRRITABILITY

con·duct·ment \kən'dəktmənt\ *n* -S *archaic* : COMMAND, LEADERSHIP

conduct money *n* : money paid or to pay for conveyance or for traveling expenses (as of a witness or a man newly enlisted); *esp* : a tax levied by Charles I to defray expenses of transporting men to the point of mobilization of the king's army — compare COAT MONEY

con·duc·tom·e·ter \,kändək'tämәd·ə(r), -ətə(r)\ *or* **con·duc·tim·e·ter** \-'tim-\ *n* -S [²*conduct* + *-o-* or *-i-* + *-meter*] : any instrument for measuring conductivity; *specif* : one for comparing the rates at which rods of different materials transmit heat

con·duc·to·met·ric *or* **con·duc·ti·met·ric** \kən¦dəktə¦me-trik\ *adj* : of, relating to, or involving the measurement of conductivity : relating to or by means of conductometry ⟨~ titration⟩

con·duc·tom·e·try \,kändək'tämə·trē, -ri\ *n* -ES [²*conduct* + *-o-* + *-metry*] : determination of the quantity of a material (as an element or salt) present in a mixture by measurement of its effect on the electrical conductivity of the mixture

con·duc·tor \kən'dəktə(r)\ *n* -S [alter. (influenced by L *conductor* lessee) of earlier *conduitour, conditour* commander, guide, fr. ME, commander, fr. MF *conduiteur* one that conducts, fr. ML *conductor* escorter, manorial manager, commander, fr. L, lessee, fr. *conductus* (past part. of *conducere* to bring together, hire) + *-or* — more at CONDUCE] **1** : one that conducts (as a person that leads or escorts) : GUIDE, ESCORT **2 a** *obs* : a commander or leader (as of an army or a ship) **b** : one in charge of a public conveyance (as a streetcar) **c** : a railroad employee who supervises the train crew and collects fares from passengers **3 a** : DOWNSPOUT **b** : LIGHTNING ROD **4** [L, lessee] : HIRER; *esp* : BAILEE, LESSEE **5** : a substance or body capable of transmitting electricity, heat, or sound **6** : a person that conducts an orchestra, chorus, or other group of musical performers **7** : a bodily part that transmits excitation (as a nerve fiber)

conductor head *n* : LEADER HEAD

con·duc·to·ri·al \¦kändək¦tōrēəl, -¦tȯr-\ *adj* : of or relating to a conductor esp. of an orchestra — **con·duc·to·ri·al·ly** \-əlē\ *adv*

con·duc·tor·less \kən'dəktə(r)lə̇s\ *adj* : having no conductor

con·duc·tress \kən'dəktrə̇s\ *n* -ES [*conductor* + *-ess*] : a female conductor; *esp, Brit* : a female bus or tram conductor

conducts *pl of* CONDUCT, *pres 3d sing of* CONDUCT

con·duc·tus \kən'dəktəs\ *n, pl* **conductus** \"\ [ML, fr. L *conductus,* past part. of *conducere* to bring together — more at CONDUCE] : a medieval vocal composition consisting of one to four voice parts the lowest of which is composed of a Latin text set to an invented melody and accompanied homophonically by the other voices

con·duit \'kän(,)düə̇t, -,dwit, -,dəwə̇t, -də̇t, *usu* -d· +V\ *n* -S [ME *condut, condit, conduit,* fr. MF *conduit,* lit., action of leading, commanding — more at CONDUCT] **1** : a natural or artificial channel through which water or other fluid passes or is conveyed : AQUEDUCT, PIPE ⟨the ~ of a volcano⟩ ⟨all the ~s of my blood froze up —Shak.⟩ **2** *archaic* : FOUNTAIN ⟨the ~s round the garden sing —D.G.Rossetti⟩ **3 a** *obs* : a passage within or between parts of a building **b** : a narrow often underground passage for private communication **4** : pipe, tube, or tile for receiving and protecting electric wires or cables (as for telephones or power lines) **5** : a means of conveying or distributing money ⟨the doctrine that corporations are a ~ for profits —J.T.Norman⟩

conduit box *n* : an electric outlet box to which a rigid or flexible conduit runs — compare JUNCTION BOX, SERVICE BOX

conduit system *n* : a system for supplying electric power to a car or locomotive by means of one or more underground contact rails

Con·du·let \'kändə,let, -dələ̇t\ *trademark* — used for a fitting resembling a pipe or box with a removable cover for access to electric conduits

con·duplicate \(')kän, kən +\ *adj* [L *conduplicatus,* past part. of *conduplicare* to double, fr. *com-* + *duplicare* to double — more at DUPLICATE] : folded lengthwise along the midrib so that the halves are applied together by their upper faces — used of leaves or petals in the bud — **con·duplication** \¦kän, kən + \ *n* -S

con·du·ran·gin \,kändə'raŋ(g)ə̇n, -'ranjə̇n\ *n* -S [ISV *condurango* + *-in*] : a bitter poisonous yellowish glucoside obtained from condurango

con·du·ran·go \-aŋ(,)gō\ *n* -S [AmerSp *condurango, cundurango,* fr. Quechua *kunturánku,* lit., condor vine] : the dried bark of a So. American vine (*Marsdenia cundurango*) used as an alterative and stomachic — see CONDURANGIN

condyl- *or* **condylo-** *comb form* [NL, fr. Gk *kondyl-, kondylo-,* fr. *kondylos* — more at CONDYLE] : joint : knob : condyle ⟨*condyl*oid⟩ ⟨*Condylo*poda⟩

con·dy·lar \'kändələ(r)\ *adj* [*condyl-* + *-ar*] : of, relating to, or associated with a condyle

con·dy·larth \'kändə,lärth\ *n* -S [NL *Condylarthra*] : an individual or fossil of the order Condylarthra

con·dy·lar·thra \,kändə'lärthrə\ *n pl, cap* [NL, fr. *condyl-* + *-arthra* (neut. pl. of *-arthrus* jointed, fr. Gk *-arthros,* fr. *arthron* joint) — more at ARTHR-] : an order or suborder of extinct Eocene ungulate mammals having many primitive characters some of which connect them with the Creodonta and being more or less plantigrade with five-toed limbs and a third trochanter — **con·dy·lar·throus** \¦==¦=thrəs\ *adj*

con·dy·lar·thro·sis \,kändə(,)lär'thrōsə̇s\ *n, pl* **condylarthro·ses** \-,sēz\ [NL, fr. *condyl-* + *arthrosis*] *anat* : articulation by means of a condyle (as that between the head and vertebral column involving the occipital condyles and the atlas)

con·dyle \'kän,dīl, -dᵊl\ *n* -S [F & L; F, fr. L *condylus* knuckle, joint, fr. Gk *kondylos* knuckle, joint, fist; akin to Lith *kánduolas* core, and perh. to Skt *kanda* bulbous root] **1** : an articular prominence on a bone — used chiefly of such as occur in pairs likened to a pair of knuckles (as those of the occipital bone for articulation with the atlas, those at the distal end of the humerus and femur, and those of the lower jaw) **2** : a rounded process of the hard integument in the articulations of the limbs of arthropods; *also* : a similar process on the mandible of some insects

con·dyl·i·on \kən'dilēən, kän'-, -lē,än\ *n* -S [NL, fr. Gk *kondylion,* dim. of *kondylos* knuckle] **1** : the lateral tip of the condyle of the lower jaw — see CRANIOMETRY illustration **2** : the posteriormost point of the articular surface of either occipital condyle of a mammal

con·dy·loid \'kändə,lȯid\ *adj* [*condyl-* + *-oid*] : shaped like or situated near a condyle : relating to a condyle

condyloid foramen *n* : a foramen in front of each condyle of the occipital bone

condyloid joint *n* : an articulation in which an ovoid head is received into an elliptical cavity permitting all movements except axial rotation

condyloid process *n* : the rounded process by which the ramus of the mandible articulates with the temporal bone

con·dy·lo·ma \,kändə'lōmə\ *n, pl* **condylomas** \-ōməz\ *or* **condyloma·ta** \-ōməd·ə\ [NL, fr. Gk *kondylōma,* fr. *kondylos* knuckle, knob — more at CONDYLE] : a new growth like a wart on the outer skin or adjoining mucous membrane usu. near the anus and genital organs —**con·dy·lom·a·tous** \¦==¦lämәd·əs, -¦lōm-\ *adj*

con·dy·lo·sto·ma \,kändələ'stōmə\ *n, cap* [NL, fr. *condyl-* + *-stoma*] : a genus of large heterotrichous ciliated protozoans having the form of a somewhat flattened ellipsoid with a truncated anterior end and being common and free-living in fresh and salt water

con·dy·lu·ra \,kändə'lu̇rə\ *n, cap* [NL, fr. *condyl-* + *-ura*] : a genus of moles having 44 small teeth and a muzzle like a snout that terminates in a fringe of cartilaginous or fleshy processes and comprising the star-nosed moles

con·dy's fluid \'kändēz-, -diz-\ *also* **condy** *n, often cap C* [after Henry Bollman *Condy,* 19th cent. Eng. manufacturing chemist] *chiefly Brit* : a common household disinfectant consisting essentially of an aqueous solution of a permanganate

¹**cone** \'kōn\ *n* -S [MF or L; MF *cone,* fr. L *conus,* fr. Gk *kōnos* — more at HONE] **1 a** : a mass of ovule-bearing or pollen-bearing scales or bracts in trees of the pine family and in cycads arranged usu. on a somewhat elongated axis : a carpellate or staminate strobilus; *esp* : the carpellate strobilus of pine and related trees — see CONIFERALES **b** : any of several flower or fruit clusters suggesting a cone (as of the hop or certain magnolias) **2 a** : a solid generated by the rotation of a right triangle about one of its legs as axis, the length of this leg being the altitude of the cone and the length of the hypotenuse of the right triangle its slant height — called also *right circular cone* **b** : a solid bounded by a circular or other closed plane base and the surface formed by line segments joining every point of the boundary of the base to a common vertex **c** : a conical surface : any surface traced by a moving straight line passing through a fixed vertex **3** : an object, part, or structure felt to resemble a geometric cone: as **a** : a natural formation built up around the crater of a volcano or the outlet of a geyser ⟨basalt ~⟩ ⟨spatter ~⟩ **b** : a steep alluvial or detrital fan ⟨talus ~⟩ ⟨gravity ~⟩ **c** : one of the short sensory end organs of the vertebrate retina that are the sole receptors present in the fovea and are scattered among the rods over most of the rest of the retina and that function chiefly or wholly in the light-adapted eye and are usu. regarded as the only visual receptors concerned in color vision **d** : any of numerous somewhat conical tropical gastropod mollusks constituting the family Conidae — see CONUS **e** : any of certain conical or conoidal parts: as (1) : CONE PULLEY (2) : an inner race for ball bearings (3) : the portion of the bore of a shotgun that lies immediately forward of the chamber (4) : a bobbin upon which yarn is wound preparatory to weaving or knitting it into a fabric; *also* : the entire package of yarn and bobbin **f** : PYROMETRIC CONE; *often* : the temperature or refractory range indicated by a particular combination of pyrometric cones **g** : an unblocked hat **h** : a cusp of a tooth esp. of the upper jaw **i** : ICE-CREAM CONE **j** : CONE SPEAKER **k** : the cone-shaped part of a gas flame that is immediately adjacent to the source of gas **l** : a cone-shaped area of illumination (as from a searchlight)

cone of red spruce

²**cone** \"\ *vb* -ED/-ING/-S *vt* **1** : to render cone-shaped : bevel like the slanting surface of a cone ⟨~ the tires of car wheels⟩ **2** : to wind on a cone ⟨~ a textile yarn⟩ ~ *vi* **1** : to form or bear cones (as of a pine tree) **2** : to form a cone (as of a whirling liquid)

cone adaptation *n* : the relatively rapid adaptation of the central portion of the retina of the eye occurring in high light intensities — compare PHOTOPIA

cone anchor *n* : a sea anchor shaped like a cone

cone-bearing \'=¦==\ *adj* : bearing cones : belonging to the Pinaceae or Cycadaceae

cone bearing *n, mech engin* : a journal bearing containing a taper sleeve capable of endwise movement for taking up wear

cone beetle *n* : any of numerous small beetles constituting the genus *Conophthorus* and having larvae that develop in and destroy the growing cones of conifers, esp. pines

cone bit *n* : a conical bit for boring

cone brake *n* : a friction brake in which the frictional surfaces are cone-shaped

cone clutch *n* : a friction clutch in which the frictional surfaces are cone-shaped

cone crusher *or* **cone mill** *n* : a mill for crushing ore into sizes suitable for grinding

cone-cut \'=¦=\ *adj* : cut from the tapered end of a log much as a pencil is sharpened ⟨certain veneers are *cone-cut*⟩

coned \'kōnd\ *adj* [¹*cone* + *-ed*] **1** : shaped like a cone or segment of a cone; *also* : having a cone **2** *of an airplane* : caught by converging searchlight beams and so a target for gunfire

coneflower \'=,==\ *n* : any of several composite plants having cone-shaped flower disks: as **a** : a plant of the genus *Rudbeckia* (esp. *R. hirta*) **b** : a plant of the genus *Ratibida* **c** : a plant of the genus *Echinacea*

cone gamba *n* : a labial organ stop with conical pipes ending in a bell

conehead \'=,=\ *n* : a plant of the genus *Strobilanthes* of the family Acanthaceae

conehead rivet *n* : a rivet having a head in the form of a truncated cylindrical cone

cone-in-cone \¦==¦=\ *n* : a small-scale geologic structure resembling a set of concentric cones piled one above another developed in sedimentary rocks under pressure with or without solution of adjacent materials

cone joint *n* : a joint made by inserting a double cone of iron into the ends of pipes and tightening by screw bolts

cone key *n* : any of usu. three taper saddle keys fitting all round a shaft to key on it a piece (as a pulley) the hole in which is too large for the shaft

cone·let \'kōnlə̇t\ *n* -S [¹*cone* + *-let*] : a little cone

con·el·rad \'känᵊl,rad, -,raa(ə)d\ *n* -S [*con*trol of *el*ectromagnetic *rad*iation] : a system for preventing an enemy from using radio signals from any particular AM station as a guide for aircraft or missiles by shifting all AM stations to either of the frequencies 640 or 1240 and having them broadcast in a group in random order for short intervals on only these frequencies

cone mandrel *n* **1** : an expanding mandrel whose diameter is varied by the shifting of conical sleeves **2** : a blacksmith's conical swage block

cone·nose \'=,=\ *also* **cone-nose bug** *or* **cone-nosed bug** \'=,=-\ *n* : any of certain large bloodsucking bugs of *Triatoma* or closely related genera of the family Reduviidae including insects capable of inflicting extremely painful bites and at least one So. American form (*Panstrongylus megistus* or *Triatoma megista*) that is a vector of Chagas' disease — called also *assassin bug, big bedbug, kissing bug*

cone number *n* : a number indicating the fusing point of a particular Seger cone

cone of origin : a clear area of cytoplasm where the axon of a neuron leaves the cell body

cone of silence : a cone-shaped region directly above a radio signal beacon in which signals from the beacon are not received by aircraft

co·ne·pa·te \,kōnə'päd·ā\ *also* **co·ne·patl** \-ăd·ᵊl\ *n* -S [MexSp, fr. Nahuatl *conepatl,* fr. *conetl* small + *epatl* fox] : HOG-NOSED SKUNK

co·ne·pa·tus \,kōnə'päd·əs\ *n, cap* [NL, fr. MexSp *conepate*] : a genus of mammals (family Mustelidae) comprising the hog-nosed skunks

cone pepper *n* **1** : a hot pepper (*Capsicum frutescens conoides*) with erect pungent conical fruits that is sometimes considered to be a variety of the cherry pepper **2** : the fruit of a cone pepper

cone-plant \'=,=\ *n* : any of certain small succulent plants constituting a genus (*Conophytum*) of the family Aizoaceae and consisting of inverted cone-shaped bodies each made up of two joined leaves with a small opening through which a stemless flower emerges

cone pulley *n* : a pulley in the form of a truncated cone : a series of pulleys forming a stepped cone or conoid that are used in pairs (as for varying the velocity ratios of shafts)

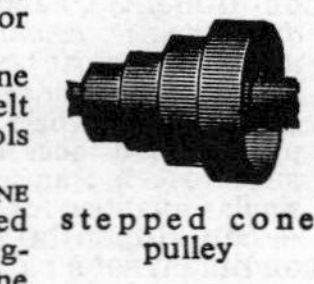

stepped cone pulley

con·er \'kōnə(r)\ *n* -S **1** : a machine operator who mats fur fibers for hat felt **2** : one that winds yarn on cones or spools (as a workman or a machine)

cones *pl of* CONE, *pres 3d sing of* CONE

cone sheet *n* : a tabular body of intruded igneous rock having the form of a segment of a downward-pointing cone : one of a group of centrally inclined sheets of igneous rock

cone shell *n* : CONE 3d; *also* : its shell

cone speaker *n* : a loudspeaker in which the vibrating diaphragm is large and conical and usu. made of paper, no horn being used

con es·pres·si·o·ne \,kōn,ə̇,sprese'ō(,)nā, ,kōn-\ *adv (or adj)* [It, lit., with expression] : with feeling — used as a direction in music

co·nes·si bark \kə'nesē-\ *n* [origin unknown] : TELLICHERRY BARK

co·nes·sine \kə'ne(,)sēn, -nesə̇n\ *n* -S [ISV *conessi (bark)* + *-ine*] : a very bitter poisonous crystalline alkaloid $C_{24}H_{40}N_2$ obtained from certain tropical trees of the family Apocynaceae (esp. *Holarrhena antidysenterica* and *Wrightia zeylandica*)

¹**con·es·to·ga** \,känə'stōgə, '==,==\ *n, pl* **conestoga** *usu cap* [Conestoga *Kanastóge,* lit., at the place of the immersed pole] **1** : SUSQUEHANNA **2** : the language of the Susquehanna people

²**conestoga** \"\ *also* **conestoga wagon** *n, usu cap C* [fr. *Conestoga,* Pa., where it originated] : a broad-wheeled covered wagon having a body curving upward toward the ends and suggesting the shape of a boat, usu. drawn by six horses, and used esp. for transporting freight

Conestoga wagon

³**conestoga** \"\ *n* -S [fr. *Conestoga,* Pa.] : BROGAN — compare STOGIE

cone tree *n* : a coniferous tree

cone valve *n* : a valve with a conical seat

cone wheat *n* [so called fr. its cone-shaped spikes] : POULARD WHEAT

co·ney *or* **co·ny** \'kōnē, -ni\ *n, pl* **coneys** *or* **conies** [ME *cony, conig, coning,* back-formation fr. *conies,* pl., fr. OF *connis, conis,* pl. of *connil, conil,* fr. L *cuniculus* rabbit, underground passage, prob. of Iberian origin; akin to Basque *untxi* rabbit, prob. fr. (assumed) *kuntxi* (whence perh. Ar dial. — Spain — *conchair* hound, dog)] **1 a** (1) : RABBIT;

esp : the European rabbit (*Oryctolagus cuniculus*) (2) : LITTLE CHIEF HARE **b** : HYRAX **2** : rabbit skin or fur; *also* : a coat made of rabbit fur clipped and usu. dyed to resemble other furs **3** *obs* : DUPE, GULL, SIMPLETON **4** *heraldry* : a rabbit borne as a charge **5** : any of several fishes: as **a** : a dusky black-spotted reddish-finned grouper (*Cephalopholis fulvus*) of the tropical Atlantic **b** : GRAYSBY **c** : INCONNU 2

coney island *n, usu cap C&I* [fr. *Coney Island*, a resort in Brooklyn, N.Y.] : a place felt to resemble the resort Coney Island esp. in blatantly entertaining quality or garish attraction

conf *abbr* **1** confederation **2** [L *confer*] compare **3** conference **4** confessor **5** confidential

[1]**con·fab** \'kän,fab, kən'f-\ *n* -s [by shortening] : CONFABULATION ⟨careful ~*s*, handshakings and organization building —*N.Y. Herald Tribune*⟩

[2]**con·fab** \kən'fab, 'kän,f-\ *vi* **confabbed; confabbed; confabbing; confabs** : CONFABULATE ⟨I would see them *confabbing* in the shed —Saul Bellow⟩

con·fab·u·lar \kən'fabyələ(r)\ *adj* [*confabulate* + *-ar*] : CONFABULATORY

con·fab·u·late \-,lāt\ *vi* -ED/-ING/-S [L *confabulatus*, past part. of *confabulari*, to talk, fr. *com-* + *fabulari* to talk, fr. *fabula* narration, account — more at FABLE] **1** : to talk familiarly together : CHAT, PRATTLE **2** : to hold discussion : CONFER, POWWOW — **con·fab·u·la·tor** \-ād·ə(r)\ *n* -s

con·fab·u·la·tion \kən,fabyə'lāshən, ,kän-\ *n* -s [ME *confabulacion*, fr. LL *confabulation-, confabulatio*, fr. L *confabulatus* + *-ion-, -io* -ion] **1 a** : familiar talk : CONVERSATION ⟨drew closer in whispered ~ —Elinor Wylie⟩; *also* : CHAT ⟨the staple of feminine ~*s* —George Santayana⟩ **b** : CONFERENCE, DISCUSSION ⟨plans and intrigues and whispered ~*s* —Max Lerner⟩ **2** : a filling in of gaps in memory by free fabrication (as in Korsakoff's syndrome) — **con·fab·u·la·to·ry** \kən'fabyələ,tōrē\ *adj*

con·far·re·a·tion \kən,farē'āshən, ,kän-\ *n* -s [L *confarreation-, confarreatio*, fr. *confarreatus* (past part. of *confarreare* to unite in marriage by a ceremony prob. including sacrifice of a spelt cake, fr. *com-* + *-farreare* — fr. *farreum* spelt cake, fr. neut. of *farreus* of spelt, fr. *farr-, far* spelt) + *-ion-, -io* -ion — more at BARLEY] : a ceremony of Roman patrician marriage that gave special sanctity to the marriage bond and until after the time of Tiberius conferred upon the husband the right of absolute control of the wife as of a daughter — see DIFFARREATION, MANUS; compare COEMPTIO

[1]**con·fect** \kən'fekt\ *vt* -ED/-ING/-S [L *confectus*, past part. of *conficere* to prepare — more at COMFIT] **1** : to put together (as ingredients in compounding a medicine) ⟨home-*confected* medicaments —S.H.Adams⟩ **2 a** : PREPARE ⟨hard sauce ~*ed* for the pudding —Silas Spitzer⟩ : PICKLE, PRESERVE **b** : to put together (as a novel) from varied and often incongruous material : form of diverse elements : make up : CONSTRUCT, CONCOCT ⟨writers busy ~*ing* best sellers⟩ ⟨the majority of attempts to ~ a poetic drama —T.S.Eliot⟩

[2]**con·fect** \'kän,fekt\ *n* -s [ML *confectum*, fr. L, neut. of *confectus*, past part. of *conficere*] : COMFIT, CONFECTION ⟨a ~ of leafy faces in a tree —Wallace Stevens⟩

con·fec·tio \kən'fekshē,ō, -ktē,ō\ *n, pl* **confecti·o·nes** \-kshē'ō,nēz, -ktē'ō,nās\ : CONFECTION 1b

[1]**con·fec·tion** \kən'fekshən\ *n* -s [ME *confeccioun*, fr. MF *confection*, fr. LL *confection-, confectio*, fr. L, preparation, making, fr. *confectus* + *-ion-, -io* -ion] **1** : MIXTURE : a preparation esp. for human consumption made by mixing diverse ingredients: as **a** : DELICACY; *usu* : a preparation of fruits, nuts, roots, or other morsels with sugar : SWEETMEAT, PRESERVE, CANDY **b** *pharmacy* (1) *obs* : a medicinal preparation made up of diverse drugs or ingredients (2) : a soft mass consisting of a vegetable drug or drugs incorporated with sugar, syrup, or honey — compare ELECTUARY **c** *obs* : a draft compounded with poison : a preparation of poison **2** : a making or preparing by combining ingredients : PREPARATION, MANUFACTURE ⟨the ~ of comedies⟩ **3** : something elaborate, complex, or ornate in makeup or form: as **a** : an artistic or literary work marked by artificiality or lack of sincerity or made up of unsuitable or incongruous elements combined without real unification or feeling of purpose ⟨an amusing ~ with several charming melodies but no real substance⟩ **b** : an elaborate architectural work; *esp* : one combining elements of style or materials that might be expected to give an incongruous effect ⟨a ~ in metal and glass, similar to the original Quai d' Orsay Station in Paris —*Architectural Rev.*⟩ **c** : any of various fancy decorative articles of women's dress or household ornament — often used in advertisements

[2]**confection** \"\ *vt* **confectioned; confectioned; confectioning** \-sh(ə)niŋ\ **confections** *archaic* : to mix or prepare as a confection

[1]**con·fec·tion·ary** \-shə,nerē, -ri\ *n* -ES [ML *confectionarius* apothecary, fr. LL *confection-, confectio* + L *-arius* -ary] **1** *archaic* : CONFECTIONER **2 a** : a place (as a preserve closet) where confections are kept **b** : CONFECTIONERY 3 **3** : CONFECTIONERY 1 **4** : the making of confections

[2]**confectionary** \"\ *adj* [*confection* + *-ary*] **1** : prepared as or being a confection **2** : of or relating to confections or their making or selling

con·fec·tion·er \-sh(ə)nə(r)\ *n* -s **1** *obs* : a compounder esp. of drugs, poisons **2** : one that deals in confections, candies, and often cakes and ice cream **3** : a candymaker or cake decorator

confectioners' sugar *n* : a highly refined finely powdered sugar

con·fec·tion·ery \-shə,nerē, -ri\ *n* -ES [[1]*confection* + *-ery*] **1** : sweet edibles (as candy, cake, pastry, candied fruits, ice cream) : things prepared and sold by a confectioner **2** : the confectioner's art or business **3** : a shop where confectionery is made, sold, or served

con·fed·er·a·cy \kən'fed(ə)rəsē, -si, *rap.* -dərs-\ *n* -ES [ME *confederacie*, fr. AF, fr. LL *confoederation-, confoederatio* agreement, compact — more at CONFEDERATION] **1** : a league or compact between two or more persons, bodies of men, or states for mutual support or common action : ALLIANCE **2** : a combination of persons to do an unlawful act or to do a lawful act by unlawful means — see CONSPIRACY **3** : the body formed by persons, bodies, states, or nations united by a league; *esp* : a union of states ⟨the U.S. was orig. a ~⟩ ⟨the Southern *Confederacy*⟩ — now usu. used to imply a looser union than *federation*

con·fed·er·al \-d(ə)rəl\ *adj* [*confederation* + *-al*] : of or relating to a confederation (as that of the U.S. under the Articles of Confederation)

con·fed·er·al·ist \-ləst\ *n* -s : a member or advocate of a confederation

[1]**con·fed·er·ate** \kən'fed(ə)rət, *rap.* -dərt; *usu* -əd· *or* -rd· +V\ *adj* [ME *confederat*, fr. LL *confoederatus*, past part. of *confoederare* to unite by a league, fr. *com-* + *foederare* to establish by treaty, fr. L *foeder-, foedus* treaty, league — more at FEDERAL] **1 a** : united in a league : allied by treaty : engaged in a confederacy or confederation : CONFEDERATED ⟨~ government⟩ **b** *of a person* (1) : ASSISTING, ABETTING (2) : CONSPIRATORIAL ⟨~ look between father and child —Elizabeth Bowen⟩ **2** *usu cap* : of or relating to the Confederate States of America ⟨the *Confederate* army⟩

[2]**confederate** \"\ *n* -s [ME *confederat*, fr. LL *confoederatus*, fr. *confoederatus*, past part. of *confoederare*] **1 a** : one united with others in a confederacy or confederation : a person or a nation in a confederacy : ALLY **b** : a member of a gang : ACCOMPLICE 1 **2** *usu cap* : an adherent of the Confederate States of America or their cause

[3]**con·fed·er·ate** \kən'fedə,rāt, *usu* -ād·+V\ *vb* -ED/-ING/-S [[1]*confederate*] *vt* : to unite (as nations) in a league, confederacy, or conspiracy : ALLY ⟨the enemy is just the enemy, regardless of how many nations he has been able to ~ —R.M. Weaver⟩ ~ *vi* : to unite in a league : join in a mutual contract or covenant : band together

confederate jasmine *n* [so called fr. its cultivation in the southern U.S.] : either of two vines of the genus *Trachelospermum*: **a** : STAR JASMINE **b** : a similar vine (*T. asiaticum*) having smaller but broader leathery leaves with blunt tips

confederate memorial day *n, cap C&M&D* : any of several days appointed in southern states for the commemoration of servicemen of the Confederacy: **a** : April 26 in Alabama, Florida, Georgia, and Mississippi **b** : May 10 in No. and So. Carolina **c** : June 3 in Kentucky, Louisiana, and Texas **d** : May 30 in Virginia

confederate rose *n, often cap C* [so called fr. its naturalization in the southern U.S.] : a Chinese mallow (*Hibiscus mutabilis*) with showy white or pink flowers that become deep red at night — called also *cotton rose*

confederate violet *n, often cap C* [prob. so called fr. the grayish appearance of the flowers, suggesting the gray uniform of the Confederate army] : a violet (*Viola papilionacea priceana*) having white flowers heavily veined with bluish violet

con·fed·er·a·tion \kən,fedə'rāshən\ *n* -s [ME *confederacioun*, fr. MF or LL; MF *confederation*, fr. LL *confoederation-, confoederatio* agreement, compact, fr. *confoederatus* + L *-ion-, -io* -ion] **1 a** : an act of confederating or a state of being confederated : a compact for mutual support : an alliance (as of nations or states) : LEAGUE **b** *archaic* : CONSPIRACY **2** : a group of independent nations, states, or tribes more or less permanently united by a treaty or alliance for joint action (as for defense against a common enemy)

con·fed·er·a·tion·ist \-sh(ə)nəst\ *n* -s : a supporter or adherent of a confederation or of a policy of confederating

con·fed·er·a·tism \kən'fed(ə)rə,tizəm\ *n* -s : the system and practice of a confederacy or confederates

con·fed·er·a·tive \kən'fed(ə)rə|d·iv, -də,rā|, |tiv\ *adj* : of, relating to, or characteristic of a confederation or confederates

confederator *n* -s *obs* : CONFEDERATE, CONSPIRATOR

con·fer \kən'fər, +V -ər-; -fə̄, +V -ər- *also* -ə̄r\ *vb* **conferred; conferred; conferring; confers** [L *conferre* to bring together, contribute, consult, fr. *com-* + *ferre* to carry — more at BEAR] *vt* **1** *obs* **a** : to bring or add together : COLLECT **b** : CONTRIBUTE **2** *obs* : COMPARE, COLLATE **3 a** : to grant or bestow esp. at a public ceremony (as a title of nobility or an academic degree) **b** : to give or yield (a characteristic or quality, esp. an advantageous one) ⟨carbon ~*s* hardness upon steel⟩ ⟨the mastery of physical nature which this science has *conferred* on its practitioners —A.J.Toynbee⟩ ~ *vi* **1** *obs* : CONTRIBUTE **2** *obs* : AGREE, CONFORM **3** : to hold conversation or conference now typically on important, difficult, or complex matters : compare views : take counsel : CONSULT, DELIBERATE

con·fer·ee \¦kän fə¦rē\ *n* -s [*confer* + *-ee*] **1** : one conferred with : one taking part in a conference **2** : one upon whom something is conferred

con·fer·ence \'känfər(ə)n(t)s, -frən-; *in sense 4* " *or* kən'fər·ən- *also* kən'fərən-\ *n* -s [MF or ML; MF *conference*, fr. ML *conferentia*, fr. L *conferent-, conferens* (pres. part. of *conferre*) + *-ia* -y] **1** *obs* : comparison of texts : COLLATION **2** : the act of consulting together usu. formally : interchange of views : DISCUSSION, DELIBERATION ⟨~ maketh a ready man —Francis Bacon⟩ ⟨the president in ~ with his advisers⟩ **3** : a meeting for consultation, discussion, or an interchange of opinions whether of individuals or groups: **a** : a meeting of the representatives of different nations to discuss international problems or determine general policy ⟨a ~ of foreign ministers⟩ ⟨a summit ~⟩ **b** : a meeting of members of the two branches of a legislature; *specif* : one to adjust differences in the provisions of a bill passed in different forms by the House of Representatives and the Senate **c** : a meeting of those members of a legislative body who belong to the same party in order to plan party policy but without binding its members to a certain course of action — compare CAUCUS **4** *also* **con·fer·rence** \kən'fər·ən- *also* -fərən-\ : conferment (as of an academic degree) **5 a** (1) : a church court of the early English Presbyterians corresponding roughly to the modern presbytery : CLASSIS (2) : a stated meeting of preachers and others in the Methodist and Mennonite churches invested with authority to act on or take cognizance of ecclesiastical matters (3) : a voluntary association of Congregational churches of a district; *also* : a district containing such churches (4) : a subdivision of a district in the United Lutheran Church (5) : a semiannual general meeting of the Church of Jesus Christ of Latter-day Saints **b** : a league or association of athletic teams esp. representing educational institutions ⟨a football ~⟩ **c** : an association of firms in the same business for carrying out a common policy — compare TRUST **6 a** : an informal meeting for purposes of intensive instruction between a teacher and a small group of students or a single student **b** : a brief and intensive course often held during a vacation emphasizing practical experience and demonstration and usu. attended by adults

con·fé·ren·cier \kōⁿfārāⁿsyā\ *n* -s [F, fr. *conférence* lecture (fr. MF *conference* comparison, discussion) + *-ier* -er] **1 a** : LECTURER **b** : a master of ceremonies of a revue **2** : one taking part in a diplomatic conference : CONFEREE

con·fer·en·tial \¦känfə¦renchəl\ *adj* [fr. *conference*, after such pairs as E *penitence: penitential*] : relating to conference or a conference

con·fer·ment \kən'fərmənt, -fə̄m-\ *n* -s : a conferring esp. of a title

con·fer·ra·ble \-fərəbəl *also* -fə̄rə-\ *adj* [*confer* + *-able*] : that may be conferred

con·fer·ral \-fərəl *also* -fə̄rəl\ *n* -s : the act of conferring : CONFERMENT

con·fer·rer *R* -fərər, -*R* -fərə(r *also* -fə̄rə(r\ *n* -s : BESTOWER, GIVER

con·fer·ru·mi·nate \¦känfə¦rüməṅət\ *also* **con·fer·ru·mi·nat·ed** \-,nād·əd\ *adj* [*conferruminatus* fr. L *conferruminatus*, past part. of *conferruminare* to solder, glue, fr. *com-* + *ferruminare* to solder, join, fr. *ferrumin-, ferrumen* solder, glue; *conferruminated* fr. L *conferruminatus* + E *-ed* — more at FERRUMINATE] : closely adherent — used chiefly of the cotyledons of some sprouting plants

con·fert·ed \kən'fərd·əd\ *adj* [L *confertus* (past part. of *confercire* to press or cram together, fr. *com-* + *-fercire*, fr. *farcire* to stuff) + *-ed* — more at FARCE] *of plant parts* : closely crowded together ⟨the ~ gills of some mushrooms⟩

con·fer·va \kən'fərvə\ *n* [NL, fr. L, a water plant, fr. *confervēre* to boil together, grow together, heal, fr. *com-* + *fervēre*, *fervere* to boil; fr. its supposed healing power — more at BURN] **1** *cap, in some esp former classifications* : a genus of filamentous green algae containing a number of species of doubtful relationship many of which are now usu. placed in the genus *Tribonema* **2** *pl* **confer·vae** \-(,)vē\ : an alga of the genus *Tribonema*; *broadly* : any of various filamentous algae that form scums in still or sluggish fresh water

con·fer·va·ce·ae \,känfə(r)'vāsē,ē\ [NL, fr. *Conferva*, type genus + *-aceae*] *syn of* ULOTRICHACEAE

con·fer·va·les \-ā(,)lēz\ *n pl, cap* [NL, fr. *Conferva* + *-ales*] *in old classifications* : CONFERVOIDEAE

con·fer·void \kən'fər,vȯid\ *adj* [ISV *conferv-* (fr. NL *Conferva*) + *-oid*] : resembling confervae esp. in being made up of branching filaments — used chiefly of algae

con·fer·voi·de·ae \,känfə(r)'vȯidē,ē\ *n pl, cap* [NL, fr. *Conferva* + *-oideae*] *in some esp former classifications* : a group comprising filamentous or mosslike green algae (as those of the genera *Chaetophora, Ulothrix*, and *Ulva*) that are now more commonly placed in Ulotrichales

[1]**con·fess** \kən'fes\ *vb* -ED/-ING/-ES [ME *confessen*, fr. MF *confesser*, fr. OF, fr. *confes* having confessed, fr. L *confessus*, past part. of *confitēri* to confess, fr. *com-* + *-fitēri* (fr. *fatēri* to acknowledge, confess); akin to L *fari* to speak — more at BAN] *vt* **1** : to tell of or make known (something private, hidden, or damaging to oneself) : ADMIT, ACKNOWLEDGE ⟨~ an error⟩ ⟨he ~*ed* his debt⟩ ⟨I ~ myself a traditionalist —R.W. Chapman⟩ **2 a** : to make known or acknowledge (one's sins) esp. to God or to a priest in order to receive absolution **b** : to relieve (oneself) of the burden of sin by confessing (as to God or a priest) **c** *of a priest* : to receive the confession of (a penitent) : administer confession to **3** : to admit as true : assent to : acknowledge esp. after a previous doubt, denial, or concealment : CONCEDE ⟨you know perfectly well you've got a stomach ache, if you'd only ~ it —W.F.de Morgan⟩ **4** : to acknowledge one's faith in : acknowledge as one's belief : AVOW ⟨he reached the conclusion . . . that the new conditions had put the South on the defensive and that a ~*ed* "Southern party" ought to be formed —N.W.Stephenson & H.W.H. Knott⟩ **5** : to disclose or reveal as an effect discloses its cause : PROVE, ATTEST, MANIFEST ⟨and let our ordered lives ~ the beauty of Thy peace —J.G.Whittier⟩ ~ *vi* **1 a** : to disclose one's sins or faults or the state of one's conscience esp. to God or to a priest **b** *of a priest* : to hear confession : SHRIVE **2** : ADMIT, OWN ⟨~ to a crime⟩ **syn** see ACKNOWLEDGE — **confess judgment** : to acknowledge that a claim is or is about to become due to another and consent that legal judgment may be entered for the amount when due and unpaid

[2]**confess** \"\ *n* -ES [prob. fr. [1]*confess*] : an English country-dance for six persons

con·fes·sant \-ˢnt\ *n* -s [F or ML; F *confessant*, fr. ML *confessant-, confessans*, pres. part. of *confessare* to confess, fr. MF *confesser*] : one who confesses esp. to a priest

con·fes·sar·i·us \,kän,fe'sa(a)rēəs\ *n, pl* **confessar·ii** \-rē,ī, -rē,ē\ [ML, fr. L *confessus* + *-arius*] : one who receives confessions; *esp* : FATHER CONFESSOR

con·fess·ed·ly \kən'fesədlē, -li\ *adv* [*confessed* (past part. of *confess*) + *-ly*] : by confession or acknowledgment : ADMITTEDLY, AVOWEDLY

con·fess·ing·ly *adv* : in the manner of one confessing ⟨testimony ~ intimate in tone⟩

con·fes·sio \kən'fes(h)ē,ō\ *n, pl* **confessi·o·nes** \kən,feshē'ō(,)nēz, -sē'ō,nās\ [ML, fr. LL, tomb of a martyr, fr. L, confession] : CONFESSION 8a(3)

con·fes·sion \kən'feshən\ *n* -s [ME *confessioun*, fr. MF *confession*, fr. L *confession-, confessio*, fr. *confessus* + *-ion-, -io* -ion] **1** : the act of confessing : ADMISSION : a statement of guilt or obligation in a matter pertaining to oneself; *also* : the contents of such a statement **2 confessions** *pl* : a usu. written statement in which hidden or intimate matters are disclosed ⟨the *Confessions* of St. Augustine⟩; *broadly* : intimately autobiographical writing or fiction intended to give the illusion of such writing **3** : acknowledgment of sins or sinfulness; *specif* : the act of disclosing sins or faults to a priest to obtain sacramental absolution or to a minister to obtain pastoral counseling **4 a** : acknowledgment of belief or profession of faith; *specif* : a personal declaration of religious faith **b** : a formal statement of doctrinal belief (as a creed or a catechism) ordinarily intended for public avowal by an individual, a group, a congregation, a synod, or a church **5** : an acknowledgment of guilt by a party accused of an offense (1) made before a judge or court in due course of legal proceedings or (2) made before an officer or other person, no confession being admissible as evidence that is not entirely voluntary and made without being induced by threats, promises, or hope of escape or favor extended by a person in authority — called also (1) *judicial confession*, (2) *extrajudicial confession*; compare ADMISSION **6** : a form (as for use in public worship) for the general acknowledgment of sinfulness ⟨a general ~⟩ **7** : a church or body of Christians having a particular confession of faith : COMMUNION **8 a** (1) [LL *confession-, confessio*, fr. L] : the tomb of a martyr (2) : an altar built over the tomb (3) : the crypt or shrine or the part of the altar or occas. a large subterranean chapel in which the relics are placed — called also *confessio* **b** : the high altar in a basilica that stands directly over the altar on a martyr's tomb **c** : the entire building enclosing these two altars

[1]**con·fes·sion·al** \-shənᵊl, -shnəl\ *n* -s [F *confessionnal*, fr. NL *confessionale*, fr. neut. of (assumed) NL *confessionalis* of confession, fr. L *confession-, confessio* confession + *-alis* -al] **1 a** : the recess, seat, or enclosed place where a priest sits to hear confessions **b** : the act or practice of confessing to a priest **2** [F *confessionnal*, modif. (prob. influenced by F *confessionnal* place where a priest sits to hear confessions) of LL *confession-, confessio* tomb of a martyr] : CONFESSION 8 **3** [[2]*confessional*] *usu cap* : a member of a confessional church

confessional 1a

[2]**confessional** \"\ *adj* [*confession* + *-al*] **1** : of, relating to, or being a confession esp. of faith ⟨a ~ statement⟩ **2** : adhering to, established on, or defined by a confession of faith ⟨creedal or ~ orthodoxy⟩ ⟨~ boundaries⟩ : associated with a confession : DENOMINATIONAL ⟨~ schools⟩ ⟨a ~ political party⟩

con·fes·sion·al·ism \-,lizəm\ *n* -s : the principle that a church should have a confession of faith : devotion or adherence to a confession of faith

confession and avoidance *n* : an admission of or failure to deny an allegation coupled with the allegation of new matter that avoids or nullifies the effect of the original allegation — used in legal pleas

[1]**con·fes·sion·ary** \-shə,nerē\ *adj* [prob. fr. (assumed) NL *confessionarius*, fr. L *confession-, confessio* + *-arius* -ary] : of or relating to confession ⟨a ~ litany⟩

[2]**confessionary** \"\ *n* -ES [NL *confessionarium*, fr. L *confession-, confessio* + *-arium* -ary] *archaic* : CONFESSIONAL

con·fes·sion·ist \-sh(ə)nəst\ *n* -s [NL *confessionista*, fr. L *confession-, confessio* + *-ista* -ist] : an adherent of a particular confession of faith

confession of faith : CONFESSION 4b

con·fes·sor \kən'fesə(r) *sometimes* 'kän,fe-, *archaic* 'känfəsə(r) *or* 'känfə,sȯ(ə)r *or* 'känfə,sȯ(ə)\ *n* -s [ME *confessor*, *confessour*, fr. OF & LL; OF *confessour*, fr. LL *confessor*, fr. L *confessus* (past part. of *confitēri* to confess) + *-or* — more at CONFESS] **1** : one who confesses : one who avows belief in someone or something esp. in a religious faith or leader **2** : a giver of heroic evidence of faith; *specif* : a Christian saint who has lived heroically for his faith esp. through a persecution without being martyred ⟨Edward the *Confessor*, King of England 1042–1066⟩ **3** : one (as a priest) who hears the confessions of others

con·fet·ti \kən'fed·|ē, -et|, |i *or in sense 1 as It* kōn'fettē\ *n pl but sing in constr* [It, pl. of *confetto*, fr. ML *confectum* sweetmeat, confection — more at CONFECT] **1** : bonbons or other candies; *also* : their plaster or paper substitutes **2** : tiny colored paper disks or paper streamers so made as to scatter readily when thrown (as at carnivals, parties, weddings) **3** : a deep pink to moderate red that is yellower and stronger than laurel pink and yellower than watermelon

con·fi·dant \'känfə,dant, -daa(ə)nt, ,==¦= *also* -dänt *or* -dȧnt; '==,dənt *also* -dᵊnt *or* -,dent\ *also* **con·fi·dent** \'==,dənt *also* -dᵊnt *or* -,dent\ *n* -s [F *confident*, fr. It *confidente*, fr. *confidente* confident, trustworthy, fr. L *confident-, confidens* confident] : a person to whom secrets (as of personal or professional matters) are confided and entrusted; *usu* : an intimate with whom one feels free to discuss private or secret matters **syn** see FRIEND

con·fi·dante *like* CONFIDANT\ *n* -s [F *confidente*, fem. of *confident*] **1** : a female confidant **2** : a sofa divided by arms into separate seats: as **a** : one at either end of which a small seat extends beyond the arm **b** : one in the shape of the letter S

confidante 2a

con·fide \kən'fīd\ *vb* -ED/-ING/-S [ME *confiden*, fr. MF or L; MF *confider*, fr. L *confidere*, fr. *com-* + *fidere* to trust — more at BIDE] *vi* **1** : to place or have faith : have confidence : TRUST ⟨we cannot ~ wholly in our own powers⟩ **2** : to share or impart secrets or intimate matters : seek advice or help (as in secret distress or perplexity) ⟨a *confiding* letter⟩ — usu. used with *in* ⟨~ in the neighbors⟩ ~ *vt* **1** : to tell confidentially ⟨he dared not ~ the secret to his family —George Meredith⟩ **2** : to give into the care or protection of : place in charge of : ENTRUST, COMMIT ⟨the defense of our island was still *confided* to the militia —T.B.Macaulay⟩ **syn** see COMMIT

[1]**con·fi·dence** \'känfədən(t)s *also* -dᵊn- *or* -,den-\ *n* -s [ME, fr. MF, fr. L *confidentia*, fr. *confident-, confidens* (pres. part. of *confidere* to confide) + *-ia* -y] **1** : the state of one that confides : TRUST, RELIANCE, BELIEF ⟨a cheerful ~ in the mercy of God —T.B.Macaulay⟩ **2** : feeling or consciousness of reliance on oneself or one's circumstances : SELF-CONFIDENCE ⟨a doctor's increasing ~ and skill⟩ ⟨painters who had . . . lost their ~ —W.B.Yeats⟩ **3** : the state of feeling sure : CERTITUDE — usu. used with *of* ⟨great ~ of success⟩ ⟨the level of ~ accepted for a given set of statistical data⟩ **4** : ASSURANCE 7, PRESUMPTION, IMPUDENCE ⟨he had that ~ which the first thinker of anything never has, for all thinkers . . . approach the truth full of hesitation and doubt. *Confidence* comes from repetition, from the breath of many mouths —W.B.Yeats⟩ **5** *archaic* : an object of faith or reliance ⟨the Lord shall be thy ~ —Prov 3:26

(AV)) **6 a :** a relation or state of trust or intimacy between persons who confide in each other ⟨take a friend into one's ~ concerning a private affair⟩ **b** *obs* **:** TRUSTWORTHINESS **c :** a communication made in confidence ⟨the ~s between lawyer and client⟩ **d :** trust in or support of the policy or action of a prime minister and his cabinet expressed by a formal vote of the legislature in a parliamentary system of government **syn** see TRUST

²confidence \"\ *adj* **:** having to do with the appropriation by a swindler of funds entrusted to him usu. by a dupe promised large and easy profits from a type of investment not generally considered ethical ⟨~ game⟩ ⟨~ man⟩

³confidence \"\ *vt* -ED/-ING/-S **:** to swindle esp. by exploiting confidence or desire for quick gain

confidence course *n* **:** OBSTACLE COURSE

confidence interval *n, statistics* **:** an interval which is based on a random sample and for which there is a given probability that it contains a given population parameter (as the mean)

confidence limit *n, statistics* **:** either end point of a confidence interval

confidency *n* -ES [L *confidentia*] *obs* **:** CONFIDENCE

¹con·fi·dent \ˈkänfədənt *also* -dᵊnt *or* -ˌdent\ *adj* [MF, fr. L *confident-, confidens*, pres. part. of *confidere* to confide] **1** *obs* **a :** TRUSTFUL, CONFIDING **b :** giving occasion for confidence **:** TRUSTWORTHY **2 :** characterized by confidence, by a strong, reliant, and bold belief in oneself, and by freedom from fear, doubt, and worry ⟨advancing from triumph to triumph with clear eye and ~ step —W.R.Inge⟩ **3 :** strongly disposed to believe in the merit or truth of something or to accept it as reliable or certain without doubt or reservation — usu. used with *of* or a dependent clause ⟨he felt ~ that he could live to see the day —O.E.Rölvaag⟩ **4 a :** characterized by an excessive belief in one's rightness, strength, or security and therefore rash or bold ⟨I have no cocksure answer . . . Of course ~ answers are common enough —C.E.Montague⟩ **b :** DOGMATIC, CONTENTIOUS, PRESUMPTUOUS **5 :** CONFIDENTIAL — obs. except as applied in Scots law to a person standing in such intimate and confidential relations as to be likely to know the state of one's business affairs

syn ASSURED, SANGUINE, SURE, SELF-CONFIDENT, SELF-ASSURED, PRESUMPTUOUS: usu. complimentary, CONFIDENT may imply an undemonstrative firm feeling of certain success ⟨a *confident* feeling of immense reserves in strength and endurance —T.E. Lawrence⟩ Sometimes it may imply ill-grounded optimism or overbearing presumption ⟨we have not realized the hopes of the eighteenth century 'illumination', when *confident* philosophers believed that humanity was shaking off its ancient chains —J.H.Robinson⟩ ⟨he swaggered up the path as if the place belonged to him and we heard his loud, *confident* peal at the bell —A. Conan Doyle⟩ ASSURED, sometimes uncomplimentary, indicates utter absence of doubt in one's ability, success, or correctness ⟨"All the boys in my class are older, but I keep at the head." Sometimes he was almost too *assured* —Ellen Glasgow⟩ ⟨[he] has *assured* carriage, walking boldly into good hotels and mixing with patrons on terms of equality —Don Marquis⟩ SANGUINE, usu. complimentary, stresses extreme optimism ⟨a surgeon's commission for the doctor, and a lieutenancy for myself, were certainly counted upon in our *sanguine* expectations —Herman Melville⟩ ⟨his *sanguine* spirit kindled with an enthusiasm which overleaped every obstacle —W.H.Prescott⟩ SURE usu. indicates a reasonable, well-grounded confidence ⟨individual members may be ill-bred; the House itself has a fine taste and breeding, and a *sure* instinct in matters of conduct —John Buchan⟩ ⟨she tempted the young man into kissing her, and later lay in his arms for two hours, entirely *sure* of herself —Sherwood Anderson⟩ SELF-CONFIDENT and SELF-ASSURED intensify suggestions of CONFIDENT and ASSURED and are often not complimentary ⟨their claim to superiority is just as stubborn as though it were well-founded, just as *self-assured* as in case of our own really superior nation —Bertrand Russell⟩ PRESUMPTUOUS always implies overconfidence and usu. suggests boldness and insolence ⟨Arheetoo had known me but two hours and as he made the proposition very coolly, I thought it rather *presumptuous* —Herman Melville⟩ ⟨to write in this way of men like Dante and Shakespeare is really less *presumptuous* than to write of smaller men —T.S.Eliot⟩

²confident *var of* CONFIDANT

con·fi·den·tial \ˌkänfəˈdenchəl\ *adj* [fr. *confidence*, after such pairs as E *penitence: penitential*] **1 :** communicated, conveyed, acted on, or practiced in confidence **:** known only to a limited few **:** not publicly disseminated **:** PRIVATE, SECRET ⟨chary of committing anything of a ~ nature to any more concrete medium than speech —William Faulkner⟩ ⟨~ remarks⟩ ⟨a ~ document⟩ — compare CLASSIFIED 2 **2 a :** showing confidence in another **:** disposed to relate or confide private or secret matters ⟨growing still more ~ . . . said that I would soon be a most important personage among them —W.H.Hudson⟩ **b :** marked by or indicative of confiding or confidence **:** indicative of intimacy, mutual trust, or willingness to confide ⟨he slipped his arm through his father's with a ~ pressure —Edith Wharton⟩ **c :** receiving confidences **:** treated with confidence **:** adjudged trustworthy ⟨he had been his ~ servant and was intimate with all his habits —Anthony Trollope⟩ **3 a :** SECRET, HIDDEN, ESOTERIC **b :** characterized by or relating to information considered prejudicial to a country's interests and advantageous to its enemies **syn** see FAMILIAR

confidential communication *n* **:** PRIVILEGED COMMUNICATION 1

confidential employee *n* **:** an employee having access in the course of his duties to confidential information on the employer's labor relations and consequently excludable from union membership

con·fi·den·tial·i·ty \ˌkänfəˌdencheˈaləd·ē, -ˌdenˈshal-\ *n* -ES **:** the quality or state of being confidential, private, or secret ⟨the ~ of birth records —*Jour. Amer. Med. Assoc.*⟩ ⟨federal law establishes the ~ of clinical records concerning voluntary patients —D.W.Maurer & V.H.Vogel⟩

con·fi·den·tial·ly \ˌkänfəˈdench(ə)lē, -li\ *adv* **:** in a confidential manner ⟨addressing him intimately and ~⟩ ⟨leaning ~ across the table —Gerald Beaumont⟩

con·fi·den·tial·ness \-chəlnəs\ *n* -ES **:** the quality or state of being confidential **:** CONFIDENTIALITY

con·fi·dent·ly *adv* **:** with confidence **:** with strong assurance **:** POSITIVELY, BOLDLY, UNHESITATINGLY

con·fi·dent·ness *n* -ES **:** CONFIDENCE

confides *pres 3d sing of* CONFIDE

confiding *adj* [fr. pres. part. of *confide*] **:** that confides **:** TRUSTFUL — **con·fid·ing·ly** *adv* — **con·fid·ing·ness** *n* -ES

con·fig·u·ral \kənˈfigyərəl, ÷ -gər-\ *adj* [*configuration* + *-al*] **:** of or relating to a configuration

con·fig·u·rate \-ˌrāt, *usu* -ād·+V\ *vt* -ED/-ING/-S [L *configuratus*, past part. of *configurare* to form from or after, fr. *com-* + *figurare* to form, fr. *figura* figure — more at FIGURE] **:** to give or assign a form to **:** FASHION, SHAPE, FORM

configurated *adj* [fr. past part. of *configurate*] **1** *astrol* **:** associated in a configuration **2** *of glass* **:** having an irregularly patterned surface

con·fig·u·ra·tion \⸗ˌ⸗⸗ˈrāshən *also* ˌkän-\ *n* -S [LL *configuration-, configuratio* comparison, shaping, fr. L *configuratus* + *-ion-, -io* -ion] **1 a** *astrol* **:** relative position or aspect of the planets **b** *astron* **:** any of several limiting apparent positions of a celestial body with respect to another (as conjunction, quadrature, opposition, and elongation) **2 :** relative disposition or arrangement of parts **:** interrelationships of constituent elements **:** CONTOUR, PATTERN, FIGURE ⟨a network of roads following the ~ of the country —John Buchan⟩ **3 :** a geometrical figure usu. consisting of points and lines and the points, lines, and planes which

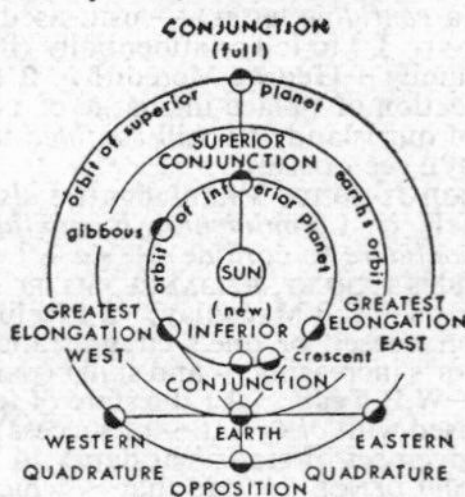

planetary configurations

may be derived from them **4 :** the structure of chemical compounds esp. with reference to the space relations of the atoms in molecules **5** [G *konfiguration*, fr. LL *configuration-, configuratio*] **:** GESTALT **syn** see FORM

con·fig·u·ra·tion·al \kənˌ⸗⸗ˈrāshənᵊl, ˌkänˌ⸗⸗ˈrā-, -shnəl\ *adj* **:** relating to or based on a configuration — **con·fig·u·ra·tion·al·ly** \-ᵊlē, -əlē\ *adv*

con·fig·u·ra·tion·ism \kənˌ⸗⸗ˈrāshəˌnizəm, ˌkän-\ *n* -S **:** GESTALT PSYCHOLOGY — **con·fig·u·ra·tion·ist** \-sh(ə)nəst\ *n* -S

con·figurative \kən +\ *adj* [*configuration* + *-ive*] **:** CONFIGURATIONAL

con·figure \kən +\ *vt* -ED/-ING/-S [ME *configuren*, fr. L *configurare*] **1 :** to shape according to some model **:** cause to conform ⟨man's nature is *configured* to the divine⟩ **2 :** to arrange in a certain form, figure, or shape **:** give a configuration to **:** SHAPE ⟨a magnet is surrounded by a *configured* field⟩

¹con·fine \kənˈfīn\ *vb* -ED/-ING/-S [MF *confiner* to lie contiguous, restrain within limits, fr. *confine*, n.] *vi, archaic* **:** to have a common boundary **:** lie contiguous ~ *vt* **:** to hold within bounds **:** restrain from exceeding boundaries: **a :** to keep in narrow cramped quarters **:** IMPRISON **b :** to prevent free outward passage or motion of **:** SECURE, ENCLOSE, FASTEN ⟨the loose cloud of hair was *confined* in two plaits —W.H.Hudson⟩ ⟨dikes *confined* the flood waters⟩ **c :** to keep from leaving accustomed quarters (as one's room or bed) under pressure of infirmity, childbirth, detention, business reasons ⟨now that he was able to employ an assistant, he was not closely *confined* to the store —Ellen Glasgow⟩ **d :** to narrow down (range of possible interest, participation, expression) and exclude from embracing various matters possible **:** make applicable only to a limited group ⟨for what reason was the Greek tragic poet *confined* to so limited a range of subjects —Matthew Arnold⟩ ⟨a rare luxury *confined* to princes and ministers —T.B. Macaulay⟩ **e :** to keep to a certain place or to a limited area **:** prevent unlimited incidence of ⟨in *confining* the disease to Memphis —W.F.Willcox⟩ ⟨the buffalo was not *confined* to the open grassland —C.D.Forde⟩ **syn** see LIMIT

²con·fine \ˈkänˌfīn, *in sense 5a usu* kənˈf-\ *n* -S [MF or L; MF *confin*, fr. L *confine*, fr. neut. of *confinis* having the same boundary, adjacent, fr. *com-* + *finis* end, border — more at FINAL] **1** *usu pl* **:** BOUNDS, BORDERS; *esp* **:** the mutual boundary with adjacent regions ⟨betwixt the ~s of night and day —John Dryden⟩ **2** *usu pl* **:** regions along or near a border **:** outlying parts ⟨the Newtonian scheme does not banish God from the universe, but it pushes him to the ~s —*Times Lit. Supp.*⟩ **3** *usu pl* **:** constricting limits (as of an area of activity or operation) **:** SCOPE ⟨Darwin had not moved entirely within the ~s of the thought of his generation —S.F.Mason⟩ ⟨lifts the story beyond a conventional ~ —*Times Lit. Supp.*⟩ **4** *usu pl* **:** enclosed or otherwise limited space or area **:** TERRITORY ⟨the future of the city lies in the eastern corner of its ~s —*Springfield (Mass.) Daily News*⟩ **5 a** *archaic* **:** RESTRICTION, CONFINEMENT ⟨the dungeon's dim ~ —Robert Burns⟩ **b** *obs* **:** PRISON, DUNGEON ⟨many ~s, wards, and dungeons —Shak.⟩

³confine *adj* [MF or L; MF *confin*, fr. L *confinis* adjacent] *obs* **:** NEIGHBORING

con·fined \kənˈfīnd\ *adj* [fr. past part. of *confine*] **:** kept in confines; *often* **:** in childbed **:** in the course of childbirth

con·fined·ly \-īn(ə)dlē\ *adv* **:** in a confined manner

con·fined·ness \-īndnəs, -īn(d)nəs\ *n* -ES **:** the quality or state of being confined

confineless *adj* [²*confine* + *-less*] *obs* **:** BOUNDLESS, LIMITLESS

con·fine·ment \kənˈfīnmənt\ *n* -S [F, fr. MF, fr. *confiner* + *-ment*] **1 :** the act of confining or state of being confined **:** restraint within limits ⟨the mind hates restraint and is apt to fancy itself under ~ when the sight is pent up —Joseph Addison⟩ **2 a :** restraint within doors by sickness ⟨after several weeks of ~ he was eager to cooperate with his doctor⟩ **b :** LYING-IN, ACCOUCHEMENT ⟨the normal ~ may often advantageously take place at home⟩

confinement system *n* **:** any system of raising poultry or other livestock in which the animals are kept from contact with the ground primarily as a sanitary measure

confiner *n* -S *obs* **:** one that lives on or within the confines **:** NEIGHBOR, INHABITANT

confining *adj* [fr. pres. part. of *confine*] **:** that confines **:** RESTRAINING, RESTRICTIVE ⟨bookkeeping is a ~ occupation⟩ ⟨glaciers flowing . . . between rugged ~ peaks —W.E.Rudolph⟩

confining bed *n, geol* **:** a comparatively impervious stratum directly above or below one bearing water or petroleum

con·fin·i·ty \kənˈfinəd·ē\ *n* -ES [MF *confinité*, fr. *confin* adjacent, neighboring + *-ité* -ity] *archaic* **:** community of limits **:** CONTIGUITY, ADJACENCY

con·firm \kənˈfərm, -fə̄m, -fəim\ *vt* -ED/-ING/-S [ME *confermen, confirmen*, fr. OF *confermer, confirmer*, fr. L *confirmare*, fr. *com-* + *firmare* to make firm, fr. *firmus* firm — more at FIRM] **1 :** to make firm **:** strengthen (as a person) in resolution, conviction, loyalty, position ⟨America would once again as a nation confound its critics and . . . ~ its friends —Barbara Ward⟩ **2 a :** to make valid by formal assent **:** complete by a necessary approval ⟨the Senate ~s a treaty⟩; *often* **:** to vote approval of (the appointment of a person to an office) ⟨the Senate ~*ed* his appointment to the Supreme Court⟩ **b :** to give formal acknowledgment of receipt of ⟨an order ~*ed* by a stockbroker⟩ **3 :** to administer the rite of confirmation to **4 :** to give new assurance of the truth or validity of **:** CORROBORATE ⟨~ a rumor⟩ ⟨~ a hypothesis or diagnosis⟩ ⟨~ a plane reservation⟩ **5 :** to make (someone or oneself) firmer or more settled in a conviction, purpose, or habit ⟨the experience ~*ed* him in his dislike of foreign cooking⟩ **6 :** to state or imply the truth of (as a rumor or forecast) **:** ASSERT, MAINTAIN — usu. used with *that* **7** *Scots law* **:** to ratify the right of (a person) to take and administer property of a deceased person as executor or administrator

syn CORROBORATE, SUBSTANTIATE, VERIFY, AUTHENTICATE, VALIDATE: these may be compared in that they signify to attest or establish usu. beyond a reasonable doubt the truth, accuracy, validity, or genuineness of something. CONFIRM and CORROBORATE both imply an attesting to something already formulated or recognized but not yet made certain. CONFIRM usu. implies the making unquestionable of something in question by means of authoritative statement or indisputable fact ⟨they are asked to *confirm* or correct facts —Evelyn Lohr⟩ ⟨there is a rumor — which cannot of course be *confirmed* —Frank Gorrell⟩ ⟨*confirm* the persistent suspicion that eggs are carriers of fowl typhoid —*Collier's Yr. Bk.*⟩ CORROBORATE suggests the buttressing or strengthening by authority or fact of something already pretty well established ⟨in general, the material illustrates and *corroborates* what has already become known from other sources —G.F.Kennan⟩ ⟨no matter how many *corroborating* tests we may adduce as proof . . . the skeptic still is not convinced —Arthur Pap⟩ ⟨these were the earliest professional sodalities in Spain, though *corroborating* documentation is lacking —G.M.Foster⟩ SUBSTANTIATE implies the presenting of evidence adequate to demonstrate or make certain ⟨individual differences within one race and culture are well *substantiated* . . . by psychological and practical tests —A.L.Kroeber⟩ ⟨reference material to support, *substantiate*, or enlarge upon the text —Frank Mortimer⟩ ⟨no proof had to be brought forward to *substantiate* the claims they made —Sherwood Anderson⟩ VERIFY implies the seeking of a close correspondence between a statement and the facts it involves or an attestation to the correctness of its logic, or, as applied to suspicions or predictions, the actualization in fact of the thing suspected ⟨he has explored most of Trans-Jordan, *verified* Biblical accounts by his findings and excavations —*Current Biog.*⟩ ⟨discouraging predictions that have not been *verified* by events —*Times Lit. Supp.*⟩ AUTHENTICATE and VALIDATE presuppose a question about genuineness or validity. AUTHENTICATE signifies to establish genuineness by or as if by expert opinion or official or legal document ⟨the painting was finally *authenticated* by experts in Barcelona and Madrid —*Time*⟩ ⟨each citizen ought to be *authenticated* as the son of his proper father —H.M.Parshley⟩ ⟨an *authenticated* copy of the Declaration —Dumas Malone⟩ VALIDATE generally involves establishing of validity, as of a document by reference to legal or official act or record or as of an opinion or policy by justifying facts or events ⟨what directors do . . . by law must be *validated* by formal board action —G.B.Hurff⟩ ⟨the sort of evidence by which one *validates* a scientific hypothesis —*Life*⟩ ⟨the expansion of demand which alone can *validate* the policy —J.A.Hobson⟩ ⟨the two performances more than *validated* the words of praise —Irving Kolodin⟩

con·firm·abil·i·ty \⸗ˌ⸗əˈbiləd·ē, -ətē, -i\ *n* -ES **:** the quality or state of being confirmable

confirmability theory *n* [*confirmability* fr. *confirmable* + *-ity*] **:** a logical empiricist theory that makes confirmability a requirement for the meaningfulness of a factual statement and typically defines the confirmability of such a statement as the reducibility of its descriptive predicates to a set of observation predicates — compare VERIFIABILITY PRINCIPLE

con·firm·able \⸗ˈ⸗əbəl\ *adj* **1 :** capable of being confirmed **2 :** susceptible to the possibility of being either theoretically or actually supported or weakened by reference to empirical facts

con·fir·mand \ˌkänfə(r)ˈmand\ *n* -S [L *confirmandus* fit to be confirmed, fr. *confirmare* to confirm] **:** a candidate for religious confirmation

con·fir·ma·tion \ˌkänfə(r)ˈmāshən\ *n* -S [ME *confirmacioun*, fr. MF *confirmation*, fr. L *confirmation-, confirmatio*, fr. *confirmatus* (past part. of *confirmare*) + *-ion-, -io* -ion] **1 :** the act of confirming or strengthening **:** the act of establishing, assuring, or upholding: **a** (1) **:** a rite of various Christian churches regarded as supplemental to the rite of baptism, held by some churches to be a sacrament, and viewed generally as confirming a person in his religious faith (2) **:** the act or ceremony of confirming or sanctioning 14 to 16 year-old boys and girls in the Jewish faith following their study of the faith and history of Judaism and their declaration of devotion to its principles; *also* **:** the synagogue service now usu. held on Shabuoth in which this religious ceremony occurs **b :** the ratification of an executive act (as a treaty or an appointment) by a legislative body **2 :** CORROBORATION, SUBSTANTIATION ⟨the report lacked ~⟩: as **a :** something that confirms **:** PROOF, SUPPORT ⟨find ~ of a theory⟩ **b :** the procedure of supporting a factual statement by means of empirical evidence **c** (1) **:** a written order or agreement that verifies or substantiates an agreement previously concluded orally (2) *in auditing* **:** written substantiation of the existence or value esp. of claims against assets, assets held by others, or assets and liabilities **3 a :** a conveyance by which a voidable estate is made sure and not voidable or by which a particular estate is increased **:** an express or implied contract by which a person makes that firm and binding which was before voidable **b** *Scots law* **:** a sentence empowering an executor upon making inventory of the movables pertaining to the deceased to recover, possess, and administer them

confirmation class *n* **:** a course of study in the fundamentals of religion designed to prepare young people for confirmation and usu. conducted by a pastor, priest, or rabbi; *also* **:** the group of young persons participating in such a class

con·fir·ma·tive \kənˈfərməd·|iv, -fə̄m-, -fəim-, -mət| *also* |əv\ *adj* [LL *confirmativus*, fr. L *confirmatus* + *-ivus* -ive] **:** tending to confirm or establish — **con·fir·ma·tive·ly** \ |əvlē, -li\ *adv*

con·fir·ma·to·ry \-məˌtōrē, -tȯr-, -ri\ *adj* [ML *confirmatorius*, fr. L *confirmatus* + *-orius* -ory] **1 :** serving to confirm **:** CORROBORATIVE **2 :** relating to the rite of confirmation

con·firmed \-md\ *adj* [ME *confermed* chronic, inveterate, fr. past part. of *confermen* to confirm] **:** made firm or established (as by stengthening, accustoming, or settling by long continuance, habitual usage, or determined or expressed preference): **a :** made resolute **:** ENCOURAGED, FORTIFIED ⟨southern zealots ~ by early successes at Bull Run⟩ **b :** given to habit so long-continued or to a way of acting or thinking so resolutely adhered to that change is unlikely ⟨~ pedestrians like my father and me —George Santayana⟩ ⟨a bore to all but a few ~ antiquarians —Lewis Mumford⟩ **c :** marked by long continuance **:** deeply ingrained **:** constantly practiced ⟨like all other ~ habits . . . easier to obey than to break —Ellen Glasgow⟩ **d :** having received the rite of confirmation **syn** see INVETERATE

confirmed credit *n* **:** LETTER OF CREDIT

con·firm·ed·ly \-mədlē, -li\ *adv* [ME *confermedly*, fr. *confermed* + *-ly*] **:** in the manner of one convinced **:** UNALTERABLY ⟨~ pro-American . . . on foreign policy —F.H.Gervasi⟩

con·firmed·ness \-mdnəs, -m(d)n-\ *n* -ES **:** the quality or state of being confirmed

confirming *pres part of* CONFIRM

con·fir·mor \ˌkänfərˈmȯ(ə)r, kənˈfərmər\ *n* -S **:** one that makes a confirmation of title to another

confirms *pres 3d sing of* CONFIRM

con·fis·ca·ble \kənˈfiskəbəl, (ˈ)känˈf-\ *adj* [prob. fr. F, fr. MF, fr. *confisquer* to confiscate (fr. L *confiscare*) + *-able*] **:** liable to confiscation

con·fis·cat·able \ˈkänfəˌskād·əbəl, -ātə-\ *adj* **:** CONFISCABLE

¹con·fis·cate \ˈkänfəˌskāt, kənˈfiskət, *usu* -d·+V\ *adj* [L *confiscatus*, past part. of *confiscare* to confiscate, fr. *com-* + *-fiscare* (fr. *fiscus* basket, purse, treasury) — more at FISCAL] **1** *archaic* **:** appropriated by the government to public use **:** FORFEITED **2 :** deprived of property by confiscation

²con·fis·cate \ˈkänfəˌskāt, *archaic* kənˈfi-, *usu* -ād·+V\ *vt* -ED/-ING/-S [L *confiscatus*] **1 :** to seize as forfeited to the public treasury **:** APPROPRIATE ⟨~ an estate⟩ ⟨a capital gains tax that *confiscated* most of the wealth accumulated since 1940 —*Current Biog.*⟩ **2 :** to seize by or as if by public authority ⟨police *confiscated* the liquor⟩ ⟨the teacher *confiscated* the notes⟩ **syn** see APPROPRIATE

con·fis·ca·tion \ˌkänfəˈskāshən, -n,fiˈ-\ *n* -S [MF or L; MF, fr. L *confiscation-, confiscatio*, fr. *confiscatus* + *-ion-, -io* -ion] **:** the act of confiscating or state of being confiscated **:** the taking of private property to the public use as being forfeited

con·fis·ca·tor \ˈkänfəˌskād·ə(r), -ātə-, *archaic* kənˈfi-\ *n* -S [²*confiscate* + *-or*] **:** one that confiscates

con·fis·ca·to·ry \kənˈfiskəˌtōrē, -tȯr-, -ri *sometimes* ˈkänfəs-\ *adj* **:** effecting or constituting confiscation **:** characterized by confiscations ⟨~ taxation⟩

con·fi·se·rie \kōⁿfēzrē\ *n* -S [F, fr. *confis-* (stem of *confire* to preserve) + *-erie* -ery — more at COMFIT] **:** CONFECTIONERY, SWEETSHOP

con·fi·tent \ˈkänfətənt\ *n* -S [L *confitent-, confitens*, pres. part. of *confitēri* to confess — more at CONFESS] **:** CONFESSANT

con·fi·te·ria \kənˌfēd·əˈrēə, ˌkänfətə-\ *n* -S [Sp *confiteria*, fr. *confite* comfit (fr. Catal *confit*, fr. ML *confectum*) + *-eria* -ery — more at CONFECT] **:** a Latin-American establishment devoted to the sale of tea, coffee, chocolate, and other beverages and sometimes other refreshments (as pastry and sandwiches)

con·fi·ture \ˈkänfəˌchu̇(ə)r\ *n* -S [F — more at COMFITURE] **1** *obs* **:** CONFECTION 1b **2 :** preserved or candied fruit **:** JAM

con·flab \ˈkänˌflab, kənˈf-\ *dial var of* CONFAB

con·fla·grant \kənˈflāgrənt\ *adj* [L *conflagrant-, conflagrans*, pres. part. of *conflagrare* to burn, be consumed by fire, fr. *com-* + *flagrare* to burn, blaze — more at BLACK] **:** BURNING, BLAZING

con·fla·grate \ˈkänfləˌgrāt\ *vb* -ED/-ING/-S [L *conflagratus*, past part. of *conflagrare*] *vi* **:** to catch fire ~ *vt* **:** to set on fire

con·fla·gra·tion \ˌkänfləˈgrāshən\ *n* -S [L *conflagration-, conflagratio*, fr. *conflagratus* + *-ion-, -io* -ion] **1 obs a :** consumption by fire **b :** INFLAMMATION, FEVER **2 :** FIRE; *esp* **:** a large disastrous fire involving numerous buildings

con·fla·gra·tor \ˈkänfləˌgrād·ə(r)\ *n* -S [L *conflagratus* + E *-or*] **:** INCENDIARY

con·flag·ra·to·ry \kənˈflagrəˌtōrē\ *adj* [*conflagrate* + *-ory*] **:** INFLAMMATORY

¹con·flate \ˈkänˌflāt, kənˈf-\ *adj* [L *conflatus*, past part. of *conflare* to blow together, fr. *com-* + *flare* to blow — more at BLOW] **:** brought together **:** assembled, blended, or consolidated into one ⟨~ readings of a text⟩

²con·flate \kənˈflāt, ˈkänˌf-\ *vt* -ED/-ING/-S [L *conflatus*] **1 :** FUSE **:** bring together **:** COLLECT, MERGE, CONFUSE **2 :** to combine (two readings of a text) into a composite whole **:** produce (a composite reading or text)

con·fla·tion \kənˈflāshən\ *n* -S [LL *conflation-, conflatio*, fr. L *conflatus* + *-ion-, -io* -ion] **:** the process or result of conflating **:** BLEND, FUSION; *esp* **:** a composite reading or text

¹con·flict \ˈkänˌflikt\ *n* -S [ME, fr. L *conflictus* act of striking together, fr. *conflictus*, past part. of *confligere* to strike together, fight, fr. *com-* + *fligere* to strike — more at PROFLIGATE] **1 a :** clash, competition, or mutual interference of opposing or incompatible forces or qualities (as ideas, interests, wills) : ANTAGONISM ⟨the convulsions of a soul storm-driven amid unreconcilable spiritual ~*s* —H.O.Taylor⟩ **b** : an emotional state characterized by indecision, restlessness, uncertainty, and tension resulting from incompatible inner needs or drives of comparable intensity **2 a** : an engagement between men under arms : STRUGGLE, CONTEST, FIGHT **b** : prolonged fighting esp. with weapons : WARFARE, STRIFE **c** : the opposition of persons or forces upon which the dramatic action depends in drama or fiction **d** : CONFLICT OF LAWS **3** : a striking or clashing together of material bodies or substances (as air currents, parts of a mechanism) : COLLISION **syn** see CONTEST, DISCORD

²con·flict \kən'flikt, 'kän,f-\ *vi* -ED/-ING/-S [ME *conflicten*, fr. L *conflictus*, past part. of *confligere* to fight] **1** : to contend with or against another in strife or warfare ⟨France ~*ed* with England⟩ ⟨the ~*ing* nations of Greece and Turkey⟩ **2** : to show variance, incompatibility, irreconcilability, or opposition : evidence variance or disharmony calling for adjustment, harmonizing, bringing into accord ⟨the two versions of the story ~⟩ ⟨nor does the French revolutionary spirit ~ with what we ordinarily mean by respect for law —W.C.Brownell⟩ **syn** see BUMP, CONTEST

conflicting *adj* [fr. pres. part. of *conflict*] : being in conflict, collision, or opposition : CONTENDING, INCOMPATIBLE — **con·flict·ing·ly** *adv*

con·flic·tion \kən'flikshən\ *n* -S [L *confliction-*, *conflictio*, fr. *conflictus* + *-ion-*, *-io* -ion] : the process of conflicting or state of being in conflict

con·flic·tive \kən'fliktiv, 'kän,f-\ *adj* : tending to conflict

conflict of interest : a conflict between an individual's private interests and his duties or actions as a government official

conflict of laws : opposition or conflict between the laws of different states or jurisdictions as respects the rights of the same individual; *also* : a branch of law that deals with the adjustment of such opposition or defines the law applicable to situations or transactions asserted to be governed by divergent local laws

con·flic·tu·al \(')kän¦flikchəwəl, kən'f-, -ksh-\ *adj* [¹*conflict* + *-ual* (as in *actual*)] : marked by, involving, or containing conflict

con·flow \kən'flō, kän-\ *vi* [*com-* + *flow*] : to flow together

confluction *n* -S [modif. of ML *confluxion-*, *confluxio*, fr. LL, abundant flow, fr. L *confluxus* (past part. of *confluere*) + *-ion-*, *-io* -ion] *obs* : CONFLUENCE

con·flu·ence \'kän,flüən(t)s\ *n* -S [LL *confluentia* act of flowing together, fr. L *confluent-*, *confluens*, pres. part. of *confluere* + *-ia* -y] **1 a** : a coming or flocking together, meeting, or gathering at one place : CONCOURSE ⟨you see this ~, this great flood of visitors —Shak.⟩ **b** : large assemblage : CROWD **2 a** : the flowing together of two or more streams ⟨an island formed by the ~ of two rivers⟩ **b** : the place of meeting of two streams ⟨Koblenz stands at the ~ of the Rhine and the Moselle⟩ **c** : the stream or body formed by the junction of two or more streams : a combined flood **3** : CONCRESCENCE 2

¹con·flu·ent \(')kän¦flüənt, kən'f-\ *adj* [L *confluent-*, *confluens*, pres. part. of *confluere* to flow together, fr. *com-* + *fluere* to flow — more at FLUENT] **1** : flowing together : meeting or coming together : combining to form one ⟨~ streams⟩ ⟨~ glaciers⟩ ⟨~ veins⟩ **2** *med* **a** : running or run together : UNITED ⟨~ pustules⟩ **b** : characterized by confluent lesions ⟨~ smallpox⟩ — compare DISCRETE 1b **3** : coming together smoothly without a notch at the point of junction ⟨~ dorsal fins of certain fishes⟩

²confluent \"\ *n* -S : a confluent stream; *broadly* : AFFLUENT, TRIBUTARY

con·flux \'kän,fləks\ *n* -ES [ML *confluxus*, fr. LL, abundant flow, fr. L *confluxus*, past part. of *confluere*] : CONFLUENCE

con·focal \(')kän+\ *adj* [*com-* + *focal*] *math* : having the same real or imaginary foci — used of conic sections and of conicoids whose principal sections are confocal conics

¹con·form \kən'fȯ(ə)rm, -ȯ(ə)m\ *vb* -ED/-ING/-S [ME *conformen*, fr. MF *conformer*, fr. L *conformare* to form, conform, fr. *com-* + *formare* to form, fr. *forma* form — more at FORM] *vt* : to make like : shape to fit : ADAPT ⟨~*s* the belt to the contour⟩ : bring into harmony or agreement ⟨~ this regulation to existing business practices —M.V.DiSalle⟩ ~ *vi* **1** : to have the same shape, outline, or contour ⟨the areas of greater rainfall ~ roughly with these forested areas —*Amer. Guide Series: Minn.*⟩ : be in agreement or harmony ⟨his way of life ~*s* to his income⟩ — used with *to* or *with* **2 a** : to be obedient : COMPLY — usu. used with *to* ⟨men are bound to obey the law of society and ~ to its harmless orders —W.M.Thackeray⟩ : act in accordance with prevailing standard or custom ⟨even without racial and religious segregation the pressure to ~ is intense and stultifying —Sidonie M. Gruenberg⟩ **b** : to comply with the usages of an established church; *esp* : to comply with the usages of the Church of England **3** *geol* : to follow in unbroken sequence of deposition **syn** see ADAPT, AGREE

²conform \"\ *adj* [ME *conforme*, fr. MF or LL; MF *conforme*, fr. LL *conformis*, fr. L *com-* + *-formis* (fr. *forma*)] : CONFORMABLE — usu. used with *to*

³conform \"\ *adv*, *Scot* : CONFORMABLY — used with *to*

con·form·abil·i·ty \kən,fȯ(r)mə'bilәd-ē, -ətē, -i\ *n* -ES [*conformable* + *-ity*] : the quality of conforming — used esp. of geological strata

con·form·able \ᵊ'ᵊᵊməbəl\ *adj* **1** : corresponding in form, character, opinions, social conventions : SIMILAR, HARMONIOUS, ADAPTED — usu. used with *to* **2** : giving compliance or obedience : SUBMISSIVE, COMPLIANT ⟨I have been to you a true and humble wife, at all times to your will —Shak.⟩ **3** *Brit* : conforming to the usages of the Church of England esp. as prescribed by the Acts of Uniformity **4** : following in unbroken sequence — used of geologic strata formed by uninterrupted deposition under the same general conditions — **con·form·ably** \-blē, -li\ *adv*

con·formal \kən, (')kän+\ *adj* [LL *conformalis* having the same shape, fr. L *com-* + *formalis* having a set form, formal — more at FORMAL] **1** *math* : conserving the size of all angles and therefore the shape of every elementary triangle — used of a depiction of one surface on another **2** *of a map* : having the same scale along both the meridian and the parallel at any point and having meridians and parallels at right angles so that the shapes of small areas around that point are true to the shape of the corresponding areas on the earth ⟨Mercator's is the best known of ~ projections⟩ — **con·formality** \,kän(,)fȯ(r)'maləd-ē\ *n* -ES

con·form·ance \kən'fȯrmən(t)s, -ȯ(ə)m-\ *n* -S : the act of conforming : CONFORMITY

conformant *adj*, *obs* : CONFORMING, CONFORMABLE

con·for·ma·tion \,kän(,)fȯ(r)'māshən, -fə(r)-\ *n* -S [L *conformation-*, *conformatio* symmetrical forming, fr. *conformatus* (past part. of *conformare*) + *-ion-*, *-io* -ion — more at CONFORM] **1** : the act of conforming or producing conformity : ADAPTATION ⟨~ of lives to duties⟩ **2** : formation of something by appropriate arrangement of parts or elements : an assembling into a whole **3 a** : agreement esp. with a model or plan **b** : STRUCTURE, FORM ⟨~ of the ocean bed⟩ **c** : the form or outline esp. of an animal or of a dressed carcass : SHAPE **d** : any of the spatial arrangements of a molecule that can be obtained by rotating the atoms or groups around one or more single bonds **syn** see FORM

con·for·ma·tor \'känfər,mād-ər\ *or* **con·for·ma·teur** \,kän,fȯrmə'tər\ *n* -S [F *conformateur*, fr. *conformer* to conform (fr. L *conformare*) + *-ateur* -ator] : an apparatus for taking the conformation of a thing (as of the head for fitting a hat)

conformed *past of* CONFORM

con·form·er \kən'fȯrmər, -ȯ(ə)mə(r\ *n* -S : one that conforms

conforming *pres part of* CONFORM

con·form·ism \kən'fȯr,mizəm, -ȯ(ə),m-\ *n* -S [prob. fr. F *conformisme*, fr. *conformiste* person inclined to conventional thoughts and actions, English person that conforms to the established Church of England (after such pairs as F *déiste* deist: *déisme* deism), fr. E *conformist* English person that conforms to the established Church of England] : the act, practice, or principle of conforming ⟨unimaginative timid ~ in key positions —K.S.Davis⟩

¹con·form·ist \-məst\ *n* -S : one who conforms esp. to an established church; *specif* : a person who conforms to the established Church of England

²conformist \"\ *adj* : CONFORMING, STANDARDIZED, STANDARDIZING

con·form·i·ty \kən'fȯ(r)məd-ē, -ətē, -i\ *n* -ES [ME *conformyte*, fr. MF *conformite*, fr. LL *conformitat-*, *conformitas*, fr. *conformis* conformable + *-itat-*, *-itas* -ity — more at CONFORM] **1 a** : correspondence in form, manner, or character : a point of resemblance (as of tastes) — usu. used with *to* **b** : HARMONY, AGREEMENT, CONGRUITY — usu. used with *with* ⟨his behavior was in ~ with his ideals⟩ **2** : the action or an act of conforming to something established (as law or fashion) : COMPLIANCE, ACQUIESCENCE **3 a** : religious or ecclesiastical compliance; *esp* : compliance with usages of the Church of England **b** : action in accordance with some specified standard or authority : OBEDIENCE, SUBMISSION — used with *to* ⟨~ to duty⟩ **4** : uninterrupted depositional sequence (as of beds or strata of rock) : CONFORMABILITY — compare UNCONFORMITY

conformly *adv* [ME *conformely*, fr. *conforme* conformable + *-ly* — more at CONFORM] *obs* : CONFORMABLY

conforms *pres 3d sing of* CONFORM

con·for·ta·ble \kōⁿfȯrtabl(ᵊ), -b(lə)\ *n*, *pl* **confortables** \"\ [F, fr. *confortable* comfortable, fr. E *comfortable*] : an all-upholstered chair of the early 19th century

con for·za \kän'fȯrt(,)sä, kōn-, -,sə\ *adv* [It] : with force — used as a direction in music

con·found *in senses other than 4* kən'faùnd *also* (')kän¦f-; *in sense 4* (')kän¦f- *sometimes* kən'f-\ *vt* -ED/-ING/-S [ME *confounden*, fr. OF *confondre*, fr. L *confundere* to pour together, confuse, fr. *com-* + *fundere* to pour — more at FOUND] **1** *archaic* : to bring to ruin : DESTROY **a** : to inflict defeat on (as an army or adversary) **b** : to cause to fail : BAFFLE ⟨~ their politics, frustrate their knavish tricks —Henry Carey⟩ **2 a** : SPOIL, CORRUPT ⟨their native speech was not ~*ed* with a vulgarized spoken Latin —M.W.Baldwin⟩ **b** *obs* : CONSUME, WASTE ⟨he did ~ the best part of an hour in changing hardiment with great Glendower —Shak.⟩ **3 a** : to put to shame : DISCOMFIT, ABASH ⟨the influence of . . . El Greco . . . lay dormant for centuries and rose to ~ the critics of later times —Bernard Smith⟩ **b** : to refute esp. by argument or demonstration : OVERTHROW ⟨this new arm of science may corroborate or ~ the theories of the universe—David England⟩ **4** : to send to perdition : DAMN — used as a mild imprecation ⟨~ it⟩ **5** : to throw (a person) into confusion : strike with amazement : STUPEFY, PERPLEX, CONFUSE ⟨attacks which ~*ed* opponents with bewildering reverses [of direction] —*Springfield (Mass.) Union*⟩ **6** : to ignore, overlook, or fail to discern a difference between (two or more things) : mistake (one thing) for another : CONFUSE, MINGLE ⟨they implored Charles not to ~ the innocent with the guilty —T.B.Macaulay⟩ **7** : to cause or to increase disorder in (an existing situation) ⟨ruin upon ruin, rout on rout, confusion worse ~*ed* —John Milton⟩ ⟨to divide Europe as the politicians have done is to invite confusion and to divide the frontier as the Europeans did is to ~ the confusion —W.P.Webb⟩ **syn** see PUZZLE

¹confounded *adj* [ME, fr. past part. of *confounden*] **1** : CONFUSED, PERPLEXED ⟨a cloudy and ~ philosopher⟩ **2** : DAMNED, CURSED, BLASTED — used as a mild imprecation ⟨this ~ weather⟩ or as an intensive ⟨close that ~ window⟩

²confounded *adv* : CONFOUNDEDLY

con·found·ed·ly *adv* : VERY, EXTREMELY, ANNOYINGLY ⟨so ~ without a clear moral purpose —Alfred Kazin⟩

con·found·ed·ness *n* -ES : the quality or state of being confounded

confounding *adj* [fr. pres. part. of *confound*] : that confounds : CONFUSING, PUZZLING — **con·found·ing·ly** *adv*

confraction *n* -S [MF & LL; MF *confraction*, fr. LL *confraction-*, *confractio*, fr. L *confractus* (past part. of *confringere* to break in pieces, fr. *com-* + *-fringere*, fr. *frangere* to break) + *-ion-*, *-io* -ion — more at BREAK] *obs* : breaking in pieces : CRUSHING

confrairy *n* -ES [MF *confrarie*, fr. ML *confratria*, fr. *confratr-*, *confrater* + L *-ia* -y] *obs* : CONFRATERNITY

con·fra·ter \kən'frād-ə(r), (')kän¦f-\ *n*, *pl* **confraters** \-ə(r)z\ *or* **con·fra·tres** \-ᵊ·ᵊ,trez, -es\ [ML, fr. L *com-* + *frater* brother — more at BROTHER] **1** : a member of a confraternity **2** : an associate of a monastery or monastic group who received certain privileges (as a share in prayers) without corresponding responsibilities (as rigorous life or restrictive vows)

con·fraternity \¦kän+\ *n* -ES [ME *confraternite*, fr. MF *confraternité*, fr. ML *confraternitat-*, *confraternitas*, fr. *confrater*, after L *frater* brother: *fraternitat-*, *fraternitas* brotherhood, fraternity] **1** : a society or body of men or of men and women united for a religious, charitable or other purpose or in a profession **2** : fraternal union or communion

con·fraternization \(¦)kän+\ *n* -S [*com-* + *fraternization*] : fraternization together : recognition as a brother

con·frere \(')kōⁿ,fre(ə)r, -fra(ə)r, 'kän,f-, 'kȯn,f-\ *n* -S [ME, colleague, fellow member esp. of a confraternity, fr. MF, fr. OF (trans. of ML *confrater*), fr. *com-* + *frere* brother, fr. L *frater*] : COLLEAGUE : a fellow worker (as in a profession or in a field of study); *broadly* : FELLOW, COMRADE

con·fre·rie \kōⁿfrarē\ *n*, *pl* **confreries** \-ē(z)\ [F *confrérie*, fr. OF *confrerie*, alter. (influenced by *frere*) of *confrarie*] : BROTHERHOOD, ASSOCIATION; *often* : those sharing a common interest or quality

con·fri·ca·tion \,känfrə'kāshən\ *n* -S [ME *confricacioun*, fr. LL *confrication-*, *confricatio*, fr. L *confricatus* (past part. of *confricare* to rub vigorously, fr. *com-* + *fricare* to rub) + *-ion-*, *-io* -ion — more at FRICTION] *archaic* : a rubbing together : FRICTION

¹con·front \kən'frənt\ *vt* -ED/-ING/-S [MF *confronter* to confront, border on, fr. ML *confrontare* to bound, fr. L *com-* + ML *-frontare*, fr. L *front-*, *frons* forehead, front) — more at BRINK] **1 a** : to stand facing or opposing esp. in challenge, defiance, or accusation : FACE : stand up to ⟨enemies ~*ing* one another⟩ ⟨~ an accuser in court⟩ **b** : to face (something dangerous or dreaded) without flinching or avoiding ⟨the test of a free society is its capacity to ~, rather than evade, the vital questions of choice —J.M.Burns⟩ **2 a** : to put or bring face to face : compel (a person) to face, take account of, or endure — usu. used with *with* ⟨~ a reader with statistics⟩ **b** : OFFEND, AFFRONT, OPPRESS — used with *with* or *by* ⟨~*ed* by . . . novels . . . frank to the point of immodesty —M.D.Geismar⟩ ⟨poor culprits . . . ~*ed* with law Latin —R.M.Weaver⟩ **3 a** : MEET, ENCOUNTER ⟨recurrent phenomena . . . can always . . . be ~*ed* experimentally —A.C.Danto⟩ **b** : to stand before or in the way of ⟨the hardships and problems ~*ing* the pioneers⟩ **4** : to set in opposition for comparison : COMPARE ⟨conclusions which can be ~*ed* with experience —Alfred Einstein⟩ **syn** see MEET

²confront *n* -S *obs* : CONFRONTING, FACING, AFFRONT

con·front·al \kən'frəntᵊl\ *n* -S : CONFRONTATION

con·fron·ta·tion \,kän(,)frən'tāshən\ *n* -S [F, fr. ML *confrontation-*, *confrontatio* comparison, boundary, fr. *confrontatus* (past part. of *confrontare* to bound) + L *-ion-*, *-io* -ion] : the act of confronting : the state of being confronted : MEETING, OPPOSITION, COMPARISON; *specif* : the bringing face to face of an accused person and his accusing witnesses — used esp. in the phrase *right of confrontation*

con·front·ment \kən'frəntmənt\ *n* -S **1** : CONFRONTATION **2** *obs* **a** : FACE, ASPECT **b** : AFFRONT

¹con·fu·cian \kən'fyüshən\ *n* -S *usu cap* [*Confucius* †ab479 B.C. Chin. philosopher + E *-an*, n. suffix] : a follower of the Chinese philosopher Confucius : an adherent of Confucianism

²confucian \"\ *adj*, *usu cap* [*Confucius* + E *-an*, adj. suffix] : of or relating to Confucius or his teaching or followers

con·fu·cian·ism \-,nizəm\ *n* -S *usu cap* : the system of teachings of Confucius and his disciples characterized by central emphasis on the practice and cultivation of the cardinal virtues of filial piety, kindness, righteousness, propriety, intelligence, and faithfulness that historically has formed the basis of much of Chinese ethics, education, statecraft, and religion

con·fu·cian·ist \-,nəst\ *adj*, *usu cap* : CONFUCIAN

con fuo·co \kän'fwȯ(,)kō, kōn-, ᵊ,fü'ō-\ *adv* [It, with fire] : FIERILY, IMPETUOUSLY — used as a direction in music

con·fus·able \kən'fyüzəbəl\ *adj* : capable of being confused — **con·fus·a·bly** \-blē\ *adv*

¹confuse *adj* [ME *confus*, fr. MF] *obs* : CONFUSED

²con·fuse \kən'fyüz\ *vb* -ED/-ING/-S [back-formation fr. *confused*] *vt* **1** *archaic* : to bring to ruin : ROUT **2 a** : to make embarrassed or embarrassed : ABASH, DISCONCERT, FLUSTER **b** : to make unclear in mind or purpose : MISLEAD, BEWILDER, PERPLEX : throw off **3 a** : to dull or make indistinct the outlines or separate elements of (as a picture, pattern, or narrative) : BLUR ⟨~ the issue in a debate⟩ **b** : to throw into disorder : jumble together : CONFOUND ⟨a . . . wind *confused* the waters —Virginia Woolf⟩ ⟨~ accounts⟩ **c** : to mistake (one person or thing) for another : fail to distinguish between (two or more separate entities) ⟨expression may be too easily *confused* with communication —Havelock Ellis⟩ ~ *vi* : to fail to discriminate ⟨I always ~ between him and Orion —W.F. de Morgan⟩

con·fused \-zd\ *adj* [ME, fr. MF *confus* confused (fr. L *confusus*, past part. of *confundere* to pour together, confuse) + ME *-ed* — more at CONFOUND] **1** : PERPLEXED, DISCONCERTED **2** : mingled so as to be indistinguishable ⟨a ~ shouting⟩ : DISORDERED, MUDDLED ⟨a ~ sea⟩ — **con·fus·ed·ly** \-zədlē, -li\ *adv* — **con·fused·ness** \-zədnəs, -z(d)n-\ *n* -S

confused flour beetle *n* [so called fr. its being confused with the red flour beetle (*Tribolium castaneum*)] : a cosmopolitan beetle (*Tribolium confusum*) that feeds both as larva and adult chiefly on damaged grain — called also *bran bug*

con·fus·ing·ly *adv* [*confusing*, adj. (fr. pres. part. of *confuse*) + *-ly*] : in a confusing way

con·fu·sio bo·no·rum \kən¦fyüz(h)ē,ōbə'nōrəm\ *n* [NL, confusion of goods] : COMMIXTURE 3

con·fu·sion \kən'fyüzhən\ *n* -S [ME, fr. OF, fr. L *confusion-*, *confusio*, fr. *confusus* + *-ion-*, *-io* -ion] **1** : OVERTHROW, DEFEAT, RUIN, DESTRUCTION ⟨the defeat and ~ of Carthage in the war with Rome⟩ ⟨~ to such a tyrant king⟩ **2 a** : a state of being discomfited, disconcerted, chagrined, or embarrassed esp. at some blunder or check ⟨his sister [was] overcome with ~ and unable to lift up her eyes —Jane Austen⟩ **b** : state of being confused mentally : lack of certainty, orderly thought, or power to distinguish, choose, or act decisively : PERPLEXITY ⟨slowly emerging from the mental ~ which followed the fall —Havelock Ellis⟩ ⟨present intellectual ~ and moral chaos of the world —John Dewey⟩ **3 a** : an act of confusing, of mixing, pouring, blending, or heaping together in disorder with identities and distinctions blended ⟨the ~ of tongues at the tower of Babel⟩ ⟨a ~ of history and poetry in his work⟩ **b** : an act of mistaking one thing for another, of failing to note distinctions, and of falsely identifying ⟨a formal ~ of poetry and painting —Irving Babbitt⟩ ⟨~ between public and private morality —D.W.Brogan⟩ **4** : a situation or condition marked by lack of order, system, arrangement : an unclear welter or muddle : an utter disorder ⟨a luxuriant crop of very long hair which . . . got itself into great ~ —W.H.Hudson⟩ ⟨the ~ of hills typical of glacial regions —*Amer. Guide Series: Minn.*⟩ ⟨the dark ~ of German history —A.L.Guérard⟩ ⟨the long uncertainty and bloody ~ that attended the breakdown of the Roman Empire —Lewis Mumford⟩ **5** *law* **a** : a merging of two rights in one or of two property or really antagonistic interests in one **b** : COMMIXTURE 3 **c** *Roman & civil law* : extinction of an obligation by a person acquiring the right from which the obligation arose

syn DISARRAY, DISORDER, CLUTTER, JUMBLE, PI, SNARL, MUDDLE, CHAOS: CONFUSION is a rather general term suggesting any mixing, blending, adding together that blurs identities and distinctions or any result of such mixing. DISARRAY suggests a disarranging — a breaking away from order, sequence, form, or discipline ⟨the *disarray* in which the Germans found themselves . . . following on the capitulation of their Italian ally —*Times Lit. Supp.*⟩ DISORDER indicates a want of order through wonted neglect of it or through some break or interruption in orderly processes or arrangements ⟨our last chance to substitute order for *disorder*, government for anarchy —E.B.White⟩ ⟨standing between the older America and the new, with the foundations disintegrating under his feet, he confused the *disorder* in his own mind with the disorder in the external world —V.L.Parrington⟩ CLUTTER implies a confused litter of the miscellaneous and adventitious, impeding free activity or clear perception ⟨what a mess this set is in! if there's one thing I hate . . . it's *clutter* —Edna St. V. Millay⟩ ⟨this essay clears one irrelevant topic from the *clutter* of symbolist criticism —*Times Lit. Supp.*⟩ JUMBLE suggests a heaping together of many incongruous things so that free use, enjoyment, or perception of any individual item is made difficult ⟨the ruptured ambulance convoy . . . a *jumble* of overturned wagons, spilled pungent powders —Irwin Shaw⟩ ⟨a vast *jumble* of incoherent erudition on which he drew for purely poetic effects —T.S.Eliot⟩ PI, in this sense from printing, sometimes designates a confusion or disarrangement of small items hard to classify or order like miscellaneous type. SNARL is likely to suggest a knotted entanglement hard to unravel, resolve, or sort out ⟨parachute cords in a *snarl*⟩ ⟨a *snarl* of traffic at the bridge entrance⟩ MUDDLE suggests a litter or welter so extreme that making order is impossible and hence a situation marked by bungling, uncertainty, and feeble, dubious, ill-directed expediency ⟨as . . . they all had to live in one small room and the kitchen, the place usually looked a *muddle* —Nigel Balchin⟩ ⟨the effort to make a distinction . . . produced such a *muddle* that it was dropped —G.B.Shaw⟩ CHAOS suggests uttermost confusion, with no order, arrangement, regularity, sequence, or predictability; it may suggest primordial formlessness or complete disintegration ⟨disorder to the point of *chaos* —B.N.Cardozo⟩ ⟨back not merely to the dark ages but from cosmos to *chaos* —B.M.Baruch⟩ ⟨such social *chaos* . . . as to make civilization impossible —Blanton Fortson⟩ **syn** see in addition COMMOTION

con·fu·sion·al \-zhənᵊl, -zhnəl\ *adj* : characterized by mental confusion

con·fut·able \kən'fyüd-əbəl\ *adj* [*confute* + *-able*] : capable of being confuted

con·fu·ta·tion \,kän(,)fyü'tāshən, -,fyə'-\ *n* -S [L *confutation-*, *confutatio*, fr. *confutatus* (past part. of *confutare*) + *-ion-*, *-io* -ion] **1** : the act or process of confuting : REFUTATION **2** : something that confutes (as an argument)

con·fu·ta·tive \kən'fyüd-əd-iv\ *adj* [L *confutatus* + E *-ive*] : adapted, designed, or tending to confute

con·fu·ta·tor \'känfyü,tād-ə(r)\ *n* -S [LL, fr. L *confutatus* + *-or*] : one that confutes

¹con·fute \kən'fyüt, *usu* -üd-+V\ *vt* -ED/-ING/-S [L *confutare*, fr. *com-* + *-futare* to beat — more at BEAT] **1** : to overwhelm by argument : refute conclusively : OVERCOME, SILENCE ⟨rugged individualism . . . is . . . *confuted* in our social legislation and social habits —*N. Y. Times*⟩ **2** *obs* : to bring to naught : CONFOUND **syn** see DISPROVE

²confute *also* **confutement** *n* -S *obs* : CONFUTATION

cong *abbr* **1** congius **2** congregation **3** congress; congressional

con·ga \'käŋgə\ *n* -S [AmerSp, fr. Sp, fem. of *congo* of the Congo, fr. *Congo*, region in Africa] **1** : a Cuban dance of African origin involving three steps followed by a kick and performed by a group usu. in single file following a leader **2** : a tall narrow-headed bass drum beaten with the hands and used to provide the rhythm for the conga dance

con·ga·ree \'käŋgə¦rē\ *n*, *pl* **congaree** *or* **congarees** *usu cap* [native name] **1** : a Siouan people in the Congaree river valley, So. Carolina **2** : a member of the Congaree people

con·gé \kōⁿzhā, 'kän,jā\ *n* -S [F, fr. OF *congié* — more at CONGEE] **1 a** : a formal permission to depart (as from one in authority) ⟨you've got your ~, and my blessing on ye —George Meredith⟩ **b** [F, fr. OF *congié*] : DISMISSAL ⟨she was given her ~ with a good deal less in the way of salary than she was entitled to —Susan Ertz⟩ ⟨he got by way of ~ a punch in the nose⟩ **2** : a ceremonious bow made as a sign of recognition or at taking one's leave ⟨shuffling forward with a hundred apish *congés* —Sir Walter Scott⟩ **3** : LEAVE-TAKING, FAREWELL ⟨we may as well make our ~*s* here . . . as under the porter's nose —A.T.Quiller-Couch⟩ ⟨the departing spirit saying his ~ dimmer and fainter as he leaves our stupidities behind —Christopher Morley⟩ **4** [F, fr. OF *congié*] *archit* : a molding of concave quarter-round profile tangent to a vertical surface and followed by a fillet parallel to that surface — see MOLDING illustration

con·geal \kən'jēl, *esp bef pause or cons* -ēəl\ *vb* -ED/-ING/-S [ME *congelen*, fr. MF *congeler*, fr. L *congelare*, fr. *com-* + *gelare* to freeze — more at COLD] *vt* **1** : to change from a fluid to a solid state by or as if by cold ⟨~*ed* the water into ice⟩ : FREEZE ⟨tundra ~*ed* forever by the arctic cold⟩ **2 a** : to make (a liquid) viscid or of a consistency like jelly : CURDLE, COAGULATE **b** *obs* : to make (a liquid) solid or crystalline **3** : to make rigid or inflexible : freeze into a pattern or system ⟨~*ing* the speculations of Aristotle into authoritarian dogma⟩ : make immobile : PARALYZE ⟨a density of two hundred people to the acre would even further ~ traffic —Lewis Mumford⟩ ~ *vi* **1** : to grow hard, stiff, or thick from cold or other causes : FREEZE, COAGULATE ⟨oil ~*s* in cold weather⟩ **2 a** *of a sentiment* : to lose all warmth ⟨his passion for the ballerina soon ~*ed*⟩ **b** : to assume a fixed, rigid, or unchanging form or character ⟨saw . . . factions cleaving classes and classes ~*ing* into castes —Will Durant⟩ ⟨thought lost its vivacity, ~*ing* into a closed system⟩

con·geal·ment \-lmənt\ *n* -s **1** : the act or action of congealing ⟨the rapid ~ of lava⟩ ⟨a tendency toward ~ of ideas —J.B.Oakes⟩ **2** : matter that has congealed ⟨a crusty ~ of frost⟩

[1]con·gee \ˈkän(ˌ)jē, kənˈjē\ *vb* **congeed; congeed; congeeing; congees** [ME *congien*, fr. MF *congier*, fr. *congié*] *vt*, *obs* : to grant permission to depart : DISMISS ~ *vi* [[2]congee] **1** *now dial* : to take one's leave ceremoniously ⟨I have *congeed* with the magistrates⟩ **2** : to make a ceremonious bow ⟨rubbing servile hands and ~*ing*⟩

[2]con·gee \ˈkän(ˌ)jē\ *n* -s [ME *congie*, fr. MF *congié*, fr. L *commeatus* going back and forth, leave of absence, furlough, fr. *commeatus*, past part. of *commeare* to go back and forth, frequent, fr. *com-* + *meare* to go — more at PERMEATE] : CONGÉ

[3]con·gee \ˈkänˌjē\ *n* -s [Tamil *kañci*] **1** : the water in which rice has been boiled and which is used esp. in India for starching clothes or for invalids' diet **2** *China* : rice or millet gruel

con·ge·la·tion \ˌkänjəˈlāshən\ *n* -s [ME, fr. MF or L; MF *congelation*, fr. L *congelation-*, *congelatio*, fr. *congelatus* (past part. of *congelare* to freeze) + *-ion-*, *-io* -ion] **1** : the action or process of alteration (as by freezing) from a fluid to a solid or semisolid state; *also* : the product of such alteration **2** : the act, process, or an instance of making numb, hard, or dead by freezing

con·ge·la·tive \ˈkänjəˌlād·iv, kənˈjelәd·iv\ *adj* [MF *congelatif*, fr. *congeler* to congeal + *-atif* -ative] : tending to congeal : CONGEALING

con·gel·i·fract \kənˈjeləˌfrakt\ *n* -s [*congeli-* (fr. L *congelare* to freeze) + *-fract* (fr. L *fractus*, past part. of *frangere* to break) — more at BREAK] : a rock fragment split off by frost action

con·gel·i·frac·tion \kənˌjeləˈfrakshən\ *n* -s [*congeli-* (fr. L *congelare*) + *fraction* (breaking)] : splitting of the soil by freezing and thawing — compare CONGELITURBATION

con·gel·i·tur·bate \kənˌjeləˈtərbət, -ˌbāt\ *n* -s [*congeli-* (fr. L *congelare*) + *-turbate* (fr. L *turbatus*, past part. of *turbare* to disturb) — more at TURBID] : earth material disturbed by frost action and usu. appearing as a rubble coarser than the underlying material

con·gel·i·tur·ba·tion \-(ˌ)tərˈbāshən\ *n* -s [*congeli-* (fr. L *congelare*) + *-turbation* (fr. L *turbation-*, *turbatio* disturbance, fr. *turbatus* + *-ion-*, *-io* -ion)] : the churning or heaving of the soil by freezing and thawing — compare CONGELIFRACTION

con·ge·na·tor \ˈkänjəˌnād·ə(r), kənˈjenəd·-\ *n* -s [by alter. (influence of L *-ator*, suffix denoting an agent) — more at -OR] : CONGENER

[1]con·ge·ner \ˈkänjənə(r), kənˈjēn-, (ˈ)känˈjēn-\ *also* **co·ge·ner** \ˈkōjən-, (ˈ)kōˈjēn-\ *n* -s [L, of the same race or kind, fr. *com-* + *gener-*, *genus* birth, kind, race — more at KIN] : one that bears relationship to another: as **a** : a member of the same genus as another plant or animal ⟨the lion and its smaller ~*s*, the lynx and domestic cat⟩ **b** : a person or thing resembling or suggesting another in nature, character, or action ⟨the living townspeople and their ~*s* in the churchyard⟩ ⟨the New England private schools and their ~*s* west of the Alleghenies —Oliver La Farge⟩ **c** : a chemical substance related to another (as a derivative or an element in the same group of the periodic table as another element) **d** : a secondary product (as an aldehyde or ester) retained in an alcoholic beverage (as whiskey) and significant in the determination of the final characteristics of the beverage — called also *congeneric* **e** : [2]COGNATE b

[2]congener \"\ *adj* [L] : CONGENERIC

[1]con·generic \ˌkän+\ *adj* [*com-* + L *gener-*, *genus* + E *-ic*] **1** : having to do with : RELATED ⟨war and its ~ industrial problems⟩ **2** : belonging to the same genus ⟨~ species⟩ **3** : belonging to the congeners of an alcoholic beverage ⟨~ substances⟩

[2]congeneric \"\ *n* -s : [1]CONGENER d

con·ge·ner·ous \kənˈjēnərəs, -jen-, (ˈ)känˈj-\ *adj* [L *congener* + E *-ous*] : akin in nature, origin, or character : RELATED, CONGENERIC

con·ge·nial \kənˈjēnyəl, -ēnēəl\ *adj* [*com-* + *genius* (person's disposition or inclination) + *-al*] **1** : having the same nature, disposition, or tastes : suited to one another : KINDRED ⟨two ~ spirits, united . . . by mutual confidence and reciprocal virtues —T.L.Peacock⟩ **2** *obs* **a** : CONGENITAL **b** : of the same genus or kind : having the same origin **3 a** : appropriate and agreeable : existing or associated together harmoniously ⟨the free system of government . . . is . . . ~ with reason, with common sense —James Madison⟩ ⟨group of ~ buildings —Lewis Mumford⟩ **b** : PLEASANT, ATTRACTIVE ⟨very ~ music, without affectation or pretense —Irving Kolodin⟩; *often* : agreeably suited (as to one's nature, tastes, or outlook) ⟨found the atmosphere of the village ~ and settled down there⟩ **c** : characterized by friendly sociability : GENIAL ⟨found in the master of the inn a most ~ host⟩ **4** : COMPATIBLE 2c(1), 2c(2) **syn** see CONSONANT

con·ge·nial·i·ty \kənˌjēnēˈaləd·ē, -ˌjēnˈya-, -ətē, -i\ *n* -ES : the quality or state of being congenial : affinity of spirit or temperament ⟨the ~ of Stoicism to the Roman mind —T.S.Eliot⟩ : mutual agreeableness ⟨an easy ~ between officers and men⟩

con·ge·nial·ly \kənˈjēnyəlē, -ēnēə-, -li\ *adv* : in a congenial manner

con·ge·nial·ness *n* -ES : CONGENIALITY

con·gen·i·tal \kənˈjenəd·ᵊl, -ətᵊl\ *adj* [L *congenitus* congenital (fr. *com-* + *genitus*, past part. of *gignere* to beget, bring forth) + E *-al* — more at KIN] **1** : existing at or dating from birth ⟨~ idiocy⟩ ⟨~ malformations⟩ : belonging to or associated with from birth : INNATE ⟨~ good health⟩ : constituting an essential characteristic : INHERENT ⟨the ~ State Department fear of newsmen —A.H.Vandenberg †1951⟩ : from birth or by nature ⟨a ~ liar⟩ **2** : acquired during development in the uterus and not through heredity — compare ACQUIRED, FAMILIAL, HEREDITARY **syn** see INNATE

congenital amputation *n* : the prenatal loss or nondevelopment of a projecting body part (as a foot or arm) esp. through constriction of the developing structure

con·gen·i·tal·ly \-ᵊlē, -ᵊli\ *adv* : in a congenital manner : from birth ⟨~ deaf⟩ : by nature or disposition ⟨~ incapable of telling the truth⟩ ⟨~ skeptical⟩

congenite *adj* [L *congenitus*] *obs* : CONGENITAL

con·ger \ˈkäŋgə(r)\ *n* [ME *congre*, *cunger*, fr. OF *congre*, fr. L *congr-*, *conger*, fr. Gk *gongros*; akin to ON *kǫkkr* ball, L *gingiva* gum of the mouth, Gk *gongros* excrescence on trees, *gongylos* round, Lith *gunga* hump, lump, ball, and perh. to MLG *kinke* kink; basic meaning: lump] **1** -s : CONGER EEL **2** *cap* [NL *Congr-*, *Conger*, fr. L] : a genus consisting of the typical conger eels — compare LEPTOCEPHALUS

con·ger·ee \ˌkäŋgəˈrē\ *n* -s [by alter.] : CONGER EEL

conger eel *n* **1 a** : a large strictly marine entirely scaleless eel (*Conger conger*) of a length sometimes as great as eight feet that is an important food fish of Europe and is found on the Atlantic coast of America and on the coasts of Asia and Africa **b** : any other member of the family Congridae some of which (as *Conger caudilimbata*) occur in the West Indies and other warm regions **2** : a California moray (*Gymnothorax mordax*)

con·ge·ries \ˈkänjə(ˌ)rēz, -ˌriz *sometimes* kənˈji(ˌ)rēz *or* -ˈjiriz *or* -ˈjirēˌēz *or* -ˈjerēˌēz\ *also* **con·ge·rie** \ˈkänjə(ˌ)rē, -ˌri\ *or* **con·ge·ry** \ˈkänjəˌrē, -ri\ *n*, *pl* **congeries** *like sing.* CONGERIES\ [*congeries* fr. L, fr. *congerere* to bring together; *congery* back-formation fr. *congeries*, pl.] : a collection or mass of entities (as objects, forces, individuals, ideas) : AGGREGATION, AGGLOMERATION ⟨a small ~ of ranches —Bernard De Voto⟩ ⟨society is not a system but a ~ of impermanent groupings —N.N.Foote⟩

conger pike *n* : a fierce large silvery scaleless eel (*Muraenesox cinereus*) with a pikelike head and numerous strong canines that is widespread and abundant in the tropical Indian and Pacific oceans and esteemed as food in adjacent lands

[1]con·gest \kənˈjest\ *vb* -ED/-ING/-S [L *congestus*, past part. of *congerere* to bring together, fr. *com-* + *gerere* to bear, carry — more at CAST] *vt* **1** *obs* : to gather into a mass : COLLECT, AMASS **2** : to overcrowd, overburden, or fill to excess so as to obstruct (as movement) or hinder (as the functioning of an organ) : CLOG, CHOKE ⟨convoys ~*ed* all arterial highways⟩ ⟨the illness ~*ed* his lungs⟩ : concentrate esp. by constricting or crowding in a small or narrow space ⟨motor transportation . . . has succeeded the railroad as the most powerful tool for either distributing or ~*ing* the population —Lewis Mumford⟩ ~ *vi* : to crowd or mass together (as in a small or narrow space) ⟨clutched each other and ~*ed* in hard knots —Robert Hazel⟩

[2]con·gest \ˈkänˌjest\ *n* -s *Irish* : an inhabitant of a congested district

con·gest·ed \kənˈjestəd\ *adj* [fr. past part. of *congest*] **1** : containing an overaccumulation of blood : HYPEREMIC ⟨~ mucous membrane⟩ **2 a** : OVERCROWDED ⟨~ slums⟩ ⟨the road was crowded, but as yet far from ~ —H.G.Wells⟩ **b** : encumbered or made turgid or difficult by an excess (as of words or ideas) ⟨a ~ prose⟩ ⟨~ reasoning⟩ **3** : set close together ⟨~ stamens⟩ ⟨~ spores⟩

con·ges·tion \kənˈjes(h)chən\ *n* -s [MF or L; MF, fr. L *congestion-*, *congestio*, fr. *congestus* + *-ion-*, *-io* -ion] **1** *obs* : ACCUMULATION, GATHERING, HEAP **2** : a condition of overcrowding ⟨traffic ~⟩ or overburdening ⟨the result was complete mental ~ and overwork —Herbert Read⟩ : an excessive accumulation ⟨his face went purple with the ~ of language which couldn't get out —R.P.Warren⟩; *specif* : an overaccumulation of blood in the blood vessels of an organ or part whether natural or artificially induced (as for therapeutic purposes)

con·ges·tive \-estiv\ *adj* : having to do with congestion

congestive heart failure *n* : heart failure in which the heart is unable to maintain an adequate circulation of blood in the tissues of the body or to pump out the venous blood returned to it by the venous circulation — compare CORONARY FAILURE

con·gi·ary \ˈkänjēˌerē\ *n* -ES [L *congiarium*, fr. *congius* + *-arium* -ary] : a present or largess (as of corn, wine, or oil) made in ancient Rome to the soldiers or the people

con·gi·o·pod·i·dae \ˌkänjē(ˌ)ōˈpädəˌdē\ *n pl*, *cap* [NL, fr. *Congiopodus*, type genus (prob. irreg. fr. NL *Conger* + Gk *pod-*, *pous* foot) + *-idae* — more at CONGER, FOOT] : a small family (type genus *Congiopodus*) of marine fishes (order Scleroparei) of the tropical southern hemisphere having a compressed elongated body, a pronounced snout, a small protractile mouth, and a head partly covered with bony plates

con·gi·us \ˈkänjēəs\ *n*, *pl* **con·gii** \-jēˌī\ [ME, fr. L, prob. modif. of Gk *konchos* conch (also, a liquid measure); akin to Gk *konchē* conch — more at CONCH] **1** : an ancient Roman unit of liquid capacity equal to ⅛ amphora or 0.84 U.S. gallon **2** *pharmacy* : GALLON — abbr. *cong* or *C*

conglaciate *vb* -ED/-ING/-S [L *conglaciatus*, past part. of *conglaciare*, fr. *com-* + *glaciare* to turn into ice, fr. *glacies* ice — more at GLACIER] *obs* : to turn into ice : CONGEAL

[1]con·glo·bate \kənˈglōˌbāt, ˈkän,g-, ˈkäŋ,g-\ *vb* -ED/-ING/-S [L *conglobatus*, past part. of *conglobare*, fr. *com-* + *globare* to conglobe, fr. *globus* globe — more at CLIP] : to form in a round mass : CONGLOBE

[2]con·glo·bate \kənˈglōbət, kän-, -ˌbāt; ˈkäŋglōˌbāt, ˈkäŋg-\ *adj* [L *conglobatus*] : collected into or forming a rounded mass or ball

con·glo·ba·tion \ˌkäŋglōˈbāshən, -äŋg-\ *n* -s [L *conglobation-*, *conglobatio*, fr. *conglobatus* + *-ion-*, *-io* -ion] **1** : the act or action of forming into a round mass **2** : a rounded mass

con·globe \kənˈglōb, kän-\ *vb* -ED/-ING/-S [L *conglobare*] : to form into a ball ⟨*conglobed* clouds⟩

[1]con·glom·er·ate \kənˈgläm(ə)rət, *usu* -əd·+V\ *adj* [L *conglomeratus*, past part. of *conglomerare* to roll together, fr. *com-* + *glomerare* to wind into a ball, fr. *glomer-*, *glomus* ball — more at CLAM] **1** : made up of parts from various sources or composed of various kinds ⟨as ~ a language as English⟩ ⟨the ~ peoples of New England⟩ **2** : densely clustered ⟨~ flowers⟩ **3** *zool* : irregularly grouped in spots ⟨~ eyes⟩

[2]con·glom·er·ate \-məˌrāt, *usu* -ād·+V\ *vb* -ED/-ING/-S [L *conglomeratus*] *vt* : to gather or collect into a mass or coherent whole : AMASS, ACCUMULATE ~ *vi* : to form into a mass or coherent whole : GATHER ⟨numbers of dull people *conglomerated* round her —Virginia Woolf⟩

[3]conglomerate *like* [1]CONGLOMERATE\ *n* -s [[1]*conglomerate*] : a mixture gathered from various sources : a composite mass ⟨a ~ of houses⟩ ⟨a shoddy ~ of people⟩; *specif* : clastic sedimentary rock composed of rounded fragments varying from small pebbles to large boulders in a cement of calcareous material, iron oxide, silica, or hardened clay — compare AGGLOMERATE, BRECCIA

conglomerate

con·glom·er·at·ic \kənˌgläməˈrad·ik, ˌkän,g-\ *also* **con·glom·er·it·ic** \-ˈrid·ik\ *adj* [*conglomeratic* fr. [3]*conglomerate* + *-ic*; *conglomeritic* irreg. fr. [3]*conglomerate* + *-ic*] : of or relating to a conglomerate

con·glom·er·a·tion \kənˌgläməˈrāshən, ˌkän,g-\ *n* -s [LL *conglomeration-*, *conglomeratio*, fr. L *conglomeratus* + *-ion-*, *-io* -ion] : a conglomerating or state of being conglomerated : COLLECTION ⟨the slow ~ of detail⟩ : something that is conglomerated ⟨a showy ~ of flowers⟩ : a mixed coherent mass ⟨a ~ of antique cars⟩

con·glutin \kən, (ˈ)kän+\ *n* -s [ISV *com-* + *glutin*; orig. formed as G *konglutin*] *biochem* : a legumin from almonds and lupines

con·glu·ti·nant \kənˈglütᵊnənt, (ˈ)känˈg-\ *adj* [L *conglutinant-*, *conglutinans*, pres. part. of *conglutinare*] : causing to adhere : promoting adhesion (as between the lips of a wound)

con·glutinate \kən, kän+\ *vb* -ED/-ING/-S [L *conglutinatus*, past part. of *conglutinare* to glue together, fr. *com-* + *glutinare* to glue, fr. *glutin-*, *gluten* glue — more at GLUTEN] *vt* : to cause to cohere ~ *vi* : COHERE

con·glutination \kən, (ˌ)kän+\ *n* -s [MF, fr. L *conglutination-*, *conglutinatio*, fr. *conglutinatus* + *-ion-*, *-io* -ion] : the act or action of conglutinating or the consequent quality or state of being conglutinated: as **a** *med* : the union or establishment of continuity of parts — now used only of abnormal adhesion of contiguous surfaces **b** : a mass esp. of things glued together : AGGLUTINATION **c** *immunol* (1) : a reaction of agglutination and lysis brought about by addition of bovine serum to antibody-treated cells (2) : agglutination brought about by serum albumin or plasma proteins when added to cells coated with blocking antibody

con·glutinin \kən, (ˈ)kän+\ *n* -s [ISV *com-* + *glutinin*, fr. *glutin* + *-in*; orig. formed as G *konglutinin*] **1** : a heat-stable component of bovine serum that combines with red blood cells which have been treated with antibody and that causes rapid strong agglutination followed by lysis **2** : a substance or substances in blood plasma possibly identical with x-protein or perhaps merely a mixture of albumin and globulin that causes clumping when added to red blood cells that are combined with blocking antibody

[1]congo \ˈkäŋ(ˌ)gō\ *adj*, *usu cap* [fr. *Congo*, territory surrounding the Congo river, West Africa] : CONGOLESE

[2]congo \"\ *n* -ES [fr. *Congo*, territory surrounding the Congo river, West Africa] **1** [AmerF, prob. fr. *Congo* (territory)] : a ballroom dance of Haitian origin **2** *South* **a** : WATER MOCCASIN **b** : CONGO SNAKE **3** *usu cap* : CONGO COPAL **4** *or* **congo brown** *often cap C* : a dark grayish yellowish brown that is stronger and slightly yellower and darker than seal and slightly redder and darker than sepia brown — called also *Antwerp brown*, *asphaltum*, *bitumen*

[3]congo \"\ *n* -s *usu cap*, *var of* KONGO

congo buffalo *n*, *usu cap C* [*Congo*, territory surrounding the Congo river, West Africa] : a rather small reddish Cape buffalo (*Syncerus caffer nanus*) from equatorial central and west Africa sometimes regarded as a distinct species (*S. nanus*)

congo copal *or* **congo gum** *n*, *usu cap Congo* : a hard insoluble colorless to amber copal derived esp. from certain trees of the genus *Copaifera* but found chiefly as a fossil resin in the Congo and used in making varnish

congo dye *n*, *usu cap C* : any of a group of direct azo dyes most of which are derivatives of benzidine — see DYE table I

congo eel *n* **1** : CONGO SNAKE **2** : WRYMOUTH **3** : MUD EEL

congo floor fly *n*, *usu cap C* : a large yellowish brown fly (*Auchmeromyia luteola*) of tropical Africa related to the blowflies and having spiny nocturnal larvae that live in the earthen floors of native huts and come out at night to suck the blood of the occupants

congo floor maggot *n*, *usu cap C* : the larva of the Congo floor fly

congo jute *n*, *usu cap C*, *chiefly in the Belgian Congo* : ARAMINA

[1]con·go·lese \ˌkäŋgōˈlēz, -ēs\ *also* **con·go·ese** \-ŋ(ˌ)gōˈē-\ *adj*, *usu cap* [*congolese* modif. (influenced by *-ese*) of F *congolais*, irreg. fr. *Congo*; *congoese* fr. *Congo* + E *-ese*] **1** : of, relating to, or characteristic of the Congo region or either of the Congo republics in Africa **2** : of, relating to, or characteristic of the Congolese

[2]congolese \"\ *also* **congoese** \"\ *n*, *pl* **congolese** *also* **congoese** *usu cap* **1** : a native or inhabitant of the Congo region or of either of the Congo republics **2** : a language native to the Congo region

congo mahoe *n*, *usu cap C* : KENAF

congoni *var of* KONGONI

congo pea *n*, *usu cap C* [*Congo*, territory in West Africa] : PIGEON PEA

congo peacock *n*, *usu cap C* : AFROPAVO 2

congo pink *n*, *often cap C* : a grayish reddish orange that is redder, lighter, and stronger than Etruscan red or hyacinth red and deeper than Persian melon

congo red *n*, *usu cap C* [trans. of G *kongorot*] : an azo dye that is red in alkaline solution and blue in acid solution and is used chiefly as an indicator and as a biological stain — see DYE table I (under *Direct Red 28*)

congo root *n*, *usu cap C* : SAMPSON SNAKEROOT

congo rubber *n*, *usu cap C* : an African rubber derived from any of several woody vines of the genus *Landolphia*

congo rubine *or* **congo rubin** *n*, *usu cap C* : a direct azo dye used esp. for dyeing cotton, wool, and silk bluish red — see DYE table I (under *Direct Red 17*)

congo snake *n* : an elongated bluish black amphibian (*Amphiuma means*) of the southeastern U.S. that has two pairs of very short limbs each with two or three toes and attains a length of three feet — called also *blind eel*, *congo eel*, *lamper eel*

congo snake

congo tobacco *n*, *usu cap C* : HEMP 1

con·gou \ˈkäŋ(ˌ)gō, -gü\ *also* **con·go** \-gō\ *n* -s [prob. fr. Chin (Amoy) *kong-hu* expenditure of time and effort, pains taken (Pek *kung*[1]-*fu*[1])] : black tea from China

con·grat·u·lant \kənˈgrachələnt, *chiefly in substand speech* -ajə-\ *adj* [L *congratulant-*, *congratulans*, pres. part. of *congratulari*] : expressive of congratulation

con·grat·u·late \-ˌlāt, *usu* -ād·+V\ *vb* -ED/-ING/-S [L *congratulatus*, past part. of *congratulari* to wish joy, fr. *com-* + *gratulari* to wish joy, fr. *gratus* pleasing — more at GRACE] *vt* **1** : to express sympathetic pleasure to on account of success or good fortune : wish joy to : FELICITATE ⟨~ herself on finding a job⟩ ⟨~ the boy for keeping a cool head⟩ ⟨~ his son upon his graduation⟩ **2** *archaic* : to express sympathetic pleasure or satisfaction at **3** *obs* : SALUTE, GREET ~ *vi* **1** *archaic* : to rejoice together : express or feel sympathetic joy **2** : to present one's expressions of sympathetic pleasure at another's good fortune

con·grat·u·la·tion \-ˈlāshən\ *n* -s [MF or L; MF, fr. L *congratulation-*, *congratulatio*, fr. *congratulatus* + *-ion-*, *-io* -ion] **1** : the act of congratulating a person or body **2** : an expression of sympathetic pleasure : FELICITATION — used chiefly in pl. ⟨~*s* on our safe arrival⟩ **3** *obs* : a grateful expression of one's joy (as at his own good fortune) : REJOICING

con·grat·u·la·tor \-ˌlād·ə(r), -ātə-\ *n* -s : one that congratulates

con·grat·u·la·to·ry \-ləˌtōrē, -tȯr-, -ri\ *adj* [ML *congratulatorius*, fr. L *congratulatus* + *-orius* -ory] : expressing or conveying congratulations ⟨~ handshake⟩ ⟨~ telegram⟩

con gra·zia \känˈgrätsēə, kōn-\ *adv* [It, with grace] : with grace : GRACEFULLY — used as a direction in music

congree *vi* **congreed; congreed; congreeing; congrees** [prob. fr. *com-* + *gree* (agree)] *obs* : AGREE

con·greet \kənˈgrēt\ *vi* -ED/-ING/-S [*com-* + *greet*] *obs* : to greet mutually

con·gre·gant \ˈkäŋgrəgənt, -reg-\ *n* -s [L *congregant-*, *congregans*, pres. part. of *congregare*] : one that congregates with others; *specif* : a member of a congregation

[1]con·gre·gate \-ˌgāt, *usu* -ād·+V\ *vb* -ED/-ING/-S [ME *congregaten*, fr. L *congregatus*, past part. of *congregare*, fr. *com-* + *gregare* to collect, fr. *greg-*, *grex* flock — more at GREGARIOUS] *vt* : to collect together into a group, crowd, or assembly ⟨the captains *congregated* their men⟩ ~ *vi* : to come together, collect, or concentrate in a particular locality or group ⟨would not have been practical to ~ in cities unless the annual food supply was well assured —Owen & Eleanor Lattimore⟩ ⟨the young men *congregated* uneasily in impermanent groups —Irwin Shaw⟩ : become situated together or in proximity to each other ⟨on Schermerhorn Street ~ many charitable institutions —*Amer. Guide Series: N. Y. City*⟩ **syn** see GATHER

[2]con·gre·gate \-ˌgət *also* -ˌgāt, *usu* -d·+V\ *adj* [ME *congregat*, fr. L *congregatus*] **1** : COLLECTED, ASSEMBLED ⟨a host of ~ angels⟩ **2** : designed for, devoted to, or housing an undifferentiated group of persons, esp. one whose institutional treatment, care, or custody is provided for through mass facilities ⟨~ prison⟩ ⟨~ methods of care⟩

con·gre·ga·tion \-ˈgāshən\ *n* -s [ME *congregacioun*, fr. MF *congregation*, fr. L *congregation-*, *congregatio*, fr. *congregatus* + *-ion-*, *-io* -ion] **1 a** : an assembly of persons : GATHERING; *esp* : an assembly of persons met for the worship of God and for religious instruction : a body of people who habitually so meet **b** (1) *obs* : the whole number or body (2) : the whole body of Christians or an organized body of believers in a particular locality; *also* : SECT, DENOMINATION **c** : a collection or gathering of animals or things ⟨a foul and pestilent ~ of vapors —Shak.⟩ ⟨a great ~ of birds flew overhead⟩ **2** : the act or an instance of congregating or bringing together : the state of being congregated **3** [LL *congregation-*, *congregatio*, trans. of Heb *gāhāl*] : the sacred community or whole body of the Jewish people **4** *sometimes cap*, *Roman Catholicism* **a** : a company or order of religious persons under a common rule either with or without vows **b** : a permanent body or committee of cardinals to which is entrusted some department of the church business **c** : a group of monasteries forming a subdivision of an order which agree to unite in closer ties of discipline and doctrine **5** : a deliberative meeting of the governing body of an English university **6** *cap* : the Protestant party in Scotland at the time of the Reformation; *also* : a local body of this party **7** : the whole body of people of a settlement, town, or parish in those No. American colonies in which the Congregational Church was established

[1]con·gre·ga·tion·al \ˌ-ˈshənᵊl, -shnəl\ *adj* **1** : of or relating to or like a congregation : conducted or participated in by a congregation : connected with a particular congregation of worshipers ⟨~ singing⟩ **2** *usu cap* : belonging to Congregationalism or to Congregationalists : INDEPENDENT ⟨a *Congregational* church⟩ **3** : of or relating to congregationalism (sense 1) — **con·gre·ga·tion·al·ly** \-ᵊlē, -əlē, \li\ *adv*

[2]congregational \"\ *n* -s : CONGREGATIONALIST

congregational christian *adj*, *usu cap both Cs* : of or relating to a denominational union of churches effected in 1931 between the Congregational Church and the Christian Church

con·gre·ga·tion·al·ism \ˌ-ˈgāshənᵊlˌizəm, -shnəˌli-\ *n* -s **1** : a system of church government in which the local congregation has full control and final authority over church matters within its own area **2** *cap* : the faith and government of those evangelical and trinitarian churches that recognize the congregation of each local church as independent of all dictation in church matters within its own area and that trace their formal beginning to England

¹con·gre·ga·tion·al·ist \-shən°ləst, -shnəl-\ *n* -s **1** *usu cap* **:** one who belongs to a Congregational church **:** one who adheres to Congregationalism — compare INDEPENDENT **2 :** an adherent to or proponent of congregationalism (sense 1)

²congregationalist \\ *adj, usu cap* **:** of, sponsored by, characteristic of, or resembling a Congregational church or Congregationalism

congregationist *n* -s *usu cap, obs* **:** CONGREGATIONALIST 1

con·gre·ga·tive \'==,gād·iv\ *adj* [LL *congregativus*, fr. L *congregatus* + *-ivus* -ive — more at CONGREGATE] **:** tending to gather into or appeal to a group ⟨~ salesmen⟩ ⟨~ piety⟩

con·gre·ga·tor \-d·ə(r)\ *n* -s [LL, fr. L *congregatus* + *-or*] **:** one that congregates

¹con·gress \'käŋgrəs *also* 'kōŋ-, *chiefly in substand speech* -ŋr-\ *n* -ES [L *congressus*, fr. *congressus*, past part. of *congredi* to go or come together, fr. *com-* + *gradi* to step, go — more at GRADE] **1 a :** the act or action of coming together **:** a meeting esp. of persons or minds ⟨he was generally to be found in intellectual ~ with Keyserling —*Newsweek*⟩ **b :** SEXUAL INTERCOURSE, COITION **2 :** a meeting of heads of states or their foreign ministers, ambassadors, or envoys for discussion and adjustment of international problems or affairs ⟨the *Congress* of Vienna⟩ ⟨parliament is not a ~ of ambassadors from different and hostile interests —Edmund Burke⟩ **3 :** the supreme legislative body of a nation and esp. of a republic ⟨in form at least the ~*es* of So. American nations resemble our own⟩ ⟨the *Congress* of the U.S.⟩ **4 :** an organization designed to promote some object of common interest to its membership and usu. made up of delegates from a group of constituent organizations **:** ASSOCIATION ⟨the Massachusetts *Congress* of Parents and Teachers, Incorporated⟩ ⟨the *Congress* for Cultural Freedom⟩ ⟨the Canada Trades and Labor *Congress*⟩ **5 :** a particular meeting of a group (as a national legislature or cultural association) **:** a session or single sitting of an organization ⟨the Seventy-first *Congress* was dominantly Republican —H. R.Penniman⟩ ⟨his committee . . . has over 3000 bills per *Congress* referred to it —*Publishers' Weekly*⟩ ⟨the Social Democratic party's ~ was held in June⟩ **6 :** a coming together or meeting of persons ⟨the rupture of the disciplined silence sent an uneasy stir among the exhausted ~ of soldiers —Jack Belden⟩ ⟨a ~ of goons and thugs —S.H.Holbrook⟩ **7 :** a seasonal assemblage of amphibians (as certain toads and frogs) for breeding purposes

²con·gress \kən'gres\ *vi* -ED/-ING/-ES **:** to come together **:** ASSEMBLE

congress cap *n, usu cap 1st C* **:** a small white cloth cap worn by members of the Congress party of India

congress gaiter *or* **congress shoe** *n, often cap C* [¹*congress*; fr. its former popularity among members of the U.S. Congress] **:** a flexible ankle-high shoe having deep elastic gussets in the sides of the upper — compare ROMEO

con·gres·sion \kən'greshən\ *n* -s [L *congression-, congressio*, fr. *congressus* (past part. of *congredi*) + *-ion-, -io* -ion — more at CONGRESS] **:** the act or action of coming together (as into assembly, combat, coition); *specif* **:** the coming together or assembling of mitotic chromosomes at the equatorial plate

con·gres·sio·nal \kən'greshən°l, -shnəl\ *adj* **:** of or relating to a legislative congress ⟨the *Congressional* Register of the U.S.⟩ ⟨~ permission to . . . check names and fingerprints —R.S.Brown⟩ — **con·gres·sio·nal·ly** \-°lē, -əl, |i\ *adv*

congressional district *n* **:** one of the territorial divisions of each state of the U.S. from which a member of the House of Representatives is elected — compare APPORTIONMENT

con·gress·ist *pronunc at* ¹CONGRESS + əst\ *also* **con·gres·sio·nal·ist** \kən'greshən°ləst, -shnəl-\ *or* **con·gres·sio·nist** \-sh(ə)nəst\ *n* -s **:** a member or adherent of a congress

con·gress·ite \'käŋgrə,sīt\ *n* -s *usu cap* **:** a member of the Indian Congress Party

con·gress·man *pronunc at* ¹CONGRESS + mən\ *n, pl* **congressmen :** a member of a congress; *esp* **:** a member of the House of Representatives of the U.S. Congress ⟨*Congressman* and Mrs. Smith were present⟩ ⟨*congressmen* quoted "The White Man's Burden" in Washington —Thomas Beer⟩

congressman-at-large \\ *n, pl* **congressmen-at-large :** a member of the U.S. House of Representatives elected by the voters of an entire state rather than by those of a single congressional district

congress money *n* **:** paper money (as that issued by the Continental Congress or by the U.S. Congress during and after the panic of 1837)

con·gress·wom·an \'käŋgrə,swu̇mən\ *n, pl* **congresswom·en** \-wimən\ **:** a woman who is a member of a congress (as of the House of Representatives of the U.S. Congress)

con·gri·dae \'käŋgrə,dē\ *n pl, cap* [NL, fr. *Congr-, Conger*, type genus + *-idae*] **:** the family of fishes (order Apodes) comprising the conger eels and extinct related forms — **con·groid** \-,grȯid\ *adj or n*

con·grio \'käŋgrē,ō\ *n* -s [Sp, fr. L *congr-, conger* — more at CONGER] **:** a large Chilean cusk eel esteemed as food

congrue *vi; pres part* **congruing** [L *congruere*] *obs* **:** to be in harmony **:** AGREE

con·gru·ence \kən'grüən|(t)s, kän'g-, 'käŋ-, 'käŋ,g-; 'käŋgrəwən|\ *n* -s [ME, fr. L *congruentia*, fr. *congruent-, congruens* + *-ia*] **1 :** the quality or state of according or coinciding **:** CONGRUITY, HARMONY **2 :** AGREEMENT 4

con·gru·en·cy \|sē, |si\ *n* -ES [ME, fr. L *congruentia*] **:** the quality or state of according or coinciding **:** CONGRUITY, CONGRUENCE ⟨the ~ of ends and means⟩; *specif* **:** the relation of congruent propositions in logic

con·gru·ent \|t\ *adj* [L *congruent-, congruens*, pres. part. of *congruere* to come together, coincide, agree] **1 a :** in agreement **:** COINCIDING, CORRESPONDING ⟨to keep imaginary characters ~ with actual models —Bernard De Voto⟩ ⟨hypotheses ~ with our experiences⟩ **b** *logic* **:** relating to or predicable of the same subject **:** differing from each other but predicable as true of the same state of things ⟨~ propositions⟩ **2** *geom* **:** superposable so as to be coincident throughout **3 :** relating to the melting point at which there coexist for a molecular compound both liquid and solid phases having the same composition — **con·gru·ent·ly** *adv*

con·gru·en·tial \',käŋ,grü'enchəl, |käŋ,-\ *adj* [fr. *congruence*, after such pairs as E *penitence: penitential*] **:** having to do with congruence; *specif* **:** characterized by agreement (sense 4)

con·gru·ism \'kän(,)grü,izəm, 'käŋ(-; 'käŋgrə,wi-\ *n* -s [F *congruisme*, fr. *congru* suitable (fr. L *congruus*) + *-isme* -ism] **:** a theory advanced by the Molinists according to which divine grace is efficacious because it is given by God in circumstances which he foreknows to be congruous and favorable to its operation

con·gru·ist \-rüəst, -rəwəst\ *n* -s [F *congruiste*, fr. *congru* + *-iste* -ist] **:** an adherent of congruism

con·gru·i·ty \kən'grüəd·ē, kän'-, käŋ'-\ *n* -ES [ME *congruite*, fr. MF *congruité*, fr. LL *congruitat-, congruitas*, fr. L *congruus* + *itat-, -itas* -ity] **1 :** the quality or state of agreeing or coinciding (as one with another or with something referred to) **:** CONFORMITY, CORRESPONDENCE ⟨~ of thought and action⟩ ⟨the ~ of God's law with natural law⟩ **2 a :** SUITABILITY, APPROPRIATENESS **:** inner harmony **:** agreement or accordance of the parts of a whole ⟨we can . . . judge the coherence and ~ of its language —C.D.Lewis⟩ ⟨a spot which returned upon the memory of those who loved it with an aspect of peculiar and kindly ~ —Thomas Hardy⟩ **b** *obs* **:** natural aptitude or fitness (as for one's work) **3 :** merit described in scholastic theology as granted through divine generosity **:** merit given rather than earned or given in excess of that which is earned — distinguished from *condignity* **4 :** an instance or point of agreement or correspondence ⟨the occasional *congruities* between fact and prophecy⟩ **5** *obs* **:** correspondence in physical structure or substance tending to promote union or mixture

con·gru·ous \'käŋgrəwəs\ *adj* [L *congruus*, fr. *congruere* to come together, coincide, agree, fr. *com-* + *-gruere* (as in *ingruere* to fall upon, attack); akin to Gk *zachreēs* attacking violently, Lith *griuti* to collapse, fall in ruins, Russ *grukhnut'sya* to fall down with a clatter] **1 a :** in agreement, harmony, or correspondence ⟨did not choose to wear the tailored clothes that would be ~ with . . . her alert, military bearing —Tennessee Williams⟩ ⟨the new psychology was ~ with the conception of man as part of an unseen and infinite spiritual universe —Sherwood Eddy⟩ **b :** conforming to the circumstances or requirements of a situation **:** REASONABLE, SUITABLE, APPROPRIATE ⟨the Old Cemetery . . . , a fenced-in burying ground on a knoll above the highway is unusually ~ here —*Amer. Guide Series: Vt.*⟩ ⟨a ~ room to work in —G.B. Shaw⟩ **2 :** marked by inner harmony, coherence, or agreement of its parts ⟨a ~, plausible story, consistent in all its details⟩ ⟨proud of appearing in such incongruous attires — proud of the fact that he always made them look ~ —G.K. Chesterton⟩ **syn** see CONSONANT

con·gru·ous·ly *adv* **:** in a congruous manner **:** AGREEABLY, FITTINGLY, APPROPRIATELY

con·gru·ous·ness *n* -ES **:** the state or quality of being congruous

con gu·sto \kän'gü(,)stō, kōn-, -'gə(-\ *adv* [It] **:** with taste — used as a direction in music

con·hy·drine \kän'hīdrən, -,drēn\ *n* -s [ISV *coniine* + *hydrate* + *-ine*] **:** a poisonous crystalline alkaloid $C_8H_{17}NO$ occurring in poison hemlock; 2-(α-hydroxy-propyl)-piperidine

coni *pl of* CONUS

¹coni- *comb form* [L *coni-*, fr. *conus* — more at CONE] **:** cone ⟨*Conirostres*⟩

²coni- *or* **conio-** *comb form* [G & NL; G *koni-* & NL *coni-, conio-*, fr. Gk *koni-* dust & MGk *konio-*, fr. Gk *konia, konis* — more at INCINERATE] **:** dust ⟨*coniosis*⟩ **:** spores ⟨*Coniophora*⟩

co·ni·bo \kə'nē(,)bō\ *n, pl* **conibo** *or* **conibos** *usu cap* [Sp, fr. Conibo] **1 a :** a Panoan people of the lower Ucayali river valley in Peru **b :** a member of such people **2 :** the language of the Conibo people

¹con·ic \'känik, -nēk *sometimes* 'kōn-\ *adj* [Gk *kōnikos*, fr. *kōnos* cone + *-ikos* -ic — more at HONE] **1 :** CONICAL **2 :** of or relating to a cone **3** *of a hand* **:** of medium size with a slightly tapering palm and fingers full at the base and slightly pointed at the tip usu. held by palmists to indicate qualities of impulse and instinct and usu. an artistic nature

²conic \"\ *n* -s **:** CONIC SECTION

con·i·cal \-nəkəl, -nēk-\ *adj* [Gk *kōnikos* + E *-al*] **:** resembling a cone **:** having the shape of a cone ⟨~ roots⟩ — see ROOT illustration — **con·i·cal·ly** \-k(ə)lē, -li\ *adv* — **con·i·cal·ness** \-kəlnəs\ *n* -ES

con·i·cal·i·ty \,==ˈkaləd·ē\ *n* -ES **:** CONICITY

conical surface *n, math* **:** the surface generated by a moving straight line which always passes through a fixed point and intersects a fixed curve

conical vault *n, archit* **:** a vault of which the curved elements, usu. arcs of circles, are larger at one extremity than at the other and whose soffit is therefore conical in form

co·ni·ca·ri \,kōnə'kärē, ,kän-, -'karē\ *n, pl* **conicari** *or* **conicaris** *usu cap* [Sp, fr. a native name] **1 :** a Taracahitian people of Sonora, Mexico **2 :** a member of the Conicari people

con·ic·e·ine \kə'nisēən; ,kōnə'sēən, ,kän-\ *n* -s [G *coniceïn*, modif. of ISV *conicine* coniine, modif. of G *koniin* — more at CONIINE] **:** any of several poisonous bases $C_8H_{15}N$ prepared from the alkaloids of poison hemlock

con·i·chal·cite \,känə'kal,sīt\ *n* -s [G *konichalzit*, fr. Gk *konia* plaster, ash, dust + *chalkos* copper + G *-it* -ite; akin to Gk *konis* dust — more at CHALC-] **:** a mineral $CaCu(AsO_4)(OH)$ consisting of basic copper calcium arsenate occurring in green masses

co·nic·i·ty \kō'nisəd·ē\ *n* -ES **:** the quality or state of being conical **:** CONICALNESS

con·i·cle \'känəkəl, 'kōn-\ *n* -s [*cone* + *-icle* (as in *particle*)] **:** a small cone

con·i·coid \-nə,kȯid\ *n* -s [*conic* + *-oid*] **:** a surface of second degree **:** QUADRIC

con·i·cop·o·ly \,känə'käpəlē\ *n* -ES [Tamil *kaṇakkappiḷḷai*, fr. *kaṇakkan* accountant (fr. Skt *gaṇaka* mathematician, astrologer, fr. *gaṇayati* he reckons, fr. *gaṇa* series, multitude) + *piḷḷai* child (respectful title of certain castes)] *in the Madras area* **:** a native accountant or clerk

conic projection *n, mapping* **:** a projection based on the principle of a hollow cone placed over a sphere so that when the cone is unrolled the line of tangency becomes the central or standard parallel of the region mapped, all parallels being arcs of concentric circles and the meridians being straight lines drawn from the cone's vertex to the divisions of the standard parallel

conic section *n* **1 :** a plane section of a right circular conical surface **2 :** a curve generated by a point which always moves so that the ratio of its distance from a fixed point to its distance from a fixed line is constant

C conic section (ellipse); *F* fixed point; *L* fixed line; P_1, P_2 points on conic section; FP_1, $P_1D_1 = FP_2$, P_2D_2

co·ni·dae \'kōnə,dē\ *n pl, cap* [NL, fr. *Conus*, type genus + *-idae*] **:** a family of mollusks (group Toxoglossa) comprising the cones

con·i·den·drin \,känə'dendrən, ,kōn-\ *n* -s [*conifer* + *dendr-* + *-in*] **:** a crystalline hydroxy lactone $C_{20}H_{20}O_6$ found esp. in waste sulfite pulp liquor — called also *tsugaresinol*

conidi- *or* **conidio-** *comb form* [*conidium*] **:** conidia ⟨*conidii*ferous⟩

conidia *pl of* CONIDIUM

co·nid·i·al \kə'nidēəl\ *also* **co·nid·i·an** \-ēən\ *adj* [NL *conidium* + E *-al* or *-an*] **:** relating to, resembling, of the nature of, or producing conidia

co·nid·i·oid \-ē,ȯid\ *adj* [*conidi-* + *-oid*] **:** CONIDIAL

co·nid·i·o·phore \-ēə,fō(ə)r\ *n* -s [ISV *conidi-* + *-phore*] **:** a structure that bears conidia; *specif, in certain fungi* **:** a specialized typically erect and aerial hyphal branch that produces successive conidia by abstriction — **co·nid·i·oph·o·rous** \kə,nidē'äf(ə)rəs\ *adj*

co·nid·io·spore \kə'nidēə,spō(ə)r\ *n* -s [*conidi-* + *spore*] **:** CONIDIUM

co·nid·i·um \kə'nidēəm\ *n, pl* **conid·ia** \-ēə\ [NL, fr. *con-* (fr. Gk *konis* dust) + *-idium* — more at INCINERATE] *biol* **:** an asexual spore produced by abstriction, budding, or septation from the tip of a conidiophore; *broadly* **:** any asexual spore not borne within an enclosing structure — compare ENDOSPORE

conies *pl of* CONY

con·i·fer \'känəfə(r) *also* 'kōn-\ *n* -s [NL *Coniferae*] **:** a plant of the order Coniferales

co·nif·er·ae \kō'nifə,rē, kə'-\ *n pl, cap* [NL, fr. L, pl. fem. of *conifer* cone-bearing, fr. *coni-* + *-fer*] *in some classifications* **:** a category of trees and shrubs treated variously as a family, order, or class coextensive with the order Coniferales

co·nif·er·a·les \=,==ˈrā(,)lēz; ,känəfə-, ,kōn-\ *n pl, cap* [NL, fr. L *conifer* + NL *-ales*] **:** an order of chiefly evergreen gymnospermous trees and shrubs having acicular to linear or lanceolate leaves and the ovulate strobilus a woody cone or fleshy aril and comprising a variable number of families of which Taxodiaceae are most generally recognized

co·nif·er·in \kō'nifərən, kə'-\ *n* -s [ISV *conifer* + *-in*; orig. formed as G *koniferin*] **:** a crystalline glucoside $C_{16}H_{22}O_8$ found esp. in the cambium of coniferous trees

co·nif·er·oph·y·ta \=,==ˈräfəd·ə, ,känəfə-, ,kōn-\ *n pl, cap* [NL, fr. L *conifer* + NL *-o-* + *-phyta*] *syn of* CONIFEROPHYTAE

co·nif·er·oph·y·tae \-fə,tē\ *n pl, cap* [NL, fr. L *conifer* + NL *-o-* + *-phytae* (pl. fem. equivalent of *-phyta*)] **:** a subclass of Gymnospermae comprising profusely branched plants with simple leaves, small pith, abundant xylem, and little cortex and including the surviving orders Ginkgoales, Coniferales, and Gnetales and the extinct order Cordaitales — compare CYCADOPHYTAE — **co·nif·er·o·phyte** \kō'nifərə,fīt, kə'-\ *n* -s — **co·nif·er·o·phyt·ic** \=;==ˈfid·ik\ *adj*

co·nif·er·ous \kō'nif(ə)rəs, kə'-\ *adj* [L *conifer* + E *-ous*] **1 :** bearing cones ⟨~ pine⟩ ⟨~ trees⟩ **2 :** of or relating to conifers ⟨~ wood⟩ **:** characterized by the predominance of coniferous trees ⟨the ~ forest belt⟩

co·nif·er·yl alcohol \=ˈ=fərəl-\ *n* [ISV *coniferyl* (fr. *coniferin* + *-yl*) + *alcohol*] **:** a white crystalline alcohol $C_{10}H_{12}O_3$ obtained by hydrolysis of coniferin with emulsin or found as an ester in benzoin and held to be involved in the formation of lignin; 4-hydroxy-3-methoxy-cinnamyl alcohol

co·ni·fi·ca·tion \,känəfə'kāshən, ,kōn-\ *n* -s [fr. ¹*cone*, after such pairs as E *code: codification*] **:** the act or process of tapering toward the top ⟨~ of the social structure⟩

co·ni·form \'kōnə,fȯrm, 'kän-\ *adj* **:** shaped like a cone

co·ni·ine \'kōnē,ēn, -ē,ēn\ *also* **co·nine** \-nən, -,nēn\ *n* -s [*coniine* fr. G *koniin*, fr. LL *conium* hemlock + G *-in* -ine; *conine* ISV, modif. of *coniine* — more at CONIUM] **:** a liquid alkaloid $C_8H_{17}N$ with a penetrating odor and burning taste that is found in the poison hemlock and is a powerful poison that paralyzes the motor nerves; 2-propyl-piperidine

co·ni·lu·rus \,kän°l'(y)u̇rəs\ *n, cap* [NL, fr. *conil-* (fr. *konilos*, erroneous reading of Gk *koniklos* rabbit, fr. L *cuniculus*) + *-urus* — more at CONEY] **:** a genus of rodents consisting of the Australian jerboa rats

coning *pres part of* CONE

conio- — see ²CONI-

co·ni·o·gram·me \,kōnēō'gra(,)mē\ *n, cap* [NL, fr. *conio-* (fr. Gk *kōnion*, dim. of *kōnos* cone) + Gk *grammē* line; akin to Gk *graphein* to write — more at HONE, CARVE] **:** a small genus of ferns (family Polypodiaceae) of the Pacific islands and Japan often grown for ornament and characterized by large entire or pinnate fronds and elongate sori lacking indusia and reaching from midrib to leaf margin — see BAMBOO FERN

coniology *var of* KONIOLOGY

coniometer *var of* KONIMETER

co·ni·oph·o·ra \,kōnē'äfərə\ *n, cap* [NL, fr. ²*coni-* + *-phora*] **:** a genus of fungi (family Thelephoraceae) of which one species (*C. cerebella* syn. *C. puteana*) often causes dry rot in the timbers of buildings

co·ni·op·ter·y·gid \,kōnē,äp'terəjəd, -ē,äptə'rij-\ *n* -s [NL *Coniopterygidae*] **:** an insect of the family Coniopterygidae — called also *dusty wing*

co·ni·op·te·ryg·i·dae \,kōnē,äptə'rijə,dē\ *n pl, cap* [NL, fr. *Coniopteryg-, Coniopteryx*, type genus (fr. ²*coni-* + *-pteryx*) + *-idae*] **:** a family of small humpbacked insects (order Neuroptera) that have pollinose wings resembling those of moths and predatory larvae which feed esp. on mites and scales

co·ni·o·se·li·num \,kōnē(,)ōsə'līnəm\ *n, cap* [NL, fr. *conio-* (fr. *Conium*) + *Selinum* (genus name formerly used for what is now called *Conioselinum*), fr. LL *selinon* celery — more at CELERY] **:** a genus of aromatic herbs (family Umbelliferae) having much-dissected leaves and compound umbels of minute white flowers — see HEMLOCK PARSLEY

co·ni·o·thyr·i·um \,kōnēō'thirēəm\ *n, cap* [NL, fr. ²*coni-* + *thyr-* (fr. Gk *thyreos* oblong shield, fr. *thyra* door) + *-ium* — more at DOOR] **:** a form genus of imperfect fungi (family Sphaeropsidaceae) with dark olivaceous spores that includes a species (*C. diplodiella*) that causes white rot of grapes

co·ni·ros·tres \,kōnə'rä(,)strēz, ,kän-\ *n pl, cap* [NL, fr. ¹*coni-* + *-rostres* (fr. L *rostrum* beak) — more at ROSTRUM] *in former classifications* **:** an artificial group of birds including the finches and weaverbirds and often the tanagers

co·ni·um \kō'nīəm, 'kōnēəm\ *n* [NL, fr. LL, hemlock, fr. Gk *kōneion*, perh. fr. *kōnos* cone — more at HONE] **1 a** *cap* **:** a genus of poisonous herbs (family Umbelliferae) having spotted stems, large decompound leaves with lanceolate pinnatifid leaflets, and white flowers **b** -s **:** any plant of the genus *Conium* **2** -s **:** the dried full-grown but unripe fruit of the poison hemlock containing the alkaloids coniine and methyl coniine and used as a narcotic and sedative

con·i·za·tion \,kōnə'zāshən, ,kän-, -,nī'z-\ *n* -s [¹*cone* + *-ization*] **:** the electrosurgical excision of a cone of tissue from a diseased uterine cervix

conj *abbr* **1** conjugation **2** conjunction; conjunctive

conject *vb* -ED/-ING/-S [ME *conjecten*, fr. L *conjectare* to throw together, conjecture, fr. *com-* + *-jectare* (fr. *jactare* to throw) — more at JET] **1** *obs* **:** CONJECTURE **2** *obs* **:** PLAN, PLOT

conjector *n* -s [alter. (influenced by L *conjector*) of ME *conjectere*, modif. (influenced by ME *-ere* -er) of L *conjector* diviner, soothsayer, fr. *conjectus* (past part. of *conjicere*) + *-or*] *obs* **:** CONJECTURER

con·jec·tur·al \kən'jekchərəl, -ksh(ə)rəl\ *adj* [L *conjecturalis*, fr. *conjectura* + *-alis* -al] **1 :** of the nature of or involving or based on conjecture ⟨~ emendations⟩ **2 :** given to conjectures ⟨a ~ critic —Samuel Johnson⟩ — **con·jec·tur·al·ly** \-lē,-li\ *adv*

¹con·jec·ture \kən'jekchə(r), -ksh-\ *n* -s [ME, fr. MF or L; MF *conjecture*, fr. L *conjectura*, fr. *conjectus* (past part. of *conjicere* to throw together, conjecture, divine, fr. *com-* + *-jicere*, fr. *jacere* to throw) + *-ura* -ure — more at JET] **1** *obs* **a :** interpretation of signs or omens; *also* **:** a conclusion so drawn **b :** SUPPOSITION ⟨now entertain ~ of a time when —Shak.⟩ **2 :** inference from defective or presumptive evidence **:** the act of making or state of being absorbed in making such inference ⟨lost in ~⟩ **3 :** an inference or conclusion drawn or deduced by surmise or guesswork ⟨a mistaken ~⟩; *specif* **:** a conjectural emendation of a text

²conjecture \"\ *vb* **conjectured; conjectured; conjecturing** \-kchəriŋ, -ksh(ə)r-\ **conjectures** [ME *conjecturen*, fr. MF *conjecturer*, fr. *conjecture*, n.] *vt* **:** to arrive at by conjecture or to make conjectures as to **:** infer by way of surmise **:** form opinions concerning on grounds confessedly insufficient to certain conclusion ~ *vi* **:** to make or form conjectures; *esp* **:** to indulge in surmise

syn CONJECTURE, SURMISE, and GUESS may be compared in that they can all signify the forming of an opinion or the arriving at a conclusion on insufficient evidence or without evidence or signify the opinion or conclusion arrived at in this way. Of the three, CONJECTURE usu., though not always, suggests some evidence although insufficient; it usu. implies a strong awareness that what evidence there may be is not really sufficient ⟨it is easy to dismiss the false Cleopatra but the true one can only be *conjectured*, for the material for a reasoned verdict is lost —John Buchan⟩ ⟨Washington *conjectured* that at least 300 of the enemy were killed —*Amer. Guide Series: Pa.*⟩ SURMISE may be used in the same way as CONJECTURE although it usu. strongly implies the flimsiness of the evidence ⟨the rest of them were on holiday supposedly attending to their religious duties, though Simon *surmised* that they would be strolling idly about —L.C.Douglas⟩ ⟨as to how they came there he could only *surmise* that they had entered through the stable yard, as otherwise he must have observed their approach —Rafael Sabatini⟩ ⟨we are not told what their business was but we may *surmise* it was the fur trade —G.F.Hudson⟩ GUESS usu. implies a complete or almost complete absence of evidence; it suggests rather the use of intuition or suspicion and a reliance upon chance for verification ⟨you would never *guess* from meeting them that anyone would pay them for their ideas —Rose Macaulay⟩ ⟨Tristram *guessed* what was passing in his friend's mind —T.B.Costain⟩ ⟨he expected this eighteen-year-old girl to *guess* his love and understand its esoteric quality, without being told —H.S.Canby⟩

con·jec·tur·er \-kchərər, -ksh-; -ksh(ə)rər\ *n* -s **:** one that conjectures

con·join \kən'jȯin, (')kän|j-\ *vb* -ED/-ING/-S [ME *conjoynen*, fr. MF *conjoindre*, fr. L *conjungere*, fr. *com-* + *jungere* to join — more at YOKE] *vt* **:** to join together (as separate entities) for a common purpose or a common end ⟨the two are historically ~*ed* but not connected in a causal way at all —*Times Lit. Supp.*⟩ ⟨belief in a transcendent God ~*ed* with belief in an afterlife —A.J.Ayer⟩ ~ *vi* **:** to join together for a common purpose or a common end ⟨a certain complex of conditions ~ to create the boom —D.M.Friedenburg⟩ **:** be in conjunction (as of celestial bodies) **syn** see JOIN, UNITE

conjoined \-nd\ *adj* [fr. past part. of *conjoin*] **1 :** being, coming, or brought together so as to meet, touch, or overlap ⟨~ heads on a coin⟩ **2** *of heavenly bodies* **:** in conjunction — **con·join·ed·ly** \-nədlē\ *adv*

conjoined in lure *heraldry* **:** joined together with their tips downward — used of two wings

¹con·joint \-ȯint\ *adj* [ME, fr. MF, past part. of *conjoindre*] **1 :** UNITED, CONJOINED **2 :** related to, made up of, or carried on by two or more in combination **:** JOINT, COMBINED, SIMULTANEOUS — **con·joint·ly** *adv*

²conjoint \"\ *n* -s **1 :** an associate in interest or obligation **2 conjoints** *pl* **:** husband and wife taken collectively (as in cases of community property)

con·joint·ment \kən'jȯintmənt\ *n* -s [¹*conjoint* + *-ment*] **:** CONJUNCTION, COMBINATION

conjoint tendon *also* **conjoined tendon** *n* **:** the common tendon of the transverse and internal oblique muscles of the abdomen extending from the linea alba to the pubic bone

con·jubilant \kən, (')kän+\ *adj* [ML *conjubilant-, conjubilans*, pres. part. of *conjubilare*, fr. L *com-* + *jubilare* to shout for joy — more at JUBILATE] **:** shouting together with joy

con·ju·ga·ble \ˈkänjəgəbəl\ *adj* [*conjugate* + *-able*] : that is capable of conjugation

con·ju·ga·cy \-gəsē\ *n* -ES [*conjugate* + *-cy*] : conjugate state : relation of conjugates

con·ju·gal \ˈkänjəgəl, -jēg-; kənˈjüg-\ *adj* [MF or L; MF, fr. L *conjugalis*, fr. *conjug-, conjux* husband, wife, consort, fr. *conjungere* to join together, unite in marriage] **1 :** of or relating to marriage, the married state, or married persons in their mutual relations : MATRIMONIAL, CONNUBIAL ⟨~ worries⟩ ⟨~ politeness⟩ **2 :** consisting of or based on the husband, wife, and their offspring as constituting the functional familial unit in a society ⟨the modern American family is of the ~ type⟩ — contrasted with *consanguine;* compare FAMILY — **con·ju·gal·i·ty** \ˌkänjəˈgaləd·ē, -jēˈ-\ *n* -ES — **con·ju·gal·ly** *pronunc at* CONJUGAL + ē *or* i\ *adv*

con·ju·ga·les \ˌkänjəˈgā(ˌ)lēz\ *n, pl, cap* [NL, fr. L, pl. of *conjugalis* of marriage] *in some classifications* : an order equivalent to Zygnematales

conjugal rights *n pl* : the sexual rights or privileges implied by and involved in the marriage relationship : the right of sexual intercourse between husband and wife

con·ju·gant \ˈkänjəgənt\ *n* -S [L *conjugant-, conjugans*, pres. part. of *conjugare* to unite] : one of a pair of conjugating gametes or organisms

con·ju·gase \-ˌgās, -āz\ *n* -S [ISV *conjug-* (fr. *conjugate*, n.) + *-ase*] : any of a group of enzymes found in blood or in certain organs (as kidney and pancreas) and in some vegetables (as potatoes) that bring about the breakdown of conjugates of pteroylglutamic acid (as pteroyl-hepta-glutamic acid)

con·ju·ga·ta \ˌkänjəˈgäd·ə\ *n, pl* **conjuga·tae** \-ˌā,tē\ [NL, fr. L, fem. of *conjugatus*] : the dorsoventral diameter of the human pelvis measured from the sacral promontory to the pubic symphysis

con·ju·ga·tae \-ā,tē\ *n pl, cap* [NL, fr. L, nom. pl. fem. of *conjugatus*] *in some classifications* : a subclass equivalent to the order Zygnematales

[1]**con·ju·gate** \ˈkänjəgət, -jēg-, -jə,gāt; *usu* -d·+V\ *adj* [ME *conjugat*, fr. L *conjugatus*, past part. of *conjugare* to unite, fr. *com-* + *jugare* to join, marry, fr. *jugum* yoke — more at YOKE] **1 :** yoked or joined together esp. in pairs : MATED, COUPLED ⟨~ relationship⟩ : acting or operating as if joined ⟨~ foci⟩ : SIMULTANEOUS ⟨~ deviation of the eyes⟩ ⟨~ effect of two forces⟩ **2 :** bearing to each other a relation characterized by having certain features in common but by being opposite or inverse in some particular ⟨~ complex numbers⟩ ⟨~ axes of a pendulum⟩ ⟨~ foci of a lens⟩ **3 a :** BIJUGATE **b :** of or relating to algae that reproduce sexually by conjugation **4** *of words in the same language* : having the same derivation and therefore usu. some likeness in meaning ⟨*just, justice, justly* are ~⟩ **5 a :** CONJUGATED 2 **b** *of acids and bases in pairs* : related by the difference of a proton ⟨the acid NH_4^+ and the base NH_3 are ~ to each other⟩ **c :** relating to layers of immiscible solutions that can exist side by side at equilibrium **6** *of two leaves of a book* : forming a single piece **7 :** so formed that one gear will drive the other with constant relative angular speed — used of a pair of gear teeth or of gear teeth profiles; *also* : relating to such gear teeth or profiles — **con·ju·gate·ly** *adv* — **con·ju·gate·ness** *n* -ES

[2]**con·ju·gate** \-jə,gāt, *usu* -ād·+V\ *vb* -ED/-ING/-S [L *conjugatus*] *vt* **1 :** to give in some prescribed order the various inflectional forms of : INFLECT — used esp. of a verb, rarely of a preposition ⟨~ the Latin verb *amare*⟩ **2 :** to join together : YOKE, COUPLE **3** *of a chemical compound* : to unite (as with the elimination of water) so that the product is easily broken down (as by hydrolysis) into the original compounds ⟨benzoic acid is *conjugated* with glycine to hippuric acid in the body⟩ ~ *vi* **1 :** to join together; *specif* : to unite in marriage **2** *biol* : to unite in pairs: **a :** to fuse esp. in conjugation **b :** to pair in synapsis

[3]**conjugate** *like* [1]CONJUGATE\ *n* -S [in sense 1, fr. L *conjugatus* etymologically related, past part. of *conjugare* to unite; in senses 2 & 4, fr. [1]*conjugate*; in sense 3, fr. NL *Conjugatae*] **1 :** a word that has the same derivation as another in the same language and that therefore usu. resembles it in meaning **2 a :** CONJUGATE AXIS **b :** CONJUGATE DIAMETER **3 :** an alga of the order Zygnematales **4** *chem* : a substance that is conjugated (sense 2a)

conjugate alphabet *n* : one of a pair of alphabets in cryptography consisting of an enciphering alphabet and its equivalent deciphering alphabet

conjugate axis *n* : the line through the center of an ellipse or a hyperbola and perpendicular to the line through the two foci

conjugate complex number *n* : one of two complex numbers differing only in the sign of the imaginary part (as $a+bi$ and $a-bi$)

conjugate conductor *n* : either of two branches of an electrical network such that a change in the impressed electromotive force of one does not produce a change in the current of the other

conjugated *adj* [fr. past part. of *conjugate*] **1 :** CONJUGATE 1 **2** *chem* **a :** formed by the union of two compounds or united with another compound ⟨some enzymes are ~⟩ ⟨~ bile acids⟩ **b (1) :** having or characterized by a special mutual influence due to proximity in the molecule — used of certain groups or bonds or of compounds or systems containing them **(2)** *organic chem* : relating to or containing a system of two double bonds separated by a single bond (as in $CH_2{=}CH{-}CH{=}CH_2$ or $CH_2{=}CH{-}CH{=}O$) — often distinguished from *allenic* and *isolated* ⟨~ double bonds⟩ ⟨~ drying oils⟩ ⟨~ fatty acids⟩ ⟨a ~ system of alternating single and double bonds⟩

conjugate diameter *n* **1 :** CONJUGATA **2 a :** one of two diameters of a central conic section each of which bisects all chords parallel to the other **b :** one of three diameters of a central quadric having as its conjugate diametral plane the plane of the other two

AB, CD conjugate diameters 2a

conjugate division *n* : division of dikaryotic cells in certain fungi in which the two nuclei divide independently, one product of each nuclear division going to each daughter cell — see DIKARYON

conjugated protein *also* **conjugate protein** *n* : a compound (as hemoglobin) of a protein (as globin) with a nonprotein substance (as heme) — distinguished from *simple protein;* compare CHROMOPROTEIN, GLYCOPROTEIN, LIPOPROTEIN, NUCLEOPROTEIN, PHOSPHOPROTEIN

conjugate hyperbola *n* : either of two hyperbolas having the same asymptotes, the conjugate axis of each being the transverse axis of the other

conjugate lines *n pl* : **1** *of a conic section* : two lines each of which passes through the pole of the other **2** *of a quadric* : two lines so arranged that each intersects the polar line of the other

conjugate planes *n pl, of a quadric* : two planes so arranged that each contains the pole of the other with respect to the quadric

conjugate point *n* **1 :** either of two points lying with respect to a conic each on the polar of the other **2 a :** one of two points in reference to a rigid body such that if an impulse is applied at either the body will start to rotate about an instantaneous axis through the other, one point becoming the center of suspension of the body considered as a pendulum and the other becoming the center of oscillation **b :** one of two points in an optical system either of which is the real or virtual focus of the other

conjugate roots *n pl* : roots of an algebraic equation that are conjugate complex numbers

conjugate triangles *n pl* : two triangles in which the vertices of each are the poles with respect to a given curve of the sides of the other

conjugating tube *n* [*conjugating* fr. gerund of *conjugate*] : a tube in various algae (as members of the genus *Spirogyra*) formed by the fusion of a process of one cell with a like process of another sexually opposite cell into a canal and used by one or both gametes in coming together for conjugation

con·ju·ga·tion \ˌkänjəˈgāshən\ *n* -S [LL & L; LL *conjugation-, conjugatio* class of verbs having same type of inflectional forms, fr. L, combining, mixture, fr. *conjugatus* (past part. of *conjugare* to unite) + *-ion-, -io* -ion — more at CONJUGATE] **1 :** the act of joining together, uniting, or combining : the state of being joined together : UNION ⟨~ of the sexes⟩ **2** *obs* : something joined together or combined **3 a :** a presentation in some prescribed order of the inflectional forms of a verb **b :** verb inflection **c :** a class of verbs having the same type of inflectional forms ⟨the strong and the weak ~⟩ ⟨the Latin second ~ with its infinitive ending in *-ēre*⟩ **d :** any of several sets of inflectional forms belonging to a verb esp. in Sanskrit and the Semitic languages including the forms of the simple verb and various derivative sets of forms that typically add to the meaning of the simple verb a passive, reflexive, causative, intensive, frequentative, or desiderative meaning **4 a :** fusion of two gametes with ultimate union of their nuclei which is the common sexual process among the lower thallophytes resulting typically in formation of a thick-walled zygote, being comparable to fertilization in higher forms though male and female are not usu. recognizable, and similarly producing a genetically distinct new generation **b :** temporary cytoplasmic union in pairs of ciliated protozoa accompanied by complex nuclear phenomena comparable to meiosis and fertilization and resulting in two individuals with new genetic constitutions **5** *chem* : the state of being conjugated (sense 2b)

con·ju·ga·tion·al \ˌkänjəˈgāshənᵊl, -shnəl\ *adj* : of or relating to conjugation — **con·ju·ga·tion·al·ly** \-ᵊl|ē, -əl|ē, |i\ *adv*

conjugation canal *n* : CONJUGATING TUBE

conjugation cell *n* : GAMETE

con·ju·ga·tive \ˈkänjə,gād·iv\ *adj* : relating to, tending to, or characterized by conjugation

con·ju·gi·al \kənˈjüjēəl\ *adj* [L *conjugialis*, fr. *conjugium* marriage (fr. *conjug-, conjux* husband, wife) + *-ialis* -ial — more at CONJUGAL] : MATRIMONIAL — used to distinguish the Swedenborgian conception of marriage as a spiritual union

[1]**con·junct** \kənˈjəŋ(k)t, (ˈ)kän|j-\ *adj* [ME, fr. L *conjunctus*, past part. of *conjungere* to join together — more at CONJOIN] **1 :** JOINED, UNITED : bound together ⟨folk tunes and texts independent or ~⟩ ⟨man . . . feels himself to be ~ with a social group —Rufus Jones⟩ **2 :** belonging to, made up of, or effected by combined elements or persons : JOINT ⟨Sicily was reduced in . . . 1806 by a brilliant ~ operation —P.G. Mackesy⟩ **3 :** being so related to a person (as an insolvent) as to be legally incompetent to act as witness or judge in matters affecting him **4** *in Irish and Welsh verb inflection* : belonging to or characteristic of a verb that is preceded by any of several particles or compounded with a preverb ⟨the ~ form⟩ ⟨a ~ ending⟩ — opposed to *absolute* **5** *music* : relating to diatonic motion — contrasted with *disjunct*

[2]**con·junct** \ˈkän,j-\ *n* -S **1 :** a person or thing joined or associated with another **2 a :** CONJUNCTURE **b** *logic* **(1) :** a component of a conjunction **(2) :** CONJUNCTION 7

conjunct degrees *n pl* : adjacent successive tones of the musical scale

con·junc·tion \kənˈjəŋ(k)shən\ *n* -S [ME *conjunctioun*, fr. MF *conjonction*, fr. L *conjunction-, conjunctio*, fr. *conjunctus* + *-ion-, -io* -ion] **1 :** the act of conjoining or state of being conjoined : UNION, ASSOCIATION, COMBINATION ⟨things not normally seen in ~⟩ ⟨the view that cause is constant ~ —E.H. Madden⟩ **2 :** an instance of conjoining or coming together : UNION, ASSOCIATION ⟨quartering . . . was the normal way of indicting a ~ of lordships —A.R.Wagner⟩ **3 :** occurrence together : concurrence esp. of events or routes ⟨from the state line route 17 proceeds in ~ with route 6 for a few miles⟩ **4** *obs* : sexual union : union in wedlock **5 a :** the apparent meeting or passing of two or more celestial bodies in the same degree of the zodiac **b :** a configuration in which two celestial bodies have their least apparent separation ⟨a ~ of Mars and Jupiter⟩ — compare OPPOSITION; see CONFIGURATION illustration **6 :** a linguistic form (as an uninflected word) that joins together words or word groups such as sentences (as *but* in "He tried. But he failed"), clauses (as *if* in "I'll go if you will"), phrases (as *and* in "over the river and through the woods"), words (as *or* in "first or last"), or a word and a phrase (as *and* in "my brother and I") **7** *logic* **a :** a statement that is true only if both its components are true — called also *joint assertion* **b :** the binary connective used in logic **c :** the logical operation of forming a conjunction

con·junc·tion·al \-shənᵊl, -shnəl\ *adj* : of or relating to or of the nature of conjunction or a conjunction — **con·junc·tion·al·ly** \-ᵊl|ē, -əl|ē, |i\ *adv*

con·junc·ti·va \ˌkän,jəŋkˈtīvə, -tēvə; kənˈjəŋ(k)təvə\ *n, pl* **conjunctivas** \-vəz\ *or* **conjuncti·vae** \-ī,vē, -ē,vī, -ə,vē, -ə,vī\ [NL, fr. LL, fem. of *conjunctivus*] **1 :** the mucous membrane that lines the inner surface of the eyelids and is continued over the forepart of the eyeball covering part of the sclerotic coat and forming epithelium over the corner — see EYE illustration **2 :** the flexible usu. infolded and membranous suture between adjoining segments of an insect's body or appendages — **con·junc·ti·val** \ˌkän,jəŋkˈtīvəl, -tēvəl, -ˈtē-; kənˈjəŋ(k)təv-\ *adj*

[1]**con·junc·tive** \kənˈjəŋ(k)tiv, -tēv *also* -təv\ *adj* [LL *conjunctivus*, fr. L *conjunctus* + *-ivus* -ive — more at CONJUNCT] **1 :** CONJOINING, CONNECTING, CONNECTIVE ⟨~ forces in society⟩ **2 :** CONJOINED, CONJUNCT : done or existing in conjunction ⟨the ~ operation of several independent factors⟩ **3 a :** being a conjunction (sense 6) ⟨a ~ particle⟩ **b :** functioning like a conjunction; *specif* : connecting the sentence or main clause in which it occurs with the preceding one and qualifying the whole sentence or clause in which it occurs rather than any single word or phrase in it ⟨~ adverbs such as *hence, yet, so, consequently, however*⟩ **4** *of the mood of a verb* : SUBJUNCTIVE **5** *of a conjunction* : COPULATIVE 1a **6** *of a pronoun form* : unstressed and closely attached to the verb as an enclitic or proclitic ⟨French *me, le, te, se* are ~⟩ — contrasted with *disjunctive* — **con·junc·tive·ly** \-tėvlē, -li\ *adv*

[2]**conjunctive** \"\ *n* -S : something conjunctive: as **a (1) :** CONJUNCTION 7 **(2) :** the connective in a conjunction **b (1) :** CONJUNCTION 6 : a word (as *moreover* in "I don't know, moreover I don't care") or word group (as the phrase *in case* in "take your umbrella in case it should rain") functioning like a conjunction **(2) :** a copulative conjunction **(3) :** the conjunctive mood of a language or a form in it

conjunctive legacy *n* : a legacy awarding under Roman law the same thing to two or more persons in one dispositive clause and giving each colegatee the right of increasing his share proportionately to his interest if the share of any other colegatee lapses or becomes vacant before it vests — distinguished from *disjunctive legacy*

conjunctive tissue *n* : sometimes lignified parenchymatous ground tissue in which the vascular bundles are imbedded in certain dicotyledons (as the beet) and in those monocotyledons in which secondary thickening occurs

con·junc·ti·vi·tis \kən,jəŋ(k)təˈvīd·əs, -ītəs\ *n* -ES [NL, fr. *conjunctiva* + *-itis*] : inflammation of the conjunctiva

conjunct motion *or* **conjunct progression** *n* : melodic movement by scale intervals

conjuncts *pl of* CONJUNCT

conjunct system *n* : a diatonic series of tones in Greek music comprising three conjunct tetrachords

conjunct tetrachords *n pl* : two adjacent tetrachords in which the highest note of one is the same as the lowest note of the other

con·junc·ture \kənˈjəŋ(k)chə(r), -)sh-\ *n* -S [F *conjoncture*, fr. ML *conjunctura*, fr. L *conjunctus* + *-ura* -ure] **1 :** CONJUNCTION, UNION, COMBINATION ⟨the ~ of realism with idealism —Frank Swinnerton⟩ **2 :** a combination or complication (as of circumstances or events) esp. producing a crisis or critical point : JUNCTURE, SITUATION, OPPORTUNITY ⟨profits made through business ~s⟩

con·ju·ra·tion \ˌkänjəˈrāshən\ *n* -S [ME *conjuracioun*, fr. MF & L; MF *conjuration* constraining of spirits or devils, fr. L *conjuration-, conjuratio* conspiracy, fr. *conjuratus* (past part. of *conjurare*) + *-ion-, -io* -ion] **1 :** a swearing together : a league by a common oath (as for a criminal purpose) : CONSPIRACY **2 :** a constraining of spirits or devils by invocation of a sacred name or by a spell : CONJURING, INCANTATION **3 a :** a magic expression used in conjuring : CHARM, SPELL **b :** a conjuring trick **4 :** the act of charging or calling upon in a sacred name or in a solemn manner usu. by appealing to something binding (as an oath) : a solemn appeal : ADJURATION

[1]**con·jure** *in senses vt 2 & vi 2* ˈkänjə(r) *also* ˈkən-; *in other senses* kənˈjü(ə)r *or* -ùə\ *vb* **conjured; conjured; conjuring** \ˈkänj(ə)riŋ, ˈkən-; kənˈjùr-\ **conjures** [ME *conjuren*, fr. OF *conjurer*, fr. L *conjurare* to swear together, conspire, fr. *com-* + *jurare* to swear — more at JURY] *vt* **1 a** *obs* : to call on or charge in a solemn manner (as by invoking a sacred name) **b :** to entreat earnestly or solemnly : IMPLORE, BESEECH ⟨I ~ you . . . to weigh my case well —Sheridan Le Fanu⟩ **2 a :** to summon or constrain (as a spirit or a devil) to appear or to obey one by invoking a spell or a sacred name **b :** to affect or effect by or as if by magic : call forth or send away by magic arts : excite, bring about, get, or convey as if by magic : create in reality or to the imagination as if by magic : IMAGINE — often used with *up* ⟨~ up an image⟩ : INVENT, CONTRIVE ⟨you've *conjured* up some scheme to get us safely away —T.B. Costain⟩ ~ *vi* **1** *obs* : to swear together : CONSPIRE ⟨when those gainst states and kingdoms do ~ —Edmund Spenser⟩ **2 a :** to summon a devil or spirit to appear or obey one by invoking a sacred name or by some spell **b :** to practice magical arts : CHARM ⟨*scientific* is the word our civilization ~s with —Ruth Benedict⟩ **c :** to use a conjurer's tricks : JUGGLE

[2]**con·jure** \ˈkänjə(r) *also* ˈkən-\ *adj* **1** *of a person* : practicing magic, esp. voodoo **2** *of a thing* : used in the practice of magic, esp. voodoo ⟨~ ball⟩ ⟨~ bag⟩

con·jur·er *or* **con·ju·ror** \ˈkänjərə(r), -j(ə)rə *also* ˈkən-\ *n* -S [*conjurer* fr. ME *conjurere*, fr. *conjuren* to conjure + *-ere* -er; *conjuror* fr. ME *conjerour*, fr. *conjeren, conjuren* + *-our* -or] **1 :** one that practices magic arts : one that pretends to act by the aid of supernatural power : WIZARD **2 :** one that performs feats of legerdemain and illusion : MAGICIAN, JUGGLER

con·jury \ˈkänj(ə)rē, -ri *also* ˈkən-\ *n* -ES [*conjure* + *-y*] : the practice of magic : CONJURING

[1]**conk** \ˈkäŋk, ˈkȯŋk\ *n* -S [prob. alter. of *conch*] **1** *slang* : NOSE **2** *slang* : HEAD

[2]**conk** \"\ *vt* -ED/-ING/-S *slang* : to hit esp. on the head : knock out

[3]**conk** \"\ *n* -S [by alter.] : CONCH 3

[4]**conk** \"\ *n* -S [prob. alter. of *conch*] **1 :** the visible fruiting body of a tree fungus : BRACKET 3c **2 :** the decay in the wood of living trees caused by a fungus — **conky** \-kē, -ki\ *adj*

[5]**conk** \"\ *vi* -ED/-ING/-S [prob. imit.] **1 :** to break down : STALL, FAIL — used esp. of an engine or motor **2 :** FAINT : pass out : black out : DIE ⟨if I should ~, I do not wish to be disinterred after the war —G.S.Patton⟩ — often used with *out* ⟨she had a shock and ~*ed* out⟩ : go to sleep — usu. used with *off* ⟨go upstairs and ~ off⟩

conk·a·nee hemp \ˈkäŋkənē-\ *n* [prob. irreg. fr. *Konkan*, coast region of Bombay state, India] : SUNN

[1]**conk·er** \ˈkäŋkə(r), -ˈkȯŋ-\ *n* -S [*conch* + *-er* (influenced by *conquer*)] **1 conkers** *pl* : a game popular in England in which each player swings a horse chestnut or orig. a snail shell threaded on a string to try to break one held by his opponent **2 :** a horse chestnut or snail shell esp. when used in conkers

[2]**conker** *var of* KUNKUR

conky \-kē\ *n* -ES [[1]*conk* + *-y*] *slang* : a person having a large or prominent nose

con mae·stà \ˌk|än,mīˈstä, ˌk|än,mä,eˈstä, |ōn-\ *adv* [It] : with majesty — used as a direction in music

con man \ˈkän,man, -maa(ə)n\ *n* [by shortening] : a confidence man

con mo·to \känˈmō,tō, kōn-\ *adv* [It, with movement] : with movement : SPIRITEDLY — used as a direction in music

[1]**conn** *also* **con** \ˈkän\ *vt* -ED/-ING/-S [alter. of *cond*, prob. taken as past tense] : to conduct or superintend the steering of (a ship or airplane) : watch the course of (a ship) and direct the helmsman how to steer

[2]**conn** \"\ *n* -S : the control exercised by one who guides or directs the movements of a ship

conn *abbr* **1** connected; connection **2** connotation; connotative

con·nach \ˈkänək\ *vt* -ED/-ING/-S [ScGael *conach* murrain; akin to IrGael, murrain, rabies, rage] *Scot* : SPOIL, WASTE

con·nacht *also* **con·naught** \ˈkä(ˌ)nȯt\ *adj, usu cap* [fr. *Connacht* or *Connaught*, Ireland] : of or from the province of Connacht, Ireland : of the kind or style prevalent in Connacht

con·na·ra·ce·ae \ˌkänəˈrāsē,ē\ *n pl, cap* [NL, fr. *Connarus*, type genus + *-aceae*] : a family of mostly tropical climbing shrubs or small trees (order Rosales) closely related to the Leguminosae but lacking stipules — **con·na·ra·ceous** \ˌ==ˈrāshəs\ *adj*

con·na·rite *also* **con·a·rite** \ˈkänə,rīt\ *n* -S [ISV *connar-, conar-* (fr. Gk *konnaros*) + *-ite*; orig. formed as G *konarit*] : a mineral consisting of hydrous nickel silicate occurring as small green crystals or grains

con·na·rus \ˈkänərəs\ *n, cap* [NL, fr. Gk *konnaros*, a kind of prickly evergreen (perh. the Christ's-thorn *Paliurus spina-christi*)] : a large genus (the type of the family Connaraceae) of tropical shrubs or trees bearing indehiscent one-seeded pods — see ZEBRAWOOD

con·na·tal \(ˈ)kä|nād·ᵊl, kəˈn-, -ātᵊl\ *adj* [*connate* + *-al*] : CONGENITAL — **con·na·tal·ly** \-ād·ᵊlē, -ātᵊlē\ *adv*

con·nate \(ˈ)kä|nāt, kəˈnāt, *usu* -ād·+V\ *adj* [LL *connatus*, past part. of *connasci* to be born together, fr. L *com-* + *nasci* to be born — more at NATION] **1 :** CONGENITAL, INNATE, INBORN ⟨~ ideas⟩ **2 :** agreeing in nature : AKIN, ALLIED, COGNATE, CONGENIAL ⟨~ spirits⟩ **3 :** born, produced, or originated together ⟨~ qualities⟩ **4** *biol* **a :** congenitally united ⟨~ leaves⟩ **b :** firmly united : FUSED ⟨~ bones⟩ — distinguished from *connivent;* compare ADNATE **5** *geol* : entrapped in sediments at the time of their deposition : originating at the same time as adjacent or intermingled materials ⟨~ water⟩ — **con·nate·ly** *adv*

con·na·tion \(ˈ)kä|nāshən, kəˈn-\ *n* -S : congenital union

con·na·tive \(ˈ)kä|nād·iv, kəˈn-, -ātiv\ *adj, obs* : CONNATE 1

con·natural \(ˈ)kä, kə+\ *adj* [ML *connaturalis*, fr. L *com-* + *naturalis* natural — more at NATURAL] **1 :** connected by nature : INBORN, INHERENT, NATURAL ⟨man's ~ sense of the good⟩ **2 :** of the same nature : ALLIED, COGNATE ⟨and mix with our ~ dust —John Milton⟩ **3** *obs* : SUITABLE, CONGENIAL — **con·naturality** \"+\ *n* -ES — **con·naturally** \"+\ *adv*

con·nect \kəˈnekt\ *vb* -ED/-ING/-S [L *connectere, conectere*, fr. *com-, co-* + *nectere* to bind — more at ANNEX] *vt* **1 :** to join, fasten, or link together usu. by means of something intervening ⟨a bus line ~s the two towns⟩ ⟨~ a garden hose to the faucet⟩ ⟨the ties that ~*ed* new Europe to old —Stringfellow Barr⟩ **2 :** to place or establish in any of various intangible relationships (as association in thought or logic, the relationship of follower, official, or employee, or a relationship of things similar in purpose, motivation, configuration, or substance) ⟨~ his success with hard work and study⟩ ⟨~ himself with a radical school of painters⟩ ⟨she could not ~ her mother's meanness with the magnitude of what had happened —Louis Auchincloss⟩ ⟨the emphasis on the subjective expression of the art of the mentally ill which ~s it with certain tendencies of modern art —H.S.Langfeld⟩ ⟨the marriage of the children ~*ed* the two families⟩ ~ *vi* **1 a :** JOIN, UNITE, COHERE ⟨one room ~s with the other by means of a hallway⟩ **b :** to have a relationship ⟨one argument ~s with the other⟩ ⟨his character seems at first not to ~ with his painting —A.M. Daintrey⟩ **2 a** *of a means of transportation* : to meet for the transference of passengers ⟨the New York and Boston trains ~ at Albany⟩ **b** *of a passenger* : to transfer esp. from one train or bus to another that covers a different part of one's route — used with *with* ⟨to ~ with the Chicago train in St. Louis⟩ **3 :** to hit solidly or successfully ⟨~ for a double⟩ ⟨~ with a knockout punch⟩; *esp* : to hit a home run **syn** see JOIN

connected *adj* **1 :** joined or linked together ⟨a ~ series⟩ **2 :** having the parts or elements logically related ⟨a ~ view of the problem⟩ or continuous ⟨~ reading from the great authors⟩ **3 :** related by blood or marriage ⟨a well-*connected* Edinburgh family —Rosemary Benét⟩ ⟨a well-*connected* Marylander — it was supposed that his grandfather was the younger brother of the Earl of Wemyss —Van Wyck Brooks⟩ **4** *chess* **a** *of pawns* : on adjacent squares **b** *of rooks* : mutually supported (as on an empty rank) — **con·nect·ed·ly** *adv* — **con·nect·ed·ness** *n* -ES

connected load *n* : the total electric power-consuming rating of all devices (as lamps or motors) connected to a distribution system

connected surface *n, math* **:** a surface from any point of which a continuous path can be drawn to any other point of it without crossing its boundary

connecter *var of* CONNECTOR

con·nect·i·cut \kə'ned·ə̇kət, -netə-, *usu* -kəd·+V\ *adj, usu cap* [fr. *Connecticut*, state in the northeastern U.S., fr. *Connecticut* river, prob. fr. Mohican *quinnitukq-ut* at the long tidal river] **:** of or from the state of Connecticut ⟨*Connecticut* flora⟩ **:** of the kind or style prevalent in Connecticut

connecticut chest *n, usu cap 1st C* **:** an early American framed chest with the front panels decorated usu. with split spindles and tulip and sunflower patterns carved in flat relief — called also *sunflower chest*

con·nect·i·cut·er \-,kəd·ə(r), -,kətə-, -,kə̇d·ə-\ *n* -S *cap* **:** a native or resident of the state of Connecticut

connecticut warbler *n, usu cap C* **:** a large wood warbler (*Oporornis agilis*) gray to greenish above and yellow below that breeds in north-central No. America and winters in Brazil

connecting filament *n* **:** OOBLAST

connecting note *or* **connecting tone** *n* **:** a note common to two successive chords

connecting rod *n* **:** a rigid rod that transmits power from one rotating part of a machine to another in reciprocating motion (as from a crankpin to a piston) — see CROSSHEAD illustration

con·nec·tion \kə'nekshən\ *n* -S [L *connexion-, connexio*, fr. *connexus* (past part. of *connectere* to connect) + *-ion-, -io* -ion — more at CONNECT] **1 a :** the act of connecting **:** a coming into or being put in contact ⟨~ with the island was made by a causeway⟩ **b :** sexual relation or intercourse ⟨had had no ~ with any other woman —John Abernethy⟩ **2 :** the state of being connected or linked **:** ALLIANCE, UNION ⟨Canada's political ~ with England⟩ ⟨~ between church and state⟩ **3 a :** relationship or association in thought (as of cause and effect, logical sequence, mutual dependence or involvement) ⟨the ~ of intelligence and success⟩ **b :** CONTEXT, REFERENCE, OCCASION ⟨in this ~ the word has a different meaning⟩ **c :** COHERENCE, CONTINUITY ⟨a confused multitude without order or ~ —John Locke⟩ **4 :** CONNECTIVE b, d **5 a :** something that connects **:** COUPLING, LINK ⟨plumbing ~*s*⟩ **b :** a means of communication ⟨telephone ~⟩ or transport ⟨the train makes ~ with the steamer⟩ ⟨to miss a ~⟩ **6 :** a person connected with others by marriage, remote blood relationship, or such a tie as a common interest ⟨he has powerful ~*s* in high places⟩ **7 :** a social, professional, or commercial relationship in a practical or active way: as **a :** POSITION, JOB **b :** a permanent or continuing arrangement to execute orders or advance interests esp. at a distance ⟨a firm's foreign ~*s*⟩ **c** *slang* **:** a source of contraband (as a narcotic drug) **8 :** a set or group of persons connected or associated together in a common interest: **a :** DENOMINATION, SECT **b :** a political faction **c** *Brit* **:** the owner of a racehorse and his associates **d :** a large family **:** CLAN **e :** a clientele esp. of a doctor or lawyer **9 :** a religious association practicing connexionalism — **con·nec·tion·al** \-kshən°l, -kshnəl\ *adj*

con·nec·tion·ism \-shə,nizəm\ *n* -S **:** a theory that learning takes place through the formation of connections or associative bonds between contiguous stimulus and response

[1]**con·nec·tive** \kə'nektiv, -tēv *also* -təv\ *adj* [L *connectere* to connect + E *-ive*] **:** tending to connect **:** CONNECTING — **con·nec·tive·ly** *adv*

[2]**connective** \"\ *n* -S **:** something that connects: **a :** the tissue connecting the pollen sacs of an anther **b :** a linguistic form that connects words or word groups; *esp* **:** a relative pronoun **:** CONJUNCTION, PREPOSITION **c :** a nerve that connects two ganglia esp. of the same side of the body **d** *logic* **:** a constant (as *or, if-then, and, not*) linking two statements or attaching to a single statement so that the truth-value of the composite is determined by the truth-value of the components

connective tissue *n* **1 :** any of various tissues of mesodermal origin having abundant intercellular substance or interlacing processes and showing little tendency for the constituent cells to aggregate in sheets or masses — compare EPITHELIUM **2 :** connective tissue made up of stellate or spindle-shaped cells with interlacing processes that pervades, supports, and binds together other tissues and organs and forms ligaments, tendons, and aponeuroses — compare ADIPOSE TISSUE, AREOLAR TISSUE, ELASTIC TISSUE, WHITE FIBROUS TISSUE

con·nec·tiv·i·ty \,kä,nək'tivəd·ē, -ətē, -i\ *n* -ES **:** the quality or state of being connective

con·nec·tor *also* **con·nec·ter** \kə'nektə(r)\ *n* -S **1 :** one who connects: **a :** a worker who couples railroad coaches **b :** a construction worker who guides and bolts structural steel members as they are hoisted into position in the framework of a building or bridge **2 :** something that connects: as **a :** a flexible tube for connecting the ends of tubes **b :** a railroad coupling **c** (1) **:** a device for detachably connecting flexible electrical conductors together (2) **:** a fitting for joining wires without splicing **d :** the part of the firing mechanism of small arms that transmits the motion of the trigger to the sear **e :** a metallic fitting for joining timbers

connector, 2 c (1)

connector neuron *n* **:** an internuncial neuron

conned *past of* CON *or of* CONN

con·nell·ite \'kän°l,īt\ *n* -S [Arthur *Connell fl*1857 Brit. chemist + E *-ite*] **:** a mineral $Cu_{19}(SO_4)Cl_4(OH)_{32}.3H_2O(?)$ consisting of hydrous copper sulfate chloride commonly in slender prisms

con·ne·ma·ra pony \,känə'märə-\ *n, usu cap C* [fr. *Connemara*, district in Connacht province, Ireland] **:** a small hardy horse of an Irish breed of uncertain origin noted for its intelligence and stamina

[1]**con·ner** \'kənə(r), 'kän-\ *n* -S [ME, fr. OE *cunnere* examiner, tempter, fr. *cunnian* to examine; akin to OE *cunnan* to be able — more at CAN] *archaic* **:** one that tests or examines ⟨election of four ale ~*s* for the City of London —*Scotsman*⟩

[2]**conner** *var of* CUNNER

[1]**connex** *n* -ES [MF *connexe* connected property, fr. *connexe*, adj., connected, related, fr. L *connexus*, past part. of *connectere* — more at CONNECT] **1** *obs* **a :** BOND, TIE **b :** a connected incident or property **2** *obs* **:** a conditional proposition in logic

[2]**con·nex** \kə'neks\ *vb* -ED/-ING/-ES [MF *connexer*, fr. *connexe* connected] **:** CONNECT

[3]**connex** \'kä(,)neks, -,niks\ *adj* [L *connexus*] **1 :** CONNECTED: as **a :** closely connected **:** linked in meaning (as *father-son, left-right*) —opposed to *disparate* **b** *of a dyadic relation* **:** connecting every two distinct members of its field ⟨in the field of positive integers, the relation *less than or equal to* is ~ for either a ≤ b or b ≤ a⟩ **2 :** belonging to or constituting one syntactical unit ⟨in *the dog barked*, the complete sentence or either or both of its constituents are ~⟩

con·nex·ion \kə'nekshən\ *chiefly Brit var of* CONNECTION

con·nex·ion·al \kə'nekshənəl, -kshnəl\ *chiefly Brit var of* CONNECTIONAL

con·nex·ion·al·ism \kə'nekshənə,lizəm\ *n* -S **:** a form of church organization esp. in mission areas where scattered churches are held together by itinerant evangelists

con·nex·i·ty \kə'neksəd·ē, -ətē, -i\ *n* -ES [F *connexité*, fr. *connexe* + *-ité* -ity] **1 :** the character of being connex **2 :** something that is connex **3 :** the state of being syntactically connex

connexive *adj* [L *connexivus*, fr. *connexus* (past part. of *connectere*) + *-ivus* -ive — more at CONNECT] **1** *obs* **:** CONDITIONAL **2** *obs* **:** CONJUNCTIVE, CONNECTIVE

con·nex·i·vum \,kä,nək'sēvəm\ *n, pl* **connexi·va** \-və\ [NL, fr. L, neut. of *connexivus*] **:** the flattened often much dilated lateral border of the abdomen of hemipterous insects

con·nie \'känē\ *n* -S [prob. by shortening & alter.] **:** INCONNU

[1]**conning** *pres part of* CON

[2]**conning** *n* -S [fr. gerund of [1]*conn*] **:** the giving of directions (as of course and speed) for steering or guiding a ship or aircraft

conning tower *n* **:** an armored pilothouse (as on a submarine) usu. having narrow horizontal slits for observation and housing the means of communication with all parts of the ship

con·nip·tion \kə'nipshən\ *or* **conniption fit** *n* -S [origin unknown] **:** a fit of rage, hysteria, or alarm ⟨to throw a ~⟩

conniption bug *n* **:** HELLGRAMMITE

con·niv·ance *also* **con·niv·ence** \kə'nīvən(t)s\ *n* -S [F or L; F *connivence*, fr. L *conniventia*, fr. *connivent-, connivens* (pres. part. of *connivēre*) + *-ia*] **1 :** the act of conniving **:** intentional failure to notice or discover a wrongdoing **:** passive consent or cooperation **2 :** corrupt or guilty assent to wrongdoing that involves knowledge of and failure to prevent or oppose it but no actual participation in it — compare ACCOMPLICE

connivancy *n* -ES [L *conniventia*] *obs* **:** CONNIVANCE

con·nive \kə'nīv\ *vb* -ED/-ING/-S [F or L; F *conniver*, fr. L *conivēre, connivēre* to close the eyes, wink, be indulgent, connive, fr. *com-* + *-nivēre* (akin to *nictare* to wink); akin to OE & OHG *hnīgan* to bow, bend, Goth *hneiwan* to bow, ON *hnīga* to bow, L *nicere* to beckon, and perh. to Lith *knibti* to break by bending] *vi* **1 :** to pretend ignorance or unawareness of something one ought morally or officially or legally to oppose **:** fail to take action against a known wrongdoing or misbehavior — usu. used with *at* ⟨~ at the violation of a law⟩ **2 a :** to be indulgent, tolerant, or secretly in favor or sympathy **:** WINK — usu. used with *at* ⟨~ at youthful follies⟩ **b :** to cooperate secretly **:** have a secret understanding — usu. used with *with* ⟨officials who were not above *conniving* with him in importing goods —J.A.Krout⟩ **3 :** CONSPIRE, INTRIGUE ⟨she loved to ~ with her friends in their amours —Helen Howe⟩ ⟨he had declared that no candidate was ever chosen without *conniving* —*Time*⟩ ~ *vt, obs* **:** to shut the eyes to **:** wink at

con·niv·ent \-vənt\ *adj* [L *connivent-, connivens*, pres. part. of *connivēre*] **1** *obs* **:** CONNIVING **2 :** converging but not fused into a single part ⟨an insect with ~ wings⟩ ⟨~ stamens⟩ — distinguished from *connate*

con·niv·er \-və(r)\ *n* -S **:** one that connives

con·niv·ery \-v(ə)rē, -ri\ *n* -ES [*connive* + *-ry*] **:** the practice of conniving

con·no·chae·tes \,känə'kēd·ēz\ *n, cap* [NL, fr. Gk *konnos* beard + NL *-chaetes*] **:** the genus of ruminants (family *Bovidae*) comprising the gnus

con·nois·seur \¦känə¦sər, -sə̄ *also* -sū(ə)r, -süə *sometimes* -syü-, '==,=\ *n* -S [obs. F (now *connaisseur*), fr. OF *connoisseor*, fr. *conoiss-* (stem of *connoistre* to know, fr. L *cognoscere*) + *-eor* -or — more at COGNITION] **1 :** one who is expert in a subject; *esp* **:** one who understands the details, technique, or principles of an art and is competent to act as a critical judge **2 :** a discriminating judge or critic of something **:** one who enjoys with discrimination and appreciation of subtleties ⟨a ~ of his own responses⟩ ⟨a ~ of rare tobaccos⟩

con·nois·seur·ship \,==¦=,ship\ *n* -S **:** expertness in a matter of taste or discrimination **:** knowledgeability esp. in aesthetic or recondite matters ⟨none of that pedantic affectation of ~ which makes a premature fuss over trifles —Irvin Stock⟩ ⟨esthetic ~ has generally displaced a creative conception of art —Walter Gropius⟩

con·no·ta·tion \,känə'tāshən, -nō't-\ *n* -S [ML *connotation-, connotatio*, fr. *connotatus* (past part. of *connotare* to connote) + *-ion-, -io* -ion] **1 a :** the conveying or suggesting a meaning by a word along with or apart from the thing it explicitly names or describes ⟨the value of ~ in poetry⟩ ⟨it was quite wrong to call it mind, the ~ was false —Willa Cather⟩ — compare DENOTATION 2 **b :** something implied or suggested by a word or sometimes by a thing **:** IMPLICATION ⟨using a literary language in which the ~*s* of words tend to overwhelm their precise significance —Walter Lippmann⟩ ⟨stayed in one place long enough for it to assume familiar ~*s* —Norman Mailer⟩ **2 :** the meaning of a word (as a word representing an emotion, a feeling, quality, a moral idea) **:** SIGNIFICATION ⟨that abuse of logic which consists in moving counters about as if they were known entities with a fixed ~ —W.R.Inge⟩ **3 :** the property or group of properties connoted by a term in logic and signified by or comprised in a concept or essential to the thing named **:** COMPREHENSION, SIGNIFICATION — contrasted with *denotation* — **con·no·ta·tion·al** \¦==¦=shən°l, -shnəl\ *adj*

con·no·ta·tive \'känə,tād·iv, -tāt|, |ēv *also* |əv; *sometimes* kə'nōd·əd·iv\ *adj* [ML *connotativus*, fr. *connotatus* + L *-ivus* -ive] **1 :** connoting or tending to connote **:** relating to connotation **:** bearing implication **2** *logic* **:** having connotation **:** denoting a subject and implying an attribute — **con·no·ta·tive·ly** \'känə,tād·əvlē, -tātəv-, -li\ *adv*

connotative definition *n* **:** a statement of the equivalence of connotation between the defined term and another expression

con·note \kə'nōt, (')kä¦nōt, *usu* -ōd· +V\ *vt* -ED/-ING/-S [ML *connotare*, fr. L *com-* + *notare* to mark, note — more at NOTE] **1** *of a word or phrase* **a :** to signify in addition to its exact explicit meaning ⟨the word *home* usu. ~*s* comfort and security⟩ **b :** to have as the sum of meanings **:** MEAN, SIGNIFY ⟨to some *Bohemian* ~*s* a slovenly crank⟩ ⟨*anabolism* is a word used to ~ building up or assimilative processes —C.H.Best & N.B.Taylor⟩ **2 a :** to arouse as an inseparably associated idea or feeling **:** IMPLY, SUGGEST ⟨unless a few desiccated potted palms ~ the Orient —Truman Capote⟩ **b :** to be associated with or inseparable from as a consequence or concomitant ⟨guilt usu. ~*s* suffering⟩ **3** *logic* **:** to imply, indicate, or involve as an attribute **:** bear as connotation — contrasted with *denote* ⟨the word *white* denotes all white things, as snow, paper, the foam of the sea, etc., and implies, or, as it was termed by the schoolmen, ~*s*, the attribute *whiteness* —J.S.Mill⟩

conns *pres 3d sing of* CONN, *pl of* CONN

con·nu·bi·al \kə'n(y)übēəl\ *adj* [L *connubialis*, fr. *connubium, conubium* marriage (fr. *com-, co-* + *-nubium*, fr. *nubere* to marry) + *-alis* -al — more at NUPTIAL] **:** of or relating to marriage or the marriage state **:** CONJUGAL ⟨I never could imagine ~ bliss till after tea —W.S.Maugham⟩ — **con·nu·bi·al·ly** \-ēəlē, -li\ *adv*

con·nu·bi·al·i·ty \=,=bē'aləd·ē, -ətē, -i\ *n* -ES **:** the married state; *also* **:** something characteristic of it

con·nu·bi·um *also* **co·nu·bi·um** \kə'n(y)übēəm\ *n, pl* **connu·bia** *also* **conu·bia** \-bēə\ [L] **1** *Roman law* **:** lawful marriage **2** *Roman law* **:** the right to intermarry — called also *jus conubii*

con·ny \'känē, -ni\ *dial Eng var of* CANNY

conny boy \"-\ *n* [origin unknown] **:** a worker who removes sludge and incrustations from refining pans and vats

cono- — see [2]CON-

con·ob \(')kä¦nōb\ *n, pl* **conob** *or* **conobs** *usu cap* **:** KANHOBAL

co·no·car·pus \¦kōnə¦kärpəs, ¦kän-\ *n, cap* [NL, fr. [2]*con-* + *-carpus*] **:** a monotypic genus of tropical American trees or shrubs (family Terminaliaceae) with dense flower heads resembling buttons — see BUTTON TREE 1

co·no·ceph·a·lum \-¦sefələm\ *n, cap* [NL, fr. [2]*con-* + *-cephalum* (irreg. fr. Gk *-kephalos* -cephalous)] **:** a small genus of liverworts (family Marchantiaceae) having conical long-stalked female receptacles

co·no·dont \'kōnə,dänt, 'kän-\ *n* -S [ISV [2]*con-* + *-odont*; orig. formed as G *konodont*] **:** a Palaeozoic fossil sometimes considered to be teeth of extinct cyclostomes but more probably the remains of an unknown invertebrate form of life

[1]**co·noid** \'kō,nȯid, 'kä,n-\ *n* -S [Gk *kōnoeides* small cone, fr. neut. of *kōnoeidēs*, adj.] **1** *math* **:** a surface generated by a straight line that is perpendicular to and intersects a fixed straight line *l*, is revolved about *l*, and at the same time is translated along *l* **2 :** something that has a conoidal form (as a rifle bullet)

[2]**conoid** \"\ *adj* [Gk *kōnoeidēs* conical, fr. *kōn-* [2]con- + *-oeidēs* -oid] **:** shaped like or nearly like a cone **:** CONOIDAL

co·noi·dal \(')kō¦nȯid°l, kə'n-, (')kä¦n-\ *adj* [Gk *kōnoeidēs* + E *-al*] **:** like a cone **:** resembling or approaching a cone in shape — **co·noi·dal·ly** \-d°lē, -li\ *adv*

conoid ligament *n* **:** the posterior fasciculus of the coracoclavicular ligament connecting the conoid tubercle and the base of the coracoid

conoid tubercle *n* **:** a prominence on the underside of the clavicle that forms one attachment of the conoid ligament

co·nol·o·phus \kə'näləfəs, kō'n-\ *n, cap* [NL, fr. [2]*con-* + Gk *lophos* crest] **:** a genus of iguanid lizards including a single large burrowing form (*C. subcristatus*) of the Galápagos islands

co·noph·o·lis \-'näfələs\ *n, cap* [NL, fr. [2]*con-* + *-pholis*] **:** a small genus of parasitic scaly herbs (family Orobanchaceae) with flowers in a thick spike — see SQUAWROOT

co·no·phor oil \'kōnəfə(r)-, 'kän-\ *n* [NL *conophorum* (specific epithet of *Tetracarpidium conophorum*), fr. Gk *kōnophoron*, neut. of *kōnophoros*, fr. *kōno-* [2]con- + *-phoros* -phorous] **:** a drying oil resembling perilla oil in properties that is obtained from the fruit of a western African vine (*Tetracarpidium conophorum*) of the family Euphorbiaceae

[1]**co·no·pid** \'kōnə,pid, 'kän-\ *adj* [NL *Conopidae*] **:** of or relating to the Conopidae

[2]**conopid** \"\ *n* -S **:** a fly of the family Conopidae

co·nop·i·dae \kə'näpə,dē, kō'n-\ *n pl, cap* [NL, fr. *Conop-, Conops*, type genus (fr. Gk *kōnōps* gnat, mosquito) + *-idae*] **:** a family of broadheaded flies (order Diptera) comprising the thickheaded flies or wasp flies

co·no·po·phag·i·dae \,kōnə(,)pō'fajə,dē, ,kän-\ *n pl, cap* [NL, fr. *Conopophaga*, type genus (fr. Gk *kōnōp-, kōnōps* gnat, mosquito + NL *-o-* + *-phaga*) + *-idae*] **:** a small family of birds (order Passeriformes) that are related to the ovenbirds and have a large head and in some cases a very short tail

co·no·rhi·nus \,kōnə'rīnəs, ,kän-\ *n* [NL, fr. [2]*con-* + *-rhinus*] *syn of* TRIATOMA

co·no·scen·te \,kōnə'shentē, ,kän-\ *var of* COGNOSCENTE

co·no·scope \'kōnə,skōp, 'kän-\ *n* -S [[2]*con-* + *-scope*] **:** a polariscope for examining the interference figures produced by crystals in convergent polarized light — **co·no·scop·ic** \¦==¦skäpik\ *adj*

co·no·tra·che·lus \,kōnə'trākələs, -trak-, -ə·trə'kēləs\ *n, cap* [NL, fr. [2]*con-* + Gk *trachēlos* neck, throat] **:** a large genus of small, dark-colored American weevils (family Curculionidae) the larvae of which develop in fruits and seeds — see PLUM CURCULIO

con ot·ta·va \¦känə¦tävə, ¦kōn-\ *adv (or adj)* [It] **:** COLL' OTTAVA

co·noy \kə'nȯi\ *n, pl* **conoy** *or* **conoys** *usu cap* [prob. fr. Algonquian *Kanawha*] **1 a :** an Indian people that dwelt between the Potomac river and Chesapeake Bay, Maryland **b :** a member of such people **2 :** a dialect of Nanticoke

conquassation *n* -S [L *conquassation-, conquassatio*, fr. *conquassatus* (past part. of *conquassare* to shake severely, fr. *com-* + *quassare* to shake) + *-ion-, -io* -ion —more at QUASH] *obs* **:** a severe shaking

con·quer \'käŋkə(r) *sometimes* 'kȯŋkə(r)\ *vb* **conquered; conquered; conquering** \-k(ə)riŋ\ **conquers** [ME *conqueren*, fr. OF *conquerre*, fr. (assumed) VL *conquaerere*, alter. (influenced by L *quaerere* to ask, search) of L *conquirere* to search for, bring together, fr. *com-* + *-quirere* (fr. *quaerere*)] *vt* **1** *obs* **:** to procure by effort; ACQUIRE, GET, GAIN **2 :** to gain or acquire by force of arms **:** take possession of by violent means **:** gain dominion over **:** SUBJUGATE **3 :** to overcome by force of arms **:** VANQUISH ⟨if we be *conquer'd* let men ~ us —Shak.⟩ **4 :** to gain or win by overcoming obstacles or opposition **:** gain mastery over (as by exploration, penetration, or surmounting) ⟨the mountain was ~*ed*⟩ **5 :** to subdue or overcome by mental or moral power **:** SURMOUNT ⟨~ difficulties⟩ ⟨~ her fear⟩ ~ *vi* **:** to gain the victory **:** make conquests **:** be victorious ⟨resolved to ~ or to die⟩ ⟨hail the ~*ing* hero⟩

syn DEFEAT, VANQUISH, OVERCOME, SURMOUNT, SUBDUE, SUBJUGATE, REDUCE, OVERTHROW, ROUT, BEAT, LICK: these verbs are all of a kind in signifying to get the better of or bring to subjection. CONQUER and DEFEAT are perhaps the most general. DEFEAT usu. signifies merely the fact of getting the better of or winning against ⟨the enemy were successfully *defeated*⟩ ⟨he *defeated* the older man in the tennis tournament⟩ ⟨a distortion of the news picture which *defeats* the whole purpose to which our system is committed —F.L.Mott⟩ CONQUER, however, usu. implies a large and significant action as of a large force in war or an action involving an all-inclusive effort and a more or less permanent result ⟨Caesar *conquered* most of Gaul⟩ ⟨culture *conquers* more surely than the sword —A.M.Young⟩ ⟨science has *conquered* yellow fever —*Amer. Guide Series: La.*⟩ ⟨the 21-year-old Englishman who *conquered* the most dangerous river in the world —*N. Y. Times Book Rev.*⟩ VANQUISH suggests a significant action of a certain dignity usu. in the defeat of a person rather than a thing and usu. carrying the suggestion of complete defeat ⟨to overthrow the enemy solely by his own strength — to *vanquish* him solely by his own effort —Lafcadio Hearn⟩ ⟨to *vanquish* an opponent in a championship match at tennis⟩ OVERCOME usu. implies an opposing, more or less fixed obstacle to be dealt with ⟨to *overcome* the enemy's shore fortifications⟩ ⟨*overcoming* difficult legal obstacles —*Americana Annual*⟩ ⟨using the airlift to *overcome* the blockade —*Collier's Yr. Bk.*⟩ ⟨to *overcome* a speech defect⟩ SURMOUNT, like OVERCOME, implies an opposing, more or less fixed obstacle but carries the idea of surpassing or exceeding rather than overcoming in face-to-face conflict ⟨the technical problems to be *surmounted* —K.F.Mather⟩ ⟨many petty faults which he is apparently unable to *surmount* —*New Republic*⟩ ⟨Simon . . . has an inner force that is capable of *surmounting* conditions —Malcolm Cowley⟩ SUBDUE, SUBJUGATE, and REDUCE all throw emphasis upon the condition of subjection resulting from defeat. SUBDUE signifies to bring under control by or as if by overpowering ⟨in 1803 Commodore Edward Preble *subdued* the Barbary Coast pirates —*Amer. Guide Series: Maine*⟩ ⟨in their last century of conquest they almost succeeded in *subduing* the whole island —Paul Blanshard⟩ ⟨all violence or recklessness of feeling has been finally *subdued* —Willa Cather⟩ ⟨the wilderness had been almost completely *subdued* by cutting down the forests and building roads and cities⟩ SUBJUGATE signifies to bring into and keep in subjection, often as a slave is in subjection ⟨authoritarian reaction which overwhelmed Italy and *subjugated* it for two centuries —R.A.Hall b.1911⟩ ⟨the heart and imagination *subjugating* the senses and understanding —Matthew Arnold⟩ REDUCE signifies surrender and submission but usu. of a town or fortress under attack or siege ⟨the town and finally the province were *reduced* by the invaders⟩ OVERTHROW is much like OVERCOME but carries the strong idea of disaster to the overthrown ⟨to *overthrow* the established government by violence⟩ ⟨to get swiftly through the field of fire and pierce and *overthrow* the enemy lines —Tom Wintringham⟩ ⟨a huge body of evidence . . . completely *overthrows* the older view —*Meanjin*⟩ ROUT always suggests a defeat so complete as to cause flight or the complete dispersion of the opposition ⟨twelve hundred French and a large force of Indians . . . were intercepted . . . and utterly *routed*, only 200 of the French escaping capture or death —R.W.Bingham⟩ ⟨Weaver with the assistance of two other gunboats *routed* a large force of Texas cavalry when they attacked Fort Butler —L.H.Bolander⟩ BEAT and LICK are mainly characteristic of a different style of expression or level of usage than the preceding verbs. BEAT means the same as and is as comprehensive as DEFEAT but usu. applies to smaller, less significant actions than, say, CONQUER or VANQUISH ⟨the local ball team won the state championship by *beating* all comers⟩ LICK, a more informal word for DEFEAT, usu. implies the complete humbling or humiliation of the person defeated ⟨the fighter must be confirmed in the belief that he can *lick* anybody in the world —A.J. Liebling⟩ ⟨with the problem growing, the railroads have redoubled their efforts to *lick it* —William Faulkner⟩

con·quer·ing·ly *adv* **:** in a conquering manner

con·quer·or \-k(ə)rə(r)\ *n* -S [ME *conquerour*, fr. OF *conquereor*, fr. *conquerre* + *-eor* -or] **1 :** one that conquers **:** one that wins a country in war, subdues or subjugates a people, or overcomes an adversary **:** WINNER, VICTOR — compare CONQUISTADOR **2** *obs* **:** deciding game **:** RUBBER

[1]**con·quest** \'käl|n,kwest, |ŋ,k- *also* -,kwəst *sometimes* 'kȯ|\ *n* -S [ME *conquest, conqueste*, fr. OF *conquest, conqueste*, fr. (assumed) VL *conquaesitus, conquaesita*, alter. of L *conquisitus* (masc.) *conquisita* (fem.), past part. of *conquirere* to search for, bring together — more at CONQUER] **1 :** the act or process of conquering or acquiring by force **:** the act of overcoming ⟨three years sufficed for the ~ of the country —W.H.Prescott⟩ **2 :** the act of gaining by or as if by struggle ⟨the ~ of liberty⟩ ⟨she came dressed for ~⟩ ⟨an army bent on ~⟩ **3** *obs* **:** the state of being conquered **4 a :** something that is conquered **:** a possession gained by physical or moral force; *esp* **:** territory definitely appropriated in war **b :** a person whose favor, heart, or hand has been won ⟨what ~ brings he home —Shak.⟩ **5** *feudal law* **:** acquisition of property by purchase or means other than inheritance **:** ACQUISITION; *also* **:** the property so acquired **syn** see VICTORY

[2]**conquest** \", kən'kwest\ *vt* -ED/-ING/-S [ME *conquesten*, fr. MF *conquester*, fr. *conquest, conqueste*, n.] **1** *archaic* **:** ACQUIRE, GAIN **2** *archaic* **:** CONQUER, VANQUISH

conquest state *n* **:** a state formed by or based upon the subjugation of the original inhabitants

con·qui·an \'käŋkēən\ *n* -S [MexSp *con quien*, fr. Sp *¿con quién?* with whom?] **:** a card game for two played with 40 cards in which each player tries to form three or four of a kind or sequences and from which all games of rummy developed

con·quin·a·mine \(ˈ)kän¦kwinə,mēn, kən'k-, -,mən\ n -s [ISV com- + quinamine; orig. formed as G konquinamin] : a crystalline alkaloid $C_{19}H_{24}N_2O_2$ found with quinamine in cinchona barks

con·qui·nine \ˈkäŋkwə,nēn, -ïnk-, -,nən\ n -s [ISV com- + quinine; orig. formed as G konquinin] : QUINIDINE

con·quis·ta·dor \kə̇n¦k(w)istə,dȯ(ə)r, (ˈ)kä¦,(ˈ)kō¦,(ˈ)kō¦, ¦ŋ-'k(w)-, -k(w)ēs-, -¦dȯ(ə)r, -¦dȯ(ə)ə, -dōə\ n, pl **conquistadores** \-¦dȯ(ə)rz,-dō(ə)rz, -dōəz; -¦dō(,)z, -dō(,)-, -(,)rās\ or **conquistadors** \-¦dȯ(ə)rz,-dō(ə)rz, -¦dȯ(ə)z,-dōəz\ [Sp, fr. conquistado (past part. of conquistar to conquer, fr. conquista conquest, fr. fem. of conquisto, past part. of conquerir to conquer, fr. L conquirere to search for, bring together) + -or — more at CONQUER] : CONQUEROR; specif : any one of the leaders in the Spanish conquest of America, esp. of Mexico and Peru, in the 16th century

con·rad·son carbon test \¦känrədsən-\ n, usu cap 1st C [after Dr. Pontus H. Conradson, 20th cent. scientist, its inventor] : a determination of the weight of carbon residue of an oil (as a lubricating oil) obtained on evaporation to dryness in a closed vessel

con·ring·ia \kän'riŋ(g)ēə, -rinjēə\ n, cap [NL, fr. Herman Conring †1681 Ger. scholar + NL -ia] : a genus of Eurasian herbs (family Cruciferae) with entire clasping leaves, small yellow flowers in racemes, and long slender pods — see HARE'S-EAR 2

cons pl of CON, pres 3d sing of CON

cons abbr **1** consecrated **2** conservative **3** consigned; consignment **4** consol; consolidated **5** consonant **6** constable **7** constitution **8** construction **9** consul **10** consulting

con·san·guine \(ˈ)kän¦saŋgwə̇n also -¦sangw-\ adj [F consanguin, fr. L consanguineus, fr. com- + sanguineus of blood — more at SANGUINE] : CONSANGUINEOUS; specif : based on an extended group of blood relations esp. of unilinear descent and constituting the functional familial unit in a society ⟨the ~ family type of the matriarchal Hopi⟩ — contrasted with conjugal; compare FAMILY

con·san·guin·eal \¦kän,saŋ¦gwinēəl, -san¦gw-\ adj [L consanguineus + E -al] : CONSANGUINE ⟨~ ties are the normal basis for the transmission of land rights —W.H.Goodenough⟩

con·san·guin·ean \-¦gwinēən\ adj [L consanguineus + E -an] Roman law : having the same father

con·san·guin·eous \-nēəs\ adj [L consanguineus] **1** : of the same blood ⟨a ~ mating⟩ : descended from the same person (as a father) or the same ancestor ⟨~ brothers⟩; also : of or relating to persons so related ⟨a ~ community⟩ — distinguished from affinal; compare CONSANGUINE **2** : of the same origin ⟨~ igneous rocks⟩ — **con·san·guin·eous·ly** adv

con·san·guin·i·ty \¦känsaŋ¦gwinəd·ē, -san¦gw- -ətē, -i\ n -ES [ME consanguinyte, fr. MF consanguinité, fr. L consanguinitat-, consanguinitas, fr. consanguineus + -itat-, -itas -ity] **1** : the quality or state of being related by blood or descended from a common ancestor : BLOOD RELATIONSHIP — distinguished from affinity and commonly expressed in degrees of consanguinity ⟨according to one scheme a person has ~ of the second degree with his grandfather, grandson, uncle, cousin-german, and nephew or with corresponding female relations⟩; compare AGNATE, COGNATE **2** : genetic relationship; specif : the spatial, chronological, and compositional relationship existing between the various rocks in a single petrographic province **3** : a close relation or connection : AFFINITY ⟨the ~ of all religions⟩

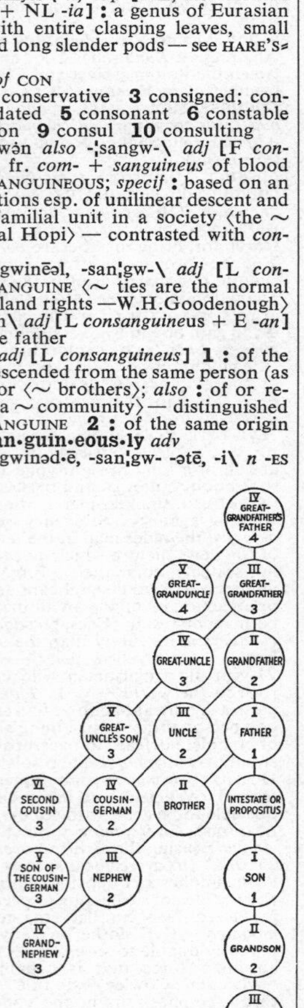

IV GREAT-GRANDFATHER'S FATHER 4 · V GREAT-GRANDUNCLE 4 · III GREAT-GRANDFATHER 3 · IV GREAT-UNCLE 3 · II GRANDFATHER 2 · V GREAT-UNCLE'S SON 3 · III UNCLE 2 · I FATHER 1 · VI SECOND COUSIN 3 · IV COUSIN-GERMAN 2 · II BROTHER 1 · INTESTATE OR PROPOSITUS · V SON OF THE COUSIN-GERMAN 3 · III NEPHEW 2 · I SON 1 · IV GRAND-NEPHEW 3 · II GRANDSON 2 · III GREAT-GRANDSON 3

diagram showing degrees of consanguinity between a given person (intestate or propositus) and lineal and collateral relations according to the common-law and canon-law computation (Arabic numerals) and the civil-law computation (Roman numerals), lineal relations being represented by the disks vertically connected, collateral relations by those at the side

consarcinate vt -ED/-ING/-S [L consarcinatus, past part. of consarcinare, fr. com- + -sarcinare (fr. sarcire to mend, patch)] obs : to patch together — **consarcination** n -S archaic

con·sarn \(ˈ)kän¦särn, kən-'s-, -sän\ vt -ED/-ING/-S [alter. of ¹concern; prob. euphemism for confound] dial : DAMN — a mild imprecation

¹con·sarned \(ˈ)kän¦särnd, kən's-, -sänd\ also **consarn** \-särn, -sän\ adj, dial : DAMNED, CONFOUNDED — a mild imprecation ⟨that ~ old thief —Kate D. Wiggin⟩

²consarned \"\ also **consarn** \"\ adv [¹consarned, consarn] dial : TERRIBLY, AWFULLY — a mild imprecation ⟨he was always ~ lucky⟩

con·science \ˈkänchən(t)s sometimes ˈkōn-\ n -S [ME, fr. OF, fr. L conscientia, fr. conscient-, consciens (pres. part. of conscire to know, be conscious, fr. com- + scire to know) + -ia -y — more at SCIENCE] **1 a** : the sense of right or wrong within the individual ⟨decide a matter according to your own ~⟩ : the awareness of the moral goodness or blameworthiness of one's own conduct, intentions, or character together with a feeling of obligation to do or be that which is recognized as good often felt to be instrumental in producing feelings of guilt or remorse for ill-doing; specif : the part of the superego in psychoanalysis of which the ego is conscious and through which the commands and admonitions of the superego are communicated to the ego **b** : the faculty, power, or principle (as in an individual, nation, or group) that guides toward the right and away from the wrong ⟨~ rather than professional loyalty was his spiritual leader⟩ ⟨the still small voice of his ~⟩ **2** obs : inmost thought or sense : knowledge of inner self : CONSCIOUSNESS ⟨a ~ of having done his duty⟩ **3 a** obs : conscientious observance : REVERENCE, REGARD — used with of or to ⟨mere ~ of royal rank⟩ **b** : observance of or loyalty to the dictates of the moral or ethical sense : CONSCIENTIOUSNESS ⟨forbidden by ~ and by law⟩ ⟨they blunder along badly enough in all ~ —Walter Lippmann⟩ **4** : sensitive regard for fairness or justice : SCRUPLE, COMPUNCTION ⟨a legal advisor with no ~ for his client's feeling⟩ ⟨a profiteer with no ~⟩ — **in all conscience** or **in conscience** adv **1** : in all reasonableness and fairness **2** : beyond a doubt

conscience clause n : a clause in a general law exempting persons whose religious scruples forbid compliance therewith (as from taking judicial oaths)

con·science·less \-ləs\ adj : lacking a conscience : not guided by conscience : UNSCRUPULOUS

conscience money n : money paid to relieve the conscience by rendering or restoring usu. anonymously what has been wrongfully acquired or withheld (as a tax payment)

con·scient \-chənt\ adj [L conscient-, consciens, pres. part. of conscire to be conscious] : CONSCIOUS

con·sci·en·tious \¦känchē¦enchəs also -änsē¦- sometimes ¦kōn-\ adj [F conscientieux, fr. ML conscientiosus, fr. L conscientia conscience + -osus -ous — more at CONSCIENCE] **1** : governed by or made in accordance with the dictates of conscience : HONEST, SCRUPULOUS ⟨a ~ public servant⟩ ⟨~ judgments⟩ ⟨too ~ to cultivate political arts that were repulsive to him —S.E.Morison & H.S.Commager⟩ **2** : marked by or done with exact or thoughtful attention : METICULOUS, CAREFUL ⟨a very ~ description of every feature —R.P.Warren⟩ ⟨~ about justifying every phrase —Leslie Rees⟩ ⟨a ~ reader of newspapers —Willa Cather⟩ **syn** see UPRIGHT

con·sci·en·tious·ly adv : in a conscientious manner

con·sci·en·tious·ness \,==ˈ==nəs\ n -ES : the quality or state of being conscientious

conscientious objection n : objection on moral or religious grounds (as to service in the armed forces or to bearing arms)

conscientious objector n : one who refuses or is exempted from service in the armed forces as contrary to his moral or religious principles; also : one who although serving in the armed forces is exempted for like reasons from bearing arms

conscionable adj [conscion- (back-formation fr. conscience, taken as pl.) + -able] : CONSCIENTIOUS

¹con·scious \ˈkänchəs sometimes ˈkōn-\ adj [L conscius, fr. com- + -scius (fr. scire to know) — more at SCIENCE] **1** : knowing secret human thoughts : noting human actions — used of inanimate things as if capable of human perception ⟨cries that fell upon the ~ air⟩ **2** : perceiving, apprehending, or noticing with a degree of controlled thought or observation : recognizing as existent, factual, or true: **a** : knowing or perceiving something within oneself or a fact about oneself ⟨~ of his own deficiencies⟩ ⟨~ of having succeeded⟩ ⟨the careful tread of one ~ of his alcoholic load —Thomas Hardy⟩ — formerly used with to and a reflexive pronoun ⟨~ to himself of being remiss⟩ **b** : recognizing as factual or existent something external ⟨Rose was ~ that she was steadily bringing the tiller over —C.S.Forester⟩ ⟨I suddenly became ~ that some one was looking at me —Oscar Wilde⟩ — formerly used with to ⟨~ to a crime⟩ **3** obs : inwardly aware of guilt : having knowledge of wrongdoing : GUILTY **4 a** : present esp. to the senses : VISIBLE ⟨the ~ grace of a thoroughbred horse⟩ **b** : subjectively perceived : personally felt ⟨~ guilt⟩ **5 a** : having rational power : capable of thought, will, design, or perception ⟨not a mindless force but a ~ one, bent upon our destruction —C.B.Nordhoff & J.N.Hall⟩ **b** : involving rational power, perception, and awareness : embodying consideration and decision ⟨our ~ actions⟩ ⟨all ~ experience has of necessity some degree of imaginative quality —John Dewey⟩ **6** : marked by self-consciousness : aware of the scrutiny of others to a point of not appearing natural or spontaneous : AFFECTED, MANNERED ⟨she is artificial . . . one can feel always the heavily ~ performer —G.J.Nathan⟩ **7** : mentally active : fully possessed of one's mental faculties : having emerged from sleep, faint, or stupor : AWAKE ⟨the patient becoming ~ as the anesthesia wears off⟩ **8 a** : marked by full recognition, candid acceptance, or frank espousal of a given role and often by pervasive conviction in filling it ⟨a deliberate and ~ artist with an abiding care for craftsmanship —Times Lit. Supp.⟩ ⟨a restrained . . . altogether ~ comedian, an artful creature of merriment —Time⟩ **b** : assumed, determined, treated, or executed with awareness, care, purpose, or consideration ⟨a half-conscious effort, like our self-deceptive pretence of jollity at a threadbare joke —Nathaniel Hawthorne⟩ ⟨the settlers in Minnesota . . . had neither leisure nor impulse for a ~ art —Amer. Guide Series: Minn.⟩ **9 a** : likely to notice, consider, or appraise ⟨a style-conscious buyer⟩ **b** : concerned with, interested in, realizing, or pondering significance or potentialities ⟨modern air-conscious businessmen⟩ **c** : marked by a strong or compulsive complex of feelings or notions ⟨an extremely class-conscious appeal⟩ **syn** see AWARE

²conscious \"\ n -ES : CONSCIOUSNESS 5

con·scious·ly adv : in a conscious manner

con·scious·ness \-nəs\ n -ES **1 a** : awareness or perception of an inward psychological or spiritual fact : intuitively perceived knowledge of something in one's inner self **b** : inward awareness of an external object, state, or fact ⟨a ~ . . . of what really is at stake in modern philosophy —Hannah Arendt⟩ **c** : concerned awareness : INTEREST, CONCERN — often used with an attributive noun ⟨tax ~⟩ ⟨class ~⟩ ⟨rank ~⟩ **2** : the state or activity that is characterized by sensation, emotion, volition, or thought : mind in the broadest possible sense : something in nature that is distinguished from the physical **3** : the totality in psychology of sensations, perceptions, ideas, attitudes, and feelings of which an individual or a group is aware at any given time or within a particular time span — compare STREAM OF CONSCIOUSNESS **4** : waking life (as that to which one returns after sleep, trance, fever) wherein all one's mental powers have returned ⟨the ether wore off and the patient regained ~⟩ **5** : the part of mental life or psychic content in psychoanalysis that is immediately available to the ego — compare PRECONSCIOUS, UNCONSCIOUS 2

con·scribe \kən'skrīb\ vt -ED/-ING/-S [L conscribere to enroll, fr. com- + scribere to write — more at SCRIBE] **1** : LIMIT, CIRCUMSCRIBE ⟨ill-health . . . conscribed the force of his intentions —Times Lit. Supp.⟩ **2** : to enlist forcibly : CONSCRIPT, IMPRESS ⟨the power to ~ everybody and everything in the case of war —Aldous Huxley⟩

¹con·script \ˈkän,skript\ adj [MF & L; MF conscript, conscrit, fr. L conscriptus, past part. of conscribere to write together, enroll, fr. com- + scribere to write — more at SCRIBE] **1** : enrolled into service by compulsion : CONSCRIPTED, DRAFTED ⟨~ soldiers⟩ ⟨a hospital served by ~ nurses⟩ **2** : made up of impressed or drafted persons ⟨~ armies⟩ ⟨a ~ labor camp⟩

²conscript \"\ n -S [trans. of F conscrit] : one that has been enrolled into service (as by arbitrary compulsion or by the dictates of law); esp : a recruit secured by conscription

³conscript \kən'skript\ vt -ED/-ING/-S [²conscript] : to enroll into service by compulsion ⟨~ soldiers⟩ ⟨a labor battalion ~ed from the ranks of political outcasts⟩ ⟨though I could ~ my body I could not ~ my mind —M.R.Cohen⟩

con·scrip·tion \kən'skripshən\ n -S [F, fr. L conscription-, conscriptio written composition, conscription, fr. conscriptus (past part. of conscribere to write together, enroll) + -ion-, -io -ion — more at CONSCRIPT] : the enlisting or procurement of services, money, property, or profits by an authority ⟨the ~ of government workers from private business⟩; esp : a compulsory enrollment of men for service in the armed forces

con·scrip·tion·ist \-nəst\ n -S : a person who favors or advocates military conscription ⟨a ~ point of view⟩

¹con·se·crate \ˈkänsə,krāt, usu -ād.+V\ adj [ME consecrat, fr. L consecratus, past part. of consecrare to consecrate, fr. com- + sacrare to consecrate, fr. sacr-, sacer sacred — more at SACRED] : CONSECRATED, HALLOWED

²consecrate \ˈkänsə,krāt, usu -ād.+V\ vb -ED/-ING/-S [ME consecraten, fr. L consecratus, past part.] vt **1 a** : to induct (a person) into a permanent office with a religious rite — usu. used with a double object ⟨~ the young prince king⟩; used in the Anglican Communion only of the induction of a bishop; compare ORDAIN **b** : to confirm officially (a rank, dignity, or office) by religious or civil ceremonies or rites ⟨the place where kings were consecrated⟩ **2 a** : to make or declare sacred or holy : effect the consecration of : set apart, dedicate, devote to the service or worship of God ⟨~ a church⟩ **b** : to effect the liturgical transubstantiation of **c** : to deliver up or give over often with or as if with deep solemnity, dedication, or devotion — used with to ⟨a gang leader who consecrated his fortune to charity⟩ ⟨a pupil who ~s himself to study⟩ **d** obs : DOOM, CONDEMN — used with to **3** : to render inviolate or venerable ⟨rules or principles consecrated by time —Edmund Burke⟩ : make memorable, significant, or consequential ⟨a slogan consecrated by the party⟩ ⟨a document consecrated by the presence of the national emblem⟩ ~ vi : to perform consecration (as of the elements in the Eucharist)

con·se·crat·ed·ness \ˈ==,===,₌ˈ===\ n -ES : CONSECRATION 1d

con·se·cra·tion \,känsə'krāshən\ n -S [ME consecracioun, fr. L consecration-, consecratio, fr. consecratus + -ion-, -io -ion] **1** : the solemn dedication (as of a person, thing, ideal) with or as if with religious rites and usu. to some high purpose, office, or function: as **a** : ordination or elevation to a sacred or high office ⟨~ of a bishop⟩ ⟨the . . . ~ of an English king —F.M. Stenton⟩ **b** : apotheosis esp. of a Roman emperor or hero of classic literature **c** : the solemn dedication in perpetuity of a church or of vessels used in the Eucharist esp. in the Roman Catholic Church **d** : devotion or appropriation to any special purpose ⟨the ~ of money to a hobby⟩ ⟨their ~ of all ingenuity to ridding the land of foreign troops⟩ ⟨complete moral ~ which is at the base of Willa Cather's work —M.D.Geismar⟩ **2** often cap : the part of a Christian liturgy in which the bread and wine are consecrated — compare TRANSUBSTANTIATION

con·se·cra·tive \ˈkänsə,krād·iv\ adj : solemnly dedicational

con·se·cra·tor \ˈkänsə,krād·ə(r), -ātə-\ n -S [LL, fr. L consecratus + -or] : one that consecrates

con·se·cra·to·ry \ˈkänsəkrə,tōrē, -tȯrē, -ri; chiefly Brit ˈ==,krātərē, -ri\ adj : serving to consecrate ⟨a ~ prayer⟩

¹con·sec·ta·ry \kən'sektərē\ n -ES [L consectarium, fr. neut. of consectarius logically following, fr. consectari to follow after, fr. com- + sectari to follow, accompany, fr. secta sect — more at SECT] : CONSEQUENCE, COROLLARY ⟨a ~ drawn from careful observations⟩

²consectary adj [L consectarius] obs : following by consequence : CONSEQUENT

con·se·cu·tion \,känsə'kyüshən\ n -S [L consecution-, consecutio, fr. consecutus (past part. of consequi to follow) + -ion-, -io -ion — more at CONSEQUENT] **1** : advance in argument from antecedent to consequent : logical sequence : chain of reasoning ⟨reading each . . . chapter separately abandoning any search for ~ of argument —Times Lit. Supp.⟩; specif, obs : the inferred part of an argument : the necessary sequence **2** : sequence esp. of events, similar harmonic intervals in music, or tenses in grammar ⟨~ of octaves⟩ : SUCCESSION ⟨~ of sins⟩

con·sec·u·tive \kən'sek(y)əd·iv, -ətiv, -əv\ adj [F consécutif, fr. L consecutus + F -if -ive] **1 a** : following esp. in a series : one right after the other often with small intervening intervals : SUCCESSIVE, SEQUENT ⟨four ~ terms in office⟩ ⟨the coastal battery scored several ~ hits⟩ **b** : having no interval or break : CONTINUOUS ⟨the most important cause . . . has run throughout post-Conquest history like a ~ thread —G.G.Coulton⟩ ⟨a ~ conversation⟩ **2** : proceeding by successive interrelated stages of thought : marked by logical sequence ⟨~ premises⟩ ⟨a ~ thinker⟩ **3 a** : expressing result ⟨a ~ conjunction⟩ — often used of a clause (as that he ran away in "he was so frightened that he ran away") **b** Semitic grammar : characterized by attachment to an imperfect verb form of a sense that otherwise would belong to the perfect or to a perfect verb form of a sense that otherwise would belong to the imperfect — used of the conjunction meaning "and" that is prefixed to such a verb form or of the verb itself — **con·sec·u·tive·ly** adv — **con·sec·u·tive·ness** n -ES

consecutive intervals n pl : a recurrence in music of the same interval between two parts or voices in successive chord progressions

con·sec·u·tives \kən'sek(y)əd·ivz, -ətivz\ n pl : CONSECUTIVE INTERVALS; esp : consecutive fifths and octaves

con·se·nes·cence \,kän(t)sə'nesən(t)s\ n -S [L consenescere to grow old together, to grow old in a profession, to become weak (fr. com- + senescere, incho. of senere to be old, fr. senex old) + E -ence — more at SENIOR] : general decay esp. from old age

con·sen·sion \kən'senchən\ n -S [L consension-, consensio, fr. consensus (past part. of consentire) + -ion-, -io -ion] : unanimity of opinion or attitude

con·sen·su·al \kən'senchəwəl\ adj [L consensus + E -al] **1** : existing or made by mutual consent without the intervention of any act of writing ⟨a ~ contract⟩ ⟨the powers of the United Nations are ~ in nature —Jour. of Internat'l Affairs⟩ **2** : involving or caused by involuntary action or movement accompanying or correlative with voluntary action or movement ⟨~ reactions⟩ — **con·sen·su·al·ly** \-wəlē, -li\ adv

con·sen·sus \kən'sen(t)səs\ n -ES [L, fr. consensus, past part. of consentire to feel together, agree — more at CONSENT] **1 a** : harmony, cooperation, or sympathy esp. in different parts of an organism **b** : group solidarity in sentiment and belief ⟨a kind of unspoken ~ . . . appeared —Henry Dicks⟩ ⟨broad group ~, as manifested in the folkways, mores, and other institutional usages —H.A.Bloch⟩ **2 a** : general agreement : UNANIMITY, ACCORD ⟨the ~ of their opinion, based on reports that had drifted back from the border —John Hersey⟩ **b** : collective opinion : the judgment arrived at by most of those concerned ⟨in the ~ of a number of critics —Current Biog.⟩ **3** : a formal statement of religious belief : CONFESSION

¹con·sent \kən'sent\ vi -ED/-ING/-S [ME consenten, fr. OF consentir, fr. L consentire to feel together, agree, consent, fr. com- + sentire to feel — more at SENSE] **1** archaic : to be in harmony or concord esp. in opinion, statement, or sentiment **2** : to express a willingness (as to accept a proposition or carry out a particular action) : give assent or approval : AGREE — usu. used with to ⟨~ to shoulder a debt⟩ ⟨~ to cross-examination⟩ **syn** see ASSENT

²consent \"\ n -S [ME, fr. OF consent, consente, fr. consentir, v.] **1 a** : compliance or approval esp. of what is done or proposed by another : ACQUIESCENCE, PERMISSION ⟨to do something without ~⟩ ⟨to find general ~ to his opinion⟩ ⟨the passionless ~ of the human mind —W.L.Sperry⟩ **b** : capable, deliberate, and voluntary agreement to or concurrence in some act or purpose implying physical and mental power and free action — distinguished from assent; see AGE OF CONSENT **2** archaic : correspondence in parts, qualities, operations : HARMONY, COHERENCE **3** : agreement among persons usu. as to a course of action or concerning a particular point of view or opinion ⟨by common ~ the host drank first⟩ ⟨by the ~ of scholars . . . it is by far the greatest —Choice & Interesting Books⟩; specif : voluntary agreement in political theory by a people to organize a civil society and give authority to the government ⟨the ~ theory meant that the people as a whole were sovereign —Russell Davenport⟩ **4** archaic : the being of one mind : ACCORD, UNANIMITY **5** obs : OPINION, FEELING — **of consent** obs : ACCESSORY ⟨some villains of my court are of consent . . . in this —Shak.⟩

con·sen·ta·ne·ous \¦känsən¦tānēəs, -sen-\ adj [L consentaneus, fr. consentire — more at CONSENT] **1** : AGREEING, SUITED ⟨perfectly ~ to scientific truth —T. L. Peacock⟩ **2** : done or made by the consent of all : UNANIMOUS ⟨~ profession of loyalty —G.P.Fisher⟩ — **con·sen·ta·ne·ous·ly** adv

consent decree n : a consent judgment by a court exercising equity jurisdiction or invoking equitable remedies

consent dividend n : an arrangement by which stockholders agree to report as income a portion of the corporation's retained profits and to pay taxes thereon

consent election n : an election to determine a bargaining agent held at the request of both union and employer

con·sen·tience \kən'sen(t)sh(ē)ən(t)s\ n -S : unity of consciousness felt as arising from sensation without regard to intellect

con·sen·tient \kən'sen(t)shənt\ adj [L consentient-, consentiens, pres. part. of consentire — more at CONSENT] **1** : united in opinion, judgment, view : UNANIMOUS ⟨such ~ reports⟩ **2** : disposed to agree with or conform to ⟨~ to adverse criticism⟩ — **con·sen·tient·ly** adv

con sen·ti·men·to \¦kän,sentə̇'men(,)tō, ¦kōn-\ adv [It] : with feeling — used as a direction in music

con·sent·ing·ly adv : with consent or aquiescence

con·sent·ing·ness n -ES : CONSENT

consent judgment n : a judgment by a court exercising common-law jurisdiction entered by consent of the parties upon stipulation or agreement

con·sent·ment \kən'sentmənt\ n -S [ME consentement, fr. MF, fr. consentir to consent + -ment — more at CONSENT] archaic : CONSENT

¹con·se·quence \ˈkän(t)sə̇,kwen(t)s, -sēk-, -,kwən- sometimes ˈkōn-\ n -S [ME, fr. MF, fr. L consequentia, fr. consequent-, consequens + -ia] **1** : something that is produced by a cause or follows from a form of necessary connection or from a set of conditions : a natural or necessary result ⟨this refined taste is the ~ of education and habit —Joshua Reynolds⟩ ⟨his training had been poor and in combat he suffered the ~s⟩ ⟨she was always quick and as a ~ received high grades⟩ **2** : a conclusion that results from reason or argument : an inference or proposition inferred from previous propositions ⟨we can deduce . . . many ~s each of which can be tested by experiment —J.B.Conant⟩; specif : a statement derivable from other statements in accordance with the transformation rules of the language system they belong to **3** obs **a** : the act or action of following in succession : SEQUENCE **b** : the rational process by which effect follows cause : logical sequence **4 a** : importance often with respect to what comes after or in power to produce an effect : VALUE, MOMENT ⟨a mistake of no ~⟩ ⟨a problem of grave international ~⟩ **b** : social importance or distinction ⟨a person of some ~⟩ ⟨she had managed to bring with her a certain urban ~ —Margery Sharp⟩ **5** : the appearance of importance esp. in demeanor : DIGNITY ⟨his voice had authority and his bearing ~⟩; esp : SELF-IMPORTANCE ⟨with all the ~ of a peacock⟩ **6 consequences** pl but sing in constr : a game in which a brief and humorous story descriptive of two people, their meeting, and its consequences is made up as the players in turn write answers to a series of questions, each one concealing what he has written before passing the paper to his neighbor for the next answer **syn** see EFFECT, IMPORTANCE — **in consequence** *adv* : as a result : CONSEQUENTLY, HENCE — **in consequence of** *prep* : by reason of : as a result of ⟨*in consequence of* their efforts a report was handed down⟩

2**consequence** *vi* -ED/-ING/-S *obs* : INFER

consequency *n* -ES [L *consequentia*] *obs* : CONSEQUENCE

1**con·se·quent** \ˈkän(t)sə̇ˌkwent, -sēˌk-, -ˌkwənt *sometimes* ˈkȯn-\ *n* -S [ME, fr. L *consequent-, consequens*] **1 a :** something that is deduced from reasoning or argumentation or follows from propositions by rational deduction : INFERENCE, CONCLUSION; *specif* : the clause in a hypothetical proposition that states what the hypothesis entails or implies (as the conclusion of a conditional sentence) **b** *obs* : something that results from a cause : CONSEQUENCE, OUTCOME **2 :** a thing or circumstance (as an event or phenomenon) that follows another in time or order without being a result or without any causal connection being implied; *specif* : the second term of a ratio **3 a** *in canon and fugue* : the musical restatement of the subject : COMES **b :** an answering phrase or section of a musical sentence or section — compare ANTECEDENT 6 **4 :** a stream or valley that has developed in harmony with the general slope of an existing land surface

2**consequent** \"\ *adj* [MF, fr. L *consequent-, consequens*, pres. part. of *consequi* to follow, fr. *com-* + *sequi* to follow — more at SUE] **1** *obs* : following in time or order : SUBSEQUENT ⟨in ~ years⟩ **2 a :** following esp. as a result or effect : RESULTANT ⟨the period of tension and the ~ need for military preparedness —D.W.Mitchell⟩ — often used with *on* or *upon* ⟨the decline in . . . trade ~ upon the growth of economic nationalism —*Encyc. Americana*⟩ **b :** following by necessary inference or rational deduction ⟨a proposition ~ to other propositions⟩ **3 :** observing the just order of cause and effect : logically consistent : RATIONAL ⟨not one could give a clear and ~ account —J.F. Brown⟩ **4 :** constituting the conclusion of a conditional sentence ⟨a ~ clause⟩ **5 :** developed in harmony with the general slope of an existing land surface ⟨a ~ stream⟩ ⟨a ~ valley⟩ — compare ANTECEDENT, OBSEQUENT, RESEQUENT, SUBSEQUENT, SUPERIMPOSED

con·se·quen·tial \ˌkän(t)sə̇ˈkwenchəl, -sēˈk- *sometimes* ˌkȯn-\ *adj* [L *consequentia* + E *-al*] **1 :** of the nature of or following as a consequence, result, or logical inference : involving logical sequence ⟨with the procedure in Committee of Supply and the ~ proceedings in Committee of Ways and Means —T.E.May⟩ **2 :** of the nature of a secondary result : INDIRECT ⟨more important is the ~ loss that can flow from destruction of records —*Financial Times (London)*⟩ **3 a :** following in due course : falling in consequence — often used with *on* or *upon* ⟨a result ~ upon bankruptcy⟩ **b :** governed or guided by logical sequence : RATIONAL ⟨any system of ~ conduct that in their most reasonable moments they might have been capable of forming —Earl of Chesterfield⟩ **4 :** of importance : of consequence : bringing about or responsible for significant changes or results ⟨reports of a ~ nature⟩ ⟨the only ~ immigrant group at first were the French —Oscar Handlin⟩ ⟨many errors have been made but hardly one as grave and ~ as this failure —E.J.Simmons⟩ **5 :** having or displaying importance or assuming distinction to a point of being pompous : SELF-IMPORTANT ⟨~ deportment⟩ ⟨a loud ~ voice⟩ — **con·se·quen·tial·ly** \-shəlē, -li\ *adv*

consequential contempt *n* : CONSTRUCTIVE CONTEMPT

consequential damages *n pl* : the damages that do not arise as an immediate or natural and probable result of the act of the party but are an incidental result of it and are generally not recoverable because remote except in case of special damages or special statutory provision

con·se·quen·ti·al·i·ty \ˌkän(t)sə̇ˌkwen(t)shēˈalədˑē, -sēˌk-, -ətē, -i\ *n* -ES : air of importance : SELF-IMPORTANCE ⟨his intolerable ~⟩

consequential loss *n* : an indirect or secondary loss occasioned by direct property loss (as that caused by a fire) and often provided for by special provisions in insurance policies or by special policies (as rent insurance or business interruption insurance)

con·se·quent·ly \ˈkän(t)sə̇ˌkwentlē, -sēˌk- -ˌkwən-, -li\ *adv* [ME, fr. MF *consequent* + ME *-ly* — more at CONSEQUENT] **1** *obs* **a :** in order : SUBSEQUENTLY ⟨fighting first in the north and ~ in the west⟩ **b :** in succession ⟨to say all her prayers ~⟩ **2 :** as a result : in view of the foregoing : ACCORDINGLY ⟨taxes were lowered and ~ complaints were fewer⟩ **3** *archaic* : in a logical manner ⟨to argue his case ~⟩

consequent pole *n* : any one of the magnetic poles that appear in a nonuniformly magnetized body excepting those poles near its ends

con·ser·tal \kənˈsərdˑᵊl\ *adj* [L *consertus* (past part. of *conserere* to connect, fr. *com-* + *serere* to bind together) + E *-al* — more at SERIES] *of an igneous rock* : of a texture in which the irregularly shaped crystals interlock : SUTURED

conservacy *n* -ES [AF *conservacie*, fr. ML *conservatia*, fr. L *conservatus* + *-ia* -y] *obs* : CONSERVATION 2

con·serv·an·cy \kənˈsərvən(t)sē, -sə̄v-, -si\ *n* -ES [alter. of *conservacy*] **1** *Brit* : a board that has jurisdiction over a river or port esp. for the regulation of fisheries and navigation ⟨the Thames *Conservancy*⟩ **2 :** conservation esp. of natural resources ⟨~ work being done on the . . . rivers to control floods —*Americana Annual*⟩; *specif* : an organization designed and often government-sponsored to conserve and protect natural resources (as trees or wildlife)

conservant *adj* [L *conservant-, conservans*, pres. part. of *conservare* to preserve] *obs* : CONSERVING, PRESERVING ⟨the procreant and ~ cause —Abraham Fraunce⟩

con·ser·va·tion \ˌkän(t)sə(r)ˈvāshən\ *n* -S [ME *conservacioun*, fr. MF *conservation*, fr. L *conservation-, conservatio*, fr. *conservatus* (past part. of *conservare* to conserve) + *-ion-, -io* -ion — more at CONSERVE] **1 :** deliberate, planned, or thoughtful preserving, guarding, or protecting : a keeping in a safe or entire state : PRESERVATION ⟨the ~ of the ideal of liberty⟩ ⟨the ~ of religious shrines⟩ ⟨the ~ of the individual's nervous energy —Ralph Linton⟩; *specif* : the repair and preservation of works of art **2 :** care or keeping and supervision of something by a governmental authority or by a private association or business: as **a :** planned management of a natural resource to prevent exploitation, destruction, or neglect ⟨wild-life ~⟩ ⟨~ of the Northwest⟩ **b :** the wise utilization of a natural product esp. by a manufacturer so as to prevent waste and insure future use of resources that have been depleted **3 :** a field of knowledge concerned with coordination and plans for the practical application of data from ecology, limnology, pedology, and other sciences that are significant to preservation of natural resources ⟨offering graduate degrees in ~⟩

con·ser·va·tion·al \ˌ==ˈvāshənᵊl, -shnəl\ *adj* : tending to conserve : PRESERVATIVE ⟨~ measures to protect wildlife⟩

con·ser·va·tion·ist \ˌkän(t)sə(r)ˈvāsh(ə)nə̇st\ *n* -S : one that advocates conservation esp. of natural resources (as forests)

conservation of electricity : a principle in physics: if two or more charges combine to form one or conversely if one charge breaks up into two or more, the algebraic sum of the partial charges equals the single charge

conservation of energy : a principle in physics: the total energy of an isolated system remains constant irrespective of whatever internal changes may take place, energy disappearing in one form reappearing in another — compare DEGRADATION OF ENERGY, DISSIPATION OF ENERGY, MASS-ENERGY EQUATION

conservation of mass : a principle in classical physics: the total mass of any material system is neither increased nor diminished by reactions between the parts — compare MASS-ENERGY EQUATION

conservation of momentum : a principle in physics: the total linear momentum of a system of particles not acted upon by external forces is constant in magnitude and direction irrespective of any reactions among the parts of the system

con·serv·a·tism \kənˈsərvədˑˌizəm, -sə̄v-,-səiv-, -vəˌtiz-\ *n* -S [*conservative* + *-ism*] **1 a :** the disposition in politics to preserve what is established ⟨twentieth century politics of New Jersey has continued to be dominated . . . by the natural ~ of the industrial and business interests —*Amer. Guide Series: N.J.*⟩ **b :** a political philosophy based on a strong sense of tradition and social stability, stressing the importance of established institutions (as religion, property, the family, and class structure), and preferring gradual development with preservation of the best elements of the past to abrupt change ⟨political ~ in the United States . . . has become identified with the business interests —Francis Biddle⟩ **2** *usu cap* **a :** the principles and policies of the Conservative party in the United Kingdom ⟨the fundamental and distinct tenets of *Conservatism* —R.A.Butler⟩ **b :** the Conservative party or its members ⟨whether *Conservatism* enjoys a long tenure of office —L.D.Epstein⟩ **3 a :** the tendency to accept an existing fact, order, situation, or phenomenon and to be cautious toward or suspicious of change : extreme wariness and caution in outlook ⟨acquired ~ which normally increases with increasing age and sagacity —H.G.Armstrong⟩ ⟨~ in banking practices⟩ ⟨~ in interpreting data⟩ **b :** strong resistance to innovation : relative freedom from change ⟨the ~ of the area . . . has helped to preserve the evidences of its past —R.W. Southern⟩; *specif* : the tendency of certain plants or animal groups (as the brachiopods) to remain narrowly adapted to a particular environment and undergo minimal evolutionary change or differentiation **4 :** CONSERVATIVE JUDAISM

con·serv·a·tist \-vədˑə̇st,-vətə̇st\ *n* -S [*conservatism* + *-ist*] : one who supports conservative forces, principles, or ideas

1**con·serv·a·tive** \kənˈsərvədˑ|iv, -sə̄v-,-səiv, -vət|iv *also* |əv\ *adj* [ME, fr. MF & LL; MF *conservatif*, fr. LL *conservativus*, fr. L *conservatus* (past part of *conservare* to conserve) + *-ivus* -ive — more at CONSERVE] **1 :** having the power or tendency to preserve in a safe and entire state : PRESERVATIVE ⟨the ~ powers of the Egyptian climate have given us priceless relics in near-perfect condition⟩ ⟨~ of all good things⟩; *specif* : designed to preserve parts or restore function ⟨~ surgery⟩ — compare RADICAL **2 a :** of or relating to a political party, point of view, or philosophy that advocates preservation of the established order and views proposals for change critically and usu. with distrust ⟨~ elements opposed to . . . further steps toward socialization or nationalization —*Collier's Yr. Bk.*⟩ **b :** of, relating to, or constituting a political party professing the principles of conservatism: as (1) *usu cap* : of or constituting one of the two major parties in the United Kingdom evolving from the 18th century Tories and in modern times associated with policies advocating support of established institutions, a close relationship with the Commonwealth and Empire, and a positive although limited role by the government in social and economic affairs ⟨the parliamentary *Conservative* party is preeminently recruited from the upper and upper-middle classes —J.F.S.Ross⟩ ⟨a handsome *Conservative* majority . . . emerged from the general election —J.A.Hawgood⟩ — compare LABOR, LIBERAL, TORY, UNIONIST, WHIG (2) *usu cap* : PROGRESSIVE CONSERVATIVE **3 a :** tending or disposed to maintain existing views, habits, conditions, or institutions : opposed to radical or basic changes : exhibiting minimal change : TRADITIONAL ⟨~ policies⟩ ⟨a ~ administration⟩ ⟨a ~ genus⟩ **b :** not in excess ⟨~ action⟩ : CAUTIOUS ⟨a ~ point of view⟩ ⟨a ~ utterance⟩ : MODERATE ⟨a ~ estimate of 200⟩ : unwilling to overreach : involving little or fearful of risk ⟨a ~ banker⟩ ⟨~ investments⟩ **c :** tending to avoid dissonance, showiness, or effects that would attract undue or immediate attention : cleaving to traditional norms of taste, elegance, or manners ⟨a ~ suit⟩ ⟨a rich but ~ architectural style⟩ **4 :** of or relating to Conservative Judaism

syn REACTIONARY, DIE-HARD, TORY: CONSERVATIVE suggests desire to retain and maintain existing institutions, procedures, and ways and to resist and suspect proposals for change ⟨although he was naturally *conservative* and did not disturb the predominance of Latin and Greek, he somewhat modified the curriculum —C.M.Fuess⟩ REACTIONARY applies to wishes to return to an older outworn order or to influences making for such a return; unlike CONSERVATIVE, it is almost always derogatory ⟨both the Reformation and the Counter Reformation were *reactionary;* though they brought the Middle Ages to an end, they themselves were medieval in spirit and method —W.R.Inge⟩ DIE-HARD implies a stubborn, truculent retention of older procedures and resistance to new ⟨some *die-hard* individual may insist on driving a horse and buggy after all the rest of his society have automobiles —Ralph Linton⟩ ⟨while the Progressive Conservative platform reflected the party's *die-hard* conservatism on most issues, it came out, in striking contrast to previous policies, for the principle of expanding international trade —*Collier's Yr. Bk.*⟩ TORY may suggest a sometimes reactionary allegiance to long-established principles and social customs ⟨to a slow-moving and *Tory* society they were radical changes shocking to men's minds —C.W.de Kiewiet⟩

2**conservative** \"\ *n* -S [ME, fr. *conservative*, adj.] **1** *archaic* : a preservative agent or principle : PRESERVER, CONSERVER ⟨the Holy Spirit is the great ~ of the new life —Jeremy Taylor⟩ **2 a :** an adherent or advocate of political conservatism ⟨it is the task of the ~ not to defeat but to forestall revolutions —H.A.Kissinger⟩ **b** *usu cap* : a member or supporter of a conservative political party; *esp* : a member of the Conservative party of the United Kingdom ⟨both *Conservatives* and Labour competed for the middle-class vote —Roy Lewis & Angus Maude⟩ **3 :** one who adheres to traditional, time-tested, long-standing methods, procedures, or views : a moderate, cautious, or discreet person ⟨a ~ in his choice of clothes⟩ ⟨the firm was always the ~ in marine architecture⟩

conservative baptist *n, usu cap C&B* : a member of one of the independent Baptist churches belonging to the Conservative Baptist Association of America which took its present name in 1946 and withdrew from the American Baptist Convention in 1951

conservative jew *n, usu cap C&J* : an adherent of Conservative Judaism

conservative judaism *n, cap C&J* : a middle-of-the-road development in Judaism that began in the 19th century in western Europe and attained a large following in the U.S. and that accepts limited modifications in liturgy and in ritual practice but stresses the historic laws of the Bible and the Talmud and also the authority and sanctity of the religious traditions of the Jewish people — compare ORTHODOX JUDAISM

con·serv·a·tive·ly *adv* : in a conservative manner

con·serv·a·tive·ness *n* -ES : CONSERVATISM

con·serv·a·tize \kənˈsərvəˌtīz\ *vb* -ED/-ING/-S [*conservative* + *-ize*] *vi* : to grow conservative ~ *vt* : to make conservative ⟨unions are being *conservatized* —Theodore Levitt⟩

con·ser·va·toire \kənˌsərvəˈtwär, =ˈ==ˌ=\ *n* -S [F, fr. It *conservatorio* — more at CONSERVATORY] : CONSERVATORY

con·ser·va·tor \ˈkän(t)sə(r)ˌvādˑə(r), -vātə-; *esp in senses 2 and 3* kənˈsərvədˑər, -sə̄vədˑə,-səivədˑə, -vətə-\ *n* -S [ME *conservatour*, fr. MF or L; MF *conservateur*, fr. L *conservator*, fr. *conservatus* (past part. of *conservare* to keep, protect) + *-or* — more at CONSERVE] **1 :** one that preserves from injury or violation : PROTECTOR, PRESERVER ⟨a fine art ~⟩ **2 :** a person, official, or institution designated (as by a court) to take over and protect the interests of an incompetent (as a minor child, an insane person, a convict) **3 :** an official charged with the protection of any of various things concerned with public welfare and interests ⟨~ of a river⟩ ⟨~ of fisheries⟩; *also* : a person placed by the secretary of the treasury in charge of a national bank whose affairs are not in a satisfactory condition **4 :** an overflow reservoir to permit expansion of a liquid (as oil in a transformer or water in a heating system)

con·ser·va·to·ri·um \kənˌsərvəˈtōrēəm, -tȯr-\ *n* -S [G *konservatorium*, modif. of It *conservatorio*] : 1CONSERVATORY 3

conservator of the peace [trans. of ML *custos pacis* or AF *gardein de la pees*] : an officer charged with maintaining the public peace or one having this power as an adjunct of another office

con·ser·va·tor·ship *pronunc at* CONSERVATOR +ˌship\ *n* -S : the office of conservator

1**con·serv·a·to·ry** \kənˈsərvəˌtōrē, -sə̄v-,-səiv, -ˌtȯr-, -ri\ *n* -ES [L *conservatus* + E *-ory*] **1** *archaic* : a place for the preservation or safekeeping of things **2 :** a greenhouse sometimes attached to a dwelling for growing or displaying plants **3** [It *conservatorio*, fr. *conservato* (past part. of *conservare* to keep, preserve, maintain) (fr. L *conservatus*) + *-orio* -ory (fr. L *-orium*)] : a school of advanced standing specializing in one of the fine arts (as music, drama, or dance) and emphasizing technical instruction and practical performance ⟨the Wilkes-Barre Municipal *Conservatory*⟩

2**conservatory** \"\ *adj* [LL *conservatorius*, fr. L *conservatus* + *-orius* -ory] : having the quality or power of conserving or preserving : PRESERVATIVE ⟨the ~ legal protection of wildlife⟩

1**con·serve** \kənˈsərv, -sə̄v,-səiv; *in sense 2 also* ˈkänˌs-\ *vt* -ED/-ING/-S [ME *conserven*, fr. MF *conserver*, fr. L *conservare*, fr. *com-* + *servare* to keep, guard, protect, preserve, observe; akin to OE *searu* weapons, armor, skill, ON *sörvi* pearl necklace, *sörvar* armed men, Goth *sarwa* weapons, armor, Gk *horminos* salvia, Av *haraiti, haurvaiti* he guards] **1 :** to keep in a safe or sound state (as by deliberate, planned, or intelligent care) : preserve from change or destruction : SAVE ⟨~ national forests⟩ ⟨~ moral standards⟩ **2 :** to preserve (as fruits) with sugar : make a conserve of

2**conserve** \ˈkänˌsərv, -sə̄v,-səiv; *Brit usu* kənˈs-\ *n* -S [ME, fr. *conserven*, v.] **1** *archaic* : a conserving agent : PRESERVATIVE ⟨his passion for Eustacia had been a sort of ~ of his whole life —Thomas Hardy⟩ **2 a :** SWEETMEAT; *esp* : a candied fruit : CONFECTION **b :** PRESERVE; *specif* : a preserve prepared from a mixture (as of rhubarb, raisins, and oranges) and sometimes with the addition of nuts **3 :** an obsolete medicinal preparation made by mixing undried vegetable drugs with sufficient powdered sugar to form a soft mass — see 1CONFECTION 1b

consgt *abbr* consignment

con·shy \ˈkänchē, -chi\ *var of* CONCHIE

con·sid·er \kənˈsidə(r)\ *vb* **considered**; **considered**; **considering** \-d(ə)riŋ\ **considers** [ME *consideren*, fr. MF *considerer*, fr. L *considerare*, lit., to observe the stars, fr. *com-* + *-siderare* (fr. *sider-, sidus* star, constellation) — more at SIDEREAL] *vt* **1 :** to reflect on : think about with a degree of care or caution ⟨before she could ~ what to do, her husband came in —Thomas Hardy⟩ ⟨~ how serious your position is⟩ **2 :** to think of, regard, or treat in an attentive, solicitous, or kindly way ⟨he ~*ed* her every wish⟩ **3 :** to look at or gaze on steadily or with earnest reflection ⟨the old gentleman ~*ed* him attentively —Edith Wharton⟩ **4 :** to think of : come to view, judge, or classify ⟨~ thrift essential⟩ ⟨~ a leader to be unwise⟩ **5** *obs* : REQUITE, REMUNERATE **6 :** to regard highly : RESPECT, ESTEEM ⟨his works are well ~*ed* abroad⟩ **7 :** to be of the opinion : SUPPOSE ⟨I ~ it's best that he left when he did⟩ **8 :** to give thought to with a view to purchasing, accepting, or adopting ⟨~ an apartment⟩ ⟨~ a trade-in on a car⟩ ~ *vi* **1** *obs* : to look attentively ⟨then the priest shall ~: and, behold, if the leprosy have covered all his flesh, he shall pronounce him clean that hath the plague —Lev 13:13 (AV)⟩ **2 :** REFLECT, DELIBERATE, PONDER ⟨paused a moment to ~⟩

syn CONTEMPLATE, STUDY, WEIGH, REVOLVE, EXCOGITATE: CONSIDER often indicates little more than *think about*. It may occasionally suggest somewhat more conscious direction of thought, somewhat greater depth and scope, and somewhat greater purposefulness ⟨glancing at that, as at something she would take up presently and *consider* —Mary Austin⟩ ⟨love she *considered*, and hate, the enduringness and the moral and spiritual consequences of each —Rose Macaulay⟩ ⟨when I came to *consider* his conduct, I realized that he was guilty of a confusion —T.S.Eliot⟩ CONTEMPLATE stresses the steady calm focussing of one's attentive thought but implies nothing about the aims, methods, or results of that thinking ⟨fine gentlemen and fine ladies are charming to *contemplate* in history —Bertrand Russell⟩ ⟨the poet "has an idea", and in the course of *contemplating* it he draws from his subconscious a string of associated ideas and images —C.D.Lewis⟩ STUDY implies sustained, purposeful effort, care for both details and significance and ramifications, and full knowledge as an end ⟨I like very naturally to think that I am being read, but the idea that I am being *studied* fills me . . . with a deepening gloom —Aldous Huxley⟩ ⟨Bryce, who had *studied* the matter so thoroughly, was wont to insist it is the smallest democracies which today stand highest in the scale —Havelock Ellis⟩ WEIGH suggests thoughtful arrival at an evaluation or decision in which evidence leading to opposite conclusions has been examined and evaluated ⟨the problem is to get them [the young] to *weigh* evidence, draw accurate inferences, make fair comparisons, invent solutions, and form judgments —C.W. Eliot⟩ ⟨the fine balance with which Johnson *weighed* and sustained his judgments of human flaws and virtues —H.V. Gregory⟩ In this sense REVOLVE suggests turning over the matter under consideration so that all facets of it may be viewed and thought about ⟨should he write to his son? For a time he *revolved* a long, tactful letter in his mind —H.G.Wells⟩ ⟨she was desperately *revolving* the risk of taking him into the front room to have out of him what his distrait presence half declared —Mary Austin⟩ EXCOGITATE suggests deep thought and is likely to connote the fact of a notion or concept having been evolved or contrived as well as the fact of the occurrence of thought ⟨the more sophisticated views on mental structure which Freud himself *excogitated* —*Times Lit. Supp.*⟩

syn REGARD, ACCOUNT, RECKON, DEEM: of this series REGARD is probably the least rich in suggestion. It may, but does not necessarily, connote viewing without reflection and, consequently, quick judgment based on appearances alone from a purely personal point of view ⟨a church . . . which *regarded* all dissentients as rebels and traitors —W.R.Inge⟩ ⟨to *regard* her passion . . . and its tragic sequel as a romantic episode of girlhood —Rose Macaulay⟩ Although often interchangeable with REGARD, CONSIDER may suggest a degree of reflection and hence a more soundly based judgment ⟨it seems, however, best to *consider* as literature only works in which the aesthetic function is dominant —René Wellek & Austin Warren⟩ ACCOUNT probably more common with plural than with singular subjects and certainly more common in passive than in active uses, most often suggests a consensus, a generality of opinion or judgment ⟨the pier . . . was *accounted* a most excellent piece of stonework —William Cowper⟩ ⟨*accounted* the best jockey of the lot —Agnes M. Cleaveland⟩ RECKON, often informal in its tone, may suggest counting or computation underlying a judgment or indicating a point of view ⟨not to be *reckoned* one character . . . but to *reckon* in the gross, in the hundred or thousand of the party —R.W.Emerson⟩ It may on the other hand suggest casual judgment or supposition or guess ⟨another field where the dominance of the method of sociology may be *reckoned* as assured —B.N.Cardozo⟩ DEEM has a wide aura of suggestion. It often sounds archaic or literary; it is likely to sound formal or pompous or, by irony therefore, modest or whimsical. It may suggest considered, judicious judgment ⟨investigation of all the facts which it *deems* relevant —H.S.Truman⟩ It also may apply to unreflective, intuitive choice ⟨*deeming* a figure of speech to be worth frequent use —C.E.Montague⟩

1**con·sid·er·a·ble** \kənˈsidər(ə)bəl, -drəb-, *rapid* *-R* -dəb-\ *adj, sometimes* -ER/-EST [ME, fr. ML *considerabilis*, fr. L *considerare* to consider + *-abilis* -able] **1** *obs* **a :** capable of being perceived or understood : PERCEPTIBLE, COGNIZABLE ⟨a ~ truth⟩ **b :** calling for consideration : requiring to be observed, borne in mind, or attended to : NOTABLE ⟨a ~ testimony⟩ **2 :** worthy of consideration : of consequence or distinction : IMPORTANT, SIGNIFICANT ⟨a series of rather ~ observations on human behavior⟩ ⟨William Faulkner is . . . the most ~ 20th-century American writer of short fiction —William Peden⟩ **3 a :** rather large in extent or degree ⟨a ~ distance⟩ ⟨a ~ number⟩ ⟨he got in ~ trouble⟩ **b :** great in size : LARGE ⟨a house with a ~ barn in back⟩ ⟨fingers, with a ~ diamond on one, a star sapphire on another —Glenway Wescott⟩

2**considerable** \"\ *n* -S **1** *obs* : a thing to be considered **2 :** a considerable amount, degree, or extent ⟨learned ~ of his life⟩ ⟨anything else the proprietor can get together and the public will stand for, which is ~ —W.L.Gresham⟩

3**considerable** \"\ *adv, now dial* : CONSIDERABLY

con·sid·er·a·bly \-blə, -bli\ *adv* **1** *obs* : in a way demanding or warranting consideration : NOTABLY **2 :** to a notable extent or degree : MARKEDLY, MUCH ⟨fallen ~ in price⟩

considerance *n* -S [ME *consideraunce*, fr. MF *considerance*, fr. L *considerantia*, fr. *considerant-, considerans* (pres. part. of *considerare*) + *-ia* -y] *obs* : CONSIDERATION

con·sid·er·ate \kənˈsid(ə)rə̇t, *usu* -dˑ+V\ *adj* [L *consideratus*, past part. of *considerare* — more at CONSIDER] **1 :** marked by or given to consideration or sober reflection : regardful of consequences or circumstances : CIRCUMSPECT, CAREFUL ⟨a cold and ~ temperament⟩ **2 :** observant of the rights and feelings of others : showing thoughtful kindness ⟨too courteous and ~ to make stubborn subordinates bend properly to his will —Allan Nevins & H. S. Commager⟩ — **con·sid·er·ate·ly** \-dər(ə)tlē, -drət-, -li\ *adv* — **con·sid·er·ate·ness** \-d(ə)rətnəs\ *n* -ES

con·sid·er·a·tion \kən,sidə'rāshən\ *n* -S [ME *consideracioun*, fr. MF *consideration*, fr. L *consideration-, consideratio*, fr. *consideratus* + *-ion-, -io* -ion] **1** *obs* : OBSERVATION, CONTEMPLATION ⟨his careful ~ of each object⟩ **2** : continuous and careful thought : DELIBERATION, ATTENTION ⟨to read a book with ~⟩ ⟨to take a matter into ~⟩ ⟨his request was under ~⟩ **3 a** : something that is considered as a ground of opinion or action : MOTIVE, REASON ⟨weighing several ~*s*⟩ **b** : a taking into account ⟨in ~ of the enormous difficulties involved⟩ **4** : thoughtful regard : sympathetic notice ⟨his ~ of the needs of others⟩; *specif* : attentive or formal respect ⟨diplomats used to the punctilious ~ of foreign officials⟩ **5** : a result of reflecting or pondering : mature opinion ⟨his ~*s* favoring one profession over another⟩ **6** : the act of regarding or weighing carefully ⟨during his ~ of the problem⟩ **7** : ESTEEM, REGARD, ESTIMATION ⟨a person of ~ in his own field⟩ **8** : something given as recompense: as **a** : PAYMENT, REWARD ⟨a ~ paid for legal services⟩ **b** (1) : something that is legally regarded as the equivalent or return given or suffered by one for the act or promise of another : an act or forbearance or the promise of it done or given by one party in return for the act or promise of another — see GOOD CONSIDERATION, VALUABLE CONSIDERATION (2) : a judgment of a court — **in consideration of** *prep* : as payment or recompense for ⟨a small fee *in consideration of* many kind services⟩

con·sid·er·a·tive \kən'sid(ə)rəd·iv\ *adj* [ME, fr. MF *consideratif*, fr. *consideration* + *-if* -ive] : CONSIDERATE 1

considered *adj* [fr. past part. of *consider*] **1** : matured by extended deliberative thought **2** : regarded with respect or esteem **syn** see DELIBERATE

¹con·sid·er·ing \kən'sid(ə)riŋ\ *prep* [ME, fr. pres. part. of *consideren* to consider] : in view of : taking into account ⟨he did well ~ his limitations⟩

²considering \"\ *conj* : inasmuch as ⟨~ he was new at the game, he did very well⟩

³considering \"\ *adv* : taking all circumstances into account ⟨the boy does well, ~⟩

con·sid·er·ing·ly *adv* : in a considering manner

considers *pres 3d sing of* CONSIDER

con·sign \kən'sīn\ *vb* -ED/-ING/-S [MF *consigner*, fr. L *consignare* to seal, vouch for, sign, fr. *com-* + *signare* to mark, seal, fr. *signum* mark, sign — more at SIGN] *vt* **1** *obs* **a** : to place a seal or sign upon **b** [MF or L; MF *consigner*, fr. LL *consignare*, fr. L] : to make the sign of the cross on or for (as at baptism or confirmation) : CONFIRM **2** *archaic* : to attest or confirm (as a truth, fact, promise) by some sign or token ⟨a pact ~*ed* by holy oaths⟩ **3** : to give over to another's charge, custody, or care : COMMISSION, ENTRUST ⟨~ her single daughters to the care of their sister —Jane Austen⟩ ⟨in spite of the thankless tasks ~*ed* to him —*Times Lit. Supp.*⟩ **4** : to give, transfer, or deliver over by or as if by signing over esp. into the possession of another or into a lasting state : commit in a formal or solemn manner ⟨~ a body to the grave⟩ ⟨after a death they ~*ed* the name of the deceased to oblivion, and never mentioned it again —J.G.Frazer⟩ ⟨~ a letter to the flames⟩ **5** : to make a legal consignation or deposit of (as money) in making a tender of payment or in surrendering money to abide the determination of the rights of competing claimants **6** : to send or address to an agent in another place to be cared for or sold or for the use of such agent ⟨~ a ship⟩ ⟨~ goods⟩ ~ *vi*, *obs* : SUBSCRIBE, AGREE, SUBMIT ⟨heaven ~*ing* to my good intents —Shak.⟩ **syn** see COMMIT

con·sig·na·tary \kən'signə,terē, -ri\ *n* -ES [*consignation* + *-ary*] : CONSIGNEE; *specif* : one who in Roman and civil law has received money on deposit (as by consignation)

con·sig·na·tion \,känsig'nāshən\ *n* -S [ML *consignation-, consignatio* sealing, marking, branding, fr. L, written proof, document, fr. *consignatus* (past part. of *consignare*) + *-ion-, -io* -ion] **1** : the act of marking with the sign of the cross **2** : a deposit of something a person owes tendered under judicial sanction by a debtor or a surrender of money by one claiming no interest therein to abide the determination of the rights of competing claimants **3** *archaic* : confirmatory indication by or as if by a sign or token ⟨the Scriptures having their ~ from God⟩ **4** *obs* : the act of consigning (as to another person or to a state) : COMMITTING, ENTRUSTING

con·sign·ee \¦kän,sī¦nē, ¦kän(t)sə¦nē, kən,sī¦nē\ *n* -S [*consign* + *-ee*] : one to whom something is consigned or shipped

con·significant \¦kän+\ *adj* [ML *consignificant-, consignificans*, pres. part. of *consignificare* to consignify] : SYNCATEGOREMATIC

con·signification \¦kän+\ *n* -S [ML *consignification-, consignificatio*, fr. *consignificatus* (past part. of *consignificare*) + *-ion-, -io* -ion] : connotative or contextual meaning : joint signification — **con·significa·tive** \¦kän+\ *adj*

con·signify \(')kän, kən+\ *vt* -ED/-ING/-ES [ML *consignificare*, fr. L *com-* + *significare* to signify — more at SIGNIFY] *archaic* : to signify in combination with something else

¹con·sign·ment \kən'sīnmənt\ *n* -S [*consign* + *-ment*] **1** : the act of consigning something ⟨the ~ of finished products to a wholesaler⟩ **2** : something that is consigned esp. in a single shipment ⟨the first ~ of new cars to reach the city⟩ — **on consignment** *adj (or adv)* : shipped to a dealer who acts as agent (as for a manufacturer) to sell, auction, or exhibit with the agreement that he may take title to and pay for what he sells, that he must remit the proceeds of sales less commission to the shipper, and that he may return anything left unsold ⟨goods shipped *on consignment*⟩

²consignment \"\ *adj* : of, relating to, or received as goods on consignment ⟨a ~ account⟩ ⟨~ marketing⟩ ⟨a ~ sale⟩ ⟨~ merchandise⟩ ⟨selling on a ~ basis⟩

consignment note *n* : AIRWAYBILL

con·sign·or \kən'sīnə(r), ¦kän,sī¦nō(ə)r, ¦kän(t)sə¦nō(ə)r, kən¦sī¦nō(ə)r, -nō(ə)r\ *also* **con·sign·er** \kən'sīnə(r)\ *n* -S : one that consigns something (as the goods of an individual shipment)

con·sil·ience \kən'silyən(t)s, -lēən-\ *n* -S [*com-* + *-silience* (as in *resilience*)] : the concurrence of generalizations from separate classes of facts in logical inductions so that one set of inductive laws is found to be in accord with another set of distinct derivation — **con·sil·ient** \-lyənt, -lēənt\ *adj*

con·similar \(')kän, kən+\ *adj* [obs. E *consimile* (fr. ME, fr. L *consimilis* entirely similar, fr. *com-* + *similis* similar) + *-ar* — more at SIMILAR] : sharing in similarity or being entirely similar; *specif* : having both valves alike ⟨~ diatoms⟩ — **con·similarity** \(')kän, kən+\ *n* -ES

¹con·sist \kən'sist\ *vi* -ED/-ING/-S [MF & L; MF *consister*, fr. L *consistere* to stand still or firm, be steadfast, exist, fr. *com-* + *sistere* to stand, cause to stand; akin to L *stare* to stand — more at STAND] **1** : to become comprised : LIE, RESIDE, INHERE — used with *in* ⟨national strength ~*s* not alone in national armies⟩ **2** *obs* : to become founded, based, or upheld — used with *on* or *upon* **3** *obs* : to have place or station : STAND, LIE — used chiefly with *in, within, between* **4** *archaic* : to exist in a fixed or permanent state (as of a body made up of parts in union) : hold together : BE **5** : to become composed or made up — used with *of* ⟨coal ~*s* mainly of carbon⟩ **6** *obs* : INSIST, URGE, DEMAND — used with *on* or *upon* **7** : to be consistent, harmonious, or in accordance — used with *with* ⟨the testimony ~*ed* with all known facts⟩ **8** *archaic* : to exist or be capable of existing — used with *with* ⟨refined tastes do not long ~ with abject poverty⟩

²consist \", 'kän,sist\ *n* -S : makeup or composition (as of coal sizes or a railroad train) by classes, types, or grades and arrangement

con·sist·ence \kən'sistən(t)s\ *n* -S [MF *consistance*, fr. *consistant*, pres. part. of *consister*] : CONSISTENCY

con·sist·en·cy \kən'sistənsē, -si\ *n* -ES **1 a** *archaic* : the condition (as of a material) of standing together or remaining fixed in union : FIRMNESS ⟨to boil a substance into a ~⟩ **b** : persistence of firmness (as in following a single or predetermined plan, method, or procedure) : singleness of purpose : PERSISTENCY ⟨Haydn's twenty sonatas are distinguished by the ~ with which their cheerful mood is maintained —A.E. Wier⟩ **2 a** : a degree of firmness, density, viscosity, or resistance to movement or separation of constituent particles ⟨the ~ of syrup⟩ **b** : the manifestation of mutual attraction of particles at different moisture contents ⟨~ of soil⟩ **c** : the percentage by weight of dry fibrous matter in a stock suspension about to be made into paper **3 a** : agreement or harmony of parts, traits, or features : uniformity among a number of things : CORRESPONDENCE ⟨a ~ of style in the furnishings and decorations of all the rooms⟩; *specif* : the characteristic of two or more propositions and derivatively of properties and propositional functions in logic that appertains if their conjunction does not result in a contradiction **b** : harmony of conduct or practice with profession : persistent adherence to moral or ethical standards in thought or action ⟨the ~ with which the foremost philosophic apostle of practicing what one preaches followed his own advice —*Americana Annual*⟩

con·sist·ent \kən'sistənt\ *adj* [L *consistent-, consistens*, pres. part. of *consistere*] **1** *archaic* : marked by unchanging position or by firmness, stiffness, solidarity, or coherence ⟨organs made ~ by cartilage⟩ : stationary, changeless, and enduring ⟨the ~ pines on the ledge⟩ **2 a** : marked by harmony, regularity, or steady continuity throughout : showing no significant change, unevenness, or contradiction ⟨in art all styles are good provided . . . they are ~ and harmonious within themselves —J.W.Krutch⟩ ⟨the influence of America should be ~ in seeking for humanity a final peace —F.D.Roosevelt⟩ **b** : marked by agreement and concord ⟨opinions ~ with each other⟩ : coexisting and showing no noteworthy opposing, conflicting, inharmonious, or contradictory qualities or trends : COMPATIBLE — usu. used with *with* ⟨drinking more hollands and water than is ~ with decorum —George Borrow⟩ ⟨is your aunt's romanticism always ~ with accuracy —Edith Wharton⟩ **c** : showing steady regular conformity to character, profession, belief, or custom ⟨a ~ advocate of a high protective tariff and was for many years president of the Protective Tariff League —A.L.Churchill⟩ **d** : jointly assertible so as to be true or not contradictory : COMPOSSIBLE **syn** see CONSONANT

consistent equations *n pl* : a set of equations possessing a common solution

consistently *adv* : in a consistent manner: as **a** : COMPATIBLY ⟨~ with standards⟩ : CONGRUOUSLY ⟨one cannot ~ defend such dishonesty⟩ **b** : in harmony with ⟨~ with our intentions⟩ **c** : in a persistent or even manner : UNIFORMLY ⟨a ~ ironic tone throughout the whole novel⟩

con·sist·om·e·ter \,känsə'stämәd·ə(r)\ *n* -S [*consistency* + *-o-* + *-meter*] : a device for measuring consistency or flow characteristics of a viscous or plastic substance (as a lubricating grease or a starch suspension)

con·sis·to·ri·al \¦känsə¦stōrēəl, -stȯr-\ *adj* [ME, fr. ML *consistorialis*, fr. LL & ML *consistorium* + L *-alis* -al] : of or having to do with a consistory

consistorian *adj* [LL & ML *consistorianus*, fr. *consistorium* + L *-anus* -an] *obs* : CONSISTORIAL

con·sis·to·ry \kən'sist(ə)rē, -ri *Brit also* 'känsist(ə)ri\ *n* -ES [ME *consistorie*, fr. MF, fr. ML & LL; ML *consistorium* church tribunal, fr. LL, place of assembly, imperial council, fr. L *consistere* to stand still or firm + *-orium* -ory — more at CONSIST] **1 a** *obs* : a place of assembly (as a council chamber) **b** : a solemn assembly : COUNCIL **2** : a church tribunal or governing body: as **a** *also* **consistory court** : a diocesan court with jurisdiction in matters (as of marriage and titles) relating to general ecclesiastical and moral discipline; *specif* : a similar court in the Church of England presided over by the bishop's chancellor or commissary and dealing only with spiritual and ecclesiastical matters **b** : a solemn meeting of Roman Catholic cardinals convoked and presided over by the pope **c** : an advisory body in the Eastern Orthodox Church assisting the ecumenical patriarch of Constantinople in the affairs of his diocese **d** : a church council in certain churches with a presbyterian polity (as the Dutch and other Reformed churches) charged with managing the general affairs of a church and composed of the ministers, the elders, and sometimes (as in the Evangelical and Reformed church) the deacons of the congregation **e** : an administrative body of clerical and lay officers appointed by civil authority to administer ecclesiastical affairs in Lutheran state churches **3 a** : the organization or a branch of the organization that confers the degrees of the Ancient and Accepted Scottish Rite of Freemasonry usu. from the 19th to the 32d inclusive; *also* : a meeting of such an organization or branch **b** : a building serving as headquarters for a Masonic consistory

¹con·so·ciate \kən'sōs(h)ēət, (')kän¦-, -shət, -shē,āt, -sē,āt, *usu* -d·+V\ *adj* [ME *consociat*, fr. L *consociatus*, past part. of *consociare* to associate, unite, fr. *com-* + *sociare* to join, unite, fr. *socius* associate, ally — more at SOCIAL] : united in fellowship : intimately associated ⟨a ~ family⟩

²con·so·ci·ate \kən'sōs(h)ē,āt, (')kän¦-, *usu* -ād·+V\ *vb* -ED/-ING/-S [L *consociatus*] *vt* : to unite or bring into association ⟨Swedenborg's best of angels . . . did not live *consociated* —Van Wyck Brooks⟩ ⟨the *consociated* Congregational churches of New England⟩ ~ *vi* : to associate esp. in fellowship or partnership : enter into intimate or close association ⟨*consociating* with the best of men⟩ ⟨the churches *consociated* to fight against their dissolution⟩

³con·so·ciate *see adj*\ *n* -S [¹*consociate*] : one who is united with another : ASSOCIATE, CONFEDERATE ⟨~*s* in a plot⟩

con·so·ci·a·tion \kən,sōsē'āshən, (')kän¦=¦=, -oshē-\ *n* -S [L *consociation-, consociatio*, fr. *consociatus* + *-ion-, -io* -ion] **1 a** : the act of uniting in fellowship or association ⟨the possibility of friendly ~ with the countess —Carl Van Vechten⟩ **b** *archaic* : intimate or close association : ALLIANCE, CONFEDERATION ⟨~ with God⟩ ⟨to enter into a ~ with friendly countries⟩ **2** : an association or confederation of churches or religious societies: as **a** (1) : a voluntary council or union of neighboring Congregational churches for cooperation in ecclesiastical matters (2) : a standing council with disciplinary authority composed of the ministers and representative laymen in a district in Connecticut Congregationalism **b** : the union of churches on a Presbyterian basis among English Puritans **3 a** : a community within an ecological association having a single dominant which is usu. one of the dominants of the association ⟨a sugar-maple ~ in a beech-maple association⟩ — compare FACIATION **b** : an association having a single dominant

con·so·ci·a·tion·al \kən¦=¦=¦āshənᵊl, (')kän-, -āshnəl\ *adj* : of or having to do with a consociation

con·so·ci·a·tion·ism \kən,=='āshə,nizəm, (')kän-\ *n* -S : the theory or practice of church consociation

con·so·cia·tive \kən'sōs(h)ē,ād·iv, (')kän¦-, -ōshəd·iv, -ōs(h)ēəd·iv\ *adj* : promoting, exhibiting, or having to do with association or fellowship ⟨~ behavior⟩ ⟨the headmaster who knew little about games, though . . . approving of their ~ virtues —V.V.Nabokov⟩

con·so·ci·es \kən'sōs(h)ē,ēz, (')kän¦-\ *n, pl* **consocies** [*consociation* + *-ies* (as in *species*)] : a consociation of plants in a developmental stage

con·sol \'kän,säl, kən'-\ *n* -S *sometimes cap, often attrib* [*consolidated* annuity] : a bond issue having no maturity date although the issuer may have the right to call for redemption; *esp* : a perpetual interest-bearing obligation first issued by the British government in 1751 ⟨the ~ market⟩ — usu. used in pl. ⟨an old dowager countess whose money was all in *Consols* —Samuel Butler †1902⟩

con·sol·a·ble \kən'sōləbəl\ *adj* : that can be consoled — **con·sol·able·ness** \-nəs\ *n* -ES — **con·sol·ably** \-blē, -bli\ *adv*

con·so·la·men·tum \kən'sōlə̇mentəm\ *n, pl* **consolamen·ta** \-tə\ [ML, fr. L *consolari* + *-mentum* -ment] : the Cathari rite of spiritual baptism usu. administered just before death making the candidate one of the perfecti

¹consolate *vt* -ED/-ING/-S [L *consolatus*] *obs* : CONSOLE

²consolate *adj* [L *consolatus*] *obs* : CONSOLED, COMFORTED

con·so·la·tion \,kän(t)sə'lāshən\ *n* -S [ME *consolacioun*, fr. MF or L; MF *consolation*, fr. L *consolation-, consolatio*, fr. *consolatus* (past part. of *consolari* to console) + *-ion-, -io* -ion] **1 a** : alleviation of distress or misery (as by sympathetic care or attention or by the soothing or mitigating effects of natural or psychological phenomena) : COMFORT, SOLACE ⟨nothing brings me so much ~ as music —Havelock Ellis⟩ ⟨he had sought the ~ of the twilight —Elinor Wylie⟩ **b** : an instance or act of comforting or being comforted ⟨~*s* to offset the inevitable physical decay that befalls most of us —Elmer Davis⟩ **2 a** : a fine paid by the loser in some card games (as ombre) **b** : a contest (as a game, match, or race) held for those who have lost in the early stages of a tournament ⟨~ match⟩ ⟨~ race⟩ **c** *or* **consolation prize** : a prize of relatively little value given to a runner-up or a loser **3** : CONSOLAMENTUM

consolator *n* -S [L, fr. *consolatus* + *-or*] *obs* : one that consoles

¹con·sol·a·to·ry \kən'sōlə,tōrē, -tȯrē, -ri; *chiefly Brit* -'sälət(ə)rē, -ri\ *adj* [ME, fr. L *consolatorius*, fr. *consolatus* + *-orius* -ory] : designed or tending to bring consolation ⟨~ words⟩ ⟨a gesture ~ to his injured pride⟩

²consolatory *n* -S *obs* : a consolatory communication

¹con·sole \kən'sōl\ *vb* -ED/-ING/-S [F *consoler*, fr. L *consolari*, fr. *com-* + *solari* to console, comfort — more at SILLY] *vt* : to soothe in distress or depression : alleviate the grief and raise the spirits of : COMFORT ⟨*consoling* advice⟩ ⟨~ herself with music⟩ ~ *vi* : to alleviate grief or disappointment : SOOTHE **syn** see COMFORT

²console \'kän,sōl\ *n* -S [F, short for MF *consolateur* consoler, carved human figure used as a bracket to support cornices, fr. L *consolator*] **1 a** : an architectural member usu. in Roman and neoclassic style having its sides nearly plane and more or less parallel and a profile of scroll shape (as an ogee curve) and projecting from a wall to form a bracket or corbel (as for the support of a cornice, window head, or bust) or from a keystone (as for ornament) — see ANCON **b** : a similar member reversed and depending upon the horizontal rather than the vertical surface and used to finish a parapet or gallery with an ornament shaped like a scroll **2** : CONSOLE TABLE **3 a** : the desk from which an organ is played and which contains the keyboards, pedal board, and other controlling mechanisms **b** : a panel or cabinet on which are mounted dials, switches, and other apparatus used in centrally controlling electrical or mechanical devices **4** : a cabinet (as for a radio or television set) often decorated and designed to rest directly on the floor and usu. against a wall

console supporting a cornice

console table *n* [²*console*] : a table fixed to a wall with its top supported by one or more consoles, front legs, or an eagle or other carved motive; *broadly* : any table to be placed against a wall (as a side or pier table)

con·so·lette \,känsə'let, '==,=\ *n* -S [²*console* + *-ette*] : a small cabinet containing a radio, television, or record player designed to be placed against a wall

18th cent. console table

¹con·sol·i·date \kən'sälə,dāt, *usu* -ād·+V\ *vb* -ED/-ING/-S [L *consolidatus*, past part. of *consolidare* to make firm, fr. *com-* + *solidare* to make firm, fr. *solidus* solid — more at SAFE] *vt* **1 a** : to join together (as two or more items into one unit, or whole) : UNITE ⟨~ various ideas⟩ ⟨~ several colleges into a university⟩ **b** *law* (1) : to cause to become united and extinguished in a superior right or estate by both becoming vested in the same person (2) : to join in or cause to proceed as a single action — used of causes of action or of actions started separately **2 a** : to make firm or secure : STRENGTHEN, CONFIRM ⟨~ their hold on first place⟩ ⟨~ the economic power of an empire with great merchant fleets⟩; *specif* : to organize and strengthen by military means (as a position or ground recently captured) **b** : to make stronger or more secure ⟨condemnation of Italy . . . *consolidated* Italian-American support for Il Duce —Oscar Handlin⟩ ⟨~ his reputation⟩ : make more tangible or effective ⟨five years . . . have only *consolidated* the paradoxes —James Cameron⟩ **3** : to make or form into a solid or hardened mass ⟨the press ~*s* fibers into board under pressures which vary from 300 to 1000 pounds a square inch —*Monsanto Mag.*⟩ ~ *vi* **1** : to become firm or hard (as by solidifying, freezing, uniting, adhering) : grow solid ⟨the mud of the roads *consolidated* in the freezing night⟩ **2** : to unite or grow into a coherent whole ⟨his ideas *consolidated* into a plan⟩; *specif* : to undergo merger (as for mutual advantage) **syn** see UNIFY

²consolidate \-,dāt, -dət\ *adj* [L *consolidatus*] : made solid, firm, or coherent : CONSOLIDATED ⟨one of Montague's earliest ~ memories —Peggy Bennett⟩

consolidated *adj* **1** : that has become firm or solid; *specif* : SOLIDIFIED ⟨a ~ lung in pneumonia⟩ — compare CONSOLIDATION 1b(1) **2** : joined together into a coherent, compact, or unified whole ⟨a ~ balance sheet⟩ ⟨a ~ European army⟩

consolidated annuities *n pl* : CONSOLS

consolidated school *n* : a school formed by merging two or more public schools usu. of the elementary level and often located in a rural district — compare UNION SCHOOL

consolidated statement *n* : a balance sheet or profit and loss statement of two or more affiliated enterprises (as a parent company and its wholly owned subsidiary companies)

consolidated stock *n* : CONSOLS

con·sol·i·da·tion \kən,sälə'dāshən\ *n* -S [ME *consolidacion*, fr. LL *consolidation-, consolidatio*, fr. L *consolidatus* + *-ion-, -io* -ion — more at CONSOLIDATE] **1 a** : the process of becoming firm or solid ⟨the ~ of fibrous matter under pressure⟩ **b** (1) : the process by which an infected lung passes from an aerated collapsible condition to one of airless solid consistency through the accumulation of exudate in the alveoli and adjoining ducts ⟨pneumonic ~⟩ (2) : tissue that has undergone consolidation ⟨areas of ~⟩ — compare RESOLUTION **c** : the passage from a loosely aggregated or liquid condition to firm rock through the effect of pressure, chemical action, or crystallization : LITHIFICATION **2** : the process of becoming or making stronger or more secure ⟨the ~ of gains⟩ ⟨his ~ of political power⟩ ⟨the year 1952 was one of ~ in physics —*Americana Annual*⟩ ⟨her more recent fiction suggests nothing more than a ~ of her previous achievement —W.S.Graham⟩ **3** : the process of uniting or the quality or state of being united : COMBINATION, UNIFICATION ⟨the ~ of several works into one volume⟩ ⟨the present ~ of rural schools⟩ ⟨the twin Communist goals of ~ of the Communist world and disintegration of the rest —J.P.Lash⟩; *specif* : the unification of two or more corporations by dissolution of existing ones and creation of a single new corporation

con·sol·i·da·tion·ist \-nəst\ *n* -S : one who advocates consolidation; *esp* : an advocate of a strong federal government

con·sol·i·da·tor \-'sälə,dād·ə(r)\ *n* -S : one that consolidates

con·sol·ing·ly *adv* : in a consoling manner

consols *pl of* CONSOL

con·so·lute \'kän(t)sə,lüt\ *adj* [LL *consolutus* dissolved together, fr. L *com-* + *solutus*, past part. of *solvere* to set free, loosen, dissolve — more at SOLVE] **1 a** : miscible in all proportions : mutually soluble — used of two or more liquids **b** : soluble in each of two nonmiscible liquids in contact with each other **2** : of or relating to liquids perfectly miscible under certain conditions

consolute temperature *n* : CRITICAL SOLUTION TEMPERATURE

con·som·mé *also* **con·som·me** \'känsə,mā, ,==='=; *Brit* kən'sämā *or* kōⁿsȯmā\ *n* -S [F *consommé*, fr. past part. of *consommer* to accomplish, consume, boil down, fr. L *consummare* to complete, finish — more at CONSUMMATE] : a soup made usu. of meat stock often in combination and condensed by boiling, highly seasoned, cleared, and strained

consomol *usu cap, var of* KOMSOMOL

con·so·nance \'kän(t)s(ə)nən(t)s\ *n* -S [ME, fr. MF, fr. L *consonantia*, fr. *consonant-, consonans* + *-ia* -y] **1** : harmony of parts : pleasing, desired, or logical agreement among components ⟨~ of thought and expression⟩ ⟨the literary conceptions which prevailed were in ~ with the social structure —V.F.Calverton⟩ ⟨she spoke with an angry . . . vehemence that was strangely out of ~ with her ordinary serenity of demeanor —William Black⟩ **2 a** : correspondence of sounds : recurrence of like or similar sounds : ACCORD ⟨a pleasing ~ among final syllables⟩ — compare ASSONANCE **b** : a combination of musical tones felt as satisfying and restful; *specif* : an interval included in a major or minor triad and its inversions — compare DISSONANCE **c** : sympathetic vibration : RESONANCE — used by some to distinguish the sympathetic vibration of independent things (as two musical strings or two electric circuits) from *resonance* **d :** recurrence or repetition of identical or similar consonants; *specif* **:** correspondence of consonants alone unaccompanied by like correspondence of vowels at the ends of two or more syllables, words, or other units of composition — called also *consonant-rhyme;* compare ALLITERATION, ASSONANCE

con·so·nan·cy \ˈkän(t)s(ə)nənsē, -si\ *n* -ES [ME *consonancie,* fr. MF & L; MF, fr. L *consonantia*] **:** the quality or state of being harmonious or congruent ⟨~ of sounds⟩ ⟨~ of related parts⟩

[1]**con·so·nant** \ˈkän(t)s(ə)nənt\ *n* -S [ME, fr. L *consonant-, consonans,* fr. pres. part. of *consonare* to sound at the same time] **1 :** one of a class of speech sounds (as *p, g, n, l, s, r, w*) characterized by constriction or closure at one or more points in the breath channel; *broadly* **:** any sound in a syllable other than the one most prominent sound (as the second element of a falling diphthong) — compare CONSONANTAL VOWEL, SEMIVOWEL, VOWEL **2 :** a letter representing a consonant — usu. used in English of all letters in the alphabet except *a, e, i, o,* and *u*

[2]**consonant** \"\ *adj* [MF, fr. L *consonant-, consonans,* pres. part. of *consonare* to sound at the same time, agree, fr. *com-* + *sonare* to sound — more at SOUND] **1 :** suiting or according with a circumstance or situation or conforming to a standard or pattern without discord or difficulty ⟨Fijians possessed a physical endurance ~ with their great stature —V.G. Heiser⟩ ⟨it is . . . more ~ with the Puritan temper to abolish a practice than to elevate it —A.T.Quiller-Couch⟩ **2 :** agreeable in sound; *specif* **:** harmonically satisfying — contrasted with *dissonant* **3 :** having like sounds ⟨~ words⟩ **4 :** CONSONANTAL **5 :** relating to or exhibiting consonance **:** RESONANT **syn** CONSISTENT, COMPATIBLE, CONGRUOUS, CONGENIAL, SYMPATHETIC: CONSONANT implies general harmony and stresses lack of factors making for discord or difficulty ⟨the book presented meditations which were so *consonant* with Christian views that its Christian readers from Alfred to Dante mistook them for Christian sentiments —H.O.Taylor⟩ ⟨even the man's start and suspicious stare as the priest went by were *consonant* enough with the vigilance and jealousy of such a type —G.K.Chesterton⟩ The implications of CONSISTENT are much the same, although it may tend to suggest accord on small details in addition to main matters ⟨Father John did not think it to be *consistent* with his dignity to answer this sally —Anthony Trollope⟩ ⟨I have decided that the course of conduct which I am following is *consistent* with my sense of responsibility as president in time of war —F.D.Roosevelt⟩ COMPATIBLE indicates capacity for existing together without discord or conflict, although not necessarily in positive agreement or harmony ⟨all systems of economy that are to be *compatible* with man's continual adaptation to a changing world must employ both the principle of order and that of freedom —M.R.Cohen⟩ ⟨in ordinary society it is notoriously difficult for people of very unequal fortune to be friends in the true sense; that beautiful relationship is not *compatible* with patronage and dependence —H.J.Mackinder⟩ CONGRUOUS suggests a more positive harmony, a suitability of things likely to make for a pleasant impression ⟨thoughts *congruous* to the nature of their subject —William Cowper⟩ ⟨the doctrine is not always quite *congruous* with itself —Havelock Ellis⟩ CONGENIAL is likely to imply pleasing concord or satisfying harmony ⟨I was brought up in the freer, less conventional atmosphere of South Australia, and this English life, with its proprieties and its primness, is not *congenial* to me —A. Conan Doyle⟩ ⟨the ideal of a Greek democracy was vastly *congenial* to his aristocratic temperament —V.L.Parrington⟩ SYMPATHETIC may apply to a milder appeal or to a less hearty acceptance, but it always indicates a strong tendency toward concord ⟨a semimystical, *sympathetic* harmony between husband and wife —Norman Cameron⟩ ⟨thus a tête-à-tête with a man of similar tastes, who is just and yet *sympathetic,* critical yet appreciative . . . this is a high intellectual pleasure —A.C. Benson⟩

con·so·nan·tal \ˌkän(t)səˈnantᵊl, -naan-\ *adj* **1 :** being or functioning as a consonant **:** of or relating to a consonant **2 :** marked by or consisting of consonants ⟨a ~ diphthong⟩ ⟨a ~ Hebrew text⟩ — **con·so·nan·tal·ly** \-tᵊlē, -li\ *adv*

con·so·nan·tal·i·za·tion \ˌkän(t)səˌnantᵊləˈzāshən\ *also* **con·so·nant·i·za·tion** \ˌkän(t)sənəntəˈz-, -ˌnant-\ *n* -S **:** the act or action of consonantalizing

con·so·nan·tal·ize \ˌkän(t)səˈnantᵊlˌīz\ *also* **con·so·nant·ize** \ˈkän(t)sənənˌtīz\ *vb* -ED/-ING/-S *vt* **:** to change into or articulate as a consonant (as when the ē in *piteous* is pronounced \y\ rather than \ē\) ~ *vi* **:** to change a vowel to a consonant ⟨the tendency to ~⟩

consonantal stem *n* **:** CONSONANT STEM

consonantal vowel *n* **:** the unstressed less prominent part of a diphthong (as the \i\ of \ȯi\ in \ˈbȯi\ *boy*)

consonant declension *n* **:** a declension characterized by the addition of case endings to a stem that ends in a consonant

con·so·nan·tic \ˌkän(t)səˈnantik\ *adj* **:** CONSONANTAL

con·so·nant·ism \ˈkän(t)sənənˌtizəm\ *n* -S **1 :** the consonant system (as of a language or dialect) **2 :** the consonants, sequence of consonants, or quality peculiar to the consonants of a word or group of related words ⟨the ~ of the 4 words hardly seems . . . to point to Scandinavian origin —Stephen Ullmann⟩

con·so·nan·tize \ˈkän(t)s(ə)nənˌtīz\ *vt* -ED/-ING/-S **:** to change into or articulate as a consonant

con·so·nant·ly *adv* **:** in a consonant manner

con·so·nant·ness *n* -ES **:** the quality or state of being consonant

consonant–rhyme \ˈ==(=)=,=\ *n* **:** CONSONANCE 2 d

consonants *pl of* CONSONANT

consonant shift *n* **1 :** the set of regular changes in consonant articulation which distinguish the Germanic languages from the other Indo-European languages and through which Indo-European voiceless stops become Germanic voiceless fricatives (as in Greek *pyr, treis, kardia* compared with English *fire, three, heart*), Indo-European voiced stops become Germanic voiceless stops (as in Old Slavic *jablŭko,* Greek *dyo, genos* compared with English *apple, two, kin*), and Indo-European voiced aspirated stops become Germanic voiced fricatives (as in Sanskrit *nābhi, madhya* "mid", Latin *helvus* compared with English *navel,* Old Norse *mithr* "mid", English *yellow*) — called also *first consonant shift, Germanic consonant shift* **2 :** the set of regular changes in consonant articulation which distinguish High German from the other Germanic languages and through which Germanic voiceless stops become High German affricates or voiceless fricatives (as in English *pound, open, ten, eat, corn, make* compared with German *pfund, offen, zehn, essen,* Upper German *kchorn,* German *machen*) and Germanic voiced stops become High German voiceless stops (as in English *rib, middle,* Dutch *egge* "edge", compared with German *rippe, mittel* "means", *ecke* "corner") — called also *second consonant shift, High German consonant shift* **3 :** the Germanic and High German consonant shifts together **4 :** any set of regular changes in consonant articulation in the history of a language or dialect ⟨the Armenian *consonant shift*⟩

consonant stem *n* **:** a word or stem belonging to a consonant declension

consopite *vt* -ED/-ING/-S [L *consopitus,* past part. of *consopire* to put to sleep, fr. *com-* + *sopire* to put to sleep — more at SOPITE] *obs* **:** to lull to sleep **:** QUIET

consopition *n* -S [L *consopitus* + E *-ion*] *obs* **:** a lulling to sleep

con sor·di·no \ˌkän(ˌ)sȯ(r)ˈdē(ˌ)nō, ˌkōn-\ *adv* [It] **:** with the mute — used as a direction in music

[1]**con·sort** \ˈkänˌsȯrt, -sȯ(ə)t, *usu* -d·+V\ *n* -S [ME, fr. MF, fr. L *consort-, consors,* fr. *com-* + *sort-, sors* lot, fate, share — more at SORT] **:** one that shares the company of or is associated with another: as **a** *obs* **:** a colleague of one's profession or official office **b :** COMPANION ⟨the criminal and his semirespectable ~*s*⟩ ⟨the second volume is in every respect a splendid ~ of the first⟩; *specif* **:** a ship accompanying another ⟨far astern . . . he could see the brown sail and the red sail of their ~*s* —C.S.Forester⟩ **c :** a wife or husband **:** SPOUSE, MATE ⟨the queen attended the opening of the exhibition with her ~⟩ — compare PRINCE CONSORT

[2]**consort** \"\ *n* -S [MF *consorte* company, fr. *consort*] **1** *obs* **:** ASSEMBLY, COMPANY, GROUP ⟨in one ~ there sat cruel revenge and rancorous despite —Edmund Spenser⟩ **2 :** concurrence or accord **:** CONJUNCTION, ASSOCIATION ⟨I can claim that poetry . . . had ~ with me through life —A.T. Quiller-Couch⟩ — often used with *in* ⟨he ruled in ~ with his father⟩ **3** [prob. by folk etymology fr. MF *concert* — more at CONCERT] **a :** a group of musicians entertaining by voice or instrument or the entertainment they afford **b** *obs* **:** harmony of sounds **c :** a set of 16th and 17th century musical instruments of the same family (as viols) played in concert

[3]**consort** \kənˈsȯ(ə)rt, -sȯ(ə)t *sometimes* ˈkänˌsȯrt, -ˌsȯ(ə)t, *usu* -d·+V\ *vb* -ED/-ING/-S [¹*consort*] *vt* **1 :** to unite esp. in affection, harmony, company, marriage **:** ASSOCIATE ⟨the ideas that naturally ~ themselves with the word civilization —Isaac Taylor⟩ **2** [²*consort* (harmony of sounds)] *obs* **:** to sound in harmony **:** HARMONIZE **3** *obs* **:** ESCORT, ATTEND, ACCOMPANY ~ *vi* **1 :** to keep company ⟨a unit's soldiery . . . ~*ing* with women —Fred Majdalany⟩ ⟨from this time on he ~*ed* more and more with Methodists —Allen Johnson⟩ **2** [²*consort* (harmony of sounds)] *obs* **:** to make harmony **:** PLAY **3** [²*consort* (accord)] **:** to be or come into accord **:** HARMONIZE ⟨except in matters of doctrine Pilgrim and Puritan ~*ed* ill together —V.L.Parrington⟩ ⟨the statement of faith . . . is so inane that . . . an apostate . . . can easily ~ to it —H.H.Savage⟩ ⟨the illustrations ~ admirably with the text —*Times Lit. Supp.*⟩

con·sor·tion \kənˈsȯrshən\ *n* -S [L *consortion-, consortio,* fr. *consort-, consors* partner + *-ion-, -io* -ion — more at CONSORT] **:** ASSOCIATION, ALLIANCE

con·sort·ism \ˈkänˌsȯrdˌizəm\ *n* -S [¹*consort* + *-ism*] **:** SYMBIOSIS

con·sor·ti·um \kənˈsȯrsh(ē)əm, -ȯrd·ēəm\ *n, pl* **consor·tia** \-rsh(ē)ə, -rd·ēə\ *also* **consortiums** \-mz\ [L, fellowship, fr. *consort-, consors* + *-ium*] **1 :** an international business or banking agreement or combination (as for the financial assistance of another nation or for the control of a particular industry in a country or countries) — compare CARTEL, TRUST **2 :** ASSOCIATION, FELLOWSHIP, CLUB, SOCIETY ⟨speaking of distinguished *consortia,* a new one called the Renaissance Society of America is announced —*N.Y. Herald Tribune Bk. Rev.*⟩ **3 a :** marital association — used chiefly in a legal action for damages for injury to a spouse or for alienation of a spouse's affections ⟨loss of ~⟩ **b :** persistent intimate association of different kinds of organisms usu. with close physical contact (as in the symbiosis of certain algae)

con·species \(ˈ)kän, kən+\ *n, pl* **conspecies** [*com-* + *species*] **:** a congeneric species

con·specific \ˈ;kän+\ *adj* [fr. *conspecies,* after such pairs as *species: specific*] **:** of the same species

con·spec·tus \kənˈspektəs, -nˈsp-\ *n* -ES [L, fr. *conspectus,* past part. of *conspicere* to perceive — more at CONSPICUOUS] **1 :** a survey (as of a comprehensive subject) usu. in brief compass or rapid topical summary and often providing an overall view or perspective ⟨a ~ of the history of human thought⟩ **2 :** OUTLINE, LIST, SYNOPSIS ⟨a brief ~ on rose diseases and their control —*Experiment Station Record*⟩ **syn** see ABRIDGMENT

con·sper·gent \kənzˈpərjənt, -nˈsp-\ *n* -S [L *conspergent-, conspergens,* pres. part. of *conspergere* to sprinkle, fr. *com-* + *spergere* (fr. *spargere* to scatter, strew) — more at SPARK] **:** a dusting powder (as lycopodium) used to coat the surface of handmade pills to prevent them from adhering to one another

con·sperse \kənzˈpərs, (ˈ)känz;-, kənˈsp-, (ˈ)kän;sp-\ *adj* [L *conspersus,* past part. of *conspergere*] **:** thickly and irregularly strewn (as with fine spots or punctures)

con·spi·cu·i·ty \ˌkänzpəˈkyüəd·ē, -än(t)sp-, -ətē, -i\ *n* -ES [*conspicuous* + *-ity*] **:** CONSPICUOUSNESS

con·spic·u·ous \kənzˈpikyəwəs, -nˈsp-\ *adj* [L *conspicuus,* fr. *conspicere* to get sight of, perceive, fr. *com-* + *-spicere* (fr. *specere* to look) — more at SPY] **1 :** obvious to the eye or mind **:** plainly visible **:** MANIFEST ⟨~ at a great distance⟩ ⟨an intention ~ only to his friends⟩ **2 :** attracting or tending to attract attention by reason of size, brilliance, contrast, station **:** STRIKING, EMINENT ⟨a ~ tower⟩ ⟨~ statesmen⟩ **3 :** undesirably noticeable by reason of violation of good taste or sense ⟨a ~ necktie⟩ ⟨against spending money for cement sidewalks, which he considered ~ waste —E.W.Smith⟩ **syn** see NOTICEABLE

conspicuous consumption *n* **:** lavish or wasteful spending regarded as establishing or enhancing social prestige

con·spic·u·ous·ly *adv* **:** in a conspicuous manner

con·spic·u·ous·ness \-nəs\ *n* -ES **:** the quality or state of being conspicuous

con·spir·a·cy \kənzˈpirəsē, -nˈsp-, -si\ *n* -ES [ME *conspiracie,* alter. (influenced by *-cie* -cy) of *conspiracioun* — more at CONSPIRATION] **1 a :** an illegal, treasonable, or treacherous plan to harm or destroy another person, group, or entity ⟨the ~ to murder Caesar⟩ ⟨his theory of the trade-union movement as a ~ against the unorganized worker —L.A. Fiedler⟩ **b :** an agreement manifesting itself in words or deeds and made by two or more persons confederating to do an unlawful act or use unlawful means to do an act which is lawful **:** CONFEDERACY **2 :** a combination of persons banded secretly together and resolved to accomplish an evil or unlawful end ⟨a ~ made up of storm troopers and disgruntled aristocrats⟩ **3 :** a striking concurrence of tendencies, circumstances, or phenomena as though in planned accord ⟨the portentous ~ of night and solitude and silence —Ambrose Bierce⟩ **syn** see PLOT

conspiracy of silence : a secret agreement to keep silent about an occurrence, situation, or subject esp. to promote or protect selfish interests ⟨local manufacturers were accused of a *conspiracy of silence* on the child-labor situation⟩

con·spir·ant \kənzˈspīrənt, -nˈsp-\ *adj* [F, fr. L *conspirant-, conspirans,* pres. part. of *conspirare*] *archaic* **:** CONSPIRING

con·spi·ra·tion \ˌkänzpəˈrāshən, -än(t)sp-\ *n* -S [ME *conspiracioun,* fr. OF *conspiration,* fr. L *conspiration-, conspiratio,* fr. *conspiratus* (past part. of *conspirare*) + *-ion-, -io* -ion] **1 :** the act or action of plotting or secretly combining ⟨an everlasting ~ against authority⟩ **2** *obs* **:** CONSPIRACY, PLOT **3 :** joint effort toward a particular end ⟨a ~ to give evidence of faith by good works⟩ — **con·spi·ra·tion·al** \ˌ==ˈ=shənᵊl, -shnəl\ *adj*

con·spir·a·tive \kənzˈpirəd·iv, -nˈsp-\ *adj* [*conspiration* + *-ive*] **:** of or having to do with conspiracy or a conspiracy ⟨the discovery of possible ~ codes and ciphers —Joseph Barnes⟩

con·spir·a·tor \kənzˈpirəd·ə(r), -nˈsp-, -ətə-\ *n* -S [ME *conspiratour,* fr. MF *conspirateor,* fr. L *conspirator,* fr. *conspiratus* (past part. of *conspirare*) + *-or*] **:** one that conspires esp. treasonably **:** PLOTTER

con·spir·a·to·ri·al \kənzˌpirəˈtōrēəl, -nˌsp-, -tȯr-\ *adj* **:** of, having to do with, or suggestive of conspiracy or a conspiracy ⟨~ propaganda⟩ ⟨~ funds⟩ ⟨~ glances⟩ — **con·spir·a·to·ri·al·ly** \-rēəlē, -li\ *adv*

con·spire \kənzˈpī(ə)r, -nˈsp-, -īə\ *vb* -ED/-ING/-S [ME *conspiren,* fr. MF *conspirer,* fr. L *conspirare* to blow together, harmonize, agree, plot, fr. *com-* + *spirare* to breathe, blow — more at SPIRIT] *vt* **1 :** PLOT, PLAN, CONTRIVE ⟨your fall and mine do they alike ~ —Robert Southey⟩ **2** *obs* **:** to unite in producing or contributing to ~ *vi* **1 :** to make an agreement with a group and in secret to do some act (as to commit treason or a crime or carry out a treacherous deed) **:** plot together ⟨~ against the state⟩ ⟨lamented that the English workers . . . had never learned to ~ —*Time*⟩ **2 :** to concur or work to one end **:** act in harmony ⟨circumstances of life have *conspired* . . . to render any fixed and authoritative belief incredible —Walter Lippmann⟩

con·spir·ing·ly *adv* **:** in a conspiring manner

con spir·i·to \kän ˈspirəd·(ˌ)ō, -änˈsp-, kōn-\ *adv* [It] **:** with spirit or animation — used as a direction in music

con·spue \kənzˈpyü, -nˈsp-\ *vt* -ED/-ING/-S [F *conspuer,* fr. L *conspuere,* fr. *com-* + *spuere* to spit — more at SPEW] **:** to spurn with contempt as if by spitting upon

const *abbr* **1** constable **2** constant **3** constituent **4** constitution **5** construction

con·sta·ble \ˈkänztəbəl, -än(t)st-; *chiefly Brit* ˈkən-\ *n* -S [ME *conestable,* fr. OF, fr. LL *comes stabuli* officer of the stable, chief equerry, marshal, fr. *comes* officer, count + *stabuli,* gen. of *stabulum* stable — more at COUNT, STABLE] **1 :** the chief officer of the household, court, or army of a nobleman or king during the middle ages who often acted as commander in chief of the army next to the king and as supreme judge of the military courts and courts of chivalry ⟨*constable* of Scotland⟩ ⟨lord high *constable* of England⟩ **2 :** the warden or governor of a royal castle or fortress or of a fortified town **3 :** a military officer esp. of the middle ages **4 a :** a public officer responsible for keeping the public peace and for certain petty judicial duties **b** *Brit* **:** a policeman of the lowest rank

constablery *n* -ES [ME *conestablerie,* fr. MF, fr. *conestable* + *-erie* -ery] *obs* **:** the office of or district under a constable

con·sta·ble·wick \-ˌwik\ *n* -S [*constable* + *wick* (village)] **:** the jurisdiction or district of a constable

[1]**con·stab·u·lary** \kənzˈtabyəˌlerē, -nˈst-, -ri\ *n* -ES [ME *constabularie,* fr. ML *constabularia,* fr. *constabularius, conestabulus* constable (fr. LL *comes stabuli*) + L *-aria* -ary, n. suffix — more at CONSTABLE] **1 :** CONSTABLEWICK **2 :** a body of constables or policemen (as of a particular town, district, country) **3 :** an armed police force organized on military lines but distinct from the regular army ⟨the Royal Irish *Constabulary*⟩

[2]**constabulary** \"\ *adj* [ML *constabularius,* fr. *constabulus* constable + L *-arius* -ary, adj. suffix] **:** of, relating to, or suggestive of a constable or constabulary ⟨~ duties⟩ ⟨possessed of a ~ power before which barbaric . . . forces will stand in awe —Sir Winston Churchill⟩

con·stance \ˈkänztən(t)s, -änst-\ *n* -S [ME *constaunce,* fr. MF *constance,* fr. L *constantia*] **1** *obs* **:** CONSTANCY 1, 3 **2 :** the relative occurrence of a kind of organism (as a species) in several examples of a particular type of ecological community based on counts of sample plots of uniform size in each example and commonly expressed as a percentage of the whole population of the sample plot

con·stan·cy \ˈkänztənsē, -än(t)st-, -si\ *n* -ES [L *constantia,* fr. *constant-, constans* (pres. part. of *constare*) + *-ia* -y] **1 a :** steadfastness or firmness of mind (as under duress, hardship, suffering) **:** FORTITUDE, ENDURANCE ⟨resolute ~ in the face of odds⟩ **b :** steadiness in attachments **:** FIDELITY, LOYALTY ⟨the Pony Express was served by the best of its men with ~ and devotion —S.H.Adams⟩ **2** *obs* **:** CERTAINTY **3 :** freedom from change **:** STABILITY, UNIFORMITY ⟨it was shown that among the characteristics of the words of science were their ~ of meaning —T.H.Savory⟩ **4 :** CONSTANCE 2 — **for a constancy** *adv* **:** as something permanent ⟨such a job would be bad *for a constancy*⟩

[1]**con·stant** \ˈkänztənt, -n(t)st-\ *adj* [ME, fr. MF, fr. L *constant-, constans,* pres. part. of *constare* to stand firm, be consistent, fr. *com-* + *stare* to stand — more at STAND] **1 :** marked by firmness, steadfastness, resolution, or faithfulness **:** not weak, yielding, vacillating, or disloyal ⟨a man ~ in adherence to his ideals⟩ ⟨a ~ friend⟩ **2 :** fixed and invariable ⟨the content of constitutional immunities is not ~ but varies from age to age —B.N.Cardozo⟩ **:** remaining unchanged **:** STEADY, UNIFORM ⟨a *constant*-flow calorimeter⟩ **3 :** marked by continual recurring or by regular occurrence, operation, or manifestation ⟨their aims and their methods have been subject to ~ scrutiny, not only by professionals, but also by parents and citizens —J.B.Conant⟩ ⟨the children running in and out of the house were a ~ annoyance⟩ **4** *obs* **:** firm and steady **:** IMMOVABLE, SOLID **5** *obs* **:** confident in opinion **:** POSITIVE, CERTAIN **syn** see CONTINUAL, FAITHFUL, STEADY

[2]**constant** \"\ *n* -S **1 :** something that does not vary or change in its relationship or in an essential relationship with other things ⟨the one ~ in all this is that each page is indelibly marked with personality —E.A.Weeks⟩ ⟨the environment should be the ~; the individual, the variable —W.H.Whyte⟩: as **a :** an abstract number or a physically dimensional quantity having a fixed or approximately fixed value (as in a situation or throughout the operation concerned) and being sometimes universal and permanent (as the circular ratio π or the constant of gravitation) or sometimes characteristic of some substance or instrument (as the refractive index of an optical glass or the sensitivity of a galvanometer) **b :** a magnitude in mathematics that is assumed not to change its value in a certain discussion, process, or stage of investigation — opposed to *variable* **c :** a term in logic with an invariant denotation **:** a symbol with fixed designation (as a connective, quantifier, or parenthesis) — contrasted with *variable* **d :** a kind of plant or animal (as a species or variety) that is regularly present in a particular ecological community (as an association) **2 :** a secondary-school subject considered of such basic importance that it is required of all pupils

con·stant·an \ˈkänztənˌtan, -n(t)st-\ *n* -S [ISV ¹*constant* + *-an*] **:** an alloy of about 55 percent copper and 45 percent nickel that is used for electrical resistors and in thermocouples

con·stan·tia \kənzˈtanch(ē)ə, kōnzˈtän(t)sēə, -nˈst-\ *n* -S *often cap* [prob. fr. Afrik *constantia-* (in *constantiawyn* Constantia wine), fr. *Constantia,* former estate near Cape Town, Union of So. Africa] **:** a white or red dessert wine produced on vineyards near Wynberg, a suburb of Cape Town, Union of So. Africa

con·stan·tine \ˈkänztənˌtēn, -än(t)st-, -ˌtīn\ *adj, usu cap* [fr. *Constantine,* Algeria] **:** of or from the city of Constantine, Algeria **:** of the kind or style prevalent in Constantine

con·stan·tin·i·an \ˌkänztənˈtinēən, -än(t)st-, -ˈtēn-, -nyən\ *adj, usu cap* [*Constantine* I †A.D.337 Roman emperor + E *-ian*] **:** of, derived from, or resembling the Roman emperor Constantine the Great or his reign (A.D. 306–337)

constantinian monogram *n, usu cap C* **:** CHI-RHO

con·stan·ti·no·ple \ˌkänzˌtantᵊnˈōpəl, -änˌsta-, -antəˈnō-, *sometimes* =ˈ=ˌ== *or* kən-\ *adj, usu cap* [fr. *Constantinople* (now Istanbul, Turkey)] **:** CONSTANTINOPOLITAN

con·stan·ti·no·pol·i·tan \(ˌ)känzˌtantᵊnōˈpälətᵊn, kən-, -nˌsta-, -antə(ˌ)nō- *also* -lətən *or* -ləd·ən\ *adj, usu cap* [LL *constantinopolitanus,* fr. *Constantinopolis* Constantinople (now Istanbul, Turkey), capital of the Byzantine Empire until 1453 and of Turkey from 1453–1922 (after LL *metropolis: metropolitanus* metropolitan), fr. LGk *Kōnstantinoupolis,* fr. *Kōnstantinou* (gen. of *Kōnstantinos* Constantine I) + Gk *polis* city — more at POLICE] **:** of, relating to, or connected with Constantinople

constant–level watering \ˈ;==;==-\ *n* **:** a system of watering plants in greenhouse beds or benches in which the water is maintained at a desired constant level usu. automatically

con·stant·ly *adv* **1** *archaic* **:** with loyalty **:** FAITHFULLY **2** *obs* **:** with confidence **:** FIRMLY **3 :** without variation, deviation, or change **:** EVER, ALWAYS ⟨to be ~ on the alert⟩ **4 :** with regular occurrence **:** INCESSANTLY ⟨write letters ~⟩

con·stant·ness *n* -ES **:** the quality or state of being constant **:** CONSTANCY

constant of aberration : the maximum apparent displacement of a star from its mean position due to the aberration of light corresponding to the earth's orbital motion and having a value of about 20.5 seconds of arc

constant of gravitation : the acceleration produced by the attraction of a unit of mass at unit distance and having a value of about 6.670×10^{-8} in cgs units

constant of nutation : the amplitude of the celestial-latitude component of the precessional nutation of the earth's axis that is equal to about 9.2 seconds of arc — compare NUTATION 2

constant of precession : the average annual rate of the precession of the equinoxes along the ecliptic amounting to about 50.26 seconds of arc

constant white *n* **:** BLANC FIXE

con·stat \ˈkänzˌtat, -nˌst-\ *n* -S [L, it is certain, 3d pers. sing. pres. indic. of *constare* to be certain, stand firm — more at CONSTANT] **:** a legal certificate showing what appears upon record touching a matter in question

con·sta·ta·tion \ˌkänztəˈtāshən, -n(t)stəˈ-\ *n* -S [F, fr. *constater* + *-ation*] **:** basic assumption **:** ASSERTION ⟨the mere ~ that a century and a half ago the family counted for much more than it does now —F.R.Leavis⟩

con·state \kənzˈtāt, -nˈst-, *usu* -ād·+V\ *vt* -ED/-ING/-S [F *constater,* fr. L *constat* it is certain] **:** to assert positively

[1]**con·stel·late** \ˈkänztəˌlāt, -än(t)st-, *usu* -ād·+V\ *vb* -ED/-ING/-S [LL *constellatus* studded with stars, fr. L *com-* + *stellatus* set with stars, fr. *stella* star + *-atus* -ate — more at STAR] *vt* **1 a** *obs* **:** to affect with stellar influence **b** *astrology* **:** to fashion or predestine esp. by an especial conjunction of planets ⟨an individual *constellated* to be great⟩ **2 :** to unite

in a cluster esp. with a radiance or display suggestive of a constellation ⟨manifestations . . . *constellated* around a single motif —A.L.Kroeber⟩ ⟨it is not strange that the 19th century is *constellated* with demonic figures —Henry Miller⟩ **3 :** to set or adorn with or as if with stars or constellations **:** STUD ⟨hills . . . *constellated* and twinkling with street lamps —J.B. Priestley⟩ **~** *vi* **:** to cluster like stars in a constellation ⟨all writers of note ~ there in the summer⟩ ⟨the tendency of symbolisms to ~ in accordance with an unconscious or intuitive logic —Edward Sapir⟩

[2]**constellate** \-ˌlāt, -ˌlət\ *adj* [LL *constellatus*] **:** CONSTELLATED

con·stel·la·tion \ˌkänztəˈlāshən, -än(t)st-\ *n* -S [ME *constellacioun*, fr. MF *constellation*, fr. LL *constellation-*, *constellatio*, fr. *constellatus* + L *-ion-*, *-io* -ion] **1 a :** the configuration of stars esp. at one's birth that in astrology determines one's fate or status in life ⟨to be born under the ~ that makes a man rich⟩ — compare HOROSCOPE **b** *obs* **:** character or constitution as determined by or as if by the stars ⟨a person of whatever profession or ~⟩ **2 :** any one of 88 arbitrary configurations of stars or an area of the celestial sphere covering one of these configurations and numbering 48 according to the 2d century A.D. catalogue of Ptolemy, each named after a mythological personage, animal, or inanimate object, the remaining 40 having been added later to fill in areas of the sky left vacant by the ancients (as in the region around the south celestial pole invisible to the Mediterranean world) **3 :** an assemblage, collection, or gathering esp. of a splendid, radiant, or excellent sort ⟨a ~ of atomic scientists⟩ ⟨the carpet was scattered with a ~ of gardenias —P.L.Fermor⟩ **4 a :** PATTERN, ARRANGEMENT ⟨the state's interpretation of welfare is set in the ~ of security, order, justice, and freedom —Asher Achinstein⟩ **b :** a determining, differentiating, or individualizing pattern or grouping ⟨the unique and flavorful ~ of qualities, the emphases and shadings of the universal human that make a Frenchman —Robert Redfield⟩ **c** (1) **:** a group of consciously related esp. emotionally significant ideas (2) **:** an assemblage or configuration of stimulus conditions or factors affecting behavior and personality development ⟨the way in which family ~ and handling of punishment influenced this particular boy —S.B.Sarason⟩ (3) **:** an assemblage or configuration of behavioral or personality traits or characteristics

con·stel·la·tion·al \¦==¦lāshənᵊl, -shnəl\ *adj* **:** of or having to do with a constellation

con·stel·la·to·ry \kənzˈteləˌtōrē, (ˈ)känz¦t-, kənˈst-, (ˈ)kän¦st-, -tȯr-, -ri\ *adj* [*constellation* + *-ory*] **:** of, having to do with, or suggestive of a constellation ⟨~ magnitude⟩ ⟨~ brilliance⟩

con·ster \ˈkän(t)stə(r)\ *vb* -ED/-ING/-S [by alter.] *archaic* **:** [1]CONSTRUE

con·ster·nate \ˈkänztə(r)ˌnāt, -än(t)st-, *usu* -ād·+V\ *vt* -ED/-ING/-S [L *consternatus*, past part. of *consternare*] **:** to fill with dismay or astonishment ⟨the colonel was not only embarrassed, he was *consternated* —Hervey Allen⟩

con·ster·na·tion \ˌkänztə(r)ˈnāshən, -än(t)st-\ *n* -S [F or L; F, fr. L *consternation-*, *consternatio*, fr. *consternatus* (past part. of *consternare* to overcome, confuse, perplex, fr. *com-* + *-sternare*, akin to ON *stara* to stare) + *-ion-*, *-io* -ion — more at STARE] **:** amazement or dismay that hinders or throws into confusion **:** confused and distressing excitement **:** grievous exasperation or distraction ⟨to flee in ~⟩ ⟨the two, father and son, stared at each other in ~, and neither knew what to do —Pearl Buck⟩ **syn** see FEAR

con·sti·pate \ˈkänztəˌpāt, -än(t)st-, *usu* -ād·+V\ *vb* -ED/-ING/-S [L *constipatus*, past part. of *constipare*, fr. *com-* + *stipare* to press together — more at STIFF] *vt* **1** *obs* **:** to make firm or hard (as by thickening, pressing together, condensing) **2** [ML *constipatus*, fr. L] **:** to make costive **:** cause constipation in **3 :** to make immobile, inactive, or dull **:** STULTIFY ⟨Paris quickens the mind, New York energizes the character, London ~*s* the soul —Cyril Connolly⟩ **~** *vi* **:** to make evacuation of the feces difficult or infrequent

con·sti·pa·tion \ˌkänztəˈpāshən, -än(t)st-\ *n* -S [LL *constipation-*, *constipatio*, fr. L *constipatus* + *-ion-*, *-io* -ion] **1** *obs* **a :** COMPRESSION, CONDENSATION **b :** CONTRACTION, CONSTRICTION **2** [MF or ML; MF, fr. ML *constipation-*, *constipatio*, fr. LL] **a :** abnormally delayed or infrequent passage of dry hardened feces associated with varying degrees of stasis of the lower bowel **b :** STULTIFICATION ⟨~ of intellectual freedom⟩

con·stit·u·en·cy \kənzˈtichəwənsē, -nˈst-, -si\ *n* -ES **1 a :** a body of citizens or voters that is entitled to elect a representative to a legislative or other public body **b :** the residents in an electoral district **c :** an electoral district **2 :** a group or body that patronizes, supports, or offers representation **:** body of supporters ⟨there was no ~ of millionaires to back him⟩ **3 :** the constituents of a linguistic construction or a compound

[1]**con·stit·u·ent** \kənzˈtichəwənt, -nˈst-\ *n* -S [F *constituant*, fr. *constituant*, adj.] **1 :** a person who appoints another to act for him as attorney-in-fact **:** PRINCIPAL **2 a :** one of a group who elects another to represent him in a legislative assembly or to a public office **b :** a citizen or resident of a district represented by one so elected **3 a :** a thing, person, or organism that along with others serves in making up a complete whole or unit **:** an essential part **:** COMPONENT ⟨matter and radiation, the two ~*s* of the physical universe —James Jeans⟩ ⟨society is held together by the mutual needs of its ~*s* —Abram Kardiner⟩ **b** (1) **:** an element or radical that is part of a chemical compound (as hydrogen or oxygen in water) (2) **:** a phase of a chemical system — compare COMPONENT 3 **c :** a part of an alloy or metallic mixture that can be distinguished microscopically **d :** one of two or more linguistic forms that enter into a construction or a compound and are either immediate and normally two in number (as *he* and *writes for the stage* in the construction "he writes for the stage") or ultimate and of any number (as *he*, *write*, *-s*, *for*, *the*, and *stage* in the same construction) **syn** see ELEMENT

[2]**constituent** \"\ *adj* [F or L; F *constituant*, fr. L *constituent-*, *constituens*, pres. part. of *constituere* to constitute — more at CONSTITUTE] **1 :** serving to form, compose, or make up a unit or whole **:** COMPONENT ⟨molecules and their ~ atoms —A.C.Morrison⟩ ⟨within the broad confines of science there are many ~ sciences —T.H.Savory⟩ **2 a :** having power to elect or appoint ⟨a ~ body⟩ **b :** having the right or power to create a government or frame or amend a constitution ⟨a ~ group⟩ ⟨a ~ assembly⟩ — **con·stit·u·ent·ly** *adv*

constituta *pl of* CONSTITUTUM

con·sti·tu·ta pe·cu·nia \¦känztə¦tüd·əpə¦k(y)ünēə, -än(t)stə¦-\ *n* [LL, lit., money agreed upon] **:** PACTUM DE CONSTITUTO

[1]**con·sti·tute** \ˈkänztəˌt(y)üt, -än(t)stəˌt(y)-, *rapid* -än(t)səˌt(y)- *or* -än(t)ˌst(y)-, *usu* -üd·+V\ *vt* -ED/-ING/-S [L *constitutus*, past part. of *constituere* to constitute, fr. *com-* + *-stituere* (fr. *statuere* to set, place) — more at STATUTE] **1 a :** to appoint to an office, function, or dignity ⟨legal authority ~*s* all magistrates⟩ ⟨*constituted* authorities⟩ **b :** to make (a person or thing) something ⟨he *constituted* himself their guide⟩ ⟨I shall ~ you skipper and pilot of the craft —William Black⟩ **2** *archaic* **:** to set or station in a situation, state, character **:** PLACE ⟨the fiery star of Mars *constituted* in the midst of heaven —John Gaule⟩ **3 :** to set up **:** ESTABLISH: as **a :** to put into force (as a law) **:** ENACT ⟨such regulations as are *constituted* by the government⟩ **b :** FOUND ⟨~ a social club for immigrants⟩ **:** formally establish ⟨~ a provisional government⟩ ⟨in 1833 Ceylon had been *constituted* a British crown colony —*Current Biog.*⟩ **c :** to give due or lawful form to (as a proceeding or document) **:** legally process ⟨an agreement *constituted* by writing⟩ **d :** to cause (as a trait) to become fixed **:** DETERMINE **4 :** to make up (the element or elements of which a thing, person, or idea is made up) **:** FORM, COMPOSE ⟨52 cards ~ a pack⟩ ⟨vivacity ~*s* her greatest charm⟩

[2]**constitute** \"\ *adj* [L *constitutus*] **1** *archaic* **:** CONSTITUTED, ESTABLISHED **2** *archaic* **:** FORMED

[3]**constitute** \"\ *n* -S [[1]*constitute*] **:** a linguistic form with more than one immediate constituent **:** CONSTRUCTION, COMPOUND

con·sti·tu·tion \ˌkänztəˈt(y)üshən, -än(t)stəˈt(y)-, *rapid* -än(t)səˈt(y)- *or* -än(t)ˈst(y)-; ˈ==ˈ==\ *n* -S [ME *constitucioun*, fr. MF *constitution*, fr. L *constitution-*, *constitutio*, fr. *constitutus* + *-ion-*, *-io* -ion] **1 a** (1) **:** an authoritative ordinance or enactment (2) **:** an enactment of a Roman emperor **b :** an established law or settled custom **:** ORDINANCE ⟨the sacred ~*s* of the church⟩ **2 :** the act of establishing, making, or setting up ⟨before the ~ of civil laws⟩ **3 a :** the whole physical makeup of the individual comprising the inherited qualities as modified by the environment **:** PHYSIQUE — compare DIATHESIS **b** *archaic* **:** the aggregate of an individual's mental powers or qualities **:** TEMPERAMENT, DISPOSITION **4 :** the mode or manner in which something is constituted, constructed, or organized **:** the structure, composition, physical makeup, or nature of anything specif. as determined by the interrelation of its atoms, elements, or parts ⟨the ~ of the sun⟩ ⟨the ~ of society⟩; *specif* **:** the structure of a compound as determined by the kind, number, and arrangement of atoms in its molecule **5 :** the mode in which a state or society is organized; *esp* **:** the manner in which sovereign power is distributed ⟨democratic ~⟩ **6 a :** the system or body of fundamental rules and principles of a nation, state, or body politic that determines the powers and duties of the government and guarantees certain rights to the people — see FLEXIBLE CONSTITUTION, RIGID CONSTITUTION, UNWRITTEN CONSTITUTION **b :** the written instrument embodying these fundamental rules and constituting the organic law of the land **c :** the basic rules governing a social or professional organization **syn** see PHYSIQUE

[1]**con·sti·tu·tion·al** \¦känztə¦t(y)üshənᵊl, -än(t)stə¦t(y)-, *rapid* -än(t)sə¦t(y)- *or* -än(t)¦st(y)-; -shnəl\ *adj* [*constitution* + *-al*] **1 a :** having to do with, inherent in, or affecting the constitution or structure of body or mind ⟨~ symptoms⟩ ⟨~ strength⟩ **b :** of benefit to or intended to benefit one's physical or mental makeup ⟨a ~ stroll⟩ **2 :** having to do with, belonging to, or forming the composition or makeup of something **:** ESSENTIAL ⟨the very ~ part of a system⟩ **3 :** in accordance with or authorized by the constitution of a state or a society ⟨~ reforms⟩ ⟨~ limitations⟩ ⟨~ rights⟩ **4 :** regulated by, dependent on, or ruling according to a constitution or constitutional forms limiting arbitrary or absolute power ⟨~ monarchy⟩ ⟨~ government⟩ ⟨~ democracy⟩ **5 :** of, relating to, or dealing with a constitution ⟨~ crisis⟩ ⟨~ theory⟩ or its interpretation, formulation, or amendment ⟨~ assembly⟩ ⟨~ court⟩ **6 :** loyal to or supporting the existing constitution or established form of government ⟨they organized a ~ fact on⟩

[2]**constitutional** \"\ *n* -S **:** a walk or other exercise taken for one's health

constitutional formula *n* **:** STRUCTURAL FORMULA

con·sti·tu·tion·al·ism \-nᵊlˌizəm, -nəˌlizəm\ *n* -S **1 :** the doctrine or system of government in which the governing power is limited by enforceable rules of law and concentration of power is prevented by various checks and balances so that the basic rights of individuals and groups are protected **2 :** adherence to the principles of constitutionalism

con·sti·tu·tion·al·ist \-ˌləst\ *n* -S **1 :** one who studies or writes on constitutionalism **2 :** an adherent or advocate of constitutionalism or of some particular constitution; *specif*, *usu cap* **:** an advocate of the U.S. Constitution about the time of its adoption

con·sti·tu·tion·al·i·ty \¦känztəˌt(y)üshəˈnaləd·ē, -än(t)stəˌt(y)-, *rapid* -än(t)səˌt(y)- *or* -än(t)ˌst(y)-; -ətē, -i\ *n* -ES **1 :** the quality or state of being constitutional ⟨with the restoration of ~, a distinguished lawyer . . . came to power —Rodrigo Niró⟩ **2 :** the quality or state of being consistent with the provisions of a constitution (as the U.S. Constitution)

con·sti·tu·tion·al·ize \ˌ=(=)ˈ=shənᵊlˌīz, -shnəˌlīz\ *vt* -ED/-ING/-S **:** to provide with a constitution or organize along constitutional principles ⟨~ the government of the church on the lines of a medieval system of representation —G.H. Sabine⟩ ⟨attempts to ~ Spain —John Gunther⟩

constitutional law *n* **:** the area of law that has to do with the subject matter and with the interpretation and construction of constitutions or that deals with the nature and organization of government, its sovereign powers and their distribution and mode of exercise, and the relation of the sovereign to the subjects or citizens; *specif* **:** the constitution of a particular state with the judicial constructions and interpretations that it has received

con·sti·tu·tion·al·ly \¦=(=)¦=shənᵊlē, -shnəlē, -li\ *adv* **1 a :** with respect to mental or spiritual makeup ⟨~ unable to grasp subtleties⟩ **b :** with respect to bodily makeup ⟨~ a weakling⟩ **2 :** in basic or essential structure or composition **:** FUNDAMENTALLY ⟨despite repeated heatings the material remained ~ the same⟩ **3 :** in accordance with the constitution or fundamental law **:** LEGALLY ⟨was not ~ eligible to fill an office⟩

constitutional psychology *n* **:** the systematic attempt to

TABLE OF CONSTELLATIONS

NAME AND PRONUNCIATION	[3]GENITIVE AND PRONUNCIATION	MEANING	DECLINATION
[1]Andromeda \anˈdrämədə\	Andromedae \-ˌdē\	*Andromeda, the Chained Lady*	40° N
Antlia (Antlia Pneumatica) \ˈantlēən(y)üˈmad·ikə\	Antliae \-ē,ē\	*Pump (Air Pump)*	35° S
Apus \ˈāpəs\	Apodis \ˈapədəs\	*Bird of Paradise*	75° S
[1]Aquarius \əˈkwa(a)rēəs\	Aquarii \-rēˌī\	*Water Carrier*	10° S
[1]Aquila \ˈakwələ\	Aquilae \-ˌlē\	*Eagle*	5° N
[1]Ara \ˈa(a)rə\	Arae \ˈa(a)ˌrē\	*Altar*	55° S
[1]Aries \ˈa(a)rēˌēz, ˈer-,ˈār, -rēz\	Arietis \əˈrīəd·əs\	*Ram*	20° N
[1]Auriga \ȯˈrīgə\	Aurigae \-īˌjē\	*Charioteer*	40° N
[1]Boötes \bōˈōd·ēz\	Boötis \-ˈōd·əs\	*Herdsman*	30° N
Caelum (Caela Sculptoris) \ˈsēləm (-lə ˌskəlpˈtōrəs)\	Caeli \-ˌlī\	*Graving Tool*	40° S
Camelopardalis \kəˌmeləˈpärdᵊləs, ˌkamə(ˌ)lōˈ-\	Camelopardalis \"\	*Giraffe*	70° N
[1]Cancer \ˈkan(t)sər\	Cancri \ˈkaŋˌkrī\	*Crab*	20° N
Canes Venatici \ˈkāˌnēzvəˈnad·əˌsī\	Canum Venaticorum \ˈkānəmvəˌnad·əˈkōrəm\	*Hunting Dogs*	40° N
[1]Canis Major \¦kānəˈsmājər, -¦a-\	Canis Majoris \-ˌsməˈjōrəs\	*Larger Dog*	20° S
[1]Canis Minor \-ˈsmīnər\	Canis Minoris \-ˌsmīˈnōrəs\	*Lesser Dog*	5° N
[1]Capricornus \¦kaprə¦kȯrnəs\	Capricorni \ˌ==ˈ=ˌnī\	*Horned Goat*	20° S
[2]Carina \kəˈrīnə\	Carinae \-ˌnē\	*Keel*	60° S
[1]Cassiopeia \ˌkasēəˈpē(y)ə\	Cassiopeiae \-pēˌ(y)ē, -ˌ(y)ī\	*Cassiopeia, the Lady in the Chair*	60° N
[1]Centaurus \senˈtȯrəs\	Centauri \-ˌrī\	*Centaur*	45° S
[1]Cepheus \ˈsēˌfyüs, -ˌfēəs\	Cephei \-ˌfēˌī\	*Cepheus, the Monarch*	70° N
[1]Cetus \ˈsēd·əs\	Ceti \-ēˌtī\	*Whale*	5° S
Chamaeleon \kəˈmēlyən, -lēən\	Chamaeleontis \-ˌmēlēˈäntəs\	*Chameleon*	80° S
Circinus \ˈsərsᵊnəs\	Circini \-nˌī\	*Pair of Compasses*	65° S
Columba (Columba Noae) \kəˈləmbəˈnōˌē\	Columbae \-mˌbē\	*Dove (Noah's Dove)*	35° S
Coma Berenices \ˈkōməˌberəˈnī(ˌ)sēz\	Comae Berenices \-(ˌ)mēˌb-\	*Berenice's Hair*	25° N
[1]Corona Australis \kəˈrōnəˌȯˈstrāləs, -al-\	Coronae Australis \-(ˌ)nēˌȯ-\	*Southern Crown*	40° S
[1]Corona Borealis \-ˌbōrēˈaləs, -ˈā-\	Coronae Borealis \-(ˌ)nēˌb-\	*Northern Crown*	30° N
[1]Corvus \ˈkȯrvəs\	Corvi \-ˌvī\	*Crow*	20° S
[1]Crater \ˈkrād·ər\	Crateris \krāˈti(ə)rəs\	*Cup*	15° S
Crux \ˈkrəks\	Crucis \ˈkrüsəs\	*Southern Cross*	60° S
[1]Cygnus \ˈsignəs\	Cygni \-ˌnī\	*Swan*	40° N
[1]Delphinus \delˈfīnəs\	Delphini \-ˌnī\	*Dolphin*	15° N
Dorado \dəˈrä(ˌ)dō\	Doradus \-ˌdəs\	*Dorado [a fish]*	60° S
[1]Draco \ˈdrāˌkō\	Draconis \drāˈkōnəs\	*Dragon*	65° N
[1]Equuleus \eˈkwülēəs\	Equulei \-lēˌī\	*Colt*	5° N
[1]Eridanus \əˈridᵊnəs\	Eridani \-nˌī\	*Eridanus, the River Po*	20° S
Fornax \ˈfȯrˌnaks\	Fornacis \fȯrˈnasəs, -ˈā-\	*Furnace*	30° S
[1]Gemini \ˈjeməˌnī\	Geminorum \ˌjeməˈnōrəm\	*Twins*	25° N
Grus \ˈgrəs, -üs\	Gruis \ˈgrüəs\	*Crane*	45° S
[1]Hercules \ˈhərkyəˌlēz\	Herculis \-yələs\	*Hercules*	30° N
Horologium \ˌhȯrəˈlōjēəm\	Horologii \-ōjēˌī\	*Clock*	50° S
[1]Hydra \ˈhīdrə\	Hydrae \-ˌdrē\	*Water Monster*	10° S
Hydrus \ˈhīdrəs\	Hydri \-ˌdrī\	*Water Snake*	70° S
Indus \ˈindəs\	Indi \-ˌdī\	*Indian*	55° S
Lacerta \ləˈsərd·ə\	Lacertae \-rˌtē\	*Lizard*	45° N
[1]Leo \ˈlē(ˌ)ō\	Leonis \lēˈōnəs\	*Lion*	15° N
Leo Minor \-ˈmīnər\	Leonis Minoris \-nəˌsmīˈnōrəs\	*Smaller Lion*	25° N
[1]Lepus \ˈlēpəs, -ˈe-\	Leporis \ˈlepərəs\	*Hare*	20° S
[1]Libra \ˈlībrə\	Librae \-ˌbrē\	*Balance*	15° S
[1]Lupus \ˈlüpəs\	Lupi \-ˌpī\	*Wolf*	40° S
Lynx \ˈliŋks\	Lyncis \ˈlinsəs\	*Lynx*	45° N
[1]Lyra \ˈlīrə\	Lyrae \-ˌrē\	*Lyre*	35° N
Mensa (Mons Mensae) \ˈmen(t)sə (ˈmänzˈmenˌsē)\	Mensae \ˈmenˌsē\	*Table (Table Mountain)*	75° S
Microscopium \ˌmīkrəˈskōpēəm\	Microscopii \-pēˌī\	*Microscope*	35° S
Monoceros \məˈnäsərəs\	Monocerotis \-ˌnäsəˈrōd·əs\	*Unicorn*	5° S
Musca \ˈməskə\	Muscae \ˈməˌsē\	*Fly*	70° S
Norma \ˈnȯrmə\	Normae \-ˌmē\	*Square (and Rule)*	50° S
Octans \ˈäkˌtanz\	Octantis \äkˈtantəs\	*Octant*	85° S
[1]Ophiuchus \ˌäfēˈ(y)ükəs\	Ophiuchi \-üˌkī\	*Serpent Holder*	0°
[1]Orion \əˈrīən\	Orionis \əˈrīənəs, ˌȯrēˈōnəs\	*Orion, the Hunter*	0°
Pavo \ˈpā(ˌ)vō, -ˈä-\	Pavonis \pəˈvōnəs\	*Peacock*	65° S
[1]Pegasus \ˈpegəsəs\	Pegasi \-əˌsī\	*Pegasus, the Winged Horse*	20° N
[1]Perseus \ˈpərˌsüs\	Persei \-rsēˌī\	*Perseus, the Rescuer or Champion*	45° N
Phoenix \ˈfēniks\	Phoenicis \fēˈnīsəs\	*Phoenix*	50° S
Pictor \ˈpiktər\	Pictoris \pikˈtōrəs\	*Painter's Easel*	55° S
[1]Pisces \ˈpiˌsēz\	Piscium \ˈpis(h)ēəm\	*Fishes*	10° N
[1]Piscis Austrinus \ˈpisəˌsȯˈstrīnəs\	Piscis Austrini \-ˌnī\	*Southern Fish*	30° S
[2]Puppis \ˈpəpəs\	Puppis \"\	*Stern*	30° S
[2]Pyxis \ˈpiksəs\	Pyxidis \-ksədəs\	*Mariner's Compass*	30° S
Reticulum \rəˈtikyələm\	Reticuli \-ˌlī\	*Net*	60° S
[1]Sagitta \səˈjid·ə\	Sagittae \-iˌtē\	*Arrow*	20° N
[1]Sagittarius \ˌsajəˈterēəs\	Sagittarii \-rēˌī\	*Archer*	30° S
[1]Scorpius \ˈskȯrpēəs\	Scorpii \-pēˌī\	*Scorpion*	30° S
Sculptor \ˈskəlptər\	Sculptoris \ˌskəlpˈtōrəs\	*Sculptor's Workshop*	30° S
Scutum \ˈsk(y)üd·əm\	Scuti \-üˌtī\	*Shield*	10° S
[1]Serpens \ˈsərpənz, -ˌpenz\	Serpentis \(ˌ)sərˈpentəs\	*Serpent*	0°
Sextans \ˈsekˌstanz\	Sextantis \sekˈstantəs\	*Sextant*	5° S
[1]Taurus \ˈtȯrəs\	Tauri \-ˌrī\	*Bull*	20° N
Telescopium \ˌteləˈskōpēəm\	Telescopii \-pēˌī\	*Telescope*	50° S
[1]Triangulum \trīˈaŋgyələm\	Trianguli \-ˌlī\	*Triangle*	30° N
Triangulum Australe \-ˌȯˈstrā(ˌ)lē\	Trianguli Australis \-ˌlīˌȯˈstrāləs\	*Southern Triangle*	65° S
Tucana \tüˈkanə, -ˈä-\	Tucanae \-ˌnē\	*Toucan*	65° S
[1]Ursa Major \ˈərsəˈmājər\	Ursae Majoris \ˈərˌsēməˈjōrəs\	*Larger Bear*	50° N
[1]Ursa Minor \ˈərsəˈmīnər\	Ursae Minoris \ˈərˌsēˌmīˈnōrəs\	*Smaller Bear*	80° N
[2]Vela \ˈvēlə\	Velorum \vēˈlōrəm\	*Sails*	45° S
[1]Virgo \ˈvərˌgō\	Virginis \-rjənəs\	*Virgin*	0°
Volans (Piscis Volans) \ˈpisəsˈvōˌlanz\	Volantis \vōˈlantəs\	*Flying Fish*	70° S
Vulpecula \ˌvəlˈpekyələ\	Vulpeculae \-ˌlē\	*Little Fox*	25° N

[1]One of the 48 constellations of Ptolemy. [2]One of the subdivisions of the Ptolemaic constellation Argo or Argo Navis \¦är(ˌ)gōˈnāvəs\ the Ship Argo, which included Carina, Puppis, Pyxis, and Vela. [3]The genitive is used in referring to the individual stars of a constellation (as α Aurigae for the star Capella).

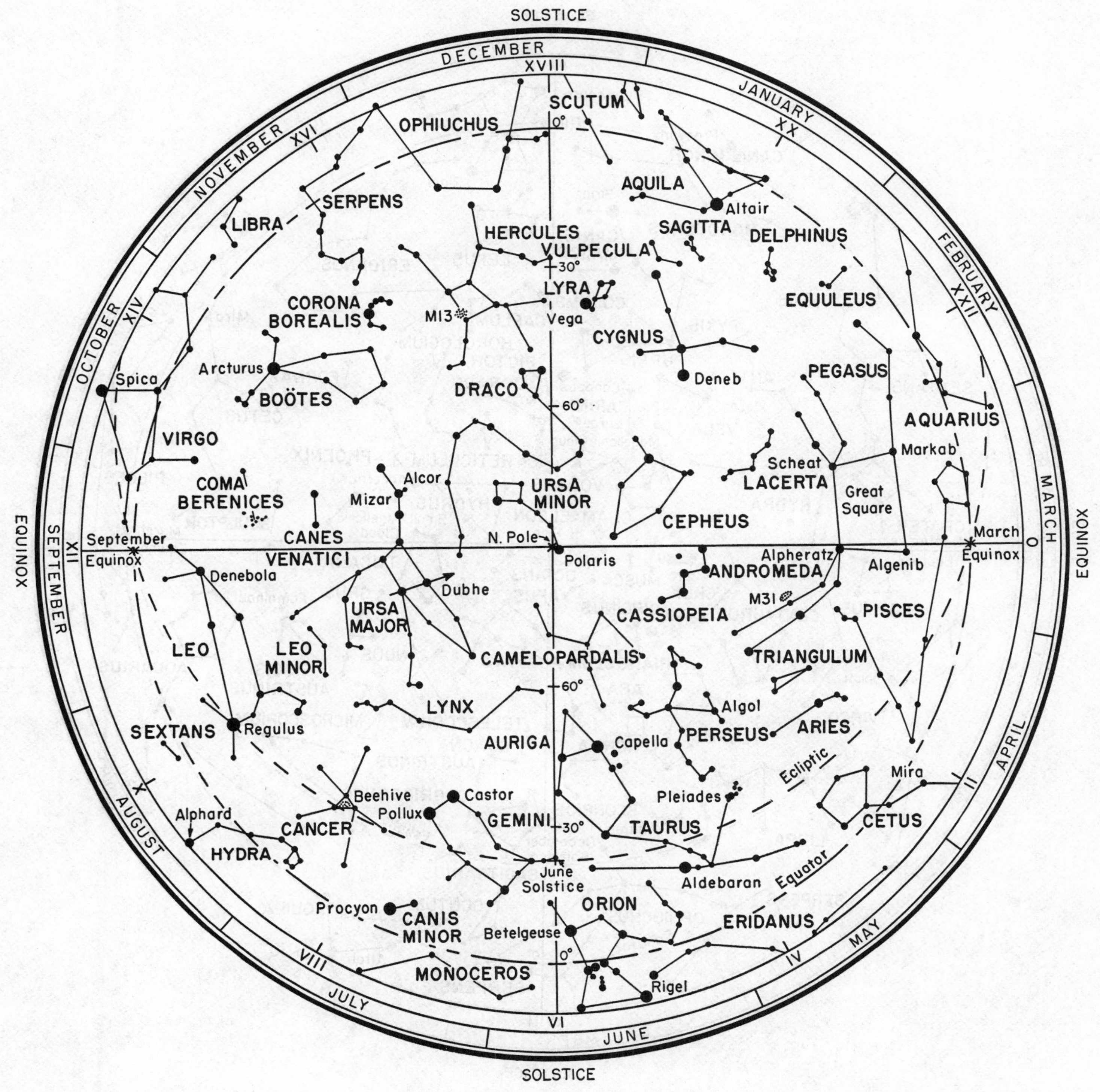
SOLSTICE
DECEMBER
JANUARY
FEBRUARY
MARCH
APRIL
MAY
JUNE
JULY
AUGUST
SEPTEMBER
OCTOBER
NOVEMBER
EQUINOX
EQUINOX
SOLSTICE
XVIII
XX
XXII
O
II
IV
VI
VIII
X
XII
XIV
XVI
SCUTUM
OPHIUCHUS
AQUILA
Altair
SERPENS
LIBRA
HERCULES
SAGITTA
DELPHINUS
VULPECULA
LYRA
Vega
M13
CORONA BOREALIS
CYGNUS
Deneb
EQUULEUS
Arcturus
BOÖTES
DRACO
PEGASUS
Spica
VIRGO
AQUARIUS
Markab
COMA BERENICES
Alcor
Mizar
URSA MINOR
Scheat
LACERTA
Great Square
CEPHEUS
CANES VENATICI
N. Pole
Polaris
Alpheratz
Algenib
March Equinox
September Equinox
Denebola
Dubhe
ANDROMEDA
M31
URSA MAJOR
CASSIOPEIA
PISCES
LEO
LEO MINOR
CAMELOPARDALIS
TRIANGULUM
LYNX
Algol
SEXTANS
Regulus
AURIGA
Capella
PERSEUS
ARIES
Ecliptic
Mira
Beehive
Castor
Pleiades
Alphard
Pollux
CANCER
GEMINI
TAURUS
CETUS
HYDRA
June Solstice
Aldebaran
Equator
Procyon
CANIS MINOR
ORION
Betelgeuse
ERIDANUS
MONOCEROS
Rigel
0°
30°
60°

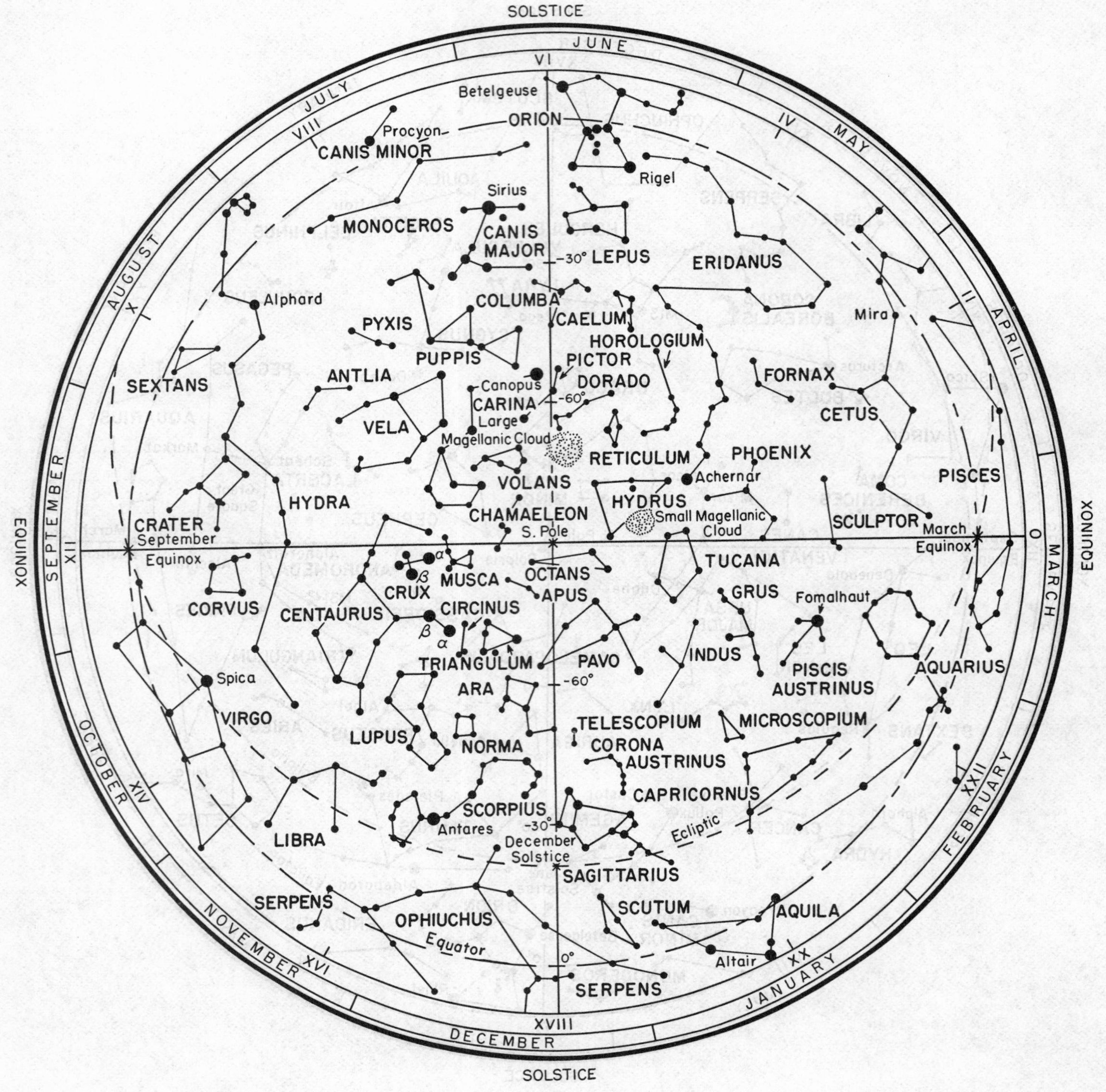
SOLSTICE
JUNE
VI
JULY
MAY
VIII
IV
Betelgeuse
ORION
Procyon
CANIS MINOR
Rigel
Sirius
MONOCEROS
CANIS
MAJOR
-30°
LEPUS
ERIDANUS
AUGUST
X
II
APRIL
Alphard
COLUMBA
CAELUM
HOROLOGIUM
Mira
PYXIS
PUPPIS
PICTOR
ANTLIA
Canopus
DORADO
FORNAX
SEXTANS
CARINA
-60°
CETUS
Large
VELA
Magellanic Cloud
RETICULUM
PHOENIX
Achernar
VOLANS
PISCES
HYDRA
HYDRUS
CHAMAELEON
Small Magellanic Cloud
SCULPTOR
SEPTEMBER
EQUINOX
CRATER
September
Equinox
S. Pole
March
Equinox
XII
O
MARCH
TUCANA
MUSCA
OCTANS
CRUX
APUS
GRUS
CORVUS
CENTAURUS
CIRCINUS
Fomalhaut
INDUS
TRIANGULUM
PAVO
PISCIS
AUSTRINUS
AQUARIUS
Spica
ARA
-60°
VIRGO
TELESCOPIUM
MICROSCOPIUM
LUPUS
NORMA
CORONA
AUSTRINUS
OCTOBER
XIV
CAPRICORNUS
XXII
FEBRUARY
SCORPIUS
Antares
-30°
December
Solstice
Ecliptic
LIBRA
SAGITTARIUS
SERPENS
SCUTUM
AQUILA
OPHIUCHUS
Equator
0°
Altair
NOVEMBER
XVI
XX
JANUARY
SERPENS
XVIII
DECEMBER
SOLSTICE

account for such psychological variables as temperament and character in terms of bodily shape and organic function
constitutional type *n* **:** bodily habitus or makeup — used esp. in coordinating bodily proportions with factors concerned in normal or abnormal physiologic or psychologic functions; compare ECTOMORPHIC, ENDOMORPHIC, MESOMORPHIC
constitutional water *n* **:** the water contained in a mineral after its temperature has been raised to 110° C and its hygrometric water driven off
con·sti·tu·tion·er \ˌ==(=)'=sh(ə)nə(r)\ *n* -s **:** a framer or supporter of a constitution
con·sti·tu·tion·ist \-nəst\ *n* -s **:** CONSTITUTIONALIST
constitution mirror *n, often cap C* **:** a mirror of Sheraton design usu. having a row of balls under the top cornice, side pilasters, and a painted panel above the looking glass — called also *tabernacle mirror*
con·sti·tu·tive \'känztəˌt(y)üd·iv, -ä̈n(t)stəˌt(y)-; kənz'tichəd·iv, -ən'sti-\ *adj* **1 a :** having the power to enact or establish **:** CONSTRUCTIVE **b :** having the character of stating a condition of the possibility of experience and hence of natural phenomena — used in Kantianism of the categories (as those of quantity and quality); contrasted with *regulative* **2 a :** that gives the essential quality or nature **:** ESSENTIAL ⟨a truly ~ ingredient⟩ **b :** tending or assisting to constitute **:** COESSENTIAL, COMPONENT ⟨reason as a ~ factor of faith —W.R.Inge⟩ ⟨for the part evidently is ~ of the whole —A.N.Whitehead⟩ **3 :** relating to or dependent on constitution (as the arrangement of atoms in a molecule) ⟨a ~ property⟩ — compare ADDITIVE 3, COLLIGATIVE — **con·sti·tu·tive·ly** \-d·ə̇vlē\ *adv*
con·sti·tu·tum \ˌkänztə'tüd·əm, -ä̈n(t)stə't-\ *n, pl* **consti·tu·ta** \-üd·ə\ [L, neut. of *constitutus*] *Roman law* **:** an agreement not made by formal stipulation whereby one promises to discharge on a given day at a fixed place an existing obligation of himself or another or to give security for its fulfillment
constitutum deb·i·ti \-'debəd·ˌī\ *n* [L, agreement concerning a debt] *Roman law* **:** a promise not founded on formal stipulation by one to pay an existing debt of himself or of another at a fixed time and place
constitutum pos·ses·so·ri·um \-ˌpōzə'sōrēəm, -sȯr-\ *n* [L, agreement of possessors] *Roman law* **:** the change in intention of one having legal possession of real or personal property whereby he remains in control but transfers the legal possession to another
constl *abbr* constitutional
constr *abbr* construction
con·strain \kənz'trān, kən'str-\ *vb* -ED/-ING/-S [ME *constrainen*, fr. MF *constraindre, constreindre*, fr. L *constringere*, fr. *com-* + *stringere* to draw tight — more at STRAIN] *vt* **1 a :** to force by stricture, restriction, or limitation imposed by nature, oneself, or circumstances and exigencies ⟨no one shall ~ me against my conscience to reveal my beliefs —Alexander Laing⟩ ⟨fate was ~*ing* him to follow Cleopatra —John Buchan⟩ **b :** to bring about by force or necessity ⟨the evidence ~*ing* belief in his guilt⟩ **c :** to restrict the motion of (a mechanical body) along a curve or surface to a particular mode ⟨a wheel is ~*ed* to rotate on its axle⟩ **2 a :** to force or force out in an artificial or unnatural way ⟨a ~*ed* polite laugh at his attempt at humor⟩ **b :** to check esp. from free or easy indication or expression **:** stifle the spontaneity of ⟨tensions ~*ed* their friendship because of the difference in station —*New Republic*⟩ **3 a :** to make fast by or as if by bonds or fetters **:** IMPRISON ⟨~*ed* to a dungeon⟩ ⟨the winds ~*ed* by magic⟩ **b :** to compress tightly **:** bind narrowly **:** SQUEEZE ⟨his clothes . . . ~ him so much that he seems rather their prisoner than their proprietor —Earl of Chesterfield⟩ **c** *obs* **:** CONSTRICT, CONSTRINGE **d :** to withhold or restrain by force **:** subject to restraint or repression ⟨~*ing* my mind not to wander from the task —Charles Dickens⟩ **e :** to cause to suffer from duress or affliction **:** DISTRESS, OPPRESS ⟨poverty constantly ~*ing* him⟩ **~** *vi* **:** to force or oblige one **:** COMPEL ⟨doctrine that enlightens but does not ~⟩ **syn** see FORCE
con·strained·ly \-n(ə̇)dlē\ *adv* **:** in a constrained manner
con·strained·ness \-nədnə̇s, -n(d)nə̇s\ *n* -ES **:** the quality or state of being constrained
con·strain·ing·ly *adv* **:** in a constraining manner
con·strain·ment \-nmənt\ *n* -s **:** CONSTRAINT
con·straint \kənz'trānt, kən'str-\ *n* -s [ME, fr. MF *constreinte, constrainte*, fr. fem. of *constreint, constraint*, past part. of *constreindre, constraindre*] **1 a :** the act or action of using force or threat of force to prevent or condition an action **b :** the quality or state of being checked, restricted, or compelled to avoid or perform some action ⟨the individual spirit anxious for freedom from ~ —W.C.Brownell⟩ ⟨the ~ and monotony of a monastic life —Matthew Arnold⟩ **c :** a constraining agency **:** a constricting, regulating, or restricting force **:** CHECK ⟨a government works only by means of external ~*s*, generally by the fear of punishment —M.R.Cohen⟩ **d :** a restriction or limitation that contains a motion or other process (as the action of a cam in machinery) **2 :** compulsion by circumstances **:** the force of necessity **:** EXIGENCY ⟨obligation is felt by the good man, whereas the bad one feels ~ —Samuel Alexander⟩ **3 a :** control over one's own feelings, behavior, or actions that is exercised either to feign or repress ⟨a youth ill brought up, without the training which teaches us that we must put some ~ upon our feelings —Matthew Arnold⟩ **b :** the sense of being constrained, checked, or inhibited **:** EMBARRASSMENT ⟨a ~ between us as if we were strangers —J.P.Marquand⟩ **4 :** the restoring force on an ion in a crystal per unit displacement constituting a measure of the forces acting between ions in a lattice **syn** see FORCE
con·strict \kənz'trikt, kən'str-\ *vb* -ED/-ING/-S [L *constrictus*, past part. of *constringere* — more at CONSTRAIN] *vt* **1 a :** to subject (as a body part) to compression **:** SQUEEZE **b :** to draw together or render narrower (as a mouth, orifice, channel, passage) **:** CONSTRINGE ⟨a hard rock obstruction which ~*ed* the valley's width from five miles to one —*Amer. Guide Series: Texas*⟩ **2 :** to stultify, stop, or cause to falter esp. under emotional or psychological duress or pressure of circumstances **:** CRAMP, INHIBIT ⟨personal stresses ~*ed* his poetry —A.C.Ward⟩ ⟨~ our generous impulses as a people —F.L. Allen⟩ **~** *vi* **1 :** to become constricted **2 :** to engage in constricting something **syn** see CONTRACT
constricted *adj* **1 a :** drawn together **:** NARROWED, CONTRACTED ⟨a ~ passageway⟩ **b** *bot* **:** contracted or compressed at regular intervals **:** MONILIFORM ⟨a ~ pod⟩ ⟨a ~ legume⟩ **2 :** CRAMPED, INHIBITED, NARROW ⟨a ~ view of life⟩
con·stric·tion \kənz'trikshən, kən'str-\ *n* -s [F or L; F *constriction*, fr. L *constriction-, constrictio*, fr. *constrictus* + *-ion-, -io* -ion] **1 a :** the act of constricting **:** COMPRESSING ⟨the slow ~ of a snake coiled around its prey⟩ **b :** temporary or permanent contraction resulting in the narrowing of a channel (as a blood vessel or ureter) and impeding passage through it **c :** a bringing of one organ of speech close enough to another so that audible friction is produced when breath of sufficient intensity passes between **2 :** the quality or state of being constricted or contracted ⟨the ~ of international trade brought on by war⟩ **3 a :** something that blocks, impedes inhibits, or hinders ⟨the swollen river piled up refuse against every ~ along the bank⟩ **b :** narrowness, repression, or inhibition esp. in emotional or intellectual activity ⟨the excessive ~ of Puritanism —E.A.Mowrer⟩ ⟨the lifelong fighter against cruelty, bigotry, and ~ —C.H.Driver⟩ **4 :** a feeling or sensation of tightness, narrowness, or compression ⟨a ~ in the throat brought on by emotion⟩ **5 :** a part that is narrowed down, compressed, or contracted ⟨a ~ in a waterway⟩
constriction disease *n* **:** a disease of peach trees caused by a fungus of the genus *Phomopsis* and having symptoms similar to those of dieback (sense 1)
¹con·stric·tive \kənz'triktiv, (')känz¦tr-, kən'str-, (')kän¦str-, -tēv *also* -təv\ *adj* [LL *constrictivus*, fr. L *constrictus* + *-ivus* -ive] **:** of, having to do with, or marked by constriction **:** tending to constrict **:** CONSTRINGENT
²constrictive \"\ *n* -s **:** FRICATIVE
con·stric·tor \kənz'triktə(r), kən'str-\ *n* -s [NL, fr. L *constrictus* + *-or* — more at CONSTRICT] **:** one that constricts: as **a :** a muscle that contracts a cavity or orifice or compresses an organ **b :** a snake that kills its prey by rhythmically compressing it in coils of the body until the heartbeat and respiration are checked; *esp* **:** a member of the Boidae (as the boa constrictor or the anaconda)

constrictor knot *n* **:** a knot that consists of a half-knot under a single turn and is used to bind a cylindrical object and keep it from expanding

constrictor knot

con·stringe \kənz'trinj, kən'str-\ *vt* -ED/-ING/-S [L *constringere* — more at CONSTRAIN] **1 :** to draw or press together **:** COMPRESS, CONSTRICT ⟨constringed between two forces⟩ **2 :** to cause to shrink ⟨cold ~*s* the pores⟩
con·strin·gent \kənz'trinjənt, kən'str-\ *adj* [L *constringent-, constringens*, pres. part. of *constringere*] **:** causing constriction
constrn *abbr* construction
con·stru·a·ble \kənz'trüəbəl, (')känz¦tr-, kən'str-, (')kän¦str-\ *adj* **:** that may be construed ⟨the made speeches ~ as promises that he would stay by the governorship —*Economist*⟩
con·stru·al \kənz'trüəl, kən'str-\ *n* -s [*construe* + *-al*] **:** an interpreting (as of facts, data, a statement) **:** INTERPRETATION ⟨in this case genealogy and taxonomy rest partly on admitted facts but partly also on ~ of fact —A.L.Kroeber⟩
¹con·struct \kənz'trəkt, (')känz¦tr-, kən'str-, (')kän¦str-\ *adj* [ME, fr. L *constructus*, past part. of *construere*] *archaic* **:** CONSTRUCTED
²construct \kənz'trəkt, kən'str-\ *vt* -ED/-ING/-S [L *constructus*, past part. of *construere* to pile up, construct, fr. *com-* + *struere* to pile up, arrange, build — more at STRUCTURE] **1** *obs* **:** to construe or interpret (as a document, statement, expression) **2 :** to form, make, or create by combining parts or elements **:** BUILD, FABRICATE ⟨in ~*ing* the new freeway⟩ ⟨~ a new dormitory⟩ ⟨a well-*constructed* blend of unimpeachable teas —*New Yorker*⟩ ⟨an elegantly ~*ed* pair of dark green trousers —Mollie Panter-Downes⟩ **3 a :** to create by organizing ideas or concepts logically, coherently, or palpably ⟨a well-*constructed* argument⟩ ⟨Proust ~*s* a moral scheme out of phenomena whose moral values are always shifting —Edmund Wilson⟩ **b** (1) **:** to arrange (words or morphemes) in a meaningful combination (2) **:** to produce (as a sentence) by such arrangement of words or morphemes **4 a :** to draw (a geometrical figure) with suitable instruments so as to fulfill certain specified conditions ⟨~ a regular octagon with sides of given length⟩ **b :** to assemble separate and often disparate elements into (an abstract or nonrepresentational sculptural creation) **5 a :** to fabricate out of heterogeneous or discordant elements ⟨by India, they mean the political unit ~*ed* by English rule —D.W.Brogan⟩ ⟨a ~*ed* international language —Edward Sapir⟩ **b** (1) **:** FEIGN ⟨~*ed* dignity —John Buchan⟩ (2) **:** to infer in law **syn** see BUILD
³construct \'känzˌtrəkt, 'känˌstr-\ *n* -s **1 :** something that is constructed esp. by a process of mental synthesis: as **a :** an object of thought constituted by the ordering or systematic uniting of experiential elements (as percepts and sense data) and of terms and relations **b :** an intellectual or logical construction **:** an operational concept; *also* **:** the result of such a construction or concept ⟨the ~*s* of science⟩ **2 a :** CONSTRUCT STATE **b :** a noun in the construct state
construct form *n* **:** CONSTRUCT STATE
con·struct·ible \kənz'trəktəbəl, kən'str-\ *adj* [²*construct* + *-ible*] **:** capable of being constructed
con·struc·tion \kənz'trəkshən, kən'str-\ *n* -s [ME *construccioun*, fr. MF *construction*, fr. L *construction-, constructio*, fr. *constructus* + *-ion-, -io* -ion] **1 a** *obs* **:** the act of construing (as in translating) **b :** the syntactical relation of a word, phrase, or clause to another **c :** the arrangement and connection of words in a sentence **:** syntactical arrangement **d :** any meaningful combination of linguistic forms — see MORPHOLOGICAL CONSTRUCTION, SYNTACTIC CONSTRUCTION **2 a :** the act of putting parts together to form a complete integrated object **:** FABRICATION ⟨during the ~ of the bridge⟩ **b** (1) **:** the form or manner in which something has been put together **:** DESIGN ⟨several ships of similar ~⟩ ⟨an analysis of the ~ of a time bomb⟩ (2) **:** the science or study of building or erection ⟨two years in college mastering ship ~⟩ **c :** something built or erected **:** STRUCTURE ⟨raw new ~*s* along a highway⟩ **3 a** (1) **:** the act of construing, interpreting, or explaining a declaration or fact **:** INTERPRETATION ⟨putting the worst ~ on things innocent —Rudyard Kipling⟩; *also* **:** the result of such an act (2) **:** the discovery and application of the meaning and intention of a statement or fact to a particular state of affairs ⟨the ~ put on a statute by a lawyer⟩ **b** (1) **:** the process of mentally uniting ideas or conceptions so as to form an organic or congruous object of thought (2) **:** a procedure in logic that utilizes contextual definition to construct or analyze an actual entity (as a table) or an inferred entity (as a subatomic particle) by translating statements containing the name of the entity into synonymous statements that eliminate it in favor of names of experientially more fundamental elements (as sense data); *also* **:** the resultant conception or mental or logical entity formed through such a procedure **4 a :** the act of constructing a geometrical figure; *also* **:** its result **b :** an abstract or nonrepresentational sculptural creation composed of separate and often disparate elements
con·struc·tion·al \kənz'trəkshənᵊl, (')känz¦tr-, kən'str-, (')kän¦str-, -shnəl\ *adj* **1 :** deduced by or dependent on interpretation **2 :** STRUCTURAL ⟨~ details⟩ ⟨~ drawings⟩ **3 :** of or having to do with construction ⟨great ~ activity in the new nation's shipyards⟩ **4 :** of, resulting from, or being constructive geological processes (as those involving deposition and volcanic eruption) ⟨half of the area . . . is made up of ~ plains, as yet mostly undissected by erosion —*Amer. Guide Series: Nebr.*⟩ — **con·struc·tion·al·ly** \-nᵊlē, -nəlē, -li\ *adv*
construction bond *n* **:** a bond furnished by a contractor for the completion of his contract for construction work
con·struc·tion·ism \kənz'trəkshəˌnizəm, kən'str-\ *n* -s **1 a :** advocacy of, reliance on, or employment of construction or constructive methods or processes **b :** a doctrine or theory based on construction **2 :** CONSTRUCTIVISM
con·struc·tion·ist \-shənə̇st\ *n* -s **:** one who construes an instrument (as the U.S. Constitution) in a specific way ⟨the Soviet Union, abandoning its usual strict ~ position, urged a broad interpretation of what constitutes "states directly concerned" —C.D.Fuller⟩ ⟨the loose, or broad, ~*s* . . . contended that the national government had all powers which could by any reasonable interpretation be regarded as implied in the letter of the granted powers —F.A.Ogg & P.O.Ray⟩ — compare IMPLIED POWER
construction loan *n* **:** a loan secured by lien on property to finance a building project until completion and issuance of the long-term mortgage
construction paper *n* **:** colored paper suitable for crayon or ink drawings and watercolors and for making cutouts — compare ART PAPER
construction wrench *n* **:** an open-end wrench used by steel construction workers and having a long handle tapering to a blunt point that is used to hold matching holes (as for bolts or rivets) in alignment
con·struc·tive \kənz'trəktiv, (')känz¦tr-, kən'str-, (')kän¦str-, -tēv *also* -təv\ *adj* [ML *constructivus*, fr. L *constructus* + *-ivus* -ive — more at CONSTRUCT] **1 :** derived from or depending on construction or interpretation **:** not directly expressed **:** INFERRED — often used in law of an act or condition assumed from other acts or conditions which are considered by inference or by public policy as amounting to or involving the act or condition assumed **2 :** of, having to do with, or promoting construction or creation ⟨~ philosophy⟩ ⟨~ work⟩ ⟨~ fingers⟩ **3 :** helpful toward further development **:** promoting improvement or advance ⟨~ criticism⟩ ⟨a ~ attitude⟩ ⟨a ~ program⟩ **4 :** CONSTRUCTIVIST
constructive catabolism *n* **:** catabolic activity that results in the production of new substances other than excretions (as nectar in flowering plants)
constructive contempt *n* **:** a contempt that is committed outside the presence of a court in session or of a judge acting in a judicial capacity and is either civil in character when in willful disobedience to a lawful order or decree made for the benefit of a party or criminal in character when tending to belittle or insult the court or judge or to interfere with or degrade or obstruct justice **:** an indirect or consequential contempt — compare CRIMINAL CONTEMPT, DIRECT CONTEMPT
constructive delivery *n* **:** a delivery not accompanied by an actual transfer of possession of the property delivered yet recognized as having been intended by the parties and as sufficient in law (as where one sells to another and agrees to hold the goods as agent for the buyer or where one delivers the documentary evidence of title to another)
constructive escape *n* **:** the obtaining by a prisoner of more liberty than the law allows
constructive eviction *n* **:** any act or acts legally equivalent to or producing the same result as an actual eviction
constructive fraud *n* **:** conduct that is based on acts, omissions, or concealments considered fraudulent and that gives one an advantage against another because such conduct though not actually fraudulent, dishonest, or deceitful demands redress for reasons of public policy (as because of some private or public trust or confidence or fiduciary relationship or because of undue influence) — see FRAUD, MISREPRESENTATION; compare DECEIT
con·struc·tive·ly *adv* **:** in a constructive manner
constructive malice *n* **:** IMPLIED MALICE
constructive mileage *n* **:** mileage that is in excess of actual distance covered by freight shipments or passengers and is used in the computation of rates and in giving allowance for expenses
con·struc·tive·ness *n* -ES **:** the quality or state of being constructive
constructive total loss *n* **:** a loss to insured property that is not total but is so great that repair would cost more than the value of the property
constructive trust *n* **:** a trust set up by a court to deal with property that has been acquired by fraud or by inequitable means; *specif* **:** a trust so formed to distribute property where distribution and enjoyment under the original transaction was against the principles of equity — compare EXPRESS TRUST, RESULTING TRUST
con·struc·tiv·ism \kənz'trəktə̇ˌvizəm, kən'str-\ *n* -s **:** attachment to or employment of construction or constructive methods or principles: as **a :** an anti-illusionistic style of stage setting that employs practical but nonrealistic arrangements of steps, platforms, and scaffolding for acting areas and that is held to form a mise en scène appropriate to an age of technological progress **b :** nonfigurative art (as that produced by the school founded in Moscow in 1920 as a secession from suprematism) concerned with formal organization of planes and expression of volume in terms of modern industrial materials (as glass and plastic)
¹con·struc·tiv·ist \kənz'trəktə̇və̇st, (')känz¦tr-, kən'str-, (')kän¦str-\ *adj* [*constructive* + *-ist*] **:** of or belonging to constructivism **:** adhering to or following a theory, method, or practice of constructivism
²constructivist \"\ *n* -s **:** an adherent or follower of a theory, method, or practice of constructivism
con·struc·tor \kənz'trəktə(r), kən'str-\ *n* -s [²*construct* + *-or*] **1 :** one that constructs ⟨the company was a ~ of automatic elevators⟩ **2 :** a naval officer supervising the construction and repair of ships — called also *naval constructor* **3 :** one that creates a constructivist work of art
constructs *pres 3d sing of* CONSTRUCT, *pl of* CONSTRUCT
construct state \'känzˌtrəkt-, 'känˌstr-\ *n* **:** a noun inflectional form typically designating what is possessed and accompanied by another noun designating the possessor (as Hebrew *ben* "son" in *ben Yishay* "son of Jesse") **:** the relation expressed by such a form — called also *construct form*; compare ABSOLUTE STATE, EMPHATIC STATE
con·struc·ture \kənz'trəkchə(r), kən'str-, -kshə(r)\ *n* -s [²*construct* + *-ure*] *archaic* **:** STRUCTURE, CONSTRUCTION
¹con·strue \kənz'trü, kən'str\ *also* \'känzˌtrü *or* 'känˌstrü\ *vb* -ED/-ING/-S [ME *construen*, fr. LL *construere*, fr. L, to construct — more at CONSTRUCT] *vt* **1 a :** to analyze the arrangement and connection of words in (a sentence or part of a sentence) **:** translate piecemeal in such an order as to show the syntactical relation of the parts **b :** to combine idiomatically ⟨the verb *trust* is sometimes *construed* with *in*⟩ **2 a :** to put a construction on **:** discover and apply the meaning and intention of with reference to a particular state of affairs ⟨freedom of the press, literally *construed*, is the freedom to publish anything at all —F.L.Mott⟩ ⟨is it within judicial power, in *construing* the amendment, to abolish segregation —*N.Y. Times*⟩ **b :** to understand usu. in a particular way **:** explain the sense or intention of often to one's own satisfaction or according to or in conformity with a given set of circumstances ⟨~ an action as one pleases⟩ ⟨energy could be *construed* as something subsidiary to matter —A.N.Whitehead⟩ **3** *obs* **:** CONSTRUCT **~** *vi* **1 a :** to construe a sentence or part of a sentence esp. in connection with translating **b** *of a sentence or part of a sentence* **:** to be construable **2** *obs* **:** INFER — used with *of*
²construe \'känzˌtrü, 'känˌstrü *sometimes* kənz'trü *or* kən'strü\ *n* -s **:** an act of construing esp. by piecemeal translation; *also* **:** the translated version resulting from such an act
constuprate *vt* -ED/-ING/-S [L *constupratus*, past part. of *constuprare*, fr. *com-* + *stuprare* to ravish] *obs* **:** RAVISH
con·substantial \¦kän+\ *adj* [LL *consubstantialis*, fr. L *com-* + *substantia* substance + *-alis* -al — more at SUBSTANCE] **:** of the same kind or nature **:** having the same substance or essence **:** COESSENTIAL ⟨Three Persons in one ~ Godhead —R.M.Benson⟩ — **con·substantially** \¦kän+\ *adv*
con·substantialism \¦kän+\ *n* -s **:** the doctrine of consubstantiality or of consubstantiation
con·substantiality \¦kän+\ *n* -ES [LL *consubstantialitas*, fr. *consubstantialis* consubstantial + L *-itas* -ity] **:** the quality or state of being consubstantial ⟨the ~ of the persons of the Trinity⟩
¹con·substantiate \¦kän+\ *vt* -ED/-ING/-S [NL *consubstantiatus*, past part. of *consubstantiare*, fr. L *com-* + NL *-substantiare* (fr. L *substantia* substance)] **:** to regard as or make to be united in one common substance or nature ⟨language *consubstantiated* with thought⟩
²con·sub·stan·ti·ate \¦kän(t)səb¦stanch(ē)ə̇t, -səb¦stan-, -ēˌāt\ *adj* [NL *consubstantiatus*] **:** CONSUBSTANTIAL
con·substantiation \¦kän+\ *n* -s [NL *consubstantiation-, consubstantiatio*, fr. *consubstantiatus* + L *-ion-, -io* -ion] **:** the theological doctrine of the actual substantial presence and combination of the body of Christ with the bread and wine of the sacrament of the Lord's Supper — distinguished from *transubstantiation*
con·sue·tude \'kän(t)swəˌt(y)üd\ *n* -s [ME, fr. L *consuetudo* — more at CUSTOM] **1 :** social usage **:** CUSTOM, HABIT ⟨the stain hath become engrained by . . . ~ —Sir Walter Scott⟩ **2 :** custom or a custom imbued with legal force ⟨a right depending upon ~⟩ ⟨the laws and ~*s* of a clan⟩
con·sue·tu·di·nal \¦==¦t(y)üdᵊnəl\ *adj* [L *consuetudin-*, *consuetudo* custom + E *-al*] **1 :** CONSUETUDINARY **2** *of a verb form or aspect* **:** denoting customary action (as in French *il vendait* "he used to sell")
¹con·sue·tu·di·nary \ˌkän(t)swə't(y)üdᵊnˌerē, -ri\ *n* -ES [ML *consuetudinarius*, fr. LL *consuetudinarius*, adj.] **:** a manual embodying the customs or usages of a particular body; *esp* **:** one containing ritualistic and ceremonial observances of monastic discipline
²consuetudinary \¦==¦==ˌ==\ *adj* [LL *consuetudinarius*, fr. L *consuetudin-, consuetudo* custom + *-arius* -ary] **:** derived from or depending on habit or custom ⟨~ law⟩
con·sue·tu·do \ˌkän(t)swə't(y)üdō\ *n, pl* **consuetudi·nes** \-dᵊnˌēz\ [L, custom] **:** a custom or usage; *esp* **:** one having essentially the force of law
¹con·sul \'kän(t)səl\ *n* -s [ME, fr. L, fr. *consulere* to consult — more at CONSULT] **1 a** (1) **:** either of the two joint chief magistrates of the Roman republic (2) **:** a high honorary official of the Roman empire **b :** a municipal magistrate (as in Italy) during the middle ages **c :** one of the chief magistrates of the French republic from 1799 to 1804 or of one of the Italian republics established upon the French pattern **2** *obs* **:** a member of a council esp. of a trading company **3 :** an official appointed by or with the authority of a government to reside in a foreign country to represent the interests of citizens of the appointing country (as in commerce)
²consul \"\ *vt* -ED/-ING/-S **:** to submit (as an invoice) to a consul for inspection and approval
con·sul·age \-lij\ *n* -s [¹*consul* + *age*] **:** a duty or tax paid for consular protection
con·sul·ar \'kän(t)s(ə)lə(r) *also* -syəl-\ *adj* [L *consularis*, fr.

consul + *-aris* -ar] **:** of, having to do with, or of the nature of a consul, his office, or his duties ⟨both Polybius and Cicero speak of the ~ power as monarchical —C.H.McIlwain⟩
consular agent *n* **:** an official assuming consular duties at a place where a full consular post is not maintained
consular court *n* **:** one of the courts presided over by a minister or consul established by treaty in certain foreign countries and assigned criminal and civil jurisdiction over actions involving nationals of the country having extraterritorial rights
consular document *n* **:** a document (as a bill of lading, consular invoice, or certificate of origin) bearing the visa of a consul of the country of destination
consular invoice *n* **:** an invoice visaed by a consular officer of the country of destination
con·sul·ary \ˈkän(t)sə,lerē, -ri *also* -syə,l-\ *adj* [LL *consularius*, fr. L *consul* + *-arius* -ary] **:** CONSULAR
¹con·sul·ate \ˈkän(t)s(ə)lət *also* -syəl- *sometimes* ,lāt, *usu* -d·+V\ *n* -s [ME *consulat*, fr. L *consulatus*, fr. *consul* + *-atus* -ate — more at CONSUL] **1 :** government by consuls ⟨at that time Rome was still under the ~⟩ **2 a :** the office of consul ⟨while Caesar held the ~⟩ **b :** the term of office of a consul ⟨during his ~⟩ **3 :** the jurisdiction of a consul **:** consular territory ⟨attended to matters within his ~⟩ **4 :** the premises or the residence of a consul ⟨a ~ of the U.S. . . . is a fairly safe place in times of disturbances —F.A.Magruder⟩
²consulate \-,lāt, *usu* -ād·+V\ *vt* -ED/-ING/-S **1 :** to conduct a consular inspection of (as an invoice) **2 :** to submit (papers or records) for consular inspection and visa
consulate general \-lət- *sometimes* -,lāt-\ *n, pl* **consulates general :** the residence, office, or jurisdiction of a consul general
consul general *n, pl* **consuls general :** a consul of the first rank stationed in an important place or having jurisdiction in several places or over several consuls
con·sul·ship \ˈkän(t)səl,ship\ *n* **:** the office or term of office of a consul **:** CONSULATE 2
¹con·sult \kənˈsəlt\ *vb* -ED/-ING/-S [MF or L; MF *consulter*, fr. L *consultare*, freq. of *consulere* to consult, fr. *com-* + *-sulere* (perh. akin to Gk *helein* to take) — more at SELL] *vt* **1** *obs* **a :** to deliberate on **:** DISCUSS **b :** to take counsel to bring about **:** DEVISE, CONTRIVE **2 a :** to ask advice of **:** seek the opinion of **:** apply to for information or instruction ⟨~ a doctor about an ailment⟩ **b :** to refer to esp. for information ⟨~ a dictionary⟩ **3 :** to have prudent regard to **:** have an eye to **:** CONSIDER ⟨~ one's pocketbook before buying⟩ ~ *vi* **:** to take counsel **:** deliberate together **:** CONFER ⟨after ~*ing* with a lawyer⟩ ⟨the three powers would ~ on how to ameliorate the internal political conflict —W.S.Vucinich⟩
²consult \ˈkän,səlt *sometimes* kənˈs-\ *n* -s [MF *consulte*, fr. *consulter*, v.] **1** *archaic* **:** the act of consulting or deliberating **2 a :** CONSULTATION ⟨their ~*s* produced resolutions of violence —Thomas Carte⟩ **b** *archaic* **:** a secret meeting for devising treasonable or seditious actions **:** CABAL
con·sul·tant \kənˈsəltᵊnt, -tənt\ *n* -s [F, fr. L *consultant-, consultans*, pres. part. of *consultare*] **1 :** one who consults another **2 :** one who gives professional advice or services regarding matters in the field of his special knowledge or training (as a consulting physician or engineer) **:** EXPERT
con·sul·ta·ry response \kənˈsəlt(ə)rē-, ˈkän(t)səl,terē-\ *n* **:** the opinion of a court of law on a special case
con·sul·ta·tion \,kän(t)səlˈtāshən\ *n* -s [ME *consultacioun*, fr. MF *consultation*, fr. L *consultation-, consultatio*, fr. *consultatus* + *-ion-, -io* -ion] **1 :** a council or conference (as between two or more persons) usu. to consider a special matter ⟨holding frequent ~*s* with his lawyer to discuss the case⟩; *specif* **:** a formal deliberation between two or more physicians on the diagnosis of a disease or its treatment in a patient **2 :** the act of consulting or conferring **:** deliberation of two or more persons on some matter ⟨the two firms were in ~ over the construction of the new airplane⟩
con·sul·ta·tive \kənˈsəltəd·|iv, -tət|iv *also* |əv; ˈkän(t)səl,tād·|iv, -tāt|iv *also* |əv\ *adj* [*consultation* + *-ive*] **:** of or having to do with consultation **:** having the privilege or right of conference **:** ADVISORY ⟨employed in a ~ capacity only⟩
con·sul·ta·to·ry \kənˈsəltə,tōrē, -tȯrē, -ri\ *adj* [L *consultatorius*, fr. *consultatus* + *-orius* -ory] **:** of or having to do with consultation **:** ADVISORY, CONSULTATIVE
con·sult·er \kənˈsəltə(r)\ *n* -s **:** one that consults
consulting *adj* **1 :** that advises **:** that aids esp. by providing professional or expert advice ⟨a ~ architect⟩ ⟨a ~ psychologist⟩ **2 :** of or having to do with consultation or a consultant ⟨the ~ room of a psychiatrist⟩ ⟨the ~ services of a law firm⟩
con·sul·tive \kənˈsəltiv, -tēv *also* -təv\ *adj* **:** CONSULTATIVE
con·sul·tor \kənˈsəltə(r)\ *n* -s [L, fr. *consultus*, past part. of *consulere* + *-or* — more at CONSULT] **:** one that consults or advises; *esp* **:** a person expert in a particular field of knowledge who is chosen by the Roman Catholic Church esp. for assisting and advising a bishop
con·sul·tory \kənˈsəlt(ə)rē; (ˈ)kän(t)səl,tōrē, -tȯrē, -ri\ *adj, archaic* **:** CONSULTATORY
con·sum·able \kənˈsüməbəl\ *adj* **:** capable of being consumed ⟨~ goods⟩
con·sume \kənˈsüm\ *vb* -ED/-ING/-S [ME *consumen*, fr. MF or L; MF *consumer*, fr. L *consumere* to take completely, consume, fr. *com-* + *sumere* to take, fr. *sub-* + *emere* to buy, obtain — more at REDEEM] *vt* **1 :** to destroy or do away with completely (as by fire, disease, famine, decomposition) ⟨the blaze *consumed* several blocks⟩ **:** cause to waste away utterly ⟨plague *consumed* an entire generation⟩ **2 a :** to spend wastefully **:** SQUANDER ⟨~ the family income on luxuries⟩ **b** (1) **:** to use up **:** EXPEND ⟨an iron furnace *consumed* thousands of cords for fuel —*Amer. Guide Series: Mich.*⟩ (2) **:** to use up (as time) ⟨hours *consumed* in reading⟩ ⟨visitors who wish to spend a brief vacation . . . and to ~ as little of it as possible in transit—*Amer. Guide Series: Vt.*⟩ **c :** to utilize (an economic good) in the satisfaction of wants or the process of production ⟨the production of nuclear energy . . . soon to ~ 10 percent of all the electricity we produce —*New Republic*⟩ **3 :** to eat or drink esp. without measure ⟨the banqueters *consumed* several kegs of beer⟩ **4 :** to engage or absorb fully the attention, interest, or energy of **:** ENGROSS ⟨when the rage and the hatred that ~ one are more than one can bear —Kay Boyle⟩ ~ *vi* **:** to waste or burn away **:** PERISH ⟨as quickly as blossoms ~ away⟩ ⟨leaves, which were quietly *consuming* in bonfires —Sylvia T. Warner⟩ **syn** see EAT, MONOPOLIZE, WASTE
con·sum·ed·ly \kənˈsümədlē, -li\ *adv* **:** EXCESSIVELY ⟨I shall miss him ~ —O.W.Holmes †1935⟩
con·sum·er \kənˈsümə(r)\ *n* -s *often attrib* **:** one that consumes ⟨the ship's boilers were great ~*s* of cordwood —*Amer. Guide Series: Minn.*⟩ ⟨~*s* of political propaganda —Louis Simpson⟩; *specif* **:** one that utilizes economic goods ⟨~ commodity⟩ ⟨~ demand⟩ ⟨~ price⟩ ⟨~ cooperative⟩ — compare PRODUCER
consumer credit *n* **:** credit (as a charge account or installment loan) that is granted to an individual esp. to finance the purchase of consumer goods or defray personal or family expenses and is usu. repaid in installments
consumer goods *also* **consumer items** *n pl* **:** economic goods that directly satisfy human wants or desires — compare PRODUCER GOODS
consumer price index *n* **:** an index measuring the change in the cost of typical wage-earner purchases of goods and services expressed as a percentage of the cost of these same goods and services in some base period — called also *cost-of-living index*
consumer sovereignty *n* **:** the economic power exercised by the preferences of consumers in a free market
consumer's surplus *also* **consumer's rent** *n* **:** the amount above the actual price of a commodity a purchaser would pay in order not to go without the commodity
con·sum·ing·ly *adv* **:** INTENSELY, DEVOTEDLY ⟨~ earnest⟩
con·sum·ing·ness *n* -ES **:** the quality or state of being consuming
¹con·sum·mate \kənˈsəmət, ˈkän(t)səm-, *usu* -ȧd·+V\ *adj* [ME *consummat*, fr. L *consummatus*, past part. of *consummare* to sum up, finish, fr. *com-* + *-summare* (fr. *summa* sum) — more at SUM] **1** *archaic* **:** brought to completion **:** FINISHED **2 :** complete in every detail **:** PERFECT ⟨a ~ little model of a clipper ship⟩ **3 :** extremely skilled and accomplished **:** supremely capable or proficient ⟨a ~ actor⟩ ⟨a ~ politician⟩ ⟨a ~ liar⟩ **4 a :** of the very highest or finest **:** supremely excellent ⟨~ wisdom⟩ ⟨a ~ performance⟩ **b :** greatest possible **:** EXTREME ⟨~ treachery⟩ ⟨~ cruelty⟩ — **con·sum·mate·ly** *adv*
²con·sum·mate \ˈkän(t)sə,māt, *usu* -ād·+V; *"consummated" in the passage "It is consummated" in some versions of the Bible is often pronounced* kənˈsəmȧd·ȧd *or* -mətȧd\ *vb* -ED/-ING/-S [L *consummatus*] *vt* **1 a :** to bring to completion **:** FINISH, COMPLETE ⟨~ a business merger⟩ ⟨~ a military alliance⟩ **b :** to bring to the highest point or degree **:** make perfect ⟨their happiness was *consummated* when they bought their house⟩ **c :** to bring about **:** ACHIEVE ⟨the opportunity to ~ such a desire⟩ ⟨annexation was *consummated* by a joint resolution —Oscar Handlin⟩ **2 :** to complete (marital union) by the first act of sexual intercourse after marriage **3** *obs* **:** to put an end to ~ *vi* **:** to come to fulfillment or perfection; *specif* **:** to engage in the first act of sexual intercourse after marriage
con·sum·ma·tion \,kän(t)səˈmāshən\ *n* -s [ME *consummacioun*, fr. MF *consommation*, fr. L *consummation-, consummatio*, fr. *consummatus* + *-ion-, -io* -ion] **1 :** the act of completing, achieving, or bringing to perfection ⟨the ~ of a contract by mutual signature⟩ ⟨production of the new model marks the ~ of this particular design⟩; *specif* **:** the consummating of a marriage **2 :** the finish or ultimate end ⟨death is the ~ of life⟩; *specif* **:** the supreme or highest goal ⟨the universal loving-kindness of Deity as the ~ of existence —W.L.Sullivan⟩
con·sum·ma·tive \ˈkän(t)sə,mād·iv, kənˈsəməd·iv\ *adj* **:** serving or tending to consummate **:** COMPLETING, FINAL — **con·sum·ma·tive·ly** \-d·əvlē\ *adv*
con·sum·ma·tor \ˈkän(t)sə,mād·ə(r)\ *n* -s [LL, fr. L *consummatus* + *-or*] **:** one that consummates
con·sum·ma·to·ry \kənˈsəmə,tōrē, -tȯrē, -ri\ *adj* **:** of or having to do with consummation **:** CONCLUDING, COMPLETING, FINISHING ⟨a ~ act⟩ ⟨art as appreciation, as ~ experience —J.L.Blau⟩ ⟨in proper sequence of preparatory, intermediate, and ~ situations —*Psychiatry*⟩
con·sumpt \kənˈsəm(p)t, -səm-\ *n* -s [by shortening] *chiefly Scot* **:** CONSUMPTION
con·sumpt·ed \-tȧd\ *adj* [*consumption* + *-ed*] *dial* **:** affected with consumption
con·sump·ti·ble \kənˈsəmptəbəl\ *n* -s [*consumption* + *-ible*] **:** an object (as an economic good) that in use is consumed (as by wear, decay, attrition)
con·sump·tion \kənˈsəmpshən\ *n* -s [ME *consumpcioun*, fr. L *consumption-, consumptio*, fr. *consumptus* (past part. of *consumere* to consume) + *-ion-, -io* -ion — more at CONSUME] **1 a :** the act or action of consuming or destroying ⟨the ~ of organic matter by fire⟩ ⟨the ~ of an entire generation of young men in a war⟩ **b :** the wasting, using up, or wearing away of something ⟨the slow ~ of a person's vitality⟩ ⟨the ~ of a fortune⟩ **2 :** the utilization of economic goods in the satisfaction of wants or in the process of production resulting in immediate destruction (as in the eating of foods), gradual wear and deterioration (as in the habitation of dwellings), no change aside from natural decay (as in the enjoyment of art objects), or transformation into other goods (as in manufacturing) — see CONSPICUOUS CONSUMPTION **3 a :** a progressive wasting away of the body; *esp* **:** the disabling wasting stage of pulmonary tuberculosis characterized by great destruction of lung tissue and systemic toxemia **b :** TUBERCULOSIS — not used technically
consumption function *n* **:** a function relating the level of consumer expenditures to national income orig. believed to be a constant but subsequently held to fluctuate under various conditions
consumption goods *n pl* **:** CONSUMER GOODS
consumption weed *n* **:** FALSE WINTERGREEN
¹con·sump·tive \kənˈsəmptiv, -tēv *also* -təv\ *adj* [*consumption* + *-ive*] **1 a :** tending to consume or be consumed **:** DESTRUCTIVE, WASTEFUL ⟨~ fires⟩ ⟨duties ~ of time and money⟩ **b :** of or having to do with the consumption of economic goods ⟨this milk which is in excess of ~ requirement . . . is termed "surplus" —A.L.Anderson⟩ **2 a :** wasted or reduced by or as if by a sickness **b** (1) **:** affected with consumption ⟨a ~ boy⟩ (2) **:** of, having to do with, or suggestive of consumption ⟨a ~ cough⟩ — **con·sump·tive·ly** \-tȧvlē, -li\ *adv*
²consumptive \"\ *n* -s **:** a person affected with consumption
consumptive's weed *n* [so called fr. its use in the relief of bronchial disorders] **:** YERBA SANTA
consumptive use *n* **:** the total seasonal water loss from an area of land due to plant growth and evaporation usu. being expressed in acre-feet
cont *abbr* **1** containing **2** contemporary **3** contents **4** continent; continental **5** continued; continuous **6** contract **7** contrary **8** control
con·ta·bes·cence \,käntəˈbesᵊn(t)s\ *n* -s [ISV *contabesc-* (fr. L *contabescere* to waste away, fr. *com-* + *tabescere* to melt gradually, to decay) + *-ence* — more at THAW] **:** abortion of an anther — **con·ta·bes·cent** \;=;ˈbesᵊnt\ *adj*
¹con·tact \ˈkän,takt\ *n* -s [F or L; F, fr. L *contactus*, fr. *contactus*, past part. of *contingere* to touch on all sides — more at CONTINGENT] **1 a :** union or junction of body surfaces **:** a touching or meeting ⟨cooled by ~ with the air⟩ ⟨sexual ~⟩ **:** IMPACT ⟨body ~ in football and hockey⟩ **b** *geom* **:** the meeting of curves or surfaces so as to have tangents or tangent planes in common **c :** the apparent touching or mutual tangency of the limbs of any two celestial bodies or of the disk of one body with the shadow of another during an eclipse, transit, or occultation **d** (1) **:** the junction or touching surface of two electrical conductors through which a current passes (2) **:** a special part (as a platinum stud) made for such a junction for temporary or momentary connection **2 a :** association or relationship (as in physical or mental or business or social meeting or communication) ⟨students and teachers in daily ~⟩ ⟨Japan's new ~*s* with Europe⟩ **:** direct experience through the senses ⟨a mental patient's infrequent ~*s* with reality⟩ **b :** a condition or an instance of meeting, connecting, or communicating ⟨ordinary men were made to feel a direct ~ with their God —H.S.Canby⟩ ⟨keep in ~ with the other members⟩ ⟨neither party had made any ~ with the other⟩ ⟨made ~ with the enemy⟩ **c :** ACCULTURATION **d :** direct visual observation of the surface of the ground or water made from an airplane esp. as an aid to judging position and properly guiding the airplane ⟨flying by ~ rather than flying by instruments⟩ **e :** an instance of establishing communication with someone ⟨a radio ~⟩ or of observing or receiving a significant signal from a person or object (as by radar or sonar) ⟨got three ~*s* on the radarscope⟩; *also* **:** a person or object with which such contact is made **3 a :** a person serving as go-between, messenger, agent, or source of special information esp. in a secret activity ⟨the ~ for the syndicate⟩ ⟨a newspaperman's ~*s* are often cabdrivers or bartenders⟩ **b :** any person or animal that has been in contact with a person or animal affected with a contagious disease **4 :** the often irregular surface that constitutes the junction of two bodies of rock different in kind, age, or origin **5 :** CONTACT LENS
²con·tact \", kənˈt-, känˈt-\ *vb* -ED/-ING/-S *vt* **:** to bring into contact **:** enter or be in contact with: **a :** to press against **:** MEET, TOUCH ⟨brake shoes ~ the inside diameter of the drum⟩ **:** JOIN ⟨where the line of ordinary low water . . . directly ~*ed* the open sea —*U.S.Code*⟩ **b :** to make connection with **:** get in communication with **:** REACH — used often where the means is not precisely specified ⟨~ your local dealer⟩ ⟨the salesman ~*ed* a few prospects⟩ **c :** to talk or confer with **:** INTERVIEW **:** apply to **:** APPROACH ⟨the first company you ~ may not . . . use your services —W.J.Reilly⟩ ⟨the department . . . was ~*ed* to learn of availability and costs —R.C.Emery⟩ ~ *vi* **:** to make contact ⟨the point at which the two surfaces ~⟩
³contact \ˈkän,takt\ *adj* **1 :** of, maintaining, or establishing contact ⟨a ~ man⟩ ⟨~ area⟩ **:** involving, permitting, or activated by contact ⟨~ weather⟩ ⟨~ fuse⟩ **2** *geol* **:** lying along or near or genetically connected with a contact ⟨a ~ deposit⟩ **3 :** characterized by or normally involving body contact between players ⟨football and hockey are ~ sports⟩ **4 :** caused or transmitted by direct or indirect contact (as with an allergen or a contagious disease) ⟨~ allergy⟩ ⟨~ transmission⟩
⁴contact \"\ *adv* **:** by direct visual observation of the earth ⟨the ceiling was so low that the patrol was flown ~ —J.L. Foley⟩
contact acid *n* **:** sulfuric acid produced by contact catalysis
con·tac·tant \kənˈtaktənt, (ˈ)kän¦-\ *n* -s [¹*contact* + *-ant*] **:** any allergen that produces manifestations of hypersensitivity at the site of contact with the skin or the mucosa
contact bed *n* **:** a watertight bed filled with coke or other coarse material and used for purifying sewage which after being run into the bed and left for some hours in contact with the material to promote bacterial action is filtered off and the bed aerated
contact block *n* **:** a block of conducting material forming one of the two surfaces of an electric contact
contact catalysis *n* **:** catalysis in which the catalyst is a solid in contact with gaseous or liquid reactants
contact clip *n* **:** the clip into which the blade of an electrical switch enters or which it embraces
contact electricity *n* **:** electricity arising on two dissimilar bodies at their surface of contact
contact flying *n* **:** navigation of an airplane by means of direct observation of landmarks — contrasted with *instrument flying*
contact lens *n* **:** a thin lens of glass or plastic designed to fit over the cornea for the correction of refractive errors; *also* **:** a similar lens or a prism employed by the ophthalmologist in eye examinations with a gonioscope
contact light *n* **:** one of a series of white marker lights placed in parallel rows on either side of an airfield runway to provide a visual aid to the pilot in landing
contact maker *n* **:** a device for making or for making and breaking an electric contact
contact metamorphic *adj* **:** formed by or associated with contact metamorphism
contact metamorphism *or* **contact metasomatism** *n* **:** metamorphosis found in the region of contact of a rock mass with an igneous intrusion
contact microphone *n* **:** a microphone designed to be used in contact with the source of sound or with a resonating or conducting surface
contact mineral *n* **:** a mineral whose origin is due to contact metamorphism
con·tac·tor \ˈkän,taktə(r), kənˈt-, känˈt-\ *n* -s **:** a device for repeatedly establishing and interrupting an electric power circuit under normal conditions
contact potential *n* **1 :** VOLTA EFFECT **2 :** grid bias in a vacuum tube due to the lodging of space-charge electrons upon the grid wires
contact print *n* **:** a photographic print made by passing light through the negative while it is held in contact with the sensitized paper, plate, or film — compare PROJECTION PRINT
contact receptor *n* **:** a receptor for a stimulus (as taste) produced by an object touching it — compare DISTANCE RECEPTOR
contact rock *n* **:** rock associated with a contact metamorphic zone — compare CONTACT METAMORPHISM
contacts *pl of* CONTACT, *pres 3d sing of* CONTACT
contact series *n* **:** an arrangement of metals so that each is positively electrified by contact with the next
contact twin *n* **:** a twin crystal in which the two individuals are joined along a plane
con·tac·tu·al \kənˈtakchəwəl, (ˈ)kän¦-\ *adj* [fr. ¹*contact*, after such pairs as E *fact: factual*] **:** of, relating to, or involving contact — **con·tac·tu·al·ly** \-wəlē, -li\ *adv*
contact vein *n* **:** a vein formed along the common boundary of two different rock formations **:** a contact deposit of tabular form
contact zone *n* **:** a zone surrounding or adjacent to an igneous intrusion in which rocks have been affected by heat or magmatic solutions and gases
contagia *pl of* CONTAGIUM
con·ta·gion \kənˈtājən\ *n* -s [ME *contagioun*, fr. MF & L; MF *contagion*, fr. L *contagion-, contagio*, fr. *contag-* (fr. *contingere* to touch, to pollute) + *-ion-, -io* -ion — more at CONTINGENT] **1 a :** the process by which disease is transmitted from one person to another by direct or indirect means **b :** a contagious disease **c :** something that serves as a medium to transmit disease **:** a virus or other infective agent that may produce disease **2 a :** POISON ⟨I'll touch my point with this ~ —Shak.⟩ **b :** contagious influence, quality, or nature ⟨to dare the vile ~ of the night —Shak.⟩ **c :** evil or corrupting influence or contact ⟨war . . . had become . . . a ~ attacking neutrals as well as belligerents —*Saturday Rev.*⟩ **3 a :** the spread or communication or the tendency to be communicated of any influence, doctrine, emotion, or emotional state ⟨the ~ of love obeys no human logic —John Erskine †1951⟩ ⟨the ~ of mob enthusiasm —H.L.Mencken⟩ **b :** an influence, doctrine, or emotion that spreads rapidly ⟨when people began to run the ~ spread and soon the whole mob was running⟩
con·ta·gion·ist \-nȧst\ *n* -s **:** one who believes in the contagiousness of certain diseases before proof is available
con·ta·gi·os·i·ty \kən,tājēˈäsəd·ē\ *n* -ES [F *contagiosité*, fr. L *contagiosus* + F *-ité* -ity] **:** the state of being contagious or the degree of contagiousness
con·ta·gious \kənˈtājəs\ *adj* [ME, fr. MF *contagieus*, fr. LL *contagiosus*, fr. L *contagio* + *-osus* -ous] **1 a :** communicable by contact **:** CATCHING ⟨~ diseases⟩ — compare INFECTIOUS **b :** bearing contagion ⟨many persons . . . are ~ long before they are aware of the presence of their disease —*Jour. Amer. Med. Assoc.*⟩ **c :** for contagious diseases ⟨a ~ ward⟩ **2** *obs* **:** causing disease **:** NOXIOUS **3 :** spreading or communicable from one to another **:** exciting similar emotions or conduct in others ⟨a ~ grin⟩ ⟨~ enthusiasm⟩ **:** exciting enthusiasm **:** exciting response ⟨~ music⟩ — **con·ta·gious·ly** *adv*
contagious abortion *n* **1 :** brucellosis in domestic animals characterized by abortion: **a :** bovine brucellosis caused by a brucella (*Brucella abortus*), contracted by ingestion, by copulation, or possibly by wound infection, and characterized by proliferation of the organism in the fetal membranes inducing abortion, subsequent invasion of the regional lymph nodes and udder with the formation of chronic foci of infection, and sometimes reinvasion of the uterus when pregnancy is reestablished, though a degree of local immunity usu. appears after one or more abortions, an affected cow carrying her calf to term even though retaining a chronic brucella infection outside the uterus **b :** any brucellosis of swine or goats having a somewhat similar course to bovine brucellosis but usu. caused by different brucellae **2 :** any of several contagious or infectious diseases of domestic animals marked by abortion (as vibrionic abortion of sheep or an acute salmonellosis of the mare)
contagious bovine pleuropneumonia *n* **:** pleuropneumonia of cattle
contagious disease *n* **:** a disease communicable by contact with one suffering from it, with a bodily discharge of such a patient, or with an object touched by such a patient or his bodily discharges — compare INFECTIOUS DISEASE; GERM THEORY
contagious distribution *n, statistics* **:** a distribution for which the number of variates in some classes is influenced by a tendency of the variates to occur in aggregates
contagious ecthyma *n* **:** SORE MOUTH
contagious epithelioma *n* **:** FOWL POX
contagious indigestion *n* **:** BLUE COMB
contagious magic *n* **:** magic based on the assumption that things once associated are able to affect one another when separated so that anything done to an object (as a garment or a hair) will affect its former owner
con·ta·gious·ness \kənˈtājəsnəs\ *n* -ES **:** the quality or state of being contagious
contagious pleuropneumonia *n* **:** pleuropneumonia of cattle
con·ta·gium \kənˈtāj(ē)əm\ *n, pl* **conta·gia** \-j(ē)ə\ [L, fr. *contingere* to touch, pollute — more at CONTINGENT] **:** a virus or living organism capable of causing a communicable disease
con·tain \kənˈtān\ *vb* -ED/-ING/-S [ME *conteinen, contenen*, fr. OF *contenir*, fr. L *continēre*, fr. *com-* + *-tinēre* (fr. *tenēre* to hold) — more at THIN] *vt* **1 :** to keep within limits **:** hold back or hold down: as **a :** RESTRAIN, CONTROL ⟨tried to ~ his tendency to argue⟩ **:** SUPPRESS ⟨unable to ~ his laughter⟩ ⟨all the appearance of ~*ed* rage⟩ ⟨not able to ~ himself⟩ **b :** CHECK, HALT, WITHSTAND, STEM ⟨~ an advancing flood⟩ ⟨economic inflation has so far been ~*ed*⟩ ⟨~*ed* the enemy's attack⟩ **c :** to confine (the enemy) to the immediate terrain or to a limited area **:** prevent (the enemy) from making a breakthrough **d :** to follow successfully a policy of containment

toward (a hostile power) **:** hold in check **2 a :** to have within **:** HOLD ⟨the box ~*ed* only some old papers and a few odds and ends⟩ **b :** to consist of wholly or in part **:** COMPRISE, INCLUDE ⟨the bill ~*s* several new clauses⟩ **:** ENCLOSE ⟨the building ~*s* classrooms and an auditorium⟩ **3 a :** to have capacity for **:** be able to hold **:** be equivalent to ⟨a bushel ~*s* four pecks⟩ **b :** to extend over **:** MEASURE, OCCUPY ⟨the farm ~*s* more than 10,000 acres⟩ **c** (1) **:** to be a multiple of or to be divisible by usu. without a remainder (2) **:** ENCLOSE, INCLUDE, BOUND **4 :** IMPLY, ENTAIL ⟨the conclusions are ~*ed* in the premises⟩ **5 a** *archaic* **:** to keep or retain under or as if under control ⟨impossible that he could at once ~ . . . every part of his wide-extended dominions —Edward Gibbon⟩ **b** *obs* **:** RETAIN, KEEP **~** *vi* **1** *obs* **:** to conduct oneself **:** BEHAVE **2 a :** to restrain oneself (as from laughter) **b** *obs* **:** to live in continence

syn HOLD, ACCOMMODATE: to CONTAIN is usu. to have within ⟨the top compartment *contains* tools most often used⟩ ⟨old river valleys . . . are still visible and usually *contain* lakes or chains of lakes —*Amer. Guide Series: Minn.*⟩ ⟨animal protein and animal fat *contained* in an ordinary mixed diet —N.C. Wright⟩ ⟨the picture *contains* strange figures⟩ To HOLD is usu. to have the capacity to contain or retain ⟨the jug, which *holds* over a gallon, contained only a pint⟩ Often, however, the two words are used interchangeably, esp. in the past tenses ⟨the compartments of the cash register *contained* the various denominations of coins but were often empty⟩ ⟨the box *held* his clothes and some small valueless trinkets⟩ To ACCOMMODATE is to hold conveniently or without crowding ⟨the bus *accommodates* about 60 passengers and the driver⟩

con·tained \kən'tānd\ *adj* [ME *conteined*, fr. past part. of *conteinen*] **1 :** RESTRAINED, CONTROLLED ⟨striking with ~ ferocity at my head —R.L.Stevenson⟩ **:** COMPOSED, CALM ⟨the ~ peace of the village⟩ — see SELF-CONTAINED **2 :** SUSTAINED, SUPPORTED — now used chiefly in compounds ⟨the Tsarist Russian land-*contained* expansion —Owen Lattimore⟩ — **contain·ed·ly** \-'tānədlē, -li\ *adv*

con·tain·er \kən'tānə(r)\ *n* -s **:** one that contains: as **a :** a receptacle (as a box or jar) or a formed or flexible covering for the packing or shipment of articles, goods, or commodities **b :** a portable usu. metal compartment in which freight is placed for convenience of movement esp. on railroad container cars

container board *n* **:** any of the various paperboards (as corrugated board, fiberboard) from which containers are made

container car *n* **:** an open-top railroad freight car specially fitted for the accommodation of containers

containing *pres part of* CONTAIN

con·tain·ment \kən'tānmənt\ *n* -s **1 :** the act of containing **:** RESTRAINT, CONSTRAINT, CONTROL **2 a :** the policy or the process of preventing the expansion beyond prescribed limits of a hostile power or ideology or inimical forces esp. by employing political, economic, and propaganda pressure and by strengthening friendly powers **b :** the result to be attained by such a policy or process

contains *pres 3d sing of* CONTAIN

contakion *var of* KONTAKION

con·tam·i·nant \kən'tamənənt\ *n* -s [L *contaminant-, contaminans*, pres. part. of *contaminare*] **:** something that contaminates

[1]**con·tam·i·nate** \kən'tamə,nāt, *usu* -ād.+V\ *vt* -ED/-ING/-S [L *contaminatus*, past part. of *contaminare* to bring into contact, contaminate; akin to L *contingere* to touch, pollute — more at CONTINGENT] **1 :** to soil, stain, corrupt, or infect by contact or association ⟨a surgical wound *contaminated* by bacteria⟩ ⟨believers *contaminated* by the presence of infidels⟩ **:** make inferior or impure by mixture **:** POLLUTE ⟨iron *contaminated* by phosphorus⟩ **2 :** to render unfit for use by the introduction of unwholesome or undesirable elements ⟨water *contaminated* by sewage⟩ ⟨~ a state the size of Maryland with radioactivity —R.E.Lapp⟩

syn TAINT, ATTAINT, POLLUTE, DEFILE: these all mean to make impure or unclean. CONTAMINATE implies an action by something external to an object which by entering into or coming in contact with the object destroys its purity ⟨the surgical wound became *contaminated*⟩ ⟨the incoming air will not be *contaminated* with exhaust or oil fumes —H.G.Armstrong⟩ ⟨you allowed your fine magazine to be *contaminated* with such a vicious, foul, and absurd writing —*Fortune*⟩ TAINT usu. suggests a less complete debasing than CONTAMINATE, often suggesting only a partial contamination, but stresses more strongly the sullied or stained quality of the thing acted upon ⟨water . . . becomes *tainted* easily through smells and impurities in the air —Henry Wynmalen⟩ ⟨the poison of greed, ambition, and vulgarity had not *tainted* the Italian air —Ann Bridge⟩ ATTAINT, less frequently used than TAINT, has come, because of etymological similarity, to be used as synonymous with TAINT though it suggests the idea of infection or of inevitable corruption following from an original sullying contact ⟨our writers have been *attainted* by the disease they must help to cure —Waldo Frank⟩ ⟨the slightest contact with them *attaints* and works corruption of the blood —G.W.Johnson⟩ POLLUTE carries strongly the idea of a completed process of contamination, esp. and usu. an offensive contamination ⟨water *polluted* by garbage and other filth⟩ DEFILE implies a willful befouling of what ought to be kept clean, clear, or bright, frequently, therefore, suggesting violation, profanation or desecration ⟨wheat which the mice ate or *defiled* —F.E.Garlough⟩ ⟨cruelty is not only the worst accusation that can be brought against a man, *defiling* the whole character —Hilaire Belloc⟩ ⟨the Sabbath should not be *defiled* —William McFee⟩

[2]**contaminate** *adj* [L *contaminatus*] *obs* **:** CONTAMINATED

con·tam·i·na·tion \kən,tamə'nāshən\ *n* -s [LL *contamination-, contaminatio*, fr. L *contaminatus* + *-ion-, -io* -ion] **1 :** the act or process of contaminating or the state of being contaminated **:** something that contaminates **:** IMPURITY **2 a :** a blending in manuscript tradition whereby a single manuscript contains readings belonging to different groups **b :** a blending of legends or stories resulting in new combinations of incident or in modifications of plot **3** [G *kontamination*, fr. LL *contamination-, contaminatio*] **:** the blending of two linguistic forms (as words or word groups) into a single new one (as *irregardless*, prob. from *irrespective* and *regardless*, *different than*, prob. from *different from* and *other than*) — compare [3]BLEND d **4 :** corruption of relatively inexperienced offenders by hardened criminals within a prison population

con·tam·i·na·tive \kən'tamə,nād·|iv, -ăt|iv *also* |əv; -'tamənəd·|iv, -nət|iv *also* |əv\ *adj* **:** tending to contaminate

con·tam·i·na·tor \kən'tamə,nād·ə(r), -ātə-\ *n* -s **:** one that contaminates

[1]**con·tango** \kən'taŋ(,)gō\ *n, pl* **contangos** *or* **contangoes** [perh. alter. of *continue*] **:** premium or interest paid on a fixed day on the London stock exchange by a buyer to the seller to be allowed to defer payment until a future settlement — compare BACKWARDATION

[2]**contango** \"\ *vi* -ED/-ING/-ES **:** to allow deferment of payment of the purchase price of stocks in consideration of a contango

con·ta·rin·ia \,käntə'rinēə\ *n, cap* [NL] **:** a large genus of gall midges (family Cecidomyiidae) including several that invade buds and flowers of economically important plants

contbd *abbr* contraband

contbg *abbr* contributing

contbn *abbr* contribution

contbr *abbr* contributor

contd *abbr* continued

[1]**conte** \'kōnt, -ōⁿt\ *n, pl* **contes** \-t(s)\ [F, fr. *conter* to relate — more at COUNT] **1 :** a short tale esp. of adventure ⟨a ~ in the old-fashioned sense, a tale of temptation and adventure, innocence and world-wickedness —Parker Tyler⟩ — compare SHORT STORY **2 :** a narrative somewhat shorter than the average novel but longer than a short story ⟨a ~ rather than a full-length novel —*John O'London's Weekly*⟩

[2]**conté** \(')kōn¦tā, -ōⁿ¦-\ *or* **conté crayon** *n, sometimes* Conté [F *crayon Conté*, after Nicolas-Jacques *Conté* †1805 Fr. chemist, its inventor] **:** a hard crayon made of a mixture of graphite and clay in white, sepia, sanguine, and black

con·temn \kən'tem\ *vt* **contemned**; **contemned** \-temd\ **contemning** \-temiŋ *sometimes* -temniŋ\ **contemns** [ME *contempnen*, fr. MF *contempner, contemner*, fr. L *contemnere*, fr. *com-* + *temnere* to slight, despise — more at STAMP] **:** to view or treat with contempt as mean and despicable **:** reject with disdain **:** DESPISE, SCORN ⟨those who have ~*ed* its visual art —David Sylvester⟩ **syn** see DESPISE

con·tem·ner *also* **con·tem·nor** \kən'temə(r), -mnə-\ *n* -s [MF *contemneur*, fr. *contemner* + *-eur* -or] **1 :** one that contemns ⟨the agrarian, the ~ of cities —*Times Lit. Supp.*⟩ ⟨the ~ of democracy who outaristocrats the aristocrats —C.C.Abbott⟩ **2** *usu* **contemnor :** one that is held to be in contempt of court

con·tem·per \kən'tempə(r)\ *vt* -ED/-ING/-S [L *contemperare*, fr. *com-* + *temperare* to temper — more at TEMPER] *archaic* **:** to moderate by mixing **:** BLEND, QUALIFY, ADAPT

contemperament *n* -s [LL *contemperamentum*, fr. L *contemperare* + *-mentum* -ment] *obs* **:** CONTEMPERATION

contemperation *n* -s [MF, fr. LL *contemperation-, contemperatio*, fr. L *contemperatus* (past part. of *contemperare*) + *-ion-, -io* -ion] *obs* **:** the act of contempering or state of being contempered **:** ACCOMMODATION; *also* **:** something that contempers **:** COMPROMISE

contemperature *n* -s [MF, fr. L *contemperatus* + MF *-ure*] *obs* **:** harmonious or proportionate mixture

con·tem·pla·ble \kən'templəbəl\ *adj* [L *contemplabilis*, fr. *contemplari* + *-abilis* -able] **:** capable of being contemplated ⟨she found the nearer past . . . framed and ~ like the pictures on the wall —Dorothy M. Richardson⟩

con·tem·plant \-plənt\ *adj* [L *contemplant-, contemplans*, pres. part. of *contemplari*] **:** CONTEMPLATING

con·tem·plate \'käntəm,plāt, -(,)tem-; *rap. often* 'känəm,-; *sporadically and old fash* kən'tem,-; *usu* -ād.+V\ *vb* -ED/-ING/-S [L *contemplatus*, past part. of *contemplari, contemplare*, fr. *com-* + *-templari, -templare* (fr. *templum* space for observation marked out by the augur) — more at TEMPLE] *vt* **1 :** to view with sustained attention **:** gaze at thoughtfully for a noticeable time **:** observe with ostensibly steady reflection ⟨a way of looking her over from beneath lowered lids while he affected to be . . . *contemplating* the tip of his shining boot —Edith Wharton⟩ **2 :** to view mentally with continued thoughtfulness, attention, or reflection **:** muse or ponder about ⟨while in your pride ye ~ your talents, power, or wisdom —William Wordsworth⟩ **3 :** to view mentally in a stated or implied way with thoughtfulness and reflection: **a :** to think about or regard from a certain viewpoint or in a certain light or respect ⟨the opinion . . . that while science, by a deliberate abstraction, ~*s* a world of facts without values, religion ~*s* values apart from facts —W.R.Inge⟩ **b :** to have in view as a purpose **:** anticipate doing or performing **:** plan on **:** INTEND, PLAN ⟨absent-mindedly feeling in their pockets as men do when *contemplating* a purchase —Kenneth Roberts⟩ **c :** to dream of as a cherished aim **:** ENVISION ⟨the moment and the act he had *contemplated* for weeks with a thrill of pleasure —Thomas Hardy⟩ **d :** to presume or imply as a concomitant or result **:** POSTULATE, PRESUPPOSE ⟨the law would seem to ~ that it should be made to the secretary of state —John Marshall⟩ **4 :** to view or regard (as an object or an objective fact) with detachment ⟨since contemplation is an intellectual exercise it cannot allow itself to be identified with the thing *contemplated* —Leon Livingstone⟩ — compare ENJOY **~** *vi* **:** PONDER, MUSE, MEDITATE ⟨to sit still and ~ — to remember the faces of women without desire —R.L.Stevenson⟩ **syn** see CONSIDER

con·tem·plat·ing·ly *adv* **:** CONTEMPLATIVELY

con·tem·pla·tion \,käntəm'plāshən, -(,)tem'-\ *n* -s [ME *contemplacioun*, fr. OF *contemplation*, fr. L *contemplation-, contemplatio*, fr. *contemplatus* + *-ion-, -io* -ion] **1 a :** meditation on spiritual things as a form of private devotion **b :** a state of mystical awareness of God's being or presence **:** an ecstatic perception of God ⟨a state of rapture . . . in which the soul is freed from its senses and organs and lost in pure ~ —Frank Thilly⟩ **2 :** an act of the mind in considering with attention **:** continued attention to a particular subject **:** MEDITATION, MUSING, STUDY **3** *obs* **:** REGARD, CONSIDERATION; *also* **:** something for which such consideration is asked **:** PETITION, PRAYER, REQUEST **4 :** the act of viewing steadfastly and attentively **:** the viewing of something (as a picture or a scene) for its own sake **5 :** the act of looking forward to an event **:** the act of intending or considering a future event **:** EXPECTATION ⟨a shooting match . . . and other sports were in ~ —S.E.White⟩

[1]**con·tem·pla·tive** \kən'templəd·|iv, -ət|iv, *also* |əv; 'käntəm,plād·|iv, -(,)tem-, -āt|iv *also* |əv\ *adj* [ME, fr. MF *contemplatif*, fr. L *contemplativus*, fr. *contemplatus* + *-ivus* -ive] **1 :** marked by or accompanied by contemplation **:** addicted to contemplation **:** suggesting or suited to contemplation **:** MEDITATIVE **2** *usu* kən'templə-\ **:** practicing or devoted to meditation (as religious meditation and prayer) ⟨the ~ life⟩ ⟨merely a ~ thinker, withdrawn from active life —Theodore Spencer⟩ **3** *obs* **a :** THEORETICAL **b :** THEORIZING — **con·tem·pla·tive·ly** \-əvlē, -li\ *adv* — **con·tem·pla·tive·ness** \-ivnəs, -ēv- *also* -əv-\ *n* -ES

[2]**contemplative** \kən'tem-\ *n* -s [ME, fr. MF *contemplatif*, fr. *contemplatif*, adj.] **:** one who practices contemplation

con·tem·pla·tor \'käntəm,plād·ə(r), -(,)tem-, -ātə-\ *n* -s [L, fr. *contemplatus* + *-or*] **1 :** a person who contemplates or is contemplative **2** *obs* **:** THEORIZER, SPECULATOR

[1]**con·tem·po·ra·ne·an** \kən¦tempə¦rānēən, (')kän-, -nyən\ *adj* [L *contemporaneus* + E *-an*] **:** CONTEMPORANEOUS

[2]**contemporanean** \"\ *n* -s **:** CONTEMPORARY

con·tem·po·ra·ne·i·ty \kən,tempərə¦nēəd·ē, (')kän-, -ətē, -i\ *n* -ES [fr. *contemporaneous*, after such pairs as E *spontaneous: spontaneity*] **:** the quality or state of being contemporaneous

con·tem·po·ra·ne·ous \kən¦tempə¦rānēəs, (')kän¦-, -nyəs\ *adj* [L *contemporaneus*, fr. *com-* + *tempor-, tempus* time + *-aneus* (as in *subterraneus* subterranean) — more at TEMPORAL] **1 :** existing or occurring during the same time (as during a year, decade, or longer span of time) ⟨the Classical Revival or Federal style, which was virtually ~ with the Regency in England —*Amer. Guide Series: Pa.*⟩ ⟨love of school is not ~ with residence therein; it is an after product —C.H.Grandgent⟩ **2 :** originating, arising, or being formed or made at the same time **:** marked by characteristics compatible with such origin ⟨the portions of the reef that are surrounded by ~, pure, fragmentary limestone —*Jour. of Geol.*⟩ **syn** see CONTEMPORARY

con·tem·po·ra·ne·ous·ly *adv* **:** at or near the same time

con·tem·po·ra·ne·ous·ness *n* -ES **:** CONTEMPORANEITY

con·tem·po·rar·i·ly \kən¦tempə¦rerəlē, (')kän¦-, -li\ *adv* **:** CONTEMPORANEOUSLY

con·tem·po·rariness \=ˈ==,=rēnəs, -rin-, =,==ˈ===\ *n* -ES **:** the quality or state of being contemporary

[1]**con·tem·po·rary** \kən'tempə,rerē, -ri\ *adj* [*com-* + L *temporarius* of time, temporary — more at TEMPORARY] **1 :** happening, existing, living, or coming into being during the same time, sometimes during the same year, decade, century, or period as something else mentioned ⟨Dante had put some ~ popes in Hell —M.R.Cohen⟩ ⟨Renaissance painting, which was ~ with the great age of exploration —Lewis Mumford⟩ and sometimes during the present ⟨we are not without ~ talent; but for works of genius we must still look to the past —Edith Wharton⟩ ⟨the avenging on the ~ woman of resentments inculcated by an earlier woman —Philip Wylie⟩ **2 a :** occurring at the same moment **:** SIMULTANEOUS ⟨~ turns of two wheels⟩ **b :** having existed through the same period **:** originating at the same time ⟨~ rock strata⟩ **3 :** of or as though of the present period **:** marked by characteristics compatible with being of the present period; *sometimes* **:** ADVANCED, MODERN, UP-TO-DATE **:** au courant ⟨peculiarly ~ in his anxiety, his longing for a faith —Alfred Kazin⟩

syn CONTEMPORANEOUS, SIMULTANEOUS, SYNCHRONOUS, COEVAL, COETANEOUS, COINCIDENT, CONCOMITANT, CONCURRENT: CONTEMPORARY, indicating, like the others, existence or incidence at the same time, is likely to be used in reference to years, decades, lifetimes, and similar time spans ⟨Faraday's work on electricity coupled with Joseph Henry's exactly *contemporary* research on the electromagnet —Lewis Mumford⟩ ⟨*contemporary* with those intermediaries, or following hard upon them, were the great missionaries or converters —H.O.Taylor⟩ There is little difference between CONTEMPORARY and the less common CONTEMPORANEOUS ⟨the A. F. of L. was closer to *contemporaneous* British labor organizations than to the American Knights of Labor —Allan Nevins & H.S.Commager⟩ SIMULTANEOUS is likely to describe occurrence of two things at precisely the same minute or within the same limited period of time ⟨the three men, deftly timing the roll, made a *simultaneous* leap aboard the schooner —Jack London⟩ ⟨control of the air involves the *simultaneous* use of two types of planes — first, the long-range heavy bomber; second, light bombers, dive bombers, torpedo planes —F.D.Roosevelt⟩ SYNCHRONOUS may describe continuing action taking place over somewhat longer periods ⟨French speech has run a similar and almost *synchronous* course with English —Havelock Ellis⟩ COEVAL may be used in reference to periods, ages, eras, eons ⟨if the meteorites represent fragments of the solar system, we may conclude that the system is *coeval* with the Earth —F.L.Whipple⟩ COETANEOUS, a close synonym of COEVAL, may suggest origination at the same time ⟨the Alleghenies and other *coetaneous* mountain chains⟩ COINCIDENT refers to occurrences, events, incidents, developments taking place at the same time but may minimize ideas of causal relationship ⟨the growth of the mine union movement was *coincident* with the growth of business and manufacturing —T.R.Hay⟩ CONCOMITANT describes a development taking place at the same time but one of subordinate incidental character ⟨a bite from any carnivorous animal is likely to lead to some measure of *concomitant* poisoning —*Discovery*⟩ ⟨*concomitant* with the creation of these new rhythms came . . . "the dance craze" —Oscar Hammerstein *b*1895⟩ CONCURRENT may add to the idea of occurrence at the same time the notion of accord, agreement, fitness between the things involved ⟨great cultural achievements have not been inevitably, or even generally, *concurrent* with great material power —Lyman Bryson⟩

[2]**contemporary** \"\ *n* -ES **1 :** one that is contemporary with another ⟨Petrarch and Chaucer were *contemporaries*⟩ **2 :** one of the same or nearly the same age as another **3 :** a newspaper or periodical contemporary with another

con·tem·po·rize \kən'tempə,rīz\ *vb* -ED/-ING/-S [LL *contemporare* (fr. L *com-* + *-temporare*, fr. *tempor-, tempus* time) + E *-ize* — more at TEMPORAL] *vt* **:** to make contemporary **~** *vi* **:** to be contemporary **:** SYNCHRONIZE

[1]**con·tempt** \kən'tem(p)t\ *n* -s [ME, fr. L *contemptus*, fr. *contemptus*, past part. of *contemnere* to despise — more at CONTEMN] **1 a :** the act of despising or the state of mind of one who despises **:** the feeling with which one regards something that is esteemed low, vile, or worthless **:** DISDAIN, SCORN **b :** the condition of having no respect, concern, or regard for something ⟨and, in ~ of heaven and hell, dies rather than bear some yoke of priests or kings —John Masefield⟩ **2 :** the state of being despised **:** DISGRACE, SHAME ⟨bring his nation into ~⟩ **3** *obs* **:** an object of contempt **4 a :** willful disobedience to or open disrespect of the valid rules, orders, or process or the dignity or authority of a court or a judge acting in a judicial capacity whether by contumacious or insolent language, by disturbing or obstructive conduct, or by mere failure to obey the orders of the court **b :** willful disobedience to a lawful order of or willful obstruction of a legislative body in the actual course of exercising its lawful legislative powers **c :** an act or expression denoting such contempt of judicial or legislative authority

[2]**contempt** \"\ *vt* -ED/-ING/-S *archaic* **:** CONTEMN

con·tempt·ibil·i·ty \kən,tem(p)tə'bilǝd·ē, -i\ *n* -ES [LL *contemptibilitas*, fr. *contemptibilis* + L *-itas* -ity] **:** the quality or state of being contemptible **:** also **:** an instance of this

con·tempt·ible \kən'tem(p)təbəl\ *adj* [ME, fr. LL *contemptibilis*, fr. L *contemptus* (past part. of *contemnere* to despise) + *-ibilis* -ible — more at CONTEMN] **1 :** worthy of contempt **:** meriting scorn and condemnation as paltry, mean, base, or vile **:** held in contempt ⟨the Christianity which these emperors aimed at suppressing was . . . philosophically ~, politically subversive, and morally abominable —Matthew Arnold⟩ **2 :** worthy of being scorned, rejected, or ignored esp. for poverty or penury **:** unworthy of consideration ⟨with that property he will never be a ~ man —Jane Austen⟩ **3** *obs* **:** SCORNFUL, CONTEMPTUOUS ⟨'tis very possible he'll scorn it, for the man . . . hath a ~ spirit —Shak.⟩

syn DESPICABLE, PITIABLE, SORRY, SCURVY, CHEAP, BEGGARLY, SHABBY: CONTEMPTIBLE means deserving of contempt for any reason ⟨a curse may, like rags and dirt, be supposed to benefit a man by making him appear vile and *contemptible* —J.G.Frazer⟩ ⟨the one disgraceful, unpardonable, and to all time *contemptible* action of my life was to allow myself to appeal to society for help and protection —Oscar Wilde⟩ DESPICABLE, a more scornful term, may indicate utter worthlessness or suggest bitterness and indignation ⟨all things are sold . . . the smallest and most *despicable* —P.B.Shelley⟩ ⟨even excellent science could and did often make *despicable* morality —Christian Gauss⟩ PITIABLE applies to that which inspires mixed contempt and pity ⟨the resorting to epithets . . . is a *pitiable* display of intellectual impotence —M.R. Cohen⟩ ⟨that *pitiable* husk of a man . . . a shadow of his former insolence and splendor —E.V.Lucas⟩ SORRY is close to PITIABLE and suggests inadequacy, wretchedness, or sordidness ⟨I am a *sorry* physician and do but aggravate a disorder which I am seeking to cure —Benjamin Jowett⟩ ⟨one bids the poor pretender take his *sorry* self, a trouble and disgrace, from out the sacred presence —Robert Browning⟩ SCURVY implies the mean and vile inspiring disgust and contempt ⟨the *scurvy* mutilation of a portrait by a noble lord who had sat for it and then did not like it —C.E.Montague⟩ ⟨since some villain robbed his mates of their pork, we'll put it out of his power to play that *scurvy* trick again —C.B.Nordhoff & J.N.Hall⟩ CHEAP and BEGGARLY imply the petty, mean, and paltry ⟨any cheap and facile gibes about the duplicity and dissimulation of that church —T.S.Eliot⟩ ⟨the South in 1800 was a land of contrasts, of opulence and squalor . . . fine mansions, *beggarly* taverns —Van Wyck Brooks⟩ CHEAP may also indicate meretricious availability ⟨the wide insatiable mouth, painted as red as a wound, and the flaunting bare knees . . . *cheap*, that was the trouble —Ellen Glasgow⟩ SHABBY connotes the tawdry, worn-out, or ignoble ⟨a *shabby* electric sign that had said *Cedar Hill* before it lost its globes —Dashiell Hammett⟩ ⟨the old story, ever *shabby*, ever pitiful, of a man for whom intrigue was a substitute for creativeness —Max Lerner⟩

con·tempt·ible·ness *n* -ES \-nəs\ **:** the quality or state of being contemptible

con·tempt·ibly \kən'tem(p)təblē, -li\ *adv* **1 :** in a contemptible manner **2** *obs* **:** CONTEMPTUOUSLY

contempt of court **:** CONTEMPT 4a

con·temp·tu·ous \kən'tem(p)chəwəs\ *adj* [L *contemptus* contempt + E *-ous*] **1 :** manifesting, feeling, or expressing contempt or disdain ⟨the crowd were actively against him, and he was utterly ~ and indifferent —Ernest Hemingway⟩ ⟨the gambler smiled a thin, ~ smile —Dashiell Hammett⟩ **2** *archaic* **:** contemptible or exciting contempt **:** DESPICABLE — **con·temp·tu·ous·ly** *adv* — **con·temp·tu·ous·ness** *n* -ES

con·tend \kən'tend\ *vb* -ED/-ING/-S [MF or L; MF *contendre*, fr. L *contendere* to stretch vigorously, to strive, contend, fr. *com-* + *tendere* to stretch — more at TEND] *vi* **1 :** to strive or vie esp. with determination and exertion in contest or rivalry or against difficulties, exigencies, or failings ⟨the Manichean theory of a good and an evil spirit ~*ing* on nearly equal terms —W.R.Inge⟩ ⟨the *African Queen* might soon be ~*ing* with difficulties of refueling —C.S.Forester⟩ **2 :** to strive in debate **:** engage in discussion **:** ARGUE ⟨stubbornly ~*ed* for what he believed to be the truth —H.E.Starr⟩ **~** *vt* **1 :** MAINTAIN, ASSERT, ARGUE ⟨~*ing* that literature must serve a moral function —C.I.Glicksberg⟩ **2 :** to struggle for **:** CONTEST ⟨she ~*ed* every point, objected to every request —Margaret Mead⟩

syn COPE, FIGHT, BATTLE, WAR: CONTEND is a general term indicating endeavoring or striving to vanquish an opponent or to overcome difficulties or adversities ⟨the lusty wrestlers shall *contend* —William Wordsworth⟩ ⟨ladies *contended* for the honor of being taken down to dinner by the brilliant French journalist —W.C.Brownell⟩ ⟨since they had left the Espanola country behind them, they had *contended* first with wind and sandstorms, and now with cold —Willa Cather⟩ COPE may imply contending with an adversary on even or better than even terms and defeating or parrying his efforts, or facing adversity, difficulty, exigency and finding expedients ⟨a boy of barely sixteen cannot stand against the moral pressure of a father and mother who have always oppressed him any more than he can *cope* physically with a powerful full-grown man —Samuel Butler †1902⟩ ⟨the National Government had to *cope* with . . . provincial separatism —Owen & Eleanor Lattimore⟩ ⟨the inadequate medical staff, without drugs, could not *cope* with the situation —W.B.Hesseltine⟩ FIGHT is likely to involve notions of more strenuous activity or even violence than CONTEND or COPE; it suggests constant vigorous effort ⟨while Spaniards *fought* back with gun and Gospel to retain control of territories painfully won —R.A. Billington⟩ ⟨the advocates of the old classical education have been gallantly *fighting* a losing battle for over half a century —W.R.Inge⟩ ⟨he had *fought* like a demon every inch of the way against poverty and discouragement —A.W.Long⟩ BATTLE and WAR are more figurative; the first suggests contending as under battle conditions, with fierce fighting, resolute attack and defense, and changing fortunes ⟨grimy rescue teams working in shifts *battled* gas and smoke tonight attempting to reach an estimated sixty men still entombed by a Christmastide mine explosion —*N. Y. Times*⟩ ⟨thou wouldst have nobly stirred thyself and *battled* for the right —William Wordsworth⟩; the second suggests sustained struggle as under war conditions ⟨to *war* against my people and my knights —Alfred Tennyson⟩ ⟨spent his life *warring* against war, and disease, and poverty —V.L.Parrington⟩ ⟨housewife that is forever *warring* with the dust —Edith Sitwell⟩ **syn** see in addition COMPETE

con·tend·er \-də(r)\ *n* -S : CONTESTANT; *esp* : a contestant for a championship or high honor ⟨the leading ~ in his class⟩

1con·tent \kən'tent\ *adj* [ME *contente, content,* fr. MF *content,* fr. L *contentus,* fr. past part. of *continēre* to contain, hold together, restrain — more at CONTAIN] **1 a** : having the desires limited to whatever one has : not disposed to complain or grumble : SATISFIED, CONTENTED ⟨~ with any food that God doth send —Edmund Spenser⟩ **b** : inclined by wish, ambition, or design to no greater state or further act or advance than that specified ⟨presidents who have been ~ to leave the active leadership . . . to . . . Congress —A.N.Holcombe⟩ ⟨~ to wait his turn⟩ **2 a** : GRATIFIED, PLEASED — archaic except in the phrase *well content* **b** *archaic* : WILLING, CONSENTING **3** : ASSENTING, AGREEING — used specif. in the British House of Lords as an affirmative response in voting

2content \"\ *vt* -ED/-ING/-S [ME *contenten,* fr. MF *contenter,* fr. *content,* adj.] **1** : to make content : appease the desires of : SATISFY ⟨my own garden must ~ me this year —A.T.Quiller-Couch⟩ **2** : to limit (oneself) in requirements for satisfaction or in immediate desires or actions — used with *with* ⟨he ~*ed* himself with threats⟩ **3** *obs* **a** : to satisfy the expectations or claims of : PAY **b** : GRATIFY, PLEASE ⟨his painted skin ~*s* the eye —Shak.⟩ **syn** see SATISFY

3content \"\ *n* -S [1*content*] **1** : the state of being content : SATISFACTION, CONTENTMENT; *esp* : freedom from dissatisfaction, anxiety, or agitation ⟨cuddles down . . . with a grunt of sleepy ~ —Stephen Crane⟩ ⟨ate to his heart's ~⟩ — formerly also used in pl. **2** *obs* : acquiescence without examination ⟨the sense they humbly take upon ~ —Alexander Pope⟩ **3** *obs* : something that contents : a means of contentment **4 a** : an expression of assent to a bill or motion in the British House of Lords **b** : a member of the House of Lords who votes assent

4content \'kän,tent *sometimes* kən't-\ *n* -S [ME, fr. *content,* adj., contained, fr. L *contentus,* past part. of *continēre* to contain — more at CONTAIN] **1** *usu pl* **a** : something that is contained : the thing, things, or substance in a receptacle or an enclosed space ⟨he emptied his pocket of its ~*s*⟩ ⟨the ~*s* of the room⟩ **b** : the topics, ideas, facts, or statements in a book, document, or letter ⟨a table of ~*s*⟩ ⟨summarize the ~*s* of a will⟩ **2 a** : the matter esp. of a book or discourse : SUBJECT MATTER, SUBSTANCE ⟨when a man has nothing to say . . . sonority without ~ is the smartest effect he can achieve —G.W.Johnson⟩ **b** : essential meaning or significance ⟨if Zionism is to have ~ and vitality, it must impose obligation —Rose L. Halprin⟩ ⟨trying to translate these words "human values" . . . into . . . technical terminology and to put some ~ into them —F.S.C.Northrop⟩ **c** : the sum of events, physical detail, and information embodied in a work of art esp. as it gives rise to ideas and emotions — often contrasted with *form* **3** *archaic* **a** : CAPACITY, SIZE ⟨the ~ of a cask⟩ **b** : quantity of space, area, or length contained in certain limits : VOLUME ⟨the solid ~ of a tree⟩ **4 a** : the matter dealt with in a field of study : the subject matter of a discipline or an educational course ⟨the ~ of a national culture⟩ ⟨the ~ of sociology is inexhaustible —F.H.Giddings⟩ **b** : something that constitutes a part or element or a series of parts considered abstractly or without precise determination ⟨~ of consciousness⟩ **5** : the amount of specified material contained, present, or yielded : PROPORTION ⟨the sulfur ~ of a sample of coal⟩ ⟨to reduce the soda ~ and increase the silica in glass⟩

content analysis *n* [4*content*] : a detailed study and analysis of the manifest and latent content of various types of communication (as newspapers, radio programs, and propaganda films) through a classification, tabulation, and evaluation of their key symbols and themes in order to ascertain their meaning and probable effect

contentation *n* -S [ME *contentacioun* payment, fr. ML *contentation-, contentatio,* fr. *contentatus* (past part. of *contentare* to pay, satisfy, fr. L *contentus*) + -*ion-, -io* -ion] **1** *obs* : a making or being contented; *also* : whatever makes one content **2** *obs* : state of contentment

con·tent·ed \kən'tentəd\ *adj* **1** : CONTENT : easy in mind : satisfied esp. with one's lot in life : characterized by or suggesting contentment ⟨leading ~ lives⟩ ⟨a ~ little sigh⟩ **2** *obs* : WILLING — **con·tent·ed·ly** *adv*

con·tent·ed·ness \-nəs\ *n* -ES : CONTENTMENT

con·ten·tion \kən'tenchən\ *n* -S [ME *contencioun,* fr. MF, fr. L *contention-, contentio,* fr. *contentus* (past part. of *contendere* to contend) + -*ion-, -io* -ion — more at CONTEND] **1** : an act or instance of contending : violent effort or struggle to obtain, resist, or compete : CONFLICT, STRIFE ⟨in spite of the violent ~*s* of the great . . . many of the cities of Italy were advancing on in prosperity —C.E.Norton⟩ **2** : strife in words : ALTERCATION, CONTROVERSY, SQUABBLING ⟨to escape the theological ~*s* in the Congregational parish —S.E.Morison⟩ — often used in the phrase *bone of contention* **3** : a point advanced or maintained in a debate or argument : the subject matter of debate or strife : CLAIM, CHARGE, THESIS ⟨supporting his ~ with biblical and mythological evidence —*Amer. Guide Series: Pa.*⟩ ⟨the ~ that the growers . . . concurred with the pricing and grading —*Farmer's Weekly (So. Africa)*⟩ **4** *archaic* : strong effort : earnest striving ⟨a study that requires effort and ~ of mind —William Whewell⟩ **5** : RIVALRY, COMPETITION ⟨too slow to keep him in ~ with even the cheapest of company —D.M.Mankiewicz⟩ **syn** see DISCORD

con·ten·tion·al \-chən°l\ *adj* : characterized by contention : CONTENTIOUS

con·ten·tious \kən'tenchəs\ *adj* [ME *contenciose,* fr. L *contentiosus,* fr. *contentio* contention + -*osus* -ose, -ous] **1 a** : given to contention : marked by an often perverse and wearisome tendency to quarrels and disputes ⟨a ~ nature⟩ **b** : engaged in, employed in, or serving to carry on contention ⟨~ language⟩ ⟨~ objection⟩ ⟨the most ~, quarrelsome, disagreeing crew —George Berkeley⟩ **2** : likely to cause contention : apt to arouse argument, conflict, or marked difference of opinion ⟨a ~ argument⟩ ⟨a ~ issue⟩ **3** : relating to or involving the litigation of differences between contending parties **syn** see BELLIGERENT

contentious jurisdiction *n* : jurisdiction over matters in controversy — compare VOLUNTARY JURISDICTION

con·ten·tious·ly *adv* : in a contentious manner

con·ten·tious·ness *n* -ES : QUARRELSOMENESS

1con·tent·less \kən'tentləs\ *adj* : DISSATISFIED

2con·tent·less \'kän,tentləs *sometimes* kən't-\ *adj* : lacking content or meaning

con·tent·ment \kən'tentmənt\ *n* -S [ME *contentement,* fr. MF, fr. *contenter* to content + -*ment* — more at CONTENT] **1** *archaic* : the act or process of making content : SATISFYING ⟨~ of avarice is impossible⟩ **2** : the quality or state of being contented **3** : something that affords content or pleasure ⟨an old man's small ~⟩ **a** *archaic* : GRATIFICATION, PLEASURE

content psychology \'=,=-\ *n* [4*content*] : the study of the components and constituents of consciousness specif. by introspective methods — contrasted with *act psychology*

contents *pres 3d sing of* CONTENT, *pl of* CONTENT

content subject *n* [4*content*] : a subject (as history, geography, science) studied in order to acquire a certain body of information rather than to achieve competence in a skill (as penmanship, typing, or composition)

con·terminal \kən, (')kän+\ *adj* [ML *conterminalis,* fr. L *com-* + *terminalis* terminal — more at TERMINAL] : CONTERMINOUS

con·terminate \kən, (')kän+\ *adj* [LL *conterminatus,* past part. of *conterminare* to border on, fr. L *com-* + *terminare* to terminate — more at TERMINATE] : CONTERMINOUS

contermine *vb* -ED/-ING/-S [F *conterminer,* fr. LL *conterminare*] *vt, obs* : to make conterminous ~ *vi, obs* : to be conterminous

con·ter·mi·nous \kən'tərm(ə)nəs, (')kän¦-, -tə̄m-\ *adj* [L *conterminus,* fr. *com-* + *terminus* boundary — more at TERM] **1 a** : having a common boundary (as with another section or country) : BORDERING, ADJACENT ⟨the side of Germany ~ with France⟩ ⟨Colorado and Utah are ~⟩ **b** *of a boundary* : COMMON, COINCIDENT ⟨states with a ~ boundary⟩ **2** : COTERMINOUS **3** : enclosed within one common boundary ⟨the 48 ~ states of the U.S.⟩ **syn** see ADJACENT

con·ter·mi·nous·ly *adv* : in a conterminous manner or position : so as to be conterminous

contes *pl of* CONTE

con·tes·sa \kən'tesə\ *n* -S [It, fem. of *conte* count, fr. L *comit-, comes* associate, companion — more at COUNT] : COUNTESS

contesseration *n* -S [LL *contesseration-, contesseratio,* fr. *contesseratus* (past part. of *contesserare* to contract friendship by means of tesserae, fr. L *com-* + *tessera* die, square tablet, token of friendship) + L -*ion-, -io* -ion — more at TESSERA] *obs* : the act of contracting friendship or union

1con·test \kən'test *also* 'kän,t-\ *vb* -ED/-ING/-S [MF *contester,* fr. L *contestari* to call to witness & *contestari (litem)* to introduce (a lawsuit) by calling witnesses, bring an action, fr. *com-* + *testari* to be a witness, fr. *testis* witness — more at TESTIS] *vt* **1** : to make the subject of dispute, contention, or battle ⟨~ a seat in congress⟩ ⟨~ an issue⟩ ⟨~ a prize⟩ ⟨~ every inch of land in their retreat⟩ **2** : to make a subject of litigation : dispute or resist by course of law : DEFEND ⟨~ a suit⟩ : CONTROVERT ~ *vi* : STRIVE, VIE ⟨~ with an opponent in argument⟩ ⟨~ against too strict regulations⟩

syn RESIST, WITHSTAND, OPPOSE, FIGHT, COMBAT, CONFLICT, ANTAGONIZE: these terms indicate a setting of one person or thing against another in a hostile or competing way and may be roughly distinguished according to the degree to which one of the things or forces takes the initiative against the other. RESIST and WITHSTAND suggest generally that the initiative lies wholly with the person or force competed against. RESIST implies an overt recognition of a hostile or threatening force and a positive effort to counteract it, repel it, or ward it off ⟨the criminal *resisted* captivity⟩ ⟨*resist* the pressure of political orthodoxy⟩ ⟨*resist* the enemy attacks⟩ WITHSTAND suggests a successful resistance so that if nothing is gained, at least nothing is lost ⟨most plants cannot *withstand* frost⟩ ⟨*withstand* the impact of humiliation and disease⟩ ⟨*withstand* the attacks by air⟩ CONTEST and OPPOSE suggest a more positive action against a threatening or objectionable force. CONTEST suggests the raising of the issue, the bringing into open question of the matter over which there is conflict ⟨the board's power to inspect private welfare agencies was later *contested* and restricted —*Amer. Guide Series: N. Y.*⟩ ⟨it is impossible to *contest* your principle —George Meredith⟩ ⟨attempt to reconcile *contesting* parties⟩ OPPOSE, perhaps the most general of the terms, can indicate almost any degree of attitude from mild objection to positive belligerence, and can suggest any action from a mere contrastive setting of one thing against another to open violence against an opposing force, although in all instances positive action is implied ⟨the chronic objector, who *opposes* every popular measure —S.M.Crothers⟩ ⟨he had been much *opposed* by women, crossed, balked, wronged, misled —Francis Hackett⟩ ⟨Whipple was said to be the only man in public life who dared *oppose* wholesale executions of the Sioux captives —*Amer. Guide Series: Minn.*⟩ ⟨human art, as *opposed* to mere tools and mechanical contrivances —Edward Clodd⟩ FIGHT and COMBAT suggest strong action. FIGHT puts the initiative clearly in the hands of the subject of the verb and stresses the forthrightness or belligerence of the action ⟨*fight* the enemy on all fronts⟩ ⟨*fight* the forces of evil⟩ ⟨*fight* extradition⟩ COMBAT stresses more the force or impact, though it says nothing about the success, of counteraction ⟨*combat* pollution in streams⟩ ⟨*combat* aggression⟩ ⟨*combat* business depressions⟩ CONFLICT and ANTAGONIZE do not fit easily into the scale. CONFLICT, never used transitively, indicates merely the fact of competition, friction, or hostility between two forces ⟨the two men *conflict* on all major principles⟩ ⟨one nation can *conflict* with another in territorial claims⟩ ⟨two logical principles often *conflict*⟩ ANTAGONIZE once carried the idea of placing oneself in opposition or in the position of antagonist but in current general use carries only the idea of arousing antagonism or making antagonistic ⟨to *antagonize* the other students in the class⟩ **syn** see in addition COMPETE

2contest \'kän,test\ *n* -S [MF *conteste,* fr. *contester,* v.] **1** : earnest struggle for superiority or victory : COMPETITION, EMULATION, STRIFE, ARGUMENT; *also* : an encounter of such nature (as in arms) ⟨what mighty ~*s* rise from trivial things —Alexander Pope⟩ ⟨reelected almost without a ~⟩ **2** : a competition in which each contestant performs without direct contact with or interference from his competitors — sometimes distinguished from *game* ⟨an oratorical ~⟩

syn CONFLICT, COMBAT, FIGHT, AFFRAY, FRAY: CONTEST is a general term applying orig. to arguments but now also to any competition or struggle ⟨boundary controversies or other *contests* between states (as, for instance, the litigation arising out of Chicago's attempted use of the waters of the Great Lakes) —Felix Frankfurter⟩ ⟨an athletic *contest*⟩ ⟨prominent among the great events which the 18th century witnessed was the *contest* between England and France for the control of the Mississippi valley —G.M.Capers⟩ CONFLICT implies a jarring clash ranging from discordant argument through any sustained active opposition up to warfare ⟨he then returned to Massachusetts with authority to enlist troops, which led to a *conflict* with the state authorities —C.R.Fish⟩ ⟨primitive competition was a *conflict* as to which should murder the other man and his wife and children; modern competition in the shape of war still takes this form —Bertrand Russell⟩ COMBAT implies an encounter, often an armed one ⟨these progressive leaders in both parties rose only after bitter struggle. They were the product of more than a lively contest. Sometimes the contests were *combats* —W.A.White⟩ ⟨he [Alexander the Great] had mastered, in defiance of fatigue, hardship, and *combat* . . . unknown Indian regions —George Grote⟩ FIGHT implies a rigorous strenuous struggle, sustained at high pitch for a time at least, and resolute and determined ⟨the *fight* at the rampart⟩ ⟨the *fight* for world peace⟩ ⟨mental *fight* means thinking against the current, not with it. That current flows fast and furious —Virginia Woolf⟩ AFFRAY, now somewhat literary in suggestion, may indicate a wild, confused, sharp fight ⟨the suppressing of riots and *affrays* —Edmund Burke⟩ ⟨*affray*.— Fighting together of two or more persons in a public place to the terror of the persons lawfully there —*General Laws of the Commonwealth of Mass.*⟩ FRAY, also somewhat literary, may apply to any fight or combat marked by quick individual action against a background of noisy confusion ⟨a *fray* is a fight in a public place to the terror of the people, in which acts of violence occur or dangerous weapons are exhibited or threatened to be used —*U.S. Manual for Courts-Martial*⟩

con·test·able \kən'testəbəl, 'kän,te-\ *adj* [F, fr. *contester* to contest + -*able* — more at CONTEST] : capable of being contested — **con·test·ably** \-blē\ *adv*

1con·tes·tant \kən'testənt *also* 'kän,-\ *n* -S [F, fr. pres. part. of *contester*] : one that participates in a contest; *specif* : one that contests or challenges an award or decision (as in election returns or in legal proceedings)

2contestant \"\ *adj* [F, pres. part.] : CONTESTING, DISPUTING ⟨the ~ parties in a court action⟩

con·tes·ta·tion \,käntə'stāshən, -(,)te's-\ *n* -S [MF & L; MF, fr. L *contestation-, contestatio,* fr. *contestatus* (past part. of *contestari* to call to witness) + -*ion-, -io* -ion — more at CONTEST] **1** : an act or instance of contesting : CONTROVERSY, COMPETITION **2** : a position assumed or a point made in controversy : CONTENTION **3** : the preface of the Mass — used in the old Gallican liturgy

contested *past of* CONTEST

contested election *n* : an election of which the legality or validity of the result is challenged by the losing candidate

con·test·ee \¦käntə¦stē, -(,)te¦s-; kən¦te¦s-\ *n* -S [1*contest* + -*ee*] : one whose election is contested

contesting *pres part of* CONTEST

contests *pres 3d sing of* CONTEST, *pl of* CONTEST

con·teur \kōn'tər, kōⁿ't-\ *n, pl* **conteurs** \-r(z)\ [F, fr. *conter* to relate, count + -*eur* -or — more at COUNT] : a reciter or composer of contes : STORYTELLER

con·text \'kän,tekst\ *n* -S [ME, fr. L *contextus* connection, coherence, fr. *contextus,* past part. of *contexere* to weave, join together, fr. *com-* + *texere* to weave — more at TECHNICAL] **1** *obs* : the weaving together of words in language; *also* : the discourse or writing so produced **2** : the part or parts of a written or spoken passage preceding or following a particular word or group of words and so intimately associated with them as to throw light upon their meaning **3** : the interrelated conditions in which something exists or occurs : ENVIRONMENT ⟨historical ~⟩ ⟨within the general ~ of world disarmament —M.W.Straight⟩ ⟨that each man have an understanding of himself and of his job in its ~ —Oscar Handlin⟩ **4** *obs* **a** : coherence in discourse **b** : CONTEXTURE **5** : things or conditions that serve to date or characterize an article (as a primitive artifact) : SURROUNDINGS **6** : the fleshy part of the pileus of a mushroom or other pileate fungus as distinguished from the hymenium

con·tex·tu·al \kən'tekschəwəl, (')kän¦-\ *adj* [*context* + -*ual* (as in *textual*)] : in, relating to, determined by, or conforming to a context — **con·tex·tu·al·ly** \-wəlē, -li\ *adv*

contextual definition *n* : a definition in which the meaning of a word, expression, or symbol is partly or wholly determined by defining the meaning of a larger expression containing the definiendum (as a definition of *legal right* by the statement "X has a *legal right* to y = X has a claim upon somebody for possession of y which the courts will sustain") — contrasted with *explicit definition;* compare RECURSIVE DEFINITION

con·tex·tu·al·ism \kən'tekschəwə,lizəm\ *n* -S : PRAGMATISM, OPERATIONALISM

con·tex·tu·al·ist \-ləst\ *n* -S : PRAGMATIST, OPERATIONALIST

con·tex·tu·al·is·tic \kən¦tekschəwə¦listik, (')kän¦-\ *adj* : of, relating to, or having the characteristics of contextualism

con·tex·tur·al \kən'tekschərəl\ *adj* : relating to or producing contexture

con·tex·ture \kən'tekschə(r)\ *n* -S [F, fr. L *contextus* + F -*ure*] **1** : the act or process of weaving or of assembling and putting together parts into a connected structure **2** : the arrangement and union of the constituent parts of a thing ⟨myriads of flies . . . rose up momentarily; then, keeping their ~ like a veil, fell into place again —Hugh McCrae⟩ : structural character of a thing ⟨a critic with no perception of the ~ of the narrative⟩ : physical constitution : TEXTURE **3** : a body or structure made by the interweaving or putting together of parts ⟨this sweet shady arbor . . . a ~ of woodbines, sweetbriar, jessamine, and myrtle —Izaak Walton⟩ : FABRIC ⟨a ~ of lies⟩ **4** : CONTEXT ⟨setting him clearly in the ~ of his time as none of the biographies has done it —*New Republic*⟩

contg *abbr* containing

con·ti·cent \'käntəsənt\ *adj* [L *conticent-, conticens,* pres. part. of *conticēre* to be silent, fr. *com-* + *tacēre* to be silent — more at TACIT] : SILENT

con·tig·na·tion \,käntəg'nāshən\ *n* -S [L *contignation-, contignatio,* fr. *contignatus* (past part. of *contignare* to join with beams, fr. *com-* + -*tignare,* fr. *tignum* beam) + -*ion-, -io* -ion — more at STAKE] **1** *archaic* : a framing together of timbers : a joining esp. of beams and boards **2** *archaic* **a** : FRAMEWORK, STRUCTURE **b** : FLOOR, STORY

con·ti·gu·i·ty \,käntə'gyüəd·ē, -ətē, -i\ *n* -ES [F or L; F *contiguité,* fr. ML *contiguitat-, contiguitas,* fr. L *contiguus* + -*itat-, -itas* -ity] **1** : the state of being contiguous : intimate association or relation : close proximity **2** *obs* : a continuous mass or series

con·tig·u·ous \kən'tigyəwəs\ *adj* [L *contiguus,* fr. *contingere* to touch on all sides — more at CONTINGENT] **1 a** (1) : touching along boundaries often for considerable distances ⟨Kentucky and Tennessee are ~⟩ ⟨a lot ~ to a road⟩ (2) *of angles* : ADJACENT 2 **b** : next or adjoining with nothing similar intervening ⟨the ~ bedroom —W.M.Thackeray⟩ ⟨two ~ benches —Jane Austen⟩ **c** : NEARBY, CLOSE : not distant ⟨while the dwelling vibrates to the din of the ~ torrent —William Wordsworth⟩ **d** : CONTINUOUS, UNBROKEN, UNINTERRUPTED : touching or connected throughout ⟨the houses . . . ~ all along from end to end of the town —Nathaniel Hawthorne⟩ **2 a** : immediately preceding or following in time or sequence : without intervening interval or item; *also* : involving items so occurring or arranged **b** : near in time or sequence **syn** see ADJACENT

con·tig·u·ous·ly *adv* : in a position or way that is contiguous

con·tig·u·ous·ness *n* -ES : CONTIGUITY

con·ti·nence \'känt(°)nən(t)s, -tənən-\ *also* **con·ti·nen·cy** \-t(°)nənsē, -tənən-, -si\ *n, pl* **continences** *also* **continencies** [*continence* fr. ME, fr. MF, fr. L *continentia,* fr. *continent-, continens* + -*ia* -y; *continency* fr. L *continentia*] **1** : self-restraint from yielding to impulse or desire ⟨he knew what to say, so he knows also when to leave off, a ~ which is practiced by few writers —John Dryden⟩ **2** : self-restraint in refraining from sexual intercourse **3** : the ability to retain a bodily discharge voluntarily ⟨fecal ~⟩

1con·ti·nent \'känt(°)nənt, -tənənt\ *adj* [ME, fr. MF, fr. L *continent-, continens,* fr. pres. part. of *continēre* to hold together, repress, contain — more at CONTAIN] **1** : exercising continence, specif. sexual continence : TEMPERATE, MODERATE, CHASTE **2** *obs* **a** : serving to restrain or limit : RESTRICTIVE **b** : CONNECTED, CONTINUOUS ⟨~ islands⟩ **3** : containing or able to contain or retain **syn** see SOBER

2continent \" *sometimes* -t°n,ent *or* -tə,ne-\ *n* -S [in senses 1, 2, & 3, fr. L *continent-, continens,* pres. part. of *continēre* to contain, hold together, be continuous; in other senses, fr. L *continent-, continens* continuous mass of land, fr. *continent-, continens,* pres. part.] **1** *archaic* **a** : whatever contains something : RECEPTACLE **b** : whatever restrains or bounds something **2** *archaic* : whatever is the seat or the external representative of something or represents the totality of a complex being **3** *obs* : CAPACITY, CONTENT **4 a** : a continuous extent or mass of land : MAINLAND **b** *obs* : the land, the earth, or the world **5 a** : one of the great divisions of land on the globe; *specif* : a large body of land differing from an island or a peninsula in its size and in its structure, which is that of a large basin bordered by mountain chains (as No. America, So. America, Europe, Asia, Africa, Australia, and Antarctica) **b** *usu cap* : the continent of Europe — used with *the* ⟨traveling on the *Continent*⟩ **6** : a large segment of the earth's outer shell including a terrestrial continent and the adjacent continental shelf

1con·ti·nen·tal \¦känt°n¦ent°l, -tə¦ne-, -təl *also rap. attrib* 'känt,ne-\ *adj* [2*continent* + -*al*] **1 a** : of or relating to the continent of Europe or the countries of the continent of Europe as distinguished from the British Isles **b** : of or relating to the continent of No. America **c** (1) *often cap* : of, relating to, or concerning the colonies or states later forming the U.S. ⟨*Continental* Congress⟩ (2) : WORTHLESS, CONFOUNDED — used in imprecation in negative expressions such as *not worth a continental damn* **d** : of, relating to, or concerning the continental U.S. **2 a** : of, relating to, or characteristic of a continent ⟨~ waters⟩ **b** : having large daily and annual ranges of temperature (as in the interior of a continent) **c** : NONMARINE — **con·ti·nen·tal·ly** \-t°lē, -li\ *adv*

2continental \"\ *n* -S **1 a** *often cap* : an American soldier of the Revolution in the Continental army **b** : a piece of the Continental paper currency **c** : an inhabitant of a continent (as the continental of Europe) **2** : the least bit : DAMN ⟨not worth a ~⟩ ⟨don't care a ~⟩

continental block *or* **continental mass** *n* : CONTINENT 6

continental breakfast *n, often cap C* : a light breakfast (as rolls or toast with coffee)

continental celtic *n, usu cap both Cs* : a division of the Celtic languages including Gaulish

continental code *n, sometimes cap 1st C* **:** the international Morse code — see MORSE CODE table

continental currency *n, usu cap 1st C* **1 :** the paper money issued by the Continental Congress during the American Revolution **2 :** a series of early American pattern dollar-size coins, struck in England in pewter, silver, and brass and bearing on the obverse the legend "Continental Currency" and the date 1776

continental divide *n* **:** a divide separating streams which flow to opposite sides of a continent

continental dollar *n, usu cap C* **1 :** a one-dollar note of Continental paper currency **2 :** a Continental currency coin

continental drift *n* **:** a hypothetical slow movement of the continents on a supposed deep-seated viscous or plastic zone within the earth — compare WEGENER HYPOTHESIS

continental glacier *n* **:** an ice sheet covering a considerable part of a continent — compare OCEANITY

continental heel *n* **:** a high slender shoe heel having a slightly curved back line and a slightly curved or straight breast line

continental island *n* **:** an island (as Great Britain) that is near and geologically related to a continent — compare OCEANIC ISLAND

con·ti·nen·tal·ism \\ˌkänt³n'ent³lˌizəm, -tə'ne-, -təˌli-\\ *n* -s **1 :** a thing (as an expression, trait, opinion) characteristic of a continent or the residents of a continent, esp. the continent of Europe **2 :** a policy favoring the restricting of relations (as political and economic) to countries of the same continent ⟨warned against a narrow nationalism or even a ~ —*New Republic*⟩

con·ti·nen·tal·ist \\-t³ləst, -təl-\\ *n* -s **:** a supporter or advocate of continentalism

con·ti·nen·tal·i·ty \\ˌkänt³nən'taləd·ē, -tə,ne-, -ətē, -i\\ *n* -ES **1 :** the quality or state of being continental **2 :** the degree to which a climate has continental qualities — compare OCEANITY

con·ti·nen·tal·ize \\ˌkänt³n'ent³lˌīz, -tə'ne-, -təˌlīz\\ *vt* -ED/-ING/-S [prob. fr. F *continentaliser*, fr. *continental* (fr. E) + *-iser* -ize] **1 :** to make continental in scope, character, culture, or ideas ⟨~ American literature as a protest against local color —Carl Van Doren⟩ **2** *sometimes cap* **:** to affect with the ways or ideas of European culture ⟨the gradual *continentalizing* of American habits of recreation —*Nation*⟩

continental morse code *n, usu cap M* **:** the international Morse code — see MORSE CODE table

continental plateau *or* **continental platform** *n* **:** a broad protuberance of the surface of the lithosphere coinciding approximately with a continent but including also the continental shelf

continental pronunciation *n, sometimes cap C* **:** a method of pronouncing Latin and Greek in which the vowel values approximate those of the languages spoken on the European continent (as \\ē\\ for the letter *ī* and \\ā\\ for the letter *ē*) and the consonants are pronounced approximately as in English

continental rummy *or* **continental rum** *n, usu cap C* **:** a game of rummy for several players in which only sequences or the entire hand but no lesser part of it may be melded

continental shelf *n* **:** a comparatively shallow submarine plain of a width varying from several to several hundred miles forming a border to a continent and typically ending in a continental slope

continental slope *n* **:** the usu. steep slope from a continental shelf to the oceanic abyss

continental sunday *n, often cap C&S* **:** Sunday as observed on the continent of Europe commonly without special restrictions on public behavior and activities as distinguished from common British and American practice

continental system *n* **:** FRENCH SYSTEM

continental tea *n* [so called fr. its alleged use as tea during the Revolution] **:** LABRADOR TEA a

continental terrace *n* **:** the submerged margin of a continent (sense 6) including both the continental shelf and the continental slope

con·ti·nent·ly *adv* [¹*continent* + *-ly*] **:** in a continent or temperate manner **:** CHASTELY

con·tin·gence \\kən'tinjən(t)s\\ *n* -s [in sense 1, fr. L *contingere* + E *-ence*, in sense 2, fr. MF] **1 :** CONTACT, TOUCHING ⟨angle of ~⟩ **2 :** CONTINGENCY

con·tin·gen·cy \\kən'tinjənsē, -si\\ *n* -ES [MF or ML; MF *contingence*, fr. ML *contingentia*, fr. LL, possibility, fr. L *contingent-*, *contingens* (pres. part. of *contingere* to touch on all sides, to happen) + *-ia*] **1 :** the quality or state of being contingent: as **a** (1) **:** the condition that something may or may not occur **:** the condition of being subject to chance (2) **:** the happening of anything by chance **:** FORTUITOUSNESS **b** (1) **:** close connection or relationship esp. of a causal nature (2) *obs* **:** CONTACT, CONTINGENCE **2** [*contingence* + *-y*] **a :** something that is contingent **:** an event or condition occurring by chance and without intent, viewed as possible or eventually probable, or depending on uncertain occurrences or coincidences ⟨the remarkable position of the queen rendering her death a most important ~ —Henry Hallam⟩ **b :** a possible future event or condition or an unforeseen occurrence that may necessitate special measures ⟨a reserve fund for *contingencies*⟩ **c :** something liable to happen as a chance feature or accompaniment of something else ⟨*contingencies* of marriage⟩ **syn** see JUNCTURE

contingency coefficient *n* **:** COEFFICIENT OF CONTINGENCY

contingency fund *n* **:** assets segregated as a fund for the purpose of meeting a specific or general contingency and usu. accompanied by a contingency reserve

contingency method *n* **:** a statistical method for computing the probability of the joint occurrence of attributes (as blue eyes and blond hair) which do not admit of refined measurement but can be roughly grouped

contingency reserve *n* **:** an appropriation of surplus or retained earnings that may or may not be funded, indicating a reservation against a specific or general contingency

contingency table *n, math* **:** a table in which the rows tabulate the frequency distribution of one variable and the columns that of another, serving therefore to indicate the existence of a contingency or correlation between the variables — compare CONTINGENCY METHOD

¹con·tin·gent \\kən'tinjənt\\ *adj* [ME, fr. MF, fr. L *contingent-*, *contingens*, pres. part. of *contingere* to touch on all sides, happen, fr. *com-* + *-tingere* (fr. *tangere* to touch) — more at TANGENT] **1** *obs* **:** in contact **:** TOUCHING **2 :** of possible occurrence **:** likely but not certain to happen ⟨a bogey's alarum of ~ grave results —George Meredith⟩ **3 a :** happening by chance **:** affected by unforeseen causes or conditions **:** not patently necessary **:** unpredictable in occurrence or outcome ⟨a ~ event⟩ ⟨floods ~ and unexpected⟩ **b :** intended for use in exigent circumstances not completely foreseen **c :** unpredictable in outcome or effect because happening by chance and modified by unseen causes and unforeseen conditions ⟨speaks so scornfully of the ~ and tentative character of scientific knowledge —Sidney Hook⟩ **4 a :** dependent on, associated with, or conditioned by something else, sometimes indirectly or remotely ⟨the continuance of the latter is wholly ~ on the presence of the former —C.H. Grandgent⟩ **b :** dependent for effect on or liable to modification by something that may or may not occur ⟨a ~ estate⟩ ⟨a ~ legacy⟩ **5** *logic* **a :** not necessary **:** not true a priori **b** *of a proposition* **:** capable of being proved true or false only by experience **:** EMPIRICAL, FACTUAL **6 :** not necessitated **:** FREE — used of human volition, action, or existence **syn** see ACCIDENTAL

²contingent \\"\\ *n* -s [in sense 1, fr. ¹*contingent;* in other senses fr. F, fr. *contingent*, adj.] **1 a :** something that is contingent **:** CONTINGENCY **b :** a chance occurrence **:** ACCIDENT **c :** an extra salesperson who is available on call **2 :** a quota (as one's part in a general contribution): as **a :** a number of personnel supplied to the armed forces from a section ⟨the Ohio ~ in the army⟩ **b :** the military forces supplied by one combatant in an allied effort ⟨the British ~ in the Low Countries campaign⟩ **3 a :** a representational group ⟨the French ~ of Olympic athletes⟩ **b :** any group distinguished from the other members of an assemblage or organization ⟨the Democratic ~ at the conference⟩

contingent annuity *n* **:** an annuity terminable upon the happening of a future event uncertain either as to the date or the possibility of occurrence

contingent beneficiary *n* **:** a secondary beneficiary under a life-insurance policy whose rights mature if the primary beneficiary predeceases the insured or dies before payment of proceeds is completed

contingent fee *n* **:** a fee for services (as of a lawyer or agent) to be paid in the event of success in a particular transaction usu. as a specified percentage of the sum realized for the client or principal

contingent fund *n* **:** CONTINGENCY FUND

contingent liability *n* **:** an amount that may or may not be owed dependent on the outcome of a contingency (as a discounted note receivable)

con·tin·gent·ly *adv* [ME, fr. ¹*contingent* + *-ly*] **:** in a contingent way or manner **:** PROVISIONALLY, ACCIDENTALLY

contingent symbiosis *n* **:** HELOTISM 2

contingent truth *n* **:** EMPIRICAL TRUTH

contingent use *n, law* **:** a use to come into operation on a future uncertain event

continua *pl of* CONTINUUM

con·tin·u·al \\kən'tinyəwəl, -yəl\\ *adj* [ME, fr. MF *continuel*, fr. L *continuus* continuous + MF *-el* -al — more at CONTINUOUS] **1 :** continuing in time **:** proceeding without stopping, interruption, or intermission **:** going on indefinitely — now used only of things ⟨the ~ dread of falling into poverty which haunts us all at present —G.B.Shaw⟩ **2 :** recurring in steady and rapid succession **:** repeated at intervals with brief perhaps regular intermissions in time ⟨~ storm . . . with frequent showers of snow —William Wordsworth⟩ **3** *obs* **a :** continuously acting or engaged **:** CONSTANT **b** *of disease* **:** CHRONIC **c :** forming a continuous series or whole **:** UNBROKEN

syn CONTINUOUS, CONSTANT, INCESSANT, UNREMITTING, PERPETUAL, PERENNIAL: CONTINUAL and CONTINUOUS indicate lasting occurrence or presence over long periods ⟨we live in a country where his Majesty's Cabinet governs subject to the *continual* superintendence, correction, and authority of Parliament —Sir Winston Churchill⟩ ⟨the new struggle was *continuous*, the old had been sporadic —Lewis Mumford⟩ CONTINUAL is somewhat more common than CONTINUOUS in describing intermittent action, but both words are well-established and satisfactory in this sense ⟨the century and a half that followed the gathering of the estates at Westminster was a time of almost *continual* war —J.R.Green⟩ ⟨*continual* and regular impulses of pleasurable surprise from the metrical arrangement —William Wordsworth⟩ ⟨*continuous* landslides raised the cost of maintenance so high that a loss was sustained each year —*Amer. Guide Series: Conn.*⟩ Unlike CONTINUAL in this respect, CONTINUOUS may apply to space as well as time ⟨the *continuous* plains of the Great Lowland overlap from the Continental and Arctic drainage of the Heartland into the east of the European peninsula —H.J.Mackinder⟩ CONSTANT strongly implies lasting steadiness, lack of change, or uniformity ⟨unfortunately, perhaps, experience does not grow at a *constant*, but at an accelerated, rate —J.W.Krutch⟩ ⟨personal goodness . . . of a very fitful cast — an occasional almost oppressive generosity rather than a mild and *constant* kindness —Thomas Hardy⟩ INCESSANT suggests virtually ceaseless uninterrupted activity ⟨his *incessant* talking and shouting and bellowing of orders had been too much —Jack London⟩ ⟨over that which we call the meaning of the words a poet uses, there goes on an *incessant* play of suggestion, caught from each user's own adventures among words —J.L.Lowes⟩ UNREMITTING indicates unceasing activity without slackening or halting ⟨sporadic outbursts are converted by the rationalization into purposive and *unremitting* activity —Aldous Huxley⟩ ⟨the men fifteen or twenty paces apart, all in concealment and under injunction of strict silence and *unremitting* vigilance —Ambrose Bierce⟩ PERPETUAL indicates lasting duration or unfailing repetition ⟨sins unatoned for and uncondoned bring purgatorial or *perpetual* torment after death, even as holiness brings eternal bliss —H.O.Taylor⟩ ⟨their heroic defense will be recorded for all time. It will be *perpetual* proof that democracy . . . can show the stuff of which it was made —F.D. Roosevelt⟩ ⟨weary . . . of *perpetual* state business and perpetual honors; he wanted a rest —Robert Graves⟩ PERENNIAL connotes either existence over a long period or certain recurrence ⟨those who have lived before such terms as "highbrow fiction", "thrillers", and "detective fiction" were invented realize that melodrama is *perennial* —T.S.Eliot⟩ ⟨to all who profess faith in the democratic ideal Jefferson is a *perennial* inspiration —V.L.Parrington⟩

con·tin·u·al·ly \\-yəlē, -yəwəlē, -li\\ *adv* [ME *continuelly*, fr. *continuel* + *-ly*] **1 :** in a continual way **:** UNCEASINGLY **2 :** continuously in time **:** without intermission **3 :** in regular or repeated succession **:** very often

con·tin·u·ance \\kən'tinyəwən(t)s\\ *n* -s [ME, fr. MF, fr. *continuant*] **1 :** a holding on or remaining in a particular state or course of action **:** permanence esp. of action, condition, habits, or abode **:** PERSEVERANCE: **a :** PROLONGATION, DURATION ⟨great plagues, and of long ~ —Deut 28:59 (AV)⟩ **b :** a continuing or remaining in some place or condition **:** ABIDING, STAY ⟨~ in office⟩ **2 :** uninterrupted succession **:** continuation esp. of a species **3** *obs* **a :** CONTINUITY **b :** DURABILITY, PERMANENCE ⟨you call in question the ~ of his love —Shak.⟩ **4 :** a continuation or sequel esp. to a novel **5 :** the adjournment of the court proceedings in a case to a future day; *also* **:** the entry of such adjournment and the grounds thereof on the record

con·tin·u·an·cy \\-wənsē, -si\\ *n* -ES **:** CONTINUANCE

¹con·tin·u·ant \\kən'tinyəwənt\\ *adj* [F or L; F *continuant*, fr. L *continuant-*, *continuans*, pres. part. of *continuare* to continue — more at CONTINUE] **1 :** CONTINUING **2** *phonetics* **:** of, being, or having the character of a continuant

²continuant \\"\\ *n* -s **:** one that continues **:** something that serves for continuation: as **a :** a consonant that may be continued or prolonged without alteration for the duration of an emission of breath **:** an open consonant: (1) *in some classifications* **:** any consonant except a stop or an affricate (2) *in some classifications* **:** any consonant except a stop, an affricate, a nasal, or a semivowel — compare SPIRANT **b** *math* **:** a determinant of which all the elements are zero except those of a principal diagonal and the two adjacent minor diagonals, one of the latter being made up of –1's **c** *philos* **:** something that continues to exist throughout some limited or unlimited period of time during which its inner states or its outer connections with other continuing existences may be changing or remaining unchanged — contrasted with *occurrent* **d :** a linguistic form descending without change or with only regular phonetic change from a form in an ancestral language or an earlier stage of the same language (as *bed* from Old English *bed*, *home* from Old English *hām*, Latin *unus* "one" from assumed Indo-European *oinos*) — compare REFLEX

¹continuate *adj* [L *continuatus*, past part. of *continuare* to continue] **1** *obs* **:** continuous without break or interruption in substance **2** *obs* **:** CONTINUOUS, UNINTERRUPTED, CHRONIC —**continuately** *adv, obs*

²con·tin·u·ate \\kən'tinyə,wāt\\ *vt* -ED/-ING/-S [L *continuatus*] *archaic* **:** to make continuous or give continuity to

con·tin·u·a·tion \\kən'tinyə'wāshən\\ *n* -s [ME *continuacioun*, fr. MF *continuation*, fr. L *continuation-*, *continuatio*, fr. *continuatus* + *-ion-*, *-io* -ion] **1 :** continuance in a state, existence, or activity **:** uninterrupted extension or succession **:** PROLONGATION ⟨~ of the war into next year⟩ **:** the causing of something to continue ⟨payments made in ~ of his obligated support⟩ **2 :** the action of carrying on or resuming after an interruption or break ⟨~ of the meeting was delayed until the next day⟩ **3 a :** something that continues, extends, increases, or supplements ⟨the border is a ~ of the central design⟩ **b continuations** *pl, obs slang* **:** TROUSERS, GAITERS **c :** a work (as a periodical or numbered monograph) issued in successive parts; *also* **:** one of the parts **4 :** CONTANGO

continuation school *n* **1 :** a school above the elementary level enabling young people in trade or industry to continue their schooling in their spare time **2 :** a small secondary school in Canada usu. in a remote rural area

¹con·tin·u·a·tive \\kən'tinyə,wād·iv, -yəwəd·iv\\ *adj* [LL *continuativus*, fr. L *continuatus* (past part. of *continuare* to continue) + *-ivus* -ive] **1 :** causing continuance or tending to continue **2 a** *of a modifier* **:** NONRESTRICTIVE **b** *of a verb form or aspect* **:** expressing continuation of an action — **con·tin·u·a·tive·ly** \\-d·əvlē\\ *adv*

²continuative \\"\\ *n* -s [LL *continuativus*, adj.] **:** something continuative: as **a :** a logical statement denoting continuance **b :** a continuative verb form **:** the continuative aspect **c** *phonetics* **:** CONTINUANT

con·tin·u·a·tor \\kən'tinyə,wād·ə(r)\\ *n* -s [F *continuateur*, fr. L *continuatus* + F *-eur* -or] **:** one that continues (as a work, a style, a tradition)

con·tin·ue \\kən'ti(,)nyü, -tinyə (*this pronunc bef a vowel or pause is esp S*); *often* -,nyəw+V\\ *vb* -ED/-ING/-S [ME *continuen*, fr. MF *continuer*, fr. L *continuare* to connect, continue, fr. *continuus* continuous — more at CONTINUOUS] *vi* **1 a :** to be steadfast or constant in a course or activity **:** keep up or maintain esp. without interruption a particular condition, course, or series of actions **:** PERSEVERE, ENDURE, PERSIST ⟨~ to go to church each Sunday⟩ **b :** to keep going **:** maintain a course, direction, or progress ⟨the boat *continued* downstream after discharging the passengers⟩ ⟨the broad beach ~*s* all the way along the promenade⟩ — often used with *on* ⟨they *continued* on for a quarter of a mile —Norman Mailer⟩ **2 :** to be permanent or durable **:** remain in existence **:** ENDURE, LAST ⟨but now thy kingdom shall not ~ —1 Sam 13:14 (AV)⟩ **3 :** to remain in a place or condition ⟨if the patient ~*s* unconscious⟩ **:** ABIDE, STAY ⟨he cannot long ~ here⟩ **4 :** to proceed to discourse esp. after intermission ~ *vt* **1 :** to carry onward or extend **:** keep up or maintain (as an activity) ⟨*continued* walking all day⟩ **:** PROLONG **:** add to or draw out in length, duration, or development ⟨~ the battle⟩; *specif* **:** to resume (as a discourse) esp. after intermission **2 :** to cause to last, endure, or keep on ⟨*continued* my subscription for another year⟩ **3 :** to allow or cause to remain (in a place or condition) **:** RETAIN ⟨the trustees were *continued*⟩ **4 :** to keep on the court calendar **:** subject to further consideration **:** postpone by a continuance — used of a legal proceeding

syn LAST, ENDURE, ABIDE, PERSIST: CONTINUE indicates a remaining or going on, often in an uninterrupted way, without ceasing or ending ⟨in *continuing* cancer research lies the ultimate hope of providing the clinician with solutions to his many diagnostic and therapeutic dilemmas —*Americana Annual*⟩ ⟨the illusion *continues* that civilization can somehow be reconciled with atomic war —D.F.Fleming⟩ LAST may focus attention on a length of existence greater than the normal or expected ⟨the work that Michelangelo did complete has *lasted* well —Stringfellow Barr⟩ ENDURE often calls attention to resistances to destructive and disintegrative forces ⟨it is only the exceptional skeleton, protected by favorable circumstances, of which the bones will *endure* for thousands of years —A.L.Kroeber⟩ ⟨the government thus established *endured* till Oregon became a Territory —Joseph Schafer⟩ ABIDE, often poetic or archaic, may suggest unchanging constancy and stability ⟨O Thou who changest not, *abide* with me —Henry Lyte⟩ ⟨notwithstanding the countless features of . . . living which were *abiding*, the changes made themselves felt —John Mason Brown⟩ PERSIST may imply continuing or recurring with or as if with resolution, doggedness, or stubbornness ⟨the idea that there exists a universal remedy which is sovereign over all diseases has *persisted* through the centuries —G.W.Gray b.1886⟩ ⟨this tribal structure, though simplified to some extent by past reforms, still *persists* —Patrick Smith⟩ ⟨these forests have reigned supreme for countless millenia, probably having *persisted* more or less unchanged for a longer period than any other contemporary forest type —W.H. Hodge⟩

continued *adj* [ME, fr. past part. of *continuen*] **1 :** stretching out in time or space esp. without interruption **:** CONSTANT, CONTINUOUS ⟨cold weather, and ~ rain —John Dryden⟩ **2 :** resumed after interruption ⟨a ~ story⟩ — **con·tin·ued·ly** *adv* — **con·tin·ued·ness** *n* -ES

continued bass *n* **:** CONTINUO

continued bond *n* **:** a bond that need not be presented for payment at maturity but may be held for a further period usu. upon specified terms

continued fraction *n* **:** an expression in the form of a fraction whose numerator is an integer and whose denominator is an integer plus a fraction whose numerator is an integer and whose denominator is an integer plus a fraction, and so on; thus:

$$a + \cfrac{b}{a' + \cfrac{b'}{a'' + \cfrac{b''}{\dots}}}$$

continued product *n* **:** a finite or infinite product of the form $(1 + a_1)(1 + a_2)(1 + a_3) \ldots (1 + a_n) \ldots$ none of whose factors are zero

continued proportion *n, math* **:** a proportion in which the consequent of each ratio is the antecedent of the next (as 4:8=8:16=16:32)

continued voyage *n* **:** CONTINUOUS VOYAGE

continues *pres 3d sing of* CONTINUE

continuing *adj* [ME, fr. pres. part. of *continuen*] **1 :** CONTINUOUS, CONSTANT **2 :** needing no renewal **:** LASTING, ENDURING ⟨a ~ contract⟩ — **con·tin·u·ing·ly** *adv*

continuing agreement *n* **:** an agreement made by a regular borrower with his lender, giving to the latter continued rights (as of collateral) for repeated transactions

con·ti·nu·is·mo \\kən,tinə'wiz(,)mō\\ *n* -s [AmerSp, fr. Sp *continuar* to continue (fr. L *continuare*) + *-ismo* -ism — more at CONTINUE] **:** the practice in some Latin-American countries of maintaining a chief executive in power beyond the legal term of his office by such methods as amending the constitution or drafting a new one exempting the incumbent from the usual prohibition against reelection

con·ti·nu·i·ty \\ˌkäntə'n(y)üəd·ē, -nt³n'(y)ü-, -ətē, -i\\ *n* -ES [MF or L; MF *continuité*, fr. L *continuitat-*, *continuitas*, fr. *continuus* + *-itat-*, *-itas* -ity] **1 a :** the quality or state of being continuous **:** uninterrupted connection or succession **:** close union of parts **:** COHESION, COHERENCE ⟨the highest percentage of cures with the least disturbance in the ~ of tissue —E.D. Osborne⟩ ⟨~ of management⟩ **b :** the quality or state of continuing without essential change **:** uninterrupted persistence of a particular quality or essential with reference to conjoint changing qualities ⟨the life of ancient Rome, its unbroken ~ through the centuries, and its connection with the life of the modern world —H.N.Fowler⟩ **c :** continuousness in time **:** duration without intermission; *specif* **:** uninterruptedness of existence (as of germ plasm) **2 :** something that shows continuity **:** a connected or unbroken course or series: as **a :** the narrative line or the thematic development of an idea in a motion picture **b :** a detailed scenario or shooting script showing dialogue, shots, and transitions **c :** the script for a radio or television program (as of the introductory and transitional material used by an announcer or master of ceremonies of a musical or variety program); *also* **:** the lines read from such a script **d :** the story and dialogue of a comic strip; *also* **:** a daily comic strip or picture strip that sustains a narrative **3 :** an individual feature, element, or unit of a connected series ⟨number of *continuities* that can be discovered in the play —R.A.Brower⟩ **4** *math* **:** the property characteristic of a continuous function; *also* **:** an example of such property — compare DISCONTINUITY 3

continuity acceptance *n* **:** a department of a broadcasting company in which program material and commercials are examined and if necessary edited to assure conformity with government regulations and company policy

continuity girl *or* **continuity clerk** *n* **:** a member of a motion-picture crew that is responsible for recording the details of a take in order to avoid discrepancies and to facilitate editing

continuity title *n* **:** a legend or subtitle inserted into a motion picture to introduce a change of time or place or supply a necessary circumstance to the narrative

con·tin·uo \\kən'tinə(,)wō *also* -inyə-\\ *n* -s [It, lit., continuous, fr. L *continuus*] **:** an instrumental part usu. for keyboard instrument accompanying solo or choral or concerted instrumental voices and consisting of a succession of bass notes with numerals and other marks placed under each note according to a system that indicates the chords that are required at each step but leaves to the player's discretion the actual arrangement of the notes constituting each successive chord — called *also figured bass, thorough bass*

con·tin·u·ous \\kən'tinyəwəs\\ *adj* [L *continuus*, fr. *continēre* to hold together — more at CONTINENT] **1 a :** characterized by uninterrupted extension in space : stretching on without break or interruption ⟨a ~ and rather spacious channel —C.H.Grandgent⟩ **b** : characterized by uninterrupted extension in time or sequence : continuing without intermission or recurring regularly after minute interruptions ⟨humanism has been sporadic, but Christianity ~ —T.S.Eliot⟩ ⟨a ~ rearrangement of electrons in the solar atoms results in the emission of light —James Jeans⟩ **2** : operated without interruption ⟨a ~ furnace⟩ ⟨a ~ retort⟩ **3** *of sculpture* : having one depicted scene following another without an obvious break **4** *of a beam, span, truss* : having three or more supports or extending over two or more panels — see BRIDGE illustration **5** *of plant spores* **a** : lacking septa **b** : merging or in protoplasmic continuity with the tissue of the cap or peridium (as in certain fungi) **6** : PROGRESSIVE 7 **7** : of the nature of a continuum **8** *math, of a function at a point* : defined at a point and having the numerical difference between the value at this point and a second nearby point made arbitrarily small by taking the second point sufficiently close to the first **syn** see CONTINUAL

continuous brake *n* : a train-brake system consisting of a series of brakes attached one to each car and operated on all the cars from one point

continuous current *n* : DIRECT CURRENT

continuous easement *or* **continuous servitude** *n, law* : an easement that does not require the act of man for its enjoyment (as an easement of drainage by a natural watercourse or a right of light or air) — compare DISCONTINUOUS EASEMENT

continuous girder *or* **continuous beam** *n* : a girder or beam having more than two supports

continuous hinge *n* : PIANO HINGE

continuous industry *n* : an industry in which most of the material is received at one point from which successive operations turn it into a finished product (as yarn spinning and paper manufacture)

continuous kiln *n* **1** : a series of connected kilns or one continuous chamber through which a fire travels, green brick being set ahead of the fire **2** : a long narrow kiln which is hottest in its middle portion and through which ware travels on cars or conveyor — called also *tunnel kiln*

con·tin·u·ous·ly *adv* : in a continuous manner ⟨a double feature alternates ~ throughout the day⟩

continuous mill *n* : a mill consisting of a series of consecutive rolls or dies; *specif* : one used in wire drawing through which a rod is passed from one set of rolls or dies to the next until finished

continuous miner *n* : a machine that cuts and loads coal in one continuous operation

continuous mixer *n* : a mixer (as of asphalt) into which the ingredients of the mix are introduced continuously, are mixed as they pass through the mixer, and are then discharged in a continuous operation — opposed to *batch mixer*

con·tin·u·ous·ness \-nəs\ *n* -ES : the quality or state of being continuous

continuous performance *n* : a performance (as of a motion-picture program) that is repeated continuously till closing so customers need not come at the beginning to see a complete showing

continuous phase *n* : DISPERSION MEDIUM

continuous pool *n* : fifteen-ball pool in which whenever 14 balls have been pocketed the frame is set up anew to be broken while or after pocketing the 15th ball

continuous spectrum *n* : a spectrum (as of light emitted by a white-hot lamp filament) having no apparent breaks or gaps throughout its wavelength range

continuous spinning *n* : rayon spinning in which extrusion, coagulation, washing, and winding are accomplished continuously on one machine

continuous variation *n, biol* : variation in which a series of intermediate types connects the extremes — compare QUANTITATIVE INHERITANCE

continuous voyage *n* : a voyage which in view of its purposes is regarded in international law as one single voyage though interrupted (as in transshipment of contraband of war) — see ULTIMATE DESTINATION

continuous watermark *n* : a watermark on stamps consisting of letters, words, or a phrase repeated continuously, only part of the mark appearing on each stamp

continuous waves *n pl* **1** : radio waves that continue with unchanging intensity or amplitude without modulation and that are used in telegraphy in which the wave is turned on and off with a key to form the dots and dashes of a code ⟨*continuous-wave* telegraphy⟩ — abbr. *CW* **2** : radio waves of which the intensity continues unchanged except for modulation — called also *modulated continuous waves;* see INTERRUPTED CONTINUOUS WAVES

con·tin·u·um \kən'tin(y)əwəm\ *n, pl* **contin·ua** \-wə\ *also* **continuums** [L, neut. of *continuus* — more at CONTINUOUS] **1** : something that is absolutely continuous and selfsame: as **a** : something of which no distinction of content can be affirmed except by reference to something else (as duration and extension which are capable of supporting distinctions only by reference to numbers or to such relations as those of *now* to *then, here* to *there, before* to *after*) **b** : something of which the only assertable variation is variation in time or space **2 a** : something in which a fundamental common character is discernible amid a series of insensible or indefinite variations ⟨a sensation ~⟩ **b** : an identity of substance uniting discrete parts; *broadly* : CONTINUITY **3** : a set that has the same transfinite cardinal number as the set of real numbers or the set of all the points of a straight line used as a number scale **4 a** : an ideal substance or medium containing no vacant spaces and devoid of discrete structure **b** : a continuous portion of a spectrum

contl *abbr* **1** continental **2** control

cont·line \'känt,līn, -ˌlən\ *or* **cant·line** \'kant-\ *or* **cunt·line** \'kənt-\ *n* -S [*contline* fr. alter. of ²*cant* + *line; cantline* fr. ²*cant* + *line; cuntline* by folk etymology (influence of *cunt*) fr. *contline*] **1** : the space between the strands on the outside of a rope **2** : the space between the bilges of two casks stowed side by side

contn *abbr* continuation

con·to \'kän(ˌ)tō\ *n* -S [Pg, lit., number, fr. LL *computus* computation — more at COUNT] *in Portugal and Brazil* : a monetary unit equal to 1,000,000 reis or to 1000 Portuguese escudos or 1000 Brazilian cruzeiros

con·to·ise \ˌkäntə'wēz\ *n* -S [by alter.] : COINTISE

¹**con·tor·ni·ate** \kən'tō(r)nēət, -ē,āt\ *adj* [It *contorniato*, fr. past part. of *contorniare* to make a circuit or outline, fr. *com-* + *torniare* to surround, measure in circuit, fr. *tornio, torno* turning lathe, circuit, fr. L *tornus* lathe — more at TURN] : encircled by a groove just inside the edge ⟨a ~ medal⟩

²**contorniate** \"\ *also* **con·tor·ni·a·to** \=ˌ=nē'äd·ō\ *n, pl* **contorniates** \-ts\ *also* **contornia·ti** \-äd·ē\ [*contorniate* fr. F, fr. It *contorniato; contorniato* fr. It, fr. *contorniato*, adj.] : a thin bronze contorniate medallion of the Roman Empire first used about the time of Constantine the Great supposedly in connection with a game like chess

con·tort \kən'tȯ(ə)rt, -ō(ə)t, *usu* -d·+V\ *vb* -ED/-ING/-S [L *contortus*, past part. of *contorquēre* to twist, fr. *com-* + *torquēre* to twist — more at TORTURE] *vt* : to twist or twist together esp. in a strained or violent manner : turn awry : BEND, DISTORT ⟨branches that had been ~*ed* and gnarled by years of struggle to survive —*New Yorker*⟩ ⟨~ spelling and grammar⟩ ~ *vi* : to twist into a strained shape or expression (as from pain or violent feeling) ⟨his face would ~ in a grimace at the heat —D.C.Jenkins⟩ ⟨fine features hardened and ~*ed* with rage⟩ **syn** see DEFORM

con·tor·tae \kən'tȯrd·ē\ [NL, fr. fem. pl of L *contortus*] *syn of* GENTIANALES

contorted *adj* **1** : twisted together : TWISTED ⟨a ~ coastline⟩ ⟨tears streaked her ~ face⟩ **2** : CONVOLUTE ⟨~ leaves in the bud⟩ — **con·tort·ed·ly** *adv*

con·tor·tion \kən'tȯrshən, -tō(ə)shən\ *n* -S [F & L; F *contorsion*, fr. L *contortion-, contortio*, fr. *contortus* + *-ion-, -io* -ion] : the act or result of contorting or the state of being contorted : a twisting into abnormal or grotesque shape : a needlessly or unduly complicated action or posture ⟨goes through tremendous ~*s* in an effort to link . . . her plots—James Yaffe⟩ — **con·tor·tion·al** \-shənᵊl, -shnəl\ *adj*

con·tor·tion·ate \kən'tȯ(r)sh(ə)nət, -ˌnāt\ *adj* : CONTORTIVE

con·tor·tion·ist \kən'tȯ(r)sh(ə)nəst\ *n* -S : one who contorts or resorts to or practices contortions; *specif* : an acrobat who specializes in throwing his body into unnatural or extraordinary postures — **con·tor·tion·is·tic** \=ˌ=shə¦nistik\ *adj*

con·tor·tive \kən'tȯrd·iv, -tō(ə)d-\ *adj* : causing or characterized by or tending to contortions or twisting

¹**con·tour** \'kän,tů(ə)r, -tůə\ *n* -S [F, modif. of It *contorno*, fr. *contornare* to surround, sketch in outline, round off, fr. L *com-* + *tornare* to turn in a lathe, fr. *tornus* lathe — more at TURN] **1** : the delimitations of a figure: **a** : the drawn or painted outline of a two-dimensional figure **b** : the periphery of a form seen two-dimensionally ⟨the ~ of a mountain silhouetted against the sky⟩ **c** : SHAPE, FORM ⟨the ~*s* of a statue⟩ ⟨the ominous ~*s* of a ravine⟩ — usu. used in pl.; used of any irregularly shaped body or uneven surface or curving line ⟨the ~*s* of the shoreline⟩ **2** : the individual features or the order or arrangement of features of anything having discernible and usu. complex structure — usu. used in pl. ⟨the ~*s* of a melody⟩ ⟨the ~*s* of the plan are beginning to emerge⟩ ⟨poetry is a discovery of ~*s* and connections —C.S.Kilby⟩ **3 a** *math* : a plotted curve : GRAPH **b** : a line or surface at all points of which a certain quantity, otherwise variable, has the same value (as lines of equal elevation on the ground or isothermal surfaces in a heat-conducting solid) : CONTOUR LINE **4** : a sequence of levels of pitch or stress typically extending over several successive words in an utterance **syn** see OUTLINE

²**contour** \"\ *vb* -ED/-ING/-S *vt* **1 a** : to draw or shape the contours of **b** : to shape (a thing) to fit the contours of something else ⟨~ the waist of a jacket⟩ **2 a** : to construct (as a road) in conformity to a contour **b** : to cultivate (land) along lines connecting points of equal elevation **c** : to provide (as a map) with contour lines ~ *vi* : to draw or plot a contour

³**contour** \"\ *adj* **1** : following the contour lines or running furrows or ridges along the contour lines to retard erosion of sloping land by runoff rainwater ⟨~ plowing⟩ **2** : made to fit the contour of something enclosed or contained ⟨~ sheet⟩

contour chair *n* [fr. *Contour*, a trademark] : a chair esp. designed to fit the form of the human body

contour feather *n* : one of the medium-sized feathers that form the general covering of a bird and determine the external contour — compare DOWN, FLIGHT FEATHER

contour interval *n* : the vertical distance between the elevations represented by adjacent contour lines on a map

contour line *n* : an imaginary line connecting the points on a land surface that have the same elevation; *also* : the line representing this on a map or chart

contour map *n* : a map showing the configuration of a surface by means of contour lines drawn at regular intervals of elevation (as one for every 20 feet)

50 40 30 20 10

contour map

con·tour·né \ˌkäntůr¦nā\ *adj* [F, past part. of *contourner* to round off, twist, fr. It *contornare* to round off] *heraldry* : turned about — used of a figure facing to the sinister

contr *abbr* **1** contract; contraction; contractor **2** contralto **3** contrary **4** control; controller

¹**con·tra** \'käntrə\ *prep* [ME, fr. L, adv. & prep. — more at COUNTER] : AGAINST — used chiefly in the phrase *pro and contra*

²**contra** \"\ *adv* [ME, fr. L] : to the contrary : CONTRARIWISE

³**contra** \"\ *n* -S **1** : CONTRARY : a thing opposite or against another **2** : OFFSET : an item on the opposite side of an account or statement — compare PER CONTRA

⁴**contra** \'käntrə, 'kōn-\ *n* -S [by shortening and alter.] : CONTREDANSE 1

contra- *prefix* [ME, fr. L *contra-, contra* against — more at COUNTER] **1** : against : contrary : contrasting : in opposition ⟨*contra*-acting⟩ ⟨*contra*indicative⟩ ⟨*contra*tenor⟩ **2** : pitched below normal bass ⟨*contra*bassoon⟩ ⟨*contra*octave⟩ ⟨*contra*posaune⟩

¹**con·tra·band** \'käntrəˌband, -baa(ə)nd\ *n* -S [It *contrabbando*, fr. ML *contrabannum*, fr. L *contra-* + ML *bannus, bannum* decree, of Gmc origin; akin to OHG *ban* command — more at BAN] **1** : illegal or prohibited traffic : SMUGGLING ⟨persons the most bound in duty to prevent ~ —Edmund Burke⟩ **2** : goods or merchandise the importation, exportation, or sometimes possession of which is forbidden; *also* : smuggled goods **3** : a Negro slave who during the Civil War escaped to or was brought within the Union lines **4** : CONTRABAND OF WAR

²**contraband** \"\ *adj* : prohibited or excluded by law or treaty : FORBIDDEN ⟨~ liquor⟩ ⟨~ cargo⟩

³**contraband** \"\ *vt* -ED/-ING/-S **1** : to import illegally (as prohibited goods) : SMUGGLE **2** : to declare prohibited : FORBID

con·tra·band·age \-dij\ *n* -S : traffic in contraband

con·tra·band·ist \-dəst\ *n* -S [Sp *contrabandista*, fr. *contrabando* contraband (fr. obs. It) + *-ista* -ist] : one engaged in contraband trade : SMUGGLER

contraband of war : something that according to international law cannot be supplied to one belligerent except at the risk of seizure and condemnation by the other

¹**con·tra·bass** \'käntrəˌbās\ *n* -ES [obs. It *contrabasso* (now *contrabbasso*), fr. *contra-* + *basso* — more at BASSO] : the largest instrument of the viol family having usu. four strings tuned in fourths and a range of about three octaves — called also *bass, bass fiddle, bull fiddle, double bass, string bass*

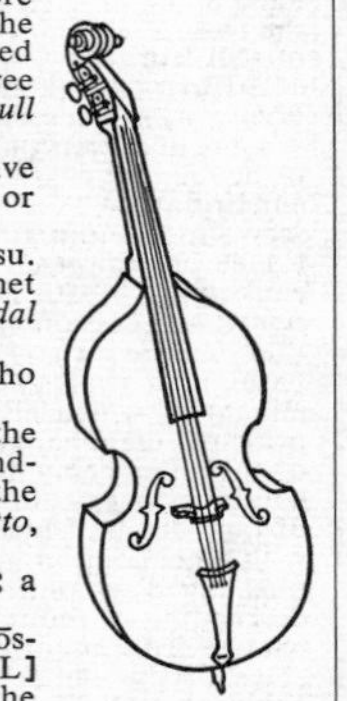

contrabass

²**contrabass** \"\ *adj* : pitched an octave below the normal bass instrumental or vocal range

contrabass clarinet *n* : a clarinet usu. pitched an octave below the bass clarinet — called also *double-bass clarinet, pedal clarinet*

con·tra·bass·ist \-səst\ *n* -S : one who plays a contrabass instrument

con·tra·bassoon \¦käntrə +\ *n* : the largest member of the oboe family sounding an octave lower in pitch than the bassoon — called also *contrafagotto, double bassoon*

con·tra·bassoonist \¦käntrə +\ *n* -S : a contrabassoon player

con·tra bo·nos mo·res \¦kōntrə¦bōnōs-¦mō(ˌ)rās, ¦kän-, -(ˌ)rāz,-rez,-rēz\ *adj* [L] : against good morals : harmful to the moral welfare of society — used of contracts, which are then void by public policy

con·tra·cep·tion \¦käntrə¦sepshən\ *n* -S [*contra-* + *conception*] : the prevention of conception or impregnation by voluntary and artificial means — compare RHYTHM METHOD

¹**con·tra·cep·tive** \¦käntrə¦septiv *also* -təv\ *adj* [*contra-* + *conceptive*] : used for or relating to contraception

²**contraceptive** \"\ *n* -S : a contraceptive agent or device

con·tra·clockwise \¦käntrə +\ *adj (or adv)* [*contra-* + *clockwise*] : COUNTERCLOCKWISE

¹**con·tract** \'kän·ˌtrakt\ *n* -S [ME, fr. L *contractus*, fr. *contractus*, past part. of *contrahere* to draw together, collect, cause, make a bargain, make a contract, fr. *com-* + *trahere* to draw — more at DRAW] **1 a** : an agreement between two or more persons or parties to do or not to do something : BARGAIN, COMPACT, COVENANT; *esp* : an agreement that is legally enforceable — see QUASI CONTRACT; compare CONSIDERATION 8b, DEED, NUDUM PACTUM, PACTUM, PAROL CONTRACT, SPECIALTY CONTRACT **b** : the act by which two persons enter into the marriage relation; *also* : the agreement so to do : BETROTHAL **c** *archaic* : a legal transaction (as a grant between private parties or a grant, charter, or franchise from the state) ⟨no State shall . . . pass any bill of attainder . . . or law impairing the obligation of contracts. . . . *U.S. Constitution*⟩ **d** : a collective agreement (as between an employer and a union) **2** *obs* : a drawing together : mutual attraction **3** : a writing made by the parties to evidence the terms and conditions of a contract **4** : the department or principles of law having to do with contracts **5** *card games* **a** : an undertaking usu. by the player or side that makes the highest bid to win a specified number of tricks or points; *also* : the number of tricks or points so undertaken **b** *contract bridge* : the final bid **c** : CONTRACT BRIDGE **6** [²*contract*] : a word or form undergoing contraction or resulting from contraction **7** : the customary unit of trading in produce exchanges ⟨one ~ in wheat is 5,000 bushels⟩ **8** : one of the installments in a course of schoolwork which a student undertakes to complete within a given time working at his own speed and under individual instruction according to a system originated in the public high school of Dalton, Mass.

²**contract** \(')kän·¦trakt', kən·'-\ *adj* [ME, fr. MF *contracte*, fr. L *contractus*, past part.] : CONTRACTED ⟨a ~ noun⟩ : SHRUNKEN, NARROWED

³**contract** *in sense 1 usu* 'kän,trakt; *in other senses usu* kən'trakt\ *vb* -ED/-ING/-S [MF *contracter* to agree upon, enter into, fr. L *contractus* contract (agreement)] *vt* **1 a** : to enter into with mutual obligations : establish or undertake by contract ⟨~*ed* an engagement with a neighboring . . . farmer —Rose Macaulay⟩ : place under contract **b** : BETROTH, AFFIANCE ⟨~*ed* his daughter with the son of an old friend⟩ **2 a** : to bring on oneself : acquire usu. involuntarily (as a habit) : CATCH ⟨~ a disease⟩ ⟨~*ed* pneumonia⟩ **b** : INCUR ⟨~ an obligation⟩ ⟨~*ed* numerous debts⟩ **3 a** : LIMIT, RESTRICT ⟨the town's limits had not been ~*ed*⟩ **b** *obs* : ABRIDGE **c** : to draw together so as to wrinkle : KNIT ⟨a frown ~*ed* his brow⟩ **d** : to draw together or nearer : CONCENTRATE ⟨~ his armies into one force⟩ **4** [L *contractus*, past part.] : to reduce to less compass or smaller size : squeeze or force together : SHORTEN, NARROW, LESSEN ⟨~ a muscle⟩ : cause to shrink ⟨reexpand the world which Bacon had so effectively ~*ed* —J.W.Krutch⟩ **5** : to shorten (as a word) by omitting one or more sounds or letters or by reducing two or more vowels or syllables to one ~ *vi* **1** : to make a contract : COVENANT, BARGAIN ⟨responsible for ~*ing* with local institutions for the confinement . . . of Federal offenders —*Current Biog.*⟩ ⟨~ for the supply of meat to the barracks⟩ **2** : to draw together so as to diminish in size or extent : SHRINK ⟨iron ~*s* in cooling⟩ : become reduced in compass, duration, or length ⟨years ~*ing* to a moment —William Wordsworth⟩; *specif, of a muscle or muscle fiber* : to shorten and broaden

syn CONDENSE, COMPRESS, CONSTRICT, DEFLATE, SHRINK: CONTRACT is a general antonym for *expand* and indicates any drawing in and limiting of area or scope ⟨the range of classical reading might extend, or from time to time *contract* —H.O.Taylor⟩ ⟨since World War II gold mining has expanded considerably while supplies of Negro labor have been *contracting* —*N.Y. Times*⟩ ⟨he sank back into his chair, seeming to *contract*, to wither before their shocked eyes —Angus Mowat⟩ CONDENSE indicates a reduction of space occupied with resulting greater compactness of original material ⟨*condense* gas into a liquid⟩ ⟨in so far as we can *condense* Langland's message into a few words, we must sum it up as a long search for three degrees of excellence in life — Do Well, Do Better, and Do Best —G.G. Coulton⟩ COMPRESS indicates a pressing, often against resistance, into smaller compass and definite shape ⟨great depths of snow are accumulated, and this weight causes lower layers to *compress* and form ice —Patricia Spring⟩ ⟨one of those tiny handkerchiefs, *compressed* into the shape of a small puffball by being clutched in the palm of a feverish hand —J.C.Powys⟩ ⟨I shall make no attempt to *compress* a history of modern philosophy within the limits of one lecture —A.N.Whitehead⟩ CONSTRICT indicates a binding, squeezing, or gripping contracting, often forced, onerous, or painful ⟨the education of this promising young aristocrat *constricted* by the anti-intellectual traditions of his class excluded him from "the two great conceptions of our day . . . artistic integrity . . . and . . . social justice" —Harry Levin⟩ ⟨from the health point of view garments should in general never be so tight as to *constrict* the tissues —Morris Fishbein⟩ DEFLATE indicates contracting brought about by the exhausting of air or gas that fills or inflates it ⟨*deflate* a balloon⟩ ⟨in his lecture on temperance he *deflated* those who felt too superior to associate with a reformed drunkard —Ruth P. Randall⟩ SHRINK indicates a contracting of length, scope, or volume but may suggest the contracting of wet fabrics ⟨as colonial empires *shrink*, Europe's horizons will too —A.E.Stevenson b.1900⟩ ⟨in 1906 he met his first sharp reverse in losses incurred by the San Francisco earthquake, but it was not until some seven years later that his modest fortune began to *shrink* —G.C.Knight⟩ **syn** see in addition PROMISE

con·tract·able \kən·'traktəbəl, (')kän·¦-\ *adj* : capable of being contracted ⟨~ diseases⟩

con·tract·ant \kən·'trakt³nt, (')kän·¦-\ *n* -S [F *contractant*, fr. pres. part. of *contracter*] : one that contracts

contract bond \'kän,trakt-\ *n* : a bond or other form of indemnity agreement to indemnify one against loss or damage by reason of the breach of a contract (as for building, construction, or supply)

contract bridge \'=,=-\ *n* : a card game for four players in two partnerships identical with auction bridge except that odd tricks do not count toward making game or scoring slam bonuses unless they are undertaken in the contract — see BRIDGE, DUPLICATE BRIDGE

contract carrier \'=,=-\ *n* : a transport line that carries persons or property under contract to one or a limited number of shippers — compare COMMON CARRIER

contracted *adj* **1 a** : agreed upon : BARGAINED ⟨a ~ peace⟩ **b** : BETROTHED **2** : ABRIDGED, CONCISE **3** : ILLIBERAL, SELFISH, NARROW ⟨a ~ mind⟩ **4** : drawn together : SHRUNKEN, WRINKLED ⟨~ brow⟩ : NARROW, SHORTENED ⟨a ~ rest period⟩ — **con·tract·ed·ly** *adv* **con·tract·ed·ness** *n* -ES

contracted foot *or* **contracted heel** *n* : a horse's foot exhibiting a shrinking or contraction of the lateral hoof walls preventing the proper expansion of the parts and producing pressure on the soft structures causing pain and lameness

contracted pelvis *n* : a pelvis that is abnormally small in one or more principal diameters and that consequently interferes with normal parturition

contract grade \'kän,trakt-\ *n* : a certain grade of a product (as wheat or cotton) defined and established by an exchange dealing in this product and assumed to be understood in every transaction between floor traders

con·tract·ile \kən·'traktəl, (')kän·¦-\ *also* **con·tract·ible** \-təbəl\ *adj* [³*contract* + *-ile* or *-ible*] : tending to contract : having the power or property of contracting : displaying or producing contraction

contractile cell *n* : one of the wall cells whose hygroscopic contraction causes the rupture of a sporangium or anther — see DEHISCENCE a (1)

contractile vacuole *n* : a vacuole in many unicellular organisms that gradually enlarges and suddenly collapses, dispersing its watery content often in regular pulsations, and that is thought to maintain the normal hydrostatic relation of the organism with its environment — see AMOEBA illustration

con·trac·til·i·ty \ˌkän·(ˌ)trak'tiləd·ē, -ətē, -i\ *also* **con·tract·ibil·i·ty** \kən·ˌtraktə'bil-, ˌkän·-\ *n* -ES : the capability or quality of shrinking or contracting; *esp* : the power of shortening or drawing into a more compact form possessed by living muscle fibers and to a less extent by many forms of living matter

contract in \'kän,trakt-\ *vi, Brit* : to consent in writing to pay to a trade union a levy for political use — compare CONTRACT OUT

contracting *pres part of* CONTRACT

con·trac·tion \kən·'trakshən\ *n* -S [L *contraction-, contractio*, fr. *contractus* (past part. of *contrahere* to draw together) + *-ion-, -io* -ion — more at CONTRACT] **1** [³*contract* (enter into) + *-ion*] : the making of a contract, agreement, or covenant ⟨the ~ of peace and friendship⟩ ⟨~ of marriage⟩ **2 a** : the action or process of becoming smaller, shorter, or pressed together ⟨the ~ of a gas on cooling⟩ : decrease of size or scope ⟨the ~ at the end of a discharge nozzle⟩ : the quality or state of being contracted : NARROWNESS ⟨complaining of monotony and the ~ of his life⟩ **b** (1) : the shortening and thickening of a muscle or muscle fiber (2) : a percussive tightening of the muscles usu. beginning in the pelvic region, affecting the whole body, and followed by release, the series constituting one of the basic movements of the modern dance **c** : a reduction in the volume of credit outstanding **d** : a reduction in business activity **3** : the act of acquiring or incurring (as a debt) or catching (as an infection) **4 a** (1) : a shortening of a word, syllable, or word group by omission of one or more sounds or letters or by the reduction of two or more vowels or syllables to one — used esp. of shortening in the interior of a word (as *e'er* for *ever*) and of shortening of enclitics (as *'ll* for *will* in *they'll*) and proclitics (as *'t* for *it* in *'t is*) — compare SYNCOPE 2a (2) **:** a form produced by such a shortening **b** (1) **:** representation of a word or part of a word by a nonalphabetic shorthand symbol (as the Latin genitive plural ending *-orum* by *4* or the *m* in Latin *cum* by a mark over the preceding letters, *cū*) — compare SUSPENSION (2) **:** a shorthand sign made up of two or more strokes and representing a word (3) **:** a conventional abbreviation; *esp* **:** one that uses the initial and final letters of a word, sometimes with one or more medial letters (as *Dr.* for *Doctor* or, in Late Latin manuscripts, *ds* for *deus*, *dns* for *dominus*) (4) **:** a braille sign representing a word of several letters (as *and*) or part of a word (as *com*) by means of a 1-cell or 2-cell character or representing a word by means of its chief consonants (as *rcv* for *receive*) **c** *classical prosody* **:** the substitution of one long syllable for two short ones — contrasted with *resolution*

con·trac·tion·al \kən-ˈtrakshənᵊl, (ˈ)kän-ˌ-, -shnəl\ *adj* **:** of, relating to, or caused by contraction

con·trac·tion·ist \-shənəst\ *n* -s **:** an advocate of contraction esp. of the U.S. paper currency — opposed to *expansionist*

contraction joint *n* **:** EXPANSION JOINT

contraction rule *n* **:** a patternmaker's rule in which the divisions are made larger (1/96 for iron, 1/64 for brass) than standard measures to allow for contraction during cooling of the metal being cast

con·trac·tive \kən-ˈtraktiv, (ˈ)kän-ˌ-, -tēv *also* -təv\ *adj* [³*contract* + *-ive*] **:** tending to produce contraction **:** CONTRACTILE — **con·trac·tive·ly** \-təvlē, -li\ *adv*

contract labor \ˈkän-ˌtrakt-\ *n* **1 :** labor based on a free but legally enforceable contract **2 :** labor imported from a foreign country under agreement to work for a particular employer

con·tract·less \ˈ=,=-ləs\ *adj* **:** lacking a contract

contract note \ˈ=,=-\ *n* **:** a brief written announcement given by a factor or broker to his principal that he has bought or sold for his principal a certain amount of merchandise or securities at the terms specified

contract of affreightment \ˈ=,=-\ **:** a charter party in which the vessel leased remains in the management of the owner

con·tract·om·e·ter \ˌkän-(ˌ)trakˈtäməd-ə(r)\ *n* -s [³*contract* + *-o-* + *-meter*] **:** an instrument that measures stresses developed in electrolytically deposited metals

contract on \kən-ˈtrakt-\ *vt* **:** to shrink on (as a steel tire to a wheel)

con·trac·tor \ˈkän-ˌtraktə(r), kən-ˈ-\ *n* -s [LL, fr. L *contractus* (past part. of *contrahere* to contract + *-or* — more at CONTRACT] **1 a :** one that contracts **:** a party to a bargain **:** one that formally undertakes to do something for another **b :** one that performs work (as a printing job) or provides supplies on a large scale (as to troops) according to a contractual agreement at a price predetermined by his own calculations **c :** one who contracts on predetermined terms to provide labor and materials and to be responsible for the performance of a construction job in accordance with established specifications or plans — called also *building contractor* **2 :** something (as a muscle) that contracts or shortens

contract out \ˈkän-ˌtrakt-\ *vi, chiefly Brit* **:** to remove oneself by contract from an incurred obligation ⟨believed that France could *contract out* of the war⟩; *specif* **:** to make formal refusal as a union member to contribute to a political levy — compare CONTRACT IN **~** *vt* **:** to send or assign outside on contract (as a part or process in manufacturing)

contract pinochle \ˈ=,=-\ *n* **:** any of various partnership pinochle games in which a player may pass and later reenter the auction

contract practice \ˈ=,=-\ *n* **:** medical service furnished by a physician or group of physicians to a group or class of individuals under an agreement (as with an industrial plant or a fraternal organization) that specifies the scope of the services to be rendered and the amount and form of the compensation — compare GROUP PRACTICE

contract quasi \ˌ=ˈ=,=\ *or* **contract uti** \-ˈyü,tī, -ˈü,tē\ *n* **:** QUASI CONTRACT

contract rummy \ˈ=,=-\ *n* **:** any of several rummy games in which restriction is placed on what a player must meld in order to go out

contracts *pl of* CONTRACT, *pres 3d sing of* CONTRACT

contract shop \ˈ=,=-\ *n* **1 :** a shop operating under a contract system **2 :** CLOSED SHOP **3 :** a shop in which conditions of employment are covered by a collective agreement

contract station \ˈ=,=-\ *n* **:** a postal station operated under contract by private employees and usu. located in a private establishment (as a drugstore) — compare CLASSIFIED STATION

contract system \ˈ=,=-\ *n* **1 :** an arrangement whereby industrial activities are carried out by a contractor intermediary between the manufacturer or entrepreneur and the workers **2 :** the system of selling to a contractor at a fixed sum per unit of time the labor of convicts to be performed within a prison under prison discipline with the contractor supervising the work and furnishing the materials — compare CONVICT LABOR SYSTEM, LEASE SYSTEM

contract tablet \ˈ=,=-\ *n* **:** an ancient Babylonian or Assyrian clay tablet on which a contract was inscribed

contract theory \ˈ=,=-\ *n* **:** a theory or the group of theories holding that society originated in a contract — compare SOCIAL CONTRACT

con·trac·tu·al \kən-ˈtrakchəwəl, (ˈ)kän-ˌ-, -kshə-\ *adj* [L *contractus* contract + E *-al* — more at CONTRACT] **:** of, relating to, or implying a contract **:** bound or secured by a contract ⟨~ obligations⟩ ⟨a ~ salary increase⟩ — **con·trac·tu·al·ly** \-wəlē, -li\ *adv*

contractual liability insurance *n* **:** insurance against loss due to liability assumed under a contract

con·trac·ture \kən-ˈtrakchə(r), -kshə-\ *n* -s [L *contractura* drawing together, fr. *contractus* (past part. of *contrahere* to draw together) + *-ura* -ure — more at CONTRACT] **1** *archit* **:** a narrowing of the girth of a column (as at the top) — compare ENTASIS **2 a :** a permanent shortening of muscle, tendon, fascia, or scar tissue producing deformity or distortion — see DUPUYTREN'S CONTRACTURE, ISCHEMIC CONTRACTURE **b :** an atypical contraction of skeletal muscle differing from the twitch and from tetanus in the slowness of its development and relaxation, in the absence of summation, and in anomalies of the associated electrical phenomena

con·trac·tus fi·du·ci·ae \kən-ˈtraktəsfiˈdükē,ī, -,fīˈd(y)üshē,ē\ *n* [L, lit., contract of trust] **:** FIDUCIA

contract verb \ˈ=,=-\ *n* [²*contract*] **:** a verb characterized by contraction (sense 4a) — used esp. in Greek grammar

contract whist \ˈ=,=-\ *n* **:** a card game in which the deal, auction, and scoring are as in contract bridge but the play is as in whist with no dummy hand exposed

contra dance *var of* CONTREDANSE

con·tra·dict \ˌkän-trəˈdikt\ *vb* -ED/-ING/-S [L *contradictus*, past part. of *contradicere* to speak against, fr. *contra-* + *dicere* to speak — more at DICTION] *vt* **1** *obs* **:** to resist or oppose in argument (as the claim or proposal of another) **2 :** to assert the contrary of **:** take issue with **:** GAINSAY, IMPUGN **:** deny the truth of ⟨please ~ anything you hear said about . . . me —Sheila Kaye-Smith⟩ **3 a** *logic* **:** to be the contradictory of **b :** to be contrary or opposed to **:** go counter to ⟨no truth can ~ another truth —Richard Hooker⟩ **:** act in a manner contrary to ⟨his practice ~*s* his principles⟩ **~** *vi* **:** to deny, dispute, or assert the contrary of something ⟨he thought it outrageous to dispute and ~ —H.G.Wells⟩ **syn** see DENY

con·tra·dict·ed·ness \ˌ==ˈ===\ *n* -ES **:** the quality or state of being contradicted

con·tra·dict·er *or* **con·tra·dic·tor** \ˌ==ˈ=tə(r)\ *n* -s **:** one who contradicts

con·tra·dic·tio in ad·jec·to \ˌkän-trəˈdiktē(ˌ)ō,inădˈyek(ˌ)tō, -ˈdikshē(ˌ)ō,ina'jek-\ *n, pl* **contradicti·o·nes in adjecto** \ˌ==ˌ==ˈō,nēz-\ [NL, lit., contradiction in what is added] **:** contradiction in terms

con·tra·dic·tion \ˌkän-trəˈdikshən\ *n* -s [ME *contradiccioun*, fr. L *contradiction-, contradictio*, fr. *contradictus* + *-ion-, -io* -ion] **1 a :** the act of opposing in speech **:** GAINSAYING **b :** assertion of the contrary to what has been said or affirmed **:** denial of the truth of a statement **2 a :** a statement or proposition containing contradictory parts ⟨both parts of a ~ cannot possibly be true —Thomas Hobbes⟩ **b :** a self-contradictory phrase or expression ⟨a round square is a ~ in terms⟩ **3 a :** logical incongruity **:** INCOMPATIBILITY ⟨many patriots found no ~ in devoting their energies to the cause . . . and . . . making a little profit on the side —Sidney Warren⟩ **b :** opposition of facts, forces, tendencies, qualities, or events ⟨the inner ~*s* of an economic system⟩ **4 a :** direct opposition of logical contradictories **b :** an instance that violates the law of contradiction

con·tra·dic·tious \ˌ==ˈ=shəs\ *adj* [*contradiction* + *-ous*] **1 a** *obs* **:** CONTRADICTORY; *also* **:** ADVERSE **b** *archaic* **:** SELF-CONTRADICTORY **2 :** inclined to contradict or cavil **:** CONTRARY ⟨when a man won't even agree with you that times are bad you know he is of an independent and ~ nature —A.J. Liebling⟩ — **con·tra·dic·tious·ly** *adv*

con·tra·dic·tive \ˌ==ˈ=diktiv, -tēv *also* -təv\ *adj* **:** CONTRADICTORY — **con·tra·dic·tive·ly** \-təvlē, -li\ *adv*

con·tra·dic·to·ri·ly \ˌkän-trəˈdiktərəlē, -k·trəlē, -li\ *adv* **:** in a contradictory manner **:** OPPOSINGLY, CONTRASTINGLY

con·tra·dic·to·ri·ness \-dikt(ə)rēnəs, -ri-\ *n* -ES **:** the quality or state of being contradictory

¹con·tra·dic·to·ry \ˌkän-trəˈdiktərē, -k·trē, -ri\ *n* -ES [ME, fr. LL *contradictorius*, adj.] **1 a :** a word, proposition, or principle that contradicts another **b :** OPPOSITE, CONTRARY ⟨it is common with princes to will *contradictories* —Francis Bacon⟩ **2** *logic* **a :** a proposition so related to another that if either of the two is true the other must be false and if either is false the other must be true **:** a proposition having the same terms as another proposition but opposite in quality and quantity ⟨"all *a* is *b*" is the ~ of "some *a* is not *b*"⟩ **b :** a term that is the exact negative of another ⟨"white" and "not white" are *contradictories*⟩ — distinguished from *contrary*

²contradictory \ˌ==ˈ=(=)=\ *adj* [LL *contradictorius*, fr. L *contradictus* + *-orius* -ory] **1 :** tending to contradict **:** having the character or qualities of contradiction ⟨schemes . . . ~ to common sense —Joseph Addison⟩ **:** given to contradiction **:** CONTRADICTIOUS ⟨an irritable ~ nature⟩ **:** involving or causing contradiction ⟨uncoordinated often ~, agricultural programs⟩ **2** *logic* **:** being or having the character of a contradictory **syn** see OPPOSITE

contradicts *pres 3d sing of* CONTRADICT

con·tra·distinct \ˌkän-trə +\ *adj* [*contra-* + *distinct*] **:** distinct by way of or by reason of contrast — **con·tra·distinctly** *adv*

con·tra·distinction \ˌkän-trə +\ *n* [*contra-* + *distinction*] **:** the act of contradistinguishing **:** distinction by contrast **:** OPPOSITION ⟨to use that term art in ~ to science —J.W. Krutch⟩

con·tra·distinctive \ˌkän-trə +\ *adj* [*contra-* + *distinctive*] **:** having the quality of contradistinction **:** serving to contradistinguish — **con·tra·distinctively** *adv*

con·tra·distinguish \ˌkän-trə+\ *vt* [*contra-* + *distinguish*] **:** to distinguish by a contrast of opposite qualities ⟨man's earlier discoveries in mathematics were made by observation of his physical surroundings, as ~*ed* from abstract reason —A.N.Whitehead⟩

con·tra·fact \ˈkän-trə,fakt\ *or* **con·tra·fac·tum** \ˈ==,=təm, ,==ˈ==\ *n, pl* **contrafacts** \-ts\ *or* **contrafac·ta** \-tə\ [NL *contrafactum*, fr. ML, neut. of *contrafactus*, past part. of *contrafacere* to counterfeit (trans. of MF contrefaire), fr. L *contra-* + *facere* to do — more at DO] **:** a 16th century musical setting of the mass or a chorale or hymn produced by replacing the text of a secular song with religious poetry — compare PARODY MASS

con·tra·fagotto \ˌkän-trə+\ *n, pl* **contrafagotti** [It, fr. *contra-* (fr. L) + *fagotto* bassoon — more at FAGOTTO] **1 :** CONTRABASSOON **2 :** a reed organ stop of 16-foot pitch

con·tra·flexure \ˌkän-trə+\ *n* [*contra-* + *flexure*] **:** a bending in opposite directions like the curve of an ogee; *also* **:** the point where this occurs **:** a point of contrary flexure or inflexion that in a fixed beam is a point of zero bending moment

con·tra·flow \ˈkän-trə + ,-\ *n* [*contra-* + *flow*] **:** COUNTERFLOW

con·tra·hent \ˈkän-trəhənt\ *adj* [L *contrahent-, contrahens*, pres. part. of *contrahere* — more at CONTRACT] **:** entering into covenant **:** CONTRACTING ⟨one of the parties ~⟩

contrahierba *var of* CONTRAYERVA

con·trail \ˈkän-,=\ *n* -s [*condensation trail*] **:** streaks of condensed water vapor created in the air by an airplane or rocket esp. at high altitudes — called also *vapor trail*

con·tra·indicate \ˌkän-trə+\ *vt* [prob. back-formation fr. *contraindication*] **:** to make (a treatment or procedure) inadvisable ⟨the ugly side of cortisone does not . . . completely ~ its use —Berton Roueché⟩ — **con·tra·indicative** \ˌkän-trə+\ *adj*

con·tra·indication \ˌkän-trə+\ *n* [*contra-* + *indication*] **:** an indication, symptom, or condition that makes inadvisable a particular treatment or procedure

con·tra-ion \ˌkän-trə+\ *n* [*contra-* + *ion*] **:** COUNTERION

¹con·trair \kən-ˈtrār, ˈkän-trər\ *adv* (*or adj*) [ME *contrare, contrair*, fr. MF *contraire*, — more at CONTRARY] *Scot* **:** CONTRARY

²contrair \"\ *vt* -ED/-ING/-S [ME *contraren*, fr. *contrare*, adj.] *Scot* **:** OPPOSE, THWART

con·tra·lateral \ˌkän-trə+\ *adj* [ISV *contra-* + *lateral*] **:** located or occurring on or acting in conjunction with similar parts on an opposite side of the body ⟨the brain cortex controls ~ muscles⟩ — compare IPSILATERAL

con·tral·to \kən-ˈtral(ˌ)tō *also* -räl-\ *n* -s *often attrib* [It, fr. *contra-* (fr. L) + *alto* — more at ALTO] **1 :** the higher of the two countertenor voices or voice parts sung or to be sung in early 4-part church music by the highest adult male voice **:** ALTO 1 **2 a :** the lowest female singing voice or a singer possessing such a voice **:** ALTO 2; *specif* **:** a woman's voice rich and powerful in the lower range with a compass of about two octaves from f upward **b :** the part sung or to be sung by such a singer

con·tra mun·dum \ˌkän-trəˈmündəm, -mən-\ *adv* (*or adj*) [NL] **:** against the world **:** in defiance of all general opinion

con·tra·octave \ˌkän-trə+\ *n* [*contra-* + *octave*] **:** the musical octave that begins on the third C below middle C — see PITCH illustration

con·tra pa·cem \ˌkän-trəˈpä(ˌ)kem, -pāsəm\ *adv* (*or adj*) [ML] **:** against the peace — used of a legal allegation once material in prosecution for trespass but now purely formal

con·tra·pás \ˌkōn-trəˈpäs\ *n, pl* **contrapa·ses** \-ä(ˌ)säs\ [Sp, fr. Catal *contrapàs*, fr. *contra-* (fr. L) + *pas* step, dance step, fr. L *passus* step — more at PACE] **:** a Catalan chain dance of ceremonial origin with grapevine steps varied in rhythm and direction according to the province

con·tra·ple·tal \ˌkän-trəˈplēd-ᵊl\ *adj* **:** polar and complementary

con·tra·plete \ˈkän-trə,plēt\ *n* -s [*contra-* + *-plete* (as in *complete*)] **:** one of the complementary relata of a polar relationship

con·tra·plex \ˈkän-trə,pleks\ *adj* [*contra-* + *-plex* (as in *duplex*)] **:** relating to or capable of sending two messages by telegraph in opposite directions at the same time — compare DIPLEX

con·tra·polarization \ˌkän-trə+\ *n* [*contra-* + *polarization*] **:** the dilating influence of strongly polarizing atoms (as Li^{+}) on closed groups (as ClO_4 or CO_3) that may even cause the group to break up

con·tra·pone \ˈkän-trə,pōn\ *vt* -ED/-ING/-S [L *contraponere* — more at CONTRAPOSITION] **:** CONTRAPOSE

con·tra·po·nend \ˈkän-trəpə,nend, -pō,-\ *n* -s [L *contraponendum* thing that is to be contraposed, neut. of *contraponendus*, gerundive of *contraponere*] *logic* **:** a proposition upon which the operation of contraposition is performed

con·tra·posaune \ˌkän-trə+\ *n* -s [G *kontraposaune*, fr. *kontra-* contra- (fr. L *contra-*) + *posaune* trombone — more at POSAUNE] **:** a powerful reed organ stop sounding an octave or sometimes two octaves lower than the ordinary posaune

con·tra·pose \ˈkän-trə,pōz\ *vt* -ED/-ING/-S [L *contrapositus*, past part. of *contraponere* to place opposite — more at CONTRAPOSITION] **1 :** to set over against (as the thumb to the fingers) **2** *logic* **:** to convert (a proposition) by contraposition

contraposed shoreline *n* **:** a shoreline along which wave action has removed a cover of marine sediments and exposed a previously buried land surface

con·tra·pos·it \ˈkän-trə,päzət\ *vt* -ED/-ING/-S [L *contrapositus*, past part.] **:** CONTRAPOSE 2

con·tra·pos·i·ta \ˌkän-trəˈpäzəd-ə\ *n pl* [L, pl. of *contrapositum* antithesis, fr. neut. of *contrapositus*] *logic* **:** the two propositions appearing in a process of contraposition

con·tra·position \ˌkän-trə+\ *n* [LL *contraposition-, contrapositio*, fr. L *contrapositus* (past part. of *contraponere* to place opposite, fr. *contra-* + *ponere* to put, place) + *-ion-, -io* -ion — more at POSITION] **1 :** a placing over against **:** OPPOSITION, ANTITHESIS **2** *logic* **:** an operation of immediate inference in which the terms of a given proposition are permutated and negated (as given the contraponend "all S is P", there follows the contrapositive "all not-P is not-S and vice versa")

¹con·tra·pos·i·tive \ˌkän-trəˈpäzəd·iv\ *adj* [*contraposition* + *-ive*] **:** of, relating to, or characterized by contraposition

²contrapositive \"\ *n, logic* **:** a proposition resulting from the operation of contraposition

con·trap·pos·to \ˌkōntrəˈpä(ˌ)stō\ *n* -s [It, contraposition, fr. *contrapposto* (past part. of *contrapporre* to oppose), fr. L *contrapositus*, past part. of *contraponere* to place opposite — more at CONTRAPOSITION] **:** a position of the depicted human body (as in late Renaissance painting and sculpture) in which a twisting of the vertical axis results in hips, shoulders, and head turned in different directions

con·tra·prop \ˈkän-trə,präp\ *n* -s [*contra-* + *prop*] **:** CONTRAROTATING PROPELLER

con·trap·tion \kən-ˈtrapshən\ *n* -s [perh. blend of *contrivance, trap*, and *invention*] **:** CONTRIVANCE **:** a newfangled or complicated device — usu. used in mild scorn or indulgence

con·tra·pun·tal \ˌkän-trəˈpəntᵊl\ *adj* [It *contrappunto* + E *-al* — more at COUNTERPOINT] **1 :** of, relating to, or according to the rules of counterpoint **2 :** POLYPHONIC **3 :** presenting a contrast of or interweaving of component elements — **con·tra·pun·tal·ly** \-tᵊlē, -li\ *adv*

con·tra·pun·tal·ist \-ləst\ *n* -s **:** CONTRAPUNTIST

con·tra·pun·tist \ˈkän-trə,pəntəst, ,==ˈ==\ *n* -s [It *contrappuntista*, fr. *contrappunto* + *-ista* -ist] **:** one skilled in counterpoint or one who writes or uses counterpoint

con·tra·pun·to \ˌkän-trəˈpən(ˌ)tō\ *n* -s [It *contrappunto*] **:** COUNTERPOINT

con·tra·remonstrance \ˌkän-trə+\ *n* [NL *contraremonstrantia*, fr. L *contra-* + NL *remonstrantia* — more at REMONSTRANCE] **:** a remonstrance to a remonstrance

con·tra·remonstrant \ˌkän-trə+\ *n* [NL *contraremonstrant-, contraremonstrans*, fr. L *contra-* + NL *remonstrant-, remonstrans* — more at REMONSTRANT] **:** one who makes a contraremonstrance

con·trar·i·ant \kən-ˈtrerēənt, (ˈ)kän-ˌt-\ *adj* [ME *contrariaunt*, fr. MF *contrariant*, fr. LL *contrariant-, contrarians*, pres. part. of *contrariare* to oppose, fr. L *contrarius*] **:** OPPOSED, ANTAGONISTIC, CONTRARY ⟨~ factions⟩ — **con·trar·i·ant·ly** *adv*

contraried *past of* CONTRARY

contraries *pl of* CONTRARY, *pres 3d sing of* CONTRARY

con·tra·ri·e·ty \ˌkän-trəˈrīəd·ē, -əte, -i\ *n* -ES [ME *contrariete*, fr. MF *contrarieté*, fr. LL *contrarietat-, contrarietas*, fr. L *contrarius* + *-tat-, -tas* -ty] **1 :** the quality or state of being contrary **:** OPPOSITION, DISAGREEMENT, INCONSISTENCY **2 :** something that is contrary to something else **:** ANTAGONISM, INCONSISTENCY, DISCREPANCY **:** ADVERSITY ⟨how can these *contrarieties* agree? —Shak.⟩ **3** *logic* **:** the relation of contraries — see OPPOSITION

con·trar·i·ly \(ˈ)kän-ˌtrerəlē, kən-ˈt- — *see* ²CONTRARY\ *adv* **:** in a contrary way **:** CONTRARIWISE, OTHERWISE

con·trar·i·ness *pronunc at* ²CONTRARY + nəs\ *n* -ES [ME *contrarinesse*, fr. *contrarie* + *-nesse* -ness] **:** the quality or state of being contrary **:** OPPOSITION, PERVERSENESS

con·trar·i·ous \kən-ˈtrerēəs, (ˈ)kän-ˌt-\ *adj* [ME, fr. OF *contrarious*, fr. ML *contrariosus*, fr. L *contrarius* contrary + *-osus* -ous — more at CONTRARY] **1** *obs* **:** contrary in tendency or character **:** OPPOSED, HOSTILE **2 a :** PERVERSE, REFRACTORY, ANTAGONISTIC ⟨~ moods⟩ **:** VEXATIOUS ⟨~ weather⟩ **b** *archaic* **:** PREJUDICIAL, HARMFUL — **con·trar·i·ous·ly** *adv*

¹con·trari·wise *pronunc at* ²CONTRARY + ,wīz\ *adv* [ME *contrarie wise*, fr. *contrarie* + *wise*, n.] **1 :** on the contrary **:** OPPOSITELY **:** on the other hand ⟨not rendering evil for evil, or railing for railing; but ~, blessing —1 Pet 3:9 (AV)⟩ **2 a :** in contrary order **:** in a contrary manner **:** CONVERSELY, VICE VERSA ⟨everything that acts upon the fluids must at the same time act upon the solids and ~ —John Arbuthnot⟩ **b :** on opposite sides or in opposite directions ⟨facing ~⟩ ⟨moving ~⟩ **3 :** PERVERSELY, CONTRARILY

²contrariwise \"\ *adj* **:** CONTRARY, PERVERSE ⟨her unexpected and ~ conversation —C.E.Craddock⟩

con·tra·rotating propeller \ˌkän-trə+...\ *n* [*contra-* + *rotating*] **:** one of a pair of propellers (as on a ship or airplane) mounted on concentric shafts, having a common drive, and turning in opposite directions to reduce the torque reaction

con·tra·rotation \ˌkän-trə+\ *n* [*contra-* + *rotation*] **:** rotation contrary to another rotation (as of a propeller)

¹con·trary \ˈkän-ˌtrer\|ē, *Brit usu & US sometimes* -trər\|ē; *sometimes* ˈkän-tr\|ē *or* kən-ˈtrer\|ē; \|i\ *n* -ES [ME *contrarie*, modif. (influenced by L *contrarius*) of OF *contraire*, fr. *contraire*, adj.] **1 :** the opposite **:** a proposition, fact, or condition incompatible with another **2 :** one of a pair of opposites (as objects, facts, qualities) ⟨thinking well of oneself . . . is the exact ~ of self-importance —F.A.Swinnerton⟩ ⟨pleasure and pain, wetness and dryness are *contraries*⟩ **3** *logic* **a :** a proposition so related to another that though both may be false they cannot both be true **:** a universal proposition affirming what another universal proposition denies or denying what another affirms (as "every vine is a tree" and "no vine is a tree") — distinguished from *converse*; compare OPPOSITION **b contrar·ies** *pl* **:** CONTRARY TERMS **4 contrar·ies** *pl, Brit* **:** foreign matter (as buttons and pins in rags or wax and bitumen in waste papers) that is removed in papermaking before pulping — **by contraries** *adv* **1 :** in a manner opposite to what is logical or expected ⟨in dreams things often go *by contraries*⟩ — **on the contrary** *adv* **1 :** on the other hand **2 :** just the opposite **:** NO ⟨"you look tired". "*On the contrary*, I feel fine"⟩ — **to the contrary** *adv* **:** to the opposite effect **:** NOTWITHSTANDING ⟨I know she's unhappy, all her brave talk *to the contrary*⟩

²contrary \", *but* kən-ˈtrer\|ē *or* \|i *is as frequent as any other pronunc for sense 4*\ *adj* [ME *contrarie*, modif. (influenced by L *contrarius* contrary) of MF *contraire*, fr. L *contrarius*, fr. *contra* against + *-arius* -ary — more at CONTRA-] **1 a :** diametrically different **:** OPPOSED ⟨a move ~ to government policy⟩ ⟨facts which point to a ~ conclusion⟩ **b :** opposite in character or nature ⟨firm in the ~ intention⟩ **:** tending to an opposite or opposing course esp. of thought or development ⟨confirmatory or ~ evidence⟩ **c :** mutually opposed **:** ANTAGONISTIC ⟨holding ~ opinions⟩ **2 :** that is the other or opposite ⟨belonging to the ~ sex⟩ **:** opposite in position or direction **:** on the other side **:** in the other way ⟨moving the ~ way⟩ **3 :** opposed to one's interests or desires **:** UNFAVORABLE, PREJUDICIAL ⟨~ to the work which ye intend —Edmund Spenser⟩ — now used only of wind or weather ⟨prevented by ~ winds from reaching port⟩ **4 a :** disposed temperamentally to oppose, contemn, or disregard the wishes or suggestions of others **:** obstinately self-willed in refusing to concur ⟨they've been in your way all these years and you've always complained of them, so don't be ~ —Willa Cather⟩ **b :** expressive of or characteristic of such a temperament **:** PERVERSE ⟨a ~ word⟩ ⟨~ act⟩

syn PERVERSE, RESTIVE, BALKY, FROWARD, WAYWARD, CANTANKEROUS, CROSS-GRAINED, ORNERY: CONTRARY indicates a self-willed opposition to others' wishes, suggestions, and advice ⟨a very *contrary* child⟩ ⟨if you was to take it into your head . . . to marry a man like that . . . you wouldn't hear a single *contrary* word out of me or your ma —Erskine Caldwell⟩ PERVERSE, sometimes a stronger word, may imply wrongheaded, determined, or cranky opposition to the right, correct, established, or normal ⟨a malicious and *perverse* refusal to be convinced by the "greatest and highest evidences" which God has condescended to give to men —Leslie Stephen⟩ ⟨Rimbaud was the rebel incarnate . . . he was *perverse*, untractable, adamant until the very last hour —Henry Miller⟩ ⟨usually the most affectionate and docile of wives, Maimiti was now in one of the *perverse* humors which accompany her condition —C.B.Nordhoff & J.N.Hall⟩ RESTIVE may imply an obstinate disinclination to follow orders or act in accordance with established custom ⟨the common man . . . is increasingly *restive* under the state of "things as they are" —Thorstein Veblen⟩ ⟨Increasingly in today's English it suggests a disinclination arising from restlessness or impatience ⟨the freemen of the Massachusetts towns were *restive* under the strict rule of the magistrates —V.L.Parrington⟩ BALKY, often applied to animals, connotes a tendency to refuse to follow certain orders or to act or function as expected ⟨examination of witnesses mostly reluctant if not downright *balky* —*Nation*⟩ FROWARD implies habitual disobedience and refusal to comply with requests ⟨Russell had always been *froward*, arrogant, and mutinous —T.B.Macaulay⟩ ⟨*froward* beyond control, the insurgent young physician refused to submit the validity of his opinions to the decision of the clergy —John Bennett⟩ WAYWARD suggests extreme self-will and preference for one's own way and often implies an almost ungovernable wantonness ⟨one of the brightest intellects of the university, but he is *wayward*, dissipated, and unprincipled. He was nearly expelled over a card scandal in his first year —A. Conan Doyle⟩ ⟨conceived . . . by a *wayward* mulatto girl in a tryst —Worth T. Hedden⟩ CANTANKEROUS suggests truculent irritability ⟨Giddy felt *cantankerous* and wanted to get a rise out of Kennedy —Willa Cather⟩ ⟨a group of people . . . who are, almost by definition, *cantankerous*, jealous, and uncooperative —James Laughlin⟩ CROSS-GRAINED stresses irascibility and perhaps moroseness ⟨*cross-grained* as a hickory knot, he even resented persuasion from Emerson to convictions he already held —Isabel Paterson⟩ ORNERY suggests crusty disagreeableness ⟨you might find that bear and try to throw him, if you feel so *ornery* —Hervey Allen⟩ ⟨he's *ornery*, hardheaded, the damnedest . . . hotheaded man you ever saw —M.W.Straus⟩ **syn** see in addition OPPOSITE

³contrary *like* ²CONTRARY\ *vt* -ED/-ING/-ES [ME *contrarien*, fr. MF *contrarier*, fr. LL *contrariare* — more at CONTRARIANT] *now dial* **:** to act contrary to **:** OPPOSE, CONTRADICT ⟨try to do as they tell you and don't ~ them —H.L.Davis⟩

⁴contrary *like* ²CONTRARY\ *adv* [ME *contrarie*, fr. *contrarie*, adj.] **:** in a contrary way or manner **:** CONTRARILY, CONTRARIWISE, COUNTER

contrary–minded *pronunc at* ²CONTRARY + ¦mīndəd\ *adj* **:** of a contrary opinion

contrary motion *n* **:** melodic progression of two voices moving in opposite directions

contrary terms *n* **:** terms that cannot both be affirmed in the same sense of the same subject (as *white* and *black*, *good* and *bad*)

contras *pl of* CONTRA

con·tra·seasonal \¦kän·trə +\ *adj* [*contra-* + *seasonal*] **:** contrary or opposite to the normal seasonal trend ⟨a ~ rise in unemployment⟩ — **con·tra·seasonally** *adv*

¹con·trast \'kän‚trast, -raa(ə)st,-raist *also* -rȧst\ *n* -S [F *contraste*, fr. *contraster*] **1** [MF *contrast*, alter. (influenced by OIt *contrasto*, fr. *contrastare*) of *contrest*, fr. *contrester*] *obs* **:** STRIFE, OPPOSITION **2 a :** diversity of adjacent elements in a work of art — opposed to *gradation*, *transition* **b :** juxtaposition of dissimilar elements in a work of art (as complementary colors or lines of different weight) **3 a :** divergence between objects belonging to or having qualities belonging to the same category or associated in an actual or assumed relationship ⟨the ~ between the British and American forms of democracy⟩ ⟨blue eyes form a striking ~ to dark hair⟩ ⟨many authors develop their characters by ~⟩ **b :** comparison of like objects by means of which dissimilar qualities are made prominent ⟨a child of average ability may appear dull by ~ with a brilliant brother⟩ **4 :** a person or thing exhibiting difference upon comparison with another ⟨as a ~ to the Queen, Ophelia brings a note of tenderness into the violent tragedy of *Hamlet*⟩ **5 a :** the quality of a photograph determined by the magnitude of the brightness differences between adjacent parts **b :** the ratio of the maximum and minimum illuminances in a scene ⟨a scene-lighting ~ of three to one⟩ **6 :** a relationship accentuating the differences rather than the similarities between simultaneously or sequentially presented stimuli ⟨a color ~⟩ **syn** see COMPARISON

²contrast \kən·'t-, 'kän‚t- *also* 'kän·'t-\ *vb* -ED/-ING/-S [F *contraster*, fr. MF, to battle, resist, alter. (influenced by OIt *contrastare*) of *contrester*, fr. (assumed) VL *contrastare*, fr. *contra-* + *stare* to stand — more at STAND] *vi* **:** to form a contrast **:** exhibit somewhat marked or noticeable difference by contrast or opposition ⟨~*ing* colors⟩ ⟨his fine words ~*ed* with his unscrupulous behavior⟩ ~ *vt* **1 :** to put in contrast **:** set off by contrast or form a contrast to **2 :** to compare in respect of differences **:** exhibit esp. antithetically the differences and relative worth of ⟨compare and ~ the American and European codes⟩ **syn** see COMPARE

con·trast·able \kən·'t...stəbəl, (')kän·¦t-\ *adj* **:** capable of being contrasted

contrast bath \'kän‚t...-\ *n* **:** a therapeutic immersion of a part of the body (as the extremities) alternately in hot and cold water

con·trast·ed·ly *adv* **:** in a contrasted manner

con·trast·ing·ly *adv* **:** in a way that makes a contrast ⟨demonstrating ~ and startlingly the infinitely greater worth of practices that derive from a spiritual view of the nature of man —J.F.Dulles⟩

con·tras·tive \kən·'trastiv, -raas-,-rais- *also* -rȧs-; (')kän·¦-; -tēv *also* -təv\ *adj* **:** forming or consisting of a contrast **:** CONTRASTING — **con·tras·tive·ly** \-təvlē, -li\ *adv*

contrastive linguistics *n* **:** a branch of linguistics concerned with showing the differences and similarities in the structure of at least two languages or dialects

contrast medium \'kän‚trast-,-raa(ə)st-,-raist- *also* -rȧst-\ *n* **:** a material comparatively opaque to X rays that is injected into a hollow organ to provide contrast with the surrounding tissue and make possible radiographic and fluoroscopic examination

con·trasty \'=¦=stē, -ti\ *adj*, *usu* -ER/-EST **:** displaying marked contrast of visual tone; *esp* **:** having or producing in photography a great difference in brightness between highlights and shadows — compare CHALKY

con·tra·suggestible \¦kän·trə +\ *adj* [*contra-* + *suggestible*] **:** likely to respond to a suggestion by doing or believing the contrary

con·tra·tab·u·lar \¦kän·trə¦tabyələ(r)\ *adj* [*contra-* + L *tabula* board, tablet, will + E *-ar* — more at TABLE] *Roman law* **:** contrary to the terms of a written instrument, usu. a will

contratabular possession *n*, *Roman law* **:** possession of a decedent's estate granted contrary to the terms of his will (as where an emancipated son is neither instituted as heir nor expressly disinherited but is given possession by the praetor)

con·trate \'kän‚trāt\ *adj* [prob. fr. *contra-* + *-ate*] **:** having gear teeth set on the face of the wheel and perpendicular to its plane **:** relating to such an arrangement — used of a wheel in timepieces having verge or platform escapements

con·tra·tempo \¦kän·trə +\ *n* -S [It *contrattempo*, fr. *contra-* (fr. L) + *tempo*] **:** SYNCOPATION 2

con·tra·tenor \¦kän·trə +\ *n* -S [It *contratenore*, fr. *contra-* + *tenore* tenor — more at TENOR] **:** COUNTERTENOR

contra trombone *n* [*contra-*] **:** a reed organ stop of 16-foot pitch in the manual organ and 32-foot pitch in the pedal organ and similar to the contraposaune but less powerful

con·tra·valid \¦kän·trə +\ *adj* [*contra-* + *valid*] **1 :** having no validity **:** FALSE, INDEFENSIBLE **2** *logic*, *of a sentence or class of sentences* **:** having every sentence in the system as a consequence **:** SELF-CONTRADICTORY — **con·tra·validity** \¦kän·trə +\ *n* -ES

con·tra·vallation \¦kän·trə +\ *n* -S [modif. (influenced by L *contra-*) of F *contrevallation*, fr. *contre-* (fr. L *contra-*) + LL *vallation-*, *vallatio* rampart, entrenchment — more at VALLATION] **:** a series of works confronting the walls of an invested place to isolate the defenders and safeguard the besiegers against sallies; *also* **:** construction of such works

con·tra·vene \‚kän·trə'vēn, '==¦=\ *vb* -ED/-ING/-S [MF or LL; MF *contrevenir*, fr. LL *contravenire*, fr. L *contra-* + *venire* to come — more at COME] *vt* **1 :** to go or act contrary to **:** obstruct the operation of **:** INFRINGE, DISREGARD ⟨~ a law⟩ **2 :** to oppose in argument **:** CONTRADICT, DISPUTE ⟨a proposition . . . not likely to be *contravened* —Robert Southey⟩ ~ *vi* **:** to make a contravention **syn** see DENY

con·tra·ven·tion \‚kän·trə'venchən, '==¦==\ *n* -S [MF, fr. LL *contraventus* (past part. of *contravenire*) + MF *-ion*] **1 :** the act of contravening **:** TRANSGRESSION, VIOLATION ⟨warrants in ~ of the acts of Parliament —T.B.Macaulay⟩ **2 a :** the lowest class of offenses in the law codes of many European countries constituted by those punishable in police courts **b** *Scots law* **:** an act in violation of the provisions of a deed resulting in a forfeiture of an estate **c** *Scots law* **:** an act in violation of a judicial bond to keep the peace **syn** see BREACH

con·tra·version \¦kän·trə +\ *n* -S [*contra-* + L *-version-*, *-versio* (fr. *versus* — past part. of *vertere* to turn — + *-ion-*, *-io* -ion) — more at WORTH] **:** a turning toward the opposite side

con·tra·vindicate \¦kän·trə +\ *vi* [L *contra vindicatus*, past part. of *contra vindicare*, fr. *contra* + *vindicare* to claim — more at VENGEANCE] **:** to make a defense or a counterclaim in a Roman legal action to recover possession of property

con·tra·wise \'kän·trə‚wīz\ *adv* [alter. (influenced by *contra-*) of *contrariwise*] **1 :** CONTRARIWISE **2 :** CONTRA

con·tra·yer·va \‚kän·trə'yərvə, ‚kȯn-, -yer-\ *or* **con·tra·hier·ba** \-trə'yerbə, -yervə\ *n* -S [Sp *contrayerba*, *contrahierba*, fr. *contra-* + *yerba*, *hierba* herb, grass, poison, fr. L *herba* herb; fr. the belief that it was a poison antidote — more at HERB] **:** a tropical American herb (*Dorstenia contrayerva*) the aromatic root of which was formerly used as a stimulant, tonic, and diaphoretic; *also* **:** any West Indian species of *Aristolochia* similarly used

con·tre basse \kōⁿ·trəbȧs, 'kän·trə‚bās\ *n* [F *contrebasse*, lit., contrabass fr. MF, fr. OIt *contrabasso* — more at CONTRABASS] **:** a wood or metal organ stop of 16-foot pitch with a string tone — called also *violone*

con·tre·coup \'kōⁿ·trə‚kü, 'kän-, ‚==ˈ=\ *n* -S [F *contre-coup*, fr. *contre-*, counter- + *coup* blow — more at COUP] **:** injury of one part of an organ (as the brain) as a result of the transmitted shock from a blow on the opposite side

con·trec·ta·tion \‚kän‚(‚)trek'tāshən\ *n* -S [L *contrectation-*, *contrectatio* act of touching, feeling, fr. *contrectatus* (past part. of *contrectare* to touch, feel, fr. *com-* + *-trectare*, fr. *tractare* to handle) + *-ion-*, *-io* -ion — more at TREAT] **:** the initial stage of the sexual act concerned with manual contact and tumescence

con·tre·dance \kōⁿ·trədäⁿs, 'kän·trə‚dan(t)s\ *or* **con·tra dance** \'kän·trə‚dan(t)s\ *n* -S [F *contredanse*, by folk etymology (influence of *contre-* counter-) fr. E *country-dance*] **1** *usu* *contra dance* **:** a folk dance in which couples face each other in two lines or in a square — compare COUNTRY-DANCE, LONGWAYS **2** *usu* *contredanse* **:** a piece of music for a contra dance characterized by strongly marked duple rhythm in repeating 8-measure units

con·tre·fort \kōⁿ·trəfōr, 'kän·trə‚fōrt\ *n* -S [F, fr. MF — more at COUNTERFORT] **:** COUNTERFORT

con·tre gambe \kōⁿ·trəgäⁿb, 'kän·trə‚gam(b)\ *n* -S [F *contre-gambe*, fr. *contre-* counter- + *gambe* viola da gamba, short for *viole de gambe*, part trans., part alter. of It *viola da gamba* — more at VIOLA DA GAMBA] **:** an organ flue stop of 16-foot pitch with a string tone

con·tre–jour \¦kōⁿ·trə¦zhü(ə)r\ *adj* [F, lit., counter-daylight] *of a photograph* **:** taken with the camera pointed toward or nearly toward the chief source of light

con·tre·temps \kōⁿ·trətäⁿ, 'kän·trə‚täⁿ\ *n*, *pl* **contretemps** \"\, -‚täⁿz\ [F, fr. *contre-* counter- + *temps* time, fr. L *tempus* — more at TEMPORAL] **1 :** an inopportune embarrassing occurrence **:** MISHAP, MISCHANCE ⟨he moves steadily from one blunder to the next ~ to the next embarrassment —H.A. Smith⟩ **2 :** SYNCOPATION

con·tre viole \kōⁿ·trəvyȯl, 'kän·trəvē‚ōl\ *n* [F *contre-viole*, lit., counter viol] **:** a 16-foot organ stop with a string tone

contributary *var of* CONTRIBUTORY

con·trib·ute \kən·'tribyət, -i(‚)byüt, *chiefly in substand speech* -‚bət; *usu* -d·+V\ *vb* **contributed** \-yəd·əd, -yətəd\ **contributed** \"\ **contributing** \-yəd·iŋ, -yətiŋ\ **contributes** \-yəts, -yüts\ [L *contributus*, past part. of *contribuere* to bring together, fr. *com-* + *tribuere* to grant, impart — more at TRIBUTE] *vt* **1 a :** to give or grant in common with others (as to a common fund or for a common purpose) **:** give (money or other aid) for a specified object ⟨~ $10 to the project⟩ **b :** to furnish or supply (as a share or part to the advance of a project or development) ⟨primitive living conditions . . . have *contributed* a lot to the drift away from these Kimberley stations —F.J.R.Rodd⟩ **:** add (as knowledge or effort) to a common interest or activity ⟨these explorers *contributed* much to our knowledge of the Arctic⟩ **2 :** to supply (as an article) for a publication ~ *vi* **1** *obs* **:** to pay tribute **2 :** to give a part to a common fund or store **:** lend assistance or aid to a common purpose **:** have a share in any act or effect ⟨they . . . *contributed* to obstruct the progress of wisdom —Oliver Goldsmith⟩ **3 :** to write and submit articles to a publication ⟨has written novels and *contributed* to magazines⟩

contributing *adj* **:** that contributes a share in anything or has a part in producing an effect **:** making a contribution to ⟨the seaport was a ~ factor in the growth of the city⟩ **:** that contributes regularly ⟨a ~ editor⟩ ⟨~ members pay the regular two-dollar dues⟩

con·tri·bu·tion \‚kän·trə'byüshən\ *n* -S [ME *contribucioun*, fr. MF *contribution*, fr. LL *contribution-*, *contributio*, dividing, distributing, assigning, fr. L *contributus* + *-ion-*, *-io* -ion] **1 :** a payment imposed upon a body of persons or on the population of a territory by civil, military, or ecclesiastical authority **:** IMPOST; *esp* **:** a tax or imposition levied on the people of a country by an army of occupation orig. as a payment for exemption from pillage but later to meet military necessity **2 :** act of contributing ⟨the ~ of funds to a campaign⟩ **3 a :** something that is contributed **:** a sum or thing voluntarily contributed ⟨a five-dollar ~ to charity⟩ **:** the portion or share that an individual contributes to the common store ⟨a great ~ to our knowledge of the stars⟩ **:** a share contributed to any act or effect ⟨a ~ to the progress of the war⟩ **b :** something written or prepared for publication esp. in a periodical **c :** the whole that is formed by the gifts of individuals ⟨the total ~ amounted to $500⟩ **4 a :** a pro rata apportionment of loss among all the insurance policies covering a property as provided for by a clause in some policies **b :** a distribution of surplus by allocating to each life-insurance policy the excess of premiums and interest earned thereon over the expenses of management, cost of insurance, and the policy value at the date of computation; *also* **:** the excess so distributed **c :** a sum paid by an employer to an unemployment or group-insurance fund or for retirement benefits for employees; *also* **:** a sum paid by employees under such a plan **5 :** a payment of an individual's share in a loss for which several are jointly liable; *also* **:** the amount so paid by one of them

con·trib·u·tive \kən·'tribyəd·iv, -yətiv\ *adj* [MF *contributif*, fr. L *contributus* + MF *-if* -ive] **:** contributing or tending to contribute — **con·trib·u·tive·ly** \-əvlē\ *adv*

con·trib·u·tor \-yəd·ə(r), -ətə-\ *n* -S [AF *contributour*, fr. L *contributus* + AF *-our* -or] **1 :** one that contributes; *specif* **:** one that contributes articles to a publication (as a periodical) ⟨a prolific ~ to magazines⟩ **2** *obs* **:** one that pays tribute

con·trib·u·to·ri·al \kən·¦tribyə¦tōrēəl\ *adj* **:** of or relating to contributing or to a contributor — **con·trib·u·to·ri·al·ly** \-əlē\ *adv*

¹con·trib·u·to·ry \kən·'tribyə‚tōrē, -ȯr-, -ri\ *also* **con·trib·u·tary** \-ter-\ *adj* [ME *contributorie*, *contributarie*, fr. L *contributus* (past part. of *contribuere* to bring together) + ME *-orie* -ory or *-arie* -ary — more at CONTRIBUTE] **1 :** subject to or contributing to a common fund or enterprise **:** subject to levy or furnishing a share or contingent ⟨~ allies⟩ **2 :** of the nature of or forming a contribution **:** entering, given, occurring, or acting as a contribution, share, or aid toward effecting an end or result ⟨~ factors in a crisis⟩ **3** *obs* **:** TRIBUTARY **4** *of an insurance or pension plan* **:** contributed to both by employers and employees

²contributory \"\ *n* -ES [ME *contributorie*, fr. *contributorie*, adj.] **1 :** one that contributes or is bound to contribute; *also* **:** a contributing factor **2** *Eng law* **:** one (as a past or present member) who is liable to contribute to the payment of the debts of a corporation with its being wound up

contributory mortgage *n*, *Brit* **:** PARTICIPATING MORTGAGE

contributory negligence *n*, *law* **:** negligence by an injured party that combines with the negligence of the injurer as a proximate and efficient cause in producing the injury and that bars recovery by the injured party at common law but may only diminish his damages in admiralty and under many statutes — compare WORKMEN'S COMPENSATION INSURANCE

con·trist \kən·¦trist\ *vt* -ED/-ING/-S [MF *contrister*, fr. L *contristare*, fr. *com-* + *tristare* to sadden, fr. *tristis* sad — more at TRISTE] **:** SADDEN

contristate *vb* -ED/-ING/-S [L *contristatus*, past part. of *contristare*] *obs* **:** SADDEN

con·trite \(')kän·¦trīt, kən·'t-, *usu* -īd·+V\ *adj* [ME *contrit*, fr. MF, fr. ML *contritus*, fr. L, bruised, fr. past part. of *conterere* to grind, bruise, fr. *com-* + *terere* to rub, grind — more at THROW] **1 :** broken down in spirit with grief and penitence for sin or shortcoming **:** REMORSEFUL **:** humbly and thoroughly penitent ⟨a ~ heart, O God, thou wilt not despise —Ps 51:17 (AV)⟩ **2 :** proceeding from contrition ⟨~ sighs⟩ **3** *obs* **:** crushed or worn from rubbing — **con·trite·ly** *adv* — **con·trite·ness** *n* -ES

con·trit·ed \kən·'trīd·əd\ *adj* [L *contritus* + E *-ed*] *archaic* **:** CONTRITE

con·tri·tion \kən·'trishən\ *n* -S [ME *contricioun*, fr. OF *contricion*, fr. LL *contrition-*, *contritio*, fr. L *contritus* + *-ion-*, *-io* -ion] **1 :** state of being contrite **:** consciousness of guilt or sin giving rise to humility and sorrow ⟨the tears of my ~ . . . repentance for things past —Edmund Spenser⟩ ⟨tears of ~ for her negligence⟩ **2** *obs* **:** the act of grinding **:** FRICTION **syn** see PENITENCE

con·trit·u·rate \kən·'trichə‚rāt\ *vt* -ED/-ING/-S [*com-* + *triturate*] **:** TRITURATE, PULVERIZE

con·triv·able \kən·'trīvəbəl\ *adj* **:** capable of being contrived

con·triv·ance \kən·'trīvən(t)s\ *n* -S **1 :** the act or faculty of contriving ⟨a ready and lively ~ of certain ideal solutions —J.P.Anton⟩ **:** inventive ability **:** skill at devising **:** INGENUITY ⟨the writer's expert ~ often becomes mere trickery⟩ **2 :** the quality or state of being contrived **:** artificial arrangement or mechanical assembling as opposed to natural or logical development ⟨at times in the story ~ is obvious and so are coming events —L.T.Bulman⟩ ⟨the lack of emotional impact which is the effect of a too careful ~ —*Times Lit. Supp.*⟩ **3 :** a thing contrived: **a :** ARTIFICE, SCHEME, PLAN ⟨telling a story honestly without dramatic ~*s*⟩ ⟨government is a ~ of human wisdom —Edmund Burke⟩ **b :** a mechanical device **:** INVENTION, APPLIANCE ⟨how prosaic the modern . . . ~*s* compared to the old boilers [fire-engines] —Elmer Rice⟩

con·triv·an·cy \-vənsē\ *n* -ES **:** the faculty or means of contriving

¹con·trive \kən·'trīv\ *vb* -ED/-ING/-S [alter. of ME *contreven*, *controven*, fr. MF *controver*, fr. LL *contropare* to compare, fr. L *com-* + LL *-tropare* (perh. fr. L *tropus* metaphor, trope, figure of speech) — more at TROPE] *vt* **1 a :** DEVISE, PLAN, PLOT ⟨~ means of meeting⟩ **b :** to fabricate as a work of art or ingenuity **:** DESIGN, INVENT ⟨from stone, wood, shell, and bone the Indians *contrived* . . . household utensils —*Amer. Guide Series: Tenn.*⟩ **2** *now dial* **:** to find out **:** UNDERSTAND **3** *obs* **:** to form, shape, lay out, or adapt by contrivance ⟨the whole shire *contrived* into 33 hundreds —John Speed⟩ **4 :** to bring about by stratagem or with difficulty **:** EFFECT, MANAGE — often followed by the infinitive ⟨he *contrived* to win the cooperation . . . of Voltaire, Buffon —*Times Lit. Supp.*⟩ ~ *vi* **:** to make devices **:** form plans, schemes, or designs **:** PLAN, SCHEME, PLOT ⟨if we were perfectly satisfied with the present we should cease to ~, to labor, and to save for the future —T.B.Macaulay⟩

syn DEVISE, INVENT, FRAME, CONCOCT: CONTRIVE may suggest ingenuity and cleverness in planning or effecting ⟨a couple of neighboring farmers in a village will *contrive* and practice as many tricks to overreach each other at the next market —Earl of Chesterfield⟩ ⟨the little dress that Maman had so cleverly *contrived* out of two Empire scarves —Anne D. Sedgwick⟩ ⟨you have come here to cast me off and artfully *contrive* that it should appear to be my doing —T.L.Peacock⟩ Sometimes it applies to a deliberate cleverness in factitious works ⟨the *contrived* simplicity of the novel —C.C.Walcutt⟩ DEVISE may suggest reflection, analysis, and experimentation continued over a considerable period ⟨Paterson gradually shifted from cotton to silk manufacture after 1840, when John Ryle *devised* a way of winding silk on a spool —*Amer. Guide Series: N.J.*⟩ ⟨a real science — as well as a real philosophy — of human nature could not be born until there were *devised* techniques of accurate observation and verified experiment —H.A.Overstreet⟩ ⟨within a year they had *devised* the "Pond alphabet" of the Sioux language —*Amer. Guide Series: Minn.*⟩ INVENT may connote more of finding, discovering, making, or making up than of ingenuity or reflection ⟨Newton *invented* the differential and the integral calculus and discovered the laws of motion —K.K.Darrow⟩ ⟨1856, when simultaneously Bessemer *invented* his converter and Siemens introduced the open-hearth process —S.F.Mason⟩ ⟨his pains to *invent* a complete, generally unlovely terminology of his own —H.J.Muller⟩ ⟨he did not know the schoolteacher's name but *invented* one for her —Sherwood Anderson⟩ ⟨I *invented* a monster called Hormuz, who lived in the woods behind the town and devoured little children —John Reed⟩ FRAME in this sense suggests a careful devising and constructing to fit a situation ⟨*framing* legislation which may make valuable contributions to a badly needed national water policy —K.S.Davis⟩ ⟨absorbed in *framing* a question that he was intent on persuading a friend, who was a member of Parliament, to ask in the House of Commons —Osbert Sitwell⟩ CONCOCT may suggest devising by ingenious or inventive combining of ingredients ⟨the most loathsome and noisome abominations that his fervid imagination could *concoct* out of his own bitter experiences and the manners and customs of his cruel times —C.W.Eliot⟩

²contrive *vt* -ED/-ING/-S [L *contriv-*, perf. stem of *conterere* to bruise, grind, consume, exhaust — more at CONTRITE] *obs* **:** to wear away **:** CONSUME **:** PASS ⟨~ time⟩

con·trived \-vd\ *adj* [fr. past part. of ¹*contrive*] **:** showing the effects of planning or devising **:** ARTIFICIAL, LABORED, UNNATURAL ⟨the layman writhes at the ~ coyness of the dialect —Bernard De Voto⟩ ⟨music — always one of the most ~ of all the arts —Winthrop Sargeant⟩ — **con·triv·ed·ly** \-vədlē, -li\ *adv*

con·triv·er \-və(r)\ *n* -S [¹*contrive* + *-er*] **:** one that contrives ⟨hasty ~ of popular fiction —A.C.Ward⟩ ⟨~*s* of leisure-time activities —Mary McCarthy⟩ ⟨an excellent ~ in housekeeping —Oliver Goldsmith⟩

¹con·trol \kən·'trōl\ *vt* **controlled**; **controlled**; **controlling**; **controls** [ME *controllen*, fr. MF *conteroller*, *contreroller*, fr. *contrerolle*, n.] **1** *obs* **:** to check by a duplicate register or account **:** REGULATE ⟨~ accounts⟩ **2 :** to check, test, or verify by counter or parallel evidence or experiments **:** verify by comparison or research ⟨~ an experiment⟩ ⟨no way to ~ his statements⟩ **3** *obs* **:** to call to account **:** CENSURE **4 a :** to exercise restraining or directing influence over **:** REGULATE, CURB ⟨*controlling* her interest in the enterprise⟩ ⟨~ one's anger⟩ **:** DOMINATE, RULE **:** have power over ⟨a single company ~*s* the entire industry⟩ **b** *obs* **:** OVERPOWER **c :** to kill (animals) when not wanted at a particular time or place; *also* **:** to kill off (a particular kind of animal) **syn** see CONDUCT

²control \"\ *n* -S *often attrib* [MF *contrerolle* copy of an account, counter-register, verification, scrutiny, fr. *contre-* counter- + *rolle* roll, catalog, account — more at ROLL] **1 a :** the act or fact of controlling ⟨man's increasing ~ over nature⟩ **:** power or authority to guide or manage **:** directing or restraining domination ⟨under parental ~⟩ ⟨the car went out of ~ on a curve⟩ **b :** effective and reliable skill in the use of a tool, instrument, technique or artistic medium ⟨have ~ of several languages⟩ ⟨the singer's ~ of her voice was perfect⟩ ⟨a poet's ~ of a variety of metrical forms⟩ ⟨a baseball pitcher needs ~ as well as speed⟩ **c :** regulation or direction in the use or application of an artistic medium resulting in proportion and appropriate emphasis **d :** reduction or regulation of wildlife population of an area by killing **e :** the regulation of economic activity esp. by government directive ⟨price ~*s*⟩ ⟨wage ~*s*⟩ ⟨rent ~⟩ — usu. used in pl. **f :** application of policies and procedures for directing, regulating, and coordinating production, administration, and other business activities in a way to achieve the objectives of the enterprise **2 :** RESTRAINT, RESERVE ⟨~ of the passions⟩ **:** SELF-RESTRAINT **:** possession and command of one's faculties ⟨her hands wrung pale in effort at ~ —Amy Lowell⟩ **3 :** a means or method of controlling : one that controls or determines: as **a :** something that affords a standard of comparison or means of verification (as an organism, culture, or group in a control experiment) : CONTROL EXPERIMENT ⟨half the dogs were injected, the others reserved as a ~⟩ ⟨a ~ group⟩ **b :** a hand-operated or automatic mechanism used to regulate or guide the operation of a machine or an apparatus or system (as a steam shovel, a radio, a heating system) — usu. used in pl. **c :** a system of relatively precise field measurements (as a traverse or a triangulation system) with which local secondary surveys may be tied in to ensure their essential accuracy **d :** a personality or spirit believed to actuate the utterances or performances of a spiritualist medium **e :** any of the physical factors (as latitude, altitude, ocean currents) determining the climate of a place **f :** any of the factors determining the nature of geological formations at a given place **g :** a recording device in the form of a letter or number or combination of letters and numbers in the margin of a sheet of British stamps printed between 1887 and 1948 **h :** a control mark on a stamp **syn** see POWER

control account *n* **:** a financial account that summarizes detailed subsidiary accounts or records — called also *controlling account*

control assay *n* **:** an exact assay (as of ore or metal); *esp* **:** one made of a sample from a shipment

control board *n* **:** a panel at which circuit changes are made (as for theater lighting)

control center *n* **:** an installation or activity from which a series of operations is directed ⟨civil defense *control center*⟩

control clock *n* **:** MASTER CLOCK

control column *n* **:** an airplane lever that operates the elevators by a fore-and-aft motion and the ailerons by turning a wheel mounted at the upper end of the lever — compare CONTROL STICK

control electrode *n* **:** the electrode in an electron tube whose voltage with respect to the voltage of the cathode determines the electron flow to the anode

control experiment *n* **:** an experiment for checking the results of other experiments by maintaining the same conditions except in some one particular and thus inferring the causal significance of this varied factor — compare BLANK DETERMINATION, CONTROLLED EXPERIMENT

control grid *n* **:** a grid usu. placed between the cathode and plate of an electron or vacuum tube to modulate the flow of electrons

control head *n* **:** a casinghead for controlling unexpected flows of oil or gas from a well which is being drilled

con·trol·la·bil·i·ty \kən-ˌtrōlə'bilədē, -ətē, -i\ *n* -ES **:** the quality or state of being controllable ⟨the ~ of forest fires⟩

con·trol·la·ble \kən-'trōləbəl\ *adj* **:** capable of being controlled — **con·trol·la·bly** \-blē, -li\ *adv*

controlled *adj* [fr. past part. of *control*] **:** restrained, managed, or kept within bounds (as of decorum or good taste) ⟨with ~ half-conscious desperation —John Hurkan⟩ **:** conducted or maintained in accordance with fixed rules, restraints, or procedures ⟨study disease under ~ conditions —V.G.Heiser⟩

controlled experiment *n* **:** a complex experiment including one or more control experiments or blank determinations along with the actual experimental tests

controlled hypotension *n* **:** low blood pressure induced and maintained to reduce blood loss or to provide a bloodless field during surgery

controlled school *n* **:** a British voluntary usu. denominational school receiving more than half of its maintenance costs from public funds and in return giving up its control over staff appointments — compare AIDED SCHOOL

con·trol·ler \kən-'trō(l)ə(r), 'kän-ˌt-\ *n* -S [ME *conterroller*, fr. MF *contrerolleur*, fr. *contrerolle* copy of an account, counter-register + *-eur* -or — more at CONTROL] **1 a :** one that keeps a duplicate record in order to control accounts **b :** an officer appointed to check expenditure (as a steward) **c :** the chief accounting officer of a business enterprise whose duties usu. include responsibility for all accounting, budgeting, costing, and internal auditing functions, the measuring of performance against previously approved plans and standards, and the interpreting and reporting thereon to other members of the management responsible for policy or executive action **d :** COMPTROLLER 2 **2 a :** one that controls or has power or authority to control **b :** an iron block usu. bolted to a ship's deck into the hollows of which the links of the cable drop as it comes aboard and thus hold fast until disengaged **c :** CONTROL 3b **d :** an electric device for governing in some predetermined way the power delivered to the apparatus (as a motor) to which it is connected **e :** an administrator of a control law (as of price controls or crop controls) **f :** one that controls the use or flight pattern of aircraft or guided missiles by means of electronic or radio communication

con·trol·ler·ship \-(r)ˌship\ *n* -S **1 :** the office of controller **2 :** the position and functions of a controller

con·trol·less \kən-'trōlləs\ *adj* **:** lacking control

controlling *pres part of* CONTROL

controlling account *n* **:** CONTROL ACCOUNT

controlling interest *n* **:** sufficient stock ownership in a corporation to exert control over policy; *also* **:** a person or group that possesses such an interest

con·trol·ling·ly *adv* **:** in a controlling manner

control mark *n* **:** a mark (as a numeral or a device) on a stamp usu. overprinted for checking on its use

con·trol·ment \kən'trōlmənt\ *n* -S [ME, fr. *controllen* to control + *-ment*] *archaic* **:** the act of controlling **:** CHECK

control number *n* **1 :** a control on a sheet of British stamps **2 :** a numerical control mark on a stamp; *also* **:** a serial or catalog number of a precanceled stamp

control panel *n* **:** PANELBOARD 3

control room *n* **:** the room (as in a broadcasting station) in which the control instruments are located

controls *pres 3d sing of* CONTROL, *pl of* CONTROL

control species *n* **:** a species of animal predator or parasite introduced into a region to prey on another kind of animal or plant that is considered undesirable

control stick *n* **:** an airplane lever that operates the elevators by a fore-and-aft motion and the ailerons by a side-to-side motion — compare CONTROL COLUMN

control surface *n* **:** a movable airfoil designed to change the attitude of an aircraft

control tower *n* **:** an elevated glass-enclosed structure which has an unobstructed view of a landing field and from which air traffic may be controlled usu. by radio

control track *n* **:** an auxiliary sound track for a motion picture usu. placed on the same film with the program material and used to control additional features of sound reproduction (as variation in amplification and use of additional speakers)

controversal *adj* [L *controversus*, turned in the opposite direction, disputed (fr. *contro-* — akin to *contra-* — + *versus*, past part. of *vertere* to turn) + E *-al* — more at WORTH] **1** *obs* **:** CONTROVERSIAL **2** *obs* **:** turning or looking opposite ways

controverse *n* -S [MF, fr. L *controversia*] *obs* **:** CONTROVERSY

con·tro·ver·sial \ˌkän·trə¦vərshəl, -vəs|, -vəi|, |sēəl *also* |shēəl\ *adj* [LL *controversialis*, fr. L *controversia* controversy + *-ialis* -ial] **1 :** subject to controversy **:** relating to or arousing controversy **:** being an object of controversy ⟨a ~ figure in public life⟩ ⟨the matter is . . . highly ~ and calculated to provoke violent dissent in many quarters —*Times Lit. Supp.*⟩ **2 :** given to controversy **:** engaging in controversy **:** DISPUTATIOUS, POLEMIC ⟨dogmatic treatises commonly were ~ . . . , directed against pagans or Jews, or Gnostics or Manicheans —H.O.Taylor⟩ — **con·tro·ver·sial·ism** \-əˌlizəm\ *n* -S — **con·tro·ver·sial·ly** \-əlē, -li\ *adv*

con·tro·ver·sial·ist \-ələst\ *n* -S **:** one who engages in controversy **:** DISPUTANT ⟨in his novels the ~ often takes precedence of the artist —B.R.Redman⟩

con·tro·ver·sion \'kän·trəˌvərzhən *also* -rsh-\ *n* -S [ML *controversion-*, *controversio*, alter. of L *controversia* controversy] **1** *obs* **:** CONTROVERSY **2 :** the act of controverting ⟨an argument in ~ of an assertion⟩ **3** [L *controversus* + E *-ion*] **:** a turning in the opposite direction ⟨a general ~ in ethics⟩

con·tro·ver·sy \'kän·trəˌvərsē, -vəs-, -vəis-, -si, *Brit also* kən·'trävə(r)si\ *n* -ES [ME *controversie*, fr. L *controversia*, fr. *contro-* (akin to L *contra-*) + *-versia* (fr. *versus*, past part. of *vertere* to turn) — more at WORTH] **1 a :** the act of disputing or contending **b** (1) **:** a cause, occasion, or instance of disagreement or contention **:** a difference marked esp. by the expression of opposing views **:** DISCUSSION, DISPUTE, DEBATE ⟨engaged in a long ~ with university officials and had denounced evolutionary teachings —*Amer. Guide Series: Minn.*⟩ (2) **:** QUARREL, STRIFE **2 :** a suit in law or equity — distinguished from *case* as not including criminal actions or proceedings ⟨the judicial power shall extend . . . to *controversies* to which the U.S. shall be a party; to *controversies* between two or more States —*U.S. Constitution*⟩ — **in controversy :** to be decided by factual evidence rather than by legal decision

con·tro·vert \'kän·trəˌvərt, -vət, -vəit, ¦==¦=, *usu* -d· +V\ *vb* -ED/-ING/-S [fr. *controversy*, after such pairs as E *conversion: convert*] *vt* **1** *obs* **:** to oppose or contest by action or argument (as possession of a property) **2 :** to dispute or oppose by reasoning **:** DENY, CONTRADICT ⟨~ a point in a discussion⟩ ~ *vi* **:** to engage in controversy **syn** see DISPROVE

controverted election *n, Brit* **:** CONTESTED ELECTION

con·tro·vert·ible \¦==¦=təbəl\ *adj* **:** capable of being controverted — **con·tro·vert·ibly** \-blē, -i\ *adv*

con·tro·vert·ist \-təst\ *n* -S **:** CONTROVERSIALIST

con·tu·ber·nal \kən-'t(y)übə(r)nᵊl\ *adj* [L *contubernalis* tentmate, fr. *com-* + *-tubernalis* (fr. *taberna* hut, booth + *-alis* -al) — more at TAVERN] **:** living together **:** INTIMATE

con·tu·ma·cious \ˌkäntə¦māshəs, -n·tyə¦-,-n·tyü¦-,-nchə¦-\ *adj* [*contumacy* + *-ous*] **:** perverse in resisting authority **:** stubbornly disobedient **:** REBELLIOUS, IRRECONCILABLE ⟨to refer the case of a ~ witness to the court for punishment —H.A. Schweinhaut⟩ **syn** see INSUBORDINATE

con·tu·ma·cious·ly *adv* **:** PERVERSELY, REBELLIOUSLY, STUBBORNLY

con·tu·ma·cy \kən-'t(y)üməsē, (')kän·¦t-, -si; 'käntəm-, -n·tyə-,-nchə-\ *n* -ES [ME *contumacie*, fr. L *contumacia*, fr. *contumac-*, *contumax* insubordinate (fr. *com-* + *-tumax*, fr. *tumēre* to swell, be proud) + *-ia* -y — more at THUMB] **1 :** stubborn resistance to authority; *specif* **:** willful contempt of court **2 :** refusal to comply ⟨the ~ of Frenchmen in stolidly remaining French —G.W.Johnson⟩

con·tu·me·li·ous \ˌkäntə¦mēlēəs, -n·tyə¦-,-n·tyü¦-,-nchə¦-\ *adj* [MF *contumelieus*, fr. L *contumeliosus*, fr. *contumelia* + *-osus* -ous] **:** exhibiting contumely **:** insolently abusive and humiliating **:** DESPITEFUL, DISDAINFUL ⟨~ taunts⟩ ⟨a ~ critic⟩ — **con·tu·me·li·ous·ly** *adv*

con·tu·me·ly \kən-'t(y)ümәlē, (')kän·¦t-, -li; 'käntə,mēlē, -n·tyə-,-nchə-, -ˌməl-; *in the Hamlet soliloquy often* 'känchəml- *or* -n·tyəml- *or* -n·ˌtyüml-\ *n* -ES [ME *contumelie*, fr. MF, fr. L *contumelia*, perh. fr. *com-* + *-tumelia* (akin to *tumēre* to swell); fr. its assumed earlier meaning of "puffed-up, arrogant speech" — more at THUMB] **1 :** rude language or treatment arising from haughtiness and contempt ⟨the book bristles with ~ and wrath —*New Yorker*⟩ **2 :** an instance or exhibition of contumely **:** INSULT ⟨their tracts got burnt or treated with even worse ~ —Samuel Butler †1902⟩ **3 :** the suffering of contumely **:** HUMILIATION ⟨a capacity for bearing ~ —Herman Wouk⟩

con·tund \kən-'tənd\ *vt* -ED/-ING/-S [L *contundere* — more at CONTUSE] *archaic* **:** POUND, BRUISE

con·tur·ba·tion \ˌkän·tə(r)'bāshən\ *n* -S [ME, fr. L *conturbation-*, *conturbatio*, fr. *conturbatus* (past part. of *conturbare* to disturb, fr. *com-* + *turbare* to disturb, fr. *turba* disorder) + *-ion-*, *-io* -ion — more at TURBID] *archaic* **:** DISTURBANCE

con·tuse \kən-'t(y)üz\ *vt* -ED/-ING/-S [MF *contuser*, fr. L *contusus*, past part. of *contundere* to beat, crush, fr. *com-* + *tundere* to beat — more at STUTTER] **1 :** to beat or pound together (as in a mortar) **2 :** to injure or disorganize (superficial or deeper tissues) with or without breaking the skin **:** BRUISE

con·tu·sion \kən-'t(y)üzhən\ *n* -S [ME *conteschown*, fr. MF *contusion*, fr. L *contusion-*, *contusio*, fr. *contusus* + *-ion-*, *-io* -ion] **1 :** the act of contusing or the state of being contused **2 :** a bruise caused by external violence and characterized by hemorrhage into and swelling of the superficial or deeper-lying tissues with or without a break in the covering skin or membrane **syn** see WOUND

con·tu·sioned \-zhənd\ *adj* **:** CONTUSED, BRUISED

conubium *var of* CONNUBIUM

con·u·lar·ia \ˌkänᵊl'a(a)rēə, -nyə'la-\ *n, cap* [NL, fr. *conulus* small cone (dim. of L *conus* cone) + *-aria* — more at CONE] **:** a genus of Paleozoic and Mesozoic tapering shells possibly of worms of uncertain relationships

con·u·lar·i·id \-ēəd\ *n* -S [NL *Conulariida*] **:** a fossil or individual of the group Conulariida

con·u·la·ri·i·da \ˌkänᵊlə'rīədə, -nyələ'-\ *n pl, cap* [NL, fr. *Conularia* + *-ida*] **:** a phylum or other group of extinct invertebrate animals of uncertain relationships known from pyramidal usu. 4-sided chitinophosphatic tests widely distributed in Devonian, Pennsylvanian, and Permian rocks

restoration of an individual conulariid

con·ule \'känᵊl, -nyəl\ *n* -S [NL *conulus*, dim. of L *conus* cone] **:** one of the somewhat conical void elevations of the body surface of certain sponges — **con·u·lose** \-nᵊlˌōs, -nyəˌlōs\ *adj*

co·nun·drum \kə'nəndrəm\ *n* -S [origin unknown] **1** *obs* **a :** CONCEIT, WHIM, FANCY **b :** PUN, QUIBBLE **2 :** a riddle based on some fanciful or fantastic resemblance between things quite unlike and forming a puzzling question whose answer is or involves a pun (as in "Why didn't the children of Israel starve in the desert? Because of the *sand which is* there") **3 a :** a question or problem to which only a conjectural answer can be made ⟨the political ~s, particularly the problem of how the richer areas . . . can be made to subsidize the poorer —Douglass Cater⟩ **b :** a puzzle or problem that is usu. intricate and difficult of solution ⟨it's been a chronic ~ where they were to pay taxes and vote: some have paid taxes to both states, some to neither —*N.Y. Times*⟩ **syn** see MYSTERY

con·ur·ba·tion \ˌkänə(r)'bāshən\ *n* -S [*com-* + L *urb-*, *urbs* town + E *-ation* — more at URBAN] **:** a great aggregation or continuous network of urban communities ⟨the Paris ~ covers the whole of the Department of the Seine and also parts of Seine-et-Oise and Seine-et-Marne —Brian Chapman⟩

con·ure \'känyə(r)\ *n* -S [NL *Conurus* (in some classifications, a genus of parrots), fr. ²*con-* + *-urus*] **:** any of several tropical American parrots (of *Aratinga* and related genera) closely related to and resembling in their brilliant coloration the macaws

co·nu·rop·sis \ˌkän(y)ə'räpsəs\ *n, cap* [NL, fr. *Conurus* + *-opsis*] **:** a genus of small American parrots including among recent forms only the extinct Carolina parakeet

co·nus \'kōnəs\ *n* [NL, fr. L, cone — more at CONE] **1** *cap* **:** a very large genus (the type of the family Conidae) of pectinibranchiate tropical marine snails comprising the cones and including many beautiful and harmless forms and a few chiefly in the southwest Pacific that are highly dangerous by biting with the radula and injecting a paralytic venom that has been known to cause death in man — see GEOGRAPHER CONE, TEXTILE CONE **2** *pl* **co·ni** \-ˌnī,-(ˌ)nē\ [NL, by shortening] **:** CONUS ARTERIOSUS

con·u·sa·ble \'kän(y)əzəbəl\ *adj* [AF, fr. OF *conissable*, fr. *coniss-*, *conoiss-* (stem of *conoistre* to know) + *-able* — more at COGNIZANCE] *law* **:** capable of being judicially examined **:** subject to legal jurisdiction ⟨the matter was particularly reserved for Parliament as being ~ by them alone —T.E.May⟩

conus ar·te·ri·o·sus \-ärˌtirē'ōsəs\ *n, pl* **coni arteriosi** \-ˌsī, -(ˌ)sē\ [NL, lit., arterial cone] **1 :** a prolongation of the ventricle of amphibians and certain fishes that is equipped with a spiral valve by which venous blood going to the pulmocutaneous arteries is separated from arterial blood going to the aorta and systemic arteries **2 :** a conical prolongation of the right ventricle in man and mammals from which the pulmonary arteries emerge

conv *abbr* **1** convalescent **2** convenient **3** convent **4** convention **5** conversation **6** converted; converter; convertible **7** convict **8** convocation

con·va·lesce \ˌkänvə'les\ *vi* -ED/-ING/-S [L *convalescere*, fr. *com-* + *valescere* to grow strong, fr. *valēre* to be strong, be well — more at WIELD] **:** to gather strength **:** recover health and strength gradually after sickness or weakness **:** RECOVER

con·va·les·cence \-sən(t)s\ *n* -S [MF, fr. LL *convalescentia*, fr. L *convalescent-*, *convalescens* (pres. part. of *convalescere*) + *-ia*] **1 :** gradual recovery of health and strength after disease ⟨a patient well advanced in ~⟩ **2 :** the time between the subsidence of a disease and complete restoration to health ⟨quiet and rest during ~⟩

con·va·les·cen·cy \-ənsē\ *n* -ES [LL *convalescentia*] *archaic* **:** CONVALESCENCE

¹**con·va·les·cent** \¦känvə¦lesənt\ *adj* [L *convalescent-*, *convalescens*, pres. part. of *convalescere*] **1 :** recovering from sickness or debility **:** partially restored to health or strength ⟨~ children nearly ready to leave the hospital⟩ **2 :** of, for, or relating to convalescence or convalescents ⟨a patient in a ~ ward⟩ — **con·va·les·cent·ly** *adv*

²**convalescent** \"\ *n* -S **:** one recovering from sickness

convalescent home *n* **:** an institution for the care of convalescing patients

convalescent serum *n* **:** serum obtained from one who has recovered from an infectious disease and considered to be esp. rich in antibodies against the infectious agent of the disease

con·val·la·mar·in \kənˌvalə'ma(a)rən, ˌkänvə'lamər-\ *n* -S [ISV *convall-* (fr. NL *Convallaria*) + *amar-* (fr. L *amarus* bitter) + *-in* — more at AMAROID] **:** a bitter poisonous glycoside extracted from the lily of the valley

con·val·lar·ia \ˌkänvə'la(a)rēə\ *n* -S [NL *Convallaria*, genus of plants having as its only species the lily of the valley, fr. L *convallis* enclosed valley (fr. *com-* + *vallis* valley) + NL *-aria* — more at VALE] **:** the dried rhizome and roots of the lily of the valley

con·val·lar·in \ˌkänvə'la(a)rən, kən'valər-\ *n* -S [ISV *convallar-* (fr. NL *Convallaria*) + *-in*; orig. formed as G *konvallarin*] **:** a poisonous glycoside extracted from the lily of the valley

con·val·la·tox·in \¦kän,valə¦täksən, -nvalə¦-\ *n* -S [NL *Convallaria* + E *toxin*] **:** a crystalline glycoside $C_{29}H_{42}O_{10}$ obtained from the flowers of the lily of the valley that acts on the heart and that on hydrolysis yields strophanthidin and rhamnose

con va·ri·a·zio·ni \¦kän,värē,ätsē¦ō(,)nē, ¦kōn-\ *adv* [It] **:** with variations — used as a direction in music

con·variety \¦kän+\ *n* -ES [*com-* + *variety*] **:** a group of cultivated varieties within a species or an interspecific hybrid ⟨the Darwin tulips constitute a ~⟩

con·vect \kən'vekt\ *vb* -ED/-ING/-S [back-formation fr. *convection*] *vi* **:** to transfer heat by convection ~ *vt* **:** to circulate (warm air) by convection **:** transfer (heat) by convection

con·vec·tion \-kshən\ *n* -S [LL *convection-*, *convectio*, fr. L *convectus* (past part. of *convehere* to bring together, fr. *com-* + *vehere* to carry) + *-ion-*, *-io* -ion — more at WAY] **1 :** the action or process of conveying or transmitting **2 :** a mechanically or thermally produced upward or downward movement of a limited part of the atmosphere that is essential to the formation of many clouds (as cumulus clouds) and is used in certain heating systems **3 a :** the circulatory motion that occurs in a fluid at a nonuniform temperature owing to the variation of its density and the action of gravity **b :** the transfer of heat by this automatic circulation of a fluid — compare CONDUCTION 5a **c :** the transfer of electricity in the form of a surface charge on a moving body (as an electrostatic-generator belt)

con·vec·tion·al \-shənᵊl, -shnəl\ *adj* **:** of, relating to, or produced by convection

convection current *n* **1 a :** a stream of fluid propelled by thermal convection **b :** thermally produced vertical air flow **2 :** a surface charge of electricity on a moving body — compare CONVECTION 3c

con·vec·tive \kən'vektiv\ *adj* [*convection* + *-ive*] **1 :** having the property or power of conveying **:** TRANSPORTING ⟨the ~ force of water⟩ **2 :** of or relating to convection

con·vec·tor \-tə(r)\ *n* -S **:** something that convects; *specif* **:** a room-heating unit in which air heated by contact with a heating device (as a radiator or finned tube) in a casing having openings at top and bottom circulates by convection

¹**convenable** *adj* [ME, fr. MF, fr. *convenir* to be suitable, convenient + *-able*] *archaic* **:** in accord with circumstances **:** PROPER

²**con·ven·able** \kən'vēnəbəl\ *adj* [*convene* + *-able*] **:** capable of being convened or assembled

con·ve·nance \kōⁿv(ə)näⁿs; 'känvənən(t)s, -ˌnän(t)s\ *n, pl* **convenances** \kōⁿv(ə)näⁿs; 'känvənən(t)səz, -ˌnän(t)-\ [F, fr. *convenant*, pres. part. of *convenir* to be suitable] **1 :** conventional usage **2** *convenances pl* **:** the things established by custom as proper to social intercourse **:** CONVENTIONS ⟨a forthright man with little regard for the ~s⟩ **syn** see FORM

con·vene \kən'vēn\ *vb* -ED/-ING/-S [ME *convenen*, fr. MF *convenir* to agree, be suitable, meet, fr. L *convenire*, fr. *com-* + *venire* to come — more at COME] *vi* **1** *of persons* **:** to come together, meet, or assemble in a group or body (as in a formal meeting for some specific purpose) ⟨the executive directors *convened* once a week⟩ **2** *of things* **:** to come, be brought, or occur together at one place or time ⟨large stars *convening* for nativity eve —Genevieve Taggard⟩ **3** *of a body of persons* **:** to meet in formal session ⟨the Seventy-Fifth Congress *convened* in January⟩ ⟨a special committee of jurists *convened* in Washington —Vera M. Dean⟩ ~ *vt* **1 :** to summon to appear before a tribunal or authority ⟨Tom was . . . *convened* before Mr. Allworthy —Henry Fielding⟩ **2 :** to cause (persons) to assemble in a group or body **:** call or gather together ⟨Mlle. Boulanger, who *convened* her bright young composers . . . in Paris —H.W. Wind⟩ **:** CONVOKE ⟨*convened* the assembly⟩ ⟨the court-martial . . . was never *convened* —Anthony Powell⟩ ⟨a world conference was *convened* in Paris⟩

con·ven·er \-nə(r)\ *or* **con·ve·nor** \", -ˌnó(ə)r,-ˌnó(ə)\ *n* -S *chiefly Brit* **:** one that convenes; *esp* **:** the chairman of a committee or other organized body of persons

con·ven·er·ship \-(r)ˌship\ *n* -S *chiefly Brit* **:** the office of official convener

¹**con·ve·nience** \kən'vēnyən(t)s, -nēən-\ *n* -S [ME, fr. MF, fr. L *convenientia*, fr. *convenient-*, *conveniens* + *-ia*] **1** *obs* **:** AGREEMENT, HARMONY, CONGRUITY, APTITUDE **2 :** fitness or suitability for performing some action or fulfilling some requirement ⟨the ~ of the new alphabet for transcribing spoken English⟩ **3 :** a favorable or advantageous condition, state, or circumstance **:** ADVANTAGE ⟨it becomes something of a virtue as well as a ~ to be domesticated —Walter de la Mare⟩ **4 :** something that provides comfort or advantage **:** something suited to one's material wants: **a :** an arrangement, appliance, device, material, or service conducive to personal ease or comfort ⟨a landscaped corner lot, handy to all ~s⟩ ⟨carry camping ~s and . . . supplies on packhorses —H.E.Scudder⟩ **b :** TOILET 5 **5 :** a convenient condition or time **:** OPPORTUNITY ⟨answer at your earliest ~⟩ **6 :** freedom from difficulty, discomfort, or trouble ⟨chairs arranged for his own ~⟩ **:** EASE, COMFORT, EFFICIENCY ⟨impressed by the greater ~ and cheapness of canal transportation⟩ ⟨buildings are not grouped like that by pure accident, though ~ probably had much to do with it —Willa Cather⟩

²**convenience** \"\ *vt* -ED/-ING/-S **:** to afford convenience to **:** ACCOMMODATE ⟨the new system of collection *convenienced* the taxpayer⟩

convenience goods *n pl* **:** articles that are purchased frequently for immediate use in readily accessible stores and with a minimum of effort (as tobacco, magazines, gum, or candy) — contrasted with *shopping goods*

convenience outlet *n* **:** a receptacle in a wall or baseboard for connection to lamps or other electrical appliances

con·ve·nien·cy \-ənsē\ *n* -ES [ME *conveniencie*, fr. L *convenientia*] *archaic* **:** CONVENIENCE

con·ve·nient \kən'vēnyənt, -nēənt\ *adj* [ME, fr. L *convenient-*, *conveniens* suitable, pres. part. of *convenire* to come together, be suitable — more at CONVENE] **1** *obs* **a :** FIT, ADAPTED, SUITABLE, CONGRUOUS ⟨feed me with food ~ for me —Prov 30:8 (AV)⟩ **b :** APPROPRIATE, BECOMING, PROPER **2 a :** suited to personal ease or comfort or to easy performance of some act or function ⟨programs broadcast at hours that are more ~ for the housewife⟩ **b :** suited to the needs or the circumstances of a particular situation ⟨he had . . . the ~ habit of discounting the sufferings of the victims of civilization on the score of their presumed insensibility —Benjamin Farrington⟩ **c :** affording accommodation or advantage ⟨Europe is so divided from Asia by deserts and mountains . . . that it is very ~ to call it a continent —Samuel Van Valkenburg & Ellsworth Huntington⟩ **:** well adapted to ready use ⟨there is no ~ experimental animal for investigating the cold virus —C.H.Andrewes⟩ **3 :** near at hand **:** easily accessible **:** HANDY ⟨the crossroads church, set . . . at a point ~ to a group of plantations —*Amer. Guide Series: Va.*⟩ — **con·ven·ient·ly** *adv*

¹con·vent \ˈkänvənt, -ˌvent\ *n* -s [alter. (influenced by ML & L *conventus*) of earlier *covent*, fr. ME, fr. OF, fr. ML *conventus* community of monks or nuns, fr. L, assembly, fr. *conventus*, past part. of *convenire* to come together — more at CONVENE] **1 :** an association or community of recluses devoted to a religious life under a superior **:** a body of monks, friars, or nuns constituting one local community — now usu. restricted to a convent of nuns **2** *obs* **:** ASSEMBLY, MEETING ⟨these . . . witches beginning to dance (which is an usual ceremony at their ~*s* or meetings) —Ben Jonson⟩ **3 :** a house or set of buildings occupied by a community of religious recluses **:** a monastery or nunnery — now usu. restricted to a nunnery

²convent *vb* -ED/-ING/-S [L *conventus*, past part. of *convenire*] *vt, obs* **:** to cause to come together **:** summon to meet **:** CONVENE, CITE ⟨command him to ~ his whole host —George Chapman⟩ ~ *vi, obs* **:** to meet together ⟨many beasts did often ~ together at some river to drink —John Guillim⟩

con·ven·ti·cal \kənˈventəkəl\ *adj* [in sense 1, fr. ¹*convent* + *-ical*; in sense 2, fr. ¹*conventicle*] **1 :** of or relating to a convent **2 :** of or relating to a conventicle — **con·ven·ti·cal·ly** \-tək(ə)lē\ *adv*

¹con·ven·ti·cle \-kəl\ *n* -s [ME *conventicle*, *conventicule*, fr. L *conventiculum*, dim. of *conventus* assembly — more at CONVENT] **1 :** an assembly, meeting, or convention esp. of a society or body of persons **2 :** an assembly or meeting of an irregular or unlawful character or regarded as having a sinister or evil purpose or tendency **3 :** an assembly for religious worship; *esp* **:** a secret meeting for worship by a group not sanctioned by civil law (as one formerly held by nonconformists in England) **4 :** a meetinghouse or meeting place of a religious group esp. of nonconformists

²conventicle \"\ *vi* -ED/-ING/-S **:** to assemble in a conventicle **:** frequent conventicles

con·ven·ti·cler \-k(ə)lə(r)\ *n* -s **1 :** one who supports or frequents conventicles **2 :** SEPARATIST — used disparagingly

con·ven·tic·u·lar \ˌkänˌvenˈtikyələ(r)\ *adj* [L *conventiculum* + E *-ar*] **:** of, relating to, or resembling a conventicle

con·ven·tion \kənˈvenchən\ *n* -s [ME *convencioun*, fr. MF or L; MF *convention*, fr. L *convention-*, *conventio*, fr. *conventus* (past part. of *convenire* to come together, be suitable, agree) + *-ion-*, *-io* -ion — more at CONVENE] **1 a :** an agreement between persons or parties **b :** an agreement between two or more states arranging for the regulation of matters affecting all of them (as postage, copyright, or the conduct of war) **c :** an agreement enforceable in law **:** CONTRACT, COVENANT **d :** a compact between commanders of opposing armies esp. concerning the exchange of prisoners or the suspension of hostilities **e :** an agreement or decision about basic concepts or principles (as geometric axioms) voluntarily but not altogether arbitrarily arrived at though based neither on physical experiments nor on a priori judgments **f :** an axiom or principle regarded as true by convention **2 a** (1) *obs* **:** a meeting or coming together by chance or plan of two or more persons (2) *obs* **:** the gathering together or union of things (3) *obs* **:** the act of summoning before a court or other authority (4) **:** the summoning or convening of an assembly ⟨forced his ~ of the council⟩ **b** (1) **:** a body or assembly of persons met for some common purpose; *esp* **:** a formal and special or regular assembly of delegates or members of a party or association met to accomplish some specific civil, social, political, or ecclesiastical object or for the exchange of ideas, views, and information of common interest to the group ⟨an annual sales ~⟩ ⟨the American Legion ~⟩ (2) **:** a special assembly of representatives or delegates convened for the purpose of framing or amending a constitution (3) **:** a meeting of the local members of an American political party or of delegates on the county, state, or national level for the purpose of formulating the party platform or of selecting candidates for office ⟨the Democratic national ~⟩ ⟨aldermanic district ~⟩ **c :** a permanent organization maintained within some Protestant denominations to carry on through duly chosen representatives benevolent, educational, and missionary work for an entire denomination or one of its state divisions ⟨the American Baptist *Convention*⟩ ⟨the North Carolina state ~⟩ **3 a :** usage, custom, or practice generally agreed on and followed esp. in social usage or moral matters ⟨words express whatever meaning ~ has attached to them —O.W.Holmes †1935⟩ ⟨rigid ~ prescribes that such meetings open with prayer —D.L.Cohn⟩ ⟨the child is trained to fit into his world, both of fact and ~ —H.A.Overstreet⟩ **b :** a rule, custom, or belief widely accepted and established by long usage ⟨this . . . is not a rule of law; it is a usage or ~ of the Commonwealth which is accepted as binding in practice by all the members —K.C.Wheare⟩ **:** a rule of conduct or behavior **:** a customary pattern of conduct ⟨a rebel against the ~*s* of education —Allen Johnson⟩ **:** a rule, mode, or principle of conduct accepted by society ⟨Henry the Fifth, who asserted that the great made their ~*s* and lesser people followed them —J.F.Wharton⟩ **c :** a practice in bidding or playing that by agreement between partners in certain card games (as bridge) conveys some information not necessarily deducible by logic **d** (1) **:** a practice, device, or mode of performance established by custom and widely recognized and accepted ⟨the ~ of the first-person narrator who observes all but is not implicated in the action⟩ ⟨singing ~*s* such as the use of falsetto and nasality⟩ ⟨putting a front-view eye into a profile face, a ~ found in all primitive art —Herbert Read⟩ **:** a representation or mode of performance recognized as a substitute for a natural form or mode ⟨the ~*s* of Renaissance iconography⟩ (2) **:** a representation (as in art or design) that simplifies, symbolizes, or substitutes for a natural form ⟨the ~ of representing vegetation by circles and slabs⟩ **syn** see FORM

con·ven·tion·al \-chənᵊl, -chnəl\ *adj* [LL *conventionalis*, fr. L *convention-*, *conventio* convention + *-alis* -al] **1 a :** based on, settled by, or formed by agreement or compact **:** STIPULATED, CONTRACTUAL — compare JUDICIAL, LEGAL ⟨~ services reserved by tenures upon grants, made out of the crown or knights' service —Matthew Hale⟩ **b :** CONVENTIONARY **2 a :** according with, sanctioned by, conforming to, or based on convention, custom, or traditional usages or attitudes ⟨a skillful . . . journalist, ~ and conformist except in a strong bent toward liberal humanitarianism —H.S.Canby⟩ **:** established and sanctioned by general agreement and usage **:** TRADITIONAL ⟨it has been ~ to regard the Horites as a legendary race of cave dwellers —E.W.K.Mould⟩ **b** (1) **:** lacking spontaneity, originality, or individuality **:** TRITE ⟨to distinguish . . . that which is organic, animated, expressive, from that which is only ~, derivative, inexpressive —Walter Pater⟩ ⟨a politician of small vision and ~ mind —*New Republic*⟩ (2) **:** commonly encountered, observed, or performed **:** COMMONPLACE, ORDINARY, USUAL ⟨dead-alive, hackneyed people . . . scarcely conscious of living except in the exercise of some ~ occupation —R.L.Stevenson⟩ **c** (1) **:** in accordance with a mode of artistic representation that simplifies or provides symbols or substitutes for natural forms **:** ABSTRACT (2) **:** based on a convention and depending for effectiveness or understanding on recognition of the convention ⟨a ~ bid in bridge indicating extraordinary strength in one suit⟩ (3) **:** of traditional design ⟨silver having a ~ pattern⟩ (4) *of a playing card back* **:** bearing a symmetrical nonpictorial design **3 :** of, like, or relating to a convention, assembly, or public meeting **syn** see CEREMONIAL

conventional heir *n* **:** one entitled by contract to be heir

con·ven·tion·al·ism \kənˈvenchənᵊlˌizəm, -chnəˌli-\ *n* -s **1 :** observance of or tendency to observe conventions ⟨such social compulsives as fear of ridicule, desire for public esteem, prestige, social habits — all that J. S. Mill included in "the authority of *Conventionalism*" —Jerome Frank⟩ **2 :** a conventional practice, usage, or principle ⟨he thanked his soldiers after a victory, but he did not order Te Deums to be sung for it; and in the absence of these ~*s* he perhaps showed more real reverence —J.A.Froude⟩ **3 :** a theory that regards the principles of logic, mathematics, or science as conventions (sense 1e) or as true by convention

con·ven·tion·al·ist \-nᵊləst, -nəl-\ *n* -s **1 :** a member or supporter of a convention (as a constitutional convention) **2 :** an observer of conventions **:** a conventional person **3 :** an adherent of philosophical conventionalism — **con·ven·tion·al·ist·ic** \kənˌvenchənᵊlˈistik, -chnəˌli-\ *adj*

con·ven·tion·al·i·ty \kənˌvenchəˈnaləd·ē, -ətē, -i\ *n* -ES **1 :** the quality or state of being conventional; *specif* **:** adherence to established or traditional social, intellectual, or artistic conventions **2 :** something that is established by conventional use **:** a conventional usage, practice, or thing

con·ven·tion·al·i·za·tion \kənˌvenchənᵊləˈzāshən, -chnəl-\ *n* -s **:** the act, practice, or product of conventionalizing

con·ven·tion·al·ize \kənˈvenchənᵊlˌīz, -nchnəˌlīz\ *vb* -ED/-ING/-S *see -ize in Explan Notes, vt* **1 :** to make conventional **:** cause to conform to conventional rules, patterns, attitudes ⟨*conventionalized* behavior⟩ **2** *in art and design* **a :** to treat in a conventional or nonnaturalistic manner ⟨flowers are *conventionalized* to serve as a motif⟩ **b :** to establish as a readily interpreted mode of representation ⟨an alphabet developing out of *conventionalized* pictographs⟩ ~ *vi* **:** to follow conventional principles

con·ven·tion·al·ly \-nᵊlē, -nəlē, -li\ *adv* **:** in a conventional manner **:** in accordance with convention

conventional mortgage *n* **:** a real-estate mortgage not underwritten by a government agency

conventional person *n* **:** JURISTIC PERSON

con·ven·tion·ary \kənˈvenchəˌnerē\ *adj* [ML *conventionarius*, fr. L *convention-*, *conventio* + *-arius* -ary] **:** acting under convention or contract **:** settled by express agreement — used now chiefly of a form of tenure existing in Cornwall and parts of Devonshire, England

convention blank *n* **:** a report form required to be filed by insurance companies with state insurance departments

con·ven·tio·neer \kənˌvenchəˈni(ə)r, -iə\ *n* -s **:** a person attending a convention

con·ven·tion·er \-ˈ‧‧nə(r)\ *n* -s **1 :** a person attending a convention **2 :** a member of a convention

con·ven·tion·ist \-nəst\ *n* -s **1 :** a member of a convention **2** *obs* **:** a party to a convention or contract

conventions *pl of* CONVENTION

con·ven·to \kōnˈven(ˌ)tō, kənˈ-\ *n* -s [PhilSp, fr. Sp, convent, fr. ML *conventus* — more at CONVENT] **:** the residence of a parish priest in the Philippines or in Spanish America

convents *pl of* CONVENT, *pres 3d sing of* CONVENT

¹con·ven·tu·al \kənˈvenchəwəl\ *adj* [ME, fr. MF or ML; MF, fr. ML *conventualis*, fr. *conventus* convent + L *-alis* -al — more at CONVENT] **1 :** of, relating to, or befitting a convent or the monastic life **:** MONASTIC ⟨in a ~ cell⟩ ⟨various ~ groups⟩ **2** *usu cap* **:** of or relating to the Friars Minor Conventual

²conventual \"\ *n* -s **:** a member of a conventual community; *specif, usu cap* **:** FRIAR MINOR CONVENTUAL

con·ven·tu·al·ly \-wəlē, -li\ *adv* **:** in a manner belonging to or befitting a convent or the monastic life **:** MONASTICALLY

conventual mass *n, usu cap C&M* **:** a daily mass celebrated for and usu. in the presence of the members of a monastic community

con·verge \kənˈvərj, -vəj, -vəij\ *vb* -ED/-ING/-S [ML *convergere*, fr. L *com-* + *vergere* to bend, incline — more at WRENCH] *vi* **1 :** to tend toward one point **:** approach nearer together ⟨the radii of a circle ~ toward the center⟩ **:** move toward a single point **:** come together **:** MEET ⟨in the Forum . . . where all the ways of the world *converged* —John Buchan⟩ ⟨she and her husband both *converged* upon the caller —H.G.Wells⟩ **2 :** to come together, meet, or join so as to form a single product or come to bear on or conclude in a single thing or place ⟨the real social forces which *converged* to bring the Nazis and Fascists to power —W.G.Carleton⟩ ⟨the demand necessarily *converged* upon banks situated in the financial centers —G.L.Harrison⟩ **3** *biol* **:** to develop or possess similar characters — compare CONVERGENCE 3 **4** *of a sequence, series, or integral* **:** to be convergent **:** approach a limit ~ *vt* **:** to cause to tend to one point **:** cause to approach nearer together **:** cause to come together

con·ver·gence \-jən(t)s\ *n* -s **1 a :** the act or condition of converging ⟨~ of two valleys⟩ **:** tending or moving toward union or uniformity ⟨~ of the earnings of skilled and unskilled workers⟩ **:** coming together or joining so as to bear on a single object or conclude in a single product ⟨~ of kindred qualities in two otherwise alien tongues —J.L.Lowes⟩ **b :** an embryonic movement that involves streaming of material from the dorsal and lateral surfaces of the gastrula toward the blastopore and concurrent shifting of lateral materials toward the mid-dorsal line and that is a process fundamental to the establishment of the germ layers **2 :** the state or property of being convergent **3 :** the development or possession of similar characters by animals or plants of different groups due to similarity in habits or environment (as the resemblance in form of body of the whales and fishes) — compare PARALLELISM, RADIATION **4** *anthrop* **:** the independent apparently accidental development of similarities between separate cultures — compare DIFFUSION, PARALLELISM **5 :** movement of the two eyes so coordinated that the images of a single point fall on corresponding points of the two retinas **6 :** overlapping synaptic innervation of a single cell by more than one nerve fiber — compare FACILITATION **7 :** the accumulation of air in a layer or region due to inflowing winds

con·ver·gen·cy \-ənsē, -si\ *n* -ES **:** the quality or state of converging **:** CONVERGENCE

con·ver·gent \-jənt\ *adj* [ML *convergent-*, *convergens*, pres. part. of *convergere* — more at CONVERGE] **1 :** tending to move toward one point or to approach each other **:** CONVERGING ⟨~ lines⟩ **:** coming together **:** JOINING ⟨great ~ movement of the nations to make a world peace —H.G.Wells⟩ **2 a :** exhibiting convergence in form, function, or development **b :** of or relating to the process of convergent evolution by which genetically distinct organisms sharing a common environment come to mimic one another — compare RADIATION **3 a** *of an improper integral* **:** really existent **b :** of or relating to an infinite series that has a sum **c :** of or relating to an infinite sequence whose *nth* term approaches a finite limit as *n* becomes infinite — see ABSOLUTELY CONVERGENT — **con·ver·gent·ly** *adv*

converging lens *n* **:** a lens whose focus for parallel rays is real — compare DIVERGING LENS

converging meniscus *n* **:** a meniscus lens of true crescent-shaped section — see LENS illustration

con·vers·able *also* **con·vers·ible** \kənˈvərsəbəl, -vəs-, -vəis-\ *adj* [MF *conversable*, fr. *converser* to converse + *-able* — more at CONVERSE] **1 :** capable of being readily conversed with **:** pleasant and easy to converse with ⟨a friendly ~ man⟩ **2** *archaic* **:** of, concerning, or suitable for social intercourse ⟨the evening was quiet and ~ —Jane Austen⟩

con·ver·sance \kənˈvərsᵊn(t)s, -vəs-,-vəis-; ˈkänvə(r)sən-\ *or* **con·ver·san·cy** \-nsē, -si; ˈkänv-\ *n, pl* **conversances** *or* **conversancies :** the quality or state of being conversant ⟨~ with a particular subject⟩

¹con·ver·sant \kənˈvərsᵊnt, -vəs-,-vəis-; ˈkänvə(r)sənt\ *adj* [ME *conversaunt*, fr. MF *conversant*, fr. L *conversant-*, *conversans*, pres. part. of L *conversari* to associate with — more at CONVERSE] **1** *archaic* **:** accustomed to dwell or stay **:** abiding for a considerable amount of time ⟨they who have been ~ abroad —Joseph Addison⟩ **2** *archaic* **:** having to do **:** BUSIED, OCCUPIED, CONCERNED — used with *in, about, with, among* ⟨long ~ in this horrid practice —Oliver Goldsmith⟩ ⟨the passions which are ~ about the preservation of the individual —Edmund Burke⟩ **3** *archaic* **:** having frequent, customary, or familiar association **:** intimately acquainted ⟨I have been ~ with the first persons of the age —John Dryden⟩ — used with *with, in, among* ⟨to be ~ in great men's families —Robert Boyle⟩ **4 :** having knowledge or experience ⟨British officers . . . must be ~ with the ways of a dozen or more castes —Christopher Rand⟩ ⟨anyone ~ with other parts of England found our neighborhood very depressing —Joyce Warren⟩ **:** familiar or acquainted by use or study **:** well-informed — used with *with*, formerly often with *in* ⟨~ with business trends⟩ ⟨deeply ~ in the Platonic philosophy —John Dryden⟩ **5** *archaic* **:** inclined to conversation

²conversant \"\ *n* -s **:** one who converses ⟨conversation recorded without the knowledge of the ~*s* —R.C.Pooley⟩

con·ver·sant·ly *adv* **:** in the manner of one who has knowledge or experience (as of a subject or a thing)

con·ver·sa·tion \ˌkänvə(r)ˈsāshən\ *n* -s [ME *conversacioun*, fr. MF *conversation*, fr. L *conversation-*, *conversatio* frequent abode in a place, intercourse, manner of life, fr. *conversatus* (past part. of *conversari* to associate with) + *-ion-*, *-io* -ion — more at CONVERSE] **1** *obs* **a :** the action of living or dwelling in a place ⟨for our ~ is in heaven —Phil 3:20 (AV)⟩ **b :** the action of living, associating, or having dealings with others ⟨my long . . . ~ with him, that continued to his death for twenty-three years —Gilbert Burnet⟩ **c :** manner of living **:** conduct or behavior ⟨be ye holy in all manner of ~ —1 Pet 1:15 (AV)⟩ **d :** those with whom one associates **:** social circle **:** COMPANY ⟨you may know the man by the ~ he keeps —Thomas Shelton⟩ **e :** occupation or association esp. with an object of study or a subject **:** close acquaintance or intimacy ⟨experience in business and ~ in books —Francis Bacon⟩ **2 :** SEXUAL INTERCOURSE — used esp. in the phrase *criminal conversation* **3 a** (1) **:** oral exchange of sentiments, observations, opinions, ideas **:** colloquial discourse ⟨in casual ~ on the street corner⟩ ⟨we had talk enough but no ~; there was nothing discussed —Samuel Johnson⟩ (2) **:** an instance of conversational exchange **:** TALK, COLLOQUY ⟨had a long ~ with his friend⟩ **b** *archaic* **:** a meeting or assembly for conversing or discussing: (1) **:** a public conference or debate (2) **:** an at home or reception **:** CONVERSAZIONE **c :** an informal exploratory discussion of an issue by diplomats of two or more governments or by officials or representatives of any institutions or groups ⟨diplomatic ~*s*⟩ ⟨~*s* among representatives of the colleges, business, and industry —H.D. Gideonse⟩ **4 :** CONVERSATION PIECE — **make conversation :** to talk or converse for the sake of conversing, with no particular purpose, and usu. under some social compulsion ⟨he was only *making conversation* while they waited for the train⟩

con·ver·sa·tion·al \ˌ‧‧ˈsāshənᵊl, -shnəl\ *adj* **1 :** inclined to converse **:** fond of or given to conversation **2 :** of, for, characteristic of, or suited to conversation or oral communication ⟨written in an easy informal ~ style⟩ ⟨a ~ method of teaching by question and answer⟩ ⟨~ talent⟩ — **con·ver·sa·tion·al·ly** \-ᵊlē, -əlē, -li\ *adv*

con·ver·sa·tion·al·ist \-ləst\ *or* **con·ver·sa·tion·ist** \-sh(ə)nəst\ *n* -s **:** one who converses much or who excels in conversation

conversation chair *n* **1 :** a small upright chair with a padded top rail on the back orig. designed in the 18th century for a man to sit in facing backwards astride the seat with his arms resting on the top rail **2 :** a double chair designed so that two people can sit side by side but facing in opposite directions **:** a tête-à-tête chair

conversation piece *n* **1** *or* **conversation picture** *also* **conversation :** a painting of a group of figures (as members of a family) shown in their customary indoor or outdoor surroundings **2 :** a piece of writing (as a play) that depends for its effect chiefly upon the wit or excellent quality of its dialogue **3 :** something that furnishes a subject of conversation (as by reason of its novel, striking, or amusing appearance) ⟨pink elephant beer mugs and Diamond Jim apron waistcoats are *conversation pieces* —Sylvia Wright⟩ ⟨set off . . . with *conversation piece* gloves trailing sweeping panels of white satin lined in champagne tulle —*Time*⟩

conversative *adj* [*conversation* + *-ive*] *obs* **:** CONVERSATIONAL

con·ver·sa·zi·o·ne \ˌkänvə(r)ˌsätsēˈō(ˌ)nē, ˌkōn-, -ˌsat-, -(ˌ)nā\ *n, pl* **conversaziones** \-ˌnēz, -ˌnāz\ *or* **conversazio·ni** \-(ˌ)nē\ [It, lit., conversation, fr. L *conversation-*, *conversatio*] **:** a meeting, reception, or assembly for conversation and social recreation or for discussion of art, literature, or science

¹con·verse \kənˈvərs, -vəs,-vəis\ *vb* -ED/-ING/-S [ME *conversen*, fr. MF *converser*, fr. L *conversari* to associate with, fr. *conversare* to turn often, freq. of *convertere* to turn around — more at CONVERT] *vi* **1** *obs* **:** to move about, live, or dwell esp. in a place ⟨impurities . . . contracted by *conversing* to and fro in a defiling world —Robert Boyle⟩ **2** *obs* **:** to have sexual intercourse **3** *archaic* **:** to become occupied or engaged (as with a subject) **:** have acquaintance or familiarity from long intercourse or study ⟨he had . . . *conversed* so much with money —Henry Fielding⟩ **4** *obs* **:** to have dealings **:** ASSOCIATE (as with another) ⟨to seek the distant hills and there ~ with nature —James Thomson †1748⟩ ⟨Indians . . . *conversed* with the islands near them —Daniel Defoe⟩ **5 :** to engage in conversation **:** exchange thoughts and opinions in speech **:** TALK ⟨they *conversed* like gentlemen, about the racing season, the hunting, the new roads —Stark Young⟩ ~ *vt, obs* **:** to associate or hold conversation with **syn** see SPEAK

²con·verse \ˈkän,v-\ *n* -s **1** *obs* **a :** intimate association **:** social intercourse **b :** CONVERSATION 1e **c :** CONVERSATION 1c **2 :** familiar discourse **:** free exchange of thoughts or views **:** TALK ⟨a freedom to resolve difference by ~ —Julian Huxley⟩ ⟨some perception of the . . . intimate ~ between instructor and student —Allen Johnson⟩ **3** *obs* **:** sexual intercourse **:** CONVERSATION 2

³con·verse \kənˈv-, (ˈ)känˈv-\ *adj* [L *conversus*, past part. of *convertere*] **:** turned about **:** reversed in order or relation **:** acting oppositely or contrarily ⟨deduction . . . runs not from the indubitable data to one's theoretical conclusions, but in the ~ direction, from the theory back to the facts —F.S.C. Northrop⟩ **:** that is the converse of something **:** with the principal terms transposed ⟨Socrates, while he said that the true tragic writer was also an artist in comedy, did not lay down the ~ proposition that the true comic writer is also an artist in tragedy —Samuel Alexander⟩ — **con·verse·ly** *adv*

⁴con·verse \ˈkän,v-\ *n* -s **1 :** something related to something else in a way that is turned about in order, its statement being derived from that of the other by transposing two principal or antithetical terms ("a rainy day and a clear night" is the ~ of "a clear day and a rainy night"): as **a :** a theorem formed by the interchange of hypothesis and conclusion in a given theorem **b :** a proposition in logic obtained by conversion ⟨the ~ of "no *S* is *P*" is "no *P* is *S*" and of "some *S* is *P*" is "some *P* is *S*"⟩ — distinguished from *contrary* **2 :** a thing that is the opposite or reverse of another ⟨proclaim him moral, as well as wise, and the pleasing ~ every-way of his disgraced cousin —George Meredith⟩

syn OBVERSE, REVERSE: these three nouns mean in common that which is the opposite in some way of another thing. Although in its chief application, that is, to statements, CONVERSE implies an interchange or transposition of the significant terms of a given proposition, in popular use it often signifies a proposition or fact that is merely antithetical or opposing in some way ⟨the relation of wife to husband is called the *converse* of the relation of husband to wife —Bertrand Russell⟩ ⟨the words "I need you" are as potent as ever, and Anthony Gilfillan had made a slip in psychology when he imagined that the *converse* "You need me" would weigh much —William McFee⟩ ⟨if the man stood to profit he would offer his services; if the *converse* were true he would avoid any involvement⟩ Applied to the two faces of a coin or medal, OBVERSE refers to the face containing the head and the principal inscription, REVERSE to the other. In strict transfer of this use, OBVERSE may signify the more apparent and intentionally conspicuous side or face of anything, REVERSE the less apparent or less conspicuous side; in common use, however, OBVERSE and REVERSE are used alike to refer to the other side or face of anything or to the opposite of anything ⟨good and evil are but the *obverse* and *reverse* sides of the same shield —M.J. Herskovits⟩ ⟨love means discrimination and preference, and the *obverse* of that is natural aversion —M.R.Cohen⟩ ⟨their rise was merely the *obverse* of the Empire's fall —A.J.Toynbee⟩ ⟨on one side of the sheet was the title; on the *reverse*, the dedication⟩

conversed *past of* CONVERSE

converses *pres 3d sing of* CONVERSE, *pl of* CONVERSE

conversi *pl of* CONVERSUS

¹con·ver·si·ble \kənˈvərsəbəl, -vəs-,-vəis-\ *adj* [L *conversibilis*, fr. *conversus* + *-ibilis* -ible] **:** capable of being converted or transposed

²conversible *var of* CONVERSABLE

conversing *pres part of* CONVERSE

con·ver·sion \kən'vərzhən, -vəzh-,-vəizh-, *Brit usu & US also* -shən\ *n* -s [ME *conversioun*, fr. MF *conversion*, fr. L *conversion-, conversio*, fr. *conversus* (past part. of *convertere* to turn round, convert) + *-ion-, -io* -ion — more at CONVERT] **1 a** (1) **:** change from one belief, view, course, party, or principle to another **:** the bringing over or persuasion of a person to a particular belief, party, or principle ⟨his ~ to, and disillusionment with, the Communist party —Sidney Hook⟩; *specif* **:** the bringing over or persuasion of a person to the Christian faith ⟨in order to help forward ~*s* among her people —I.B. Richman⟩ (2) **:** a change of one's feelings or one's point of view from a state marked by indifference or opposition to one of zealous acceptance, liking, or devotion ⟨Melville's sudden passionate ~ to Shakespeare —K.S.Davis⟩; *specif* **:** such a change in one's religious orientation marked also by a concomitant change in belief **b** (1) **:** change from one form, state, or character into another ⟨turtles . . . await ~ into canned meat and soup —*Amer. Guide Series: Fla.*⟩ ⟨the company's ~ to war production⟩ (2) **:** translation (as of a literary text) from one language into another (3) **:** structural change or remodeling usu. to increase efficiency or usefulness ⟨~ of the aircraft carrier will include strengthening of the flight deck and increasing the fuel capacity⟩ (4) **:** the transformation of an unconscious mental conflict into a symbolically equivalent bodily symptom (5) **:** a change in type of forest management (as from coppice forest system to seedling forest system) (6) **:** the making of a score on a try for point after touchdown in football or a free throw in basketball **c :** an appropriation of and dealing with the property of another as if it were one's own without right ⟨the ~ of a horse⟩ **d :** change from one use or purpose to another ⟨~ of the electronic eye, then used mainly to open doors . . . into an anticrime device —Alan Hynd⟩; *also* **:** the thing so converted (as a hunting rifle converted from a military rifle) **2** *obs* **:** the action of revolving (as on an axis) or turning (as from one position or direction to another) ⟨the ~ of the needle to the north —Sir Thomas Browne⟩ **3 a :** the act of interchanging the terms of a proposition (as by putting the subject in place of the predicate or the contrary) — see CONVERSION PER ACCIDENS, SIMPLE CONVERSION **b :** a change or reduction of the form of a mathematical proposition or expression ⟨the ~ of equations⟩ ⟨the ~ of proportions⟩; *esp* **:** reduction by clearing of fractions **c :** change from one thing to another by substitution **:** EXCHANGE ⟨~ on the railroad from steam to diesel locomotives⟩ **d :** the exchange of property of one nature to property of another nature (as of real to personal, heritable to movable, or the reverse) sometimes considered for legal purposes as having taken place although no actual exchange has been made (as where a trustee has been directed to sell real estate and buy bonds but fails to do so) **e** (1) **:** the exchange of outstanding currency for a new monetary unit as part of the reconstruction of a currency system (2) **:** the change of one or more security issues into a single new issue (3) **:** the exchange of one kind of security for another **f :** the act of converting an insurance policy **4** *in compounding interest* **:** the creation at each interest period of a new principle sum by adding the accrued interest to the principal of the preceding period **5 :** the amount (as of a hydrocarbon oil) converted in a chemical reaction or decomposition **6 :** the transferring of information from one code to another usu. with a simultaneous transfer from one recording medium to another

con·ver·sion·ary \-nerē\ *adj* **:** of or relating to conversion (sense 1c) ⟨commit a ~ act⟩

conversion cost *n* **:** the combined total of direct labor cost and burden incurred in processing raw materials to a finished state

conversion hysteria *or* **conversion reaction** *n* **:** a psychoneurosis manifested by somatic conversion symptoms

con·ver·sion·ist \-nəst\ *n* -s **:** one devoting himself to converting others (as to a belief in Christianity)

conversion per accidens *n, logic* **:** the transposing of the subject and predicate of a proposition involving the limitation of quantity from universal to particular, valid of universal affirmatives ⟨"some *P* is *S*" is the *conversion per accidens* of "all *S* is *P*"⟩

conversion privilege *n* **:** the contractual right to exchange one security for another at the owner's option (as the right to exchange bonds to common stock of the issuer at a fixed ratio)

conversion table *n* **:** a table of equivalents for changing units of measure or weight into other units

con·ver·sive \kən'vərsiv, -vəs-,-vəis-\ *adj* [F *conversif*, fr. *conversion* + *-if* -ive] **:** CONSECUTIVE 3b

con·ver·so \kən'ver(,)sō, kōn-\ *n* -s [Sp, convert, fr. *converso* converted, fr. ML *conversus*] **:** a Jew who publicly recanted his faith and adopted Christianity under the pressure of the Spanish Inquisition

con·ver·sus \kən'vərsəs, -vəs-, -vəis-; -ver-\ *n, pl* **conver·si** \-,sī, -(,)sē\ [ML, fr. L, past part. of *convertere*] **1 :** a lay brother **2 :** an administrator of episcopal or monastic property

[1]**con·vert** \kən'vərt, -vət, -vəit, *usu* -d·+V\ *vb* -ED/-ING/-S [ME *converten*, fr. OF *convertir*, fr. ML *convertere*, fr. L, to turn around, employ, transform, fr. *com-* + *vertere* to turn — more at WORTH] *vt* **1 a** (1) **:** to bring over or persuade (a person or group) to a particular belief, view, course, party, or principle often from a previously held position ⟨he was ~*ed* to the Copernican theory by . . . the professor of astronomy —S.F.Mason⟩ ⟨~ young people to the pleasures of reading⟩ ⟨an ex-Tory who . . . had gone to give a Socialist editor a good piece of her mind and come away ~*ed* —N.F.Busch⟩; *specif* **:** to bring over or persuade to the Christian faith ⟨no attempt was made to ~ the Moslems —W.H.Prescott⟩ (2) **:** to bring about a spiritual conversion in (as a religious conversion in a person or group) **b** (1) **:** to change or turn from one state to another **:** alter in form, substance, or quality **:** TRANSFORM, TRANSMUTE ⟨sheepskins are ~*ed* into parchment⟩ ⟨ideas . . . ~*ed* into deeds —John Mason Brown⟩ (2) **:** to turn (iron) into steel by the Bessemer process **:** turn (matte) into copper **:** make (Bessemer steel) from iron **:** make (copper) from matte (3) **:** to change the chemical nature of (as by changing starch into dextrose) (4) **:** to finish (gray goods) by dyeing, bleaching, or printing (5) **:** to score on a try for point after touchdown in football or a free throw in basketball) (6) **:** to process (paper) as by gumming or waxing; *also* **:** to fabricate (paper) into finished products ⟨~ paper into envelopes or paperboard into cartons⟩ **c** (1) **:** to change or turn from one use, purpose, or function to another ⟨~*ing* some newly unpacked article . . . into a missile against the head of some unfortunate servant —T.L.Peacock⟩ ⟨every possible industry was ~*ed* to produce war goods —Morris Sayre⟩ (2) **:** to remodel in order to accommodate to a new manner of operation or change from one type to another ⟨~ a coal furnace to oil⟩ ⟨a trawler ~*ed* into a minesweeper⟩ (3) **:** to appropriate dishonestly or illegally ⟨~*ing* to its own . . . use 80,000 bushels of corn stored for the Commodity Credit Corp. —*Time*⟩ **2 a** *obs* **:** to cause to turn **:** TURN, DIRECT ⟨which way shall I first ~ myself —Ben Jonson⟩ **b** *obs* **:** to turn back **:** cause to return **:** turn in the opposite direction **3** [ME *converten*, fr. OF *convertir*, fr. LL *convertere* to convert, fr. L, to turn around, transform] **a** *obs* **:** to translate into another language ⟨which story . . . Catullus more elegantly ~*ed* —Ben Jonson⟩ **b** *logic* **:** to make a conversion of (a proposition) **c :** to exchange for a specified equivalent ⟨~ stock holdings into cash⟩ **d :** to create a situation that causes (property of one nature) to be deemed in equity changed into property of another nature — compare CONVERSION 3d **e :** to exchange (one security) for another under a conversion privilege or an offer made by the issuer **f :** to turn (one type of money) into another in the market or merely for purposes of calculation ⟨~ francs into dollars⟩ **g :** to exchange (an insurance policy) for one of a different type ~ *vi* **1 :** to make or undergo a conversion **:** undergo physical, moral, or functional change ⟨let grief ~ to anger —Shak.⟩ ⟨factories were ~*ing* to war production⟩ ⟨a sofa that ~*s* into a bed⟩ **2 :** to make a score on a try for point or a free throw **syn** see TRANSFORM

[2]**con·vert** \'kän,v-\ *n* -s **:** a person or group that is converted to a religious faith or to a particular belief, attitude of mind or feeling, course, party, or principle ⟨a ~ and disciple of Saint Paul⟩ ⟨the first American novelist to become a . . . ~ to naturalism —Malcolm Cowley⟩; *esp* **:** one who has experienced conversion

converted *past of* CONVERT

converted rice *n* [fr. *Converted*, a trademark] **:** rice that has been processed to retain its natural mineral and vitamin content and to have improved keeping qualities

con·ver·tend \'känvə(r),tend\ *n* -s [L *convertendum* thing that is to be converted, neut. of *convertendus*, gerundive of *convertere* — more at CONVERT] **:** a proposition in logic subjected to the process of conversion

con·vert·er \kən'vər|d·ə(r), -vȯ|,-vəi|, |tə-\ *n* -s **:** one that converts a thing, person, or group ⟨is the steer that eats eight pounds of wheat, corn, and soybeans to give us one pound of meat an efficient food ~ —George Poindexter⟩: as **a :** a workman or machine that performs a step or series of steps in the transformation of materials into a manufactured product (as a furnace in which air is blown through crude metal or matte to refine it or the operator of such a furnace) **b** *or* **conver·tor** \"\ **:** a device for changing energy from one form to another (as formerly a transformer or now a machine employing mechanical rotation) — see MOTOR CONVERTER, SYNCHRONOUS CONVERTER **c :** a businessman or firm that buys unfinished goods for finishing; *specif* **:** one that buys gray goods and finishes them by dyeing, bleaching, or printing **d :** a radio device usu. consisting of an oscillator and mixing tube that is used in superheterodyne receivers or other equipment where a change of signal frequency is desired **e** (1) **:** a cipher machine; *esp* **:** an electric one adaptable to automatic operation (2) **:** a machine that transfers information from one code to another and usu. from one recording medium to another **f :** an auxiliary device for adapting a television receiver to receive channels for which it was not orig. designed

converter plant *n* **:** an indicator plant capable of absorption of selenium or copper and sometimes leaving a residue of it in upper layers of the soil

con·vert·ibil·ity \kən,vər|d·ə'biləd·ē, -vȯ|,-vəi|, |tə'-, -ətē, -i\ *n* -ES **1 :** the quality of being convertible; *specif* **:** the ability of currency to be exchanged for gold or other currencies without restriction ⟨a bilateral ~ of the currencies of the two friendly countries⟩ **2 :** the ability, the freedom, or the right to exchange a currency for gold or other currencies without restriction ⟨the two countries adopted a mutual ~⟩

[1]**con·vert·ible** \kən'vər|d·əbəl, -vȯ|,-vəi|, |təb-\ *adj* [ME, fr. MF, fr. ML *convertibilis*, fr. L, changeable, fr. *convertere* to turn round, transform + *-ibilis* -ible — more at CONVERT] **:** capable of being converted: as **a :** interchangeable in meaning ⟨*synonymous* and *equivalent* are ~ terms⟩ **b :** capable of being changed in form, properties, type, or use **:** capable of being adapted to more than one use ⟨heat ~ into electricity⟩ ⟨an afternoon dress ~ for evening wear⟩: as (1) **:** capable of being worn in more than one way ⟨a ~ collar worn open or closed⟩ (2) *of an automobile* **:** having a top that may be folded back, lowered, or removed ⟨a ~ coupe⟩ ⟨a ~ sedan⟩ **c** *logic* **:** capable of being transposed by conversion **d :** capable of being converted to a belief, opinion, or principle ⟨a man not easily ~ to strange manners and morals⟩ **e** (1) **:** capable of being exchanged for a specified equivalent (as property, value, or obligation of another kind) ⟨preferred stock ~ at an agreed ratio into common⟩ (2) *of currency* **:** capable of being exchanged without restriction for currency of another kind ⟨francs ~ into dollars⟩ — **con·vert·ible·ness** *n* -ES

[2]**convertible** \"\ *n* -s **:** something that is convertible: as **a :** a convertible term in a logical proposition **b :** a convertible automobile — compare HARDTOP CONVERTIBLE

con·vert·ibly \-blē,-bli\ *adv* **:** INTERCHANGEABLY

converting *pres part of* CONVERT

con·vert·i·plane *or* **con·vert·a·plane** \kən'vərd·ə,plān\ *n* [[1]*convert* + connective *-i-* or *-a-* + *-plane*] **:** an aircraft combining the vertical takeoff of the helicopter with the greater forward speed of the airplane, having a rotating airfoil for vertical lift, and capable of conversion to a fixed-wing configuration for forward flight

con·ver·tive \kən'vərd·iv\ *adj* **:** tending to convert **:** CONVERTING

converts *pres 3d sing of* CONVERT, *pl of* CONVERT

con·veth \'kän,veth\ *n* -s [ML *conveth, cuneveth*, of Celt origin; akin to MIr *connmedh* quarterage, billeting — more at COYNYE] **:** a burden upon land under the Scottish tribal chiefs orig. of a night's entertainment of the chief and his followers

[1]**con·vex** \(')kän¦veks, kən'v-\ *adj* [MF or L; MF *convexe*, fr. L *convexus* vaulted, arched, convex, concave, fr. *com-* + *-vexus* (akin to *vacillare* to sway, stagger) — more at VACILLATE] **1 :** curved or rounded as the exterior or a section of a spherical or circular form — used of a spherical surface or curved line viewed from without; opposed to *concave* **2 :** arched up **:** bulging out — used of that side of a curve or surface on which the tangent line or plane lies or on which normals at neighboring points diverge; opposed to *concave* — **con·vex·ly** *adv* — **con·vex·ness** *n* -ES

[2]**con·vex** \(')kän¦v-\ *n* -ES *archaic* **:** a convex body, surface, or part (as a vault or arch seen from without); *specif* **:** the vault of the sky ⟨half heaven's ~ glitters with the flame —Thomas Tickell⟩

[3]**con·vex** \'kän,v-, kən'v-\ *vb* -ED/-ING/-ES **:** to bend convexly **:** bow outward in a convex curve

con·vex·i·ty \kən'veksəd·ē, kän-, -ətē, -i\ *n* -ES [MF or L; MF *convexité*, fr L *convexitat-, convexitas*, fr. *convexus* convex + *-itat-, -itas* -ity] **1 :** the quality or state of being convex ⟨a degree of ~⟩ **2 :** a convex surface, curve, part, or body ⟨a man . . . with a ripe ~ under his waistcoat —Leslie Charteris⟩

con·vexo–concave \kən¦veksō +\ *adj* [[1]*convex* + *-o-* + *concave*] **1 :** convex on one side and concave on the other **2 :** having the convex side of greater curvature than the concave

con·vexo–convex \kən¦veksō +\ *adj* [[1]*convex* + *-o-* + *convex*] **:** BICONVEX

convex polygon *n* **:** a polygon each of whose angles is less than a straight angle

[1]**con·vey** \kən'vā\ *vb* -ED/-ING/-S [ME *conveyen*, fr. OF *conveier*, fr. (assumed) VL *conviare*, fr. L *com-* + *-viare* (fr. *via* way) — more at VIA] *vt* **1** *obs* **:** to accompany as a guide or escort **:** LEAD, CONDUCT ⟨~ him to the tower —Shak.⟩ **2 a :** to bear from one place to another **:** CARRY, TRANSPORT ⟨the Irish mail was ~*ed* by coach to Holyhead —O.S.Nock⟩ **b :** to impart or communicate either directly by clear statement or indirectly by suggestion, implication, gesture, attitude, behavior, or appearance ⟨words will not ~ what is in my heart —H.S.Truman⟩ ⟨something . . . which ~*ed* the idea that he could say more if he chose —Samuel Butler †1902⟩ **c** (1) *archaic* **:** STEAL (2) *obs* **:** to carry or take away or remove usu. secretly **d :** to transfer or deliver (as property) to another; *specif* **:** to transfer (as real estate) or pass (a title, as to real estate) by a sealed writing **e :** to serve as a channel or medium for in carrying or in aiding passage from one place or person to another **:** cause to pass from one place or person to another **:** TRANSMIT ⟨an infection ~*ed* by food⟩ ⟨a pipe for ~*ing* water⟩ ⟨~ this message to your brother⟩ **3** *obs* **:** to derive by succession or descent **4** *obs* **:** to manage or conduct (as affairs) esp. with privacy or craft ⟨~ the business as I shall find means —Shak.⟩ ~ *vi, law* **:** to make conveyance **syn** see CARRY

[2]**convey** *n* -s *obs* **:** a convoy or protective escort

con·vey·al \-āəl\ *n* -s **:** CONVEYING, CONVEYANCE

con·vey·ance \-āən(t)s\ *n* -s **1 :** the action of conveying: as **a :** the communication or transmission of thought, idea, or meaning ⟨~ of the meaning . . . through speech —A.T. Davison⟩ **b :** CARRYING, TRANSPORTING, TRANSPORTATION ⟨the railways are . . . suited to the ~ of heavy loads at high speed —O.S.Nock⟩ **:** a serving as a means of transportation ⟨~ of irrigation water⟩ **c :** the act by which the title to property (as real estate) is transferred **:** the transfer of ownership — compare CONVEYANCING 2 **d** *archaic* **:** a carrying off or removal (as feloniously or by stealth) **:** THEFT **e** *obs* (1) **:** the act or manner of conducting or managing (2) **:** crafty or dishonest management **:** underhanded work or practice **:** TRICK, ARTIFICE **2 :** a means or way of conveying: as **a** *obs* **:** a way or means of communicating (as thought or meaning) or passing (as from place to place) **b :** an instrument in writing (as a deed or mortgage) by which the title to property is conveyed from one person to another **c** *obs* **:** a channel or passage for conduction or transmission (as of fluids or electricity) ⟨these pipes and these ~*s* of our blood —Shak.⟩ **d :** a means of carrying or transporting something (as persons as passengers) **:** VEHICLE ⟨all . . . who had horses and ~*s* of any sort —Kenneth Roberts⟩

con·vey·anc·er \-ənsə(r)\ *n* -s **1 :** one that conveys something **2 :** one whose business is conveyancing; *esp* **:** a lawyer who specializes in the conveyancing of properties

con·vey·anc·ing \-ənsiŋ\ *n* -s **1** *obs* **:** crafty management or practice **2 :** the act or business of drawing deeds, leases, or other writings for transferring the title to property **:** the branch of law having to do with titles and their transference

con·vey·er *or* **con·vey·or** \kən'vāə(r)\ *n* -s **1 :** one that conveys: as **a :** one that carries or transmits ⟨a ~ of bold new ideas⟩ **b** *obs* **:** THIEF **c :** a person who transfers property **2 a** *usu conveyor* **:** a mechanical apparatus for carrying packages or bulk material from place to place: as (1) *or* **conveyor belt :** an endless moving belt (as of canvas, rubber, metal) on which items, packages, or material to be moved may be placed and which operates over terminal pulleys or rollers together with receiving and delivery appliances — called also *band conveyor, belt conveyor* (2) **:** a set of arms or trays for carrying that travel on an endless chain (3) **:** two or more slow-moving chains on which bulky parts of work in process are placed so that smaller parts may be added as the work passes — called also *chain conveyor* (4) **:** containers (as baskets or carriages) or hooks attached to a moving chain or cable suspended by rollers from overhead supports (5) **:** a series of horizontal rollers spaced close together and turned by power in the same direction (6) **:** buckets attached to or forming a continuous moving chain — called also *bucket conveyor* (7) **:** wooden or steel plates attached to endless chains and running in a trough through which material to be moved is dragged (8) **:** an enclosed single-plate or double-plate helix formed about a turning shaft that moves material along a trough or tube — called also *auger conveyor, screw conveyor* (9) **:** air pumps or blowers arranged to draw or force material to be moved and air through a hose or pipe usu. to a separator where the solid material falls to the bottom — called also *pneumatic conveyor, wind conveyor* **b :** one that operates a conveyor

conveying *pres part of* CONVEY

conveyor belt *n* **:** CONVEYER 2a (1)

conveyor–belt \⸗'⸗⸗¦⸗\ *adj* [*conveyor belt*] **:** of, relating to, or characteristic of mass production ⟨*conveyor-belt* uniformity⟩ ⟨*conveyor-belt* shoddiness —Roy Lewis & Angus Maude⟩

con·vey·or·ize \kən'vāə,rīz\ *vt* -ED/-ING/-S **1 :** to equip with a conveyor ⟨*conveyorized* assembly lines⟩ ⟨~ an industrial plant⟩ **2 :** to do, achieve, or effect by means of a conveyor ⟨*conveyorized* . . . heat-treatment of gears —*Chem. Abstracts*⟩ ⟨the *conveyorized* assembly of radios⟩

conveys *pres 3d sing of* CONVEY, *pl of* CONVEY

[1]**con·vict** \kən'vikt\ *adj* [ME, fr. L *convictus*] *archaic* **:** CONVICTED

[2]**convict** \"\ *vt* -ED/-ING/-S [ME *convicten*, fr. L *convictus*, past part. of *convincere* to convict, prove — more at CONVINCE] **1 a :** to find or declare guilty of an offense or crime by the verdict or decision of a court or other authority ⟨he was tried, ~*ed*, and fined $50⟩ **b :** to show or prove to be guilty of something blamable (as wrong or error) ⟨their writings ~ them of an ignorance of history⟩ **2 a** *obs* **:** to demonstrate by proof or evidence **:** PROVE **b :** to convince of error or sinfulness ⟨~ us of sin⟩ **c** *archaic* **:** to prove to be false or in the wrong **:** REFUTE

[3]**con·vict** \'kän,v-\ *n* -s [[1]*convict*] **1 :** a person pronounced guilty by a competent tribunal of a criminal offense; *esp* **:** a person convicted of and under sentence for a felony or serious crime ⟨~*s* transported to the colonies for life⟩ **2 :** a person serving a prison sentence usu. for a long term ⟨~ labor⟩ ⟨~ uniforms⟩ **3** *or* **convict fish** [so called fr. the resemblance of their striped skin to the traditionally striped garb of convicts] **:** any of various striped or barred fishes **syn** see CRIMINAL

con·vict·ed \-təd\ *adj* [*conviction* + *-ed*] **:** conscious of and repentant for one's sin **:** CONVERTED

convict goods \'⸗,⸗-\ *n pl* [[3]*convict*] **:** goods produced by convict labor

con·vic·tion \kən'vikshən\ *n* -s [ME *conviccioun*, fr. LL *conviction-, convictio* proof, fr. L *convictus* + *-ion-, -io* -ion — more at CONVICT] **1 :** the act of proving, finding, or adjudging a person guilty of an offense or crime ⟨~ of the prisoner for burglary⟩; *specif* **:** the proceeding of record by which a person is legally found guilty of any crime esp. by a jury and on which the judgment is based **2** *obs* **:** demonstration or proof; *esp* **:** the proof or exposure of error **3 a :** the act of convincing a person of error or of compelling the admission of a truth **b** (1) **:** the state of being convinced of error or compelled to admit the truth ⟨all his tedious talk is but vain boast, or subtle shifts ~ to evade —John Milton⟩ (2) **:** the state of being convinced of and repentant for one's sin — often used with *under* ⟨making them think in order to bring them to ~ of sin —G.B.Shaw⟩ ⟨unaware that for a month he had been under ~⟩ **4 a :** a strong persuasion or belief ⟨the ~ that the next man he would meet . . . would be his father —E.J.Simmons⟩ ⟨~ that learning was essential for godliness —K.B.Murdock⟩ **b :** the state of being convinced (as of the truth or rightness of one's belief or acts) ⟨he was an internationalist by ~⟩ **:** a feeling or awareness of the rightness, truth, or certainty of what is thought, spoken, or done ⟨the actors played with great ~⟩ ⟨not enough ambition to shape his thought, nor enough ~ to give rhythm to his style —W.B. Yeats⟩ **c convictions** *pl* **:** strongly held beliefs or views ⟨certain thoughts sustain us in defeat . . . and it is these thoughts . . . that we call ~*s* —W.B.Yeats⟩ **syn** see OPINION

con·vic·tion·al \-shənᵊl, -shnəl\ *adj* **:** of or concerning conviction

con·vict·ism \'kän(,)vik,tizəm\ *n* -s [[3]*convict* + *-ism*] **:** the policy or practice of transporting convicts to colonial penal settlements

con·vic·tive \kən'viktiv\ *adj* [L *convictus* + E *-ive*] **:** producing or tending to produce conviction **:** CONVINCING ⟨a ~ answer⟩ — **con·vic·tive·ly** \-tə̇vlē\ *adv*

convict labor system *n* **:** a plan or system for utilizing convict labor often authorized by law — compare CONTRACT SYSTEM, LEASE SYSTEM, PIECE PRICE SYSTEM, PUBLIC ACCOUNT SYSTEM, PUBLIC WORKS AND WAYS SYSTEM, STATE USE SYSTEM

con·vic·tor \-tə(r)\ *n* -s [L, fr. *convictus* (past part. of *convivere* to live with, feast together, fr. *com-* + *vivere* to live) + *-or* — more at QUICK] *archaic* **:** a table companion **:** COMMONER

con·vince \kən'vin(t)s\ *vt* -ED/-ING/-S [L *convincere* to refute, convict, prove, fr. *com-* + *vincere* to conquer — more at VICTOR] **1 a** *obs* **:** to overcome by argument **:** CONFUTE ⟨Satan stood . . . confuted and *convinced* —John Milton⟩ **:** prove to be wrong or in error **:** demonstrate the fallacy of ⟨God never wrought miracle to ~ atheism because his ordinary works ~ it —Francis Bacon⟩ **b** *obs* **:** OVERPOWER, OVERCOME, SUBDUE **2 a** *obs* **:** to prove guilty **:** CONVICT ⟨which of you *convinceth* me of sin —Jn 8:46 (AV)⟩ **b** *obs* **:** DEMONSTRATE, PROVE ⟨to ~ the honor of my mistress —Shak.⟩ **3 :** to bring to or cause to have belief, acceptance, or conviction ⟨this ruse succeeded in *convincing* his pursuers that he was drowned —S.P.B.Mais⟩ **:** bring by argument to give assent or have belief ⟨it is difficult to ~ people that . . . we would also gain something —Vera M. Dean⟩

convinced *adj* **:** having or feeling strong belief or conviction ⟨he was a ~ and fanatical pacifist —W.A.White⟩ **:** CERTAIN, SURE ⟨~ that it would be to their advantage to join —A.P. Ryan⟩ — **con·vinced·ly** \-sədlē, -stlē, -li\ *adv* — **con·vinced·ness** \-sədnəs, -s(t)n-\ *n* -ES

con·vince·ment \-smənt\ *n* -s **:** the action of convincing or the state of being convinced; *esp* **:** religious conviction or conversion ⟨many of the first ~*s* by Quaker missionaries —*Times Lit. Supp.*⟩

con·vinc·er \-sə(r)\ *n* -s **:** one that convinces; *specif* **:** a particular act or argument that brings conviction ⟨the offer of $15 was the ~⟩

convincing *adj* **1 :** satisfying or assuring by argument or proof ⟨one very ~ test which so strongly supports the tradition that it seems conclusive —Hilaire Belloc⟩ **2 :** having the power to convince one of the truth, rightness, or reality of what is done or stated **:** PLAUSIBLE ⟨the dialogue is most ~ —G.C. Sellery⟩ ⟨more ~ than most spy novels —Anthony Boucher⟩ **syn** see VALID

con·vinc·ing·ly *adv* : in a convincing manner

con·vive \kōⁿvēv, 'kän,vīv\ *n, pl* **convives** \kōⁿvēv, 'kän-,vīvz\ [F, fr. L *conviva* one who lives with another, eats with another, fr. *com-* + *-viva* (fr. *vivere* to live) — more at QUICK] : a fellow banqueter or feaster : a comrade at table

con·viv·i·al \kən'vivēəl, -vyəl\ *adj* [LL *convivialis*, fr. L *convivium* banquet (fr. *com-* + *-vivium*, fr. *vivere* to live) + *-alis* -al — more at QUICK] : of, relating to, or occupied with feasting, drinking, and good company ⟨the lighthearted cup and the ~ jest for them —W.S.Gilbert⟩ : fond of good company and of festivity ⟨Virginians of the ~ sort, sportsmen, lovers of scenery, lovers of horses —Van Wyck Brooks⟩ **syn** see SOCIAL

con·viv·i·al·i·ty \kən,vivē'aləd·ē, -ətē, -i\ *n* -ES **1** : convivial quality esp. of spirit or humor ⟨his ~, warmth, and good nature were irresistible⟩ **2** : convivial activities or behavior ⟨evenings spent in ~⟩

con·viv·i·al·ly \kən'vivēəlē, -vyəl-, -li\ *adv* : in a convivial manner

con·viv·i·um \-vēəm\ *n, pl* **conviv·ia** \-vēə\ [L] **1** : a convivial gathering : BANQUET **2** [NL, fr. L] : a subdivision of a commiscuum comprising a group of organisms that are set apart by characters other than interfertility and are maintained by some isolating mechanism other than intersterility and usu. equivalent in scope to a taxonomic subspecies or variety

con·vo·cate \'känvə,kāt\ *vt* -ED/-ING/-S [L *convocatus*, past part. of *convocare*] *archaic* : to call together : CONVOKE

con·vo·ca·tion \,känvə'kāshən, -nvō'-\ *n* -S [ME *convocacioun*, fr. MF *convocation*, fr. L *convocation-*, *convocatio*, fr. *convocatus* (past part. of *convocare* to convoke) + *-ion-*, *-io* -ion — more at CONVOKE] **1 a** : an assembly or meeting of persons convoked ⟨the Accession Council, the oldest governmental ~ in England —*Time*⟩; *also* : the people so assembled **b** (1) : an assembly of representatives of Church of England clergy that is constituted by statute to consult on ecclesiastical affairs (2) : a meeting of an organization in the Protestant Episcopal Church that is composed of the clergy and some of the laity of a territorial division of a diocese to promote interest in such matters as diocesan missions; *also* : the organization itself which is a purely voluntary one with no legislative functions or the territorial division (3) : the annual meeting in the Protestant Episcopal Church of the bishop, clergy, and lay delegates of a missionary jurisdiction which not being a diocese cannot hold a diocesan convention **c** *at some British universities* (1) : a deliberative, advisory, or elective body composed usu. of graduates or of those with the degree of M.A.; *also* : an assembly of this body (2) : a purely social group open to all graduates who pay a membership fee **d** (1) : an assembly of the members of a college or university to observe a particular ceremony (as the opening of the academic year or the announcing of prizes, awards, and honors) (2) *at some Canadian universities* : COMMENCEMENT 2 **e** : a meeting of a chapter of Royal Arch Masons or a reunion of Scottish Rite for the conferring of degrees **2** : the act of calling or assembling by summons ⟨at the time of the ~ of the parliament⟩

con·vo·ca·tion·al \¦==¦=shənᵊl, -shnəl\ *adj* : of or relating to a convocation — **con·vo·ca·tion·al·ly** \-ᵊlē, -əlē\ *adv*

con·voke \kən'vōk\ *vt* -ED/-ING/-S [MF *convoquer*, fr. L *convocare*, fr. *com-* + *vocare* to call — more at VOICE] : to call together : summon to meet : assemble by summons (as a parliament, council, or other official body) ⟨the government *convoked* a congress of physicists⟩

con·vo·lu·ta \,känvə'lüd·ə\ *n, cap* [NL, fr. L, fem. of *convolutus*] : a genus of marine acoelous flatworms (the type of the family Convolutidae) including a number of forms having symbiotic algae in the parenchyma

¹con·vo·lute \'känvə,lüt *also* -əl,yüt, *usu* -üd.+V\ *vb* -ED/-ING/-S [L *convolutus*, past part. of *convolvere* to enfold, enwrap — more at CONVOLVE] *vt* **1** : to twist or coil around (an object) **2** : to make convolute : TWIST ⟨*convoluting* and entangling his phrases —George Saintsbury⟩ ~ *vi* : TWIST, COIL : assume twisted or tangled form ⟨grief had *convoluted* into monomania —Edgar Saltus⟩

²convolute \"\ *adj* [L *convolutus*] : rolled or wound together one part upon another : COILED — used esp. of cotyledons, of flowers or leaves in the bud, or of discoid shells having the inner whorls somewhat concealed by the outer — **con·vo·lute·ly** *adv*

convoluted *adj* **1** : folded in curved or tortuous windings : having convolutions : COILED ⟨a highly ~ brain —*No. Amer. Rev.*⟩ ⟨beaks recurved and ~ like a ram's horn —Thomas Pennant⟩ **2** : complicated and involved ⟨~ form⟩ ⟨his ~ later stories have more layers of meaning . . . than Henry James' —DeLancey Ferguson⟩ : having intricate and complexly related detail ⟨a ~ process of reasoning⟩

convoluted tubule *n* **1** : PROXIMAL CONVOLUTED TUBULE **2** : DISTAL CONVOLUTED TUBULE

con·vo·lu·tion \,känvə'lüshən\ *n* -S [L *convolutus* + E *-ion*] **1 a** : a tortuous or sinuous winding, fold or design (as of something rolled or folded upon itself) : COIL, WHORL, FOLD, SINUOSITY ⟨the ~s of the intestines⟩ **b** : one of the irregular ridges upon the surface of the brain, esp. of the cerebrum, of some animals : GYRUS **c** : TWISTING, WINDING : a complication or intricacy of form, design, or structure ⟨as a lover, as a writer, as a soldier, as an aesthete, and as a public official his life was of an almost inconceivable ~ —*Times Lit. Supp.*⟩ **2** : the act or action of convoluting or of following a convoluted course ⟨o'er the sea in ~s swift, the feathered eddy floats —James Thomson †1748⟩

con·vo·lu·tion·al \¦==¦=shənᵊl, -shnəl\ *adj* : of, relating to, or resembling a convolution

convolution of bro·ca \-(')brō¦kä, -'brōkə\ *usu cap B* [trans. of F *circonvolution de Broca*, after Paul *Broca* †1880 Fr. surgeon] : a brain center associated with the motor control of speech usu. in the left but sometimes in the right inferior frontal convolution

con·volve \kən'välv\ *vb* -ED/-ING/-S [L *convolvere*, fr. *com-* + *volvere* to roll — more at VOLUBLE] *vt* **1** *obs* : ENFOLD, ENWRAP, ENCLOSE **2** : to roll together : roll or twist (one part) on another : WRITHE ⟨*convolving* his chin and cheek in a rapid series of pursed lips and horrible squints —Thomas Wolfe⟩ ~ *vi* : to roll together or circulate involvedly ⟨the sweeping brushstrokes ~ like thunderclouds —R.C.Peace⟩

con·vol·vu·la·ce·ae \kən,välv(y)ə'lāsē,ē\ *n pl, cap* [NL, fr. *Convolvulus*, type genus + *-aceae*] : a family of twining vines, erect herbs, shrubs, or trees (order Polemoniales) comprising the morning-glory family and having alternate leaves and regular pentamerous flowers with plaited corollas — **con·vol·vu·la·ceous** \=¦==¦=shəs\ *adj*

con·vol·vu·lin \=ˈ==lən\ *n* -S [G *konvolvulin*, fr. NL *Convolvulus* (genus name of *Convolvulus schiedanus*) + G *-in*] : an ether-insoluble glucosidic constituent of true jalap resin

con·vol·vu·lus \-ləs\ *n* [NL, fr. L, bindweed, fr. *convolvere* to enfold, enwrap — more at CONVOLVE] **1** *cap* : a genus of erect trailing or twining herbs and shrubs (family Convolvulaceae) having the style undivided or merely cleft at its apex and with two linear stigmas — see BINDWEED, MORNING GLORY **2** *pl* **convolvuluses** \-ləsəz\ *or* **convolvu·li** \-,lī, -,lē\ : a plant of the genus *Convolvulus*

¹con·voy \'kän,vói, kən'v-\ *vt* -ED/-ING/-S [ME *convoyen*, fr. MF *convoier*, *conveier* — more at CONVEY] **1 a** : ACCOMPANY, ESCORT ⟨~ him out across the terrace —D.C.Peattie⟩ : GUIDE, CONDUCT **b** : to accompany or escort for protection ⟨he is . . . ~ed by Secret Service agents —*Newsweek*⟩; *specif* : to provide protective escort for (as a group of merchant ships) ⟨tankers ~ed by destroyers and aircraft⟩ **2** *obs* : CARRY, CONVEY

²con·voy \'kän,vói\ *n* -S *often attrib* [MF *convoi*, fr. *convoier*] **1** : one that convoys, escorts, or accompanies: as **a** : a funeral train **b** : a protective force (as of troops or warships) escorting ships, persons, or goods moving by sea or land : ESCORT ⟨a Dutch man-of-war of forty guns, which was ~ to the . . . fleet —Richard Steele⟩ **c** : CONDUCTOR, GUIDE ⟨Oh be some god his ~ to our shore —Alexander Pope⟩ **2** : the act of convoying, accompanying, or escorting esp. for protection ⟨they vanished quietly upstairs in ~ of the manager's wife —Arnold Bennett⟩ ⟨to obtain the ~ of a man-of-war —T.B.Macaulay⟩ **3** : an individual or group that is convoyed or a group organized for convenience or protection in moving: as **a** : a train of vehicles transporting goods under armed escort : a group of persons or vehicles traveling under escort **b** : a body of merchant ships sailing under the protection of an armed escort ⟨each ~ escorted by seven warships⟩ **c** : a body of persons or vehicles organized into a unit for the purpose of orderly or efficient movement ⟨a storm was raging . . . and cars had to fight their way through in ~ —G.R.Stewart⟩

¹con·vul·sant \kən'vəlsᵊnt\ *adj* [¹*convulse* + *-ant*] : causing convulsions : CONVULSIVE

²convulsant \"\ *n* -S : an agent that produces convulsions

con·vulse \kən'vəls\ *vb* -ED/-ING/-S [L *convulsus*, past part. of *convellere* to tear loose, dislocate, fr. *com-* + *vellere* to pluck, pull — more at VULNERABLE] *vt* **1** : to shake violently : agitate greatly : throw into confusion ⟨the world is *convulsed* by the agonies of great nations —T.B.Macaulay⟩ ⟨the ferment of change that has *convulsed* . . . our twentieth-century world —A.E.Stevenson †1965⟩ **2** : to affect with violent and irregular contractions of the muscles : shake with irregular spasms (as in agony from grief or pain) ⟨she writh'd about, *convuls'd* with scarlet pain —John Keats⟩ **3** : to cause to laugh violently ⟨he . . . *convulsed* the country with the famous kitten-and-coat saga —Scott Fitzgerald⟩ ~ *vi* : to become affected with convulsions ⟨some will ~ as a result of high fever⟩ **syn** see SHAKE

con·vul·sed·ly \-sədlē, -li\ *adv* : with spasmodic shaking

con·vul·sion \kən'vəlshən\ *n* -S [MF or L; MF *convulsion*, fr. L *convulsion-*, *convulsio*, fr. *convulsus* + *-ion-*, *-io* -ion] **1 a** *obs* : spasmodic contraction of the muscles : CRAMP **b** : an abnormal, violent, and involuntary contraction or series of contractions of the muscles — often used in pl. ⟨a patient suffering from ~s⟩ **2** *obs* : WRENCHING, TEARING **3 a** : a forceful wrenching, distorting, or upheaving seismic action ⟨the ~s which physical nature has always in reserve . . . , earthquakes of Lisbon, eruptions of Mount Pelée —Samuel Alexander⟩ **b** : a period of violent social or political stress, strain, surging action, and confusion ⟨the vast social ~s of a continent in travail —Reinhold Niebuhr⟩ **c** : an uncontrolled fit : a powerful emotional upheaval ⟨a ~ of grief and anger⟩ : PAROXYSM ⟨~s of sobbing —Joseph Conrad⟩ ⟨literally throwing themselves down on the ground in ~s of unholy mirth —Rudyard Kipling⟩ **syn** see COMMOTION

¹con·vul·sion·ary \-,nerē\ *n* -ES [F *convulsionnaire*, fr. *convulsion* + *-aire* -ary] **1** : one who has convulsions esp. as a result of religious mania or ecstasy **2** *usu cap* : one of a body of Jansenist fanatics in France in the early 18th century who exhibited convulsions esp. at the tomb of the Jansenist François de Paris in the cemetery of St.-Médard at Paris

²convulsionary \"\ *adj* [*convulsion* + *-ary*] **1** : of, relating to, or resembling a convulsion ⟨~ struggles —Sir Walter Scott⟩ **2** *usu cap* : of or relating to the Convulsionaries

con·vul·sion·ist \-,nəst\ *n* -S *sometimes cap* [F *convulsionniste*, fr. *convulsion* + *-iste* -ist] : CONVULSIONARY

convulsion root *or* **convulsion weed** *n* : INDIAN PIPE

con·vul·sive \kən'vəlsiv, -sēv *also* -səv\ *adj* [F *convulsif*, fr. *convulsion* + *-if* -ive] **1** : producing or accompanied by convulsion ⟨~ disorders⟩ : affected by or having convulsions ⟨~ children⟩ : accompanying or resembling convulsion ⟨~ motions⟩ **2** : resembling convulsion in being violent, sudden, frantic, or spasmodic ⟨the nation . . . made a ~ effort to free itself from military domination —T.B.Macaulay⟩ ⟨he had a ~ drive, a boundless and explosive fervor —S.N.Behrman⟩ ⟨a ~ little hug —Agnes S. Turnbull⟩ — **con·vul·sive·ly** \-səvlē, -li\ *adv* — **con·vul·sive·ness** \-sivnəs, -sēv- *also* -səv-\ *n* -ES

convulsive therapy *n* : SHOCK THERAPY

cony *var of* CONEY

cony-catch *vb* [back-formation fr. *conycatcher*] *obs* : DECEIVE, CHEAT, TRICK

conycatcher *n* [*cony* + *catcher*] *obs* : CHEAT, SHARPER, SWINDLER

co·ny·rine \'känə,rēn, -,rən\ *n* -S [ISV, alter. (influenced by *pyridine*) of *coniine*; orig. formed as G *konyrin*; fr. the fact that conyrine stands in the same chemical relationship to coniine as does pyridine to piperidine] : an oily base $C_8H_{11}N$ obtained as a decomposition product of coniine; 2-propyl-pyridine

¹coo \'kü\ *vi* **cooed; cooed; cooing; coos** [imit.] **1 a** : to make the low soft cry of a dove or pigeon ⟨in the coconut palms overhead doves were gloomily ~*ing* —John Dos Passos⟩ ⟨~*ing* like a dove to summon a great peace conference —A.L.Guérard⟩ **b** : to make a similar sound sometimes fatuously often in showing affection or pleasure or in seeking to placate **2** : to talk fondly or amorously ⟨such ~*ing* and kissing among us that indeed it is scandalous —John Dryden⟩

²coo \"\ *n* -S **1** : a soft low cry; *typically* : the call of a dove or pigeon ⟨the grave ~ of a dove —Sidney Lanier⟩ **2** : a sound or expression similar to a coo often in indication of or implying affection, fondness, or peaceful intent

³coo \"\ *interj* [origin unknown] *Brit* — used to express surprise, surprised pleasure, or wonder ⟨~, what an evening that was —Clemence Dane⟩

coob \'küb\ *n* -S [by alter.] *South* : ¹COOP 1

coo·ba *or* **coo·bah** \'kübə, -(,)bä\ *n* -S [native name in Australia] : an Australian wattle (*Acacia salicina*) with foliage resembling willow — called also *native willow*

cooch *or* **cootch** \'küch\ *n* -ES [by shortening & alter. fr. earlier *hootchy-kootchy*] : a pseudo-Oriental female dance common in carnivals and fairs and marked by a sinuous and often suggestive twisting and shaking of the torso and limbs ⟨a roving carnival ~ dancer —Frank Barton⟩ ⟨a circus ~ show⟩

¹coo·ee *also* **coo·ey** \'kü¦ē\ *n* -S [origin unknown] *chiefly Austral* : a cry to attract attention or give warning — **within cooee** : within hailing distance : not unapproachable

²cooee *also* **cooey** \"\ *vi, chiefly Austral* : to call cooee

coo·ee bird \'küē,-\ *n* [native name in Australia, prob. of imit. origin] : an Australian koel (*Eudynamys scolopacea*)

coof \'küf\ *n* -S [perh. alter. of *goff*] *chiefly Scot* : a stupid fellow : DOLT, LOUT

coohee *cap, var of* COHEE

cooing *adj* : uttering coos ⟨~ voice⟩ ⟨~ baby⟩ : fondly amorous — **coo·ing·ly** *adv*

¹cook \'ku̇k\ *n* -S *often attrib* [ME *cooke*, *coke*, fr. OE *cōc*; akin to OHG *koch*, OS *kok*; all fr. a prehistoric WGmc word borrowed fr. L *cocus*, *coquus*, fr. *coquere* to cook; akin to OE *āfigen* fried, Gk *pessein* to cook, digest, W *pobi* to bake, Serb *peći*, Lith *kepti*, Skt *pacati* he cooks] **1 a** : one who prepares food for the table (as in a private home, public eating place, or institution) **b** : one who prepares a particular kind of food ⟨a pastry ~⟩ **2 a** : one who cooks meats, fruits, fish, vegetables, or other foods for commercial canning **b** : a packing-house worker who cooks meats to prepare them for smoking, molding, or packing **3 a** : an often technical or industrial process comparable to cooking food ⟨a 20-minute ~⟩; *specif* : the cooking of cellulosic raw materials in papermaking **b** : substance or material so treated : a product thus obtained **c** : one who conducts such a cook **4 a** : a previously unrecognized or unrecorded series of moves in a chess or checkers game prepared as a surprise for an opponent esp. in tournament play **b** : a solution to a chess or checker problem unforeseen by the composer

²cook \"\ *vb* -ED/-ING/-S [ME *coken*, fr. *coke*, n.] *vi* **1** : to do the work of a cook : prepare food for the table **2 a** : to undergo the action of being cooked ⟨the rice is ~*ing* now⟩ **b** : to suffer through the effects of noticeable or great heat ⟨~*ing* in the heat of the city⟩ **3** : DEVELOP, EVOLVE, OCCUR, HAPPEN ⟨find out what was ~*ing* in the committee⟩ ~ *vt* **1** : to make up : devise or fabricate often factitiously as an expedient : PREPARE, CONCOCT, IMPROVISE — usu. used with *up* ⟨if she hadn't any problems, I said, she could ~ up some —J.B.Benefield⟩ ⟨we ~ed up a scheme to buy some desert land —W.A.White⟩ **2** : to prepare for eating by a heating process (as boiling, roasting, or baking) **3** : to alter to convey an untrue impression : FALSIFY, DOCTOR, ANGLE, MANIPULATE ⟨an old hand at company manipulation, he prepares to ~ the books —*Punch*⟩ **4 a** : to bring decisively to a bad end : UNDO, RUIN, KILL ⟨my chances were ~ed by this decision⟩ **b** *Brit* : to wear out : EXHAUST, FATIGUE ⟨too ~ed to leave camp again —J.H.Williams⟩ **5 a** : to expose to fire, heat, or some agency felt to be similar in a technical process ⟨a coke brazier was ~*ing* rivets —George Farwell⟩ ⟨~*ing* TNT —Stanley Frank⟩ **b** : to make radioactive ⟨put into a nuclear reactor and ~ed⟩ **6** : to enervate, make suffer, or parch with excessive heat ⟨the sun ~*ing* the dry plains⟩ — **cook one's goose** : to settle, undo, or ruin (a person) irretrievably — **cook with gas** *slang* : to perform excellently : do very well; *also* : to be on the right track

³cook \"\ *vi* -ED/-ING/-S [perh. of Scand origin; akin to Icel *kūka* to defecate, Sw & Norw dial. *kukka* to defecate, Shetland Norse *kuk* dried excrement; perh. akin to G *kauchen* to crouch] *Scot* : to crouch down in hiding : take cover

cook·able \-kəbəl\ *n* -S : foodstuff to be cooked

cookbook \'=,=\ *n* [perh. trans. of G *kochbuch* or D *kookboek*] : a book of directions and recipes for cooking

cook cheese *n* : a cheese made of skim milk, the curd being cured a few days, heated to honey consistency, and poured into hot containers — see CUP CHEESE

cook·ee \'ku̇kē, ='=\ *n* -S [¹*cook* + *-ee*] : a cook's helper esp. in a logging camp

cooke·ite \'ku̇,kīt\ *n* -S [Josiah P. *Cooke* †1894 Am. chemist + E *-ite*] : a micaceous mineral related to lepidolite

cook·er \'ku̇kə(r)\ *n* -S **1** : a utensil, device, or apparatus for cooking **2** : an eatable for cooking as opposed to being served or eaten raw ⟨we had better grade those apples as ~s⟩ **3** : one that cooks or attends the cooking process of foods or of ingredients of commercial products: as **a** : one that cooks grain meal to prepare a mash that will be distilled into high wine for use in gin, whiskey, and commercial alcohol **b** : one that cooks veneer by steam pressure to harden the glue **c** : a worker who uses mixing, cooking, and cooling equipment to process cereals **d** : a worker who cooks ground cottonseed or linseed meal in steam kettles prior to its being formed into cakes and pressed **4** *Brit* : COOKSTOVE

cook·ery \'ku̇k(ə)rē, -ri\ *n* -ES [ME *cokerie*, fr. *coken* to cook + *-erie* -ery] **1** : the art, science, process, or practice of cooking **2** : an establishment or apparatus for cooking : a place for cooking

cookery-book \'=(=)=,=\ *n, chiefly Brit* : COOKBOOK

cook-general \'=,-\ *n, pl* **cooks-general** *Brit* : a servant who does both cooking and general housework

cookhouse \'=,=\ *n* **1 a** : a compartment or building for cooking **b** : a circus tent for cooking **2** : a ship's galley

¹cook·ie *or* **cooky** *also* **cook·ey** \'ku̇kē, -ki\ *n, pl* **cookies** *also* **cookeys** *often attrib* [D *koekje*, *koekie*, dim. of *koek* cake, fr. MD *coeke*; akin to OHG *kuocho* cake — more at CAKE] **1** : any of various small sweet cakes either flat or slightly raised, cut from rolled dough, dropped from a spoon, or cut into pieces after baking **2** : a moderate brown that is yellower, lighter, and stronger than bay or auburn and lighter, stronger, and slightly redder than chestnut brown **3** : an appliance or strip of material (as of leather or metal) inserted in a shoe over the insole from heel to shank to support the arch **4 a** : a little girl : CHILD, SWEETHEART — used usu. as an affectionate term of address **b** *slang* : PERSON, GUY ⟨tough ~⟩ ⟨smart ~⟩ **5 cookies** *pl, slang* : the contents of one's stomach : what one has recently eaten ⟨she got sick and tossed her *cookies*⟩

²cookie *var of* COOKY

cookie cutter *n* : a sharp-bladed device for cutting cookies in particular shapes from rolled dough

cookie press *n* : an implement consisting of a hollow barrel to hold cookie dough, a plunger, and interchangeable plates of various designs through which the dough is pressed onto a sheet for baking

cookie pusher *n* : a careerist (as a diplomat) attentive to form and protocol but generally pliant and without force; *broadly* : a vacuous person without force who is given to an active but innocuous social life

cookie sheet *n* : a flat rectangle of metal with a rolled edge on one, two, or three sides designed for the baking of cookies or biscuits

cooking *adj* [fr. gerund of ²*cook*] **1** : fit for being cooked : useful in cooking ⟨~ apples⟩ ⟨~ salt⟩ ⟨~ sherry⟩ **2** : used in cooking : designed to serve in cooking ⟨~ utensils⟩

cook·less \'ku̇kləs\ *adj* : not having a cook : not being cooked

cook off *vi, of a cartridge* : to fire as a result of being allowed to rest in the chamber of an overheated weapon

cook·out \'ku̇,kau̇t\ *n* -S [fr. *cook out*, v.] : an outing at which a meal is cooked and served in the open; *also* : the meal cooked at such an outing

cookroom \'=,=\ *n* : KITCHEN, GALLEY

cooks *pl of* COOK, *pres 3d sing of* COOK

cookshack \'=,=\ *n* : a shack used for cooking; *sometimes* : a portable kitchen

cookshop \'=,=\ *n* : a shop supplying or serving cooked food : EATING HOUSE

cook's tour \'ku̇ks-\ *n, usu cap C* [after Thomas *Cook* †1892 Eng. tourist agent] : a quick tour in which attractions are viewed very briefly and cursorily : a quick cursory scanning ⟨a 15-hour *Cook's tour* of the Philippines —*Newsweek*⟩

cookstove \'=,=\ *n* : a stove for cooking

cookware \'=,=\ *n* : utensils used in cooking

cook wrasse *n* : a wrasse (*Crenilabrus mixtus*) of English waters

¹cooky *var of* COOKIE

²cooky *or* **cookie** \'ku̇kē, ='=\ *n, pl* **cookies** [¹*cook* + *-y*, *-ie*] : a cook esp. on a ranch, at a camp, or on a ship; *sometimes* : a female cook

¹cool \'kül\ *adj* -ER/-EST [ME *cole*, fr. OE *cōl*; akin to OHG *kuoli* cool, OE *calan* to get cold, *cald*, *ceald* cold — more at COLD] **1 a** : moderately cold : between tepid and chill : lacking in warmth ⟨a ~ wind⟩ ⟨water a little too ~ for swimming⟩ ⟨preferred to drink coffee when it was ~ rather than hot⟩ **b** : CHILLY ⟨shivering in the ~ air of the evening⟩ **c** : having refrigeration facilities : under refrigeration **2 a** : unaffected by passion, agitation, alarm, perturbation, unsteadying tension : showing calmness, steadiness, impassiveness, resolution, or control ⟨"never shoot in a passion", the excellent advice went on; "only a ~ hand is steady" —Joseph Hergesheimer⟩ ⟨he was very ~ outwardly, but was nervous all the same —Bram Stoker⟩ **b** : free from excitement, strong feeling, passion, or confusion : marked by deliberate judgment and temperate moderation ⟨the heated personal disputes . . . gave way to ~ negotiations —G.B.Shaw⟩ **c** : EXPERIENCED, SOPHISTICATED **3** : lacking ardor, enthusiasm, warmth, friendliness, or affability : unresponsive and apathetic or unfriendly and antagonistic ⟨he received a very ~ reception⟩ ⟨"a pity you take on so . . .", the young lady said, with a ~, slightly sarcastic air —W.M.Thackeray⟩ **4** *of a scent* : WEAK, FAINT ⟨the trail of the fox is ~⟩ **5 a** : as indicated : CERTAIN, POSITIVE : not scant or bare : WHOLE, FULL ⟨a ~ million in gambling debts⟩ **b** : gained, lost, executed, or reckoned calmly or deliberately without excitement or fuss ⟨he made a ~ $100,000 by his investment schemes⟩ **6** : marked by deliberate unabashed effrontery, presumption, or lack of due deference, respect, or discretion ⟨a ~ reply⟩ ⟨a ~ pleasure in stripping the Indians of their horses or silver or blankets —Willa Cather⟩ **7 a** : facilitating or suggesting pleasurable sensations of comfort or ease at relief from heat ⟨a ~ dress⟩ ⟨a ~ air-conditioned room⟩ ⟨the ~ beauty of freshwater lakes —*Amer. Guide Series: Mich.*⟩ **b** : marked by lack of fervor, dash, or excitement : RESTFUL, UNEMOTIONAL, STUDIED ⟨simple ~ clear prose⟩ ⟨~ jazz⟩ ⟨sweet ~ paintings that are more refreshing than stimulating —*Time*⟩ **c** *of a color* : producing an impression of coolness; *specif* : of a hue in the range violet through blue to green **d** *of a musical tone* : relatively lacking in timbre or resonance **8** *slang* : GREAT, EXCELLENT; *esp* : showing a mastery of the latest in approved technique and style ⟨as an actor he's real ~⟩ ⟨a ~ performance⟩

syn COMPOSED, COLLECTED, UNRUFFLED, IMPERTURBABLE, NONCHALANT: COOL implies general self-control uninfluenced by excitement or emotion ⟨my work, I am often told, is *cool* and serene, entirely reasonable and free of passion —Havelock Ellis⟩ ⟨this wonder, that when near her he should be *cool* and composed, and when away from her wrapped in a tempest of desires —George Meredith⟩ It may also imply calm courage, deliberateness, effrontery, or indifference ⟨*cool* and deliberate, he gave his orders in a voice devoid of alarm —J.J.Floherty⟩ ⟨the sudden change in her voice, from *cool* imperial arrogance to terrified pleading —Robert Graves⟩ COMPOSED refers to absence of indications of agitation or tension ⟨she was *composed* without bravado —Agnes Repplier⟩ ⟨did he appear . . . *composed*, or was he agitated and alarmed —C.B.Nordhoff & J.N.Hall⟩ COLLECTED implies a concentration of faculties to avoid or overcome distraction ⟨they did not look very unhappy, though Mrs. Hawthorne wore her *collected* Sunday expression —Archibald Marshall⟩ UNRUFFLED implies an accustomed calmness even in exciting situations ⟨on the one hand, feeling at its keenest edge and highest tension; on the other the low, placid, *unruffled* level of our normal moods —J.L.Lowes⟩ ⟨the familiar estate of marriage was preserved in the *unruffled* calm of their bedroom as in an embalming fluid —Ellen Glasgow⟩ IMPERTURBABLE implies extreme and accustomed calm, rendering one unlikely to be disconcerted, disturbed, or alarmed ⟨Irving, the pleasure-loving, genial, *imperturbable* traveler and gentle hedonist —Saxe Commins⟩ ⟨at her side sat a rosy-cheeked *imperturbable* nurse in a stiff white uniform —W.H.Wright⟩ NONCHALANT suggests easy casualness and an appearance of detached indifference or carefreeness ⟨at the back [of the ambulance], haughty in white uniform, *nonchalant* on a narrow seat was The Doctor —Sinclair Lewis⟩

2**cool** \"\ *vb* -ED/-ING/-S [ME *colen*, fr. OE *cōlian* to become cool, fr. *cōl* cool] *vi* **1 :** to become cool **:** lose heat or warmth **:** lose some characteristic likened to heat (as force or activity) ⟨the summer ~*ed* into autumn —Arnold Bennett⟩ ⟨the material exposed to radiation was left alone to ~ for a long time⟩ — sometimes used with *off* or *down* ⟨~*ing* off in the evening breezes⟩ **2 a :** to lose ardor or passion **:** become less fervent, zealous, impassioned, angry, or affectionate **:** lose intensity **:** MODERATE ⟨his anger ~*ed*⟩ — often used with *off* or *down* ⟨give those hotheads a chance to ~ off —L.C.Douglas⟩ **b :** to lose enthusiasm or interest and to become tepid, indifferent, suspicious, or inimical — used with *on*, *to*, or *toward* ⟨its main backers have ~*ed* on the project⟩ **c :** to become less hot **:** allow enough time to pass for a lessening of the police's efforts to capture one — usu. used with *off* ⟨hiding out to ~ off⟩ ~ *vt* **1 a :** to impart a feeling of coolness or cold to; *often* **:** to refresh by countering the effects of heat ⟨the breeze ~*ed* them⟩ — often used with *off* or *down* ⟨a swim ~*ed* us off a little⟩ **b :** to make less hot or warm **:** cause loss of heat in **:** reduce in temperature often to a satisfactory or pleasurable point ⟨~ the milk before storing it⟩ ⟨~ the vegetables with refrigeration⟩ ⟨an engine ~*ed* with water⟩ ⟨~ the room with a fan⟩ ⟨~ the emotions and restore peace —*N.Y. Times*⟩ — sometimes used with *off* or *down* ⟨the agitation was ~*ed* down —J.A.Froude⟩ **2 :** to moderate the heat or excitement of **:** ALLAY ⟨~ her growing anger⟩ **:** MODERATE, CALM **3 a :** to check decisively **:** rob of force or effectiveness **:** STOP **b :** to knock out; *also* **:** KILL ⟨the gangsters ~*ed* him for squealing⟩ — **cool one's heels :** to wait esp. for a long time **:** be kept waiting from or as if from disdain or discourtesy ⟨forced to *cool his heels* outside for 40 minutes —*Newsweek*⟩

3**cool** \"\ *n* -S [ME *cole*, fr. *cole*, adj.] **1 :** a cool time, place, occasion, or situation ⟨the ~ of evening⟩ **2 :** COOLNESS

4**cool** \"\ *adv* [1*cool*] **:** in a cool manner **:** COOLLY ⟨play it ~⟩

coo·la·bah *or* **coo·li·bah** \'külə,bä\ *n* -S [native name in Australia] **:** any of several Australian gum trees (as *Eucalyptus coolabah*, *E. microtheca*, or *E. largiflorens*)

coo·la·mon \'külə,män, -,mən\ *also* **coo·la·man** *or* **coo·li·man** \-,man, -,mən\ *n* -S [native name in Australia] **:** an Australian vessel of bark or wood that resembles a basin and is used for carrying and holding water

cool·ant \'külənt\ *n* -S [2*cool* + *-ant*] **:** a cooling usu. fluid agent (as a liquid applied to the edge of a cutting tool to carry off frictional heat or a circulating fluid for cooling an engine)

cool bath *n* **:** a bath in which the temperature of the water is between 65° and 80° F

1**cooler** *comparative of* COOL

2**cool·er** \'külə(r)\ *n* -S **1 :** one that cools **:** one that either brings about loss of heat or protects from heat: as **a :** a vessel or container in which water, milk, or other liquids are cooled or kept cool ⟨a wine ~⟩ **b :** a device, implement, or machine by means of which food is cooled or kept cool **c :** a refrigerated room or box kept at a moderately cold temperature for the storing of perishables (as meat) **d :** AIR CONDITIONER **2 a :** one that abates or damps excitement, passion, fervor, optimism, or happiness ⟨putting a ~ on his hopes⟩ **b :** LOCKUP, JAIL; *esp* **:** a prison cell for the confinement of violent or refractory prisoners **3 a :** a cooling drug or agent **:** REFRIGERANT — compare SURFACE COOLER **b :** a tall chilled nonalcoholic drink (as lemonade) **c :** a thirst-quenching drink consisting of gin, rum, whiskey, or wine to which are added grenadine or other flavoring ingredients and sugar and served iced with the spirally cut rind of a lemon or other citrus fruit in a tall glass **4 a :** one that operates a cooling device or machine **b :** a worker who stacks hot bread on racks or conveyors for removal to a cooling room **c :** one that cools charges of artificial graphite electrodes by gradual removal of insulating material from the electrothermal furnace **5 :** COOLER NAIL **6 :** a light blanket or wrap used to protect a horse while cooling out

coolerman \'==,man\ *n, pl* **coolermen 1 :** one who tends refrigeration equipment or a refrigerated storage room **2 :** an operator of equipment for cooling molasses in a sugar refinery

cooler nail *n* **:** a wire nail similar in shape to a common nail but slenderer and usu. cement-coated to increase its holding power

coolest *superlative of* COOL

cooley *var of* 1COULEE 1

coo·ley's anemia *also* **cooley's disease** \'külēz-\ *n, usu cap C* [after Thomas B. *Cooley* †1945 Am. pediatrician] **:** THALASSEMIA

coolhouse \'=,=\ *n* **:** a greenhouse maintained at a cool temperature for the forcing of hardy plants or the winter storage of dormant plants

coo·lidg·e·an \(')kü¦lijēən\ *adj, usu cap* [Calvin *Coolidge* †1933 30th president of the U.S. + E *-an*] **:** of, relating to, or reminiscent of Calvin Coolidge or his times or policies

coo·lidge tube \'külij-\ *n, usu cap C* [after William D. *Coolidge* *b*1873 Am. physicist] **:** a vacuum tube for the generation of X rays in which the cathode consists of a spiral filament of incandescent tungsten and the target which also serves as anode is of massive tungsten, the temperature of the cathode determining the intensity of the X rays while the applied voltage determines wavelength

1**coo·lie** *also* **coo·ly** \'külē, -li\ *n, pl* **coolies** [Hindi *kulī, qulī*, prob. of Dravidian origin; akin to Tamil *kūli* wages] **1 :** an unskilled laborer, carrier, or porter or a semiskilled menial usu. in or from the Far East hired for low or subsistence wages **2** *Africa* **:** a person of Indian origin or descent

2**coolie** *var of* 1COULEE 1

coo·lie·ism \'külē,izəm\ *n* -S [1*coolie* + *-ism*] **:** exploitation of imported coolies at substandard wages; *also* **:** any similarly exploitative system

cooliman *var of* COOLAMON

cooling *pres part of* COOL

cooling board *n, chiefly South* **:** a board on which a corpse is laid during preparation for burial

cool·ing·ly *adv* **:** in a cooling manner

cooling-off *adj* **:** designed to allow intemperate feeling to abate and to permit negotiation between contestants (as between a call to strike and its taking effect or as between the start of a dispute between nations and their resorting to force) ⟨a *cooling-off* period⟩ ⟨a *cooling-off* agreement⟩ ⟨*cooling-off* legislation⟩

cooling time *n* **:** a lapse of time that under all the circumstances of a case ought to produce a subsiding of passion previously provoked so that the provocation cannot then be set up as a defense for subsequent acts

cooling tower *n* **:** a structure over which circulated water that is to be reused as a coolant is trickled to reduce its temperature by partial evaporation

cool·ish \'külish, -lēsh\ *adj* **:** somewhat cool ⟨gray fog and ~ to cold weather —John Steinbeck⟩

cool·ly \'kül(l)ē, -i\ *or* **cooly** \-lē, -li\ *adv* [1*cool* + *-ly*] **1 :** in a cool manner **:** without heat or excessive cold **2 a :** without passion or ardor **:** CALMLY, DELIBERATELY **b :** with indifference **:** IMPUDENTLY

cool·ness \'külnəs\ *n* -ES **:** the quality or state of being cool: as **a :** CHILLINESS ⟨the ~ of the night⟩ **b :** CALMNESS, SELF-POSSESSION ⟨showed great ~ and courage in a desperate conflict —L.C.Hatch⟩ **c :** lack of ardor, enthusiasm, or friendly warmth ⟨a long-standing ~ between the two families⟩ **d :** SELF-ASSURANCE ⟨takes possession of the territory with all the ~ of a usurper —Mary Cowden-Clarke⟩

cool-off \'=,=\ *n* -S [fr. *cool off*, v.] **:** a cooling-off period

cool out *vt* **:** to cause (a horse) to move about quietly after heavy exercise until sweating has ceased and relaxation is attained

cools *pres 3d sing of* COOL, *pl of* COOL

coolth \'külth\ *n* -S [*cool* + *-th* (as in *warmth*)] **:** the state or occasion of being cool

coolweed \'=,=\ *n* [1*cool* + *weed;* fr. its habit of growing in cool places] **:** RICHWEED 1

coolwort \'=,=\ *n* **1 :** FALSE MITERWORT **2 :** TOOTHWORT 2 **3 :** FAIRY CUP 3

1**cooly** *var of* COOLIE

2**cooly** *var of* COOLLY

cooly sore *n* [1*cooly*] **:** TROPICAL ULCER 2

1**coom** *or* **coomb** \'küm\ *n* -S [ME *culme* — more at CULM] **1** *dial Brit* **a :** SOOT, SMUT **b :** coal dust or coal slack **2 :** grease exuding from axle boxes or bearings

2**coom** *or* **coomb** \"\ *n* -S [origin unknown] *Scot* **:** the wooden centering or frame on which a masonry arch is built

1**coomb** *or* **coombe** \'küm, 'kōm\ *var of* COMBE

2**coomb** *or* **coom** \'küm\ *n* -S [ME *combe*, fr. OE *cumb*, a liquid measure; akin to MLG *kump* bowl, vessel, MHG *kumpf* bowl, Pers *gumbed* arch, dome, drinking vessel, OE *cofa* room — more at COVE] **:** an English unit of capacity equal to 4 imperial bushels or 4.13 U.S. bushels

coombe *or* **coom** \'küm\ *dial var of* 4CULM 2

1**coon** \'kün\ *n* -S [short for *raccoon*] **1 :** RACCOON **2 :** a rustic, eccentric, or undignified person **3 :** a supporter or member of the American Whig party **4 :** NEGRO — usu. taken to be offensive

2**coon** \"\ *vb* -ED/-ING/-S *vt* **1** *dial* **:** to crawl or creep along (a place of insecure footing) ⟨he ~*ed* a log that spanned the stream⟩ **2** *slang* **:** STEAL ⟨every man that had ~*ed* a horse in the county was in cahoots with them —Howard Troyer⟩ ~ *vi, dial* **:** to crawl or creep in a place of insecure footing

coon bear *n* **:** GIANT PANDA

coon bug *n* **:** a black-and-white Australian bug (*Oxycarenus luctuosus*) having the immature stages bright red and feeding on the foliage of native and cultivated plants often causing serious defoliation

coon·can \'kün,kan\ *or* **coon king** *n* -S [by folk etymology fr. MexSp *con quien*, fr. Sp *¿con quién?* with whom?] **:** a game of rummy derived from conquian and played by two or more with two packs including two jokers — called also *double rum*

coon cat *n* **1 :** *chiefly NewEng* **:** ANGORA CAT **2 :** CACOMISTLE **3 :** COATI

coon dog *n* **:** a sporting dog trained to hunt raccoons

coon·er \'künə(r)\ *n* -S **:** COON DOG

coon grape *n* **1 :** a woody vine (*Ampelopsis cordata*) of the southeastern U. S. with inedible bluish fruit and foliage like that of the grape **2 :** a fox grape (*Vitis labrusca*)

coonhound \'=,=\ *n* **:** COON DOG; *specif* **:** a large black-and-tan hound with a short dense coat of a breed developed esp. for use as coon dogs

coonier *comparative of* COONY

cooniest *superlative of* COONY

coon·i·ly \'künᵊlē, -nəlē\ *adv* **:** in a coony manner

coon·i·ness \-nēnəs\ *n* -ES **:** CAGEYNESS, CANNINESS ⟨a sort of slang that . . . will impart to the user an appearance of savviness, ~, and general know-how —W.H.Whyte⟩

1**coon·jine** \'kün,jīn\ *vb* -ED/-ING/-S [origin unknown] **:** to walk, dance, or carry with a sidling waddling shuffle

2**coonjine** \"\ *n* -S **1 :** a step or dance suggestive of the rhythmic shuffle of riverboat loaders **2 :** a song accompanying the coonjine

coon oyster *n* **1 :** MANGROVE OYSTER **2 :** an oyster undersized and inferior because of growth in a crowded situation

coonroot \'=,=\ *n* [short for *puccoonroot*, fr. *puccoon* + *root*] **:** BLOODROOT 1

coon's age *n* **:** a long while ⟨been sick for a *coon's age*⟩

coon shouter *n* [1*coon* (Negro)] **:** one that sings in the manner of a blackface minstrel — compare COON SONG, SHOUT SONG

coonskin \'=,=\ *n* **1 :** the skin or pelt of the raccoon **2 :** a coat, cap, or other article made of coonskin

coon song *n* [1*coon* (Negro)] **:** a typically ragtime and usu. sentimental popular song of the 19th century derived from or related to the songs of the southern Negro

coonskin cap

coon-striped shrimp \'=¦=-\ *n* **:** a large edible shrimp (*Pandalus danae*) common in moderately deep water from San Francisco to Alaska

coontail \'=,=\ *n* **:** HORNWORT

coon·tie \'küntē\ *or* **comp·tie** \'kämptē\ *n* -S [Seminole *kunti* coontie flour] **:** any of several tough woody plants of the genus *Zamia* of Florida and tropical America whose roots and half-buried stems yield an arrowroot

coony \'künē\ *adj* -ER/-EST [1*coon* + *-y*] **:** showing astute and clever closeness **:** CAGEY, CANNY ⟨a ~ candidate remaining mum⟩

1**coop** \'küp *also and S usu* 'ku̇p\ *n* -S [ME *cupe*, akin to OE *cȳpa*, *cȳpe* basket — more at KIPE] **1 a :** a cage or small enclosure for poultry or other small animals **:** PEN; *also* **:** a small building for housing poultry **b :** a poorly made or ramshackle structure with holes or cracks in the walls **2 :** a confined area **:** a narrow constricted space: as **a :** JAIL **b :** quarters in which voters were cooped **c :** a small booth or gallery ⟨reporters in the press ~⟩

coop 1a

2**coop** \"\ *vt* -ED/-ING/-S **1 :** to confine in a narrow restricted often crowded area **:** deprive of free motion by cramped quarters — often used with *up* ⟨poor emigrants, ~*ed* up in their steerage quarters —Ruth Park⟩ **2 :** to place or keep in a coop **:** PEN — often used with *up* ⟨rabbits ~*ed* up in their hutches⟩ **3 :** OBSTRUCT, RESTRAIN, INHIBIT — often used with *up* ⟨~*ing* up the mind in dogma⟩ **4** *slang* **:** to hold (voters that are often unqualified or bribed) in seclusion under guard until election day **syn** see ENCLOSE

3**coop** \'küp, 'ku̇p, 'kōp, 'käp\ *v imper* [contr. of *come up*] *dial* **:** COME — a call to domestic animals

4**coop** \'küp\ *n* -S [by alter.] *substand* **:** COUPÉ

co-op *also* **coop** \'kō,äp, ='= *also* 'küp\ *n* -S [by shortening] **:** COOPERATIVE

1**coop·er** \'küpə(r), 'ku̇p-\ *n* -S [ME *couper*, *cowper*, fr. MD *cūper* (fr. *cūpe* cask + *-er*) or MLG *kūper* (fr. *kūpe* cask + *-er*); MD *cūpe* and MLG *kūpe*, fr. ML *copa*, alter. of L *cupa* — more at HIVE] **1 a :** one that makes or repairs wooden casks or tubs — called also *cooperer* **b :** a shipboard artisan who repairs casks and other vessels **2 :** an English tradesman who samples, bottles, or retails wine **3** [so called fr. the daily allotment of stout and porter to coopers at breweries] **:** porter and stout in equal parts

2**cooper** \"\ *vb* **coopered; coopered; coopering** \-p(ə)riŋ\ **coopers** *vt* **1 a :** to do the work of a cooper on **:** engage in the manufacture or repair of (barrels or casks) **:** secure with hoops **b :** to put into proper or presentable shape or form — used with *up* or *out* **2 :** to pack or stow in casks or barrels **3 :** SPOIL, RUIN ⟨the dodge was ~*ed* by the police⟩ **4 :** to cover holes and cracks inside (a freight car) to prevent leakage of bulk grain ~ *vi* **:** to work at or do coopering

3**cooper** \", 'kōp-\ *or* **cop·er** \'kōp-\ *n* -S [prob. modif. of D *koper* buyer, fr. *kopen* to buy (fr. MD *cōpen*) + *-er;* akin to OHG *koufōn* to buy — more at CHEAP] **:** a ship equipped to supply liquor and tobacco to fishing fleets in the North sea in the 19th century

coop·er·age \'küp(ə)rij, 'ku̇p-\ *n* -S [1*cooper* + *-age*] **1 :** a cooper's place of business **2 a :** a cooper's work **b :** the products of a cooper's work **:** casks and tubs **3 :** pay for cooperage **4 :** casks for draft beer or bulk wine

co·op·er·ant \(')kō¦äp(ə)rənt\ *adj* [LL *cooperant-*, *cooperans*, pres. part. of *cooperari*] **:** working in cooperation ⟨man and nature intimately ~ —John Collier b.1884⟩

1**co·op·er·ate** \kō'äpə,rāt, '=¦==,=, *usu* -ād·+V\ *vi* -ED/-ING/-S [LL *cooperatus*, past part. of *cooperari*, fr. L *co-* + *operari* to work — more at OPERATE] **1 :** to act or work with another or others to a common end **:** operate jointly ⟨marines and navy men *cooperated* in the attack⟩ ⟨the police force always ~s with the fire department⟩ **2 :** to act together **:** produce an effect jointly ⟨heavy rains and rapid thaws *cooperated* to bring disastrous floods⟩ **3 :** to associate with another or others for mutual often economic benefit ⟨many nations *cooperated* in the trade agreement⟩ **syn** see UNITE

2**cooperate** \(')kō¦äp(ə)rət *also* (')kō¦äpə,rāt, *usu* -d·+V\ *adj* **:** made cooperative **:** brought into working together ⟨~ forces⟩

co·op·er·a·tion \kō,äpə'rāshən, (')=,==¦==\ *n* -S [ME *cooperacioun*, fr. L *cooperation-*, *cooperatio*, fr. *co-* + *operation-*, *operatio* work, operation — more at OPERATION] **1 :** the act of cooperating **:** a condition marked by cooperating **:** joint operation **:** common effort or labor ⟨the river was dredged by the two states acting in ~⟩ **2 :** association of persons for their common often economic benefit **:** association in a venture (as an industry, credit group, consumer group) the profits or benefits of which are shared **:** collective action for common well-being or progress **3** *biol* **:** a dynamic social process associated with organisms living in some degree of aggregation (as in communities or colonies) and characterized by sufficient mutual benefit to outweigh disadvantages (as competition) associated with crowding; *esp* **:** PROTOCOOPERATION

co·op·er·a·tion·ist \-nəst\ *n* -S **:** one who advocates or practices cooperation

1**co·op·er·a·tive** \(')kō¦äp(ə)rəd·iv, -rətiv: (')kō¦äpə,rād·iv, -ātiv, -ēv *also* -əv\ *adj* [LL *cooperativus*, fr. *cooperatus* + L *-ivus* -ive] **1 a :** marked by cooperation **:** marked by working together or by joint effort toward a common end ⟨the work demanded ~ organization⟩ ⟨wherever there was a prospect of a steady return to ~ agriculture, ceorls tended to live together —F.M.Stenton⟩ **b :** given to or marked by willingness and ability to work with others in a common effort **:** not motivated entirely by selfish individual aims **:** refraining from malingering, lowering morale, or obstructing accomplishment ⟨the professor was not promoted because he was not ~⟩ ⟨the historians are more ~ than they used to be; they engage in joint projects and have common standards —*Times Lit. Supp.*⟩ **2 a :** of, relating to, or organized as a cooperative ⟨a ~ business enterprise⟩ **b :** belonging to or undertaken by a cooperative ⟨~ producers⟩ ⟨~ farming⟩ ⟨~ marketing⟩ **c :** favoring the organization of cooperatives ⟨the ~ movement⟩ **3 :** showing organized diversification of student activities to include practical work (as in industry, agriculture, social welfare, or in college maintenance activities and domestic chores like cooking and cleaning) ⟨the ~ plan at various universities⟩ ⟨~ courses requiring outside work in industry —*Mass. Inst. of Technology Bull.*⟩ ⟨a ~ dormitory⟩ **syn** see SOCIAL

2**cooperative** \"\ *n* -S **:** an enterprise or organization owned by and operated for the benefit of those using its services ⟨marketing ~s⟩ ⟨a consumers' ~⟩

cooperative bank *n* **:** SAVINGS AND LOAN ASSOCIATION

co·op·er·a·tive·ly \-əvlē, -li\ *adv* **:** in a cooperative manner ⟨other groups acted ~⟩ **:** according to a cooperative plan or arrangement ⟨farmers selling milk ~⟩

co·op·er·a·tive·ness \-əvnəs\ *n* -ES **:** the quality or state of being cooperative

co·op·er·a·tor \kō'äpə,rād·ə(r), -ātə- *also* (')kō¦ä-\ *n* -S [LL, fr. *cooperatus* + *-or* — more at COOPERATE] **1 :** one that cooperates: **a :** COWORKER, COLLEAGUE, COLLABORATOR ⟨the ~s with whom he worked⟩ **b :** one who follows with thoroughness the directions or suggestions of a government, governmental agency, or political party ⟨soil conservation programs gaining more ~s⟩ **2 :** a member of a cooperative **:** an advocate of cooperative principles and practices

co·oper·cu·lum \,kōə'perk(y)ələm, -pər-\ *n, pl* **coopercu·la** \-lə\ [L, cover, lid, fr. *cooperire* to cover — more at COVER] **:** the cover of a pyx

coopered joint *n* **:** a joint in a curved part of a wooden object (as a piece of furniture) made to resemble a joint made in a barrel

coop·er·er \'küp(ə)rə(r), 'ku̇p-\ *n* -S **:** COOPER

coop·er-hew·itt lamp \¦küpə(r)¦hyüət-\ *n, usu cap C&H* [fr. *Cooper Hewitt*, a trademark] **:** a commercial mercury-vapor lamp

1**coo·pe·ria** \kü'pirēə\ *n, cap* [NL, fr. Daniel *Cooper* †1842 Eng. botanist + NL *-ia*] **:** a small genus of bulbous herbs (family Amaryllidaceae) having solitary fragrant white flowers with erect anthers — see RAIN LILY

2**cooperia** \"\ *n, cap* [NL, fr. A. R. *Cooper*, 20th cent. Can. helminthologist + NL *-ia*] **:** a genus of small reddish brown nematode worms (family Trichostrongylidae) including several species infesting the small intestine of sheep, goats, and cattle and sometimes held responsible for marked catarrhal inflammation, anemia, and diarrhea — **coop·er·id** \'küp(ə)rəd\ *n* -S

coopering *n* -S **:** the work or trade of a cooper

coop·er·ite \'küpə,rīt\ *n* -S [R. A. *Cooper fl ab*1920, who first described it + E *-ite*] **:** a steel-gray mineral PtS of metallic luster consisting of a sulfide of platinum belonging to the tetragonal system and occurring usu. in irregular grains

coopers *pl of* COOPER, *pres 3d sing of* COOPER

cooper's flag *or* **cooper's reed** *n* [1*cooper*] **:** the cattail whose long leaves are sometimes used between barrel staves to make the barrel watertight

cooper's hawk *or* **cooper hawk** *n, usu cap C* [after William *Cooper* †1864 Am. naturalist] **:** a common American hawk (*Accipiter cooperii*) resembling in color but larger than the sharp-shinned hawk and like it inclined to prey on domestic poultry

cooper's ligament *n, usu cap C* [after Sir Astley P. *Cooper* †1841 Eng. surgeon] **:** a strong ligamentous band extending upward and backward from the base of Gimbernat's ligament along the iliopectineal line to which it is attached

coop·ery \'küp(ə)rē, 'ku̇p-, -ri\ *n* -ES [1*cooper* + *-y*] **:** COOPERAGE

cooping *pres part of* COOP

coops *pl of* COOP, *pres 3d sing of* COOP

co-ops *pl of* CO-OP

co-opt \kō'äpt, '=,=\ *vt* -ED/-ING/-S [L *cooptare*, fr. *co-* + *optare* to choose — more at OPINE] **1 :** to choose or elect into a body or group as a fellow member ⟨outside persons may be *co-opted* to committees —W.A.Robson⟩ **2 a :** to appoint usu. as a colleague **b :** to appoint or deputize summarily; *sometimes* **:** PREEMPT, COMMANDEER

co-op·tate \kō'äp,tāt, '=¦=,=\ *vt* -ED/-ING/-S [L *cooptatus*, past part. of *cooptare*] **:** CO-OPT, CHOOSE

co-op·ta·tion \,kō(,)äp'tāshən, '=(,)=¦==\ *n* -S [L *cooptation-*, *cooptatio*, fr. *cooptatus* + *-ion-*, *-io* -ion] **:** election or selection usu. to a body or group by vote of its own members

co-optative \(')kō +\ *adj* **:** practicing or chosen by co-optation **:** of or relating to co-optation

co-option \(')kō +\ *n* -S [*co-opt* + *-ion*] **:** CO-OPTATION

co-op·tive \(')kō¦äptiv\ *adj* **:** CO-OPTATIVE

1**co·or·di·nate** \(')kō¦ȯrd(ᵊ)nət, -ȯdᵊn-, -ȯ(ə)dn-, -dᵊn,āt, -d,nāt, *usu* -d· +V\ *adj* [back-formation fr. *coordination*] **1 a :** equal in rank, quality, or significance **:** similar in order or nature **:** not subordinate ⟨keeping the branches of government ~⟩ **b :** being of equal rank in a compound sentence ⟨~ clauses⟩ **:** standing in the same rank or relation in a sentence ⟨*by sea* and *by land* are ~ in "they travel by sea and by land"⟩ **2 a :** of or marked by coordination **:** marked by related actions or processes cooperating **:** composed of things of equal rank or order **:** COORDINATED **b** *chem* **:** relating to or formed by coordination ⟨6-*coordinate* complexes⟩ **c :** COORDINATING **3 a** *of a university* **:** giving degrees to both men and women taught by the same faculty but in separate classes and sometimes on separate campuses **b** *of a college* **:** being one of the colleges of a coordinate university, esp. the women's branch — **co·or·di·nate·ly** *adv* — **co·or·di·nate·ness** *n* -ES

2**coordinate** \-dᵊn,āt, *usu* -ād· +V\ *vb* -ED/-ING/-S [back-formation fr. *coordination*] *vt* **1 :** to make coordinate **:** put in the same order or rank ⟨~ the two groups in classification⟩ **2 :** to bring into a common action, movement, or condition **:** regulate and combine in harmonious action **:** HARMONIZE ⟨~ the work of various bureaus⟩ ⟨~ the divergent Gospel stories

—*America*⟩ ⟨~ muscular movements⟩ **3 a :** to attach so as to form a coordination complex ⟨a *coordinated* group⟩ ⟨a *coordinated* molecule⟩ **b :** to constitute by such attachment ⟨*coordinated* salts⟩ ~ *vi* **1 :** to be or become coordinate **:** act together in a smooth concerted way ⟨muscles of spastics do not ~⟩ **2** *chem* **:** to combine by means of a coordinate bond

³coordinate *as at adj*\ *n* -s [¹*coordinate*] **1 :** one who is of equal rank, authority, or importance with another ⟨in the federal system each of the ~s has equal power⟩ **2 a :** any one of a set of numbers used in specifying the location of a point on a line, in space, or on a given plane or other surface ⟨latitude and longitude are ~s of a point on the earth's surface⟩ **b :** any one of a set of variables or parameters used in specifying the state of a substance (as temperature, pressure, or entropy) or the motion of a particle (as position, velocity, or momentum)

coordinate bond *or* **coordinate covalence** *n* **:** a covalent bond typical of coordination complexes that is held to consist of a pair of electrons donated by only one of the two atoms it joins [as in the compound $(C_2H_5)_3N{:}BF_3$ formed from triethylamine $(C_2H_5)_3N{:}$ and boron fluoride BF_3] — called also *dative bond, semipolar bond*

coordinated *adj* **:** dexterous in the use of more than one set of muscle movements to a single end ⟨she was usually good with her hands and well ~ —Mary McCarthy⟩

coordinate geometry *n* **:** ANALYTIC GEOMETRY

coordinate paper *n* **:** GRAPH PAPER

coordinate space *n* **:** space in the usual sense of three-dimensional geometry as distinguished from various symbolic phase spaces

coordinate system *n, math* **:** a system of coordinates

coordinating *adj, of a conjunction* **:** joining together words or word groups of equal grammatical rank as sentences (as *and* in "He tried. And he succeeded"), clauses (as *but* in "he speaks French but I don't"), phrases (as *or* in "by night or by day"), words (as *and* in "comes and goes"), or a word and a phrase (as *or* in "now or in the future")

co·or·di·na·tion \kō,ȯ(r)dᵊn'āshən, (')ₛ,ₛₛ'ₛₛ\ *n* -s [F or LL; F *coordination*, fr. LL *coordination-, coordinatio*, fr. L *co-* + *ordination-, ordinatio* arranging, ordination — more at ORDINATION] **1 :** a making or being coordinate **:** arrangement in the same order, class, rank, or dignity **:** coordinate relation ⟨~ of the executive, legislative, and judicial authority⟩ **2 :** combination in suitable relation for most effective or harmonious results **:** the functioning of parts in cooperation and normal sequence ⟨demand a single national military policy, proper ~ of our armed services —D.D.Eisenhower⟩

coordination complex *n* **:** a compound or ion that contains a central usu. metallic atom or ion combined by coordinate bonds with a definite number of surrounding ions, groups, or molecules, that retains its identity more or less even in solution, and that may be nonionic {as tri-ammine-trinitro-cobalt $[Co(NH_3)_3(NO_2)_3]^0$}, cationic {as hex-ammine-cobalt-(III) $[Co(NH_3)_6]^{+++}$}, or anionic {as hexachloroplatinate-$[PtCl_6]^{--}$} — see ¹CHELATE

coordination compound *n* **:** a compound in which atoms are combined with each other by coordinate bonds; *esp* **:** a coordination-complex compound

coordination number *n* **1 :** the number of attachments being usu. four or six to the central atom in a coordination complex **2 :** a number used in classifying various arrangements in space of constituent groups of crystals, the number being a function of the relative sizes and polarization properties of oppositely charged ions forming the solid crystal lattice

co·or·di·na·tive \(')kō¦ȯ(r)dᵊnəd-iv, -ətiv; -dᵊn,ād·iv, -ātiv\ *adj* [*coordination* + *-ive*] **1** *of a conjunction* **:** COORDINATING **2 :** that coordinates ⟨a ~ mechanism⟩ **:** having reference to coordination ⟨~ duties⟩ **3** *linguistics* **:** having two or more heads — used of an endocentric construction (as *books and papers*); opposed to *subordinative*

co·or·di·na·tor \kō'ȯ(r)dᵊn,ād·ə(r), -ātə- *also* (')kō¦ō-\ *n* -s **1 :** one that coordinates; *esp* **:** one that expedites by recommending although often not supervising measures which eliminate confusion **2 :** an educator who is responsible for coordinating academic instruction with the on-the-job activities of employed students and the vocational requirements encountered by employed graduates **3 :** a coordinating conjunction

coorg \'kü(ə)rg\ *n* -s *usu cap* [fr. *Coorg*, region of India] **:** one of a Dravidian people in southwest India — called also *Kadaga*

coo·rie \'küri\ *vi* -ED/-ING/-S [freq. of *coor*, var. of *cower*] *chiefly Scot* **:** CROUCH, COWER, STOOP

¹coos *pres 3d sing of* COO, *pl of* COO

²coos \'küs\ *n, pl* **coos** *usu cap* **1 a :** a Kusan people of Oregon **b :** a member of such people **2 :** the language of the Coos people

coos·er \'küsər, 'kəs-\ *n* -s [alter. of ¹*courser*] *chiefly Scot* **:** STALLION

co·ossification \(')kō + \ *n* -s [*co-* + *ossification*] **:** the process of coossifying

co·ossify \(')kō + \ *vi* -ED/-ING/-ES [*co-* + *ossify*] **:** to grow together by ossification (as of bones or parts of a bone) **:** ANKYLOSE

coost \'küst\ *Scot past of* CAST

¹coot \'küt, *usu* -üd·+V\ *n* -s [ME *coote*; akin to D *koet* coot] **1 :** any of certain sluggish slow-flying slaty-black birds that somewhat resemble ducks, have lobed toes and the upper mandible prolonged on the forehead as a horny frontal shield, and constitute a genus (*Fulica*) of the family Rallidae, the No. American representative (*F. americana*) being distinguished from the common one of the Old World (*F. atra*) by a white wing patch **2 :** any No. American scoter; *sometimes* **:** any of several other American ducks — often used with a qualifying word ⟨mud ~⟩ **3 :** a person often old and harmless and sometimes not bright ⟨poor old ~ with no one to look after him —Ruth Park⟩ ⟨crazy as a ~⟩ **4 :** a large purplish blue rail (*Porphyrio porphyrio*) widely distributed in Australia and the islands of the southwestern Pacific esp. in marshland and about forest margins — called also *bald coot, swamphen*

²coot \'kœ̄t\ *n* -s [MLG *kote* hoof, fetlock; akin to MD *cote* knuckle, knucklebone, OFris *kāte* knuckle, MLG *kūt* entrails, calf of the leg — more at KYTE] *Scot* **:** the ankle joint; *also* **:** ¹FOOT 1

coo·ta·mun·dra wattle \,küd·ə'məndrə-\ *also* **cootamundra** *n, usu cap C* [fr. *Cootamundra*, N. S. W., Australia] **:** a small Australian tree (*Acacia baileyana*) with delicate feathery foliage and golden-yellow flowers

cootch *var of* COOCH

¹coo·ter \'kütə(r)\ *dial Eng var of* COLTER

²coo·ter \'küd·ə(r), 'kú-\ *n* -s [of African origin; akin to Bambara and Malinke *kuta* turtle] *chiefly South & Midland* **:** any of several turtles or tortoises of the southern and eastern U.S.; *esp* **:** the slider turtle (*Pseudemys concinna*) and certain closely related forms

³cooter \"\ *vi* -ED/-ING/-S *chiefly South* **:** LOITER, IDLE

cooter grass *n* [²*cooter*] **:** WATER SHIELD 2

¹coot·ie \'küte\ *n* -s [alter. of Sc *coodie*, dim. of *cood* tub, fr. ScGael *cùdainn* large tub, prob. fr. ON *kūtr* cask; akin to ON *kot* cottage — more at COT] *Scot* **:** a wooden bowl or vessel

²cootie *or* **cooty** \'küd·ē, -üte\ *adj* -ER/-EST [²*coot* + *-ie, -y*] *Scot, of fowls* **:** FEATHER-LEGGED

³cootie \"\ *n* -s [perh. modif. of Malay *kutu* louse] **1 :** a body louse **2 :** a game in which players compete to finish the pictorial and stylized representation of a cootie, the markings on a die representing its parts and the representation being added to according to throws of the die

¹cop \'käp\ *n* -s [ME, fr. OE *copp* top, summit; perh. akin to Norw dial. *kup* humpback, Sw dial. *kupa* beehive, OE *cȳpa* basket — more at KIPE] **1** *chiefly dial Eng* **:** TOP, HEAD, CREST **2 :** a cylindrical, conical, or conical-ended mass of thread, yarn, or roving wound upon a quill or tube **3 :** a tube or quill upon which thread, yarn, or roving is wound **4 :** a heap or pile: **a** *dial Eng* **:** a bank of earth (as earth thrown up from digging a ditch and left as a hedge bank) **b :** the bank of a golf bunker

²cop \"\ *vt* **copped; copped; copping; cops :** to wind on a cop

³cop \"\ *vt* **copped; copped; copping; cops** [alter. of *cob* (to strike)] *dial Eng* **:** to strike (a person) esp. on the head

⁴cop \"\ *vb* **copped; copped; copping; cops** [perh. fr. D *kapen* to steal, plunder, fr. Fris *kāpia* to take away, buy, fr. OFris, to buy; akin to OHG *koufōn* — more at CHEAP] *vt* **1** *slang* **:** CATCH, CAPTURE ⟨~ a prize⟩ **:** get hold of ⟨they *copped* the best seats⟩ **:** TAKE **2** *slang* **:** to steal esp. on the spur of the moment **:** SWIPE ⟨somebody *copped* my watch⟩ ~ *vi, slang* **:** WIN ⟨there's 20 bucks extra in it for you if you ~⟩ **syn** see STEAL — **cop a plea** *slang* **:** to plead guilty to a lesser charge in order to avoid standing trial for a more serious one — compare BARGAIN PLEA — **cop it** *slang* **:** to get beaten, scolded, punished **:** catch it; *sometimes* **:** get killed

⁵cop \"\ *n* -s *slang Brit* **:** CAPTURE, ARREST ⟨it's a fair ~. I'll go quiet —Arthur Morrison⟩

⁶cop \"\ *n* -s [short for ⁵*copper*] **:** POLICEMAN

cop *abbr* **1** copper **2** copulative **3** copy **4** copyright

co·pa \'kōpə, -(,)pä\ *n* -s [AmerSp (Panama) *copá*] *in Panama* **:** YAYA a

co·pa·cet·ic *or* **co·pe·set·ic** \¦kōpə¦sed·ik, -sēd-·\ *adj* [origin unknown] *slang* **:** very satisfactory **:** fine and dandy ⟨everything is ~ with me this morning⟩

co·pa de oro \,kōpədā'ō(,)rō, -dē'-\ *n* [AmerSp, lit., cup of gold] **:** CUPFLOWER 3

co·pa·ene \kō'pā,ēn, 'ₛₛ,ₛ\ *n* -s [*copaiba* + *-ene*] *chem* **:** an oily tricyclic sesquiterpene $C_{15}H_{24}$ occurring in certain essential oils (as oil of supa)

¹co·pai·ba \kō'pībə, -pābə\ *n* -s [Sp & Pg; Sp, fr. Pg *copaiba*, of Tupian origin; akin to Guarani *cupaiba* copaiba, Tupi *copaiba, copaiiva*] **1** *also* **copaiba balsam :** the oleoresin obtained from several So. American trees of the genus *Copaifera* as a viscid transparent pale yellow or brown liquid of aromatic odor that has a stimulant action on mucous membranes **2 a :** a tree of the genus *Copaifera* **b :** the wood of one of these trees or sometimes of certain related trees

²copaiba \"\ [NL, fr. Sp & Pg] *syn of* COPAIFERA

copaiba oil *n* **:** a colorless or pale yellow essential oil obtained from copaiba and used chiefly as an odor fixative in soaps and perfumes

copaiba resin *n* **:** the resin that remains after distilling off the essential oil from copaiba

co·pa·if·era \,kōpä'if(ə)rə\ *n* [NL, fr. *copai-* (fr. ISV *copaiba*) + *-fera* (fem. of *-fer* -ferous)] **1** *cap* **:** a genus of tropical American and African trees (family Leguminosae) with pinnate leaves, racemose apetalous flowers, strong durable wood of moderate weight and density, and an oily liquid of commercial importance — see ¹COPAIBA **2** -s **:** ¹COPAIBA 1

co·pain \kȯpaⁿ\ *n* -s [F, alter. of OF *compain*, fr. LL *companio* — more at COMPANION] **:** COMRADE, PAL

co·pai·va \kō'pīvə, -pävə\ [NL, fr. Sp *copaiba* or Pg *copaiba*] *syn of* COPAIFERA

co·pai·yé family \kō'pī(,)yā-, -pā(,)-\ *n* [AmerSp *copaiyé* (*Vochysia guianensis*), fr. Macusi *kopai-ye*] **:** VOCHYSIACEAE

copaiyé wood *n* [AmerSp *copaiyé*] **:** the compact wood of a So. American tree (*Vochysia guianensis*)

co·pal \'kōpəl, -,pal\ *n* -s [Sp, fr. Nahuatl *copalli* resin] **:** a resinous exudation from various tropical trees that is collected from living trees or dug from the ground as a fossil, that when hard must be rendered soluble in alcohol and other organic solvents by heating, and that is used chiefly in making varnishes and printing ink — see CONGO COPAL, KAURI 3, MANILA COPAL

co·pal·che \,kōpəl'chā, 'ₛₛ,ₛ, kə'pal(,)chā\ *or* **co·pal·chi** \,kōpəl'chē, 'ₛₛ,ₛ, kə'pal(,)chē\ *n* -s [AmerSp *copalché, copalchi*] **1 :** either of two So. American trees (*Strychnos pseudo-quina* and *Croton niveus*) having bitter medicinal bark used locally as a febrifuge **2 :** a Mexican shrub or small tree (*Coutarea latiflora*) of the family Rubiaceae having fragrant white flowers and bark that is used locally as a febrifuge

co·pal·co·co·te \,kōpəlkə'kōd·(,)ā\ *also* **co·pal·jo·co·te** \-pəlhə'-\ *n* -s [MexSp, fr. Nahuatl *copalxocotl*, fr. *copalli* gum, resin + *xocotl* acid fruit] **:** a Mexican tree (*Cyrtocarpa procera*) of the family Anacardiaceae with yellow fruits that resemble plums and are used locally as a remedy for leprosy

co·pal·if·er·ous \¦kōpə¦lif(ə)rəs\ *adj* [*copal* + *-i-* + *-ferous*] **:** yielding or producing copal

co·pal·ite \'kōpə,līt\ *also* **co·pal·ine** \-,lēn, -lən\ *n* -s [*copalite* fr. *copal* + *-ite*; *copaline*, ISV *copal* + *-ine*] **:** a resinous substance that is apparently a vegetable resin and that is partly mineralized by remaining in the earth

co·palm \'kō,päm\ *n* -s [LaF *copalm*, *copal*, fr. MexSp *copalme*] **1 :** STORAX 2b **2 :** SWEET GUM 1

copal tree *n* **:** any of several trees (as of the genus *Copaifera*) that yield fragrant resins

co·parcenary \(')kō + \ *n* -ES [*co-* + *parcenary*] **1 :** partnership in inheritance **:** joint heirship **2 :** joint ownership

co·parcener \(')kō + \ *n* -s [*co-* + *parcener*] **:** a joint heir

co·part \'kō + ,-\ *n* -s [*co-* + *part*] **:** a joint or coordinate part

copartment *obs var of* COMPARTMENT

co·partner \(')kō + \ *n* [*co-* + *partner*] **1 :** PARTNER **:** fellow partner ⟨the authority of a partner to bind his ~s —*Encyc. Britannica*⟩ **2** *obs* **:** COPARCENER

co·partnership \(')kō + \ *n* -s **1 :** the state or right of a copartner ⟨a ~ to employees⟩ **2 :** a company of copartners **:** PARTNERSHIP

co·part·nery \(')kō¦pärtnərē, -pȧt-, -ri\ *n* -ES **:** COPARTNERSHIP

copatain *var of* COPINTANK

¹cope \'kōp\ *n* -s [ME, fr. OE *-cāp*, fr. ML *capa*, fr. LL *cappa* — more at CAP] **1 a** *archaic* **:** a long cape or cloak esp. for outdoor wear **b :** an orig. hooded ecclesiastical vestment in the form of a long semicircular cloak open in front except at the top where it is united by a band or clasp **2 :** something felt to resemble a cope (as by concealing or covering over) **:** a vault or canopy (as the vault, arch, or expanse of heaven) ⟨the dark sky's starry ~ —P.B.Shelley⟩ **3 :** COPING **4 :** a muzzle for a ferret **5 a :** the top part of a flask, mold, or pattern; *also* **:** the brick structure in which the outer surface of a loam mold is formed **b :** the outer case in bell founding

bishop with *1* cope, *2* crosier, *3* miter

²cope \"\ *vb* -ED/-ING/-S [ME *copen*, fr. *cope*, n.] *vt* **:** to dress, cover, or furnish with a cope **:** cover as if with a cope or a coping ~ *vi* **:** to form a cope or arch **:** BEND, ARCH

³cope \"\ *vb* -ED/-ING/-S [ME *copen*, *coupen*, fr. MF *couper* to strike, cut, cut off, cut, fr. OF, fr. *coup* blow, fr. LL *colpus*, fr. L *colaphus* blow with the fist, fr. Gk *kolaphos* buffet; akin to Gk *klan* to break — more at HALT] *vi* **1** *obs* **:** STRIKE, FIGHT **2 a :** to maintain a contest or combat usu. on even terms or with success — used with *with* ⟨how effectively he can ~ with local law-enforcement agencies —D.W.Maurer⟩ **b :** to face or encounter and to find necessary expedients to overcome problems and difficulties ⟨he died before the war. He couldn't have *coped* now —Rose Thurburn⟩ — often used with *with* ⟨~ intelligently with weighty problems of public policy —C.H.Grandgent⟩ **3** *archaic* **:** MEET, ENCOUNTER ~ *vt* **1** *obs* **:** to meet in combat ⟨he yesterday *coped* Hector in the battle —Shak.⟩ **2** *obs* **:** come in contact with **:** MEET **3** *obs* **:** MATCH ⟨three thousand ducats due unto the Jew we freely ~ your courteous pains withal —Shak.⟩ **syn** see CONTEND

⁴cope \"\ *vb* -ED/-ING/-S [ME *copen* to buy, fr. MD; akin to OHG *koufōn* to buy — more at CHEAP] *dial Eng* **:** EXCHANGE, BARTER

⁵cope \"\ *vt* -ED/-ING/-S [prob. fr. F *couper* to cut] **1 :** to notch or cut away a part of (as a timber or a structural-steel flange) to fit or give clearance for some other member **2 :** to cut or shape (the end of a structural member or a molding) to fit a coping or conform to the shape of another member; *also* **:** to make (a joint) by so shaping a joining part

copeck *var of* KOPECK

cope cutter *n* [¹*cope* (coping)] **:** a cutter for undercutting the shoulder of a tenon

co·pe·han \kō'pə(h)ən\ *n, pl* **copehan** *or* **copehans** *usu cap* **1 :** a language family of the Penutian stock in California comprising Patwin and Wintun **2 :** WINTUN 2

co·pei \kō'pāē\ *n* -s [AmerSp *copey*, fr. Taino] **:** PITCH APPLE

co·pe·la·ta \,kōpə'lād·ə\ *or* **co·pe·la·tae** \-d·(,)ē\ [NL, fr. Gk *kōpēlatēs* rower, fr. *kōpē* oar + *-latēs* (fr. *elaunein* to drive) — more at COPEPODA, ELASTIC] *syn of* LARVACEA

co·pel·li·dine \kō'pelə,dēn, kə'-, -,dən\ *n* -s [fr. ISV *collidine*, after such pairs as ISV *pyridine*: *piperidine*; orig. formed as G *kopellidin*] **:** any of several liquid bases $C_8H_{17}N$; hexahydro-collidine

cope·man \'kōpmən\ *n, pl* **copemen** [D *koopman*, fr. *koop* trade (fr. MD *coop*) + *man*, fr. MD; akin to OHG *kouf* trade and to OHG *man* — more at CHEAP, MAN] *archaic* **:** CHAPMAN

cope·mate \'kōp,māt\ *or* **copes·mate** \-p,sm-\ *n* -s [*copemate*, fr. ³*cope* + *-mate*; *copesmate*, alter. (influenced by obs. E *copesman, copeman* merchant) of *copemate*] **1** *obs* **:** ANTAGONIST **2** *obs* **:** PARTNER, COMRADE, ASSOCIATE ⟨misshapen Time, copesmate of ugly Night —Shak.⟩

co·pen \'kōpən\ *or* **copen blue** *n* -s [*copen*, short for ²*copenhagen; copen blue* fr. *copenhagen blue*] **:** a variable color averaging a moderate blue that is redder, lighter, and stronger than pompadour, bluebird, azurite blue, or Dresden blue and greener, lighter, and stronger than luster blue

co·pe·na \kə'pēnə\ *adj, usu cap* [conical *piles* + *-ena* (as in *Adena*)] **:** of or belonging to an ancient culture in northern Alabama characterized by conical burial mounds

¹co·pen·ha·gen \¦kōpən¦hāgən, -häg-\ *adj, usu cap* [fr. *Copenhagen*, Denmark] **:** of or from Copenhagen, the capital of Denmark **:** of the kind or style prevalent in Copenhagen

²copenhagen \"\ *or* **copenhagen blue** *n* -s **:** a grayish blue that is redder and paler than electric, redder, stronger, and slightly lighter than Gobelin, stronger and slightly greener than old china, and redder, lighter, and stronger than average shadow blue

co·pen·ha·gen·er \,ₛₛ'ₛgənə(r)\ *n* -s *cap* [*Copenhagen*, Denmark + E *-er*] **:** a native or resident of Copenhagen

co·pe·og·na·tha \,kōpē'ägnəthə\ [NL, fr. *copeo-* (fr. Gk *kopeus* chisel) + *-gnatha*; akin to Gk *koptein* to smite, cut off — more at CAPON] *syn of* CORRODENTIA

¹co·pe·pod \'kōpə,päd\ *adj* [NL *Copepoda*] **:** of or belonging to the Copepoda

²copepod \"\ *n* -s **:** one of the Copepoda

co·pep·o·da \kō'pepədə\ *n pl, cap* [NL, fr. Gk *kōpē* oar + NL *-poda*; akin to L *capere* to take, seize — more at HEAVE] **:** a subclass of Crustacea comprising minute aquatic forms abundant in both fresh and salt waters and including the order Eucopepoda of which the members are chiefly free-living and important as fish food and the order Branchiura which is parasitic on the skin and gills of fish — **co·pep·o·dan** \(')kō¦pepədən\ *adj or n* — **co·pep·o·dous** \-dəs\ *adj*

co·pep·o·did \kō'pepədə̇d\ *n* -s [²*copepod* + *id*] **:** a free-swimming larval stage of certain parasitic copepods

¹cop·er \'kōpə(r)\ *n* -s [⁴*cope* + *-er*] *Brit* **:** a dealer or bargainer; *specif* **:** a horse dealer esp. if dishonest

²coper \"\ *var of* COOPER

³coper \"\ *n* -s [⁵*cope* + *-er*] **:** one that copes **:** a machine for coping or notching girders **:** a coping machine

¹co·per·ni·can \kō'pərnəkən, kə'-, -pən-\ *adj, usu cap* [Nicolaus *Copernicus* (Kopernik) †1543 Pol. astronomer + E *-an*] **1 :** of, relating to, or being the astronomic system of Copernicus in which the sun is taken as the center of the planets **2 :** of radical or major importance or degree ⟨a ~ revolution in psychologic theory⟩ — **co·per·ni·can·ism** \-kə,nizəm\ *n* -s *usu cap*

²copernican \"\ *n* -s *usu cap* **:** a believer in the Copernican system of astronomy usu. as opposed to the Ptolemaic

copernican system *n, usu cap C* **:** the system of planetary motions maintained by Copernicus according to which the earth rotates on an axis once each day and revolves around the sun once each year while the other planets have orbits also centered near the sun

co·per·ni·cia \,kōpə(r)'nish(ē)ə\ *n* [NL, fr. Nicolaus *Copernicus* + NL *-ia*] **1** *cap* **:** a small genus of lofty tropical American fan palms having cup-shaped flowers followed by a one-seeded drupe — see CARNAUBA **2** -s **:** a palm of the genus *Copernicia*

coperose *obs var of* COPPERAS

copes *pl of* COPE, *pres 3d sing of* COPE

copesetic *var of* COPACETIC

copesmate *var of* COPEMATE

cope·stone \'ₛ,ₛ\ *n* [¹*cope* (coping) + *stone*] **1 :** COPING STONE **2 :** CROWN, FINISHING TOUCH

co·pey oak \kō'pā(ē)-\ *n, usu cap C* [AmerSp *copey* (also, copei) — more at COPEI] **:** a large Central American white oak (*Quercus copeyensis*) that reaches a height of 125 feet or more and a diameter of 8 feet

coph *var of* QOPH

co·phasal \(')kō + \ *adj* [*co-* + *phasal*] **:** having the same phase — **co·phasally** \(')kō + \ *adv*

co·pi·a·pite \kōpēə,pīt\ *n* -s [G *copiapit*, fr. *Copiapó*, Chile, its locality + G *-it* -ite] **:** a mineral composed of a basic iron sulfate $(Fe,Mg)Fe_4(SO_4)_6(OH)_2.20\,H_2O$, of yellow color and metallic taste (hardness 2.5, sp. gr. 2.10)

copied *past of* COPY

cop·i·er \'käpēə(r)\ *n* -s **1 :** one that copies **:** TRANSCRIBER, COPYIST **2 :** one that imitates an example **:** IMITATOR

copies *pl of* COPY, *pres 3d sing of* COPY

co·pigment \(')kō + \ *n* [*co-* + *pigment*] **:** one of a group of colorless or pale substances (as certain tannins and anthoxanthins) that affect the color of flowers by combining with anthocyanins thereby increasing the blue tone of these pigments

co·pi·hue \kə'pē(,)wā\ *n* -s [AmerSp, fr. Araucan *copiu*] **:** CHILE-BELLS

co·pilot \(')kō + \ *n* [*co-* + *pilot*] **:** a qualified airplane pilot who assists or relieves the pilot but is not in command of the airplane

¹cop·ing \'kōpiŋ\ *n* -s [fr. gerund of ²*cope* (bend)] **:** the highest or covering course of a wall often of tile and usu. with a sloping top to carry off water and commonly cut with a drip

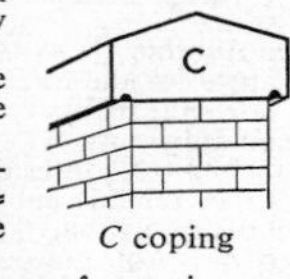

C coping

²coping \"\ *n* -s [fr. gerund of ⁵*cope*] **:** the operation of sawing stone with an abrasive wheel

coping saw *n* [¹*coping*] **:** a saw blade of ribbon shape held under tension in a U-shaped frame and used for cutting intricate patterns in wood

coping stone *n* [¹*coping*] **:** one of the stones of a coping

copintank *or* **copertank** *n* -s [origin unknown] *obs* **:** a sugar-loaf hat

co·pi·os·i·ty \,kōpē'äsəd·ē, -ətē, -i\ *n* -ES [MF *copiosité*, fr. LL *copiositat-, copiositas*, fr. L *copiosus* + *-itat-, -itas* -ity] **:** COPIOUSNESS

co·pi·ous \'kōpēəs\ *adj* [ME, fr. L *copiosus*, fr. *copia* abundance, fr. *co-* + *-opia* (fr. *ops* power, wealth) — more at OPULENT] **1 a :** having or yielding an abundance or plenty **:** ABOUNDING ⟨~ springs⟩ **b :** plentiful in number **2 a :** full of thought, information, matter ⟨Shakespeare whose soul was so ~ —Gilbert Highet⟩ **b :** profuse or exuberant in words, expression, or style **3 :** present in large quantity **:** PLENTIFUL, ABUNDANT, LAVISH ⟨~ footnotes⟩ ⟨the ~ matter of my song —John Milton⟩ ⟨~ amounts of beer and sandwiches consumed —Robert Shaplen⟩ **syn** see PLENTIFUL

co·pi·ous·ly *adv* **:** in a copious manner **:** ABUNDANTLY, RICHLY, AMPLY ⟨he dined slowly and ~⟩

co·pi·ous·ness \-nə̇s\ *n* -ES **:** PLENTY, RICHNESS, FULLNESS

copist *n* -s [MF *copiste* — more at COPYIST] *obs* **:** COPIER 1

co·planar \(')kō + \ *adj* [*co-* + *planar*] **:** lying or acting in the same plane — **co·planarity** \¦kō + \ *n* -ES

cop·lin jar \'käplən-, 'kōp- \ *or* **coplin staining jar** *n, cap C* [after William M. L. *Coplin* †1928 Am. physician] **:** a covered glass vessel that is rectangular in cross section and grooved inside for holding microscope slides vertical during processing

co·plowing \(')kō + \ *n* [*co-* + *plowing*] **:** cooperative plowing

co·polymer \(')kō + \ *n* [*co-* + *polymer*] **:** a product of copolymerization ⟨GR-S is a ~ of butadiene and styrene⟩

co·polymeride \(')kō + \ *n* [*co-* + *polymeride*] **:** COPOLYMER

co·polymerization \(')kō + \ *n* **:** the act or process of copolymerizing

co·polymerize \(')kō\ *vb* [*co-* + *polymerize*] **:** to polymerize together — used of two or more polymerizing substances that together form complex molecules usu. of high molecular weight (as plastics and synthetic rubber)

cop out *vi* [⁴*cop*] **1** *slang* **:** to meet failure or death **2** *slang* **:** to cop a plea

cop·pa \'käpə\ *n* -s [It, lit., cup, fr. LL *cuppa;* fr. its shape — more at CUP] **:** an Italian sausage made chiefly of pork butts and seasoned with cayenne pepper

copped \'käpt\ *adj* [ME, fr. ¹*cop* + *-ed*] **:** rising to a top or head **:** CONICAL, PEAKED ⟨~ hills —Shak.⟩

¹cop·per \'käpə(r)\ *n* -s [ME *coper,* fr. OE; akin to MD *koper,* OHG *kupfar,* ON *koparr;* all fr. a prehistoric WGmc-NGmc word borrowed fr. LL *cuprum* copper, fr. L *cyprum,* fr. (*aes*) *Cyprium,* lit., metal of Cyprus, fr. *aes* metal + *Cyprium,* neut. of *Cyprius* of Cyprus, fr. Gk *Kyprios,* fr. *Kypris* Cyprus (island in the Mediterranean)] **1 :** a common reddish chiefly univalent and bivalent metallic element that is ductile and malleable and one of the best conductors of heat and electricity, that is the only metal that occurs native abundantly in large masses, being found also in various ores (as chalcopyrite, chalcocite, bornite, cuprite, and malachite), that is used in industry, engineering, and the arts both in the pure state and in brass, bronze, and other alloys, and that is an important trace element in animal and plant nutrition — symbol *Cu;* see ELEMENT table **2 a :** a coin or token made of copper **b :** a minor coin made of bronze (as a U.S. cent or a British halfpenny, penny, or farthing) **3 :** copper sheathing of a vessel **4 a** *chiefly Brit* **:** a large boiler (as for cooking or laundering) now often of iron ⟨a soap ~⟩ **b coppers** *pl* **:** the boilers and cooking vessels in a ship's galley **5 a** *or* **copper red :** a grayish reddish orange that is redder and darker than Etruscan red or hyacinth red and yellower and darker than Persian melon — called also *carnelian, wax red* **b :** a moderate reddish orange to brownish orange **6 :** SOLDERING IRON **7 :** the mouth and throat — used esp. in *hot coppers, cool one's coppers,* implying a parched condition due to excessive drinking **8 :** any of various small butterflies of the family Lycaenidae with copper-colored wings; *esp* **:** AMERICAN COPPER **9 :** the token used in coppering in the game of faro **10 :** a copper sheet like a shield with a T-shaped ridge across it that was used as a symbol of wealth or distinction in ceremonial exchange among the Indians of the northwestern coast of No. America

²copper \"\ *adj* **1 :** of copper ⟨~ wire⟩ **2 :** relating to copper, copper mining, or copper smelting **3 :** having the characteristic color of copper ⟨a hot and ~ sky —S.T.Coleridge⟩ **4 :** of the color copper or copper brown

³copper \"\ *vt* **coppered; coppered; coppering** \-p(ə)riŋ\ **coppers 1 :** to cover, coat, or sheathe with or as if with copper **2 :** to treat with copper or a copper compound **3 a :** to lay a copper cent or token upon or against (a card or bet) in the game of faro to indicate that the player bets against its winning **b :** HEDGE

⁴copper \"\ *n* -s [²*cop* + *-er*] **:** one that cops **:** an operator of a copping machine

⁵copper \"\ *n* -s [⁴*cop* + *-er*] *slang* **:** POLICEMAN

copper acetate *n* **:** an acetate of copper: as **a :** the normal salt $Cu(C_2H_3O_2)_2$ forming dark green crystals — called also *cupric acetate* **b :** any of several basic salts derived from this — see VERDIGRIS 2

copper age *n, usu cap C&A* **:** the aeneolithic age

cop·per·as \'käp(ə)rəs\ *n* -ES [alter. of ME *coperose,* fr. MF *coperose, couperose,* fr. (assumed) VL *cuprirosa,* fr. LL *cupri-* (fr. *cuprum* copper) + L *rosa* rose — more at ROSE] **1** *obs* **:** VITRIOL 1a **2 :** green ferrous sulfate heptahydrate **3** *archaic* **:** a green obtained by use of copperas in dyeing — used attributively esp. of trousers

copperas black *n* **:** a black obtained by the use of logwood with copperas as a mordant in dyeing cloth

copper barilla *n* **:** a native copper concentrate

copper beech *n* **:** a beech that is a variety (*Fagus sylvatica atropunicea*) of the European beech with copper-colored shining leaves — called also *purple beech*

copper-belly \'==,==\ *n* **1 :** COPPERHEAD 1 **2 :** the common American water snake (*Natrix sipedon*)

copper bit *n* **:** the copper head of a soldering iron to which an iron shank is attached; *also* **:** SOLDERING IRON

copper blight *n* [so called fr. the coppery sheen of the diseased leaves] **:** a leaf-spot disease of tea caused by a fungus (*Guignardia camelliae*)

copper blue *n* **:** AZURITE BLUE

copperbottom \'==,==\ *vt* **:** to make copper-bottomed

copper-bottomed \¦==¦==\ *adj* **:** having a bottom of copper ⟨*a copper-bottomed* boiler⟩ or sheathed with copper ⟨*a copper-bottomed* ship⟩

copper brown *n* **:** a variable color averaging a strong brown that is stronger and slightly yellower and darker than average russet, duller and slightly yellower than rust, and deeper and slightly redder than gold brown

copper butterfly *n* **:** COPPER 8

copper cent *n* **1 :** a large U.S. cent of the series coined 1793–1857 and made of copper **2 :** MITE, WHIT, TRIFLE, PARTICLE **3 :** a bronze cent

copper chloride *n* **:** a chloride of copper: **a :** a white poisonous powder CuCl made by reducing cupric chloride and used chiefly as a catalyst and as an absorbent of carbon monoxide — called also *copper(I) chloride, cuprous chloride* **b :** a yellowish brown deliquescent anhydrous powder $CuCl_2$ made by heating copper in chlorine or a green crystalline dihydrate $CuCl_2.2H_2O$ made by evaporating cupric oxide in hydrochloric acid, both being used chiefly as a mordant in dyeing and printing and in some metallurgical processes — called also *copper(II) chloride, cupric chloride* **c :** any of various basic chlorides (as a brown powder $CuCl_2.3CuO$) or mixtures formed on exposure of cupric chloride to air used as pigments and fungicides — called also *copper oxychloride*

copper chromite catalyst *n* **:** a catalyst composed essentially of oxides of copper and chromium and used in the hydrogenation of organic compounds

copper citrate *n* **:** a green or bluish green crystalline powder used as an astringent and antiseptic — called also *cupric citrate*

copper cyanide *n* **:** a cyanide of copper; *specif* **:** a white crystalline poisonous powder CuCN made by reaction of cuprous chloride with sodium cyanide and used chiefly in electroplating because of its ability to form complex cyanides

coppered *past of* COPPER

copper-faced \¦==¦=\ *adj* **1 :** faced or covered with copper ⟨*copper-faced* type⟩ **2 :** having a face like copper **:** BRAZEN

copper finch *n* **:** CHAFFINCH

copper glance *n* **:** CHALCOCITE

copper green *n* **1 :** MINERAL GREEN 1a **2 :** MALACHITE GREEN 2

copperhead \'==,=\ *n* **1 a :** a pit viper (*Agkistrodon contortrix,* syn. *mokasen*) widely distributed in upland areas of the eastern U.S. that attains a length of three feet, is coppery brown above with dark transverse blotches that render it inconspicuous among fallen leaves, and is usu. regarded as much less dangerous than a rattler of comparable size **b :** a very venomous but sluggish Australian elapid snake (*Denisonia superba*) **c :** a harmless Indian colubrid snake (*Elaphe radiata*) **2 a :** a person in the northern states who sympathized with the South during the Civil War **b :** one whose loyalty is questioned **3 :** a ground squirrel (*Citellus lateralis*) of the western U.S. having a yellowish head and shoulders and conspicuously striped body **4 a :** AMERICAN GOLDENEYE **b :** YELLOW-HEADED BLACKBIRD **5** *or* **copperhead bream :** BLUEGILL

cop·per·head·ism \"+,izəm\ *n* -s **:** sympathy for the Confederate cause in the Civil War **:** disloyalty to the Union

copper hydroxide *n* **:** a hydroxide or hydrated oxide of copper; *specif* **:** the hydroxide $Cu(OH)_2$ obtained as a blue precipitate by the action of alkali on cupric salt solutions or as blue crystals and used chiefly as a mordant and in preparing cuprammonium solution

copper indian *n, cap I* **:** YELLOWKNIFE

coppering *pres part of* COPPER

copper iris *n* **:** an herb (*Iris fulva*) of the southern U.S. with a reddish brown flower

cop·per·ish \'käpərish\ *adj* **:** resembling or suggesting copper **:** somewhat coppery

cop·per·ize \-,rīz\ *vt* -ED/-ING/-S **:** to impregnate or plate with copper **:** treat with copper or a copper compound

copperleaf \'==,=\ *n* [so called fr. the color of the matured plant] **:** a plant of the genus *Acalypha* (esp. *A. virginica*)

copper loss *n* **:** electrical energy wasted as heat in a copper conductor

copper luster *n* **:** a metallic luster on pottery obtained by firing a copper-salt glaze applied to the pottery surface

copper naphthenate *n* **:** a green cupric salt of a commercial naphthenic acid used on textiles and in paints to prevent growth of fungi and barnacles

copper nickel *n* **:** NICCOLITE

coppernose \'==,=\ *n* [prob. by folk etymology fr. F *couperose* copperose, copperas — more at COPPERAS] **1 :** an inflamed nose such as that of acne rosacea or that sometimes produced by habitual drunkenness **2 a :** AMERICAN SCOTER **b :** BLUEGILL

coppernosed bream \'==¦=-\ *also* **coppernosed sunfish** *n* **:** BLUEGILL

copper number *n* **:** a number that expresses the amount of copper reduced from the cupric to the cuprous state (as in Fehling solution) by a given amount of cellulose material and that is useful as a measure of purity esp. in relation to strength and resistance to chemical deterioration of paper and other cellulose products

copper oxide *n* **:** any oxide of copper: as **a :** the oxide Cu_2O that occurs naturally as cuprite and is obtained as red or yellow crystals or powder by oxidation of copper in a furnace or by electrolysis and that is used chiefly as a pigment (as in ceramics and in antifouling paints) and as a seed disinfectant and fungicide — called also *copper(I) oxide, cuprous oxide, red copper oxide* **b :** the monoxide CuO that occurs naturally as paramelaconite and tenorite, is obtained usu. in black amorphous form by oxidizing copper, and is used chiefly in preparing cuprammonium solution, as a pigment in ceramics, as a catalyst for hydrogenations, and in chemical analysis — called also *black copper oxide, copper(II) oxide, cupric oxide*

copper oxychloride *n* **:** COPPER CHLORIDE c

¹copperplate \'==¦=\ *n* [¹*copper* + *plate*] **1 a :** a plate of polished copper on which a design or writing is engraved or etched **b :** a printed impression taken from such a plate **c :** a print or printing made by an intaglio process from a copperplate **d :** copperplate engraving or printing **2 :** a handwriting based on models engraved in copper with a burin and characterized by lines of sharply contrasting thickness achieved through the use of a very fine pen applied with varying pressure

²copperplate \"\ *vt* -ED/-ING/-S **1 :** to engrave on a copperplate **2 :** to print from a copperplate

copperplate press *n* **:** a manually operated printing press used for making prints from intaglio metal plates

copper pyrites *n* **:** CHALCOPYRITE

copper red *n* **:** ¹COPPER 5a

copper-rose \'==,=\ *var of* COPROSE

copper rust *n* **:** VERDIGRIS 3

coppers *pl of* COPPER, *pres 3d sing of* COPPER

copper·skin \'==,=\ *n* **:** an American Indian

coppersmith \'==,=\ *n* [ME *copresmyth,* fr. *copre, coper* copper + *smyth* smith] **1 :** one who makes objects (as kettles, coils, tubing, and fittings) from sheet copper and brass **:** a worker in copper **2 :** a barbet (*Megalaima haemacephala*) of India, southeast Asia, and islands of the southwest Pacific having a characteristic ringing note

coppersmithing \'==,==\ *n* -s **:** the work or occupation of a coppersmith

copper snake *n* **:** any of certain somewhat copper-colored snakes: as **a :** a coppery brown Australian venomous snake (*Pseudechis cupreus*) related to the Australian black snake **b :** a small harmless colubrid snake (*Storeria occipitomaculata*) of eastern No. America

copper spot *n* **:** a disease of lawn and golf-green grasses caused by a fungus (*Gloeocercospora sorghi*) and producing dead areas of a coppery red color

copper sulfate *n* **:** any sulfate of copper; *specif* **:** the normal sulfate $CuSO_4$, white when anhydrous but best known as the blue crystalline pentahydrate $CuSO_4.5H_2O$, that is made by roasting copper sulfide ores and by the action of sulfuric acid on copper or copper oxide and that is used chiefly as a fungicide and algicide, in dyeing and printing, in making pigments and other compounds, and in electric batteries — see BORDEAUX MIXTURE

copper sulfide *n* **:** any sulfide of copper: as **a :** the black crystalline sulfide Cu_2S occurring naturally as chalcocite — called also *cuprous sulfide* **b :** the black, bluish black, or brownish black crystalline sulfide CuS occurring naturally as covellite and precipitated by hydrogen sulfide from a solution of a cupric salt — called also *cupric sulfide*

copper tan *n* **:** a light reddish brown that is duller and slightly yellower than peach tan and duller and yellower than monkey skin

coppertip \'==,=\ *n* **:** a bulbous African herb (*Crocosma aurea*) of the family Iridaceae of branching habit that is often cultivated for its bright yellow panicled flowers

copper vitriol *n* **:** COPPER SULFATE

copperweed \'==,=\ *n* [so called fr. the copper-colored flowers] **:** a tall shrubby herb (*Oxytenia acerosa*) of the family Compositae that is troublesome esp. in the Western U.S. as a plant poisonous to stock

cop·pery \'käp(ə)rē, -ri\ *adj* **:** mixed with copper **:** containing copper **:** like copper (as in color or taste)

copper yellow *n* **:** QUINCE YELLOW

coppery snake *n* **:** a small harmless colubrid snake (*Prosymna sundevallii*) occurring in southern Africa

¹cop·pice \'käpəs\ *n* -s [MF *copeiz, coupeiz,* fr. *couper* to cut — more at COPE] **1 :** a thicket, grove, or growth of small trees that are cut on a short rotation **:** COPSE **2 a :** wood cut from coppice growth **b :** UNDERWOOD, BRUSHWOOD **3 :** a forest originating mainly from sprouts or root suckers as opposed to one derived from seed

²coppice \"\ *vb* -ED/-ING/-S *vt* **:** to cause to grow in the form of a coppice **:** cut back so as to produce shoots from old stumps ~ *vi* **:** to form a coppice **:** sprout freely from the base

coppice oak *n* **:** bark from roots of the kermes oak

coppice shoot *n* **:** a young tree that has grown from a sucker and not from seed

cop·ping \'käpiŋ\ *n* -s [¹*cop* (thread wound on a spindle) + *-ing*] **:** the forming of the cop in spinning

coppled *adj* [obs. E *copple* crest on a bird's head (fr. AF *copel* top of the head, top of a plant, dim. of OF *cope* drinking vessel, fr. LL *cuppa*) + *-ed* — more at CUP] **1** *obs* **:** CONICAL, COPPED **2** *obs* **:** CRESTED

¹cop·py \'käpi\ *n* -ES [by shortening & alter.] *dial Eng* **:** COPPICE

²coppy \"\ *n* -ES [prob. fr. ¹ *coppy*] *dial Eng* **:** a low stool

copr- *or* **copro-** *comb form* [NL, fr. Gk *kopr-, kopro-,* fr. *kopros;* akin to Lith *šikti* to void excrement, Skt *śakṛt* dung] **1 :** dung **:** feces ⟨*copr*emia⟩ ⟨*copro*lite⟩ **2 :** filth **:** obscenity ⟨*copro*lalia⟩ **3** *usu* **copro- :** related to coprostanol

copr *abbr* copyright

co·pra \'kōprə, 'käp-\ *n* -s [Pg, fr. Malayalam *koppara,* prob. fr. Hindi *khoprā*] **:** coconut meat dried esp. for export before the coconut oil is pressed out

copra beetle *also* **copra bug** *n* **:** the red-legged ham beetle

copra cake *n* **:** COCONUT CAKE

copra itch *n* **:** GROCER'S ITCH

copra meal *n* **:** COCONUT MEAL

copra oil *n* **:** coconut oil pressed out from copra

co-precipitate \¦kō+\ *vb* [*co-* + *precipitate*] **:** to precipitate together

co-precipitation \¦kō+\ *n* **:** the process of coprecipitating

co·presence \(')kō+\ *n* [*co-* + *presence*] **:** occurrence of two or more things together in the same place and time

cop·ri·nus \'käprənəs, kə'prīnəs\ *n, cap* [NL, fr. Gk *koprinos* of dung, fr. *kopros* dung; fr. the habitat of some species — more at COPR-] **:** a genus of black-spored agarics of the family Agaricaceae in which the pileus breaks down at maturity into an inky fluid — see SHAGGYMANE

copro·culture \¦käprə+\ *n* [ISV *copr-* + *culture*] **:** culture of feces (as for detection of pathogenic microorganisms)

cop·ro·dae·al *or* **cop·ro·de·al** \¦käprə¦dēəl\ *adj* [NL *coprodaeum, coprodeum* + E *-al*] **:** relating or belonging to the coprodaeum

cop·ro·dae·um *or* **cop·ro·deum** \,käprə'dēəm, '==,==\ *n* -s [NL, fr. *copr-* + *-odaeum, -odeum* (fr. Gk *hodaion,* neut. of *hodaios* on the way, fr. *hodos* way) — more at CEDE] **:** the innermost division of the cloaca of birds or reptiles

co-product \(')kō+\ *n* [*co-* + *product*] **:** BY-PRODUCT 1

co·ro·lag·nia \,käprə'lagnēə, '==,===\ *n* -s [NL, fr. *copr-* + *-lagnia*] **:** sexual excitement produced by contact with feces — **cop·ro·lag·nist** \-nəst\ *n* -s

cop·ro·la·lia \-'lālēə\ *n* -s [NL, fr. *copr-* + *-lalia*] **1 :** obsessive or uncontrollable use of obscene language **2 :** the use of obscene (as scatological) language as sexual gratification

cop·ro·lite \'käprə,līt\ *n* -s [*copr-* + *-lite*] **:** fossil excrement being often a valuable source of information about the food and habits of extinct animals — **cop·ro·lit·ic** \¦==¦lid·ik\ *adj*

cop·ro·lith \'käprə,lith\ *n* -s [NL *coprolithus,* fr. *copr-* + *-lithus* -lith] **:** a mass of hard fecal matter in the intestine

co·prol·o·gy \kə'prälәjē\ *n* -ES [ISV *copr-* + *-logy*] **1 :** SCATOLOGY **2 :** PORNOGRAPHY

co·proph·a·gan \kə'präfəgən\ *n* -s [NL *Coprophaga* (former subfamily of beetles containing the dung beetle, fr. *copr-* + *-phaga,* neut. pl. of *-phagus* -phagous) + E *-an*] **:** one that feeds on excrement; *specif* **:** DUNG BEETLE

cop·ro·pha·gia \,käprə'fāj(ē)ə, '==,=(=)=\ *n* -s [NL, fr. *copr-* + *-phagia*] **:** COPROPHAGY — **cop·ro·phag·ic** \¦==¦fajik\ *adj* — **co·proph·a·gous** \kə'präfəgəs\ *adj*

co·proph·a·gist \kə'präfəjəst\ *n* -s **:** one that practices coprophagy

co·proph·a·gy \-jē\ *n* -ES [ISV *copr-* + *-phagy*] **:** the feeding on or eating of dung or excrement that is normal behavior among many insects, birds, and other animals but in man is a symptom of some forms of insanity

cop·ro·phil·ia \,käprə'filēə, '==,==\ *n* -s [NL, fr. *copr-* + *-philia*] **:** marked interest in excrement; *esp* **:** use of feces or filth for sexual excitement — **cop·ro·phil·i·ac** \¦==¦filē,ak\ *n* -s

cop·ro·phil·ic \¦käprə¦filik\ *adj* [in sense 1, fr. NL *coprophilia* + E *-ic;* in sense 2, fr. *copr-* + *-philic*] **1 :** relating to coprophilia **2 :** COPROPHILOUS

co·proph·i·lous \kə'präfələs\ *adj* [*copr-* + *-philous*] **1 :** growing or living on dung ⟨~ fungi⟩ ⟨~ beetles⟩ **2 :** fond of pornography

cop·ro·porphyrin \¦käprə+\ *n* -s [ISV *copr-* + *porphyrin*] **:** any of four isomeric porphyrins $C_{20}H_6N_4(CH_3)_4(CH_2CH_2COOH)_4$ of which types I and III are found in feces and urine esp. in certain pathological conditions and also in yeast

cop·ro·porphyrinuria \¦käprə+\ *n* -s [NL, fr. ISV *coproporphyrin* + NL *-uria*] **:** excretion of coproporphyrin in the urine

co·proprietor \¦kō+\ *n* [*co-* + *proprietor*] **:** a joint owner — **co·proprietorship** \¦kō+\ *n*

cop·rose \'kä,prōz\ *n* -s [perh. modif. of D *klaproos,* fr. *klappen* to clap, chat (fr. MD *clappen*) + *roos* rose, fr. MD *rôse, rose,* fr. L *rosa* — more at CLAP, ROSE] *dial Brit* **:** CORN POPPY

co·pros·ma \kə'präzmə\ *n* [NL, fr. *copr-* + *-osma*] **1** *cap* **:** a genus of shrubs or small trees of the family Rubiaceae found in New Zealand, Australia, and Hawaii and having shining often variegated leaves and small flowers with revolute corolla lobes **2** -s **:** a plant of the genus *Coprosma*

cop·ro·stane \'käprə,stān\ *n* -s [ISV *copr-* + *-stane* (as in *cholestane*)] **:** a crystalline steroid hydrocarbon $C_{27}H_{48}$ stereoisomeric with cholestane

co·pros·ta·nol \kə'prästə,nōl, -nōl\ *n* -s [*coprostane* + *-ol*] **:** a crystalline sterol $C_{27}H_{47}OH$ formed by bacterial reduction of cholesterol in the intestines and present in feces — called also *3-coprostanol, coprosterol*

co·pros·ter·ol \-tə,rōl, -rōl\ *n* -s [*copr-* + *sterol*] **:** COPROSTANOL

cop·ro·zo·ic \¦käprə¦zōik\ *adj* [*copr-* + *-zoic*] *of an animal* **:** COPROPHILOUS — **cop·ro·zo·on** \,=='zō,än, '==,=(,)=\ *n, pl* **copro·zoa** \-zōə\

¹cops *or* **copse** \'käps\ *n, pl* **copses** [ME *cops, copse, cospe* shackle, hasp, fr. OE *cops, cosp* shackle; akin to OS *-cosp* shackle] *dial Eng* **:** a hasp, clevis, or similar coupling device

²cops *pl of* COP, *pres 3d sing of* COP

cops and robbers *n* **:** children's play in which the players imitate the chasing, shooting, and capturing of criminals by police

¹copse \'käps\ *n* -s [by alter.] **:** COPPICE ⟨near yonder ~ where once the garden smiled —Oliver Goldsmith⟩

²copse \"\ *vb* -ED/-ING/-S **:** COPPICE

copse laurel *n* **:** SPURGE LAUREL

copsewood \'=,=\ *n* **1 :** COPSE **2 :** the underwood of a copse

cops·ing \'käpsiŋ\ *n* -s [¹*copse* + *-ing*] **:** COPSEWOOD, COPPICE

copsy \'käpsē, -si\ *adj* [¹*copse* + *-y*] **:** abounding in copses

copt \'käpt\ *n* -s *cap* [Ar *quft, qift, qubt, qibt* Copts, *qufṭī, qifṭī, qubṭī, qibṭī* Coptic, fr. Copt *gyptios, kyptaios* Egyptian, fr. Gk *aegyptios* — more at EGYPTIAN] **:** an Egyptian of the native race descended from the ancient Egyptians; *esp* **:** a member of the Coptic church

cop·ter \'käptə(r)\ n -s [by shortening] **:** HELICOPTER

¹cop·tic \'käptik, -tēk\ *adj, usu cap* [*Copt* + *-ic*] **1 :** relating or belonging to the Copts, to Coptic, or to the Egyptian Christian church **2** *fine art* **:** produced in Egypt during the Christian period; *specif* **:** having to do with the distinctive art of Christian Egypt which reached its apex in the 6th century

²coptic \"\ *n* **1** *cap* **:** an Afro-Asiatic language descended from ancient Egyptian and used by the Egyptians from about the 3d century A.D. to about 1500 when it was superseded by Arabic and became a dead language except for continued liturgical use in the Coptic church **2** -s **:** OXBLOOD

cop·tis \'käptəs\ *n, cap* [NL, irreg. fr. Gk *koptein* to cut off; fr. the divided leaves — more at CAPON] **:** a genus of small herbs of the family Ranunculaceae that are found in the north temperate zone and have basal divided or compound leaves, a slender rootstock, and white flowers on a scape — see GOLDTHREAD

cop·u·la \'käpyələ\ *n, pl* **copulas** \-ləz\ *also* **copu·lae** \-,lē\ [L, bond — more at COUPLE] **1 :** something that connects **:** LINK: as **a :** the connecting link or relation between the subject and predicate of a strictly formulated proposition; *esp* **:** such a link when it is a form of the verb *to be* (as in "he is a shoemaker" instead of "he makes shoes") — see BE, PREDICABLE **b :** a linguistic form that links a subject with its predicate and sometimes has some additional meaning of its own (as *looks* in "that looks good," *got* in "he got sleepy") and sometimes not (as *is* in "that is right") **c :** any of certain connecting structures; *specif* **:** a basibranchial or basihyal bone or cartilage **2 :** sexual union **:** COPULATION — used chiefly in law **3 :** COUPLER 1c **4 :** a descant having a florid cadential passage usu. in the plainsong tenor **5** *obs* **:** a chemical compound that joins itself to another

cop·u·la·ble \-ləbəl\ *adj* [²*copulate* + *-able*] *chem* **:** able to couple or be coupled

cop·u·lar \-lə(r)\ *adj* [*copula* + *-ar*] **:** relating to or of the nature of a copula

¹cop·u·late \-lət, -,lāt\ *adj* [ME *copulat,* fr. L *copulatus,* past part. of *copulare* to bind, fr. *copula*] **:** JOINED, COUPLED

²copulate \'käpyə,lāt, *usu* -ād·+V\ *vi* -ED/-ING/-S [L *copulatus*] **1 :** to join or unite **2 a :** to unite in sexual intercourse **:** engage in coitus **b** *of gametes* **:** to fuse permanently — compare CONJUGATE

cop·u·la·tion \,käpyə'lāshən\ *n* -s [ME *copulacioun,* fr. MF *copulation,* fr. L *copulation-, copulatio,* fr. *copulatus* + *-ion-, -io* -ion] **1 :** the act of coupling or joining **:** the state of being coupled or joined **:** UNION, CONJUNCTION ⟨wit, you know, is the unexpected ~ of ideas —Samuel Johnson⟩ **2 a :** sexual union **:** COITUS **b :** permanent fusion of gametes — compare CONJUGATION **3 :** the joining of subject and predicate by a copula **4 :** COUPLING — compare COUPLE vi 2b

copulation path *n* **:** the intracytoplasmic course followed by the male pronucleus in approaching the female pronucleus during fertilization and often delineating the direction of the first cleavage furrow

¹cop·u·la·tive \'käpyə,lād·|iv, -ləd·|, -,lāt|, -lət|, |ēv\ *adj* [ME *copulatif,* fr. MF or LL; MF, fr. LL *copulativus,* fr. L *copulatus* + *-ivus* -ive] **1 a** *of a conjunction* **:** joining together coordinate words or word groups and expressing addition of their meanings ⟨*and* in "bread and meat" is ~⟩ — contrasted with *disjunctive* **b :** containing words or word groups joined by a copulative conjunction ⟨~ sentences⟩ **c** *of a verb* **:** being a copula (sense 1b) **d** *of a compound* **:** belonging to the dvandva class **2 :** relating to or serving for copulation ⟨~ organs⟩ **3 :** of or relating to coupling of chemical compounds or radicals — **cop·u·la·tive·ly** \|əvlē, -li\ *adv*

²**copulative** \"\ *n* -s **1 :** a copulative conjunction **2 :** a compound belonging to the dvandva class

cop·u·la·to·ry \ˈkäpyələ,tōrē, -tȯrē, -ri\ *adj* **:** relating to or used in copulation ⟨~ organs⟩ **:** tending or serving to unite **:** COPULATIVE

co·punctal \(ˈ)kō+\ *adj* [*co-* + *punctal*] *geom* **:** having a point in common **:** relating to a point at which lines or planes meet **:** ¹CONCURRENT 1

¹**copy** \ˈkäpē, -pi\ *n* -ES [ME *copie*, fr. MF, fr. ML & L; ML *copia* imitation, transcript, fr. L, abundance, number, ability, power — more at COPIOUS] **1** *obs* **:** PLENTY, COPIOUSNESS **2 :** an imitation, transcript, or reproduction of an original work (as of a letter, an engraving, a painting, a statue, a piece of furniture, a dress) **3** *English law* **a :** the transcript of the roll of the manorial court containing the entries made by the steward of the admissions of tenants to land according to custom under the tenure thence called copyhold **b :** a holding or estate by copyhold **4 :** one of a series of esp. mechanical reproductions of the same original text, engraving, or photograph **:** an individual example of a series of identical impressions (as of type, a printing plate) ⟨a book printed in 500 *copies*⟩ ⟨a rag-paper ~ of a newspaper⟩ ⟨a presentation ~⟩ **5 a** *archaic* **:** something that is or is to be imitated or transcribed **:** an example (as of penmanship) **:** MODEL, PATTERN **b :** a picture that is to be photographically reproduced **6 a :** matter to be set up for printing or photoengraving (as a draft of a news story, an author's manuscript, or a picture) ⟨this is dirty ~⟩ **b :** something considered printable or newsworthy — used in the singular and without an article ⟨crime makes good ~⟩ **c :** the text of an advertisement — **by copy** *English law* **:** by copy of the manorial court roll

²**copy** \"\ *vb* -ED/-ING/-ES [ME *copien*, fr. MF *copier*, fr. ML *copiare*, fr. *copia*] *vt* **1 :** to make a copy of **:** write, print, engrave, or paint after an original **:** DUPLICATE, REPRODUCE, TRANSCRIBE; *specif* **:** to duplicate (a document) by pressing in a copying press **2 :** to attempt to resemble **:** follow esp. in manners or course of life ⟨when art *copies* nature⟩ ~ *vi* **1 :** to make a copy ⟨he *copies* from Rembrandt⟩ **2 :** to undergo copying ⟨the document did not ~ well⟩

syn IMITATE, MIMIC, APE, MOCK, BURLESQUE: COPY applies to the making of duplications of originals with resemblances as close as circumstances will permit ⟨you gave natives bits to *copy* under all possible threats against lapses of accuracy —Mary Austin⟩ ⟨later examples of the Greek revival travestied the classic style rather than *copied* it —*Amer. Guide Series: Mass.*⟩ IMITATE suggests following a pattern or model in overall qualities or in some specific characteristics, without precluding considerable variation ⟨she slept for hours in the daytime, *imitating* the cats —Jean Stafford⟩ ⟨plaster was originally painted to *imitate* marble —*Amer. Guide Series: Minn.*⟩ ⟨their pots seem to *imitate* leather vessels —V.G.Childe⟩ MIMIC may suggest a copying either exact in emulation of or fidelity to the original or heightened for making sport of or satirizing ⟨he learned to call wild turkeys with a piece of bone through which he was able to *mimic* the notes of the bird —Van Wyck Brooks⟩ ⟨he attends even to their air, dress, and motions, and imitates them liberally and not servilely; he copies but does not *mimic* —Earl of Chesterfield⟩ APE likewise may apply to close copying in emulation; often it suggests inept, presumptuous, or servile copying of a better or more worthy original ⟨the pride that *apes* humility —F.M.Ford⟩ ⟨feudal principalities each *aping* sovereignty —Will Durant⟩ ⟨the lower classes *aped* the rigid decorum of their "betters" with laughable results —Harrison Smith⟩ MOCK usu. applies to imitation or repetition with scornful derisive intent ⟨she contended every point, objected to every request, shirked her work, fought with her sisters, *mocked* her mother —Margaret Mead⟩ ⟨half a dozen jackals went through the compound singing and a hyena stood afar off and *mocked* them —Rudyard Kipling⟩ BURLESQUE applies to imitation designed to ridicule by grotesque exaggeration ⟨she read these letters aloud, *burlesquing* them in spite of protests —Katherine Mansfield⟩ ⟨most of the local humor is corny, but it's shrewd, earthy, and droll, *burlesquing* in its extravagance the pompousness of our national self-esteem —Bergen Evans⟩

copyboard \ˈ==,=\ *n* **:** the backing on which the original to be reproduced is positioned in front of the camera in photoengraving

¹**copybook** \ˈ==,=\ *n* **1 :** a book containing copies (as of accounts) **2 :** a book formerly used in elementary schools containing samples of penmanship (as in the form of proverbs or moral precepts) for the learner to imitate

²**copybook** \"\ *adj* **:** characterized by conventionality or triteness ⟨old-fashioned standards of morality and ~ virtues —Lucius Garvin⟩ ⟨~ maxims⟩

copyboy \ˈ==,=\ *n* **:** one who carries copy and runs errands (as in a newspaper office or publishing house)

¹**copycat** \ˈ==,=\ *n* [²*copy* + *cat*] **:** one who slavishly imitates or adopts the behavior or practice of another

²**copycat** \"\ *vb* **copycatted; copycatted; copycatting; copycats** *vi* **:** to act as a copycat ~ *vt* **:** IMITATE

copy cutter *n* **:** a newspaper employee who divides copy into takes and apportions them to compositors

copydesk \ˈ==,=\ *n* **:** the desk in a newspaper editorial office at which copyreaders edit copy and write headlines

copy editor *n* **1 :** COPYREADER **2 a :** an editor who prepares copy for the printer **b :** an editor in charge of a copydesk and copyreaders on a newspaper

copyfit \ˈ==,=\ *vt* **:** to fit (printer's copy) to the required space (as by cutting or expanding the copy or the space and by the use of different-size typefaces, measures, and leading) — **copyfitter** \ˈ==,==\ *n*

copy·graph \ˈkäpē,graf\ *n* -s [¹*copy* (manuscript) + *-graph*] **:** HECTOGRAPH — **copy·graphed** \-ft\ *adj*

copyhold \ˈ==,=\ *n* [ME, fr. *copy*, *copie* copy (transcript) + *hold*] **1 :** a tenure of land in England and Ireland until largely abolished by the Copyhold Act of 1894 by copy of court roll, at the will of the lord, and according to the custom of the manor of which the land was a part **2 :** an estate held by copyhold

¹**copyholder** \ˈ==,==\ *n* [*copyhold* + *-er*] **:** one holding land in copyhold

²**copyholder** \"\ *n* [¹*copy* + *holder*] **1 :** a device for holding copy that is being typed, typeset, or photographically reproduced **2 :** one who assists a proofreader by reading copy aloud or following copy as the proofreader reads aloud

copyholding \ˈ==,==\ *n* **:** the work of a copyholder (sense 2)

copying *pres part of* COPY

copying ink *n* **:** ink suitable for writing or typing that is to be copied by direct transfer (as in a copying press)

copying paper *n* **:** thin unsized paper used for taking copies by direct transfer (as in a copying press)

copying press *n* **:** an obsolescent device in which an original (as a letter) in copying ink is transferred in reverse by being pressed against an absorbent translucent sheet which is read from the reverse side — called also *letterpress*

copy·ism \ˈkäpē,izəm\ *n* -s **:** the act or practice of copying esp. mechanically or unthinkingly

copy·ist \-ēəst\ *n* -s [alter. of earlier *copist*, fr. MF *copiste*, fr. *copier* to copy + *-iste* -ist — more at COPY] **1 :** one who is employed to make copies (as of instrumental scores) **:** COPIER, TRANSCRIBER **2 :** IMITATOR, PLAGIARIST, COPYCAT **3 a :** one who makes paper novelties according to pattern **b :** a hand sewer who copies hats **c :** one who copies or adapts clothing designs by sketching or making models

copy·man \-ē,man, -maa(ə)n\ *n*, *pl* **copymen :** COPYCUTTER

copy number *n* **:** a numeral placed on a book to distinguish it from other copies of the same title

copy paper *n* **:** COPYING PAPER

copy·read \ˈkäpē,rēd\ *vt* **:** to edit (as manuscript or copy) for printing

copy·reader \-də(r)\ *n* **1 :** a publishing-house editor who reads and corrects manuscript copy and sometimes specifies size and style of type and the positioning of illustrations; *also* **:** one who edits copy and adds headlines for a newspaper **2 :** one who reads and evaluates usu. unsolicited manuscripts for publication

¹**copyright** \ˈ==,=\ *n* [¹*copy* + *right*] **:** the exclusive, legally secured right to reproduce (as by writing or printing), publish, and sell the matter and form of a literary, musical, or artistic work (as by dramatizing, novelizing, performing or reciting in public, or filming) for a period in the U. S. of 28 years with a right of renewal for another 28 years — see LITERARY PROPERTY; compare PATENT, TRADEMARK

²**copyright** \"\ *adj* **:** secured by copyright **:** COPYRIGHTED

³**copyright** \"\ *vt* -ED/-ING/-S **:** to secure a copyright on

copy·right·able \ˈ==,rīd·əbəl, -ītə-\ *adj* **:** capable of being copyrighted

copywriter \ˈ==,==\ *n* **:** a writer of advertising or publicity copy

coq *or* **coque** \ˈkäk\ *n* -s [F *coq*, fr. OF *coc* — more at COCKEREL] **:** ¹COCK; *specif* **:** a trimming of cock feathers on a woman's hat

coque \"\ *n* -s [F, lit., shell, fr. L *coccum* excrescence on a tree; fr. their original shell-like appearance — more at COAK] **:** a loop of ribbon or feathers used in trimming hats

coque·ci·grue \ˈkäksə,grü, ,==ˈ=\ *n* -s [F, fr. MF] **:** an imaginary creature regarded as an embodiment of absolute absurdity

co·quei·ro \kü'kärü; kəˈka(a)rü, -rō, -rə\ *n* -s [Pg, fr. *côco* coconut — more at COCO] **:** OURICURY

co·que·li·cot \ˈkäklə,kō, ˈkōk-\ *n* -s [F, cry of a cock, cock, poppy, of imit. origin; fr. a comparison of the flower to the comb of a cock] **1 a :** any of several poppies of the genus *Papaver*; *esp* **:** CORN POPPY **b :** a mallow (*Callirrhoë papaver*) of the southern U. S. that resembles a poppy **2 :** PONCEAU

¹**co·quet** \kōˈket\ *n* -s [F, dim. of *coq* cock — more at COQ] **1** *obs* **:** a man who indulges in coquetry **2 :** COQUETTE

²**coquet** \(ˈ)=ˈ=\ *adj* [F, fr. *coquet*, n.] **1** *obs* **:** boldly amorous in manner **2 :** COQUETTISH

³**co·quet** *or* **co·quette** \kōˈket, *usu* -ed· +V\ *vb* **coquetted; coquetted; coquetting; coquets** *or* **coquettes** [partly fr. ¹*coquet*, partly fr. *coquette*, n.] *vt*, *obs* **:** to treat coquettishly **:** flirt with ⟨you are *coquetting* a maid of honor —Jonathan Swift⟩ ~ *vi* **1 :** to trifle in love **:** play the coquette ⟨she *coquetted* with the solid husbands of her friends —Dorothy Parker⟩ ⟨the courtiers stood around . . . *coquetting* and making their pretty speeches —Francis Hackett⟩ **2 :** deal playfully instead of seriously **:** PLAY, DALLY — used with *with* ⟨we have *coquetted* with a serious matter⟩

coque·toon \ˈkäkə,tün, ,==ˈ=\ *n* -s [native name in western Africa] **:** GRIMME

co·quet·ry \ˈkōkətrē, -ri *sometimes* kōˈket-\ *n* -ES [F *coquetterie*, fr. *coquette* + *-erie* -ery] **1 :** the conduct or art of a coquette **:** effort or action intended to attract admiration, gallantry, or affection without responsive feeling **:** a trifling in love **2 :** a dallying or trifling attention or consideration (as to a cause) without serious espousal **3 :** delicate charm of a type distinctive of coquettes ⟨lack of ~ — in the sense of a lighthearted desire to please — is a lack of charity, of natural kindness —*English Digest*⟩

co·quette \kōˈket, *usu* -ed· +V\ *n* -s [F, fem. of *coquet*] **1 :** a woman who endeavors without affection to attract men's amorous attention **:** FLIRT ⟨instruct the eyes of young ~s to roll —Alexander Pope⟩ — sometimes, with *male*, used of a man **2 :** any of several tropical hummingbirds (of *Lophornis* and related genera) with crested head and metallic-tinted neck feathers **3 :** a moderate to strong yellowish pink that is yellower and paler than coral blush

co·quett·ish \(ˈ)kōˈked·ish, -eti-, -ēsh\ *adj* **:** having the air or nature of a coquette or coquetry **:** practicing or exhibiting coquetry ⟨heartless, ~ women, who put self first and played with fire —Margaret A. Barnes⟩ — **co·quett·ish·ly** *adv* — **co·quett·ish·ness** *n* -ES

co·qui \ˈkōkwē\ *or* **coqui partridge** *n* -s [Sechuana, quail] **:** a small francolin (*Francolinus coqui*) widely distributed in African grasslands

co·quil·lage \,kōkəˈläzh, ˈ==,=\ *n* -s [F, shellfish, shellfish used as decorations, fr. *coquille* + *-age*] **:** decoration imitating shells

co·quil·la nut \kəˈkilə,-, kōˈkē(l)yə,-\ *n* [modif. of Pg *coquilho*, dim. of *côco* coconut — more at COCO] **:** the nut of a piassava palm (*Attalea funifera*) of Brazil having a hard hazel-brown shell much used like vegetable ivory by turners

co·quille \kōˈkil, kəˈ-, -kēl; *F* kōkēʸ\ *n* -s [F, lit., shell — more at COCKLE] **1 :** SHELL: as **a :** a shell-like dish in which food is served **:** SCALLOP **b :** the expansion of the guard of a sword or dagger **c :** a ruching or edging gathered and fulled in a shell-like design and used for clothing or millinery trimming **2 a** *or* **coquille board :** an artist's white drawing board with stippled texture that produces a dotted drawing that looks like a half tone but may be reproduced as a line cut **b :** a drawing technique involving the use of coquille board

coquille lens *n* [*coquille*] **:** an oval glass of curved surface and uniform thickness used in eyeglasses

co·quim·bite \kōˈkim,bīt, kəˈ-\ *n* -s [G *coquimbit*, fr. *Coquimbo* province in Chile (where it was discovered) + G *-it* -ite] **:** a mineral consisting of a hydrous ferric sulfate $Fe_2(SO_4)_3 \cdot 9H_2O$ occurring in white or slightly colored masses

co·qui·na \kōˈkēnə, kəˈ-\ *n* -s [Sp, prob. irreg. dim. of *concha* shell — more at CONCHA] **1 :** a small marine clam of the genus *Donax* (esp. *D. variabilis*) used for broth or chowder **2 :** a soft whitish limestone formed of broken shells and corals cemented together that is found in the southern U. S. and used for roadbeds and for building

co·qui·ta \-ˈkēd·ə\ *n* -s [AmerSp, fr. Sp *coquito*] **:** the strong cordage fiber of the coquito palm

co·qui·to \-d·ō\ *also* **coquito palm** *n* -s [Sp *coquito*, dim. of *coco* coco palm, fr. Pg *côco* — more at COCO] **:** a pinnate-leaved palm (*Jubaea spectabilis*) of Chile whose sap is used in making palm honey, seeds for sweetmeats, and fiber for cordage

¹**cor** *var of* KOR

²**cor** *n* -s [origin unknown] *obs* **:** salt fish; *esp* **:** COD

³**cor** \ˈkȯ(ə)r\ *n*, *pl* **cordia** \-rdēə\ [L — more at HEART] **:** HEART

cor- — see COM-

¹**cor** *abbr* **1** corner **2** cornet **3** coroner **4** coronet **5** corpus

²**cor** *or* **corr** *abbr* **1** correct; corrected; correction **2** correlative **3** correspondence; correspondent; corresponding **4** corrigendum **5** corrugated **6** corrupt; corruption

¹**co·ra** \ˈkōrə, ˈkȯrə\ *n* -s [origin unknown] **:** a gazelle (*Gazella arabica*) found from Persia to No. Africa

²**cora** \"\ *n*, *cap* [NL, perh. fr. Gk *korē* girl, doll, pupil of the eye; fr. its circular shape; akin to L *crescere* to grow — more at CRESCENT] **:** a genus of basidiolichens superficially resembling the bracket fungi and widely distributed on soil and trees in Central and So. America

³**cora** \"\ *n*, *pl* **cora** *or* **coras** *usu cap* [Sp, of AmerInd origin] **1 a :** a Taracahitian people of the states of Jalisco and Nayarit, Mexico including the Cora proper and the Coano, **b :** a member of such people **2 :** the language of the Cora people

co·ra·be·ca \,kōrəˈbekə, ,kȯr-, -ˈbākə\ *or* **co·ra·ve·ca** \-ˈvē-, -ˈvā-\ *n*, *pl* **corabeca** *or* **corabecas** *or* **coraveca** *or* **coravecas** *usu cap* [AmerSp *corabeca*, of AmerInd origin] **1 a :** an extinct people of Bolivia **b :** a member of such people **2 :** the language of the Corabeca people considered by some Americanists as an independent linguistic family and by others as Otoquian or uncertain — **co·ra·be·can** *or* **co·ra·ve·can** \ˈ==ˈ==\ *adj* or *n*

co·ra·ci·ae \kōˈrāsē,ē, kəˈ-\ [NL, pl. of *Coracias*] *syn of* CORACII

co·ra·ci·as \kōˈrāsēəs, kəˈ-\ *n*, *cap* [NL, fr. Gk *korakias*, a kind of chough; akin to Gk *korax* raven — more at RAVEN] **:** a genus of vigorous active brightly colored birds related to and somewhat resembling the kingfishers and being the type of a widespread Old World family Coraciidae

cor·a·cid·i·um \,kȯrəˈsidēəm\ *n*, *pl* **coracid·ia** \-dēə\ [NL, fr. Gk *korak-*, *korax* raven, anything hooked like a raven's beak + NL *-idium*] **:** the onchosphere of a tapeworm at about the time of hatching while still surrounded by the embryophore which in Pseudophyllidea is ciliated

co·ra·cii \kōˈrāsē,ī, kəˈ-\ *n pl*, *cap* [NL, pl. of *Coracius* (syn. of *Coracias*, fr. Gk *korakias*)] **:** the suborder of Coraciiformes that includes the rollers, hoopoes, wood hoopoes, and related birds

cor·a·ci·idae \,kȯrəˈsīə,dē\ *n pl*, *cap* [NL, fr. *Coracias*, type genus + *-idae*] **:** a family (order Coraciiformes) of Old World birds including the common roller and certain related birds

co·ra·ci·iform \kəˈrāsēə,fȯrm, ˈkȯrəˈsīə,-\ *adj* [NL *Coraciiformes*] **:** of or relating to the Coraciiformes

co·ra·ci·ifor·mes \kə,rāsēəˈfȯr,mēz, ,kȯrə,sīəˈf-\ *n pl*, *cap* [NL, fr. *Coracii* + *-formes*] **:** an order of chiefly arboreal birds comprising the rollers, kingfishers, hornbills, hoopoes, motmots, and related forms and formerly containing also the hummingbirds, woodpeckers, swifts, and owls

cor·a·cite \ˈkȯrə,sīt\ *n* -s [Gk *korak-*, *korax* raven + E *-ite*; fr. its black color] **:** URANINITE

cor·a·cle \ˈkȯrəkəl, ˈkär-\ *n* -s [alter. of earlier *corougle*, fr. W *corwgl*, *cwrwgl*, fr. *corwg*, *cwrwg*, fr. MW *corwc*; akin to MIr *curach* boat, L *corium* leather — more at CUIRASS] **1 :** a small boat made by covering a wicker frame with hide or leather and used by the ancient Britons **2 :** a boat made of broad hoops covered with horsehide or tarpaulin and used in parts of the British Isles

coracles

coraco- *comb form* [NL, fr. *coracoides* coracoid] **:** coracoid and ⟨*coraco*costal⟩

cor·a·co·bra·chi·a·lis \,kȯrə(,)kō,brākēˈāləs, -brak-\ *n*, *pl* **coracobrachiales** \-,lēz\ [NL, fr. *coraco-* + L *brachialis* brachial] **:** a muscle extending between the coracoid process and the middle of the shaft of the humerus

¹**cor·a·coid** \ˈkȯrə,kȯid\ *adj* [NL *coracoides*, fr. Gk *korakoeidēs*, lit., like a raven, fr. *korak-*, *korax* raven + *-oeidēs* -oid — more at RAVEN] **:** relating to the coracoid bone or process

²**coracoid** \"\ *n* -s **:** a cartilage bone of the shoulder girdle of many vertebrates that extends from the scapula to or toward the sternum and is well-developed in most reptiles, in the birds and monotremes, but in the higher mammals including man is rudimentary and represented by the coracoid process of the scapula

cor·a·coid·al \ˈkȯrəˈkȯidᵊl\ *adj* **:** CORACOID

coracoid ligament *n* **:** the transverse ligament of the scapula which bridges over the suprascapular notch

coracoid process *n* **:** the rudimentary coracoid bone of most mammals ankylosed with and forming a process of the scapula and in man extending upward and inward from the scapula and then curving forward and finally outward

cor·a·co·ra·di·a·lis \,kȯrə(,)kō,rādēˈāləs\ *n*, *pl* **coracoradiales** \-,lēz\ [NL, fr. *coraco-* + ML *radialis* radial — more at RADIAL] **:** the short head of the biceps muscle

co·rail \kəˈrā(ə)l, kōˈ-\ *n* -s [F (*bois de*) *corail*, (*bois*) *corail*, lit., coral wood; *corail* coral, fr. MF *coral*] **:** AFRICAN PADAUK

¹**cor·al** \ˈkȯrəl, ˈkär- *sometimes* ˈkōr-\ *n* -s [ME, fr. MF, fr. L *corallum*, *corallium*, fr. Gk *korallion*] **1 a :** a skeletal deposit produced esp. by certain anthozoan polyps: (1) **:** the richly red precious coral secreted by a gorgonian (*Corallium nobile*) (2) **:** any marine deposit like coral resulting from vital activities of various organisms (as hydrocorals, stony corals, certain algae, or bryozoans and worms) **b :** a polyp or polyp colony together with its membranes and skeleton, the majority being compound animals resembling small sea anemones united into branching, encrusting, or more or less solid colonies by a continuous sheet of tissue that together with the basal epidermis of the individual polyps secretes the largely calcareous skeletal framework, the colony enlarging by asexual reproduction of the individual polyps and new colonies being established by motile planulae produced by sexual reproduction — often used with a qualifying term ⟨rose ~⟩ ⟨mushroom ~⟩ ⟨brain ~⟩ **2 :** a piece of coral; *esp* **:** a piece of coral or other material often fitted with small bells and given to infants as a plaything or teething ring **3 :** something bright red in color: as **a :** a bright-reddish ovary (as that of a lobster or scallop); *also* **:** the cooked roe of a lobster **b :** a variable color averaging a deep pink that is yellower and duller than fiesta or begonia and yellower and darker than sweet William **c** *of textiles* **:** a strong pink that is yellower and stronger than carnation rose, bluer, stronger, and slightly lighter than rose d'Althaea, and lighter, stronger, and slightly yellower than sea pink

coral 1b: portion of a colony of red coral with polyps expanded

²**coral** \"\ *adj* **1 :** of coral **2 :** of the color coral red or coral

³**coral** \"\ *vt* -ED/-ING/-S [²*coral*] **:** to make coral red or coral in color

coral bead *n* **1 :** JEQUIRITY BEAN **2 :** the red fruit of the Carolina moonseed; *also* **:** CAROLINA MOONSEED

coral bean *n* **1 :** MESCAL BEAN 2a **2** *or* **coral bean tree :** either of two tropical American coral trees: **a :** a small chiefly West Indian tree (*Erythrina corallodendron*) with deep scarlet flowers and black-spotted red seeds **b :** CEIBO 1

coralbells \ˈ==,=\ *n pl but sing or pl in constr* **:** a perennial herb (*Heuchera sanguinea*) of the western U.S. that has flowers in feathery spikes and is used as an ornamental

coralberry \ˈ==- — *see* BERRY\ *n* **1 :** an American dwarf shrub (*Symphoricarpos orbiculatus*) bearing clusters of small white flowers succeeded by red berries **2 :** any of certain plants of the genus *Ardisia* (esp. *A. crenulata*)

coral blow *n* **:** CORAL PLANT 2c

coral blush *n* **:** a moderate to strong yellowish pink

coralbush \ˈ==,=\ *n* **:** an Australian shrub (*Templetonia retusa*) with brilliant scarlet flowers

coral cod *n* **:** a brilliant red-and-blue percoid food fish (*Plectropomus leopardus*) of Australian coral reefs

coral crab *n* **1 :** either of two large yellow or reddish spider crabs (*Mithrax cornutus* and *M. hispidus*) widely distributed in shallow water from the Carolinas to southern Brazil **2 :** the queen crab and related forms

coral creeper *n* **:** CORAL PEA

coral drops *n pl but sing or pl in constr* **:** a half-hardy Mexican bulbous herb (*Bessera elegans*) of the family Liliaceae that is often cultivated for its showy red and white flowers

coral evergreen *n* **:** a ground pine (*Lycopodium clavatum*)

coral fish *n* **:** any of numerous bright-colored fishes living among coral reefs (as members of the families Chaetodontidae, Apogonidae, and Pomacentridae)

coralflower \ˈ==,==\ *n* **1 :** CORAL PEA **2 :** CHRIST'S-THORN

coral fungus *n* [so called fr. its growing in masses like coral] **:** any fungus of the family Clavariaceae

coral gem *n* **:** a small much-branched shrub (*Lotus bertheletii*) of the Canary islands

coral greenbrier *n* **:** a vine (*Smilax walteri*) of the southern U.S. with smooth branches and coral-red berries

coral head *n* **:** a rounded often knobby protuberance of coralline material on the submerged portion of a coral reef or in close proximity to it

coral honeysuckle *n* **:** TRUMPET HONEYSUCKLE

coral insect *n* **:** a coral polyp

corall- *or* **coralli-** *or* **corallo-** *comb form* [NL, fr. L *corallium* — more at CORAL] **:** coral ⟨*coralli*form⟩ ⟨*corall*oid⟩ ⟨*Corallorhiza*⟩

coralla *pl of* CORALLUM

co·ral·lic \kəˈralik\ *adj* [L *corall*um, *corall*ium coral + E *-ic*] **:** of or like coral

co·ral·li·dae \kəˈralə,dē\ [NL, fr. *Corallium*, type genus + *-idae*] *syn of* CORALLIIDAE

cor·al·lig·e·na \-ˈlijənə\ *n pl*, *cap* [NL, fr. *corall-* + *-gena* (neut. pl. of *-genus* -genous)] **:** a formerly recognized group more or less equivalent to Anthozoa and comprising coral-forming coelenterates

cor·al·li·idae \,kȯrəˈlīə,dē\ *n pl*, *cap* [NL, fr. *Corallium*, type genus + *-idae*] **:** a family of erect branching corals (order Gorgonacea) having a dense skeletal axis free or nearly free from horny material — see CORALLIUM

coral lily *n* **:** an Asiatic bulbous lily (*Lilium pumilum*) having scarlet showy flowers

coral limestone *n* **:** a rock consisting of the calcareous skeletons of corals often cemented by calcium carbonate

cor·al·li·na \,kȯrəˈlīnə\ *n*, *cap* [NL, fr. LL, fem. of *corallinus* coral-red] **:** a genus of red algae typifying the family Corallinaceae

cor·al·li·na·ce·ae \,==lə'nāsē,ē\ *n pl, cap* [NL, fr. *Corallina*, type genus + *-aceae*] **:** a family of red algae (order Cryptonemiales) of which the thallus becomes hard and brittle from the deposition of calcium carbonate which sometimes forms beautifully colored deposits like coral and contributes to reef formation — **cor·al·li·na·ceous** \¦==lə¦nāshəs\ *adj*

1cor·al·line \'kȯrə,līn, 'kär-, -,lən\ *adj* [F *corallin*, fr. MF, fr. LL *corallinus*, fr. L *corallium* coral + *-inus* -ine — more at CORAL] **1 :** like coral in color or form **:** of the color coral red or coral **2 :** composed of coral or corallines **3** [NL *Corallina*] **:** belonging to or resembling the genus *Corallina* or the family Corallinaceae

2coralline \"; *in sense 3 usu* -,lēn, -lən\ *n* -s [F, fr. MF, fr. fem. of *corallin*, adj.] **1 :** a calcareous alga of the family Corallinaceae **2 :** any animal that resembles a coral; *esp* **:** a bryozoan or hydroid that forms delicate somewhat branching or frondose growths **3** *also* **cor·al·lin** \-ələn\ -s **a :** a poisonous yellow dye consisting of the sodium salt of aurin — called also *yellow coralline* **b :** AURIN **c :** ROSOLIC ACID **a d :** a red dye derived from aurin — called also *red coralline*

coralline limestone *n* **:** CORAL LIMESTONE

cor·al·li·ta *or* **cor·al·i·ta** \,kȯrə'lēd·ə\ *n* -s [modif. of AmerSp *coralito, coralillo*, dim. of Sp *coral*, fr. L *corallum* — more at CORAL] **:** CORALVINE

cor·al·lite \'kȯrə,līt\ *n* -s [ISV *corall-* + *-ite*] **:** the skeleton of a single coral polyp consisting of a septate investing wall or theca and an underlying basal plate and being imbedded in the general structure of the corallum

co·ral·li·um \kə'ralēəm\ *n, cap* [NL, fr. L, coral — more at CORAL] **:** a genus (the type of the family Coralliidae) of corals having the skeletal axis very hard and red or pink and including the red coral of commerce

cor·al·loid \'kȯrə,lȯid, 'kär-\ *or* **cor·al·loid·al** \¦==¦lȯidᵊl\ *adj* [ISV *corall-* + *-oid, -oidal*] **:** having the form or appearance of coral **:** branching like coral ⟨a ~ root⟩

cor·al·lo·rhi·za \,kȯrə(,)lō'rīzə\ *n, cap* [NL, fr. *corall-* + *-rhiza*] **:** a genus of leafless root-parasitic or saprophytic orchids of wide distribution in temperate regions having small purplish or yellowish racemose flowers with an entire or lobed lip

co·ral·lum \kə'raləm\ *n, pl* **coral·la** \-lə\ [L *corallum, corallium* coral — more at CORAL] **:** the entire skeleton of a compound coral — compare CORALLITE

co·ral·lus \-ləs\ [NL, prob. fr. L *corallum* coral] *syn of* BOA

coral orchid *n* **:** a plant of the genus *Corallorhiza*

coral pea *n* **:** an Australian plant of the genus *Kennedya* having scarlet flowers (esp. *K. prostrata*)

coral pink *n* **:** a moderate yellowish pink that is redder, lighter, and stronger than dusty pink, redder and darker than peach pink, and redder and deeper than average peach

coral plant *n* **1** *obs* **:** a coral like a plant **2 a :** a much-cultivated East Indian plant (*Jatropha multifida*) with showy scarlet flowers and deeply incised leaves **b :** any plant of the genus *Erythrina* (esp. *E. corallodendron*) **c :** an essentially leafless Mexican shrub (*Russelia equisetiformis*) like a rush with bright-red flowers — called also *coral blow*

coral rag *n* **:** a calcareous rock composed largely of coral-reef deposits and used locally in Britain as a building stone

coral red *n* **:** a variable color averaging a strong reddish orange that is redder and deeper than fire red and yellower and paler than paprika or poppy — compare CORAL 3b

coral reef *n* **:** a reef often of great extent made up chiefly of fragments of corals, coral sands, algal and other organic deposits, and the solid limestone resulting from their consolidation — see ATOLL

coral-reef limestone \'==¦=-\ *n* **:** a limestone composed of reef-forming coral **:** a fossil coral reef

coralroot \'==,=\ *n* **:** a plant of the genus *Corallorhiza*

coral rose *n* **:** a variable color averaging a deep yellowish pink to moderate reddish orange

corals *pl of* CORAL, *pres 3d sing of* CORAL

coral shrub *n* **:** a low New Zealand shrub (*Helichrysum coralloides*) with stout tubercled white-woolly stems

coral snake *n* **1 :** any of a number of venomous elapid snakes with some red in their pattern: as **a :** any of several brilliantly banded in red, black, and yellow or white and extremely venomous but sluggish and retiring New World snakes (genus *Micrurus*) widely distributed in So. and Central America with two species (*M. fulvius* and *M.*, or *Micruroides, euryxanthus*) extending into the southern U.S. — called also *harlequin snake* **b :** any snake of an Indian genus (*Callophis*) that is reddish beneath with variously patterned dorsal surface **c :** a small venomous but harmless Australian snake (*Rhynchoelaps australis*) brilliantly marked with black and white on a red ground **d :** a small widely distributed arboreal snake (*Aspidelaps lubricus*) of southern Africa handsomely banded with black and orange bars **2 :** any of several nonvenomous snakes resembling those of the genus *Micrurus:* as **a :** KING SNAKE **b :** a common So. American aniliid (*Anilius scytale*)

coral spot *n* **:** a disease of trees and shrubs caused by a fungus (*Nectria cinnabarina*) which produces cankers on the twigs and branches

coral sumac *n* **:** POISONWOOD 1

coral tree *n* **:** any of numerous trees and shrubs constituting the genus *Erythrina*, having scarlet to coral red flowers and often bright red seeds, and being cultivated in warm regions as an ornamental: as **a :** a small thorny tree (*E. indica*) of tropical Asia and northern Australia **b :** CORAL BEAN 2a **c :** KAFFIR BOOM

coralvine \'==,=\ *n* **:** a West Indian climbing plant (*Antigonon leptopus*) grown widely as an ornamental, in some areas being evergreen, and having cordate leaves and clusters of pinkish flowers succeeded by brightly colored veiny fruit

coralwood \'==,=\ *n* **:** RED SANDALWOOD 2

coralwort \'==,=\ *n* **1 :** any plant of the genus *Dentaria* having a knotted white rootstock; *esp* **:** a common European toothwort (*D. bulbifera*) **2 :** CORALROOT

Cor·a·mine \'kȯrə,mēn, 'kōr-, -,mən\ *trademark* — used for nikethamide

co·ram ju·di·ce \¦kō(,)ram¦yüdə,kā, -ōrəm-, -¦jüdə,sē\ *adv (or adj)* [L, lit., before a judge] **:** before a judge having jurisdiction

1coram no·bis \-¦nōbəs\ *adj (or adv)* [NL, lit., before us] **1** *obs, of a writ of error* **:** for the review in the King's Bench of its own judgments as to errors of fact **2 :** based upon an alleged error of fact — used of a writ of review in some jurisdictions

2coram nobis \"\ *n* **:** a writ of error or a writ of review coram nobis ⟨some doubt as to the continued availability of *coram nobis* in the federal courts —*Harvard Law Rev.*⟩

coram non judice \-¦nōn¦-, -nän-\ *adv (or adj)* [ML, lit., before one not a judge] **:** before a judge not competent or without jurisdiction

coram pa·ri·bus \-¦pärēbüs, -pa(a)r-, -bəs\ *adv (or adj)* [ML] **:** before one's peers

coram po·pu·lo \-¦pōpü,lō, -päp-, -p(y)ə,-\ *or* **coram pu·bli·co** \-¦püblē,kō, -pəb-, -lə,-\ *adv (or adj)* [L] **:** in public ⟨I did not . . . tear my hair *coram populo* over my loss —Joseph Conrad⟩

cor an·glais \,kȯrō(n)n'glā, ,ȯ(r)'-\ *n* [F] **1 :** ENGLISH HORN **2 :** an organ stop with tone quality similar to that of the English horn

cor·a·nine \'kȯrə,nīn, -,nən, -,nēn\ *n, pl* **coranine** *or* **cor·anines** *usu cap* **:** COREE

1co·ran·to \kə'ran(,)tō, kō'-, -rän-\ *n, pl* **corantos** *or* **co·rantoes** [modif. of F *courante*] **:** COURANTE

2coranto *n, pl* **corantos** *or* **corantoes** [modif. of F *courant* — more at COURANT] *obs* **:** 1COURANT

coras *pl of* CORA

coraveca *usu cap, var of* CORABECA

-co·rax \kō,raks, kə,-\ *n comb form* [NL, fr. Gk *korax* — more at RAVEN] **:** crow **:** raven ⟨Phalacrocorax⟩

cor·ban *or* **kor·ban** \'kȯr,ban, -bän, ='=\ *n* -s [Heb *qorbān* offering] *among the ancient Hebrews* **:** any sacrifice or oblation; *specif* **:** an offering devoted to God particularly in fulfillment of a vow and therefore not to be appropriated to any other purpose

cor·beau \(')kȯ(r)¦bō\ *n* -s [F, crow, raven, fr. OF *corbel*] **:** a greenish black

cor·beil *or* **cor·beille** \'kȯ(r)bəl, *F* kȯrbeʸ\ *n* -s [F *corbeille*, lit., basket, fr. LL *corbicula*, dim. of L *corbis* basket; perh. akin to Gk *karphos* dry stalk — more at HARP] **1 :** a sculptured basket of flowers or fruit as an architectural decoration **2** *usu corbeille* **:** a basket of flowers or fruit

1cor·bel \'kȯ(r)bəl\ *n* -s [ME, fr. MF, dim. of *corp* raven, fr. L *corvus* — more at RAVEN] **:** an architectural member which projects from within a wall and supports a superincumbent weight; *esp* **:** one that is stepped upward and outward from a vertical surface

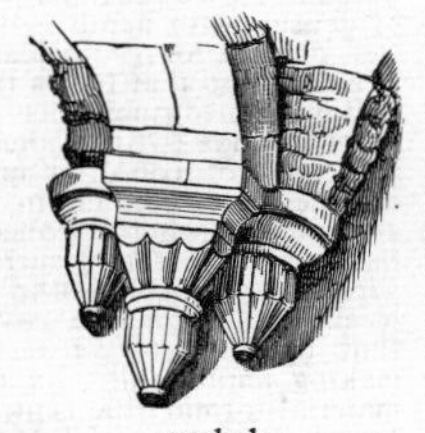
corbels

2corbel \"\ *vb* **corbeled** *or* **corbelled; corbeled** *or* **corbelled; corbeling** *or* **corbelling** \-b(ə)liŋ\ **corbels** *vt* **:** to furnish with or make into a corbel for decoration or as a support — often used with *out* ⟨resting on two rows of ~*ed* brick courses —*Amer. Guide Series: Minn.*⟩ ⟨with oak posts ~*ed* to form bold brackets —*Antiques*⟩ ~ *vi* **:** to project from a vertical surface on corbels or upward and outward in the manner of a stepped corbel ⟨a pulpit ~*ing* out over our heads⟩

corbel arch *or* **corbeled arch** *n* **:** a structure which spans an opening like an arch by having successive courses of masonry project farther inward as they rise on each side of the gap

corbeling *or* **corbelling** *n* -s **1 a :** a member that serves as a corbel; *esp* **:** continuous corbeled masonry **b :** ornamental molding having steps like a corbel **2 a :** the use of the corbel as a supporting member **b :** the act of constructing a stepped corbel

corbel-step \'==,=\ *n* [by alter.] **:** CORBIESTEP

corbel table *n* **:** a projecting course (as of masonry) resting on a horizontal row of corbels

corbel vault *n* **:** a corbeled covering like a vault

1cor·bic·u·la \kȯ(r)'bik(y)ələ\ *n, pl* **corbicu·lae** \-,lē, -,lī\ [NL, fr. LL, little basket — more at CORBEIL] **:** POLLEN BASKET

2corbicula \"\ *n, cap* [NL, fr. LL, little basket] **:** a genus (the type of the family Corbiculidae of the suborder Submytilacea) of small edible mussels native to fresh or brackish waters of eastern Asia but also introduced in parts of California

cor·bic·u·late \(')kȯ(r)¦bik(y)ələt, -,lāt\ *adj* [NL 1*corbicula* + E *-ate*] **:** having corbiculae

1cor·bie \'kȯrbi\ *n* -ES [ME, modif. (influenced by *-ie*) of OF *corbin*, fr. L *corvinus* of a raven — more at CORVINE] *chiefly Scot* **:** RAVEN, CARRION CROW

2corbie \'kȯ(r)bē\ *n* -s [prob. native name in Tasmania] **:** the subterranean larva of a Tasmanian ghost moth (*Oncopera intricata*) that feeds on the roots of grasses and is a destructive pest of pastureland

corbie gable *n* [*corbiestep* + *gable*] **:** a gable having corbiesteps

cor·bie·step \'kȯ(r)bē,-\ *n* [1*corbie* + *step*] **:** one of a series of steps which rise toward the ridgepole of a building and terminate the upper part of a gable wall

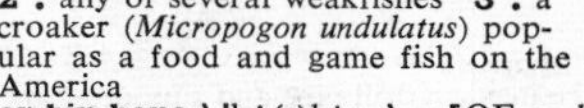
gable with corbiesteps

cor·bi·na \kȯ(r)'bēnə\ *or* **cor·vi·na** \-'vē-\ *n* -s [MexSp, fr. Sp, an acanthopterygian fish, fr. fem. of *corvino* of a raven, ravenlike, fr. L *corvinus;* fr. the color — more at CORVINE] **1 :** a bluish gray dark-spotted whiting (*Menticirrhus undulatus*) that is favored by surf casters along the California coast **2 :** any of several weakfishes **3 :** a croaker (*Micropogon undulatus*) popular as a food and game fish on the Atlantic coast of No. America

cor·bin bone \'kȯ(r)bən,-\ *n* [OF *corbin* raven] **:** the caudal segment of the sternum of a deer

cor bo·vi·num \,kȯrbō'vīnəm\ *n* [NL, lit., ox heart] **:** a greatly enlarged heart

cor·bu·li·dae \kȯr'byülə,dē\ *n pl, cap* [NL, fr. *Corbula*, type genus (fr. L *corbula* little basket, dim. of *corbis* basket) + *-idae* — more at CORBEIL] **:** a family of bivalve mollusks (suborder Myacea) comprising the basket shells

cor·cass \'kȯrkəs\ *n* -ES [modif. of IrGael *corcach*, fr. MIr; akin to Gk *koryza* nasal mucus — more at CORYZA] *Ireland* **:** a marsh or mud flat along the bank of a tidal river

cor·cho·rus \'kȯ(r)kərəs\ *n, cap* [NL, fr. L, a kind of pulse, fr. Gk *korchoros*, a kind of pimpernel (*Anagallis*)] **:** a widely distributed genus of tropical herbs or undershrubs (family Tiliaceae) having large leaves and yellow flowers in cymose clusters

cor·cir \'kȯ(r)kə(r)\ *or* **corke** \'kȯ(ə)rk, -ō(ə)k\ *or* **cor·ker** \'kȯ(r)kə(r)\ *n* -s [ScGael *corcur* purple, fr. L *purpura* — more at PURPLE] **:** ARCHIL 3

1cord \'kȯ(ə)rd, -ō(ə)d\ *n* -s [ME, fr. OF *corde*, fr. L *chorda* catgut, chord, cord, fr. Gk *chordē* — more at YARN] **1 a :** a long slender flexible roughly cylindrical construction usu. of several threads or yarns twisted or woven together and used for tying, binding, or connecting **:** a small rope **:** STRING **b :** the hangman's rope ⟨O, the charity of a penny ~ —Shak.⟩ **c** (1) **:** any of various strings for communicating motion in a pattern-weaving or a Jacquard loom (2) **:** a space on a design paper representing a warp thread **d :** a heavy string used as a material (as in braid or cordonnet) **e :** any of the heavy strings or small hemp ropes usu. four to six in number which extend across the backbone of a book, which are usu. attached to the board of the cover, and to which the sections are handsewn — called also *band* **f :** a heavy thread or firm yarn made by tightly twisting together two or more threads or plied yarns and used often in the manufacture of heavy-duty fabrics **g :** one of the round plies forming a multistrand thread ⟨sewing thread is usually 3-*cord* or 6-*cord*⟩ **2 :** a moral, spiritual, or emotional bond or influence by which one is held, drawn, or sustained as if by a cord ⟨the interwoven ~*s* of affection and confidence that wind between her and her husband —Roger Angell⟩ **3 a :** an anatomical structure resembling a cord; *esp* **:** TENDON, NERVE — see SPERMATIC CORD, SPINAL CORD, UMBILICAL CORD, VOCAL CORDS **b :** a small flexible insulated electrical cable usu. consisting of a pair of insulated stranded wires twisted together and having a plug at one or both ends used to connect a lamp, electric iron, toaster, or other appliance with a receptacle **c :** STRIA 3 **4 a :** any of various units of quantity for wood cut for fuel or pulp; *esp* **:** a unit equal to a stack 4x4x8 foot or 128 cubic feet **b :** a unit for rough building stone equal to 128 cubic feet **5 a :** a rib like a cord on a textile **b** (1) **:** a fabric made with such ribs or a garment made of such a fabric — compare CORDUROY, WHIPCORD (2) **cords** *pl* **:** trousers made of such fabric **c :** CORD TIRE **d :** a composition and fabric material used in the outsole of a work shoe or sport shoe

2cord \"\ *vt* -ED/-ING/-S [ME *corden*, fr. *cord*, n.] **1 :** to tie, bind, fasten, or connect with a cord ⟨package already . . . ~*ed* lengthwise —R.V.Morse⟩ **2 :** to pile up (as wood) in cords; *also* **:** to pile deeply ⟨rooms ~*ed* nine feet deep with gold and emeralds —Bernard DeVoto⟩ **3 :** to ornament or finish with cord **4 :** to connect the treadles of (a hand loom) by cords with the leaves of the heddles so as to produce the pattern

cord·age \-dij, -dēj\ *n* -s [MF, fr. *corde* + *-age*] **1 :** ropes or cords; *esp* **:** the ropes in the rigging of a ship **2 :** the number of cords (as of wood) on a given area

cordage tree *n* **:** an Australasian tree (*Plagianthus pulchellus*) the bark of which was formerly used esp. for tying fence posts and rafters

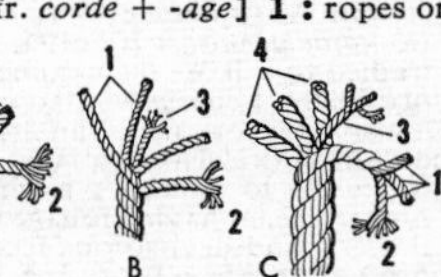

cordage 1: hawser-laid rope, *A;* shroud-laid rope, *B;* typical three-strand four-hawser cable, *C; 1* strands; *2* yarns; *3* core; *4* ropes

cor·dai·ta·ce·ae \,kȯ(r)dā,ī'tāsē,ē, -,dī't-\ *n pl, cap* [NL, fr. *Cordaites*, type genus + *-aceae*] **:** a family of chiefly Paleozoic plants (order Cordaitales) of which *Cordaites* is the chief and typical genus — **cor·dai·ta·ceous** \¦kȯ(r)dā,ī¦tāshəs, -,dī¦t-\ *adj*

cor·dai·ta·les \,kȯ(r)dā,ī'tā,lēz, -,dī't-\ *n pl, cap* [NL, fr. *Cordaites* + *-ales*] **:** an order of extinct gymnospermous plants first known from the Pennsylvanian and probably extinct since the Mesozoic that had tall arborescent trunks structurally comparable to or more advanced than those of cycads and branched in the upper part, long simple parallel-veined leaves spirally arranged, and separate male and female strobili — see CORDAITACEAE — **cor·dai·ta·le·an** \¦=(=),=¦tālēən\ *adj*

cor·dai·te·an \¦kȯ(r)dā¦īd·ēən, (')kȯ(r)¦dīd-\ *adj* [NL *Cordaites* + E *-an*] **:** of, relating to, or characteristic of the genus *Cordaites*

cor·dai·tes \,kȯ(r)dā'īd,ēz, kȯ(r)'dīd-\ *n, cap* [NL, fr. August K.J.*Corda* †1849 Bohemian botanist + L *-ites* -ite] **:** the type genus of Cordaitaceae comprising tall Paleozoic forest trees that superficially resembled the modern screw pines but structurally were intermediate in some respects between the cycadophytes and the more advanced coniferophytes

cor·date \'kȯ(r)dət, -,dāt\ *adj* [NL *cordatus*, fr. L *cord-, cor* heart + *-atus* -ate — more at HEART] **1 :** shaped like a heart ⟨a ~ shell⟩ **2 :** having a rounded base with a notch at the point of attachment ⟨a ~ leaf⟩ — see LEAF illustration — **cor·date·ly** *adv*

cor·dax \'kȯ(r),daks\ *var of* KORDAX

cord connector *n* **:** CONNECTOR 2c(1)

corde \kȯ(r)'dā\ *n* -s [F *cordé*, past part. of *corder* to cord, fr. *corde*, n., cord — more at CORD] **:** cord that is usu. covered with silk or rayon and used esp. for crocheting handbags

cord·ed \'kȯ(r)dəd\ *adj* [ME, fr. past part. of *corden*] **1 a :** made of or provided with cords or ridges or markings ⟨a ~ ladder —Shak.⟩; *specif* **:** having muscles or tendons standing up in ridges like cords ⟨face . . . drawn and pallid, with a ~ neck —Ellen Glasgow⟩ **b** *of muscles* **:** tense or taut ⟨the ~ muscles relaxed⟩ **c** *of ply cordage* **:** with the plies given an extra amount of twist **2 :** bound, fastened, or wound about with cords **3 a :** striped, ribbed, or otherwise decorated with cord or lines like cords **:** TWILLED ⟨a ~ cloth⟩ **:** finished with cord ⟨a ~ seam⟩ ⟨~ lace⟩ **b** *of pottery* **:** having a decoration made by pressing cords into the clay before firing

cor·de·lière \,kȯ(r)dᵊl'ye(ə)r\ *n* -s [F, fr. MF, knotted rope worn by Cordeliers, fr. *Cordelier*, a kind of Franciscan friar, fr. *cordel*, dim. of *corde* cord, rope — more at CORD] *heraldry* **:** a knotted cord (as around the escutcheon of a widow)

1cor·delle \¦kȯ(r)'del, '=,=, '=dᵊl\ *n* -s [F, dim. of *corde*] **:** a towline esp. as used on keelboats on U.S. and Canadian rivers

2cordelle \"\ *vb* -ED/-ING/-S **:** to tow by a cordelle

cor·de-nuit \,kȯ(r)dən'wē, -dᵊn-\ *n* -s [F, lit., night horn] **:** a soft-toned labial organ stop of metal or wood usu. of 8-foot pitch

cord·er \'kȯ(r)də(r)\ *n* -s **1 :** one that cords; *specif* **:** one that stitches cord or braid on fabric **2 :** TUCKER 1a(2)

cord foot *n* **:** a quantity of wood equal to a stack 4x4x1 foot or 16 cubic feet

cord glottis *n* **:** the opening between the vocal cords proper as distinguished from the whisper glottis — called also *voice glottis*

cordgrass \'=,=\ *n* **:** a grass of the genus *Spartina*

1cordia *pl of* COR

2cor·dia \'kȯ(r)dēə\ *n, cap* [NL, fr. Euricius *Cordus* †1535 and his son Valerius *Cordus* †1544 Ger. scholars + NL *-ia*] **:** a large genus of chiefly tropical shrubs and trees (family Boraginaceae) that have fleshy often edible fruits and wood varying from dense, heavy, and dark to spongy, light, and pale, that are often pleasantly scented, and that have considerable use in cabinetmaking and general construction

1cor·dial \'kȯ(r)jəl; *US sometimes and Brit usu* 'kȯ(r)dyəl *or* -dēəl\ *adj* [ME, fr. ML *cordialis*, fr. L *cord-, cor* heart + *-ialis* -ial — more at HEART] **1 :** of, belonging to, or proceeding from the heart **:** VITAL ⟨opened my left side and took from thence a rib with ~ spirits warm and life-blood streaming fresh —John Milton⟩ **2 :** tending to revive, cheer, or invigorate ⟨a ~ medicine or drink⟩ ⟨drink this ~ wine —S.T.Coleridge⟩ **:** invigorating or cheering ⟨for fainting age what ~ drop remains —Alexander Pope⟩ **3 a :** sincerely or deeply felt **:** HEARTFELT, HEARTY ⟨showed a ~ regard for his visitor's comfort⟩ ⟨a ~ and active dislike for both his parents —Samuel Butler †1902⟩ **b :** showing warm and often hearty friendliness, favor, or approval ⟨they gave us a ~ reception, and a hearty supper, and we sat up talking until a late hour —Herman Melville⟩ ⟨relations between white and black . . . are not merely good: they are ~ —*Economist*⟩ ⟨his argument had ~ support from the experts⟩ **syn** see GRACIOUS

2cordial \"\ *n* -s **1 a :** an invigorating and stimulating medicine, food, or drink ⟨the peppermint water and other ~*s* —Thomas DeQuincey⟩ **b :** something that comforts, gladdens, and exhilarates ⟨charms to my sight, and ~*s* to my mind —John Dryden⟩ **2 :** LIQUEUR; *sometimes* **:** a somewhat sharp and spicy drink or one made by infusion of fruit juice or wine with spirits

cor·dial·i·ty \,kȯ(r)jē'aləd·ē, kȯ(r)'jal-, -ətē, -i; *US sometimes and Brit usu* ,kȯ(r)dē'al- *or* -d'yal-\ *n* -ES [F *cordialité*, fr. MF, fr. *cordial* (fr. ML *cordialis*) + *-ité* -ity] **:** cordial quality **:** sincere affection and kindness **:** warmth of regard ⟨the ~ of his greeting was pleasant to his guests⟩ **:** good will or good feeling **:** FAVOR ⟨the city's ~ to new industry⟩

cor·dial·ly \'kȯ(r)jəlē, -li; *US sometimes and Brit usu* 'kȯ(r)dyə- *or* -dēə-\ *adv* **1 :** in a cordial manner **:** with sincere good will ⟨welcomed his friends ~⟩ ⟨~ yours⟩ **2 :** with zeal **:** vigorously and sincerely **:** EMPHATICALLY ⟨Jefferson and Hamilton ~ disliked each other —H.E.Scudder⟩

cor·dial·ness \-əlnəs\ *n* -ES **:** the quality or state of being cordial **:** CORDIALITY

cordier *comparative of* CORDY

cor·di·er·ite \'kȯ(r)dēə,rīt\ *n* -s [F, fr. Pierre L. A. *Cordier* †1861 Fr. geologist, who first described it + F *-ite*] **:** an orthorhombic mineral of various shades of blue with vitreous luster and strong dichroism consisting of a silicate of aluminum, iron, and magnesium $(Mg,Fe)_2Al_4Si_5O_{18}$ easily altered by exposure (hardness 7–7.5, sp. gr. 2.60–2.66)

cordiest *superlative of* CORDY

cor·di·form \'kȯrdə,fȯrm\ *adj* [F *cordiforme*, fr. L *cord-, cors* heart + F *-iforme* -iform — more at HEART] **:** shaped like a heart

cordiform tendon *n* **:** the central tendon of the diaphragm

cor·dil·le·ra \,kȯ(r)dᵊl'erə, -l'ye- *also* kȯ(r)'dilərə\ *n* -s [Sp, fr. *cordilla*, dim. of *cuerda* rope, string, line of mountain peaks, fr. L *chorda* cord — more at CORD] **:** a group of mountain ranges forming a mountain system of great linear extent often consisting of a number of more or less parallel chains ⟨the No. American ~ includes all the mountains from the eastern face of the Rocky mountains to the Pacific ocean —W.J.Miller⟩ — **cor·dil·le·ran** \¦kȯ(r)dᵊl¦erən, -l¦ye-, (')=¦dilər-\ *adj*

cording *n* -s **1 :** cord often covered with fabric for decorative effects **2 :** the act or result of ornamenting with cord

cording quires *n* **:** the two outside quires of a ream of paper

cord·ite \'kȯr,dīt\ *n* -s [1*cord* + *-ite*] **:** a smokeless powder composed of nitroglycerin, guncotton, and mineral jelly usu. gelatinized by the addition of acetone and pressed out into cords resembling brown twine

cordleaf \'=,=\ *n* **:** any plant of the family Restionaceae; *esp* **:** a plant of the genus *Restio*

cord moss *n* **:** any moss of the genus *Funaria; esp* **:** the common moss (*F. hygrometrica*) that is particularly frequent on recently burned-over soil and that has a twisted hygroscopic seta which uncoils when moist

1cór·do·ba *or* **cor·do·ba** \'kȯ(r)dəbə, -əvə; -(,)bä, -(,)vä\ *adj, usu cap* [fr. *Córdoba*, Spain & *Córdoba*, Argentina] **1** *or* **cor·do·va** \"\ **:** of or from the city of Córdoba, Spain **:** of the kind or style prevalent in Córdoba, Spain **:** CORDOVAN **2 :** of or from the city of Córdoba, Argentina **:** of the kind or style prevalent in Córdoba, Argentina

2cordoba \"\ *n, pl* **cordobas** [Sp *córdoba*, after Francisco Fernández de *Córdoba* †1526 Sp. explorer] **1 :** the basic monetary unit of Nicaragua — see MONEY table **2 :** a silver coin struck in 1912 representing one cordoba but later withdrawn from circulation **3 :** a currency note representing one cordoba

¹cor·do·bán \ˌkȯ(r)dəˈbän; ˈ==(ˌ)bän, -(ˌ)vän, -bən, -vən\ *n* -s [Sp — more at CORDOVAN] : cordovan leather

²cordoban \"\ *adj, usu cap* [Sp *cordobán*, fr. *Córdoba*, Argentina + *-án* (as in *cordobán* of Córdoba, Spain)] : of or belonging to Córdoba, Argentina

¹cor·don \ˈkȯrdᵊn, -ȯ(ə)d-, -ˌdän; *in senses 2a–c usu* -dᵊn\ *n* -s [MF, dim. of *corde* string, rope — more at CORD] **1 a** : an ornamental cord, braid, lace, or string used esp. on costumes: as (1) : an ornamental cord encircling a heraldic shield esp. of an ecclesiastical dignitary (2) : a cord or ribbon worn as a badge of honor or as a decoration of an order of knighthood — see GRAND CORDON **b** : STRINGCOURSE **2 a** : a line or series of troops or of military posts placed at intervals and enclosing an area to prevent passage **b** : a barrier of any kind operating to close off, restrict, or control access or communication ⟨a traffic ~ around the business center of a city⟩ ⟨protected from the mainland by a ~ of seven hills —Horace Sutton⟩ **c** : a line or circle of persons or objects around any person or place ⟨a ~ of police kept back the crowd⟩ ⟨a ~ of ramshackle market stalls was thrown around the circular facade to accommodate the provision merchants —Lewis Mumford⟩ **d** : CORDON SANITAIRE **3** : an espalier trained to a single horizontal shoot or to two opposed shoots so as to form one line

²cordon \-dᵊn, -ˌdän; *in sense 2 usu* -dᵊn\ *vt* -ED/-ING/-S [MF *cordonner*, fr. *cordon*, n.] **1** : to ornament with a cordon **2** : to form a protective or restrictive cordon around (an area) : close to communication with the outside by a cordon — often used with *off* ⟨were not allowed inside the front yard, which was ~ed off by the police —Marcia Davenport⟩

cor·do·na·zo \ˌkȯ(r)dᵊnˈä(ˌ)sō\ *n* -s [MexSp, short for Sp *cordonazo de San Francisco* autumnal storm, lit., lash of St. Francis (around whose birthday — Oct. 4 — such storms occur); *cordonazo* fr. *cordón* rope worn by friars (fr. OSp, fr. OF *cordon*) + *-azo* (suffix denoting a blow) — more at CORDON] : a southerly hurricane wind that occurs along the west coast of Mexico when a tropical cyclone passes northward offshore

cor·don bleu \ˌkȯrdōⁿˈblœ̄; *esp in senses 2 and 3* ˌkȯrdᵊnˈblü *or* -(ˌ)dänˈ-\ *n, pl* **cordon bleus** \-œ̄(z), -üz\ *also* **cordons bleus** \"\ [F, lit., blue cordon] **1** : the blue ribbon worn as a decoration by members of the old order of the Holy Ghost **2 a** : a person eminent for his rank or authority; *specif* : a cook of great skill **3** *also* **cordon bleu finch** : any of several African waxbills (genus *Uraeginthus*) that have a clear bright blue breast and tail and drab back and underparts and that are often kept as cage birds

cor·don·net \ˌkȯ(r)dᵊnˈet, -nˈā, ˈ==,=\ *n* -s [F, dim. of *cordon*] : a thread or small cord used to edge braid, to make tassels and fringes, or to outline the design of lace and embroidery

cor·don sa·ni·taire \kȯrdōⁿsänēter\ *n, pl* **cordon sanitaires** *also* **cordons sanitaires** \"\ [F, lit., sanitary cordon (quarantine line)] : a chain of nations designed as a protection or buffer against a nation considered potentially aggressive or ideologically dangerous

cordotomy *var of* CHORDOTOMY

cordova *usu cap, var of* CORDOBA

¹cor·do·van \ˈkȯ(r)dəvən\ *adj* [OSp *cordován* (now *cordobán*), Mozarabic alter. of OSp *cordovano*, fr. *Córdova* (now *Córdoba*), Spain + Sp *-ano* -an] **1** *usu cap* : of or belonging to Córdoba, esp. Córdoba, Spain **2** : made of cordovan leather

²cordovan \"\ *n* -s [Sp *cordobán*, fr. *cordobán*, adj.] **1** *cap* : a native or resident of Córdoba, esp. Córdoba, Spain **2 a** : a soft fine-grained colored leather manufactured of split horsehides, goatskins, or pigskins **b** : leather tanned from the inner layer of horsehide from the rump area and distinguished for its nonporosity, density, and long-wearing qualities — called also *shell cordovan* **3 a** : a dark grayish brown that is yellower than average chocolate brown and yellower and slightly less strong than African brown **b** : a variable color averaging a dark grayish red that is darker and slightly yellower than average rose brown

cords *pl of* CORD, *pres 3d sing of* CORD

cord switch *n* : a snap switch mounted at the end of a cord suspended from a ceiling fixture — called also *pendant switch*

cord tire *n* : a pneumatic tire having a carcass constructed of cords running parallel to each other and crossed by small threads

cor·du·la \kȯ(r)ˈd(y)üla; ˈkȯ(r)d(y)əla, -(r)jəla\ *n, cap* [NL, prob. irreg. fr. LGk *kordylē* club, fr. Gk, bump, swelling; prob. fr. the shape of the column — more at CARDINAL] : a large genus of tropical Old World terrestrial orchids resembling the common lady's-slippers

¹cor·du·roy \ˈkȯ(r)dəˌrȯi *sometimes* -(r)dyə,- *or* -(r)jə,-\ *n* -s *often attrib* [earlier *corderoy*, perh. fr. the name *Corderoy*] **1 a** : a cut-pile fabric with vertical ribs or wales usu. made of cotton in plain or twill weave in various weights with up to 22 wales per inch and used for clothing and interior decoration ⟨a ~ jacket⟩ **b corduroys** *pl* : trousers of corduroy **2 a** : CORDUROY ROAD **b** : the material or structure of such a road **c** : a road surface ribbed transversely

²corduroy \"\ *vt* -ED/-ING/-S **1** : to build (a road) of logs laid side by side transversely **2** : to build a corduroy road across (as a swamp)

corduroy road *n* : a road built of logs laid side by side transversely and usu. used in low or swampy places

cord·wain \ˈkȯrdˌwān\ *n* -s [ME *cordwane*, fr. MF *cordoan*, fr. OSp *cordován* (now *cordobán*) — more at CORDOVAN] *archaic* : cordovan leather

cord·wain·er \-nər\ *n* -s [ME *cordewaner*, fr. OF *cordoanier*, fr. *cordoan*] **1** *archaic* : a worker in cordovan leather **2** : SHOEMAKER

cord·wain·ery \-nərē\ *n* -ES : SHOEMAKING

cord·wind·er \ˈkȯrdˌwīndər\ *n* -s [by folk etymology] : CORDWAINER

cordwood \ˈ=,=\ *n* [¹*cord* (measure) + *wood*] : wood piled up or sold in cords : wood for fuel cut to the length of four feet so as to be readily measurable in cords; *also* : standing timber of such size and quality as to be fit only for burning as fuel

cordy \ˈkȯrdē, -ȯ(ə)dē, -di\ *adj* -ER/-EST **1** : of or like cord : having cords or parts resembling cords **2** : of a thready or striated appearance

cor·dy·ceps \ˈkȯ(r)dəˌseps\ *n, cap* [NL, irreg. fr. LGk *kordylē* club (fr. Gk, bump, swelling) + L *-ceps* (fr. *caput* head) — more at CARDINAL, HEAD] : a genus of ascomycetous fungi (family Hypocreaceae) parasitic in insect larvae and ultimately converting the whole body into a sclerotium — see AWETO

cor·dyl·i·dae \kȯ(r)ˈdiləˌdē\ *n pl, cap* [NL, fr. *Cordylus*, type genus (fr. Gk *kordylos* water newt) + *-idae*; prob. akin to Gk *kordylē* bump, swelling — more at CARDINAL] : a small family of spiny ovoviviparous African lizards somewhat resembling tiny crocodiles

cor·dy·li·ne \ˌkȯ(r)dᵊlˈī(ˌ)nē\ *n* [NL, irreg. fr. LGk *kordylē* club, fr. Gk, bump, swelling; fr. the stout caudex] **1** *cap* : a genus of tropical Old World plants (family Liliaceae) having a creeping rhizome and often included in the genus *Dracaena* but distinguished by the single ovule in each cell of the ovary and by the solitary pedicles — see TI; compare DRACAENA **2** -s : any tree of the genus *Cordyline*

cor·dyl·ite \ˈkȯ(r)dᵊlˌīt\ *n* -s [ISV *cordyl-* (fr. LGk *kordylē* club) + *-ite*; orig. formed as G *kordylit*] : a mineral (Ce,La)$_2$Ba(CO$_3$)$_3$F$_2$ consisting of a carbonate and fluoride of cerium, lanthanum, and barium

cor·dy·lo·bia \ˌkȯ(r)dᵊlˈōbēə\ *n, cap* [NL] : a genus of true flies (family Calliphoridae) including the African tumbu fly

cor·dy·lu·ri·dae \ˌkȯ(r)dᵊlˈ(y)ürəˌdē\ [NL, fr. *Cordylura*, type genus (fr. LGk *kordylē* club + Gk *oura* tail) + *-idae* — more at -UROUS] *syn of* SCATOPHAGIDAE

¹core \ˈkō(ə)r, -ōə,-ō(ə),-ȯ(ə)r\ *n* -s [ME] **1** : the central and often foundational part of a body, mass, or construction usu. distinct from the enveloping part by a difference in nature or by being cut out or separated ⟨the ~ of a storm⟩ ⟨~ of a city⟩ ⟨~ of a flame⟩: as **a** : the central portion in certain fruits (as the hard central section of a pineapple); *esp* : the papery or leathery carpels composing the ripened ovary in fruits of the apple family **b** : a hard unburned central part of a piece of coal or limestone; *also* : an unburned or overburned piece of limestone found in hydrated lime **c** : the necrotic slough in the central part of a boil **d** : the central or axial interior part of a structure (as a column or wall) often made of inferior material **e** : a separate portion of a foundry mold which shapes the interior of a hollow casting or which makes a hole in or through a casting; *also* : a part of the mold made separately and inserted for shaping some part of the casting **f** : a portion removed from the interior of a mass usu. to determine the interior composition or hidden condition ⟨the holes bored in the ice provided ~s for determination of the variation of density with depth —Valter Schytt⟩ ⟨took a ~ from the well drilling for geological and chemical analysis⟩ **g** : the bony process that forms the central axis of the horns of the hollow-horned ruminants **h** : the central strand around which other strands twist in some kinds of rope — called also *heart* **i** : a mass of iron often made up of thin plates or wires and enclosed in a coil (as in an electromagnet, transformer, or armature) serving to concentrate and intensify the magnetic field resulting from a current in the coil **j** : the conducting wire with its insulation in an electric cable but not including mechanical protective covering **k** : a nodule of obsidian, flint, or other stone from which flakes have been struck for making implements **l** : a wall or structure of impervious material forming the central part of an embankment or dike (as a dam) the outer parts of which are pervious **m** : a hollow space in the body of a large metal type or in the metal base of a stereotype or electrotype; *also* : a hollow stereotype mount **n** : the unaffected interior of a carburized or case-hardened piece of metal **o** : the central part of the earth having a radius of about 2100 miles and displaying notably different physical properties from the surrounding mantle and crust **p** : the cylindrical portion of a lock which rotates when the key is turned **q** : a stiff tube on which paper or other material may be wound ⟨paper toweling wound on a paperboard ~⟩ **r** (1) : the central layer of wood on which veneers are glued in making plywood or veneered wood for cabinetwork (2) : the center ply of a piece of plywood **s** : CENTRUM **t** : the remainder of an atom after the removal of the valency electrons — called also *rumpf* **u** : an arrangement of a course of studies that combines under certain basic topics material from subjects conventionally separated and aims to provide a common background for all students, to integrate the individual student's program, and to relate the work of the school to experience and to society ⟨~ curriculum⟩ ⟨~ program⟩ **v** : the shield of a continent **w** : the plug or neck of a volcano **x** : the central part of an anticlinal or domal structure or of mountains having a folded or completely crumpled structure **y** : the part of an automobile radiator in which most of the cooling of the water takes place **z** : the center or base portion of a clad product **aa** : the place in a nuclear reactor where fission occurs **2** : the part (as of an individual, a class, an entity) that is basic, essential, vital, or enduring as distinct from the incidental or transient ⟨a hard ~ of perhaps 10 percent of those who have been in the party for 15 years —A.M.Schlesinger b.1917⟩ ⟨carrier task forces are the ~ of the Navy —T.K. Finletter⟩ : the essential meaning or gist ⟨the ~ of the book is thus an attempt to comprehend the nature of total war —*Times Lit. Supp.*⟩ : the inmost or most intimate part ⟨their theory of life had its ~ of soundness —George Eliot⟩ ⟨his wife was Victorian to the ~ —Robert Payne⟩ **syn** see CENTER

²core \"\ *vt* -ED/-ING/-S **1** : to take out the core of ⟨~ an apple⟩ **2** : to drill through the core of : remove the axial portion of ⟨~ the barrel after casting it⟩ **3** : to take a core from as a sample of interior composition ⟨~ an oil well⟩ ⟨~ a salt formation⟩ **4** : to form (as a hole in a casting) by means of a core

³core \ˈkō(ə)r, -ōə\ *n* -s [alter. of ME *chore* chorus, choir, company, fr. L *chorus* — more at CHORUS] **1** *chiefly Scot* : a company (as of players in a curling match) **2** *dial Eng* **a** : a gang of miners in one shift **b** : underground working time or shift esp. in a mine

⁴core *var of* KOR

corean *usu cap, var of* KOREAN

core barrel *n* **1** : a tube inside a drill pipe and supported by a bit to receive the core in core boring **2** : a tube usu. of iron on which a foundry loam core is formed

core bit *n* : a hollow cylindrical bit that is the cutting part of a core drill

corebox \ˈ=,=\ *n* : an open box in which a foundry core is formed

co·recreation \(ˈ)kō+\ *n* [*co-* + *recreation*] : recreation engaged in jointly by both sexes

cored *adj* **1** : having the core removed ⟨~ apples⟩ **2** : cast or made with a hollow core ⟨metal type with a ~ base⟩ **3** : having a core composed of a specified material or character and esp. differing from that of the outer part ⟨carbon arcs ~ with various salts⟩ ⟨black-*cored* pottery⟩

cored carbon *n* : a carbon for arc lights that has a small core of softer material to keep the crater central

co·redeem \ˌkō+\ *vt* [*co-* + *redeem*] : to share in the process or function of redeeming

co·redemption \ˌkō+\ *n* [*co-* + *redemption*] : participation in the act or process of redemption

co–redemptrix \ˌkō+\ *n, often cap C&R* [NL, fr. *co-* + *redemptrix*, fem. of L *redemptor* redeemer — more at REDEMPTOR] : a female sharer in the redemption of the human race (as the Virgin Mary among some Roman Catholics)

core diameter *n* : MINOR DIAMETER

core drill *n* : a drill that removes a cylindrical core from the drill hole — compare DIAMOND DRILL, SHOT DRILL — **core drilling** *n*

co·ree \ˈkō(ˌ)rē\ *n, pl* **coree** *or* **corees** *usu cap* **1** : an extinct Indian people of the coast of No. Carolina of uncertain linguistic affinities **2** : a member of the Coree people

cor·e·go·nid \ˌkȯrəˈgōnəd\ *n* -s [NL *Coregonidae*] : WHITEFISH 1a

cor·e·go·ni·dae \ˌ==ˈgōnəˌdē\ *n pl, cap* [NL, fr. *Coregonus*, type genus + *-idae*] *in some classifications* : a family of fishes (order Isospondyli) comprising the freshwater whitefishes and now usu. included among the Salmonidae

cor·e·go·nine \ˌkȯrəˈgōˌnīn, -ˌnən\ *adj* [NL *Coregonus* + E *-ine*] : of or belonging to the genus *Coregonus* or to freshwater whitefishes

cor·e·go·nus \ˌ==ˈgōnəs\ *n, cap* [NL, fr. Gk *korē* pupil of the eye + NL *-gonus* (fr. Gk *gōnia* angle) — more at CRESCENT, DIAGONAL] : a genus of plainly colored salmonid fishes comprising the typical whitefishes of the lakes of Europe, Asia, and No. America — see WHITEFISH

¹core·id \ˈkȯrēəd\ *adj* [NL *Coreidae*] : of or relating to the Coreidae

²coreid \"\ *n* -s : any true bug of the family Coreidae

co·re·i·dae \kəˈrēəˌdē\ *n pl, cap* [NL, fr. *Coreus*, type genus (fr. Gk *koris* bedbug) + *-idae*; akin to Gk *keirein* to cut — more at SHEAR] : a large family of true bugs (order Hemiptera) comprising the squash bugs and leaf-footed bugs and including many that are injurious to cultivated plants

co·relate \ˌkō+\ *vt* [back-formation fr. *corelation*] *now chiefly Brit* : to relate to each other : CORRELATE

co·relation \ˌkō+\ *n* [*co-* + *relation*] *now chiefly Brit* : CORRELATION

core·less *pronunc at* ¹CORE + lə̇s\ *adj* : not having a core

co·religionist *also* **co·religionary** \ˌkō+\ *n, pl* **coreligionists** *also* **coreligionaries** [*co-* + *religion* + *-ist* or *-ary*] : one having the same religion ⟨Mohammedans did not like to hold their ~s in slavery —C.S.Forester⟩

co·rel·la \kəˈrelə\ *n* -s [native name in Australia] : any of certain Australian cockatoos; *esp* : a long-billed cockatoo (*Kakatoe tenuirostris*) often kept as a cage bird and readily trained to talk — see BARE-EYED COCKATOO

core loss *n* : energy wasted by hysteresis and eddy currents in a magnetic core (as of an armature or transformer)

co·re·ma \kōˈrēmə, kəˈ-\ *n, cap* [NL, fr. Gk *korēma* broom, fr. *korein* to sweep] : a small genus of low shrubs (family Empetraceae) having foliage resembling heath, small apetalous flowers, and drupaceous fruits — see BROOM CROWBERRY

coremaker \ˈ=,=\ *n* **1** : one that makes sand cores for metal castings or clay cores for iron pipe or metal cores for building tile **2** : an operator of a machine that winds tubular paperboard cores for rolls of paper

co·re·mi·um \kōˈrēmēəm, kəˈ-\ *n, pl* **core·mia** \-mēə\ [NL, fr. Gk *korēma* broom + NL *-ium*] : a fruiting body characteristic of certain imperfect fungi (as the Stilbellaceae) and consisting of a sterile stalk of parallel or fascicled hyphae and a terminal head of fertile or spore-bearing branches — compare SYNNEMA

core oil *n* : oil used to bind sand for foundry cores

co·re·op·sis \ˌkōrēˈäpsəs, ˌkȯr-\ *n* [NL, fr. *core-* (fr. Gk *koris* bedbug) + *-opsis*; fr. the shape of the achene — more at COREIDAE] **1** *cap* : a genus of herbs (family Compositae) many of which are used in cultivation and which have showy flower heads with involucral bracts in two distinct series of eight each, the outer being commonly connate at the base **2** *pl* **coreopsis** : a plant of the genus *Coreopsis* — called also *tickseed*; compare CALLIOPSIS

core oven *n* : an oven in which foundry cores are baked

core print *n* : the part of a foundry pattern which makes an opening in a mold to receive a core and to support it while the metal is being poured

co·requisite \(ˈ)kō+\ *n* [*co-* + *requisite*] : a formal course of study required to be taken simultaneously with another

cor·er \ˈkōrə(r), ˈkȯr-\ *n* -s **1** : an instrument for taking out cores ⟨an apple ~⟩ ⟨a ~ for taking geological samples⟩ **2** : a tube or cylinder impelled into the sea bottom to obtain samples of its composition and the animal life inhabiting it

cores *pl of* CORE, *pres 3d sing of* CORE

co·respondent \ˌkō+\ *n* [*co-* + *respondent*] : a joint respondent; *specif* : a person charged with adultery in a divorce suit and proceeded against together with the respondent

core tool *n* : a stone age tool made by striking flakes from a nodule — compare FLAKE TOOL

core wall *n* : CORE 1*l*

corf \ˈkȯ(ə)rf, ˈkȯ(ə)f\ *n, pl* **corves** \-vz\ [ME, basket, fr. MD *corf* or MLG *korf*, prob. fr. L *corbis* — more at CORBEIL] **1** *Brit* : a basket, tub, or truck used in a mine for conveying ore or coal to the pit mouth **2** *Brit* : a cage like a basket used by fishermen for keeping live lobsters or other catch

cor·fi·ote \ˈkȯ(r)fēˌōt\ *n* -s *cap* [F, fr. *Corfou* Corfu (Greek island in the Ionian sea) + F *-i-* + *-ote*] : a native or resident of the island of Corfu, off the coast of southwest Albania

corge \ˈkȯ(ə)rj, -ȯ(ə)j\ *n* -s [Pg *corja*, prob. fr. Malayalam *kōṭi*] *India* : a unit of 20 : SCORE

corgi *n* -s [W, fr. *cor* dwarf + *-gi* (fr. *ci* dog); akin to Corn & Bret *ki* dog, OIr *cū*, OE *hund* — more at HOUND] : WELSH CORGI

coria *pl of* CORIUM

co·ri·a·ceous \ˌkōrēˈāshəs, ˌkȯr-\ *adj* [LL *coriaceus* — more at CUIRASS] : like leather in appearance, texture, or quality : TOUGH ⟨a ~ leaf⟩

co·ri·al \ˌkōrēˈäl, ˈ==,=\ *n* -s [AmerSp, of Arawakan or Cariban origin; akin to Arawak *kuljara* corial, Macusi *kulial*] : a Guianan native dugout canoe

co·ri·a·myr·tin \ˌkōrēəˈmərtᵊn, ˌkȯr-, ˈ===,==\ *n* -s [ISV *coriamyr-* (fr. NL *Coriaria myrtifolia*, a species of shrubs) + *-in*; orig. formed as F *coriamyrtine*] : a bitter poisonous crystalline compound $C_{15}H_{18}O_5$ found in an Old World dye plant (*Coriaria myrtifolia*)

co·ri·an·der \ˌkōrēˈandə(r), ˌkȯr-, -aand-\ *n* -s [ME *coriandre*, fr. OF, fr. L *coriandrum*, fr. Gk *koriandron, koriannon*, fr. *koris* bedbug; fr. its odor — more at COREIDAE] **1** : an Old World herb (*Coriandrum sativum*) with aromatic fruits **2** *or* **coriander seed** : the ripened dried fruit of coriander used for flavoring esp. of pickles, curries, confectioneries, and liquors

coriander oil *n* : a colorless or pale-yellow essential oil obtained from the dried ripe fruit of coriander and used chiefly as a flavoring agent

co·ri·an·drol \ˌkōrēˈanˌdrȯl, ˌkȯr-, -ˌdrōl\ *n* -s [ISV *coriandr-* (fr. L *coriandrum*) + *-ol*; orig. formed as G *koriandrol*] : dextrorotatory linalool

co·ri·an·drum \-ˈandrəm\ *n, cap* [NL, fr. L] : a genus of slender annual herbs (family Umbelliferae) with pinnately dissected leaves and white flowers in compound umbels and with the petals of the outer flowers in each umbel enlarged and like rays

co·ri·ar·ia \ˌkōrēˈa(a)rēə, ˌkȯr-\ *n, cap* [NL, fr. L, fem. of *coriarius* useful for tanning leather, fr. *corium* leather + *-arius* -ary; fr. the use of the leaves in tanning — more at CUIRASS] : a small widely distributed genus (coextensive with the family Coriariaceae of the order Sapindales) of shrubs or subshrubs having small opposite leaves, terminal racemes of very small flowers, and purplish fruit — see TUTU — **co·ri·ar·i·a·ceous** \ˌ==ˌ=rēˈāshəs\ *adj*

cori ester \ˈkōrē-\ *n, usu cap C* [after Carl F. *Cori* b1896 and his wife Gerty T. *Cori* †1957 Am. biochemists] : GLUCOSE PHOSPHATE a

cor·i·me·lae·na \ˌkȯrəməˈlēnə\ *n, cap* [NL, fr. *cori-* (fr. Gk *koris* bedbug) + *melaena* (fr. Gk *melaina*, fem. of *melas* black) — more at COREIDAE, MULLET] : a genus of small black bugs comprising the negro bugs

co·rin·don \kəˈrindən\ *n* -s [F, fr. Tamil *kurundam*] : CORUNDUM

co·rinne \kəˈrin\ *n* -s [origin unknown] : the common gazelle (*Gazella dorcas*)

cor·inth \ˈkȯrən(t)th, ˈkär-\ *n* -s [obs. E *corinth* currant, alter. (influenced by Greek city name *Corinth*) of *currant*] : any of certain usu. red dyes (as Congo corinth G)

¹co·rin·thi·an \kəˈrin(t)thēən\ *n* -s *cap* [L *Corinthiensis*] **1** : a native or resident of Corinth, Greece **2 a** : a gay profligate licentious man **b** : a fashionable man-about-town : SPORTSMAN **c** : an amateur yachtsman or sailor

²corinthian \"\ *adj, usu cap* [L *Corinthiensis*, adj. & n., fr. *Corinthus* Corinth, city in ancient Greece, fr. Gk *Korinthos*] **1 a** : of, relating to, or characteristic of Corinth **b** : of, relating to, or characteristic of Corinthians **2** : of or belonging to the lightest and most ornate of the three Greek orders that is characterized esp. by its bell-shaped capital enveloped with acanthuses — see CAPITAL illustration **3** : of or belonging to the type of decorative painting on vases practiced in Corinth in the 7th century B.C. and characterized by ornamentation with figures in black and purple and many details rendered by incision (as the engraving of fine lines in the dark silhouette) **4** : elegant and ornate in style or manner, esp. in literary style

A B

Corinthian order: Greek Corinthian order, *A;* Roman Corinthian order, *B*

corinthian atrium *n, usu cap C* : an atrium having a peristyle

co·rin·thi·an·ism \-ˌnizəm\ *n* -s *usu cap* **1** : Corinthian profligacy or elegance **2** : amateur yachting

corinthian pink *n, often cap C* : a moderate pink to light grayish red that is very slightly darker than lilac (sense 3b)

corinthian purple *n, often cap C* : a grayish purplish red that is redder and deeper than average rose plum, redder and slightly less strong than Aztec maroon, and redder and duller than tourmaline pink

corinthian red *n, often cap C* : a grayish red that is bluer and duller than bois de rose or Pompeian red, yellower and duller than appleblossom, and deeper than livid brown

co·ri·o·lis acceleration \(ˈ)kōrēˌōlə̇s-\ *n, usu cap C* [after Gaspard G. *Coriolis* †1843 Fr. civil engineer] : a quantity that must be added vectorially to the acceleration of a body with respect to another accelerated body to get the true acceleration of the former ⟨*Coriolis acceleration* applies to the motion of a long-range projectile with respect to the rotating earth⟩

coriolis force *n, usu cap C* [after G. G. *Coriolis*] : the force corresponding to the Coriolis acceleration of a body equal to the product of the mass by the Coriolis acceleration and responsible as a result of the earth's rotation for the deflection of projectiles and the motion of the winds to the right in the northern hemisphere and to the left in the southern hemisphere

co·ri·ta \kə'rēd·ə\ *n* -s [MexSp] : a small boat resembling a coracle used by the Indians of southern California

co·ri·um \'kōrēəm, 'kȯr-\ *n, pl* **co·ria** \-rēə\ [NL, fr. L, leather — more at CUIRASS] **1** : DERMIS 1 **2** : the layer of the mucous membranes corresponding to the dermis **3** : the chief or middle division of the thickened portion of the hemelytra of true bugs (order Hemiptera)

corival *var of* CORRIVAL

co·rixa \kə'riksə\ *n, cap* [NL, irreg. fr. Gk *koris* bedbug — more at COREIDAE] : a genus (the type of the family Corixidae) of carnivorous aquatic bugs comprising the boat bugs and having the hind pair of legs modified into elongated swimming organs which resemble oars — **co·rix·id** \-səd\ *n or adj*

co·riz·i·dae \kə'rizə,dē\ [NL, fr. *Corizus*, type genus (fr. Gk *koris* bedbug) + *-idae*] *syn of* COREIDAE

¹cork \'kȯ(ə)rk, 'kȯ(ə)k\ *n* -s [ME *corke* cork (bark), cork sandal, prob. fr. Ar *qurq*, fr. L *cortic-, cortex* bark, cork — more at CUIRASS] **1 a** : the outer tissues of the stem of the cork oak that in young stems consists of epidermis, cortical tissue, and periderm and in older stems of secondary phloem and periderm, that attains great thickness, and that is used commercially for cork stoppers and insulation — see VIRGIN CORK **b** : PHELLEM **2** : a piece of cork : something made from a piece of cork: as **a** : a usu. tapering or cylindrical stopper cut out of cork for a bottle, jug, or other container; *also* : a similar stopper of other material ⟨a rubber ~⟩ **b** : a float for a fishing line **3** *Scot* : a small employer : OVERSEER **4** : a light brown that is yellower and darker than blush, yellower and deeper than alesan, and yellower and slightly lighter than French beige **5** : a disease of apples and related plants (as pear and quinces) caused by boron deficiency and characterized by internal brown, dry, spongy or corky, bitter-tasting flecks in the fruits — called also *corky core*

²cork \"\ *vb* -ED/-ING/-S *vt* **1** : to furnish or fit with cork ⟨fishermen ~ their nets⟩ **2** : to stop up with a cork ⟨~ the bottle⟩ : seal (the contents) in a container by means of a cork ⟨~ the wine securely⟩ **3** : to close up or seal off (as a passage) ⟨for Charleston's ~*ed* with a Northern fleet —S.V. Benét⟩ : seal against escape : press down ⟨keeping his emotions ~*ed* up inside him⟩ **4** : to blacken (as one's face) with burnt cork ⟨minstrels with ~*ed* faces⟩ **5** : to develop corky tissue over (wounds or cuts) — used of a plant or tuber ~ *vi, of a plant or tuber* : to develop corky tissue over wounds or cuts

³cork \"\ *vb* -ED/-ING/-S [by folk etymology] : CALK, CAULK

⁴cork \"\ *n* -s [by folk etymology] : CALK

⁵cork \"\ *adj, usu cap* [fr. *Cork*, county in Ireland] **1** : of or from the city of Cork, Ireland : of the kind or style prevalent in Cork **2** : of or from County Cork, Ireland : of the kind or style prevalent in County Cork

cork·age \'kȯrkij, -ō(ə)k-, -kēj\ *n* -s **1** : the corking or uncorking of bottles **2 a** : a charge made by a hotel or restaurant for serving bottles of wine or other liquor bought elsewhere **b** : a charge made by a restaurant for every bottle of liquor served

cork-bark elm *n* : ROCK ELM 1a

cork black *n* : a black pigment made by charring cork

corkboard \'=,=\ *n* : a heat-insulating material made of granulated cork compressed in sheets or blocks and baked

cork cambium *n* [¹*cork*] : PHELLOGEN

cork carpet *n* : a floor covering similar to linoleum and made of ground cork, rubber, and linseed oil

corke *or* **corker** *var of* CORCIR

corked *adj* [fr. past part. of ²*cork*] *of wine or brandy* : having the unpleasant odor and taste resulting from corking

cork elm *n* **1** : ROCK ELM 1a **2** : WINGED ELM

cork·er \'kȯrkər, 'kȯ(ə)kə(r\ *n* -s **1** : one that corks bottles or other containers **2** *slang* : a person or thing of excellent or remarkable quality ⟨the story is amazingly good — a ~⟩ **3** : CAPPER 5 **4** *or* **corker nail** : COOLER NAIL

cork fir \'=,=\ *also* **corkbar fir** \'=,='=\ *n* : an evergreen tree (*Abies arizonica*) of Arizona and New Mexico with yellowish white thick corky bark

corkier *comparative of* CORKY

corkiest *superlative of* CORKY

¹corking *adj* [fr. pres. part. of ²*cork* (influenced in meaning by CORKER)] : extremely fine : extraordinarily good ⟨a ~ satire . . . which I conjure you to read —H.J.Laski⟩ ⟨a pitcher with a ~ fast ball⟩

²corking \"\ *n* -s [fr. gerund of ²*cork*] : impairment of the quality of wine or brandy usu. by the action of an injurious microorganism and perhaps resulting from a tainted cork or a seal that is not airtight

corking pin *n* [*corking* perh. alter. of *calkin*] *dial* : a large pin

cork·ite \'kȯr,kīt\ *n* -s [F, fr. *Cork*, county in Ireland, its locality + F *-ite*] : a phosphate-sulfate-hydroxide of lead and iron $PbFe_3(PO_4)(SO_4)(OH)_6$ that is isomorphous with beudantite

cork jacket *n* : a sleeveless canvas jacket with slabs of cork sewn into pockets on the front and back and used as a life preserver

cork leg *n* [¹*cork*] : an artificial leg

corkline \'=,=\ *n* : the upper line of a gill net having cork or other floats at intervals to give the net buoyancy — compare LEAD LINE 1b

cork oak *n* : an oak (*Quercus suber*) of southern Europe and northern Africa and esp. abundant in Spain and Portugal, attaining a height of 40 feet and furnishing the cork of commerce which is cut off in large plates at intervals of from 12 to 15 years

cork·o·ni·an \(')kȯ(r)k'kōnēən, -nyən\ *n* -s *cap* [*Cork*, county & city in Ireland + E *-onian* (as in *Oxonian*)] : a native or resident of Cork, Ireland

cork paint *n* : a coating of fine cork embedded in the base coat of paint on steel parts of ships to prevent sweating

cork paper *n* : a heavy wrapping paper surfaced with powdered cork and used to protect fragile articles

cork pine *n* [¹*cork*] : lumber sawed from mature specimens of a common white pine (*Pinus strobus*)

corks *pl of* CORK, *pres 3d sing of* CORK

¹cork·screw \'=,=\ *n* **1** : a pointed spiral piece of metal having a handle and used for drawing corks from bottles **2 a** : an imperfection in silk filament **b** : a defect in unevenly twisted yarns resembling the spiral of a corkscrew

²corkscrew \"\ *adj* : having the shape or taking the course of a corkscrew : SPIRAL ⟨a ~ curl⟩ ⟨the ~ motion of the ship over the heavy swell⟩

³corkscrew \"\ *vt* **1** : to cause to proceed in a spiral or winding course : WIND ⟨the road ~*ed* its way in and out of a gully —Ngaio Marsh⟩ **2** : to elicit (as information) with difficulty or by roundabout questioning ⟨every word had to be ~*ed* out of him⟩ **3** : to twist into a spiral ⟨~ copper tubing⟩ ~ *vi* : to move spirally or in a twisting or winding course ⟨the plane ~*ed* down toward the earth⟩ : take a winding or spiraling course ⟨the road ~*s* up the steep valley⟩

corkscrew

corkscrew flower *n* : SNAILFLOWER 1

corkscrew grass *n* : an Australian grass (*Stipa setacea*) that is like a corkscrew in the lower part of its fruiting awn

cork tan *n* : a light brown that is yellower and darker than blush and darker and slightly redder than cork

cork tile *n* : an elastic noiseless flooring tile made of cork shavings compressed and baked

cork tree *n* **1** : CORK OAK **2** *Austral* : a prickly Australian coral tree (*Erythrina vespertilis*) with soft spongy wood **3** : an Asiatic tree (*Phellodendron amurense*) with compound leaves, a turpentine odor when bruised, and deeply fissured corky bark **4** *West Indies* : PORTIA TREE

corkwing \'=,=\ *or* **corkwing wrasse** *n* : a small variably colored European wrasse (*Cremilabrus melops*)

corkwood \'=,=\ *or* **corkwood tree** *n* : any of various chiefly tropical American or Australian trees and shrubs having light-weight or corky wood; *esp* : a small tree or coarse shrub (*Leitneria floridana*) of the southeastern U.S. that has a swollen base, pale fissured bark, somewhat lanceolate and hairy leaves, and extremely soft light wood weighing about 12½ pounds to the cubic foot

corkwood elm *n* : ROCK ELM 1a

corkwood family *n* : LEITNERIACEAE

corky \'kȯrkē, 'kȯ(ə)k-, -ki\ *adj* -ER/-EST [¹*cork* + *-y*] **1** : resembling cork: as **a** : shriveled up : DRY, WITHERED ⟨bind fast his ~ arms —Shak.⟩ **b** : light or buoyant in spirits : LIVELY, SKITTISH ⟨a jovial ~ fellow⟩ **c** *of cheese* : firm, hard, without plasticity, and tending to break up under pressure **2 a** *of wine or brandy* : CORKED **b** : peculiar to or suggestive of a beverage spoiled by corking ⟨~ taste or odor⟩ **3** *of dogs* : compactly built and lively

corky core *also* **corky pit** *n* : ¹CORK 5

corky ring spot *n* : INTERNAL BROWN SPOT

corky scab *n* : POTATO SCAB

corm \'kȯ(ə)rm, 'kȯ(ə)m\ *n* -s [NL *cormus*] : a rounded thick modified underground stem base bearing membranous or scaly leaves and buds and acting as a vegetative reproductive structure in certain monocotyledonous plants (as gladiolus and crocus) — distinguished from *bulb*; compare TUBER

corm of crocus

corm- *or* **cormo-** *comb form* [NL, fr. Gk *korm-, kormo-* tree trunk, fr. *kormos* — more at CORMUS] : tree trunk : stem ⟨*Cormophyta*⟩

C or M *abbr* cost or market

cor·ma·tose \'kȯrmə,tōs\ *adj* [*corm* + *-atose* (as in *comatose*)] : having or producing corms

cor·mel \'kȯrməl\ *n* -s [*corm* + *-el*] : one of the small or secondary corms produced annually by an old corm — called also *bulblet*

cor·mid·i·um \kȯr'midēəm\ *n, pl* **cormid·ia** \-ēə\ [NL, fr. Gk *kormos* tree trunk + NL *-idium*] : the entire body or colony of a compound animal; *sometimes* : one of the clusters of zooids usu. consisting of a helmet-shaped bract, a gastrozooid, and one or more gonophores often functioning as swimming bells and arising from the main stem of a calycophoran — used chiefly of the Siphonophora

cor·moid \'kȯr,mȯid\ *adj* : like a corm

cor·moph·y·ta \kȯr'mäfəd·ə\ *n pl, cap* [NL, fr. *corm-* + *-phyta*] *in older classifications* : a division comprising all plants that have a stem and root

cor·mo·phyte \'kȯrmə,fīt\ *n* -s [NL *Cormophyta*] : a plant of the division Cormophyta

cor·mo·phyt·ic \;kȯrmə;fid·ik\ *adj* [NL *Cormophyta* + E *-ic*] : of, relating to, or characteristic of the Cormophyta

cor·mo·rant \'kȯrm(ə)rənt, 'kȯ(ə)m-; -mə,rant, -raa(ə)nt\ *n* -s [ME *cormeraunt*, fr. MF *cormorant, cormaran*, fr. OF *cormareng*, fr. *corp* raven (fr. L *corvus*) + *marenc* of the sea, fr. L *marinus* — more at RAVEN, MARINE] **1** : any of various dark-colored web-footed sea birds (family Phalacrocoracidae) that have a long neck, stiff wedge-shaped tail, slender hooked bill, and a patch of bare often brightly colored distensible skin under the mouth, that occur on most tropical and temperate seacoasts of the world but more abundantly in the southern hemisphere, that are used in parts of eastern Asia for catching fish by having a band placed about the throat to prevent them from swallowing their catch, and that are such voracious eaters of fish that they have become an emblem of gluttony **2** : a gluttonous, greedy, or rapacious person ⟨the bead-eyed ~*s* of lost estates, who love to rummage into fusty rooms —Howard Griffin⟩ ⟨[a place seeker's] ~ appetite for office —John Quincy Adams⟩

cor·mose \'kȯr,mōs\ *or* **cor·mous** \'kȯrməs\ *adj* : bearing or producing corms

cor·mus \'kȯrməs\ *n, pl* **cor·mi** \-,mī, -,mē\ [NL, corm, cormus, fr. Gk *kormos* tree trunk, fr. *keirein* to shear — more at SHEAR] : the entire body or colony of a compound animal

¹corn \'kȯ(ə)rn, 'kȯ(ə)n\ *n* -s *often attrib* [ME, fr. OE; akin to OHG & ON *korn* grain, Goth *kaurn*, L *granum*, Gk *gēras* old age, Skt *jīrṇa* worn out, frail, old; basic meaning: ripening] **1** *now chiefly dial* : a small hard particle : GRAIN ⟨a ~ of salt⟩ ⟨a ~ of gunpowder⟩ **2** : a small hard seed (as of an apple, a pepper, or a coffee cherry) **3 a** : the seeds of any of the cereal grasses used for food; *esp* : the seeds of the important cereal crop (as wheat, oats, or Indian corn) of a particular region **b** *Brit* : WHEAT **c** *Scot & Irish* : OATS **d** *Canad & Austral* : INDIAN CORN **4** : the kernels of sweet corn or maize served as a vegetable while still soft and milky ⟨a dish of ~⟩ — see CORN ON THE COB **5 a** : a plant that produces corn — now used of the grain crop, the stalks and ears after reaping, or the ears ready for threshing **b corns** *pl, obs* : kinds or crops of grain : CEREALS **c** *obs* : the stalk of a cereal plant ⟨playing on pipes of ~ —Shak.⟩ **6** : CORN WHISKEY **7** : a moderate yellow that is redder and deeper than colonial yellow, greener, lighter, and stronger than brass, and redder, lighter, and stronger than mustard yellow **8** : something (as writing, music, or acting) that is corny ⟨plot dealing with . . . Greek gods, nymphs, and shepherds, and a soccer . . . that has become dreadfully familiar as dinner music. . . . One false move and it would degenerate into intolerable ~ —Winthrop Sargeant⟩ ⟨it's corny, but ~ is the staff of entertainment life —Yasha Frank⟩ **9** : CORN SNOW — **acknowledge the corn** : to admit or confess a charge, fault, error, or failure ⟨when his error was proved he had to *acknowledge the corn*⟩

²corn \"\ *vb* -ED/-ING/-S *vt* **1** : to form into grains : GRANULATE ⟨~ gunpowder⟩ **2 a** : to preserve or season with salt in grains : cure by salting : sprinkle with salt **b** : to salt lightly in brine containing preservatives, sweetening, and sometimes spices ⟨you can ~ beef in a few weeks⟩ ⟨~ a tongue⟩ **3** : to plant (land) with corn ⟨~*ing* my land to death —Russell Lord⟩ **4** : to feed with corn or grain ⟨~ horses⟩ ~ *vi* **1** *obs* : to become granular **2** : to form or fill with the corn or seed — used of cereals or pulse or their ears or pods

³corn \"\ *n* -s [ME *coorne*, fr. MF *corne* horn, fr. L *cornu* — more at HORN] **1** : a horny hardening and thickening of the epidermis at some point (as on a toe) produced by friction or pressure and formed into a central conical mass extending into the dermis — called also *clavus*; compare CALLOSITY **2** : a reddish painful discoloration of the sole of the fore hoof of a horse usu. caused by pressure resulting from improper shoeing and resultant bruises of the velvety tissue overlying the horn which diffuse blood into it **3** : the abnormal growth on the feet of poultry affected with bumblefoot

¹-corn \-,kȯrn, -,kȯ(ə)n\ *n comb form* -s [L *-cornis* -horned, fr. *cornu* horn] : one having (such or so many) horns ⟨*unicorn*⟩

²-corn \"\ *adj comb form* [L *-cornis*] : having (such or so many) horns : horned

cor·na·ce·ae \kȯr'nāsē,ē\ *n pl, cap* [NL, fr. *Cornus*, type genus + *-aceae*] : a family of mainly temperate-region trees, shrubs, or herbs (order Umbellales) comprising the dogwoods and related plants and having small clustered flowers, an inferior ovary, and drupaceous fruit — **cor·na·ceous** \(')kȯr-nāshəs\ *adj*

cor·na·da \kȯr'nädə, *or as Sp*\ *n* -s [Sp, fr. *corn-* (fr. *cuerno* horn, fr. L *cornu*) + *-ada* (fr. L *-ata*) — more at -ADE] : a wound inflicted by a bull's horn in formal bullfighting

corn aphid *or* **corn aphis** *n* : CORN LEAF APHID

cornball \'=,=\ *n, often attrib* [*corn ball* "ball of popped corn and molasses" (influenced in meaning by ¹*corn* "something corny" & *screwball, meatball*)] *slang* : an unsophisticated person : RUBE, HICK; *also* : something corny

corn beef *n* : corned beef

corn belt *n* : an area in which more land is used for the cultivation of corn than for any other single crop (as the central portion of the U.S. from western Ohio into Nebraska and Kansas including northern Missouri, eastern So. Dakota, and southwestern Minnesota)

corn billbug *n* : any of several billbugs that feed on maize

cornbind \'=,=\ *n, Brit* : CORN BINDWEED

corn binder *n* : an implement for harvesting standing corn or other tall crops grown in rows comprising a cutter and a device for packing and tying the stalks into bundles — called also *corn harvester, row binder*

corn bindweed *n* : a bindweed of grainfields (as black bindweed and field bindweed)

corn borer *n* : any of several insects that bore in maize: as **a** : the larva of an Old World moth (*Ostrinia nubilalis*) of the family Pyraustidae introduced into and now widespread in eastern No. America where it is a major pest in the stems and crowns of maize, dahlias, potatoes, and many other plants — called also *European corn borer* **b** : a larval pyralidid moth (*Diatraea grandiosella*) of similar habits native to Mexico but now widespread in the southwestern U.S. — called also *southwestern corn borer* **c** : SOUTHERN CORNSTALK BORER **d** : GRANARY WEEVIL

cornbottle \'=,=\ *n* [¹*corn* + *bluebottle*] : CORNFLOWER 1b

corn bran *n* : the hull of the grain of Indian corn separated during milling and used as livestock feed

corn bread *n* : bread made with cornmeal: as **a** : cornmeal mixed with shortening and water and baked or fried **b** : cornmeal mixed with wheat flour, eggs, milk, and leavening and baked

corn broom *n* : a broom made from the panicles of broomcorn

corn bunting *n* : a grayish brown streaked bird (*Emberiza calandra*) of marshy fields or brushland of Europe

corn buttercup *n* : CORN CROWFOOT

corn cake *n* [¹*corn* (maize) + *cake*] : corn bread baked in a pan in an oven or as small cakes on a griddle

corn catchfly *n* : a European annual herb (*Silene armeria*) adventive as a garden escape in No. America

corn centaury *n* : CORNFLOWER 1b

corn chamomile *n* : FIELD CHAMOMILE

corn chandler *n, Brit* : a retailer of grain and allied products

corn chop *n* : coarse feed consisting of bran, husk, and germ fragments removed from corn which is being ground into meal — often used in pl.

corn chrysanthemum *n* : CORN MARIGOLD

corncob \'=,=\ *n* **1** : the axis on which the kernels of Indian corn are arranged **2** : an ear of Indian corn

corncob pipe *also* **corncob** *n* : a tobacco pipe with a bowl made from a corncob or made to resemble a corncob

corn cockle *or* **corn campion** *n* : an annual hairy weed (*Agrostemma githago*) common in grainfields and having purplish red flowers — called also *crown-of-the-field*

corncracker \'=,==\ *n* **1 a** : KENTUCKIAN — used as a nickname **b** : CRACKER 5 **2** : a mill, machine, or device for the coarse grinding of corn

corncrake \'=,=\ *n* [ME, fr. *corn* + *crake*] : a common Eurasian short-billed rail (*Crex crex*) that frequents grainfields — called also *land rail*

corncrib \'=,=\ *n* : a crib for holding or storing ears of Indian corn

corn crowfoot *n* : a common European crowfoot (*Ranunculus arvensis*) with pale yellow flowers and spiny achenes

corncrusher \'=,==\ *n* : a machine or device for crushing grain

corncutter \'=,==\ *n* [³*corn*] : CHIROPODIST

corn cutter *n* [¹*corn*] **1** : a machine for cutting up stalks of Indian corn as food for cattle **2** : a knife (as a sickle) or a machine for cutting down the stalks of Indian corn

corn dance *n* : a No. American Indian ceremonial dance expressing supplication or thanksgiving for the maize crop and held at such stages as the planting, ripening, or harvesting of the grain — called also *green corn dance*; compare ⁴BUSK, RAIN DANCE

corn dodger *n* [¹*corn* (maize) + *dodger* (cake)] *chiefly South & Midland* : a cake of corn bread often shaped by hand and fried on a griddle, baked in an oven, or boiled as a dumpling with ham and cabbage or with greens

corn drake *n, dial Eng* : CORNCRAKE

corn dumpling *n* : a boiled corn dodger

corne- *or* **corneo-** *comb form* [F *corné-, cornéo-*, fr. *corné* corneous (fr. L *corneus*), *cornée* cornea (fr. ML *cornea*)] **1** : corneous : corneous and ⟨*corneo*calcareous⟩ **2** : cornea ⟨*corneitis*⟩ : corneal and ⟨*corneo*sclerotic⟩

¹cor·nea \'kȯ(r)nēə\ *n* -s [ML, fr. L, fem. of *corneus* horny — more at CORNEOUS] **1** : the transparent part of the coat of the eyeball which covers the iris and pupil and admits light to the interior, which is of mesodermic origin and is covered externally by the ectodermic conjunctival epithelium, and which is composed of layers of interlacing fibers continuous with those of the sclerotic coat and united by a cementing substance — see EYE illustration **2** : the outer transparent covering of the compound eyes of arthropods which is divided into small facets, each acting as a lens

²cornea *pl of* CORNEUM

cor·nea·gen \'kȯ(r)nēə,jen\ *or* **cor·ne·ag·e·nous** \;kȯ(r)nē-;ajənəs\ *adj* [*cornea* + *-gen*, n. suffix (here in attributive use) or *-genous*] : secreting cornea — used of the hypodermal cells that underlie the ocelli and ommatidia in insects

cor·ne·al \'kȯ(r)nēəl\ *adj* : of or related to the cornea

corneal transplant *n* : the transplanting of a piece of transparent cornea from a donor eye into the space made by excision of a piece of a patient's opaque cornea to provide a clear window for vision; *also* : the piece transplanted

corn earworm *n* : the large smooth longitudinally striped yellow-headed destructive larva of a noctuid moth (*Heliothis zea*) that is worldwide in distribution but esp. destructive in warm regions and that feeds on many cultivated plants usu. (as on maize) by entering at the tip of the ear, feeding on the developing kernels, and befouling the area in which it lodges with frass and debris — called also *bollworm, tobacco budworm, tomato fruitworm, vetchworm*

corned *past of* CORN

cor·ne·in \'kȯ(r)nēən\ *n* -s [ISV *corne-* (fr. L *corneus* horny) + *-in*; orig. formed as G *kornein*] : an iodized nitrogenous substance showing some protein reactions and constituting the organic basis of corals

cor·ne·itis \,kȯ(r)nē'īd·əs\ *n* -ES [NL, fr. *corne-* + *-itis*] : KERATITIS

cor·nel \'kȯrnᵊl, -,nel\ *n* -s [prob. fr. (assumed) obs. LG *kornelle*, fr. MLG *kornelle*, fr. OF *cornelle, cornolle*, fr. (assumed) VL *cornulla*, dim. of (assumed) VL *corna*, alter. of L *cornum* cornel cherry, fr. *cornus* cornel tree; akin to Gk *kranos* cornel tree, Lith *Kirnis*, god of cherries, Gk *kerasos* cherry tree] : a plant of *Cornus* or a related genus: as **a** : CORNELIAN CHERRY **b** : RED DOGWOOD 1 **c** : DWARF CORNEL **d** : FLOWERING DOGWOOD

cor·ne·lian \kȯ(r)'nēlyən\ *n* -s [alter. of ME *corneline*, fr. MF, perh. fr. *cornelle* cornel cherry + *-ine*; fr. its color] : CARNELIAN

cornelian cherry \"-\ *n* [*cornel* + *-ian*] **1** : a European shrub or small tree (*Cornus mas*) **2** : the berry borne on the cornelian cherry tree

cornelian red *n* : COPPER 5a

cor·ne·muse \'kȯ(r)nə,myüz *or as F*\ *n* -s [ME, fr. MF, back-formation fr. *cornemuser* to play the cornemuse, fr. *corne* horn (fr. L *cornu*) + *muser* to play the bagpipe — more at HORN, MUSETTE] : a French bagpipe

corneo- — see CORNE-

cor·ne·ous \'kȯ(r)nēəs\ *adj* [L *corneus* horny, fr. *cornu* horn — more at HORN] : of a texture resembling horn : HORNY

¹cor·ner *R* 'kȯrnər *sometimes* 'kōnər; *–R* 'kȯ(ə)nə(r\ *n* -s [ME, fr. OF *cornere, corniere*, fr. *corne* corner, horn, fr. L *cornu* horn, end, point] **1 a** : the point or place where converging lines, edges, or sides meet : ANGLE ⟨the ~ of a square⟩ ⟨~ of a box⟩ ⟨the ~*s* of his eyes and mouth⟩ **b** : an angular part at the meeting point of two of the sides or edges of something ⟨lift up the ~*s* of the tablecloth⟩; *also* : a small piece separated (as by tearing off) or separate from something but including such an angular part **c** : the place of intersection of two streets or roads **d** : a stake, tree, or other mark designating the point of intersection of two boundary lines of a piece of land **e** : a piece designed to form, occupy, mark, protect, or ornament a corner of something (as a leather or metal cap for the corner of a book); *also* : a design for a corner ornament or a device (as type or a stamp) for impressing it **f** : a corner kick in soccer or a free hit from an opponent's defensive corner in field hockey **g** : the area or edge of home plate nearest or farthest from the batter ⟨the inside ~ is that closest to the batter, the outside ~ is that farthest from him⟩ **h** : one of the two pairs of opponents in a 4-hand card game ⟨play for 10 cents a ~⟩ — distinguished from *side* **2 a** : the space between meeting lines, walls, or borders close to the vertex of the angle ⟨the southwest ~ of the state is hilly⟩ **b (1)** : a secret place or place of secrecy ⟨dark deeds done in ~*s*⟩

: an out-of-the-way place remote from ordinary life or affairs ⟨a quiet ~ of a small New England town⟩ : a small part or area (as of one's mind); *esp* : one that is secret, private, or little known ⟨kept a ~ of their minds free from the strict rule of logic —G.G.Coulton⟩ ⟨every ~ of his inoffensive life was open to the day —Dorothy Sayers⟩ ⟨he had a soft ~ in his heart for Valentine —F.M.Ford⟩ (2) : any place or part (as of the world) whether far or near ⟨starlings are found in every ~ of England⟩ : the remotest extremity ⟨the power of England extended to all ~*s* of the world⟩ : a part or area esp. of a field of activity ⟨establishing frequency modulation in every ~ of the . . . electronics industry —C.B.Fisher⟩ (3) : a point of view : an observer or critic of the scene ⟨this ~ believes that the music should be of prime interest to the collector —Howard Taubman⟩ : a place of observation; *specif* : a regular column in a periodical devoted to a particular interest or activity ⟨verses from his pen had appeared in the poet's ~ of the . . . *Journal* —W.B.Parker⟩ **c** : a position from which escape or retreat is difficult or impossible : a position of danger, difficulty, or embarrassment ⟨he was daring but not imprudent and never got himself into such a tight ~ that he could not escape⟩ **d** (1) : the angle of the ring in which a boxer rests and is worked on by his seconds during the periods between rounds (2) : the party of supporters, well-wishers, or adherents associated with a contestant or with one engaged in some effort, struggle, or controversy ⟨he will have most of the businessmen in his ~ in his fight for the nomination⟩ **3** *obs* : a direction from which the wind blows ⟨sits the wind in that ~ —Shak.⟩ **4 corners** *pl* : CHARACTERISTICS, TRAITS, MANNERS; *esp* : rough, rude, or uncultivated manners or ways ⟨a year or two at a good school will round off some of his rough ~*s*⟩ **5 a** : the critical moment in any series of events; *esp* : the moment marking a turning point from failure to success — used esp. in the phrase *turn the corner* ⟨the business has turned the ~ after three years of losses⟩ **b** : the halfway point toward game on a cribbage board **6 a** : control or ownership by an individual or group of enough of the available supply of a commodity or a security to permit manipulation of the selling price ⟨made a fortune from a ~ in cotton⟩ — compare TRUST **b** : possession of the whole amount or supply of something ⟨a ~ on vigor and virtue —H.J.Muller⟩ : the unique possession of a privilege or ability ⟨a ~ on sales of out-of-town papers —H.H.Martin⟩ **7** : the adjacent dancer standing at a right angle in a square dance ⟨the man's ~ is the woman to his left; his partner is on his right⟩ **8** : CORNER TOOTH — **around the corner** : about to be met, to occur, or to be realized : IMMINENT : at hand ⟨promised that better times were just *around the corner*⟩

²corner \"\ *vb* **cornered; cornered; cornering** \-n(ə)riŋ\ **corners** [ME *corneren*, fr. *corner*, n.] *vt* **1 a** : to drive into a corner or into a position where escape is difficult or impossible : bring to bay ⟨largest known eel . . . not usually aggressive, but dangerous when ~*ed* —J.L.B.Smith⟩ **b** : to force into a position of difficulty or embarrassment ⟨the prosecutor ~*ed* the witness and forced out the truth⟩ : catch and hold the attention of (a person) esp. so as to force an interview ⟨he ~*s* the secretary on his way to lunch . . . and says what he has to say right in his ear —Clarence Woodbury⟩ **2** : to get command of a large part of the supply of (as a stock or a commodity) so as to be able to dictate one's own price ⟨~ the common stock of a railroad⟩ ⟨~ the rye market⟩ : get a corner on ⟨you have not ~*ed* all the good ideas —Beatrice S. Rossell⟩ — compare ENGROSS **3** : to cut with an ax a wide chip from each half or each corner of (a box) in turpentine orcharding ~ *vi* **1** : to meet or converge at a corner or angle ⟨the spot where three states ~⟩ **2** *of an automobile* : to turn to one side or the other ⟨a car that ~*s* at high speed without skidding, swerving, or excessive leaning⟩

³corner \"\ *adj* [¹*corner*] **1** : situated at a corner; *specif* : situated at a street corner or an intersection ⟨the ~ grocer, druggist or other small merchant —*Time*⟩ **2** : used or fitted by shape or design for use in or on a corner ⟨a ~ brace⟩ ⟨a triangular ~ table⟩

cornerball \ˈ==,=\ *n* : a game in which each team occupying half of a court with one man stationed in each far corner of the opponents' side tries to seize the ball when it is thrown up at the center line and throw it over the opponents' heads to one of its corner men

corner bead *n* **1** : a bead having a quirk on each side and worked on or fixed to the angle of any architectural work esp. for protecting an angle of a wall **2** : STAFF ANGLE

cornerbind \ˈ==,=\ *n* : a hook or chain used in binding logs, timber, or lumber on vehicles

corner bit brace *or* **corner brace** *n* : ANGLE BRACE 2

corner boy *n, chiefly Irish* : one who loafs at street corners

corner card *n* : RETURN CARD 2

corner chair *n* : a chair whose curved or angular back is set around one corner of its seat and extends on each side to another corner — called also *roundabout chair, writing chair*

corner chair

corner chisel *n* : a chisel having two cutting edges at right angles to each other for cutting mortise corners or angles

corner clump *n, Brit* : CORNER QUAD

corner cupboard *n* : a cupboard fitting into a corner of a room

cornered *adj* [ME, fr. ¹*corner* + *-ed*] **1** : having corners of a specified number or type ⟨three-*cornered* hat⟩ ⟨sharp-*cornered*⟩ **2** : involving a specified number of participants ⟨a three-*cornered* contest for mayor⟩ **3** : brought to bay : TRAPPED ⟨savage as a ~ rat⟩ : in a position of difficulty ⟨he answered reluctantly, feeling ~⟩

corner influence *n* : the additional value to land resulting from its location at or near a street intersection

cornering *n* -s [¹*corner* + *-ing*] : the construction of a corner in building; *also* : CORNER ⟨dovetailed or square ~*s*⟩

cornering tool *n* : a tool with a curved cutting edge used by woodworkers for rounding sharp corners and edges

corner kick *n* : a free kick in soccer from close to the point of intersection of the goal line and a touchline allowed to the opposite side when a player has sent the ball behind his own goal line

corner lady *n* : the woman at a man's left in a square-dance set — called also *left-hand lady;* compare OPPOSITE LADY, PARTNER, RIGHT-HAND LADY

cornerpiece \ˈ==,=\ *n* : CORNER 1e

corner quad *n, printing* : an L-shaped quad commonly used as an inside support for a mitered corner

corners *pl of* CORNER, *pres 3d sing of* CORNER

cornerstone \ˈ==,=\ *n* [ME *cornerston*, fr. *corner* + *ston* stone] **1** : a stone forming a part of a corner or angle in a wall and esp. lying at the foundation of a principal angle; *specif* : such a stone laid at the formal inauguration of the erection of a building, usu. inscribed with the date or other matters, and often hollowed out to receive records, documents, or relics **2** : the event, fact, or thing that forms the principal foundation or support upon which an achievement is based or from which a development makes its beginning ⟨this first bill is the ~ of the administration's economic policy⟩ : the principal or fundamental element, feature, or part of something ⟨natural selection remains the ~ of evolutionary theory —E.W.Sinnott⟩

corner tooth *n* : one of the third or outer pair of incisor teeth of each jaw of a horse

corner tree *n* : a tree marking a surveyor's corner

cornerwise \ˈ==,=\ *or* **cor·ner·ways** \ˈ==,wāz\ *adv* : with the corner set in front : DIAGONALLY

¹cor·net \(ˈ)kȯrˈnet, -ō(ə)r;-, *usu* -ed+V; *Brit usu* ˈkō(ə)nit\ *n* -s [ME *cornette*, fr. MF *cornet*, fr. OF, dim. of *corn* horn, fr. L *cornu* — more at HORN] **1 a** *often* **cor·nett** \"\ : a Renaissance woodwind with a cup mouthpiece and tapered wooden or ivory body with no flare, six finger holes, and one thumb hole used esp. with church choral music — called also *zinke;* compare SERPENT **b** : a valved brass instrument primarily used in bands that resembles the trumpet in shape and pitch range but has a less brilliant quality — called also *cornopean* **c** (1) : a cornet player (2) : the part played by or written for a cornet player **d** : one of several organ stops **2** : something rolled or formed in the shape of a cone: as **a** : a piece of paper rolled into a cone shape and twisted at the end for use as a container **b** *also* **cor·nette** \"\ : a metallic bead flattened out and made into a roll for treatment with acid in assaying **c** : a cone-shaped pastry shell that is often filled with whipped cream **d** *Brit* : ICE-CREAM CONE **e** : a thin slice (as of meat or smoked salmon) rolled into a cone shape

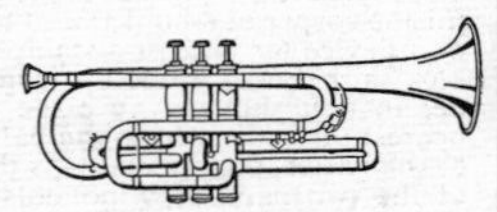

cornet 1b

²cornet \"\ *n* -s [MF *cornette*, fr. *corne* horn (fr. L *cornu*) + *-ette*] **1** *also* **cornette a** : a woman's cap or headdress varying in style from the 15th through the 18th centuries and usu. made of delicate materials with lappets of lace or ribbon **b** : a lappet of such a headdress **2 a** : the standard of a troop of cavalry **b** : a troop of cavalry **c** (1) : the onetime fifth grade of commissioned officer in a British cavalry troop who carried the standard (2) : the onetime lowest commissioned rank in the U. S. cavalry

cor·net-à-pis·tons \-,äˈpistənz, -,ä|, -,ə|, |(,)pēˈstōⁿ *or as F*\ *n, pl* **cornets-à-pistons** \", -nets- *or as F*\ [F, lit., cornet with valves] : ¹CORNET 1b

cor·net·cy \ˈkȯ(r)nətsē, -si\ *n* -ES [²*cornet* (officer) + *-cy*] : the office, rank, or commission of a cornet

cornetfish \(ˈ)=ˈ=,=\ *n* [so called fr. the long snout] : any of several slender elongated fishes (family Fistulariidae) of tropical seas having an elongated tubular snout and the scales replaced by bony plates — called also *flutemouth*

cor·net·ist *or* **cor·net·tist** \(ˈ)kȯ(r)ˈned·əst, -etə-\ *n* -s : a performer on the cornet

cor·ne·tite \ˈkȯ(r)nə,tīt\ *n* -s [F, fr. Jules *Cornet* †1929 Belgian geologist + F *-ite*] : a mineral consisting of basic copper phosphate $Cu_3(PO_4)(OH)_3$

cor·net·ti·no \,kȯ(r)nəˈtē(,)nō\ *n* -s [It, lit., small cornet, dim. of *cornetto*] : a 2-foot reed organ stop

cor·net·to \kȯ(r)ˈned·(,)ō\ *n, pl* **cornet·ti** \-d·(,)ē\ [It, dim. of *corno* horn, fr. L *cornu*] : ¹CORNET 1a

cor·ne·um \ˈkȯ(r)nēəm\ *n, pl* **cor·nea** \-ēə\ [NL, fr. L, neut. of *corneus* horny, fr. *cornu* horn — more at HORN] : STRATUM CORNEUM

corn–fed \ˈ=,=\ *adj* **1** : fed or fattened on corn or other grain ⟨*corn-fed* hogs⟩ **2** : well fed : PLUMP, HEALTHY ⟨a husky, *corn-fed* youth of twenty-eight . . . addicted to thick, rare beefsteaks —W.A.White⟩

cornfield \ˈ=,=\ *n* : a field in which corn is grown

cornfield ant *n* : a dark brown No. American ant (*Lasius alienus*) that colonizes the corn-root aphid on maize and cotton

cornfield meet *n, slang* : a head-on collision of railroad trains

cornfield pea *n, South* : COWPEA

corn flag *n* **1** : a plant of the genus *Gladiolus* (esp. *G. segetum*) **2** : a yellow iris (*Iris pseudacorus*) of Europe naturalized in the eastern U. S.

cornflakes *n pl* : a breakfast cereal made from the coarse meal of hulled corn by moistening, heating, and rolling it into flakes that are subsequently dried and usu. toasted

corn flea beetle *n* : a common flea beetle (*Chaetocnema pulicaria*) destructive to maize foliage in the eastern U. S.

corn flour *n* **1** : white, finely ground, and bolted cornmeal **2** *Brit* : CORNSTARCH

cornflower \ˈ=,==\ *n* [so called fr. its growth in grainfields] **1 a** : CORN COCKLE **b** : a European plant (*Centaurea cyanus*) having flower heads with blue, pink, or white rays that is often cultivated in No. America — called also *bluebottle* **c** : a dogtooth violet (*Erythronium americanum*) **2** *or* **cornflower blue** : a variable color averaging a moderate purplish blue that is redder, lighter, and stronger than marine blue, redder, stronger, and slightly lighter than gentian blue, and lighter and stronger than old glory blue

cornflower aster *n* : STOKES' ASTER

corn fodder *n* : the entire Indian-corn plant cut and used either fresh or dry-cured for forage; *also* : the leaves and tops dry-cured for use as a stock feed — compare STOVER

corn fodder disease *n* : CORNSTALK DISEASE

corn gallon *n* : an old unit of capacity equal to 272¼ cubic inches or 4.46 liters

corn gluten *n* : a protein-rich product separated from starch in the wet-milling process

corn gluten feed *n* : a by-product of the wet-milling process consisting of corn gluten meal and other fractions (as bran)

corn gluten meal *n* : a high-protein feed consisting chiefly of corn gluten

corn god *n* : any one of a class of deities believed to promote crop growth and to share the annual growth, decay, and rebirth of vegetable life

corn grass *n* **1** : SILKY BENT GRASS **2** : a panic grass (*Panicum clandestinum*)

corn grits *n pl* : HOMINY — compare ¹GRITS 2

corn gromwell *n* : an annual or biennial herb (*Lithospermum arvense*) with inconspicuous white flowers growing as a weed in fields — called also *field gromwell*

corn harvester *n* : CORN BINDER

corn–hog ratio *n* : a measure of the relative profitability of producing market pork at different times expressed as the number of bushels of maize equal in market value to 100 pounds of live hogs ⟨a profitable *corn-hog ratio* is 11: 1 or higher⟩

cornhouse \ˈ=,=\ *n, New Eng & South* : CORNCRIB

cornhusking \ˈ=,==\ *n* : the husking of corn; *specif* : HUSKING BEE

corni *pl of* CORNO

¹cor·nice \ˈkȯrnəs, ˈkō(ə)n-, *esp by builders* ÷-nish *or* ÷-nesh\ *n* -s [MF *corniche, cornice*, fr. It *cornice*, perh. modif. (influenced by *cornice* crow, fr. L *cornic-, cornix*) of L *coronis* curved line, fr. Gk *korōnis*, fr. *korōnē* anything curved — more at CROWN, RAVEN] **1 a** : the typically molded and projecting horizontal member that crowns an architectural composition; *specif* : the uppermost of the three members of a classic entablature — see ENTABLATURE illustration **b** : the top course of the wall when treated as a finish or crowning member **c** : a member in a piece of furniture resembling a cornice **2** : a decorative band of metal or wood used to conceal curtain fixtures — compare VALANCE 1 **3** : an overhanging mass of snow, ice, or rock usu. on a ridge or at the top of a couloir

C cornice 1a

²cornice \"\ *vt* -ED/-ING/-S : to furnish or crown with or as if with a cornice

cornice brake *n* : ⁴BRAKE 5

cor·niche \ˈkȯr|nish, |nēsh, kȯrˈnēsh, -ō(ə)|\ *or* **corniche road** *n* -s [*corniche* fr. F, lit., cornice; *corniche road* part trans. of F *route en corniche*] : a road built along the edge of an overhanging precipice or along the face of a cliff

cor·ni·cle \ˈkȯ(r)nəkəl\ *n* -s [L *corniculum*, dim. of *cornu* horn — more at HORN] : a little horn or horn-shaped process; *specif* : either of two protruding dorsal tubes in aphids that secrete a waxy fluid and were formerly believed to discharge honeydew

cor·nic·u·late \kȯ(r)ˈnikyələt\ *adj* [L *corniculatus*, fr. *corniculum* + *-atus* -ate] : having horns or small horn-shaped processes

corniculate cartilage *n* : a small nodule of yellow elastic cartilage articulating with the apex of the arytenoid

cor·nic·u·lum \-ləm\ *n, pl* **cornicu·la** \-lə\ [L, little horn] : a small horn-shaped part or process

cor·nic·u·lus \-ləs\ *n, pl* **cornicu·li** \-,lī, -,lē\ [NL, alter. of L *corniculum*] : one of the horny tips of the ovipositor of an orthopterous insect

corni di bassetto *pl of* CORNO DI BASSETTO

corni di caccia *pl of* CORNO DI CACCIA

cornier *comparative of* CORNY

corniest *superlative of* CORNY

cor·nif·ic \(ˈ)kȯ(r)ˈnifik\ *adj* [L *cornu* horn + E *-i-* + *-fic*] : producing horns : forming horn

cor·ni·fi·ca·tion \,kȯ(r)nəfəˈkāshən\ *n* -s [L *cornu* horn + E *-i-* + *-fication*] **1** : conversion into horn or a horny substance or tissue **2** : the conversion of the vaginal epithelium from the columnar to the squamous type

cor·ni·form \ˈkȯrnə,fȯrm\ *adj* [L *cornu* horn + E *-iform*] : shaped like a horn

cor·ni·fy \-,fī\ *vi* -ED/-ING/-ES [L *cornu* horn + E *-i-* + *-fy*] : to become converted or changed into horn or horny tissue

cor·nig·er·ous \(ˈ)kȯrˈnijərəs\ *adj* [L *corniger* horn-bearing (fr. *cornu* horn + *-i-* + *-ger*, fr. *gerere* to bear) + E *-ous* — more at JEST] : having horns

corni inglesi *pl of* CORNO INGLESE

corn·ily \ˈkȯ(r)nᵊlē, -nəl|, |ī\ *adv* [*corny* + *-ly*] : in a corny manner

cor·nin \ˈkȯrnən\ *n* -s [L *cornus* cornel + E *-in* — more at CORNEL] **1** : VERBENALIN **2** : CORNUS 2

corn·i·ness \ˈkȯ(r)nēnəs, -nin-\ *n* -ES [*corny* + *-ness*] : the quality or state of being corny ⟨a musical revue marked by banality and ~⟩

corning *pres part of* CORN

¹cor·nish \ˈkȯrnish, -ō(ə)n-, -nēsh\ *adj, usu cap* [*Corn*wall, county in southwest England + E *-ish*] **1 a** : of, relating to, or characteristic of Cornwall, England **b** : of, relating to, or characteristic of Cornishmen **2** : of, relating to, or characteristic of the Cornish language

²cornish \"\ *n* -ES *usu cap* **1** : a Celtic language of Cornwall, England, extinct since the late 18th century — see INDO-EUROPEAN LANGUAGES table **2 a** : an English breed of domestic fowls with pea combs, very close feathering, and compact sturdy bodies **b** : a bird of the Cornish breed now much used in cross-breeding for meat production

³cornish \"\ *dial var of* CORNICE

cornish chough *n, usu cap 1st C* [¹*cornish*] **1** : a red-billed chough (*Pyrrhocorax pyrrhocorax*) now rare in England but found in mountainous parts of Europe and northern Africa **2** : the heraldic representation of a Cornish chough with black feathers and red legs and beak

cornish diamond *n, usu cap C* : a quartz crystal from Cornwall

cornish elm *n, usu cap C* : a narrow-pyramidal tree (*Ulmus stricta*) long cultivated for its graceful habit and ascending branches

cornish heath *n, usu cap C* : a low bushy shrub (*Erica vagans*) common on the moors of Cornwall and in southwestern Europe and often cultivated elsewhere

cor·nish·man \-mən\ *n, pl* **cornishmen** *cap* : a native or resident of Cornwall, England

cornish pasty *n, usu cap C* : cooked meat and vegetables encased in pastry and baked

cornish stone *n, usu cap C* : china stone found in extensive beds in Cornwall and Devonshire, England, and much used in English ceramics

corn juice *n* : WHISKEY; *esp* : CORN WHISKEY

corn kale *n* [so called fr. its frequent occurrence as a weed in fields of grain] : CHARLOCK

corn knife *n* : a long heavy knife used in chopping down Indian cornstalks in harvesting by hand

corn·land \ˈkȯrn,land\ *n* [ME, fr. ¹*corn* + *land*] : land used for or suitable for the growing of corn

corn law *n* : a law regulating trade in grain; *specif, usu cap C&L* : one of a series of laws in force in Great Britain before 1846 that prohibited or laid heavy duties upon the importation of foreign grain for home consumption except when the price rose above a certain rate

corn leaf aphid *n* : a dusky greenish or brownish aphid (*Rhopalosiphum maidis*) that feeds on the foliage and flowers of maize and other commercially important grasses

corn lily *n* **1** : HEDGE BINDWEED **2** : FIELD BINDWEED **3** : WANDFLOWER 1 **4** : a plant of the genus *Ixia* **5** : a tall white hellebore (*Veratrum californicum*) with broad plaited leaves and panicles of greenish flowers that is a characteristic floral element of moist upland meadows of the Sierra Nevada of California

corn liquor *n* : CORN WHISKEY

cornloft \ˈ=,=\ *n* : GRANARY

corn maggot *n* **1** : SEED-CORN MAGGOT **2** : the larva of the gout fly

corn marigold *n* : a European herb (*Chrysanthemum segetum*) with bright yellow rays that is common in grainfields — called also *field marigold*

corn mayweed *n* **1** : FIELD CHAMOMILE **2** : a European weed (*Matricaria inodora*) with white flowers and finely divided leaves that is naturalized and sometimes cultivated in eastern No. America

cornmeal \ˈ=,=\ *n* : meal made from white or yellow corn

corn mill *n* **1** *Brit* : a flour mill **2** : a mill for grinding corn

corn mint *n* : a European mint (*Mentha arvensis*) naturalized in No. America with a pubescent stem and flowers in subglobose axillary clusters — called also *field mint*

cornmonger \ˈ=,==\ *n, archaic* : a grain dealer

corn mustard *n* : CHARLOCK

cor·no \ˈkȯr(,)nō\ *n, pl* **cor·ni** \-nē\ [It, horn, fr. L *cornu* — more at HORN] : FRENCH HORN

corno di bas·set·to \ˈ=(,)=(,)dēbəˈse,tō\ *n, pl* **corni di bassetto** \ˈ=(,)=-\ [It] **1** : BASSET HORN **2** : an 8-foot reed organ stop of clarinet quality

corno di cac·cia \-,dēˈkä(,)chä\ *n, pl* **corni di caccia** [It, lit., hunting horn] : NATURAL HORN

corno flute *n* [It *corno* horn + E *flute*] : a soft 8-foot organ stop

corn oil *n* : a yellow semidrying fatty oil obtained from the germs of corn kernels and used chiefly as a salad oil and in soft soaps — called also *maize oil*

cor·no in·gle·se \ˈkȯr(,)nō|iŋˈglāse, -inˈg-, -ā(,)sā, -āsē\ *n, pl* **cor·ni in·gle·si** \-r(,)nē|...ā(,)sē, -āzē\ [It] : ENGLISH HORN

corn on the cob : corn cooked and eaten on the cob

cor·no·pe·an \,kȯrnəˈpēən, kȯrˈnōpē-\ *n* -s [perh. fr. It *corno* horn + *pean* paean, fr. L *paean*] **1** *Brit* : ¹CORNET 1b **2** : a powerful 8-foot reed organ stop

corn oyster *n* : a fritter containing young corn cut from the cob and cooked on a griddle

corn parsley *n* : a wild parsley (*Petroselinum segetum*) found as a weed in European grainfields

corn picker *n* : a machine for gathering the ears and removing the husks from standing Indian corn

corn pink *n* : CORN COCKLE

corn plant *n* : any of several plants of the genus *Dracaena* with broad leaves either green or variously striped (esp. *D. fragrans* and *D. deremensis*)

corn planter *n* : any of various mechanical devices for planting Indian corn in furrows or hills

corn plow *n, chiefly Midland* : a machine for cultivating corn

corn pone *n, South & Midland* : corn bread often made without milk or eggs, shaped in irregular ovals by the palm of the hand, and baked or fried on a griddle

corn popper *n* : any of various utensils used in popping corn

corn poppy *n* : an annual red-flowered poppy (*Papaver rhoeas*) common in European grainfields and cultivated in several varieties — called also *field poppy*

corn pudding *n* : a pudding made with sweet corn canned or cut from the cob, eggs, milk, and other ingredients

corn–root aphid *n* : a destructive aphid (*Anuraphis maidiradicis*) that feeds on the roots esp. of maize or cotton and is dependent on the cornfield ant for distribution and care

corn rootworm *n* : the root-eating larva of any of several cucumber beetles of the genus *Diabrotica* — used esp. when the larvae are found on the roots of maize

corn rose *n* **1** : CORN POPPY **2** : CORN COCKLE

corns *pl of* CORN, *pres 3d sing of* CORN

-corns *pl of* -CORN

cornsack \ˈ=,=\ *n, chiefly Austral* : a burlap bag : GUNNYSACK

corn salad *n* [so called fr. its occurrence as a weed in fields of grain] : a plant of the genus *Valerianella*; *esp* : a low European herb (*V. olitoria*) that is widely cultivated as a salad plant and potherb

corn sap beetle *n* : a small brown beetle (*Carpophilus dimidiatus*) with truncate wing covers that is related to the dried-fruit beetle, that is sometimes a destructive pest of sweet corn, and that feeds on decaying fruits and vegetation and sometimes swarms in rice mills

corn sheller *n* **1** : a machine or device that separates the kernels of corn from the cob **2** *slang* : a repeating firearm ⟨defending himself with a *corn sheller*⟩

corn shucking *n* : CORNHUSKING

corn silk *n* : the silky styles on an ear of Indian corn

corn smut *n* : a smut attacking Indian corn — compare BOIL SMUT, HEAD SMUT

corn snake *n* [so called fr. its being found in corncribs and cornfields] **:** a large harmless No. American snake (*Elaphe guttata*) brightly blotched with scarlet on a grayish ground — called also *red rat snake*
corn snakeroot *n* **:** BUTTON SNAKEROOT
corn snapdragon *n* **:** a European wild snapdragon (*Antirrhinum orontium*)
corn snapper *n* **:** a machine that snaps the ear of corn from the stalk but does not husk it
corn snow *n* **:** granular snow formed by alternate thawing and freezing — called also *spring corn, spring snow*
corn speedwell *n* **:** a small annual or winter annual speedwell (*Veronica arvensis*) of Europe and America found in fields and waste places and having median and upper leaves entire or toothed
corn spurry *or* **corn spurrey** *n* **:** a small European weed (*Spergula arvensis*) with whorled leaves and white flowers
cornstalk \ˈ=,=\ *n* **1 :** a stalk of Indian corn **2** *slang Austral* **:** AUSTRALIAN; *specif* **:** a native of New So. Wales
cornstalk disease *also* **cornstalk poisoning** *n* **1 :** a severe frequently fatal intoxication of cattle fed on corn fodder that resembles pasteurellosis but is usu. considered due to abnormalities in the nitrogen content of the fodder **2 :** an acute encephalitic disease of horses fed on moldy corn fodder
cornstalk pine *n* **:** LOBLOLLY PINE 1
cornstalk weed *or* **cornstalk pondweed** *n* **:** a river weed (*Potamogeton lucens*) with shining elongated leaves
cornstarch \ˈ=,=\ *n* **:** starch resembling a fine white flour made from corn and used chiefly in foods as a thickening agent (as in puddings and gravies), in making corn syrup and sugars, and in the manufacture of adhesives and sizes for paper and textiles
corn stick *n* **:** a corn bread baked in a special muffin pan having cups shaped like ears of corn
cornstock \ˈ=,=\ *n* **:** CORNSTALK
corn sugar *n* **:** DEXTROSE; *esp* **:** dextrose made by complete hydrolysis of cornstarch
corn syrup *n* **:** a transparent thick syrup containing dextrins maltose, and dextrose that is obtained by partial hydrolysis of cornstarch and is used chiefly in foods (as in bakery products and candy) and in the brewing industry — called also *glucose, starch syrup*
corn thistle *n* **:** CANADA THISTLE
cor·nu \ˈkȯr(,)n(y)ü\ *n, pl* **cor·nua** \-nyəwə\ [L, horn — more at HORN] **:** something shaped like or resembling a horn; *esp* **:** a bodily structure suggesting a horn in form (as either of the lateral divisions of a bicornuate uterus, one of the lateral processes of the hyoid bone, or one of the gray columns of the spinal cord) — **cor·nu·al** \-nyəwəl\ *adj*
cor·nu·co·pia \,kȯ(r)n(y)əˈkōpēə *sometimes* -nēˈk- *or* -niˈk-\ *n* -S [LL, fr. L *cornu copiae* horn of plenty, fr. *cornu* horn + *copiae*, gen. of *copia* abundance, plenty — more at COPIOUS] **1 :** a curved goat's horn from the mouth of which fruit and ears of grain overflow used as a decorative motif in art, architecture, and design (as on furniture, porcelain, and silver work), emblematic of abundance, and representing the horn of the Greek nymph Amalthea that was endowed with the virtue of becoming filled with whatever its possessor wished — called also *horn of plenty* **2 :** something that produces an overflowing and inexhaustible supply esp. of desirable things ⟨American consumption . . . allows mass production to continue with safety its outpouring of goods from its miraculous ~ —P.M.Mazur⟩ **:** an inexhaustible store **:** ABUNDANCE ⟨a pair of books that . . . add up to a 550-page ~ of humor —Bernard Kalb⟩ **3 :** a receptacle shaped like a horn or cone (as a paper horn filled with candy or a pastry filled with whipped cream) **4 :** a protrusion of the choroid plexus into each lateral recess of the fourth ventricle of the brain

cornucopia 1

cor·nu·co·pi·an \,==ˈ=pēən\ *adj* **:** resembling a cornucopia **:** existing in or producing abundance ⟨~ industry⟩ **:** marked by abundance ⟨~ markets⟩
cornucopia sofa *n* **:** an early 19th century sofa with arms carved in the form of cornucopias
cor·nu·da \kȯrˈnüdə\ *n* -S [AmerSp, fr. Sp, fem. of *cornudo* horned, fr. L *cornutus*] **:** HAMMERHEAD 3a
cor·nule \ˈkȯr(,)nyül\ *n* -S [LL *cornulum* small horn, dim. of L *cornu* horn] **:** a small horny plate or process; *specif* **:** one of those that serve as teeth in the lower jaw of the duckbill
cor·nu·li·tes \,kȯrnyəˈlīd·ēz\ *n, cap* [NL, fr. LL *cornulum* + NL *-ites* -ite] **:** a genus of extinct tubicolous annelids known from trumpet-shaped tubes with annulations and longitudinal striations found in Ordovician and Silurian strata
corn up *vt, slang* **:** to make corny **:** introduce corny elements into ⟨*corn up* a story⟩
cor·nu·pete \ˈkȯrnyə,pēt\ *adj* [LL *cornupeta*, fr. L *cornu* horn + LL *-peta* (fr. L *petere* to go to, head for, attack) — more at FEATHER] **:** goring or attacking with the horns — used of a bull represented in sculpture or painting
cor·nus \ˈkȯrnəs\ *n* [NL, fr. L, cornel — more at CORNEL] **1** *cap* **:** a genus of shrubs and small trees of the family Cornaceae usu. having very hard wood and perfect flowers with a 2-celled ovary — see CORNEL, DOGWOOD; compare KINNIKINNICK **2** -ES **:** the dried bark of the root of the flowering dogwood containing a bitter principle sometimes used as a mild astringent and stomachic
cor·nu spiral \(ˈ)kȯrˈn(y)ü-\ *n, usu cap C* [after Marie Alfred *Cornu* †1902 Fr. physicist] **:** a spiral of two oppositely coiled branches obtained by plotting as abscissas and ordinates respectively the corresponding values of a certain two integrals and used to afford graphical solution of various problems in diffraction of light
¹cor·nute \(ˈ)kȯrˈn(y)üt\ *vt* -ED/-ING/-S [L *cornutus* horned, fr. *cornu* horn] *archaic* **:** to bestow horns upon **:** make a cuckold of **:** CUCKOLD
²cornute \ˈ"\ *n* -S [L *cornutus* horned] **:** something forked or having horns: as **a :** ¹CUCKOLD 1 — compare HORN 4b **b** [LL *cornutus*, fr. L] **:** DILEMMA; *esp* **:** a sophistical dilemma
³cornute \ˈ"\ *adj* [L *cornutus*] *bot* **:** CORNUTED
cor·nut·ed \-üdəd\ *adj* [fr. past part. of *cornute*] **:** bearing or having horns or shaped like a horn
cor·nu·to \kȯrˈnü,tō\ *n* -S [It, fr. L *cornutus* horned] **:** CUCKOLD — compare HORN 4b
corn violet *n* **:** a European herb (*Specularia speculum-veneris*) with purple flowers
corn·wall \ˈkȯrn,wȯl, -,wəl\ *adj, usu cap* [fr. *Cornwall*, county in England] **:** of or from the county of Cornwall, England **:** of the kind or style prevalent in Cornwall **:** CORNISH
corn·wal·lis \kȯrnˈwälə̇s, -wȯl-\ *n* -ES [after Charles, 1st Marquis *Cornwallis* †1805 Eng. soldier] **:** a muster in masquerade formerly held in New England and believed to commemorate the surrender of Lord Cornwallis at Yorktown
corn·wall·ite \ˈkȯrn,wȯ,līt, -,wə,l-\ *n* -S [G *cornwallit*, fr. *Cornwall*, county in southwest England, its locality + G *-it* -ite] **:** a mineral consisting of a basic copper arsenate $Cu_5(AsO_4)_2(OH)_4.H_2O$ resembling malachite
cornwall stone *n, usu cap C* **:** CORNISH STONE
corn weevil *n* **1 :** GRANARY WEEVIL **2 :** a billbug attacking maize
corn whiskey *n* **:** whiskey distilled from corn mash; *specif* **:** whiskey distilled from a mash made up of not less than 80 percent corn and aged in uncharred or used charred oak containers — compare BOURBON 4
corn wil·lie \(ˈ)kȯrnˈwilē\ *n* [*corn* (as in *corn beef*) + *Willie*, nickname for *William*] *slang* **:** canned corned beef esp. as an army ration
corn woundwort *n* [so called fr. its growth in cultivated areas] **:** a European weed (*Stachys arvensis*) naturalized in No. America and in Australia — called also *shiverweed*
¹corny \ˈkȯrnē, ˈkō(ə)n-, -ni\ *adj, usu* -ER/-EST [ME, fr. ¹*corn* + *-y*] **1** *archaic* **:** tasting strongly of malt **2 :** of or relating to corn **:** producing, abounding in, or full of corn ⟨the ~ ear —Matthew Prior⟩ **3 :** using familiar and stereotyped formulas believed to appeal to the unsophisticated **:** TRITE ⟨the American satirizing the Englishman and the Englishman satirizing the American reach their *corniest* and most obvious depths —Stephen Potter⟩ ⟨a play full of ~ music and ~ jokes⟩ **:** mawkishly sentimental ⟨fantasy about a blue kitten . . . in less talented hands . . . could have been painfully ~ —*Atlantic*⟩ **:** OLD-FASHIONED ⟨TV sets are selling poorly because their styling is a little backward, sort of ~ —*Time*⟩ **:** characterized by threadbare moralizing, exaggerated theatricality, or grandiose but commonplace sentiments ⟨especially eloquent in a slightly ~ way, with the wide gestures and grandiloquent intonations of a U.S. senator —F.L.Allen⟩
²corny \ˈ"\ *adj, usu* -ER/-EST [³*corn* + *-y*] **1 :** relating to corns **2 :** having corns on the feet
co·ro·a·do \,kȯrəˈwä(,)dō\ *n, pl* **coroado** *or* **coroados** *usu cap* [Pg, lit., crowned one, fr. *coroado* (past part. of *coroar* to crown), fr. L *coronatus*, past part. of *coronare* to crown; fr. their crown-shaped hairdress — more at CROWN] **1 :** BORORO **2 :** the Caingang people of São Paulo, southeastern Brazil
co·ro·di·ary *or* **cor·ro·di·ary** \kəˈrōdē,erē\ *n* -ES [ML *corrodiarius*, fr. *corrodium* + L *-arius* -ary] **:** the recipient of a corody
cor·o·dy *or* **cor·ro·dy** \ˈkȯrədē\ *n* -ES [ME *corodie*, fr. ML *corrodium, corredium, conredium*, irreg. fr. OF *corroi, conroi, conrei* order, arrangement, fr. *corroyer, correer, conreer* to prepare, arrange, furnish — more at CURRY] **1 a :** the right of free quarters due a lord on circuit from his vassals **b :** an allowance of food, clothing, or other commodities due from a religious house to the crown and assigned to one of its subjects **2 :** an allowance of provisions for maintenance (as food or clothing) that is dispensed as a charity
corojo *var of* COROZO
co·rol·la \kəˈrälə\ *n* -S [NL, fr. L, small garland, dim. of *corona* — more at CROWN] **:** the inner set of floral leaves that immediately surround the sporophylls, consist of separate or fused petals, and are often highly colored in contrast to the calyx but sometimes inconspicuous or even absent
cor·ol·la·ceous \ˌkȯrəˈlāshəs, ˌkär-\ *adj* [*corolla* + *-aceous*] **:** of or resembling a corolla
¹cor·ol·lary \ˈkȯrə,lerē, ˈkär-, -eri, *Brit usu* kəˈräləri\ *n* -ES [ME *corolarie*, fr. LL *corollarium*, fr. L, gratuity, garland, fr. *corolla* small garland + *-arium* -ary — more at COROLLA] **1 a :** a proposition that follows upon one just demonstrated and that requires no additional proof **b :** a deduction, consequence, or additional inference more or less immediate from a proved proposition **2** *obs* **a :** something appended to a speech or writing **:** APPENDIX, CONCLUSION **b :** something beyond what is due **:** something added or superfluous **3 a :** something that naturally follows **:** a practical consequence **:** RESULT ⟨the war has . . . paved the way for an economic and, as a ~, a semipolitical internationalism —Edward Sapir⟩ ⟨love was a stormy passion, and jealousy its normal ~ —Ida Treat⟩ **b :** something that incidentally or naturally attends or accompanies **:** ACCOMPANIMENT, EQUIVALENT ⟨only after the physical impossibility of the revolutionary goals had been demonstrated did its political ~ find acceptance —H.A.Kissinger⟩ ⟨a ~ to the problem of the number of vessels to be built was that of the types of vessels to be constructed —Daniel Marx⟩

open flower of the cinnamon rose showing corolla

²corollary \ˈ"\ *adj* **:** constituting a corollary: **a :** derived from a proposition **:** CONSEQUENTIAL **b :** that follows from or derives naturally from a circumstance or phenomenon **:** RESULTING ⟨a sound economy and the ~ prosperity⟩ **c :** occurring together with or accompanying another phenomenon **:** ASSOCIATED, SUPPLEMENTARY ⟨five years after the Emancipation Proclamation the Fourteenth Amendment was established as a ~ measure⟩ ⟨expansion of the knowledge of atomic energy leading to ~ experimentation . . . in power generation —*Americana Annual*⟩
co·rol·late \kəˈräl,āt, ˈkȯrəl, \|,lət\ *or* **co·rol·lat·ed** \|,lād·əd\ *adj* [*corollate*, ISV *coroll-* (fr. NL *corolla*) + *-ate*; *corollated* fr. *corollate* + *-ed*] **:** having a corolla
corolla tube *n* **:** TUBE 1b(2)
cor·ol·lif·er·ous \ˌkȯrəˈlif(ə)rəs\ *adj* [ISV *coroll-* (fr. NL *corolla*) + *-i-* + *-ferous*; prob. orig. formed as F *corollifère*] **:** bearing or having a corolla
co·rol·li·form \kəˈrälə,fȯrm\ *adj* [ISV *coroll-* (fr. NL *corolla*) + *-iform*; prob. orig. formed as F *corolliforme*] **:** having the form of a corolla
co·rol·line \kəˈrä,līn, ˈkȯrə,-\ *adj* [*corolla* + *-ine*] **1 :** relating to or resembling a corolla **2 :** borne on a corolla
cor·o·man·del \,kȯrəˈmandᵊl\ *n* -S *often cap* [*Coromandel* coast, southeast India] **:** COLCOTHAR 2
coromandel ebony \,==ˈ==-\ *also* **coromandel** \,==ˈ=\ *n, usu cap C* **:** an East Indian timber tree (*Diospyros melanoxylon*) with a hard dark-colored wood
coromandel gooseberry *n, usu cap C* **:** CARAMBOLA
coromandel screen *n, often cap C* [so called fr. its being formerly brought to Europe by way of the Coromandel coast] **:** a Chinese lacquered folding screen
coromandel wood *n* **:** CALAMANDER WOOD
¹co·ro·na \kəˈrōnə\ *n* -S [L, garland, crown, cornice — more at CROWN] **1 :** the projecting part of a classic cornice the underside of which is often cut with a drip **2 :** something suggesting a crown: as **a** (1) **:** a usu. colored circle often seen around and close to a luminous body (as the sun or moon) caused by diffraction produced by suspended droplets or occas. particles of dust — see HALO 1 (2) **:** the tenuous outermost part of the atmosphere of the sun extending for millions of miles from its surface, containing very highly ionized atoms of iron, nickel, and other gases that indicate a temperature of millions of degrees, and appearing to the naked eye as a pearly gray halo around the moon's black disk during a total eclipse of the sun but observable at other times with a coronagraph; *also* **:** a similar portion of the atmosphere of a star (3) **:** a circle of light made by the apparent convergence of the streamers of the aurora borealis about a spot in the heavens toward which the dipping needle points **b** [NL, fr. L] **:** the upper portion of a body part (as of a tooth or of the skull) **c** [NL, fr. L] **:** CROWN 12a **d** [ML, fr. L] **:** a crown or circlet suspended from the roof or vaulting of churches to hold tapers lighted on solemn occasions **e** [NL, fr. L] **:** an appendage or series of united appendages borne on the inner side of the corolla in certain flowers (as in the daffodil, jonquil, and milkweed) and often resembling an additional whorl of the perianth **f** [ML, fr. L] (1) **:** a circlet (as of gold) on an ecclesiastical vestment for the head (2) **:** the tonsure of a cleric **g :** a faint glow adjacent to the surface of an electrical conductor at sufficiently high voltage that results from electrical discharge and indicates an early stage of electric breakdown in the surrounding air or gas **h :** a usu. radial zone of minerals surrounding another mineral or occurring at the contact between certain minerals (as olivine and feldspar) **i** [NL, fr. L] **:** the group of cells at the apex of the oogonium in stoneworts **j** [NL, fr. L] **:** the ciliated trochal disk of rotifers and some other organisms **3** [NL, fr. L] **:** MEDULLARY SHEATH 2 **4** [It, lit., crown, fr. L] **:** a mark ⌒ used in musical notation to indicate a hold or a pause **:** FERMATA **5 :** ¹KRONE **6 :** ROSARY **7** [fr. *La Corona*, a trademark] **:** a long cigar having the sides straight to the unsealed end and roundly blunt at the sealed end **8** [NL, fr. L] **:** the main part of the calcareous test of a sea urchin excluding the apical system of plates **9** [Sp, lit., crown, fr. L] **:** a saddle blanket shaped to the saddle and bound at the margin with a fold of different color

flower of a narcissus showing a corona

²corona \ˈ"\ *n*, [NL, fr. L, garland, crown — more at CROWN] *syn of* CORONATAE
cor·o·nach \ˈkȯrənək, -nək\ *n* -S [ScGael *corranach* & IrGael *coranach*, fr. MIr *com-* together + (assumed) MIr *rānach* outcry, weeping — more at CO-] **:** a lamentation for the dead as sung or played on the bagpipes in Scotland and Ireland **:** DIRGE
corona discharge *n* [¹*corona*] **:** the discharge of electricity causing a corona (sense 2g)
cor·o·na·dite \,kȯrəˈnä,dīt\ *n* -S [Francisco Vásquez *Coronado* †1554 Sp. explorer + E *-ite*; fr. its occurrence in the Coronado vein, Greenlee county, southeast Arizona] **:** a lead and manganese oxide $MnPbMn_6O_{14}$ that is an important constituent of manganese ore, occurs in black massive form with fibrous structure, and is isostructural with hollandite
¹cor·o·na·do \-ä(,)dō\ *n* -S [AmerSp, fr. Sp (past part. of *coronar* to crown), fr. L *coronatus*, past part. of *coronare* to crown; fr. the yellow band on its side — more at CROWN] **:** AMBERJACK
²coronado \ˈ"\ *n, pl* **coronado** *or* **coronados** *usu cap* [AmerSp, fr. Sp, past part. of *coronar* to crown; fr. their crown-shaped hairdress] **1 :** CAINGANG **2 :** MATACO **3 :** ABIPÓN
co·ro·na·graph *or* **co·ro·no·graph** \kəˈrōnə,graf\ *n* -S [*coronagraph* alter. of *coronograph*, fr. ¹*corona* + *-o-* + *-graph*] **:** a telescope designed to facilitate observations of the sun's corona without benefit of a total solar eclipse, usu. containing a monochromatic objective lens and a series of diaphragms to eliminate scattered light, and used with a monochromatic filter matching one of the wavelength regions of the bright emission lines of the corona — **co·ro·na·graph·ic** *or* **co·ro·no·graph·ic** \kə,rōnəˈgrafik\ *adj*
¹cor·o·nal *also* **cor·o·nel** \ˈkȯrənᵊl, ˈkär-\ *n* -S [ME *coronal, coronell*, fr. AF *coronal*, fr. L *coronalis* of a crown, fr. *corona* crown + *-alis* -al] **1 :** a circlet for the head esp. implying rank or dignity **:** CROWN, CORONET; *also* **:** such a circlet around a helmet **2 :** a garland of flowers or leaves for the head
²cor·o·nal \ˈkȯrənᵊl, ˈkär- *or, especially when referring to something familiarly known as "corona",* kəˈrōn-\ *adj* [MF or L; MF *coronal*, fr. L *coronalis*] **1 :** of or relating to a corona or crown (as a king's crown, the corona of a flower, the sun's corona, the crown of a tooth) ⟨the law and his ~ oath require his . . . assent to what laws the Parliament agree upon —John Milton⟩ **2** *anat* **:** lying in the direction of the coronal suture **:** of or relating to the frontal plane which passes through the long axis of the body **3** *phonetics* **:** RETROFLEX
cor·o·na·le \,kȯrəˈna(,)lē, -nä-,-nā-\ *n* -S [NL, fr. L, neut. of *coronalis* coronal] **:** the point of the coronal suture marking the greatest diameter of the frontal bone
coronal root *n* **:** an adventitious root that springs from the stem just above the surface of the ground (as in wheat) — compare SEMINAL ROOT
coronal suture *n* **:** a suture extending across the skull between the parietal and frontal bones
co·ro·na ra·di·a·ta \kəˈrōnə,rādēˈäd·ə\ *n, pl* **co·ro·nae ra·di·a·tae** \-,nē, . . . ˈā,tē\ [NL, lit., rayed crown] **1 :** the zone of small follicular cells immediately surrounding the ovum in the Graafian follicle and accompanying the ovum on its discharge from the follicle **2 :** a large mass of medullated nerve fibers radiating from the internal capsule to the cerebral cortex
¹cor·o·nary \ˈkȯrə,nerē, ˈkär-, -ri\ *adj* [L *coronarius*, fr. *corona* garland, crown + *-arius* -ary] **1 :** of, relating to, or being a crown or coronal **:** forming or designed to form a crown or coronal **2** *anat* **a :** resembling a crown or circlet **:** encircling another part **b :** relating to or involving the coronary vessels of the heart; *broadly* **:** of or relating to the heart
²coronary \ˈ"\ *n* -ES **1 :** CORONARY ARTERY **2 a :** CORONARY OCCLUSION **b :** CORONARY THROMBOSIS
coronary artery *n* **1 :** either of the two arteries, right and left, which arise from the aorta immediately above the semilunar valves and supply the tissues of the heart itself **2 :** one of various arteries encircling the lips **3 :** the artery passing along the lesser curvature of the stomach
coronary bone *n* **:** the small pastern bone of the horse and related animals
coronary cushion *also* **coronary band** *or* **coronary ring** *n* **:** a thickened band of extremely vascular tissue that lies at the upper border of the wall of the hoof of the horse and related animals and that plays an important part in the secretion of the horny walls
coronary disease *also* **coronary artery disease** *or* **coronary heart disease** *n* **:** a condition (as sclerosis or thrombosis) that reduces the blood flow through the coronary arteries to the heart muscle
coronary failure *n* **:** heart failure in which the heart muscle is deprived of the blood necessary to meet its functional needs as a result of narrowing or blocking of one or more of the coronary arteries
coronary insufficiency *n* **:** cardiac insufficiency of relatively mild degree
coronary ligament *n* **1 :** the folds of peritoneum connecting the posterior surface of the liver and the diaphragm **2 :** a part of the capsular ligament of the knee connecting each semilunar fibrocartilage with the margin of the head of the tibia
coronary occlusion *n* **:** the partial or complete blocking of a coronary artery (as by a thrombus or by spasm or sclerosis of the artery)
coronary sclerosis *n* **:** sclerosis of the coronary arteries of the heart
coronary sinus *n* **:** a venous channel that is derived from the sinus venosus, is continuous with the largest of the cardiac veins, receives most of the blood from the walls of the heart, and opens into the right atrium
coronary sulcus *n* **:** a depression surrounding the heart at the atrioventricular junction and giving passage to coronary arteries, veins, and sinus
coronary thrombosis *n* **:** the formation of a thrombus in a coronary artery of the heart
coronary valve *n* **:** the fold of endocardium at the opening of the coronary sinus into the right atrium
coronary vein *n* **1 a :** any of several veins that drain the tissues of the heart and empty into the coronary sinus **b :** CARDIAC VEIN — not used technically **2 :** a vein draining the lesser curvature of the stomach and emptying into the portal vein
coronas *pl of* CORONA
cor·o·na·ta \,kȯrəˈnäd·ə, -ād·ə\ [NL, fr. L, neut. pl. of *coronatus*] *syn of* CORONATAE
cor·o·na·tae \-d·(,)ē\ *n pl, cap* [NL, fr. L, fem. pl. of *coronatus*] **:** an order of Scyphomedusae comprising rather larg pelagic or deep-sea jellyfishes that have marginal tentacles and the bell margin divided into lappets
¹cor·o·nate \ˈkȯrə,nāt, ˈkär-\ *vt* -ED/-ING/-S [L *coronatus*, past part. of *coronare* to crown, fr. *corona* garland, crown] **:** CROWN
²coronate \ˈ"\ *adj* [L *coronatus*] **:** CROWNED, CORONATED
cor·o·nat·ed \-ād·əd\ *adj* [fr. past part. of ¹*coronate*] **:** CROWNED; *specif* **:** having a crown, crest, corona, or some similar structure — used esp. of univalve shells when the spire is surrounded by a row of spines or tubercles
cor·o·na·tion \,kȯrəˈnāshən, ,kär-\ *n* -S *often attrib* [ME *coronacioun*, fr. MF *coronation*, fr. *coroner* to crown + *-ation* — more at CROWN] **1 :** the act or occasion of crowning: as **a :** the ceremony of investing a sovereign or his consort with the royal crown **b :** the ceremony of enthroning or of celebrating the official accession of a sovereign ⟨~ festivities of the present emperor of Japan —Edwin Strawbridge⟩ **c :** the crowning or ceremonious installation of a person that is chosen as the principal in a celebration or other function or that is the winner of a contest (as a beauty contest) ⟨the ~ of the queen of the lilac festival⟩ ⟨the ~ of this year's Miss America⟩ **2 :** a culminating act or event **:** an act or event that brings to completion ⟨the victory is a ~ of all our efforts⟩ **3 :** the official accession to the highest office among a group or the ceremony marking such an accession ⟨the anniversary of the pope's ~ —*Springfield (Mass.) Daily News*⟩ ⟨the Iowan tribe . . . council put off scheduling a ~ —*Life*⟩
coronation oath *n* **:** an oath taken by a sovereign at coronation
coronel *var of* CORONAL
cor·o·nene \ˈkȯr-ə-,nēn\ *n* -S [L *corona* crown + E *-ene*] **:** a pale yellow very high-melting fluorescent hydrocarbon $C_{18}H_{12}$ having a molecular structure like a crown with six benzene rings fused together
cor·o·ner \ˈkȯrənə(r), ˈkär-\ *n* -S [ME *coroner, corowner*, fr. AF *corouner*, fr. OF *corone, coroune* crown (fr. L *corona*) + AF *-er* (fr. L *-arius*) — more at -ER] **1 :** an officer of an earlier time in England whose duty was to keep a record of the pleas of the crown in a county and guard the royal revenues arising from them **2 :** a public officer whose principal duty is to inquire by an inquest held in the presence of a jury into the cause of any death which there is reason to suppose is not due to natural causes — compare MEDICAL EXAMINER **3 :** a chief constable of a sheading in the Isle of Man

[1]**cor·o·net** \ˌkȯrəˌnet, ˈkär-, *usu* -ed.+V; *esp Brit* ˈ==ˌnət\ *n* -s [MF *coronette*, fr. OF *coronete*, fr. *corone* crown + -*ete* -ette] **1 a :** a small or lesser crown usu. signifying a high rank below that of a sovereign **b :** CROWN **2 :** something resembling or suggesting a coronet: as **a :** an ornamental wreath, circlet, or band for the head usu. for wear by women on formal occasions **b :** a small structure resembling a crown: (1) **:** the lower part of a horse's pastern where the horn terminates in skin (2) **:** the burr of an antler (3) **:** a terminal circle of small spines or hairs (as on the genitalia of certain arthropods) **3 :** a card sequence in some card games (as vint) consisting of three or more cards in any suit or three or four aces held in one hand **4 :** a white band in the habit of certain Catholic sisterhoods that encircles the face and to which a black veil is pinned

British coronets: duke, *A*; marquess, *B*; viscount, *C*; baron, *D*; earl, *E*

[2]**coronet** \"\ *vt* **coroneted** *or* **coronetted; coroneted** *or* **coronetted; coroneting** *or* **coronetting; coronets :** to provide with a coronet: **a :** to raise to a rank or position that warrants the wearing of a coronet; *esp* **:** to raise to such a rank in an official ceremony ⟨the ~*ing* of a May queen⟩ **b :** to decorate or adorn with a coronet ⟨a heraldic shield bearing a ~*ed* miter⟩ ⟨plain and ~*ed* designs —Charles Hasler⟩

coronet boot *n* **:** a shield of heavy leather or rubber placed over the hoof wall and coronet of the rear hooves of a racehorse to prevent injury from blows by the front shoes

coroneted *or* **coronetted** *adj* [[1]*coronet* + -*ed*] **:** of noble birth or rank ⟨the princess and her ~ companions⟩

cor·o·nilla *in sense 1* ˌkȯrəˈnilə, *in sense 2* -nē(y)ə\ *n* [NL, irreg. fr. L *corona* crown; fr. the flower clusters — more at CROWN] **1 a** *cap* **:** a genus of Old World often woody herbs (family Leguminosae) having purple, pink, or yellow flowers in long-stalked axillary heads or umbels — see AXSEED, SCORPION SENNA **b** -s **:** any plant of the genus *Coronilla* **2** *also* **co·ro·ni·llo** \-nē(ˌ)(y)ō\ -s [AmerSp *coronilla, coronillo*, fr. Sp *coronilla* crown of the head, dim. of *corona* crown, fr. L] **:** a valuable timber tree (*Gleditsia amorphoides*) of Argentina the bark of which yields a saponin

cor·o·nil·lin \-nilən\ *n* -s [ISV *coronill-* (fr. NL *Coronilla*) + -*in*] **:** a poisonous yellow glucoside from seeds of plants of the genus *Coronilla* that affects the heart like digitalis

co·ro·ni·on \kəˈrōnēˌän, -ēən\ *n, pl* **coro·nia** \-ēə\ [NL, irreg. fr. Gk *korōnē* crow; akin to Gk *korax* raven — more at RAVEN] **:** the tip of the coronoid process of the mandible — see CRANIOMETRY illustration

co·ro·nis \kəˈrōnəs\ *n* -ES [L, fr. Gk *korōnis*, fr. *korōnē* anything curved — more at CROWN] **:** a mark ʼ used in Greek over a vowel to indicate contraction

cor·o·ni·tis \ˌkȯrəˈnīdəs\ *n* -ES [NL, fr. *coron-* (fr. E *coronary cushion*) + -*itis*] **:** inflammation of the coronary cushion of animals

co·ro·ni·um \kəˈrōnēəm\ *n* -s [NL, fr. L *corona* + NL -*ium*] **:** a hypothetical chemical element thought to have been detected in the solar corona whose spectrum showed a number of lines later identified as belonging to iron, nickel, and other elements highly ionized at the extreme solar temperatures

cor·o·no- *comb form* [prob. fr. F, fr. *coronal*, adj.] *anat* **:** coronal and ⟨ *coronobasilar*⟩ ⟨*corono*facial⟩

cor·o·no·frontal \ˌkȯrəˌnō, kəˈrō(ˌ)nō +\ *adj* **:** of or relating to the forehead and crown of the head

coronograph *var of* CORONAGRAPH

cor·o·noid \ˈkȯrəˌnȯid\ *adj* [ISV *coron-* (fr. Gk *korōnē* coronoid process, anything curved) + -*oid*] **:** of, relating to, or indicating the coronoid process or coronoid fossa ⟨~ teeth⟩

coronoid fossa *n* **:** a depression of the humerus into which the coronoid process fits when the arm is flexed

coronoid process *n* **1 :** the anterior process of the superior border of the ramus of the mandible **2 :** a flared process of the lower anterior part of the upper articular surface of the ulna fitting into the coronoid fossa when the arm is flexed

co·ron·o·pus \kəˈränəpəs, -rōn-\ *n, cap* [NL, fr. Gk *korōnopous* hartshorn plantain, fr. *korōno-* (fr. *korōnē* crow) + *pous* foot — more at FOOT] **:** a small genus of widely distributed ill-smelling herbs (family Cruciferae) with pinnately divided leaves and compact racemes of minute whitish flowers along the depressed stems — see SWINE CRESS

cor·o·nule \ˈkȯrəˌnyül, kəˈrō-\ *n* -s [NL *coronula*, fr. ML, fr. L *corona* crown + -*ula* -ule] **:** the peripheral ring of spines on the shells of some diatoms (as members of the genus *Stephanodiscus*)

cor·o·plast \ˈkȯrəˌplast\ *n* -s [Gk *koroplastēs*, fr. *koro-* (fr. *koros* boy, puppet) + *plastēs* molder, modeler (fr. *plassein* to form, mold) — more at CRESCENT, PLASTIC] **:** a modeler of wax or terra-cotta figurines (as of young women) of ancient Greece

co·ro·zo \kəˈrō(ˌ)sō\ *or* **co·ro·jo** \-rōˌhō\ *also* **co·ro·so** \-rō(ˌ)sō\ *n* -s [AmerSp, fr. Sp *corozo, corojo* fruit pit, fr. (assumed) VL *carudium*, fr. Gk *karydion* small nut, dim. of *karyon* nut — more at CAREEN] **1** *also* **corozo palm :** any of several tropical American palms: as **a :** IVORY PALM **b :** COHUNE PALM **c :** COYOL 1 **d :** any of several palms of the genus *Cocos* **2** *also* **corozo nut :** the seed of the ivory palm **3** *also* **corozo fiber :** a strong leaf fiber obtained from a coyol (*Acrocomia lasiospatha*) and used for making ropes

corp \ˈkȯrp\ *dial var of* CORPSE

corp *abbr* **1** corporal **2** corporation

corpora *pl of* CORPUS

[1]**cor·po·ral** \ˈkȯrp(ə)rəl, ˈkȯ(ə)p-\ *n* -s [ME *corporale*, fr. MF *corporal*, fr. ML *corporale*, fr. L, neut. of *corporalis* of the body; fr. the doctrine that the bread of the Eucharist becomes or represents the body of Christ] **:** a linen cloth on which the sacred elements are consecrated in the Eucharist or with which they are covered — called also *communion cloth*

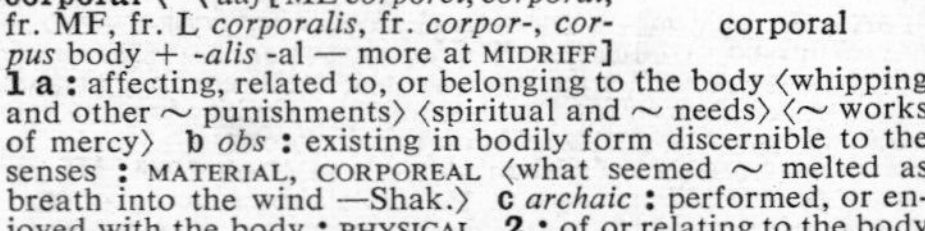
corporal

[2]**corporal** \"\ *adj* [ME *corporel, corporal*, fr. MF, fr. L *corporalis*, fr. *corpor-, corpus* body + -*alis* -al — more at MIDRIFF] **1 a :** affecting, related to, or belonging to the body ⟨whipping and other ~ punishments⟩ ⟨spiritual and ~ needs⟩ ⟨~ works of mercy⟩ **b** *obs* **:** existing in bodily form discernible to the senses **:** MATERIAL, CORPOREAL ⟨what seemed ~ melted as breath into the wind —Shak.⟩ **c** *archaic* **:** performed, or enjoyed with the body **:** PHYSICAL **2 :** of or relating to the body as distinguished from the head and limbs **syn** see BODILY

[3]**corporal** \"\ *n* -s [MF, lowest noncommissioned officer, alter. (prob. influenced by *corps* body) of *caporal*, fr. It *caporale*, fr. *capo* head, chief (after such pairs as It *tempo* time: *temporale* temporal), fr. L *caput* head — more at HEAD] **1 a :** a noncommissioned army officer just below a sergeant and above a private first class **b :** a noncommissioned marine officer just below a sergeant and above a lance corporal **2 :** a fallfish (*Semotilus corporalis*) **3 :** an assistant to a precinct police sergeant

corporal forbes \-ˈfȯrbz, -rbəs\ *n, usu cap C&F* [prob. by folk etymology] *India* **:** CHOLERA MORBUS

cor·po·ral·i·ty \ˌkȯ(r)pəˈraləd.ē\ *n* -ES [ME *corporalite*, fr. LL *corporalitas*, fr. L *corporalis* + -*itat-, -itas* -ity] **:** the quality or state of being or having a body or a material or physical existence

cor·po·ral·ly \ˈkȯ(r)p(ə)rəlē, -li\ *adv* **:** in a corporal manner

corporal major *n* [[3]*corporal*] **:** the highest noncommissioned officer in the British household cavalry; *also* **:** his office or rank

corporal oath *n* [[2]*corporal*] **:** an oath solemnized by actually touching a sacred object (as the Bible)

corporal punishment *n* [[2]*corporal*] **1 :** punishment applied to the body of an offender including the death penalty, whipping, and imprisonment **2 :** punishment administered by an adult (as a parent or a teacher) to the body of a child ranging in severity from a slap to a spanking

corporal's guard *n* [[3]*corporal*] **:** a small group of persons (as of followers or adherents) ⟨scarcely more than a *corporal's guard* of these talented men are left —S.H.Holbrook⟩

cor·po·ral·ship \ˈkȯ(r)p(ə)rəlˌship\ *n* -s [[3]*corporal* + -*ship*] **1** *obs* **:** a body of soldiers under a corporal's command **2** *or* **corporalcy** -ES [*corporalcy* fr. [3]*corporal* + -*cy*] **:** a corporal's office or position **:** the rank of corporal

corpora lutea *pl of* CORPUS LUTEUM

cor·po·ra pe·dun·cu·la·ta \ˌkȯrp(ə)rəpəˌdəŋkyəˈlād.ə, -lä-\ *n pl* [NL, lit., pedunculate bodies] **:** a pair of stalked bodies on the dorsal part of the insect forebrain believed to function as association centers

corpora quad·ri·gem·i·na \-ˌkwädrəˈjemənə\ *n pl* [NL, lit., fourfold bodies] **:** two pairs of colliculi on the dorsal surface of the midbrain composed of white matter externally and gray matter within, the superior pair containing correlation centers for optic reflexes and the inferior pair containing correlation centers for auditory reflexes

corpora striata *pl of* CORPUS STRIATUM

[1]**cor·po·rate** \ˈkȯrp(ə)rət, ˈkȯ(ə)p-, *usu* -əd.+V\ *adj* [L *corporatus*, past part. of *corporare* to make into a body, fr. *corpor-, corpus* body — more at MIDRIFF] **1 a :** formed into or forming a body by legal enactment **:** united in an association and endowed by law with the rights and liabilities of an individual **:** INCORPORATED ⟨a ~ town⟩ ⟨a new federal agency, set up in ~ form to insure state school . . . bonds —Edgar Fuller⟩ **b :** of or relating to a corporation or to corporations in general ⟨a plan to reorganize the ~ structure⟩ ⟨whether the tax should be applicable to business (particularly ~ business) as such —H.M.Groves⟩ **:** of or relating to an incorporated body ⟨the ~ powers of the municipality⟩ **2** *obs* **:** having a body **:** MATERIAL **3 a :** of or relating to a unified body made up of individuals or particulars **:** AGGREGATE ⟨the student experiences as part of his training the ~ life of the college⟩ **:** made or performed as a body or in a body rather than individually ⟨human law arises by the ~ action of a people —G.H.Sabine⟩ **b :** combined, united, or grouped together into one usu. cohesive body ⟨the yeomen . . . were a ~ society like the country gentry —Adrian Bell⟩ ⟨the immunities and good fellowship with which the Senate, as a ~ group, cushions conflicts within its own circle —Charles McKinley⟩ **c :** of or relating to the whole group as distinguished from the individual members ⟨sacrifice their individual rights for . . . the ~ good —Rebecca West⟩ **d :** consisting of two or more persons jointly responsible (as for the authoring of a novel) ⟨a ~ author⟩ **:** consisting of a group or corporation ⟨a ~ defendant⟩ ⟨a ~ person⟩ **4 :** CORPORATIVE 2 — **cor·po·rate·ly** *adv*

[2]**cor·po·rate** \ˈkȯ(r)pəˌrāt, *usu* -ād.+V\ *vt* -ED/-ING/-S [L *corporatus*] **:** INCORPORATE

corporate colony *n* **:** a charter colony (as Connecticut or Rhode Island) having a royal charter granted to the inhabitants as a corporate body

corporate county *n* **:** COUNTY 3a

corporate member *n* **:** an actual or voting member of a corporation as distinct from an associate or honorary member

corporate name *n* **:** the legal name of a corporation

cor·po·rate·ness *n* -ES **:** the quality or state of being a corporate body

corporate stock *n* **1 :** stock issued by a corporate business enterprise **2** *chiefly Brit* **:** MUNICIPAL SECURITY

corporate suretyship *or* **corporate bonding** *n* **:** the business of issuing fidelity and surety bonds engaged in by a corporation (as a casualty insurance company)

corporate trust *n* **:** a trust in which the cestui que trust is a corporation — opposed to *personal trust*

cor·po·ra·tion \ˌkȯ(r)pəˈrāshən\ *n* -s *often attrib* [ME, fr. ML *corporation-, corporatio*, fr. L *corporatus* + -*ion-, -io* -ion] **1 :** a body of persons associated for some purpose (as standardization of conditions): as **a** *obs* **:** a group of merchants or traders united in an association **:** a trade guild **b :** the body of municipal authorities of a town or city ⟨the *Corporation* of the City of London⟩ **2** *Roman & civil law* **a :** a group of persons or objects treated by the law as an individual or unity having rights or liabilities distinct from those of the persons or objects composing it **:** UNIVERSITY — called also *body corporate* **b :** a single person or object treated by the law as having a legal individuality or entity other than that of a natural person **:** ARTIFICIAL PERSON **3** *or* **corporation aggregate** *English & US common & statute law* **:** a body formed and authorized by law to act as a single person and endowed by law with the capacity of succession **:** an entity recognized by law as constituted by one or more persons and as having various rights and duties together with the capacity of succession ⟨a ~ is an artificial being, invisible, intangible, and existing only in contemplation of law —John Marshall⟩ — see COMPANY 3, ECCLESIASTICAL CORPORATION, MUNICIPAL CORPORATION, PRIVATE CORPORATION, PUBLIC CORPORATION, PUBLIC SERVICE CORPORATION, QUASI CORPORATION **4 :** the area governed by a municipal corporation ⟨within the ~ limits of Chicago⟩ **5 :** an association of employers and employees in a basic industry or of members of a profession organized as an organ of political representation in a corporative state and responsible for supervision and control of production, wages, working conditions, and all matters pertaining to that industry or profession — see CORPORATISM **6 :** a fat or protuberant belly **:** POTBELLY

cor·po·ra·tion·al \ˌkȯ(r)pəˈrāshənᵊl, -shnəl\ *adj* **:** of or relating to a corporation

corporation cock *or* **corporation stop** *n* **:** a water or gas cock by means of which utility-company employees connect or disconnect service lines to a consumer

corporation lawyer *n* **:** an attorney who specializes in cases that involve the law as it pertains to corporations **:** one whose practice is confined to the legal affairs of a corporation

corporation life insurance *n* **:** life insurance purchased by a corporation on the lives of officers, employees, or principal stockholders and of which the corporation is the beneficiary

corporation sole *n* **:** a corporation consisting of only one person; *esp* **:** ECCLESIASTICAL CORPORATION

corporation stock *n, chiefly Brit* **:** MUNICIPAL SECURITY

cor·po·rat·ism *or* **cor·po·ra·tiv·ism** *pronunciations at* [1]CORPORATE & CORPORATIVE + ˌizəm\ *n* -s **:** a system or principle in which a whole society is organized into industrial and professional corporations serving as organs of political representation and controlling to a large extent the persons and activities within their jurisdiction with emphasis on labor-management cooperation ⟨the *corporativism* of Fascist Italy —A.J.Bruwer⟩

cor·po·rat·ist *pronunc at* [1]CORPORATE + əst\ *adj* **:** based upon or favoring corporatism ⟨~ doctrines⟩

cor·po·ra·tive \ˈkȯ(r)pəˌrād.iv, ˈkȯ(r)p(ə)rəd.-, -ət|, -ət|, |ēv *also* |əv\ *adj* [[1]*corporate* + -*ive*] **1 :** of, relating to, or consisting of a corporation **2 :** based on, organized according to, or favoring the principles of corporatism **:** CORPORATE ⟨a ~ state⟩ ⟨a ~ government⟩ ⟨a ~ parliament⟩

cor·po·ra·tor \ˈkȯ(r)pəˌrād.ə(r), -ātə-\ *n* -s [[2]*corporate* + -*or*] **1 :** a corporation member (as an official of a municipal corporation) **:** a corporation stockholder **2 :** INCORPORATOR a

corpora vilia *pl of* CORPUS VILE

cor·po·re·al \(ˈ)kȯ(r)ˈpōrēəl, -pȯr-\ *adj* [L *corpore*us of the body (fr. *corpor-, corpus* body) + E -*al* — more at MIDRIFF] **1 :** having, consisting of, or relating to a physical material body: as **a :** not spiritual ⟨some few traces of a diviner nature which look out through his ~ baseness —Robert Browning⟩ **b :** not immaterial or intangible **:** SUBSTANTIAL ⟨that which is created is of necessity ~ and visible and tangible —Benjamin Jowett⟩ **2** *archaic* **:** of, relating to, or affecting the human body **:** CORPORAL **3 :** tangible and palpable **:** not insubstantial **:** MATERIAL ⟨~ property⟩ ⟨~ hereditaments, mainly land and large savings⟩ **syn** see BODILY, MATERIAL

cor·po·re·al·ist \=ˈ===əst\ *n* -s **:** MATERIALIST

cor·po·re·al·i·ty \(ˌ)=ˌ==ˈaləd.ē\ *n* -ES **:** the quality or state of being corporeal **:** corporeal existence

cor·po·re·al·ize \=ˈ==əˌlīz\ *vt* -ED/-ING/-s **:** to make corporeal

cor·po·re·al·ly \(ˈ)kȯ(r)ˈpōrēəlē, -pȯr-, -li\ *adv* **:** in a corporeal manner **:** in the body

cor·po·re·als \=ˈ==əlz\ *n pl* **1 :** material things **2** *law* **:** corporeal property

cor·po·re·i·ty \ˌkȯ(r)pəˈrēəd.ē\ *n* -ES [ML *corporeitat-, corporeitas*, fr. L *corporeus* corporeal + -*itat-, -itas* -ity] **:** the quality or state of having or being a body **:** the state of being corporeal **:** physical nature **:** MATERIALITY

cor·por·i·fy \kȯ(r)ˈpȯrəˌfī\ *vt* -ED/-ING/-ES [L *corpor-, corpus* body + E -*ify*] **:** to form into a body **:** EMBODY, INCORPORATE, SOLIDIFY

cor·po·sant \ˈkȯ(r)pəˌsant *also* -ˌza-\ *n* -s [Pg *corpo-santo*, lit., holy body, fr. *corpo* body (fr. L *corpus*) + *santo* holy, fr. L *sanctus* — more at SAINT] **:** SAINT ELMO'S FIRE

corps \ˈkō(ə)r|, -ō(ə)r|, -ȯ(ə)r|, -ȯ(ə)|\ *n, pl* **corps** \|z\ [F, fr. L *corpus* body] **1 a :** an organized subdivision of the military establishment ⟨the Marine *Corps*⟩ ⟨the Ordnance *Corps*⟩ **b :** a tactical unit usu. consisting of two or more divisions and auxiliary arms and services **c** (1) **:** a local unit of the Salvation Army that administers a Salvation Army center (2) **:** such a center established for the propagation of the Gospel and the administration of welfare services **2 a :** a body of persons associated together or acting under common direction ⟨his ~ of laborers⟩ **b :** a body of persons having a common activity or occupation ⟨a ~ of trained lifeguards⟩ ⟨the press ~⟩ ⟨the English . . . succeeded in building up a remarkable public service ~ —C.J.Friedrich⟩ **c :** an association of German university students binding its members to strict adherence to certain customs and a fixed code of honor **3 :** CORPS DE BALLET

corps area *n* **:** a territorial division of the U.S. for purposes of administration and training of the army

corps·bru·der \ˈkōrˌbrüdər, ˈkȯr-\ *n, pl* **corpsbruders** \-ərz\ *or* **corps·brü·der** \-ˌbrüdər\ [G *korpsbruder*, fr. *korps* corps (fr. F *corps*) + *bruder* brother, fr. OHG *bruoder* — more at BROTHER] **1 :** a comrade in a German student corps **2 :** a close comrade

corps de bal·let \ˌkōrdə(ˌ)baˈlā, ˌkȯr-\ *n, pl* **corps de ballet** \"\ [F] **:** the ensemble or chorus of a ballet company as distinguished from soloists and principals

corps d'elite \-dāˈlēt\ *n, pl* **corps d'elite** \"\ [F *corps d'élite*] **1 :** a body of picked troops **2 :** a group of the best men of any category ⟨thirteen reporters — the *corps d'elite* of a great newspaper —*N.Y. Herald Tribune*⟩

corps di·plo·ma·tique \ˌ=ˌdipləˌmaˈtēk\ *n, pl* **corps diplomatique** \"\ [F] **:** the body of diplomatic officers accredited to a government

[1]**corpse** \ˈkȯ(ə)rps, -ȯ(ə)ps\ *n* -s [ME *corps*, fr. MF, fr. L *corpus* — more at MIDRIFF] **1** *obs* **:** a human or animal body whether living or dead **2 a :** a dead body esp. of a human being **b :** something that has been forgotten or discarded or that is no longer active, vital, or effective ⟨it was an awful thing to look at the ~ of a city . . . that once had been so beautiful and gay —*Nat'l Geographic*⟩ **3** *obs* **:** the main portion or substance **:** the collective whole **:** BODY ⟨one . . . uniform ~ of law —Francis Bacon⟩ **4 :** an endowment belonging to a prebend or other ecclesiastical office

[2]**corpse** \"\ *vt* -ED/-ING/-s **1** *dial Brit* **:** KILL **2 :** to confuse (an actor) in performance **:** spoil (an actor's speech or a scene) by cutting in or by blundering

corpse candle *n* **:** a luminous appearance resembling the flame of a candle sometimes seen in churchyards and thought to presage someone's death

corpse plant *also* **corpse light** *n* **:** INDIAN PIPE

corps·man \ˈkōr(z)mən, ˈkȯr-\ *n, pl* **corpsmen :** HOSPITAL CORPSMAN

corps of cadets : a body of cadets under instruction and military discipline and control at a school, college, or service academy

corps troops *n pl* **:** troops assigned or attached to a corps but not part of one of the divisions in the corps

corpsy \ˈkȯrpsē\ *adj* -ER/-EST [[1]*corpse* + -*y*] **:** like or suggesting a corpse ⟨a cool ~ smell —Christopher Morley⟩ ⟨looking a bit ~⟩

cor·pu·lence \ˈkȯ(r)pyələn(t)s\ *n* -s [MF *corpulence*, fr. L *corpulentia*, fr. *corpulentus* + -*ia*] **:** bulkiness of body; *usu* **:** excessive fatness **:** FLESHINESS, OBESITY

cor·pu·len·cy \-nsē, -si\ *n* -ES [L *corpulentia*] **:** CORPULENCE

cor·pu·lent \-nt\ *adj* [ME, fr. L *corpulentus*, fr. *corpus* body + -*ulentus* -ulent] **1 :** having a large bulky body **:** fat and heavy **:** OBESE ⟨a ~ giant, over six feet in height, and . . . as big round as a hogshead —Herman Melville⟩ **:** LARGE, MASSIVE ⟨his money belt was . . . ~ —Elinor Wylie⟩ **2** *archaic* **:** CORPOREAL, MATERIAL **syn** see FAT

cor·pu·lent·ly *adv* **:** in a corpulent manner ⟨a ~ constructed man⟩

cor·pu·lent·ness *n* -ES **:** CORPULENCE

cor pul·mo·na·le \ˌkȯrˌpu̇lməˈnalˌ(ˌ)lē, -ˌpəl-, -nā-ˌ -nä-\ *n, pl* **cor·dia pulmona·lia** \ˈkȯrdēəˌp...|ˌlēə\ [NL, lit., pulmonary heart] **:** heart disease secondary to disease of the lungs or their blood vessels **:** pulmonary heart disease

cor·pus \ˈkȯrpəs, -ȯəp-\ *n, pl* **corpo·ra** \-p(ə)rə\ [ME, fr. L] **1 :** the body of a man or animal esp. when dead **2 a :** the main part or body of a structure or organ ⟨the ~ of the jaw⟩ ⟨the ~ of the uterus⟩ **b :** the main body or corporeal substance of a thing; *specif* **:** the principal of a fund or estate as distinct from income or interest **c :** the main body, the substance, or the essential element of a thing ⟨a ferocious metaphysical dispute. The ~ of the dispute was a squirrel —William James⟩ **3 a :** the whole body or total amount of writings of a particular kind or on a particular subject (as the total production of a writer or the whole literature of a subject) ⟨the Dickens ~⟩ ⟨judging the ~ of American literature in the light of these standards —C.I.Glicksberg⟩ **b :** a collection or body esp. of knowledge or evidence ⟨a sizable ~ of opinion⟩; *specif* **:** the collection of recorded utterances that is used as a basis for the descriptive analysis of a language or dialect **4** *in the tunica-corpus theory* **:** the inner of the two growth regions into which the apical meristem is considered divisible consisting of a core of cells which divide at various angles and provide for increase in bulk

corpus al·bi·cans \-ˈalbəˌkanz\ *n, pl* **corpora albican·tia** \-ˌalbəˈkanchēə\ [NL, lit., whitish body] **1 :** MAMMILLARY BODY **2 :** the white fibrous scar remaining in the ovary after resorption of the corpus luteum that replaces a discharged Graafian follicle

corpus cal·lo·sum \-(ˌ)kaˈlōsəm, -kəˈl-\ *n, pl* **corpora callo·sa** \-sə\ [NL, lit., callous body] **:** the great band of commissural fibers uniting the cerebral hemispheres in man and in the higher mammals — see BRAIN illustration

corpus ca·ver·no·sum \-ˌkavərˈnōsəm\ *n, pl* **corpora caverno·sa** \-sə\ [NL, cavernous body] **:** a mass of erectile tissue with large interspaces capable of being distended with blood; *esp* **:** one of those that form the bulk of the body of the penis or of the clitoris

[1]**corpus christi** \ˌkȯrpəˈskristē\ *n, pl* **corpus christis** *usu cap both Cs* [ME. fr. ML, lit., body of Christ] **:** a Roman Catholic festival in honor of the Eucharist observed on the Thursday after Trinity Sunday

[2]**corpus christi** \"\ *adj, usu cap both Cs* [fr. *Corpus Christi*, city of Texas] **:** of or from the city of Corpus Christi, Texas ⟨*Corpus Christi* refineries⟩ **:** of the kind or style prevalent in Corpus Christi

cor·pus·cle \ˈkȯ(r)ˌpəsəl *also* -ˌp-\ *n* -s [L *corpusculum*, dim. of *corpus* body] **1 :** a minute or elementary particle; *specif* **:** ELECTRON **2 a :** a living cell; *usu* **:** one that is somewhat isolated and not aggregated into continuous tissues (as red and white blood cells or cells isolated in the matrix of cartilage or bone) — compare BLOOD, LYMPH **b :** any of various small circumscribed bodies composed of many cells — usu. used with a qualifying term ⟨the tactile ~*s*⟩ ⟨Malpighian ~*s*⟩

corpuscle of has·sall *or* **corpuscle of has·sal** \-ˈhasəl\ *usu cap H* [after Arthur H. Hassall †1894 Eng. physician] **:** one of the small usu. concentrically striated bodies in the thymus body representing remains of the epithelial tissue found in early stages of development

corpuscle of herbst \-ˈhe(ə)rpst\ *usu cap H* [trans. of G *herbstsches körperchen*, after Ernst F. Herbst †1893 Ger. physician] **:** any of certain tactile organs found in birds related to Pacinian corpuscles

corpuscle of krause *usu cap K* **:** KRAUSE'S CORPUSCLE

corpuscle of meissner *usu cap M* **:** MEISSNER'S CORPUSCLE

corpuscle of the spleen : MALPIGHIAN CORPUSCLE 2

corpuscle of va·ter \-ˈfätər\ *usu cap V* [trans. of G *vatersches körperchen*, after Abraham *Vater* †1751 Ger. anatomist] **:** PACINIAN CORPUSCLE

cor·pus·cu·lar \(ˈ)kȯ(r)ˈpəskyələ(r)\ *adj* [L *corpusculum* + E -*ar*] **:** relating to, dealing with, or composed of corpuscles

corpuscular philosophy *n* **:** the philosophy that attempts to account for the phenomena of nature by the characteristics (as motion, figure, rest, position) of minute particles of matter

corpuscular theory *n* **:** a theory in physics: light consists of material particles sent off in all directions from luminous bodies

cor·pus·cu·lat·ed \-ˌlād·əd\ *adj* [L *corpuscul*um + E *-ate* + *-ed*] **:** furnished with or containing corpuscles

cor·pus·cule \kȯ(r)ˈpəˌskyül\ *n* -s [F *corpuscule*, fr. L *corpusculum*] **:** CORPUSCLE

cor·pus·cu·lum \kȯ(r)ˈpəskyələm\ *n, pl* **corpuscu·la** \-lə\ [L] **:** CORPUSCLE

corpus de·lic·ti \-dəˈlikˌtī, -k(ˌ)tē\ *n, pl* **corpora delicti** [NL, lit., body of the crime] **1 :** the substantial and fundamental fact or facts (as, in murder, actual death and its occurrence as a result of criminal agency) necessary to prove the commission of a crime **2 :** the material substance (as the body of the victim of a murder) upon which a crime has been committed

corpus ju·ris \-ˈju̇rəs\ *n, pl* **corpora juris** [LL] **:** a body of law **:** a comprehensive collection of the law of a country or jurisdiction

corpus lu·te·um \-ˈlüd·ēəm\ *n, pl* **corpora lu·tea** \-ēə\ [NL, lit., yellowish body] **1 :** a reddish yellow endocrine body consisting of pale secretory cells derived from granulosa cells and filling the cavity of a Graafian follicle following discharge of the ovum and regressing rather quickly if the ovum is not fertilized but persisting throughout the ensuing pregnancy if it is fertilized **2 :** the fresh substance of the corpora lutea of the hog or cow dried and powdered and used in the treatment of conditions due to ovarian dysfunction

corpus stri·a·tum \-ˌstrīˈād·əm\ *n, pl* **corpora stria·ta** \-d·ə\ [NL, lit., striated body] **:** either of a pair of masses of nervous tissue beneath and external to the anterior cornua of the lateral ventricles of the brain and forming part of their floor, each mass containing two large nuclei of gray matter that are separated by sheets of white matter to give the mass a striated appearance in section

corpus vi·le \-ˈvī(ˌ)lē\ *n, pl* **corpora vil·ia** \-ˈvilēə\ [NL, lit., worthless body] **:** something felt to be of so little value that it may be experimented with or upon without concern for loss or damage ⟨literature may come to be used as a *corpus vile* for acute dons to sharpen their wits upon —*Times Lit. Supp.*⟩

corr *abbr* — see COR

cor·rade \kəˈrād, kȯˈ-\ *vb* -ED/-ING/-S [L *corradere* to scrape together, fr. *com-* + *radere* to scrape — more at RASE] *vt* **:** to wear away by abrasion ⟨a stream ~*s* its banks⟩ **~** *vi* **:** to crumble away through abrasion

1**cor·ral** \kəˈral, kȯˈ-\ *n* -s [Sp, fr. (assumed) VL *currale* enclosure for vehicles, fr. L *currus* cart, fr. *currere* to run — more at CURRENT] **1 a :** a pen or enclosure for confining or capturing livestock **b :** an enclosure that resembles a corral ⟨spectators were held in a roped-off ~ until they could be seated⟩ **c :** a fish trap resembling a corral in shape **2 :** an enclosure made with wagons as a place of defense for an encampment

2**corral** \"\ *vb* **corralled; corralled; corralling; corrals** *vt* **1 :** to enclose in a corral or similar pen or yard **:** round up (as cattle) and drive into a corral **2 :** to arrange (wagons) so as to form a corral **3 a :** to get hold of, get control over, catch, or gather up (something wandering or elusive) **:** get possession of ⟨~ a new desk for his secretary⟩ ⟨taxi drivers *corralling* customers for a hotel⟩ ⟨the winning candidate is the man who can ~ the most votes⟩ **b :** to bring together in one place ⟨~ all the passengers in the lounge⟩ **:** restrict to a particular place ⟨reporters *corralled* the congressman in a corner of the lobby⟩ **:** restrict the movement of ⟨boys quickly *corralled* a small brush fire and put it out⟩ **~** *vi* **:** to form a protective corral around an encampment ⟨the train probably would ~ by alternate wagons, the first wagon turning right, the second left . . . until the circle was formed —W.F.Harris⟩ **syn** see ENCLOSE

cor·ra·sion \kəˈrāzhən, kȯˈ-\ *n* -s [ISV *corras-* (fr. L *corrasus*, past part. of *corradere*) + *-ion*] **:** the wearing away of rocks and soil by the abrasive action of material moved along by wind, waves, streams, or glaciers **:** one of the several processes of erosion

cor·ra·sive \-āsiv, -āziv\ *adj* [ISV *corras-* (fr. L *corrasus*) + *-ive*] **:** producing or tending to produce corrasion

cor·rea \kəˈrēə, -rāə\ *n* [NL, after José F. *Correa* da Serra †1823 Port. statesman and botanist] **1** *cap* **:** a small genus of Australian shrubs (family Rutaceae) most of which have tubular scarlet, yellow, or white flowers **2** -s **:** any plant of the genus *Correa* — called also *native fuchsia*

cor·re·al \(ˈ)kȯ¦rē(ə)l, ˈkȯrē-\ *adj* [LL *correus* joint criminal (fr. L *com-* + *reus* accused person, prob. fr. *res* lawsuit, thing) + E *-al* — more at REAL] *civil law* **:** having or constituting a joint obligation or right that may be enforced in full against any one of several joint debtors or by any one of several joint creditors against a single debtor

cor·re·al·i·ty \ˌkȯrēˈaləd·ē\ *n* -ES **:** the quality or state of being correal

1**cor·rect** \kəˈrekt, *rap.* ˈkre-\ *vb*-ED/-ING/-S [ME *correcten*, fr. L *correctus*, past part. of *corrigere* to make straight, correct, fr. *com-* + *-rigere* (fr. *regere* to lead straight, guide, rule) — more at RIGHT] *vt* **1 a :** to make or set right **:** remove the faults or errors from **:** AMEND ⟨~ some of the mistaken ideas about farming —C.R.Hope⟩ ⟨his answer was wrong and he at once ~*ed* himself⟩ ⟨legislative action designed to ~ existing difficulties —*U. S. Code*⟩ ⟨~ abuses in the city prison⟩ **b :** to counteract or neutralize by means of opposite qualities or tendencies — used esp. of what is undesirable ⟨the good philosopher was leaning a little in the other direction to ~ the excess of my hellenizing zeal —A.N.Whitehead⟩ **c :** to alter or adjust so as to bring to some standard or required condition ⟨~ a reading of a gas volume for temperature and pressure⟩ ⟨~ a lens for spherical aberration⟩ ⟨~ the timing in a motor⟩ **2 a :** to rebuke or to punish or discipline for some fault or lapse (as from propriety) ⟨the older woman ~*ed* the man for taking liberties⟩ **b :** to point out for amendment the errors or faults of ⟨the student had to be ~*ed* several times during her recitation⟩ ⟨~ proof by indicating the changes to be made in type⟩ ⟨a teacher ~*s* examination papers⟩ **3** *obs* **:** to bring order to **:** TAME **~** *vi* **:** to make corrections

syn RECTIFY, EMEND, REMEDY, REDRESS, AMEND, REFORM, REVISE: these verbs mean, in common, to right what is wrong. One CORRECTS something by altering what is inaccurate, untrue, or imperfect in it or about it so that it is accurate, true, or perfect, or by putting against it or substituting for it what is accurate, true, or perfect ⟨to *correct* a false accusation⟩ ⟨to *correct* a wrong address on a package⟩ ⟨to *correct* a serious fault of character⟩ ⟨to *correct* spelling errors⟩ One RECTIFIES a mistake or an injustice or a deviation from a standard by the elimination or nullification of the mistake or injustice or by making the deviation conform to the standard ⟨an incredible, disgraceful blunder, which should be *rectified* at the earliest possible moment —*New Republic*⟩ ⟨to have exploited, rather than tried to *rectify* . . . misunderstandings —*Times Lit. Supp.*⟩ ⟨set himself to *rectify* the spiritual and physical poverty of his people — Green Peyton⟩ One EMENDS by freeing from error or defect, esp. a statement that misrepresents a speaker's intention or a piece of writing that contains doubtful readings ⟨to *emend* a financial report hastily and inaccurately compiled⟩ ⟨to *emend* a transcription of an ancient religious scroll⟩ One REMEDIES a cause of trouble, harm, or evil by rendering it innocuous or substituting for it what is good, right, or helpful ⟨the crime can never be *remedied*, it can only be expiated —C.D.Lewis⟩ ⟨done much to *remedy* the confusion —*Amer. Guide Series: Vt.*⟩ ⟨must *remedy* their deficiencies —*Loyola Univ. Bull.*⟩ One REDRESSES an unfairness, injustice, or imbalance sometimes by elimination of it but usu. by making a reparation or providing compensation ⟨trying to *redress* the serious dislocations resulting from . . . bad policies —E.B. George⟩ ⟨to *redress* the imbalance in American politics —M.W.Straight⟩ ⟨the wrongs that were to be righted, the grievances to be *redressed*, the abuses to be done away with —Malcolm Muggeridge⟩ ⟨the *redress* of certain social inequities —W.R.Inge⟩ One AMENDS something by making such corrections or alterations as will better it ⟨to *amend* her life⟩ ⟨the work once done he could not or would not *amend* it —W.B.Yeats⟩ ⟨to *amend* local traffic regulations⟩ One REFORMS something by making drastic alterations for the better, usu. so that it acquires a new form or character ⟨to *reform* an inefficient administrative system⟩ ⟨*reformed* the rules of procedure of the mayor's court —M.L.Bonham⟩ ⟨to *reform* sloppy habits of study⟩ One REVISES something when he makes changes that presumably improve it without drastically altering the character of the whole, usu. after looking it over carefully ⟨to *revise* a manuscript story⟩ ⟨to *revise* his opinions⟩ ⟨to *revise* a business organization⟩ **syn** see in addition PUNISH

2**correct** \"\ *adj, sometimes* -ER/-EST [ME, corrected, fr. L *correctus*] **1 :** adhering or conforming to an approved or conventional standard: as **a** *of literary or artistic style* **:** conforming to recognized conventions or an established mode ⟨a ~ Palladian portico⟩ **b :** suiting or conforming to conventionally recognized principles of thought, behavior, or taste ⟨the ~ tip is sixpence —Richard Joseph⟩ ⟨Soviet criticism . . . tried to rule on the attitude of the author as ~ or incorrect —Edmund Wilson⟩ **c :** scrupulously in accord with social proprieties ⟨rebuffed or evaded with dry ~ civilities —John Hurkan⟩ **:** placing high value on propriety ⟨a careful and ~ young man⟩ **d** *of speech or writing* **:** conforming to the generally accepted rules of grammar or to what is regarded as the best usage **2 a :** conforming to or agreeing with fact **:** ACCURATE ⟨have a ~ answer to the problem⟩ **:** conforming to logical or proven principles or agreeing with known truth ⟨it would be ~ to call it the best possible treaty⟩ ⟨the ~ way to hold the tool⟩ **b** *of a copy or reproduction* **:** free from errors **:** identical in relevant characteristics **:** EXACT **3 :** conforming to or agreeing with a set figure (as the price established for an article of merchandise) ⟨sent the ~ return postage⟩

syn ACCURATE, EXACT, PRECISE, NICE, RIGHT: CORRECT means hardly more than freedom from fault or error, often as judged by some conventional or acknowledged standard ⟨it is our custom at Shangri-La to be moderately truthful, and I can assure you that my statements about the porters were almost *correct* —James Hilton⟩ ⟨the more *correct* social circles of Boston and Cambridge —Florence H. Bullock⟩ ACCURATE implies positive and careful fidelity to fact or truth ⟨the phrases are good enough for statesmen, who identify order with orders and creation with regulations, but the poet-writer must be more *accurate* than that —E.M.Forster⟩ ⟨a solecism of this kind . . . would have seemed a shocking thing to . . . so *accurate* a scholar —L.P.Smith⟩ EXACT, sometimes interchangeable with PRECISE, generally emphasizes the strictness of the agreement or conformity with fact, standard, or truth ⟨not less than a hundred and thirty feet surely . . . a hundred and twenty-eight, to be *exact* —Dorothy Sayers⟩ ⟨sciences are not vague. On the contrary they are *exact*. They are based on fact, proven fact —T.B.Costain⟩ PRECISE carries the idea of sharpness of definition or delimitation or scrupulous exactness ⟨I saw the outside of the note, addressed in straggling, irregular characters, very unlike Holmes' usual *precise* hand —A. C. Doyle⟩ ⟨only an endlessly patient, careful, laborious, *precise* investigator could set up the new revolutionary conceptions needed to replace these traditions and preconceptions —Havelock Ellis⟩ NICE, in the sense pertinent here, implies great, sometimes excessive, precision or delicacy as in discrimination of terms, or the adjustment of interrelated parts ⟨the small provincial gentry of the West, as drawn by Miss Austen . . . are *nice* in their gentility almost to a fault —G.M.Trevelyan⟩ ⟨it was a time of revolution, when *nice* legal distinctions are meaningless —John Buchan⟩ ⟨the detail of the cornices, the delicate fanlight and *nice* disposition of carved ornament on the white exterior —*Amer. Guide Series: Vt.*⟩ RIGHT, very close in meaning to CORRECT, has a more positive suggestion, often implying more than mere avoidance of error ⟨the *right* practice of "art for art's sake" was the devotion of Flaubert or Henry James —T.S.Eliot⟩ ⟨where water from wells has just that *right* degree of permanent hardness to favor brewing —L.D.Stamp⟩ **—correct in the mouth** *Brit, of sheep* **:** having the full adult complement of permanent teeth

cor·rect·able \-təbəl\ *adj* **:** capable of being corrected

cor·rec·tant \kəˈrektənt\ *n* -s [1*correct* + *-ant*] **:** CORRECTIVE

corrected *past of* CORRECT

corrected establishment *n* [*corrected* fr. past part. of *correct*] **:** the mean of all high-water lunitidal intervals for at least a month used in navigation to find the approximate time of high water by adding it to the time of the moon's upper transit as shown in the nautical almanac

corrected grain *n* **:** leather that has been lightly buffed or skived to remove grain defects

corrected time *n* **:** a ship's elapsed time less her time allowance in yacht racing

correcting *pres part of* CORRECT

cor·rect·ing·ly *adv* **:** in a correcting manner

cor·rec·tion \kəˈrekshən, *rapid* ˈkre-\ *n* -s [ME *correccion*, fr. MF *correction*, fr. L *correction-*, *correctio*, fr. *correctus* (past part. of *corrigere* to make straight, correct) + *-ion-*, *-io* -ion — more at CORRECT] **1 :** the action or an instance of correcting: as **a :** the action or an instance of remedying or removing error or defect **:** AMENDMENT, RECTIFICATION ⟨the ~ of stream pollution by the treatment of sewage⟩ ⟨~ of inaccuracies in accounting⟩ **b :** the act or an instance of calling attention to, reproving, or punishing faults or deviations from propriety or rectitude **:** REBUKE ⟨kept an iron potlid by him as a projectile for the ~ of Mrs. Cruncher in case he should observe any symptoms of her saying grace —Charles Dickens⟩ **c :** the action or an instance of making that right which was wrong or of bringing into conformity with a standard ⟨the ~ of injustice⟩ ⟨small frontier ~*s* were made by the conference of nations⟩ **d :** the action or an instance of counteracting or neutralizing something harmful or undesirable ⟨~ of acidity⟩ ⟨~ of visual defects with eyeglasses⟩ **e :** the action or an instance of adjusting or altering so as to produce a particular condition or result ⟨~ of photographic lenses⟩ **f :** a reversal of an exaggerated trend in a market or industry; *esp* **:** a decline in market price or in business activity following a protracted sharp rise **2 a :** something that is or should be substituted in place of what is wrong ⟨mark ~*s* on an examination paper⟩; *specif* **:** an indication on a proof of a change to be made by the printer **b :** a quantity applied by way of correcting (as for inaccuracy in an instrument or of its adjustment); *specif* **:** the quantity that must be algebraically added to the result of a measurement to obtain the correct value — compare ERROR 5 **3 :** the treatment of offenders through a program involving penal custody, parole, and probation ⟨disabilities from which the field of ~ has suffered —*Yale Law Jour.*⟩ ⟨two prison wards under the *Correction* Department —*N.Y. Times*⟩ — often used in pl. ⟨training in the techniques of casework, probation and parole, and the general field of ~*s* —L.J. Sharp⟩ ⟨the ~*s* worker who has the interest and courage to look at his own work objectively —C.C.Scott⟩ — **under correction :** subject to correction ⟨I am speaking *under correction*, for only the editors know . . . how much . . . were usable —H.L.Savage⟩

cor·rec·tion·al \-shənᵊl,-shnəl\ *adj* **:** of or relating to correction; *esp* **:** dealing with or charged with the administration of corrections **:** concerned with or providing corrections ⟨a ~ court⟩ ⟨a ~ institution⟩ ⟨a ~ probation service was instituted⟩

correction line *n* **:** one of a set of parallels of latitude 24 miles apart that is used for laying out nominally square sections and townships in the public land survey

cor·rec·ti·tude \-təˌtüd,-tə·ˌtyüd\ *n* -s [blend of 2*correct* and *rectitude*] **:** correctness or propriety of conduct

1**cor·rec·tive** \kəˈrektiv, -tēv *also* -təv; *rapid* ˈkre-\ *adj* [MF *correctif*, fr. ML *correctivus*, fr. L *correctus* + *-ivus* -ive] **:** tending to correct ⟨~ lenses⟩ ⟨~ punishment⟩ **:** having the power or property of correcting, counteracting, or restoring to a normal condition ⟨~ exercises⟩ **:** CORRECTIONAL — **cor·rec·tive·ly** \-tə̇vlē, -li\ *adv* — **cor·rec·tive·ness** \-tivnə̇s, -tēv- *also* -təv-\ *n* -ES

2**corrective** \"\ *n* -s **1 :** something that corrects **:** a corrective agent ⟨uses criticism as a ~ of abuses⟩ ⟨phenobarbital is a ~ of ephedrine⟩ **:** REMEDY ⟨his speech was a timely ~ for national complacency⟩ **2** *obs* **:** a change that corrects

corrective justice *n* **:** RETRIBUTIVE JUSTICE

cor·rect·ly *adv* **:** in a correct manner

cor·rect·ness *n* -ES **:** the quality or state of being correct

cor·rec·tor \-tə(r)\ *n* -s [ME *correctour*, fr. MF *correcteur*, fr. L *corrector*, fr. *correctus* + *-or*] **1 :** one that corrects ⟨a ~ of abuses⟩ ⟨time is a great ~ of taste⟩ ⟨hire someone to be a ~ of incoming manuscripts⟩ **2** *or* **corrector of the press** *Brit* **:** PROOFREADER

corrects *pres 3d sing of* CORRECT

cor·reg·i·dor \kəˈregəˌdȯ(ə)r, *or as Sp*\ *n, pl* **corregidors** \-rz\ *or* **corregido·res** \kəˌregəˈdōrēz, *or as Sp*\ [Sp, corrector, magistrate, fr. *corregir* to correct, fr. L *corrigere*] **:** a Spanish magistrate; *esp* **:** the chief magistrate or governor of a town in Spain or the Spanish colonies

1**cor·re·late** \ˈkȯrəˌlāt, ˈkär-, *usu* -ād·+V\ *n* -s [back-formation fr. *correlative* & *correlation*] **1 :** either of two things so related that one directly implies or is complementary to the other (as husband and wife) **2 :** one of two related things viewed in terms of its relationship to the other **:** CORRELATIVE ⟨expressing himself in . . . works of art that are the objective ~ of his inner emotional tensions —Herbert Read⟩ **3 :** a phenomenon that accompanies another, usu. also paralleling it (as in form, type, development, or distribution) and being related in some way to it ⟨the tribal division coincides with geographic features and has a linguistic ~⟩

2**correlate** \" *sometimes* ˌ==ˈ=\ *vb* -ED/-ING/-S *vi* **:** to bear reciprocal or mutual relations ⟨doctrine and worship ~ as theory and practice —E.B.Tylor⟩ **~** *vt* **1 :** to establish a definite stratigraphic relationship between ⟨~ the faunas or formations of two areas⟩ **2 a :** to establish a mutual or reciprocal relation of ⟨non-science and nonsense are nearly synonymous to many who highly ~ science and sense —Harlow Shapley⟩ **:** relate as necessary or invariable accompaniments with or without the implication of causality ⟨~ emotional states with physiological changes⟩ **b :** to determine, establish, or show a usu. causal relationship between ⟨~ their environment with the health of the children —*Times Lit. Supp.*⟩ **3 :** to establish a one-to-one correspondence of (two sets or series of things) **:** relate so that to each member of one set or series a corresponding member of another is assigned ⟨the scores made by high school juniors . . . on seven standard . . . tests were *correlated* with teachers' ratings of those pupils on dramatic talent —*Quarterly Jour. of Speech*⟩ **4 a :** to put in relation with each other **:** connect systematically **:** present or set forth so as to show relationship ⟨he ~*s* the findings of the scientists, the psychologists, and the mystics —Eugene Exman⟩ **b :** to bring into complementary relationship with each other **:** organize so as to advance effectively a common program ⟨~ the activities of the college and the . . . organizations for rural improvement —*Amer. Guide Series: Mich.*⟩

3**correlate** \ˈ==ˌ=\ *adj* **1 :** CORRELATED **2** *geol* **:** belonging to the same stratigraphic horizon ⟨~ strata⟩

correlated *adj* [fr. past part. of *correlate*] **1 :** closely, systematically, or reciprocally related ⟨human faculties form a ~ whole; and this composite human nature seeks to act, to function —H.O.Taylor⟩ **2 :** related as a universal accompaniment whether causally connected or not ⟨nest building is ~ with a precise physiological state —E.A.Armstrong⟩ **3 :** relating to or indicating the relationship between the attributes in a mathematical correlation

cor·re·la·tion \ˌ==ˈlāshən\ *n* -s [ML *correlation-*, *correlatio*, fr. L *com-* + *relation-*, *relatio* relation — more at RELATION] **1 :** the act or process of correlating **:** the condition or fact of being correlated ⟨the exact ~ of tempo, emphasis, and climax —Parker Tyler⟩; *specif* **:** the relation of phenomena as invariable accompaniments of each other whether causally connected or not ⟨the assumption is that there is a positive ~ between performance and pay —Kermit Eby⟩ **2 :** reciprocal or mutual relation in the occurrence (as of deafness in blue-eyed white cats or the expression of apical dominance in plants) of different structures, characteristics, or processes in organisms **3 :** an interdependence between mathematical variables esp. in statistics **4 :** determination of synchrony, of homotaxis, or of relation to the scale of geologic time — usu. used in the comparison of geologic formations or of fossil faunas or floras belonging to different districts

cor·re·la·tion·al \¦==¦=shənᵊl, -shnəl\ *adj* **:** of or concerning correlation **:** employing correlation ⟨metaphysics is a basic and ~ discipline —V.C.Aldrich⟩

correlation coefficient *n* **:** a number that serves to measure the degree of correlation between two mathematical variables, being the quotient of the arithmetic mean of the products of the corresponding deviations (from their means) of the values of the variables in question divided by the product of the corresponding standard deviations of the two variables

correlation curve *n* **:** CORRELOGRAM

correlation ratio *n* **:** a number other than the correlation coefficient that measures the degree of correlation between two mathematical variables

1**cor·rel·a·tive** \kəˈreləd·¦iv, -lət¦, ¦ēv *also* kȯˈ- *or* ¦əv\ *adj* [ML *correlativus*, fr. L *com-* + LL *relativus* relative — more at RELATIVE] **1 :** naturally related (as by occurring in conjunction) **:** CORRESPONDING ⟨points of view toward the contemporary world always imply ~ points of view toward . . . a dozen crucial issues in past centuries —Paul Farmer⟩ **2 :** having, indicating, or involving a reciprocal relation **:** being a correlate ⟨linked the continuing progress of our system to a ~ development in the economies of all democratic peoples —N.A.Rockefeller⟩ **:** reciprocally related esp. so that each directly implies the existence of the other ⟨the ~ rights and duties between shareholders, directors, and executives —G.B. Hurff⟩ **3** *of paired words or expressions* **:** regularly used together but typically not adjacent to each other ⟨the ~ conjunctions *either . . . or*⟩ ⟨the ~ demonstratives *the former . . . the latter*⟩ **4** *biol* **:** exhibiting correlation — **cor·rel·a·tive·ly** \¦ə̇vlē, -li\ *adv*

2**correlative** \"\ *n* -s **:** CORRELATE: as **a :** either of two correlative words or expressions **b :** a word denoting a correlate (sense 1)

cor·rel·a·tiv·i·ty \kəˌreləˈtivəd·ē, (ˌ)kȯˌ-\ *n* -ES **:** the quality or state of being correlative

cor·rel·o·gram \kəˈreləˌgram\ *n* -s [*correl*ation + *-o-* + *-gram*] **:** a curve plotted to exhibit the assumed correlation between two mathematical variables — called also *correlation curve*

cor·ren·te \kəˈrentē, kȯˈ- *or as It*\ *n* -s [It, modif. of MF *courante* — more at COURANTE] **:** COURANTE

cor·re·spond \ˌ¦kȯrə¦spänd, ¦kär-\ *vi* -ED/-ING/-S [MF or ML; MF *correspondre*, fr. ML *correspondēre*, fr. L *com-* + *respondēre* — more at RESPOND] **1 a :** to be in conformity or agreement **:** SUIT, AGREE ⟨incomes do not always ~ with the efforts or skill that appear to be involved —J.A.Hobson⟩ **:** match or compare closely ⟨the man whose consciousness does not ~ to that of the majority is a madman —G.B.Shaw⟩ ⟨the numbers of the paragraphs ~ with numbers on the map⟩ **b :** to be equivalent ⟨government budgets, in their final form . . . ~ to "intention surveys" of expenditure —G.W. Mitchell⟩ **:** be parallel **:** be the counterpart ⟨the English parish may be said to ~ closely to the French rural commune —G.M.Harris⟩ **2 a** *obs* **:** to have communication, communion, or intercourse with persons or affairs **b :** to communicate with a person by exchange of letters ⟨~*ed* regularly with friends⟩ **3** *archaic* **:** to make a return **:** RESPOND ⟨Matilda might not ~ to his passion —Horace Walpole⟩ **4 :** to be connected by means of a geometrical transformation or by means of a functional relation (as of the values $x = 2$ and $y = ½$ in the relation $y = \frac{1}{x}$) **syn** see AGREE

cor·re·spon·dence \ˌ==ˈ=dən(t)s\ *n* -s [ME, fr. MF or ML; MF *correspondence*, *correspondance*, fr. ML *correspondentia*, fr. *correspondent-*, *correspondens* + L *-ia*] **1 a :** the state or condition of agreement of things or of one thing with another **:** relation of congruity **:** resemblance or similarity of detail ⟨Joyce elaborates a point-to-point ~ between the spiritual movements of a little Dublin city-dweller and the mythical wanderings of Ulysses —Francis Fergusson⟩ **b :** an instance or point of agreement, similarity, or analogy ⟨many ~*s* between the two plays⟩ **c** *math* **:** definite association of certain members of one aggregate with each member of a second and of certain members of the second with each member of the first **2 a** *archaic* **:** relations between persons or groups **:** social or business relations or communication **b :** the communication between persons by an exchange of letters ⟨a long ~ between the two friends⟩; *also* **:** any communication by letter ⟨application should be made by ~ or in person at our offices⟩ **c :** the letters exchanged by correspondents ⟨publication of the Holmes-Laski ~⟩ **d :** the news, information, or opinion contributed by a correspondent to a newspaper or periodical **e :** study or instruction carried on by written communication between student and a correspondence school

correspondence principle *n* **:** a principle of spectroscopy: the characteristics of spectral series are in approximate agreement with both the classical electromagnetic theory and the quantum theory of electron transitions, the correspondence becoming closer as the quantum numbers involved become greater

correspondence school *n* **:** a school often connected with a university extension that teaches nonresident students by mailing to them lessons and exercises which upon completion are returned to the school for grading

correspondence theory *n* **:** a theory holding that truth consists in agreement between judgments or propositions and an independently existing reality — contrasted with *coherence theory*

cor·re·spon·den·cy \-dənsē, -si\ *n* -ES [ML *correspondentia*] **1 :** CORRESPONDENCE 1 **2** *obs* **:** CORRESPONDENCE 2

¹**cor·re·spon·dent** \¦=‚=¦=dənt\ *adj* [ME, fr. MF or ML; MF *correspondent, correspondant,* fr. ML *correspondent-, correspondens,* pres. part. of *correspondēre* — more at CORRESPOND] **1 :** having a relation of likeness **:** being similar or analogous to something ⟨you tell of . . . preparing books — I have nothing ~. I am fooling around . . . dabbling in philosophy —O.W.Holmes †1935⟩ **:** CORRESPONDING ⟨each advantage having ~ disadvantages⟩ **2 :** being in agreement **:** SUITING, FITTING — used with *with* or *to* ⟨the outcome was entirely ~ with my wishes⟩ **3** *obs* **:** OBEDIENT, SUBMISSIVE

²**correspondent** \"\ *n* -S **1 :** something that corresponds **:** something equivalent or similar ⟨this fish, the Oriental ~ of the celebrated tarpon of the western Atlantic —H.M. Smith⟩ **2 a :** one who communicates with another by letter esp. as part of a regular exchange **b** *archaic* **:** one who communicates with another esp. secretly **:** ACCOMPLICE **c :** one who has regular commercial relations with another esp. with a concern at a distance ⟨the New York ~ of a San Francisco brokerage house⟩ **d :** one who communicates information or comment to a newspaper by letter ⟨no letter to the editor will be printed unless it bears the ~'s name and address⟩ **e :** one employed by a newspaper or broadcasting company to contribute regular news reports or interpretations from a location distant from the home office **f :** a clerk who handles correspondence for a business concern

cor·re·spon·dent·ly *adv* **:** in a correspondent manner

corresponding *adj* [fr. pres. part. of *correspond*] **1 a :** agreeing in kind, degree, position, function, or other respects ⟨the figures are large but the ~ totals next year will be larger⟩ **b :** RELATED, DERIVED, ACCOMPANYING ⟨all rights carry with them ~ responsibilities —W.P.Paepcke⟩ **2 :** charged with the duty of writing letters ⟨~ secretary⟩ **:** participating or serving at a distance and by mail ⟨~ member of the society⟩

cor·re·spond·ing·ly *adv* **:** in a corresponding manner ⟨is less than one inch long and is ~ small in its other dimensions —Morris Fishbein⟩

corresponding points *n pl* **:** points on the retinas of the two eyes which when simultaneously stimulated normally produce a single visual impression

corresponding states *n pl, physical chem* **:** the states of two or more substances in which their pressures are proportional to their critical pressures, their temperatures to their critical temperatures, and their volumes to their critical volumes

corresponds *pres 3d sing of* CORRESPOND

cor·re·spon·sive \¦=‚=¦spän(t)siv\ *adj* [fr. *correspond,* after E *respond: responsive*] **:** mutually responsive **:** CORRESPONDING

co·rri·da \kō'rrēthä\ *n* -S [Sp (often in the combination *corrida de toros* bullfight), lit., act of running, fr. fem. of *corrido,* past part. of *correr* to run, fr. L *currere* — more at CURRENT] **:** BULLFIGHT

co·rri·do \-(‚)thō\ *n* -S [Sp, prob. fr. past part. of *correr* to run] **:** a Mexican narrative folk ballad usu. on a topical subject

cor·ri·dor \'kȯrədə(r), 'kär- *also* -‚dȯ(ə)r *or* -ȯ(ə)\ *n* -S [MF, fr. OIt *corridore,* fr. *correre* to run, fr. L *currere*] **1 a :** a usu. covered passageway; *esp* **:** one into which compartments or rooms open (as in a hotel or on certain types of trains) **b :** a gallery or passageway connecting several apartments of a building **c :** a place of gossip or intrigue outside a meeting hall ⟨it was assumed around legislative ~s that the bill would be defeated⟩ **2 a :** a usu. narrow passageway or route ⟨the Rhineland . . . has been the usual ~ of German attack —A.H. Vandenberg †1951⟩ **b :** a narrow strip of land through foreign-held territory providing access to a place ⟨Vienna, . . . ninety miles behind the Iron Curtain, is connected with the western world by two official ~s, each one containing a railroad line and a highway —Joseph Wechsberg⟩ or joining a country to its seaport ⟨the Polish ~ across Germany to Danzig⟩ **c :** an open or cleared strip ⟨fire hazard is reduced by frequent ~s cut through the forest —*Amer. Guide Series: Ark.*⟩ **d :** a restricted lane for air traffic **e :** a pair of parallel ridges and the valley between them esp. when the longer axis of the valley is parallel to and in line with the route of advance of an attacking force

cor·rie *also* **cor·ry** \'kȯrē\ *n, pl* **corries** [ScGael *coire,* lit., kettle; akin to OIr *coire* kettle; akin to OE & OHG *hwer* kettle, ON *hverr,* Skt *caru*] **:** CIRQUE

cor·rie·dale \-‚dā(ə)l\ *n* -S *usu cap* [*Corriedale,* ranch in New Zealand where the breed was developed] **:** a member of a dual-purpose breed of rather large usu. hornless sheep developed in New Zealand from the Lincoln, Leicester, and Merino breeds

cor·ri·gan pulse \'kȯrəgən-\ *n, usu cap* [after Sir Dominic J. *Corrigan* †1880 Irish physician, who described it] **:** a pulse characterized by a sharp rise to full expansion followed by immediate collapse that is seen in aortic insufficiency — called also *water-hammer pulse*

cor·ri·gen·dum \‚kȯrə'jendəm, ‚kär-\ *n, pl* **corrigen·da** \-də\ [L, neut. of *corrigendus,* gerundive of *corrigere*] **1 :** an error to be corrected; *esp* **:** an error in a printed work discovered after printing and shown with its correction on a separate sheet bound with the original **2 :** a list of errors in a printed work, with corrections — sometimes pl. but sing. in constr.

cor·ri·gent \'=rəjənt\ *n* -S [L *corrigent-, corrigens,* pres. part. of *corrigere*] **:** a substance added to a medicine to modify its action or counteract a disagreeable effect

cor·ri·gi·bil·i·ty \‚kȯrəjə'biləd·ē, ‚kär-, -rej-, -ətē, -i *sometimes* kə‚rij-\ *n* -ES **:** the quality or state of being corrigible

cor·ri·gi·ble \'kȯrəjəbəl, 'kär-, -rej- *sometimes* kə'rij-\ *adj* [ME *corrigabill,* fr. MF *corrigible,* fr. ML *corrigibilis,* fr. L *corrigere* to correct + *-ibilis* -ible — more at CORRECT] **1 a :** capable of being set right, amended, or reformed **:** CORRECTABLE ⟨a ~ defect⟩ **b :** capable of being modified or corrected as a result of empirical or experimental observation ⟨the ~ nature of the findings of experimental science⟩ **2** *obs* **:** deserving chastisement **:** PUNISHABLE **3** *obs* **:** having the power to correct **:** CORRECTIVE ⟨~ authority —Shak.⟩ — **cor·ri·gi·bly** \-blē, -i\ *adv*

cor·rig·i·o·la \kə‚rijē'ōlə\ *n, cap* [NL, fr. LL, a plant (perh. *Polygonum aviculare*), dim. of L *corrigia* shoelace, prob. of Celt origin; akin to OIr *cuimrech* fetter, fr. a prehistoric compound whose first and second constituents respectively are akin to L *com-* and to MHG *ric* bond, fetter, knot, W *rhwym* bond, obligation, OE *rǣw* row — more at COM-, ROW] **:** a genus of low herbs having alternate entire stipulate leaves and small white or greenish flowers succeeded by one-seeded utricles that is placed in the family Caryophyllaceae or sometimes in the Illecebraceae or is made the type of a separate family

cor·rig·i·o·la·ce·ae \kə‚rijēə'lāsē‚ē\ *n pl, cap* [NL *Corrigiola,* type genus + *-aceae*] *in some classifications* **:** a family of plants typified by the genus *Corrigiola*

¹**cor·ri·val** \kə'rīvəl, kō'-‚kō'-\ *n* -S [MF *corrival,* fr. L *corrivalis,* fr. *com-* + *rivalis* rival — more at RIVAL] **:** RIVAL, COMPETITOR

²**corrival** \"\ *adj* **:** having rivaling claims **:** RIVAL

¹**cor·rob·o·rant** \kə'räb(ə)rənt\ *adj* [L *corroborant-, corroborans,* pres. part. of *corroborare*] *of a medicine, archaic* **:** STRENGTHENING, INVIGORATING

²**corroborant** \"\ *n* -S *archaic* **:** an invigorating medicine **:** TONIC

¹**cor·rob·o·rate** \kə'räbə‚rāt, *usu* -ād·+V\ *vb* -ED/-ING/-S [L *corroboratus,* past part. of *corroborare,* fr. *com-* + *roborare* to strengthen, fr. *robor-, robur* strength — more at ROBUST] *vt* **1** *obs* **:** to make strong or strengthen in body or construction **2 :** to establish or make firm ⟨~ his authority⟩ **:** establish legally or by law **3 :** to provide evidence of the truth of **:** make more certain **:** CONFIRM ⟨the authority of religion and science did not ~ Bellamy's high view of man —Joseph Schiffman⟩ ~ *vi* **:** to give evidence or confirmation **syn** see CONFIRM

²**cor·rob·o·rate** \-b(ə)rət\ *adj* [L *corroboratus*] *archaic* **:** CORROBORATED

cor·rob·o·ra·tion \kə‚räbə'rāshən\ *n* -S [MF or LL; MF *corroboration,* fr. LL *corroboration-, corroboratio,* fr. L *corroboratus* + *-ion-, -io* -ion] **1 :** the act of corroborating **2 :** a strengthening or confirming ⟨sought ~ for his views⟩ **:** something that corroborates

¹**cor·rob·o·ra·tive** \kə'räbə‚rād·|iv, -ät|, -b(ə)rəd·|, -b(ə)rət|, |ēv *also* |əv\ *adj* [MF *corroboratif,* fr. *corroborer* to strengthen (fr. L *corroborare*) + *-atif* -ative] **:** serving or tending to corroborate **:** CONFIRMATORY ⟨~ details⟩ — **cor·rob·o·ra·tive·ly** \|əvlē, -li\ *adv*

²**corroborative** \"\ *n* -S *archaic* **:** CORROBORANT

cor·rob·o·ra·tor \-bə‚rād·ə(r), -ātə-\ *n* -S **:** one that corroborates

cor·rob·o·ra·to·ry \-b(ə)rə‚tōrē, -tȯr-, -ri\ *adj* [¹*corroborate* + *-ory*] **:** CORROBORATIVE

¹**cor·rob·o·ree** \kə'räbərē\ *n* -S [native name in New South Wales, Australia] **1 a :** a nocturnal festivity with songs and symbolic dances by which the Australian aborigines celebrate events of importance **b :** a song or chant made for such a festivity **2** *Austral* **a :** a festivity or social gathering; *esp* **:** a gathering of noisy or uproarious character **b :** TUMULT, UPROAR

²**corroboree** \"\ *vi* **corroboreed; corroboreed; corroboreeing** \-(‚)rēiŋ\ **corroborees :** to hold or take part in a corroboree

cor·rode \kə'rōd\ *vb* -ED/-ING/-S [ME *corroden,* fr. L *corrodere* to gnaw to pieces, fr. *com-* + *rodere* to gnaw — more at RAT] *vt* **1 :** to eat away by degrees as if by gnawing ⟨*corroded* by consumption and indigence⟩ **:** wear away or diminish by gradually separating or destroying small particles or converting into an easily disintegrated substance; *esp* **:** to eat away or diminish by acid or alkali reaction or by chemical alteration ⟨the metal was *corroded* beyond repair by exposure⟩ ⟨the caustic substance *corroded* the material so that it fell apart in the hands⟩ **2** *obs* **:** to eat or gnaw away **3 :** to weaken or destroy (as spirit, strength, or force) by a gradual process of impairment ⟨manners and miserliness that ~ the human spirit —Bernard DeVoto⟩ ~ *vi* **1 :** to act corrosively ⟨certain chemicals will ~ if left on bare metal⟩ **2 :** to undergo corrosion ⟨the bare metal began to ~ after a few weeks of exposure to the weather⟩

cor·ro·dent \kə'rōdᵊnt\ *adj or n* [L *corrodent-, corrodens,* pres. part. of *corrodere*] **:** CORROSIVE

cor·ro·den·tia \‚kȯrə'denchēə\ *n pl, cap* [NL, fr. L neut. pl. of *corrodent-, corrodens*] **:** an order of small soft-bodied insects having chewing mouthparts and either two pairs of wings held over the back like a roof or no wings at all, the best-known members of the order being the book lice

corrodiary *var of* CORODIARY

cor·rod·ibil·i·ty \kə‚rōdə'biləd·ē\ *n* -ES **:** capability of being corroded ⟨the relative ~ of different kinds of atmospheres —*Mill & Factory*⟩

cor·rod·i·ble \kə'rōdəbəl\ *adj* **:** capable of being corroded ⟨all metals are ~ under the proper circumstances —*Bell System Technical Jour.*⟩

corroding lead \-¦led\ *n* [*corroding* fr. gerund of *corrode*] **:** lead sufficiently pure to be used in making white lead by a process of corroding

corrody *var of* CORODY

cor·ro·si·ble \kə'rōsəbəl, -ōzə-\ *adj* [*corros-* (as in *corrosive*) + *-ible*] **:** CORRODIBLE

cor·ro·sion \kə'rōzhən\ *n* -S [ME *corosion,* fr. LL *corrosion-, corrosio* act of gnawing, fr. L *corrosus* (past part. of *corrodere*) + *-ion-, -io* -ion] **1 :** the action, process, or effect of corroding: as **a :** the action or process of corrosive chemical change not necessarily accompanied by loss of form or compactness; *typically* **:** a gradual wearing away or alteration by a chemical or electrochemical essentially oxidizing process (as in the atmospheric rusting of iron) **b :** a gradual weakening, loss, or destruction (as of spirit or force) ⟨the ~ of faith and the corruption of moral standards —*Times Lit. Supp.*⟩ **c :** erosion of land or rock; *specif* **:** the removal of soil or rock by the solvent or chemical action of running water — compare CORRASION **2 a :** a product of corrosion ⟨a hard ~ of white lead⟩ **b :** a study specimen of an organ or other structure prepared by injection of hollow parts (as blood vessels) with a plastic and subsequent removal of the surrounding tissue by corrosion

cor·ro·sion·al \-nᵊl\ *adj* **:** resulting from corrosion ⟨~ grooving in a steam boiler⟩

corrosion border *or* **corrosion zone** *n* **:** RESORPTION BORDER

corrosion fatigue *n* **:** the fatigue of a material that is accompanied and aggravated by corrosion and that may cause fracture of the material much below the ordinary fatigue limit

¹**cor·ro·sive** \kə'rōs|iv, |ēv *also* -ōz| *or* |əv; *archaic* 'kȯrə-\ *adj* [ME *corosif,* fr. MF or ML; MF *corrosif,* fr. ML *corrosivus,* fr. L *corrosus* + *-ivus* -ive] **:** having the power to corrode **:** CORRODING: as **a :** bringing about or causing chemical corrosion ⟨a ~ alkali⟩ ⟨a ~ dampness⟩ **b :** weakening and destroying by a gradual process of breaking down or wearing away ⟨that most ~ instrument of disintegration the European world has yet known: class warfare —Sir Thomas Beecham⟩ **c :** having the power to wound the feelings **:** SARCASTIC ⟨~ satire⟩ **:** tending to cut deeply or affect powerfully and usu. unfavorably **:** BITING ⟨Veblen's ~ and coruscating observations on society —C.E.Lindblom⟩

²**corrosive** \"\ *n* -S [ME *corosif,* prob. fr. *corosif,* adj.] **1 a :** a substance that corrodes **:** CAUSTIC **2 :** something that weakens or destroys ⟨criminal ~s against . . . society —Marjorie Grene⟩

cor·ro·sive·ly \|əvlē, -li\ *adv* **:** in a corrosive manner ⟨dialogue that is ~ revealing —*Time*⟩

cor·ro·sive·ness *n* -ES **:** the quality or state of being corrosive **:** the tendency to corrode

corrosive sublimate *n* **:** MERCURY CHLORIDE b

cor·ro·siv·i·ty \‚kō(‚)rō'sivəd·ē\ *n* -ES **:** the quality of being corrosive

¹**cor·ru·gate** \'kȯrə‚gāt, 'kär- *sometimes* -ryə-; *usu* -ād·+V\ *vb* -ED/-ING/-S [L *corrugatus,* past part. of *corrugare,* fr. *com-* + *rugare* to wrinkle, fr. *ruga* wrinkle — more at ROUGH] *vt* **:** to form or contract into wrinkles or folds ⟨*corrugated* his brows in thought —John Buchan⟩ **:** shape into alternating ridges and grooves **:** FURROW ⟨the wind ~s the surface of the sea⟩ ⟨the roots *corrugated* the path⟩; *specif* **:** to shape (sheet metal or other material) into straight, parallel, regular, and equally curved ridges and hollows ~ *vi* **:** to become corrugated ⟨surfaces speedily rutted and *corrugated* — N.C.Rockwood⟩

²**cor·ru·gate** \-gət\ *adj* [L *corrugatus*] *archaic* **:** CORRUGATED

corrugated *adj* [fr. past part. of ¹*corrugate*] **1 :** formed into folds or furrows **:** having a ridged or furrowed surface ⟨angry face and ~ brow⟩ ⟨~ waves of the dunes⟩ **:** having even parallel ridges and furrows ⟨~ fabric⟩ ⟨~ steel rollers⟩ **2 :** made of material (as metal or paper) with corrugations ⟨~ hut⟩ ⟨~ boxes⟩

corrugated bar *n* **:** a steel bar for reinforcing concrete having spiral or transverse ridges or nubs at short intervals on each face to provide a bond with the concrete

corrugated board *n* **:** a paperboard having permanent corrugations; *also* **:** such a sheet with an adherent flat board on one or both sides

corrugated fastener *n* **:** a small corrugated strip of steel sharp on one of the long edges and hammered in as a fastener across wood joints in rough carpentry

corrugated iron *n* **:** usu. galvanized sheet iron or sheet steel shaped into straight parallel regular and equally curved ridges and hollows

corrugated lens *n* **:** a lens in which concentric portions are cut out from the surface so as to lessen the weight without affecting the focal power

corrugated paper *n* **:** a thick coarse paper corrugated to give it elasticity and used as a protective wrapper

corrugated pottery *n* **:** coil pottery usu. with indentations on the surface of the coils typical of modified Basket Maker culture and common in later stages of the Anasazi culture

1 2

corrugated lens: *1* inner face cut away; *2* outer face cut away

cor·ru·ga·tion \‚=‚='gāshən\ *n* -S [ML *corrugation-, corrugatio,* fr. L *corrugatus* + *-ion-, -io* -ion] **1 :** the act of corrugating or state of being corrugated **2 :** a ridge or groove of a corrugated surface ⟨gravel roads with ~s and potholes⟩ **3 :** a small furrow used for the distribution of irrigation water

cor·ru·ga·tor \'=‚=‚gād·ə(r), -ātə-\ *n* -S [NL, fr. L *corrugatus* + *-or*] **:** one that corrugates: as **a :** a muscle that contracts the skin into wrinkles **b :** an implement for furrowing land for irrigation **c :** a machine or a workman that makes corrugations in material (as paperboard)

¹**cor·rupt** \kə'rəpt\ *vb* -ED/-ING/-S [ME *corrupten,* fr. L *corruptus,* past part. of *corrumpere,* fr. *com-* + *rumpere* to break — more at REAVE] *vt* **1 a :** to change from good to bad in morals, manners, or actions **:** make base **:** PERVERT ⟨there is an opposite error . . . and that is the belief that children are naturally virtuous, and are only ~*ed* by . . . their elders' vices —Bertrand Russell⟩; *specif* **:** to make subject to improper influence (as bribery) ⟨~ the offices of state⟩ **b :** to degrade with unsound principles or moral values ⟨enslave America with machines . . . and ~ it with materialism —Brooks Atkinson⟩ **:** WEAKEN, PERVERT ⟨such behavior ~s party discipline⟩ **:** SPOIL, RUIN ⟨that fevered imagination which ~*ed* everything that touched me —W.H.Hudson⟩ **2 :** to spoil or make putrid by decomposition or rotting **:** taint or infect with infectious or putrefying matter ⟨a city ~*ed* with the plague⟩ **3 :** to subject (a person) to corruption of blood **4 a :** to change (a language) in such a way that standard forms become different from earlier forms regarded as better or purer — not used technically **b :** to change (as a word) often by substitution of the familiar for the unfamiliar or by adaptation to the sound system of a language ⟨Dutch *koolsla* was ~*ed* to English *coldslaw*⟩ — not used technically **5 :** to alter from the original or correct form or version (as by error, omission, or addition) ⟨the text was ~*ed* by careless copyists⟩ ~ *vi* **1 a :** to become tainted, rotten, or putrid ⟨leaving the bodies to ~ on the field⟩ **b :** to become morally debased, perverted from right principles, weakened, or unsound ⟨power tends to ~ and absolute power ~s absolutely —J.E.E.Dalberg-Acton⟩ **2 :** to cause disintegration, spoiling, or ruin ⟨lay not up for yourselves treasures upon earth, where moth and rust doth ~ —Mt 6:19 (AV)⟩ **syn** see DEBASE

²**corrupt** \"\ *adj, sometimes* -ER/-EST [ME, fr. MF or L; MF, fr. L *corruptus*] **1 a :** DEPRAVED, EVIL **:** perverted into a state of moral weakness or wickedness ⟨humanity they knew to be ~ and incompetent from the day of Adam's creation —Henry Adams⟩ **b :** of debased political morality **:** characterized by bribery, the selling of political favors, or other improper political or legal transactions or arrangements ⟨~ judges⟩ ⟨~ and incompetent city government⟩ **2** *archaic* **:** tainted by decomposition or rotting **:** PUTRID **3 a :** adulterated or debased by change from an original condition of purity or excellence **:** debased or contaminated by the addition of undesirable elements ⟨forsook classic . . . plays for . . . melodramas that culminated in the ~ . . . imitations known as thrillers and tearjerkers —*Amer. Guide Series: N.J.*⟩; *specif* **:** altered from the original or correct condition (as by error) ⟨many of the original Scarlatti . . . notations have been deleted . . . by editors . . . simply because they were copying an edition already ~ —D.D. Boyden⟩ **b** *of a language* **:** changed from an earlier form regarded as better or purer — not used technically **c** *of a word or other linguistic form* **:** characterized by having undergone linguistic change — not used technically **4 :** affected by corruption of blood **syn** see VICIOUS

cor·rupt·ed·ly *adv* **:** in a corrupt manner

cor·rupt·ed·ness *n* -ES **:** the quality or state of being corrupted

cor·rupt·er \-tə(r) *or* **cor·rup·tor** \" *also* -‚tȯ(ə)r *or* -ȯ(ə)\ *n* -S **:** one that corrupts

cor·rupt·ibil·i·ty \kə‚rəptə'biləd·ē, -ətē, -i\ *n* -ES [F or LL; F *corruptibilité,* fr. LL *corruptibilitat-, corruptibilitas,* fr. *corruptibilis* + L *-itat-, -itas* -ity] **:** capability of being corrupted **:** liability to corruption

cor·rupt·ible \kə'rəptəbəl\ *adj* [ME, fr. MF or LL; MF, fr. LL *corruptibilis,* fr. L *corruptus* + *-ibilis* -ible] **1 :** capable of being corrupted **2 :** subject to corruption **:** PERISHABLE

cor·rupt·ing·ly *adv* **:** in a corrupting manner — **cor·rupt·ible·ness** *n* -ES — **cor·rupt·ibly** \-blē, -bli\ *adv*

cor·rup·tion \kə'rəpshən\ *n* -S [ME *corrupcioun,* fr. MF *corruption,* fr. L *corruption-, corruptio,* fr. *corruptus* + *-ion-, -io* -ion] **1 a :** impairment of integrity, virtue, or moral principle **:** DEPRAVITY ⟨the luxury and ~ . . . among the upper classes —W.N.Ewer⟩ **b** (1) **:** decay or decomposition of matter (as by rotting or by oxidation) ⟨~ of the bone⟩ ⟨~ of metal⟩ (2) **:** decay of the body after death ⟨death had apparently devoted the body to ~ —Mary W. Shelley⟩ **c :** inducement (as of a political official) by means of improper considerations (as bribery) to commit a violation of duty ⟨the ~ of officials by gambling bosses⟩ ⟨exposing ~ in city politics⟩ **d :** the changing or state of being changed for the worse **:** a departure from what is pure or correct or from the original ⟨the ~ of every art form⟩ ⟨the ~ of the text introduced by copyists⟩ **2** *archaic* **:** an agency or influence that corrupts ⟨the love of money is the ~ of states —Benjamin Jowett⟩ **3** *now dial* **:** a product of decomposition or putrefaction **:** putrid matter **:** PUS **4 a :** an instance of making or becoming corrupt **:** a result of perversion ⟨modern ~s of religious faith —Reinhold Niebuhr⟩; *specif* **:** an erroneous reading in a text ⟨a manuscript full of ~s⟩ **b** (1) *of a word or other linguistic form* **:** change in form often consisting of substitution of the familiar for the unfamiliar or adaptation to the sound system of a language — not used technically (2) **:** a word or form resulting from such a change — not used technically **c** (1) *of a language* **:** change from an earlier form regarded as better or purer — not used technically (2) **:** a language or dialect resulting from such a change — not used technically **5** *dial Brit* **:** evil or irascible nature **:** TEMPER

cor·rup·tion·ist \-sh(ə)nəst\ *n* -S **:** one who practices or defends corruption esp. in a position of public trust

corruption of blood : a legal taint that was one of the results of a conviction by attainder, that barred the attainted person from inheriting, retaining, or transmitting any estate, rank, or title, and that was abolished in England in 1870 and never was recognized in the U.S. ⟨the Congress shall have power to declare the punishment of treason, but no attainder of treason shall work *corruption of blood* or forfeiture except during the life of the person attainted —*U.S. Constitution*⟩

cor·rup·tive \-ptiv, -tēv *also* -təv\ *adj* [MF or LL; MF *corruptif,* fr. LL *corruptivus,* fr. L *corruptus* + *-ivus* -ive] **:** producing or tending to produce corruption — **cor·rup·tive·ly** \-təvlē, -li\ *adv*

cor·rupt·less \kə'rəptləs, *rapid* -pl-\ *adj* **:** INCORRUPTIBLE

cor·rupt·ly \-ptlē, -li, *rapid* -pl-\ *adv* **:** in a corrupt manner **:** by corruption

cor·rupt·ness \-p(t)nəs\ *n* -ES **:** the quality or state of being corrupt

corruptor *var of* CORRUPTER

corrupt practices act *n* **:** any of various statutes in the U.S. limiting the amount and source of political campaign contributions and requiring detailed reports of expenditures

corrupts *pres 3d sing of* CORRUPT

corry *var of* CORRIE

cors *pl of* COR

cor·sac *or* **cor·sak** \'kȯr‚sak, =¦=\ *n* -S [Russ *korsak,* fr. Kirghiz *karsak*] **:** a small yellowish brown bushy-tailed fox (*Vulpes corsac*) of central Asia — called also *Afghan fox*

cor·sage \kȯr'säzh, kȯ(ə)'-, -säj, '=‚= *also* |j *or* kə(r)'s-\ *n* -S [F, upper part of the body, bust, bodice, fr. OF, upper part of the body, fr. *cors* body (fr. L *corpus*) + *-age* — more at

MIDRIFF] **1 :** the waist or bodice of a woman's dress **2 :** an arrangement of flowers to be worn as a costume accessory (as on the bodice or at the waist)

cor·sair \R 'kȯr,sa(a)(ə)r, -se(ə)r; -R 'kȯ(ə),sa(a)|ə, -se|ə, +V" *or* |(ə)r\ *n* -S [MF & OIt; MF *corsaire* pirate, fr. OProv *corsari,* fr. OIt *corsaro, corsare, corsale,* fr. ML *cursarius,* fr. L *cursus* course + *-arius* -ary — more at COURSE] **1 :** a privateer of the Barbary coast authorized by his government to prey upon the commerce and harry the shores of Christian nations **2 :** a pirate of any kind or period **3 :** a California rockfish (*Sebastomus rosaceus*) **4 :** any of several large nocturnal reduviid bugs not normally bloodsuckers but capable of inflicting an extremely painful bite

¹corse \'kȯ(ə)rs\ *n* -S [ME *cors,* fr. OF, body] *archaic* **:** a dead body **:** CORPSE ⟨that thou, dead ~, again in complete steel, revisits thus the glimpses of the moon —Shak.⟩

²corse \"\ *vt* -ED/-ING/-S [ME *corsen*] *archaic* **:** BARTER

³corse *Scot var of* CROSS

¹corse·let *also* **cors·let** \'kȯrslət\ *n* -S [MF *corselet,* dim. of *cors* waist of a garment, body] **1 a :** a usu. tight-fitting garment covering the trunk but usu. not the arms or legs **b** *usu corslet* (1) **:** a piece of armor for the trunk usu. consisting of a breastplate and backpiece (2) **:** a pikeman's armor including helmet (3) *usu corslet* **:** a soldier wearing a corslet **c :** a sash or close-fitting midriff section of a woman's dress **2** [F, fr. MF] **a :** the hard prothorax of a beetle **b :** an area of enlarged scales surrounding the body immediately behind the head in certain mackerels and related fishes **c :** the bony exoskeleton of a turtle

²cor·se·let *or* **cor·se·lette** \¦kȯrsə¦let\ *n* -S [fr. *Corselette,* a trademark] **:** a foundation garment combining girdle and brassiere

corse·pres·ent \'ˌ=,=\ *n* [ME *corspresent,* fr. *cors* corpse + *present*] **:** a gift made to the clergy from the goods of the deceased at the time of a funeral

¹cor·set \'kȯrsət, 'kȯ(ə)s-, *usu* -əd.+V\ *n* -S [ME, fr. OF, dim. of *cors*] **1 :** a medieval jacket usu. close-fitting and often laced **2 a :** a woman's close-fitting boned supporting undergarment often hooked and laced, extending from above or beneath the bust or from the waist to below the hips, and having garters attached — sometimes used in pl. **b :** a support for injured bones or muscles or for correcting deformities of the spine or thorax

²corset \"\ *vt* -ED/-ING/-S **1 :** to dress in or fit with a corset **2 :** to restrict closely or control rigidly ⟨most governments ~ed their countries in trade controls —*Wall Street Jour.*⟩

corset cover *n* **:** a woman's undergarment worn over a corset

cor·se·tiere \¦kȯ(r)sə¦ti(ə)r, -sə,tye(ə)r\ *also* **cor·se·tier** \-sə¦ti(ə)r, -sə,tyā\ *n* -S [*corsetiere* fr. F *corsetière,* fem. of *corsetier; corsetier* fr. F, fr. *corset* + *-ier* -er] **:** one who makes, fits, or sells corsets, girdles, brassieres

cor·set·less \'kȯ(r)sətləs\ *adj* **:** not having a corset

cor·set·ry \'kȯ(r)sətrē\ *n* -ES **1 :** the art of making or fitting corsets, girdles, and brassieres **2 :** corsets, girdles, and brassieres

¹cor·si·can \'kȯ(r)səkən, -sēk-\ *adj, usu cap* [*Corsica,* French island in the Mediterranean + E *-an*] **1 :** of, relating to, or characteristic of the island of Corsica in the Mediterranean sea **2 :** of, relating to, or characteristic of Corsicans

²corsican \"\ *n* -S *cap* **1 :** a native or inhabitant of Corsica **2 :** the dialect of Italian spoken in Corsica

corsican mint *n, usu cap C* **:** a minute low creeping mint (*Mentha requienii*) with tiny pale purple flowers

corsican moss *n, usu cap C* **:** a small red alga (*Alsidium helminthocorton*) of the Mediterranean formerly much used as an anthelminthic — called also *worm moss*

corsican pine *or* **corsican fir** *or* **corsican larch** *n, usu cap C* **:** a European pine (*Pinus laricio*) of symmetrical growth that is closely related to the Austrian pine and is the source of a large quantity of resin from which turpentine and Burgundy pitch are made

corsing *pres part of* CORSE

corsive *obs var of* CORROSIVE

corslet *var of* CORSELET

cor·so \'kȯr(,)sō\ *n* -S [It, lit., course, fr. L *cursus* — more at COURSE] **:** STRUT; *esp* **:** PROMENADE

cor·ta·de·ria \,kȯrdə'dirēə\ *n, cap* [NL, fr. AmerSp *cortadera* plant with sharp-edged leaves (fr. Sp, hot chisel, fr. *cortar* to cut, fr. L *curtare* to shorten, fr. *curtus* short) + NL *-ia* — more at CURT] **:** a genus of So. American grasses with tall stems and large silky panicles — see PAMPAS GRASS

cor·te \'kȯr,tā\ *n* -S [AmerSp (Argentina), gracefulness, good breeding, corte, fr. Sp, court] **:** a dip or backward step in ballroom dancing with knee bend by the man or the corresponding forward step by the woman

cor·tege *also* **cor·tège** \'kȯr,tezh, -ō(ə),-, ='=\ *n* -S [F *cortège,* fr. It *corteggio,* fr. *corteggiare* to court, fr. *corte* court, fr. L *cohort-, cohors* enclosure, court — more at COURT] **1 :** a train of attendants **2 :** a procession of mourners at a funeral

cor·tes \'kȯr,tez, -ō(ə),-, -es\ *n, pl* **cortes** \"\ [Sp & Pg, pl. of *corte* court, fr. L *cohort-, cohors*] **:** a Spanish parliament

cor·tex \'kȯr|,teks, -ō(ə)|\ *n, pl* **cor·ti·ces** \|d·ə,sēz\ *or* **cortex·es** \|,teksəz\ [L, bark — more at CUIRASS] **1 a :** the bark of various plants used medicinally (as cinchona bark or cotton-root bark) **b :** the peel of any of several fruits — used esp. in the writing of medical prescriptions **2 a :** the outer or superficial part of an organ or structure (as the kidney, adrenal gland, or a hair); *esp* **:** the outer layer of gray matter of the cerebrum and cerebellum that contains most of the higher nervous centers (as those concerned with the interpretation and correlation of sensory impressions) **b :** the outer part of certain organisms (as some protozoans) — compare MEDULLA **3 a :** the cylinder of primary tissue surrounding the stele of a vascular plant, extending from endodermis, pericycle, or vascular tissue on the inside to the epidermis or into the bark on the outside, and consisting in its simplest form of thin-walled parenchyma cells which function in photosynthesis and food storage but often esp. in herbaceous plants consisting at least in part of collenchyma or sclerenchyma cells or both which function in support and sometimes where much secondary growth occurs consisting of crowded and crushed cells that eventually slough off partially or wholly; *broadly* **:** all tissues outside the xylem — see SECONDARY CORTEX **b :** the layer of nearly cubical cells surrounding the central core of certain brown algae immediately beneath the superficial layer **c :** a layer of compacted and often somewhat fused fungal hyphae on either or both surfaces of many lichens that is often limited externally by an outer dermal layer — called also *pseudocortex* **d :** the peridium of a fungus

cor·tex·one \'ko(r),tek,sōn\ *n* -S [*cortex* + *-one*] **:** DEOXYCORTICOSTERONE

cor·tez \kȯr'tez, -es\ *n* -ES [AmerSp] **1** *in Panama* **:** TIBOURBOU **2 :** any of several Central American timber trees of the genus *Tabebuia* (esp. *T. chrysantha*)

corti apparatus *n, usu cap C* [after Alfonso *Corti* — more at ARCH OF CORTI] **:** ORGAN OF CORTI

cor·ti·cal \'kȯ(r)d·ə̇kəl, -)t|, |ēk-\ *adj* [NL *corticalis,* fr. L *cortic-, cortex* + *-alis* -al] **1 a :** of, relating to, or located in or on the outer part of something ⟨~ secretion⟩ ⟨~ cells of a fruit⟩ **b :** of, relating to, or consisting of cortex **2 a :** involving or resulting from the action or condition of the cerebral cortex as distinguished from the more peripheral parts (as sense organs) ⟨~ blindness⟩ ⟨~ deafness⟩ **b :** mental as opposed to sensory — **cor·ti·cal·ly** \|ək(ə)lē, |ēk-, -li\ *adv*

cortical rhythm *n* **:** the apparently inherent rhythmic electrical oscillations taking place in the brain in the absence of evident external stimulation

cor·ti·cate \'kȯ(r)d·ə̇,kāt, -,kət\ *adj* [L *corticatus,* fr. *cortic-, cortex* + *-atus* -ate] **:** covered with bark or with a cortex or specially developed external investment

cor·ti·cat·ed \-,kād·əd\ *adj* [L *corticatus* + E *-ed*] **:** CORTICATE

cor·ti·cif·u·gal \¦kȯ(r)d·ə¦sifyəgəl\ *adj* [L *cortic-, cortex* bark, cortex + E *-i-* + *-fugal*] **:** originating within and passing away from the cortex ⟨a ~ nerve fiber⟩

cor·ti·cip·e·tal \-¦sipəd·ᵊl\ *adj* [L *cortic-, cortex* + E *-i-* + *-petal*] **:** originating without and passing to or toward the cerebral cortex ⟨a ~ nerve fiber⟩

cor·ti·ci·um \kȯ(r)'tis(h)ēəm\ *n, cap* [NL, fr. L *cortic-, cortex* bark + NL *-ium* — more at CUIRASS] **:** a genus of basidiomycetous fungi (family Thelephoraceae) that are distinguished by a simple smooth-surfaced prostrate or resupinate sporophore and that include a number of forms parasitic on wood or on economic crops — see BOTTOM ROT 1, PINK DISEASE, RHIZOCTONIA

cortico- *comb form* [L *cortic-, cortex* bark] **1 :** cortex; *esp* **:** cerebral cortex ⟨corticoefferent⟩ **2 :** cortical and ⟨corticospinal⟩

cor·ti·co·adrenal \¦kȯrd·ə̇,kō+\ *adj* **:** of or relating to the adrenal cortex — compare ADRENAL GLAND

cor·ti·co·ad·re·nal·o·trop·ic \¦kȯrd·ə,kō¦ə¦drēnᵊlō¦träpik\ *or* **cor·ti·co·ad·re·no·trop·ic** \-rēnō¦t, -ren-\ *adj* [*corticoadrenal* or *corticoadrenal* + *-o-* + *-tropic*] **:** ADRENOCORTICOTROPHIC

cor·ti·co·afferent \¦kȯrd·ə̇,kō+\ *adj* **:** CORTICIPETAL

cor·ti·co·efferent \"+\ *adj* **:** CORTICIFUGAL

¹cor·ti·coid \'kȯrd·ə̇,kȯid\ *adj* [L *cortic-, cortex* bark, cortex + E *-oid*] **:** relating to or similar (as in activity) to a corticoid

²corticoid \"\ *n* -S **:** any of various steroids several of which are hormones (as corticosterone, cortisone, and aldosterone) extracted from the adrenal cortex

cor·tic·o·line \kȯr'tikə,līn\ *or* **cor·tic·o·lous** \-ləs\ *also* **cor·ti·cole** \'kȯrd·ə,kōl\ *adj* [*corticoline* fr. *corticole* + *-ine; corticolous* irreg. fr. F *corticole* corticoline + E *-ous; corticole* irreg. fr. F *corticicole,* fr. L *cortic-, cortex* bark + F *-i-* + *-cole* -colous] **:** growing on bark ⟨~ lichens⟩ ⟨~ fungi⟩

cor·ti·co·peduncular \¦kȯrd·ə,kō+\ *adj* **:** of or relating to the cerebral cortex and peduncles

cor·ti·co·pontocerebellar \"+\ *adj* [*cortico-* + *pontocerebellar*] **:** of or indicating a tract of nerve fibers or a path for nervous impulses that passes from the cerebral cortex through the internal capsule to the pons to the white matter and cortex of the cerebellum

cor·ti·co·ru·bral tract \"+¦rübrəl-\ *n* [*cortico-* + L *rubr-, ruber* red + E *-al* — more at RED] **:** a conducting path of the brain extending from the cortex of the frontal lobe to the red nucleus

cor·ti·co·spinal \¦kȯrd·ə,kō+\ *adj* **:** of or relating to cerebral cortex and spinal cord or to the pyramidal tract

corticospinal tract *n* **:** PYRAMIDAL TRACT

cor·ti·co·steroid \"+\ *n* -S [ISV *cortico-* + *steroid*] **:** CORTICOID

cor·ti·cos·ter·one \,kȯrd·ə̇'kästə,rōn, -ə,kō'sti,rōn\ *n* -S [*cortico-* + *sterol* + *-one*] **:** a colorless crystalline steroid hormone $C_{21}H_{30}O_4$ extracted from the adrenal cortex or made synthetically; 11,21-dihydroxy-progesterone

cor·ti·co·striate \¦kȯrd·ə,kō+\ *adj* [*cortico-* + *-striate* (fr. *corpus striatum*)] **:** relating to or connecting the corpus striatum and the cerebral cortex

cor·ti·cothalamic \"+\ *adj* **:** of or relating to the cerebral cortex and the thalamus

cor·ti·co·troph·ic \¦kȯrd·ə,kō¦träfik\ *or* **cor·ti·co·trop·ic** \-träpik\ *adj* **:** influencing a cortex; *specif* **:** influencing or stimulating the adrenal cortex ⟨~ pituitary fractions⟩

cor·ti·co·troph·in \,=,='=fən\ *or* **cor·ti·co·trop·in** \-trōpən\ *n* -S [*cortico-* + *-trophin, -tropin* (fr. *-trophic, -tropic* + *-in*)] **:** a preparation of the adrenocorticotrophic hormone extracted from the anterior pituitary of certain domesticated animals and used esp. in the treatment of rheumatoid arthritis and rheumatic fever

cor·ti·le \kȯr'tē,lā\ *n, pl* **corti·li** \-(,)lē\ [It, fr. (assumed) VL *cohortile,* fr. L *cohort-, cohors* enclosure, court — more at COURT] **:** an open courtyard enclosed by the walls of a building or buildings (as a cloister garth)

cor·tin \'kȯrtᵊn\ *n* -S [*cortex* + *-in*] **1 :** the active principle of the adrenal cortex now known to consist of several hormones **2 :** an aqueous hormone-containing extract of the adrenal cortex — compare CORTICOID

cor·ti·na \kȯr'tīnə, -tēnə\ *n, pl* **corti·nae** \-ī,nē, -ē,nī\ [NL, fr. LL, curtain — more at CURTAIN] **:** the cobwebby remnants of the veil which in mature specimens of certain fungi (order Agaricales) hang from the border of the pileus

cor·ti·nar·i·ous \,kȯrtᵊn¦a(a)rēəs, -ȯrd·ə¦na-\ *adj* [NL *cortina* + E *-arious* (fr. L *-arius*) — more at -ARY] **:** CORTINATE

cor·ti·nar·i·us \,=,='=rēəs\ *n, cap* [NL, fr. *cortina* + L *-arius* -ary; fr. the prominent cortina] **:** a large genus of rusty-spored agarics having a pileus of various colors, powdery gills, and a prominent cortina

cor·ti·nate \'kȯrtᵊn,āt, -rd·ə,nāt\ *adj* [NL *cortina* + E *-ate*] **:** characterized by a cortina

cortine *obs var of* CURTAIN

cor·ti's ganglion \'kȯrd·ēz-, -r,tēz-\ *n, usu cap C* [after Alfonso *Corti* — more at ARCH OF CORTI] **:** a mass of bipolar nerve cells occupying the spiral canal in the modiolus of the cochlea and containing the axons that comprise the cochlear division of the eighth cranial nerve

cor·ti·sol \'kȯrd·ə,sȯl, -sōl\ *n* -S [*cortisone* + *-ol*] **:** HYDROCORTISONE

cor·ti·sone \'kȯ(r)d·ə,sōn, -)tə-, -,zōn\ *n* -S [alter. of *corticosterone*] **:** a colorless crystalline steroid hormone $C_{21}H_{28}O_5$ of the adrenal cortex prepared from the adrenal glands of certain domesticated animals or made synthetically that acts chiefly on carbohydrate metabolism, is usu. administered in the form of its 21-acetate in the treatment esp. of rheumatoid arthritis, rheumatic fever, and certain allergic diseases, and is also used locally in certain inflammatory diseases of the eye; 17-hydroxy-11-dehydrocorticosterone

corti's organ *n, usu cap C* [after Alfonso *Corti*] **:** ORGAN OF CORTI

cort·landt·ite \'kȯ(r)tlən,dīt, -n,tīt\ *n* -S [*Cortlandt* township, Westchester county, N.Y. + E *-ite*] **:** a variety of peridotite consisting essentially of hornblende and olivine

co·ru·co \kə'rü(,)kō\ *n* -S [MexSp] **:** ADOBE BUG

coru·mi·na·ca \kə,rümə'näkə\ *n, pl* **coruminaca** *or* **coruminacas** *usu cap* [native name] **1 a :** an Otuke people **b :** a member of such people **2 :** the language of the Coruminaca people formerly considered to constitute the Coruminacan language family

co·ru·mi·na·can \kə¦rümə¦näkən\ *adj, usu cap* [*Coruminaca* + E *-an*] **:** of, relating to, or characteristic of the Coruminaca people

co·ru·na \kə'rün(y)ə\ *or* **co·ru·ña** \-ünyə\ *or* **co·run·na** \-'rənə\ *adj, usu cap* **:** LA CORUNA

co·run·doph·i·lite \kə,rən'däfə,līt, ,kȯ(,)rə-\ *n* -S [*corundum* + *-o-* + *-phil* + *-ite;* fr. its occurrence together with corundum in one locality] **:** a chlorite $(Mg,Fe)_3(Al,Fe)_3(Si,Al)_4O_{10}(OH)_8$ consisting of magnesium, iron, aluminum hydroxyl silicate

co·run·dum \kə'rəndəm\ *n* -S [Tamil *kuruntam;* akin to Skt *kurunvinda* ruby] **:** aluminum oxide Al_2O_3 occurring in native massive and as variously colored rhombohedral crystals including the gems ruby, sapphire, oriental amethyst, oriental emerald, and oriental topaz, synthesized both in gem and industrial quality, extremely tough and with a hardness exceeded only by a few substances (as silicon carbide and diamond), and used industrially as an abrasive (hardness 9, sp. gr. 3.95–4.10)

co·rus·cant \kə'reskənt; 'kȯrə-, 'kär-\ *adj* [ME, fr. L *coruscant-, coruscans,* pres. part. of *coruscare*] **:** GLITTERING, GLEAMING, CORUSCATING

cor·us·cate \'kȯrə,skāt, 'kär-, *usu* -ād.+V\ *vi* -ED/-ING/-S [L *coruscatus,* past part. of *coruscare* to flash, vibrate; perh. akin to Gk *skairein* to gambol — more at CARDINAL] **1 :** to gleam with intermittent flashes **:** GLITTER, SPARKLE ⟨polished brass, *coruscating* helmets and horses shining like table silver —Edith Wharton⟩ **2 :** to be brilliant or showy in technique or style ⟨an ornate style that *coruscated* with verbal epigrams —Aldous Huxley⟩ **:** be brilliant or keen in intelligence or wit ⟨far-darting, restlessly *coruscating* soul —Thomas Carlyle⟩

cor·us·cat·ing·ly *adv* [*coruscating,* adj. (fr. pres. part. of *coruscate*) + *-ly*] **:** in a flashing, brilliant, or keen manner

cor·us·ca·tion \,=='skāshən\ *n* -S [MF or LL; MF *coruscation,* fr. LL *coruscation-, coruscatio,* fr. L *coruscatus* + *-ion, -io* -ion] **1 :** the act of coruscating or the light so produced **:** GLITTER, SPARKLE ⟨a ~ of lights burned like . . . rubies set in the silver shield of the night —H.G.Wells⟩ **2 :** a brilliant flash of wit **:** the play of intellectual brilliance ⟨continuous verbal ~ sometimes makes attention difficult, so that the line of the play . . . is obscured —*New Republic*⟩

cor·vée \kȯr'vā, '=,=\ *n* -S [ME *corvee,* fr. MF, fr. ML *corrogata,* fr. LL, contribution, collection, fr. L, fem. of *corrogatus,* past part. of *corrogare* to bring together by entreaty, fr. *com-* + *rogare* to ask, request — more at RIGHT] **1 :** unpaid labor (as on roads) for a day or longer period due from a vassal to his lord **2 :** unpaid or partially paid labor exacted usu. in lieu of taxes by public authorities (as for the construction or repair of highways, bridges, or canals) **3 :** an onerous or unpleasant and unavoidable task ⟨the daily ~ of bringing . . . the women in to shop —A.J.Liebling⟩

corves *pl of* CORF

cor·vette \(')kȯr¦vet\ *n* -S [F, fr. MF, prob. fr. MD *corf* basket (or, a ship) — more at CORF] **1 :** a warship with flush deck ranking in the old sailing navies next below a frigate and having usu. only one tier of guns **2 :** a highly maneuverable orig. British and Canadian escort ship that is smaller than a destroyer, armed with antisubmarine and antiaircraft guns and depth charges, and equipped with detection devices

cor·vi·dae \'kȯrvə,dē\ *n pl, cap* [NL, fr. *Corvus,* type genus + *-idae*] **:** a large and widely distributed family of typical passerine birds having a stout moderately long cultrate bill and including the ravens, crows, choughs, magpies, and jays

cor·vi·form \'kȯrvə,fȯrm\ *adj* [L *corvus* + E *-iform*] **:** like a crow in form **:** CORVINE

corvina *var of* CORBINA

cor·vine \'kȯr,vīn\ *adj* [L *corvinus,* fr. *corvus* + *-inus* -ine] **:** of or relating to the crow **:** resembling a crow

cor·void \-vȯid\ *adj* [L *corvus* + E *-oid*] **:** resembling a crow or other member of the Corvidae

cor·vus \-vəs\ *n, cap* [NL, fr. L, raven — more at RAVEN] **:** a widely distributed genus (the type of the family Corvidae) of large active harsh-voiced usu. dark-colored birds including the common crows and ravens

cor·vus·ite \-və,sīt\ *n* -S [L *corvus* + E *-ite;* fr. its color] **:** a hydrous vanadium oxide $V_7O_{17}.nH_2O$ of blue-black to brown color

cor·y·bant \'kȯrə,bant, 'kär-, -rē,-, -baa(ə)nt\ *n, pl* **cory·bants** \-ts\ *or* **cory·ban·tes** \,=='ban(,)tēz, -baan-\ *usu cap* [L *Corybant-, Corybas,* fr. Gk *Korybant-, Korybas,* prob. alter. of *Kyrbant-, Kyrbas*] **1 :** one of the attendants of the Greek nature goddess Cybele who were supposed to accompany her with wild dances and music **2 :** one of the priests of Cybele who act as Corybants with orgiastic processions and rites

cor·y·ban·tic \¦=¦=¦tik, -tēk\ *adj* [Gk *Korybantikos,* fr. *Korybant-, Korybas* + *-ikos* -ic] **:** like or in the spirit of a Corybant; *specif* **:** WILD, FRENZIED ⟨excited by the ~ mood of the gathering⟩

cor·y·bul·bine \,kȯrə'bəl,bēn, -,bən\ *n* -S [ISV *cory-* (fr. NL *Corydalis*) + *bulb-* (fr. NL *bulbosa* — former specific epithet of *Corydalis cava* — fr. L, fem. of *bulbosus* bulbous) + *-ine* — more at BULBOUS] **:** a crystalline alkaloid $C_{21}H_{25}NO_4$ obtained from the roots of species of *Corydalis*

co·ry·ci·um \kə'ris(h)ēəm\ *n* -S *often cap* [NL] **:** a globular object from Finnish Precambrian rocks thought to be the fossil remains of an unknown life-form

co·ryd·a·line \kə'ridᵊl,ēn, -ᵊlən\ *n* -S [G *korydalin,* fr. NL *Corydalis* + G *-in* -ine] **:** a bitter crystalline alkaloid $C_{22}H_{27}NO_4$ obtained from the root of species of *Corydalis*

¹co·ryd·a·lis \-ᵊləs\ *n* [NL, fr. Gk *korydallis* crested lark; fr. the shape of the flowers; akin to L *cornu* horn — more at HORN] **1 a** *cap* **:** a large genus of herbs (family Fumariaceae) that are native to north temperate regions and southern Africa and have decompound leaves, racemose irregular flowers, and a several-seeded capsular fruit **b** -ES **:** any plant of this genus **2** -ES **:** the dried tubers of squirrel corn and Dutchman's-breeches containing the alkaloid corydaline and formerly used as a tonic

²corydalis \"\ [NL, alter. (influenced by Gk *korydallis*) of *Corydalus*] *syn of* CORYDALUS

corydalis green *n* **:** a grayish yellow green that is yellower and paler than average sage green, greener, lighter, and stronger than mermaid, and yellower, lighter, and stronger than palmetto

co·ryd·a·lus \-ᵊləs\ *n, cap* [NL, fr. L, crested lark, fr. Gk *korydalos;* akin to L *cornu* horn — more at HORN] **:** a genus (the type of the family Corydalidae) of large megalopterous insects that includes the dobsons and in some classifications is placed in the family Sialidae

cor·y·dine \'kȯrə,dēn, -,dən\ *n* -S [ISV *coryd-* (fr. NL *Corydalis*) + *-ine*] **:** a crystalline alkaloid $C_{20}H_{23}NO_4$ obtained esp. from the roots of plants of the genus *Corydalis*

co·ryd·o·ras \kə'ridərə\ *n* -S [back-formation fr. *Corydoras,* taken as a plural] **:** any of various small catfishes often kept as scavengers in the tropical aquarium

co·ryd·o·ras \-dərəs\ *n, cap* [NL] **:** a genus (family Callichthyidae) comprising small often brightly colored tropical catfishes often less than an inch in adult length

cor·y·la·ce·ae \,kȯrə'lāsē,ē\ *n pl, cap* [NL, fr. *Corylus,* type genus + *-aceae*] *in some classifications* **:** a family coextensive with the Betulaceae

cor·y·la·ceous \¦kȯrə¦lāshəs\ *adj* [NL *Corylaceae* + E *-ous*] **:** of or relating to the genus *Corylus* **:** BETULACEOUS

cor·y·lop·sis \-'läpsəs\ *n, cap* [NL, fr. *Corylus* + *-opsis*] **:** a small genus of shrubs (family Hamamelidaceae) of the temperate regions of Asia having racemose flowers — compare HAMAMELIS

cor·y·lus \'kȯrələs\ *n, cap* [NL, fr. L *corylus, corulus* hazel or filbert shrub — more at HAZEL] **:** a genus of shrubs or small trees (family Betulaceae) comprising the hazels and having the nut enclosed in a leafy involucre — see FILBERT

cor·ymb \'kȯ,rim(b), 'kä,-, -,rəm(b)\ *n, pl* **corymbs** \-mz\ [F *corymbe,* fr. L *corymbus* cluster of fruits, cluster of flowers, fr. Gk *korymbos* summit, cluster of fruits or flowers; prob. akin to L *cornu* horn — more at HORN] **:** a flat-topped inflorescence; *specif* **:** a flower cluster or inflorescence in which the flower stalks arise at different levels on the main axis and reach about the same height so that there results a somewhat flat-topped cluster in which the outer flowers open first, the inflorescence being indeterminate — compare CYME

corymb

cor·ymbed \-md\ *adj* **:** having corymbs

cor·ym·bif·er·ous \¦kȯrəm¦bif(ə)rəs, ¦kär-, -,rim-\ *adj* [NL *corymbifer* (fr. L, bearing clusters of berries, fr. *corymbi-* — fr. *corymbus* — + *-fer*) + E *-ous*] **:** bearing corymbs

cor·ym·bose \'=(,)=,bōs, kə'rim-\ *adj* [NL *corymbosus,* fr. L *corymbus* corymb + *-osus* -ose] **:** resembling a corymb **:** borne in a corymb — **cor·ym·bose·ly** *adv*

co·rym·bous \kə'rimbəs, kō'-\ *adj* [*corymb* + *-ous*] **:** CORYMBOSE

cor·y·ne·bacteriaceae \¦kȯrə,nē+\ *n pl, cap* [NL, fr. *Corynebacterium,* type genus + *-aceae*] **:** a family (order Eubacteriales) of chiefly gram-positive and nonmotile pleomorphic rod-shaped bacteria that include important parasites as well as saprophytes of soil and dairy products — see CORYNEBACTERIUM, ERYSIPELOTHRIX, LISTERIA

cor·y·ne·bacterial \"+\ *adj* [NL *Corynebacterium* + E *-al*] **:** of, relating to, or caused by bacteria of the genus *Corynebacterium*

cor·y·ne·bacterium \"+\ *n* [NL, fr. Gk *korynē* club + NL *bacterium;* akin to L *cornu* horn — more at HORN] **1** *cap* **:** a large genus (the type of the family Corynebacteriaceae) of usu. gram-positive aerobic to microaerophilic nonmotile bacteria that occur as irregular or branching rods often banded with metachromatic granules and include a number of important parasites of man, lower animals, and plants — see DIPHTHERIA, RING ROT **2** *pl* **corynebacteria :** any bacterium of the genus *Corynebacterium*

co·ryn·e·form \kə'rinə,fȯrm\ *adj* [*coryne-* (fr. NL *Corynebacterium*) + *-form*] **:** resembling bacteria of the genus *Corynebacterium*

cor·y·ne·um \,kȯrə'nēəm, kə'rinē-\ *n, cap* [NL, fr. Gk *korynē* club] **:** a large form genus of imperfect fungi of the family Melanconiaceae having dark-colored fusiform sometimes dry spores with long stalks and several septa — see CALIFORNIA BLIGHT

cor·y·no·car·pus \ˌkȯrənō'kärpəs\ *n, cap* [NL, fr. *coryno-* (fr. Gk *korynē* club) + *-carpus*] **:** a genus (coextensive with a family Corynocarpaceae of the order Sapindales) comprising trees of New Zealand and Polynesia with smooth entire leaves and small white flowers having glandular scales alternating with the petals

cor·y·no·mor·pha \-ō'mȯrfə\ *n, cap* [NL, fr. *coryno-* (fr. Gk *korynē*) + *-morpha*] **:** a genus of solitary marine hydrozoans

cor·y·pha \'kȯrəfə\ *n, cap* [NL, fr. Gk *koryphē* top, summit] **:** a small genus of very large East Indian and Australian fan palms that have a spineless trunk and that die after once fruiting — see BOOK PALM, GEBANG PALM, TALIPOT

cor·y·phae·ni·dae \ˌkȯrə'fēnəˌdē\ *n pl, cap* [NL, fr. *Coryphaena*, type genus (fr. Gk *koryphaina* dolphin, prob. fr. *koryphē*) + *-idae*] **:** a family (coextensive with the genus *Coryphaena*) of large active pelagic percoid fishes comprising the dolphins (sense 2) — **cor·y·phae·noid** \-ˌnȯid\ *adj*

cor·y·phae·noi·di·dae \-ˌfē'nȯidəˌdē\ [NL, fr. *Coryphaenoides*, type genus (fr. *Coryphaena* + *-oides* -oid) + *-idae*] *syn of* MACRURIDAE

cor·y·phae·us \ˌkȯrə'fēəs\ *n, pl* **cory·phaei** \-ēˌī\ [L, leader, fr. Gk *koryphaios* leader, leader of the chorus, fr. *koryphē* top, summit; akin to L *cornu* horn — more at HORN] **1 :** the leader of a chorus — see CHORAGUS 2 **2 :** the leader of a party, school of thought, or other group of persons

cor·y·phée \ˌkȯrə'fā, ˌkär-, -rē;-\ *n* -s [F, fr. L *coryphaeus*] **:** a ballet dancer who dances in a small group instead of in the corps de ballet or as a soloist; *broadly* **:** a dancer in the chorus **:** CHORUS GIRL

cor·y·phene \'kȯrəˌfēn\ *n* -s [F *coryphène*, fr. NL *Coryphaena*] **:** a fish of the genus *Coryphaena* — compare DOLPHIN 2

co·ryph·o·don \kə'rifəˌdän\ *n* [NL, fr. Gk *koryphē* point, top + NL *-odon*] **1** *cap* **:** a genus of extinct mammals (order Pantodonta) from the Lower Eocene of Europe and America varying in size between the tapir and rhinoceros and having short plantigrade 5-toed feet like the elephant and sometimes small or rudimentary horns **2** -s **:** any animal or fossil of the genus *Coryphodon* — **co·ryph·o·dont** \-nt\ *adj or n*

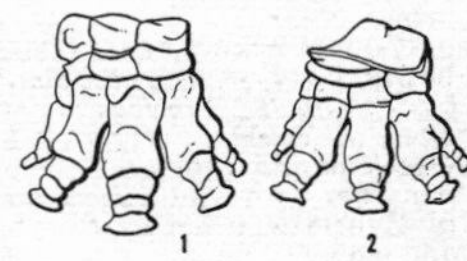

coryphodon: *1* forefoot, *2* hind foot

co·ryth·o·sau·rus \kəˌrithə'sȯrəs\ *n, cap* [NL, fr. *corytho-* (fr. LGk *korythos* crested, fr. Gk *koryth-*, *korys* helmet) + *-saurus*; akin to L *cornu* horn — more at HORN] **:** a genus of duck-billed dinosaurs (suborder Ornithopoda) having a thin domed bony crest capping the skull and found in Upper Cretaceous formations of western No. America

cor·y·tu·ber·ine \ˌkȯrə'tübəˌrēn, -ə'tyü-, -bərən\ *n* -s [ISV *cory-* (fr. NL *Corydalis*) + *tuber-* (fr. NL *tuberosa* — former specific epithet of *Corydalis cava* — fr. L, fem. of *tuberosus* tuberous) + *-ine* — more at CORYDALIS, TUBEROUS] **:** a crystalline alkaloid $C_{19}H_{21}NO_4$ obtained from the roots of certain fumeworts (as members of the genus *Corydalis*)

co·ry·za \kə'rīzə\ *n* -s [LL, fr. Gk *koryza* nasal mucus; akin to OE *hrot* thick fluid, OHG *hroz* nasal mucus, ON *horr* nasal mucus, Skt *kardama* mud, dirt] **:** an acute inflammatory contagious disease involving the upper respiratory tract: **a :** COMMON COLD **b :** such a disease in domestic animals characterized by inflammation of and discharge from the mucous membranes of the upper respiratory tract, sinuses, and eyes; *esp* **:** such a disease in chickens usu. caused by a bacterium (*Hemophilus gallinarum*) — called also *roup* — **co·ry·zal** \-zəl\ *adj*

cos *n* **:** COS LETTUCE

cos *abbr* **1** cosine **2** consul; consulship

COs *pl of* CO

COS *abbr* **1** cash on shipment **2** chief of section **3** chief of staff **4** condemned or suppressed

co sa *abbr* [It *come sopra*] as above

co·sa·lite \'kōzəˌlīt, -ōsə,-\ *n* -s [fr. *Cosalá*, Sinaloa, Mexico + E *-ite*] **:** a lead-gray or steel-gray mineral $Pb_2Bi_2S_5$ composed of lead, bismuth, and sulfur (sp. gr. 6.39–6.75)

co·saque \kō'zäk, kə'-, -zak\ *n* -s [F, lit., Cossack, fr. Russ *kazak* & Ukrainian *kozak* — more at COSSACK] **:** CRACKER 2c

cos·cet \'käsət\ *n* -s [prob. alter. of OE *cotsæta* cottager, fr. *cot* cottage + *-sæta* resident (fr. the stem of *sittan* to sit) — more at COT, SIT] **:** a class of medieval English peasant landholders — see ¹COTTER 2

cos·ci·no·dis·ca·ce·ae \ˌkäsə(ˌ)nōdi'skāsēˌē\ *n pl, cap* [NL, fr. *Coscinodiscus*, type genus + *-aceae*] **:** a family of diatoms (order Centrales) having the characteristics of *Coscinodiscus*

cos·ci·no·dis·cus \-'diskəs\ *n, cap* [NL, fr. Gk *koskinon* sieve + NL *-discus*] **:** a large genus (the type of the family Coscinodiscaceae) of chiefly marine disk-shaped diatoms that are often abundant in the plankton — see CYCLOTELLA

cos·ci·no·man·cy \'käsənōˌmansē\ *n* -ES [LL *coscinomantia*, fr. Gk *koskinomanteia*, fr. *koskinon* sieve + *-manteia* -mancy] **:** divination by the mode of sieve and shears

cos·co·ro·ba \ˌkäskə'rōbə\ *n* -s [Sp] **:** a large white So. American bird (*Coscoroba coscoroba*) of the family Anatidae that is intermediate in several respects between the ducks and swans

cose \'kōz\ *vi* -ED/-ING/-S [back-formation fr. *cosy*] **:** to make oneself cozy **:** be cozy

co·secant \(')kō+\ *n* -s [NL *cosecant-*, *cosecans*, fr. L *co-* + *secant-*, *secans*, pres. part. of *secare* to cut — more at SAW] **:** the distance between the vertex of an angle and any other point on its terminal side divided by the nonzero ordinate of this point, the vertex coinciding with the origin of a plane rectangular coordinate system and the initial side of the angle coinciding with the positive x-axis — abbr. *cosec* or *csc*

co·seism \(')kō +\ *n* -s [*co-* + *seism*] **:** a line drawn about an epicenter through all the coseismal points — called also *coseismal line*

¹**co·seismal** *or* **co·seismic** \(')kō +\ *adj* [*co-* + *seismal*, *seismic*] **:** simultaneously affected by the same phase of any particular seismic shock **:** relating to or being such simultaneous affection

²**coseismal** \"\ *n* -s **:** COSEISM

co·session \(')kō +\ *n* -s [*co-* + *session* (Christ's sitting)] **:** the theological doctrine of the enthronement of the ascended Christ at the right hand of the Father

¹**co·sey** *or* **co·sie** \'kōzē, -zi\ *archaic var of* ¹COZY

²**cosey** *var of* ²COZY

¹**cosh** \'käsh, 'kōsh\ *adj* [origin unknown] **1** *chiefly Scot* **:** COMFORTABLE, SNUG **2** *chiefly Scot* **:** TIDY, NEAT **3** *chiefly Scot* **:** STILL, QUIET

²**cosh** \'käsh\ *n* -ES [perh. fr. Romany *kosh*, *koshter* stick, skewer] *slang Brit* **:** a weighted weapon usu. similar to a blackjack; *also* **:** an attack with a cosh

³**cosh** \"\ *vt* -ED/-ING/-ES **:** to strike or assault with or as if with a cosh

cosh *abbr* [*cosine* + *hyperbolic*] hyperbolic cosine

cosh·er \'käshə(r), 'kōsh-\ *vb* **coshered; coshered; coshering** \-sh(ə)riŋ\ **coshers** [IrGael *cōisir* feast, banquet] *vi* **1** *Irish* **:** to lodge and eat at the expense of dependents or tenants **2** *Irish* **:** to live at another's expense **:** SPONGE **3** *Irish* **:** to make a visit **:** have a friendly chat ~ *vt* **:** PET, PAMPER

cosh·er·er \-sh(ə)rə(r)\ *n* -s **:** one that coshers

cosh·ery \-sh(ə)rē, -ri\ *n* -ES **:** coshering or entertainment so exacted

cosier *comparative of* COSY

cosiest *superlative of* COSY

co·signatory \(')kō +\ *n* -ES [*co-* + *signatory*] **:** one of the joint signers of a document (as a treaty)

cosily *var of* COZILY

cos·in·age \'kəzənij\ *n* -s [ME — more at COUSINAGE] **:** COUSINHOOD — see WRIT OF COSINAGE

co·sine \'kō +,-\ *n* -s [NL *cosinus*, fr. ML *sinus* sine] **:** the abscissa of any point, except the vertex, on the terminal side of an angle, divided by the distance between the vertex and the point, the vertex coinciding with the origin of a plane rectangular coordinate system and the initial side of the angle coinciding with the positive x-axis — abbr. *cos*

cosine curve *n* **:** a curve whose equation in Cartesian coordinates is of the form $y = a \cos x$

cosine law *n* **:** either of two laws of radiation: **a :** the radiant flux emitted in a given direction from a given small area of a perfectly diffusing surface varies as the cosine of the angle of emission **b :** the irradiation by parallel rays falling on a surface varies as the cosine of the angle of incidence

cosiness *var of* COZINESS

cosing *pres part of* COSE

cos lettuce \'käs-\ *n, sometimes cap C* [fr. *Cos*, *Kos*, Greek island of the Dodecanese in the Aegean sea] **:** a variety (*Lactuca sativa longifolia*) of lettuce having long spoon-shaped leaves with large midribs and columnar heads — called also *romaine lettuce*

cosm- *or* **cosmo-** *comb form* [ME (in *cosmographie* cosmography), fr. L *cosm-*, LL *cosmo-*, fr. Gk *kosm-*, *kosmo-*, fr. *kosmos*] **:** world **:** universe ⟨*cosmorama*⟩ ⟨*cosmogenesis*⟩

-cosm \ˌkäzəm\ *n comb form* -s [ME *-cosme*, fr. MF, fr. ML *-cosmus*, fr. Gk *kosmos*] **:** world ⟨micro*cosm*⟩ ⟨loxo*cosm*⟩

cos·ma·tesque \ˌkäzmə'tesk\ *adj, sometimes cap* [It *cosmatesco*, fr. *Cosmati* + *-esco* -esque] **:** of, relating to, or resembling Cosmati work

cos·ma·ti work \(')käz'mäd·ē-, (')kōz'-\ *n, usu cap C* [after *Cosmati*, a group of It. artists active in Rome and vicinity from *ab*1150–1320, pl. of the name *Cosmas*; fr. the fact that many members of the group had the given name *Cosmos* (*Cosimo*)] **:** a style of fine mosaic inlay in geometric patterns made of colored marbles, glass paste, and gold leaf developed during the 12th and 13th centuries

cos·me·col·o·gy \ˌkäzmə'käləjē\ *n* -ES [*cosm-* + *ecology*] **:** the science that considers the earth in its relation to cosmic phenomena

¹**cos·met·ic** \käz'med·ik, -etik, -ēk\ *n* -s [in sense 1, fr. Gk *kometikē*, fr. fem. of *kosmētikos*, adj.; in sense 2, fr. Gk *kosmētikos*, adj.] **1** *archaic* **:** the art of beautifying the body — sometimes used in pl. **2 :** a preparation (except soap) to be applied to the human body for beautifying, preserving, or altering the appearance of a person (as for theatricals) or for cleansing, coloring, conditioning, or protecting the skin, hair, nails, lips, eyes, or teeth

²**cosmetic** \(')=ˈ=\ *adj* [Gk *kosmētikos* skilled in arrangement or adornment, fr. *kosmētos* well-arranged (fr. *kosmein* to arrange, adorn, fr. *kosmos* order, ornament) + *-ikos* -ic] **:** relating to or making for beauty esp. of the complexion **:** BEAUTIFYING ⟨~ salves⟩; *also* **:** correcting defects esp. of the face ⟨~ surgery⟩

cos·met·i·cal \(')käz'med·əkəl, -etə-\ *adj* [Gk *kosmētikos* + E *-al*] **:** relating to cosmetics or to physical appearance — **cos·met·i·cal·ly** \-ək(ə)lē, -li\ *adv*

cos·me·ti·cian \ˌkäzmə'tishən\ *n* -s [¹*cosmetic* + *-ician* (as in *physician*)] **:** one who is expert in the use of cosmetics **:** a makeup artist

cos·me·tol·o·gist \-'täləjəst\ *n* -s **:** one who gives beauty treatments (as to skin and hair) — called also *beautician*

cos·me·tol·o·gy \-'täləjē\ *n* -ES [F *cosmétologie*, fr. *cosmétique* cosmetic (fr. E *cosmetic*) + *-o-* + *-logie* -logy] **:** the art or practice of cosmetic treatment of the skin, hair, and nails and professional application of cosmetics

cos·mic \'käzmik, -mēk\ *adj* [Gk *kosmikos* of the universe, fr. *kosmos* order, universe + *-ikos* -ic] **1 :** of, from, or relating to the cosmos, the extraterrestrial vastness, or the universe in contrast to the earth alone; *sometimes* **:** of, from, or relating to the cosmos as an ordered system or the cosmos outside the solar system ⟨in addition to these general ~ theories there were particular problems, above all that of the diurnal rotation of the earth —Douglas Bush⟩ ⟨the misty radiance of a setting sun, whose streamers are like the spokes of some gigantic ~ wheel —J.L.Lowes⟩ **2 :** characteristic of the cosmos **:** of a magnitude universally transcending or subsuming **:** VAST, UNFATHOMED, INFINITE, GRAND, GRANDIOSE ⟨anthropomorphism . . . making man the central aim or goal of the whole ~ process —M.R.Cohen⟩ ⟨an abiding illness of the 20th century democratic man — a ~ boredom —Albert Hubbell⟩ **3 :** relating to cosmism **syn** see UNIVERSAL

cos·mi·cal \'käzməkəl\ *adj* [Gk *kosmikos* + E *-al*] **1** *obs* **:** relating to the terrestrial world **2 :** COSMIC — **cos·mi·cal·ly** \-k(ə)lē, -li\ *adv*

cos·mi·cal·i·ty \ˌkäzmə'kaləd·ē\ *n* -ES **:** the quality or state of being cosmic

cosmic dust *n* **:** very fine particles of solid matter in any part of the universe including meteoric dust and zodiacal light particles in the solar system, interstellar matter that absorbs starlight and forms the vast dark nebulae of the Milky Way galaxy, and lanes of dark matter in other galaxies

cosmic noise *or* **cosmic static** *n* **:** GALACTIC NOISE

cosmic philosophy *n* **:** COSMISM

cosmic radiation *n* **:** radiation made up of cosmic rays

cosmic ray *n* **:** a stream of atomic nuclei of heterogeneous extremely penetrating character that enter the earth's atmosphere from outer space at speeds approaching that of light and with energies ranging from a few billion to at least 10^7 billion electron volts and that bombard atmospheric atoms to produce mesons as well as secondary particles possessing some of the original energy

cosmic-ray shower \'==ˌ=-\ *n* **:** a shower of ionizing particles originating in bombardment by a single cosmic ray that reveals itself by leaving tracks in a cloud chamber or by actuating a counting tube

cosmic-ray telescope *n* **:** a set of counting tubes so arranged as to register by simultaneous ionic discharge only those cosmic rays coming from a selected direction in space

cosmic year *n* **:** the estimated time required for a star at the sun's distance from the center of the Milky Way galaxy to make one trip around it in a circular orbit, about 200 million years

cos·mine \'käzˌmēn, -mən\ *n* -s [Gk *kosmos* order, arrangement + E *-ine*] **:** a bony material infiltrated by vascular channels that resembles dentin and underlies the ganoin in certain primitive ganoid scales

cos·mism \'käzˌmizəm\ *n* -s [*cosm-* + *-ism*] **:** a philosophy of the cosmos or of cosmic evolution esp. as interpreted teleologically by John Fiske — **cos·mist** \-məst\ *n* -s

cosmo- — see COSM-

cos·mo·chemistry \ˌkäzmō, ˌkäzmə +\ *n* [*cosm-* + *chemistry*] **:** the study of the chemical composition of and changes in the universe

cos·mo·genesis \" +\ *n, pl* **cosmogeneses** [NL, fr. *cosm-* + *-genesis*] **:** COSMOGONY — **cos·mo·genetic** \" +\ *adj*

cos·mog·e·ny \käz'mäjənē, -ni\ *n* -ES [Gk *kosmogeneia*, fr. *kosm-* cosm- + *-geneia* -geny] **:** COSMOGONY

cos·mo·gon·ic \ˌkäzmə'gänik, -nēk\ *or* **cos·mo·gon·i·cal** \-nəkəl\ *also* **cos·mog·o·nal** \(')käz'mägənəl\ *adj* [*cosmogony* + *-ic*, *-ical* or *-al*] **:** relating to or dealing with cosmogony

cos·mog·o·nist \käz'mägənəst\ *n* -s [NL *cosmogonia* + E *-ist*] **:** one specializing in or occupied with cosmogony

cos·mog·o·ny \-'mägənē, -ni\ *n* -ES [NL *cosmogonia*, fr. Gk *kosmogonia*, fr. *kosm-* cosm- + *-gonia* -gony] **1 :** the creation, origination, or manner of coming into being of the world or universe **2 :** a theory or account of the origination of the universe ⟨a primitive ~⟩ **3 :** a part of the science of astronomy that deals with the origin and development of the universe and its components

cos·mog·ra·pher \-'mägrəfə(r)\ *n* -s [*cosmography* + *-er*] **1 :** one skilled or occupied in cosmography **2** *obs* **:** GEOGRAPHER

cos·mo·graph·ic \ˌkäzmə'grafik\ *or* **cos·mo·graph·i·cal** \-fəkəl\ *adj* [F *cosmographique*, fr. *cosmographie* (fr. LL *cosmographia*) + *-ique* -ic, -ical] **:** concerned with or relating to cosmography — **cos·mo·graph·i·cal·ly** \-fək(ə)lē\ *adv*

cos·mog·ra·phist \käz'mägrəfəst\ *n* -s [*cosmography* + *-ist*] **:** COSMOGRAPHER

cos·mog·ra·phy \-fē, -fi\ *n* -ES [ME *cosmographie*, fr. LL *cosmographia*, fr. Gk *kosmographia*, fr. *kosm-* cosm- + *-graphia* -graphy] **1 :** a general description of the world or of the universe **:** a recital of cosmic principles or speculations **2 :** the science that deals with the constitution of the whole order of nature or the figure, disposition, and relation of all of its various parts

cos·moid \'käzˌmȯid\ *adj* [*cosmine* + *-oid*] **:** indicating a ganoid scale that contains a cosmine layer

cos·mo·labe \'käzməˌlāb\ *n* -s [MF, fr. *cosm-* + *-labe*] **:** an instrument resembling the astrolabe formerly used for measuring angular distances between heavenly bodies

cos·mo·line \'käzməˌlēn, -lən\ *vt* -ED/-ING/-S **:** to smear with Cosmoline grease (as for storage) ⟨Tokyo fell and the guns were *cosmolined* —John Scarne⟩

Cosmoline \"\ *trademark* — used for petrolatum

cos·mo·log·ic \ˌkäzmə'läjik, -jēk\ *or* **cos·mo·log·i·cal** \-jəkəl\ *adj* [*cosmology* + *-ic* or *-ical*] **:** of or relating to cosmology — **cos·mo·log·i·cal·ly** \-jək(ə)lē, -li\ *adv*

cos·mol·o·gist \käz'mäləjəst\ *n* -s [*cosmology* + *-ist*] **:** one skilled in, occupied with, or propounding a cosmology

cos·mol·o·gy \-'mäləjē, -ji\ *n* -ES [NL *cosmologia*, fr. *cosm-* + *-logia* -logy] **1 :** a branch of systematic philosophy that deals with the character of the universe as a cosmos by combining speculative metaphysics and scientific knowledge; *esp* **:** a branch of philosophy that deals with the processes of nature and the relation of its parts — compare ONTOLOGY **2 :** a particular theory or body of doctrine relating to the natural order **3 :** astronomy dealing with the origin, structure, and space-time relationships of the universe

cos·mo·naut \'käzməˌnȯt, -ˌnät\ *n* -s [part trans. of Russ *kosmonavt*, fr. Gk *kosmos* + Russ *-navt* (as in *aeronavt* aeronaut)] **:** a traveler beyond the earth's atmosphere **:** ASTRONAUT

cos·mo·plastic \ˌkäzmə +\ *adj* [Gk *kosmoplastēs* molder of the world (fr. *kosm-* cosm- + *plastēs* molder, fr. *plassein* to mold) + E *-ic* — more at PLASTIC] **:** of a molding force regarded as operative in the formation of the world independently of God **:** world-forming ⟨~ and hylozoic atheisms —Ralph Cudworth⟩

cos·mo·poi·et·ic \ˌkäzmōˌpȯi'ed·ik, -mə,-\ *adj* [Gk *kosmopoiētikos*, fr. *kosm-* cosm- + *poiētikos* capable of making, creative, poetical — more at POETIC] **:** cosmos-producing **:** world-creating

cos·mop·o·lis \käz'mäpələs\ *n* -ES [NL, fr. F *cosmopolitain* & E *cosmopolitan*, after F *métropolitain* & E *metropolitan*: LL *metropolis*] **1 :** a community of citizens of the world bound by juridical or moral principles **2 :** a city of world importance or inhabited by many nationalities

¹**cos·mo·pol·i·tan** \ˌkäzmə'pälət°n *also* -ətən *or* əd·ən\ *adj* [F *cosmopolitain*, fr. MF, fr. *cosmopolite* + *-ain* (as in MF *métropolitain* metropolitan)] **1 :** marked by interest in, familiarity with, or knowledge and appreciation of many parts of the world **:** not provincial, local, limited, or restricted by the attitudes, interests, or loyalties of a single region, section, or sphere of activity **:** worldwide rather than regional, parochial, or narrow ⟨the softened ~ teaching of the prophets of the captivity and the rigid national teaching of the instructors of Israel's youth —Matthew Arnold⟩ ⟨his ~ benevolence, impartially extended to all races and to all creeds —T.B.Macaulay⟩ **2 :** marked by sophistication and savoir faire arising from urban life and wide travel ⟨the instructor began to put on the airs of the city. He wanted to appear ~ —Sherwood Anderson⟩ **3 :** composed of persons, constituents, or elements from all parts of the world or from many different places or levels ⟨that queer, ~, rather sinister crowd that is to be found around the Marseilles docks —Rose Macaulay⟩ **4 :** widely distributed and common **:** found in most parts of the world and under varied ecological conditions — used of kinds of organisms ⟨the coccidia are ~ parasites⟩ **syn** see UNIVERSAL

²**cosmopolitan** \"\ *n* -s **:** one that is cosmopolitan

cos·mo·pol·i·tan·ism \-ˌizəm\ *n* -s **1 :** the quality or state of being cosmopolitan **:** cosmopolitan character **2 a** (1) **:** the theory or advocacy of the formation of a world society or cosmopolis (sense 1) ⟨advocates of internationalism who decry the sovereignty or need of state organization . . . are called proponents of ~ —F.L.Burdette⟩ (2) **:** a climate of opinion distinguished by the absence of narrow national loyalties or parochial prejudices and by a readiness to borrow from other lands or regions in the formation of cultural or artistic patterns ⟨a genial ~ was the hallmark of that enlightened age⟩ ⟨the literary ~ was followed by an artistic ~ which transcended all frontiers —Paul Wescher⟩ **b :** excessive admiration and imitation of the cultural traits or achievements of others at the expense of the cultural identity or integrity of one's own land or region ⟨a "divine provincialism" . . . is but ill replaced by a ~ lacking in virtue and distinction —Agnes Repplier⟩

cos·mo·pol·i·tan·ize \-ˌīz\ *vt* -ED/-ING/-S **:** to make cosmopolitan

cosmopolitan justice *n* **:** a theory of criminal jurisdiction whereby any state having before it a criminal who has committed a grave offense anywhere in the world may punish him without regard to his citizenship or where he acted or what state was injured

cos·mo·pol·i·tan·ly *adv* **:** in a cosmopolitan manner

¹**cos·mop·o·lite** \käz'mäpəˌlīt\ *n* -s [NL *cosmopolites*, fr. Gk *kosmopolitēs*, fr. *kosm-* cosm- + *politēs* citizen — more at POLICE] **1 :** one that is at home in every country **:** a citizen of the world **:** one without national prejudices or attachments **2 a :** a cosmopolitan organism **b :** a literary form (as a tale, proverb, or maxim) occurring in many different languages or areas **3 :** PAINTED LADY

²**cosmopolite** \(')=ˈ=ˌ=\ *adj* **:** COSMOPOLITAN

cos·mo·political \ˌkäzmō, ˌkäzmə +\ *adj* **:** of the nature of universal polities or interests

cos·mop·o·lit·ism \käz'mäpəˌlīdˌizəm, -ī,tiz-\ *n* -s **:** COSMOPOLITANISM

cos·mo·ra·ma \ˌkäzmə'ramə, -rämə, '==ˌ==\ *n* -s [*cosm-* + *panorama*] **:** an exhibition of views of various parts of the world made to appear realistic by mirrors, lenses, and illumination — **cos·mo·ram·ic** \ˌ=='ramik\ *adj*

cos·mor·gan·ic \ˌkäzˌmȯ(r)'ganik\ *adj* [*cosm-* + *organic*] **:** relating to or implying an organic cosmos ⟨a ~ evolution⟩

cos·mos \'käzməs; *in senses 1 & 2 also* -ˌmōs *or* -ˌmäs\ *n* [G *kosmos*, fr. Gk, order, ornament, universe] **1** -ES **a :** the universe conceived as an orderly and harmonious system — contrasted with *chaos* **b :** ORDER, HARMONY **2** -ES **:** a self-inclusive system characterized by order and harmony amid complexity of detail **3** *cap* [NL, fr. Gk *kosmos*] **:** a genus of tropical American herbs (family Compositae) having opposite leaves, flowers solitary in loose corymbose panicles, and flower heads with prominent rays most cultivated varieties of which are derived from a Mexican species (*C. bipinnatus*) and are popular fall-blooming annuals **4** *pl* **cosmos** *also* **cosmoses :** any plant or flower of the genus *Cosmos*

cos·mos·o·phy \käz'mäsəfē\ *n* -ES [ISV *cosm-* + *-sophy*] **:** a body of belief or theory about the cosmos

cos·mo·sphere \'käzmə +,-\ *n* -s [*cosm-* + *-sphere*] **1 :** the material universe **2 :** an apparatus for showing the position of the earth at any given time with respect to the fixed stars that consists of a hollow glass globe on which are depicted the stars and constellations and within which is a terrestrial globe

cos·mo·tellurian \ˌkäz(ˌ)mō, ˌkäzmə +\ *adj* [*cosm-* + *tellurian*] **:** relating to or affecting both heavens and earth

cos·mo·the·ism \'käzmə(ˌ)thēˌizəm, ˌ=='th-\ *n* -s [*cosm-* + *-theism*] **:** ascription of divinity to the cosmos **:** identification of God with the world **:** PANTHEISM — **cos·mo·the·ist** \'käzməˌthēəst, -ˌthēˌist, ˌ=='thēəst\ *n* -s — **cos·mo·the·is·tic** \ˌ==thē'istik\ *adj*

cos·mo·thet·ic \ˌkäzmə'thed·ik\ *adj* [*cosm-* + Gk *thetikos* positive, fr. *thet-* (stem of *tithenai* to set, place, assume) + *-ikos* -ic — more at DO] *philos* **:** positing the external world — compare COSMOTHETIC IDEALISM

cosmothetic idealism *n* **:** a theory that posits a real external world but denies that mind has immediate cognizance of matter — compare REPRESENTATIONALISM

cos·mo·zo·ic \ˌkäzmə'zōik\ *adj* [*cosm-* + *-zoic*] **:** of or relating to the hypothetical origination of life in or from outer space ⟨~ theories⟩

cos·mo·zo·ism \ˌkäzmə'zōˌizəm, '==ˌ==\ *n* -s [*cosm-* + *zoism*] **:** the theory or conception of the cosmos as animate

-cosms *pl of* -COSM

co·solvent \(')kō+\ *n* [*co-* + *solvent*] **:** a solvent that in conjunction with another solvent can dissolve a solute ⟨ether and alcohol are ~s for pyroxylin⟩

co·sovereignty \(')kō+\ *n* [*co-* + *sovereignty*] **:** joint sovereignty

co·specific \ˌkō+\ *adj* [*co-* + *specific*] **:** of the same species

co·sponsor \(')kō+\ *n* [*co-* + *sponsor*] **:** a joint sponsor

cos·sack \ˈkäˌsak *also* -sək\ *n* -s *sometimes cap* [Russ *kazak* & Ukrainian *kozak*, fr. Turk *kazak* free, independent person, adventurer, vagabond] **1 :** a member of a favored military caste of Russian frontiersmen and border guards in Czarist Russia, esp. in the Ukraine, who played an important part in Russian expansion in the Ukraine and eastward into southeastern Russia, the Caucasus, and Siberia **2 :** a member of an armed contingent (as company police) using force to suppress or break up some activity (as a strike or demonstration)

cossack green *n* **:** a dark yellowish green that is yellower and duller than holly green (sense 1), lighter and stronger than deep chrome green, and yellower and paler than average hunter green

cossack post *n, sometimes cap C* **:** a onetime 4-man outguard that posted a single sentinel

cos·sae·an \kəˈsēən\ *n* -s *cap* [L *Cossaeus* (fr. Gk *Kossaios*, fr. *Kossaia*, land of the Kassites) + E *-an*] **:** KASSITE 1

cosse green \ˈkäs-\ *n* [F *cosse* pod, fr. (assumed) VL *coccia*, alter. (influenced by L *coccum* kermes berry, excrescence on a plant) of L *cochlea* snail — more at COCHLEA, COCC-] **:** a strong yellow green that is yellower and slightly duller than viridine yellow and yellower, lighter, and stronger than parrot green

¹cos·set \ˈkäsət, *usu* -d.+V\ *n* -s [origin unknown] **:** a lamb reared without the aid of the dam **:** a pet lamb **:** PET

²cosset \"\ *vt* -ED/-ING/-S **:** to treat as a pet **:** FONDLE, PAMPER, CODDLE ⟨my complaint is that my life is too ~*ed* and padded —John Buchan⟩ ⟨one who ~*ed* his health —Joyce Cary⟩

cos·sette \käˈset, kəˈ-, ˈkäsət\ *n* -s [F, dim. of *cosse* pod — more at COSSE GREEN] **:** a strip or slice (as of sugar beet or potato) **:** CHIP

¹cos·sid \ˈkäsəd\ *n* -s [Hindi *qāṣid*, fr. Ar] *India* **:** a mounted messenger

²cossid \"\ *adj* [NL *Cossidae*] **:** of or belonging to the family Cossidae

cos·si·dae \ˈkäsəˌdē\ *n pl, cap* [NL, fr. *Cossus*, type genus + *-idae*] **:** a family of nocturnal moths with heavy spindle-shaped bodies and strong narrow wings including the goat moths, carpenter moths, and related forms and having larvae that bore in the wood of living trees

cos·sus \ˈkäsəs\ *n, cap* [NL, fr. L, a kind of larva under the bark of trees; perh. akin to Gk *skedannynai* to scatter — more at SHATTER] **:** the type genus of Cossidae including a number of moths the larvae of which were once highly esteemed as food and are still eaten by Australian aborigines — see WITCHETTY GRUB

cos·sy·rite \ˈkäsəˌrīt\ *n* -s [G *cossyrit*, fr. *Cossyra*, island near Sicily (now *Pantelleria*) + G *-it* -ite] **:** a variety of aenigmatite occurring in minute crystals in lava

¹cost \ˈkȯst *also* ˈkäst\ *n* -s [ME, fr. OF, fr. *coster*, v.] **1 a :** the amount or equivalent paid or given or charged or engaged to be paid or given for anything bought or taken in barter or for service rendered **:** CHARGE, PRICE **b :** whatever must be given, sacrificed, suffered, or forgone to secure a benefit or accomplish a result ⟨to retain life at the ~ of honor⟩ **2 :** loss, deprivation, or suffering as the necessary price of something gained or as the unavoidable result or penalty of an action ⟨knowledge is gained at the ~ of innocence⟩ ⟨he found him, to his ~, a dangerous enemy⟩ **3 :** the expenditure or outlay of money, time, or labor ⟨to spare no ~ in furnishing a house⟩ ⟨to live *cost*-free⟩ **4 costs** *pl* **:** expenses incurred in litigation: as **a :** those payable to the attorney or counsel by his client esp. when fixed by law **b :** those given by the law or the court to the prevailing against the losing party in equity and frequently by statute — called also *bill of costs* **5 :** an item of outlay incurred in the operation of a business enterprise (as for the purchase of raw materials, labor, services, supplies) including depreciation and amortization of capital assets — see ACTUAL COST, CONVERSION COST, DIRECT COST, DISTRIBUTION COST, HISTORICAL COST, INDIRECT COST, PREDETERMINED COST, PRIME COST, PRODUCTION COST, STANDARD COST **6 :** something that is sacrificed to obtain something else — see ALTERNATIVE COST, REAL COST

²cost \"\ *vb* **cost; cost; costing; costs** [ME *costen*, fr. MF *coster*, fr. L *constare* to stand with or at, cost, agree — more at CONSTANT] *vi* **1 :** to require expenditure or payment **2 :** to require effort, suffering, or loss ~ *vt* **1 a :** to have a price of ⟨the book ~*s* five dollars⟩ **b :** to cause or require the expenditure or loss of ⟨riots between natives and foreigners ~ some lives —*Encyc. Americana*⟩ ⟨to prepare oneself for this ~*s* some trouble —I.A.Richards⟩ **2 :** to cause to pay, suffer, or lose something ⟨it will ~ you about $10 each way —Richard Joseph⟩ ⟨long wait had ~ him his dinner —T.B.Costain⟩ ⟨rear guard action that ~ the British dearly —F.V.W.Mason⟩

³cost \"\ *vb* -ED/-ING/-S [prob. fr. ¹*cost*] *vt* **:** to estimate or figure on the cost of ⟨some colleges try to ~ menus before they use them —*College and Univ. Business*⟩ ~ *vi* **:** to estimate or figure on costs ⟨standardize ~*ing* in an industry⟩

⁴cost \"\ *n* -s [MF *coste*, lit., rib — more at COAST] **:** RIBBON 2a

cost- *or* **costi-** *or* **costo-** *comb form* [F, fr. L *costa*] **:** rib **:** costa ⟨*cost*ectomy⟩ ⟨*costi*form⟩ **:** costal and ⟨*costo*radial⟩ ⟨*costo*sternal⟩

cos·ta \ˈkästə\ *n, pl* **cos·tae** \-(ˌ)stē, -ˌstī\ [L, rib — more at COAST] **:** a rib or a bodily structure resembling a rib: as **a** *anat* **:** the side or border of a part **b** *bot* **:** a leaf vein; *esp* **:** MIDRIB **c** *zool* **:** any of various ridged or thickened linear parts; *specif* **:** the anterior vein of an insect's wing

cost accountant *n* **:** one skilled in the technique of cost accounting **:** one whose business or vocation is accounting for costs

cost accounting *n* **1 :** the branch of accounting that deals with systematically classifying, recording, analyzing, and summarizing in those books of account constituting a cost system the cost elements of material, labor, and burden incident to production or to the rendering of a service **2 :** the art of devising and installing cost systems

¹cos·tal \ˈkästᵊl\ *adj* [F, fr. MF, fr. *coste* side, rib + *-al* — more at COAST] **:** of or relating to a costa or rib; *also* **:** relating to or situated near ribs ⟨a ~ scale or plate⟩ ⟨a *costal*-veined leaf⟩

²costal \"\ *n* -s **:** a costal element (as a plate or nerve)

costal cartilage *n* **:** any of the cartilages that connect the distal ends of the ribs with the sternum and by their elasticity permit of the movements of the walls of the chest in respiration — see THORAX

cos·tal·ly \ˈkästəlē\ *adv* **:** in a costal position or direction; *specif* **:** toward or at the costal vein or adjoining margin of an insect's wing

costal-nerved \ˈ==ˌ=\ *adj, bot* **:** costal-veined — see ¹COSTAL

costal process *n* **1 :** the ventral or anterior root of the transverse process of a cervical vertebra **2 :** a process of the sternum of many birds with which the ribs articulate

costal respiration *n* **:** inspiration and expiration produced chiefly by movements of the ribs — distinguished from *diaphragmatic respiration*

cost analysis *n* **1 :** the act of breaking down a cost summary into its constituents and studying and reporting on each factor **2 :** the comparison of costs (as of standard with actual or for a given period with another) for the purpose of disclosing and reporting on conditions subject to improvement

cost and freight *n* **:** a charge or quotation made in waterborne export trade by a seller to a buyer that includes the price of the goods and all transportation costs to a designated destination — abbr. *C and F*

cos·ta·no·an \kəˈstänəwən, kōˈ-\ *n, pl* **costanoan** *or* **costanoans** *usu cap* [*Costano*, a division of the Costanoan (fr. Sp *costeño*, lit., coastman, fr. *costa* coast, fr. L *costa* rib, side) + E *-an* — more at COAST] **1 a :** an Indian people of coastal California from San Francisco Bay to Monterey **b :** a member of such people **2 :** a language of the Costanoan people **3 :** a language family of the Penutian stock comprising only the Costanoan language or languages

¹co·star \ˈkō+\ *n* [*co-* + *star*] **:** a star whose role in a motion picture or a play is equal in importance to that of another leading player

²costar \(ˈ)kō+\ *vi* **:** to appear with another star in a motion picture or a play ~ *vt* **:** to employ or present (a player) as one of two or more leading players in a motion picture or play

cos·tard \ˈkästə(r)d, ˈkȯs-; *Brit usu* ˈkəs-\ *n* -s [ME, perh. fr. OF *coste* rib + ME *-ard*; fr. its ribbed appearance — more at COAST] **1 :** any of several large oval strongly ribbed English cooking apples — compare CODLING, PIPPIN **2** *archaic* **:** PATE ⟨whether your ~ or my ballow be the harder —Shak.⟩

costardmonger *archaic var of* COSTERMONGER

cos·ta ri·ca \ˌkästəˈrēkə, ˌkȯs-, ˌkōs-\ *adj, usu cap C&R* [fr. *Costa Rica*, country in Central America] **:** of or from Costa Rica **:** of the kind or style prevalent in Costa Rica **:** COSTA RICAN

¹cos·ta ri·can \-kən\ *adj, usu cap C&R* [*Costa Rica*, the country + E *-an*] **1 :** of, relating to, or characteristic of Costa Rica **2 :** of, relating to, or characteristic of Costa Ricans

²costa rican *n, pl* **costa ricans** *cap C&R* **:** a native or inhabitant of Costa Rica

cos·ta·ta \käˈstād·ə\ *n pl, cap* [NL, fr. L, neut. pl. of *costatus*] *in certain classifications* **:** a suborder of Salientia comprising the frogs and toads with ribs that is nearly coextensive with the family Discoglossidae — compare PHANEROGLOSSA

cos·tate \ˈkäˌstāt, -stət\ *adj* [L *costatus*, fr. *costa* rib + *-atus* -ate — more at COAST] **:** having ribs: as **a :** having one or more longitudinal ribs or nerves ⟨a ~ leaf⟩ **b :** having ridges on the surface ⟨a ~ shell⟩

cos·tated \-ˌstād·əd\ *adj* [L *costatus* + E *-ed*] **:** COSTATE

cost bond *n* **:** a bond filed by plaintiff guaranteeing payment of court costs

cost book *n, Brit* **:** a book made up every 16 weeks containing the names of the shareholders and the number of shares held by each partner and particulars of all transactions in a partnership formed for working a mine

cost card *n* **:** COST SHEET

cost center *n* **:** the most appropriate production unit (as a single machine, a group of machines or workers, or a department) into which manufacturing operations may be divided to facilitate the allocation and application of cost factors

cost clerk *n* **1 :** one who computes the cost of producing or selling goods or of any phase of business operations **2 :** a clerk who checks the cost of each item purchased against the seller's price list

cost control *n* **:** use by management of cost analyses and their interpretation in corrective measures toward increasing efficiency and economy of operation

cos·tean *or* **cos·teen** \käˈstēn, ˈ=ˌ=\ *vi* -ED/-ING/-S [fr. (assumed) Corn *costēn*, prob. fr. *codha* to fall, happen + *stēn* tin; akin to ON *hitta* to hit, find — more at HIT, STANNUM] *Brit* **:** to dig trenches or small pits through the surface soil or debris to the underlying rock in place for the purpose of exposing the outcrop of a mineral deposit and determining its course

cos·ter \ˈkästə(r)\ *n* -s [by shortening] *Brit* **:** COSTERMONGER

costermonger \ˈkästə(r)+ˌ-\ *n* [*coster* (alter. of *costard*) + *monger*] **1** *archaic Brit* **:** a street seller of fruit **2** *Brit* **:** a hawker of fruit or vegetables from a street stand, barrow, or cart

cost factor *n* **:** an element or condition related to a unit of product or to an activity or to a service for which money must be spent (as raw material, direct labor, and burden)

cost finding *n* **:** COST ACCOUNTING

cost·ful \ˈkȯstfəl\ *adj* [ME, fr. ¹*cost* + *-ful*] *archaic* **:** COSTLY

costi- — see COST-

cos·ti·a·sis \käsˈtīəsəs\ *n, pl* **costia·ses** \-ˌsēz\ [NL, fr. *Costia* (genus name of *Costia necatrix*) + *-iasis*] **:** a frequently fatal disease of freshwater fishes due to invasion of the skin by a flagellated protozoan (*Costia necatrix*)

costing *n* -s [fr. gerund of ³*cost* (estimate cost)] **1** *chiefly Brit* **:** COST ACCOUNTING **2 :** the calculating, recording, and allocating of current costs and determining of prospective costs for the guidance of management in regulating operations

cost, insurance, and freight *adj* **:** subject to agreement that cost of transportation and insurance be paid by the seller of goods to the named point of destination — abbr. *CIF*

cos·tive \ˈkästiv, ˈkȯs-\ *adj* [ME *costif*, modif. of MF *costivé*, past part. of *costiver* to bind, constipate, fr. L *constipare* — more at CONSTIPATE] **1 a :** CONSTIPATED **b :** causing constipation **2 a :** slow or stiff in action or expression **:** SLUGGISH ⟨the system . . . was so ~ that no new design could ever be expected —*Economist*⟩ ⟨readers now wearied by the ~ pronouncements —*Times Lit. Supp.*⟩ **b :** NIGGARDLY — **cos·tive·ly** \-stəvlē\ *adv*

cos·tive·ness \-nəs\ *n* -ES [ME *costyfnes*, fr. *costyf*, *costif* costive + *-nes* -ness] **:** CONSTIPATION

cost keeper *n* **:** COST ACCOUNTANT

cost ledger *n* **:** one of the books of account in a cost system to which entries are posted from books of original entry, the various accounts therein showing the accumulated costs classified as to order, process, type of expense, and department

cost·less \ˈkȯstləs *also* ˈkäs-, *rap.* -s(t)l-\ *adj* **:** costing nothing

cost·li·ness \ˈkȯstlēnəs, -lin- *also* ˈkäs-, *rap.* -s(t)l-\ *n* -ES **:** the quality or state of being costly **:** high price or value **:** EXPENSIVENESS

cost·ly \ˈkȯstlē, -li *also* ˈkäs-, *rap.* -s(t)l-\ *adj* -ER/-EST [ME, ¹*cost* + *-ly*] **1 :** of great cost or value **:** FINE, RICH, SPLENDID ⟨they are clad in very ~ robes of silk; they are girdled like queens —Lafcadio Hearn⟩ **2 :** involving excessive expenditure **:** necessitating considerable loss or sacrifice ⟨to encourage me in litigation and to make it as protracted and ~ as he can —G.B.Shaw⟩ **3 :** EXTRAVAGANT, PRODIGAL, LAVISH ⟨~ entertainment⟩ ⟨~ habits⟩

syn COSTLY, EXPENSIVE, DEAR, VALUABLE, PRECIOUS, INVALUABLE, PRICELESS: COSTLY stresses high price and may suggest elegance, sumptuousness, or luxury ⟨the curtains and upholstery of the chairs and sofas and the hangings of my bed are of the *costliest* and most beautiful fabrics, and must have been of fabulous value when they were made —Bram Stoker⟩ ⟨walls, columns, and arches seem a quarry of precious stones, so beautiful and *costly* are the marbles with which they are inlaid —Nathaniel Hawthorne⟩ EXPENSIVE may imply a cost above a purchaser's means or above intrinsic valuation ⟨the father was unable to give the child as *expensive* an education as he had desired —J.A.Froude⟩ DEAR indicates a high cost, often one greatly increased because of scarcities ⟨the lively affection seamen have for strong drink is well known; but in the South Seas, where it is so seldom to be had, a thoroughbred sailor deems scarcely any price too *dear* which will purchase his darling "tot" —Herman Melville⟩ VALUABLE may suggest hope or chance of great gain or usefulness or of high price in sale or exchange ⟨how *valuable* these lands were to become Congress could hardly guess, nor did it suspect that the grants in the northern part of the state were to be worth millions in timber and iron —*Amer. Guide Series: Minn.*⟩ PRECIOUS may stress extremely great value, often value brought about by rareness or scarcity ⟨a *precious* thing, a treasure beyond diamonds or rubies —Jack London⟩ ⟨we of the Bounty's launch had been so accustomed to thinking of wine and spirits as the most *precious* of commodities, to be taken only a spoonful at a time —C.B.Nordhoff & J.N.Hall⟩ In other than monetary matters, these words keep more or less the same connotations COSTLY, DEAR, and EXPENSIVE may describe great expenditure of resources, materials, or effort ⟨in order to finance the ever more *costly* equipment and maintenance of the new paid soldiery, the rulers of Europe had recourse to the financier —Lewis Mumford⟩ ⟨their stout resistance was destined to cost them *dear* . . . many thousand citizens were ruined, many millions of property confiscated —J.L.Motley⟩ DEAR and PRECIOUS are often used in matters of emotion ⟨and measureless sweet I deem her, and *dear* she is to mine eyes —William Morris⟩ ⟨his child, his *precious* possession —W.F. de Morgan⟩ ⟨*precious* Savior, still our refuge —Joseph Scriven⟩ VALUABLE often describes things or conditions quite advantageous or useful ⟨that the release of the information at the time it is received will not prove *valuable* to the enemy —F.D. Roosevelt⟩ INVALUABLE and PRICELESS may describe any thing or condition of such great worth that evaluation is practically impossible ⟨this *invaluable* liquor was of a pale golden hue, like other of the rarest Italian wines —Nathaniel Hawthorne⟩ ⟨control of the sea was a *priceless* asset to the Union. the navy maintained communications with Europe, cut off those of the South, captured important coastal cities —S.E.Morison & H.S.Commager⟩

cost·mary \ˈkȯstˌmerē, -ˌma(a)rē, -ˌmārē, -ri *also* ˈkäst-\ *n* -ES [ME *costmarie*, fr. *coste* costmary (fr. OE *cost*, fr. L *costum*, fr. Gk *kostos* costusroot) + *Marie* Mary (the Virgin *Mary*)] **1 :** a tansy-scented herb (*Chrysanthemum balsamita*) that has yellow flowers shaped like buttons and is used as a potherb and salad plant and now less commonly in flavoring ale and beer — called also *alecost, bible leaf* **2 :** the common tansy (*Tanacetum vulgare*)

costo- — see COST-

cos·to·central \ˌkästə, ˌkästō+\ *adj* [*cost-* + *central*] **:** relating to or joining a rib and a vertebral centrum

cos·to·chondral \"+\ *adj* [*cost-* + *chondral*] **:** relating to or joining a rib and costal cartilage

cos·to·clavicular \"+\ *adj* [*cost-* + *clavicular*] **:** of or relating to a ligament connecting the costal cartilage of the first rib with the clavicle

cos·to·coracoid \"+\ *adj* [*cost-* + *coracoid*] **:** relating to or joining the ribs and coracoid process or bone

costocoracoid membrane *n* **:** a strong fascia that ensheathes and extends between the subclavius and pectoralis minor muscles and that protects the axillary vessels and nerves

cost of living : the cost of purchasing those goods and services which are included in an accepted standard level of consumption

cost-of-living index \ˌ=ˈ=ˌ==-\ *n* **:** CONSUMER PRICE INDEX

cost of money : rate of interest or dividend payment on borrowed capital

cost of sales 1 *in retailing* **:** the purchase cost or inventory value of merchandise sold during a stated period plus the cost of direct work thereon (as alterations or workroom charges) **2** *in manufacturing* **:** the production cost or inventory value of goods sold during a stated period

cos·ton light \ˈkȯstən-, ˈkäs-\ *n, usu cap C* [after B. F. *Coston* *fl*1840, its inventor] **:** a signal made by burning lights of different colors that is used by ships at sea and in the life-saving service

cos·to·transverse \ˌkästə, ˌkästō+\ *adj* [*cost-* + *transverse*] **:** relating to or connecting a rib and the transverse process of a vertebra

cos·to·xiphoid \"+\ *adj* [*cost-* + *xiphoid*] **:** relating to or connecting a costal cartilage and the xiphoid process

cost-plus *adj* **:** providing for calculation of payment for work done under contract by adding to actual cost either a fixed fee or a percentage of the cost as profit

cos·trel \ˈkästrəl\ *n* -s [ME, fr. MF *costerel*, fr. *costier* at the side (fr. *coste* rib, side) + *-el* (dim. suffix) — more at COAST] *now dial Eng* **:** a leather, earthenware, or wooden container for liquids having ears by which it may be hung up; *specif* **:** a small wooden keg

costs *pl of* COST, *pres 3d sing of* COST

cost sheet *n* **:** a sheet on which detailed cost elements relating to a specific production order or process are assembled — called also *cost card*

cost system *n* **:** books of account specif. designed for purposes of cost accounting **:** a cost-accounting system

cos·tu·la \ˈkäschələ, -styə-\ *or* **cos·tule** \-schəl, -styəl\ *n, pl* **costu·lae** \-ˌlē, -ˌlī\ *or* **costules** [NL *costula*, fr. L *costa* rib + NL *-ula* — more at COAST] *zool* **:** a small ridge (as one of those that make up the sculpture of a mollusk shell) — **cos·tu·lation** \ˌ==ˈlāshən\ *n* -s

¹cos·tum·bris·ta \ˌkōstəmˈbristə, ˌkäs-, -rēs-\ *n* -s [Sp, fr. *costumbre* custom (fr. L *consuetudin-*, *consuetudo*) + *-ista* -ist — more at CUSTOM] **:** a Spanish or Latin-American writer whose work is marked by usu. realistic depiction of local or regional customs and types

²costumbrista \ˌ==ˈ==\ *adj* **:** depicting local or regional customs, scenes, or types in literature or art ⟨a ~ novel⟩ ⟨a ~ picture⟩

¹cos·tume \ˈkäˌst(y)üm, *sometimes* ˈ=ˌ= *or* =ˈ= *or* ˈkästəm *or sporadically* ˈkäschəm\ *n* -s [F, fr. It *costume* custom, dress, fr. L *consuetudin-*, *consuetudo* custom — more at CUSTOM] **1** *archaic* **:** custom or style with respect to manners, dress, arms, and other surroundings of a place or period depicted in a painting **2 :** the distinctive style and prevailing fashion of personal adornment including the style of wearing the hair, jewelry, and apparel of all kinds characteristic of any period, country, class, occupation, or occasion **3 :** the distinctive dress of a particular period, locality, or occupation worn in the drama, at fancy-dress balls, or for festivals or carnivals **4 :** the chiefly outer garments worn by a person at any one time; *esp* **:** a woman's ensemble of dress with coat or jacket

²costume \"\ *vt* -ED/-ING/-S **:** to provide with a costume ⟨*costumed* in medieval armor⟩ **:** design costumes for ⟨~ a play⟩

³costume \"\ *adj* **1 a :** characterized by the use of costume (sense 3) ⟨a ~ ball⟩ **b :** depicting or portraying a subject taken from a bygone age or set in an exotic locale and usu. marked by the display or depiction of colorful costumes or pageantry ⟨a ~ movie⟩ ⟨a ~ novel⟩ **2 :** suitable for or enhancing the effect of a particular costume ⟨a ~ handbag⟩

costume jewelry *n* **:** jewelry for wear with current fashions usu. made of inexpensive materials (as metal, shells, plastics, wood) often set with imitation or semiprecious stones

cos·tum·er \-mə(r)\ *n* -s [¹*costume* + *-er*] **1 :** one that makes or deals in costumes (as for stage or fancy-dress events) **2 :** CLOTHES TREE

cos·tum·ery \-m(ə)rē, -ri\ *n* -ES [¹*costume* + *-ery*] **1 :** articles of costume **:** a quantity of costumes **2 :** the art of costuming

cos·tum·ier \ˌkästəmˈyā, ˈ=ˌ=ˌ=, (ˈ)käˈst(y)ümēə(r), ˈkästəmə(r)\ *n* -s [F, fr. *costume* costume + *-ier* -er — more at COSTUME] **:** one that makes, sells, or rents costumes

cost unit *n* **:** a unit of a commodity or service selected as the appropriate unit for cost purposes

cos·tus oil \ˈkȯstəs-, ˈkäs-\ *n* [*costus*root + oil] **:** a light yellow essential oil obtained from costusroot

cos·tus·root \ˈkȯstəs, ˈkästəs+\ *n* [Gk *kostos* costusroot + E *root*] **:** the fragrant root of an annual herb (*Saussurea lappa*) native to Kashmir that yields a volatile oil used in perfumery, in sachets, and for preserving furs

co·surety \(ˈ)kō+\ *n* [*co-* + *surety*] **:** a person who is a surety with another

co·suretyship \(ˈ)kō+\ *n* [*co-* + *suretyship*] **:** joint liability with another as surety on the same obligation

co·swearer \(ˈ)kō+\ *n* [*co-* + *swearer*] **:** one bound by a common oath with another; *specif* **:** COMPURGATOR

cosy *var of* COZY

¹cot \ˈkät, *usu* -äd.+V\ *n* -s [ME, fr. OE; akin to MHG *kūz* pit as a place of execution, ON *kot* small hut, Goth *qithus* stomach, L *guttur* throat, Gk (Maced dial.) *goda* intestines, Skt *guḍa* bowel, rectum; basic meaning: round, curved] **1 :** a small house **:** a cottage or hut **2 :** COTE 3 **3 :** a cover or sheath: as **a :** the cloth covering of a drawing roller in a spinning frame **b :** a protective cover for a finger

²cot \"\ *vt* **cotted; cotted; cotting; cots :** to provide shelter for **:** put in a cot

³cot *or* **cott** \"\ *n* -s [ME *cot*, fr. AF, perh. fr. ML *cottum* quilt] **:** a matted or felted lock of wool or hair (as in the fleece of a sheep or the fur of a cat) **:** refuse wool

⁴cot \"\ *vi* **cotted; cotted; cotting; cots :** to form cots **:** MAT

⁵cot \ˈkät, ˈkȯt\ *n* -s [IrGael *coite*] *Irish* **:** a small boat

⁶cot \ˈkät, *usu* -äd.+V\ *n* -s [Hindi *khāṭ* bedstead, bier, fr. Skt *khaṭvā*, of Dravidian origin; akin to Tamil-Malayalam *kaṭṭil* bedstead, bier] **1** *India* **:** a light bedstead **:** CHARPOY **2 :** a small bed that is often collapsible and that is used typically for camping or by a child

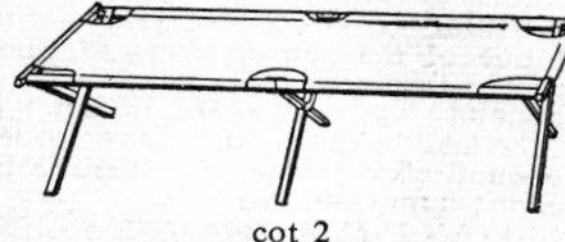

cot 2

3 : a bed made of canvas stretched on a frame, suspended like a hammock, and formerly used on shipboard esp. by officers and sick persons **4 :** a wheeled stretcher for hospital, mortuary, or ambulance service

⁷cot \"\ *n* -s [by shortening] **:** APRICOT

cot *abbr* cotangent

co·ta *or* **cot·ta** \ˈkōd·ə, -ōˌtä\ *n* -s [Tag, Bisayan & Taw-Sug *kutà* fort, of Dravidian origin; akin to Tamil *koṭṭai* fort] **:** a fort formerly common in parts of the Philippines

co·tangent \(ˈ)kō+\ *n* [NL *cotangent-*, *cotangens*, fr. *co-* + *tangent-*, *tangens* tangent] **:** the abscissa of any point except the vertex on the terminal side of an angle divided by the nonzero ordinate of the point, the vertex coinciding with the origin of a plane rectangular coordinate system and the initial side of the angle coinciding with the positive x-axis — abbr. *cot* or *ctn*

co·tar·i·us \kə'ta(a)rēəs, kō'-\ *n, pl* **cotarii** \-rē,ī\ [ML — more at COTTER] : ¹COTTER 2

co·tar·nine \kō'tär,nēn, -nən\ *n* -s [ISV, anagram of *narcotine;* prob. orig. formed as G *kotarnin*] : a crystalline alkaloid $C_{12}H_{15}NO_4$ obtained by the oxidation of narcotine and used chiefly in the form of its chloride in checking bleeding esp. from small blood vessels

cot bed *n* [⁶*cot*] : a light narrow single bed

¹cotch \'käch\ *vb* -ED/-ING/-ES [by alter.] *dial* : ¹CATCH

²cotch \"\ *n* -ES [Malay *kachu* — more at CATECHU] : CATECHU

¹cote \'kōt, *usu* -ōd·+V; *sometimes esp in senses 3 & 4* 'kät\ *n* -s [ME, fr. OE; akin to OE *cot* cottage — more at COT] **1** *now dial Eng* : ¹COT 1 **2** : the ancient holding of a cotter consisting typically of a house or hut and five acres of land **3** : a shed or coop for small domestic animals; *specif* : a structure for pigeons **4** : a sheltering structure ⟨a bell ~⟩

²cote *vt* -ED/-ING/-S [prob. fr. MF *cotoyer*, fr. OF *costoier*, fr. *coste* side, coast — more at COAST] *obs* : to pass by

³côte \'kōt\ *n* -s [F, slope, side, rib, fr. OF *coste* — more at COAST] : a French hillside vineyard or series of hillside vineyards — often used prepositively in compounds (as *Côte Rotiè*) naming such vineyards and their wines — compare CHÂTEAU 3, CLOS

cote–armour *n, pl* **cotes–armours** [ME *cote armure*, fr. MF *cote a armeure*, coat with (heraldic) arms] *obs* : COAT OF ARMS

co·teau \kō'tō, kō'-\ *n, pl* **co·teaux** \-'tō(z)\ [CanF, fr. F, slope of a hill, small hill, fr. OF *costel* slope, dim. of *coste* slope, side, rib] **1** : a hilly upland including the divide between two valleys : DIVIDE **2** : the side of a valley

co·teen \kä'tēn, kō't-, '=,='=\ *n* -s [¹*cot* + *-een*] *Irish* : ¹COT

co·te·har·die \(')kōd·¦ärdē, -ōt¦ä-, -ōt¦hä-\ *n* -s [MF *cote hardie*, lit., bold tunic] : a long-sleeved medieval garment that was usu. thigh-length and belted for men and full-length for women and that was made to fit closely often by buttoning or lacing

cô·te·lé \¦kōd·ᵊl¦ā\ *adj* [F, lit., ribbed, fr. MF *costelé*, fr. *costel* small rib (dim. of *coste* rib) + *-é* (fr. L *-atus* -ate) — more at COAST] *in decorative art* : having a broken outline of straight or curved portions

côte·lette \kōt'let\ *n* -s [F — more at CUTLET] : CUTLET

co·tenancy \(')kō+\ *n* [*co-* + *tenancy*] : JOINT TENANCY

co·tenant \(')kō+\ *n* [*co-* + *tenant*] : JOINT TENANT

co·ten·tion \(')kō¦tenchən\ *n* -s [*co-* + *attention*] : a mode of attention or sustained interest undisturbed by the intrusion of affect — compare DITENTION

cotehardie

co·ten·tive \-entiv\ *adj* [fr. *cotention*, after E *attention: attentive*] : of, relating to, or marked by cotention

co·tenure \(')kō+\ *n* [*co-* + *tenure*] : joint tenure

cot·er·ell \'käd·ərəl\ *n* -s [ME *coterel*, fr. OF & ML; OF *coterel*, fr. ML *coterellus*, dim. of *cotarius* cotter] : ¹COTTER 2

co·te·rie \'kō|d·ə·rē, |tərē, -ri; ,=='rē; *esp archaic* ¦kä|\ *n* -s *often attrib* [F, fr. MF, association of peasant tenants, fr. (assumed) *cotier* cottager (fr. ML *cotarius*) + MF *-ie* -y — more at COTTER] : an intimate often exclusive group of persons having a binding common interest or purpose : CLIQUE ⟨the aristocratic ~ finally got the upper hand —Edith Hamilton⟩

co·ter·mi·nous \(')kō¦tərmənəs, -¦tōm-\ *adj* [alter. of *conterminous*] **1** : having the same or coincident boundaries : covering or involving the same area ⟨the city of Washington and the District of Columbia are ~⟩ **2** : coincident or coextensive in range, scope, limit, time, or duration ⟨the 35 year period . . . ~ with the career of the hardy Champlain —Allan Nevins & H.S.Commager⟩ : identical with ⟨since folk culture has always existed, a study of its origins is ~ with the study of the origins of culture itself —S.W.Mintz⟩ **syn** see ADJACENT

co·ter·mi·nous·ly *adv* : in a coterminous manner : so as to be coterminous

¹cotes *pl of* COTE, *pres 3d sing of* COTE

²côtes *pl of* CÔTE

coth *abbr* [*co*tangent + *h*yperbolic] hyperbolic cotangent

coth·a·more \'kōt(h)ə,mōr\ *n* -s [IrGael *cōta mōr*, lit., big coat] : a frieze overcoat made in Ireland

coth·er·stone \'kəthə(r)stən\ *n* -s *usu cap* [fr. *Cotherstone*, Yorkshire, England] : a rennet cheese of cow's milk resembling Stilton

cothouse \'=,=\ *n* [¹*cot* + *house*] *chiefly Scot* : COT, COTTAGE

co·thurn \'kō,thərn, ='=\ *n* [F & L; F *cothurne*, fr. L *cothurnus*] : COTHURNUS

co·thur·nal \(')kō¦thərnəl\ *adj* [L *cothurnus* + E *-al*] **1** : of or relating to the cothurnus **2** : of, relating to, or characteristic of tragedy

co·thur·nus \kō'thərnəs, kə'-\ *n, pl* **cothur·ni** \-,nī\ [L, fr. Gk *kothornos*] **1** : a thick-soled laced boot reaching halfway to the knees worn by actors in the Greek and Roman tragic drama — called also *buskin* **2** : the dignified and somewhat stilted spirit of ancient tragedy

co·tidal \(')kō+\ *adj* [*co-* + *tidal*] : marking or indicating an equality in the tides or a coincidence in the time of high or low tide ⟨~ lines on a chart⟩

co·til·lion \kō'tilyən, kə'-\ *also* **co·til·lon** \", kótēyōⁿ\ *n* -s [F *cotillon*, lit., petticoat, fr. OF, fr. *cote* coat — more at COAT] **1** : a ballroom dance for couples that resembles the quadrille and is possibly based on French peasant dances **2** : an elaborate dance executed under the leadership of one couple at formal balls and marked by the giving of favors and frequent changing of partners : GERMAN **3** : a formal ball (as one at which debutantes are presented to society)

co·tin·ga \kō'tiŋgə, kə'-\ *n* [NL, fr. F *cotinga*, of Tupian origin; akin to Tupi *coting* to wash, *tinga* white] **1** *cap* : the type genus of Cotingidae **2** -s : a bird of the genus *Cotinga* or family Cotingidae

cotinga purple *n, often cap C* : IMPERIAL 10

co·tin·gi·dae \kō'tinjə,dē, kə'-\ *n pl, cap* [NL, fr. *Cotinga*, type genus + *-idae*] : a family of birds (suborder Tyranni) of tropical America related to the manakins

cot·i·nus \'kät'nəs\ *n, cap* [NL, fr. L *cotinus*, a kind of shrub furnishing a purple color] : a genus of shrubs or small trees (family Anacardiaceae) that are sometimes included in *Rhus* but distinguished by plumose sterile pedicels in the fruiting panicles — see SMOKE TREE

¹cot·ise *also* **cot·ice** *or* **cot·tise** *or* **cot·tice** \'käd·əs\ *n* -s [MF *cotice*, *costice*, fr. *coste* rib + *-ice* — more at COAST] *heraldry* : one of a pair of narrow stripes borne one along each side of but slightly separated from a bend, fess, bar, pale, or chevron

²cotise \"\ *vt* -ED/-ING/-S *heraldry* : to put cotises along the sides of

cotised *adj, heraldry* : borne between cotises ⟨a fess ~⟩

co·titular \(')kō+\ *n* [*co-* + *titular*] : one of the patron saints to whom a church is jointly dedicated

cotised bend

cot·land \'kätlənd\ *n* [ME, fr. ¹*cot* + *land*] : the land belonging to a cot or cotter

cot·man \'kätmən\ *n, pl* **cotmen** [ME, fr. ¹*cot* + *man*] *chiefly Scot* : COTTAGER, COTTER

¹co·to \'kōd·ō\ *or* **coto bark** *n* -s [Sp *cotocoto*, fr. Quechua *kkhotokkhótó*] : the bark of an unidentified tree of northern Bolivia formerly used as an astringent and stomachic

²coto \"\ *n, pl* **coto** *or* **cotos** *usu cap* [Sp, of AmerInd origin] **1 a** : a Tucano people of eastern Ecuador **b** : a member of such people **2** : the Tucano language of the Coto people

³coto \"\ *also* **coc·to** \'kōk(,)tō, 'käk-\ *n, pl* **coto** *or* **cotos** *also* **cocto** *or* **coctos** *usu cap* [Sp, of AmerInd origin] **1 a** : a Chibchan people of Costa Rica **b** : a member of such people **2** : the Chibchan language of the Coto people

co·to·in \'kōd·əwən\ *n* -s [ISV ¹*coto* + *-in*; orig. formed as G *kotoin*] : a crystalline ketone $C_{14}H_{12}O_4$ occurring in true coto bark and formerly used in intestinal disorders; 2,6-dihydroxy-4-methoxy-benzophenone

co·to·na·me \,kōd·ə'nä(,)mā\ *or* **co·to·nam** \'==,näm, -,nam\ *n, pl* **cotoname** *or* **cotonames** *or* **cotonam** *or* **cotonams** *usu cap* [Sp *cotoname*, of AmerInd origin] **1 a** : an Indian people of northeastern Mexico **b** : a member of such people **2** : the Coahuiltecan language of the Cotoname people

co·to·ne·as·ter \kə,tōnē'astə(r), =='==,== *also* 'kät'n,ēst-\ *n* [NL, fr. L *cotoneum*, *cydoneum* quince + NL *-aster* — more at QUINCE] **1** *cap* : a genus of Old World shrubs (family Rosaceae) with small, numerous, and mostly entire leaves and fruit a pome containing two to five nutlets **2** -s : any shrub of the genus *Cotoneaster*

co·ton·er·ol A \kō¦tänə,rō'lä, -rō'-\ *n, usu cap C* [origin unknown] : a direct dye — see DYE table I (under *Direct Black 22*)

co·to·nier \,kōtən'yā, ,kót-, '==,=\ *n* -s [LaF *cotonnier*, fr. F, cotton plant, fr. *coton* cotton + *-ier* -er — more at COTTON] *dial* : a sycamore (*Platanus occidentalis*)

cot·quean \'kät,kwēn\ *n* -s [¹*cot* + *quean* (woman)] **1** *obs* : the wife of a cotter **2** *archaic* **a** : a coarse masculine woman **b** : a man who busies himself with affairs properly feminine

co–tradition \¦kō +\ *n* [*co-* + *tradition*] : the entire cultural history of an area in which a number of cultures have been interrelated over a period of time

cot·rine \'kä·trən, -,trēn\ *n* -s [origin unknown] : a dark orange yellow to light yellowish brown that is very slightly redder than spruce yellow

co·trustee \(¦)kō +\ *n* [*co-* + *trustee*] : a joint trustee

cots *pl of* COT, *pres 3d sing of* COT

cots·wold \'kät,swōld, -,swəld\ *n* -s *usu cap* [fr. *Cotswold* hills, Gloucestershire, England, where the breed developed] : a sheep of an English breed of large long-wooled sheep

cott *var of* COT

¹cot·ta \'käd·ə, -ätə\ *n* -s [ML, of Gmc origin; akin to OHG *kozza* coarse mantle — more at COAT] : a short white ecclesiastical vestment worn by various clerics, altar boys, and choristers — compare SURPLICE

²cot·ta *var of* COTA

cot·tage \'käd·ij, -ätij, -ēj\ *n* -s [ME *cotage*, fr. (assumed) AF, fr. ME ¹*cot* + OF *-age*] **1** : the dwelling of a rural laborer, small farmer, or miner : COT **2** : a small structure built as a temporary or occasional shelter typically for shepherds or hunters : HUT, SHACK **3** : a detached one-family house; *esp* : a frame house of no more than one or two stories **4 a** : one of several detached dwelling units forming part of a resort hotel, sanatorium, hospital, or school : GUESTHOUSE; *specif* : one of several small detached dwelling units that house neglected or delinquent children and are designed to reproduce a noninstitutional familial environment **b** : a small house designed typically for summer use

cotta

cottage bonnet *n* : a woman's bonnet of a shape fashionable in England in the first half of the 19th century

cottage cheese *n* : a soft uncured cheese made from soured skim milk — called also *Dutch cheese, pot cheese, smearcase*

cottage curtains *n pl* : a double set of straight-hanging window curtains, one for each sash, the upper set often made with ruffles and tiebacks and usu. overlapping the lower set

cottage fried potatoes *n pl* : raw or cooked potatoes sliced and fried in a heavy skillet — called also *home fried potatoes*

cottage hospital *n* **1** *Brit* : a small hospital that is served by local general practitioners **2** : a hospital consisting of or including several detached or semidetached cottages

cottage industry *n* : an industry based upon the family unit as a labor force in which workers using their own equipment at home process goods usu. belonging to a merchant employer and supplement their income from small agricultural holdings

cottage lily *n* : MADONNA LILY

cottage loaf *n, Brit* : a loaf of bread consisting of a smaller round part on top of a larger round part

cottage nail *n* : a small cut nail similar to a shingle nail and available in lengths ¾ in. to 1½ in.

cottage organ *n* : a small reed organ

cottage or·né \-(')ȯr¦nā\ *n, pl* **cottages ornés** \-"\ [F, lit., ornate cottage] : a picturesquely designed small country house of 19th century England

cottage period *n* : a period in a country's economic development when its industry is primarily cottage industry

cottage piano : a small upright piano of the 19th century

cottage pie *n* : SHEPHERD'S PIE

cottage pink *n* : a very fragrant tufted pink (*Dianthus plumarius*) with solitary flowers having petals deeply cleft and rose or pink-colored with a striate or darker center

cottage pudding *n* : plain cake covered with a hot sweet sauce

cot·tag·er \'käd·ijə(r), -äti-, -ēj-\ *n* -s **1** : ¹COTTER 2 **2** *Brit* : a rural laborer **3** : one who resides in a cottage at a resort

cottage rose *n* : a European rose (*Rosa alba*) or any of several forms derived from it having broad serrate nonglandular leaves and flowers with a smooth hypanthium

cottage style *n* : a book cover design made of panels with sides resembling gables developed by the 17th century English binder Samuel Mearne

cottage tulip *n* : any of various tall-growing tulips that flower in May as distinguished from the very early-flowering and the late-flowering tulips — compare DARWIN TULIP

cot·tagey \-jē\ *adj* : resembling or suggesting a cottage

cot·ta grass \'käd·ə-\ *n* [modif. of NL *Cottea*, genus name of *Cottea pappophoroides*] : an erect branching perennial grass (*Cottea pappophoroides*) of the southwestern U.S. with narrow attenuate leaves

cotte \'kät, 'kȯt\ *n* -s [F, fr. OF *cote*, *cotte* — more at COAT] : a tight-fitting garment resembling the cotehardie

cotted *past of* COT

¹cot·ter *or* **cot·tar** \'käd·ə(r), -ätə-\ *n* -s [ME *cottar*, *cotar*, fr. ML *cottarius*, *cotarius*, fr. ME ¹*cot* + L *-arius* -ary — more at COT] **1 a** : COTTIER 2 **b** : COTTIER 3 **2** : a peasant of a class of medieval English villeins ranking next above the slaves and below the bordars and usu. including the coscets **3** *in Scotland* **a** : a peasant occupying a small holding orig. in return for services **b** : a peasant tenant similar to the Irish cottier

²cotter \"\ *vb* -ED/-ING/-S [prob. freq. of ⁴*cot*] **1** *dial Brit* **a** : MAT, ENTANGLE **b** : CLOT, CONGEAL, COAGULATE **2** *dial Eng* : SHRIVEL, SHRINK, PUCKER, WITHER — often used with *up*

³cotter *also* **cottar** \"\ *n* -s [short for *cotterel*] **1 a** : a wedge-shaped or tapered piece used to fasten together parts of a machine or structure by being driven into a tapered opening through one or all the parts — called also *key* **b** : COTTER PIN **2** : TOGGLE

⁴cotter \"\ *vt* -ED/-ING/-S : to fasten with a cotter

cotter drill *n* [³*cotter*] : TRAVERSE DRILL

cot·ter·el \'kätər(ə)l, -trəl\ *n* -s [origin unknown] **1** *dial Eng* : ³COTTER **2** *dial Eng* : a bar, crane, or pothook for a fireplace

a cotter fastening parts *b* and *c*

cotter mill *n* [³*cotter*] : a milling cutter for forming grooves, slots, or keyways

cotter pin *n* [³*cotter*] : a half-round metal strip bent into a pin whose ends can be flared after insertion through a slot or hole

cotterway \'==,=\ *n* [³*cotter* + *way*] : a slot or hole that receives a cotter : KEYWAY

cot·tid \'käd·əd\ *n* -s : a fish of the family Cottidae

cot·ti·dae \'käd·ə,dē\ *n pl, cap* [NL, fr. *Cottus*, type genus + *-idae*] : a family of fishes (order Scleroparei) comprising the sculpins and related forms all of which have a tapering body, wide mouth, and large head and occur in fresh and salt water in the cold and temperate parts of the northern hemisphere

¹cot·ti·er \'käd·ēə(r), -ätē-\ *n* -s [fr. (assumed) MF *cotier* — more at COTERIE] **1** : ¹COTTER 2 **2** : a tenant in Ireland formerly renting a small farm under the rack-rent system, the land being let to the highest bidder **3** : a peasant farmer

²cottier *comparative of* COTTY

cottiest *superlative of* COTTY

cotting *pres part of* COT

cottise *or* **cottice** *var of* COTISE

cot·tle \'käd·ᵊl, -ät'l\ *n* -s [origin unknown] **1** : a band or wall typically of clay that encircles an object to be molded and determines the outer extremity of the completed mold **2** : a cylinder usu. of waterproof paper used for retaining plaster-of-paris slurry around a mold or form

¹cot·ton \'kät'n\ *n* -s *often attrib* [ME *coton*, fr. MF, fr. Ar dial. *quṭun*, fr. Ar *quṭn*] **1** : a soft fibrous usu. white substance that clothes the seeds of various plants esp. of the genus *Gossypium*, is composed of unicellular hairs forming fine twisted fibers from ½ inch to over 2 inches long when mature, and is used extensively in the making of threads, yarns, and fabrics **2** : any plant of the genus *Gossypium* characterized by an erect and freely branching habit, alternate lobed leaves, and large creamy white or yellow flowers that soon turn red and are subtended by a cup-shaped involucre and produce a capsular fruit that bursts open when ripe thereby exposing the seeds and attached hairs — see SEA ISLAND COTTON, UPLAND COTTON **3 a** : a fabric made of cotton **b** : a garment made of cotton **4 a** : any of the various yarns spun from the short carded fiber and the long combed fiber of cotton **b** : any of the various hard-twisted or loose-twisted threads of cotton used for sewing, embroidery, and crocheting **5** : any downy substance resembling cotton produced by such plants as the silk-cotton tree and cottonwood **6** : a woolen fabric resembling frieze and made in England in the 16th and 17th centuries **7** : CELLULOSE NITRATE 2

cotton: *1* flowering branch; *2* unopened fruit; *3* fruit partly open

²cotton \"\ *vb* **cottoned; cottoned; cottoning** \-t(ᵊ)niŋ\ **cottons** [ME *cotonen*, fr. *coton*, n.] *vt* **1** *obs* : to furnish with a down or nap **2** : to wrap as if in cotton : CODDLE ~ *vi* **1** *obs* **a** : to rise with a nap **b** : to go on prosperously : develop well : SUCCEED **2 a** : to harmonize in action or association : AGREE **b** : to make friends : FRATERNIZE ⟨a quarrel will end in one of you being turned off, in which case it will not be easy to ~ with another —Jonathan Swift⟩ **3** : to become attached by or as if by personal liking : TAKE — used with *to* ⟨he rather ~*s* to the idea —John Galsworthy⟩ **4** : UNDERSTAND, PERCEIVE, TUMBLE — used with *to* or *on to* ⟨could ~ on to the fact that it was my car —Nigel Balchin⟩ **5** : to curry favor : TOADY

cot·ton·ade \,kät'n'ād, '==,=\ *n* -s [F *cotonnade*, fr. *coton* cotton (fr. MF) + *-ade*] : a heavy coarse twilled cotton fabric made to resemble woolen fabric and used for work clothes

cotton anthracnose *n* : a destructive disease of cotton caused by an ascomycete (*Glomerella gossypii*) that produces reddish brown to light-colored or necrotic spots on seedling parts and on leaves, stems, and bolls

cotton aphid *n* : a small widely distributed and variably colored aphid (*Aphis gossypii*) that attacks the leaves of various plants and is esp. injurious to cotton, cucurbits to which it transmits certain mosaic diseases, and citrus

cotton ball *n* : a disease of the cranberry caused by a fungus (*Sclerotinia oxycocci*) that forms a cottony mass of mycelium in the center of affected berries

cotton–boll weevil \'==¦=-\ *n* : BOLL WEEVIL

cotton bollworm *n* : CORN EARWORM — used of the worm when feeding in cotton bolls

cotton bur *n* : the dried cotton boll and attached pedicel of snapped or stripped cotton after the lint and seed are removed

cottonbush \'==,=\ *n, Austral* : either of two low Australian forage shrubs (*Kochia villosa* and *Bassia bicornis*)

cotton cake *n* : COTTONSEED CAKE

cotton candy *n* : a candy made in a special machine by spinning sugar that has been boiled to a high temperature

cotton dauber *n* : either of two lygus bugs (*Lygus elesius* and *L. oblineatus*) that attack cotton plants in the southwestern U.S.

cotton dye *n* : any of various direct dyes — see DYE table I (under *Direct Brown 57, Direct Blue 41, Direct Yellow 26*)

cottoned out *adj* : deprived of its crop-producing capacity by continuous cropping with cotton

cotton fern *n* : a Californian fern (*Notholaena newberryi*) characterized by a hairy covering on the fronds

cottonfish \'==,=\ *n* [so called fr. the sticky threads it exudes] **1** : BOWFIN **2** *Austral* : COTTON SPINNER

cotton fleahopper *n* : a small green No. American mirid bug (*Psallus seriatus*) that feeds on the young squares and new growth of cotton and on many other cultivated and wild plants

cotton gin *n* : a machine that separates the seeds, hulls, and foreign material from cotton

cotton grass *or* **cotton rush** *n* [so called fr. the tufted heads] : any sedge of the genus *Eriophorum*

cotton gum *n* [so called fr. the tufts of cottony hairs on the seeds] : TUPELO GUM

cot·ton·ize \'kät'n,īz\ *vt* -ED/-ING/-S : to make like cotton; *specif* : to reduce (flax, hemp) to short cottony fiber

cotton leafworm *n* : the slender greenish black-and-white-marked larva of a tropical American noctuid moth (*Alabama argillacea*) that migrates northward as far as southeastern Canada in the spring and deposits its eggs on cotton leaves on which the larvae feed often thereby defoliating the plants — called also *cotton leaf caterpillar*

cot·ton·less \-ləs\ *adj* : being without cotton

cotton moth *n* : any moth whose larva feeds on cotton; *esp* : the adult of the cotton leafworm

cotton mouse *n* : a rather large dark field mouse (*Peromyscus gossypinus*) widely distributed in the southeastern U. S.

cottonmouth \'==,=\ *also* **cottonmouth moccasin** *n* [so called fr. the white interior of the mouth] : WATER MOCCASIN

cotton mule *n* : a small mule suitable for the cultivation of cotton — distinguished from *sugar mule*

cotton picker *n* : a machine for gathering the ripe lint and seed of cotton from the standing stalk

cotton–picking \¦==,==\ *adj* : DAMNED — often used as a generalized expression of disapproval

cotton powder *n* : an explosive (as tonite) in which guncotton is a prominent ingredient

cotton press *n* **1** : a press for baling ginned cotton **2** : a building where cotton is baled

cotton rat *n* : a destructive long-haired burrowing rat (*Sigmodon hispidus*) native to the southern U.S. and Central America that in a typical subspecies (*S. h. hispidus*) has recently proved valuable in poliomyelitis research

cotton rock *n* **1** : decomposed chert **2** : a magnesian limestone

cotton–root bark \'==¦=-\ *n* : the recently gathered air-dried bark of the roots of various cultivated cottons (esp. *Gossypium herbaceum*) formerly used as an emmenagogue

cotton root rot *n* : a destructive wilting and browning disease of cotton and other plants in the Southwest caused by a fungus (*Phymatotrichum omnivorum*)

cotton rose *n* **1** : CONFEDERATE ROSE **2** : FILAGO 2; *esp* : an annual herb (*Filago germanica*) with capitate clusters of woolly heads — called also *herba impia*

cotton rust *n* **1** : a disease of cotton caused by a rust fungus (*Puccinia stakmanii*) that produces slightly elevated greenish yellow or orange aecia chiefly on the undersurface of the leaves **2** : a potash-deficiency disease of cotton that produces a rusty brown color in the leaves

cottons *pl of* COTTON, *pres 3d sing of* COTTON

cottonseed \'==,=\ *n* : the seed of the cotton plant

cottonseed cake *n* : the solid mass remaining after the oil has been expressed from cottonseeds — called also *cotton cake*

cottonseed feed *n* : a mixture of cottonseed hulls and cottonseed meal containing less than 36 percent protein

cottonseed foots *n pl* : residue from cottonseed-oil refining

cottonseed hulls *n pl* : the outer covering of cottonseeds used as a roughage for feeding cattle

cottonseed meal *n* : a meal high in protein obtained in the production of cottonseed oil usu. by grinding cottonseed cake and used as a feed for livestock and as a fertilizer

cottonseed oil *n* : a semidrying fatty oil that is obtained from cottonseed by expression or solvent extraction, is pale yellow after refining, contains principally glycerides of linoleic, oleic, and palmitic acids, and is used chiefly in salad and cooking oils and after hydrogenation in shortenings and margarine

cotton shrimp *n* **:** a condition of shrimp in which the animal appears bluish and the flesh soft, white, and cottony
cotton shrub *n* **1 :** ¹COTTON 2 **2 :** a half-buried low Australian shrub (*Dryandra nivea*) of the family Proteaceae
cotton–sick \ˈ==,=\ *adj* **:** unable to produce cotton because infested with cotton pests — used of land
cotton sled *n* **:** a box-shaped machine with a V-shaped opening that when drawn over cotton plants pulls off the bolls and directs them into the box
cotton spinner *n* **:** a sea cucumber (esp. *Holothuria forskali*) that ejects a mass of white Cuvierian organs when disturbed
cotton spirits *n* **:** a solution of a stannic salt; *esp* **:** the chloride used as a mordant for cotton
cotton stainer *n* **:** any of several red and black or dark brown bugs (genus *Dysdercus*) that are economic pests of cotton and oranges and other fruits in warmer areas; *specif* **:** a red and dark brown bug (*D. suturellus*) that injures cotton in the southern U.S. by puncturing the developing bolls thereby causing an exudation that stains the lint
cotton stripper *n* **:** STRIPPER 3b
cotton sweep *n* **:** a small wide-bladed tool used for the surface cultivation of soils growing cotton
cottontail \ˈ==,=\ *n* **1** *or* **cottontail rabbit :** any of several rather small No. American rabbits (genus *Sylvilagus*) sandy brown in color with a white-tufted underside of the tail **2 :** the tail of a cottontail rabbit

cottontail

cotton teal *n* [prob. so called fr. the white cottony patches on the wings of the male] **:** the Indian pygmy goose (*Nettapus coromandelianus*)
cotton thistle *n* **:** a biennial white-tomentose prickly Eurasian herb (*Onopordon acanthium*) with pale purple flowers that is naturalized in No. America — called also *Scotch thistle*
cotton tie *n* **:** a band of steel used to encircle a bale of cotton and thus hold it together
cottontop \ˈ==,=\ *n* **:** COTTON GRASS
cotton tree *n* **1 :** any of various trees belonging to the genera *Bombax* and *Ceiba; esp* **:** CEIBA 2a **2 :** WAYFARING TREE 1 **3 :** either of two cottonwoods (*Populus balsamifera* and *P. heterophylla*) **4 :** BLACK POPLAR 1 **5** *Austral* **:** MAJAGUA a
cotton waste *n* **:** WASTE 4a(1)
cotton wax *n* **:** a wax occurring as a coating on raw cotton fibers
cottonweed \ˈ==,=\ *n* **1 :** CUDWEED a **2 :** a common milkweed (*Asclepias syriaca*) with dull purplish flowers **3 :** a plant of the genus *Diotis* (family Compositae) having cottony foliage **4 :** INDIAN MALLOW 1 **5 :** PEARLY EVERLASTING
cotton whig *n, usu cap C&W* **:** member of the northern Whig party about 1850 esp. in Massachusetts who favored a conciliatory policy toward the South
cotton wilt *n* **1 :** a disease of cotton caused by the growth of a fungus (*Fusarium vasinfectum*) in the water-conducting vessels and characterized by wilting, yellowing, blighting, and death **2 :** a blight of cotton caused by a fungus (*Verticillium alboatrum*) and characterized by pale yellow mottled areas on the leaves
cottonwood \ˈ==,=\ *n* **1 :** any of several American trees of the genus *Populus* having a tuft of cottony hairs on the seed; *esp* **:** a common poplar (*P. deltoides*) of the eastern and central U.S. that is often cultivated for its rapid growth and luxuriant foliage or in Europe as a timber tree — see TREE illustration **2 :** WHITE BASSWOOD **3 :** an Australian tree (*Bedfordia salicina*) of the family Compositae having abundant down on its leaves **4 :** PAULOWNIA 2
cottonwood leaf beetle *n* **:** an oval yellowish or reddish black-marked beetle (*Chrysomela scripta*) having a dusky blackish larva that feeds on and defoliates cottonwood
cotton wool *n* **1 a :** raw cotton; *esp* **:** cotton batting **b :** excessive protection or comfort ⟨a *cotton wool* existence⟩ **2** *Brit* **:** ABSORBENT COTTON
cotton worm *n* **:** COTTON LEAFWORM
cot·tony \ˈkät(ᵊ)nē, -ni\ *adj* **1 :** covered with hairs or pubescence **:** DOWNY, NAPPY, WOOLLY **2 :** resembling cotton in appearance or character; *esp* **:** SOFT
cottony–cushion scale \ˈ=(=)=ˈ==-\ *n* **:** a scale (*Icerya purchasi*) introduced into the U.S. from Australia that infests citrus and other plants — see VEDALIA
cottony houseleek *n* **:** COBWEB HOUSELEEK
cottony leak *n* **:** a soft watery rot of cucumbers caused by a phycomycete (*Pythium aphanidermatum*)
cottony maple scale *n* **:** a brown oval soft scale (*Pulvinaria innumerabilis*) that in summer becomes covered with a white cottony secretion beneath which its eggs are laid, that is widespread in No. America, and that attacks and often kills various native and cultivated trees and shrubs
cottony rot *also* **cottony mold** *n* [so called fr. the fluffy white masses appearing on the rotted tissue] **:** a fungous disease of various plants caused by a fungus (*Sclerotinia sclerotiorum*) that produces wilt and rot of the stem and often of other parts
cot·trel \ˈkätərl, -trəl\ *var of* COTTEREL
cot·trell process \kəˈtrel-, käˈtrel-\ *n, usu cap C* [after Frederick G. Cottrell †1948 Am. chemist, its inventor] **:** electrostatic precipitation in which both the charging and precipitation are carried out in a single piece of equipment
cotts *pl of* COTT
cot·tus \ˈkädəs\ *n, cap* [NL, fr. Gk *kottos*, a kind of river fish] **:** the type genus of the family Cottidae
cot·ty \ˈkädē\ *adj, usu* -ER/-EST [³*cot* + -*y*] **:** ENTANGLED, MATTED
cot·u·la \ˈkächələ, -ädᵊlə, -ätᵊlə, -ätyələ\ *n* -S [NL, fr. L, small vessel, fr. Gk *kotylē* cup, small vessel, anything hollow — more at KETTLE] **:** MAYWEED
co·tun·nite \kəˈtəˌnīt\ *n* -S [G *cotunnit*, fr. *Cotunnius* (latinization of Domenico *Cotugno* †1822 Ital. anatomist) + G -*it* -ite] **:** a mineral consisting of lead chloride $PbCl_2$ that is soft and of white to yellowish color (sp. gr. 5.24)
co·tur·nix \kəˈtərniks\ *n, cap* [NL, fr. L, quail] **:** a genus of birds (family Phasianidae) containing the common European and other Old World quails
cotwal *var of* KOTWAL
co–twin \(ˈ)kō+\ *n* -S **:** the birth partner of a twin
cotyl- *or* **cotyli-** *or* **cotylo-** *comb form* [Gk *kotyl-*, *kotylo-*, fr. *kotylē*] **:** cup **:** organ or part like a cup ⟨*cotyloid*⟩ ⟨*cotyliform*⟩ ⟨*Cotylosauria*⟩ **:** acetabular and ⟨*cotylosacral*⟩
-cot·yl \ˌkädᵊl, -ätᵊl\ *n comb form* -S [*cotyledon*] **:** cotyledon ⟨*dicotyl*⟩ ⟨*epicotyl*⟩
cot·y·la \ˈkädᵊlə\ *or* **cot·y·le** \-l(ˌ)ē\ *n* -S [NL *cotyla*, fr. L *cotyla*, *cotula* small vessel — more at COTULA] **:** COTULA
cot·y·lar \-lə(r)\ *adj* [NL *cotyla* + E -*ar*] **:** of or relating to a cotyla
cot·y·le·don \ˌkädᵊlˈēdᵊn, -ätᵊlˈ-, ˈ==,==\ *n* [NL, fr. L, navelwort, fr. Gk *kotylēdōn* cup-shaped hollow, navelwort, fr. *kotylē* cup, anything hollow — more at KETTLE] **1** -S **:** a placental lobule with its included and complexly branched villous tree — used esp. of the discrete placental lobules typical of ruminants **2** -S **:** the first leaf or one of the first pair or whorl of leaves developed by the embryo in seed plants and in ferns and related plants that functions primarily to make stored food in the endosperm available to the developing young plant but in some cases acts as a storage or photosynthetic organ — called also *seed leaf;* see SCUTELLUM 1b **3 a** *cap* **:** a large genus of herbaceous succulent southern African plants (family Crassulaceae) having a gamopetalous corolla of five petals and usu. twice as many stamens as petals **b** -S **:** any plant of this genus
cot·y·le·don·al \ˌ==ˈēdᵊnᵊl, -ˈed-\ *or* **cot·y·le·don·ar** \-nə(r)\ *adj* [NL *cotyledon* + E -*al* or -*ar*] **:** belonging to or resembling a cotyledon
cot·y·le·don·ary \-nˌerē\ *or* **cot·y·le·don·ous** \-nəs\ *adj* [NL *cotyledon* + E -*ary* or -*ous*] **:** consisting of, having, or resembling cotyledons
co·tyl·i·form *or* **ko·tyl·i·form** \kəˈtiləˌfȯrm, ˈkädᵊlə,-\ *adj* [*cotyl-* or Gk *kotyl-* + E -*iform*] **:** ACETABULAR
cot·y·lig·er·ous \ˌkädᵊlˈijərəs\ *adj* [*cotyl-* + -*gerous*] **:** having cuplike cavities or cotyledons
cot·y·loid \ˈkädᵊlˌȯid\ *adj* [Gk *kotyloeidēs* cup-shaped, fr. *kotyl-* cotyl- + -*oeidēs* -oid] **:** ACETABULAR
cotyloid bone *n* **:** a small bone forming part of the acetabulum of some mammals
cotyloid cavity *n* **:** ACETABULUM 2a
cotyloid notch *n* **:** ACETABULAR NOTCH
cot·y·loph·o·ra \ˌkädᵊlˈäf(ə)rə\ [NL, fr. *cotyl-* + -*phora*] *syn of* PECORA
cot·y·loph·o·rous \ˌ==ˈäf(ə)rəs\ *adj* [*cotyl-* + -*phorous*] **:** having a cotyledonary placenta
cot·y·lo·saur \ˈkädᵊləˌsȯ(ə)r\ *n* -S [NL *Cotylosauria*] **:** a reptile of the order Cotylosauria
cot·y·lo·sau·ria \ˌkädᵊlōˈsȯrēə\ *n pl, cap* [NL, fr. *cotyl-* + -*sauria*] **:** an order of Anapsida comprising extremely primitive late Paleozoic and early Triassic reptiles with short legs and massive bodies — **cot·y·lo·sau·rian** \-rēən\ *adj or n*
co·type \ˈkō+\ *n* [*co-* + *type*] **1 :** SYNTYPE 1 **2 :** PARATYPE 1 **:** ISOTYPE 1b (1) — compare HOLOTYPE
couac \ˈkwak, ˈkwäk\ *n* -S [F, of imit. origin] **:** the strident tone sometimes produced by a reed instrument when the reed is out of order or when the instrument is blown incorrectly
cou·cal \ˈküˌkal\ *n* -S [F, perh. fr. *coucou* cuckoo (of imit. origin) + *alouette* lark, fr. OF *aloete*, dim. of *aloe*, fr. L *alauda*, fr. Gaulish] **:** any of various large long-tailed, brown-and-black cuckoos (genus *Centropus*) of Africa, southern Asia, and Australia that resemble pheasants esp. in plumage pattern and habits — see CROW PHEASANT
¹**couch** \ˈkau̇ch; *in sense 9 usu* ˈküch\ *vb* -ED/-ING/-ES [ME *couchen*, fr. MF *couchier*, *coucher* to lay down, put to bed, fr. L *collocare* to lay, put, place, fr. *com-* + *locare* to place — more at LOCATE] *vt* **1 a** *obs* **:** to set over **:** OVERLAY, INLAY **b :** to embroider by laying an outlining thread along the surface and fastening it with small stitches at regular intervals **2 a :** to compose, settle, or recline for sleep or rest ⟨at the end of the day's journey the camels needed no urging to be ~*ed* —John Sköllе⟩ — used of an animal usu. reflexively or passively ⟨a lion ~*ing* himself by the tree⟩ **b :** to compose for sleep **:** cause to lie down **:** BED — used of a person usu. reflexively or passively ⟨~*ed* on the ground⟩ **c :** to place, locate, or settle esp. in a position suggesting security, protection, or repose **:** place in a particular setting or background ⟨~*ed* in the magnificence of gorgeous and elaborate costumes —Faubion Bowers⟩ **3** *archaic* **:** to lay or deposit in a bed or layer (as in building or gardening) **:** BED **4 :** to place or hold in a position level and pointed forward ready or as if ready for use ⟨advancing with spears ~*ed*⟩ ⟨~*ing* his lance, he seated himself firmly in his saddle —W.S.Maugham⟩ **5 :** EXPRESS: **a :** to place or compose in a specified kind of language **:** WORD, PHRASE ⟨prayer, ~*ed* in the idiom of the Bible —Edna Ferber⟩ **b :** to include or imply obscurely or so as to make comprehension difficult ⟨all this and more . . . lies naturally ~*ed* under this allegory —Roger L'Estrange⟩ **6** *archaic* **:** to place in hiding or ambush **:** set in hiding or lurking — usu. used reflexively or in the passive **7 :** to treat (a cataract or a person having a cataract) by an operation intended to restore partial vision by displacing the lens of the eye into the vitreous **8 :** to bring down **:** LOWER, DEPRESS, CONTRACT ⟨some of the quills ~*ed*, some still erect⟩ **9 a :** to press (a wet sheet of new handmade paper still on the mold) onto a felt **b :** to press (a sheet of paper stock) on the wire of a cylinder machine and transfer onto a felt for further pressing and drying **c :** to press water from (a sheet) on a couch roll of a fourdrinier machine or extract it by a suction couch preparatory to transferring to a felt ~ *vi* **1 :** to lie down for or as if for sleep or rest **a** *of a person* **:** to recline on or as if on a bed; *sometimes* **:** to couple in sexual intercourse ⟨a goddess ~*ing* with a mortal —Andrew Lang⟩ **b** *of an animal* **:** to lie down, recline, or kneel for or as if for rest ⟨boars ~*ing*⟩ ⟨the odd way a camel ~*es*⟩ **c :** to lie or be situated ⟨the deep that ~*es* beneath —Deut 33:13 (RSV)⟩ **2 :** to bend down low: **a :** to kneel, stoop, or bow esp. in obeisance, subserviency, or submission **b :** to lie or lurk in concealment or ambush ⟨~*ing* in the wood to waylay the traveler⟩ **3** *of leaves* **:** to lie in a heap or mass while decomposition or fermentation proceeds **syn** see LURK
²**couch** \ˈkau̇ch; *in sense 3 often and in sense 4 usu* ˈküch\ *n* -ES *often attrib* [ME *couche*, fr. MF, fr. OF *culche*, *couche*, fr. *couchier*] **1 a** *archaic* **:** BED **b** *archaic* **:** a piece of furniture or other arrangement on which one sleeps **c :** an article of furniture for sitting or reclining; *specif* **:** a piece of upholstered furniture that is long enough to lie down on or that can seat several persons and that has sometimes a headrest at one end or sometimes a raised back and arms at both ends **:** SOFA **d :** a psychiatrist's or psychoanalyst's couch on which patients recline **2 a :** the den of an animal **b :** the burrow of an otter **3 :** a layer or stratum that is preliminary in some fine arts processes to later layers **4 :** a board covered with felt or flannel on which the sheets of pulp for handmade paper are pressed — compare COUCH ROLL
³**couch** *var of* COUCH GRASS
couch·an·cy \ˈkau̇chənsē\ *n* -ES **:** a lying down for repose esp. by an animal
couch·ant \ˈkau̇chənt, *sometimes* küshäⁿ\ *adj* [ME, fr. MF, fr. pres. part. of *coucher*] **1 :** COUCHING ⟨an animal lying ~⟩ **2 :** lying down with the head up — used of a heraldic lion or other beast; distinguished from *dormant* **syn** see PRONE
couchant and levant *adj* [ME — more at LEVANT AND COUCHANT] **:** LEVANT AND COUCHANT
cou·ché \(ˈ)küˈshā\ *adj* [F, fr. past part. of *coucher* to lay down — more at COUCH] *heraldry* **:** INCLINED **:** not erect ⟨a ~ shield with its sinister angle uppermost⟩
couched *adj* [fr. past part. of ¹*couch*] **:** COUCHÉ
couched harp *n* **:** SPINET
cou·chee \küˈshā, ˈ=,=\ *n* -S [F *couchée*, fr. fem. of *couché*, past part. of *coucher*] **:** a reception given late in the evening esp. by royalty or nobility
couch·er \ˈküchər; *in sense 2 sometimes* ˈkau̇ch-\ *n* -S [¹*couch* + -*er*] **1** *Scot* **:** COWARD **2 :** one that couches handmade paper
couches *pres 3d sing of* COUCH, *pl of* COUCH
couch grass \ˈkau̇ch-, ˈküch-\ *also* **couch** *n* -ES [alter. of *quitch* (*grass*)] **1 :** any of various grasses having creeping rhizomes by which they spread rapidly: as **a :** a European grass (*Agropyron repens*) naturalized throughout No. America as a weed — called also *quack grass, quick grass, quitch grass, scutch grass, twitch grass, witchgrass* **b :** a redtop (*Agrostis alba*) **c :** SLENDER FOXTAIL **2** *Austral* **:** BERMUDA GRASS
¹**couching** *pres part of* COUCH
²**couch·ing** \ˈkau̇chiŋ\ *n* -S [ME, fr. gerund of *couchen*] **:** a style of embroidery in which a flat or raised design is made by laid threads or cords fastened down by small stitches at regular intervals

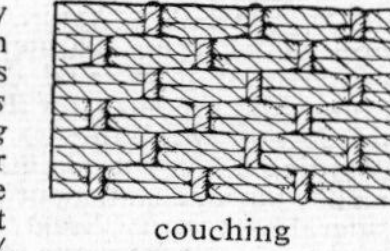

couching

couch roll \ˈküch- *sometimes* ˈkau̇ch-\ *n* [¹*couch*] *papermaking* **:** a large roll that removes water from the wet web as it leaves the wire and is guided onto the felt
couchy \ˈkau̇chē, ˈküchē\ *adj* -ER/-EST [³*couch* + -*y*] **:** infested with or resembling couch grass
¹**coudé** \küˈdā, ˈ=,=\ *n* -S [F, fr. *coudé*, adj.] **:** a coudé telescope
²**coudé** \(ˈ)=ˈ=\ *adj* [F, fr. past part. of *couder* to bend like an elbow, fr. *coude*, elbow, fr. L *cubitum* — more at HIP] **1 :** bent like an elbow — used of instruments ⟨~ catheter⟩ **2 a** *of a telescope* **:** constructed so that the light is reflected along the polar axis to come to a focus at a fixed place where the plateholder or a spectrograph may be permanently mounted **b :** of or relating to such a telescope ⟨~ form⟩ ⟨~ focus⟩ ⟨~ image⟩ ⟨~ spectrograph⟩
cou·dière \küdˈye(ə)r, ˈ=,=\ *n* -S [F, fr. *coude* elbow] **:** CUBITIERE
coué·ism \küˈāˌizəm, ˈ==,==\ *n* -S *cap* [F *couéisme*, fr. Émile *Coué* †1926 Fr. pharmacist & psychotherapist, its originator + F -*isme* -ism] **:** a system of psychotherapy based upon autosuggestion of health and general well-being and improvement
cou·ette flow \küˈet-\ *n, usu cap C* [F *couette* machine bearing, lit., feather bed, fr. OF *coute*, *cuilte* quilt, mattress — more at QUILT] **:** the shearing flow of a fluid between two parallel surfaces in relative motion (as of the oil in a cylindrical bearing)
cou·gar \ˈkügə(r), -ˌgär, -ˌgä(r\ *also* **cou·guar** \", -ˌgwär, -ˌgwä(r\ *n, pl* **cougars** *also* **cougar** [F *couguar*, modif. (influenced by *jaguar*) of NL *cuguacuarana*, modif. of Tupi *suasuarana*, *çuçuarana*, lit., false deer, fr. *suasú*, *suusú* deer + *rana* false; fr. its color] **:** a large powerful tawny brown unspotted cat (*Felis concolor*) longer limbed and less bulky than the jaguar and formerly widespread over most of the Americas but now extinct in much of the U. S. and eastern Canada — called also *American lion, catamount, mountain lion, panther, puma*
¹**cough** \ˈkȯf *also* ˈkäf\ *vb* -ED/-ING/-S [ME *coughen*, fr. (assumed) OE *cohhian* (of which *cohhettan* is a freq.); akin to MD *cochen* to cough, MHG *kūchen* to breathe heavily, prob. of imit. origin] *vi* **1 :** to expel air from the lungs suddenly with an explosive noise usu. in a series of efforts **2 :** to make a noise like that of coughing: as **a :** to fire in a single short burst or series of separate bursts ⟨the machine gun ~*ed* once⟩ **b** *of an engine* **:** to go through an operation cycle without continuous firing ⟨the engine began to ~ on the hill⟩ ~ *vt* **1 :** to expel by coughing — used with *up* or *out* ⟨~ up mucus⟩ **2 :** DISCLOSE — used with *up* or *out* ⟨~ up all he knows⟩
²**cough** \"\ *n* -S *often attrib* [ME *coughe*, fr. *coughen*, v.] **1 :** a condition marked by repeated coughing **:** an ailment manifesting itself by frequent coughing ⟨he has a bad ~⟩ **2 :** an explosive expulsion of air from the lungs acting as a protective mechanism to clear the air passages or as a symptom of pulmonary disturbance **3 :** a single burst of firing **:** a single firing or irregular bursts of firing in the cylinders of a motor
cough drop *n* **:** a lozenge or troche used to relieve coughing
coughroot \ˈ=,=\ *n* [so called fr. its use as a remedy for coughs] **:** a wake-robin (*Trillium cernuum*) of north eastern No. America having nodding flowers almost hidden by the leaves
cough syrup *n* **:** any sweet usu. medicated liquid used as a remedy for cough
cough up *vt* **:** to hand over **:** give up **:** DELIVER, PAY, CONTRIBUTE ⟨*cough up* the money for the tickets⟩
coughweed \ˈ=,=\ *n* **:** GOLDEN RAGWORT
coughwort \ˈ=,=\ *n* [so called fr. its use as a remedy for coughs] **:** COLTSFOOT a
cou·gnar \ˈkünˌyär, ˈku̇n,-\ *n* -S [Malay *chunya*] **:** a three-masted square-rigged Malay ship
couhage *var of* COWAGE
coul \ˈkōl, ˈkül, ˈkau̇(ə)l\ *dial var of* COWL
coul *abbr* coulomb
could *or archaic 2d sing* **couldst** [alter. (influenced by *should* and *would*) of ME *coude*, *couthe*, fr. OE *cūthe;* akin to OHG *konda* could, ON *kunna*, Goth *kuntha* — more at CAN] *past of* CAN — used in auxiliary function in the past tense ⟨he found he ~ go⟩, in the past conditional ⟨he said he would go if he ~⟩, and as an alternative to *can* suggesting less force or certainty or as a polite form in the present ⟨~ you do this for me⟩ and the present conditional ⟨if you ~ come we would be pleased⟩
could·est \ˈku̇dəst\ *archaic past 2d sing of* CAN
couldn't **:** could not
cou·lé \küˈlā, ˈ=,=\ *n* -S [F, fr. *coulé*, past part. of *couler*] **1 a :** a slur in music **b :** one of several graces usu. of two or three sliding notes indicated by a dash **c :** a sliding from one note or one string to another (as on a banjo) **2 :** a gliding dance step
¹**cou·lee** \ˈkülē, -li *sometimes* küˈlā *or* ˈ=,=\ *n* -S [CanF *coulée*, fr. F, flowing, flow of lava, fr. fem. of *coulé*, past part. of *couler* to flow, glide, fr. L *colare* to strain, purify, fr. *colum* sieve — more at HEDGE] **1** *also* **cou·lie** \ˈkülē, -li\ *chiefly West* **a :** a small often intermittent stream **:** a dry creek bed sometimes running in a wet season **b :** a steep-walled valley or ravine varying widely in size and often having a stream at the bottom **c :** a small valley or low-lying area **2** [F] **:** a thick sheet or stream of lava esp. when solidified
²**cou·lée** \küˈlā, ˈ=,=\ *n* -S [F, short for *écriture coulée*, lit., flowing writing, fr. *écriture* writing + *coulée*, fem. of *coulé*, past part. of *couler* to flow] **:** a French commercial and official hand based partly on bâtarde
cou·lee cricket \ˈkülē-\ *n* [¹*coulee* (valley) + *cricket*] **:** a large wingless cricket (*Peranabrus scabricollis*) of the northwestern U. S. sometimes destructive to crops
cou·leur \küˈlər, -ˈlə\ *n* -S [F, fr. L *color* — more at COLOR] **1 :** ¹COLOR 1 **2 :** the color of the first card dealt in the winning row in the game of rouge et noir — compare INVERSE
¹**couleur de rose** \(ˈ)=ˈ=dəˈrōz\ *n* [F] **:** ROSE **:** rose color
²**couleur de rose** \(ˈ)=ˈ==ˈ=\ *adj* **:** ROSY, ROSEATE
cou·lier \ˈkülyə(r)\ *n* -S [prob. fr. F *coulière*, lit., sliding, gliding, fr. *couler* to slide, glide, flow — more at COULEE] **:** the cam motion that controls delivery of yarn over needles on a full-fashioned knitting machine
cou·lisse \küˈlēs\ *n* -S [F (also, groove, door, window, or partition that slides in a groove), fr. OF *couleice* portcullis, short for *porte couleice*, lit., sliding door, fr. *porte* door + *couleïce*, fem. of *couleïz* slidable, penetrating, fr. *couler* to slide, flow — more at COULEE] **1 a :** a side scene of the stage in a theater or the space between the side scenes **b :** a place behind the scenes **c :** a lobby, corridor, or other place where informal discussion is likely **2 :** a piece of timber having a groove in which something slides (as an upright of a sluice)
cou·loir \külˈwär\ *n* -S [F, lit., colander, fr. LL *colatorium* sieve, fr. L *colatus* (past part. of *colare* to strain) + -*orium* -ory — more at COULEE] **1 :** a deep gorge **:** a gully on a mountainside esp. in the Swiss Alps **2 :** PASSAGE, GANGWAY, CORRIDOR
cou·lomb \ˈküˌläm, -ˌlōm, =ˈ=\ *n* -S *sometimes cap* [after Charles A. de *Coulomb* †1806 Fr. physicist] **1 :** the practical mks unit of electric charge equal to the quantity of electricity transferred by a current of one ampere in one second and now taken as the standard in the U.S. **2 :** a unit of electric charge equal to 0.999835 coulomb and formerly taken as the standard — called also *international coulomb*
coulomb field *n, sometimes cap C* **:** a field of coulomb force (as due to an electric charge)
coulomb force *n, sometimes cap C* **:** any of the forces of attraction or repulsion that obey the inverse-square law and are derived from a Newtonian potential — compare NEWTONIAN FORCE
cou·lom·bi·an \(ˈ)küˈlämbēən, -ˈlōm-\ *also* **cou·lom·bic** \-bik\ *adj, often cap* [C. A. de *Coulomb* + E -*ian* or -*ic*] **:** of or relating to the discoveries or laws of C. A. de Coulomb
cou·lomb·me·ter \ˈkü(ˌ)läm,mēd·ə(r), -(ˌ)lōm,-, =ˈ=,-\ *n* [ISV *coulomb* + -*meter*] **:** COULOMETER
coulomb's law *n, cap C* [after C. A. de *Coulomb*] **:** a statement in physics: the force of attraction or repulsion acting along a straight line between two electric charges or two magnetic poles is directly proportional to the product of the charges or pole strengths and inversely to the square of the distance between them
cou·lom·e·ter \küˈlämədə(r), kəˈ-\ *n* [alter. of *coulombmeter*] **:** VOLTAMETER; *sometimes* **:** one in which a metal other than silver is deposited or gas is evolved
cou·lo·met·ric \ˌküləˈme·trik\ *adj* **:** of or relating to coulometry — **cou·lo·met·ri·cal·ly** \-trək(ə)lē\ *adv*
coulometric titration *n* **:** a method of titration in which the titrating agent is produced in a solution by electrolysis and the required amount of the agent is determined by measuring the number of coulombs used in preparing it
cou·lom·e·try \küˈlämə·trē, kəˈ-\ *n* -ES [*coulomb* + -*metry*] **:** chemical analysis performed by determining the amount of a substance released in an electrolysis by measuring the number of coulombs used
cou·lom·mi·ers \kəˌləməˈā\ *n, usu cap* [F, fr. *Coulommiers*, town in central France where it is produced] **:** a small mold-ripened fresh or cured Brie cheese
coul·son·ite \ˈkōlsəˌnīt\ *n* -S [Arthur L. *Coulson* b 1898 geologist in India + E -*ite*] **:** vanadoan magnetite
coulter *var of* COLTER
coul·ter·neb \ˈkōltə(r)ˌneb\ *n* -S [*coulter* + *neb;* fr. the shape of the bill] *dial Brit* **:** PUFFIN
coul·ter pine \ˈkōltə(r)-\ *or* **coulter's pine** *n, usu cap C* [after Thomas *Coulter* †1843 Irish botanist] **:** a tall pine (*Pinus coulteri*) of the southwestern U. S. with cones 9 to 15 inches long and consisting of stout sharp-pointed scales — called also *big-cone pine*
cou·ma \ˈkümə\ *n* -S [NL, genus to which the couma belongs, fr. F, fr. Tupi *cumá*] **1 :** a tropical So. American tree (*Couma utilis*) of the family Apocynaceae — see COW TREE, SORVA **2 :** the edible sweet fruit of the couma

cou·ma·lic acid \(ˈ)küˈmalik-, -mā-\ *also* **cu·mal·ic acid** \(ˈ)kyü-\ *n* [ISV *coumalic*, blend of *coumarin* and *malic*] **:** a white crystalline acid $C_6H_4O_4$ formed by heating malic acid with sulfuric acid or zinc chloride; 5-coumalin-carboxylic acid

cou·ma·lin *also* **cu·ma·lin** \ˈk(y)ümələn\ *n* -s [ISV *coumalic* + *-in*] **:** pyrone (sense 1a) or any of its derivatives

cou·ma·ran \ˈk(y)üməˌran\ *n* -s [ISV *coumarin* + *-an*; prob. orig. formed as G *kumaran*] **:** a colorless oil C_8H_8O formed by reducing coumarone of which it is the dihydride

cou·ma·ra nut \ˈkümərə-\ *n* [alter. of *coumarou*] **:** TONKA BEAN

cou·ma·rin *also* **cu·ma·rin** \ˈk(y)ümərən, -ˌrēn\ *n* -s [F *coumarine*, fr. *coumarou* + *-ine*] **:** a toxic white crystalline lactone $C_9H_6O_2$ with an odor of new-mown hay that is found in many plants (as the tonka bean and clover), is made synthetically, and is used in perfumery and soap, in the synthesis of dicoumarol, and formerly in flavoring; 1,2-benzopyrone; *also* **:** any derivative (as umbelliferone) of this compound

cou·ma·rone *or* **cu·ma·rone** \-ˌrōn\ *n* -s [ISV *coumarin* + *-one*; prob. orig. formed as G *kumaron*] **:** a heavy oily compound C_8H_6O present in solvent naphtha and made synthetically; *also* **:** any derivative of this compound — called also *benzofuran*

coumarone-indene resin *also* **coumarone resin** *n* **:** any of a group of thermoplastic resins obtained by polymerization of mixtures of coumarone and indene (as those obtained from solvent naphtha) and used chiefly in coatings, paints, printing ink, and asphalt tile — called also *paracoumarone-indene resin*

cou·ma·rou \ˌk(y)üməˈrü\ *or* **cu·ma·ra** \ˈ=mərə\ *or* **cu·ma·ru** \ˌ=məˈrü\ *n* -s [F, fr. Sp or Pg; Sp *cumarú*, fr. Pg, fr. Tupi *cumarú*, *commarú*] **1 :** the tonka-bean tree **2 :** the seeds of the tonka-bean tree

coumbite *var of* COMBITE

coun *abbr* **1** council **2** counsel

[1]**coun·cil** \ˈkau̇n(t)səl\ *n* -s [ME *counceil*, *conceil* (influenced in meaning by ME *counseil*, *conseil* counsel, council), fr. OF *concile* assembly, ecclesiastical assembly, fr. LL & L; LL *concilium* ecclesiastical assembly, fr. L, *assembly*, fr. *com-* + *-cilium* (fr. *calare* to call) — more at COUNSEL, LOW] **1 a :** an assembly of ecclesiastics or church representatives convened to consider matters of doctrine, discipline, law, morals, or the relation of the Christian church to world problems ⟨seven widely recognized ecumenical (or general) ~*s* of the Christian church are those held at Nicaea, 352; Constantinople, 381; Ephesus, 431; Chalcedon, 451; Constantinople, 553; Constantinople, 680; Nicaea, 787⟩ **b :** a meeting of the Sanhedrin or of a similar minor assembly with limited jurisdiction ⟨the Pharisees went out and held a ~ against him —Mt 12:14 (AV)⟩ **2 :** a deliberative assembly ⟨the department is under a prefect and an elected general ~ of 36 members —*Statesman's Yr. Bk.*⟩ **:** an assembly or meeting held for consultation, advice, or discussion ⟨a ~ among the leaders⟩ **:** a meeting for discussion **3 :** a somewhat permanent group elected or appointed to constitute an advisory body or a body with a degree of legislative power ⟨a privy ~⟩ ⟨a ~ of state⟩ ⟨a governor's ~⟩ **4 :** an administrative body: as **a :** a local governing instrumentality (as of a town, borough, city, or county) ⟨county ~*s* in England⟩ ⟨borough ~*s* in U.S.⟩ **b :** a collegial executive body ⟨the Federal *Council* of Switzerland⟩ **c :** one of three governing bodies of a British university composed chiefly of persons not otherwise connected with the institution and charged with administrative functions — compare COURT 4c, SENATE **d :** SOVIET **e :** a governing body consisting of voting delegates from local labor unions united in a federation **5 :** the deliberation carried on in a council or council chamber **:** CONSULTATION ⟨summoned to ~⟩; *sometimes* **:** COUNSEL **6 a :** a federation of or a central body uniting a group of organizations **b :** a local chapter of an organization **c :** CLUB, SOCIETY, ASSOCIATION

[2]**council** \"\ *vi* **counciled** *or* **councilled; counciled** *or* **councilled; counciling** *or* **councilling** \-s(ə)liŋ\ **councils :** to hold a council **:** meet and deliberate in council — used esp. of the councils of American Indians

[3]**council** \"\ *adj* **1 :** used for councils esp. by or with No. American Indians ⟨a ~ ground⟩ **2** *Brit* **:** built, maintained, or operated by a local governing agency ⟨a ~ house⟩ ⟨~ flats⟩

council board *or* **council table** *n* **:** the table around which a council holds consultation; *also* **:** the council itself in deliberation

council fire *n* **:** the ceremonial fire kept burning during a council of No. American Indians; *also* **:** the council itself — compare LONG HOUSE 2

council-general \ˌ==ˌ=(=)=\ *n, pl* **councils-general** [trans. of F *conseil général*] **:** a deliberative body of a French administrative department

coun·cil·lor *also* **coun·cil·or** \ˈkau̇n(t)s(ə)lə(r)\ *n* -s [alter. (influenced by *council*) of *counsellor*, *counselor*] **:** a member of a council **:** one appointed or elected to advise or supervise

coun·cil·lor·ship \-ˌship\ *n* -s **:** the position or function of a councillor

coun·cil·man \ˈkau̇n(t)səlmən\ *n, pl* **councilmen :** a member of a council, esp. of a city council

council-manager plan *n* **:** a method of municipal government in which legislative and policy-determining powers are held by an elected council that employs a city manager who is responsible to the council for city administration — compare COMMISSION PLAN

coun·cil·man·ic \ˌkau̇n(t)səlˈmanik\ *adj* [irreg., fr. *councilman* + *-ic*] **:** of, by, or for a council or councilman

council of ministers *often cap C&M* [trans. of F *conseil des ministres*] **:** CABINET ⟨the French *Council of Ministers*⟩

council of state : an administrative or deliberative body for state matters **:** a governmental council considering high policy matters

council of war 1 : an assembly of officers usu. of high rank called to consult with the commander on questions of importance or emergency **2 :** a deliberation to concert measures

council school *n, Brit* **:** a nondenominational elementary or secondary school provided and maintained by a local education authority — called also *county school;* compare PUBLIC SCHOOL, VOLUNTARY SCHOOL

council tool *n* **:** a long-handled combination hoe and rake of which the blade consists of mowing-machine blade sections attached to a piece of angle iron

councilwoman \ˈ==ˌ==\ *n, pl* **councilwomen :** a female member of a council

[1]**counsel** \ˈkau̇n(t)səl\ *n* -s [ME *counseil*, *conseil*, fr. OF *conseil*, fr. L *consilium*, fr. *com-* + *-silium* (perh. akin to Gk *helein* to take) — more at SELL] **1 a :** OPINION, ADVICE, DIRECTION **:** instruction or recommendation esp. as given as a result of consultation ⟨his own more wary followers took heed to his ~ —W.H.Prescott⟩ **b :** a policy or plan of action or behavior ⟨observe the sixth commandment, not as a precept of divine law but as a ~ of profitable prudence —W.L.Sullivan⟩ **2 :** DISCUSSION, DELIBERATION, CONSULTATION **:** interchange of opinion esp. on possible procedure **3** *obs* **:** PRUDENCE, THOUGHTFULNESS **:** faculty or exercise of deliberate judgment **4** *archaic* **:** INTENTION, PURPOSE **:** plan arrived at through deliberation ⟨the ~ of the Lord stands for ever —Ps 33:11 (RSV)⟩ **5 a** *archaic* **:** secret purpose or opinion **:** SECRET **:** private confidence ⟨did you ne'er hear say, two may keep ~, putting one away —Shak.⟩ **b :** reflection, thought, intent, or plan discreetly and carefully guarded from being known — used in the phrase *keep one's own counsel* ⟨chary and given to keeping his own ~⟩ **6 :** ADVISER: **a** *sing or pl in constr* **:** a person professionally engaged in the trial or management of a cause in court **:** BARRISTER ⟨his ~ is able⟩ ⟨the arguments of ~⟩ **b** *sing or pl in constr* **:** a legal advocate managing a case at law ⟨to have the assistance of ~ for his defense —*U.S.Constitution*⟩ ⟨if ~ are familiar with the rules of this court⟩ — compare ATTORNEY **c :** a lawyer appointed or engaged to advise and represent in legal matters a particular client, public officer, or public body — called also *legal counsel* **d :** COUNCILLOR **:** one called on to advise **:** CONSULTANT

[2]**counsel** \"\ *vb* **counseled** *or* **counselled; counseled** *or* **counselled; counseling** \-s(ə)liŋ\ *or* **counselling; counsels** [ME *counseilen*, *conseillen*, fr. OF *conseillier*, fr. L *consiliari*, fr. *consilium*] *vt* **1 :** to advise esp. seriously and formally after consultation ⟨~*ed* them to avoid rash actions —George Orwell⟩; *esp* **:** to advise (students) on personal or vocational problems **2 :** to recommend esp. as the best or most expedient act, course, or policy ⟨~ great caution⟩ ⟨he wrote to his father ~*ing* further delay —T.E.Lawrence⟩ ~ *vi* **:** CONSULT, DELIBERATE **:** take counsel ⟨~*ing* about the problem⟩

coun·sel·able *or* **coun·sel·la·ble** \ˈkau̇n(t)s(ə)ləbəl\ *adj* **:** willing to receive advice; *also* **:** ADVISABLE

coun·sel·ee \ˌkau̇n(t)səˈlē, -)ˈslē\ *n* -s **:** one who is being counseled

counseling *n* -s [ME *counseilling*, *conseilling* advising, fr. gerund of *counseilen*, *conseillen* to counsel] **:** a practice or professional service designed to guide an individual to a better understanding of his problems and potentialities by utilizing modern psychological principles and methods esp. in collecting case history data, using various techniques of the personal interview, and testing interests and aptitudes ⟨industrial ~⟩ ⟨vocational ~⟩ ⟨pastoral ~⟩

counsellor seal *n* [so called fr. the long whitish hair of the head that suggests a lawyer's wig] **:** a large So. Pacific hair seal (*Arctocephalus cinereus*)

counsel of perfection 1 : instruction given for the attainment of perfection **2 :** an unrealizable ideal

coun·sel·or *or* **coun·sel·lor** \ˈkau̇n(t)s(ə)lə(r)\ *n* -s [ME *conseiler*, *counseilour*, fr. OF *conseilleor*, fr. L *consiliator*, fr. *consiliatus* (past part. of *consiliari* to counsel) + *-or* — more at COUNSEL] **1 :** one that counsels **:** ADVISER **2 :** one that gives advice in law and manages cases for clients in court **:** COUNSEL 6 **3 :** COUNCILLOR **4 :** one of the two aids to a president of any unit in the Mormon Church **5 a :** a faculty member assigned to advise students on personal, academic, and vocational matters **b :** one who engages in or whose profession is counseling **c :** an official who directs a group of camp members in some recreational activity (as swimming, dramatics, handicrafts) **6 :** a diplomatic official at an embassy or legation ranking just below an ambassador or minister

counselor-at-law \ˈ=(=)=(ˌ)=ˈ=\ *n, pl* **counselors-at-law :** COUNSELOR 2

counsels *pl of* COUNSEL, *pres 3d sing of* COUNSEL

[1]**count** \ˈkau̇nt\ *vb* -ED/-ING/-S [ME *counten*, fr. MF *conter*, *compter*, fr. L *computare* to reckon, compute, fr. *com-* + *putare* to consider, think — more at PAVE] *vt* **1 a :** to indicate, name, or separate (units out of a body of units) one by one or group after group to find the total number of units involved or concerned **:** NUMBER, TALLY, RECKON ⟨~ the pages of a manuscript⟩ — sometimes used with *up* or *over* ⟨~ up the money in the register⟩ **b :** to tell over or name the numbers in regular order up to and including (a specified number) ⟨~ ten before answering⟩ **c :** to include in a tallying and reckoning ⟨about 100 people present, ~*ing* women and children⟩ **d :** to compute or tally mechanically and record a total ⟨a machine that ~*s* cars crossing the bridge⟩ **e :** to call aloud (beats or time units) esp. in the practicing of a musical composition ⟨~ eighth notes⟩ **f** (1) **:** to recollect or keep track of the number of cards that have been played in (a specified suit) ⟨~ trumps⟩ (2) **:** to estimate or mentally reconstruct the distribution of cards in (another player's hand) (3) **:** to count the points in (a hand of cards) — compare POINT COUNT **2 a :** CONSIDER, ACCOUNT, REGARD, JUDGE ⟨~ oneself lucky⟩ ⟨the true dignity of man . . . is ~*ed* folly —W.E.Channing⟩ **b :** ESTIMATE, ESTEEM ⟨he ~*ed* it nothing that his follower had sacrificed his life⟩ **c :** to record as of a particular opinion or persuasion ⟨~ me as uncommitted⟩ ⟨stand and be ~*ed*⟩ **d** *dial* **:** SUPPOSE, GUESS, RECKON ⟨I ~ there's three of them coming⟩ ~ *vi* **1** *archaic* **:** to think much of something **:** care about something **:** take account ⟨no man ~*s* of her beauty —Shak.⟩ **2 a :** to recite or indicate the numbers in order one by one or group by group ⟨a little child who could not ~⟩ ⟨~ by fives⟩ **:** count the units in a group ⟨interrupted while he was ~*ing*⟩ **b :** to mark the time by counting aloud the beats in a musical composition **3 a :** to rely or depend on someone or something in plans or calculations — used with *on* or *upon* ⟨the man they ~*ed* on in this crisis —Stuart Cloete⟩ **:** look forward to, expect, or plan on something with assured confidence ⟨~ on clear weather⟩ ⟨~*ing* on his car to get him there on time⟩ **b :** to expect, predict, or take something into consideration — usu. used with *on* ⟨they ~ on winning⟩ ⟨he had not ~*ed* on paying and had brought no money⟩ **4** *English law*, *obs* **3 :** to plead in court **:** state a complaint in court **5 :** to add up **:** amount in number **:** TOTAL — sometimes used with *up* ⟨they ~*ed* 30 —Lord Byron⟩ ⟨it ~*s* up to a sizable sum⟩ **6 a :** to have value, meaning, weight, significance, or importance ⟨landscape ~*s* in the character of a place, but people ~ more —H.L.Davis⟩ **:** merit consideration **:** be of consequence or account ⟨these are the men who really ~⟩ **b :** to be of account **:** have status or rank **:** become classed or regarded ⟨achievements such as the TVA have ~*ed* for far more . . . than our military power —M.W.Straight⟩ ⟨the things that ~*ed* so much with us when we were young —Louis Bromfield⟩ **7 :** to make a score ⟨~*ed* twice in the third inning⟩

syn TELL, ENUMERATE, NUMBER: COUNT is likely to call attention to the finding of a total without minimizing the notion of numbering units or groups in the process of attaining to that total ⟨as many as 30 bonfires could be *counted* within the whole bounds of the district —Thomas Hardy⟩ TELL, now archaic in suggestion, may center attention on the fact of units being counted ⟨*telling* one's beads⟩ ⟨a shepherd *telling* his sheep⟩ ENUMERATE may suggest counting up or totaling with specific and clear treatment of each item ⟨Pliny *enumerates* among the trees of Syria the date, pistachio, fig, cedar, juniper, terebinth, and sumac —P.K.Hitti⟩ ⟨among the *enumerated* powers, we do not find that of establishing a bank or creating a corporation —John Marshall⟩ NUMBER may suggest either limited allotting or precise ordering in sequence ⟨the days of every man are *numbered*⟩ ⟨to *number* the volumes on the shelf⟩ **syn** see in addition RELY

—**count coup** *of an American Indian* **:** to make a coup; *also* **:** to relate the story of one's coups — **count heads** *or* **count noses :** to count the number (as of persons) present

[2]**count** \"\ *n* -s [ME *counte*, fr. MF *conte*, *compte*, fr. LL *computus* computation, fr. L *computare* to reckon, compute] **1 :** the act or process of numbering, counting, or reckoning ⟨completing the ~ of the ballots⟩ **2 a** *archaic* **:** a reckoning of money, goods, or conduct ⟨call to ~ —Edmund Spenser⟩ **:** ACCOUNT; *specif* **:** a statement of stewardship or managing **b :** formulation of a total arrived at by examination of a sample ⟨a ~ of white corpuscles⟩ **c :** population enumeration **:** CENSUS **3** *archaic* **:** consideration as important **:** ESTIMATION, REGARD **4 :** number or sum total obtained by counting **:** ENUMERATION, TALLY ⟨the official ~ came to over a hundred⟩ **5 a :** ALLEGATION, CHARGE; *specif* **:** a particular allegation or charge separately stating the cause of action or prosecution in a legal declaration or indictment ⟨the jury found him innocent on the first ~, guilty on the second and third⟩ ⟨guilty on all ~*s*⟩ **b :** the declaration in common-law pleading when the plaintiff has but one cause of action and makes but one statement of it **c :** a specific point under consideration **:** ISSUE ⟨disagreeing on this ~⟩ **6 a :** the calling off of the seconds from one to ten when a boxer has been knocked down ⟨took a ~ of nine before getting up⟩ **b :** the number of balls and strikes charged to a baseball batter at one turn ⟨a full ~ of 3 and 2⟩ **c :** the number of bowling pins knocked down with the first bowl of a frame that is added to a spare in the previous frame **d :** an estimate of the number of cards in each suit that were orig. dealt to or are still held by another player ⟨take a ~ on the opponents' hands⟩ **e :** point count in bridge **f :** a point or points scored in a game or the total points that have been scored up to any particular time ⟨the ~ now stands at 15-30⟩ **7 a :** an oyster, terrapin, or food fish of a size reckoned as standard or above a specified minimum size — used chiefly in selling by the number **b :** a stem bearing nine or more hands of bananas **c :** the number of sheets of paper or board that make up a given weight or unit **8 a :** a system of measuring yarns by the number of hanks or yards per pound and indicating size or fineness **b :** the number of warp yarns and weft yarns per inch in a textile fabric — compare [5]PICK 2b **9 :** an indication by an enumerating device of an ionizing event (as the arrival of a cosmic-ray particle) or of the total number of such events in a given period; *also* **:** a single ionizing event — compare COUNTING TUBE

[3]**count** \"\ *n* -s [MF *conte*, *comte*, fr. LL *comit-*, *comes*, fr. L, associate, companion, one of the imperial court or train, lit., one who goes with another, fr. *com-* + *-it-*, *-es* (fr. *ire* to go) — more at ISSUE] **:** a European nobleman whose rank corresponds to that of an English earl

[1]**count·able** \ˈkau̇ntəbəl\ *adj* [ME, fr. MF *contable*, *comptable*, fr. *conter*, *compter* to count + *-able* — more at COUNT] **1** *archaic* **:** liable for an account **:** ACCOUNTABLE, RESPONSIBLE **2 :** capable of being counted

[2]**countable** \"\ *n* -s **1 :** something that is countable **2 :** COUNT NOUN

countdown \ˈ=ˌ=\ *n* -s [*count down*, v.] **:** an audible backward counting off in fixed units (as seconds) from an arbitrary starting number (as 10) to mark the diminishing time remaining before the execution of an operation ⟨the ~ concluded, "four, three, two, one," and then the firing button was pushed⟩; *also* **:** the length of time marked by such a counting or required by the entire sequence of steps in readying a missile for flight — compare ZERO HOUR

[1]**coun·te·nance** \ˈkau̇nt(ᵊ)nən(t)s, -tən-\ *n* -s [ME *countenaunce*, fr. MF *contenance* behavior, demeanor, fr. ML *continentia*, fr. L, continence, restraint, fr. *continent-*, *continens* (pres. part. of *continēre* to hold together, restrain, contain) + *-ia* -y — more at CONTAIN] **1** *obs* **a :** BEARING, DEMEANOR **b :** BEHAVIOR, COMPORTMENT **c :** bearing or behavior as indicative of goodwill or ill will **2 a :** calm expression **:** facial expression indicating composure ⟨he kept his ~ so well that he had the air of having made a finished speech —G.B.Shaw⟩; *also* **:** mental composure ⟨startled and also somewhat out of ~ —Arnold Bennett⟩ **b :** the expressive appearance of one's face **:** LOOK, EXPRESSION ⟨a ~ which expressed both good humor and intelligence —Sir Walter Scott⟩ **3** *archaic* **a :** ASPECT, SEMBLANCE **b** (1) **:** a mere appearance or show (2) **:** a feigned or assumed appearance **:** PRETENSE **4 :** FACE, VISAGE; *esp* **:** the face as an indication of mood, emotion, or character ⟨good-looking and gentlemanlike, he had a pleasant ~ —Jane Austen⟩ **5** *archaic* **:** the appearances that one maintains **:** STANDING, DIGNITY **6 a** *obs* **:** CREDIT, ESTEEM **b :** appearance of favor **:** bearing or expression appearing or calculated to approve or encourage **:** SANCTION **:** moral support **:** GOODWILL ⟨his having had no support or ~ in accepted tradition —F.R.Leavis⟩ ⟨give the hussy no ~ —S.E.Morison & H.S. Commager⟩ **c** *obs* **:** confidence arising from favor and encouragement **:** TRUST **syn** see FACE

[2]**countenance** \"\ *vt* -ED/-ING/-S [MF *contenancer*, fr. *contenance*, n.] **:** to give countenance to **:** extend approval or toleration to **:** ENCOURAGE, SANCTION, SUPPORT, FAVOR, CONDONE ⟨asked his family to ~ her⟩ ⟨although militant, he never *countenanced* violence⟩ **syn** see FAVOR

coun·te·nanc·er \-sə(r)\ *n* -s **:** one that countenances **:** ENCOURAGER

[1]**count·er** \ˈkau̇ntə(r)\ *n* -s [ME *countour*, fr. MF *comptouer*, *comptoir*, fr. ML *computatorium*, computing place, place of accounts, fr. L *computatus* (past part. of *computare* to compute) + *-orium* -ory — more at COUNT] **1 a :** an article used in reckoning; *esp* **:** a piece (as of metal, ivory, wood, bone) used in keeping accounts and in playing games of chance **b :** one of a set of small objects (as disks or squares of wood, plastic, bone) with which a game (as a board game) is played **2** *obs* **:** a prison esp. for debtors that is attached to a city court **3 a :** an imitation often in base metal of a coin **b :** TOKEN **c :** money in general or a particular coin **d :** a possession or attribute of value in bargaining ⟨the Guam fortifications were intended as a bargaining ~ in possible future negotiations —*New Republic*⟩ ⟨to use sex as a ~ rather than value it as either a means of self-expression or communication —Margaret Mead⟩ **:** ASSET **4 a :** a table, shelf, or other level surface usu. of a height convenient for a person standing before it and over which transactions may be conducted **:** a table, case, or shelf on which goods are displayed and over which payment for purchases is made **:** any article of business, store, or institutional furniture that separates clientele from personnel and over which transactions are made **b :** a long and somewhat narrow serving area flanked by a row of stools ⟨eating at the ~ rather than taking a table⟩ **:** flat working space on the top of kitchen equipment or furnishings **5 :** COUNTERWORD ⟨a cliché, a worn ~ of a word, with its original meaning all effaced —Havelock Ellis⟩ — **over the counter** *adv* **:** in or through a broker's office rather than through a stock exchange ⟨bought stock *over the counter*⟩ — **under the counter** *adv* **:** in a stealthy or surreptitious manner **:** illicitly and privately **:** according to an arrangement that does not apply to a total clientele

[2]**count·er** \"\ *n* -s [ME *countere*, *countour*, fr. MF *conteor*, fr. *conter* to count + *-eor* -or — more at COUNT] **:** one that counts: as **a :** a worker who counts units of materials in process or finished products for purposes of inspection, record keeping, or distribution **b :** one that counts votes **c :** SPEED COUNTER **d** (1) **:** an instrument for recording the number of repetitions of an operation (as the revolution of a shaft) or of things produced (as copies printed on a printing press) (2) **:** a device, unit, or circuit in a business machine (as a cash register or bookkeeping machine) that automatically performs certain mathematical operations and records the results (as the automatic totaling of certain classes of figures entered in the machine or the counting of certain classes of operations performed on the machine) **e :** a device for detecting the passage of ionizing particles whose presence is recorded in the form of electrical impulses **f :** CLASSIFIER 2

[3]**coun·ter** \"\ *vb* -ED/-ING/-S [ME *countren*, partly short for *encountren* to encounter, partly fr. MF *contre* against, contrary — more at ENCOUNTER] *vt* **1 a :** to act or operate in opposition to **:** argue against **:** contend with or against **:** OPPOSE, COMBAT ⟨~*ing* the claim for damages⟩ **b :** CHECK, OFFSET, NULLIFY ⟨~*ing* the trend towards decentralization⟩ ⟨means to ~ or neutralize an enemy's sea mines and torpedoes —*N.Y. Times*⟩ **2 a :** to fight against **:** encounter in opposition **:** meet in combat ⟨~*ing* the foe valiantly⟩ **b :** to adduce in answer to another's contention ⟨he ~*ed* that his warnings had been ignored⟩ **3** *obs* **:** to perform variations upon (a song or instrumental composition) ~ *vi* **1 :** to meet attacks or arguments step by step with appropriate defensive or retaliatory steps ⟨~*ing* with surprise sallies against the besiegers⟩ ⟨~*ing* with appeals to other authorities⟩ **2 :** to deliver a blow while receiving or parrying one (as in boxing) ⟨he ~*ed* with his left⟩ **3 :** to sing a counter or accompanying voice part to a principal melody

[4]**coun·ter** \"\ *adv* [ME *countre*, fr. MF *contre*, fr. L *contra* against, fr. OL *com* with (whence L *cum*) + *-tra* (comparative suffix) — more at COM-] **1 :** in an opposite direction **:** in the wrong direction **:** in a reverse way **:** contrary to the true or indicated course ⟨a *hound* running ~⟩ **2 :** in a contrary or opposite trend or direction **:** to a different result or effect **:** in antagonism or opposition — often used with *go* or *run* ⟨moral obligations or interests which persistently go ~ to our general pleasure-seeking tendencies —Joseph Margolis⟩

[5]**coun·ter** \"\ *n* -s [[4,6]*counter*] **1 :** the direction opposite to that taken by the game in hunting ⟨the hounds taking the ~⟩ **2 :** the after portion of a boat from the waterline to the extreme outward swell or stern overhang — see SHIP illustration **3 :** the breast of a horse **4** [It *contro*, fr. *contro*, prep., against, var. of *contra*, fr. L] **a :** a circular parry in fencing in which the blade follows that of the opponent and meets it again where the former engagement was, diverting the point **b :** the act of giving a blow when receiving or parrying one (as in boxing); *also* **:** the blow so given **c :** a second diagonal tension member commonly having a turnbuckle and provided in certain panels of a truss where the stress in the main diagonal is subject to reversal under change of load **5** [short for *counterfort*] **:** a stiffener of leather, fiber, or other material shaped and skived to a soft edge and intended to give permanent form to a boot or shoe upper around the heel

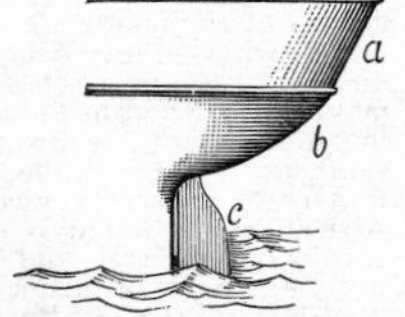

a stern, *b* counter, *c* rudder

6 [by shortening] : COUNTERTENOR **7** : CONTRARY, OPPOSITE ⟨promising the ~⟩ ⟨believing the ~ of what was said⟩ **8 :** an agency, move, or force that offsets, checks, neutralizes, or otherwise acts in opposition : ANSWER, REJOINDER, PARRY, CHECK, DEFENSE ⟨this salutary ~ to the baleful influence of our philosophical extremists —J.A.Mourant⟩ ⟨the dramatic ~ to an unexpected thrust —E.M.Lustgarten⟩ ⟨a football formation used as a ~ to an overshifted defense⟩ **9 a :** CROSS LODE **b** [by shortening] : COUNTERSHAFT **c** [by shortening] : COUNTERSEAL **10 a :** any of the areas in the faces of printing type that are less than type high and enclosed by the strokes of the letter — see TYPE illustration **b :** the matching counterpart of a die (sense 6h(1)), usu. of softer and less permanent material — called also *force* **11 :** a 3-lobed school skating figure performed on either edge and either forward or backward in which the skater executes a turn at each junction of the three lobes against the natural rotation of the curve being skated and remains on the same edge throughout — compare ROCKER

⁶**coun·ter** \"\ *adj* [⁴*counter*] **1 :** marked by or tending toward an opposite direction, motion, or effect : OPPOSED, CONTRARY: **a :** moving in an opposite direction ⟨a ship slowed down by ~ tides⟩ **b :** serving to answer, check, offset, or challenge the action of another (as an opponent) : RETALIATORY ⟨a sally of the tongue may invite a ~ sally of the fists —V.L.Parrington⟩ ⟨the westward expansion of the southern slave power in search of unexhausted land, or the ~ expansion of the free-soil movement —Ellen Semple⟩ **c :** given to or marked by opposition, hostility, or antipathy ⟨from being current with his times and his fellow men he seemed to become ~ —H.S. Canby⟩ **d :** situated opposite : lying opposite ⟨and clambered halfway up the ~ side —Alfred Tennyson⟩ **e :** NULLIFYING, COUNTERMANDING ⟨~ orders from the colonel⟩ **2 :** duplicate and serving as a tally or check ⟨a ~ list⟩ **syn** see ADVERSE

⁷**coun·ter** \"\ *vt* -ED/-ING/-S [⁵*counter*] : to furnish with a counter ⟨~*ing* a shoe⟩

counter- *prefix* [ME *countre-*, fr. MF *contre-*, *contre* — more at COUNTER (adv.)] **1 a :** contrary : opposite : adverse ⟨*counter*current⟩ ⟨*counter*order⟩ **b :** opposing : retaliatory : answering ⟨*counter*blow⟩ ⟨*counter*weapon⟩ **2 :** complementary : corresponding : alternate ⟨*counter*weight⟩ ⟨*counter*part⟩ ⟨*counter*theme⟩ **3 :** duplicate : substitute ⟨*counter*foil⟩

coun·ter·act \ˌkau̇ntəˈrakt\ *vt* -ED/-ING/-S [*counter-* + *act*] : to act in opposition to : make ineffective by opposite force : mitigate ill effects of : CHECK, OFFSET, NEUTRALIZE, NULLIFY ⟨the spontaneous physiological processes which ~ disease before medical science comes into play —Havelock Ellis⟩ **syn** see NEUTRALIZE

coun·ter·ac·tant \-tənt, -tᵊnt\ *adj* : COUNTERACTING

coun·ter·act·ing·ly *adv* : in a counteracting manner

coun·ter·action \ˈkau̇ntər+\ *n* -S **1 :** contrary action : OPPOSITION, RESISTANCE ⟨scheming ~⟩ **2 :** act or action of counteracting : a counteracting agency ⟨the ~ of centripetal forces on centrifugal tendencies⟩

¹**coun·ter·active** \"+\ *adj* [*counteract* + *-ive*] : tending to counteract **syn** see ADVERSE

²**counteractive** \"\ *n* -S : a counteractive agency

coun·ter·agent \ˈkau̇ntər+,-\ *n* [*counter-* + *agent*] : one that counteracts

coun·ter·approach \"+\ *n* [trans. of F *contre-approches*] : approaches (sense 4b) advanced from defensive works to meet hostile approaches

¹**coun·ter·arch** \"+\ *n* [*counter-* + *arch*] : an opposite and strengthening arch

²**counterarch** \ˌkau̇ntər+\ *vt* : to supply with a counterarch

counterargument \"+\ *n* [*counter-* + *argument*] : an opposing or answering argument

¹**coun·ter·attack** \ˈkau̇ntər+\ *n* [*counter-* + *attack*] **1 :** an attack against an enemy attacking force usu. with limited tactical objectives (as to regain a key position) — compare COUNTEROFFENSIVE **2 :** an aggressive action in defense : an attack on one attacking ⟨a ~ on his detractors⟩

²**counterattack** \ˈ≈≈+\ *vi* : to make a counterattack : attack in reprisal or retaliation ⟨the defenders have ~*ed* with the charges that the critics themselves are fascist —Paul Woodring⟩ ~ *vt* : to make a counterattack against

¹**coun·ter·balance** \ˈkau̇ntə(r)+\ *n* [*counter-* + *balance*] **1 :** a weight that balances another : COUNTERPOISE **2 :** an agency, force, or power that balances, offsets, checks, or neutralizes an opposing force ⟨his chary caution serving as a ~ to her impetuousness⟩

A counterbalance of locomotive driving wheel

²**counterbalance** \ˌ≈≈+\ *vt* **1 :** to serve as a counterbalance to : oppose with an equal weight : BALANCE, COUNTERPOISE, COUNTERVAIL ⟨the inward thrust is *counterbalanced* by the outer⟩ **2 :** to oppose with equal force or significance : CHECK, OFFSET, NEUTRALIZE, BALANCE, COMPENSATE ⟨those two opposite causes seem to ~ one another —Adam Smith⟩ **3 :** to equip with counterbalances ⟨two *counterbalanced* cable cars⟩

counterbalanced window *n* : a double-hung window in which the upper and lower sashes are so connected that they balance

coun·ter·battery \ˈkau̇ntə(r)+\ *n* [trans. of MF *contre-batterie*] : artillery fire directed against enemy artillery ⟨guns assigned to a ~ mission⟩

coun·ter·blast \"+\ *n* [*counter-* + *blast*] : a check, offset, balance, or counteraction marked by strength, vigor, explosiveness, and lack of restraint ⟨the secretary's tirade drew a ~ from the opposition leader⟩

coun·ter·blow \"+\ *n* [*counter-* + *blow*] : a return blow : a reprisal measure : RETALIATION ⟨the ~ delivered against the aggressor —*Soviet Russia Today*⟩

¹**coun·ter·bore** \ˌkau̇ntə(r)+\ *vt* [*counter-* + *bore*] : to form a counterbore in : enlarge (part of a hole) by means of a counterbore

²**counterbore** \ˈ≈≈+,-\ *n* **1 :** a flat-bottomed enlargement of the mouth of a cylindrical bore **2 :** a drill for making a counterbore — compare COUNTERSINK

count·er·boy \ˈkau̇ntə(r)+,-\ *n* [¹*counter* + *boy*] : a boy who does the work of a counterman

¹**coun·ter·brace** \ˈkau̇ntə(r)+,-\ *n* [*counter-* + *brace*] : a brace counteracting the strain of another brace: **a :** the brace of the fore-topsail on the leeward side of a ship **b :** ⁵COUNTER 4c

²**counterbrace** \ˌ≈≈+\ *vb* [*counter-* + *brace*] : to brace in opposite directions ⟨~ a ship's yards⟩; *also* : to brace so that opposite stresses are resisted

coun·ter·brand \ˈkau̇ntə(r)+,-\ *n* [*counter-* + *brand*] : a brand put on cattle to supersede a previous brand

¹**counterbuff** *n* [*counter-* + *buff*] *obs* : COUNTERBLOW, REBUFF

²**counterbuff** *vt, archaic* : to strike back at : REBUFF

counter card *n* [¹*counter*] : an advertising placard for use on or in a store counter

countercast *n* -S [*counter-* + *cast*] *obs* : an antagonistic trick or artifice

countercaster *n* -S [¹*counter* (piece used in keeping account) + *caster*] *obs* : a reckoner of accounts : BOOKKEEPER

coun·ter·cathexis \ˌkau̇ntə(r)+\ *n, pl* **countercathexes** [*counter-* + *cathexis*] : the act by the ego of blocking from consciousness objectionable notions and impulses of the id

¹**coun·ter·change** \ˈ≈≈+,-\ *n* [part trans. of MF *contrechange*, fr. *contre-* counter- + *change* exchange change — more at CHANGE] **1** *obs* : EXCHANGE, RECIPROCATION, ALTERNATION **2 :** the contrast of a dark area against a light ground with a light area against a dark ground in a painting

²**counterchange** \ˌ≈≈+\ *vt* [part trans. of MF *contrechanger*, fr. *contrechange*, n.] **1 :** to cause to change places or characteristics : SHIFT, TRANSPOSE **2 :** to make checkered (as with contrasting colors) ⟨elms that ~ the floor of this flat lawn with dusk and bright —Alfred Tennyson⟩ **3** *heraldry* **a :** to depict (charges or a charge borne on a party or varied field) in the tincture of the opposite part of the field from that on which each charge or each part of a charge lies **b :** to reverse the two tinctures of (a varied field) on the opposite sides of a line of partition

counterchanged *adj* **1** *heraldry* : each one or each part having the tincture of the opposite portion of the field — used of charges or a charge borne so as to lie on both tinctures of a party or varied field **2** *heraldry* : having the two tinctures reversed on the opposite sides of a line of partition — used of a varied field

¹**coun·ter·charge** \ˌkau̇ntə(r)+\ *vt* [*counter-* + *charge*] : to charge in opposition, contradiction, or reply

²**countercharge** \ˈ≈≈+,-\ *n* : an opposing or retaliatory charge

¹**coun·ter·check** \ˈkau̇ntə(r)+,-\ *n* [*counter-* + *check* (n.)] **1** *obs* : a rebuke in answer to another **2 :** a check or restraint often operating against something that itself exercises a restraining force

²**countercheck** \ˌ≈≈+\ *vt* [*counter-* + *check* (v.)] **1 :** CHECK, COUNTERACT **2 :** to check a second time for verification

counter check *n* [¹*counter*] : a blank check obtainable at a bank esp. to be cashed only at the bank by the drawer

¹**coun·ter·claim** \ˈkau̇ntə(r)+\ *n* [*counter-* + *claim* (n.)] : an opposing claim; *esp* : a law claim of matter constituting a distinct cause of action made by a defendant in an action as an offset to a claim made on him and distinct from his defense, being in effect a distinct action that is sometimes allowed to be brought in order to reduce amount and cost of litigation

²**counterclaim** \ˌ≈≈+\ *vb* [*counter-* + *claim* (v.)] *vi* : to enter or plead a counterclaim ~ *vt* : to ask in a counterclaim

¹**coun·ter·clockwise** \ˌkau̇ntə(r)+\ *adv* [*counter-* + *clockwise*] : in a direction opposite to that in which the hands of a clock rotate : from horizontal left down or nearer and then upwards to horizontal right — opposed to *clockwise*

²**counterclockwise** \"\ *adj* : moving or directed counterclockwise : LEFTHANDED, LEVOROTATORY

coun·ter·colored \ˌkau̇ntə(r)+\ *adj* [*counter-* + *colored*] *heraldry* : COUNTERCHANGED

coun·ter·com·po·ny \ˌkau̇ntə(r)kəmˈpōnē\ *adj* [trans. of F *contre-componé*] *heraldry* : composed of a double row of small squares of alternating tinctures

coun·ter·couchant \"+\ *adj* [*counter-* + *couchant*] *heraldry* : couchant with heads in opposite directions

coun·ter·courant \"+\ *adj* [*counter-* + *courant*] *heraldry* : running in opposite directions ⟨two stags ~⟩

coun·ter·cry \ˈkau̇ntə(r)+,-\ *n* [*counter-* + *cry*] : an answering cry ⟨cries of "Espionage" and *countercries* of "Nonsense" —*Time*⟩

¹**coun·ter·current** \ˈkau̇ntə(r)+,-\ *n* [*counter-* + *current* (n.)] : a current flowing in a direction opposite to that of another one ⟨an oceanic ~⟩

²**countercurrent** \ˌ≈≈+\ *adj* [*counter-* + *current* (adj.)] **1 :** flowing in an opposite direction **2 :** involving flow of materials in opposite directions ⟨acetylene dissolved by ~ treatment with water⟩

³**countercurrent** \ˌ≈≈+\ *or* **coun·ter·currently** \"+\ *adv* : in a direction opposite to that in which something else is flowing ⟨a gas passed ~ to a fluid running through a tube⟩

coun·ter·cyclical \ˌkau̇ntə(r)+\ *adj* [*counter-* + *cyclical*] : calculated to check excessive developments in a business cycle : COMPENSATORY ⟨~ budget policies of the government⟩

coun·ter·dike \ˈ≈≈+,-\ *n* [*counter-* + *dike*] : a second or reserve dike

¹**coun·ter·disengage** \ˌ≈≈+\ *vi* [*counter-* + *disengage*] *fencing* : to disengage into the previous line and at the moment when one's adversary disengages — **coun·ter·disengagement** \"+\ *n* -S

²**coun·ter·disengage** \ˈkau̇ntə(r)+\ *n* : the act of counterdisengaging

coun·ter·earth \ˈkau̇ntər+,-\ *n* [*counter-* + *earth*; trans. of Gk *antichthōn*] : a planet supposed in Pythagoreanism to accompany the earth in its revolutions and to shield it from the fire at the center of the universe

countered *past of* COUNTER

counter electromotive force *n* [⁶*counter*] : the electromotive force that develops in some circuits from chemical or magnetic effects of the current and that opposes the impressed electromotive force producing the current — called also *back electromotive force*

coun·ter·embattled \ˌkau̇ntər+\ *adj* [*counter-* + *embattled*] *heraldry* : embattled on opposite sides with the battlement or merlon on one side opposed to the embrasure on the other

coun·ter·embowed \"+\ *adj* [*counter-* + *embowed*] *heraldry* : bent or curved one to the dexter and the other to the sinister

¹**coun·ter·enamel** \ˈkau̇ntər+\ *n* [*counter-* + *enamel* (n.); trans. of F *contre-émail*] : enamel on the reverse side of an enameled plate, plaque, or shield

²**counterenamel** \ˌ≈≈+\ *vt* [*counter-* + *enamel* (v.); trans. of F *contre-émailler*] : to enamel on the reverse side

coun·ter·espionage \ˌkau̇ntər+\ *n* [*counter-* + *espionage*; part trans. of F *contre-espionnage*] : the activity concerned with the discovery and defeat of enemy espionage

¹**coun·ter·etch** \ˌkau̇ntər+\ *vt* [*counter-* + *etch*] : to clean (a lithographic plate) with dilute acid solution

²**counteretch** \ˈ≈≈+,-\ *n* : the cleaning (as of a lithographic plate) by counteretching; *also* : the solution used for such cleaning

coun·ter·exposition \ˌkau̇ntər+\ *n* [*counter-* + *exposition*] : a secondary exposition of a musical fugue with the subject and answer usu. in reverse order

¹**coun·ter·factual** \ˌkau̇ntə(r)+\ *adj* [*counter-* + *factual*] : contrary to fact — **coun·ter·factually** \"+\ *adv*

²**counterfactual** \"+\ *n* -S : a logical conditional whose antecedent is or is presumed to be contrary to fact (as *if he had come*)

coun·ter·faller \ˈkau̇ntə(r)+,-\ *n* -S [*counter-* + *faller*] : a wire in a spinning mule that lifts the yarn when it is not depressed by a faller so as to keep tension uniform

counterfeisance *n* -S [part trans. of MF *contrefaisance*, fr. *contrefaisant*, pres. part. of *contrefaire* to imitate — more at COUNTERFEIT] *obs* : COUNTERFEITING, IMPOSTURE

¹**coun·ter·feit** \ˈkau̇ntə(r),fit, *usu* -id.+V; *Brit also* -,fēt\ *vb* -ED/-ING/-S [ME *countrefeten*, fr. MF *contrefait*, past part.] *vt* **1** *obs* : IMPERSONATE **2 :** to put on the false appearance of : FEIGN, SIMULATE ⟨~ sorrow and mask inward glee⟩ **3 a :** to endeavor or succeed in having the appearance or characteristics of without attempt to deceive or delude : IMITATE, COPY ⟨fiction that seeks to ~ reality —Bernard De Voto⟩ **b :** to imitate fraudulently : copy with intent to deceive : make a fraudulent copy or replica of (something of value, as a coin, bill, note, or signature) ⟨a gang ~*ing* $50 bills⟩ **4 a** *archaic* : to use as a model : seek to imitate : EMULATE **b** *obs* : to cause to have a false or misleading appearance : DISGUISE ~ *vi* **1 :** to try to deceive by pretending or dissembling : SIMULATE, FEIGN **2 :** to practice counterfeiting of valuables ⟨held on charges of ~*ing*⟩ **syn** see ASSUME

²**counterfeit** \"\ *adj* [ME *countrefet*, fr. MF *contrefait*, past part. of *contrefaire* to imitate, draw, paint, fr. *contre-* counter- + *faire* to make, fr. L *facere* — more at DO] **1 a :** SPURIOUS : not genuine or authentic; *esp* : not composed by the author indicated or under the circumstances ascribed ⟨a ~ gospel rejected as apocryphal⟩ **b :** made in fraudulent imitation : produced with intent to deceive : FORGED ⟨a ~ diamond made of paste⟩; *esp* : made fraudulently in imitation of a government issue ⟨a ~ stamp⟩ ⟨a ~ bill⟩ **2 a :** FEIGNED : assumed with calculation to mislead ⟨a ~ joy at her friend's engagement⟩ **b :** marked by false pretense : SHAM, PRETENDED ⟨an impostor, a ~ prince⟩ **3** *archaic* : represented in a picture or by means of a picture : PORTRAYED ⟨look here upon this picture and on this, the ~ presentment of two brothers —Shak.⟩

syn SPURIOUS, BOGUS, FAKE, SHAM, PSEUDO, PINCHBECK, PHONY: COUNTERFEIT applies to something made or fabricated in quite close imitation of something else, esp. to something genuine or original and with intent to deceive ⟨a *counterfeit* coin⟩ ⟨a *counterfeit* passport⟩ ⟨the austere word of genuine religion is: save your soul! The degenerate counsel of a *counterfeit* religion is: salve your soul! —W.L.Sullivan⟩ SPURIOUS applies to what is not genuine, authentic, or true without necessarily implying fraudulent purpose or deceiving imitation ⟨the French look on us English monk-made knights as *spurious* and adulterine, unworthy of the name of knight —Charles Kingsley⟩ ⟨it is certain that the letter, attributed to him, directing that no Christian should be punished for being a Christian, is *spurious* —Matthew Arnold⟩ BOGUS is likely to imply fraud, imposture, or deception, sometimes self-deception ⟨in red cambric and *bogus* ermine, as some kind of king —Mark Twain⟩ ⟨*bogus* naturalization of immigrants and repeating at elections were now carried to hitherto unknown lengths —A.F.Harlow⟩ ⟨nostalgia can be the trickiest of maladies. It invests the past with *bogus* glamour —W.C. Richards⟩ FAKE implies a false fabrication or fraudulent manipulation ⟨a *fake* ruby⟩ ⟨a *fake* cure-all⟩ ⟨another source of quick money was selling life memberships in *fake* yacht clubs —Alva Johnston⟩ ⟨any Americans who cling to illusions about communism and its *fake* Utopia—A.E.Stevenson b.1900⟩ SHAM may suggest thinness and obviousness of the disguise, naïveté of the deception, or lack of intent to imitate exactly ⟨a garden adorned with *sham* ruins and statues —L.P.Smith⟩ ⟨he [Euripides] looked at war and he saw through all the *sham* glory to the awful evil beneath —Edith Hamilton⟩ ⟨not one officer among them whose experience of war extended beyond a drill on muster day and the *sham* fight that closed the performance —Francis Parkman⟩ PSEUDO (often appearing as a combining form) may apply to either pretentious, spurious imitation or to imitation to deceive ⟨the cottage seemed very small and horribly 'arty-crafty'. 'Everything looks so *pseudo*,' said Lucy —Frances Towers⟩ ⟨those democrats who wholeheartedly are democrats and not *pseudo*-democrats —*Fortnightly*⟩ ⟨these *pseudo*-evangelists pretended to inspiration —Thomas Jefferson⟩ PINCHBECK may apply to a cheap imitation, often to a poor copy of something costly or grand ⟨*pinchbeck* imitations of the glory of ancient Rome —*Manchester Guardian Weekly*⟩ ⟨greater numbers could afford the *pinchbeck* splendor of organizations like the Colonial Order of the Crown —J.D.Hart⟩ PHONY, more forceful than most in this group, stigmatizes anything spurious ⟨the *phony* aura of romance which travel bureaus are wont to attach to the West Indies —Gladwin Hill⟩ ⟨the Germans were deceiving us at that very moment with a *phony* show of strength —F.E.Fox⟩

³**counterfeit** \"\ *n* -S [ME *countrefet*, fr. *countrefet*, adj.] **1 a :** an imitation or replica markedly close or faithful to an original and typically made to deceive for gain ⟨the $10 bill turned out to be a ~⟩ **b :** a close approximation likely to be confused with reality or with the genuine ⟨that temporary ~ of fame which is publicity —Irwin Edman⟩ **2** *archaic* : a representation, counterpart, or picture : an art work closely similar to its subject ⟨fair Portia's ~ —Shak.⟩ **3** *archaic* : PRETENDER, IMPOSTOR **syn** see IMPOSTURE

coun·ter·feit·er \-,fid·ə(r), -fitə-, -fētə-\ *n* -S [ME *countrefetere*, fr. *countrefeten* + *-ere* -er] : one that forges or makes fraudulent imitations of current money; *also* : one that copies or imitates with either good or bad intent

coun·ter·feit·ly *adv* : in a counterfeit manner : by use of counterfeits

coun·ter·feit·ness *n* -ES : the quality or state of being counterfeit

coun·ter·flashing \ˈkau̇ntə(r) +,-\ *n* [*counter-* + *flashing* (metal strips)] : a strip of sheet metal in the form of an inverted L built into a vertical wall of masonry and bent down over the flashing to make it watertight

coun·ter·flood \ˌ≈≈ +\ *vt* [*counter-* + *flood*] : to flood compartments in (a ship) to counterbalance listing and loss of trim resulting esp. from already flooded compartments

coun·ter·flory *also* **coun·ter·fleury** \ˈ≈≈ +\ *adj* [part trans. of MF *contrefleuri*, fr. *contre-* counter- + *fleuri* fleury — more at FLEURY] *heraldry* : flory on opposite sides so that the middles of the flowers are apparently covered by a part of the charge — used of an ordinary

coun·ter·flow \" +,-\ *n* [*counter-* + *flow*] : flow in opposite directions or the opposite direction — used esp. of fluids in adjacent parts of an apparatus (as a heat exchanger)

coun·ter·foil \ˈkau̇ntə(r) +,-\ *n* -S [*counter-* + *foil*] : a form giving main particulars of something treated in more detail on another and detachable form : a detachable stub usu. serving as a record or receipt (as on a check or ticket)

coun·ter·force \" +,-\ *n* [*counter-* + *force*] : a force, power, activity, or trend that opposes or counters another

coun·ter·fort \" +,-\ *n* -S [part trans. of MF *contrefort*, fr. *contre-* counter- + *fort* strength, force, fr. *fort*, adj., strong — more at FORT] : a buttress built against or integral with a wall (as a retaining wall or dam) but on the back or thrust-receiving side

coun·ter·fugue \" +,-\ *n* [trans. of F *contre-fugue*] : a fugue in which the answer is an inverted imitation of the subject

coun·ter·gambit \"+,-\ *n* [*counter-* + *gambit*] : a chess gambit offered by the second player

counter game *n* [¹*counter*] : any of various games usu. played with dice on a store counter in which a customer attempts to win a prize

coun·ter·gauge *or* **coun·ter·gage** \ˈkau̇ntə(r)+,-\ *n* [*counter-* + *gauge, gage*] : an adjustable gauge with double points for transferring measurements from one piece of lumber to another

count·er·girl \"+,-\ *n* [¹*counter* + *girl*] : a girl counterman

coun·ter·glow \"+,-\ *n* [*counter-* + *glow*; trans. of G *gegenschein*] : GEGENSCHEIN

coun·ter·guard \"+,-\ *n* [part trans. of MF *contre-garde*, fr. *contre-* counter- + *garde* guard, fr. OF *guarde* — more at GUARD] : an outwork protecting from a breaching fire the faces of a bastion, ravelin, or similar work

counter hoop *n* [⁶*counter*] : the outer hoop that clamps and tightens a drumhead

countering *pres part of* COUNTER

coun·ter·intelligence \ˌkau̇ntər+\ *n* [*counter-* + *intelligence*] : organized activity of an intelligence service designed to block an enemy's sources of information by concealment, camouflage, censorship, and other measures, to deceive the enemy by ruses and misinformation, to prevent sabotage, and to gather political and military information

coun·ter·ion \ˈ≈≈+,-\ *n* [*counter-* + *ion*] : an ion having a charge opposite to that of the substance with which it is associated (as in an electric double layer)

¹**coun·ter·irritant** \ˈ≈≈+,-\ *n* [*counter-* + *irritant*] : an agent applied locally to produce superficial inflammation with the object of reducing inflammation in deeper adjacent structures (as a mustard plaster applied to the chest in bronchitis); *broadly* : an additional irritation or discomfort that diverts attention from another

²**counterirritant** \"\ *adj* : having the properties of a counterirritant : dealing with or marked by counterirritants

coun·ter·irritate \ˈkau̇ntər +,-\ *vt* [*counter-* + *irritate*] : to irritate as an offset to adjacent inflammation : treat with counterirritants — **coun·ter·irritation** \"+,-\ *n*

count·er·jumper \ˈkau̇ntə(r) +,-\ *n* [¹*counter* + *jumper*] : a store clerk

¹**coun·ter·lath** \"+,-\ *n* [*counter-* + *lath*] **1 :** a batten laid lengthwise between two rafters to afford a bearing for laths laid crosswise **2 :** any lath laid without actual measurement between two gauged laths **3 :** any of a series of laths nailed to the timbers to raise the sheet lathing above their surface to afford a key for plastering **4 :** one of many laths used in preparing one side of a partition or framed wall when the other side has been covered in and finished

²**counterlath** \"\ *vt* : to furnish with counterlaths

coun·ter·lode \ˈkau̇ntə(r) +,-\ *n* [*counter-* + *lode*] : CROSS LODE

count·er·man \ˈkau̇ntə(r),man, -,maa(ə)n *also* -,mən\ *n, pl* **countermen** [¹*counter* + *man*] **1 :** one that tends a counter; *specif* : one that serves food over the counter of a cafeteria or lunchroom **2 :** a marker in a laundry or cleaning and dyeing establishment **3 :** one that sells or directs the sale of automobile parts; *sometimes* : a manufacturer's representative **4 :** a clerk in charge of stockroom supplies

¹**coun·ter·mand** \ˈkau̇ntə(r),mand, -,månd, ˌ≈≈ˈ≈\ *vt* -ED/-ING/-S [ME *countermaunden*, fr. MF *contremander*, fr. *contre-* counter- + *mander* to command, fr. L *mandare* — more at MANDATE] **1 :** to revoke (a former command) : cancel or rescind (an order) by giving a contrary order ⟨~ an order for goods⟩ **2 :** to recall or order back by a superseding contrary order ⟨~ reinforcements⟩ **3 :** to stop or prohibit by revoking an order or issuing a contrary order ⟨~ a payment⟩ **4** *obs* **a :** to oppose or go counter to a command of **b :** FRUSTRATE, COUNTERACT

2countermand \"\ *n* -s [part trans. of MF *contremand*, fr *contremander*] **:** a contrary order **:** revocation of an order or command; *specif* **:** a legal revoking order or act ⟨halting and retreating according to the ~ of the first orders⟩

1coun·ter·march \ˈkau̇ntə(r)+,-\ *n* [*counter-* + *march* (n.)] **:** a marching back; *specif* **:** a march by troops back over ground recently passed over **:** an evolution by which a unit reverses direction while marching but keeps the same order

2countermarch \ˌ⸗⸗+\ *vi* [*counter-* + *march* (v.)] **:** to march back; *specif* **:** execute a countermarch

1coun·ter·mark \ˈ⸗⸗+,-\ *n* [part trans. of MF *contremarque*] **1 :** an added mark designed to secure greater safety or more complete identification: **a :** a mark put on a package of goods belonging to several persons to show that it may not be opened except in the presence of all **b :** a hallmark added to that of the artificer of gold or silver work **2 :** an artificial cavity formerly made in the teeth of horses to disguise their age — compare 3BISHOP **3 a :** a mark on a coin that is not part of the original design but that has been added as indication of a change in the coin's value, in its issuing authority, or in its country of circulation **b :** a mark on a coin added as attestation of purity or standard value **:** CHOP MARK

2countermark \ˌ⸗⸗+\ *vt* [trans. of F *contremarquer*] **:** to apply a countermark to ⟨~ silverware⟩

coun·ter·measure \ˈ⸗⸗+,-\ *n* [*counter-* + *measure*] **:** a measure, means, or expedient calculated to counter, check, or offset another

coun·ter·melody \"+,-\ *n* [*counter-* + *melody*] **:** a secondary melody sounded or to be sounded simultaneously with the principal one

coun·ter-memorial \ˌkau̇ntə(r)+\ *n* [*counter-* + *memorial*] **:** an answer admitting, denying, or commenting on charges in a memorial in international law

1coun·ter·mine \ˈ⸗⸗+,-\ *n* [*counter-* + *mine* (subterranean passage)] **1 :** a tunnel for intercepting an enemy mine **2 :** a stratagem for defeating an attack **:** COUNTERPLOT

2countermine \ˌ⸗⸗+\ *vt* **1 :** to frustrate or combat by secret means ⟨know exactly the play of another in order to ~ him —Henry Fielding⟩ **2 :** to oppose by means of a countermine **:** intercept with a countermine **:** destroy (a laid mine or a minefield) with an explosion **~** *vi* **:** to make or lay down countermines

coun·ter·mortar \"+\ *adj* [*counter-* + *mortar*] **:** directed against enemy mortars ⟨~ fire⟩

coun·ter·move \ˈkau̇ntə(r)+,-\ *n* [*counter-* + *move*] **:** an action designed to check, offset, or counter another

coun·ter·movement \"+,-\ *n* [*counter-* + *movement*] **:** a movement in an opposite direction

1coun·ter·mure \ˈkau̇ntə(r)+,-\ *n* [alter. of earlier *contremeur*, fr. MF *contremur*, fr. *contre-* counter- + *mur* wall — more at MURE] **1 :** a second or supplementary wall **:** a wall raised behind another that might be breached **2 :** a wall raised by besiegers confronting a defense wall

2countermure \ˌ⸗⸗+\ *vt* -ED/-ING/-S **:** to protect or fortify with a countermure

coun·ter·naiant \"+\ *adj* [*counter-* + *naiant*] *heraldry* **:** swimming in opposite directions

coun·ter·offensive \ˈkau̇ntər +\ *n* [*counter-* + *offensive*] **:** a military offensive operation that is undertaken by a defending force on a large scale and usu. embodies a general shift from defense to attack with important objectives (as the destruction of the enemy's forces) — compare COUNTERATTACK

coun·ter·opening \" + ,-\ *n* [*counter-* + *opening*] **:** an aperture on the opposite side or in a different place; *specif* **:** a surgical opening made opposite another to facilitate drainage (as of an abscess)

coun·ter·order \" + ,-\ *n* [*counter-* + *order*] **:** a contradicting or countermanding order

counterpace *n* [*counter-* + *pace*] *obs* **:** COUNTERMOVEMENT

1counterpane *n* -s [ME *contrepane*, fr. *contre-* counter- + *pane*, *pan* piece, part, piece of cloth, coverlet — more at PANE] *obs* **:** COUNTERPART

2coun·ter·pane \ˈkau̇ntə(r),pān *also chiefly Brit* -,pin\ *n* -s [by folk etymology (influence of *pane* coverlet) fr. obs. E *counterpoint*, fr. ME *countrepointe*, by folk etymology (influence of *countre-* counter-) fr. MF *coute pointe*, fr. OF, fr. *coute* quilt + *pointe* (fem. of *point*, past part. of *poindre* to prick, stitch), fr. L *puncta*, fem. of *punctus*, past part. of *pungere* to prick — more at QUILT, PUNGENT] **:** BEDSPREAD

1coun·ter·part \ˈkau̇ntə(r) + ,-\ *n* [*counter-* + *part*] **1 :** one of two corresponding copies of a legal instrument (as an indenture) **:** DUPLICATE **2 a :** a thing that may be applied to another thing so as to fit perfectly (as a seal to its impression) **b :** something that serves to complete or complement **:** COMPLEMENT ⟨retain export controls . . . only where needed as a ~ of domestic distribution controls —*U.S.Code*⟩ **c :** one playing opposite in a play ⟨Miss Doe as heroine served as an adequate ~ to the lead role⟩ **3 a :** one remarkably similar to another **:** a person or thing so like another that it seems a duplicate ⟨mistook a feverish flush as the ~ of healthy color⟩ **b :** EQUIVALENT **:** something or someone having the same use, role, office, or characteristics often in a different sphere or period ⟨metal knives and axes came into use promptly, replacing their stone ~*s* —E.H.Spicer⟩ ⟨such laws in psychology he thought to be the ~ of the laws of mechanics in physics —S.F. Mason⟩

2counterpart \"\ *adj* **:** of or relating to a fund set up by a nation receiving economic aid from another, the fund being in the currency of the former and its amount being equal to the value of the goods and services received ⟨~ funds⟩ ⟨~ francs⟩

coun·ter·passant \ˌkau̇ntə(r) +\ *adj* [part trans. of F *contre-passant*, fr. *contre-* counter- + *passant* — more at PASSANT] *heraldry* **:** passant in opposite directions ⟨two lions ~⟩

coun·ter·plan \ˈ⸗⸗ + ,-\ *n* [*counter-* + *plan*] **:** a plan countering another **:** an alternate or substitute plan

coun·ter·plea \" + ,-\ *n* [*counter-* + *plea*] **:** a replication to a legal plea **:** an answering plea

1coun·ter·plot \" + ,-\ *vb* [*counter-* + *plot* (v.)] *vi* **:** to plot against one that has given himself to plotting **:** INTRIGUE **~** *vt* **:** to intrigue against (a plotter) **:** contend against or foil with plots ⟨~ the wily courtiers⟩

2counterplot \"\ *n* [*counter-* + *plot* (n.)] **:** a plot or artifice opposed to another

1coun·ter·point \ˈkau̇ntə(r) + ,-\ *n, often attrib* [earlier *conterpoint*, fr. MF *contrepoint*, fr. *contre-* counter- + *point* dot, musical note — more at POINT] **1 a :** one or more independent melodies added as accompaniment to a primary melody (as the cantus firmus) **b :** the combination of two or more related but independent melodies into a single harmonic texture in which each retains its linear or horizontal character **c :** melodic part writing **:** POLYPHONY — see DOUBLE COUNTERPOINT, QUADRUPLE COUNTERPOINT, SINGLE COUNTERPOINT, TRIPLE COUNTERPOINT **2 a :** a foil or contrasting element **:** a matching, complementing, or contrasting item **:** OPPOSITE, ANTITHESIS ⟨this subtle novelist employs another symbolic situation to serve as ~ to the basic one —Robert Humphrey⟩ **b :** any artistic arrangement or device using significant contrast or interplay of distinguishable elements ⟨the ~ of two interwoven dramatic plots⟩; *specif* **:** motions in dance juxtaposed rhythmically and visually against the music or against other motions by parts of the body or groups of dancers

2counterpoint \"\ *vt* **1 a :** to compose or arrange in counterpoint **b :** to compose in counterpoint rhythm **2 :** to set off, emphasize, or enliven by contrast or juxtaposition (as in fiction, film cutting, painting) **:** set in contrast ⟨a deep streak of conventionality that is ~*ed* by an intense sensuality —C.J. Rolo⟩

counterpoint rhythm *n* **:** rhythm including so much metrical inversion that the prevailing cadence ceases at times to prevail and so that a complex rhythm results from the concomitance of the basic cadence with its inversion ⟨if . . . reversal is repeated in two feet running . . . it . . . is . . . the superinducing . . . of a new rhythm upon the old . . . [so that] two rhythms are in some manner running at once . . . and this is *counterpoint rhythm* —G.M.Hopkins⟩

1coun·ter·poise \ˌkau̇ntə(r) +\ *vt* [alter. (influenced by *poise*) of ME *countrepesen*, *counterpeisen*, fr. MF *contrepeser*, fr. *contre-* counter- + *peser* to weigh — more at POISE] **1 :** to counteract equally **:** equal in weight, effect, or power **:** COMPENSATE, OFFSET ⟨sorrow *counterpoising* happiness at the event⟩ **2 a :** to bring into a condition of equilibrium or stability ⟨all parts of the sphere were nicely *counterpoised*⟩ **b :** to bring into balance by or as if by addition of weight on an opposite side **:** COUNTERBALANCE ⟨scales in which the weight on one side must be *counterpoised* by a weight in the other —Richard Jefferies⟩ **3** *archaic* **:** CONSIDER, PONDER; *esp* **:** to weigh (one consideration) against another — used with *with*

2counterpoise \ˈ⸗⸗ +\ *n* [alter. (influenced by *poise*) of ME *countrepeis*, fr. MF *contrepeis*, *contrepois*, fr. *contre-* counter- + *peis*, *pois* weight — more at POISE] **1 :** a weight acting against another **:** COUNTERWEIGHT: as **a :** that part of the mechanism in some scales that is suspended from the end of a beam upon which weights are placed to counterbalance load on a platform **b :** any weight used to counterbalance some other part of a scale **2 :** an equivalent power **:** an equal force acting in opposition **:** COUNTERBALANCE, CHECK ⟨his robust strength was a ~ to the disease⟩ **3 :** a state of balance **:** EQUILIBRIUM ⟨the ~ of day and night⟩ **4 :** balance of a horseman in his saddle **5 :** a system of wires or other conductors except the ground forming the lower plate of a radio condenser antenna **6 :** an earth conductor usu. buried below a transmission line for protection of the line against lightning

coun·ter·poison \" + ,-\ *n* [part trans. of MF *contrepoison*, fr. *contre-* counter- + *poison*] **1** *obs* **:** ANTIDOTE **2 :** a poison that counteracts another poison

coun·ter·pole \" + ,-\ *n* [*counter-* + *pole*] **:** an exact opposite **:** ANTITHESIS

coun·ter·pose \ˌkau̇ntə(r) +\ *vt* [*counter-* + *-pose* (as in *compose*); trans. of L *contraponere*] **:** to place counter to **:** juxtapose in opposition, for contrast, or in equilibrium ⟨the view that *counterposed* "formal democracy" to "real democracy" —Sidney Hook⟩ — **coun·ter·position** \" +\ *n*

coun·ter·potent \ˌkau̇ntə(r) +\ *n* [*counter-* + *potent*] **:** a variety of the heraldic fur potent in which each pane stands head to head or foot to foot with one of the same tincture above or below it

coun·ter·preparation \" +\ *n* [*counter-* + *preparation*] **:** preparation to meet something being prepared; *specif* **:** prearranged fire against an enemy that is preparing for attack

coun·ter·pressure \ˈ⸗⸗ + ,-\ *n* [*counter-* + *pressure*] **:** pressure countering that exerted **:** force in a contrary or reverse direction

coun·ter·proof \" + ,-\ *n* [*counter-* + *proof*] **:** a reversed print taken from an ordinary fresh proof by contact impression and used to study the state of the engraved plate

coun·ter·proposal \ˈkau̇ntə(r) +\ *n* [*counter-* + *proposal*] **:** a countering proposal **:** a rejoinder to something proposed

coun·ter·prove \ˌ⸗⸗ +\ *vt* [*counter-* + *prove*] **:** to take a counterproof of

counter·pull \ˈ⸗⸗ + ,-\ *n* [*counter-* + *pull*] **:** a countering attraction or force

coun·ter·punch \" + ,-\ *n* [*counter-* + *punch*] **1 :** a support beneath metal being hammered or punched from above **2 :** a punch in boxing thrown after an opponent's lead; *broadly* **:** any countering blow or attack ⟨the enemy air forces seeking to deliver a ~⟩

coun·ter·puncher \" + ,-\ *n* **:** a boxer who uses the counterpunch as his characteristic style **:** one that counterattacks

coun·ter·puncture \ˈkau̇ntə(r) + ,-\ *n* [*counter-* + *puncture*] **:** a surgical counteropening

coun·ter·quartered \ˌ⸗⸗ +\ *adj* [*counter-* + *quartered*] *heraldry, of a grand quarter* **:** divided again into quarters

coun·ter–rampant \" +\ *adj* [*counter-* + *rampant*] *heraldry* **:** rampant and facing each other — used of two animals ⟨two lions *counter-rampant*, supporting a dexter hand gules⟩; compare COMBATANT

counter rate *n* [1*counter* + *rate*] **:** the rate at which a bank makes loans to its regular customers

coun·ter·reaction \ˌkau̇ntə(r) +\ *n* [*counter-* + *reaction*] **:** a chemical reaction opposing the main action

coun·ter·recoil \" +\ *n* [*counter-* + *recoil*] **:** the return of an artillery piece to the firing position after recoil

coun·ter·reconnaissance \ˈkau̇ntə(r) +\ *n* [*counter-* + *reconnaissance*] **:** measures taken to prevent an enemy's reconnaissance

coun·ter·reformation \" +\ *n* [*counter-* + *reformation*; trans. of G *gegenreformation*] **:** a reformation countering or counteracting another ⟨the *Counter-Reformation* regained much . . . for Roman Catholicism —J.S.Roucek⟩

coun·ter·remonstrant \" +\ *n* [*counter-* + *remonstrant*; trans. of D *contra-remonstrant*] **:** a remonstrant of an opposing party or movement

coun·ter·revolution \" +\ *n* [*counter-* + *revolution*; trans. of F *contre-révolution*] **:** a revolution in opposition to a current or earlier revolution

1coun·ter·revolutionary \ˌkau̇ntə(r) +\ *adj* [*counter-* + *revolutionary*] **:** marked by opposition or antipathy to a current or earlier revolution ⟨arrested for ~ tendencies⟩

2counterrevolutionary \"\ *n* **:** one that abets, encourages, sympathizes with, or takes part in a counterrevolution

coun·ter·revolutionist \ˌkau̇ntə(r) +\ *n* [*counter-* + *revolutionist*] **:** COUNTERREVOLUTIONARY

coun·ter·riposte \ˈkau̇ntə(r) +\ *n* [*counter-* + *riposte*; part trans. of F *contre-riposte*] **:** a riposte delivered after parrying the adversary's riposte

coun·ter·rotating propeller \ˌ⸗⸗ + . . . -\ *n* [*counter-* + *rotating*] **:** CONTRAROTATING PROPELLER

coun·ter·rotation \"+\ *n* [*counter-* + *rotation*] **:** counterclockwise rotation

counters *pl of* COUNTER, *pres 3d sing of* COUNTER

coun·ter·salient \" +\ *adj* [*counter-* + *salient*; trans. of F *contre-saillant*] *heraldry* **:** leaping in opposite directions

coun·ter·scarp \ˈkau̇ntə(r) + ,-\ *n* [part trans. of MF *contrescarpe*, fr. *contre-* counter- + *escarpe* scarp — more at SCARP] **:** the exterior slope or wall of the ditch in a work of fortification

coun·ter·sea \" + ,-\ *n* [*counter-* + *sea*] **:** a sea running counter to the wind or to another sea

coun·ter·seal \" + ,-\ *n* [*counter-* + *seal*] **1 :** a seal that is imposed upon the reverse of a main or usu. larger seal **2 :** the reverse die of a double seal

coun·ter·secure \ˌkau̇ntə(r) +\ *vt* [*counter-* + *secure*] **1** *of a borrower* **:** to give a security to (one who has become a bond for the borrower) to protect against default by the borrower **2 :** to give additional security to or for

coun·ter·selection \" +\ *n* [*counter-* + *selection*] **:** selection opposed in its effects to natural selection: as **a :** preservation of the unfit **:** dysgenic selection (as forced on man by social customs) **b :** selection in plant or animal breeding against a quality undesirable from the point of view of the breeder though likely to be retained in a state of nature ⟨~ against low milk production in cattle⟩

coun·ter·sense \ˈkau̇ntə(r) + ,-\ *n* [*counter-* + *sense*; trans. of F *contresens*] **:** a meaning or interpretation opposed to the original or intended meaning

coun·ter·shading \ˌkau̇ntə(r) +\ *n* [*counter-* + *shading*] **:** coloration (as of an animal) with parts normally in shadow being light or parts normally illuminated being dark — compare PROTECTIVE COLORATION

coun·ter·shaft \ˈ⸗⸗ + ,-\ *n* [*counter-* + *shaft*] **1 :** a mechanism used to transmit motion and power from a main driving shaft to an individual machine, typically mounted by hangers on a ceiling, and driven by one belt from the main shaft and in turn driving the machine by another belt **2 :** a short shaft in a machine (as an automobile) carrying intermediate gears to transmit motion usu. with change of speed or direction or both from one set of gears to another — **coun·ter·shaft·ing** *n*

1coun·ter·sign \" + ,-\ *n* [*counter-* + *sign* (n.); trans. of F *contresigne*] **1 a :** a special mark for identifying or authenticating **:** COUNTERMARK **b :** the signature of a secretary or other person to attest authenticity of a piece of writing already signed by another **2 :** a sign used in reply to another; *specif* **:** a military secret signal (as a word or phrase) that must be given by anyone wishing to pass

2coun·ter·sign \ˈ⸗⸗ +ˌ\ *vt* [*counter-* + *sign* (v.); trans. of F *contresigner*] **1 :** to add one's signature to (a document) after another's to attest authenticity **2 :** CONFIRM, CORROBORATE, SANCTION

coun·ter·signature \" +\ *n* [fr. 2*countersign*, after such pairs as E *sign: signature*] **:** the signature of one that countersigns

1coun·ter·sink \ˌkau̇ntə(r) +\ *vt* [*counter-* + *sink*] **1 :** to make a countersink on (a hole) **2 :** to set the head of (as a screw) at or below the surface esp. by means of a countersink

2countersink \ˈ⸗⸗ + ,-\ *n* **1 :** a funnel-shaped enlargement at the outer end of a drilled hole usu. for the reception of a screw, bolt, or rivet head **2 :** a bit or drill for making such an enlargement — compare COUNTERBORE

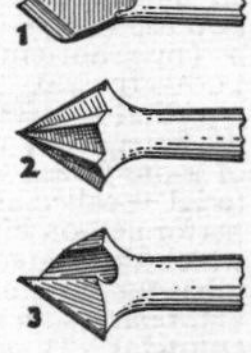

countersinks: *1* flat, *2* rose, *3* snail

coun·ter·sinker \" + ,-\ *n* **:** a worker that countersinks drilled holes

coun·ter·slope \" + ,-\ *n* [*counter-* + *slope*] **:** a slope in an opposite direction

coun·ter·spy \" + ,-\ *n* [*counter-* + *spy*] **:** one who spies against spies **:** one who investigates and seeks to check the activities of spies, espionage agents, and subversives

1coun·ter·stain \ˈkau̇ntə(r) + ,-\ *n* [*counter-* + *stain* (n.)] **:** a stain used to color parts of a microscopy specimen not affected by another stain; *esp* **:** a cytoplasmic stain used to contrast with or enhance a nuclear stain

2counterstain \ˌ⸗⸗ +\ *vt* [*counter-* + *stain* (v.)] **:** to stain (a tissue or microscopy specimen) with an additional usu. contrasting color

1coun·ter·stamp \ˌkau̇ntə(r) +\ *vt* [*counter-* + *stamp* (v.)] **1 :** to stamp or impress (something already stamped or signed) — compare COUNTERSIGN **2 a :** to countermark (a coin) **b :** to stamp (a different coin design or a countermark) onto a coin ⟨~ a coin of Heraclius on a coin of Justinian⟩ ⟨~ a Texan 8-real piece on a Mexican 5-real piece⟩

2counterstamp \ˈ⸗⸗ + ,-\ *n* [*counter-* + *stamp* (n.)] **1 :** a stamp or impression put upon something (as a check or paper) that has already been stamped **2 :** a numismatic countermark

coun·ter·statement \" + ,-\ *n* [*counter-* + *statement*] **:** a statement opposing or denying another statement **:** REJOINDER

coun·ter·stroke \" + ,-\ *n* [*counter-* + *stroke*] **:** a stroke in return **:** COUNTERBLOW

coun·ter·subject \" + ,-\ *n* [*counter-* + *subject*] **:** a contrasting or secondary melody in contrapuntal music

coun·ter·sun \" + ,-\ *n* [*counter-* + *sun*] **:** ANTHELION

coun·ter·sunk \ˈkau̇ntə(r)+ˌ-\ *adj* [fr. past part. of 1*countersink*] **1 :** having a countersink at the top ⟨a ~ hole⟩ **2 :** having the head set in a countersink ⟨a ~ screw⟩

countersway *n* [*counter-* + *sway*] *obs* **:** force in an opposite direction

coun·ter·tenor \ˈkau̇ntə(r)+\ *n* [ME *cownturtenur*, fr. MF *contreteneur*, fr. *contre-* counter- + *teneur*, *tenour* tenor — more at TENOR] **1 :** one of the middle parts in music between the tenor and the soprano **2 a :** a tenor with an unusually high range and tessitura **b :** a man's countertenor voice

countertenor clef *n* **:** ALTO CLEF

coun·ter·theme \"+,-\ *n* [*counter-* + *theme*] **1 :** COUNTERSUBJECT **2 :** a theme or thesis controverting another theme or thesis

coun·ter·thrust \"+,-\ *n* [*counter-* + *thrust*] **:** a thrust offsetting or opposing another force

counter timber *n* [5*counter*] **:** one of the short vertical timbers between the stern timbers in the counter of a square-stern wooden boat

coun·ter·tonic \ˌkau̇ntə(r) +\ *adj* [*counter-* + *tonic*] *of a syllable or vowel* **:** between tonic and atonic in stress **:** bearing secondary stress

coun·ter·trades \ˈ⸗⸗+,-\ *n pl* [*counter-* + *trades*, pl. of 1*trade* (wind)] **:** the westerly winds above the trade winds

coun·ter·transference \ˌ⸗⸗+\ *n* [*counter-* + *transference*] **1 :** transference evidenced by the psychoanalyst during the course of treatment; *esp* **:** the psychoanalyst's reactions to his patient's transference **2 :** the complex of feelings of a therapist toward his patient

counter tube *n* [2*counter*] **:** COUNTING TUBE

coun·ter·turn \ˈ⸗⸗+,-\ *n* [*counter-* + *turn*] **1** [trans. of Gk *antistrophe*] **:** an unexpected turn or development in the action of a play esp. at the climax **2 :** a turn in the opposite direction ⟨amid the turns and ~*s*, the strife and various trials of our complex being —William Wordsworth⟩

coun·ter·type \"+,-\ *n* [*counter-* + *type*] **:** a corresponding type **:** EQUIVALENT

1coun·ter·vail \ˈkau̇ntə(r),vāl, ,⸗⸗ˈ⸗, *esp before pause or cons* -āəl\ *vb* -ED/-ING/-S [ME *countrevailen*, fr. MF *contrevaloir*, fr. *contre-* counter- + *valoir* to be worth, fr. L *valēre* to be strong, healthy, to be worth — more at WIELD] *vt* **1 :** to compensate for **:** make up for **:** furnish or serve as an equivalent to **2** *archaic* **:** EQUAL, MATCH **3 :** to oppose or exert force against **:** COUNTERACT, OFFSET ⟨the absence of fuss . . . ~*ed* any tendency to self-importance —Sylvia T. Warner⟩ **~** *vi* **:** to exert force against an opposing side ⟨~*ing* military power —D.D.Eisenhower⟩

2countervail *n* [ME *countervaille*, fr. *countrevailen*, v.] *archaic* **:** a countervailing power or value **:** EQUIVALENT

countervailing duty *n* **1 :** a duty or surtax imposed on imports to offset an excise or inland revenue tax put upon articles of the same class manufactured at home **2 :** a duty imposed to offset the advantage to foreign producers derived from a subsidy that their government offers for the production or export of the article taxed

coun·ter·vair \ˈkau̇ntə(r)+,-\ *n* [part trans. of F *contrevair*, fr. *contre-* counter- + *vair* — more at VAIR] **:** a heraldic vair in which each pane stands broad edge to broad edge or point to point with one of the same tincture above or below it

coun·ter·view \"+,-\ *n* [*counter-* + *view*] **1** *archaic* **:** view from opposite viewpoints **:** confrontation or juxtaposition for the sake of contrast **2 :** an opposite view **:** an opposing opinion

counter voltage *n* [6*counter*] **:** COUNTER ELECTROMOTIVE FORCE

coun·ter·weigh \ˌkau̇ntə(r)+\ *vb* [ME *countreweyen*, fr. *countre-* counter- + *weyen* to weigh — more at WEIGH] *vt* **:** COUNTERBALANCE **~** *vi* **:** to act as a counterpoise

1coun·ter·weight \ˈ⸗⸗+,-\ *n* [*counter-* + *weight*] **:** an equivalent weight **:** COUNTERPOISE, COUNTERBALANCE; *specif* **:** a weight that is placed on a mechanism that is out of balance at a place opposite to the heaviest point and that is just sufficiently heavy to restore the balance of the mechanism

2counterweight \ˌ⸗⸗+\ *vt* **:** to equip with a counterweight **:** balance by means of a counterweight **:** COUNTERBALANCE

counterweighted window *n* **:** a window with vertical sliding sashes whose weights are balanced by sash weights

counterweight system *n* **:** a system for flying stage scenery by means of adjustable counterweights that are connected by cables running over loft blocks to battens which support the scenery

count·er·word \ˈkau̇ntə(r)+,-\ *n* [1*counter* (table) + *word*] **:** a word that has a broad and vague range of meaning through widespread use in many markedly different situations (as *case, awfully, fix, job, payoff*)

1coun·ter·work \ˈ⸗⸗+,-\ *n* [*counter-* + *work* (n.)] **1 :** any work done counter to another work **2 counterworks** *pl* **:** fortifications constructed to counteract the effect of fortifications of the enemy

2coun·ter·work \ˌ⸗⸗+\ *vb* [*counter-* + *work* (v.)] *vi* **:** to work in opposition **~** *vt* **:** to work against **:** have a contrary effect on **:** COUNTERACT ⟨~*ing* his rival's designs⟩

count·ess \ˈkau̇ntəs\ *n* -ES [ME *cuntesse*, *contesse*, fr. OF *contesse*, fem. of *conte* count — more at COUNT] **1 a :** the wife or widow of an earl in the British peerage **b :** the wife or widow of a count in the Continental nobility **2 :** a woman who holds in her own right the rank of earl or count

countfish \ˈ⸗,⸗\ *n* [1*count*; fr. its use as a gauge to determine what fish shall count as being large enough to be sold at a certain price per dozen] **:** SNAPPER

coun·ti·an \ˈkau̇ntēən\ *n* -S [1*county* + *-an*] **:** a native or resident of a particular usu. specified county

counties *pl of* COUNTY

count in *vt* [1*count*] **:** INCLUDE; *specif* **:** to consider as a participant ⟨if there is going to be a game *count me in*⟩

counting *pres part of* COUNT

counting cell *or* **counting chamber** *n* **:** an accurately sized chamber in a microslide designed to accommodate a definite volume of fluid and usu. ruled into divisions to facilitate the counting under the microscope of contained cells or bacteria

counting frame *also* **counting rail** *n* **:** a frame strung with movable beads on wires and used in teaching elementary number concepts **:** ABACUS

counting glass *n* **:** a magnifying glass used in counting threads per inch in fabrics

countinghouse \ˈ==,=\ *n* [ME *counting hous*] **:** a building, room, or office in which a banker, merchant, trader, or manufacturer keeps books and transacts business

counting-out rhyme \ˈ==ˌ=-\ *n* **:** one of the meaningless rhymes (as "eeny, meeny, miney, mo") traditionally used to count out a player in a child's game

counting room *n* **:** COUNTINGHOUSE

counting scales *n* **:** weighing scales calibrated to count the units in a quantity being weighed

counting tube *n* **:** an ionization chamber designed to respond to passage through it of fast-moving ionizing particles and usu. connected to some device (as a Geiger counter) for counting the particles

count·less \ˈkau̇ntləs\ *adj* [²*count* + *-less*] **:** of such great number as to defy counting or recalling **:** INNUMERABLE, MYRIAD, MANY ⟨the ~ halls in some palace of the Arabian Nights —Nathaniel Hawthorne⟩ ⟨for ~ centuries Mars has been the star of war —H.G.Wells⟩

count noun *n* [²*count*] **:** a noun that forms a plural and is used with a numeral, with words such as *many* or *few*, or in English with the indefinite article *a* or *an* (as *bean, stick, sheet, beer* in "a dark beer") — contrasted with *mass noun*

count off *vi* **:** to call in turn from right to left or front to rear numbers determining individual positions in a military or similar formation usu. at command by the persons in the formation ~ *vt* **:** to separate into parts or divisions by or as if by counting **:** select or designate as members of a group by or as if by counting ⟨*counted off* three men to help with the job⟩

coun·tour *or* **coun·tor** \ˈkau̇ntə(r)\ *n* -s [ME *countour* (also, accountant), fr. OF *conteor* — more at COUNTER (one that counts)] **:** a pleader in an English court; *specif* **:** SERGEANT-AT-LAW

count out *vt* **1 :** to consider or list as nonparticipating **:** omit from consideration as unimportant, insignificant, or impracticable **:** EXCLUDE ⟨*count* one *out* of a poker hand⟩ ⟨help from such sources can be *counted out*⟩ **2 :** to indicate (a player) for a special role in or for exclusion from a child's game by pointing on recitation of the last syllable of a rhyme **3 :** to bring about or declare adjournment of (the House of Commons) by ascertaining that a quorum is not present **4 :** to signalize the knockout of (a boxer who is down) by completing an audible count of 10 seconds before the boxer rises **5 :** to clarify the rhythmical ordering of (the musical notes of a piece) by counting orally the beats in each bar **6 a :** to defraud (a winning candidate) of office by a false return or count of votes **b :** to reject (certain votes) from an official election count ~ *vi* **:** to announce before the completion of play in certain card games that one has already achieved a score sufficient to win the game

count palatine *n, pl* **counts palatine** [³*count*] **1 a :** a count having supreme judicial authority in the later Roman Empire **b :** a count granted the right to exercise certain imperial powers in his own domain under the German Emperors **2 :** the earl or proprietor of a county palatine in England or Ireland

coun·tree *or* **coun·trie** \ˈkəntrē, =ˈ=\ *archaic var of* COUNTRY

coun·tri·fied *also* **coun·try·fied** \ˈkəntrəˌfīd, -trē,-\ *adj* [¹*country* + *-fy*] **1 :** marked by country rather than city ways and fashions **:** PROVINCIAL, RUSTIC, UNSOPHISTICATED ⟨so very rural and silly as I always have been . . . you yourself notice my ~ ways — Thomas Hardy⟩ **2 :** like or suggestive of the country **:** RURAL, BUCOLIC, NATURAL ⟨how ~ the sparrows and the leaves are —Charles Dickens⟩

¹**coun·try** \ˈkən-trē, -ri\ *n* -ES [ME *cuntree, contree*, fr. OF *contrée*, fr. ML *contrata* landscape, country, lit., that which is situated opposite the beholder, fr. L *contra* against, on the opposite side + *-ata* (fem. of *-atus* -ate) — more at COUNTER] **1 a :** an expanse of land of undefined but usu. considerable extent **:** REGION, DISTRICT ⟨the North ~⟩ **b :** a district or area marked by some distinguishing feature ⟨hill ~⟩ ⟨Indian ~⟩ ⟨tobacco ~⟩ ⟨bad ~ for walking⟩ **c :** LAND ⟨much ~ sown to grass⟩ **2 a :** the land of a person's origin, birth, residence, or citizenship **:** motherland or home region ⟨in my own ~⟩ **b :** a political state or nation **:** the territory of a usu. independent nation that is distinct as to name and the characteristics or attributes of its people ⟨the ~ of Mexico⟩ **c :** area of interest or affiliation **:** SPHERE ⟨the borderline ~ between aesthetics and psychology —Kathleen Raine⟩ **3 a :** the people of a state or district **:** POPULACE, CITIZENRY ⟨the Hunt Fête . . . drew the entire ~ —Elizabeth Bowen⟩ **b :** the jury by which a defendant is tried — used esp. in legal phrases ⟨the litigant puts himself upon his ~⟩ ⟨tried by God and his ~⟩ **c :** the electorate regarded as the authority to which political controversy may be appealed ⟨the government will go to the ~ with this issue⟩ **4 :** rural regions as distinguished from city, town, or other thickly inhabited and built-up areas ⟨walk out in the ~⟩ **5 a :** a region of the ocean **b :** the part of a ship esp. in the U. S. Navy near officers' cabins ⟨wardroom ~⟩ ⟨admiral's ~⟩ **6** *cricket* **:** OUTFIELD **7** *or* **country rock :** the rock in which a mineral deposit or intrusion is enclosed — **across country** *adj* **:** ³CROSS-COUNTRY

²**country** \ˈ"\ *adj* [ME *cuntree, contree*, fr. *cuntree, contree*, n.] **1 a** *obs* **:** of one's own country **:** NATIVE **b** *India* **:** of or belonging to India or an adjacent land ⟨three European ships and a ~ ship⟩ **2 a :** living, located, or operating in the country **:** of, belonging, or appropriate to rural regions **:** suitable to or suggestive of the country rather than the city ⟨a ~ school⟩ ⟨one big rawboned ~ preacher —Eudora Welty⟩ ⟨expensive and decorative ~ clothes —Susan Ertz⟩ **b :** prepared, processed, or preserved with farmhouse supplies and procedures rather than those employed in industrial plants ⟨~ butter⟩ ⟨~ sugar⟩ ⟨~ ham⟩

country almond *n* **:** MALABAR ALMOND

country bank *n* **:** a commercial bank not in a reserve or central reserve city

country beam *n* **:** a setting of the headlights of an automobile to illuminate the road far ahead — compare DIMMER

country bishop *n* **:** CHOREPISCOPUS

country borage *n* **:** an aromatic fleshy herb (*Coleus aromaticus*) of India and Ceylon

country-bred \ˈ==ˌ=\ *adj* **:** bred or reared in the country

country club *n* **:** an upper-class suburban or outlying club or clubhouse for social life, golf, and other recreation

country cousin *n* **:** a country visitor ingenuously unfamiliar with city ways and sights

country damage *n* **:** depreciation of cotton or other commodities by weather, excessive or careless handling, or transit

country-dance \ˈ==,=\ *n* **1 :** any native English social dance in which dancers form square or circular figures or partners in rows face each other and which usu. has its origin in gatherings of rural folk — compare CONTREDANSE **2 :** a piece of music written or customarily played for a country-dance

country desk *n* **:** a state department subbranch dealing with a particular country

country fever *n, South & Midland* **:** MALARIA

countryfied *var of* COUNTRIFIED

country fig *n* **1 :** a western African tree (*Nauclea esculentus*) of the family Rubiaceae with bark formerly reputed to have astringent and febrifugal properties **2 :** CLUSTER FIG

countryfolk \ˈ==,=\ *n pl* **1 :** fellow countrymen **2 :** country dwellers **:** RUSTICS

country gentleman *n* **1 :** a well-to-do country resident **:** an owner of a country estate **2 :** one of the English landed gentry

country hide *n* **:** a hide usu. of inferior quality removed by a farmer, ranchman, or local butcher — compare PACKER HIDE

country house *n* **:** a house or mansion in the country; *specif* **:** COUNTRYSEAT — compare TOWN HOUSE

country jake *n* **:** RUSTIC, YOKEL

coun·try·man \ˈkəntrēmən, -trəm-; *in sense 3 often* -ˌman, -ˌmaa(ə)n\ *n, pl* **countrymen** [ME *contreeman*, fr. *contree* country + *man*] **1 :** an inhabitant or native of a specified country ⟨a north ~⟩ **2 :** one born, residing, or holding citizenship in the same country as another **:** COMPATRIOT ⟨liked abroad but hated by his *countrymen*⟩ **3 :** one living in the country **:** HUSBANDMAN, FARMER; *also* **:** one marked by country ways **:** RUSTIC ⟨some great gawk of a ~ —Donagh MacDonagh⟩

country mile *n* **:** a long distance ⟨loud enough to be heard a *country mile*⟩

country music *n* **:** HILLBILLY MUSIC

country pay *n* **:** rural commodities used in lieu of money in transactions

countrypeople \ˈ==,==\ *n, pl in constr* **:** COUNTRYFOLK

country road *n* **:** a usu. unpaved rural road off the main highway

country rock *n* **1 :** COUNTRY 7 **2 :** the common rock of a region

country sausage *n* **:** fresh pork sausage orig. prepared on the farm and usu. sold in bulk to be made into patties but also available in links both fresh and smoked

country school *n* **:** a school in a rural district; *specif* **:** a one-room rural school in which all elementary grades are taught by one teacher

country-seat \ˈ==ˌ=\ *n* **:** a country mansion or estate; *esp* **:** the country residence of an English person of rank or of a country gentleman

country-side \ˈ==,=\ *n* **1 :** a particular rural district **:** a country neighborhood **:** country as contrasted with city ⟨he returned to his native ~ —I.M.Price⟩ ⟨the ~ bright with wild flowers⟩ **2 :** citizenry or inhabitants of a countryside ⟨the whole ~ had risen solid against the invader —E.H.Stuart-Jones⟩

country store *n* **:** a retail store carrying widely diversified goods, supplies, and equipment orig. for serving a sparsely populated region

country town *n* **:** a town usu. small and concerned primarily with serving the surrounding rural area

coun·try·ward \ˈkəntrēwərd, -trə,-, -ˌwȯd\ *adv* [ME *contreewarde*, fr. *contree* country + *-warde* -ward] **:** toward the country

coun·try·wide \ˈ==ˌwīd\ *adj* **:** extended throughout the whole country

countrywoman \ˈ==,==\ *n, pl* **countrywomen** [ME *contreewoman*, fr. *contree* country + *woman* woman] **1 :** a woman compatriot **2 :** a woman resident of the country

counts *pl of* COUNT, *pres 3d sing of* COUNT

count·ship \ˈkau̇nt,ship\ *n* [³*count* + *-ship*] **1 :** the rank or office of a count **2 :** the domain or territory of a count

count wheel *n* [²*count*] **:** the notched wheel that in some clocks regulates the number of strokes in sounding the hour

¹**coun·ty** \ˈkau̇ntē, -ti\ *n* -ES [ME *counte, cunte*, fr. AF *counté*, fr. OF *cunté, conté* domain of a count, fr. ML *comitatus*, fr. LL, office of a count, fr. *comit-, comes* count + L *-atus* -ate — more at COUNT] **1** *obs* **:** COUNTY COURT **2 :** the domain of a European count or earl **3 :** one of the territorial divisions of Great Britain and Ireland constituting the chief units for administrative, judicial, and political purposes and comprising the districts that were formerly Anglo-Saxon shires and other areas which never were shires: as **a** *or* **county corporate :** one of certain districts consisting of cities and towns with neighboring territories separated out of the older shires and given the status of county — called also *corporate county* **b :** the largest administrative unit for local government in Great Britain and Northern Ireland — called also in England and Wales *administrative county* and in Scotland *civil county* **c** *or* **county borough :** a borough of at least 100,000 inhabitants that has been given the status of an administrative county **4 a :** the people of a county **b** *Brit* **:** the gentry of an English county ⟨never happier than when they were entertaining the ~ —W.S. Maugham⟩ **5 a :** the largest division for local government within a state of the U. S. with administrative functions differing from state to state — compare MUNICIPAL CORPORATION, PARISH, QUASI CORPORATION, TOWN, TOWNSHIP **b** *in Rhode Island* **:** a judicial district **c :** the county government regarded as a source of poor relief or other services esp. for the destitute ⟨throwing his money away and if we don't get a guardian for him he'll be on the ~ —Willard Robertson⟩ **6 :** the largest local administrative unit in various countries esp. in the British Commonwealth

²**county** \ˈ"\ *adj* **1 :** of, for, or relating to a county ⟨a ~ treasurer⟩ **:** concerned in county affairs **:** administered by a county **2** *chiefly Brit* **:** of, belonging to, or appropriate to the county gentry ⟨her mother's clothes being excessively ~ —Michael Arlen⟩ ⟨a ~ family⟩

³**county** *n* -ES [modif. of MF *conte* count — more at COUNT] *obs* **:** ³COUNT

county agent *n* **:** a consultant and advisor employed jointly by the federal and state governments to provide information concerning proper methods in agriculture and home economics by means of lectures, demonstrations, and discussions in rural areas and to assist in the solution of problems related thereto — called also *agricultural agent, extension agent*

county attorney *n* **:** a district attorney for a county

county board *n* **:** the elected administrative body of a U.S. county

county clerk *n* **:** an elected county official whose duties vary widely but are likely to include serving as secretary to the county board, issuing licenses, keeping records, and acting as county auditor or comptroller

county college *n* **:** a British continuation school for persons under 18 not receiving full-time education elsewhere

county commissioner *n* **:** a county administrator **:** a member of a county board

county court *n* **1 :** the court formerly assembled for an English county that was presided over by the sheriff and attended by suitors who represented all the lands in the county or shire and were the doomsmen of the court and that had jurisdiction as a court of first instance in both civil and criminal cases and as a court of appeal from the minor courts and had also certain administrative and legislative powers **2 :** any of various English judicial courts for civil actions established by the County Courts Act of 1846 mainly for the recovery of small debts **3 :** a court having a designated jurisdiction usu. both civil and criminal within the limits of a U.S. or British colonial county

county fair *n* **:** a fair usu. held annually at a set location in a county esp. to exhibit local agricultural products

county farm *n* **:** the poor farm of a county

county home *or* **county house** *n* **:** the poorhouse of a county

county library *n* **:** a library unit supported by public taxation for the use of all or part of a county

county manager *n* **:** the chief executive of a county having a system of government similar to the council-manager plan

county palatine *n* **:** the dominion or territory of a count palatine **:** a county in England of which the earl or lord orig. had royal powers with exclusive civil and criminal jurisdiction

county rate *n, Brit* **:** a tax levied upon the county and collected by county officers

county road *n* **:** a highway maintained by a county

county school *n, Brit* **:** COUNCIL SCHOOL

county seat *or* **county site** *n* **:** a town which is the seat of county administration and in which the county offices, courthouse, and jail are located

county sessions *n, Brit* **:** the general quarter sessions of the peace for each county held four times a year

county solicitor *n* **:** DISTRICT ATTORNEY

county town *n, now chiefly Brit* **:** COUNTY SEAT

county unit system *n* **:** a system of voting in a primary election in Georgia whereby each county is allotted a certain number of unit votes so that the candidate winning the highest popular vote in the county receives all that county's unit votes and the one who receives a majority of the state's unit votes is nominated

coun·ty·wide \ˈkau̇ntēˌwīd, -tə̇ˈ-\ *adj* **:** extending over the whole county **:** present throughout the county

¹**coup** \ˈkau̇p, ˈkōp, ˈkəu̇p\ *vt* -ED/-ING/-S [ME *coupen* to pay for, fr. ON *kaupa* to buy — more at CHEAP] *dial Brit* **:** EXCHANGE, BARTER

²**coup** \ˈkəu̇p\ *n* -S [ME *caupe* blow, fr. MF *coup* — more at COPE] *chiefly Scot* **:** FALL, TUMBLE, UPSET

³**coup** \ˈ"\ *vb* -ED/-ING/-S [ME *cowpen* to strike, fr. MF *couper* — more at COPE] *vt* **1** *chiefly Scot* **:** OVERTURN, UPSET **2** *chiefly Scot* **:** to drink off **:** DRAIN ~ *vi, chiefly Scot* **:** UPSET, CAPSIZE

⁴**coup** \ˈkü\ *n, pl* **coups** \-üz\ [F — more at COPE] **1 a :** BLOW, STROKE **b :** the act practiced by some American Indians (as the Plains Indians) of striking or touching an enemy in warfare in such a manner as is by custom considered a deed of bravery **c :** any of various acts recognized by custom as laudatory **2 a** *English billiards* **:** the pocketing of the cue ball without its touching another ball **b :** a roll of a roulette wheel, cast of dice, deal of cards, or similar event after which bets are settled **c :** an end play in bridge in which declarer trumps to reduce his trump holdings to avoid being forced to lead from his own hand at an inopportune later time **d :** a particularly brilliant or skilled play in a board game or card game **3 a :** a highly successful stroke, action, plan, or stratagem **:** a clever device ⟨a clever fraud which, like many other ~*s* of history, used religion as its chief vehicle —R.W.Murray⟩ **b :** COUP D'ETAT

⁵**coup** \ˈ"\ *vt* **couped** \-üd\ **couped** \ˈ"\ **couping** \-üiŋ\ **coups** \-üz\ **:** to execute a bridge coup in playing (a hand)

cou·page \(ˈ)küˈpäzh\ *n* -S [F, act of cutting, fr. MF, fr. *couper* to cut + *-age* — more at COPE] **:** the process of unhairing skins

coup-cart \ˈ=,=\ *n* [³*coup* + *cart*] *chiefly Scot* **:** DUMPCART

coup d'ar·chet \ˌküˌdärˈshā\ *n, pl* **coups d'archet** \ˈ"\ [F] **:** a stroke of the bow in violin playing

coup de fou·dre \ˌküdəˈfüdr(ᵊ), -d(rə)\ *n, pl* **coups de foudre** \ˈ"\ [F, lit., clap of thunder] **:** an astonishing occurrence; *esp* **:** overwhelming love at first sight

coup de glotte \-ˈglät\ *n, pl* **coups de glotte** \ˈ"\ [F] **:** the glottal stop esp. in singing and elocution as a prefixion to words that in ordinary pronunciation begin with a vowel sound

coup de grace \-ˈgräs\ *n, pl* **coups de grace** \ˈ"\ [F *coup de grâce*] **1 :** a death blow or shot administered in mercy to end the suffering of a person or animal mortally wounded **2 :** a decisive finishing blow **:** an act or event that puts an end to something ⟨an incident that gave the *coup de grace* to Harriet's Calvinist faith —Edmund Wilson⟩

coup de main \-ˈmaⁿ\ *n, pl* **coups de main** \ˈ"\ [F, lit., hand stroke] **:** a sudden attack in force **:** vigorous attack **:** sudden forceful development

coup de poing \-ˈpwaⁿ\ *n, pl* **coups de poing** \ˈ"\ [F, lit., blow with the fist] **:** a biface stone hand ax typical of the Abbevillian epoch

coup de re·pos _rəˈpō\ *n, pl* **coups de repos** \ˈ"\ [F, lit., stroke of rest] **:** a chess move leaving the main features of a position unchanged when the adversary can change these only to his disadvantage

coup d'e·tat \ˌkü(ˌ)dāˈtä, -tä *also* -üdə-\ *n, pl* **coups d'etat** \ˈ"\ *also* **coup d'etats** \-äz,-äz\ [F *coup d'état*, lit., stroke of state] **1 :** a sudden decisive exercise of localized or concentrated force unseating the personnel of a government **2 :** a coup violently and unexpectedly reformulating state policy **:** an unexpected or sudden measure of state often involving force or threat of force

coup de the·atre \ˌküdə(ˌ)tāˈä·tr(ᵊ), -t(rə)\ *n, pl* **coups de theatre** \ˈ"\ [F *coup de théâtre*, lit., stroke of theater] **:** a sudden and sensational turn in a play; *also* **:** a sudden dramatic and unexpected stroke or turn of events

coup d'oeil \küˈdəry, -ˈdə̄y\ *n, pl* **coups d'oeil** \ˈ"\ [F, lit., stroke of the eye] **:** a glance embracing a wide view **:** a survey accomplished with a glance ⟨his penetrating *coup d'oeil* which makes him a master at rapid chess —A.J.Liebling⟩

¹**coupe** *obs var of* COOP

²**cou·pé** *or* **coupe** \(ˈ)küˈpā, *in sense 2b often* ˈküp\ *n* -S [F *coupé*, fr. past part. of *couper* to cut, cut off; in senses 2 & 3, fr. F *coupé*, prob. fr. *carrosse coupé*, lit., cut-off coach, fr. *carrosse* coach + *coupé*, past part. of *couper*] **1** *ballet dancing* **:** a quick sharp cut finishing with an extension **2 a :** a 4-wheeled closed horse-drawn carriage for two persons inside with an outside seat for the driver in front **b** *usu coupe* **:** a closed 2-door automobile with one seat compartment and a separate luggage compartment — see CLUB COUPE **3 a :** the front or after compartment of a Continental stagecoach **b** *Brit* **:** an end compartment of a railway carriage often with a seat on one side only **4 :** CUTOVER 2

coupé 2a

³**coupe** \ˈküp\ *n* -S [F, cup, fr. LL *cuppa* — more at CUP] **1 a :** a dessert commonly served in a glass and consisting of ice cream or an ice topped with mixed fruit, whipped cream, or other garnish **b :** the glass for serving this dessert; *esp* **:** a footed glass having a deep lower cup and a wide shallow upper cup **2 :** a rimless plate or wide shallow rimless bowl

¹**couped** *past of* COUP

²**couped** \ˈküpt\ *adj* [F *coupé* (fr. past part. of *couper*) + E *-ed*] **1** *heraldry* **:** cut off smoothly — used esp. of the head or limb of an animal; compare ERASED **2** *heraldry* **:** cut off short at the ends so as not to extend to the edges of the field

coupe de ville \(ˈ)küˌpādəˈvil, ˌküpdə-\ *n, pl* **coupes de ville** \-ˌpāzdəˈvil, -psd-; -ˌpādəˈvilz, -pd-\ [F *coupé de ville* town coupé] **:** a convertible coupe in which the top may be adjusted to cover either both seats or the back seat alone

¹**coup·er** \ˈkəu̇pər, ˈküp-\ *n* -S [¹*coup* + *-er*] *chiefly Scot* **:** a dealer esp. in horses and cattle

²**couper** \ˈkau̇pə(r), ˈkōp-\ *n* -S [prob. fr. ³*coup* (overturn) + *-er*] **:** a lever in a loom for lifting the harness

coup·ette \(ˈ)küˈpet\ *n* -S [³*coupe* (glass) + *-ette*] **:** a small coupe used in serving cold seafood appetizers, fruit, or ices

couping *pres part of* COUP

coup·ist \ˈküəst\ *n* -S [⁴*coup* + *-ist*] **:** one that attempts or supports a coup d'etat

coupette

¹**cou·ple** \ˈkəpəl\ *vb* **coupled; coupled; coupling** \ˈkəp(ə)liŋ, -lēŋ\ **couples** [ME *couplen* to join, connect, fr. OF *copler, coupler*, fr. L *copulare*, fr. *copula* bond] *vt* **1 :** to connect for consideration together **:** join together for combined effect or consideration ⟨supported the bill . . . and *coupled* it with a demand for national reclamation —P.C. Phillips⟩ **:** unite or link esp. abstract or immaterial things ⟨individuality of expression *coupled* with the spice of novelty —J.L.Lowes⟩ ⟨trade-union pressure *coupled* with unemployment —H.B.Parkes⟩ **2 :** to fasten together **:** JOIN, LINK ⟨*coupling* his holdings and his deceased brother's⟩: as **a :** to fasten with a leash ⟨*coupling* the hounds⟩ **b :** to connect with a coupling ⟨*coupling* the freight cars⟩ **c :** to connect (as two or more keys or keyboards of an organ) by a coupler **d** (1) **:** to bring (two physical systems) into such relation that the performance of one influences the performance of the other (as in suspending two pendulums from different points on the same horizontal rope) (2) **:** to bring (two electric circuits) into such close proximity as to permit mutual influence (3) **:** to join (electric circuits or devices) into a single circuit **e :** to cause (as an aromatic diazonium compound) to unite with another compound usu. with the elimination of a simple molecule (as of hydrochloric acid in the formation of an azo dye) — compare CONJUGATE 3 **f :** to record on opposite sides of a phonograph record or in the same series of records ⟨his first symphony being *coupled* with his third⟩ **3 a :** to join in marriage or sexual union **b :** to bring into association (as friendship, companionship, partnership, opposition, or rivalry) **c :** to cause (domestic animals) to breed or copulate ~ *vi* **1 :** to unite in sexual union — often used with *with* **2 a :** to come together **:** JOIN **b** *of chemical compounds or radicals* **:** to unite usu. with elimination of a simple molecule (as of hydrochloric acid)

²**couple** \ˈ"; *"a couple of" is often* əˈkəplə(v)\ *n, pl* **couples** *also* **couple** [ME, pair, bond, fr. OF *cople, couple*, fr. L *copula* bond, band, fr. (assumed) L *co-apula*, fr. L *co-* + (assumed) L *-apula* (fr. L *apere* to fasten, tie) — more at APT] **1 a :** a man and his wife **:** a man and woman married or engaged ⟨she and Jon would make a lovely ~ —John Galsworthy⟩ **b :** a man and woman paired as partners in any work, recreation, or other activity **c :** a man and wife employed together to perform usu. related jobs in a single establishment (as butler and cook in a household) **d :** any two persons

paired together in some work, enterprise, or activity **2 :** MATING, COPULATION ⟨birds in ~⟩ **3 a :** a pair of animals often of different sexes **b :** a pair of hounds **c :** a ewe and lamb **4 :** something that joins or links two things together: as **a** *couples pl* **:** a pair of collars joined by a chain for coupling two hounds together **b :** COUPLER 1c **5 a :** two of the same kind considered together **:** PAIR **b** COUPLE-CLOSE 2 **c :** two equal and opposite forces that act along parallel lines **d :** VOLTAIC COUPLE **e :** BINARY STAR — **a couple of :** two or an indefinite small number of **:** FEW ⟨*a couple of* days ago⟩ ⟨for *a couple of* centuries — the fourth to the sixth —I.M.Price⟩ ⟨I only had *a couple of* drinks⟩

³couple \"\ *adj* **:** TWO — used with *a* ⟨a ~ more oaths⟩ ⟨a ~ nights ago⟩

couple–beggar *n* [¹*couple* + *beggar*] *obs* **:** a marrier of beggars **:** a performer of clandestine or irregular marriages

couple–close \ˈ==ˌklōs\ *n* -s [²*couple* + *close*] **1** *heraldry* **:** a cotise paralleling a chevron **2 :** a pair of rafters framed together with a tie fixed at their feet or with a collar beam

coupled *adj* [ME, joined, fr. past part. of *couplen* to couple, join — more at COUPLE] **1** *of a quadrupedal mammal* **:** having a coupling of a specified sort — usu. used in combination ⟨long-*coupled*⟩ ⟨well-*coupled*⟩ **2 :** entered in a horse race as a single entry ⟨two of that stable's horses ~ in the third race⟩ **3** *of a fighting cock* **:** crippled specif. by a back wound paralyzing the legs **4 a :** mechanically or electrically connected **b** *of a photographic range finder* **:** connected to the focusing mechanism so that operation of the finder focuses the lens

coupled column *n, archit* **:** one of a pair of columns set nearer together than others of the same order or forming one of many groups of two used esp. in the neoclassic art of the 17th century and later

coupled engine *n* **:** a locomotive engine having two or more driving wheels on either side joined by a coupling rod

cou·ple·ment \ˈkəpəlmənt\ *n* -s [MF, fr. *coupler* to couple, join + *-ment* — more at COUPLE] *archaic* **:** the act or result of coupling

cou·pler \ˈkəplə(r)\ *n* -s **1 a :** one that couples (as a link, ring, or shackle that connects cars or the ends of a chain belt) **b :** COUPLING **c :** a contrivance on a keyboard instrument by which any two or more of the manuals or a manual and the pedal keyboard or keys of the same keyboard an octave apart are connected so as to act together when one is played **d :** a radio device coupling two electric circuits **e :** an agent (as a mutual solvent) that renders two nonmiscible liquids miscible or aids in the formation of emulsions (as of oils in soap solutions) — called also *coupling agent* **2 :** a compound in a color-photography emulsion or developer solution that combines with the oxidized developer to form a dye — compare COLOR DEVELOPER

coupler developer *n* **1 :** COUPLER 2 **2 :** a photographic developer solution having a coupler as one of its constituents

cou·pler·ess \ˈkəplərəs\ *n* -ES **:** PROCURESS

couples *pres 3d sing of* COUPLE, *pl of* COUPLE

cou·plet \ˈkəplət\ *n* -s [MF, dim. of *couple* pair — more at COUPLE] **1 :** two successive lines of verse usu. having some unity greater than that of mere contiguity (as that provided by rhythmic correspondence, rhyme, or the complete inclusion of a grammatically or rhetorically independent utterance) **:** DISTICH — see CLOSED COUPLET, OPEN COUPLET **2 a :** PAIR, COUPLE **:** a pair born together **:** TWINS **b :** a pair of items of the same kind occurring together **3 :** a window of two lights **4 :** one of the musical episodes alternating with the main theme (as in the early French rondos)

cou·pling \ˈkəpliŋ, -lēŋ\ *n* -s [ME, fr. gerund of *couplen* to couple, join] **1 :** the act of bringing together **:** PAIRING **:** a coming together; *specif* **:** sexual union **2 :** a device that serves to couple or connect the ends of adjacent parts or objects ⟨a belt ~⟩ ⟨a car ~⟩ ⟨a shaft ~⟩ ⟨a pipe ~⟩ — see FLUID COUPLING **3 :** the joint together with its supporting structures between the last lumbar vertebra and the sacrum that joins the hindquarters to the trunk; *broadly* **:** the part of the body or the conformation and proportionate length of the part of the body that joins the hindquarters to the forequarters — used of a horse, dog, or other mammalian quadruped **4 a :** an arrangement of two electric circuits by means of which the electromotive force and current in one circuit are influenced by the electromotive force and current in the other **b :** an interaction between two systems or parts of the same system, esp. between parts of atomic or molecular systems (as the mutual magnetic influence of two spinning electrons) **5 :** the tendency of certain genetic characters to be inherited together presumably because of linkage of the dominant genes that control their expression — compare REPULSION

coupling box *n* **:** JUNCTION BOX

coupling coefficient *n, physics* **:** an abstract number representing the degree in which the performance of either of two coupled systems influences that of the other

coupling rein *n* **:** the short rein that runs from the inner side of the bridle of one horse of a pair to the draft rein of the other horse

coupling rod *n* **:** a link connecting two or more cranks or their equivalents (as the side rod of a locomotive)

cou·pon \ˈk(y)üˌpän\ *n* -s [F, fr. OF *coupon, copon* piece, fr. *couper, coper* to cut — more at COPE] **1 :** a statement of due interest to be cut from a bearer bond when payable and presented for payment **2 :** a form, slip, or section of a paper resembling a bond coupon in that it may be surrendered in order to obtain some article, service, or accommodation: as **a :** one of a series of attached tickets or certificates often for accommodations or services to be detached and presented as needed ⟨a railroad ticket with many ~*s*⟩ **b :** a ticket or form authorizing purchases of rationed commodities as indicated ⟨a clothing ~⟩ ⟨the three ~*s* required for the gasoline⟩ **c :** a token or certificate given with a purchase and redeemable in merchandise or cash — compare TRADING STAMP **d :** a trademark, wrapper, box top, or similar evidence of a purchase for which premium articles are given **e :** a part of a printed advertisement designed to be cut or torn off for use as an order blank or as a form for inquiry **f :** a leaf of a credit account booklet to be removed to accompany installment payments and identify the customer **g :** a form or check indicating a credit against future purchases or expenditures **h** *Brit* **:** a blank for entering one's choices in a sports pool ⟨filling out his football ~⟩ **3 :** a test sample ⟨taking off a ~ of the steel plate⟩ **4 :** a party recommendation given to a candidate for parliament in acknowledgment of his pledge to the party leader

coupon bond *n* **:** a bond on which interest is paid by coupons

coupon clipper *n* **:** a wealthy and idle person whose chief labor is clipping and cashing bond coupons

cou·pon·less \-ləs\ *adj* **:** not having a coupon

coups *pres 3d sing of* COUP, *pl of* COUP

coupstick *n* [⁴*coup* + *stick*] **:** a stick or switch used in counting a coup in warfare or symbolically on ceremonial occasions

cour *chiefly Scot var of* COWER

cour·age \ˈkər·ij, ˈkə·r, ǀəj\ *n* -s [ME *corage*, fr. OF *corage, curage*, fr. *cuer* heart (fr. L *cor*) + *-age* — more at HEART] **1** *obs* **:** the heart as the seat of intelligence or feeling ⟨this soft ~ makes your followers faint —*Shak.*⟩ **2** *obs* **:** INCLINATION, INTENTION ⟨I'd such a ~ to do him good —*Shak.*⟩ **3** *obs* **:** a proud and angry temper **:** high spirit **4 :** mental or moral strength enabling one to venture, persevere, and withstand danger, fear, or difficulty firmly and resolutely ⟨I would define true ~ to be a perfect sensibility of the measure of danger and a mental willingness to endure it —W.T.Sherman⟩ **5 :** confidence that encourages and sustains ⟨a ~ resting on God —Daniel Defoe⟩ ⟨the ~ of his convictions⟩

syn METTLE, SPIRIT, RESOLUTION, TENACITY: COURAGE is the firmness of spirit that faces danger or extreme difficulty without flinching or retreating ⟨*courage* to fight for our ideals although we are certain they shall never be realized —Paul Eldridge⟩ ⟨*courage* to act on limited knowledge, *courage* to make the best of what is here and not whine for more —Robert Frost⟩ METTLE suggests an ingrained capacity for meeting strain or difficulty without fear or with fortitude and resilience of spirit or mind ⟨difficulties calculated to test the *mettle* of even the bravest men⟩ ⟨showed his *mettle* in two strenuous European campaigns⟩ SPIRIT, like METTLE in suggesting a quality of temperament, implies an ability to hold one's own, fight for one's principles, or keep up one's morale when opposed, interfered with, or checked ⟨to show his *spirit* by fighting to the last ditch⟩ ⟨a man of considerable *spirit* standing virtually alone in defense of his rights as a citizen⟩ RESOLUTION, like COURAGE, implies firmness of spirit but puts stress upon determination to achieve one's end rather than upon the facing of danger without flinching ⟨she sat for twenty minutes or more ere she could summon *resolution* to go down to the door, her courage being lowered to zero by her physical lassitude —Thomas Hardy⟩ ⟨a man of a strong *resolution* and a set purpose; a man not desirable to be met rushing down a narrow pass with a gulf on either side, for nothing would turn the man —Charles Dickens⟩ TENACITY adds to RESOLUTION the idea of stubborn persistence or unwillingness to recognize defeat ⟨all his convictions were strong and he held them with an unswerving *tenacity* —F.T.Persons⟩ ⟨the roots insinuate themselves into the rocks with such demoniac *tenacity* that only dynamite will dislodge them permanently —Norman Douglas⟩

cou·ra·geous \kəˈrājəs\ *adj* [ME *corageous*, fr. OF *corageus*, fr. *corage* + *-eus* -ous] **:** having or characterized by courage **:** marked by bold resolution in withstanding the dangerous, alarming, or difficult **:** BRAVE ⟨a frank ~ heart and buoyant spirit triumphed over pain —William Wordsworth⟩ ⟨a ~ rescue⟩ ⟨a ~ example⟩ **syn** see BRAVE

cou·ra·geous·ly *adv* **:** in a courageous manner

cou·ra·geous·ness *n* -ES **:** the quality or state of being courageous

¹cou·rant \ˈkərənt, ˈkə·rənt *sometimes* ˈkùrənt *or* k(y)ùˈrant *or* -ùˈränt\ *n* -s [prob. fr. F *courante*, fr. fem. of *courant* current, running, fr. pres. part. of *courir* to run] **:** NEWSPAPER — obs. except in names of newspapers

²cou·rant \ˈkùrənt; kùˈrant, -änt\ *adj* [F, fr. pres. part. of *courir* to run, fr. L *currere* — more at CURRENT] *heraldry* **:** RUNNING ⟨a stag ~⟩

³cou·rant \kəˈrant\ *vi* -ED/-ING/-S [*courante*] **1** *dial Eng* **:** ROMP, CAPER **2** *dial Eng* **:** to go about gossiping

cou·rante *also* **cou·rant** \küˈränt, -ant\ *n* -s [MF *courante*, fr. fem. of *courant*, pres. part. of *courir* to run] **1 a :** a dance of Italian origin marked by quick running steps **b :** a similar but graver and more formal dance developed in France in the 17th century **2 :** music for a courante or having the rhythm of a courante that is in rather quick ³⁄₂ measure and is characterized by dotted notes and shifts to ⁶⁄₄ measure **3** *dial Eng* **:** an adventurous frolic **:** ROMP, CAROUSE

cou·ra·ta·ri \ˌkùrəˈtärē\ *n* -s [NL, fr. Galibi *couratary* couratari tree] **1 :** a tropical So. American tree (*Couratari tauari*) of the family Lecythidaceae **2 :** the laminated inner bark of the couratari that occurs in the form of thin whitish sheets and is used for rough clothing, wrapping, and cordage

courb \ˈkù(ə)rb\ *vb* -ED/-ING/-S [ME *courben*, fr. MF *courber* — more at CURB] *archaic* **:** BEND, BOW

cour·ba·ril \ˈkùrbərəl, ˌkùrbəˈril\ *n* -s [F, fr. Island Carib *kurbaril*] **1 :** a West Indian locust tree (*Hymenaea courbaril*) with a very hard tough wood **2** *or* **courbaril copal :** the resin from the courbaril tree

courbash *var of* KURBASH

courbe *adj* [ME, fr. MF — more at CURB] *obs* **:** BENT

cour·bette \(ˈ)kùrˈbet\ *n* -s [F, fr. MF, fr. *courber* to bend + *-ette*] **:** CURVET

cour d'hon·neur \ˌkùr,dóˈnər\ *n, pl* **cours d'honneur** \"\ [F, lit., court of honor] **:** a monumental forecourt to a building

cou·reur de bois \küˈrərdəbˈwä\ *n, pl* **coureurs de bois** \"\ [CanF, lit., woods runner] **:** a French or French and Indian half-breed trapper, woodsman, or hunter of No. America and esp. of Canada

courge \ˈkù(ə)rzh\ *n* -s [F, lit., gourd, fr. MF dial., fr. L *cucurbita* — more at GOURD] **:** an elongated basket for holding sand eels and other live bait in sea fishing

courge green *n* [F *courge* gourd] **:** a moderate yellow green that is yellower, lighter, and slightly stronger than average moss green, yellower and duller than average pea green, and yellower and lighter than spinach green

cou·ri·da \küˈrēdə\ *n* -s [native name in Brit. Guiana] **:** BLACK MANGROVE 1

courie *var of* COWRIE

cou·ri·er \ˈkùrēə(r), ˈkər·ē-, ˈkə·rē-, ˈkürē *sometimes* ˈkōrē-\ *n* -s *often attrib* [MF *courrier*, fr. OIt *corriere*, fr. *correre* to run (fr. L *currere*) + *-iere* -er (fr. OF *-ier*) — more at CURRENT] **1 :** one that carries messages, news, or information either with urgent haste or in accordance with a regular schedule **:** MESSENGER ⟨a ~ who will carry the tidings of distress —B.N.Cardozo⟩ ⟨~ communication nearly equivalent to postal service —F.B Warren⟩: as **a :** a member of a diplomatic service entrusted with bearing messages ⟨~*s* who carry official despatches possess the right of inviolability —G.H.Stuart⟩ **b :** an espionage agent transferring secret information; *sometimes* **:** a runner of contraband or illicit materials **:** an underworld liaison man **c :** a member of the armed services whose duties include carrying mail, information, or supplies **2 :** a traveler's paid attendant **:** a servant who facilitates travel arrangements; *often* **:** a tourists' guide employed by a travel agency **3** *Canad* **:** a mail carrier **4 :** a plane or other conveyance used in courier duties

cour·lan \ˈkùrlən, (ˈ)kùrˈlän\ *n* -s [F, alter. of *courliri*, fr. Galibi *kurliri*] **:** a long-billed bird (*Aramus guarana*) intermediate in some respects between the cranes and the rails that occurs in much of So. and Central America and is represented in Florida, Cuba, and Jamaica by the limpkin

cou·ronne \küˈrón\ *n* -s [F, lit., crown, fr. L *corona* — more at CROWN] **:** a loop added to the cordonnet on the edge of point lace or in the body of the pattern

¹course \ˈkō(ə)rs, -ó(ə)rs,-ōəs,-ó(ə)s\ *n* -s [ME *cours, course*, fr. OF *cors, cours, corse, course*, fr. L *cursus*, fr. *cursus*, past part. of L *currere* to run] **1 a :** the act or action of moving in a particular path from point to point ⟨the planets in their ~*s*⟩ **b** *obs* **:** RUN, GALLOP **c** *archaic* **:** a charge by opposing knights **:** ONSET **:** passage at arms **:** BOUT **d :** a life regarded as a race **:** LIFE HISTORY **:** CAREER ⟨ending his ~ with fame and wealth⟩ **e :** the pursuit of game by hounds — usu. used with *of* or *at* ⟨the ~ at the deer⟩ **f :** RACE ⟨a prize for winning the ~⟩ **g :** a progressing or proceeding along a straight line without change of direction ⟨the ship made many ~*s* sailing through the islands⟩ **2 :** the path over which something moves or the way which something extends **:** the line or way described by some motion, progression, or series **:** the direction taken or the ground traversed **:** TRACK, WAY ⟨the ~ of an ocean current⟩ ⟨the ~ of a mountain range⟩ ⟨his ~ was straight east⟩: as **a :** RACECOURSE **b** (1) **:** the track or way taken by a ship or the direction of flight of an airplane **:** the way projected and assigned usu. measured as a clockwise angle from north — see COMPASS COURSE, MAGNETIC COURSE, TRUE COURSE (2) **:** a point of the compass **c** *obs* **:** a fashionable place or way for riding or driving **d :** a channel through which water flows **:** WATERCOURSE **e :** GOLF COURSE **f :** horizontal direction of a geological structure **:** STRIKE **3 a :** accustomed procedure **:** customary action **:** usual method of proceeding ⟨the law taking its ~⟩ ⟨to die according to the ~ of nature⟩ **b :** policy chosen **:** manner of conducting oneself **:** conduct esp. when reprehensible **:** way of acting **:** BEHAVIOR ⟨persisting in his evil ~*s*⟩ ⟨our wisest ~ is to retreat⟩ **c :** progress or progression through a series (as of acts or events) or through a development or a period ⟨watching man's hesitant ~ through . . . this time of trouble —Herrymon Maurer⟩ ⟨a highway in ~ of construction⟩ ⟨in the ~ of his service he rose to the rank of colonel⟩ **4 :** an ordered continuing process, succession, sequence, or series ⟨following the ~ of the argument⟩ ⟨the ~ of history⟩ ⟨the ~ of the hearings⟩: as **a :** the series of prayers used in the daily canonical hours **b courses** *pl* **:** MENSTRUATION **c** (1) **:** an educational unit usu. at the high school, college, or university level consisting of a series of instruction periods (as lectures, recitations, and laboratory sessions) dealing with a particular subject ⟨an English ~⟩ ⟨a ~ in trigonometry⟩ (2) **:** a series of such courses coordinated to constitute a curriculum and leading typically to a degree ⟨a premedical ~⟩ ⟨a commercial ~⟩ **d :** a series of doses or medicaments usu. administered over a designated period of time ⟨a ~ of three doses daily for five days⟩ **e :** the series of changes or the shifting path through a series of changes that a single bell makes in change ringing **f :** a sequence of different crops in crop rotation **g :** a series of rounds fired at a target or at a series of targets under specified conditions **5 :** a single member of a sequence **:** one item in a series: as **a :** a division of a meal **:** the part of a meal served at one time with its accompaniments ⟨a seven-*course* meal⟩ ⟨the main ~ was roast beef⟩ **b :** ROW, LAYER: as (1) **:** a horizontal layer forming one of a series (as of concrete in road making, of lumber in a lumber pile, or of shingles on a roof) (2) **:** a continuous level range of brick or masonry throughout a wall (3) **:** a lode of ore (4) **:** a horizontal row of loops or stitches in knitted fabrics formed by one passage of the yarn or thread — compare WALE (5) **:** a strake of plating on a ship's hull **c** (1) **:** the lowest sail on any square-rigged mast of a ship ⟨the fore ~⟩ (2) **:** a length esp. of a rope or cable **d** *obs* **:** a time or occasion coming to each individual **:** TURN ⟨the older generation dying in its ~⟩ **e :** a set of persons appointed to hold some office or perform some duty ⟨the ~ of priests then performing the rites⟩ **f** *archaic* **:** each one of several attacks in series **g :** a set of things made or used together ⟨a ~ of candles⟩ **h :** one of two or more strings (as of the lute) tuned in unison or octaves and played together for increased volume **6 :** faculty or opportunity of moving, flowing, or circulating ⟨that the word of the Lord may have free ~ —2 Thess 3:1 (AV)⟩ **syn** see WAY — **as of course** *law* **:** as a thing to be granted upon a mere showing of the usual grounds and as not within the discretion of the judge to withhold — **in course** *adv* **1 a** *obs* **:** in turn **b :** in regular succession **:** in the usual or natural order **2 :** as a result of study and examination ⟨a degree taken *in course*, not an honorary one⟩ **3** *now dial* **:** of course **:** as might be expected — **in due course** *adv* **:** after natural passage of time **:** without modification of usual procedure **:** REGULARLY — **in full course :** moving or operating rapidly, at maximum speed, or without check or restraint — **in short course** *adv* **:** after a short period **:** BRIEFLY — **of course 1 :** of or following the ordinary way or procedure **:** NATURAL ⟨a thing *of course*⟩ ⟨a matter *of course*⟩ **2 :** as might be expected **:** without question **:** NATURALLY, CERTAINLY ⟨*of course* we will go⟩ **3 :** on the other hand **:** BUT

²course \"\ *vb* -ED/-ING/-S [ME *coursen*, fr. *cours, course*, n. — more at ¹COURSE] *vt* **1 a :** to hunt or pursue (game) with hounds ⟨*coursing* the stag⟩ **b :** to chase (game) with dogs by sight rather than scent ⟨~ a hare⟩ **c :** to cause (dogs) to chase after game **2 :** to follow close upon **:** PURSUE, RUN, CHASE ⟨we *coursed* him at the heels —*Shak.*⟩ **3** *obs* **:** to drive with blows **:** BLUDGEON, TROUNCE **4 a :** to run or move swiftly through or over **:** take one's course through **:** TRAVERSE ⟨jets *coursed* the area daily⟩ **b :** to cause (dogs) to run in a race **:** RACE **5 a :** to follow the course of (a stream) ⟨*coursing* the river⟩ **b :** to trace (a bee) by observing flight direction ⟨*coursing* the bee to its hive⟩ **6 :** to lay or form in courses ⟨~ bricks⟩ ⟨*coursing* the lumber⟩ **7 :** to divert and direct (an air current) along a certain route through a mine ~ *vi* **1 a :** to run or gallop esp. in a tournament or race or in hunting **b :** to take a course **:** pursue a certain course ⟨*coursing* along the coast⟩ **c :** to run or drive rapidly and steadily often over a set course or through a certain channel ⟨two Zuni runners . . . *coursed* over the sand with the fleetness of young antelope —Willa Cather⟩ **d :** to traverse or flow strongly or rapidly esp. on or as if on a certain path **:** PULSATE, SURGE ⟨blood *coursing* through his veins⟩ ⟨sap *coursing* through the young trees⟩ **2** *of a bell* **:** to move in change ringing steadily up or down in the striking order through a series of changes ⟨the biggest bell *coursing*⟩ **syn** see RUN

³course *obs var of* COARSE

coursed *adj* [fr. past part. of ²COURSE] **1 :** hunted with dogs ⟨a ~ hare⟩ **2 :** arranged in courses ⟨~ masonry⟩

coursed ashlar *n* **:** ashlar masonry in which the stones in a course are of the same height

coursed rubble *n* **:** masonry composed of roughly shaped stones fitting approximately on level beds

course of sprouts [prob. so called fr. the use of sprouts as switches in flogging] **:** a course of instruction marked by corporal punishment, hazing, rigorous discipline, or grueling tests or by thoroughness or difficulty

course of study 1 : the total number of courses offered by a school or college or by one of its branches **:** CURRICULUM **2 :** COURSE 4c

course protractor *n* **:** a navigation instrument for measuring bearings and comparing them against chart courses

¹cours·er \ˈkōrsər, ˈkór-, -ōəsə(r, -ó(ə)sə(r\ *n* -s [ME, fr. OF *coursier*, fr. *cours* course, run + *-ier* -er — more at COURSE] **:** a swift or spirited horse **:** WAR-HORSE, CHARGER

²courser \"\ *n* -s [*course* + *-er*] **1 :** a dog for coursing **2 :** one that courses **:** HUNTSMAN **3 :** any of a small group of birds that are related to the plovers and that inhabit Africa and southern Asia and are remarkable for their speed in running

courses *pl of* COURSE, *pres 3d sing of* COURSE

coursing *n* -s [fr. gerund of ²*course*] **:** conduction of the air current of a mine in different directions by means of doors and stoppings

coursing joint *n* **:** the mortar joint between two courses of bricks or stones

¹court \ˈkō(ə)r\|t, -ó(ə)r\|t,-ōə\|t,-ó(ə)\|t, *usu* \|d.+V\ *n* -s [ME, fr. OF, fr. L *cohort-, cohors* enclosure, court, thing enclosed, crowd, fr. *co-* + *-hort-, -hors* (akin to L *hortus* garden) — more at YARD] **1 a :** the residence or establishment of a sovereign or similar dignitary and his retinue **:** the meeting place of a sovereign and his retinue, officers, or councillors ⟨riding to the king's ~⟩ **b :** a sovereign's formal assembly of his councillors and officers for administrative deliberation ⟨faced with these difficulties the king held a general ~⟩ **c :** the sovereign and his officers and advisers as constituting the governing power ⟨the ~ has decided against the alliance⟩ **d :** the family, officers, councillors, attendants, and retinue of a sovereign ⟨the ~ were enjoying the tournaments⟩ **:** the structure of social life revolving around a sovereign ⟨the gaiety of the ~⟩ **e :** an assembly held by a sovereign for diplomatic or social purposes **:** a state reception ⟨the ~ was held on Thursday⟩ ⟨being presented at ~ was the culmination of her social career⟩ **f :** an assembly of one given the title of sovereign and his or her attendants ⟨the college May queen and her ~⟩ **:** a session in which one honored or prominent receives, is visited by, or talks freely with those seeking him out ⟨the old coach holding ~ in the locker room after the game⟩ **2 a :** a manor house, castle, or large building or group of buildings surrounded by its usu. enclosed grounds — now usu. used in the names of buildings or manors ⟨Hampton *Court*⟩ **b :** a group of cottages or cabins often in a formal arrangement **:** MOTEL **c :** an open space enclosed wholly or partly by buildings, walls, or fences **:** YARD; *sometimes* **:** an open area circumscribed on all sides by a single building ⟨the ~ at the center of the palace⟩ **d :** a quadrangular space either walled or marked off for playing one of various games with a ball (as lawn tennis, racquets, handball, or basketball); *also* **:** a division marked off in such a court ⟨a service ~⟩ ⟨the back ~⟩ **e :** an open area about a Jewish tabernacle or sanctuary **f :** an often paved yard opening off a street and built around with houses **:** a wide alley with only one opening onto a street **g :** a section of an exhibition or museum devoted to a particular exhibit or group of exhibits **h :** a place on or within a plant that provides circumstances suitable for some biological process (as infection or decay) to get a start **3 a :** the persons duly assembled under authority of law for the administration of justice **:** an official assembly legally met together for the transaction of judicial business **:** a judge or judges sitting for the hearing or trial of cases **b :** a session of such a court ⟨~ is now adjourned⟩ **c :** a chamber, hall, building, or other place for the administration of justice ⟨not enough seats in the ~ to accommodate the crowd⟩ **d :** a judge or judges in session viewed as individual persons ⟨restoratives were applied and the ~ was able to gasp "twenty dollars" —D.D.Martin⟩ ⟨the ~ was inconsistent in his rulings⟩ **e :** a faculty or agency whereby judgment or evaluation is made ⟨condemned in the ~ of human reason —M.R.Cohen⟩ **f :** a body of citizens convened to try a case ⟨condemned by the Athenian ~⟩ **g :** a body exercising the self-assigned role of judging and imposing punishments ⟨an investigating committee becoming a de facto ~⟩ **4 a :** an assembly or board vested with legislative or administrative as well as judicial powers ⟨many county governing boards are called ~*s* —J.E.Pate⟩ **b :** PARLIAMENT, LEGISLATURE ⟨the laws enacted by the high ~ of the land⟩

⟨the Great and General *Court* of Massachusetts⟩ **c :** a body of directors, managers, or delegates qualified to superintend the general affairs of an organization ⟨~ of a university⟩ **:** a body exercising judicial powers over its members or the members of a body represented by it ⟨commissioner's ~⟩ ⟨an ecclesiastical ~⟩; *also* **:** the assembly of such a body **5 :** ATTENTIONS: **a :** respectful deference **:** conduct or address calculated to win favor or dispel hostility **:** HOMAGE ⟨pay ~ to the king⟩ **b :** attentions intended to attract affection **:** wooing devices and techniques ⟨to pay ~ to a wealthy widow⟩ **6 :** a local chapter or lodge of any of various organizations **7** [short for *court shoe*] *Brit* **:** ³PUMP — **in open court :** with opportunity for public knowledge **:** not covertly or privately **:** OPENLY ⟨a judgment read *in open court*⟩ — **out of court 1 :** without a court hearing **:** by private arrangement ⟨settling the dispute *out of court*⟩ **2 :** out of consideration **:** extraneous to a discussion **:** too ill-advised or ridiculous to be considered ⟨the nationalists . . . have put themselves *out of court* as desirable rulers of African communities —A.P.Ryan⟩

²**court** \"\ *vb* -ED/-ING/-S *vt* **1 a :** to seek to win, gain, or achieve ⟨~ opportunity⟩ ⟨~ the favor of her professional associates —Tennessee Williams⟩ **b** (1) **:** to allure with attractions **:** INVITE, TEMPT, ATTRACT ⟨mountain streams ~*ing* the fishermen⟩ (2) **:** to act so as to invite, induce, call forth, or provoke ⟨~*ing* a disastrous defeat⟩ ⟨one ~*s* derision by imitating a classic without improving it —D.S.Berkeley⟩ **2 a :** to seek the affections of **:** make love to **:** WOO; *specif* **:** to seek to marry **b** *of an animal* **:** to perform actions to attract for mating ⟨a male bird ~*ing* a female⟩ **3 a :** to seek to attract by paying court **:** serve with attentions and courtesies **:** treat with blandishments and flatteries ⟨young nobles ~*ing* the dowager queen⟩ **b :** to seek the goodwill of **:** offer advantages and rewards to for support or alliance ⟨both candidates ~*ing* the independent voter⟩ ~ *vi* **1 :** to engage in social activities leading to engagement and marriage ⟨how the two met, how they ~*ed*, how they married —Quentin Reynolds⟩ **2** *of an animal* **:** to engage in play, display, and similar activity leading to mating ⟨a pair of robins ~*ing* in the trees⟩

³**court** \"\ *adj* **:** of, relating to, or appropriate to a court: as **a :** of, relating to, appropriate to, or frequenting a royal court; *sometimes* **:** FORMAL ⟨a ~ ball⟩ **b :** of or appropriate to a legal court; *sometimes* **:** LEGALISTIC, FORMALISTIC **c :** of a court game (as basketball or tennis) ⟨a ~ star⟩

court art *n* **:** art forms that exemplify or illustrate the elegant tastes or customs of a royal court — often opposed to *folk art*

court baron \'ˌ=ˈ==\ *n, pl* **courts baron** *or* **court barons** [AF *court baron*, lit., baron's court] **:** an inferior manorial court presided over by its lord or his steward that had jurisdiction over certain cases (as petty offenses) arising on the manor and affecting its tenants and that was abolished in England in 1867 after having fallen into disuse and was early abolished in New York, Pennsylvania, and Maryland where it existed briefly

court bond *n* **:** a surety bond required of litigants to insure payment of costs or the meeting of other obligations

court bouillon \(ˌ)kůr, (ˌ)kōr, (ˌ)kȯr+; *South often* ¦kübe¦än *or* -¦ōn *or* -¦ōⁿ\ *n* [F *court-bouillon*, fr. *court* short (fr. L *curtus* shortened) + *bouillon* — more at SHEAR] **:** a fish stock usu. containing seasonings, vegetables, and wine

court card *pronunc at* ¹COURT + ˌ-\ *n* [by folk etymology (influence of ¹*court*) fr. *coat card*] **:** FACE CARD

court christian *n, often cap both Cs* [trans. of AF *court cristiene*] **:** ECCLESIASTICAL COURT

court circular *n, usu cap both Cs* **:** the bulletin issued daily by the court of Great Britain to the press containing news of the court and the royal family

court clinic *n* **:** a clinic making psychiatric diagnosis of legal offenders in order to provide the judge with information and advice

courtcraft \'=ˌ=\ *n* **:** the art or craft of conducting the affairs of a court **:** skill at improvising and implementing policy

court cupboard *n* [prob. fr. ¹*court*] **:** a cupboard of the 16th and 17th centuries in two sections the upper of which is closed with a door or doors and the lower open — compare PRESS CUPBOARD

court cupboard

court dance *n* **:** a grave and stately dance suitable for court functions — distinguished from *folk dance*

court day *n* [ME *corte day*, fr. *corte, court* court + *day*] **:** a day on which a court is in session

court dress *n* **:** formal dress prescribed for those appearing at a royal court

courted *past of* COURT

courte-échelle \¦kůrd·(ˌ)ā¦shel\ *n, pl* **courte-échelles** \-l(z)\ [F *courte échelle*, lit., short ladder] **:** a mountaineering maneuver in which a climber clambers on the body or head of another in order to reach a hold

cour·te·ous \'kər|d·ēəs, 'kə̄|,'kəi|, |tēəs, *esp Brit* 'kȯ| *or* |·tyəs\ *adj* [alter. (influenced by *-eous*) of earlier *curtes, curtayse*, fr. ME *curteis, corteis*, fr. OF, fr. *court, cort* court — more at COURT] **1 :** marked by polished manners, gallantry, or ceremonial usage of a court **:** befitting a chevalier, courtier, or cosmopolitan ⟨presentation at St. James's had made him ~ —Jane Austen⟩ ⟨this love was ~, delicately ceremonial, precise —H.O.Taylor⟩ **2 :** marked by respect for and consideration of others **:** observing gentle or polished forms of social conduct often with inner sincerity **:** WELL-MANNERED ⟨too ~ and considerate to make stubborn subordinates yield —Allan Nevins & H.S.Commager⟩ ⟨most ~ and helpful in assisting me —Ellsworth Huntington⟩ **syn** see CIVIL

cour·te·ous·ly *adv* [alter. (influenced by *courteous*) of earlier *curtysely*, fr. ME *curteisly*, fr. *curteis* + *-ly*] **:** in a courteous manner

cour·te·ous·ness *n* -ES [ME *curteisnesse*, fr. *curteis* courteous + *-nesse* -ness] **:** the quality or state of being courteous **:** gracious civility **:** POLITENESS, COURTESY

cour·te·san *also* **cour·te·zan** \'kȯr|d·əzən, 'kər|,'kə̄ə|,'kȯ|, 'kə̄|,'kəi|, |tə-, -əsən *also* -ˌzan *or* -ˌsan *or* -aa(ə)n, *esp Brit* ˌ==ˈzan\ *n* -S [MF *courtisane*, fr. OIt *cortigiana* woman courtier, fem. of *cortigiano* courtier, fr. *corte* court (fr. L *cohort-, cohors*) + *-igiano* (suffix denoting origin, fr. *-ese* — fr. L *-ensis* — + *-ano* -an) — more at COURT] **:** a prostitute or kept woman often with a clientele drawn from a court or from the wealthy or the upper class

¹**cour·te·sy** \'kər|d·əsē, 'kə̄|,'kəi|, |tə-, *esp Brit* 'kȯ|; *sense 4 and* ³COURTESY *are* " *or like* CURTSY\ *n* -ES [ME *curteisie, corteisie*, fr. OF, fr. *curteis, corteis* courteous + *-ie* -y] **1 a :** courteous behavior **:** well-mannered conduct indicative of respect for or consideration of others ⟨here was true ~ — the civil deed that shows the good heart —E.M.Forster⟩ **b :** a courteous act or expression **:** a favor courteously performed ⟨rising to receive him with every refinement of manner known to the time and with all the engaging graces and *courtesies* —Charles Dickens⟩ **c** *archaic* **:** a conventional expression of respect (as a bow) **2 a :** the sanction of general allowance or acceptance with goodwill despite facts or official regulation **:** INDULGENCE ⟨mountains they are called . . . but they are such by ~ only, for . . . the largest rises little more than 1300 feet —Hodding Carter⟩ **b :** consideration, cooperation, and generosity in providing or according (as a gift, loan, or privilege) **:** GRATUITY, GIFT ⟨the flowers were placed in the church through the ~ of the florist⟩ ⟨the player's costumes are by ~ of the department store⟩; *also* **:** AGENCY, MEANS ⟨all . . . swung obligingly into place . . . by ~ of a revolving stage —Robert Lawrence⟩ **3 :** CURTESY **4 :** ¹CURTSY

²**courtesy** \"\ *adj* **1 :** granted or performed as a courtesy or by way of courtesy ⟨a ~ letter⟩ ⟨~ visit⟩ **:** acting as or performing a courtesy **2 :** popularly conceded but not legally valid ⟨a ~ rank⟩ **:** done or performed as a ceremony usu. without official significance ⟨~ inspections⟩ **3 :** enjoying privileges of membership without officially belonging ⟨a hospital's ~ staff of doctors⟩ **:** conveying or granting privileges of membership to nonmembers

³**courtesy** \"\ *vb* -ED/-ING/-ES **:** ²CURTSY

courtesy book *n* **1 :** a medieval or Renaissance book designed to prepare the young nobleman for the proper pursuit of his courtly duties and pleasures **2 :** a book designed to prepare a young gentleman for public duties and conduct **:** a book of advice about social conduct

courtesy call *n* **:** a social call made for reasons of general courtesy and without a more specific purpose

courtesy card *n* **:** a card entitling its holder to some special privilege (as purchasing on credit or enjoying guest privileges)

courtesy literature *n* **:** literature comprising courtesy books and similar pieces

courtesy of the port : the extension to a passenger returning from a foreign port of the privilege of immediate customs examination of his baggage

courtesy title *n* **1 :** a title granted by usage and in some cases royal permission to certain lineal relatives of British peers: as **a :** a title in the style of a peerage borne by an heir in the direct line of a duke or marquess and by the eldest son of an earl and consisting in the case of the eldest son of the father's secondary title and in the case of the eldest son of the eldest son of another minor title attached to the peerage (as of the eldest son of the duke of Devonshire titled Marquess of Hartington and the eldest son of the marquess titled Earl of Burlington) **b :** a title consisting of the prefix "Lord", "Lady", or "the Honourable" added to the Christian name of other children of British peers **2 :** a title taken by the user and commonly accepted without consideration of official right (as *professor* for any teacher or *colonel* for any notable citizen)

court game *n* **:** an athletic game played on a court

court gray *n* **:** a very pale green that is yellower and paler than tourmaline and bluer and duller than emerald tint — called also *starling's-egg green*

court guide *n* **:** a directory of persons (as those received at court) who have status in British society

court hand *n* [¹*court* (of law) + *hand*] **:** the hand formerly used in charters, deeds, and other legal documents

court holy water *n* [¹*court*] *obs* **:** empty or insincere fair words **:** FLATTERY

courthouse \'=ˌ=\ *n* [ME, fr. ¹*court* + *hous* house] **1 :** a building in which established courts are held **:** the principal building in which county offices are housed and in which county administrative affairs are conducted and which often contains also the county jail **2 :** COUNTY SEAT — used chiefly in place names in Virginia and some nearby states ⟨Appomattox *Courthouse*⟩; abbr. *C. H.*

cour·tier \'kōr|d·ēər, 'kȯr-; 'kōə|d·ēə(r, 'kȯ(ə)|; |tēə-,|tyə- *also* |chə(r) *sometimes* 'kůr| *or* 'kůə| *or* |ˌchi(ə)r *or* |ˌchiə *or* ˌ='ti(ə)r *or* ˌ='tiə\ *n* -S [ME *courteour*, fr. (assumed) AF *courteour*, fr. OF *corteier* to be at the court of a prince (fr. *cort, court* court + *-our* -or) — more at COURT] **1 :** a gentleman attendant or habitué of a sovereign's court; *sometimes* **:** a ruler's satellite esp. given to flattery, soliciting favor, and connivance **2** *archaic* **:** one that courts or woos

cour·tier·ly *adj* **:** like a courtier **:** having the characteristics of a courtier

courting *pres part of* COURT

courting chair *n* **:** LOVE SEAT

courting mirror *n* **:** a usu. small mirror having a narrow wooden frame with insets of painted glass

court lands *n pl, English law* **:** land kept in demesne

court leet *n, pl* **courts leet** *also* **court leets :** a court formerly held in England and the colonies with jurisdiction over civil matters and petty offenses and surviving in England only for ceremonial purposes

courtlike \'=ˌ=\ *adj* **:** ELEGANT, COURTLY

court·li·ness \'kōrtlēnəs, 'kōət-,'kȯ(ə)rt-, -lin-\ *n* -ES **:** the quality of being courtly **:** ELEGANCE, DIGNITY

court·ling \'kōrtliŋ, 'kȯrt-,'kōət-,'kȯ(ə)t-, -lēŋ\ *n* -S [¹*court* + *-ling*] **:** a courtier esp. when young or insignificant

¹**court·ly** \-lē,-li\ *adj* -ER/-EST [ME, fr. ¹*court* + *-ly*] **1 a :** marked by highbred polish, stateliness, and ceremony **:** characteristic of court usage or of courtiers ⟨and the stately Spanish men . . . with their ~ foreign grace —Alfred Tennyson⟩ **b :** marked by elegance, richness, wit, or refinement befitting a court ⟨luxury and all manner of conceits are part and parcel of such a ~ civilization —George Santayana⟩ ⟨the ~ wit of the Cavalier —V.L.Parrington⟩ **2 a :** belonging to a court **:** appropriate to or suggestive of a court ⟨a ~ manor⟩ **:** participating in or serving at court functions ⟨the ~ guard⟩ **b :** favoring a court party or faction or its policies ⟨the plans of the ~ adherents⟩ **3 a :** strongly marked by formality and ceremony ⟨~ addresses⟩ **b :** utterly lacking in sincerity **:** FLATTERING, UNCTUOUS, OBSEQUIOUS ⟨~ protestations⟩ **syn** see CIVIL

²**courtly** \"\ *adv* **:** in a courtly manner **:** POLITELY

courtly love *n* **:** a late medieval highly conventionalized code prescribing conduct and emotions of ladies and their lovers and providing the theme of an extensive medieval courtly literature

court·man \'=mən, -ˌman\ *n, pl* **courtmen** [ME, fr. ¹*court* + *man*] **:** COURTIER

¹**court-martial** \'=¦==\ *n, pl* **courts-martial** *also* **court-martials** [alter. of earlier *martial court*] **1 :** a court consisting of commissioned officers and in the U. S. in some instances other personnel of the armed forces for the trial of offenders who are members of the armed forces or are within the jurisdiction of the armed forces and for the trial of offenses against military law **2 :** a session of a court-martial **:** a trial by court-martial

²**court-martial** \"\ *vt* **court-martialed** *also* **court-martialled; court-martialed** *also* **court-martialled; court-martialing** *also* **court-martialling** \-sh(ə)liŋ\ **court-martials :** to subject to trial by court-martial

court-noué \¦kůr,nü¦ā, -rnə¦wā\ *n* -S [F, fr. *court* short (fr. L *curtus* shortened) + *noué* knotted, past part. of *nouer* to tie, knot, fr. OF *noer* — more at SHEAR, DENOUEMENT] **:** a disease of the grape characterized by shortening of internodes, by small leaves, and by decline of vigor — called also *roncet*

court of admiralty : ADMIRALTY 3

court of appeal 1 *or* **court of appeals :** a court hearing appeals from the decisions of lower courts — compare APPELLATE, COURT OF FIRST INSTANCE **2** *usu cap C&A* **:** an appellate court usu. exercising final jurisdiction over civil cases in England and Wales from which appeal may be taken only to the House of Lords — compare HIGH COURT OF JUSTICE

court of cassation *often cap both Cs* [trans. of F *cour de cassation*] **:** the highest court of appeal esp. in various European countries

court of chivalry 1 *often cap both Cs* **:** an English court orig. dealing with military discipline but at various times trying cases concerning prisoners of war, high treason and rebellion, peerage claims, offenses against the honor of other persons, and usurpation or unlawful assumption of honors and still retaining jurisdiction in cases involving the right to armorial bearings — see COURT OF HONOR 1b, COURT OF THE CONSTABLE AND MARSHAL, EARL MARSHAL'S COURT **2 :** COURT OF HONOR

court of claims : a court having jurisdiction over claims (as against a government) ⟨the U.S. *Court of Claims*⟩

court of common pleas *often cap both Cs&P* **1 :** a former superior court of English common law at Westminster having jurisdiction over the ordinary civil suits between subject and subject and now forming part of the Court of King's Bench **2 :** a court of intermediate rank in some American states usu. having civil and criminal jurisdiction

court of criminal appeal *usu cap both Cs&A* **:** an appellate court usu. exercising final jurisdiction over criminal cases in England and Wales and from which appeal may be taken only to the House of Lords

court of delegates *often cap C&D* **:** a former English high court of appeal composed of commissioners appointed by the Crown and having jurisdiction over ecclesiastical cases now heard by the Judicial Committee of the Privy Council

court of domestic relations : a court having jurisdiction of family disputes that involve the rights and duties of husband and wife and parent and child esp. in matters affecting support, custody, and welfare of children and often having advisory and investigative powers and the assistance of psychiatrists, physicians, and other experts — called also *family court;* compare JUVENILE COURT

court of dustyfoot \-'==ˌ=\ **:** COURT OF PIEPOUDRE

court of equity *also* **court of conscience :** a court having jurisdiction over suits in equity and administering justice and providing remedies according to the rules and principles of equity

court of errors : a court having jurisdiction to hear appeals on error

court of exchequer *usu cap C&E* **:** EXCHEQUER 2

court of first instance : the court first taking jurisdiction of a case — compare COURT OF APPEAL

court of honor 1 a : a tribunal to investigate questions of personal honor (as a military court investigating questionable acts) **b :** a court of chivalry (sense 1) in the exercise of its function esp. in the 17th century as a tribunal for trial of slanders against people of honor and for usurpation or unlawful assumption of armorial ensigns or of privileges of rank or office **2 a :** a troop committee in the British boy scout and girl guide movements that is composed of the troop leader or the guider and the patrol leaders and that deals with internal matters of discipline, expenditure, and general administration **b** (1) **:** a local or national group of authorized officials of the Boy Scouts of America that grants to scouts certificates of promotion and honor medals (2) **:** a meeting of or a ceremony conducted by this group **c :** the planning body of a girl scout troop composed of troop officers and adult leader **3 :** a group of outstanding usu. noncompeting exhibits in a stamp exhibit

court of inquiry : a military court to inquire into and report on some military matter (as the conduct of an officer)

court of king's bench *or* **court of queen's bench** *usu cap C&K&B&Q* **:** a former superior court presided over by the sovereign of England and following his person and now forming the King's Bench or Queen's Bench Division of the High Court of Justice entertaining as a superior court of record criminal cases on its crown side and civil cases on its plea side and embracing the jurisdiction of the former Court of Common Pleas and Court of Exchequer

court of last resort : a court of final appeal

court of law : a court that hears cases and decides them on the basis of statutes or the common law — compare EQUITY 2

court of love : a court of ladies supposed to have been held in medieval times to pass on questions of courtesy and courtly love

court of pie·pou·dre *or* **court of pie·pow·der** \-'pī,paůdə(r)\ [alter. of earlier *court of pipowders*, fr. ME *court of pepowders*, fr. ¹*court* + *of* + *pepowders, pipowdres*, pl. of *pipoudre* itinerant trader, fr. AF *piepoudrous*, fr. OF *pied, pié* foot (fr. L *ped-, pes*) + AF *poudrous* dusty, fr. OF *poudre* dust + *-ous, -eus* -ous — more at FOOT, POWDER] **1 :** an English summary court of record incident by the common law to every fair or market to administer justice for commercial injuries at that fair or market **2 :** a U.S. small-debts court

court of record [ME, fr. ¹*court* + *of* + *record*] **:** a court whose acts and judicial proceedings are written down for a perpetual memorial and hence are established and proved by the record

court of requests : an English court for the recovery of small debts

court of review : an appellate court

court of session *usu cap C&S* **:** the supreme civil court of Scotland

court of sessions : a court with power to hold sessions of the peace; *specif* **:** any of various U.S. state criminal courts of record

court of the constable and marshal *usu cap both Cs & M* **:** the English court of chivalry at the period when both the lord high constable and the earl marshal presided in it — compare EARL MARSHAL'S COURT

court of the lord lyon *usu cap C & both Ls* **:** LYON COURT

court of wards *or* **court of wards and liveries** *usu cap C&W &L* **:** an English court of record under the feudal system having jurisdiction over matters dealing with estates held of the Crown including their transfer from a deceased tenant to his heir and the payment of taxes and rents due the Crown from such estates

cour·toi·sie \¦kür·ˌtwä¦zē\ *n* -S [F, fr. MF *corteisie* — more at COURTESY] **:** COURTLINESS; *esp* **:** the code of courtly love

court order *n* **:** an order issuing from a competent court requiring a person to do or abstain from doing a certain act

court painter *n* **:** an artist holding the official position of painter to a royal court

court party *n* **:** a faction or party supporting the royal court esp. in political matters

court plaster *n* [so called fr. its cosmetic use by ladies at royal courts] **:** an adhesive plaster usu. of silk coated with a mixture of isinglass and glycerin that was formerly used for medical and cosmetic purposes — see ¹PATCH 2

court reporter *n* **:** a stenographer who records and transcribes a verbatim report of all proceedings in a law court

court roll *n* [ME *corte rolle*, fr. *corte, court* court + *rolle* roll] **:** a roll used in the records of a court

courtroom \'=ˌ=\ *n* **:** a room in which a court of law is held

courts *pl of* COURT, *pres 3d sing of* COURT

courts baron *pl of* COURT BARON

court·ship \'kōr|t,ship, 'kȯr|,'kōə|,'kȯ(ə)|, |ˌchip\ *n* **1** *obs* **:** conduct appropriate to a court or courtier **:** COURTLINESS, COURTESY **:** a courtier's state or condition ⟨gallants full of ~ and of state —Shak.⟩ **2 a** *obs* **:** the act of paying court **:** performance of ceremonial or complimentary courtesies ⟨his ~ to the common people —Shak.⟩ **b** *obs* **:** practice of a courtier's arts **:** use of diplomacy, flattery, finesse, and connivance **3 a :** the process of paying court to or showing attention to and affection for another person with intentions that involve marriage or other intimacy **b :** the relationship between a couple from awakening of deep interest to formal engagement **:** the period of such relationship **4 :** the act of trying to gain support or goodwill **:** solicitation and enticement **:** the endeavor to win, gain, or attain ⟨the duke's ~ of factions as yet uncommitted⟩ **5 :** the somewhat stereotyped and often complicated behavior culminating in copulation in many animals

court shoe *n* [so called fr. its use as a part of court dress] *Brit* **:** ³PUMP

courts leet *pl of* COURT LEET

courts-martial *pl of* COURT-MARTIAL

court tennis *n* **:** an ancient and complicated game played with a ball and rackets in an enclosed court that is usu. a covered building of peculiar construction, there being used in play besides a specially marked-out floor with a net crossing it the main walls, lower inner walls with sloping roof, various openings (as the dedans, grille, and winning gallery), and a projection in the main wall — see HAZARD SIDE, SERVICE SIDE, TAMBOUR; RACKET illustration

courtyard \'=ˌ=\ *n* **:** a court or enclosure adjacent to or attached to a house, castle, palace, or other building; *specif* **:** a service area adjoining an apartment building, hotel, or commercial structure

cous \'kaů(ə)s\ *also* **cow·ish** \'kaůish\ *n* -ES [perh. fr. Nez Percé *kowish*] **:** an herb (*Lomatium cous*) of the northwestern U.S. having edible roots

cous·cous \'kü,skiis\ *or* **cus·cou·su** *or* **cus·cu·su** \¦küskə·¦sü\ *or* **cus·cus** \'kü,skiis\ *n, pl* **couscouses** *or* **cuscousous** *or* **cuscusus** *or* **cuscuses** [F *couscous, couscoussou*, fr. Ar *kuskus*, fr. *kaskasa* to pound, pulverize] **:** a No. African dish consisting variously of cracked wheat steamed and eaten as a cereal or with meat and vegetables as a main dish or with fruits and nuts as a dessert

cousen *obs var of* COZEN

¹**cous·in** \'kəzᵊn\ *n* -S [ME *cosin*, fr. OF *cosin, cousin*, fr. L *consobrinus* child of a mother's sister, cousin, fr. *com-* + *sobrinus* cousin on the mother's side, fr. *soror* sister — more at SISTER] **1 a** *obs* (1) **:** someone collaterally related more remotely than a brother or sister (as a nephew) (2) **:** one that is legally next of kin whether collaterally or lineally related except parent or child **b :** a child of one's uncle or aunt — called also *first cousin, full cousin, own cousin;* see CROSS-COUSIN, PARALLEL COUSIN **c :** a relative descended from one's grandparent or from a more remote ancestor by two or more steps and in a different line, a distinction often being made between (1) those descended an equal number of steps and (2) those descended an unequal number of steps from a common ancestor ⟨the children of first ~*s* are second ~*s* to each other, the children of second ~*s* are third ~*s*, etc.⟩ ⟨the child of one's first ~ is one's first ~ once removed, the latter's child is one's first ~ twice removed, etc., though these are often called also second and third ~*s* respectively⟩ **d :** a kinsman having some distant

relationship usu. by blood **2 :** one marked by relationship, resemblance, or similar position or status **:** one readily associated with or thought of in connection with another **:** EQUIVALENT, COMPLEMENT, COUNTERPART, OPPOSITE NUMBER ⟨rural children deserve as good an education as their city ~s get —Benjamin Fine⟩ ⟨the sonic barrier and its higher-speed ~, the thermal barrier —B.K.Thorne⟩ **3 —** used as a title by a sovereign in addressing or formally naming a nobleman of his own country or another sovereign and in English writs and commissions issued by the crown to refer to earls and peers of higher rank ⟨my noble lords and ~s all, good morrow —Shak.⟩ **4 a :** FRIEND, COMRADE, ASSOCIATE **b** *obs* **:** FOOL, GULL, DUPE **c :** a competitor who is frequently and easily defeated or thwarted by an opponent not clearly superior ⟨a pitcher who is a ~ to a certain batter⟩ **d :** an acquaintance of long, intimate, or informal standing **5 :** a person of a race or people ethnically or culturally related or similar ⟨our English ~s⟩ ⟨today's islanders resemble their mainland ~s —*Nat'l Geographic*⟩

²cousin \" \ *vi* **cousined; cousined; cousining** \ˈkəz(ᵊ)niŋ\ **cousins** *NewEng* **:** to visit relatives esp. when distant

cous·in·age \ˈkəz(ᵊ)nij\ *n* -S [ME *cosinage*, fr. MF *cousinage*, fr. OF, fr. *cosin, cousin* + *-age*] **1 :** relationship of cousins **:** KINSHIP **2 :** a collection of cousins **:** KINSFOLK

cous·in·ess \-zᵊnəs\ *n* -ES [ME *cosiness*, fr. *cosin* + *-ess, -esse* -ess] **:** a female cousin **:** KINSWOMAN

cousin-german \ˈ==ˌ==\ *n, pl* **cousins-german** [ME *cosin germain*, fr. MF, fr. OF, fr. *cosin* + *germain* related by descent from a common ancestor, having the same parents — more at GERMAN] **:** COUSIN 1b

cous·in·hood \ˈkəzᵊnˌhu̇d\ *n* -S **1 :** KINSFOLK, KINSMEN **2 :** the relationship of cousins **:** the condition of being a cousin

cousin-in-law \ˈ===ˌ=\ *n, pl* **cousins-in-law** **1 :** a wife or husband of one's cousin **2 :** a cousin of one's wife or one's husband

cousin jack \ˈ==ˈjak\ *n, pl* **cousin jacks** *usu cap C&J* [¹*cousin* + *Jack* (the name)] **:** CORNISHMAN; *esp* **:** a Cornish miner

cous·in·ly *adj* **:** like or becoming a cousin ⟨shyly gave her a ~ kiss⟩

cous·in·ry \ˈkəzᵊnrē\ *n* -ES **:** a body of cousins or kinsfolk

cous·in·ship \-ᵊnˌship\ *n* -S **:** relationship of cousins **:** the fact of being a cousin **:** KINSHIP

cous·si·net \ˌküsᵊnˈā, -ᵊnˈet\ *n* -S [F, fr. OF, small cushion, dim. of *coissin* cushion — more at CUSHION] **1 :** a stone placed on the impost of a pier for receiving the first stone of an arch **2 :** the bolster or cushion of an Ionic capital

cou·tel \(ˈ)küˈtel\ *n* -S [MF, knife, fr. L *cultellus*, dim. of *culter* knife, plowshare — more at COLTER] **:** a medieval short knife or dagger

¹couth \ˈküth\ *adj* -ER/-EST [ME, pleasant, familiar, known, fr. OE *cūth* familiar, known; akin to OHG *kund* known, ON *kunnr*, Goth *kunths*; all fr. past part. of a prehistoric Gmc verb represented by OE *cunnan* to know, be able — more at CAN] *Scot* **:** COUTHIE

²couth \" \ *adj* -ER/-EST [back-formation fr. *uncouth*] **:** marked by finesse, polish, grooming, breeding, or sophistication **:** SMOOTH

couth·ie \-thē\ *adj* -ER/-EST [¹*couth* + Sc *-ie* -y (adj. suffix)] **1** *chiefly Scot* **:** PLEASANT, KINDLY, FRIENDLY **2** *chiefly Scot* **:** COMFORTABLE, SNUG

cou·til \küˈtē(ə)l, -til\ *n* -S [F, fr. OF, smooth tightly woven cloth used for covering mattresses, fr. *coute* quilt, mattress — more at QUILT] **:** a firm durable cotton or cotton and rayon fabric that is usu. woven in herringbone twill and is used esp. for foundation garments and suitings

cou·ture \küˈtu̇(ə)r *or as F*\ *n* -S [F, sewing, dressmaking, fr. OF *cousture* sewing, seam, fr. (assumed) VL *consutura*, fr. L *consutus* (past part. of *consuere* to sew together, fr. *com-* + *suere* to sew) + *-ura* -ure — more at SEW] **:** the business of designing, making, and selling fashionable expensive custom-made women's clothing; *collectively* **:** the designers and establishments engaged in this business

cou·tu·rier \küˈtu̇rēər; küˈtu̇rēˌā, (ˌ)=ˌ==ˈ=; küˈtu̇rˌyā, ˌ=ˌ=ˈ=\ *n* -S [F, dressmaker, fr. OF *cousturier* tailor's assistant, fr. *cousture* + *-ier* -er] **:** an establishment engaged in the business of couture; *also* **:** the proprietor of or designer for such an establishment

cou·tu·riere \küˈtu̇rēər; küˈtu̇rēˌe(ə)r, (ˌ)=ˌ==ˈ=; küˈtu̇rˌye(ə)r, ˌ=ˌ=ˈ=\ *n* -S [F *couturière*, fr. OF *cousturiere* seamstress, fem. of *cousturier*] **:** a female couturier

cou·vade \küˈväd\ *n* -S [F, fr. MF, cowardly inactivity, fr. *couver*, *cover* to sit on (as a female bird on eggs), brood over + *-ade* — more at COVEY] **:** a custom among primitive peoples in many parts of the world in accordance with which when a child is born the father takes to his bed as if he himself had suffered the pains of childbirth, cares for the child, and submits himself to fasting, purification, or various taboos

cou·vert \(ˈ)küˈve(ə)r\ *n* -S [F, fr. MF, fr. OF *covert, couvert* covered, past part. of *covrir, couvrir* to cover — more at COVERT] **1 :** a table cover **2 :** COVER CHARGE

cou·verte \(ˈ)küˈve(ə)rt\ *n* -S [F, fr. fem. of *couvert* covered (past part. of *couvrir* to cover), fr. OF *covert, couvert*] **:** hard porcelain glaze

cou·xia \ˈküshēə\ *or* **cou·xio** \ˈküshēˌü, -ēˌō\ *n* -S [Tupi *cuchiu, cuxiu*] **:** SAKI

co·valence *or* **co·valency** \(ˈ)kō+\ *n* [*co-* + *valence, valency*] **:** nonionic valence characterized by the sharing of electrons usu. in pairs by two atoms in a chemical compound; *also* **:** the number of pairs of electrons an atom can share with its neighbors — distinguished from *electrovalence*

co·valent \"+\ *adj* **:** of relating to, or characterized by covalence — **co·va·lent·ly** *adv*

covalent bond *n* **:** a nonionic chemical bond formed by shared electrons, usu. a pair belonging orig. each to a different atom or both to one atom — distinguished from *electrovalent bond*; see COORDINATE BOND

co·va·re·ca \ˌkōvəˈrākə\ *n, pl* **covareca** *or* **covarecas** *usu cap* [AmerSp, prob. fr. Covareca] **1 a :** an extinct Otukian people of Paraguay **b :** a member of such people **2 :** the language of the Covareca people formerly considered to constitute a language family

co·variance \(ˈ)kō+\ *n* [*co-* + *variance*] **:** the arithmetic mean or the expected value of the product of the deviations of corresponding values of two variables from their respective mean values

co·variant \"+\ *adj* [ISV *co-* + *variant*] **:** changing along with something else so as to preserve certain mathematical interrelations unchanged

co·variation \"+\ *n* [*co-* + *variation*] **:** coincident variation

¹cove \ˈkōv\ *n* -S [ME, den, cave, fr. OE *cofa* den, small room; akin to OHG *chubisi* hut, ON *kūfr* heap, Gk *gypē* cave, Skt *guda* rectum — more at COT] **1** *Scot* **:** a hollow in a rock formation **:** CAVERN **2 :** a concavity or recessed place in a structure: as **a :** a member (as a molding) with a concave cross section **b :** a hollow slot in a spar into which the boltrope on a sail slides as a means of securing the sail to the spar **c :** a recess or trough for concealed lighting at the upper part of a wall **3 a :** a small sheltered inlet or bay ⟨an irregular shoreline broken by many ~s —*Amer. Guide Series: Mich.*⟩ **b :** a shallow tidal stream or arm of the sea **:** a backwater near the mouth of a tidal stream **4 :** a deep recess or small valley in the side of a mountain **:** a level area sheltered by hills or mountains **5 :** a basin or hollow where the surface of the land has caved in (as from solution of underlying rock)

²cove \" \ *vt* -ED/-ING/-S **1 :** to make or build in a hollow concave form **2 :** to provide (as a ceiling) with a cove

³cove \" \ *n* -S [Romany *kova* thing, person] *slang Brit* **:** MAN, CHAP, FELLOW, BLOKE

cove ceiling *n* **:** a ceiling the part of which next the wall is constructed in a cove

coved vault *n* **:** CLOISTER VAULT

cove lighting *n* **:** indirect interior lighting from incandescent or fluorescent lamps concealed in a reflecting trough near the ceiling

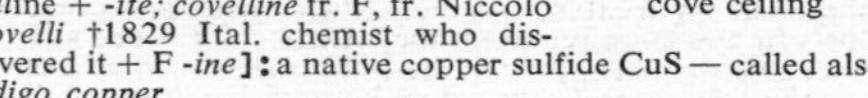
cove ceiling

co·vel·lite \kōˈveˌlīt, ˈkōvəˌ-\ *also* **co·vel·line** \-ˌlēn\ *n* -S [*covellite* fr. *covelline* + *-ite*; *covelline* fr. F, fr. Niccolò *Covelli* †1829 Ital. chemist who discovered it + F *-ine*] **:** a native copper sulfide CuS — called also *indigo copper*

cov·en \ˈkəvən, ˈkōv-\ *n* -S [ME *covin* troop, band — more at COVIN] **:** a congregation or assembly of witches; *specif* **:** a band of 13 witches

¹cov·e·nant \ˈkəvənənt *sometimes* -vnə-\ *n* -S *often attrib* [ME, fr. OF, fr. pres. part. of *covenir* to agree, be suitable, meet, fr. L *convenire* — more at CONVENE] **1 a :** an agreement that is usu. formal, solemn, and intended as binding **:** COMPACT ⟨international law, which depends upon the sanctity of ~s between rulers —G.H.Sabine⟩ ⟨the ~ among the people to defend their religion⟩ **b :** a particular stipulation in a covenant — obs. except in law **2** *obs* **:** SECURITY, PLEDGE **3 a :** an undertaking or promise of legal validity: as (1) **:** a contract under seal distinguished from other specialties by the promise or undertaking contained in it (2) **:** a particular agreement contained in a specialty or deed incidental to its main purpose — see USUAL COVENANTS (3) **:** the document or writing containing the terms of the agreement or promise **b :** the common-law form of action to recover damages for breach of such a contract **4 :** a solemn compact between members of a church to maintain its faith and discipline; *also* **:** the document recording such a compact **5 :** the promises of God as revealed in the Scriptures conditioned on certain terms on the part of man (as obedience, repentance, and faith); *specif* **:** an agreement regarded as having been made between God and his people Israel (as represented by Abraham, David, and others) whereby Israel was to be faithful to God and God was to protect and bless his faithful people

²covenant \", *before a syllable-increasing inflectional suffix usu* -vəˌnant *or* -vəˌnaa(ə)nt\ *vb* -ED/-ING/-S [ME *covenanten*, fr. *covenant*, n.] *vt* **1 :** to promise solemnly by or as if by a covenant **:** pledge in formal agreement ⟨~*ing* that their hostages would be present⟩ ⟨~*ing* to sell only to certain buyers⟩ **2 :** to lay down as a condition **:** STIPULATE ⟨before signing, he ~*ed* that he would remain in possession⟩ ~ *vi* **1 :** to enter into a covenant **:** to come to formal agreement **:** CONTRACT ⟨his retainers ~*ing* in loyalty to the king⟩ **syn** see PROMISE

cov·e·nan·tal \ˌkəvəˈnantᵊl, -naan-\ *adj* **:** of or relating to a covenant ⟨the . . . purposes of a ~ God —N.H.Snaith⟩ — **cov·e·nan·tal·ly** \-ᵊlē, -ᵊli\ *adv*

covenanted *adj* [fr. past part. of *covenant*] **1 :** bound by a covenant: **a** *of an official of the Indian Civil Service* **:** bound by a covenant with the East India Company or later with the British government to observe certain regulations and assume certain obligations **b :** having subscribed to a covenant ⟨a ~ king⟩ **2 :** established by a covenant

cov·e·nan·tee \ˌkəvəˌnanˈtē, -naan-; ˌkəv(ə)nən-\ *n* -S **:** the person to whom a promise in the form of a covenant is made

¹cov·e·nan·ter \ˈkəvəˌnantə(r), -naan-, *in sense 2 often* ˌ==ˈ==; ˈkəv(ə)nən-\ *n* -S **1 :** one that makes a covenant **2** *usu cap* **a :** a signer or adherent of the Scottish National Covenant of 1638; *esp* **:** one of those who steadfastly held to the principles of this Covenant during the persecution under Charles II and James II (1661–1687) **b :** CAMERONIAN **c :** a member of a Reformed Presbyterian church

²covenanter \" \ *adj, usu cap* **:** of or relating to the Covenanters ⟨with their Scotch-Irish fire and Covenanter background — F.S.Mead⟩

covenanting *adj* [fr. pres. part. of *covenant*] **1 :** belonging to a covenant **2 :** entering into a covenant

covenant of salt [so called fr. its being ratified by eating a meal, the preservative quality of the salt perh. symbolizing a long-lasting agreement] **:** an inviolable covenant

cov·e·nan·tor \like COVENANTER, *or* ˌ==(ˌ)=ˈtó(ə)r *or* ˌ==ˈtó(ə)r *or* -ˈtó(ə)r\ *n* -S **:** the party to a covenant who is bound to perform the obligation expressed in it

covenant theology *n* **:** FEDERAL THEOLOGY

covens *pl of* COVEN

¹cov·en·try \ˈkävəntrē, -ri, *more often in US than Brit speech* ˈkəv-\ *adj, usu cap* [fr. *Coventry*, city and county borough, Warwickshire, England] **:** of or from the city of Coventry, England **:** of the kind or style prevalent in Coventry

²coventry \" \ *n* -ES *usu cap* **:** a state of ostracism or exclusion from the society of one's fellows (as for objectionable conduct) ⟨sent to *Coventry*⟩

coventry bell *n, usu cap C* **1 :** a Eurasian perennial herb (*Campanula trachelium*) **2 :** CANTERBURY BELL **3 :** EUROPEAN PASQUEFLOWER

coventry blue *n, usu cap C* [fr. *Coventry*, England, where it was first made] **:** a blue embroidery thread

co-venture \(ˈ)kō+\ *n* -S **:** a cooperative that terminates after a certain project has been completed

¹cov·er \ˈkəvə(r)\ *vb* **covered; covered; covering** \ˈkəv(ə)riŋ, -rēŋ\ **covers** [ME *coveren*, fr. OF *covrir*, fr. L *cooperire*, fr. *co-* + *operire* to cover, fr. (assumed) L *opverire*, fr. L *op-* (akin to L *ob* to, before, against) + (assumed) L *verire* to cover — more at EPI-, WEIR] *vt* **1 a :** to guard from attack **:** protect by interposition as a defending element **:** guard the safety and further the success of by aggressive action precluding attack ⟨units ~*ing* the retreat of the main army⟩ ⟨ships ~*ing* approaches to the harbor⟩ ⟨~*ing* the landing with a naval bombardment⟩ **b** (1) **:** to serve as a defense unit or center for **:** have within the range of one's guns **:** COMMAND ⟨forts ~*ing* the city⟩ ⟨artillery ~*ing* the channel⟩ (2) **:** to have within direct range of an aimed or drawn firearm ⟨the deputy ~*ed* the wounded gangster⟩ (3) **:** to protect by being in position and readiness to fire at a possible attacker ⟨the others in the patrol were ~*ing* the leader⟩ **c** (1) **:** to afford protection or security to typically by means of some stated provision **:** insure against a specified risk **:** guarantee indemnification to ⟨a policy ~*ing* the traveler in all kinds of accidents⟩ ⟨~ teachers by the retirement plan⟩ (2) **:** to afford protection against or compensation or indemnification for ⟨~ any storm losses⟩ ⟨~ loss of time due to illness⟩ (3) **:** to protect (oneself) against the consequences of possible loss or incrimination ⟨they felt themselves to be exposed to unnecessary risk, and they started to ~ themselves —Roy Lewis & Angus Maude⟩ ⟨~ himself with an alibi⟩ **d** (1) **:** to guard (as an opponent) in order to obstruct a play ⟨~*ing* the ends on a forward pass⟩ ⟨keeping the wings ~*ed* in hockey⟩ (2) **:** to station oneself so as to be able to receive a throw to (a base in baseball) ⟨the pitcher ~*ed* first on the bunt⟩ **e** (1) **:** to guard against or make provision for (a demand or charge) by means of a reserve stock or deposit ⟨a balance to ~ the check⟩ ⟨money to ~ his debts⟩ (2) **:** to maintain a check on by patrolling or watching ⟨motorcycle police ~*ing* the roads⟩ (3) **:** to protect by contrivance or expedient ⟨otherwise slavers could ~ themselves by that flag with impunity —S.F. Bemis⟩ **2 a** (1) **:** to hide from sight or knowledge **:** prevent observation or knowledge of **:** divert attention from **:** conceal the impression of by a device for masking **:** CONCEAL ⟨a show of his old arrogance to ~ his embarrassment —Agnes S. Turnbull⟩ ⟨the shrewd purpose, ~*ed* over with pretentious rhetoric —V.L.Parrington⟩ (2) **:** to conceal or mask as blameworthy or illicit ⟨fanaticism ~*s* a weakness of moral position —Weston La Barre⟩ — often used with *up* or *over* ⟨~ up a scandal⟩ ⟨~*ing* up his own lack of trust⟩ (3) **:** to divert attention from (another who is engaged in something criminal or unethical) (4) **:** to obliterate from knowledge or remembrance (as through complete forgiveness) ⟨blessed is he . . . whose sin is ~*ed* —Ps 32:1 (AV)⟩ (5) **:** to block (an actor or a stage property) from being seen by an audience or photographed by a camera (6) **:** MAKE *vt* 13b (7) **:** ²BLANKET 3d **b :** to envelop or lie over or around so as to present an ornamental, disguising, or protecting exterior ⟨all that beauty that doth ~ thee —Shak.⟩ **3 :** to put, lay, or spread something over, on, or before (as for protecting, enclosing, or masking) **:** OVERLAY ⟨~*ing* the seed bed with straw⟩ ⟨~*ing* the bruise with salve⟩ **4 a :** to lie over **:** spread over **:** be placed on or often over the whole surface of **:** ENVELOP, FILM, COAT ⟨snow ~*ing* the highways⟩ ⟨new paint ~*ing* the old⟩ ⟨~*ed* with oil⟩ ⟨a badly wounded man ~*ed* with blood⟩ **b :** to extend thickly over conspicuously or dominatingly **:** abound over **:** occupy the whole surface of ⟨locusts ~*ing* the plains⟩ ⟨armadas ~*ing* the sea⟩ ⟨invaders ~*ing* the land⟩ **c :** to appear here and there on the surface of **:** DOT, DAPPLE — usu. used with *with* ⟨a resort area ~*ed* with lakes⟩; often in Brit. use with *in* ⟨the backs of his huge hands were ~*ed* in thick black hair —George Bellairs⟩ **5 :** to protect or conceal (one's body or a part of it) from view typically with an article of clothing or bedding ⟨~ her nakedness⟩ ⟨~ your head⟩ ⟨~ your mouth while coughing⟩ **6 :** to equip with a cover **:** place or set a cover over permanently or temporarily ⟨~ a book with leather⟩ ⟨~ a couch with mohair⟩ ⟨~ a pan with a lid⟩ **7 :** to put a surface layer over usu. completely ⟨a tent ~*ed* with skins⟩ ⟨~*ing* the old roof with new shingles⟩ ⟨~*ing* the page with ink⟩ **8 a :** to fill (a blank surface) completely ⟨~*ing* the sheet of paper with marks⟩ ⟨~*ing* the silk with embroidery⟩ **b :** to spread a cloth over in preparing to serve a meal **9 :** to rise above and immerse ⟨floodwaters ~*ing* the town⟩ ⟨enough water to ~ the vegetables⟩ **10 a :** to copulate with (a female) **:** SERVE — usu. used of an animal (as a horse) ⟨a horse ~*s* a mare⟩ **b :** to sit on and incubate (eggs) **:** BROOD **11 :** to bring upon or earn for (a person) a large or excessive amount of something usu. immaterial ⟨~*ed* with shame at his failure⟩ ⟨~*s* himself with glory in the battle⟩ **12 a :** to play a higher-ranking card immediately after or on (a previously played card) ⟨North ~*ed* West's jack with the queen⟩ **b :** to be higher in rank than (the previously played card) ⟨the king from the dummy ~*ed* the queen led by East⟩ **13 a :** to have width or scope enough to include or embrace ⟨an examination ~*ing* the year's work⟩ ⟨we must remember that no laws can be provided to ~ every contingency —F.D.Roosevelt⟩ **b :** to comprise, include, or embrace in an effective scope of treatment or operation ⟨policy clauses ~*ing* the situation⟩ ⟨plans ~*ing* unexpected enemy attacks⟩ **14 :** to subsume in an overall class, significance, or meaning ⟨people are so intensely for anything ~*ed* by the word *democratic* —M.R.Cohen⟩ ⟨a formula which should ~ everything I wished to include —T.S.Eliot⟩ **15 :** to treat or deal with; *often* **:** DISCUSS ⟨material ~*ed* in the first chapter⟩ ⟨a talk ~*ing* an important question⟩ **16 a :** to serve often with scope or inclusiveness in an indicated or expected way ⟨bus lines ~*ing* the area⟩ **:** operate in **b :** to have (a locality or a group of persons) as one's territory or field of activity (as in selling the merchandise or promoting the interests of a company or in rendering social or business service) ⟨one salesman ~*s* the whole state⟩ **17 a :** to pass over at an indicated speed **:** journey through while executing one's mission **:** TRAVEL, TRAVERSE ⟨~*ing* 10 miles that day⟩ ⟨~*ing* the distance to the city in two hours⟩ ⟨prospectors who ~*ed* this range⟩ **b :** to be found over or in **:** INHABIT ⟨tribes that ~ these areas⟩ **c :** to travel to or through as a sightseer **:** visit as a sightseer ⟨~*ing* three states in two days⟩ ⟨the trip ~*ed* the museum that afternoon⟩ **18 :** to be adequate to defray or compensate **:** defray the cost of **:** pay for **:** BALANCE ⟨a reserve fund to ~ unexpected expenses⟩ ⟨a special grant to ~ the research program⟩ **19 :** to place one's money or stake upon or in equal jeopardy with (the money or stake of one's opponent) in a bet **:** answer to (a similar offer or challenge) **:** accept an offered bet by (a person) **20 :** to extend a treatment over **:** range in treatment through or over ⟨a series of medical examinations ~*ing* three weeks⟩ ⟨a novel ~*ing* three generations⟩ **21 :** to buy securities or commodities for delivery against (an earlier short sale) ⟨~*ing* his shorts⟩ ⟨~ his sales⟩ **22 :** to report news about **:** investigate, watch, and check on for newsworthy material **:** be responsible for information about **:** take news pictures of ⟨reporters and radio commentators ~*ing* the campaign⟩ **23 :** to extend over (an indicated area) ⟨a park ~*ing* 50 acres⟩ ~ *vi* **1 a** *obs* **:** to spread a table for a meal **b :** to put one's hat back on after having stood bareheaded **2 :** to spread over a surface ⟨this paint ~*s* well⟩ **3 :** to buy stocks or commodities for delivery on a date fixed by a previously contracted sale ⟨~*ing* at a loss⟩ **4 a :** to guard a player, play, or position (as in basketball) **b :** to play a higher-ranking card on a lower-ranking one **5** *of a bird or mammal* **:** to become covered with feathers or hair (as after a molt) **6 a :** to conceal something illicit, blameworthy, or embarrassing from notice **:** prevent one from being censured for error, laxity, or omission — usu. used with *up* ⟨~ up for a careless friend⟩ **b :** to act as a substitute or replacement to prevent loss or disaster during an absence ⟨a fire company ~*ing* for another answering a call⟩ ⟨a stand-in ~*ing* for an injured star⟩ **c :** to assume a defensive position (as in boxing) that protects the face and midriff — often used with *up* ⟨the challenger ~*ed* up⟩ — **cover one's tracks** *or* **cover up one's tracks :** to conceal traces to elude pursuit **:** hide or mask evidences of usu. blameworthy or illicit activity ⟨he was guilty but he *covered his tracks* too well to be convicted⟩ — **cover the ground** *or* **cover ground 1 :** to traverse a course or distance with satisfying speed ⟨that new outfielder can really *cover the ground*⟩ ⟨a bulldozer that *covers the ground* well⟩ **2 :** to embrace or treat a subject or to perform or execute an assignment esp. with thoroughness and efficiency ⟨the lecturer *covered the ground* well⟩ ⟨the book *covers* a lot of *ground*⟩

²cover \" \ *n* -S *often attrib* [ME, fr. *coveren* to cover] **1 :** something that protects, shelters, or guards ⟨run for ~ when the fight starts⟩: as **a** (1) **:** a place of natural shelter for an animal or bird esp. when sought as game ⟨foxes in a ~⟩ (2) **:** the factors that provide natural shelter and protection for wild animals (as suitable arrangements of vegetation, denning sites, or rock formations) (3) **:** plants and their residues covering the ground and retarding runoff and erosion of soil **b** (1) **:** a position or situation affording protection from enemy fire ⟨as the gunners ducked behind ~ —C.S.Forester⟩ ⟨the platoon sergeant crawls and slithers from ~ to ~ —Burtt Evans⟩ ⟨~ and concealment⟩ (2) **:** the protection offered by aircraft in tactical support of a military operation ⟨landing on the beach under heavy air ~⟩ **c** (1) **:** a deposit or sum of money sufficient to secure against loss or to meet an obligation (2) **:** insurance coverage **d** (1) **:** COVER POINT (2) **covers** *pl* **:** cover point and extra cover point ⟨a drive through the ~*s*⟩ **2 :** something that is placed over or about another thing **:** something that covers: **a :** LID, TOP ⟨a box ~⟩ **b** (1) **:** a binding or case for a book or the comparable outer part of a pamphlet or magazine; *also* **:** either rectangular portion of this cover extending from the backbone and forming the front or the back ⟨front ~⟩ (2) **:** JACKET 3f (1) **c :** an overlay or outer layer esp. for protection ⟨a mattress ~⟩ **d** (1) [trans. of F *couvert*] **:** a tablecloth and the other table fittings; *esp* **:** the table fittings for use of one person at a meal ⟨~*s* were laid for 50 guests⟩ (2) **:** COVER CHARGE **e :** COPULATION **:** an act of covering — usu. used of animals (as horses) **f :** ROOF ⟨exhibits under ~⟩ **g** (1) **:** a cloth used on a bed for warmth or for decoration (as a quilt, blanket, bedspread, or coverlet) (2) **:** bedclothes for covering a person in bed — usu. used in pl. **h** *Brit* **:** an automobile tire tread **i :** something that covers the ground: (1) **:** VEGETATION ⟨a thick forest ~ in these areas⟩ (2) **:** snow esp. for skiing ⟨the lodge area had a good ~⟩ **j :** a large shallow salt pan with a movable roof used for making salt from brine by evaporation in the sun **k :** COVER STONE **l :** the overburden or cap rock above a deposit (as of ore, oil, or coal) **m :** full obscuration of the sky by clouds **:** the extent to which clouds obscure the sky ⟨clear weather with only ¹⁄₁₀ ~⟩ **3 :** something that conceals or obscures **:** CONCEALMENT: as **a :** the total factors making for hiding or obscuring ⟨a crime committed under ~ of darkness⟩ **b :** a masking device or pretext **:** SCREEN, GUISE ⟨the club was a ~ for a subversive group⟩ ⟨we may admit that our conventional morality often serves as a ~ for hypocrisy and selfishness —Lucius Garvin⟩ ⟨under ~ of altruism he took greedy advantage of the wartime misfortunes —Ann F. Wolfe⟩ ⟨a spy with a ~ name⟩ **c** (1) **:** an envelope or wrapper that contains or has contained mail matter (2) **:** an envelope, wrapper, letter sheet, or postal card bearing stamp and postmark or other markings showing that it has passed through the mails — see FLOWN COVER, STAMPLESS **4 a :** the uniform appearance of plain closely woven goods with threads evenly spaced **b :** the nap on fabric **5 :** the whole width of a horseshoe ⟨a shoe with a ~ of 6 inches⟩ — **from cover to cover** *of a book* **:** from the front cover through to the back cover **:** COMPLETELY, THOROUGHLY ⟨read *from cover to cover*⟩ — **off cover** *of a stamp* **:** having been removed from the cover (sense 3c(2)) — **on cover** *of a stamp* **:** remaining on the cover (sense 3c(2)) — **under cover 1 :** in an envelope or wrapper **2 :** enclosed within a missive addressed to a person other than the intended recipient **3 :** under concealment **:** in secret

cover address *n* **:** an address to which mail can be sent for forwarding to the real addressee and which is used to conceal the name or address of the addressee or in the case of illicit correspondence to avoid arousing the suspicion of the postal authorities

cov·er·age \ˈkəv(ə)rij, -rēj\ *n* -S [¹*cover* + *-age*] **1 :** the act or fact of including or treating : a thing that covers : COVER: as **a** : INSURANCE : protection by insurance policy : inclusion within the scope of a protective or beneficial plan ⟨~ against liability claims⟩ ⟨~ for librarians in the teachers' retirement system⟩ **b** : the amount (as of gold) available to meet liabilities ⟨a 40 percent gold ~ of outstanding bank notes⟩ **c** : treatment to publicize or make known ⟨the ~ of the subject in his botany text⟩: (1) : news reporting and comment ⟨~ of the state department involves certain technical problems⟩ (2) : amount of news reporting ⟨the revolution was given scant ~ abroad⟩ ⟨the dictator demanded better ~ for his domestic program⟩ **d** : provision of cover by aircraft **e** : vegetation covering the ground : GROUND COVER **2** : whatever is covered : scope or extent of covering : aggregate of items covered: as **a** : the area that may be covered with a gallon of paint, varnish, or other surface cover — distinguished from *hiding power* **b** : extent of covering by plant sprays **c** : the aggregate of risks covered by the terms of a contract of insurance ⟨a policy with extensive ~⟩ **d** (1) : the number of persons or the population area reached or served by a communication or a medium of communication : percentage of potential customers covered ⟨an advertisement with wide ~⟩ ⟨a radio station with more power and greater ~⟩ (2) : the circulation of a newspaper or periodical in a given area or throughout a class of people **e** : the area of the subject that is or can be included clearly in a photographic image **f** : percentage of ground area occupied by buildings

cover·all \ˈ==,=\ *n* -S [¹*cover* + *all*] : an outer garment worn to protect other garments; *esp* : a one-piece combination of overalls and shirt — usu. used in pl.

cover-all \"\ *adj* [¹*cover* + *all*] : COMPREHENSIVE ⟨*cover-all* provisions⟩

coveralls

cover charge *n* : a charge made by a restaurant or nightclub for service or entertainment in addition to the charge for food and drink ⟨a 2-dollar *cover charge* per person⟩

cov·er·chief \ˈkəvə(r)-; *last syll like that of* HANDKERCHIEF\ *n* [ME *coverchief, keverchief* — more at KERCHIEF] : a covering for the head; *also* : HANDKERCHIEF

cover crop *n* : a crop (as rye or clover) planted in orchards or in otherwise bare fields to prevent soil erosion and to help soil improvement

covered *adj* [ME, having a cover, fr. past part. of *coveren* to cover] **1** : with contracted throat : not open : CLOSED, THIN — used esp. of a tone in the upper register **2** : included in the group with respect to which a particular contract or agreement is in force ⟨domestic service is now a ~ job under the social-security law⟩

covered bridge *n* : a bridge that has its roadway protected by a roof and enclosing sides

covered dish *n* : CASSEROLE

covered-dish supper *n* : a community meal to which each guest brings one dish, all dishes being shared by all

covered fifth *n* : HIDDEN FIFTH

covered octave *n* : HIDDEN OCTAVE

covered smut *n* : a smut disease of grains in which the spore masses are covered or held together for some time by the persistent grain membrane and glumes — compare LOOSE SMUT

covered wagon *n* **1** : a broad-wheeled wagon with a canvas top supported by bows ⟨the *covered wagon* of the pioneers⟩ — see ²CONESTOGA, PRAIRIE SCHOONER **2** *Brit* : BOXCAR

covered way *n* : a corridor running along the top of a counterscarp and protected by an embankment whose outer slope forms the glacis

cov·er·er \ˈkəvərə(r)\ *n* -S [ME, fr. *coveren* to cover + *-er, -ere* -er] : a factory workman who puts a cover or wrapping on manufactured articles

cover girl *n* : a usu. beautiful girl whose picture appears on a magazine cover

cover glass *n* **1** : a piece of very thin glass used to cover microscopic preparations mounted on glass slides **2** : a sheet of plain glass used to protect the surface of a transparency to which it is bound

cover in *vt* **1** : to finish the covering over of; *esp* : complete a roof over **2** : to cover into

¹**cov·er·ing** \ˈkəv(ə)riŋ, -rēŋ\ *n* -S [ME *coveringe*, fr. *coveren* to cover + *-inge, -ing* -ing (n. suffix)] : something that covers or conceals: as **a** : COVER 2g **b** : purchases by short sellers in security and commodity markets to close out their commitments

²**covering** \"\ *adj* [fr. pres. part. of *cover*] : that covers: as **a** : protecting or supporting a position or a force ⟨~ fire for the platoon that was moving up⟩ **b** : containing explanation, additional information, and often recommendation of an accompanying communication ⟨a ~ letter⟩ ⟨a ~ note⟩

covering disease *n* : DOURINE

covering power *n* : the extent of the field over which a photographic lens can give a sharp image often expressed as an angle

cover into *vt* **1** : to transfer to : enter into the receipt records of : assign to the control of ⟨funds *covered into* the treasury by the bill⟩ **2** : to cause to be included or embraced within or under a particular system or category ⟨the power to *cover into* the civil service any minor government office⟩

cov·er·less \ˈkəvə(r)ləs\ *adj* : not having a cover

cov·er·let \ˈkəvə(r)lət *also* -,le|t *or* -,li|t; *usu* |d·+V\ *n* -S [ME, by folk etymology (influence of ME *-let*) fr. *coverlite*, fr. AF *coverelyth*, fr. *covere-* (fr. OF *covrir* to cover) + *lyth, lit* bed, fr. L *lectus* — more at COVER, LIE] **1** : a bedspread sometimes quilted or of heavy material **2** *archaic* : COVER

cov·er·lid \-,lid, -,ləd\ *n* -S [ME, by folk etymology (influence of ME *lid*) fr. *coverlite* coverlet] *dial* : BEDSPREAD

cover memory *n* : SCREEN MEMORY

cover note *n, Brit* : a preliminary memorandum or binder for insurance

cover paper *n* : a strong durable printable paper of a type suitable for booklet or magazine covers

cover plate *n* **1** : a cover, hood, or head used to close in or cover over the end or top of a receptacle, chamber, or section of a structure **2** : a plate riveted to the flange of a steel beam, girder, or column to increase its strength — called also *flange plate*

cover point *n* [¹*cover* + *point*] **1 a** : a cricket fielding position between point and mid off **b** : a player in this position **2 a** : a lacrosse position between point and first defense **b** : a player in this position

covers *pres 3d sing of* COVER, *pl of* COVER

cover-shame \ˈ==,=\ *n* [¹*cover* + *shame*] **1** *obs* : a device for masking something shameful ⟨put on holy garments for a *cover-shame* of lewdness —John Dryden⟩ **2** [so called fr. its use to induce abortion] : SAVIN

cover shot *n* : a wide-angle photographic shot including a whole scene

cover slip *n* : COVER GLASS 1

coverslut \ˈ==,=\ *n* [¹*cover* + *slut*] : an outer garment worn to conceal untidy clothes

cover spray *n* : a pesticidal spray applied esp. to fruit trees at intervals after the petals fall in order to provide a protective coverage for the foliage

cover stone *n* : the coarse mineral aggregate strewn over the surface of a bituminous bound or treated pavement

cover story *n* : a story accompanying a magazine-cover illustration

cover symbol *n* : a symbol standing for two or more related phonemes (as *V* or *C* in *VCV*, meaning vowel + consonant + vowel)

¹**cov·ert** \ˈkəvə(r)|t, ˈkōvə(r)|t, -ō,vər|t, -ō,vəˈ|t, -ō,vəi|t, *usu* |d·+V\ *adj* [ME, fr. OF (past part. of *covrir* to cover), fr. L *coopertus*, past part. of *cooperire* to cover — more at COVER] **1 a** : marked by or as if by concealment : kept private : not open, overt, or avowed : HIDDEN, VEILED ⟨ostensibly in sympathy but with ~ malice⟩ **b** : of hidden or doubtful meaning ⟨the ~ wording of the message⟩ **c** : performed or expressed surreptitiously, with reluctance to admit or avow, or with attempt at concealment ⟨listening to the long story with ~ yawns⟩ ⟨at first in ~ conversation and now more openly in published works —W.H.Camp⟩ **2** *obs* : SECRETIVE, DECEITFUL **3** : covered over, sheltered, and secluded esp. in sylvan surroundings ⟨starting from some ~ place, saluted the chance comer on the road —William Wordsworth⟩ **4** *of a woman* : married and under cover, authority, or protection of the husband — see FEME COVERT **5 a** : subconsciously motivated : implicit rather than explicit : UNDERLYING ⟨~ behavior⟩ ⟨~ needs⟩ **b** : not sanctioned or allowed open social expression ⟨~ cultural configurations and values⟩ **syn** see SECRET

²**cov·ert** \ˈkəvə(r)|t, ˈkōvə(r)|t, *usu* |d·+V; *Brit often* ˈkəvə(r\ *n* -S [ME, fr. MF, fr. *covert*, adj.] **1 a** : hiding place : SHELTER, REFUGE ⟨soldiers firing from ~*s*⟩ **b** : a coppice affording cover for game : a hiding place in such a coppice ⟨the king shot a stag as it broke from ~ —S.P.B.Mais⟩ **c** : a masking or concealing device ⟨deliberation as a ~ for their inactivity⟩ **2** *archaic* : something that covers : COVERING ⟨the thick ~ on a walnut⟩ ⟨a bed without ~*s*⟩ **3** : a feather covering the bases of the quills of the wings and tail of a bird — called also *tectrix*; see BIRD illustration **4** *or* **covert cloth** : a firm durable twilled sometimes waterproofed coating and suiting usu. made of mixed-color yarns that give a flecked effect; *also* : a similar cotton or rayon fabric for sportswear

¹**covert-baron** \ˈ=(,)=ˈ==\ *adj* [AF *couverte baroun*, alter. of *coverte de baron*, lit., covered by a husband] : ¹COVERT 4

²**covert-baron** \"\ *n, pl* **coverts-baron** : the status of one married, usu. a woman

covert brown *n* [²*covert* + *brown*] : a variable color averaging a grayish olive that is redder and duller than average olive drab and redder and lighter than bronzesheen

cover text *n* : a text in clear language within which a ciphertext is concealed (as by a grille)

covert gray *n* [²*covert* + *gray*] : a variable color averaging a light olive gray that is deeper and slightly greener than piping rock and paler and slightly greener than slate tan

cover title *n* : the title lettered on the cover (as of a book, magazine, or catalog)

co·vert·ly *adv* [ME, fr. ¹*covert* + *-ly*] **1** : in a covert manner ⟨glancing ~ over his shoulder⟩ **2** : with suggestive implication rather than direct expression

co·vert·ness *n* -ES : the quality or state of being covert

covert tan *n* [²*covert* + *tan*] : a light grayish olive color that is redder and stronger than Quaker gray, lighter and slightly redder and less strong than hemp, and redder, lighter, and stronger than twine

cov·er·ture \ˈkəvər,chů(ə)r, -,chər\ *n* -S [ME, fr. OF, fr. *covert* (past part. of *covrir* to cover) + *-ure*] **1 a** : a decorative or protective covering **b** : SHELTER, PROTECTION, DISGUISE **2** : the legal status of a woman during marriage and under the cover, authority, and protection of her husband

cover type *n* : the plant growth characteristic of an area

cover-up \ˈ==,=\ *n* -S [fr. *cover up*, v.] : a device or stratagem for masking, concealing, or preventing investigation, incrimination, or discovery ⟨a *cover-up* for incompetence and wishful thinking —Herbert Elliston⟩ ⟨using a contrived accident as a *cover-up* for murder⟩

coves *pl of* COVE, *pres 3d sing of* COVE

cov·et \ˈkəvət, *usu* ·əd·+V\ *vb* -ED/-ING/-S [ME *coveiten*, fr. OF *coveitier*, fr. *coveitié* covetousness, desire, fr. (assumed) VL *cupidietat-, cupidietas*, alter. of L *cupiditat-, cupiditas*, fr. *cupidus* desirous (fr. *cupere* to desire) + *-itat-, -itas* -ity; akin to MHG *verwepfen* to become moldy, Icel *hvap* dropsical flesh, Goth *afhwapjan* to choke, extinguish, L *vapor* steam, vapor, Gk *kapnos* smoke, Skt *kupyati* he swells with rage, is angry; basic meaning: smoking, boiling] *vt* **1** : to wish for earnestly : crave possession or enjoyment of : long for ⟨winning ~*ed* honors⟩ ⟨her invitations came to be ~*ed* by people who were desirous of moving in good society —G.B.Shaw⟩ **2** : to desire (another's possession or attribute) inordinately or culpably ⟨neither shalt thou ~ thy neighbor's house, his field, or his manservant —Deut 5:21 (AV)⟩ ⟨this region originally belonged to the Sioux but was ~*ed* for its rich resources by the Chippewa —*Amer. Guide Series: Minn.*⟩ ~ *vi* : to feel or cherish inordinate desire or craving for another's possession or attributes ⟨you should be content with what you have . . . it is a sin to ~ —Edna S. V. Millay⟩ — formerly used with *for* or *after* ⟨the wealth that many had ~*ed* after was willed to various charities⟩ **syn** see DESIRE

cov·et·able \ˈkəvəd·əbəl\ *adj* [ME *covaytabill*, modif. (influenced by ME *coveiten* to covet) of MF *covoitable*, fr. OF *coveitable*, fr. *coveitier* to covet + *-able*] : DESIRABLE

cov·et·ing·ly *adv* : in a coveting manner

covetise *n* -S [ME *coveitise*, fr. OF, alter. (influenced by *-ise* as in *marcheandise* merchandise) of *coveitié*] *obs* : inordinate desire : COVETOUSNESS

cov·e·tive·ness \ˈkəvəd·ivnəs\ *n* -ES [*covet* + *-ive* + *-ness*] : an inclination or desire to acquire and possess esp. as indicated phrenologically

cov·e·tous \ˈkəvəd·əs, -ətəs, *Brit also* ÷ -vəchəs\ *adj* [ME *coveitous*, fr. OF, fr. *coveitié* + *-ous*] : given to, marked by, or arising from coveting: **a** : marked by craving and deep desire to own wealth or possessions ⟨it's on your account that he's been so particular about money of late, he was never ~ before —G.B.Shaw⟩ **b** : having a craving for possession — used with *of*, formerly with *for* ⟨a man ~ of honors⟩ **c** : marked by inordinate, culpable, or envious desire for another's possessions ⟨throwing ~ eyes out of their forests on the fields and vineyards of their neighbors —J.A.Froude⟩

syn GREEDY, ACQUISITIVE, GRASPING, AVARICIOUS: COVETOUS stresses strength of desire, usu. for what is rightfully another's and generally with envy ⟨France, jealous as it was of his greatness and *covetous* of his Gascon possessions —J.R.Green⟩ ⟨first settlers brought fine hunting dogs . . . of which the Indians were so *covetous* that a day was set each year when settlers traded dogs —*Amer. Guide Series: Va.*⟩ GREEDY stresses lack of restraint ⟨a child *greedy* for candy⟩ ⟨with eyes by the gold lust blinded, with the *greedy* griping hand —William Morris⟩ ⟨he loved learning; he was *greedy* of all writings and sciences —G.G.Coulton⟩ ACQUISITIVE implies not only eagerness to possess but aptitude for acquiring and retaining ⟨one of those strenuous, *acquisitive* women —E.A.Weeks⟩ ⟨our present *acquisitive* society, in which our craving for material things seems never to be satisfied —R.E.Baber⟩ GRASPING always implies an unashamed selfishness in acquiring, usu. by any quick means ⟨a *grasping* old miser⟩ ⟨*grasping* commercialism —George Nobbe⟩ AVARICIOUS implies eagerness and the capacity for indiscriminate acquisition befitting a grasping person and strongly suggests stinginess ⟨an *avaricious* black-market profiteer⟩ ⟨dust and ashes, and fiery lava are sufficient to satisfy the most *avaricious* thrill seeker —E.B. Branson & W.A.Tarr⟩ ⟨the *avaricious* old man lived in squalor, keeping his money hidden in odd places around his house⟩

cov·e·tous·ly *adv* [ME *coveitously*, fr. *coveitous* + *-ly*] : in a covetous manner

cov·e·tous·ness *n* -ES [ME *coveitousnesse*, fr. *coveitous* + *-nesse* -ness] : the state of being covetous : AVARICE

¹**cov·ey** \ˈkəvē, -vi\ *n* -S [ME, fr. MF *couvee, covee*, fr. OF *covee*, fr. fem. of *covée*, past part. of *cover* to sit on (as a female bird on eggs), brood over, fr. L *cubare* to lie down — more at HIP] **1** : a brood of birds : a mature bird or pair of birds with a brood of young : a small flock or number of birds of the same kind — used typically of partridges and certain related birds; compare BEVY **2 a** : COMPANY, CROWD, BAND, CREW ⟨a ~ of friends —John Buchan⟩ ⟨a ~ of schoolgirls —H.V.Morton⟩ ⟨a ~ of suspicious nuns —Earle Birney⟩ **b** : a number of things of the same kind : GROUP ⟨barricades and a ~ of tanks —Virginia A. Oakes⟩ ⟨a ~ of queries answered for about-to-be brides —*Mademoiselle*⟩ ⟨a ~ of conferences —*Economist*⟩

²**cov·ey** \ˈkōvi\ *n* -S [³*cove* + *-y*] *slang Brit* : a young fellow

cov·in *also* **cov·ine** \ˈkəvən, ˈkōv-\ *n* -S [ME *covin, covine*, fr. MF *covin* band, affair, *covine* affair, fr. ML *convenium* agreement, arrangement, fr. L *convenire* to agree — more at CONVENE] **1** *archaic* : CREW, BAND, CONFEDERACY **2 a** : collusive agreement between two or more persons to the detriment of a third : CONSPIRACY **b** : *archaic* : FRAUD, TRICKERY **3** : COVEN

coving *n* -S [³*cove* (molding) + *-ing*] : COVE; *specif* : the molding or members that form a cove

cov·i·nous \ˈkəvənəs, ˈkōv-\ *adj* [*covin* + *-ous*] : marked by covin : COLLUSIVE, FRAUDULENT — **cov·i·nous·ly** *adv*

covin-tree \ˈ==,=\ *n* [*covin* + *tree*] : a tree in front of a Scottish mansion beneath which a laird or owner formerly met his visitors or his retainers

¹**cow** \ˈkau̇\ *n, pl* **cows** *or archaic* **kine** \ˈkīn\ [ME *cou* (pl.

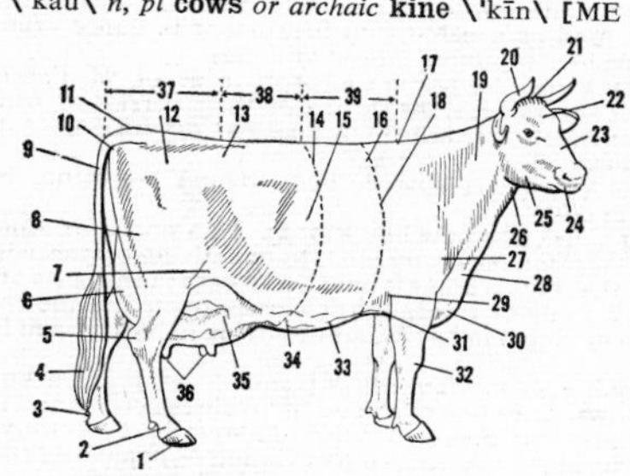

cow: *1* hoof, *2* pastern, *3* dewclaw, *4* switch, *5* hock, *6* rear udder, *7* flank, *8* thigh, *9* tail, *10* pinbone, *11* tail head, *12* thurl, *13* hip, *14* barrel, *15* ribs, *16* crops, *17* withers, *18* heart girth, *19* neck, *20* horn, *21* poll, *22* forehead, *23* bridge of nose, *24* muzzle, *25* jaw, *26* throat, *27* point of shoulder, *28* dewlap, *29* point of elbow, *30* brisket, *31* chest floor, *32* knee, *33* milk well, *34* milk vein, *35* fore udder, *36* teats, *37* rump, *38* loin, *39* chine

ky, kyn), fr. OE *cū* (pl. *cȳ, cȳe*, gen. *cūna, cȳna*); akin to OHG *kuo* cow, ON *kȳr*, L *bos* ox, cow, Gk *bous* head of cattle, cow, Skt *go* bull, cow] **1 a** : the mature female of wild or domestic cattle of the genus *Bos* or of any of the various animals the male of which is called *bull* (as the moose, certain seals, or the alligator) — see HEIFER **b** : a domestic bovine animal regardless of its sex or age ⟨bring home the ~*s*⟩ **2** : a person clumsy, obese, coarse, or otherwise unpleasant; *sometimes* : PROSTITUTE **3** *slang Austral* : a troublesome or unpleasant person or thing ⟨shot by some silly ~ with a gun⟩ — compare FAIR COW **4** *slang* : MILK

²**cow** \"\ *n* -S [origin unknown] *Scot* : GOBLIN, BUGBEAR

³**cow** \"\ *vt* -ED/-ING/-S [alter. of ³*coll*] **1** *chiefly Scot* : to cut short : POLL, CROP **2** *Scot* : OVERTOP, EXCEED

⁴**cow** \"\ *n* -S [origin unknown] **1** *chiefly Scot* : a bare twig of heather or broom **2** *chiefly Scot* : a brush of twigs : BESOM

⁵**cow** \"\ *vt* -ED/-ING/-S [prob. of Scand origin; akin to Dan *kue* to subdue, Sw & Norw *kuva*, obs. Sw & Norw *kuv* hump] : DAUNT, AWE : intimidate with threats, show of strength, or impressiveness : dispirit into inactivity or submission ⟨he flung them back, commanded them, ~*ed* them with his hard, intelligent eyes, like a tamer among beasts —Arthur Morrison⟩ ⟨frightfulness inaugurated by the military chiefs to ~ the inhabitants —A.D.H.Smith⟩ **syn** see INTIMIDATE

⁶**cow** \"\ *n* -S *Scot* : FRIGHT, SCARE, ALARM

⁷**cow** \"\ *n* -S [alter. of ¹*cowl* (chimney pot)] *dial Eng* : a chimney cowl

cow·age *also* **cow·hage** *or* **cou·hage** \ˈkau̇ij\ *n* -S [Hindi *kavāc, kāvāc*, prob. fr. Skt *kapikacchu*, fr. *kapi* monkey (of Hamitic origin; akin to Egypt *gif*, an eastern African ape) + *kacchu* itch, of Dravidian origin; akin to Kanarese *kajji* itch] **1** : a tropical woody vine (*Mucuna pruritum*) having crooked pods covered with barbed brittle hairs that cause severe itching **2** : the hairs of the cowage mixed with honey or other vehicle used as a vermifuge **3** : TRUMPET CREEPER

cow·an \ˈkau̇ən\ *n* -S [Sc, fr. *cowan* unskilled worker at masonry, of unknown origin] : one who is not a Freemason; *esp* : one who would pretend to Freemasonry or intrude upon its secrets

cow·an·young \ˈkau̇ən,yəŋ\ *n* -S [prob. native name in Australia] : a horse mackerel (*Trachurus novaezelandiae*) of Australia and New Zealand often canned for food

¹**cow·ard** \ˈkau̇(ə)rd, |əd\ *n* -S [ME *coward, cuard*, fr. OF *coart, cuart*, adj & n., fr. *coe, coue* tail (fr. L *cauda*) + *-art* -ard; fr. the idea of a coward retreating to the tail end of an army, or fr. the idea of a frightened animal with its tail between its legs] : one who shows ignoble fear : a basely timid, easily frightened, and easily daunted person ⟨a ~, irresolute, impulsive in any crisis —Walter de la Mare⟩ ⟨is an arrant ~ and shows the white feather at the slightest display of pluck in his antagonist —John Burroughs⟩

²**coward** \"\ *adj* [ME *coward, cuard*, fr. OF *coart, cuart*, adj. & n.] **1 a** : having or arising from a coward's nature : TIMID, FAINTHEARTED, COWARDLY ⟨that craven ~ knight —Edmund Spenser⟩ ⟨neither altogether ~ nor brave —John Reed⟩ **b** : of or characteristic of a coward or cowardice ⟨~ cries⟩ ⟨~ deceit⟩ **2** *heraldry* : borne in the escutcheon with his tail doubled between his legs ⟨a lion ~⟩ **syn** see COWARDLY

³**coward** *vt* -ED/-ING/-S [ME *cowarden*, fr. ¹*coward*] *obs* : to make timorous : FRIGHTEN : cause to show cowardice

cow·ard·ice \-dəs *sometimes* -,dīs\ *n* -S [ME *cowardise*, fr. OF *coardise, cuardise*, fr. *coart, cuart* coward + *-ise* -ice] : the quality of a coward : ignoble timidity : fainthearted lack of courage; *also* : lack of resolution in the face of hostile sentiments of others ⟨there was no mean between foolhardiness and ~ —G.L.Dickinson⟩ ⟨to abandon that logic was to abandon clearness of mind: it was mental ~ —F.M.Ford⟩

cow·ard·li·ness \-dlēnəs, -lin-\ *n* -ES : the quality or state of being cowardly

¹**cow·ard·ly** \-dlē, -li\ *adv* [ME, fr. ²*coward* + *-ly*] : in a cowardly manner

²**cowardly** \"\ *adj* [¹*coward* + *-ly*] : like or befitting a coward : showing a coward's nature : marked by or arising from utter lack of courage : ignobly timid and faint-hearted ⟨~ dogs, ye will not aid me then —P.B.Shelley⟩ ⟨if you want to make charges, make them openly. I will not listen to ~ hints —Sinclair Lewis⟩

syn COWARD, PUSILLANIMOUS, POLTROON, CRAVEN, DASTARDLY, RECREANT: COWARDLY, the most general term of this group, and COWARD indicate weak and ignoble timidity ⟨a timid and *cowardly* man, who, according to one account, now surrendered Lothian to King Malcolm for fear that he might avenge the victories won over him by his brother —E.A.Freeman⟩ ⟨you are an incompetent *cowardly* rascal, sir! damn me if you're not! are you afraid of a crowd of bloody savages whilst you have arms in your hands —C.B.Nordhoff & J.M.Hall⟩ ⟨you laughed in my face as you are trying to laugh now, only your *coward* heart cannot keep your lips from twitching —A. Conan Doyle⟩ PUSILLANIMOUS connotes abjectness and contemptibility ⟨I lived in a continual indefinite pining fear; tremulous, *pusillanimous*, apprehensive of I knew not what —Thomas Carlyle⟩ POLTROON, uncommon as an adjective, suggests complete cowardice ⟨we had to make a show of impotence, which gave them to understand that the Arabs were too *poltroon* to cut the line near Maan and keep it cut —T.E.Lawrence⟩ CRAVEN implies extreme defeatism and complete lack of resistance ⟨your prayers will do more for me . . . than the swords of the *craven* sycophants would have done had they remained true —Alfred Tennyson⟩ ⟨a man whom a *craven* fear had made insensible to shame —T.B.Macaulay⟩ DASTARDLY is used in references to situations and personalities blending utter cowardice with the treacherous or outrageous ⟨since the unprovoked and *dastardly* attack by Japan on Sunday, December 7th —F.D.Roosevelt⟩ ⟨they'll spare the women; but my man tells me they have taken an oath to give no quarter to the men —the *dastardly* cowards —W.M.Thackeray⟩ RECREANT, currently more common in the meaning of *apostate*, implies abject lack of resistance ⟨when I was bewildered and *recreant* and was inclined to go back upon all my fiercest convictions —Victoria Sackville-West⟩

cow·ard·ness *n* -ES [ME *cowardnesse*, fr. *coward* + *-nesse* -ness] : the quality or state of being coward : COWARDICE

cowbane \ˈ=,=\ *n* [¹*cow* + *bane*] : any of several poisonous plants of the family Umbelliferae: as **a** (1) : the European water hemlock (2) : an American water hemlock; *esp* : SPOTTED COWBANE **b** : a hog fennel (*Oxypolis rigidior*) that is widespread in wet lowlands in the eastern and central U.S.

cow bean *n* : COWPEA

cow beet *n* : MANGEL-WURZEL

cowbell \ˈ=,=\ *n* **1 a** : a bell hung about the neck of a cow to make a sound by which it can be located **b** : a bell without a clapper used as a percussion instrument in dance orchestras **2** : a bladder campion (*Silene latifolia*)

cowberry \'⸗- — *see* BERRY\ *n* [prob. trans. of NL *Vaccinium*] : any of several pasture shrubs or their berries or fruits: as **a** : MOUNTAIN CRANBERRY **b** : MARSH CINQUEFOIL **c** : PARTRIDGEBERRY 1

cowbind \'⸗,⸗\ *n* [1*cow* + *bind* (bine)] : a white bryony (*Bryonia alba*)

cowbird \'⸗,⸗\ *also* **cow blackbird** *n* **1** : a small No. American blackbird (*Molothrus ater*) that frequently associates with cattle and that builds no nest but lays its eggs in the nests of other birds **2** : any of several birds closely related to the cowbird and resembling it in habits but occurring in Mexico and further south

1cowboy \'⸗,⸗\ *n, often attrib* [1*cow* + *boy*] **1** : a boy that tends cows **2 a** : one of a band of loyalist guerillas and irregular cavalry that operated mostly in Westchester county, New York, during the American Revolution — compare SKINNER 2 **b** : an outlaw or gangster in the early days of the U.S. West **3 a** : one who tends and drives herds of cattle particularly in western U.S. and Canada; *typically* : a distinctively accoutered horseman tending large herds of beef cattle — called also *cowpuncher, puncher* **b** : a usu. mounted cattle ranch hand **c** (1) : a rodeo rider : a performer who gives exhibitions of roping, riding, bulldogging (2) : an actor whose usual role is that of a cowboy, a gunman, or adventurer in a western **4** : NEW BRONZE **5** : one given to display or to recklessness; *esp* : an automobile driver who violates rules of safety and law ⟨a cautious highway cyclist, though; no ~ stuff —W.L.Gresham⟩

2cowboy \"\ *vi* -ED/-ING/-S : to drive an automobile recklessly

cowboy boot *n* : a boot made with a high arch, a high Cuban heel, and usu. fancy stitching and worn esp. by American cowboys

cowboy hat *n* : a wide-brimmed hat with a large soft crown of the type worn by western ranch hands

cowboy pool *n* : pool played with a cue ball and three object balls numbered 1, 3, and 5, the object being to score exactly 90 points by caroms and by pocketing the object balls, 10 points more by caroms only, and finally a single point by pocketing the cue ball after contact with the number one ball

cowboys and indians *n, usu cap I* : a children's game involving mock pursuits, gunfights, and killings as though between cowboys and Indians

cowboy suit *n* : a child's outfit typically with colored shirt, wide belt, and chaps simulating the dress of a cowboy

cowbrute \'⸗,⸗\ *n, chiefly Midland* : a cow or steer esp. when range-bred and wild

cow calf *n* : HEIFER

cow camp *n* : a cowboy camp : a roundup headquarters

cow cane *n, Austral* : a sugarcane grown for silage

cowcatcher \'⸗,⸗⸗\ *n* **1** : PILOT 4a **2** : a brief radio and television commercial given just before a program and advertising a secondary product of the program's sponsor

cow clover *n* : ZIGZAG CLOVER

cow cockle *n* : COWHERB

cow cocky *n, chiefly Austral* : a small dairy farmer

cow college *n* **1** : a college devoted to agriculture : a university school of agriculture **2** : a freshwater or provincial college or university that lacks culture, sophistication, and tradition

cow corn *n* : POD CORN

cow cress *n* : FIELD CRESS

cow·cum·ber \'kaů,kəm(b)ə(r)\ *dial var of* CUCUMBER

cow·die \'kaůdē\ *n* -S [modif. of Maori *kawri*] : KAURI

cow·dria \'kaůdrēə\ *n, cap* [NL, fr. Edmund V. *Cowdry* *b*1888 Am. scientist + NL -*ia*] : a genus of small pleomorphic intracellular rickettsias known chiefly from ticks but including the causative organism (*C. ruminantium*) of heartwater disease of ruminants

cowed *past of* COW

co·ween \kə'wēn, kō'-\ *n* -S [of Algonquian origin; akin to Malecite *ku-wĕs* mallard, Pequot *ungowáums* old squaw duck, Narragansett *queequeekum* duck] : OLD-SQUAW

cow·er \'kaůə(r)\ *vb* **cowered**; **cowered**; **cowering** \-aů(ə)riŋ\ **cowers** [ME *couren*, of Scand origin; akin to Norw *kura* to cower, OSw *kūra* to sit still, Dan *kure* to sit or lie still; akin to MHG & MLG *kūren* to lie in wait, lurk, ON *kārr* curly hair, Gk *gyros* round, MIr *gūaire* hair, Lith *gauras* body hair, and perh. to ON *kot* small hut — more at COT] *vi* **1** *now dial Eng* : to crouch down : SQUAT **2** : to shrink away or cringe usu. in abject fear of something menacing or domineering and sometimes from cold ⟨they all ~*ed* silently in their places, seeming to know in advance that some terrible thing was about to happen —George Orwell⟩ ⟨~*ing* in their huts like so many rabbits in their burrows, listening in fear —Charles Kingsley⟩ ~ *vt, chiefly Scot* : to bend down

cowfish \'⸗,⸗\ *n* **1 a** : any of various small cetaceans (as the grampus and species of porpoises and dolphins) **b** : SIRENIAN **2** : any of various boxfishes having projections resembling horns over the eyes

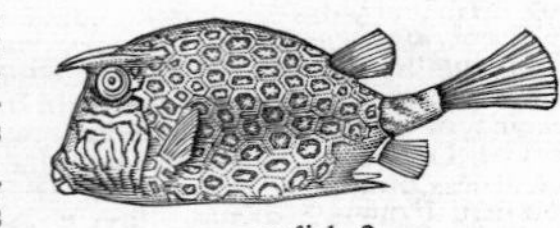
cowfish 2

cow fulani *n, pl* **cow fulani** *or* **cow fulanis** *usu cap C&F* [1*cow*] : one of a nomadic group of the Fulani people of West Africa

cowgate \'⸗,⸗\ *n* -S [back-formation fr. earlier *kynegates*, fr. *kine* (*archaic* pl. of 1*cow*) + *gates*, pl. of *gate* (way)] : a right to pasture one cow on common land ⟨a cottager having two ~*s* on the common⟩

cowgirl \'⸗,⸗\ *n* **1** : a girl who tends cows **2** : a girl or woman working, performing, or acting as a cowboy

cowgram \'⸗,⸗\ *n* -S [1*cow* + *gram* (chick-pea)] : CHICK-PEA

cowgrass \'⸗,⸗\ *n, Austral* : RED CLOVER

cowhage *var of* COWAGE

cowhand \'⸗,⸗\ *n* [1*cow* + *hand* (laborer)] : a man engaged to assist with ranch work and the care of range cattle : COWBOY

cow·heart·ed \'kaů¦härd·əd\ *adj* -ER/-EST [influenced in meaning by *coward*] : COWARDLY

cow·heel \'⸗,⸗\ *n* : the foot of a cow or ox stewed into a jelly

cow–heifer \'⸗,⸗⸗\ *n, Brit* : a young cow up to the time of attaining a full set of adult teeth

cow·herb \'⸗,⸗\ *n* : a European soapwort (*Saponaria vaccaria* or *Vaccaria pyramidata*) with pale rose-colored flowers

cowherd \'⸗,⸗\ *n* [ME *cowherde*, fr. OE *cūhyrde*, fr. *cū* cow + *hyrde* herder — more at COW, HERD] : one who tends cows

1cowhide \'⸗,⸗\ *n* [1*cow* + *hide*] **1** : the hide of a cow **2** : leather made of the hide of a cow or other adult bovine animal **3 a** : a coarse whip made of rawhide or of braided leather **b** : a shoe or boot of cowhide

2cowhide \"\ *vt* -ED/-ING/-S : to flog with a cowhide whip

cow hitch *n, naut* : a clumsy or slippery hitch

cow hock *n* : a hock of a horse or dog that turns or bends inward like that of a cow so that the shanks of the hind legs are very close

cow–hocked \'kaů¦häkt\ *adj* : having cow hocks

cow horse *n* : COW PONY

cowhouse \'⸗,⸗\ *n* : a barn for cows

cow hunt *n* : ROUNDUP 2

cow·i·chan \'kaůəchən\ *n, pl* **cowichan** *or* **cowichans** *usu cap* **1** : a Salishan people of Vancouver Island **2** : a member of the Cowichan people

cowier *comparative of* COWY

cowiest *superlative of* COWY

cowing *pres part of* COW

1cowish *var of* COUS

2cowish \'kaůish\ *adj* **1** : like a cow : BOVINE **2** *obs* : FEARFUL, COWARDLY

cow·itch \'kaůich\ *n* -ES [by folk etymology] : COWAGE

cow keeper *n* **1** : one that keeps cows **2** *obs* : one appointed by a town or village to superintend pasturing of cows and sometimes distributing milk

cow killer *n* : the wingless female of certain wasps of the family Mutillidae; *esp* : the large red and black velvet ant (*Dasymutilla occidentalis*) that has a severe sting

1cowl \'kaůl, *esp before pause or consonant* -aůəl\ *n* -S [ME *cowle*, fr. OE *cugele*, fr. LL *cuculla* monk's hood, fr. L *cucullus* hood, perh. of Celt origin; akin to OIr *cūl* hiding place; akin to Gk *keuthein* to conceal — more at HIDE] **1 a** : a usu. sleeveless garment composed of a hood attached to a gown or robe and worn as the typical garb of a monk **b** : a hood esp. of a monk **c** : the symbol of a monk or of things monastic : the condition of a monk or fact of being a monk ⟨abandoning the ~ to assume a layman's life⟩; *sometimes* : MONK **d** : a part of a garment modeled after some part of the monk's cowl; *esp* : a draped neckline on a woman's garment **2 a** *Scot* : a cap worn in the house : NIGHTCAP **b** *dial Eng* : a swelling on the head : BOIL **3** : something resembling a cowl in shape : HOOD: as **a** : a chimney covering designed to improve the draft by directing the smoke out horizontally often by use of a revolving metal hood **b** : a curved hood or a cap on a ventilator pipe to improve the draft : a covered air exhaust **c** : the top portion of the front part of an automobile body forward of the two front doors to which are attached the windshield and instrument board **d** : COWLING

C
C cowl 1b

2cowl \"\ *vt* -ED/-ING/-S **1 a** : to garb with a cowl; *specif* : to make a monk of **b** : to cover as if with a cowl ⟨peaks ~*ed* in clouds⟩ **2** : to equip or cover with a cowl ⟨an airplane engine ~*ed* in⟩

3cowl \'kōl, 'kül, 'kaů(ə)l\ *n* -S [ME *cowle, cuvel*, fr. OE *cȳfel, cūfel*, fr. ONF *cuvele* small vat, fr. LL *cupella*, dim. of L *cupa* tub, cask — more at HIVE] *now dial Eng* : a large tub or vessel; *esp* : a vessel with two handles to facilitate carrying

cowle \'kaů(ə)l\ *n* -S [Hindi *qawl*, fr. Ar *qawl* saying] *India* : a grant or engagement in writing esp. of safe-conduct or amnesty

cowled *adj, biol* : shaped like a hood : HOODED, CUCULLATE

cowled seal *n* : COUNSELLOR SEAL

cow·ley father \'kaůlē, -li *also* 'kül-\ *n, cap C&F* [fr. *Cowley*, suburb of Oxford, England] : a member of the Society of Mission Priests of St. John the Evangelist, an Anglican religious community founded at Oxford in 1865 by the Rev. R. M. Benson (1824–1915)

cowlick \'⸗,⸗\ *n* : a lock or tuft of hair growing in a different direction from the rest of the hair and usu. turned up or awry as if licked by a cow

cowlicks \'⸗,⸗\ *n pl but sing or pl in constr* : SILVER BELL

cow·like \'kaů,līk\ *adj* : resembling, suggestive of, or having the characteristics of a cow

cow lily *n* **1** : a marsh marigold (*Caltha palustris*) **2** : SPATTERDOCK

cowl·ing \'kaůliŋ\ *n* -S [1*cowl* + -*ing*] : a removable metal covering that houses the engine and sometimes also a portion of the fuselage or nacelle of an aircraft; *broadly* : a metallic cover over or around any engine

cow·litz \'kaůləts\ *n, pl* **cowlitz** *or* **cowlitzes** *usu cap* [fr. the *Cowlitz* river in southwestern Wash.] **1 a** : a Salishan people of the Cowlitz river valley in southwestern Washington **b** : a member of such people **2** : the language of the Cowlitz people

cowlstaff *as at* 3COWL + ,-\ *n* [ME *cuvelstaf*, fr. *cuvel* vessel + *staf* staff — more at COWL, STAFF] *now dial Eng* : a staff from which a vessel is suspended by its handles and carried between two persons

cow·man \'kaůmən *also* -,man\ *n, pl* **cowmen** **1** : one who tends cows **2** : a cattle owner : cattle rancher

cow–nosed ray *or* **cow–nose ray** \'⸗¦⸗-\ *n* : a large sting ray of the genus *Rhinoptera* (esp. *R. bonasus* of the eastern coast of America)

cow oak *n* [so called fr. the fact that its acorns are relished by cows] : BASKET OAK

co–worker \(')kō+\ *n* [*co-* + *worker*] : one who works with another : a fellow worker

co·worship \(')kō+\ *n* [*co-* + *worship*] : worship within two distinctive religious faiths at the same time

cow parsley *n* : WILD CHERVIL 1

cow parsnip *n* : a plant of the genus *Heracleum* (esp. the English *H. sphondylium* or the No. American *H. lanatum*)

cow pat *n* : a dropping of cow dung

cow·pea \'⸗,⸗\ *n* **1 a** : a sprawling herb (*Vigna sinensis*) found throughout the tropics of the Old World, more nearly related to the bean than to the pea, and cultivated in the southern U.S. for forage and green manure **b** : the seed of this plant used for food esp. in the southern U.S. — called also *blackeye, blackeye bean, black-eyed pea* **2** : MEADOW PEA

cowpea aphid *n* : a widely distributed shiny black aphid (*Aphis craccivora*) feeding esp. on cowpeas and other legumes

cowpea weevil *n* : a small nearly cosmopolitan weevil (*Callosobruchus maculatus*) having larvae that eat the interior of cowpeas, common peas, and beans

cow pen *n* : a pen for cows; *specif* : the enclosed area adjoining or surrounding a cow shed or cow barn

cow·pen \'⸗,⸗\ *vt* : to pen cows upon (ground) for fertilization

cow·per·i·tis \,kaůpə'rīd·əs, ,küp-, -ītəs\ *n* -ES [NL, fr. William *Cowper* + NL -*itis*] : inflammation of Cowper's glands

cow·per's gland \'kaůpə(r)z-, 'küp-\ *n, usu cap C* [after William *Cowper* †1709 Eng. surgeon, its discoverer] : either of two small glands discharging into the male urethra — called also *bulbourethral gland*

cow pilot *n* : SERGEANT MAJOR 4

cow poison *n* : a tall mountain larkspur (*Delphinium trollifolium*) of the American Pacific coast that is poisonous to stock

cowpoke \'⸗,⸗\ *n* [prob. alter. (influenced by *poke*, "to *punch*") of *cowpuncher*] : COWBOY 3a

cow pony *n* : a light saddle horse trained and used for herding cattle

cowpox \'⸗,⸗\ *n* -ES **1** : a mild eruptive disease of cattle (as cows) that when communicated to man (as by vaccination or natural inoculation) protects against smallpox : VACCINIA **2** : an eruptive disease in cows that when communicated to man (as during milking) causes nodules on the hands — called also *false cowpox;* compare MILKER'S NODULES

cowpuncher \'⸗,⸗⸗\ *n* : COWBOY 3a

1cow·rie *or* **cow·ry** *also* **cou·rie** \'kaůrē\ *n, pl* **cowries** *also* **couries** [Hindi *kauṛī*, fr. Skt *kaparda*, of Dravidian origin; akin to Tamil-Malayalam *kavaṭi* cowrie] : any of numerous marine gastropod mollusks of a family (Cypraeidae) widely distributed in warm seas with shells that are beautifully polished, often brightly colored, and much used for ornament or as money; *also* : a cowrie's shell

money cowrie: *a* dorsal side, *b* ventral side

2cowrie *var of* KAURI

cow·roid \'kaů,ròid\ *n* -S [1*cowrie* + -*oid*] : an inscribed Egyptian seal in the shape of a cowrie

cows *pl of* COW, *pres 3d sing of* COW

cow·shard \'⸗,⸗\ *n* -S *now dial Eng* : a dropping of cow dung

cow shark *n* : a shark of the family Hexanchidae; *esp* : a large shark (*Hexanchus griseus*) having six gill openings on each side and being widely distributed in warm and temperate seas

cow·sharn \'⸗,⸗\ *n* -S *now dial Eng* : cow dung

1cowskin \'⸗,⸗\ *n* [1*cow* + *skin*] **1** : cow leather : COWHIDE **2** : a cowhide whip

2cowskin \"\ *vt* : COWHIDE

cow·slip \'⸗,⸗\ *n* -S *often attrib* [ME *cowslyppe*, fr. OE *cūslyppe*, lit., cow dung, fr. *cū* cow + *slyppe, slypa* pulp, paste — more at COW, SLIP] **1 a** : a primrose (*Primula veris*) that is common in the British isles and has umbels of fragrant yellow or sometimes purplish flowers that appear in early spring **b** : a marsh marigold (*Caltha palustris*) **c** : SHOOTING STAR **d** : VIRGINIA COWSLIP **2** : ZINC ORANGE

cow·son \'kaů(z)(,)sən\ *n* -S *Brit* : BASTARD — a generalized term of abuse

cow sorrel *n* : SHEEP SORREL

cow's–tail \'⸗,⸗\ *or* **cow tail** *n* : a frayed end of a line where the strands have come unlaid

cowsucker \'⸗,⸗⸗\ *n* [so called fr. the belief that they milk cows] : any of various No. American harmless colubrid snakes

cow·tail \'⸗,⸗\ *n* : a wool of the coarsest grade sheared from the hind legs of the sheep

cowth·wort \'kü,thwərt\ *n* [origin unknown] : MOTHERWORT 1

cowtongue \'⸗,⸗\ *n* : YELLOW CLINTONIA

cow town *n* : a small cattle center that is typically provincial or unruly ⟨wide-open *cow towns* —Ross Santee⟩ ⟨a typical small *cow town*, with the usual single crooked street —P.E.Lehman⟩

cow tree *n* **1** [trans. of AmerSp *árbol de vaca*] **a** : a So. American tree (*Brosimum galactodendron*) yielding a rich milky juice sometimes used as food **b** : any of several other trees (as the balata and the couma) yielding a similar juice **c** : a Guatemalan tree (*Couma guatemalensis*) related to the cow tree **2** [so called fr. the use of its leaves as food for cattle] : KARAKA

cow vetch *n* : TUFTED VETCH

cow waddy *n* : COWBOY 3a

cowwheat \'⸗,⸗\ *n* : an herb of the genus *Melampyrum* (esp. *M. arvense*) found as a weed in European wheat fields

cowy \'kaůē\ *adj* -ER/-EST [1*cow* + -*y*] **1** : suggestive of a cow **2** : marked with a taste or flavor strongly suggestive of a cow ⟨fresh warm ~ milk⟩

cow yard *n, dial* : COW PEN, BARNYARD

1cox *obs var of* COKES

2cox \'käks\ *n* -ES [euphemism for *God*] : 5COCK

3cox \"\ *n* -ES [by shortening] : COXSWAIN

4cox \"\ *vb* -ED/-ING/-ES : to steer or direct as coxswain

coxa \'käksə\ *n, pl* **cox·ae** \-,sē, -,sī\ [L, hip; akin to OHG *hāhsina* hock, OIr *coss* foot, Skt *kakṣa* armpit] **1** : the hip joint : HIP **2** [NL, fr. L] : the first segment of the leg of an insect or other arthropod by which the leg articulates with the body

cox·al \'käksəl\ *adj* [prob. fr. F, fr. L *coxa* + F -*al*] : of, relating to, or near a coxa

coxal cavity *n* : one of the cavities on the lower surface of the body of arthropods in which the coxae of the limbs articulate

cox·al·gia \käk'salj(ē)ə\ *also* **cox·al·gy** \'⸗,⸗jē\ *n, pl* **coxalgias** *also* **coxalgies** [NL *coxalgia*, fr. L *coxa* + NL -*algia*] **1** : pain in the hip **2** : hip-joint disease — **cox·al·gic** \(')⸗¦⸗jik\ *adj*

coxal gland *n* : one of certain paired glands with ducts opening in the coxal region of arthropods and in some forms (as spiders) functioning as excretory organs

cox and box *usu cap C&B, var of* BOX AND COX

cox·bones \'käks+,-\ *n pl* [ME *cokkes bones*, euphemism for *Goddes bones* God's bones] : 5COCK

cox·comb \'käks+,-\ *n* -S [ME *cokkes comb* cock's comb — more at COCKSCOMB] **1 a** *obs* : a jester's cap adorned with a strip of red **b** *archaic* : PATE, HEAD **2 a** *obs* : FOOL **b** : a vain conceited foolish usu. male person that is falsely proud of his achievements and foppish or finical about his dress **3** : a cleat near the end of a yardarm to afford a lead in hauling out reef earings **4** : a hinge with the scrolled ends of each half resembling a cock's comb made in the 17th century

cox·comb·i·cal \(')käk¦skōməkəl, -käm-\ *also* **cox·comb·ic** \-mik\ *adj* : marked by a coxcomb's characteristics : FOPPISH, VAIN, DANDYISH

cox·comb·ly \'⸗,skōmlē\ *adj, archaic* : resembling a coxcomb esp. in manner or dress

cox·comb·ry \-mrē\ *n* -ES **1** : the behavior or manners of a coxcomb : FOPPERY **2** : a trait or characteristic of a coxcomb ⟨a ~ of his to affect the modish⟩

cox·i·el·la \,käksē'elə\ *n, cap* [NL, fr. Herald R. *Cox* *b*1907 Am. scientist + NL -*i-* + -*ella*] : a genus of small pleomorphic rickettsias occurring intercellularly in ticks and intracellularly in the cytoplasm of vertebrates and including the causative organism (*C. burnetii*) of Q fever

cox·ite \'käk,sīt\ *n* -S [NL *coxa* + E -*ite*] : one of a pair of lamellate structures on the underside of each abdominal segment in insects of the order Thysanura

cox·i·tis \käk'sīd·əs\ *n, pl* **cox·it·i·des** \-sid·ə,dēz\ [NL, fr. L *coxa* hip + NL -*itis* — more at COXA] : inflammation of the hip joint

cox·o·femoral \¦käksə+\ *adj* [*coxo-* (fr. L *coxa*) + *femoral*] : of or relating to the hip and thigh

coxon *n* [by alter.] *obs* : COXSWAIN

cox·op·o·dite \käk'säpə,dīt\ *n* -S [*coxo-* (fr. NL *coxa*) + -*podite*] : the basal or first joint of a crustacean limb

cox·sack·ie virus \(,)kůk,säkē-, -sak-; (,)käk,sa-\ *n, usu cap C* [fr. *Coxsackie*, N.Y., home of the patient in whom the virus was first found] : any of several related but serologically distinct viruses apparently related to the virus of poliomyelitis and associated with certain diseases of man — compare EPIDEMIC PLEURODYNIA, HERPANGINA

1cox·swain *also* **cock·swain** \'käksᵊn *also* -,swān\ *n* -S [ME *cokswayne*, fr. *cok*, a kind of boat + *swayne* servant — more at COCK, SWAIN] **1** : a sailor who has charge of a ship's boat and its crew and who usu. steers **2** : a steersman of a racing shell who usu. directs the crew

2coxswain \"\ *vb* -ED/-ING/-S *vt* : to steer or direct as coxswain ~ *vi* : to act as coxswain

coxwell chair *often cap 1st C, var of* COGSWELL CHAIR

1coxy \'käksi\ *adj* -ER/-EST [alter. of *cocks*, pl. of 1*cock* (in the phrase *cocks of the game* fighting cocks) + -*y*] *Brit* : CONCEITED, IMPUDENT, ARROGANT

2coxy *also* **cox·ey** \'käksē\ *n, pl* **coxies** *also* **coxeys** [modif. of NL *coccidiosis*] : avian coccidiosis

1coy \'kòi\ *adj* -ER/-EST [ME, fr. MF *coi* calm, tranquil, fr. L *quietus* quiet, calm — more at QUIET] **1** *obs* : QUIET, STILL ⟨the court became ~⟩ **2 a** : shrinking bashfully from familiarity : SHY : modestly or warily rejecting approaches or overtures ⟨like a lot of wild young colts, very inquisitive, but very ~ and not to be cajoled easily —Samuel Butler †1902⟩ ⟨the moon was a ~ or a wanton maiden, who either fled from or pursued the sun —J.G.Frazer⟩ **b** *archaic* : INACCESSIBLE, SECLUDED ⟨a sequestered ~ retreat⟩ **c** : archly affecting shy or demure reserve : marked by cute, coquettish, or artful playfulness ⟨using ~ tricks to awaken interest⟩ ⟨the combination of the adult and childish in the style will seem a bit too ~ —Louise S. Bechtel⟩ **d** : showing marked often playful or irritating reluctance to make a definite or committing statement ⟨a politician ~ about his intentions⟩ **syn** see SHY

2coy \"\ *vb* -ED/-ING/-S [ME *coyen* to calm, caress, coax, fr. *coy*, adj.] *vt, obs* : CARESS ~ *vi* **1** *archaic* : to act coyly — sometimes used with *it* ⟨a shy maiden ~*ing* it⟩ **2** : DEMUR, WITHDRAW

coy *abbr* company

coy·dog \'kī, 'kòi+,-\ *n* [*coyote* + *dog*] : a hybrid between a coyote and a feral dog found in parts of the northeastern U.S.

coy·ly *adv* : in a coy manner

coy·ness *n* -ES : the quality or state of being coy

coy·nye \'kòin(y)ē\ *or* **coyne** \-n\ *or* **coi·gny** \-n(y)ē\ *n* -S [ME *coynee*, fr. MIr *coinnemh;* akin to MIr *connmedh* quarterage, billeting] : an Irish chieftain's exaction of food and drink from his tenants for his soldiers — compare BONAGHT

co·yo \'kō(,)yō\ *n* -S [AmerSp *coyó*, fr. Maya] **1** : a Mexican and Central American avocado (*Persea schiedeana*) **2** : the fruit of the coyo

co·yol \(')kō¦yōl, kə'y-\ *also* **coyol palm** *n* -S [MexSp *coyol*, fr. Nahuatl *coyoli*, lit., bell; fr. the shape of the fruit and the rattle made by the dried fruit when shaken] **1** : any of several tropical American palms of the genus *Acrocomia* (esp. *A. vinifera*) **2** : the fiber of a coyol

1coy·ote \'kī,ōt *also* -,yōt *sometimes* 'kòi,-, *usu* -ōd·+V; kī'ōd·(,)ē, -'ō(,)tē *also* -'yō- *sometimes* kòi'- *or* kə'- *or* kē'-\ *n, pl* **coyotes** *or* **coyote** [MexSp, fr. Nahuatl *coyotl*] **1** : a small wolf (*Canis latrans*) native to the western part of No. America and well established northward in Alaska and eastward at least as far as New York state — called also *prairie wolf* **2** : an objectionable person : CHISELER

2coyote \"\ *vi* **coyoteed** \-d·(,)ēd\ *or* **coyoted** \-d·əd, -d·(,)ēd\ **coyoteed** *or* **coyoted**; **coyoteing** *or* **coyoting** \-d·iŋ\ **coyotes** \-ts, -d·(,)ēz\ *West* : to mine by sinking small shallow shafts with drifts running in several directions — compare GOPHER

3coyote \"\ *adj* : marked by shallow excavation or digging suggestive of a coyote's hole ⟨a ~ shaft⟩ ⟨a ~ cellar⟩

coyote blast *n* **:** blasting in a coyote hole
coyote brush *also* **coyote bush** *n* **:** a prostrate spreading or erect smooth evergreen shrub (*Baccharis pilularis*) of the southwestern U.S. having ovoid flower heads in a leafy panicle made up of sessile clusters — called also *kidneywort*
coyote dance *n* **:** a dance mimetic of the coyote; *esp* **:** a Yaqui Indian prowling dance by three members of the warriors' society
coyote getter *n* **:** a device used to kill coyotes by shooting cyanide into the mouth when the animal disturbs the bait
coyote hole *n* **:** a short T-shaped blasthole — compare [2]COYOTE
co·yo·te·ro \ˌkōyəˈte(ˌ)rō\ *n* -s *usu cap* [MexSp, fr. *coyote* + *-ero* -er; fr. their reputation for eating coyote meat] **:** an Indian of an Apache division comprising the Pinal White Mountain and Tonto groups
coyote willow *n* **:** SANDBAR WILLOW b
co·yo·til·lo \ˌkōyəˈtilō, -tē(ˌ)lō, -tēl(ˌ)yō\ *n* -s [MexSp, dim. of *coyote*] **:** a low poisonous shrub (*Karwinskia humboldtiana*) of the southwestern U.S. and Mexico
coy·pu *also* **coy·pou** \ˈkȯi(ˌ)pü, ·ˈ·\ *n* -s [AmerSp *coipú*, fr. Araucan *coypu*] **1 :** a So. American aquatic rodent (*Myocastor coypus*) with webbed feet and dorsally located mammae that has been introduced into other regions for the sake of its fur and is now thoroughly naturalized on the U.S. Gulf Coast and Pacific Northwest and is a pest in parts of England because of its destruction of marsh vegetation **2 :** NUTRIA 1b
coystrill *var of* COISTREL
coz \ˈkəz\ *n, pl* **cozes** *or* **coz·zes** \-əzəz\ [by shortening & alter.] **:** COUSIN
[1]**coze** \ˈkōz\ *n* -s [prob. fr. F *causer* to chat] **:** CHAT
[2]**coze** \"\ *vi* -ED/-ING/-s [F *causer*, fr. OF, to plead a case, fr. L *causari*, fr. *causa* cause — more at CAUSE] **:** CHAT, GOSSIP
coz·en \ˈkəzᵊn\ *vb* **cozened; cozened; cozening** \-z(ᵊ)niŋ\ **cozens** [obs. It *cozzonare* to act like a horse trader or knave, to cheat, fr. *cozzone* horse trader, matchmaker, fr. L *coction-, coctio, cocion-, cocio* horse trader] *vt* **1 :** to deceive by artful wheedling or tricky dishonesty **:** CHEAT, DEFRAUD ⟨*~ing* his unsuspecting and unsophisticated brother⟩ **2 :** to beguile craftily **:** victimize by chicanery **:** DELUDE, DECEIVE ⟨he had *~ed* the world by fine phrases —T.B.Macaulay⟩ **3 :** to bring about, induce, or obtain by artful wheedling or tricky dishonesty ⟨*~ing* the old man into signing the paper⟩ ⟨with a conscious knowledge of their art, *~ed* their supper out of Mrs. Torrelli —John Steinbeck⟩ **~** *vi* **:** to act with artful deceit **:** CHISEL ⟨cheated and plundered by gentlemen who prospered in *~ing* —V.L.Parrington⟩ **syn** see CHEAT
coz·en·age *also* **coz·in·age** \-z(ᵊ)nij\ *n* -s **1 :** the art or practice of cozening **:** ARTIFICE, FRAUD ⟨a thievish rogue expert at *~*⟩ **2 :** an act of cozening **:** an instance of deception ⟨his frauds and *~s*⟩
co·zey *or* **co·zie** \ˈkōzē, -zi\ *archaic var of* COZY
cozier *n* [MF *couseor* seamster, tailor, fr. (assumed) VL *consuator*, fr. L *consuere* to sew together (fr. *com-* + *suere* to sew) + *-ator* — more at SEW] *obs* **:** SHOEMAKER, COBBLER
co·zi·ly *or* **co·si·ly** \ˈkōz(ə)lē, -li\ *adv* **:** in a cozy manner **:** SNUGLY, INTIMATELY
co·zi·ness *or* **co·si·ness** \ˈkōzēnəs, -zin-\ *n* -ES **:** the quality or state of being cozy **:** SNUGNESS
co·zonal \(ˈ)kō+\ *adj* [*co-* + *zonal*] **:** TAUTOZONAL
[1]**co·zy** *or* **co·sy** \ˈkōzē, -zi\ *adj* -ER/-EST [prob. of Scand origin; akin to Norw *kose* (*sig*) to be snug, *koselig* snug, cozy] **1 :** enjoying, affording, or suggesting warmth, homey ease, and freedom from care and inconvenience often within smallish or compact quarters ⟨he felt ~ watching the hearth fire⟩ ⟨~ blankets⟩ ⟨a ~ lakeside cabin⟩ ⟨the happy life that pair had led in the ~ studio in Montmartre —W.S.Maugham⟩ **2 a :** marked by or suggestive of the warm and understanding intimacy of the family or the friendly familiarity of a close group **:** lacking restraint or cold formality ⟨desirous of living on the ~ footing of a father-in-law —Herman Melville⟩ ⟨the *coziest* picture of Johnson working, no longer "in the gloom of solitude" but surrounded by friends —J.W.Krutch⟩ ⟨a ~, first-person, family kind of democracy —Ruth Gruber⟩ **b :** showing or suggesting close association often for devious connivance ⟨the ~ prewar cartel which was profitable to them and their fellow industrialists —*America*⟩ **3 :** marked by or suggestive of a discreet and cautious attitude or procedure that avoids anything forthright, novel, or extreme ⟨a ~ waiting game⟩ ⟨instead of acting ~, the scheduled airlines have fought . . . at every turn —*Air Transportation*⟩ **syn** see COMFORTABLE
[2]**cozy** *adv* **:** in a cautious manner — often used in the phrase *play it cozy* ⟨play it ~ and wait for the other team to make a mistake —Bobby Dodd⟩
[3]**cozy** *or* **cosy** *also* **co·sey** \"\ *n* -ES [prob. fr. [1]*cozy*] **:** a covering or holder for food; *esp* **:** a holder for keeping tea, eggs, or muffins warm
co·zymase \(ˈ)kō+\ *n* [*co-* + *zymase*] **:** DIPHOSPHOPYRIDINE NUCLEOTIDE
cozy up *vi* [[1]*cozy*] **:** to attain or try to attain to familiarity, friendship, or intimacy **:** ingratiate oneself — usu. used with *to* ⟨*cozying up* to the party leaders⟩ ⟨trying to *cozy up* to the boss's secretary⟩
cp *abbr* **1** centipoise **2** compare **3** coupon
CP *abbr* **1** candlepower **2** carriage paid **3** cerebral palsy **4** charter party **5** chemically pure **6** civil procedure **7** code of procedure **8** [It *colla parte*] with the solo part **9** command post **10** common pleas **11** common prayer **12** communist party **13** court of probate **14** custom of port
CPA *abbr or n* -s certified public accountant
CPC *abbr* **1** chronic passive congestion **2** crafts, protective, custodial
CPC and N *abbr* certificate of public convenience and necessity
CPCU *abbr* chartered property casualty underwriter
cpd *abbr* compound
CPD *abbr* **1** charterers pay dues **2** contact potential difference
CPFF *abbr* cost plus fixed fee
CPI *abbr* constitutional psychopathic inferior
cpl *abbr* **1** complete **2** corporal
CPM *abbr* **1** common particular meter **2** cycles per minute
CPO *abbr* chief petty officer
c power supply \ˈsē-\ *n, usu cap C* **:** a battery or voltage-divider section supplying direct voltage in the grid circuit of an electron tube — compare A POWER SUPPLY, B POWER SUPPLY; C BATTERY
cpr *abbr* copper
CPS *abbr* **1** constitutional psychopathic state **2** cycles per second
cpt *abbr* **1** captain **2** counterpoint
cptr *abbr* carpenter
CQ \(ˈ)sēˈkyü\ [abbr. for *call to quarters*] — communication code letters used at the beginning of radiograms of general information or safety notices or by shortwave amateurs as an invitation to talk to other shortwave amateurs
CQ *abbr* **1** charge of quarters **2** commercial quality **3** conceptual quotient
cr *abbr* **1** center **2** circular **3** commander **4** councillor **5** crate **6** created **7** credit; creditor **8** creed **9** creek **10** crescendo **11** crew **12** crochet **13** crown **14** cruiser **15** cruzeiro
CR *abbr* **1** carrier's risk **2** change of rating **3** class rate **4** commodity rate **5** company's risk **6** conditioned reflex; conditioned response **7** creditable record **8** critical ratio **9** crossroad **10** currency regulation **11** current rate
Cr *symbol* chromium
[1]**crab** \ˈkrab, -aa(ə)b\ *n* -s [ME *crabbe*, fr. OE *crabba*; akin to OHG *krebiz* crab, ON *krabbi*, OE *ceorfan* to cut — more at CARVE] **1 a :** any of a number of chiefly marine largely carnivorous rather stocky and broadly built crustaceans: (1) **:** any member of the tribe Brachyura distinguished by a short broad and usu. flattened carapace, a small abdomen that curls forward beneath the body and fits into a groove in the thorax, short antennae, and the anterior pair of limbs modified as pincers or grasping organs (2) **:** any of various members of the tribe Anomura resembling the brachyurans in having the abdomen reduced and permanently flexed — see HERMIT CRAB, PURSE CRAB **b :** KING CRAB **2 :** any of various machines or apparatus esp. for raising or hauling heavy weights: as **a :** a winch mounted (as on skids) so that it can be moved **b :** the part of an overhead traveling crane that rolls along the track and carries the load **c :** a claw for anchoring a portable machine **d :** a machine for textile crabbing **3 crabs** *pl* **:** a losing throw of two or three in the game of hazard — compare CRAP 1 **4 :** failure to raise an oar clear of the water on recovery of a stroke or missing the water altogether when attempting a stroke — used esp. in the phrase *to catch a crab* **5 a** (1) [so called fr. the hooked feet resembling those of a crab] **:** CRAB LOUSE (2) **crabs** *pl* **:** PEDICULOSIS — usu. used with *the* **b :** the larva of a stone fly **6 :** apparent sideways motion esp. of an airplane headed into a crosswind
[2]**crab** \"\ *vb* **crabbed; crabbed; crabbing; crabs** *vt* **1 :** to cause to move sideways or in an indirect or diagonal manner ⟨on the upstream trip broadside winds *crabbed* the boat close to the riverbank⟩; *specif* **:** to head (an airplane or glider) by means of the rudder into a crosswind to counteract drift and thus give the aircraft apparent sidewise motion with respect to the ground **2 :** to subject to crabbing **~** *vi* **1 a** (1) **:** to move sideways indirectly or diagonally ⟨at high speed the car would ~ around corners⟩ (2) *of a pilot* **:** to crab an airplane or glider **b :** to scuttle or scurry sideways like a crab ⟨jumping aboard and *crabbing* along the gunwale to the controls —K.M.Dodson⟩ **2 :** to fish for or catch crabs
[3]**crab** \"\ *adj, music* **:** moving backwards
[4]**crab** \"\ *n* -s [ME *crabbe*, perh. fr. *crabbe* crab (the crustacean) — more at [1]CRAB] **1 :** CRAB APPLE **2 :** a cudgel of crab-tree wood **:** CRABSTICK
[5]**crab** \"\ *vb* **crabbed; crabbed; crabbing; crabs** [ME *craben, crabben*, prob. back-formation fr. *crabbed*] *vt* **1** *archaic Brit* **:** ANGER, IRRITATE **2 :** to make sullen **:** SOUR ⟨old age had *crabbed* his nature⟩ ⟨then what's *crabbing* you? —S.H.Adams⟩ **3 :** to complain about **:** criticize peevishly or petulantly **:** pull to pieces ⟨~ the conduct of a neighbor⟩ ⟨each side tended to ~ the weapon of the other —Bernard Brodie⟩ **4 :** SPOIL, RUIN ⟨~ a deal⟩ ⟨an unknown . . . might have *crabbed* his own act if he had started clobbering a war hero —James Marlow⟩ ⟨the author's writing . . . is not so much *crabbed* by technical jargon as by a pedantic style —*Infantry Jour.*⟩ **~** *vi* **1 :** to be ill-tempered **:** GROUSE ⟨she'd always be *crabbing* without cause⟩ **2 :** to criticize in a petty, peevish, or petulant manner **:** COMPLAIN ⟨~ at a person⟩ ⟨his boss *crabbed* about him⟩
[6]**crab** \"\ *n* -s **1 :** a sour ill-tempered person **:** CROSSPATCH **2 :** an instance of critical carping **:** testy objection ⟨the boarder's chief ~ was that his room was cold⟩
[7]**crab** \"\ *vb* **crabbed; crabbed; crabbing; crabs** [D *krabben* to scratch, claw, fr. MD *crabben*; akin to OE *crabba* crab — more at [1]CRAB] *of hawks* **:** SCRATCH, FIGHT
[8]**crab** \"\ *var of* CARAPA
crab apple *n* [[4]*crab*] **1 :** a small wild sour apple: **a** *Brit* **:** the wild form of the common apple (*Malus sylvestris*) **b :** any of several American trees of the genus *Malus* (as *M. ioensis* and *M. cornaria*) **c :** SIBERIAN CRAB **2 :** any of several cultivated apples having long petioles and rather small usu. highly colored acid fruit and used chiefly for jelly and preserves — see FLOWERING CRAB **3 :** a moderate reddish orange that is lighter, stronger, and slightly yellower than flamingo, redder, lighter, and stronger than coral red, and redder, lighter, and stronger than burnt ocher
crab·bed \ˈkrabəd\ *adj* [ME, partly fr. *crabbe* (crustacean), partly fr. *crabbe* (crab apple) + *-ed*] **1 a :** perversely obstinate **:** INTRACTABLE, CONTRARY ⟨he sets out his theory with such ingenuity . . . that it would be a ~ mind indeed that didn't respond —R.J.Cruikshank⟩ **b :** out of humor **:** CROSS, PETULANT ⟨the only audible response in this country should be a ~ and jaundiced bickering —*Economist*⟩ **2 :** characterized by harshness or roughness **:** BITTER ⟨a ~ satirist⟩ ⟨~ wit⟩ **3** *obs* **:** CROOKED, GNARLED, ROUGH **4 :** difficult to understand **:** INTRICATE, OBSCURE ⟨~ style⟩ ⟨the ~ complexities of fine automotive machinery —*Newsweek*⟩ ⟨his mature compositions are generally considered the more cerebral and ~ —Sarah R. Watson⟩ **5** *of handwriting* **:** difficult to read ⟨wrote laboriously in his old man's ~ hand —Verne Athanas⟩ **syn** see SULLEN
crab·bed·ly *adv* [ME, fr. *crabbed* + *-ly*] **:** in a crabbed manner
crab·bed·ness *n* -ES [ME *crabbydnesse*, fr. *crabbyd, crabbed* + *-nesse* -ness] **:** the quality or state of being crabbed
[1]**crab·ber** \ˈkrabə(r)\ *n* -s [[1]*crab* + *-er*] **1 a :** one that fishes for or catches crabs **b :** a boat used in crab fishing **2 :** WINCHMAN **3** [[2]*crab* + *-er*] **:** an operator of a machine for crabbing
[2]**crabber** \"\ *n* -s [[5]*crab* + *-er*] **:** one that carps or complains
crab·bery \-b(ə)rē, -ri\ *n* -ES [[1]*crab* + *-ery*] **:** a place where crabs abound or are fished for
crabbing *n* -s [fr. gerund of [2]*crab*] **:** a finishing process for setting the warp and weft threads of woolen and worsted fabrics by winding the cloth under tension on rollers and subjecting it to boiling water or steam which is followed by a cooling process
crab·bit \ˈkrabət\ *chiefly Scot var of* CRABBED
[1]**crab·by** \ˈkrabē, -bi\ *adj* -ER/-EST [in sense 1, fr. [4]*crab* + *-y*; in sense 2, fr. [6]*crab* + *-y*] **1** *obs* **:** CROOKED, ROUGH, PERPLEXING **2 :** CROSS, CHURLISH, ILL-NATURED
[2]**crabby** \"\ *adj* -ER/-EST [[1]*crab* + *-y*] **1 :** resembling a crab **2 :** abounding in crabs
crab cactus *n* **:** a So. American cactus (*Zygocactus truncatus*) with red flowers — called also *Christmas cactus*
crab canon *n* [[3]*crab*] **:** a canon with a theme that is repeated backward — called also *canon cancrizans*
crab claw *n* **1 :** a claw or clutch for grappling or fastening **:** PAWL **2 :** an Oceanian lateen sail
crab·eater \ˈ·ˌ··\ *n* **1 :** any of several fishes and birds reputed to eat crabs (as the sergeant fish and various herons) **2 :** CRABEATER SEAL **3 :** CRAB-EATING RACCOON **4 :** COBIA
crabeater seal \"-\ *or* **crab-eating seal** \ˈ·ˌ··-\ *n* **:** a silvery gray antarctic seal (*Lobodon carcinophaga*) subsisting largely on crustaceans
crab-eating fox *or* **crab-eating dog** *n* **:** a wild dog (*Dusicyon cancrivorus*) of northern So. America
crab-eating macaque *n* **:** a macaque (*Macaca irus*) of southeastern Asia, Borneo, and the Philippines — called also *croo monkey*
crab-eating opossum *n* **:** a So. American opossum (*Didelphis marsupialis*)
crab-eating raccoon *n* **:** a So. American raccoon (*Procyon cancrivorus*)
crab float *n* **:** a live-box in which crabs are kept
crab form *n* [[3]*crab*] **:** the placing of the notes of a musical theme, voice part, or twelve-tone row in reverse order in either direct or inverted imitation
crabgrass \ˈ·ˌ·\ *n* **1 :** any of several grasses that have creeping or decumbent stems which root freely at the nodes and that are often pests in turf or cultivated lands: as **a :** any of several grasses of the genus *Digitaria*; *esp* **:** LARGE CRABGRASS **b :** YARD GRASS **c :** EGYPTIAN GRASS **2 :** KNOTGRASS I **3 :** a glasswort (*Salicornia europaea*) supposed to be a food for crabs
crabhole \ˈ·ˌ·\ *n* **:** the hole in which a crab (as a land crab) lives
cra·bier \ˌkrab(ē)ˈyā, ˈ··(ˌ)·\ *n* -s [F, fr. *crabe* crab (fr. MF, fr. MD *crabbe*) + *-ier* -er; akin to OE *crabba* crab — more at CRAB] **:** any of several crab-eating birds of the Caribbean area (as the great blue heron)
crab line *n* **:** a soft-laid rope of ¼-inch diameter or less used as net mending and trawl twine and as bait line (as by inserting bait between strands in the crab-fishing industry)
crab locomotive *n* **:** a small mine locomotive on which is mounted a power-driven winch
crab louse *n* [[1]*crab*] **:** a louse (*Phthirus pubis*) infesting the human body in the pubic region

crabgrass (*Digitaria sanguinalis*)

crab·man \ˈkrabˌman, -mən\ *n, pl* **crabmen :** a seller of crabs
crab nut *n* [[8]*crab*] **:** the seed of the carapa
crab plover *n* **:** a bird (*Dromas ardeola*) like a plover widely distributed along the east coast of Africa and the southern shores of Asia where it feeds chiefly on crabs and burrows into sandbanks to deposit its single white egg
crab pot *n* **:** a wickerwork trap for crabs
crab reel locomotive *n* **:** CRAB LOCOMOTIVE
crabs *pl of* CRAB, *pres 3d sing of* CRAB
crab's claw *n* **:** WATER SOLDIER
crab's-eye \ˈ·ˌ·\ *n* **1 :** a hard calcareous mass found in the stomach of certain crustaceans (as the European crayfish) that was formerly used in medicine — compare GASTROLITH **2 :** JEQUIRITY
crab's-eye vine *n* **:** INDIAN LICORICE
crab spider *n* **:** any of the numerous spiders that make up the family Thomisidae and resemble crabs in attitude and in ability to run sideways
crab·stick \ˈ·ˌ·\ *n* [[4]*crab* + *stick*] **1 :** a stick, cane, or cudgel of crab-tree wood **2 :** a crabbed ill-natured person
crab stock *n* **:** a seedling of the common apple that is used as a stock
[1]**crab tree** *n* [[4]*crab*] **1 :** a crab-apple tree **2** *Austral* **:** NATIVE QUINCE
[2]**crab tree** *n* [[8]*crab*] **:** CARAPA
crabwise \ˈ·ˌ·\ *adv* [[1]*crab* + *-wise*] **1 :** SIDEWAYS ⟨the battleship was pushed several feet ~ by its nine-gun broadside⟩ **2 :** in a sidling or cautiously indirect manner ⟨Canada has moved ~ toward socialism —W.G.Hardy⟩
[1]**crabwood** \ˈ·ˌ·\ *n* [[8]*crab* + *wood*] **:** a timber tree (*Carapa guianensis*) of tropical So. America
[2]**crabwood** \"\ *n* [prob. fr. [4]*crab* + *wood*] **:** a tree (*Gymnanthes lucida*) of the West Indies and southern Florida that contains a poisonous juice
crab yaws *n pl* **:** secondary lesions of yaws characterized by thickening of the skin on the soles of the feet and formation of fissures and ulcers which causes a waddling gait
crac·ca \ˈkrakə\ [NL, fr. L, a kind of leguminous plant, perh. vetch] *syn of* TEPHROSIA
crac·i·dae \ˈkrasəˌdē\ *n pl, cap* [NL, fr. *Crac-, Crax*, type genus + *-idae*] **:** a family of gallinaceous birds of the warmer parts of America that comprises the curassows, guans, and chachalacas and is related to the megapodes
-cracies *pl of* -CRACY
[1]**crack** \ˈkrak\ *vb* -ED/-ING/-s [ME *crakken*, alter. (influenced by *crak*, n.) of *craken*, fr. OE *cracian*; akin to OE *cearcian* to creak, gnash, OHG *krahhōn* to crack, Skt *garjati* he roars, OE *cran* crane — more at CRANE] *vi* **1 :** to make a loud sharp sudden sound or series of such sounds (as the snap of a whip, a rifle shot) **:** give forth a report ⟨wood *~ing* in a fire⟩ ⟨his high yell of laughter *~ed* out when he thought of something funny —Virginia D. Dawson & Betty D. Wilson⟩ **2 :** to snap asunder ⟨the ropes *~ed* under pressure⟩ **:** open in chinks **3 a** *chiefly Scot* **:** TALK, CHAT, GOSSIP **b** *now dial* **:** to speak pompously **:** BRAG, BOAST **4 :** to become ruined or impaired **:** FAIL: as **a :** to lose control or effectiveness esp. when working or competing under pressure ⟨his reserve *~ed*⟩ ⟨any pitcher is liable to ~ during a tight game⟩ — often used with *up* ⟨if he doesn't rest he'll ~ up completely⟩ **b :** to fail in tone production **:** become discordant or harsh ⟨his voice *~ed*⟩ **c :** to smash up a vehicle esp. by losing control — used with *up* ⟨he *~ed* up taking a curve⟩ **5** *archaic* **:** to go or travel at good speed; *specif* **:** to proceed under or as if under full sail or steam — used with *on* **6 a** *of chemical compounds* **:** to break up into simpler compounds usu. as a result of heating **:** undergo pyrolysis **b** *of an emulsion* **:** BREAK *vi* 7 f (2) **7** *of hot syrup* **:** to break when dropped into cold water and subjected to moderate pressure **~** *vt* **1 :** to break or burst: as **a :** to break (something brittle or hollow) with a sharp or explosive sound ⟨~ a nut⟩ **b :** to break (anything hard or brittle) so that clefts, chinks, or fissures appear on the surface ⟨the fall *~ed* the cup across the bottom⟩ ⟨the storm broke a dozen windowpanes and *~ed* many others⟩ **2 a :** to utter esp. suddenly and sententiously **:** tell strikingly ⟨~ a jest⟩ ⟨~ a joke⟩ **b :** to cry up **:** EXTOL, PRAISE — used with *up* ⟨the car wasn't all the dealer *~ed* it up to be⟩ ⟨he *~ed* up Whitehead to the stars —H.J.Laski⟩ **3 :** to strike with a sharp noise **:** SLAP, BANG ⟨~ a person over the head⟩ **4 :** to put on (as full sail, steam, speed) **:** clap on — used with *on* ⟨he liked everything about this convoy: he liked its air of purpose as it *~ed* on speed —Nicholas Monsarrat⟩ **5 :** to break open or into: as **a :** to open (as a bottle) and usu. drink ⟨~ a fifth⟩ **b :** to puzzle out and solve, expose, or reveal the mystery of ⟨~ an enemy code⟩ ⟨~ a garbled message⟩ ⟨~ a crime syndicate wide open⟩ ⟨~ the logic of an argument⟩ **c :** to break into ⟨~ a safe⟩; *specif, Brit* **:** to break into (a house) — often used in the phrase *crack a crib* **d :** to open slightly ⟨~ a door⟩ ⟨~ a window⟩ ⟨~ a throttle⟩ ⟨~ a valve⟩ **e :** to enter or win recognition by (an exclusive profession, coterie, society) ⟨it has been extremely difficult . . . for foreign artists . . . to ~ the Parisian art front without going there to live —J.T.Soby⟩ **f :** to open (a book) for the purpose of study ⟨~ a physics text⟩ ⟨several students were up . . . *~ing* the books beyond midnight —Jack Edison⟩ **6 :** VIOLATE, DAMAGE, DESTROY: as **a :** to impair often irreparably **:** WRECK, RUIN ⟨~ a bat⟩ ⟨~ an opponent's courage⟩ — often used with *up* ⟨~ a new car up⟩ **b :** to make (the voice) discordant or harsh **:** destroy the tone of **c :** DISORDER, CRAZE ⟨worry had *~ed* his otherwise expansive personality⟩ ⟨~ the heartstrings with sorrow⟩ **d :** to interrupt (as a settled usage, condition, continuity, tradition) sharply or abruptly ⟨his criticism *~ed* our complacency⟩ ⟨~ a winning streak with four straight losses⟩ **7 :** to cause to make a sharp noise ⟨~ one's knuckles⟩ **8 a** (1) **:** to subject (hydrocarbon oils or gases) to cracking (2) **:** to produce by cracking — usu. used in past participle ⟨*~ed* gasoline⟩ **b :** to break up (chemical compounds) into simpler compounds usu. by means of heat **:** subject to pyrolysis **9 a** *in contract bridge* **:** DOUBLE **b** *in poker* **:** OPEN ⟨~ the pot⟩ **syn** see BREAK — **crack a smile :** SMILE — **crack the whip :** to adopt sometimes suddenly or unexpectedly an authoritative, tyrannical, or threatening pose or policy ⟨he has made great industrial corporations jump . . . when he *cracks the whip* —*Time*⟩ — **crack wise** [by analysis fr. [1]*wisecrack*] *slang* **:** to make a smart remark
[2]**crack** \"\ *n* -s [ME *crak*; akin to OHG *krach* loud noise, OE *cracian*, v.] **1 a :** a loud earsplitting roar or peal ⟨a ~ of thunder⟩ ⟨the ~ of trumpets⟩ ⟨the ~ of a cannon⟩ — often used interjectionally **b :** a sudden sharp noise **:** a brief intense report **:** BANG ⟨the jug hit the floor with a terrible ~⟩ ⟨the chair went over with a ~⟩ ⟨the ~ of a rifle⟩ — often used interjectionally ⟨~! went the whip⟩ **c :** the breaking or broken tone of the voice (as when changed at puberty) **2 a** *now dial Brit* **:** boasting or an instance of boasting **b** *chiefly dial Brit* (1) **:** TALK, CONVERSATION, GOSSIP (2) **:** TALE, STORY, JOKE (3) **cracks** *pl* **:** NEWS **c :** a sharp, cutting, or sarcastically witty remark **:** QUIP ⟨Washington was not famous for saying funny things but sometimes he got off a ~ that was widely appreciated —Roger Butterfield⟩ **3 a :** a narrow break or thin slit (as in or across a surface) sometimes caused by incomplete joining, drying, or setting, by strain or decay, or by a blow or fall not sufficiently violent to cause a complete break **:** FISSURE ⟨a windowpane full of *~s*⟩ ⟨trip over a ~ in the ice⟩ **b :** a narrow opening ⟨you can leave the outer door open a ~ so you can hear if anyone comes —John Steinbeck⟩ **c :** an open crosswise streak in woven fabrics **4 a :** a weakness or flaw caused by decay, age, or deficiency **:** UNSOUNDNESS ⟨a ~ in a person's mind⟩ ⟨little rifts and *~s* . . . in the whole bland, ecclesiastical facade of Victorian England —C.D.Lewis⟩ **b :** a crazy or erratic person **:** CRACKPOT ⟨the *~s* who . . . interest themselves . . . in every sensational murder case —D.L. Champion⟩ **5** *obs* **:** a roguish boy **:** WAG **6** *slang Brit* **:** a thing or person of superior excellence or ability ⟨Australia sent a couple of *~s* to defend the trophy⟩ **7** *archaic* **:** PROSTITUTE **8 :** MOMENT, INSTANT ⟨I'll be there in a ~⟩ ⟨at the ~ of dawn⟩ **9 a** *archaic* **:** BURGLAR **b :** HOUSEBREAKING, BURGLARY ⟨a successful ~⟩ **10 :** a sharp resounding blow ⟨a ~ on the head⟩ **11 :** a concerted effort or try ⟨to get rid of a job at one ~⟩ ⟨he said he didn't know how to swim but would take a ~ at it⟩ **12 :** the stage at which syrup from boiling sugar breaks with a snap when chilled by being dripped from a spoon or dropped into water **13 :** a poultry egg with a

noticeably cracked shell but with unbroken membrane — contrasted with *check*

syn FISSURE, CREVICE, CHINK, CLEFT, CRANNY: CRACK is likely to indicate a line of breaking or splitting in a continuing surface with or without perceptible separation into an opening that resembles a slit ⟨a *crack* in a pane of glass⟩ ⟨*cracks* in the parched mud⟩ FISSURE usu. indicates a narrow opening of some depth as a result of some rending or breaking force ⟨a *fissure* in the stone floor, like a *crack* in china, which was plastered up with clay —Willa Cather⟩ CREVICE indicates an opening like a fissure but less strongly suggests forceful recent cleavage and may lend itself to use in situations involving accumulation, deposit, growth, or concealment within ⟨the cross formed by snow in the *crevices* of the rock⟩ ⟨intolerance can always find some *crevice* in the administration of the law —Zechariah Chafee⟩ CHINK suggests a space or hole, often a slit, permitting one to see through or to utilize in escape, evasion, or deft attack ⟨I felt as if I had slipped through some *chink* in the veil of the past and become a medieval student —John Buchan⟩ ⟨Republicans . . . had independently been studying the Truman armor for new *chinks* —*Atlantic*⟩ CLEFT suggests a V-shaped indention, as though made with a splitting wedge, in some formation ⟨Dover, an English seaport . . . occupies a wide *cleft* in the chalk hills formed by the valley of the river Don —*Chambers's Encyc.*⟩ CRANNY suggests a slit, niche, or recess, often one in a wall or enclosed structure and often small and easy to overlook ⟨they explored every nook and *cranny* of the West, seeking out passes through mountain barriers —R.A.Billington⟩ **syn** see in addition JOKE

[3]**crack** \"\ *adj* [[2]*crack* (something excellent)] **:** of superior excellence or ability ⟨a ~ ship⟩ ⟨a ~ tennis player⟩ ⟨a ~ regiment⟩ ⟨~ maintenance and cargo specialists —B.M. Bowie⟩

crackajack *var of* CRACKERJACK

crackaloo *var of* CRACK-LOO

crack arrester *n* **1 :** a plate on a ship riveted over a crack in another plate or over a stressed area where a crack might start **2 :** a hole drilled or a slot cut at the apex of a crack in the plate of a ship to stop the crack from spreading or at a point of stress to stop a crack from starting

crackbrain \'ˌ=\ *n* **:** a person of unbalanced or erratic tendencies or ideas **:** CRACKPOT

crackbrained \'ˌ=\ *adj* **:** ERRATIC, UNREASONABLE, CRAZY ⟨a ~ genius⟩ ⟨a ~ feminist⟩ ⟨a ~ scheme⟩

crack down *vi* **:** to take punitive action **:** enforce strict conformance with or increase the severity of regulations or restrictions — usu. used with *on* ⟨the government *cracked down* on violators⟩

crackdown \'ˌ=\ *n* -S [*crack down*] **:** an act or instance of cracking down

cracked *adj* [ME *crackyd*, fr. past part. of *crakken* to crack] **1 a :** broken (as by a sharp blow) so that the surface is fissured ⟨~ china⟩ **b :** broken into coarse particles ⟨~ wheat⟩ ⟨~ ice⟩ **c :** marked by harsh or discordant notes or by failure to sustain tones ⟨a ~ voice⟩ ⟨a ~ laugh⟩ **2 a :** DAMAGED, FLAWED ⟨a ~ reputation⟩ **b** *obs* **:** BANKRUPT **c :** mentally disturbed **:** CRAZY; *also* **:** intensely preoccupied **:** having a fixed idea **:** ENTHUSIASTIC — **cracked·ness** \'krak(t)nə̇s\ *n* -ES

cracked cocoa *n* **:** CACAO NIBS

cracked heels *n* **:** grease heel of the horse

cracked plate *n* **:** a postage stamp showing a mark or line not part of the original design and due to a crack or flaw in the printing plate

cracked stem *n* **:** a boron-deficiency disease of celery characterized by brownish leaf mottling and brittleness and crosswise cracking of the leafstalks

crack·er \'krakə(r)\ *n* -S **1** *chiefly dial* **a :** bragging liar **:** BOASTER **b :** LIE **c :** one that quips or relates wittily ⟨a ~ of jokes⟩ **2 :** anything that makes a cracking or snapping noise: as **a :** FIRECRACKER **b :** the cracking or snapping part at the end of a whiplash **:** SNAPPER **c :** a paper cylinder-shaped holder for a party favor containing an explosive that discharges when the ends are pulled sharply **3 :** one that cracks esp. into pieces: **a crackers** *pl* **:** NUTCRACKER **b :** one that softens and breaks down slabs of milled rubber so that they can be more easily cut for feeding into the tubing machine **4 :** a small dry bakery product made of flour and water with or without leavening and shortening and salted, semisweet, or plain **5** [prob. fr. *cracker* "boaster"] **a** *South* **:** POOR WHITE — usu. used disparagingly **b :** GEORGIAN — used as a nickname **c :** FLORIDIAN — used as a nickname **6** *Brit* **:** a rapid pace **7 :** a light yellowish brown that is redder and slightly lighter and stronger than khaki, duller than walnut brown, less strong and slightly yellower and lighter than cinnamon, and duller and slightly redder than manila **8 :** the equipment in which cracking is carried out

cracker–barrel \'==,==\ *adj* [fr. *cracker barrel*; fr. its being formerly a popular feature of the country store where discussions on any and all subjects are carried on] **:** suggestive of the intimate homespun nature of a country store ⟨the *cracker-barrel* democracy of rural life —W.R.Goldschmidt⟩

crackerberry \'==— *see* BERRY\ *n* [so called fr. the noise produced when it is eaten] **:** DWARF CORNEL

[1]**crack·er·jack** \'krakə(r),jak\ *also* **crack·a·jack** \-kə,j-\ *n* -S [prob. fr. [1]*crack* (to go fast) + -*er* + *jack* (fellow)] **1 :** an exceptionally skilled person ⟨a good student and a ~ on the football field⟩ ⟨the humor she was a ~ at —Saul Bellow⟩ **2 :** a thing of highest excellence ⟨a ~ of a book —Fitzhugh Green⟩

[2]**crackerjack** *also* **crackajack** \"\ *adj* **:** of striking ability or excellence ⟨a ~ revolver shot⟩ ⟨a ~ bicycle⟩

Cracker Jack *trademark* — used for a confection of popcorn and sometimes shelled peanuts coated with syrup

cracker mill *n* **:** a mill made of large disks covered with projecting teeth set face to face and rotating in opposite directions and used to crush previously softened grain

cracker–off \'==ˌ=\ *n, pl* **crackers–off** [fr. *crack off*, v.] **:** a glassworker that trims glass chemical ware with a flame and diamond or removes the blowpipe from the neck of a glass object **:** WETTER-OFF

[1]**crack·ers** \'krakə(r)z\ *n pl but sing or pl in constr* [so called fr. the cracking noise produced by the seeds when the berries are eaten] **:** BLACK HUCKLEBERRY

[2]**crackers** \"\ *adj* [fr. pl. of *cracker* (influenced in meaning by *cracked*, *crackbrain*)] *slang Brit* **:** CRAZY ⟨I'm here to tell you that you're driving me ~ —Noel Coward⟩; *also* **:** intensely enthusiastic **:** CRACKED ⟨we went ~ about them —Clarence Woodbury⟩

crack·et \'krakə̇t\ *dial Brit var of* CRICKET

crackhalter *n* [[1]*crack* + *halter*] *obs* **:** GALLOWS BIRD

crackhemp *n* [[1]*crack* + *hemp*] *obs* **:** GALLOWS BIRD

crackier *comparative of* CRACKY

crackiest *superlative of* CRACKY

[1]**crack·ing** \'krakiŋ, -kēŋ\ *adj* [fr. pres. part. of [1]*crack*] **:** GREAT, SMASHING ⟨his dying was ~ relief —Elizabeth Bowen⟩ ⟨a ~ regimental salute —Geoffrey Household⟩

[2]**cracking** \"\ *adv* **:** SUPERLATIVELY — usu. used with *good* ⟨a ~ good show⟩

[3]**cracking** \"\ *n* -S [fr. gerund of [1]*crack*] **:** a process in which relatively heavy hydrocarbons (as fuel oils and naphthas from petroleum) are broken up into lighter products (as gasoline and ethylene) by means of heat and usu. pressure and sometimes catalysts — see CATALYTIC CRACKING, THERMAL CRACKING

crackjaw \'ˌ=\ *adj* [[1]*crack* + *jaw*] **:** hard to pronounce **:** JAWBREAKING ⟨a ~ name⟩

[1]**crack·le** \'krakəl\ *vb* **crackled; crackled; crackling** \-k(ə)liŋ\ **crackles** [freq. of [1]*crack*] *vi* **1 a :** to make small sharp sudden repeated noises ⟨a fire *crackling* in the hearth⟩ ⟨the dry leaves *crackled* along the walk⟩ **b :** to be alive (as with animation, enthusiasm, excitement, suspense) **:** SPARKLE ⟨an anthology that ~*s* with wit and wisdom —Bennett Cerf⟩ ⟨the very air, charged by an invisible generator, ~*s* with new business —Clifton Fadiman⟩ **2 :** to develop a surface network of fine cracks ⟨varnish applied over wet paint is likely to ~⟩ **:** become cracked ⟨his face was so dry and grimy that he thought he could feel his skin ~ —Stephen Crane⟩ ~ *vt* **1 :** to crush or crack with a series of sharp snapping noises ⟨thrust her hand between a sheaf of loosened papers and *crackled* them —Rosamond Langbridge⟩ **2 :** to detach or curtail (a note or chord) in lute music

[2]**crackle** \"\ *n* -S **1 a :** the noise of slight and frequent cracks or reports ⟨the ~ of small arms⟩ ⟨the ~ of laughter⟩ ⟨the ~ as he folded his newspaper⟩ **b :** SPARKLE, EFFERVESCENCE ⟨the dry ~ of Yankee wit —Clifton Fadiman⟩ **2 a :** a network of fine cracks on an otherwise smooth surface (as on pottery and glassware) — compare CRAZE **b :** a painted surface in which numerous fine cracks have been caused by superimposition of layers which contract differently in the process of drying **3 :** CRACKLING 2b

crack·led \'krakəld\ *adj* **1 :** having the rind crisp and brittle ⟨~ roast pork⟩ **2 :** covered with or as if with minute cracks ⟨pottery with a ~ finish⟩

crack·less \'krakləs\ *adj* **:** not having a crack

crack·le·ware \'==,=\ *n* [[2]*crackle* + *ware*] **:** glazed ceramic ware with a crazed finish

[1]**crack·ling** \'krak(ə)liŋ\ *adj* **1 :** that crackles ⟨~ sounds⟩ ⟨~ wit⟩ **2** *of wine* **:** mildly sparkling **:** PÉTILLANT

[2]**crackling** \"; *in sense 2 & 3 often* -lə̇n\ *n* -S **1 :** a series of small sharp cracks or reports (as from frozen snow being walked over or rifle fire at a distance) **2 a :** refuse of tallow melting used as food for dogs — usu. used in pl. **b :** the crisp residue left after the fat has been separated from the fibrous tissue in rendering lard or frying or roasting the skin of pork, turkey, duck, or goose — usu. used in pl.; compare CRACKLING BREAD **3** *dial Eng* **:** CRACKNEL 1 — usu. used in pl.

crackling bread \'krakliŋ-, -klən-\ *or* **crack·lin bread** \-lən-\ *n, chiefly South* **:** corn bread made with cracklings

crack–loo \'kra,klü\ *also* **crack·a·loo** \-akə,lü\ *n* -S [*crack-loo* fr. [2]*crack* + *loo*; *crackaloo* fr. [2]*crack* + connective -*a*- + *loo*] **:** a gambling game in which players toss up coins and consider the winner the one whose coin falls and rests nearest to a crack in the floor

crack·ly \'krak(ə)lē, -li\ *adj* -ER/-EST **:** inclined to crackle **:** crisp and brittle

crack·nel \'kraknəl\ *n* -S [ME *krakenelle*, perh. modif. of MF *craquelin*, fr. MD *crākelinc*, fr. *crāken* to crack; akin to OE *cracian* to crack — more at CRACK] **1 :** a hard brittle biscuit **2 :** CRACKLING 2 — usu. used in pl.

crackowe *var of* CRAKOW

crack·pot \'ˌ=\ *n, often attrib* [[1]*crack* + *pot* "head"] **:** one given to erratic, impractical, or lunatic ideas or notions ⟨a new crop of ~*s* determined to lead the country into chaos —Bill Mauldin⟩ ⟨~ ideas⟩ — **crack·pot·ism** \"+,izəm\ *n* -S

crackrope \'ˌ=\ *n* [ME *crakraip*, fr. *craken*, *cracken* to crack + *raip*, var. of *rope*] **1** *archaic* **:** GALLOWS BIRD **2 :** ROGUE, WAG

cracks *pl of* CRACK, *pres 3d sing of* CRACK

crackskull \'ˌ=\ *n* [[1]*crack* + *skull*] *archaic* **:** CRACKBRAIN

cracks·man \'kraksmən\ *n, pl* **cracksmen** [*cracks* (pl. or gen. sing. of [2]*crack* "burglary") + *man*] **:** BURGLAR, HOUSEBREAKER; *also* **:** SAFECRACKER

crack–the–whip \ˌ==ˈ=\ *n* **:** a game in which players join hands in a line and rush forward together until the leader's sudden turn causes the line to swing around rapidly often throwing off players at the opposite end

crack–up \'ˌ=\ *n* -S [fr. *crack up*, v.] **:** an instance of cracking up: as **a :** NERVOUS BREAKDOWN **b :** a wrecking or smashing (as of a vehicle); *specif* **:** an accident involving serious but repairable structural damage to an aircraft **c :** COLLAPSE, BREAKDOWN ⟨the *crack-up* of a political coalition⟩

crack willow *n* **1 :** a common and widely cultivated Old World willow (*Salix fragilis*) — called also *brittle willow*, *snap willow* **2 :** any of several willows closely related to the crack willow

[1]**cracky** \krakē, -ki\ *adj* -ER/-EST [[2]*crack* + -*y*] **1 a :** having cracks **b :** inclined to crack **2** *chiefly dial Eng* **:** CRACKBRAINED

[2]**cracky** \"\ *interj* [alter. of *crickey*, *crikey*] — a mild oath; used in the phrase *by cracky*

cracky wagon *n* [prob. fr. [2]*crack* (noise) + -*y*] **:** a light wagon without springs drawn by one horse

cra·co·vi·enne \krə,kōvē'en, =ˌ==ˌ=\ *n* -S [F, fr. fem. of *cracovien* of Cracow, fr. *Cracovie* (Cracow), Poland + F -*ien* -ian] **:** KRAKOWIAK

cra·cow *or* **kra·kow** \'krä,kaů, -ra,-, -rā,-, -(,)kō; 'krä,küf, -,kōf\ *adj, usu cap* [fr. *Cracow* (*Kraków*), Poland] **:** of or from the city of Cracow, Poland **:** of the kind or style prevalent in Cracow

cracowe *var of* CRAKOW

crac·ti·ci·dae \krak'tisə,dē\ *n pl, cap* [NL, fr. *Cracticus*, type genus (fr. Gk *kraktikos* noisy, fr. assumed Gk *kraktos*, verbal of Gk *krazein* to croak) — + Gk -*ikos* -ic + -*idae* — more at ROOK] **:** a small family of Australasian oscine birds that were formerly included in the family Laniidae — see STREPERA

-cra·cy \krəsē, -si\ *or* **-oc·ra·cy** \ˈäkrəsē, -si\ *n comb form* -ES [MF & LL; MF -*cratie*, fr. LL -*cratia*, fr. Gk -*kratia*, fr. *kratos* strength, power — more at HARD] **1 :** form of government; *also* **:** state having such a form ⟨*democracy*⟩ ⟨*mobocracy*⟩ ⟨*squirocracy*⟩ **2 :** social or political class (as of powerful persons) ⟨*plutocracy*⟩ ⟨*snobocracy*⟩ **3 :** theory of government or of social organization ⟨*technocracy*⟩

[1]**cra·dle** \'krād[ə]l\ *n* -S [ME *cradel*, fr. OE *cradol* cradle, cot; akin to OHG *kratto* basket, Skt *grantha* knot, ON *karmr* breastwork, L *grumus* pile of earth scratched together, Gk *grypos* bent, Skt *guṇa* rope, string; basic meaning: turning, twisting] **1 a :** a bed or cot for a baby usu. oscillating on rockers or swinging on pivots ⟨rock a ~⟩ **b :** the earliest period of life **:** INFANCY ⟨from the ~ to the grave⟩ **c :** a place where something began to develop **:** region of origin ⟨the Nile valley conceived of as the ~ of civilization⟩ **2 :** a resting place, framework, container, or grip felt to resemble the restraining or supporting nature of a baby's cradle or of its shape: as **a** (1) **:** a framework of bars and rods joined by crosspieces (as a workman's suspended scaffold or the ribbing of a vaulted ceiling to be covered with plaster) (2) **:** a supporting foundation usu. of concrete for maintaining the proper gradient of a pipe drain located on a subgrade not capable of supporting it (3) **:** a frame in which the treads and risers of stairs are glued together (4) **:** a framework of ribs often joined by crosspieces and attached to the back of a painted panel to prevent warping or splitting (5) **:** the support for a telephone receiver or handset **b** (1) **:** an implement with rods like fingers attached to a scythe and used formerly esp. for harvesting grain (2) **:** a device in weaving consisting of curved metal pieces fastened beneath the cylinders to catch the cards of a jacquard head as they fall **c** (1) **:** a wooden frame supporting a ship when launched — called also *launching cradle* (2) **:** a wooden or metal framework on a ship (as under a lifeboat or machinery) used to support in a fixed position or facilitate in moving from one place to another (3) **:** a frame of timber or blocks for the support of large rounded objects (as boats, tanks, pipes) so that they do not roll esp. while being transported (4) **:** the part of a gun carriage that supports the tube and upon which the tube recoils (5) **:** a low frame on casters used by mechanics to support themselves while working under an automobile — called also *creeper* **d** (1) **:** a frame to keep the bedclothes from contact with an injured part of the body (as in fractures, wounds, burns) (2) **:** a frame placed on an animal's neck by a veterinarian to keep the animal from biting an injury or sore **e :** a device on the string of a stonebow to hold a missile **f :** CAT'S CRADLE **g :** a grip by which a wrestler holds an opponent in a doubled-up position by circling his head and one leg and interlocking his own hands **3 :** anything that rocks or may be rocked in the manner of a baby's cradle: as **a :** a rocking device used by miners in washing out auriferous earth by hand — called also *rocker* **b :** a tool used in mezzotint engraving that by a rocking motion raises burrs on the surface of the plate

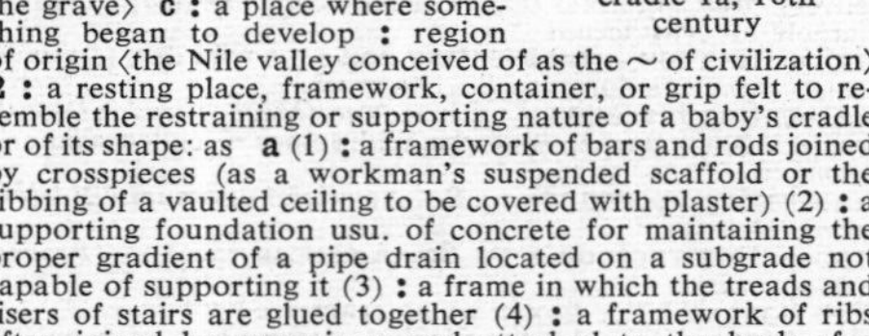
cradle 1a, 18th century

cradle 2b(1)

[2]**cradle** \"\ *vb* **cradled; cradled; cradling** \-d([ə])liŋ\ **cradles** *vt* **1 a :** to place or keep (a baby) in or as if in a cradle ⟨they *cradled* their youngest on the sun porch⟩ ⟨an occasional Paiute woman with baby *cradled* on her back —*Amer. Guide Series: Nev.*⟩ **b :** SHELTER, REAR ⟨while Italy was *cradling* the strange Etruscan culture —Jacquetta & Christopher Hawkes⟩ **c :** to support protectively or intimately **:** hold closely ⟨*cradled* his head on his folded arms —MacKinlay Kantor⟩ ⟨*cradling* a cup of coffee in his hand —Luke Short⟩ **2 :** to cut (as grain) with a cradle scythe **3 a :** to place in or provide with a special or suitable form or container ⟨~ a boat⟩ ⟨~ the receiver of a telephone⟩ ⟨~ machinery for shipment⟩ **b :** to furnish or reinforce with a ribbed framework ⟨~ a painting⟩ ⟨~ a panel⟩ **4 :** to wash in a miner's cradle ⟨~ out a few grains of gold⟩ **5 :** to keep (a lacrosse ball) in the pocket of the crosse with rotating motions ~ *vi* **1** *obs* **:** to rest in or as if in a cradle **2 :** to wash out ore in a cradle **3 :** to cut grain with a cradle scythe

cradleboard \'==,=\ *n* **:** a board or flat framework to which American Indians traditionally and often today bind a child during the infant stage of growth

cradle cannon *n* **:** a cannon in billiards made when the balls are close beside a pocket

cradle cap *n* **:** eczema of the crown of the head in infants marked by greasy, gray, or dark brown adherent scaly crusts that often coalesce to form a covering resembling a cap

cradle knoll *n* **:** a small knoll (as on a logging road) that requires grading

cradleland \'==,=\ *n* **:** the land or region of origin

cra·dler \'krād(ə)lə(r)\ *n* -S [[2]*cradle* (to mow) + -*er*] **:** one that cradles (as in reaping wheat)

cradle roll *n* **:** a listing kept by a church of the names of very young children esp. those of members

cradle roof *n* **:** a timber roof much used in the middle ages with the rafters, collar beams, and braces of each truss combined into a form approaching that of an arch and thus giving the effect of a series of arches or when ceiled of a barrel vault — compare COMPASS ROOF

cradles *pl of* CRADLE, *pres 3d sing of* CRADLE

cradle scythe *n* **:** a scythe equipped with a cradle

cradle snatcher *n* **:** one that weds or associates with one of the opposite sex who is comparatively very young

cradlesong \'==,=\ *n* [ME *cradyl songe*, fr. *cradyl* cradle + *songe* song] **:** LULLABY, BERCEUSE

cradle vault *n* **:** BARREL VAULT

cradlewalk *n*, *obs* **:** a walk covered by arching trees

cradling *n* -S **1 :** the act of using a cradle **2 :** the placing of the cables of a suspension bridge closer together at the center of span than at the supporting towers **3 :** a wooden or iron framework **:** structural work in the form of a cradle or cradles; *specif* **:** a framework in arched or coved ceilings to which the laths are nailed

[1]**craft** \'kraft, -raa(ə)ft, -raift, -râft\ *n* -S *see sense 6* [ME, fr. OE *cræft* strength, skill — more at CRAVE] **1** *obs* **:** STRENGTH, FORCE **2 :** skillfulness in planning, making, or executing **:** artistic dexterity ⟨great ~ in catching fish⟩ ⟨manual ~⟩ — often used in combination ⟨stage*craft*⟩ ⟨siege*craft*⟩ ⟨wine*craft*⟩ ⟨campaign*craft*⟩ **3 a :** an occupation, trade, or pursuit requiring manual dexterity or the application of artistic skill ⟨the carpenter's ~⟩ ⟨the ~ of playwriting⟩ ⟨learn a ~ from the ground up⟩ **b :** any one of the seven divisions of Camp Fire Girl activities **4 a** *obs* **:** EXPEDIENT, TRICK, ARTIFICE **b :** skill in deceiving for the promotion of one's own ends **:** CUNNING, GUILE ⟨an enemy of great ~ and subtlety⟩ ⟨Henry, out of a lifetime of political ~, coached Cranmer how to turn the tables on his accusers —Francis Hackett⟩ **5 a :** the members of a particular trade or an association of these **:** GUILD ⟨the ~ of ironmongers⟩ **b** *often cap* **:** the brotherhood of Freemasons **6** *pl usu* **craft a :** a boat esp. of small size ⟨a seaworthy ~⟩ ⟨these fascinating ~ that floated downstream —*Amer. Guide Series: Ind.*⟩ ⟨storm warnings put up for small ~⟩ **b :** AIRCRAFT ⟨helicopter delivery service . . . using four ~ —*Tide*⟩ **7** [origin unknown] **:** the equipment for catching and killing fish **syn** see ART

[2]**craft** \"\ *vt* -ED/-ING/-S **:** to make or construct esp. by or as if by hand ⟨scale models he has ~*ed* —*Newsweek*⟩

[3]**craft** \'kraft\ *chiefly Scot var of* [1]CROFT

craft·i·ly \'kraftəlē, -raaf-,-raif-,-râf-, -li\ *adv* [ME, fr. OE *cræftiglice*, fr. *cræftig* + -*lice* -ly] **1** *archaic* **:** SKILLFULLY **2 :** SLYLY, ARTFULLY ⟨a ~ devised trap⟩

craft·i·ness \-tēnə̇s, -tin-\ *n* -ES **:** the quality or state of being crafty

craft·less \-tləs\ *adj* **:** not having a craft

crafts·man \-f(t)smən\ *n, pl* **craftsmen** [ME *craftes man*, fr. *craftes* (gen. sing. of [1]*craft*) + *man*] **1 :** one who practices some trade or handicraft (as a bricklayer, woodcarver, plumber) **:** ARTISAN **2 :** one who creates or performs with skill or dexterity esp. in the manual arts ⟨jewelry made by Old World *craftsmen*⟩ **3 :** one who does work of consistently high quality ⟨as a novelist he was a consummate ~⟩ — **crafts·man·ship** \-,ship\ *n*

craftsmaster *n* [*crafts* (gen. of [1]*craft*) + *master*] *obs* **:** a skilled craftsman

craftswoman \'==,=\ *n, pl* **craftswomen :** a female craftsman

craft union *n* **:** a labor union whose membership is limited to workmen following the same craft — compare INDUSTRIAL UNION

craftwork \'==,=\ *n* **:** work usu. done by hand that exhibits artistry and individuality ⟨~ in metal⟩; *also* **:** a product of such work ⟨pottery and other imported ~⟩

crafty \-ftē, -ti\ *adj, usu* -ER/-EST [ME, fr. OE *cræftig* strong, skillful, fr. *cræft* + -*ig* -y] **1** *dial chiefly Brit* **:** SKILLFUL, CLEVER, INGENIOUS **2** *obs* **:** showing skill **:** skillfully made **3 :** adept at deceiving others **:** CUNNING, WILY **syn** see SLY

[1]**crag** \'krag, -raa(ə)g,-raig\ *n* -S [ME, of Celt origin; akin to OIr *crec* crag, OW *creik* rock; perh. akin to OE *heard* hard — more at HARD] **1 :** a steep rugged rocky eminence **:** a rough broken cliff or projecting point of rock **2 a** *archaic* **:** a sharp detached fragment of rock **b :** a sedimentary rock found in Norfolk, Suffolk, and Essex, England, and composed of fragments of shells mingled with sand

[2]**crag** \"\ *n* -S [ME *crag*, *crage*, fr. MD *crāghe*; akin to ME *crawe* craw — more at CRAW] **1** *chiefly Scot* **:** NECK **2** *chiefly Scot* **:** THROAT

crag and tail *n* **:** an elongate hill having at one end a steep face of ice-smoothed rock and at the other a gentle slope of rock or glacial drift

crag–fast \'ˌ=\ *adj* **:** stranded on or as if on a crag and unable to ascend or descend ⟨~ sheep⟩

crag·gan \'kragən\ *n* -S [ScGael *cragan*, akin to MIr *crocān* pot, prob. fr. OE *crocca* — more at CROCK] **:** a rude earthenware vessel for domestic use made in the Hebrides

crag·ged \'kragə̇d, -raag-,-raig-\ *adj* **:** CRAGGY

crag·ged·ness *n* -ES **:** CRAGGINESS

crag·gi·ly \-gəlē, -li\ *adv* **:** in a craggy manner

crag·gi·ness \-gēnə̇s, -gin-\ *n* -ES **:** the quality or state of being craggy

crag·gy \-gē,-gi\ *adj, usu* -ER/-EST [ME, fr. [1]*crag* + -*y*] **1 :** full of or abounding in crags ⟨~ slopes⟩ **2 :** ROUGH, RUGGED ⟨~ facial features⟩ ⟨a ~ personality⟩

crag martin *n* **:** ROCK SWALLOW

cra·go \'krāgō\ *n, cap* [NL, alter. of *Crangon*] **:** a genus (the type of the family Crangonidae) of large shrimps including the black-tailed shrimp (*C. nigricauda*) of the Pacific coast of No. America

crags·man \'kragzmən\ *n, pl* **cragsmen :** one expert in climbing crags or cliffs

craich \'krāk\ *var of* CREAGH

crai·chy \'krāchi\ *adj* [origin unknown] **1** *dial Eng* **:** DILAPIDATED **2** *dial Eng* **:** INFIRM, AILING

[1]**craig** \'krāg\ *n* -S [ME *crag* — more at CRAG (rock)] *Scot* **:** [1]CRAG

[2]**craig** \"\ *also* **craig·ie** *or* **craigy** \-gi\ *n, pl* **craigs** *also* **craigies** [*craig* fr. ME *crag*, *crage*; *craigie*, *craigy*, dim. of *craig* — more at CRAG (neck)] *Scot* **:** [2]CRAG

craik \'krāk\ *Scot var of* CRAKE

crai·sey \'krāzi\ *var of* [3]CRAZY

[1]**crake** \'krāk\ *n, pl* **crakes** *also* **crake** [ME, prob. fr. ON *krāka* crow or *krākr* raven — more at CROW] **1** *dial Brit* **:** CROW, ROOK **2 :** any of various rails; *esp* **:** the corncrake and other short-billed kinds **3 :** the corncrake's cry

2crake \"\ *vi* -ED/-ING/-S [ME *craken*, prob. of imit. origin] **1 :** to cry out harshly and loudly ⟨crows *craking* in a field⟩ **2** *dial Brit* **:** COMPLAIN, FRET
3crake \"\ *vi* -ED/-ING/-S [ME *craken* — more at CRACK] *dial Brit* **:** 1CRACK *vi* 3
crakeberry \ˈ=,— *see* BERRY\ *n* [1*crake* + *berry*] **:** CROWBERRY 1a
cra·kow *also* **cra·kowe** *or* **crac·kowe** *or* **cra·cowe** \ˈkrä,kaů, -ra,-, -rā,-, -(,)kō\ *n* -S [ME *crakowe*, fr. *Cracow* (*Kraków*) Poland whence they came] **:** a shoe, boot, or slipper made with an extremely long pointed toe and worn in Europe in the 14th and 15th centuries
1cram \ˈkram, -raa(ə)m\ *vb* **crammed; crammed; cramming; crams** [ME *crammen*, fr. OE *crammian*; akin to OHG *krimman* to press, ON *kremja* to squeeze, L *gremium* lap, Skt *grāma* multitude, pile, village, L *grex* herd — more at GREGARIOUS] *vt* **1 :** to fill esp. forcibly with more than is necessary or appropriate **:** pack tight **:** load to overflowing **:** JAM ⟨~ a suitcase with clothes⟩ ⟨a *crammed* schedule⟩ ⟨a novel *crammed* with surprises⟩ **2 a :** to fill with food to satiety **:** OVERFEED, STUFF; *esp* **:** to feed forcibly in order to fatten (poultry) either through a tube inserted into the crop or by thrusting long strips of dough down the gullet by hand **b :** to eat voraciously or clumsily **:** BOLT ⟨rebuke a child for *cramming* his food⟩ **3 :** to thrust, jam, or drive in or as if in a rough, clumsy, willful, or unsuitable manner ⟨he *crammed* the letters in his pocket⟩ ⟨~ lies down another's throat⟩ **4 a :** to put (a person) hastily through a course of memorizing esp. in preparation for an examination **b :** to study (a subject) under pressure ⟨~ physics for the final examination⟩ ~ *vi* **1 :** to eat greedily or to satiety **:** STUFF **2 :** to study intensively or under pressure esp. for an examination — often used with *up* ⟨~ up on mathematics⟩ **syn** see PACK
2cram \"\ *n* -S **1 :** a compressed multitude or crowd **:** CRUSH ⟨there was such a ~ in the church that the procession had almost to fight its way to the high altar —Bruce Marshall⟩ **2 :** studying or instructing under pressure or limitations of time esp. for a coming examination ⟨he got through his senior year finally by sheer ~⟩ ⟨students attending ~ courses before their exams⟩
3cram \"\ *n* -S [G, Sw, Dan & Norw *kram* trifles, small wares, rubbish; G, fr. MHG *krām* stretched out cloth, tent covering, merchandise booth, fr. OHG *crām* market booth; Sw, Dan & Norw, fr. MLG *krām* market booth, tent covering, small wares; akin to MD *crāme*, *craem* tent flap, market booth, small wares] *dial* **:** anything unwanted or in the way **:** JUNK
cram·a·sie *or* **cram·a·sy** \ˈkraməzē\ *archaic var of* CRAMOISIE
1cram·be \ˈkrambē\ *n, cap* [NL, fr. L, cabbage, fr. Gk *krambē*; akin to LGk *krambos* dry, withered — more at RUMPLE] **:** a genus of chiefly Old World mostly annual herbs (family Cruciferae) having coarse lyrate leaves and panicled white flowers — see SEA KALE
2crambe *vi* -ED/-ING/-S [obs. E *crambe* crambo — more at CRAMBO] *obs* **:** to play crambo
cram·ber·ry \ˈkram,berē, -b(ə)rē, -ri — *see* BERRY\ *now dial var of* CRANBERRY
1cram·bid \ˈkrambəd\ *adj* [NL *Crambidae*] **:** of or relating to the Crambidae
2crambid \"\ *n* -S **:** any moth of the family Crambidae
cram·bi·dae \ˈkrambə,dē\ *n, pl, cap* [NL, fr. *Crambus*, type genus + *-idae*] *in some esp former classifications* **:** a family that comprises small moths which wrap the wings about the body when at rest and that is now usu. made a subfamily of Pyralididae — compare CHILO, CORN BORER, GRASS MOTH
cram·ble *or* **cram·mel** \ˈkraməl\ *vi* -ED/-ING/-S [fr. obs. E, to crawl, of unknown origin] *dial Eng* **:** to walk or move stiffly or with difficulty **:** HOBBLE
cram·bling rocket \ˈkramb(ə)liŋ-\ *n* [prob. fr. pres. part. of obs. E *cramble* to crawl] **:** a European herb (*Reseda lutea*) resembling the common garden mignonette
cram·bo \ˈkram(,)bō\ *n* -ES [alter. of earlier *crambe*, fr. L, cabbage — more at CRAMBE] **1 :** a game in which one player gives a word or line of verse that is to be matched in rhyme by other players **2 :** ineffectual, fatuous, or second-rate rhyme or rhyming ⟨his verse was nothing but ~⟩
crambo clink *or* **crambo jingle** *n, Scot* **:** DOGGEREL, CRAMBO
cram·bus \ˈkrambəs\ *n, cap* [NL, fr. LGk *krambos* dry, withered — more at RUMPLE] **:** a genus of small moths (family Pyralididae) that have fringed hindwings and include several economic pests with larvae that are webworms
crame \ˈkrām\ *n* -S [ME, fr. MD *crāme* or MLG *krāme*; akin to OHG *crām* market booth] *Scot* **:** a booth, stall, or tent where goods are sold (as at a fair)
cram–full \ˈ=ˈ=\ *adj* [2*cram*] **:** as full as can be **:** OVERFLOWING ⟨a novel *cram-full* of suspense⟩
cra·mi·gnon \krámēnyōⁿ\ *n* -S [F] **:** a festive dance of southern France in which the dancers are in chain formation
cram·mer \ˈkramə(r)\ *n* -S **:** one that crams: as **a :** an apparatus for cramming poultry **b** *Brit* **:** a school or instructor that crams students (as for college, a branch of the armed forces, a profession, a civil-service examination)
1cram·oi·sie *or* **cram·oi·sy** \ˈkraməzē, krəˈmȯi-, ˈkra,mȯi-\ *n, pl* **cramoisies** [ME *cremesye*, *crammasy*, fr. MF *cremosi*, *cramoisi*, adj.] **:** crimson cloth
2cramoisie *or* **cramoisy** \"\ *adj* [ME *crymysy*, *cramysse*, fr. MF *cremosi*, *cramoisi*, fr. Ar *qirmizī* red of the kermes — more at CRIMSON] **:** CRIMSON
1cramp \ˈkramp, -raa(ə)mp, -raimp\ *n* -S [ME *crampe*, fr. MF, of Gmc origin; akin to MD *crampe* cramp, hook] **1 a** (1) **:** a spasmodic painful involuntary contraction of a muscle ⟨a ~ in the leg⟩ (2) **:** a case or instance of such a contraction ⟨suffering from the ~⟩ **b :** a temporary paralysis of certain muscles from overuse — see WRITER'S CRAMP **c** (1) **:** a sharp abdominal pain — usu. in pl. (2) **cramps** *pl* **:** painful menstruation **2 cramps** *pl* **a :** a partial paralysis of the hindquarters occasionally seen in pregnant animals **b :** the condition of birds unable to fly as a result of narrow confinement
2cramp \"\ *n* -S [obs. D *krampe* hook (fr. MD *crampe*) or LG, fr. MLG; akin to OHG *kramph* bent, ON *kreppa* to clench, Latvian *grumbt* to become wrinkled, OE *cradol* cradle — more at CRADLE] **1 a :** a device usu. of iron bent at the ends or of dovetail form used to hold together blocks (as of stone or timbers) **b :** 1CLAMP 1 **c :** a piece of wood used in the manufacture of shoes and having a curve corresponding to that of the upper part of the instep on which the upper leather of a boot is stretched — called also *crimp* **2 a :** something that confines or contracts **:** RESTRAINT, SHACKLE ⟨authoritarian ~s on free thinking⟩ **b :** the quality or state of being confined or compressed **:** CONSTRAINT ⟨the ~ and pettiness of bourgeois life⟩

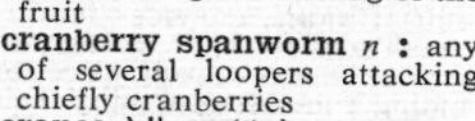
cramp 1a

3cramp \"\ *vb* -ED/-ING/-S [partly fr. 1*cramp*, partly fr. 2*cramp*] *vt* **1 :** to cause to have a cramp **:** affect with or as if with cramp ⟨gout ~*ing* his limbs⟩ ⟨his hands were ~*ed* for lack of movement⟩ **2 :** COMPRESS, RESTRAIN, CONFINE ⟨prisoners ~*ed* in fetters⟩ ⟨a spirit ~*ed* with dogma⟩ ⟨they ~*ed* the livestock in ancient barns⟩; *also* **:** to restrain from free expression of one's tastes or skill **:** dampen the spirits of — used esp. in the phrase *cramp one's style* **3 :** to turn (the front wheels of a vehicle) to right or left ⟨~ the wheels into the curb . . . when parked —C.P.Taylor⟩ **4 a :** to fasten or hold with a cramp **b :** to form on a cramp ⟨~ bootlegs⟩ ~ *vi* **:** to suffer from or as if from cramps
4cramp \"\ *adj* [prob. fr. 3*cramp*] **1 :** KNOTTY, DIFFICULT ⟨not to add any of the ~ reasons for this opinion —S.T. Coleridge⟩ **2 :** CONTRACTED, NARROW, CONFINED ⟨a ~ corner⟩
cramp bark *n* [1*cramp*] **1 :** CRANBERRY BUSH 2 **2 :** the dried bark of the cranberry tree used as an antispasmodic
cramp bone *n* [1*cramp*] **:** the patella of a sheep formerly used as a charm for the cramp
cramp colic *n* [1*cramp*] *South & Midland* **:** APPENDICITIS
cramped odds *n pl* **:** odds in court tennis that place a limitation on play instead of on the score only
cramp·er \-pə(r)\ *n* -S **1 :** one that cramps **2** *obs* **:** CRAMP IRON
cramp·ette *also* **cramp·et** \ˈkrampət\ *n* -S [ME *crampette*, fr. MD *crampe* hook + ME *-ette* — more at CRAMP] **1 :** the chape of a sword scabbard; *specif* **:** a conventionalized representation of such a chape used as a charge in heraldry **2** *usu* **crampet a** *obs* **:** FERRULE **b :** CRAMPIT
crampfish \ˈ=,=\ *n* [1*cramp* + *fish*; fr. its ability to give electric shocks] **:** ELECTRIC RAY
cramp·ing·ly *adv* **:** in a cramping manner
cramp iron *n* **1 :** 2CRAMP 1a **2 :** a metal piece attached at each side of a horse-drawn vehicle where a front wheel may rub when cramped
cramp·it \ˈkrampət\ *n* -S [alter. of *crampette*] **:** a sheet of iron on which a player stands to deliver his stone in curling
cram·pon \ˈkram,pän; *US also & Brit usu* -,pən\ *also* **cram·poon** \-,pün, =ˈ=\ *n* -S [MF, *crampon*, of Gmc origin; akin to MD *crampe* hook — more at CRAMP] **1 :** a form of hooked clutch or dog for raising heavy objects (as stones, lumber, blocks of ice) **:** GRAPPLING IRON — used usu. in pl. **2 :** a steel frame provided with spikes and attached to a boot with straps for use as a climbing iron on ice and snow

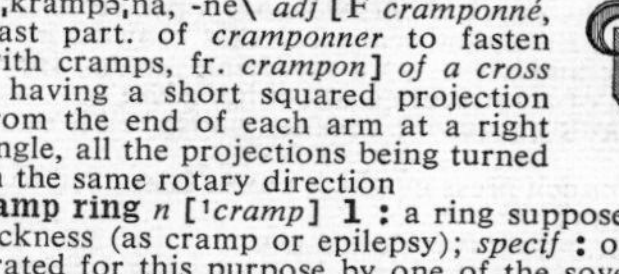
crampon 1

cram·po·née *also* **cram·po·née** \ˌkrampəˈnā, -nē\ *adj* [F *cramponné*, past part. of *cramponner* to fasten with cramps, fr. *crampon*] *of a cross* **:** having a short squared projection from the end of each arm at a right angle, all the projections being turned in the same rotary direction
cramp ring *n* [1*cramp*] **1 :** a ring supposed to avert or cure sickness (as cramp or epilepsy); *specif* **:** one formerly consecrated for this purpose by one of the sovereigns of England on Good Friday **2** *obs* **:** FETTER, SHACKLE
cramps *pl of* CRAMP, *pres 3d sing of* CRAMP
crampy \ˈkrampē, -raim-, -pi\ *adj* -ER/-EST [1*cramp* + *-y*] **:** affected with, resembling, or marked by a cramp **:** productive of cramps; *specif* **:** STRINGHALTED ⟨a ~ horse⟩
crams *pres 3 sing of* CRAM, *pl of* CRAM
1cran \ˈkran\ *n* -S [ME, crane — more at CRANE] *Scot* **:** a common swift (*Apus apus*)
2cran \"\ *n* -S [ScGael *crann* tree, lot, measure of herring; akin to OIr *crann* tree — more at HURST] **:** British unit of capacity for fresh herrings equal to 37½ imperial gallons
cran·age \ˈkrānij, -nēj\ *n* -S [ME, fr. *cran* crane + *-age*] **1 :** the use of a crane (as for loading and unloading ships) **2 :** the price paid for the use of a crane
1cran·ber·ry \ˈkran,berē, -raan-, -b(ə)rē, -ri *also* ÷ -am(,)- — *see* BERRY\ *n* -ES [part modif., part trans. of LG *kraanbere*, *kroonbere*, fr. *kraan*, *kroon* crane (fr. MLG *krān*, *krāne*) + *bere* berry; akin to OE *cran* crane — more at CRANE] **1 :** the bright red acid berry produced by any of several plants of the genus *Vaccinium* (as *V. oxycoccus* and *V. macrocarpon*) — see AMERICAN CRANBERRY, EUROPEAN CRANBERRY **2 :** any plant that produces cranberries — see OXYCOCCUS **3 :** any of numerous plants having fruit resembling a cranberry — see AUSTRALIAN CRANBERRY **4 a :** BOG BILBERRY **b :** MOUNTAIN CRANBERRY **5 :** a dark red that is bluer, lighter, and stronger than average garnet, bluer and slightly lighter and stronger than pomegranate, and bluer, lighter, and stronger than average wine
2cranberry \"\ *vi* **:** to gather or seek cranberries ⟨the whole family was ~*ing* all day⟩
cranberry bog *or* **cranberry marsh** *n* **:** a low periodically flooded area in which cranberries are grown
cranberry bush *n* **1 :** any plant bearing cranberries **2** *or* **cranberry tree :** a shrub or tree (*Viburnum trilobum*) of No. America and Europe with prominently 3-lobed leaves and red fruit — called also *highbush cranberry*; see GUELDER ROSE
cranberry fruitworm *n* **:** the larva of a small snout moth (*Acrobasis vaccinii*) that feeds in and destroys the growing fruits of cranberry and blueberry
cranberry gall *n* **:** a disease of the cranberry and related species caused by a fungus (*Synchytrium vaccinii*) and producing reddish galls on stem, leaves, flowers, and fruits
cranberry gourd *n* **1 :** a So. American tuberous-rooted herbaceous vine (*Abobra tenuifolia*) with 5-lobed or much divided leaves and small greenish fragrant flowers **2 :** the small fruit of the cranberry gourd at first white and later carmine used for ornament
cranberry rake *or* **cranberry scoop** *n* **:** a scoop with teeth on the front edge for harvesting cranberries
cranberry scald *or* **cranberry blast** *n* **:** a disease of the cranberry caused by a fungus (*Guignardia vaccinii*) producing a blasting of the flowers and scalding and rotting of the fruit
cranberry spanworm *n* **:** any of several loopers attacking chiefly cranberries

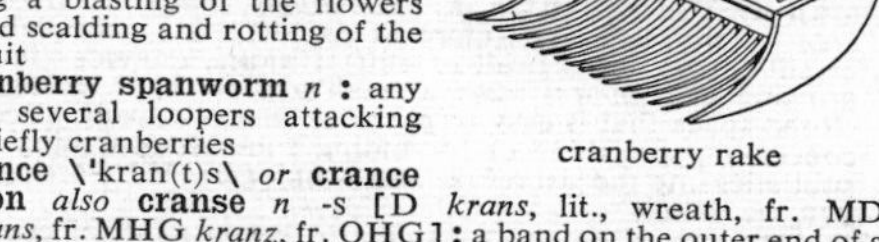
cranberry rake

crance \ˈkran(t)s\ *or* **crance iron** *also* **cranse** *n* -S [D *krans*, lit., wreath, fr. MD *crans*, fr. MHG *kranz*, fr. OHG] **:** a band on the outer end of a bowsprit to which the bobstays and bowsprit shrouds are fastened
cranch *var of* CRAUNCH
cran·dall·ite \ˈkrandəl,īt\ *n* -S [M. L. *Crandall*, 20th cent. Am. mining engineer + E *-ite*] **:** a mineral consisting of hydrous calcium-aluminum phosphate $CaAl_3(PO_4)_2(OH)_5H_2O$ occurring in white to grayish fine-fibrous masses
1crane \ˈkrān\ *n, pl* **cranes** *or* **crane** [ME *cran*, fr. OE; akin to OHG *krano* crane, ON *trani*, Gk *geranos*, L *grus* crane, Skt *jarate* he cries, it sounds; basic meaning: croaking] **1 :** any bird of the family Gruidae (order Gruiformes) consisting of a small group of tall wading birds superficially resembling the herons but structurally more nearly related to the rails and being usu. larger than the herons and differing from them in having a schizognathous skull, plumage more compact, partly naked head, obtuse bill with large nostrils near the middle, and elevated hind toe **2 a** *Midland* **:** GREAT BLUE HERON **b** (1) **:** the common heron (2) **:** CORMORANT **3** *pl* **cranes :** a projection often horizontal swinging about a vertical axis or having at one end a bend suggestive of a crane's neck: as **a :** a machine for raising and lowering heavy weights and transporting them through a limited horizontal distance while holding them suspended and usu. having a jib of timber or steel sometimes affixed to a rotating post held by guys or having the hoisting apparatus supported by a trolley running on an overhead track **b :** a siphon or bent pipe for drawing liquid out of a ship **c :** a davit for handling lifeboats, anchors, or heavy weights — used usu. in pl. **d :** an iron arm with horizontal motion attached to the side or back of a fireplace and used for supporting kettles over a fire **e :** WATER CRANE **f :** a device or machine for weighing goods **g :** MAIL CRANE **h :** a boom of considerable size used in the motion-picture and television industry for holding a camera and sometimes a cameraman **4** *or* **crane gray :** a purplish gray that is bluer and duller than dove gray, bluer and slightly less strong than granite, darker and slightly redder than zinc, and bluer and darker than cinder gray — called also *Prince gray*

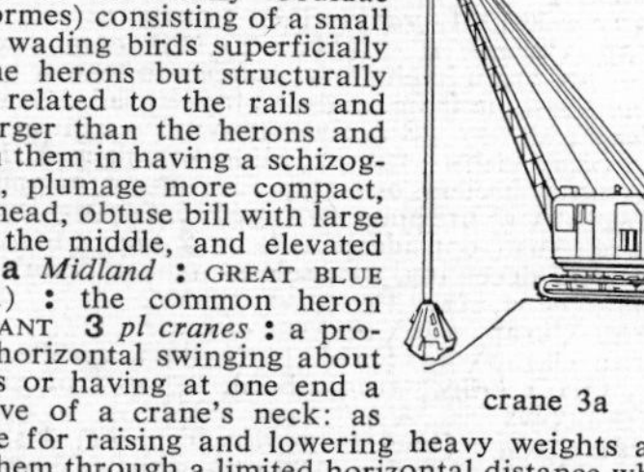
crane 3a

2crane \"\ *vb* -ED/-ING/-S *vt* **1 :** to raise or lift by or as if by a crane ⟨~ up building material⟩ **2 :** to stretch (the neck) forward ⟨~ one's neck to get a better view⟩ ⟨~ one's neck out a window⟩ ~ *vi* **1 :** to stretch out one's neck **:** bend forward with head and neck in order to see better ⟨people in the seats were *craning* back to look at him —T.B.Costain⟩ **2 a :** to stop at an obstacle in hunting and look over before leaping **b :** to look before one leaps **:** HESITATE
3crane \"\ *n* -S [MF *crâne*, fr. ML *cranium* — more at CRANIUM] *archaic* **:** CRANIUM
crane·ber·ry \"- — *see* BERRY\ *archaic var of* CRANBERRY
crane fly *n* **1 :** any of numerous long-legged slender two-winged flies (family Tipulidae) that resemble large mosquitoes but do not bite, that produce larvae which usu. live in the ground or sometimes in water, and that are destructive to the roots of native and cereal grasses — see RANGE CRANE FLY **2 :** any of various flies somewhat similar in form to the crane fly
crane–fly orchid \ˈ=ˈ=,=-\ *n* **:** a small orchid (*Tipularia discolor*) of the eastern U.S.
crane follower *n* **:** a worker who assists with the grappling of a load by a crane and who follows it to help with its deposition — called also *burdenman*, *groundsman*, *slingman*, *spotter*
crane line *n* **1 :** one of the lines running from the spritsail topmast of a sailing ship to the middle of the forestay to steady the former or one of the small lines for preventing the lee backstays from chafing against the yards **2 :** a small line joining the backstays on a sailing ship — usu. used in pl.
crane·man \ˈkrān,man, -,mən\ *n, pl* **cranemen 1 :** a crane operator **2 :** a worker who assists a drop-hammer operator to reduce the size of hot steel blooms by hoisting them into position
cranes·bill \ˈkrānz,bil\ *n* **:** a plant of the genus *Geranium* (as *G. dissectum*, *G. maculatum*, *G. robertianum*)
crane ship *n* **:** a ship equipped with cranes for handling heavy weights
crane shot *n* **:** BOOM SHOT
cranet *n* -S [modif. of MF *crinete* mane — more at CRINET] *obs* **:** CRINET
crane·way \ˈ=,=\ *n* **1 a :** the part of an area served by a crane **b :** the beams on which a crane trolley travels **2 :** the opening in the end of an industrial building which allows cranes to pass from the interior to the yard
crane willow *n* **:** BUTTONBUSH
crang *var of* KRENG
cranging hook *var of* KRENGING HOOK
cran·gon \ˈkran,gän, -,gōn\ [NL, fr. Gk *krangōn* shrimp, prawn; perh. akin to Gk *keras* horn — more at HORN] *syn of* CRAGO
cran·gon·i·dae \kranˈgänə,dē, -ˈgōn-\ *n pl, cap* [NL, fr. *Crangon*, type genus + *-idae*] **:** a large family of shrimps that have the first two pairs of legs chelate and the first pair enlarged and usu. unsymmetrical — see SNAPPING SHRIMP
crani- *or* **cranio-** *comb form* [*cranium*] **:** cranium ⟨*cranio*stosis⟩ ⟨*cranio*metry⟩ **:** cranial and ⟨*cranio*spinal⟩
1crania *pl of* CRANIUM
2cra·nia \ˈkrānēə\ *n, cap* [NL, fr. ML *cranium* + NL *-ia*] **:** a genus of inarticulate brachiopods attached by the surface of the ventral valve
-cra·nia \ˈkrānēə, -nyə\ *n comb form* -S [NL, fr. ML *cranium* + L *-ia* -y] **:** -skulledness ⟨platy*crania*⟩ **:** condition of the skull or head ⟨amphi*crania*⟩
cra·ni·acromial \ˈkrānē+\ *adj* [*crani-* + *acromial*] **:** having to do with the cranium and acromion
cra·ni·ad \ˈkrānē,ad\ *adv* [*crani-* + *-ad*] **:** toward the head or anterior end ⟨dissected out the growth as far ~ as the base of the hyoid⟩
cra·ni·al \ˈkrānēəl, -nyəl\ *adj* [*cranium* + *-al*] **1 :** of or belonging to the skull **2 :** of or belonging to the cranium proper **3 :** CEPHALIC 1 ⟨the ~ end of the spinal column⟩
cranial bones *n pl* **:** those bones of the skull that enclose the brain — compare CRANIAL SEGMENT
cranial capacity *n* **:** the cubic capacity of the braincase estimated for the living by a formula based on head measurements and determined for the skull by filling the cranial cavity with particulate material (as mustard seed or small shot) and measuring the volume of the latter
cranial flexure *n* **:** the middle of the three anterior flexures of a vertebrate embryo
cranial fossa *n* **:** one of the three large depressions in the posterior, middle, and anterior aspects of the floor of the cranial cavity which lodge respectively the cerebellum and the temporal and frontal lobes of the two hemispheres of the cerebrum
cra·ni·al·gia \ˌkrānēˈalj(ē)ə\ *n* -S [NL, fr. *crani-* + *-algia*] **:** pain occurring within the skull **:** HEADACHE
cranial index *n* **:** the ratio multiplied by 100 of the maximum breadth of the skull to its maximum height — compare CEPHALIC INDEX
cra·ni·al·ly \ˈkrānēəlē, -nyəl, -əli\ *adv* **:** in a cranial position or relation ⟨a duct opening ~ into the nasopharynx⟩
cranial module *n* **:** a measure of the external size of the skull obtained by averaging its length, breadth, and auricular height
cranial nerve *n* **:** any of the nerves that arise from the vertebrate brain, pass through openings in the skull to the periphery of the body (as the head), comprise 12 pairs in reptiles, birds, and mammals and usu. 10 in fishes and amphibians, and are sensory, motor, or mixed in constitution — see ABDUCENS NERVE, ACCESSORY NERVE, AUDITORY NERVE, FACIAL NERVE, GLOSSOPHARYNGEAL NERVE, HYPOGLOSSAL NERVE, OCULOMOTOR NERVE, OLFACTORY NERVE, OPTIC NERVE, TRIGEMINAL NERVE, TROCHLEAR NERVE, VAGUS NERVE
cranial segment *n* **:** any of three annular segments into which the bones of the cranium proper may be grouped: **a :** an occipital segment consisting of the basioccipital, exoccipital, and supraoccipital bones **b :** a parietal segment consisting of the basisphenoid, alisphenoid, and parietal bones **c :** a frontal segment consisting of the presphenoid, orbitosphenoid, and frontal bones
cra·ni·a·ta \ˌkrānēˈād·ə\ [NL, fr. *crani-* + *-ata*] *syn of* VERTEBRATA
1cra·ni·ate \ˈkrānēət, -ē,āt\ *adj* [in sense 1, fr. NL *Craniata*; in sense 2, fr. *crani-* + *-ate*] **1 :** of or relating to the Vertebrata **:** VERTEBRATE ⟨the lowest ~ fishes⟩ **2 :** having a skull or cranium
2craniate \"\ *n* -S **:** a craniate animal
cra·nic \ˈkrānik\ *adj* [prob. fr. F *crânique*, fr. *crâne* cranium + *-ique* -ic — more at CRANE] **:** CRANIAL
cra·nid·i·um \krəˈnidēəm\ *n, pl* **cranid·ia** \-dēə\ [NL, fr. LGk *kranidion* small skull, dim. of *kranion* skull — more at CRANIUM] **:** the central part of the cephalon of a trilobite bounded by the facial sutures
cra·ni·ec·to·mize \ˌkrānēˈektə,mīz\ *vt* -ED/-ING/-S **:** to perform a craniectomy on
cra·ni·ec·to·my \ˌkrānēˈektəmē\ *n* -ES [ISV *crani-* + *-ectomy*; prob. orig. formed as F *craniectomie*] **:** the surgical removal of a portion of the skull
cranies *pl of* CRANY
craning *pres part of* CRANE
cranio- — see CRANI-
cra·ni·o·cele \ˈkrānēə,sēl\ *n* -S [*crani-* + *-cele*] **:** ENCEPHALOCELE
cra·ni·o·cerebral \ˌkrānēō, -nēə+\ *adj* [*crani-* + *cerebral*] **:** involving both cranium and brain ⟨a ~ wound⟩
cra·ni·o·cla·sis \ˌkrānēōˈklāsəs, -nēˈäkləsəs-\ *n, pl* **cranioclases** \-,sēz\ [NL, fr. *crani-* + *-clasis*] **:** the crushing of the fetal head in difficult delivery
cra·ni·o·facial index \ˌkrānēō, -nēə+...-\ *n* [*crani-* + *facial*] **:** the ratio of the breadth of the cranium to the breadth of the face
cra·ni·o·graph \ˈkrānēə,graf, -räf\ *n* [ISV *crani-* + *-graph*] **:** an instrument used for the accurate depiction of a skull in outline
cra·ni·og·ra·pher \ˌkrānēˈägrəfə(r)\ *n* -S [*crani-* + *-grapher*] **:** a specialist in descriptive craniology
cra·ni·o·log·i·cal \ˌkrānēəˈläjəkəl\ *adj* **:** of or belonging to craniology — **cra·ni·o·log·i·cal·ly** \-jək(ə)lē\ *adv*
cra·ni·ol·o·gist \ˌkrānēˈäləjəst\ *n* -S **:** a specialist in craniology
cra·ni·ol·o·gy \-jē\ *n* -ES [prob. fr. G *kraniologie*, fr. *kranio-* crani- + *-logie* -logy] **1** *obs* **:** PHRENOLOGY **2 :** a science dealing with variations in size, shape, and proportions of skulls esp. as characterizing the different races of men — compare CRANIOMETRY
cra·ni·om·e·ter \ˌkrānēˈämәd·ə(r)\ *n* [ISV *crani-* + *-meter*; prob. orig. formed as F *craniomètre*] **:** an instrument for measuring skulls
cra·ni·o·met·ric \ˌkrānēəˈme·trik, -nēō,-\ *also* **cra·ni·o·met·ri·cal** \-trəkəl\ *adj* **:** of or belonging to craniometry — **cra·ni·o·met·ri·cal·ly** \-rək(ə)lē\ *adv*
craniometric point *n* **:** LANDMARK 2c (2)
cra·ni·om·e·trist \ˌkrānēˈämə·trəst\ *n* -S **:** a student or practitioner of craniometry

cra·ni·om·e·try \-rē\ *n* -s [ISV *crani-* + *-metry*] **:** a science dealing with measuring the skull esp. for determining the dimensions and proportions characteristic of a particular race, sex, developmental stage, or somatotype — distinguished from *cephalometry*

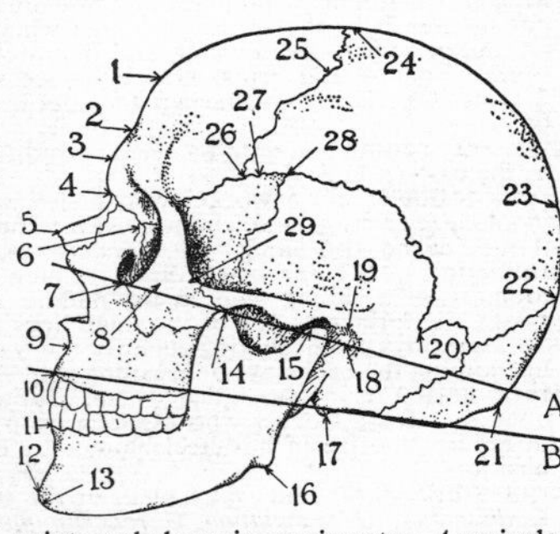

points and planes in craniometry: *A* auriculo-infraorbital plane; *B* alveolocondylean plane; *1* metopion; *2* ophryon; *3* glabella; *4* nasion; *5* rhinion; *6* dacryon; *7* orbital point; *8* malar point; *9* acanthion; *10* alveolar point or prosthion; *11* symphysion; *12* pogonion; *13* gnathion; *14* coronion; *15* condylion; *16* gonion; *17* mastoidale; *18* auricular point; *19* supra-auricular point; *20* entomion, at arrow, left; asterion at junction of sutures, right; *21* inion; *22* lambda; *23* obelion; *24* bregma; *25* stephanion; *26* sphenion; *27* pterion; *28* crotaphion; *29* jugal point

cra·ni·op·a·gus \ˌkrānēˈäpəgəs\ *n, pl* **cra·niopa·gi** \-əˌjē, -ˌjī\ [NL, fr. *crani-* + *-pagus*] **:** a pair of twins joined at the heads

cra·ni·o·phore \ˈkrānēəˌfō(ə)r\ *n* -s [ISV *crani-* + *-phore;* orig. formed in F] **:** a device for holding skulls in position (as for taking measurements)

cra·ni·o·plas·ty \-ˌplastē\ *n* -ES [ISV *crani-* + *-plasty*] **:** the surgical correction of skull defects

cra·ni·o·ra·chis·chi·sis \ˌkrānē(ˌ)ōrəˈkiskəsəs\ *n, pl* **cranio·rachischi·ses** \-ˌsēz\ [NL, fr. *crani-* + *rachi-* + *-schisis*] **:** a congenital fissure of the skull and spine

cra·ni·o·sacral \ˌkrānēō, -nēə+\ *adj* [*crani-* + *sacral*] **1 a :** of or belonging to the cranium and the sacrum **b :** supplied with nerves from these areas **2 :** PARASYMPATHETIC

cra·ni·os·chi·sis \ˌkrānēˈäskəsəs\ *n, pl* **cranioschi·ses** \-ˌsēz\ [NL, fr. *crani-* + *-schisis*] **:** a congenital fissure of the skull

cra·ni·o·scop·ic \ˌkrānēōˌskäpik, -nēə-\ *also* **cra·ni·o·scop·i·cal** \-pəkəl\ *adj* **:** of or belonging to cranioscopy

cra·ni·os·co·pist \ˌkrānēˈäskəˌpist\ *n* -s **:** a specialist in cranioscopy

cra·ni·os·co·py \-kəpē\ *n* -ES [*crani-* + *-scopy*] **:** observations on or examination of the human skull

cra·ni·o·ta \ˌkrānēˈōdə\ [NL, alter. of *Craniata*] *syn of* VERTEBRATA

cra·ni·o·tabes \ˌkrānēə, -nēō+\ *n* [NL, fr. *crani-* + *tabes*] **:** a thinning and softening of the infantile skull in spots usu. due to rickets or syphilis

cra·ni·o·tome \ˈkrānēəˌtōm\ *n* -s [ISV *crani-* + *-tome*] **:** an instrument used in performing craniotomy

cra·ni·ot·o·my \ˌkrānēˈädəmē\ *n* -ES [ISV *crani-* + *-tomy*] **1 :** the operation of cutting or crushing the fetal head to effect delivery **2 :** surgical opening of the skull

cra·ni·o·topography \ˌkrānē(ˌ)ō, -nēə+\ *n* [*crani-* + *topography*] **:** a science that deals with the relations of the skull surface to the parts of the brain

cra·ni·um \ˈkrānēəm\ *n, pl* **craniums** \-mz\ *or* **cra·nia** \-nēə\ [ML, fr. Gk *kranion;* akin to Gk *kara* head — more at CEREBRAL] **1 :** SKULL; *specif* **:** the part of the skull that encloses the brain and is composed of continuous cartilage in the embryos of all craniate vertebrates and in certain lower vertebrates or of distinct bones more or less fused together in adult higher vertebrates **:** CALVARIUM, BRAINCASE — see CHONDROCRANIUM **2** [NL, fr. ML] **:** EPICRANIUM 1

¹crank \ˈkraŋk, -raiŋk\ *n* -s [ME *cranke,* fr. OE *cranc-* (as in *crancstæf,* a weaving instrument); akin to OHG *krankolōn* to stumble, become weak, MHG *kranc* weak, OE *crincan* to fall in battle, OE *cradol* cradle — more at CRADLE] **1 :** a part of an axis bent at right angles: as **a** (1) **:** a bent part of an axle or shaft or an arm keyed at right angles to the end of a shaft by which circular motion is imparted to or received from it or by which reciprocating motion is changed into circular motion or vice versa — see BELL CRANK (2) **:** DISK CRANK **b :** an elbow-shaped brace, bracket, or support **c :** a machine consisting of a disk that can be revolved by hand with some effort and that was formerly used as a means of disciplinary exercise in prisons **d :** a fireclay stand (as in glost firing) **2 :** something crooked or out of line: as **a** *archaic* **:** a bend, turn, or winding (as in a road, channel, path) **b :** a twist or turn of speech **:** a conceit consisting of a fantastic change of the form or meaning of a word — used esp. in the phrase *quips and cranks* **c** (1) **:** a fantastic, fanciful, or impractical turn of mind or action **:** WHIM ⟨a man subject to unpredictable ~*s*⟩ (2) **:** a person with a fanciful, impractical, or crackbrained obsession or project **:** one overenthusiastic or overly active and attentive in some particular field or activity ⟨~ adherents of a lost cause⟩ ⟨a gun ~⟩ ⟨~ letters⟩ ⟨a ~ on the subject of tax reform⟩ **d :** a bad-tempered often quarrelsome person **:** GROUCH, CROSSPATCH

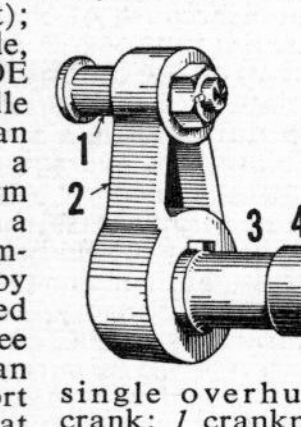

single overhung crank: *1* crankpin, *2* web, *3* journal, *4* crankshaft

²crank \"\ *vb* -ED/-ING/-S *vi* **1 :** to run or move with a winding course **:** wind and turn **:** ZIGZAG ⟨the river comes ~*ing* into the town⟩ ⟨the hare ~*ed* and doubled⟩ **2 :** to turn a crank (as in starting an automobile engine) **~** *vt* **1 :** to bend into the shape of a crank **:** bend back or down **2 :** to furnish or fasten with a crank **3 :** to move or operate by a crank **:** start or attempt to start (an engine) by use of a crank — often used with *up*

³crank \"\ *adj* -ER/-EST [prob. fr. ¹*crank*] **1** *now chiefly Scot* **a :** DISTORTED, BENT ⟨a ~ tree trunk⟩ **b :** AWKWARD, DIFFICULT ⟨a ~ word to pronounce⟩ **2 :** out of kilter **:** working with difficulty **:** LOOSE ⟨~ machinery⟩

⁴crank \"\ *n* -s [perh. fr. ¹*crank;* fr. the creaking sound made by a windlass] **:** a grating or creaking sound

⁵crank \"\ *vi* -ED/-ING/-s **:** to make a creaking or raucous sound

⁶crank \"\ *adj* -ER/-EST [ME *cranke*] **1** *obs* **:** LUSTY, VIGOROUS **2** *now dial* **a :** MERRY, HIGH-SPIRITED **b :** inclined to exult **:** COCKY, CONFIDENT

⁷crank \"\ *adv, obs* **:** LUSTILY, VIGOROUSLY, BOLDLY

⁸crank \"\ *n* -s [D or LG *kranke* sick person, fr. *krank* sick, fr. MD *cranc* and MLG *krank* sick, weak; akin to MHG *kranc* weak — more at ¹CRANK] *obs* **:** a person who pretends to have epilepsy in order to get sympathy and money

⁹crank \"\ *adj* -ER/-EST [short for *crank-sided*] **:** very easily tipped by any external force (as that of the wind on the sails) — used of a boat; compare STEADY, STIFF

crank arm *n* **:** CRANK WEB; *specif* **:** the offset portion of a crankshaft to which connecting rod and piston are attached

crank axle *n* **1 :** a driving axle formed with a crank or cranks **2 :** a carriage axle bent twice at a right angle near the ends to allow a low body with large wheels

crank brace *n* **:** a brace having a shank bent in the form of a crank by which it is rotated

crankcase \ˈ=,=\ *n* **:** the housing of the crankshaft of an engine (as in an automobile)

cranked \ˈkraŋkt, -raiŋ-\ *adj* [¹*crank* + *-ed*] **:** formed with or having a bend or crank **:** provided with a crank ⟨a ~*ed* axle⟩

crank·er \-kə(r)\ *n* -s [²*crank* + *-er*] **:** one that cranks; *specif* **:** one who arranges ceramic flatware on cranks

crank·ery \-k(ə)rē\ *n* -ES [¹*crank* (crotchety person) + *-ery*] **:** the practices or ideas of a crank or crackpot

crank hanger *n* **1 :** a support for a bell crank **2 :** BRACKET 2b

crank·i·ly \-kəlē, -li\ *adv* [¹*cranky* + *-ly*] **:** in a cranky manner ⟨~ individualistic artists⟩

crank·i·ness \-kēnəs, -kin-\ *n* -ES [¹*cranky* + *-ness*] **:** the quality or state of being cranky: as **a :** irritable or unreasonable temper ⟨the fussy ~ of the dyspeptic⟩ **b :** emotional or intellectual perversity or idiosyncrasy ⟨the reader can sometimes glimpse a sort of perverse . . . ~ at work —*Canadian Forum*⟩

crank·ish \-kish\ *adj* [¹*crank* + *-ish*] **:** FREAKISH, CRACKPOT, PERVERSE ⟨the word . . . occurs with a ~ and verbally impoverished tastelessness about 200 times —Mary McCarthy⟩

crank·ism \-ˌkizəm\ *n* -s [¹*crank* + *-ism*] **:** the attitude or activity of a crank or crackpot

¹cran·kle \ˈkraŋkəl\ *vb* -ED/-ING/-s [freq. of ²*crank*] *vt, obs* **:** to break into turns, bends, or angles **:** CRINKLE **~** *vi, archaic* **:** BEND, TURN, WIND, ZIGZAG

²crankle \"\ *n* -s **:** BEND, TURN, TWIST, CRINKLE ⟨the ~*s* of a brook⟩

crank·less \ˈkraŋkləs, -raiŋ-\ *adj* **:** not having a crank

crank·ous \ˈkraŋkəs\ *adj* [¹*crank* + *-ous*] *Scot* **:** FRETFUL, PEEVISH

crank out *vt* [²*crank*] **:** to produce esp. in a mechanical or unfeeling manner ⟨he *cranked out* two novels per year⟩

crankpin \ˈ=,=\ *n* **:** the cylindrical piece that projects from a crank web or disk and serves as a revolving journal for the bearing at the end of a connecting or coupling rod

crank plane *or* **crank planer** *n* **:** a planer whose bed is crank-driven

crank press *n* **:** a punch press in which power is applied to the slide through a crank

cranks *pl of* CRANK, *pres 3d sing of* CRANK

crankshaft \ˈ=,=\ *n* **:** a shaft driven by or driving a crank

crankshaft with four double cranks: *1, 1, 1, 1* crankpins

crank-sided \ˈ=ˌ=\ *adj* [*crank-* perh. irreg. fr. D *krengen* to careen, fr. MD *crenghen* to cause to turn, causative fr. the root of *cringhen* to turn; akin to MHG *krinc* ring — more at CRINGE] **1 :** ⁹CRANK **2 :** on one side **:** ASKEW, LOPSIDED ⟨knocked *crank-sided* off its foundation⟩

crank tail *n* **:** a short crooked tail (as that of a bulldog) resembling a crank handle

crank throw *n* **1 :** CRANK ARM, CRANK WEB **2 :** the radial displacement from crankshaft center to crankpin center

crank·um \ˈkraŋkəm\ *n* -s [¹*crank* (whim) + L *-um* (neut. n. ending)] **:** an eccentric turn **:** CROTCHET, VAGARY

crank web *n* **:** the portion of a crank between the crankpin and the shaft or between adjacent crankpins — called also *crank arm, crank throw*

¹cranky \ˈkraŋkē, -raiŋ-, -ki\ *adj* -ER/-EST [D or LG *krank* sick + E *-y* — more at CRANK (person pretending epilepsy)] *dial* **:** SICKLY, AILING, INFIRM

²cranky \ˈkraŋki\ *adj* -ER/-EST [⁶*crank* + *-y*] *dial chiefly Eng* **:** ⁶CRANK 2

³cranky \ˈkraŋkē, -raiŋ-, -ki\ *adj* -ER/-EST [¹*crank* + *-y*] **1** *dial* **:** SILLY, IMBECILE, CRAZY, INSANE **2 a :** out of working order **:** in bad condition ⟨a ~ old wagon⟩ **b :** uncertain in operation **:** likely to miscarry, operate peculiarly, or break down **:** needing especial attention or ingenuity to operate **:** UNPREDICTABLE, ERRATIC ⟨a rickety sled pulled by a ~ tractor —*Nat'l Geographic*⟩ **3 a :** marked by capricious eccentricity or wrongheadedness ⟨fighting for a European and ripened and wise philosophy against an insular and immature and ~ one —*Times Lit. Supp.*⟩ **b :** given to fretful fussiness **:** CROTCHETY, IRRITABLE ⟨a ~ old man⟩ **4 :** full of twists and turns **:** CROOKED, TORTUOUS ⟨a ~ road⟩ **syn** see IRASCIBLE

⁴cranky \"\ *adj* -ER/-EST [⁹*crank* + *-y*] *of a boat* **:** liable to heel or tip **:** CRANK

cranky fan *n* [³*cranky;* fr. its erratic flight] **:** a grayish Australian fantail (*Rhipidura flabellifera*)

cran·nage \ˈkranij\ *n* -s [²*cran* + *-age*] **:** amount of herrings in crans

cran·nied \ˈkranēd, -nəd\ *adj* [ME *cranyyd,* fr. *crany* cranny + *-ed*] **1 :** having crannies, chinks, or fissures ⟨~ earth⟩ **2** *obs* **:** of the form of a cranny

cran·nock \ˈkranək\ *n* -s [ML *crannoca, crannocus,* of Celt origin; akin to W *crynog* crannock] **:** an old unit of capacity once used in the west of England and in Wales and Ireland and equal to two, four, or more bushels

cran·nog \ˈkranəg\ *n* -s [ScGael *crannag* & IrGael *crannōg,* fr. MIr *crannōc* wooden structure, fr. OIr *crann* tree — more at HURST] **:** an artificial fortified island constructed in a lake or marsh orig. in prehistoric Ireland and Scotland

¹cran·ny \ˈkranē, -ni\ *n* -ES [ME *cranie, crany,* fr. MF *cran, cren* notch + ME *-y* — more at CRENEL] **1 :** a small break or slit (as in a rock wall or cliff) **:** NICHE, CREVICE ⟨flowers growing in *crannies*⟩ **2 :** a small obscure cleft, corner, or closed space that is easy to overlook and is a likely place for concealing something or for hiding **:** RECESS ⟨pursuing their subtleties into the last refuge and ~ of logic —V.L.Parrington⟩ **syn** see CRACK

²cranny \"\ *vi* -ED/-ING/-ES **1 :** to become full of crannies **:** form crannies ⟨earth ~*ing* in the hot sun⟩ **2 :** to enter or penetrate by or as if by crannies ⟨the rain *crannied* into the old house⟩

cran·reuch \ˈkran(ˌ)rük\ *n* -s [alter. of earlier *cranra, crainroch,* prob. modif. of ScGael *crannreotha, crannreothadh,* perh. fr. *crann* to wither + *reotha, reodhadh* frost; perh. akin to OIr *crann* tree and to OE *frēosan* to freeze — more at HURST, FREEZE] *Scot* **:** HOARFROST, RIME

crans *pl of* CRAN

cranse *var of* CRANCE

crants *n* -ES [D *krans* — more at CRANCE] *obs* **:** GARLAND, WREATH

crany *n* -ES [ML *cranium*] *obs* **:** CRANIUM

¹crap \ˈkrap\ *n* -s [ME, fr. MD *crap, crappe* pork chop, greaves, grain in chaff, fr. *crappen* to tear or break off] **1** *dial Eng* **:** residue from rendered fat — used usu. in pl. **2** *archaic slang* **:** MONEY **3 a :** EXCREMENT — usu. considered vulgar **b :** DEFECATION — usu. considered vulgar **4** *slang* **:** something deceitful, useless, or empty **:** NONSENSE, RUBBISH

²crap \"\ *vb* **crapped; crapped; crapping; craps** *vi* **1 :** DEFECATE — usu. considered vulgar **2** *slang* **:** to behave or act in a foolish, deceiving, or useless manner ⟨don't ~ around like that⟩ **~** *vt, slang* **:** DECEIVE, BEFOOL

³crap \ˈkrap, -räp\ *dial var of* CROP

⁴crap \ˈkräp\ *n* -s [prob. fr. G dial *krape* clamp for torturing, fr. OHG *krāpo, krāpfo* hook — more at CRAVE] *slang Brit* **:** GALLOWS

⁵crap \"\ *n* -s [back-formation fr. *craps*] **1 :** CRAPS ⟨~ game⟩ **2 :** a throw of 2, 3, or 12 in the game of craps that causes the shooter to lose the bet unless he has a point — called also *craps;* compare NATURAL

⁶crap \"\ *vi* **crapped; crapped; crapping; craps 1 :** to throw a crap **2 :** to throw a seven while trying to make a point — usu. used with *out*

cra·paud \kraˈpō, ˈ=(ˌ)=\ *n* -s [ME *crepaude, crapaulde,* fr. MF *crapaud, crapot* toad, prob. fr. *crape* hook, of Gmc origin; akin to OHG *krāpo, krāpfo* hook; fr. the appearance of the feet — more at CRAP] **1** *obs* **:** a jewel or precious stone supposed to come from the head of a toad **2 :** a large toad (*Leptodactylus pentadactylus*) esteemed as food in parts of the Caribbean area

¹crap·au·dine \ˌkrapəˈdēn, ˈ==ˌ=\ *n* -s [F, fr. MF, fr. *crapaud* toad + *-ine*] **:** an ulcer on the coronet of a horse

²crapaudine \ˌ==ˈ=\ *adj* [F (*à la*) *crapaudine,* lit., in a toadlike manner, fr. *crapaud* toad + *-ine*] *cookery, of small birds* **:** prepared by splitting down the back and flattening the breast — often used postpositively ⟨pigeon ~⟩

¹crape \ˈkrāp\ *n* -s [alter. of earlier *crespe,* fr. obs. F (now *crêpe*), fr. MF, fr. *crespe,* adj., curly, fr. OF, fr. L *crispus* — more at CRISP] **1 :** CREPE **2** *archaic* **:** a thin worsted stuff formerly used for the gowns of clergymen and sometimes considered to be a symbol of the clergy **3 :** a piece of black crepe used for a specific purpose: as **a :** a band of crepe worn on a hat or sleeve as a sign of mourning **b :** a piece of crepe worn over the face as a disguise

²crape \"\ *vt* -ED/-ING/-s **:** to drape, cover, or shroud with or as if with crape ⟨dark clouds *craping* the sun⟩ ⟨a widow *craped* in the latest fashion⟩

³crape \"\ *vt* -ED/-ING/-s [F *crêper,* fr. MF *cresper,* fr. *crespe,* adj.] **:** to make (the hair) curly

crape fern *n* **:** a New Zealand fern (*Todea superba*) of the family Osmundaceae with a short trunk, pinnate fronds, and densely woolly stalks

crapehanger *var of* CREPEHANGER

crape jasmine *n* **:** a cultivated shrub (*Ervatamia coronaria*) of the family Apocynaceae having crimped or wavy corollas — called also *Adam's apple*

crape moss *n* **:** SPANISH MOSS

crape myrtle *also* **crepe myrtle** *or* **crêpe myrtle** *n* **:** an ornamental East Indian shrub (*Lagerstroemia indica*) commonly planted in the southern U.S. for its white, pink, red, or purplish flowers

crape needle *n* **:** LADY'S-COMB

cra·pette \kraˈpet, krə-\ *n* -s [F] **:** RUSSIAN BANK

crap out *vi* [²*crap*] **1** *slang* **a :** to pass out (as from an injury) **b :** to fall asleep (as from exhaustion) **2** *slang* **:** to avoid assigned duty or obligations

crap·per \ˈkrapə(r)\ *n* -s [²*crap* + *-er*] **:** TOILET, PRIVY — usu. considered vulgar

crap·pie \ˈkräpē, -pi *sometimes* -rap-\ *also* **crop·pie** \-räp-\ *n* -s [CanF *crapet*] **:** either of two No. American sunfishes most abundant in the Great Lakes region and Mississippi valley and introduced elsewhere — see BLACK CRAPPIE, WHITE CRAPPIE

crap·pin \ˈkrapən\ *n* -s [Sc ³*crap* (crop of a bird) + *-in* (alter. of E *-ing*)] *chiefly Scot* **:** CROP, STOMACH

crap·pit head \ˈkrapət-\ *n* [*crappit* prob. fr. past part. of Sc *crap* to cram, fr. ³*crap* (top)] *Scot* **:** stuffed haddock head

crap·po \ˈkrapō\ *n* -ES [by alter.] **:** CARAPA 2

crap·py \ˈkrapē, -pi\ *adj* -ER/-EST [¹*crap* + *-y*] *slang* **:** markedly inferior in quality **:** LOUSY

craps \ˈkraps\ *n pl but usu sing in constr* [LaF, fr. F *crabs, craps,* fr. E *crabs* lowest throw at hazard, fr. pl. of ¹*crab*] **1 :** a gambling game in which a player rolls two dice and wins his bet if the throw is 7 or 11, loses it if the throw is 2, 3, or 12, or gets a point if the throw is 4, 5, 6, 8, 9, or 10, in which case he continues to throw until he wins by throwing his point again or loses both bet and dice by throwing 7 **2 :** ⁵CRAP 2

crapshooter \ˈ=ˌ==\ *n* [⁵*crap* + *shooter*] **:** one that plays craps

crap shooting *n* [⁵*crap*] **:** the game or playing of craps

crap table *n* [⁵*crap*] **:** a high table that is used for playing craps and that has a raised rim against which the dice must be thrown

crap·u·lence \ˈkrapyələn(t)s\ *n* -s **1** *archaic* **:** sickness occasioned by intemperance (as in food or drink) **2 :** great intemperance esp. in drinking

crap·u·lent \-lənt\ *adj* [LL *crapulentus,* fr. L *crapula* intoxication] *archaic* **:** suffering from excessive eating or drinking

crap·u·lous \ˈkrapyələs\ *adj* [LL *crapulosus,* fr. L *crapula* intoxication (fr. Gk *kraipalē* intoxication, drunken headache) + *-osus* -ous; prob. akin to Gk *kara* head, and to Gk *pallein* to shake, quiver — more at CEREBRAL, POLEMIC] **1 :** intemperate esp. in drink ⟨a ~ old reprobate⟩ **2 :** suffering the effects of, derived from, or suggestive of intemperance esp. in drink ⟨a ~ stomach⟩ ⟨~ slumber⟩ ⟨~ stupidities⟩ — **crap·u·lous·ly** *adv*

crapy \ˈkrāpē, -pi\ *adj* -ER/-EST [¹*crape* + *-y*] **:** of, resembling, or draped in crape ⟨a ~ fabric⟩ ⟨a ~ procession⟩

cra·que·lé \(ˈ)kraˌklā\ *adj* [F, fr. past part. of *craqueler* to crack, crackle, fr. *craquer* to crack, crackle, of imit. origin] **:** CRACKLED ⟨a ~ glaze⟩

cra·que·lure \kraˈklü(ə)r, ˈ=ˌ=\ *n* -s [F, fr. *craqueler* + *-ure*] **:** a cracking (as of varnish, color, or enamel) on a work of plastic art

crare *var of* CRAYER

¹crash \ˈkrash, -raa(ə)sh, -raish\ *vb* -ED/-ING/-ES [ME *crasschen,* perh. alter. of *crasen* to break — more at CRAZE] *vt* **1 a :** to break into pieces violently and noisily **:** SMASH, SHATTER ⟨~ a glass against a wall⟩ **b :** to bring (an airplane) down in such a manner that damage is sustained in landing **2 a :** to cause to make a loud noise **:** make a loud shattering or clattering noise with **b :** to force (as one's way) with loud crashing noises ⟨~ one's way through brush⟩ **3** *obs* **:** to snap (the teeth) together **:** GNASH **4 a :** to enter or attend without invitation or credentials or without paying ⟨~ a dance⟩ ⟨~ an executive's office⟩ **b :** to gain acceptance, position, or recognition in usu. suddenly and spectacularly ⟨the murder ~*ed* the headlines⟩ ⟨when television ~*ed* the retail market⟩ **~** *vi* **1 a :** to break or go to pieces esp. with or as if with violence and noise ⟨the national economy ~*ed*⟩ **b :** to crash an airplane **2 :** to make a loud smashing or shattering noise ⟨~*ing* thunder⟩ **3 a :** to move with or as if with a crashing noise ⟨the doors ~*ed* open⟩ ⟨he ~*ed* into the room⟩ **b :** to force one's way with or as if with a crash ⟨he ~*ed* through the line for a touchdown⟩ — **crash the gate :** to enter without paying or without authority or permission ⟨all the kids used to sneak in . . . they had a million ways of *crashing the gate* —J.T. Farrell⟩ **:** enter successfully **:** make the grade ⟨he was the boy who made good, the outsider who *crashed* all *the gates* of Philadelphia —H.S.Commager⟩

²crash \"\ *n* -ES **1 :** a loud sound (as of many hard things smashing or shattering) **:** SMASH ⟨a ~ of thunder⟩ ⟨the ~ of a military band⟩ ⟨a ~ of applause⟩ ⟨a ~ of static⟩ — often used interjectionally ⟨~ went the lamp against the floor⟩ **2 :** a breaking to pieces esp. by or as if by collision **:** a smashing esp. of or as if of heavy bodies; *also* **:** an instance of crashing ⟨an airplane ~⟩ ⟨the ~ of a falling tree⟩ **3 a :** a sudden failure esp. of a business **:** a sudden widespread business collapse ⟨stock market ~⟩ **b :** the period of heavy mortality and sharp decline in numbers of an animal with strongly developed population cycles; *also* **:** the decline in population during such a period **4** *archaic* **:** SPELL, BOUT, TURN — used esp. in the phrase *have a crash at* **5 :** a basket of glass or pottery fragments used in the theater to imitate the sound of breaking glass

³crash \"\ *adj* **:** designed to meet emergency conditions esp. in the shortest possible time by maximum utilization of resources ⟨a ~ program⟩ ⟨~ priority⟩ ⟨do a ~ job of making the most needed changes —G.C.Smith⟩

⁴crash \"\ *n* -ES [prob. modif. of Russ *krashenina* colored linen, fr. *krashenie* dyeing, fr. *krasit'* to color, beautify, fr. *krasa* beauty; prob. akin to Skt *carkṛti* praise — more at CADUCEUS] **1 a :** a coarse fabric made in plain weave of uneven linen, rayon, cotton, or jute and cotton yarns and used for draperies, toweling, and table linen and often in smooth-finished form for clothing **b :** a fabric covering for a carpeted floor (as for use during a dance) **2 :** a grayish yellow that is greener and duller than chamois, slightly greener and less strong than old ivory, and greener and duller than flax

crash boat *n* **:** a fast motorboat used to rescue survivors of a plane crash at sea

crash cover *n* **:** an airmail cover that has been in an airplane crash

crash cymbal *n* **:** a single cymbal suspended by a cord and struck with a drumstick

crash dive *n* **:** a dive made by a submarine (as in avoiding attack) in the least possible time

crash-dive \ˈ=ˌ=\ *vi, of a submarine* **:** to submerge in the shortest possible time **~** *vt* **:** to dive into ⟨hit by flak, the plane . . . rolled over . . . in an attempt to *crash-dive* the escort carrier —*Time*⟩

crash finish *n* [⁴*crash*] **:** a finish esp. of paper resembling coarse linen

crash helmet *n* **:** a usu. plastic or leather helmet that is worn (as by auto racers, bobsledders, motorcycle policemen) as protection for the head in an accident

crashing *adj* [fr. pres. part. of ¹*crash*] **1 :** OUT-AND-OUT, UTTER ⟨a ~ bore⟩ ⟨a ~ cliché⟩ **2 :** SUPERLATIVE, STUNNING ⟨a ~ virtuoso⟩ ⟨a ~ effect⟩

crash-land \ˈ=ˌ=\ *vt* **:** to land (an airplane) under conditions (as damaged landing gear or the absence of an adequate landing area) that result in structural damage usu. extensive enough to prevent takeoff **~** *vi* **:** to crash-land an airplane — **crash landing** *n*

crash pad *n* **:** padding (as on the inside of a tank or car) to protect the occupants from injury in the event of an accident or sudden jolt

crash truck *or* **crash wagon** *n* **:** a specially equipped truck designed to rescue survivors of an airplane crash

cra·sis \ˈkrāsəs\ *n, pl* **cra·ses** \-ˌsēz\ [NL, fr. Gk *krasis* mixing, combination, fr. *kerannynai* to mix — more at CRATER] **1 a** *obs* **:** a blend or combination of constituents **b** *archaic* **:** CONSTITUTION **2 :** a contraction of two vowels or diphthongs esp. in Latin and Greek at the end of one word and the beginning of an immediately following word into one long vowel or diphthong (as in Latin *cogo* for *coago* and in Greek *kan* for *kai an*)

cras·pe·da·cus·ta \ˌkraspədəˈküstə, -ˈkəs-\ *n, cap* [NL, irreg. fr. *craspedon* velum + Gk *kystis* bladder — more at CYST] **:** a cosmopolitan genus of minute freshwater hydrozoan medusae — see MICROHYDRA

cras·pe·do·ta \ˌ==ˈdōd·ə\ *n pl, cap* [NL, irreg. fr. *craspedon* velum, fr. Gk *kraspedon* edge, border, fr. *kras-* head + *pedon* ground; akin to Gk *kara* head and to Gk *pod-, pous* foot — more at CEREBRAL, FOOT] **:** the velate medusae regarded as a natural group more or less equivalent to Hydrozoa — **cras·pe·do·tal** \ˌ==¦dōd·ᵊl\ *adj*

cras·pe·dote \ˈkraspəˌdōt\ *adj* [NL *Craspedota*] **:** VELATE — used chiefly of hydrozoan medusae

crass \ˈkras, -raa(ə)s, -rais\ *adj* -ER/-EST [L *crassus* thick, fat, gross — more at HURDLE] **1** *archaic, of the texture or makeup of a substance* **:** THICK, DENSE, COARSE **2 :** lacking delicacy **:** devoid of refined sensitivity **:** GROSS, UNFEELING, STUPID ⟨~ butchery⟩ ⟨~ avarice⟩ ⟨a ~ misreading of a statement⟩ **syn** see STUPID

cras·sa·men·tum \ˌkrasəˈmentəm\ *n, pl* **crassamentums** \-mz\ *or* **crassamen·ta** \-tə\ [NL, fr. L, sediment, dregs, fr. *crassare* to make thick (fr. *crassus*) + *-mentum* -ment] **:** the clot formed in coagulation of blood **:** COAGULUM

cras·sa ne·gli·gen·tia \ˌkrasəˌneglәˈjenchēə\ *n* [LL] **:** GROSS NEGLIGENCE

cras·si·so·ma \ˌkrasəˈsōmə\ *n, cap* [NL, fr. L *crassi-* (fr. *crassus* thick, fat) + NL *-soma*] **:** a genus of hookworms including the only worm (*C. urosubulatum*) commonly infesting swine in No. America

cras·si·tude \ˈkrasəˌt(y)üd\ *n* -S [ME, fr. L *crassitudo*, fr. *crassus* + *-i-* + *-tudo* -tude] **1** *obs* **:** thickness (as of a solid body) **2 :** crass quality or state **:** GROSSNESS; *also* **:** an instance of grossness

crass·ly *adv* **:** in a crass manner

crass negligence *n* **:** GROSS NEGLIGENCE

crass·ness \ˈkrasnəs, -raas-, -rais-\ *n* -ES **:** the quality or state of being crass ⟨the arrogance and ~ of the industrial millionaires —Edmund Wilson⟩

cras·sos·trea \krəˈsästrēə\ *n, cap* [NL, fr. L *crassus* thick, fat + *ostrea* oyster — more at OYSTER] **:** a genus of bivalve mollusks comprising those oysters that discharge their reproductive products directly into the water and have no larval development in the gills of the parent, and now usu. including the Virginia oyster — compare GRYPHAEA 1, OSTREA

cras·su·la \ˈkras(y)ələ\ *n* [NL, fr. ML, stonecrop, orpine, fr. L *crassus* + *-ula* (dim. suffix)] **1** *cap* **:** a genus of chiefly So. African succulent herbs (family Crassulaceae) having opposite leaves and flowers with petals separate or connate only at the base **2** *pl* **crassu·lae** \-ˌlē, -ˌlī\ *also* **crassulas :** a plant of the genus *Crassula* **3** *pl* **crassulae :** a thickening of the middle lamella and primary wall between or around bordered pits or pit fields esp. prominent on the radial walls of tracheids in gymnosperm wood — called also *bar of Sanio, rim of Sanio, Sanio's beam*

cras·su·la·ce·ae \ˌ==ˈlāsēˌē\ *n pl, cap* [NL, fr. *Crassula*, type genus + *-aceae*] **:** a family of mostly fleshy herbs and subshrubs (order Rosales) having a scalelike gland at the base of each of the three or more connate pistils — compare SEDUM, STONECROP — **cras·su·la·ceous** \ˌ==¦lāshəs\ *adj*

-crat \ˌkrat, *usu* -ad·+V\ *or* **-ocrat** \əˌkrat, ōˌ-, *usu* -ad·+V\ *n comb form* -S [F *-crate*, back-formation fr. *-cratie* -cracy & *-cratique* -cratic] **1 :** advocate or partisan of a theory of government ⟨*democrat*⟩ ⟨*physiocrat*⟩ ⟨*theocrat*⟩ **2 :** member of a (specified) dominant class ⟨*bureaucrat*⟩ ⟨*plutocrat*⟩ **3 :** member or supporter of a political party or faction ⟨*Dixiecrat*⟩ — **-crat·ic** \ˌkrad·ik, -atˌik, ¦ëk\ *adj comb form* [MF *-cratique*, fr. ML *-craticus*, fr. Gk *-kratikos*, fr. *kratos* strength, power + *-ikos* -ic — more at HARD]

cra·tae·gus \krəˈtēgəs\ *n, cap* [NL, fr. Gk *krataigos*, prob. fr. *kratos* strength + *-aigos* (akin to Gk *aigilōps* Turkey oak) — more at HARD, OAK] **:** a genus of usu. thorny shrubs and small trees (family Rosaceae) having usu. stipulate leaves, an inferior ovary, and mature carpels that are hard and bony with a pulpy fruit — see HAWTHORN

cra·tae·va \-ēvə\ *n, cap* [NL, irreg. after *Cratevas* (Gk *Krateuas*), 1st cent. B.C. Gk. herbalist] **:** a small genus of tropical shrubs (family Capparidaceae) having trifoliolate leaves, flowers with stalked petals, and striped berries — see GARLIC PEAR

cratch \ˈkrach\ *n* -ES [ME *cracche, crecche*, fr. OF *creche* manger, of Gmc origin; akin to OHG *krippa* manger — more at CRIB] **1** *dial Brit* **:** a crib or rack esp. for fodder; *also* **:** GRATING, FRAME **2** *archaic* **:** MANGER

¹crate \ˈkrāt, *usu* -ād·+V\ *n* -S [L *cratis* wickerwork, hurdle — more at HURDLE] **1 :** a container used to transport wares: as **a :** a rigid shipping structure that consists usu. of a wood frame of which the size and shape are usu. determined by the article to be shipped, the structure often being built around the article, and which is often not completely enclosed but is often reinforced with sheathing **b :** a similar structure used esp. for agricultural products and having a frame covered by thin boards with openings left between for ventilation ⟨an orange ~⟩ **2 :** a lead grating used in making white lead **3 :** an obsolete, patched-up, or badly used vehicle ⟨his car was an old ~⟩ ⟨to replace plane losses they built spare-parts ~*s* from wrecked machines —*Time*⟩

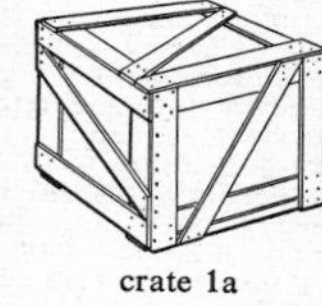

crate 1a

²crate \"\ *vt* -ED/-ING/-S **:** to pack in a crate or case esp. for transportation

¹cra·ter \ˈkrād·ə(r), -ātə-\ *n* -S [L, mixing bowl, mouth of a volcano, fr. Gk *kratēr*, fr. *kerannynai* to mix; akin to Skt *śrīta* mixed, and prob. to OE *hrēran* to stir, OHG *hruoren*, ON *hrœra*] **1 :** a hole at the top of a cone-shaped object: as **a** (1) **:** the depression above or around the orifice of a volcano that often appears as a funnel-shaped pit maintained by successive explosions at the top of a built-up cone (2) **:** the flaring or bowl-shaped opening of a geyser (3) **:** a depression formed by the impact of a meteorite (4) **:** any of thousands of formations on the lunar surface ranging in size from small pocks less than a mile in diameter to walled plains nearly 150 miles across and thought by many astronomers to be caused by the impact of huge meteorites and by others to be of igneous origin **b :** a hole in the ground made by the explosion of a projectile, bomb, or charge **c :** the cup-shaped cavity formed at the end of the positive carbon of a direct-current arc lamp **d :** an eroded crateriform lesion of a wall or surface (as the site of an ulcer of the stomach or duodenal wall) **2 :** KRATER

²crater \"\ *vb* -ED/-ING/-S *vi* **:** to form a crater ⟨the surface ~*ed* with the constant dropping of water⟩ ~ *vt* **:** to form or make a crater in ⟨artillery ~*ed* the roads⟩

³crat·er \"\ *n* -S [²*crate* + *-er*] **:** one that packs articles into crates for shipment **:** one that builds crates around large objects (as pianos)

cra·ter·al \ˈkrād·ərəl\ *or* **cra·ter·ine** \-əˌrīn\ *or* **cra·ter·ous** \-ərəs\ *adj* [¹*crater* + *-al* or *-ine* or *-ous*] **:** of or belonging to a crater

cra·tered \-ə(r)d\ *adj* [¹*crater* + *-ed*] **:** having a crater or craters **:** full of craters ⟨the ~ moon⟩

cra·ter·el·lus \ˌkrād·əˈreləs\ *n, cap* [NL, irreg. fr. L *crater*] **:** a genus of fleshy or membranous white-spored mushrooms (family Thelephoraceae) having the shape of a club, shelf, or funnel and resembling *Cantharellus* but having the hymenium at most only rugose and not in prominent gills

cra·ter·i·form \ˈkrād·ərəˌfȯrm, krəˈterə-\ *adj* [ISV ¹*crater* + *-iform*] **:** having the form of a crater; *specif* **:** of the form of a bowl or saucer ⟨a flower with a ~ corolla⟩

cra·ter·less \ˈkrād·ə(r)ləs, -ātə-\ *adj* **:** not having a crater

cra·ter·let \ˈkrād·ə(r)lət, -ātə-\ *n* -S **:** a little crater

-cratic — see -CRAT

cra·tic·u·lar \krəˈtikyələ(r)\ *adj* [L *craticula* fine hurdlework, gridiron (dim. of *cratis* hurdle) + E *-ar* — more at HURDLE] *bot* **:** having to do with a resting stage in diatoms during which new valves are formed within the old ones

c ration \ˈsē-\ *n, usu cap C* **:** a canned field ration of the U.S. Army

cra·ton \ˈkrāˌtän\ *n* -S [G *kraton*, modif. of Gk *kratos* strength, power — more at HARD] **:** a stable relatively immobile area of the earth's crust that forms the nuclear mass of a continent or the central basin of an ocean — compare SHIELD — **cra·ton·al** \(ˈ)krāˈtänᵊl\ *or* **cra·ton·ic** \-nik\ *adj*

-crats *pl of* -CRAT

cra·tur \ˈkrātər\ *Scot & Irish var of* CREATURE

¹craunch \ˈkrȯnch, -rän-\ *also* **cranch** \-rän\ *vb* -ED/-ING/-ES [prob. of imit. origin] **:** CRUNCH

²craunch \"\ *also* **cranch** \"\ *n* -ES **1 :** act or action of craunching **:** CRUNCH **2 :** anything that is craunched **:** material to craunch

¹cra·vat \krəˈvat, *usu* -ad·+V\ *n* -S [F *cravate* cravat, linen scarf worn in 17th cent. by Croatian mercenaries, fr. *Cravate* Croatian, fr. G (dial.) or Serbo-Croatian; G (dial.) *Krawat*, fr. Serbo-Croatian *Hrvat*; akin to OSlav *Chŭrvatinŭ* Croatian] **1 a :** a band or scarf of fine cloth often trimmed with lace and formerly worn around the neck tied in a bow or knotted so that the ends hung down in front **b :** NECKTIE **2 :** a wrinkle of flesh on the neck esp. of a dog **3 :** a bandage made by folding the point of a triangular piece of material toward the base, folding the base over the point, and folding the whole again

²cravat \"\ *vt* **cravatted; cravatted; cravatting; cravats :** to dress with or as if with a cravat ⟨a handsomely *cravatted* young man⟩

crave \ˈkrāv\ *vb* -ED/-ING/-S [ME *craven*, fr. OE *crafian*; akin to ON *krefja* to crave, OE *cræft* strength, skill, OHG *kraft* strength, skill, *krāpo, krāpfo* hook, ON *kraptr* strength, skill, OE *cradol* cradle — more at CRADLE] *vt* **1 a :** to ask authoritatively **:** DEMAND ⟨~ a hearing before a court⟩ **b** *chiefly Scot* **:** DUN ⟨~ a debtor⟩ **2 a :** to ask earnestly **:** BEG, BESEECH, IMPLORE ⟨~ a person's pardon⟩ ⟨~ the indulgence of an audience⟩ **b** *obs* **:** to ask to know **3 a :** to want greatly **:** NEED ⟨~ sweets⟩ ⟨~ fresh air⟩ **b :** to yearn for **:** REQUIRE ⟨an ego *craving* flattery⟩ **4 :** to demand as necessary or expedient **:** REQUIRE ⟨orders *craving* immediate attention⟩ ~ *vi* **:** to have a strong or inward desire ⟨~ after inspiration⟩ ⟨~ for good food⟩ **syn** see DESIRE

¹cra·ven \ˈkrāvən\ *adj* [alter. of ME *cravant*, perh. fr. OF *crevant*, pres. part. of *crever* to burst, cause to burst, fr. L *crepare* to crack, creak, break — more at RAVEN] **1 :** DEFEATED, VANQUISHED — used in the phrase *to cry craven* acknowledging defeat **2 :** lacking even the rudiments of courage **:** characterized by abject defeatism **:** contemptibly fainthearted ⟨a ~ proposal for putting up the white flag —F.L.Allen⟩ **syn** see COWARDLY

²craven \"\ *n* -S **1 :** an avowed coward **:** a weakhearted person **2 :** a cock that lacks courage or shows little or no inclination to fight

³craven \"\ *vt* -ED/-ING/-S *archaic* **:** to make cowardly or timid

cra·ven·ette \ˌkrāvəˈnet, ˈ==ˌ=; *also* -rav-\ *vt* -ED/-ING/-S [fr. *Cravenette*, a trademark] **:** to make (a textile) water-repellent ⟨*cravenetted* khaki⟩

cravenhearted \¦==¦==\ *adj* **:** COWARDLY, CRAVEN

cra·ven·ly *adv* **:** in a craven manner

cra·ven·ness \-ən(n)əs\ *n* -ES **:** the quality of being craven **:** feebleness of courage **:** COWARDICE

crav·er \ˈkrāvə(r)\ *n* -S [ME, fr. *craven* to crave + *-er*] **:** one that craves

¹craving *n* -S [ME, fr. gerund of *craven* to crave] **1** *obs* **:** urgent asking **:** ENTREATING **2 a :** an urgent need for gratification ⟨a ~ for tobacco⟩ **b :** the desire to satisfy a vague inner need **:** LONGING, YEARNING ⟨a ~ to be understood⟩ ⟨the deepest ~*s* of his being — to create and, as Byron says, in creating live —C.S.Kilby⟩

²craving *adj* [fr. pres. part. of *crave*] **1** *obs* **:** urgently entreating **:** BEGGING **2 :** desiring deeply or inwardly ⟨~ passion⟩ — **crav·ing·ly** *adv* — **crav·ing·ness** *n* -ES

cra·vo \ˈkravō\ *n* -ES [origin unknown] **:** OPAH

¹craw *Scot var of* CROW

²craw \ˈkrȯ\ *n* -S [ME *crawe*, fr. (assumed) OE *crawa*; akin to MHG *krage* neck, throat, ON *kragi* collar, OIr *brāgae* neck, Gk *bronchos* trachea, L *vorare* to devour — more at VORACIOUS] **1 :** the crop of a bird or insect **2 :** the stomach esp. of a lower animal

craw–craw \ˈkrȯˌkrȯ\ *n* -S [prob. modif. & redupl. of D *krauwen* to scratch, fr. MD; akin to OHG *krouwōn* to scratch — more at CRUMB] **:** an itching skin disease produced by the young of a filarial worm (*Onchocerca volvulus*) migrating in the subcutaneous tissues — compare ONCHOCERCIASIS

craw·dad \ˈkrȯˌdad\ *also* **craw·dab** \-ˌdab\ *n* -S [alter. of *crawfish*] *chiefly Midland* **:** CRAYFISH

¹craw·fish \ˈkrȯ+ˌ-\ *n* [by folk etymology fr. ME *crevis* — more at CRAYFISH] **1 :** CRAYFISH **2 :** SPINY LOBSTER **3** *in California* **:** GHOST SHRIMP

²crawfish \"\ *vi* **:** to retreat from a position **:** back out — usu. used with *out* ⟨we'll just have to ~ out of shaking hands with them —Sally Benson⟩

¹crawk \ˈkrȯk\ *vi* -ED/-ING/-S [imit.] **:** to utter a harsh squawk ⟨the crows ~*ing* overhead⟩

²crawk \"\ *n* -S **:** a sound-effects man who imitates animals (as for radio programs)

¹crawl \ˈkrȯl\ *vb* -ED/-ING/-S [ME *crawlen*, fr. ON *krafla* to crawl, creep; akin to ON *krabbi* crab — more at CRAB] *vi* **1 :** to move or go slowly (as an insect, snake, turtle) with the body close to the ground **:** CREEP **2 :** to move, progress, or advance slowly or laboriously **:** drag along ⟨hardly able to ~⟩ ⟨the hours ~*ed* by⟩ ⟨tanks and amphibian tractors were ~*ing* up on the beach —H.L.Merillat⟩ **3 :** to advance servilely, abjectly, or furtively ⟨~ into favor⟩ **4** *of plants* **:** to spread by extending stems, branches, or tendrils **:** CREEP, TRAIL **5 a :** to be alive or swarming with or as if with a great number of creeping things ⟨a kitchen ~*ing* with ants⟩ ⟨a living room ~*ing* with bric-a-brac⟩ **b :** to have an unpleasant sensation as if insects were creeping over one **:** become unnaturally upset, perturbed, or anguished ⟨his flesh was ~*ing* with the need of alcohol —Eddie Doherty⟩ **6 :** to swim a crawl ⟨~ across the pool in record time⟩ **7 :** to fail to stay evenly spread **:** draw into puddles or dense areas — used of paint, varnish, glaze ~ *vt* **1 :** to move upon in or as if in a creeping manner ⟨the meanest person who ever ~*ed* the earth⟩ **2** *slang* **:** to reprove with severity ⟨they got no good right to ~ me for what I wrote —Marjorie K. Rawlings⟩

²crawl \"\ *n* -S **1 a :** the act or action of crawling ⟨a dangerous ~ up a roof⟩ **b :** slow or laborious motion or progress ⟨will speed up the gluey ~ of the Sunday driver —Lewis Mumford⟩ **c** *chiefly Brit* **:** a leisurely progress from one bar to another — used usu. in combination ⟨beer ~⟩ **2 :** a prone speed swimming stroke consisting of a double overarm stroke combined with a flutter kick usu. in a ratio of six leg kicks to two arm strokes — called also *American crawl*; see AUSTRALIAN CRAWL, TRUDGEN CRAWL **3** *or* **crawl box :** a revolving drum on which lettering can be affixed in producing creeper titles in motion pictures and television **4 :** a pulley block that has sheaves that roll laterally along a rope and is used for transporting a suspended load

³crawl \"\ *n* -S [D *kraal* — more at KRAAL] **:** an enclosure (as one used in shallow waters to confine lobsters or turtles)

crawl·er \ˈkrȯlə(r)\ *n* -S **1 :** one that crawls: as **a** (1) **:** a newly hatched or first-stage insect that has not lost the ability to crawl about **:** TRIUNGULIN (2) **:** HELLGRAMMITE **b** *Austral* **:** a servile person **c** (1) *Brit* **:** a cruising taxi (2) **:** a Caterpillar tractor **d** (1) **:** either of the treads of a crawler tractor (2) **:** CREEPER TITLE **2 :** a garment similar to overalls and suitable for wear by children while crawling — usu. used in pl. ⟨gabardine ~*s*⟩; compare CREEPER

crawler crane *n* **:** a crane mounted on and operating from a crawler tractor

crawler wheel *n* **:** either of a pair of wheels carrying and running on an endless metal belt (as on a crawler tractor)

craw·ley root \ˈkrȯlē-\ *n* [by folk etymology] **:** a coralroot (*Corallorrhiza odontorhiza*) of dry woodlands in eastern and central No. America that produces a scape of small white to purple crimson-spotted flowers and has an irregular perennial rootstock which is sometimes collected for use as a diaphoretic

craw·lie \ˈkrȯlē\ *n* -S [prob. fr. ¹*crawl* + *-ie*] **:** YABBY

crawling *n* -S [fr. gerund of ¹*crawl*] **:** an undesirable drawing together or lumping of a surface finish (as of paint, enamel, glaze)

crawl·ing·ly *adv* **:** in a crawling manner

crawl·ing·ness *n* -ES **:** the quality or state of being crawling

crawls *pl of* CRAWL, *pres 3d sing of* CRAWL

crawl space *n* **:** a space about two feet high provided in a building in order to enable workmen to gain access to plumbing, wiring, and other equipment

crawly \ˈkrȯlē, -li\ *adj* -ER/-EST [¹*crawl* + *-y*] *adj* **:** CREEPY

craws *pl of* CRAW

craw·thump·er \ˈkrȯˌthəmpə(r)\ *n, usu cap* [fr. *Crawthumper*, a nickname for Roman Catholics] **:** MARYLANDER — used as a nickname

crax \ˈkraks\ *n, cap* [NL, modif. of Gk *krex*, a kind of long-legged bird — more at CREX] **:** the type genus of Cracidae

cray \ˈkrā\ *n* -S [short for *crayfish*] **:** a spiny lobster (*Jasus lalandii*) of Australia

crayer \ˈkra(a)(ə)r\ *n* -S [ME *crayer*, fr. MF *crayer, croyer*, fr. OF *croier*] **:** a former small sailing cargo boat

cray·fish \ˈkrā+ˌ-\ *n* [by folk etymology fr. ME *crevis*, fr. MF *crevice*, of Gmc origin; akin to OHG *krebiz* crab — more at CRAB] **1 :** any of numerous freshwater crustaceans of the tribe Astacura resembling the lobster but usu. much smaller in size, all those of the northern hemisphere belonging to a single family (Astacidae) which includes the genera *Astacus* with species in Europe, Asia, and western No. America, and *Cambarus* to which most No. American forms belong **2 :** SPINY LOBSTER

crayfish

cray·let \ˈkrālət\ *n* -S [*cray* + *-let*] **:** any of several small anomuran crustaceans of Australia belonging to the genus *Galathea* and resembling lobsters

¹cray·on \ˈkrāˌän, -āən *also* ˈkran *or* -rān\ *n* -S [F, crayon, pencil, dim. of *craie* chalk, fr. L *creta*] **1 a :** a stick of white or colored chalk used for drawing **b :** a stick of colored wax composition used for drawing and coloring **c :** LITHOGRAPHIC CRAYON **d :** CONTÉ **e :** a cosmetic in stick or pencil form used esp. for coloring eyebrows **2 :** a crayon drawing

²crayon \"\ *vt* -ED/-ING/-S [F *crayonner*, fr. *crayon*] **1 :** to draw or color with a crayon ⟨~ a portrait⟩ **:** cover or decorate with crayon work ⟨a wall ~*ed* with colorful designs⟩ **2 :** to sketch out **:** draw up ⟨a plan carefully ~*ed out*⟩

crayon board *n* **:** cardboard with a surface for crayon drawing

crayon green *n* **:** a light yellowish green that is yellower and paler than apple green (sense 2), greener, lighter, and stronger than pistachio, and greener and deeper than ocean green

cray·on·ist \-nəst\ *n* -S **:** a specialist in the use of crayons

crayon manner *n* **:** a manner of etching in which the ground is perforated with various needles, roulettes, or mattoirs to produce the effect of crayon or chalk drawing on the print — called also *chalk manner*

crayon sauce *n* **:** powdered crayon used for retouching in photography

crayonstone \ˈ=(ˌ)=ˌ, ˈ=(=)+ˌ-\ *n* **:** a lithographic drawing made directly upon the stone

cray·thur \ˈkrāthər\ *Irish var of* CREATURE

¹craze \ˈkrāz\ *vb* -ED/-ING/-S [ME *crasen*, of Scand origin; akin to OSw *krasa* to crush, smash, Norw, to crush, smash, crunch, prob. of imit. origin] *vt* **1** *obs* **:** to break to pieces **:** CRUSH, SMASH **2 a** *now dial Brit* **:** to break without separation of parts **:** CRACK ⟨*crazing* the jug⟩ **b :** to produce minute cracks on the surface or glaze of — compare ²CRACKLE 2 **3** *archaic* **:** to weaken or injure physically **:** make infirm **4 :** to derange the intellect of **:** make insane or as if insane ⟨*crazed* by drink⟩ ⟨they were *crazed* by the famine and pestilence of that last bitter winter —*Amer. Guide Series: Wash.*⟩ ~ *vi* **1** *archaic* **:** SHATTER, BREAK **2 :** to become crazed **:** go mad **3 :** to develop a mesh of fine cracks — used of solid plastics, surface coating (as pottery glazing), and adhesives

²craze \"\ *n* -S **1** *obs* **a :** BREAK, FLAW, DEFECT **b :** physical weakness **:** INFIRMITY **2 :** a transient infatuation **:** FAD, MANIA ⟨his ~ for easy money⟩ ⟨the cocktail ~⟩ ⟨a ~ for internal improvements spread over the country —Isaac Lippincott⟩ **3 :** CRAZINESS, INSANITY ⟨writhing in a ~ of pain⟩ **4 a :** cracking of ceramic glaze due to unequal contraction of body and glaze — compare ²CRACKLE 2 **b :** hairline cracks on the surface (as of paint) **syn** see FASHION

craz·ed·ly \ˈkrāzədlē, -li\ *adv* **:** in a crazed manner **:** CRAZILY

craz·ed·ness \-zədnəs\ *n* -ES **:** the quality or state of being crazed

cra·zi·ly \ˈkrāz(ə)lē, -li\ *adv* **:** in a crazy manner

cra·zi·ness \-zēnəs, -zin-\ *n* -ES **:** the quality or state of being crazy

crazing *n* -S [fr. gerund of ¹*craze*] **:** the formation of minute cracks (as on glaze, enamel, varnish) usu. attributed to shrinkage or sometimes to moisture

¹cra·zy \ˈkrāzē, -zi\ *adj* -ER/-EST [²*craze* + *-y*] **1 a :** full of cracks or flaws **:** DAMAGED, UNSOUND ⟨a ~ old building⟩ ⟨embarked in a ~ dugout canoe —*Nat'l Geographic*⟩ **b :** not straight or upright **:** CROOKED, ASKEW ⟨a ~ tower⟩ ⟨~ little cow paths —T.H.Fielding⟩ **c :** not in order **:** JUMBLED DISORDERED ⟨a ~ pile of equipment⟩ **d** *of livestock brands* **:** UPSIDE-DOWN — see BRAND illustration **2** *archaic* **:** broken down in health **:** AILING, INFIRM, FRAIL **3 a :** broken or as if broken in mind **:** INSANE ⟨yelling like a ~ man⟩ ⟨~ with hatred⟩ ⟨go ~ with drink⟩ **b :** arising from, produced by, or suggestive of insanity ⟨a ~ leer and giggle⟩ ⟨~ turmoil⟩ **c :** devoid of common sense: as (1) **:** IMPRACTICAL ⟨a ~ plan⟩ ⟨a ~ idealist⟩ (2) **:** ERRATIC ⟨a ~ driver⟩ **d :** out of the ordinary **:** ODD, UNUSUAL ⟨a ~ taste in hats⟩ ⟨a cart pushed by a ~ little old man⟩ **4 a :** distracted with desire or excitement ⟨a thrill-*crazy* mob⟩ **b :** absurdly fond **:** INFATUATED ⟨~ over a girl⟩ **c :** passionately preoccupied **:** OBSESSED ⟨~ about new cars⟩ **d :** wildly or intensely eager ⟨~ to try out a new boat⟩ **5 :** WILD 8 — often used in the names of card games similar to stops in which a card of a specified rank is wild ⟨~ jacks⟩

²crazy \"\ *adv* **1** *slang* **:** VERY, EXTREMELY ⟨~ mean neighbors drove him to violence —G.S.Perry⟩ ⟨a ~ mad policeman⟩ ⟨a ~ drunk individual⟩ **2** *slang* **:** MADLY, FURIOUSLY ⟨soldiers yelling ~ in the distance —Shelby Foote⟩

³crazy *also* **cra·zey** \"\ *n, pl* **crazies** *also* **crazeys** [origin unknown] *dial Eng* **:** any of several plants of the family Ranunculaceae: as **a :** BUTTERCUP 1 **b :** a marsh marigold (*Caltha palustris*)

crazy ant *n* **:** a very active ant (*Paratrechina longicornis*) native to the tropics and now found in buildings and protected areas in many temperate regions

crazy bone *n* **:** FUNNY BONE

crazy chick disease *also* **crazy chick** *n* **:** a nervous disease of young chickens caused by inadequate intake of vitamin E and marked by severe muscular incoordination and tremors followed by paralysis and by renal congestion and failure — called also *nutritional encephalomalacia*

crazy eights *n pl but sing in constr* **:** EIGHT 8

crazy house *n* **1 :** an insane asylum **2 :** a building in an amusement park containing fun-provoking devices (as distortion mirrors, compressed-air jets, chute-the-chutes)

crazy quilt *n* **1 :** a patchwork quilt made without a design or pattern **2 :** an incoherently pieced-together entity **:** JUMBLE, PATCHWORK ⟨our *crazy quilt* divorce laws⟩ ⟨his body a *crazy quilt* of cuts and bruises —*Newsweek*⟩

crazy top *n* **:** any of several plant diseases in which the top growth undergoes characteristic alteration: as **a :** a disease of citrus that occurs on alkaline soils, that is marked by loss of mature leaves, stiff brushy terminal growth, and abnormal fruits, and that may be related to or a form of stubborn disease **b :** a disease of corn that is prob. due to a virus and that is characterized by the appearance of vegetative shoots often in bunches in place of floral organs **c :** a disease of almonds that is probably caused by a virus and is characterized by growth failure of many flower and leaf buds resulting in a sparse open tree with little fruit

crazyweed \ˈ⸗,⸗\ *n* [so called fr. its toxic effect upon horses and cattle] **1 :** LOCOWEED **2 :** WHITE LOCOWEED

cre- *or* **creo-** *also* **kreo-** *comb form* [G *kreo-*, fr. Gk *kre-*, *kreo-*, fr. *kreas* — more at RAW] **:** flesh ⟨*cre*odont⟩ ⟨*creo*phagous⟩ ⟨*kreo*toxism⟩

crea·chy \ˈkrēchi\ *var of* CRAICHY

creagh \ˈkrāk\ *n* -S [ScGael *creach*; akin to MIr *crech* raid] **1** *chiefly Scot* **:** a plundering raid **2** *chiefly Scot* **:** PLUNDER, BOOTY

creaght \ˈkrā(k)t\ *n* -S [IrGael *caoraidheacht*, fr. MIr *caeraigheacht*, fr. OIr *caera* sheep; prob. akin to L *caper* goat — more at CAPRIOLE] **1** *Irish* **:** a herd of cattle driven about for pasture or with a warring band **2** *Irish* **:** RAPPAREE

¹creak \ˈkrēk\ *vi* -ED/-ING/-S [ME *creken* to utter a harsh cry, of imit. origin] **1** *obs* **a :** CROAK **b :** to speak querulously **2 :** to make a prolonged grating or squeaking sound ⟨doors upon their hinges ~*ed* —Alfred Tennyson⟩ ⟨~*ing* saddles⟩ **3 :** to proceed on or as if on worn wheels, springs, or joints ⟨the story ~*s* along to a dull conclusion⟩

²creak \"\ *n* -S **:** a high typically subdued rasping or grating noise (as of an ungreased axle or hinge or of the movement of worn joints of furniture)

creak·i·ly \-kəlē, -li\ *adv* **:** with creaks **:** with creaking

creak·ing·ly *adv* **:** in a creaking manner

creaky \ˈkrēkē, -ēki\ *adj* -ER/-EST **1 :** apt to creak **:** marked by creaking **:** SQUEAKY ⟨~ shoes⟩ **2 :** DILAPIDATED, DECREPIT ⟨a ~ plot⟩ ⟨a ~ old house⟩

¹cream \ˈkrēm\ *n* -S [ME *creme, creime*, fr. MF *cresme* & ONF *craime*; MF *cresme*, fr. OF, alter. (influenced by *cresme* chrism, fr. LL *chrisma*) of (assumed) OF *craime* (ONF *craime*), fr. LL *cramum*, of Celt origin; akin to W *cramen* scab, MIr *screm* surface; akin to MHG *schram* gash, ON *skrāma* wound, Lith *kramas* scurf, Gk *keirein* to cut — more at SHEAR, CHRISM] **1 :** the yellowish part of milk containing from 18 to about 40 percent butterfat that rises to the surface on standing or is separated by centrifugal force **2 a :** a food or substance made from or containing cream ⟨~ of celery soup⟩ — usu. used with a qualifying word ⟨Bavarian ~⟩ ⟨tapioca ~⟩ **b :** a solid or liquid substance resembling or suggesting cream in appearance or consistency: as (1) **:** any of a class of cosmetic preparations used esp. for cleansing, softening, smoothing, and protecting the skin ⟨emollient ~⟩ ⟨finishing ~⟩ — see COLD CREAM, SHAVING CREAM, VANISHING CREAM (2) **:** any of various medicinal preparations usu. classed as ointments (3) **:** a sweet or candy of a consistency suggesting cream ⟨a box of chocolate ~*s*⟩ (4) **:** ICE CREAM ⟨bring along a quart of vanilla ~⟩ (5) **:** the part of an emulsion or suspension that rises and collects on the surface **3 :** the best, most desirable, or choicest part of something ⟨the ~ of society⟩ ⟨the ~ of the crop⟩ **:** QUINTESSENCE ⟨the ~ of the jest⟩ **4 :** CREAMER 2 **5 :** a pale yellow that is lighter, slightly greener, and very slightly stronger than ivory, paler than straw, and greener and paler than leghorn **6 :** a cream-colored animal (as a horse or rabbit)

²cream \"\ *vb* -ED/-ING/-S [ME *cremen*, fr. *creme*, n.] *vi* **1 a :** to form cream ⟨let the milk stand till it ~*s*⟩ **b :** to become covered with cream ⟨beer ~*ing* in a glass⟩ **c :** to become like cream **:** FOAM, FROTH ⟨waves ~*ing* on the rocks⟩ **d :** to undergo creaming **2 :** to proceed with foamy spray and wake (as of a ship) ~ *vt* **1 a :** to draw off by skimming **:** take the cream off (milk) **b :** to take or remove (the choicest part) — often used with *off* ⟨~ off the best of a country's production by export⟩ **2 a :** to furnish with or as if with cream **:** prepare with cream or a cream sauce **b :** to rub, stir, or beat (as butter) until of a light creamy consistency **c :** to blend (as butter and sugar) by stirring or beating **d** *slang* **:** BEAT, LAMBASTE **3 a :** to cause or allow cream to form on (milk) **b :** to cause to froth or foam ⟨the ship's wake ~*ed* the waves⟩ **c :** to bring about creaming of ⟨rubber latex is ~*ed* by salts of alginic acid⟩ **4 :** to apply a cosmetic cream to ⟨~*ing* her face daily⟩

³cream \"\ *adj* [¹*cream*] **1 a :** having the consistency and appearance of cream ⟨~ soup⟩ **b :** having cream added **2 :** of the color cream

cream·able \-məbəl\ *adj* **:** having the quality necessary for creaming ⟨~ lard⟩

cream beige *n* **:** SANDSTONE 2

cream buff *n* **:** a pale to grayish yellow that is slightly greener than Naples yellow and redder and stronger than wine yellow

cream bun *n*, *Brit* **:** a bun filled with cream **:** CREAM PUFF

creambush \ˈ⸗,⸗\ *n* [so called fr. the white flowers] **:** OCEAN SPRAY

cream cheese *n* **1 :** an unripened cheese made from whole sweet milk enriched with cream or by working cream into a skimmed-milk curd and often containing as high as 50 percent fat **2** *dial* **:** CHEDDAR CHEESE; *esp* **:** one that is made from whole milk

creamcups \ˈ⸗,⸗\ *n pl but sing or pl in constr* [so called fr. the appearance of the flower] **1 :** any of several Californian annuals of the family Papaveraceae (esp. *Platystemon californicus*) **2 :** OCEAN SPRAY

cream·er \ˈkrēmə(r)\ *n* -S **1 :** a can or pan in which milk is set to form cream **:** a cream separator **2 :** a small pitcher or jug for serving cream

cream·ery \ˈkrēm(ə)rē, -ri\ *n* -ES [¹*cream* + -*ery*] **1 :** an establishment where butter and cheese are made or where milk and cream are sold or processed; *also* **:** the work of such an establishment **2 :** a building where milk and other dairy products are stored **:** DAIRY

cream–faced \ˈ⸗,⸗\ *adj* **:** PALE ⟨*cream-faced* from fear⟩

cream ice *n*, *Brit* **:** ICE CREAM

cream·i·ly \ˈkrēməlē, -li\ *adv* [*creamy* + -*ly*] **1 :** in the manner of or with the appearance of cream ⟨swift waters dashing ~ over the falls⟩ **2 :** SOFTLY, SUAVELY, BLANDLY ⟨~ venomous politeness —*Time*⟩

cream·i·ness \ˈkrēmēnəs, -min-\ *n* -ES **:** the quality or state of being creamy in texture or color

creaming *n* -S [fr. gerund of ²*cream*] **:** reversible separation of an emulsion or suspension by rising or settling of the dispersed particles (as oil droplets or suspended solids) ⟨~ of rubber latex⟩

cream laid *n* -S *chiefly Brit* **:** a cream-colored laid writing paper

cream·less \-mləs\ *adj* **:** not having cream

cream line *n* **:** the place where the risen cream meets the milk, esp. as seen in a transparent milk bottle

cream nut *n* [prob. so called fr. the rich flavor] **1 :** BRAZIL NUT **2 :** the nut of the cauchillo

cream of lime 1 : a scum of calcium carbonate formed on a solution of milk of lime by combination with the carbon dioxide of the air **2 :** a mixture of slaked lime and water

cream of tartar [prob. so called fr. its being the choicest or most essential ingredient in tartar] **:** a white crystalline salt $KHC_4H_4O_6$ with a pleasant acid taste found in grapes and in tartars from wine making, prepared esp. from argols and also synthetically from tartaric acid, and used chiefly in foods (as baking powder and hard candy) and in certain treatments of metals (as in the electrolytic tinning of iron and steel); potassium hydrogen tartrate — called also *potassium acid tartrate, potassium bitartrate*

cream–of–tartar tree *n* [so called fr. the taste of the fruit] **:** a desert tree (*Adansonia gregorii*) of northern Australia that produces an agreeably acid fruit — called also *Australian baobab, sour gourd*

cream puff *n* **1 :** a round shell of light pastry filled with whipped cream or a cream filling **2** *slang* **a :** a timid, weak, ineffectual, or oversensitive person ⟨no namby-pamby, *cream puff* fighter —*Sporting Life*⟩ **b :** something trifling or inconsiderable ⟨the play is a diverting *cream puff*⟩

creams *pl of* CREAM, *pres 3d sing of* CREAM

cream sauce *n* **:** WHITE SAUCE

cream soda *n* **:** a carbonated soft drink flavored with vanilla and sweetened with sugar

cream soup *also* **cream–soup bowl** *n* **:** a two-handled soup bowl

cream–soup spoon *n* **:** a round-bowled spoon slightly shorter than a standard soup spoon

creamware \ˈ⸗,⸗\ *n* **:** cream-colored pottery

cream wove *n* -S *chiefly Brit* **:** a cream-colored wove writing paper

creamy \ˈkrēmē, -mi\ *adj* -ER/-EST [¹*cream* + -*y*] **1 :** full of or containing cream **2 :** resembling cream in nature, appearance, color, or taste **:** soft and smooth **:** LUSCIOUS

cre·ance \ˈkrēən(t)s\ *n* -S [ME *creaunce* trust, confidence, leash for a hawk, fr. MF *creance*, fr. (assumed) VL *credentia* trust, belief (whence ML *credentia* promise, security given, credit, belief) — more at CREDENCE] **:** a fine line used to leash a hawk during training

¹crease \ˈkrēs\ *n* -S [prob. alter. of earlier *creaste*, fr. ME *creste* crest] **1 a :** a line, groove, or ridge that is made by or as if by folding a pliable substance and is generally larger or longer than a wrinkle and not so deep as a fold **b :** a similar mark on the skin esp. about the face or neck ⟨a ~ between the eyes⟩ — usu. used in pl. ⟨many ~*s* about her mouth —Eve Langley⟩ **c :** the front or back edge of a man's trouser leg esp. when pressed — often used in pl. **2 a :** the diagonal ventral fold marking the anterior and medial margin of junction of either leg and the trunk in man **b :** the medial cleft between the buttocks **3 :** a specially marked area in various field sports: **a** (1) **:** POPPING CREASE (2) **:** BOWLING CREASE (3) **:** RETURN CREASE (4) **:** GROUND 5h(2) **b :** an area surrounding the goal (as in lacrosse and hockey) forbidden to attacking players unless the ball or puck is in it — called also *goal crease*; see ICE HOCKEY illustration **4 :** the longitudinal groove on the ventral surface of certain grains (as of wheat)

²crease \"\ *vb* -ED/-ING/-S *vt* **1 :** to make a crease in or on **:** WRINKLE ⟨a frown *creased* his forehead⟩ **2 a :** to stun (as a wild horse wanted alive) by placing a grazing shot that does not cause permanent injury **b :** to wound slightly esp. by grazing ⟨the bullet *creased* him⟩ **:** GRAZE ⟨*creased* his head⟩ ~ *vi* **:** to become creased or wrinkled ⟨this dress material will not ~ easily⟩

³crease *var of* KRIS

crease·less \-ləs\ *adj* **:** not having a crease

creas·er \ˈkrēsə(r)\ *n* -S **:** one that creases: as **a :** a tool or a sewing-machine attachment for making lines or creases on leather or cloth as guides to sew by **b :** a tool for making creases or beads (as in sheet iron) **c :** a tool for making the band impression distinct on the backbones of books or for making blind lines or creases on the cases of books

creashaks *n, pl* **creashaks** [origin unknown] **:** BEARBERRY 1

creas·ing \ˈkrēsiŋ\ *n* -S [prob. fr. E dial. *crease* ridge tile (prob. alter. of earlier E *creast* crest, fr. ME *creste*) + E -*ing* (n. suffix)] **:** one or more courses of bricks or tiles, each course projecting slightly, crowning a wall or chimney

creasol *var of* CREOSOL

creasote *var of* CREOSOTE

creasy \ˈkrēsē, -si\ *adj* -ER/-EST [¹*crease* + -*y*] **:** having or forming creases

cre·at \(ˈ)krēˈat\ *n* -S [Hindi *kariyāt, kiryāt*] **:** an East Indian herb (*Andrographis paniculata*) having a juice that is a strong bitter tonic variously used in local medicine

creat- *or* **creato-** *comb form* [F *créat-*, fr. Gk *kreas* — more at RAW] **:** flesh ⟨*creat*ine⟩ ⟨*creato*phagous⟩

¹cre·ate \krēˈāt\ *adj* [ME *creat*, fr. L *creatus*, past part. of *creare* to create — more at CRESCENT] *archaic* **:** CREATED

²cre·ate \(ˈ)krē¦āt, *usu* -ād.+V\ *vb* -ED/-ING/-S [ME *createn*, fr. L *creatus*] *vt* **1 :** to bring into existence **:** make out of nothing and for the first time ⟨God *created* the heaven and the earth —Gen 1:1 (AV)⟩ **2 :** to cause to be or to produce by fiat or by mental, moral, or legal action: as **a :** to invest with a new form, office, or rank **:** constitute by an act of law or sovereignty ⟨~ one a peer⟩ ⟨~ a new administrative post⟩ **:** APPOINT ⟨~ one a judge⟩ **b :** to produce or effect as an act of grace ⟨~ in me a clean heart —Ps 51:10 (AV)⟩ **c :** to bring about by a course of action or behavior ⟨~ an impression of invincibility⟩ ⟨~ an opportunity to talk to someone⟩ ⟨~ a demand for a product by advertising⟩ ⟨~ a disturbance⟩ **3 :** to cause or occasion — used of natural or physical causes and esp. of social and evolutionary or emergent forces ⟨a famine ~*s* high food prices⟩ ⟨modern science, which *created* this dilemma, is also capable of solving it —Bruce Bliven b. 1889⟩ **4 a :** to produce (as a work of art or of dramatic interpretation) along new or unconventional lines ⟨*created* a new Hamlet⟩ **b :** to design (as a costume or a dress) ~ *vi* **1 :** to make or bring into existence something new (as something of an imaginative or artistic character) **:** INVENT ⟨quick to imitate but powerless to ~⟩ **2** *slang Brit* **:** to complain loudly **:** carry on **:** GRIPE ⟨don't go near him while he's *creating*⟩

cre·at·ed·ness \krēˈādədnəs, -ātə-\ *n* -ES **:** the quality or state of being created

cre·at·ic \(ˈ)krē¦ad·ik\ *adj* [*creat-* + -*ic*] **:** relating to or caused by flesh or animal food ⟨~ nausea⟩

cre·atine \ˈkrēə,tēn, -,tən\ *n* -S [ISV *creat-* + -*ine*; orig. formed as F *créatine*] **:** a white crystalline compound $NH_2C(=NH)N(CH_3)CH_2COOH$ found esp. in the muscles of vertebrates both as phosphocreatine and as the free form and also in the blood and obtained from meat extracts; 1-methylguanidine-acetic acid

creatine phosphate *or* **creatine phosphoric acid** \"+\ *n* **:** PHOSPHOCREATINE

cre·at·i·nine \krēˈatᵊn,ēn, -tᵊnən\ *n* -S [G *kreatinin*, fr. *kreatin* creatine + -*in* -ine] **:** a white crystalline strongly basic compound $C_4H_7N_3O$ formed from creatine by dehydration and found esp. in muscle, blood, and urine

cre·atin·uria \,krēətᵊn(y)u̇rēə\ *n* -S [NL, fr. ISV *creatine* + NL -*uria*] **:** the presence of creatine in urine; *esp* **:** an increased or abnormal amount of it therein ⟨marked ~ may accompany some endocrine disorders⟩

cre·ation \krēˈāshən\ *n* -S [ME *creacioun*, fr. MF or L; MF *creation*, fr. L *creation-, creatio*, fr. *creatus* (past part. of *creare* to create) + -*ion-*, -*io* -ion] **1 :** the act of creating; *esp* **:** the act of bringing into existence from nothing the universe or the world or the living and nonliving things in it **2 :** the act or practice of making, inventing, devising, fashioning, or producing: as **a :** the act of investing with a new rank or office ⟨a baron of recent ~⟩ ⟨the ~ of a special committee⟩ **b :** the presentation of a new conception in an artistic embodiment; *esp* **:** the first dramatic representation of a role ⟨Jefferson's ~ of Rip Van Winkle⟩ **3 :** something that is created: as **a :** WORLD **b :** creatures singly or as an aggregate ⟨throughout all ~⟩ **c :** an original work of art or of the imagination ⟨the question of whether folk songs are the ~*s* of groups or individuals⟩ **d :** an article of attire of new and striking design

cre·ation·al \(ˈ)krē¦āshənᵊl, -shnəl\ *adj* **:** of or relating to creation

cre·ation·ary \krēˈāshə,nerē\ *adj* **:** of the nature of or relating to creation

cre·ation·ism \-,nizəm\ *n* -S **1 :** a doctrine or theory of creation holding that matter, the various forms of life, and the world were created by a transcendent God out of nothing — compare EVOLUTIONISM **2 :** the theological doctrine that the human soul is separately created in each individual born — compare INFUSIONISM, TRADUCIANISM

cre·ation·ist \-sh(ə)nəst\ *n* -S **:** a believer in creationism — **cre·ation·is·tic** \krē,āshə¦nistik, ,krē,ā⸗ˈ⸗\ *adj*

cre·ative \(ˈ)krē¦ād·|iv, -āt|, |ēv *also* |əv *sometimes* ˈkrēəd·| *or* -ēət|\ *adj* **1 :** having the power or quality of creating **:** given to creation **2 :** PRODUCTIVE — used with *of* ⟨events ~ of alarm⟩ **3 :** having the quality of something created rather than imitated or assembled **:** expressive of the maker **:** IMAGINATIVE ⟨~ art⟩ ⟨~ writing⟩ — **cre·ative·ly** *adv*

creative evolution *n* **:** evolution conceived as a creative rather than a mechanically explicable process — see BERGSONISM; compare ÉLAN VITAL, EMERGENT EVOLUTION

cre·ative·ness *n* -ES **:** CREATIVITY

creative play *n* **:** children's play (as modeling or painting) that tends to satisfy the need for self-expression as well as to develop manual skills

cre·ativ·i·ty \,krē,āˈtivəd·ē, -rēəˈ-, -ətē, -i\ *n* -ES **:** the quality of being creative **:** ability to create ⟨the ~ of generations of immigrants —D.D.McKean⟩

creato- — see CREAT-

cre·ator \(ˈ)krē¦ād·ə(r), -ātə-; krēˈā,tȯ(ə)r, -tȯ(ə)\ *n* -S [ME *creatour*, fr. OF, fr. L *creator*, fr. *creatus* (past part. of *creare* to create) + -*or*] **:** one that creates, produces, or constitutes **:** MAKER, AUTHOR, INVENTOR

cre·atress \(ˈ)krē¦ā·trəs\ *n* -ES [*creator* + -*ess*] **:** a woman that creates (as a dramatic role)

cre·atrix \-triks\ *n, pl* **cre·atri·ces** \krēˈā·trə,sēz, ,krēə·ˈtrī-(,)sēz\ [L, fem. of *creator*] **:** CREATRESS

creats *pl of* CREAT

crea·tur·al \ˈkrēch(ə)rəl\ *adj* **:** belonging to or of the nature of a creature ⟨~ sensibilities⟩

crea·ture \ˈkrēchə(r), *dial* ˈkrid·ə(r) *or* ˈkrēd·- *or* ˈkrād·-\ *n* -S [ME, fr. OF, fr. LL *creatura*, fr. L *creatus* + -*ura* -ure] **1 :** something whether animate or inanimate regarded as created: as **a** *obs* **:** WORLD, CREATION, UNIVERSE **b** *archaic* **:** something (as food or drink) that serves man's material comfort ⟨were put to it to reconcile the phrase good ~*s* . . . with the fare set before us —Charles Lamb⟩ **c** *chiefly dial* **:** SPIRITS; *esp* **:** WHISKEY — usu. used with *the* ⟨a drop o' the ~⟩ **2 a :** one of the lower animals ⟨visited in their haunts the wild ~*s* of the woods⟩; *esp* **:** a farm animal — compare CRITTER **b :** a human being ⟨fellow ~*s*⟩ **:** PERSON ⟨the dearest ~ in the world⟩ ⟨the poor ~ has had a hard life⟩ — often used in disparagement ⟨I'll never speak to that ~ again⟩ **c :** a being of anomalous, unspecified, or uncertain aspect or nature ⟨strange fearsome ~*s*, neither man nor beast⟩ ⟨a world of fancy peopled by ~*s* unknown to man⟩ **3 a :** one that owes existence or position to another and is therefore subject to control or undue influence **:** a servile dependent **:** INSTRUMENT, MINION ⟨the Governor was a mere ~ of the Senator's⟩ ⟨the bank is a ~ of Congress⟩ **b :** one whose will is not free ⟨a ~ of habit⟩ ⟨the individual who is simultaneously the creator, the carrier, and the ~ of all institutions —Abram Kardiner⟩

creature comfort *n* **:** something (as food or warmth) that gives bodily comfort

crea·ture·li·ness \ˈkrēchə(r)lēnəs, -lin-\ *n* -ES **:** the quality or state of being a creature esp. in sharing kinship with the animals

crea·ture·ly \-lē, -li\ *adj* **:** characteristic of a creature **:** CREATURAL

creb·ri·ty \ˈkrebrəd·ē\ *n* -ES [L *crebritat-, crebritas*, fr. *crebr-*, *creber* frequent + -*itat-*, -*itas* -ity; akin to L *crescere* to grow — more at CRESCENT] **:** FREQUENCY

crèche \ˈkresh, -rāsh\ *n* -S [F, fr. OF *creche* manger, crib — more at CRATCH] **1 :** a day nursery **2 :** a foundling hospital **3 :** a representation of the stable at Bethlehem with the infant Jesus surrounded by Mary, Joseph, the oxen and asses, and adoring shepherds and magi

cré·cy \ˈkrāsē, krāˈsē, ˈkresē\ *adj, usu cap* [F *crécy* carrot of a choice variety, fr. *Crécy*, commune in northern France where it is grown] **:** prepared with carrots — used esp. of soups, eggs, entrees

credal *var of* CREEDAL

cre·dence \ˈkrēdᵊn(t)s\ *n* -S [ME, fr. MF or ML; MF *credence* trust, confidence, fr. ML *credentia* promise, security given, credit, belief, fr. (assumed) VL *credentia* trust, belief, fr. L *credent-, credens* (pres. part. of *credere* to trust, believe) + -*ia* -y — more at CREED] **1 :** acceptance (as of a story or statement) as true **:** BELIEF ⟨to give ~ to gossip⟩ ⟨to withhold ~ from the miracles of Scripture⟩ **2 :** TRUSTWORTHINESS, RELIABILITY ⟨the words of a man of ~⟩ ⟨the ~ of the senses⟩ **3 :** CREDENTIALS — now used only in the phrase *letters of credence* **4** [MF, fr. OIt *credenza*] **:** a sideboard, elaborate cupboard, or buffet of the Renaissance period used chiefly for valuable plate and vessels — see CREDENZA **5** *or* **credence table** [F *crédence* table for bread and wine beside the communion table, sideboard or buffet of the Renaissance period, fr. MF *credence* sideboard or buffet of the Renaissance period] **:** a small table, shelf, or niche beside the communion table where the bread and wine rest before consecration **syn** see BELIEF

cre·den·da \krəˈdendə, krēˈ-\ *n pl* [L, neut. pl. of *credendus*, gerundive of *credere* to believe] **:** doctrines to be believed **:** articles of faith — distinguished from *agenda*

cre·den·dum \-dəm\ *sing of* CREDENDA

cre·dent \ˈkrēdᵊnt\ *adj* [L *credent-, credens*, pres. part. of *credere*] **1** *archaic* **:** giving credence **:** CONFIDING ⟨if with too ~ ear you list his songs —Shak.⟩ **2** *obs* **:** CREDIBLE

¹cre·den·tial \krəˈdenchəl, krēˈ-\ *adj* [ML *credentialis*, fr. *credentia* + L -*alis* -al] **:** giving a title or claim to credit or confidence **:** ACCREDITING — used chiefly in the phrase *credential letters*

²credential \"\ *n* -S **1 :** something that gives a title to credit or confidence **2 credentials** *pl* **:** testimonials showing that a person is entitled to credit or has a right to exercise official power (as the letters given by a government to an ambassador) **3 a :** a document, issued to a college or university student upon leaving the institution, that testifies to his academic achievement and his personal character ⟨evaluating ~*s* of students from foreign countries⟩ **b :** DEGREE, DIPLOMA, CERTIFICATE

cre·den·tialed \-ld\ *adj* **:** having or furnished with credentials

credentials committee *n* **:** a committee (as at a national party convention) for examining the credentials of delegates and deciding upon contested claims to represent certain groups of the membership

cre·den·za \krəˈdenzə, krēˈ-\ *n* -S [It, lit., belief, confidence, fr. ML *credentia* security given, belief; fr. the practice of placing a lord's food and drink on a sideboard or buffet to be tasted by a servant before being put on the lord's table in order to make sure that it contained no poison] **1 :** CREDENCE 4 **2 :** a sideboard, buffet, or bookcase patterned after the credence of the Renaissance period; *esp* **:** one without legs whose base rests flat on the floor

20th century credenza

cre·dé's method \krəˈdāz-\ *n, cap C* [trans. of G *credésche methode*, after Karl S.F. *Credé* †1892 Ger. gynecologist] **1 :** the dropping of silver nitrate solution into the eyes of newborn infants to prevent the development of gonorrheal ophthalmia **2** *also* **credé's maneuver :** expression of the placenta after birth by manual compression of the uterus through the abdominal wall

cred·i·bil·i·ty \,kredəˈbiləd·ē, -ətē, -i\ *n* -ES [ML *credibilitat-*, *credibilitas*, fr. L *credibilis* + -*itat-*, -*itas* -ity] **:** the quality or power of inspiring belief ⟨an account lacking in ~⟩ **:** worthiness of belief ⟨doubts the ~ of the story⟩ **:** capacity for belief ⟨strains her reader's ~ —*Times Lit. Supp.*⟩

cred·i·ble \ˈkredəbəl\ *adj* [ME, fr. L *credibilis*, fr. *credere* + -*ibilis* -ible] **1 :** capable of being credited or believed **:** worthy of belief ⟨~ information⟩ **:** entitled to confidence **:** TRUSTWORTHY ⟨a ~ witness⟩ **2** *obs* **:** CREDULOUS **3** *obs* **:** CREDITABLE, REPUTABLE — **cred·i·bly** \-blē, -li\ *adv*

cred·i·ble·ness \-nəs\ *n* -ES **:** the quality of being credible

¹cred·it \ˈkredət, *usu* -əd·+V\ *n* -S [MF, reputation, commercial credit, fr. OIt *credito*, fr. L *creditum* loan, fr. neut. of *creditus*, past part. of *credere*] **1 a :** the balance in a person's favor in an account; *also* **:** an amount or limit to the extent of which a person may receive goods or money for payment in the future **b :** an amount or sum placed at a person's disposal by a bank **:** a loan of money **c :** time given for payment for goods or services sold for future payment ⟨long-term ~⟩ **d** (1) **:** an entry on the right-hand side of an account constituting an addition to a revenue, net worth, or liability account (2) **:** a deduction from an expense or asset account **e :** any one of or the sum of the items entered on the right-hand side of an account — abbr. *cr.*; opposed to *debit* **f :** a sum of money (as to meet unexpected demands) voted by the British parliament for use during the fiscal year by the administration

⟨votes of ~⟩ **g :** a deduction from an amount otherwise due ⟨a tax ~ for dividends received⟩ ⟨a ~ for returned goods⟩ **2 a :** reliance on the truth or reality of something **:** BELIEF, FAITH, TRUST ⟨give no ~ to these idle rumors⟩ **b** *obs* **:** something believed **:** a believed report **3 a :** influence or power derived from enjoying the confidence of another or others **:** STANDING ⟨I will use my ~ with her to persuade her to go⟩ **b :** reputation esp. when favorable **:** good name **:** ESTEEM ⟨he lived with ~ in the village⟩; *also* **:** financial or commercial trustworthiness **:** reputation entitling one to be trusted with money or goods advanced **4** *archaic* **:** the quality of being believed or of being worthy of belief **:** authority causing belief **:** CREDIBILITY **5 :** a source of honor ⟨he was a ~ to his family⟩ **6 a :** something that gains or adds to reputation or esteem **:** HONOR ⟨he took no ~ for his generous act⟩ ⟨it is to his ~ that he acknowledged his error⟩ **b :** RECOGNITION, ACKNOWLEDGMENT, ASCRIPTION ⟨he did not actually write the book, but he got ~ for it⟩ **c :** a printed or spoken acknowledgment of the authorship, source, or ownership of material used in a publication or in a play, motion picture, or radio or television program **d :** a recognition by name of a person contributing to a performance (as the author, director, or producer of a broadcast, telecast, or stage play) **e :** recognition by a school or college typically measured in credit hours that a student has fulfilled a requirement leading to a degree (as by completing a course) **syn** see BELIEF, INFLUENCE

[2]**credit** \"\ *vt* -ED/-ING/-S [partly fr. L *creditus* (past part. of *credere*); partly fr. [1]*credit*] **1 a :** to supply goods on credit to **b** *obs* **:** ENTRUST **2 :** to trust in the truth of **:** BELIEVE ⟨if we can ~ ancient reports⟩ **3** *archaic* **:** to bring credit or honor upon **4 :** to enter upon the credit side of an account **:** give credit for **:** place to the credit of — opposed to *debit* **5 :** to give credit to: as **a :** to consider usu. favorably as the source, author, motivating agent, or performer of an action or as possessor of a trait — usu. used with *with* ⟨Rivera, who is ~*ed* with introducing the spermaceti industry to the colonies —*Amer. Guide Series: R.I.*⟩ ⟨we are ~*ed* with hospitality, good nature, and high sexual morality —H.L.Carter⟩ **b :** to attribute (as an act or a trait) to some person — usu. used with *to* ⟨they ~ the invention to him⟩ **syn** see ASCRIBE

cred·it·abil·i·ty \ˌkredəd·əˈbiləd·ē, -edətə-, -lətē, -i\ *n* -ES **:** the quality or state of being worthy of belief or acceptance; *also* **:** a believable thing

cred·it·able \ˈkredəd·əbəl, -ətəbəl\ *adj* [partly fr. L *creditus* (past part. of *credere*) + E *-able*; partly fr. [2]*credit* + *-able*] **1 :** worthy of belief **2 a :** sufficiently good to bring reputation or esteem **:** deserving of judicious praise **:** REPUTABLE ⟨a ~ performance⟩ **b :** SUITABLE, RESPECTABLE ⟨born of ~ parents⟩ **3 :** worthy of having commercial credit **4 :** capable of being credited or ascribed ⟨victory was directly ~ to his efforts⟩ ⟨5 years of ~ service toward a retirement eligibility⟩ — **cred·it·ably** \-blē, -li\ *adv*

cred·it·able·ness \-nəs\ *n* -ES **:** the quality of being creditable

credit card *n* **1 :** a small card (as one issued by hotels, restaurants, stores, or petroleum companies) authorizing the person or company named or its agent to charge goods or services **2 :** a record in a mercantile credit department of a credit customer's purchases and payments used to check credits on orders received from him

credit hour *n* **:** the unit of measuring educational credit usu. consisting of one weekly period lasting approximately one hour of classroom work or a given number of periods of laboratory work throughout one semester or term

credit instrument *n* **:** a document (as a check, letter of credit, or bond) other than paper money that evidences a debt

credit insurance *n* **:** insurance against excessive loss due to default of debtors

cred·it·less \ˈkredətləs\ *adj* **:** having no credit

credit life insurance *n* **:** insurance on the life of a debtor under an installment purchase contract relieving the debtor's estate of further payments in event of his death

credit line *n* **1 :** a line, note, or name that accompanies and acknowledges the source of an item (as a news dispatch, a published article, or a television program) **2 :** the amount fixed as the limit of the credit to be extended to a customer

credit man *n* **:** one who investigates the financial standing of an individual or a firm to determine what credit should be extended

credit manager *n* **:** one in charge of the credit department of a business organization; *also* **:** CREDIT MAN

credit memorandum *n* **:** a document issued by a seller as confirmation to a customer that a credit adjustment has been made to his account (as for merchandise returned or for errors)

credit money *or* **credit currency** *n* **:** money accepted because of the credit of the issuer rather than for its intrinsic commodity value

cred·i·tor \ˈkredəd·ə(r), -ətə-\ *n* -S [ME *creditour*, fr. MF *crediteur*, fr. L *creditor*, fr. *creditus* (past part. of *credere* to trust) + *-or*] **1 :** one who gives credit in business matters **:** one to whom money is due — opposed to *debtor* **2** *Roman law* **:** any person to whom a debt is owed, who has a civil cause of action for anything due him, or who has a right to enforce a duty owed to him under any obligation arising out of a contract, quasi contract, delict or quasi delict

creditor nation *n* **:** a nation whose investments abroad exceed in value the investments made in it by foreign countries — compare DEBTOR NATION

creditor's bill *n* **:** a bill in equity filed by one or more creditors, usu. in behalf of all who may become parties to the action, to collect or protect debts where an execution at law would not be available for the purpose

cred·i·tor·ship \-ə(r),ship\ *n* -S **:** the state or fact of being a creditor ⟨assets of ~⟩

credit rating *n* **:** an estimate of the amount of credit that can safely be extended to a person or company as determined usu. by a mercantile agency or a credit man on the basis of financial resources, ability to repay advances, and record in paying debts

credits *pl of* CREDIT, *pres 3d sing of* CREDIT

credit slip *n* **1 :** DEPOSIT SLIP **2 :** a slip issued as evidence of a credit given for the value of merchandise returned

credit union *n* **:** a cooperative association that makes small loans to its members at low interest rates

cred·ner·ite \ˈkrednə,rīt\ *n* -S [G *crednerit*, fr. K. F. Heinrich *Credner* †1876 Ger. geologist + G *-it* -ite] **:** a grayish to black foliated mineral $CuMn_2O_4$ consisting of copper, manganese, and oxygen

cre·do \ˈkrē(,)dō, ˈkrā-\ *n* -S [ME, fr. L, I believe, 1st pers. sing. pres. indic. of *credere*] **1** *often cap* **a :** a confession of faith said or sung in Christian liturgies **b :** a choral setting of the Apostles' Creed or the Nicene Creed **2 :** a strongly held or frequently affirmed belief or conviction; *esp* **:** a generality or system adopted as a guide to action or achievement **:** TENET, DOCTRINE ⟨an artist's ~⟩ ⟨a ~ of usefulness to society⟩

credo play *n, usu cap C* **:** a medieval play based on the Apostles' Creed acted at York, England, at Lammastide

cre·du·li·ty \krəˈd(y)üləd·ē, krē'-,kre'-, -ətē, -i *sometimes* -ˈjü-\ *n* -ES [ME *credulite*, fr. MF or L; MF *credulité*, fr. L *credulitat-, credulitas*, fr. *credulus* + *-itat-, -itas* -ity] **:** belief or readiness of belief esp. on slight or uncertain evidence **:** GULLIBILITY ⟨ready ~ in the face of repeated assertions is one of the curses of the modern world —Bertrand Russell⟩ ⟨to strain ~ to the breaking point —T.S.Eliot⟩

cred·u·lous \ˈkrejələs\ *adj* [L *credulus*, fr. *credere*] **1 :** ready or inclined to believe esp. on slight or uncertain evidence; easily imposed upon ⟨a boy very ~ of life —Sinclair Lewis⟩ **2 :** based upon or proceeding from credulity ⟨~ superstition⟩ — **cred·u·lous·ly** *adv* — **cred·u·lous·ness** *n* -ES

[1]**cree** \ˈkrē\ *vt* **creed; creed; creeing; crees** [F *crever* to cause to burst — more at CRAVEN] *dial Eng* **:** to soften (grain) into a pulpy mass by boiling

[2]**cree** \"\ *n, pl* **cree** *or* **crees** *usu cap* [short for earlier *Christenaux, Christeno*, fr. CanF *Christianaux, Christino*, prob. fr. Ojibwa *Kenistenoag*] **1 a :** an Indian people ranging from James Bay in Ontario to the Saskatchewan river in Saskatchewan and south into Montana **b :** a member of such people **2 :** an Algonquian language of the Cree, Montagnais, and Naskapi peoples **3 :** a syllabic writing system used in writing Cree and other languages

[1]**creed** \ˈkrēd\ *n* -S [ME *crede*, fr. OE *crēda*, fr. L *credo* (first word of the Apostles' and Nicene Creeds), 1st pers. sing. pres. indic. of *credere* to believe; akin to OIr *cretim* I believe, Av *zrazdā-* to believe, Skt *śrad-dadhāti* he believes, *śraddhā* belief, confidence; all fr. a prehistoric IE combination whose first constituent means "magic power" and is akin to OIr *cretar* holy relic and whose second constituent is the verb represented by Skt *dadhāti* he puts, places — more at DO] **1 :** a brief authoritative doctrinal formula beginning with such words as "Credo", "Credimus", "I believe", "We believe", intended to define what is held by a Christian congregation, synod, or church to be true and essential and exclude what is held to be false belief **2** *cap* **:** that portion of a Christian liturgy in which a profession of faith is corporately recited ⟨the sermon follows the ~⟩ **3 a :** a formulation or system of religious faith ⟨a religion of usage and sentiment rather than of ~ —John Buchan⟩; *esp* **:** one definitively stated (as for affirmation or confession) ⟨drew up a ~ whose acceptance was required of all believers⟩ **b :** a religion or religious sect ⟨men of all races and ~*s*⟩ **c :** a formulation or epitome of principles, rules, opinions, and precepts formally expressed and seriously adhered to and maintained **:** a notion or complex of notions viewed as so expressed or adhered to ⟨that general distrust of logic and dethroning of reason . . . formulated into a ~ by D. H. Lawrence —C.D.Lewis⟩ ⟨the devotion to work . . . became a ~ and the principal article of economic faith —W.P. Webb⟩ **syn** see RELIGION

[2]**creed** *vb* -ED/-ING/-S [L *credere* to believe] *obs* **:** BELIEVE

creed·al *also* **cre·dal** \ˈkrēdᵊl\ *adj* [*creedal* fr. [1]*creed* + *-al*; *credal* prob. fr. *credo* + *-al*] **:** of or relating to a creed

creed·al·ism \-ᵊl,izəm\ *n* -S **:** undue insistence upon traditional statements of belief

creed·ed \-dəd\ *adj* [[1]*creed* + *-ed*] **:** having a creed

creed·ite \ˈkrē,dīt\ *n* -S [*Creede* quadrangle (U.S. Geol. Survey), southwest Colorado, its locality + E *-ite*] **:** a mineral $Ca_3Al_2F_4(OH, F)_6(SO_4).2H_2O$ consisting of hydrous calcium aluminum fluoride with calcium sulfate, occurring in white to colorless grains, and radiating crystalline masses (hardness 2, sp. gr. 2.7)

creed·less \ˈkrēdləs\ *adj* **:** not having a creed

creed·more \ˈkrēd,mō(ə)r\ *n* -S [fr. *Creedmoor*, a trademark] **:** a man's heavy blucher shoe with gusset and laces

creeds·man \ˈkrēdzmən\ *n, pl* **creedsmen :** one who follows a creed

[1]**creek** \ˈkrēk, ˈkrik — ˈkrik *is less frequent in the South than in the rest of the US and less frequent in urban than in rural areas*\ *n* -S [ME *creke, crike*, fr. ON *-kriki* bend, concavity; akin to ON *krīkr* bend, bay, *krōkr* hook — more at CROOK] **1 a** *chiefly Brit* **:** a small inlet or bay narrower and extending farther into the land than a cove **:** a narrow recess in the shore of the sea, a river, or a lake ⟨each ~ and cavern of the dangerous shore —William Cowper⟩ — used in the U.S. only in names given during the earliest period of English colonization **b :** a saltwater estuary of a small river or stream emptying on a low coast or into the lower reaches of a wide river **2 :** a natural stream of water normally smaller than and often tributary to a river — compare BRANCH, BROOK, RUN **3** *archaic* **:** a narrow commonly winding strip of comparatively flat land between hills or mountains **4** *dial chiefly Brit* **:** a narrow or winding passage **:** a concealed or secret corner ⟨each ~ and cranny of his chamber —Thomas Gray⟩ — **up the creek** *adv* **:** in a difficult or perplexing position

[2]**creek** \ˈkrēk\ *n, pl* **creek** *or* **creeks** *usu cap* [prob. so called fr. the numerous streams in the territory of the Creek Confederacy] **1 a :** CREEK CONFEDERACY **b :** a member of any of the peoples of the Creek Confederacy **2 :** MUSKOGEE 2

creek broadbill *n* [[1]*creek*] **:** LESSER SCAUP

creek chub *n* **:** a common chub (*Semotilus atromaculatus*) of small streams of eastern No. America

creek confederacy *n, usu cap both Cs* [[2]*creek*] **:** an American Indian confederacy organized around the Muskogee and including the Hitchiti, Alabama, and Koasati that dominated most of Georgia, Alabama, and northwestern Florida before their removal to Oklahoma

creek duck *n* [[1]*creek*] **:** GADWALL

creek fern *n* [[1]*creek*] **:** a stout New Zealand fern (*Lomaria fluviatilis*) with a large crown of numerous pinnate fronds

creekfish \ˈ=,=\ *n* **:** CHUB SUCKER

creek grass *n* **:** a No. American pondweed (*Potamogeton epihydrus*) with linear submerged and elliptical floating leaves

creek gum *n* **:** any of several Australian eucalypts (as *Eucalyptus gunnii* and *E. rostrata*)

creek nettle *n* **:** a tall nettle (*Urtica holosericea*) growing along streams on the Pacific coast of the U. S.

creek·ol·o·gy \krēˈkäləjē, kri'-\ *n* -ES [[1]*creek* + *-o-* + *-logy*] **:** any method of searching for oil based on a limited knowledge of geology and practiced esp. by wildcat prospectors

creek sedge *n* **:** a salt-marsh grass (*Spartina alterniflora glabra*) common along the Atlantic coast of No. America

creekstuff \ˈ=,=\ *n* **:** a grass (*Spartina cynosuroides*) growing along creeks and in salt marshes

creek thatch *n* [[1]*creek*] **:** any grass of the genus *Spartina*

[1]**creel** \ˈkrēl, *esp before pause or consonant* -ēəl\ *n* -S [ME *crele, crelle, creille*, prob. fr. (assumed) MF *creille* small gridiron (OF & MF *greille*), fr. L *craticula*, dim. of *cratis* wickerwork — more at HURDLE] **1 :** a wickerwork receptacle: as **a :** a basket for carrying fish or peat on the back **b :** an angler's basket **c :** a trap for fish or lobsters **2** *dial Eng* **:** a framework of varying form (as a rack for plates or a frame on which to slaughter pigs or shear sheep) **3** *textile manuf* **:** a bar or set of bars with skewers for holding paying-off bobbins (as in the roving machine or mule); *also* **:** any frame for holding the bobbins or spools — **in a creel** *adv, Scot* **:** in a state of temporary confusion

creel 1b

[2]**creel** \"\ *vt* -ED/-ING/-S **1 :** to put (fish) in a creel **:** CATCH, TAKE ⟨the number of trout ~*ed* per angler⟩ **2 :** to set up the creel on (a textile machine)

creel census *n* **:** the collection of data concerning the number of fish caught by sport fishermen (as on a particular stream or in a particular area) used esp. in determining effects of stocking and in planning future limits for various species

creel·er \-ēlə(r)\ *n* -S [[1]*creel* + *-er*] **:** a textile worker who replaces empty spools in the creel of a warping machine

creeling *n* -S [[1]*creel* + *-ing* (n. suffix)] *Scot* **:** a hazing ceremony in which a newly married man is made to carry a creel of stones until released by his wife

creem \ˈkrēm\ *vt* -ED/-ING/-S [perh. irreg. fr. OE *crimman* to cram; akin to OHG *krimman* to scratch, press, OE *crammian* to cram — more at CRAM] *dial Eng* **:** to squeeze or hug (as in wrestling) **:** CRUSH, MASH

[1]**creep** \ˈkrēp\ *vb* **crept** \-krept\ **crept; creeping; creeps** [ME *crepen*, fr. OE *crēopan*; akin to ON *krjūpa* to creep, MLG *kruppen* to bend, Lith *grubinėti* to stumble, Gk *grypos* bent — more at CRADLE] *vi* **1 :** to move along with the body prone and close to or touching the ground **:** move slowly on all fours **:** CRAWL ⟨watched the foxes ~ into their den⟩ **2 a :** to go very slowly ⟨the hours *crept* by⟩ ⟨~*ing* like snail, unwillingly to school —Shak.⟩ **:** to go timidly or cautiously or so as to escape notice or attention ⟨~ away into retirement⟩ **b :** to go or enter stealthily and secretly **:** STEAL ⟨~ and intrude into the fold —John Milton⟩ **:** to advance or enter unnoticed little by little **:** insinuate itself or oneself ⟨age ~*s* upon us⟩ ⟨a note of irritation had *crept* into his voice⟩ **c :** to move or behave with servility or exaggerated humility **:** CRINGE ⟨you'll come ~*ing* back when your money is gone⟩ **3 a** *of a liquid* **:** to spread slowly and steadily over a surface **b** *of sand or loose soil* **:** to shift or advance slowly ⟨sand dunes ~*ing* inland year by year⟩ **c** *of a plant* **:** to spread or grow over the ground or other surface by rooting at intervals or clinging with tendrils, stems, or aerial roots **4 a :** to move or stir slightly by swelling or shrinking (as the skin of the body) ⟨the thought makes my flesh ~⟩ **b :** to slip, slide, or gradually shift position (as a belt on a pulley, a bearing on an axle, a steel rail on a supporting surface) because of strain or vibration **c** *of a film of paint or emulsion* **:** to slide or sag on drying **d :** to change shape permanently from prolonged stress or exposure to high temperatures or both (as turbine blades or flooring material) **5** *Brit* **:** to drag in deep water with creepers (as to recover a cable) — used with *for* **6 a :** to slip or become slightly displaced **b** *of railroad rails* **:** to shift longitudinally **7 :** to rise above the surface of a solution upon the walls of a vessel ⟨salt crystals ~ in a voltaic cell⟩ **8** *of an arrow* **:** to edge forward just before release **9 a** *of a belt* **:** to slip or slide backwards on a pulley by reason of the extension or contraction of the belt as the tension is changed in passing from the tight side to the slack side or vice versa **b** *of metal* **:** to undergo creep ~ *vt, archaic* **:** to creep along or over

[2]**creep** \"\ *n* -S **1 :** the act of creeping **:** a movement of or like creeping **:** a very slow pace ⟨traffic moving at a ~⟩ ⟨the ~ of the centuries⟩ **2 a :** a tightening of the skin of the body caused by horror, disgust, or fear esp. of the strange or supernatural **:** SHIVER, SHUDDER — usu. used in pl. ⟨snakes give me the cold ~*s*⟩ **b :** a strong sensation (as of unease, revulsion, or fear) induced in a person by some other person or thing — usu. used in pl. ⟨he's crazy . . . he gives me the ~*s* —Carson McCullers⟩ **3 :** a pen or other enclosure so fenced that young animals can enter while adults are excluded and used esp. to supply special or supplementary feed **4 :** GRAPNEL, DRAG, CREEPER **5 a :** a slow longitudinal movement of the rails of a track under traffic **b :** gradual retrograde movement (as of a belt on a pulley or a tire on a wheel) **c :** the drawing together of the edges of two metal parts as a result of expansion from the heat due to welding; *also* **:** the amount the edges are drawn together **d :** the play or slack in the trigger mechanism of a firearm before it releases the hammer or firing pin **6 :** a gradual usu. downhill movement (as of loose rock, soil, sand, or shale) that is due mainly to gravity together with freezing and thawing or wetting and drying **7 a :** a slow rising of the floor of a mining gallery occasioned by the pressure of incumbent strata upon the pillars or sides; a gradual movement of mining ground **b :** a slight sometimes audible movement of rock along a fault without producing a perceptible earthquake **8 :** the slow change of dimensions of an object (as of wood, rubber, plastics) due to prolonged exposure to high temperature or stress: as **a :** deformation of a concrete structure or a casting under sustained stress **b :** progressive plastic flow of a metal under constant or nearly constant stress — usu. used of slow deformation of hot metal under a long-sustained load of magnitude less than would deform it in a brief time **9 creeps** *pl* **:** a deficiency disease esp. of sheep and cattle associated with abnormal calcium-phosphorus ratio in the diet and characterized by progressive anemia, painful softening of the bones, and a stiff slow gait **10** *slang* **a :** a sneak thief that works in or in connivance with a cheap hotel or flophouse ⟨he was rolled by a ~⟩; *also* **:** a stealthy snooper (as for facts useful for blackmail) **b :** an unpleasant, unattractive, obnoxious, or insignificant person **11 :** RELAXATION 6

creep·age \ˈkrēpij\ *n* -S **:** gradual movement **:** CREEP: as **a :** leakage of electricity over a surface of a dielectric **b :** the creeping of an electrolyte up the sides and parts of a cell **c :** the slow spreading or movement of a substance (as oil along a shaft or rust over a surface)

creep·er \-pə(r)\ *n* -S [ME *crepere*, fr. OE *crēopere*, fr. *crēopan* to creep + *-ere* -er — more at CREEP] **1 :** one that creeps; *esp* **:** an animal (as an insect or reptile) having a creeping gait or locomotion **2 a** *archaic* **:** a servile opportunist **b** *obs* **:** a reporter of odd bits for newspapers **:** a free-lance hack writer **3 :** any plant that creeps: as **a :** HEDGE BINDWEED **b :** WILD CUCUMBER c **c :** TRUMPET CREEPER **d :** VIRGINIA CREEPER **4 :** any of various rather small birds that creep or clamber over trees and bushes searching for insects: as **a :** any member of the family Certhiidae **b :** any of several American warblers — see HONEYCREEPER, TREE CREEPER, WALL CREEPER **5 :** any of various tools or implements designed to assist a man, animal, or machine to advance or climb: as **a :** a fixture with iron points worn on the shoe to prevent slipping (as on ice) — usu. used in pl. **b :** CLIMBING IRON — usu. used in pl. **c :** CLIMBER 2b **6 :** GRAPNEL **7 :** a device for supplying or moving material in a steady flow: as **a :** an endless belt or chain conveyor **b :** a spiral or screw conveyor (as for grain) **8 creepers** *pl* **:** CROCKETS **9 a :** a genetic anomaly of the domestic fowl marked by shortening and thickening of the long bones in the heterozygote and completely lethal when homozygous — compare ACHONDROPLASIA **b** *or* **creeper fowl :** an individual exhibiting this anomaly **10 :** a garment similar to a romper and suitable for wear by children while creeping — usu. used in pl.; compare CRAWLER **11 :** a small frame or platform mounted on casters, used for supporting the knees when scrubbing floors or the body when working under an automobile **12** *cricket* **:** a bowled ball that rolls along the ground after pitching

creeper 5a

creep·ered \-ə(r)d\ *adj* **:** overgrown with creeping plants

creeper lane *n* **:** an extra lane provided on an uphill grade for the use of slow-moving vehicles on a superhighway

creep·er·less \-ə(r)ləs\ *adj* **:** having no creeper **:** being without a creeper

creeper title *or* **creeping title** *n* **:** a long title on a movie or television screen that moves continuously into view from below while it is being read

creep–feed \ˈ=,=\ *vt* **:** to feed (young animals) in a creep

creep feeder *n* **:** CREEP 3

creephole \ˈ=,=\ *n* **1 :** a retreat through or into which an animal creeps (as to escape notice) **2 :** SUBTERFUGE, EXCUSE

creep·ie \ˈkrēpē\ *n* -S [[1]*creep* + *-ie*] *dial Brit* **:** a low three-legged stool **:** CUTTY STOOL

creepier *comparative of* CREEPY

creepiest *superlative of* CREEPY

creep·i·ly \ˈkrēpəlē, -li\ *adv* **:** in a creepy manner ⟨footsteps sounding ~ in a lonely house⟩

creep·i·ness \ˈkrēpēnəs, -pin-\ *n* -ES **:** the quality or state of being creepy **:** EERINESS

[1]**creeping** *n* -S [ME *crepinge*, gerund of *crepen* to creep] **1 a :** the action of one that creeps **b :** an instance of such action **2 :** a running together of the lines in a photoengraving causing a distorted image

[2]**creeping** *adj* [ME *crepinge*, pres. part. of *crepen* to creep] *of a plant* **:** tending to spread over the ground or other substrate: as **a :** PROSTRATE, PROCUMBENT, TRAILING **b :** spreading by rhizomes or stolons

creeping barrage *n* **:** ROLLING BARRAGE

creeping bellflower *n* **:** an erect European herb (*Campanula rapunculoides*) with creeping rootstocks

creeping bent *also* **creeping bentgrass** *n* **:** a common pasture or lawn grass (*Agrostis palustris*) that spreads by long stolons

creeping bur *n* **1 :** BUR CLOVER **2 :** GROUND PINE 2

creeping buttercup *n* **:** CREEPING CROWFOOT

creeping char·lie \-ˈchärlē\ *n, cap 2d C* **1 :** a stonecrop (*Sedum acre*) **2 :** MALLOW **3 :** MONEYWORT **4 :** GROUND IVY

creeping crowfoot *n* **:** a perennial European crowfoot (*Ranunculus repens*) with long creeping stolons

creeping cucumber *n* **:** a small herbaceous vine (*Melothria pendula*) bearing oblong green fruits

creeping devil cactus *n* **:** a prostrate much-branched very spiny cylindrical cactus (*Machaerocereus eruca*)

creeping disk *n, zool* **:** the smooth adhesive lower surface of the foot or sometimes of the entire body of mollusks and some other invertebrates on which they creep along

creeping eruption *n* **:** a human skin disorder that is characterized by a red line of eruption which fades at one end as it progresses at the other and that is usu. caused by insect or worm larvae and esp. those of the dog hookworm burrowing in the subdermal tissue

creeping fern *n* **:** CLIMBING FERN

creeping fescue *n* **:** RED FESCUE

creeping fig *n* **:** a prostrate or climbing Asiatic fig (*Ficus pumila*) commonly cultivated in greenhouses

creeping forget–me–not *n* **:** a low perennial European herb (*Omphalodes verna*) of the family Boraginaceae

creeping greenhead *n* **:** CLUSTERED BLUET

creeping hemlock *n* **:** GROUND HEMLOCK

creeping indigo *n* **:** a suberect or prostrate herb (*Indigofera endecaphylla*) that is woody at the base and has red flowers in dense axillary racemes

creeping jen·nie \-ˈjenē\ *n, usu cap J* **1 :** MONEYWORT **2 :** WILD CUCUMBER c **3 :** GROUND PINE **4 :** FIELD BINDWEED

creeping juniper *n* **1 :** SAVIN 1 **2 :** an American juniper (*Juniperus horizontalis*) with prostrate or procumbent rooting stems

creeping lawyer *n* **:** a small half-buried prickly New Zealand blackberry (*Rubus parvus*) with large juicy fruit

creeping loosestrife *n* **:** MONEYWORT

creep·ing·ly *adv* **:** in a creeping manner

creeping oxeye *n* **:** a West Indian maritime semiprostrate herb (*Wedelia triloba*) of the family Compositae with bright yellow flowers

creeping paralysis *or* **creeping palsy** *n* **1 :** a disease (as locomotor ataxia) characterized by gradual and spreading loss of muscular function **2 :** any gradual loss of effectiveness or vigor ⟨a *creeping paralysis* in a nation's intellectual life⟩

creeping phlox *n* **:** a perennial phlox (*Phlox stolonifera*) with long creeping leafy runners

creeping pine *n* **1** *in Europe* **:** MUGHO PINE **2** *West* **:** WHITEBARK PINE

creeping sailor *n* **1 :** STRAWBERRY GERANIUM **2 :** a stonecrop (*Sedum acre*)

creeping sal·ly \-ˈsalē\ *n, usu cap S* **:** MONEYWORT

creeping snowberry *n* **:** an American prostrate woody vine (*Gaultheria hispidula*) with white berries

creeping sow thistle *n* **:** PERENNIAL EUROPEAN SOW THISTLE

creeping spear grass *n* **:** WIRE GRASS a

creeping spike rush *n* **:** a cylindrical-stemmed sedge (*Eleocharis palustris*)

creeping strawberry *n* **:** DEWDROP 2

creeping thistle *n* **:** CANADA THISTLE

creeping thyme *n* **:** WILD THYME

creeping wheat grass *n* **:** COUCH GRASS 1 a

creeping willow *n* **:** a small Eurasian trailing or straggling bush (*Salix repens*) of which several varieties are cultivated

creeping wintergreen *n* **:** any prostrate plant of the genus *Gaultheria* (esp. *G. procumbens* in eastern No. America and *G. humifusa* in the Rocky mountains)

creeping zinnia *n* **:** a low branching leafy annual (*Sanvitalia procumbens*) with heads of flowers resembling zinnias

creep joint *n* **1 :** a gambling establishment that changes its location each night **2 :** a brothel in which a patron's clothes are rifled **3 :** any place of unsavory reputation (as one frequented by homosexuals)

creepmouse \ˈ=,=\ *n* **:** a creeping mouse; *also* **:** a motion or tickling suggestive of a creepmouse

cree potato *or* **cree turnip** *n, usu cap C* **:** BREADROOT

creeps *pres 3d sing of* CREEP, *pl of* CREEP

creepy \ˈkrēpē, -pi\ *adj* -ER/-EST **1 :** marked by creeping or slow motion ⟨man had to pass through a ~, slimy, slithery, finny, furry past —Waldemar Kaempffert⟩ **2 :** having or producing a sensation as if insects are creeping on the skin **:** inducing a nervous, shivering apprehension **:** CRAWLY, EERIE ⟨~ dark things crawled over them —C.E.W.Bean⟩ **3 :** causing horror esp. by suggestion ⟨a ~ tale⟩ **:** UNNATURAL, WEIRD, UNCANNY ⟨there is something ~ about him⟩

crees *pres 3d sing of* CREE, *pl of* CREE

creese *var of* KRIS

creesh \ˈkrēsh\ *n* -ES [ME *cresche*, fr. MF *creisse*, *cresse*, *craisse*, fr. (assumed) VL *crassia* — more at GREASE] *chiefly Scot* **:** GREASE

creesh·ie *or* **creeshy** \-shi\ *adj, chiefly Scot* **:** GREASY

cree·tur \ˈkrēd·ə(r)\ *dial var of* CREATURE

creish \ˈkrēsh, ˈkrash\ *var of* CREESH

cré·mant \krāmäⁿ, ˈkremənt\ *adj* [F, fr. pres. part. of *crémer* to become covered with cream or foam, fr. MF *cremer*, fr. *creme*, *cresme* cream — more at CREAM] *of wine* **:** mildly sparkling **:** CRACKLING — see PÉTILLANT

cre·mas·ter \krəˈmastə(r), krēˈ-\ *n* -S [NL, fr. Gk *kremastēr*, fr. *kremannynai* to hang; prob. akin to Lith *karti* to hang with a rope] **1 :** a thin muscle consisting of loops of fibers derived from the internal oblique muscle and descending upon the spermatic cord to surround and suspend the testicle **2 :** a usu. hooked process of the posterior end of the lepidopterous pupa that serves to suspend the pupa — **crem·as·te·ri·al** \ˌkreməˈstirēəl\ *adj* — **crem·as·ter·ic** \-ˈsterik\ *adj or n*

cre·mate \ˈkrē,māt *also* krēˈ- *or* krəˈ-; *usu* -ād·+V\ *vt* -ED/-ING/-S [L *crematus*, past part. of *cremare* — more at HEARTH] **:** to reduce (a dead body) to ashes by the action of fire either directly or in an oven or retort ⟨ritual pits whose contents included charcoal and *cremated* human bones —*Notes & Queries*⟩

cre·ma·tion \krēˈmāshən, krəˈ-\ *n* -S [L *cremation-*, *crematio*, fr. *crematus* + *-ion-*, *-io* -ion] **1 :** the act or practice of cremating the dead **2 :** the destruction of records or documents (as expired bonds or coupons) by several fire ⟨watch the ~ of a batch of canceled securities —*New Yorker*⟩

cre·ma·tion·ism \-,nizəm\ *n* -S **:** the advocacy or practice of cremation

cre·ma·tion·ist \-nəst\ *n* -S **:** one advocating or practicing cremation

cre·ma·tor \ˈkrē,mād·ə(r), -ātə-; krēˈ-, krəˈ-\ *n* -S [LL, fr. L *crematus* + *-or*] **1 :** one that cremates corpses **2 :** CREMATORY

cre·ma·to·ri·um \ˌkrēməˈtōrēəm, ˌkrem-, -tȯr-\ *n, pl* **crema·to·ria** \-rēə\ *or* **crematoriums** [NL] **:** CREMATORY

¹cre·ma·to·ry \ˈ==,=ē, -ri\ *n* -ES [NL *crematorium*, fr. L *crematus* + *-orium* -ory] **1 a :** a furnace for cremating the bodies of the dead **b :** a building containing such a furnace **2 :** INCINERATOR

²crematory \"\ *adj* [*cremate* + *-ory* (adj. suffix)] **:** of or relating to cremation

crème \ˈkrem, ˈkrām, ˈkrēm\ *n, pl* **crèmes** \-m(z)\ [F, fr. OF *cresme* — more at CREAM] **1 :** cream or cream sauce as used in cookery **2 :** a sweet liqueur — usu. used with the flavor specified **3 :** CREAM 2 b

crème d'a·na·nas \ˌkrem,dänäˈnä, ¦krām-, ¦krēm-, -nəˈ-\ *n, pl* **crèmes d'ananas** [F, lit., cream of pineapples] **:** a liqueur flavored with pineapple

crème de ba·nanes \¦=dəbäˈnän, -bəˈ-\ *n, pl* **crèmes de bananes** [F, lit., cream of bananas] **:** a liqueur flavored with bananas

crème de ca·cao \¦kremdəˈkō(,)kō; ¦kremdə,käkäˈō, ¦krām-, -kəˈō\ *n, pl* **crèmes de cacao** [F, lit., cream of cacao] **:** a relatively sweet liqueur flavored with cacao beans and vanilla used as an after-dinner cordial and as a cocktail ingredient esp. in an Alexander or pousse-café

crème de café \-dəkäˈfā, -kəˈfā\ *n, pl* **crèmes de café** [F, lit., cream of coffee] **:** a coffee-flavored liqueur

crème de cas·sis \-dəkäˈsēs, -kəˈ-\ *n, pl* **crèmes de cassis** [F, lit., cream of black currants] **:** a black-currant liqueur

crème de la crème \ˌkremdəläˈkrem, -ləˈ-; ¦krām . . . ¦krām\ *n* [F, lit., cream of the cream] **:** the very best **:** the highest elite ⟨these dinings and winings, mostly among the *crème de la crème* of the literati —E.F.Payne⟩

crème de menthe \ˌkremdəˈmenth, -mint; ¦kremdəˈmäⁿt, ¦krām-\ *n, pl* **crèmes de menthe** [F, lit., cream of mint] **:** a relatively sweet green or white liqueur flavored with various mints, principally peppermint

crème de mo·ka \ˌkremdəmōˈkä, ¦krām-; ¦krēmdə¦mōkə\ *n, pl* **crèmes de moka** [F, lit., cream of mocha] **:** a liqueur flavored with coffee essence and other aromatic substances

crème de no·yau \ˌkremdə¦nwäˈyō, ¦krām-; ¦krēmdən¦wīˈō\ *n, pl* **crèmes de noyau** [F, lit., cream of kernel] **:** a liqueur with a brandy base flavored primarily with essential oils derived from the kernels of peaches, plums, and cherries or from almonds, the predominant flavor being that of bitter almonds

crème de vio·lette \ˌkremdə¦vyōˈlet, ¦krām-; ¦krēmdəˈvī(ə)lət\ *n, pl* **crèmes de violette** [F, lit., cream of violet] **:** a sweet violet-flavored liqueur — compare CREME YVETTE

cré·me·rie \ˈkrēm(ə)(,)rē; ˈkrem-, ˈkrām-, ,=(=)ˈ=\ *n* -S [F, fr. *crème* cream + *-erie* -ery] **:** a small shop for dairy products **:** DAIRY LUNCH

Crème Yvette \ˌkremēˈvet, -rām-, -rēm-\ *trademark* — used for a bluish violet-flavored liqueur

cremnitz white *usu cap C, var of* KREMNITZ WHITE

crem·o·carp \ˈkremə,kärp, -rēm-\ *n* -S [ISV *cremo-* (fr. Gk *kremannynai* to hang) + *-carp*; prob. orig. formed as F *crémocarpe*] **:** a dry dehiscent fruit characteristic of plants of the family Umbelliferae that consists of two indehiscent one-seeded mericarps which split apart at maturity and remain pendent from the summit of the carpophore

cremona *var of* CROMORNA

cre·mone bolt \krəˈmōn-, krāˈ-\ *n* [F *crémone*, prob. fr. *Crémone* (Cremona), city in northern Italy] **:** a fastening used on double doors and casement windows that has vertical rods moved up and down so that the ends of the bolts engage the top and bottom of the frame

cre·morne bolt \-ˈmȯ(ə)rn-\ *n* [*cremorne* modif. of F *crémone*] **:** CREMONE BOLT

crems white *usu cap C, var of* KREMS WHITE

cren- *or* **creno-** *comb form* [Gk *krēn-*, *krēno-*, fr. *krēnē* spring; perh. akin to OE *hærn*, *hræn* sea, ON *hrönn* wave] **1 :** spring **:** mineral spring ⟨*crenic*⟩ ⟨*creno*therapy⟩ **2 :** crenic acid ⟨*crenite*⟩

cre·na \ˈkrēnə, -renə\ *n, pl* **cre·nae** \-(,)nē, -,nī\ [ML, fr. *crenare* to split] **:** NOTCH, INDENTATION, CLEFT, SCALLOP

cre·nate \ˈkrē,nāt, -re,-, -,nət\ *adj* [NL *crenatus*, fr. ML, past part. of *crenare* to split — more at CRENEL] **:** having the margin cut into rounded scallops — used esp. in botany of foliar structures ⟨a bi*crenate* leaf⟩ and in physiology of shrunken red blood corpuscles; see CRENATION — **cre·nate·ly** *adv*

cre·nat·ed \-,nād·əd\ *adj* [NL *crenatus* + E *-ed*] **:** CRENATE

cre·na·tion \krēˈnāshən, -reˈ-,-rəˈ-\ *n* -S [*crenate* + *-ion*] **1 a :** one of a series of rounded projections forming an edge (as of a leaf or a coin) **b :** the quality or state of being crenate **2 :** shrinkage or the shrunken condition of red blood cells exposed to hypertonic solutions in which the cell margins become crenate

cremone bolt

cren·a·ture \ˈkrenəchə(r), -rēn-\ *n* -S [*crenate* + *-ure*] **:** CRENATION; *also* **:** a notch or indentation (as between crenations)

¹cren·el \ˈkrenᵊl\ *also* **cre·nelle** \krəˈnel\ *n* -S [MF *crenel*, fr. OF, dim. of *cren* notch, fr. *crener* to notch, fr. ML *crenare*, fr. (assumed) VL *crinare* to split, perh. of Celt origin; akin to OIr *criathar* sieve; akin to Gk *krinein* to separate — more at CERTAIN] **:** one of the embrasures alternating with merlons in a battlement — see BATTLEMENT illustration

²crenel \"\ *vt* **creneled** *or* **crenelled**; **creneled** *or* **crenelled**; **creneling** *or* **crenelling** \ˈkren(ᵊ)liŋ\ **crenels** [F *créneler*, fr. OF *creneler*, fr. *crenel*] **:** CRENELLATE

cré·ne·lé *or* **cre·nel·lé** *also* **cre·ne·lee** \¦krānᵊl¦ā, -ren-\ *adj* [MF *crenelé*, fr. past part. of *creneler* to crenellate] *heraldry* **:** having the upper edge crenellated **:** EMBATTLED

cren·el·et \ˈkrenᵊlət, -ᵊl,et\ *n* -S [¹*crenel* + *-et*] **:** a small crenel or an imitation of one (as in a design)

¹cren·el·late *also* **cren·el·ate** \ˈkrenᵊl,āt, *usu* -ād·+V\ *vt* -ED/-ING/-S [¹*crenel* + *-ate* (vb. suffix)] **:** to furnish (as a wall or a manor house) with battlements **:** CASTELLATE

²crenellate *or* **crenelate** \", -lət\ *adj* [¹*crenel* + *-ate* (adj. suffix)] **:** CRENELLATED

cren·el·lat·ed *or* **cren·el·at·ed** \ˈkrenᵊl,ād·əd\ *adj* [fr. past part. of *crenellate*] **1 :** having battlements **:** CASTELLATED **2 :** embattled or having repeated indentations like those in a battlement ⟨a ~ pattern⟩ **3** *bot* **:** minutely crenate **4 :** having crenations; *esp, of a coin* **:** having crenations on the edge of the hole made by cutting out the center

crenellated molding *n* **:** a molding of embattled or indented pattern common in medieval buildings

cren·el·la·tion *or* **cren·el·a·tion** \ˌkrenᵊlˈāshən\ *n* -S **1 :** the act of crenellating **2 :** BATTLEMENT **3 :** CRENEL

crenellated molding

cre·nit·ic \krəˈnid·ik\ *adj* [cren- + *-ite* + *-ic*] **:** relating to or resulting from the raising of mineral matter from subterranean sources through the action of springs

creno- — *see* CREN-

cren·o·cyte \ˈkrenə,sīt, -rēn-\ *n* -S [*crenate* + *-o-* + *-cyte*] **:** a red blood cell with notched serrated edges (as that resulting from crenation)

cren·o·thrix \-,thriks\ *n, cap* [NL, fr. *cren-* + *-thrix*] **:** a genus (the type of the family Crenotrichaceae) usu. regarded as including a single species (*C. polypora*) of attached sheathed unbranched chlamydobacteria that are a frequent nuisance in water pipes and iron-containing springs and that have cylindrical or spherical cells which divide in three planes to form nonmotile spherical conidia

cren·u·la \ˈkrenyələ, -nᵊlə\ *n, pl* **crenu·lae** \-nyə,lē, -nᵊl,ē, -nyə,lī\ [NL, dim. of ML *crena*] **:** CRENULATION

cren·u·late \-nyələt, -nᵊlət, -nyə,lāt, -nᵊl,āt\ *adj* [NL *crenulatus*, fr. *crenula* + L *-atus* -ate] **:** minutely crenate ⟨~ leaf edge⟩ ⟨a ~ shoreline⟩

cren·u·lat·ed \-nyə,lād·əd, -nᵊl,ā-\ *adj* [*crenulate* + *-ed*] **:** minutely crenate

cren·u·la·tion \ˌkrenyəˈlāshən, -nᵊlˈā-\ *n* -S [*crenulate* + *-ion*] **1 :** a minute crenation **2 :** the state of being minutely crenate

creo- — see CRE-

¹cre·o·dont \ˈkrēə,dänt\ *adj* [NL *Creodonta*] **:** of or relating to the Creodonta

²creodont \"\ *n* -S [NL *Creodonta*] **:** any mammal of the suborder Creodonta

cre·o·don·ta \ˌkrēəˈdäntə\ *n pl, cap* [NL, fr. *cre-* + *-odonta*] **:** a suborder of extinct primitive mammals (order Carnivora) showing relationship to the early ungulates and known from fossil remains in Eocene and Oligocene formations — compare HYAENODON

¹cre·ole \ˈkrē,ōl\ *n* -S [F *créole*, fr. Sp *criollo*, fr. Pg *crioulo* slave born in his master's house, Negro born in the colonies, white person born in the colonies, prob. dim. of *cria* slave brought up in his master's house, fr. *criar* to bring up, fr. L *creare* to create, beget — more at CRESCENT] **1** *usu cap* **:** one of native birth but of European descent — used in the West Indies, in Spanish America, and formerly in French settlements of No. America **2** *usu cap* **:** a white person descended from early French or sometimes Spanish settlers of the southern U.S. esp. in the Gulf states and preserving a characteristic form of French speech and culture **3** *usu cap* **a :** a person of mixed French and Negro or Spanish and Negro descent speaking a dialect of French or Spanish — used esp. in Mississippi, Alabama, and Florida **b** *Alaska* **:** a person of mixed Russian and Eskimo or Indian descent **4** *usu cap* **:** any of several creolized languages: as **a :** the creolized French spoken by many Negroes in southern Louisiana **b :** the creolized French spoken by the great majority of the inhabitants of Haiti — called also *Haitian Creole* **5** *or* **creolefish :** a serranoid market fish (*Paranthias furcifer*) from tropical America **syn** see DIALECT

²creole \"\ *adj* **1** *usu cap* **:** being a Creole **:** of or belonging to the Creole group or culture ⟨~ landowners⟩ **2** *sometimes cap, in Louisiana & the West Indies* **:** of native origin or production **:** of the local variety ⟨~ cattle⟩ ⟨~ vegetables⟩ **3** *often cap* **:** being or having the characteristics of a creolized language ⟨a ~ dialect⟩ ⟨the ~ French of Saint Lucia⟩ **4** *sometimes cap* **:** of, belonging to, or characteristic of native-born people of European (as Spanish) descent resident esp. in Spanish America ⟨a ~ culture neither Indian nor Iberian —G.M. Foster⟩ **5** *of food* **:** prepared in a style characterized by the use of rice, okra, tomatoes, peppers, and high seasonings ⟨~ sauce⟩ ⟨lobster ~⟩

creole lily *n, usu cap C* **:** an Easter lily that has rather short foliage giving it a columnar habit, that has flowers shorter than those of the Croft lily, and that is much used for forcing

cre·o·lite \ˈkrēə,līt\ *n* -S [perh. fr. ¹*creole* + *-ite*] **:** a jasper with red and white bands found in California

cre·ol·i·za·tion \ˌkrēələˈzāshən, -ē(,)ōl-\ *n* -S **:** the act or process of creolizing

cre·ol·ize \ˈkrēə,līz, -ēō,-\ *vt* -ED/-ING/-S **1 :** to make Creole **:** cause to adopt Creole qualities or customs ⟨*creolized* immigrants⟩ **2 :** to cause to become a creolized language ⟨pidgin which has existed over several centuries without becoming *creolized* —C.F.Hockett⟩

creolized language *also* **creole language** *n* **:** a language resulting from the acquisition by a subordinate group of the language of a dominant group, with phonological changes, simplification of grammar, and an admixture of the subordinate group's vocabulary, and serving as the mother tongue of its speakers, not solely for communication between people of different languages — compare PIDGIN

cre·oph·a·gous \(ˈ)krēˈäfəgəs\ *adj* [Gk *kreophagos*, fr. *kre-* cre- + *-phagos* -phagous] **:** CARNIVOROUS

cre·oph·a·gy \=ˈ=fəjē\ *n* -ES [Gk *kreophagia*, fr. *kre-* cre- + *-phagia* -phagy] **:** the use of flesh as food

cre·o·sol *also* **cre·a·sol** \ˈkrēə,sōl, -,sȯl\ *n* -S [ISV *creosote* + *-ol*; prob. orig. formed as G *kreosol*] **:** a colorless aromatic phenol $CH_3O(CH_3)C_6H_3OH$ obtained from beechwood tar and guaiacum resin; 2-methoxy-*para*-cresol

cre·o·so·tate \ˈkrēə,sōd·,āt, -ə,sō,tāt, -əsə,tāt\ *n* -S [*creosote* + *-ate*] **:** a mixture or compound with creosote

¹cre·o·sote \ˈkrēə,sōt, *usu* -ōd·+V\ *n* -S [G *kreosot*, fr. *kre-* cre- + Gk *sōtēr* preserver, fr. *sōzein* to preserve; akin to L *tumēre* to swell — more at THUMB] **1** *also* **creasote** \"\ **:** a colorless or yellowish oily liquid that has a burning smoky taste, contains a mixture of phenolic compounds (as guaiacol), is obtained by the distillation of wood tar, esp. that of beechwood, and is used chiefly as an expectorant in chronic bronchitis and as a collector and frother in ore flotation — called also *wood creosote* **2 :** CREOSOTE OIL 2

²creosote \"\ *vt* -ED/-ING/-S **:** to impregnate (wood) with creosote oil

creosote bush *n* [so called fr. the odor of its foliage] **:** a desert shrub (*Larrea tridentata*) of the southwestern U.S. and adjacent Mexico having persistent resinous aromatic foliage and small bright-yellow flowers — see SONORA GUM

creosote carbonate *n* **:** a yellow oily liquid consisting of a mixture of the carbonates of the constituents of creosote used esp. as an expectorant in chronic bronchitis

creosote oil *n* **1 :** the part of the wood-tar distillate from which creosote is obtained by refining **2 :** a yellowish to dark-colored heavy oil that consists chiefly of liquid and solid aromatic hydrocarbons, tar acids, and tar bases, is obtained by distillation of coal tar, and is used as a preservative for wood, as an insecticide, and in ore flotation — called also *coal-tar creosote*

cre·o·sot·ic \¦krēə¦säd·ik, -sōd-\ *adj* **:** of or relating to creosote

crep·ance \ˈkrepən(t)s, -rēp-\ *n* -S [modif. of It *crepaccio*, aug. of *crepa* crack, fr. *crepare* to crack, burst, fr. L, to crack, creak, break — more at CRAVEN] **:** an injury to a horse's leg caused by interference

¹crepe *or* **crêpe** \ˈkrāp; *in sense 3 also* -rep\ *n* -S [F *crêpe* — more at CRAPE] **1 :** a lightweight fabric of various fibers (as silk or cotton) with a crinkled surface obtained by using hard-twisted yarns, by printing with caustic soda, by weaving with varied tensions, or by embossing **2 :** CRAPE 3 **3 :** a small very thin pancake **4 :** CREPE RUBBER

²crepe *or* **crêpe** \ˈkrāp\ *vt* -ED/-ING/-S **:** to make (as paper) crinkly like crepe **:** CRINKLE

³crepe \"\ *adj* **1 :** of highly twisted yarns used for dullness and durability in hosiery and for crinkled effects in woven fabrics **2 :** of fancy weaves producing a pebbly or rough grainy surface on fabrics **3 :** made of crepe rubber

crepe-back \ˈ=,=\ *adj, of reversible satins* **:** having a crepe surface on the back and a satin surface on the front

crepe de chine \ˌkrāpdəˈshēn\ *n, pl* **crepes de chine** \-p(s)də-\ *or* **crepe de chines** \-nz\ *often cap 2d C* [F *crêpe de Chine*, lit., China crepe] **1 :** a silk fabric woven in the gum **2 :** a soft fine clothing crepe with a smoother face than other crepes that is woven of silk, rayon, cotton, or wool in plain weave

crepe hair *n* **:** artificial hair used as stage makeup

crepehanger *also* **crape·hanger** \ˈkrāp+,-\ *n* [¹*crepe* or ¹*crape* + *hanger*] **:** one who takes a pessimistic view of things **:** KILLJOY ⟨man is doomed, say the ~s, to overpopulate his planet —*Time*⟩

crepe marocain *n* [F *crêpe marocain*, lit., Moroccan crepe] **:** MAROCAIN

crepe myrtle *or* **crêpe myrtle** *var of* CRAPE MYRTLE

crepe paper *n* **:** paper with a crinkled or puckered texture

crepe rubber *n* **:** crude rubber in the form of nearly white to brown crinkled sheets prepared by passing coagulated latex through grooved rollers and used esp. for shoe soles

crepe su·zette \ˌkrāp(,)süˈzet, -rep-, -(,)swˈ-\ *n, pl* **crepes suzette** \-p(s)(,)s-\ *or* **crepe suzettes** \-ts\ [F *crêpe Suzette*, fr. *crêpe* (pancake) + *Suzette* (dim. of the name *Suzanne* Susan)] **:** a small thin pancake folded in quarters or rolled, heated in a sauce of butter, sugar, orange or lemon juice, grated rind, and a liqueur (as curaçao) to which is added a pony or two of cognac and cointreau, and usu. set ablaze before serving

crep·ey *or* **crepy** \ˈkrāpē, -pi\ *adj* -ER/-EST [¹*crepe* + *-y*] **:** like crepe **:** CRINKLY

cre·pid·u·la \krəˈpijələ, -idyələ, -idᵊlə\ *n, cap* [NL, fr. L, small sandal, dim. of *crepida* sandal, fr. Gk *krēpid-*, *krēpis* boot; akin to OIr *cairem* shoemaker, Lith *kurpe* shoe, and prob. Gk *keirein* to cut — more at SHEAR] **:** a genus of marine gastropods (suborder Taenioglossa) comprising the typical slipper limpets

crep·i·ness \ˈkrāpēnəs, -pin-\ *n* -ES **:** the quality or state of being crepey

cre·pip·o·da \krəˈpipədə\ [NL, fr. *crepi-* (perh. fr. Gk *krēpis* boot) + *-poda*] *syn of* AMPHINEURA

cre·pis \ˈkrēpəs\ *n* [NL, fr. L, a plant, fr. Gk *krēpis*, lit., boot] **1** *cap* **:** a genus of herbs (family Compositae) with alternate or basal chiefly pinnatifid leaves and heads of yellow or orange colored flowers — see HAWK'S-BEARD **2 crepis** *pl* **:** a plant of the genus *Crepis*

crep·i·tant \ˈkrepəd·ənt, -ətənt *also* -ətᵊnt\ *adj* [L *crepitant-*, *crepitans*, pres. part. of *crepitare*] **:** having or making a crackling sound **:** CRACKLING, RATTLING ⟨~ dead leaves⟩ ⟨a ~ radio static⟩ ⟨a ~ joint⟩

crepitant rale *n* **:** a peculiar crackling sound audible with inspiration in pneumonia and other lung diseases

crep·i·tate \ˈkrepə,tāt, *usu* -ād·+V\ *vi* -ED/-ING/-S [L *crepitatus*, past part. of *crepitare* to rattle, crackle, fr. *crepitus*, past part. of *crepare* to crack — more at RAVEN] **:** to make a series of small sharp rapidly repeated explosions or sounds **:** CRACKLE

crep·i·ta·tion \ˌ==ˈtāshən\ *n* -S [LL *crepitation-*, *crepitatio*, fr. L *crepitatus* + *-ion-*, *-io* -ion] **1 :** the act or an instance of crepitating **:** a crackling noise **:** CRACKLING **2** *med* **:** a grating or crackling sound or sensation (as that produced by the fractured ends of a bone moving against each other or as that in tissues affected with gas gangrene) ⟨~ in the arthritic knee⟩ **:** CREPITANT RALE

crep·i·tus \ˈkrepəd·əs, -ətəs\ *n, pl* **crepitus** [L, fr. *crepitus*, past part. of *crepare*] *med* **:** CREPITATION

creplich *var of* KREPLACH

cre·pon \ˈkrā(,)pän, -re(,)-\ *n* -S [F, fr. *crêpe* crepe — more at CRAPE] **:** a heavy crepe fabric characterized by a crinkled puckered face

crept *past of* CREEP

cre·pus·cu·lar \krəˈpəsk(y)ələ(r)\ *adj* [L *crepusculum* + E *-ar*] **1 :** of, relating to, or like twilight **:** GLIMMERING **:** imperfectly luminous **:** DIM ⟨~ depths of personality —William James⟩ **2 :** active in the twilight ⟨~ insects⟩

crepuscular light *n* **:** a faint light (as of a slightly illuminated sky)

crepuscular ray *n* **:** a streak of light that seems to radiate from the sun shortly before or after sunset when sunlight shines through a break in the clouds or a notch in the horizon line and illuminates atmospheric haze or dust particles

cre·pus·cule \krəˈpə,sk(y)ü(ə)l, ˈkrep-\ *or* **cre·pus·cle** \krəˈpəsəl\ *n* -S [L *crepusculum*, fr. *creper* dusky, dark] **:** a time of half-light; *specif* **:** TWILIGHT

crepy *var of* CREPEY

¹cre·scen·do \krəˈshen(,)dō, -ˈse-; krāˈsh-, kreˈsh-\ *n, pl* **crescendos** *or* **crescendoes** [It, fr. *crescendo* (verbal of *crescere* to grow), fr. L *crescendum*] **1 a :** a swelling in volume of sound esp. in playing or singing music **b :** a passage so performed **2 a :** any gradual increase (as in physical or emotional force or intensity) ⟨a ~ of irritation⟩ ⟨a ~ of attacks upon the town⟩ ⟨a ~ of color spread over the sky⟩ **b :** the peak of such an increase ⟨the gale reached its ~ in the evening⟩

²crescendo \"\ *adj (or adv)* [It, lit., growing, fr. L *crescendum*, gerund of *crescere* to grow] **:** with an increase in volume — used as a direction in music and often indicated by the abbr. *cresc* or the symbol <

³crescendo \"\ *vi* -ED/-ING/-ES **:** to grow esp. in volume of

sound or in emotional intensity ⟨chants that . . . had ~*ed* to a wild frenzy —Hendrik de Leeuw⟩
crescendo pedal *n* **:** an organ pedal by which most of the stops comprising the organ may be gradually thrown on or off in proper order as to quality and volume
[1]**cres·cent** \ˈkresᵊnt *sometimes* ˈkrezᵊnt\ *n* -s [ME *cressant, cressent*, fr. MF *croissant, creissant* crescent, time between the new and full moon, fr. pres. part. of *creistre, croistre* to increase, grow, fr. L *crescere;* akin to OE *hersewæstm* millet grain, OS *hirsi* millet, OHG *hirsi, hirso* millet, L *creare* to create, produce, beget, bring forth, Gk *koros* boy, puppet, *korē* girl, virgin, pupil of the eye, Lith *šerti* to feed, Alb *thjer* acorn; basic meaning: growing, feeding] **1 a** (1) **:** the aspect presented by the moon at any stage between new moon and first quarter and between last quarter and the succeeding new moon (2) **:** any of the similar aspects of Venus and Mercury when less than half of the illuminated hemisphere is visible **b :** the shape or figure defined by a convex and a concave edge **2 a :** a representation of the crescent moon used as an ornament, emblem, or badge **b :** a heraldic charge that consists of the figure of the crescent moon with the horns directed upward and is often used as a cadency mark to distinguish a second son and his descendants **3 :** an object shaped like a crescent: as **a :** ROLL, BUN, COOKIE **b :** a raised cordonnet used in needlepoint laces for separating or outlining a portion of the design **c :** an anatomical structure or section **d :** the concave in the edge of a roller in a lever escapement to allow passage of the guard pin — called also *passing hollow* **e :** PAVILLON CHINOIS **4 a :** an area shaped like a crescent ⟨the industrial ~ along the Gulf coast⟩ **b :** a semicircular row of houses or the street serving such a row ⟨the bedlam of roads, ~*s*, drives . . . that form the suburbs of Dublin —*Irish Digest*⟩ **5 :** the gametocyte of the falciparum malaria parasite that is shaped like a crescent and constitutes a distinguishing character of malignant tertian malaria

crescent 1b

[2]**crescent** \"\ *adj* [L *crescent-, crescens*, pres. part. of *crescere*] **1 :** INCREASING, GROWING ⟨there was a ~ humming on the rails —Thomas Wolfe⟩ **2 :** having the shape or outline of a crescent **:** MENISCOID ⟨New Orleans . . . built on a ~ sweep of the Mississippi —Allan Nevins & H. S. Commager⟩
[3]**crescent** \"\ *or* **crescent spot** *or* **crescent spot butterfly** *n* -s [[1]*crescent*] **:** any of numerous small butterflies (genera *Phyciodes* and *Melitaea*) having white spots on the wings
cre·scen·tia \krəˈsensh(ē)ə\ *n, cap* [NL, fr. Pietro Crescenzi (Petrus de *Crescentiis*) †1310? Ital. writer on agriculture + NL *-ia*] **:** a genus of tropical American trees (family Bignoniaceae) distinguished chiefly by short trunk, crooked limbs, often drooping branches, purplish blotched flowers, and large globose fruits — see CALABASH
cres·cen·tic \krəˈsentik\ *adj* **:** resembling or suggesting a crescent ⟨~ patterns of meandering channels —P.E.James⟩
crescentic lobe *n* **:** SEMILUNAR LOBE
crescent of gia·nuz·zi \-jəˈnütsē\ *usu cap G* [after Giuseppe *Giannuzzi* †1876 Ital. physiologist] **:** DEMILUNE
cres·cent·oid \ˈkresᵊnˌtȯid\ *adj* **:** CRESCENTIC
crescent stretcher *n* **:** a curved stretcher peculiar to American Windsor chairs of the 18th and early 19th centuries
crescent terrapin *n* **:** a common No. American turtle (*Graptemys pseudogeographica*) olive with black blotches and a yellow crescent behind each eye
cres·cive \ˈkresiv\ *adj* [L *crescere* + E *-ive*] **:** INCREASING, GROWING **:** capable of growth ⟨the emergence of a ~ American culture —Louis Wirth⟩ — **cres·cive·ly** \-sə̇vlē\ *adv*
cres·co·graph \ˈkreskəˌgraf\ *n* -s [L *crescere* + E *-o-* + *-graph*] **:** an instrument for making perceptible the growth of plants — **cres·co·graph·ic** \ˌ⸗⸗ˈgrafik\ *adj*
cre·sol \ˈkrēˌsōl, -ˌsȯl\ *n* -s [ISV *cres-* (irreg. fr. *creosote*) + *-ol;* prob. orig. formed as G *kresol*] **1 :** any of three poisonous colorless crystalline or liquid isomeric phenols $CH_3C_6H_4OH$ distinguished as *ortho*-cresol, *meta*-cresol, and *para*-cresol, obtained usu. from coal tar, and used chiefly as disinfectants, in making phenolic resins and plasticizers, and in organic synthesis; methyl-phenol **2 :** a mixture of isomeric cresols obtained from coal tar
cresol red *n* **:** a dye $C_{21}H_{18}O_5S$ of the sulfonephthalein series derived from *ortho*-cresol that is obtained as a reddish brown crystalline powder and is used as an acid-base indicator
cre·sor·ci·nol \krəˈsȯrsᵊnˌōl, -ˌȯl\ *n* -s [ISV *cresol* + *orcinol*] **:** crystalline phenol $CH_3C_6H_3(OH)_2$ isomeric with orcinol; 4-methyl-resorcinol
cre·so·tate \ˈkrēsəˌtāt, -res-\ *also* **cre·sot·i·nate** \krəˈsätᵊnˌāt\ *n* -s [ISV *cresotic* (in *cresotic acid*) + *-ate*] **:** a salt of cresotic acid
cre·sot·ic acid \krəˈsäd·ik-\ *n* [ISV *cresotic* (fr. *cresot-* — prob. irreg. fr. *creosote* — + *-ic*) + *acid*] **:** any of 10 isomeric acids $CH_3C_6H_3(OH)COOH$ derived from the cresols; hydroxy-toluic acid
cre·so·tine yellow G \ˌkresəˌtēn-\ *n, usu cap C&Y* [*cresotine*, fr. *cresotic* + *-ine*] **:** a direct dye — see DYE table I (under *Direct Yellow 20*)
cre·so·tin·ic acid \ˌkresəˈtinik-, -rēs-\ *n* [ISV *cresotinic* (fr. *cresot-* + *-in* + *-ic*) + *acid*; prob. orig. formed as G *kresotinsäure*] **:** CRESOTIC ACID
cres·oxide \krəs, kres+\ *n* [*cresol* + *oxide*] **:** a salt of cresol
cresoxy- *comb form* [ISV *cresol* + *oxy-*] **:** TOLOXY-
cress \ˈkres\ *n* -ES [ME *cresse*, fr. OE *cressa, cresse, cærse;* akin to MD *kersse* cress, OHG *kresso, kressa*, and perh. to L *gramen* grass, Gk *grastis* green fodder, *gran* to gnaw, Skt *grasati* he eats, devours; basic meaning: eating, nibbling] **1 :** any of numerous plants of the family Cruciferae whose moderately pungent leaves are used in salads and garnishes: as **a :** WATERCRESS **b :** GARDEN CRESS **2 :** any plant that resembles a true cress — usu. used with a qualifying word ⟨Peter's ~⟩
cres·set \ˈkresə̇t\ *also* **cris·set** \-ris-\ *n* -s [ME, fr. MF *cresset, craisset*, fr. OF *craisset*, fr. *craisse* grease, fr. (assumed) VL *crassia* — more at GREASE] **1 :** an iron vessel or basket used for holding burning oil, pitchy wood, or other illuminant and mounted as a torch or suspended as a lantern **:** a fire basket ⟨blazing ~*s*, fed with naphtha and asphaltus —John Milton⟩ **2** *or* **cres·et** \-res-\ **:** a small furnace or iron fire cage used in coopering to heat and so bend staves to shape

cresset

cress green *n* **:** a moderate yellow green that is greener and deeper than average moss green, yellower and darker than average pea green, and yellower and duller than apple green (sense 1) — called also *cresson, watercress*
cres·son \kreˈsäⁿ, kresōⁿ\ *n* -s [F, cress, of Gmc origin; akin to OHG *kresso* cress] **:** CRESS GREEN
cress rocket *n* **:** a yellow-flowered Spanish herb (*Vella pseudocytisus*) of the family Cruciferae
cressweed \ˈ⸗ˌ⸗\ *n* **:** SAND ROCKET
cresswort \ˈ⸗ˌ⸗\ *n* **:** a plant of the family Cruciferae
cres·sy \ˈkresē\ *adj* -ER/-EST **:** abounding in cresses
[1]**crest** \ˈkrest\ *n* -s [ME, fr. MF *creste*, fr. L *crista;* akin to OE *hrisian* to shake, OHG *hris* twig, ON *hrista* to shake, Goth *afhrisjan* to shake off, MIr *cressaim* I shake, OPruss *craysi* blade of grass, straw, L *curvus* curved — more at CROWN] **1 a :** a usu. ornamental tuft or process on the head of a bird or animal; *specif* **:** COCKSCOMB — see BIRD illustration **b** (1) **:** the plume of feathers, painted metal fan, modeled emblem, or other decoration worn on a knight's helmet; *esp* **:** one indicating the identity of the wearer (2) **:** the apex of a helmet ⟨on his ~ sat horror plumed —John Milton⟩ (3) **:** a heraldic device that represents the crest formerly borne upon the helmet of a knight, is depicted in a full achievement of arms upon the helmet, and is also used separately as an ornament or cognizance (as for plate or liveries) (4) **:** a heraldic device depicted above the escutcheon but not upon a helmet — used esp. in the official heraldry of the New World (5) **:** an escutcheon of arms (6) **:** a complete coat of arms — not used technically (7) **:** an emblem, badge, device, or other object regularly used as a symbol (as of a family, tribe, or nation) — usu. used only of emblems employed among peoples who do not practice the European system of heraldry ⟨the Indians . . . mark off the hunting ground selected by them by blazing the trees with their ~*s* —*Amer. Anthrop. Assoc. Memoir*⟩ (8) **:** an identifying mark usu. consisting of painted rings placed near the vanes of an arrow (9) **:** high spirits or self-confidence **:** PRIDE, COURAGE, TEMPER **c :** a process or prominence on any part of the body of an animal: as (1) **:** the upper curve or ridge of the neck of a horse or other quadruped (2) **:** the mane borne by such a crest (3) **:** a ridge esp. when longitudinal and median or serrated or tuberculated (as that on the back of certain lizards) — compare BASILISK (4) **:** a ridge esp. on a bone ⟨the ~ of the tibia⟩ ⟨the ~ of the ilium⟩ — see FRONTAL CREST, OCCIPITAL CREST **2 :** the top of a structure or natural formation: as **a :** the highest point of a mountain **:** SUMMIT **:** the highest line of a range of mountains or hills or fold of rock ⟨the ~ of a watershed⟩ ⟨the ~ of an anticline⟩ **b :** the top edge of a dam or weir **c :** the ridge of a roof **3 a** *physics* (1) **:** the highest part of the oscillating surface in a gravity wave or a ripple on a liquid at any instant — contrasted with *trough* (2) **:** the maximum attained by a wave variable during the passage of a complete cycle **:** PEAK ⟨~ voltage⟩ **b :** the highest stage of a river in flood **4 a :** one of the high points of an action or process marked by a periodic alternation of rise and fall ⟨at the ~ of each breath, weeping threatened her —Elizabeth Taylor⟩ **b :** the culmination of an action or process **:** CLIMAX ⟨the ~ of a civilization⟩ ⟨at the ~ of his fame⟩ ⟨the ~ of the evening's excitement⟩ **5 :** a structure terminating or crowning an organ (as the persistent style forming a partial aril in plants of the genus *Sanguinaria*) **6 :** the outermost part of a screw thread often in the form of a rounded or flat-surfaced helical ridge
[2]**crest** \"\ *vb* -ED/-ING/-S [ME *cresten*, fr. *crest*, n.] *vt* **1 :** to furnish with a crest **:** serve as a crest for **:** TOP, CROWN **2 :** to reach the crest of (as a mountain or wave) **~** *vi* **1** *obs* **:** to bear oneself proudly or erectly **2 :** to form or rise to a crest ⟨the river is expected to ~ at noon⟩
crest·al \ˈkrestəl\ *adj* **:** at, near, on, or relating to a crest
crest clearance *n* **:** the radial clearance between the crest of a screw thread and the root of the thread mating with it
crest coronet *n* **1 :** a coronet supporting the crest in some coats of arms either instead of the wreath or additional to and resting upon it **2 :** DUCAL CREST CORONET
crest·ed \ˈkrestə̇d\ *adj* [ME, fr. [1]*crest* + *-ed*] **1 :** having a crest ⟨a ~ bird⟩ — often used in combination ⟨fan-*crested*⟩ ⟨golden-*crested*⟩ **2 :** emblazoned with a crest **:** COMBED ⟨a cock argent ~ gules⟩
crested auklet *or* **crested auk** *n* **:** an auklet (*Aethia cristatella*) with a recurved frontal crest
crested barbet *n* **:** a large barbet (*Trachyphonus raillantii*) of southern and eastern Africa that is brightly marked with red and yellow and has a small crest of dusky feathers
crested cariama *n* **:** a cariama (*Cariama cristata*) of the campos of southern Brazil that is yellowish gray mottled with dark brown on the back and somewhat striped below and has a large frontal crest of stiff filamentous feathers
crested coralroot *n* **:** a leafless scaly-stemmed orchid (*Hexalectris spicata*) with a spike of brownish purple striped flowers
crested dogstail *n* **:** a European grass (*Cynosurus cristatus*) used for pasture and forage and also in lawns and bearing flowers in stiff panicles resembling spikes
crested duck *n* **:** a long-legged short-necked So. American duck (*Lophonelta specularoides*) related to the sheldrakes
crested fern *n* **:** CREST FERN
crested flycatcher *n* **:** any of various flycatchers having a prominent crest; *esp* **:** an eastern No. American flycatcher (*Myiarchus crinitus*) that is olive brown above with gray chest, yellow belly, and reddish brown tail and is nearly as large as the robin — called also *great crested flycatcher*
crested guinea fowl *n* **:** a game bird (*Guttera edouardi*) of northern West Africa
crested hair grass *n* **:** JUNE GRASS 2
crested hamster *n* **:** a cat-sized nocturnal arboreal African rodent (*Lophiomys imhassi*) having a bushy tail and a crest of erectile hair on the back
crested hen *n, usu cap C&H* **:** a Danish hopping dance for two women and a man
crested iris *also* **crested dwarf iris** *n* **:** a low-growing herb (*Iris cristata*) that spreads by rhizomes and rootless stolons and has pale lilac flowers with an orange-tipped white crest
crested lark *n* **:** a common stout-bodied lark (*Galerida cristata*) of Europe sometimes kept as a cage bird
crested leaf monkey *n* **:** a Malaysian leaf monkey (*Presbytis mitratus*) having a black crest and pale abdomen
crested oriole *n* **:** a So. American cacique (*Xanthornus decumanus*)
crested penguin *n* **:** ROCK HOPPER
crested pig *n* **:** a wild swine (*Sus cristata*) of eastern Asia that is blackish brown and has a crest of stiff black bristles
crested screamer *n* **1 :** a screamer (genus *Chauna*) distinguished from the horned screamer by a feathery crest on the back of the head; *esp* **:** CHAJA **2 :** CARIAMA
crested shield fern *n* **:** CREST FERN
crested shrimp *n* **:** a large shrimp (genus *Eusicyonia*) of the tropical Atlantic ocean
crested titmouse *or* **crested tit** *n* **:** a European titmouse (*Parus cristatus*) with a speckled black and whitish crest
crested wheat grass *n* **:** a European grass (*Agropyron cristatum*) grown in the U.S. for forage and erosion control and having flowers in a short spike resembling a comb
crested wren *n* **:** KINGLET
crestfallen \ˈ⸗ˌ⸗⸗\ *adj* **1 :** with drooping crest or hanging head **:** DISPIRITED, DEJECTED, COWED ⟨let it make thee ~ —Shak.⟩ **2** *of a horse* **:** having the upper part of the neck hanging to one side — **crest·fall·en·ly** *adv* — **crest·fall·en·ness** \ˈ⸗ˌfȯlən(n)ə̇s\ *n* -ES
crest fern *or* **crested fern** *n* **:** a tall woodland fern (*Dryopteris cristata*) of No. America, Europe, and Asia
crest·ing \ˈkrestiŋ\ *n* -s [[1]*crest* + *-ing*] **1 :** an ornamental crest (as on the ridge of a roof or at the top of a clock) **2 a :** the members that form the crest **b :** the ornamentation (as carving or fretwork) on a top member (as on the crest rail of a chair)
crest·less \ˈkres(t)lə̇s\ *adj* **:** without a crest; *specif* **:** of low birth ⟨the ~ churls of England —Sir Walter Scott⟩
crest line *n* **:** an elongate crest or a linear series of crests ⟨a wave with a long *crest line*⟩ ⟨the *crest line* of the mountains⟩
crest·more·ite \ˈkres(t)mōˌrīt, -mȯ,-\ *n* -s [*Crestmore*, Calif. + E *-ite*] **:** a mineral consisting of hydrated calcium silicate occurring in compact snow-white masses
crest rail *n* **:** the top rail of a chair back esp. when distinctively carved or shaped
crests *pl of* CREST, *pres 3d sing of* CREST
crest table *n* **:** a crested or saddleback coping used for the top of a wall
crest tile *n* **:** one of the tiles made to cover the ridge of a roof by fitting upon it like a saddle
crest voltmeter *n* **:** PEAK VOLTMETER
cres·well·i·an \(ˈ)krezˈwelēən\ *adj, usu cap* [*Creswell* Crags, northeast Derbyshire, England + E *-ian*] **:** of or relating to a Mesolithic development of the Aurignacian in Great Britain
cres·yl \ˈkresəl, -rēs-\ *n* -s [ISV *cresol* + *-yl*] **:** TOLYL
cres·yl·ate \ˈkresəˌlāt, -ˌlə̇t\ *n* -s [*cresyl* + *-ate*] **:** a salt of cresol or cresylic acid — used chiefly commercially
cre·syl·ic \krəˈsilik\ *adj* [ISV *cresyl* + *-ic*] **:** relating to, containing, or derived from cresol or creosote
cresylic acid *n* **1 :** CRESOL; *esp* **:** a crude mixture of the three cresols **2 :** a mixture of phenols (as cresols and xylenols) obtained from coal tar or cracked petroleum oils
cres·yl·ite \ˈkresəˌlīt\ *n* -s [ISV *cresyl* + *-ite;* orig. formed as F *crésylite*] **:** an explosive consisting of trinitrocresol or of trinitrocresol and picric acid
cre·ta \ˈkrēd·ə\ *n* -s [L] **1 :** CHALK **2 :** FULLER'S EARTH
[1]**cre·ta·ceous** \krəˈtāshəs\ *adj* [L *cretaceus*, fr. *creta* chalk] **1 :** relating to, having the characteristics of, or abounding in chalk **:** CHALKY ⟨~ formations⟩ **2** *usu cap* **:** of or relating to the last period of the Mesozoic era and the corresponding system of rocks, the deposits of the period including the larger part of the known chalk beds, greensand marl, and most of the coal of the U.S. west of the Great Plains, the vegetation of the period having approached the modern temperate and subtropical flora in general aspect, and the reptiles of the period having remained dominant on the land and in the sea, ganoid fishes for the first time having become subordinate to teleosts — see GEOLOGIC TIME table — **cre·ta·ceous·ly** *adv*
[2]**cretaceous** \"\ *n* -ES *usu cap* **:** the Cretaceous period or system of rocks
cre·tac·ic \krəˈtasik\ *adj, usu cap* [ISV *cretaceous* + *-ic*] **:** CRETACEOUS
[1]**cre·tan** \ˈkrētᵊn\ *adj, usu cap* [L *cretanus*, fr. *Creta* Crete (fr. Gk *Krētē*) + *-anus* -an] **1 :** of, relating to, or characteristic of Crete, an island in the eastern part of the Mediterranean sea **2 :** of, relating to, or characteristic of Cretans
[2]**cretan** \"\ *n* -s *cap* [L *cretanus*, fr. *cretanus*, adj.] **:** a native or inhabitant of Crete
cretan bear's-tail *n, usu cap C* **:** a tall European herb (*Celsia arcturus*) with elongate clusters of long-stalked flowers
cretan dittany *also* **crete dittany** *n, usu cap C* **:** an herb (*Origanum dictamnus*) native to Crete having drooping spikes of pink flowers and a once-believed power to expel arrows from the body
cretan hemp *n, usu cap C* **:** BASTARD HEMP 1
cretan mullein *n, usu cap C* **:** an erect herb (*Celsia cretica*) with broad oblong leaves and irregular short-stalked flowers in loose elongate clusters found along the Mediterranean
cretan rockrose *n, usu cap C* **:** a southern European rockrose (*Cistus creticus*) that is one of the sources of labdanum
cretan spikenard *n, usu cap C* **:** an Asiatic valerian (*Valeriana phu*) sometimes cultivated as a substitute for the true spikenard
cre·te·fac·tion \ˌkrēd·əˈfakshən\ *n* -s [*crete-* (fr. L *creta* chalk) + *-faction*] **:** CRETIFICATION
cre·tic \ˈkrēd·ik\ *n* -s [LL *creticus* constituting an amphimacer, fr. Gk *krētikos* amphimacer, fr. *krētikos* (adj.) Cretan, fr. *Krētē* + *-ikos* -ic] **:** AMPHIMACER
cre·ti·fi·ca·tion \ˌkrēd·əfə̇ˈkāshən, ˈ⸗⸗⸗,⸗⸗\ *n* -s [L *creta* chalk + E *-i-* + *-fication*] **:** the process or an instance of cretifying
cre·ti·fy \ˈkrēd·əˌfī\ *vt* -ED/-ING/-ES [L *creta* chalk + E *-i-* + *-fy*] **:** to convert into chalk **:** infiltrate with calcium salts **:** CALCIFY
cre·tin \ˈkrētᵊn; *Brit usu* -ret-\ *n* -s [F *crétin*, fr. F dial. *cretin* Christian, human being, kind of deformed idiot found in the Alps, fr. L *christianus* Christian; fr. the desire to indicate that such idiots were after all human — more at CHRISTIAN] **:** one afflicted with cretinism; *broadly* **:** a person showing marked mental deficiency
cre·tin·ism \-ᵊnˌizəm\ *n* -s [F *crétinisme*, fr. *crétin* + *-isme* -ism] **:** a condition originating during fetal life or early infancy characterized by stunted physical and mental development and caused by severe thyroid deficiency — called also *infantile myxedema;* compare MONGOLISM, MYXEDEMA
cre·tin·ize \-ᵊnˌīz\ *vt* -ED/-ING/-S [F *crétiniser*, fr. *crétin* + *-iser* -ize] **:** to reduce to the condition of a cretin
cre·tin·oid \-ᵊnˌȯid\ *adj* [ISV *cretin* + *-oid*] **:** like a cretin **:** resembling cretinism
cre·tin·ous \-ᵊnəs\ *adj* [ISV *cretin* + *-ous*] **1 :** relating to a cretin **2 :** being a cretin or affected with cretinism
cre·tion \ˈkrēshən\ *n* -s [L *cretion-, cretio*, fr. *cretus* (past part. of *cernere* to cern, discern) + *-ion-, -io* -ion — more at CERTAIN] **1** *Roman law* **:** an act before a magistrate by which an outside heir declares his acceptance of the succession **2** *Roman law* **:** the time allowed an heir to make his decision of cretion — compare JUS DELIBERANDI — **cre·tion·ary** \-əˌnerē\ *adj*
cre·to–mycenaean \ˌkrēd·ō+\ *adj, usu cap C&M* [*Crete* + E *-o-* + *mycenaean*] **:** characterizing the civilization prob. originating in Crete but first widely known through discoveries at Mycenae — compare MYCENAEAN
cre·tonne \ˈkrēˌtän, krəˈ-; *Brit usu* kreˈ- *or* ˈkreˌ-\ *n* -s [F, fr. *Creton*, village in Normandy where it was made] **:** a strong unglazed cotton or linen fabric similar to chintz but usu. printed with larger floral designs, woven in plain or fancy weaves, and used esp. for curtains and upholstery
creutzer *var of* KREUZER
cre·val·le \krəˈvalē, -lə, -lā\ *also* **cre·val·ly** \-lē\ *n, pl* **crevalles** *also* **crevallies** [alter. of *cavalla*] **:** CAVALLA; *esp* **:** a carangid fish (*Caranx hippos*) important as a food fish along the west coast of Florida, widely but sparsely distributed elsewhere in the western Atlantic, and represented in the Pacific by the same or a closely related species
cre·vasse *also* **cre·vass** \krəˈvas, -aa(ə)s *sometimes* -väs *or* -vəs *or* ˈkrevə̇s\ *n, pl* **crevasses** [F, fr. OF *crevace*] **:** a break, opening, or chasm of some width and considerable depth: as **a :** a split or cleavage through massed ice, glacier, snow field, or earth after earthquakes **b** [AmerF, fr. F] **:** a breach in the levee of a river
creve·coeur \ˈkrev,kər, ⸗ˈ⸗\ *n* -s *often cap* [F *crèvecœur*, prob. fr. *Crèvecœur*, Calvados dept., France] **:** a domestic fowl of a French breed that is black and crested and has a V-shaped comb
cre·vette \krəˈvet\ *n* -s [F, shrimp, fr. MF, lit., little goat, prob. irreg. fr. (assumed) MF dial. (northern) *kevre* she-goat (fr. L *capra*, fem. of *capr-, caper* goat) + MF *-ette;* fr. its habit of leaping — more at CAPRIOLE] **:** a strong yellowish pink that is redder and very slightly darker than average salmon, redder and darker than salmon pink, and deeper than melon — called also *prawn*
crev·ice \ˈkrevə̇s\ *n* -s [ME *crevice, crevace*, fr. MF *crevace*, fr. OF, fr. *crever* to break, burst, fr. L *crepare* to crack, break — more at CRAVEN] **:** a narrow opening of some depth caused esp. by a split or cleavage **:** a narrow recess like a slit ⟨hidden in a ~ under a cliff⟩ **syn** see CRACK
crev·iced \-st\ *adj* [*crevice* + *-ed*] **:** having a crevice
cre·vic·u·lar \krəˈvikyələ(r)\ *adj* [irreg. fr. *crevice* + *-ular*] *anat* **:** of, relating to, or involving a crevice, esp. the gingival crevice
[1]**crew** *chiefly Brit past of* CROW *vi* 1
[2]**crew** \ˈkrü\ *n* -s [ME *crue* reinforcement, body of soldiers, fr. MF *creue* increase, fr. OF, fem. of *creu*, past part. of *creistre* to grow — more at CRESCENT] **1** *archaic* **:** a band or force of armed men ⟨that fair ~ of knights —Edmund Spenser⟩ **2 :** a company of people temporarily associated together **:** ASSEMBLAGE, THRONG, RETINUE ⟨mirth, admit me of thy ~ —John Milton⟩ **3 a :** a group of people regarded as associated by common traits, interests, or purpose **:** SET, GANG, MOB ⟨that crooked politician and his ~ of heelers⟩ **b :** a company or squad of men working on one job or under one foreman **:** GANG ⟨lumbering ~⟩ ⟨wrecking ~⟩ ⟨stage ~⟩ **c :** a group of men organized to serve or operate a machine, vehicle, or other apparatus (as a fieldpiece, railroad train, or tank) ⟨mortar ~⟩ **4 a :** the company of seamen who man a ship **:** the whole company belonging to a ship sometimes including the officers and master **b :** a small body or gang of men on a ship who work under the direction of some petty officer or who are assigned to some particular duty ⟨the galley ~⟩ **c :** the body of men manning a racing shell ⟨a college ~⟩ ⟨~ practice⟩; *also* **:** ROWING ⟨his chief activities were wrestling and ~⟩ **d :** the persons who man an aircraft in flight — called also *flight crew* **5 :** a subdivision of an explorer unit of the Boy Scouts of America made up of two or more explorers and corresponding to a boy scout patrol
[3]**crew** \"\ *vb* -ED/-ING/-S *vi* **:** to act as a member of a crew ⟨~ on the winning sailboat⟩ **~** *vt* **:** to serve on (a ship or aircraft) as a crew member ⟨any man who has ~*ed* both conventional fighters and jets —*Aero Digest*⟩
[4]**crew** \"\ *n* -s [partly fr. ME, fish trap, fr. ScGael *crō* pen for animals, hut; partly fr. W *crau* pigpen & Corn *crow;* akin to OIr *crāu* stable, hut — more at CRYPT] *dial Brit* **:** a pen for cattle, swine, or sheep
crew chief *n* **:** a noncommissioned officer (as in the U.S. Air Force) who supervises a ground crew of airplane mechanics
crew cut *or* **crew haircut** *n* **:** a very short hair style copied from a style worn by oarsmen with the hair more or less resembling the bristle surface of a brush
crewe *n* -s [MF *crue, cruie* — more at CRUET] *obs* **:** CRUSE, POT
crew·el \ˈkrüəl, *Brit usu* -ü,il\ *n* -s [ME *crule*] **1 :** worsted slackly twisted yarn used for embroidery **2 :** CREWELWORK
crewel needle *n* **:** a long-eyed needle used esp. for embroidery
crewel stitch *n* **:** STEM STITCH
crewelwork \ˈ⸗⸗ˌ⸗\ *n* **:** embroidery consisting of simple

stitches (as stem stitch, chain stitch, buttonhole stitch) worked with crewel in floral and scroll patterns on plain material often of linen or cotton and used for interior decoration

crew·er \'krüə(r)\ *n* -s [origin unknown] **:** one that curves tongues for spring clips and harness buckles

crewet *var of* CRUET

crew·less \'krüləs\ *adj* **:** being without a crew

crew·man \'krümən\ *n, pl* **crewmen :** a member of a crew

crew neck *or* **crew neckline** *n* [²crew] **:** a straight neckline like a slit that runs from shoulder to shoulder adapted from the pullovers worn by oarsmen

crew-served \'⸗,⸗\ *adj* [²crew] *of a weapon* **:** operated by two or more men

crex \'kreks\ *n, cap* [NL, fr. Gk *krex*, a long-legged bird; akin to Gk *kirkos* hawk — more at CIRCAETUS] **:** a genus of birds (family Rallidae) including the corncrake

cri·ant \'krīənt, krēäⁿ\ *adj* [F, fr. pres. part. of *crier* to cry out, fr. OF — more at CRY] **:** attracting attention by gaudiness **:** GARISH, LOUD ⟨~ wallpaper⟩

¹crib \'krib\ *n* -s [ME, manger, stall, fr. OE *cribb* manger; akin to OHG *krippa* manger, MHG *krebe* basket, ON *kjarf* bundle, sheaf, Gk *griphos* reed basket, Skt *grapsa* bunch, tuft, OE *cradol* cradle — more at CRADLE] **1 a :** MANGER; *esp* **:** a barred or slatted manger for the feeding of hay or other bulky fodder **b** *obs* **:** an osier or wickerwork basket **c :** BIN, CRATE, BOX **d** *archery* **:** a box topped with netting or perforated board in which to stand arrows **e** *slang* **:** SAFE 1 b **2 :** an enclosure esp. of framework: as **a :** a stall for an ox or other stabled animal **b :** a small bedstead with high enclosing usu. slatted sides for a child; *also* **:** CRADLE 1a **c :** a heavy supporting or strengthening framework (as for a roof or a house being moved or a shaft) **d :** a frame of logs or beams to be filled with heavy material (as stones or rubble) and sunk as a foundation or retaining wall in the building of docks, piers, dams, and similar structures **e :** a wooden framework with upright rods used as a drying rack **f** *archaic* **:** JAIL **g :** an enclosure in a workshop or factory where tools or supplies are issued to workers **h :** a structure enclosing a water intake and filter offshore in a lake (as one of the Great Lakes) **i :** an enclosure in shallow water (as at the edge of a lake) where small children may play in safety **3 a :** HUT, HOVEL; *sometimes* **:** a small narrow room **b** *slang* **:** a building (as a house or store) considered with a view to unlawful entry — used chiefly in the phrase *crack a crib* **c :** a house of prostitution; *esp* **:** a room or shack where a prostitute plies her trade as contrasted with a more extensive establishment **d :** a building usu. of open or slat construction for the storing of grain (as corn) **e :** CABOOSE 3 **4 a :** the cards discarded for the dealer to use in scoring in cribbage **b** *slang* **:** CRIBBAGE **5 a :** a small theft **:** something stolen **b :** PLAGIARISM **c** (1) **:** a literal translation of a foreign text used by a student in preparing or reciting a language lesson often to simulate fluency — compare PONY, TROT (2) **:** a key to an understanding of a literary work; *esp* **:** an explication that follows a text line by line or page by page (3) **:** a phrase of probable words determining some of a cipher key **d :** a device or object used for cheating in an examination **6 :** CRÈCHE 3 **7** *chiefly Brit* **:** LUNCH — used esp. of the meal that a workman carries with him to eat at his place of employment **8 :** something forming a barrier: as **a :** WEIR **b :** a barrier for reducing the flow of water downstream but extending only part way from shore and thence upstream so as to form a sheltered area (as for storing logs) **c :** a retaining wall of logs used to protect road cuts **9 :** the space between two adjacent railroad ties

crib 2b

²crib \"\ *vb* **cribbed; cribbed; cribbing; cribs** *vt* **1 :** to confine to a small area or within narrow limits **:** CAGE, CRAMP, RESTRAIN ⟨now am I cabin'd, *cribbed*, confined —Shak.⟩ **2 a :** to provide with a crib; *esp* **:** to line or support with a framework of timber **b :** to put (as grain) into a crib **3 :** to surround (floating logs) with a boom and draw on to a raft **4 :** PILFER, PURLOIN, STEAL; *esp* **:** to appropriate (as a passage or idea) and use as one's own **:** PLAGIARIZE ⟨the screen writers were able to ~ a few useful lines from Christopher Marlowe —*Newsweek*⟩ ~ *vi* **1 a :** STEAL, PILFER, PLAGIARIZE **b :** to use a crib in preparing a lesson or taking an examination **:** CHEAT ⟨pupils charged that *cribbing* had been going on at the school for years⟩ **2 :** CRIB-BITE **3** *slang Brit* **:** COMPLAIN, GRIPE

crib·bage \'kribij, -bēj\ *n* -s [*crib* (discarded cards) + *-age*] **:** a card game for two and sometimes three or four players each of whom is dealt six cards one or two of which are discarded before play to form an extra hand counting for the dealer, the object of the game being to form various counting combinations in the hand and in the cards played

cribbage board *n* **:** a cribbage scoring board usu. in the form of a narrow rectangle having holes by which each player can count with pegs up to 121 usu. twice around

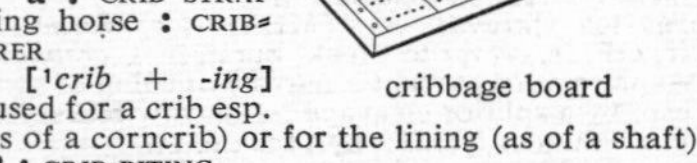
cribbage board

crib·ber \'kribə(r)\ *n* -s **:** one that cribs: as **a :** CRIB STRAP **b :** a crib-biting horse **:** CRIB-BITER **c :** SHORER

cribbing *n* -s [¹crib + *-ing*] **1 a :** material used for a crib esp. for the sides (as of a corncrib) or for the lining (as of a shaft) **b :** CRIB 2 c **2 :** CRIB-BITING

crib-bite \'⸗,⸗\ *vi* [back-formation fr. *crib-biter* & *crib-biting*] **:** to be addicted to crib-biting — **crib-biter** \'⸗,⸗⸗\ *n*

crib-biting \'⸗,⸗⸗\ *n* -s **:** the habit of some horses of making peculiar movements with the head, gnawing at the manger or other object with the teeth, and slobbering and salivating while so doing — called also *cribbing*; compare WIND SUCKING

¹crib·ble \'kribəl\ *n* -s [MF *crible*, fr. LL *criblum*, alter. of L *cribrum* — more at CRIBELLUM] **1 :** SIEVE, STRAINER **2** *obs* **:** coarse flour or meal

²cribble \"\ *vt* **cribbled; cribbled; cribbling** \-b(ə)liŋ\ **cribbles** [F *criblé*, adj.] **:** to cover (a surface) with small round holes or dots; *specif* **:** to make a pattern of small round punctures in (a block or plate) in engraving

cribbled *adj* **:** having a surface pattern composed of small round holes or dots; *specif* **:** CRIBLÉ

crib·el·la·tae \,kribə'lād,(,)ē, -läd-\ *n pl, cap* [NL, fr. *cribellum* + L *-atae* (fem. pl. of *-atus* -ate)] *in some classifications* **:** a division of arachnomorph spiders comprising those that have a cribellum

crib·el·late \'kribəlát, lāt\ *also* **crib·el·lat·ed** \'⸗⸗,lād·əd\ *or* **cri·bel·lar** \krə'belə(r)\ *adj* [NL *cribellum* + E *-ate, -ated* or *-ar*] **1 :** of, having, or relating to a cribellum **2** [NL *Cribellatae*] **:** of or relating to the Cribellatae

cri·bel·lum \krə'beləm\ *n, pl* **cribel·la** \-lə\ [NL, fr. LL, small sieve, dim. of L *cribrum* sieve; akin to L *cernere* to sift, discern — more at CERTAIN] **1 :** a special spinning organ having numerous fine perforations and situated in front of the ordinary spinning organs that is found only in spiders of certain families **2 :** a chitinous plate with perforations which constitute the openings of minute ducts leading from certain glands of insects

cri·blée *also* **cri·blée** \(')krē¦blā\ *adj* [F *criblé*, masc., & *criblée*, fem., fr. *crible* sieve — more at CRIBBLE] *of an engraving* **:** having a background pattern composed of small white dots produced by cribbling the plate — see MANIÈRE CRIBLÉE

cri·bo \'krē(,)bō\ *n* -s [origin unknown] **:** a large harmless snake (*Drymarchon corais corais*) that is closely related to the No. American indigo snake and widely distributed in the West Indies and tropical America where it is of some importance as a destroyer of venomous snakes

crib·ral \'kribrəl\ *adj* [L *cribrum* + E *-al*] **:** of or relating to a sieve or structure like a sieve **:** CRIBROSE

crib·rate \'kri,brāt, -brət\ *adj* [L *cribrum* sieve + E *-ate* — more at *cribellum*] **:** like a sieve — **crib·rate·ly** *adv*

cri·bra·tion \krə'brāshən\ *n* -s [L *cribratus* (past part. of *cribrare* to sift, fr. *cribrum* sieve) + E *-ion*] **:** the act or an instance of sifting (as drugs)

crib·ri·form \'kribrə,fȯrm\ *adj* [L *cribrum* sieve + E *-iform*] **:** pierced with small holes like a sieve ⟨a ~ bone⟩

cribriform fascia *n* **:** the perforated fascia covering the saphenous opening in the fascia lata of the thigh and giving passage to various blood and lymph vessels

cribriform plate *n* **:** the horizontal plate of the ethmoid bone perforated with numerous foramina for the passage of the olfactory nerve filaments from the nasal cavity

crib·rose \'kri,brōs\ *adj* [ISV *cribr-* (fr. L *cribrum* sieve) + *-ose*] **:** CRIBRIFORM, PERFORATED

cribs *pl of* CRIB, *pres 3d sing of* CRIB

crib strap *n* **:** a strap fitted closely about the throat of a horse to prevent crib-biting or wind sucking

cribwork \'⸗,⸗\ *n* -s **1 :** a framework formed by or as if by logs arranged as in a crib **:** a structure made with cribs **2 :** CRIB 2c, 2d

¹cri·ce·tid \krə'sēd·əd, -sed-\ *adj* [NL *Cricetidae*] **:** of or relating to the family Cricetidae

²cricetid \"\ *n* -s **:** a rodent of the family Cricetidae

cri·cet·i·dae \krə'sed·ə,dē\ *n pl, cap* [NL, fr. *Cricetus*, type genus + *-idae*] **:** a family of myomorph rodents comprising the New World mice, the lemmings, voles, hamsters, and related forms that are mostly small, resemble mice or rats, and have three molar teeth on each side whose cusps in the upper series are arranged in transverse pairs

cric·e·tine \'krisə,tīn\ *n* -s [NL *Cricetinae*, subfamily of rodents, fr. *Cricetus*, type genus + *-inae*] **:** a rodent of the Cricetidae

cri·ce·tu·lus \krə'sēd·ᵊləs, -sed-\ *n, cap* [NL, dim. of *Cricetus*] **:** a large genus of small short-tailed Asiatic hamsters that resemble the New World white-footed mice

cri·ce·tus \-'sēd·əs, -'sed-\ *n, cap* [NL, of Slav origin; akin to Czech *křeček* hamster, Pol *skrzeczek*] **:** the type genus of Cricetidae comprising Old World hamsters of moderate to large size and including the golden hamster

¹crick \'krik\ *n* -s [ME *cryk, crykke*] **:** a painful spasmodic condition of a muscle (as of the neck or back)

²crick \"\ *vt* -ED/-ING/-S **1 :** to cause a crick in (as the neck) **:** WRENCH **2 :** to turn or twist (as the head) esp. into a strained position ⟨~*ing* her head sideways —Elizabeth Bowen⟩

³crick \"\ *n* -s [ME *crike* — more at CREEK] *dial* **:** CREEK 2

⁴crick \"\ *vi* -ED/-ING/-S [imit.] **:** to make a slight abrupt sound

⁵crick \"\ *n* -s [F *cric* jackscrew, fr. MF, fr. MHG *kriec*] **:** a small jackscrew

¹crick·et \'krikət, *usu* -əd·+V\ *n* -s [ME *criket*, fr. MF *criquet*, of imit. origin] **1 :** any of certain saltatorial insects that constitute a family Gryllidae, that are noted for the chirping notes of the males produced by rubbing together specially modified parts of the fore wings, and that include the European house cricket (*Acheta domestica*) which is naturalized in parts of America and lives in human dwellings and the common large black American field cricket (*A. assimilis*) which also enters houses — see MOLE CRICKET, TREE CRICKET **2 :** any of various insects other than crickets; *esp* **:** GRASSHOPPER — usu. used with a qualifying word; see MORMON CRICKET, SAND CRICKET **3 :** something making a sound like the chirp of a cricket: as **a :** a roller in the bit of a horse **b :** a small metal toy or signaling device that makes a sharp click or snap when pressed **4 :** a person regarded as like a cricket (as in smallness and briskness or in rusticity) **5 :** a small false roof or a canted part of a roof to throw off water from behind an obstacle (as a chimney) **6 :** a low wooden footstool

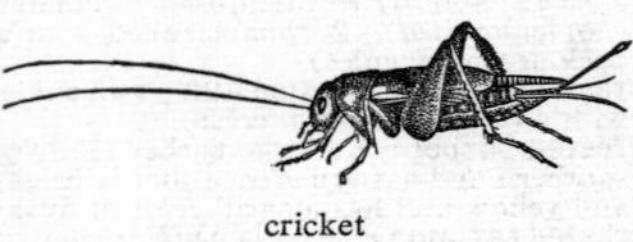
cricket

²cricket \"\ *n* -s [MF *criquet* goal stake in old games of bowls, perh. fr. *criquer* to crack, of imit. origin; fr. the sound of the balls striking the stakes] **1 :** a game played with a ball and bat by two sides of usu. 11 players each on a large field centering upon two wickets pitched 22 yards apart and defended each by a batsman for one over against a bowler, a run being scored each time the two batsmen exchange their wicket positions on hit or passed balls without either being out — see INNING **2 :** fair and honorable behavior like that of a sportsman **:** proper and gentlemanly conduct

typical positions of cricket players in the field: *1* bowler, *2* wicketkeeper, *3* first slip, *4* second slip, *4A* third man, *5* point, *6* cover point, *6A* extra cover, *7* mid off, *8* long off, *9* long on, *10* mid on, *11* short leg, *11A* square leg, *11B* long leg; *B* batsman, *U* umpire

³cricket \"\ *vi* -ED/-ING/-S **:** to play cricket

cricket ball *n* [²cricket] **:** the ball with a dark hard leather cover about 9 inches in circumference used in cricket

cricket bat *n* [²cricket] **:** the bat usu. made of willow with a long rectangular blade shaped like a paddle and a short handle used in cricket

cricket-bat willow \'⸗⸗¦⸗-\ *n* **:** a Eurasian tree (*Salix alba caerulea*) having ascending branches and smooth foliage

cricket bird *n* **:** GRASSHOPPER WARBLER

cricket chair *n* **:** a small armchair or rocker usu. of maple with turned legs and posts, a padded seat and a back cushion, and usu. a cloth skirt dropping down from the seat cushion

crick·et·er \'krikəd·ə(r)\ *n* -s [²cricket + *-er*] **:** one that plays cricket

cricket frog *n* [¹cricket; from its chirping] **:** a small American tree frog (*Acris gryllus*)

crick·ety \'krikəd·ē\ *adj* **:** like a cricket esp. in liveliness or sound

cricks *pl of* CRICK, *pres 3d sing of* CRICK

crico- *comb form* [NL, fr. *cricoides* cricoid] **:** cricoid ⟨*cricotomy*⟩ **:** cricoid and ⟨*cricothyroid*⟩

¹cri·coid \'krī,kȯid\ *n* -s [NL *cricoides*, fr. Gk *krikoeidēs* ring-shaped, fr. *krikos* ring + *-oeidēs* -oid — more at CIRCLE] **:** a cartilage of the larynx which articulates with the lower cornua of the thyroid cartilage and with which the arytenoid cartilages articulate

²cricoid \"\ *adj* **:** being or relating to the cricoid

cri·co·ne·ma \,krīkə'nēmə\ *n, cap* [NL, fr. *crico-* + Gk *nēma* thread — more at NEEDLE] **:** the type genus of Criconematidae including short stout strongly annulated nematode worms with the annular cuticle prolonged into posteriorly directed scales or spines

cri·co·ne·mat·i·dae \,krī(,)kōnə'mad·ə,dē\ *n pl, cap* [NL, fr. *Criconemat-, Criconema*, type genus + *-idae*] **:** a family of nematode worms (suborder Tylenchina) that includes a number of saprophagous and rhizophagous forms and a few plant parasites

cri de coeur *or* **cri du coeur** \,krēdə'kər\ *n, pl* **cris de coeur** *or* **cris du coeur** \,krē(z)d-\ [F, lit., cry from the heart] **:** passionate protest, appeal, or complaint

cried *past of* CRY

cri·er *or* **cry·er** \'krī(ə)r, -īə\ *n* -s [ME *criere*, fr. MF *crieor*, fr. *crier* to cry, shout + *-eor* -or — more at CRY] **:** one that cries: **a :** an officer who proclaims the orders or directions of a court **b :** a person appointed to make public proclamations in a loud voice **:** TOWN CRIER **c :** a person who cries goods for sale **:** HAWKER, AUCTIONEER

cries *pres 3d sing of* CRY, *pl of* CRY

crig \'krig\ *n* -s [IrGael *criogān* bruise, sore] **:** ⁵BLOW 1a

cri·key \'krīkē\ *or* **crick·ey** \'krikē\ *or* **crick·ety** \-kəd·ē\ *or* **cricky** \-kē\ *interj* [euphemism for *Christ*] — a mild oath, often in the phrase *by crikey*

crile \'krīl\ *n* -s [obs. D *kriel* hunchback, dwarf, collection of small items; akin to MD *crauwel, crouwel* hook, OHG *krouwōn* to scratch — more at CRUMB] *chiefly Scot* **:** a short deformed person **:** DWARF

¹crime \'krīm\ *n* -s [ME, fr. MF, fr. L *crimen* accusation, fault, crime; perh. akin to OHG *scrīan* to cry out — more at SCREAM] **1 a :** an act or the commission of an act that is forbidden or the omission of a duty that is commanded by a public law of a sovereign state to the injury of the public welfare and that makes the offender liable to punishment by that law in a proceeding brought against him by the state by indictment, information, complaint, or similar criminal procedure **:** an offense against public law (as a misdemeanor, felony, or act of treason) providing a penalty against the offender but not including a petty violation of municipal regulation — compare DELICT, MALICE, MALUM IN SE, MALUM PROHIBITUM, TORT, WRONG **b :** an offense against the social order or a violation of the mores that is dealt with by community action rather than by an individual or kinship group **2** *obs* **:** CHARGE, ACCUSATION **:** cause for accusation or reproach **3 a :** a gross violation of law — distinguished from *misdemeanor, trespass* **b :** a grave or aggravated offense against or departure from moral rectitude **4 :** criminal activity **:** conduct in violation of the law **5 a :** an evil act **:** SIN **:** a violation of divine law; *esp* **:** a grievous sin **b :** sinful conduct **:** WRONGDOING **6 :** something reprehensible, foolish, indiscreet, or disgraceful ⟨it's a ~ to waste good food⟩ ⟨the bishop's ~ was that he dogmatized —Walter Moberly⟩

²crime \"\ *vt* -ED/-ING/-S *slang Brit* **:** to indict and punish (a soldier) for a minor infraction of military rules

crime against humanity : atrocity (as extermination, enslavement, or deportation under inhuman conditions) that is directed esp. against an entire population or segment of a population on specious grounds and without regard to individual guilt or responsibility even on such grounds

crime against nature : a sexual act that is regarded by the law as abnormal **:** SODOMY, BUGGERY

cri·me·an \(')krī¦mēən, krə'-\ *adj, usu cap* [*Crimea*, peninsula in southern Russia + E *-an*] **:** of, relating to, or originating in Crimea

crimean gothic *n, usu cap C&G* **:** a dialect of the Gothic language known only from a list of words in use in the Crimea in the 16th cent.

crimean pine *n, usu cap C* **:** an evergreen tree (*Pinus nigra caramanica*) of Asia Minor with esp. the lower branches sharply ascending and rigid twisted glossy leaves

crimean snowdrop *n, usu cap C* **:** a bulbous herb (*Galanthus plicatus*) of the Crimea with bluish green foliage

crimean wheat *n, usu cap C* **:** any of several wheats introduced from the Crimean region of Russia and grown extensively in the Great Plains area and in Canada

crime·ful \'krīmfəl\ *adj* **:** marked by crime or notable for crimes **:** CRIMINAL ⟨feats so ~ and so capital in nature —Shak.⟩

crime·less \-ləs\ *adj* **:** INNOCENT; *esp* **:** free of crime ⟨I am loyal, true, and ~ —Shak.⟩

cri·men \'krīmən, -(,)men\ *n, pl* **crim·i·na** \'krimənə\ [L — more at CRIME] **:** CRIME

crimen ex·tra·or·di·nar·i·um \-¦ekstrə¦ȯ(r)də¦na(a)rēəm\ *n, pl* **crimina extraordinaria** [LL, lit., extraordinary crime] **:** a crime in Roman law that was considered extraordinary in that punishment was not fixed by earlier written law but was left to the discretion of the judge

crimen fal·si \-'fȯl(t),sī\ *n* [LL, crime of falsifying] **:** FALSI CRIMEN

crime of passion 1 : a crime committed in the heat of passion **2 :** CRIME PASSIONEL

crime pas·si·o·nel *also* **crime pas·si·on·nel** \,krēm,päsēə'nel\ *n, pl* **crimes passionels** \"\ [F, lit., crime of passion] **:** a crime due to sexual motives

crime wave *n* **:** a transitory but marked and relatively widespread increase in crime

¹crim·i·nal \'krimənᵊl, -mnəl\ *adj* [ME *cryminall*, fr. MF or LL; MF *criminel*, fr. LL *criminalis*, fr. L *crimin-, crimen* crime + *-alis* -al — more at CRIME] **1 :** involving or being a crime ⟨~ carelessness⟩ **2 :** relating to crime or its punishment ⟨a ~ action⟩ — distinguished from *civil* **3 :** guilty of crime or serious offense ⟨he created a government that was frankly ~ —Eric Linklater⟩ ⟨~ in the sight of God and man⟩ **4 a :** REPREHENSIBLE, BLAMEWORTHY, DISGRACEFUL ⟨she was a ~ idiot to marry a man with his record⟩ ⟨it was one of those ~ adventures that marked the road of the Communist International during the twenties —D.J.Dallin⟩ **b :** EXCESSIVE, EXTORTIONATE ⟨saddle horses to be had not too far from the campus, but the rates were absolutely ~ —Edward Newhouse⟩ **5 :** of or suitable to a criminal ⟨the twists of the ~ mind⟩ **6 :** concerned with crime or criminal law

²criminal \"\ *n* -s [F *criminel*, fr. *criminel*, adj.] **1 :** one that has committed a crime **:** MALEFACTOR **2 :** a person who has been convicted of one or more crimes ⟨habitual ~s⟩

syn FELON, CONVICT, MALEFACTOR, CULPRIT, DELINQUENT: these words mean, in common, one guilty of a transgression or an offense, esp. against the law. CRIMINAL designates one who commits some serious violation of the law, of public trust, or common decency, as vicious unwarranted attack, embezzlement, or murder. FELON, the legal term for one popularly called a criminal, designates one guilty of a felony, which usu. with legal exactness covers all lawbreaking punishable by death or prolonged confinement (as in a state penitentiary) and is distinguished from a misdemeanor ⟨men were transported with the worst *felons* for poaching a few hares or pheasants —G.B.Shaw⟩ ⟨the casual or accidental *felon* who is impelled into a misdeed by force of circumstances —R.S.Banay⟩ CONVICT designates one convicted of a crime or felony but has come more generally to signify any person serving a long prison term ⟨the stranger turned out to be a *convict* who had escaped on the way to prison⟩ ⟨a riot among *convicts* in a state penitentiary⟩ MALEFACTOR signifies one who has committed an evil deed or serious offense but suggests little or no relation to courts or punishment ⟨most of our *malefactors*, from statesmen to thieves —T.S.Eliot⟩ ⟨a *malefactor* robbing small stores at night and setting fire to them⟩ CULPRIT often carries the weakened sense of one guilty of a crime ⟨after the series of crimes, the police tried for several weeks to find the *culprit*⟩ but more generally either suggests a trivial fault or offense, esp. of a child ⟨the *culprits* were two boys, one about 12 years old, the other about 10 —Green Peyton⟩ or applies to a person or thing that causes some undesirable condition or situation ⟨another group of supposed *culprits* who are being blamed for the present inflationary situation —T.O.Waage⟩ ⟨the *culprit* holding up world peace and understanding —W. A. Lydgate⟩ DELINQUENT applies to an offender against duty or the law esp. in a degree not constituting crime; in its present semilegal use, in application to juvenile offenders against civil or moral law, it usu. implies a habitual tendency to commit certain offenses and contrasts with CRIMINAL in implying a sociological or psychological rather than judicial attitude toward the offender ⟨whether a customer who has missed a payment is . . . a habitual *delinquent* —C.W.Phelps⟩ ⟨we label as *delinquents* those who do not conform to the legal and moral codes of society—*Federal Probation*⟩

criminal abortion *n* **:** ILLEGAL ABORTION

criminal anthropology *n* **:** CRIMINOLOGY; *specif* **:** Lombrosian doctrines

criminal assault *n* **:** a violent physical attack upon a person esp. with sexual contact or attempt at sexual contact **:** RAPE

criminal conspiracy *n* **:** CONSPIRACY 1b

criminal contempt *n* **1 :** contempt that is committed in the presence of a court in session or a judge acting in a judicial capacity or so near to either of these as to interfere with the proceedings and that tends to belittle or insult the judge or to degrade or obstruct justice **:** a direct contempt not affecting a civil remedy of a party — compare CONSTRUCTIVE CONTEMPT **2 :** contempt that tends to interfere directly with a legislature or one of its committees exercising its lawful powers or that constitutes disrespect for its authority in the course of its lawful proceedings

criminal conversation *n* **:** unlawful intercourse with a married woman **:** adultery considered as a tort — abbr. *crim. con.*

criminal court *n* **:** a court established with jurisdiction to try and punish offenders against the criminal laws

crim·i·nal·ism \'krimənᵊl,izəm, -mnə,li-\ *n* -s [prob. fr. F *criminalisme,* fr. LL *criminalis* criminal + F *-isme* -ism] **:** the tendency to criminality; *also* **:** habitual criminality

crim·i·nal·ist \-mənᵊləst, -mnəl-\ *n* -s [F *criminaliste* or G *kriminalist,* fr. NL *criminalista,* fr. L *criminalis* + *-ista* -ist] **1 :** a specialist in criminal law **2 :** a specialist in criminology

crim·i·nal·is·tic \¦krimənᵊl¦istik, -mnə¦li-\ *adj* **:** tending to criminality

crim·i·nal·is·tics \-ks\ *n pl but sing in constr* [G *kriminalistik,* fr. *kriminalist* criminalist + *-ik* -ics] **:** scientific crime detection **:** the application of techniques from the physical sciences and psychology to the problems of criminal identification and apprehension

crim·i·nal·i·ty \,krimə'naləd·ē, -ətē, -i\ *n* -ES [F or ML; F *criminalité,* fr. ML *criminalitat-, criminalitas,* fr. LL *criminalis* criminal + L *-itat-, -itas* -ity — more at CRIMINAL] **1 :** the quality or state of being guilty of crime or of being criminal **2 :** an act or practice that constitutes a crime **3 :** the criminal class ⟨prohibition opened up a world of profits to organized ~ —*Newsweek*⟩

criminal law *n* **:** a branch of jurisprudence that relates to crimes — distinguished from *civil law*

criminal lawyer *n* **:** a lawyer who specializes in cases that involve the law as it relates to crime

crim·i·nal·ly \'krimənᵊlē, -mnəlē, -i\ *adv* [1*criminal* + *-ly*] **1 :** according to criminal law ⟨to proceed against him ~⟩ **2 :** in a criminal manner **:** in violation of law **:** WICKEDLY ⟨~ involved with gamblers⟩ **3 :** REPREHENSIVELY, DISGRACEFULLY, SHAMEFULLY ⟨the lawns were ~ kept —J.T.Jackson⟩ ⟨he calls our schools ~ superficial and ill-disciplined⟩

crim·i·nal·ness \-mənᵊlnəs, -mnəl-\ *n* -ES **:** CRIMINALITY

crim·i·nal·oid \-mənᵊl,ȯid, -mnə,lȯid\ *n* -s [2*criminal* + *-oid*] **:** a person with some criminal characteristics **:** an occasional criminal

criminals *pl of* CRIMINAL

criminal syndicalism *n* **:** a statutory crime in many states of the U.S. consisting of acts of violence or of advocating violence or other illicit means of bringing about political change or alterations in government

crim·i·nate \'krimə,nāt, *usu* -ād·+V\ *vt* -ED/-ING/-S [L *criminatus,* past part. of *criminari* to accuse, fr. *crimin-, crimen* crime — more at CRIME] **1 a :** to accuse of or charge with a crime **b :** INCRIMINATE **2 :** to accuse or represent as criminal **:** censure by charging or implying something criminal **syn** see ACCUSE

crim·i·na·tion \,krimə'nāshən\ *n* -s [L *crimination-, criminatio,* fr. *criminatus* + *-ion-, -io* -ion] **:** the act of criminating **:** ACCUSATION ⟨an attitude of cold determined ~⟩

crim·i·na·tive \'krimə,nād·iv, -mənəd·-\ *adj* **:** leading to or involving crimination **:** charging with crime

crim·i·na·tor \-,nād·ə(r)\ *n* -s [L, fr. *criminatus* + *-or*] **:** one that criminates

crim·i·na·to·ry \'krimənə,tōrē, -,tȯrē, -ri\ *adj* **:** relating to or involving crimination **:** ACCUSING ⟨a ~ conscience⟩

crim·i·ne *or* **crim·i·ni** *or* **crim·i·ny** \'krimənē, -rīm-\ *interj* [prob. euphemism for Christ] — used chiefly to express surprise

criming *pres part of* CRIME

crim·i·no·genesis \¦krimə(,)nō+\ *or* **crim·o·genesis** \¦krīmə+\ *n* [*criminogenesis,* NL, fr. L *crimin-, crimen* crime + NL *-o-* + *-genesis; crimogenesis,* NL, alter. of *criminogenesis*] **:** the origin of crime

crim·i·no·gen·ic \¦krimə(,)nō¦jenik\ *or* **crim·o·gen·ic** \¦krīmə¦-\ *adj* [*criminogenic* fr. L *crimin-, crimen* + E *-o-* + *-genic; crimogenic* alter. of *criminogenic*] **:** producing or leading to crime or criminality

crim·i·no·log·i·cal \¦krimənə¦läjəkəl\ *also* **crim·i·no·log·ic** \-¦läjik\ *adj* **:** of or relating to criminology — **crim·i·no·log·i·cal·ly** \-jək(ə)lē\ *adv*

crim·i·nol·o·gist \,==¦näləjəst\ *n* -s **:** one that specializes in criminology

crim·i·nol·o·gy \-jē, -ji\ *n* -ES [It *criminologia,* fr. L *crimin-, crimen* crime + It *-o-* + *-logia* -logy] **:** the scientific study of crime as a social phenomenon, of criminal investigation, of criminals, and of penal treatment

crim·i·no·sis \,krimə'nōsəs\ *n, pl* **crimino·ses** \-,sēz\ [NL, fr. L *crimin-, crimen* crime + NL *-osis*] **:** psychoneurotic behavior taking the form of criminal or antisocial acts; *also* **:** a tendency toward such behavior

crim·i·not·ic \¦==¦näd·ik\ *adj* [fr. NL *criminosis,* after such pairs as NL *hypnosis*: E *hypnotic*] **:** suffering from criminosis ⟨a ~ individual⟩ **:** marked by criminosis ⟨~ behavior⟩

crim·i·nous \'krimənəs\ *adj* [MF *crimineux,* fr. ML *criminosus,* fr. L, reproachful, slanderous, fr. *crimin-, crimen* crime + *-osus* -ous] **1 a** *obs* **:** deserving punishment **:** CRIMINAL **b :** guilty of crime ⟨~ clerks⟩ **2 :** concerned with crime ⟨an hysterical ~ tale⟩ ⟨the author's ~ reputation —Anthony Boucher⟩

crimmer *var of* KRIMMER

crim·my \'krimē, -mi\ *adj* [prob. alter. of E dial. *creemy,* fr. 1*creem* + *-y*] *NewEng* **:** COLD, CHILLY

1**crimp** \'krimp\ *vb* -ED/-ING/-S [D or LG *krimpen* to shrink, shrivel; akin to ON *kreppa* to clench — more at CRAMP] *vi* **:** to acquire, assume, or exhibit a creased or wavy appearance **:** WRINKLE ⟨hair that ~s easily⟩ ~ *vt* **1 :** to cause to become wavy, crinkled, bent, or warped ⟨lumber ~*ed* by exposure to weather⟩: as **a :** to wave or curl (hair) usu. with a hot iron **b :** to cause the muscles of (a fresh fish) to contract by gashing or slashing; *also* **:** GASH, CUT **c :** to fix (cloth) in small pleats or folds **d :** to form (leather) into a desired shape (as in making boot uppers or saddles) **e :** to give (synthetic fibers) a curl like that of natural fibers **f :** to draw or pinch in or together in glass manufacturing to form a neck, produce fluting, or set off a base (as in the making of a vase) **g :** to roll or curl the edge of (as a steel panel) **h :** CORRUGATE ⟨~*ing* sheet iron⟩ **2 :** to close, unite, or make continuous by crimping, pinching together, or folding: as **a :** to fold inward (as the edge of a tin can or a shotgun shell) to retain a head or other cover **b :** to pinch or press together (as the margins of a pie crust) in order to seal **3 :** to press in in order to contract (as the end of a pipe) **4 :** to put a crimp in **:** CRAMP, INHIBIT ⟨~*ing* sales by credit controls⟩ ⟨stern knights ~*ed* by their armor⟩

2**crimp** \"\ *n* -s **1 :** something produced by or as if by crimping: as **a :** a section of hair artificially waved or curled — usu. used in pl. ⟨her head covered with ~*s*⟩ **b :** the succession of waves in wool fiber ⟨a fine ~ is typical of the best wools⟩; *also* **:** induced waviness of a synthetic fiber (as nylon) **c :** disordering of fibers in wood (as by too rapid drying) **d :** 2CRAMP 1c **e :** the fold formed by crimping esp. on a can or cartridge **f :** an offset in a structural steel member (as a web stiffener) that adapts it to fit over another member **g :** a slight bend or crease put in a playing card in order to identify it **2 :** an interfering element **:** something that cramps or inhibits **:** OBSTACLE, CURB — used chiefly in the phrase *put a crimp in* ⟨strikes last year put a serious ~ in production —*Time*⟩

3**crimp** \"\ *adj* [perh. fr. LG *krimp* crooked, shrunken; akin to LG & D *krimpen* to shrink, shrivel] **1** *archaic* **:** easily crumbled **:** FRIABLE **2 :** CRIMPED, CRINKLED — **crimp·ness** *n* -ES

4**crimp** \"\ *n* -s [D or LG *krimp,* perh. fr. *krimpen* to shrink, shrivel] **:** an old game of cards

5**crimp** \"\ *n* -s [perh. fr. 1*crimp*] **:** a person who entraps or forces men into shipping as sailors or enlisting in an army or navy against their will or while insensible — compare PRESS

6**crimp** \"\ *vt* -ED/-ING/-S **:** to trap into military or sea service **:** IMPRESS

crimp·age \-pij\ *n* -s [5*crimp* + *-age*] *archaic* **:** money paid to a crimp for his services

crimped *adj* [fr. past part. of 1*crimp*] **:** marked or affected by crimping; *esp* **:** CRAMPED, HANDICAPPED, STRAITENED ⟨cash-crimped savings banks —*Newsweek*⟩ ⟨exposing briefly their ~ personalities and petty goals —*Time*⟩

1**crimp·er** \'krimpə(r)\ *n* -s [1*crimp* + *-er*] **:** one that crimps (as bottle tops)

2**crimper** \"\ *n* -s [6*crimp* + *-er*] **:** 5CRIMP

crimping iron *n* [fr. pres. part. of 1*crimp*] **:** a fluted block or die for crimping

crim·ple \'krimpəl\ *n* -s [2*crimp* + *-le*] **:** 2CRIMP; *esp* **:** CURL, WAVE

crimpy \'krimpē, -pi\ *adj* -ER/-EST [1*crimp* + *-y*] **1 :** having a crimped appearance **:** FRIZZY ⟨~ hair⟩ **2** *of weather* **:** UNPLEASANT **:** raw and cold

1**crim·son** \'krimzən *also* -m(p)sən\ *n* -s [ME *cremesin, crimisin,* fr. OSp *cremesin,* fr. Ar *qirmizī* red of the kermes, fr. *qirmiz* kermes, perh. of Indic origin; akin to Skt *kṛmi* worm; akin to Lith *kirmis* worm, OIr *cruim*] **1 a :** any of several deep or vivid reds or purplish reds of rather indefinite range **b :** a pigment or dye that colors crimson **2 :** something crimson ⟨a coat of fine-woven ~⟩

2**crimson** \"\ *adj* [ME *cremesin, crimisin,* fr. *cremesin, crimisin,* n.] **1 :** of the color crimson **2 :** resembling the color crimson; *esp* **:** BLOODY **3 :** flushed from embarrassment or anger **4 :** VIOLENT, LURID ⟨writes of ~ deeds and barbaric days —Andrea Parke⟩ ⟨circulating ~ rumors⟩ — **crim·son·ly** *adv* — **crim·son·ness** \-ᵊn(n)əs\ *n* -ES

3**crimson** \"\ *vb* -ED/-ING/-S *vt* **:** to make crimson **:** dye with crimson ~ *vi* **:** to become crimson: **a :** BLUSH, FLUSH **b :** RIPEN ⟨apples ~*ing* in the fall⟩

crimson antimony *n* **:** ANTIMONY VERMILION

crimson climbing rata *n* **:** a New Zealand woody vine (*Metrosideros diffusa*) that produces a profusion of brilliant red flowers

crimson clover *n* **:** a European annual clover (*Trifolium incarnatum*) that has cylindrical spiky heads of crimson flowers and that is extensively cultivated in the U.S. as a forage plant

crimson flag *n* **:** a South African herb (*Schizostylis coccinea*) of the family Iridaceae with clustered fleshy roots, narrow leaves, and a slender stalk bearing a number of crimson flowers shaped like a bell

crimson-fronted bullfinch \¦==¦==-\ *n* **:** HOUSE FINCH

crimson glory vine *n* **:** a Japanese grape (*Vitis kaempferi*) with very colorful autumnal foliage

crimson haw *n* **:** SCARLET HAW

crimson lake *n* **1 a :** a lake that is made from cochineal and that is similar to carmine — called also *Florentine lake* **b :** lake that is made from redwood **2 :** a moderate red that is yellower than cerise, yellower and slightly darker than claret (sense 3a), and bluer and very slightly lighter than Turkey red — called also *sultan*

crimson madder *n* **:** MADDER CRIMSON

crimson manuka *n* **:** a usu. shrubby red-flowered New Zealand tea tree (*Leptospermum scoparium*)

crimson rambler *n* **:** a well-known hardy climbing rose (*Rosa barbierana*) originating as a hybrid between *R. wichuraiana* and *R. cathayensis*

crimson sage *n* **:** a coarse herb (*Ramona grandiflora*) of the western U.S. with showy crimson flowers

crimson tragopan *n* **:** a crimson Indian tragopan (*Tragopan satyra*) that has the feathers ocellated with white and that is a favorite game bird

crim·sony \'krimzənē *also* -m(p)sənē\ *adj* **:** tinged with or resembling crimson

crin \'krin\ *n* -s [by shortening] **:** CRINOLINE 1

cri·nal \'krīnᵊl\ *adj* [L *crinalis,* fr. *crinis* hair + *-alis* -al; akin to L *crista* crest — more at CREST] **:** of or relating to the hair

crine \'krīn\ *vb* -ED/-ING/-S [ScGael *crìon* to wither; akin to OIr *crīn* withered, L *caries* decay — more at CARIES] *vi, Scot* **:** SHRINK, SHRIVEL ~ *vt, Scot* **:** to cause to dry up, shrink, or shrivel

crined \'krīnd\ *adj* [MF *crin* hair (fr. L *crinis*) + E *-ed* — more at CRINAL] **:** emblazoned with hair ⟨a unicorn argent ~ or⟩

crin·et \'krinət\ *n* -s [MF *crinete, crignete* mane, fr. OF *crignete,* dim. of *crin* hair, horsehair, mane] **:** articulated armor protecting the upper surface of the neck of a medieval war horse

1**cringe** \'krinj\ *vb* -ED/-ING/-S [ME *crengen,* causative fr. the root of OE *cringan* to fall, yield; akin to MHG *krinc* ring, circle, ON *kringr* circle, OE *cradol* cradle — more at CRADLE] *vi* **1 :** to draw in or contract one's muscles involuntarily **:** SHRINK, HUDDLE, CROUCH ⟨we ~ under the blasting wind —C.S.Houston⟩ **2 :** to shrink in fear or servility **:** bend or crouch with base humility **3 :** to make court in a degrading or servile manner **:** to approach with fawning and self-abasement ~ *vt* **1** *obs* **:** to draw in or together **:** cause to shrink or wrinkle **:** CONTRACT, CONTORT **2** *archaic* **:** to meet, greet, or escort with cringes ⟨hence, and bow and ~ him here —Lord Byron⟩

2**cringe** \"\ *n* -s **1 :** excessive deference **:** SERVILITY, FAWNING ⟨the provincial tends to suffer a cultural ~ toward urban centers⟩ **2 :** a cringing act; *specif* **:** an excessive or servile bow ⟨performing ~*s* and congees like a court chamberlain —W.M.Thackeray⟩

cringe·ling \-jliŋ\ *n* -s **:** CRINGER

cring·er \-jə(r)\ *n* -s **:** one that cringes

cringing *adj* **1 :** that shrinks in fear or servility ⟨a ~ rascal⟩ **2 :** ABJECT, SERVILE ⟨~ caution⟩ — **cring·ing·ly** *adv* — **cring·ing·ness** *n* -ES

crin·gle \'kriŋgəl\ *n* -s [LG *kringel,* dim. of *kring* ring, circle, fr. MLG *kring, krink;* akin to MHG *krinc* ring, circle] **:** a ring or loop for holding or fastening something: as **a :** TERRET **b :** a thimble, grommet, eyelet, or rope loop worked into or attached to the edge of a sail and used for making fast various ropes and lines

cringle b

crin·gle-cran·gle \¦kriŋgəl¦kraŋgəl\ *adv* (*or adj*) [prob. alter. of *crinkle-crankle*] **:** in a zigzag manner

crini- *comb form* [L, fr. *crinis*] **:** hair ⟨*crini*culture⟩ ⟨*crini*parous⟩

cri·nière \krēn'ya(a)(ə)r\ *n* -s [F, fr. MF, fr. *crin* hair, horsehair, mane — more at CRINED] **:** CRINET

Crin·i·ger \'krinəjə(r)\ *n, cap* [NL, fr. L *criniger* long-haired, fr. *crini-* + *-ger* -gerous; fr. the hairlike filaments on some of the feathers] **:** a genus of thick-billed harsh-voiced Asiatic and African bulbuls

crin·i·on \'krinē,än\ *n* -s [NL, fr. L *crinis* hair + Gk *-ion* (dim. suffix) — more at CRINOL] **:** TRICHION

1**cri·nite** \'krī,nīt, -ri,-\ *adj* [L *crinitus,* past part. of *crinire* to provide with hair, fr. *crinis* hair] **:** covered or provided with hairy growths **:** like hair or a hair

2**crinite** \"\ *n* -s [ISV *crinoid* + *-ite*] **:** a fossil crinoid

1**crink** \'kriŋk\ *n* -s [LG *krink* circle, ring; akin to MHG *krinc* circle, ring — more at CRINGE] *dial Eng* **:** BEND, TWIST

2**crink** \"\ *vt* -ED/-ING/-S *dial Eng* **:** BEND, TWIST, WRENCH

3**crink** \"\ *vi* -ED/-ING/-S [imit.] **:** to make or emit a thin abrupt metallic or crackling sound ⟨cicadas ~*ing* in the heat⟩

1**crin·kle** \'kriŋkəl\ *vb* **crinkled; crinkled; crinkling** \-k(ə)liŋ\ **crinkles** [ME *crynkelen, crenklen, crounkilen;* akin to MD *crinkelen* to crinkle, OE *cringan* to fall, yield — more at CRINGE] *vi* **1 a :** to form many short bends or turns **:** TURN, WIND **b :** to move in waves **:** WRINKLE, RIPPLE **2** *now dial Eng* **:** CRINGE; *also* **:** to turn aside or draw back from a purpose or promise **3 :** to give forth a thin metallic or crackling sound **:** RUSTLE ⟨stiff silk *crinkling* and swishing about her ankles⟩ ~ *vt* **:** to cause to crinkle ⟨the damp air *crinkled* her hair about her face⟩ **:** WRINKLE, RIPPLE, CURL ⟨a breeze barely *crinkling* the ripening wheat⟩

2**crinkle** \"\ *n* -s **1 :** WINDING, TURN, WRINKLE, CORRUGATION, FOLD **2 a :** cork (sense 5) when marked by internal necrotic regions **b :** potato mosaic in which puckered crinkly-edged downward-curved leaves occur **c :** any of several diseases characterized by crinkling of leaf margins (as strawberry crinkle)

crinkle·awn \'kriŋkəl,ȯn\ *n* -s **:** a grass (*Trachypogon montufari*) of the southwestern U.S. having spiky racemes and long awns

crinkle-bush \'==,=\ *n* **:** the dyed sprays of an Australian shrub (*Lomatia silaifolia*) used by decorators and florists for ornament

crin·kle-cran·kle \¦kriŋkəl¦kraŋkəl\ *n* -s [*crinkle* + *crankle*] **:** a winding in and out **:** SINUOSITY, ZIGZAG

crinkled *also* **crinkle** *adj* **:** having crinkles: as **a** *of a fabric* **:** woven or processed so as to produce a wholly or partially puckered surface — compare SEERSUCKER **b** *of a finish* **:** having a roughened surface thrown into fine wrinkles ⟨finished in ~ black enamel⟩

crinkle·root \'==,=\ *n* **:** an American plant of the genus *Dentaria* (esp. *D. diphylla*)

crin·kly *also* **crin·kley** \'kriŋk(ə)lē, -li\ *adj* -ER/-EST **1 :** full of crinkles **:** WAVY, WRINKLY **2 :** CRACKLY, RUSTLING

crin·kum-cran·kum \¦kriŋkəm¦kraŋkəm\ *n* -s [alter. (influenced by L nouns ending in *-um*) of *crinkle-crankle*] *archaic* **:** something full of twists and turns **:** a thing fancifully or excessively intricate and elaborate

1**cri·noid** \'krī,nȯid, -ri,-\ *adj* [NL *Crinoidea*] **:** of or relating to the Crinoidea **:** CRINOIDAL

2**crinoid** \"\ *n* -s **:** one of the Crinoidea **:** SEA LILY

cri·noi·dal \(')krī¦nȯidᵊl, krə'-\ *adj* **:** of or relating to crinoids **:** consisting of or containing crinoids ⟨~ limestone⟩

Cri·noi·dea \krə'nȯidēə, -rī'-\ *n pl, cap* [NL, fr. Gk *krinon* lily + NL *-oidea*] **:** a large class of chiefly tropical or fossil echinoderms that have a more or less cup-shaped body provided with five or more feathery arms commonly bifurcated or many-branched and bearing pinnules, a mouth lying between the arms on the concave upper surface, and opposite the mouth usu. a long jointed stalk fixed to the base of the body and having its opposite end divided into rhizoid processes that anchor the animal to the sea bottom — compare COMATULID, SEA LILY — **cri·noi·de·an** \krə'nȯidēən, (')krī¦-\ *adj or n*

1**crin·o·line** \'krinᵊlən, -ᵊl,ēn *also* ¦=ᵊ¦ēn *sometimes* '=ᵊl,īn\ *n* -s [F, fr. It *crinolino,* fr. *crino* horsehair (fr. L *crinis* hair) + *lino* flax, linen, fr. L *linum* — more at CRINAL, LINEN] **1 a :** a stiffened open-weave fabric of horsehair or cotton used for interlinings and millinery and for underskirts to expand the overskirts; *also* **:** this fabric without stiffening used for surgical purposes (as in bandages impregnated with plaster of paris) **2 a :** HOOPSKIRT **b :** a full stiff skirt or underskirt

2**crinoline** \"\ *adj* **1 :** of or relating to crinoline ⟨~ bandage⟩ **2 :** suggesting, typified by, or having a crinoline **:** belonging to the crinoline era; *esp* **:** OUTDATED, OLD-FASHIONED

crin·o·lined \-nd\ *adj* **1 :** wearing a crinoline ⟨a pretty ~ miss⟩ **2 :** stiffened with crinoline ⟨a ~ petticoat⟩

cri·nos·i·ty \krī'näsəd·ē, krə'-\ *n* -ES [L *crinis* hair + E *-osity*] **:** HAIRINESS

crins *pl of* CRIN

cri·num \'krīnəm\ *n* [NL, fr. L *crinum, crinon,* lily, fr. Gk *krinon*] **1** *cap* **:** a large genus of chiefly tropical bulbous herbs (family Amaryllidaceae) that are often cultivated for their umbels of showy and often fragrant white flowers which are frequently tinged or banded with red **2** -s **:** any plant of the genus *Crinum*

-cri·nus \¦krīnəs\ *n comb form* [NL, fr. Gk *krinon* lily] **:** a crinoid — in generic names of Crinoidea ⟨Actino*crinus*⟩ ⟨Penta*crinus*⟩

crin ve·ge·tal \,kraⁿ,vāzhə'täl\ *n, pl* **crins vegetal** *or* **crin vegetals** \"\ [F *crin végétal,* lit., vegetable hair] **:** the fiber of the European hemp palm

cri·o·bo·li·um \,krīə'bōlēəm\ *also* **cri·ob·o·ly** \krī'äbəlē\ *n, pl* **criobo·lia** \-lēə\ *also* **criobolies** [LL *criobolium,* fr. LGk *kriobolion,* fr. Gk *krios* ram + *-bolion* (fr. Gk *ballein* to throw); akin to L *cornu* horn — more at HORN, DEVIL] **:** a ceremony in the cult of certain Mediterranean deities (as Cybele and Attis) in which a ram was sacrificed so that the blood fell on the devotee — compare TAUROBOLIUM

Cri·oc·er·as \krī'äsərəs\ *n, cap* [NL, fr. Gk *krios* ram + NL *-ceras*] **:** a genus of Cretaceous ammonites with complexly plicated septa — **cri·o·cer·a·tite** \,krīə'serə,tīt\ *n* -s — **cri·o·cer·a·tit·ic** \¦==¦==¦tid·ik\ *adj*

Cri·oc·er·is \krī'äsərəs\ *n, cap* [NL, fr. Gk *krios* ram + NL *-ceris* (alter. of *-ceras*)] **:** a large cosmopolitan genus of beetles (family Chrysomelidae) including the asparagus beetle

cri·ol·la \krē'ōl(y)ə\ *n* -s *sometimes cap* [Sp, fem. of *criollo*] **:** a female criollo

cri·ol·lis·mo \krēō'liz(,)mō\ *n* -s [Sp, fr. *criollo* + *-ismo* -ism] **:** preoccupation in the arts and esp. the literature of Latin America with native scenes and types; *esp* **:** nationalistic preoccupation with such matter

1**cri·ol·lo** \krē'ōl(y)ō\ *n* -s *sometimes cap* [Sp — more at CREOLE] **1 a :** a person of pure Spanish descent born in Spanish America — compare CREOLE **b :** any person born and usu. raised in a Spanish-American country; *esp* **:** one of Spanish descent **2** [AmerSp, fr. Sp] **:** an animal of any of various breeds or strains of domestic animals developed in Latin America: as **a :** a small vigorous usu. dun or light brown So. American horse developed by judicious interbreeding of native and Arab stock **b :** a long-wooled sheep of Spanish origin now restricted to the Andes and adjacent Argentina **c :** any of several local strains of cattle some of predominantly dairy type, others of beef **3 :** any of various cacaos with very rough but thin-shelled pods and white seeds of superior quality — compare FORASTERO

2**criollo** \"\ *adj, sometimes cap* [Sp, fr. *criollo,* n.] **1 :** of, relating to, or being a criollo **2 :** native to a Spanish-American country as opposed to European **:** not alien to Spanish America

cri·o·phore \'krīə,fō(ə)r\ *n* -s [F, carrying a ram, fr. Gk *kriophoros,* fr. *krios* ram + *-phoros* -phorous] **:** a statue, figurine, or other representation in ancient art of a man carrying a ram

1**crip** \'krip\ *n* -s [by shortening] **:** CRIPPLE — often taken to be offensive

2**crip** \"\ *adj* **:** such as a cripple could perform **:** EASY ⟨a ~ course⟩ ⟨a ~ shot in basketball⟩

cripes \'krīps\ *also* **cripe** \-p\ *interj* [euphemism for *Christ*] — a mild oath

1**crip·ple** \'kripəl\ *n* -s [ME *cripel,* fr. OE *crypel;* akin to MLG *kropel, krepel,* cripple, ON *kryppill,* OE *cryppan* to bend, *crēopan* to creep — more at CREEP] **1 a :** one that has lost or never has had the use of a limb or limbs or has lost a greater part of such use **:** a lame person or animal **:** one that creeps, halts, or limps **b :** a person disabled, deficient, or ineffective in a specified manner or fashion ⟨a heart ~⟩ ⟨social and mental ~*s*⟩ **c :** a game bird or mammal injured but not recovered by the hunter **2 :** SUPPORT; *esp* **:** a temporary staging used in washing or painting windows **3 a :** something flawed or imperfect (as a badly done job, a damaged railway car, or a cake marred in the baking) **b** *dial* **:** swampy or low wet ground usu. covered with brush or thickets **4 :** a baseball pitch delivered without much stuff on it esp. when the count favors the batter (as at three balls and no strikes) ⟨hit the ~ for a double⟩ **5 :** a unit in a building frame that is shorter than is usual for such a unit (as a stud reaching only from a window opening to a ceiling beam)

2**cripple** \"\ *adj* [ME *cripel,* fr. *cripel,* n.] **:** being a cripple **:** LAME; *also* **:** worn out **:** INFERIOR

3**cripple** \"\ *vb* **crippled; crippled; crippling** \-p(ə)liŋ\ **cripples** [ME *criplen,* fr. *cripel,* n.] *vt* **:** to make a cripple of: as **a :** to deprive of the use of a limb (as a leg or foot) **:** LAME ⟨those sorry thousands *crippled* by arthritis⟩ **b :** to deprive of strength, efficiency, wholeness, or capability for service ⟨strikes are *crippling* our basic industries⟩ ⟨such a sea would ~ any boat⟩ ~ *vi* **:** to be, become, or act like a cripple: **a :** to walk lamely **:** HOBBLE, HALT **b :** to become disabled, incapacitated, or weakened **syn** see MAIM, WEAKEN

crip·ple·dom \-(,)dəm\ *n* -s **:** CRIPPLEMENT

crip·ple·ment \-mənt\ *n* -s **:** crippled condition **:** LAMENESS

crip·pler \-p(ə)lə(r)\ *n* -s **1 :** one that cripples; *esp* **:** a disease that results in crippling ⟨polio is still a major ~ of children⟩ **2 :** a wooden tool used in graining leather

1**crippling** *adj* [fr. pres. part. of 3*cripple*] **1 :** that cripples ⟨a ~ sense of personal inferiority⟩ **2 :** caused by crippling ⟨~ losses of game by careless hunters⟩ — **crip·pling·ly** *adv*

2**crippling** *n* -s [fr. gerund of 3*cripple*] **1 :** the state of being or process of becoming crippled; *specif* **:** the failure of the webs of steel beams or girders by buckling due to excessive loading **2 :** shoring for the side of a building

crips \'krips\ *adj* -ER/-EST [ME — more at CRISP] *dial* **:** CRISP

crise \'krēz\ *n* -s [F, fr. L *crisis*] **:** a moment of risk or stress **:** CRISIS; *also* **:** a state of perturbation

cri·sic \'krīsik\ *adj* [*crisis* + *-ic*] **:** of or relating to a crisis

cri·sis \'krīsəs\ *n, pl* **cri·ses** \-,sēz\ *also* **crisises** \-səsəz\ [L, fr. Gk *krisis,* fr. *krinein* to separate — more at CERTAIN] **1 a :** the turning point for better or worse in an acute disease or fever; *esp* **:** a sudden turn for the better (as sudden abatement in severity of symptoms or abrupt drop in temperature)

— compare LYSIS **b :** a paroxysmal attack of pain, distress, or disordered function ⟨tabetic ~⟩ ⟨cardiac ~⟩ **c :** an emotionally significant event or radical change of status in a person's life **2 a :** the point of time when it is decided whether an affair or course of action shall proceed, be modified, or terminate **:** decisive moment **:** turning point **b :** such a point in the course of the action of a play or other work of fiction — compare CLIMAX, RESOLUTION **c :** the immediate sequel to the culminating point of a period of prosperity and rising markets at which the business organism is severely strained and forced liquidation occurs — see BUSINESS CYCLE **3 a :** an unstable state of affairs in which a decisive change is impending ⟨recurrent cabinet *crises* trouble France⟩ **b :** a psychological or social condition characterized by unusual instability caused by excessive stress and either endangering or felt to endanger the continuity of the individual or his group; *esp* **:** such a social condition requiring the transformation of existing cultural patterns and values **syn** see JUNCTURE

crisis theologian *n* **:** an adherent of crisis theology

crisis theology *n* **:** neoorthodoxy esp. in its pessimistic view of human nature that holds that man and all human institutions are inevitably confounded by their own inner contradictions and that the resultant crisis forces man to despair of his own efforts and possibly to turn to divine revelation and grace in faith

¹crisp \ˈkrisp\ *adj* -ER/-EST [ME *crisp, crips* curly, fretted, fr. OE *crisp* curly, fr. L *crispus;* akin to MHG *rispen* to curl, OHG *hrispahi* bush, thicket, ON *rispa* to scratch, W *crych* curly, L *curvus* curved — more at CROWN] **1 a** (1) **:** CURLY, WAVY; *also* **:** having close stiff curls or waves or being somewhat wiry and stiff ⟨the short ~ hair of the natives⟩ (2) **:** having or made up of crisp hair ⟨a ~ hairdo⟩ ⟨the bull is commonly ~*er* about the forehead than his cows⟩ **b :** having the surface roughened into small folds or curling wrinkles ⟨~ whitecaps blown up by the wind⟩ **c :** CURLED **2 a :** having such a texture as to break apart easily and with a clear-cut fracture **:** BRITTLE, FRIABLE ⟨~ snow crackling underfoot⟩ **b** *of pastry* **:** SHORT **c :** firm and fresh **:** not flabby and wilted ⟨~ lettuces with the dew still on them⟩ **3 :** exhibiting or suggesting some combination of qualities characteristic of or attributable to that which is crisp: **a :** sharp, clean-cut, and clear ⟨a ~ illustration⟩ **:** concise and orderly to the point of terseness ⟨~ military reports⟩ ⟨a ~ reply⟩ **b :** noticeably neat and spruce in appearance or deportment **:** well-groomed **c :** SPRIGHTLY, BRISK, VIVACIOUS ⟨a ~ manner⟩ **:** lively and sparkling ⟨~ repartee⟩ ⟨dialogue as ~ as Shaw at his best⟩ **d :** COLD, FROSTY, SNAPPY ⟨~ winter weather⟩; *also* **:** fresh and invigorating ⟨a ~ odor of pines⟩ ⟨a ~ autumn breeze⟩ **e** *of a trigger* **:** releasing the firing mechanism smoothly and easily — compare ²CREEP 5d **syn** see INCISIVE

²crisp \ˈ"\ *vb* -ED/-ING/-S [ME *crispen,* fr. *crisp,* adj.] *vt* **1 a :** CURL, CRIMP ⟨~ her hair⟩ ⟨~ the nap of cloth⟩ **b :** to cause to ripple or undulate irregularly **:** WRINKLE ⟨a lake ~*ed* by the west wind⟩ **c :** to make crisp ⟨~*ing* celery in ice water⟩ **2 :** to cause to crackle ⟨the wheels ~ the gravel⟩ **3 :** to fold (cloth) into lengths **~** *vi* **1 :** CURL, RIPPLE ⟨her fingers ~*ed* on the tablecloth —Rebecca West⟩ ⟨leaves ~*ing* and fluttering in the sunlight⟩ **2 :** to become crisp ⟨bread ~*ing* in the oven⟩ ⟨the ground ~*ed* with frost⟩

³crisp \ˈ"\ *n* -s [¹*crisp*] **:** something crisp or brittle ⟨dinner burned to a ~⟩: as **a** *slang* **:** BANK NOTE **b** *chiefly Brit* **:** POTATO CHIP — usu. used in pl.

cris·pate \ˈkriˌspāt, -ˌspət\ *or* **cris·pat·ed** \-ˌspādəd\ *adj* [*crispate* fr. L *crispatus,* past part. of *crispare* to curl, fr. *crispus* curly; *crispated* fr. L *crispatus* + E *-ed*] **:** having a crisped appearance **:** irregularly curled or crinkled **:** CRISPED

cris·pa·tion \kriˈspāshən\ *n* -s [L *crispatus* + E *-ion*] **1 :** the act or process of curling **:** the state of being curled **:** UNDULATION **2 :** a slight shrinking or spasmodic contraction ⟨few men can look down from a great height without creepings and ~*s* —O.W.Holmes †1894⟩

crisped *adj* [ME, curled, fr. past part. of *crispen* to curl — more at CRISP] **1 :** made crisp **:** curled esp. in ringlets **:** RIPPLED **2 :** contorted or twisted ⟨the ~ leaves of the cabbage⟩

crisp·en \ˈkrispən\ *vb* -ED/-ING/-S [¹*crisp* + *-en*] *vt* **:** to make crisp ⟨celery ~*ed* by frost⟩ **~** *vi* **:** to become crisp ⟨a pasty ~*ing* in the oven⟩

crisp·er \ˈkrispə(r)\ *n* -s **:** one that crisps; *specif* **:** a closed container intended to prevent loss of moisture from fresh produce stored in a mechanical refrigerator

cris·pin \ˈkrispən\ *n* -s [after St. *Crispin* †*ab*287 patron saint of shoemakers] **:** SHOEMAKER, COBBLER

crisp·i·ness \ˈkrispēnəs, -pin-\ *n* -ES **:** CRISPNESS, BRITTLENESS, FLAKINESS

crisply *adv* **:** in a crisp manner ⟨never spoke or wrote except ~ —R.H.Rovere⟩

crisp·ness \ˈkrispnəs\ *n* -ES [ME *cryspeness,* fr. *cryspe, crisp* + *-ness*] **:** the quality or state of being crisp

crispy \ˈkrispē, -pi\ *adj* -ER/-EST [ME, curly, fr. ¹*crisp* + *-y*] **:** CRISP

criss \ˈkris\ *n* -ES [alter. of ¹*crest*] **:** a wooden stand with a curved top on which crest tiles are shaped

cris·sal \ˈkrisəl\ *adj* [NL *crissalis,* fr. *crissum* + L *-alis* -al] **:** relating to or having a crissum — used chiefly in vernacular names of birds ⟨a ~ bunting⟩

crissal thrasher *n* **:** a thrasher (*Toxostoma crissalis*) occurring in the southwestern U.S. and distinguished by colored crissal feathers

¹criss·cross \ˈkriˌskrȯs *also* -rȧs\ *n* -ES [alter. of *christcross*] **1 :** CHRISTCROSS; *esp* **:** MARK 2b(1) **2** *archaic* **:** TICKTACKTOE **3 :** a crisscross pattern or something made up of one **:** NETWORK ⟨a ~ of greenery overhead —*New Yorker*⟩ **4 :** something disordered or at cross purposes **:** confused state ⟨the fallacy which leads to this ~ of interpretations and opinions is the familiar one of confusing what the poet creates with what he represents —Susanne K. Langer⟩ ⟨a depressing ~ of figures⟩ **5 :** a play in football in which the paths of two offensive players cross; *also* **:** a pass pattern in which two receivers cross to opposite sides of the field

²crisscross \ˈ"\ *vb* -ED/-ING/-ES *vt* **1 :** to mark or score with intersecting lines ⟨~ the fat with a sharp knife⟩ **2 :** to pass back and forth through or over ⟨British ships ~*ed* the seas⟩ **~** *vi* **1 :** to go or pass back and forth ⟨birds ~*ing* in the blue⟩ **2 :** to run toward opposite sides of the football field (as on a pass pattern) ⟨had the ends ~ downfield to confuse the pass defenders⟩

³crisscross \ˈ"\ *also* **criss·crossed** \ˈ⸗ˌ⸗\ *adj* **:** marked or characterized by crisscrossing ⟨his ~ course⟩ **:** so arranged that constituent parts cross ⟨a ~ bodice⟩ ⟨~ fires⟩ **:** disposed in or made up of crossing lines ⟨~ threads⟩ ⟨a ~ pattern⟩

⁴crisscross \ˈ"\ *adv* **1 :** in opposite directions **:** in a way to cross something else **:** by crossing one another **2 :** with opposition or hindrance **:** at cross-purposes **:** AWRY, ASKEW, CONTRARILY ⟨things go ~⟩

criss·crossing \ˈ⸗ˌ⸗⸗\ *also* **crisscross breeding** *n* **:** a system of breeding domestic animals involving the use of purebred sires of two breeds alternately or crossbred females of the same breeds in such an order that the females are always bred to the males with which they have least blood in common — compare ROTATION CROSSING

crisscross inheritance *n* **:** inheritance of sex-linked characters transmitted from fathers to daughters or from mothers to sons

crisscross-row \ˈ⸗ˌ⸗-\ *n* [alter. of *christcross-row*] **:** ALPHABET

crisset *var of* CRESSET

cris·sum \ˈkrisəm\ *n, pl* **cris·sa** \-sə\ [NL, fr. L *crissare, crisare* to wiggle the backside while having sexual intercourse (said of a woman); akin to OE *hrith* fever, *scrīthan* to go, move around, OHG *hritto* fever, *scrītan* to go, step, ON *hrīth* storm, attack, *skrītha* to creep, glide, W *cryd* fever, *ysgryd* shiver, Lith *skrytis* felly of a wheel, and prob. to L *curvus* curved — more at CROWN] **:** the part of a bird surrounding the cloacal opening; *also* **:** the feathers covering that region **:** the under tail coverts

cris·ta \ˈkristə\ *n, pl* **cris·tae** \-ˌstē, -ˌstī\ [L — more at CREST] **:** CREST, RIDGE: as **a :** the keel of a carinate sternum **b :** CRISTA ACUSTICA **c :** a membranous spiral fold running the length of the body of certain spirochetes **d :** an elevation of the surface of a bone for the attachment of a muscle or tendon

crista acus·ti·ca \-əˈküstəkə\ *n, pl* **cristae acusti·cae** \-təˌkē, -ˌsē, -ī\ [NL, lit., acoustic crest] **1 :** one of the areas of specialized sensory epithelium in the ampullae of the semicircular canals of the ear serving as end organs for the labyrinthine sense **2 :** an auditory organ on the fore tibia of certain insects (as most grasshoppers)

cris·tate \ˈkriˌstāt, -ˌstət *also* **cris·tated** \-ˌstādəd\ *adj* [L *cristatus,* fr. *crista* crest + *-atus* -ate] **:** having a crista or crest **:** CRESTED

cris·ta·tel·la \ˌkristəˈtelə\ *n, cap* [NL, fr. L *cristatus* + NL *-ella*] **:** a genus (class Phylactolaemata) comprising freshwater bryozoans that form elongated creeping gelatinous colonies with the zooids restricted to the upper surface

cris·ti·spi·ra \-ˈspīrə\ *n, cap* [NL, fr. *cristi-* (fr. L *crista* crest) + L *spira* coil, twist — more at CREST, SPIRE] **:** a genus of large flexuous coarsely spiral bacteria (family Spirochaetaceae) parasitic in mollusks and having a crista along one side of the body

cris·ti·vomer \ˌkristə +\ *n, cap* [NL, fr. *cristi-* + *vomer*] **:** the genus (family Salmonidae) to which the lake trout belongs

cris·to·bal·ite \kriˈstōbəˌlīt\ *n* -s [G *cristobalit,* fr. Cerro San *Cristóbal,* Pachuca, Mexico + G *-it* -ite] **:** silica occurring in white octahedra stable at high temperature — compare QUARTZ, TRIDYMITE

cristy \ˈkristē\ *n* -ES *often cap* [by shortening and alter.] **:** CHRISTIANIA

crit *abbr* critical; criticism; criticized

critch \ˈkrich\ *n* -ES [origin unknown] *dial Eng* **:** an earthenware dish **:** CROCK

cri·te·ri·ol·o·gy \krīˌtirēˈäləjē\ *n* -ES [*criterion* + *-logy*] **:** the part of logic dealing with the establishment of criteria

cri·te·ri·on \krīˈtirēən *sometimes* krəˈ-\ *n, pl* **crite·ria** \-rēə\ *also* **criterions** [Gk *kritērion,* fr. *kritēs* judge, fr. *krinein* to separate, decide — more at CERTAIN] **1 :** a characterizing mark or trait ⟨increased speed, climb, and ceiling, three of the four basic *criteria* of air combat —*Science News Letter*⟩ ⟨a special constitutional ~ of that person —*Jour. Amer. Med. Assoc.*⟩ **2 :** a standard on which a decision or judgment may be based ⟨the accepted *criteria* of adequate diet⟩ **:** a standard of reference **:** YARDSTICK **:** an identifying indication ⟨what then are the *criteria* of a desirable organization of utilities —*Harper's*⟩ **:** a basis for discrimination **:** GROUND **3 :** an expression by whose value varieties of a mathematical form may be distinguished ⟨~ of a conic⟩ **syn** see STANDARD

cri·te·ri·um \-rēəm\ *n, pl* **crite·ria** \-rēə\ [LL, fr. Gk *kritērion*] **:** CRITERION

crith \ˈkrith\ *n* -s [Gk *krithē* barleycorn (or, a small weight); akin to Gk *kri* barley — more at HORDEUM] **:** the weight of a liter of hydrogen at 0° C and 760 millimeter pressure (0.08987 gram)

cri·thid·ia \krəˈthidēə\ *n* [NL, fr. Gk *krithidion,* dim. of *krithē* barleycorn] **1** *cap* **:** a genus of flagellates (family Trypanosomatidae) that are exclusively parasites of invertebrates esp. in the digestive tract of insects and that occur typically as elongated forms morphologically like trypanosomes but pass through developmental stages all in a single host in which they are indistinguishable from typical leptomonads and leishmanias **2** -s **a :** any flagellate of the genus *Crithidia* **b :** any flagellate of the family Trypanosomatidae when exhibiting a typical crithidial form

cri·thid·i·al \-dēəl\ *adj* [NL *Crithidia* + E *-al*] **:** of, like, or relating to crithidias **:** CRITHIDIFORM

cri·thid·i·form \-dəˌfȯrm\ *adj* [NL *Crithidia* + E *-form*] **:** resembling a crithidia in structure

crith·mene \ˈkrithˌmēn\ *n* -s [ISV *crithm-* (fr. NL *Crithmum* — genus name of the samphire *Crithmum maritimum* — fr. Gk *krēthmon* samphire) + *-ene;* orig. formed as It *critmene*] **:** TERPINENE b

¹crit·ic \ˈkrid·ik, -itik, -ēk\ *n* -s [MF & L; MF *critique,* fr. L *criticus,* fr. Gk *kritikos,* fr. *kritikos,* adj., able to discern or judge, fr. *kritos* (verbal of *krinein* to judge, discern) + *-ikos* -ic — more at CERTAIN] **1 a :** one who expresses a reasoned opinion on any matter (as a work of art or a course of conduct) involving a judgment of its value, truth, or righteousness, an appreciation of its beauty or technique, or an interpretation **b :** one who engages often professionally in the analysis, artistic evaluation, or appreciation of works of art (as literary or dramatic works) **2 :** one given to harsh or captious judgment **:** CARPER, CAVILER ⟨~*s* using hindsight in the best tradition of Monday morning quarterbacks⟩

²critic \ˈ"\ *adj* [MF & L; MF *critique,* fr. L *criticus,* fr. Gk *kritikos*] **:** CRITICAL

³critic \ˈ"\ *vb* **criticked; criticked; criticking; critics** [¹*critic*] *vi* **:** to act as a critic **~** *vt, obs* **:** to pass judgment on **:** CRITICIZE

⁴critic \ˈ"\ *n* -s [partly fr. ¹*critic;* partly fr. Gk *kritikē,* fr. fem. of *kritikos*] **1** *archaic* **:** CRITICISM **2** *archaic* **:** CRITIQUE

crit·i·cal \ˈkrid·əkəl, -itək-, -ēk-\ *adj* [¹*critic* + *-al*] **1 a :** inclined to criticize severely and unfavorably **:** given to noticing faults and imperfections ⟨cooler and more ~ in temper; hard to please —Willa Cather⟩ **b :** consisting of, marked by, being, or involving criticism ⟨the ~ writings of Swinburne⟩ ⟨a ~ biography⟩ ⟨his ~ insight⟩; *also* **:** of or in the judgment of critics ⟨the book won wide ~ praise⟩ ⟨the play was a ~ success⟩ **c :** exercising or involving careful judgment or judicious evaluation **:** DISCRIMINATING, CAREFUL, EXACT ⟨a ~ weighing of all the factors leaves no doubt that the countryman labors under real disadvantages⟩ ⟨a cautious ~ mind⟩ **d :** including variant readings and scholarly emendations ⟨a ~ edition⟩ — compare VARIORUM **2 :** of, relating to, or being a turning point or specially important juncture: **a :** indicating or being the stage of a disease at which an abrupt change for better or worse may be anticipated with reasonable certainty ⟨the ~ phase of a fever⟩ **b :** relating to, indicating, or being a state in which or a measurement or point at which some quality, property, or phenomenon suffers a finite change or undergoes drastic alteration ⟨the parabola is a ~ curve through which a conic section passes from an ellipse into a hyperbola⟩ **c :** CRUCIAL, DECISIVE ⟨a ~ analogy between sound and light⟩ ⟨this will be the ~ test in the series⟩ **d :** indispensable for the weathering, the solution, or the overcoming of a crisis; *specif* **:** essential for the conduct of war but available only in short supply ⟨~ materials⟩ **e :** in or approaching a crisis esp. through economic disorders or by virtue of a disaster ⟨a ~ area⟩ **3 a :** of doubtful issue **:** attended by risk or uncertainty ⟨our situation became ~ with the early freeze⟩ **b** *of kinds of organisms* (1) **:** so nearly related as to be distinguished with difficulty ⟨two ~ species⟩ (2) **:** rare and diminishing in numbers ⟨a ~ element in the local flora⟩ **4 :** of sufficient size to sustain or to be capable of sustaining a chain reaction — used of a mass of fissionable material

syn HYPERCRITICAL, CENSORIOUS, FAULTFINDING, CARPING, CAPTIOUS, CAVILING: CRITICAL may describe a disposition to find and to stress faults ⟨the attitude of Euripides . . . is so . . . frankly *critical* that a recent writer has even gone so far as to maintain that his main object . . . was to discredit the myths —G.L.Dickinson⟩ Unlike the other words in this list, CRITICAL may describe fair, judicious evaluation ⟨the exemplars of . . . the *critical* spirit, discriminators between the false and the true —P.E.More⟩ The other words in the list are all close in suggestion and are often interchangeable. HYPERCRITICAL and CENSORIOUS indicate a tendency to discover and stress errors and imperfections ⟨exceedingly difficult to please, not . . . because he was *hypercritical* and exacting, but because he was indifferent —Arnold Bennett⟩ ⟨"do you mean that you heard a fellow doubt my wife . . .?" "The world's very *censorious,* old boy" —W.M.Thackeray⟩ FAULTFINDING, sometimes implying lack of background and discrimination, describes a temperament that is exacting and almost impossible to satisfy. CARPING and CAPTIOUS may imply perverse ill-natured faultfinding ⟨these criticisms of a book that is a labor of love may seem ungracious or even *carping* —M.R.Cohen⟩ ⟨after reading a work of such amplitude it seems *captious* to protest that the motivating forces . . . are inadequately analyzed —Geoffrey Bruun⟩ CAVILING suggests frequent petty objections ⟨those *caviling* critics who snipe from the musty back rooms of libraries —Charles Ramsdell⟩ **syn** see in addition ACUTE

critical angle *n* **1 :** the least angle of incidence at which total reflection takes place when a ray of light or other electromagnetic radiation passes through one medium toward another that is less refracting **2** *or* **critical angle of attack** *aeronautics* **:** the angle of attack at which the flow about an airfoil changes abruptly with corresponding abrupt changes in the lift and drag, an airfoil possibly having two or more critical angles one of which usu. corresponds to the angle of maximum lift

critical angle: *AOB, AO′B′, AO″B″* angles of incidence; *AOC* refracted ray, *AO″C″* totally reflected ray; *AO′B′* critical angle

critical apparatus *n* **:** APPARATUS CRITICUS

critical coefficient *n* **:** the ratio of the critical temperature to the critical pressure

critical constant *n* **:** the critical temperature, critical pressure, or critical density of any one substance — usu. used in pl.

critical density *n* **:** the density of a substance in its critical state

critical flicker frequency *or* **critical fusion frequency** *n* **:** the threshold at which light from an intermittent source is seen half the time as flickering and half the time as fused or continuous

critical idealism *n* **:** TRANSCENDENTAL IDEALISM

crit·i·cal·i·ty \ˌ⸗⸗ˈkaləd·ē, -ətē, -i\ *n* -ES **:** a critical quality or condition — used esp. of fissionable material

crit·i·cal·ly \ˈ⸗⸗k(ə)lē, -li\ *adv* **:** in a critical manner **:** with criticism

crit·i·cal·ness \-kəlnəs\ *n* -ES **:** the quality or state of being critical ⟨the ~ of the situation called for quick action⟩

critical philosophy *n* **:** Kantianism esp. with reference to the critical establishment of necessary presuppositions for knowledge

critical point *n* **1** *math* **:** a point on the graph of a function where the derivative of the function is zero or infinite **2 :** TRANSFORMATION TEMPERATURE **3 a :** the point on a phase diagram of a pure substance that corresponds to its critical state **b :** CRITICAL STATE

critical potential *n* **:** either the radiation potential or the ionization potential of an atom

critical pressure *n* **:** the pressure exerted by a substance in its critical state

critical ratio *n* **:** the ratio of any one deviation from the mean in a set of observed values of the same statistical variable to the standard deviation of the set or to the corresponding probable error

critical realism *n* **:** a system of philosophical realism that incorporates features approximating to the Kantian theory of knowledge (as that of a group of American realists in 1920)

critical realist *n* **:** one who adheres to or advocates critical realism

critical size *n* **:** the size corresponding to the critical mass

critical solution temperature *n* **:** the temperature at which complete miscibility is reached as the temperature is raised or in some cases lowered — used of two liquids that are partially miscible under ordinary conditions; called also *consolute temperature*

critical state *n* **:** a state attainable by every chemically stable pure substance in which the liquid and the vapor phases have the same density

critical temperature *n* **1 a :** the temperature of a substance in its critical state **:** the highest temperature at which it is possible to separate substances into two fluid phases (vapor and liquid) **b :** the transition temperature of a solid from one allotropic form to another (as the Curie point of a metal) **2 :** TRANSFORMATION TEMPERATURE

critical value *n, math* **:** the value of the argument or independent variable corresponding to a critical point of a function

critical velocity *n* **:** the greatest velocity with which a fluid can flow through a given conduit without becoming turbulent

critical volume *n* **:** the specific volume of a substance in its critical state **:** the reciprocal of the critical density

crit·ic·as·ter \ˈ⸗⸗ˌkastə(r), ˌ⸗⸗ˈ⸗⸗\ *n* -s [¹*critic* + *-aster*] **:** an inferior or contemptible critic ⟨should make real critics proud of their vocation and the ~*s* ashamed of their presumption —W.H.Gardner⟩

crit·i·cism \ˈkrid·əˌsizəm, -itə,-\ *n* -s [¹*critic* + *-ism*] **1 a :** the act of criticizing usu. unfavorably **:** faultfinding disapproval and objection **b :** CRITIQUE **2** *obs* **:** a subtle point or fine distinction **:** NICETY, SUBTLETY **3 :** the art of evaluating or analyzing with knowledge and propriety works of art or literature ⟨the first principle of ~, which is, to consider the nature of the piece, and the intent of its author —Alexander Pope⟩; *broadly* **:** similar consideration of other than literary matters (as moral values or the soundness of scientific hypotheses and procedures) **4 :** the scientific investigation of literary documents (as the Bible) in regard to such matters as origin, text, composition, character, or history **5 :** CRITICAL PHILOSOPHY

crit·i·ciz·able \ˌ⸗⸗ˈsīzəbəl\ *adj* **:** that may be criticized **:** subject to criticism

crit·i·cize \ˈ⸗⸗ˌsīz\ *vb* -ED/-ING/-S *see -ize in Explan Notes* [¹*critic* + *-ize*] *vi* **1 :** to act as a critic **:** consider and estimate worth or value ⟨the man who did not ~ or reflect —G.L. Dickinson⟩ **2 :** to find fault **:** stress faults, errors, or demerits ⟨an unpleasant person, always *criticizing*⟩ **~** *vt* **1 :** to consider the merits and demerits of and judge accordingly **:** EVALUATE ⟨Dr. Burney *criticized* the manuscript very favorably —Elizabeth Lee⟩ **2 :** to stress the faults and demerits of **:** cavil at ⟨we are trying to get away from the word "management" because it has been lambasted, ridiculed, *criticized,* and blasted —*Personnel Jour.*⟩

syn REPREHEND, REPROBATE, BLAME, CENSURE, CONDEMN, DENOUNCE: CRITICIZE, among more erudite persons, is likely to indicate measured judgment or evaluation ⟨he does not *criticize,* he denounces —*Times Lit. Supp.*⟩ Often it means focusing attention on weak points, demerits, failings, and delighting in pointing them out ⟨newspaper policy is attacked, display advertising is *criticized,* features are ridiculed —*Public Relations Jour.*⟩ REPREHEND, now more commonly used with grammatical objects designating things, actions, or qualities than persons, may imply a severe rebuke decided on after deliberate judgment ⟨being to advise or *reprehend* any one, consider whether it ought to be in public or in private . . and in reproving show no signs of choler —George Washington⟩ ⟨the thing to be *reprehended* is the confusing misuse of the word "verse" —C.H.Grandgent⟩ REPROBATE may suggest strong disapproval and firm rejection or final refusal to tolerate or sanction ⟨those peaceful and friendly conferences between capitalists and trade-union leaders which are so *reprobated* by Marxist critics —H.B.Parkes⟩ ⟨he *reprobated* the "paltry jealousy" manifested toward Congress —H.R. Warfel⟩ BLAME is now likely to indicate the placing of responsibility for something bad or unfortunate on a person or thing although it is still sometimes used as a general antonym of *praise* ⟨the general was *blamed* for the defeat⟩ ⟨Heine . . . cared . . . whether people praised his verses or *blamed* them —Matthew Arnold⟩ CENSURE indicates disapproval delivered sternly, often as a reprimand from someone in an authoritative or competent position ⟨the *Times* published an article . . . in which . . . all contemporary literature was *censured* —E. M.Forster⟩ CONDEMN may suggest a severe, unmitigated, final, or definitive judgment which is wholly unfavorable ⟨vice, on this view, is *condemned* because it is a frustration of nature —G.L.Dickinson⟩ ⟨the entire week before election was a holiday and was *condemned* by ministers as a time "to meet, to smoke, to drink, carouse, and raise the devil" —*Amer. Guide Series: N.H.*⟩ DENOUNCE suggests stigmatizing publicly with force, vehemence, or conviction ⟨members of the owning classes, who *denounce* alike the encroachment of the state and of organized labor upon the wealth which they have "made" —J.A.Hobson⟩ ⟨in all ages, priests and monks have *denounced* the growing vices of society —Henry Adams⟩

crit·i·ciz·er \-zə(r)\ *n* -s **:** CRITIC

criticked *past of* CRITIC

criticking *pres part of* CRITIC

critics *pl of* CRITIC, *pres 3d sing of* CRITIC

critic teacher *n* **:** a secondary or elementary school teacher who supervises the practice teaching of a student teacher

[1]**cri·tique** \kri'tēk *also* krē'- *or* krə'-\ *n* -s [alter. (influenced by F *critique*) of [4]*critic*] **:** an act of criticizing; *esp* **:** a critical examination or estimate of a thing or situation (as a work of art or literature) with a view to determining its nature and limitations or its conformity to standards

[2]**critique** \"\ *vt* -ED/-ING/-S **:** CRITICIZE, REVIEW

critize *vt* -ED/-ING/-S [[1]*critic* + *-ize*] *obs* **:** CRITICIZE

crit·ter *or* **crit·tur** \'krid·ə(r) -itə-\ *n* -s [alter. of *creature*] **1** *dial* **:** CREATURE **2 a** *dial* **:** ANIMAL **b** *dial* **:** a domestic animal; *esp* **:** a horse or a cow **c** *chiefly South* **:** HORSE **d** *North* **:** BULL

[1]**criz·zle** \'krizəl\ *vb* -ED/-ING/-S [origin unknown] *vi, dial* **:** to become rough or crumpled (as of the surface of freezing water) ~ *vt, chiefly dial* **:** to roughen or crumple the surface of

[2]**crizzle** \"\ *n* -s *now dial* **:** a roughened surface (as of the skin when exposed to sun and wind)

criz·zling \'kriz(ə)liŋ\ *n* -s **:** the blemish on a surface (as of glass) due to crumpling or roughening

cro \'krō\ *n* -ES [ME *cro, croy*, fr. ScGael *crō*, lit., blood; akin to MIr *crū, crō* blood, L *cruor* — more at RAW] **:** satisfaction in an amount suitable to the rank of the parties involved made in early Scottish law for the killing of a man

[1]**croak** \'krōk\ *vb* -ED/-ING/-S [ME *croken*, of imit. origin] *vi* **1 a :** to make a deep harsh sound ⟨the frogs ~*ed*⟩ **b :** to speak in a hoarse throaty raucous voice ⟨I tried to ask . . . but my voice just ~*ed* indistinguishably —Kenneth Roberts⟩ **2 a :** to protest dismally or dolefully **:** grumble dourly **:** COMPLAIN ⟨a querulous patient always ~*ing* about the hospital⟩ **b :** to predict evil **:** talk dismally ⟨misanthropists always ~*ing* about man's demerits⟩ **3** *slang* **:** DIE ~ *vt* **1 :** to forebode, announce, or utter in a hoarse raucous voice ⟨the raven . . . that ~*s* the fatal entrance of Duncan —Shak.⟩ **2** *slang* **:** to kill esp. with brutal violence **syn** see COMPLAIN

[2]**croak** \"\ *n* -s **1 :** the hoarse harsh cry of a frog or raven or a similar sound ⟨the ~ of an old woman⟩ ⟨a strange ~ of a laugh⟩; *esp* **:** an expiring gasp ⟨his last ~⟩ **2 :** an asthmatic disease affecting the hawk — usu. used in pl.

croak·er \-kə(r)\ *n* -s **1 :** an animal that croaks (as a frog) **2 :** any of various fishes esp. of the family Sciaenidae that produce croaking or grunting noises (as certain grunts and surf fishes): as **a :** ATLANTIC CROAKER **b :** FRESHWATER DRUM **c :** QUEENFISH **3 :** one that murmurs, grumbles, or complains unreasonably; *esp* **:** one that habitually forbodes evil ⟨it didn't turn out as bad as the ~*s* thought⟩ **4** [[1]*croak* (to kill) + *-er*] *slang* **:** DOCTOR

croaker family *n* **:** SCIAENIDAE

croaking gourami *n* **:** a rare East Indian green and gold freshwater labyrinth fish (*Ctenops vittatus*) sometimes kept in the tropical aquarium and noted for its ability to make croaking sounds when removed from the water

croaking lizard *n* **:** a gecko (*Thecadactylus rapicadus*) occurring in the West Indies and Central and So. America

croaking sac *n* **:** VOCAL SAC

croaky \'krōkē, -ōki\ *adj* -ER/-EST **:** deeply hoarse **:** CROAKING ⟨a ~ voice⟩

croat \'krō|ət *sometimes* 'krō,a|t, *usu* |d·+V\ *n* -s *cap* [NL *Croata*, fr. Serbo-Croatian *Hrvat*] **1 :** CROATIAN **2 :** a member of a former French light cavalry regiment made up largely of Croatians

cro·atan \¦krōə¦tan\ *also* **croatan indian** *n* -s *usu cap C&I* [fr. *Croatan*, island, off the coast of No. Carolina] **:** one of a group of people of mixed Indian, white, and Negro ancestry in southern No. Carolina and adjoining sections of So. Carolina — sometimes used disparagingly

[1]**cro·atian** \krō'āshən\ *n* -s *cap* [*Croatia*, region of southeastern Europe and federated republic of Yugoslavia + E *-ian*] **1 :** a native or inhabitant of the former Austrian province of Croatia or of the federal republic of Croatia in Yugoslavia **2 a** (1) **:** a south Slavic people that settled in Croatia in the 7th century and who are closely akin to the Serbs (2) **:** a member of such people — compare SERB, SERBO-CROATIAN, YUGOSLAV **b :** a south Slavic language spoken by the Croatian people and distinct from Serbian only in its use of the Latin alphabet and in certain minor dialect differences

[2]**croatian** \(')¦=¦=\ *adj, usu cap* **1 a :** of, relating to, or characteristic of Croatia **b :** of, relating to, or characteristic of Croatians **2 :** of, relating to, or characteristic of the Croatian language

croc \'kräk\ *n* -s [by shortening] **:** CROCODILE

croc·ard *also* **crock·ard** \'kräkərd, krō'kärd\ *n* -s [ME *crocarde*, fr. MF *crocard*, perh. fr. *croc* hook (of Scand origin; akin to ON *krōkr* hook) + *-ard* — more at CROOK] **:** a coin of base metal that circulated in England at two to the penny during the 13th century and until its circulation was prohibited in 1310 — compare POLLARD I

cro·ce·an *also* **cro·ci·an** \'krōchēən\ *adj, usu cap* [Benedetto *Croce* †1952 Ital. philosopher & statesman + E *-an*] **:** of, having to do with, or suggesting Croce or his idealist philosophy of the spirit or his liberalism

cro·ce·ic acid \(')krō¦sēik-\ *n* [*crocein* + *-ic*] **:** CROCEIN ACID

cro·ce·in \'krōsēən\ *or* **cro·ce·ine** \", -ē,ēn\ *n* -s *usu cap* [ISV *croce-* (fr. L *croceus* of saffron) + *-in, -ine*] **:** any of several red or orange acid azo dyes — see DYE table I (under *Acid Orange 12, Acid Red 25*)

crocein acid *or* **croceine acid** *n* **:** a crystalline acid $HOC_{10}H_6SO_3H$ used as an intermediate in making azo dyes; 2-naphthol-8-sulfonic acid — called also *Bayer's acid*

croceine scarlet MOO \-,e,mō'ō, -,em,dəbə'lō\ *n, usu cap C&S* **:** BRILLIANT CROCEIN

cro·ce·tin \'krōsət°n\ *n* -s [ISV *croc-* (fr. *crocin*) + *-et-* + *-in*; prob. orig. formed as G *krozetin*] **:** red crystalline dicarboxylic carotenoid acid $C_{20}H_{24}O_4$ obtained by hydrolysis of crocin — called also *alpha-crocetin*

cro·ce·us \'krōsēəs\ *n* -ES [L, adj., of saffron, saffron-colored, fr. *crocus* saffron — more at CROCUS] **:** SAFFRON 3

croche \'krōsh\ *n* -s [MF *croche*, lit., hook] **:** a little knob at the top of a deer's antler

[1]**cro·chet** \(')krō¦shā\ *n* -s [F, hook, crochet work, fr. MF dim. of *croche* hook, of Scand origin; akin to ON *krōkr* hook — more at CROOK] **1 a :** needlework consisting of the interlocking of looped stitches formed with a single thread and a hooked needle ⟨~ work⟩ ⟨~ hook⟩ ⟨she looked up from her ~ —Alma Stone⟩ **b :** a stitch used in crochet **2 :** a hook or hooked process: as **a :** one of a series of minute hooks on the apical surface of the proleg of a caterpillar **b :** CROTCHET 2c(1)

position of thread and needle in crochet work

[2]**crochet** \"\ *vb* -ED/-ING/-S *vt* **:** to make of crochet ⟨Meggie . . . returned to the counterpane she was ~*ing* — Ellen Glasgow⟩ ~ *vi* **:** to work with crochet

cro·chet·er \-āə(r)\ *n* -s **:** one that crochets; *specif* **:** one that crochets trimmings by machine on knitted garments

crochet file *n* **:** a thin flat file rounded on the edges and tapering to a point

crocheting *n* -s **1 :** the act or action of one that crochets **2 :** crochet work

croci *pl of* [1]CROCUS

cro·cid·o·lite \krō'sid°l,īt\ *n* -s [G *krokydolith*, fr. Gk *krokyd-, krokys* nap on cloth + G *-o-* + *-lith* -lite] **:** a lavender-blue or leek-green mineral of the amphibole group that is a variety of riebeckite and occurs in silky fibers and in massive and earthy form — called also *blue asbestos*; see TIGEREYE

croc·i·du·ra \,kräsə'd(y)ùrə, ,krōs-\ *n* [NL, fr. *crocid-* (fr. Gk *krokyd-, krokys* nap on cloth) + *-ura*; akin to Gk *krekein* to weave — more at REEL] **1** *cap* **:** a genus including the Old World house shrew or musk shrew **2** *pl* **crociduras** \-əz\ *or* **crocidu·rae** \-ù,rē\ **:** any member of the genus *Crocidura*

cro·cin \'krōs°n, -sən\ *n* -s [ISV *croc-* (fr. L *crocus* saffron) + *-in*; prob. orig. formed in G — more at CROCUS] **:** a yellow glycoside $C_{44}H_{64}O_{24}$ of crocetin occurring in species of crocus (as saffron) and gardenia that is active in inducing sexual change in certain algae

[1]**crock** \'kräk\ *n* -s [ME *crocke*, fr. OE *crocc*; akin to OS *krūka* pot, ON *krukka*, OE *crūce* pot, pitcher, MHG *krūche* crock, pitcher, and perh. to OHG *kriochan* to creep — more at CRUTCH] **1 :** a thick earthenware pot or jar **2** *dial Eng* **:** a potsherd used esp. to cover the hole in a flowerpot **3 :** a broken piece of earthenware **4** *dial* **:** loose black particles collected from combustion (as on cooking utensils or in a chimney) **:** SOOT, SMUT **5 :** coloring matter that rubs off from cloth or dyed leather

[2]**crock** \"\ *vb* -ED/-ING/-S *vt* **1 :** to put in a crock ⟨~ butter⟩ **2 :** to provide drainage in (a flowerpot) by means of a crock **3** *dial* **:** to soil with crock **:** SMUDGE ~ *vi, of dye or dyed fabric or leather* **:** to transfer color under rubbing **:** rub off ⟨a suede that will not ~⟩

[3]**crock** \"\ *n* -s [ME *crok*, prob. of Scand origin; akin to Norw dial. *krokje* broken-down horse or person, Icel *kraki* delicate boy, LG *krakke* broken-down horse, D *kraak* broken-down cow or person, and perh. to ON *krōkr* hook, corner — more at CROOK] **1** *dial Brit* **:** an old or barren ewe **2 :** an old or broken-down animal; *esp* **:** an old or broken-down horse **3 :** one that is broken down, disabled, or impaired ⟨over three quarters of all the ships were ~*s* —*Yale Rev.*⟩ ⟨an old ~ of 104 who does nothing but sit by the fire —Richard Joseph⟩ ⟨the poor old ~ who feels tired every afternoon at three, from a complicated set of physical and psychological causes —Martin Mayer⟩

[4]**crock** \"\ *vb* -ED/-ING/-S *vt* **:** to cause to become impaired **:** put out of commission **:** DISABLE ⟨~ his thumb⟩ — often used with *up* ⟨a *crocked*-up athlete⟩ ~ *vi* **:** to become impaired **:** break down ⟨his physical vigor ~*ed*⟩ ⟨the mare soon ~*ed*⟩

crockard *var of* CROCARD

crocked *adj* [prob. fr. past part. of [4]*crock*] *slang* **:** DRUNK

crock·ery \'kräk(ə)rē, -ri\ *n* -ES **:** vessels formed of fired clay esp. for domestic use **:** EARTHENWARE

crock·et \'kräkət\ *n* -s [ME *croket*, fr. ONF *croquet* shepherd's crook, dim. of *croc* hook, of Scand origin; akin to ON *krōkr* hook — more at CROOK] **1 :** an ornament usu. in the form of curved and bent foliage used on the edge of a gable or spire **2 :** CROCHE

crock·et·ed *also* **crock·et·ted** \-əd·əd\ *adj* **:** furnished with crockets ⟨a ~ spire⟩

crock·et·ing *also* **crock·et·ting** \-əd·iŋ\ *n* -s **:** ornamentation with crockets

crocking *n* -s [fr. gerund of [2]*crock*] **1 :** the transfer or rubbing off of leather-finishing materials or color onto materials coming into contact with the leather **2 :** the tendency of a painted surface to show color irregularity on rubbing

crocket

crock tile *n* **:** a hard-burned glazed clay drain tile with or without bell-shaped ends

crocky \'kräkē\ *adj* -ER/-EST [[3]*crock* + *-y*] **:** impaired in one's powers **:** physically frail

[1]**croc·o·dile** \'kräkə,dīl\ *n* -s *see sense 1* [alter. (influenced by L *crocodilus*) of ME *cocodrille*, fr. OF, fr. ML *cocodrillus*, alter. of L *crocodilus, corcodillus*, fr. Gk *krokodeilos, krokodilos*, alter. of (assumed) *krokodrilos*, fr. *krokē* pebble + *drilos* worm; akin to Skt *śarkara* pebble — more at SUGAR] **1** *pl sometimes* **crocodile a :** any of several large thick-skinned long-bodied aquatic reptiles of tropical and subtropical waters constituting *Crocodylus* and one or two closely related genera and including certain voracious forms (as the Nile crocodile [*C. niloticus*] or the very large estuarine crocodile [*C. porosus*] of eastern Asia and the Pacific islands) that do not hesitate to attack man **b :** a reptile of the order Loricata — see ALLIGATOR **c :** crocodiles' skin tanned for use in manufacturing (as of handbags, shoes, luggage, and belts) **2** *archaic* **:** one who hypocritically affects sorrow — compare CROCODILE TEARS **3** *chiefly Brit* **:** a number of persons moving in a long file; *esp* **:** the file formed by the members of a school out for a walk

[2]**crocodile** \"\ *vi* -ED/-ING/-S *of paints* **:** ALLIGATOR

crocodile bird *n* **:** an African plover (*Pluvianus aegypticus*) that alights upon the crocodile and devours its insect parasites and reputedly even enters its open mouth in pursuit of flies

crocodile clip *n* **:** ALLIGATOR CLIP

crocodile shears *n pl* **:** LEVER SHEARS

crocodile squeezer *n* **:** a squeezer consisting of a lever device with powerful jaws between which metal is placed for shingling

crocodile tears *n pl* [so called fr. the ancient belief that crocodiles shed tears over their victims and make moaning sounds to attract prey] **1 :** false or affected tears **:** hypocritical sorrow **2 :** a disorder characterized by a profuse flow of tears initiated by chewing or the taste of food and occurring in facial paralysis

croc·o·dil·ia \,kräkə'dilēə\ [NL, fr. *Crocodilus* + *-ia*] *syn of* [2]LORICATA

[1]**croc·o·dil·ian** \¦kräkə¦dilēən, -lyən\ *adj* [[1]*crocodile* + *-ian*] **1 :** FALSE, INSINCERE ⟨~ grief⟩ ⟨a ~ lament⟩ **2 a :** of, relating to, or characteristic of a crocodile ⟨a ~ walk⟩ **b :** LORICATE

[2]**crocodilian** \"\ *n* -s [NL *Crocodilia* + E *-an*] **:** any of an order (Loricata) of reptiles including the crocodiles, alligators, and related extinct forms

croc·o·dil·i·dae \,kräkə'dilə,dē\ [NL, fr. *Crocodilus* + *-idae*] *syn of* CROCODYLIDAE

croc·o·dil·oid \,kräkə'di,lȯid, 'kräkə,dī,-\ *adj* **:** like a crocodile

croc·o·di·lus \,kräkə'dīləs\ [NL, fr. L, crocodile] *syn of* CROCODYLUS

croc·o·dyl·i·dae \-'dilə,dē\ *n pl, cap* [NL, fr. *Crocodylus*, type genus + *-idae*] **:** a family of the order Loricata variously construed as including all recent and some fossil crocodilians or as comprising only the true crocodiles, the alligators, caimans, and gavials being excluded

croc·o·dy·loi·dea \-,də'lȯidēə\ *n pl, cap* [NL, fr. *Crocodylus* + *-oidea*] *in some classifications* **:** a suborder of Loricata containing recent crocodiles and related forms

croc·o·dy·lus \-'dīləs\ *n, cap* [NL, alter. of L *crocodilus* crocodile] **:** the type genus of Crocodylidae

croc·o·ite \'krākə,wīt\ *or* **croc·oi·site** \'kräkwə,zīt\ *n* -s [*crocoite* fr. G *krokoit*, alter. of *krokoisit*; *crocoisite* fr. G *krokoisit*, fr. F *crocoise* (fr. Gk *krokoeis* saffron-colored, fr. *krokos* saffron) + G *-it* -ite — more at CROCUS] **:** a mineral $PbCrO_4$ consisting of native lead chromate in monoclinic crystals — called also *red lead ore*

cro·con·ic acid \krə'känik-\ *n* [part trans. of G *krokonsäure*, fr. *krokon-* (irreg. fr. Gk *krokos* crocus, saffron) + *säure* acid] **:** a yellow crystalline hydroxy ketone $C_5O_3(OH)_2$ obtained from rhodizonic acid and various other oxygen derivatives of benzene and that forms yellow or orange-colored salts

crocs *pl of* CROC

[1]**cro·cus** \'krōkəs\ *n* [NL, fr. L, fr. Gk *krokos*, of Sem origin; akin to Assyr-Bab *kurkanū* saffron, crocus, Heb *karkōm*, Aram *kurkĕmā*, Ar *kurkum*] **1 a** *cap* **:** a large genus of perennial herbs (family Iridaceae) native chiefly to the Mediterranean region but widely cultivated for their solitary long-tubed flowers that arise with the slender linear leaves from a fibrous-coated corm **b** *pl* **crocuses** \-səz\ *also* **cro·ci** \-ō,sī, ō,kī\ *or* **crocus :** a bulb, plant, or flower of the genus *Crocus* **2** *pl* **crocuses a :** a deep yellow or red powder that is usu. the oxide of some metal; *esp* **:** a dark red ferric oxide obtained similarly to colcothar and used for polishing metals — called also *crocus mar·tis* \¦krōkə'smärd·əs\, *crocus of Mars* \-ōkəsəv'märz\ **b :** SAFFRON 2 **3** *pl* **crocuses a :** a pale to grayish reddish purple that is less strong than Argyle purple **b :** a light reddish purple that is redder, lighter, and stronger than rose purple

[2]**cro·cus** \'krōkəs\ *n* -ES [origin unknown] *chiefly South* **:** coarse sacking (as gunny or burlap) ⟨~ bag⟩ ⟨a bushel of potatoes in a ~ sack⟩

[3]**crocus** \"\ *n* -ES [alter. of *croaker* (doctor)] **:** a quack doctor

[4]**crocus** \"\ *n* -ES [by alter.] **1 :** ATLANTIC CROAKER **2 :** FRESHWATER DRUM

crocus cloth *n* [[1]*crocus* (powder)] **:** cloth that has finely divided ferric oxide glued to one side and is used for fine abrading or polishing

crocus of antimony : a brownish yellow product mainly sodium thioantimonite Na_3SbS_3 or potassium thioantimonite K_3SbS_3 obtained as a slag in refining antimony

cro·cu·ta \krō'kyüd·ə\ *n, cap* [NL, fr. L *crocuta, corocottas*, a kind of wild animal, perh. the hyena, fr. Gk *krokottas, korokottas*] **:** the genus consisting of the African spotted hyena

croes *pl of* CRO

croe·sus \'krēsəs\ *n, pl* **croesuses** \-ēsəsəz\ *also* **croe·si** \-ē,sī\ *usu cap* [after *Croesus* †546B.C. wealthy king of ancient Lydia, fr. L, fr. Gk *Kroisos*] **:** a very rich man ⟨the arrogant *Croesus* of the neighborhood who was brought down to size . . . by the parish drunk —*N.Y. Times Book Rev.*⟩

[1]**croft** \'krȯft, *Brit usu & US also* -ä-\ *n* -s [ME, fr. OE; akin to MD *krocht* hill, field of dunes, OE *crēopan* to creep — more at CREEP] **1** *chiefly Brit* **:** a small enclosed field usu. adjoining a house **2** *chiefly Brit* **:** a small farmhold usu. of 5 to 10 acres that is worked by a tenant

[2]**croft** \"\ *vb* -ED/-ING/-S *vt, Brit* **:** to expose (as linen) on the grass for bleaching in the sun ~ *vi, Brit* **:** to live as a crofter

[3]**croft** \"\ *n* -s [ME *crofte*, fr. MD *crofte, crochte*, fr. ML *crupta*, fr. L *crypta* — more at CRYPT] **:** CRYPT, VAULT, CAVERN

croft·er \-tə(r)\ *n* -s [[1]*croft* + *-er*] *chiefly Brit* **:** one that rents and works a croft

croft·ing \-tiŋ\ *n* -s [[1]*croft* + *-ing*] **1** *chiefly Brit* **a :** the quality or state of being successively cropped **b :** the land so cropped **2** *chiefly Brit* **:** the system of tenancy of crofters ⟨~ townships⟩ ⟨the ~ problem⟩

croft lily \'krȯft- *also* -ä-\ *n, usu cap C* [after Sydney *Croft*, †*ab* 1940 Am. horticulturist] **:** an Easter lily characterized by short stems, long leaves, and pure white flowers with strongly recurved perianth tips

crof·ton weed \'krȯftən- *also* -räf-\ *n, often cap C* [origin unknown] **:** an herb (*Eupatorium riparium*) native to the New World but now common in Australia that is a troublesome weed on rangelands

crohn's disease \'krōnz-\ *n, usu cap C* [after Burill B. *Crohn* *b*1884 Am. physician] **:** REGIONAL ILEITIS

croisade [MF — more at CRUSADE] *obs var of* CRUSADE

croise *vt* -ED/-ING/-S [ME *croisen*, fr. OF *croisier*, fr. *crois* cross, fr. L *cruc-, crux* — more at RIDGE] *obs* **:** to make the sign of the cross on or over (a person) esp. in sanctification of a vow to fight the foes of Christianity

[2]**croi·sé** \krə¦wä¦zā, (')krwä-\ *adj* [F, fr. past part. of *croiser* to cross, fr. OF *croisier*] **:** with the legs crossed and the body at an oblique angle to the audience — used of a ballet pose

crois·es \'krȯizəz\ *n pl* [F *croisés*, pl. of *croisé*, fr. OF *croisié*, fr. past part. of *croisier*] *archaic* **:** persons croised as crusaders

crois·sant \krə¦wä¦sän, (')krwä-\ *n, pl* **croissants** \-än(z)\ [F, lit., crescent — more at CRESCENT] **:** a rich crescent-shaped roll ⟨reading the newspaper with my coffee and ~ —Noel Barber⟩

croix·an \'krȯiən\ *adj, usu cap* [fr. *Croixan*, subdivision of the American Cambrian, fr. Saint *Croix*, county & river in Wisconsin + E *-an*] **:** of or relating to a subdivision of the American Cambrian — see GEOLOGIC TIME table

cro·jack \'kräjik\ *n* -s [by alter.] **:** CROSSJACK

cro·ker sack \'krōkə(r)-\ *n* [alter. of [2]*crocus*] *chiefly South* **:** a sack made of crocus **:** a burlap bag

cro·ki·nole \'krōkə,nōl\ *n* -s [F *croquignole* fillip, fr. MF, irreg. fr. *croquer* to crunch] **:** a game resembling squails ⟨a ~ board⟩ ⟨a ~ party⟩

cro–magnon \krō'magnən, -maig- *also* -g,nän *or* -manyən *or* -märy- *or* -n,yän; *or as F*\ *n* -s *usu cap C&M* [fr. *Cro-Magnon*, a cave near Les Eyzies, Dordogne dept., France, where type specimens were found] **1 :** a tall erect race of men having large faces and deep-set eyes known from skeletal remains found with Aurignacian artifacts chiefly in southern France and regarded by some anthropologists as the substratum of the modern European population or even as surviving in comparative purity in local areas ⟨*Cro-Magnon* race⟩ ⟨*Cro-Magnon* skeletons⟩ **2 :** an Upper Paleolithic European man including such diverse forms as the Brünn and Grimaldi races

crom·bec \'kräm,bek\ *n* -s [F, fr. Afrik *krombek*, fr. *krom* crooked (fr. MD *crom*) + *bek* beak, fr. MD *bec*, fr. OF; akin to OHG *krump, krumpf* crooked — more at CRUMP, BEAK] **:** any of numerous small short-tailed African warblers constituting a genus (*Sylvietta*) of the family Sylviidae and widely distributed in dry open country

crome \'krōm\ *n* -s [ME *crome, crombe, cromp*, prob. fr. MD *crampe* hook, cramp — more at CRAMP] *now dial Eng* **:** HOOK; *also* **:** a fork or staff with a hook at the end

cromeski *or* **cromesqui** *var of* KROMESKI

crom·lech \'kräm,lek, -ek\ *n* -s [W, fr. *crom* (fem. of *crwm* bent) + *llech* slate, flat stone; akin to LGk *krambos* dry, withered and to OIr *lie* stone, Bret *lia* — more at RUMPLE] **1 :** DOLMEN **2 :** a circle of monoliths usu. enclosing a dolmen or mound

cro·mor·na \krō'mȯrnə, krə'-\ *also* **cre·mo·na** \krə'mōnə\ *n* -s [modif. of F *cromorne*] **:** a reed stop in the organ usu. of 8-foot pitch

cro·morne \krō'mȯrn, krə'-\ *n* -s [F, fr. G *krummhorn*, fr. *krumm* crooked (fr. OHG *krump*) + *horn*, fr. OHG — more at CRUMP, HORN] **1 :** CROMORNA **2 :** KRUMMHORN

crom·wel·li·an \(')kräm¦welēən\ *adj, usu cap* [Oliver *Cromwell* †1658 "lord protector" of England + E *-ian*] **1 :** of, relating to, or suggestive of Cromwell or the period of Puritan ascendancy in England or to its politics or methods **2 :** of or relating to a style of furniture in vogue under the Protectorate and early Restoration characterized by straight lines, refined moldings, and simplicity of ornament

cromwellian chair *n, usu cap 1st C* **:** a square low-backed chair of simple design having turned legs and usu. covered with leather fastened by metal nails

cro·nar·ti·um \krō'närshēəm, -rd·ēəm\ *n, cap* [NL] **:** a genus of rust fungi (family Melampsoraceae) having aecia produced in raised or swollen sori and teliospores borne in waxy pillars or columns — see WHITE PINE BLISTER RUST

crone \'krōn\ *n* -s [ME, fr. ONF *carogne* carrion, hag, fr. (assumed) VL *caronia* — more at CARRION] **1 :** a withered old woman esp. in humble circumstances ⟨an old half-witted ~ whom peasants called a witch —Ernest Poole⟩ **2 :** an old man useless or womanish from senility **3** [prob. fr. obs D *karonje*, *kronje* old ewe, hag (now "hussy"), fr. MD *cronghe* hag, fr. ONF *carogne*] **:** an old ewe

Cromwellian chair

[1]**cronk** \'kräŋk, 'krȯŋk\ *n* -s [imit.] **:** a hoarse croak (as of a raven) or honk (as of a wild goose)

[2]**cronk** \"\ *vi* -ED/-ING/-S **:** to make a croaking or honking noise ⟨the wild-goose wedge . . . ~*s* harsh —W.P.Johnston⟩

[3]**cronk** \"\ *adj* [Yiddish or G *krank*, fr. MHG *kranc* weak — more at CRANK] **1** *slang Austral* **a :** SICK, AILING **b :** INFIRM, UNSOUND **2** *slang Austral* **:** FRAUDULENT, DISHONEST

cron·stedt·ite \'krän,stedˌīt\ *n* -s [G *cronstedit*, fr. Baron Axel F. *Cronstedt* †1765 Sw. mineralogist + G *-it* -ite] **:** a mineral consisting of a black hydrous iron silicate of the chlorite group, crystallizing in hexagonal prisms with perfect basal cleavage, and showing a dark green streak (sp. gr. 3.34–3.35)

[1]**cro·ny** \'krōnē, -ni\ *n* -ES [fr. earlier *chrony* (university slang), perh. fr. Gk *chronios* long-lasting, fr. *chronos* time] **:** an intimate companion esp. of long standing **:** a familiar friend **:** an old chum

[2]**crony** \"\ *vi* -ED/-ING/-ES **:** to associate intimately ⟨~ with a person⟩

cro·ny·ism \-nē,izəm, -ni,iz-\ *n* -s **:** partiality to cronies esp. as evidenced in the appointing of political hangers-on to office without due regard being taken of their qualifications

[1]**crooch** \'krüch\ *vb* -ED/-ING/-ES [ME *crouchen* — more at CROUCH] *dial* **:** [1]CROUCH

[2]**crooch** \"\ *n* -ES *dial* **:** [2]CROUCH

crood \'krüd\ *vi* -ED/-ING/-S [imit.] *Scot* **:** COO

[1]**croo·dle** \'krüd°l\ *vi* -ED/-ING/-S [freq. of *crood*] *dial Brit* **:** to make a low murmuring sound

[2]**croodle** \"\ *vi* -ED/-ING/-S [prob. freq. of Sc *crood* to crowd, fr. ME *crouden* — more at CROWD] **1** *dial Brit* **:** to huddle together (as from cold); *also* **:** CUDDLE, SNUGGLE **2** *dial Brit* **:** COWER, CROUCH

[1]**crook** \'krůk\ *n* -s [ME *crok*, fr. ON *krōkr* hook; akin to OHG *krācho* hook-shaped tool, ON *kraki* pole with a hook, Gk *gyrgathos* wicker basket, Latvian *gredzens* ring, OE *cradol* cradle — more at CRADLE] **1 :** any implement having a bent or hooked form: as **a** *obs* **:** SICKLE **b :** hook (as a pothook) **c :** the hinge of a gate or door **d** *archaic* **:** (1) the staff used by a shepherd (2) CROSIER 2 **2 a** *obs* **:** a piece of trickery **:** ARTIFICE, SUBTERFUGE **b :** a person given to crooked or fraudulent practices **:** SWINDLER, THIEF ⟨what the insurance ~ does is always the same: fakes an accident and claims . . . damages —Henry La Cossitt⟩ **3 a** *obs* **:** a bending of the knee or body in reverence **b :** the act or action of bending **4 a :** a portion of something that is hook-shaped, curved, or bent ⟨the ~s of a river⟩ ⟨the ~ of an umbrella handle⟩ **b** (1) **:** a small tube inserted in the tube of a trumpet or horn to change its pitch or key (2) **:** the curved tube carrying the mouthpiece of a bassoon **c :** a longitudinal warp in a piece of lumber determined by its deviation from a straight line drawn from one edge at one end to the corresponding edge at the opposite end **5 :** an angular or odd-shaped bit of land **6** *usu pl, obs* **:** BRACKET 4b

crook 1d (1)

[2]**crook** \"\ *vb* **crooked** \-kt\ **crooked** \"\ **crooking; crooks** [ME *croken*, fr. *crok*, n.] *vt* **1 :** to turn from a straight line **:** BEND ⟨*crooked* his neck in order to get a better view —Hamilton Basso⟩ **2** *obs* **:** to twist perversely **:** MISAPPLY **3** *slang* **a :** to make dishonest or ineffective **:** cause to go wrong ⟨~ a deal⟩ **b :** CHEAT ⟨you wouldn't ~ a friend, would you?⟩ **c :** to obtain or manipulate dishonestly or by fraud ⟨he was living pretty much from supplies ~*ed* from the army⟩ ~ *vi* **1 :** BEND, CURVE, WIND ⟨a river ~*ing* through a valley⟩ ⟨sunflowers, ~*ing* over in the sun —William Goyen⟩ **2** *archaic* **:** to bow (as in obeisance) **3** *obs* **:** to turn from a straight or direct course

[3]**crook** \"\ *adj* [perh. alter. of [3]*cronk*] **1** *Austral* **a :** physically unwell **:** SICK ⟨~ with the flu⟩ **b :** out of sorts **:** ANGRY, ILL-HUMORED, IRRITABLE — often used with *go* ⟨he's going ~ at the men for not working⟩ **2** *Austral* **a :** out of order **:** not in proper working condition ⟨something ~ with the car⟩ **b :** poorly suited **:** UNSATISFACTORY ⟨a ~ place for a dance —not enough girls —Nevil Shute⟩

crookback \'=,=\ *n* **1** *obs* **:** a crooked back **2** *obs* **:** HUNCHBACK

crookbacked \'=,=\ *adj* **:** HUMPBACKED ⟨those poor babes their ~ uncle murdered —H.H.Milman⟩

crookbill \'=,=\ *n* **:** WRYBILL

crook·ed \'krůkəd\ *adj, sometimes* -ER/-EST [ME *croked*, partly fr. *crok*, n. + *-ed*, partly fr. past part. of *croken* to crook] **1 :** having or distinguished by a crook or curve **:** not straight **:** BENT, TWISTED ⟨a ~ road⟩ ⟨the pictures on a wall are ~⟩ ⟨an aged man with a ~ frame⟩ **2 :** not straightforward **:** deviating from rectitude ⟨~ dealings⟩; *esp* **:** FRAUDULENT, DISHONEST ⟨~ politicians⟩ ⟨a ~ business⟩ ⟨~ profits⟩ — **crook·ed·ly** *adv*

crooked-foot \'==,=\ *n* **:** a deformity of a horse's hoof due to irregular growth induced by improper trimming and shoeing

crook·ed·ness \-kədnəs\ *n* -ES [ME *crokednesse*, fr. *croked* + *-nesse* -ness] **1 :** the quality or state of being crooked **2 :** DISHONESTY

crooked stick \'==,'=\ *n, dial* **:** a worthless or idle man; *esp* **:** one not fitting into society ⟨she picked up a *crooked stick* for a husband⟩

crooked-wood \'==,=\ *n* **:** BUTTONBUSH

crook·en \'krůkən\ *vb* -ED/-ING/-S [[1]*crook* + *-en*] *dial Brit* **:** BEND, CROOK ⟨a . . . *crookened*-limbed speck of a dwarf —*Irish Statesman*⟩

crook·ery \'krůkərē, -ri\ *n* -ES [[1]*crook* (swindler) + *-ery*] **:** crooked dealings or practices ⟨all the ~ exposed in the Internal Revenue Bureau —*New Orleans States*⟩ ⟨unmasks the ~ of a fellow journalist —*Time*⟩

crookes dark space \'krůks-\ *n, usu cap C* [after Sir William *Crookes* †1919 Eng. physicist] *physics* **:** a dark space between the cathode glow and the negative glow — called also *cathode dark space*

crookes glass *n, usu cap C* [after Sir Wm. *Crookes*] **:** one of several types of glass designed to diminish the transmission of ultraviolet rays

crookes·ite \'krůk,sīt\ *n* -s [F, fr. Sir Wm. *Crookes* + F *-ite*] **:** a mineral $(Cu,Tl,Ag)_2Se$ consisting of selenide of copper, thallium, and silver occurring in lead-gray metallic-looking masses (sp. gr. 6.9)

crookes tube *n, usu cap C* [after Sir Wm. *Crookes*] **:** a vacuum tube evacuated to a pressure of about .04 mm of mercury for demonstrating the properties of cathode rays

crookneck \'=,=\ *n* [[1]*crook* + *neck*] **1 :** any of numerous bush or vining squashes that are characterized by elongated tapering recurved necks: as **a :** SUMMER CROOKNECK **b :** WINTER CROOKNECK **2 a :** a disease of tobacco producing one-sided development of the midribs of the leaves **b :** a copper and zinc deficiency disease of pineapples

crooks *pl of* CROOK, *pres 3d sing of* CROOK

crool \'krül\ *vi* -ED/-ING/-S [imit.] **:** to make a repeated low, liquid, or gurgling sound ⟨a ~*ing* dove⟩

croo·mia \'krümēə\ *n* [NL, fr. H. B. *Croom* †1837 Amer. botanist + NL *-ia*] **1** *cap* **:** a genus of herbs (family Stemonaceae) of the southern U.S. having horizontal rootstocks, leaves near the top of the stem, and nodding flowers **2** -s **:** a plant of the genus *Croomia*

croo monkey \'krü-\ *n* [origin unknown] **:** CRAB-EATING MACAQUE

[1]**croon** \'krün\ *vb* -ED/-ING/-S [ME *croynen* to bellow, fr. MD *cronen;* akin to OHG *krōnen* to chatter, beat, L *gingrire* to honk (of geese), Gk *gingras* Phoenician flute, MIr *grith* cry, Skt *jarate* he cries — more at CRANE] *vi* **1** *chiefly Scot* **a :** to make a continuous hollow sound **:** low (as of cattle) **:** boom (as of a bell) **b :** LAMENT, WAIL, MOAN ⟨~*ing* for her lost child⟩ **2 a :** to make a continued moaning sound ⟨with the doctor's fiddle ~*ing* away down the corridor —Hervey Allen⟩ ⟨the wind ~*ing* in the trees⟩; *specif* **:** to sing in a gentle murmuring manner and often wordlessly ⟨~ over a baby⟩ **b :** to sing in half voice esp. into a closely held microphone ~ *vt* **1 :** to sing (as a lullaby, song, or lament) in a crooning manner ⟨~ a hit song⟩ **2 :** to sing to in a soft composing manner **:** LULL ⟨~ a child to sleep⟩

[2]**croon** \"\ *n* -s **1 :** the sound made in crooning (as low murmuring, humming, or singing) **:** LAMENT **2 :** a song that is crooned or adapted to crooning

croon·er \-nə(r)\ *n* -s **:** one that croons; *specif* **:** a singer of popular songs who uses a soft-voice technique adapted to amplifying systems

croose *var of* CROUSE

[1]**crop** \'kräp\ *n* -s [ME, fr. OE *cropp* craw, cluster, head of a plant; akin to OHG *kropf* goiter, craw, ON *kroppr* torso, body, OE *crēopan* to creep — more at CREEP] **1 a** *now Scot* **:** the top, head, or highest part orig. of an herb, flower, or tree **b :** FINIAL **c :** the upper part of a whip **:** the stock or handle of a whip; *specif* **:** a riding whip with a short straight stock and a loop **d :** OUTCROP **2 a :** an enlargement of the gullet of many birds that forms a pouch which serves as a receptacle for the food and for its preliminary maceration **b** *dial, of a human* **:** STOMACH; *also* **:** THROAT **c :** an enlargement of the gullet of some animals (as insects) **3 :** something that has been cut or trimmed or that is the result of cutting and trimming: as **a :** the part of the chine of a quadruped (as a domestic cow) lying immediately behind the withers — usu. used in pl.; see COW illustration **b** *dial* **:** a cut of meat from this region **:** short ribs or spareribs **c :** the portion of tanned hide resulting from cutting in half along backbone and then trimming off the belly **4 a :** an earmark on an animal; *esp* **:** one made by a straight cut squarely removing the upper part of the ear **b** [[2]*crop*] **:** a close cut of the hair; *also* **:** a style of wearing the hair cut short **5 :** the end or ends of an ingot, billet, slab, bar, or other semifinished metallic mill product cut off and discarded because of defects **6 a** (1) **:** a plant or animal or plant or animal product that can be grown and harvested extensively for profit or subsistence ⟨an apple ~⟩ ⟨a maple-sugar ~⟩ ⟨a ~ of foals⟩ (2) *in turpentine orcharding* **:** the working unit generally equal to 10,000 boxes and usu. coming from a tract of timber of some 250 acres comprising about 5000 trees **b :** the product or yield of anything formed together ⟨a ~ of garnets⟩ ⟨the ice ~⟩ **c :** a batch or lot (as of something produced during a particular cycle) **:** COLLECTION ⟨a ~ of lies⟩ ⟨a ~ of war babies⟩ ⟨it was there the more unscrupulous whaling captains got their bumper ~ of hands —H.A.Chippendale⟩ ⟨a bumper ~ of best stories —Bennett Cerf⟩ **7 :** the total yearly production from a specified area ⟨the local grange reported that the county corn ~ had never been better⟩

[2]**crop** \"\ *vb* **cropped; cropped; cropping; crops** [ME *croppen*, fr. *crop*, n. (top)] *vt* **1 a :** to cut off (as the top or upper or outer parts of a tree or plant) **:** lop off ⟨~ branches⟩; *specif* **:** to trim esp. by the cutting off of grass, leaves, buds, or twigs ⟨~ a hedge⟩ ⟨*cropped* lawns⟩ **b** (1) **:** to clip off the tops of (the ears) as a means of identifying animals or formerly as a punishment for criminals (2) **:** to trim (the wattles of a bird) — compare DUB **c :** to shear (cloth) **d :** to cut (the hair) close ⟨these Indians *cropped* their hair above the eyebrows and along the nape of the neck —Alfred Métraux & Curt Nimuendajú⟩ **e** (1) **:** to trim (as a book) too close to the printed matter (2) **:** to cut off or mask out unwanted parts of (as a photograph that is to be engraved or an overlarge halftone cut) (3) **:** to trim down arbitrarily **:** excise to suit one's purposes ⟨he relied on *cropped* passages from the Old Testament —*Time*⟩ **2 a** *now dial Brit* **:** to gather (as flowers) **:** PLUCK **b :** to gather by or as if by cutting **:** REAP, HARVEST ⟨a continuous *cropping* of forest lands —E.S.Mason⟩ ⟨the number of trout *cropped* each year⟩ **3 :** to feed or graze on esp. by biting off the tenderer shoots **:** BROWSE ⟨sheep *cropping* a meadow⟩ **4 a :** to cause (land) to bear produce **:** PLANT, CULTIVATE ⟨after the land has been *cropped* for about three years it is allowed to revert to bush —Madeline Manoukian⟩ **b :** to grow as a crop ⟨potatoes are *cropped* in the valley⟩ ~ *vi* **1 :** to feed on grass **:** GRAZE ⟨it was so quiet that I could hear the sheep *cropping* —Mary Webb⟩ **2 a :** to yield a crop ⟨the berry bushes were in their first season but *cropped* well⟩ **b :** FARM, CULTIVATE ⟨he ~s far more heavily than in the North —*McGill News*⟩; *specif* **:** to farm as a sharecropper ⟨I tried to get hold of Tom . . . and found he was *cropping* at a Mr. Bannerman's —Caroline Gordon⟩ **3 a :** to appear at the surface **:** OUTCROP ⟨the rocks which ~ out on the Allegheny plateau —*Jour. of Geol.*⟩ **b :** to turn up or appear unexpectedly or casually ⟨problems kept *cropping* up⟩ ⟨the naïveté that ~s out in his work⟩

[1]**crop-bound** \'=,=\ *adj, of poultry* **:** having the crop distended and paralyzed from overeating or from swallowing coarse fibrous matter

[2]**crop-bound** \"\ *n* **:** the condition of crop-bound poultry

crop duster *n* **:** one that sprays crops with fungicidal or insecticidal dust from a low-flying airplane ⟨ex-Air Force pilot who has become a *crop duster* —Henry Cavendish⟩

crop-dusting \'=,==\ *n* **:** the application of fungicidal or insecticidal dusts to crops esp. from an airplane

crop-ear \'=,=\ *n* **:** a person or animal whose ears have been cropped

crop-eared \'=¦=\ *adj* **1 :** having the ears cropped ⟨a *crop-eared* horse⟩ **2 :** having the hair cropped so that the ears are conspicuous — used esp. of the English Puritans

crop-full \'=¦=\ *adj* **:** having a full crop or stomach **:** OVERFULL ⟨a person *crop-full* of news —Scott Fitzgerald⟩

crop grass *n* **1 :** YARD GRASS **2 :** a crab grass (*Digitaria sanguinalis*) ⟨struggled all summer to rid the lawn of *crop grass*⟩

crophead \'=,=\ *n* **:** the top of an ingot

crop-headed \'=¦==\ *adj* **:** having the hair of the head cut close

crop index *n* **:** the number that expresses the relative yield of the crops on a particular area with the average yield over an entire region being taken as 100

crop insurance *n* **:** insurance available to farmers against loss or damage to growing crops as a result of natural hazards (as hail, drought, flood, insects)

cropland \'=,land, -aa(ə)nd\ *n* **:** land that is suited to or used for crops

crop·man \-,man, -,mən\ *n, pl* **cropmen :** a scrap remover in a rolling mill

crop mark *n* **:** any of the marks used to indicate places where a drawing or photograph is to be cropped

crop meter *n* **:** an instrument connected to an automobile speedometer and used to register mileage of fields of each crop growing adjacent to a road

crop-milk \'=,=\ *n* **:** a secretion resembling milk that is produced in the crop of certain pigeons and doves and used to feed the young

crop pasture *n* **:** a field on which a crop (as corn, soybeans, or peanuts) is allowed to become fairly mature before animals are grazed on it

cropped *past of* CROP

[1]**crop·per** \'kräpə(r)\ *n* -s [ME, fr. *croppen* to crop + *-er*] one that crops: as **a** (1) **:** one that raises produce; *specif* **:** SHARECROPPER ⟨returned to the soil as ~s and later as tenants —*Amer. Guide Series: Tenn.*⟩ (2) **:** a market gardener who raises special crops out of season **b :** a plant that yields a crop ⟨this raspberry is a good ~⟩ **c :** a worker who cuts hides into crops and butt bends — called also *carver* **d** (1) **:** any of various workers who shear textiles, metals, or leather (2) **:** a machine for doing this work

[2]**cropper** \"\ *n* -s [[1]*crop* (gullet) + *-er*] **:** a pigeon resembling the pouter

[3]**cropper** \"\ *n* -s [perh. fr. [1]*crop* (neck) + *-er*] **1 :** a severe fall ⟨first time in the saddle he got an awful ~⟩ **2 :** a sudden or violent failure or collapse ⟨his delusions and the ~s they cost him —Edmund Wilson⟩ — often used with *come* ⟨to see their betters come a ~ —Tyrone Guthrie⟩

croppie *var of* CRAPPIE

cropping *pres part of* CROP

crop·py \'kräpē\ *n* -ES [[2]*crop* + *-y*] **:** one of the Irish rebels of 1798 who wore their hair cut close to the head as a token of sympathy with the French Revolution

crop rotation *n* **:** the practice of growing different crops in succession on the same land chiefly to preserve the productive power of the soil

crops *pl of* CROP, *pres 3d sing of* CROP

crop seed *n* **:** small sweet potatoes culled from the regular crop for use as seed stock — compare SLIP SEED

cropsick \'=,=\ *adj* [[1]*crop* (stomach) + *sick*] *now dial Eng* **:** sick from excess in eating or drinking

cropweed \'=,=\ *n* **:** KNAPWEED

crop worm *n* **:** any of several nematode worms (as members of the genus *Capillaria*) that invade the mucosa of the crop of domestic poultry

[1]**cro·quet** \(')krō¦kā\ *n* -s [F dial., hockey stick, fr. ONF, shepherd's crook — more at CROCKET] **1 :** a game in which players drive wooden balls with mallets through a series of wickets set out on a lawn in a particular order — compare ROQUE **2 :** the driving away of another's ball in the game of croquet by striking one's own placed in contact with it

[2]**croquet** \"\ *vb* -ED/-ING/-S *vt* **:** to drive away (another's ball) in the game of croquet by striking one's own ball placed against the other ball ~ *vi* **:** to croquet another's ball

croquet set

cro·quette \(')krō¦ket, *usu* -ed·+V\ *n* -s [F, fr. *croquer* to crunch (of imit. origin) + *-ette*] **:** a small cone-shaped or rounded mass consisting usu. of minced fowl, meat, or vegetable coated with egg and bread crumbs and fried in deep fat ⟨sweet potato ~s⟩ ⟨chicken ~s⟩

cro·qui·gnole \'krōkə,nōl *also* -kən,yōl\ *n* -s [F, a kind of biscuit, irreg. fr. *croquer* to crunch] **:** a method used in waving the hair by winding it on curlers from the ends of the hair toward the scalp

cro·quill \'krō,kwil\ *n* -s [by alter.] **:** CROW QUILL

cro·quis \(')krō¦kē\ *n, pl* **croquis** \-ē(z)\ [F, fr. *croquer* to crunch, know a person slightly, sketch] **:** a sketch or study; *esp* **:** a preparatory drawing or design for a projected work of art ⟨the design and layout started with ~ or thumbnail sketches —Fred Freeman⟩

crore \'krō(ə)r\ *n, pl* **crores** *also* **crore** [Hindi *karor*] **:** ten million ⟨100 ~ of rupees⟩; *specif* **:** a unit of value equal to ten million rupees or 100 lakhs

cro·sier *or* **cro·zier** \'krōzhə(r)\ *n* -s [ME *croser*, fr. MF *crossier* staff bearer, fr. *crosse* pastoral staff (fr. OF *croce*, of Gmc. origin; akin to OHG *krucka* crutch) + *-ier* -er — more at CRUTCH] **1** *obs* **a :** the bearer of the pastoral staff of a bishop **b :** the bearer of a cross before an archbishop **2 :** the pastoral staff of a bishop, abbot, or abbess resembling a shepherd's crook and borne as a symbol of the pastoral office; *also* **:** the processional cross or cross-staff of an archbishop in the Church of England **3 :** any botanical structure with a curled, coiled, or circinate end (as the young frond of a fern)

cro·siered \'krōzhə(r)d\ *adj* **:** bearing or having a crosier

crosnes *also* **crosne** \'krōn\ *n, pl* **crosnes** \-nz\ [F, fr. *Crosnes*, town near Corbeil, France, where it was first cultivated] **:** CHINESE ARTICHOKE

crosier 2

[1]**cross** \'krȯs *also* 'kräs\ *n* -ES [ME *cros, crosse*, fr. OE *cros*, fr.

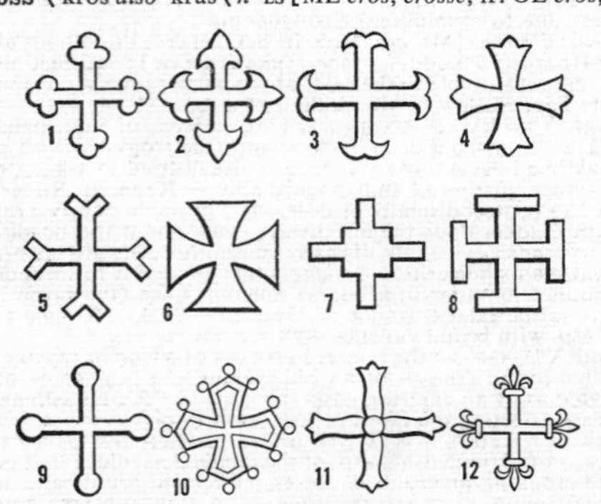

crosses 5a: *1* botonée, *2* fleury, *3* moline, *4* patonce, *5* fourchée, *6* formée, *7* quadrate, *8* potent, *9* pommée, *10* clechée, *11* avellan, *12* fleurettée

ON or OIr; ON *kross*, fr. (assumed) OIr *cross* (whence MIr), fr. L *crux* — more at RIDGE] **1 a :** a structure usu. consisting of an upright with a transverse beam used esp. by the ancient Romans as a means of execution ⟨the slave who revolted was fastened to a ~⟩ — see CRUCIFY, CRUX COMMISSA, CRUX DECUSSATA, CRUX IMMISSA **b** *often cap* **:** the cross on which Jesus Christ was crucified ⟨the day when Jesus died on the *Cross*⟩ **2 a :** CRUCIFIXION ⟨the penalty of the ~⟩; *specif* **:** the crucifixion and death of Jesus Christ regarded as the culmination of his mission of redemption ⟨by thy *Cross* and Passion . . . Good Lord, deliver us —Litany in *Bk. of Com. Prayer*⟩ **b :** the gospel of redemption through the death of Jesus Christ ⟨the doctrine of the ~, as the one great rule and hope of the world —G.A. Poole⟩ **3 :** an affliction or trial regarded as a test of Christian steadfastness, patience, or virtue — often used in the phrase *bear one's cross, take one's cross,* or *take up one's cross* with allusion to such biblical passages as Mt 10: 38, 16: 24, 27: 32; *broadly* **:** any affliction, trial, or trouble ⟨it was Ian's ~ to be a social coward —Hamilton Basso⟩ **4 :** SIGN OF THE CROSS **5 a :** a device or emblem composed essentially of an upright bar traversed by or joined at the top to a horizontal one but found in many varying types and used by people of various cultures as a symbol having any of various meanings, or as an amulet, and adopted by Christians because of its resemblance to the instrument of Jesus' crucifixion as a symbol of the culmination of his mission of redemption through his death or as a symbol of the Christian faith, a Christian people, or Christendom, and also widely used without specific religious symbolism in countries having a predominantly Christian background — see CALVARY CROSS, CELTIC CROSS, CROSS-CROSSLET, CROSS OF LORRAINE, GREEK CROSS, LATIN CROSS, MALTESE CROSS, PAPAL CROSS, PATRIARCHAL CROSS, SAINT ANDREW'S CROSS, TAU CROSS **b :** something that this device or emblem symbolizes (as Christianity or Christendom) ⟨to fight for the ~⟩ **6 a :** a cross-shaped badge, ornament, or article of ecclesiastical furniture used as a religious emblem **b :** a staff surmounted by a cross or crucifix borne in religious processions; *specif* **:** CROSS-STAFF 1 **7 a :** a monument or other structure in the form of a cross or surmounted by a cross ⟨a boundary ~⟩ ⟨a ~ over a grave⟩; *esp* **:** a cross set up in the center or market place of a town **b** *now Scot* **:** MARKET **8 :** a figure or mark formed by two intersecting lines or bars usu. of equal or approximately equal length and crossing at or about their midpoints (as + or ×) ⟨written in warm terms with plenty of ~*es* indicating kisses —L.A.Norris⟩ ⟨the morning star, represented by a ~ —L.H.Appleton⟩ ⟨a single ~ placed opposite one of the party names and counted as a vote —F.A.Ogg & P.O.Ray⟩; *specif* **:** such a cross (as in ink or pencil) used as a signature — see CHRISTCROSS **9 a :** a badge or emblem of an order of chivalry or a decoration of honor having the form of a cross or of a number of rays, often more or less than four, radiating from a common center — compare CROSS OF FOURTEEN POINTS **b :** one entitled to wear such a badge or emblem ⟨he is a Victoria *Cross*⟩ **10** *archaic* **a :** a cross-shaped impression on a coin **b :** a coin having such an impression **11** *heraldry* **:** an ordinary having the form of a pale and a fess combined intersecting in the center of the field **12 :** a pipe fitting with four branches the axes of which usu. form right angles **13 :** a piece of fur made of sections or of whole skins sewed in the form of a cross **14 :** any device or emblem of an extensive category that includes not only the cross (sense 5a) in all of its varieties but also various other devices of which a cross forms a part (as the swastika) or which are analogous to the cross ⟨as early as 317 B.C., the coins of Sicily bear the three-armed ~ as a symbol —E.S.Holden⟩ — see ANKH; compare TRISKELION **15** *obs* **:** a transverse part of an object (as the cross guard of a sword or dagger, the stock of an anchor, or the cross stroke on a letter *t*) **16** *obs* **:** a position wherein one thing rests over another in the form of a cross — used with *in* or *on* **17** *archaic* **:** the intersection of two ways or lines **:** CROSSING **18 :** an accidental contact between two electrical conductors **19 :** THWARTING, VEXATION, ANNOYANCE ⟨a ~ in love⟩ **20 a :** an act of crossing (as between breeds, races, or kinds of individuals) ⟨his first ~ of radish and cabbage was unsuccessful⟩ **b :** a crossbred individual or kind **:** a product of crossing ⟨the blue-gray ~ resulting from breeding a Galloway cow to a white Shorthorn bull exhibits outstanding beef conformation⟩ **c :** one that combines characteristics of two different types or individuals ⟨a ~ between a hiss and a spit —H.J.Laski⟩ **21 a :** something that is not honest or fair (as a contest) **:** something fraudulent or predeterminedly dishonest ⟨I never fought a ~ or struck a foul blow in my life —G.B.Shaw⟩ **b :** dishonest or illegal practices — used esp. in the phrase *on the cross* ⟨he earned money mostly on the ~⟩; see DOUBLE CROSS **22 :** a motion that intersects or goes across: as **a :** a movement from one part of the stage of a theater to another or from one side to the other **b :** a hook crossed over the opponent's lead in boxing — usu. used with *right* or *left* ⟨I caught him off guard with . . . a lucky right ~ —G.A.Hamid⟩ **syn** see TRIAL — **in cross 1** *of four heraldic bearings* **:** two in upright and two in horizontal position so as to approach or join at a common center ⟨four lozenges conjoined *in cross*⟩ **2** *of four or more heraldic bearings* **:** arranged as if along the arms of a cross ⟨four mullets *in cross*⟩ — **per cross** *heraldry* **:** divided into four parts by an upright and a horizontal line crossing each other **:** QUARTERLY

[2]**cross** \"\ *vb* **crossed** *also* **crost; crossed** *also* **crost; crossing; crosses** [ME *crossen*, fr. *cros*, n.] *vt* **1 a :** to lie or be situated across ⟨the bandoliers ~*ed* his chest⟩ ⟨the point where the two braces ~ each other⟩ **b :** INTERSECT ⟨the two lines ~ each other at right angles⟩; *specif* **:** to intersect (one another) as pairs so that each member of one pair meets each

member of the other — used in mathematics of two pairs of lines in space **2 :** to fasten (a sail or yard) across a mast ⟨the sails were ~*ed* and the voyage begun⟩ **3 a :** to make the sign of the cross upon or over : BLESS ⟨pilgrims ~*ed* by a bishop⟩ ⟨the communicants ~*ed* themselves devoutly and knelt in prayer⟩ **b :** to place a coin in (the hand of a gypsy fortune-teller) when paying for a consultation **c :** to place (one's fingers) in a crossed position (as the middle finger over the index finger) as a gesture intended to bring good luck, to free one from responsibility while telling a lie, or to indicate private reservations when making a statement **d :** to draw a cross over (one's heart) with one's finger as a gesture intended to indicate the absolute truthfulness of a statement **4 a :** to cancel by or as if by marking a cross on or drawing a line through : strike out : ERADICATE — usu. used with *off* or *out* ⟨~ out a bad debt⟩ ⟨~ names off a list⟩ ⟨~ out portions of a text⟩ **b** *obs* **:** to cut off : DEBAR **5 a :** to lay or place crosswise usu. with one above and almost parallel to the other ⟨~ the arms⟩ — often used with *over* ⟨he sat down and ~*ed* one leg over the other⟩ **b :** to arrange in a crisscross pattern ⟨to start a fire first ~ some dry twigs⟩ **c :** to place one's leg over (as a horse or saddle) : sit astride : RIDE ⟨the best pony that was ever ~*ed*⟩ **6 a** (1) **:** to run counter to : OPPOSE ⟨he was ugly if ~*ed*⟩ : THWART ⟨~*ed* in love⟩ (2) **:** to deny the validity of : CONTRADICT ⟨~ a person's statement⟩ **b** (1) *obs* **:** to encounter hostilely : engage in combat with (2) **:** to confront in a troublesome or bothersome manner : OBSTRUCT ⟨the ship was ~*ed* by contrary winds⟩ **c** (1) **:** to spoil completely : DISRUPT — used with *up* ⟨his not appearing ~*ed up* the whole program⟩ (2) **:** to deceive, betray, or turn against — used with up ⟨~ someone up on a deal⟩ **7 a :** to extend from one edge or corner of to the other : TRAVERSE ⟨a highway ~*ing* the entire state⟩ ⟨a forest that ~*es* the length of a valley⟩ **b :** to reach or attain ⟨only two runners ~*ed* the finish line⟩ ⟨the number of accidents ~*ed* the 1000 mark in July⟩ **c** (1) **:** to go from one side of to the opposing side ⟨~ a street⟩ ⟨~ a mine field⟩ (2) **:** to pass over on (as an elevated structure) from one side to the other ⟨~ a bridge⟩ ⟨~ a trestle⟩ **8 a :** to draw a line across or on (as something already drawn) ⟨~ one's *t's*⟩ ⟨~ line A at right angles with a second line B⟩ **b :** to mark or figure with or as if with lines : STREAK ⟨a mineral ~*ed* with irregular yellow lines⟩ **c** *Brit* **:** to draw two parallel lines across the face of (a check) often with *& Co* written between them in order to indicate that payment is to be made only through a bank ⟨if a check is sent it should be ~*ed* and made nonnegotiable —*Australian Home Beautiful*⟩ or to write or print between two parallel lines drawn across the face of (a check) the name of the particular bank through which payment is to be made ⟨checks . . . should be made payable to "The Times Publishing Co., Ltd.," and ~*ed* "Barclays Bank Ltd." —*Times Lit. Supp.*⟩ **9 :** to cause (an animal or plant) to interbreed with another animal or plant of a different race or kind : HYBRIDIZE, CROSS-POLLINATE ⟨improvements were made by ~*ing* mongrel sows with imported boars —E.D.Ross⟩ **10 :** to occur to ⟨an idea ~*ed* me once that he might be an actor —G.B.Shaw⟩ — often used with *mind* ⟨misgivings of every sort ~*ed* my mind⟩ **11 a :** to come upon : MEET ⟨~ an acquaintance on the street⟩ **b :** to meet and pass on the way because of setting out or being sent out at approximately the same time ⟨our letters must have ~*ed* each other⟩ **12 a :** CROSS-PLOW **b** (1) **:** to intersect the path in front of (the bows) of another ship ⟨a destroyer ~*ed* the bows of the transport⟩ (2) **:** to ride across the course of (another horse) in horse racing or polo **13 a :** to carry, transport, or take across ⟨a man bold enough to take his chances could ~ livestock to the Texas side of the river —F.B.Gipson⟩ **b :** to transfer (as from one side to another) — usu. used with *under* or *over* ⟨to tie the knot ~ the right hand under the left⟩ **14 :** to name as trump (a suit) of a different color from the card turned in the game of euchre ~ *vi* **1 a** *obs* **:** to run counter : be at odds — used with *upon* or *with* **b :** to ride across the course of another horse ⟨the jockey claimed there was too much bumping and ~*ing* in the race⟩ **2 :** to move, pass, or extend across something ⟨a path that ~*es* through the garden⟩ ⟨a throw that ~*ed* from left field to first base⟩ ⟨the ship ~*ed* over the equator⟩; *specif* **:** to pass from one side of the theater stage to another — used with *over* **3 :** to lie or be athwart each other ⟨the two highways ~ nearby⟩ **4 :** to meet in passing esp. from opposite directions ⟨our letters ~*ed* in the mail⟩ **5 :** to interbreed (as of two races) : HYBRIDIZE; *specif, of a gene* **:** to pass from one homologous chromosome to another — used with *over;* see CROSSING-OVER — **cross a person's palm** *or* **cross a person's hand** *slang* **:** BRIBE ⟨his palm had been amply ~*ed*⟩ — **cross swords :** to come to grips : be drawn into combat or altercation ⟨*cross swords* with one's landlady over the rent⟩ — **cross the floor** *Brit* **:** to vote with the opposing party on a legislative measure proposed by one's own party — **cross the line** *also* **cross over the line :** to take up status as a white ⟨the place where hundreds of light-skinned persons with a modicum of colored blood *crossed over the line* —Hamilton Basso⟩ — **cross the T :** to maneuver warships in a surface battle so that one's line of ships passes across the bow of the enemy's line of ships and thus all of one's own broadsides can be concentrated on the leading ship of the enemy

³cross \"\ *adj* -ER/-EST [¹*cross*] **1 a :** lying across or athwart ⟨the crazy tangle of ~ wires —H.J.Muller⟩ : extending from one side to the other ⟨~ members should be all steel or metal or equivalent strength —*Bookmobile Specifications*⟩ **b :** moving across : traversing from one side to the other ⟨~ ventilation⟩ ⟨~ traffic⟩ **2** *archaic* **:** not accordant with what is wished or expected : THWARTING, PERVERSE, UNFAVORABLE ⟨bowed down by a ~ fortune⟩ ⟨~ weather⟩ **3 :** running counter : OPPOSING, OPPOSITE ⟨a ~ wind⟩ ⟨tugging on some issues in ~ directions —*N.Y.Times*⟩ ⟨ideas ~ to those of most other people⟩; *specif* **:** mutually opposed ⟨working at ~ purposes⟩ **4 :** involving mutual interchange : RECIPROCAL ⟨a system of ~ payments was worked out by the two governments⟩ **5 a** *archaic* **:** CONTENTIOUS, FRACTIOUS, PERVERSE, CONTRARIOUS **b :** marked by bad temper and irritable disposition : easily vexed : SNAPPISH, GRUMPY, PEEVISH ⟨a woman who feels that her future is uncertain . . . can be . . . ~ with her husband and children —Harrison Smith⟩ ⟨a ~ answer⟩ **6 :** extending over, covering, or treating several categories, groups, conditions, or classes — used chiefly in adjective-noun compounds ⟨a *cross*-cultural perspective⟩ ⟨~ sample records of . . . 1800 children —*Amer. Child*⟩ **7 :** CROSSBRED, HYBRID; *specif* **:** heterozygous for a recessive character **syn** see IRASCIBLE

⁴cross \"\ *prep* [by shortening] **:** ACROSS ⟨the daily flight of an eagle back and forth ~ the river to its nest —*Amer. Guide Series: Texas*⟩

⁵cross \"\ *adv* [in sense 1, short for *across;* in other senses, partly fr. ¹*cross,* partly, fr. ³*cross*] **1** *archaic* **:** from side to side : ACROSS, ATHWART **2** *archaic* **:** CONTRARIWISE, UNFAVORABLY **3 :** not parallel : CROSSWISE, CRISSCROSS — used chiefly with verbs ⟨to *cross*-wind wire on a spool⟩

cross- *or* **crosso-** *comb form* [NL, fr. Gk *krossoi* tassels, fringe; akin to OE *ofer*hrǣgan to tower above, MHG *ragen* to tower up, stick up, MD *raghen,* Gk *krossai* coping of a parapet, OIr *crich* end, furrow, Russ *krokva* pole, rafter; basic meaning: jutting out, sticking up] **:** fringe ⟨*Cross*aster⟩ ⟨*crosso*pterygian⟩ ⟨*Crosso*soma⟩

cross·abil·i·ty \ˌkrȯsəˈbiləd·ē *also* ˌkräs-\ *n* **:** the ability of different species or varieties to cross with each other

cross·able \'⸗səbəl\ *adj* **:** capable of being crossed ⟨a river ~ at several points⟩; *specif* **:** capable of crossing : admitting of being crossed ⟨a plant ~ with other varieties⟩

cross action *n* **:** a legal action by a party sued made against the person who has sued him and upon the same subject matter

cross agglutination *n* **:** agglutination of cells of one species by serum of an animal immunized against another usu. closely related species — called also *group agglutination*

cross aisle *n, obs* **:** TRANSEPT

cross and english bond *n, usu cap E* **:** a bond formed by laying the inner part of a wall in one way and the outer part in another

cross and pile *n* [ME; *pile* reverse of a coin, fr. MF, pillar, pier of a bridge, device for stamping coins, reverse of a coin — more at PILE] **1** *archaic* **:** HEADS OR TAILS **2** *archaic* **:** MONEY

crossarm \'⸗,⸗\ *n* **:** an arm fastened at right angles to an upright (as the horizontal member of a cross or a traverse on a telephone pole)

cros·sas·ter \krȯ'sastə(r)\ *n, cap* [NL, fr. *cross-* + *-aster*] **:** a widely distributed genus (family Solasteridae) of brightly colored starfishes including the circumpolar rose star (*C. papposa*)

cross axle *n* **1 :** a shaft, windlass, or roller worked by levers at opposite ends (as in the copperplate printing press) **2 :** a driving axle with cranks set at an angle of 90 degrees

cross-back \"\ *n* [fr. *cross back,* v.] **1 :** the act or action of breeding back a crossbred individual to one of the parent breeds **2 :** the offspring of such breeding

crossband \"\ *adj* **:** *of a twist in textile manufacture* **:** left-hand or S-shaped — compare OPENBAND

crossbanded \'⸗¦⸗⸗\ *adj* **1 :** having or utilizing a crossband ⟨~ construction⟩ **2 :** having crossbanding ⟨a ~ and inlaid table⟩

crossbanding \'⸗¦⸗⸗\ *n* **1** *also* **crossband** \'⸗,⸗\ **:** a piece of veneer (as in a 5-ply panel) glued between the core and an outer ply and having the grain at right angles to that of the core **2 :** a veneer border (as on furniture) with its grain at right angles to the grain of the adjacent wood

crossbar \'⸗,⸗\ *n* **:** a traverse bar: as **a :** the horizontal member of a cross **b :** a horizontal brace : RUNG, ROUND **c :** a traverse bar or stripe esp. on fabrics ⟨a ~ design⟩ **d** (1) **:** a bar within a printer's chase running from top to bottom or from side to side and used to strengthen the chase and facilitate locking (2) **:** a horizontal stroke in a letter (as that joining the upright strokes in A and H) — see TYPE illustration **e** (1) **:** the horizontal bar across the goalposts in football and soccer (2) **:** a loose horizontal bar on uprights used in high jumping (3) **:** HORIZONTAL BAR **f :** the top bar of a bicycle frame **g :** a bar of insulating material to which the blades of a multipole knife switch are attached

cross-barred shell \'⸗,⸗-\ *n* **:** any mollusk of the genus *Cancellaria* or family Cancellariidae — called also *crossbar*

crossbar shot *n* **1 :** a round shot with two projections so that it appears to have a bar running through its center **2 :** an obsolete projectile that folds into a sphere for loading but that on leaving the gun opens into a cross with a quarter ball at the end of each arm

crossbeak \'⸗,⸗\ *n* **:** CROSSBILL

crossbeam \'⸗,⸗\ *n* **:** a traverse beam (as a structural girder or the horizontal member of a cross)

crossbearer \'⸗,⸗⸗\ *n* **:** one that bears a cross: as **a :** an attendant who carries a cross in a religious procession or ceremony : CRUCIFER **b :** a device of transverse bars for supporting the grate bars of a furnace or the planking or roadway of a bridge

cross bearings *n pl* [³*cross*] **:** compass bearings of two or more points taken simultaneously to fix a position (as of a ship)

cross-bedded \'⸗¦⸗⸗\ *adj* [⁵*cross*] **:** having minor beds or laminae lying oblique to the main beds of stratified rock ⟨*cross-bedded* sandstone⟩

cross-bedding \'⸗¦⸗⸗\ *n* **1 :** the quality or state of being cross-bedded **2 :** a cross-bedded structure

crossbelt \'⸗,⸗\ *n* [³*cross* + *belt*] **:** a double belt passing over both shoulders and crossing at the breast or a single belt passing obliquely across the breast ⟨sergeants wearing ~*s* and sidearms⟩

crossbench \'⸗,⸗\ *n, often attrib* [³*cross* + *bench*] **:** one of the benches in the House of Lords of the British parliament which is set at right angles to other benches and on which neutral or independent members sit ⟨a ~ mind⟩ — **crossbencher** \'⸗,⸗⸗\ *n*

cross-bill \'⸗,⸗\ *n* [³*cross*] **1 :** a bill in equity by a defendant against a plaintiff respecting the matter in question in a suit **2 :** a bill of exchange given in return for another

²crossbill \"\ *n* **:** any of several finches constituting a genus (*Loxia*), having a bill adapted to the extraction of seeds from fruits and tree cones by means of strongly curved and overlapping mandibles, and inhabiting coniferous forests of the northern hemisphere — see RED CROSSBILL, WHITE-WINGED CROSSBILL

crossbill

cross-bind \'⸗¦⸗\ *vt* [⁵*cross*] **1 :** to bind or grip (a creeping rail) by placing the outside spikes in advance of inside ones in the direction of creep so that any movement in the tie end caused by the creeping rail will cramp both the inside and outside spikes against the rail **2 :** to arrange (spikes) in such a way as to cross-bind a railroad rail

cross bit *n* **:** a rock drill made with cruciform cutting edges and used in mining

crossbite \'⸗,⸗\ *vt* [⁵*cross* + *bite*] *archaic* **:** to cheat in return : OUTWIT, COZEN

cross-blocking \'⸗¦⸗⸗\ *n* [³*cross*] **:** mechanical thinning of sugar beets or other crops with an implement carrying knives or sweeps driven across the rows

cross-body ride *n* [³*cross*] **:** a wrestling position in which a contestant has a scissors hold on the opponent's near leg and underhooks or overhooks the opponent's far arm

crossbolt \'⸗,⸗\ *n* [³*cross* + *bolt*] **:** a double bolt in a lock having two parts that can be shot simultaneously in opposite directions

crossbolt safety *n* **:** a safety device on certain firearms that utilizes a metal bar which can be positioned to act as a positive block to trigger movement

cross bond *n* [³*cross*] **1 :** a masonry bond in which courses of Flemish bond alternate with courses of stretchers **2 :** an electrical connection between the ground feeder or conductor and the rails of an electric railway or between rails of one or more tracks for equalizing the return current flowing in the rails and for bridging around possible open joint bonds

cross-bond \'⸗¦⸗\ *vt* [*cross bond*] **:** to provide with a cross bond

crossbones \'⸗,⸗\ *n pl* **:** two leg or arm bones placed or depicted crosswise — see SKULL AND CROSSBONES

crossbow \'⸗,⸗\ *n* [ME *crosbowe,* fr. *cros* cross + *bowe* bow (weapon)] **:** a weapon having a short bow mounted crosswise near the end of a wooden stock that resembles the stock of a modern rifle and that is often provided with a mechanical device by which the string is drawn back and fixed and being usu. shot from the shoulder by means of a trigger that releases the string and discharges a quarrel lying in a groove in the stock — see ARBALEST

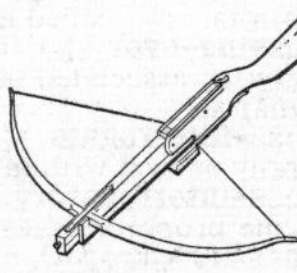

a modern crossbow

crossbowman \'⸗¦⸗mən\ *n, pl* **crossbowmen :** a man (as a soldier or hunter) whose weapon is a crossbow

cross brace *n* **:** a crosspiece that transmits, diverts, or resists weight or pressure

cross bracing *n* **1 :** any system of bracing by means of cross struts or ties; *specif* **:** CROSS BRIDGING **2 :** bracing consisting of two diagonal members which intersect or cross each other

cross break *n* [³*cross*] **:** a separation of wood cells across the grain

¹crossbred \'⸗,⸗\ *adj* [⁵*cross* + *bred*] **1 :** produced by crossing : HYBRID; *specif* **:** produced by interbreeding two pure but different breeds, strains, or varieties **2 :** subjected to cross-breeding

²crossbred \'⸗,⸗\ *n* -S **1 :** a crossbred individual **2 :** CROSS-BRED WOOL

crossbred wool *n* **:** wool from crossbred sheep

¹crossbreed \'⸗¦⸗\ *vb* [⁵*cross* + *breed* (v.)] **:** HYBRIDIZE, CROSS; *esp* **:** to breed between two varieties or breeds of the same species — compare INBREED, INTERBREED, INTERCROSS, LINE-BREED, OUTBREED, OUTCROSS

²crossbreed \'⸗,⸗\ *n* **:** a strain or an individual produced by crossbreeding : HYBRID

cross bridging *n* [³*cross*] **:** traverse rows of small diagonal braces or struts set in pairs and crossing each other between the timbers (as of a floor)

crossbuck \'⸗,⸗\ *n* [¹*cross* + *buck* (as in *sawbuck*)] **:** an X-shaped highway warning sign at a highway-railroad intersection

cross buck *n* [³*cross*] **:** an offensive play in football in which a back faking to receive the ball charges into the line of scrimmage diagonally across the path of the ball carrier

cross-buttock \'⸗¦⸗⸗\ *n* [³*cross*] **:** a throw in wrestling in which a wrestler turns his side to his opponent, places his leg across both legs of his opponent, and pulls him forward over his hip

cross calvary *n, usu cap 2d C* **:** CALVARY CROSS

cross cell *n* [³*cross*] **:** any of certain cells found just below the hypodermis of the wheat grain having long axes at right angles to the pericarp and thin walls with transverse pits and in young grains containing chlorophyll

¹cross-check \'⸗¦⸗\ *vt* [⁵*cross*] **1 :** to obstruct in ice hockey by holding or thrusting one's stick held in both hands across an opponent's face or body **2 :** to check (as data, reports, statements) from various angles or sources to determine accuracy or validity

²cross-check \"\ *n* **1 a :** an illegal cross-checking of an opposing player **b :** an illegal stopping of an opponent by holding the handle of the stick across his body or face in the game of lacrosse **2 a :** an act or action of cross-checking ⟨a *cross-check* made by comparing foreign and domestic news accounts⟩ **b :** a means of cross-checking ⟨lists used as *cross-checks*⟩

cross claim *n* [³*cross*] **:** a claim made by the defendant against the plaintiff and raised in the defendant's answer

cross cleavers *n pl but sing in constr* [so called fr. the fact that its leaves are arranged in sets of four that resemble crosses] **:** a wild licorice (*Galium circaezans*)

cross code *n* **:** a method of communication with the deaf-blind in which taps and strokes in various numbers, combinations, and positions on an imaginary cross usu. on the back of the hand stand for the letters of the alphabet

cross complaint *n* [³*cross*] **:** a complaint used in code pleading whereby a defendant by his answer or separate pleading sets up a claim against a codefendant or a third person arising out of the same subject matter of the original complaint

cross-compound \(¦)⸗+ *pronunc at* COMPOUND *adj* \ *adj* [⁵*cross*] *of a compound engine* **:** having cylinders side by side

cross-connection \'⸗¦⸗⸗\ *n* [³*cross*] **:** a connection in a plumbing installation through which water may possibly pass to or come in contact with another part (as a water inlet in a bathtub that may at times be below the water level of the tub)

cross correspondence *n* [³*cross*] **:** agreement or coherence of messages reputed to have been received by two spiritualist mediums as if fragments from the same control

cross counter *n* [³*cross*] **:** ¹CROSS 22b

¹cross-country \'⸗¦⸗⸗\ *adj* [⁴*cross*] **1 :** extending or moving across a country ⟨a *cross-country* railroad⟩ ⟨a *cross-country* concert tour⟩ **2 a :** proceeding over countryside (as across fields and through woods) and not by roads or paths ⟨a *cross-country* race⟩ **b :** having to do with cross-country sports ⟨a *cross-country* champion⟩

²cross-country \"\ *n* **:** cross-country sports ⟨interest in *cross-country* is growing in eastern colleges⟩; *specif* **:** a cross-country event (as in skiing, horse racing, distance running) — compare LANGLAUF

³cross-country \"\ *adv* **:** across the countryside ⟨a river meandering *cross-country*⟩; by a course going directly over the countryside ⟨a group of tanks moving *cross-country*⟩

cross-cousin \'⸗¦⸗⸗\ *n* [³*cross*] **:** one of two cousins esp. of different sex who are respectively the children of a brother and of a sister ⟨the institution of *cross-cousin* marriage⟩ — compare PARALLEL COUSIN

cross-crosslet \'⸗¦⸗⸗\ *n, pl* **cross-crosslets** *or* **crosses crosslet** [ME *cros croslette,* fr. *cros* cross + *croslette* crosslet] **1 :** CROSSLET 1a **2** *heraldry* **:** a cross wth a crossbar near the end of each arm

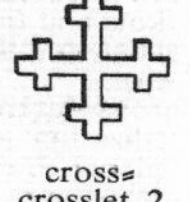

cross-crosslet 2

cross-cultural \'⸗¦(⸗)⸗\ *adj* [⁵*cross*] **:** dealing with or offering comparison between two or more different cultures or cultural areas ⟨assembling data for a *cross-cultural* survey⟩ ⟨a *cross-cultural* investigation of the psychological significance of drama in war among primitive peoples —Lucile H. Charles⟩

crosscurrent \'⸗¦⸗⸗\ *n* [³*cross* + *current*] **1 :** a current traverse to the general forward direction (as of water in a river) **2 :** a conflicting tendency — usu. used in pl. ⟨the political ~*s* that disrupt the business of government⟩

¹crosscut \'⸗¦⸗\ *vt* [⁵*cross* + *cut* (v.)] **:** to cut (something) traversely: as **a :** to cut (as wood) with a crosscut saw **b :** to go or move across ⟨a stream which ~*s* the country from north to south —*Harper's*⟩ **c** (1) **:** INTERSECT ⟨dimensions ~ one another, levels imply parallelism —A.L.Kroeber⟩ (2) **:** to enter into (as a different category) : impinge on ⟨a legal document that ~*s* medical knowledge⟩ **d :** to break up (as an association) : DIVIDE ⟨dissension and jealousy *crosscutting* a political party⟩ **e :** to subject (a film or the lines of action of a film) to crosscutting ⟨the scenario and the technical feat of *crosscutting* the stories are things ingeniously accomplished —Parker Tyler⟩

²crosscut \"\ *adj* **1 :** made or used for crosscutting ⟨a saw with ~ teeth⟩ **2 :** cut across or traversely ⟨a ~ incision⟩

³crosscut \'⸗,⸗\ *n* **1 :** something that cuts through traversely (as a path cutting across countryside or a cut sawed through a log) ⟨a ~ through the park⟩; *specif* **:** a mine working driven horizontally and at right angles to an adit, drift, or level or across or toward a vein or ore body or across the general trend of the rock formation **2 :** CROSS SECTION ⟨a novel that gives a ~ of American business activity⟩ **3 :** an instance of crosscutting in the editing of motion-picture film **4 :** a gemstone cut so that the arrangement of the facets produces an effect resembling that of a cross **5** [¹*crosscut*] **:** a tool that crosscuts; *esp* **:** CROSSCUT SAW

crosscut file *n* **:** a file of uniform width that has a blunt rounded edge on one side tapering to a thin edge on the other and that is used for sharpening saw teeth having straight sides and round gullets

crosscut saw *n* **:** a saw designed chiefly to cut across the grain of wood — compare RIPSAW

crosscut shank *n* **:** a retail cut from the fore shank of a beef — see BEEF illustration

crosscutter \'⸗¦⸗⸗\ *n* **1 :** one that cuts stock lumber into lengths, cuts out imperfections, or squares the ends **2 :** BUCKER b

crosscutting \'⸗¦⸗⸗\ *n* **:** a technique of motion-picture film editing in which fragments of two or more lines of action are intermingled so as to appear alternately in the finished picture

cross-date \'⸗¦⸗\ *vb* [⁵*cross*] *vi* **:** to show by close similarity of spacing, cell structure, and related criteria that certain of the annual rings of two or more different trees or pieces of wood were produced in the same year ~ *vt* **:** to establish (trees or pieces of wood) as cross-dating with each other — compare DENDROCHRONOLOGY

cross dating *n* **:** the correlation of distinctive traits between two or more sites or levels in different localities for purposes of chronology; *specif* **:** the establishment of the date of an archaeological site or level by comparing its distinctive traits with those of another site or level of known date that is assumed to be of similar age

cross direction *n* [³*cross*] **:** the dimension at right angles to the machine direction of a sheet of paper

¹cross-dye \'⸗¦⸗\ *vt* [⁵*cross* + *dye* (v.)] **:** to dye by the process of cross-dyeing

²cross-dye \"\ *n* **1 :** the dye used in cross-dyeing **2 :** a fabric that has been cross-dyed

³cross-dye \'⸗¦⸗\ *adj* **:** treated by or resulting from cross-dyeing ⟨~ rayon⟩ ⟨~ effects⟩

cross dye black RX \-,ä'reks\ *n, usu cap C&D&B* **:** a sulfur dye — see DYE table I (under *Sulfur Black 2*)

cross-dyeing \'⸗¦⸗⸗\ *n* **:** the production by either of two methods of multicolored effects on fabrics woven of more than one kind of fiber (as animal and vegetable fibers) having different affinities for dyes: **a :** the dyeing of a fabric by dyeing one or more kinds of fiber in the fabric with or without subsequent dyeing of the other fibers present **b :** the dyeing of one kind of fiber (as wool) after it has been woven with other fiber (as cotton) already dyed in the form of yarn

crosse \ˈkrȯs *also* ˈkräs\ *n* -s [F, lit., crosier (pastoral staff) — more at CROSIER] **:** the stick used in lacrosse

crossed *past of* CROSS

crossed belt *n* **:** a pulley belt whose sides cross each other so that the direction of rotation is reversed

crossed nicols *n pl, often cap N* **:** two nicol prisms placed one in front of the other and so oriented that their transmission planes for plane-polarized light are at right angles with the result that light transmitted by one is stopped by the other unless modified by some intervening body

crossed paralysis *or* **crossed palsy** *n* **:** paralysis affecting the extremities of one side and the face on the opposite side or the arm on one side and the leg on the other

crossed pyramidal tract *n* **:** a tract of motor nerve fibers in the lateral column of the spinal cord

crossed specially *adj, Brit* **:** bearing the name of the bank by which payment of a check is to be made — compare ²CROSS 8c

cross education *n* [³*cross*] **:** improvement of one side of the body in a performance which is practiced by the other

¹**cross·er** \-sə(r)\ *comparative of* CROSS

²**crosser** \ˈ"\ *n* -s [²*cross* + *-er*] **:** one that crosses; *specif* **:** ²STICKER 2

crosses *pl of* CROSS *or of* CROSSE, *pres 3d sing of* CROSS

crossest *superlative of* CROSS

cross·ette \(ˈ)krȯ¦set\ *n* -s [F *crossette*, dim. of *crosse* crosier (pastoral staff) — more at CROSIER] **1 :** a projection at a corner of the architrave of a door or window — called also *ancon, ear, elbow* **2 :** a projection in a voussoir (as of a flat arch) fitting into a corresponding recess in the adjacent voussoir

cross-examination \ˌ==,==ˈ==\ *n* **:** a careful examination ⟨a little *cross-examination* seldom fails to reveal that he desires art to reproduce only certain aspects of the natural world —Hunter Mead⟩; *specif* **:** a questioning designed esp. to check the accuracy of answers to prior questions ⟨under *cross-examination* the witness admitted his information was all secondhand⟩

cross-examine \ˌ==ˈ==\ *vt* [⁵*cross*] **:** to examine by a series of questions designed to check the accuracy of answers to previous questions **:** examine closely or repeatedly; *specif* **:** to examine (a witness who has testified for the other side in a legal action) esp. in order to disprove testimony already given

cross-examiner \ˈ"+ə(r)\ *n* **:** one that cross-examines

cross-eye \ˈ=,=\ *n* [³*cross*] **1 :** squint in which the eye turns inward toward the nose — called also *esotropia;* compare WALLEYE **2 cross-eyes** \ˈ=¦=\ *pl* **:** eyes affected with cross-eye ⟨the use of muscle exercises in the treatment of *cross-eyes*⟩

cross-eyed \ˈ=¦=\ *adj* [³*cross*] **1 :** affected with cross-eye **:** having cross-eyes ⟨a *cross-eyed* child⟩ **2 :** COCKEYED 2b ⟨to attempt to investigate both at the same time (to say nothing of all six) would be a *cross-eyed* procedure —Anna G. Hatcher⟩

cross facet *n* **:** SKEW FACET

¹**cross-fade** \ˈ=¦=\ *vt* [⁵*cross* + *fade*] **:** to fade in (a sound or image) in a motion picture or a radio or television program while fading out another sound or image ⟨the scream of the charlady . . . was *cross-faded* into the shriek of a nearby train —Lewis Herman⟩; *also* **:** to fade in (a camera or piece of sound equipment) while fading out another camera or piece of sound equipment — compare DISSOLVE

²**cross-fade** \ˈ=,=\ *n* **1 :** an act or instance of cross-fading **2 :** the technique of cross-fading

crossfall \ˈ=,=\ *n* [³*cross* + *fall*] **:** the transverse sloping of a roadway toward the shoulder or gutter on either side

cross fault *n* [³*cross*] **:** a dip fault or oblique fault

¹**cross-feed** \ˈ=,=\ *n* [³*cross* + *feed* (n.)] **:** a feeding mechanism that acts transversely to the longitudinal axis of the machine bed — see ²FEED 5

²**cross-feed** \ˈ=,=\ *vb* **:** to feed into a machine transversely

cross-fertile \ˈ=¦=(,)=\ *adj* **:** fertile in a cross ⟨the true pumpkins and the summer squashes are generally *cross-fertile*⟩

cross-fertilizable \ˈ=¦==,===\ *adj* **:** capable of cross-fertilization

cross-fertilization \ˈ=,=(,)=ˈ==\ *n* **1** *in seed plants* **a :** fertilization between gametes produced by separate individual plants **b :** fertilization between different kinds of individuals (as species or varieties) resulting in the production of hybrids **2 :** CROSS-POLLINATION — not used technically **3 :** the fertilization of the eggs of an animal by spermatozoa of another individual esp. in potentially hermaphroditic forms **4 :** interchange or interplay (as between different ideas, cultures, or categories) esp. of a vitalizing, broadening, or productive nature ⟨the best work in the field of the novel came from the *cross-fertilization* of realism with the movement of regionalism —R.A.Hall b.1911⟩

cross-fertilize \ˈ=ˈ==,=\ *vb* [⁵*cross* + *fertilize*] *vt* **:** to accomplish cross-fertilization of ~ *vi* **:** to undergo cross-fertilization

cross file *n* [³*cross* + *file* (tool)] **:** CROSSING FILE

¹**cross-file** \ˈ=¦=\ *vb* [⁵*cross* + *file* (to rub)] **:** to file by applying pressure against the work with no pressure on the return

²**cross-file** \ˈ"\ *vb* [⁵*cross* + *file* (to arrange)] *vi* **:** to register as a candidate in the primary elections of more than one political party ~ *vt* **:** to register (a person) as a candidate for more than one party ⟨is nominally *cross-filed* as a Republican —Gladwin Hill⟩

cross-fingering \ˈ=¦=(=)=\ *n* [³*cross*] **:** fingering out of serial order (as in producing certain chromatic tones) in the playing of certain wind instruments

cross fire *n* [³*cross*] **1 a :** firing in combat from two or more points so that the lines of fire cross ⟨gaps in the barrier of artillery . . . filled by the *cross fires* of . . . machine guns —M.H.Armor⟩ **b** (1) **:** a position or situation wherein the forces of opposing factions meet or cross ⟨a son caught in the emotional *cross fire* of his parents⟩ (2) **:** rapid or heated interchange ⟨the *cross fire* of question and answer⟩ **2 :** noise or interfering current set up in a telephone or telegraph circuit by the operation of a neighboring circuit — compare CROSS TALK **3 :** a sidearm pitch in baseball that cuts across the plate at an angle **4** *or* **cross figure :** a pattern in the figure of certain woods caused by distortion of the wood fibers and characterized usu. by parallel mottled bands at right angles to the grain

cross-fire \ˈ=¦=\ *vb* [*cross fire*] *vi* **1 :** to set up or cause cross fire **2 :** to overreach by striking the opposite forefoot — used of horses (as pacers) **3 a :** to aim over the left or the right barrel of a double-barreled shotgun instead of over the center rib ⟨he overcame a tendency to *cross-fire*⟩ **b :** to fire upon an adjacent target rather than on one's own ~ *vt* **:** to burn (the leg of a horse) with a firing iron in a checkerboard pattern for therapeutic purposes

cross-firing \ˈ=¦==\ *n* **:** a method of radiation therapy in which the rays are directed from different points to meet at the same point in the patient

cross flute *n* **:** TRANSVERSE FLUTE

cross flux *or* **cross field** *n* [³*cross*] **:** a component of flux at right angles to that produced by field magnets (as in a dynamo)

cross-fold \ˈ=,=\ *n* [³*cross*] **:** a secondary geological fold at right or nearly right angles to a primary fold

crossfoot \ˈ=¦=\ *vt* [⁵*cross* + *foot* (to sum up)] **:** to add (figures) across instead of up or down

crossfooter \ˈ"+ə(r)\ *n* **:** any device on a bookkeeping or other office machine that crossfoots; *specif* **:** the key that actuates this operation on the machine or the device that registers or makes visible the result

cross fox *n* [³*cross*] **:** a melanistic color phase of the red fox or sometimes of the common European fox characterized by a somewhat definite dark cross-shaped mark on the back and shoulders; *also* **:** fox fur or a fox pelt in such a color phase

cross-fur \ˈ=¦=\ *vt* [⁵*cross*] **:** to apply traverse furring to (as ceiling joists)

cross-garnet \ˈ=,==\ *n, archaic* **:** a T-shaped hinge

cross-gartered \ˈ=¦==\ *adj* [⁵*cross*] **:** wearing garters crossed along the leg (as in some ancient or medieval costumes)

cross grain *n* [³*cross*] **1 :** a grain running transversely to the regular grain or not parallel to the long axis of the piece (as in certain wood) **2 :** interweaving grain in lumber

cross-grained \ˈ=¦=\ *adj* **1 :** having the grain or fibers running diagonally, transversely, or irregularly **2 a :** difficult to deal with, handle, or master ⟨a *cross-grained* problem⟩ ⟨the story . . . *cross-grained* in its structure —D.L.Morgan⟩ **b :** morosely irascible **:** grumpy and intractable **:** perversely contrary ⟨a spiteful *cross-grained* old woman⟩ **syn** see CONTRARY

cross-grain·ed·ness \(ˈ)=ˈ=nədnəs\ *n* -ES **:** the quality or state of being cross-grained **:** PERVERSITY

cross guard *n* **:** a sword or bayonet guard consisting of a short bar which crosses the blade at its junction with the hilt

crosshackle \ˈ=¦==\ *vt* [⁵*cross* + *hackle*] **:** to cross-question esp. annoyingly

cross hair *n* **:** one of the fine wires or spider lines mounted as a reticle in the focus of the eyepiece of optical instruments and used as a reference line in the field or for marking the instrumental axis

¹**cross-handed** \ˈ=¦==\ *adj* [⁵*cross*] **:** with the hands crossed or in reverse of the usual position ⟨a *cross-handed* grip on a ball bat⟩

²**cross-handed** \ˈ"\ *adv* **:** in a cross-handed manner ⟨using a canoe paddle *cross-handed*⟩

¹**crosshatch** \ˈ=¦=\ *vb* [⁵*cross* + *hatch*] **:** to mark with or as if with crosshatch ⟨a slum ~*ed* with dismal streets⟩; *esp* **:** to shade with crosshatch ⟨a drawing with shadows ~*ed* in⟩ — compare HACHURE

²**crosshatch** \ˈ=,=\ *n* **:** a pattern made up of one series of parallel lines crossing (as at right angles or obliquely) another series of parallel lines with the space between the lines in one series usu. being identical to the space between the lines in the other series ⟨abrupt gradients on these maps are indicated by ~⟩ ⟨a ~ of branches⟩

cross-hatching \ˈ=¦==\ *n* **1 a :** the process of marking with crosshatch **b :** the effect produced by such a process **2 :** a pottery design that consists of two series of parallel lines intersecting each other usu. at an oblique angle and is typical of Hopewell pottery

¹**crosshaul** \ˈ=¦=\ *n* [³*cross* + *haul*] **1 a :** a loading device consisting of a chain having each end fastened to opposing sides of a vehicle (as a sled or wagon) and the resulting loop passed under the object to be loaded (as a log) and back to a source of power that rolls the object usu. up a ramp onto the vehicle **b** *also* **crosshauling** \ˈ=¦==\ **:** the method of loading employing this device **2 :** an instance where the transportation of goods promotes or creates crosshauling ⟨millions of railroad car miles . . . saved by the elimination of ~*s* —K.A.Solmssen⟩

²**crosshaul** \ˈ"\ *vb* **:** to transport under conditions that promote or create crosshauling

crosshauling \ˈ=¦==\ *n* **:** the regular transportation (as by railroad) of goods away from a locality while similar or corresponding goods are transported into the locality ⟨efforts to eliminate ~ of farm produce⟩

crosshead \ˈ=,=\ *n* [³*cross* + *head*] **1 :** a beam or bar across the head or end of a rod or a block attached to it and carrying a knuckle pin; *esp* **:** a block guided so as to move in a straight line and serving as a connection between the piston rod and the connecting rod of a steam engine **2 :** a heavy rectangular guide frame attached to the hoisting cable just above the bucket in a mine **3 :** *also* **crossheading** \ˈ=¦==\ **:** a heading centered in a column and preceding text or (as in a long newspaper article) between portions of text

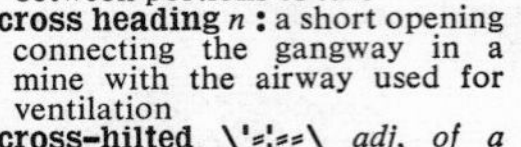

A crosshead, *B* guide, *C* piston rod, *D* connecting rod, *E* wrist pin

cross heading *n* **:** a short opening connecting the gangway in a mine with the airway used for ventilation

cross-hilted \ˈ=¦==\ *adj, of a sword* **:** having a cross guard and thus forming with the blade a Latin cross

cross-immunity \ˌ==ˈ===\ *n* [³*cross*] **:** immunity toward one of a pair of antigens following immunization toward the other that is used to assess the relationship between certain antigens

cross-immunization \ˌ=+\ *n* [³*cross*] **:** the act or action of effecting cross-immunity

¹**cross-index** \ˈ=ˈ==\ *vb* [⁵*cross* + *index* (v.)] *vt* **1 a :** to refer by means of a note at one place to matter at another place ⟨all items in the biology file are *cross-indexed* to related material in the zoology file⟩ **b :** to refer from (a variant or subordinate entry) to a main entry ⟨"public sanitation" should be *cross-indexed* to "public health"⟩ **2 :** to provide (as the body of a text, an index, or a file) with cross-references ⟨a *cross-indexed* report⟩ ~ *vi* **:** to function as or become provided with a cross-referring note or index ⟨most variants *cross-index* to main entries⟩ ⟨all annotations for the most part *cross-index*⟩

²**cross-index** \ˈ"\ *n* **:** a note, series of notes, or index that cross-indexes ⟨each *cross-index* is written on a blue slip⟩ ⟨a text with a *cross-index* in footnotes as well as a general index in the back⟩

cross infection *n* [³*cross*] **:** infection esp. between the newborn

crossing *n* -s **1 :** the act or action of crossing: as **a** *archaic* **:** the making of the sign of the cross **b :** a traversing or going across ⟨a channel ~⟩ ⟨a ~ made without incident⟩ ⟨the troops effected a ~ under fire⟩ **c** (1) **:** a drawing of lines across esp. in canceling — often used with *out* or *off* ⟨a letter full of mispellings and ~*s* out⟩ (2) *Brit* **:** the crossing of a check ⟨fraudulent ~*s*⟩ **d :** an opposing, blocking, or thwarting esp. in an unfair or dishonest manner ⟨a jockey fined for ~ and bumping⟩ **e :** INTERBREEDING, HYBRIDIZING, CROSS-POLLINATING **2 a :** a place or structure that crosses or is crossed: as **a** (1) **:** a place or structure (as on a street or over a river) on which pedestrians or vehicles cross ⟨the right to build additional Hudson river ~*s* —*N.Y. Times*⟩; *esp* **:** CROSSWALK (2) **:** INTERSECTION ⟨at the ~ of Main street and State⟩ **b :** the place in a church where the transept crosses the nave **c** (1) **:** the point at which a railroad track crosses another track or a highway at grade (2) **:** a structure consisting of four connected frogs used where two railroad tracks intersect at grade to permit traffic to move along either track

crossing file *n* **:** a file similar to a half-round file but convex on both faces — called also *cross file*

crossing-over \ˈ==ˈ==\ *n* **:** interchange of genes or segments between associated parts of homologous chromosomes during synapsis

cross-interrogate \ˌ==ˈ==,=\ *vt* [⁵*cross*] **:** to cross-question orally or by a written interrogatory

cross-interrogatory \ˌ==ˈ==,==\ *n* **:** CROSS-QUESTION; *esp* **:** one propounded as an interrogatory in taking a deposition

cross·ite \ˈkrȯ,sīt\ *n* -s [Whitman *Cross* †1949 Am. geologist + E *-ite*] **:** an amphibole intermediate in composition between glaucophane and riebeckite

cross·jack \ˈkräjik, ˈkrȯs,jak\ *n* [³*cross* + *jack* (flag)] **:** a now rarely used square sail set on the lower yard of the mizzenmast — see SAIL illustration, SHIP illustration

cross keys *n pl but sing in constr* [³*cross*] **:** a heraldic representation of two keys laid crosswise in saltire

cross kick *n* [³*cross*] **:** a lateral kick in rugby; *esp* **:** one from a wing toward the center of the field

cross-laminated \ˈ=¦==,==\ *adj* [⁵*cross*] **:** CROSS-BEDDED

cross-lamination \ˈ=,==ˈ==\ *n* [³*cross*] **:** CROSS-BEDDING

cross-leaved heath *also* **cross-leaf heath** \ˈ=,=-\ *n* **:** a low perennial European shrub (*Erica tetralix*) of bogs and marshy ground that is often used for ornament

cross-legged *esp US* ˈ=¦legəd, *esp Brit* -gd\ *adj* (*or adv*) [⁵*cross*] **1 :** with the legs crossed and the knees spread wide ⟨beside her sitting *cross-legged* on the ground there was a child —Olive H. Prouty⟩ **2 :** with one leg placed over and across the other ⟨sat *cross-legged* beating time in the air with his free foot⟩

crosslegs \ˈ=,=\ *adv* [³*cross* + *legs*] **:** in a cross-legged position

¹**crosslet** *n* -s [ME *crosselette*, fr. OF *croisol* lamp (fr. — assumed — VL *croceolus*, dim. of a word of Gmc origin) + ME *-ette;* akin to ON *krōkr* hook — more at CROOK] *obs* **:** CRUCIBLE

²**cross·let** \ˈkrȯslət *also* -räs-\ *n* -s [ME *croslette*, fr. *cros* cross + *-lette* -let] **1 a** *heraldry* **:** a small cross orig. of no fixed shape but in the late medieval period usu. botonée as also in the 20th century in the work of some artists but since the 16th century usu. in the form of a Greek cross with a crossbar near the end of each arm — called also *cross-crosslet* **b :** a Greek cross with a crossbar near the end of each arm used in architecture or design or as an ornament **2 :** a small cross used as an ornament **3 :** a small cross sometimes found attached to a letter or figure (as the right end of the horizontal stroke of the figure 4 in the date) on any of various issues of coins

cross-level \ˈ=¦==\ *vt* [⁵*cross*] **:** to level (as a surveyor's transit) at right angles to the principal line of sight

cross liability *n* [³*cross*] **:** liability of each of the two or more vessels involved in a collision when both or all are to blame

cross license *n* [*cross license*] **:** a license that is granted by a patent holder to another (as a competitor) who reciprocates with a similar license and that is designed to control the marketing of the products involved or to further their development

cross-license \ˈ=¦==\ *vb* [⁵*cross* + *license* (v.)] *vt* **:** to give a license to another to use (a patent or invention) in return for a similar license ~ *vi* **:** to practice cross-licensing

cross-lift \ˈ=¦=\ *vt* [⁵*cross*] **:** to raise (a gun or other object) by crossing handspikes under from opposite sides

crosslight \ˈ=,=\ *n* [³*cross* + *light*] **1 :** a light that crosses the path of another light and illuminates what the other leaves dark **2 :** something that indirectly casts light on or aids in comprehension ⟨new material . . . throws a *crosslight* on Chinese history —Owen & Eleanor Lattimore⟩ — **cross-lighted** \ˈ=¦==\ *adj*

crosslighting \ˈ=¦==\ *n* **:** the lighting of an object from the side

¹**crossline** \ˈ=,=\ *n* [²*cross* + *line*] **1 :** a line that crosses something: as **a :** a trotline set across a stream **b :** a subhead (as between banks) in a newspaper

²**crossline** \ˈ"\ *adj* [³*cross* + *line* (n.)] **:** of, relating to, or being the offspring resulting from the crossbreeding of two pure lines ⟨~ pigs⟩

¹**cross-link** \ˈ=,=\ *n* [³*cross* + *link* (n.)] **:** a comparatively short connecting unit (as a chemical bond or a chemically bonded atom or group) between neighboring chains of atoms in a complex chemical molecule (as a polymer) — used esp. in relation to thermosetting plastics, vulcanized rubber, and proteins

²**cross-link** \ˈ=¦=\ *vt* **:** to join by cross-links ⟨*cross-linked* polymers⟩ ~ *vi* **:** to form cross-links

cross-linkage \ˈ=¦==\ *n* [³*cross*] **1 :** CROSS-LINK **2 :** the process of cross-linking

cross lode *n* [³*cross*] **:** a geological vein that intersects a principal lode — called also *counterlode*

cross-lots \ˈ=,=\ *adv* [⁴*cross*] **:** by a short cut (as across the fields or vacant lots instead of by the road or sidewalk) — often used with *cut* ⟨going home they cut *cross-lots*⟩

cross-lot strut *n* **:** a bracing timber or steel strut extending across an excavation

cross·ly *adv* **:** in a cross manner

cross-magnetizing field *n* [⁵*cross*] **:** CROSS FLUX

cross matching *n* [³*cross*] **:** the testing of the compatibility of the bloods of transfusion donor and recipient by mixing the serum of each with the red cells of the other to determine the absence of agglutinative reactions

cross-mate \ˈ=¦=\ *vb* [⁵*cross*] **:** CROSSBREED

cross modulation *n* [³*cross*] **:** electrical intermodulation in which there are produced frequencies equal to the sums and differences of a desired and an undesired frequency or of their harmonics

cross moline *n, pl* **crosses moline :** a cross with the end of each arm forked and recurved and often used in heraldry as a cadency mark for the eighth son

cross multiplication *n* [³*cross*] **:** the multiplying of a numerator of one fraction by the denominator of another (as in clearing an equation of fractions)

cross·ness *n* -ES **:** the quality or state of being cross **:** PEEVISHNESS ⟨some breeds of bees are notorious for their ~, especially when there is thunder in the air —Robert Lynd⟩

crosso- — see CROSS-

cross of calvary *usu cap 2d C* **:** CALVARY CROSS

cross of con·stan·tine \-ˈkänztən‚tēn, -ān(t)stə-, -‚tīn\ *usu cap 2d C* [after *Constantine* I (the Great) A.D. †337 Roman emperor] **:** CHI-RHO

cross of eight points : MALTESE CROSS 1b

cross of fourteen points : an emblem consisting of seven bars radiating from a center, broadening toward the end, and having each end indented in the form of a V

cross of lor·raine \-ləˈrān, -lȯˈ-, -lōˈ-\ *usu cap L* [fr. *Lorraine*, region in western Europe] **1 :** a cross with two crossbars having the upper one intersecting the upright above its middle and the lower one which is longer than the upper one intersecting the upright below its middle **2 :** a patriarchal cross sometimes depicted botonée

cross of Lorraine 1

cross of mal·ta \-ˈmȯltə\ *usu cap C & M* **:** MALTESE CROSS 1b

cross of st. andrew *usu cap S&A* **:** SAINT ANDREW'S CROSS

cross of st. anthony *usu cap S&A* **:** SAINT ANTHONY'S CROSS

cross of the resurrection *usu cap R* **:** a slender cross with a pennant at the junction of the bars

cros·so·po·dia \‚kräsəˈpōdēə, -rȯs-\ *n pl* [NL, fr. *cross-* + *-podia*, pl. of *-podium*] **:** sinuous markings on certain sedimentary rocks that are supposed to be trails left by creeping marine animals

cros·sopt \ˈkrä‚säpt, -rȯ‚-\ *adj or n* [by shortening] **:** CROSSOPTERYGIAN

cros·sop·te·ryg·ia \(‚)krä‚säptəˈrijēə, -rȯ‚-\ [NL] *syn of* CROSSOPTERYGII

¹**cros·sop·te·ryg·i·an** \¦=¦=təˈrij(ē)ən\ *adj* [NL *Crossopterygii* + E *-an*] **:** of or relating to the Crossopterygii

²**crossopterygian** \ˈ"\ *n* -s **:** a fish of the superorder Crossopterygii

cros·sop·te·ryg·ii \(‚)=‚=təˈrijē‚ī\ *n pl, cap* [NL, fr. *cross-* + *-pterygii*] **1 :** a superorder of Choanichthyes comprising the lobe-finned fishes that have existed since the Devonian but are now largely extinct, that have paired fins somewhat resembling limbs with a scaly axis fringed on one or both sides by dermal rays, and that are generalized fishes in some respects resembling elasmobranchs and in others foreshadowing terrestrial vertebrates which may have evolved from unknown early members of the group — compare LATIMERIA **2** *in some classifications* **:** a division of fishes coextensive with Choanichthyes or comprising Choanichthyes together with Cladistia — compare ACTINISTIA, RHIPIDISTIA

cross order *n* [³*cross*] **:** an order in a stock exchange to buy matched with an order to sell at the same price so that execution on the open market is unnecessary

cross or pile *n, archaic* **:** CROSS AND PILE

cros·so·so·ma \‚kräsəˈsōmə, -rȯs-\ *n, cap* [NL, fr. *cross-* + *-soma*] **:** a small genus of shrubs (constituting the family Crossosomataceae) restricted to the southwestern U.S. and Mexico and having small simple leathery leaves that are often clustered on short branches and solitary terminal flowers — **cros·so·so·ma·ta·ceous** \¦=‚sōmə¦tāshəs\ *adj*

cros·so·the·ca \‚==ˈthēkə\ *n, cap* [NL, fr. *cross-* + *-theca*] **:** a form genus of fossil plants that are known from fructifications bearing pendulous sporangia in epaulet-shaped clusters and occurring on pecopteroid plant remains and that are usu. considered to be seed ferns

cross-out test \ˈ=,=-\ *n* [fr. *cross out*, v.] **:** a mental test in which the task is to cancel items that are superfluous or incongruous

¹**crossover** \ˈ=,==\ *n* [fr. *cross over*, v.] **1 a :** CROSSING 2a (1) **b :** a diagonal railroad track affording passage between two parallel lines **c :** the duct leading from one stage to the adjoining stage (as in a pump or turbine) **2 a :** an instance of the process of crossing-over **b :** a character or an individual having characters inherited by crossing-over **3 a** (1) **:** an exchange of dance places by partners esp. when face to face in open position (2) **:** a dance movement in which the man

transfers the woman from one arm across in front of him to the other **b :** a ball bowled by a right-hander that hits to the left of the kingpin

²crossover \"\ *adj* **:** having two pieces that cross esp. one over the other ⟨a ~ shawl⟩ ⟨a ~ collar⟩

crossover network *n* **:** a circuit that separates the range of frequencies in an audio signal into two or more parts so that each part may be delivered to a different speaker

crosspatch \ˈ=,=\ *n* [³*cross* (ill-humored) + *patch* (fool)] **:** an ill-natured person ⟨an old ~⟩

cross peen *n* [³*cross*] **:** the wedge-shaped edge of a hammer-head running crosswise to the direction of the handle — see PEEN illustration

crosspiece \ˈ=,=\ *n* [³*cross* + *piece*] **:** a horizontal member of a figure or structure (as the crossbar of the letter H, the arm of a cross, or the bar connecting two bitts or knightheads on a boat)

cross-plow *or* **cross-plough** \ˈ=ˌ=\ *vb* [⁵*cross*] *vi* **:** to plow across an earlier plowing ~ *vt* **:** to plow (a field) so that the furrows cross those of an earlier plowing

cross-point \ˈ=,=\ *vt* [⁵*cross* + *point*] **:** to point (a rope) by plaiting the nettles or seizing crosswise

cross-pollinate *or* **cross-pollinize** \ˈ=ˈ==,=\ *vt* [⁵*cross*] **:** to subject to the operation of cross-pollination

cross-pollination \ˈ=,===ˈ==\ *n* **:** the transfer of pollen from one flower to the stigma of another by various devices in the structure of the plant, by the agency of wind or insects, or artificially; *often* **:** the artificial transfer of pollen from one flower to another of a different variety in order to induce hybridization

cross product *n* [³*cross*] **:** the vector product of two vectors

cross-purpose \ˈ=ˈ==\ *n* [³*cross*] **1** *usu pl* **a :** a purpose usu. unintentionally or innocently contrary to another purpose of oneself or of someone else ⟨the terrible *cross-purposes* at work in modern society —Nicolás Monjo⟩ — often used with *at* ⟨the two men were always working at *cross-purposes*⟩ **b :** a subject different from and often ludicrously mistaken for the intended subject — used with *at* ⟨to talk at *cross-purposes*⟩ **2** *pl but sing in constr* **:** a game in which questions and answers are made so as to involve ludicrous combinations of ideas

cross quarters *n pl but sing in constr* **:** an architectural ornament consisting of a cruciform flower in tracery

¹cross-question \ˈ=ˈ==\ *n* **:** a question that is put in cross-examination

²cross-question \"\ *vt* [⁵*cross* + *question* (v.)] **:** to subject to close questioning; *specif* **:** CROSS-EXAMINE

crossrail \ˈ=,=\ *n* [³*cross* + *rail*] **1 :** the horizontal member (as of a planer) supporting the toolheads and on which the toolheads traverse **2 :** a horizontal structural member in a chair back or piece of case furniture

cross rate *n* [³*cross*] **:** the rate of exchange of two foreign currencies based on their quotation in a third market ⟨the sterling-dollar *cross rate* in francs in Paris⟩

cross ratio *n* [³*cross*] **:** an anharmonic ratio in mathematics

cross-reaction \ˈ=ˌ=ˈ==\ *n* [³*cross*] **:** the immunological phenomenon wherein one antigen reacts toward antibodies developed against another and which has been used to study relationships between viruses

cross-refer \ˌ==ˈ=\ *vb* [⁵*cross*] *vt* **:** to refer (a reader) from one place to another (as in a book, list, or catalog) ~ *vi* **:** to make a cross-reference

¹cross-reference \ˈ=ˈ=(=)=\ *n* [³*cross*] **1 :** a notation or direction at one part of a work referring to pertinent information at another part of the work ⟨a file system complete with *cross-references* and bibliographies⟩ **2 :** a grammatical agreement consisting of the use of a substantive and an equivalent pronoun or other substitute in the same construction (as *Marie* and *elle* in French *Marie où est-elle?* "where is Mary"? and as *John* and *he* in substandard English "John he went home")

²cross-reference \"\ *vt* **1 :** to supply with cross-references ⟨*cross-reference* a catalog⟩ **2 :** to refer from (as one subject) to a related subject ⟨a book given coherence by *cross-referenced* paragraphs⟩ ~ *vi* **:** CROSS-REFER

cross-reference code *n* **:** TWO-PART CODE

cross relation *n* [³*cross*] **:** FALSE RELATION

cross remainder *n* [³*cross*] **:** either of two or more remainders left by law to two or more persons so that upon failure of one his share goes to the other or others

cross-rhythm \ˈ=ˌ==\ *n* [³*cross*] **:** the simultaneous use of contrasting rhythmic patterns

cross-rib \ˈ=,=\ *n* [³*cross*] **:** an arch supporting and strengthening a vault

crossroad \ˈ=,=\ *also* ˈ=ˈ=\ *n, often attrib* [³*cross* + *road*] **1 :** a road that crosses a main road or runs across country between main roads ⟨he came by way of a ~⟩ **2** *often pl but sing or pl in constr* **:** the place of intersection of two or more roads ⟨traffic stalled at a ~⟩ ⟨a remote ~*s* hamlet⟩ ⟨the . . . travelers reached a ~*s* marked by a signpost —F.V.W.Mason⟩ **3** *usu pl but sing or pl in constr* **a :** a small community located at a crossroads and often serving as the meeting place of the inhabitants of the surrounding countryside ⟨the small general store at any ~*s* —J.M.Mogey⟩ ⟨physicians then were to be found . . . even at some of the ~*s* —*Jour. Amer. Med. Assoc.*⟩ **b :** a central meeting place **:** FOCAL POINT ⟨like Broadway for showmen or Wall Street for financiers, it is a ~*s* for army men —Green Peyton⟩ ⟨England will be uncomfortable while confusion lasts in Europe for a world ~*s* community —Griffin Barry⟩ **4** *usu pl but sing or pl in constr* **:** a crucial or critical point or place esp. where a decision or choice must be made ⟨it is generally realized that defense policy is at the ~*s* —Lewis Hastings⟩

cross roll *n* **:** a figure-skating movement made by crossing the free foot onto the outside edge behind the outside edge of the skating foot — called also *Dutch roll*

crossrow *n* [¹*cross* + *row*; fr. its formerly being printed with a cross preceding it] *obs* **:** ALPHABET

¹crossruff \ˈ=,=\ *n* [³*cross* + *ruff*] **:** a series of plays in some card games in which partners alternately trump different suits and lead to each other for that purpose

²crossruff \"\ *vt* **:** to effect a crossruff by leading (two specified suits) alternately ⟨~ spades and hearts⟩ ~ *vi* **:** to effect a crossruff

cross saltire *n* **:** SALTIRE

cross sea *n* [³*cross*] **:** a choppy sea in which the waves run in different directions (as from a change in the wind or to a certain extent from a change in tide)

cross section *n* [³*cross*] **1 a :** a cutting or section across **:** a section at right angles to esp. the longer axis of anything **b :** a piece of something cut off in a direction at right angles to an axis **c :** a view, diagram, or drawing representing such a cutting **2 :** a measure of the probability of an encounter between particles such as will result in a specified effect (as ionization or capture) and commonly expressed as the effective area that one particle presents to the other as a possible target for such encounter — compare BARN **3 :** a composite representation typifying the constituents of a thing in their relations ⟨a *cross section* of the people⟩ — **cross-sectional** \ˈ=ˈ=(=)=\ *adj*

cross-section \ˈ=ˈ==\ *vt* [*cross section*] **1 :** to represent in cross section **:** make a cross section of ⟨*cross-section* a ship⟩ **2 :** to cut or divide into cross sections ⟨a city *cross-sectioned* by canals⟩ ⟨*cross-section* a heart to show its chambers⟩ **3 :** to take at regular intervals levelings across (as a railroad or highway embankment) for the purpose of plotting transverse contours in the estimation of earthwork

cross-section paper *n* **:** paper ruled vertically and horizontally in squares (as for drawings or plans)

cross signal *n* [³*cross*] **:** a signal blast usu. forbidden because of the danger of collision that is made by one ship approaching another in the opposite direction and indicates a desire to pass on the side opposite to that orig. signaled by the other ship

cross skip *n* [³*cross*] **:** a skip with the free foot crossed in front

cross slide *n* [³*cross*] **:** a member of a machine (as of a lathe) on which the tool carriage moves at right angles to its principal direction of travel

cross-spale *also* **cross-spall** \ˈ=,=\ *n* [³*cross*] **:** a temporary wooden brace used in shipbuilding secured horizontally across a frame to hold it in position until the deck beams are in place

cross spider *n* **:** the common European garden spider (*Araneida diadema*) that has a cross-shaped mark on its abdomen

cross springer *n* [³*cross*] **:** DIAGONAL RIB

cross-staff \ˈ=,=\ *n* **1 a :** a processional staff usu. with a cross or crucifix borne before an archbishop in his own province **b :** CROSIER **2 :** an instrument once used at sea for taking the altitudes of celestial bodies, esp. of the sun **3 :** a surveying instrument for laying off offsets perpendicular to the main course and consisting of two pairs of sights at right angles to each other on a staff sharp at the end

cross-sterile \ˈ=ˈ=(,)=\ *adj* **:** sterile in a particular cross ⟨plants of widely different geographic origin are often *cross-sterile* even though closely related⟩ — **cross-sterility** \ˌ==ˈ===\ *n*

¹cross-stitch \ˈ=,=\ *n* [³*cross*] **1 :** any needlework stitch that forms an X **2 :** work having cross-stitch

²cross-stitch \ˈ=,=\ *vt* **:** to sew cross-stitch on ~ *vi* **:** to work with cross-stitch

cross-stitch

cross-stone \ˈ=,=\ *n* **1 :** CHIASTOLITE **2 :** STAUROLITE

cross street *n* [²*cross*] **:** a street intersecting a main thoroughfare esp. at right angles and continuous on both sides of it — compare SIDE STREET

cross string *n* [³*cross*] **:** one of the horizontal strings running across the head of a racket

cross suit *n* [³*cross*] **:** a suit of different color from the trump suit

cross tag *n* [²*cross*] **:** a game of tag in which the player who is it must chase any player who passes between him and the one he is pursuing

cross talk *n* [³*cross*] **1 a :** voice sounds heard in a telephone receiver which are induced in the receiver circuit by a neighboring telephone circuit **b :** interference in radiotelephony caused by received waves of frequency other than that to which the receiving set is tuned **c :** the transfer of a recorded signal from one layer of a magnetic tape to another while the tape is wound on a reel **2 a :** CONVERSATION ⟨the one-color groups form, but *cross talk* between them is not uncommon —Walter Goodman⟩ **b** *Brit* **:** REPARTEE ⟨snatches of *cross talk*, lifted wholesale from a current . . . show —Nicholas Monsarrat⟩

cross tau *n* **:** TAU CROSS — used esp. in blazoning heraldic arms

cross·tie \ˈ=,tī\ *n* [³*cross* + *tie*] **:** a tie placed across something for support; *specif* **:** a railroad tie — **cross·tied** \-,tīd\ *adj*

cross timber *n* [³*cross*] **:** a strip of woodland chiefly of oaks stretching across grassland esp. in Texas

cross-tolerance \ˈ=ˈ=(=)=\ *n* [³*cross*] **:** a tolerance or resistance to the action of a drug brought about by the development of a tolerance to another drug of similar pharmacologic action that has been in continued use

cross tongue *n* [³*cross*] **:** a cross-grained tongue of wood used to give additional strength to a tenoned frame

¹crosstown \ˈ=ˈ=\ *adv* [⁴*cross* + *town*] **:** in a direction extending or running across town ⟨taxis cruising ~⟩

²crosstown \ˈ=ˈ=\ *adj* **1 :** situated at opposite points of a town ⟨~ neighbors⟩ **2 :** extending across a town ⟨a ~ street⟩ **3 :** running across a town esp. traverse to main thoroughfares ⟨a ~ bus⟩

crosstree \ˈ=(,)=\ *n* [³*cross* + *tree*] **:** two horizontal crosspieces of timber or metal supported by trestletrees at a masthead that spread the upper shrouds in order to support the mast — usu. used in pl.; see SHIP illustration

cross turret *n* [³*cross*] **:** a lathe turret whose motion is horizontal and at right angles to the ways of the lathe

cross vault *or* **cross vaulting** *n* [³*cross*] **:** a vault formed by the intersection of two or more simple vaults — see VAULT illustration

crossvein \ˈ=,=\ *n* [³*cross* + *vein*] **1 :** a vein (as in a mine) that crosses or intersects an older, larger, or more productive vein **2 :** any vein in an insect's wing extending transversely to the longitudinal veins

cross vine *n* **1 :** a woody vine (*Bignonia capreolata*) of the southern U. S. with stems that often show a conspicuous cross in a transverse section **2 :** TRUMPET CREEPER **3 :** PEPPER VINE 2

cross-voting \ˈ=ˈ==\ *n* [³*cross*] **1 :** voting in which individuals of one party vote with another **2 :** a list system permitting a voter to select names from more than one party list — compare PANACHAGE

crosswalk \ˈ=,=\ *n* [³*cross* + *walk*] **:** a specially paved or marked path for pedestrians crossing a street or road

crossway \ˈ=,=\ *n* [ME *cros waye*, fr. *cros* cross + *waye* way] **:** CROSSROAD ⟨the aerial ~ of the southern Caribbean area —*Americana Annual*⟩ — often used in pl. ⟨at that point came definite ~*s*, and a call for final choice —G.G.Coulton⟩

cross-ways \ˈ=,=\ *adv* [¹*cross* + *-ways*] **:** CROSSWISE, DIAGONALLY ⟨two boards nailed over a door ~⟩ ⟨parallel and not ~⟩

crossweed \ˈ=,=\ *n* [so called fr. the cruciate flowers] **:** either of two plants of the genus *Diplotaxis* (*D. tenuifolia* or *D. muralis*) that are related to and resemble mustards

crosswind \ˈ=,=\ *n* [³*cross* + *wind*] **:** a wind blowing in any direction not parallel to a course (as of an airplane or projectile) ⟨~ landing⟩ ⟨~ takeoff⟩

crosswind force *n* **:** the component perpendicular to the lift and to the drag of the total air force on an airplane or any part thereof

cross wire *n* **:** CROSS HAIR

¹crosswise \ˈ=,=\ *adv* [ME *croswise*, fr. *cros* cross + *-wise*] **1** *archaic* **:** in the form or figure of a cross ⟨a chapel built ~⟩ **2 :** so as to cross something **:** ACROSS ⟨placed ~⟩ **3 :** in a way contrary to what is right or purposed ⟨things are going ~⟩

²crosswise \"\ *adj* **1 :** TRAVERSE, CROSSING ⟨a ~ street⟩ **2 :** DIAGONAL ⟨a ~ brace⟩

crossword \ˈ=,=\ *or* **crossword puzzle** *n* [³*cross* + *word*] **:** a puzzle in which words are filled into a pattern of numbered squares in answer to correspondingly numbered clues and in such a way that they read across and down and so that usu. most letters appear as part of two words

cross·word·er \ˈ=,wərdər\ *n* **:** one who solves crossword puzzles

crosswort \ˈ=,=\ *n* **:** any of several plants having leaves in whorls of four or opposite and 2-ranked: as **a :** BONESET 1 **b :** LOOSESTRIFE **c :** a weedy yellow-flowered European bedstraw (*Galium cruciatum*) that is occas. cultivated

crost *past of* CROSS

crostarie *n* -s [ScGael *crois-tàra*, prob. fr. *crois* cross + *tàir* contempt, reproach; akin to MIr *cross* and to MIr *tár* contempt — more at CROSS] **:** FIERY CROSS 1

¹cro·tal \ˈkrōtᵊl, -ōdᵊl\ *n* -s [L *crotalum* rattle, castanet, fr. Gk *krotalon*, fr. *krotein* to clap; akin to OE *hrindan* to thrust, ON *hrinda* to push] **1 :** CROTALUM **2 :** a small spherical metal rattle (as on a harness)

²crotal *var of* CROTTLE

³crot·al \ˈkrädᵊl\ *adj* [²*crotal*] **1 :** reddish brown ⟨a suit of ~ tweed⟩ **2 :** of or relating to crottle ⟨a ~ dye⟩

cro·ta·lar·ia \ˌkrōdᵊlˈa(a)rēə, -räd-\ *n* [NL, fr. L *crotalum* + NL *-aria*; fr. the rattling of the ripe seeds in the pod when shaken] **1** *cap* **:** a very large genus of mainly tropical herbs (family Leguminosae) with chiefly simple leaves and showy yellow flowers in racemes — see SUNN **2** -s **:** any plant of the genus *Crotalaria*; *specif* **:** any of several plants of this genus used for pasture and green-manure crops

cro·ta·lar·i·o·sis \ˌ==,rarēˈōsə̇s\ *n, pl* **crotalario·ses** \-ˌsēz\ [NL, fr. *Crotalaria* (genus name of *Crotalaria dura*, which ingested causes the disease) + *-osis*] **:** CROTALISM

cro·tale \ˈkrōtᵊl, -ōdᵊl\ *n* -s [F, fr. L *crotalum*] **:** CROTALUM

cro·tal·ic \(ˈ)krōˈtalik\ *adj* [NL *Crotalus* + E *-ic*] **:** of or relating to rattlesnakes

¹cro·ta·lid \ˈkrōdᵊləd\ *adj* [NL *Crotalidae*] **1 :** of or belonging to the family Crotalidae ⟨~ snakes⟩ **2 :** typical of a pit viper ⟨~ venom⟩

²crotalid \"\ *n* -s **:** a crotalid snake

cro·tal·i·dae \krōˈtaləˌdē\ *n pl, cap* [NL, fr. *Crotalus*, type genus + *-idae*] **:** a family of venomous snakes sometimes regarded as a viperid subfamily (Crotalinae) comprising the pit vipers

cro·tal·i·form \(ˈ)=ˈtaləˌfȯrm\ *adj* [NL *Crotalus* + E *-iform*] **:** resembling a rattlesnake

cro·ta·lin \ˈkrōdᵊlən, -räd-\ *n* -s [NL *Crotalus* + E *-in*] **:** rattlesnake venom

cro·ta·line \-ᵊl,īn, -ᵊlən\ *adj* [NL *Crotalus* + E *-ine*] **:** CROTALID

cro·ta·lism \ˈkrōdᵊl,izəm, -räd-\ *n* -s [NL *Crotalaria* (genus name of *Crotalaria sagittalis*) + E *-ism*] **:** the poisoning or poisoned condition of animals caused from eating rattlebox (*Crotalaria sagittalis*) or other crotalarias in the field or as hay — called also *crotalariosis*

cro·ta·lo \-ᵊl(,)ō\ *n* -ES [It, fr. L *crotalum*] **:** CROTAL

cro·ta·loid \-ᵊl,ȯid\ *adj* [ISV *crotal-* (fr. NL *Crotalus*) + *-oid*] **:** resembling the Crotalidae, esp. the rattlesnakes

cro·ta·lum \-ᵊləm\ *n, pl* **crota·la** \-ᵊlə\ [L — more at CROTAL] **:** one of a pair of small cymbals or rods used like castanets by dancers in antiquity

cro·ta·lus \-ᵊləs\ *n, cap* [NL, alter. of L *crotalum* rattle, castanet] **:** the type genus of the Crotalidae — see RATTLESNAKE

cro·taph·i·on \krōˈtafē,än\ *n* -s [NL, fr. Gk *krotaphion*, neut. of *krotaphios* of the temples, fr. *krotaphos* temple] *anthrop* **:** a point at the tip of the greater wing of the sphenoid — see CRANIOMETRY illustration

cro·ta·phy·tus \ˌkrōdəˈfīdəs, ˌkräd-\ *n, cap* [NL, modif. of Gk *krotaphitēs* of the temples, fr. *krotaphos* temple + *-itēs* -ite; akin to Gk *krotein* to clap — more at CROTAL] **:** a genus of lizards (family Iguanidae) of the southern and western U.S. including the collared lizard

¹crotch \ˈkräch\ *n* -ES [prob. alter. of ¹*crutch*] **1 a :** a pole having a fork on one end and used esp. as a prop **b :** a stanchion on a ship with two arms or a hollowed top (as for supporting a boom or spare yards) **:** CRUTCH **c :** ALLIGATOR 6b **2 a :** something in the form of an angle usu. less than a right angle formed by the parting (as from a trunk or body) of two legs, branches, or members ⟨the ~ of a human being⟩ ⟨the ~ of a tree⟩ ⟨the ~ of the letter Y⟩ **b :** something from, between, or at the intersection of an object in the form of a crotch: as (1) **:** wood taken from the section just below the fork of a tree and used chiefly for its swirl-figured grain in the manufacture of furniture ⟨~ veneer⟩ ⟨~ mahogany⟩ (2) **:** the section of a garment where the leg seams meet ⟨the ~ of a pair of pants⟩; *specif* **:** a detachable piece of cloth forming the crotch section of a garment (3) **:** a 4½-inch square at each corner of a billiard table **3 a :** a wrestling hold in or near an opponent's crotch **b :** the situation in billiards when both object balls lie within the same crotch and allow only three counts unless one of the balls is forced out

²crotch \"\ *vb* -ED/-ING/-ES *vt* **1 :** to provide with a crotch ⟨a ~*ed* stick⟩ **:** give the form of a crotch to; *esp* **:** to notch (a log) on opposite sides to provide a grip for the dogs in hauling **2 :** MARRY, SPLICE ⟨~ two rope ends that have been opened in the form of a crotch⟩ **3 :** to play (an object ball) into a crotch in billiards ~ *vi* **1 :** to play on balls lying in the crotch in billiards **2 :** to take a position or lie within a crotch — used of the object balls in billiards

crotch-buck \ˈ=,=\ *also* **crotch-horn buck** \ˈ=ˌ=-\ *n* **:** a buck deer with at least one antler forked

crotch chain *n* **:** a tackle for loading a log sideways on a sled or skidway

¹crotch·et \ˈkrächət, *usu* -əd·+V\ *n* -s [ME *crochet* hook, crocket, quarter note, fr. MF — more at CROCHET] **1 :** CROCHET 1 **2** *obs* **a :** a small hook or hooked instrument **b :** BROOCH **c** *zool* (1) **:** a process or organ shaped like a hook or fork; *specif* **:** a simple curved seta that is notched at the distal end and that is found in annelids (2) **:** CROCHET 2a **3 a :** an out-of-the-ordinary attitude or habit **:** an opinion usu. of little ultimate importance and often serving to mark off a person from others **:** WHIM, PECULIARITY ⟨his political ~*s*⟩ ⟨~*s*, though plentiful, had not yet snatched away the reins of his judgment —Marvin Lowenthal⟩ **b :** a strange or peculiar trick, dodge, or device ⟨bookkeeping full of unorthodox ~*s*⟩ ⟨fainting was just one of her ~*s*⟩ ⟨a prose style burdened with Victorian ~*s*⟩ **4** *chiefly Brit* **:** QUARTER NOTE **5** *now Brit* **:** BRACKET 4a

²crotchet \"\ *vb* **crotcheted** *also* **crotchetted**; **crotcheted** *also* **crotchetted**; **crotcheting** *also* **crochetting**; **crochets** **:** to provide or adorn with crockets

³crotchet \"\ *n* -s [¹*crotch* + *-et*] *archaic* **:** CROTCH

crotch·e·teer \ˌkrachəˈti(ə)r\ *n* -s [¹*crotchet* (whim) + *-eer*] **:** one who has a crotchet or who thrusts his crotchets on others

crotch·ety \ˈkrächəd·ē, -ətē, -i\ *adj* [¹*crotchet* + *-y*] **1 :** given to crotchets **:** subject to whims, crankiness, or ill temper ⟨a ~ old man⟩ **2 :** full of or arising from crotchets ⟨a ~ style⟩

crotch tongue *n* **:** a V-shaped part joining the front and rear sleds of a logging sled

crotchy \ˈkrächē, -chi\ *adj* **:** full of crotches ⟨a ~ tree⟩

crotesco *obs var of* GROTESQUE

-crot·ic \ˈkräd·ik, -ēk\ *adj comb form* [NL *-crotus* (fr. Gk *-krotos*, fr. *krotos* beat, clapping) + E *-ic*; akin to Gk *krotein* to clap — more at CROTAL] **:** having (such) a heartbeat or pulse ⟨poly*crotic*⟩

cro·tin \ˈkrōtᵊn\ *n* -s [NL *Croton* (genus name of *Croton tiglium*) + E *-in*] **:** a mixture of poisonous proteins found in the seeds of a small Asiatic tree (*Croton tiglium*) related to the spurges

-cro·tism \krə,tizəm, krō,-\ *n comb form* -s [*-crotic* + *-ism*] **:** condition of having (such) a heartbeat ⟨di*crotism*⟩

cro·ton \ˈkrōtᵊn\ *n* [NL, fr. Gk *krotōn* tick, castor-oil plant] **1** *cap* **:** a genus of herbs and shrubs of the spurge family with stellate-pubescent foliage and small dioecious flowers — see CASCARILLA, CROTON OIL **2** -s **a :** a plant of the genus *Croton* **b :** a plant of the related genus *Codiaeum* (esp. *C. variegatum*)

cro·ton·aldehyde \ˌkrōtᵊn +\ *n* [ISV *crotonic* + *aldehyde*] **:** a pungent liquid aldehyde $CH_3CH{=}CHCHO$ obtained by dehydration of aldol and used chiefly as an intermediate in organic synthesis and as a warning agent in fuel gases; β-methyl-acrolein

cro·ton·ate \ˈkrōtᵊn,āt, -ᵊnət\ *n* -s [ISV *crotonic* + *-ate*] **:** a salt or ester of crotonic acid

croton bug \ˈkrōtᵊn-\ *n, usu cap C* [fr. *Croton* river, Westchester co., N.Y., used as a water supply by New York City] **:** a small active winged cockroach (*Blattella germanica*) prob. of African origin but common aboard ships and in urban buildings wherever food and moisture are available — called also *German cockroach, water bug*

cro·ton·ic acid \(ˈ)krōˈtänik-\ *n* [F *crotonique*, fr. NL *Croton* + F *-ique* -ic] **:** an unsaturated aliphatic acid $CH_3CH{=}CHCOOH$ existing in cis and trans forms; β-methyl-acrylic acid; *esp* **:** the colorless crystalline trans form obtained in the carbonization of wood, made by oxidation of crotonaldehyde, and used chiefly in making synthetic resins and coatings

crotonic aldehyde *n* **:** CROTONALDEHYDE

croton oil *n* **:** a viscid acrid yellow to brown fatty oil obtained from the seeds of a small Asiatic tree (*Croton tiglium*) that acts as a drastic cathartic, vesicant, and pustulant

cro·ton·o·yl \krōˈtänə,wil, -,wēl\ *n* -s [*crotonic* + *-o-* + *-yl*] **:** the univalent radical $CH_3CH{=}CHCO-$ of crotonic acid

cro·to·nyl \ˈkrōtᵊn,il, -,ēl\ *n* -s [ISV *crotonic* + *-yl*] **1 :** CROTONOYL **2 :** CROTYL

cro·toph·a·ga \krōˈtäfəgə\ *n, cap* [NL, fr. Gk *krotōn* tick + NL *-phaga*] **:** a genus of birds consisting of the anis

cro·toph·a·gine \-,jīn, -jən\ *adj* [NL *Crotophaga* + E *-ine*] **:** of or relating to birds of the genus *Crotophaga*

cro·tox·in \krōˈtäksən\ *n* [blend of NL *Crotalus* (genus name of *Crotalus terrificus*) and E *toxin*] **:** a crystalline neurotoxin obtained from the venom of the cascabel

crot·tels \ˈkrädᵊlz\ *n pl* [pl. of *crottel*, fr. MF *crote* (of Gmc origin; akin to MHG dial. *krotz* spot, obs. D *krotte* spot on clothes) + E *-el* (var. of *-le*)] **:** excrement esp. of hares

crot·tle *also* **crot·tal** *or* **crot·al** \ˈkrädᵊl\ *n* -s [ScGael *crotal*; akin to IrGael *crotal* kernel, rind, crottle] *Scot* **:** any of several lichens from which dyes are made; *esp* **:** a member of the genus *Parmelia* that yields reddish brown or purple dye — often used in pl.

cro·tyl \ˈkrōdᵊl, -ō,til\ *n* -s [ISV *crotonic* + *-yl*] **:** the butenyl radical $CH_3CH{=}CHCH_2-$ — called also *2-butenyl*

¹crouch \ˈkrau̇ch\ *vb* -ED/-ING/-ES [ME *crouchen*, perh. fr. MF *crochir* to become hook-shaped, fr. *croche* hook — more at CROCHET] *vi* **1 a** *obs* **:** to bend low as a sign of reverence or deference ⟨~ to the crucifix⟩ **b :** to stoop with the limbs close to the body ⟨beside the kitchen fires, old women ~*ed* as they turned the spit —Van Wyck Brooks⟩ **c** : to lie close to the ground with the legs bent (as of a wildcat) **d** : to lower the body stance esp. by flexing the legs ⟨a tackle ~*ing* at the line of scrimmage⟩ ⟨the sprinter ~*ed* and waited for the gun⟩ **2** : to bend or bow servilely : stoop meanly : FAWN, CRINGE ⟨made black Jove to kneel and ~ to me —Christopher Marlowe⟩ ~ *vt* : to bow esp. in humility or fear : BEND ⟨~ one's head⟩ ⟨~ the knee⟩

²crouch \"\ *n* -ES **1** : the act or action of crouching **2** : the position of crouching ⟨a boxer who fights mostly in a ~⟩

crouch·ant \'krau̇chənt\ *adj* [¹*crouch* + *-ant* (as in *couchant*)] : CROUCHING

crouchback *n* [ME *crouchbak*, fr. *crouchen* to crouch + *bak* back] *obs* : HUNCHBACK

crouch·er \'krau̇chə(r)\ *n* -S : one that crouches esp. in a servile or flattering manner

crouch ware \'krau̇ch-\ *n* [origin unknown] : an early Staffordshire pottery made of clay and sand and glazed with salt

¹croup \'krüp\ *n* -S [ME *croupe*, fr. OF *crope, croupe*, of Gmc origin; akin to OHG *kropf* craw — more at CROP] **1 a** : the part of the back above the hind limbs of a quadruped (as a horse) : RUMP, CRUPPER — see HORSE illustration **b** : the place behind the saddle **2** *obs* : BUTTOCKS **3** : the part of a side horse to the right of the pommels

²croup \"\ *vi* -ED/-ING/-S [prob. of imit. origin] **1** *now dial Brit* **a** : to cry hoarsely ⟨the raven ~*s*⟩ **b** : to speak hoarsely **2** : to cough with the hoarse ringing cough of croup

³croup \"\ *n* -S **1** : a spasmodic laryngitis in infants and children characterized by episodes of difficult breathing and hoarse metallic cough that occur esp. at night and may be relieved by steam inhalations **2** *in domestic animals* : any of several diseases or inflammatory conditions in which pseudomembranous deposits are formed in hollow organs

crou·pade \krü'päd, ˈ=ˌ=\ *n* -S [F (trans. of It *groppata*), fr. *croupe* hindquarters (fr. OF *crope, crupe*) + *-ade* — more at CROUP] : a curvet with the hind legs of the horse well under his belly

crou·pi·er \'krüpēə(r), -ē,ā\ *n* -S [F, lit., one who rides behind another on a horse, fr. *croupe* hindquarters + *-ier* -er] **1** : an assistant and adviser to a person engaged in a gambling game — now used only in connection with certain games (as baccarat and chemin de fer) **2 a** : an employee of a gambling casino who watches, collects, and pays bets and assists the tourneur or dealer in charge of the table **b** : a representative of a gambling house or casino who officiates at a gaming table **3** : one who at a public dinner party sits at the lower end of the table as assistant chairman

croup kettle *n* [³*croup*] : a kettle for the production of steam or medicated vapor for treating croup or bronchitis

crou·pon \'krüpən\ *n* -S [F, aug. of *croupe* hindquarters] : untanned cattlehide from which belly and shoulder areas have been trimmed

croup·ous \'krüpəs\ *adj* [³*croup* + *-ous*] **1** : relating to or resembling croup ⟨pneumonia which . . . was lobar in distribution and ~ in character —*Science*⟩ **2** : attended with the formation of a deposit or membrane ⟨~ enteritis⟩

croupous pneumonia *n* **1** : LOBAR PNEUMONIA **2** : shipping fever of cattle

croup tent *n* [³*croup*] : a covering or shelter over the head and shoulders within which a stream of medicated vapor is maintained for the relief of some respiratory conditions

croupy \'krüpē, -pi\ *adj* -ER/-EST [³*croup* + *-y*] : of, arising from, like, or indicating croup ⟨a ~ cough⟩

¹crouse \'krüs\ *adj* [ME, prob. fr. MLG *krūse* confused, mixed-up, curly; akin to MHG *krūs* curly, OHG *krol* — more at CURL] **1** *chiefly Scot & Irish* **a** : BOLD, CONFIDENT **b** : COCKY **2** *chiefly Scot & Irish* : BRISK, LIVELY, CHEERFUL — **crouse·ly** *adv*

²crouse \"\ *adv, chiefly Scot & Irish* : BOLDLY, BRISKLY — often used with *craw* or *crack* ⟨he wouldn't have crawed so ~ if he'd known⟩

crou·stade \krü'städ, ˈ=ˌ=\ *n* -S [F, fr. Prov *croustado* — more at CUSTARD] : a crisp shell (as of toasted or fried bread) in which to serve food

croûte \'krüt\ *n* -S [F, lit., crust, fr. OF *crouste* — more at CRUST] : a slice of toasted or fried bread cut in fancy shape and used as a foundation in serving food

crouth *var of* CRWTH

crou·ton \'krü,tän, =ˈ=\ *n* -S [F *croûton*, dim. of *croûte*] : a small cube of bread toasted or fried crisp and used in soups and garnishing

¹crow \'krō\ *n* -S [ME *crowe*, fr. OE *crāwe*; akin to OHG *krāwa, krāja* crow, OS *krāja*, MD *crā, craie*, OE *crāwan*, v.] **1** : any of various large usu. entirely glossy black birds of *Corvus* and related genera noted for their alertness and intelligence: as **a** : CARRION CROW **b** *Brit* : the rook represented in different regions by distinct subspecies — see EASTERN CROW **c** : the common crow (*C. brachyrhynchos*) of No. America **2** : any bird of the family Corvidae — used chiefly in combination; see FISH CROW, HOODED CROW, PIPING CROW **3 a** : a bar of iron with a beak, crook, or claw; *esp* : CROWBAR **b** : a yoke applied to a street water main to hold the drill for tapping the main **4** *archaic* : a grapnel used esp. in siege operations **5** *obs* : a door knocker **6** : a slightly violet black seen on a glossy surface **7** : NEGRO — usu. taken to be offensive; compare JIM CROW **8** *usu cap* **a** (1) : a Siouan people inhabiting the region between the Platte and Yellowstone rivers — called also *Absaroka* (2) : a member of such people **b** : the language of the Crow people **9** *slang* : the eagle worn on the sleeves of petty officers of the U.S. naval forces — **as the crow flies** : in a straight line : by a direct course ⟨by rail today is 80½ miles, whereas it is only 49 miles *as the crow flies* —O.S. Nock⟩ — **crow to pull** *or* **crow to pluck** *or* **crow to pick 1** : a fault to find ⟨no *crow to pull* with him⟩ **2** : a disagreeable or embarrassing matter to settle ⟨brothers with a *crow to pluck*⟩

²crow \"\ *vb* **crowed** \'krōd\ *also in vi sense 1 chiefly Brit* **crew** \'krü\ **crowed; crowing; crows** [ME *crowen*, fr. OE *crāwan*; akin to OHG *krāen* to crow, MLG *krēien*, OSlav *grajati* to croak, OE *cran* crane — more at CRANE] *vi* **1** : to make the loud shrill sound characteristic of a cock ⟨the second time the cock *crew* —Mk 14:72(AV)⟩ ⟨a cockerel *crew* from a blossoming apple bough —W.B.Yeats⟩ **2** *archaic* : to utter a sound expressive of joy or pleasure (as of a baby or child) **3 a** : to shout esp. in exultation, exuberance, or defiance ⟨550 people who had crowded into the old New Orleans dance hall . . . stamped and ~*ed* —*Time*⟩ **b** : EXULT ⟨~*ing* over a recent success⟩ **c** : BRAG ⟨~ over one's ancestors⟩ ⟨he had nothing to ~ about⟩ ~ *vt* : to greet or wake by crowing — often used with *up* ⟨roosters ~*ing* the sleeping barnyard up⟩ **syn** see BOAST

³crow \"\ *n* -S **1** : the cry of the cock ⟨an old cock . . . with . . . a faltering ~ —W.M.Thackeray⟩ **2** : a triumphant cry : an exultant outburst ⟨she gave a little ~ of happiness and gaiety —Charles Reade⟩

⁴crow \"\ *n* -S [perh. by folk etymology fr. D *kroos*, fr. MD *croos* intestine; akin to MHG *krœse*, OHG *chrōse*, a kind of fritter, MHG *krūs* curly — more at CROUSE] : the mesentery of an animal esp. when used as food

crowbait \ˈ=ˌ=\ *n* : a worn-out emaciated horse : a horse of poor quality and conformation

crowbar \ˈ=ˌ=\ *n* [prob. so called fr. the forked end it sometimes has, likened to a crow's foot] : a usu. bent iron or steel bar that is usu. wedge-shaped at the working end and is used esp. as a pry or lever — compare PINCH BAR

crowbells *n pl* **1** *obs* : DAFFODIL **2** *obs* : BLUEBELL

crowberry \ˈ=- — *see* BERRY\ *n* **1** : any of several heaths or related plants: **a** : an undershrub (*Empetrum nigrum*) of arctic and alpine regions with an insipid black berry **b** : BEARBERRY 1 **c** : AMERICAN CRANBERRY **d** : WHORTLEBERRY 1 **2 a** : the fruit of a crowberry **b** : RED CROWBERRY 2

crowberry family *n* : EMPETRACEAE

crowbill \ˈ=ˌ=\ *n* [¹*crow* + *bill*] : a conical arrowhead made of horn — compare ¹PILE 4a

crow corn *n* : COLICROOT

¹crowd \'krau̇d\ *vb* -ED/-ING/-S [ME *crouden*, fr. OE *crūdan* to press, hasten, drive; akin to MLG *krūden* to annoy, MHG *kroten* to press, crowd, annoy, OE *crod* multitude, Norw *kryda* to swarm, MIr *gruth* curds] *vi* **1 a** : to press on : HURRY ⟨~ on one's way⟩ ⟨the ships ~*ed* northward⟩ **b** : to force a way : appear in an oppressive or importunate manner ⟨darkness of evening ~*ed* in⟩ ⟨his heart ~*ed* up into his breast —Pearl S. Buck⟩ **c** : to press close ⟨the players ~*ed* around the coach⟩ ⟨new cheap labor ~*ing* on the heels of earlier comers —*Amer. Guide Series: Minn.*⟩ **2** : to collect in numbers : THRONG ⟨memories ~ in from every stage of the journey —Barbara Ward⟩ ⟨policemen warning people not to ~⟩ ~ *vt* **1** : ENCUMBER, BURDEN, CRUSH, OPPRESS ⟨~ a person's patience with solicitations⟩ ⟨a person ~*ed* to death with titles and honors⟩ **2 a** : to fill by pressing or thronging together : fill or occupy to excess or obstruction ⟨~ a bus with children⟩ ⟨10,000 spectators ~*ing* a stadium⟩ ⟨his mind was ~*ed* with the detail he observed —Nevil Shute⟩ **b** : to press, force, or thrust esp. into a small space or little time : COMPRESS, COMPACT, CRAM ⟨~ children into a bus⟩ ⟨the same wish to ~ meaning is responsible for a good many slurred references —John Berryman⟩ ⟨a multitude of things were ~*ed* together⟩ **3** *obs* : to confine forcibly : IMPRISON — usu. used with *in* **4** : PUSH, MOVE, FORCE — usu. used with *off* or *out* ⟨~ a person off the sidewalk⟩ ⟨we have allowed a false creed to ~ out the real American tradition —Bradford Smith⟩ **5 a** : to urge on : HURRY ⟨we ~*ed* the motor to ten knots —Clifford Gessler⟩ ⟨I ~*ed* him until streams of sweat ran —J.H.Stuart⟩ **b** (1) : to put on (sail) in excess of the usual amount so as to attain maximum speed (2) : INCREASE ⟨the engineer ~*s* steam in the cylinders —Frederick Way⟩ — often used with *on* ⟨~ on speed⟩ **6** : to put pressure upon (as by solicitation) : dun unreasonably or harshly ⟨I'd never ~*ed* him with questions —J.B.Benefield⟩ **7** : THRONG, JOSTLE ⟨changes . . . ~ each other in a whirl of confusing images —N.M.Butler⟩ **8 a** : to press close to ⟨one car ~*ing* the car in front⟩ ⟨~*ing* thirty and still not married⟩ **b** : to be a close second to : nearly overtake **c** : to stand close to (the plate) when batting in baseball **9** : to count on or trust to (luck) unreasonably ⟨~*ing* his luck for all it was worth —F.B. Gipson⟩ **syn** see PACK, PRESS

²crowd \"\ *n* -S **1 a** : a large number of persons esp. when collected into a somewhat compact body without order : THRONG ⟨a ~ of little children⟩ **b** : an unorganized aggregate of people temporarily united in response to a common stimulus or situation in which the individuality of the participants is submerged — compare MOB **2** : the great body of the people : POPULACE ⟨no man more hated and feared by the ~, the generality of mankind —Edith Sitwell⟩ ⟨all our ideas are ~ ideas —T.H.Ferril⟩ **3** : a large number of things collected or closely pressed together : MULTITUDE ⟨~*s* of fine silver dust —G.H.Johnston⟩ ⟨an exciting ~ of incidents —H.C.Webster⟩ ⟨a ~ of wasps, hornets, flies, and gnats —Ellen Glasgow⟩ **4** : a group of people with something (as a habit, interest, occupation) in common : an exclusive company : SET, CLIQUE ⟨the cocktail ~⟩ ⟨the Hollywood ~⟩ ⟨I don't like him or his ~⟩ ⟨in with the wrong ~⟩ **5 a** : the impressed forward movement of the dipper of a power shovel that forces it into the material to be moved **b** : the mechanism that does the forcing

syn THRONG, PRESS, CRUSH, MOB, ROUT, HORDE: CROWD indicates a massed group of persons, often closely pressed and often with subordination of individualities involved ⟨the *crowd* came pouring out with a vehemence that nearly took him off his legs —Charles Dickens⟩ ⟨we get the real sense of a *crowd* of human beings, animated, as a *crowd*, by an instinct and a genius different from that of any of its particular members —Laurence Binyon⟩ THRONG is closely synonymous with CROWD; occas. it may suggest surging motion or bustling confusion ⟨summer tourists come to join the shopping *throngs* on summer evenings —*Amer. Guide Series: N.H.*⟩ ⟨sailors hung from yards and bowsprits to shout the names of vessels to the bewildered, harried *throng* —Kenneth Roberts⟩ PRESS, not now used so much as formerly, may suggest compact concentration in which movement is difficult ⟨they could not come nigh unto him for the *press* —Mk 2:4 (AV)⟩ CRUSH more strongly stresses compact concentration and difficulty of passage through; it is rarely used without connotation of discomfort ⟨the *crush* was terrific for that time of day . . . for the street was blocked —Virginia Woolf⟩ ⟨a *crush* of dancing couples packed the floor —Hamilton Basso⟩ MOB, usu. derogatory, is likely to indicate a rough crowd composed of lower elements, often one disposed to disorder, riot, or other antisocial action and one abrogating any finer feeling ⟨Oliver was burned in effigy, and Hutchinson's town house was gutted by the *mob* —C.L.Becker⟩ ⟨the *mob*, loudly as they clamored for their own rights, cared nothing for the rights of others —J.A.Froude⟩ ROUT is sometimes a close synonym of MOB; it may suggest a concentration of hectic or disorderly activity in a circumscribed space ⟨the busy *rout* of the street could be seen. He loved the changing panorama of the street —Theodore Dreiser⟩ ⟨a kind of jollity and recklessness which was born in the fort, at the old *routs* and balls —Bruce Hutchison⟩ ⟨a flying *rout* of suns and galaxies, rushing away from the solar system and from one another —E.M.Forster⟩ HORDE may apply to a large surging mass or crowd of rough or savage individuals disposed to predatory or destructive action ⟨*hordes* of desperadoes and gunmen who found the river at this point a convenient crossing —*Amer. Guide Series: Texas*⟩ ⟨*hordes* of sturdy rogues and vagrants —G.E.Fussell⟩ ⟨a *horde* of heavily armed buffoons in big boots went stamping round my decks for hours, poking their great stupid faces into everything —*Times Lit. Supp.*⟩

³crowd \", 'krüd\ *n* -S [ME *crowde, crouth*, fr. (assumed) MW *crwth* (whence W *crwth* fiddle); akin to MIr *crott* harp, L *curvus* curved — more at CROWN] **1** : CRWTH **2** *dial Eng* : FIDDLE

⁴crowd \"\ *vi* -ED/-ING/-S *dial Eng* : FIDDLE

crowded *adj* **1** : filled with numerous things or people often overly compacted or concentrated ⟨a ~ valley⟩ ⟨a ~ program⟩ ⟨a brilliant, ~, highly colored book —Gerald Bullett⟩ ⟨a ~ theater⟩ **2** : COMPRESSED, COMPACTED ⟨St.-Étienne, ~ within a series of narrow valleys —James Bird⟩ : resting or placed close together ⟨small ~ freckles⟩ **3** : full of or rich in events or experience ⟨a ~ life⟩ ⟨a ~ career⟩ — **crowd·ed·ly** *adv* — **crowd·ed·ness** *n* -ES

¹crowd·er \'krau̇də(r), -rüd-\ *n* -S [ME *crowdere*, fr. *crowde* fiddle + *-ere* -er] **1** : one that plays a crowd **2** *dial Eng* : FIDDLER

²crowd·er \'krau̇də(r)\ *n* -S [¹*crowd* + *-er*] **1** : one that crowds ⟨that type of fighter, a ~ with both hands milling at all times —*Ring*⟩ **2** *Brit* : a worker who loads handmade bricks on barrows

crowder pea *n* [²*crowder*] : any cowpea in which the seeds are produced in long narrow pods and closely crowded during development

crowd grass *n* [¹*crowd*; fr. its tendency to crowd out other plants] : CHARLOCK

crowding engine *or* **crowding motor** *n* : the engine on a power shovel that forces the dipper into the material

crowds *pres 3d sing of* CROWD, *pl of* CROWD

crowdweed \ˈ=ˌ=\ *n* [¹*crowd* + *weed*; fr. its tendency to crowd out other plants] **1** : CHARLOCK **2** : FIELD CRESS

crow·dy *also* **crow·die** \'krōdē, -üdē, -üdē\ *n, pl* **crowdies** [origin unknown] *chiefly Scot* : a thick gruel of oatmeal and water or milk : PORRIDGE

crowed *past of* CROW

crow fig *n* : NUX VOMICA 1

crowflower \ˈ=ˌ=\ *n* [*crow* + *flower*; fr. the shape of the leaf] : RAGGED ROBIN

crowfoot \ˈ=ˌ=\ *n, pl* **crowfeet** *see sense 1* **1** *pl usu* **crowfoots** : any of numerous plants having leaves pedately lobed; *specif* : a plant of the genus *Ranunculus* **2** : any of several plants with flowers or other structures suggestive of a bird's foot (as the male orchis, the wild hyacinth, and certain club mosses) **3** : CROW'S-FOOT **a** — usu. used in pl. ⟨eyes . . . edged with *crowfeet* wrinkles —*Time*⟩ **4** *on a boat* **a** : a number of small lines rove through a long block **b** : an iron stand fastened at one end to a mess table and at the other to a beam above and used to hang articles on **5** : CALTROP 2a **6** : a brace end consisting of branching parts: as **a** : a brace end in boilers having each of its branching parts fastened to the shell **b** : the crosspiece that holds a manhole or handhole plate in place **7** : a mark used on drawings esp. to limit a dimension or indicate a note

crowfooted \ˈ=ˌ=\ *adj* : having corbiesteps — used esp. of a gable

crowfoot family *n* : RANUNCULACEAE

crowfoot grass *n* : CRABGRASS 1

crowfoot violet *n* : BIRD'S-FOOT VIOLET

crow garlic *n* [ME *crawegarlek*, fr. *crawe, crowe* crow + *garlek* garlic] : a wild onion (*Allium vineale*) having no bulblets in the flower cluster and with narrow terete leaves that extend one-third way to halfway up the stiff stem — called also *field garlic, wild garlic*

crowhop \ˈ=ˌ=\ *n* **1** : a short quick jump (as that of a startled crow) **2** : a stiff-legged hop made by a horse often with the back arched

crow–hop \"\ *vi* [*crow hop*] **1** : to hop or jump like a crow **2** *of a horse* : to buck without violence and with a series of short stiff-legged jumps

crowing *pres part of* CROW

crowing area *or* **crowing ground** *or* **crowing territory** *n* : the mating site selected and defended by a cock pheasant — compare TERRITORIALITY

crowkeeper \ˈ=ˌ=\ *n, now dial Eng* : a person employed to scare off crows

¹crowl \'krōl, -ül\ *n* -S [origin unknown] *Scot & Irish* : a dwarfed person

²crowl \"\ *vt* -ED/-ING/-S *Scot & Irish* : STUNT, DWARF

¹crown \'krau̇n\ *n* -S [ME *coroune, croun, crowne*, fr. OF *corone, curune*, fr. L *corona* garland, wreath, crown, fr. Gk *korōnē* anything curved, tip of a bow, stem of a ship, kind of crown, fr. *korōnos* curved; akin to L *curvus* curved, Gk *skairein* to dance, MIr *cruind* round, Skt *krīḍati* he dances, plays, OE *hrīth* storm, *hrith* fever, OHG *hrito* fever, ON *hrīth* attack, storm, period of time; basic meaning: turning, bending] **1** : a reward of victory or mark of honor ⟨the ~ of life everlasting⟩ ⟨a ~ of glory⟩; *esp* : the title representing the championship in a sport ⟨to win the heavyweight boxing ~⟩ ⟨contending for the intercollegiate football ~⟩ **2** : a royal or imperial headdress or cap of sovereignty worn by monarchs and usu. made of precious metals and adorned with precious stones : DIADEM — see CORONET

imperial state crown of England

3 : the highest part of something: as **a** (1) : the topmost part of the skull or head (2) : HEAD 1 **b** : the summit of a mountain **c** (1) : the head of foliage in a tree or shrub (2) : CROWN CANOPY **d** : CORONA 1 **e** : the vertex or top part of an arch or arched surface (as a street or deck rounding toward the middle); *specif* : the difference in elevation between the center and edges of a rounded roadway **f** (1) : the part of a hat or other headgear covering the crown of the head (2) : the piece of harness that in a bridle passes over the head — called also *crownpiece* **g** : the branched portion of an antler **h** (1) : the part of a tooth external to the gum — see TOOTH illustration (2) : an artificial substitute for the natural crown of a tooth **i** : the tuft of leaves at the apex of a pineapple **j** : the portion of a brilliant above the girdle — compare PAVILION **k** : the dome of a furnace, gas retort, or brick kiln **l** : the crest of a bird **4** : a wreath, band, or circular ornament for the head that is made of flowers, fabric, or metal and worn as a decorative clothing accessory or as a mark of prestige, preeminence, or accomplishment **5** : something felt to resemble the form or shape of a wreath or crown: as **a** : CORONA 2a(1) **b** : a circlet of tapers **c** : the entire body of a crinoid **d** : the knurled cap on top of the stem for winding a watch **e** (1) : CROWN GLASS (2) : CROWN LENS **f** *also* **crown cap** *or* **crown cork** : a metal cap usu. lined (as with cork), used as a closure for a narrow-necked container (as a bottle), and locked in place by its fluted rim being crimped down and around the rounded lip of the container **6** *often cap* **a** (1) : imperial or regal power or dominion : SOVEREIGNTY (2) : the government under a constitutional monarchy **b** : one entitled to wear a crown; *esp* : the monarch in his official capacity as supreme ruler **7** : something that imparts beauty, splendor, honor, or finish : high point : CULMINATION ⟨whatever the beginnings of religion, Jesus is the ~ and climax —J.C.Swaim⟩ ⟨your companionship was the ~ of his life —H.J.Laski⟩ **8** : something bearing a representation of a crown: as **a** (1) : any of several old gold coins with a crown as part of the device (as an English crown of the rose) — compare CROWN GOLD (2) : an English coin worth 5 shillings issued since 1551 but now struck only on special occasions and orig. made of silver but since 1946 of cupronickel (3) : any dollar-size silver coin **b** : a size of paper orig. watermarked with a crown and now measuring usu. 15 x 20 or 15 x 19 inches **c** : a green or blue symbol resembling a crown that marks the fifth suit in some five-suit packs of playing cards **9 a** : a unit of value equivalent to the value of a crown **b** (1) : KORUNA (2) : KRONA (3) : KRONE (4) : KROON **10** : the highest quality or state of something **11** : a representation of a crown (as a heraldic bearing, watermark, hallmark) **12 a** : the region of a seed plant usu. at ground level at which stem and root merge **b** : the thick arching end of the shank of an anchor where the arms are joined to it — see ANCHOR illustration **c** *in carding* : the crossbar connecting the prongs of card teeth at back of the card clothing **13** : the bit of a diamond drill **14 a** : COURONNE **b** (1) : a knot formed in the strands of a rope to prevent untwisting (2) : an interweaving of the strands of a rope to add a finish to a wall knot — see WALL AND CROWN **15** : the colon esp. of a domestic animal

²crown \"\ *vb* -ED/-ING/-S [ME *corounen, crounen*, fr. OF *coroner*, fr. L *coronare*, fr. *corona* crown] *vt* **1 a** : to place a crown or wreath upon the head of ⟨the May queen ~*ed* each child⟩; *specif* : to place a crown upon in order to invest with regal dignity and power — often used with a double object ⟨~ a person king⟩ **b** : to encircle or encompass ⟨perspiration ~*ed* his forehead⟩ — often used with *with* ⟨his head was ~*ed* with thorns⟩ **c** : to recognize officially as ⟨he was ~*ed* heavyweight boxing champion⟩ — often used with a double object ⟨the association ~*ed* him athlete of the year⟩ **2** : to imbue or endow : ENRICH, ADORN — usu. used with *with* ⟨a man ~*ed* with wisdom⟩ ⟨she ~*ed* all about her with beauty⟩ **3** : to surmount, top, or cap ⟨a sun helmet ~*ing* an impressively big head —Earle Birney⟩ ⟨patches of clay ~ the higher slopes —L.D.Stamp⟩; *esp* : to top (a checker) with a checker to make a king **4 a** : to bring to a happy, suitable, or successful conclusion : round off : finish off : CLIMAX ⟨Christmas dinner . . . was ~*ed* . . . by a sleek jet-black plum pudding —Silas Spitzer⟩ ⟨you can ~ your trip to Europe with a wonderful side trip —*Saturday Rev.*⟩ **b** : to form or provide the finishing element of : COMPLETE ⟨each stanza is ~*ed* with a couplet⟩ ⟨to ~ all, none of the trucks would start⟩ **5** : to provide with something like a crown: as **a** : to fill so that the surface forms a crown ⟨he ~*ed* each tankard⟩ **b** : to put an artificial crown upon (a tooth) **c** : to provide (a road) with a crown **d** : to place the cap on (a bottle) **6** : to inflict a blow or bruise on the crown of : hit on the head ⟨getting ~*ed* with a beer bottle by a South African trooper —Hal Lehrman⟩ **7** : TOP ⟨~ a plant⟩ ~ *vi* **1** *of a checker man* : to become a king ⟨a single man ~*s* on reaching the king row —*New Complete Hoyle*⟩ **2** *in childbirth* : to appear at the vaginal opening — used of the first portion (as the crown of the head) of the infant to appear ⟨a low spinal anesthetic was given when the head ~*ed* —*Jour. Amer. Med. Assoc.*⟩ **3** *of fire* : to sweep to or through the crown canopy of a forest

³crown \'krün, -rau̇n\ *vt* -ED/-ING/-S [back-formation fr. ²*crowner*] *now dial* : to hold a coroner's inquest on

crown agent *n, usu cap C&A* **1** : an agent for the British crown; *specif* : a solicitor under the lord advocate in charge of criminal proceedings in Scotland **2** : an agent in England acting in behalf of the business and financial interests of a British colony

crown·al \'krau̇nᵊl\ *n* -S [alter. (influenced by ¹*crown*) of ¹*coronal*] *archaic* : CORONET, CROWN, WREATH

crown aloes *n pl* : a commercial variety of aloes

crown and anchor *n* : chuck-a-luck played with three dice having faces bearing a crown, an anchor, and the four aces and with a cloth or board marked with similar figures on which the players place their bets

crown antler *n* **:** the topmost branch or tine of an antler

crown·ation \krü'nāshən, -raü'-\ *n* -s [by alter. (influenced by ¹*crown*)] *now dial Eng* **:** CORONATION 1

crownbeard \'=,=\ *n* [so called fr. the appearance of the flowers] **:** any plant of the genus *Verbesina*

crown bird *n* **:** CROWNED CRANE

crown block *n* **:** a timber or steel pulley support connecting at the top the derrick posts of an oil well

crown bud *n* **:** the first flower bud that is formed normally on an untopped chrysanthemum plant and that is accompanied by vegetative buds

crown canker *n* **:** canker disease of roses caused by an imperfect fungus (*Cylindrocladium scoparium*)

crown canopy *n* **:** the cover formed by the top branches of trees in a forest

crown cap *or* **crown cork** *n* **:** CROWN 5f

crown class *n* **:** any of several classes into which a forest of even age can be classified according to the height and relative density of and amount of light received by its crown canopy

crown colony *n, often cap both Cs* **:** a colony of the British Commonwealth over which the crown (as through an appointed governor) retains some control

crown daisy *n* **:** a shrubby annual composite herb (*Chrysanthemum coronarium*) of the Mediterranean region with dissected foliage and yellowish white flower heads

crown dancers *n pl* [so called fr. the yucca crowns they wear] **:** GAHE

crown debt *n* **:** a debt due under English law to the crown and upon which if on record the crown has the remedy of extent

crown density *n* **:** the relation of the area of the crown canopy of a forest to the land area determined esp. by the distance apart of the trees and the compactness of the crowns of the individual trees

crown derby *n, usu cap C&D* [so called fr. the crown it once bore as an identifying mark] **:** Derby china manufactured under a royal warrant

crowned \'kraünd\ *adj* [ME *crouned,* fr. past part. of *crounen* to crown] **1 a :** invested with or as if with the royal crown ⟨a ~ sovereign⟩ ⟨Death the ~ phantom —Thomas De Quincey⟩ **b :** arising from, based on, or peculiar to the royal crown ⟨~ authority⟩ ⟨~ tyranny⟩ **2 :** provided with or as if with a crown ⟨a ~ seal⟩ ⟨a ~ decoration⟩ — often used in combination ⟨a high-*crowned* hat⟩ ⟨an orange-*crowned* bird⟩

crowned crane *n* **:** any crane of an African genus (*Balearica*) distinguished by a stiff bristly yellow crest on the back of the head — called also *crown bird*

crowned eagle *n* **:** a large forest-dwelling African eagle (*Stephanoaetus coronatus*) that has a yellowish-marked crest and the breast feathers yellow tipped with black and that feeds chiefly on monkeys and small antelopes

crowned pigeon *n* **:** any of several pigeons constituting a genus (*Goura*) native to New Guinea and adjacent islands having a high fan-shaped erect crest of lacy feathers and slaty-blue plumage and being occas. as large as geese

crow needle *n, often pl but sing or pl in constr* [so called fr. the long beaks of the fruit] **:** LADY'S-COMB

¹crown·er \'kraünə(r)\ *n* -s [ME *crounere,* fr. *crounen* to crown + *-ere* -er] **1 :** one that crowns: as **a :** a crowning or consummating act ⟨we slipped our cables, as a ~ to our fun ashore —R.H.Dana⟩ **b :** a fall or bruise on the crown of the head **2 :** an inspector of shoes; *esp* **:** one who looks for flaws that may have occurred in the lasting department

²crown·er \'krünə(r), -raün-\ *n* -s [ME, alter. (influenced by *croun, crowne* crown) of *coroner, corowner* — more at CORONER] *now dial* **:** CORONER

crown·et \'kraünət\ *n* -s [ME, alter. (influenced by ME *croun, crowne* crown) of *coronette* — more at CORONET] *archaic* **:** CORONET

crown fire *n* **:** a forest fire that advances often at great speed from crown to crown often well in advance of the fire on the ground

crown flower *n* **:** a large shrub (*Calotropis gigantea*) with white and pale lavender flowers used for leis in Hawaii

crown gall *n* **1 :** a disease of various plants esp. destructive to pome and stone fruits, grapes, and roses caused by a bacterium (*Agrobacterium tumefaciens*) which forms tumorous enlargements mainly just below ground on the stem — see BLACK KNOT 4, HAIRY ROOT **2 :** CROWN WART

crown gate *n* **:** the head gate (as of a lock of a canal)

crown gear *n* **:** a gear whose teeth project parallel to the axis and whose pitch surface is a plane — see CROWN WHEEL

crown girdler *n* **:** STRAWBERRY ROOT WEEVIL

crown glass *n* **1 :** glass blown and whirled into the form of a flat disk having a bull's-eye in the center **2 :** alkali-lime silicate optical glass having relatively low index of refraction and low dispersion value — compare FLINT GLASS **3 :** CROWN LENS

crown gold *n* **:** gold eleven-twelfths fine that was used in the minting of the crown of the rose from 1526 and adopted in 1634 as the standard for other English gold coins

crown graft *n* **1** *Brit* **:** BARK GRAFTING **2 :** a plant graft made at the level of the crown

crown gum *n* **:** a crude coagulated latex taken from certain Central American trees and used as a substitute for chicle

crown head *n* **:** KING ROW

crown imperial *n* **:** a Eurasian spring-blooming herb (*Fritillaria imperialis*) having at the top of the stalk a cluster of pendent bell-shaped flowers surmounted by a whorl of leaves

¹crown·ing \'kraüniŋ, -nēŋ\ *n* -s [ME *coruning, crouning,* fr. gerund of *corunen, crounen* to crown — more at CROWN] **:** the act or action of bestowing or providing with a crown ⟨the ~ of the May queen⟩ ⟨the ~ of a road⟩; *esp* **:** the marriage ceremony in the Eastern Church in which the officiating priest places crowns on the heads of bride and bridegroom

²crowning \"\ *adj* [fr. pres. part. of ²*crown*] **1 :** TOPPING, SURMOUNTING ⟨a . . . pavilion with ~ gable pediment —*Amer. Guide Series: Maine*⟩ **2 :** SUPREME, ULTIMATE ⟨her ~ glory⟩ ⟨a ~ achievement⟩

crown jewels *n pl* **:** the jewels (as crown, scepter, and other precious objects of symbolic value) appendant to the office of a sovereign; *specif* **:** the jewels belonging to a sovereign's regalia

crown knot *n* **:** a knot tied in the unlaid strands at the end of a rope and used chiefly as part of other knots

crown knot

crown land *n* **1 :** land belonging to the crown and yielding revenues that the reigning sovereign is entitled to **:** the crown's domain or estate ⟨the conqueror inherited . . . a considerable revenue, derived in the main from *crown lands* —F.M.Stenton⟩ **2 :** public land in some British dominions or colonies ⟨*crown lands* of Australia⟩

crownland \'=,land\ *n* [trans. of G *kronland*] **:** one of the provinces of the old Austro-Hungarian Empire

crown law *n* **:** the part of English common law that applies to criminal prosecutions

crown leather *n* **:** a strong leather used esp. for belting, washers, valve cups, and belt laces and tanned usu. by drumming with warm fats and other materials

crown lens *n* **:** the crown glass component of an achromatic lens

crown·less \-ləs\ *adj* **:** being without a crown

crown monkey *n* **:** BONNET MONKEY

crown office *n* **1 :** the office of the Court of King's Bench in English law in which certain procedure formerly took place on the criminal-law side and in matters relating to the prerogative writs of quo warranto, mandamus, and prohibition **2 :** a department for the King's Bench division in the central office of the High Court of Justice in English law **3** *in English law* **a :** the Chancery Office in which the great seal is generally affixed **b :** the former office of the common-law side of the Chancery Court

crown-of-the-field \'=,==',=\ *n* **:** CORN COCKLE

crown of the rose [¹*crown* (coin); fr. the rose on its face] **:** an English gold coin first struck by Henry VIII in 1526

crown of thorns 1 [so called fr. the wreath placed on Jesus' head by Roman soldiers who mocked him as "King of the Jews" prior to his crucifixion] **:** a severe infliction **:** unmerited injury **2 a :** a somewhat climbing bushy spurge (*Euphorbia milii*) of Madagascar that has long thick woody stems covered with stout spines, few leaves mostly restricted to the new growth, and flowers subtended by brilliant scarlet bracts and that is sometimes cultivated in the greenhouse **b :** CARAUNDA

crown palm *n* **:** a West Indian pinnate-leaved palm (*Englerophoenix caribaea*) related to the coconut palm

crownpiece \'=,=\ *n* **:** a piece or part forming the crown or top of something; *specif* **:** CROWN 3f(2)

crown post *n* **:** KING POST

crown prince *n* **1 :** the heir apparent to a crown or throne ⟨the customary title of the Belgian *crown prince,* Duke of Brabant —*Current Biog.*⟩ **2 :** a person esp. prepared or favored to fill a forthcoming vacancy ⟨the former president's handpicked *crown prince* —*Springfield (Mass.) Union*⟩

crown princess *n* **1 :** the wife of a crown prince **2 :** a female heir apparent or heir presumptive to a crown or throne

crown pulley *n* **:** a pulley in the crown block of an oil-well derrick

crown roast *n* **:** a fancy roast of lamb, veal, or pork made from the rib portions of two loins by trimming off the backbone and skewering the ends together in a circle with the bones outside

crown roast

crown rot *n* **:** any rot affecting the part of a plant at or near the ground level and caused in the sugar beet by boron deficiency or in rhubarb by a fungus (*Phytophthora parasitica*) — compare COLLAR ROT

crown-rump length *n* **:** SITTING HEIGHT

crown rust *n* [so called fr. the crown of blunt teeth surmounting the terminal cells of the teliospores of the causal fungus] **:** a leaf rust of oats and other grasses characterized by rounded light-orange uredinia and buried telia

crowns *pl of* CROWN, *pres 3d sing of* CROWN

crown saw *n* **:** a saw for cutting round holes having its teeth at the edge of a hollow cylinder — called also *cylinder saw, hole saw*

crown saw attached to arbor

crown's evidence *n* **:** KING'S EVIDENCE

crownshaft \'=,=\ *n* **:** the extension that rises above the flower cluster of the shaft of many palms, is composed of the erect sheathing petioles of the crown leaves, and resembles a trunk

crown sheet *n* **1** *also* **crown plate :** the plate that forms the top of the furnace or firebox of an internally fired steam boiler **2 :** one of the upper steel plates in an oil still

crown shell *n* **:** ACORN BARNACLE

crown side *n* **:** the criminal-law side in English law

crown vent *n* **:** a vent for a plumbing fixture in which the vent pipe is connected at the top of the curve in the pipe that forms the trap

crown vetch *n* **:** AXSEED

crown wart *n* **:** a disease of alfalfa caused by a fungus (*Urophlyctis alfalfae*) which produces large dirty-white excrescences at the stem base

crown wheel *n* **:** a crown gear of light construction: as **a :** the crown-shaped horizontal escape wheel of a verge escapement timepiece **b :** a contrate wheel in the winding mechanism of a watch that drives the ratchet wheel and is itself driven by the winding-stem pinion

crownwort \'=,=\ *n* [so called fr. the arrangement of the petals] **:** a plant of the genus *Malesherbia*

crownwort family *n* **:** MALESHERBIACEAE

crow onion *n* **:** CROW GARLIC

crow pheasant *n* **:** the common coucal (*Centropus sinensis*) of India and China that is a large cuckoo of terrestrial habits

crow poison *n* **1 :** a small American plant (*Nothoscordum bivalve*) poisonous to stock **2 :** FLY POISON

crow quill *n* [¹*crow* + *quill* (of which they were formerly made)] **:** a narrow flexible artist's pen that is circular in section at the holder end and that produces a very fine line which can be thickened by slight pressure

crows *pl of* CROW, *pres 3d sing of* CROW

crow's ash *n* **:** either of two Australian timber trees of the genus *Flindersia*: **a :** FLINDOSA **b :** a closely related tree (*Flindersia bennettiana*)

crow's-bill \'=,=\ *n, pl* **crow's-bills :** CORACOID PROCESS

crow's-foot \'=,=\ *n, pl* **crow's-feet :** something felt to resemble a crow's foot or the outline of a crow's footprint: as **a :** a set of wrinkles around the outer corners of the eyes resulting from age, mental distress, or habitual squinting — usu. used in pl. **b :** CROWFOOT 4 **c :** CALTROP 2a **d :** a triangular figure filled with interlacing stitches and used as a finish or decoration on tailored garments **e :** CROWFOOT 7 **f :** CROWFOOT 1 **g** *aeronautics* (1) **:** a system of diverging short ropes for distributing the pull of a single rope (2) **:** an arrangement in which the strands of a cord are opened out so that they can be effectively cemented to a fabric surface **h** (1) **:** BIRD'S-MOUTH (2) **:** the veining in a streaked stone (as marble)

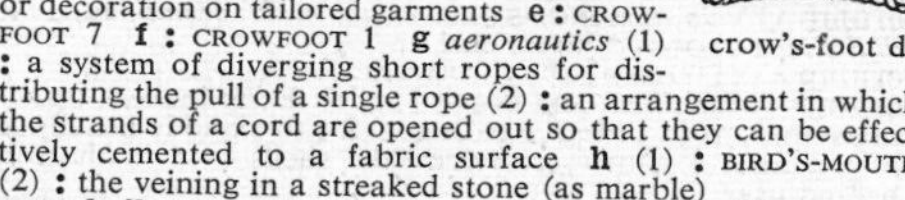

crow's-foot d

crow shrike *n* **:** PIPING CROW **:** an Australian bird closely related to the piping crow

crow's nest *n* **1 a :** a partly enclosed platform for a lookout on a boat usu. placed well up on the foremast **b :** an elevated platform (as on a traffic-control tower, oil derrick, or coast-guard lookout) **c :** a maneuverable bucket-shaped platform on a crane (as used by workers trimming off high tree branches) **d :** the cupola in a caboose **2 :** WILD CARROT

crow-soap \'=,=\ *n* **:** SOAPWORT

crowstep \'=,=\ *n* **:** CORBIESTEP — **crow·stepped** \'=,stept\ *adj*

crow tit *n* **:** any of various small birds of *Paradoxornis* or related genera of southeastern Asia that resemble tits

crowtoe \'=,=\ *n* **1 :** a toothwort (*Dentaria laciniata*) of the eastern U.S. **2 :** a bird's-foot trefoil (*Lotus corniculatus*) **3** *Brit* **:** WOOD HYACINTH **4** *Brit* **:** MALE ORCHIS **5** *Brit* **:** BUTTERCUP

crow-tread *vt* [¹*tread* (copulate); fr. the belief that crows tread hens against their will] *obs* **:** to treat ignominiously

crow-victuals \'=,==\ *n pl but sing or pl in constr* **:** GROUND IVY

croy \'krȯi\ *n* -s [ML *croya, croa* fish trap, fr. ScGael *crō* pen for animals, hut — more at CREW] **:** a barrier built out in a stream as a fish shelter or means of allaying bank erosion

croy·don \'krȯid°n\ *adj, usu cap* [fr. *Croydon,* Surrey, England] **:** of or from the county borough of Croydon, Surrey, England **:** of the kind or style prevalent in Croydon

¹croze \'krōz\ *n* -s [prob. fr. MF *crues* cavity, hole, groove; akin to OProv *croza* hole, cave, It dial. *croso* deep] **1 :** the groove near either end of a barrel stave in which the barrelhead is inserted **2 :** a plane or machine for cutting the croze in staves

²croze \"\ *vt* -ED/-ING/-S **1 :** to make a croze in (a stave) **2 :** to fold and refold (felt hat bodies) during sizing

croz·er \'krōzə(r)\ *n* -s **:** one that crozes; *specif* **:** CHUCKER 2

crozier *var of* CROSIER

crt *abbr* **1** court **2** crate

CRT *abbr* cathode-ray tube

cru \'krü, -rǣ\ *n, pl* **crus** \-üz,-ǣ(z)\ [F, quantity in which something is produced, production, producing field, graded field, fr. *crû* (past part. of *croître* to grow) fr. OF *crëu* — more at CREW] **:** a French vineyard producing wine grapes; *esp* **:** one formally graded as to the quality of its annual production ⟨a claret from one of the better ~*s*⟩

¹crub \'krüb, -rəb\ *dial var of* CRIB

²crub \"\ *dial var of* CURB

cruce *n* -s [by shortening] *obs* **:** CRUCIBLE

cruces *pl of* CRUX

cru·cet·house \'krüsət,haüs\ *n* [OE *crucethūs,* fr. *crucet-* (fr. L *cruciatus* torture, fr. *cruciatus,* past part. of *cruciare* to torture, fr. *cruc-, crux* cross) + *hūs* house — more at RIDGE, HOUSE] **:** a chest used in medieval torture

cru·cial \'krüshəl\ *adj* [F, fr. L *cruc-, crux* cross + F *-ial*] **1** *archaic* **:** characteristic of or having the form of a cross **:** CRUCIFORM, CRUCIATE, CROSSED, INTERSECTING ⟨a ~ scar⟩ **2 :** important or essential as decisive or as resolving a crisis **:** marked by final determination of a doubtful issue ⟨a ~ decision⟩ ⟨a ~ operation⟩ ⟨the ~ game of a series⟩; *broadly* **:** SEVERE, TRYING, TESTING ⟨a ~ experience⟩ ⟨a ~ moment⟩ **syn** see ACUTE

cru·ci·al·i·ty \,krüshē'alədē, krü,shal-, -ətē, -i\ *n* -ES **:** the quality or state of being crucial ⟨the episodes chosen by Homer have no evident ~ for the course of the war —S.G.F. Brandon⟩

cru·cial·ly \'krüshəl|ē, |i, *rapid* -shl|\ *adv* **:** in a crucial manner **:** to a crucial degree ⟨~ necessary⟩ ⟨~ tested in a laboratory⟩

cru·cian carp \'krüshən-\ *also* **crucian** *n* -s [modif. of LG *karuse, kruske* (fr. MLG *karuske, karusse*) or Fris *krūsken* both fr. Lith *karušis, karōsas*; akin to Russ *karas'* crucian carp, Pol *karaś,* and perh. to Skt *kilāsa* spotted, leprous] **:** a European carp (*Carassius vulgaris* syn. *C. carassius*)

cru·cia·nel·la \,krüshə'nelə\ *n, cap* [NL, irreg. dim. of L *cruci-, crux* cross; fr. the arrangement of the leaves] **:** a genus of herbs or low shrubs (family Rubiaceae) with opposite or whorled leaves and small tubular flowers in close clusters

¹cru·ci·ate \'krüshē,āt\ *adj* [NL *cruciatus,* fr. L *cruci-, crux* cross + *-atus* -ate] **:** cross-shaped or marked with a cross ⟨a ~ bandage⟩: **a :** having leaves or petals in the form of a cross **:** CRUCIFORM **b :** CROSSING — used esp. of the wings of some insects — **cru·ci·ate·ly** *adv*

²cruciate \"\ *vt* -ED/-ING/-S [L *cruci-, crux* cross + E *-ate*] **:** to mark with a cross

cruciate ligament *n* **:** any of several more or less cross-shaped ligaments: as **a :** a V-shaped arrangement of fibers over the extensor tendons of the ankle **b :** either of two ligaments in the knee joint that cross each other from femur to tibia **c :** a complex ligament made up of the transverse ligament of the atlas and vertical fibrocartilage extending from the odontoid process to the border of the foramen magnum

cru·ci·ble \'krüsəbəl\ *n* -s [ME *corusible,* fr. ML *crucibulum, crucibolum* small lamp, earthen pot for melting metals, prob. by folk etymology (influence of L *cruc-, crux* cross, and *turibulum* thurible) fr. OF *croiseul* — more at CRUSIE] **1 :** a vessel or melting pot of some very refractory material (as clay, graphite, porcelain, or a relatively infusible metal) that may vary in size from a small laboratory utensil for chemical analysis to very large industrial equipment and that is used for melting and calcining a substance (as metal and ore) which requires a high degree of heat **2 :** something that tests as if by fire **:** a severe test or trial ⟨~ of affliction⟩ ⟨~ of war⟩

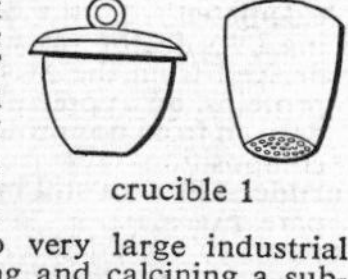

crucible 1

crucible furnace *n* **:** a furnace for heating material contained in crucibles

crucible steel *n* **:** hard cast steel (as for dies and cutting tools) made in pots that are lifted from the furnace before the metal is poured into molds

cru·cib·u·lum \krü'sibyələm\ *n, cap* [NL, fr. ML, earthen pot — more at CRUCIBLE] **:** a genus of bird's-nest fungi (family Nidulariaceae) with the peridium consisting of one layer and opening by a deciduous yellow tomentose membrane

cru·ci·fer \'krüsəfə(r)\ *n* -s [LL, fr. L *cruci-, crux* cross + *-fer* — more at CROSS] **1 :** one that carries a cross (as at the head of an ecclesiastical procession) **2** [NL *Cruciferae*] **:** any plant of the family Cruciferae **:** CRESS

Cru·cif·er·ae \krü'sifə,rē\ *n pl, cap* [NL, fr. L *cruci-, crux* + *-ferae* (fem. pl. of *-fer*)] **:** a family of herbs (order Rhoeadales) characterized by cruciate tetramerous flowers and by the fruit which is a silique or a silicle — see BRASSICA

cru·cif·er·ous \(')krü'sif(ə)rəs\ *adj* [L *cruci-, crux* + E *-ferous*] **1 :** bearing a cross **2** [NL *Cruciferae* + E *-ous*] **:** belonging to or having the characteristics of the mustards or related plants

cru·ci·fi·er \'krüsə,fī(ə)r, -īə\ *n* -s [ME, fr. *crucifien* + *-er*] **:** one that crucifies

cru·ci·fix \-,fiks\ *n* -ES [ME, fr. ML & LL; ML *crucifixus* representation of Christ on the cross, fr. LL, the crucified Christ, fr. *crucifixus,* past part. of *crucifigere* to crucify, fr. L *cruci-, crux* cross + *figere* to fasten — more at RIDGE, DIKE] **1 :** a representation of Christ on the cross usu. painted in the Eastern Church or sculptured or molded and affixed in the Western Church ⟨the cross, too, by degrees became the ~ —H.H.Milman⟩; *also* **:** the cross itself as a Christian emblem **2** *obs* **:** the crucified Christ **3 :** a gymnastic stunt in which a performer supports himself on the rings by his hands with his arms held rigid in a horizontal position

crucifix fish *n* **:** any of several saltwater catfishes (genus *Arius*) of the Caribbean area with the bones of the lower part of the skull arranged in the form of a crucifix

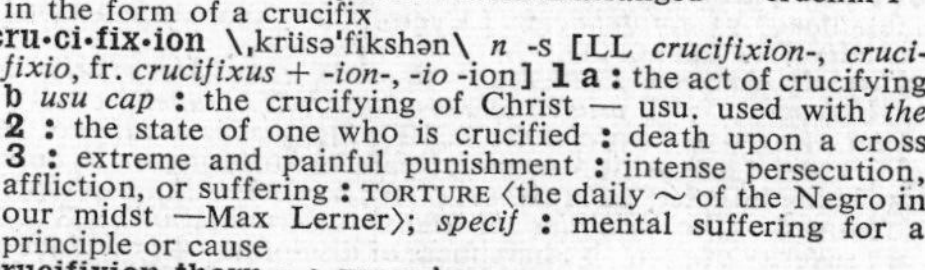

crucifix 1

cru·ci·fix·ion \,krüsə'fikshən\ *n* -s [LL *crucifixion-, crucifixio,* fr. *crucifixus* + *-ion-, -io* -ion] **1 a :** the act of crucifying **b** *usu cap* **:** the crucifying of Christ — usu. used with *the* **2 :** the state of one who is crucified **:** death upon a cross **3 :** extreme and painful punishment **:** intense persecution, affliction, or suffering **:** TORTURE ⟨the daily ~ of the Negro in our midst —Max Lerner⟩; *specif* **:** mental suffering for a principle or cause

crucifixion thorn *n* **:** CHRIST'S-THORN

¹cru·ci·form \'krüsə,fȯrm\ *adj* [L *cruci-, crux* cross + E *-form* — more at RIDGE] **:** forming or arranged in a cross **:** CRUCIATE ⟨a ~ aircraft wing⟩ — **cru·ci·form·ly** *adv*

²cruciform \"\ *n* -s **:** a figure representing or resembling a cross **:** CROSS ⟨the ground plan is a ~⟩

cruciform ligament *n* **:** CRUCIATE LIGAMENT c

cru·ci·fy \'krüsə,fī\ *vt* -ED/-ING/-ES [ME *crucifien,* fr. OF *crucifier,* fr. LL *crucifigere* — more at CRUCIFIX] **1 :** to put to death by nailing or binding the hands and feet to a cross **2 :** to destroy the power or ruling influence of **:** subdue completely **:** MORTIFY ⟨they that are Christ's have *crucified* the flesh —Gal 5:24(AV)⟩ **3 a :** to treat cruelly (as in severe punishment) **:** TORMENT, TORTURE **b :** to harry, persecute, or pillory esp. for some cause or principle **:** DENIGRATE ⟨a ~ a political leader⟩

cruck \'krək\ *n* -s [ME *crokke,* prob. var. of *crok* crook — more at CROOK] **:** one of a pair of curved timbers forming a principal support of a roof in primitive English house construction

¹crud \'krəd, 'krüd\ *n* -s [ME *crudd* — more at CURD] **1** *dial* **:** ¹CURD **2 :** a deposit or incrustation of filth, grease, or refuse **:** an impurity or unwanted foreign substance **3 :** a usu. ill-defined or imperfectly identified bodily disorder ⟨jungle ~⟩ — **crud·dy** \-dē\ *adj*

²crud \"\ *vb* **crudded; crudded; crudding; cruds** [ME *crudden* — more at CURD] *dial* **:** ²CURD

crud·dle \'krəd°l, -rüd-\ *vb* -ED/-ING/-S [freq. of ²*crud*] *dial* **:** CURDLE

¹crude \'krüd\ *adj* -ER/-EST [ME, fr. L *crudus* raw — more at RAW] **1 :** in a natural state **:** not cooked or prepared by fire or heat **:** not altered or prepared for use by any process **:** RAW ⟨~ flesh⟩ **:** not refined ⟨~ sugar⟩ ⟨~ rubber⟩ **2** *obs* **:** UNDIGESTED **:** not digestible **:** not brought into a form to give nourishment **3** *obs* **:** UNRIPE **:** not mature or perfect **:** IMMATURE, UNDEVELOPED ⟨I come to pluck your berries harsh and ~ —John Milton⟩ **4 :** marked by the primitive, gross, or elemental or by the most readily apprehended **:** wanting subtlety, nuance, or complexity **:** low in perception, analysis, or appreciation ⟨a ~ notion⟩ ⟨a ~ theory⟩ ⟨it was there that the ~ dogmatism of New England was refined and humanized —H.L.Mencken⟩ **5 :** marked by uncultivated simplicity **:** wanting in elegance, discrimination, or polish esp. in choice of words or figures ⟨*cruder,* because less capable of expressing complicated, subtle, and surprising emotions —T.S.Eliot⟩ **:** noticeable or offensive for vulgarity ⟨~ barracks conversations⟩ **:** harshly loud **:** GRATING **:** unpleasant through lack of modulation or relief ⟨the China asters smear their ~ colors —Amy Lowell⟩ **6 :** quite oblivious or contemptuous of the refined or elevated ⟨the ~ masses of Teutondom which poured into Provincia to be leavened by its culture —H.O.Taylor⟩ **7 :** rough or inexpert in plan or execution **:** wanting advanced technical skill in contrivance and elegance in effect ⟨the *cruder* means of transportation, by wooden ships propelled by the wind . . . by oxcart —A.C.Morrison〉 **8 :** lacking any covering, glossing, concealing, or masking **:** lacking mitigation, alleviation, or reservation **:** OBVIOUS, SHEER, UTTER, BALD, STARK 〈~ facts〉 〈~ necessity〉 〈~ sensation〉 〈not the ~ beauty of the eye. It was not beauty pure and simple —Virginia Woolf〉 **9** *archaic* **:** constituting the part of a word that remains constant or nearly constant throughout a paradigm **:** being the base to which inflectional affixes are attached 〈the stem or ~ form of a word〉 **10** *of statistics* **:** tabulated without breaking down into classes 〈~ death rate〉 **11** *of animal feedstuffs* **:** reacting like members of a particular class of nutrients to certain identifying tests though not necessarily chemically a member of such class 〈~ protein includes all the nitrogenous compounds of a feed〉 〈~ fat is high in this analysis but digestible fats are low〉 **syn** see RUDE

²**crude** \"\ *n* -S **:** a substance in its natural unprocessed state: as **a :** CRUDE OIL **b :** initial products of distillation of crude oil without cracking or other treatment **c :** a crude substance (as benzene, toluene, xylene, cresol, naphthalene, anthracene, or carbazole) distilled from coal tar

crude drug *n* **:** a plant or animal drug occurring in either the fresh or dried condition and either whole or reduced in particle size by cutting or grinding

crude fiber *n* **:** the chiefly cellulose material obtained as a residue in the chemical analysis of vegetable substances (as foods and animal feeds)

crude·ly *adv* **:** in a crude manner **:** ROUGHLY, SIMPLY, APPROXIMATELY, BLUNTLY

crude·ness *n* -ES **:** the quality or state of being crude

crude oil *or* **crude petroleum** *n* **:** petroleum as it occurs naturally, as it comes from an oil well, or after extraneous substances (as entrained water, gas, and minerals) have been removed

crude protein *n* **:** the approximate amount of protein in foods calculated from the determined nitrogen content by multiplying by a factor (as 6.25 for many foods and 5.7 for wheat) derived from the average percentage of nitrogen in the food proteins, an appreciable error thus resulting if the nitrogen is derived from nonprotein material or from a protein of unusual composition

crude still *n* **:** a still in which crude oil is first distilled — compare TAR STILL

cru·di·ty \ˈkrüdəd·ē, -ətē, -i\ *n* -ES [MF or L; MF *crudité*, fr. L *cruditat-, cruditas*, fr. *crudus* raw + *-itat-, -itas* -ity — more at RAW] **1 :** the quality or state of being crude **:** lack of polish, refinement, or subtlety **:** RAWNESS, ROUGHNESS, HARSHNESS **2 :** something (as undigested matter) that is crude **:** something that is unfinished or undeveloped or offensive to refined taste **:** IMPOLITENESS, IMPERFECTION 〈*crudities* of speech and behavior〉

cru·dle \ˈkrədᵊl, -rüd-\ *vb* -ED/-ING/-S [freq. of ²*crud*] *dial* **:** CURDLE

cruds *pl of* CRUD, *pres 3d sing of* CRUD

¹**cru·el** \ˈkrüəl, -üəl *also* -ü(ə)l *also esp Brit* |(,)il\ *adj* **crueler** *or* **crueller; cruelest** *or* **cruellest** [ME, fr. OF, fr. L *crudelis*, irreg. fr. *crudus* raw — more at RAW] **1 a :** disposed to inflict pain esp. in a wanton, insensate, or vindictive manner **:** pleased by hurting others **:** SADISTIC **:** devoid of kindness **b :** RAPACIOUS, RAVENING **:** given to killing and mangling or to tormenting prey **c :** arising from or indicative of an inclination to enjoy another's pain or misfortune 〈~ epigrams〉 〈~ slanders〉 **2 a :** bitterly conducted **:** devoid of mildness **:** causing or conducive to injury, grief, or pain 〈a ~ struggle for existence〉 **b :** stern, rigorous, and grim **:** unrelieved by leniency or softness 〈a monastic regula stern and ~〉 **c :** bitterly ironical **3 :** SEVERE, DISTRESSING **:** extremely painful **:** EXTREME **syn** see FIERCE

²**cruel** \"\ *adv, now dial* **:** CRUELLY, EXTREMELY 〈a ~ hard job〉

³**cruel** \"\ *vt* -ED/-ING/-S *slang Austral* **:** to destroy all chance of success **:** SPOIL 〈that ~*ed* the experiment〉

cruel and unusual punishment *n* **:** punishment to include torture, barbarous punishments, degrading punishments not known to the common law, and punishments so disproportionate to the offense as to shock the general moral sense 〈excessive bail shall not be required, nor excessive fines imposed, nor *cruel and unusual punishments* inflicted —*U.S. Constitution*〉

cruelhearted \ˌ==ˈ==, ˈ=ˌ==\ *adj* **:** having a cruel heart

cru·el·ly *pronunc at* CRUEL + ē *or* i\ *adv* [ME, fr. ¹*cruel* + *-ly*] **1 :** so as to cause pain or hurt 〈~ done to death〉 **2 :** EXTREMELY, SEVERELY 〈the rooms are ~ overcrowded with furniture —F.A.Swinnerton〉

cru·el·ness *n* -ES [ME *cruelnes*, fr. *cruel* + *-nes* -ness] **:** CRUELTY

cruel plant *n* [so called fr. the fact that insects become entangled in the flowers] **:** any of several plants of the genera *Araujia, Schubertia,* or *Cynanchum* (family Asclepiadaceae)

cru·els \ˈkrüəlz\ *n pl* [MF *escroele, escroelle*, fr. OF, fr. (assumed) VL *scrofellae*, fr. LL *scrofulae* — more at SCROFULA] *chiefly Scot* **:** SCROFULA

cru·el·ty *pronunc at* CRUEL + tē *or* ti\ *n* -ES [ME *cruelte*, fr. OF *crueltė*, fr. L *crudelitat-, crudelitas*, fr. *crudelis* cruel + *-itat, -itas* -ity — more at CRUEL] **1 :** the quality or state of being cruel **:** disposition to inflict pain or suffering or to enjoy its being inflicted **:** INHUMANITY **2 :** a cruel action **:** inhuman treatment 〈the *cruelties* of racial discrimination〉 **3** *obs* **a :** severity of pain **b :** harshness of discipline **4 :** conduct of either party in a divorce action that endangers the life or health of the other; *also* **:** acts that cause mental suffering or fear

cru·en·ta·tion \ˌkrüˌenˈtāshən, -üən-\ *n* -S [LL *cruentation-, cruentatio* staining with blood, fr. L *cruentatus* (past part. of *cruentare* to make bloody, fr. *cruentus* bloody) + *-ion-, -io* -ion; akin to L *cruor* blood — more at RAW] **:** the oozing of blood from a corpse after incision or according to superstitious belief in the presence of the murderer

cruentous *adj* [L *cruentus*, fr. *cruor* blood] *obs* **:** BLOODY

cru·et *also* **crew·et** \ˈkrüət\ *n* -S [ME *cruette*, fr. AF *cruet*, dim. of OF *crue, cruie*, of Gmc origin; akin to OS *krūka* pot — more at CROCK] **:** a usu. glass bottle or vessel used to hold vinegar, oil, or other condiments for table use or to hold wine or water for altar service

cruet

¹**cruise** \ˈkrüz\ *vb* -ED/-ING/-S [D *kruisen* to make a cross, move crosswise, cruise, fr. MD *crucen*, fr. *crūce* cross, fr. L *cruc-, crux* — more at RIDGE] *vi* **1 :** to sail about touching at a series of ports as distinguished from voyaging to a set destination **2** *slang* **:** to be on one's way **:** GO 〈you ~ right along and cheer her up —J.C.Lincoln〉 **3 :** to travel for the sake of traveling without destination or other definite purpose **4 :** to go about at random but on the lookout for possible developments (as of a taxicab or a police car) **5 a** *of an airplane* **:** to fly at the most efficient operating speed of the engine **b** *of an automobile* **:** to travel at a speed suitable for maintaining steadily for long distance; *sometimes* **:** to go at or near the highest speed that can be safely and steadily maintained ~ *vt* **1 :** to cruise over or about 〈*cruising* the Mediterranean in a yacht〉 **2 :** to explore with reference to the possible lumber yield 〈~ a section of land〉 〈~ the timber in a holding〉 **3 :** to fly (an airplane) or drive (a car or truck) at cruising speed 〈the car can be *cruised* at 70 mph〉

²**cruise** \"\ *n* -S **1 :** the act of cruising **:** a journeying from or as if from port to port 〈the ~ of a trapper for game〉 **2 a :** the trip of a ship cruising **b :** any casual trip

cruise car *n* **:** SQUAD CAR

cruis·er \-zə(r)\ *n* -S [D *kruiser*, fr. *kruisen* to cruise + *-er*] **1 :** a boat or vehicle (as a taxicab or police car) that cruises **2 :** any of certain warships: **a :** an 18th century privateer **b :** a large fast moderately armored and gunned warship usu. of 6000 to 15,000 tons displacement — see GUIDED MISSILE CRUISER, HEAVY CRUISER, LIGHT CRUISER **3 :** a powerboat equipped with cabin, permanent berths, fixed plumbing, and other arrangements necessary for cooking and living aboard — called also *cabin cruiser* **4 :** a person who cruises: **a :** one who estimates the volume and value of marketable timber on a tract of land and maps it out for logging **b** *slang* **:** PROSTITUTE **c :** TRAVELER **5 :** a high-topped laced boot used by lumbermen in cruising timber **6 :** FASHION GRAY **7** [by shortening] **:** CRUISERWEIGHT

cruiser stern *n* **:** a stern on high-speed naval vessels designed without overhang to give maximum immersed length

cruiserweight \ˈ==ˌ=\ *n* [so called fr. the comparison of the second-heaviest boxing class (light-heavyweight) to the traditionally second heaviest warship (cruiser)] *chiefly Brit* **:** a light-heavyweight boxer or class

crui·sie *var of* CRUSIE

cruising radius *n* **1 :** the maximum distance that the fuel capacity of a naval vessel or an airplane will allow it to go and return from at cruising speed **2 :** the distance an animal may move from an initial point (as a den) in the course of a day

cruis·keen \(ˈ)krüshˈkēn\ *or* **cruis·ken** \ˈkrüskən\ *n* -S [IrGael *crūiscīn* & ScGael *crūisgean*, both fr. (assumed) MD *croeskijn*, dim. of MD *croese, crose* jug, pitcher — more at CRUSE] *Irish & Scot* **:** a small pitcher or jug for holding liquor

cruive \ˈkrǣv\ *n* -S [ME (Sc dial) *cruﬁe, crove*, prob. fr. ScGael *crō* pen for animals, hut — more at CREW] *Scot* **:** a small rude enclosure (as a hovel or a pen for animals)

crul·ler \ˈkrələ(r)\ *n* -S [D *krulle*, a kind of twisted cake, fr. *krul* curly, fr. MD *crulle;* akin to MHG *krol, krul* curly — more at CURL] **1 :** a small sweet cake made of a rich egg batter formed into twisted strips and fried brown in deep fat **2** *North & Midland* **:** an unraised doughnut **:** FRIEDCAKE

crum *archaic var of* CRUMB

¹**crumb** \ˈkrəm\ *n* -S [ME *cromme*, fr. OE *cruma;* akin to MHG *krume* crumb, MD *crume*, Icel *krumur* soft inside, OHG *krouwōn* to scratch, L *grumus* pile of dirt, Gk *grymea* bag, trash, fish remnants, Alb *grime* crumb; basic meaning: something scratched together; akin to OE *cradol* cradle — more at CRADLE] **1 :** a small fragment or piece; *esp* **:** a very small piece of bread or other food broken or rubbed off **2 :** a little **:** BIT 〈a ~ of comfort〉 **3 :** the soft part of bread — opposed to *crust* 〈if you can't get ~, you'd best eat crust〉 **4 :** any material resembling bread crumb: as **a :** loose friable soil **b :** shredded alkali cellulose **5 a :** BODY LOUSE **b** *slang* **:** a worthless person **6 crumbs** *pl* **:** a mixture of sugar, butter, and flour used as a topping on pastry (as coffee cake) — **to a crumb :** to the last detail

²**crumb** \"\ *vt* -ED/-ING/-S [ME *crummen*, fr. *crumme*, n.] **1 :** to break into crumbs 〈~ bread〉 **2 :** to cover, thicken, or dress with crumbs **3 :** to remove crumbs from 〈~ the table〉

crumbcloth \ˈ=ˌ=\ *n* **1 :** a cloth often of damask formerly laid under a dining table to receive falling fragments **2 :** a heavy damask suitable for embroidery

crumb·i·ness \ˈkrəmēnə̇s, -in-\ *n* -ES **:** the quality or state of being crumby

¹**crum·ble** \ˈkrəmbəl\ *vb* **crumbled; crumbled; crumbling** \-b(ə)liŋ\ **crumbles** [alter. (influenced by ¹*crumb*) of earlier *crimble*, fr. ME *kremelen*, freq. of OE *gecrymian* to crumble, fr. *cruma* crumb — more at CRUMB] *vt* **:** to break into or cause to fall in small pieces ~ *vi* **:** to fall into small pieces 〈stone that ~*s* quickly〉 **:** fall to decay or ruin **:** DISINTEGRATE, COLLAPSE 〈*crumbling* walls〉 **syn** see DECAY

²**crumble** \"\ *n* -S **1** *dial* **:** CRUMB **2 :** crumbling substance **:** fine debris

crum·bli·ness \ˈkrəmb(ə)lēnə̇s, -lin-\ *n* -ES **:** the quality or state of being crumbly

crum·bling·ness \-b(ə)liŋnə̇s\ *n* -ES **:** the quality or state of being crumbling

crum·blings \ˈkrəmbliŋz\ *n pl* **:** crumbled particles **:** CRUMBS

crum·bly \-b(ə)lē, -bli\ *adj* **:** easily crumbled **:** FRIABLE 〈~ soil〉

crumb-of-bread sponge *n* **:** a common encrusting sponge (*Halichondria panicea*) lacking microscleres and having the megascleres irregularly arranged

cru·men \ˈkrümən, -ˌmen\ *or* **cru·me·na** \krüˈmēnə, -ˈmänə\ *n, pl* **crumens** \-ənz, -enz\ *or* **crumenas** \-ēnəz, -ānəz\ *or* **crume·nae** \-ē,nē, -ā,nī\ [L *crumena, crumina* purse, bag, modif. of Gk *grymea* bag, trash — more at CRUMB] *zool* **:** POUCH: as **a :** the suborbital gland that secretes a waxy substance and is present in many deer and antelopes **b :** one into which the mouthparts of certain bugs can be retracted

crum·mie *or* **crum·my** \ˈkrəmi\ *n, pl* **crummies** [Sc *crum*, *crumb* crooked (fr. ME *crumb*, fr. OE) + *-ie, -y;* akin to OE *crump* crooked — more at CRUMP] *chiefly Scot* **:** COW; *esp* **:** one with crumpled horns

crum·mock \ˈkrəmək\ *n* -S [ScGael *cromag* anything bent, fr. *crom* crooked; akin to OIr *cromm*, OE *gehrumpen* wrinkled — more at RUMPLE] *chiefly Scot* **:** a staff with a crooked head

¹**crum·my** *or* **crumby** \ˈkrəmē, -mi\ *adj* -ER/-EST [*crummy* fr. obs. E *crumme* crumb (fr. ME) + E *-y* — more at CRUMB] **1** *obs* **:** FRIABLE, CRUMBLY **2** *slang* **a :** MISERABLE, FILTHY **b :** CHEAP, WORTHLESS **3** *Brit* **:** PLUMP, BUXOM

²**crummy** \"\ *n* -ES [prob. fr. ¹*crummy;* fr. the fact that food is eaten there and that it is traditionally untidy] *slang* **:** CABOOSE

¹**crump** \ˈkrump, ˈkrəmp\ *adj* [ME *crumb, crump*, fr. OE; akin to OS *crumb* crooked, OHG *krump, krumpf* crooked, *kramph* bent — more at CRAMP] *chiefly dial Brit* **:** CROOKED, BENT

²**crump** \"\ *vb* -ED/-ING/-S [ME *crumpen*, fr. *crump*, adj.] *now dial Eng* **:** CROOK, CURVE **:** curl up

³**crump** *n* -S [¹*crump*] *obs* **:** HUMPBACK

⁴**crump** \ˈkrəmp\ *vi* -ED/-ING/-S [imit.] **1 :** to make a crunching sound (as in eating) **:** CRUNCH **2 :** to explode heavily (as of a bomb) **:** THUMP, THWACK 〈the shells ~*ed* in the road behind us〉

⁵**crump** \"\ *n* -S **1 :** a crunching sound **2** *Brit* **:** BLOW, THUMP **3 a :** the explosion of a heavy shell or bomb **b :** SHELL, BOMB

⁶**crump** \"\ *adj* [perh. alter. (influenced by ⁴*crump*) of ³*crimp*] *chiefly Scot* **:** BRITTLE, FRIABLE, CRISP

crum·pet \ˈkrəmpə̇t\ *n* -S [perh. fr. ME *crompid* (*cake*) wafer (lit., curled-up cake), fr. *crompid, crumped*, past part. of *crumpen* to curve, curl up — more at CRUMP] **:** a small round cake made of rich unsweetened batter cooked on a griddle and usu. served split and toasted

crump hole *n* [⁵*crump*] **:** a bomb crater

¹**crum·ple** \ˈkrəmpəl\ *vb* **crumpled; crumpled; crumpling** \-p(ə)liŋ\ **crumples** [fr. (assumed) ME *crumplen*, freq. of *crumpen* to crump — more at CRUMP (to crook)] *vt* **1 :** to press or twist into folds or wrinkles 〈~ a paper〉 **:** RUMPLE **:** make creases in 〈a smile *crumpled* his face〉 **:** bend and crush out of shape 〈the crash *crumpled* both fenders badly〉 **2 :** to cause to collapse **:** break the resistance of 〈swearing always *crumpled* her〉 ~ *vi* **1 :** to show wrinkles after crushing 〈tinfoil ~*s* readily〉 **2 :** to collapse as if crumpled 〈at the sound of the shot the figure suddenly *crumpled*〉 — often used with *up* 〈he lay there all *crumpled* up〉

²**crumple** \"\ *n* -S **:** a wrinkle, fold, or crease made by crumpling or squeezing **:** a crumpled part of something

crumpled *adj* [ME *crumpled, crompled*, past part. of (assumed) *crumplen*] **1 :** wrinkled, creased, or bent out of shape by or as if by pressing, folding, or crushing 〈a ~ pack of cigarettes〉 **2 :** bent spirally **:** CURVED 〈the cow with the ~ horn〉

crum·pler \-p(ə)lə(r)\ *n* -S **:** one that crumples

crump·ling \ˈkrəmpliŋ, -rəm-\ *n* -S [¹*crump* + *-ling*] *dial Eng* **:** something stunted or shriveled (as an apple or cucumber)

crump·ly \ˈkrəmp(ə)lē, -li\ *adj* **:** full of crumples **:** having a tendency to crumple

crump·sall yellow \ˈkrəm(p)səl-\ *n, usu cap C* [fr. *Crumpsall*, suburb of Manchester, England, where chemicals are manufactured] **:** a mordant dye — see DYE table I (under *Mordant Yellow 20*)

¹**crunch** \ˈkrənch\ *vb* ED/-ING/-ES [alter. of ¹*craunch*] *vi* **1 :** to chew with a crushing or grinding noise **2 :** to grind or press with a noise of crushing **3 :** to move or proceed with a crunching sound ~ *vt* **1 :** to bite with a crushing noise **2 :** to crush or grind (as under a foot or wheel) with a noise 〈~*ed* the crisp snow〉

²**crunch** \"\ *n* -ES **1 :** the act of crunching **2 :** a sound made by crunching 〈hear the ~ of his saddle shoes on the gravel lane —A.W.Turnbull〉 **3 :** a piece made or separated by crunching

crunch·er \-chə(r)\ *n* -S *slang* **:** a finishing blow

crunch·i·ness \ˈkrənchēnə̇s, -chin-\ *n* -ES **:** the quality or state of being crunchy **:** CRISPNESS

crunch·ing·ly *adv* **:** in a crunching manner

crunch·ing·ness *n* -ES **:** the quality or state of being crunching

crunchweed \ˈ=ˌ=\ *n* **:** CHARLOCK

crunchy \ˈkrənchē, -chi\ *adj* -ER/-EST **:** that crunches **:** CRUNCHING, CRISP

crun·kle \ˈkrəŋkəl, -əŋk-\ *vt* -ED/-ING/-S [ME *crounkilen* — more at CRINKLE] *dial Brit* **:** CRUMPLE, WRINKLE

cruor *n* -S [L, blood — more at RAW] *obs* **:** the clotted portion of coagulated blood

crup·per \ˈkrəpə(r), -rüp-,-rüp-\ *n* -S [ME *croper, cruper*, fr. OF *cropiere, crupiere*, fr. *crope, crupe* hindquarters + *-iere* -er — more at CROUP] **1 :** a leather loop passing under a horse's tail and buckled to the saddle to keep it from slipping forward — see HARNESS illustration **2 :** the rump of a horse **:** CROUP; *broadly* **:** HINDQUARTERS, BUTTOCKS

crura *pl of* CRUS

cru·ral \ˈkrürəl\ *adj* [MF or L; MF *crural*, fr. L *cruralis*, fr. *crur-, crus* leg + *-alis* -al] **:** relating to the thigh or leg or any of the crura; *specif* **:** FEMORAL 〈~ artery〉 〈~ nerve〉

crural arch *n* **:** POUPART'S LIGAMENT

crural septum *n* **:** a thin fascia that normally closes the femoral ring and prevents descent of abdominal viscera into the femoral canal

cruro- *comb form* [NL, fr. L *crur-, crus* leg] **:** crural and 〈*cruro*inguinal, *cruro*tarsal〉

¹**crus** \ˈkrüs, ˈkrəs\ *n, pl* **cru·ra** \ˈkrürə\ [L; akin to Arm *srunk* shinbones, calves of the legs] **1 :** the part of the hind limb between the femur or thigh and the ankle or tarsus **:** SHANK **2 :** any of various parts likened to a leg or to a pair of legs: as **a :** either of the diverging proximal ends of the corpora cavernosa **b :** the tendinous attachments of the diaphragm to the bodies of the lumbar vertebrae forming the sides of the aortic opening — often used in pl. **c** *crura, pl* **:** the peduncles of the cerebrum — called also *crura ce·re·bri* \-ˈserə,brī, -ˈkerə,brē\ **d** *crura, pl* **:** the peduncles of the cerebellum **e** *crura, pl* **:** the posterior pillars of the fornix — called also *crura for·ni·cis* \-ˈfȯrnə,sis, -ə,kis\ **f :** either of a pair of basal processes on the brachidia of certain brachiopods — see BRACHIOPOD illustration

²**crus** *pl of* CRU

¹**cru·sade** \(ˈ)krüˈsād\ *n* -S [blend of earlier *croisade* & *crusado; croisade* fr. MF, modif. (influenced by OProv *crozada*) of OF *croisée*, fr. fem. of past part. of *croiser* to take up the cross, fr. *crois* cross; *crusado* modif. of Sp *cruzada* (after Prov *crozada*), fr. fem. of past part. of *cruzar* to take up the cross, fr. *cruz* cross; OF *crois* and Sp *cruz* fr. L *cruc-, crux* — more at RIDGE] **1** *usu cap* **:** an expedition undertaken for a declared religious purpose (as recovering Jerusalem from the Muslims in the middle ages) **:** a campaign or war sanctioned by the church against unbelievers or heretics **2 :** any remedial activity pursued with zeal and enthusiasm 〈a ~ against drinking〉

THE CHIEF CRUSADES

NAME	DATE	OUTCOME
First	1096–99	Took Jerusalem
Second	1147–49	Unsuccessful
Third	1189–92 (or 91)	Conquest of Acre
Fourth	1202–04	Established Latin Empire in East
Fifth	1228–29	Jerusalem taken, but lost, finally, 1244
Sixth	1248–54	Unsuccessful
Seventh	1270	Unsuccessful

²**crusade** \"\ *vi* -ED/-ING/-S **:** to engage in a crusade **:** attack zealously **:** strive to further a cause 〈a newspaper *crusading* against corruption〉

cru·sad·er \-də(r)\ *n* -S **:** one engaged in a crusade

¹**cru·sa·do** \krüˈzä(ˌ)dō, -)thü, -ˈsä(ˌ)dō, -ˈsā(ˌ)dō\ *also* **cru·za·do** \-ˈzä(ˌ)dō, -)thü\ *n, pl* **crusadoes** *or* **crusados** [Pg *cruzado*, lit., marked with a cross, fr. past part. of *cruzar* to mark with a cross, fr. *cruz* cross, fr. L *cruc-, crux* — more at RIDGE] **:** an old gold coin of Portugal orig. issued by Alfonso V (1438-81) having a cross on the reverse in commemoration of the king's crusading struggle against the Muslims of No. Africa; *also* **:** a similar Portuguese coin in silver first issued by John IV (1640-56)

²**cru·sa·do** \-ˈsā(ˌ)dō\ *n, pl* **crusados** *or* **crusadoes** [modif. of Sp *cruzada* — more at CRUSADE] *archaic* **:** CRUSADE

cruse \ˈkrüz, -üs\ *n* -S [ME *cruse, crowse*, prob. fr. MD *croese* jug, pitcher; akin to MHG *krūse* pitcher, OE *crūse*] **:** a small vessel (as a jar, pot) for holding a liquid (as water, oil, honey)

¹**crush** \ˈkrəsh\ *vb* -ED/-ING/-ES [ME *crusshen*, fr. MF *cruisir, croissir*, of Gmc origin; akin to MLG *krossen* to crush, OSw *krusa, krosa* to crush, *krysta* to gnash, Goth *kriustan* and perh. to Gk *brychein* to gnash, Lith *griūti* to collapse] *vt* **1 :** to press between two hard bodies 〈~ grapes〉 **:** squeeze or force by pressure so as to damage or destroy the structure of **:** force together into a mass 〈~ clothes into a box〉 〈~ out a cigarette〉 〈~*ed* under the wheels of a truck〉 **2 :** to press or cause to press closely **:** embrace strongly **:** HUG, SQUEEZE 〈~*ed* her child to her breast〉 **3 :** to reduce to particles by pounding or grinding **:** COMMINUTE, BRAY 〈~ rock〉 **4 a :** to suppress or overwhelm as if by pressure or weight 〈truth, ~*ed* to earth, shall rise again —W.C.Bryant〉 **b :** to oppress or burden grievously 〈a ~*ing* burden of debt〉 **c :** to subdue completely **:** EXTINGUISH, STIFLE 〈the rebellion was ~*ed*〉 〈poverty ~*ed* his spirit〉 〈a ~*ing* retort〉 **5 :** CROWD, PUSH 〈~*ed* into the elevator〉 **6** *archaic* **:** to drink up **:** finish off 〈come and ~ a cup of wine —Shak.〉 **7 a :** to subject (paper in process) to greater than usual roller pressure accidentally or deliberately 〈the mottled appearance of a ~*ed* finish〉 **b :** to flatten out the grain of (as leather) by ironing or pressing **8** *also* **crush-dress** \ˈ=ˌ=\ **:** to form or dress (an abrasive wheel) by forcing to revolve against a hardened steel roll ~ *vi* **1** *obs* **:** CRASH **2 :** to become crushed 〈an eggshell ~*es* easily〉 **3 :** to advance with or as if with crushing 〈several men ~*ed* ruthlessly toward the door〉

syn QUELL, EXTINGUISH, SUPPRESS, QUENCH, QUASH: CRUSH indicates the utter destruction of effectiveness by heavy ruthless pressure and force smashing resistance and strangling growth 〈the sternest of those iron proconsuls who were employed by the House of Austria to *crush* the lingering public spirit of Austria —T.B.Macaulay〉 〈to *crush* the individual by its demand for unwavering obedience, total loyalty, and absolute uniformity —Oscar Handlin〉 QUELL now indicates overwhelming completely and reducing to inactivity or passivity 〈the nation obeyed the call, rallied round the sovereign, and enabled him to *quell* the disaffected minority —T.B. Macaulay〉 〈police *quelling* the disturbance〉 〈peace depends on the existence of organized power to *quell* transgressors of the peace —Bruce Bliven b.1889〉 EXTINGUISH suggests a total ending as sudden, thorough, and decisive as putting out a fire with water 〈lives that were to be *extinguished* in Hitler's gas chambers —Isaac Deutscher〉 〈the Black Death itself had *extinguished* many painfully acquired patrimonies —Roy Lewis & Angus Maude〉 〈we must not let such embers of freedom as existed in Eastern Europe and the Balkans be *extinguished* in the hour of liberation —Vera M. Dean〉 SUPPRESS may suggest rendering ineffective or nonexistent by the power of governmental, legal or legalistic, or social pressure 〈to provide for calling forth the militia to execute the laws of the Union, *suppress* insurrections, and repel invasions —*U. S. Constitution*〉 〈President Lincoln authorized searches and arrests without warrants, caused newspapers to be *suppressed*, declared martial law even in regions where the regular courts were open —F.A.Ogg & P.O.Ray〉 〈*suppressing* gambling and prostitution〉 QUENCH suggests a checking of force, impetus, effectiveness, or ardor by or as if by drenching, dampening, cooling, or slaking 〈his misfortunes never *quenched* his sprightly spirit —R.M.Lovett〉 〈the rising of the Speaker of the House *quenches* all voices and decides all quarrels —J.P. Martin〉 〈nothing could be farther from me than a desire to *quench* the imagination, on the contrary I would preserve it —George Santayana〉 QUASH indicates summary and decisive extinction or subduing 〈the poverty-stricken Hitler, whom the death of his mother deprived of a home and whose hope to study architecture had been *quashed* —G.N.Shuster〉 〈he foresaw that the dreadful woman . . . would *quash* his last chance of life —Charles Dickens〉

²**crush** \"\ *n* -ES **1** *obs* **:** clashing noise **:** CRASH **2 :** the act of crushing **:** violent compression **:** DESTRUCTION, RUIN 〈the ~ of worlds —Joseph Addison〉 **3 :** the amount of material crushed or prepared as if crushed (as for further treatment in a manufacturing process); *specif* **:** the quantity of cottonseed crushed for the extraction of oil in a given period **4** *obs* **:** BRUISE **5 a :** a violent crowding (as of people or animals)

: a crowd that produces uncomfortable pressure ⟨a ~ in the subway⟩ **b** : a large reception or party **6** : an intense and usu. passing attachment or infatuation ⟨have a ~ on someone⟩ ⟨her schoolgirl ~*es*⟩; *also* : the object of one's attachment **7** : a fenced passage narrow at one end that is used in Australia esp. in handling cattle (as for branding or vaccination) **syn** see CROWD

crush·able \-shəbəl\ *adj* : that can be crushed; *esp* : that can be crushed without harm ⟨a ~ dress material⟩

crush breccia *n* : a breccia of cataclastic texture formed by mechanical crushing in earth-crust movements

crush conglomerate *n* : an altered crush breccia whose fragments have been rounded by attrition

crushed *past of* CRUSH

crushed leather *n* : leather that has had its grain pattern accentuated by boarding, plating, or other process

crushed levant *or* **crushed morocco** *n* : a smooth-surfaced strong flexible leather obtained by crushing a coarse-grained goatskin

crushed steel *n* : an abrasive made by suddenly cooling steel and then reducing it to powder

crushed strawberry *n* : a deep to strong yellowish pink

crush·er \-shə(r)\ *n* -s **1** : one that crushes: as **a** : a machine for crushing rock, oilseeds, grapes, or other material **b** : a worker tending a crushing machine **2 a** : a crushing blow : KNOCKOUT **b** : a conclusive or overwhelming fact, realization, or retort

crushes *pres 3d sing of* CRUSH, *pl of* CRUSH

crush hat *n* : a hat that may be crushed, bent, or folded without injury (as a soft felt hat); *specif* : OPERA HAT

crushing *adj* [fr. pres. part. of *crush*] : OVERWHELMING, DEVASTATING ⟨a ~ retort⟩ : DECISIVE, FINISHING ⟨a ~ blow⟩

crush·ing·ly *adv* : in a crushing manner : OVERWHELMINGLY, WITHERINGLY

crushing strength *n* : the greatest compressive stress that a brittle solid (as stone or concrete) can sustain without fracture

crush-out \'ˌ=,=\ *n* [fr. *crush out*, v.] *slang* : a prison break

crush-room \'ˌ=,=\ *n*, *chiefly Brit* : the foyer of a theater or opera house

crush syndrome *n* : the physical responses to severe crushing injury of muscle tissue involving esp. shock and partial or complete renal failure; *also* : the renal failure associated with such responses

crush zone *also* **crush plane** *n*, *geol* : the zone of crushing along a fault characterized by the presence of fault breccia, gouge, mylonite

cru·sie \'krüzē, -ēzē\ *n* -s [modif. of MF *creuset*, alter. of *croiseul*, fr. OF *crosel, cruisel*] *Scot* : a rude iron lamp or candlestick

cru·si·ly *or* **cru·sil·ly** \'krüsəlē, -üzə-\ *adj* [MF *crusillié, crusillé*, fr. *croisille*, dim. of *crois* cross, fr. L *cruc-, crux* — more at RIDGE] *heraldry* : sprinkled with cross-crosslets

cru·soe \'krü(,)sō *sometimes* -)zō\ *n* -s *usu cap* [after Robinson *Crusoe*, shipwrecked hero of the novel *Robinson Crusoe* (1719) by Daniel Defoe †1731 Eng. journalist & novelist] : a solitary castaway : one that lives or survives by his own unaided effort and ingenuity — called also *Robinson Crusoe* — **cru·so·ni·an** \(')krü¦sōnēən, -¦zō\ *adj*, *usu cap*

¹crust \'krəst\ *n* -s [ME *crouste, cruste*, fr. MF & L; MF *croste, crouste*, fr. L *crusta* shell, crust, inlaid work; akin to OE *hrūse* earth, ground, OHG *hrosa, hroso* ice, crust, ON *hrjōsa* to shudder, Gk *kryos, krymos* icy cold, frost, *krystallos* ice, crystal, Latvian *kruvesis* frozen mud, L *cruor* blood — more at RAW] **1 a** : the hardened exterior or surface part of bread — opposed to *crumb* **b** : a piece of this or of any bread grown dry or hard : a remnant of food : a bare living ⟨what does he do to earn his ~⟩ **2** : the pastry portion of a pie **3** : a hard or brittle external coat or covering of something : a hard exterior surface : outer shell : INCRUSTATION: as **a** : the hard surface layer formed on many soils esp. when dry or on snow, mud, or lava **b** : the outer part of the earth composed essentially of crystalline rocks and varying in thickness from place to place but prob. nowhere more than a few score miles thick as distinguished from the underlying zones composed of denser but less rigid matter **c** : the horny outer wall of a hoof (as of the horse) **d** : a deposit built up on the interior surfaces of a wine bottle during a long period of aging **e** (1) : a wound covering composed primarily of serum and blood dried into a hardened mass — called also *scab* (2) : an encrusting deposit of serum, cellular debris, and bacteria present over or about lesions of certain skin diseases (as impetigo or eczema) **4 a** : a defensive simulation or covering or hardness in behavior ⟨a ~ of indifference⟩ **b** *slang* : aggressiveness obtuse to the feelings of others : NERVE ⟨he had the immortal ~ to ask me for a loan⟩ **5** *archaic* : a crusty or surly person **6** : the state of rough-tanned hides or skins before they are dyed; *also* : a skin in this state

²crust \"\ *vb* -ED/-ING/-S [ME *crousten*, fr. MF *crouster, croster*, fr. *crouste, croste*] *vi* : to form a crust : become encrusted ⟨~*ing* had begun over the wound⟩ ⟨lava ~*s* as it cools⟩ ~ *vt* : to form a crust on : cover (a surface) with incrustation ⟨ice ~*ed* the pond⟩

¹crus·ta \'krəstə\ *n*, *pl* **crus·tae** \-ˌstē, -tī\ [L, shell, crust, inlaid work] **1** : something prepared (as an engraved gem or a plate embossed in low relief) for inlaying or applying (as to a vase) **2** *anat* : the lower or ventral of the two parts into which the substantia nigra divides the cerebral peduncles

²crusta \"\ *n* -s [irreg. fr. ¹*crust*] : a cocktail containing an alcoholic liquor, flavored variously with bitters, curaçao, and lemon juice, and served in a glass lined with lemon or orange peel and frosted with powdered sugar ⟨rum ~⟩ ⟨gin ~⟩

crus·ta·cea \ˌkrə'stāsh(ē)ə\ *n pl* [NL, fr. neut. pl. of *crustaceus* crustaceous] **1** *cap* : a large class of Arthropoda comprising the majority of the marine or freshwater arthropods (as lobsters, shrimps, crabs, water fleas, and barnacles) and some terrestrial forms (as the wood lice) all having a body that is divided into segments of head, thorax, and abdomen of which the first two often consolidate into a cephalothorax and that is enclosed in a chitinous integument often hardened with calcareous matter into a firm exoskeleton, having a pair of appendages which are variously differentiated into mouthparts, walking legs, and swimmerets associated with each segment, and having two pairs of antennae — compare BRANCHIOPODA, CIRRIPEDIA, COPEPODA, MALACOSTRACA, TRILOBITA **2** : members of the class Crustacea : CRUSTACEANS

¹crus·ta·cean \ˌkrə¦stāshən\ *also* **crus·ta·ceal** \-sh(ē)əl\ *adj* [NL *Crustacea* + E *-an* or *-al*] : belonging or relating to the Crustacea : CRUSTACEOUS

²crustacean \"\ *n* -s : an animal of the class Crustacea

crus·ta·ce·ol·o·gy \ˌkrəˌstāshē'äləjē\ *n* -ES [ISV *crustaceo-* (fr. NL *Crustacea*) + *-logy*] : a branch of zoology that treats of crustaceans

crus·ta·ceous \ˌkrə¦stāshəs\ *adj* [NL *crustaceus*, fr. L *crusta* shell, crust + *-aceus* -aceous — more at CRUST] **1** : of the nature of, having, or suggesting a crust or shell **2** : ²CRABBY 1, CRUSTY 1a(2) **3** : belonging to the Crustacea : CRUSTACEAN **4** *bot* **a** : having a brittle crust **b** *of a lichen* : having a crusty thallus adhering inseparably to rocks, bark, soil

crust·al \'krəstᵊl\ *adj* [L *crusta* shell, crust + E *-al*] : relating to a crust esp. of the earth or the moon

crus·ta·tion \ˌkrə'stāshən\ *n* -s [L *crustatus* (past part. of *crustare* to cover with a shell, fr. *crusta* shell) + E *-ion*] **1** : the act or process of forming a crust ⟨soil ~⟩ **2** : a thin coating or layer : DEPOSIT

crust·ed \'krəstəd\ *adj* [ME, fr. *cruste* crust + *-ed*] **1** : covered with a crust : hardened on the surface (as by freezing or congealing) **2** : having an adhering deposit or layer ⟨~ with salt⟩ : having the accretion of age ⟨~ port⟩ ⟨a ~ conservative⟩

crust fold *n*, *geol* : a fold of large dimensions perhaps involving much minor folding and faulting such as would produce an entire mountain chain or an oceanic deep

crus·tif·ic \(')krə¦stifik\ *adj* : forming a crust

crus·ti·fi·ca·tion \ˌkrəstəfə'kāshən\ *n* -s : INCRUSTATION; *specif* : a mineral deposit formed in successive layers or crust by crust usu. in a cavity or fissure

crus·ti·fied \'krəstəˌfīd\ *adj* : formed by or filled with successively deposited layers of minerals

crust·i·ly \-tələ̄, -li\ *adv* : in a crusty or surly manner

crust·i·ness \'krəstēnəs, -tin-\ *n* -ES : SURLINESS, IRRITABILITY

crusting *pres part of* CRUST

crust·less \-s(t)ləs\ *adj* : being without a crust

crus·tose \'krəˌstōs\ *adj* [L *crustosus* crusted, fr. *crusta* crust + *-osus* -ose — more at CRUST] : forming a thin brittle crust; *specif*, *of a lichen* : having a thin thallus adhering closely to the substratum of rock, bark, or soil

crust roan *n* : a sheepskin tanned with sumac and dried but not dyed or grained

crusts *pl of* CRUST, *pres 3d sing of* CRUST

crusty \'krəstē, -ti\ *adj* -ER/-EST [ME, fr. *cruste* crust + *-y*] **1 a** (1) : having a crust (2) : having or forming a crisp dry outer layer **b** *of wine* : CRUSTED : old and mellow ⟨a flagon ~ —W.M.Thackeray⟩ **2** : genuinely or apparently abrupt, surly, and uncivil in address or disposition and often crude in appearance ⟨a ~ old fellow, as close as a vise —Nathaniel Hawthorne⟩ **3** : FILTHY, VILE ⟨~ jokes⟩ **syn** see BLUFF

crut \'krət\ *n* -s [by alter.] *substand* : ¹CRUD 2,3

¹crutch \'krəch\ *n* -ES [ME *crucche*, fr. OE *crycc*; akin to OS *krukka* crutch, OHG *krucka*, Norw dial. *krykkia* crutch, OHG *kriochan* to creep, OIr *gruc* wrinkle, OE *cradol* cradle — more at CRADLE] **1 a** : a support to aid the disabled in walking made usu. of a split staff long enough to reach to the armpit and fitted at the top with a curved crosspiece and another crosspiece at hand level **b** : any prop, support, or assisting device **2 a** : the raised part at either end of a saddle **b** (1) : the part of a saddletree that supports the pommel (2) : a forked leg rest constituting the pommel of a sidesaddle **3** : the crotch of a human being or of an animal (as a sheep) **4** : something resembling a crutch in shape or use: as **a** : a support made by joining inclined timbers near the top **b** : the depending forked rod by which the pendulum of a clock is moved **c** (1) : a breasthook at the stern of a ship (2) : a forked or 2-legged support for a fore-and-aft boom when its sail is stowed (3) : a forked stanchion to support any spar or rail when not in use **d** *chiefly Brit* : ROWLOCK **e** : a bar with a crosspiece at the end used for stirring (as formerly in making soap)

crutches 1

²crutch \"\ *vb* -ED/-ING/-ES *vt* **1** : to support on or as if on crutches : prop up **2** : to stir or mix with or as if with a crutch; *specif* : to mix (soap) with other substances in a crutcher **3** : to clip (a sheep or wool from a sheep) so as to remove the urine-stained or daggy locks from around the crutch ~ *vi* : to go on crutches

crutched \'krəcht\ *adj* **1** : supported upon or as if upon a crutch ⟨a ~ invalid⟩ **2** : caught or fixed in or as if in a forked crutch ⟨it is there that we see ourselves ~ between love grown old and indifference —George Meredith⟩ **3** : furnished with a crutch or a handle like a crutch ⟨a ~ umbrella⟩

crutch·er \-chə(r)\ *n* -s : a usu. steam-jacketed mixing device for incorporating fillers and perfume into soap

crutching *n* -s [fr. gerund of ²*crutch* (to clip wool)] : removal of wool from the crutch of a sheep; *also* : the wool crutched

crutch strike *n* : blowfly strike in or about the sheep's crutch

cruth *var of* CRWTH

crut·ter \'krəd·ə(r)\ *n* -s [E dial. *crut* passage in a mine cut across strata of rock + E *-er*] : one that drills and prepares a blasting charge in a coal mine; *also* : one who clears away blasted rock

crux \'krəks *also* -rüks\ *n*, *pl* **cruxes** \-ksəz\ *also* **cru·ces** \'krüˌsēz\ [L, cross, torture — more at RIDGE] **1 a** : a puzzling, confusing, or difficult problem : an unsolved question ⟨a scholarly ~ about the meaning of a line in Shakespeare⟩ **b** : a determinative point at issue : a pivotal or essential point requiring resolution or resolving an outcome ⟨the ~ of the problem⟩ **2** : a main or central feature (as of an argument or plan) ⟨he discarded all but the essential ~*es* of his argument —Carl Van Doren⟩

crux an·sa·ta \-ˌan'sād·ə, -sä-\ *n*, *pl* **cruces ansa·tae** \-ā,tē, -ä,tī\ [NL, lit., cross with a handle] : ANKH

crux ca·pi·ta·ta \-ˌkapə'tād·ə, -tä-\ *n*, *pl* **cruces capita·tae** \-ā,tē, -ä,tī\ [NL, lit., cross having a head] : CRUX IMMISSA

crux com·mis·sa \-kə'misə, -'kä,m-\ *n*, *pl* **cruces commis·sae** \-ˌsē, -ˌsī\ [NL, lit., connected cross] **1** : a cross of crucifixion in which the upright shaft does not extend higher than the transverse beam — compare CRUX DECUSSATA, CRUX IMMISSA **2** : TAU CROSS 1

crux de·cus·sa·ta \-ˌdekə'sād·ə, -äd·ə\ *n*, *pl* **cruces decussa·tae** \-ā,tē, -ä,tī\ [NL, lit., decussate cross] **1** : a supposed variety of the cross of crucifixion consisting of two intersecting beams set up in the form of an X : a decussate cross — compare CRUX COMMISSA, CRUX IMMISSA **2** : SAINT ANDREW'S CROSS

crux gam·ma·ta \-gə'mād·ə, -äd·ə\ *n*, *pl* **cruces gamma·tae** \-ā,tē, -ä,tī\ [NL, lit., gamma cross] : GAMMADION

crux im·mis·sa \-i'misə, -'i,m-\ *n*, *pl* **cruces immis·sae** \-ˌsē, -ˌsī\ [NL, lit., cross hanging down] **1** : a cross of crucifixion in which the top of the upright shaft extends above the transverse beam — called also *crux capitata*; compare CRUX COMMISSA, CRUX DECUSSATA **2** : LATIN CROSS 1

crux stel·la·ta \-ste'lād·ə, -äd·ə\ *n*, *pl* **cruces stella·tae** \-ā,tē, -ä,tī\ [NL, lit., starred cross] : a cross with arms that end in stars

cruzado *var of* CRUSADO

cru·zei·ro \krü'zā(ˌ)rō, -)rü\ *n* -s [Pg, fr. *cruz* cross + *-eiro* -er — more at CRUSADO] **1** : the basic monetary unit of Brazil — see MONEY table **2** : a coin representing one cruzeiro

crwth *also* **cruth** *or* **crouth** \'krüth\ *n* -s [W — more at CROWD] : an ancient Celtic musical instrument with a shallow body and a varying number of strings that were orig. plucked but later played with a short bow — called also *crowd*

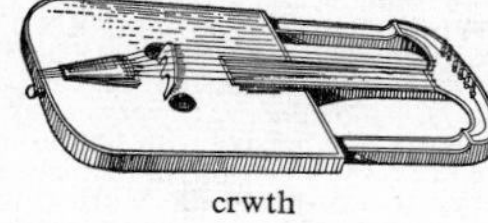

crwth

¹cry \'krī\ *vb* **cried; cried; crying; cries** [ME *crien*, fr. OF *crier*, fr. L *quiritare* to cry out for help (from a citizen), to scream, shriek, fr. *Quirit-, Quiris*, Roman citizen — more at QUIRITARIAN] *vi* **1** : to call loudly : call out (as from pain, anger, or in asking for help or mercy) : SHOUT **2** : to express grief, pain, or distress by sobbing and weeping : WAIL, WEEP, LAMENT ⟨she could not stop ~*ing* and the sobbing had a strangled sound —Carson McCullers⟩ **3 a** *of an animal* : to utter a characteristic sound or call ⟨the blown spume, and the sea gulls ~*ing* —John Masefield⟩ **b** *of a hound* : to yelp in the chase : give tongue **4** *of things* : to require or suggest strongly a given disposition or remedy ⟨the occasion ~*ing* for a new man —Francis Hackett⟩ — often used with *out* ⟨a hundred things which ~ out for planning —Roger Burlingame⟩ ~ *vt* **1** : to ask for earnestly or excitedly : BEG, BESEECH — now used chiefly in the phrase *cry quarter* **2** : to utter loudly : call out : SHOUT ⟨I heard a voice *cry* "Murder"—Shak.⟩ : declare publicly : PROCLAIM ⟨voice . . . ~*ing* in the wilderness, Prepare ye the way of the Lord —Mk 1:3 (AV)⟩ — often used with *out* **3 a** : to make public proclamation of or about : ADVERTISE, PUBLICIZE ⟨a popular TV performer to ~ their wares —*Atlantic*⟩ **b** *dial* : to publish the banns of marriage of ⟨be *cried* in the kirk on Sunday —D.M.Moir⟩ **4 a** *Scot* : SUMMON **b** *obs* : DEMAND : call for **5** *obs* : PRAISE, EXTOL **syn** see EXCLAIM — **cry halves** : to claim an equal share — **cry harrow** *or* **cry haro** : DENOUNCE ⟨you may *cry haro* upon me for a cynic —G.A.Sala⟩ — **cry havoc** : to sound an alarm : warn of disaster — **cry one's eyes out** : to weep excessively — **cry over spilled milk** : to express vain regrets for what cannot be recovered or undone : complain uselessly — **cry quits** : to call matters even (as in a contest) : propose truce : QUIT : leave off ⟨kept up the applause after the majority had *cried quits* —*N.Y. Times*⟩ — **cry wolf** [so called fr. the fable of the shepherd boy who gave the alarm of "wolf" in fun] : to give alarm without occasion

²cry \"\ *n* -ES [ME, fr. OF *cri*, fr. *crier*, v.] **1 a** : the utterance of the emotion of affliction or distress esp. when inarticulate ⟨the ~ of the children —Elizabeth B. Browning⟩ **b** *obs* : OUTCRY, CLAMOR ⟨confused ~ —Edmund Spenser⟩ **2** : a loud vehement utterance of a sound expressing strong or sudden emotion ⟨*cries* of rage and pain⟩ **3 a** *obs* : a proclamation, summons, or announcement made publicly and usu. orally **b cries** *pl*, *Scot* : banns of marriage **4** : ENTREATY, APPEAL ⟨deaf to their *cries*⟩ **5** : a loud shout (as expressing excitement or urgency) ⟨there was a ~ of "man overboard"⟩ **6 a** : a word or phrase used as a watchword, a battle cry, or a slogan repeated by a faction or party ("death to the invader" was the ~⟩ **b** : a vendor's habitual words used in announcing his wares **7 a** : common report : RUMOR ⟨the ~ goes that you shall marry her —Shak.⟩ **b** : a general opinion or belief : prevailing fashion ⟨to be in the tradition is now the ~ —F.J.Mather⟩ **8** : the utterance of the general opinion, feeling, or desire : the public voice raised in anger, protest, or approval ⟨repeated droughts brought a ~ for water⟩ **9** : an act of shedding tears : a fit of weeping ⟨a good ~ made her feel better⟩ **10 a** : an inarticulate vocal sound characteristic of an animal ⟨a hawk's ~⟩ **b** : the yelping of hounds in the chase **c** : a pack of hounds **11** : a noise resembling the crying of a man or animal ⟨the ~ in an overloaded loudspeaker⟩ ⟨a brace block's creaking ~ —John Masefield⟩; *specif* : the characteristic noise made by block tin and certain other metals under bending **syn** see FASHION — **a far cry** : a great distance : a long way — **in full cry** : in full pursuit : in full career — **out of all cry** : beyond reckoning : beyond reason : EXCESSIVELY

cry- *or* **cryo-** *also* **kryo-** *comb form* [G *kryo-*, fr. Gk, fr. *kryos* icy cold — more at CRUST] : cold : freezing ⟨*cry*anesthesia⟩ ⟨*cryo*gen⟩ ⟨*kryo*konite⟩

crybaby \'=,==\ *n* : one who cries or complains easily or often

crybaby tree *n* : a Brazilian coral tree (*Erythrina crista-galli*) with small red-orange flowers commonly cultivated esp. under glass in the U.S.

cry back *vi* : to revert to a former type (as after crossbreeding)

cry down *vt* : DISPRAISE, DISPARAGE, DEPRECIATE ⟨I no longer feel obliged to *cry down* Great Britain in order to exalt the U.S. —Hamlin Garland⟩

cryer *var of* CRIER

¹crying *adj* [ME, fr. pres part. of *crien* to cry] **1** : calling for notice : ACUTE ⟨a ~ need⟩ **2** : NOTORIOUS, HEINOUS ⟨a ~ shame⟩ **syn** see PRESSING

²crying *or* **crying out** *n* -s *now chiefly Scot* : CHILDBIRTH, CONFINEMENT

crying bird *n* : LIMPKIN

crying hare *n* : PIKA

crym- *or* **crymo-** *comb form* [NL, fr. Gk *krym-, krymo-*, fr. *krymos* icy cold — more at CRUST] : cold : frost ⟨*crymo*therapy⟩

cry·mo·therapy \¦krīmō+\ *or* **cryo·therapy** \¦krīō+\ *n* [ISV *crym-* or *cry-* + *therapy*; prob. orig. formed as F *crymothérapie*] : therapeutic use of cold to reduce sensitivity to pain, to check shock or hemorrhage, or to control psychopathic excitement — compare REFRIGERATION

cry·oc·o·nite \krī'äkəˌnīt\ *n* -s [ISV *cry-* + *con-* (fr. Gk *konis* dust) + *-ite*; orig. formed as Sw *krykonit* — more at NIT] : dust that is found on the surface of a glacier (as the Greenland ice cap) esp. on the bottom of small depressions and is formed as a result of differential melting of the ice

cry off *vt* : to call off (as a bargain) ~ *vi*, *chiefly Brit* : to excuse oneself (as from a promise or agreement) : beg off : obtain release (as from punishment)

cry·o·gen \'krīōjən, -ˌjen\ *n* -s [*cry-* + *-gen*] : a substance for obtaining low temperatures : REFRIGERANT : freezing mixture

cry·o·gen·ic \¦krīō¦jenik\ *adj* [*cry-* + *-genic*] : of or relating to the production of very low temperatures

cry·o·gen·ics \ˌ=¦=¦=niks\ *n pl but usu sing in constr* : the branch of physics that relates to the production and effects of very low temperatures — formerly called *cryogeny*

cryo·globulin \¦krīō+\ *n* [*cry-* + *globulin*] : any of several proteins similar to gamma globulins (as in molecular weight) that precipitate usu. in the cold from blood serum esp. in pathological conditions (as multiple myeloma) and that redissolve on warming

cryo·hydrate \¦krīō+\ *n* [*cry-* + *hydrate*] : a crystalline solid of constant composition and definite freezing point that is obtained by freezing a saturated solution and contains the same ratio of solute and solvent as were present in the saturated solution — compare EUTECTIC

cryo·hy·dric \¦krīō¦hīdrik\ *adj* [*cryohydrate* + *-ic*] : of or relating to a cryohydrate or the temperature at which it freezes

cry·o·lite \'krīəˌlīt\ *n* -s [ISV *cry-* + *-lite*; orig. formed as G *chryolith*] : a mineral consisting of sodium-aluminum fluoride Na_3AlF_6 found in Greenland usu. in white cleavable masses of waxy luster and used in making soda and aluminum (hardness 2.5, sp. gr., 2.95–3.0)

cry·o·lith·i·o·nite \ˌkrīō'lithēəˌnīt, -ˌlə'thīə-\ *n* -s [alter. of earlier *kryolithionite*, fr. *kryo-* cry- + *lithionite* (obs. syn. of *lepidolite*), fr. G *lithonit*, fr. obs. NL *lithion* (now *lithia*) + G *-it* -ite] : a mineral composed of a fluoaluminate of sodium and lithium $Na_3Li_3(AlF_6)_2$ found in the Ural mountains

cry·ol·o·gy \krī'äləjē\ *n* -ES [*cry-* + *-logy*] **1** : the study of snow and ice; *sometimes* : GLACIOLOGY **2** : the science of refrigeration

cryo·magnetic \¦krīō+\ *adj* [*cry-* + *magnetic*] : relating to or dependent on the production of very low temperatures by the adiabatic demagnetization of certain salts

cry·om·e·ter \krī'ämәd·ə(r)\ *n* [ISV *cry-* + *-meter*] : an instrument for the measurement of low temperatures

cry·om·e·try \-mə·trē\ *n* -ES [ISV *cry-* + *-metry*] : the measurement of low temperatures

cryo·pedologic \¦krīō+\ *adj* : caused by or associated with permanently frozen ground or intensive frost action

cryo·pedology \¦=+\ *n* [*cry-* + *pedology* (science of soil)] : the study of frozen ground and intensive frost action

cry·o·phile \'krīəˌfīl\ *n* -s [*cry-* + *-phile*] : a cryophilic microorganism

cry·o·phil·ic \¦krīə¦filik\ *adj* [*cry-* + *-phile* + *-ic*] *biol* : preferring low temperatures; *specif*, *of bacteria* : developing best at temperatures below 10° C

cry·o·phor·ic \¦krīə¦fōrik\ *adj* [NL *cryophorus* + E *-ic*] : of or relating to the process of freezing water by its own evaporation

cry·oph·o·rus \krī'äfərəs\ *n* -ES [NL, fr. *cry-* + *-phorus* -phore] : an instrument that illustrates the freezing of water by its own evaporation

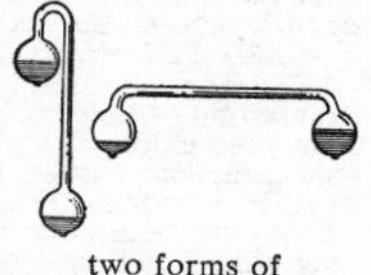

two forms of cryophorus

cry·o·phyl·lite \ˌkrīō'fiˌlīt\ *n* -s [*cry-* + Gk *phyllon* leaf + E *-ite* — more at BLADE] : a lithium mica related to zinnwaldite

cryo·planation \¦krīō+\ *n* [*cry-* + *planation*] : the modification of a land surface by intensive frost action that generally decreases the steepness of slopes and lowers the tops of hills and mountains

cry·o·scope \'krīəˌskōp\ *n* [back-formation fr. *cryoscopy*] : an instrument for determining freezing points (as of milk for detection of added water)

cry·o·scop·ic \¦krīə¦skäpik\ *or* **cry·o·scop·i·cal** \-pəkəl\ *adj* [ISV *cryoscopy* + *-ic*, *-ical*] : of or relating to cryoscopy — **cry·o·scop·i·cal·ly** \-ək(ə)lē\ *adv*

cry·os·co·py \krī'äskəpē\ *n* -ES [ISV *cry-* + *-scopy*; prob. orig. formed as F *cryoscopie*] : the determination of freezing points produced in liquid by dissolved substances in order to determine molecular weights of solutes and certain properties (as concentration or osmotic pressure) of solutions

cry·o·sel \'krīōˌsel\ *n* -s [F, fr. *cry-* + *sel* salt, fr. L *sal* — more at SALT] : CRYOHYDRATE

cry·o·stat \-ˌstat\ *n* -s [ISV *cry-* + *-stat*] : an apparatus for maintaining a constant low temperature esp. below 0° C (as by means of liquid helium)

cryotherapy *var of* CRYMOTHERAPY

cry·o·tron \'krīəˌträn\ *n* -s [*cry-* + *-tron*] : a device performing some of the functions of an electron tube and consisting of a straight wire and another wire wound in a coil around it kept at a temperature near absolute zero, the straight wire being superconducting at the low temperature but becoming nonsuperconducting when a current passes through the coil wire

cry out *vi* : to protest or complain loudly or vigorously ⟨those who *cry out* against federal interference⟩

¹crypt \'kript\ *n* -s [L *crypta* vault, cavern, fr. Gk *kryptē*, fr. fem. of *kryptos* hidden, fr. *kryptein* to hide; akin to ON *hreysar* heap of stones, OIr *crāu* stable, hut, Lith *krauti* to pile up] **1 :** a vault or other chamber wholly or partly underground; *esp* **:** a vault under the main floor of a church **2** [NL *crypta*, fr. L] *anat* **:** PIT, DEPRESSION **:** a simple gland, glandular cavity, or tube **:** FOLLICLE

²**crypt** \ˈkrip(t)\ *n* -s [in sense 1, short for *cryptogram;* in sense 2, short for *cryptography & cryptanalysis*] **1** *slang* **:** CRYPTOGRAM; *esp* **:** one favored by puzzlers **2** *slang* **:** CRYPTOGRAPHY, CRYPTANALYSIS

crypt- *or* **crypto-** *also* **krypt-** *or* **krypto-** *comb form* [NL, fr. Gk *kryptos*] **1 :** hidden **:** covered ⟨*crypto*branch⟩ ⟨*crypto*porticus⟩ **2 :** invisible **:** latent ⟨*crypto*crystalline⟩ ⟨*cryp*tomere⟩ **3 :** occult ⟨*crypt*esthesia⟩ **4 :** secret **:** private ⟨*crypto*gram⟩ ⟨*crypto*nym⟩ **5 :** hidden by dissembling **:** unavowed ⟨*crypto*fascist⟩ ⟨*crypto*rationalism⟩

crypt·al \ˈkript³l\ *adj* **:** of, like, or relating to a crypt

crypt·analysis \ˌkript+\ *n* [*crypto*gram + *analysis*] **1 :** the solving of cryptograms or cryptographic systems **2 :** the theory of solving cryptograms or cryptographic systems **:** the art of devising methods for this — called also *cryptanalytics*

crypt·analyst \(ˈ)kript+\ *n* [fr. *cryptanalysis*, after E *analysis: analyst*] **:** one who does cryptanalysis esp. as a profession

crypt·analytic \ˌkript+\ *adj* [fr. *cryptanalysis*, after E *analysis: analytic*] **:** of or relating to cryptanalysis ⟨information gained by ~ work⟩

crypt·analytics \ˌkript+\ *n pl* **:** CRYPTANALYSIS 2

crypt·analyze \(ˈ)kript+\ *vt* [fr. *cryptanalysis*, after E *analysis: analyze*] **:** to solve by cryptanalysis

cryp·ta·rithm \ˈkriptəˌrithəm, -thəm\ *n* -s [*crypto*gram + *arithmetic*] **:** a cryptogram in which letters represent digits and the key is obtained by studying arithmetical operations so written

crypt·ed \ˈkriptəd\ *adj* **:** VAULTED

cryp·te·ro·ni·a·ce·ae \ˌkriptəˌrōnēˈāsēˌē\ *n pl, cap* [NL, fr. *Crypteronia*, type genus (irreg. fr. *crypt-* + Gk *eros* love) + *-aceae;* akin to Gk *erōs* love — more at EROS] **:** a family (coextensive with the genus *Crypteronia*) of East Indian trees of uncertain affinities within the order Myrtales that have long finger-shaped clusters of greenish white flowers and capsular fruits

crypt·esthesia *or* **crypt·aesthesia** \ˌkript+\ *n* [NL, fr. *crypt-* + *esthesia, aesthesia*] **:** CLAIRVOYANCE — **crypt·esthetic** \"+\ *adj*

cryp·tic \ˈkriptik, -tēk\ *also* **cryp·ti·cal** \-təkəl, -tēk-\ *adj* [LL *crypticus*, fr. Gk *kryptikos*, fr. *kryptos* hidden + *-ikos* -ic, -ical — more at CRYPT] **1 :** HIDDEN, SECRET, OCCULT ⟨a ~ language⟩ **2 :** ENIGMATIC, MYSTERIOUS ⟨~ prophecies⟩ ⟨a ~ remark⟩ **3 :** of the nature of a crypt **4 :** serving to conceal — used esp. of the pattern or coloring of an animal **5** *med* **:** UNRECOGNIZED **6 :** BRIEF, CURT, ABBREVIATED ⟨a ~ syllogism⟩ **7 :** employing cipher or code **syn** see OBSCURE

cryp·ti·cal·ly \-tək(ə)lē, -tēk-, -li\ *adv* **:** in a cryptic way **:** MYSTERIOUSLY, ENIGMATICALLY

cryptic species *n* **:** one of two or more morphologically indistinguishable biological groups that are incapable of interbreeding — compare PHYSIOLOGIC RACE

cryp·ti·tis \kripˈtīdəs\ *n* -ES [NL, fr. *crypta* crypt (gland) + *-itis* — more at CRYPT] **:** inflammation of a crypt (as an anal crypt)

¹**cryp·to** \ˈkrip(ˌ)tō\ *n* -s [*crypt-*] **:** one who adheres or belongs secretly to a party, sect, or other group ⟨fellow travelers and ~s⟩ ⟨the ~ vote⟩

²**crypto** \"\ *adj* [by shortening] **:** CRYPTOGRAPHIC ⟨teletype, either ~ or in clear⟩

cryp·to·batholithic \ˌkrip(ˌ)tō\ *adj* [*crypt-* + *batholithic*] **:** of or relating to ore deposits formed near a batholith that is not exposed at the surface

cryp·to·biotic \"+\ *adj* [*crypt-* + *-biotic*] **:** living in concealment — used of insects or other animals that live in secluded situations (as underground or in wood)

cryp·to·blast \ˈkriptəˌblast\ *n* -s [*crypt-* + *-blast*] **:** a sterile conceptacle (as in plants of the genus *Fucus*)

cryp·to·bran·chia \ˌkriptəˈbraŋkēə\ *also* **cryp·to·bran·chi·a·ta** \-ˌbraŋkēˈädə, -ādə\ *n pl, cap* [NL, fr. *crypt-* + *-branchia, -branchiata*] **:** any of various groups of animals having concealed gills — **cryp·to·bran·chi·ate** \ˌkriptəˈbraŋkēət, -ēˌāt\ *adj*

¹**cryp·to·bran·chid** \ˌkriptəˈbraŋkəd\ *adj* [NL *Cryptobranchidae*] **:** belonging or relating to the Cryptobranchidae

²**cryptobranchid** \"\ *n* -s **:** one of the Cryptobranchidae

cryp·to·bran·chi·dae \ˌkriptəˈbraŋkəˌdē\ *n pl, cap* [NL, fr. *Cryptobranchus*, type genus + *-idae*] **:** a family of large aquatic salamanders including the American hellbenders and the Asiatic giant salamanders, all distinguished by amphicoelous vertebrae, external fertilization, and the absence of eyelids and of lacrimal and septomaxillary bones and with Hynobiidae forming a suborder of Caudata comprising primitive salamanders with relatively generalized skeletons

cryp·to·bran·chus \-ŋkəs\ *n, cap* [NL, fr. *crypt-* + Gk *branchos* gill; prob. akin to Gk *bronchos* windpipe, throat — more at CRAW] **:** the type genus of Cryptobranchidae comprising the hellbenders

cryp·to·car·ya \-ˈka(a)rēə\ *n, cap* [NL, fr. *crypt-* + *-carya* (fr. Gk *karyon* nut) — more at CAREEN] **:** a genus of tropical trees (family Lauraceae) having flowers with nine fertile and three sterile stamens and with the ripened ovary embedded in the succulent calyx tube

cryp·to·ceph·a·la \-ˈsefələ\ *n pl, cap* [NL, fr. *crypt-* + *-cephala*] *in some classifications* **:** a primary division of Polychaeta in which the peristomium is greatly developed and the prostomium is reduced — compare PHANEROCEPHALA

cryp·to·ce·ra·ta \ˌkriptōsəˈrädə, -ādə\ *n pl, cap* [NL, fr. *crypt-* + *-cerata* (fr. Gk *kerat-*, *keras* horn) — more at HORN] **:** a division of Heteroptera comprising chiefly aquatic bugs (as the boat bugs) with the antennae shorter than the head and usu. hidden in cavities beneath the eyes — compare GYMNOCERATA — **cryp·to·cer·ous** \(ˈ)kripˈtäsərəs\ *adj*

cryp·to·clas·tic \ˌkriptəˈklastik\ *adj* [ISV *crypt-* + *clastic;* orig. formed as G *kryptoklastisch*] *of a rock* **:** made up of microscopic fragmental particles

cryp·to·coc·co·sis \ˌkriptə(ˌ)käˈkōsəs\ *n, pl* **cryptococco·ses** \-ōˌsēz\ [NL, fr. *Cryptococcus* (genus name of *Cryptococcus neoformans*) + *-osis*] **:** a chronic or subacute infectious disease caused by a fungus (*Cryptococcus neoformans*) and marked by the production of nodular lesions or abscesses in the lungs, subcutaneous tissues, joints, and esp. the brain and meninges

cryp·to·coc·cus \ˌkriptəˈkäkəs\ *n* [NL, fr. *crypt-* + *-coccus*] **1** *cap* **:** a genus (the type of the family Cryptococcaceae) of yeastlike budding imperfect fungi that includes a number of saprophytes and a few serious pathogens and is often treated as a synonym of *Torula* or of *Torulopsis* — see CRYPTOCOCCOSIS, EPIZOOTIC LYMPHANGITIS **2** *pl* **cryp·to·coc·ci** \-ˈkäˌkī, -äkē, -äkˌsī, -äksē\ **:** any organism of the genus *Cryptococcus; broadly* **:** TORULA 1a

cryp·to–communist \ˌkrip(ˌ)tō+\ *n, usu cap 2d C* [*crypt-* + *Communist*] **:** one who secretly sympathizes with communism or is secretly a member of the Communist party

cryp·to·cor·y·ne \ˌkriptəˈkórəˌnē\ *n* [NL, fr. *crypt-* + Gk *korynē* club, knobby bud; perh. akin to Gk *kara* head — more at CEREBRAL] **1** *cap* **:** a genus of aquatic herbs (family Araceae) that have broad leaves and long slender spathes and are often used as aquarium plants **2** -s **:** any plant of the genus *Cryptocoryne*

cryp·to·crystalline \ˌkrip(ˌ)tō+\ *adj* [ISV *crypt-* + *crystalline;* orig. formed as G *kryptokrystallinisch*] *of a rock* **:** indistinctly crystalline **:** having a structure that, though crystalline, is so fine that no distinct particles are recognizable even under the microscope

cryp·to·di·ra \ˌkriptəˈdīrə\ *n pl, cap* [NL, fr. *crypt-* + *-dira* (fr. Gk *deirē* neck); akin to L *vorare* to devour — more at VORACIOUS] *in some classifications* **:** a suborder of Thecophora comprising turtles that bend the neck in a vertical plane in order to retract it into the shell — **cryp·to·di·ran** \ˌ==ˈ=rən\ *adj or n* — **cryp·to·dire** \ˈ==ˌdī(ə)r\ *n* -s — **cryp·to·di·rous** \ˌ==ˈdīrəs\ *adj*

cryp·to·fascist \ˌkrip(ˌ)tō+\ *n* [*crypt-* + *fascist*] **:** one who has secret fascist sympathies but is not an avowed fascist

crypt of lieberkühn *usu cap L* [trans. of G *Lieberkühnsche krypte*, after Johann N. *Lieberkühn* †1756 Ger. anatomist] **:** LIEBERKÜHN'S GLAND

crypt of mor·ga·gni \-mórˈgänyē\ *usu cap M* [trans. of It *critta di Morgagni*, after Giovanni B. *Morgagni* †1771 It. physician] **:** any of the pouched cavities of the rectal mucosa immediately above the anorectal junction, intervening between vertical folds of the rectal mucosa

cryp·to·gam \ˈkriptəˌgam\ *n* -s [F *cryptogame*, fr. NL *Cryptogamia*] **:** a plant reproducing by means of spores and not producing flowers or seed (as ferns, mosses, algae, or fungi) — see CRYPTOGAMIA

cryp·to·gam·ia \ˌkriptəˈgamēə, -ām-\ *n, cap* [NL, fr. *crypt-* + *-gamia* (fr. Gk *-gamia* -gamy)] *in former classifications* **:** a class or subkingdom embracing all cryptogams — compare PHANEROGAMIA

cryp·to·gam·ic \ˌkriptəˈgamik\ *also* **cryp·to·gam·i·cal** \-məkəl\ *or* **cryp·tog·a·mous** \(ˈ)kripˈtägəməs\ *or* **cryp·to·gam·i·an** \ˌkriptəˈgamēən, -ām-\ *adj* [NL *Cryptogamia* + E *-ic, -ical* or *-ous* or *-an*] **:** belonging or relating to the nonflowering plants or to the old group Cryptogamia

cryp·to·genetic \ˌkriptō+\ *adj* [ISV *crypt-* + *genetic*] **:** CRYPTOGENIC

cryp·to·gen·ic \ˌkriptəˈjenik\ *adj* [*crypt-* + *-genic*] **:** of obscure or unknown origin — used chiefly of diseases; opposed to *phanerogenic*

cryp·to·gram \ˈkriptəˌgram, -raa(ə)m\ *n* -s [F *cryptogramme*, fr. *crypt-* + *-gramme* -gram] **1 :** a writing in cipher or code **2 :** a figure or representation having a hidden significance — **cryp·to·gram·mic** \ˌ==ˈgramik\ *adj*

cryp·to·gram·ma \ˌkriptəˈgramə\ *n, cap* [NL, fr. *crypt-* + Gk *gramma* letter, line of a drawing, fr. *graphein* to scratch, write, draw; prob. fr. the lines of sporangia, sometimes hidden by the reflexed margin of the frond — more at CARVE] **:** a genus of ferns (family Polypodiaceae) of arctic and north temperate regions having indusia formed by the revolute margins of fertile fronds that are much taller and have narrower divisions than the sterile ones — see ROCK BRAKE

¹**cryp·to·graph** \ˈkriptəˌgraf, -raa(ə)f, -raif, -räf\ *n* -s [back-formation fr. *cryptography*] **1 :** CRYPTOGRAM **2 :** a device for enciphering and deciphering **:** a simple cipher machine

²**cryptograph** \"\ *vt* **:** to convert (a text) into code or cipher

cryp·tog·ra·pher \kripˈtägrəfə(r)\ *n* -s [NL *cryptographia* + E *-er*] **:** one that practices cryptography: as **a :** a cryptographic clerk **b :** one who devises cryptographic methods or systems **c :** CRYPTANALYST

cryp·to·graph·ic \ˌkriptəˈgrafik, -fēk\ *adj* **:** belonging or relating to cryptography ⟨~ methods⟩ **:** relating to a code or cipher system or to knowledge gained from a decipher or a decode ⟨~ information⟩ **:** employing cryptography ⟨~ writing⟩ — **cryp·to·graph·i·cal·ly** \-fək(ə)lē, -fēk-, -li\ *adv*

cryp·tog·ra·phist \kripˈtägrəfəst\ *n* -s **:** one who practices secret writing

cryp·tog·ra·phy \-fē, -fi\ *n* -ES [NL *cryptographia*, fr. *crypt-* + *-graphia* -graphy] **1 :** secret writing **:** cryptic symbolization **2 a :** the art or practice of preparing or reading messages in a form intended to prevent their being read by those not privy to secrets of the form; *also* **:** the science of devising methods and means for this — compare CIPHER 2, CODE 3 **b :** CRYPTANALYSIS

cryp·to·halite \ˌkriptō+\ *n* [ISV *crypt-* + *halite;* orig. formed as It *criptolite*] **:** a rare mineral consisting of ammonium fluosilicate $(NH_4)_2SiF_6$

cryp·to·lae·mus \ˌkriptəˈlēməs\ *n, cap* [NL, fr. *crypt-* + *-laemus* (fr. Gk *laimos* throat, gullet)] **:** a genus of small predacious coccinellid beetles including an Australian species (*C. montrouzieri*) that has been widely introduced to control mealybug infestations on citrus

cryp·to·lite \ˈkriptəˌlīt\ *n* -s [ISV *crypt-* + *-lite;* orig. formed as G *kryptolith*] **:** MONAZITE

cryp·tol·o·gist \kripˈtäləjəst\ *n* -s **:** CRYPTOGRAPHER b

cryp·tol·o·gy \-jē, -ji\ *n* -ES [NL *cryptologia*, fr. *crypt-* + *-logia* -logy] **:** the scientific study of cryptography and cryptanalysis

cryp·to·medusoid \ˌkrip(ˌ)tō+\ *adj* [*crypt-* + *medusoid*] **:** relating to the final stage in the reduction of the medusa or free-swimming generation of a hydroid to a rudiment bearing the sex cells within the gonophore

cryp·to·melane \ˌkriptə+\ *n* -s [*crypt-* + *-melane*] **:** a mineral consisting of an oxide of manganese and potassium, prob. $KMn_8O_{16}.H_2O$, common in manganese ores

cryp·to·mere \ˈkriptəˌmi(ə)r\ *n* -s [*crypt-* + *-mere*] **:** a gene or factor (as a heterozygous recessive) not detectable by inspection of the individual carrying it but demonstrable by suitable crosses — **cryp·tom·e·rism** \kripˈtäməˌrizəm\ *n* -s

cryp·to·me·ria \ˌkriptəˈmirēə\ *n* [NL, fr. *crypt-* + Gk *meros* part + NL *-ia;* fr. the concealment of the seeds of the cones within bracts — more at MERIT] **1** *cap* **:** a monotypic genus of evergreen trees (family Pinaceae) with verticillate branches, subulate leaves, and globose cones — see JAPANESE CEDAR **2** -s **:** any tree of the genus *Cryptomeria*

cryp·tom·er·ous \(ˈ)kripˈtämərəs\ *adj* [*crypt-* + *-merous*] *of a rock* **:** very finely crystalline

cryp·tom·e·ter \kripˈtämədə(r)\ *n* -s [*crypt-* + *-meter*] **:** an instrument for determining the hiding power of a paint

cryp·to·mitosis \ˌkrip(ˌ)tō+\ *n, pl* **cryptomitoses** [NL, fr. *crypt-* + *mitosis*] **:** a type of nuclear division in certain protozoa characterized by formation of a modified achromatic spindle and by absence of differentiated chromosomes

cryp·tom·ne·sia \ˌkripˌtämˈnēzhə\ *n* -s [NL, fr. *crypt-* + *-mnesia*] **:** the appearance in consciousness of memory images which are not recognized as such but which appear as original creations — **cryp·tom·ne·sic** \-ēzik, -ēsik\ *adj*

cryp·tom·o·nad \kripˈtäməˌnad\ *n* -s [NL, fr. *Cryptomonad-, Cryptomonas*] **:** a flagellate of the order Cryptomonadina

cryp·to·mon·a·da·les \ˌkriptōˌmänəˈdā(ˌ)lēz\ *n pl, cap* [NL, fr. *Cryptomonad-, Cryptomonas* + *-ales*] **:** an order of algae that is coextensive with Cryptomonadina and is usu. included among the Pyrrophyta or placed in the class Flagellatae

cryp·to·mo·nad·i·da \ˌkrip(ˌ)tōməˈnadədə\ *n pl, cap* [NL, fr. *Cryptomonad-, Cryptomonas* + *-ida*] *syn of* CRYPTOMONADINA

cryp·to·mo·nad·i·dae \-nadəˌdē\ *n pl, cap* [NL, fr. *Cryptomonad-, Cryptomonas*, type genus + *-idae*] **:** a large family (order Cryptomonadina) of chiefly freshwater and holophytic plantlike flagellates with the anterior end truncate and two anterior flagella — see CHILOMONAS

cryp·to·mon·a·di·na \-ˌmänəˈdīnə, -dēnə\ *n pl, cap* [NL, fr. *Cryptomonad-, Cryptomonas* + *-ina*] **:** a small order of plantlike flagellates having one or two flagella and usu. yellow-brown chromatophores — see CRYPTOMONADALES, CRYPTOMONADIDAE

cryp·tom·o·nas \kripˈtämənəs, -ˌnas\ *n, cap* [NL, fr. *crypt-* + *-monas*] **:** the type genus of Cryptomonadidae comprising small elliptical freshwater protozoans with two chromatophores

cryp·to·mys \ˈkriptəˌmis\ *n, cap* [NL, fr. *crypt-* + *-mys*] **:** a genus of blind burrowing mole rats of southern Africa

cryp·to·ne·mi·a·les \ˌkriptəˌnēmēˈā(ˌ)lēz\ *n pl, cap* [NL, fr. *crypt-* + Gk *nēma* thread + NL *-i-* + *-ales* — more at NEEDLE] **:** an order of red algae (class Rhodophyceae) having the auxiliary cells borne on filaments that differ markedly from the vegetative filaments (as in lacking chromatophores and in being filled with dense protoplasm)

cryp·to·neu·rous \ˌkriptōˈn(y)ůrəs\ *adj* [NL *cryptoneurus*, fr. *crypt-* + *-neurus* (fr. Gk *neuron* nerve) — more at NERVE] **:** having no distinct or recognizable nervous system

cryp·to·nym \ˈkriptəˌnim\ *n* -s [prob. fr. F *cryptonyme*, fr. *crypt-* + *-onyme* -onym] **:** a secret name — **cryp·ton·y·mous** \(ˈ)kripˈtänəməs\ *adj*

cryp·to·perthite \ˌkriptō+\ *n* -s [ISV *crypt-* + *perthite;* orig. formed as G *kryptoperthit*] **:** a perthite with lamellae of submicroscopic dimensions, such lamellae being observable by X-ray diffraction or by the electron microscope — **crypto·perthitic** \ˌ==+\ *adj*

cryp·to·phy·ce·ae \ˌkriptəˈfīsēˌē, -fis-\ *n pl, cap* [NL, fr. *crypt-* + *-phyceae*] **:** a class of motile usu. brownish green algae that are sometimes included among the Pyrrophyta and that have asymmetrical compressed cells enclosed in a firm periplast and with the two slightly unequal flagella inserted laterally or terminally

cryp·to·phyte \ˈkriptəˌfīt\ *n* -s [prob. fr. F, fr. *crypt-* + *-phyte*] **:** a plant that produces its buds underwater or underground on corms, bulbs, or rhizomes — **cryp·to·phyt·ic** \ˌ==ˈfidik\ *adj*

cryp·to·pine \ˈkriptəˌpēn, -ˌpən\ *n* -s [*crypt-* + *opium* + *-ine*] **:** a colorless crystalline alkaloid $C_{21}H_{23}NO_5$ obtained from opium and plants of the genus *Corydalis*

cryp·to·por·ti·cus \ˌkriptōˈpōrdəkəs\ *n, pl* **cryptoporticus** [L, fr. *crypt-* + *porticus* portico — more at PORCH] **:** a porch, gallery, or ambulatory in ancient Roman architecture that was wholly or partly concealed, had few openings, and served for private communication

cryp·to·pyrrole \ˌkriptō+\ *n* -s [ISV *crypt-* + *pyrrole*] **:** a liquid homologue $C_8H_{13}N$ of pyrrole formed during reduction of hemin or phylloporphyrin with hydriodic acid; 2, 4-dimethyl-3-ethyl-pyrrole

¹**cryp·tor·chid** \kripˈtórkəd\ *also* **cryp·tor·chis** \-kəs\ *n, pl* **cryptorchids** *also* **cryptorchises** [NL *cryptorchid-, cryptorchis*, fr. *crypt-* + *orchid-, orchis* testicle, fr. Gk — more at ORCHIS] **:** one affected with cryptorchidism

²**cryptorchid** \(ˈ)=ˈ==\ *adj* **:** exhibiting or affected with cryptorchidism

cryp·tor·chi·dism \kripˈtórkəˌdizəm\ *also* **cryp·tor·chism** \-ˌkizəm\ *n* -s [NL *cryptorchidismus, cryptorchismus*, fr. *crypt-* + *-orchidismus, -orchismus* -orchism] **:** a condition in which one or both testes fail to descend normally

cryp·to·rhyn·chus \ˌkriptəˈriŋkəs\ *n, cap* [NL, fr. *crypt-* + *-rhynchus*] **:** a large cosmopolitan genus of weevils including numerous pests of economic plants (as the poplar borer)

cryptos *pl of* CRYPTO

cryp·to·si·pho·nia \ˌkriptōˌsīˈfōnēə\ *n, cap* [NL, fr. *crypt-* + *siphon-* + *-ia*] **:** a genus of marine Pacific red algae (order Cryptonemiales) including one that is common on the coast and has a compressed tubular thallus with few branches and many short branchlets disposed along them

cryp·to·ste·gia \ˌkriptəˈstējēə\ *n, cap* [NL, fr. *crypt-* + Gk *stegē* roof + NL *-ia;* fr. the concealment of the corona within the tube of the corolla; akin to Gk *stegein* to cover — more at THATCH] **:** a genus of chiefly tropical African woody vines (family Asclepiadaceae) that have large polished leaves and funnel-shaped flowers and are important as a source of rubber — see INDIA-RUBBER VINE

cryp·tos·ter·ol \kripˈtästəˌrōl, -rōl\ *n* -s [ISV *crypt-* + *sterol*] **:** LANOSTEROL

cryp·to·sto·ma·ta \ˌkriptəˈstōmədə\ *n pl, cap* [NL, fr. *crypt-* + *-stomata*] **:** a group of Paleozoic bryozoa (class Gymnolaemata) in which the true apertures of the zooecia are concealed at the bottom of vestibular tubes — **cryp·to·stome** \ˈ==ˌstōm\ *adj or n*

cryp·to·termes \ˌkrip(ˌ)tō+\ *n, cap* [NL, fr. *crypt-* + *Termes*] **:** a cosmopolitan genus of dry-wood termites that is sometimes considered a subgenus of *Kalotermes* — see POWDER-POST TERMITE

cryp·to·volcanic \ˌkrip(ˌ)tō+\ *adj* [*crypt-* + *volcanic*] *of a rock structure* **:** produced by completely concealed volcanic activity — **cryp·to·volcanism** \"+\ *n* — **cryp·to·volcano** \"+\ *n*

cryp·to·xanthin \ˌkriptō+\ *n* [ISV *crypt-* + *xanthin*] **:** a red crystalline carotenoid alcohol $C_{40}H_{55}OH$ that occurs in many plants (as yellow Indian corn and papaya), in blood serum, and in some animal products (as butter and egg yolk) and that is a precursor of vitamin A; 3-hydroxy-β-carotene — called also *cryptoxanthol*

cryp·to·zoa \ˌkriptəˈzōə\ *n pl* [NL, fr. *crypt-* + *-zoa*] **1 :** the animals that live a cryptobiotic life among the organic debris of a forest floor **2 :** structures in Precambrian rocks thought to be the remains of primitive life — compare CRYPTOZOON

cryp·to·zo·ic \ˌkriptəˈzōik\ *adj* [*crypt-* + *-zoic*] **1 :** CRYPTOBIOTIC **2** *of a geologic eon* **:** prior to the beginning of the Cambrian period — compare PHANEROZOIC

cryp·to·zo·ite \ˌkriptəˈzōˌīt\ *n* -s [*crypt-* + *-zoite* (as in *sporozoite*)] **:** a malaria parasite that develops in tissue cells from the sporozoite, ultimately giving rise to the forms that invade the blood cells

cryp·to·zo·nia \-ōnēə\ *n pl, cap* [NL, fr. *crypt-* + Gk *zōnē* girdle + NL *-ia* — more at ZONE] *in some classifications* **:** a division of starfishes having the marginal plates inconspicuous and being nearly equal to the orders Spinulosa and Forcipulata combined — opposed to *Phanerozonia*

cryp·to·zo·on \-ōˌän\ *n, cap* [NL, fr. *crypt-* + *-zoon*] **:** a form genus of Cambrian and Precambrian reef-forming fossils that are usu. considered to be the remains of mats of filamentous calcareous algae

cryp·to·zy·gous \ˌkriptəˈzīgəs, (ˈ)kripˈtäzəgəs\ *adj* [*crypt-* + *-zygous*] **:** having a wide skull and a narrow face so that the zygomatic arches are concealed when the skull is viewed from above — **cryp·to·zy·gy** \ˈkriptəˌzīgē, kripˈtäzəj, |jē\ *n* -ES

crypts *pl of* CRYPT

crysal *var of* CHRYSAL

¹**crys·tal** \ˈkrist³l\ *n* -s [ME *cristal*, fr. OF, fr. L *crystallum*, fr. Gk *krystallos* — more at CRUST] **1** *obs* **:** clear ice **2 :** quartz that is transparent or nearly so and that is either colorless or only slightly tinged; *also* **:** a piece of this material (as one cut for personal ornament or for use in magic art) — called also *rock crystal;* compare CAIRNGORM, PEBBLE 2; CRYSTAL GAZING **3 :** something (as clear water) resembling crystal in transparency and colorlessness **4 a :** a body formed by the solidification under favorable conditions of a chemical element, a compound, or an isomorphous mixture and having a regularly repeating internal arrangement of its atoms; *esp* **:** such a body that has natural external plane faces as a result of the internal structure **b :** a substance having certain properties of crystals — see LIQUID CRYSTALS **5 a :** glass of superior quality and often with ornamental cutting **:** FLINT GLASS; *also* **:** a piece of this material ⟨a fine dinner set of ~⟩ **b :** a colorless transparent diamond **6 :** the glass or transparent plastic that covers the dial of a watch or clock **7 a :** a crystalline material used in a sharply tuned electromechanical transducer often as a frequency-determining element **:** a quartz plate **b :** a class of detector in a radio receiver

²**crystal** \"\ *adj* [ME *cristal*, fr. *cristal*, n.] **1 :** consisting of or resembling crystal **:** CRYSTALLINE, CLEAR, TRANSPARENT, LUCID ⟨~ streams⟩ ⟨the ~ clearness of his arguments⟩ **2 a :** relating to or using a crystal ⟨a ~ radio receiver⟩ **b :** utilizing a Rochelle salt or other crystal as the basic conversion mechanism — used esp. of a microphone, phonograph pickup, or cutting head

³**crystal** \"\ *vt* **crystaled** *or* **crystalled; crystaled** *or* **crystalled; crystaling** *or* **crystalling; crystals :** to make into crystal **:** cover with crystal ⟨the frost that ~*ed* it over⟩

crystal ball *n* **1 :** a sphere esp. of quartz crystal traditionally used by fortune-tellers **2 :** a means or method of divining or predicting future events ⟨used history as his *crystal ball*⟩ ⟨in spite of the precise technique now available . . . only the *crystal ball* of guesswork is consulted —L.P.Crespi⟩

crystal clock *n* **:** QUARTZ-CRYSTAL CLOCK

crystal detector *n, radio* **:** a detector that depends for its operation on the rectifying action of the surface of contact between certain crystals (as of galena) and a metallic electrode

crystal flower *n* **:** a low No. American herb (*Mitella nuda*) with basal rounded leaves and greenish flowers

crystal gazer *n* **:** one that practices crystal gazing

crystal gazing *n* **1 :** the art or practice of concentrating upon a glass or crystal globe with the aim of inducing a psychical state in which divination can be performed **2 :** the attempt to predict future events or developments or to make difficult judgments esp. without adequate data

crystal glass *n* **:** a clear glass with a high refractive index; *esp* **:** such glass containing lead

crystal globe *n* **:** GAZING GLOBE

crystal grating *n* **:** a diffraction grating for X rays or gamma rays utilizing the natural spacing of a crystal lattice as the grating space

crystal gray *n* **:** CINDER 5

crystall- *or* **crystallo-** *comb form* [Gk *krystall-*, *krystallo-*, fr. *krystallos* ice, crystal — more at CRUST] **:** crystal ⟨*crystal*liferous⟩ ⟨*crystall*uria⟩ ⟨*crystallo*genic⟩

crystal lattice *n* **:** the arrangement of atoms, molecules, or ions of a crystal in the form of a space lattice

crys·tal·lic \(ˈ)kriˈstalik\ *adj* **:** relating to crystals or crystallization

crys·tal·lif·er·ous \ˌkristəˈlif(ə)rəs\ *adj* [ISV *crystall-* + *-i-* + *-ferous;* prob. orig. formed as F *cristallifère*] **:** producing or bearing crystals

crys·tal·li·form \kri'stalə,fȯrm\ *adj* [*crystall-* + *-iform*] **:** having crystalline form

crys·tal·lig·er·ous \,kristə'lijərəs\ *adj* [*crystall-* + *-i-* + *-gerous*] **:** CRYSTALLIFEROUS

crys·tal·lin \'kristələn\ *n* -s [G & Sw; G *kristallin*, fr. Sw, fr. *kristall-* crystall- + *-in*] *biochem* **:** either of two globulins in the crystalline lens

crys·tal·line \'kristələn, -,līn *sometimes* -,lēn, *archaic* kri'stal-\ *adj* [ME *cristallin*, fr. MF & L; MF *cristallin*, fr. L *crystallinus*, fr. Gk *krystallinos*, fr. *krystallos* ice, crystal + *-inos* -ine — more at CRUST] **1 :** made of crystal **2 :** resembling crystal: as **a :** TRANSPARENT, PURE, PELLUCID ⟨the ~ sky —John Milton⟩ **b :** CLEAR-CUT ⟨~ sharpness of outline —John Buchan⟩ **3 a :** of the nature of or relating to a crystal **:** formed by crystallization **:** having regular arrangement of the atoms in a space lattice — opposed to *amorphous* **b :** having the internal structure though not necessarily the external form of a crystal ⟨granite is only ~, while quartz crystal is perfectly crystallized⟩ **4** *of rock* **:** composed of crystals or fragments of crystals

crystalline cone *n* **:** a transparent conical refractive body that functions as a lens in each ommatidium of the compound eye of many arthropods

crystalline flake *n* **:** graphite in flaky form either in rock matrix or separated from it

crystalline glaze *n* **:** a pottery glaze that on cooling permits the formation of crystals

crystalline heaven *or* **crystalline sphere** *n* **:** either of two transparent spheres imagined in the Ptolemaic system of astronomy to exist between the region of the fixed stars and the primum mobile in order to explain certain observed movements of the heavenly bodies

crystalline lens *n* **:** the lens of the eye in vertebrates

crystalline solution *n* **:** SOLID SOLUTION

crystalline style *or* **crystalline stylet** *n* **:** a long cylindrical or tapered translucent gelatinous rod in the digestive tract of many bivalve mollusks

crystalline veratrine *n* **:** CEVADINE

crys·tal·lin·i·ty \,kristə'linəd·ē\ *n* -ES [ISV *crystalline* + *-ity*] **:** the quality or state of being crystalline **:** degree of crystallization

crystal liquid *n* **:** LIQUID CRYSTAL

crys·tal·lite \'kristə,līt\ *n* -s [G *kristallit*, fr. *kristall-* crystall- + *-it* -ite] **1 a :** a minute mineral form like those common in glassy volcanic rocks and some slags usu. not referable to any mineral species but marking the first step in the crystallization process **b :** a single grain in a polycrystalline medium; *also* **:** a crystallographically homogeneous domain within such a grain **2 a :** any part of a plant-cell wall in which the chain molecules of cellulose lie parallel **b :** MICELLE — used esp. of the structural units of fibers (as cellulose) and other high polymers (as rubber) **c :** an oriented or crystalline region (as of high lateral order in natural and synthetic fibers) — **crys·tal·lit·ic** \¦==¦lid·ik\ *adj*

crys·tal·liz·able \'==,līzəbəl, ,==ˈ===\ *adj* **:** capable of forming or of being formed into crystals

crys·tal·li·za·tion \,kristələ'zāshən, -,līz-\ *n* -s **1 :** the process of crystallizing **2 :** a form of body resulting from crystallizing — compare CRYSTAL SYSTEM

crys·tal·lize *also* **crys·tal·ize** \'kristə,līz\ *vb* -ED/-ING/-S *see -ize in Explan Notes* [*crystall-* or ¹*crystal* + *-ize*] *vt* **1 :** to cause to form crystals or assume crystalline form; *esp* **:** to cause to assume perfect or large crystals **2 :** to cause to take a fixed and definite form ⟨tried to ~ his thoughts⟩ **3 :** to coat with crystals esp. of sugar ⟨~ cherries⟩ ~ *vi* **1 :** to become converted into crystals **:** assume crystalline form **:** solidify by crystallizing **:** deposit crystals — often used with *out* **2 :** to become fixed and definite in form — often used with *out* ⟨opinion has *crystallized* out into two sharply opposed viewpoints —S.F.Mason⟩

crystallized *adj* **1 :** formed into crystals **2 :** coated with crystals esp. of sugar **:** CANDIED **3 :** definite in form ⟨failure to distinguish between ~ and uncrystallized opinion —*Psychological Abstracts*⟩

crys·tal·liz·er \-zə(r)\ *n* -s **:** one that crystallizes: as **a :** an apparatus for carrying out crystallization (as by cooling, evaporation, or the use of a vacuum) **b :** a reagent that causes or promotes crystallization

crystallo- — see CRYSTALL-

crys·tal·lo·blast \'kristəlō,blast, kri'stalə,-\ *n* -s [back-formation fr. *crystalloblastic*] **:** one of the components of a crystalloblastic rock or rock mass

crys·tal·lo·blas·tic \¦kristəlō¦blastik\ *adj* [ISV *crystall-* + *-blastic*; orig. formed as G *kristalloblastisch*] **1** *of a rock* **:** of or relating to any crystalline texture resulting from metamorphism **2 :** denoting a structure produced by crystals growing in a solid solution

crys·tal·lo·genesis \,kristəlō+\ *n* [NL, fr. *crystall-* + L *genesis*] **:** the production or formation of crystals

crys·tal·lo·gen·ic \¦===¦jenik\ *or* **crys·tal·lo·gen·i·cal** \-¦jenəkəl\ *also* **crys·tal·lo·ge·net·ic** \-jə¦ned·ik\ *adj* [ISV *crystall-* + *-genic*, *-genical* (fr. *-genic* + *-al*) or *-genetic*] **:** crystal-producing ⟨~ attraction⟩

crys·tal·log·e·ny \,kristə'läjənē\ *n* -ES [ISV *crystall-* + *-geny*] **:** the formation of crystals as a branch of crystallography

crys·tal·lo·gram \'kristəlō,gram, kri'stalə,-\ *n* -s [*crystall-* + *-gram*] **:** a photographic record of crystal structure obtained through the use of X rays

crys·tal·log·ra·pher \,kristə'lägrəfə(r)\ *n* -s [*crystallography* + *-er*] **:** a specialist in crystallography

crys·tal·lo·graph·ic \¦kristəlō¦grafik\ *or* **crys·tal·lo·graph·i·cal** \-fəkəl\ *adj* **:** relating to or dealing with crystallography or crystals ⟨~ textures⟩ ⟨~ axes⟩ — **crys·tal·lo·graph·i·cal·ly** \-fək(ə)lē\ *adv*

crys·tal·log·ra·phy \,kristə'lägrəfē\ *n* -ES [F or NL; F *cristallographie*, fr. NL *crystallographia*, fr. *crystall-* + *-graphia* -graphy] **:** the science of crystallization dealing with the system of forms among crystals, their structure, and their forms of aggregation

¹**crys·tal·loid** \'kristə,lȯid\ *adj* [ISV *crystall-* + *-oid*; prob. orig. formed as F *cristalloïde*] **:** having some or all of the properties of crystal

²**crystalloid** \"\ *n* -s [ISV, fr. ¹*crystalloid*] **1 :** a substance (as a salt or sugar) that forms a true solution, in solution diffuses readily through a membrane, and is capable of being crystallized — compare COLLOID **2 :** one of the minute particles resembling crystals and consisting of protein that are found in certain cells esp. of oily seeds (as the Brazil nut and castor bean) — called also *protein crystal*

crys·tal·loi·dal \¦kristə¦lȯidᵊl\ *adj* **:** having the properties of or relating to a crystalloid

crys·tal·lo·luminescence \¦kristə(,)lō+\ *n* [*crystall-* + *luminescence*] **:** the emission of light by certain substances while crystallizing (as by common salt while precipitating from a hot solution of alcohol) — **crys·tal·lo·luminescent** \"+\ *adj*

crys·tal·lo·magnetic \"+\ *adj* [*crystall-* + *magnetic*] **:** relating to the magnetic properties of crystals and crystal structure

crys·tal·lo·man·cy \'kristəlō,man(t)sē\ *n* -ES [*crystall-* + *-mancy*] **:** divination by crystal gazing **:** CRYSTAL GAZING

crys·tal·lu·ria \,kristə'l(y)ürēə\ *n* -s [NL, fr. *crystall-* + *-uria*] **:** the presence of crystals in the urine indicating renal irritation (as that caused by sulfa drugs)

crystal-palace blue *n* **:** a deep blue that is greener and duller than Yale blue and greener and paler than royal (sense 8b)

crystal-palace green *n* **:** STONE GRAY

crystal pickup *n* **:** a phonograph pickup in which stylus movements generate a voltage by bending or twisting a Rochelle salt or other crystal

crystals *pl of* CRYSTAL, *pres 3d sing of* CRYSTAL

crystal sand *n* **:** very minute crystals that are scattered through the tissue of most plants and are of the same nature and origin as raphides but not needle-shaped

crystal set *n* **:** a radio receiver having a crystal detector and no vacuum tubes

crystals of ve·nus \-'vēnəs\ *usu cap V* **:** crystallized copper acetate

crystal spectrometer *n* **:** an X-ray spectrometer employing a crystal grating

crystal system *n* **:** any of the six or sometimes seven main

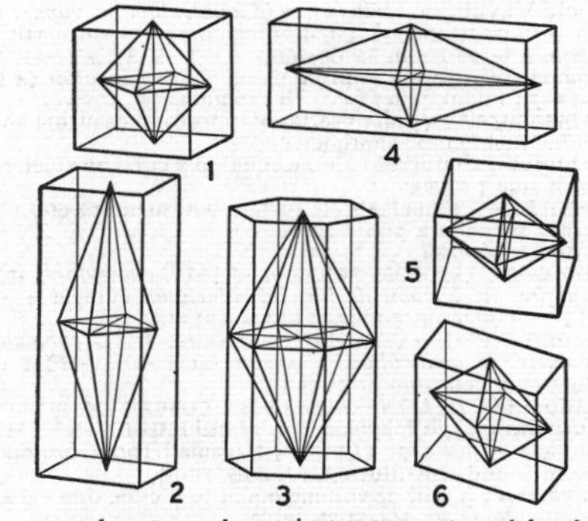

crystal systems shown in transparent models of forms analogous to the cube and the octahedron of the isometric system: *1* isometric, *2* tetragonal, *3* hexagonal, *4* orthorhombic, *5* monoclinic, *6* triclinic

groups into which crystals are commonly classified according to the relative lengths and inclinations of their axes or according to their respective symmetries — see HEXAGONAL SYSTEM, ISOMETRIC SYSTEM, MONOCLINIC SYSTEM, ORTHORHOMBIC SYSTEM, RHOMBOHEDRAL SYSTEM, TETRAGONAL SYSTEM, TRICLINIC SYSTEM, TRIGONAL SYSTEM

crystal tea *n* **1 :** a No. American cinquefoil (*Potentilla tridentata*) with trifoliolate 3-toothed leaflets and small white cymose flowers **2 :** LABRADOR TEA a

crystal vinegar *n* **:** vinegar that has been decolorized by distillation or filtration

crystal violet *n, often cap C&V* **:** a basic triphenylmethane dye consisting essentially of hexamethyl-pararosaniline chloride and used similarly to methyl violet and in medicine as an anthelmintic and bactericide and in the treatment of burns — called also *gentian violet, methylrosaniline chloride*; see DYE table I (under *Basic Violet 3* and *Solvent Violet 9*)

crystalwort \'==,=\ *n* **1 :** a plant of the order Ricciales (esp. of the genus *Riccia*) **2 :** a hepatica (*Hepatica americana*) having reniform leaves

crys·to·le·um \kri'stōlēəm\ *n* -s [*crystal* + L *oleum* oil — more at OIL] **:** an obsolete process in which a photograph was transferred to glass, the paper backing removed, and the image layer colored by the application of colors to the back

crys·to·sphene \'kristə,sfēn\ *n* -s [*cryst-* (irreg. fr. Gk *krystallos* ice) + *-o-* + Gk *sphēn* wedge — more at CRYSTAL, SPOON] **:** a buried sheet of ice under the tundra of northern America formed by the freezing of spring water which rises from the rock beneath alluvial deposits or under swamps and spreads laterally at the zone of freezing

cry up *vt* **:** to enhance the value or reputation of by public praise **:** EXTOL ⟨will hear him generally *cried up* as the most attentive and best of brothers —Jane Austen⟩

cs *abbr* **1** case **2** census **3** centistoke **4** consciousness **5** consul

CS *abbr* **1** capital stock **2** chief of staff **3** civil service **4** [It *colla sinistra*] with the left hand **5** common serjeant **6** conditioned stimulus **7** cooperative society **8** court of sessions **9** current series

Cs *symbol* cesium

c's *or* **cs** *pl of* C

csardas *var of* CZARDAS

csc *abbr* cosecant

csch *abbr* [F *cosécant hyperbolique*] hyperbolic cosecant

c-scroll \'=,=\ *n, cap C* **:** a carved shaped ornamental motive in the form of the letter C that is used decoratively esp. on furniture

CSF *abbr* cerebrospinal fluid

csg *abbr* casing

c-shaped \'=,=\ *adj, usu cap C* **:** having the shape of a capital C

c sharp \'='=\ *n, usu cap C* **1 :** the keynote of C-sharp major or C-sharp minor **2 :** the tone a half step above C

c-sharp major \'=,='==\ *n, usu cap C* **:** the major musical key having a signature of seven sharps

c-sharp minor \'=,='==\ *n, usu cap C* **:** the minor musical key having a signature of four sharps

csk *abbr* **1** cask **2** countersink

c spring *n, cap C* **:** a leaf spring the ends of which are formed in a large curve roughly resembling the letter C

CSR *abbr* certified shorthand reporter; chartered stenographic reporter

CST *abbr* central standard time

c-stage resin *n, usu cap C* **:** RESITE

cstg *abbr* casting

ct *abbr* **1** carat **2** carton **3** caught **4** cent **5** centum **6** circuit **7** count **8** county **9** court **10** current

CT *abbr* **1** cable transfer **2** central time **3** certificated teacher; certified teacher **4** code telegram **5** combat team **6** commercial traveler **7** current transformer

CTA *abbr* [L *cum testamento annexo*] with the will annexed

cten- *or* **cteno-** *comb form* [NL, fr. Gk *kten-*, *kteno-*, fr. *kten-*, *kteis* — more at PECTINATE] **:** comb ⟨*ctenacanthus*⟩ ⟨*ctenophore*⟩

cten·acan·thus \,tenə'kan(t)thəs, ,tēn-\ *n, cap* [NL, fr. *cten-* + *-acanthus*] **:** a genus of Upper Devonian and Lower Permian sharks related to *Cladoselache* and known chiefly from its very stout fin spines

cte·nac·o·don \tə'nakə,dän\ *n, cap* [NL, fr. *cten-* + Gk *akē* point + NL *-odon* — more at EDGE] **:** a genus of small primitive mammals (order Multituberculata) from the Upper Jurassic of Europe and No. America

ctene \'tēn\ *n* -s [Gk *kten-*, *kteis* comb] **:** COMB 4c

cte·nid·i·al \tə'nidēəl\ *adj* [NL *ctenidium* + E *-al*] **:** relating or belonging to a ctenidium

cte·nid·i·um \-ēəm\ *n, pl* **ctenid·ia** \-ēə\ [NL, fr. *cten-* + *-idium*] **1 :** the gill of a mollusk consisting typically of a respiratory structure that resembles a comb or feather, has a main stem with lateral lamellae, and is developed from the inner side of the mantle — distinguished from *ceras* **2 :** a structure consisting of a row of spines resembling the teeth of a comb on the head or thorax, or both, of certain fleas

cten·ii \'tenē,ī, 'tēn-\ *n pl* [NL, fr. Gk *kten-*, *kteis* comb — more at PECTINATE] **:** spinules or teeth on the posterior margin of a ctenoid scale

¹**cten·i·zid** \'tenəzəd\ *adj* [NL *Ctenizidae*] **:** of or relating to the family Ctenizidae

²**ctenizid** \"\ *n* -s **:** a spider of the family Ctenizidae

cte·niz·i·dae \tə'nizə,dē\ *n pl, cap* [NL, fr. *Cteniza*, type genus (fr. Gk *ktenizein*, dim. of *kten-*, *kteis* comb) + *-idae* — more at PECTINATE] **:** a family of large burrowing spiders — see TRAP-DOOR SPIDER

cteno·ce·phal·i·des \,tenōsə'falə,dēz\ *n, cap* [NL, fr. *cten-* + *cephal-* + Gk *-idēs* (patronymic suffix)] **:** a genus of fleas (family Pulicidae) including the dog flea (*C. canis*) and cat flea (*C. felis*)

cteno·ceph·a·lus \-'sefələs\ [NL, fr. *cten-* + *-cephalus*] *syn of* CTENOCEPHALIDES — a prior usage invalid as a homonym

cteno·cyst \'tenə,sist\ *n* [*cten-* + *-cyst*] **:** a characteristic sensory or balancing organ of Ctenophora situated at the aboral pole of the body

cteno·dac·tyl·i·dae \,tenō,dak'tilə,dē\ *n pl, cap* [NL, fr. *Ctenodactylus*, type genus (fr. *cten-* + Gk *daktylos* finger) + *-idae*] **:** a family of African rodents of uncertain systematic relationships that are distinguished by the presence of strong stiff bristles on the hind feet — see GUNDI

cteno·dip·te·ri·ni \¦tenō,diptə'rī,nī\ *n pl, cap* [NL, fr. *cteno-* (fr. *Ctenodus*) + *Dipterus* + *-ini*] *in some classifications* **:** an order of late Paleozoic dipnoan fishes with small and numerous cranial bones

cten·odus \'tenədəs\ *n, cap* [NL, fr. *cten-* + *-odus*] **:** a genus of Carboniferous dipnoan fishes whose dental plates have radiating tuberculated ridges

cten·oid \'te,nȯid, 'tē,-\ *adj* [ISV, fr. Gk *ktenoeidēs* comblike, fr. *kten-*, *kteis* comb + *-oeidēs* -oid — more at PECTINATE] **1 :** having the margin toothed like a comb ⟨~ scales are characteristic of spiny-rayed fishes⟩ **2 :** consisting of scales with ctenoid margins ⟨~ scalation⟩; *often* **:** having such scales ⟨~ fishes⟩

cte·noi·dei \tə'nȯidē,ī\ *n pl, cap* [NL, fr. Gk *ktenoeidēs* comblike] **:** an artificial group formerly regarded as an order that includes fishes with ctenoid scales and is more or less exactly coextensive with Acanthopterygii

cte·noph·o·ra \tə'näfərə\ *n pl, cap* [NL, fr. *cten-* + *-phora*] **:** a small phylum sometimes esp. formerly considered a class of Coelenterata and consisting of widely distributed and at times very abundant marine hermaphroditic solitary animals that superficially resemble jellyfishes, are usu. more or less ellipsoidal with decided biradial symmetry, and swim by means of eight meridional bands of transverse ciliated plates, each plate representing a row of large modified cilia — compare NUDA, TENTACULATA; COMB 4c; VENUS'S-GIRDLE — **cte·noph·o·ral** \-rəl\ *adj* — **cte·noph·o·ran** \-rən\ *n or adj* — **cten·o·phor·ic** \¦tenə¦fȯrik\ *adj* — **cte·noph·o·rous** \tə'näfərəs\ *adj*

cte·noph·o·rae \tə'näfə,rē\ *syn of* CTENOPHORA

cteno·phore \'tenə,fō(ə)r\ *n* -s [NL *Ctenophora*] **:** one of the Ctenophora

cteno·pla·na \,tenə'plānə\ *n, cap* [NL, fr. *cten-* + L *plana*, fem. of *planus* flat, level — more at FLOOR] **:** a genus of ctenophores consisting of a single species of small degenerate bottom-dwelling forms lacking ciliated swimming plates that are widely distributed in the Indian and Pacific oceans

cteno·sto·ma·ta \,tenə'stōməd·ə\ *n pl, cap* [NL, fr. *cten-* + *-stomata*] **:** an order of Bryozoa (class Gymnolaemata) having a circle of processes resembling bristles that close the aperture when the tentacles are retracted — **cteno·stom·a·tous** \¦tenə¦stämad·əs\ *adj* — **cteno·stome** \'tenə,stōm\ *n* -s

cte·tol·o·gy \tə'tälәjē\ *n* -ES [*cteto-* (fr. Gk *ktētos* that may be acquired, fr. *ktasthai* to acquire) + *-logy* — more at CHECK] **:** a branch of biology that deals with the origin and development of acquired characters

ctenophore: *1* tentacle extended, *2* tentacle partially contracted, *3* tentacle sheath, *4* funnel, *5* pole plate, *6* excretory pores, *7* axial funnel tube, *8* tentacular canal, *9* paragastric canal, *10* stomodaeum, *11* mouth

ctf *abbr* certificate

ctge *abbr* cartage

c3 \'sē¦thrē\ *adj, usu cap C* **1** *Brit* **:** assigned to a classification for recruits of the lowest grade of physical fitness for military service in World War I **2** *Brit* **:** very inferior in quality or state **:** THIRD-RATE

ctl *abbr* cental

CTL *abbr* constructive total loss

ctmo *abbr* **1** centesimo **2** centimo

ctn *abbr* **1** carton **2** cotangent

cto *abbr* concerto

-c·to·nus \ktənəs\ *n comb form* [NL, fr. Gk *ktonos* murder; akin to Gk *kteinein* to slay, Skt *kṣaṇoti* he wounds, injures, OPer a-*ḫshata* unhurt] **:** killer — in generic names esp. of insects ⟨*Dendroctonus*⟩

C to S *abbr* carting to shipside

ctr *abbr* **1** center **2** counter

ctss *abbr* countess

c-tumor \'=¦==\ *n* **:** a swelling or proliferation produced in plant tissue by a c-mitotic agent (as certain insecticides and herbicides)

ctvo *abbr* centavo

cu *abbr* **1** cubic **2** cumulative

CU *abbr* close-up

Cu *symbol* [L *cuprum*] copper

cua·dri·lla \kwä'drē(y)ə, -ēlyə\ *n* -s [Sp, division of an army into 4 parts for distribution of booty, group of horsemen at a tourney, bullfighter's retinue, dim. of *cuadra* square, fr. L *quadra*; akin to L *quattuor* four — more at FOUR] **:** the team assisting the matador in the bullring

cua·dri·lle·ro \,kwädrə(l)'ye(,)rō\ *n* -s [Sp, fr. *cuadrilla* + *-ero*] **:** a member of the cuadrilla

cua·gua·yo·te \,kwägwə'yōd·ē\ *n* -s [MexSp *cuaguayote*, *cuahuayote*, fr. Nahuatl *cuauhayotli*, lit., tree gourd, fr. *cuauh-* (fr. *cuahuitl* tree) + *ayotli* gourd] **:** a small Mexican tree (*Pileus mexicanus*) of the family Caricaceae having leaves and fruit that yield a proteolytic enzyme

cuamuchil *var of* HUAMUCHIL

cuan·do \'kwän(,)dō\ *n* -s [AmerSp, fr. Sp, when, fr. L *quando*; fr. the fact that each strophe of the song originally sung to accompany this dance began with *cuando* — more at QUANTITY] **:** an Argentine dance resembling a minuet

cua·pi·nole \'kwäpə,nōl\ *n* -s [Sp *cuapinol*, *guapinol*, fr. Nahuatl *cuauhpinolli*, lit., flour tree, fr. *cuauh-* (fr. *cuahuitl* tree) + *pinolli* flour; fr. the floury powder found in its pods] **:** COURBARIL

cuar·tel \kwär'tel\ *n, pl* **cuarte·les** \-'tā,lās\ [Sp, fr. MF *quartier* — more at QUARTER] **:** BARRACKS

cuar·te·la·zo \,kwärd·ᵊl'ä(,)sō\ *n* -s [AmerSp, fr. Sp *cuartel* + *-azo* (suffix denoting a blow)] **:** a military coup usu. originating in a single barracks **:** seizure of power by an army — used chiefly of Latin-American army revolts

cua·tro-ojos \,kwä·trō'ō(,)hōs, -hōz\ *n, pl* **cuatro-ojos** \-hōz\ [AmerSp, fr. Sp *cuatro* four (fr. L *quattuor*) + *ojos*, pl. of *ojo* eye, fr. L *oculus* — more at FOUR, EYE] **:** FOUR-EYES

¹**cub** \'küb, 'kəb\ *n* -s *dial Eng* **:** a stall for cattle (obs.), thatched roof, fish trap, fish basket, fr. MD *cubbe*; akin to MHG *kobe* pigpen, cage, OE *cofa* room, cave — more at COVE] *now dial Eng* **:** to shut up **:** CONFINE

²**cub** \'kəb\ *n* -s *often attrib* [origin unknown] **1 a :** a young carnivorous mammal (as a fox or bear) **b :** a young shark **2 :** a young person; *esp* **:** an awkward or ill-mannered boy ⟨I began to envy those young ~s at the university —Sir Winston Churchill⟩ **3 :** APPRENTICE ⟨a ~ pilot on a steamboat⟩; *esp* **:** a young and inexperienced newspaper reporter **4 :** CUB SCOUT

³**cub** \"\ *vb* **cubbed; cubbed; cubbing; cubs 1 :** to bring forth — used of those animals of which the young are commonly called cubs **2 :** to hunt fox cubs

Cub \"\ *trademark* — used for a light low-horsepower high-wing airplane

cub- *or* **cubi-** *or* **cubo-** *comb form* [NL, fr. Gk *kyb-*, *kybo-*, fr. *kybos* — more at CUBE] **1 a :** cube ⟨*cubo*ctahedron⟩ ⟨*cubi*form⟩ ⟨*cubo*mancy⟩ **b :** of the third algebraic degree ⟨*cub*invariant⟩ ⟨*cubo*cubic⟩ **2** *cubo-* **:** cuboid and ⟨*cubo*metatarsal⟩

¹**cu·ba** \'kyübə\ *adj, usu cap* [fr. *Cuba*, island in the West Indies] **:** of or from Cuba **:** of the kind or style prevalent in Cuba **:** CUBAN

²**cuba** \"\ *n* -s *often cap* [fr. *Cuba*, island in the West Indies] **:** WALLFLOWER 4

cuba bark *or* **cuba bast** *n, usu cap C* **:** the coarse strong bast fiber found in any of certain plants of the genus *Hibiscus* and esp. in majagua and used in tropical America for making twine and ropes

cub·age \'kyübij\ *n* -s [¹*cube* + *-age*] **:** cubic content, volume, or displacement

cuba grass *n, usu cap C* **:** JOHNSON GRASS

cu·ba·laya \,kyübə'lāə\ *n* -s *often cap* [blend of *Cuba* and *Malaya*] **:** a fowl of a breed of Cuban origin from oriental ancestry that resembles the Sumatra but is much smaller

cu·ba li·bre \,kyübə'lēbrə\ *n, pl* **cuba libres** [AmerSp, lit., free Cuba (originally a drink of water and sugar or honey drunk by insurrectionists during the Cuban War of Independence)] **:** a tall drink made from lime juice, rum, and a cola beverage iced and usu. garnished with lime peel

¹cu·ban \'kyübən\ *adj, usu cap* [Sp *cubano*, adj. & n., fr. *Cuba*, island in the West Indies + Sp *-ano* -an] **1 :** of, relating to, or characteristic of Cuba **2 :** of, relating to, or characteristic of Cubans

²cuban \"\ *n* [Sp *cubano*, adj. & n.] **1** *cap* **:** a native or inhabitant of Cuba **2** *also* **cuban tobacco** *usu cap C* **:** a chiefly filler-leaf tobacco derived from seed obtained from Cuba — compare BROADLEAF 2, HAVANA SEED

cuban bast *n, usu cap C* **:** the bast fiber of the mountain mahoe

cuban blindfish *n, usu cap C* **:** either of two blindfishes (*Lucifuga subterranea* and *Stygicola dentata*) of the family Brotulidae found in cave streams in Cuba

cuban cedar *n, usu cap 1st C* **:** SPANISH CEDAR

cuban crocodile *n, usu cap 1st C* **:** a small crocodile (*Crocodylus rhombifer*) found only in the island of Cuba

cuban ebony *n, usu cap C* **:** GRANADILLA TREE

cuban eight *n, usu cap C* **:** an acrobatic maneuver by an airplane consisting of three-quarters of a normal loop, a half roll, three quarters of another normal loop, and another half roll followed by recovery from the dive to straight level flight

cuban heel *n, usu cap C* **:** a broad medium-high heel with a moderately curved back and a straight breast line

cu·ban·ite \'kyübə,nīt\ *n* -s [G *cuban* cubanite (fr. Sp *cubano* Cuban) + E *-ite*] **:** a bronze-yellow copper-iron sulfide $CuFe_2S_3$

cu·ban·ize \-īz\ *vt* -ED/-ING/-s *often cap* **:** to make Cuban in quality or in interests

cuban lily *n, usu cap C* **:** a bulbous plant (*Scilla peruviana*) of the Mediterranean region

cuban macaw *n, usu cap C* **:** a large macaw (*Ara tricolor*) that formerly inhabited Cuba but is now exterminated

Cuban heel

cuban oysterwood *n, usu cap C* **:** a thin cross section of a West Indian tree (*Gymnanthes lucida*) used as a veneer — used esp. in the lumber trade

cuban pine *n, usu cap C* **:** CARIBBEAN PINE

cuban sand *n, often cap C* **:** a light grayish yellowish brown that is yellower and paler than almond brown and less strong than gravel

cuban spinach *n, usu cap C* **:** INDIAN LETTUCE 3

cuban vanilla *n, usu cap C* **:** a West Indian shrub (*Eupatorium dalea*)

cu·ba·rithm slate \'kyübə,rithəm-, thəm-\ *n* [¹*cube* + *arithmetic*] **:** a braille slate consisting of a box divided into square compartments into which cubes bearing on each face a number in braille dots may be placed in the usual pattern for performing arithmetical problems

cu·ba·ture \'kyübə,chü(ə)r\ *n* -s [¹*cube* + *-ature* (as in *quadrature*)] **1 :** determination of cubic contents **2 :** CUBIC CONTENT, VOLUME

cubbed *past of* CUB

cub·ber \'kəbə(r)\ *n* -s [*cub* (*scout*) + *-er*] **:** an adult who is active in the cub-scouting program of the Boy Scouts of America

¹cubbing *pres part of* CUB

²cubbing *n* -s [²*cub* + *-ing*] *Brit* **:** the hunting of young foxes esp. as a means of training the hounds

cub·bish \'kəbish\ *adj* **:** resembling a cub **:** AWKWARD, UNCOUTH — **cub·bish·ly** *adv*

cub·by \-bē\ *n* -ES [obs. E *cub* pen, stall + *-y* — more at CUB] **1 :** a snug or confined place (as for hiding) **:** a small room **:** a cramped space ⟨a little ~ of an office⟩ **2 :** a small closet or cupboard for storage **3 :** CUBBY PEN

cubbyhole \'==,=\ *n* **1 :** CUBBY 1, 2 **2 :** PIGEONHOLE 6

cubbyhouse \'==,=\ *n* **:** PLAYHOUSE

cubby locker *n, Brit* **:** GLOVE COMPARTMENT

cubby pen *n* **:** a small baited enclosure (as of upright sticks or sometimes stones) with traps so arranged that an animal cannot reach the bait without being caught by a trap

¹cube \'kyüb\ *n* -s [MF, fr. L *cubus*, fr. Gk *kybos* cube, cubical die, vertebra, hollow before the hip (in cattle) — more at HIP] **1 a :** the regular solid of six equal square sides — see VOLUME table **b :** the product got by taking a number or quantity three times as a factor ⟨2×2×2=8, the ~ of 2⟩ **c :** CUBAGE **2 :** a block or set for road paving **3 :** one of the geometric forms into which a natural object is resolved in cubist art **4** *slang* **:** DIE — usu. used in pl. ⟨throw the ~s⟩ **5 :** the crystal form in the isometric system that consists of six like, mutually perpendicular faces and differs from the geometrical cube in that the six faces need not be square but must only bear like relations to the internal structure of the crystal **6 :** a cubic portion of morphine

cube 1a

²cube \"\ *vt* -ED/-ING/-s **1 :** to raise to the third power **:** form the cube of **2 :** to measure the cubic content of ⟨~ a house⟩ **3 :** to form into a cube **:** cut into cubes ⟨~ carrots⟩ **4 :** to cut partly through one or both surfaces of (a steak) in a checkered pattern in order to increase tenderness by breaking the fibers

³cu·be *or* **cu·bé** \'kyü,bā, ='=\ *n* -s [AmerSp *cubé*] **1 :** any of several tropical American shrubs or climbers used as fish poisons and in the manufacture of insecticides; *esp* **:** any of certain plants of the genus *Lonchocarpus* (esp. *L. utilis* and *L. urucu*) the roots of which contain rotenone **2 :** the material from cube used as a fish poison or also in ground and refined form as an insecticide — called also *barbasco, timbo*

cu·beb \'kyü,beb\ *n* -s [MF *cubebe*, fr. OF, fr. ML *cubeba*, fr. Ar *kubābah, kabābah*] **1 a :** the dried unripe nearly full-grown fruit of the Java pepper which is crushed and smoked in cigarettes for catarrh and from which there is prepared an oleoresin formerly used medicinally **b :** one of these fruits **2** *or* **cubeb cigarette :** a cigarette containing cubeb **3 :** JAVA PEPPER

cubeb oil *n* **:** a colorless or greenish essential oil that is obtained from cubebs, has an odor resembling pepper, and is used in lozenges

cube·let \'kyüblət\ *n* -s **:** a little cube

cub·er \'kyübə(r)\ *n* -s **:** one that cubes; *esp* **:** a device or machine that cuts food into cubes or scores slices of meat to break the tough fibers

cu·be·ra \k(y)ü'berə\ *n* -s [Sp] **:** a large coarse snapper (*Lutjanus cyanopterus*) of the tropical western Atlantic esp. abundant about Cuba

cube root *n* **:** a number or quantity whose cube is the given number or quantity ⟨3 is a *cube root* of 27⟩

cube spar *n* **:** ANHYDRITE

cube steak *n* **:** a steak that has been made tender by any of several means; *esp* **:** a small thin slice of a tough cut of beef shaped round or square that has been cubed

cube sugar *n* **:** white granulated sugar moistened with white syrup, molded into cubes, and dried

cub–hunting \'=,==\ *n* **:** CUBBING

cubi- — see CUB-

¹cu·bic \'kyübik, -bēk\ *adj* [MF or L; MF *cubique*, fr. L *cubicus*, fr. Gk *kybikos*, fr. *kybos* cube + *-ikos* -ic — more at HIP] **1 :** having the form of a cube **:** CUBICAL **2** *mineralogy* **a :** relating to the cube considered as a crystal form ⟨a ~ face⟩ **b :** ISOMETRIC **3 a :** THREE-DIMENSIONAL **b :** being the volume of a cube whose edge is a specified unit ⟨64 ~ inches⟩ **4** *math* **:** of third degree, order, or power — **cu·bic·ly** \-bəklē, -bēk-, -li\ *adv*

²cubic \"\ *n*, **:** a cubic curve, equation, or polynomial

cu·bi·cal \'kyübəkəl, -bēk-\ *adj* **1 :** CUBIC; *esp* **:** shaped like a cube **2** *physics* **:** relating to volume ⟨~ expansion⟩ — **cu·bi·cal·ly** \-k(ə)lē, -li\ *adv*

cubic centimeter *n* **:** a unit of volume equal to a cube one centimeter long on each side — see METRIC SYSTEM table

cubic content *n* **:** VOLUME 4

cubic coordination *n* **:** HEXAHEDRAL COORDINATION

cubic determinant *n* **:** a mathematical form analogous to a square determinant but with constituents forming a cube

cubic equation *n* **:** a polynomial equation in which the highest sum of exponents of variables in any term is three

cubic foot *n* **:** a unit of volume equal to a cube one foot long on each side — see MEASURE table

cubic foot bottle *n* **:** a metal container having a capacity of one cubic foot for use in the testing of gas-meter provers and precision gas meters

cubic inch *n* **:** a unit of volume equal to a cube one inch long on each side — see MEASURE table

cu·bic·i·ty \kyü'bisəd-ē\ *n* -ES **:** the quality or state of being cubic

cu·bi·cle \'kyübəkəl, -bēk-\ *n* -s [L *cubiculum*, fr. *cubare* to lie down — more at HIP] **1 :** a sleeping compartment partitioned off from a large room ⟨a dormitory ~⟩ **2 a :** a small room or compartment often approximately square in plan ⟨a bathhouse ~⟩ ⟨a bank teller's ~⟩ **b :** CARREL

cubic measure *n* **:** a unit or series of units for measuring volume (as cubic inch, cubic centimeter)

cubic meter *n* **:** a unit of volume equal to a cube one meter long on each side **:** STERE

cubic surface *n* **:** an algebraic surface whose intersection by an arbitrary plane is a cubic curve

cubic ton *n* **:** TON 2c

¹cu·bic·u·lar \kyü'bikyələ(r)\ *n* -s [ME *cubiculer*, fr. MF *cubiculaire*, fr. L *cubicularius*, fr. *cubiculum* cubicle + *-arius* -ary] **:** a chamber attendant **:** CHAMBERLAIN

²cubicular \(')=¦===\ *adj* [F *cubiculaire*, fr. L *cubicularius, cubicularis*, fr. *cubiculum* + *-arius* -ary, *-aris* -ar] **:** of or relating to a bedroom or cubicle

cubiculo *n* [It, fr. L *cubiculum*] *obs* **:** CUBICULUM, BEDROOM

cu·bic·u·lum \kyü'bikyələm\ *n, pl* **cubicu·la** \-lə\ [ML, fr. L, cubicle — more at CUBICLE] **:** a small room provided in catacombs and constituting a family vault

cubic yard *n* **:** a unit of volume equal to a cube one yard long on each side — see MEASURE table

cu·bi·form \'kyübə,fȯrm\ *adj* [*cub-* + *-iform*] **:** of the shape of a cube

cub·ism \'kyü,bizəm\ *n* -s *sometimes cap* [F *cubisme*, fr. *cube* + *-isme* -ism — more at CUBE] **1** *fine art* **a :** the typically monochromatic expression of natural forms in terms of simplified planes and lines and basic geometric shapes sometimes organized to depict the subject simultaneously from several points of view — compare ANALYTICAL **b :** the arbitrary arrangement and interrelation of contours and fragments of contours on a picture surface without necessary reference to natural objects or their structure — compare SYNTHETIC **2 :** a French abstract art movement embracing analytical cubism from about 1906 to 1912 and synthetic cubism from 1913 into the following decade **3 :** a technique of writing that attempts to exploit abstract structural relationships of things by using bizarre associations and dissociations in imagery, the simultaneous evocation of several points of view toward the material, and other devices

¹cub·ist \'kyübəst\ *n* -s *often cap* [F *cubiste*, fr. *cube* + *-iste* -ist] **:** an adherent or follower of a theory, method, or practice of cubism

²cubist \"\ *adj* **1 :** relating to or characteristic of cubism **2 :** composed of or decorated with geometric forms or patterns **:** GEOMETRIC, CUBISTIC

cu·bis·tic \(')kyü¦bistik, -tēk\ *adj* **1 :** CUBIST; *esp* **:** of or resembling cubist painting **2 :** of excessively intricate or contrived geometric design ⟨the ~ panels of the thirties —Kay Boyle⟩

cu·bit \'kyübət, *usu* -əd-+V\ *n* -s [ME *cubite*, fr. L *cubitus, cubitum* elbow, cubit — more at HIP] **1 :** any of various ancient units of length based on the length of the forearm from the elbow to the tip of the middle finger and usu. equal to about 18 inches but sometimes to 21 or more **2 :** CUBITUS

¹cu·bi·tal \-bəd-ᵊl\ *adj* [ME, fr. L *cubitalis*, fr. *cubitus, cubitum* elbow, cubit + *-alis* -al] **:** of or relating to a cubitus ⟨~ nerve⟩

²cubital \"\ *n* -s **1** *obs* **:** a sleeve covering the forearm **2 a :** CUBITUS **b :** SECONDARY 6a

cu·bi·tale \,kyübə'ta(,)lē, -ā(,)lē, -ä(,)lē\ *n, pl* **cubital·ia** \-lēə\ [NL, fr. L, neut. of *cubitalis* cubital] **:** any of the cuneiform bones

cubital fossa *n* **:** the anterior depression at the elbow

cubit arm *n, heraldry* **:** a hand and arm couped at the elbow

cu·bi·tiere \¦kyübə¦tye(ə)r\ *n* -s [F *cubitière*, fr. L *cubitum* elbow + F *-ière* -er — more at HIP] **:** an elbow guard in medieval armor

cubito- *comb form* [F, fr. L *cubitus* elbow] **:** cubital and ⟨*cubitocarpal*⟩

cu·bi·tus \'kyübəd-əs\ *n, pl* **cubi·ti** \-bə,tī\ [L, elbow, cubit — more at CUBIT] **1 a :** FOREARM, ANTEBRACHIUM **b :** ULNA **2** [NL, fr. L] **:** one of the primary veins of an insect's wing, located between the media and the anal vein

cubmaster \'=,==\ *n* [*cub* (*scout*) + *master*] **:** a male adult leader of a cub-scout pack of the Boy Scouts of America

cubo- — see CUB-

cub·octahedral \¦(')kyü¦b+,-\ *adj* [*cub-* + *octahedral*] **:** of or relating to a cuboctahedron

cub·octahedron \"+\ *also* **cu·bo-octahedron** \¦kyü,bō+\ *n* [*cub-* + *octahedron*] **:** one of the 13 Archimedean solids having as faces six equal squares and eight equal regular triangles and formed by cutting off the corners of a cube

¹cu·boid \'kyü,bȯid\ *adj* [NL *cuboides*, fr. Gk *kyboeidēs* cubelike, fr. *kybos* cube + *-oeidēs* -oid — more at CUBE] **:** approximately cubic in shape; *specif* **:** being the outermost of the distal row of tarsal bones of many of the higher vertebrates that supports the fourth and fifth metatarsals and is considered as representing the fused fourth and fifth distal tarsal bones

²cuboid \"\ *n* -s [NL *cuboides*, fr. *cuboides*, adj.] **1 :** a rectangular parallelepiped **2 :** the cuboid bone

cu·boi·dal \(')kyü¦bȯidᵊl\ *adj* **1 :** relating to or like a cuboid **2 :** relating to or being a more or less cubical structure

cuboidal epithelium *n* **:** epithelial tissue made up of small polygonal cells much shorter than columnar cells but not thin and flat like squamous cells

cu·bo·man·cy \'kyübə,man(t)sē\ *n* -ES [F *cubomancie*, fr. *cub-* + *-mancie* -mancy] **:** divination with dice

cu·bo·medusae \¦kyü(,)bō+\ *n pl, cap* [NL, fr. *cub-* + *Medusae*] **:** an order or suborder of Scyphozoa with a 4-sided cup-shaped umbrella and four perradial tentaculocysts — **cu·bo·medusan** \"+\ *adj or n*

cubs *pres 3d sing of* CUB, *pl of* CUB

cub scout *n* **:** a member of the scouting program of the Boy Scouts of America for boys of the age range 8–10 — compare BOY SCOUT, EXPLORER; see BEAR, BOBCAT, LION, WEBELOS, WOLF

cub shark *n* **:** a stout sluggish bottom-dwelling shark (*Carcharhinus leucas*) widely distributed along the western Atlantic shores and commonly entering fresh water; *also* **:** the young of various other sharks

cu·ca \'kükə\ *n* -s [Quechua *kúka*] **:** COCA

cu·ca·ra·cha \,kükə'rächə\ *n* -s [fr. (*La*) *Cucaracha* The Cockroach, Mexican popular song to which it is danced] **:** a Mexican ballroom and nightclub dance

cu·chia \'küchēə\ *n* -s [NL, fr. Beng *kūciyā*] **:** a sluggish fish (*Amphipnous cuchia*) resembling an eel, inhabiting swamps in Bengal, and having membranous vascular sacs enabling it to breathe air and most fins absent or vestigial

cuck *vt* -ED/-ING/-s [back-formation fr. *cucking stool*] *obs* **:** to punish by the cucking stool

cuck·hold \'kək,hōld, 'kə,kō-\ *n* -s [perh. fr. E dial. *cuck* muck (alter. of E ²*cack*) + E *hold*, v.] **:** a concave shovel for cutting off the tempered clay coming from the pugmill in brickmaking

cuck·ing stool \'kəkiŋ-\ *n* [ME *cucking stol*, lit., defecating chair, fr. *cucking* (fr. pres. part. of *cukken* to defecate, alter. of *cakken*) + *stol* chair — more at CACK, STOOL] **:** a chair in which such offenders as scolds, prostitutes, or dishonest tradesmen were formerly fastened for punishment by public exposure or ducking in water — compare DUCKING STOOL

cuck·le \'kəkəl\ *dial var of* ¹COCKLE

¹cuck·old \'kəkəld *sometimes* 'kük-\ *n* -s [ME *cukeweld, cokewold*] **1 :** a man whose wife is unfaithful **:** the husband of an adulteress — see ¹HORN 4b **2 a :** COWFISH 2 **b :** COWBIRD

²cuckold \"\ *vt* -ED/-ING/-s **:** to make a cuckold of (a husband)

³cuck·old \'kəkəl(d)\ *also* **cuckold bur** *n* -s [*cuckold* prob. alter. of ¹*cockle*; *cuckold bur* prob. alter. of *cocklebur*] **1 :** any of several plants of the genus *Bidens*; *esp* **:** an erect annual No. American beggar-tick (*B. connata*) with small barbed fruits **2 :** COCKLEBUR 1

cuckoldly *also* **cuckoldy** *adj, obs* **:** having the qualities of a cuckold

cuck·ol·dom \-dəm\ *n* -s **1 :** the state of being a cuckold **2 :** ADULTERY, CUCKOLDRY

cuck·old·ry \-drē, -ri\ *n* -ES **:** the practice of making cuckolds

¹cuck·oo \'kü(,)kü, 'kủ(,)-\ *n* -s [ME *cuccu, cuckow*, of imit. origin like MLG *kukuk*, MD *coecoec*, OF *cucu*, L *cuculus*, Gk *kokkyx*, Skt *kokila*] **1 a :** a familiar European bird (*Cuculus canorus*) that is grayish brown above and white barred with dusky on the underparts and is noted for its characteristic two-syllabled whistle and for its habit of laying its eggs in the nests of other birds for them to hatch **b :** any member of the large family (Cuculidae) to which this bird belongs — see ANI, BLACK-BILLED CUCKOO, COUCAL, ROADRUNNER **2 a :** the call of the cuckoo **b :** any repeated vapid calling or utterance **3** *music* **:** a whistle that imitates the song of the cuckoo **4 :** a silly or slightly crackbrained person **:** one erratic in behavior

²cuckoo \"\ *vb* -ED/-ING/-s *vt* **:** to repeat monotonously as a cuckoo does its call ~ *vi* **:** to utter the call of the cuckoo or a sound like it

³cuckoo \"\ *adj* **1 a :** of or resembling the cuckoo **b** *of a domestic fowl* **:** barred like the underparts of the cuckoo **2 a :** SILLY, STUPID, CRAZY **b :** dazed or unconscious esp. from a blow ⟨knocked him ~⟩ **3 a :** like a cuckoo in habits **b** *of certain ants* **:** living as social parasites

cuckoo bee *n* **:** any of various apoid bees (as members of the family Nomadidae) that live esp. in the larval stage as inquilines or parasites in the nests of other bees

cuckoo–bread \'=(,)=,=\ *n* **:** WOOD SORREL 1a

cuckoo–buds \'=(,)=,=\ *n pl but sing or pl in constr* **1 :** a common Old World crowfoot (*Ranunculus bulbosus*) **2 :** CUCKOOPINT

cuckoo–button \'=(,)=,==\ *n* **:** a burdock (*Arctium minus*)

cuckoo clock *n* **:** a wall or shelf clock that announces the hours by sounds resembling a cuckoo's often also with the appearing of an imitation cuckoo

cuckoo clover *n* **:** CUCKOOFLOWER 1

cuckoo dove *n* **:** any of several large chiefly ground-dwelling doves of a genus (*Macropygia*) distinguished by an elongated graduated tail, widely distributed in southeast Asia, the Pacific Islands, and Australia, and feeding chiefly on seeds, small fruits, and grain

cuckoo falcon *n* **:** any of numerous falcons of a genus (*Aviceda*) distinguished by a crested head and doubly notched bill and commonly resembling cuckoos in color and pattern

cuckooflower \'=(,)=,=\ *n* **1 :** a bitter cress (*Cardamine pratensis*) of Europe and America **2 :** RAGGED ROBIN **3 :** WOOD SORREL 1a

cuckoo clock

cuckoo froth *n* [so called fr. the frothy secretion on the stem popularly believed to be cuckoo spittle] **:** CUCKOOFLOWER

cuckoo gillyflower *n* **:** RAGGED ROBIN

cuckoo lamb *n* [so called fr. its being born in the mating season of the cuckoo] **:** a late-born lamb

cuckoo–meat \'=(,)=,=\ *n* **:** WOOD SORREL 1a

cuck·oo·pint \'=(,)=,pint\ *n, pl* **cuckoopint** [short for *cuckoopintle*, fr. ME *cokkupyntel*, fr. *cokku*, *cuckow* cuckoo + *pyntel* pintle (penis); fr. the shape of the spadix] **:** a common European arum (*Arum maculatum*) with lanceolate erect spathe and short purple spadix

cuckoo ray *n* **:** a European ray (*Raja noevus*)

cuckoo shrike *n* **:** any of numerous Old World birds somewhat like flycatchers in habits constituting the family Campephagidae but formerly often included in the family Laniidae and differing from the true shrikes esp. in their undulating flight resembling that of the cuckoo

cuckoo's–leader \'=(,)=¦==\ *n, pl* **cuckoo's–leaders** [so called fr. the belief that it arrives in the spring shortly before the cuckoo] *dial Eng* **:** WRYNECK

cuckoo sorrel *n* **:** WOOD SORREL 1a

cuckoo spit *n* **1** *also* **cuckoo spittle a :** a frothy secretion exuded upon plants by the nymphs of spittle insects — called also *frog spit, snake spit, toad spit* **b :** an insect secreting this **:** SPITTLE INSECT **2 a :** COCKOOFLOWER 1 **b :** CUCKOOPINT **c :** WOOD ANEMONE b

cuckoo's–sandy \'=(,)=,==\ *n, pl* **cuckoo's–sandies** [so called fr. its nest being favored by the cuckoo] **:** MEADOW PIPIT

cuckoo wasp *n* **:** any of certain usu. brilliantly metallic-green or metallic-blue wasps that constitute the family Chrysididae or the superfamily Chrysidoidea and lay their eggs in the provisioned larval cells of other hymenopterous insects

cuckoo wrasse *n* **:** a brilliantly colored European wrasse (*Labrus mixtus*) the male orange or yellow banded with bright blue and the female reddish brown blotched with black

cuckquean *n* -s [*cuckold* + *quean*] *obs* **:** a woman whose husband is unfaithful to her

cucks *pres 3d sing of* CUCK

cuck·stool \'kək,stül\ *n* [ME *cukstol*, lit., defecating chair, fr. *cukken* to defecate (alter. of *cakken*) + *stol* chair — more at CACK, STOOL] **:** CUCKING STOOL

cu·cu·ba·no \kü'kübə,nō\ *n* -s [AmerSp (Puerto Rico) *cucubano*] **:** a large luminous click beetle (*Pyrophorus luminosus*) of the West Indies having a larva also luminous that is predacious on other insects

¹cu·cu·jid \kə'küyəd, kə'k(y)üjəd\ *adj* [NL *Cucujidae*] **:** of or relating to the family Cucujidae

²cucujid \"\ *n* -s **:** a cucujid beetle

cu·cu·ji·dae \-üyə,dē, -üjə-\ *n pl, cap* [NL, fr. *Cucujus*, type genus (prob. fr. Sp *cocuyo*, *cucuyo* fire beetle) + *-idae*] **:** a family of small flattened elongated beetles (suborder Polyphaga) that live mostly under the bark of trees — compare SAW-TOOTHED GRAIN BEETLE

cu·cu·jo \-ü(,)yō, -ü(,)jō\ *n* -s [modif. of Sp *cocuyo, cucuyo*, fr. Taino, fr. *cuyo* fire] **:** a luminous click beetle (*Pyrophorus noctilucus*) related to the cucubano and having a similar distribution

cu·cu·li \'k(y)üky,lī\ *n pl, cap* [NL, fr. L, pl. of *cuculus* cuckoo — more at CUCKOO] **:** a suborder of Cuculiformes coextensive with the family Cuculidae

cu·cu·li·dae \kə'k(y)ülə,dē\ *n pl, cap* [NL, fr. *Cuculus*, type genus + *-idae*] **:** a family of birds (order Cuculiformes) that comprises the cuckoos, including the anis and roadrunners

cu·cu·li·form \-lə,fȯrm\ *adj* [L *cuculus* cuckoo + E *-iform*] **:** like or belonging to the cuckoos or the Cuculiformes

cu·cu·li·for·mes \=,=lə'fȯr(,)mēz\ *n pl, cap* [NL, fr. *Cuculus* + *-iformes*] **:** a small order of birds comprising the cuckoos, touracos, various related birds, and formerly the parrots and having 10 primaries and the feet zygodactyl except in the touracos in which the outer toe is reversible

cu·cu·line \'k(y)ük(y)ə,līn\ *adj* [L *cuculus* cuckoo + E *-ine*] **:** of, like, or relating to the cuckoos

cu·cul·la \kə'külə, kyü'kələ\ *n* -s [ML, fr. LL, cowl — more at COWL] **:** a loose sleeveless garment put on over the head and used esp. to protect other garments; *specif* **:** a monk's scapular

cu·cul·lar·is \,kyükə'la(a)rəs\ *n, pl* **cucullar·es** \-(,)rēz\ [NL, fr. L *cucullus* cap + *-aris* -ar] **:** TRAPEZIUS

cu·cul·late \'kyükə,lāt, kyü'kələt\ *also* **cu·cul·lat·ed** \'kyükə,lād-əd\ *adj* [ML *cucullatus*, fr. L *cucullus* cap, hood + *-atus* -ate — more at COWL] **1 :** shaped like a hood ⟨the posterior sepal in the flower of aconite is ~⟩ **:** having the basal edges rolled inward ⟨~ leaves⟩ **2 :** having the prothorax elevated so as to form a sort of hood receiving the head — used of certain insects — **cu·cul·late·ly** *adv*

cu·cul·li·form \kyü'kələ,fȯrm\ *adj* [ISV *cucull-* (fr. L *cucullus* cap, hood) + *-iform* — more at COWL] **:** CUCULLATE

cu·cul·lus \kyü'kələs\ *n, pl* **cucul·li** \-,lī\ [NL, fr. L, cap, hood — more at COWL] **:** the anterior dorsal shield of the cephalothorax in pseudoscorpions and Ricinulei

cu·cu·lus \'k(y)ük(y)ələs\ *n, cap* [NL, fr. L, cuckoo — more at CUCKOO] **:** the type genus of Cuculidae comprising the typical cuckoos

cu·cu·mar·ia \,kyük(y)ə'ma(a)rēə\ *n, cap* [NL, fr. L *cucumis* cucumber + NL *-aria* — more at CUCUMBER] **:** the type genus of Cucumariidae

cu·cu·ma·ri·idae \,kyük(y)əmə'rīə,dē\ *n pl, cap* [NL, fr. *Cucumaria*, type genus + *-idae*] **:** a large family of shallow-water sea cucumbers (order Dendrochirota) having a number of intricately branched oral tentacles, an internal madreporite, and a well-developed respiratory tree

cu·cum·ber \'kyü,kəmbə(r) *sometimes* '=,== *or* ='==; *archaic or humorous* 'kaủ(,)-\ *n* -s [ME *cucumer, cucumber*, fr. MF & L;

MF *cocombre, concombre,* fr. L *cucumer-, cucumis,* prob. (like Gk *sikyos* cucumber) of non-IE origin] **1 a :** the succulent fruit of a vine (*Cucumis sativus*) cultivated from earliest times as a garden vegetable, having a smooth or warty surface, and varying in shape from cylindrical to globular — see GHERKIN **b :** the annual trailing or climbing vine that bears cucumbers — see CUCUMIS **c :** any of several other plants of the genus *Cucumis* or the family Cucurbitaceae — usu. with qualifying word ⟨bitter ~⟩ ⟨snake ~⟩ **2 :** CUCUMBER TREE **3 :** SEA CUCUMBER

cucumber angular leaf spot *n* **:** a leaf spot of cucumber caused by a bacterium (*Pseudomonas lachrymans*)

cucumber beetle *n* **:** any of several leaf beetles that are esp. injurious to cucumbers and squashes, attacking the leaves as adults and the roots and stems as larvae — see SPOTTED CUCUMBER BEETLE, STRIPED CUCUMBER BEETLE; compare CORN ROOTWORM

cucumber family *n* **:** CUCURBITACEAE

cucumber fly *n* **:** MELON FLY

cucumber magnolia *n* **:** CUCUMBER TREE 1

cucumber melon *or* **cucumber apple** *n* **:** MANGO MELON

cucumber mildew *n* **1 :** either of two fungi destructive to cucumbers and melons: **a :** a downy mildew (*Peronoplasmopara cubensis*) **b :** a powdery mildew (*Erysiphe cichoracearum*) **2 :** a disease caused by cucumber mildew

cucumber mosaic *n* **:** a virus disease of cucumbers and related fruits transmitted by the melon aphid and producing characteristic mottling of the foliage and smooth pale fruits often with swellings or warts

cucumber root *n* **:** INDIAN CUCUMBER

cucumber scab *n* **:** a disease of the cucumber caused by a fungus (*Cladosporium cucumerinum*) characterized by spotting and blighting of the leaves and dark sunken cavities on the fruit

cucumber tree *n* **1 :** any of several American magnolias (esp. *Magnolia acuminata*) having fruit like a small cucumber **2 :** TULIP TREE **3** *India* **:** BILIMBI

cu·cu·mis \'kyük(y)əmə̇s\ *n, cap* [NL, fr. L, cucumber — more at CUCUMBER] **:** a genus of plants (family Cucurbitaceae) that are native to the warmer parts of the world, that include the cucumbers and muskmelons, and that have small sepals and a corolla with five petals

cu·curb \kyü'kərb\ *n* -s [by shortening] **:** CUCURBIT 2

cu·cur·bit \kyü'kərbət, *attrib* (')=¦==\ *n* -s [ME *cucurbite,* fr. MF, fr. L *cucurbita* gourd] **1** [so called fr. its shape] **:** a vessel or flask used in distillation as a part of or in conjunction with an alembic **:** MATRASS — see ALEMBIC illustration **2** [NL *Cucurbita*] **:** any plant of the genus *Cucurbita* or of the family Cucurbitaceae

cu·cur·bi·ta \-bəd·ə\ *n, cap* [NL, fr. L, gourd — more at GOURD] **:** the type genus of Cucurbitaceae comprising tropical herbaceous vines that have a bell-shaped gamopetalous corolla five-lobed to the middle or a little lower, coherent stamens, and a many-seeded fleshy fruit with a hard rind, that include the squashes, pumpkins, vegetable marrows, and certain gourds, and that are now nearly cosmopolitan in cultivation

cu·cur·bi·ta·ce·ae \(,)kyü,kərbə'tāsē,ē\ *n pl, cap* [NL, fr. *Cucurbita,* type genus + *-aceae*] **:** a family of chiefly herbaceous tendril-bearing vines (order Campanulales) that are characterized by an inferior ovary and anthers usu. united and that include food plants (as the cucumber, melon, squash, and pumpkin), drug plants (as the colocynth), and ornamental plants (as the gourds) — **cu·cur·bi·ta·ceous** \(;)=;==¦tāshəs\ *adj*

cu·cur·bi·tar·i·a·ce·ae \(,)kyü,kərbə,ta(a)rē'āsē,ē\ *n pl, cap* [NL, fr. *Cucurbitaria,* type genus (fr. L *cucurbita* gourd + NL *-aria*) + *-aceae*] **:** a family of ascomycetous fungi (order Sphaeriales) having the perithecia in caespitose clusters on the stroma

cucurbit mosaic *n* **:** CUCUMBER MOSAIC

cucurbit wilt *n* **:** a disease of cucumbers and related plants characterized by sudden wilting of affected plants and caused by a motile bacterium (*Erwinia tracheiphila*)

¹cud \'kəd *also* 'küd\ *n* -s [ME *cudde,* fr. OE *cwidu, cwudu, cudu* cud, gum mastic; akin to OHG *kuti* glue, ON *kvātha* resin, MIr *bethe, beithe* box (tree), Skt *jatu* lac, gum; basic meaning: resin] **1 :** the portion of food that is brought up into the mouth by ruminating animals from their first stomach to be chewed a second time **2 :** something ruminated ⟨chewing on the ~ of old problems⟩ **3 :** a portion of chewing tobacco or chewing gum

²cud \"\ *vi* **cudded; cudded; cudding; cuds :** to chew the cud

cu·da \'küdə\ *n* -s [short for *barracuda*] **:** GREAT BARRACUDA

cud·bear \'kəd,ba(a)(ə)r\ *n* -s [irreg. (pron. spelling) after Dr. *Cuthbert* Gordon, 18th cent. Scot. chemist] **:** a coloring matter prepared from lichens similarly to archil and sometimes considered a form of archil, obtained as a red or purple powder, and used in coloring pharmaceutical preparations

cudden *n* -s [origin unknown] *obs* **:** FOOL, DOLT

¹cud·dle \'kəd[ə]l\ *vb* **cuddled; cuddled; cuddling** \'kəd(ə)liŋ\ **cuddles** [origin unknown] *vt* **:** to hold close for warmth or comfort or in affection **:** FONDLE, HUG ~ *vi* **:** to lie close or snug **:** NESTLE, SNUGGLE

²cuddle \"\ *n* -s **:** a close embrace **:** the act of nestling

³cuddle \"\ *now dial var of* ¹CUTTLE

cud·dle·some \'kəd[ə]lsəm\ *adj* **:** fit for or inviting cuddling **:** LOVABLE ⟨a ~ and merry girl —J.B.Cabell⟩

cud·dly \'kəd(ə)lē, -li\ *adj* -ER/-EST **:** CUDDLESOME

¹cud·dy \'kədē\ *n* -ES [origin unknown] **1 :** a small cabin formerly under the poop deck; *also* **:** the galley or pantry of a small ship **2 :** a small room or closet (as a cupboard)

²cud·dy \'küdi, 'kədi\ *or* **cuddie** *n, pl* **cuddies** [perh. fr. *Cuddy,* nickname for *Cuthbert*] **1** *dial Brit* **:** ASS, DONKEY **2** *dial Brit* **:** BLOCKHEAD, LOUT

cuddyhole \'=,=\ *n* **:** ¹CUDDY 2

¹cud·gel \'kəjəl\ *n* -s [ME *kuggel,* fr. OE *cycgel;* akin to MD *cōghele* stick with a rounded end, MHG *kugele* ball, OHG *coccho* rounded ship, Lith *gugà* pommel, hump, hill; basic meaning: ball; akin to OE *cot* cottage, den — more at COT] **1 :** a short heavy stick that is shorter than a quarterstaff and is used as an instrument of punishment or a weapon **2 cudgels** *pl* **:** CUDGEL PLAY

²cudgel \"\ *vt* **cudgeled** *or* **cudgelled; cudgeled** *or* **cudgelled; cudgeling** *or* **cudgelling** \-j(ə)liŋ\ **cudgels :** to beat with or as if with a cudgel **:** BELABOR, THRASH, DRUB, RACK ⟨~*ed* his brains for a rhyme⟩

cudgel play *n* **:** a fighting or sporting contest with cudgels

cud·ger·ie \'kəjərē\ *n* -s [native name in Australia] **:** BUNJI-BUNJI

cudweed \'=,=\ *n* **:** any of several composite plants with silky or woolly foliage: as **a :** a European perennial herb (*Gnaphalium sylvaticum*) sometimes cultivated and widely naturalized as an escape in temperate No. America; *broadly* **:** any plant of the genus *Gnaphalium* **b :** LADIES' TOBACCO **c :** COTTON ROSE 2 **d :** WORMWOOD 1

cudweed mugwort *n* **:** PRAIRIE SAGE

¹cue \'kyü\ *n* -s [ME *cu*] **1 :** the letter *q* **2** *dial Eng* **:** the shoe of an ox

²cue \"\ *n* -s [prob. fr. *q, qu,* abbr. (used as a direction in actors' copies of plays) of L *quando* when — more at QUANTITY] **1 a :** a word, phrase, or bit of stage business in a play serving as a signal to the actor who is to act or speak next that it is time for him to begin **b :** a similar signal to a member of the stage crew to begin a particular operation (as producing a sound effect or lighting change) **c :** a musical passage from another instrumental or voice part inserted usu. in smaller type in an instrumental or accompanying part to signal a place of entrance or to permit substitution or doubling **2 a :** a signal to begin an action **:** STIMULUS **b :** a hint, intimation, or suggestion as to what course of action to take or when to take it ⟨the Cairo press, which takes its ~ carefully from the government in political affairs —R.C.Doty⟩ **c :** an item or feature acting as an indication of the nature of the object or situation perceived ⟨a subliminal hearing ~⟩ ⟨foreshortened lines in a picture are ~*s* to depth perception⟩ **3 :** the part one has to perform in or as if in a play ⟨was it my ~ to fight? —Shak.⟩ **4** *archaic* **:** attitude of mind **:** MOOD, TEMPER, HUMOR ⟨nobody was in the ~ to dance —Nathaniel Hawthorne⟩

³cue \"\ *vt* **cued; cued; cuing** *or* **cueing; cues 1 :** to give a cue to (as in a play) **:** PROMPT **2 :** to insert (a musical passage) as or provide (a musical score) with a cue — usu. used with *in* **3 :** CUE-BID **4 :** to insert or provide for the insertion of into a continuous performance — usu. used with *in* or *into* ⟨~ a duet into the scene⟩ ⟨~ in a sound effect⟩

⁴cue \"\ *n* -s [F *queue,* lit., tail, fr. OF *cöe, coue* — more at COWARD] **1 :** QUEUE 2 **2 a :** a leather-tipped tapering rod used to strike the ball in billiards and other games **b :** a long-handled instrument with a concave head used to shove the disks in shuffleboard

⁵cue \"\ *vb* **cued; cued; cuing** *or* **cueing; cues** *vt* **1 :** to form into a queue **:** BRAID, TWIST **2 :** to strike (as a billiard ball) with a cue ~ *vi* **1 :** to line up in a queue — usu. used with *up* **2 :** to use a cue **:** strike with a cue

cue ball *n* [⁴*cue*] **1 :** the ball that a player strikes with his cue in billiards and pool as distinguished from any of the other balls on the table — compare OBJECT BALL **2 :** either of the two white balls used in ordinary billiards — see SPOT BALL

cue bid *n* [²*cue*] **1 :** a bid in contract bridge in a suit previously bid by an opponent made with the purpose of showing an ace or a void in that suit **2 :** a bid in contract bridge showing the ace or less often a void or a king in the suit

cue–bid \'=¦=\ *vb* [*cue bid*] *vi* **:** to make a cue bid ~ *vt* **:** to indicate possession of (an ace, void, or king) by bidding the suit

cue·ca \'kwākə\ *n* -s [AmerSp, short for *zamacueca*] **:** a So. American esp. Chilean courtship dance — called also *zamacueca*

cue·ist \'kyüə̇st\ *n* -s [⁴*cue* + *-ist*] **:** BILLIARDIST

cue·man \'kyümən\ *n, pl* **cuemen** [⁴*cue* + *man*] **:** one who uses a cue **:** a billiard player — **cue·man·ship** \-,ship\ *n* -s

cuena *var of* QUENA

cuer·da \'kwerdə, -rthə\ *n* -s [AmerSp, fr. Sp, cord, rope, fr. L *chorda* catgut, chord, cord — more at CORD] **:** a Puerto Rican unit of land measure equal to 0.97 acre

cuerda se·ca \,==¦sākə, 'sekə\ *n* [Sp, lit., dry cord] **:** a technique used to simulate mosaic and cloisonné enamel effects in colored ceramic tiles

cue sheet *n* [²*cue*] **:** a detailed outline of a television or radio program giving cues and timing for each item

cues·ta \'kwestə, -wās-\ *n* -s [Sp, fr. L *costa* side, rib — more at COAST] **1** *Southwest* **:** a sloping plain esp. with the upper end at the crest of a cliff **:** a hill or ridge with a steep face on one side and gentle slope on the other **2 :** a landform commonly found in regions of gently tilted sedimentary rocks and consisting of an inclined upland the slope of which conforms with the dip of a resistant bed or series of beds and a relatively steep escarpment descending abruptly from its crest

cue·va \'kwāvə\ *n, pl* **cueva** *or* **cuevas** *usu cap* [Sp] **1 a :** a Cunan people of Panama **b :** a member of such people **2 :** a Chibchan language of the Cueva people

¹cuff \'kəf\ *n* -s [ME *coffe, cuffe,* perh. modif. of MF *coife, coiffe* coif — more at COIF] **1 a :** the part of a glove covering the wrist and sometimes the forearm **b :** EPIMANIKION **c :** a covering (as of stiff paper) for the forearm to prevent soiling the sleeves **2 a :** a band used to finish the end of a sleeve either by turning back a part of the sleeve or by attaching a separate piece **b :** the part of a sleeve at the wrist (as a coat sleeve that is finished by a hem) **c :** any of various separate bands worn at the wrist **d :** the turned-back hem of a trouser leg **3 a :** a piece of leather or other material sewn outside on the top of a shoe upper usu. for ornament **:** a wide collar **b :** the top band of a sock or stocking **4 :** HANDCUFF — usu. used in pl. **5 :** something resembling or likened to a cuff for the wrist (as the ferrule on a tool handle) **6 :** an inflatable band that is wrapped about an extremity to control the flow of blood through the part when recording blood pressure with the sphygmomanometer — **off the cuff** *adj* (*or adv*) **:** SPONTANEOUS, UNPREPARED, AD-LIB, INFORMAL — **on the cuff** *adj* (*or adv*) **1 :** on credit **2 :** on the house **:** GRATIS

²cuff \"\ *vt* -ED/-ING/-S **1 :** to furnish with a cuff **2 :** HANDCUFF

³cuff \"\ *vb* -ED/-ING/-S [perh. fr. obs. E *cuff* glove, fr. ME *cuffe*] *vt* **:** to strike with the palm of the hand or in a manner suggesting such a blow **:** BUFFET ⟨~ a boy over the ears⟩ ⟨~*ed* by the gale —Alfred Tennyson⟩ ~ *vi* **:** FIGHT, SCUFFLE **syn** see STRIKE

⁴cuff \"\ *n* -s **:** a blow with the hand esp. when open **:** SLAP ⟨gave him a good ~⟩

⁵cuff \"\ *n* -s [prob. modif. of Romany *kova* thing, person — more at COVE] **:** an old codger; *esp* **:** an old miser

⁶cuff \"\ *n* -s [perh. alter. of ¹*scuff*] *Scot* **:** ³SCRUFF

¹cuff·er \'kəfə(r)\ *n* -s [¹*cuff* + *-er*] **:** one that stitches cuffs to various articles of clothing or who folds the top of short hose

²cuffer \"\ *n* -s [E dial. *cuff* to talk over, gossip (perh. fr. ⁵*cuff*) + E *-er*] *Brit* **:** a preposterous story **:** YARN

cuf·fin \'kəfə̇n\ *n* -s [prob. modif. of Romany *kova* thing, person] **:** FELLOW, CHAP — see QUEER CUFFIN

cuff link *n* **:** a usu. ornamental device consisting of two pieces like buttons joined by a shank, chain, or bar for passing through buttonholes to fasten a cuff without overlapping the cuff ends — usu. used in pl.

cuff links

cufic *usu cap, var of* KUFIC

cui bo·no \kwē'bō(,)nō, ¦küē-\ *n* [L, to whose advantage?] **1 :** the principle that probable responsibility for an act or event lies with one who had something to gain by it ⟨a *cui bono* approach to an investigation⟩ **2 :** usefulness or utility as a principle in estimating the value of an act or policy

cui·ca \'kwēkə\ *n* -s [Pg, lit., cavy, fr. Guarani; fr. its squealing sound] **:** a Brazilian rhythm instrument consisting of a drumhead vibrated by oscillating a rosined string that has been placed through a hole made in it

cui·ca·tec \'kwēkə,tek, ,==¦=\ *or* **cui·ca·te·co** \,kwēkə'tā-(,)kō\ *n, pl* **cuicatec** *or* **cuicatecs** *or* **cuicateco** *or* **cuicatecos** *usu cap* [Sp *cuicateco,* of AmerInd origin] **1 a :** an Indian people of the district of Cuicatlan in the Mexican state of Oaxaca **b :** a member of such people **2 :** the Mixtecan language of the Cuicatec people

cui·chun·chul·li \,kwēchən'chülē\ *n* -s [modif. of AmerSp *cuichunchulo,* fr. Quechua *quichay* to open + *chunchulo* bowels] **:** the root of a So. American shrub (*Ionidium glutinosum*) of the family Violaceae used locally as an emetic

cu·ie·jo \kü'yā(,)hō\ *n* -s [modif. of AmerSp *cuyeo*] **:** a tropical American nighthawk (*Nyctidromus albicollis*) the dried and ground bones of which are highly esteemed in parts of its range as a love potion — called also *pauraque*

cuif \'küf, 'küef\ *var of* COOF

cui in vi·ta \,kwē(,)in'wē,tä\ *n* [ML, lit., to whom in life] **:** a writ of entry by means of which a widow sought to recover lands which had belonged to her but had been transferred by her husband during his lifetime

cuing *pres part of* CUE

cuir \'kwi(ə)r\ *n* -s [F, lit., leather, fr. L *corium*] **:** DORADO 2

¹cui·rass \kwē'ras, kwi-,kyù-,kyü-, -raa(ə)s, '=,=\ *n* -ES [ME *curas,* fr. MF *curasse, cuirasse,* fr. LL *coriacea,* fem. of *coriaceus* leathern, fr. L *corium* skin, hide + *-aceus* -aceous; akin to OE *heortha* deerskin, OHG *herdo* fleece, sheepskin, ON *hörundr* skin, Goth *hairthra* intestines, MIr *curach* skin boat, L *cortic-, cortex* bark, cork, Skt *kṛtti* hide, Gk *keirein* to cut — more at SHEAR] **1 a :** a piece of armor made orig. of leather and covering the body from neck to girdle; *esp* **:** one consisting of a coupled breastplate and backpiece — usu. used in pl. ⟨a pair of ~*es*⟩ **b :** the breastplate of such a piece **c :** any ancient close-fitting body armor **2 :** protecting armor plate (as of a ship) **3** *zool* **:** an armor of bony plates or other protective structure that is felt to resemble a cuirass **4 a :** a plaster cast for the trunk and neck **b :** a respirator that covers the chest or the chest and abdomen and provides artificial respiration by means of an electric pump

²cuirass \"\ *vt* -ED/-ING/-ES **:** to cover or armor with or as if with a cuirass

cui·ras·sier \,kwirə'si(ə)r, ¦kyùr-\ *n* -s [F, fr. *cuirasse* + *-ier* -er] **:** a mounted soldier wearing a cuirass; *specif* **:** a soldier of a certain type of heavy cavalry in the French and other European armies

cuir-bouil·li \¦kwir(,)bü¦yē\ *n* -s [F *cuir bouilli,* lit., boiled leather] **:** leather softened by soaking, pressed, molded, or stamped to shape, and hardened by drying and used for armor in the middle ages and for decorative objects (as book covers)

cuir ci·se·lé \¦kwir,sēz(ə)¦lā, -,siz-\ *n, pl* **cuir ciselés** [F, lit., chiseled leather] **:** an ancient style of decoration made on leather book covers by outlining with a knife and stippling the uncut background; *also* **:** an object so decorated

cui·sine \kwə̇'zēn, kwē'-\ *n* -s [F, lit., kitchen, fr. LL *coquina* — more at KITCHEN] **:** manner of preparing food **:** style of cooking ⟨the inn's ~ is American, not French⟩

cui·si·nier \¦kwē(,)zēn¦yā\ *n* -s [F, fr. *cuisine* + *-ier* -er] **:** COOK, CHEF 2

cui·si·nière \-¦ye(ə)r\ *n* -s [F, fem. of *cuisinier*] **:** a female cuisinier

cuis·sard *or* **cuis·sart** \kwē'sär\ *n* -s [F, fr. *cuisse* + *-ard*] **:** CUISSE

cuisse \'kwis\ *also* **cuish** \-ish\ *n* -s [back-formation fr. ME *cusseis, cushies,* fr. MF *cuissaux,* pl. of *cuissel,* fr. *cuisse* thigh, fr. L *coxa* hip, thigh — more at COXA] **:** defensive plate armor for the thighs esp. in front — see ARMOR illustration

cuit *or* **cute** *n* -s [ME *cute,* adj., boiled down (of wine), fr. MF *cuit,* fr. past part. of *cuire* to boil, cook, fr. L *coquere* to cook — more at COOK] *obs* **:** new wine boiled down

cuit·la·tec \'kwitlə,tek, 'kwēt-, ,==¦=\ *or* **cuit·la·te·co** \,==¦tā(,)kō\ *n, pl* **cuitlatec** *or* **cuitlatecs** *or* **cuitlateco** *or* **cuitlatecos** *usu cap* [Sp *cuitlateco,* of AmerInd origin] **1 a :** a people of unknown affiliations in Guerrero and Michoacán, Mexico **b :** a member of such people **2 :** the language of the Cuitlatec people

cuit·tle \'küt[ə]l, 'kət-\ *vt* -ED/-ING/-S [origin unknown] *Scot* **:** COAX, WHEEDLE

cui·vré \(')kwēv¦rā\ *adj* [F, fr. past part. of *cuivrer* to play with a brassy tone, fr. *cuivre* copper, fr. OF, fr. (assumed) VL *coprium,* fr. L *cyprium*] **:** OVERBLOWN — used as a direction in music for brass instruments (as the muted horn)

cuke \'kyük\ *n* -s [by shortening and alter.] **:** CUCUMBER

-cular — see -CLE

cu·lasse \kyü'las\ *n* -s [F, fr. *cul* bottom, backside] **:** CULET 1

cul·bert·son system \'kəlbə(r)tsən-\ *n, usu cap C* [after Ely *Culbertson* †1955 Amer. authority on contract bridge] **:** a system of bidding in contract bridge characterized by the use of approach and forcing bids, limited no-trump bids, and ace-showing no-trump bids — called also *approach-forcing system*

culch *var of* CULTCH

cul·dee \'kəl,dē\ *n* -s *often cap* [NL *culdei* (pl.), alter. (influenced by NL *cultores Dei* worshipers of God) of ML *keldei, keledei,* fr. OIr *cēle Dē,* lit., companion of God, fr. *cēle* companion + *Dē,* gen. of *Dia* God; akin to L *civis* citizen and to L *deus* god — more at CEMETERY, DEITY] **1** *archaic* **:** one of a class of religious recluses appearing first in Ireland in the 7th century **2** *archaic* **:** an Irish or Scottish monk

cul-de-four \¦kəldə¦fù(ə)r *also* ¦kùl-, *F* küdfüür\ *n, pl* **culs-de-four** \"\ [F, lit., bottom of an oven] **1 :** a vault shaped like a quarter sphere or like a hemisphere **2 :** VAULT — compare SEMIDOME

cul-de-lampe \¦kəldə¦lamp *also* ¦kùl-, *F* küdlääⁿp\ *n, pl* **culs-de-lampe** \"\ [F, lit., lamp bottom] **1 :** any of various ornaments or parts resembling the conical bottom of ancient lamps (as a pendant from a roof or an isolated corbel supporting an oriel, column, or turret) **2 :** TAILPIECE

cul-de-sac \¦kəldə¦sak, -dē;- *also* ¦kùl- *sometimes* -sək *or* -sák, *F* küdsák\ *n, pl* **culs-de-sac** *or* **cul-de-sacs** \-ks\ [F, lit., bottom of the bag] **1** *anat* **a :** a blind diverticulum or pouch (as the cecum); *also* **:** the closed end of such a pouch **b** *or* **cul-de-sac of douglas** *usu cap 2d D* [after James *Douglas* †1742 Scot. physician and anatomist] **:** POUCH OF DOUGLAS **2 :** a passage or alley with no exit forward **:** BLIND ALLEY; *esp* **:** a street that is closed at one end but usu. has a circular area for turning around at that end **3 :** a point beyond which further advance or progress is or seems to be impossible ⟨worked himself into a *cul-de-sac* within three or four hundred feet of the top —Andrew Hamilton & Chandler Harris⟩ ⟨his own investigations into the substantiality of matter lead him into a *cul-de-sac* —Leslie Paul⟩

culdo- *comb form* [*cul*-de-sac of Douglas] **:** pouch of Douglas ⟨*culdocentesis*⟩

Cul·do·scope \'kəldə,skōp, 'kùl-\ *trademark* — used for a specialized endoscope employed in culdoscopy

cul·do·scop·ic \¦=¦=skäpik\ *adj* [*culdoscopy* + *-ic*] **:** of, relating to, or involving culdoscopy

cul·dos·co·py \,kəl'däskəpē, ,kùl-\ *n* -ES [*cul*-de-sac of Douglas + *-scopy*] **:** a technique for endoscopic visualization and minor operative procedures on the female pelvic organs in which the instrument is introduced through a puncture in the wall of the pouch of Douglas

cu·let \'kyülə̇t\ *n* -s [F, dim. of *cul* bottom, backside, fr. L *culus;* akin to OFris *skūl* hiding place, MLG *schūl,* ON *skjōl* hiding place, refuge, barn, OIr *cūl* hiding place, W *cil,* OE *hȳdan* hide — more at HIDE] **1 :** the small flat facet at the bottom of a brilliant parallel to the table — called also *collet;* see BRILLIANT illustration **2 :** a piece of plate armor covering the buttocks

cu·lex \'kyü,leks\ *n, cap* [NL, fr. L, gnat; akin to OIr *cuil* gnat and prob. to Skt *sūla* spit, spear, sharp pain, L *cuneus* wedge] **:** a large cosmopolitan genus of mosquitoes that includes the common house mosquito (*C. pipiens*) of Europe and No. America, a widespread tropical mosquito (*C. quinquefasciatus* or *C. fatigans*) which transmits certain filarial worms parasitic in man, and other mosquitoes which have been implicated as vectors of virus encephalitides and possibly of other diseases of man and animals — compare ANOPHELES

cul·gee \¦kəl¦gē\ *n* -s [Hindi *kalgī,* fr. Per *kalgī* jeweled plume] **:** a jeweled plume worn in India on the turban

culic- *or* **culici-** *comb form* [NL, fr. L *culic-, culex*] **:** gnat **:** mosquito ⟨*Culicidae*⟩ ⟨*culicifuge*⟩

¹cu·li·cid \'kyüləsə̇d, -,sid; kyü'lisə̇d\ *adj* [NL *Culicidae*] **:** of or relating to the Culicidae

²culicid \"\ *n* -s **:** one of the Culicidae **:** MOSQUITO

cu·lic·i·dae \kyü'lisə,dē\ *n pl, cap* [NL, fr. *Culic-, Culex,* type genus + *-idae*] **:** a family of slender long-legged two-winged flies having the body and appendages partly covered with hairs or scales and the mouthparts adapted for piercing and sucking, comprising the mosquitoes, and having active aquatic larvae known as wrigglers

cu·li·cide \'kyülə,sīd\ *n* -s [blend of *culic-* and *-cide*] **:** an insecticide that destroys mosquitoes

cu·lic·i·dol·o·gist \kyü,lisə'däləjə̇st\ *n* -s [NL *Culicidae* + E *-ologist* (as in *bacteriologist*)] **:** one specializing in the study of mosquitoes

¹cu·li·cine \'kyülə,sīn, -,sə̇n\ *adj* [NL *Culic-, Culex* + E *-ine*] **:** of, involving, or affecting mosquitoes of *Culex* or many related genera (as *Aedes*) — compare ANOPHELINE

²culicine \"\ *n* -s **:** a culicine mosquito

cu·li·la·wan \,külē'läwən\ *or* **culilawan bark** *n* -s [Malay *kulit lawang,* fr. *kulit* bark + *lawang* cinnamon] **:** the aromatic bark of a tree (*Cinnamomum culilawan*) of the Moluccas

cu·li·nar·i·an \,kələ'nerēən, ,kyül-\ *n* -s [*culinary* + *-an*] **:** COOK, CHEF

cu·li·nary \'kələ,nerē, 'kyül-, -ri\ *adj* [L *culinarius,* fr. *culina* kitchen + *-arius* -ary — more at KILN] **:** of or relating to the kitchen or cookery ⟨~ art⟩ **:** suited for cooking ⟨~ herbs⟩

cu·li·no \kü'lē(,)nō, -)nü\ *n, pl* **culino** *or* **culinos** *usu cap* [Pg, of AmerInd origin] **1 :** an Indian people of western Brazil that is closely related to the Arauá **2 :** a member of the Culino people

¹cull \'kəl\ *vt* -ED/-ING/-S [ME *cullen, colen,* fr. MF *cuillir, coillir* to pick, gather, fr. L *colligere* to gather, collect — more at COLLECT] **1 a :** GATHER, PLUCK ⟨~ flowers⟩ **b :** to pick out and collect **:** CHOOSE ⟨~*ed* the best passages from the poet's works⟩ **2 a :** to subject (as a field) to culling **b :** to identify and remove culls from (a flock or herd) **3 :** to select or separate out as inferior or worthless

²cull \"\ *n* -s **1** *obs* **:** the act of culling **:** SELECTION **2 :** something rejected esp. as being inferior or worthless (as a cow from the herd, diseased plants from healthy ones, or nonlaying hens from a flock) — usu. used in pl. **3 a :** a grade of lumber below the lowest common grade **b :** PECKY CYPRESS

³cull \"\ *adj* [²*cull*] **:** culled out esp. as inferior **:** being a cull; *specif* **:** being a low grade of animal carcass used for processed meat food products

⁴cull \"\ *vt* -ED/-ING/-S [by alter.] *now dial* **:** ¹COLL

⁵cull \", 'kùl\ *n* -s [perh. short for *cullion*] *dial Brit* **:** DUPE, GULL, SIMPLETON

cul·lage \'kəlij\ n -s [¹cull + -age] : material eliminated in culling

cull board n [¹cull] : a table used for culling (as on an oyster boat)

cullender var of COLANDER

cul·len earth \'kələn-\ n [alter. of Cologne earth] : VANDYKE BROWN 2

cull·er \'kələ(r)\ n -s : one that culls: as a : one who inspects barrel staves b : one who examines poultry to detect inferior layers c : a scaler of logs d : one who picks out imperfect cookies or cakes in a bakery

cul·let \'kələt\ n -s [perh. fr. F cueillette act of gathering, picking, fr. L collecta — more at COLLECT] : broken or refuse glass that is generally added to a batch of new material to facilitate melting in glass manufacturing

cul·li·bil·i·ty \,kələ'biləd·ē\ n -ES [¹cully + -bility] : GULLIBILITY

culling n -s : something culled out : CULL — usu. used in pl.

cul·lion \'kəlyən\ n -s [ME coillon, colyoun testicle, fr. MF coillon, couillon, fr. (assumed) VL coleon-, coleo, fr. L coleus scrotum, perh. fr. colum sieve, strainer; fr. the shape of a straining bag — more at HEDGE] 1 obs : TESTIS 2 archaic : a mean or base fellow 3 : ORCHID 1

cul·lion·ly adj, archaic : MEAN, BASE

¹cul·lis \'kələs\ n -ES [ME colis, colice, fr. MF coleïs, fr. coler to strain, fr. L colare, fr. colum sieve — more at HEDGE] : a strong clear broth of meat (as for invalids)

²cullis \"\ n -ES [F coulisse groove, gutter — more at COULISSE] : a gutter in a roof : CHANNEL, GROOVE

¹cul·ly \'kəlē\ n -ES [perh. alter. of cullion] 1 archaic : one easily tricked or imposed on : DUPE, GULL 2 slang : COMPANION, MATE

²cully \"\ vt -ED/-ING/-ES : to impose on : TRICK, CHEAT, DECEIVE

¹culm \'kəlm, 'kau̇m\ n -S [ME culme; prob. akin to ME col coal — more at COAL] 1 : refuse coal screenings often piled in heaps : SLACK 2 a : a shoal-water deposit of conglomerates, sandstones, and shales in which marine fossil-bearing beds alternate with those containing plant remains b also **culm measures** : a Lower Carboniferous formation consisting of such deposits that in parts of Europe underlies the productive coal measures and has the stratigraphic position elsewhere occupied by the mountain limestone

²culm \"\ adj, usu cap [fr. Culm, division of the European Carboniferous, fr. ¹culm] : of or relating to a division of the Carboniferous of Europe — see GEOLOGIC TIME table

³culm \"\ n -S [modif. of L culmen — more at HILL] obs : CULMEN

⁴culm \"\ n -S [L culmus stalk — more at HAULM] 1 : the jointed stem of a grass usu. hollow except at the often swollen nodes and usu. herbaceous except in the bamboos and other arborescent grasses; also : one of the solid stems of sedges, rushes, and similar monocotyledonous plants 2 **culms** pl, Brit : rootlets of brewer's malt often used as a feed

cul·mann's diagram \'külmənz-, -,mänz-\ n, usu cap C [after Karl Culmann †1881 Ger. engineer] : FUNICULAR POLYGON 2

culm bank n [¹culm] : a storage dump of culm

cul·men \'kəlmən\ n, pl **culmens** \-nz\ or **cul·mi·na** \-nə\ [L — more at HILL] 1 : ACME, CULMINATION 2 [NL, fr. L] : the dorsal ridge of a bird's bill

culmi- comb form [L culmus — more at HAULM] : stalk : culm ⟨culmicolous⟩ ⟨culmiferous⟩ ⟨culmigenous⟩

culm·ide \'kəl,mīd\ adj, usu cap [fr. Culmide, mountain-making episode, fr. Culm, division of the European Carboniferous + E -ide] : of or relating to mountain-making movements in the Carboniferous era — see GEOLOGIC TIME table

cul·mi·nant \'kəlmənənt\ adj [ML culminant-, culminans, pres. part. of culminare to culminate] 1 : being at greatest altitude or on the meridian 2 : fully developed ⟨the blow was not the expression of any ~ rebellion —J.B.Clayton⟩

cul·mi·nate \-,nāt, usu -ād·+V\ vb -ED/-ING/-S [ML culminatus, past part. of culminare, fr. LL, to crown, fr. L culmin-, culmen top — more at HILL] vi 1 of a celestial body : to reach the highest altitude : come to the meridian; also : to be directly overhead 2 a : to rise to or form a summit (as of a mountain or wave) ⟨a helmet culminating in a crest⟩ b : to reach the highest point (as of rank or power) ⟨the house of Burgundy was rapidly culminating —J.L.Motley⟩ c : to reach a climactic or decisive point ⟨the troubles of the year culminated in rioting in November⟩ ~ vt : to bring to a head : be the culminating point of : CLIMAX, CAP ⟨the agreement culminated a long controversy —Newsweek⟩

cul·mi·na·tion \,kəlmə'nāshən\ n -S [ML culminatus + E -ion] 1 : the highest point reached by a celestial body in its diurnal revolution; also : the lowest point reached by a circumpolar celestial body 2 : that in which something culminates : culminating position : SUMMIT, ACME, CONSUMMATION, CLIMAX ⟨the ~ of a brilliant career⟩ ⟨the ~ of years of effort⟩

cu·lotte \(')k(y)ü¦lät\ n -S [F, lit., breeches, dim. of cul bottom, backside — more at CULET] 1 : hair on the thighs of an animal (as a Pomeranian dog) : BREECHING 2 : a divided skirt; also : a garment having a divided skirt — often used in pl.

cul·pa \'ku̇lpə, 'kəl-\ n, pl **cul·pae** \-ül,pī, -əl,pē\ [L, guilt, fault; prob. akin to OIr col sin, blame, W cwl] 1 Roman & civil law : actionable negligence or fault; specif : the failure to use the care and diligence demanded by the special relationship between the plaintiff and defendant under the particular circumstances that arises from inattention, careless conduct, or want of care — distinguished from dolus 2 Roman & civil law : all actionable fault or misconduct including both negligence and willful or wanton wrongs arising from malice, fraud, or a desire for wrongful gain 3 : CULPA LEVIS

cul·pa·bil·i·ty \,kəlpə'biləd·ē, -ətē, -i\ n -ES : the quality or state of being culpable : BLAMEWORTHINESS

cul·pa·ble \'kəlpəbəl\ adj [ME coupable, culpabil, fr. MF coupable, culpable, fr. L culpabilis, fr. culpare to blame (fr. culpa) + -abilis -able] 1 obs : GUILTY, CRIMINAL 2 : meriting condemnation or censure esp. as criminal ⟨~ plotters⟩ ⟨~ homicides⟩ or as conducive to accident, loss, or disaster ⟨~ negligence⟩ ⟨is it not . . . ~ and unworthy, thus beforehand to slur her honor —P.B.Shelley⟩ **syn** see BLAMEWORTHY

cul·pa·ble·ness n -ES [ME coupablenesse, fr. coupable + -nesse -ness] : the quality or state of being culpable : CULPABILITY

cul·pa·bly \-blē, -li\ adv : in a manner or to a degree deserving blame or censure : REPREHENSIBLY

culpa la·ta \¦==¦läd·ə, -lā-\ or **culpa mag·na** \-'magnə, -mag-\ n [LL, lit., great negligence] Roman & civil law : the absence of the degree of care even inattentive or thoughtless persons would exercise under all the circumstances : GROSS NEGLIGENCE

culpa le·vis \-'levəs\ n [NL culpa levis, lit., slight negligence] Roman & civil law : ordinary or slight negligence arising from failure to exercise such care as a diligent father is accustomed to observe in his own affairs under all the circumstances

culpa levis in ab·strac·to \-,inəbz'trak(,)tō, -,i,nab-, -b'st-\ n [NL, lit., slight negligence in the abstract] Roman & civil law : ordinary negligence arising from the failure to exercise the very high degree of care that men of good business or very prudent persons would exercise under all the circumstances

culpa levis in con·cre·to \-,in,kän'krē,tō\ n [NL, lit., slight negligence in the concrete] Roman & civil law : ordinary negligence arising from one's failure to exercise such care in the interest of another as he exercises in his own affairs

culpa le·vis·si·ma \-le'visəmə\ n [NL, lit., slightest negligence] Roman & civil law : negligence arising from the slightest fault : very slight negligence arising from the failure to exercise the most exact care which a most diligent father would exercise under all the circumstances

cul·pa·to·ry \'kəlpə,tōrē\ adj [L culpatus (past part. of culpare to blame, fr culpa fault, blame) + E -ory — more at CULPA] : CENSORIOUS, ACCUSING

cul·peo \kül'pā(,)ō\ n -S [Sp, fr. Araucan culpeu] : a So. American mammal (Dusicyon magellanicus) that was formerly considered a true dog (genus Canis); also : any of several closely related species

cul·prit \'kəlprət also -,prit; usu -d·+V\ n -S [AF cul. (abbr. of culpable guilty) + prit, prist, prest ready (i.e., to prove it), fr. L praestus — more at PRESTO] 1 a : one accused of or arraigned for a crime b : one accused of a fault 2 a : one guilty of a crime b : one guilty of a fault **syn** see CRIMINAL

culs-de-four pl of CUL-DE-FOUR

culs-de-lampe pl of CUL-DE-LAMPE

culs-de-sac pl of CUL-DE-SAC

cult \'kəlt\ n -S [F & L; F culte, fr. L cultus care, cultivation, culture, adoration, fr. cultus, past part. of colere to till, cultivate, dwell, inhabit, worship — more at WHEEL] 1 : religious practice : WORSHIP 2 : a system of beliefs and ritual connected with the worship of a deity, a spirit, or a group of deities or spirits ⟨the ~ of Apollo⟩ ⟨the earth ~⟩ 3 a : the rites, ceremonies, and practices of a religion : the formal aspect of religious experience ⟨dissent occurs in all three fields of expression of religious experience, in doctrine, in ~, and organization —Joachim Wach⟩ b Roman Catholicism : reverence and ceremonial veneration paid to God or to the Virgin Mary or to the saints or to objects that symbolize or otherwise represent them (as the crucifix or a statue) — called also cultus; compare DULIA, HYPERDULIA, LATRIA 4 : a religion regarded as unorthodox or spurious ⟨the exuberant growth of fantastic ~s⟩; also : a minority religious group holding beliefs regarded as unorthodox or spurious : SECT ⟨provided a haven for persecuted ~s⟩ 5 : a system for the cure of disease based on the dogma, tenets, or principles set forth by its promulgator to the exclusion of scientific experience or demonstration 6 a : great or excessive devotion or dedication to some person, idea, or thing ⟨the ~ of success⟩; esp : such devotion regarded as a literary or intellectual fad or fetish ⟨the ~ of art-for-art's sake⟩ b : the object of such devotion ⟨square dancing has developed into something of a ~ —R.L.Taylor⟩ c (1) : a body of persons characterized by such devotion ⟨America's growing ~ of home fixer uppers —Wall Street Jour.⟩ (2) : a usu. small or narrow circle of persons united by devotion or allegiance to some artistic or intellectual program, tendency, or figure (as one of limited popular appeal) ⟨the exclusive ~ of those that profess to admire his esoteric verse⟩ **syn** see RELIGION

cultch or **culch** \'kəlch\ n -ES [perh. fr. a F dial. form of F couche couch, bed, fr. OF culche, couche — more at COUCH] 1 a : material (as oyster shells) laid down on oyster grounds to furnish points of attachment for the spat; also : similar material provided for any other shellfish b : a horny or gelatinous egg mass of a mollusk 2 chiefly NewEng : TRASH, RUBBISH

cul·tel·la·tion \,kəltə'lāshən\ n -S [F, fr. L cultellus + F -ation] : the transferring in surveying of the exact location of a point from a higher level (as an overhanging cliff) to a lower by dropping a sharp-pointed marking pin

cul·tel·lus \kəl'teləs\ n, pl **cultel·li** \-e,lī, -(,)lē\ [NL, fr. L, small knife, dim. of culter knife, plowshare — more at COLTER] : one of the sharp pointed cutting organs (as mandibles and maxillae) of many bloodsucking flies

culti pl of CULTUS

cul·tic \'kəltik\ adj : of or relating to a cult ⟨a temple that became the ~ center of the entire province⟩

cul·ti·cut·ter \'kəltə,kəd·ə(r)\ n [cultivator + cutter] : a cultivator with blades that cut into sod or cover crop

cul·ti·gen \'kəltəjən, -,jen\ n -S [cultivated + -gen] 1 : a cultivated organism (as maize) of a variety or species for which a wild ancestor is unknown 2 : CULTIVAR — not used technically

cul·ti·pack \'kəltə,pak\ vt [cultivate + pack] : to firm and pulverize (a seedbed) with a corrugated roller

cul·ti·pack·er \-kə(r)\ n [fr. Cultipacker, a trademark] : a corrugated roller used to break clods and firm a seedbed

cul·ti·ros·tral \¦kəltə¦rästrəl\ adj [NL Cultirostres + E -al] : having a cultrate bill : of or relating to the Cultirostres

cul·ti·ros·tres \,==¦=(,)strēz\ n pl, cap [NL, fr. culti- (fr. L culter knife, plowshare) + -rostres (fr. L rostrum beak) — more at COLTER, ROSTRUM] in old classifications : a group including the storks, herons, cranes, and various other large birds with pointed sharp-edged bills

cult·ish \'kəltish\ adj : of, relating to, or suggesting a cult ⟨a ~ belief that such composers . . . could hardly be represented on the modern grand —Irving Kolodin⟩

cult·ism \'kəl,tizəm\ n -S 1 : devotion to the doctrine or practice of a cult ⟨however foolish the ~ of those who systematized his half-truths —P.T.Homan⟩ : a cultish tendency or outlook ⟨to avoid any taint of ~, each issue will have a different editor —Time⟩ : a tendency to form or embrace a cult ⟨America's intellectual history is rich in ~, faddism, and large-scale self-deception —R.H.Rovere⟩ 2 : WORSHIP, VENERATION ⟨lived in a world of antiquities and were actuated by . . . ~ of the dead —J.P.Marquand⟩

cult·ist \'kəltəst\ n -S : a devotee or practitioner of a cult : SECTARIAN

cul·ti·va·bil·i·ty \,kəltəvə'biləd·ē\ n -ES : the quality or state of being cultivable

cul·ti·va·ble \'kəltəvəbəl\ adj [F, fr. MF, fr. cultiver, coutiver to cultivate (fr. OF) + -able — more at CULTIVATE] : capable of being cultivated

cul·ti·var \'kəltə,vär\ n -S [cultivated variety] : an organism of a kind (as a variety, strain, or race) that has originated and persisted under cultivation

cul·ti·vat·able \'kəltə,vād·əbəl, -ātə-\ adj : CULTIVABLE

cul·ti·vate \'kəltə,vāt, usu -ād·+V\ vt -ED/-ING/-S [ML cultivatus, past part. of cultivare, fr. OF cultiver, coutiver, fr. culti, couti cultivable, fr. ML cultivus, fr. L cultus (past part. of colere to till, cultivate, dwell, inhabit) + -ivus -ive — more at WHEEL] 1 : to prepare for the raising of crops : prepare and use for such a purpose : TILL ⟨~ the soil⟩; specif : to loosen or break up the soil about (growing crops or plants) for the purpose of killing weeds and modifying moisture retention of the soil esp. with a cultivator 2 : to protect and encourage the growth of: a : to till or labor over; esp : to apply methods of culturing to ⟨~ oysters⟩ ⟨~ yeasts⟩ b : to improve by labor, care, or study : bring to culture, civilization, or refinement ⟨writers who ~ style⟩ 3 : to cause to grow by special attention or by studying, advancing, developing, practicing, or publicizing : FURTHER, ENCOURAGE ⟨Italy, where law and medicine were cultivated, and the North, where theology with logic and metaphysics were supreme —H.O. Taylor⟩ 4 : to seek the society of : make friends with ⟨outraged constantly by the odd assortment of people my father cultivated —Elsa Maxwell⟩ **syn** see NURSE

cultivated adj 1 a of a plant : grown or developed by human care : DOMESTICATED ⟨~ varieties of roses⟩ b of a field : under cultivation : in crops 2 of a person, quality, or faculty : socially well-trained : CULTURED, REFINED, EDUCATED ⟨~ speech⟩ ⟨~ tastes⟩ ⟨~ voices⟩

cultivated pearl n : CULTURED PEARL

cul·ti·va·tion \,kəltə'vāshən\ n -S 1 : the act or art of cultivating: as a : the art or process of agriculture : TILLAGE; esp : intertillage to destroy weeds and loosen soil ⟨fields brought under ~⟩ b : CULTURE 6 c : a fostering or practicing esp. of a branch of learning : a training and developing (as of taste, mind, manners) d : assiduous development of personal relations ⟨~ of new friendships⟩ 2 : something produced by cultivating : CULTURE, REFINEMENT, CIVILIZATION ⟨a man of charm and ~⟩ 3 : land being cultivated ⟨villagers working on the headman's ~s⟩

cul·ti·va·tor \'kəltə,vād·ə(r), -ātə-\ n -S 1 : one that cultivates (as the soil, an art, a discipline) : FARMER; esp : one that cultivates the soil as a mode of life ⟨by contrast with their nomadic neighbors these Indians are ~s and skilled craftsmen⟩ 2 : an implement (as a hand tool or a large wheeled horse-drawn or tractor-drawn vehicle) that consists usu. of a frame upon which are fastened shares, discs, or tines and that is used for breaking up the soil surface esp. among growing crops in order to aerate the soil, conserve moisture, and control weeds — compare GO-DEVIL, SULKY

cultivator 2

cultivator shield n : an attachment to a cultivator to prevent damage to the crop

cult object n : an object of religious devotion, veneration, or ritualistic and symbolic value within a system of worship

cult of the dead : ANCESTOR CULT

cul·trate \'kəl·,trāt\ also **cul·trat·ed** \-ād·əd\ adj [cultrate fr. L cultratus knife-shaped, fr. cultr-, culter knife + -atus -ate; cultrated fr. L cultratus + E -ed — more at COLTER] : sharp-edged and pointed : shaped like a pruning knife ⟨a crow's beak is ~⟩

cults pl of CULT

cul·tu·al \'kəlch(ə)wəl\ adj [F cultuel, fr. culte cult + -uel (as in mutuel mutual) — more at CULT] : of or relating to cult or worship

cul·tur·able \'kəlch(ə)rəbəl\ adj [²culture + -able] : capable of culture : CULTIVABLE

cul·tur·al \'kəlch(ə)rəl, +V also -chərl\ adj [¹culture + -al] 1 : of or relating to the artistic and intellectual aspects or content of human activity ⟨a person of broad ~ interests⟩ ⟨organized ~ activity at the camp includes theatricals and study circles⟩ 2 a : produced by breeding ⟨a ~ variety⟩ b : of or relating to the culture of a plant : HORTICULTURAL 2 3 a : dealing with culture data ⟨~ anthropology⟩ ⟨Portuguese ~ influences in Brazil⟩ ⟨all humans are strongly influenced by ~ inheritance as well, which is transmitted outside the body, such as language, custom, education, and so on —L.C.Dunn⟩ b : of, relating to, or being the complex of institutionalized traits learned and transmitted by man as a member of society 4 : MAN-MADE ⟨~ features of the landscape⟩

cultural anthropology n : the division of anthropology that deals with the study of culture in all its aspects and that utilizes the methods, concepts, and data of archaeology, ethnology and ethnography, folklore and linguistics, and sometimes those of the sociological and psychological sciences — distinguished from physical anthropology

cultural change n : modification of a society through innovation, invention, discovery, or contact with other societies

cultural drift n 1 : the spread of culture traits throughout an area 2 : the tendency of a culture or its institutions to manifest cumulative variation in certain directions

cultural evolution n : EVOLUTION 6b

cultural history n 1 : the history of a culture or culture area ⟨a cultural history of the Southwest⟩; specif : a history treating one or a number of historic world cultures as an integrated unit for purposes of cross comparison with others and for analysis of the forces presumed to be in operation as regards cultural growth, development, fruition, and decay 2 : history that esp. by contrast with narrative political history concentrates upon the social, intellectual, and artistic aspects or forces in the life of a people or nation — compare SOCIAL HISTORY

cul·tur·al·ist \-ch(ə)rələst\ n -S 1 : one that emphasizes the importance of culture in determining behavior 2 : a specialist in the study of culture; specif : a cultural anthropologist

cul·tur·al·ized \-ch(ə)rə,līzd\ adj : deriving from or imposed or conditioned by culture

cultural lag n : a relatively slower advance or change of one aspect of a culture; esp : the slower development of nonmaterial as contrasted with material or technological culture traits

cul·tur·al·ly \'kəlch(ə)rəlē, -li\ adv 1 : with regard to culture ⟨~ the period was one of rapid advance⟩ : in a cultural manner ⟨will seek every evening to do something that is ~ satisfying and significant —Current Biog.⟩ 2 : according to the prevailing culture ⟨handled and fed, clothed and cared for in ~ approved ways —Grace De Laguna⟩ 3 : according to the principles of culture for a plant or crop

cultural nature n : HUMAN NATURE a

cultural sociology n [trans. of G kultursoziologie] : the sociological study of the historical processes involved in cultural phenomena (as art, philosophy, religion)

¹cul·ture \'kəlchə(r)\ n -S [ME, fr. MF, fr L cultura, fr. cultus (past part. of colere to till, cultivate) + -ura -ure — more at WHEEL] 1 a : the art or practice of cultivating : the manner or method of cultivating : TILLAGE ⟨we ought to blame the ~, not the soil —Alexander Pope⟩ b obs : cultivated land : a cultivated area 2 : the act of developing by education, discipline, social experience : the training or refining of the moral and intellectual faculties 3 a : the cultivation or rearing of a particular product or crop or stock for supply ⟨the ~ of the vine⟩ ⟨bee ~⟩ b : steady endeavor at improvement of or in a special line ⟨~ of the sonnet⟩ c : professional or expert care and training ⟨voice ~⟩ ⟨beauty ~⟩ 4 a : the state of being cultivated; esp : the enlightenment and excellence of taste acquired by intellectual and aesthetic training : the intellectual and artistic content of civilization : refinement in manners, taste, thought b : acquaintance with and taste in fine arts, humanities, and broad aspects of science as distinguished from vocational, technical, or professional skill or knowledge 5 a : the total pattern of human behavior and its products embodied in thought, speech, action, and artifacts and dependent upon man's capacity for learning and transmitting knowledge to succeeding generations through the use of tools, language, and systems of abstract thought b : the body of customary beliefs, social forms, and material traits constituting a distinct complex of tradition of a racial, religious, or social group ⟨a nation with many ~s⟩ ⟨Plains Indian ~⟩ ⟨but to many men today the most interesting thing about society is its ~ . . . that complex whole that includes knowledge, belief, morals, law, customs, opinions, religion, superstition, and art —Preserved Smith⟩ c : a complex of typical behavior or standardized social characteristics peculiar to a specific group, occupation or profession, sex, age grade, or social class ⟨youth ~⟩ ⟨middle class ~⟩ d : a recurring assemblage (as of artifacts, house types, methods of burial, and other evidences of a way of life) that differentiates a group of archaeological sites 6 a : cultivation of living material (as bacteria or tissues) in prepared nutrient media; also : an instance of such cultivation or a growth that is the intended product of it b : any inoculated nutrient medium whether or not it contains living organisms — see MEDIUM 8; PURE CULTURE 7 : the details of a map in the aggregate that represent cultural features (as canals, buildings, roads)

²culture \"\ vt **cultured; cultured; culturing** \-ch(ə)riŋ\ **cultures** [MF culturer, fr. culture, n.] 1 : CULTIVATE 2 biol a : to grow (as microorganisms or tissues) in a prepared medium b : to start a culture from ⟨~ soil⟩; also : to make a culture of ⟨cultured milk⟩

culture and personality n : an area of investigation within anthropology concentrating upon the psychological orientation of culture and the dynamic structure of personality developed within it

culture area n : a contiguous geographic area comprising a number of societies that possess the same or similar traits or that share a dominant cultural orientation ⟨the cattle complex serves to delimit the East African culture area⟩

culture-bound \'==,=\ adj : limited by or valid only within a particular culture ⟨intelligence tests are commonly culture-bound to some degree⟩

culture center n : the region of a culture area showing the greatest concentration of traits peculiar to or typical of the area

culture complex n : ³COMPLEX 1a

culture conflict n : the conflict of behavior patterns and values that results when different cultures are incompletely assimilated; esp : the conflict that may find expression in high rates of criminality and delinquency

culture contact n, chiefly Brit : ACCULTURATION

cultured adj 1 : being under culture : CULTIVATED ⟨~ fields⟩ 2 : well-educated : URBANE, POLISHED : having refined taste, speech, and manners 3 : grown or produced under artificial conditions ⟨bacteria ~ for vaccine production⟩

cultured milk or **cultured buttermilk** n : the product resulting from the souring of skimmed or partially skimmed milk by the addition of a culture of lactic acid bacteria

cultured pearl also **culture pearl** n : a natural pearl grown under controlled conditions (as by inserting a seed pearl into the mantle of an oyster and keeping the oyster in a sea bed for some years)

culture feature n : a man-made feature (as a town, road, bridge, or house) of a region

culture hero n 1 : a legendary figure variously represented as a beast, bird, man, or demigod to whom a people attributes the factors that appear most essential to its existence and culture (as important inventions, the overcoming of major obstacles, the exercise of divine leadership, and the origin of itself, mankind, natural phenomena, or the world) **2 :** one that symbolizes the ideal of a people or a group

culture-historical \ˌ⸗⸗⸗ˌ⸗⸗⸗\ *adj* [trans. of G *kulturhistorisch*] **:** being or relating to the theory and methods of the Vienna school of ethnology

culture language *n* **:** a language that is learned by many members of other speech communities for the sake of access to the culture of which it is the vehicle

culture myth *n* **:** a myth accounting for the discovery of arts and sciences

culture trait *n* **:** TRAIT 4

cul·tur·ist \ˈkəlch(ə)rəst\ *n* -s **1 :** one engaged in a culture **2 :** an advocate of culture or of a particular method of cultivating mind or body **3 :** one that breeds or raises animals esp. of kinds not usu. regarded as domesticated (as fishes or game birds)

cul·tur·o·log·i·cal \ˌkəlch(ə)rəˈläjəkəl\ *adj* **:** of or relating to culturology **:** of, relating to, or applying a methodology that regards culture as an autonomous self-determined process and explains human behavior in terms of that process — **cul·tur·o·log·i·cal·ly** \-jək(ə)lē\ *adv*

culturologist *n* -s **:** a specialist in or advocate of culturology

cul·tur·ol·o·gy \-jē\ *n* -ES [¹*culture* + *-o-* + *-logy*] **:** the science of culture; *specif* **:** a methodology esp. associated with the American anthropologist Leslie A. White that treats culture as a self-contained self-determined process and regards cultural traits (as technologies, ideologies, and institutions) as the products of antecedent and concomitant cultural elements and as developing independently of other data (as climatic environment, human physical type, or human wishes and purposes)

¹**cul·tus** \ˈkəltəs\ *n, pl* **cultuses** \-təsəz\ *or* **cul·ti** \-ˌtī, -ˌtē\ [NL, fr. L, adoration — more at CULT] **1 :** organized religious practice or system of worship **:** the practical aspect of a religion embodying the aggregate of its ritual forms, sacred ceremonies, liturgies, rites, and all acts expressive of veneration or worship **2 :** CULT 3b

²**cultus** \"\ *or* **cultus cod** *n* -ES [Chinook *kúltus* worthless] **:** LINGCOD

cultus image *or* **cultus statue** *n* [¹*cultus*] **:** an image or statue that is a direct object of worship

¹**cul·ver** \ˈkəlvə(r), ˈku̇l-\ *n* -s [ME, fr. OE *culfre, culufre,* fr. (assumed) VL *columbra,* fr. L *columbula,* dim. of *columba* dove — more at COLUMBA] **:** DOVE, PIGEON; *specif, Brit* **:** WOOD PIGEON

²**cul·ver** \ˈkəlvə(r)\ *n* -s [by shortening] **:** CULVERIN

culverfoot \ˈ⸗⸗ˌ⸗\ *n, pl* **culverfoots** [ME *culverfot,* fr. ¹*culver* + *fot* foot; fr. the shape of the leaves] **:** any of several plants of the genus *Geranium; esp* **:** the small-flowered European cranesbill (*G. columbinum*) — compare DOVE'S-FOOT

culverhouse \ˈ⸗⸗ˌ⸗\ *n* [ME *culverhous,* fr. ¹*culver* + *hous* house] **:** DOVECOTE

cul·ve·rin \ˈkəlvərən\ *also* **cul·ve·ring** \-riŋ\ *n* -s [ME, fr. MF *coulevrine, couleuvrine,* fr. *couleuvre* adder, snake (fr. L *colubra,* fem. of *colubr-, coluber* snake) + *-ine* — more at COLUBER] **:** a firearm that was orig. a rude musket but was in the 16th and 17th centuries a long cannon (as an 18-pounder) with serpent-shaped handles

cul·ver·key \ˈkəlvə(r),kē\ *n* [¹*culver* + *key*] **1** *dial Eng* **:** WOOD HYACINTH **2** *dial Eng* **:** COWSLIP 1a

cul·ver's root \ˈkəlvə(r)z-\ *or* **culver's physic** *also* **culvers** *n, usu cap C* [after a Dr. *Culver fl* before 1716 Am. physician who used it for medicinal purposes] **1 :** a tall perennial herb (*Veronicastrum virginicum*) common in eastern No. America **2 :** the rhizome and roots of Culver's root used as a cathartic

¹**cul·vert** \ˈkəlvə(r)t, *chiefly in dial or substand speech* -lbə-; *usu* |d·+V\ *n* -s [origin unknown] **1 :** a transverse drain or waterway (as under a road, railroad, or canal) **2 :** a conduit for a culvert **3 :** a bridge over a culvert

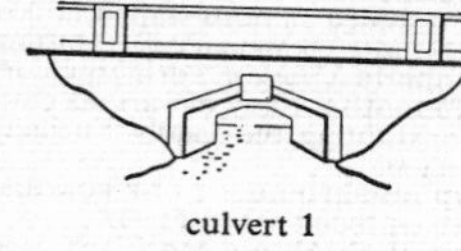
culvert 1

²**culvert** \"\ *vt* -ED/-ING/-S **1 :** to provide (a road) or bridge (a stream) with a culvert **2 :** to channel (a river) underground

cul·vert·age \ˈkəlvə(r)d·ij\ *n* -s [OF, fr. *culvert* serf (fr. L *collibertus* fellow freedman, fr. *com-* + *libertus* one made free, fr. *liber* free) + *-age* — more at LIBERAL] **:** VILLENAGE; *also* **:** reduction to villenage with forfeiture of estate

culverwort \ˈ⸗⸗ˌ⸗\ *n* [¹*culver* + *wort*] **:** GARDEN COLUMBINE

¹**cum** \(ˌ)ku̇m, (ˌ)kəm\ *prep* [L; akin to L *com-* — more at CO-] **:** WITH **:** combined with ⟨the entertainment-*cum*-profit motive —*Newsweek*⟩ **:** INCLUDING **:** along with ⟨house-*cum*-farm⟩ ⟨the members of this orchestra-*cum*-ballet —*New Yorker*⟩

²**cum** \ˈ⸗\ *adj* (*or adv*) [in sense 1, by shortening; in sense 2, fr. ¹*cum*] **1 :** CUM LAUDE **2 :** including dividend ⟨the ~ price of a stock⟩

cum- *or* **cumo-** *comb form* [*cumin*] **:** cumic **:** cumin ⟨*cum*aldehyde⟩ ⟨*cumo*quinol⟩

cum *abbr* cumulative

cu·ma·cea \kyüˈmāshēə\ *n pl, cap* [NL, fr. *Cuma,* type genus (irreg. fr. Gk *kyma* sprout, wave, anything swollen) + *-acea* — more at CYME] **:** an order of small sessile-eyed malacostracan marine crustaceans (division Peracarida) having a carapace formed by fusion of the first three or four thoracic segments with the head — **cu·ma·cean** \(ˈ)⸗ˈ⸗shən\ *adj or n* — **cu·ma·ceous** \-shəs\ *adj*

cu·ma·gloia \ˌkyüməˈglȯiə\ *n, cap* [NL, irreg. fr. Gk *kyma* sprout, wave, anything swollen + *gloia,* var. of *glia* glue — more at CLAY] **:** a genus of marine red algae (family Helminthocladiaceae) occurring commonly along the Pacific coast of No. America as a summer annual, the mature thallus consisting of a disk-shaped holdfast and a simple or sparsely branched upper portion with numerous fine cylindrical branches

cu·mal·de·hyde \kyüˈmaldəˌhīd\ *n* [*cum-* + *aldehyde*] **:** an aromatic oily aldehyde $(CH_3)_2CHC_6H_4CHO$ found in cumin oil and other essential oils and used in perfumes and flavors; *para*-isopropyl-benzaldehyde — called also *cuminaldehyde*

cumalic acid *var of* COUMALIC ACID

cumalin *var of* COUMALIN

cu·man \k(y)üˈmän, ˈ⸗ˌ⸗\ *or* **co·man** \kōˈ-, ˈ⸗ˌ⸗\ *or* **ku·man** \k(y)üˈ-, ˈ⸗ˌ⸗\ *n, pl* **cuman** *or* **cumans** *or* **coman** *or* **comans** *or* **kuman** *or* **kumans** *usu cap* [ML *Cumani* (pl.), fr. MGk *Koumanoi*] **1 a :** a Turkic people who occupied parts of southern Russia and the Moldavian and Wallachian steppes during the 9th, 10th and 11th centuries and were driven out by the Tatar and Mongol invasions and some of whom passed into Hungary where they were absorbed **b :** a member of such people **2 :** the Turkic language of the Cuman people

cu·ma·na·go·to \kü,mänəˈgōd·(ˌ)ō\ *n, pl* **cumanagoto** *or* **cumanagotos** *usu cap* [Sp, of AmerInd origin] **1 a :** a Cariban people of Venezuela **b :** a member of such people **2 :** the language of the Cumanagoto people

cu·ma·ni·an \kyüˈmānēən\ *n* -s *usu cap* [*Cuman* + *-ian*] **:** CUMAN

cumara *or* **cumaru** *var of* COUMAROU

cumarin *var of* COUMARIN

cumarone *var of* COUMARONE

cu·mat·o·phyte \kyüˈmad·əˌfīt\ *also* **cu·ma·phyte** \ˈkyüməˌ-\ *n* -s [*cumatophyte* irreg. fr. Gk *kymato-* (fr. *kymat-, kyma* wave) + E *-phyte; cumaphyte* irreg. fr. Gk *kyma* wave + E *-phyte* — more at CYME] **:** a plant adapted for growth under surf conditions **:** SURF PLANT — **cu·mat·o·phyt·ic** \(ˈ)kyüˌmad·əˈfid·ik\ *also* **cu·ma·phyt·ic** \ˌkyüməˈ⸗\ *adj*

cu·may \küˈmā, ˌkēmə'ē\ *n* -s [Pg *cumai, cumahy,* fr. Tupi *cumá*] **:** a small tree or shrub (*Zschokkea arborescens*) of the family Apocynaceae of the Amazon valley; *also* **:** its gum

cum·bent \ˈkəmbənt\ *adj* [L *-cumbent-, -cumbens,* pres. part. of *-cumbere* to lie (as in *recumbere* to lie down) — more at RECUMBENT] **:** RECUMBENT

¹**cum·ber** \ˈkəmbə(r)\ *vt* **cumbered; cumbered; cumbering** \-b(ə)riŋ\ **cumbers** [ME *cumbren, combren,* perh. fr. OF *combrer* to prevent, hinder, fr. (assumed) OF *combre* abatis — more at ENCUMBER] **1** *obs* **a :** to destroy utterly **:** DEFEAT **b :** TROUBLE, HARASS ⟨Martha was ~*ed* about much serving —Luke 10:40 (AV)⟩ **2 :** to hinder or bother by being in the way ⟨~*ed* with heavy clothing⟩ **3 :** to weigh down needlessly **:** burden uselessly **:** clutter up ⟨~ the memory with trivial facts⟩ ⟨an old walnut tree . . . had perished a long time ago, but still stood and was ~*ing* the earth —A.E.Coppard⟩ **syn** see BURDEN

²**cumber** \"\ *n* -s [ME *cumbre, combre,* fr. *cumbren, combren,* v.] **:** something that cumbers: as **a** *archaic* **:** CARE, WORRY **b** *archaic* **:** TROUBLE, INCONVENIENCE **c :** HINDRANCE, BURDEN, ENCUMBRANCE

cum·ber·land \ˈkəmbə(r)lənd\ *adj, usu cap* [fr. *Cumberland* county, England] **:** of or from the county of Cumberland, England **:** of the kind or style prevalent in Cumberland **:** CUMBRIAN

cum·ber·some \ˈkəmbə(r)səm\ *adj* **1 a** *obs* **:** difficult of passage or access **b** *chiefly dial* **:** BURDENSOME, TROUBLESOME **2 :** awkward, inconvenient, or difficult to handle, carry, or manage **:** of an excessive size, shape, or length ⟨plants wrapped for carrying are sometimes ~⟩ **:** CLUMSY, UNWIELDY ⟨~ technical terms⟩ **3 :** slow-moving **:** PONDEROUS, LUMBERING ⟨~ administrative procedures⟩ ⟨the grizzly bear looked ~ and awkward⟩ **syn** see HEAVY

cum·ber·some·ly \-lē, -li\ *adv* **:** in a cumbersome manner

cum·ber·some·ness \-nəs\ *n* -ES **:** the quality or state of being cumbersome

cumb·ly \ˈkəmlē, -li\ *n* -ES [Hindi *kamlī,* fr. Skt *kambala* woolen blanket] *India* **:** a blanket made of wool or goat's hair; *also* **:** the material of such blankets

cum·brance \ˈkəmbrən(t)s\ *n* -s [ME *cumbraunce, combraunce,* fr. *cumbren, combren* to cumber + *-aunce* -ance] **:** ENCUMBRANCE, TROUBLE

¹**cum·bri·an** \ˈkəmbrēən\ *adj, usu cap* [NL *Cumbria* Cumberland county (fr. ML, ancient Celtic kingdom in northwestern Britain, of Celt origin; akin to W *Cymro* Welshman) + E *-an*] **1 :** CUMBERLAND **2 :** of, relating to, or characteristic of Cumbrians

²**cumbrian** \"\ *n* -s *cap* **:** a native or inhabitant of Cumberland

cum·brous \ˈkəmbrəs\ *adj* [ME, fr. *cumbren* to cumber + *-ous*] **1** *obs* **a :** difficult to pass through or over **:** hard to reach **b :** giving trouble **:** VEXATIOUS **2 :** making action or motion difficult **:** UNWIELDY, CLOGGING, CUMBERSOME **syn** see HEAVY

cum·brous·ly *adv* [ME, fr. *cumbrous* + *-ly*] **:** in a cumbrous way **:** CLUMSILY, PONDEROUSLY

cum·brous·ness *n* -ES **:** the quality or state of being cumbrous

cum·bu \ˈkəm(ˌ)bü\ *n* -s [Kaunada & Telugu *kambu* or Tamil *kampu*] **:** PEARL MILLET 1

cum dividend \ku̇m-, kəm-\ *adv* (*or adj*) [¹*cum*] **:** with the value of a pending dividend included in the sale price of a security, the buyer being entitled to the dividend when paid — opposed to *ex dividend*

cu·mene \ˈkyü(ˌ)mēn\ *n* -s [ISV *cum-* + *-ene;* orig. formed as F *cumène*] **:** a colorless oily hydrocarbon $(CH_3)_2CHC_6H_5$ obtained by acid-catalyzed alkylation of benzene with propylene and used as an additive for high-octane motor fuel; isopropyl-benzene

cumene hydroperoxide *n* **:** an oily liquid made by oxidation of cumene with air and used as a polymerization catalyst (as in making synthetic rubber) and as a source material for the production of phenol and acetone

cu·men·gite *also* **cu·men·geite** \kyüˈmen,jīt, -ˌgīt\ *n* -s [G *cumengit,* fr. Édouard *Cumenge* †1902 Fr. mining engineer + G *-it* -ite] **:** a mineral $Pb_4Cu_4Cl_8(OH)_8.H_2O$ consisting of a basic lead-copper chloride occurring in deep blue tetragonal crystals

cu·me·nyl \ˈkyüməˌnil\ *n* -s [*cumene* + *-yl*] **:** any of three univalent radicals $(CH_3)_2CHC_6H_4$— derived from cumene by removal of one hydrogen atom; isopropyl-phenyl

cumfrey *var of* COMFREY

cu·mic acid \ˈkyümik-\ *n* [*cum-* + *-ic*] **:** a white crystalline acid $(CH_3)_2CHC_6H_4COOH$ obtained by oxidation of cumin oil; *p*-isopropyl-benzoic acid

cumic aldehyde *n* **:** CUMALDEHYDE

cu·mi·dine \ˈkyüməˌdēn, -dən\ *n* -s [ISV *cum-* + *-idine;* orig. formed as G *kumidin*] **:** any of three isomeric liquid bases $C_3H_7C_6H_4NH_2$ derived from cumene; isopropylaniline; *esp* **:** the para isomer made by nitration of cumene followed by reduction

cum·in *also* **cum·min** \ˈkəmən\ *n* -s [ME *comin, cummin,* fr. OE *cymen;* akin to OHG *kumīn* cumin, MLG *kōmen,* all fr. a prehistoric WGmc word borrowed fr. L *cuminum,* fr. Gk *kyminon,* of Sem origin; akin to Ar *kammūn* cumin, Heb *kammōn*] **:** a dwarf plant (*Cuminum cyminum*) of the family Umbelliferae that is native to Egypt and Syria and has long been cultivated for its aromatic seeds which are used in flavoring

cum·i·nal·de·hyde \ˌkəməˈnaldəˌhīd\ *n* [ISV *cumin* + *aldehyde*] **:** CUMALDEHYDE

cu·min·ic acid \(ˈ)kyüˈminik-\ *n* [ISV *cumin* + *-ic*] **:** CUMIC ACID

cumin oil *also* **cummin oil** *n* **:** a colorless to yellow essential oil obtained from cuminseeds

cu·min·o·in \kyüˈminəwən\ *n* -s [ISV *cumin* + *-oin* (as in *benzoin*); orig. formed as G *kuminoin*] **:** a white crystalline compound $C_{20}H_{24}O_2$ prepared from cumaldehyde and analogous to benzoin

cu·mi·nol \ˈkyüməˌnȯl, -nōl\ *n* -s [ISV *cumin* + *-ol*] **:** CUMALDEHYDE

cuminseed *or* **cumminseed** \ˈ⸗⸗ˌ⸗\ *n* **:** the seed of the cumin plant

cu·mi·nyl \ˈkyüməˌnil\ *n* -s [ISV *cumin* + *-yl*] **:** the univalent radical $(CH_3)_2CHC_6H_4CH_2$— derived from the para isomer of cymene; *para*-isopropyl-benzyl

cum lau·de \ku̇mˈlau̇də, -dē, -dā; kəmˈlȯd-\ *adv* (*or adj*) [NL, with praise] **:** with distinction — used as a mark of meritorious achievement in the academic requirements for graduation from school or college; compare MAGNA CUM LAUDE, SUMMA CUM LAUDE

cum·ly \ˈkəmlē, -li\ *var of* CUMBLY

cum·mer \ˈkəmər\ *n* -s [ME *commare* godmother, fr. MF *commere,* fr. LL *commater,* fr. L *com-* + *mater* mother — more at MOTHER] **1** *chiefly Scot* **:** GODMOTHER **2** *chiefly Scot* **:** an intimate female friend **3** *chiefly Scot* **:** a woman or girl; *also* **:** WITCH **4** *chiefly Scot* **:** MIDWIFE

cum·mer·bund \ˈkəmə(r)ˌbənd\ *n* -s [Hindi *kamarband,* fr. Per, fr. *kamar* waist, loins + *band* band, bandage; akin to Av *bandō* band, fetter, Skt *bandha* binding — more at BAND] **:** a broad sash worn as a waistband by men in India; *also* **:** a similar waistband worn in place of a vest with men's dress clothes and adapted in various styles for women's clothes

cummerbund

cum·ming·ton·ite \ˈkəmiŋtəˌnīt\ *n* -s [*Cummington,* Mass. + E *-ite*] **:** a mineral (Fe, $Mg)_7Si_8O_{22}(OH)_2$ consisting of an iron-magnesium amphibole isomorphous with anthophyllite

cum·mock \ˈkəmək\ *var of* CAMMOCK

cumo- — see CUM-

cu·mol \ˈkyüˌmȯl, -mōl\ *n* -s [ISV *cum-* + *-ol;* prob. orig. formed as G *kumol*] **:** CUMENE

cu·mo·yl \ˈkyüməˌwil\ *n* -s [*cum-* + *-yl*] **:** the radical $(CH_3)_2CHC_6H_4CO$— of cumic acid

cum pri·vi·le·gio \ˌku̇m,privəˈlāgē(ˌ)ō, ˌkəm-, -lē-, -jē-\ *adv* [NL] **:** with privilege — used esp. in a published book to indicate that the issue is duly licensed or authorized

cumquat *var of* KUMQUAT

¹**cum·shaw** *also* **cum·sha** \ˈkəmˌshȯ\ *n* -s [Chin (Amoy) *kam sia* & (Pek.) *kan³ hsieh⁴* grateful thanks (a phrase used by beggars)] **:** PRESENT, BONUS, GRATUITY, TIP

²**cumshaw** \"\ *vt* -ED/-ING/-S **:** to make a present of ⟨resigned to ~*ing* ten cents an hour to any stevedore foreman who would give them a short job —N.C.McDonald⟩

cumul- *or* **cumuli-** *or* **cumulo-** *comb form* [NL, fr. L *cumulus* heap, mass — more at CUMULATE] **1 :** cumulus and ⟨*cumulo*cirrus⟩ **2 :** cumulus ⟨*cumul*ous⟩ **3 :** heap **:** mass ⟨*cumul*ose⟩

cu·mu·lant \ˈkyümyələnt, ÷-mə-\ *n* -s [L *cumulant-, cumulans,* pres. part. of *cumulare* to heap up] **:** any of the statistical coefficients that arise in the series expansion in powers of *x* of the logarithm of the moment-generating function

cu·mu·lar \-lə(r)\ *adj* [L *cumularis,* fr. L. *cumulus* heap + *aris* -ar] **:** CUMULOUS

¹**cu·mu·late** \ˈkyümyəˌlāt, ÷ -mə-, *usu* -ād·+V\ *vb* -ED/-ING/-S [L *cumulatus,* past part. of *cumulare* to pile up, fr. *cumulus* heap, mass; akin to L *cavus* hollow — more at CAVE] *vt* **1 :** to gather or pile up into a heap **:** heap together **:** ACCUMULATE **2 a :** to combine (as votes, law actions, or penalties) into one; *specif* **:** to combine (the entries of preceding issues) in successive issues (as of an index or catalog) **b :** to enlarge (a collection) by addition of new material ⟨~ an index⟩ ~ *vi* **:** to become massed **:** form into a cumulus **:** ACCUMULATE ⟨sets up tensions which ~ —P.M.Gregory⟩

²**cumulate** \-lət, -ˌlāt\ *adj* [L *cumulatus*] **:** heaped up **:** gathered in a heap

cu·mu·lat·ed \-ˌlād·əd\ *adj, of the molecule of an organic compound* **:** characterized by two double bonds on the same atom (as C—C—C) — compare CONJUGATED

cu·mu·la·tion \ˌ⸗⸗ˈlāshən\ *n* -s **1 :** a heaping together **:** a gradual building up ⟨~ of effect of a drug⟩ ⟨the ~ of a body of jurisprudence⟩ **2 :** the product or result of cumulating ⟨three ~s of the index were published yearly⟩

cu·mu·la·tive \ˈ⸗⸗lā|d·iv, -ˌlā|, |tiv, -ēv\ *adj* **1 :** increasing in size or strength by successive additions without corresponding loss ⟨the ~ effect of small daily doses⟩ ⟨a ~ weight of evidence⟩ **2 a** *of evidence* **:** tending to prove the same point to which other evidence has been offered **b** *of a legacy* **:** given by the same testator to the same legatee **3** *criminal law* **a** *of a sentence* **:** to be carried into effect after the convict has suffered a punishment to which he has already been sentenced **b** *of a penalty* **:** increasing in severity with repetition of the offense **4 a** *of preferred dividends or contingent interest* **:** to be added if not paid when due to the next payment or a future payment **b** *of stock* **:** bearing such a dividend **5 :** formed by the addition of new material of the same kind as that already collected ⟨~ record⟩; *specif* **:** having reference to or prepared according to a system whereby additional entries for books or periodical articles are integrated in a later issue of a printed index to maintain the original order of arrangement (as alphabetically by subject) ⟨~ book index in the reference library⟩ **6 :** ¹COPULATIVE 1a — **cu·mu·la·tive·ly** \-əvlē, -li\ *adv*

cumulative error *n* **:** an error whose degree or significance gradually increases in the course of a series of measurements or connected calculations; *specif* **:** an error that is repeated in the same sense or with the same sign

cumulative intercession *n* **:** the assumption of liability for another's debt by the addition of a new debtor or security

cu·mu·la·tive·ness *pronunc at* CUMULATIVE + nəs\ *n* -ES **:** the quality or state of being cumulative

cumulative scoring *n* **:** a scoring of duplicate bridge that ranks contestants by the sum of all points scored by each on all boards played — called also *total-point scoring;* compare MATCH POINT

cumulative temperature *n* **:** the algebraic sum for a week, month, or other considerable period of the daily or other unit interval departures of the average temperature of the air from any arbitrary value, commonly 42° F

cumulative voting *n* **:** proportional representation that allocates to each voter as many votes as there are persons to be voted for and permits him to cast these votes for one person or to distribute them among the candidates as he pleases

cu·mu·lene \ˈkyümyəˌlēn\ *n* -s [*cumulated* + *-ene*] **:** a hydrocarbon containing cumulated double bonds

cumuli- *or* **cumulo-** — see CUMUL-

cu·mu·li·form \ˈkyümyələˌfȯrm\ *adj* [*cumul-* + *-form*] **:** of the form of a cumulus

cu·mu·lo·cirrus \ˌkyümyə(ˌ)lō, ÷ -mə-+\ *n* [NL, fr. *cumul-* + *cirrus*] **:** a small cumulus cloud at a high altitude having the whiteness and delicacy of the cirrus

cu·mu·lo·nimbus \"+\ *n* [NL, fr. *cumul-* + *nimbus*] **:** a mountainous cumulus cloud often spread out in the shape of an anvil extending to great heights and topped with a fibrous veil of ice crystals **:** THUNDERCLOUD — see CLOUD illustration

cu·mu·lose \ˈkyümyəˌlōs, ÷-mə-\ *adj* [*cumul-* + *-ose*] **1 :** full of heaps **2** *of a soil deposit* **:** consisting chiefly of accumulated organic matter

cu·mu·lo·stratus \ˌkyümyə(ˌ)lō, ÷-mə-+\ *n* [NL, fr. *cumul-* + *stratus*] **:** a cumulus whose base extends horizontally as a stratus cloud

cu·mu·lous \ˈkyümyələs, ÷-mə-\ *adj* [*cumul-* + *-ous*] **1 :** resembling cumulus **2 :** CUMULATIVE

cu·mu·lo·volcano \ˌkyümyə(ˌ)lō, ÷-mə-+\ *n* [*cumul-* + *volcano*] **:** a dome-shaped volcano formed by the extrusion of highly viscous lava

cu·mu·lus \ˈkyümyələs, ÷-mə-\ *n, pl* **cumu·li** \-ˌlī, -ˌlē\ [L, heap — more at CUMULATE] **1 :** the acme of an accumulation **:** HEAP, ACCUMULATION ⟨what a tremendous lot of stuff makes up the ~ called "the home" —E.B.White⟩ **2** [NL, fr. L] **:** a massy cloud form usu. occurring in the low or middle cloud regions at elevations between 2,000 and 15,000 feet, having a flat base and rounded outlines often piled up like a mountain, commonly appearing in the early afternoon on warm days, and sometimes affording rain or thunder gusts — see CLOUD illustration **3** *or* **cumulus ooph·o·rus** \-ōˈäf(ə)rəs\ [*cumulus,* NL, fr. L; *cumulus oophorus,* NL, lit., ovarian heap] *anat* **:** the projecting mass of granulosa cells that bears the developing ovum in a Graafian follicle

cumulus con·ges·tus \-kənˈjestəs\ *n, pl* **cumuli conges·ti** \-ˌstī, -(ˌ)stē\ [NL, lit., pressed together, thick cumulus] **:** a swelling cumulus cloud of cauliflower appearance

cumulus hu·mi·lis \-ˈhyüməlǝs\ *n, pl* **cumuli humi·les** \-ˌlēz\ [NL, lit., low cumulus] **:** a small white cumulus cloud appearing in fine weather

cu·myl \ˈkyüməl\ *n* -s [ISV *cum-* + *-yl*] **1 :** CUMOYL **2 :** CUMINYL **3 :** CUMENYL

cu·na \ˈkünə\ *n, pl* **cuna** *or* **cunas** *usu cap* [Sp, of AmerInd origin] **1 a :** a Cunan people of the Republic of Panama **b :** a member of such people **2 :** the Chibchan language of the Cuna people

cu·nab·u·la \kyüˈnabyələ\ *n pl* [L, fr. *cunae* cradle — more at CEMETERY] **:** INCUNABULA

cu·nan \ˈkünən\ *n, pl* **cunan** *or* **cunans** *usu cap* [*Cuna* + *-an*] **1 :** a language family of the Chibchan stock including Coiba, Cueva, Cuna, and San Blas **2 a :** the peoples speaking Cunan languages **b :** a member of one of such peoples

cunc·ta·tion \kəŋkˈtāshən\ *n* -s [L *cunctation-, cunctatio,* fr. *cunctatus* (past part. of *cunctari* to hesitate) + *-ion-, -io* -ion — more at ¹HANG] **:** DELAY, PROCRASTINATION

cund *var of* COND

cun·de·a·mor \ˌkün(ˌ)dāəˈmȯ(ə)r\ *n* -s [AmerSp, prob. fr. Sp *cunde* (3d sing. pres. indic. of *cundir* to spread, swell) + *amor* love, fr. L — more at AMOROUS] **:** CYPRESS VINE 1

cun·dy \ˈkəndē\ *n* -ES [by alter.] *chiefly Scot* **:** CONDUIT

cu·ne·al \ˈkyünēəl\ *adj* [NL *cunealis,* fr. L *cuneus* wedge + *-alis* -al — more at COIN] **:** relating to a wedge **:** shaped like a wedge

cu·ne·ate \ˈkyünēˌāt, -ēət\ *also* **cu·ne·at·ed** \-ˌād·əd\ *adj* [L *cuneatus,* fr. *cuneus* wedge + *-atus* -ate, -ated — more at CULEX] **:** shaped like a wedge **:** narrowly triangular with the acute angle toward the base ⟨a ~ leaf⟩ — see LEAF illustration — **cu·ne·ate·ly** *adv*

cuneate lobe *n* **:** CUNEUS 3

cu·ne·at·ic \ˌkyünēˈad·ik\ *adj* [L *cuneatus* + E *-ic*] **:** CUNEIFORM

¹**cu·ne·i·form** \kyüˈnēəˌfȯrm, ˈkyünēə-, ˈkyünə-\ *adj* [prob. fr. F *cunéiforme,* fr. MF, fr. L *cuneus* wedge + MF *-iforme* -iform — more at CULEX] **1 :** of, relating to, or being any of several somewhat wedge-shaped chiefly skeletal elements: as **a :** any of three small bones of the tarsus lying between the navicular and the first three metatarsals **b :** the pyramidal bone of the wrist **c :** either of a pair of rods of yellow elastic cartilage lying in the aryepiglottic folds of the larynx **2** *of a human skull* **:** wedge-shaped as viewed from above — used of a head type not uncommon in the Mediterranean subrace **3 a :** composed of strokes having the form of a wedge or arrowhead — used of the characters employed in a system of writing in which the strokes are formed by the impression of a stylus in soft clay or are written in some other medium but with strokes in imitation of ones impressed on clay **b :** written in cuneiform characters — used of a document or of a language **c :** made up of cuneiform characters ⟨tablets . . . were written in an alphabetic ~ script —L.A.Weigle⟩

²cuneiform \"\ *n* **1** : cuneiform writing **2** : a cuneiform part; *specif* : a cuneiform bone or cartilage

cuneiform

cu·ne·i·form·ist \-məst\ *n* -s : a student of or an expert in the deciphering or study of cuneiform

cu·ne·o- \ˌkyünē(ˌ)ō, -ēə\ *comb form* [NL, fr. L *cuneus* wedge] : cuneiform and ‹*cuneo*cuboid›

cu·nette \kyü'net\ *n* -s [F, fr. It *cunetta*, alter. (resulting from incorrect division, *la*- being taken as *la*, fem. def. art.) of *lacunetta*, dim. of *lacuna* pond, fr. L — more at LAGOON] **1** : a channel of small cross section dug in the bottom of a much larger channel or conduit to concentrate the flow at low-water stages **2** : a reinforcement of a canal bank constructed of piles and planking

cu·ne·us \'kyünēəs\ *n, pl* **cunei** \-ēˌī\ [L, wedge — more at CULEX] **1** : WEDGE : something shaped like a wedge **2** : one of the wedge-shaped blocks of seats into which the cavea of the ancient Roman theater was divided by stairways **3** [NL, fr. L] : a convolution of the mesial surface of the occipital lobe of the brain above the calcarine fissure that forms a part of the visual cortex

cun·ge·boi \'kənjəˌbȯi\ *or* **cun·ge·voi** \-ˌvȯi\ *n* -s [native name in Australia] *Austral* : an ascidian of the family Cynthiidae that grows upon rock and is used for bait

cu·nic \'kyünik\ *also* **cunic mixture** *n* -s [LL *cuprum* copper + E *nicotine* — more at COPPER] : a mixture of copper sulfate and nicotine sulfate administered to livestock as an anthelmintic

cu·nic·u·lus \kyü'nik(y)ələs\ *n* [L, rabbit, rabbit burrow — more at CONY] **1** *pl* **cunicu·li** \-ˌlī, -ˌlē\ : an underground passage (as a burrow or mine); *specif* : one of the prehistoric underground drains about ancient Rome **2** *cap* [NL, fr. L] **a** : a genus of pacas **b** *in some classifications* (1) : DICROSTONYX (2) : ORYCTOLAGUS **3** *pl* **cuniculi** [NL, fr. L] : the burrow of an itch mite in the skin

cu·nit \'kyünət\ *n* -s [*1C* (100) + *unit*] : a unit of volume that is sometimes used for pulpwood and is equal to 100 cubic feet of solid wood

cun·je·voi \'kənjəˌvȯi\ *n* -s [native name in Australia] : a large Australian aroid (*Alocasia macrorrhiza*) whose poisonous juice is similar in its action to that of dumb cane

¹**cun·ner** \'kənə(r)\ *also* **con·ner** \", 'kän-\ *n* -s [origin unknown] : either of two wrasses: **a** : an English wrasse (*Crenilabrus melops*) **b** : an American wrasse (*Tautogolabrus adspersus*) that is abundant on the rocky shores of New England and is a good though generally small food fish

²**cunner** \"\ *n* -s [prob. alter. of ¹*canoe*] : a sailing canoe made of logs that was formerly common in Chesapeake Bay

cun·ni·lin·gu·ism \ˌkənə'liŋgəˌwizəm\ *n* -s [NL *cunnilingus* + E -*ism*] : the practice or habit of cunnilingus

cun·ni·lin·gus \-'liŋgəs\ *or* **cun·ni·linc·tus** \-ŋktəs\ *n* -ES [*cunnilingus*, NL, fr. L, one who licks the vulva, fr. *cunni*- (fr. *cunnus* vulva) + -*lingus* (fr. *lingere* to lick); *cunnilinctus*, NL, fr L *cunni*- + *linctus* act of licking, fr. *linctus*, past part. of *lingere* to lick — more at LICK] : stimulation of the vulva or clitoris with the lips or tongue

¹**cun·ning** \'kəniŋ, -nēŋ\ *adj, often* -ER/-EST [ME, fr. pres. part. of *cunnen* to know — more at CAN] **1** *obs* **a** : possessed of or marked by knowledge, learning, or lore **b** : possessing occult or magical knowledge **2** : marked by dexterous or crafty use of some special skill, knowledge, or other resource ‹gnomes and the brownies, the ~ little people who know how to use the bellows, the forge, the hammer and the anvil —Lewis Mumford› ‹the birds . . . were found singularly ~ and repeatedly eluded the aim of these prime shots —George Meredith› **3** : marked by keen insight, practical analytic intelligence, resourcefulness, or ability to anticipate, escape, elude ‹the same ~ artist Daedalus who planned the Labyrinth —J.G. Frazer› ‹his ~ knowledge of the weaknesses of the human heart —T.S.Eliot› **4** : marked by wiles, craftiness, artfulness, or trickery in attaining ends ‹the ~ contrivance of traps and pitfalls —Lewis Mumford› ‹this ~ subterfuge of, Januslike, looking two ways at once —C.C.Furnas› **5** : appealing (as by reason of smallness, prettiness, quaintness, or archness) : FETCHING ‹a ~ little baby› ‹a ~ little kitten› **syn** see CLEVER, SLY

²**cunning** \"\ *n* -s [ME, fr. ger. of *cunnen* to know] **1** *obs* : KNOWLEDGE, LEARNING **2** *obs* : ART; *esp* : magic art **3** : SKILL, DEXTERITY ‹let my right hand forget her ~ —Ps 137:5 (AV)› **4** : skill in devising or using indirect or subtle methods : ability to mislead, trap, or escape an enemy or opponent : SLYNESS, CRAFT **syn** see ART, DECEIT

cun·ning·ham·ia \ˌkəniŋ'hamēə, -ŋ'am-\ *n, cap* [NL, fr. Allan *Cunningham* †1839 or his brother Richard †1835 Eng. botanists + NL -*ia*] : a small genus of decorative Asiatic evergreen trees (family Pinaceae) having flat leaves arranged spirally and singly along the whorled branches

cun·ning·ly *adv* [ME, fr. ¹*cunning* + -*ly*] : with cunning : in a dexterous, subtle, or ingenious way : CLEVERLY, ARTFULLY ‹a trap ~ placed in the trail› ‹a ~ wrought brass figure›

cun·ning·ness *n* -ES [ME *cunningnesse*, fr. *cunning* + -*nesse* -ness] : the quality or state of being cunning

cun·nus \'kənəs\ *n, pl* **cun·ni** \-ˌnī, -(ˌ)nē\ [L; akin to L *cutis* skin — more at HIDE] : the female external genitals : VULVA

¹**cun·ny-thumb** \'kənē+ˌ\ *adv* [obs. *cunny* woman, rabbit (alter. of *cony*) + *thumb*] *marbles* : with the thumb bent in behind the second finger of the closed hand : INEXPERTLY

²**cunny-thumb** \"\ *vb, marbles* : to shoot inexpertly

cu·no·nia \kyü'nōnēə\ *n, cap* [NL, fr. John C. *Cuno*, 18th cent. Dutch botanist + NL -*ia*] : a genus (the type of the family Cunoniaceae) of shrubs or small trees with pinnate leaves, racemose white flowers, and bark that is used for tanning

cu·no·ni·a·ce·ae \kyüˌnōnē'āsēˌē\ *n pl, cap* [NL, fr *Cunonia*, type genus + -*aceae*] : a family of trees and shrubs (order Rosales) that are sometimes placed in the family Saxifragaceae but are distinguished by opposite or verticillate leaves and small flowers borne in dense clusters — **cu·no·ni·a·ceous** \ˌ=ˌ==ˈāshəs\ *adj*

cunt \'kənt\ *n* -s [ME *cunte*; akin to OFris & MLG *kunte* female pudenda, MD *conte*, Norw & Sw dial. *kunta*, MLG *kutte* female pudenda, MHG *kotze* prostitute, and perh. to OE *cot* cottage — more at COT] : the female pudenda : a woman regarded as a sexual object; *also* : COITUS — usu. considered obscene

cuntline *var of* CONTLINE

cun·yie \'kənē\ *or* **cun·zie** \-nzē\ *n* -s [ME (Sc dial.) *cunye*, fr. a MF dial. word akin to MF *coing*, *coin* wedge, stamp corner — more at COIN] *Scot* : COIN, MONEY

cu·on \'kyüˌän\ *n, cap* [NL, modif. of Gk *kyōn* dog — more at HOUND] : a genus of Asiatic wild dogs (family Canidae) characterized by the absence of the usual last lower molar and including the dhole

cu·o·rin \'kyü(ə)rən\ *n* -s [ISV *cuor*- (fr. It *cuore* heart, fr. L *cor*) + -*in* — more at HEART] : an amorphous phosphatide obtained from heart muscle and soybeans that resembles cephalin and is held to be a mixture

¹**cup** \'kəp\ *n* -s [ME *cuppe*, fr. OE; akin to OFris *kopp* head, cup, MLG *kopp* drinking vessel, MD *coppe*, OHG *kopf*; all fr. a prehistoric WGmc word borrowed fr. LL *cuppa* cup, alter. of or akin to L *cupa* vat, tub — more at HIVE] **1** : a usu. open bowl-shaped drinking vessel often having a handle and a stem and base and sometimes a lid ‹finely made wine ~s› : CHALICE; *specif* : a handled vessel of china or glass that is set on a saucer and used for hot liquids (as coffee, tea, or soup) **2 a** : the containing part of a drinking vessel that has a stem and a foot **b** : a drinking vessel and its contents : the beverage or food contained in a cup ‹a second ~ of coffee› **c** : the consecrated wine of the Communion **3** : something (as an experience or sensation) that is to be enjoyed or endured : something that falls to one's lot : PORTION ‹his ~ of bitterness is full› **4 cups** *pl* : prolonged or convivial drinking ‹thence from ~s to civil broils —John Milton› **5** *sometimes cap* : an ornamental cup offered as a prize esp. when symbolic of a championship ‹the ~ race for large yachts›; *often* : a prize other than or in addition to money **6** : something felt to resemble a cup esp. in shape or use: as **a** : a socket or recess in which something turns (as the hipbone or the recess in which a capstan spindle turns) **b** : a metal or earthenware receptacle that is shaped like a flowerpot and that is attached to a tree in turpentine orcharding to collect the resin **c** (1) : an athletic supporter reinforced with metal for providing extra protection to the wearer in certain strenuous sports (as boxing, hockey, football) (2) : either of the two parts of a brassiere that are shaped like and fit over the breasts **d** *med* : a small bell-shaped glass formerly used in cupping **e** : a cap of metal shaped like the femoral head and used in plastic reconstruction of the hip joint **f** : the metal case inside a hole in golf; *also* : the hole itself **g** : an annular trough filled with water at the base of each section of a telescopic gas holder into which fits the grip of the section next outside **7 a** : a cup-shaped organ or part of a plant (as an apothecium or peridium, a volva, or in seed plants a cupule, a calyx, or corolla) **b** : a cup-shaped structure; *esp* : a cup-shaped external skeleton (as the theca of a coral or the calyx of a crinoid) **8** : a usu. iced beverage resembling punch in its ingredients but served from a pitcher rather than a bowl ‹claret ~› ‹cider ~› ‹champagne ~› **9** : a curve across the grain or width of a piece of lumber **10** : CUPFUL **11** : a food served in a cup-shaped usu. footed vessel ‹fruit ~› — **in one's cups** : in a state of intoxication : DRUNK ‹blurted out the story while *in his cups*›

²**cup** \"\ *vb* **cupped**; **cupped**; **cupping**; **cups** *vt* **1** [ME *cuppen*, fr. *cuppe*, n.] *med* : to subject to cupping **2** : to make or curve into a hollow or cup shape ‹*cupping* his hand to his ear› **3** : to receive, take, or place in or as if in a cup ‹~ water from a stream› ‹*cupping* his chin in his hand› ‹a town *cupped* by surrounding hills› **4** : to provide a cup for catching latex or sap from the trunk of (a tree) in rubber and turpentine culture ~ *vi* **1 a** : to grow or become cup-shaped **b** *of a board* : to warp crosswise **2** : to undergo or perform cupping **3** : to make a depression in the ground with the club when hitting a golf ball

³**cup** \'ku̇p, 'kəp\ *var of* ³COOP

cu·pa·lo *n* -s [by alter] : CUPOLA

cup and ball *n* **1** : a bilboquet having a cup; *also* : the game of maneuvering the bilboquet so as to catch the ball in the cup **2** : the cross-parting in columnar igneous rocks in which one face of the parting is concave and the other convex (as in the columnar basalt of the Giant's Causeway on the north coast of Ireland)

cup-and-ball joint *n* : BALL-AND-SOCKET JOINT

cup and cone *n* : BELL AND HOPPER

cup and ring *n* : a cup-shaped pit surrounded by a ring or rings cut in stone found in bronze age cup sculpture

cup-and-saucer \ˌ=ˌ=ˈ==\ *n* [so called fr. the shape of the flower] : a plant that is a cultivated variety (*Campanula medium calycanthema*) of the Canterbury bell

cup-and-saucer limpet *also* **cup-and-saucer** *n* [so called fr. the shape of the inverted shell, the inner shelf of which resembles a cup sitting on the saucer-shaped outer shell] : a mollusk of the family Calyptraeidae

cup-and-saucer vine *n* [so called fr. the shape of the flower] : CATHEDRAL BELLS

cu·pa·nia \kyü'pānēə\ *n, cap* [NL, fr. Francesco *Cupani* †1711 Sicilian botanist + NL -*ia*] : a genus of tropical American timber trees (family Sapindaceae) with greenish or white paniculate flowers and capsular fruit — see GUARA

cu·pay \kü'pä, -'pī\ *also* **cu·pey** \-'pā\ *n* -s [Sp *cupey*, *copey*, fr. Taino] : PITCH APPLE

cup baller *n* : ⁵BATTER 2a(1)

cup barometer *n* : a barometer consisting of a graduated glass tube about 34 inches long filled with mercury and inverted in a cup containing mercury, the column of mercury in the tube descending until balanced by the pressure of the atmosphere, its rise and fall being a measure of change of atmospheric pressure

cupbearer \'=ˌ==\ *n* [ME *copberer*, fr. *cop* cup (var. of *cuppe*) + *berer* bearer] : one whose office it is to fill and hand the cups in which wine is served

¹**cup·board** \'kəbə(r)d\ *n* [ME *cupbord*, fr. *cuppe* cup + *bord* board, table — more at BOARD] **1 a** : a board or shelf for cups and dishes **b** : ³BUFFET 2 **2** *obs* : a set of dishes as kept on a sideboard **3** : a closet with shelves to receive cups, dishes, or food; *also* : any small closet

²**cupboard** \"\ *vt* -ED/-ING/-S : to put away or collect in or as if in a cupboard

cupboard love *n* : insincere love professed for the sake of gain — **cupboard lover** *n*

cupcake \'=ˌ=\ *n* : a small cake baked in any cup-shaped container or utensil (as a paper cup or a muffin pan)

cup cheese *n* : cook cheese that is poured into china cups

cup coral *n* : a cup-shaped coral formed by a single polyp

cup custard *n* : custard baked in and usu. served in cup-shaped ceramic or glass cookware

cup drill *n* : a grain drill having a cup-shaped attachment by which grasses and legumes can be seeded with the grain

¹**cu·pel** \kyü'pel, 'ˌ=ˌpel, 'ˌ=pəl\ *n* -s [F *coupelle*, dim. of *coupe* cup, fr. LL *cuppa* — more at CUP] **1** : a small shallow porous refractory cup esp. of bone ash used in assaying to separate precious metals from lead **2** : the hearth of a small furnace used in commercial separation of precious metals from lead

²**cupel** \"\ *vt* **cupeled** *or* **cupelled**; **cupeled** *or* **cupelled**; **cupeling** *or* **cupelling**; **cupels** [F *coupeller*, fr. *coupelle*, n.] : to refine by means of a cupel — **cu·pel·er** *or* **cu·pel·ler** \-lə(r)\ *n* -s

cu·pel·la·tion \ˌkyüpə'lāshən\ *n* -s [²*cupel* + -*ation*] : refinement (as of gold or silver) in a cupel by melting the metallic charge and then exposing it to a blast of air, the lead, copper, tin, and other unwanted metals being oxidized and partly sinking into the porous cupel and partly being swept away by the blast

cu·pe·ño \kə'pān(ˌ)yō\ *n, pl* **cupeño** *or* **cupeños** *usu cap* [Sp, fr. *Kupa*, a Cupeño town] **1** : a Shoshonean people of California **2** : a member of the Cupeño people

cup fern *n* [so called fr. its cup-shaped indusium] : HAY-SCENTED FERN

cup·fer·ron \'kəpfəˌrän, 'k(y)üp-\ *n* -s [ISV *cupric* + *ferric* + -*on*] : a colorless crystalline salt $C_6H_5N(NO)ONH_4$ that is a precipitant for copper and iron from solutions and is used also in the analysis of other metals esp. of the uranium group : the ammonium salt of *N*-nitroso-*N*-phenyl-hydroxylamine

cupflower \'=ˌ=\ *n* **1** : NIEREMBERGIA 2 **2** : a Chilean plant (*Scyphanthus elegans*) of the family Loasaceae with yellow flowers **3** : a Mexican shrub (*Solandra guttata*) of the family Solanaceae

cup·ful \'kəpˌfu̇l\ *n, pl* **cupfuls** *also* **cupsful** \-pˌfu̇lz, -psˌfu̇l\ **1** : as much as a cup will hold **2** *cookery* : a half pint : eight ounces

cup fungus *n* [so called fr. the cup-shaped ascoma] : a fungus of the order Pezizales — compare DISCOMYCETES

cup grass *n* [so called fr. the shape of the callus] : any of several grasses constituting a genus (*Erichloa*) of annual and perennial grasses chiefly of warm or tropical regions; *esp* : a common weedy annual grass (*E. contracta*) of the eastern and central U.S. that has villous spikelets and the second glume acuminate

cup grease *n* : a grease used in grease cups; *esp* : a mixture of a mineral oil and lime or soda soap with or without other ingredients (as rosin, oil, graphite, mica)

cu·phea \'kyüfēə\ *n, cap* [NL, irreg. fr. Gk *kyphos* hump; fr. the protuberance on the calyx tube; akin to OE *hūfe* hood, Gk *kyptein* to bend forward, stoop, Skt *kakubha* high, eminent, OE *hēah* high — more at HIGH] : a large genus of American plants (family Lythraceae) with opposite leaves and solitary slightly irregular flowers — see CIGAR FLOWER, WAXWEED

cupholder \'=ˌ==\ *n* : a sports contestant successful in the latest trial for a cup

cup hook *n* : a screw hook that usu. has a collar at the base of the thread and that is used esp. for hanging up cups by their handles

cu·pid \'kyüpəd\ *n* -s [after *Cupid*, Roman god of love, fr. ME *Cupide*, fr. L *Cupido*] : a naked usu. winged infantile figure representing the god of love and often holding a bow and arrow : CHERUB 3

cu·pid·i·ty \kyü'pidəd·ē, -ətē, -i\ *n* -ES [ME *cupidite*, fr. MF *cupidité*, fr. L *cupiditat-*, *cupiditas*, fr. *cupidus* desirous + -*itat-*, -*itas* -ity — more at COVET] **1** *archaic* : strong desire : ardent longing : LUST **2** : inordinate desire for wealth : AVARICE, GREED ‹these reports . . . inflamed . . . curiosity and ~ all the more —R.W.Murray›

syn CUPIDITY, GREED, RAPACITY, AVARICE can signify in common an inordinate desire for wealth or possessions. CUPIDITY stresses the intensity of the desire, strongly suggesting covetousness ‹the vast *cupidity* of business in preempting the virgin resources of California —V.L.Parrington› ‹the poverty-stricken man gazed at the silverware and jewels with *cupidity* shining intensely in his face› GREED implies inordinate desire as a controlling passion and usu. connotes both meanness and covetousness ‹[his] face and green-gray eyes mirrored a low, incessant, gnawing *greed* . . . for power, for money, for destruction —W.A.White› ‹the craving for more than she needs is a symptom of neurotic *greed* —Leo Gurko› ‹their whole being made over to desire for an iced cake or a caramel. It was an honest *greed* —Audrey Barker› RAPACITY implies not only cupidity but the actual seizing of the thing desired or of anything that will satisfy greed, often suggesting extortion, plunder, or oppressive exactions ‹the *rapacity* of the tax collectors was nothing to the greed of the landlords› ‹the *rapacity* of the first foreign conquest on this continent —Russell Lord› ‹the *rapacity* of the warlords —Nathaniel Peffer› AVARICE stresses both greed and miserliness ‹life . . . was a sort of furnace in which all the elements of human nature were transmuted into a single white flame, an incandescence of the passion of *avarice* —Van Wyck Brooks› ‹economy approached the border of *avarice* —Ellen Glasgow›

cu·pi·don \'kyüpəˌdän, -dᵊn\ *n* -s [F, fr. *Cupidon*, Roman god of love, fr. L *Cupido*] : CUPID

cupid's bow *n, usu cap C* : the classical form of bow; *also* : a line like it esp. as seen in shapely lips

cupid's-dart \ˈ==ˌ=\ *n, pl* **cupid's-darts** *usu cap C* [so called fr. the belief that it is efficacious as a love philter] : BLUE SUCCORY

cupid's darts *n pl but usu sing in constr, usu cap C* [so called fr. the red shafts in the crystals] : ONEGITE

cupid's-delight \ˈ===ˌ=\ *n,pl* **cupid's-delights** *usu cap C* : WILD PANSY

cu·pis·ni·que \ˌküpēz'nē(ˌ)kā, -ē'sn-\ *adj, usu cap* [fr. *Cupisnique*, valley on the northern coast of Peru, where the remains were found] : of or relating to the coastal section of the Chavin culture of ancient Peru

cu·pi·u·ba \ˌküpē'übə\ *n, pl* **cupiuba** [Pg *cupiúba*] : a tropical American tree (*Goupia glabra*) of the family Celastraceae with hard heavy reddish brown wood that is used for furniture, railroad ties, and general construction — called also *kabukalli*

Cupid's bow

cup joint *n* : BELL-AND-SPIGOT JOINT

cup jolly *n* : a jollier that makes cups

cup leather *n* : a packing (as in hydraulic cylinders and pumps) that consists of a ring of leather of a U-shaped or cup-shaped cross section and that is made tight by the pressure of the fluid on the hollow side

cup·less \'kəpləs\ *adj* : being without a cup

cup lichen *also* **cup moss** *n* : a lichen having cup-shaped fruiting bodies or stalks (as *Lecanora tartarea* and various species of *Cladonia*)

cuplike \'=ˌ=\ *adj* : resembling a cup esp. in having or forming a rounded smooth-walled hollow

cup·man \'kəpmən\ *n, pl* **cupmen** : TOPER

cupmate \'=ˌ=\ *n* : drinking companion

cup moth *n* : any of various chiefly tropical New World moths constituting the family Eucleidae — see SADDLEBACK CATERPILLAR

cup mushroom *n* : CUP FUNGUS

cup nutseed *n* : CUPSEED

cup of elijah *usu cap E* : ELIJAH'S CUP

cup of flame : CALIFORNIA POPPY

cup of gold : CUPFLOWER 3

cup of tea **1** : something one likes or excels in : something or someone suited to one's taste ‹mathematics is not my *cup of tea*› **2** : a thing to be reckoned with : MATTER, AFFAIR

¹**cu·po·la** \'kyüpələ, ÷-pəˌlō *sometimes* ÷'kü- *or* ÷-pyə-\ *n* -s [It, fr. L *cupula* little tub, small burying vault, dim. of *cupa* tub — more at HIVE] **1 a** : a rounded vault raised on a circular or other base and forming a roof or a ceiling — compare DOME **b** : a small structure built on top of a roof to provide interior lighting, to serve as a lookout, or for ornamental purposes : LANTERN **2** : a vertical cylindrical furnace for melting iron in the foundry having tuyeres and tapping spouts near the bottom **3** : CUPULA **4** : DOME 4f **5** : BEEHIVE KILN **6** : a geological dome projecting from a batholith **7 a** : a revolving armored turret of a tank or pillbox for fire or observation **b** : BLISTER 8b **8** : an observation post in the roof of a railroad caboose used by brakemen to keep watch over a train while it is in motion

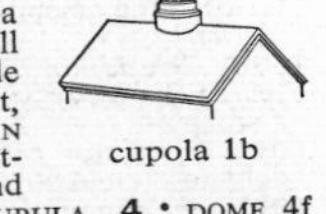
cupola 1b

²**cupola** \"\ *vt* -ED/-ING/-S : to furnish with a cupola

cu·po·lat·ed \-ˌlād·əd\ *adj* : having a cupola

cu·po·lo *n* -s [by alter.] : CUPOLA

cupped *adj* **1** : formed like a cup : cup-shaped ‹calling through ~ hands› **2** : having cup-shaped depressions (as those worn in stairs by use) **3** *of a golf ball* : lying in a small depression

cup·pen *or* **cup·pin** \'kəpən\ *n* -s [by alter.] *dial* : COWPEN

cupping *n* -s [fr. gerund of ²*cup*] **1** : a technique formerly employed for drawing blood to the surface of the body for producing counterirritation or for bloodletting by application of a glass vessel from which air had been evacuated by heat, forming a partial vacuum **2** : vibration of a band saw causing it to cut lumber of uneven thickness **3** : a concave depression in a body organ; *also* : the formation of such a depression

cupping glass *n* : a small glass cup in which a partial vacuum is produced for cupping

cup plant *n* : a tall yellow-flowered herb (*Silphium perfoliatum*) of the U.S. whose upper leaves are connate at the base and form a cup around the stem

cup plate *n* : a small usu. glass ornamental plate, formerly used to hold a cup after the hot beverage had been poured into a deep saucer for cooling and drinking

cup·py \'kəpē, -pi\ *adj* -ER/-EST **1** : HOLLOW : like a cup **2** : full of small depressions ‹a ~ lie for a golf ball› ‹a ~ racetrack› **3** *of timber* : marred by ring shakes

cupr- *or* **cupro-** *comb form* [LL *cupr-*, fr. *cuprum* — more at COPPER] **1 a** : copper ‹*cupr*ite› **b** : copper and ‹*cupro*nickel› **2** *cupro-* : containing univalent copper : cuprous ‹*cupro*cyanide›

cu·pram·mo·ni·um \ˌk(y)üprə'mōnēəm, -nyəm\ *n* -s [*cupr-* + *ammonium*] **1** : any of certain complex ammino radicals or cations containing copper and ammonia; *esp* : the bivalent tetrammine-copper cation $Cu(NH_3)_4$ compounds of which are formed by the action of ammonia on ordinary cupric compounds **2** : CUPRAMMONIUM SOLUTION **3** : CUPRAMMONIUM RAYON

cuprammonium rayon *n* : a rayon made from cellulose dissolved in cuprammonium solution

cuprammonium solution *n* : a deep blue solution of cupric hydroxide or cupric oxide in aqueous ammonia used as a solvent for cellulose (as in making cuprammonium rayon) — called also *Schweizer's reagent*

cu·prea bark \'k(y)üprēə-\ *n* [AmerSp *cuprea*, any of several rubiaceous plants (including *Remijia purdieana*), fr. LL, fem. of *cupreus* cupreous] : the coppery-red bark of either of two So. American trees (*Remijia pedunculata* and *R. purdieana*) that yields quinine

cu·pre·ine \'k(y)üprēˌēn, -ēən\ *n* -s [*cuprea* (*bark*) + -*ine*] : a crystalline alkaloid $C_{19}H_{22}N_2O_2$ that occurs in cuprea bark and cinchona bark closely related to quinine

cu·prene \'k(y)üˌprēn\ *n* -s [ISV *cupr-* + -*ene*; prob. orig. formed as F *cuprène*] : a light yellow to dark brown inert insoluble solid obtained by polymerization of acetylene (as by heating in the presence of copper or copper oxides)

cu·pre·ous \'k(y)üprēəs\ *adj* [LL *cupreus*, fr. *cuprum* copper — more at COPPER] **:** containing or resembling copper **:** COPPERY

cu·pres·sa·ce·ae \,k(y)üprə'sāsē,ē\ *n pl, cap* [NL, fr. *Cupressus*, type genus + *-aceae*] *in some classifications* **:** a family of coniferous trees and shrubs comprising the cedars and junipers and including all members of Pinaceae with leaves decussate or in three ranks and usu. resembling flat scales

cu·pres·sin·e·ous \¦==¦sinēəs\ *adj* [NL *Cupressineae*, tribe including the cypress (fr. *Cupressus* + *-ineae*) + E *-ous*] **:** relating to or resembling the cypress or family Cupressaceae

cu·pres·si·nox·y·lon \k(y)ü,presə'näksə,län\ *n* [NL, fr. *cupressino-* (fr. L *cupressinus* of cypress, fr. *cupressus* cypress + *-inus* -ine) + *-xylon*] **1** *cap* **:** a genus of fossil plants having an internal structure similar to that of present-day *Cupressus* and related genera **2** -s **:** any fossil wood having this structure

cu·pres·sus \k(y)ü'presəs\ *n* [NL, fr. L, cypress — more at CYPRESS] **1** *cap* **:** a genus of evergreen trees (family Pinaceae) having small scaly appressed leaves similar to those of the juniper and globose cones composed of peltate scales — see MONTEREY CYPRESS **2** -ES **:** any tree of the genus *Cupressus* — see CYPRESS 1

cupri- *comb form* [*cupr-* + *-i-*] **1 :** copper ⟨*cupri*ferous⟩ **2** [ISV, fr. *cupric*] **:** containing bivalent copper **:** cupric ⟨*cupri*tartrate⟩

cu·pric \'k(y)üprik\ *adj* [LL *cupr*um copper + E *-ic* — more at COPPER] **:** of, relating to, or containing copper in the bivalent state

cupric acetate *n* **:** COPPER ACETATE a

cupric ammonia complex *n* **:** the cuprammonium cation $Cu(NH_3)_4$

cupric chloride *n* **:** COPPER CHLORIDE b

cupric citrate *n* **:** COPPER CITRATE

cupric hydroxide *n* **:** the copper hydroxide $Cu(OH)_2$

cupric oxide *n* **:** COPPER OXIDE b

cupric sulfate *n* **:** the copper sulfate $CuSO_4$

cupric sulfide *n* **:** COPPER SULFIDE b

cu·prif·er·ous \(')k(y)ü¦prif(ə)rəs\ *adj* [*cupri-* + *-ferous*] **:** containing copper

cu·prite \'k(y)ü,prīt\ *n* -s [G *kuprit*, fr. *kupr-* cupr- + *-it* -ite] **:** an important ore of copper, cuprous oxide, or red copper oxide Cu_2O occurring massive or in isometric crystals or sometimes in capillary forms — called also *red copper ore, ruby copper ore*

cuprobismutite *n* [*cupr-* + *bismutite*] *obs* **:** a mineral consisting of an intimate mixture of bismuthinite and emplectite

cu·pro·copiapite \¦k(y)üprō+\ *n* [*cupr-* + *copiapite*] **:** a mineral $CuFe_4(SO_4)_6(OH)_2.20H_2O$ consisting of a hydrous basic sulfate of copper and iron

cu·pro·cyanide \"+\ *n* [*cupr-* + *cyanide*] **:** a compound of copper and cyanogen with another element or other elements

cu·proid \'k(y)ü,pròid\ *n* -s [ISV *cupr-* + *-oid;* orig. formed as G *kuproid*] *crystallog* **:** a solid related to a tetrahedron and having 12 equal triangular faces

cu·pro·nickel \¦k(y)üprō+\ *n* [*cupr-* + *nickel*] **:** an alloy of copper and nickel; *esp* **:** the alloy containing about 70 percent copper and 30 percent nickel used esp. to make condenser plates and tubes for evaporators and heat exchangers

cu·pro·ri·va·ite \¦==¦rēvə,īt, -ri-, -,vīt\ *n* -s [*cupr-* + *rivaite* (syn. of *wollastonite*), fr. Dr. Carlo *Riva* Ital. mineralogist + E *-ite*] **:** a mineral approximately $CaCuSi_4O_{10}.H_2O$ consisting of a hydrous silicate of calcium and copper

cu·pro·sklodowskite \¦k(y)üprō+\ *n* [*cupr-* + *sklodowskite*] **:** a mineral $Cu(UO_2)_2Si_2O_7.6\text{–}7H_2O$ consisting of hydrous copper uranyl silicate

cu·pro·tungstite \"+\ *n* [*cupr-* + *tungstite*] **:** a mineral $Cu_2(WO_4)(OH)_2$ consisting of cupric tungstate

cu·pro·uranite \"+\ *n* [ISV *cupr-* + *uranite*] **:** TORBERNITE

cu·prous \'k(y)üprəs\ *adj* [*cupr-* + *-ous*] **:** of, relating to, or containing copper in the univalent state

cuprous chloride *n* **:** COPPER CHLORIDE a

cuprous cyanide *n* **:** the copper cyanide CuCN

cuprous oxide *n* **:** COPPER OXIDE a

cuprous sulfide *n* **:** COPPER SULFIDE a

cu·prum \'k(y)üprəm\ *n* -s [LL — more at COPPER] **:** COPPER — symbol *Cu*

cups *pres 3d sing of* CUP, *pl of* CUP

cup sculpture *n* **:** a bronze age sculpture in stone characterized by pits within circles, concentric circles, and spirals

cupseed \'=,=\ *n* **:** a woody vine (*Calycocarpum lyoni*) of the family Menispermaceae of the southern U.S. having the stone of the fruit hollowed out on one side like a shallow cup

cupsful *pl of* CUPFUL

cup shake *n* **:** RING SHAKE

cup–shot *or* **cup–shotten** *adj, obs* **:** TIPSY, INTOXICATED

cup sponge *n* **:** a cup-shaped sponge

cup·stone \'=,=\ *n* **:** a stone or rock surface bearing cup sculpture

cup tie *n* **:** a deciding contest in a competition for a cup

cup towel *n* **:** DISH TOWEL

cu·pu·la \'kyüp(y)ələ\ *n, pl* **cupu·lae** \-,lē\ [NL] **:** CUPULE, CUP: as **a :** the bony apex of the cochlea **b :** the peak of the pleural sac covering the apex of the lung

cu·pu·late \-,lāt, -,lət\ *also* **cu·pu·lar** \-lə(r)\ *adj* [NL *cupula* + E *-ate*] **:** shaped like a cupule **:** having or bearing a cupule

cu·pule \'kyü,p(y)ül\ *n* -s [NL *cupula*, fr. LL, small tub, dim. of L *cupa* tub, cask — more at HIVE] **1 a :** a cup-shaped involucre in which the bracts are indurated and coherent and which is esp. characteristic of the oak **b :** the ascoma of a discomycete **c :** a cup-shaped outgrowth of the thallus of certain liverworts (order Marchantiales) **d :** a cup-shaped corolla **2 :** a small cup-shaped depression **3 :** a small sucker (as on the feet of certain male flies)

cu·pu·lif·er·ae \,kyüp(y)ə'lifə,rē\ *n pl, cap* [NL, fr. *cupula* + *-i-* + *-ferae* (fem. pl. of *-fer* -ferous)] *in some classifications* **:** an order or family of catkin-bearing trees including oaks, chestnuts, beeches, birches, and others that are now usu. divided among the families Betulaceae and Fagaceae — **cu·pu·lif·er·ous** \¦==¦lif(ə)rəs\ *adj*

cu·pu·li·form \'==lə,fòrm\ *adj* [ISV *cupuli-* (fr. NL *cupula*) + *-form*] **:** CUPULATE

cu·pu·lo \"\ *n* -s [by alter.] **:** CUPOLA

cup wheel *n* **:** a cup-shaped grinding wheel

cur \'kər, +V 'kər·; 'kə̄, +V ", 'kər· *also* 'kōr\ *n* -s [ME *curre*, short for *kurdogge*, fr. (assumed) ME *curren* to growl + ME *dogge* dog; akin to MLG *kurren* to growl, MHG *kurren* to grunt, ON *kurra* to grumble, OE *cran* crane — more at CRANE] **1 :** DOG: **a** *dial chiefly Brit* **:** SHEEP DOG, WATCHDOG **b** *also* **cur dog :** a mongrel or inferior dog **c :** a dog other than a foxhound — used by fox hunters **2 :** an objectionable often surly, low, or cowardly person **3** *dial chiefly Brit* **:** GOLDENEYE 1a

cur *abbr* **1** currency **2** current

cur·abil·i·ty \,kyůrə'biləd·ē, -ətē, -i\ *n* -ES **:** the quality or state of being curable

cur·able \'kyůrəbəl\ *adj* [ME, fr. MF or L; MF *curable*, fr. L *curabilis*, fr. *curare* to take care of, heal + *-abilis* -able — more at CURE] **:** capable of being cured **:** susceptible to remedy — **cur·able·ness** *n* -ES — **cur·ably** \-blē,-bli\ *adv*

cu·ra·ca \kü'räkə\ *n* -s [Sp, fr. Quechua] **:** a member of the Inca provincial nobility often acting as administrator or ruler over an ayllu or group of ayllus

cu·ra·çao \¦k(y)ůrə¦saů, *esp Brit* -sō\ *also* **cu·ra·çoa** \,=='sōə, ¦==¦sō\ *n* -s [D *curaçao*, short for *curaçao-oranjeappel* curaçao orange, out of which it was made, fr. *Curaçao*, island in Netherlands Antilles] **1 :** an orange-flavored liqueur that is made from the dried peel of the sour orange and that varies in color from yellow to brown but is sometimes colorless **2** *also* **curaçao orange** *or* **curaçoa orange :** SOUR ORANGE

cu·ra·cy \'kyůrəsē, -si\ *n* -ES [fr. *curate*, after such pairs as E *legate: legacy*] **:** the office or employment of a curate

cur·agh *var of* CURRAGH

cu·ra·re \k(y)ü'rärē\ *or* **cu·ra·ra** \-ärə\ *n* -s [Pg & Sp *curare*, fr. Carib *kurari*] **1 :** any of certain complex arrow poisons of So. American Indians that have a paralytic action, include varied plant and animal ingredients, and usu. depend for their effectiveness on aqueous extracts of plants of the genus *Strychnos* (esp. *S. toxifera*) **2 :** a dried aqueous extract of the woody vine (*Strychnos toxifera*) or of certain closely related plants that is rich in alkaloids which act on the neuromuscular junction of skeletal muscle or on cardiac muscle producing paralysis — see CALABASH CURARE **3 :** a purified extract of a So. American menispermaceous vine (*Chondodendron tomentosum*) that is used medicinally to produce muscular relaxation during shock therapy for certain mental diseases and as an adjunct to anesthesia in surgery — called also *tube curare;* see TUBOCURARINE

cu·ra·ri·form \k(y)ü'rärə,fòrm, -'rar-\ *adj* [*curare* + *-iform*] **:** producing the muscular relaxation characteristic of curare

cu·ra·rine \k(y)ü'rärən, -ä,rēn\ *n* -s [ISV *curare* + *-ine*] **:** any of several alkaloids obtained from curare: as **a :** one of three alkaloids from calabash curare — usu. used with a preceding *C* and a following Roman numeral ⟨C-*curarine* I⟩ ⟨C-*curarine* III⟩ **b :** TUBOCURARINE

cu·ra·ri·za·tion \k(y)ü,rärə'zāshən\ *n* -s **:** administration of curare or one of its derivatives to induce relaxation of voluntary muscles (as in spastic disorders) or as an adjunct to certain anesthetics; *also* **:** the state resulting from such treatment

cu·ra·rize \k(y)ü'rä,rīz\ *vt* -ED/-ING/-S **:** to bring under the influence of curare; *esp* **:** to induce curarization

cu·ras·sow \'kyůrə,sō\ *n* -s [alter. of *Curaçao*, island of Netherlands Antilles] **:** any of several large arboreal birds of So. and Central America that are distantly related to the domestic fowl, that constitute *Crax* and related genera of the family Cracidae, and that are highly esteemed as game and for food

cu·rat·age \'kyůrəd·ij\ *n* -s [*curate* + *-age*] **:** the residence of a curate

[1]**cu·rate** \'kyůrət\ *n* -s [ME *curat*, fr. ML *curatus*, fr. *cura* cure of souls (fr. L, care) + L *-atus* -ate — more at CURE] **1 :** one who has the care of souls **:** CLERGYMAN **2 :** an assistant or a deputy of a rector or vicar in the churches of the Anglican communion and in the Roman Catholic Church

[2]**cu·rate** \kyə'rāt, 'kyů,r-\ *vt* -ED/-ING/-S [back-formation fr. *curator*] **:** to act as curator of

curate's assistant *n* **:** MUFFIN STAND

cu·rat·ess \'kyůrəd·əs\ *n* -ES **:** a curate's wife

cu·ra·tial \kyə'rāshəl, *attrib* " *or* 'kyů,r-\ *adj* **:** of curatic status

cu·rat·ic \kyə'rad·ik\ *also* **cu·rat·i·cal** \-d·əkəl\ *adj* **:** of or relating to a curate

cu·ra·tion \kyə'rāshən\ *n* -s [ME *curacioun*, fr. MF *curation*, fr. OF, fr. L *curation-*, *curatio*, fr. *curatus* (past part. of *curare* to take care of, heal) + *-ion-*, *-io* -ion — more at CURE] **:** CURE

cu·ra·tive \'kyůrəd·|iv, -ət|\ *adj* [MF *curatif*, fr. OF, fr. *curer* to take care of, heal + *-atif* -ative — more at CURE] **:** relating to or used in the cure of diseases **:** tending to cure — **cu·ra·tive·ly** \|əvlē, -li\ *adv*

cu·ra·tor \kyə'rā|d·ə(r), 'kyů,rā|, 'kyůrə|, 'kyü,rā|, |tə-\ *n* -s [ME *curatour* guardian, curate, fr. MF *curateur*, fr. OF, fr. L *curator* manager, overseer, guardian, fr. *curatus* + *-or*] **1 a** *Roman law* **:** a person corresponding nearly to the guardian of English law and appointed to manage the affairs of a person past the age of puberty while he is a minor or of any such person when legally incompetent (as a spendthrift or a lunatic) **b :** a similar guardian in various modern legal systems (as the Scots law or Roman Dutch law) appointed for minors or others past the age of pupillarity **2** [L] **a :** a person having the care and superintendence of something **:** OVERSEER, MANAGER, STEWARD **b :** one in charge of the exhibits, research activities, and personnel of a museum, zoo, or other place of exhibit **c :** one in charge of a single collection or subject of study in such an institution ⟨~ of manuscripts⟩ ⟨~ of birds⟩ **3 a :** a member of a board of trustees charged with administering the business of a university or a division thereof ⟨~*s* of the university⟩ ⟨~*s* of the university library⟩ **b :** a member of a body that elects certain professors at Scottish universities ⟨the patronage of seventeen chairs, previously in the gift of the Town Council, was transferred to seven ~*s* —*Edinburgh Univ. Cal.*⟩ **c :** the director of an educational fund who is entrusted with selecting and advising holders of fellowships under that fund ⟨~ of fellowships⟩ **4 :** a cricket groundsman

curator bo·nis \-'bōnəs\ *n, pl* **curators bonis** [NL, lit., curator for goods] *Scots law* **:** a guardian in charge of the goods, property, or person of a minor or incompetent person

cu·ra·to·ri·al \¦kyůrə¦tōrēəl, -tòr-\ *adj* [L *curatorius* + E *-al*] **:** of or relating to a curator or his work

cu·ra·tor·ship *pronunc at* CURATOR +,ship\ *n* -s **:** the office, position, duties, or jurisdiction of a curator ⟨appointed a new man to the ~ of the museum⟩ ⟨fulfilled his ~ with efficiency and care⟩ ⟨the ~ of the international committee extended over the disputed territory⟩

cu·ra·tory \kyə'rād·ərē, 'kyůrə,tōrē\ *n* -ES [ME *curatorie*, fr. LL *curatoria*, fr. L *curator* + *-ia*] **1 :** CURATORSHIP **2 :** a body of curators

cu·ra·trix \kyə'rā·triks\ *n, pl* **curatri·ces** \kyə'rā·trə,sēz, ,kyůrə·'trī(,)sēz\ [LL, fem. of L *curator*] **:** a female curator

[1]**curb** \'kərb, -ə̄b, -əib\ *vi* -ED/-ING/-S [ME *courben*, fr. MF *courber*, fr. L *curvare*, fr. *curvus* bent, curved — more at CROWN] *archaic* **:** BEND, BOW, CRINGE

[2]**curb** \"\ *n* -s *often attrib* [partly fr [1]*curb;* partly fr MF *courbe* curve, curved piece of wood or iron, fr *courbe* crooked, curved, bent, fr L *curvus*] **1 :** a chain or strap attached to the upper part of the branches of a bit and used to restrain a horse — see BIT illustration **2 :** a usu. curved enclosing frame, border, or edging; *specif* **:** the framing round the mouth of a well or of a shaft or at the change of slope in a roof **3 :** a swelling on the back of the hind leg of a horse just behind the lowest part of the hock joint that is due to strain or rupture of the ligament and generally causes lameness **4 :** CHECK, RESTRAINT, CONTROL ⟨a ~ on rising prices⟩ ⟨a ~ on their unruliness⟩ ⟨the ~ of his mother's will had held him —Margaret Deland⟩ **5 :** a raised edge or margin **:** a wall or casing to strengthen or confine **a :** a crib for molding a block of concrete **b :** the casing of a turbine wheel **c :** the curved guide for directing water against the buckets or floats of a breast wheel **d :** a flat ring usu. of wood on which a complete section of brickwork lining for a shaft or well is built **e :** a lead flashing for the curb plate of a curb roof **f :** the lower of the two slopes of a mansard roof **g** *Brit* **:** a massive ornamental fireplace fender without a plane horizontal top **h :** an iron border to the incorporating bed of a gunpowder mill **i :** a timber nosing for a brick step **6 :** a siding (as of stone or concrete) built along the edge of a street to form part of a gutter **7** *or* **curb plate :** a circular frame or plate around an opening to strengthen it (as the casing for a skylight, the wall plate at the springing of a dome, or the race of a windmill) **8 :** the walls of a chamber in which sulfuric acid is manufactured **9 a :** a sidewalk market **:** a street market **b** *also* **curb market** [so called fr. the fact that it orig. transacted its business on the street] **:** a market for trading in securities not listed on the N. Y. Stock Exchange; *also* **:** the personnel, organization, or facilities of such a market

[3]**curb** \"\ *vt* -ED/-ING/-S **1 :** to put a curb on (a horse) **:** check (a horse) with a curb **2 a :** to bring to a stop and halt the forward course or progress of usu. sharply ⟨attempts to ~ lynching by legislation have taken various forms —F.W. Coker⟩ **b .** to restrain, abate, or moderate the course or force of **:** GUIDE, CONTROL, MANAGE ⟨the sober scientific method does not stimulate the imagination; it ~*s* it —S.M.Crothers⟩ **3 a :** to furnish (a street) with a curb **b :** build a curb around ⟨~ a well⟩ **4 :** to make (telegraph signals) shorter and sharper by reducing retardation thus increasing speed **5 :** to lead (a dog) to the gutter or other suitable place for defecation **syn** see RESTRAIN

[4]**curb** \"\ *adj* [[3]*curb*] **:** used in or concerned with sending curbed telegraph signals

curbash *var of* KURBASH

curb bit *n* **:** a stiff bit having branches by which a leverage is obtained upon the jaws of a horse — see BRIDLE illustration

curb box *n* **:** a vertical cast-iron pipe extending from curb or sidewalk level down to the shutoff at the water-main connection

curb chain *n* **1 :** a flat chain hooked into the eyes of a curb bit and passed under the chin of a horse where it augments the leverage of the bit **2 :** a jewelry chain composed of round links slightly twisted to make them lie flat and close together

curb edger *n* **:** a tool used in cement work for finishing edges (as of cement walks) — compare TROWEL

curb·ing \-biŋ,-bēŋ\ *n* -s [[2]*curb* (rim) + *-ing*] **1 :** the material of which a curb is made **2 :** CURB

curbline \'=,=\ *n* **:** the boundary between a roadway and a sidewalk area

curb pin *n* **:** REGULATOR PIN

curb roof *n* **:** a roof with a ridge at the center and a double slope on each of its two sides — compare GAMBREL ROOF, MANSARD ROOF

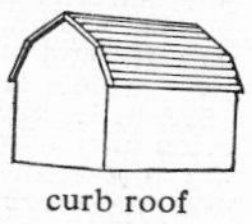

curb roof

curbs *pres 3d sing of* CURB, *pl of* CURB

curb service *n* **1 :** service extended to persons sitting in parked automobiles esp. at a street curb ⟨the store offered *curb service*⟩ **2 :** any special service or favor

curbside \'=,=\ *n* **1 :** the side of a pavement bordered by a curb ⟨trees set at intervals along the ~ —Kay Boyle⟩ **2 :** SIDEWALK ⟨~ interview⟩

[1]**curbstone** \'=,=\ *n* [[2]*curb* (rim) + *stone*] **:** a stone set along a margin as a limit and protection — called also *edgestone*

[2]**curbstone** \"\ *adj* **1 :** operating in a curb market or on the street without maintaining an office ⟨a ~ broker⟩ **2 :** based on chance impression, random observation, or hunches ⟨~ advice⟩ ⟨~ opinion⟩ **:** not having the benefit of training or experience **:** AMATEURISH ⟨a ~ engineer⟩ ⟨a ~ commentator⟩

curb·ston·er \"+ə(r)\ *n* **:** a curbstone broker or vendor

curby \-bē\ *adj* -ER/-EST [[2]*curb* (swelling) + ●] *of an equine hock* **:** affected with curb; *also* **:** liable to become affected with curb esp. by reason of being thick, coarse, or overbent

cur·cas oil \'kərkəs-\ *n* [NL *curcas* (specific epithet of *Jatropha curcas*), fr. Sp *curcaso*] **:** a colorless to yellowish cathartic fatty oil that contains a toxic principle, is obtained from physic nuts, and is used chiefly in medicine and soap-making

curch \'kərch\ *n* -ES [ME *curch*, *courche*, prob. back-formation fr. *courcheis*, pl., fr. MF *couvrechiés*, pl. of *couvrechef* kerchief — more at KERCHIEF] *Scot* **:** KERCHIEF 1

cur·chie *or* **cur·chy** \'kərchē\ *dial var of* CURTSY

cur·cu·lio \(,)kər'kyülē,ō\ *n* [NL, fr. L, grain weevil; prob. akin to L *curvus* curved — more at CROWN] **1** *cap* **:** the type genus of Curculionidae including a number of typical weevils most of which feed in nuts **2** -s **:** any of various weevils; *esp* **:** one that injures fruit (as the plum curculio)

[1]**cur·cu·li·on·id** \(,)kər¦kyülē¦änəd, ¦kər,k-\ *adj* [NL *Curculionidae*] **:** of or relating to the Curculionidae

[2]**curculionid** \"\ *n* -s **:** a beetle of the family Curculionidae

cur·cu·li·on·i·dae \(,)kər,kyülē'änə,dē\ *n pl, cap* [NL, fr. *Curculion-*, *Curculio*, type genus + *-idae*] **:** a family of snout beetles (suborder Rhynchophora) consisting of the typical weevils and including many that injure fruits and crops

cur·cu·ma \'kərkyəmə\ *n* [NL, fr. Ar *kurkum* saffron, crocus] **1 a** *cap* **:** a genus of Old World tropical herbs (family Zingiberaceae) having tuberous roots and spicate flowers, some members having roots that yield starch — see TURMERIC, ZEDOARY **b** -s **:** any plant of the genus *Curcuma* **2** -s **a :** an arrowroot obtained from a curcuma **b :** TURMERIC 1a(2)

curcuma paper *n* **:** TURMERIC PAPER

curcuma starch *n* **:** TIKOR

cur·cu·min \'kərkyəmən\ *n* -s [G, fr. NL *Curcuma* (genus name of *Curcuma longa*) + G *-in*] **:** an orange-yellow crystalline compound $C_{21}H_{20}O_6$ constituting the coloring principle of turmeric and used chiefly in coloring foods

curcumin S *n, usu cap C* [ISV *Curcum-* (fr. NL *Curcuma*, genus that produces it) + *-in*] **:** a direct yellow dye — see DYE table I (under *Direct Yellow 11*)

[1]**curd** \'kərd, -ə̄d,-əid\ *n* -s *often attrib* [ME *curd*, *crudd;* prob. akin to OE *crūdan* to press — more at CROWD] **1 a :** the part of milk coagulated by souring or being treated with certain enzymes, consisting mainly of casein, and used as food either as produced or as made into cheese — distinguished from *whey;* often used in pl. ⟨~*s* and cream⟩ ⟨~*s* and whey⟩ **b :** a food resembling milk curd in form or appearance ⟨soybean ~⟩ **c :** a gray or whitish coagulant; *specif* **:** the precipitate formed when soap is used in hard water **2 :** the granular mass of soap that separates from the lye and rises when salt is added to the boiled mixture of lye and fat in soapmaking **3 :** the undeveloped or partially developed flower head or aggregation of flower heads that forms the edible part of certain brassicas (as cauliflower and broccoli)

[2]**curd** \"\ *vb* -ED/-ING/-S [ME *curden*, *crudden*, fr. *curd*, *crudd*, n.] *vt* **:** to cause to thicken or congeal **:** COAGULATE, CURDLE ~ *vi* **:** to become coagulated or thickened **:** separate into curds and whey

curd cheese *n* **:** COTTAGE CHEESE

curd knife *n* **:** a device consisting of fine wires or blades stretched in a steel frame and used to cut soft curd into cubes to facilitate drainage of whey

curdle \'kərdᵊl, -ə̄d-,-əid-\ *vb* **curdled; curdled; curdling** \-d(ᵊ)liŋ\ **curdles** [freq. of [2]*curd*] *vt* **1 :** to change (milk) into curds **:** cause curds to form in (milk) ⟨the milk is *curdled*⟩ **2 :** to cause to coagulate **:** CONGEAL, FREEZE ⟨~ the whites of eggs⟩ **3 :** SPOIL, ADDLE, SOUR, EMBITTER ⟨disappointments *curdling* his previously gay disposition⟩ ~ *vi* **1 :** to form curds **:** change into curd **:** COAGULATE ⟨the milk has *curdled*⟩ **2 :** to appear as though covered with curds **:** accumulate scurf **3 :** CONGEAL, FREEZE ⟨the latex ~*s* in small lumps⟩ **4 :** to become bitter **:** go bad or wrong **:** SPOIL, SOUR ⟨envy soon ~*s* into hate —J.A.Froude⟩ ⟨how ambition frustrated will ~ —Robert Hatch⟩ — **curdle the blood :** to fill with horror ⟨his account fairly *curdled my blood*⟩

cur·dly \-d(ᵊ)lē\ *adj* **:** CURDLED **:** having a curdled appearance

curd mill *n* **:** a machine that cuts slabs of cheddared curd into pieces of uniform size

cur dog *n* **:** CUR b

curd soap *n* **:** soap separated as curds by addition of salt during saponification; *also* **:** a solidified neat soap of open finish

curdwort \'=,=\ *n* **:** YELLOW BEDSTRAW

curdy \-dē\ *adj* -ER/-EST **:** resembling curds in consistency and appearance **:** coagulating into curds

[1]**cure** \'kyů(ə)r, -ůə\ *n* -s [ME (also, care), fr. OF, fr. ML & L; ML *cura* cure of souls, fr. L, care, medical attendance, healing; akin to OL *coiraveront* they cared for, Paelignian *coisatens*, and perh. to Goth us*haista* needy] **1 a :** spiritual charge of a parish **:** the office of a parish priest or of a curate **b :** CURACY, PARISH **2 a** *obs* **:** a medical course of treatment for a bodily ailment — used without implication of success **b :** recovery from a disease ⟨his ~ was complete⟩; *also* **:** remission of signs or symptoms of a disease ⟨clinical ~⟩ esp. during a prolonged period of observation ⟨5-year ~ of cancer⟩ **:** return to freedom from an infecting agent ⟨biologic ~ of typhoid⟩ — compare ARREST, QUIESCENCE, REMISSION **c :** a drug, treatment, regimen, or other agency that cures a disease ⟨water ~⟩ ⟨quinine is a ~ for malaria⟩ **d :** a course or period of treatment; *esp* **:** one designed to interrupt an addiction or compulsive habit ⟨take a ~ for alcoholism⟩ or to improve general health ⟨an annual ~ at a spa⟩ **e :** SPA ⟨one of the fashionable ~*s*⟩ **3 :** REMEDY **:** a procedure or agency that heals or permanently alleviates a troublesome or harmful situation ⟨the attractively plausible idea that the ~ for negative attitudes and misinformation is information —W.H.Whyte⟩ **4 :** a process or method involving aging, seasoning, washing, drying, heating, smoking, or otherwise treating whereby a product is preserved, perfected, or readied for use **5** *maritime law* **:** the medical care awarded a merchant seaman injured or taken sick in the course of his duties **syn** see REMEDY

[2]**cure** \"\ *vb* -ED/-ING/-S [ME *curen* to take care of, heal, fr. MF *curer* to take care of, heal, cleanse, fr. L *curare* to take care of, heal, fr. *cura*, n.] *vt* **1 :** HEAL **a :** to restore to health, soundness, or normality ⟨~ him of his illness⟩ ⟨*curing* his patients rapidly by new procedures⟩ ⟨a child *cured* of lisping⟩ **b :** to bring about recovery from **:** REMEDY ⟨any physician can ~ a clean wound⟩ ⟨antibiotics ~ many formerly intractable infections⟩ **2 a :** to treat so as to remove, eliminate, or rectify ⟨every fact you learn ~*s* ignorance or confusion —J.M. Barzun⟩ ⟨no amount of sweeping and clean mats could ~ the bedbugs⟩ **b :** to free or relieve (a person) from an objectionable or harmful condition or inclination ⟨the loss *cured* him of his gambling⟩ ⟨a rebuff that *cured* him of his brash aggressiveness⟩ **3 :** to subject to a preservative process ⟨~ meat by salting⟩ ⟨drying the hay to ~ it⟩ ⟨*curing* tobacco by aging it⟩ **:** perfect by chemical change (as rubber by vulcanizing, plastics by treating with heat or chemicals to make them infusible and insoluble, or green concrete by maintaining proper condi-

tions of moisture and temperature) **4 :** to clear (land) for cultivation or other use **5 :** to make acceptable in legal procedure (the appearance of objectionable evidence, the omission of relevant matter, or supposed error in charging the jury) by admission of certain evidence giving charges considered under the law to nullify any effect prejudicial to the appellant that any defective evidence or charges might have ~ *vi* **1 :** *of a product* **:** to undergo a preservative process **2 a :** to effect a cure ⟨careful living ~s more often than it kills⟩ **b :** to take a cure (as in a sanatorium or at a spa)

syn HEAL, REMEDY: CURE and HEAL may apply, literally and often interchangeably, to wounds or diseases ⟨mind and will are so powerful they can *heal* the sick —C.A.Dial⟩ CURE, however, more commonly applies to restoration of a healthy or normal condition of body or organism ⟨*cure* a headache⟩ ⟨*cure* a cold⟩ HEAL commonly applies to restoration to soundness of an affected part after a wound or lesion ⟨*heal* an open sore⟩ ⟨*heal* a cut in the hand⟩ Figuratively, one *cures* a bad condition of things, but *heals* a breach as in human relations ⟨*cure* him of his faults —Douglas Stewart⟩ ⟨went far toward *curing* the cynicism of youth —Dixon Wecter⟩ ⟨half a century's estrangement between the farmers and the townsmen may yet be *healed* —Roy Lewis & Angus Maude⟩ ⟨*heal* a split in his own Liberal Party —*Time*⟩ REMEDY applies to the use of any means of correction or relief of a morbid or evil condition ⟨*remedy* the common cold⟩ ⟨anxieties would be *remedied* —J.A. Pike⟩ ⟨*remedy* the breakdown of international prestige —Max Ascoli⟩ ⟨the theory that better religion, better houses, or larger prisons can *remedy* the badly functioning brain —*Atlantic*⟩

[3]**cu·ré** \kyə'rā, 'kyü,rā, *F* küřā\ *n* -s [F, fr. OF, fr. *cure* cure of souls (after ML *curatus* parish priest)] **:** a parish priest

cure–all \'⸗,⸗\ *n, pl* **cure–alls** **1 :** a remedy for all diseases or ills **:** PANACEA **2 :** any of several plants of reputed medicinal value: as **a :** a balm (*Melissa officinalis*) **b :** WATER AVENS **c :** HEAL-ALL 2

cure·less \'⸗ləs\ *adj* **:** being without a cure

cur·er \'kyůrə(r)\ *n* -s **1 :** HEALER, SHAMAN **2 :** one that cures (as fish, meat, leather, rubber)

cures *pl of* CURE, *pres 3d sing of* CURE

cu·rete \kyə'rēt\ *n* -s *usu cap* [L *Curetes* (pl.), fr. Gk *Kourētes*] **:** a priest of the Cretan goddess Rhea

cu·rett·age \kyə'red·ij, ¦kyůrə¦täzh\ *n* -s [F, fr. *curette* + *-age*] **:** scraping of a bodily cavity by means of a curette to clean its surface, to obtain material for diagnostic purposes, or to remove a lesion or foreign body

[1]**cu·rette** *or* **cu·ret** \kyə'ret, *usu* -ed·+V\ *n* -s [F *curette*, fr. *curer* to cure. cleanse + *-ette* — more at CURE] **:** a scoop, loop, or ring used as a scraper in performing curettage

[2]**curette** *or* **curet** \"\ *vt* **curetted; curetted; curetting; curettes** *or* **curets :** to scrape with a curette

cu·rette·ment *also* **cu·ret·ment** \kyə'retmənt\ *n* -s **:** CURETTAGE

[1]**cur·few** \'kər(,)fyü, -ə(-,-əi(-\ *n* -s *often attrib* [ME *corfeu, curfew*, fr. MF *cuevrefeu, covrefeu*, signal given in the evening to put out or bank the fire in the hearth, curfew, fr. *covrir* to cover + *feu* fire, fr. L *focus* fireplace, hearth — more at COVER, FOCUS] **1 a :** an order or regulation enjoining withdrawal of persons (as juveniles, military personnel, or other specified classes) from the streets or the closing of business establishments or places of assembly at a stated hour usu. of the evening **b :** the sounding of a bell or other signal to announce the beginning of a time of curfew **c :** the bell or other signal so used **d :** the hour at which curfew becomes effective **e :** the period of time during which a curfew is in effect **2** *obs* **:** a morning signal bell **3 :** a utensil for covering a hearth fire esp. to permit its burning safely overnight

[2]**curfew** \"\ *vt* -ED/-ING/-S **:** to impose a curfew upon ⟨the only . . . nightclub that remains open in an otherwise ~*ed* town —Herbert Kubly⟩

cur·fuf·fle \kər'fəfəl\ *var of* CARFUFFLE

cu·ria \'kyůrēə\ *n, pl* **curi·ae** \-ē,ē, 'kůrē,ī\ [L, fr. (assumed) OL *coviria*, fr. L *co-* + (assumed) OL *-viria* (fr. L *vir* man) — more at VIRILE] **1 a :** a political subdivision comprising several gentes of the tribe in early Rome — compare GENS **b :** the place of assembly of one of these subdivisions **c :** a division of the people or the senate in Italian cities under Roman rule **2** [ML, fr. L] **:** a feudal assembly or court of justice; *esp* **:** a court held in the king's name **3** *often cap* [ML, fr. L] **:** the full body of organized congregations, tribunals, and offices that aid the pope in the administration and government of the Roman Catholic Church

[1]**cu·ri·al** \-ēəl\ *adj* [ME, fr. MF or ML & L; MF *curial*, fr. ML *curialis* of a feudal or ecclesiastic curia, fr. L, of a Roman curia, fr. *curia* + *-alis* -al] **:** of or relating to a curia

[2]**curial** \"\ *n* -s [L *curialis*, fr. *curialis*, adj.] **:** a member of an ancient curia

cu·ri·al·ism \-,lizəm\ *n* -s **:** the view or doctrine of the ultramontane party in the Latin church **:** the system or policy of the Roman curia **:** VATICANISM, ULTRAMONTANISM

cu·ri·al·ist \-ləst\ *n* -s **:** a supporter of curialism

cu·ri·al·is·tic \¦kyůrēə¦listik\ *adj* **:** of or relating to curialism or curialists

cu·ri·al·i·ty \,kyůrē'aləd·ē\ *n* -ES *Scots law* **:** CURTESY

cu·ria·ra \,k(y)ůrē'ärə\ *n* -s [AmerSp, of Cariban origin; akin to Carib *culiala* dugout canoe] **:** a So. American dugout canoe

curia re·gis \¦⸗⸗⸗'rējəs\ *n, pl* **curiae regis** *usu cap C&R* [ML, lit., king's curia] **:** a small permanent council in medieval England composed of those members of the great council serving as officers of the royal household

cu·ri·bo·ca \,k(y)ůrə'bōkə\ *n* -s [Pg *cariboca, curiboca*, fr. Tupi] **:** a dark-complexioned Brazilian of mixed white and Indian or Indian and Negro blood

cu·rie \'kyůrē, -ů,rē, kyə'rē; *in the open compounds that follow, the last two pronunciations are more frequent than for the measure*\ *n* -s [after Mme. Marie *Curie* (Marja Sklodowska) †1934 Pol.-Fr. chemist] **1 :** a unit quantity of radon that in radioactive equilibrium contains one gram of radium **2 :** a quantity of any radioactive nuclide in which exactly 3.7×10^{10} disintegrations occur per second **3 :** a unit of radioactivity equal to 3.7×10^{10} disintegrations per second

curie point *or* **curie temperature** *n, usu cap C* [after Pierre *Curie* †1906 Fr. chemist] **1 :** a temperature at which there is a transition in a substance from one phase to another of markedly different magnetic properties; *specif* **:** the temperature at which there is a transition between the ferromagnetic and paramagnetic phases — compare CURIE-WEISS LAW **2 :** a temperature at which the anomalies that characterize a ferroelectric substance disappear **:** either the upper or the lower temperature limit of the ferroelectric state

curie's law *n, usu cap C* [after P. *Curie*] **:** a law of magnetism now replaced by the Curie-Weiss law: the susceptibility of a paramagnetic substance is inversely proportional to the absolute temperature

cu·rie·therapy \¦kyůrē+\ *n* -ES [F *curiethérapie*, fr. Pierre & Marie *Curie* + *-thérapie* -therapy] **:** RADIOTHERAPY

curie–weiss law \-'wīs-,-'vīs-\ *n, usu cap C&W* [after Pierre *Curie* & Pierre-Ernest *Weiss* †1940 Fr. physicists] **:** a law of magnetism: the susceptibility of a paramagnetic substance is inversely proportional to the excess of its temperature above the Curie point, below which it ceases to be paramagnetic

cu·rine \'kyů,rēn\ *n* -s [ISV *curare* + *-ine*; orig. formed as G *kurin*] **:** a crystalline alkaloid $C_{36}H_{38}N_2O_6$ obtained from tube curare **:** levorotatory bebeerine

curing *pres part of* CURE

cu·rio \'kyůrē,ō\ *n* -s [short for *curiosity*] **:** something arousing interest as being novel, rare, or bizarre **:** CURIOSITY ⟨the priceless paintings, the tapestries, and the ~*s* that adorn the rooms —A.B.Osborne⟩ ⟨as an unwed woman traveling alone, she was treated as a ~ —Galbraith Welch⟩

cu·ri·o·log·ic \¦kyůrēə¦läjik\ *or* **cu·ri·o·log·i·cal** \-jəkəl\ *adj* [*curiologic* fr. LGk *kyriologikos* in an obvious sense, fr. *kyriologia* obvious language (fr. Gk *kyrios* ruling, literal — fr. *kyros* power, might — + *-logia* -logy) + Gk *-ikos* -ic; akin to Skt *śūra* powerful, L *cavus* hollow; *curiological* fr. *curiologic* + *-al* — more at CAVE] **:** representing things by their pictures instead of by symbols — used of hieroglyphic writing — **cu·ri·o·log·i·cal·ly** \-jək(ə)lē\ *adv*

cu·ri·o·log·ics \,⸗⸗⸗'jiks\ *n pl but sing in constr* **:** curiologic writing

cu·ri·o·sa \,kyůrē'ōsə, -ōzə\ *n pl* [NL (influenced in meaning by E *curio* and *curious*), fr. L, neut. pl. of *curiosus* careful, inquisitive — more at CURIOUS] **1 :** CURIOSITIES, RARITIES **2 :** books strange or unusual in subject or treatment; *specif* **:** FACETIAE, PORNOGRAPHY, EROTICA

curiosa fe·li·ci·tas \-fə'lisə,tas\ *n, pl* **curio·sae felicita·tes** \-ō,sēfə,lisə'täd·əz, -ō,zē-\ [L, careful felicity] **:** a studied felicity of expression

cu·ri·os·i·ty \,kyůrē'äsəd·ē, -ür-, -s(ə)tē, -i\ *n* -ES [ME *curiosite*, fr. MF *curiosité*, fr. L *curiositat-, curiositas*, fr. *curiosus* + *-itat-, -itas* -ity] **1 :** desire to know: **a** *archaic* **:** a blamable tendency or desire to inquire into or seek knowledge (as of sacred matters) or to inquire too minutely into any subject **b :** NOSINESS **:** inquisitiveness about others' concerns ⟨to escape the ~ of prying neighbors⟩ **c :** desire to investigate **:** interest leading to inquiry ⟨intellectual ~⟩ ⟨his own ~ to know what really happened long ago —G.M.Trevelyan⟩ **d** *archaic* **:** scientific or artistic interest **:** desire to evaluate and appreciate **2** *archaic* **a :** careful workmanship **:** accuracy or perfection in construction **b :** undue nicety, subtlety, or fastidiousness **c :** proficiency acquired by careful practice **:** INGENUITY **3 a** *obs* **:** a matter (as a question, argument, theory, or experiment) that is curious and ingenious **b :** one that arouses curiosity **:** one that arouses attention or awakes interest esp. for strange, uncommon, or exotic characteristics ⟨an architectural ~⟩ ⟨his uncommon illness was a medical ~⟩ ⟨exploiting the poet as a ~⟩ **c :** an unusual knickknack (as a travel souvenir) **d :** ability to arouse curiosity esp. through novelty **:** INTEREST, PIQUANCY ⟨the ~ of the operation⟩ **e :** curious trait or aspect ⟨another ~ observable in these verbs with separable suffixes —Charlton Laird⟩

cu·ri·o·so \-ē'ō(,)sō, -)zō\ *n* -s [It, curious or inquisitive person, fr. *curioso*, adj., curious, fr. L *curiosus*] **:** one that makes a practice of inquiring into esoteric matters; *specif* **:** a collector of curios or objets d'art

cu·ri·ous \'kyůrēəs, -ür-\ *adj, sometimes* -ER/-EST [ME, fr. MF *curios*, fr. L *curiosus* careful, inquisitive, fr. *curi-* (fr. *cura* care) + *-osus* -ous — more at CURE] **1 a** *archaic* **:** made or prepared with careful skill **:** elaborately or exquisitely executed **:** DAINTY, ELABORATE, RECHERCHÉ **b** *obs* **:** minutely searching **:** ABSTRUSE, RECONDITE **c** *archaic* **:** marked by precise accuracy or careful ingenuity **d** *now dial* **:** CHOICE, EXCELLENT, SUPERLATIVE **2 a :** marked by desire to investigate and learn **:** showing interest in finding or searching out information **:** INQUISITIVE ⟨a rationalist who was ~ and had a sort of scientific interest in life —D.H.Lawrence⟩ ⟨a man, like a cat, is ~ about his environment and keeps investigating it —Stuart Chase⟩ **b :** given to investigating concerns other than one's own ⟨an apprentice ~ of his master's secrets⟩; *often* **:** marked by inquisitiveness about others' concerns **:** PRYING, NOSY ⟨~ about the neighbors' doings⟩ **c** *archaic* **:** having a connoisseur's or virtuoso's interests **3 a** *now dial* **:** difficult to please **:** FASTIDIOUS **b** *archaic* **:** CAREFUL, SOLICITOUS, CHARY, CAUTIOUS **4 a** *archaic* **:** accompanied by feelings of interest **:** INTERESTING **b :** exciting attention, inquiry, speculation, or surprise as strange, hard to explain, unusual, or novel **:** awakening inquisitiveness **:** EXTRAORDINARY ⟨whatever we're thoroughly unfamiliar with is apt to seem to us odd . . . or ~ —J.L.Lowes⟩ **c** *of a book* **:** EROTIC, PORNOGRAPHIC

syn INQUISITIVE, PRYING, SNOOPY, NOSY: CURIOUS always suggests an eager desire to learn and may or may not imply such objectionable qualities as intrusiveness or impertinence ⟨a *curious* person, who searches into things under the earth and in heaven —Benjamin Jowett⟩ ⟨anyone who is prematurely *curious* to see the difference in treatment between different centuries —Henry Adams⟩ ⟨it was as if listening to her I had taken advantage of having seen her poor, bewildered, scared soul without its veils. But I was *curious* too . . . I was anxious, anxious to know a little more —Joseph Conrad⟩ INQUISITIVE implies habitual and perhaps impertinent search for information, sometimes about matters secret and unrevealed ⟨we were in plain sight of everybody passing; and therefore we had no lack of visitors among such an idle, *inquisitive* set as the Tahitians —Herman Melville⟩ ⟨well, this Elsie, she was a bit *inquisitive*, as girls are, and one day . . . she managed to take a peep through a keyhole or something of that kind, and caught the old lady just in the act of putting the stuff away —Dorothy Sayers⟩ PRYING implies officious meddling ⟨in Texas the fearful, thirsty citizen may be afraid to have a drink on his front porch because of the *prying* eyes of his bluenosed neighbor across the hedge —Stanley Walker⟩ ⟨and down in one corner of the chest, safe from the *prying* eyes of my messmates, was a velvet-lined box from Maiden Lane. It contained a bracelet and necklace —C.B.Nordhoff & J.N.Hall⟩ To this SNOOPY adds the suggestion of slyness or sneaking ⟨the businessman sufficiently *snoopy* to discover what Jones has saved —*Atlantic*⟩ NOSY, suggesting a dog's procedure, implies desire for full information about any new situation ⟨doesn't want *nosy* state officials or city slickers prying into its manners and morals —*Fortnight*⟩ **syn** see in addition STRANGE

cu·ri·ous·ly *adv* [ME, fr. *curious* + *-ly*] **:** in a curious manner; *esp* **:** in a way or to a degree inspiring curiosity

cu·ri·ous·ness *n* -ES [ME, fr. *curious* + *-ness*] **:** the quality of being curious: as **a** *obs* **:** CAREFULNESS, PAINSTAKING **b :** curious workmanship **:** ingenuity of contrivance **c :** INQUISITIVENESS, CURIOSITY **d :** NOVELTY, ODDITY

cu·rite \'kyů,rīt\ *n* -s [F, fr. Pierre *Curie* †1906 Fr. chemist + F *-ite*] **:** a radioactive mineral $2PbO.5UO_3.4H_2O$ occurring in orange acicular crystals and supposed to be a hydrous lead uranyl uranate

cu·ri·ti·ba \¦k(y)ůrə¦tēbə\ *adj, usu cap* [fr. *Curitiba*, Brazil] **:** of or from the city of Curitiba, Brazil **:** of the kind or style prevalent in Curitiba

cu·ri·um \'kyůrēəm\ *n* -s [NL, fr. Marie & Pierre *Curie* + NL *-ium* — more at CURIE] **:** a metallic radioactive trivalent element artificially produced (as by bombardment of plutonium with high-energy helium nuclei) — symbol *Cm*; see ELEMENT table

[1]**curl** \'kərl, *esp before pause or consonant* 'kər-əl; 'kəl, 'kəil\ *vb* -ED/-ING/-S [ME *curlen, crullen*, fr. *crolle, crulle* curly, prob. fr. MD; akin to OHG *krol* curly, Norw *krull*, MHG *krūs*, OE *crēas* fine, elegant, *cradol* cradle — more at CRADLE] *vt* **1 :** to twist or form into coils or ringlets (as the hair) **2 :** to form into a curved shape **:** make a curve or curves in or on **:** TWIST ⟨~*ed* one leg about the other⟩ **3 :** to furnish with or as if with curls ⟨a head ~*ed* with graceful locks⟩ **4 :** to contort in a grimace or similar expression of feeling ⟨~*ing* his lips in a sneer⟩ ⟨she looked at him contemptuously and then ~*ed* her mouth up in anger —Liam O'Flaherty⟩ **5 :** to cut so thinly as to create a twisted or ringed effect ⟨~*ed* bacon⟩ ⟨~*ed* celery stalks⟩ ~ *vi* **1 :** to grow in coils or spirals ⟨her hair ~*s* naturally⟩ ⟨a ~*ing* vine⟩ **:** form ripples, crinkles, or ringlets ⟨her hair ~*s* only in damp weather⟩ ⟨bacon ~*s* when fried⟩ ⟨the crisp white edge of a ~*ing* wave —F.J.Mather⟩ **2 :** to move or progress in curves or spirals ⟨the lanes ~ and wind into a . . . sort of labyrinth —Faubion Bowers⟩ **:** form into rings or curves ⟨the snake lashed and ~*ed* —William Beebe⟩ **:** roll or move in ripples ⟨his laughter ~*ed* round his sentences —Virginia Woolf⟩ **3 :** to twist or contort (as in a grimace) ⟨his lip ~*ed* in scorn⟩ **4 :** to play the game of curling **syn** see WIND — **curl the hair :** FRIGHTEN, STUN, NONPLUS, AMAZE ⟨it's enough to *curl your hair* to watch his acrobatic stunts⟩

[2]**curl** \"\ *n* -s **1 :** a lock of hair that coils **:** RINGLET **2 :** something having a curling or coiling shape (as a shaving of wood) **:** COIL, SPIRAL **3 :** the action or fact of curling **:** the state of being curled ⟨keep the hair in ~⟩ **4 a :** an eddy in a stream **b** *South* **:** a bend in a stream **5 :** an abnormal rolling or curling of leaves; *also* **:** a malformation caused by the feeding of aphids or other sucking insects — compare LEAF CURL, LEAF ROLL **6 a** *archery* **:** a sudden turn in the grain of a bow **b :** a curved or spiral marking in the grain of wood **7 :** TENDRIL **8** *math* **:** the vector product of the operator *del* and the vector **9 :** the degree to which a sheet of paper departs from a plane when freely exposed to the atmosphere

curl cloud *n* **:** a cirrus cloud

curled \-ld\ *adj* [ME *curled, crulled*, past part. of *curlen, crullen* to curl — more at CURL] *bot* **:** having crisped leaves ⟨~ lettuce⟩

curled cress *n* **:** WINTER CRESS

curled dock *n* **:** a European dock (*Rumex crispus*) with curled leaves that has become naturalized as a weed in the U.S.

curled hair *n* **:** hair of the manes and tails of horses prepared for upholstery and cushioning purposes

curled mallow *n* **:** a European mallow (*Malva verticillata crispa*) with curled and twisted leaves

curled mustard *n* **:** an Asiatic herb (*Brassica juncea crispifolia*) whose crispy curled foliage is used for greens

curled·ness \'kərldnəs, 'kəl-,'kəil-, -l(d)nəs\ *n* -ES **:** the quality or state of being curled

curled–toe paralysis *n* **:** ariboflavinosis of young chickens and turkeys marked by retarded growth, weakness of the legs with a squatting shuffle, and the turning inward of the toes

curl·er \'kərlər; 'kəlø(r, 'kəil-\ *n* -s **1 :** one that curls: **a :** a worker who curves the brims of felt hats **b :** a worker who shapes feathers into curls **c :** a metal or plastic pin on which hair is wound for curling **2 :** a player of the game of curling

cur·lew \'kər(,)lü *also* -rl(,)yü\ *n, pl* **curlews** *or* **curlew** [ME *corlewe, curlewe*, fr. MF *corlieu, courlis*, of imit. origin] **:** any of a number of wide-ranging chiefly migratory birds (family Scolopacidae) esp. of the genus *Numenius* having long legs, a long slender bill that curves downward, and plumage variegated with brown and buff

curlewberry \'⸗(,)⸗— *see* BERRY\ *n* **1 :** CROWBERRY 1a **2 :** the fruit of the curlewberry

curlew bug *n* **:** CORN BILLBUG

curlew jack *n* **:** WHIMBREL

curlew sandpiper *n* **:** a sandpiper (*Calidris ferruginea*) that is widely distributed in the Old World and has a curved bill like that of a curlew

[1]**cur·li·cue** *also* **cur·ly·cue** *or* **cur·le·cue** \'kərlē,kyü, -əl-,-əil-, -lə,-\ *or* **car·la·cue** \'kärl-, -ál-\ *n* -s [*curly* + *cue* (queue)] **:** a fancifully curved or spiral figure (as a flourish in writing)

[2]**curlicue** \"\ *vb* -ED/-ING/-S *vi* **:** to form curlicues ⟨the words *curlicued* almost illegibly across the brown-edged paper —Nancy Cardozo⟩ ~ *vt* **:** to decorate with curlicues ⟨houses *curlicued* in exuberant outburst of Tyrolean design —Claudia Cassidy⟩

cur·lie·wur·ly \¦kərlē¦wərlē\ *n, pl* **curliewurlies** [redupl. of *curly*] **:** something fantastically circular or curly

curl·i·ly \'kərlələ̄, 'kəl-,'kəil, -əli\ *adv* **:** in a curly manner

curl·i·ness \-lēnəs, -lin-\ *n* -ES **:** the quality or state of being curly

curl·ing \'kərliŋ, -əl-,-əil-, -lēŋ\ *n* -s [ME, act of curling, fr. gerund of *curlen* to curl] **:** a game developed in Scotland in which two teams of four men each send stones spinning over a stretch of ice about 42 yards long toward a target circle in an attempt to place a stone nearest the center

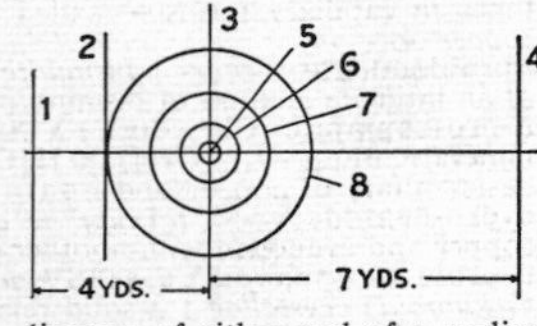

diagram of either end of a curling rink: *1* foot score, *2* back score, *3* sweeping score, *4* hog score, *5* tee, *6* 2-ft. circle, *7* 4-ft. circle, *8* 6-ft. circle (outer limit of parish)

curling dies *n pl* **:** a set of shaping tools consisting of a die and a punch that bends the edges or ends of the work into a form having a circular cross section

curling iron *n* **:** a rod-shaped usu. metal instrument which is heated by direct flame or electricity and around which a lock of hair to be curled or waved is wound

curling machine *n* **:** a machine made with one or more sets of curling dies and used to curl or crimp the ends of cans

curling stone *n* **:** a stone or sometimes iron ellipsoid with a gooseneck handle for delivery in the game of curling

curlpaper \'⸗,⸗⸗\ *n* **:** a strip or piece of paper around which a lock of hair is wound for curling — usu. used in pl.

curling stone

curls *pres 3d sing of* CURL, *pl of* CURL

curl up *vi* **1 :** to roll oneself into the shape of a ball, a coil, or a curl ⟨*curl up* in a chair⟩ **2 :** to give up **:** COLLAPSE, SLUMP ⟨on the battlefield they would surely lie down and *curl up* —Dorothy C. Fisher⟩

curly \'kərlē, -əl-,-əil-, -li\ *adj* -ER/-EST [[2]*curl* + *-y*] **1 :** curling or tending to curl **:** having curls **:** full of ripples **:** CRINKLED **2 a** *of the grain of wood* **:** having fibers that curve in and out without crossing and often form alternating light and dark lines ⟨~ maple⟩ **b :** having such grain **3 :** having a tilde

curly birch *n* **:** YELLOW BIRCH

curly clematis *n* **:** a shrubby climber (*Clematis crispa*) having nodding urn-shaped flowers with open flaring top and with recurved crisped sepals

curly–coated retriever \'⸗⸗,⸗⸗-\ *n* **1** *usu cap both Cs&R* **:** a breed of sporting dogs having a long head, dark eyes, deep chest and shoulders, and a black or liver coat of short crisp curly hair **2 :** a dog of the Curly-Coated Retriever breed

curly dock *n* **:** CURLED DOCK

curly dwarf *n* **:** a phase of rugose mosaic involving dwarfing and leaf curling often without mottled symptoms

curly grass *n* **:** a rare small fern (*Schizaea pusilla*) with slender spiraling fronds

curlyhead \'⸗⸗,⸗\ *n* **1 :** a person with curly hair **2 curlyheads** *pl but sing or pl in constr* \'⸗⸗,⸗\ **:** something suggestive of curly hair; *specif* **:** a clematis (*Clematis ochroleuca*) of the eastern U.S.

curly indigo *n* **:** SENSITIVE JOINT VETCH

curly leaf *n* **:** a plant disease characterized by curling of the leaves: as **a :** curly top of the beet **b :** RASPBERRY MOSAIC

curlylocks \'⸗⸗,⸗\ *n pl but sing in constr* **:** one having curly hair

curly mesquite *also* **curly mesquite grass** *n* **:** a valuable creeping pasture grass (*Hilaria belangeri*) of the southwestern U.S.

curly n *n* **:** the letter *n* with tilde (as *ñ*)

curly–pate \'⸗⸗,⸗\ *n* **:** a curly-headed person

curly–toe \'⸗⸗¦⸗\ *n* **:** CURLED-TOE PARALYSIS

curly top *n* **:** a destructive virus disease esp. of beets and particularly the sugar beet but also of other plants (as tomato, bean, or squash) that is transmitted in the western U.S. by the beet leafhopper and causes prompt death in plants affected when young and a curling and puckering of the leaves in plants affected when half grown or older and some necrosis of the phloem in all parts

curly wolf *n, slang* **:** a tough objectionable character

cur·mud·geon \(,)kər'məjən, 'kər,m-\ *n* -s [origin unknown] **1** *archaic* **:** a grasping avaricious man **:** MISER **2 :** a crusty, ill-tempered, or difficult and often elderly person **:** CHURL ⟨grew up into something of a top brass ~ —*Time*⟩ ⟨a cantankerous old ~⟩

cur·mud·geon·ish \-nish\ *adj* **:** somewhat curmudgeonly ⟨made him feel mean and small and ~ —Cora Jarrett⟩

cur·mud·geon·ly \-nlē\ *adj* **:** like or characteristic of a curmudgeon esp. in being crotchety, surly, or cantankerous **:** CHURLISH ⟨whose temper was not so ~ as that of his famous friend —Edith Sitwell⟩ **syn** see STINGY

cur·mur·ring \kər'məriŋ\ *n* -s [fr. pres. part. of *curmurr* to rumble, fr. Sc *cur-* (intensive prefix) + *murr* to purr] *Scot* **:** rumbling esp. in the bowels

curn *or* **curran** \'kərn\ *n* -s [ME *curn*; akin to ME *corn* grain — more at CORN] **1** *Scot* **:** GRAIN, CORN **2** *Scot* **:** a small number **:** FEW

cur·ney *or* **cur·nie** \'kərnē\ *n, pl* **curneys** *or* **curnies** [*curn* + *-ey -ie* (dim. suffix)] *Scot* **:** a company esp. of persons

cur·nock \'kərnək\ *n* -s [ME *carnok*, of Celt origin; akin to W *crynog* crannock] **:** CRANNOCK

cur·pin \'kərpən\ *n* -s [alter. of *croupon*, fr. ME, fr. OF, aug. of *croupe* rump — more at CROUP] *chiefly Scot* **:** RUMP, BUTTOCKS; *also* **:** CRUPPER

cur·ple \'kərpəl\ *n* -s [ME (Sc dial.) *courpale*, alter. of *croper, crupere* crupper — more at CRUPPER] *Scot* **:** CRUPPER; *also* **:** BUTTOCKS

curr \'kər(·)\ *vi* -ED/-ING/-S [imit.] **:** to make a murmuring sound (as of doves) ⟨the owlets ~ —William Wordsworth⟩

cur·rack *or* **cur·rach** \'kərək, -rək\ *n* -s [modif. of ScGael *curran*] *Scot* **:** a wicker pannier

cur·ragh *or* **cur·rach** \ˈkərə(k̲)\ *n* -s [partly fr. ME *currok*, fr. ScGael *curach;* partly fr. IrGael *currach;* akin to MIr *curach* coracle — more at CORACLE] **1** *Irish* **:** marshy waste-land **2** *Irish & Scot* **:** CORACLE

currajong *var of* KURRAJONG

currance *n* -s [L *curr*ere to run + E *-ance* — more at CURRENT] *obs* **:** CURRENT, FLOW

cur·rant \ˈkər·ənt, ˈkə·rə-\ *n* -s *often attrib* [ME *rayson of Coraunte*, a variety of small raisin principally grown in Greece, lit., raisin of Corinth, fr. AF *raisin de Corauntz*, fr. *Corauntz* Corinth, Greece, fr. L *Corinthus*, fr. Gk *Korinthos*] **1 :** a small seedless raisin grown chiefly in the Levant and used extensively in cookery and confectionery **2 :** the acid edible fruit of several plants of the genus *Ribes* used chiefly for jams and jellies — see BLACK CURRANT, RED CURRANT, WHITE CURRANT **3 :** a plant of the genus *Ribes* that bears currants **4** *or* **currant red :** GOYA

currant aphid *n* **:** an aphid (*Cryptomyzus ribis*) that is very destructive to the new leaves of currants in spring

currant borer *n* **:** the larva of a small yellow clearwing moth (*Ramosia tipuliformis*) that bores longitudinal tunnels in the canes of currants and gooseberries and often kills them

currant bush *n* **1 :** CURRANT 3 **2** *in Australia* **:** a shrub (*Apophyllum anomalum*) of the family Capparidaceae that bears small berries and serves as a browse plant

currant-leaf \ˈ==,=\ *n* **:** MITERWORT

currant leaf spot *n* **:** any of three fungous diseases of the currant: **a :** an angular leaf spot caused by an imperfect fungus (*Cercospora angulata*) **b :** an anthracnose characterized by small brownish or black spots and caused by a discomycete (*Pseudopeziza ribis*) **c :** a grayish-centered leaf spot caused by an ascomycetous fungus (*Mycosphaerella grossulariae*)

currant rust *n* **:** any of several rusts affecting currants; *esp* **:** WHITE PINE BLISTER RUST

currant spanworm *n* **:** a larval moth (*Itame ribearia*) that is extremely injurious to the leaves or fruit of the currant

currant stem girdler *n* **:** the larva of a sawfly (*Janus integer*) that feeds in and frequently girdles the shoots of the currant and gooseberry

currant tomato *n* **1 :** a Peruvian plant (*Lycopersicon pimpinellifolium*) bearing its spherical small scarlet fruits in long racemes **2 :** the fruit borne on the currant tomato

currantworm \ˈ==,=\ *n* **:** any of various insect larvae that feed on the leaves or the developing fruit of the currant: as **a :** any of several sawfly larvae that feed on currant leaves **b :** CURRANT SPANWORM **c :** a maggot (*Epochra ribearia*) that feeds in the fruit **d :** a caterpillar (*Zophodia convolutella*) that attacks the fruit of currants and gooseberries — see IMPORTED CURRANTWORM

cur·ra·wong \ˈkərə,wȯŋ, -wäŋ\ *n* -s [native name in Australia] **:** any of several loud-voiced fruit-eating Australian birds constituting the genus *Strepera* of the family Cracticidae — called also *bell magpie*

cur·ren·cy \ˈkər·ənsē, ˈkə·rə-, -si\ *n* -ES *often attrib* [ML *currentia* flowing, fr. L *current-*, *currens* (pres. part. of *currere* to run) + *-ia*] **1 a :** circulation as a medium of exchange ⟨the ~ of these coins⟩ **b :** CIRCULATION **:** general use **:** general acceptance **:** the fact of being commonly accepted, used, and repeated **:** PREVALENCE ⟨a story that enjoyed wide ~⟩ ⟨a version that gained ~⟩ — used chiefly of reports, sayings, and ideas **c :** the time of such currency **:** the time during which something is current ⟨a test to ensure that he can do a satisfactory weld . . . throughout the ~ of the work —S.C.Robertson⟩ **2 a :** something that is in circulation as a medium of exchange including coin, government notes, and bank notes ⟨the silver ~⟩ ⟨the note ~⟩ ⟨the use of beads as minor ~ in Africa —*advt*⟩ **b :** paper money in circulation ⟨the gift purse contained both coin and ~⟩ **c** (1) **:** the amount of paper and metallic money in circulation (2) **:** the amount of paper money in circulation **d :** a common article for bartering ⟨tobacco being the ~ of the colony⟩ ⟨furs as ~ in dealing with the natives⟩ **e :** a medium of intellectual exchange or expression ⟨ideas are the ~ of the few —Roy Lewis & Angus Maude⟩ ⟨neither side possessed any ~ but clichés —Jan Struther⟩ ⟨sadism is the ~ in which every activity is expressed when its organized forms are . . . frustrated —Abram Kardiner⟩ **f :** a set of values and designations used in certain British colonies instead of the legal values and proper designations of the English coinage system ⟨six pence in ~ equals three pence in sterling⟩ **3 :** a native-born Australian ⟨his ~ sons and daughters⟩

currency bond *n* **:** a bond payable as to both interest and principal in any form of money that is legal tender within the country of issue — compare GOLD BOND

currency declaration *n* **:** a statement of currency ownership made by a traveler on entering or by a shipper on sending parcels to a country (as one having foreign-exchange control)

currency doctrine *or* **currency principle** *n* **:** the principle that banks should issue notes only against coin or bullion — compare BANKING DOCTRINE

currency dollar *n* **:** CONTINENTAL DOLLAR

currency unit *n* **:** MONETARY UNIT

[1]**cur·rent** \ˈkər·ənt, ˈkə·rə-\ *adj* [ME *curraunt*, *coraunt*, fr. OF *corant*, *curant*, pres. part. of *corre*, *courre* to run, fr. L *currere;* akin to MHG *hurren* to hurry, OIr & MW *carr* vehicle, Gk epi*kouros* hastening to aid, and perh. to OE & OHG *horsc* wise, quick, ON *horskr*] **1 a** *archaic* **:** RUNNING, FLOWING, MOVING **b** *archaic* **:** FLUENT **:** flowing easily and smoothly **c** (1) **:** presently elapsing ⟨the ~ fiscal year⟩ ⟨the ~ month⟩ (2) **:** occurring in or belonging to the present time **:** in evidence or in operation at the time actually elapsing ⟨the ~ crisis⟩ ⟨~ excitement over elections⟩ ⟨~ services⟩ (3) *of a serial publication* **:** most recent ⟨the ~ number of a quarterly magazine⟩ **2 a :** being in use as a medium of exchange **:** circulating as money ⟨the ~ coin of the realm⟩ **b** *obs* **:** not counterfeit or spurious **:** GENUINE **3 a :** in general knowledge, acceptance, use, or practice **:** PREVALENT, ACCUSTOMED, GENERAL **:** commonly accepted, engaged in, followed, used, or practiced **:** in vogue **:** CONTEMPORARY ⟨~ fashions⟩ ⟨~ customs⟩ ⟨~ beliefs⟩ ⟨~ theories of education⟩ **b** *math* **:** varying from point to point **:** GENERAL **syn** see PREVAILING

[2]**current** \"\ *n* -s [ME *curraunt*, fr. MF *curant*, fr. *curant*, adj.] **1 a :** the part of a fluid body (as air or water) moving continuously in a certain direction **:** STREAM **b :** the swiftest part of a stream **c :** a tidal or nontidal movement often horizontal of lake or ocean water **:** DRIFT **d :** condition of flowing **:** flow marked by force or strength **:** FLOW, FLUX ⟨the violent ~ of the mountain stream⟩ **e :** the velocity of flow of a fluid in a stream ⟨measured the ~ and temperature in the sea just off the ice shelf —Valter Schytt⟩ **2 :** inclination given a channel or a surface shedding water **:** PITCH, TILT ⟨the ~ of the gutter⟩ **3 :** course of events **:** TENOR, TREND, TENDENCY **:** flux of forces ⟨in the deep emotional and creative ~*s* that produced the Renaissance —G.C.Sellery⟩ ⟨strong ~*s* of public opinion⟩ ⟨an adventure that changed the whole ~ of his life —Sherwood Anderson⟩ **4 a :** ELECTRIC CURRENT **b :** the intensity of an electric current **syn** see FLOW, TENDENCY

current account *n* **1 a :** an account between two parties having a series of transactions not covered by evidences of indebtedness (as notes or certificates) and usu. subject to settlements at stated intervals (as monthly or quarterly) — called also *account current*, *book account*, *open account*, *running account* **b :** a statement or transcript of such an account **2 :** an open account with a balance not yet due **3 :** CHECKING ACCOUNT — distinguished from *deposit account*

current assets *n pl* **:** assets of a short-term nature (as cash, accounts receivable, or merchandise) — contrasted with *capital assets*

current balance *n* **:** an instrument for measuring electric currents by weighing the mechanical force exerted

current-bedded \ˌ==ˌ==\ *adj* **:** relating to or exhibiting stratification features produced by currents

current bedding *n* **:** cross-bedding produced by water currents or air currents

current cost *n* **:** a cost whose factors are valued at present-day acquisition and production costs

current density *n* **:** the current per unit area of cross section perpendicular to flow in a region through which an electric current is flowing

PRINCIPAL OCEAN CURRENTS, DRIFTS, STREAMS

NAME	OCEAN	DESCRIPTION
Agulhas current	Indian	warm; partly a continuation of Mozambique current; flows SW along SE coast of Africa, turns E at about 40° S
Alaska current	Pacific	cold; a branch of Aleutian current; flows N from about 45° N and counterclockwise in Gulf of Alaska
Aleutian current	Pacific	cold; flows E at about 45° N; branches into Alaska and California currents
Antarctic West Wind drift	Atlantic-Indian-Pacific	cold; encircles Antarctica S of about 50° S
Antilles current	Atlantic	warm; flows NW along N coast of Greater Antilles; joins Florida current
Arctic current *or* Arctic stream: Labrador current		
Australia current: East Australian current; West Australian current		
Benguela current	Atlantic	cold; flows N along W coast of southern Africa
Black current *or* Black stream: Kuroshio current		
Brazil current	Atlantic	warm; flows S along E coast of So. America to about 40° S, then turns E into So. Atlantic current
California current	Pacific	cold; a branch of Aleutian current; flows SE along coast of No. America from about 45° N to about 20° N; joins No. Equatorial current
Canaries current *or* Canaries drift	Atlantic	cold; flows SW from about 40° N along coast of west Africa to about 20° N; joins No. Equatorial current
Cape Horn current	Pacific-Atlantic	cold; flows E off S tip of So. America
Caribbean current	Atlantic	warm; formed by joining of part of No. Equatorial current and a branch of So. Equatorial current; flows NW along N coast of So. America into Caribbean sea
Chilean current: Peru current		
East Australian current	Pacific	warm; flows S along E coast of Australia, then counterclockwise in Tasman sea and E from New Zealand
East Greenland current	Arctic-Atlantic	cold; flows SW along E coast of Greenland
El Niño	Pacific	warm; periodic; flows S from Colombia along coast of So. America between Peru current and the shorelines
Equatorial countercurrent	Pacific-Indian	warm; flows E along equator; affected by monsoons
Falkland current	Atlantic	cold; flows NE along coast of Argentina; joins Brazil current turning E into So. Atlantic current
Florida current	Atlantic	warm; a part of the Gulf stream from Straits of Florida to Cape Hatteras
Guinea current	Atlantic	warm; flows E in Gulf of Guinea along S coast of west Africa
Gulf drift: No. Atlantic drift		
Gulf stream	Atlantic	(1) the warm current flowing along coast of No. America from Cape Hatteras to the Grand Banks, formed by merging of Florida and Antillean currents; (2) the entire stream from the Straits of Florida to the NW coast of Europe, including the Florida current and No. Atlantic drift
Gulf Stream drift: No. Atlantic drift		
Humboldt current: Peru current		
Japan current *or* Japan stream *also* Japanese current: Kuroshio current		
Kurile current: Oyashio current		
Kuroshio current	Pacific	warm; flows NE from E coast of Philippines along E coast of Japan; turns E at about 40° N, becomes part of No. Pacific drift
Labrador current	Atlantic	cold; flows S from Baffin Bay through Davis strait to Newfoundland; E branch joins No. Atlantic drift flowing E; W branch flows into Gulf of St. Lawrence
Monsoon current *or* Monsoon drift	Indian	warm; N of equator; direction of flow dependent on monsoons
Mozambique current *also* Natal current	Indian	warm; flows SW along SE coast of Africa through Mozambique channel; see Agulhas current
No. Atlantic drift *or* No. Atlantic current	Atlantic	warm; continuation of Gulf stream joined by E branch of Labrador current in region of Grand Banks; flows NE to NW coast of Europe
No. Equatorial current	Atlantic-Pacific	warm; flows W, N of equator
No. Pacific drift *or* No. Pacific current	Pacific	warm; formed by merging of Japan and Oyashio currents; flows E to W coast of No. America at about 40° N; branches into Alaska and California currents
Norwegian current	Atlantic	warm; continuation of No. Atlantic drift; flows NE along coast of Norway into Arctic ocean
Oyashio current *or* Oya Siwo current *also* Okhotsk current	Pacific	cold; flows SW from Bering sea along Kurile islands and E coast of Japan; meets Kuroshio current at about 40° N
Peru current *also* Peruvian current	Pacific	cold; flows N and NW along coast of N Chile, Peru, and Ecuador; turns W to join So. Equatorial current
So. Atlantic current	Atlantic	cool; flows E from So. America toward southern tip of So. Africa, between latitude 35° S and 45° S, as part of the Antarctic West Wind drift
So. Equatorial current	Atlantic-Pacific-Indian	warm; flows W just S of the equator; in the Atlantic it branches, forming the Brazil and Caribbean currents
So. Indian drift *or* So. Indian current: Antarctic West Wind drift		
So. Pacific current *or* So. Pacific drift: Antarctic West Wind drift		
Subarctic current: Aleutian current		
Tsushima current: Kuroshio current		
West Australian current	Indian	cold; flows N along W coast of Australia; one branch turns W to join the So. Equatorial current, the other continues NE along N coast of Australia
West Greenland current	Atlantic	cold; continuation of East Greenland current; flows NW along SW coast of Greenland
West Wind drift: Antarctic West Wind drift		

cur·ren·te ca·la·mo \kə¦rentēˈkalə,mō\ *adv* [L, lit., with running pen] **:** OFFHAND **:** without deep reflection ⟨written *currente calamo*⟩

current events *n pl but sing or pl in constr* **:** contemporary developments in local, national, or world affairs; *also* **:** the organized study of such developments

current intensity *or* **current strength** *n* **:** the magnitude of an electric current as measured by the quantity of electricity crossing a specified area of equipotential surface per unit time

current liability *n* **:** a liability that arises in the ordinary course of business and must be met in a comparatively short time (as an account payable or an accrual of interest not yet due)

current limiter *n* **:** a fuse to break a circuit when a predetermined current is exceeded

current-limiting reactor \ˈ==,===-\ *n* **:** an electrical inductance made up of a number of turns of wire of low ohmic resistance and inserted in series with a line to limit the current that can flow under short circuit

cur·rent·ly *adv* **1 :** FLUENTLY, READILY ⟨reading 16th century writing as ~ . . . as we read our own is an illusion —Virginia Woolf⟩ **2 :** at present ⟨~ engaged in scientific research⟩ ⟨~ running at the local theater⟩

currently insured *adj* **:** entitled to retirement payments under federal old-age and survivors insurance or at death having at least 6 quarters of coverage within the 3 years immediately preceding

current meter *n* **:** an instrument for measuring the velocity of flow of a fluid (as water) in a stream

current money *n* **:** lawful or universally acceptable money

cur·rent·ness *n* -ES **:** the state of being current **:** CURRENCY

current of action : ACTION CURRENT

current of rest : an electric current that is due to a difference of potential between two inactive parts of an organism (as between two regions on an unstimulated nerve) and that is modified when excitation occurs

current ratio *n* **:** the ratio between current assets and liabilities used in appraising credit worthiness of a business

current ripple *or* **current mark** *n* **:** an asymmetrical ripple mark formed by currents of water on the surface of sediments (as river bars, tidal flats, beaches, or sand dunes) — compare OSCILLATION RIPPLE

current tap *n* **:** a device permitting the attachment of a branch electrical circuit to a main circuit by means of an attachment plug or cap

current transformer *n* **:** a transformer whose primary carries the whole of an alternating current to be measured or controlled and whose secondary is connected to a measuring or control device

current yield *n* **:** the rate of return given by a bond on its current price without allowance for the fact that it will be paid at par at maturity

cur·ri·cle \ˈkərəkəl\ *n* -s [L *curriculum* running, racecourse, chariot] **:** a 2-wheeled chaise usu. drawn by two horses

cur·ric·u·lar \kəˈrikyələ(r)\ *adj* [*curricul*um + *-ar*] **:** of or relating to the curriculum **:** of or relating to academic courses of study

cur·ric·u·lum \-ləm\ *n, pl* **curricu·la** \-lə\ *also* **curriculums** [NL, fr. LL, course of a year, fr. L, running, racecourse, chariot, fr. *currere* to run — more at CURRENT] **1 :** the whole body of courses offered by an educational institution or one of its branches ⟨widening the college ~⟩ **2 :** any particular body of courses set for various majors ⟨the ~ in engineering⟩ ⟨the premedical ~⟩ **3 :** all planned school activities including besides courses of study organized play, athletics, dramatics, clubs, and home-room program **4 a :** general education and breeding ⟨people who had not learned courtesy in the course of an elaborate ~⟩ **b :** a work schedule

cur·ric·u·lum vi·tae \kə¦rikələmˈwē,tī, -kyələmˈvī,tē\ *n, pl* **curricu·la vitae** \-ləˈ-\ [L, course of (one's) life] **:** a brief account of one's life **:** a brief statement including biographical data ⟨applications should include a *curriculum vitae* —*Science*⟩

[1]**cur·ri·er** \ˈkər·ēə(r), ˈkə·rē-\ *n* -s [alter. (influenced by [1]*curry*) of ME *corier*, fr. MF, fr. L *coriarius*, fr. *corium* leather + *-arius* -ary — more at CUIRASS] **:** one that curries: as **a :** a worker who performs any of the operations (as oiling, softening, or rolling) necessary to bring tanned hides or skins to salable form **b :** one that curries a horse

[2]**currier** *n* -s [origin unknown] **:** a 16th century firearm resembling the harquebus

cur·ri·ery \ˈkər·ēərē, ˈkə·rē-, -əri\ *n* -ES [[1]*curry* + *-ery*] **1 :** the trade of a currier of leather **2 :** a place where currying is done

curring *pres part of* CURR

cur·rish \ˈkər·|ish, |ēsh *-R also* ˈkər|\ *adj* [ME, fr. *curre* cur + *-ish*] **:** like a cur **:** MONGREL; *also* **:** BASE, MEANSPIRITED, IGNOBLE — **cur·rish·ly** *adv*

currs *pres 3d sing of* CURR

[1]**cur·ry** \ˈkər·|ē, ˈkə·r|, |i\ *vb* -ED/-ING/-ES [ME *currayen*, *corien*, fr. OF *correer*, *conreer* to prepare, arrange, furnish, curry, fr. (assumed) VL *conredare*, fr. L *com-* + (assumed) VL *redare* to provide — more at ARRAY] *vt* **1 :** to comb the hair or coat of (as a horse) with a currycomb **2 :** to incorporate oils and greases into (heavy leathers) in order to increase strength, water repellency, and pliability **3 :** BEAT, DRUB, THRASH **4 :** to make presentable **:** DRESS, ARRANGE, COMB, GROOM ⟨a courtier well *curried*⟩ ~ *vi, archaic* **:** to engage in flattery, blandishment, and cajolery — **curry fa·vor** \-ˈfāvə(r)\ [alter. (influenced by *favor*, n.) of ME *currayen favel* to curry a chestnut horse, trans. of MF *estriller fauvel*] **:** to seek to gain favor by flattery or attentions

[2]**curry** \"\ *also* **cur·rie** \"\ *n* -ES [Tamil-Malayalam *kaṟi*] **1 :** CURRY POWDER **2 :** a food seasoned with curry powder ⟨vegetable ~⟩ ⟨lamb ~⟩ ⟨shrimp ~⟩

3curry \"\ *vt* -ED/-ING/-ES **:** to flavor or cook (a food) with curry

4curry *vi* -ED/-ING/-ES [perh. back-formation fr. *currier*, obs. var. of *courier*] *obs* **:** COURSE, SCURRY

1currycomb \ˈ==,=\ *n* [¹*curry* + *comb*] **:** a comb made of rows of metallic teeth or serrated ridges and used esp. in currying a horse

currycomb

2currycomb \"\ *vt* **:** to comb (as a horse) with a currycomb **:** CURRY

curry leaf *n* [²*curry*] **:** the pungent leaf of an Asiatic shrub (*Murraya koenigii*)

curry powder *also* **currie powder** *n* [²*curry*] **:** a condiment consisting of ground spices blended according to the type of food (as egg or vegetable) to be curried

curs *pl of* CUR

1curse \ˈkərs, -ōs,-əis-\ *n* -s [ME *curs*, fr. OE] **1 a :** a calling to a deity to visit evil on one **:** a solemn pronouncement or invoking of doom or great evil on one **:** an imprecation for harm **b :** any utterance marked by malediction or execration **:** OATH **c :** evil effects brought about by a curse or by or as if by something cursed ⟨a witch putting a ~ on them⟩ ⟨an ancient house and family on which a ~ had long rested⟩ **2 :** excommunication or anathema **:** formal and extreme church censure **3 :** something that is cursed or worthy of being cursed **:** an evil, misfortune, or source of harm **:** SCOURGE ⟨intolerance is the greatest ~ of every land —Kenneth Roberts⟩ ⟨such ~*s* as yaws and malaria —Robert Trumbull⟩ **4 :** MENSTRUATION — used with *the*

2curse \" *or, as a vi & in vt sense 2c*, ˈkəs\ *vb* -ED/-ING/-S [ME *cursen*, fr. OE *cursian*, fr. *curs*, n.] *vt* **1 :** to rail at typically impiously and profanely **:** BLASPHEME ⟨*cursing* his god⟩ ⟨*cursing* his wretched fate⟩ **2 a :** to utter words calculated to consign to great evil **:** assign to an evil fate **:** DAMN, DOOM ⟨a blasphemer *cursed* by his gods⟩ **b :** to pronounce a formal curse on **:** ANATHEMATIZE, EXCOMMUNICATE ⟨an act *cursed* by the high church council⟩ **c :** to swear at **:** call on fate to visit with dire misfortune and evil **:** invoke divine vengeance or anger against — sometimes used with *out* ⟨he *cursed* out his treacherous ally⟩ ⟨*cursing* his servant for his stupidity⟩ **3 :** to bring evil on **:** visit with retribution **:** punish with wrath sometimes divine **:** endow to one's detriment **:** AFFLICT, HARASS ⟨*cursed* with misfortunes⟩ ⟨*cursed* by society as always outcast⟩ ⟨*cursed* by misplaced loyalties⟩ **~** *vi* **:** to utter curses, oaths, and imprecations **:** SWEAR ⟨rebuked for his *cursing*⟩ ⟨he ~*s* too much⟩ **syn** see EXECRATE

cursed \ˈkərsəd, -ōs-,-əis-, -st — *in sense 1 -st is rare except in poetry; in sense 2, either* -səd *or* -st *but* -st *is usual nonattributively; in sense 3* -st *is usual*\ *also* **curst** \-st\ *adj, sometimes* -ER/-EST [ME *cursd, cursed, curste*, fr. past part. of *cursen*] **1 :** worthy of being cursed **:** execrable, wicked, hateful, or obnoxious ⟨his ~ stupidity⟩ **2 :** under a curse ⟨villagers shun the place believing it to be ~⟩ **3** *now chiefly dial* **:** of a vicious or irritable disposition **:** CANTANKEROUS, SHREWISH

cursed crowfoot *n* **:** an annual or short-lived perennial herb (*Ranunculus sceleratus*) growing in marshy places and having stems hollow and basal leaves reniform with the upper ones smaller and marked with three linear segments

curs·ed·ly \-sədlē, -li\ *adv* [ME, fr. *cursed* + *-ly*] **:** INTENSELY, DAMNABLY, BITTERLY ⟨~ hard job⟩ ⟨~ cold weather⟩

curs·ed·ness \-sədnəs\ *n* -ES [ME *cursednes*, fr. *cursed* + *-nes* -ness] **:** the quality or state of being hateful, vicious, or perverse **:** bad temper **:** bad disposition

cursed thistle *n* **1 :** BLESSED THISTLE **2 :** CANADA THISTLE

curse of scot·land \-əvz'kätlənd, -əv'sk-\ *cap S* [so called fr. its similarity to the coat of arms of Sir John Dalrymple, 1st Earl of Stair †1707 Scot. lawyer, as lord advocate partly responsible for the massacre of the MacDonald clan at Glencoe, Scotland, in 1692] **:** the nine of diamonds in playing cards

cursitor *n* -s [AF & ML; AF *coursetour*, fr. ML *cursitor* runner, alter. of L *cursor* — more at CURSOR] *obs* **:** COURIER

1cur·sive \ˈkərsiv\ *adj* [F or ML; F *cursif*, fr. ML *cursivus*, lit., running, fr. L *cursus* (past part. of *currere* to run) + *-ivus* -ive] **:** RUNNING, COURSING**:** as **a** *of writing* **:** flowing often with the strokes of successive characters joined and the angles rounded ⟨children are still taught ~ writing —Marcia Winn⟩ **b :** having a flowing, easy, impromptu character ⟨the ~ quality of a rapid sketch —Tatiana Proskouriakoff⟩ **:** done in an offhand or casual manner without great attention to detail ⟨a somewhat free and ~ rendering of Horace —Cyril Connolly⟩

2cursive \"\ *n* -s **1 :** a manuscript written in cursive writing **2 :** a style of printed letter imitating handwriting — sometimes used of letters that do not join each other and thereby distinguished from *script*

Italian curſive

cursive 2

cur·sive·ly *adv* **:** in a cursive style or manner

cur·sive·ness *n* -ES **:** the quality of being cursive

cur·sor \-sə(r), -,sȯ(ə)r, -ō(ə)\ *n* -s [obs. E, runner, fr. ME, fr. L, fr. *cursus* (past part. of *currere* to run) + *-or* — more at CURRENT] **:** a part of a mathematical instrument that moves back and forth upon another part

cursorary *adj* [obs. E *cursor* + *-ary*] *obs* **:** CURSORY

cur·so·res \,kərˈsōr(,)ēz\ *n pl, cap* [NL, fr. L, pl. of *cursor* runner] **1** *in some esp former classifications* **:** any of certain groups of long-legged birds **2** *in some esp former classifications* **:** a group consisting of the wolf spiders and other forms that make no web but pursue their prey

cur·so·ria \-ōrēə\ *n pl, cap* [NL, fr. LL, neut. pl. of *cursorius* of running, fr. L *cursus* running, course (fr. *cursus*, past part.) + *-orius* -ory] *in some classifications* **:** a suborder of Orthoptera including cockroaches, mantes, and stick insects comprising those that progress by running and not leaping — compare SALTATORIA

cur·so·ri·al \,kərˈsōrēəl\ *adj* [LL *cursorius* of running + E *-al*] **1 :** adapted to running ⟨~ insects⟩ **:** having limbs adapted to running and not to prehension ⟨a ~ horse⟩ — opposed to *fossorial* **2 a** [NL *Cursores* + E *-ial*] **:** of or relating to the Cursores **b** [NL *Cursoria* + E *-al*] **:** of or relating to the Cursoria

cur·so·ri·ly \ˈkərs(ə)rəlē, -ōl,-əil, -li *sometimes* |z(-\ *adv* **:** in a cursory manner

cur·so·ri·ness \-)rēnəs, -rin-\ *n* -ES **:** the quality of being cursory

cur·so·ri·us \,kərˈsōrēəs\ *n, cap* [NL, fr. LL *cursorius* of running] **:** a genus of birds (family Glareolidae) comprising the typical coursers — compare GLAREOLA

cur·so·ry \ˈkərs(ə)rē, -ōl,-əil, -ri *sometimes* |z(-\ *adj* [LL *cursorius* of running] **:** rapidly often superficially performed with scant attention to detail **:** marked by hurried passing over or through something that invites exhaustive treatment **:** HASTY ⟨investigations were ~ to the point of being slapdash —Norman Moss⟩ ⟨studied three months in a ~ fashion —C.G. Bowers⟩ ⟨issued either no reports at all or only extremely ~ ones —John Brooks⟩

curst *var of* CURSED

cur·sus \ˈkərsəs\ *n, pl* **cursus** [ML, fr. L, course — more at COURSE] **:** movement or flow of style; *specif* **:** a pattern of cadence at the end of a sentence or phrase in medieval Latin prose which aimed by varying rhythm to avoid stressing the ultimate syllable

curt \ˈkər|t, -ōl,-əil, *usu* |d.+V\ *adj* -ER/-EST [L *curtus* shortened — more at SHEAR] **1 a** *of speech or writing* **:** brief or concise **:** sparing of words **:** CONDENSED, TERSE ⟨wrote with ~ realistic precision —Carl Van Doren⟩ ⟨a ~, clean, and complete account⟩ **b :** marked by such shortness of speech, writing, or manner as to suggest discourtesy, displeasure, or peremptoriness **:** LACONIC, TERSE ⟨a ~ message . . . bade her return at once to Rome —John Buchan⟩ **:** BRUSQUE, ABRUPT ⟨a ~ nod⟩ **2 :** short in linear extent **:** SHORTENED **syn** see BLUFF

curt *abbr* current

1cur·tail \,kərˈtāl, |kō|-, |kəi|-, kə(r)ˈt-, *esp before pause or consonant* -āl\ *vt* -ED/-ING/-S [by folk etymology fr. earlier *curtal* to make a curtal of, fr. *curtal*, n.] **1 a :** to cut off the end or any part of **:** shorten in linear extent **:** reduce in area or amount ⟨whether the hair is ~*ed* or long and upswept —*New Yorker*⟩ ⟨its area — it had extended . . . southward to the Ohio and westward to the Mississippi — was greatly ~*ed* —B.K. Sandwell⟩ **b :** to diminish (intangible objects or values) **:** shorten in duration or scope **:** ABRIDGE, REDUCE ⟨~ the power of feudal militarists —Vera M. Dean⟩ ⟨~ the working day⟩ **2 :** to deprive, dock, or rob (a person) of a right, privilege, or possession as indicated — used with *of* ⟨~*ed* of his heritage⟩ ⟨~*ed* of one's citizenship⟩ **syn** see SHORTEN

2curtail \ˈ=,=\ *n* -s [prob. by folk etymology fr. *curtal*, n.] **:** the scroll end of any architectural member (as a step at the foot of a flight)

cur·tailed·ness \(,)=ˈtālədnəs, -l(d)n-\ *n* -ES **:** the quality or state of being curtailed

cur·tail·ment \(,)=ˈ= mənt\ *n* -s **:** the act of curtailing **:** the fact of being curtailed

1cur·tain \ˈkər|tᵊn, -ōl,-əil *sometimes* |tən *or* |d·ən\ *n* -s *often attrib* [ME *curtine, cortine, curteyne*, fr. OF *curtine, cortine*, fr. LL *cortina* (trans. of Gk *aulaia*, fr. *aulē* court, hall), fr. L *cort-* (*cohort-*), *cors* (*cohors*) enclosure, court + *-ina* -ine — more at COURT] **1 a :** a piece of material finished with hems, ruffles, pleats, or casings and hung usu. by the top edge on rods or poles at windows or sometimes on beds for decoration, privacy, and control of light and drafts **b :** any similar material that serves to screen, divide, protect, conceal, or decorate ⟨a plastic shower ~⟩ ⟨isinglass side ~*s* on a car⟩ **2 a :** SCREEN **:** a device that hides or masks **:** an agency that conceals **:** a check to clear perception, understanding, or communication ⟨the rebel fort, less than a mile away, was wholly lost behind ~*s* of rain —Kenneth Roberts⟩ ⟨a ~ of reserve which she meant to draw again across her features —Marcia Davenport⟩ **b :** an arrangement of moving items or particles serving to screen or protect ⟨a ~ of bullets around the outpost⟩; *specif* **:** a protective sheet or spray of water thrown by a fire hose or sprinkler **c :** a barrier to free communication or exchange of information typically implemented by rigid censorship and restriction on travel and trade **:** a line demarcating the operation of such a barrier ⟨an iron ~⟩ ⟨a security ~⟩ **3 a :** the part of a bastioned front that connects two neighboring bastions — see BASTION illustration **b :** a similar stretch of plain wall **c :** a geological formation similar in effect **4 a :** the screen separating the stage from the auditorium of a theater **b :** the ascent of the curtain at the beginning of a play ⟨~ is at 8:30⟩ **c :** the descent of the curtain at the end of a scene or act of a play **d :** a theatrical effect just prior to the descent of the curtain **e :** the final situation or line of an act; *esp* **:** the closing scene of a play **f :** music used to signal the end of a scene or act of a radio or television program **g curtains** *pl* **:** END **:** definitive conclusion; *esp* **:** DEATH — used as a predicate noun ⟨it was ~*s* for him when his treason was discovered⟩ **5 a :** the part of a wall of a building that is between two pavilions or towers **b :** an exterior wall that serves to enclose rather than to support **6 :** a floating boom to protect a riverbank **7** *chiefly dial* **:** SHADE 7g

2curtain \"\ *vb* **curtained**; **curtained**; **curtaining** \-t(ᵊ)niŋ, -tən-,-d·ən-\ **curtains** [ME *curtinen, cortinen, curteynen*, fr. *curtine, cortine, curteyne*, n.] *vt* **1 :** to enclose with or as if with curtains **:** furnish with curtains **2 :** to veil with or as if with a curtain ⟨an area ~*ed* off from the rest of the world⟩ ⟨Father had never ~*ed* his eyes —Isa Glenn⟩ **~** *vi, of paint* **:** to sag or droop because of too heavy application

curtain board *n* **:** a partition of noncombustible material fitting tightly against a ceiling and intended to prevent or retard the spread of fire and heat

curtain call *n* **:** an appearance by a performer (as at the final curtain of a play) in response to the applause of the audience

curtainfall \ˈ==,=\ *n* **:** the fall of a curtain at the end of a play **:** CONCLUSION

cur·tain·ing \-t(ᵊ)niŋ, -tən-,-d·ən-\ *n* -s **:** material for curtains

curtain lecture *n* **:** a censorious lecture by a wife to her husband in privacy, often in bed

cur·tain·less *pronunc at* ¹CURTAIN +ləs\ *adj* **:** being without a curtain

curtain line *n* **:** the final line of an act or play

curtain raiser *also* **curtain lifter** *n* **1 :** a short play usu. of one scene with few characters used to open a performance **2 :** a usu. short and unimportant preliminary to a main or significant event

curtain shutter *n* **:** a focal-plane photographic shutter

curtain speech *n* **1 :** the last speech of an act or play **2 :** any speech in front of the curtains by author, actor, or manager

curtain stretcher *n* **:** an adjustable rigid frame to which curtains are attached for drying after laundering in order to restore their original dimensions and smoothness

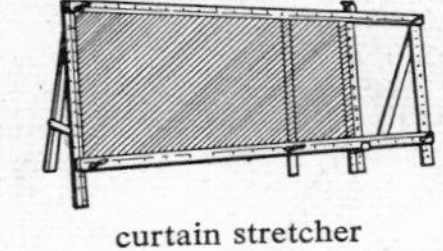
curtain stretcher

curtain wall *n* **1 :** CURTAIN 5 **2 :** a nonbearing wall between columns or piers that is not supported by the girders or beams of a skeleton frame — called also *enclosure wall*

1cur·tal \ˈkərd·ᵊl\ *n* -s [MF *courtault, courtaud* horse with its ears and mane cut short, fr. *courtault, courtaud*, adj.] **1** *obs* **:** a short-barreled cannon **2** *archaic* **:** an animal with a docked tail **3** *obs* **:** a short-coated rogue **4 a :** a tenor or bass musical instrument of the shawm or oboe type — called also *dulcian* **b :** an organ stop imitating the tone of this instrument — compare DULCIANA

2curtal \"\ *adj* [MF *courtault, courtaud*, fr. *court* short, fr. L *curtus* shortened — more at SHEAR] **1** *obs* **:** having a docked tail **2** *obs* **:** made or being short **:** CURTAILED, CURT, BRIEF **3** *archaic* **:** wearing a short frock

curtal ax \ˈkərd·ᵊl,aks\ *or* **cur·tle ax** \"\ *n* [by folk etymology fr. MF *coutelas* — more at CUTLASS] **:** CUTLASS

curtal sonnet *n* **:** a curtailed or contracted sonnet; *specif* **:** a sonnet of eleven lines rhyming *abcabc dcbdc* or *abcabc dbcdc* with the last line a tail

cur·tate \ˈkər,tāt\ *adj* [L *curtatus*, past part. of *curtare* to shorten, fr. *curtus* shortened — more at SHEAR] **:** comparatively short or shortened ⟨~ expectation of life⟩; *specif, of an annuity* **:** payable to the end of each complete year survived but not for part of a year

curtate distance *n* **:** the distance of a planet or comet from the sun or earth as measured in the plane of the ecliptic or the distance from the sun or earth to that point where a perpendicular let fall from the planet upon the plane of the ecliptic meets that plane

curted *adj* [L *curtus* + E *-ed*] *obs* **:** SHORTENED **:** made curt

curter *comparative of* CURT

curtest *superlative of* CURT

cur·te·sy \ˈkərd·əsē\ *or* **curtesy initiate** *n, pl* **curtesies** *or* **curtesies initiate** [ME *curtasy, curteisie, corteisie* curtesy, courteous behavior — more at COURTESY] **:** the future potential interest that a husband has in all real estate in which his wife has an estate of inheritance arising upon the birth to them of a child alive and capable for an instant of inheriting from her the interest at common law and that is as often defined by statute, a life estate for his life or sometimes a one-third interest in fee which becomes consummate upon his surviving his wife and thereby having the right of enjoyment

cur·ti·lage \ˈkərd·ᵊlij\ *n* -s [ME, fr. OF *cortillage*, fr. *cortil* court, courtyard (fr. *cort* court, yard) + *-age* — more at COURT] **:** a yard, courtyard, or other piece of ground included within a fence surrounding a dwelling house

cur·tis·ite \ˈkərd·ə,sīt\ *n* -s [P. L. *Curtis*, 20th cent. American who discovered it + E *-ite*] **:** a mineral consisting of a hydrocarbon compound $C_{24}H_{18}$ found at Skaggs Springs, California

cur·tis stage \ˈkərd·əs-\ *n, usu cap C* [after Charles Gordon *Curtis* †1953 Amer. inventor] **:** a stage in the high-pressure section of a turbine consisting of two rows of impulse blades with intermediate reversing buckets

cur·ti·us rearrangement \ˈkürtsēəs-\ *n, usu cap C* [after Theodor *Curtius* †1928 Ger. chemist] **:** the conversion by heat of an acid azide $RCON_3$ into nitrogen and an isocyanate RNCO

curt·ly *adv* **:** in a curt manner

curt·ness *n* -ES **:** the quality of being curt **:** shortness of speech or manner ⟨the ~ of the refusal⟩

1curt·sy *or* **curt·sey** \ˈkərtsē, -ōt-,-əit-, -si\ *n, pl* **curtsies** *or* **curtseys** [alter. of *courtesy*] **:** an act of civility, respect, or reverence made mainly by women and consisting of a slight dropping of the body with bending of the knees ⟨*curtsies* from all the . . . ladies of the train —Sir Walter Scott⟩ **:** a gesture of courteous recognition

2curtsy *or* **curtsey** \"\ *vb* **curtsied** *or* **curtseyed**; **curtsied** *or* **curtseyed**; **curtsying** *or* **curtseying**; **curtsies** *or* **curtseys** *vi* **:** to make a curtsy — often used with *to* ⟨~*ing* to the queen⟩ **~** *vt* **1** *obs* **:** to make a curtsy to **2** *archaic* **:** to express by curtsying

cu·ru·ba \kəˈrübə\ *n* -s [Pg, fr. Tupi] **1 :** SWEET CALABASH **2 :** CASSABANANA

cu·ru·cu·cu \ˌsürəkə¦kü, ¦kür-, -rəkü¦kü\ *n* -s [modif. of Pg *çurucucú, surucucú*, fr. Tupi *surucucú*] **:** BUSHMASTER

cu·rule \ˈkyü,rül, -ür,yül, ˈkyü,rül\ *adj* [L *curulis, currulis* of a chariot (as in *sella curulis* curule chair), fr. *currus* chariot, fr. *currere* to run — more at CURRENT] **1 :** of or relating to a style of seat reserved in ancient Rome for the use of the highest dignitaries and usu. made like a campstool with curved legs **:** having or consisting of tangent semicircular segments forming legs, backs, or other structural members ⟨a ~ chair⟩ **:** having or consisting of one such segment ⟨a ~ leg⟩ **2 :** privileged to sit in a curule chair because of high rank or dignity ⟨a ~ magistrate⟩

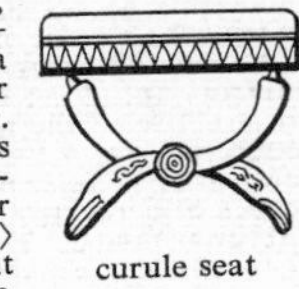
curule seat

cu·ru·pay \ˌkürəˈpī\ *n* -s [AmerSp, fr. Guarani] **1 :** ANGICO **2 :** the hard heavy reddish brown wood of the angico

cu·ru·ro \kəˈrü(,)rō\ *n* -s [Sp, modif. of Araucan *curi*] **:** a small burrowing hystricomorph rodent (*Spalacopus poeppigi*) of Chile

cur·va·ceous *also* **cur·va·cious** \ˌkərˈvāshəs, ¦kō¦-, ¦kəi¦-\ *adj* [³*curve* + *-aceous, -acious*] **:** having a well-proportioned feminine figure marked by pronounced curves **:** marked by sex appeal — **cur·va·ceous·ness** *n*

cur·va·tion \ˌkərˈvāshən\ *n* -s [L *curvation-, curvatio*, fr. *curvatus* (past part. of *curvare* to bend, curve, fr. *curvus* curved) + *-ion-, -io* -ion — more at CROWN] **:** CURVATURE

cur·va·ture \ˈkərvə,chü(ə)r, -ōv-,-əiv-, -üə *sometimes* -və-,tyü-\ *n* -s [L *curvatura*, fr. *curvatus* + *-ura* -ure] **1 a :** CURVE **:** curved part **b :** the act of curving or the state of being curved **2** *of a plane curve* **:** the rate of change per unit of arc length of the angle through which the tangent turns in rolling round from point to point of the curve **3 a :** an abnormal curving ⟨~ of the spine⟩ — see KYPHOSIS, SCOLIOSIS **b :** a curved surface of an organ ⟨the lesser ~ of the stomach⟩

curvature of field : a defect in an optical system that results in points on an object plane perpendicular to the axis being imaged on a curved surface rather than on a plane

1curve \ˈkərv, -ōv,-əiv\ *adj* [L *curvus* bent, curved — more at CROWN] *archaic* **:** CURVED

2curve \"\ *vb* -ED/-ING/-S [L *curvare*, fr. *curvus*] *vi* **:** to have or take a turn, change, or deviation from a straight line or course or from a level surface typically with a rounded gradual effect and without sharp breaks or angularity ⟨the road ~*s* around the town⟩ **~** *vt* **1 :** to cause to curve **:** form into a curving surface **:** BEND ⟨*curving* the line gracefully⟩ ⟨*curving* the strips slightly⟩ **2 a :** to throw or propel (as a ball) so that a course follows curves or appears to curve ⟨*curving* the next pitch⟩ **b :** to throw a curve ball to (a batter)

syn BEND, TWIST: CURVE describes any deviation or swerving from the straight or level that suggests an arc of a circle or an ellipse ⟨his lips were *curved* in a smile —Kenneth Roberts⟩ ⟨over the roof a few swallows were *curving* —Ellen Glasgow⟩ BEND is likely to refer to an angular turning or curving at a certain point under a degree of force or pressure ⟨*bend* the steel strips as required⟩ ⟨*bend* the glass tube at the point indicated⟩ Figuratively BEND may imply some forcing or distortion of materials or of facts, or some pressure on or persuasion of people ⟨was somewhat prone to *bend* logic to meet the demands of argument —E.S.Bates⟩ ⟨not all prescriptive speech aims purely and typically at *bending* the hearer's attitudes to those of the speaker —W.D.Falk⟩ TWIST is likely to suggest a force having a spiraling effect throughout the object involved rather than an effect at one point ⟨the light steel rods *twisted* together by the explosion⟩ Figuratively TWIST suggests a more extreme distortion than BEND ⟨an unconquerable confidence . . . which understates or *twists* into a wry joke the fatal moment of war —*Times Lit. Supp.*⟩

3curve \"\ *n* -s [¹*curve*] **1 :** a line or surface that curves **:** a bending without angles **:** BEND, FLEXURE ⟨a train going around a ~⟩ ⟨the stream describing many ~*s* through the valley⟩ **2 :** something curved**:** as **a :** a curving line of the human body; *esp* **:** a curving line characteristic of an attractive feminine figure — usu. used in pl. **b :** FRENCH CURVE **c curves** *pl* **:** PARENTHESES **3 a** *or* **curve ball :** a baseball pitch in which the ball swerves or appears to swerve from its normal or expected course of flight because of a spin put on it in delivery — compare INSHOOT, OUTSHOOT **b :** a ball bowled by a right-handed bowler that starts to the right and then veers to the left — compare HOOK **c :** TRICK, DECEPTION **:** the act of deluding or breaking a promise **4 :** GRAPH**:** as **a :** a usu. curved line representing graphically a variable element as affected by one or more conditions ⟨the price ~ mounts to a peak in summer⟩ **b :** an indication of development or progress **:** COURSE, RATE, TREND **5 a :** a line that may be precisely defined by an equation in such a way that the coordinates of its points are functions of a single independent variable or parameter **b** (1) **:** the intersection of two geometrical surfaces (2) **:** the path of a moving point **6 :** a teacher's arrangement of grades purporting to represent the distribution of excellent, medium, and poor performances that may be expected in a certain assignment or over a certain period ⟨a teacher marking on a ~ will give more C's than A's or D's⟩ **7 :** CHARACTERISTIC CURVE

curve–billed thrasher \ˈ=,=-\ *n* **:** a light brownish gray thrasher (*Toxostoma curvirostre curvirostre*) of southwestern No. America having white wing bars and black tail tipped with white

curved bar *n, usu cap C&B* **:** the highest rank in the Girl Scout intermediate program symbolized by a red, green, and gold pin bearing the Girl Scout trefoil and motto and surmounting a curved bar

curved knife–tooth harrow *n* **:** ACME HARROW

curved·ly \-vədlē, -vd-\ *adv* **:** in a curved manner

curved·ness \-vədnəs, -v(d)n-\ *n* -ES **:** the quality or state of being curved

curve–drawing meter \ˈ=,==-\ *n* **:** RECORDING METER

curved runner *n* **:** a furrow opener for a corn or cotton planter adapted to soil free from trash

curve fitting *n* **:** the determination of a curve of assigned character (as an exponential curve) that approaches most closely or fits best a number of points in a plane

curve of areas : a curve that is composed in its forward half of a curve of versed sines and in its after half of a trochoid and is used in distributing the displacement in the design of a ship

curve of pursuit : a curve described by a point moving always directly toward or from a second point that is itself moving according to some law

curves *pres 3d sing of* CURVE, *pl of* CURVE

curve·some \ˈkərvsəm\ *adj* **:** CURVACEOUS

1cur·vet \ˌkərˈve|t, ˌkərˈve|t *also* ˈkərvə|t; *usu* |d.+V\ *n* -s [modif. of It *corvetta*, fr. OIt, fr. MF *courbette*, fr. *courber* to bend, curve (fr. L *curvare*) + *-ette* — more at CURVE] **:** a leap of a horse in which he raises both forelegs at once equally advanced and as they are falling raises his hind legs so that for an instant all his legs are in the air at the same time

2curvet \"\ *vi* **curvetted** *or* **curveted**; **curvetted** *or* **curveted**; **curvetting** *or* **curveting**; **curvets** [It *corvettare*, fr. *corvetta*] **1 :** to make a curvet **:** LEAP, BOUND **2 :** PRANCE, CAPER, GYRATE

curvi- *comb form* [MF or LL; MF, fr. LL, fr. L *curvus*] **:** curved; bent ⟨*curviform*⟩ ⟨*curvifoliate*⟩ ⟨*curvirostral*⟩

cur·vi·linear *or* **cur·vi·lineal** \ˌkərvə+\ *adj* [*curvi-* + *linear* or *lineal*] **1 :** consisting of or bounded by curved lines ⟨a ~ angle⟩ **:** following a curve ⟨~ motion⟩ **:** represented by a curved line **2 :** marked by flowing tracery and showing relationships to French flamboyant styles ⟨~ Gothic⟩ **3 :** CURVACEOUS — **curvilinearity** \"+\ *n* -ES — **curvilinearly** \"+\ *adv*

curvilinear coordinates *n pl* **:** a system of geometrical coordinates in which if only one of the coordinates is allowed to vary the locus may be a plane or twisted curve

curvilinear motion *n* **:** motion in which the direction of the velocity of a body is variable and the path of the body is a curved line

curving *pres part of* CURVE

cur·vi·ty \'kərvəd·ē\ *n* -ES [MF or LL; MF *curvité,* fr. LL *curvitat-, curvitas,* fr. L *curvus* curved + *-itat-, -itas* -ity — more at CROWN] *archaic* **:** CURVATURE, CURVE

cur·vom·e·ter \,kər'vämәd·ər\ *n* -S [*curve* + *-o-* + *-meter*] **:** an instrument for measuring the length of a curve, the simplest form consisting essentially of a wheel that is rolled tangentially along the curve and a recording dial

curvy *also* **curv·ey** \'kərvē\ *adj* -ER/-EST **:** CURVED; *esp* **:** CURVACEOUS

cur·wil·let \,kər'wilət\ *n* -S [imit.] *dial Eng* **:** SANDERLING

cus·co bark *or* **cuz·co bark** \'kü(,)skō-\ *n* [fr. *Cuzco,* Peru] **:** cinchona bark from a common cinchona (*C. pubescens*)

cus·co·hygrine *or* **cus·ko·hygrine** \;kü(,)skō+\ *n* -S [G *cuskohygrin,* fr. *cusko* cusco bark + *hygrin* hygrine] **:** an oily base $C_{13}H_{24}N_2O$ occurring with hygrine in the leaves of the cusco-bark tree and in coca leaves

cus·co·nine \'küskə,nēn, -,nən\ *n* -S [ISV *cusco (bark)* + connective *-n-* + *-ine, -in;* prob. orig. formed as G *cuskonin*] **:** a crystalline alkaloid $C_{23}H_{26}N_2O_4$ found in cusco bark

cuscousou *or* **cuscusu** *var of* COUSCOUS

[1]cus·cus \'kəskəs\ *n* -ES [NL, fr. a native name in New Guinea] **:** any of several bright-colored woolly-haired arboreal marsupials (genus *Phalanger*) that superficially resemble monkeys and are common in New Guinea and tropical northern Australia

[2]cuscus *var of* KHUSKHUS

[3]cuscus *var of* COUSCOUS

cus·cu·ta \(,)kə'sk(y)üd·ə\ *n, cap* [NL, fr. ML, dodder, fr. Ar *kushūth, kashūta, kashūtha*] **:** a large and widely distributed genus of twining leafless parasitic herbs (family Convolvulaceae) comprising the dodders and having whitish or yellow filamentous stems

cu·sec \'kyü,sek\ *n* -S [*cu*bic foot per *sec*ond] **:** a volumetric unit of flow equal to a cubic foot per second

[1]cush \'kush, 'küsh\ *n* -ES [of African origin; akin to Hausa *ku³sha¹* thin cake made of peanuts, Efik *kus³kus¹* couscous, both fr. Ar *kuskus* couscous] *South* **:** a dish made of seasoned corn meal dough fried, baked with meat, or dropped into pot liquor and boiled

[2]cush \'kush\ *also* **cusha** \-shə\ *n, pl* **cushes** *also* **cushas** [prob. fr. E dial., a call to cows; akin to ON *kussi* calf, G dial. *küse*] *dial Eng* **:** COW

[3]cush \'kush\ *n* -ES [origin unknown] *slang* **:** MONEY

[4]cush \'kush\ *n* -ES [Hindi *kuś,* love grass (*Eragrostis cynosuroides*), fr. Skt *kuśa* grass, sacred grass; perh. akin to ORuss *kustŭ* bush, Lith *kuokštas*] *India* **:** SORGHUM

cush·ag \'kü,shag, -,shəg\ *n* -S [modif. of Manx *cuishag vooar,* lit., big stalk] *Isle of Man* **:** TANSY RAGWORT

cush·at \'kəshət, 'küsh-,'küsh-\ *also* **cush·ie** \-shē\ *n* -S [ME *cowscott, cowschote,* fr. OE *cūscote, cūcsceote*] *chiefly Scot* **:** RINGDOVE 1

cushat lily *n* **:** INDIAN CUCUMBER

cu·shaw \kə'shȯ, kü'-, 'kü,shȯ, 'kü,shȯ\ *also* **ca·shaw** \kə'shȯ\ *n* -S [perh. of Algonquian origin; akin to *escushaw* it is green (in some Algonquian language of Virginia)] **:** WINTER CROOKNECK; *esp* **:** one (as a butternut squash) having the body of the fruit much enlarged

cush-cush \'küsh,küsh\ *n* -ES [origin unknown] **:** a tropical American yam (*Dioscorea trifida*) with small yellow-skinned edible tubers

cushier *comparative of* CUSHY

cushiest *superlative of* CUSHY

cush·i·ly \'küshəlē, -li\ *adv* **:** in a cushy manner

cush·ing's disease *or* **cushing's syndrome** \'küshiŋz-\ *n, usu cap C* [after Harvey *Cushing* †1939 Amer. surgeon] **:** a disease characterized by obesity esp. of the head, neck, and trunk, brownish streaks on the abdominal wall, muscular weakness, and porosity of bone and associated with dysfunction of the adrenal cortex or of the anterior lobe of the pituitary body

[1]cush·ion \'küshən *sometimes* -shin\ *n* -S *often attrib* [ME *cuisshin, cusshin,* fr. MF *coissin, cussin, coussin,* fr. (assumed) VL *coxinus,* fr. L *coxa* hip + *-inus* -ine — more at COXA] **1 a :** a bag or case made typically of cloth, upholstery, or matting that is stuffed with a soft or resilient material and used for sitting, reclining, or kneeling **:** PILLOW, PAD **b :** the cushion on the seat of a ruler or judge often regarded as a symbol of his office **c :** the cushion on which a Bible or other book rests on a lectern **d :** a cushion regarded as a symbol of ease and luxury **2 :** a part resembling a pad: as **a :** the fleshy part of the rump of the horse or pig **b** (1) **:** the frog of a horse's hoof (2) **:** the pad just above the hoof **c :** the fleshy foreface or top lips of certain animals (as the bulldog) **d :** PULVILLUS **e :** the ball of the thumb **f :** the soft feathers about the base of the tail of a hen esp. when present in excess **g :** STRAWBERRY COMB **h :** a boned shoulder of pork or lamb with a pocket for stuffing **3 :** something resembling a cushion in properties or use: as **a :** PILLOW 3 **b :** PINCUSHION **c :** RAT 3 **d :** BUSTLE **e :** the pad of springy rubber affixed along the upper part of the inside of the rim of a billiard table or pool table — called also *bank* **f :** the head of a drill brace **g :** a padded insole **:** a padded insert in a shoe at the ball or heel **h :** a strip of soft resilient rubber between the breaker and carcass of a pneumatic tire to secure the adhesion of carcass to tread and assist in protecting the former **i** (1) **:** an architectural part (as a frieze) that projects convexly — compare CUSHION CAPITAL (2) **:** the top stone of a pier supporting an arch **j :** an artificial pool provided to absorb the kinetic energy of falling water and so prevent erosion **k :** an elastic body (as of air or steam) for reducing shock; *esp* **:** the steam allowed to remain in an engine cylinder after exhaust in order to avoid shock by reducing the momentum of the reciprocating parts **l :** a layer of fine material (as sand, granulated slag, bituminous mastic, or stone screenings) placed on top of a foundation for a block pavement **m** *or* **cush·ion·ing** \-sh(ə)niŋ, -shin-\ **:** a structure or material used to separate and protect goods in transit from shock and damage **n :** a felt mat laid under a large rug to ease the effect of wear **o :** a pad on which gold leaf is placed to be cut **4** *obs* **:** a swelling like that of pregnancy **5 a :** something serving to mitigate the effects of economic disturbances ⟨public works to provide jobs as a ~ against unemployment⟩ **:** a factor that lessens adverse developments in the economy and limits price declines in markets; *esp* **:** a monetary reserve for use in special circumstances ⟨a thickened ~ of liquid assets for protection —*N.Y. Herald Tribune*⟩ **b :** MARGIN **:** reserve supply ⟨a ~ of resources⟩ **6 :** a medical method, procedure, or drug that eases a patient's discomfort without necessarily affecting his basic condition **7 :** program material that can be lengthened, shortened, or omitted entirely to make a radio or television program end exactly on time

[2]cushion \"\ *vt* **cushioned; cushioned; cushioning** \-sh(ə)niŋ, -shin-\ **cushions 1 :** to seat (a person) on a cushion **:** prop up or make comfortable with cushions ⟨nurses ~*ing* his injured shoulder⟩ **2 a :** to suppress by ignoring ⟨~*ing* the scandalous occurrence⟩ **b :** to mitigate the effects of **:** PALLIATE **:** protect by absorbing or checking harmful force or shock **:** keep from harm or shock as if with a cushion ⟨~*ing* the blow⟩ ⟨~*ing* the public from disappointment⟩ **3 :** to provide or equip with a cushion or cushions **:** PAD ⟨~ the wooden seats⟩ **:** protect from jarring effects with or as if with a cushion ⟨soft tires that ~ the ride⟩ **4 :** to check gradually so as to minimize shock due to the inertia of moving parts ⟨~ a piston by leaving some steam in the cylinder after exhaust⟩

cushion aloe *n* **:** a plant of the genus *Haworthia*

cushion capital *n* **1 :** an architectural capital so sculptured as to look like a cushion pressed down by the weight of its entablature **2 :** a capital esp. in the Romanesque style modeled like a bowl whose upper part is cut away on four sides

cushion carom *also* **cushion shot** *n* **1 :** a billiard carom in which the cue ball goes to a cushion before touching the second object ball **2 cushion caroms** *pl but sing in constr* **:** any of the billiard games in which one or more cushions must be touched before completion of a carom

cushion comb *n* **:** STRAWBERRY COMB

cushion cut *n* **:** STEP CUT

cushion dance *n* **:** an old English round dance in which a dancer and the partner of his choice knelt and kissed on a cushion that he placed before her

cushionflower \'==,=\ *n* **:** an Australian shrub (*Hakea laurina*) with large globose crimson-yellow flowers

cushion head *n* **:** a lined paper pad used for protecting the facing layer of apples in a barrel

cush·ion·less \-ləs\ *adj* **:** being without a cushion

cushion pink *n* **:** MOSS CAMPION

cushion plant *n* **:** any plant that grows in a dense cushiony tuft (as many xerophilous and alpine plants) thereby preventing excessive transpiration

cushions *pl of* CUSHION, *pres 3d sing of* CUSHION

cushion sole *n* **:** a special shoe insole having a padded surface facing the foot

cushion star *n* **:** any of numerous thickened more or less globose pentamerous starfishes belonging to *Goniaster* and related genera

cush·iony \'küshənē, -shinē, -ni\ *adj* **:** like a cushion **:** SOFT, CUSHY **:** serving as a cushion **:** equipped with cushions

[1]cush·ite \'kə,shīt\ *n* -S *cap* [*Cush* (Kush), ancient country in the Nile valley adjoining Egypt + E *-ite*] **:** a native or inhabitant of ancient Cush

[2]cushite \"\ *adj, usu cap* **:** of or relating to ancient Cush

[1]cush·it·ic \,kə'shid·ik\ *n* -S *cap* [[1]*Cushite* + *-ic*] **:** a subfamily of the Afro-Asiatic language family comprising a number of languages spoken in East Africa and esp. in Ethiopia and Somaliland — see AFRO-ASIATIC LANGUAGES table

[2]cushitic \;=;==\ *adj, usu cap* **1 :** of, relating to, or characteristic of the Cushites **2 :** of, relating to, or characteristic of the Cushitic languages

cush·la·mo·chree *or* **cush·la·ma·chree** \,küshləmə'krē, -'krē\ *n* -S [IrGael *cuisle mo chroidhe,* lit., vein of my heart] *chiefly Irish* **:** DARLING

cushy \'küshē, -shi\ *adj* -ER/-EST [modif. of Hindi *khush* pleasant, fr. Per *khūsh*] **:** SOFT, PLEASANT, COZY, COMFORTABLE **:** entailing little hardship or difficulty ⟨a ~ job with a high salary in the home office⟩

cusk \'kəsk\ *n, pl* **cusk** *or* **cusks** [prob. alter. of *tusk*] **1 :** a large edible marine fish (*Brosme brosme*) related to the cod — called also *tusk* **2 :** the New World burbot

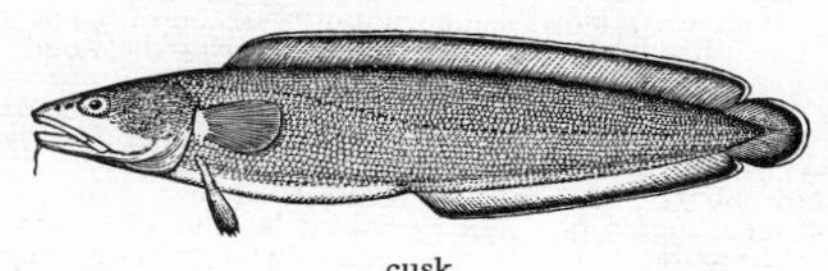

cusk

cusk eel *n* **:** a fish of the family Ophidiidae

cuskohygrine *var of* CUSCOHYGRINE

cusp \'kəsp\ *n* -S [L *cuspis* point] **1 :** the beginning or first entrance of any house in astrological nativity calculations **2 :** POINT, APEX ⟨the ~ of a cone⟩ ⟨the ~ of a peak⟩: as **a :** either horn of the crescent moon or other crescent-shaped luminary **b :** a fixed point on a mathematical curve at which a point tracing the curve would exactly reverse its direction of motion, the tangents to the two parts of a cusp coinciding at the cusp **c :** an ornamental pointed projection (as from the intrados of a Gothic arch) formed by or arising from the intersection of two arcs or foils **d** (1) **:** a point or projection on the occlusal surface of a tooth (2) **:** one of various folds or flaps forming a cardiac valve **e** *bot* **:** a sharp and rigid point **3 :** a landform characterized by a projection with indentations of crescent shape on either side (as along a shoreline or in a mountain front) **4 :** a skate mark left on the ice in executing a half-turn from edge to edge

cusp 2c: *1* cusp

cus·par·ia bark \,kə'spa(a)rēə-\ *n* [AmerSp *cusparia, cuspare,* of Cariban origin; akin to Galibi *cuspare,* the tree from which it is obtained] **:** ANGOSTURA BARK

cus·pa·rine \'kəspə,rēn, -,rən\ *n* -S [F, fr. NL *Cusparia* genus of So. Amer. trees (fr. AmerSp) + *-ine*] **:** a crystalline alkaloid $C_{19}H_{17}NO_3$ found in angostura bark

cus·pate \'kə,spā|t, -,spə|t, *usu* |d·+V\ *also* **cus·pat·ed** \-,spād·əd\ *adj* [*cusp* + *-ate*] **:** having a cusp; *also* **:** shaped like a cusp ⟨a ~ shoreline⟩

cus·pid \'kəspəd\ *n* -S [back-formation fr. *bicuspid*] **:** CANINE TOOTH

cus·pi·dal \'kəspəd[ə]l\ *adj* [L *cuspid-, cuspis* point + E *-al*] **:** constituting or resembling a cusp **:** having or relating to a cusp

cuspidal cubic *n* **:** a plane cubic of the third class with one cusp, one point of inflexion, and no node

cuspidal curve *n* **:** a mathematical curve marking a sharp ridge on a surface corresponding to a cusp on a plane curve

cuspidal locus *n, math* **:** the locus of the cusps of a family of curves

cuspidal point *n, math* **1 :** CUSP 2b **2 :** a point on a ruled surface where a generator or ruling intersects a consecutive ruling

cus·pi·date \-,dāt, *usu* -ād·+V\ *or* **cus·pi·dat·ed** \-,dād·əd\ *adj* [*cuspidate* fr. L *cuspidatus,* past part. of *cuspidare* to make pointed, fr. *cuspid-, cuspis* point; *cuspidated* fr. L *cuspidatus* + E *-ed*] **:** having a cusp **:** terminating in a point ⟨a ~ leaf⟩ — see LEAF illustration

cus·pi·da·tion \,kəspə'dāshən\ *n* -S **:** decoration with cusps ⟨the ~ of an arch⟩

cus·pi·dine \'kəspə,dēn, -dīn\ *n* -S [It *cuspidina,* fr. L *cuspid-, cuspis* point + It *-ina* -ine] **:** a mineral $Ca_4Si_2O_7(F,OH)_2$ consisting of a basic silicate of calcium

cus·pi·dor *also* **cus·pa·dore** \'kəspə,dō(ə)r, -ō(ə)r,-ōə,-ō(ə)\ *n* -S [Pg *cuspidouro* place for spitting, fr. *cuspir* to spit, fr. L *conspuere* — more at CONSPUE] **:** SPITTOON

cusp·ing \'kəspiŋ\ *n* -S [*cusp* + *-ing*] **:** cuspate ornamentation

cus·pule \'kə,spyül\ *n* -S [*cusp* + *-ule*] **:** a small tubercle on the occlusal surface of a tooth

[1]cuss \'kəs\ *n* -ES [alter. of [1]*curse*] **1 :** CURSE, OATH, SWEARWORD ⟨has yet to . . . utter his first ~ —*Atlantic*⟩ **2 :** FELLOW ⟨poor little ~⟩ ⟨an independent ~, but he's awful good —Bill Mauldin⟩ ⟨a crotchety, antic, and lovable old ~ —*New Yorker*⟩

[2]cuss \"\ *vb* -ED/-ING/-ES [by alter.] *vt* **:** CURSE — often used with *out* ⟨~*ing* out the driver ahead⟩ **~** *vi* **:** CURSE ⟨in the habit of ~*ing*⟩

cuss·ed \'kəsəd\ *adj* [fr. past part. of [2]*cuss*] **1 :** CURSED **2 :** PERVERSE, OBSTINATE, CANTANKEROUS — **cuss·ed·ly** *adv*

cuss·ed·ness *n* -ES **:** disposition to willful perversity **:** CANTANKEROUSNESS, OBSTINACY

cus·ser \'küsər, 'kəs-\ *Scot var of* [1]COURSER

cus·so \'kü(,)sō, 'kül,'kə|\ *n* -S [Amharic *kussu*] **:** BRAYERA

cussword \'=,=\ *n* **1 :** CUSS **2 :** a term of abuse **:** a derogatory term ⟨in its lexicon, "academic" and "bookish" are sort of ~s —W.L.Miller⟩

cus·tard \'kəstə(r)d\ *n* -S *often attrib* [ME *custarde, crustade,* a kind of pie, prob. modif. of OProv *croustado,* fr. *crosta* crust (fr. L *crusta*) + *-ado-* ate — more at CRUST] **1 :** a sweetened mixture of milk and eggs that is baked, boiled, or frozen **2 :** a dish prepared with a custard base ⟨corn ~⟩

custard apple *n* **1 a :** any of various fruits of trees of the genus *Annona; esp* **:** BULLOCK'S-HEART **b :** a tree of this genus (as a bullock's-heart or sweetsop) **2 :** PAPAW 2

custard-apple family *n* **:** ANNONACEAE

custard cheeses *n pl* **:** CHEESE 4

custard cup *n* **:** a heat-resistant cup of porcelain or glass in which an individual custard is baked

custard-pie \;==;=\ *adj* [so called fr. the frequent pie-throwing battles waged in early motion-picture comedies] **:** SLAPSTICK **:** relating to or marked by broadest comedy ⟨~ antics⟩

cus·te·nau \kü'stä,naü\ *n, pl* **custenau** *or* **custenaus** *usu cap* [Sp, of AmerInd origin] **1 a :** an Arawakan people of the Xingú river valley, Brazil **b :** a member of such people **2 :** the language of the Custenau people

cus·ter·ite \'kəstə,rīt\ *n* -S [*Custer* co., Idaho + E *-ite*] **:** CUSPIDINE

cus·tock \'kəstək\ *var of* CASTOCK

cu·sto·de \kü'stōdē, -,dā\ *n, pl* **custodes** \-ēz,-āz\ *or* **custo·di** \-(,)dē\ [It, fr. L *custod-, custos* — more at CUSTODY] **:** CUSTODIAN

cus·to·dee \;kəstə;dē\ *n* -S **:** one to whom custody is given

custodes *pl of* CUSTOS

cus·to·dia \(,)kə'stōdēə\ *n, pl* **custodi·ae** \-dē,ē, -dē,ī\ [ML, fr. L, guarding, keeping — more at CUSTODY] **:** CUSTODIAL

[1]cus·to·di·al \;kə;stōdēəl, ,kə's-\ *adj* [L *custodia* + E *-al*] **:** relating to or marked by guardianship or maintaining safety; *specif* **:** marked by or given to watching and protecting rather than seeking to cure ⟨~ care rather than a therapeutic program⟩

[2]custodial \"\ *n* -S [ML *custodia* + E *-al*] **:** a receptacle for sacred objects (as the Host)

cus·to·di·am \(,)kə'stōdēəm, -ē,am\ *n* -S [L, acc. of *custodia*] **:** a grant of land in possession of the English crown to a person who acts as custodee or lessee

cus·to·di·an \(,)kə'stōdēən\ *n* -S [*custody* + *-an*] **1 a :** one that guards and protects or maintains **:** one entrusted officially with guarding and keeping (as property, artifacts, or records) or with custody or guardianship (as of a prisoner, inmate, or ward) ⟨the ~ of the manor and the park⟩ ⟨the ~ in charge of a prison camp⟩ **b :** a monitor preserving a cherished intangible often with or as if with a vested proprietary right ⟨I trust we acquit ourselves worthily as ~s of this sacred mystery —Elinor Wylie⟩ ⟨~s of very glorious traditions and the trustees of a spiritual wealth —W.R.Inge⟩ **2 a :** BUILDING SUPERINTENDENT **b :** one who takes charge of the recording, safekeeping, and release of all valuables that come into the hands of the police department **3 :** an agency that takes care of securities including collection of income but without authority to buy and sell

cus·to·di·an·ship \-,ship\ *n* **:** the office or duty of a custodian ⟨the sense of ~ of a faith received —R.M.French⟩

cus·to·di·er \-dēər\ *n* -S [ME, fr. L *custodia* custody + ME *-er*] *now chiefly Scot* **:** CUSTODIAN

cus·to·dy \'kəstədē, -di\ *n* -ES [ME *custodie,* fr. L *custodia* guarding, keeping, fr. *custod-, custos* guardian keeper + *-ia;* perh. akin to Gk *keuthein* to hide — more at HIDE] **1 a :** the act or duty of guarding and preserving (as by a duly authorized person or agency) **:** SAFEKEEPING ⟨the Serials Division has ~ of newspapers, unbound periodicals, and government and other serials —L.H.Evans⟩ **b :** protection, care, maintenance, and tuition **:** GUARDIANSHIP ⟨orphans in the ~ of their uncle⟩ **2 :** judicial or penal safekeeping **:** control of a thing or person with such actual or constructive possession as fulfills the purpose of the law or duty requiring it **:** imprisonment or durance of persons or charge of things ⟨a man held in police ~⟩ ⟨a suspect in protective ~⟩ **3 :** a territorial division of the Franciscan order smaller than a province

[1]cus·tom \'kəstəm\ *n* -S [ME *custume, custom, costome,* fr. OF *custume, costume,* fr. L *consuetudin-, consuetudo,* fr. *consuetus,* past part. of *consuescere* to accustom, fr. *com-* + *suescere* to become accustomed, accustom; akin to L *suus* one's own — more at SUICIDE] **1 a :** a form or course of action characteristically repeated under like circumstances **:** a usage or practice that is common to many or to a particular place or class or is habitual with an individual ⟨one of the many gracious ~s of the late Queen —G.W.Talbot⟩ **b** (1) **:** long-established, continued, peaceable, reasonable, certain, and constant practice considered as unwritten law and resting for authority on long consent **:** a usage that has by long continuance acquired a legally binding force (2) **:** the usage of a country or particular locality having the force of law in that country or locality ⟨the ~ of London⟩ **c :** repeated practice ⟨~ makes all things easy —Jean Ingelow⟩ **d :** the whole body of usages, practices, or conventions that regulate social life **:** usual manner and method of living and doing **:** social habit ⟨the icy chains of ~ —P.B.Shelley⟩ — compare FOLKWAY **2** *obs* **:** a due or rent in money, in kind, or in services that a feudal tenant was bound to render to his lord **:** the obligation to render or right to receive such due or rent **3 customs** *pl* **a :** duties, tolls, or imposts imposed by the sovereign law of a country on commodities imported into or exported from the country — compare RATE **b** *usu sing in constr* **:** the agency, establishment, or procedure for collecting such customs **4 a :** business patronage **:** personal and often habitual patronage of an establishment **:** habit of purchasing or buying services **:** amount of business ⟨the town shopkeepers sought his ~ —Adrian Bell⟩ ⟨paying personal calls on likely firms to try to obtain their ~ —F.W.Crofts⟩ **b :** CUSTOMERS ⟨the ~ liked the new line⟩ **5 :** CELEBRATION; *esp* **:** a celebration formerly held by the Dahomeans and Ashanti and attended with much human sacrifice **6 :** a custom-built automobile

syn see HABIT

[2]custom \"\ *vt* -ED/-ING/-S [ME *customen,* fr. MF *costumer,* fr. *costume* custom] **1** *archaic* **:** ACCUSTOM **2** *obs* **:** to deal with as a customer

[3]custom \"\ *adj* [[1]*custom*] **1 a :** made or performed according to personal order usu. to individual specifications ⟨a ~ suit⟩ ⟨a ~ set of silver⟩ **b :** performed or effected by an owner of machinery or facilities according to special personal order ⟨the ~ work I did for the neighbors with the tractor plowing and with the cornpicker picking corn —John Dos Passos⟩ ⟨doing ~ smelting for small companies⟩ **2 :** specializing in custom work or operation ⟨a ~ tailor⟩ ⟨a ~ cabinetmaker⟩ ⟨a ~ sawmill⟩

cus·tom·able \-məbəl\ *adj* [ME, fr. MF *costumable,* fr. *costumer* to accustom + *-able*] *archaic* **:** subject to the payment of customs **:** DUTIABLE

customal *var of* CUSTUMAL

cus·tom·ar·i·ly \;kəstə;merəlē, -li\ *adv* **:** by custom **:** in a customary manner

cus·tom·ar·i·ness \-rēnəs, -rin-\ *n* -ES **:** the quality or state of being customary

[1]cus·tom·ary \'kəstə,merē, -ri\ *adj* [ML *customarius,* fr. OF *costumier,* fr. LL *consuetudinarius,* fr. L *consuetudin-, consuetudo* habit + *-arius* -ary — more at CUSTOM] **1** *law* **a :** liable or subject to, or holding by payment of, customs or dues ⟨~ tenure⟩ ⟨~ lands⟩ **:** fixed by custom ⟨~ rent⟩ **b :** holding, held by, or owing its validity as law to custom ⟨~ tenants⟩ ⟨~ services⟩ **2 :** agreeing with custom **:** established by custom **:** commonly practiced, used, or observed **:** familiar through long use or acquaintance ⟨events that are familiar and ~ are those we are least likely to reflect upon —John Dewey⟩ ⟨incensed at a refusal of ~ marks of courtesy —W.R. Inge⟩ **3** *of a verb form or aspect* **:** expressing habitual action

syn see USUAL

[2]customary \"\ *n* -ES [ML *customarium,* fr. neut. of *customarius,* adj.] **1 :** a book or body of customary laws (as of a manor or district) **2 :** CONSUETUDINARY **3 :** the customary aspect of a verb **:** a customary form of a verb

customary constitution *n* **:** UNWRITTEN CONSTITUTION

customary court *n* **:** a court that was formerly a part of a court baron and that exercised jurisdiction over the transfer, surrender, admittance, incidents, and tenures of copyhold estates

custom-built \;==;=\ *adj* **:** built to individual specifications rather than as part of a mass-production plan **:** MADE-TO-ORDER, TAILOR-MADE

cus·tom·er \'kəstəmə(r)\ *n* -S [ME *custumer, costomer,* partly fr. MF *costumier, custumier* tax collector, fr. OF, fr. *costume, custume* custom + *-ier* -er; partly fr. ME *custume, custom, costome* custom + *-er* — more at CUSTOM] **1** *obs* **a :** customs collector **:** a customhouse official **2 a :** one that purchases some commodity or service ⟨she had never seen that ~ before⟩; *esp* **:** one that purchases systematically or frequently ⟨these countries are the largest ~s of U.S. products⟩ ⟨lost most of her ~s through neglect and rudeness⟩ **b :** one that patronizes or uses the services (as of a library, restaurant, or theater) **:** CLIENT **3** *obs* **:** PROSTITUTE **4 :** an individual usu. having some specified distinctive trait or traits that one has or may have some dealing, encounter, or relationship with ⟨what sort of a ~ is he?⟩ ⟨compact of bone and gristle and grim insensitiveness, dangerous ~s every one —Dorothy C. Fisher⟩ ⟨the mule deer buck is an ugly ~ —D.C.Peattie⟩ ⟨a smooth ~, could look after himself —Rex Ingamells⟩ **5 :** a fox that affords good sport in a hunt

customer agent *n* **:** a foreign purchaser who buys goods outright for resale to his trade

customer ownership *n* **:** the partial or complete ownership of a concern (as a public utility) by those who buy or use its output or merchandise

customer's broker *or* **customer's man** *n* **:** a broker's employee who takes buying and selling orders and seeks to induce trading by advising customers and maintaining friendly relations with them

customhouse *also* **customshouse** \ˈ⸗⸗,⸗\ *n* [ME *custom-hous*, fr. ¹*custom* + *hous* house] **:** a building where customs and duties are paid or collected and where vessels are entered and cleared

customhouse broker *n* **:** an agent who acts for merchants in entering and clearing goods and vessels

cus·tom·ize \ˈkəstə,mīz\ *vt* -ED/-ING/-S [³*custom* + *-ize*] **:** to build, fit, or alter according to individual specifications ⟨*customizing* an automobile⟩ ⟨*customized* hair styling⟩

custom-made \ˌkəstə(m)ˌmād\ *adj* **:** CUSTOM-BUILT, TAILOR-MADE, MADE-TO-ORDER

custom of kent \-ˈkent\ *usu cap K* [fr. *Kent* county, England] **:** GAVELKIND

custom of merchants : LAW MERCHANT

customs *pl of* CUSTOM, *pres 3d sing of* CUSTOM

customs bond *n* **:** a bond given by an importer for payment of damage resulting from failure to comply with the customs laws and regulations

customs union *n* **:** a union between two or more states that have abolished tariffs and other restrictions on their interstate trade and have adopted a common commercial policy toward other states

custom-tailor \ˌ⸗⸗ˌ⸗⸗\ *vt* **:** to treat, alter, plan, or build according to individual specifications or needs ⟨new tenants . . . find that they live in a model city, *custom-tailored* to their needs —*Dupont Mag.*⟩

cus·tos \ˈkə,stäs, -tōs; ˈku̇,stōs, ˈkü,-\ *n, pl* **cus·to·des** \(,)kəˈstō(,)dēz; ku̇ˈstō,dās, kü-\ [ME, guardian, fr. L — more at CUSTODY] **1 :** KEEPER, CUSTODIAN, GUARD **2 :** DIRECT 1 **3** [ML, fr. L] **:** a superior of a Franciscan province or custody

custos ro·tu·lo·rum \-,rächəˈlōrəm, -äd-ᵊlˈō-,-ōd-ᵊlˈō-\ *n, pl* **custodes rotulorum** [NL, keeper of the rolls] **:** the principal justice of the peace in an English county who is also keeper of the rolls and records of the sessions of the peace

custrel *n* -s [ME *custrell*, prob. modif. of MF *coustillier* soldier carrying a short sword, squire of a knight — more at COISTREL] *obs* **:** an armor-bearer to a knight

cus·tu·mal \ˈkəstəməl, -schəm-\ *or* **cus·tom·al** \-stəm-\ *n* -s [ML (*liber*) *custumalis*, fr. L *liber* book + ML *custumalis* of customs, fr. OF *costumal*, fr. *costume* custom + *-al* — more at CUSTOM] **:** a written collection of the customs of a monastery, a manor, or a locality

¹**cut** \ˈkət, *usu* -əd·+V\ *vb* **cut; cut; cutting; cuts** [ME *cutten, kitten;* perh. akin to Sw dial. *kata* to cut] *vt* **1 a :** to penetrate with or as if with an edged instrument **:** CLEAVE, PIERCE **:** make an incision in **:** GASH, SLASH ⟨~ one's hand with a knife⟩ **b** (1) **:** to operate on **:** castrate (as a domestic animal) (2) **:** to perform lithotomy upon **c :** to hurt the feelings of ⟨sarcasm ~*s* him to the quick⟩ **d :** to strike sharply with a cutting effect ⟨~ him across the legs with a whip⟩ **e :** to slice or enter into with an effect like that of an edged instrument ⟨icy blasts that ~ one to the marrow⟩ **f :** to score the surface of (a cylinder or bearing) by moving other parts over it usu. without sufficient lubrication **g :** to experience the growth of (a tooth) through the gum **2 :** to reduce by or as if by severing a part: as **a :** TRIM, PARE ⟨~ one's nails⟩ **b :** to shorten (as for reading or presentation) by omissions ⟨~ a manuscript⟩ **c :** to reduce the intensity of: (1) **:** to cause to be less thick, viscous, or tenacious **:** DISSOLVE, DILUTE ⟨alcohol ~*s* shellac⟩ (2) **:** to dilute or adulterate (liquor) by adding water or other nonalcoholic liquid **:** reduce the concentration or strength of **d :** to reduce in amount **:** LOWER, DIMINISH ⟨~ prices⟩ **e :** to trim (book edges) slightly in order to loosen leaves for reading, produce pleasing margins, or bring the book to the size desired **f :** to remove (excess metal) with an edged tool or an oxidizing flame **g :** to trim and join (motion-picture shots or sound tracks) **:** edit (a film) by rearrangements and omissions **h :** to take away show points from (an animal being shown) for a fault (as of conformation or color) **3 a** (1) **:** MOW, REAP ⟨~ hay⟩ (2) **:** to sever from the growing plant ⟨~ flowers⟩ (3) **:** to yield as a crop ⟨that field ~*s* several tons of hay⟩ **b** (1) **:** to divide into parts or to sever a part from by an edged tool ⟨~ bread⟩ (2) **:** to separate or remove by an edged tool ⟨~ a slice of bread⟩ (3) **:** to divide for distribution or apportionment **:** CARVE ⟨~ meat⟩ **c :** FELL, HEW ⟨~ timber⟩ **d :** to slit (folded but untrimmed pages of a book) **e :** to separate (a person) from an organization ⟨a coach who ~ two men from his football squad⟩ **:** DETACH **:** single out and remove, extract, or isolate — often used with *out* ⟨*cutting* these steers out from the herd⟩ **f :** to uncouple (two railroad cars or a car and locomotive) **g** (1) **:** to hit (a ball) with a glancing blow so as to deflect it and put a spin on it ⟨~ a tennis ball with an inclined racket⟩ (2) *cricket* **:** to deflect (a bowled ball) to the off with a chopping stroke (3) **:** to hit and propel (an object ball in pool or billiards) at a marked angle by a very fine contact **h :** to cause to move along (as a timber, roller, or gun) by prying or driving each end alternately sideways **i :** to change the direction of **:** TURN ⟨the driver ~ the wheels sharply⟩ **j :** to proceed with a very near approach to **:** SKIRT **4 a :** to divide into segments **:** separate into parts with an action or result suggestive of that of an edged instrument **:** divide off or up **b :** INTERSECT, CROSS ⟨the lines ~ one another⟩ **c :** to describe (an intersecting line) ⟨*cutting* a diagonal across the state⟩ **d :** BREAK, INTERRUPT, SEVER **:** make the use of for travel, transportation, or communication impossible **:** break the continuity of ⟨the enemy had ~ our communication lines⟩ **e** (1) **:** to divide or separate (a deck of cards) esp. into two portions by removing cards from the top (2) **:** to draw (a card) from the deck esp. for the purpose of deciding the deal **f :** to salt out (as soap) **g :** to cut apart (full printed sheets of text, maps, or illustrations) in preparation for binding **h :** to divide (as spoils or profits) into shares **:** SPLIT **i** *of a pitched baseball* **:** to pass over (a part of the plate) ⟨a fast ball that ~ the inside corner⟩ **5 a :** STOP, CEASE **:** desist from ⟨~ the nonsense⟩ **b :** to break off an acquaintance with **:** OSTRACIZE ⟨friends ~ him as news of the scandal spread⟩ **:** refuse to recognize (an acquaintance) ⟨~ him dead in the street⟩ **c :** to absent oneself usu. without excuse from (a lecture, recitation, or other academic function or an engagement) **d :** to stop (a motor or engine) by opening a switch or closing a throttle valve **:** turn off **:** adjust to a lesser or minimal speed or intensity **e :** to terminate the photographing of (a motion-picture scene) **f :** to terminate the transmission of (part of a radio or television program) **g :** to ignore an admonition or direction of and proceed ⟨~ a red light⟩ **6 a :** to make by or as if by cutting **:** give form or shape to by cutting: as (1) **:** to carve (as a statue) (2) **:** to shape (as by grinding facets) ⟨~ a diamond⟩ (3) **:** to engrave (as a woodcut) (4) **:** to shear out (5) **:** to hollow out (as by erosion), bore, or excavate ⟨floodwaters ~ new channels⟩ ⟨~ a tunnel⟩ (6) **:** to pierce (as by excavation) ⟨~ a dike⟩ **b :** to record a speech, musical selection, or other sound on (a phonograph record) **c :** to type (a stencil) **:** type on a stencil ⟨army orders being ~⟩ **7 a :** to engage in (a grotesque, frolicsome, or mischievous action) — used esp. in the phrases *cut a caper* and *cut didoes* **b :** to give the appearance or impression of **:** MAKE — usu. used with *figure* as object ⟨tall and stately, he ~ a fine figure as a senator⟩ ~ *vi* **1 a :** to do the work or as if of an edged tool **:** serve in or as if in dividing or gashing ⟨a knife that ~*s* well⟩ **b :** to permit of being cut **:** admit of incision or severance ⟨cheese ~*s* easily⟩ **c :** to perform the operation of dividing, severing, incising, or intersecting **:** use a cutting instrument ⟨a tailor busy *cutting*⟩ **d :** to pierce through incisively **e** *of a horse* **:** to interfere slightly esp. by brushing the inner aspect of the corona of a hoof **f :** to make a stroke with a whip, sword, or other weapon ⟨a duelist *cutting* at his adversary⟩ **:** inflict a sharp painful stroke ⟨a heavy whip that ~*s* deep⟩ **g :** to wound feelings or sensibilities ⟨remarks that ~⟩ **h :** to cut in surgery **:** OPERATE **i :** to have constricting and chafing effects ⟨a coat that ~*s* at the armpits⟩ **j :** to be of effect, influence, or significance ⟨an analysis that ~*s* deep⟩ **2 a** (1) **:** to divide a pack of cards into two or more portions in order to decide the deal or trump, change the order of the cards, or settle a bet as to who will have the highest (2) **:** to draw a card from the pack in order to decide the deal or choice of seats or partners **b :** to divide spoils **:** SPLIT **3 a :** to go, pass, or proceed esp. with dispatch ⟨~ along a side road⟩ ⟨a launch *cutting* across the harbor⟩ **b :** to go across rather than around **:** make a short cut **:** proceed obliquely from a straight course ⟨~ across the campus⟩ ⟨~ down the alley⟩ **c :** to move away quickly **:** leave hurriedly **d :** to execute a dancing coupé **e :** to move swiftly as if passing through — usu. with *through* ⟨a yacht *cutting* through the water⟩ **f :** to describe an often oblique or diagonal line ⟨a road that ~*s* through the swamp⟩ **g :** to change in direction **:** VEER, SWERVE, TURN ⟨the carriage ~ to the right⟩; *esp* **:** to swerve sharply from one's original direction so as to elude an opponent ⟨an end who ~*s* in to receive a pass⟩ ⟨a wing who must ~ in order to get around the defense⟩ **h :** to make an abrupt transition from one sound or image to another in motion pictures, radio, or television **i :** to stop a dancing couple and take the place of one of the partners — usu. used with *in* **4** *of a color in a painting* **:** to stand out prominently **5 a :** to absent oneself from an appointment or academic session **b :** to cease photographing motion pictures **c** *of an engine or machine* **:** to fail or cease operation

syn CARVE, SLIT, SLASH, CHOP, HEW: CUT is a general term without much connotational force and is generally interchangeable with the others in this group. CARVE, in earlier English likewise general in meaning, is likely now to suggest purposive, deft, and careful cutting with a sharp knife or chisel to achieve a desired form or shape ⟨*carve* a figure from wood⟩ ⟨a statue *carved* from granite⟩ SLIT indicates a narrow lengthwise cutting with a sharp instrument, often with some skill or dexterity ⟨the surgeon *slit* the abdominal wall above the appendix⟩ ⟨*slit* a sealed envelope⟩ CARVE and SLIT may indicate care, skill, deftness, and restraint; SLASH, CHOP, and HEW are likely to suggest violent forceful action. SLASH may suggest swinging sweeping strokes made forcefully or fiercely without precision in direction and inflicting gashes with a long blade as of a sword, machete, or straight razor ⟨his face was *slashed* with dueling scars⟩ ⟨*slashing* their way through the jungle⟩ CHOP involves cutting with rough heavy blows made without precision with a heavier tool like a hatchet or chopping knife ⟨*chopping* the wood into stove lengths⟩ ⟨the workmen *chopped* down the tree⟩ HEW may suggest sustained great energy in cutting with a heavy tool like an ax or large chisel through something large or difficult ⟨*hew* down a forest⟩ ⟨*hew* a crypt out of the rock⟩

— **cut adrift :** to sever the connections of **:** leave or become independent or derelict — **cut a feather** *of a ship* **:** to cause the water to rise in a feathery foam or spray on each side of the stem when under way — **cut and run 1 :** to cut mooring cables and sail before the wind **2 :** to hurry off abruptly ⟨hearing the alarm, the gang *cut and ran*⟩ — **cut a rug** *slang* **:** DANCE; *esp* **:** JITTERBUG — **cut a rusty :** to be clever or otherwise noticeable — **cut a swathe :** to make an impression **:** have an effect **:** attract attention — **cut both ways** *or* **cut two ways :** to have a mixed effect **:** have both favorable and unfavorable results or implications **:** avail for either of two counterarguments or implications ⟨a fact that *cuts both ways* in the case⟩ — **cut corners** *also* **cut a corner :** to perform some action in the quickest, easiest, or cheapest way **:** cut out inessentials **:** neglect strict requirements for the sake of expediency ⟨the factory has increased profits 10 per cent by *cutting corners* wherever possible⟩ ⟨*cut a corner* in simplifying the inspection⟩ — **cut fine :** to be precise or meticulous in treating **:** allow no leeway concerning **:** proceed in by finical consideration ⟨to allow only 90 seconds for this operation is *cutting it fine*⟩ — **cut flush :** to trim the edges and covers of (a book) to the same size — **cut ice :** to have weight or influence **:** be of importance — usu. used in negative constructions ⟨his opinion *cuts* no *ice* with them⟩ ⟨a speech that did not *cut* much *ice*⟩ — **cut into 1 :** DIMINISH, DECREASE ⟨late votes for Doe were *cutting into* Roe's early lead⟩ ⟨the decline of the neighborhood *cut into* the value of his house⟩ ⟨new competitors would *cut into* existing markets⟩ **2 :** to join (a card game) by cutting in — **cut loose 1 :** to free from custody, contact, restraint, or check **2 :** to free oneself from domination, control, restraint, inhibition, or influence ⟨he *cut loose* from his domineering father⟩ **3 :** to act, proceed, or perform with abandon or wildness ⟨the rattled pitcher *cut loose* with a wild pitch⟩ **:** celebrate or enjoy oneself with carefree abandon and lack of restraint ⟨convention delegates *cutting loose* at night⟩ — **cut one's eye :** to glance obliquely — **cut one's eyeteeth** *or* **cut one's wisdom teeth :** to acquire wisdom or sophistication — **cut one's teeth on** *or* **cut one's eyeteeth on :** to learn, do, or perform as a beginning or at the start of one's career **:** start with **:** do while young and inexperienced ⟨he *cut his eyeteeth on* algebra at the age of eight⟩ — **cut one's throat :** to injure irreparably **:** DESTROY, RUIN — **cut short 1 :** to arrest or check abruptly **:** INTERRUPT ⟨his words being *cut short* by the disturbance in the audience⟩ **2 :** to terminate usu. in an untimely or premature manner **:** END ⟨illness *cutting short* his career⟩ — **cut square :** to cut (a postage stamp) from a cover with margins forming a square or rectangle — **cut stick** *or* **cut one's stick** *dial* **:** to run away **:** ESCAPE — **cut the buck :** to act efficiently or rapidly **:** do well what is expected of one — **cut the ground from under :** to deprive of foundation or basis **:** destroy claims or appearances of the validity of **:** destroy the effectiveness or cogency of ⟨a fact that *cuts the ground from under* his argument⟩ — **cut the gun :** to close the throttle of an airplane engine — **cut the knot :** to resolve a difficulty by prompt arbitrary action — see GORDIAN KNOT — **cut the muster** *or* **cut the mustard** *slang* **:** to achieve the standard of performance necessary for success ⟨in our work . . . those of our fellow workers who can't or won't *cut the mustard* must of necessity be shoved out —*Atlantic*⟩ — compare PASS MUSTER — **cut the pan :** to salt out (soap) — **cut to pieces :** to impose crushing defeat and loss upon **:** DECIMATE ⟨a unit *cut to pieces* by the enemy fire⟩ — **cut to shape :** to cut (a stamp) from a cover leaving no margins at all — **cut to the bone :** to reduce to the barest minimum **:** divest of anything that could be regarded as nonessential, extra, or extrinsic — **cut up touches :** to exchange comments **:** CHAT

²**cut** \"\ *n* -s **1 :** something that is cut or cut off **:** a severed

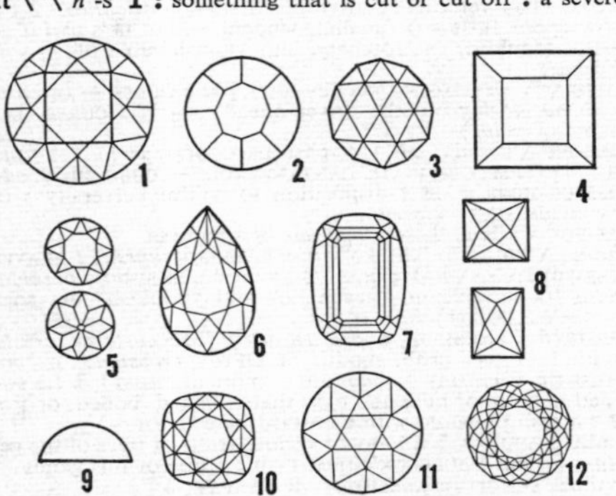

cut 5c: *1* brilliant; *2* single; *3* rose; *4* table; *5* Swiss, top and back; *6* pendeloque; *7* emerald; *8* French; *9* cabochon; *10* Lisbon; *11* star; *12* Portuguese

part or portion **:** DIVISION, SEGMENT, PIECE: as **a** [ME *cut, cutte*, fr. *cutten*, v.] **:** one of a number of straws or sticks cut in uneven lengths and used to draw lots **b :** a slice of food (as of meat or bread) **c :** a unit indicating yarn size based on the number of fixed-length hanks per pound ⟨a 1-*cut* asbestos or glass yarn has one 100-yard hank to the pound; a 4-*cut* has four 100-yard hanks per pound⟩ ⟨a 1-*cut* woolen yarn has 300 yards per pound; a 6-*cut* has 1800 yards per pound⟩ **d** (1) **:** a length of cloth as cut from a loom or packaged for selling varying from 40 to 100 yards in length (2) **:** a section cut from such a length of cloth ⟨he sold 5-yard ~*s* for dresses⟩ **e :** a field under cultivation **:** a specified part of such a field **f :** LUNCH, SNACK **g :** a part of a tree bough from which rails and board may be split **h :** the yield of products that are cut (as grain, timber, or lumber) during a specified period or operation **i :** a segment or section of a meat animal carcass **:** a piece from such a segment ⟨a rib ~⟩ **j cuts** *pl* **:** persons who have cut each other socially **:** former friends now not speaking **k :** a part of a band of animals that has been separated from a main herd **l :** a fraction separated in the course of a process (as distilling) ⟨the lighter ~*s* of petroleum⟩ **m :** SHARE **:** portion of gain, profit, or loot **:** allotment from some often illicit venture **n cuts** *pl* **:** hard candies broken into irregular shapes and sizes **o :** a dispersion of a certain number of pounds of shellac or resin per gallon of volatile liquid paint **p :** a part of salable size cut off from a sponge too large to be marketable **q :** the material removed by a cutting tool **:** the thickness of the chip removed ⟨a ~ of ⅛ inch⟩ **r :** needles per inch in latch-needle circular or flat knitting machines **:** the relative fineness of fabric therefrom **s :** one or more scoring points taken from a show animal for a fault **t :** two or more cars coupled together or to a locomotive but not conforming to specifications for a train **u :** a compass bearing line or a set of intersecting bearing lines that indicate a ship's position **2 a** [ME, fr. *cutten*, v.] *now dial* **:** a man or woman who is disliked; *specif* **:** TROLLOP **b** *obs* **:** PLOW HORSE, CART HORSE **3 :** the effect produced by cutting: as **a :** a notch, creek, channel, or inlet made by excavation or worn by natural action (as of water) ⟨a ~ or canal⟩ **b :** an opening made with an edged instrument **:** CLEFT, GASH, SLASH **:** a wound made by cutting ⟨a ~ in the thigh⟩ **c** *obs* **:** an ornamental slash in a garment **d :** a natural cleft resembling a cut ⟨the ~*s* of a maple leaf⟩ **e :** a surface or outline left by cutting ⟨a clean or smooth ~⟩ **f :** a passage cut as a roadway ⟨a railway ~⟩ **g :** a grade or step (as in a social or economic scale) ⟨be a ~ above one's neighbor⟩ ⟨a few lads several ~*s* above the ordinary —J.F.Powers⟩; *also* **:** a social stratum **h :** a narrow opening in the floor of a theater stage for the passage of scenery **i** *also* **cut point** (1) **:** a mathematical division **:** something that divides into two classes (2) *in the aggregate of rational numbers* **:** a partition or border constituted by an irrational number **j :** the notchings made in a key **k** (1) **:** a printing surface used for a pictorial illustration or matter not readily reproducible in type (as a line or halftone engraving or an electrotype or stereotype molded therefrom) — called also *block* (2) **:** a print or impression from a cut; *also* **:** any printed illustration **4 :** the act or an instance of cutting: as **a :** a gesture or expression that wounds the feelings (as a harsh criticism or sarcastic remark); *esp* **:** personal discourtesy in neglecting to recognize an acquaintance **b :** a straight or easy passage or course ⟨took a ~ through the woods⟩ **c** (1) **:** a stroke with the edge of a fencing weapon — distinguished from *thrust* (2) **:** the motion of giving a cut **d :** a stroke or blow with the edge of a knife or other edged tool **:** the lash of a whip **e :** the act of removing a part (as of a composition) or reducing or dividing as if by use of a knife ⟨make ~*s* in a drama⟩ ⟨a ~ in prices⟩ ⟨salary ~*s* and other retrenchments⟩ **f :** a quick replacement of one foot by the other in dancing — compare COUPÉ **g** *of a horse* **:** the action of cutting **:** INTERFERING **h :** act or turn of cutting cards; *also* **:** the result of cutting **:** a card so obtained **i** (1) **:** a student's voluntary absence from a regular academic class or function at which attendance is expected (2) **:** an instructor's or other official's absenting himself from class or other academic function and thereby canceling its meeting ⟨giving his class a ~ when he was out of town⟩ **j** (1) **:** a stroke that cuts a ball; *also* **:** the spin imparted by such a stroke (2) **:** such a cricket stroke on the off side between point and the wicket; *also* **:** a cricketer who plays this stroke — see LATE CUT (3) **:** a swing by a batter at a pitched baseball **k :** an exchange of captures in checkers **l :** an abrupt transition from one sound or image to another in motion pictures, radio, or television **5 a :** the shape and style in which a thing is cut, formed, or made; *esp* **:** the distribution of material or the design characterizing a garment ⟨clothes of the latest ~⟩ **b :** PATTERN, TYPE, APPEARANCE ⟨an odd ~ of a dog⟩ ⟨others of her ~⟩ **c :** style of cutting a gem **d** [by shortening] **:** HAIRCUT — **cut of one's jib :** the appearance of one's face **:** COUNTENANCE ⟨I like the *cut of your jib*, or you wouldn't be sitting there opposite me —G.N.Boothby⟩

³**cut** \"\ *adj* [ME *cutt, kitt*, fr. past part. of *cutten, kitten* to cut] **1 :** subjected to cutting **:** formed or fashioned by cutting: **a :** detached by cutting; *specif* **:** cut from a growing plant ⟨~ flowers⟩ **b :** sliced, chopped, or shredded; *specif* **:** shredded for use in smoking ⟨~ tobacco⟩ **c** *archaic* **:** showing ornamental cuts or slashes ⟨a ~ doublet⟩ **d** [ME, fr. *cutt* cut (castrated)] **:** CASTRATED ⟨a ~ horse⟩ **e :** cut from a coin of larger denomination — used esp. of metallic money (as pieces of eight) circulated in the West Indies and in parts of the American mainland in the 18th and early 19th centuries **2 :** INCISED, LOBED ⟨a flower with ~ leaves⟩ **3 :** DRUNK ⟨~ last night and unable to remember⟩

cut- *or* **cuti-** *comb form* [NL, fr. L *cuti-*, fr. *cutis* skin — more at HIDE] **:** skin ⟨*cutin*⟩ ⟨*cuticolor*⟩ ⟨*cutigeral*⟩ **:** cuticle ⟨*cutification*⟩

cut across *vt* **1 :** to avoid following or being subsumed, defined, or determined by or in accordance with **:** COUNTER, TRANSCEND ⟨an issue that *cuts across* party lines⟩ **2 :** to include within the scope of effect or significance ⟨a development that *cuts across* all strata of society⟩

cut-and-come-again \ˌ⸗⸗ˌ⸗⸗\ *n* -s **:** TEN-WEEK STOCK

cut-and-cover \ˌ⸗⸗ˈ⸗⸗\ *adj* **:** constructed in a cut or trench and after completion covered as with some of the excavated material or paving ⟨a *cut-and-cover* conduit⟩

cut-and-dried *also* **cut-and-dry** \ˌ⸗⸗ˈ⸗\ *adj* **:** in accordance with a plan, set procedure, or formula **:** without spontaneity, freshness, interest, or novel development **:** ROUTINE ⟨their plans were *cut-and-dried*, down to the smallest detail —E.A. Peers⟩ ⟨a *cut-and-dried* committee meeting⟩

cut and fill *n* **1 :** the leveling or gradational process whereby waves, currents, streams, or winds erode material from one place and deposit it near by until the surfaces of erosion and deposition become continuous and uniform in grade; *esp* **:** the action of a meandering stream in cutting from its concave banks and depositing within its loops **2 :** the excavating of material in one place and the depositing of it nearby (as in building a road or canal) ⟨wholly obscured by the construction of two later highways, demanding a considerable amount of *cut and fill* —G.R.Stewart⟩

cut and thrust *n* **1 :** cutting and thrusting with a sword **2 :** the interplay of a sharp struggle ⟨the inevitability of war between the two . . . powers was implicit . . . in the *cut and thrust* necessarily concealed at the time —*Times Lit. Supp.*⟩

cut-and-try \ˌ⸗⸗ˈ⸗\ *adj* **:** marked by experimental procedure **:** EMPIRICAL ⟨there were no analytical procedures to help him, but although he had to work by *cut-and-try* methods, he thrived —C.E.Waters⟩

cu·ta·ne·al \kyüˈtānēəl\ *adj* [NL *cutaneus* + E *-al*] **:** CUTANEOUS

cutaneo- *comb form* [F *cutanéo-*, fr. *cutané* cutaneous, fr. NL *cutaneus*] **:** skin and ⟨*cutaneo*visceral⟩

cu·ta·ne·ous \kyüˈtānēəs\ *adj* [NL *cutaneus*, fr. L *cutis* skin — more at HIDE] **:** of or relating to the skin **:** existing on or affecting the skin ⟨a ~ nerve⟩ ⟨a ~ infection⟩ ⟨~ test⟩ — **cu·ta·ne·ous·ly** *adv*

cutaneous sensation *n* **:** a sensation (as of warmth, cold, contact, or pain) aroused by stimulation of end organs in the skin

¹**cutaway** \ˈ⸗⸗,⸗\ *adj* [fr. past part. of *cut away*, v.] **1 :** having parts cut away **:** made or styled quite trim or scant as if to suggest that some materials have been cut off or away ⟨a dress with ~ shoulders⟩ **2 :** having a cutting action ⟨a ~ harrow⟩ **3 :** illustrating or conforming to a style of pictorial presentation in which an outer surface or cover is not fully shown and in which inner details are made apparent ⟨a ~ picture of the street showing the subway below⟩

²**cutaway** \"\ *n* -s **1** *also* **cutaway coat :** a coat with skirts cut on a tapering line from the front waistline to form tails at the back — compare TAILCOAT **2 :** a disc harrow with notched discs **3 a :** a cutaway picture or representation **b :** a shot that interrupts the main action of a film or television program to take up a related subject or to depict action supposed to be going on at the same time as the main action **4 :** a back dive in which the head is lowered toward the board after the takeoff — compare BACKWARD DIVE, GAINER

cutaway coat

cut back *vt* **1 :** to shorten by cutting off the end ⟨*cut back* a word⟩ **:** PRUNE ⟨*cut back* the shoots of a plant⟩ **2 :** to return (a distillate) to a still (as in petroleum refining); *also* **:** to thin (as asphalt) by the addition of lighter oils **3 :** REDUCE, DECREASE; *sometimes* **:** ELIMINATE, ABOLISH ⟨*cut back* military expenditure⟩ ⟨*cut back* reforestation work⟩ **~** *vi* **:** to interrupt the sequence of a plot by introducing events prior to those last presented ⟨then the script *cut back* to the old man's childhood⟩

cutback \ˈ=,=\ *n* -s [*cut back*] **1 :** something that is cut back; *specif* **:** a product (as asphalt) thinned or made less viscous by the addition of lighter oils **2 :** a reduction (as in rate, amount, or number) ⟨a ~ in orders or in production⟩ ⟨budget limitation required ~s in personnel allowances⟩ **:** discontinuance before full quota or fulfilment is achieved **3 :** a shift from a chronological order in narration to events earlier than those last presented **:** a motion picture or television shot in which previously depicted action is reverted to and continued — compare FLASHBACK **4 :** a market animal rejected or put in a lower class than its fellows because of inferior condition or size **5 :** any football play in which the runner cuts back **6 :** a part of a word or pronunciation printed (as in a dictionary) to represent the whole word or pronunciation the missing part of which is given elsewhere

cutbank \ˈ=,=\ *n, West* **:** a steep bare slope formed typically by stream erosion

cut bone *n* **:** raw bone coarsely ground and used chiefly as a feed for poultry

cut card *n* **:** a guide or other card of a card series equipped with a tab for use in filing

cut–card work *n* **:** relief ornament of silverware common in the 12th century consisting of a thin sheet of silver cut into a pattern and soldered onto the surface of the piece usu. around a spout, handle, or finial

¹**cutch** *also* **kutch** \ˈkəch\ *n* -ES [modif. of Malay *kachu* — more at CATECHU] **1 :** CATECHU **2 :** a tanning extract derived from any of several mangrove barks of Borneo and the Philippines

²**cutch** \"\ *n* -ES [modif. of F *caucher,* fr. *caucher* to press, trample, alter. (influenced by F dial. *cauquer*) of OF *chaucher,* fr. L *calcare* to tread on, trample, fr. *calc-, calx* heel — more at CALK] **:** a packet of vellum or tough paper leaves in which gold is first beaten into thin sheets

³**cutch** \"\ *n* -ES [alter. of *quitch*] **:** COUCH GRASS 1a

⁴**cutch** *var of* CULTCH

cut·chery *or* **cut·chery** \(,)kəˈcherē, ˈkəchərē\ *n* -ES [Hindi *kacahrī,* fr. *kaca-* (prob. fr. Prakrit *kacca,* fr. Skt *kṛtya*) + *-hri* (prob. fr. Prakrit *ghara* house, hearth); akin to Skt *kṛtyā* act, action, *karman* act, work and to Skt *gharma* heat — more at KARMA, WARM] *India* **:** a public office for administrative or judicial business **:** COURTHOUSE; *also* **:** any administrative office (as of a planter)

cut down *vt* **1 a :** to remodel by removing extras or furnishings and fittings not completely necessary; *specif* **:** RAZEE **b :** to remake in a smaller size ⟨*cutting down* her older sister's dress⟩ **2 :** to strike down and kill, incapacitate, or take out of activity ⟨the swordsman *cut down* his foe⟩ ⟨was *cut down* by the voters of Washington —Murray Kempton⟩ **3 :** to diminish the scope, volume, or intensity of **:** REDUCE, CURTAIL ⟨*cut down* expenses⟩ ⟨*cut down* the accident rate⟩ **4 :** to separate into parts in ore dressing ⟨*cut down* a sample of ore⟩ **~** *vi* **:** to lessen or retard volume or activity ⟨*cut down* on smoking⟩ — **cut down to size :** to reduce from an inflated or exaggerated importance to true or suitable stature ⟨the challenger looks impressive, but stiffer competition will *cut* him *down to size*⟩

cutdown \ˈ=,=\ *n* [*cut down*] **1 :** DECREASE, REDUCTION ⟨a ~ in production⟩ ⟨a ~ in employment⟩ **2 :** incision of a superficial blood vessel (as a vein) to facilitate insertion of a catheter (as for administration of fluids)

¹**cute** *var of* CUIT

²**cute** \ˈkyüt, *usu* -üd.+V\ *adj* -ER/-EST [short for ¹*acute*] **1 :** marked by acuteness and shrewdness **:** INGENIOUS, CLEVER, SHARP ⟨a most particular ~ lawyer —T.C.Haliburton⟩ ⟨the apprehension of the ~ practical man —Francis Hackett⟩ **2 :** ATTRACTIVE, PRETTY — a generalized expression of approval sometimes suggesting daintiness, fine features, deftness, or delicacy ⟨a ~ kid with pigtails bound in red ribbons —W.A. White⟩ ⟨young, dark and small, with pretty features as regular as if they had been cut by a die. "He's ~," I said —Dashiell Hammett⟩ ⟨a ~ little bungalow⟩ ⟨a ~ wristwatch⟩ **3 :** obviously straining for effect **:** mawkish through affected archness, prettiness, or contrivance **:** ARTIFICIAL, MANNERED ⟨~, self-conscious, and elaborate in its use of trick devices —C.M. Smith⟩ ⟨a bad book, shallow, corny, and unmercifully ~ —L.A.Fiedler⟩ — **cute·ly** *adv*

cute·ness *n* -ES **:** the quality or state of being cute ⟨the delicacy and taste of a fairy story told without ~ —Brooks Atkinson⟩

cu·ter \ˈkyüd·ə(r)\ *n* -S [alter. of *quarter*] **:** a 25-cent piece **:** QUARTER

cu·te·re·bra \,kyüd·əˈrēbrə, kyüˈterəbrə\ *n, cap* [NL, fr. L *cutis* skin + *terebra* borer — more at HIDE, THROW] **:** the type genus of Cuterebridae comprising large usu. dark-colored botflies with larvae that form tumors under the skin of rodents, cats, and other small mammals

cu·te·re·brid \-brəd\ *n* -S [NL *Cuterebridae*] **:** a botfly of the family Cuterebridae

cu·te·reb·ri·dae \,kyüd·əˈrebrə,dē\ *n pl, cap* [NL *Cuterebra,* type genus + *-idae*] **:** a family of chiefly New World botflies that occur under the skin or sometimes in the throat or nasal sinuses of various mammals and that include a botfly (*Dermatobia hominis*) that normally parasitizes man — see CUTEREBRA

cu·te·re·brine \ˌkyüd·əˈrēbrən, (ˌ)kyüˈterəb-, -,brīn\ *adj* [NL *Cuterebra* + E *-ine*] **:** of or relating to the genus *Cuterebra* or family Cuterebridae

cutes *pl of* CUTIS

cutey *var of* CUTIE

cut film *n* **:** SHEET FILM

cut flower *n* **:** a flower cut from the plant for use in decoration

cut gear *n* **:** a gear whose teeth have been machined

cut glass *n* **:** glassware usu. made of flint glass that is ornamented with patterns cut into its surface by an abrasive wheel and polished

cut–grass \ˈ=,=\ *n* **:** a grass having minute hooked bristles along the edges of the leaf blade; *specif* **:** a species of *Leersia* — see RICE CUT-GRASS

cu·thae·an *or* **cu·the·an** \kyüˈthēən\ *n* -S *usu cap* [*Cuthah,* ancient city of Babylonia whence many Cuthaeans were taken according to 2 Kings 17:24 + E *-an*] **:** a member of a group of people of ancient Babylonia who were sent as colonists to Samaria

cuti– — see CUT-

cu·ti·cle \ˈkyüd·əkəl, -üt|, |ēk-\ *n* -S [L *cuticula,* dim. of *cutis* skin — more at HIDE] **1 :** SKIN, PELLICLE, MEMBRANE, INTEGUMENT: as **a :** an external membranous or hardened noncellular investment secreted by the cells of the epidermis or by the outer surface of the body (as in arthropods) **b :** the epidermis of man or other animals lacking a noncellular integument **c :** the cell wall of a unicellular animal **2** *bot* **:** a thin continuous noncellular film of fatty substances secreted by epidermal and other cells on the external surface of many leaves, stems, fruits, and other plant organs, functioning in preventing desiccation **3 :** dead or cornified epidermis (as that surrounding the base and sides of a fingernail or toenail) **4 :** a thin skin formed on the surface of a liquid **5 :** an outermost layer (as the bloom on the shell of an egg or the scaly outer layer of a wool fiber)

cu·ti·col·or \ˈkyüd·ə,kələ(r)\ *adj* [*cut-* + *color*] **:** having the color of flesh

cu·tic·u·la \kyüˈtikyələ\ *n, pl* **cuticu·lae** \-,lē\ [L] **:** CUTICLE 1a; *specif* **:** the outer body wall of an insect, secreted by the hypodermis

cu·tic·u·lar \(ˈ)kyüˈtikyələ(r)\ *adj* [L *cuticula* + E *-ar*] **:** of or relating to a cuticle or cuticula **:** EPIDERMAL

cu·tic·u·lar·i·za·tion \kyü,tikyələrəˈzāshən\ *n* -S **:** the state of being or process of becoming cuticularized ⟨heavy root ~⟩ ⟨gradual ~ of the vaginal mucosa⟩

cu·tic·u·lar·ized \=ˈ===,rīzd\ *adj* **1 :** covered with or altered into cuticle ⟨a ~ surface⟩ ⟨~ cells⟩ **2 :** CUTINIZED

cuticular transpiration *n* **:** the transpiration of gases or vapor directly through the external membranes

cu·tic·u·late \-lət, -,lāt\ *adj* [L *cuticula* + E *-ate*] **:** possessing a cuticle

cu·ti·dure \ˈkyüd·ə,d(y)ù(ə)r\ *also* **cu·ti·du·ris** \,kyüd·əˈd(y)ürəs\ *n, pl* **cuti·dures** \-,d(y)ù(ə)rz, -ˈd(y)ù(,)rēz\ [*cutidure* fr. F, fr. *cut-* + *dure,* fem. of *dur* hard, fr. L *durus, cutiduris* fr. NL, fr. F *cutidure* — more at DURE] **:** CORONARY CUSHION

cut·ie *or* **cut·ey** \ˈkyüd·|ē, -üt|, |i\ *n, pl* **cuties** *or* **cuteys** [*cute* + *-ie, -ey*] **1 :** an attractive person; *esp* **:** a pretty girl **2 :** an athlete who attempts to outthink and outmaneuver an opponent

cutie pie *n* **1** *slang* **:** a cute person **:** SWEETHEART **2 :** a portable gamma-radiation detecting and measuring and beta-radiation detecting instrument that includes an ionization chamber and a direct-reading microammeter with a pointer

cu·ti·fi·ca·tion \,kyüd·əfəˈkāshən\ *n* -S [*cuticle* + *-fication*] **:** formation of cuticle

cu·tig·er·al \(ˈ)kyüˈtijərəl\ *adj* [ISV *cut-* + L *gerere* to bear + ISV *-al* — more at CAST] **:** bearing skin

cutigeral cavity *n* **:** the depression on the inner superior border of a horse's hoof

cut in *vi* **1 :** to thrust oneself usu. with abruptness or force into a position between others or belonging to another; *specif* **:** to drive a vehicle rapidly into place in a moving line of vehicles ⟨there was a steady flow of traffic on the avenue, but we managed to *cut in*⟩ **2 :** to join a card game previously begun by other persons **3 :** to interrupt **:** interpose sharply **:** join in anything suddenly — often used with *on* ⟨*cutting in* on the conversation⟩ **4 :** to interrupt a dancing couple and take one of them for one's partner — often used with *on* **5 :** to become connected or started in operation usu. automatically ⟨when more power is needed, the auxiliary motor *cuts in*⟩ **6 :** to cut blubber from a newly killed whale **~** *vt* **1 :** to cut up (a whale) to obtain blubber **2 :** to mix (as fat and flour for pastry) with cutting motions of a knife, spatula, or blender **3 :** to introduce into a number, group, or sequence ⟨*cut in* titles in a motion picture⟩ **4 :** to connect (a piece of electrical apparatus) into a circuit **:** to connect (as a part or an engine) to a mechanical apparatus so as to permit or facilitate its operation ⟨*cut in* a spare fuel tank⟩ ⟨*cut in* a rocket engine⟩ **5 :** INCLUDE; *specif* **:** to include among those benefiting or favored — often used with *on* ⟨*cut* them *in* on the profit⟩

¹**cut–in** \ˈ=,=\ *n, pl* **cut–ins** [*cut in*] **:** something cut in: as **a :** a shot inserted in a motion picture or television program in interruption of the main action **b :** a radio or television announcement or advertising message originating locally and introduced into a network program **c :** a share in another's royalties or profits ⟨a singer receiving a *cut-in* from publisher and author⟩ **:** a person receiving such a share **d :** a heading or illustration placed in a space provided by beginning or ending consecutive lines of text short of the column edge

²**cut–in** \"\ *adj* [*cut in*] **1 :** inserted by or as if by cutting **2 :** marked by cutting in on dancing partners ⟨a *cut-in* affair⟩ **3 :** occupying space left by lines shorter than the full-length lines of a column or paragraph ⟨a *cut-in* heading or illustration⟩

cu·tin \ˈkyüt°n\ *n* -S [ISV *cut-* + *-in;* orig. formed as F *cutine*] **:** the insoluble water-impermeable complex aggregate of waxes, fatty acids, soaps, higher alcohols, and resinous material that is found as a continuous external lamella on the outer wall of the epidermis in leaf and stem of plants — compare CUTICLE, SUBERIN

cu·tin·i·za·tion \,kyüt°nəˈzāshən\ *n* -S [ISV *cutinize* + *-ation*] **:** infiltration of plant cell walls with cutin — compare CUTICULARIZATION, SUBERIZATION

cu·tin·ized \ˈ==,īzd\ *adj* [*cutin* + *-ized*] **:** infiltrated with cutin ⟨~ epidermal cells⟩

cu·tis \ˈkyüd·əs\ *or* **cutis ve·ra** \ˌ=ˈ=ˈvirə\ *n, pl* **cu·tes** \ˈkyü,tēz\ *or* **cutises** *or* **cutes ve·rae** \ˌkyü,tēzˈvi,rē\ [*cutis* fr. L, skin; *cutis vera* fr. L, lit., true skin — more at HIDE] **:** the dermis of the skin

cutis an·se·ri·na \ˌ==,an(t)səˈrīnə\ *n, pl* **cutes anseri·nae** \-ī,nē\ [NL, lit., goose skin] **:** GOOSEFLESH

cutis plate *n* **:** DERMATOME 2a

cut·lash \ˈkət,lash\ *n* -ES [by folk etymology] **:** CUTLASS

cut·lass *also* **cut·las** \ˈkətləs\ *n* -ES [alter. of earlier *coutelace,* fr. MF *coutelas,* aug. of *coutel* knife, fr. L *cultellus* small knife, dim. of *culter* knife — more at COLTER] **1 a :** a short heavy curving cutting sword formerly used by sailors on war vessels **2 :** MACHETE

cutlass 1

cutlass fish *n* **:** any fish of the family Trichiuridae; *esp* **:** a long thin fish (*Trichiurus lepturus*) often occurring on the coasts of the southern U.S. and the West Indies

cut–leaved \ˈ=ˈ=\ *also* **cut–leaf** \ˈ=,=\ *adj* **:** having leaves that are more than normally divided ⟨*cut-leaved* maple⟩

cut·ler \ˈkətlə(r)\ *n* -S [ME, fr. MF *coutelier,* fr. LL *cultellarius,* fr. L *cultellus* small knife + *-arius* -ary — more at CUTLASS] **:** a person that makes, deals in, or repairs cutlery

cut·le·ria \,kətˈlirēə\ *n, cap* [NL, fr. Manasseh *Cutler* †1823 Am. clergyman and botanist + NL *-ia*] **:** a genus (the type of the family Cutleriaceae) of marine brown algae characterized by true alternation of generations, the gametophyte being an upright plant with a broad flat forking thallus and the sporophyte a flat lobed disk — **cut·le·ri·a·ceous** \ˌkət¦lirēˈāshəs\ *adj*

cut·le·ri·a·ce·ae \ˌ=ˌ==ˈāsē,ē\ *n pl, cap* [NL, fr. *Cutleria,* type genus + *-aceae*] **:** a family of algae coextensive with the order Cutleriales

cut·le·ri·a·les \-ˈā(,)lēz\ *n pl, cap* [NL, fr. *Cutleria* + *-ales*] **:** an order of marine brown algae (class Phaeophyta) having a flattened blade-shaped or discoid thallus in which growth is partially or entirely trichothallic

cut·ler·ite \ˈkətlə,rīt\ *n* -S *usu cap* [Alpheus *Cutler,* 19th cent. Am. theologist, its organizer + E *-ite*] **:** a member of the Church of Jesus Christ organized in 1853

cut·lery \ˈkətlərē, -ri\ *n* -ES [ME *cutellerie,* fr. MF *coutelerie,* fr. OF, fr. *coutel* knife + *-erie* -ery — more at CUTLASS] **1 :** edged or cutting tools (as shears, knives, surgical instruments); *specif* **:** implements for use in cutting, serving, and eating food — compare FLATWARE **2 :** the business of making or selling cutlery

cut·let \ˈkətlət, *usu* -əd.+V\ *n* -S [F *côtelette,* fr. OF *costelette,* dim. of *coste* rib, side, fr. L *costa* — more at COAST] **1 :** VEAL CUTLET **2 :** a small slice of meat cooked by broiling or frying ⟨pork ~⟩ **3 :** a food mixture shaped to resemble a meat cutlet ⟨cheese ~⟩

cutline \ˈ=,=\ *n* [²*cut* (printing block) + *line*] **:** LEGEND, CAPTION

cut·ling \ˈkətliŋ, ˈkəd·°liŋ\ *n* -S [*cutler* + *-ing*] **:** the occupation of a cutler

cut·lings \ˈkùtlənz, ˈkət-\ *n pl* [¹*cut* + *-lings* (pl. of *-ling*)] *dial Eng* **:** grits of oatmeal or barley

cutlip minnow \ˈ=,=-\ *n, or* **cutlips** \ˈ=,=\ *n pl but sing or pl in construction* **:** an olive-colored cyprinid fish (*Exoglossum maxillingua*) of the northeastern U. S. and adjoining Canada having the lower lip 3-lobed

cut man \ˈ=,=\ *n* **:** a newspaperman in charge of advertising and layout cuts

cutmeter \ˈkət,mēd·ə(r)\ *n* **:** a hand tachometer for determining the cutting speed of machine tools

cut money *n* **:** a currency circulating in the West Indies and in parts of the American mainland in the 18th and early 19th centuries, obtained by cutting the Spanish American dollar or its fractions into halves, quarters, or eighths to obtain small change — compare³ BIT 2b

cut nail *n* **:** a nail cut or stamped from sheet metal

cu·to·cellulose \ˌkyüd·(,)ō+\ *n* [*cutin* + *-o-* + *cellulose*] **:** cellulose associated with cutin in the cuticle of certain plants

cut off *vt* **1 :** DETACH **:** strike off **:** SEVER ⟨*cut off* 20 years of his life⟩ **2 :** to cause the death of **:** end life **:** bring to an untimely end ⟨suddenly *cut off* by a fever in the plenitude of health, vigor, and aspirations —George Grote⟩ **3 :** INTERCEPT, STOP **:** stop the passage of ⟨*cut off* supplies from a beleaguered town⟩ ⟨*cutting off* communications between the defenders⟩ **4 :** to shut off **:** BAR ⟨the fence *cut off* his view⟩ ⟨the river *cutting off* their retreat⟩ ⟨a scandal *cutting* her *off* from society⟩ ⟨*cut off* from one another by miles of moorland —L.D.Stamp⟩ **5 a :** to end suddenly **:** break off **:** terminate abruptly **:** interrupt and silence ⟨*cutting off* hope of reconciliation⟩ ⟨*cutting off* the prisoner's protests⟩ **b :** to turn off **:** stop the operation of ⟨*cut off* the engine⟩ **6 :** SEPARATE, ISOLATE ⟨*cut* himself *off* entirely⟩ ⟨*cut* herself *off* from her family⟩ **7 :** DISINHERIT; *sometimes* **:** to bequeath to (a person) a ridiculously paltry sum (as to indicate displeasure with the legatee) ⟨*cut off* his scapegrace son with a hundred dollars⟩ **8 :** INTERRUPT, STOP **:** turn off **:** stop the operation of ⟨*cut off* a motor⟩ ⟨*cut off* a radio program⟩; *specif* **:** to stop or interfere with (someone speaking on a telephone) by breaking the connection ⟨he had spoken only a dozen words when the operator *cut* him *off*⟩ **9 :** to intercept (a baseball thrown from the outfield usu. toward home plate) **~** *vi* **:** to cease operating ⟨a motor may *cut off* if it is overtaxed⟩

¹**cutoff** \ˈ=,=\ *n* -S [*cut off*] **1 :** the action or act of cutting off: **a :** the act of shutting off admission of working fluid to an engine cylinder **b :** CESSATION **:** suspension of activity, operation, or established trend ⟨a firm ~ in wage boosts had to be made somewhere —*Time*⟩ **c** *music* (1) **:** GENERAL PAUSE (2) **:** a conductor's gesture (as an abrupt sweep of the hand) commanding a sharp cessation of playing **d :** interception by an infielder of a baseball thrown from the outfield to home plate **2 a :** the new and relatively short channel formed when a stream cuts through the neck of an oxbow **b :** any route that cuts away from a main or accustomed course in order to shorten passage **:** SHORTCUT, BYPASS **c :** a channel made to straighten a stream (as for the facilitation of log driving) **3 :** a device for cutting off: as **a :** a mechanism for shutting off the admission of a working fluid (as steam) to an engine cylinder — compare VALVE GEAR **b :** a device in the mechanism of magazine rifles that when in active use prevents the feeding of cartridges from the magazine into the chamber with the gun then being used as a single-loader **c :** any device for stopping or changing a current (as of grain in a chute or water in a spout) **d :** FIRE STOP **e :** a wall or similar structure to stop or reduce seepage and percolation of water **f :** a device to stop passage of light **:** HOOD, SHUTTER **g :** a device for eliminating undesirable sound frequencies **h** *or* **cutoff rule :** a horizontal rule or its imprint separating discontinuous printed matter **4 :** something that is cut off; *specif* **:** the crescent-shaped body of water cut off from a channel when a stream cuts through an oxbow **5 :** the point, date, or period for a cutoff: as **a :** the point in a cycle of operations of an engine at which a cutoff occurs **b :** a date marking the end of a period or operation (as for the submission of offers or the filing of applications for tax refunds) **c :** a point or date where an accounting period ends and settlement or closing is made

²**cutoff** \"\ *adj* [partly fr. *cut off;* partly fr. past part. of *cut off*] **1 :** that is cut off or serves to cut off ⟨~ valve⟩ **2** *of a shoe vamp* **:** cut off at the line at which the toe cap is stitched on

cutoff saw *n* **1 :** a circular, band, or power-driven hacksaw for cutting off metal bars, pipes, or lumber **:** SWING SAW **2 :** a carpenter's crosscut handsaw

cut oil *n* **:** an emulsion of water in petroleum; *esp* **:** one of natural origin

cut on *vt, chiefly South* **:** to turn on ⟨*cut on* the light⟩

¹**cut out** *vt* **1 :** to cut so as to remove **:** remove by cutting ⟨a surgeon *cutting out* diseased tissue⟩ **2 :** to form by erosion **:** EXCAVATE, CARVE ⟨valleys *cut out* by swift rivers⟩ **3 :** to form or shape by cutting ⟨a dressmaker *cutting out* a garment⟩ **4 a :** PLAN, PROJECT ⟨tasks *cut out* for the week⟩ **b :** to form or assign through necessity ⟨have one's work *cut out* for one⟩ **5 :** to take the place of (as a rival) **:** SUPPLANT, ELIMINATE ⟨*cutting out* her other boyfriends⟩ **6 :** DEBAR, EXCLUDE **7 a :** REMOVE, OMIT ⟨*cutting out* the needless explanation in the speech⟩ **b** (1) **:** ELIMINATE ⟨wasteful expenditure that must be *cut out*⟩ (2) **:** to stop or desist from ⟨the children were told to *cut out* the noise⟩ **8 :** to capture (a ship) by cutting off possible defenses or means of escape ⟨*cutting out* a sloop of war from the enemy fleet⟩ **9 :** DEPRIVE, DEFRAUD ⟨*cutting* him *out* of his share⟩ **10 a :** to separate (an animal) from a herd **b :** to thin out ⟨*cutting out* carrot seedlings⟩ **11 :** DISCONNECT **:** detach and separate **:** remove from a series or circuit ⟨*cut out* a car from a train⟩ **:** make inoperative ⟨*cut out* the number 3 motor⟩ **~** *vi* **1 :** to clear out **:** depart in haste ⟨the rest of the gang *cut out* for safety⟩ **2 :** to withdraw from a card game as a result of another player's cutting in **:** cut too low to be one of a card-playing group **3 :** to cease operating or operating effectively ⟨one of the airplane's engines *cut out*⟩ **4 :** to swerve out of a traffic line

²**cut out** *adj* [fr. past part. of ¹*cut out*] **:** naturally fitted **:** endowed with suitable characteristics ⟨not *cut out* to be a lawyer⟩ ⟨*cut out* for stage work⟩

¹**cutout** \ˈ=,=\ *n* -S [¹*cut out*] **1 a :** something cut out or off from something else: as (1) **:** a picture or figure (as of a doll, animal, or building) cut from or designed to be cut from paper or cardboard for children to play with — usu. used in pl. (2) **:** a shape or design (as a printed or lithographed representation of an advertised article) cut out of or designed to be cut out of cardboard, wood, or similar material and used as a holder or background for display of merchandise **b** (1) **:** a piece of painted scenery from which parts have been cut out so as to form apertures or outlines (2) **:** an aperture or an object thus formed **c :** a notable break designed in an otherwise continuing line or surface **d :** a flat pictorial presentation done in metal **e :** an animal cut out from a herd **2 :** one that cuts out (as by interrupting, closing off, or conducting outward): as **a :** a device (as a switch, circuit breaker, valve, or clutch) for interrupting or closing a connection **b :** a valve in the exhaust pipe of an internal-combustion engine through which the exhaust gases may escape without going through the muffler **c** *also* **cutout block** *or* **cutout base :** a fuse block **3 a :** the act or an instance of cutting out **b** *Austral* **:** the end of sheep shearing

²**cutout** \"\ *adj* [partly fr. ¹*cut out;* partly fr. past part. of ¹*cut out*] **1 :** having for its function cutting out ⟨a ~ valve⟩ **2 :** made by cutting out **:** prepared for cutting out ⟨~ designs⟩ **3 :** having parts cut out ⟨a ~ shoe⟩

cutout box *n* **:** a fireproof box or cabinet with hinged door or doors that houses the switches and fuses for the various leads of an electrical wiring system

cutout switch *n* **:** an electric switch that isolates a circuit or piece of equipment after the current has been interrupted by other means

cut over *vt* **1 :** to cut most or all of the merchantable timber of (a forest) **2 :** to open one set of connections on (a machine) and simultaneously to close another set so as not to interfere with normal functioning

¹**cutover** \ˈ=,==\ *n* -S [*cut over*] **1 :** land the timber of which has been cut over **2 :** a disengage in fencing executed over the adversary's foil followed immediately by a lunge **3 :** a change from one procedure or service to another (as from direct to alternating current or from manual to dial telephones) **:** the period of such change

²**cutover** \"\ *adj* [fr. past part. of *cut over*] **:** having been cut over in lumbering ⟨a ~ area⟩

cut plug *n* **:** a cake of pressed tobacco used for chewing

cut point *n* **:** ²CUT 3i

cut proud *adj, of animals* **:** imperfectly castrated

cutpurse \ˈ=,=\ *n* [ME *cutpurs,* fr. *cutten* to cut + *purs* purse] **1 :** a thief who cuts purses from girdles **2 :** PICKPOCKET

cut–rate \ˈ=¦=\ *adj* **:** marked by, offering, or making use of a reduced rate or price ⟨a *cut-rate* store⟩ ⟨*cut-rate* commodities⟩ ⟨*cut-rate* passengers⟩; *sometimes* **:** poor in quality **:** SECOND=

RATE, CHEAP, IMITATION ⟨a mountebank caesar, a *cut-rate* dictator⟩
cut round *vi* **:** to act demonstratively ⟨she shouted and laughed and *cut round*⟩
cuts *pres 3d sing of* CUT, *pl of* CUT
cut square *n* **:** a usu. nonadhesive postage stamp that has been cut square
cut stone *n* **:** stone dressed smooth with a chisel or saw
cut string *n* **:** OPEN STRING
cut sugar *n* **:** CUBE SUGAR
cut·ta·ble \ˈkəd·əbəl\ *adj* [ME, fr. *cutten* to cut + *-able*] **:** capable of being cut
cut·tage \ˈkəd·ij\ *n* -s **:** the practice or method of propagating plants by means of cuttings — compare GRAFTAGE
cut–tail \ˈ⸗,⸗\ *n* -s **:** a tall eucalypt (*Eucalyptus fastigiata*) of Australia
cut·ta·nee \kəˈtänē\ *n* -s [Hindi *kattānī*, fr. Ar *kattān* flax, linen] **:** piece goods of fine linen or of silk and cotton mixed made in India
cut·teau \,kəˈtō\ *n* -s [modif. of F *couteau* knife, fr. OF *coutel* — more at CUTLASS] *archaic* **:** a large knife used in carving or fighting
cut·ted \ˈkəd·əd, -d·ət\ *adj* [ME, fr. past part. of *cutten* to cut] **1** *now dial* **:** cut or cut short; *also* **:** having the skirts cut short **2** *now dial* **:** cut short in expression **:** CONCISE, CURT
¹**cut·ter** \ˈkəd·ə(r), ˈkətə-\ *n* -s *often attrib* [ME, fr. *cutten* to cut + *-er*] **1 :** one that cuts: **a :** one whose work is cutting or involves cutting: as (1) **:** one that castrates animals ⟨a horse ~⟩ (2) **:** one that cuts cloth or fur to measure in making garments (3) **:** one that cuts flat glass or grinds designs on glass (4) **:** an operator of a machine for pulverizing crushed ore samples into powder for chemical analysis (5) **:** a miner who uses hand tools to extract coal in underground areas (6) **:** one that cuts and shapes gems (7) **:** one that cuts or carves building and monumental stone (8) **:** one that edits individual motion-picture shots and assembles them into a finished motion picture **b** (1) **:** an instrument that cuts **:** a machine, machine part, or tool that cuts (2) **:** a rotary cutting tool with many cutting edges (3) **:** a device for vibrating a cutting stylus in exact accord with electrical input in disc recording (4) **:** the cutting stylus **:** the sapphire or diamond point of a stylus **2** *obs* **a :** BRAVO, BULLY **b :** CUTTHROAT, HIGHWAYMAN **3 a :** a cutting comment **b :** one that cuts an acquaintance **4 :** a fore tooth **:** INCISOR — distinguished from *grinder* **5 a :** a boat, usu. broad and square sterned, motor powered or rowed, carried aboard large ships for carrying stores or passengers **b :** a fore-and-aft rigged sailing boat with jib, forestaysail, and mainsail, the single mast now usu. stepped further aft than that of a sloop, the hull formerly being typically of extreme length and depth but now not usu. distinguished from that of a sloop **c :** a small armed boat in the government service, in the U.S. Coast Guard being over 83 feet in length and not classed as an auxiliary **d :** a boat carrying coaches, trainers, and officials at a boat race **6 :** a light sleigh drawn by one or two horses **7 :** a soft brick that can be cut or rubbed to shape **8 :** an inferior grade of carcass beef of which only the ribs and loins are sometimes marketed as cuts, the remainder being boned out for processing into beef products (as sausage) **9 :** a leaf of flue-cured tobacco pulled from the higher portion of the lower half of the stalk **10** *slang* **:** REVOLVER

cutter 5b

²**cut·ter** \ˈku̇tə(r), ˈkət-\ *vi* -ED/-ING/-S [prob. of imit. origin like MHG *kuteren* to giggle, coo] *dial Brit* **:** to talk confidentially or in a low voice
³**cut·ter** \ˈkəd·ə(r), ˈkətə-\ *vt* -ED/-ING/-S *usu cap* [*Cutter (number)*] **:** to assign a Cutter number to
cutter bar *n* [¹*cutter*] **1 :** a bar on a chucking lathe that fits a tool holder at one end and supports a cutting tool at the other **2 :** a bar with pointed guards along which the knife runs in a mowing machine or along which a sickle blade runs in a combine or binder
cutter bounce *n* [¹*cutter*] **:** a tendency of the recording cutter to move up and down continuously during disc recording and produce a groove varying in depth
cutter brig *n* [¹*cutter*] **:** a vessel rigged like a yawl but having square topsails on the mainmast
cutter classification *n*, *usu cap 1st C* [after Charles A. *Cutter* †1903 Amer. librarian] **:** EXPANSIVE CLASSIFICATION
cutterhead \ˈ⸗⸗,⸗\ *n* [¹*cutter* + *head*] **:** any head (as on a lathe) for holding rotating or other cutting tools
cut·ter·man \ˈ⸗⸗mən, -,man\ *n*, *pl* **cuttermen** [¹*cutter* + *man*] **1 :** an operator of a machine for cutting rolls of paper or cellophane to length **2 :** an operator of a power-driven press that cuts out envelope blanks from sheets of paper **3 :** an operator of a machine for cutting strands of smokeless powder into grains to produce explosives having uniform ballistic qualities **4 :** CLUTCHMAN
cut·ter number \ˈkəd·ə(r)-, ˈkətə(r)-\ *n*, *usu cap C* [after Charles A. *Cutter* †1903 Am. librarian] **:** a combination of characters representing an author's surname, composed of the initial letter or the first letters followed by numbers (as M62 = Milne, M64 = Milton), chosen to make the numerical order of the symbols correspond to the alphabetical order of the names, and used to arrange books in the same class alphabetically by authors
cut terrace *n*, *geol* **:** a bench or platform cut by waves at the base of a cliff — applied esp. after the bench has emerged
cutters *pl of* CUTTER, *pres 3d sing of* CUTTER
cutter yacht *n* [¹*cutter*] **:** a yacht built like a cutter
¹**cutthroat** \ˈ⸗,⸗\ *n* [¹*cut* + *throat*] **1 :** one likely to cut throats **:** MURDERER **:** a murderous character **:** a hired killer; *sometimes* **:** one fierce and unprincipled ⟨a band of ~s that terrorized the area⟩ **2** *or* **cutthroat finch :** a small African bird (*Amadina fasciata*) resembling a finch and having a deep crimson band about the throat and the rest of the plumage grayish brown marked with white **3** [by shortening] **:** CUTTHROAT TROUT **4 a :** any cutthroat game **b :** CUTTHROAT CONTRACT **5 :** straight razor **6 :** KOSHER HIDE
²**cutthroat** \ˈ"\ *adj* **1 :** having the characteristics of a cutthroat **:** MURDEROUS, CRUEL ⟨a ~ rogue⟩ **2 :** marked by fierce and unprincipled practices **:** MERCILESS, RUTHLESS ⟨~ competition⟩ **:** difficult to win, gain from, or compete against ⟨~ stocks⟩ **3 :** characterized by each player playing for himself rather than having a permanent partner — used esp. of partnership games adapted for three players ⟨~ bridge⟩ ⟨~ pinochle⟩
cutthroat contract *n* **1 :** contract bridge in which partnerships are determined by the bidding **2 :** any of various three-hand forms of contract bridge
cutthroat trout *n* **:** a large trout (*Salmo clarki*) native to cold lakes and rivers from northern California to southern Alaska, attaining a maximum weight of 65 pounds, and typically having numerous rounded black spots and a red mark under the jaw, a pattern subject to great variation in local races
cutties *pl of* CUTTY
cut time *n* **:** ²ALLA BREVE
¹**cutting** *n* -s [ME, fr. gerund of *cutten* to cut] **1 :** something cut or cut off, out, or over: as **a :** a section of a plant of stem, root, or leaf origin capable of sending out roots and used for propagation; *specif* **:** a stem cutting **b** (1) **:** a crop (as of indigo, grain, or hay) that has been cut esp. at a single mowing (2) **:** FELLING **c** *chiefly Brit* **:** an excavation or cut (as for a canal, railway, or highway) **d** *chiefly Brit* **:** a clipping (as from a newspaper or magazine) **e cuttings** *pl* **:** rock particles brought to the surface in well drilling **2** *obs* **:** TALLAGE **3 :** something made by cutting; *esp* **:** RECORDING
²**cutting** *adj* [ME, fr. pres. part. of *cutten*] **:** given to or designed for cutting: as **a :** EDGED, SHARP **:** made for cutting, severing, or dividing ⟨a ~ blade⟩ **b :** marked by sharp piercing cold ⟨the ~ winds of January⟩ **c :** marked by or given to penetrating sarcastic asperity wounding the feelings of others ⟨disagreeably arrogant or contemptuous in a ~ way —Edmund Wilson⟩ **d :** grown or cultivated for cutting ⟨flowers from the ~ garden⟩ **e :** SHARP, INTENSE **:** demanding attention ⟨a ~ whistle⟩ **syn** *see* INCISIVE
cutting angle *n* **:** the angle between the cutting face of a cutting tool and the surface of the work back of the tool
cutting board *n* **:** a board on which material (as leather or cloth) is laid for cutting
cutting fluid *n* **:** a fluid used esp. for cooling, lubrication, rust prevention, or chip flushing in a machine metal-cutting operation or for other special effects in other metal working operations
cutting grass *n* **1** *Austral* **:** any of several sedges of the genera *Gahnia* and *Cladium*; *esp* **:** a widely distributed sedge (*C. psittacorum*) with sharp-edged triquetrous leaves — called also *cutty grass* **2 :** a sedge of the genus *Scleria*; *esp* **:** a high-climbing tropical American sedge (*S. flagellum-nigrorum*) with cutting stems
cutting head *n* **:** CUTTER 1b(3)
cutting horse *n* **:** a quick light saddle horse trained for use in separating cattle from a herd — compare QUARTER HORSE
cut·ting·ly \-ŋlē, -li\ *adv* **:** in a cutting manner
cutting oil *n* **:** an oil or oily preparation used as a cutting fluid; *esp* **:** a water-insoluble oil (as a mineral oil containing a fatty oil) — compare SOLUBLE OIL 2
cutting pliers *n* **:** pliers that have a cutting blade on the side of the jaws
cutting press *n* -s **:** a device for trimming book edges and boards for covers
cutting rule *n* **:** a sharp steel rule slightly more than type-high to be placed in a form in a printing press or in a cutting and creasing machine for cutting paper or cardboard
cutting shoe *n* **:** a horseshoe having a narrow inner branch with nail holes at the toe only used for shoeing horses that interfere
cutting stage *or* **cutting–in stage** *n* **:** a stage rigged over the side of a whaler to support men engaged in cutting blubber
cutting stick *n* **:** a strip of wood countersunk in the table of a paper-cutting machine to receive the knife edge as it completes cutting the sheets
cutting stylus *n* **:** a cutting tool used in disc recording to engrave grooves in the original record
cutting torch *also* **cutting blowpipe** *n* **:** a blowpipe by which metal is preheated with a flame and then oxidized rapidly and removed by a jet of oxygen issuing centrally through the preheating flame
¹**cut·tle** \ˈkəd·ᵊl, ǀtᵊl\ *n* -s [ME *cotul*, *codull*, fr. OE *cudele*; akin to MHG *kutel* tripe, OHG *kiot* bag, pocket, OE *codd* husk, scrotum — more at COD] **:** CUTTLEFISH
²**cuttle** *n* -s [origin unknown] *obs* **:** BULLY, RUFFIAN
³**cut·tle** \ˈkəd·ᵊl, ǀtᵊl\ *vt* -ED/-ING/-S [fr. *cuttle*, n., "folded layer of cloth", of unknown origin] **:** to fold (cloth) in pleats after it has been finished
cuttlebone \ˈ⸗⸗,⸗\ *n* [¹*cuttle* + *bone*] **:** the shell or bone of cuttlefishes used for making polishing powder or for hanging in bird cages to supply lime and salts
cuttlefish \ˈ⸗⸗,⸗\ *n* [¹*cuttle* + *fish*] **:** a 10-armed marine cephalopod mollusk of the family Sepiidae (order Decapoda) differing from a squid in possessing a calcified internal shell; *broadly* **:** any of various other cephalopods (as the squids and octopuses) — see SEPIA

cuttlefish

cut·tler \ˈkəd·ᵊlə(r), ǀt(ᵊ)l-\ *n* -s **:** one that cuttles
¹**cut·ty** \ˈkəd·ē, ˈku̇ǀ, ǀtē, -i\ *adj* [²*cut* + *-y*] *dial chiefly Brit* **:** SHORT, SHORTENED, STUBBY
²**cutty** \ˈ"\ *n* -ES **1** [short for *cutty spoon*] *chiefly Scot & Irish* **:** a short spoon **2** [short for *cutty pipe*] *chiefly Brit* **:** a short tobacco pipe **3** *chiefly Scot* **a :** a small or mischievous girl **b** [perh. fr. ²*cut* (trollop) + *-y*] **:** a woman of loose morals **:** BAGGAGE **4** *dial Brit* **:** WREN **5** *Scot* **:** HARE
cutty grass \ˈ"-\ *n* [by alter.] *Austral* **:** a cutting grass (*Cladium psittacorum*)
cut·ty·hunk \ˈkəd·ē,həŋk\ *n* -s [fr. *Cuttyhunk* Island, Mass.] **:** a handlaid twisted linen fishing line suitable for deep-sea sport fish; *broadly* **:** any twisted linen fishing line
cutty sark *n* [¹*cutty*] **1** *chiefly Scot* **:** a short garment (as a shirt, slip, or skirt); *sometimes* **:** a woman's short undergarment **2** *chiefly Scot* **:** WOMAN, HUSSY
cutty stool *n* [¹*cutty*] **1** *chiefly Scot* **:** a low stool **2 :** a seat in old Scottish churches where offenders esp. against chastity were made to sit for public rebuke
cutty wren *n* [²*cutty*] *dial Brit* **:** WREN
¹**cut–under** \ˈ⸗,⸗⸗\ *adj* [fr. past part. of *cut* + *under* (adv.)] **:** so made that front wheels can go under the body in turning — used esp. of a carriage or wagon
²**cut–under** \ˈ"\ *n*, *pl* **cut–unders :** a cut-under vehicle
cut under *vt* **:** UNDERSELL
cut up *vt* **1 a :** to cut into parts or pieces ⟨*cut up* a steer⟩ ⟨*cut up* a log into timbers⟩ **b :** to inflict great loss on **:** cut to pieces ⟨the attackers being *cut up* by the stalwart defense⟩ **c :** to chop into parts **:** destroy the continuity of ⟨his sleep being *cut up* by the noise⟩ **d :** to wound deeply **:** GRIEVE, DISTRESS, HURT, CHAGRIN ⟨*cut up* by the adverse criticism⟩ ⟨*cut up* by her jilting him⟩ **2 :** to damage by or as if by cutting **:** GASH, SLASH ⟨the new lawn was *cut up* by the heavy truck⟩ **3 :** to sever at the bottom or root ⟨*cut up* weeds⟩ **4 :** to shape by cutting esp. after a pattern (as cloth) **5 :** to criticize adversely **:** subject to carping hostile criticism **:** CENSURE ⟨revenged himself by *cutting up* the author's next publication⟩ ⟨an underlying sentiment among lawyers against being *cut up* by outsiders —John Galsworthy⟩ **6 :** PERFORM, EXECUTE ⟨*cutting up* mischief⟩ **~ vi 1 :** to admit of being cut up ⟨this wood *cuts up* readily⟩ **2 :** to behave in a comic, boisterous, or unruly manner **:** show off **:** CLOWN **:** demand attention by unsanctioned behavior ⟨the average cowboy was a young fellow and he *cut up* plenty, meaning no harm to anyone —S.E.Fletcher⟩ ⟨she *cut up* with other men and after about a year ran off entirely —Danforth Ross⟩
cutup \ˈ⸗,⸗\ *n* -s [*cut up*] **:** one that cuts up and clowns or acts boisterously **:** SHOW-OFF
cut velvet *n* **:** a brocaded fabric with a background of chiffon or voile and a pattern of velvet
cutwater \ˈ⸗,⸗⸗\ *n* **1 :** the forepart of a ship's stem — see SHIP illustration **2 :** a structure built around or upstream from a bridge pier with an angle or edge to resist better the action of water, ice, or flotsam **:** the sharpened end of the pier itself **3 :** BLACK SKIMMER
cutweed \ˈ⸗,⸗\ *n* **:** any of various marine algae: as **a :** BLADDER WRACK 1 **b :** SEA GIRDLE 2
cutwork \ˈ⸗,⸗\ *n* **1 :** an embroidery usu. on linen in which a design is outlined in buttonhole stitch and the intervening material is then cut away **2 :** a method of making lace by supporting it on a fabric foundation
cutworm \ˈ⸗,⸗\ *n* **:** any of certain smooth-bodied chiefly nocturnal caterpillars (family Noctuidae) that hide by day in soil and debris and feed at night on plant stems near ground level or climb into trees to feed on flower buds and that mature in midsummer into egg-laying moths
cu·vee *also* **cu·vee** \(ˈ)k(y)üǀvā, *F* küvā\ *n* -s [F *cuvée*, fr. *cuve* tub, vat] **1 :** bulk wine; *esp* **:** wine in casks or vats so blended by the vintner as to ensure uniformity and marketability — usu. used of French wine (as Burgundy) **2 :** a blend of still wines prepared for use in secondary fermentation in the production of champagne
cu·vette \(ˈ)k(y)üǀvet\ *n* -s [F, dim. of *cuve* tub, vat, fr. OF, fr. L *cupa* — more at HIVE] **1 :** a small often transparent vessel (as a tube or basin) that is used in scientific research **2 :** a carved semiprecious or precious stone with raised design (as a figure like a cameo) on the floor of a hollowed-out background
cu·vie·ri·an \(ˈ)k(y)üǀvirēən, ǀk(y)üvēǀir-\ *adj*, *usu cap* [Georges L. C. *Cuvier* †1832 Fr. naturalist + E *-ian*] **:** of or relating to Cuvier or his classification of animals
cuvierian organ \ˈ"-\ *or* **cu·vier's organ** \ˈk(y)üvē,āz-, küvyāz-\ *n*, *usu cap C* **:** a glandular tubule of uncertain function that can be extruded from the cloaca of certain holothurians
cuvierian vein *n*, *usu cap C* **:** CARDINAL VEIN
cuy·a·hoga red \(ˈ)kīǀhǀōgə, ǀkīəǀhǀ,kəˈhǀ, ǀägə,ǀōgə\ *n*, *often cap C* [prob. fr. *Cuyahoga* river or *Cuyahoga* county, Ohio] **:** OLD ROSELEAF
cuzco bark *var of* CUSCO BARK
cv *or* **cvt** *abbr* convertible
CV *abbr* **1** *often not cap* chief value **2** *often not cap* [It *colla voce*] with the voice **3** common version
c virus *n*, *cap C* **:** COXSACKIE VIRUS
cw *abbr* clockwise
CW *abbr* **1** chemical warfare **2** child welfare **3** churchwarden **4** cold water **5** commercial weight **6** continuous wave
cwm \ˈküm\ *n* -s [W, valley; akin to Gk *kymbē* drinking cup — more at HUMP] **:** CIRQUE 3
CWO *abbr* **1** cash with order **2** chief warrant officer **3** commissioned officer from warrant rank **4** commissioned warrant officer
cwt *abbr* [L *centum* + E *weight*] hundredweight
cx *abbr* convex
-cy \-sē, -si\ *n suffix* -ES [ME *-cie*, fr. OF, fr. LL *-cia*, fr. L *-tia*, partly fr. L *-t-* (as final stem consonant) + *-ia* -y, partly fr. Gk *-teia*, *-tia*, fr. *-t-* (as final stem consonant) + *-eia*, *-ia* -y] **:** act **:** action **:** practice **:** function ⟨pira*cy*⟩ ⟨prophe*cy*⟩ **:** rank **:** office ⟨baronet*cy*⟩ ⟨chaplain*cy*⟩ ⟨general*cy*⟩ **:** body **:** class ⟨aristocra*cy*⟩ **:** state **:** quality ⟨accura*cy*⟩ ⟨bankrupt*cy*⟩ ⟨normal*cy*⟩ — orig. and still often replacing a final *-t* or *-te* of the base noun or adjective
cy *abbr* **1** capacity **2** county **3** currency **4** cycle
cy·am·e·lide \sīˈamə,līd, -ləd\ *n* -s [ISV *cya-* (fr. *cyan-*) + *melam* + *-ide*] **:** a white amorphous compound $(CNOH)_x$ formed by the polymerization of cyanic acid
cy·an \ˈsī,an, -īən\ *n* -s [Gk *kyanos*] **:** any of a group of colors of greenish blue hue, medium lightness, and high saturation; *specif* **:** one of the subtractive primaries
cyan– *or* **cyano–** *comb form* [G *cyan-*, *zyan-*, fr. Gk *kyan-*, *kyano-*, fr. *kyanos* dark blue enamel, lapis lazuli] **1 :** dark blue **:** blue ⟨*cyano*type⟩ ⟨*cyan*osis⟩ **2 a :** cyanogen (sense 1) ⟨*cyan*amide⟩ ⟨*cyano*phoric⟩ — compare ISOCYAN- **b** *now usu cyano-* **:** containing cyanogen in place of hydrogen — in names of organic compounds ⟨*cyano*benzoic acid⟩ **c** *now usu cyano-* **:** containing cyanogen regarded as replacing hydroxyl or oxygen or as coordinated to a central atom — in names of inorganic acids and salts ⟨*cyano*auric acid⟩ ⟨*cyano*ferrate⟩ **3 :** cyanide ⟨*cyano*genetic⟩
–cy·an \ˈsī,an, -īən\ *n comb form* -s [Gk *kyanos*] **:** blue pigment ⟨algo*cyan*⟩ ⟨leuco*cyan*⟩
cy·an·a·mide \sīˈanəməd, -,mīd\ *also* **cy·an·a·mid** \-məd\ *n* -s [ISV *cyan-* + *amide*, *amid*; orig. formed as G *cyanamide*] **1 :** a colorless crystalline acidic compound $CNNH_2$ obtained by the action of ammonia gas on cyanogen chloride and by acidification of calcium cyanamide **2 :** CALCIUM CYANAMIDE — used esp. of the commercial products
cyanamide process *n* **:** a nitrogen-fixation process in which calcium cyanamide is formed from calcium carbide and nitrogen at high temperature
Cy·an·throl \,sīəˈnan,thrōl, -rōl\ *trademark* — used for an acid dye; see DYE table I (under *Acid Blue 47*)
cy·a·nas·tra·ce·ae \,sīə,naˈstrāsē,ē\ *n pl*, *cap* [NL, fr. *Cyanastrum*, type genus (fr. *cyan-* + L *astrum* star, fr. Gk *astron*) + *-aceae* — more at STAR] **:** a small family (order Xyridales) consisting of a single genus (*Cyanastrum*) of tropical African bog or aquatic herbs with tuberous rootstocks and paniculate or racemose flowers
cy·a·nate \ˈsīə,nāt, -nət\ *n* -s [ISV *cyan-* + *-ate*; prob. orig. formed as G *zyanat*] **:** a salt or ester of cyanic acid
cyan blue *n* **:** a moderate bluish green to greenish blue that is paler than gendarme and less strong than parrot blue
cy·an·ea \sīˈanēə, -ān-\ *n*, *cap* [NL, fr. L, fem. of *cyaneus* dark blue, fr. Gk *kyaneos*, fr. *kyanos* dark blue enamel, lapis lazuli] **:** a genus of scyphozoan jellyfishes chiefly of temperate and arctic seas that includes the common red stinging jellyfish (*C. capillata*) of the No. Atlantic coast which reputedly attains a maximum diameter of over seven feet
cy·an·e·ous \-ēəs\ *or* **cy·an·e·an** \-ēən\ *adj* [*cyaneous* fr. L *cyaneus* dark blue; *cyanean* fr. L *cyaneus* + E *-an*] **1 :** CERULEAN **2 :** of a dark blue
cyanhydrin *var of* CYANOHYDRIN
cy·an·ic \(ˈ)sīǀanik, -nēk\ *adj* [ISV *cyan-* + *-ic*] **1 :** relating to or containing the cyanogen radical — used esp. of certain acids and their derivatives **2** [F *cyanique*, fr. *cyan-* + *-ique* -ic] **:** having a blue color; *specif* **:** having blue color in at least part of the flower — compare XANTHIC
cyanic acid *n* [ISV *cyanic* + *acid*; orig. formed as G *zyansäure*] **:** a strong acid HOCN or HNCO obtained by heating cyanuric acid as a mobile and very volatile liquid that is stable below 0° C but at ordinary temperature rapidly polymerizes to cyamelide and cyanuric acid — see ISOCYANIC ACID
cy·a·ni·da·tion \,sīənəˈdāshən, -īə,nīˈd-, (,)sī,anəˈd-\ *n* -s [*cyanide* + *-ation*] **:** the act or process of cyaniding; *esp* **:** CYANIDE PROCESS
¹**cy·a·nide** \ˈsīə,nīd, -,nəd\ *n* -s [ISV *cyan-* + *-ide*] **1 :** a compound of cyanogen usu. with a more electropositive element or radical **:** a salt or ester of hydrocyanic acid — see NITRILE **2 a :** POTASSIUM CYANIDE **b :** SODIUM CYANIDE
²**cy·a·nide** \-,nīd\ *vt* -ED/-ING/-S **:** to treat with a cyanide: as **a :** to subject to the cyanide process **b :** to treat (iron or steel) by immersion in molten cyanide in order to produce a hard surface by causing carbon and nitrogen to be taken up in a thin outer layer — see CASE HARDEN **c :** to fumigate (as greenhouses or flour) with hydrogen cyanide gas
cyanide mill *n* **:** a mill in which the cyanide process is used
cyanide process *n* **:** a method of extracting gold and silver from ores by treatment with a dilute solution of sodium cyanide or calcium cyanide, the dissolved metal being afterwards precipitated from the solution and cast into ingots
cy·an·i·din \sīˈanədən\ *n* -s [ISV *cyan-* + *-idin*] **:** an anthocyanidin occurring widely in the form of glycosides (as cyanin) and usu. obtained as the brown-red crystalline chloride $C_{15}H_{11}ClO_6$ (as by hydrolysis of cyanin or by synthesis from pyrocatechol derivatives)
cy·a·ni flower \ˈsīə,nī-\ *n* [NL *cyani*, fr. *cyanus* (specific epithet of *centaurea cyanus*), fr. Gk *kyanos* dark blue enamel] **:** the blue flower of a bachelor's button (*Centaurea cyanus*) used to color sachet powders
cy·a·nin \ˈsīənən\ *n* -s [*cyan-* + *-in*] **:** a violet crystalline anthocyanin pigment $C_{27}H_{30}O_{16}$ found esp. in the petals of the rose, cornflower, and dahlia; cyanidin 3,5-diglucoside
cy·a·nine \ˈsīə,nēn, -nən\ *n* -s [ISV *cyan-* + *-ine*] **1** *or* **cyanine dye :** any of a large class of usu. unstable dyes that are important in photography for sensitizing film to light from the green, yellow, red, and infrared regions of the spectrum and that are characterized by a structure containing two heterocyclic rings derived from quinoline or a related base (as benzothiazole) and typically joined by one or more carbon atoms — see CARBOCYANINE **2 :** any of a class of cyanine dyes in which the two heterocyclic rings are joined by only one carbon atom (as in =CH—); *specif* **:** any such dye containing two quinoline rings — called also *monomethine*, *simple cyanine* **3** *also* **cy·a·nin** \-nən\ *or* **cyanine blue a :** a blue cyanine dye (sense 2) $C_{29}H_{35}IN_2$ obtained from quinoline, lepidine, and isoamyl iodide; 1,1′-di-isoamyl-4,4′-cyanine iodide — called also *quinoline blue* **b :** a homologue (as the diethyl compound) of this dye — called also *quinoline blue*
cyanine blue *n* **1 a :** a strong blue that is greener and deeper than Sèvres and redder and darker than cerulean blue (sense 1b) — called also *Leitch's blue* **b :** a deep purplish blue that is less strong and very slightly redder than sapphire (sense 2a) and bluer and duller than hyacinth blue or Mazarine blue **2** *also* **cyanine :** a blue pigment consisting of a mixture of cobalt blue and Prussian blue — called also *Leitch's blue* **3 :** CYANINE 3
cy·a·nite \ˈsīə,nīt\ *also* **ky·a·nite** \ˈkī-\ *n* -s [G *zyanit*, fr. *zyan-* cyan- + *-it* -ite] **:** a mineral Al_2SiO_5 consisting of an aluminum silicate occurring commonly in blue thin-bladed triclinic crystals and crystalline aggregates — called also *disthene* — **cy·a·nit·ic** \ǀsīəǀnid·ik\ *adj*

cy·a·nize \ˈsīə,nīz\ *vt* -ED/-ING/-S [ISV *cyan-* + *-ize*] **:** to convert into cyanide

cyanmethemoglobin *var of* CYANOMETHEMOGLOBIN

cy·a·no \ˈsīə(,)nō\ *adj* [*cyan-*] **:** relating to or containing the cyanogen group — used esp. of organic compounds; compare CYAN- 2

cyano- — see CYAN-

cy·a·no·acetate \¦sīə(,)nō+\ *n* [*cyan-* + *acetate*] **:** a salt or ester of cyanoacetic acid

cy·a·no·acetic acid \¦sīə,nō+ . . .-\ *n* [ISV *cyan-* + *acetic*] **:** a colorless hygroscopic crystalline acid $CNCH_2COOH$ obtained by treating chloroacetic acid with sodium cyanide and used in organic synthesis

cy·a·no·auric acid \¦==(,)=+ . . .-\ *n* [*cyan-* + *auric*] **:** a white crystalline acid $H[Au(CN)_4].3H_2O$ that on heating decomposes into gold, cyanogen, and hydrogen cyanide — called also *tetracyanoauric acid*

cy·a·no·benzene \¦sīə(,)nō+\ *n* [*cyan-* + *benzene*] **:** BENZONITRILE

cy·a·noch·ro·ite \,sīəˈnäkrə,wīt\ *n* -S [modif. of It *cianocrome* (fr. *ciano-* cyan- + *-crome*, fr. Gk *chrōma* color) + E *-ite* — more at CHROMATIC] **:** a mineral $K_2Cu(SO_4)_2.6H_2O$ consisting of a hydrous sulfate of potassium and copper found rarely at Vesuvius

cy·a·no·cit·ta \,sīə(,)nōˈsid·ə\ *n, cap* [NL, fr. *cyan-* + Gk *kitta, kissa* jay; akin to OE *higora, higore* magpie, jay, MLG *heger* jay, OHG *hehara* jay, Skt *kiki, kikidīvi* blue jay] **:** a genus of American jays largely blue in color — see BLUE JAY 1

cy·a·no·cobalamin \¦sīə(,)nō+\ *n* -S [*cyan-* + *cobalamin*] **:** VITAMIN B_{12} (1)

cy·a·noc·o·rax \,sīəˈnäkə,raks\ *n, cap* [NL, fr. *cyan-* + LL *corax* raven, fr. Gk *korax* — more at RAVEN] **:** a genus of mostly green and yellow Central and So. American jays — see GREEN JAY

cy·a·no·crystallin \¦sīə(,)nō+\ *n* -S [*cyan-* + *crystallin*] **:** the blue pigment of the shells and eggs of lobsters and crabs turned red by acids or boiling water

cy·a·no·ethylation \"+\ *n* [*cyan-* + *ethylation*] **:** the introduction of the beta-cyano-ethyl group $CNCH_2CH_2-$ into a compound usu. by means of acrylonitrile ⟨~ of cotton⟩

cy·an·o·gen \sīˈanəjən, -,jen\ *n* -S [F *cyanogène*, fr. *cyan-* + *-gène* -gen] **1 :** a univalent radical —CN present in hydrogen cyanide and other simple and complex cyanides (as ferricyanides) — called also *cyano group;* compare ISOCYANO **2 :** a colorless flammable poisonous gas $(CN)_2$ having an odor like that of peach leaves, variously formed (as by heating mercuric cyanide), and polymerizing readily — called also *dicyanogen*

cyanogen bromide *n* **:** a colorless crystalline poisonous compound CNBr having a pungent irritating vapor and used in organic synthesis

cyanogen chloride *n* **:** a colorless very pungent poisonous low-boiling liquid compound CNCl obtained by the action of chlorine on hydrocyanic acid or a cyanide and polymerizing on storage to cyanuric chloride

cy·a·no·genet·ic \¦sīə,nō+\ *also* **cy·a·no·gen·ic** \¦sīə,nō¦jenik\ *adj* [*cyan-* + *-genetic* or *-genic*] **:** capable of producing cyanide (as hydrogen cyanide) ⟨~ plants⟩ ⟨~ glycosides⟩

cyano group *n* **:** CYANOGEN 1

cy·a·no·guanidine \¦sīə(,)nō+\ *n* [*cyan-* + *guanidine*] **:** DICYANDIAMIDE

cy·a·no·hy·drin \,sīə(,)nōˈhīdrən\ *also* **cy·an·hy·drin** \,sī,anˈ-, -īənˈ-\ *n* -S [ISV *cyan-* + *-hydrin*] **:** any of a class of organic compounds containing both cyano and alcoholic hydroxyl groups usu. made by the addition of hydrogen cyanide to an aldehyde or ketone **:** a hydroxy nitrile; *esp* **:** an alpha-hydroxy nitrile

cy·a·no·maclurin \¦sīə(,)nō+\ *n* -S [*cyan-* + *maclurin*] **:** a colorless crystalline compound $C_{15}H_{12}O_6$ found in jackwood

cy·a·nom·e·ter \,sīəˈnämәd·ə(r)\ *n* -S [F *cyanomètre*, fr. *cyan-* + *-mètre* -meter] **1 :** an instrument for measuring degrees of blueness (as of the sky) **2 :** an apparatus for determining cyanogen or a cyanide

cy·a·no·methemoglobin \¦sīə,nō+\ *or* **cy·an·methemoglobin** \¦sī,an, -īən+\ *n* -S [ISV *cyan-* + *methemoglobin;* orig. formed as G *zyanmethämoglobin*] **:** a bright red crystalline compound formed by the action of hydrogen cyanide on methemoglobin in the cold or on oxyhemoglobin at body temperature

cy·a·no·met·ric \¦sīə(,)nō¦me·trik\ *adj* **:** of or relating to cyanometry

cy·a·nom·e·try \,sīəˈnäma·trē\ *n* -ES **1 :** measurement of the blueness of light **2 :** determination of or with cyanogen or a cyanide **:** the use of the cyanometer

cy·a·nope \ˈsīə,nōp\ *n* -S [Gk *kyanōpēs* dark-eyed, fr. *kyan-* cyan- + *-opēs* (fr. *ōp-, ōps* eye, face) — more at EYE] **:** a person with fair hair and brown eyes — compare GLAUCOPE

cy·an·o·phile \sīˈanə,fīl\ *also* **cy·an·o·phil** \-,fil\ *n* -S [ISV, back-formation fr. *cyanophilous*] **:** a cyanophilous tissue element

cy·a·noph·i·lous \¦sīə¦näfələs\ *also* **cy·a·no·phil·ic** \¦sīənō¦filik\ *adj* [ISV *cyan-* + *-philous, -philic;* orig. formed as G *zyanophil*] **:** having an affinity for blue or green dyes — used of cells or tissues

cy·a·no·phor·ic \¦sīə,nō¦fórik\ *adj* [*cyan-* + *-phore* + *-ic*] **:** CYANOGENETIC

cy·a·no·phy·ce·ae \,sīə,nōˈfīsē,ē, -fis-\ [NL, fr. *cyan-* + *-phyceae*] *syn of* MYXOPHYCEAE

[1]cy·a·no·phy·cean \¦sīə,nō¦fishən\ *also* **cy·a·no·phy·ceous** \-shəs\ *adj* [NL *Cyanophyceae* + E *-an* or *-ous*] **:** MYXOPHYCEAN

[2]cyanophycean \"\ *n* -S **:** any member of the Myxophyceae **:** BLUE-GREEN ALGA

cy·a·no·phy·cin \,sīə,nōˈfīsᵊn\ *n* -S [ISV *cyanophyc-* (fr. NL *Cyanophyceae*) + *-in*] **:** granular protein material forming food reserve in the cells of blue-green algae and concentrated esp. in the peripheral region of the cell

cy·a·noph·y·ta \,sīəˈnäfəd·ə\ *n pl, cap* [NL, fr. *cyan-* + *-phyta*] **:** a division or other category of lower plants coextensive with the class Myxophyceae

cy·a·no·platinite \¦sīə(,)nō+\ *n* -S [*cyan-* + *platinite*] **:** PLATINOCYANIDE

cy·a·nose \ˈsīə,nōs *also* -ōz\ *also* **cy·an·o·site** \sīˈanə,sīt\ *n* -S [*cyanose* fr. F, fr. *cyan-* + *-ose; cyanosite* fr. *cyanose* + *-ite*] **:** CHALCANTHITE

cy·a·nosed \ˈsīə,nōzd, -ōst\ *adj* [NL *cyanosis* + E *-ed*] **:** affected with cyanosis

cy·a·no·sis \,sīəˈnōsəs\ *n, pl* **cyano·ses** \-ō,sēz\ [NL, fr. Gk *kyanōsis* dark blue color, fr. *kyan-* cyan- + *-ōsis* -osis] **:** a dusky bluish or purplish discoloration of skin or mucous membranes due to deficient oxygenation of the blood either locally (as in certain vasomotor disturbances) or systemically (as in some congenital heart defects)

cy·a·no·spi·za \,sīə,nōˈspīzə\ [NL, fr. *cyan-* + Gk *spiza* chaffinch] *syn of* PASSERINA

cy·a·not·ic \¦sīə¦näd·ik\ *adj* [fr. NL *cyanosis*, after such pairs as NL *chlorosis:* E *chlorotic*] **:** relating to or associated with cyanosis ⟨~ heart disease⟩ **:** CYANOSED

cy·a·not·ri·chite \,sīəˈnä·trə,kīt\ *n* -S [G *zyanotrichit*, fr. *zyan-* cyan- + Gk *trich-, thrix* hair + G *-it* -ite — more at TRICHINA] **:** a mineral $Cu_4Al_2(SO_4)(OH)_{12}.2H_2O$ occurring as a hydrous basic copper aluminum sulfate in bright blue fibrous forms

cy·an·o·type \sīˈanə,tīp\ *n* [*cyan-* + *-type*] **:** BLUEPRINT

cyans *pl of* CYAN

-cyans *pl of* -CYAN

cy·a·nu·ra·mide \,sīəˈn(y)ůrə¦,mīd, (,)sī,anyəˈra¦, ¦_məd\ *n* -S [G *zyanuramid*, fr. *zyanursäure* cyanuric acid + *amid* amide] **:** MELAMINE

cy·a·nu·rate \,sīəˈn(y)ů,rāt, -_rət\ *n* -S [ISV *cyanuric* + *-ate*] **:** a salt or ester of cyanuric acid

cy·an·u·ret \sīˈanyə,ret\ *n* -S [*cyan-* + *-uret*] **:** CYANIDE

cy·a·nu·ric \¦sīə¦n(y)ůrik\ *adj* [ISV *cyan-* + L *urea* + ISV *-ic* — more at UREA] **:** relating to derivatives of symmetrical triazine formed by polymerization of certain cyanogen compounds (as cyanic acid and cyanogen chloride)

cyanuric acid *n* [part trans. of G *zyanursäure*, fr. *zyanur-* (fr. *zyan-* cyan- + NL *urea*) + *säure* acid] **:** a crystalline weak acid $C_3N_3(OH)_3$ usu. made by hydrolysis of cyanuric chloride and yielding cyanic acid when heated; *s*-triazine-2,4,6-triol

cyanuric chloride *n* **:** a crystalline compound $C_3N_3Cl_3$ made by polymerization of cyanogen chloride and used in organic synthesis; 2,4,6-trichloro-*s*-triazine

cy·aph·e·nine \sīˈafə,nēn, -_nən\ *n* -S [ISV *cyan-* + *phenine;* orig. formed as G *zyaphenin*] **:** a white crystalline compound $C_{21}H_{15}N_3$ formed esp. by the polymerization of benzonitrile; 2,4,6-triphenyl-*s*-triazine

cyath- *or* **cyatho-** *comb form* [NL, fr. Gk *kyath-, kyatho-*, fr. *kyathos* — more at CYATHUS] **:** cup **:** cup-shaped ⟨*Cyathaspis*⟩ ⟨*cyatholith*⟩

cy·a·thas·pis \,sīəˈthaspəs\ *n, cap* [NL, fr. *cyath-* + *-aspis*] **:** a genus of small Upper Silurian ostracoderms having the dorsal shield composed of a median plate and three smaller pieces

cy·ath·ea \sīˈathēə\ *n, cap* [NL, irreg. fr. Gk *kyatheion* little cup, dim. of *kyathos* cup — more at CYATHUS] **:** the type genus of the family Cyatheaceae

cy·ath·e·a·ce·ae \(,)sī,athēˈasē,ē\ *n pl, cap* [NL, fr. *Cyathea*, type genus + *-aceae*] **:** a family of tropical tree ferns having the sporangia crowded, stalked, and either naked or more often with a cup-shaped indusium — compare SILVER TREE FERN — **cy·ath·e·a·ceous** \(ˈ)sī¦athē¦āshəs\ *adj*

cy·ath·i·form \sīˈathə,fórm\ *adj* [ISV *cyath-* + *-iform;* prob. orig. formed as F *cyathiforme*] **:** shaped like a cup

cy·ath·i·um \sīˈathēəm\ *n, pl* **cyath·ia** \-ēə\ [NL, fr. Gk *kyathion, kyatheion*, dim. of *kyathos* cup] **:** an inflorescence consisting of a cuplike involucre with the flowers arising from its base (as in the poinsettia)

cy·a·tho·phyl·li·dae \,sīə,thōˈfilə,dē\ *n pl, cap* [NL, fr. *Cyathophyllum*, type genus (fr. *cyath-* + *-phyllum*) + *-idae*] **:** a family of Paleozoic tetracorals esp. abundant in the Devonian — **cy·a·tho·phyl·loid** \¦sīə,thō¦fi,lȯid\ *adj or n*

cy·a·tho·zooid \¦sīə(,)thō+\ *n* [*cyath-* + *zooid*] **:** the imperfect primary zooid of certain compound tunicates (as those of the genus *Pyrosoma*) from which the secondary zooids bud

cy·a·thus \ˈsīəthəs\ *n* [L & Gk; L *cyathus*, fr. Gk *kyathos;* akin to Gk *koilos* hollow — more at CAVE] **1** *or* **ky·a·thos** \ˈkīə,thäs\ *pl* **cya·thi** \-,thī\ *or* **kya·thoi** \-,thȯi\ **:** a long-handled cup or earthenware ladle used esp. in ancient Greece for filling drinking cups with wine **2** *pl* **cyathi** [NL, fr. L] **:** any small cup-shaped cavity or organ of a plant; *esp* **:** CUPULE 1c **3** *cap* [NL, fr. L] **:** a genus of bird's-nest fungi having the fruit body narrowed at the base and flaring at the top — compare NIDULARIACEAE

cy·ber·net·ic \¦sībə(r)¦ned·ik *sometimes* -nē- — *see* CYBERNETICS\ *adj* [back-formation fr. *cybernetics*] **:** of, relating to, or involving cybernetics

cy·ber·net·i·cist \,sībə(r)ˈned·əsəst *sometimes* -nē-\ *also* **cy·ber·ne·ti·cian** \-)nəˈtishən\ *n* -S **:** a specialist in cybernetics

cy·ber·net·ics \,sībə(r)ˈned·iks; *sometimes* -nē-, *a pronunc advocated by the introducer of the term*\ *n pl but sing or pl in constr* [Gk *kybernētēs* steersman, governor (fr. *kybernan* to steer) + E *-ics* — more at GOVERN] **:** the comparative study of the automatic control system formed by the nervous system and brain and by mechanoelectrical communication systems and devices (as computing machines, thermostats, photoelectric sorters)

cy·bis·tax \səˈbi,staks, ˈsibə,s-\ *n, cap* [NL] **:** a genus of tropical American trees (family Bignoniaceae) having digitate leaves with five to nine leaflets and greenish or yellow flowers in terminal clusters

cy·bis·ter \səˈbistə(r), ˈsibəs-\ *n, cap* [NL, modif. of Gk *kybistētēr* diver, tumbler, fr. *kybistan* to turn a somersault; prob. akin to Gk *kyphos* bent — more at CYPHELLA] **:** a genus of large diving beetles destructive to young fishes in hatcheries

cyb·o·tac·tic \¦sibə¦taktik\ *adj* [fr. NL *cybotaxis*, after such pairs as NL *taxis:* E *tactic*] **:** of or relating to cybotaxis

cyb·o·tax·is \,sibəˈtaksəs\ *n, pl* **cybotax·es** \-k(,)sēz\ [NL, fr. *cybo-* (fr. Gk *kybos* cube) + *-taxis* — more at CUBE] **:** a transient orientation of molecules in a liquid revealed by X-ray diffraction effects analogous to those produced by crystals — compare LIQUID CRYSTAL

cyc *abbr* **1** cycle; cycling **2** cyclopedia **3** cyclorama

cy·cad \ˈsīkəd, -,kad\ *n* -S [NL *Cycad-, Cycas* — more at CYCAS] **1 :** any plant of the family Cycadaceae **2 :** a fossil cycadean trunk

cy·ca·da·ce·ae \,sīkəˈdāsē,ē, ,sik-\ *n pl, cap* [NL, fr. *Cycad-, Cycas*, type genus + *-aceae*] **:** a family of very ancient tropical gymnospermous plants (order Cycadales) resembling palms but showing a close relationship to ferns and lower groups in that fertilization takes place by means of spermatozoids — **cy·ca·da·ceous** \¦==¦dāshəs\ *adj*

cy·ca·da·les \,=='dā(,)lēz\ *n pl, cap* [NL, fr. *Cycad-, Cycas* + *-ales*] **:** an order of gymnospermous plants abundant in the Mesozoic but now reduced to a few localized and widely scattered tropical forms that have an unbranched trunk which is tall and arborescent or squat and tuberous with a large pith and starchy cortex and that bears a terminal crown of long pinnate leaves together with one or more very large cones — see CYCADACEAE

cy·ca·de·an \¦sīkə¦dēən, ¦sik-\ *adj* [*cycad* + *-ean*] **:** of, relating to, or characteristic of the order Cycadales

cy·cad·e·oid \sīˈkadē,ȯid, səˈ-\ *adj* [NL *Cycadeoidea*] **:** resembling or related to a cycad or a plant of the fossil genus *Cycadeoidea*

cy·cad·e·oi·dea \=,=ēˈȯidēə\ *n, cap* [NL, fr. *Cycadeae* (subfamily of *Cycadaceae*) (formerly used as syn. of *Cycadaceae*) (fr. *Cycad-, Cycas*, type genus + *-eae*) + *-oidea*] **:** a genus of fossil gymnospermous plants of the Mesozoic era (family Bennettitaceae) having short stout trunks clothed in a dense armor of spirally arranged leaf bases and topped by a crown of fronds

cycad family *or* **cycas family** *n* **:** CYCADACEAE

cycad fern *n* **:** any fossil plant of the order Cycadofilicales

cy·cad·i·form \sīˈkadə,fórm, səˈ-\ *adj* [*cycad* + *-iform*] **:** having the form of a cycad

cy·ca·do·filicales \¦sīkə(,)dō, ¦sik-+\ *n pl, cap* [NL, fr. *cycado-* (fr. *Cycadales*) + *Filicales*] **:** an order of fossil gymnospermous trees or climbing plants first known from the Devonian that had foliage like that of ferns, definite seeds borne on modified leaves rather than in strobili or cones, and secondary wood like the higher gymnosperms but primary wood resembling that of ferns — see SEED FERN

cy·ca·do·filices \"+\ [NL, fr. *cycado-* (fr. *Cycadales*) + *Filices*] *syn of* CYCADOFILICALES

cy·ca·doph·y·ta \,sīkəˈdäfəd·ə, ,sik-\ [NL *cycado-* (fr. *Cycadales*) + *-phyta*] *syn of* CYCADOPHYTAE

cy·ca·doph·y·tae \,=='=fə,tē\ *n pl, cap* [NL, fr. *cycado-* (fr *Cycadales*) + *-phytae* (pl. fem. equivalent of *-phyta*)] **:** a subclass of Gymnospermae comprising unbranched plants with pinnate leaves, large pith, little xylem, and a thick cortex and including the surviving order Cycadales and the extinct orders Bennettitales and Cycadofilicales — compare CONIFEROPHYTAE — **cy·cad·o·phyte** \sīˈkadə,fīt, səˈ-\ *n* -S — **cy·cad·o·phyt·ic** \(ˈ)sī¦kadə¦fid·ik, sə¦-\ *adj*

cy·cas \ˈsī,kas, -_kəs\ *n, cap* [NL, perh. fr. Gk *kykas*, MS var. of *koïkas*, acc. pl. of *koïx* doom palm (*Hyphaene thebaica*)] **:** a genus (the type of the family Cycadaceae) of widely distributed tropical trees having pinnate leaves and columnar stems covered with the persisting bases of the old leaves — see SAGO PALM

cycl- *or* **cyclo-** *comb form* [NL *cyclo-*, fr. Gk *kykl-, kyklo-*, fr. *kyklos* circle, wheel — more at WHEEL] **1 :** circle **:** ring ⟨*cyclo*meter⟩ ⟨*cyclo*tron⟩ **2 :** cycle ⟨*cyclo*grapher⟩ **3 :** cyclic compound ⟨*cyclo*heptane⟩ ⟨*cyclo*olefin⟩ **4 :** ciliary body (of the eye) ⟨*cyclo*dialysis⟩ ⟨*cycl*itis⟩

cy·clad·ic \səˈkladik, (ˈ)sī¦k-\ *adj, usu cap* [*Cyclades*, Greek islands in the Aegean sea (fr. L, fr. Gk *Kyklades*) + E *-ic*] **:** of or relating to the Cyclades islands; *specif* **:** of or relating to the pre-Mycenaean culture that prevailed there — compare MINOAN

cyc·la·mate \ˈsiklə,māt, ˈsīk-\ *n* -S [*cyclo*hexyl-sulf*amate*] **:** a cyclohexyl-sulfamate ⟨~ sodium $C_6H_{11}NHSO_3Na$ is a sweetening agent⟩

cy·cla·men \ˈsīkləmən *also* ˈsik-\ *n* [NL, fr. Gk *kyklaminos, kyklamis* (*Cyclamen graecum*), prob. fr. *kyklos* circle, wheel — more at WHEEL] **1** *cap* **:** a small genus of widely cultivated Eurasian plants (family Primulaceae) having centrally depressed rounded tubers, basal leaves, and nodding white, pink, or purplish flowers with reflexed petals **2** -S **a :** a plant or flower of the genus *Cyclamen* **b :** SHOOTING STAR **3** -S **:** a very dark reddish purple

cyclamen aldehyde *n* **:** a colorless liquid aldehyde $C_3H_7C_6H_4$-$CH_2CH(CH_3)CHO$ having a lily-of-the-valley odor, made synthetically, and used in perfumes esp. for soap; *p*-isopropyl-α-methyl-hydrocinnamaldehyde

cyclamen mite *n* **:** a minute translucent greenish mite (*Steneotarsonemus pallidus*) living on the leaves of the cyclamen and other greenhouse plants and in western No. America being a serious pest of strawberries that causes general dwarfing and death of flowers and fruit

cy·cla·min \ˈ==mən\ *n* -S [It *ciclamina*, blend of *ciclamino* cyclamen (fr. NL *cyclamin-, cyclamen*) and *-ina* -in] **:** a white amorphous saponin constituting the active principle of the root of a cyclamen (*Cyclamen europaeum*) and formerly used as an emetic and purgative

cyc·la·mine \ˈ==,mēn, -_mən\ *n* -S [*cycl-* + *-amine*] **:** a cyclic nitrogenous base (as pyrrole)

cyc·lam·mo·ni·um \,sikləˈmōnēəm, -nyəm\ *n* [*cycl-* + *ammonium*] **:** the substituted ammonium radical corresponding to a cyclamine

cyc·lane \ˈsi,klān, ˈsī,-\ *n* -S [ISV *cycl-* + *-ane*] **:** CYCLOPARAFFIN

cyc·la·nor·bi·dae \,sikləˈnȯrbə,dē, ,sīk-\ *n pl, cap* [NL, fr. *Cyclanorbis*, type genus + *-idae*] *in some classifications* **:** a small family of primitive African and Asiatic turtles related to and commonly included in Trionychidae

cyc·lan·tha·ce·ae \,si,klanˈthāsē,ē, ,sī-\ *n pl, cap* [NL, fr. *Cyclanthus*, type genus + *-aceae*] **:** a small family of plants (order Cyclanthales) that resemble palms and have monoecious flowers in dense alternating spirals or whorls around a fleshy spadix — **cyc·lan·tha·ceous** \¦=,=¦thāshəs\ *adj*

cyc·lan·tha·les \-ā(,)lēz\ *n pl, cap* [NL, fr. *Cyclanthus* + *-ales*] **:** an order of tropical monocotyledonous plants that is coextensive with the family Cyclanthaceae and is sometimes included in the order Palmales

cy·clan·thus \səˈklan(t)thəs, sīˈ-\ *n* [NL, fr. *cycl-* + *-anthus*] **1** *cap* **:** a small genus of tropical American acaulescent plants (family Cyclanthaceae) having milky juice, equitant reedlike leaves, and unisexual flowers **2** *pl* **cyclan·thi** \-n,thī\ **:** any plant of the genus *Cyclanthus*

cy·clar \ˈsīk(ə)lə(r), ˈsiklə-\ *adj* [[1]*cycle* + *-ar*] **:** CYCLIC

cyc·lar·thro·sis \,si,klärˈthrōsəs, ,sī-,\ *n, pl* **cyclarthro·ses** \-ō,sēz\ [NL, fr. *cycl-* + *arthrosis*] **:** PIVOT JOINT

[1]cyc·las \ˈsikləs\ *n, pl* **cyc·lades** \-lə,dēz\ [ML, fr. L, woman's robe with a border around it, fr. Gk *kyklas*, fr. *kyklas*, adj., encircling, fr. *kyklos* circle, wheel — more at WHEEL] **1 :** a sleeveless tunic shorter in front than behind and worn esp. in the 14th century by knights over their armor **2 :** a full-length garment similar to a cyclas but worn by women

[2]cyclas \"\ [NL, fr. L] *syn of* SPHAERIUM

[1]cy·cle \ˈsīkəl, *in sense 6* " *or* ˈsik-\ *n* -S *often attrib* [F or LL; F *cycle*, fr. LL *cyclus*, fr. Gk *kyklos* ring, circle, cycle, wheel — more at WHEEL] **1 :** an interval of time during which one sequence of a regularly recurring succession of events or phenomena is completed: as **a :** a recurrent period of time that is used as a basis of chronology usu. beginning and ending by occurrence of the same natural phenomenon (as the passage of a comet) **b :** a period of time during which something becomes established, reaches a peak, and declines ⟨the early mining ~*s* of gold and silver in the west⟩ **2 a :** a recurrent sequence of events which occur in such order that the last event of one sequence immediately precedes the recurrence of the first event in a new series — compare LIFE CYCLE **b :** a complete course of operations or events returning upon itself and restoring the original state ⟨the common ~ of birth, growth, senescence, and death —T.C.Schneirla & Gerard Piel⟩ ⟨the sporogonic ~ of the malaria mosquito⟩ **c** (1) **:** one complete performance of a vibration, electric oscillation, current alternation, or other periodic process (2) **:** CYCLES PER SECOND — compare HERTZ **d :** a series of operations at the end of which a working substance is returned to its original state usu. with accompanying conversion of heat into mechanical work or vice versa **e :** the sequence of activities repeated in each performance of an operation or task — used chiefly in connection with time and motion studies **f :** BUSINESS CYCLE **g :** a series of changes usu. but not necessarily leading back to the starting point ⟨the ~ of nitrogen in the living world⟩ ⟨the geochemical ~ of an element passing through various processes which may lead to repetition⟩ **h :** a regular periodic fluctuation in the abundance of certain kinds of animals ⟨the peak of the grouse ~⟩ **3 :** a circular or spiral arrangement: as **a** (1) **:** an imaginary circle or orbit in the heavens (2) **:** CELESTIAL SPHERE **b** (1) *in phyllotaxy* **:** a section or turn of the spiral between one member and the next immediately over or below it (2) **:** a whorl of floral leaves **c :** RING 22 **d :** a set of septa or tentacles of like age in a coral or sea anemone **e :** a set of regularly recurring values of a periodic variable **4 :** a long period of time **:** AGE ⟨better fifty years of Europe than a ~ of Cathay —Alfred Tennyson⟩ **5 a :** a group or series of poems, plays, novels, or songs treating the same theme ⟨a sonnet ~⟩ **b :** the complete series of poetic or prose narratives dealing typically with the exploits of a legendary hero and his followers ⟨the Arthurian ~⟩ **6** [by shortening] **a :** BICYCLE **b :** TRICYCLE **c :** MOTORCYCLE **7 :** the series of a single, double, triple, and home run hit by one player during one baseball game ⟨hit for the ~⟩

[2]cy·cle \ˈsīkəl, *in sense 2* " *or* ˈsik-\ *vb* **cycled; cycled; cycling** \-k(ə)liŋ\ **cycles** *vi* **1 a :** to pass through a cycle of changes ⟨the machine automatically ~*s* —*Industrial Equipment News*⟩ **b :** to recur in cycles ⟨prosperity goes *cycling* on from generation to generation⟩ **2 :** to ride a cycle (as a bicycle) ~ *vt* **:** to cause to go through a cycle ⟨~*s* the dry gas back to the natural reservoir —H.L.Ickes⟩

cycle billing *n* **:** a system of billing in which a proportionate fraction of the customers of an organization are billed on each working day of the month to equalize the work involved

cy·cle·car \ˈsīkəl,=, ˈsik-\ *n* [motor*cycle* + *car*] **:** a small 3-wheeled or 4-wheeled motor-driven vehicle

cycle form *n* **:** CYCLICAL FORM

cy·clene \ˈsī,klēn, ˈsi,-\ *n* -S [ISV *cycl-* + *-ene*] **1 :** CYCLOOLEFIN **2 :** TRICYCLENE

cycle of erosion : the sequence of changes in a landscape from the start of its erosion by running water, waves and currents, or glaciers until it has been reduced to the baselevel of erosion which limits the activity of the agents concerned — called also *geomorphic cycle*

cycle of indiction : INDICTION 1a

cycle of the sun *or* **cycle of sundays** *usu cap Sundays* **:** a period of 28 years at the end of which the days of the month according to the Julian calendar return to the same days of the week — called also *solar cycle*

cy·cler \ˈsīk(ə)lə(r), ˈsik-\ *n* -S **:** one that rides or travels on a cycle

cycles *pl of* CYCLE, *pres 3d sing of* CYCLE

cycles per second : the number of recurrences of a periodic vibration or other wave-form activity occurring in the course of a second

cycle time *n* **:** the time required to complete a cycle — used esp. in connection with time and motion studies

cycli *pl of* CYCLUS

cy·cli·ae \ˈsīklē,ē, ˈsik-\ *n pl, cap* [NL, fr. Gk *kykliai*, fem. pl. of *kyklios* round, fr. *kyklos* circle, wheel — more at WHEEL] *in some classifications* **:** a subclass of Cyclostomi coextensive with the genus *Palaeospondylus*

cyc·li·an \ˈsiklēən\ *adj* [Gk *kyklios* round, cyclic + E *-an*] **:** CYCLIC

[1]cy·clic \ˈsīklik, -lēk *also* ˈsik-\ *adj* [F or L; F *cyclique*, fr. L *cyclicus*, fr. Gk *kyklikos*, fr. *kyklos* cycle, circle + *-ikos* -ic — more at WHEEL] **1 a :** of, relating to, or belonging to a cycle **b :** moving in cycles ⟨~ time⟩ **c :** being a cycle ⟨the ~ fate of the individual life —H.G.Wells⟩ **2 a :** of, belonging to, or relating to a cycle of writings ⟨a ~ narrative⟩ **b :** being concerned with the production of cyclic writings ⟨a ~ poet⟩ **3** *classical prosody* **:** being of shortened time value in verse analyzed as logaoedic in rhythm — used esp. of a dactylic foot; compare TROCHAIC DACTYL **4** *of a plant* **:** having the floral leaves arranged in cycles **5 a :** recurrent at definite or stated periods ⟨~ phenomena⟩ ⟨~ breathing⟩ **b** *of animals* **:** subject to cycle (sense 2h) — compare IRRUPTIVE **6 :** of, relating to, or characterized by a ring of atoms ⟨benzene and pyridine are ~ compounds⟩ — see CARBOCYCLIC, HETEROCYCLIC, ISOCYCLIC

²cyclic \"\ *n* -s **:** a cyclic chemical compound

cy·cli·cal \ˈsīklə̇kəl, ˈsik-, -lēk-\ *adj* [F *cyclique* or L *cyclicus* + E *-al*] **1 :** CYCLIC **2 a :** related to or caused by a business cycle ⟨~ unemployment⟩ ⟨a period of ~ expansion⟩ **b :** relating to or esp. subject to the influence of recurring economic fluctuations ⟨a ~ industry⟩

cyclical form *n* **1 :** musical composition consisting of several movements (as a sonata, suite, or symphony) **2 :** musical composition that employs the same theme in several movements

cy·cli·cal·i·ty \ˌsīklə̇ˈkaləd·ē, ˌsik-\ *n* -ES **:** CYCLICITY

cy·cli·cal·ly \ˈsīklə̇k(ə)lē, ˈsik-, -lēk-, -)li\ *adv* **:** in a cyclical manner

cyclic chorus *n* **:** the chorus that sang and danced to the dithyrambic odes round the altar of Dionysus in ancient Greece

cyclic curve *n* **1 a :** the intersection of a sphere and a quadric surface — called also *spherical cyclic curve* **b :** the stereographic projection of such an intersection — called also *plane cyclic curve* **2 :** a curve (as a cycloid or epicycloid) generated by any point on a circular disk as it rolls along a given curve

cyclic function *n* **:** a mathematical function that changes in value by an additive constant whenever its variable arguments pass continuously through a cycle of values

cy·cli·cism \ˈsīklə̇ˌsizəm, ˈsik-\ *n* -s **:** CYCLICITY

cy·clic·i·ty \sīˈklisəd·ē, sə̇ˈk\ *n* -ES **:** the quality or state of being cyclic ⟨an absolute ~ with which men go down into extinction every generation, to be replaced by a new crop of germ cell bearing tyros —E.R.Bentley⟩

cy·cli·cize \ˈsīklə̇ˌsīz, ˈsik-\ *vt* -ED/-ING/-S **:** CYCLIZE

cy·clic·ly *adv* **:** in a cyclic manner

cyclic permutation *n* **:** a permutation in which a set of symbols is rearranged by putting the first for the last (as in *ABC, BCA, CAB, ABC*) or vice versa

cyclic-pitch control *n* **:** control of the lateral and longitudinal motion of a helicopter by means of an adjustable device that varies the pitch of the rotor blades during each rotation cycle so that there can be forward, backward, or lateral motion

cyclic poets *n pl* **1 :** the poets who followed Homer and composed epics on the Trojan war and its heroes **2 :** a series or coterie of poets writing on one subject

cyclic rate *n* **:** the rate of fire of an automatic weapon usu. expressed as number of rounds fired per minute

cyclics *pl of* CYCLIC

cyclic salt *n* **:** sodium chloride and other soluble salts carried inland by wind from a body of salt water and ultimately returned to the sea by rivers

cyclic train *n* **:** a system of gearing in which at least one axis has itself a motion of rotation about a fixed axis (as an epicyclic gear train)

cycling *n* -s **1 :** the action or practice of riding a cycle (as a bicycle) **2 :** cyclic movement; *esp* **:** movement through a circular course **3 :** the cyclic variation due to the lag behind the action of a device (as a thermostat) that is intended to maintain constant automatic control

cy·clist \ˈsīk(ə)lə̇st, ˈsik-\ *n* -s **:** one that rides a cycle ⟨lodging facilities . . . are available to all ~s, as to all other sportsmen who travel under their own steam —*Cycling Handbook*⟩

cy·cli·tis \sə̇ˈklīd·ə̇s, sī-\ *n* -ES [NL, fr. *cycl-* + *-itis*] **:** inflammation of the ciliary body

cy·cli·tol \ˈsīklə̇ˌtōl, ˈsik-, -ōl\ *n* -s [*cycl-* + *-itol* (as in *inositol, quebrachitol*)] **:** an alicyclic polyhydroxy compound (as inositol, quebrachitol)

cy·cli·za·tion \ˌsīk(ə)lə̇ˈzāshən, ˌsiklə̇-\ *n* -s [ISV *cyclize* + *-ation*] **:** formation of one or more rings ⟨~ of open-chain hydrocarbons gives naphthenes or aromatic hydrocarbons⟩ — compare AROMATIZATION

cy·clize \ˈsīˌklīz, ˈsīkəˌlīz, ˈsiˌklīz\ *vb* -ED/-ING/-S [ISV *cycl-* + *-ize*] *vt* **:** to subject to cyclization ~ *vi* **:** to undergo cyclization

cyclized rubber *n* **:** rubber obtained in the form of a white powder or of chips by cyclization usu. in the presence of a catalyst (as stannic chloride) and used chiefly in making adhesives, coatings for paper, printing ink, and paint — called also *cyclorubber*

cyclo- *in pronunciations below,* ˈ==ˈ=ˈsī|(ˌ)klō *or* ˈsi|- *or* -ˌklə\ — see CYCL-

cy·clo·aliphatic \ˈ== *at* CYCLO-+\ *adj* [*cycl-* + *aliphatic*] **:** ALICYCLIC

cy·clo·alkane \"+\ *n* [*cycl-* + *alkane*] **:** CYCLOPARAFFIN

cy·clo·alkene \"+\ *n* [ISV *cycl-* + *alkene*] **:** a cycloolefin of the formula C_nH_{2n-2}

cy·clo·alkyl \"+\ *n* [*cycl-* + *alkyl*] **:** any univalent radical (as cyclohexyl) formed by removal of one hydrogen atom from a cycloalkane

cy·clo·barbital \"+\ *n* [*cycl-* + *barbital*] **:** a white crystalline compound $C_{12}H_{16}N_2O_3$ used as a sedative and hypnotic; 5-(1-cyclohexen-1-yl)-5-ethyl-barbituric acid

cy·clo·both·ra \ˌ==ˈbäthrə\ *n* -s [NL, fr. *cycl-* + Gk *bothros* pit; perh. akin to OE *bedd* bed — more at BED] **:** a Mexican herb (*Calochortus flavus*) often cultivated for its yellow flower

cy·clo·butane \ˈ== *at* CYCLO-+\ *n* [ISV *cycl-* + *butane*] **:** a saturated cyclic hydrocarbon C_4H_8 obtained synthetically as an easily condensable gas — called also *tetramethylene*

cy·clo·chae·ta \ˌ==ˈkēd·ə\ *n, cap* [NL, fr. *cycl-* + *-chaeta*] **:** a genus of peritrichous ciliates that have marginal cirri about a ventral disk armed with chitinous hooks, are commensals or ectoparasites on aquatic animals, and include one (*C. domerguei*) which is sometimes destructive to freshwater fishes in hatcheries or aquariums

cy·clo·coe·li·dae \ˌ==ˈsēlə̇ˌdē\ *n pl, cap* [NL, fr. *Cyclocoelum*, type genus (fr. *cycl-* + *-coelum*, neut. of *-coelus* -coelous) + *-idae*] **:** a family of flattened digenetic trematodes that are parasites in the respiratory organs of birds and that have no oral and often no ventral sucker, an anterior mouth, and intestinal ceca fused posteriorly

cy·clo·converter \ˈ== *at* CYCLO- + \ *n* [*cycl-* + *converter*] **:** an electronic device for controlling the speed of a synchronous motor by supplying it with alternating current of grid-controlled frequency

cy·clo·dehydration \"+\ *n* [*cycl-* + *dehydration*] **:** cyclization involving chemical dehydration

cy·clo·dehydrogenation \"+\ *n* [*cycl-* + *dehydrogenation*] **:** DEHYDROCYCLIZATION

cy·clo·dialysis \"+\ *n* [NL, fr. *cycl-* + *dialysis*] **:** surgical detachment of the ciliary body from the sclera to reduce tension in the eyeball in some cases of glaucoma

cy·clo·diathermy \"+\ *n* [*cycl-* + *diathermy*] **:** partial or complete destruction of the ciliary body by diathermy to relieve certain conditions characterized by increased tension within the eyeball

cy·clo·ganoidei \"+\ *n pl, cap* [NL, fr. *cycl-* + *Ganoidei*] *in some classifications* **:** a group of ganoid fishes having cycloid scales, closely approaching the teleosts in structure, and including the bowfin as the only living example

cy·clo·genesis \"+\ *n* [NL, fr. *cyclo-* (fr. E *cyclone*) + L *genesis*] **:** the process of development or intensification of a cyclone

cy·clo·gen·ic \ˈ== *at* CYCLO- + ˈjenik\ *adj* [*cycl-* + *-genic*] **:** of or relating to life cycles **:** having phases in the course of development ⟨a ~ bacterium⟩

cy·clog·e·ny \sīˈkläjənē\ *n* -ES [*cycl-* + *-geny*] **:** LIFE CYCLE

cy·clo·gi·ro *also* **cy·clo·gy·ro** \ˈ== *at* CYCLO- + ˈjī(ˌ)rō\ *n* -s [*cycl-* + *giro, gyro*] **:** a rotary-wing aircraft whose support in the air is normally derived from airfoils arranged like the paddles of a paddle wheel, mechanically rotated about horizontal axes perpendicular to the plane of symmetry of the aircraft, and having an angle of attack that is always less than the stalling angle

cy·clo·gram \ˈ==ˌgram\ *n* -s [*cycl-* + *-gram*] **:** a photograph made by taking intermittent exposures of a moving object to which a light has been attached and serving to project the motion of that object in dotted curves

cy·clo·heptane \ˈ== *at* CYCLO-+\ *n* [ISV *cycl-* + *heptane*] **:** an oily saturated cyclic hydrocarbon C_7H_{14}

cy·clo·heptanone \"+\ *n* [ISV *cycl-* + *heptanone*] **:** a colorless liquid ketone $C_7H_{12}O$ with a peppermint odor — called also *suberone*

cy·clo·hexane \"+\ *n* [ISV *cycl-* + *hexane*] **:** a colorless

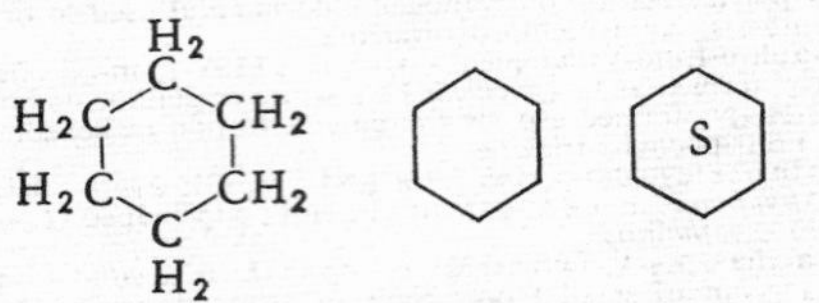

structural formula for cyclohexane (three methods of representation, S denoting saturation)

liquid saturated cyclic hydrocarbon C_6H_{12} having a pungent odor, found in petroleum, made synthetically by hydrogenation of benzene, and used chiefly as a solvent (as for resins and waxes) and in organic synthesis esp. in making adipic acid; hexahydrobenzene — see NAPHTHENE

cy·clo·hex·a·nol \ˌ==ˈheksəˌnōl, -ōl\ *n* -s [ISV *cyclohexane* + *-ol*] **:** a colorless oily alcohol $C_6H_{11}OH$ that has an odor like camphor, is made by the catalytic hydrogenation of phenol or oxidation of cyclohexane, and is used chiefly as a solvent, as a stabilizer for emulsions, and in the manufacture of adipic acid; hexahydro-phenol

cy·clo·hex·a·none \-ˌnōn\ *n* -s [ISV *cyclohexane* + *-one*] **:** a liquid ketone $C_6H_{10}O$ made by the oxidation of cyclohexanol or cyclohexane and used chiefly as a solvent and in organic synthesis

cy·clo·hexene \ˈ== *at* CYCLO-+\ *n* [ISV *cycl-* + *hexene*] **:** a colorless liquid unsaturated cyclic hydrocarbon C_6H_{10} made by dehydrating cyclohexanol — called also *tetrahydrobenzene*

cy·clo·hex·i·mide \ˌ==ˈheksəˌmīd, -ˌmə̇d\ *n* -s [*cyclohexanone* + *imide*] **:** a colorless crystalline antibiotic $C_{15}H_{23}NO_4$ isolated from streptomycin-producing strains of a soil bacterium (*Streptomyces griseus*) that is effective against several yeasts and harmful fungi

cy·clo·hexyl \ˈ==+\ *n* [ISV *cycl-* + *hexyl*] **:** a univalent radical C_6H_{11} formed by removal of hydrogen from cyclohexane

cy·clo·hex·yl·a·mine \ˌ==ˌhekˈsiləˌmēn, -ˈheksələ-, -ˌmə̇n\ *n* [ISV *cyclohexyl* + *amine*] **:** a colorless liquid amine $C_6H_{11}NH_2$ having a strong fishy odor, made usu. by catalytic hydrogenation of aniline, and used chiefly in organic synthesis

¹cy·cloid \ˈsīˌklȯid\ *n* -s [F *cycloïde*, fr. Gk *kykloeidēs*, adj., circular, fr. *kykl-* cycl- + *-oeidēs* -oid] **1 :** a curve traced by any point on the circumference of a circle that rolls without sliding on a straight line **2 :** CYCLOTHYME

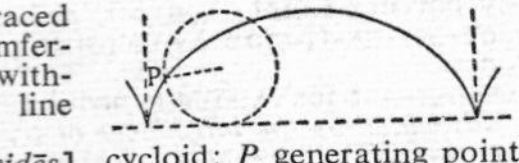

cycloid: *P* generating point

²cycloid \"\ *adj* [Gk *kykloeidēs*] **1 :** arranged or progressing in circles **:** CIRCULAR ⟨~ protoplasmic movements⟩ **2 :** having concentric lines of growth and a smooth margin and surface ⟨~ scales are characteristic of soft-rayed fishes⟩ **:** consisting of scales of this type ⟨~ scalation⟩ **:** having scales of this type ⟨~ fishes⟩ — compare CTENOID **3 :** CYCLOTHYMIC

cy·cloi·dal \(ˈ)sīˈklȯidᵊl\ *adj* **1 :** of, relating to, or resembling a cycloid **2 :** ²CYCLOID 2

cycloidal pendulum *n, physics* **:** a heavy particle constrained to frictionless oscillation under gravity along the arc of a cycloid and having a period that is strictly independent of amplitude

cycloidal propeller *n* **:** a vertical axis marine propeller sometimes used on shallow draft vessels

cy·cloi·dei \sīˈklȯidēˌī\ *n pl, cap* [NL, fr. *cycl-* + *-oidei*] *in former classifications* **:** a group of fishes including those with cycloid scales (as most teleosts) — **cy·cloi·di·an** \(ˈ)sīˈklȯidēən\ *adj or n*

cy·clo·lith \ˈ== *at* CYCLO- + ˌlith\ *n* -s [*cycl-* + *-lith*; trans. of W *cromlech*] **:** CROMLECH 2

cy·clol·y·sis \sīˈkläləsə̇s\ *n, pl* **cycloly·ses** \-əˌsēz\ [NL, fr. *cyclo-* (fr. E *cyclone*) + *-lysis*] **:** the process of decay of a cyclone

cy·clom·e·ter \sīˈkläməd·ə(r)\ *n* -s [*cycl-* + *-meter*] **1 :** an instrument used to measure arcs of circles **2 :** a contrivance for recording the revolutions of a wheel and often used for registering distance traversed by a wheeled vehicle

cy·clo·mor·phic \ˈ== *at* CYCLO- + ˈmȯrfik\ *adj* [*cycl-* + *-morphic*] **:** exhibiting cyclomorphosis

cy·clo·mor·pho·sis \ˌ==ˈmȯrfəsə̇s *sometimes* -ˌmȯrˈfōs-\ *n, pl* **cyclomorpho·ses** \-ˌsēz\ [NL, fr. *cycl-* + *-morphosis*] **:** cyclically recurrent polymorphism occurring esp. in marine planktonic animals possibly in response to seasonal changes in environmental salinity

cy·clo·my·ar·ia \ˌ==ˌmīˈa(a)rēə\ *n pl, cap* [NL, fr. *cycl-* + *-myaria*] **:** a suborder of Thaliacea comprising tunicates with a barrel-shaped body — compare DOLIOLUM — **cy·clo·my·ar·i·an** \ˈ==ˈ=ˈrēən\ *adj*

cy·clone \ˈsīˌklōn\ *n* -s [modif. of Gk *kyklōma* wheel, coil of a snake, fr. *kyklos* wheel, circle — more at WHEEL] **1 a :** a storm or system of winds that rotates about a center of low atmospheric pressure clockwise in the southern hemisphere and counterclockwise in the northern, advances at a speed of 20 to 30 miles an hour, is often violent in the tropics and usu. moderate elsewhere, often brings abundant precipitation, and usu. has a diameter of 50 to 900 miles — see ANTICYCLONE, EXTRATROPICAL CYCLONE, TROPICAL CYCLONE **b** *chiefly Midwest* **:** TORNADO **2 :** something felt to resemble a cyclone esp. in violence or intensity ⟨his story provoked a ~ of laughter⟩ **3** *or* **cyclone collector** *also* **cyclone separator :** any of certain centrifugal devices for separating solid material from gases or liquids (as dust particles from air or skins and seeds from fruit juice) **syn** see WIND

Cyclone \"\ *trademark* — used for a chain link fence

cyclone burner *n* **:** a swirling combustion device for utilizing low-grade pulverized coal as fuel and producing the ash as fluid slag

cyclone cellar *n* **:** a cellar or covered excavation for refuge from a cyclone or other dangerous windstorm

cyclone center *n* **:** the region of lowest barometric pressure about which cyclonic winds are blowing

cyclone plant *n* **:** WINGED PIGWEED

cy·clon·ic \(ˈ)sīˈklänik, -nēk\ *also* **cy·clon·i·cal** \-nə̇kəl, -nēk-\ *adj* **1 :** of, relating to, or having the characteristics of a cyclone **2 :** resembling a cyclone esp. in violence and vigor ⟨a man given to ~ rages⟩ ⟨a voluble, ~, half-mad painter —Roland Gelatt⟩

cy·clon·i·cal·ly \-nə̇k(ə)lē, -nēk-, -li\ *adv* **:** in the manner of a cyclone

cyclonic region *n* **:** the area covered by a cyclone

cyclonic storm *n* **:** CYCLONE 1a

cy·clo·nite \ˈsīkləˌnīt, ˈsik-\ *n* -s [*cyclo*-trimethylene-tri*nitramine*] **:** a powerful high explosive consisting of colorless crystals of symmetrical hexahydro-trinitro-triazine used esp. in detonators, bombs, and shells — called also *RDX*

cy·clo·octa·tet·ra·ene \ˈ== *at* CYCLO- + ˌäktəˈte·trəˌēn\ *n* -s [ISV *cycl-* + *octa-* + *tetra-* + *-ene*] **:** a liquid unsaturated cyclic hydrocarbon C_8H_8 that resembles benzene in its cyclic completely conjugated structure but is much more reactive than benzene and is usu. made by catalytic polymerization of acetylene under pressure

cy·clo·olefin \ˈ==+\ *n* [ISV *cycl-* + *olefin*] **:** an alicyclic hydrocarbon containing an unsaturated ring; *esp* **:** any cyclic hydrocarbon of the formula C_nH_{2n-2} containing only one double bond in the ring

cy·clo·paraffin \"+\ *n* [*cycl-* + *paraffin*] **:** a saturated cyclic hydrocarbon of the formula C_nH_{2n} **:** a member of the series starting with cyclopropane and cyclobutane or an alkyl derivative of one of these — called also *cycloalkane;* compare NAPHTHENE

cy·clo·pe·an \ˌsīkləˈpēən, (ˈ)sīˈklōpēən\ *also* **cy·clo·pi·an** \(ˈ)sīˈklōp-\ *adj* [*cyclopean* (fr. LL *Cyclopeus* (fr. Gk *Kyklōpeios*, fr. *Kyklōps* Cyclops) + E *-an*; *cyclopian* fr. L *Cyclopius* (fr. Gk *Kyklōpios*, fr. *Kyklōps*) + E *-an* — more at CYCLOPS] **1 a** *often cap* **:** relating to the Cyclopes **:** like or like that of a Cyclops **b :** fit for a Cyclops **:** vast and rough **:** MASSIVE, HUGE **2 :** of or relating to a style of stone construction marked typically by the use of large irregular blocks without mortar **3 a :** having or relating to a single median eye or a medially united pair of eyes **b :** of or relating to cyclopia **syn** see HUGE

cyclopean concrete *n* **:** concrete with embedded large stones

cy·clo·pe·dia *also* **cy·clo·pae·dia** \ˌsīkləˈpēdēə\ *n* -s [short for *encyclopedia, encyclopaedia*] **1** *obs* **:** the full compass of human learning **2 :** a work containing information in all departments of knowledge or on all subjects in a particular department **:** ENCYCLOPEDIA ⟨a general ~⟩ ⟨a ~ of mechanics⟩

cy·clo·pe·dic *also* **cy·clo·pae·dic** \ˌsīkləˈpēdik, -dēk\ *adj* [*cyclopedia, cyclopaedia* + *-ic*] **1 :** being a cyclopedia **2 :** of great range or extent **:** INCLUSIVE ⟨a man of ~ knowledge⟩ — **cy·clo·pe·di·cal·ly** \-də̇k(ə)lē, -dēk-, -li\ *adv*

cy·clo·pe·dist *also* **cy·clo·pae·dist** \ˌsīkləˈpēdə̇st\ *n* -s [*cyclopedia, cyclopaedia* + *-ist*] **:** a maker of or writer for a cyclopedia

cy·clo·pentadiene \ˈ== *at* CYCLO- +\ *n* -s [ISV *cycl-* + *pentadiene* (fr. *pent-* + *di-* + *-ene*)] **:** a colorless liquid unsaturated cyclic hydrocarbon C_5H_6 that is obtained by distillation of coal tar, that polymerizes to its stable dimer on standing, and is used in making plastics and insecticides

cy·clo·pentane \"+\ *n* [ISV *cycl-* + *pentane*] **:** a liquid saturated cyclic hydrocarbon C_5H_{10} found in petroleum — called also *pentamethylene;* see NAPHTHENE

cy·clo·pen·ta·none \ˌ==ˈpentəˌnōn\ *n* -s [ISV *cyclopentane* + *-one*] **:** a liquid ketone C_5H_8O with an odor like that of peppermint

cy·clo·pentene \ˈ==+\ *n* [ISV *cycl-* + *pentene*] **:** a liquid unsaturated cyclic hydrocarbon C_5H_8

¹cyclopes *pl of* CYCLOPS

²cy·clo·pes \sīˈklō(ˌ)pēz\ *n, cap* [NL, fr. L, pl. of L *Cyclops*] **:** a genus of edentate mammals including only the So. American silky anteater

cy·clo·pho·rase \ˌ== *at* CYCLO- + ˈfōˌrās, -āz\ *or* **cyclophorase system** *n* -s [*cycl-* + *phor-* + *-ase*] **:** a complex of enzymes associated with mitochondria (as of the liver and kidney) that catalyzes oxidations (as of acids participating in the Krebs cycle), oxidative phosphorylation, and various syntheses (as of hippuric acid)

cy·clo·pho·ria \ˌ==ˈfōrēə\ *n* -s [NL, fr. *cycl-* + *-phoria*] **:** a form of heterophoria in which the vertical axis of the eye rotates to the right or left due to weakness of the oblique muscles — **cy·clo·phor·ic** \ˈ==ˈfōrik\ *adj*

cy·cloph·o·rus \sīˈkläfərəs\ *n, cap* [NL, fr. Gk *kyklophoros*, adj., circular, fr. *kykl-* cycl- + *-phoros* -phorous] **:** a genus of tropical Old World ferns (family Polypodiaceae) having closely crowded circular sori and no indusia

cy·clo·phre·nia \ˌ== *at* CYCLO- + ˈfrēnēə\ *n* -s [NL, fr. *cycl-* + *-phrenia*] **:** MANIC-DEPRESSIVE PSYCHOSIS

cy·clo·phyl·lid·ea \ˌ==fəˈlidēə\ *n pl, cap* [NL, fr. *cycl-* + *phyll-* + *-idea*] **:** an order of Cestoda that consists of tapeworms with four suckers on the scolex and the vitelline glands condensed into a mass adjacent to the ovary and that includes most of the medically and economically important tapeworms of the higher vertebrates — **cy·clo·phyl·lid·e·an** \ˈ===ˈ=dēən\ *adj or n*

cy·clo·pia \sīˈklōpēə\ *also* **cy·clo·py** \ˈsīklə̇pē\ *n, pl* **cyclopias** *also* **cyclopies** [NL *cyclopia*, fr. L *Cyclop-, Cyclops* + NL *-ia*] **:** a developmental anomaly characterized by the presence of a single median eye

cyclopian *var of* CYCLOPEAN

cy·clop·ic \(ˈ)sīˈkläpik\ *adj* [L *Cyclop-, Cyclops* + E *-ic*] **:** CYCLOPEAN 3

cy·clo·ple·gia \ˌ== *at* CYCLO- + ˈplēj(ē)ə\ *n* -s [NL, fr. *cycl-* + *-plegia*] **:** paralysis of the ciliary muscle of the eye

¹cy·clo·ple·gic \ˈ==ˈplējik\ *adj* [NL *cycloplegia* + E *-ic*] **:** producing cycloplegia ⟨a ~ agent⟩ **:** involving cycloplegia ⟨~ refraction⟩ **:** being cycloplegic ⟨~ effects⟩

²cycloplegic \"\ *n* -s **:** a cycloplegic agent

¹cy·clo·poid \ˈsīkləˌpȯid, sīˈklōˌ-\ *adj* [NL *Cyclop-, Cyclops* genus of copepods + E *-oid*] **:** resembling a water flea — compare CYCLOPS 3

²cyclopoid \"\ *n* -s **:** a free-swimming larva of many parasitic copepods that resembles a water flea

cy·clo·propane \ˈ== *at* CYCLO- +\ *n* [ISV *cycl-* + *propane*] **:** a colorless flammable gaseous saturated cyclic hydrocarbon C_3H_6 made usu. from symmetrical dichloro-propane and zinc and used as a general anesthetic by inhalation — called also *trimethylene*

cy·clops \ˈsīˌkläps\ *n* [L, fr. Gk *Kyklōps*, fr. *kykl-* cycl- + *ōps* eye, face — more at EYE] **1** *pl* **cyclo·pes** \sīˈklō(ˌ)pēz\ *usu cap* **:** one of a race of giants in Greek mythology with a single eye in the middle of the forehead **2** [NL, fr. L] *pl* **cyclopes :** an individual or fetus abnormal in having a single eye or the usual two orbits fused **3** *cap* [NL, fr. L] **:** a genus of minute free-swimming copepods that have a large median eye, a pear-shaped body tapering posteriorly, and long antennules used in swimming, that are widely distributed and abundant in fresh waters, that are important elements in certain aquatic food chains, and that directly affect man as intermediate hosts of certain parasitic worms — see GUINEA WORM **4** *pl* **cyclops** [NL, fr. L] **:** a copepod of the genus *Cyclops* **:** WATER FLEA

cy·clop·ter·i·dae \ˌsīˌkläpˈterəˌdē\ *n pl, cap* [NL, fr. *Cyclopterus*, type genus (fr. *cycl-* + *-pterus*) + *-idae*] **:** a family of scorpaenoid fishes having the pelvic fins absent or united and modified into a sucking disk — compare LUMPFISH — **cy·clop·te·roid** \(ˈ)sīˈkläptəˌrȯid\ *adj or n* — **cy·clop·ter·ous** \-tərəs\ *adj*

cyclopy *var of* CYCLOPIA

cy·clo·ra·ma \ˌsīkləˈramə, -ämə, -àmə\ *n* -s [*cycl-* + *-orama* (as in *panorama*)] **1 :** a large pictorial representation encircling the spectator and often having real objects as a foreground **2 :** a curved cloth or wall forming the back of many modern stage settings and used to eliminate shadows and to suggest unlimited space (as of the sky) **3 :** something felt to resemble a cyclorama ⟨his last novel a ~ of bawdiness and confusion⟩ ⟨with the ~ of the mountains rising into view as they paddled slowly up the lake⟩ — **cy·clo·ram·ic** \ˈ==ˈramik\ *adj*

cy·clor·ha·pha \sīˈklȯrəfə\ *syn of* CYCLORRHAPHA

cy·clor·rha·pha \"\ *n pl, cap* [NL, fr. *cycl-* + Gk *rhaphē* seam (akin to *rhaptein* to sew) — more at RHAPSODY] **:** a suborder or other major division of Diptera that comprises flies lacking mandibles and first maxillae and having acephalous larvae and coarctate pupae and that includes the botflies and the common houseflies — **cy·clor·rha·phous** \(ˈ)sīˈklȯrəfəs\ *adj*

cy·clo·rubber \ˈ== *at* CYCLO- +\ *n* [*cycl-* + *rubber*] **:** CYCLIZED RUBBER

cy·clo·serine \"+\ *n* [*cycl-* + *serine*] **:** an antibiotic $C_3H_4NO_2NH_2$ derived from isoxazole that is esp. active against the tubercle bacillus and is produced by an actinomycete (*Streptomyces orchidaceus*)

cy·clo·silicate \"+\ *n* [*cycl-* + *silicate*] **1 :** a class of polymeric silicates sometimes considered a subclass of sorosilicates in which the silicon-oxygen tetrahedral groups are linked by sharing oxygen atoms so as to form rings containing 3, 4, or 6 silicon atoms and 9, 12, or 18 oxygen atoms respectively (as in benitoite or beryl) — called also *ring-silicate;* compare INOSILICATE, NESOSILICATE, PHYLLOSILICATE, SOROSILICATE, TECTOSILICATE **2 :** any mineral belonging to the class of cyclosilicates

cy·clo·sis \sīˈklōsə̇s\ *n, pl* **cyclo·ses** \-ōˌsēz\ [NL, fr. Gk *kyklōsis* act of surrounding, enveloping, fr. *kykloun* to encircle (fr. *kyklos* ring, circle) + *-ōsis* -osis — more at WHEEL] **:** the circulatory movement or streaming of protoplasm within a cell

cy·clo·spon·dy·li \ˌ== *at* CYCLO- + ˈspändəˌlī\ *n pl, cap* [NL, fr. *cycl-* + *-spondyli*] *in some classifications* **:** the sharks having cyclospondylic vertebrae regarded as a natural group

cy·clo·spon·dyl·ic \ˈ==ˌspänˈdilik\ *also* **cy·clo·spon·dy·lous** \ˈ==ˈspändələs\ *adj* [NL *Cyclospondyli* + E *-ic* or *-ous*] **:** having a single calcified cylinder surrounding the notochord in each vertebral centrum — used esp. of certain sharks

cy·clo·spo·ra·les \ˌ==spəˈra(ˌ)lēz\ [NL, fr. *cycl-* + *spor-* + *-ales*] *syn of* FUCALES

cy·clo·spo·re·ae \ˌ==ˈspōrēˌē\ *n pl, cap* [NL, fr. *cycl-* + *spor-* + *-eae* — more at SPORE] **:** a class of brown algae coextensive with the order Fucales and made up of forms having only a sporophytic generation — **cy·clos·po·rous** \(ˈ)sīˈkläspərəs; ˈ== *at* CYCLO- + ˈspōrəs\ *adj*

cy·clo·spo·ri·nae \ˌ≈≈ *at* CYCLO- + spəˈrī(ˌ)nē\ [NL, fr. *cycl-* + *spor-* + *-inae*] *syn of* CYCLOSPOREAE

cy·clo·stage \ˈ≈≈+ˌ-\ *n* [*cycl-* + *stage*] **:** a stage in a bacterial life cycle

¹cy·clos·to·ma \sīˈklästəmə\ *n, cap* [NL, fr. *cycl-* + *-stoma*] **:** a large genus of operculate pulmonate land snails widely distributed chiefly in tropical areas

²cyclostoma \"\ [NL, fr. *cycl-* + *-stoma*] *syn of* ²CYCLOSTOMATA

³cyclostoma \"\ [NL, fr. *cycl-* + *-stoma*] *syn of* CYCLOSTOMI

¹cy·clo·sto·ma·ta \ˌ≈≈ *at* CYCLO- +ˈstōməd·ə, -täm-\ [NL, fr. *cycl-* + *-stomata*] *syn of* CYCLOSTOMI

²cyclostomata \"\ *n pl, cap* [NL, fr. *cycl-* + *-stomata*] **:** an order of bryozoans (class Gymnolaemata) comprising colonial forms with tubular calcareous zooecia having circular apertures without opercula and lacking both avicularia and vibracula

cy·clos·to·mate \(ˈ)sīˈklästəmət\ *also* **cy·clo·stom·a·tous** \ˌ≈≈ *at* CYCLO- +ˈstäməd·əs, -tōm-\ *adj* [in sense 1, fr. *cycl-* + *-stomate* or *-stomatous;* in sense 2, *cyclostomate* fr. NL *Cyclostomata; cyclostomatous* fr. NL *Cyclostomata* + E *-ous*] **1 :** having a circular mouth **2 :** of or relating to the Cyclostomata or Cyclostomi

¹cy·clo·stome \ˈ≈≈ *at* CYCLO- +ˌstōm\ *adj* [NL *Cyclostomi* or *Cyclostomata*] **1 :** of or relating to the Cyclostomi or Cyclostomata **2 :** being a cyclostome

²cyclostome \"\ *n* -s **:** one of the Cyclostomi

cy·clos·to·mes \sīˈklästəˌmēz\ [NL, fr. *cycl-* + *-stomes* (fr. Gk *stoma* mouth) — more at STOMACH] *syn of* CYCLOSTOMI

cy·clos·to·mi \-ˌmī\ *n pl, cap* [NL, fr. *cycl-* + *-stomi*] **:** a class of lowly vertebrates formerly an order or subclass of Pisces but now segregated with certain extinct related forms in a superclass Agnatha that are elongated creatures resembling eels with a large jawless sucking mouth, no limbs or paired fins, a wholly cartilaginous skeleton with persistent notochord, and 6 to 14 pairs of gill pouches supported by a system of cartilaginous rods rudimentary in the hagfishes and that include the lampreys and the hagfishes

cy·clos·to·mous \(ˈ)sīˈklästəməs\ *adj* [*cycl-* + *-stomous*] **:** CYCLOSTOMATE

cy·clo·stroph·ic \ˈ≈≈ *at* CYCLO- +ˈsträfik\ *adj* [*cycl-* + LGk *strophikos* fit to be turned, turned, fr. Gk *stroph-* (stem of *strephein* to turn) + *-ikos* -ic — more at STROPHE] **:** of cyclic compulsion — used of the component of the deflective force of a wind that is due to the curvature of its path

¹cy·clo·style \ˈ≈≈+ˌstīl\ *n* -s [fr. *Cyclostyle,* a trademark] **:** a manifolding machine that utilizes a stencil cut by a graver whose tip is a small rowel

²cyclostyle \"\ *vt* -ED/-ING/-S **:** to manifold by cyclostyle

³cyclostyle \"\ *n* -s [*cycl-* + *-style* (as in *peristyle*)] **:** a structure composed of a circular row of columns about an open court — compare PERISTYLE

cy·clo·system \ˈ≈≈+ˌ-\ *n* [*cycl-* + *system*] **:** a gastropore of a hydrocoral surrounded by a circle of dactylopores

cy·clo·tel·la \ˌ≈≈ˈtelə\ *n, cap* [NL, irreg. fr. *cycl-* + L *-ella* (dim. suffix)] **:** a genus of disk-shaped solitary free-floating diatoms (family Coscinodiscaceae) often causing aromatic odors in water

cy·clo·them \ˈ≈≈ˌthem\ *n* -s [*cycl-* + Gk *thema* something laid down — more at THEME] **:** a stratigraphic unit consisting of a series of beds deposited during a single sedimentary cycle

cy·clo·thu·rus \ˌ≈≈ˈth(y)u̇rəs\ [NL, irreg. fr. Gk *kyklōtos* rounded + NL *-urus*] *syn of* CYCLOPES

cy·clo·thyme \ˈ≈≈ˌthīm\ *also* **cy·clo·thym** \-ˌthim\ *n* -s [back-formation fr. NL *cyclothymia*] **:** a cyclothymic individual

cy·clo·thy·mia \ˌ≈≈ˈthīmēə\ *n* -s [NL, fr. G *zyklothymie,* fr. *zyklo-* cycl- + *-thymie* -thymia] **:** a temperament characterized by alternation of lively and depressed moods believed to predispose the individual toward manic-depressive insanity — opposed to *schizothymia;* compare EXTROVERSION

¹cy·clo·thy·mic \ˌ≈≈ˈthīmik\ *adj* [NL *cyclothymia* + E *-ic*] **:** of, relating to, or marked by cyclothymia — compare SYNTONIC

²cyclothymic \"\ *n* -s **:** CYCLOTHYME

cy·clot·ic \(ˈ)sīˈkläd·ik\ *adj* [fr. NL *cyclosis,* after such pairs as NL *neurosis:* E *neurotic*] **:** exhibiting or being cyclosis ⟨~ movement⟩

cy·clo·tom·ic \ˌ≈≈ *at* CYCLO- +ˈtämik\ *adj* **:** of or relating to cyclotomy

cy·clot·o·my \sīˈkläd·əmē\ *n* -ES [*cycl-* + *-tomy*] **1 :** the mathematical theory of the division of the circle into equal parts or of the construction of regular polygons or analytically of the extraction of the *n*th roots of 1 **2 :** incision or division of the ciliary body

cy·clo·to·sau·rus \sīˌklōd·əˈsȯrəs\ *n, cap* [NL, fr. Gk *kyklōtos* rounded (fr. *kyklos* circle, ring) + NL *-saurus* — more at WHEEL] **:** a genus of labyrinthodonts from the Trias of Germany

cy·clo·tron \ˈsīkləˌträn\ *n* -s [*cycl-* + *-tron;* fr. the circular movement of the particles] **:** an accelerator in which particles (as protons, deuterons, or ions) are propelled by means of an alternating electric field between electrodes in a constant magnetic field

cy·clus \ˈsīkləs\ *n, pl* **cy·cli** \-ˌklī\ [LL — more at CYCLE] **:** CYCLE

cy·der \ˈsīdə(r)\ *chiefly Brit var of* CIDER

cy·dip·pe \sīˈdipē\ [NL, fr. L, a mythological girl tricked into marriage by a suitor, fr. Gk *Kydippē*] *syn of* PLEUROBRACHIA

cy·dip·pea \-pēə\ [NL, fr. *Cydippe*] *syn of* CYDIPPIDA

cy·dip·pid \-pəd\ *n* -s [NL *Cydippida*] **:** a larval ctenophore resembling an adult of the Cydippida

cy·dip·pi·da \-pədə\ *n pl, cap* [NL, fr. *Cydippe* + *-ida*] **:** an order of Ctenophora comprising forms having two long slender tentacles and unbranched meridional and stomodaeal vessels

cy·dip·pid·ea \ˌsīdəˈpidēə\ [NL, fr. *Cydippe* + *-idea*] *syn of* CYDIPPIDA

cyd·nid \ˈsidnəd\ *adj* [NL *Cydnidae*] **:** of or relating to the family Cydnidae ⟨~ bugs⟩

cyd·ni·dae \-nəˌdē\ *n pl, cap* [NL, fr. *Cydnus,* type genus (fr. Gk *kydnos* glorious, renowned, fr. *kydos* glory, renown) + *-idae;* fr. their bright colors — more at KUDOS] **:** a widely distributed family of chiefly tropical bugs that are related to the stinkbugs and include a number of burrowing bugs with the first two pairs of legs modified for digging in soil

cy·do·nia \sīˈdōnēə\ *n, cap* [NL, fr. L, quince — more at QUINCE] **:** a monotypic genus of small Asiatic trees (family Rosaceae) having crooked branches, blackish bark, large solitary white or pink flowers, and a fragrant yellow fuzzy fruit somewhat resembling a small apple — see QUINCE; compare CHAENOMELES

¹cy·do·nian \(ˈ)sīˈdōnēən, -ōnyən\ *adj, usu cap* [*Cydonia,* city of ancient Crete + E *-an*] **1 :** of, relating to, or characteristic of ancient Cydonia **2 :** of, relating to, or characteristic of Cydonians

²cydonian \"\ *n* -s *cap* **:** a native or inhabitant of ancient Cydonia

cy·do·ni·um \sīˈdōnēəm\ *n* [NL, fr. L *cydoneum* (*malum*), quince — more at QUINCE] *pharmacy* **:** quince seed

cy·e·sis \sīˈēsəs\ *n, pl* **cy·e·ses** \-ēˌsēz\ [NL, fr. Gk *kyēsis,* fr. *kyein* to be pregnant + *-ēsis* -esis; akin to Gk *koilos* hollow — more at CAVE] **:** PREGNANCY ⟨two cases of full-term abdominal ~ are described —*Jour. Amer. Med. Assoc.*⟩

cyg·ne·ous \ˈsignēəs\ *adj* [L *cygneus, cycneus,* fr. *cygnus, cycnus* swan] **:** curved like the neck of a swan

cyg·net \-nət\ *n* -s [ME *signett,* fr. MF *cygne* swan (fr. L *cygnus, cycnus,* fr. Gk *kyknos*) + ME *-et;* perh. akin to Skt *śuci* white, shining, Av *saochint-* burning] **:** a young swan

cyg·nus \-nəs\ *n, cap* [NL, fr. L, swan] **:** a genus of birds comprising the typical swans

cyke \ˈsīk\ *n* -s [by shortening & alter.] *slang* **:** CYCLORAMA 2

cyl *abbr* cylinder

cy·las \ˈsīləs\ *n, cap* [NL] **:** a genus of chiefly tropical weevils including the sweet-potato weevil

cylices *pl of* CYLIX

cyl·i·co·stome \ˈsilə(ˌ)kōˌstōm\ *n* -s [NL *Cylicostomum* genus of worms, fr. Gk *kylik-, kylix* cup + NL *-stomum;* akin to Gk *kalyx* calix, bud — more at CHALICE] **:** any of several small nematode worms (family Strongylidae) infesting the digestive tract of horses and other equines — called also *small strongyle;* compare STRONGYLE

cyl·in·der \ˈsiləndə(r)\ *n* -s *often attrib* [MF or L; MF *cylindre,* fr. L *cylindrus,* fr. Gk *kylindros,* fr. *kylindein* to roll; akin to OE *sceol* wry, squinting, OHG *scelah,* ON *skjalgr* wry, squinting, L *scelus* crime, wickedness, Gk *skolios* curved, crooked, *skelos* leg, Alb *tshalë* lame; basic meaning: turning, bending] **1** *math* **a :** the surface traced by any straight line moving parallel to a fixed straight line and intersecting a fixed curve **b :** the space bounded by any such surface and two parallel planes cutting all the elements — see VOLUME table **2 :** a cylindrical body: as **a** (1) **:** the turning chambered breech of a revolver (2) **:** one type of choke boring — see ²CHOKE 3 **b** (1) **:** a cylindrical chamber in an engine in which a piston is impelled by the pressure or expansive force of the working fluid (2) **:** the analogous though not cylindrical part in certain abnormal types of engines **c :** a chamber in a pump from which the piston expels the fluid **d :** the rapidly rotating spiked drum of a threshing machine **e** (1) **:** PLATE CYLINDER (2) **:** IMPRESSION CYLINDER (3) **:** BLANKET CYLINDER **f :** CYLINDER SEAL **g :** a cylindrical clay object inscribed with cuneiform inscriptions **h :** a typewriter platen **i :** a cylindrical record of a phonograph or dictating machine **j :** the portion of a cylinder lock that contains the tumblers and keyhole **3 :** a pivoted hollow steel shell upon which the balance of a watch is mounted and which is cut away to permit the passage of the rim of the escape wheel **4 :** the square prism carrying the cards to the needles in a jacquard loom

cylinder

cylinder block *n* **:** ¹BLOCK 1j

cyl·in·dered \-də(r)d\ *adj* **:** having a cylinder or cylinders ⟨a 6-*cylindered* engine⟩

cylinder front *n* **:** a desk front having a one-piece lid or cover resembling a longitudinal section of a cylinder

cylinder glass *n* **:** glass blown in the shape of a cylinder then split and flattened into a sheet

cylinder head *n* **:** the closed end of an engine or pump cylinder

cylinder lock *n* **:** a lock with both keyhole and tumbler mechanism in a cylinder separate from the case

cylinder machine *n* **:** a paper machine in which the sheet is formed on a wire-covered cylinder revolving in a vat of the stock; *esp* **:** such a machine having several vats and used for making boards each of which is built up by combining as many layers as there are vats

cylinder man *n* **1 :** a worker who cures bricks and cinder blocks in steam pressure cylinders to hasten hardening **2 :** an optical glass worker who grinds cylinder-shaped lens blanks

cylinder number *n* **:** the serial number of the cylindrical printing plate on a sheet of rotary-printed British stamps

cylinder oil *n* **:** a heavy grade of mineral lubricating oil; *esp* **:** such an oil used for steam-engine cylinders and valves

cylinder planer *n* **:** a wood surfacer having 1 or 2 rotating cutter cylinders and usu. from 2 to 8 feed rolls for guiding the wood

cylinder press *n* **:** a printing press in which a rotating cylinder rolls the paper against a printing surface lying on a flat usu. horizontal reciprocating bed — compare ROTARY PRESS

cylinder saw *n* **:** CROWN SAW

cylinder scale *n* **:** an automatic indicating scale in which the graduations are on a rotatable cylindrical chart — called also *barrel scale, drum scale*

cylinder seal *n* **:** a cylinder of stone or other hard material engraved in intaglio upon the curved surface and used esp. in ancient Mesopotamia to roll an identifying impression on wet clay (as in sealing a jar or writing tablet)

cylinder snake *n* **:** any of several Asiatic burrowing snakes constituting a genus (*Cylindrophis*) of the family Aniliidae

cylindr- *or* **cylindro-** *comb form* [NL, fr. Gk *kylindr-, kylindro-,* fr. *kylindros* — more at CYLINDER] **:** cylindrical **:** cylindrical and ⟨*cylindr*arthrosis⟩ ⟨*cylindro*cephalic⟩

cyl·in·dra·ceous \ˌsilənˈdrāshəs\ *adj* [*cylindr-* + *-aceous*] **:** somewhat like a cylinder

cyl·in·drar·thro·sis \ˌsilənˌdrärˈthrōsəs, səˌlin-\ *n, pl* **cyl·indrarthro·ses** \-ōˌsēz\ [NL, fr. *cylindr-* + *arthrosis*] **:** a joint in which the articular surfaces are approximately round

cy·lin·dri·cal \səˈlindrəkəl, -rēk-\ *or* **cy·lin·dric** \-drik, -rēk\ *adj* [*cylindrical* fr. F or Gk; F *cylindrique* (fr. Gk *kylindrikos,* fr. *kylindros* cylinder + *-ikos* -ic) + E *-al; cylindric* fr. F *cylindrique* or Gk *kylindrikos* — more at CYLINDER] **:** relating to or having the form or properties of a cylinder — **cy·lin·dri·cal·i·ty** \səˌlindrəˈkaləd·ē\ *n* -ES — **cy·lin·dri·cal·ly** \səˈlindrək(ə)lē, -rēk-, -li\ *adv* — **cy·lin·dri·cal·ness** \-kəlnəs\ *n* -ES

cylindrical coordinate *n, math* **:** any of the coordinates in space obtained by constructing in a plane a polar coordinate system and on a line perpendicular to the plane at the pole a linear coordinate system

cylindrical epithelium *n* **:** COLUMNAR EPITHELIUM

cylindrical harmonic *n* **:** BESSEL FUNCTION

cylindrical projection *n* **:** a projection (as of a sphere or a spheroid) on the surface of a cylinder; *specif* **:** any of numerous map projections of the terrestrial sphere on the surface of a cylinder that is then unrolled as a plane, the parallels and meridians appearing as straight lines perpendicular to each other if the cylinder is tangent over the sphere at the equator and all parallels as well as the points of the poles if shown appearing as the same length as the equator

cylindrical vault *n* **:** BARREL VAULT

cyl·in·dric·i·ty \ˌsilənˈdrisəd·ē\ *n* -ES [prob. fr. F *cylindricité,* fr. *cylindrique* cylindric + *-ité* -ity] **:** the quality or state of being cylindrical

cyl·in·drite \ˈsilənˌdrīt, səˈlin-\ *n* -s [ISV *cylindr-* + *-ite;* orig. formed as G *kylindrit*] **:** a mineral $Pb_3Sn_4Sb_2S_{14}$ consisting of sulfur, lead, antimony, and tin and being dark gray with metallic luster

cy·lin·dro·cap·sa \səˌlindrōˈkapsə\ *n, cap* [NL, fr. *cylindr-* + L *capsa* box — more at CASE] **:** a genus (the type of the family Cylindrocapsaceae) of freshwater green algae with filaments in which the cells have stratified walls

cy·lin·dro·cap·sa·ce·ae \-ōˌkapˈsāsēˌē\ *n pl, cap* [NL, fr. *Cylindrocapsa,* type genus + *-aceae*] **:** a family of algae (order Ulotrichales) having unbranched filaments and oogamous sexual reproduction

cy·lin·dro·cellular \səˈlindrō+\ *adj* [*cylindr-* + *cellular*] **:** made up of cylindrical cells

cy·lin·dro·conical \"+\ *adj* [*cylindr-* + *conical*] **:** cylindrical with one end tapering to a point

¹cyl·in·droid \ˈsilənˌdrȯid, səˈlin-\ *n* -s [*cylindr-* + *-oid*] **:** a cylinder with elliptic right sections

²cylindroid \"\ *also* **cyl·in·droi·dal** \ˌsilənˈdrȯidᵊl\ *adj* **:** CYLINDRACEOUS

cy·lin·dro·ju·lus \səˌlindrōˈ(ˌ)yüləs\ *n, cap* [NL, fr. *cylindr-* + L *iulus* catkin, fr. Gk *ioulos* (also, downy hair, sheaf of grain); akin to Gk *oulos* curly, *eilyein* to enwrap, enfold — more at VOLUBLE] **:** a genus of millipedes of the family Julidae including a species (*C. londinensis*) sometimes reported to damage potato crops in Europe

cy·lin·dro·spo·ri·um \səˌlindrōˈspōrēəm\ *n, cap* [NL, fr. *cylindr-* + *-sporium*] **:** a genus of imperfect fungi (family Melanconiaceae) producing hyaline filiform conidia in acervuli and including many forms that cause leaf and fruit spot diseases and some that are now known to be stages in the life cycles of other fungi — compare COCCOMYCES

cyl·in·dru·ria \ˌsilənˈdrurēə\ *n* -s [NL, fr. ISV *cylindroid* + NL *-uria*] **:** the presence of casts in the urine

cylix *var of* KYLIX

cym- *or* **cymo-** *also* **kym-** *or* **kymo-** *comb form* [F *cym-, cymo-,* fr. Gk *kym-, kymo-,* fr. *kyma*] **1 :** wave ⟨*cymo*scope⟩ **2 :** cyme **:** cluster ⟨*cym*oid⟩

cy·ma *also* **ci·ma** *or* **si·ma** \ˈsīmə\ *n* -s [Gk *kyma* wave, waved molding — more at CYME] **1 :** a projecting molding whose profile is a double curve: **a** *or* **cyma rec·ta** \ˌ≈≈ˈrektə\ [NL, lit., straight cyma] **:** such a molding with the upper part concave **b** *or* **cyma re·ver·sa** \-rəˈvərsə\ [NL, lit., reversed cyma] **:** such a molding with the upper part convex **2 :** a double curve formed by the union of a concave line and a convex line

cymagraph *var of* CYMOGRAPH

cymar *var of* SIMAR

cy·ma·rin \ˈsīmərən, ˈsim- *also* səˈma(a)r-\ *n* -s [fr. *Cymarin,* a trademark] **:** a cardiac glycoside $C_{30}H_{44}O_9$ occurring esp. in plants of the genus *Apocynum*

cy·ma·rose \-(ˌ)rōs *also* -rōz\ *n* -s [ISV *cymar*in + *-ose*] **:** a sugar $C_7H_{14}O_4$ occurring as a constituent of certain cardiac glycosides (as cymarin); the 3-methyl ether of digitoxose

cy·ma·ti·idae \ˌsīməˈtīəˌdē, ˌsim-\ *n pl, cap* [NL, fr. *Cymatium,* type genus (fr. Gk *kymation*) + *-idae*] **:** a family of large chiefly tropical gastropod mollusks (suborder Taenioglossa) that includes the typical tritons

cy·ma·ti·um \sīˈmāsh(ē)əm, səˈ-\ *n, pl* **cyma·tia** \-sh(ē)ə\ [L, fr. Gk *kymation,* dim. of *kyma*] **:** a crowning molding in classic architecture; *esp* **:** CYMA

cym·ba \ˈsimbə\ *n, pl* **cym·bae** \-(ˌ)bē, -ˌbī\ [NL, fr. L, boat, fr. Gk *kymbē* boat, bowl, cup] **1 :** the upper part of the concha of the ear **2 :** a woody durable boat-shaped spathe or other cover around the flower and fruit cluster of certain palms

cym·bal \ˈsimbəl\ *n* -s [ME, fr. OE *cymbal* and MF *cymbale,* both fr. L *cymbalum,* fr. Gk *kymbalon,* fr. *kymbē* boat, bowl, cup — more at HUMP] **1 a :** a large concave brass plate producing a brilliant clashing tone of indefinite pitch and used esp. to accompany the bass drum either in pairs rubbed or struck glancingly together or suspended or mounted singly and struck by drumsticks **b :** a high-pitched mixture stop of an organ **2 a :** CROTALUM **b :** a small tunable cup-shaped instrument used in pairs — called also *ancient cymbals* **3 :** TRIANGLE 3c; *specif* **:** such an instrument with attached rings **4** *archaic* **:** DOUGHNUT

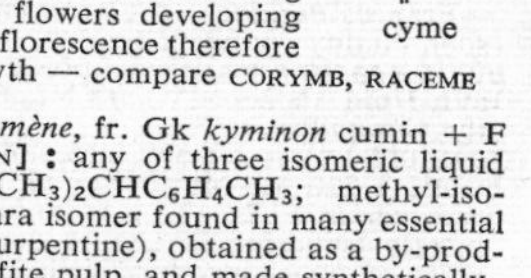

cymbals 1a

cym·bal·ist \-b(ə)ləst\ *n* -s **:** a performer on cymbals

cymbalom *or* **cymbalon** *var of* CIMBALOM

cym·bid \ˈsimbəd\ *n* -s [NL *Cymbidium*] **:** CYMBIDIUM 2

cym·bid·i·um \simˈbidēəm\ *n* [NL, fr. L *cymba* boat (fr. Gk *kymbē* boat, bowl, cup) + NL *-idium* — more at HUMP] **1** *cap* **:** a genus of tropical Old World orchids that are frequently cultivated for their boat-shaped flowers and have narrow leaves and a drooping inflorescence **2** *pl* **cymbidiums** \-mz\ *or* **cymbid·ia** \-dēə\ **:** a plant or flower of the genus *Cymbidium*

cym·bi·form \ˈsimbəˌfȯrm\ *adj* [NL *cymbiformis,* fr. L *cymba* boat + *-iformis* -iform] **:** BOAT-SHAPED **:** convex and keeled ⟨a ~ leaf⟩

cym·bi·um \-bēəm\ *n, cap* [NL, fr. L *cymbium* small cup, fr. Gk *kymbion,* dim. of *kymbē* boat, bowl, cup — more at HUMP] **:** a genus of marine snails (family Volutidae) comprising the melon shells

cymbling *also* **cymblin** *var of* CYMLING

cym·bo·cephalic *or* **cym·bo·cephalous** \ˌsimbō +\ *adj* [*cymbo-* (fr. L *cymba* boat) + *-cephalic, -cephalous*] *of a head or skull* **:** having a disproportionately prolonged receding forehead and a projecting occiput — **cym·bo·ceph·a·ly** \" + ˈsefəlē\ *n* -ES

cym·bo·pet·al·um \ˌsimbōˈped·ᵊləm\ *n, cap* [NL, fr. *cymbo-* (fr. L *cymba* boat) + *petalum* petal — more at PETAL] **:** a genus of tropical American shrubs and small trees (family Annonaceae) with fine-textured green or yellowish wood that includes the sacred earflower of Mexico and Central America

cym·bo·po·gon \-bəˈpōˌgän\ *n, cap* [NL, fr. *cymbo-* (fr. L *cymba* boat) + *-pogon;* fr. the shape of the bracts] **:** a genus of grasses occurring in warm regions of the Old World and having compound flower clusters of paired racemes enclosed by bracts that resemble spathes — see CITRONELLA GRASS, LEMONGRASS

cyme \ˈsīm\ *n* -s [NL *cyma,* fr. L, young sprout of cabbage, fr. Gk *kyma* wave, young sprout, fetus, anything swollen, fr. *kyein* to be pregnant; akin to *koilos* hollow — more at CAVE] **1 :** an inflorescence in which the main and secondary axes always terminate in a single flower whether one flower is produced (as in the wood anemone) or the inflorescence is continued by secondary and tertiary axes (as in the buttercup) **2 :** any flower cluster of the cyme type containing several or many flowers (as in pink or phlox) with the first-opening central flower terminating the main axis, subsequent flowers developing from lateral buds, and the inflorescence therefore exhibiting determinate growth — compare CORYMB, RACEME

cyme

cyme·let \-lət\ *n* -s **:** CYMULE

cy·mene \-ˌmēn\ *n* -s [F *cymène,* fr. Gk *kyminon* cumin + F *-ène* -ene — more at CUMIN] **:** any of three isomeric liquid aromatic hydrocarbons $(CH_3)_2CHC_6H_4CH_3$; methyl-isopropyl-benzene; *esp* **:** the para isomer found in many essential oils (as pine oil and spruce turpentine), obtained as a by-product in the production of sulfite pulp, and made synthetically

cym·ling \ˈsimliŋ\ *or* **cymb·ling** \-m(b)l-\ *also* **cym·lin** \-mlən\ *or* **cymb·lin** *or* **cim·lin** \-m(b)l-\ *n* -s [prob. alter. of *simnel*] **:** a summer squash having a scalloped edge

cymo- — see CYM-

cy·mod·o·ce·a·ce·ae \sīˌmädəsēˈāsēˌē\ *n pl, cap* [NL, fr. *Cymodocea,* type genus (fr. L *Cymodoce,* a Nereid) + *-aceae*] **:** a small family of tropical submerged marine plants (order Naiadales) with slender linear leaves and tiny greenish flowers

cy·mo·gene \ˈsīməˌjēn\ *n* -s [ISV *cymene* + *-o-* + *-gene*] **:** a flammable easily condensable gaseous petroleum product consisting chiefly of normal butane

¹cy·mo·graph *or* **cy·ma·graph** \ˈ≈≈ˌgraf\ *n* -s [*cym-* or *cyma* + *-graph*] **:** an instrument for making tracings of contours (as of profiles or moldings) — **cy·mo·graph·ic** \ˌ≈≈ˈfik\ *adj*

²cymograph *var of* KYMOGRAPH

¹cy·moid \ˈsīˌmȯid\ *adj* [*cyma* + *-oid*] **:** like a cyma

²cymoid \"\ *adj* [*cyme* + *-oid*] **:** like a cyme

cy·mo·phane \ˈsīməˌfān\ *n* -s [F, fr. *cym-* + *-phane*] **:** CHRYSOBERYL; *esp* **:** an opalescent chrysoberyl

cy·mose \ˈsīˌmōs\ *also* **cy·mous** \-məs\ *adj* [*cyme* + *-ose, -ous*] **1 :** being, having the form of, or derived from a cyme ⟨~ branching⟩ **2 :** of, relating to, or bearing a cyme — **cy·mose·ly** *adv*

cy·mot·ri·chous \(ˈ)sīˈmä·trəkəs\ *adj* [*cym-* + *-trichous*] **:** having the hair wavy ⟨a ~ race⟩ — **cy·mot·ri·chy** \-kē\ *n* -ES

¹cym·ric \ˈkəmrik, ˈkim- *sometimes* ˈsim-\ *also* **kym·ric** \ˈkəm-, ˈkim-\ *adj, usu cap* [W *Cymry* + E *-ic*] **1 :** of, relating to, or characteristic of the non-Gaelic Celtic people of Britain; *specif* **:** WELSH 1b **2 :** of, relating to, or characteristic of the language of the Cymric people; *specif* **:** WELSH 2

²cymric *also* **kymric** \"\ *n* -s *cap* **:** BRYTHONIC; *specif* **:** the Welsh language

cym·rite \ˈkəmˌrīt, ˈkim-, *also* ˈsim-\ *n* -s [W *Cymru* Wales + E *-ite*] **:** a rare mineral $BaAlSi_3O_8OH$ consisting of a basic aluminosilicate of barium and belonging to the zeolite family

cym·ry *also* **kym·ry** \ˈkəmrē, ˈkim-, -ri\ *n pl, cap* [W *Cymry,* pl. of *Cymro* Welshman, prob. fr. (assumed) OW *combrog* fellow countryman, Welshman, prob. fr. OW *com-* com- + (assumed) OW *brog* region (whence W *bro*); akin to L *com-* and to L *margo* border — more at MARK] **:** the Brythonic Celts; *specif* **:** WELSH

cy·mule \ˈsīˌmyül\ *n* -s [*cyme* + *-ule*] **:** a small cyme or one of very few flowers forming part of a compound cyme

cyn- *or* **cyno-** *comb form* [ME *cyno-,* fr. L, fr. Gk *kyn-, kyno-,* fr. *kyn-, kyōn* dog — more at HOUND] **:** dog ⟨*cyn*iatrics⟩

cyn *abbr* cyanide

cy·nan·chum \səˈnaŋkəm\ *n* [NL, fr. Gk *kynanchon* dogbane (*Marsdenia erecta*), fr. *kyn-* cyn- + *-anchon* (fr. *anchein* to choke) — more at ANGER] **1** *cap* **:** a genus of twining vines (family Asclepiadaceae) with opposite hanging leaves, small greenish or purplish flowers, and long smooth pods **2** -s **:** the roots of several vines of the genus *Cynanchum* formerly used as an emetic

cyn·a·ra \ˈsinərə\ *n, cap* [NL, fr. Gk *kynara, kinara,* a kind of artichoke] **:** a genus of herbs (family Compositae) having pinnatifid spiny leaves and large flower heads with fleshy receptacles — see ARTICHOKE, CARDOON — **cyn·a·ra·ceous** \ˌ≈≈ˈrāshəs\ *adj* — **cy·nar·e·ous** \səˈna(a)rēəs\ *adj* — **cyn·a·roid** \ˈsinəˌrȯid\ *adj*

cyn·e·get·ic \ˌsinəˈjed·ik\ *adj* [Gk *kynēgetikos*] **:** of or relating to hunting

cyn·e·get·ics \-iks\ *n pl but sing in constr* [L *Cynegetica*, title of a poem (fr. LGk *Kynēgetika*, fr. neut. pl. of Gk *kynēgetikos* of hunting, fr. *kynēgetēs* hunter, fr. *kyn-* cyn- + *hēgeisthai* to lead) + E *-s* — more at SEEK] **:** HUNTING **:** ²CHASE 1b

cyng·ha·nedd \kəŋˈhä(ˌ)neth\ *n, pl* **cyng·a·nedd·ion** \ˌkəŋəˈnethyən\ [W, fr. *cym-* com- (fr. OW *com-*) + *canu* to sing + *-edd* (n. suffix); akin to L *com-* and to L *canere* to sing — more at CHANT] **1 :** a strict intricate system of alliteration and rhyme used in Welsh poetry ⟨the knowledge of ~ is shared by farm laborer and village craftsman as well as the schoolmaster and parson —Wyn Griffith⟩ **2 :** alliteration or alliteration and rhyme in any of the four patterns of cynghanedd ⟨one rule is common to all the "24 measures": there must be ~ in every line —A.S.D.Smith⟩

¹cyn·ic \ˈsinik, -nēk\ *n* -s [MF or L; MF *cynique*, fr. L *cynicus*, fr. Gk *kynikos*, lit., doglike (prob. influenced in meaning by *Kynosarges*, a gymnasium where Antisthenes taught), fr. *kyn-*, *kyōn* dog + *-ikos* -ic — more at HOUND] **1** *usu cap* **:** a member or follower of a school of philosophers founded by Antisthenes (born *ab*444 B.C.) that taught that virtue is the only good, its essence lying in self-control and independence, and that later developed into a coarse opposition to social customs and current philosophical opinions — contrasted with *Cyrenaic* **2 a :** one who holds views resembling those of the Cynics **b :** one who believes that human conduct is motivated wholly by self-interest **:** a person who expects nothing but the worst of human conduct and motives **:** MISANTHROPE

²cynic \"\ *adj* **1** *usu cap* **:** of or relating to the Cynics **:** resembling the doctrines of the Cynics **2 :** CYNICAL **3** [Gk *kynikos*] **:** like or like that of a dog — now used chiefly in the phrase *cynic spasm*

cyn·i·cal \-nəkəl, -nēk-\ *adj* [¹*cynic* + *-al*] **1 :** having the qualities of a cynic **:** given to faultfinding, sneering, and sarcasm ⟨the younger sister grew more ~, not to say acid, in her ways —Rudyard Kipling⟩ **2 :** given to or affecting disbelief in commonly accepted human values and in man's sincerity of motive or rectitude of conduct **:** accepting selfishness as the governing factor in human conduct ⟨provide a smashing answer for those ~ men who say that a democracy cannot be honest and efficient —F.D.Roosevelt⟩ **3 :** exhibiting feelings ranging from distrustful doubt to contemptuous and mocking disbelief ⟨but people nowadays are so ~ — they sneer at everything that makes life worthwhile —L.P.Smith⟩

syn MISANTHROPIC (or MISANTHROPICAL), PESSIMISTIC, MISOGYNIC (or MISOGYNOUS): CYNICAL often implies a disbelief in sincerity, benevolence, rectitude, or competence ⟨the loneliness which breathes in words like these has often begotten in great rulers a *cynical* contempt of men and the judgments of men —J.R.Green⟩ ⟨he was *cynical* that any good could come of democracy —J.T.Farrell⟩ ⟨the *cynical* opinion, which dissents and says that the less we understand one another the better, will not be considered here —I.A.Richards⟩ MISANTHROPIC suggests dislike and distrust of human beings in general and discomfort at or aversion to their society ⟨he had been the laughingstock of the school even before that day for his inability to conform to their standards, but after that day his loathing for every aspect of youthful high spirits hardened into a *misanthropic* mania —J.C.Powys⟩ PESSIMISTIC connotes a gloomy view of life in general, one without joy or hope ⟨the *pessimistic* sects which despair of social progress and look for a catastrophic ending of the present world order —W.L. Sperry⟩ ⟨official Whig leaders went politically to sleep in their country seats, muttering *pessimistic* prophecies of the impossibility of conquering Napoleon —G.M.Trevelyan⟩ MISOGYNIC and its variants indicate a distrust of and aversion to women on man's part ⟨an old-fashioned bachelor whose *misogynic* views and prejudice against matrimony have been conjecturally traced to his brother Perses having a wife as extravagant as himself —James Davies⟩ ⟨in spite of this modest status of woman, the Greeks were profoundly *misogynous* —H.M. Parshley⟩

cyn·i·cal·ly \-nək(ə)lē, -nēk-, -li\ *adv* **:** in a cynical manner **:** with cynicism

cyn·i·cism \-nəˌsizəm\ *n* -s **1** *usu cap* **:** the doctrine of the Cynics **2 a :** cynical quality ⟨developed the salty ~ that stayed with him throughout his newspaper and political career —Frances Perkins⟩ **b :** an expression of or characteristic of such quality ⟨pungent ~*s*⟩

cynic spasm *n* **:** RISUS SARDONICUS

¹cyn·i·pid \ˈsinəpəd\ *adj* [NL *Cynipidae*] **:** of or relating to the Cynipidae

²cynipid \"\ *n* -s **:** any insect of the family Cynipidae

cy·nip·i·dae \səˈnipəˌdē\ *n pl, cap* [NL, fr. *Cynip-*, *Cynips*, type genus + *-idae*] **:** a large family of small hymenopterous insects (superfamily Cynipoidea) comprising the gall wasps most of which produce galls on plants (as oaks and rosebushes) in which their larvae develop — see CYNIPS

cyn·i·poid \ˈsinəˌpȯid\ *adj* [NL *Cynipoidea*] **:** of, relating to, or resembling the gall wasps or the Cynipoidea — compare CYNIPIDAE

cyn·i·poi·dea \ˌ⸗⸗ˈpȯidēə\ *n pl, cap* [NL, fr. *Cynip-*, *Cynips* + *-oidea*] **:** a superfamily of hymenopterous insects (suborder Clistogastra) that are distinguished by greatly reduced wing venation and a coiled retractile ovipositor and that include the gall wasps and several families of parasites of other insects — see CYNIPIDAE

cyn·ips \ˈsinəps\ *n, cap* [NL, prob. fr. L *cinyphes*, *cinyphum* gnat, modif. of Gk *knips* insect infesting fig and oak trees; akin to Gk *sknips*, a kind of small worm, ME *nippen* to nip — more at NIP] **:** a genus (the type of the family Cynipidae) of small gall wasps including a number that form galls on oaks

cyn·ism \ˈsiˌnizəm\ *n* -s [F *cynisme*, fr. LL *cynismus*, fr. Gk *kynismos*, fr. *kyn-* + *-ismos* -ism — more at CYNIC] **:** CYNICISM

cyno- — see CYN-

cyn·o·cephalous *also* **cyn·o·cephalic** \ˌsinō, ¦sīnō, -nə +\ *adj* [*cynocephalous* fr. Gk *kynokephalos; cynocephalic* fr. Gk *kynokephalos* + E *-ic*] **:** having a head or face like that of a dog

cyn·o·cephalus \¦⸗⸗ +\ *n* [L, fr. Gk *kynokephalos*, fr. *kynokephalos*, adj., fr. *kyn-* cyn- + *-kephalos* -cephalous] **1** *pl* **cynocephali :** a dogheaded being**: a :** one of a fabled race of dogheaded men **b :** BABOON **2** *cap* [NL, fr. L] **a :** a genus of mammals containing the flying lemurs **b** *in former classifications* **:** ¹PAPIO

cyn·o·cram·ba·ce·ae \ˌ⸗⸗ˌkramˈbāsēˌē\ *n pl, cap* [NL, fr. *Cynocrambe*, type genus + *-aceae*] **:** a family of herbs (order Caryophyllales) coextensive with the genus *Cynocrambe* — **cyn·o·cram·ba·ceous** \¦⸗⸗¦⸗ˈbāshəs\ *adj*

cyn·o·cram·be \ˌ⸗⸗ˈkram(ˌ)bē\ *n, cap* [NL, fr. Gk *kynokrambē* dog's mercury (*Mercurialis perennis*), fr. Gk *kyn-* cyn- + *krambē* cabbage — more at CRAMBE] **:** a small genus of Old World fleshy herbs constituting a family (Cynocrambaceae) and having simple petioled leaves, inconspicuous apetalous flowers, and globose fruit with a crustaceous pericarp

cyn·o·des·mus \ˌ⸗⸗ˈdezməs\ *n, cap* [NL, fr. *cyn-* + Gk *desmos* bond — more at DIADEM] **:** a genus of extinct Miocene carnivores apparently derived from *Cynodictis* and on the direct ancestral line of the true dogs and wolves

cy·o·dic·tis \ˌ⸗⸗ˈdiktəs\ *n, cap* [NL, fr. *cyn-* + *-dictis* (fr. Gk *diktys*, an unknown Libyan animal mentioned by Herodotus)] **:** a genus of extinct carnivores from the Eocene and Oligocene of Europe that were long-bodied short-legged creatures resembling weasels with retractile claws and presumably ancestral to dogs, foxes, and related forms

cyn·o·don \ˈ⸗⸗ˌdän\ *n, cap* [NL, fr. Gk *kynodōn* canine tooth, fr. *kyn-* cyn- + *odōn* tooth — more at TOOTH] **:** a genus of creeping grasses having short flat leaves and digitate spikes of one-flowered spikelets — see BERMUDA GRASS

¹cyn·o·dont \ˈ⸗⸗ˌdänt\ *adj* [Gk *kynodont-*, *kynodōn* canine tooth] **1** *of teeth* **:** having small pulp cavities **2 :** having cynodont teeth ⟨man like the higher apes is ~⟩ **3** [NL *Cynodontia*] **:** of or belonging to Cynodontia

²cynodont \"\ *n* -s **1 :** a reptile or fossil of the group Cynodontia **2 :** a canine tooth

cyn·o·don·tia \ˌ⸗⸗ˈdänsh(ē)ə\ *n pl, cap* [NL, fr. Gk *kynodont-*, *kynodōn* canine tooth + NL *-ia*] **:** a division of Triassic Therapsida comprising a number of small carnivorous reptiles often with cusps on the teeth that resemble those of mammals

cyn·o·don·tin \ˌ⸗⸗ˈdänt[ə]n, -ntən\ *n* -s [NL *cynodontis* (specific epithet of *Helminthosporium cynodontis*, fr. Gk *kynodont-*, *kynodōn* canine tooth) + E *-in*] **:** a brown crystalline phenolic pigment $C_{15}H_{10}O_6$ derived from anthraquinone that is obtained from fungi of the genus *Helminthosporium* (as *H. cynodontis*)

cy·nog·a·le \səˈnägəlē, sīˈ-\ *n, cap* [NL, fr. *cyn-* + Gk *galē*, *galeē* weasel — more at GALEA] **:** a genus of mammals consisting of the mampalon

cyn·o·glos·si·dae \ˌsinōˈgläsəˌdē, ˌsīn-, -nə'-, -lȯs-\ *n pl, cap* [NL, fr. *Cynoglossus*, type genus (fr. Gk *kynoglōssos*, a kind of fish, fr. *kyno-* cyn- + *-glōssos*, fr. *glōssa* tongue) + *-idae* — more at GLOSS] **:** a family of flatfishes comprising the tonguefishes and having small eyes on the left side of the head and the long dorsal and anal fins fused with the caudal fin

cyn·o·glos·sum \ˌ⸗⸗ˈ⸗səm\ *n; cap* [NL, fr. Gk *kynoglōsson*, fr. *kyn-* cyn- + *-glōsson* (fr. *glōssa* tongue) — more at GLOSS] **:** a large genus of tall rough herbs (family Boraginaceae) found in most temperate and subtropical regions — see HOUND'S-TONGUE

cy·nog·na·thus \səˈnägnəthəs, sīˈ-\ *n, cap* [NL, fr. *cyn-* + *-gnathus* -gnathous] **:** a genus of large carnivorous therapsid reptiles (suborder Theriodontia) that greatly resembled mammals in form, were presumably near the direct ancestral line of the true mammals, and are known chiefly from remains found in the Karroo formation of the Triassic

cy·noid \ˈsīˌnȯid, ˈsiˌ-\ *adj* [Gk *kynoeidēs*, fr. *kyn-* cyn- + *-oeidēs* -oid] **1 :** resembling a dog **2** [NL *Cynoidea*] **:** of, relating to, or belonging to the Cynoidea

cy·noi·dea \səˈnȯidēə, sīˈ-\ *n pl, cap* [NL, fr. *cyn-* + *-oidea*] *in some classifications* **:** a division of Carnivora comprising mammals that resemble dogs as distinguished from those that resemble bears, the two groups being now usu. combined as the Arctoidea

cy·nol·o·gist \səˈnäləjəst, sīˈ-\ *n* -s **:** one that specializes in the care and training of dogs

cy·nol·o·gy \-jē\ *n* -ES [*cyn-* + *-logy*] **:** scientific study of the dog esp. in respect to its natural history

cyn·o·mol·gus \ˌsinəˈmälgəs, ˌsīn-\ *n, pl* **cynomol·gi** \-ˌgī\ [NL, alter. of *cynamolgus*, fr. L, member of an ancient tribe in Libya, fr. Gk *Kynamolgos*, lit., dog-milker, fr. *kyn-* cyn- + *-amolgos* (fr. *amelgein* to milk) — more at MILK] **:** MACAQUE; *esp* **:** CRAB-EATING MACAQUE — used chiefly in technical literature concerned with poliomyelitis

cyn·o·mo·ri·a·ce·ae \ˌsinōˌmōrēˈāsēˌē, ˌsīn-, -nə-, -mȯr-\ *n pl, cap* [NL, fr. *Cynomorium*, type genus + *-aceae*] **:** a family of plants (order Myrtales) coextensive with the genus *Cynomorium*

cyn·o·mo·ri·um \ˌ⸗⸗ˈ⸗rēəm\ *n, cap* [NL, fr. L *cynomorion* broomrape, fr. Gk *kynomorion* dodder, fr. *kyn-* cyn- + *morion* part, member, dim. of *moros* fate, lot — more at MERIT] **:** a genus (the type of the family Cynomoriaceae) of bright red leafless parasitic plants that belong to the order Myrtales, have unisexual flowers borne in heads, and produce edible underground stems which have been used as a dysentery remedy

cyn·o·morph \ˈ⸗⸗ˌmȯrf\ *adj* [NL *Cynomorpha*] **:** of or belonging to Cercopithecidae

cyn·o·mor·pha \ˌ⸗⸗ˈ⸗fə\ *n pl, cap* [NL, fr. *cyn-* + *-morpha*] *in some classifications* **:** a group coextensive with Cercopithecidae — **cyn·o·mor·phic** \¦⸗⸗¦⸗fik\ *adj* — **cyn·o·mor·phous** \-fəs\ *adj*

cy·o·mys \ˈ⸗⸗ˌmis\ *n, cap* [NL, fr. *cyn-* + *-mys*] **:** a genus of rodents comprising the prairie dogs

cy·noph·i·list \səˈnäfələst, sīˈ-\ *n* -s [*cyn-* + *-phile* + *-ist*] **:** a dog fancier **:** one that is favorably disposed toward dogs

cyn·o·pi·the·ci·dae \ˌsinōpəˈthesəˌdē, ˌsīn-, -nəp-, -ēkə-\ [NL, fr. *Cynopithecus*, type genus + *-idae*] *syn of* CERCOPITHECIDAE

cy·c·pi·the·cus \ˌ⸗⸗pəˈthēkəs, -ˈpithək-\ *n, cap* [NL, fr. *cyn-* + *-pithecus*] **:** a genus of Old World monkeys (family Cercopithecidae) including only the black ape of Celebes

cy·nos·ci·on \səˈnäsēˌän, sīˈ-, -ēən\ *n, cap* [NL, fr. *cyn-* + *-scion* (modif. of Gk *skiaina*, a sea fish)] **:** a genus of marine fishes (family Sciaenidae) containing the weakfishes and related forms

cy·no·sure \ˈsīnəˌshu̇(ə)r, ˈsin-, -u̇ə; *Brit usu* ˈsinəˌzyu̇- *also* ˈsīn- *or* -ˌzh(y)u̇- *or* -ˌsyu̇-\ *n* -s [MF & L; MF, Ursa Minor, guide, fr. L *cynosura* Ursa Minor, fr. Gk *kynosoura* dog's tail, Ursa Minor, fr. *kynos* (gen. of *kyōn* dog) + *oura* tail; akin to Gk *orrhos* backside — more at HOUND, ASS] **1** *archaic* **:** one that serves to direct or guide **2 :** one that attracts **:** a center of attraction or interest ⟨the council too was a ~ of the nation's hopes —*Time*⟩ ⟨for tradition and digging the ~ of the Wichitas is Devil's Canyon —J.F.Dobie⟩

cy·no·su·rus \ˌsinəˈs(h)u̇rəs, ˌsīn-\ *n, cap* [NL, fr. Gk *kynosoura* dog's tail] **:** a small genus of European grasses with several-flowered spikelets in panicles — see CRESTED DOGSTAIL

cyn·thia \ˈsinthēə\ [NL, fr. *Cynthia*, goddess of the moon, fr. L, fr. Gk *Kynthia*] *syn of* TETHYUM

cynthia moth *n* **:** a large Asiatic silkworm moth (*Samia cynthia* or *S. walkeri*) introduced into No. America in the 19th century and having a larva that feeds chiefly on the ailanthus

cyn·thi·id \ˈsinthēəd\ *adj or n* [NL, *Cynthiidae*] **:** TETHYID

cyn·thi·idae \sinˈthīəˌdē\ [NL, fr. *Cynthia*, type genus + *-idae*] *syn of* TETHYIDAE

cy·on \ˈsīˌän, -ən\ [NL, alter. of *Cuon*] *syn of* CUON

¹cyp \ˈsip, ˈsīp, ˈsēp\ *also* **cy·pre** \-pə(r)\ *n* -s [Haitian Creole] **:** PRINCEWOOD 1

²cyp \"\ *n* -s [by shortening] **:** CYPRIPEDIUM 2

cyp·er·a·ce·ae \ˌsipəˈrāsēˌē, ˌsīp-\ *n pl, cap* [NL, fr. *Cyperus*, type genus + *-aceae*] **:** a large family of monocotyledonous plants (order Graminales) distinguished chiefly by having achenes, solid stems, and 3-ranked stem leaves — compare GRAMINEAE; see SEDGE — **cyp·er·a·ceous** \¦⸗⸗¦rāshəs\ *adj*

cyp·er·a·les \-ˈrā(ˌ)lēz\ *n pl, cap* [NL, fr. *Cyperus* + *-ales*] *in some classifications* **:** an order of monocotyledonous plants coextensive with the family Cyperaceae

cy·pe·rus \sīˈpirəs, səˈ-\ *n, cap* [NL, fr. L *cyperos*, a kind of rush, fr. Gk *kypeiros*, prob. of Sem. origin; akin to Heb *kōper*, a resin] **:** a genus of plants (family Cyperaceae) having the scales of the spikelet 2-ranked, the flowers all perfect, and the spikelets alike — see CHUFA, PAPYRUS, UMBRELLA PLANT

cy·phel·la \sīˈfelə, sīˈ-\ *n* [NL, fr. Gk *kyphella*, pl., hollows of the ears; akin to OE *hūfe* head covering, OHG *hūba*, OS *hūva*, ON *hūfa* hood, cap, bonnet, Gk *kyphos* crooked, bent, ORuss *kubŭ* drinking vessel, OE *hēah* high — more at HIGH] **1** *pl* **cyphel·lae** \-(ˌ)lē\ **:** a small cuplike pit on the lower surface of the thallus of certain lichens (as those of the genus *Sticta*) prob. functioning as a pore **2** *cap* **:** a genus of cup-shaped basidiomycetous fungi (family Thelephoraceae) having the hymenial lining on the inner surface

cy·phel·late \səˈfelət, (ˈ)sī¦-, -(ˌ)lāt\ *adj* [NL *cyphella* + E *-ate*] **:** having cyphellae

cy·pher \ˈsīfə(r)\ *chiefly Brit var of* CIPHER

cy·pho·man·dra \ˌsīfəˈmandrə, ˌsif-\ *n, cap* [NL, fr. Gk *kyphōma* hump (fr. *kyphos* crooked, bent) + NL *-andra* — more at CYPHELLA] **:** a genus of So. American shrubs or trees (family Solanaceae) having large simple or divided leaves and rotate or bell-shaped flowers — see TREE TOMATO

cy·pho·nau·tes \-ˈnȯd·(ˌ)ēz\ *n, pl* **cyphonau·tae** \-(ˌ)ā\ [NL, fr. Gk *kyphos* crooked, bent + *nautēs* sailor, fr. *naus* ship — more at NAVE] **:** the free-swimming bivalve larva of certain bryozoans

cy·praea \sīˈprēə, səˈ-\ *n, cap* [NL, fr. L *Cypria* or LL *Cypris*, a name for Venus-Aphrodite, goddess of love, fr. Gk *Kypris*, fr. *Kypros* Cyprus, island in the Mediterranean, her reputed birthplace] **:** a genus (the type of the family Cypraeidae) of gastropod mollusks comprising the typical cowries with smoothly polished often brightly colored shells covered in life by the reflected lobes of the mantle

cy·prae·i·dae \-əˌdē\ *n pl, cap* [NL, fr. *Cypraea*, type genus + *-idae*] **:** a family of marine gastropod mollusks (suborder Taenioglossa) comprising the cowries — see CYPRAEA

cy·prae·i·form \-əˌfȯrm\ *adj* [NL *Cypraea* + E *-iform*] **:** shaped like a cowrie

cy pres \(ˈ)sē¦prā\ *adv (or adj)* [*cy pres (doctrine)*] **:** in accordance with cy pres doctrine

cy pres doctrine *n* [AF *cy pres* as near, so near] **:** the doctrine in the law of charities whereby when it becomes impossible, impracticable, or illegal to carry out the particular purpose of the donor a scheme will be framed by a court or under prerogative powers of a sovereign to carry out the general intention by applying the gift to charitable purposes that are closely related or similar to the original purposes

¹cy·press \ˈsīprəs\ *n* -ES *often attrib* [ME *cipres*, *cypress*, fr. OF *ciprès*, *cyprès*, fr. L *cyparissus*, fr. Gk *kyparissos*, fr. the non-IE source of L *cupressus* cypress] **1 :** a tree of the genus *Cupressus* **2 :** branches or sprigs of cypress used as a symbol of mourning ⟨let the king dismiss his woes . . . and take the ~ from his brows —Matthew Prior⟩ **3 :** any of several coniferous trees related to cypress: as **a :** PORT ORFORD CEDAR **b :** YELLOW CEDAR **c :** BALD CYPRESS **d :** a Central-American timber tree (*Podocarpus coriacea*) that produces a fine-grained gray wood **e** *North* **:** JACK PINE 1 **4 :** the wood of cypress **5 :** any of various chiefly herbaceous plants that are not conifers but have flat scaly foliage like that of members of the genus *Cupressus* **6** *or* **cypress green :** a moderate olive green that is greener and duller than forest green (sense 2), greener, darker, and slightly less strong than Lincoln green, and greener and duller than holly green (sense 2)

²cypress \"\ *also* **cy·prus** \-rəs\ *n* -ES [ME *cipres*, *cyprus*, fr. *Cyprus*, island in the Mediterranean] **1 :** any of various rich fabrics imported from or through Cyprus in medieval times; *specif* **:** a rich satin **2 a** *also* **cypress lawn :** a silk or cotton gauze orig. made in Cyprus, usu. dyed black, and used esp. for mourning **b :** a piece of this fabric; *esp* **:** a kerchief worn as a badge of mourning

cy·pressed \-rəst\ *adj* [¹*cypress* + *-ed*] **:** having a growth of cypresses

cypress gilia *n* **:** an herb (*Gilia rubra*) with foliage like that of a cypress

cypress grass *n* **:** a common sedge (*Cyperus diandrus*) of the eastern U.S.

cypress knee *n* **:** one of the outgrowths from the roots of bald cypress that are presumed to aerate the submerged root system

cypress koromiko *n* **:** a New Zealand shrub (*Veronica cupressoides*) with very slender much-forked branches, minute leaves, and tiny flowers

cypress moss *n* **1 :** a moss (*Hypnum cupressiforme*) with foliage like that of a cypress **2 :** a club moss (*Lycopodium alpinum*) growing on mountains of Europe and America

cypress oil *n* **:** a yellowish essential oil from the leaves and young branches of Italian cypress used as an inhalant in whooping cough

cypress pine *n* **:** a tree of the genus *Callitris*

cypress spurge *n* **:** a spurge (*Euphorbia cyparissias*) with foliage resembling that of a cypress that is native to the Old World but is now established as a weed in the eastern U.S.

cypress trout *n* **:** BOWFIN

cypress vine *n* **1 :** a tropical American plant (*Quamoclit pennata*) with red or white tubular flowers and finely dissected leaves that is naturalized in the southern U.S. and used elsewhere as an ornamental garden plant **2 :** CLIMBING FUMITORY

¹cyp·ri·an \ˈsiprēən\ *n* -s [L *Cyprius* native of Cyprus, fr. *Cyprius*, adj. (fr. Gk *Kyprios*, fr. *Kypros* Cyprus) + E *-an*] **1** *often cap* [so called fr. *Cyprus*' being the reputed birthplace of Aphrodite, goddess of love] **:** a lewd person; *specif* **:** PROSTITUTE **2** *usu cap* **:** CYPRIOT **3** *or* **cyprian bee** *usu cap C* **:** a bright yellow fierce-tempered honeybee little raised in the U.S.

²cyprian \"\ *adj* [L *Cyprius* of Cyprus + E *-an*] **1** *often cap* **:** LICENTIOUS **2** *usu cap* **:** CYPRIOT

cyprian earth *or* **cyprian green** *n, often cap C* **:** TERRE VERTE 2

cyp·ri·an·ic \¦⸗⸗¦anik\ *adj, usu cap* [St. Cyprian (Thascius C. Cyprianus) †258 martyred bishop of Carthage + E *-ic*] **:** of, belonging to, or based on the thought of St. Cyprian

cyprian turpentine *n, usu cap C* **:** TURPENTINE 1a

cyp·rid \ˈsiprəd\ *n* -s [NL *Cyprid-*, *Cypris* & NL *Cyprididae*, fr. *Cyprid-*, *Cypris*, type genus + *-idae*] **1 :** a member of the genus *Cypris* or family Cyprididae **2 :** CYPRIS 2

cyprides *pl of* CYPRIS

cyp·ri·di·na \ˌsiprəˈdīnə, -dēnə\ *n, cap* [NL, fr. LL *Cyprid-*, *Cypris*, a name for Venus + NL *-ina* — more at CYPRAEA] **:** a genus (the type of the family Cyprididae) of commonly bioluminescent marine crustaceans (subclass Ostracoda) having three eyes and a deep anterior notch in the shell — **cy·prid·i·noid** \səˈprid[ə]nˌȯid\ *adj*

cyp·rine \ˈsiprən, -ˌprēn, -ˌprīn\ *n* -s [G *zyprin*, fr. L *cyprum* copper + G *-in* -ine — more at COPPER] **:** a variety of idocrase that is colored blue by copper

¹cyp·ri·nid \ˈsiprəˌnid; səˈprīnəd, -rīn-\ *adj* [NL *Cyprinidae*] **:** of or belonging to Cyprinidae

²cyprinid \"\ *n* -s **:** a cyprinid fish

¹cy·prin·i·dae \səˈprinəˌdē, -rīn-\ *n pl, cap* [NL, fr. *Cyprinus* type genus + *-idae*] **:** a large family (order Ostariophysi) of freshwater fishes (as the carps, barbels, tenches, breams, goldfishes, chubs, dace, shiners, and most of the freshwater minnows) that have a single dorsal fin, a somewhat protractile mouth destitute of teeth except for a few on the pharyngeal bones, the body nearly always covered with cycloid scales, and the air bladder large and divided into two parts

²cyprinidae \"\ *n pl, cap* [NL, fr. *Cyprina*, type genus + *-idae*] *in some classifications* **:** a family of thick-shelled marine bivalve mollusks (suborder Submytilacea) comprising the black quahog and certain related mollusks

cy·prin·o·don \-əˌdän\ *n, cap* [NL, fr. L *cyprinus*, a kind of carp + NL *-odon* — more at CYPRINUS] **:** the type genus of Cyprinodontidae comprising killifishes of tropical fresh and brackish waters that may be an important factor in mosquito control in certain areas

¹cy·prin·o·dont \-əˌdänt\ *adj* [NL *Cyprinodont-*, *Cyprinodon* & *Cyprinodontia* & *Cyprinodontes*] **:** of or belonging to *Cyprinodon*, the Cyprinodontidae, or the Microcyprini

²cyprinodont \"\ *n* -s **:** a cyprinodont fish **:** a killifish, topminnow, or related small soft-finned fish

cy·prin·o·don·tes \⸗,⸗⸗ˈdän(ˌ)tēz\ [NL, fr. *Cyprinodont-*, *Cyprinodon*] *syn of* MICROCYPRINI

cy·prin·o·don·ti·dae \-ˈdäntəˌdē\ *n pl, cap* [NL, fr. *Cyprinodont-* *Cyprinodon*, type genus + *-idae*] **:** a large family (order Microcyprini) of small scaly-headed soft-finned fishes that feed on water plants and insects and include the typical killifishes of the northern hemisphere

¹cyp·ri·noid \ˈsiprəˌnȯid; səˈpri-, -rī-,-\ *adj* [NL *Cyprinoidea*] **:** like or relating to a carp or the Cyprinoidea

²cyprinoid \"\ *n* -s **:** a cyprinoid fish

cyp·ri·noi·dea \ˌsiprəˈnȯidēə\ *n pl, cap* [NL, fr. *Cyprinus* + *-oidea*] **:** a suborder or other division of Ostariophysi comprising the carps and certain related fishes (as suckers and loaches) — **cyp·ri·noi·de·an** \¦⸗⸗¦⸗dēən\ *adj or n*

cy·pri·nus \səˈprīnəs, -rēn-\ *n, cap* [NL, fr. L, carp, fr. Gk *kyprinos*; perh. akin to Skt *śaphara* carp, Lith *šapalas*] **:** the type genus of the family Cyprinidae now usu. restricted to the typical carp

¹cyp·ri·ot \ˈsiprēət, -ēˌät *sometimes* ˈsīp-\ *or* **cyp·ri·ote** \", -ēˌōt\ *n* -s *cap* [F *cypriote*, adj. & n., fr. *Cyprus* + F *-i-* + *-ote*] **1 :** a native or inhabitant of Cyprus, an island in the eastern part of the Mediterranean sea **2 :** the ancient or modern Greek dialect of Cyprus

²cypriot *or* **cypriote** \"\ *adj, usu cap* [F *cypriote*] **1 a :** of, relating to, or characteristic of Cyprus **b :** of, relating to, or characteristic of Cypriots **2 :** of, relating to, or characteristic of the Cypriot language

cypriot syllabary *n, usu cap C* **:** a syllabary prob. of Aegean origin in which ancient Cypriot is preserved

cy·pri·pe·di·um \ˌsiprəˈpēdēəm\ *n* [NL, fr. LL *Cypris*, a name for Venus + NL *-pedium* (modif. of Gk *pedilon* sandal); fr. the shape of the flower; akin to Gk *pod-*, *pous* foot — more at CYPRAEA, FOOT] **1** *cap* **:** a genus of leafy-stemmed terrestrial orchids having large drooping usu. showily colored or marked flowers with a lip that forms an inflated pouch **2** *pl* **cypripe·dia** \-dēə\ **:** a plant or flower of the genus *Cypripedium* or of the genus *Cordula* — see LADY'S SLIPPER **3 :** the dried rhizome and roots of an orchid (*C. parviflorum*) formerly used as a nervine and antispasmodic

cy·pris \ˈsīprəs\ *n* [NL, fr. LL *Cypris,* a name for Venus — more at CYPRAEA] **1** *cap* **:** a genus (the type of the family Cyprididae) of small ostracod crustaceans that live in stagnant fresh water **2** *pl* **cyp·ri·des** \ˈsiprə,dēz\ **:** a developmental form of a barnacle in which the shell is bivalved as in members of the genus *Cypris*

cypro- *comb form, usu cap* [Gk *Kypro-,* fr. *Kypros* Cyprus] **:** Cyprian (and) ⟨*Cypro*-Phoenician⟩

cy·pro·lith·ic \ˌsīprəˈlithik, ˈsi-, -prəˈ-\ *adj, usu cap* [*cypro-* + *-lithic*] **:** AENEOLITHIC

¹cy·prus \ˈsīprəs\ *adj, usu cap* [fr. *Cyprus,* island in the Mediterranean sea] **:** of or from Cyprus **:** of the kind or style prevalent in Cyprus **:** CYPRIOT

²cyprus *var of* CYPRESS

cyprus cedar *n* [fr. *Cyprus,* island in the Mediterranean] **:** a cedar (*Cedrus libani brevifolia*) of the eastern Mediterranean region that differs from the cedar of Lebanon chiefly in its dwarf habit of growth, shorter leaves, and smaller cones

cyprus earth *or* **cyprus umber** *n, often cap C* **:** RAW UMBER 2

cyprus green *n, often cap C* **:** a strong yellowish green that is yellower and lighter than shamrock yellower, lighter, and stronger than emerald (sense 2b)

cyps *pl of* CYP

cyp·se·la \ˈsipsələ\ *n, pl* **cypse·lae** \-ˌlē\ [NL, fr. Gk *kypselē* hollow vessel, chest, box; akin to Gk *kyphos* bent, crooked — more at CYPHELLA] **:** an achene developed from an inferior bicarpellary ovary fused with the calyx tube (as in the sunflower) — see FRUIT illustration

cyp·sel·i·dae \sipˈselə,dē\ [NL, fr. *Cypselus,* type genus + *-idae*] *syn of* APODIDAE

cyp·se·li·form \(ˈ)sipˈselə,fȯrm, ˈsipsəl-\ *adj* [NL *Cypseliformes,* group of birds including the swift, fr. *Cypselus* + *-iformes*] **:** resembling a swift

cyp·se·line \ˈsipsə,līn\ *adj* [Gk *kypselos* swift + E *-ine*] **:** of or relating to the swifts

cyp·se·loid \-ˌlȯid\ *adj* [Gk *kypselos* swift + E *-oid*] **:** resembling a swift

cyp·se·lus \-ləs\ [NL, fr. L, a kind of swallow, fr. Gk *kypselos* sand martin, swift] *syn of* APUS

¹cyr·e·na·ic \ˌsirəˈnāik, ˌsīr-\ *adj, usu cap* [L *Cyrenaicus,* fr. Gk *Kyrēnaïkos,* adj. & n., fr. *Kyrēnaïka,* ancient region in Libya (fr. *Kyrēnē*) & *Kyrēnē* Cyrene, ancient Greek city in Libya] **1 a :** of, relating to, or characteristic of Cyrenaica, a region in Libya, Africa **b :** of, relating to, or characteristic of the people of Cyrenaica **2 a :** of, relating to, or characteristic of Cyrene, a city and in ancient times the capital city of Cyrenaica **b :** of, relating to, or characteristic of the people of Cyrene **3 :** of, relating to, or characteristic of the school of philosophers founded by Aristippus of Cyrene

²cyrenaic \ˮ\ *n* -s **1** *cap* **:** a native or resident of Cyrenaica **2** *cap* **:** a native or resident of Cyrene **3** *usu cap* **a :** a member or a follower of a school of philosophers founded by Aristippus of Cyrene who taught that pleasure is the chief end of life — contrasted with *cynic* **b :** one who holds views resembling those of a Cyrenaic

cyr·e·na·i·cism \ˌ≠≠ˈnāə,sizəm\ *n* -s *often cap* **:** the doctrine of the Cyrenaics **:** Cyrenaic hedonism

cy·re·ni·an *or* **cy·re·nae·an** \(ˈ)sīˈrēnēən\ *adj or n, usu cap* [*Cyrene* + E *-ian, -aean*] **:** CYRENAIC

cy·ril·la \səˈrilə\ *n* [NL, after Domenico Cirillo *or Cyrillo* †1799 It. physician] **1** *cap* **:** a small genus of shrubs and trees (family Cyrillaceae) that have flowers with acute twisted petals and wingless fruit **2** -s **:** a shrub or tree of the genus *Cyrilla*

cyr·il·la·ce·ae \ˌsirəˈlāsē,ē\ *n pl, cap* [NL, fr. *Cyrilla,* type genus + *-aceae*] **:** a family of shrubs and trees (order Sapindales) with entire coriaceous leaves, small white flowers in racemes, and capsular fruit — **cyr·il·la·ceous** \ˌ≠≠ˈlāshəs\ *adj*

¹cy·ril·li·an \səˈrilēən\ *also* **cy·ril·lic** \-lik\ *adj, usu cap* [*Cyrillus* (Cyril) †444 archbishop of Alexandria + E *-ian* or *-ic*] **:** of, relating to, or based on the thought of Cyril of Alexandria or his followers in his controversy with Nestorius

²cyrillian \ˮ\ *n* -s *cap* **:** a follower of Cyril of Alexandria

cy·ril·li·an·ism \-lēə,nizəm\ *n* -s *often cap* **:** the doctrine of Cyril of Alexandria and his followers that Christ had a thoroughly unified divine-human nature

cy·ril·lic \səˈrilik\ *adj, often cap C* [*Cyrillus* (Cyril) †869 apostle of the Slavs, reputed inventor of the Cyrillic alphabet + E *-ic*] **:** constituting or written in the Cyrillic alphabet

cyrillic alphabet *n, usu cap C* **:** the alphabet based principally on the Greek uncials that was orig. used for writing Old Church Slavonic and that in its modern form with minor variations among the different languages is the alphabet used for Russian and many other Slavic languages and for some non-Slavic languages of the Soviet Union — compare GLAGOLITIC

cyr·o·mys \ˈsirə,mis\ [NL, fr. Gk *kyros* power, might + NL *-mys* — more at CURIOLOGIC] *syn of* UROMYS

cyrt- *or* **cyrto-** *comb form* [NL, fr. Gk *kyrt-, kyrto-,* fr. *kyrtos* bulging, convex; akin to L *curvus* curved — more at CROWN] **:** bent **:** curved ⟨*cyrto*pia⟩ ⟨*cyrto*style⟩ **:** something curved ⟨*cyrto*meter⟩

cyr·ti·dae \ˈsərd·ə,dē\ *n pl, cap* [NL, fr. *Cyrtus,* type genus (fr. Gk *kyrtos* bulging, convex) + *-idae*] **:** a family of two-winged flies with small head and greatly enlarged convex thorax whose larvae are parasitic on spiders

cyr·toc·er·a·cone \sərˈtäsərə,kōn\ *n* -s [NL *Cyrtoceras* + E *cone*] **:** a nautiloid cephalopod shell curved like those of *Cyrtoceras* — **cyr·toc·er·a·con·ic** \ˌ≠≠≠rəˈkänik\ *adj*

cyr·toc·er·as \≠ˈ≠≠rəs\ *n, cap* [NL, fr. *cyrt-* + *-ceras*] **:** a genus of Paleozoic nautiloid cephalopods having a conical slightly curved shell with a large body chamber

cyr·to·cer·a·tite \ˌsərd·əˈserə,tīt\ *n* -s [NL *Cyrtocerat-, Cyrtoceras* + E *-ite*] **:** a fossil cephalopod of the genus *Cyrtoceras* — **cyr·to·cer·a·tit·ic** \ˌ≠≠≠rəˈtid·ik\ *adj*

cyr·toi·dae \sərˈtȯi(ˌ)dē\ *n pl, cap* [NL, fr. *cyrt-* + *-idae*] **:** a family of radiolarians widely distributed and often employed as a paleontological index group — compare INDEX FOSSIL

cyr·to·lite \ˈsərd·əl,īt\ *n* -s [*cyrt-* + *-lite*] **:** a mineral related to zircon but containing uranium, yttrium, and other rare earths

cyr·tom·e·ter \sərˈtäməd·ər\ *n* -s [ISV *cyrt-* + *-meter;* orig. formed as F *cyrtomètre*] **:** an instrument used for delineating or measuring the dimensions of curved surfaces esp. of the chest and head

cyr·to·mi·um \-ˈtōmēəm\ *n, cap* [NL, fr. Gk *kyrtōma* bulge, convexity (fr. *kyrtos* bulging, crooked, convex) + NL *-ium* — more at CYRT-] **:** a small genus of tropical Asiatic greenhouse ferns (family Polypodiaceae) with anastomosing veins

cyr·to·pia \-ˈtōpēə\ *n* -s [NL, fr. *Cyrtopia,* genus of crustaceans, fr. *cyrt-* + *-opia;* fr. the resemblance of these larvae to crustaceans of this genus] **:** a larva of certain crustaceans (subclass Ostracoda) characterized by a lengthening of the first pair of antennae and loss of swimming function in the second pair

cyr·to·sis \-ˈtōsəs\ *n, pl* **cyrto·ses** \-ˌsēz\ [NL, fr. Gk *kyrtōsis* bulging, fr. *kyrt-* cyrt- + *-ōsis* -osis] **:** a virus disease of cotton characterized by dwarfing, distortion, discolorations, and abnormal branching

cyr·to·style \ˈsərd·ə,stīl\ *n* -s [*cyrt-* + *-style*] **:** a circular projecting columned portico

cy·rus \ˈsīrəs\ *n* -ES [by alter.] **:** SARUS

¹cyst \ˈsist\ *n* -s [NL *cystis,* fr. Gk *kystis* bladder, pouch; akin to Gk *kysthos* vulva — more at HOARD] **1 :** a sac lacking an opening but having a distinct membrane and developing abnormally in a natural cavity of the body, in the substance of an organ, or in an abnormal structure (as a tumor) **2 a :** a resting spore formed in many algae (as blue-green algae and desmids) by the breaking up of portions of the filaments or by the enclosing of a cell or cell group and their investment by a sheath or envelope — compare STATOSPORE **b :** an air vesicle in certain algae (as the common rockweed) **c :** a structure comparable to a spore formed by certain slime molds **d** (1) **:** a capsule or round sheath formed about certain cells (as some bacteria) when going into a resting stage or becoming transformed into spores (2) **:** the whole structure including the contents of the capsule **3 :** a sac or capsule produced by an animal: as **a :** one that many protozoans and other minute animals secrete about themselves as a prelude to a resting or a specialized reproductive phase **b :** a resistant covering about a parasite produced by the parasite, the host, or by interaction of both

²cyst \ˮ\ *n* -s [alter. (prob. influenced by ¹*cyst*) of ¹*cist*] **:** CIST

cyst- *or* **cysti-** *or* **cysto-** *comb form* [F, fr. Gk *kyst-, kysto-,* fr. *kystis* bladder, pouch] **1 a :** gall bladder ⟨*cysto*colostomy⟩ **b :** urinary bladder ⟨*cyst*itis⟩ ⟨*cysto*tomy⟩ **2 :** sac **:** pouch **:** cyst ⟨*cyst*enchyma⟩ ⟨*cysti*form⟩ ⟨*cysto*phore⟩

-cyst \ˌsist\ *n comb form* -s [NL *-cyste, -cystis,* fr. Gk *kystis*] **:** bladder ⟨chole*cyst*⟩

cyst·adenoma \ˌsist +\ *n, pl* **cystadenomas** *or* **cystadenomata** [NL, fr. *cyst-* + *adenoma*] **:** an adenoma marked by a cystic structure — **cyst·adenomatous** \ˌsist +\ *adj*

cyst·a·thionine \ˌsistə +\ *n* -s [*cysteine* + *-a-* + *methionine*] **:** a diamino dicarboxylic acid $C_7H_{14}N_2O_4S$ held to be formed as an intermediate in the conversion of methionine to cysteine in the animal organism

cys·tec·to·my \siˈstektəmē\ *n* -ES [ISV *cyst-* + *-ectomy*] **:** the surgical excision of a cyst; *specif* **:** the removal of all or a portion of the urinary bladder

cys·te·ic acid \ˈsistēik-\ *n* [ISV *cysteine* + *-ic*] **:** a crystalline amino acid $HO_3SCH_2CH(NH_2)COOH$ formed by oxidation of cysteine or cystine (as in the outer layers of sheep's wool) and yielding taurine on decarboxylation; *β*-sulfo-alanine

cys·teine \ˈsi,stēn, -stē,ēn, ˈsistən *also* siˈstēən\ *n* -s [ISV, blend of *cystine* and *-eine;* orig. formed as G *zystein*] **:** a crystalline amino acid $HSCH_2CH(NH_2)COOH$ occurring as a constituent of many proteins and of glutathione and readily oxidizable to cystine; *β*-mercapto-alanine

cys·tic \ˈsistik, -tēk\ *adj* [F *cystique,* fr. NL *cysticus,* fr. *cystis* cyst + L *-icus* -ic — more at CYST] **1 a :** of or relating to a cyst **b :** of or relating to the urinary bladder or gallbladder **2 :** being a cyst **:** made up of cysts ⟨~ tissue⟩ **3 :** containing a cyst or cysts ⟨a ~ tumor⟩ **:** involving the formation of cysts ⟨~ degeneration⟩ **4 :** enclosed in a cyst **:** ENCYSTED ⟨a ~ worm larva⟩

cys·ti·ca \ˈsistəkə\ *n pl, cap* [NL, fr. *cyst-* + *-ica* (neut. pl. of *-icus* -ic)] *in former classifications* **:** the larval tapeworms regarded as constituting a natural order

cystic duct *also* **cystic canal** *n* **:** the duct from the gallbladder that unites with the hepatic to form the common bile duct — see DIGESTION illustration

cys·ti·cercal \ˌsistə +\ *adj* [NL *cysticercus* + E *-al*] **:** of, relating to, or caused by a cysticercus or cysticerci

cys·ti·cer·ci·a·sis \ˌsistəsərˈsīəsəs\ *n, pl* **cysticercia·ses** \-ˌsēz\ [NL, fr. *cysticercus* + *-iasis*] **:** CYSTICERCOSIS

cys·ti·cer·coid \-əˈsər,kȯid\ *n* -s [ISV *cysticerc-* (fr. NL *cysticercus*) + *-oid*] **:** a larval tapeworm having an invaginated scolex and solid tailpiece — compare COENURUS, CYSTICERCUS, ECHINOCOCCUS

cys·ti·cer·co·sis \-əsərˈkōsəs\ *n, pl* **cysticerco·ses** \-ō,sēz\ [NL, fr. *cysticercus* + *-osis*] **:** infestation with or disease caused by cysticerci

cys·ti·cercus \ˌsistə +\ *n* [NL, fr. *cyst-* + *-cercus* (fr. Gk *kerkos* tail)] **1** *cap, in former classifications* **:** a genus of parasitic animals comprising the cysticerci when these were not understood to be tapeworm larvae — now often used as though a generic name when referring specif. to the larva ⟨*Cysticercus cellulosae* is the larva of *Taenia solium*⟩ **2** *pl* **cysticerci :** a tapeworm larva consisting of a scolex invaginated into a fluid-filled sac lying in the tissues of an intermediate host and capable of developing into an adult tapeworm when consumed by a suitable definitive host — called also *bladder worm, measle;* compare COENURUS, CYSTICERCOID, ECHINOCOCCUS, PLEROCERCOID

cystic fibrosis *n* **:** MUCOVISCIDOSIS

cys·ti·cid·al \ˌ≠≠ˈsīdᵊl\ *adj* [*cyst-* + *-cide* + *-al*] **:** killing or tending to kill an encysted stage of an organism ⟨a ~ agent such as chlorine⟩

cys·tid \ˈsistəd\ *n* -s [NL *Cystidea*] **:** any fossil or echinoderm of the class Cystoidea

cys·tid·ea \siˈstidēə\ [NL, fr. *cyst-* + *-idea*] *syn of* CYSTOIDEA

cys·tid·e·an \(ˈ)siˈstidēən\ *adj or n* [NL *Cystidea* + E *-an*] **:** CYSTOIDEAN

cys·tid·i·um \siˈstidēəm\ *n, pl* **cystid·ia** \-dēə\ *or* **cystidiums** [NL, fr. *cyst-* + *-idium*] **:** one of the large inflated and thick-walled cells of the hymenial layer projecting beyond the basidia and paraphyses in certain basidiomycetous fungi

cys·tig·er·ous \(ˈ)siˈstijərəs\ *adj* [*cyst-* + *-gerous*] **:** containing or producing cysts ⟨~ tissue⟩

cys·tine \ˈsi,stēn, -stən\ *n* -s [*cyst-* + *-ine;* fr its discovery in urinary calculi] **:** a colorless crystalline amino acid $[-SCH_2CH(NH_2)COOH]_2$ occurring as a constituent of most proteins (as the keratins in hair, wool, and horn) from which it can be obtained by hydrolysis and yielding cysteine on reduction; *β,β′*-dithio-di-alanine

cys·ti·nu·ria \ˌsistəˈn(y)u̇rēə\ *n* -s [NL, fr. E *cystine* + NL *-uria*] **:** a familial metabolic defect characterized by the excretion of excessive amounts of cystine in the urine and sometimes resulting in the formation of stones in the urinary tract — **cys·ti·nu·ric** \ˌ≠≠≠ˈrik\ *adj or n*

-cys·tis \ˈsistəs\ *n comb form, pl* **-cystides** [NL, fr. Gk *kystis*] **:** one having (such) a bladder or pouch — esp. in generic names ⟨Macro*cystis*⟩

cys·tit·ic \(ˈ)siˈstid·ik\ *adj* [NL *cystitis* + E *-ic*] **:** characteristic of or affected with cystitis

cys·ti·tis \siˈstīd·əs\ *n, pl* **cystit·i·des** \-tid·ə,dēz\ [NL, fr. *cyst-* + *-itis*] **:** inflammation of the urinary bladder

cysto- — see CYST-

cys·to·carp \ˈsistə,kärp, -stō,-\ *n* -s [ISV *cyst-* + *-carp*] **:** the fruiting structure produced in the red algae after fertilization; *esp* **:** such a structure having a special protective envelope (as in *Polysiphonia*) — **cys·to·car·pic** \ˌ≠≠ˈ≠pik\ *adj*

cys·to·cele \-ˌsēl\ *n* -s [*cyst-* + *-cele*] **:** hernia of a bladder, esp. the urinary bladder **:** vesical hernia

cys·to·cer·cous \ˌ≠≠ˈsərkəs\ *adj* [*cyst-* + *-cercous* (fr. Gk *kerkos* tail)] *of a cercaria* **:** having a space in the tail into which the body can be retracted

cys·to·flagellata \ˌ≠≠ +\ *n pl, cap* [NL, fr. *cyst-* + *flagellata*] **:** a small suborder of Dinoflagellata comprising a few naked flagellates without furrows and lacking a transverse flagellum that are remarkably medusoid in form — **cys·to·flagellate** \ˮ +\ *adj or n*

cys·tog·e·nous \(ˈ)siˈstäjənəs\ *adj* [*cyst-* + *-genous*] **:** cyst-producing ⟨~ glands of a cercaria⟩

cys·to·gram \ˈsistə,gram, -stō,-\ *n* -s [*cyst-* + *-gram*] **:** a roentgenogram made by cystography

cys·tog·ra·phy \siˈstägrəfē\ *n* -ES [F *cystographie,* short for *cystoradiographie,* fr. *cyst-* + *radiographie* radiography] **:** roentgenography of the urinary bladder after injection of a contrast medium

¹cys·toid \ˈsi,stȯid\ *adj* [ISV *cyst-* + *-oid;* prob. orig. formed as F *cystoïde*] **1 :** like a bladder **2** [NL *Cystoidea*] **:** CYSTOIDEAN

²cystoid \ˮ\ *n* -s **1 :** a cystoid structure; *specif* **:** a mass resembling a cyst but lacking a membrane **2 :** CYSTOIDEAN

cys·toid·ea \siˈstȯidēə\ *n pl, cap* [NL, fr. *cyst-* + *-oidea*] **:** a class of Paleozoic short-stemmed or stemless pelmatozoan echinoderms formerly considered an order of Crinoidea having the body commonly somewhat globular or egg-shaped and enclosed in calcareous plates that are usu. pierced by a series of pores possibly respiratory in function

¹cys·toi·de·an \(ˈ)≠ˈ≠dēən\ *adj* [NL *Cystoidea* + E *-an*] **:** of or relating to the Cystoidea

²cystoidean \ˮ\ *n* -s **:** a fossil or echinoderm of the class Cystoidea

cys·to·lith \ˈsistə,lith, -stō,-\ *n* -s [G *zystolith,* fr. *zyst-* cyst- + *-lith*] **1 :** a calcium carbonate concretion commonly stalked and arising from the cellulose wall of certain cells of higher plants esp. from modified epidermal cells of some flowering plants — compare LITHOCYST **2 :** a urinary calculus — **cys·to·lith·ic** \ˌ≠≠ˈthik\ *adj*

cys·to·lithiasis \ˌ≠≠ +\ *n* [NL, fr. ISV *cystolith* + NL *-iasis*] **:** the presence of calculi in the urinary bladder

cys·to·ma \siˈstōmə\ *n, pl* **cystomas** \-məz\ *or* **cystoma·ta** \-məd·ə\ [NL, fr. *cyst-* + *-oma*] **:** a tumor containing cysts — **cys·tom·a·tous** \(ˈ)siˈstäməd·əs, -tōm-\ *adj*

cys·tom·e·ter \siˈstäməd·ə(r)\ *n* -s [*cyst-* + *-meter*] **:** an instrument designed to measure pressure within the urinary bladder in relation to its capacity — **cys·to·met·ric** \ˌsistəˈmetrik\ *adj* — **cys·tom·e·try** \siˈstämətrē\ *n* -ES

cys·to·met·ro·gram \ˌsistəˈmetrə,gram, -stō-, -trō-,\ *n* -s [ISV *cystometro-* (fr. *cystometer*) + *-gram*] **:** a graphic recording of a cystometric measurement — compare CYSTOMETER

cys·to·nec·tae \ˌ≠≠ˈnek(ˌ)tē\ *n pl, cap* [NL, fr. *cyst-* + *-nectae*] *in some classifications* **:** a suborder of siphonophores including only the Portuguese man-of-war — **cys·to·nec·tous** \-ktəs\ *adj*

cys·toph·o·ra \siˈstäfərə\ *n, cap* [NL, fr. *cyst-* + *-phora;* fr. the hoodlike sac on the head] **:** a genus of carnivorous mammals including solely the hooded seal

cys·to·phore \ˈsistə,fō(ə)r\ *n* -s [*cyst-* + *-phore*] **:** the branched stalk that bears the cysts of myxobacteria

cys·top·ter·is \siˈstäptərəs\ *n, cap* [NL, fr. *cyst-* + *-pteris*] **:** a genus of ferns (family Polypodiaceae) of the north temperate zone having a hooded or arched indusium partly under the roundish sori — see BLADDER FERN, FRAGILE FERN

cys·to·pus \ˈsistəpəs\ [NL, fr. *cyst-* + *-pus*] *syn of* ALBUGO

cys·to·pyelitis \ˌsistə, -stō +\ *n* [NL, fr. *cyst-* + *pyelitis*] **:** inflammation of the urinary bladder and of the pelvis of one or both kidneys

cys·to·pyelography \ˮ +\ *n* -ES [*cyst-* + *pyelography*] **:** roentgenography of the urinary bladder, the ureter, and the pelvis of the kidney after injection of these organs with a contrast medium

cys·to·pyelonephritis \ˮ +\ *n* [NL, fr. *cyst-* + *pyelonephritis*] **:** inflammation of the urinary bladder and of the cortex and pelvis of one or both kidneys

¹cys·to·scope \ˈsistə,skōp\ *n* -s [ISV *cyst-* + *-scope;* orig. formed as G *zystoskop*] **:** an instrument that permits visual examination of the bladder and the use of operative devices under visual control — **cys·to·scopic** \ˌ≠≠ˈskäpik\ *adj* — **cys·tos·co·pist** \siˈstäskəpəst\ *n* -s — **cys·tos·co·py** \-pē\ *n* -ES

²cystoscope \ˮ\ *vt* -ED/-ING/-s **:** to perform cystoscopy on (a patient)

cys·to·spore \ˈsistə,spō(ə)r\ *n* -s [ISV *cyst-* + *-spore*] **:** an encysted zoospore (as in certain chytridiales)

cys·to·tome \-ˌtōm\ *n* -s [ISV *cyst-* + *-tome*] **1 :** an instrument used in incising the urinary bladder **2 :** an instrument used in opening the capsule of the lens in cataract operations — **cys·tot·o·my** \siˈstäd·əmē\ *n* -ES

cys·to·ureteritis \ˌsistə, -stō +\ *n* [NL, fr. *cyst-* + *ureter-* + *-itis*] **:** combined inflammation of the urinary bladder and ureters

cys·to·urethrogram \ˮ +\ *n* [*cyst-* + *urethrogram*] **:** a roentgenogram of the urinary bladder and urethra made after injection of these organs with a contrast medium

cyst·ous \ˈsistəs\ *adj* [¹*cyst* + *-ous*] **:** CYSTIC

cysts *pl of* CYST

-cysts *pl of* -CYST

cyt- *or* **cyto-** *comb form* [G *zyt-, zyto-,* fr. Gk *kyto-,* fr. *kytos* hollow vessel — more at HIDE] **1 :** cell ⟨*cyt*ase⟩ ⟨*cyto*plasm⟩ **2 :** cytoplasm ⟨*cyt*ode⟩ ⟨*cyto*some⟩

cy·tase \ˈsī,tās, -āz\ *n* -s [ISV *cyt-* + *-ase;* orig. formed as G *zytase*] **:** any of several enzymes found in the seeds of various plants (as cereals) that have the power of making soluble the material of cell walls by hydrolyzing mannan, galactan, xylan, and araban

cy·tas·ter \(ˈ)sīˈtastə(r)\ *n* [ISV *cyt-* + *aster* (achromatic substance); orig. formed as G *zytaster*] **1 :** ASTER 3 **2 :** an accessory aster not associated with the chromosomes

cyte \ˈsīt\ *n* -s [*-cyte*] **:** CELL 5; *specif* **:** a maturing germ cell — compare OOCYTE, SPERMATOCYTE

-cyte \ˌ≠\ *n comb form* -s [NL *-cyta,* fr. Gk *kytos* hollow vessel] **:** cell ⟨leuko*cyte*⟩ ⟨peri*cyte*⟩

cyth·er·ea \ˌsithəˈrēə\ [NL, fr. L, epithet of Venus-Aphrodite, fr. Gk *Kythereia,* fr. *Kythēra* Cythera, Greek island associated with Aphrodite] *syn of* CALYPSO

¹cyth·er·e·an \-ən\ *n* -s *usu cap* [L *Cytherea,* epithet of Venus + E *-an*] **:** a votary of Aphrodite

²cytherean \ˌ≠≠ˈ≠\ *adj, usu cap* [L *Cytherea* + E *-an*] **:** of or relating to the goddess Venus or to the planet Venus

cyth·er·el·la \ˌsithəˈrelə\ *n, cap* [NL, dim. of L *Cytherea,* epithet of Venus] **:** a genus of crustaceans (subclass Ostracoda) with biramous second antennae used for swimming

cyt·i·dine \ˈsid·ə,dēn, -dən\ *n* -s [ISV *cyt-* + *-idine*] **:** a crystalline nucleoside $C_9H_{13}N_3O_5$ obtained by hydrolysis of ribonucleic acid and cytidylic acid; 1-D-ribosyl-cytosine

cyt·i·dyl·ic acid \ˌsid·əˈdilik-\ *n* [ISV *cytidine* + *-yl* + *-ic*] **:** a crystalline nucleotide $C_9H_{14}N_3O_8P$ known in various isomeric forms and obtained by hydrolysis of ribonucleic acid; cytidine monophosphate

cyt·i·nus \ˈsitᵊnəs\ *n, cap* [NL, fr. Gk *kytinos* flower of the pomegranate, fr. *kytos* hollow vessel, skin + *-inos* -ine — more at HIDE] **:** a genus of reddish or yellow fleshy root parasitic herbs (family Rafflesiaceae) comprising one African and three European species that grow on the roots of plants of the genus *Cistus*

cyt·i·sine \ˈsid·ə,sēn, -ˌzēn, -ˌsən\ *n* -s [NL *Cytisus* + E *-ine*] **:** a bitter crystalline very poisonous alkaloid $C_{11}H_{14}N_2O$ found in many plants of the pea family and formerly used as a cathartic and diuretic — compare ULEXINE

cyt·i·sus \-səs, -zəs\ *n* [NL, fr. L, a shrub (*Medicago arborea*), fr. Gk *kytisos*] **1** *cap* **:** a large genus of stiff or spiny shrubs (family Leguminosae) native to Europe, northern Africa, and western Asia and having showy racemose flowers with a 2-lipped calyx — see BROOM 1 **2** *pl* **cytisi :** a plant of the genus *Cytisus*

cy·to- *in pronunciations below,* ˌ≠≠ = ˌsīd·ō *or* ˌsīd·ə *or* ˌsītō *or* ˌsītə\ — see CYT-

cy·to·architectonic \ˌ≠≠ +\ *adj* [*cyt-* + *architectonic*] **:** CYTOARCHITECTURAL

cy·to·architectonics \ˌ≠≠ +\ *n pl but sing or pl in constr* **:** CYTOARCHITECTURE

cy·to·architectural \ˌ≠≠ +\ *adj* **:** of or relating to cytoarchitecture — **cy·to·architecturally** \ˌ≠≠ +\ *adv*

cy·to·architecture \ˌ≠≠ +\ *n* [*cyt-* + *architecture*] **:** the cellular makeup of a bodily tissue or structure

cy·to·blast \ˈ≠≠,blast\ *n* -s [G *zytoblast,* fr. *zyt-* cyt- + *-blast*] **1 :** NUCLEUS 2a **2 :** ALTMANN'S GRANULES **3 :** PROTOPLAST

cy·to·blastema \ˌ≠≠ +\ *n* [NL, fr. *cyt-* + *blastema*] **:** the formative material from which cells formerly were thought to arise — **cy·to·blastemal** \ˌ≠≠ +\ *adj*

cy·to·centrum \ˌ≠≠ +\ *n* [NL, fr. *cyt-* + L *centrum* center — more at CENTER] **:** CENTRAL APPARATUS

cy·to·chemical \ˌ≠≠ +\ *adj* [*cyt-* + *chemical*] **:** of, relating to, or used in cytochemistry ⟨~ methods⟩

cy·to·chemistry \ˌ≠≠ +\ *n* [*cyt-* + *chemistry*] **1 :** microscopical biochemistry **2 :** the chemistry of cells

cy·to·chon·dria \ˌ≠≠ˈkändrēə\ *n pl* [NL, fr. *cyt-* + *chondr-* + *-ia*] **:** formed bodies in the cytoplasm of a cell — compare MITOCHONDRION

cy·to·chrome \ˈ≠≠ +,-\ *n* -s [*cyt-* + *-chrome*] **:** any of several respiratory pigments that occur in animal and plant cells, play a major role in intracellular oxidations (as by oxidizing flavoproteins and being in turn oxidized by means of cytochrome oxidase), and are related chemically to hemoglobin in that they are complexes of iron, a porphyrin, and a protein; *esp* **:** CYTOCHROME C

cytochrome c *n, often cap 2d C* **:** the most abundant and stable of the cytochromes obtained from various sources (as beef heart or yeast)

cytochrome oxidase *n* **:** an iron-porphyrin enzyme important in cell respiration because of its ability to catalyze the oxidation of reduced cytochrome c in the presence of oxygen — called also *respiratory enzyme*

cy·to·chy·le·ma \ˌ≠≠ +\ *n* -s [NL, fr. *cyt-* + *-chylema* (as in *enchylema*)] **:** HYALOPLASM

cy·toc·i·dal \(ˈ)sīˈtäsədᵊl\ *adj* **:** killing or tending to kill individual cells

cy·tode \ˈsī,tōd\ *n* -s [ISV *cyt-* + *-ode* (fr. Gk *-ōdēs* like); orig. formed as G *zytode* — more at -ODES] **1 :** an anucleate mass of protoplasm **2 :** an organism normally assuming the form of a cytode (as a bacterium)

cy·to·dendrite \ˌ≠≠ *at* CYTO- +\ *n* [*cyt-* + *dendrite*] **:** a dendrite given off from the body of a nerve cell — distinguished from *axodendrite*

cy·to·diagnosis \¦== +\ *n* [NL, fr. *cyt-* + *diagnosis*] **:** diagnosis based upon the examination of cells found in the tissues or fluids of the body — **cy·to·diagnostic** \¦== +\ *adj*

cy·to·dieresis \¦== +\ *n, pl* **cytodiereses** [NL, fr. *cyt-* + *dieresis* dividing, fr. Gk *diairesis* — more at DIAERESIS] **:** CYTOKINESIS — **cy·to·dieretic** \¦== +\ *adj*

cy·tog·a·my \sīˈtägəmē\ *n* -ES [*cyt-* + *-gamy*] **:** cell fusion **:** CONJUGATION 4

cy·to·gene \ˈ== *at* CYTO- +ˌ-\ *n* [*cyt-* + *gene*] **:** a self-duplicating cytoplasmic gene or determinant (as those of certain plant plastids) — compare PLASMAGENE — **cy·to·genic** \¦== +\ *adj*

cy·to·genetic *also* **cy·to·genetical** \¦== +\ *adj* [ISV *cyt-* + *-genetic, -genetical*] **:** of, relating to, concerning, or by the methods of cytogenetics — **cy·to·genetically** \¦== +\ *adv*

cy·to·geneticist \¦== +\ *n* **:** one specializing in cytogenetics

cy·to·genetics \¦== +\ *n pl but sing or pl in constr* [ISV *cyt-* + *genetics*] **:** a branch of biology that deals with the study of heredity and variation by the methods of both cytology and genetics

cy·tog·e·nous \(ˈ)sī¦täjənəs\ *adj* [*cyt-* + *-genous*] **:** producing cells — used specif. of lymphatic tissue

cy·to·geography \¦== *at* CYTO- +\ *n* [*cyt-* + *geography*] **:** a branch of biogeography dealing with the distribution of gene complexes among related populations

cy·to·globin \¦== +\ *n* [ISV *cyt-* + *globin;* orig. formed as G *zytoglobin*] **:** a nucleoprotein obtainable from many cells and glandular organs

cy·to·histological *also* **cy·to·histologic** \¦== +\ *adj* **:** of, relating to, or by the methods of cytohistology ⟨~ zonation⟩ ⟨~ diagnosis⟩

cy·to·histology \¦== +\ *n* [*cyt-* + *histology*] **:** the integrated study of cells and tissues

cy·to·kinesis \¦== +\ *n* [NL, fr. *cyt-* + *kinesis*] **1 :** the cytoplasmic changes accompanying karyokinesis **2 :** cleavage of the cytoplasm into daughter cells following nuclear division — **cy·to·kinetic** \¦== +\ *adj*

cy·to·lei·chus \ˌ==ˈlīkəs\ *n, cap* [NL, fr. *cyt-* + *-leichus* (prob. fr. Gk *leichein* to lick, lick up) — more at LICK] **:** a genus (the type of the family Cytoleichidae) of parasitic mites including only the air-sac mite (*C. nudus*)

cy·to·logical *or* **cy·to·logic** \¦== +\ *adj* **:** of, relating to, or by the methods of cytology — **cy·to·logically** \¦== +\ *adv*

cytologic diagnosis *n* **:** cytodiagnosis esp. for the detection of cancer

cy·tol·o·gist \sīˈtäləjəst\ *n* -S **1 :** one specializing in the study of cells **2 :** a pathologist using cytological techniques in the differential diagnosis of neoplasms

cy·tol·o·gy \-jē, -ji\ *n* -ES [ISV *cyt-* + *-logy*] **1 :** the branch of biology concerned with the study of cells as vital units with reference to their structure, function, multiplication, pathology, and life history ⟨as a procedure for differentiating benign from malignant lesions ~ offers a more precise method of diagnosis than roentgenologic and endoscopic study —*Jour. Amer. Med. Assoc.*⟩ — distinguished from *histology* **2 :** the cytological aspects of a phenomenon, process, or structure considered collectively ⟨the ~ of cancer⟩ ⟨the ~ of mitosis⟩ ⟨the ~ of the normal kidney⟩

cy·to·lymph \ˈ== *at* CYTO- +ˌ-\ *n* [ISV *cyt-* + *lymph;* orig. formed as G *zytolymphe*] **:** HYALOPLASM

cy·tol·y·sin \sīˈtäləsən, ¦sīd·əˈlīsᵊn\ *n* -S [ISV *cytolys-* (fr. NL *cytolysis*) + *-in*] **:** a substance (as a hemolysin or one of certain constituents of snake venom) producing cytolysis

cy·tol·y·sis \sīˈtäləsəs\ *n* [NL, fr. *cyt-* + *-lysis*] **:** the dissolution or disintegration of cells esp. as a pathological process — **cy·to·lytic** \¦sīd·ᵊl¦id·ik\ *adj*

cy·tol·y·zate \sīˈtäləˌzāt, -ˌzət\ *n* -S [*cytolyze* + *-ate*] **:** the products resulting from cytolysis

cy·to·lyze \ˈsīd·ᵊlˌīz\ *vt* -ED/-ING/-S [fr. NL *cytolysis*, after such pairs as ML *analysis:* E *analyze*] **:** to cause to undergo cytolysis

cy·tome \ˈsīˌtōm\ *n* -S [ISV *cyt-* + *-ome;* orig. formed in F] **1 :** the formed inclusions of the cytoplasm **:** chondriome together with ergastic substances **2 :** CHONDRIOME

cy·to·mere \ˈsīd·əˌmi(ə)r\ *n* -S [ISV *cyt-* + *-mere;* orig. formed as G *zytomer*] **1 :** one of the cells resulting from the division of the schizont in certain coccidia **2 :** the cytoplasmic component of a spermatozoon

cy·tom·e·ter \sīˈtäməd·ə(r)\ *n* -S [ISV *cyt-* + *-meter*] **:** an apparatus for counting and measuring cells

cy·to·microsome \¦== *at* CYTO- +\ *n* [ISV *cyt-* + *microsome;* orig. formed as G *zytomikrosom*] **:** a cytoplasmic microsome **:** MITOCHRONDRION

cy·to·morphosis \¦== +\ *n, pl* **cytomorphoses** [NL, fr. *cyt-* + *-morphosis*] **:** the series of developmental changes undergone by a cell during its life

cy·ton \ˈsīˌtän\ *also* **cy·tone** \-ˌtōn\ *n* -S [*cyt-* + *-on, -one*] **:** CELL; *esp* **:** NERVE CELL

cy·to·path·ic \¦== *at* CYTO- +¦pathik\ *adj* [*cyt-* + *-pathic*] **:** CYTOPATHOLOGIC

cy·to·pathogenic \¦== +\ *adj* [*cyt-* + *pathogenic*] **:** pathologic for or destructive to cells ⟨~ virus⟩ ⟨~ effects⟩

cy·to·pathologic *also* **cy·to·pathological** \¦== +\ *adj* **:** of, relating to, or involving the methods of cytopathology — **cy·to·pathologically** \¦== +\ *adv*

cy·to·pathology \¦== +\ *n* [ISV *cyt-* + *pathology*] **:** a branch of pathology that deals with manifestations of disease on the cellular level

cy·to·pe·nia \ˌ==ˈpēnēə\ *n* -S [NL, fr. *cyt-* + *-penia*] **:** a deficiency of cellular elements of the blood; *usu* **:** deficiency of a specific element (as granulocytes in granulocytopenia) — **cy·to·pe·nic** \¦==¦=nik\ *adj*

cy·toph·a·ga \sīˈtäfəgə\ *n* [NL, fr. *cyt-* + *-phaga*] **1** *cap* **:** a genus of long flexuous pointed bacteria (order Myxobacterales) showing creeping motility, forming neither fruiting bodies nor microcysts, and being saprophytes of soil and water that vigorously hydrolyze cellulose and aid in the breakdown of plant remains **2** -S **:** any bacterium of the genus *Cytophaga*

cy·to·phag·ic \¦sīd·ə¦fajik\ *also* **cy·toph·a·gous** \(ˈ)sī¦täfəgəs\ *adj* [*cyt-* + *-phagic* (fr. *-phagy* + *-ic*) or *-phagous*] **:** of, relating to, or involving phagocytosis ⟨a ~ test⟩ — **cy·toph·a·gy** \sīˈtäfəjē\ *n* -ES

cy·to·pharynx \¦== *at* CYTO- +\ *n* [ISV *cyt-* + *pharynx*] **:** a channel leading from the surface into the protoplasm of certain unicellular organisms and functioning in ciliates as a gullet

cy·to·phil \ˈ==ˌfil\ *adj* [ISV *cyt-* + *-phil;* prob. orig. formed as G *zytophil*] **:** having affinity for cells

cy·to·phore \ˈ==ˌfō(ə)r\ *n* -S [F, fr. *cyt-* + *-phore*] **:** the residual mass of cytoplasm associated with each cluster of spermatozoa in certain invertebrates

cy·to·plasm \ˈ== +ˌ-\ *n* -S [ISV *cyt-* + *-plasm;* orig. formed as G *zytoplasma*] **1 a** *archaic* **:** the fluid ground substance of protoplasm **:** HYALOPLASM **b :** PROTOPLASM — used rarely in modern cytology **2 :** the part of the protoplasm of a protoplast that lies external to the nuclear membrane — distinguished from *karyoplasm, nucleoplasm;* see HYALOPLASM — **cy·to·plasmatic** \¦==+\ *adj* — **cy·to·plasmic** \¦==+\ *adj* — **cy·to·plasmically** \¦==+\ *adv*

cytoplasmic heredity *or* **cytoplasmic inheritance** *n* **:** the transmission of characters from parent to offspring through the cytoplasm of the germ cell; *also* **:** the characters so transmitted — compare PLASMAGENE, PLASTOGENE

cy·to·plast \ˈ==ˌplast\ *n* -S [*cyt-* + *-plast*] **:** the cytoplasmic content of a cell — compare PROTOPLAST — **cy·to·plas·tic** \¦==¦=stik\ *adj*

cy·to·poi·e·sis \ˌ==ˌpȯiˈēsəs\ *n, pl* **cytopoie·ses** \-ˌsēz\ [NL, fr. *cyt-* + *-poiesis*] **:** production of cells

cy·to·proct \ˈ==ˌpräkt\ *n* -S [*cyt-* + Gk *prōktos* buttocks — more at PROCT-] **:** CYTOPYGE

cy·to·pyge \ˈ==ˌpīj\ *n* -S [ISV *cyt-* + Gk *pygē* rump; orig. formed as G *zytopyge* — more at PYG-] **:** the point esp. if permanently identifiable at which waste is discharged from the protozoan body

cy·to·reticulum \¦==+\ *n* [NL, fr. *cyt-* + *reticulum*] **1 :** a relatively solid mesh or framework in which the hyaloplasm is suspended according to some theories of protoplasmic structure **2 :** a meshwork of cells and cell processes (as in connective tissues)

cy·to·ryc·tes *also* **cy·tor·rhyc·tes** \ˌ==ˈrikˌtēz\ *n, pl* **cytoryctes** *or* **cytorrhyctes** [NL, fr. *cyt-* + Gk *oryktēs* digger, fr. *orychein, oryssein* to dig — more at ROUGH] **:** any of certain inclusion bodies (as the Guarnieri bodies) orig. considered to constitute a distinct protozoan genus

cy·to·sine \ˈ==ˌsēn, -ˌzēn, -ˌsən\ *n* -S [ISV *cyt-* + *-ose* + *-ine;* orig. formed as G *zytosin*] **:** a crystalline pyrimidine base $C_4H_5N_3O$ obtained esp. by hydrolysis of nucleic acids and also made synthetically; 4-amino-2(1*H*)-pyrimidin-one

cy·to·skeleton \¦== +\ *n* [*cyt-* + *skeleton*] **:** the oriented submicroscopic framework of complex protein fibrils that is believed to be responsible for the mechanical properties of protoplasm

cy·to·some \ˈ==ˌsōm\ *n* -S [ISV *cyt-* + *-some;* orig. formed as G *zytosom*] **:** the cytoplasmic portion of the cell — distinguished from *nucleus*

cy·tos·po·ra \sīˈtäspərə\ *n, cap* [NL, fr. *cyt-* + *-spora*] **:** a form genus of parasitic imperfect fungi (family Phyllostictaceae) that produce their spores in pycnidial cavities within a stroma that is either subepidermal or subcortical in the host

cy·tos·po·ri·na \=ˌ==ˈrīnə, -ˈrēnə\ *n, cap* [NL, fr. *Cytospora* + *-ina*] **:** a form genus of imperfect fungi resembling and sometimes included in *Cytospora* but having longer spores

cy·tos·to·mal \(ˈ)sī¦tästəməl\ *adj* **:** of or relating to a cytostome

cy·to·stome \ˈ== *at* CYTO- +ˌstōm\ *n* -S [ISV *cyt-* + *-stome;* orig. formed as G *zytostom*] **:** the mouth of a unicellular organism

cy·to·taxonomic *also* **cy·to·taxonomical** \¦== +\ *adj* **:** of, relating to, or employing the methods of cytotaxonomy — **cy·to·taxonomically** \¦== +\ *adv*

cy·to·taxonomist \¦== +\ *n* **:** one specializing in cytotaxonomy

cy·to·taxonomy \¦== +\ *n* [*cyt-* + *taxonomy*] **1 :** the study of the natural relationships and classification of organisms by methods combining classical systematic techniques with comparative studies of chromosomes **2 :** the karyologic makeup of a kind of organism ⟨the ~ of *Oenothera*⟩

cy·to·toxic \¦== +\ *adj* [in sense 1, fr. *cytotox*in + *-ic;* in sense 2, fr. *cyt-* + *toxic*] **1 :** of or relating to a cytotoxin **2 :** toxic to cells — **cy·to·toxicity** \¦== +\ *n* -ES

cy·to·toxin \¦== +\ *n* [ISV *cyt-* + *-toxin;* prob. orig. formed as G *zytotoxin*] **:** a substance having a toxic effect upon cells

cy·to·trophoblast \¦== +\ *n* [*cyt-* + *trophoblast*] **:** the inner cellular layer of the trophoblast of an embryonic placental mammal that gives rise to the plasmodial syntrophoblast covering the placental villi — called also *Langhans' layer* — **cy·to·trophoblastic** \¦== +\ *adj*

cy·to·trophoderm \¦== +\ *n* [*cyt-* + *trophoderm*] **:** CYTOTROPHOBLAST

cy·to·tropic \¦== +\ *adj* [*cyt-* + *-tropic*] **1 :** exhibiting cytotropism **2 :** attracted to cells ⟨a ~ virus⟩

cy·tot·ro·pism \sīˈtä·trəˌpizəm\ *n* -S [ISV *cyt-* + *-tropism;* orig. formed as G *zytotropismus*] **:** the tendency of isolated cells and cell masses to move toward or away from one another

cy·to·zoic \¦== *at* CYTO- +\ *adj* [*cyt-* + *-zoic*] **:** parasitic within a cell — used esp. of protozoans

cy·to·zoon \¦== +\ *n, pl* **cytozoa** [*cyt-* + *-zoon*] **:** a cytozoic animal

cy·to·zyme \ˈ==ˌzīm\ *also* **cy·to·zym** \-ˌzim\ *n* -S [F *cytozyme*, fr. *cyt-* + *-zyme* (fr. Gk *zymē* leaven) — more at ZYME] **:** THROMBOPLASTIN

cyt·tar·ia \səˈta(a)rēə\ *n, cap* [NL, fr. Gk *kyttaros* cell of a honeycomb + NL *-ia;* fr. the pitted appearance of the fungi] **:** a genus of ascomycetous fungi typifying the family Cyttariaceae and comprising the beech fungi that are parasitic on certain evergreen beeches of the southern hemisphere and that have apothecia sunken in the surface of stalked often brightly colored subspherical stromata which are gelatinous at maturity and used as food by the natives of southern So. America

cyt·tar·i·a·ce·ae \=ˌ=rēˈāsēˌē\ *n pl, cap* [NL, fr. *Cyttaria*, type genus + *-aceae*] **:** a family of ascomycetous fungi (order Helotiales) that form a pear-shaped stroma with numerous apothecial cavities — see CYTTARIA

cyw·ydd \ˈkəˌwith\ *n, pl* **cywydd·au** \kəˈwəˌthī\ [W] **1 :** a Welsh verse form in couplets or occas. triplets with rhyme and cynghanedd; *esp* **:** verse consisting of couplets of 7-syllable lines with varying cynghanedd and terminal rhyme that falls alternately on accented and on unaccented syllables **2 :** a poem written in cywydd ⟨found among his loose papers . . . the autograph of a Welsh poem, a ~ by Hopkins himself —W.H.Gardner⟩

cza·pek–dox medium \¦chä(ˌ)pek¦däks-\ *or* **czapek medium** *n, usu cap C&D* [after Friedrich *Czapek* †1921 Czech botanist & Arthur W. *Dox b*1882 Am. chemist] **:** a culture medium for various fungi consisting essentially of a balanced and buffered mixture of inorganic salts, a sugar, and water and being used (1) as a solution or (2) with added agar as a solid — called also respectively (1) *Czapek solution, Czapek-Dox solution,* (2) *Czapek agar*

czar \ˈz¦är, ˈz¦å(r *sometimes* ˈts¦\ *n* -S [obs. Pol *czar* (now *car*), fr. Russ *tsar'*, fr. ORuss *tsĭsarĭ, tsěsarĭ*, emperor, fr. Goth *kaisar*, fr. Gk or L; Gk, fr. L *Caesar* — more at CAESAR] **1** *or* **tsar** *also* **tzar** \ˈz¦ *also* ˈts\ [*tsar, tzar* fr. Russ *tsar'*] **:** an emperor or king having absolute authority; *specif* **:** the ruler of Russia before the 1917 revolution **2** *also* **tsar** [*tsar* fr. Russ *tsar'*] **:** one having great power or absolute authority **:** BOSS, DICTATOR ⟨gambling ~*s* established a mass of dummy charities to comply with the law —V.W.Peterson⟩; *esp* **:** a person to whom great authority is delegated ⟨his salary as movie ~ ran into six figures —G.W.Johnson⟩

czar·das *or* **csar·das** \ˈchärˌdäs(h) *also* zä- *or* -ˌdas *or* -ˌdəs\ *n, pl* **czardas** *or* **csardas** [Hung *csárdás*] **1 :** a Hungarian couple dance to music in duple time that starts very slowly and ends in a rapid whirl **2 :** music for or suited to the czardas

czar·dom *also* **tsar·dom** *pronunc at* CZAR + dəm\ *n* -S **1 :** the territory ruled by a czar ⟨the ~ of Moscow . . . became aware of itself as the heir of Constantinople —R.M. French⟩ **2 :** the office or authority of a czar ⟨the memorable revolt . . . against the ~ of Speaker Cannon —Allan Nevins⟩

czar·e·vitch *also* **tsar·e·vitch** \ˈz¦ärəˌvich, ˈts¦, ¦år-\ *n* -ES [Russ *tsarevich*, fr. *tsar'* + *-evich* (patronymic suffix)] **:** a son of a Russian czar

cza·rev·na *also* **tsa·rev·na** \=ˈrevnə\ *n* -S [Russ *tsarevna*, fr. *tsar'* + *-evna* (fem. patronymic suffix)] **1 :** a daughter of a Russian czar **2 :** the wife of a czarevitch

cza·ri·na *also* **tsa·ri·na** \-ˈrēnə\ *n* -S [prob. modif. of G *zarin*, fr. *zar* tsar (fr. Russ *tsar'*) + *-in* (fem. suffix)] **:** the wife of a Russian czar

czar·ish *also* **tsar·ish** *pronunc at* CZAR + ish *or* ēsh\ *adj* **:** CZARIST

czar·ism *also* **tsar·ism** \" + ˌizəm\ *n* -S **:** autocratic rule; *esp* **:** the government of Russia under the czars

[1]**czar·ist** *also* **tsar·ist** \ˈz¦ärəst, ˈz¦år- *sometimes* ˈts¦\ *or* **czar·is·tic** *or* **tsar·is·tic** \(ˈ)=¦ristik\ *adj* **:** of, relating to, or characteristic of a czar or czarism ⟨the ~ autocracy —Walter Lippmann⟩ ⟨comparisons . . . between the immediate security objectives of the Soviet Union and those of the ~ regime —C.E.Black⟩ **:** DICTATORIAL ⟨gives Bevin ~ powers to shift men and women as he will —*Fortune*⟩

[2]**czarist** *also* **tsarist** \"\ *n* -S **:** a supporter of a czar or of czarism

cza·rit·za *also* **tsa·rit·za** \z¦äˈritsə, ts¦, ¦åˈ-, -ˈrēt-\ *n* -S [Russ *tsaritsa*, fem. of *tsar'*] **:** CZARINA

[1]**czech** *also* **čech** \ˈchek\ *adj, usu cap* [*Czech* alter. (prob. influenced by Pol *czech*) of earlier *Tshekh, Tschech*, fr. Czech *čech; Čech*, fr. Czech] **1 :** [1]CZECHOSLOVAK 1 **2 :** of, relating to, or characteristic of the Czechs **3 :** of, relating to, or characteristic of the language of the Czechs (sense 1a)

[2]**czech** \"\ *n* -S *cap* **1 a :** a native or inhabitant of Bohemia or Moravia and Silesia, provinces of Czechoslovakia **b :** [2]CZECHOSLOVAK **2 :** the Slavic language of the Czechs (sense 1a)

czech·ish \-kish, -kēsh\ *adj, usu cap* **:** CZECH

czech·ize \-ˌkīz\ *vt* -ED/-ING/-S *often cap* **:** to make Czech **:** cause to acquire Czech traits or characteristics

[1]**czech·o·slo·vak** \¦chekə¦slōˌväk, -kō¦-, -ˌvak,-ˌvåk\ *or* **czech·o·slo·va·ki·an** \¦==(ˌ)=¦=kēən\ *adj, usu cap* [*Czechoslovak* fr. *Czech* + *Slovak; Czechoslovakian* fr. *Czechoslovakia* + E *-an*] **1 :** of, relating to, or characteristic of Czechoslovakia **2 :** of, relating to, or characteristic of the people of Czechoslovakia

[2]**czechoslovak** *or* **czechoslovakian** \"\ *n* -S *cap* **:** a native or inhabitant of Czechoslovakia

czech·o·slo·va·kia \¦==(ˌ)=¦=kēə\ *adj, usu cap* [fr. *Czechoslovakia*, country in central Europe] **:** of or from Czechoslovakia **:** of the kind or style prevalent in Czechoslovakia **:** CZECHOSLOVAK

cze·sto·cho·wa \¦ches(t)stə¦kōvə\ *adj, usu cap* [fr. *Częstochowa*, Poland] **:** of or from the city of Czestochowa, Poland **:** of the kind or style prevalent in Czestochowa

1d \'dē\ *n, pl* **d's** *or* **ds** \'dēz\ *often cap, often attrib* **1 a :** the fourth letter of the English alphabet **b :** an instance of this letter printed, written, or otherwise represented **c :** a speech counterpart of orthographic *d* (as *d* in *did, raider, Edgar,* or French *duc*) **2 :** 500 — see NUMBER table **3 a :** the keynote of D major or D minor **b :** the tone D **4 :** a printer's type, a stamp, or some other instrument for reproducing the letter *d* **5 :** someone or something arbitrarily or conveniently designated *d* esp. as the fourth in order or class **6 a :** a grade assigned by a teacher or examiner rating a student's work as poor in quality ⟨barely passed geometry with a *D*⟩ **b :** one graded or rated with a D ⟨a *D* student⟩ ⟨a *D* movie⟩ ⟨the theme was a *D*⟩ **7 :** something having the shape of the capital letter D; *specif* **:** a semicircle on a pool table that is about 22 inches in diameter and is used esp. in snooker games

2d *abbr, often cap* **1** dam **2** dame **3** damn **4** date **5** daughter **6** day **7** deacon **8** dead **9** dean **10** deceased **11** deci- **12** deciduous **13** defeated **14** degree **15** dele; delete **16** democratic **17** demy **18** [L *denarius; denarii*] penny; pence **19** density **20** depart; departure **21** department **22** deputy **23** deserted; deserter **24** diameter **25** died **26** differential **27** dime **28** dimensional **29** dinar **30** diopter **31** director **32** discharged **33** distance **34** dividend **35** division **36** doctor **37** dog **38** dollar **39** dominus **40** dorsal **41** dose **42** double **43** dowager **44** drachma **45** driving **46** drizzling **47** duchess; duchy; duke **48** dyne

3d *symbol* **1** *cap* Deuteronomy — used in biblical criticism to designate esp. redactions of biblical material made under the editorship of Deuteronomic writers **2** *cap* deuterium **3** deuteron **4** *cap* D day ⟨wounded in the stomach on the morning of *D* plus three —Laurence Critchell⟩ **5** *cap* duodecimo

d- \(ˌ)dē\ *prefix* [ISV, fr. *dextr-*] **1 :** dextrorotatory — usu. printed in italic ⟨*d*-tartaric acid⟩; compare DEXTR- 2 **2 :** having a similar configuration at a selected asymmetric carbon atom in an optically active molecule to the configuration of dextrorotatory glyceraldehyde — usu. printed as a small capital ⟨D-fructose⟩

1-d *abbr* 1-ED — used esp. in standard abbreviations of the past and past participle forms of certain verbs (as recd for *received,* chgd for *charged,* ltd for *limited*)

2-d *symbol* — used after the figure 2 or the figure 3 to indicate the ordinal number *second* or *third* or any ordinal number ending with *second* or *third* ⟨May 2d⟩ ⟨33d St.⟩; compare -ND, -RD

d' \"*d'y*" is d(ə)y *or* y *or* j *in sense 1,* j *in sense 2*\ *vb* [by contr.] **1 :** 1DO ⟨*d'*you know what he wants?⟩ **2 :** DID ⟨*d'*you see what I saw?⟩

-'d \d\ *vb suffix or adj suffix* [by contr.] **:** 1-ED — now esp. in forms derived from words ending in a vowel ⟨the flicker of one mascara'*d* eyelash —Leslie Charteris⟩

'd \(ə)d\ *vb* [contr. of *had, would, did*] **1 :** HAD ⟨they'*d* gone⟩ **2 a :** 1WOULD ⟨he'*d* go⟩ **b :** SHOULD **3 :** DID ⟨what'*d* you say?⟩ ⟨where'*d* he go?⟩ ⟨'*d* you see what I saw?⟩

1da \'dä\ *n* -s [Bambara] **:** KENAF

2da \"\ *n* -s *sometimes cap* [short for *dada*] *dial Brit* **:** FATHER ⟨trying to make himself look like my ~ —Frank O'Connor⟩

3da *abbr* daughter

DA *abbr* **1** days after acceptance **2** deposit account **3** direct action **4** discharge afloat **5** district attorney **6** documentary bill for acceptance **7** documents against acceptance; documents for acceptance **8** documents attached

1dab \'dab, 'daa(ə)b\ *n* -s [ME *dabbe,* prob. of imit. origin] **1 a :** a sudden blow, thrust, or slap **:** POKE, PROD; *also* **:** PECK **b :** a gentle touch or stroke **:** PAT **2 :** an instrument (as a center punch) for dabbing or marking something

2dab \"\ *vb* **dabbed; dabbed; dabbing; dabs** [ME *dabben,* fr. *dabbe,* n.] *vt* **1** *archaic* **a :** to strike with a sudden motion **b :** STAB, PIERCE **c :** PECK **2 a :** to strike or touch lightly **:** PAT ⟨she *dabbed* her eyes with her pocket handkerchief —Rudyard Kipling⟩ **b :** to cause to strike ⟨~ a paintbrush against the surface⟩ **:** apply lightly to (as with a dabber) **3 a** *dial* **:** THROW, THRUST **b** *West* **:** to throw (as a rope) so as to fasten ⟨cowpunchers could ~ their lines on anything that moved —Ross Santee⟩ **4** *also* **daub :** to dress the face of (stone) by picking or fretting **5 :** to apply ink to (a printing surface) with an ink-ball ~ *vi* **1 :** to make a dab ⟨she *dabbed* at her eyes with a . . . handkerchief —*Time*⟩ **2 :** to use a dabber (as in etching) **3 :** DABBLE *vi* 2

3dab \"\ *vt* **dabbed; dabbed; dabbing; dabs** [by alter.] **:** DAUB 1

4dab \"\ *n* -s [alter. of *daub*] **1 :** 2DAUB **2 :** a small amount or portion ⟨a little ~ of peas on a plate⟩ **3** *archaic* **:** a wet or dirty cloth

5dab \"\ *n* -s [AF *dabbe*] **:** FLATFISH; *esp* **:** any of several flounders of the genus *Limanda* — often used in combination ⟨sand ~⟩

6dab \"\ *n* -s [perh. alter. (influenced by 1 & 2*dab*) of *adept* (*a dab* resulting from incorrect division of *adept*)] *chiefly Brit* **:** a skillful hand **:** EXPERT ⟨a ~ at rationalizing —C.H. Glover⟩

7dab *also* **dabb** \"\ *n* -s [Ar *ḍabb* lizard] **:** a large spinytailed agamoid lizard (*Uromastix spinipes* or related species) of Arabia, Egypt, and No. Africa

dab·ber \-bə(r)\ *n* -s **1 :** one that dabs **2 :** a utensil for dabbing: as **a :** a pad used by etchers or engravers to apply ink, ground, or color evenly to a surface **b :** a brush used by stereotypers to force the damped matrix material into the interstices of the matter being molded **c :** a similar brush used in gilding or photography **d :** INK-BALL

dab·ble \'dabəl\ *vb* **dabbled; dabbled; dabbling** \-b(ə)liŋ\ **dabbles** [perh. freq. of 3*dab*] *vt* **:** to wet by splashing or by little dips or strokes **:** SPATTER, SPLASH, SPRINKLE ⟨boots *dabbled* with mud⟩ ⟨the moon hung over the harbor *dabbling* the waves with gold —Katherine Mansfield⟩ ~ *vi* **1 a :** to paddle, splash, or play in or as if in water ⟨~ with his fingers in the sand —W.F.Davis⟩ **b** *of a duck* **:** to tilt the body forward and downward in shallow water to obtain food from the bottom **2 :** to work or concern oneself in a superficial way or intermittently according to whim — usu. used with *in* ⟨~ in politics⟩ ⟨eternally *dabbling* in diets —Lois Long⟩ **3** *archaic* **:** TAMPER, MEDDLE

dab·bler \-b(ə)lə(r)\ *n* -s **1 :** one that concerns himself only superficially with something **:** one that merely dips into something **:** DILETTANTE **2 :** a duck that frequents shallow water and feeds by dabbling — compare DIVING DUCK

dab·bling·ly *adv* **:** in a dabbling manner

dab·by \-bē\ *adj, usu* -ER/-EST [3*dab* + -*y*] *archaic* **:** wet and adhesive ⟨~ clothes⟩ **:** MOIST, DAMP

dabchick \'dab+,-\ *n* [earlier *dapchick,* prob. fr. alter. of *dop* (to dive) + *chick*] **1 :** any of several small grebes: as **a :** LITTLE GREBE **b :** PIED-BILLED GREBE **c :** a small Australian grebe (*Podiceps novae-hollandiae*) **2** *dial Eng* **:** the common gallinule of Europe

dab·er locks \'dabə(r),-\ *n pl but sing or pl in constr* [by alter.] **:** BADDERLOCKS

dab-hand *n* [6*dab*] *chiefly Brit* **:** EXPERT

da·boia \də'bȯiə\ *n* [Hindi *daboyā,* lit., lurker, fr. *dabnā* to be pressed down, lurk] **1** *also* **da·boya** \"\ -s **:** RUSSELL'S VIPER **2** *cap* [NL, fr. Hindi *daboyā*] *in some esp former classifications* **:** a genus of vipers containing solely the Russell's viper

dabs *pl of* DAB, *pres 3d sing of* DAB

dab·ster \'dabstə(r)\ *n* -s [prob. fr. 6*dab* + -*ster*] **1** *chiefly dial* **:** one that is esp. skilled **:** EXPERT **2** [prob. influenced in meaning by *dabble*] **:** a dabbler at anything **:** an unskilled hand

1da ca·po \(ˈ)dä'kä(ˌ)pō, də'k-\ *adv (or adj)* [It] **:** from the beginning — used as a direction in music to repeat; abbr. *D.C.*

2da capo \"\ *n, pl* **da capos :** a part repeated or to be repeated da capo in a piece of music

da capo aria *n* **:** ARIA DA CAPO

dac·ca \'dakə, 'dȧkə\ *adj, usu cap* [fr. *Dacca,* Pakistan] **:** of or from the city of Dacca, Pakistan **:** of the kind or style prevalent in Dacca

dace \'dās\ *n, pl* **dace** *or* **daces** [ME *dace, darce,* fr. MF *dars,* fr. ML *darsus*] **1 :** a small European cyprinoid fish (*Leuciscus leuciscus*) inhabiting chiefly clear quiet streams **2 :** any of many small No. American freshwater fishes of various genera of the family Cyprinidae (as the fallfish or golden shiner) — see HORNED DACE

da·ce·lo \də'sē(ˌ)lō\ *n, cap* [NL, anagram of *Alcedo*] **:** a genus of Australasian kingfishers including the kookaburra

da·cent \'dāsᵊnt\ *dial Brit var of* DECENT

1da·cha *or* **dat·cha** \'dächə\ *n* -s [Russ *dacha,* lit., act of giving, paying; akin to Ukrainian *dača* gift, Serbo-Croatian *dača* funeral meal, Russ *dat'* to give, Skt *dadāti* he gives — more at DATE] **:** a country house, a summer house, or a villa in Russia

2dacha *var of* DAGGA

da·chi·ar·dite \ˌdäkē'är,dīt\ *n* -s [It, fr. Antonio *d'Achiardi* †1902 Ital. mineralogist + It *-ite*] **:** a mineral $(Ca,K_2,Na_2)_3Al_4Si_{18}O_{45}.14H_2O$ belonging prob. to the zeolite group

dachs \'däks, 'dȧks *also* 'daks\ *n, pl* **dachs** *or* **dachses** [by shortening] **:** DACHSHUND

dachs·hund \'däks,hu̇nt, 'dȧk-, -k,su̇-, -ünd, -ksənt,-ksənd *also* 'dak- *or* -ks,hənd *or* -k,sənd; ÷'dashənd, ÷'daash-, ÷'daish-, ÷-sh,hau̇nd\ *n, pl* **dachshunds** \-nts,-n(d)z\ *or* **dachshun·de** \-ündə\ [G, fr. *dachs* badger (fr. OHG *dahs*) + *hund* dog, fr. OHG *hunt* — more at TECHNICAL, HOUND] **:** a small dog of a breed of German origin having long drooping ears, commonly a short sleek coat, and the legs short in comparison with the body length and being courageous and tenacious, well adapted for following game (as badgers and foxes) into burrows, and also satisfactory as a house dog

dachs·ie \-ksē\ *n* -s **:** DACHSHUND

1da·cian \'dāshən\ *adj, usu cap* [*Dacia,* ancient Roman province of central Europe (fr. L) + E *-an*] **:** of or relating to Dacia or to the inhabitants of Dacia

2dacian \"\ *n* -s *cap* **:** a native or inhabitant of Dacia

da·cite \'dā,sīt\ *n* -s [G *dazit,* fr. *Dazien* Dacia + G *-it* -ite] **:** an extrusive rock that is sometimes partly glassy and is composed of plagioclase and quartz with biotite, hornblende, or pyroxene — **da·cit·ic** \(ˈ)dā¦sid·ik\ *adj*

da·co- \'dākō, -kə\ *comb form, usu cap* [ISV, fr. *Dacia*] **:** Dacian ⟨*Daco*-Romanian⟩

da·coit \də'kȯit\ *n* -s [Hindi *ḍakait,* perh. fr. Skt *dakṣa* clever, akin to Skt *dakṣiṇa* right — more at DEXTER] **:** one of a class of criminals in India and Burma who rob and murder in roving gangs

da·coity \-ȯid·ē, -ȯitē, -i\ *n* -ES [Hindi *ḍakaitī,* fr. *ḍakait* dacoit] **:** robbery by dacoits — now used in the Indian penal code of robbery by an armed gang of not less than five men

dacota *or* **dacotah** *usu cap, var of* DAKOTA

dac·que's principle \dä'kāz-\ *n, usu cap D* [after Edgar *Dacqué* †1945 Ger. paleontologist] **:** the theory that different biological groups tend to evolve in the same direction at the same time

Da·cron \'dā,krän, 'da,- *sometimes* -,krən\ *trademark* **1** — used for a polyester fiber made in filament and staple form, characterized by its great resilience, and often blended with other fibers in fabrics **2 :** a yarn or fabric made of Dacron fiber

dacry- *or* **dacryo-** *comb form* [NL, fr. Gk *dakry-, dakryo-,* fr. *dakry, dakryon* tear — more at TEAR] **:** of a tear or tears **:** lacrimal ⟨*dacryoma*⟩ ⟨*dacryocystitis*⟩

da·cryd·i·um \də'kridēəm\ *n, cap* [NL, fr. Gk *dakrydion* scammony, lit., little tear, dim. of *dakry* drop, tear; fr. the resinous drops exuded] **:** a genus of Australasian shrubs and trees (family Taxaceae) that resemble those of the genus *Podocarpus* but have orthotropous seeds — see HUON PINE, MOUNTAIN PINE, RIMU

dac·ry·my·ces \ˌdakrə'mī,sēz\ *n, cap* [NL, fr. *dacry-* + *-myces*] **:** the type genus of Dacrymycetaceae comprising basidiomycetous fungi with a bifurcate basidium that lacks septa

dac·ry·my·ce·ta·ce·ae \ˌdakrə,mīsə'tāsē,ē\ *n pl, cap* [NL, fr. *Dacrymycet-, Dacrymyces,* type genus + *-aceae*] **:** a family of basidiomycetous fungi (order Tremellales) all of which have basidia similar to those of the type genus *Dacrymyces* — see DACRYMYCETALES

dac·ry·my·ce·ta·les \-'tā(ˌ)lēz\ *n pl, cap* [NL, fr. *Dacrymycet-, Dacrymyces* + *-ales*] *in some classifications* **:** an order of basidiomycetous fungi coextensive with the family Dacrymycetaceae

dac·ry·o·cyst \'dakrē(ˌ)ō, -rēə+,-\ *n* [ISV *dacry-* + *cyst*] **:** LACRIMAL SAC

dac·ry·o·cystitis \ˌ≠≠(ˌ)≠+\ *n* [NL, fr. ISV *dacryocyst* + NL *-itis*] **:** inflammation of the lacrimal sac

dac·ry·on \'dakrē,än\ *n, pl* **dacrya** \-rēə\ [NL, fr. Gk *dakryon* tear — more at TEAR] **:** the point of junction of the anterior border of the lacrimal bone with the frontal bone — see CRANIOMETRY illustration

dac·ry·o·stenosis \ˌdakrē(ˌ)ō, -rēə+\ *n* [NL, fr. *dacry-* + *stenosis*] **:** a narrowing of the lacrimal duct

dac·tyl \'daktᵊl\ *n* -s [ME *dactile,* fr. L *dactylus,* fr. Gk *daktylos,* lit., finger; fr. the fact that the syllables of the metrical foot are three in number like the joints of the finger] **1 :** a metrical foot of three syllables, the first being stressed and the last two being unstressed (as in "take her up tenderly") **:** a trisyllabic falling cadence — symbol -⏑⏑ for long, short, short in classical prosody or stressed, unstressed, unstressed in English prosody; also óoo; compare ANAPEST **2** [NL *dactylus,* fr. Gk *daktylos* finger, toe] **a :** a finger or toe **b :** DACTYLUS

dactyl- *or* **dactylo-** *comb form* [Gk *daktyl-, daktylo-,* fr. *daktylos*] **:** finger **:** toe **:** digit ⟨*dactyl*itis⟩ ⟨*dactylo*logy⟩

dac·ty·lar \'daktələ(r)\ *adj* [*dactyl-* + *-ar*] **:** of or relating to a dactylus

dactyli *pl of* DACTYLUS

-dac·tyl·ia \ˌdak¦tilēə, -lyə\ *n comb form* -s [NL, fr. Gk *daktylos* + NL *-ia*] **:** condition of having (such or so many) digits ⟨hexa*dactylia*⟩ ⟨sclero*dactylia*⟩

1dac·tyl·ic \(ˈ)dak¦tilik, -lēk\ *adj* [L *dactylicus,* fr. Gk *daktylikos,* fr. *daktylos* dactyl + *-ikos* -ic] **:** having the form of a dactyl ⟨a ~ foot⟩ **:** of or consisting of dactyls ⟨~ verse⟩ — **dac·tyl·i·cal·ly** \-lək(ə)lē, -li\ *adv*

2dactylic \"\ *n* -s **:** a dactylic verse or measure

dactylic pentameter *n* **:** ELEGIAC PENTAMETER

-dactylies *pl of* -DACTYLY

dactylio- *comb form* [prob. fr. F, fr. Gk *daktylio-,* fr. *daktylios,* fr. *daktylos* finger] **1 :** finger ring ⟨*dactylio*logy⟩ **2 :** gem ⟨*dactylio*graphy⟩

dac·tyl·i·o·man·cy \dak'tilēə,man(t)sē\ *n* -ES [prob. fr. F *dactyliomancie,* fr. Gk *daktylio-* dactylio- + F *-mancie* -mancy] **:** divination by means of finger rings

dac·tyl·i·on \-'tilē,än\ *n* -s [NL, fr. Gk *daktylos* finger + *-ion* (dim. suffix)] **:** the tip of the middle finger

dac·tyl·i·o·the·ca \dak¦tilēə¦thēkə\ *n, pl* **dactyliothecas** \-kəz\ *or* **dactyliothe·cae** \-(ˌ)sē\ [L, fr. Gk *daktyliothēkē,* fr. *daktylio-* dactylio- + *thēkē* case, cover — more at TICK] **1 :** a case for a collection (as of rings, gems, or seals) **2 :** a book reproducing illustrations of or cataloging a collection of gems and rings

dac·ty·lis \'daktələs\ *n, cap* [NL, fr. Gk *daktylos* finger; fr. its fingerlike spikelets] **:** a genus of two or three perennial chiefly Eurasian grasses having the 2- to 6-flowered spikelets arranged in a one-sided panicle — see ORCHARD GRASS

-dac·tyl·ism \ˌdaktə,lizəm\ *n comb form* -s [NL, fr. Gk *daktylos* finger, toe + ISV *-ism*] **:** -DACTYLIA

dac·ty·lo·gnathite \ˌdaktə(ˌ)lō, -təlō +\ *n* [*dactyl-* + *gnathite*] **:** the distal segment of a maxilliped

dac·tyl·o·gram \dak'tilə,gram; '≠tə(ˌ)lō,-, -təlō,-\ *n* -s [ISV *dactyl-* + *-gram*] **:** an impression taken from a finger **:** FINGERPRINT

dac·tyl·o·graph \-,graf\ *n* -s [*dactyl-* + *-graph*] **:** DACTYLOGRAM

dac·ty·log·ra·pher \ˌdaktə'lägrəfə(r)\ *n* -s **:** a specialist in dactylography

dac·tyl·o·graph·ic \(ˈ)dak¦tilə¦grafik; ¦≠tə(ˌ)lō¦-, -təlō¦-\ *adj* **:** of or relating to dactylogram or to dactylography

dac·ty·log·ra·phy \ˌ≠≠'lägrəfē\ *n* -ES [*dactyl-* + *-graphy*] **:** the scientific study of fingerprints as a means of identification — compare SIGNALMENT

dac·tyl·oid \'daktə,lȯid\ *adj* [Gk *daktyloeidēs,* fr. *daktyl-* dactyl- + *-eidēs* -oid] **:** resembling a finger in shape

dac·ty·lol·o·gy \ˌ≠≠'läləjē\ *n* -ES [Gk *daktyl-* dactyl- + E *-logy*] **:** the art of communicating ideas by signs made with the fingers (as in the manual alphabets of the deaf

dac·ty·lom e·tra \-'lämətrə\ *n, cap* [NL, fr. *dactyl-* + *-metra* (fr. Gk *metron* measure) — more at MEASURE] **:** a genus of tropical scyphozoan jellyfishes having a sting that is very painful and that may be dangerous to man — compare FIRE MEDUSA

dac·ty·lo·pi·us \-'lōpēəs\ *n, cap* [NL, fr. *dactyl-* + *-pius* (prob. fr. Gk *piōn* fat); fr. the form of the body] **:** a genus of scales containing the cochineal insect and formerly those mealybugs that are now placed in *Pseudococcus*

dac·tyl·op·o·dite \-'läpə,dīt\ *n* [ISV *dactyl-* + *-podite*] **:** the distal segment of certain limbs of arthropods (as the ambulatory limbs of a decapod)

dactylology: one-hand alphabet

dac·tyl·o·pore \dak'tilə,pō(ə)r, 'daktəl-\ *n* [ISV *dactyl-* + *pore*] **:** one of the pores in hydrozoan corals through which in life the dactylozooids protrude

dac·ty·lop·si·la \ˌ≠≠'läpsələ\ *n, cap* [NL, fr. *dactyl-* + *-psila* (fr. Gk *psilos* bare); fr. the bare toes — more at PSIL-] **:** a genus of mammals consisting of the striped opossums

dac·ty·lo·pter·i·dae \ˌdaktə(ˌ)lō'terə,dē, -təlō'-\ *n pl, cap* [NL, fr. *Dactylopterus,* type genus (fr. *dactyl-* + *-pterus*) + *-idae*] **:** a family (type genus *Dactylopterus*) of the order Scleroparei comprising marine fishes with greatly elongated pectoral fins — see FLYING GURNARD

dac·tyl·o·scop·ic \(ˈ)dak¦tilə¦skäpik; ¦≠tə(ˌ)lō¦-, -təlō¦-\ *adj* **:** of or relating to dactyloscopy

dac·ty·los·co·pist \ˌ≠≠'läskəpəst\ *n* -s **:** one who practices dactyloscopy

dac·ty·los·co·py \-'läskəpē\ *n* -ES [ISV *dactyl-* + *-scopy*] **:** identification by comparison of fingerprints; *also* **:** classification of fingerprints — compare SIGNALMENT

dac·ty·lo·sternal \ˌdaktə(ˌ)lō +\ *adj* [*dactyl-* + *sternal*] *of turtles* **:** having marginal processes suggesting fingers and joining the plastron to the carapace

dac·tyl·o·style \dak'tilə,stīl, '≠tə(ˌ)lō,-\ *n* -s [*dactyl-* + *-style*] **:** one of a series of minute spicules on the wall of a dactylopore

dac·ty·lo·symphysis \ˌdaktə(ˌ)lō+\ *n* [NL, fr. *dactyl-* + *symphysis*] **:** SYNDACTYLISM

dac·tyl·o·tome \dak'tilə,tōm, '≠tələ,-\ *n* -s [*dactyl-* + *-tome*] **:** one of a series of shallow slits by which dactylopores open into their associated gastropore

dac·ty·lous \'daktələs\ *adj* [NL *dactylus*] **:** of or relating to a dactylus

-dac·ty·lous \¦≠≠≠\ *adj comb form* [Gk *-daktylos,* fr. *daktylos* finger, toe] **:** having (such or so many) fingers or toes ⟨iso*dactylous*⟩ ⟨mono*dactylous*⟩

dac·ty·lo·zooid \ˌdaktə(ˌ)lō, -təlō+\ *n* [ISV *dactyl-* + *zooid*] **:** a tentacular mouthless zooid in certain hydrozoans that performs tactile and protective functions for the colony

dac·ty·lus \'daktələs\ *n, pl* **dac·ty·li** \-,lī\ [NL, fr. Gk *daktylos* finger, toe] **1 :** DACTYLOPODITE **2 :** the part consisting of one or more joints of the tarsus of certain insects following the enlarged and modified first joint

-dac·ty·ly \ˌdaktəlē, -li\ *n comb form* -ES [NL *-dactylia* — more at -DACTYLIA] **:** -DACTYLIA

da·cus \'dākəs\ *n, cap* [NL, fr. Gk *dakos* noxious animal, fr. *daknein* to bite — more at TONGS] **:** a genus of trypetid fruit flies of warm regions including several important pests of cultivated plants (as the melon fly, the oriental fruit fly, and the olive fly)

1dad \'dad, 'daa(ə)d\ *n* -s [prob. baby talk, like OHG *todo* father, L *tata,* W *tad,* Gk *tata, tetta,* Skt *tata*] **:** FATHER

2dad \"\ *interj, often cap* [euphemism for *God*] — used as a mild oath

3dad \"\ *vb* **dadded; dadded; dadding; dads** [prob. of imit. origin] *chiefly Scot* **:** BEAT, POUND

4dad \"\ *n* -s **1** *chiefly Scot* **:** a heavy blow **:** THUMP **2** *chiefly Scot* **:** LUMP, CHUNK

DAD *abbr* deputy assistant director

1dada \'dä(ˌ)da, 'dä(ˌ)dä *sometimes* 'dadə\ *n* -s [baby talk — more at DAD] **:** FATHER

2da·da \'dä(ˌ)dä\ *or* **da·da·ism** \'dä(ˌ)dä,izəm, 'dä,diz-\ *n* -s *usu cap* [*dada* fr. F, fr. (baby talk) *dada* hobby horse, hobby (arbitrarily chosen symbol of the movement), redupl. of *da, dia* giddap; *dadaism* fr. F *dadaïsme,* fr. *dada* + *-isme* -ism] **1 :** the principles or practice in the arts and esp. painting that flourished chiefly in France, Switzerland, and Germany from 1916 to about 1920 and that were based on deliberate irrationality, anarchy, cynicism, and negation of laws of beauty and social organization **2 :** the cult of Dada

da·da·ist \'dä(ˌ)dä,ist, 'dä,däəst, 'dädəst\ *n* -s *often cap* **:** a follower of Dada — **da·da·is·tic** \ˌdä(ˌ)dä¦istik\ *adj*

dad·ap \'dadəp\ *n* -s [Malay *dēdap*] **:** any of several Indian trees of the genus *Erythrina* planted for the nitrogen-fixing bacteria on their roots

1dad-burned \'dad,bərnd\ *adj* [euphemism] **:** 1DAMNED 2a,2b

2dad-burned \"\ *adv* [euphemism] **:** 2DAMNED

1dad·dle \'dadᵊl, 'dād-\ *dial Brit var of* DAWDLE

2dad·dle \'dadᵊl\ *n* -s [perh. irreg. fr. 3*dad*] *dial Brit* **:** HAND, FIST

dad·dock \'dadək\ *n* -s [origin unknown] *dial* **:** rotten wood — **dad·docky** \-kē\ *adj, dial*

dad·dy \'dadē, 'daad-, -di\ *n* -ES [1*dad* + *-y*] **1 :** FATHER ⟨there comes a time to do what our *daddies* did —Hodding Carter⟩ **2** *slang* **:** SUGAR DADDY

daddy longlegs \ˌ≠≠'≠,≠\ *n pl but sing or pl in constr* **:** any of various animals with long slender legs: as **a :** CRANE FLY **b :** HARVESTMAN

dad·dy·nut \'dadē,nət\ *also* **daddynut tree** *n* **:** AMERICAN BASSWOOD

dade \'dād\ *vt* -ED/-ING/-S [origin unknown] *now dial Brit* **:** to lead and support

1da·do \'dā(ˌ)dō *sometimes* 'dä(-\ *n* -ES [It, die, cube, plinth, perh. fr. Ar *dad* game] **1 a :** the part of a pedestal of a column included between the base and the surbase — called also *die* **b :** the part of the basement of a wall included between the surbase and the base course **c :** the lower part of an interior wall when adorned with moldings or otherwise specially decorated or faced; *also* **:** the molding, facing, or other decoration adorning this part of a wall **2** [2*dado*] **:** a groove made by dadoing **3 :** a plane or other tool for dadoing **:** DADO PLANE, DADO HEAD

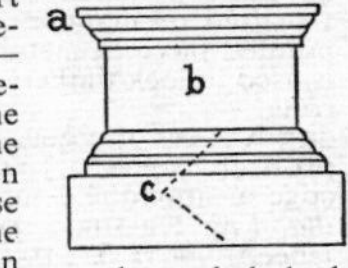

a surbase, *b* dado 1, *c* base

2dado \"\ *vt* **dadoed; dadoed; dadoing; dadoes** *or* **dados 1 :** to furnish with a dado ⟨a ~*ed* living room⟩ **2 :** to secure by fitting into a groove **:** set into a groove ⟨~ the shelves of the bookcases to make them solider⟩ **3 :** to cut a rectangular groove in (as a plank)

dado cap *n* **:** a molding that caps an interior dado; *often* **:** CHAIR RAIL

dado head *n* **:** a power-saw tool made up of two circular saws of equal diameter and one or more chippers and used for cutting flat-bottomed grooves

dado plane *n* **:** a narrow rabbet plane that has two spurs and often an adjustable fence and that is used for making flat-bottomed grooves in woodwork

dado rail *n* **:** CHAIR RAIL
da·dox·y·lon \dəˈdäksə,län, -ˌlən\ *n, cap* [NL, fr. Gk *daid-, dais* firebrand, pine wood (fr. *daiein* to kindle, burn up) + NL *-xylon* — more at TEEN] **:** a form genus of chiefly Paleozoic fossils based on a heterogeneous group of woods which are now known to belong to various families and which are all characterized by alternate pitting on tracheid walls
dads *pl of* DAD, *pres 3d sing of* DAD
dae \ˈdā\ *Scot var of* DO
dae·dal \ˈdēdᵊl\ *adj* [L *daedalus,* fr. Gk *daidalos* — more at CONDOLE] **1 a :** ingeniously formed or working **:** like a maze **:** INTRICATE ⟨this immense, ~ system of artificial segments, of facades, and paths, and bridges —Florence Gould⟩ **b :** SKILLFUL, ARTISTIC, INGENIOUS ⟨words made accessible in a novel and ~ way —*Publishers' Weekly*⟩ **2 :** adorned with many things **:** RICH ⟨through that ~, pristine world sailor and poet spread their fame —John Lehman⟩
dae·da·lea \dēˈdālēə\ *n, cap* [NL, fr. L, fem. of *Daedaleus* of Daedalus, fr. *Daedalus*] **:** a genus of tough pore fungi (family Polyporaceae) of Europe and America usu. growing on dead wood and distinguished from members of the genus *Polyporus* by the labyrinthine lamellae formed by the pores
dae·da·li·an \(ˈ)dēˈdālēən, -lyən\ *or* **dae·da·le·an** \-lēən\ *adj, usu cap* [*Daedalus,* mythical craftsman and inventor of ancient Greece noted esp. for the construction of a labyrinth to contain the Minotaur and for the invention of wings with which he escaped imprisonment (fr. L, fr. Gk *Daidalos*) + E *-ian, -ean*] **1 :** of, relating to, or suggesting the mythological Daedalus ⟨*Daedalian* wings of escape —Curtis Bradford⟩ **2 :** DAEDAL
dae·dal·ic \dēˈdalik\ *adj, usu cap* [*Daedalus* + E *-ic*] **:** DAEDALIAN 1
daemon *var of* DEMON
dae·mon·e·lix \dēˈmänə,liks\ *n, cap* [NL, fr. LL *daemon* + Gk *helix* spiral — more at HELIX] *in some classifications* **:** a genus of large spiral fossils of uncertain systematic position and nature comprising the devil's corkscrews
dae·mo·ni·an \(ˈ)dēˈmōnēən\ *var of* DEMONIAN
daemonic *var of* DEMONIC
daemonology *var of* DEMONOLOGY
dae·na \ˈdänə\ *n* -s [Av *daēnā*] **1** *Zoroastrianism* **:** the moral element in personality **:** CONSCIENCE, SELF **2** *Zoroastrianism* **:** the moral life of man **:** RELIGION
dae·va *or* **de·va** \ˈdāvə\ *or* **dev** \ˈdāv\ *n* -s [*daeva, deva* fr. Av *daēvō; dev* fr. Per *dēv,* fr. Av *daēvō;* akin to Skt *deva* god — more at DEITY] *Zoroastrianism* **:** a maleficent supernatural being **:** an evil spirit **:** DEMON
daf·a·dar *or* **duf·fa·dar** \ˌdəfəˈdär\ *n* -s [Hindi *dafadār* officer, fr. Per *daf'adār,* fr. Ar *daf'ah* time, turn + Per *-dār* holder — more at BHUMIDAR] **:** a noncommissioned officer in the former Indian army or police
¹daff \ˈdaf\ *vi* -ED/-ING/-S [obs. E *daff* fool, coward, fr. ME *daffe;* akin to ME *dafte* gentle, stupid — more at DAFT] *chiefly Scot* **:** to talk or act sportively **:** DALLY, PLAY
²daff \ˈ"\ *vt* -ED/-ING/-S [alter. of ¹*doff*] **1** *archaic* **:** to put, turn, or thrust aside — used esp. in the phrase *to daff the world aside* **2** *obs* **:** ¹DOFF 1
daf·fa·dil·ly \ˈdafəˌdilē, -li\ *or* **daf·fa·down·dil·ly** \ˌ==ˌdaün¦dil-\ *or* **daf·fo·dil·ly** \ˌ==¦dil-\ *or* **daf·fo·down·dil·ly** \ˌ==ˌdaün¦dil-\ *n* -ES [alter. (influenced by *lily*) of *daffodil; daffadowndilly, daffodowndilly* alter. of *daffadilly, daffodilly*] *chiefly dial* **:** DAFFODIL
daff·ing \ˈdafiŋ, -fən\ *also* **daff·ery** \-fəri\ *n* [*daffing* fr. gerund of ¹*daff; daffery* fr. ¹*daff* + *-ery*] *chiefly Scot* **:** FUN, GAIETY, MERRIMENT
daf·fo·dil \ˈdafə,dil\ *n* -s [prob. fr. D *de affodil* the asphodel, fr. *de,* masc. def. article (fr. MD) + *affodil* asphodel, fr. MF *afrodille,* fr. L *asphodelus;* akin to OHG *thaz,* neut. def. article — more at THAT, ASPHODEL] **1 :** a plant of the genus *Narcissus; esp* **:** any of numerous such plants of which the flowers have a large corona elongated into a trumpet (as plants derived from the species *N. pseudo-narcissus*) — called also *trumpet narcissus;* see JONQUIL 1 **2** *or* **daf·fo·dile** \-,dīl\ **:** a variable color averaging a brilliant yellow that is greener, lighter, and stronger than lemon yellow (sense 1b) and greener, stronger, and slightly darker than butter yellow — called also *jonquil*
daffodil garlic *n* **:** a European onion (*Allium neapolitanum*) with white flowers
daffodil lily *n* **:** ATAMASCO LILY
daffodil yellow *n* **1 :** DAFFODIL 2 **2 :** CADMIUM YELLOW 2
¹daf·fy \ˈdafē, -fi\ *n* -ES [short for *Daffy's elixir,* an infants' medicine containing gin, after Thomas *Daffy* †1680 Eng. clergyman who first compounded it] **:** a drop of gin **:** GIN
²daffy \ˈ"\ *n* -ES [by shortening] **:** DAFFODIL
³daffy \ˈ", ˈdāf-\ *adj* -ER/-EST [obs. E *daff* fool + *-y* — more at DAFF] *slang* **:** CRAZY, IMBECILE, DAFT ⟨the story is slight, but it has a ~ kind of logic —*N.Y.Times Bk. Rev.*⟩
daf·la \ˈdäflə\ *n, pl* **dafla** *or* **daflas** *usu cap* **1 a :** a primitive people in the Himalaya mountain region of Assam noted for their long houses that hold from 50 to 80 people **b :** a member of such people **2 :** the language of the Dafla people
daft \ˈdaft, ˈdaa(ə)ft, ˈdaift, ˈdäft\ *adj, often* -ER/-EST [ME *dafte* gentle, stupid; akin to OE *gedæfte* mild, gentle, *gedæftan* to put in order, *gedafen* fit, suitable, *gedēfe* suitable, gentle, ME *defte* deft, ON *dafna* to thrive, Goth *gadaban* to happen, *gadofs* fitting, proper, L *faber* smith, OSlav *dobrŭ* good, Arm *darbin* smith] **1 a :** SILLY, FOOLISH ⟨communicating with his friends in his own way . . . making ~ little beckonings and esoteric signals —Osbert Sitwell⟩; *esp* **:** foolishly fond ⟨a man ~ about women⟩ **b :** out of one's mind **:** MAD, INSANE ⟨they had given me so many instructions that I was nearly ~ —Mary Lavin⟩ ⟨in this ~ confusion of inverted values, it soon becomes impossible to determine when virtue is sin and sin, moral perfection —R.K.Merton⟩ **2** *Scot* **:** gay and frivolous **:** FROLICSOME — **daft·ly** \-ftlē, -li\ *adv* — **daft·ness** \-f(t)nəs\ *n* -ES
daf·tar \ˈdəftə(r)\ *n* -s [Hindi, record, office, fr. Per, fr. Ar *daftar, diftar,* fr. Gk *diphthera* prepared hide, parchment, leather — more at DIPHTHERIA] **1** *India* **:** a bundle of official papers **2** *India* **:** a business office
daf·tar·dar *or* **duf·ter·dar** \ˌdəftərˈdär\ *n* -s [Hindi *daftardār,* fr. Per, finance officer, fr. *daftar* + *-dār* holder — more at BHUMIDAR] **:** a revenue officer in India
daft·berry \ˈdaft- — *see* BERRY\ *n* [so called fr. its poisonous and narcotic properties] **:** BELLADONNA 1
daft days \ˈdaft-\ *n pl, Scot* **:** a time of gaiety and merrymaking; *specif* **:** the Christmas season
daft lamb *or* **daft lamb disease** \ˈdaft-\ *n* **:** an abnormality of lambs marked by congenital lesions of the cerebellar cortex by some regarded as genetic anomalies but by others as the result of deficiencies in the maternal diet
¹dag \ˈdag, ˈdaa(ə)g, ˈdaig\ *n* -s [ME *dagge*] **1** *also* **dagge** \ˈ"\ **a :** a hanging end or shred **b :** a division in the serrated or foliated edge of a medieval garment **:** an ornamental appliqué attached loosely to a medieval garment **2** *Brit* **:** matted or manure-coated wool — usu. used in pl. **3 :** a pointed piece of metal that resembles a dagger point and that is used to lock timbers together or for a tooth on coal-breaking rolls
²dag \ˈ"\ *vb* **dagged; dagged; dagging; dags** [ME *daggen,* prob. fr. *dagge,* n.] *vt* **1 :** to finish with a jagged or slashed edge or squared end of medieval garments **2** *now dial Eng* **:** BEMIRE, SOIL **3** *Brit* **:** to cut off the dags from (sheep) ~ *vi* **1 :** DAGGLE **2** *Brit* **:** to remove dags
³dag \ˈ"\ *vt* **dagged; dagged; dagging; dags** [ME *daggen,* prob. back-formation fr. *dagger*] *obs* **:** DAGGER, STAB
⁴dag \ˈ"\ *n* -s [origin unknown] **:** an obsolete form of large pistol
⁵dag \ˈ"\ *n* -s [F *dague,* fr. MF, lit., dagger — more at DAGGER] **:** PRICKET 2b
dag *abbr* decagram
dagaba *var of* DAGOBA
da·ga·me *or* **de·ga·me** \dəˈgä(ˌ)mā\ *n* -s [AmerSp *dagame*] **:** a tropical American timber tree (*Calycophyllum candidissimum*) whose wood is used esp. for building and tools and constitutes one of the lancewoods of commerce
dag·ba·ne *also* **dag·ba·ni** \däg'bänē, -nə\ *n* -s *usu cap* **:** DAGOMBA
dag·en·ham \ˈdag(ə)nəm\ *adj, usu cap* [fr. *Dagenham,* England] **:** of or from the municipal borough of Dagenham, England **:** of the kind or style prevalent in Dagenham

dagesh *var of* DAGHESH
¹dag·ga \ˈdagə, ˈdägə\ *also* **da·cha** \ˈdakə, ˈdäkə\ *n* -s [Afrik *dagga,* fr. Hottentot *daga-b*] **1** *Africa* **:** HEMP 1 **2 :** either of two relatively nontoxic So. African herbs (*Leonotis leonurus* and *L. orata*) smoked like tobacco — called also *Cape dagga, red dagga, wilde dagga*
²dag·ga \ˈ"\ *n* -s [Afrik *dagha* mud, mortar, fr. Bantu *daka*] **:** a mortar used in So. Africa that consists chiefly of clay wetted and packed hard
¹dag·ger \ˈdagə(r), ˈdaag-, ˈdaig-\ *n* -s [ME, prob. modif. of MF *dague,* fr. OProv or OIt *daga*] **1 a :** a short weapon used for stabbing — see ANLACE, DIRK, MISERICORD, PONIARD, STILETTO; compare BOWIE KNIFE **b :** something resembling or suggesting a dagger esp. in shape: as (1) **:** the character † used typically to mark the name of a person who is dead and as the second in series of the reference marks — called also *obelisk* (2) **:** the projecting part of a loom rod acting as a stopping device — compare FROG 3i **2 daggers** *pl* **:** HOSTILITY ⟨there's ~s in men's smiles —Shak.⟩ **3 :** DOGSHORE **4 :** DAGGER PLANK — **at daggers drawn** *also* **at daggers drawing** *or* **at daggers :** at the point of fighting **:** openly hostile — **look daggers :** to look angrily or as if ready to do violence ⟨they *looked daggers* at each other across the table⟩ — **speak daggers :** to speak angrily or with intent to hurt

daggers 1a

²dagger \ˈ"\ *vt* -ED/-ING/-S **1 :** to pierce with a dagger **:** STAB **2 :** to mark with the dagger used in printing
dagger board *also* **dagger plate** *n* **:** a narrow centerboard in some small boats that slides up and down in the trunk instead of pivoting and that can be completely removed when not in use
daggerbush \ˈ==ˌ=\ *n* **:** a plant of the genus *Furcraea*
dagger cocklebur *n* **:** SPINY CLOTBUR
dag·gered \ˈdagə(r)d\ *adj* [ME, fr. ¹*dagger* + *-ed*] *archaic* **:** armed with a dagger
dagger fern *n* **:** CHRISTMAS FERN
dagger moth *n* **:** any of several noctuid moths of *Acronicta* and related genera some of which have a mark suggesting a dagger near the anal angle of the fore wings
dagger plank *n* **:** a diagonal member holding together and bracing launching poppets — called also *dagger*
dagger plant *n* **:** SPANISH BAYONET
dagger rudder *n* **:** a narrow usu. deep rudder
dagging *n* -s [fr. gerund of ²*dag*] **1 :** the act of removing dags **2 :** DAG 2 — usu. used in pl.
dag·gle \ˈdagəl\ *vb* -ED/-ING/-S [freq. of ²*dag*] *vt* **1** *archaic* **:** to wet and soil (as a garment) by dragging in mire **2** *archaic* **:** to make wet by sprinkling or splashing **:** DRAGGLE ⟨clothes *daggled* by the splash of passing vehicles⟩ ~ *vi, archaic* **:** to trail or drag about (as through mud or slush)
dag·gy \-gē\ *adj* -ER/-EST [¹*dag* + *-y*] *of sheep* **:** having dags
¹da·ghesh *also* **da·gesh** \ˈdä(ˌ)gesh, -ˌgəsh *also* -(ˌ)gāsh\ *n* -ES [Heb *dāghēsh*] **:** a point placed in a consonant in pointed writing in the Hebrew alphabet to denote that (1) it is pronounced as a stop rather than as a spirant or that (2) it is pronounced doubled — called also respectively (1) *daghesh lene,* (2) *daghesh forte*
²daghesh *also* **dagesh** \ˈ"\ *vt* -ED/-ING/-ES **:** to mark with a daghesh
da·ghe·stan \ˌdagəˈstan, ˌdägəˈstän\ *n* -s *usu cap* [fr. *Daghestan, Dagestan,* autonomous Soviet republic in the Caucasus] **:** a Caucasian rug distinguished by medium pile, fine weave, geometric designs, and mellow colors
da·ghur \däˈgü(ə)r\ *n, pl* **daghur** *or* **daghurs** *usu cap* **1 :** a Mongol people inhabiting northwest Manchuria **2 :** a member of the Daghur people
daglock \ˈ=ˌ=\ *n* [¹*dag* + *lock*] **:** a dirty or matted lock of fur, hair, or wool **:** TAGLOCK — see ¹DAG
da·go \ˈdā(ˌ)gō\ *n, pl* **dagos** *or* **dagoes** *sometimes cap* [alter. of earlier *Diego,* fr. *Diego,* a common Spanish given name] **:** a person of Italian or Spanish birth or descent — usu. taken to be offensive
da·go·ba *also* **da·ga·ba** \ˈdägəbə\ *n* -s [Singhalese *dāgoba, dāgaba,* fr. Pali *dhātugabbha,* fr. Skt *dhātugarbha,* lit., having relics inside, fr. *dhātu* element, elemental bodily substance, relics (fr. *dadhāti* he places) + *garbha* womb, interior — more at DO, CALF] **:** a shrine for sacred relics in the Far East
da·gom·ba \dəˈgämbə\ *n* -s *usu cap* **1 :** a Negroid people in the Northern Territories, Ghana, identified primarily by possession of a common language **2 :** a Gur language of the Dagomba people — called also *Dagbane*
dago red *n* [so called fr. its being typically made and drunk by Italians] *slang* **:** an inexpensive red wine
¹dags *pl of* DAG, *pres 3d sing of* DAG
²dags \ˈdagz\ *n pl* [prob. alter. of *dares,* pl. of *dare*] *slang Brit* **:** feats of skill **:** TRICKS — usu. used in the phrase *to do one's dags*
dag-tailed \ˈ=¦=\ *adj* [¹*dag*] **:** having dags about the tail
da·guer·re·an \dəˈgerēən\ *adj* [Louis J.M.*Daguerre* †1851 French painter and inventor + E *-an*] **1** *usu cap* **:** of or relating to Daguerre **2 :** of or relating to the daguerreotype
¹da·guerre·o·type \dəˈgerə,tīp, -rō,-, -rēə,-, -rēō,-\ *n* -s [F *daguerréotype,* fr. L.J.M.*Daguerre* + F *-o-* + *-type*] **1 :** a photograph produced on a silver plate or a silver-covered copper plate which is made sensitive by the action of iodine or iodine and bromine and from which after exposure in the camera a latent image is developed by the vapor of mercury **2 :** the process of producing daguerreotype pictures — **da·guerre·o·typ·ic** \=¦=rə¦tipik, -rēə¦-\ *adj*
²daguerreotype \ˈ"\ *vt* -ED/-ING/-S **1 :** to produce or represent by the daguerreotype process **2 :** to impress with great distinctness ⟨the . . . universe around us, all ready to be *daguerreotyped* upon our souls —Benjamin Fine⟩
da·guerre·o·typ·er \-ˌtīpə(r)\ *or* **da·guerre·o·typ·ist** \-ˌtīpəst\ *n* -s **:** one that makes daguerreotypes
da·guerre·o·typy \-ˌtīpē\ *n* -ES **:** the art or process of producing daguerreotypes
¹dah \ˈdä\ *or* **dao** \ˈdaü\ *n* -s [Burmese *dā*] **:** a large heavy knife used by the Burmese
²dah \ˈ"\ *n* -s [imit.] **:** a dash in radio or telegraphic code — used by operators as an oral representation of the transmitted sound ⟨many a shortwave radio enthusiast soon may fling his dits and ~s to remote points of the world —*Science News Letter*⟩
da·ha·be·ah \ˌdä(h)əˈbēə\ *also* **da·ha·bee·yah** \-ēyə\ *or* **da·ha·bi·ah** \-ēə\ *or* **da·ha·bi·eh** \", -ēe\ *n* -s [Ar *dhahabīyah,* lit., golden one] **:** a long light-draft houseboat used on the Nile that is lateen-rigged and is often propelled wholly or partly by engines
da·hi \ˈdə,hē\ *n* -s [Hindi *dahī,* fr. Skt *dadhi* sour milk; akin to OPruss *dadan* milk, Alb *djathë* cheese, all by redupl. fr. the root of Skt *dhayati* he sucks — more at FEMININE] **:** the curd of soured curdled milk
¹dahl·ia \ˈdalyə *also* ˈdäl- *or* ˈdāl- *sometimes* -lēə; *Brit usu & US sometimes* ˈdāl-\ *n* [NL, fr. Anders *Dahl* †1789 Swedish botanist + NL *-ia*] **1** *cap* **:** a genus of Mexican and Central American tuberous-rooted herbs (family Compositae) having opposite pinnate leaves and rayed flower heads with a pappus of scales, teeth, or awns that are not retrorsely barked **2** -s **:** any plant of the genus *Dahlia,* most of the horticultural varieties being derived from a Central American species (*D. pinnata*) **3** *also* **dahlia violet** -s **a :** one of the methyl violets; *also* **:** a mixture of a methyl violet and fuchsine **b :** one of Hofmann's violets **4** -s **:** a moderate purple that is redder and duller than heliotrope (sense 4a), redder and paler than average amethyst or manganese violet, and bluer and paler than cobalt violet — compare DAHLIA PURPLE
²dahlia \ˈ"\ *also* **dahlia wartlet** *n* -s **:** a common large sea anemone (*Tealia crassicornis*) of the Atlantic coasts of Europe
dahlia carmine *n* **:** a dark purplish red that is bluer and less strong than pansy purple, bluer, stronger, and slightly lighter than raisin, and bluer, lighter, and stronger than Bokhara
dahlia purple *n* **1 :** a dark purplish red that is bluer and duller than pansy purple or Bokhara and redder and darker than raisin **2** *of textiles* **:** a deep purple that is redder and deeper than hyacinth violet, deeper than petunia violet, and bluer and stronger than imperial purple (sense 2)

dahlia sunflower *n* **:** a double-flowered horticultural form of a wild sunflower (*Helianthus decapetalus*) of eastern No. America
dahll·ite \ˈdä,līt\ *n* -s [prob. fr. G *dahllit,* fr. Tellef and Johann *Dahll,* 19th cent. Norw. geologists and mineralogists + G *-it* -ite] **:** CARBONATE-APATITE
¹da·ho·me·an \dəˈhōmēən\ *also* **da·ho·man** \-mən\ *or* **da·ho·mey·an** \-mēən, -māən\ *adj, usu cap* [*Dahomey,* republic in west Africa + E *-an*] **:** of or relating to Dahomey or its inhabitants
²dahomean *also* **dahoman** *or* **dahomeyan** \ˈ"\ *n* -s *usu cap* **:** a member of the chiefly Ewe-speaking Dahomean people
da·ho·mey \dəˈhōmē\ *adj, usu cap* [*Dahomey,* republic in west Africa] **:** of or relating to Dahomey **:** of the kind or style prevalent in Dahomey **:** DAHOMEAN
da·hoon \dəˈhün\ *also* **dahoon holly** *n* -s [origin unknown] **:** an evergreen shrub (*Ilex cassine*) of the southern U.S. — called also *yaupon*
da·hu·ri·an larch \dəˈh(y)ürēən-\ *n* [*Dahuria,* region of southern Siberia + E *-an*] **:** a Siberian tree of very irregular growth habit that is sometimes cultivated for its bright green foliage
¹dai·dle \ˈdādᵊl\ *chiefly Scot var of* DAWDLE
²daidle \ˈ"\ *also* **dai·dlie** \-d(ᵊ)li\ *n* -s [*daidle,* origin unknown; *daidlie* fr. *daidle* + *-ie*] *Scot* **:** APRON; *esp* **:** PINAFORE
daigh \ˈdāk\ *n* -s [ME (northern dial.) *dagh,* fr. OE *dāg, dāh* — more at DOUGH] *Scot* **:** DOUGH
daik·er \ˈdākər\ *vt* -ED/-ING/-S [prob. fr. F *décorer* to decorate, fr. L *decorare* — more at DECORATE] *Scot* **:** to put in order **:** DECORATE ⟨the chaise . . . was elegantly ~*ed* out with evergreens —W.D.Latto⟩
dai·kon \ˈdīkən\ *n* -s [Jap, fr. *dai* big + *kon* root] **:** a radish (*Raphanus sativus longipinnatus*) of Japan with long hard durable roots that are eaten cooked or raw
dail \ˈdāl\ *Scot var of* DEAL
dai·li·ness \ˈdālēnəs, -lin-\ *n* -ES **:** the quality of daily occurrence **:** the quality of being regular, routine, or humdrum
¹dai·ly \ˈdālē, -li\ *adj* [ME *dayly,* fr. OE *dæglīc,* fr. *dæg* day + *-līc* -ly — more at DAY] **1 :** occurring or being made, done, or acted upon every day ⟨his ~ work⟩ **:** issued every day or every weekday ⟨a ~ newspaper⟩ **:** of or for every day ⟨a ~ schedule⟩ **2 a :** reckoned by the day ⟨average ~ wage⟩ **b :** covering the period of a day **:** based on a day ⟨~ statistics⟩
²daily \ˈ"\ *adv* [ME *dayly,* fr. *dayly,* adj.] **:** every day **:** day by day **:** every weekday ⟨go to the store ~⟩
³daily \ˈ"\ *n* -ES [¹*daily*] **1 :** a newspaper published every weekday **2** *Brit* **:** a female domestic employee not a resident of the house in which she works **3 dailies** *pl* **:** RUSH 7
daily bread *n* **:** food or provisions necessary for day-to-day survival
daily double *n* **:** a system of betting on horse or dog races in which the bettor must pick the winners of two stipulated races in order to win, such bets forming a pool separate from the ordinary bets
daily dozen *n* [so called fr. its being orig. a set of 12 exercises] **1 :** a series of setting-up exercises to be performed daily **:** WORKOUT **2 :** a set of routine duties or tasks
daim \ˈdam, ˈdām\ *n* -s [F, fr. OF *dain,* fr. (assumed) VL *damus,* alter. of L *dama, damma*] **:** FALLOW DEER
dai·men \ˈdemin, ˈdām-\ *adj* [origin unknown] *chiefly Scot* **:** OCCASIONAL ⟨a ~ one here and there⟩
dai·mi·ate \ˈdīmē,ăt, -ēət\ *also* **dai·mi·ote** \-ē,ōt\ *n* -s [*daimio* + *-ate*] **:** the office, power, or territory of a daimyo
dai·mon \ˈdī,mōn\ *n, pl* **dai·mo·nes** \-ˌmə,nēz\ *also* **daimons** \-,mōnz\ *sometimes cap* [Gk *daimōn* — more at DEMON] **:** DEMON 1,4 — **dai·mon·ic** \(ˈ)dīˈmänik, -ˈmōn-\ *adj*
dai·mo·ni·on \dīˈmōnē,än\ *n* -s [Gk, fr. neut. of *daimonios* of a demon, fr. *daimon-, daimōn* demon] **:** an inward mentor conceived as partaking of the nature of a demon or inspired by one
dai·myo *or* **dai·mio** \ˈdīmē,ō, -m(ˌ)yō\ *n, pl* **dai·myos** *or* **daimyo** *or* **dai·mios** *or* **daimio** [Jap *daimyō,* fr. Chin (Pek) *ta⁴ ming²* great name, fr. *ta⁴* great + *ming²* name] **:** one of the former feudal barons of Japan who were vassals of the shogun but had extensive powers in their own baronies
dain·cha *or* **dhain·cha** \ˈdīnchə\ *n* -s [Beng *dhaincā*] **:** a valuable forage or green-manure plant (*Sesbania aculeata*) planted in tropical regions for soil improvement
daint *adj or n* [by shortening] *obs* **:** DAINTY
dain·ti·fy \ˈdāntə,fī\ *vt* -ED/-ING/-ES [²*dainty* + *-fy*] **:** to make dainty
dain·ti·ly \-tᵊlē, -tәlē, -li\ *adv* [ME, fr. ²*dainty* + *-ly*] **:** in a dainty manner: as **a :** with nice attention to taste in food or to personal comfort ⟨sold into a rich house so that she can eat ~ —Pearl Buck⟩ **b :** with nice attention to detail ⟨invitation cards, ~ got up in white and silver —Agnes M. Miall⟩
dain·ti·ness \-tēnəs, -tin-\ *n* -ES **:** the quality or state of being dainty
dain·tith \ˈdāntith\ *n* -s [ME, fr. OF *deintiet, deintié*] *Scot* **:** DELICACY, DAINTY
¹dain·ty \ˈdāntē, -ti\ *n* -ES [ME *deinte* worthiness, pleasure, delicacy, fr. OF *deintié,* fr. L *dignitat-, dignitas* worthiness — more at DIGNITY] **1 :** something delicious to the taste **:** DELICACY ⟨a London ~ — a pyramid of jelly —Virginia Woolf⟩ ⟨the various *dainties* served at supper —E.H.Collis⟩ **2 :** something that arouses favor or excites pleasure **:** something choice or pleasing ⟨sloe-eyed *dainties* in satin skirts and magenta saris —P.C.Jain⟩ **3** *obs* **:** FASTIDIOUSNESS, FUSSINESS
²dainty \ˈ"\ *adj* -ER/-EST [ME *deinte,* fr. *deinte,* n.] **1 a** *now dial Brit* **:** pleasant and agreeable **:** FINE ⟨a ~ lass⟩ ⟨~ weather⟩ **b** *obs* **:** UNCOMMON, SCARCE **2 a :** good-tasting **:** SAVORY, PALATABLE ⟨~ bits make rich the ribs —Shak.⟩ **b :** attractively prepared and prettily served to or as if to stimulate a jaded, finicky, or very slight appetite ⟨the ~ crumpets at the tearoom⟩ **3 :** marked by fragile tender beauty, nice or diminutive form, or quaint charm ⟨a ~ Spanish sword —S.P.B.Mais⟩ ⟨~ teacups⟩ **4** *obs* **:** CHARY, SPARING, LOATH, RELUCTANT — used with *of* ⟨let us not be ~ of leave-taking —Shak.⟩ **5 a :** marked by or given to fastidious discrimination and choice or by finical taste **:** shunning anything crude or excessive **:** gently careful and particular ⟨the hungry cannot be ~ —Mary W. Shelley⟩ ⟨the spirit of romance, gross and tawdry in vulgar minds, ~ and refined in the more cultivated —V.L.Parrington⟩ **b :** showing unmanly avoidance of anything rough **:** OVERNICE, SQUEAMISH, PRISSY ⟨steps ~ as those of a French dancing master —George Meredith⟩ ⟨gentry too ~ to risk blisters on their hands —G.W.Johnson⟩ **syn** see CHOICE, NICE
dai·qui·ri \ˈdīkərē, ˈdak- *sometimes* -krē\ *n* -s *often cap* [fr. *Daiquiri,* district in El Caney municipality, Cuba] **:** a cocktail made of rum, lime or sometimes lemon juice, and sugar
dai·ren \(ˈ)dī¦ren\ *adj, usu cap* [fr. *Dairen,* Manchuria] **:** of or from the city of Dairen, now forming part of Port Arthur-Dairen, Manchuria **:** of the kind or style prevalent in Dairen
dairy \ˈderē, ˈda(a)r-, ˈdār-, -ri\ *n* -ES *often attrib* [ME *dayerie, deyerie,* fr. *deye* female servant, dairymaid (fr. OE *dǣge* kneader of bread) + *-erie* -ery; akin to ON *deigja* dairymaid; fr. the root of OE *dāg* dough — more at DOUGH] **1 :** a room, building, or establishment where milk is kept and butter or cheese is made ⟨the village cheese ~ —*Nat'l Geographic*⟩ **2 :** the department of farming or of a farm that is concerned with the production of milk, butter, and cheese ⟨~ products⟩ ⟨~ farming⟩ **3 :** a dairy farm; *collectively* **:** the cows of a farm **4 :** an establishment for the sale or distribution of milk and milk products
dairy breed *n* **:** a cattle breed developed primarily for the production of milk rather than meat (as the Holstein-Friesian, Jersey, Guernsey, or Ayrshire) and characterized by the ability to convert a large proportion of their food into milk, by angular bodies that do not take on flesh readily, and by comparatively long legs and neck — compare BEEF BREED, DUAL-PURPOSE
dairy cattle *n pl* **:** cattle suitable for milk production; *esp* **:** cattle of one of the dairy breeds
dairy·ing \-rēiŋ,-riiŋ\ *n* -s **:** the business of conducting a dairy
dairy lunch *or* **dairy bar** *n* **:** a restaurant specializing in simple dishes made from dairy products
dairymaid \ˈ==ˌ=\ *n* **:** a woman employed on a dairy farm or in a dairy — called also *milkmaid*
dairy·man \-mən, -ˌman, -ˌmaa(ə)n\ *n, pl* **dairymen :** one who operates a dairy farm or one who works in the dairy industry

dairy shorthorn *n, usu cap D&S* : MILKING SHORTHORN
dairy·wom·an \-,wu̇mən\ *n, pl* **dairywom·en** \-,wimən\ : a woman who attends to a dairy or sells dairy products
dais \'dāəs *also* 'dīəs *or sometimes* 'dās *or* 'dīs\ *n* -ES [ME *deis, dees* fr. OF *deis*, fr. L *discus* quoit, dish — more at DISH] **1** : a platform raised usu. above the floor of a hall or large room to give distinction or prominence to those occupying it ⟨the principal speakers were seated on the ~⟩ **2** : a raised terrace out of doors ⟨an elevated observation point with a concrete ~ —*Amer. Guide Series: Texas*⟩ **3** : DEAS **4** *archaic* : a canopy over a throne or other seat of state
daise \'dāz\ *chiefly Scot var of* DAZE
daisee *or* **daisee jute** *var of* DESI
dai·sied \'dāzēd\ *adj* : full of daisies : adorned with daisies ⟨~ lawns⟩
dais·ing \'dāziŋ, -zən\ *n* -S [prob. fr. gerund of *daise*] *Scot* : ¹PINE 3
dai·sy \'dāzē, -zi\ *n* -ES [ME *daisie, dayeseye*, fr. OE *dægesēge, dægesēage*, fr. *dæg* day + *ēage* eye — more at DAY, EYE] **1** : any of numerous composite plants having flower heads with well-developed ray flowers usu. arranged in a single whorl or a few whorls: as **a** : a low scapose European herb (*Bellis perennis*) having flower heads with small white or pink ray flowers and yellow disk flowers — called also *English daisy* **b** : a rather tall leafy-stemmed perennial herb (*Chrysanthemum leucanthemum*) having larger flower heads than the English daisy and long white ray flowers and being often a troublesome weed esp. in parts of the U. S. — called also *oxeye daisy, white daisy* **c** *Austral* (1) : SWAN RIVER DAISY (2) : any plant of the genus *Vittadinia* **d** *New Zealand* : a plant of the genus *Lagenophora* **e** : any of several wild plants of the genera *Aster* and *Erigeron* **f** : any of various other composite plants — usu. used wth a qualifying term; see AFRICAN DAISY, MICHAELMAS DAISY, SHASTA DAISY **2** : the flower head of any daisy **3** *slang* : a person or thing that is first-rate of its kind ⟨he's a real ~⟩ **4** : a tall drink of a spirituous liquor, lime juice or lemon juice, grenadine or raspberry syrup or curaçao, and carbonated water chilled with cracked or shaved ice and garnished with fruit or mint ⟨rum ~⟩ ⟨gin ~⟩ **5 a** *usu* **daisy ham** : a boned and smoked piece of pork from the shoulder **b** : a cheddar cheese of a certain style and weight
daisybush \'⸗⸗,⸗\ *n* : any of certain frost-tender shrubs of the Australasian composite genus *Olearia* with leathery evergreen leaves and flower heads resembling daisies; *esp* : a bushy half-hardy New Zealand shrub (*O. haastii*) sometimes cultivated for its fragrant white flower heads
daisy chain *n* **1** : a string of daisies with stems linked to form a chain; *specif* : such a chain carried by chosen students at a class day or other celebration in some women's colleges **2** : an interlinked series (as of events, items, or steps) ⟨a *daisy chain* of middlemen —*Christian Science Monitor*⟩
daisy cutter *n* **1** *slang* : a horse that carries its feet low in trotting **2** *slang* : a ball (as in cricket or baseball) so batted or bowled that it skims along the ground **3** *slang* : a fragmentation bomb or an antipersonnel bomb
daisy-cutting \'⸗⸗,⸗⸗\ *adj* : having the characteristics of a daisy cutter
daisy family *n* : COMPOSITAE
daisy fleabane *n* : any of several white-rayed American plants of the genus *Erigeron* (esp. *E. annuus* and *E. strigosus*)
daisy tree *n* : DAISYBUSH
¹**dak** \'däk *also* 'dȯk\ *n* -S [Hindi *ḍāk*] **1** : transport or post by relays of men and horses **2** : a post station or traveler's rest house located orig. on post roads ⟨a ~ bungalow⟩
²**dak** *var of* DHAK
da·kar \(')da¦kär, (')dä¦-, də'-\ *adj, usu cap* [fr. *Dakar*, French West Africa] : of or from Dakar in Senegal : of the kind or style prevalent in Dakar
da·ker \'dākə(r)\ *n* -S [MF *dacre*, fr. OF, fr. MD *daker;* akin to MLG *dēker* quantity of ten (hides) — more at DICKER] : ¹DICKER 1
da·ker-hen \" + ,-\ *n* [origin unknown] : CORNCRAKE
dakh·ma \'däkmə\ *n* -S [Per, fr. MPer *dakhmak*, fr. Av *daxma-* funeral place] : TOWER OF SILENCE
da·kin's solution \'dākənz-\ *n, usu cap D* [after Henry D. *Dakin* †1952 Eng. chemist] : an antiseptic solution developed during World War I for the treatment of wounds and consisting essentially of an aqueous solution containing from 0.5 percent to 0.6 percent of sodium hypochlorite with 0.4 percent of boric acid added to reduce the alkalinity
¹**da·ko·ta** *also* **da·co·ta** *or* **da·co·tah** \də'kōd·ə, -ōtə\ *n, pl* **dakota** *or* **dakotas** *usu cap* [Dakota (Santee dial.) *Dakota*, lit., allies] **1 a** : a Siouan people of the northern Mississippi valley commonly called Sioux and divided into an eastern or forest group comprising the Mdewakanton, Wahpeton, Wahpekute, and Sisseton and a western or prairie group comprising the Yankton, Yanktonai, and Teton **b** : a member of such people **2** : the language of the Dakota people
²**dakota** \" *or* **da·ko·tan** \-t³n, -d·ən, -tən\ *adj, usu cap* [in sense 1, fr. ¹*Dakota;* in sense 2, fr. *Dakota* territory, former region of the U.S. including No. & So. Dakota, fr. the *Dakota* Indians] **1** *also* **dacota** *or* **dacotah** *pron at* DAKOTA\ *or* **da·co·tan** *pron at* DAKOTAN\ : of or relating to the Dakota people or their language **2 a** : of or relating to the Dakota territory **b** : of or from the state of No. Dakota or the state of So. Dakota : of the kind or style prevalent in No. Dakota or So. Dakota **c** : of, relating to, or constituting a division of the Cretaceous — see GEOLOGIC TIME table
dakota millet *n, usu cap D* **1** : FOXTAIL MILLET **2** : MILLET 1a
dakotan \" *n* -S *cap* [*Dakota (territory)* + E -*an*] : a native or resident of the Dakota territory or No. Dakota or So. Dakota
dak runner *n* [¹*dak*] *India & Burma* : MAIL CARRIER
da–kua \'däk(ə)wə, 'dak-\ *n* -S [Fijian] **1** : a kauri pine (*Agathis vitiensis*) of the Fiji islands **2** *also* **dakua wood** : the usu. white wood of the dakua used for masts, spars, booms, and flooring
dal \'däl\ *var of* DHAL
dal *abbr* decaliter
da·lag \də'läg, 'dä,l-\ *n* -S [Tag] *Philippines* : MURRAL
da·lai la·ma \'dä,lī'lämə, 'da,-,'dä,-, -'lämə *also* -(,)lä'l- *or* -(,)lē'l- *or* -,lə'l-; də'lī'l-\ *n, pl* **dalai lamas** *usu cap D&L* [Mongolian *dalai* ocean] : the spiritual head of Tibetan Buddhism
dal·ber·gia \dal'bərj(ē)ə, -rgēə\ *n, cap* [NL, fr. Nils *Dalberg* †1819 Swedish physician + NL -*ia*] : a large genus of tropical trees (family Leguminosae) with pinnate leaves and paniculate flowers — see BLACKWOOD b
¹**dale** \'dāl, *esp before pause or consonant* -āəl\ *n* -S [ME, fr. OE *dæl;* akin to OHG *tal* valley, ON *dalr*, Goth *dal* valley, Gk *tholos* rotunda, OSlav *dolŭ* pit; basic meaning: curving] **1** *chiefly Brit* : a river valley running between hills or through high land **2** : VALE, VALLEY
²**dale** \" *n* -S [ME, fr. OE *dāl* — more at DEAL] *Brit* : a portion of land; *specif* : a portion of an undivided common field set off by markers
³**dale** \" *n* -S [F *dalle* gutter, stone slab, fr. MF, fr. ON *dæla;* akin to ON *dalr* valley] : a tube, trough, or pipe esp. from a ship's pump
da·lea \'dālēə\ *n* [NL, after Samuel *Dale* †1739 Eng. physician and botanist] **1** *cap* : a genus of American herbs or shrubs (family Leguminosae) with pinnate leaves and spikes or heads of mostly purple flowers **2** -S : any plant of the genus *Dalea*
dale–backed \'⸗¦⸗\ *adj* [¹*dale*] : SWAYBACKED
dal·e·car·li·an \¦dalə¦kärlēən\ *adj, usu cap* [*Dalecarlia* (Dalarna), region in central Sweden + E -*an*] : of or relating to Dalecarlia in Sweden
d'a·lem·bert's principle \¦dalәm¦be(ə)rz-\ *n, usu cap A* [after Jean LeRond *d'Alembert* †1783 Fr. mathematician, its formulator] : a principle in mechanics: the reaction due to the inertia of an accelerated body (as a baseball) is equal and opposite to the force causing the acceleration (as the blow of a bat upon the baseball) and results in a condition of kinetic equilibrium — compare LAW OF MOTION 3
da·ler \'dälə(r)\ *n* -S [Dan & Sw, fr. LG, fr. G *taler* — more at DOLLAR] : a Danish or Swedish dollar : RIGSDALER, RIKSDALER
dales \'dā(ə)lz\ *n* [so called fr. its having developed in the eastern valleys of the Pennine range, England] **1** *usu cap* : a breed of sturdy sure-footed ponies native to northeast England used for farm work and as pack horses **2** *pl* **dales** *often cap* : any animal of the Dales breed
dales·man \'dālzmən, -,man\ *n, pl* **dalesmen** *Brit* : one living or born in a dale; *specif* : one of the inhabitants of the river valleys in the north of England
da·leth \'dä,leth, -,lət\ *also* **da·let** \-,let, -,lət\ *n* -S [Heb *dāleth*, prob. pausal form of *deleth* door] **1** : the fourth letter of the Hebrew alphabet — symbol ד; see ALPHABET table **2** : the letter of the Phoenician or of any of various other Semitic alphabets corresponding to Hebrew daleth
da·li·esque \¦dälē¦esk, ¦dal-,¦däl-\ *adj, usu cap* [Salvador *Dali* *b*1904 Span. painter + E -*esque*] : resembling or suggesting the painting of the surrealist artist Dali : befitting the exotic contents of such painting ⟨a pair of feathers stuck at a *Daliesque* angle in holes pierced in each nostril —*Time*⟩ ⟨a *Daliesque* landscape of stunted pines, twisted cripples of the tree world, and strangely shaped gray-black rocks —Maud Oakes⟩
dal·las \'daləs, *esp S* -lis\ *adj, usu cap* [fr. *Dallas*, Texas] : of or from the city of Dallas, Texas ⟨*Dallas* stores⟩ : of the kind or style prevalent in Dallas
dallas grass *n, usu cap D* : DALLIS GRASS
dal·las·ite \-,sīt\ *n* -S *cap* [*Dallas*, Texas + E -*ite*] : a native or resident of Dallas, Texas
dalles \-lz\ *n pl* [F, pl. of *dalle* gutter — more at DALE] : the rapids in a river confined between walls of a canyon or gorge
dal·li \'dä(,)lē, 'da(-\ *n* -S [prob. of Arawakan origin; akin to Wapisiana *dali* dalli] : any of certain tropical trees of the genus *Virola* of the family Myristicaceae (esp. *V. surinamensis*) that has wood which is used for staves and hard seeds which resemble nutmegs and yield a wax or solid oil
dal·li·ance \'dalēən(t)s, -lyə-\ *n* -S [ME *dalyaunce*, fr. *dalyen* to dally + -*aunce* -ance] **1** : PLAY, SPORTIVENESS; *esp* : amorous play (as flirting or caressing) ⟨amatory ~ —R.H.Lowie⟩ **2** : frivolous action : TRIFLING ⟨this short ~ with revolutionary ideas —John Mason Brown⟩
dal·lis grass \'daləs-\ *n, usu cap D* [perh. alter. of *Dallas*, Tex.] : a tall tufted perennial grass (*Paspalum dilatatum*) introduced from the tropics and now common as a pasture and forage grass in the southern U.S.
dallop *var of* DOLLOP
dall porpoise \'dȯl-\ *or* **dall's porpoise** *n, usu cap D* [after William H. *Dall* †1927 Am. naturalist] : a common porpoise (*Phocoenoides dalli*) of the coastal waters of western No. America that reaches a length of six feet and is black above with much white on the sides and ventral surface
dall sheep *or* **dall's sheep** *n, usu cap D* [after W.H.*Dall*] : a large white wild sheep (*Ovis montana dalli* or *O. dalli*) of northwestern No. America
¹**dal·ly** \'dalē, -li\ *vb* -ED/-ING/-ES [ME *dalyen*, fr. AF *dalier*, perh. of Gmc origin; akin to 16th cent. G *dallen, tallen* to talk foolishly, act frivolously; perh. akin to OE *dol* foolish — more at DULL] *vi* **1 a** : to act playfully : PLAY, SPORT, TOY ⟨~*ing* with a glass of wine —Victoria Sackville-West⟩ ⟨the winter that merely *dallies* and trifles —Alfred Buchanan⟩; *esp* : to play amorously ⟨*dallied* with a young Mexican girl —Green Peyton⟩ **b** : to play mockingly ⟨~*ing* with a serious proposition⟩ **2 a** : to waste time (as in frivolity, idleness, or trifling) **b** : LINGER, DELAY, TARRY ⟨while the men *dallied*, the dogs set off —J.T.McNish⟩ ~ *vt* **1** *obs* : to evade or delay by trifling **2** *archaic* : to consume or spend (as time) in dalliance or by dallying — used with *away* **syn** see DELAY
²**dally** \", 'däl-\ *vb* -ED/-ING/-ES [Sp *¡dale (vuelta)!* give it a turn!] *vi* : to twist a rope around the saddle horn in roping an animal ⟨his saddle stayed on better when he was ~*ing* if the cinch was attached at the center —S.E.Fletcher⟩ ~ *vt* : to twist (a rope) in a dally ⟨*dallied* the pack-horse rope around his saddle horn —A.B.Guthrie⟩
³**dally** \" *n* -ES : a temporary twisting of the rope around the saddle horn in roping an animal
dal·ly·ing·ly *adv* : in a dallying manner
dal·ly·man \'⸗⸗,man, -,mən\ *n, pl* **dallymen** : a cowboy who uses the daily method of roping
dal·ly wel·ta \¦⸗⸗¦weltə\ *n, pl* **dally weltas** [by folk etymology fr. Sp. *¡dale vuelta!*] : ³DALLY
dally wel·ter \-tə(r)\ *n* [*dally welta* + -*er*] : DALLYMAN
dal·ma·ni·tes \¦dalmə¦nīd·(,)ēz\ *n, cap* [NL, fr. Johan W. *Dalman* †1826 Swedish naturalist + L -*ites* -ite] : a large genus of trilobites found from the Ordovician to the Devonian in Europe, America, and India
¹**dal·ma·tian** \(')dal¦māshən\ *adj, usu cap* [*Dalmatia*, region on the Adriatic sea now included in Yugoslavia + E -*an*] : of or relating to Dalmatia
²**dalmatian** \" *n* -S **1** *cap* : a native or inhabitant of Dalmatia **2** *also* **dalmatian dog** *often cap Dalmatian* : a large dog of a breed supposed to have originated in Dalmatia having a white short-haired coat with black or brown spots varying from dime to half-dollar size, standing from 19 to 23 inches high, and weighing from 35 to 50 pounds — called also *coach dog* **3** *cap* : a Romance language developed from colloquial Latin and extinct by the late 19th century that was spoken on the Dalmatian coast and Adriatic islands from Veglia to Ragusa
dalmatian cherry *n, usu cap D* : MARASCA
dalmatian insect powder *n, usu cap D* : pyrethrum (sense 2a) derived from a Dalmatian pyrethrum
¹**dal·mat·ic** \(')dal¦mad·ik, -atik\ *adj, usu cap* [L *Dalmaticus*, fr. *Dalmatia* + L -*icus* -ic] : ¹DALMATIAN ⟨a ~ robe⟩
²**dalmatic** \⸗'⸗⸗\ *also* **dal·mat·i·ca** \-'mad·əkə, -atə-\ *n* -S [LL *dalmatica*, fr. fem. of L *Dalmaticus*] **1** : an ecclesiastical outer vestment worn in religious ceremonies orig. by a deacon but now also by some prelates (as bishops) **2 a** : a loose unbelted medieval garment with full sleeves and often with slits up the sides **b** : a similar robe of rich materials worn on state occasions by an English king; *esp* : such a robe worn by a king at his coronation
da·lo \'dä(,)lō\ *n* -S [Fijian] : TARO 1
dal·ra·di·an \(')dal¦rādēən\ *adj, usu cap* [*Dalrad-* (alter. of *Dalriada*, ancient region of Scotland) + E -*ian*] : of, relating to, or constituting a division of the Precambrian — see GEOLOGIC TIME table
dal se·gno \däl'sān(,)yō, dal'-,dȧl'-\ *adv* [It] : from the sign — used as a direction in music for the performer to return to the sign that marks the beginning of a repeat

dalmatic 1

dal·to·ni·an \(')dȯl¦tōnēən, (')däl¦-\ *adj, usu cap* [John *Dalton* †1844 Eng. chemist and physicist + E -*ian*] : of or relating to the English chemist Dalton, his theory of atoms, or his law of multiple proportions
dal·ton·ide \'dȯlt³n,īd, 'däl-\ *n* -S [John *Dalton* + E -*ide*] : a chemical compound (as sodium chloride) that conforms to the law of definite proportions : a stoichiometric compound — distinguished from *berthollide*
dal·ton·ism \-³n,izəm\ *n* -S *usu cap* [F *daltonisme*, fr. John *Dalton* †1844 + F -*isme* -ism] **1** : red-green blindness occurring in man as a recessive sex-linked genetic anomaly **2** : COLOR BLINDNESS
dalton's law *n, usu cap D* [after John *Dalton*, its formulator] : LAW OF PARTIAL PRESSURES
dal·yell·ia \dal'yelēə\ *n, cap* [NL, fr. John G. *Dalyell* †1851 Scot. naturalist + NL -*ia*] : a common genus (the type of the nearly cosmopolitan family Dalyelliidae) of widely distributed rhabdocoel turbellarians with anterior mouth and large dilated pharynx
¹**dam** \'dam, 'daa(ə)m\ *n* -S [ME, lady, dam, var. of *dame* — more at DAME] : a female parent — used esp. of domestic animals and poultry but sometimes archaically and usu. disparagingly of women
²**dam** \" *n* -S [ME; akin to OE *for*demman to dam up, MHG *tam* dam, OHG *temmen* to dam, Goth *faur*dammjan to put a stop to, and perh. to Gk *themeilia* foundations, *tithenai* to place, set — more at DO] **1** : a barrier preventing the flow of water ⟨a lava ~⟩ ⟨beaver ~s⟩ ⟨a ~ of drift or other deposits across a valley fed with meltwater —R.F.Flint⟩; *esp* : a barrier (as a bank of earth or a wall of masonry or wood) built across a watercourse to confine and keep back flowing water **2** : a body of water confined or held by a dam (as a millpond or reservoir) ⟨wild geese . . . would rise from the waters of the ~ at my approach —H.V.Morton⟩ ⟨swimming in this ~ is prohibited⟩ **3** : a barrier or obstruction intended to check the flow of liquid, gas, or air: as **a** : a thin sheet of rubber that is stretched around a tooth to keep it dry during dental work **b** : a partition for excluding water, fire, or gas from a section of a mine **c** : a firebrick wall or a stone forming the front of the hearth of a blast furnace **4** *chiefly Brit* : a portable water tank filled from a hose and used in fire fighting
³**dam** \" *vt* **dammed; dammed; damming; dams** **1** : to provide with a dam : obstruct or restrain the flow of (water) by means of a dam ⟨~ a stream⟩ — often used with *up* **2** : to stop up : block up ⟨the strait pass was *dammed* with dead men —Shak.⟩ : OBSTRUCT, IMPEDE ⟨the futility of trying to ~ the flow of history⟩ — often used with *up* or *back* ⟨~ up an emotion⟩ ⟨~ back his tears⟩ ⟨the tensions *dammed* up by the depression —Oscar Handlin⟩ **syn** see HINDER
⁴**dam** \" *n* -S [back-formation fr. *dams*] *Scot* : a piece in checkers; *esp* : KING
dam *abbr* decameter
da·ma \'dāmə\ *n* [NL, fr. L *dama, damma* fallow deer, antelope, chamois, perh. of Celt origin; akin to OIr *dam* ox, *dam allaid* stag, W *dafad* sheep, OCorn *dauat;* akin to Gk *damalēs* young bull, Skt *damya* young bull, *dāmyati* he tames — more at TAME] **1** *cap* : a genus of deers consisting of the fallow deer **2** -S [NL (specific epithet of *Gazella dama*), fr.L, fallow deer] : ADDRA
da·ma de no·che \¦dämə,dä'nō,chā\ *n, pl* **damas de noche** \-məs,-, -maz,-\ [AmerSp, lit., lady of the night] : a West Indian shrub (*Cestrum nocturnum*) with sweet scented yellowish red flowers
¹**dam·age** \'damij, -mēj\ *n* -S [ME, fr. OF, fr. *dam* damage (fr. L *damnum* damage, fine) + -*age* — more at DAMN] **1** : loss due to injury : injury or harm to person, property, or reputation : HURT, HARM ⟨flood ~⟩ ⟨~ resulting from upheavals of nature⟩ ⟨items that may be canceled without ~ to the essential plan⟩ ⟨my poor parents were afraid of social ~ to their child —Rose Macaulay⟩ **2** *obs* : a thing to be regretted : MISFORTUNE, DISADVANTAGE **3 damages** *pl* : the estimated reparation in money for detriment or injury sustained : compensation or satisfaction imposed by law for a wrong or injury caused by a violation of a legal right ⟨bring a suit for ~s⟩ ⟨was awarded compensatory ~s of $4000⟩ — compare DAMNUM ABSQUE INJURIA; see COMPENSATORY DAMAGES, GENERAL DAMAGES, NOMINAL DAMAGES, PUNITIVE DAMAGES, SPECIAL DAMAGES **4** : EXPENSE, COST, CHARGE **syn** see INJURY
²**damage** \" *vb* -ED/-ING/-S [ME *damagen*, fr. MF *damagier*, fr. OF, fr. *damage*, n.] *vt* : to do or cause damage to : HURT, INJURE, IMPAIR ⟨rehabilitation centers for men *damaged* by war⟩ ⟨*damaged* his case by overstating it⟩ ⟨frost severe enough to ~ fruit trees⟩ ~ *vi* : to become damaged ⟨a sturdy cloth that does not ~ easily⟩ **syn** see INJURE
dam·age·able \-jəbəl\ *adj* [MF, fr. OF, fr. *damagier* + -*able*] **1** *obs* : causing damage : HURTFUL **2** : capable of being injured : liable to damage
damage control *n* : procedures and skills employed to maintain or restore watertight integrity, stability, or offensive power in a warship or airplane ⟨the *damage-control* officer⟩
damaging *adj* : causing or able to cause damage : INJURIOUS, DETRIMENTAL ⟨~ though wholly circumstantial evidence⟩ ⟨it discredits the authority of science but it is equally ~ to religion —W.R.Inge⟩
dam·ag·ing·ly *adv* : in a damaging manner
dam·an \'damən\ *n* -S [Ar *damān* (*Isrā'īl*), lit., sheep of Israel] : the Syrian hyrax
dama pademelon *n* [*dama* + *pademelon*, native name in Australia] : a dark stocky thick-coated and now rare wallaby (*Thylogale eugenii*) of southern and western Australia
damar *var of* DAMMAR
da·ma·ra \'damərə, də'märə\ *n, pl* **damara** *or* **damaras** *usu cap* **1** : a people of South-West Africa including the Herero **2** : a member of the Damara people
¹**dam·a·scene** \'damə,sēn *also* ,⸗⸗'⸗\ *n* -S [ME, fr. L *Damascenus*, adj. & n., fr. Gk *Damaskēnos*, fr. *Damaskos* Damascus, Syria] **1** *cap* : a native or inhabitant of Damascus **2** : DAMASK 2b **3** [ME — more at DAMSON] : DAMSON PLUM
²**damascene** \" *adj* **1** : of or relating to damask or the art of damascening **2** *usu cap* [L *Damascenus*, adj. & n.] **a** : of, relating to, or characteristic of Damascus **b** : of, relating to, or characteristic of the Damascenes
³**damascene** \" *vt* -ED/-ING/-S [alter. (influenced by ¹*damascene*) of earlier *damaskine* — more at DAMASKEEN] **1** : to ornament with wavy patterns (as by welding together bars of iron and steel in the manufacture of Damascus blades) **2** : to ornament (as iron or steel) with inlaid work of precious metals ⟨a Kurdish flintlock *damascened* . . . with gold arabesques —*N.Y. Herald Tribune*⟩
damascened \-nd\ *adj* **1 a** : decorated with wavy patterns ⟨~ swords⟩ **b** : decorated with inlaid work of precious metals ⟨paintings with ~ gold backgrounds⟩ **2** : having an interwoven texture that resembles the markings of a damascened gun barrel — used esp. of certain volcanic glasses
dam·a·scen·er \-nə(r)\ *n* -S : one that damascenes
da·mas·cus \də'maskəs, -maas-, -mäs-\ *adj, usu cap* [fr. *Damascus*, Syria] : of or from Damascus, the capital of Syria : of the kind or style prevalent in Damascus
damascus barrel *n, usu cap D* : a shotgun barrel for use esp. with black-powder cartridges usu. made of strips or rods of iron or steel coiled in a spiral to form a tube and with a speckled or mottled pattern that often runs at right angles to the bore — compare WIRE-WOUND GUN
damascus blade *or* **damascus sword** *n, usu cap D* : a sword made of Damascus steel
damascus iron *or* **damascus twist** *n, usu cap D* : iron made by gunmakers by piling and welding together several bars or wires of iron and steel
damascus steel *or* **damask steel** *n, usu cap Damascus* : steel ornamented with wavy patterns, noted for its hardness and elasticity, and formerly used esp. for making sword blades
damascus ware *n, usu cap D* : a Turkish pottery made with a clear glaze over a white engobe and decorated under the glaze in rich colors
¹**dam·ask** \'daməsk *sometimes* də'mask\ *n* -S [ME *damaske*, fr. ML *damascus*, fr. *Damascus*, Syria, where such fabrics were first produced] **1** : a firm lustrous fabric made with flat conventional patterns in satin weave on a plain-woven ground on the right side and a plain-woven pattern on a satin ground on the reverse side, made on jacquard looms usu. of linen, cotton, silk, rayon, or combinations of these fibers, and used for household linen, interior decoration, and clothing **2 a** : DAMASCUS STEEL **b** : the peculiar markings of such steel — compare WATER 7c **3** [*damask (rose)*] : a grayish red that is bluer than bois de rose, bluer, lighter, and stronger than blush rose, and bluer and deeper than Pompeian red or appleblossom
²**damask** \" *adj* **1** : made of or resembling damask ⟨~ table linen⟩ **2** : made of or resembling Damascus steel **3** [*damask (rose)*] : of the color damask
³**damask** \" *vt* -ED/-ING/-S **1** : DAMASCENE **2** : to weave or adorn with ornamentation characteristic of damask : decorate with variegated pattern or color ⟨on the soft downy bank ~*ed* with flowers —John Milton⟩ ⟨the ~*ed* barge —Elinor Wylie⟩ **3** : to furnish with damask or damask hangings ⟨the colonned, ~*ed*, oppressively genteel mansion —Catherine M. Brown⟩ **4** : to make of the color damask **5 a** : to deface (as a book) by marking with lines or figures **b** : to make (a seal) invalid by defacing with a hammer blow
dam·a·skeen \,damə,skēn *also* ,⸗⸗'⸗\ *vt* -ED/-ING/-S [fr. earlier *damaskine*, fr. MF *damasquiner*, fr. *damasquin* of Damascus, fr. OIt *damaschino*, fr. *Damasco* Damascus (fr. L *Damascus*) + -*ino* (fr. L -*inus* -ine)] : DAMASCENE
damask rose *n* [fr. obs. *Damask* of Damascus, fr. obs. *Damask* Damascus, fr. ME *Damaske*, fr. L *Damascus*, fr. Gk *Damaskos*] : a large hardy very fragrant pink rose (*Rosa damascena*) of unknown origin that is largely cultivated in Asia Minor as a source of attar of roses and is a parent of many hybrid perpetual roses
damask violet *n* [fr. obs. *Damask* of Damascus] : DAME'S VIOLET
¹**da·mas·sé** \,damə'sā, '⸗⸗,⸗\ *n* -S [F, adj. & n., fr. past part. of *damasser* to damask (weave) fr. MF, fr. *damas* damask, fr. OF, fr. *Damas* Damascus, fr. L *Damascus*] : a damassé fabric esp. of linen

²**damassé** \¦==¦=\ *adj* [F] **:** woven like damask
dam·bo \'dăm(,)bō, 'dam-\ *n* -s [native name in Africa] **:** a small grassy floodplain of central Africa
dam·brod \'dam,(b)räd\ *n* -s [Sc ⁴*dam* + *brod* board, fr. ME (Scot. dial.) *brodd*, alter. of *bord* — more at BOARD] *Scot* **:** CHECKERBOARD
dame \'dām\ *n* -s [ME, fr. OF, fr. L *domina* mistress, lady, fem. of *dominus* master, lord; akin to L *domus* house — more at TIMBER] **1 :** a woman of rank, station, or authority: **a :** the female ruler or head of a body or institution (as a nunnery); *also* **:** a member of certain religious orders of women — used also as a title **b** *archaic* **:** the mistress of a household **:** HOUSEWIFE, WIFE — used also as a title **c :** the wife or daughter of a lord — used formerly also as a form of address but now only as a title prefixed to personified abstractions ⟨*Dame* Care⟩ ⟨*Dame* Fortune⟩ **d** *archaic* **:** the wife or widow of a knight or baronet — used prefixed to prename and surname as a legal title ⟨the will of *Dame* Margaret Murray, widow of Sir John Murray, Bart. —C.R.Hudleston⟩, not as a title of courtesy or a form of address; compare LADY **e :** the mistress of a school — used chiefly in the phrase *dame school* **f :** a matron in charge of a boarding house at Eton College — used also of men **g :** a female member of certain orders of knighthood or of chivalry — used also as a title ⟨*Dame* Myra Hess⟩; compare KNIGHT **2 a :** an elderly woman **:** MATRON ⟨the ancient ~ whose friendship I had so curiously made —William Baucke⟩ ⟨more and more old gaffers and ~*s* hanging loose on society —J.W.Krutch⟩ **b** *Scot* **:** a young unmarried woman **:** GIRL **c** *slang* **:** WOMAN, FEMALE ⟨whiskey, dice, and ~*s* speed the undertaker —Shields McIlwaine⟩ **3 :** a female parent **:** DAM — now used only of animals **4** [MF] *chess, obs* **:** QUEEN **5** *usu cap* **:** a female character in English pantomime played by a male comedian
dame de com·pa·gnie \dȧmdəkōⁿpȧnyē\ *n, pl* **dames de compagnie** \"\ [F, lit., lady of companionship] **:** a woman who acts as a paid companion
dame school \'dām-\ *n* **:** a school in which the rudiments of reading and writing were taught to small children by a woman in her own home ⟨the other girls in the *dame school* which she attended —S.H.Adams⟩
dame's violet \-mz-\ *also* **dame's gilliflower** *or* **dame's rocket** *n* **:** a Eurasian perennial plant (*Hesperis matronalis*) that is widely cultivated for its spikes of showy, single or double, and white or purple flowers which are fragrant in the evening
dame·wort \'dām + ,-\ *n* -s **:** DAME'S VIOLET
¹**dam·fool** \,dam, ¦daa(ə)m+\ *n* [alter. of *damned fool*] **:** one who is extremely foolish — not often in formal use ⟨stand around and let these two ~*s* kill each other —James Jones⟩
²**damfool** *or* **dam·foolish** \"+\ *adj* **:** extremely foolish or stupid ⟨asking ~ questions with ardor —Claud Cockburn⟩ — not often in formal use
dam·i·ana \,damē'anə, -'änə *also* -'ānə\ *n* -s [AmerSp] **:** the dried leaf of a plant (*Turnera diffusa*) of tropical America, California, and Texas formerly used as a tonic and aphrodisiac
da·mine \'dā,mīn, -mən\ *adj* [NL *Dama* + E *-ine*] **:** belonging to or like the fallow deer; *usu* **:** having or being antlers palmate near the tip like those of the fallow deer
dam·kjern·ite \'damkyə(r),nīt\ *n* -s [G *damkjernit*, fr. *Damkjern*, Telemark, Norway, where it was discovered + G *-it* -ite] **:** a melanocratic dike rock with phenocrysts of biotite, pyroxene and barkevikitic hornblende in a groundmass of pyroxene, green hornblende, olivine, magnetite, and considerable calcite
dam·mar *or* **dam·ar** *also* **dam·mer** \'damə(r)\ *n* -s [Malay *damar*] **1 :** any of various hard resins derived esp. from evergreen trees of the genus *Agathis* — compare COPAL, KAURI **2 :** any of various semifossil or recent chiefly East Indian resins; *esp* **:** a soft clear to yellow recent resin obtained chiefly in Malaya from trees of the family Dipterocarpaceae (esp. genera *Shorea*, *Balanocarpus*, and *Hopea*) and used largely in varnishes and printing inks — called also *gum dammar*; see BATU, EAST INDIA RESIN
dammar pine *n* **:** a tree of the genus *Agathis*
dam·me \'damē\ *interj* [alter. of *damn me*] — used as a mild imprecation
dammed *past of* DAM
damming *pres part of* DAM
dam·mit \'damət\ *interj* [alter. of *damn it*] — used as a mild imprecation
¹**damn** \dam, 'daa(ə)m\ *vb* -ED/-ING/-S [ME *dampnen*, fr. OF *dampner*, fr. L *damnare* to condemn, fr. *damnum* damage, fine, harm, loss; perh. akin to ON *tafn* sacrifice, L *daps* sacrificial feast, Gk *dapanē* expenditure, *daptein* to devour, Skt *dayate* he apportions — more at TIDE] *vt* **1 a** *obs* **:** to adjudge (a person) guilty or culpable **:** sentence judicially **b :** to condemn to a punishment or fate **:** DOOM ⟨if we fail, then we have ~*ed* every man to be the slave of fear —B.M. Baruch⟩ **2 a :** to doom to everlasting punishment in the future world **:** consign to perdition **:** CURSE **b :** to bring about the damnation of **3 :** to condemn as invalid, illegal, immoral, bad, or harmful **:** pronounce adverse judgment upon ⟨~*ing* movies for corrupting the minds of young innocents⟩ ⟨spent three months there and returned with a most ~*ing* report —A.G.N.Flew⟩; *specif* **:** to condemn (a work of art) as a failure **4 :** to bring condemnation or ruin upon **:** RUIN ⟨the story of a . . . minister ~*ed* by his recognition of the mean emotionalism of his church —J.D.Hart⟩ ⟨a democracy is ~*ed* when its leaders are slaves; it is safe when its leaders are not afraid to be free —*New Republic*⟩ **5 :** to invoke damnation upon **:** swear at by using *damn* **:** CURSE — often used to express annoyance, disgust, or surprise ⟨~ him, he ought to have been careful⟩ ⟨well, I'll be ~*ed*⟩ ~ *vi* **:** CURSE, SWEAR — often used interjectionally esp. to express annoyance, disgust, or surprise
syn see EXECRATE
²**damn** \"\ *n* -s **1 :** the utterance of the word *damn* as a curse **2 :** something of little value — used in various slang or profane phrases ⟨didn't give a ~⟩ ⟨not worth a ~⟩
³**damn** \"\ *adj* [by shortening] **:** ¹DAMNED 2a, 2b
⁴**damn** \"\ *adv* [by shortening] **:** ²DAMNED ⟨Americans . . . will write letters to editors about ~ near anything —*New Yorker*⟩
damna *pl of* DAMNUM
dam·na·bil·i·ty \,damnə'bilәd·ē, ,daam-, -ətē, -i\ *n* -ES **:** the quality or state of being damnable **:** liability to damnation
dam·na·ble \'=nəbəl\ *adj* [ME *dampnable*, fr. MF *damnable*, fr. LL *damnabilis*, fr. L *damnare* + *-abilis* -able] **1 :** liable to damnation **2 :** deserving condemnation **3 :** deserving imprecation **:** DETESTABLE, EXECRABLE ⟨a ~ lie⟩ — often used as a generalized expression of disapproval ⟨a ~ shame⟩ ⟨~ weather⟩ — **dam·na·ble·ness** *n* -ES — **dam·na·bly** \-blē, -bli\ *adv*
damn all *n, slang Brit* **:** NOTHING ⟨hadn't . . . the courage to tell Yeats that he knew *damn all* about the Russian writer —Sean O'Casey⟩
dam·na·tion \dam'nāshən, daam'-\ *n* -s [ME *dampnacioun*, fr. OF *dampnation*, *damnation*, fr. L *damnation-*, *damnatio*, fr. *damnatus* (past part. of *damnare* to condemn) + *-ion-*, *-io* -ion — more at DAMN] **1 :** the act of damning or the state of being damned — often used interjectionally esp. to express annoyance or disgust **2 a :** condemnation to everlasting punishment in the future state **b :** the punishment resulting from such condemnation ⟨how can ye escape the ~ of hell —Mt 23:33 (AV)⟩ **3 :** a cause or occasion of damnation **:** a sin leading to or deserving of everlasting punishment ⟨stressing that crime is sin and sin ~ —A.C.Ward⟩ **4** *Roman law* **:** condemnation, sentence, or judgment esp. to pay damages — used esp. in the phrase *legacy by damnation* with reference to the obligation of the heir to do something for or give something to another person
dam·na·tory \'=nə,tōrē, -tȯrē, -ri\ *adj* [L *damnatorius*, fr. *damnatus* + *-orius* -ory] **1 a :** expressing or imposing condemnation **:** CONDEMNATORY ⟨the ~ vehemence we were used to in him —Thomas Carlyle⟩ ⟨the comprehensive, ~ term *parliamentarism* —H.R.Spencer⟩ **b :** occasioning condemnation **:** DAMNING, RUINOUS **2 :** containing, imposing, or consigning to damnation ⟨the ~ clauses of the Athanasian Creed⟩
¹**damned** \'damd, 'daa(ə)md *also in sense 2* -m; *archaic also* -mnəd\ *adj, sometimes* **damned·er** \-mdə(r)\ *usu* **damned·est** *or* **damnd·est** \-mdəst\ [ME *dampned*, fr. past part. of *dampnen* to damn — more at DAMN] **1 :** doomed or condemned esp. to eternal punishment ⟨~ souls⟩ **2 a :** deserving condemnation **:** calling for execration **:** DAMNABLE, EXECRABLE — often used as a generalized expression of disapproval ⟨a ~ fool⟩ **b :** UNMITIGATED, COMPLETE, UTTER ⟨acted like a ~ idiot⟩ ⟨~ nonsense⟩ — often used as an intensive **c :** EXTRAORDINARY, INCREDIBLE, OUTRAGEOUS — used in the superlative ⟨the *damndest* ruckus you ever heard —Roark Bradford⟩; not often in formal use
²**damned** \-m(d)\ *adv* **:** EXTREMELY, VERY, QUITE ⟨a ~ cold day⟩ ⟨~ glad to see you⟩ ⟨a job ~ well done⟩ ⟨too ~ particular⟩
damned·est *or* **damnd·est** \-mdəst\ *n* -s [fr. superl. of *damned*] **:** UTMOST, BEST — used chiefly in the phrase *do one's damnedest* ⟨dared them to do their damnedest⟩ ⟨doing his ~ to win⟩
dam·ni·fi·ca·tion \,damnəfə'kāshən, ,daamn-\ *n* -s [F, fr. MF, damage, harm, fr. ML *damnification-*, *damnificatio*, fr. LL *damnificatus* (past part. of *damnificare*) + L *-ion-*, *-io* -ion] **:** the action of damnifying **:** an infliction of injury or loss
dam·ni·fy \'==,fī\ *vt* -ED/-ING/-ES [MF *damnifier*, *damnefier*, fr. OF, fr. LL *damnificare*, fr. L *damnificus* injurious, fr. *damnum* damage, fine + *-i-* + *-ficus* -fic — more at DAMN] **:** to cause loss or damage to **:** DAMAGE, INJURE, WRONG — now chiefly dial. except in law
damn·ing \'damiŋ, -mēŋ *sometimes* -mn-\ *adj* [fr. pres. part. of ¹*damn*] **1 :** bringing damnation ⟨a ~ sin⟩ **2 :** causing or leading to condemnation or ruin ⟨~ evidence of guilt⟩ — **damn·ing·ly** *adv*
dam·no·sa he·re·di·tas *or* **damnosa hae·re·di·tas** \dam¦nōsəhə'redə,tas\ *n* [L, lit., damaging inheritance] **1** *Roman law* **:** an inheritance from a person who dies insolvent and whose debts the heir is bound to discharge **2 :** a harmful or burdensome inheritance ⟨a *damnosa hereditas* from an imperfectly socialized . . . condition —*Times Lit. Supp.*⟩
dam·nous \'damnəs\ *adj* [L *damnosus* hurtful, fr. *damnum* + *-osus* -ous] **:** of, relating to, or involving a damnum — **dam·nous·ly** *adv*
damns *pres 3d sing of* DAMN, *pl of* DAMN
dam·num \'damnəm\ *n, pl* **dam·na** \-nə\ [L — more at DAMN] **:** detriment either to character or property whether involving legal wrong or not **:** harm or loss
damnum abs·que in·ju·ria \-¦abzkwē(,)in'yu̇rēə\ *n* [L, lit., damage without wrongdoing] **:** damage without violation of a legal right for which no legal action will lie — compare INJURIA, INJURIA ABSQUE DAMNO
damnum fa·ta·le \-fə'tā(,)lē\ *n* [L, lit., damage through fate] **:** loss arising from inevitable accident — compare ACT OF GOD
damnum in·fec·tum \-(,)in'fektəm\ *n* [L, lit., damage not done] **:** loss or damage threatened or anticipated but not yet sustained
damn well *adv* [⁴*damn*] **:** beyond doubt or question **:** CERTAINLY ⟨had never done it and *damn well* wasn't going to start⟩ ⟨we had better *damn well* be sure⟩ ⟨accustomed to doing as he *damn well* pleased⟩
damnyankee *var of* DAMYANKEE
dam·o·cle·an \,damə¦klēən\ *adj, usu cap* [*Damocles*, 4th cent. B.C. courtier in the retinue of Dionysius the Elder of Syracuse + E *-an* — more at SWORD OF DAMOCLES] **1 :** of or relating to Damocles **2 :** involving imminent danger ⟨the *Damoclean* threat of surpluses and swiftly descending prices —*N.Y.Times*⟩
dam·oi·seau \,damə'zō, '==,=\ *n, pl* **damoi·seaux** \"\ [MF, fr. OF *damoisel*, fr. (assumed) VL *domnicellus* young aristocrat, dim. of L *dominus* master, lord — more at DAME] *archaic* **:** a young noble not yet made a knight
dam·oi·selle \,damə'zel, '==,=\ *archaic var of* DAMSEL
damosel *or* **damozel** *var of* DAMSEL
da·mour·ite \də'mu̇,rīt\ *n* -s [F *damourite*, fr. A. A. *Damour* †1902 Fr. chemist + F *-ite*] **:** a variety of muscovite
¹**damp** \'damp, 'daa(ə)mp, 'daimp\ *n* -s [MD or MLG, vapor; akin to OHG *damph* vapor, *demphen* to cause to steam, MHG *dampf*, *tampf* vapor, *dimpfen* to steam, smoke, OE *dim* — more at DIM] **1 :** a noxious or stifling gas or vapor; *esp* **:** such a gas occurring in coal mines — usu. used in pl; compare BLACKDAMP, FIREDAMP **2** *obs* **:** a dazed or stupefied state **:** STUPOR, INSENSIBILITY **3** MOISTURE: **a :** DAMPNESS, HUMIDITY ⟨*damp*-resisting flour⟩ ⟨that old hostel, rotting down with ~ and time —John Galsworthy⟩ **b** *archaic* **:** FOG, MIST **4 a :** DISCOURAGEMENT, CHECK, DAMPER ⟨no sentiment of shame gave a ~ to her triumph —Jane Austen⟩ ⟨uncertainties that cast a ~ upon trade⟩ **b** *archaic* **:** a depression or dejection of mind or spirit ⟨a secret ~ of grief comes o'er my soul —Joseph Addison⟩ **5 :** a period of humid weather favorable for the moistening and softening of cured tobacco so that it can be handled
²**damp** \"\ *vb* -ED/-ING/-S *vt* **1 a :** to affect with or as if with a noxious gas or vapor **:** CHOKE, STIFLE, EXTINGUISH **b :** to check combustion in (a furnace) while keeping the fire alive: (1) **:** to cover (a fire in a furnace) with damp coal, ashes, or cinders to diminish the generation of heat or steam (2) **:** to stop (a blast) by closing up all the openings in a blast furnace — usu. used with *down* **c** (1) **:** to diminish progressively the vibration or oscillation of (as a string or voltage) (2) **:** to provide (as piano strings) with dampers **2 :** CHECK, RESTRAIN ⟨nothing could ~ his enthusiasm —George Meredith⟩ **:** RETARD ⟨the demand may be ~*ed* by increases in costs —M.D.Ketchum⟩ **:** DEPRESS ⟨nothing could ~ him — even years of failure —Robert Westerby⟩ **3** *obs* **:** to make (mental powers) stupid or dull **:** DAZE **4 :** to make damp **:** MOISTEN ⟨felt the sweat . . . ~*ing* the palms of his hands —Marcia Davenport⟩; *specif* **:** to sprinkle (laundry work) with water and fold for the ironers — usu. used with *down* ~ *vi* **1 :** to become damp **2 :** to diminish progressively in extent of vibration or oscillation ⟨the wave ~*ed* out⟩
³**damp** \"\ *adj* -ER/-EST **1** *obs* **:** belonging to or having the characteristics of a noxious gas or vapor **2 a** *archaic* **:** DAZED, STUPEFIED **b :** having or showing lack of vitality or dejection of spirits **:** DEPRESSED, DULL ⟨the thoughtful expression of a serious able musician, but I thought it a bit ~ —*New Yorker*⟩ ⟨their meandering witless conversations and their ~ love affairs —*Time*⟩ **3 :** slightly or moderately wet **:** MOIST, HUMID ⟨~ weather⟩ ⟨a ~ day⟩ ⟨wipe with a ~ sponge⟩ **syn** see WET
damp course *n* **:** a damp-resisting layer in a masonry wall
damp·en \-pən, -pᵊm\ *vb* **dampened** \-pənd, -pᵊmd\ **dampened** \"\ **dampening** \-p(ə)niŋ\ **dampens** \-pənz, -pᵊmz\ [³*damp* + *-en*] *vt* **1 :** to check or diminish the activity or vigor of **:** DEPRESS, DEADEN, DULL ⟨~*ed* our enthusiasm⟩ ⟨any downturn . . . of the nation's business could ~ the railroad boom —*N.Y.Times*⟩ ⟨nothing here to ~ courage or blunt the zest for life —M.R.Cohen⟩ **2 :** to make slightly wet **:** MOISTEN **:** make damp ⟨~ a sponge⟩ ⟨ground barely ~*ed* by showers⟩ **3 :** DAMP *vt* 1c ~ *vi* **1 :** to become damp **:** gather moisture ⟨during the night the ground ~*ed*⟩ **2 :** to become deadened or dulled ⟨soon found their ardor ~*ing*⟩
damp·en·er \-p(ə)nə(r)\ *n* -s **:** one that dampens: as **a :** a device for dampening cloth (as in a laundry) **b :** a worker that dampens articles in preparation for further processing: (1) **:** one that tempers shoe outsoles to facilitate cutting, shaping, and stitching — called also *muller* (2) **:** one that dampens textiles (as hosiery or cloth) for boarding or ironing (3) **:** one that softens hides in warm water **c :** a device for retarding the oscillations of a spring when a load is suddenly applied or removed **d :** any of the rollers on an offset printing press that convey water to nonprinting areas of the printing surface
damp·er \-pə(r)\ *n* -s **1 :** one that checks, lessens, or depresses **:** a dulling or deadening influence, agent, or device ⟨news that put a ~ on the stock market⟩ ⟨served as an effective ~ on further development⟩: as **a :** a valve or movable plate in the flue or other part of a stove, furnace, or fireplace for regulating the draft or in a duct for regulating the flow of air or other gas **b :** one of a set of felted blocks resting on a piano string to keep it silent except when the key is pressed or when the entire set is lifted by a pedal **c :** a device designed to bring a mechanism or a part thereof to rest with minimum oscillation **d** *Brit* **:** SHOCK ABSORBER **2 :** one that moistens (as a device for damping or wetting or a worker that dampens articles) **3** *slang* **:** CASH REGISTER **4** *Austral* **:** a baking-powder bread formed into flat cakes and usu. baked over a campfire

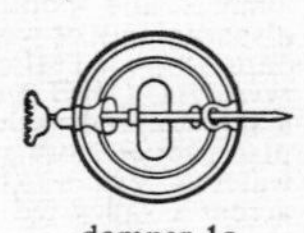

damper 1a

damper pedal *n* **:** the pedal that controls the set of dampers on a piano — called also *loud pedal*, *sustaining pedal*
damper winding *n* **:** a short-circuited squirrel-cage winding placed in the pole faces and around the pole shoes of synchronous machines, the currents induced in the winding by the periodic variations in synchronous speed having the effect of a damper — called also *amortisseur*
damping *pres part of* DAMP
damping capacity *n* **:** the ability of a material to absorb vibrations ⟨lead has high *damping capacity*⟩ ⟨a tuning fork has low *damping capacity*⟩
damping-off \'==¦=\ *n* -s **:** a diseased condition of seedlings or cuttings caused by certain parasitic fungi that invade the plant tissues near the ground and produce wilting usu. associated with rotting of the stem esp. near the ground level
damp·ish \-pish, -pēsh\ *adj* **:** somewhat damp **:** tending to dampness — **damp·ish·ly** *adv*
damp·ly *adv* **:** in a damp manner
damp·ness \-pnəs\ *n* -ES **:** the quality or state of being damp
damp off *vi* **:** to undergo damping-off
¹**damp·proof** \'=¦=\ *adj* [¹*damp* + *proof*] **:** impervious to water vapor or to liquid water when under only slight pressure
²**dampproof** \'=,=\ *vt* -ED/-ING/-S **:** to make dampproof
damp·proof·er \-fə(r)\ *n* **:** one that dampproofs: **a :** a worker that dampproofs masonry walls — called also *waterproofer* **b :** a dampproofing material
damps *pl of* DAMP, *pres 3d sing of* DAMP
damp sheet *n* **:** a curtain in a mine gallery for directing air currents and preventing accumulation of gas
damp-treat \'=,=\ *vt* **:** to treat with a dampproofing material
damp-wood termite *n* **:** any of numerous termites that live in damp decaying wood or moist living wood and do not require a connection with the soil
dampy \-mpē, -pi\ *adj* [¹*damp* + *-y*] **:** affected with damp **:** DAMPISH
¹**dams** *pl of* DAM, *pres 3d sing of* DAM
²**dams** \'damz\ *n pl but sing in constr* [alter. of earlier *dames*, fr. MF (*jeu de*) *dames*, lit., game of ladies] *Scot* **:** CHECKERS
¹**dam·sel** \'damzəl, 'daam-\ *n* -s [ME *damesel*, fr. OF *dameisele*, *damoisele*, fr. (assumed) VL *domnicella* young noblewoman, dim. of L *domina* mistress, lady — more at DAME] **1** *also* **dam·o·sel** *or* **dam·o·zel** \'=mə,zel, ,=='=\ **:** a young woman: **a** *archaic* **:** a young unmarried woman of noble or gentle birth **b** *obs* **:** a maid in waiting **:** female attendant **c :** GIRL, MAIDEN, LASS **2 :** an attachment to a millstone spindle for shaking the hopper
²**damsel** \"\ *n* -s [by folk etymology] *dial* **:** DAMSON 1,2
damsel-errant \'==='==\ *n, pl* **damsels-errant :** a female knight-errant
damselfish \'==,=\ *n* **:** any of numerous often brilliantly colored marine fishes of the family Pomacentridae that live almost entirely along coral reefs — called also *demoiselle*
damselfly \'==,=\ *n* **:** any of numerous slender-bodied insects that constitute the suborder Zygoptera of the order Odonata and that are characterized by laterally projecting eyes and by petiolate wings which are folded above the body when at rest
damsite \'=,=\ *n* [²*dam* + *site*] **:** a site for a dam
dam·son \'damzᵊn, 'daam-\ *n* -s [ME *damascene*, *damesene*, *damson*, fr. L (*prunum*) *Damascenum*, lit., plum of Damascus, fr. neut. of *Damascenus* of Damascus — more at DAMASCENE] **1 :** a rather small compact plum (*Prunus insititia* or *P. domestica insititia*) that has small usu. somewhat acid and dark purple fruits, is native to Asia Minor but now nearly cosmopolitan in cultivation, and is grown in several horticultural forms **2 :** the fruit of the damson **3 :** a moderate violet that is bluer and less strong than Roman purple, redder and darker than Parma violet (sense 2a), and redder and less strong than prelate
damson cheese *n* **:** a preserve made of damson plums peeled, stoned, and cooked with sugar to a consistency of soft cheese
damson plum *n* **:** DAMSON 2; *esp* **:** any comparatively sweet damson that suggests the typical plums in flavor
dam·yankee *also* **damn·yankee** \(')dam, (')daam + '==\ *n* -s [contr. of *damned yankee*] **:** a native or inhabitant of the northern states of the U. S. as distinguished from a Southerner — not often in formal use ⟨blaming our troubles, if we were southern, more on the ~ —Lillian Smith⟩ ⟨the South is considered with what seems to this ~ extraordinary fairness —Clifton Fadiman⟩
¹**dan** \'dan, 'daa(ə)n\ *n* -s *usu cap* [ME *dan*, *daun*, *daunz*, an honorable title for members of religious orders, fr. MF *dan*, *danz*, fr. OF, fr. ML *domnus*, fr. L *dominus* lord, master — more at DAME] — used archaically as a title for deities and poets ⟨*Dan* Cupid⟩ ⟨*Dan* Chaucer⟩
²**dan** \", 'dän\ *n, pl* **dan** *or* **dans** *usu cap* **:** a people of the border region between the Ivory coast and Liberia
dan·a·id \'danēid, -nā,-\ *n* -s [NL *Danaidae*] **:** one of the Danaidae; *esp* **:** MONARCH BUTTERFLY
da·na·i·dae \də'nāə,dē\ *n pl, cap* [NL, fr. *Danaus*, type genus + *-idae*] **:** a small family of large chiefly tropical butterflies having the first pair of legs degenerate in the adult and usu. a disagreeable taste that serves to protect them from predators
da·na·ite \'dānə,īt\ *n* -s [J. Freeman *Dana* †1827 Am. chemist + E *-ite*] **:** a mineral consisting of cobaltiferous arsenopyrite
da·na·kil \'danə,kil, ¦==¦kēl, də'nä,kēl\ *also* **dan·ka·li** \dän'kä(,)lē\ *n, pl* **danakil** *or* **danakils** *also* **dankali** *or* **dankalis** *usu cap* **1 a :** a Hamitic people of northeast Ethiopia **b :** a member of such people **2 :** ²AFAR 2
da·na·lite \'dānə,līt\ *n* -s [James D. *Dana* †1895 Am. geologist + E *-lite*] **:** a mineral $(Fe,Zn,Mn)_8Be_6Si_6O_{24}S_2$ that consists of a reddish or gray silicate and sulfide of iron and beryllium usu. containing also zinc and manganese and that is isomorphous with helvite and genthelvite
dan·a·us \'danēəs, -nāəs\ *n, cap* [NL, after *Danaus*, mythical king of Argos who ordered his daughters to murder their husbands, fr. L, fr. Gk *Danaos*] **:** the type genus of Danaidae comprising the monarch and several other predominantly black-and-orange butterflies chiefly of subtropical regions
dan buoy \'dan +,-\ *n, sometimes cap D* [origin unknown] **:** a floating temporary marker buoy (as one used on fishing grounds or in minesweeping and antisubmarine-warfare operations)
dan·bur·ite \'danbə,rīt\ *n* -s [*Danbury*, Conn., its locality + E *-ite*] **:** a mineral $CaB_2(SiO_4)_2$ consisting of a calcium borosilicate that is transparent to translucent and in crystal habit resembles topaz
¹**dance** \'dan(t)s, 'daa(ə)n-,'dain-,'dăn-\ *vb* -ED/-ING/-S [ME *dauncen*, fr. OF *dancier*, perh. fr. (assumed) VL *deantiare*, fr. LL *deante* in front of, fr. L *de* from + *ante* in front — more at DE-, ANTE-] *vi* **1 :** to perform either alone or with others a rhythmic and patterned succession of steps usu. to music **2 :** to move or seem to move nimbly and quickly up and down or about (as from excitement or emotion) **:** LEAP, SPRING, SKIP ⟨a blow that made him ~ with pain⟩ ⟨*danced* for joy at the news⟩ ⟨heart *dancing* with happiness⟩ **3 :** to bob up and down (as in the air or on the surface of water) ⟨motes *dancing* in a beam of light⟩ ~ *vt* **1 :** to perform, execute, or take part in as a dancer ⟨~ a polka⟩ ⟨*danced* the title role in the ballet⟩ **2 a :** to cause to dance **:** lead in a dance **b :** to cause to move up and down with a bouncing jerky motion **:** DANDLE ⟨~ a baby on his knee⟩ **3 :** to bring or accompany into a specified condition or position by dancing ⟨*danced* himself into the favor of the queen⟩ ⟨*danced* the new year in⟩ ⟨*danced* his youth away⟩ — **dance attendance :** to attend assiduously and obsequiously **:** be in waiting or at beck and call **:** court favor — **dance on nothing :** to be hanged — **dance to another tune :** to follow a changed course of action esp. involuntarily
²**dance** \"\ *n* -s *often attrib* [ME *daunce*, fr. OF *dance*, fr. *dancier* to dance] **1 :** rhythmic movement having as its aim the creation of visual designs by a series of poses and tracing of patterns through space in the course of measured units of time, the two components, static and kinetic, receiving varying emphasis (as in ballet, natya, and modern dance) and being executed by different parts of the body in accordance with temperament, artistic precepts, and purpose **:** the art of dancing **2 a :** a round or turn of dancing **b :** a social gathering

for the purpose of dancing **3 :** the figure or pattern of a particular form of dancing **:** a coherent series of movement patterns **4 a :** a piece of music by which dancing may be guided (as a jig, minuet, or waltz) **b :** any musical composition in a dance rhythm **5 :** a ceremony among American Indians in which dancing and singing play a conspicuous part — see CORN DANCE, SNAKE DANCE, SUN DANCE, WAR DANCE **6 :** a sequence of more or less rhythmic stereotyped movements habitually made by an animal in response to a particular stimulus ⟨the courting ~ of a prairie chicken⟩; *specif* **:** a series of special steps and turns whereby worker honeybees communicate the whereabouts of food to their fellow workers **7 :** a rhythmic or lively movement suggestive of dancing **8 :** a zigzag fess

dance·abil·i·ty \ˌ⸗sə'biləd·ē\ *n* -ES **:** the quality or state of being danceable

dance·able \'⸗səbəl\ *adj* **:** suitable for dancing ⟨tuneful and eminently ~ scores —Winthrop Sargeant⟩

danced *past of* DANCE

dance drama *n* **:** drama conveyed by dance movements sometimes accompanied by dialogue

dance fly *n* **:** a fly of the family Empididae

dance hall *n* **:** a large room set aside or suitable for dances; *esp* **:** a public hall offering facilities for dancing

dance of death : DANSE MACABRE

dance palace *n* **:** a showy dance hall

danc·er \-sə(r)\ *n* -S [ME *dauncer,* fr. *dauncen* to dance + *-er*] **1 :** one that dances; *specif* **:** a professional performer of dances **2 dancers** *pl, slang* **:** STAIRS **3 dancers** *pl, chiefly Scot* **:** AURORA BOREALIS

danc·ery \-s(ə)rē\ *n* -ES **:** a place of entertainment (as a nightclub or dance hall) providing facilities for dancing

dances *pres 3d sing of* DANCE, *pl of* DANCE

dance society *n* **:** a society often found within the communal life of primitive peoples whose function is to perform a ceremonial or ritual dance

¹dan·cet·té *or* **dan·cet·tée** \(ˈ)danˌsed·(ˌ)ā, ˈdan(t)sə'tā\ *or* **dan·cety** \(ˈ)danˈsed·ē\ *adj* [prob. modif. of F *denché,* fr. MF, fr. *dent* tooth, fr. L *dent-, dens* — more at TOOTH] *heraldry* **:** having large indentations usu. three in number ⟨a fess ~⟩

²dan·cette \dan'set, ˈ⸗ˌ⸗\ *n* -S [alter. of ¹*dancetté*] **:** an architectural molding or group of moldings with a zigzag pattern in the design **:** CHEVRON MOLDING

dance–walk \ˈ⸗ˌ⸗\ *n* **:** a ballroom step consisting of a simple rhythmic walk

dancing *pres part of* DANCE

dancing disease *n* **:** TARANTISM

dancing girl *n* **:** a girl that dances professionally **:** DANSEUSE; *esp* **:** a female professional dancer of any of several Asiatic countries

dancing–girls \ˈ⸗⸗ˌ⸗\ *n pl but sing or pl in constr* [so called fr. the fancied resemblance of the flowers to ballet dancers] **:** an East Indian herb (*Mantisia saltatoria*) sometimes cultivated in greenhouses for its purple-and-yellow flowers

danc·ing·ly *adv* **:** in a dancing manner

dancy *pron at* DANCE + ē, i\ *adj* -ER/-EST **:** given to or suggestive of dancing esp. when lively ⟨whether the music is dainty . . . or ~ and vigorously expository —Virgil Thomson⟩

dand \'dand\ *n* -S [by shortening] *dial Brit* **:** ²DANDY

d&c color \ˌdēən'sē-\ *n, cap D & 1st C* [abbr. of drug and cosmetic] **:** any of the synthetic dyes that in certified batches are permitted for use in drugs and cosmetics — see DYE table II

dan·de·li·on \'dandᵊlˌīən, 'daan-, -dəˌlī-, -dēˌlī-, ÷ -ˌlīn\ *n* -S [fr. earlier *dent de lion,* fr. MF, lit., lion's tooth; trans. of ML *dens leonis;* fr. its sharply indented leaves] **1 :** a plant of the genus *Taraxacum* (esp. *T. officinale*) abundant as a weed in meadows, lawns, and cultivated ground throughout Europe, Asia, and No. America **2 :** any of several plants related to and resembling the dandelion — see FALL DANDELION, KRIGIA **3 a :** a brilliant yellow resembling sunflower yellow **b :** a vivid yellow resembling goldenrod (sense 2a)

dandelion coffee *n* **:** a beverage made from the dried roots of the dandelion

¹dan·der \'dan(d)ə(r)\ *vi* -ED/-ING/-S [origin unknown] **1** *dial Brit* **:** to walk at a leisurely pace **:** SAUNTER, IDLE **2** *dial Brit* **:** to wander mentally

²dander \-ər\ *n* -S *chiefly Scot* **:** a leisurely walk **:** STROLL

³dan·der \'dandə(r), 'daan-\ *n* -S [alter. of earlier *dandruff, dandro*] **1 :** DANDRUFF; *specif* **:** minute scales from hair, feathers, or skin that may act as allergens **2 :** ANGER, TEMPER ⟨finally, she got her ~ up and wrote direct to the president —S.V.Benét⟩

⁴dan·der \'dan(d)ə(r)\ *n* -S [origin unknown] *dial Brit* **:** a piece of slag **:** a calcined cinder — usu. used in pl. ⟨~*s* from the fire⟩

D and H *abbr* dressed and headed

dan·di·a·cal \(ˈ)dan'dīəkəl\ *adj* [fr. ²*dandy,* after such pairs as E *prosody: prosodiacal*] **:** of, relating to, or suggestive of a dandy **:** DANDIFIED ⟨~ elegance⟩ ⟨a ~ pose⟩ **:** characterized by dandyism — **dan·di·a·cal·ly** \-k(ə)lē\ *adv*

dan·die din·mont terrier \ˌdandēˌdinˌmänt-, -ˌmənt-\ *n, usu cap both Ds* [after *Dandie Dinmont,* character owning 2 such dogs in the novel *Guy Mannering* by Sir Walter Scott †1832 Scottish writer] **:** a terrier of a breed originating on the border between Scotland and England having short legs, long body, pendulous ears, and rough coat, ranging in height from 8 to 11 inches and in weight from 14 to 24 lbs., and being silvery gray or cream to yellowish tan in color and distinctive for its very full topknot of silky light-colored hair

dan·di·fi·ca·tion \ˌdandəfə'kāshən, ˌdaan-, -ndēf-\ *n* -S **1 :** the action of dandifying or the state of being dandified **2 :** something that dandifies

dan·di·fied \ˈ⸗⸗ˌfīd\ *adj* **1 :** having the dress or manners of a dandy ⟨~ in youth, he became theatrical in later life⟩ **2 :** made or done in the style of a dandy **:** suggestive of dandies ⟨a ~ costume⟩ ⟨walked with a ~ gait⟩

dan·di·fy \-ˌfī\ *vt* -ED/-ING/-ES [²*dandy* + *-fy*] **:** to cause to resemble a dandy **:** make characteristic or suggestive of a dandy

dan·di·ly \-ndəlē, -li\ *adv* **:** in the style or manner of a dandy

dan·di·prat \'dandēˌprat\ *n* -S [origin unknown] **1 :** an English silver coin of the 16th century prob. worth twopence **2 a :** a little, insignificant, or contemptible person **:** DWARF, PYGMY **b :** a small boy **:** URCHIN

dan·di·zette *or* **dan·di·sette** \ˌdandē'zet\ *n* -S [*dandy* + *-ette, -sette* (as in *grisette*)] **:** a female dandy

¹dan·dle \'dandᵊl, 'daan-, ÷ -nᵊl\ *vb* **dandled; dandled; dandling** \-n(d)(ᵊ)liŋ\ **dandles** [origin unknown] *vt* **1 :** to move (as a baby) up and down in one's arms or on one's knee **:** toss up and down in or as if in affectionate play **2 :** to treat fondly (as a child) **:** make much of **:** PAMPER, PET ⟨editors, scholars, merchants, even the noble lords and ladies feted and *dandled* him —Max Eastman⟩ **3** *obs* **:** to play or trifle with ~ *vi* **1 :** DANGLE ⟨one leg, even if the hose wrinkle a little, must ~ over the other —Christopher Morley⟩ **2 :** TRIFLE, TOY, PLAY ⟨*dandled* with one art after another⟩

²dandle \"\ *n* -S *NewEng* **:** SEESAW 2

dan·dling·ly *adv* **:** in a dandling manner

D and M *abbr* dressed and matched

D and P *abbr* developing and printing

dan·druff \'dandrəf, 'daan-\ *n* -S [prob. fr. *dand-* (origin unknown) + *-ruff,* of Scand origin; akin to ON *hrūfa* crust on a wound, scab, Norw *ruva,* ON *hrjūfr* scabby, scurvy; akin to OE *hrēof* rough, scabby, leprous, OHG *riob* leprous, *hriūpi* scabies, *hruf* pock, scurf, Latvian *kraūpa* scurf, wart, Lith *kraupùs* rough] **:** a scurf of white or grayish usu. greasy scales forming on and shed from skin surfaces esp. of the scalp — **dan·druffy** \-əfē, -fi\ *adj*

dands *pl of* DAND

¹dan·dy *or* **dan·di** \'dandē, 'dan-\ *n, pl* **dandies** *or* **dandis** [Hindi *ḍāḍī,* fr. *ḍāḍ* oar, pole, staff, fr. Skt *daṇḍa* stick] **1 :** a boatman on the Ganges river **2 :** a palanquin used in India and made with a pole projecting at each end

²dan·dy \'dandē, 'daan-, -ndi\ *n* -ES [prob. short for *jack-a-dandy*] **1 :** a man who gives fastidious and exaggerated attention to dress or personal appearance (as by always dressing in the height of fashion or by adopting carefully affected styles of dress) ⟨he became a ~ given to lavender-colored suits with long jackets and brief double-breasted waistcoats —Walter Marsden⟩ **2 :** something esp. excellent in its class ⟨a ~ — good-natured, willing and awfully good at his job —D.B. Putnam⟩ ⟨a little ~ of a tent —*New Yorker*⟩ ⟨this novel is a ~⟩ — not often in formal use **3** [by shortening] **:** DANDY ROLL **4 :** a small 2-masted sailboat with a modified ketch rig **5 :** a device resembling a small capstan used to hoist the trawl in fishing **6 :** a large pail or can usu. mounted on wheels and used for pouring tar or asphalt in road building

³dandy \"\ *adj, usu* -ER/-EST **1 :** of, relating to, or suggestive of a dandy **:** FOPPISH ⟨gave himself ~ airs⟩ ⟨a ~ sort of fellow⟩ **2 :** very good **:** FIRST-RATE, FINE ⟨a ~ new bicycle⟩ ⟨a ~ place for a picnic⟩ ⟨~ weather⟩ — not often in formal use

dandy brush *n* [prob. fr. ²*dandy*] **:** a stiff brush used in cleaning and grooming animals

dan·dy·dom \-dəm\ *n* -S [²*dandy* + *-dom*] **1 :** the state of being a dandy **2 :** the world of dandies

dandy fever \'dandē-\ *n* [prob. fr. a West Indian Creole word of African origin; akin to Swahili *kidinga* (*popo*) dengue — more at DENGUE] **:** DENGUE

dandy funk \"-\ *n* [origin unknown] **:** hardtack soaked in water and baked with grease and molasses

dandy horse *n* [²*dandy*] **:** an early 2-wheeled velocipede propelled by pushing with the feet against the ground — called also *hobbyhorse*

dandy horse

dan·dy·ish \'dandēish, 'daan-, -ndi-\ *adj* [²*dandy* + *-ish*] **:** suggestive of a dandy in manner or appearance **:** FOPPISH — **dan·dy·ish·ly** *adv*

dan·dy·ism \-ndēˌizəm, -diˌiz-\ *n* -S [²*dandy* + *-ism*] **1 :** the style or conduct of a dandy **2 :** the literary or artistic style often associated with the English and French decadents of the last of the 19th century and marked esp. by preciosity of language and refined emotionalism of subject matter

dan·dy·ize \-ndēˌīz, -diˌīz\ *vb* -ED/-ING/-S [²*dandy* + *-ize*] *vt* **:** DANDIFY ~ *vi* **:** to act like a dandy

dandy line *n* [²*dandy* (fishing device)] **:** a fishing line to which are attached crosspieces of whalebone carrying a hook at each end

dan·dy·ling \-ndēliŋ, -dil-\ *n* -S [²*dandy* + *-ling*] **:** an insignificant fop **:** petty dandy

dan·dy·prat *obs var of* DANDIPRAT

dandy roll *also* **dandy roller** *n* [³*dandy*] **:** a light wire-covered roll that rides on the wet web of paper on a fourdrinier machine to compact the sheet and sometimes impress a watermark

dane \'dān\ *n* -S [ME *Dan,* fr. ON *Danr*] **1** *cap* **:** a Norseman of Viking times **:** VIKING **2** *cap* **a :** a native or inhabitant of Denmark **b :** a person of Danish descent **3** *usu cap* **:** GREAT DANE 2

danebrog *usu cap, var of* DANNEBROG

dane·geld \'dānˌgeld\ *also* **dane·gelt** \-lt\ *n* -S *often cap* [ME *Danegeld,* fr. *Dane* (gen. pl. of *Dan* Dane) + *geld* tribute, payment, fr. OE *gield;* akin to OE *gieldan* to pay, pay for, reward — more at DANE, YIELD] **:** an annual tax believed to have been imposed orig. to buy off the ravages of Danish invaders in England or to maintain forces to oppose them but continued as a land tax usu. of two shillings upon each hide of land

dane gun *n, often cap D* [so called fr. its introduction into Africa by Danish traders] *West Africa* **:** a firearm of obsolete design orig. of European and now of native-village manufacture

dane·law \'dānˌlȯ\ *also* **dane·la·ga** \-lägə\ *or* **dane·lagh** \-lȯ\ *n* -S *usu cap* [ME *Dene lawe,* fr. OE *Dena lagu,* lit., Danes' law, fr. *Dena* (gen. of *Dene,* pl., Danes, of Scand. origin; akin to ON *Danr* Dane) + *lagu* law — more at LAW] **1 :** the Danish law formerly in force in the northeastern part of England held by the Danes **2 :** the part of England formerly under the Danelaw

dane's–blood \ˈ⸗ˌ⸗\ *n, pl* **dane's–bloods** *usu cap D* [prob. so called fr. the belief that they grow where Danish blood was spilled] **1** *dial Eng* **:** DANEWORT **2** *dial Eng* **:** PASQUEFLOWER

daneweed \ˈ⸗ˌ⸗\ *n, often cap* **:** DANEWORT

danewort \ˈ⸗ˌ⸗\ *n, usu cap* **:** a dwarf herbaceous elder (*Sambucus ebulus*) of Europe having pink flowers and a nauseous odor

¹dang \'daŋ, -ai-\ *vt* -ED/-ING/-S [euphemism] **:** DAMN vt 5

²dang \-ŋ\ *or* **danged** \-ŋ(d)\ *adj* (*or adv*) [euphemism] **:** DAMNED

³dang \-ŋ\ *n* -S [euphemism] **:** DAMN

⁴dang [ME] *dial past of* DING

⁵dang \'daŋ\ *vb* -ED/-ING/-S [by alter.] *dial Brit* **:** ¹DING

danga·rik \'daŋ(g)əˌrik\ *n, pl* **dangarik** *or* **dangariks** *usu cap* **1 :** a Pathan people living in the southern Chitral sector of the northwest frontiers of Pakistan **2 :** a member of the Dangarik people

¹dan·ger \'dānjə(r)\ *n* -S [ME *daunger* power, jurisdiction, liability, reluctance, fr. OF *dangier* power, jurisdiction, alter. (influenced by OF *dam* damage, fr. L *damnum*) of *dongier,* fr. (assumed) VL *domniarium, dominiarium* authority, fr. L *dominium* ownership (fr. *dominus* master) + *-arium* -ary — more at DAME, DAMN] **1 a** *archaic* **:** power or authority of a master **:** JURISDICTION ⟨you stand within his ~, do you not? —Shak.⟩ **b** *obs* **:** reach or range esp. of a weapon or missile ⟨out of the shot and ~ of desire —Shak.⟩ **2** *obs* **:** HARM, INJURY, DAMAGE ⟨a sting in him that at his will he may do ~ with —Shak.⟩ **3 :** the state of being exposed to harm **:** liability to injury, pain, or loss **:** PERIL, RISK ⟨pronounced out of ~ the second day after the operation⟩ ⟨a place where children could play without ~⟩ ⟨in ~ of losing his life's savings⟩ **4 :** a case or cause of danger ⟨the ~*s* of the sea⟩

syn DANGER, PERIL, JEOPARDY, HAZARD, and RISK can mean, in common, either the state of being threatened with serious loss or injury or the cause or source of such a threat. DANGER, the general term, implies the contingent evil ⟨troubled by the *danger* that the manuscript might be lost —Carl Van Doren⟩ ⟨realizing that the buffalo in the United States were in *danger* of becoming extinct —*Amer. Guide Series: N.H.*⟩ ⟨the *dangers* of travel by air⟩ ⟨the *danger* of lowering one's standards⟩ PERIL implies more strongly the imminence and fearfulness of the danger ⟨the ship was in deadly *peril* of seizure by mutineers —C.C.Cutler⟩ ⟨the trickle of a clear spring water which is beyond all *peril* of drought —Louis Bromfield⟩ ⟨one fears to say anything when the *peril* of misunderstanding puts a warning finger to the lips —B.N.Cardozo⟩ ⟨the *perils* of modern warfare⟩ JEOPARDY implies exposure to or the position of special susceptibility to extreme danger, as of a man in court accused of a serious offense ⟨to place one's life in *jeopardy* by driving too fast⟩ ⟨one's moral and emotional balance is always in *jeopardy* during wartime⟩ HAZARD, not as strong as *jeopardy,* implies danger from something fortuitous or beyond one's control ⟨needless to say, there are *hazards* connected with brain surgery —H.R.Litchfield & L.H.Dembo⟩ ⟨the protection by insurance or otherwise, against the *hazards* of unemployment, sickness, and old age —*Amer. Guide Series: N.Y.*⟩ ⟨the steeple, with heavy iron cross, is so tall that some consider it a dangerous *hazard* —*Amer. Guide Series: La.*⟩ RISK implies a voluntary placing of oneself in circumstances of doubtful and possibly adverse outcome ⟨to fool around with dynamite to the *risk* of life and limb⟩ ⟨life is a *risk* and all individual plans precarious, all human achievements transient —Irwin Edman⟩ ⟨countries here who want to see the *risk* of another world war extinguished here and now —Benjamin Welles⟩ ⟨for many Americans the *risks* of city life outweighed the attractions —Oscar Handlin⟩

²danger \"\ *vt* -ED/-ING/-S [ME *daungeren,* fr. *daunger,* n.] **1** *obs* **:** to make liable **2** *archaic* **:** ENDANGER

danger angle *n* **:** the angle between two known points as observed from a point marking the limit of safe approach of a ship to a reef, shoal, or other obstruction which can then be passed safely by keeping the known points at an angle, as observed from the ship in her course, greater or less than the danger angle

danger bearing *n* **:** a limiting bearing of any object the passing of which bearing will cause a ship to run into danger

dangerful *adj, obs* **:** DANGEROUS

dan·ger·less \ˈ⸗⸗ləs\ *adj* **:** free from danger **:** lacking danger

danger line *n* **:** a real or imaginary boundary beyond which danger will be encountered

dan·ger·ous \'dānj(ə)rəs\ *adj* [ME *daungerous* haughty, trouble-making, hard to please, fr. OF *dangereus* trouble-making, hard to please, fr. *dangier* + *-eus* -ous] **1 :** exposing to danger **:** involving risk **:** demanding caution or care as extremely unsafe **:** HAZARDOUS, PERILOUS ⟨a little learning is a ~ thing —Alexander Pope⟩ ⟨a ~ climb⟩ ⟨~ occupations⟩ ⟨a ~ crossing⟩ **2 :** able or likely to inflict injury **:** causing or threatening harm ⟨a ~ lunatic⟩ ⟨an animal ~ when wounded⟩ **3** *now dial* **:** gravely ill **:** in critical condition ⟨he's in bed but he's not ~⟩

syn HAZARDOUS, PRECARIOUS, PERILOUS, RISKY: DANGEROUS applies to persons or things to be avoided or treated carefully as generally unsafe and likely to cause or be attended by danger ⟨a wide circuit must be made, to avoid a fierce and *dangerous* tribe called Snake Indians —Francis Parkman⟩ ⟨the most *dangerous* waters in the world, the fog-shrouded, berg-haunted Grand Banks, with their swift currents and steep, short seas —*Amer. Guide Series: Mass.*⟩ HAZARDOUS may imply greater operation of chance than DANGEROUS; it is used in reference to situations involving great or continuous risk ⟨life consists largely of *hazardous* leaps in the dark —M.R. Cohen⟩ ⟨the *hazardous* game of secret service in enemy country —Alexander Forbes⟩ Established with the meaning of *insecure* or *uncertain,* PRECARIOUS often adds the implication of attendant dangers ⟨the unorganised mass of London dock laborers who struggled with each other for *precarious* jobs at the dockyard gates —G.M.Trevelyan⟩ ⟨the British army, its communications thus rendered *precarious,* was forced to retreat —Allan Nevins & H.S.Commager⟩ PERILOUS suggests imminent danger ⟨thousands of ships and planes guarding the long, *perilous* sea lanes —F.D.Roosevelt⟩ ⟨burglars who have done a good . . . business are, as a rule, only too glad to enjoy the proceeds in peace and quiet without embarking on another *perilous* undertaking —A. Conan Doyle⟩ RISKY often joins to this suggestion the notion that the danger or risk has been realized in advance and willingly accepted ⟨the control of our universities by propertied interests makes a free and radical inquiry into social affairs a *risky* business for any professor —M.R.Cohen⟩ ⟨so *risky* was travel that the Indiana legislature specifically permitted travelers to carry concealed weapons of any kind —Carl Sandburg⟩

dan·ger·ous·ly *adv* **:** in a manner or to a degree involving danger or risk ⟨was charged with driving ~⟩ ⟨~ wounded⟩

dan·ger·ous·ness \-snəs\ *n* -ES **:** the quality or state of being dangerous

dangerous semicircle *n* **:** the half of the nearly circular area of a cyclonic storm in which the velocity of rotation is added to the velocity of translation and in which a vessel tends to be drawn into the path of the storm center

dangers *pl of* DANGER, *pres 3d sing of* DANGER

dan·ger·some \-jə(r)səm\ *adj, now dial* **:** DANGEROUS

danging *pres part of* DANG

¹dan·gle \'daŋgəl\ *vb* **dangled; dangled; dangling** \-g(ə)liŋ\ **dangles** [prob. of Scand origin; akin to Dan *dangle* to dangle, Sw *dangla,* prob. of imit. origin] *vi* **1 :** to hang loosely esp. with a swinging or jerking motion ⟨hands relaxed and *dangling* over their knee bones —Marjory S. Douglas⟩ ⟨caught hold of the eaves and swung *dangling* there —V.G. Heiser⟩ **2 :** to be a hanger-on **:** hang about as or as if a dependent ⟨a flirt, who liked to keep several beaus *dangling*⟩ —often used with *after* ⟨spent his youth in *dangling* after the ladies⟩ **3 :** to become hanged **4 :** to occur in a sentence esp. at or near the beginning without standing in some normally expected syntactic relation to the rest of the sentence and esp. without modifying the subject (as *lying* in "lying awake, memories crowded into his mind" or *tired* and *happy* in "tired but happy, the bus whisked us home") ⟨*dangling* participle⟩ ⟨*dangling* modifier⟩ ~ *vt* **1 :** to cause to dangle **:** SWING ⟨*dangling* his feet in the water⟩ **2 :** to keep (as hopes) hanging uncertainly **:** hold suspended ⟨*dangling* to them the lures of levity and life —Max Beerbohm⟩

²dangle \"\ *n* -S **1 :** the action of dangling **2 :** something that dangles

dangleberry \ˈ⸗-— *see* BERRY\ *n* **:** a huckleberry (*Gaylussacia frondosa*) of the eastern U.S. with pink flowers and sweet blue fruit

dan·gle·ment \ˈ⸗⸗mənt\ *n* -S **:** DANGLE

dan·gler \-g(ə)lə(r)\ *n* -S **:** one that dangles ⟨ear clips, some with diamond ~*s* —*New Yorker*⟩; *esp* **:** a person who dangles about or after a woman

dangle stick *n* **:** a forked green stick used as a pothook in cooking over a campfire — called also *dingle stick*

dan·glin \dăŋ'glēn\ *n* -S [Tag *danglin*] **:** a Philippine tree (*Grewia multiflora*) yielding a coarse bast fiber used for cordage

dan·gling·ly *adv* **:** in a dangling manner

dangs *pl of* DANG, *pres 3d sing of* DANG

da·ni·an \'dānēən\ *adj, usu cap* [ML *Dania* Denmark, where typical formations are found (fr. LL *Dani* Danes — of Gmc origin; akin to ON *Danr* Dane — + L *-ia* -y) + E *-an*] **:** of or relating to a subdivision of the European Cretaceous — see GEOLOGIC TIME table

da·nic \'dānik *also* 'dan-\ *adj, usu cap* [ML *Danicus,* fr. LL *Dani* Danes + L *-icus* -ic] **:** DANISH

da·ni·cism \'dānəˌsizəm\ *n* -S *often cap* [*Danish* + *-icism* (as in *Gallicism*)] **:** a characteristic feature of Danish occurring in another language

dan·iel \'danyəl, *archaic & dial* -nᵊl\ *n* -S *cap* [after *Daniel,* Hebrew prophet captive in Babylon, famous for his interpretation of Nebuchadnezzar's dreams (Dan 2 & 4) and of the handwriting on the wall before Belshazzar (Dan 5), fr. Heb *Dānīʼēl, Dānīyēl*] **:** an exemplary judge ⟨a *Daniel* come to judgment —Shak.⟩

dan·iell cell \'danyəl-\ *n, usu cap D* [after John F. *Daniell* †1845 Eng. chemist and physicist, its inventor] **:** a primary cell with a constant electromotive force of about 1.1 volts having as its electrodes copper in a copper sulfate solution and zinc in dilute sulfuric acid or zinc sulfate, the two solutions being separated by a porous partition

da·nio \'dānēˌō\ *n* -S [NL *Danio,* in older classifications, a genus of cyprinid fishes] **:** any of several small brightly colored cyprinid fishes of southeastern Asia often kept in the tropical aquarium

¹dan·ish \'dānish, -nēsh *sometimes* 'dan-\ *adj, usu cap* [ME *Danysshe,* alter. (influenced by *Dan* Dane) of *Denshe,* fr. OE *Denisc,* fr. *Dene* Danes + *-isc* -ish — more at DANE, DANELAW] **1 a :** of, relating to, or characteristic of Denmark **b :** of, relating to, or characteristic of the Danes **2 :** of, relating to, or characteristic of the Danish language

²danish \"\ *n* -ES *cap* **:** the Germanic language of the Danes — see INDO-EUROPEAN LANGUAGES table

³danish \"\ *or* **danish pastry** *n, usu cap D* **:** a rich pastry made of dough raised with yeast with the shortening rolled in

danish seine *n, usu cap D* **:** a seine arranged to be drawn through the water by a boat somewhat in the manner of a trawl

dan·ism \-ˌnizəm\ *n* -S *often cap* [*Danish* + *-ism*] **:** DANICISM

dan·ite \'daˌnīt\ *n* -S *usu cap* [*Dan,* 5th son of Jacob (Gen 30:6), the eponymous ancestor of the Danites (Judg 13:2) + E *-ite*] **1 :** a member of the Hebrew tribe of Dan **2 :** a member of a secret association of Mormons held to have been pledged to use violent means to destroy their enemies

¹dank \'daŋk\ *adj* -ER/-EST [ME *danke,* adj. & n., prob. of Scand origin; akin to ON *dǫkk* pit, pool, Sw (dial.) *dunken* moist; akin to OHG *tunkal* dark, obscure, ON *dǫkkr* dark, Latvian *danga* mudhole, Hitt *dankuiš* dark, OE *dim* — more at DIM] **1 :** wet or moist esp. in a disagreeable way **:** DAMP, HUMID ⟨~ caves⟩ ⟨the air came up cold and ~ from the surface of the water —Dorothy Sayers⟩ ⟨the ~ hot lowlands of Amazonia⟩ **2 :** RANK ⟨a ~ smell of rotting vegetation⟩ ⟨~ horror, foul and leering —Claudia Cassidy⟩ **syn** see WET

²dank \"\ *n* -S [ME *danke*] **1 :** MOISTURE, WETNESS ⟨the raw ~ of the November afternoon —Marguerite Steen⟩ **2 :** a wet place **:** MARSH ⟨a ~ crisscrossed by the numerous streams of the Pearl river delta —*Amer. Guide Series: La.*⟩

dankali *usu cap, var of* DANKAKIL

dank·ish \-kish, -kēsh\ *adj* : somewhat dank

dank·ly *adv* : in a dank manner ⟨the cloth stuck ~ to their bodies —Norman Mailer⟩

dank·ness \-knəs\ *n* -ES : the quality or state of being dank

dan·li \dän'lē\ *n* -S [Tag *danglin*] : DANGLIN

dan·ne·brog *or* **dan·e·brog** \'danə,bräg\ *n* -S *usu cap* [D *Dannebrog*, fr. *Danne* Danes (fr. ON *Dana*, gen. pl. of *Danr* Dane) + *brog* cloth, fr. ON *brōk* — more at BREECH] **1** : a red swallow-tailed ensign bearing a white cross and being the national flag of Denmark **2** : the red rectangular Danish merchant flag

dan·ne·mo·rite \,danə'mōr,īt\ *n* -S [Sw *dannemorit*, fr. *Dannemora*, Sweden, + Sw *-it* -ite] : a mineral $(Fe,Mn,Mg)_7Si_8O_{22}(OH)_2$ consisting of a columnar or fibrous amphibole containing iron, magnesium, and manganese

dan·ner process \'danə(r)-\ *n*, *usu cap D* [after Edward *Danner* †1952 Am. inventor] : a process for producing glass cane or tubing by continuous drawing from a rotating refractory cylinder, the diameter of the tubing being determined by the pressure of air passed through the center of the cylinder, the temperature of the glass, and the drawing speed

dan·nock \'danək\ *n* -S [origin unknown] *dial Eng* : a hedger's glove of thick untanned leather

dano- *comb form*, *cap* [ISV *Dan-* (fr. LL *Dani* Danes) + *-o-*] : Danish and ⟨*Dano*-Eskimo⟩

dans *pl of* DAN

dan·sant \dänˈsänˈ\ *n*, *pl* **dansants** \-z\ [F, fr. pres. part. of *danser* to dance, fr. OF *dancier* — more at DANCE] **1** : an informal or small dance **2** [short for *thé dansant*] : TEA DANCE

danse d'é·cole \däⁿsdākōl\ *n*, *pl* **danses d'école** \"\ [F, lit., school dance] : ballet that adheres to traditional rules : classical ballet

danse du ven·tre \däⁿsdüeväⁿtr(ᵊ), -t(rə)\ *n*, *pl* **danses du ventre** \"\ [F, lit., belly dance] : BELLY DANCE

danse ma·ca·bre \däⁿsmákäbr(ᵊ), -b(rə)\ *n*, *pl* **danses macabres** \"\ [F, lit., macabre dance] **1** : a medieval dance or procession in which a skeleton representing death leads other skeletons or living persons to the grave — called also *dance of death* **2** : something that evokes horror as would a danse macabre

dan·seur \(')dänˈsər(·), -sə̄(r, *F* däⁿsœr\ *n*, *pl* **danseurs** \-ərz,-ə̄z,-œr\ [F, lit., dancer, fr. OF, fr. *danser*, *dancier* to dance + *-eur* -or — more at DANCE] : a male ballet dancer

dan·seur no·ble \däⁿsœrnóbl(ᵊ), -b(lə)\ *n*, *pl* **danseurs nobles** \"\ [F, lit., noble dancer] : the male dancing partner of a ballerina

dan·seuse \(')dänˈsə(r)z, -sə̄z, 'dänˌsüz, *F* däⁿsœz\ *n*, *pl* **dan·seuses** \-ə(r)z(əz),-ə̄z(əz),-üzəz,-œz\ [F, fem. of *danseur*] : a female ballet dancer

dan·sker \'dankə(r), -n(t)sk-\ *n* -S *cap* [Dan, fr. *dansk*, adj., Danish, fr. ON *danskr*, fr. *Danr* Dane + *-skr* -ish] *obs* : DANE ⟨enquire me first what *Danskers* are in Paris —Shak.⟩

dan·ta \'dantə, 'dän-\ *n* -S [Pg & Sp; Pg, tapir, elk, buckskin, fr. Sp *de anta* of buckskin (in such phrases as *adarga de anta* shield of buckskin), fr. *de* of (fr. L, from, down, away) + *anta* tapir, elk, buckskin — more at DE-, ANTA] : TAPIR

¹dan·te·an \'dantēən, 'dän-, ˌ=ˈ==\ *adj*, *usu cap* [*Dante* Alighieri †1321 It. poet + E *-an*] : DANTESQUE

²dantean \"\ *n* -S *usu cap* : a student or admirer of Dante

dan·te chair \'dantē-, 'dän-\ *n*, *usu cap D* [after *Dante* Alighieri] : a folding X-shaped chair of Italian Renaissance style having heavy curved legs and arms and cloth or leather seat and back

dan·tesque \(')danˈtesk, (')dän;-\ *adj*, *usu cap* [It *dantesco*, fr. *Dante* Alighieri + It *-esco* -esque] : of, relating to, or resembling Dante or his writings ⟨arouse in the reader's mind the memory of some *Dantesque* scene —T.S.Eliot⟩

dan·tho·nia \dan'thōnēə\ *n* [NL, irreg. fr. Étienne *Danthoine*, 19th cent. Fr. botanist & NL *-ia*] **1** *cap* : a large genus of tufted erect perennial grasses chiefly of the southern hemisphere and No. America with narrow leaves and small terminal panicles or racemes of densely crowded florets **2** -S : any plant of the genus *Danthonia*

dan·tist \'dantəst, 'dän-\ *n* -S *usu cap* [It *dantista*, fr. *Dante* Alighieri + It *-ista* -ist] : a Dante scholar

dan·ton·esque \ˌdantə'nesk\ *adj*, *usu cap* [Georges J. *Danton* †1794 Fr. revolutionist + E *-esque*] : resembling or in the style of Danton ⟨*Dantonesque* audacity⟩

dan tuck·er \(')dan'təkə(r)\ *n*, *usu cap D&T* [prob. fr. (*Old*) *Dan Tucker*, song by Daniel D. Emmett †1904 Amer. composer, to the accompaniment of which it was danced] : an American rustic dance in which extra men singing a song choose partners from a circle formed at a signal by those dancing

dan·ube green \'da(,)nyüb-\ *n*, *often cap D* [fr. the *Danube* river, central Europe] : a dark grayish green to dark yellowish green that is greener than Empire green

da·nu·bi·an \(')dan(y)übēən, də'n-\ *adj*, *usu cap* [LL *Danubius* Danube (fr. L *Danuvius*) + E *-an*] **1** : of, relating to, characteristic of, or bordering on the Danube river **2** : of, relating to, or characteristic of the nations or peoples near the Danube river **3** : of, relating to, or characteristic of a prehistoric Neolithic culture in the Danube basin

danubian goose *n*, *usu cap D* : SEBASTOPOL GOOSE

danubian reed *n*, *usu cap D* : GIANT REED

da·nysz phenomenon \'dänish-\ *also* **danysz effect** *n*, *usu cap D* [after Jan *Danysz* †1928 Pol.-Fr. physician] : the exhibition of residual toxicity by a mixture of toxin and antitoxin in which the toxin has been added in several increments to an amount of antitoxin sufficient to completely neutralize it if it had been added as a single increment

dan·za \'dän(t)sə, -nzə\ *n* -S [Sp, fr. OSp *dança*, fr. OF *dance* — more at DANCE] : DANCE; *specif* : a formal or courtly dance

dan·zig \'dan(t)sig, 'dän-, -nzi-, -ik\ *or* **gdansk** \gə'dänzk, -dan-, -n(t)sk\ *adj*, *usu cap* [fr. *Danzig* (*Gdańsk*), city of Poland] : of or from the city of Danzig, Poland : of the kind or style prevalent in Danzig

danzig brandy *n*, *usu cap D* : DANZIGER GOLDWASSER

dan·zig·er \-igə(r)\ *n* -S *cap* [G, fr. *Danzig* + *-er*] : a native or resident of Danzig

dan·zig·er gold·was·ser \G 'däntsigər'gōlt,väsər\ *n*, *usu cap D&G* [G, lit., Danzig goldwater] : a colorless aromatic liqueur mixed with tiny flecks of gold leaf and flavored with citrus peel and various herbs — called also *Goldwasser*, *goldwater*

danzig fir *n*, *usu cap D* : SCOTCH PINE

dan·zón \dän'sōn\ *n*, *pl* **danzo·nes** \-sō,nās\ [AmerSp, aug. of Sp *danza* dance — more at DANZA] : a peasant dance; *specif* : a native Cuban dance of African origin now popularized in Vera Cruz, Mexico

¹dao *var of* DAH

²dao \'dä(,)ō, 'daù\ *n* -S [Tag & Bisayan] **1** : a very large Philippine tree (*Dracontomelon dao*) of the family Anacardiaceae with edible fruit and a fibrous bark used for cordage **2** : the rather heavy hard strong wood of the dao characterized by dark brown markings on a lighter ground and much used for veneers and cabinetwork

¹dap \'dap\ *vb* **dapped**; **dapped**; **dapping**; **daps** [perh. alter. of *²dab*] *vi* **1** : to drop bait or fish by dropping bait gently on the water : DIB ⟨had considerable success *dapping* with the natural fly —John Buchan⟩ **2** : to dip gently or quickly into water ⟨out in the bay innumerable craft *dapped* and sailed —Sean O'Dwyer⟩ **3** : REBOUND, BOUNCE, SKIP ~ *vt* **1** : to cause to jump or skip on or along the surface of water ⟨*dapping* stones⟩ ⟨*dapping* her homemade flies in an English chalk stream —E.L.Peterson⟩ **2** : to produce (cup-shaped forms in sheet metal) by the use of special dies and punches **3** : to cut and form a recess in (timbers) for making a joint

²dap \"\ *n* -S **1** : a bounce esp. of a ball : a skip esp. of a stone over water **2** : the bait used in dapping **3** : a notch cut in one timber to receive another

dap-dap \'dap,dap\ *n* -S [Tag *dapdáp*] *Philippines* : a coral tree (*Erythrina indica*)

da·pe·di·us \də'pēdēəs\ *n*, *cap* [NL, fr. Gk *dapedon* level surface, ground, fr. *da-* (akin to Gk *domos* house) + *pedon* ground, earth — more at TIMBER, PEDION] : a genus of Mesozoic ganoid fishes of the order Cycloganoidei having a deep laterally compressed body

daph·ne \'daf(,)nē\ *n* [NL, fr. L, laurel, fr. Gk *daphnē*; akin to the non-IE source of L *laurus* laurel] **1** *cap* : a genus of Eurasian shrubs (family Thymelaeaceae) having tetramerous often fragrant apetalous flowers with a colored calyx resembling a corolla — see MEZEREON, SPURGE LAUREL **2** -S : any plant of the genus *Daphne*

daph·ne·an \'dafnēən, (')=ˈ==\ *adj*, *usu cap* [*Daphne*, bashful nymph who was pursued by Apollo and upon her prayer for help was changed into a laurel (fr. L, fr. Gk *Daphnē*, fr. *daphnē* laurel) + E *-an*] : of, relating to, or suggestive of the nymph Daphne : SHY, BASHFUL

daphne lilac *n* : a small shrub (*Syringa microphylla*) with small leaves that are pubescent beneath and lilac pink blossoms in small loose pubescent panicles

daphne pink *n* : a grayish purplish red that is redder, lighter, and stronger than average rose plum, bluer, lighter, and stronger than Aztec maroon, and redder and deeper than tourmaline pink

daphne red *n* : a grayish to moderate purplish red that is bluer and lighter than heather (sense 2b)

daph·ne·tin \'dafnətən\ *n* -S [ISV, blend of *daphnin* and *-et-*] : a yellow crystalline compound $C_9H_6O_4$ obtained by hydrolysis of daphnin; 7,8-dihydroxy-coumarin

daph·nia \'dafnēə\ *n*, *cap* [NL, perh. fr. *Daphne*, the nymph + NL *-ia*] : a genus of minute freshwater branchiopod crustaceans (order Cladocera) having imperfect segmentation, very large biramous antennae that are the chief locomotor organs, and a transparent carapace enclosing the body — **daph·ni·oid** \-nē,ȯid\ *adj* — **daph·noid** \-,nȯid\ *adj*

daph·nid \'dafnəd\ *n* -S [NL *Daphnidae*, family of water fleas, fr. *Daphnia*, type genus + *-idae*] : any of numerous small active water fleas; *esp* : any member of *Daphnia* or a related genus, many of which are used as feed for aquarium fishes

daph·nin \-nən\ *n* -S [NL *Daphne* + E *-in*] : a bitter crystalline glucoside $C_{15}H_{16}O_9$ occurring esp. in plants of the genus *Daphne* (as *D. mezereum*)

daph·nite \-,nīt\ *n* -S [ISV *daphn-* (fr. Gk *daphnē* laurel) + *-ite*; fr. its appearance; orig. formed as G *daphnit* — more at DAPHNE] : a mineral $(Mg,Fe)_3(Fe,Al)_3(Si,Al)_4O_{10}(OH)_8$ consisting of a basic aluminosilicate of magnesium, iron, and aluminum belonging to the chlorite group

dap joint *n* : a joint made by dapping two timbers

dapped *past of* DAP

dap·pen dish \'dapən-\ *also* **dappen glass** *n* [origin unknown] : a small heavy 10-sided piece of glass each end of which is ground into a small cup for mixing dental medicaments or fillings

¹dap·per \'dapə(r)\ *adj*, *often* -ER/-EST [ME *dapyr*, fr. MD *dapper* quick, agile, energetic, strong; akin to OHG *tapfar* heavy, weighty, ON *dapr* sad, OSlav *debelŭ* thick] **1 a** : neat and trim in appearance : SPRUCE, SMART ⟨~ in a brown suit and green bow tie —M.W.Straight⟩ **b** : excessively spruce and stylish ⟨this old giant, intellectually and spiritually shaggy and unkempt . . . makes his splendid sons seem almost ~ —Dorothy C. Fisher⟩ **2** : alert and lively in movement and manners : BRISK, JAUNTY ⟨a ~ wave of the hand⟩ — usu. used of persons small or slight of build — **dap·per·ly** *adv* — **dap·per·ness** *n* -ES

²dapper \"\ *n* -S [¹*dap* + *-er*] : one that daps: as **a** : one that fishes by dapping **b** : BUFFLEHEAD **c** : a circular saw that daps timbers

dap·per·ling \'==,liŋ\ *n* -S [¹*dapper* + *-ling*] : a little dapper fellow

dapping *pres part of* DAP

¹dap·ple \'dapəl\ *adj* [ME *dappel* (in *dappel-gray*) — more at DAPPLE-GRAY] : DAPPLED ⟨a ~ horse⟩

²dapple \"\ *n* -S **1** : one of numerous usu. cloudy and rounded spots or patches of a color or shade different from their background ⟨the distinctive markings of each horse . . . flecks, ~*s*, stockings —Harry Disston⟩ ⟨clouds and sun throwing gigantic ~*s* over the varicolored green of the treetops —Tom Marvel⟩ **2** : the quality or state of being dappled : mottled appearance ⟨the ~ of the leaf-filtered light —Anthony West⟩ **3** : a dappled animal (as a horse)

³dapple \"\ *vb* **dappled**; **dappled**; **dappling** \-p(ə)liŋ\ **dapples** *vt* : to mark or variegate with spots or patches of different shade or color ⟨beach plums ~ our dunes and fields with snowy drifts —*Christian Science Monitor*⟩ ⟨rings of sunlight . . . *dappled* the dark grass —Truman Capote⟩ ~ *vi* : to become dappled ⟨sunlight *dappling* through the great cedar and hemlock tops —Hugh Fosburgh⟩

dappled *adj* [ME, fr. *dappel* (in *dappel-gray*) + *-ed*] : marked with small spots, patches, or dots contrasting in color or shade with the background ⟨warm and a fine ~ sky —Thomas Gray⟩ ⟨a ~ fawn⟩ **syn** see VARIEGATED

dapple-gray *also* **dappled-gray** \'=ˌ=ˈ=\ *adj* [ME *dappel-gray*, perh. alter. (influenced by ON *depill* spot) of (assumed) ME *appel-gray*, lit., apple-gray, prob. trans. of ON *apalgrār*] : gray variegated with spots or patches of a different shade — used esp. of horses

¹daps \'daps\ *n pl* [origin unknown] *now dial Eng* : distinctive characteristics : HABITS, LOOKS, MANNERISMS ⟨the very ~ of my old aunt⟩

²daps *pres 3d sing of* DAP, *pl of* DAP

¹dar \'där\ *dial var of* DARE

²dar \"\ *n* -S [Nepali *dār*, prob. fr. Skt *dāru* wood — more at TREE] : an Indian timber tree (*Boehmeria rugulosa*) with soft red wood that is used in Bengal by wood carvers

da·ra·buk·ka \də'räbəkə, ˌdarə'bükə\ *n* -S [Ar *darābukkah*, *dirbakkah*, *darbūkkah*] : a kettledrum of northern Africa

da·rak \də'räk\ *n* -S [Tag *darák*] *Philippines* : RICE BRAN

da·rap·skite \də'rap,skīt\ *n* -S [G *darapskit*, fr. L. *Darapsky*, 19th cent. Chilean scientist + G *-it* -ite] : a mineral $Na_3(NO_3)(SO_4).H_2O$ consisting of a hydrous nitrate and sulfate of sodium

darb \'därb\ *n* -S [perh. alter. of ⁶*dab*] *slang* : something superlative ⟨a ~ of a black eye⟩ ⟨a regular little ~⟩

dar·bha \'därbə\ *n* -S [Skt *darbha* tuft of grass — more at TURF] : KUSA

dar·bies \'därbēz\ *n pl* [prob. short for obs. (*father*) *Derbies* (or *Darbies*) *bonds* rigidly bonded indebtedness] *Brit* : HANDCUFFS

¹darby \'därbē\ *n* -ES [prob. fr. the name *Derby* or *Darby*]

darby 1

1 : a plasterer's float consisting of a long narrow strip of wood with two handles **2** : a trowel with a handle elevated above the blade for use as a darby

²darby \"\ *vt* -ED/-ING/-ES : to smooth with a darby

dar·by and joan \ˌdärbēən'jō(ə)n, -jō'an\ *n*, *usu cap D&J* [prob. fr. *Darby* and *Joan*, stereotypical old married couple in a popular 18th cent. Brit. song] : a happily married couple esp. of advanced years

dar·by·ism \'därbē,izəm\ *n* -S *usu cap* [J. N. *Darby* + E *-ism*] : the doctrine and practices of the Plymouth Brethren

dar·by·ite \-ˌīt\ *n* -S *usu cap* [John N. *Darby* †1882 Eng. theologist + E *-ite*] : one of the Plymouth Brethren following closely the teachings of J. N. Darby

dar·cy \'därsē\ *n* -S [after Henri P.G. *Darcy* †1858 Fr. hydraulic engineer] : a unit of porous permeability in physics equal to the permeability of a medium through which the rate of flow of a fluid having one centipoise viscosity under a pressure gradient of one atmosphere per centimeter would be one cubic centimeter per second per square centimeter cross section — compare DARCY'S LAW

dar·cy's law \'därsēz-\ *n*, *usu cap D* [after H.P.G. *Darcy*, its formulator] : a statement in fluid dynamics: the velocity of flow of a liquid through a porous medium due to difference in pressure is proportional to the pressure gradient in the direction of flow

dard \'därd\ *n*, *pl* **dard** \-d\ *or* **dards** \-dz\ *also* **dardi** \-(,)dē\ *usu cap* **1** : a member of the stocky broad-shouldered moderately fair frequently brown-haired Indo-Aryan people in the upper valley of the Indus **2** *or* **dar·dic** \-rdik\ -S : the complex of languages spoken by the Dards and including Shina, Khowar, Kafiri, Kashmiri, and Kohistani — see INDO-EUROPEAN LANGUAGES table

dar·dan \'därdᵊn\ *adj or n*, *usu cap* [L *Dardanus*, adj., fr. Gk *Dardanos*, adj.] *archaic* : TROJAN

dar·da·ni \'därdᵊn,ī, -,ē\ *n pl*, *usu cap* [L, fr. Gk *Dardanoi*] : an ancient Illyrian people esp. noted for their successful raids on Macedonia and the Roman provinces during the 1st century B.C.

dar·da·nian \(')därˌdānēən, -ānyən\ *adj*, *usu cap* [L *Dardanius* Trojan, fr. Gk *Dardanios* (fr. *Dardanos* Dardanus, legendary eponymous ancestor of the Trojans) + E *-an*] : TROJAN

¹dare \'da(a)(ə)r, 'de|, |ə\ *vb* **dared** *or archaic & dial* **durst** \'dərst, 'dəst, 'dəist\ **dared**; **daring**; **dares** *or* **dare**; *substand pres sing & plural* **dast** \'dast, 'daa(ə)st, 'daist\ *archaic pres 2d sing* **darst** \'därst, 'dast\ [ME *dar* (1st & 3d pers. sing. pres. indic. of *durren*, *daren*, past *dorste*, *durste*), fr. OE *dear* (infin. — assumed — *durran*, past *dorste*); akin to OHG *gitar* (1st & 3d pers. sing. pres. indic.) dare, Goth *gadars* (infin. *gadaursan*), L *infestus* hostile, Gk *tharsein*, *tharrein* to be bold, Skt *dharṣati* he is bold] *vi* : to have sufficient courage : be bold enough : be unafraid : VENTURE ⟨try it if you ~⟩ ~ *vt* **1** : to have the bravery, boldness, or fortitude to contend against, venture, or try ⟨the actress *dared* the title role⟩ **2 a** : to confront boldly : invite the opposition of fearlessly : DEFY ⟨*daring* the wrath of the family⟩ **b** : to challenge to perform an action : provoke or goad (a person) into demonstrating courage, power, or skill ⟨to what further frenzies would the gods ~ their victim —Virginia Woolf⟩ ⟨the other boys *dared* him to dive from the bridge⟩ ~ *verbal auxiliary* : to be sufficiently bold, brave, or courageous to : be daring enough to ⟨he ~*s* not pronounce that repentance is followed by full forgiveness in this life —*Rev. of Religion*⟩ ⟨a few twisted thorn trees . . . which no man ~ cut down —O.S.J.Gogarty⟩ ⟨the *durst* not stay for fear of some treachery —*Ballad Book*⟩ **syn** see FACE

²dare \"\ *n* -S **1** : an invitation to contend : a challenge to do something dangerous, foolhardy, or unusual ⟨a ~ which it was hard for their rough, pioneer neighbors to resist —M.R. Werner⟩ — often used with *take* ⟨so foolish he'd always take a ~⟩ **2** : DARING : imaginative or vivacious boldness; *esp* : VERVE ⟨with a little more ~, the second collection should be better —*Time*⟩ ⟨each heavenward leap, each architectural ~ —*Forum*⟩

³dare \"\ *n* -S [ME *dar*, alter. (*darce* being taken as pl.) of *darce* — more at DACE] *archaic* : DACE 1

¹daredevil \'=ˌ==\ *n* [¹*dare* + *devil*] : a person who without apparent fear faces, accepts, or carries out anything unusually dangerous or foolhardy

²daredevil *adj* : being or befitting a daredevil ⟨a ~ driver⟩ ⟨a ~ escapade⟩ ⟨a ~ attitude toward life⟩ **syn** see ADVENTUROUS

dare·dev·il·ish \'=ˌ=v(ə)lish, -lēsh\ *adj* : resembling, befitting, or suggesting a daredevil ⟨a ~ type of person⟩ ⟨a hazardous and ~ action⟩

dare·dev·il·try \'=ˌ=vəl·trē, -ri\ *also* **dare·dev·il·ry** \-vəlr-\ *n* : reckless wildness ⟨the apparent ~ of the circus⟩

dareful *adj*, *obs* : DARING

daren't \'da(a)|r(ə)nt, ˌde|,|ənt\ : dare not

daresay \ˌ=ˈ=\ *vb* [ME (*I*) *dar sayen* I venture to say] *vt* : venture to say : think probable : BELIEVE — used in the pres. 1st sing. ⟨I ~ I would have forgotten about the whole thing⟩ ~ *vi* : SUPPOSE, PRESUME, AGREE — used in the pres. 1st sing. ⟨yes, I ~⟩

dares·n't \'da(a)r|sᵊn(t), 'der|,'där|,'da̤|,'da|,'daa|,'dai| *also* |zᵊn-\ [partly contr. of (*thou*) *darst not* (fr. ME), partly contr. of (*he*) *dares not*] *dial* : dare not

darg \'därg\ *n* -S [ME *dawerk*, *daywork*, fr. OE *dægweorc*, fr. *dæg* day + *weorc* work — more at DAY, WORK] *chiefly Scot* **1** : a day's work **2** : a fixed amount of work : TASK

dar·ghin \'därgən\ *n*, *pl* **darghin** *or* **darghins** *usu cap* **1** : a member of a subdivision of the Lezghians of Eastern Dagestan in Ciscaucasia **2** *or* **dar·ghin·i·an** \där'ginēən\ -S : a North Caucasic language

da·ri \'därē\ *n* -S [Ar *dhurah*] : DURRA

dar·ic \'darik\ *n* -S [Gk *Dareikos*, prob. fr. *Dareios* Darius I †486 B.C. king of Persia + Gk *-ikos* -ic] : a small gold coin of ancient Persia

¹daring *adj* [fr. pres. part. of ¹*dare*] **1 a** : ready, able, or prone to assume or face anything dangerous, risky, or arduous ⟨~ pioneers⟩ ⟨~ acrobats⟩ **b** : suggestive of, arising from, or prompted by boldness, fearlessness, or audacity ⟨a ~ promise⟩ ⟨a ~ attempt⟩ **2 a** : deviating from or contrasting with the conventional or traditional : NOVEL, STRIKING ⟨a ~ yacht designer⟩ ⟨a ~ intellect⟩ **b** : attracting attention by being brazenly different or loudly unconventional ⟨a ~ neckline⟩ ⟨a ~ exposé⟩ **syn** see ADVENTUROUS

²daring *n* -S [fr. gerund of ¹*dare*] : the quality or state of being bold, courageous, or fearless ⟨small in body, he possessed tremendous energy and ~ —E.K.Alden⟩

dar·ing·ly *adv* : in a daring manner

dar·ing·ness *n* -ES : the quality or state of being daring

dar·i·ole \'da(a)rē,ōl\ *n* -S [F, fr. MF, a pastry filled with cream, perh. fr. an assumed dial. word akin to MF *dorer* to gild + *-ole* — more at DORY] : a shell of pastry or mold of aspic filled with sweet or savory food

dar·jee·ling \där'jēliŋ\ *also* **darjeeling tea** \(')=ˌ==-\ *n* -S *usu cap* [fr. *Darjeeling*, district in West Bengal, India] : a tea regarded as of high quality grown esp. in the mountainous districts of northern India

¹dark \'därk, 'dák\ *adj* -ER/-EST [ME *derk*, fr. OE *deorc*; akin to OHG *tarchannen* to hide, MIr *derg* red, L *fraces* dregs of oil, Gk *thrassein*, *thrattein* to trouble, disturb, and prob. to Lith *darga* rainy weather] **1 a** : destitute or partially destitute of light : not receiving, reflecting, transmitting, or radiating light ⟨a ~ room⟩ ⟨~ as night⟩; *also* : having no lights burning ⟨the theater was totally ~⟩ **b** : transmitting only a portion of light, brilliance, or glare ⟨a ~ lampshade⟩ ⟨~ glasses⟩ **2 a** : wholly or partially black : somberly hued : of a deep shade ⟨~ earth⟩ ⟨a *dark*-haired girl⟩ ⟨the ~ robes of the clergy⟩; *specif*, *of color* : of low or very low lightness **b** : made of whole wheat flour ⟨a loaf of ~ bread⟩ or of white flour darkened with spices or other ingredients ⟨~ fruitcake⟩ **3 a** : arising from, exhibiting, or motivated by evil traits or desires : WICKED, INIQUITOUS ⟨the ~ side of his character⟩ ⟨the ~ powers that lead to war⟩ **b** : destitute of sunniness or cheer : GLOOMY, DISMAL, SAD ⟨he's always looking at the ~ side of things⟩ ⟨the ~ days of the war⟩ **c** : destitute of knowledge or culture : spiritually or intellectually retarded, backward, or primitive : UNREFINED, IGNORANT ⟨the ~ age of poetry among us is almost over —H.A.Overstreet⟩ **4** : not readily perceptible: as **a** *of a celestial body*, *archaic* : barely visible : DIM **b** : not clear to the understanding : OBSCURE ⟨that which makes much which was ~ quite clear to me —John Galsworthy⟩ **5** *now dial* : unable to see : BLIND ⟨what way would I see . . . and I a ~ woman since the seventh year of my age —J.M.Synge⟩ **6 a** *of the human complexion* : not fair : DUSKY, SWARTHY ⟨brick-red face grew ~*er* —Kenneth Roberts⟩ ⟨nor had she lost her ~ good looks —*Irish Digest*⟩ **b** : having or characterized by a skin rich in melanoid pigments ⟨the ~ races⟩ **c** : not known to the public — used chiefly with *keep* **7 a** : SECRET : not known to the public ⟨he kept his plans ~⟩; see DARK HORSE **b** : MYSTERIOUS ⟨an imagination that was ~ and rich⟩ **c** : SECRETIVE, RETICENT ⟨he was always quite ~ about the matter⟩ **8 a** *of sound* : possessing depth and somberness ⟨a woman with a beautifully ~ contralto⟩ ⟨everywhere the ~ laughter of the Negro is to be heard —*Amer. Guide Series: Va.*⟩ **b** *of an l sound* : formed with the tip of the tongue on the teethridge and the rest of the tongue in a position similar to that of a back vowel — compare ¹CLEAR 2b **c** *of a vowel* : articulated with the back of the tongue higher than its rest position ⟨\ō\ and \ü\ are ~⟩ **9** *of tobacco* : fire-cured or dark air-cured

syn DIM, DUSKY, DUSK, DARKLING, OBSCURE, MURKY, OPAQUE GLOOMY: DARK, the most general and common term of this group, implies a lack or deficiency of light or illumination of whatever kind ⟨it looked *dark* as pitch, so I gave him to understand that he must strike a light —Herman Melville⟩ ⟨telling me that they were waiting till it was *dark* to speak to him; that they did not dare to speak to him during the light —Anthony Trollope⟩ DIM suggests darkness enough to render outlines indistinct and shadowy ⟨"Shall I light a taper?" "There is no need. I love this *dim* light of evening —C.B.Nordhoff & J.N.Hall⟩ ⟨the *dim* grassy bank amid the tossing trees purple with twilight —G.K.Chesterton⟩ DUSKY and the uncommon

DUSK signify a twilight condition and suggest approaching darkness ⟨but comes at last the dull and *dusky* eve —William Cowper⟩ ⟨during the short period of a total eclipse bright stars may appear in a *dusky* sky —R.M.Sutton⟩ ⟨the *dusk* heavens —John Keats⟩ DARKLING may connote the mysterious, ominous, or uncanny ⟨the *darkling* night, lit only as it was by the slender moon —H.G.Wells⟩ ⟨as on a *darkling* plain swept with confused alarms of struggle and flight, where ignorant armies clash by night —Matthew Arnold⟩ OBSCURE is likely to imply darkness and also concealment, covering, or overshadowing ⟨it does not matter to real culture whether a book be lucid as transparent air, or sullenly *obscure* as pitch-black midnight —J.C.Powys⟩ ⟨a small room, *obscure* because it was heavily curtained —Arnold Bennett⟩ Orig. connoting intense darkness, MURKY now often suggests a blanketing thickness or heaviness ⟨London seemed last winter like an underground city; as if its low sky were the roof of a cave, and its *murky* day a light such as one reads of in countries beneath the earth —L.P. Smith⟩ ⟨a coarse, cheap, and offensive-smelling tobacco. The air was thick and *murky* with the smoke of it —Jack London⟩ OPAQUE, comparatively poor in suggestion, means impervious to light, opposed to *transparent* and *translucent* ⟨*opaque* from rain drawn in slant streaks by wind and speed across the pane, the window of the railway carriage lets nothing be seen but stray flashes of red lights —Richard Jefferies⟩ GLOOMY implies interference with free radiation of light and usu. connotes a pervading cheerlessness ⟨their *gloomy* pathway tended upward, so that, through a crevice, a little daylight glimmered down upon them, or even a streak of sunshine peeped into a burial niche —Nathaniel Hawthorne⟩ **syn** see in addition OBSCURE

²**dark** \"\ *n* -s [ME *derk*, fr. *derk*, adj.] **1 :** absence of light **:** DARKNESS ⟨stumbling about in the ~⟩ **:** a place where or the time when there is little or no light ⟨the fugitives moved into the ~ and waited⟩ **:** NIGHT, NIGHTFALL ⟨we'd better wait till ~ —Zane Grey⟩ **2 a :** something devoid of or not predominantly light, bright, or brilliant **:** something somber or subdued ⟨though still early fall light clothes had given way to winter ~*s*⟩ **b :** a dark or somber hue **:** deep color ⟨in water color the darkest tones can be darker than in fresco, but attempts to rival the ~*s* of oil always looks forced —C.W.H. Johnson⟩ **3 darks** *pl but sing or pl in constr* **:** broadleaf or Havana seed tobacco used for cigar binders — **in the dark 1 :** in secrecy ⟨mostly such transactions were made *in the dark*⟩ **2 :** in ignorance ⟨*in the dark* about a person's intentions⟩

³**dark** \"\ *vb* -ED/-ING/-S [ME *derken*, fr. OE *deorcian* to become dark, grow dim, fr. *deorc* dark] *vi* **1** *obs* **:** to grow dark **:** DARKEN; *specif* **:** to undergo eclipse **2** *dial Eng* **:** EAVESDROP ~ *vt* **:** to make dark **:** DIM, CLOUD ⟨the folk whose shadows ~*ed* the blinds —John Masefield⟩

⁴**dark** \"\ *adv* [¹*dark*] *archaic* **:** DARKLY

dark adaptation *n* **:** the phenomena including dilatation of the pupil, increase in retinal sensitivity, shift of the region of maximum luminosity toward the blue, and regeneration of visual purple by which the eye adapts to conditions of reduced illumination; *sometimes* **:** the time required for the occurrence of these phenomena — compare LIGHT ADAPTATION

dark–adapted \ˈ≈,≈≈\ *adj* **:** adjusted for vision in dim light **:** having undergone dark adaptation

dark beaver *n* **:** a grayish to moderate brown that is redder and lighter than autumn brown — called also *nutmeg, praline, Santos*

dark box *n* **:** a box from which light is wholly excluded and which is used for storing light-sensitive photographic equipment (as films, plates, paper)

dark cardinal *n* **:** a dark red that is yellower, less strong, and slightly darker than cranberry, lighter, stronger, and slightly yellower than average garnet, and bluer, stronger, and slightly lighter than average wine

dark current *n* **:** the current through a photoelectric or photoconductive cell when an electromotive force is applied in the absence of light

dark·en \ˈdärkən, ˈdȧk-\ *vb* **darkened; darkened; darkening** \-k(ə)niŋ\ **darkens** [ME *derknen, darknen*, fr. *derk*, adj., dark + *-nen* -en] *vi* **1 a :** to grow dark by diminution of light ⟨the theater ~*ed* and the play began⟩ ⟨a cold winter evening ~*ing* down⟩ ⟨suddenly it ~*ed* up and started to rain⟩ **b :** to become obscured ⟨the memory of it ~*s*⟩ **2 :** to undergo or exhibit an emotional, spiritual, or facial change usu. of a disturbed or lowering nature ⟨his expression ~*ed* with anger⟩ ⟨his voice ~*ed* with the words⟩ ⟨his face ~*ing* with suspicion —Dorothy Sayers⟩ **3 :** to grow dark or darker in shading or color ⟨paper ~*ing* at the margins⟩ ~ *vt* **1 a :** to make dark or darker by depriving of light ⟨a cloud of locusts ~*ed* the sky⟩ ⟨~ a room by turning off the light⟩ **b :** to lessen (the illumination) by concealing or standing in the way ⟨a figure ~*ed* the lamplight on the porch —Ellen Glasgow⟩ **2 :** TAINT, TARNISH, BEFOUL ⟨covetousness ~*ed* his mind⟩ ⟨~*ing* a reputation with lies⟩ ⟨an evil genius to ~ the conscience of men and women —V.L.Parrington⟩ **3 :** to make less clear **:** OBSCURE ⟨uncertainty ~*s* the future of radio and television —E.D.Canham⟩; *specif* **:** to hinder or retard the receptivity or vision of ⟨superstitions ~*ing* their minds⟩ **4 :** to deprive (the eyes) in whole or in part of sight ⟨age ~*ing* his eyes⟩ **5 :** to cast a gloom over ⟨~ mirth⟩ ⟨~ his hopes⟩ **:** make unhappy or miserable ⟨a life ~*ed* by afflictions⟩; *specif, obs* **:** to put (a person) in a position bereft of glory or recognition **6 :** to give a dark shade to **:** turn into a dark color ⟨fumes from nearby chimneys had ~*ed* the statehouse dome⟩ ⟨a sun-*darkened* plainsman —R.A.Billington⟩ **syn** see OBSCURE —**darken one's door** *or* **darken the door :** to make an appearance ⟨the first salesman to *darken our door*⟩ — used sometimes with object in pl. ⟨he never *darkened the doors* of the office again⟩

dark·en·er \-k(ə)nə(r\ *n* -s **:** one that darkens

darkening *n* -s **:** an act or instance of becoming or making dark; *specif, chiefly Scot* **:** TWILIGHT, GLOAMING, DUSK

darker *comparative of* DARK

darkest *superlative of* DARK

dark field *n* **:** the dark area that serves as the background for objects viewed in an ultramicroscope

dark–field \ˈ≈ˌ≈\ *adj* [*dark field*] **:** producing, involving the use of, or relating to a dark field ⟨*dark-field* illumination⟩ ⟨*dark-field* examination⟩ — see ULTRAMICROSCOPE

dark–field microscope *n* **:** ULTRAMICROSCOPE

dark–fired \ˈ≈ˌ≈\ *adj* **:** FIRE-CURED

dark–ground \ˈ≈ˌ≈\ *adj* **:** DARK-FIELD

dark horse *n* **1 :** a racehorse whose ability and chances of success in a race are not generally known **2 :** a contestant (as a political candidate) that wins unexpectedly or that although little known is thought to be able to win or make a very good showing

darkie *or* **darkey** *var of* DARKY

darking *pres part of* DARK

dark·ish \ˈdärkish, ˈdȧk-, -kēsh\ *adj* [ME *derkysshe*, fr. *derk*, adj., dark + *-ysshe* -ish] **:** somewhat dark **:** DUSKY

dark lantern *n* **:** a lantern with a single opening which may be closed to conceal the light — called also *bull's-eye*

dar·kle \-kəl\ *vi* **darkled; darkled; darkling** \-k(ə)liŋ\ **darkles** [back-formation fr. ²*darkling*] **1 :** to lurk in the dark **:** lie concealed in or as if in the dark ⟨children playing tag *darkled* in the corners⟩ **2 a :** to grow dark **:** fade into darkness ⟨she watched the last bright-colored daylight ~ slowly against the hills—Agnes S. Turnbull⟩ **b :** to become clouded or gloomy ⟨his face *darkling* with anger⟩

dark lightning *n* **:** a lightning that gives black photographic streaks where white ones ordinarily occur — compare CLAYDEN EFFECT

dark–line spectrum *n* **:** a line spectrum produced by the passage of white light through an ionized gas or vapor

¹**dark·ling** \-kliŋ *also* -kəl- *also* **dark·lings** \-ŋz\ *adv* [ME *derkelyng*, fr. *derke, derk* dark + *-lyng* -ling — more at DARK] **:** in the dark ⟨must helpless man . . . roll ~ down the torrent of his fate —Samuel Johnson⟩

²**dark·ling** \"\ *adj* **1 :** done or taking place in the dark ⟨a ~ journey⟩ **2 :** deeply shadowed or shaded **:** DARK, DUSKY ⟨friendly ~ hills —Thomas Wood †1950⟩; *esp* **:** mysteriously, threateningly, or uncannily dark or obscure ⟨a ~ glance⟩ ⟨secret operatives and ~ conspiracies —Archibald MacLeish⟩ **syn** see DARK

darkling beetle *or* **darkling ground beetle** *n* **:** any of numerous mostly hard-bodied black sluggish terrestrial plant-eating beetles (family Tenebrionidae) that are often incapable of flight

dark·lins \-k(ə)lənz\ *adv* [alter. of *darklings*] *dial Brit* **:** DARKLING

dark·ly \-klē, -li\ *adv, sometimes* -ER/-EST [ME *derkly*, fr. OE *deorclice* (attested only in the meaning "horridly, foully"), fr. *deorc* dark + *-lice* -ly] **:** in a dark manner: as **a :** OBSCURELY, VAGUELY, MYSTERIOUSLY ⟨~ sensing the presence of someone⟩ **b :** with dimmed or obscured vision **:** DIMLY ⟨seeing a ship but ~ against the horizon⟩ **c :** with a dark or blackish color ⟨the storm clouds gathered ~⟩ **d :** with a dark, gloomy, or menacing look or manner ⟨glancing ~ at his opponent⟩ **e :** in the dark **:** SECRETLY ⟨thoughts held ~ in his mind⟩

dark meat *n* **:** dark-colored meat esp. in poultry or game (as the thigh of chicken)

dark·ness *n* -ES [ME *derknesse*, fr. OE *deorcnysse*, fr. *deorc* dark + *-nysse* -ness — more at DARK] **:** the quality or state of being dark: as **a :** the absence in part or in whole of light **:** BLACKNESS, GLOOM ⟨the ~ of night⟩ ⟨the ~ of a cave⟩ **b** (1) **:** absence of moral, religious, or cultural values **:** spiritual backwardness **:** IGNORANCE ⟨peoples living in ~ and superstition⟩ (2) **:** WICKEDNESS, INIQUITY ⟨the powers of ~⟩ **c :** deprivation of sight **:** BLINDNESS **d :** dark quality in shade or color ⟨the somber ~ of pines —*Amer. Guide Series: Vt.*⟩ **e :** PRIVACY, SECRECY ⟨questions of policy kept in ~⟩ **f** (1) **:** lack of clarity **:** OBSCURITY ⟨the ~ of certain passages in a text⟩ (2) **:** imperfect vision or understanding ⟨fanatical ~ of a mind that glimpsed light but could not win it —Carlos Baker⟩ **g** (1) **:** distress caused by misfortune or affliction **:** TROUBLE ⟨my personal life had taken a turn towards ~—Karl Polanyi⟩ (2) **:** GLOOM ⟨Brahms songs, with their decided ~ of mood —Irving Kolodin⟩

dark of the moon 1 *astron* **:** the period of about a week at the time of a new moon when the moon's light is absent from the nighttime sky **2 :** a period when the moon is not shining or when it is obscured

dark pine *n* **:** a large cypress pine (*Callitris robusta*) of Western Australia that has dark brown furrowed bark and is an important timber tree

dark plaster *n* **:** a plaster made by calcining gypsite without previous grinding

dark reaction *n* **:** a chemical reaction in the absence of light as contrasted with a photochemical reaction

dark red silver ore *n* **:** PYRARGYRITE

darkroom \ˈ≈,≈\ *n* **:** a room freed from light or lighted by a safelight for handling and processing light-sensitive materials (as plates, films, and paper)

darks *pl of* DARK, *pres 3d sing of* DARK

darkskin \ˈ≈,≈\ *n* **:** one that has skin of dark brown, red, or black color — **dark–skinned** \ˈ≈ˈ≈\ *adj*

dark slide *n* **1 :** the removable slide that covers a photographic plate or film in a holder **2 :** a photographic plateholder or sheet-film holder

dark·some \ˈdärksəm, ˈdȧk-\ *adj* [²*dark* + *-some*] **1 :** gloomily somber ⟨a ~ path⟩ ⟨~ prophecies⟩ **:** mysteriously or forbiddingly dark or obscured ⟨a ~ castle⟩ **2** *archaic* **:** not readily understood **:** OBSCURE

dark space *n* **:** any of several regions or layers in the visible glow discharge of a gas-filled cold-cathode electron tube that remain nonluminous or exhibit low light intensity until the ions in such spaces acquire sufficient energy to excite fluorescence in the tube gas — see ASTON DARK SPACE, CROOKES DARK SPACE, FARADAY DARK SPACE

dark star *n* **:** an invisible but luminous member of a double or multiple system of stars; *esp* **:** the star that causes the primary eclipse in an eclipsing variable

darktown \ˈ≈,≈\ *n* **:** a usu. urban area inhabited by Negroes — often taken to be offensive

dark wedgwood *n, often cap W* **:** a grayish to moderate purplish blue — distinguished from *light Wedgwood;* called also *flame blue*

dark whites *n pl* **:** swarthy or brunet white people

dark·ie *also* **dark·ie** *or* **dark·ey** \ˈdärkē, ˈdȧk-, -ki\ *n, pl* **darkies** *also* **darkeys** [¹*dark* + *-y, -ie, -ey*] **:** NEGRO — often taken to be offensive

¹**dar·ling** \ˈdärliŋ, ˈdȧl-, -lēŋ\ *n* -s [ME *derling*, fr. OE *dēorling*, fr. *dēore* dear + *-ling* — more at DEAR] **1 a :** a dearly beloved **:** the object of one's love ⟨she was the ~ of his life⟩ — often used as a term of endearment **b :** a favorite esp. of one in power or of a particular power, faction, or group ⟨the cultural ~ of the Communist party⟩ ⟨the king's ~⟩ ⟨Cromwell, more than ever the ~ of his soldiers —T.B. Macaulay⟩ **2 :** something looked upon with especial favor ⟨energy and matter were the scientific ~*s* of the nineteenth century—Norbert Wiener⟩ ⟨cotton shirts will be the ~ of most sportswear departments —*Women's Wear Daily*⟩

²**darling** \"\ *adj, sometimes* -ER/-EST **1 :** dearly beloved **:** FAVORITE ⟨the organization of public balls . . . was another ~ topic of his heart —Sacheverell Sitwell⟩ **2 :** delightfully pleasing **:** SWEET, CUTE, CHARMING ⟨a ~ living room⟩ ⟨a ~ little short story⟩ — **dar·ling·ly** *adv* — **dar·ling·ness** *n* -ES

darling lily \"-\ *n, usu cap D* [fr. *Darling* river, southeastern Australia] **:** an Australian herb (*Crinum flaccidum*) with white flowers and bulbs that yield a substance like arrowroot

darling pea *n, usu cap D* [fr. *Darling* river] **:** either of two Australian plants of the genus *Swainsona* (*S. galegifolia* and *S. greyana*) that have racemose flowers and are poisonous to sheep — called also *poison bush*

darling plum *n, usu cap D* [prob. fr. ²*darling*] **1 :** RED IRONWOOD 1 **2 :** the small black egg-shaped fruit of the red ironwood

dar·ling·to·nia \ˌdärliŋˈtōnēə, -nyə\ *n, cap* [NL, fr. William *Darlington* †1863 Amer. botanist + NL *-ia*] **:** a genus of Californian insectivorous plants (family Sarraceniaceae) characterized by arched and hooded leaves and solitary flowered scapes — see PITCHER PLANT

darm·stadt \ˈdärm,shtät, -,stat\ *adj, usu cap* [fr. *Darmstadt*, Germany] **:** of or from the city of Darmstadt, Germany **:** of the kind or style prevalent in Darmstadt

¹**darn** \ˈdärn, ˈdȧn\ *var of* DERN

²**darn** \"\ *vb* -ED/-ING/-S [prob. fr. F dial. (Channel Islands) *derner, darner* to darn, mend, patch, perh. fr. F dial. (Norman) *darne* piece, fr. Bret *darn*; akin to W *darn* piece, Skt *dīrna* torn, OE *teran* to tear — more at TEAR] *vt* **1 :** to mend (a hole or tear in cloth) with interlacing stitches usu. in plain weave ⟨~ woolen socks with matching yarn⟩ **2 :** to embroider by filling in a design or background with geometric patterns or parallel lines of long running or interlacing stitches ⟨the lace was formed by ~*ing* a leaf pattern on a net ground⟩ ~ *vi* **:** to do darning

³**darn** \"\ *n* -s **:** a place darned ⟨a sweater full of ~*s*⟩

⁴**darn** \"\ *or* **durn** \ˈdərn, ˈdə̄n, ˈdəin\ *vb* -ED/-ING/-S [euphemism] *vt* **:** ¹DAMN *vt* 5 ⟨~ him, he won't even try to help⟩ ⟨~ it all⟩ ⟨I'll be ~*ed* if I know⟩ ~ *vi* **:** DAMN

⁵**darn** \"\ *or* **durn** \"\ *adj* [euphemism for ³*damn*] **:** ¹DAMNED 2a, 2b ⟨one ~ thing after another⟩

⁶**darn** \"\ *or* **durn** \"\ *adv* [euphemism for ⁴*damn*] **:** ²DAMNED ⟨he came ~ near killing him⟩

⁷**darn** \"\ *or* **durn** \"\ *n* -s [euphemism] **:** ²DAMN 2

¹**dar·na·tion** \därˈnāshən, dȧˈ-\ *n* -s [euphemism] **:** DAMNATION — often used as a mild imprecation

²**darnation** \(ˈ)≈ˈ≈\ *adj* **:** ¹DAMNED 2a, 2b ⟨that ~ pump never worked⟩

³**darnation** \"\ *adv* **:** ²DAMNED ⟨a ~ fine time we had⟩

darnd·est *or* **darned·est** \ˈdärndəst, ˈdȧn-\ *or* **durn·dest** *or* **durned·est** \ˈdərn-, ˈdə̄n-, ˈdəin-\ *n* -s [euphemism] **:** DAMNEDEST

¹**darned** \ˈdärnd, ˈdȧnd\ *or* **durned** \ˈdərnd, ˈdə̄nd, ˈdəind\ *adj, sometimes* **darneder** *or* **durneder** *usu* **darndest** *or* **darnedest** *or* **durndest** *or* **durnedest** [euphemism] **:** ¹DAMNED 2

²**darned** \"\ *or* **durned** \"\ *adv* [euphemism] **:** ²DAMNED

dar·nel \ˈdärnᵊl, ˈdȧn-\ *n* -s [ME, prob. fr. an (assumed) MF word akin to F dial. *darnelle, darnèle, daurnale* darnel, cockle, prob. of Gmc origin; akin to MHG *tōre* fool, OE *dysig* foolish — more at DIZZY] **:** any of several grasses of the genus *Lolium*; *esp* **:** BEARDED DARNEL

darn·er \-nə(r)\ *n* -s **1 :** one that darns (as a darning machine) **2 :** DARNING NEEDLE **3 :** a darning egg or similar device

darnick *var of* DORNICK

darning *n* -s **:** articles or parts of articles that have been darned or are to be darned

darning egg *n* **:** an egg-shaped or round object that often has a wood or plastic handle and is used as a support for a curved area during darning

darning needle *n* **1 :** a long needle with a large eye for use in darning **2 :** DRAGONFLY, DAMSELFLY

da·ro·ga *also* **da·ro·gha** \dəˈrōgə\ *n* -s [Hindi *daroga*, fr. Per *dārogā*] *India* **:** a chief officer; *esp* **:** the head of a police, customs, or excise station

dar·rein \dəˈrān, (ˈ)daˈr-\ *adj* [AF *dreyn, derreyn*, fr. OF *darrain, derrein*, fr. (assumed) VL *deretranus*, fr. LL *deretro* back, behind (fr. L *de-* + *retro* back, backward) + *-anus* -an — more at RETRO-] *law* **:** LAST, FINAL

dars *pl of* DAR

dar·sham fern \ˈdärshəm-\ *n, usu cap D* [fr. *Darsham*, Suffolk, England] **:** CREST FERN

¹**dar·shan** \ˈdärshən\ *n, pl* **darsha·nim** \därˈshänəm, -shōn-\ [Heb *darshān* interpreter, fr. *darāsh* to inquire, expound] **:** a preacher who expounds Jewish law or scriptures

²**dar·shan** \ˈdärshən, ˈdər-\ *n* -s [Hindi *darśan*, fr. Skt *darśana* act of seeing, view, fr. *dṛś* to see; akin to Gk *derkesthai* to look — more at DRAGON] **:** a blessing held by various Hindus to consist in the viewing of an eminent person (as a religious leader)

dar·so \ˈdär(,)sō\ *n* -s [*dwarf red sorghum*] **:** a hybrid grain sorghum of doubtful origin but resulting supposedly from a natural crossing of a sorgo and a kafir and resembling kafir

d'ar·son·val current \ˈdärsᵊn,vȯl-, -val-\ *n, usu D'Arsonval* [after Jacques A. *d'Arsonval* †1940 Fr. physicist] **:** a high-frequency oscillating current of low voltage and high amperage used in diathermy

d'arsonval galvanometer *n, usu D'Arsonval* **:** a moving-coil galvanometer whose coil is provided with a filament suspension or with pivots and hairspring and rotates about a stationary soft-iron core between the poles of a strong permanent magnet

darst *archaic pres 2d sing of* DARE

¹**dart** \ˈdär|t, ˈdȧ|, *usu* |d.+V\ *n* -s [ME, fr. MF, of Gmc origin; akin to OE *daroth* dart, OHG *tart*, ON *darrathr*; perh. akin to Gk *thoos* sharp, Skt *dhārā* blade] **1 a** *archaic* **:** a light spear **:** JAVELIN **b** *archaic* **:** ARROW **c :** a small missile usu. with a shaft pointed and weighted at one end and feathered on the other (as one used in a blowgun or one thrown by hand at a target in the game of darts) **2 a :** something projected with sudden speed; *esp* **:** a sharp glance ⟨the ~ that shot from his eyes was of aggressive honesty —Winston Churchill⟩ **b :** something that sharply or suddenly wounds or pains ⟨~*s* of sarcasm⟩ **3 :** something with a slender pointed shaft or outline: as **a :** a small sharp-pointed shaft of carbonate of lime secreted in the dart sac of a land snail **b :** the guard pin in a watch **c :** a stitched tapering fold used esp. in fitting garments to the curves of the body **d :** an Australian pompano (*Trachinotus botla*) **e :** a pointed element in a wave traced in an electroencephalogram esp. in epilepsy **4 :** a quick movement **:** a sudden jump ⟨she fluttered round, making helpless little ~*s* —Dorothy Sayers⟩ **5** *slang Austral* **a :** PLAN, SCHEME **b :** something particularly to one's taste **6 darts** *pl but sing in constr* **:** a game in which darts are thrown at a target and scored according to their nearness to the bull's-eye

dart 1c

²**dart** \"\ *vb* -ED/-ING/-S [ME *darten*, fr. *dart*, n.] *vt* **1** *obs* **:** to pierce with or as if with a dart **2 :** to throw (an object) with a sudden movement ⟨~ a javelin at the foe⟩ **3 :** to thrust or move with sudden speed ⟨the snake ~*ing* its head this way and that⟩ ⟨who made man, with powers which ~ him from earth to heaven in a moment —Laurence Sterne⟩ ⟨she ~*ed* out her hand like a flash —W.H.Hudson †1922⟩; *specif* **:** to cast (as one's eyes) with suddenness or haste ⟨he shivered and ~*ed* a look over his shoulder —Ellery Queen⟩ **4 :** to furnish with a dart (as the waist of a garment in tapering) ~ *vi* **:** to move, spring, or jump with suddenness or impetuosity ⟨his tongue ~*s* about like a dragonfly —Walter de la Mare⟩ ⟨green eyes ~*ing* over the impassive faces of the judges —Earle Birney⟩ ⟨streets that ~ out at odd angles —*Amer. Guide Series: Ark.*⟩

dart board *n* **:** a large circular board (as of cork) used as a target in the game of darts

dart·er \|d.ə(r),|tə(r)\ *n* -s **1 a :** SNAKEBIRD 1 **b :** BLUE DARTER **2 :** any of numerous small American freshwater fishes closely related to the perches and constituting a subfamily of the family Percidae

dart·ford warbler \ˈdärtfərd-\ *n, usu cap D* [fr. *Dartford*, Kent, England] **:** a dark-colored long-tailed warbler (*Sylvia undata*) of western and southern Europe including the south coast of England

dart·ian \ˈdärd.ēən\ *n* -s *usu cap* [Raymond A. *Dart* b1893 Australian-born anatomist in Union of So. Africa + E *-ian*] **:** AUSTRALOPITHECINE

dart·ing *adj* **1 :** THROWING, CASTING ⟨anger-*darting* eyes⟩ **2 :** making short quick movements ⟨~ fish⟩ **3 :** QUICK, VOLATILE ⟨a ~ intelligence⟩ ⟨a glib, ~ manner of speech —Christopher Rand⟩ — **dart·ing·ly** *adv* — **dart·ing·ness** *n* -ES

dar·tle \ˈdär|d.ᵊl, ˈdȧ|, |tᵊl\ *vb* **dartled; dartled; dartling** \|d.ᵊliŋ, |t(ᵊ)liŋ\ **dartles** [freq. of ²*dart*] *vt* **:** to thrust at repeatedly ⟨flames *dartled* the horizon⟩ ~ *vi* **:** to move back and forth repeatedly ⟨an adder's *dartling* tongue⟩

dart·man \ˈdärtmən\ *n, pl* **dartmen :** a soldier armed with darts

dart·moor \ˈdärt,mu̇(ə)r, -mō(-\ *n* -s *usu cap* [fr. *Dartmoor*, region in southwestern England] **:** one of a breed of English hornless long-wooled sheep having a long whitish face similar to that of the Leicester

dartmoor pony *n, usu cap D* [fr. *Dartmoor*, region in England] **:** one of an old breed of hardy English ponies developed in Devonshire

dar·tos \ˈdär,täs, -rd·əs\ *n* -ES [NL, fr. Gk *dartos* flayed, verbal of *derein* to flay — more at TEAR] **:** a thin layer of vascular contractile tissue that contains unstriped muscle fibers but no fat and is situated beneath the skin of the scrotum or beneath that of the labia majora

dar·trose \ˈdär,trōs *also* -ōz\ *n* -s [F, fr. *dartre* herpes, tetter (fr. MF *dertre*, fr. L *derbita*, of Celt origin; akin to MBret *dervoeden* herpes, W *darwden, tarwden* ringworm) + *-ose*; akin to OE *teter* tetter, OHG *zittaroh* herpes, tetter, Skt *dadru*, a kind of leprosy, skin eruption, OE *teran* to tear — more at TEAR] **:** a disease of the potato and tomato caused by a fungus (*Colletotrichum atramentarium*) and characterized by destruction of the stems esp. towards the base, by yellowing and drying of the foliage, and by development of numerous small black sclerotia in the diseased stem tissue — called also *black dot, black speck*

darts *pl of* DART, *pres 3d sing of* DART

dart sac *n* **:** an eversible appendage of the female reproductive organs in certain land snails

dart thrower *n* **:** THROWING-STICK

dar·vesh \ˈdärvish\ *or* **dar·wish** *also* **dar·wesh** \-rwish\ *n* -ES [Per *darvīsh*] **:** DERVISH

dar·win barberry \ˈdärwən-, ˈdȧw-\ *n, usu cap D* [after Charles R. *Darwin* †1882 Eng. naturalist] **:** a half-evergreen or evergreen shrub (*Berberis darwinii*) native to So. America but much grown in England that has entire spiny-toothed leaves and orange-yellow flowers in long racemes succeeded by dark purple berries

darwin glass *n, usu cap D* [fr. Jukes-*Darwin*, mining field in western Tasmania] **:** a group of glass objects found in Tasmania and believed to be glassy meteorites

¹**dar·win·i·an** \(ˈ)därˈwinēən, (ˈ)dȧˈ-\ *adj, usu cap* [C. R. *Darwin* + E *-ian*] **:** of or relating to the naturalist Darwin, his theories, or his followers

²**darwinian** \"\ *n* -s *usu cap* **:** one who accepts or advocates Darwinism

darwinian theory *n, usu cap D* **:** DARWINISM

dar·win·ism \ˈdärwə,nizəm, ˈdȧw-\ *n* -s *usu cap* [C. R. *Darwin*, its promulgator + E *-ism*] **:** the theory of the origin and perpetuation of new species of animals and plants holding that organisms tend to produce offspring varying slightly from their parents, that the process of natural selection tends to favor the survival of individuals whose peculiarities render them best adapted to their environment, and that chiefly by the continued operation of these factors new species not only have been and may still be produced but organisms of widely differing groups may have arisen from common ancestors; *broadly* **:** biological evolutionism — compare EVOLUTION 5b, NEO-DARWINISM; LAMARCKISM, MUTATION

[1]**dar·win·ist** \ˈ-ˌnə̇st\ *n* -s *usu cap* [C. R. *Darwin* + E *-ist*] **:** [2]DARWINIAN

[2]**darwinist** \"\ *or* **dar·win·is·tic** \ˌ;==ˈnistik, -tēk\ *adj, often cap* **:** [1]DARWINIAN — **dar·win·is·ti·cal·ly** \-tə̇k(ə)lē, -tēk-, -li\ *adv, often cap*

dar·win·ize \ˈ==ˌnīz\ *vb* -ED/-ING/-S *often cap* [C. R. *Darwin* + E *-ize*] *vi* **:** to think in Darwinian terms or ways ⟨a philosopher with a tendency to *Darwinize*⟩ ~ *vt* **:** to convert to or imbue with a Darwinian point of view ⟨Ibsen was *Darwinized* to the extent of exploiting heredity on the stage —G.B.Shaw⟩

darwin's frog *n, usu cap D* [after C. R. *Darwin*] **:** a small Chilean frog (*Rhinoderma darwini*) of the family Brevicipitidae characterized by the male's carrying of the fertilized eggs in his vocal sac

darwin's sheep *n, usu cap D* **:** a central Asiatic wild sheep that is a variety (*Ovis ammon darvini*) of the argali

darwin's tubercle *n, usu cap D* **:** the slight projection occas. present on the edge of the external human ear and assumed by some scientists to represent the pointed part of the ear of quadrupeds

darwin tulip *n, usu cap D* **:** a late-flowering tulip that is single-flowered and tall-growing and has self-colored flowers with a more or less rectangular base

dar·zi \dərˈzē, ˈdär,zē\ *or* **dur·zee** \dərˈzē\ *n* -s *usu cap* [Hindi *darzī*, fr. Per] **:** a tailor or an urban caste of tailors in Hindu society in India

[1]**das** \ˈdas, ˈdäs\ *n, pl* **dases** *or* **dasses** [Afrik — more at DASSIE] **:** DASSIE 1

[2]**das** \ˈdäs\ *n* -ES [Skt *dāsa* demon, enemy, infidel, slave; prob. akin to Per *dāh* servant, Av *dahyn-, daińhu-, danghu-* land, OPer *dahyn-* land, province, Skt *dasyu* demon, barbarian] **:** a Hindu slave or servant

[3]**das** *pl of* DA

DAS *abbr* delivered alongside ship

da·se·hra *or* **da·sa·ra** *or* **dus·se·rah** \ˈdəsərə\ *or* **da·sa·ha·ra** \ˌdəs(h)əˈhərə\ *or* **da·sa·hra** \ˈdəsərə\ *n* -s *usu cap* [Skt *daśaharā*, lit., one taking away ten (sins), fr. *daśa* ten + *harā*, fem. of *hara* carrier, fr. *harati* he carries, takes; akin to Gk *chortos* pasturage, grass, enclosure — more at TEN, YARD] **:** a 10-day Hindu festival orig. in honor of the Ganges but later of Durga and held in the month Asin

da·sein \ˈdä,zīn, G ˈdäˌ-\ *n* -s *usu cap* [G, lit., existence, being, fr. *dasein* to be present, fr. *da* there, here (fr. OHG *dār*) + *sein* to be (fr. MHG *sīn*, fr. OHG — more at THERE, IS] *existentialism* **:** factual reality or existence within the spatiotemporal realm

[1]**dash** \ˈdash, -aa(ə)-,-ai-\ *vb* -ED/-ING/-ES [ME *dasshen*, prob. of imit. origin] *vt* **1 :** to knock, hurl, or thrust impetuously, violently, or destructively ⟨~ away your tears⟩ ⟨they ~*ed* water into his face to revive him⟩ ⟨the storm ~*ed* the boat against a reef⟩ ⟨he ~*ed* the door open . . . and fled down the hall —Herbert Gold⟩ ⟨the fury of Pontiac's army ~*ed* itself in vain against the palisades of Detroit —*Amer. Guide Series: Ind.*⟩ **2 :** to break, crush, or smash by striking or knocking ⟨flowers ~*ed* by rain⟩ ⟨the statue was ~*ed* to pieces when it fell⟩ **3 a :** SPLASH, SPATTER ⟨clothes ~*ed* with mud⟩ **b :** BESMIRCH, SULLY ⟨a reputation ~*ed* with rumor⟩ **c :** to spread over carelessly **:** BLOTCH, BESPECKLE ⟨a painting ~*ed* with bright colors⟩ **4 a :** to bring to naught **:** RUIN, FRUSTRATE ⟨the weather ~*ed* his hopes of making the trip⟩ **b :** to put to shame **:** CONFOUND, CONFUSE ⟨~*ed* by her scorn⟩ **c :** to cast down **:** put out of sorts **:** DEPRESS ⟨never one to be ~*ed* when a partridge gets away —Earle Birney⟩ **5 :** MIX, TEMPER ⟨happiness ~*ed* with bitterness⟩; *esp* **:** to enliven, season, or adulterate by adding something of a different quality ⟨a glass of milk was put to his lips, and a new voice said, "I've ~*ed* it with brandy" —Ellen Glasgow⟩ **6** *archaic* **:** CANCEL, ERASE — used with *out* **7 :** to complete, execute, or finish off with haste or rapidity — used with *down* or *off* ⟨~ down a few notes⟩ ⟨~ off a short story⟩ ⟨~ off a drink⟩ **8** [euphemism] **:** [1]DAMN *vt* 5 ~ *vi* **1 a :** to advance suddenly and quickly **:** hurl forward esp. in repeated thrusts ⟨storm clouds ~*ing* low across the sky⟩ ⟨waves ~*ed* against the breakwater⟩ **b :** to move with sudden speed ⟨cars ~*ing* down the highway⟩ ⟨~ upstairs⟩ ⟨the Japanese boat made another attempt to ~ downstream —Nora Waln⟩ **2 :** to make a show of dressing stylishly and acting in a spirited or romantic manner **:** cut a fancy figure **:** appear dashing ⟨a fellow whose only concern is to dress and ~⟩ **syn** see RUSH

[2]**dash** \"\ *n* -ES [ME *dasshe*, fr. *dasshen*, v.] **1 a** *archaic* **:** a violent impact **:** BLOW, STROKE — often used in the phrases *at first dash, at a dash, at one dash* **b :** a sudden impetuous burst or splash or the sound it produces ⟨a ~ of water⟩ ⟨a ~ of rain⟩ **2** *obs* **:** a sudden demoralizing, crushing, or depressing blow **3 a :** a stroke of a pen esp. when made as a flourish in writing or when drawn through a word to cancel it **b :** the punctuation mark — used to indicate an abrupt shift in the structure of a sentence (as in *the man whom I — but first let me say this*), termination of a sentence when it is syntactically incomplete (as in "*You know very well he —*"), or faltering utterance (as in "*It shows — that he is — clumsy*"), to mark the end of an introductory series and the beginning or resumption of the main structure of the sentence (as in *his colleagues, his friends, his family — all tried to dissuade him*), to set off a repetitive or reinforcing phrase or clause (as in *it was a success — a brilliant success — but it gave him little satisfaction*), a preliminary word group (as in *legend and history — where are we to draw the line between them?*), or a supplementary word group, esp. an afterthought (as in *the object of this organization is to carry on scientific research — on a nonprofit basis*), to set off and emphasize a final word or word group (as in *he never offends anyone — unintentionally*), an appositive (as in *a single blunder — the use of unreliable production figures — invalidates all his conclusions*), or a parenthetical word or word group (as in *the book — though written in haste — reads well*), to separate question and answer (as in *why did he do this? — because he found it necessary*), to indicate change of speaker in dialogue, to join the name of a writer to a quotation or the name of a source to an extract, to introduce explanatory matter, a quotation, or a list, to separate the items in a list, or to set off a heading from the rest of its paragraph or the salutation from the body of a letter **c :** the sign — used to indicate ellipsis or omission (as in *my friend H—, d—d nonsense*, or *1911— —*), to serve as a ditto mark indicating the same author or continuation of the same entry in lists such as bibliographies or catalogs, to join proper names (as in *the Brooklyn—Pittsburgh game*), or to join letters or numbers that indicate the beginning and end points of an inclusive series (as in *A—C, 22—30, 1897—1905*, usu. read as "A to C", "22 to 30", "1897 to 1905") **d :** a mark ˈ in a musical score denoting that the note over or under which it is placed is to be played very staccato **e :** a graphic character in printing consisting typically of a single horizontal line longer than a hyphen and by printers commonly named according to its width ⟨en ~⟩ ⟨em ~⟩ ⟨2-em ~⟩ **4 :** a small quantity of something added to or giving a particular character or individuality to another **:** TOUCH ⟨his ancestry was chiefly English, with some Scotch and a ~ of both French and Dutch —V.L.Kellogg⟩; *specif* **:** a very small quantity of liquid or dry ingredients variously interpreted as ranging from 3 drops to ¼ teaspoonful added to food or drink **5 :** ostentatious display **:** flashy showiness — usu. used in the phrase *cut a dash* ⟨such a car would cut a ~ anywhere⟩ ⟨the couple cut quite a ~ on the promenade⟩ **6 :** energy in style and action **:** ANIMATION, SPIRIT ⟨the verve and ~ of an old-time cavalry regiment⟩ ⟨the two sisters were not beautiful . . . but they had the ~ . . . that a later generation came to call sex appeal —Robert Shaplen⟩ **7 a :** a sudden onset, rush, or attempt ⟨the dog made a ~ at the passing car⟩ ⟨make a ~ for cover⟩ ⟨established three depots of supplies . . . for a ~ to the Pole —C.O.Paullin⟩ **b** (1) **:** a race short enough to allow the contestants to cover the entire distance at top speed **:** a short swift race or trial of speed ⟨a 100-yard ~⟩ (2) **:** a harness race decided in a single heat **8 a :** a somewhat prolonged click about the duration of three dots on a telegraph sounder forming a letter or part of a letter (as in the Morse code); *also* **:** a correspondingly long buzz by a radiotelegraph transmitter or long blast of a whistle — compare DOT 5b **b :** a wave of a flag through an arc of 90 degrees to the left from vertical as a unit of code in signaling — compare WIGWAG **c :** a flash of a beam from a somewhat prolonged opening of the shutter of a signal light for about the duration of three dots and representing a letter or part of a letter in a communication system (as the Morse code) — compare DOT 5c **9** [by shortening] **:** DASHBOARD 2 **10 :** a horizontal rule varying in length and used to separate decks of a newspaper headline or to indicate divisions between or within stories **11 :** a mixture (as of mortar) prepared to be dashed against a moist surface to make a finishing coat **syn** see VIGOR

[3]**dash** \"\, ˈdäsh\ *n* -ES [perh. fr. Pg *das*, 2d pers. sing. of *dar* to give, fr. L *dare* — more at DATE] *Africa* **:** GIFT ⟨~*es* given regularly to his native servant⟩

[4]**dash** \"\ *vt* -ED/-ING/-ES *Africa* **:** to give a gift to (as a native employee)

dashboard \ˈ=,=\ *n* [[1], [2]*dash* + *board*] **1 :** a screen of wood or leather placed on the forepart of a horse-drawn carriage, sleigh, or other vehicle to intercept water, mud, or snow thrown up by the heels of the horses **2 :** a panel extending across an automobile or airplane below the windshield and usu. containing dials, controls, and accessories — called also *instrument board*

dashboard 1

[1]**dashed** \ˈdasht, -aa(ə)-,-ai-\ *adj* [[2]*dash* (mark) + *-ed*] **1** [euphemism] **:** [1]DAMNED 2a, 2b **2 :** made up of a series of dashes ⟨a ~ line⟩ ⟨a ~ pattern⟩

[2]**dashed** \-sht\ *also* **dash·ed·ly** \-shə̇dlē\ *adv* [euphemism] **:** [2]DAMNED

da·sheen \daˈshēn, dəˈ-\ *n* -s [origin unknown] **:** TARO

dash·er \ˈdashə(r), ˈdaash-,ˈdaish-\ *n* -s **:** one that dashes: as **a :** a man or woman who acts in a stylishly clever, forward, or showy manner **b :** a device that usu. consists of a shaft to which paddles are attached and that is used to agitate liquids or semisolids ⟨the ~ of a churn⟩ ⟨the ~ of an ice-cream freezer⟩ — see CHURN illustration **c :** DASHBOARD 1 **d :** an iron plate inside a boiler to prevent the entering cold water from impinging upon the tubes

dasher block *n* **:** a small block situated at the end of the spanker gaff and used for hoisting a ship's colors or signals

dashes *pres 3d sing of* DASH, *pl of* DASH

dashing *adj* [fr. pres. part. of [1]*dash*] **1 :** beating violently **:** SPLASHING ⟨~ waves⟩ **2 :** vigorously active **:** smartly energetic **:** SPIRITED ⟨a ~ young officer⟩ ⟨the most sheerly ~ of all jazz —Wilder Hobson⟩ **3 :** stylishly or elegantly showy ⟨the then gay, ~, and reckless capital of Ireland —Wilmot Harrison⟩ **:** having a smartly impressive appearance ⟨~, newfangled bicycles —*Irish Digest*⟩ **:** brilliantly carried off ⟨a ~ piece of teaching that illuminates his own cast of thought —Charlotte Devree⟩ — **dash·ing·ly** *adv*

dash·ke·san·ite \ˌdashkəˈsaˌnīt\ *n* -s [Russ *dashkesanit*, fr. *Dashkesan*, Azerbaijan, U.S.S.R., its locality + Russ *-it* -ite] **:** a mineral consisting of a chloroaluminosilicate of sodium, potassium, iron, and magnesium $(Na,K)Ca_2(Fe,Mg)_5(Si,Al)_8O_{22}Cl_2$ and belonging near hastingsite in the amphibole group

dash light *n* [[2]*dash* (dashboard)] **:** a light on the dashboard of an automobile

dashpot \ˈ=,=\ *n* **1 :** a device used for cushioning or damping a movement to avoid shock and consisting essentially of a cylinder containing air or a liquid and a piston moving in it **2 :** a device for damping or checking the vibrations of an automatic-indicating scale

dashy \ˈda\|shē, ˈdaa\|,ˈdai\|\ *adj* -ER/-EST [[1]*dash* + *-y*] **:** DASHING 3

da·si \ˈdä(ˌ)sē\ *n* -s [Skt *dāsī*, fem of *dāsa* demon, enemy, infidel, slave — more at DAS] **:** a female Hindu slave or servant **:** a Hindu woman of low caste

dask \ˈdask\ *Scot var of* DESK

das·n't *or* **dass·n't** *also* **das·sent** \ˈda\|sᵊn(t), ˈdaa\|,ˈdai\|,ˈdȧ *also* \|zᵊn-\ [partly contr. of (*thou*) *darst not* (fr. ME), partly contr. of (*he*) *dares not*] *dial* **:** dare not

dass \ˈdas\ *var of* DESS

dasses *pl of* DAS

das·sie \ˈdasē, ˈdäsē\ *n* -s [Afrik *dassie*, dim. of *das* hyrax, badger, fr. MD, badger; akin to OHG *dahs* badger, Gk *tektōn* carpenter — more at TECHNICAL] **1 :** a hyrax (genus *Procavia*) of southern Africa — called also *das* **2 :** a small sparid fish (*Diplodus sargus*) of African coasts and estuaries that is highly regarded as a sport and table fish and is silvery when young but becomes darker with age and possesses a black spot at the base of the tail — called also *blacktail*

dassie rat *n* **:** a sand-colored diurnal hystricomorph rodent (genus *Petromus* or *Petromys*) of southern African uplands having long silky fur, a bushy tail, and a head suggesting that of a squirrel

dast \ˈdast, -aa(ə)-,-ai-,-ȧ-\ *substand pres sing & pl of* DARE

das·tard \ˈdastə(r)d\ *n* -s [ME, perh. fr. ON *dæstr* exhausted (past part. of *dæsa* to groan, lose one's breath) + ME *-ard*; akin to ON *dasask* to become exhausted — more at DAZE] **1** *obs* **:** DULLARD **2 :** one who shrinks from danger **:** COWARD; *esp* **:** one who carries out malicious or sneaky acts without exposing himself to danger ⟨like a ~ and a treacherous coward —Shak.⟩

das·tard·ize \-tə(r),dīz\ *vt* -ED/-ING/-S *archaic* **:** to make cowardly **:** INTIMIDATE, COW

das·tard·li·ness \-tə(r)dlēnə̇s, -lin-\ *n* -ES **:** COWARDICE, TREACHERY

das·tard·ly \-lē,-li\ *adj* **:** treacherously cowardly ⟨the ~ brute had trampled on him when he could not turn against him —Anthony Trollope⟩ **:** insidiously or despicably mean ⟨the flood waters have done many ~ things to our residents —K.K.Coleman⟩ **:** BASE ⟨choosing the safe side . . . appeared to me to be playing a rather ~ part —George Borrow⟩ **syn** see COWARDLY

das·tardy \-tə(r)dē\ *n* -ES *archaic* **:** DASTARDLINESS

[1]**da·stur** \dəˈstü(ə)r\ *n* -s [Hindi *dastūr* custom, fr. Per] *India* **:** CUSTOM; *also* **:** customary fee

[2]**dastur** \"\ *n* -s [Per *dastūr*] **:** a Parsi high priest

da·stu·ri \-ürē\ *n* -s [Hindi *dastūrī*, fr. Per, fr. *dastūr*] *India* **:** FEE, GRATUITY

dasy- *comb form* [NL, fr. Gk, fr. *dasys* — more at DENSE] **1 :** thick with hair or leaves **:** shaggy **:** woolly ⟨*dasy*phyllous⟩ **2 :** density ⟨*dasy*meter⟩

das·ya \ˈdasēə\ *n, cap* [NL, fr. Gk *dasys*] **:** a widely distributed genus (the type of the family Dasyaceae) of marine red algae having a filiform sympodially branched thallus — see CHENILLE WEED

dasy·at·i·dae \ˌdasēˈadəˌdē\ *n pl, cap* [NL, fr. *Dasyatis*, type genus (irreg. fr. *dasy-* + Gk *batis* ray, skate) + *-idae*] **:** a family of elasmobranchs (type genus *Dasyatis*) comprising most of the common stingrays

das·y·cla·da·ce·ae \ˌdasəklaˈdāsēˌē\ *n pl, cap* [NL, fr. *Dasycladus*, type genus (fr. *dasy-* + Gk *klados* sprout, branch) + *-aceae* — more at GLADIATOR] **:** a family of coenocytic green algae that are included in Siphonocladales or now more often isolated in a separate order and that have the filaments arranged in whorls about a central axis which is often encrusted with lime — **das·y·cla·da·cean** \ˌ;==;=ˈshən\ *adj* — **das·y·cla·da·ceous** \-shəs\ *adj*

das·y·li·ri·on \ˌdasəˈlirēən\ *n* [NL, fr. *dasy-* + Gk *leirion* lily — more at LILY] **1** *cap* **:** a genus of plants (family Liliaceae) related to *Yucca* and *Dracaena* that are native to Mexico and the southwestern U.S. and have a woody stem, stiff sword-shaped leaves, and small white flowers **2** -s **:** any plant of the genus *Dasylirion*

da·sym·e·ter \daˈsimədə(r), dəˈ-\ *n* -s [ISV *dasy-* + *-meter*; prob. orig. formed in G] **:** a thin glass globe weighed in gases to measure their density

das·y·neu·ra \ˌdasəˈn(y)u̇rə\ *n, cap* [NL, fr. *dasy-* + *-neura*] **:** a large widely distributed genus of midges that are typically gall midges having larvae which feed chiefly on plant buds, in leaf curls, or in galls and sometimes cause the destruction of reproductive structures of various plants — see CLOVER SEED MIDGE

das·y·pel·ti·dae \ˌdasəˈpeltəˌdē\ *n pl, cap* [NL, fr. *Dasypeltis*, type genus (fr. *dasy-* + Gk *peltē* small shield) + *-idae* — more at PELTA] **:** an African family of egg-eating snakes containing a single species (*Dasypeltis scaber*) having the hypapophyses of the cervical vertebra extending into the esophagus where they form a rasp used in breaking eggshells — see ELACHISTODONTIDAE

das·y·phyl·lous \ˌdasəˈfiləs\ *adj* [ISV *dasy-* + *-phyllous*] **1 :** having leaves thick or thickly set **2 :** having woolly leaves

[1]**da·syp·o·did** \daˈsipədə̇d, dəˈ-\ *or* **das·yp·o·doid** \-pəˌdȯid\ *adj* [*dasypodid* fr. NL *Dasypodidae*; *dasypodoid* fr. NL *Dasypod-*, *Dasypus* + E *-oid*] **:** of or relating to the Dasypodidae

[2]**dasypodid** \"\ *n* -s **:** one of the Dasypodidae

das·y·pod·i·dae \ˌdasəˈpädəˌdē\ *n pl, cap* [NL, fr. *Dasypod-, Dasypus*, type genus + *-idae*] **:** a family of mammals (order Edentata) that comprises the armadillos

das·y·proc·ta \ˌdasəˈpräktə\ *n, cap* [NL, fr. *dasy-* + [2]*-procta*] **:** a genus (the type of the family Dasyproctidae) of hystricomorph rodents comprising the agoutis and having relatively long legs and but three toes on the hind feet — compare PACA — **das·y·proc·tid** \ˌ;==ˈ=tə̇d\ *adj or n* — **das·y·proc·tine** \-ˌtīn\ *adj*

das·y·pus \ˈdasəpəs\ *n, cap* [NL, fr. *dasy-* + *-pus*] **:** a genus (the type of the family Dasypodidae) of armadillos that includes the peba and other common armadillos

das·yu \ˈdəs(ˌ)yü\ *n* -s *often cap* [Skt, lit., demon, barbarian — more at DAS] **:** one of the dark-skinned Dravidian aborigines of India that opposed the invasion of the Aryans

dasy·ure \ˈdasē,yu̇(ə)r\ *n* -s [NL *Dasyurus*] **:** an arboreal carnivorous marsupial of the genus *Dasyurus* — compare NATIVE CAT

dasy·u·rid \ˌdasēˈyu̇rə̇d\ *n* -s [NL *Dasyuridae*] **:** one of the Dasyuridae

dasy·u·ri·dae \ˌdasēˈyu̇rəˌdē\ *n pl, cap* [NL, fr. *Dasyurus*, type genus + *-idae*] **:** a family of polyprotodont marsupials (type genus *Dasyurus*) that includes the native cats, pouched mice, banded anteater, Tasmanian devil, and related forms

dasy·u·roi·des \ˌdasēyəˈrȯi(ˌ)dēz\ *n, cap* [NL, fr. *Dasyurus* + L *-oides* -oid] **:** a small genus of Australian pouched mice

dasy·u·rus \ˌdasēˈyu̇rəs\ *n, cap* [NL, fr. *dasy-* + *-urus*] **:** a genus of carnivorous more or less arboreal marsupials of Australia and Tasmania that includes several moderate-sized active animals that have white-spotted dark coats and somewhat resemble weasels or martens — see NATIVE CAT

dat *abbr* dative

data *pl of* DATUM

dat·able *or* **date·able** \ˈdād·əbəl, -ātə-\ *adj* **:** that may be assigned a date ⟨a concrete and ~ happening —C.W.Shumaker⟩

[1]**dat·al** \ˈdādᵊl, -ātᵊl\ *adj* [[2]*date* + *-al*] **:** containing a date ⟨the ~ clause of a charter⟩

[2]**da·tal** \ˈdātᵊl\ *n* -s [by alter.] **:** DAYTALE

da·tana \dəˈtanə, -ānə *also* -ānə\ *n* [NL] **1** *cap* **:** an American genus of moths (family Notodontidae) that have the proboscis short and that include several with social larvae that feed on economically important plants — see WALNUT CATERPILLAR, YELLOW-NECKED CATERPILLAR **2** -s **:** any insect of the genus *Datana*

[1]**da·ta·ry** \ˈdād·ərē\ *n* -ES [fr. (assumed) ML *datarius* datary, official of the Roman Curia who added dates to papal letters (whence NL), fr. LL *data* date of a letter + L *-arius* -ary (person) — more at DATE] **:** the cardinal who is head of the datary

[2]**datary** *n* -ES [fr. (assumed) ML *dataria* datary, office of the Roman Curia where dates were added to papal letters (whence NL), fr. LL *data* date of a letter + L *-aria* -ary (thing)] **:** an office of the Roman Curia charged esp. with investigating the fitness of candidates for papal benefices

datch \ˈdach\ *dial Eng var of* THATCH

datcha *var of* DACHA

[1]**date** \ˈdāt, *usu* -ād·+V\ *n* -s [ME, fr. OF, modif. of OIt *dattero* or OProv *datil*, fr. L *dactylus*, fr. Gk *daktylos*, lit., finger] **1 :** the oblong fruit of a palm (*Phoenix dactylifera*) that constitutes a staple food for the people of northern Africa and western Asia and is also largely imported into other countries **2** *or* **date palm :** a tall tree with pinnate leaves and large clusters of dioecious flowers that yields the date and is cultivated esp. in many parts of the tropics **3 :** WASHINGTON PALM

[2]**date** \"\ *n* -s [ME, fr. MF, fr. LL *data*, fr. *data* (as in *data Romae* given at Rome), fem. of L *datus*, past part. of *dare* to give; akin to Gk *didonai* to give, Skt *dadāti* he gives] **1 :** a statement or formula affixed (as to a piece of writing, inscription, or coin) that specifies the time (as day, month, and year) and often the place of execution or making ⟨a letter bearing the ~ 3 January 1856⟩ **2 :** the point of time at which a transaction or event takes place or is appointed to take place **:** a given point of time ⟨preparations were sometimes in progress far ahead of the eventful ~ —Della Lutes⟩ ⟨Easter occurs on any ~ between March 22 and April 25⟩ **3 a :** the extent of time that something lasts **:** DURATION ⟨the short ~ of all things sweet —Rebecca P. Parkin⟩ **b** *archaic* **:** TERMINATION, END **4 :** the period of time to which something belongs esp. historically ⟨sculptures of an early ~⟩ ⟨a style belonging to a later ~⟩ **5 a :** an appointment or engagement usu. for a specified time ⟨has a ~ with his lawyer to discuss the sale of a house⟩; *esp* **:** an appointment between two persons of the opposite sex for the mutual enjoyment of some form of social activity ⟨make a ~ with his girl⟩ **b :** an occasion (as an evening) of social activity arranged in advance between two persons of opposite sex **c :** a person of the opposite sex with whom one enjoys such an occasion of social activity ⟨his ~ at the school dance⟩ **syn** see ENGAGEMENT — **to date :** up to the present moment ⟨no election returns have come in *to date*⟩ — **up to date** *also* **down to date 1 :** so as to account for or include present facts or knowledge ⟨the second edition brings the first *up to date*⟩ **2 :** up to the modern or present standard or style ⟨the house was brought *up to date* by the addition of new fixtures⟩ — compare OUT-OF-DATE, UP-TO-DATE

[3]**date** \"\ *vb* -ED/-ING/-S [ME *daten*, fr. MF *dater*, fr. ML *datare*, fr. LL *data*, n.] *vt* **1 a :** to determine or fix the date of origination, fabrication, composition, or occurrence of ⟨~ an early American antique⟩ **:** assign to a particular time or period of time ⟨the start of the Counter Reformation is to be *dated* from this time —R.A.Hall b.1911⟩ **b :** to assign a chronology to ⟨method for *dating* geological periods⟩ **2 :** to note down, record, or mark with the date ⟨bills are *dated* on the day they are made out⟩ ⟨~ the arrival of each new bird⟩ ⟨engine blocks *dated* as they pass off the assembly line⟩; *specif* **:** to write and date ⟨the news dispatch was *dated* from New York⟩ **3** *obs* **:** to put an end to **4 :** to make a date with ⟨she was *dated* several times by her boss⟩ ⟨he didn't go to the dance because all the girls he knew were *dated* up⟩ **:** go on a date with ⟨she *dated* several boys of his acquaintance⟩ **5 a :** to mark strongly or essentially with the qualities typical of a particular period ⟨the manner in which the brushwork is handled ~*s* the work of the great artists⟩ **b :** to make (as a style, an art work, or an artist) only briefly fashionable or artistically appealing **:** limit artistically to a short period of time esp. time in the past **:** quickly deprive of artistic originality or freshness ⟨sentimentality ~*s* most 19th century novelists⟩ ⟨a flashy architectural style ~*s* a house⟩ **6 :** to show up plainly the age of ⟨his button shoes surely ~ him⟩ ~ *vi* **1 :** to estimate or record the date or chronology ⟨the historian ~*s* by years, the geologist by millions of years⟩ ⟨a machine that ~*s*, weighs, and wraps automatically⟩ **2 :** to become dated and written — usu. used with *from* ⟨a report *dating* from headquarters⟩ **3 a :** ORIGINATE ⟨furniture *dating* as far back as the Revolution⟩ ⟨the manuscript ~*s* not later than the latter half of the 14th century⟩ **b :** to continue in existence **:** EXTEND ⟨a friendship *dating* from college days⟩ ⟨pioneer stock *dating* back to 1640⟩ **4 :** to become dated ⟨a fashion that never seems to ~⟩ ⟨the novel, now a half century old, shows no signs of *dating*⟩

dateable *var of* DATABLE

datebook \ˈ=,=\ *n* **:** a newspaper editor's record of news events to be covered in the future

dated *adj* **1** *obs* **:** having a limit or termination **2 :** provided with a date ⟨~ and stamped documents⟩ **3 a :** spoiled or made invalid or useless by subsequent events or phenomena : OBSOLETE ⟨houses bum down, roads are changed, new bridges are built, and a map soon becomes ~ —*Infantry Jour.*⟩ **b** : marked by often hackneyed features, materials, or techniques associated with the immediate and usu. discounted past ⟨a ~ novelist⟩ ⟨~ jazz music⟩ ⟨I find her conclusions ~. She smacks too much of feminism and the selfish twenties —Rhona R. Wilber⟩

date·less \'dātləs\ *adj* **1 a** : having no fixed term : ENDLESS ⟨the ~ rise and fall of the tides⟩ **b** : bearing no date ⟨a ~ letter⟩ **c** : of an age or duration so great as to preclude the possibility of being assigned a date : IMMEMORIAL ⟨~ customs⟩ ⟨a spiritual rule of ~ antiquity derived from Rome —G.M. Trevelyan⟩ **d** : of continuously living interest : not subject to the adverse effects of the passage of time : TIMELESS ⟨few characters are more ~ than Hamlet⟩ **e** : being without a social partner ⟨some of the boys had come to the party ~⟩ **2** *dial Eng* : having mental faculties impaired by old age : FOOLISH ⟨a poor ~ old man⟩

date letter *n* : the alphabetical punch mark placed on pieces of English silver to show the year in which they are assayed

¹dateline \'=,=\ *n* [²*date* + *line*] **1** : a line in a written document or a printed publication presenting the date of composition or issue: as **a** : the line at the beginning of a nonlocal news story giving its date and place of origin **b** : a line or space in a publication giving the date of issue, the volume number, and the issue number **2** *usu* **date line** : a hypothetical line on the earth's surface coinciding with the 180th meridian except where it is deflected between north latitudes 48° and 75° and between south latitudes 15° and 51° to avoid dividing places in close intercourse and designated arbitrarily as the place where each calendar day first begins **3** : DEADLINE 3

²dateline \"\ *vt* : to provide with a dateline ⟨a dispatch *datelined* Chicago⟩

datemark \'=,=\ *n* : a marking that indicates the date of a thing; *specif* : a mark on gold and silver plate indicating date of manufacture

date mussel *also* **date shell** *n* [¹*date;* fr. its shape and color] : a rock-boring bivalve mollusk of the genus *Lithophaga*

date line, indicated in chart by heavy line

date of record *finance* : the last date for registered holders of corporate stocks to be entitled to receive a dividend, right, or other benefit

date palm *n* : ¹DATE 2

date plum *n* : PERSIMMON; *esp* : an Asiatic persimmon (*Diospyros lotus*) sometimes cultivated for its small yellow or purplish edible fruits

dat·er \'dād·ə(r), -ātə-\ *n* -s : one that dates; *specif* : an instrument for stamping dates

dates *pl of* DATE, *pres 3d sing of* DATE

date slip *n* : a slip of paper pasted to an end-paper of a circulating library book on which is stamped the date the book is loaned or the date it is due back

date stamp *n* **1** : an implement or device for stamping a date and often (as on postal matter) related information (as place of origin or receipt) **2** : the date and related information stamped by a date stamp

dater

date-stamp \'=,=\ *vt* [*date stamp*] : to stamp with a date ⟨the post office *date-stamps* outgoing mail⟩ ⟨he *date-stamped* each letter when he opened it⟩

da·til \'dä,tēl\ *n, pl* **dati·les** \-ä·dā,lās, -äd·ē,läs\ [AmerSp *dátil,* fr. Sp, date (fruit), fr. Catal *dàtil,* fr. L *dactylus* — more at DATE] : any of several plants and their leaf fibers used for baskets or hats: as **a** : a So. American palm (*Cocos datil*) **b** : a Mexican yucca (*Yucca australis*)

dating *n* -s [fr. gerund of ³*date*] : an extension of credit by postdating of a bill or by not dating it until an agreed time

dating nail *n* : a broad-headed nail driven into the upper face of a railroad tie or utility pole bearing an indication of the date when the tie was laid

da·tion \'dāshən\ *n* -s [F or L; F, fr. L *dation-, datio* act of giving, fr. *datus* (past part. of *dare* to give) + *-ion-, -io* -ion — more at DATE] : the legal act of giving or conferring

da·tion in pay·ment \'dāshənən'pāmənt\ *or* **da·tion en paie·ment** \däsyōⁿnäⁿpeymäⁿ\ [F *dation en paiement*] *civil law* : a mode of discharging a debt or claim by the debtor's giving to the creditor with the latter's consent something in full satisfaction of the obligation but of a character different from that orig. called for by the obligation

da·tis·ca \də'tiskə\ *n, cap* [NL] : a genus (the type of the family Datiscaceae) of tall herbs resembling hemps and having flowers in clusters in the axils of the leafy branches

dat·is·ca·ce·ae \,dad·ə'skāsē,ē\ *n pl, cap* [NL, fr. *Dastica* type genus + *-aceae*] : a small family of herbs or trees (order Parietales) having regular often dioecious and apetalous flowers in racemes or spikes and a one-seeded capsule — **dat·is·ca·ceous** \¦==¦skāshəs\ *adj*

da·ti·val \dā'tīvəl, də'- *sometimes* 'dād·ə̇vəl *or* 'dat¦ *or* ¦ēv-\ *adj* [²*dative* + *-al*] : connected with the dative case or any of the relations frequently expressed by it; of or relating to the dative case

¹da·tive \'dād·iv, -ät¦, ¦ēv *also* ¦əv\ *adj* [ME *datif,* fr. L *dativus,* fr. *datus* (past part. of *dare* to give) + *-ivus* -ive — more at DATE] **1** [L *dativus,* trans. of Gk *dotikos*] **a** *of a grammatical case* : marking typically the indirect object of a verb (as Latin *mihi* in *da mihi panem* "give me bread" or German *ihm* in *sie gaben ihm wein* "they gave him wine"), the only object of any one of a limited group of verbs (as German *mir* in *er hilft mir* "he helps me"), the object of any of certain prepositions (as German *mir* in *mit mir* "with me" or *ihr* in *zu ihr* "to her"), or a possessor (as German *ihr* in *er küsst ihr die hand* "he kisses her hand") **b** *of a word or word group* : standing in any grammatical or semantic relation (as indirect object) that in certain inflected languages is characteristically marked by a dative case form even when this relation is not marked by any inflectional element (as *his son* in "he gave his son a dog") — not now used technically **c** : of or relating to the dative case ⟨a ~ ending⟩ **2 a** : capable of being disposed of as one wishes ⟨a ~ office⟩ **b** [ML *dativus,* fr. L] *of an officer* : REMOVABLE — distinguished from *perpetual* **c** : given or appointed and not cast by law upon a person or group; *specif* : given or appointed by a magistrate or court or having to do with such an appointment **3** *of chemical bonds* : formed by contribution of a pair of electrons by one atom — **da·tive·ly** \'ə̇vlē, -li\ *adv*

²dative \"\ *n* -s [L *dativus,* fr. *dativus,* adj.; trans. of Gk *dotikē* (*ptōsis*)] : the dative case of a language or a dative form

dative bond *n* : COORDINATE BOND

da·to *or* **dat·to** \'dä(,)tō\ *or* **da·tu** \-)tü\ *n* -s [*dato, datto* fr. Sp *dato,* fr. Tag *dató; datu* fr. Malay] : a local headman in many parts of central Malaysia and the southern Philippines

dat·o·lite \'dad·ᵊl,īt\ *n* -s [G *datolith,* fr. Gk *dateisthai* to divide + G *-lith;* fr. its granular structure — more at TED] : a mineral $Ca_2B_5SiO_9(OH)_5$ consisting of a basic calcium borosilicate commonly occurring in glassy greenish crystals — **dat·o·lit·ic** \¦dad·ᵊl¦id·ik\ *adj* : of or relating to datolite

dat·tock \'dad·ək\ *n* -s [Wolof *detah, ditah*] **1** : a tropical African tree (*Detarium senegalense*) of the family Leguminosae having rounded to oval pods with a sweet edible pulp and a single oily edible seed **2** : the hard dark reddish brown intricately figured wood of the dattock

da·tum \'dā¦d·əm, 'da¦,'dä¦,'dȧ¦, ¦təm\ *n, pl* **da·ta** *see sense 2* \¦d·ə,¦tə\ [L, something given, fr. neut. of *datus,* past part. of *dare* to give — more at DATE] **1 a** : something that is given either from being experientially encountered or from being admitted or assumed for specific purposes : a fact or principle granted or presented : something upon which an inference or an argument is based or from which an intellectual system of any sort is constructed ⟨a ~ of experience⟩ ⟨given this ~ it follows that⟩; *specif* : SENSE-DATUM **b** (1) *data pl but often sing in constr* : material serving as a basis for discussion, inference, or determination of policy ⟨no general appraisal can be hazarded . . . until more *data* is available —*Publishers' Weekly*⟩ (2) : detailed information of any kind **2 a** *pl usu* **datums** : a point, line, or surface with reference to which positions (as elevations) are measured or indicated (as a permanent bench mark in leveling or mean sea level in a topographical survey); *specif* : the mean low-water mark of all tides assumed as a basis of reckoning but not admitting rigorous scientific determination **b** *pl often* **datums** : a magnitude, figure, or relation supposed to be given, drawn, or known in a mathematical investigation from which other magnitudes, figures, or relations are to be deduced **3** : DATE **4** : the sensory basis of a perception or judgment — see SENSE-DATUM

da·tu·ra \də'türə, də·tyü-\ *n* [NL, fr. Hindi *dhatūrā* jimsonweed, fr. Skt *dhattūra*] **1** *cap* : a genus of widely distributed strong-scented herbs, shrubs, or trees (family Solanaceae) with large funnel-shaped flowers succeeded by spiny capsules — see JIMSONWEED, THORN APPLE; CAPSULE illustration **2** -s : any plant or flower of the genus *Datura*

da·tu·ric \-rik\ *adj* [NL *Datura* + E *-ic*] : of or relating to the genus *Datura*

dau *abbr* daughter

¹daub \'dȯb, 'däb\ *vb* -ED/-ING/-S [ME *dauben,* fr. OF *dauber* to whitewash, plaster, prob. fr. (assumed) VL *dalbare,* alter. of L *dealbare,* fr. *de-* + *-albare* (fr. *albus* white) — more at ELF] *vt* **1** : to cover or coat (as lath, a wall, a building) with soft adhesive matter (as plaster, pitch, mud) : PLASTER, CLOSE, SMEAR ⟨~ the crack with plaster⟩ ⟨~ a surface with glue⟩ **2** : to coat with something that smirches or stains ⟨~*ed* his fingers with ink⟩ : SOIL ⟨generally ~*s* himself with soup and grease —Earl of Chesterfield⟩ **3** *obs* : to cover with a specious or deceitful exterior ⟨he ~*ed* his vice with show of virtue —Shak.⟩ **4** *dial Eng* : to array tastelessly esp. in a gaudy manner **5** : to apply paint or other coloring material crudely, hastily, or unskillfully to ⟨their faces ~*ed* a savage black —T.B.Costain⟩ ⟨~*ed* her lips with lipstick⟩ : apply (colors) in such a way ⟨like an artist ~*ing* unimportant touches of paint on a finished picture —Winifred Bambrick⟩ ~ *vi* **1** *now dial* : to put on a false exterior in order to make an impression **2** : to paint or apply colors in a crude, amateur, or unskillful manner ⟨Awful Arts Club . . . which has been ~*ing* for ten years —Joseph Alger⟩

²daub \"\ *n* -s [ME *dawbe,* fr. *dauben,* v.] **1** : material (as plaster, mortar, clay, mud) used with straw or hay or rough-cast to daub walls ⟨old house . . . built of wattle and ~ —G.E. Fussell⟩ — compare WATTLE **2** : the act or an instance of daubing ⟨a few hasty ~*s* and the picture was ready⟩ **3 a** : something daubed on; *esp* : a viscous sticky application or a daubed spot, smear, or patch of paint **b** : something resembling or suggestive of a hastily or crudely applied touch, smear, or splash of paint ⟨great ~*s* of brilliant-colored fabrics were stretched out on tables —Winifred Bambrick⟩ **4** : a picture coarsely and unskillfully executed

³daub \"\ *var of* DAB

daube \'dōb\ *n* -s [F] : a braised meat stew

dau·ben·to·nia \,dōbən·'tōnēə\ *n, cap* [NL, fr. Louis J. M. *Daubenton* †1800 Fr. naturalist + NL *-ia*] : a genus (coextensive with the family Daubentoniidae) of lemuriform primates comprising solely the aye-aye of Madagascar

dau·ben·ton's plane \'dōbən-,tōⁿz-, dōbäⁿtōⁿz-\ *n, usu cap D* [after L. J. M. *Daubenton*] *anthrop* : a plane that passes through the opisthion and the orbital points on a skull

daub·er \'dȯbə(r), 'däb-\ *n* -s [ME, fr. AF *daubour,* fr. OF *dauber* to plaster + *-our* -or — more at DAUB] **1** : one that daubs: as **a** : PLASTERER **b** : a worker who seals with clay the doors of kilns in which brick and tile are burned **c** : LUTER **d** : a crude unskillful painter **e** *slang* : SPIRITS, COURAGE ⟨just keep your ~ up an' your mouth shut —Harold Sinclair⟩ ⟨the boys were depressed . . . their ~ was down —Ring Lardner⟩ **f** : MUD WASP **2** : something (as a brush or pad) used for daubing

daub·ery \-b(ə)rē\ *also* **daub·ry** \-brē\ *n* -ES [¹*daub* + *-ery, -ry*] **1** : the act of daubing **2 a** *archaic* : a dauber's work **b** *obs* : a misuse of or misrepresentation by words : mystifying action

daubing *n* -s [ME, fr. gerund of *dauben* to daub] **1 a** : the material (as clay or mortar) with which something is daubed **b** : ¹DUBBIN **2** : the action of daubing **3 a** : the action of painting unskillfully or crudely **b** : a painting crudely or unskillfully done **4** *obs* : insincere praise : FLATTERY

daub·ing·ly *adv* : in a daubing manner

dau·bree·ite *or* **dau·bre·ite** \'dȯbrē,īt, dō'brā,-\ *n* -s [F *daubréite,* fr. Gabriel A. *Daubrée* †1896 Fr. geologist and mineralogist + F *-ite*] : a mineral BiO(OH,Cl) consisting of a yellowish earthy bismuth oxychloride

dau·bree·lite \-ē,līt, -ā,l-\ *n* -s [G.A. *Daubrée* + E *-lite*] : a mineral $FeCr_2S_4$ consisting of a black chromium iron sulfide occurring in some meteoric irons (sp. gr. 5.01)

daub·ster \'dȯbztə(r), 'däb-, -bst-\ *n* -s [¹*daub* + *-ster*] : a bungler in painting : DAUBER

dauby \'dȯbē, 'däb-\ *adj, usu* -ER/-EST **1** : of the nature of or like daub or a daub **2** : crudely executed ⟨a ~ painting⟩ : SMEARY, ADHESIVE ⟨~ wax⟩

dau·cus \'dȯkəs\ *n, cap* [NL, fr. L *daucus, daucum,* a kind of parsnip or wild carrot, fr. Gk *daukos, daukon;* perh. akin to Gk *daiein* to ignite, burn; fr. the sharp taste or fr. the combustible sap some species exude — more at TEEN] : a genus of chiefly Old World herbs (family Umbelliferae) having compound umbels of mostly white flowers and having prickly fruit — see CARROT, WILD CARROT

daud \'dȧd, 'dōd\ *var of* ³,⁴DAD

dau·er·lauf \'dau̇(ə)r,lau̇f\ *n, pl* **dauerlaufs** \-fs\ *or* **dauer·läu·fe** \-lōifə\ [G, fr. *dauer-* long-lasting (fr. *dauern* to last, fr. MHG *dūren, tūren,* fr. MLG *dūren,* fr. L *durare*) + *lauf* race, run, running, fr. OHG *louf* — more at DURE, LEAP] : a long-distance cross-country ski race of approximately 35 miles — compare LANGLAUF

dauer·modification \¦dau̇(ə)r +\ *or* **dauer·modi·fi·ka·tion** \+ mōdēfēkät'sē'ōn\ *n, pl* **dauermodifications** \-shənz\ *or* **dauermodifikati·o·nen** \-ē'ōnən\ [G *dauermodifikation,* fr. *dauer-,* long-lasting, permanent + *modifikation* modification, fr. F *modification* — more at MODIFICATION] : an acquired character transmitted through the cytoplasm to several succeeding generations but not incorporated into the permanent heredity of the strain

¹daugh·ter \'dȯ¦d·ə(r), 'dä¦, ¦tə-, *archaic* 'da¦ *or* 'dȧ¦\ *n* -s [ME *doughter,* fr. OE *dohtor;* akin to OHG *tohter* daughter, ON *dōttir,* Goth *dauhtar,* Gk *thygatēr,* Skt *duhitṛ*] **1** : a human female having the relation of child to a parent **2** : a human female descended from remote ancestors : female descendant : girl or woman of a given lineage **3** : a female subject to the authority or love of a parent — used esp. as a term of address indicating affectionate interest by an elder **4** : a female offspring of an animal — used chiefly of pedigreed stock or bloodstock **5** : something derived from its source or origin as if feminine ⟨the United States is a ~ of Great Britain⟩ **6** *archaic* : a young woman : MAIDEN ⟨as the lily among thorns, so is my love among the ~*s* —*Song of Sol* 2:2 (AV)⟩ **7 a** : a female native of a specified place or land ⟨~*s* of Egypt⟩ **b** : a female in a spiritual kinship analogous to the physical ⟨~*s* of the church⟩ **8** : the atomic species that is the immediate product of the radioactive decay of a given element ⟨radon, the ~ of radium⟩

²daughter \"\ *adj* **1** : having the characteristics of a daughter or relationship of or as if of a daughter **2** : having the relation of offspring of the first generation : resulting from a primary division — used without reference to sex ⟨~ cell⟩ **3 a** *of a manuscript, text, or reading* : immediately derived from a previous manuscript, text, or reading **b** *of a language* : related to another language in a way that implies a common beginning

daughter-in-law \-ə(r)ən,lȯ, -ərn-\ *n, pl* **daughters-in-law** \-ə(r)zən-\ [ME *doughter in lawe*] : the wife of one's son

daugh·ter·li·ness *pronunc at* DAUGHTERLY + nəs\ *n* -ES : the quality or state of being daughterly

daugh·ter·ly \-ərlē, -li, -*R* -əl- *or* -ᵊl-\ *adj* : befitting a daughter : FILIAL

daughter of mary *usu cap D&M* [after the Virgin *Mary*] : GUASTALLINE

daunch \'dȯnch, -ä-,-á-\ *adj* [ME *daunche*] *now dial* : SQUEAMISH

dauncy \'dȯn(t)sē, 'dän-\ *var of* DONSIE

daun·der *or* **dau·ner** \'dän(d)ər, 'dōn-\ *Scot var of* ¹,²DANDER

¹daunt \'dȯnt, -ä-,-á-\ *vt* -ED/-ING/-S [ME *daunten* (also, to tame), fr. OF *danter,* alter. (prob. influenced by OF *dangier* power, jurisdiction) of *donter,* fr. L *domitare* to tame, fr. *domitus,* past part. of *domare* to tame, conquer — more at DANGER, TAME] **1** *now dial* : to get the better of : CONQUER, SUBDUE **2** : to sap the courage of and subdue through fear : DISCOURAGE, INTIMIDATE ⟨obstacles that would have ~*ed* a man of less intrepid mind —Adeline Adams⟩ **syn** see DISMAY

²daunt \", -a-\ *n* -s [ME, fr. *daunten,* v.] *now dial Eng* : DISCOURAGEMENT

daunt·ing·ly *adv* : in a manner or to a degree that daunts ⟨~ difficult —Philip Toynbee⟩

daunt·less \'dȯntləs, -'ä-,-'á-\ *adj* : marked by courageous resolution : incapable of being daunted, intimidated, or subdued ⟨a ~ captain⟩ ⟨a ~ spirit⟩ **syn** see BRAVE

daunt·less·ly *adv* : in a dauntless manner

daunt·less·ness *n* -ES : the quality of being dauntless : COURAGE, BRAVERY

daun·ton \'dȯntᵊn, -'ä-,-'a-\ *vt* -ED/-ING/-S [by alter.] *archaic Scot* : ¹DAUNT

dau·phin \'dȯfən, 'dō,faⁿ, 'dō,faⁿ\ *n* -s *often cap* [alter. (influenced by F *dauphin,* fr. OF *dolfin*) of earlier *daulphin, dolphin,* fr. ME *dolphyn,* fr. MF *dalfin, dalphin,* fr. *Dalfin, Dolphin,* the surname of certain lords in medieval southeastern France] **1** : a feudal lord of a French territory or province **2** [MF *dalfin, dalphin;* fr. the fact that the assumption of this title by the eldest sons of the kings of France was a condition of the cession of the Dauphiné to the house of Valois in the 14th cent.] : the eldest son of the king of France — used as a title for the eldest sons from the 14th century to 1830

¹dau·phine \dō'fēn, dō'-, '=,=\ *n* -s *often cap* [F, fr. MF *daufine, dalfine,* fem. of *dalfin*] : DAUPHINESS

²dau·phi·né \¦dōfō¦nā, ¦dōf-\ *adj* [F (*à la*) *Dauphiné,* lit., in the manner of Dauphiné, region in southeastern France] *of potatoes* : mashed, shaped into balls, and fried usu. in deep fat

dau·phin·ess \'dȯfənəs\ *n, pl* **dauphinesses** *often cap* [fr. earlier *daulphinesse, dolphinesse,* fr. *daulphin, dolphyn* dauphin + *-esse* -ess] : the wife of the dauphin

¹daur \'dȧr\ *Scot var of* DARE

²daur \'dau̇(ə)r\ *n, pl* **daur** \"\ *or* **dau·ri** \-)rē\ *usu cap* : a member of certain Manchu-Tungus peoples of the Amur basin related to the Manchus

dau·ri·an \'dau̇rēən\ *n* -s *usu cap* [²*Daur* + E *-ian*] : DAUR

daur·na \'dȧrnə\ [¹*daur* + *na*] *chiefly Scot* : dare not

daut *or* **dawt** \'dȧt, -ō-\ *vt* [origin unknown] *chiefly Scot* : to make much of : FONDLE, CARESS

daut·ie *or* **dawt·ie** \-ti\ *n* -s [*daut, dawt* + *-ie*] *chiefly Scot* : DARLING, DEAR

daut·it \-tət\ *past of* DAUT

dauw \'dau̇\ *n* -s [obs. Afrik (now *dou*), fr. a native word in southern Africa] : BURCHELL'S ZEBRA

dav·ach *or* **dav·och** \'davək\ *n* -s [ME (Sc dial.), fr. ScGael *dabhach* (also, tub); akin to OIr *dabach* tub, land measure] *archaic* : any of various ancient Scottish units of land area said to have averaged 416 acres

da·vai·nea \də'vānēə\ *n* [NL, after Casimir J. *Davaine* †1882 Fr. physician] **1** *cap* : a genus of very small taenioid tapeworms infesting the intestine of gallinaceous birds and occas. of man **2** -s : any tapeworm of the genus *Davainea* — **da·vai·ne·id** \-ēəd\ *adj or n*

dav·ai·ne·i·dae \,davə'nēə,dē\ *n pl, cap* [NL, fr. *Davainea,* type genus + *-idae*] : a family of small primitive cyclophyllidean tapeworms (type genus *Davainea*) that are chiefly parasites of birds and that have an armed cushion-shaped rostellum, the suckers also often with hooks, and the larva a cysticercoid — see RAILLIETINA

da·val·lia \də'valēə\ *n* [NL, fr. Edmund *Davall* †1798 Eng. botanist in Switzerland + NL *-ia*] **1** *cap* : a genus of Old World tropical ferns (family Polypodiaceae) having scaly creeping rhizomes and ample pinnate or pinnately decompound fronds with marginal sori and cuplike indusia which open toward the leaf apex **2** -s : any plant of the genus *Davallia*

da·vao \'dä,vau̇, də'v-\ *adj, usu cap* [fr. *Davao,* Philippines] : of or from the city of Davao, Philippines : of the kind or style prevalent in Davao

da·ven \'dävən, 'dȯv-\ *vi* -ED/-ING/-S [Yiddish *davnen* to pray, worship] : to recite the prescribed prayers in the daily and festival Jewish liturgies

dav·en·port \'davən,pȯr¦t, 'davᵊm,p-, 'dabᵊm,p-, -ȯr¦,-ōə¦, -ȯ(ə)¦, *usu* ¦d· +V\ *n* -s [origin unknown] **1** : a small writing desk **2** : a large upholstered sofa often convertible into a bed

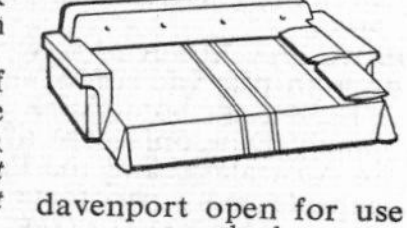

davenport open for use as a bed

¹da·ver \'dāvər\ *vb* [perh. freq. of *deave*] *vi* **1** *chiefly Scot* : to move about as if in a stupor : STAGGER **2** *Scot* : to wander in mind ~ *vt* **1** *Scot* : STUN, DAZE **2** *Scot* : CHILL, BENUMB

²da·ver \'dāvə(r), 'dəv-\ *vi* [origin unknown] *dial Eng* : FADE, WITHER

¹da·vid·ian \də'vidēən, dā'-\ *n* -s *usu cap* [*David* (Jan) Joris (Joriszoon) †1556 Flemish Anabaptist + E *-ian*] : DAVIDIST 2

²da·vid·ian \də'vidēən, dā'-,dä'-, -vēd-\ *adj, usu cap* [Jacques Louis *David* †1825 Fr. painter + E *-ian*] : of, relating to, or like Jacques Louis David or his paintings

da·vid·ic \(')dā¦vidik, də'v-\ *adj, usu cap* [*David* †*ab* 973B.C. king of Judah and Israel + E *-ic*] : of or relating to King David or his family

da·vid·ist \'dāvədəst\ *n* -s *usu cap* [in sense 1, fr. *David* of Dinant *fl* 1200 Belgian scholastic philosopher + E *-ist;* in sense 2, fr. *David* Joris + E *-ist;* in sense 3, fr. Francis *David* †1579 Transylvanian theologist + E *-ist*] **1** : a follower of the philosopher David of Dinant **2** : a follower of the theologist David Joris — called also *Davidian, Jorist* **3** : a follower of the anti-Trinitarian theologist Francis David

david's-harp \'==,=\ *n, pl* **david's-harps** *usu cap D* [after King *David,* who once charmed King Saul with his harp (1 Sam 16:23—AV); fr. the similarity of its flowering stalk to David's harp in old Biblical illustrations] : a Solomon's seal (*Polygonatum multiflorum*)

da·vid·son·ite \'dāvədsə,nīt, ÷ -vəs-\ *n* -s [Thomas *Davidson* †1885 Brit. paleontologist who discovered it near Aberdeen, Scotland + E *-ite*] : a greenish variety of beryl

da·vid·son's plum \-sənz-\ *n* [fr. the name *Davidson*] **1** : the fruit of an Australian tree (*Davidsonia pruriens*) of the family Cunoniaceae having a sharply acid reddish blue juice **2** : the tree that bears the Davidson's plum

da·vid's squirrel \dä'vēdz-, 'dāvədz-\ *n, usu cap D* [after Abbé Armand *David* †1900 Fr. missionary and naturalist] : a grayish cliff-dwelling ground squirrel (*Sciurotamias davidianus*) occurring in several races in mountainous southern China

da·vie·ly \'dāvili\ *adv* [perh. alter. of Sc *davert* (past part. of ¹*daver*) + *-ly*] *Scot* : LISTLESSLY

da·vie·sia \dā'vēzh(ē)ə, də'-\ *n, cap* [NL, fr. Hugh *Davies* †1821 Brit. botanist + NL *-ia*] : a large genus of Australasian shrubs (family Leguminosae) having small yellow or purple flowers succeeded by short triangular pods

da·vies·ite \'dāvē,zīt, -və,sīt\ *n* -s [Thomas *Davies* †1891 Eng. mineralogist + E *-ite*] : a mineral consisting of a lead oxychloride occurring in minute colorless orthorhombic crystals

da·vi·son·ite \'dāvəsə,nīt\ *n* -s *usu cap* [John M. *Davison* †1915 Amer. chemist and mineralogist + E *-ite*] : a mineral $Ca_3Al(PO_4)_2(OH)_3.H_2O(?)$ consisting of a hydrous basic phosphate of calcium and aluminum

da·vit \ˈdāvət *also* ˈdav-; *by most speakers* -vəd· *when a vowel immediately follows, and by seamen sometimes* -ăvəd *in all positions*\ *n* -s [alter. of earlier *david*, prob. fr. the name *David*] **:** a fixed or movable crane that projects over the side of a ship or over a hatchway and is used esp. for hoisting ship's boats, anchors, or cargo

1, 1, davits

davoch *var of* DAVACH

da·vy \ˈdāvē\ *n* -ES [by shortening & alter.] *slang* **:** AFFIDAVIT

da·vy jones's locker \ˌdāvēˈjōnz(əz)-\ *n, usu cap D&J* [after *Davy Jones*, legendary spirit of the sea] **:** the bottom of the ocean **:** a grave in the sea ⟨gone down to *Davy Jones's locker*⟩

da·vy lamp \ˈdāvē-\ *n, usu cap D* [after Sir Humphry *Davy* †1829 Eng. chemist, its inventor] **:** an early safety lamp

davy's gray *n, often cap D* [prob. after Sir Humphry *Davy*] **:** STEEL GRAY

¹daw \ˈdȯ, ˈdō\ *vi* **dawed** \-ȯd, -ōd\ *or sometimes* **dew** \ˈd(y)ü\ **daw·en** \ˈdȯən, ˈdōən\ *or sometimes* **dawed; dawing; daws** [ME *dawen, dagen*, fr. OE *dagian;* akin to OHG *tagēn* to dawn, ON *daga*, denominatives fr. the root of E *day*] *chiefly Scot* **:** DAWN

²daw \ˈdȯ, *Scot* ˈdä *or* ˈdō\ *n* -S [ME *dawe;* akin to OHG *taha* jackdaw] **1 :** JACKDAW **2** *obs* **:** NITWIT, SIMPLETON, FOOL **3** *Scot* **a :** a lazy person **:** SLUGGARD **b :** a slovenly woman **:** SLATTERN

³daw *vt* -ED/-ING/-S [short for *adaw*] *obs* **:** DAUNT

⁴daw \ˈdō\ *n* -S [IrGael & ScGael *dath* color, dye, stain, fr. OIr *dath* color; akin to OIr *date* agreeable] **:** the pinkish yellow color of the eyes of some game fowls

¹daw·dle \ˈdȯdᵊl\ *vb* **dawdled; dawdled; dawdling** \-ȯd-(ᵊ)liŋ\ **dawdles** [origin unknown] *vi* **:** to waste time in idle lingering **:** spend more time than is necessary or usual in doing something (~ over your work) **:** LOITER ⟨*dawdled* about in the vestibule —Jane Austen⟩ ~ *vt* **:** to spend fruitlessly **:** WASTE ⟨*dawdled* my time with . . . symbolic logic —M.R.Cohen⟩ **:** spend lackadaisically ⟨~ away their vacation —Angus Wilson⟩ ⟨~ away four years in college⟩ **syn** see DELAY

²dawdle \ˈ"\ *n* -S **1 :** DAWDLER **2 :** the act or an instance of dawdling ⟨a . . . ~ over some of the book catalogs —O.W. Holmes †1935⟩

daw·dler \-ȯd(ᵊ)lə(r)\ *n* -S **:** one that dawdles **:** IDLER

daw·dling·ly *adv* **:** in a dawdling manner

daw·dling·ness *n* -ES **:** the quality or state of being dawdling

dawes' limit \ˈdȯz(əz)-\ *n, usu cap D* [after William R. *Dawes* †1868 Eng. astronomer] **:** an approximate value of the resolving power of a telescope based on the theoretical size of the spurious disk being equal in seconds of arc to 4.56 divided by the aperture of the telescope expressed in inches

¹dawn \ˈdȯn, ˈdän\ *vi* -ED/-ING/-S [ME *dawnen*, prob. back-formation fr. *dawning*] **1 :** to begin to grow light in the morning **:** grow light with or as if with the light of the rising sun ⟨the day ~*s*⟩ **2 :** to make an initial appearance **:** begin to develop ⟨the day of mammals had ~*ed* —W.E.Swinton⟩ ⟨a watery smile ~*ed* on Joe's face —Marguerite Steen⟩ **3 :** to become apparent **:** begin to be perceived or understood — usu. used with *on* ⟨it ~*ed* on me that he was an utter fool⟩ ⟨the truth ~*ed* on him at last —T.B.Costain⟩

²dawn \ˈ"\ *n* -S **1 :** the first appearance of light in the morning **:** show of approaching sunrise **:** morning twilight **:** DAYBREAK ⟨by the ~*'s* early light —F.S.Key⟩ **2 :** first appearance **:** OPENING, BEGINNING ⟨~ of the Renaissance⟩ ⟨~ of human consciousness —W.J.Reilly⟩ **3 :** a moderate pink that is yellower and less strong than arbutus pink and bluer and stronger than hydrangea pink

dawn blue *n* **:** a pale blue that is redder and paler than average powder blue or Sistine and greener and paler than average cadet gray

dawn gray *n* **:** a medium gray that is very slightly darker than platinum

dawn–horse \ˈ⸗,⸗\ *n* [trans. of NL *Eohippus*] **:** a member of the genus *Eohippus*

dawn·ing \ˈdȯniŋ, ˈdän-, -nēŋ\ *n* -S [ME *dawning, dawening*, alter. (influenced by ME *evening*) of *dawing*, fr. OE *dagung*, fr. *dagian* to dawn + *-ung* -ing — more at DAW] **1 :** DAYBREAK, DAWN ⟨in the gray of cold ~ —Ethel Wilson⟩ **2 :** BEGINNING ⟨the ~ of the Gilded Age —J.D.Hart⟩

dawn man *n, often cap D&M* [trans. of NL *Eoanthropus*] **1 :** a primitive extinct man **2 :** PILTDOWN MAN

dawn patrol *n* **1 :** a reconnaissance flight made in the early morning usu. to observe enemy positions or movements **2 :** station personnel who prepare and put on very early morning radio or television programs

dawn pink *n* **:** a grayish purplish pink that is redder, less strong, and slightly darker than average orchid mist and redder and less strong than cameo pink

dawn redwood *n* **:** a Chinese redwood (*Metasequoia glyptostroboides*) resembling the American Coast redwood but having ascending branches and deciduous foliage

dawn stone *n* **:** EOLITH

daw·ny \ˈdȯni, ˈdäni\ *adj* [IrGael *donaidhe;* akin to MIr *dona* wretched] **1** *Irish* **:** in poor health **:** SICKLY **2** *Irish* **:** SMALL, PUNY

daws *pres 3d sing of* DAW, *pl of* DAW

daw·so·nia \dȯˈsōnēə, -nyə\ *n, cap* [NL, fr. *Dawson* Turner †1858 Eng. botanist + NL *-ia*] **:** a genus (the type of the family Dawsoniaceae) of large tufted erect mosses occurring in Australasia and the East Indies and having a dorsiventral capsule and a peristome subtended by numerous filamentous hairs — see DAWSONIALES, GIANT MOSS

daw·so·ni·a·les \(ˌ)dȯ,sōnēˈā(ˌ)lēz\ *n pl, cap* [NL, fr. *Dawsonia* + *-ales*] **:** an order of musci that is closely related to and sometimes included in the order Polytrichales from which it differs chiefly in the form of the capsule and in the size of the gametophore and that is coextensive with the genus *Dawsonia*

daw·son·ite \ˈdȯsᵊn,īt\ *n* -S [Sir John W. *Dawson* †1899 Canad. geologist + E *-ite*] **:** a mineral $NaAl(CO_3)(OH)_2$ consisting of a basic aluminum sodium carbonate occurring in white bladed crystals (sp. gr. 2.40)

dawt *var of* DAUT

dawtie *var of* DAUTIE

dawt·it \ˈdätət, ˈdȯt-\ *past of* DAWT

¹day \ˈdā\ *n* -S [ME, fr. OE *dæg;* akin to OHG *tag* day, ON *dagr*, Goth *dags*, OE *dōgor* day, ON *døgr, døgn* twelve-hour period, day, night; all prob. fr. a prehistoric Gmc blend of a form or forms akin to Skt *ahn-, ahar* twelve-hour period, day, night and a form or forms akin to L *fovēre* to warm, Gk *tephra* ashes, Skt *dahati* he burns] **1 :** the time of light or interval between one night and the next **:** the time between sunrise and sunset or from dawn to darkness **2 :** the period of the earth's rotation on its axis ordinarily divided into 24 hours, measured by the interval between two successive transits of a celestial body over the same meridian, and taking a specific name from that of the body — see SOLAR DAY, MEAN SOLAR DAY, SIDEREAL DAY **3 a :** CIVIL DAY **b** *among most modern nations* **:** the mean solar day of 24 hours beginning at mean midnight **4 a :** a day set aside for a particular purpose ⟨rent ~⟩ ⟨Monday is wash ~⟩ **b** *sometimes cap* (1) **:** a date on which some notable event occurred or on which the occurrence of a notable event is celebrated ⟨your wedding ~⟩ ⟨New Year's *Day*⟩ (2) **:** a particular day that is identified by reference to or that is commonly associated with some unique historical event ⟨Pearl Harbor *Day*⟩ **c :** the conflict or contention of the day ⟨he was confident he could carry the ~⟩ **d** *archaic* **:** one's set day of the week or month for receiving callers **e** *Scot* **:** TODAY — used with *the* **f** *sometimes cap* **:** a date on which some major event is expected to occur — used with *the* ⟨socialists of the eighties and nineties who . . . yearned for The *Day* —E.R. Bentley⟩ **5 :** DAYLIGHT ⟨at the break of ~⟩ **6 a :** the period of the existence or prominence of a person or thing **:** AGE — usu. used in pl. ⟨in the ~*s* of sailing ships⟩ **b :** the term of one's career, activity, or life **:** LIFETIME ⟨grandfather's stories about sports in his ~⟩ **:** the time during which one's life continues — usu. used in pl. ⟨the general's last ~*s*⟩ **7 a :** the distance usu. traversed in an ordinary day's travel ⟨a ship two ~*s* out of port⟩ **b :** a unit consisting of the labor or output of one individual in one day **8** *obs* **a :** a period of grace esp. for debtors **b :** a space of time **9 a :** the hours or the daily recurring period established by usage or law for work ⟨an 8-hour ~⟩ **b :** a trading session on an exchange ⟨a 3,000,000-share ~⟩ **c :** a conventional unit for calculating pay of railroad employees based on hours worked and distance run **10 :** a division of a window **:** LIGHT **11 :** the time required by a celestial body in turning once on its axis ⟨the moon's ~ is 27 solar days⟩ **12 :** the surface of the ground over a mine — **day after day :** continuously over a period of time measured in days ⟨watching the horizon for a sail *day after day*⟩ **:** for an indefinite or seemingly endless number of days — **day in, day out :** for an indefinite number of successive days without interruption, change, or rest ⟨he does nothing but work *day in, day out*⟩ — **from day to day 1 :** in such a way as to be noticeable or measurable each successive day ⟨he improves *from day to day*⟩ **2 :** without looking further than one day ahead **:** from one day to the next — **this day week :** the same day a week after or before — **without day :** sine die

²day \ˈ"\ *vt* -ED/-ING/-S *archaic* **:** to measure by the day

day·ak *also* **dy·ak** \ˈdīˌak, -īək\ *n, pl* **dayak** *or* **dayaks** *usu cap* [Malay *dayak* up-country] **1 a :** any of several Indonesian peoples in the interior regions of Borneo — compare IBAN, KENYA, LAND DAYAK, NGADJU **b :** a member of any of such peoples **2 :** the language of the Dayak peoples

da·yan \däˈyän, dī-, -yȯn\ *n, pl* **daya·nim** \-nəm\ *also* **dayans** \-nz\ [Heb *dayyān*] **:** a judge in a rabbinical court **:** an expert in Jewish law to whom rabbis in orthodox Jewish communities refer questions about matters of religious observance

day beacon *n* **:** any of various unlighted structures (as a masonry tower) serving as a daytime aid to navigation

daybed \ˈ⸗,⸗\ *n* **1 :** a chaise longue of the type made 1680–1780 **2 :** a couch with low head and foot pieces often like chair backs

18th century daybed

day·ber·ry \ˈdā— *see* BERRY\ *n* [fr. earlier *dabberry, deberry*] *dial Eng* **:** a wild gooseberry

day blindness *n* **:** HEMERALOPIA

daybook \ˈ⸗,⸗\ *n* **1 :** DIARY, JOURNAL **2 :** a book formerly used in accounting in which details of transactions of the day are recorded chronologically in diary form

day boy *n* **:** a day student at a boys' boarding school esp. in Great Britain

daybreak \ˈ⸗,⸗\ *n* **:** the first appearance of light in the morning or the time of such appearance **:** DAWN

day–by–day \ˌdā(ˌ)bīˌdā, -bə-\ *adj* [ME *day by day* daily, adv.] **:** occurring on each successive day **:** DAILY ⟨*day-by-day* labors of thousands of men and women —H.S.Truman⟩

day camp *n* **:** a camp providing activities and care for children during the daytime only

day coach *n* **:** COACH 1c

daydawn \ˈ⸗,⸗\ *n, archaic* **:** DAYBREAK

day degree *n* **:** one degree above or below a temperature adopted as a standard (as 42° F for the temperature at which vegetation commences) for a period of 24 hours or its equivalent (as 2° for 12 hours or 4° for 6 hours)

¹daydream \ˈ⸗,⸗\ *n* [*day* + *dream*] **:** a dream experienced while awake; *esp* **:** a gratifying reverie usu. of wish fulfillment **syn** see FANCY

²daydream \ˈ"\ *vi* **:** to engage in daydreams ⟨the chance to ~ about a world which has never existed —Maurice Edelman⟩ ~ *vt* **:** to transport (oneself) by or as if by daydreams ⟨the handyman and the little dancer ~ themselves into the leading parts . . . of the ballet —George Amberg⟩ **:** imagine in or as if in a daydream

day·dream·er \-mə(r)\ *n* **:** one that daydreams

day·dreamy \-mē, -mi\ *adj* **1 :** having the quality of a daydream **2 :** given to daydreams

day drift *n, mining* **:** a drift with one end at the surface so that daylight is admitted

day fighter *n* **:** a short-range fighter-interceptor designed for high-speed interception of enemy aircraft in conditions of good visibility and daylight

dayflower \ˈ⸗,⸗\ *n* **:** any of several flowers that soon perish: as **a :** a plant of the genus *Commelina; esp* **:** a troublesome weed (*C. communis*) **b :** SPIDERWORT **c :** a rockrose (*Cistus ladaniferus*) of southern Europe with large white yellow-spotted flowers

day gate *n* **:** an inner grating used while a safety vault is open

day in court 1 : a day or opportunity for appearance in a lawsuit **2 :** an opportunity to present one's point of view or argument ⟨Republicans had apparently not bothered to prepare for their biggest *day in court* —*Time*⟩

day jessamine *n* **:** a West Indian aromatic shrub (*Cestrum diurnum*) whose white flowers are sweet-scented by day

day labor *n* [ME *dai labour*] **1 :** labor performed as a daily task **:** labor done or paid for by the day **2 :** laborers hired by the day — usu. used of persons without special training

day laborer *n* **:** one that works by the day or for daily wages esp. as an unskilled laborer

day·less \ˈdāləs\ *adj* **:** lacking daylight

day letter *n* **:** a telegram sent during the day that has a lower priority than a regular telegram

¹daylight \ˈ⸗,⸗\ *n* [ME, fr. *day* + *light*] **1 :** the light of day as opposed to the darkness of night **:** the light of the sun plus the sky as opposed to that of the moon or to artificial light; *often* **:** the diffused and reflected light of the sun and the sky as distinguished from sunlight and from artificial light **2 :** the time of daylight **:** DAYBREAK ⟨arise before ~⟩ **3 a :** knowledge or understanding of something that has been obscure or of something that could not be foretold ⟨the professor's lecture threw some ~ on the problem⟩ **b :** OPENNESS, PUBLICITY ⟨the new diplomacy . . . has to operate in ~ —Dag Hammarskjöld⟩ **4 daylights** *pl, archaic slang* **:** EYES **5 :** a clear or open space ⟨you could see ~ between the cracks⟩; *esp* **:** the maximum distance between the chase bed and the platen of a platen press **6 daylights** *pl, slang* **:** vital organs **:** INSIDES; *also* **:** WITS ⟨scare the ~*s* out of you —E.A.McCourt⟩ ⟨walloped the ~*s* out of him —Dan Polier⟩

²daylight \ˈ"\ *vb* **daylighted; daylighted** *also* **daylit; daylighting; daylights** *vt* **:** to provide or light up (as a classroom) with daylight ~ *vi* **:** to supply daylight

daylight blue *n* **1 :** a pigment prepared by mixing Prussian blue with barium sulfate **2 :** the color of average daylight considered a blue if skylight under average noon sunlight is taken as gray or neutral but closely approximating gray if according to the practice of recent years overcast skylight or sunlight outside the earth's atmosphere is taken as the neutral gray

daylight factor *n* **:** the ratio of the illumination from windows at any point indoors to that out in the open, the test surface being horizontal in each case — called also *window-efficiency ratio*

daylight glass *n* **:** a bluish glass often colored with cobalt that is used with incandescent lamps to absorb the excess radiations in the red part of the spectrum and thus give the effect of daylight

daylight lamp *n* **:** an incandescent or fluorescent lamp that gives an artificial light whose energy distribution approximates that of daylight

daylight saving time *also* **daylight saving** *or* **daylight time** *n* **:** time that is ahead of standard time usu. by one hour but sometimes by two hours and that is used in some places esp. in spring, summer, and fall for the purpose of utilizing all the daylight hours for daytime activities — abbr. *DST*

daylight train *n* **:** DAY TRAIN

daylight vision *n* **:** vision adapted to daylight **:** photopic vision

day lily *n* [so called fr. the fact that each blooms for only one day] **1 a :** a plant of the genus *Hemerocallis* being native to Europe and Asia but cosmopolitan in cultivation and as escapes, having complex tuberous roots and long narrow basal leaves, and bearing short-lived flowers that resemble lilies and are yellow or tawny orange in the wild but under cultivation have developed pinkish and mahogany to purplish forms **b :** the flower of a day lily **2 :** PLANTAIN LILY

day loan *n* **:** a bank loan maturing within a day usu. on an unsecured promissory note — called also *clearance loan, morning loan*

¹daylong \ˈ⸗,⸗\ *adj* **:** lasting all day ⟨a ~ parade⟩

²daylong \ˈ⸗,⸗\ *adv* **:** during the entire day ⟨light of the sun pours ~ into the saw grass —Marjory S. Douglas⟩

day·man \ˈdāmən, -ˌman\ *n, pl* **daymen 1 :** a worker paid by time rather than piecework **:** DAY LABORER **2 :** one (as a stagehand or sailor) who works during the daytime

daymare \ˈ⸗,⸗\ *n* -S [¹*day* + *-mare* (as in *nightmare*)] **:** distress while awake like that experienced in nightmare

daymark \ˈ⸗,⸗\ *n* **:** a marker visible to pilots as a navigation guide in daylight

daynet *n, obs* **:** CLAPNET

day nettle *n* [*day* prob. by folk etymology fr. a word of Scand origin; akin to ON akr*dāi* hemp nettle, Faroese *dāi*, Norw *dåe, dæe*, Sw *då;* akin to ON *dā* senselessness, *deyja* to die — more at DIE] **:** HEMP NETTLE

day neutral *adj* **:** developing and maturing regardless of relative length of alternating exposures to light and dark periods — compare PHOTOPERIODISM

day nursery *n* **:** a public center for the care and training of young children; *often* **:** NURSERY SCHOOL

day of atonement *usu cap D&A* [trans. of Heb *yōm kippūr*] **:** YOM KIPPUR

day of fire : a unit of ammunition based on the average expenditure of a weapon in a day of combat

day of judgment *usu cap D&J* [trans. of Heb *yōm haddīn* (the) day (of) the judgment] **1 :** JUDGMENT DAY **2 :** ROSH HASHANAH

day of memorial *usu cap D&M* [trans. of Heb *yōm hazzikkārōn* (the) day (of) the memorial] **:** ROSH HASHANAH

day of reckoning : a time when the consequences of a course of mistakes or misdeeds are felt ⟨the flow of wealth . . . hurried overstocking and brought the *day of reckoning* nearer —R.A. Billington⟩

day of supply : a quantity (as of food, clothing or ammunition) taken as the average daily requirement of a body of troops in a given situation

day of the covenant *usu cap D&C* **:** December 16 observed in So. Africa as a legal holiday celebrating the anniversary of the defeat of the Zulu chieftain Dingaan by Dutch immigrants in 1838

day of the lord *usu cap L* [ME] **:** a day inaugurating the eternal universal rule of God: **a** *in the Old Testament* **:** an eschatological day of ultimate judgment bringing final deliverance or doom — called also *day of Yahweh* **b** *in the New Testament* **:** the triumphant day of Christ's return to earth in glory

day order *n* **:** a customer's order to a broker that expires automatically at the close of the day on which it is made if it is not executed or canceled — compare OPEN ORDER

day owl *n* **:** an owl that is partially or wholly diurnal; *esp* **:** SHORT-EARED OWL

day–peep \ˈ⸗,⸗\ *n, archaic* **:** DAYBREAK

day rate *n* **:** the prescribed amount of pay for a specified job of work paid for by the day or hour

dayroom \ˈ⸗,⸗\ *n* **:** a room (as in a military barracks) fitted up for reading, writing, and recreation

day rule *n* **:** a former order of court in English law allowing a prisoner on civil process to go beyond the prison limits for a single day

days \ˈdāz\ *adv* [ME *dayes*, fr. OE *dæges*, gen. of *dæg* day — more at DAY] **:** in the daytime repeatedly ⟨works ~ and goes to school nights⟩ **:** on any day

day school *n* **:** an elementary or secondary school held on weekdays; *specif* **:** a private school without boarding facilities

day's duty *n* **:** a 24-hour tour of duty on ship

day shift *n* **:** a shift of workers who work during daylight hours

dayshine \ˈ⸗,⸗\ *n* **:** DAYLIGHT

dayside \ˈ⸗,⸗\ *n* **:** the staff that works on an afternoon edition of a newspaper — contrasted with *nightside*

day–sign \ˈ⸗,⸗\ *n* **:** a Maya calendar sign designating one of the 20 successive days making up a uinal

days in bank [so called fr. its originally being the practice of the Court of Common Bank in England] *English law* **:** certain days for the return of writs and the appearance of parties

days·man \ˈdāzmən\ *n, pl* **daysmen 1** [ME *daysemen*, fr. *dayes* (gen. of *day* day set for arbitration) + *-man*] *archaic* **:** UMPIRE, ARBITER ⟨neither is there any ~ betwixt us —Job 9: 33 (AV)⟩ **2** *archaic* **:** DAY LABORER

days of awe *usu cap D&A* [trans. of Heb *yāmīm nōrāʼīm*, lit., fearful days] **:** the 10-day period of the Jewish high holidays including Rosh Hashanah and Yom Kippur

days of grace [trans. of L *dies gratiae*] **1 :** the days that immediately follow the day on which a bill or note becomes due on its face and that are allowed to the debtor in which to make payment **2 :** GRACE PERIOD

dayspring \ˈ⸗,⸗\ *n* [ME, fr. *day* + *spring*] **1** *archaic* **:** the beginning of day **:** DAWN **2 :** the beginning of a new era or order of things ⟨the ~ of their youth —W.B.Yeats⟩

daystar \ˈ⸗,⸗\ *n* [ME *daysterre*, fr. OE *dægsteorra*, fr. *dæg* day + *steorra* star — more at DAY, STAR] **1 :** MORNING STAR **2 :** SUN 1a(1)

day student *also* **day scholar** *n* **:** a student at a residential school or college who attends classes and other academic exercises but does not live in the institution

day's work *n* **1 :** the amount of work during one day prescribed or required on a given job **:** the legal amount of work in terms of hours as governed by statute or by agreement **2 :** the reckoning and observations made for 24 hours from noon to noon to determine a ship's position

day·tale \ˈdātᵊl\ *n* [*day* + *tale* (count)] *dial Eng* **:** the reckoning esp. of work or wages by the day ⟨a ~ laborer⟩

day tank *n* **:** a tank furnace in which 5 to 10 tons of glass are melted and refined in one day to be hand-shaped the next day

day ticket *n, Brit* **:** a railway ticket good for only one day

daytime \ˈ⸗,⸗\ *n* **:** the time during which there is daylight

daytimes \-mz\ *adv* [*daytime* + *-s* (adv. suffix)] **:** during the hours of daylight

day–to–day \ˈdādə,dā, ˈdātə-\ *adj* **1 :** a day at a time in unbroken succession **:** DAILY ⟨newspapers report *day-to-day* events⟩ **2 :** a day at a time without provision for continuance thereafter ⟨life . . . lived on an aimless, *day-to-day* basis —Siegfried Giedion⟩

day–to–day loan *or* **day–to–day money** *n, Brit* **:** CALL LOAN

day·ton \ˈdātᵊn\ *adj, usu cap* [fr. *Dayton*, Ohio] **:** of or from the city of Dayton, Ohio **:** of the kind or style prevalent in Dayton

day·to·ni·an \(ˈ)dā¦tōnēən\ *n* -S *cap* [*Dayton*, Ohio + E *-ian*] **:** a native or resident of Dayton, Ohio

day train *n* **:** a train scheduled to complete its journey during daylight hours — called also *daylight train*

daywoman *var of* DEYWOMAN

daywork \ˈ⸗,⸗\ *n* **1 :** work paid for at a rate per unit of time worked as distinguished from work done under a wage incentive plan **2 :** work on a day shift

dayworker \ˈ⸗,⸗⸗\ *n* **:** one engaged in daywork

daywrit \ˈ⸗,⸗\ *n* **:** DAY RULE

¹daze \ˈdāz\ *vt* -ED/-ING/-S [ME *dasen*, fr. ON *dasa* (as in *dasask* to become exhausted); akin to D *dazen* to hesitate, MHG *dæsic* quiet, stupid, ON *dāsi* lazy person, and prob. to OE *demm* injury, loss, L *fames* hunger] **1 :** to stupefy esp. by a blow **:** make numb **:** STUN ⟨he swung at him, *dazed* him, and drove him along the bar —Morley Callaghan⟩ **2 :** to confuse or dazzle with light ⟨the whiteness of the walls ~*s* me⟩

syn DAZE, STUN, BEMUSE, STUPEFY, TORPIFY, BENUMB, PARALYZE, and PETRIFY can apply, in common, to a forcefully disturbing experience or influence and mean, in common, to dull or deaden the powers of the mind. DAZE usu. implies a bewilderment or confusion from a blow, a shock, a sudden excess of light, and so on ⟨too stunned and *dazed* by the suddenness with which events had happened during the last twenty-four hours to be able to realize his position —Samuel Butler †1902⟩ ⟨*dazed* by the lantern glare —Rudyard Kipling⟩ ⟨a grief-*dazed* mother⟩ STUN usu. suggests the deprivation of powers of thought, or a usu. momentary loss of consciousness, from a heavy blow or something conceived of as resembling a heavy blow ⟨I was knocked headlong across the floor against the oven handle and *stunned*. I was insensible for a long time

—H.G.Wells⟩ ⟨the swing doors burst open with a crash. There was an instant's *stunned* silence —Nevil Shute⟩ ⟨a world *stunned* and only just beginning to awaken from the stupefying effect of war —Aneurin Bevan⟩ ⟨*stunned* by a sudden declaration of love⟩ BEMUSE implies an addling or muddling of the mind, typically through intoxication ⟨an alcohol-*bemused* tramp⟩ ⟨the noise of London *bemused* her more than the noise of the sea —Ngaio Marsh⟩ ⟨so *bemused* by theories of meaning that we have lost sight of what men do in fact mean —Iredell Jenkins⟩ STUPEFY heightens the implication of stupor or stupidity, implying not so much a blow or shock as some cause like an injury, intoxication, or long-continued grief or anxiety ⟨the ship . . . reeled, trembled, and stopped her way, as if [the heavy sea] had *stupefied* her —Frederick Marryat⟩ ⟨half *stupefied* with sleep and fatigue —Elizabeth Goudge⟩ ⟨a dull misery *stupefied* her thoughts —Ellen Glasgow⟩ TORPIFY is close to STUPEFY but stresses torpor of body resulting in torpor of mind and usu. implying a physical cause ⟨a drug that *torpifies* the rational faculties⟩ BENUMB applies usu. to the effect of cold in deadening the sensations or immobilizing muscle action; in extension, it strongly suggests this effect ⟨it is so cold, so dark, my senses are so *benumbed* —Charles Dickens⟩ ⟨her senses remained *benumbed* by toil —Ellen Glasgow⟩ ⟨Charlotte's cold resolution *benumbed* her courage, and she could find no immediate reply —Edith Wharton⟩ PARALYZE is often used to imply an inability to act or function that results from some dire event ⟨why does danger *paralyze* the will and intelligence of some men —Bernard De Voto⟩ ⟨the grim panic which *paralyzed* business and agriculture in the West —R.A.Billington⟩ PETRIFY emphasizes an immediate strong, figuratively paralyzing effect, usu. of fear, suggesting complete inability to move, think, or speak, and lending itself easily to conversational hyperbole ⟨the *petrifying* effect of fear —E.A.Armstrong⟩ ⟨a tiger, serenely gazing at me barely twenty yards away. I was *petrified* at first —Suresh Vaidya⟩ ⟨I was *petrified* to think my wallet had been lost⟩

[2]daze \"\ *n* -s **1 :** the state of being dazed ⟨went about in a ~⟩ **2 :** mica or any glittering stone

dazed \'dāzd\ *adj* [fr. past part. of E dial. *daze* to become rotten or spoiled, fr. ME *dasen* to stun] *dial Eng* **:** SPOILED, ROTTEN ⟨~ eggs⟩

daz·ed·ly \'dāzədlē\ *adv* **:** in a dazed manner

daz·ed·ness \-zədnəs\ *n* -ES [ME *dasednes*, fr. *dased* + *-nes* -ness] **:** the quality or state of being dazed **:** DAZE

[1]daz·zle \'dazəl\ *vb* **dazzled; dazzled; dazzling** \-z(ə)liŋ\ **dazzles** [freq. of [1]*daze*] *vi* **1 :** to lose clear vision **:** become dim esp. from looking at light that is too bright ⟨the stranger's eyes *dazzled* with the . . . light —Ralph Gustafson⟩ **2 a :** to excite admiration by brilliancy **:** be impressive because of splendor ⟨he ~*s* rather than charms —F.J.Mather⟩ **b :** SHINE ⟨the woods *dazzled* whitely —Truman Capote⟩ **:** REFLECT ⟨the heat ~*s* up from the white slab —R.P.Warren⟩ ~ *vt* **1 :** to overpower (the vision) with light ⟨I *dazzled* his eyes with the brightness of my blade —Padraic Colum⟩ **2 :** to impress deeply, overpower, or confound with showy performance or brilliance ⟨*dazzled* millions with oratory —J.D.Hart⟩ **3** *archaic* **:** eclipse with greater brilliance **:** OUTSHINE — usu. used with *down* or *out*

[2]dazzle \"\ *n* -s **1 :** the action of dazzling **2 :** something that dazzles ⟨the ~ of the river —Elizabeth Goudge⟩

daz·zle·ment \-zəlmənt\ *n* -s **1 :** the action of dazzling **2 :** the state or condition of being dazzled ⟨drew her hand across her eyes to wipe the ~ away —Kay Boyle⟩

daz·zler \-z(ə)lə(r)\ *n* -s **:** one that dazzles ⟨that dress is a ~⟩

dazzle system *n* **:** a system of painting by which a ship's lines are given a distorted appearance and the course she is steering is made difficult to ascertain (as from a submarine)

daz·zling·ly \-z(ə)liŋlē\ *adv* **:** in a dazzling manner **:** to a dazzling degree

db *abbr* **1** debenture **2** decibel

DB *abbr* daybook

DBA *abbr* doing business as

DBH *abbr, often not cap* diameter at breast height

dbk *abbr* drawback

dbl *abbr* double

DBN *abbr, often not cap* de bonis non

DC *abbr* **1** [It *da capo*] from the beginning **2** decimal classification **3** deputy chief **4** deputy consul **5** deviation clause **6** direct current **7** district court **8** double column **9** *often not cap* double crochet

DCL *abbr or n* -s **:** a doctor of civil law

DD *abbr or n* -s **:** a doctor of divinity

dd *abbr* **1** dated **2** delivered

DD *abbr* **1** days after date **2** days after delivery **3** day's date **4** [L *dedicavit*] he dedicated **5** delayed delivery **6** delivered at docks **7** demand draft **8** [L *Deo dedit*] he gave to God **9** deputy director **10** dishonorable discharge **11** [L *dono dedit*] he gave as a gift

d day *n, usu cap 1st D* [[2]*d* (abbr. for *day*)] **:** the day set for launching a specific tactical operation

d-day force *n, usu cap 1st D* **:** the force that is trained, equipped, and ready to fight on the day war begins **:** force in being — used esp. of air forces

DDD \ˌdē,dē'dē\ *n* -s [*d*ichloro-*d*iphenyl-*d*ichloro-ethane] **:** an insecticide $(ClC_6H_4)_2CHCHCl_2$ closely related chemically to DDT and similar in properties — called also *TDE*

DDD *abbr* **1** [L *dat, dicat, dedicat*] he gives, devotes, and dedicates **2** direct distance dialing **3** [L *dono dedit dedicavit*] he gave and dedicated as a gift

DDS *abbr or n* -s **:** a doctor of dental science **:** a doctor of dental surgery

DDSc *abbr or n* -s **:** a doctor of dental science

DDT \ˌdē(ˌ)dē'tē\ *n* -s [*d*ichloro-*d*iphenyl-*t*richloro-ethane] **:** a colorless odorless water-insoluble crystalline insecticide $(ClC_6H_4)_2CHCCl_3$ usu. made from chloral and chlorobenzene and used esp. against body lice, houseflies, mosquitoes, and agricultural pests — called also *chlorophenothane, dicophane*

d duct *n, usu cap 1st D* **:** a duct placed in a double-skinned leading edge of an airfoil in order to supply hot air for thermal anti-icing

de *var of* DEE

de- *prefix* [ME, fr. OF *de-, des-*, partly fr. L *de-* from, down, away (fr. *de*) and partly fr. L *dis-*; L *de* akin to OIr *di* from, Gk *dē* now, then, OE *tō* to — more at TO, DIS-] **1 a :** do the opposite of **:** reverse (a specified action) ⟨*de*centralize⟩ ⟨*de*code⟩ **b :** reverse of ⟨*de*calescence⟩ **2 :** remove (a specified thing or things) from ⟨*de*horn⟩ ⟨*de*louse⟩ **:** remove from (a specified thing) ⟨*de*throne⟩ **3 :** reduce **:** make lower ⟨*de*rate⟩ **4** [L] **:** something derived or compounded from (a specified thing) ⟨*de*compound, n.⟩ **:** derived or compounded from something (of a specified nature) ⟨*de*compound, adj.⟩ — often in grammatical terms (nouns or adjectives) ending in *-al* or *-ative* ⟨*de*adjectival⟩ ⟨*de*verbative⟩ **5 :** get off of (a specified thing) ⟨*de*bus⟩ ⟨*de*train⟩ **6 :** having a molecule characterized by the removal of one or more atoms of (a specified element) — in combining forms occurring in names of chemical compounds ⟨*de*hydro-⟩ ⟨*de*oxy-⟩ **7 :** cause to cease to (perform a specified action) ⟨*de*-emanate⟩

DE *abbr* **1** deckle edged **2** destroyer escort **3** double entry

dea *abbr* deacon

de·acetylate \(ˌ)dē+\ *vt* [*de-* + *acetylate*] **:** to remove acetyl from (a compound) usu. by hydrolysis — **de·acetylation** \"+\ *n*

de·acidification \ˌdē+\ *n* **:** the process of deacidifying

de·acidify \"+\ *vt* [*de-* + *acidify*] **:** to remove acid from **:** reduce the acidity of (as by neutralization)

[1]dea·con \'dēkən *sometimes* -kəŋ\ *n* -s [ME *dekne, dekene*, fr. OE *dīacon, dēacon*, fr. LL *diaconus*, fr. Gk *diakonos diēkonos*, lit., servant, fr. *dia-, diē-* (alter. of *dia-*) + *-konos* (akin to Gk *enkonein* to be active in service); akin to L *conari* to attempt — more at DIA-] **1 :** a subordinate officer in a Christian church **:** as **a** *Roman Catholicism* (1) **:** a cleric in major orders ranking above a subdeacon and below a priest and having as a principal function close assistance of the celebrant at solemn High Mass and other solemn services (2) **:** one serving as a deacon at solemn High Mass or other solemn services **b** *Anglicanism* **:** one in orders next below that of priest and now usu. a candidate for ordination to the priesthood **c** *Congregationalism* **:** a layman having some duties similar to those of a ruling elder in Presbyterian churches **d** *Lutheranism* (1) **:** a layman in an office subordinate to that of pastor and elder (2) **:** an assistant minister of a church in which there are several ministers **e** *Mormonism* **:** one ordained to the lowest grade of the Aaronic priesthood who serves as assistant to the teacher **2** *Scot* **a :** the president of an incorporated trade or craft **b :** a proficient workman **:** MASTER **3 :** one of two officers in a Masonic lodge ⟨senior ~⟩ ⟨junior ~⟩ **4 :** a young calf esp. when too young for veal; *also* **:** the hide from such a calf

[2]deacon \"\ *vt* **deaconed; deaconed; deaconing** \-k(ə)niŋ\ **deacons** **1** [so called fr. the former custom in New England Congregational churches of a deacon's reading aloud each line of a hymn before it was sung by the congregation] **:** to read aloud each line of before singing (a psalm or hymn) **2 :** to practice sly deception with usu. short of illegality **3 a :** to pack (fruit or vegetables) with the finest specimens on top **b :** to alter the boundaries of (land) **c :** to adulterate or doctor (an article to be sold) **4 :** to kill (a calf) at or very soon after birth

dea·con·al \-kənᵊl\ *adj* **:** DIACONAL

dea·con·ate \-kənət\ *n* -s **:** DIACONATE

dea·con·ess \-kənəs\ *n* -ES [fr. earlier *deaconisse*, modif. of LL *diaconissa* fr. LGk *diakonissa*, fr. Gk *diakonos* deacon + *-issa* -ess] **1 :** one of an order of women in the early church whose duties resembled those of deacons **2 :** a woman assigned to church work by a bishop of the Church of England or the Protestant Episcopal Church **3 :** a woman serving as a chosen helper in church work (as among the Methodists) **4 :** a member of a sisterhood devoted to works of religion and charity founded at Kaiserswerth in 1836 by Pastor Theodor Fliedner of the German Protestant Church **5 :** a woman in one of various Protestant denominations who has entered an order or sisterhood of deaconesses, who is commissioned or consecrated to a life of service to the church, and who is typically assigned to work as a nurse in a hospital, a benevolent institution, or on a mission field

dea·con process \'dēkən-\ *n, usu cap D* [after Henry *Deacon*, 19th cent. Eng. chemist] **:** a method of obtaining chlorine gas by passing air and hydrogen chloride over a heated catalyst (as copper chloride)

dea·con·ry \-kənrē\ *n* -ES [ME *dekenry*, fr. *dekne, dekene* deacon + *-ry*] **1 :** DIACONATE **2** *Roman Catholicism* **:** a chapel in the city of Rome under the care of a cardinal deacon; *also* **:** the charitable institution to which it was formerly attached

deacons' court *n* **:** a court in some Presbyterian churches consisting of the minister or ministers, elders, and deacons of a congregation

deacon seat *n* **:** a bench usu. of split logs extending along the front of the bunks in a lumberjack's bunkhouse

de·activate \(ˈ)dē+\ *vt* [*de-* + *activate*] **1 :** to make inactive or ineffective **2 a :** to break up (as a military unit) by discharging or reassigning personnel **:** INACTIVATE **b :** to put (as a bomb or mine) in a condition that makes detonation impossible **c :** to deprive of chemical activity ⟨~ a compound by introducing substituents⟩ ⟨~ a catalyst or enzyme⟩ — **de·activation** \(ˌ)dē+\ *n* -s — **de·activator** \(ˈ)dē+\ *n* -s

[1]dead \'ded\ *adj, sometimes* -ER/-EST [ME *deed*, fr. OE *dēad*; akin to OHG *tōt* dead, ON *dauthr*, Goth *dauths*; derivative fr. the root of ON *deyja* to die — more at DIE] **1 :** deprived of life **:** having ended existence as a living or growing thing — used of organisms or any of their parts or organs ⟨a ~ wasp⟩ ⟨a ~ rabbit⟩ ⟨~ leaves⟩ ⟨~ of scarlet fever⟩ ⟨~ by his own hand⟩ **2 a** (1) **:** having the appearance of death or of being dead **:** DEATHLY ⟨in a ~ faint⟩ **:** INSENSIBLE ⟨~ to the world⟩ (2) **:** without power to move, feel, or respond **:** NUMB ⟨my arm feels ~⟩ **b :** completely exhausted **:** very tired ⟨after two hours of hiking they were just ~⟩ **c** (1) **:** incapable of feeling or of being stirred emotionally or intellectually **:** impervious esp. to pleas or arguments **:** UNRESPONSIVE ⟨a girl with a heart ~ to pity⟩ ⟨completely ~ and deaf to his father's advice⟩ **:** lacking sensitivity or delicacy of feeling ⟨~ to all sense of honor⟩ (2) *of a sentiment* **:** grown cold **:** EXTINGUISHED ⟨a ~ passion⟩ ⟨a ~ love⟩ **3 a :** not naturally endowed with life **:** INANIMATE, INERT ⟨~ matter⟩ **b :** not producing or sustaining life **:** BARREN, INFERTILE ⟨~ soil⟩ ⟨a ~ rocky waste⟩ **c :** no longer producing or functioning **:** EXHAUSTED, WORKED-OUT ⟨a ~ oil well⟩ ⟨a ~ mine⟩ ⟨a ~ battery⟩ **4 a :** lacking power or effect ⟨a ~ law⟩ **:** no longer of concern **:** no longer having interest, relevance, or significance ⟨a ~ issue⟩ **b** (1) **:** lacking currency **:** DEFUNCT, OBSOLETE ⟨a ~ custom⟩ (2) *of a language* **:** no longer in ordinary spoken use **c :** no longer active **:** EXTINCT ⟨a ~ volcano⟩ **d :** lacking in fervor or warmth ⟨a ~ description⟩ **:** lacking in gaiety, animation, or amusing quality ⟨a very ~ party⟩ **e** (1) **:** lacking in commercial activity **:** QUIET ⟨a ~ produce market⟩ (2) **:** commercially idle or unproductive ⟨~ capital⟩ **:** lacking in salability **:** being unsold ⟨~ stock⟩ **f :** lacking responsiveness or elasticity ⟨a ~ tennis ball⟩ ⟨a ~ string on a viol⟩ **g :** out of action or out of use ⟨a ~ electric circuit⟩ ⟨a ~ telephone line⟩ ⟨~ storage⟩ **h** (1) *of a ball* **:** out of play ⟨in football the ball is ~ after an incompleted forward pass⟩ (2) *of a player* **:** temporarily forbidden to play or make a certain play ⟨a croquet player may be ~ on another player's ball⟩ **i** *printing* (1) **:** being something that has been used or is not to be used ⟨~ copy⟩ ⟨~ type⟩ ⟨~ artwork⟩ (2) **:** being something that is routed or to be routed off as not meant to print ⟨*dead*-metal areas in engravings and electrotypes⟩ **j :** out of play **:** not usable ⟨a hand that is not eligible to win is ~⟩ **k :** having a density greater than water — used of oils distilled from tar **l :** having lost the qualities required for workability ⟨~ plaster will not set hard when mixed with water⟩ ⟨~ stone, yielding a dull thud when struck with the sculptor's hammer⟩ **5 a :** not running or circulating **:** STAGNANT ⟨~ water⟩ ⟨~ air⟩ **b :** not turning ⟨the ~ center of a lathe⟩ ⟨cut between a ~ knife blade and a turning one⟩ **c** *of mail* **:** undeliverable and unreturnable — see DEAD LETTER **6 a :** having no fire, warmth, or glow ⟨a ~ cigar⟩ ⟨a ~ fire⟩ **b :** lacking brilliance or luster **:** DULL ⟨a ~ glossy finish⟩ **c :** lacking tang or taste ⟨a ~ wine⟩ **d :** MUFFLED, DEADENED ⟨a ~ sound⟩ **7 :** having a quality of completeness or finality **8 a** (1) **:** unrelieved by any breaks or deviations **:** absolutely uniform — often used in the phrase *dead level* ⟨the ~ level of a prairie⟩ ⟨reducing all to a ~ level of mediocrity⟩ (2) **:** characterized by the utmost exertion of effort, physical or mental ⟨a ~ pull⟩ **b** (1) **:** completely certain to perform or be effective ⟨a ~ shot with a rifle⟩ **:** EXACT ⟨hit the ~ center of the target⟩ (2) **:** as good as dead **:** DOOMED ⟨a ~ pigeon⟩ (3) **:** IRREVOCABLE, UNRECOVERABLE ⟨a ~ loss⟩ **c :** marked by complete and sudden cessation (as of motion or action) **:** ABRUPT ⟨brought to a ~ stop⟩ ⟨stopped him ~ in his tracks⟩ **d :** COMPLETE, TOTAL, ABSOLUTE ⟨a ~ silence fell⟩ ⟨spoke with ~ certainty of his return⟩ **9 :** being abandoned by its former human occupants **:** DESERTED ⟨a ~ mining town⟩ ⟨~ villages⟩ **10 :** characterized by high absorption of sound **:** ANECHOIC ⟨a ~ wall⟩ **11 :** free from any connection to a source of voltage and free from electric charges **:** having the same potential as that of the ground — used of current-carrying apparatus or circuits that may at other times be alive **12 a :** lacking motion ⟨the ~ spindle of a lathe⟩ **b :** not imparting motion or power although otherwise functioning ⟨the ~ rear axle of a floating transmission⟩ **c :** having the principal function in abeyance ⟨the ~ time between power strokes⟩ **d :** marked by a delay in operation or by inactivity between operations or actions — used in referring to a mechanical or electronic device ⟨~ time of a counter⟩

[2]dead \"\ *n, pl* **dead** [ME *deed*] **1 :** one that is dead — now usu. used collectively ⟨the ~ and the living⟩ **2 :** the time of greatest quiet **:** the period of profoundest inertness or gloom ⟨the ~ of winter⟩ ⟨when the drum beat at ~ of night —Thomas Campbell⟩ **3 :** something dead: as **a** *dead pl* **:** refuse from a mine **b** *slang* **:** an article of dead mail

[3]dead \"\ *vb* -ED/-ING/-S [ME *deden*, fr. OE *dēadian* to die, fr. *dēad*, adj.] *vi, obs* **:** DIE ~ *vt, chiefly dial* **:** DEADEN

[4]dead \"\ *adv* [[1]*dead*] **1 a :** to a degree or in a manner resembling or characteristic of death **:** to the last degree **:** ABSOLUTELY, UTTERLY, ENTIRELY, EXACTLY ⟨~ ripe⟩ ⟨*dead*-tired⟩ ⟨~ certain⟩ **b** *dial Brit* **:** EXTREMELY, VERY ⟨it seems to me ~ strange —C.J.Dennis⟩ **2 :** with suddenness and completeness ⟨he stopped ~⟩ **3 :** DIRECTLY ⟨the police were ~ against the plan⟩ ⟨a *dead*-square opening⟩

[5]dead \'ded, -ē-,-ā-\ *n* -s [ME *dede, deed*, prob. alter. (influenced by *deed*, adj.) of *deeth* — more at DEATH] *dial Brit* **:** DEATH

dead ahead *adj (or adv)* **1 :** directly ahead **2 :** on a forward extension of the fore-and-aft line of a ship

dead air *n* **1** *mining* **:** air deficient in oxygen or containing sufficient carbon dioxide to be unfit for breathing **2 :** silence occurring during a radio or television broadcast

dead-air space *n* **:** a sealed or unventilated air space (as in a hollow wall or ceiling)

dead-alive \ˌdedᵊlˌīv, -edəˌlīv\ *also* **dead-and-alive** \ˌdedᵊnəˌlīv\ *adj* **:** alive but as if dead **:** DULL, SPIRITLESS

dead angle *n* **:** an angle outside of a fortification that cannot be reached by the direct fire of the defenders

dead-arm \'=,=\ *n* **:** a fungous disease of the grape caused by an ascomycete (*Cryptosporella viticola*) conspicuous from the death of the main lateral branches — called also *necrosis*

dead asset *n* **:** property carried on accounting books that has neither present nor prospective value — usu. used in pl.

dead axle *n* **:** an axle that carries a road wheel but has no provision for driving it

dead-ball line *n* **:** either of two lines drawn parallel to and not more than 25 yards behind the goal lines to mark the extreme limits of a rugby playing field — see RUGBY illustration

[1]deadbeat \'=,=\ *adj* [[1]*dead* + *beat* (oscillation)] **1** *of an escapement* **:** without recoil **2 :** APERIODIC — used esp. of highly damped indicators on electrical measuring instruments

[2]deadbeat \'=,=\ *n* [prob. fr. [4]*dead* + *beat* (v.)] **1** *chiefly Austral* **:** a man without financial resources **2 :** one that habitually fails to pay his debts or to pay his way **:** SPONGE

dead beat \'=,=\ *adj* [[4]*dead* + *beat* (past part. of *beat*)] **:** completely beat **:** tired out or hopelessly defeated

dead bird *n* **1 :** a bird or other target (as in trapshooting) regarded as killed **2 :** a mark regarded as already hit **:** SURE THING **3 :** one whose death or failure is or seems inescapable

dead block *n* **:** a buffer on the ends of passenger-train cars and locomotives to absorb shock impacts

dead bolt *n* **:** a lock bolt that is moved positively by turning the knob or key without action of a spring

deadborn \'=,=\ *adj* [ME *deedborn*, fr. *deed* dead + *born*] *archaic* **:** STILLBORN

dead-bright \'=,=\ *adj, metalworking* **:** polished so that all tool marks are obliterated **:** BURNISHED

dead-burn \'=,=\ *vt* **:** to calcine (as a carbonate rock) at a higher temperature and for a longer time than usual with the production of a dense refractory material (as by driving off all carbon dioxide) ⟨*dead-burned* dolomite⟩

dead cat *n* **:** a piece of violent or jeering criticism **:** an insulting or abusive expression of disapproval ⟨the government received a barrage of *dead cats*⟩

dead center *n* **1 :** the position of a crank when the turning moment exerted on it is zero; *esp* **:** either of the two positions at the ends of a stroke in a crank and connecting rod when the crank and rod are in the same straight line **2 :** a center that does not revolve in a machine tool

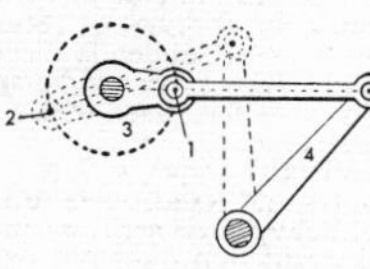
1, 2, dead centers, *3* crank, *4* lever

dead clothes *n pl* [[2,5]*dead*] *Scot* **:** the shroud of a corpse

dead deal *n* [[2]*dead*] *Scot* **:** the board on which a corpse is laid

dead dog *n* **:** something no longer important ⟨waste time beating a *dead dog*⟩

dead-doing *adj, obs* **:** KILLING, MURDEROUS

dead-drunk \'=,=\ *adj* **:** so drunk as to be unconscious or unable to move — **dead-drunkenness** \'=,===\ *n* -ES

dead duck *n* **1 :** a person or thing that has so deteriorated or depreciated as to be practically worthless **2 :** one that is as good as done for ⟨without big advertisers that magazine is a *dead duck*⟩

deaded *past of* DEAD

dead·en \'dedᵊn\ *vb* **deadened; deadened; deadening** \-ed(ᵊ)niŋ\ **deadens** [[1]*dead* + *-en*] *vt* **1 :** to make as if dead **:** impair in vigor, force, activity, or sensation **:** BLUNT ⟨~*ed* his feelings⟩ ⟨~ a sound⟩ **2 a :** to lessen the velocity or momentum of **:** RETARD ⟨~ a ship's headway⟩ **b :** to deprive of gloss or brilliancy **:** OBSCURE ⟨~ gilding by a coat of size⟩ **c :** to make vapid or spiritless ⟨~ wine⟩ **d :** to render (as a wall) impervious to sound **:** DEAFEN 3 **e :** to convert (metallic mercury) into a gray powder consisting of minute globules (as by shaking with chalk or a fatty oil) — compare FLOUR 3 **3 a :** to deprive of life **:** KILL **b :** to kill (trees) by girdling **:** clear (land) by thus killing the trees ~ *vi* **:** to become dead **:** to lose life, force, or vigor

dead end \'=,=\ *n* **1 :** an end (as of a street, pipe, or power line) that has no exit or continuation **2 :** a course of action or policy that leads to nothing further **:** BLIND ALLEY, CUL-DE-SAC

[1]dead-end \'=,=\ *adj* [*dead end*] **1 :** leading nowhere **:** lacking possibilities for advance, progress, or further action ⟨a *dead-end* job⟩ ⟨a *dead-end* policy⟩ **2 :** living in or characteristic of city slums or back streets **:** TOUGH ⟨*dead-end* kids⟩ ⟨a *dead-end* background⟩ **3 :** having a dead end ⟨a *dead-end* street⟩

[2]dead-end \'=,=\ *vb* [*dead end*] *vt* **:** TERMINATE ⟨*dead-end* electric transmission lines⟩ ~ *vi* **:** to come to a dead end **:** TERMINATE

dead·en·er \'ded(ᵊ)nə(r)\ *n* -s **:** a log with spikes in the butt end so arranged over a skidway as to retard logs that pass under it

deadening *n* -s **1 :** action that deadens **2 :** something that deadens: as **a :** material used to render a surface (as a wall, floor, or ceiling) impervious to sound **:** PUGGING **b :** a coating (as of glue) to deprive a surface of gloss or brilliancy **3 :** an area on which the trees have been killed esp. by girdling

deadening felt *n* **:** a heavy coarse paper used in building construction to reduce noises

[1]dead·er \'dedə(r)\ *comparative of* DEAD

[2]deader \"\ *n* -s [[1]*dead* + *-er*] *slang* **:** CORPSE

deadest *superlative of* DEAD

deadeye \'=,=\ *n* -s **1 :** a rounded wood block that is encircled by a rope or an iron band and pierced with holes to receive the lanyard and is used to set up shrouds and stays and for other purposes **2 :** a dead shot ⟨he's a ~ with that rifle⟩

deadfall \'=,=\ *n* **1 :** a trap constructed so that a gate, log, or other weight falls upon the animal and kills or disables it; *broadly* **:** TRAP, PITFALL **2 :** a gambling den or saloon esp. when crooked **3 :** a forest tree that has fallen from age or decay; *collectively* **:** such fallen trees or branches ⟨making his way through the ~⟩ — compare WINDFALL

dead finish *n, Austral* **:** any of several trees or shrubs (as of the genera *Albizzia* and *Acacia*) that form impenetrable thickets

dead fire *n* [[5]*dead*] **:** SAINT ELMO'S FIRE

dead flat *n* **:** the portion of a ship's transverse form that has the same form as the midship or largest section — called also *straight-of-breadth*

deadeyes

dead fold *n* **:** a fold (as in soft foil) that does not unfold spontaneously

dead freight *n* **1 :** the amount paid by or recoverable from a charterer of a ship for such part of the ship's capacity as he has contracted for but fails to occupy; *also* **:** the unoccupied space in such a ship **2 :** bulky nonperishable freight

dead-front switchboard *n* **:** a switchboard with no live or energized parts on the operating side

dead furrow *n* **:** a double furrow left in the middle of a field or between two lands in plowing

deadgrass \'=,=\ *n* **:** a deep yellow with a brownish cast — used of a Chesapeake Bay retriever

dead ground *n* **1 :** a low-resistance connection between an electric circuit and the earth **2 :** DEAD SPACE 1

dead hand *n* **1 :** MORTMAIN **2 :** the influence esp. when felt to be oppressive of the dead on the living or of the past on the present

dead handle *n* **:** DEADMAN'S HANDLE

[1]deadhead \'=,=\ *n* [[1]*dead* + *head*] **1 a :** one that has not paid for a ticket (as for admission to a show or passage on a train); *sometimes* **:** the ticket so received **b** (1) **:** an employee (as of a railroad) riding as a passenger to an assigned point (2) **:** a vehicle (as a freight car or a truck) riding empty **c :** one that does not contribute to the activity of a business or organization ⟨we have several ~*s* on the board of directors⟩ **d :** one who is unfitted or unwilling to advance to a higher rank **2 :** a wholly or partly sunken log **3 :** TAILSTOCK **4 a :** a block of wood used as a buoy **b :** a heavy post on a wharf to which to fasten a hawser **:** BOLLARD

²deadhead \"\ *adj* **:** composed of deadheads **:** acting as a deadhead ⟨~ train runs are necessary in the early morning hours⟩

³deadhead \"\ *vb* -ED/-ING/-S *vi* **1 :** to act or behave as a deadhead **2 a :** to make a return trip without a load — used esp. of a truck **b :** to drive or ride on a truck making such a trip ~ *vt* **:** to drive or haul (a truck, car, locomotive) as a deadhead

deadheart \ˈ=,=\ *n* **:** a deformed stunted plant of certain crop grasses (as maize and sugarcane) caused by borer attack on the region immediately behind the growing bud and characterized by bushy blanched distorted growth beyond the damaged area

dead heat *n* **:** a race with no single winner

dead-heat \ˈ=ˈ=\ *vi* [*dead heat*] **:** to run a dead heat

dead hole *n* **:** a hole (as in a casting) that does not pass entirely through

dead horse *n* **1 :** advance wages for work ⟨working off a *dead horse*⟩ **:** an old debt ⟨paying for a *dead horse*⟩ **2 :** an exhausted or profitless topic or issue ⟨arguing this question would be beating a *dead horse*⟩ — compare DEAD DOG

deadhouse \ˈ=,=\ *n* [*²dead* + *house*] *archaic* **:** MORGUE, MORTUARY

deading *pres part of* DEAD

dead·ish \ˈdedish\ *adj* [ME *dedisshe*, fr. *deed* dead + *-isshe* -ish] **:** somewhat dead **:** DULL ⟨a ~ sound⟩

de-adjectival \(ˌ)dē+\ *adj* [*de-* + *adjective* + *-al*] **:** derived from an adjective (as *weaken* from *weak*) ⟨a *de-adjectival* verb⟩

dead key *n* **:** a typewriter key (as for an accent or a diacritical mark) that prints when struck but does not move the carriage

deadlatch \ˈ=,=\ *n* **:** a spring-bolt latch in which the bolt is deadlocked against end pressure but may be retracted by either the knob or the key

dead latitude *n* **:** latitude found by dead reckoning

dead leaf *n* **:** FEUILLE MORTE

dead-leaf butterfly *n* **:** any of several tropical Asiatic butterflies (genus *Kallima*) with underside of wings suggesting dead leaves when at rest — compare LEAF BUTTERFLY

dead letter *n* **1 :** something that has lost its force or authority or has fallen into disuse without being formally abolished or declared useless ⟨that law has become a *dead letter*⟩ **2 :** a letter that is received by a post office but that is undeliverable (as on account of insufficient address) and unreturnable because of absence of return address or returnable only when address of sender is discovered upon opening

dead lift *n* **1** *archaic* **:** a situation taxing one's utmost effort or power — usu. used with *at* **2 :** a direct lift without mechanical assistance

deadlight \ˈ=,=\ *n* **1 a :** a metal cover or shutter fitted to air ports and fixed ports to keep out light and water **b :** a piece of heavy glass set in a ship's deck or hull to admit light **2 :** a skylight that does not open **3** *Scot* **:** a luminosity seen over graves **:** CORPSE CANDLE **4 deadlights** *pl, slang* **:** EYES

¹deadline \ˈ=,=\ *n* [*²dead* + *line*] **1 :** a line drawn within or around a prison that a prisoner passes only at the risk of being instantly shot **2 :** a line or mark made on the bed of a cylinder press to indicate the limit to which the printing surface may extend **3 :** a fixed time limit **:** a date or time before which something must be done and after which the opportunity passes or a penalty follows ⟨the ~ for filing income tax returns⟩; *specif* **:** the time limit after which copy is not accepted for use in a particular issue of a publication ⟨3 a.m. was the ~ for the newspaper's morning edition⟩ **4 :** a group of military vehicles put aside for repair or periodic maintenance

²deadline \ˈ=,=\ *vt* **:** to put aside (as a motor vehicle) for repair or maintenance

dead·li·ness \ˈdedlēnəs, -lin-\ *n* -ES [ME *deedlinesse*, fr. *deedly* deadly + *-nesse* -ness] **:** the state or quality of being deadly

dead load *n* **1 :** a constant load that in structures (as a bridge, car, building, or machine) is due to the weight of the members, the supported structure, and permanent attachments or accessories — compare IMPOSED LOAD, LIVE LOAD **2 :** factory orders prepared by a central control office but not released to the factory for production **:** BACKLOG

¹deadlock \ˈ=,=\ *n* [*¹dead* + *lock*] **1 :** a counteraction of things producing entire stoppage **:** a state of inaction or of neutralization caused by the opposition of persons or of factions (as in a government or in a voting body) **:** STANDSTILL **2 :** a device for locking or holding securely together the point and stock rails in a railroad point switch **3 :** a lock having a dead bolt — distinguished from *spring lock* **4 :** a tie score of a game or contest

²deadlock \"\ *vt* **:** to bring to a deadlock ~*vi* **:** to reach a deadlock

¹dead·ly \ˈdedlē, -li\ *adj* -ER/-EST [ME *deedlich*, *deedly*, fr. OE *dēadlic*, fr. *dēad* dead + *-lic* -ly — more at DEAD] **1** *obs* **a :** subject to death **b :** being in danger of dying **:** likely to die **c :** INANIMATE **2 :** tending to produce death **:** productive of death ⟨among the Indians, measles, scarlatina, and whooping cough were as ~ as typhus or cholera —Willa Cather⟩ **3 a :** aiming to kill or destroy or involving such an aim ⟨two brave vessels matched in ~ fight —William Wordsworth⟩ **:** lacking possibility of an amicable solution **:** IMPLACABLE ⟨a ~ quarrel⟩ **b :** tending to enervate, vitiate, or smother all force, vitality, influence, or activity ⟨the neglect of form . . . was even *deadlier* to poetry —Peter Viereck⟩ **:** extremely pernicious ⟨the ~ effects of malicious gossip⟩ **:** PENETRATING, DEVASTATING ⟨containing some ~ exposure of human folly or frailty —Daniel George⟩ **4 :** characteristic or suggestive of death or the dead ⟨a ~ paleness spread over her features⟩ **5 :** marked by great precision **:** UNERRING ⟨stories hurled with ~ aim —Green Peyton⟩ **6 :** marked by extreme seriousness and single-minded determination ⟨goes in for careermanship in an impassive, ~ sort of way —James Kelly⟩ **:** notably effective **:** UNFAILING ⟨the ~ efficiency of the famed police force⟩ **:** marked by complete lack of trifling or flippancy ⟨he spoke with ~ seriousness⟩ **7 :** very great **:** COMPLETE, EXTREME ⟨a ~ silence⟩ ⟨a ~ bore⟩ ⟨~ fear⟩

syn MORTAL, LETHAL, FATAL, DEATHLY: DEADLY applies to anything bound or likely to cause death ⟨so poisonous that the drinking of it is *deadly* to all but serpents and hippopotami —Llewelyn Powys⟩ ⟨Hands and his companion locked together in *deadly* wrestle, each with a hand upon the other's throat —R.L.Stevenson⟩ In this sense MORTAL differs from DEADLY only in that it may occur somewhat more frequently in retrospect, in reference to situations in which death has occurred ⟨till that young life being smitten in midheaven with *mortal* cold passed from her —Alfred Tennyson⟩ LETHAL, the strongest word, indicates that which by its quality or quantity is designed esp. to make death certain ⟨the morphia he gave was a full *lethal* dose, and presently the body on the deck found peace —Nevil Shute⟩ FATAL comes between DEADLY and LETHAL in inevitability and may refer to other calamities than death ⟨regarding strychnine, toxicology gives us a very wide range as to *lethal* dosage, depending on the condition and age of the patient. The average *fatal* dose for an adult is, I should say, two grains, though death has resulted from administrations of one grain —W.H.Wright⟩ ⟨the *fatal* policy by which the Empire invited its doom while striving to avert it, the policy of matching barbarian against barbarian —J.R. Green⟩ DEATHLY, once a synonym for DEADLY, is now commonly an intensive meaning "as of death" or "resembling death" ⟨she had a *deathly* fear of Quintal and with reason —C.B.Nordhoff & J.N.Hall⟩

²deadly \"\ *adv* [ME *deedliche*, *deedly*, fr. OE *dēadlice*, fr. *dēadlic*, adj.] **1** *archaic* **:** in a manner to occasion death **:** MORTALLY **:** to death ⟨the groanings of a ~ wounded man —Ezek 30:24 (AV)⟩ **2 :** in an implacable manner **:** to the death **3 :** in a manner or degree produced by or as if produced by death ⟨turned ~ pale⟩ **4 :** in a dead manner **:** as if dead **:** LIFELESSLY **5 :** EXTREMELY, EXCESSIVELY ⟨~ dull⟩

deadly agaric *n* **:** a very poisonous mushroom (as the fly agaric or death cup)

deadly amanita *n* **:** DEATH CUP 2

deadly carrot *n* **:** a large European herb (*Thapsia garganica*) the root of which is emetic and cathartic

deadly nightshade *n* **1 :** BELLADONNA 1 **2 :** BLACK NIGHTSHADE

deadly parallel *n* **:** a comparison of two things part by part (as in parallel columns) that reveals an underlying relationship (as in a case of plagiarism) or a damaging discrepancy

deadly sin *n* **:** one of seven sins of pride, covetousness, lust, anger, gluttony, envy, and sloth regarded by some as the source of other sins and as fatal to spiritual progress

dead mail *n* **:** mail that is undeliverable because of faulty or illegible address and is unreturnable to the sender or that is unclaimed after a certain period of time and that must be sent to the dead-letter branch in the case of first-class mail or to the dead parcel-post branch for disposal

dead·man \-,man, -aa(ə)n\ *n, pl* **deadmen** [ME *deedman*, fr. *deed* dead + *man*] **1 :** CORPSE — now used as one word in place names only ⟨*Deadman's* Bay⟩ **2 :** a buried log serving as an anchor (as for a guy rope) **:** ANCHOR LOG; *also* **:** a stout timber or log used as an anchorage (as for a boom) **3 :** a support that resembles a crutch and is used to hold a pole temporarily while it is being erected or lowered and so permit the workmen to take a fresh grip on the pole **4 :** a fallen tree on the shore **5** *deadmen pl, obs* **:** reef or gasket ends carelessly left dangling under the yard when the sail is furled **6** *or* **deadman control :** a device (as a brake) for controlling a vehicle or machine in case the operator becomes incapacitated

dead man *n* **1 :** the inedible gill filaments of a crab that are discarded in cleaning boiled crabs **2 :** a bottle emptied of beer, wine, or liquor; *also* **:** an empty beer can

deadman brake *n* **:** an automatic emergency brake that goes into action when the driver of a vehicle removes his foot from a pedal

dead man's eye *n, obs* **:** DEADEYE 1

dead-man's-fingers \,=ˈ=,=\ *or* **dead-men's-fingers** *n pl but sing or pl in constr* **1 :** any of several European orchids (genus *Orchis*) having pale digitate roots (esp. *O. mascula*, *O. maculata*, *O. latifolia*, and *O. morio*) **2 :** any of several other plants: as **a :** BIRD'S-FOOT TREFOIL 1a **b :** CUCKOOPINT **c :** MEADOW FOXTAIL GRASS **3 :** the fruiting bodies of fungi of the genus *Xylaria* (esp. *X. polymorpha*) **4 a :** a fleshy alcyonarian (*Alcyonium digitatum*) usu. lobed or digitate in form **b :** a white or grayish digitately branching sponge (*Chalina arbuscula*) of the Atlantic coast **5 :** DEAD MAN 1

dead man's float *n* **:** a prone floating position with arms extended forward — called also *prone float*

deadman's hand *n* **1 a** *or* **deadman's thumb :** MALE ORCHIS **b :** MALE FERN **c** *also* **deadman's toe :** a palmately branching seaweed (*Laminaria digitata*) **2 :** a poker hand with two pairs either aces and eights or jacks and eights

deadman's handle *n* **:** a handle on a machine having a small button on it which must be kept pressed down by the hand to continue contact so that if the operator is incapacitated contact is broken and the machine stops — called also *dead handle*

dead march \ˈ=ˈ=\ *n* [*²dead*] **:** a piece of solemn funereal music intended to accompany or to suggest a funeral procession

dead marine *n* **:** DEAD MAN 2

¹deadmelt \ˈ=ˈ=\ *vt, steel manuf* **:** to keep molten until bubbling ceases and the liquid becomes quiet

²deadmelt \"\ *n* **:** the state of deadmelted metal

deadmen's bells *or* **deadman's bells** *n pl, Scot* **:** FOXGLOVE 1

deadmen's bones *n pl but sometimes sing in constr* **:** a toadflax (*Linaria vulgaris*)

deadmen's lines *n pl but sing in constr* **:** SEA LACE

de ad·men·su·ra·ti·o·ne \ˌdāad,men(t)sə,rȧd·ēˈō,nā, -ˌnē\ *adj* [ML, of admeasurement] **:** commanding admeasurement of dower — used of a writ

dead metaphor *n* **:** a word or phrase that was once metaphoric but that has lost its metaphoric force in common use (as *the head of the house*, *room and board*, *time is running out*)

dead mouth *n, of a horse* **:** a mouth no longer sensitive to the bit

dead·ness *n* -ES **:** the quality or state of being dead

dead nettle *n* **1 :** a plant of the genus *Lamium* having leaves resembling those of the nettle but destitute of stinging hairs **2 :** HEMP NETTLE **3 :** HEDGE NETTLE **4 :** RICHWEED 1

dead oil *n* **:** any of various heavy oils (as creosote oil)

de·a·dose \ˈdāə,dōs\ *n, pl* **deadose** *or* **deodoses** *usu cap* **1 :** a Tunican people of south central Texas **2 :** a member of the Deadose people

dead pan \ˈ=ˈ= *in sense 1*, ˈ=,= *in sense 2*\ *n* **1 :** a completely expressionless immobile face ⟨wears a *dead pan* on and off the ice —*Newsweek*⟩ **2 :** a deadpan manner of behavior or of presentation (as of comedy) ⟨a master of *dead pan*⟩

¹deadpan \ˈ=,=\ *adj* [*dead pan*] **1 :** having or communicated with an assumed air of earnestness or gravity ⟨~ humor⟩ ⟨an infinitely irritating ~ mockery⟩ ⟨a ~ elegy on a turtle⟩ **2 :** marked by complete absence of expression or mobility ⟨a ~ face⟩ **:** WOODEN, STOLID ⟨gave his accusers a ~ stare⟩ **:** giving no sign of emotional or personal commitment or involvement **:** DETACHED, IMPERSONAL ⟨a ~ presentation of concentration-camp horrors⟩ ⟨a ~ style⟩

²deadpan \ˈ=,=\ *adv* **:** in a deadpan manner **:** with deadpan absence of expression ⟨played his role completely ~⟩

³deadpan \ˈ=,=\ *vi* **:** to maintain a deadpan manner **:** act in a deadpan manner ⟨*deadpanned* throughout the whole play⟩ ~ *vt* **:** to speak or write in a deadpan manner

dead parking *n* **:** the keeping of a vehicle standing without a driver or operator in attendance

dead pigeon *n* **:** DEAD BIRD

dead plate *n* **:** a stationary steel plate placed at the end of an automatic-stoker grate next to the fire door to collect clinkers

dead pledge *n* **:** MORTGAGE

dead point *n* **:** DEAD CENTER

dead rail *n* **:** one of two rails that are laid across a railroad track-scale platform but not connected with the weighing beam and that permit a locomotive or other load exceeding the capacity of the scale to move across the scale

dead reckoning *n* **1 :** the determination without the aid of celestial observations of the position of a ship or aircraft deduced from the record of the courses sailed or flown, the distance made, and the known or estimated drift **2 :** a procedure attempting to locate something in space or in time (as a goal, a target, an historical event) by deduction unaided by direct observation or direct evidence; *broadly* **:** GUESSWORK

dead rent *n* **:** a fixed rent; *esp* **:** one imposed upon a concessionaire without regard to the yield of his concession

dead rise *n* **:** the rise of the bottom of a midship frame from the keel to the bilge usu. given in inches per foot

dead-rise model *n* **:** a small usu. high-speed power yacht having a flat floor with extreme dead rise and straight sides

dead rising *also* **dead rise line** *n* **:** a curved fore-and-aft line in the sheer plan of a ship passing through the floorheads and showing the dead rise of each head

dead-roast \ˈ=ˈ=\ *vt* **:** to roast (ore) until free from sulfur, arsenic, or other volatile components

dead rope *n* **:** a rope that does not pass over a sheave or reeve through a block

deads *pl of* DEAD, *pres 3d sing of* DEAD

dead sea *n* [fr. the *Dead sea*, salt lake in Palestine, its prototype; trans. of LL *Mare Mortuum*, trans. of Gk *Nekra Thalassa*] **:** a body of water from which beds of rock salt, gypsum, or other evaporites have been precipitated

dead sea apple *n, usu cap D&S* [fr. the *Dead sea*] **1** *or* **dead sea fruit :** APPLE OF SODOM 1a **2 :** a gallnut coming from Asiatic Turkey caused by a gallfly (*Cynips insana*) — called also *mad apple*

dead set *n* **1 :** the position of a hunting dog in pointing his prey **2 :** a determined effort esp. to win or gain a clearly identified objective — usu. used with *at* ⟨made a *dead set* at him and married him⟩ **3 :** an attitude of fixed hostility

dead sheave *n* **:** a hole in the heel of a topmast to receive a top pendant

dead shore *n* **:** an upright shore left in a wall after completion of repairs or alterations

dead short circuit *n* **:** an electrical short circuit of great magnitude arising from large firm contact

dead slow *adv* (*or adj*), *naut* **:** so slow as to have only steerageway

dead-smooth \ˈ=ˈ=\ *adj* **1 :** extremely smooth **2 :** smoother than most other implements of the same class ⟨a *dead-smooth* file⟩

dead-soft \ˈ=ˈ=\ *adj* **1** *of steel* **:** very soft; *specif* **:** very low in carbon **2** *of steel* **:** annealed until as soft as possible

dead soldier *n* **:** DEAD MAN 2

dead space *n* **1 :** space that cannot be reached by fire from a given weapon or a given point — called also *dead ground* **2 :** the portion of the respiratory system which is external to the bronchioles and through which air must pass to reach the bronchioles and alveoli — called also *physiologic dead space* **3 :** a space left in the body as the result of a surgical procedure (as that in the chest following excision of a lung or that in an improperly closed surgical wound) **4 :** space (as in a truck or steamer) that is not utilized or occupied

dead's part *n* [*²dead*] *Scots law* **:** the part of a married man's personal property that he may dispose of by will, the rest going to the widow and children — compare JUS RELICTAE, LEGITIM

dead spot *n* **1 :** a locality where activity lags **2 :** a region of poor or no radio reception **:** BLIND SPOT

dead stick *n*, **:** an airplane propeller that has ceased to revolve because the engine has stopped

dead stock *n* **:** farm tools and equipment — opposed to *livestock*

dead-stroke \ˈ=,=\ *adj, of a mechanical device* **:** making a stroke without recoil

dead-stroke hammer *n* **:** a power hammer having a spring interposed between the driving mechanism and the hammer-head or helve to lessen the recoil and reduce the shock

dead thraw *or* **dead throw** *n* [*⁵dead*] *Scot* **:** death throe

dead time *n* **1 :** the short interval which is required for a counting tube to recover its sensitivity after any one discharge and during which it is incapable of further response **2 :** the time lag between a stimulus given to an instrument and the resulting response **3 :** DOWNTIME 2a

deadtongue \ˈ=,=\ *n* [so called fr. its paralyzing effect on the speech organs] *dial Eng* **:** a European water dropwort (*Oenanthe crocata*)

dead to rights *adj* **:** without possibility of escape, excuse, or palliation (as from a charge of guilt) **:** RED-HANDED ⟨we had him *dead to rights* on a bribery charge⟩ ⟨caught *dead to rights* on a bribery charge⟩

dead track *n* **1 :** a car or railway track that is no longer used but that has not been removed **2 :** a short section of track usu. at a crossing that is isolated by insulated joints from the track signal circuits

dead wagon *n* [*²dead*] **:** a wagon used to carry the dead

dead wall *n* **:** a wall without openings

dead watch *n* [*³dead*] **:** DEATHWATCH

dead water *n* **1 :** standing or still water **2 :** SLACK WATER, NEAP TIDE **3 :** the mass of eddying water formed along a ship's sides in her progress through the water

deadweight \ˈ=ˈ=\ *n* **1** *often* **dead weight :** the unrelieved weight of any inert mass **:** a heavy or oppressive burden **2 :** DEAD LOAD 1 **3 :** a ship's lading including the total weight of cargo, fuel, stores, crew, and passengers

deadweight capacity *or* **deadweight tonnage** *n* **:** the carrying capacity of a ship in tons of 2240 pounds **:** the difference between a ship's displacement light and her displacement loaded

deadweight safety valve *n* **:** a safety valve in which the pressure is caused by a weight acting directly on the valve

deadwood \ˈ=,=; *in sense 1* " *or* ˈ=ˈ=\ *n* **1 :** wood dead on the tree **:** dead branches **2 :** useless personnel or material (as inefficient members of an organization, unsalable stock, or outworn methods) ⟨a definite campaign against human ~ still clogging the system —Ezra Pound⟩ **3 :** solid timbers usu. horizontal and built in at the extreme bow and stern of a ship where the breadth is not such as to permit framing **4 :** bowling pins that have been knocked down but remain on the alley **5 a :** unmatched cards in gin or knock rummy **b :** useless cards (as those that have been discarded) **6 :** type or spacing matter temporarily keyboarded or inserted in typeset matter to make room for something (as a vertical rule in a table) to be inserted later **7** *chiefly West* **:** unquestioned advantage — used esp. in the expression *have the deadwood on* ⟨we've got the ~ on you on a forgery charge —Erle Stanley Gardner⟩

deadwood fence *n, Austral* **:** a heavy fence made of felled trees, heaped logs, or branches

dead wool *n* **1 :** FALLEN WOOL **2 :** wool from dead sheep

dead work *n* **1 :** work which must be done to prepare for future operations but from which there is no direct return (as stripping the surface to expose rock which is to be quarried) **2 dead works** *pl, archaic* **:** UPPERWORKS 1

de ae·qui·ta·te \ˌdē,ekwəˈtād·ē, ˌdā,īkwəˈtäd·ē\ *adv* (*or adj*) [L, from equity] *law* **:** according to the principles of equity — distinguished from *de jure*

de·aerate \(ˈ)dē +\ *vt* [*de-* + *aerate*] **:** to remove air or gas (as oxygen) from — **de·aeration** \(ˌ)dē +\ *n* -s — **de·aerator** \(ˈ)dē +\ *n* -s

¹deaf \ˈdef, *archaic & dial* -ē-\ *adj* -ER/-EST [ME *deef*, fr. OE *dēaf*; akin to OHG *toub* deaf, stupid, ON *daufr* deaf, Goth *daufs* unreceptive to impressions, Gk *typhlos* blind, *typhein* to smoke, L *fumus* smoke — more at FUME] **1 :** lacking or deprived of the sense of hearing either wholly or in part **:** unable to perceive sounds **:** having a sense of hearing that is inadequate for the purposes of daily living **2 :** unwilling to hear or listen **:** determinedly inattentive ⟨none so ~ as those that will not hear⟩ **:** not to be persuaded as to facts, argument, or exhortation — used with *to* ⟨~ to reason⟩ **3** *obs, of a sound* **:** MUFFLED, STIFLED, DEADENED ⟨mocks the dull ear of Time with ~ abortive sound —William Wordsworth⟩ **4** *dial Brit* **:** incapable of bearing **:** having no fruit or kernel **:** STERILE, INFERTILE, BARREN ⟨~ eggs⟩ ⟨~ nutmegs⟩

²deaf \"\ *vt* -ED/-ING/-S [ME *deffen*, fr. *deef*, *deff*, adj.] *archaic* **:** DEAFEN

deaf adder *n* **1 :** any of various harmless snakes; *esp* **:** HOGNOSE SNAKE **2 :** the venomous copperhead **3** *Brit* **:** BLINDWORM 1

deaf-aid \ˈ=,=\ *n* **:** HEARING AID

deaf and dumb *adj* **:** DEAF-MUTE

deaf-and-dumb alphabet *n* **:** MANUAL ALPHABET

deaf ear *n* **:** whitened and empty heads of cereals (as those caused by wheat scab) — usu. used in pl.

deaf-ear crab *n* [so called fr. the belief that juices pressed from this crab will cure deafness] **:** a West Indian fiddler crab (*Uca pugnax vapax*)

deaf·en \ˈdefən\ *vb* **deafened; deafened; deafening** \-f(ə)niŋ\ **deafens** *vt* **1 :** to make deaf **:** deprive esp. temporarily of the power of hearing **:** daze with noise ⟨~*ed* by the roar of escaping steam⟩ **2** *obs* **:** to make inaudible **:** drown out (a sound) **3 :** to make (a wall, floor, ceiling) impervious to sound (as by filling or lining with sound-absorbent material) ~ *vi* **:** to cause deafness **:** stun with noise ⟨fell with a ~*ing* clap⟩

deafened *adj* **:** having become deaf after hearing normally and esp. after learning to speak

deafening *n* -s **1 :** the action or process of making a floor or wall impervious to sound **2 :** the material with which spaces are filled in the process of soundproofing — called also *pugging*

deaf·en·ing·ly *adv* **:** in a deafening manner

de·af·fer·en·ta·tion \ˌdē,afə,renˈtāshən\ *n* -s [*de-* + *afferent* + *-ation*] **:** the freeing of a motor nerve from sensory components by severing the dorsal root central to the dorsal ganglion

deaf·ish \ˈdefish\ *adj* **:** slightly deaf **:** HARD-OF-HEARING

deaf·ly *adv* [ME *defly*, fr. *deef*, *def* deaf + *-ly*] **:** in a deaf manner **:** without hearing **:** without listening

¹deaf-mute \ˈ=ˈ=\ *adj* [trans. of F *sourd-muet* or G *taubstumm*] **:** lacking the sense of hearing and the ability to speak — **deaf-mute·ness** *n*

²deaf-mute \"\ *n* **:** a person who is deaf-mute — compare LIPREADING, ORAL METHOD

deaf-mut·ism \-ˈmyüd·,izəm\ *n* **:** the condition of being a deaf-mute

deaf·ness *n* -ES [ME *deefnesse*, fr. *deef* deaf + *-nesse* -ness — more at DEAF] **:** congenital or acquired lack, loss, or impairment of the sense of hearing whether due to defects in (1) the sound-transmitting mechanism, (2) the organ of Corti or auditory nerve, or (3) the interpretative centers of the brain —

called also respectively (1) *transmission deafness, conduction deafness,* or *conductive deafness,* (2) *perceptive deafness* or *nerve deafness,* and (3) *central deafness, cortical deafness,* or *psychic deafness*
deaf nettle *n* : a dead nettle (*Lamium purpureum*)
deaf nut *n* **1** : a nut with no kernel **2** : a thing without profit
de·air \(ˈ)ˌ=ˈ=\ *vt* [*de-* + *air* (n.)] : to remove air from (wet clay) by pugging under vacuum thereby increasing wet strength and density
[1]**deal** \ˈdēl, *esp before pause or consonant* -ēəl\ *n* -s [ME *deel, del,* fr. OE *dǣl;* akin to OE *dāl* division, portion, OHG *teil* part, ON *deild* share, Goth *dails* part] **1** *obs* : PART, PORTION, SHARE **2** : an indefinite quantity, degree, or extent ⟨it makes a good ~ of difference⟩ ⟨it means a great ~ to him⟩ ⟨he hasn't got a great ~ of money⟩ **3 a** : the act, process, or method of distributing cards to players in a card game **b** : the privilege or duty of acting as dealer ⟨it's my ~⟩ **c** : a period in the play of a card game embracing all phases from the shuffle through the determination or scoring of the result — compare HAND 10a(4) **4** : a large quantity : LOT ⟨a ~ of years —Raymond Moley⟩
[2]**deal** \"\ *vb* **dealt** \ˈdelt\ **dealt** \"\ **dealing** \ˈdēliŋ\ **deals** \ˈdē(ə)lz\ [ME *delen,* fr. OE *dǣlan;* akin to OHG *teilen* to divide, ON *deila,* Goth *dailjan;* denominative fr. the root of E [1]*deal*] *vt* **1** *obs* : DIVIDE, SEPARATE, SEVER **2 a** : to give as one's share or portion : DISTRIBUTE, APPORTION, METE ⟨*dealt* justice to all men⟩ — usu. used with *out* ⟨*dealt* out three sandwiches apiece⟩ **b** (1) : to distribute (one or more playing cards) to a player or the players in a card game (2) : to distribute the cards for (a specified card game) ⟨~ poker⟩ (3) : to act as dealer in (a specified game) ⟨~ craps⟩ **3** : ADMINISTER, DELIVER, BESTOW ⟨~ the boy a scolding⟩ ~ *vi* **1** *obs* : to be a sharer : SHARE **2 a** : to distribute the cards in a card game **b** : to have the function or duty of distributing cards to the players in a card game **c** : to act as a dealer in a gambling game **3 a** : to have to do : concern oneself : TREAT — used with *with* ⟨the book ~*s* with all aspects of the subject⟩ **b** : to become occupied or busy — used with *in* ⟨~*ing* in matters of no concern to him⟩ ⟨fond of ~*ing* in large generalities⟩ **4** : to act toward a person or regarding a thing : DO — used with *by* or *with* ⟨return . . . and I will ~ well with thee —Gen 32:9 (AV)⟩ **5** *archaic* : to have dealings — used with *with* ⟨~*ing* with witches —Shak.⟩ **6** *archaic* : to act as intermediary : make arrangements : NEGOTIATE — used with *with* or *between* **7** : to do a retailing or distributing business : TRADE, TRAFFIC — used with *in* before a thing ⟨he ~*s* in flour⟩ and with *with* before a person ⟨he ~*s* fairly with all his customers⟩ **8** *obs* : CONTEND, STRUGGLE, QUARREL — used with *with* **9** : to take action (as in regard to some object, problem, or source of difficulty) : come to grips — used with *with* ⟨he may ~ as he pleases with his own property⟩ ⟨had to ~ with a catastrophic inflation⟩ ⟨*dealt* with his problems as they arose⟩ ⟨*dealt* harshly with the rebels⟩ **syn** see DISTRIBUTE, TREAT
[3]**deal** \"\ *n* -s **1** *obs* : DEALINGS, INTERCOURSE **2 a** : an act of buying and selling : an offering of a combination of products at a special price ⟨a package ~⟩ : a reciprocal arrangement or agreement : BARGAIN **b** : treatment received in a transaction from another ⟨a raw ~⟩ or from impersonal forces or circumstances ⟨a rough ~⟩ **c** *usu cap* : a particular policy of national administration esp. of economic or politico-economic affairs ⟨Theodore Roosevelt's Square *Deal*⟩ ⟨the New *Deal*⟩ ⟨the Fair *Deal*⟩ **3** : an often clandestine arrangement to gain mutual advantage for those interested : a negotiated settlement of an issue (as a lawsuit) ⟨law . . . has a way of beginning with ideals and ending with ~*s* —H.A.Overstreet⟩
[4]**deal** \"\ *n* -s [MD or MLG *dele* plank; akin to OHG *dili, dilla* plank, plank floor — more at THILL] **1 a** *Brit* : a board of fir or pine cut to any of several specified sizes — see DEAL END, SLIT DEAL, STANDARD DEAL, WHOLE DEAL **b** *in the U.S. export trade* : sawed yellow-pine lumber nine inches and wider and three, four, or five inches thick **2** : pine or fir wood : deals in the aggregate ⟨a floor of ~⟩
[5]**deal** \"\ *adj* : made of deal; *broadly* : made of plain unfinished wood ⟨a ~ table⟩
deal apple *n* [[4]*deal*] : the cone of the white pine or of the fir
de·alate \dēˈā,lāt, -ˌlət\ *n* -s [*de-* + *alate*] : a dealated insect : a mature sexual individual of a kind of insect that undergoes dealation
de·alat·ed \-ˌlād·əd\ *adj* [*de-* + *alated*] : divested of the wings — used of postnuptial adults of certain insects (as ants and termites) that drop their wings after a nuptial flight — **de·ala·tion** \(ˌ)dē,āˈlāshən\ *n* -s
de·al·bate \dēˈal,bāt, -ˈōl-\ *adj* [L *dealbatus,* past part. of *dealbare* to whitewash — more at DAUB] *bot* : covered with an opaque white powder
deal board *n* [[4]*deal*] : a fir or pine board : DEAL
deal end *n* [[4]*deal*] : a deal board less than six feet long — usu. used in pl.
deal·er \ˈdēlə(r)\ *n* -s [ME *delere,* fr. OE *dǣlere,* fr. *dǣlen* to divide + *-ere* -er — more at DEAL] **1** : one that divides, distributes, or delivers **2** *obs* : NEGOTIATOR, AGENT, GO-BETWEEN **3** : one that acts or conducts himself in some specified way toward others ⟨noted as a plain ~⟩ **4** : one that does business : TRADER, TRAFFICKER, MIDDLEMAN : a person who makes a business of buying and selling goods esp. without altering their condition ⟨a ~ in dry goods⟩ ⟨~ in stocks⟩ ⟨an automobile ~⟩ — compare MANUFACTURER **5** : one that buys and sells (as securities, commercial paper, or foreign exchange) on his own account — compare BROKER 1b **6 a** *Brit* : STOCKJOBBER a — distinguished from *broker* **b** : a member of a stock exchange who buys and sells as principal rather than as agent for a customer **7 a** (1) : a person who deals cards (2) : a machine or device for dealing cards **b** (1) : a gambler or employee of a gambling house who officiates at a game or gaming table (as a stickman, tourneur, croupier, or cashier) (2) : the chief among such persons : the person in charge of the table (as the stickman in craps or the tourneur at roulette)
dealer acceptance *n* : purchase by a retail merchant because of a known demand
dealer help *n* : promotional aid (as samples, counter or window displays, briefings for clerks) that is furnished retailers by manufacturers and wholesalers to stimulate sales of advertised products or to gain retailers' goodwill and continued patronage
dealer's choice *n* : a card game (as poker) in which the dealer may designate the variant to be played and set the stakes
deal·er·ship \-ˌship\ *n* -s : an authorized sales agency : the business of a distributor ⟨an automobile ~⟩ ⟨a ~ for planes⟩
dealfish \ˈ=,=\ *n* [[4]*deal* + *fish*] : any of several long thin fishes of the genus *Trachypterus* inhabiting the deep sea — called also *ribbonfish*
deal frame *n* [[4]*deal*] : LOG FRAME
deal in *vt* : to include (a specified player) among those to whom cards are dealt ⟨*deal* me *in*⟩
dealing *n* -s [ME *deling,* fr. gerund of *delen* to deal] **1** : INTERCOURSE, TRAFFIC — usu. used in pl. ⟨~*s* with the devil⟩ **2** : method of business or manner of conduct ⟨underhand ~⟩
dealing box *n* : [2]BOX 13
de·alkalization \(ˌ)dē+\ *n* -s : the process of dealkalizing
de·alkalize \(ˈ)dē+\ *vt* [*de-* + *alkalize*] : to remove alkali from : reduce the alkalinity of (as by neutralization)
de·alkylate \(ˈ)dē+\ *vt* [*de-* + *alkylate*] : to remove alkyl groups from (a compound) — **de·alkylation** \(ˌ)dē+\ *n* -s
deal lugger \ˈdē(ə)l-\ *n, usu cap D* [fr. *Deal,* municipal borough on the Strait of Dover, Kent, England] : a lugger formerly common on the southeast coast of England esp. in the ship-tender service
deal off *vi* : to deal the last hand of a poker game or the last hand in which one intends to participate
deal out *vt* : to omit (a specified player) from those to whom cards are dealt
deal pine *n* [[4]*deal*] : WHITE PINE 1a
deals *pl of* DEAL, *pres 3d sing of* DEAL
dealt *past of* DEAL
de·am·bu·la·tion \(ˌ)dē,ambyəˈlāshən\ *n* [L *deambulation-, deambulatio,* fr. *deambulatus* (past part. of *deambulare* to walk abroad or about), fr. *de-* + *ambulare* to walk) + *-ion-, -io* -ion — more at AMBLE] : the act of walking abroad or about : PROMENADE
de·ambulatory \dē+\ *n* [LL *deambulatorium,* fr. L *deambulatus* + *-orium* -ory] : AMBULATORY
de·amidate \(ˈ)dē+ *or* **des·amidate** \(ˈ)des+\ *vt* [*de-* or *des-* + *amidate*] : to remove the amido group from (a compound) — **de·amidation** \(ˌ)dē+ *or* **des·amidation** \(ˌ)des+\ *n* -s
de·amidization \(ˌ)dē+\ *or* **des·amidization** \(ˌ)des+\ *n* -s : the process of deamidizing : DEAMIDATION
de·amidize \(ˈ)dē+\ *or* **des·amidize** \(ˈ)des+\ *vt* [*de-* or *des-* + *amide* + *-ize*] : DEAMIDATE
de·am·i·nase \(ˈ)dēˈamə,nās, -āz\ *also* **des·am·i·nase** \(ˈ)deˈsam-\ *n* -s [*de-* or *des-* + *amin-* + *-ase*] : an enzyme that hydrolyzes amino compounds (as amino acids) with the removal of the amino group
de·aminate \(ˈ)dē+\ *vt* [*de-* + *aminate*] : to remove the amino group from (a compound)
de·amination \(ˌ)dē+\ *or* **des·amination** \(ˌ)des+\ *n* : the process of deaminating ⟨the enzymatic oxidative ~ of glycine to glyoxylic acid and ammonia⟩ — compare AMINOLYSIS 2
de·aminization \(ˌ)dē+\ *n* -s : the process of deaminizing : DEAMINATION
de·aminize \(ˈ)dē+\ *vt* [*de-* + *aminize*] : DEAMINATE
[1]**dean** *var of* [1]DENE
[2]**dean** \ˈdēn\ *n* -s [ME *deen,* fr. MF *deien,* fr. LL *decanus,* lit., chief of ten, fr. L *decem* ten + *-anus* -an — more at TEN] **1** *obs* : a chief of 10 men : TITHINGMAN 1 **2 a** : a head over 10 monks in a monastery **b** : the head of the chapter or body of canons or prebendaries in a collegiate or cathedral church **c** : a priest of the Roman Catholic Church appointed by a bishop to supervise the affairs of a group of parishes within the diocese — called also *vicar forane* **3 a** : a resident fellow at an English university charged with the discipline rather than the instruction of undergraduates **b** : the head of one of the divisions, faculties, colleges, or schools of a university ⟨the ~*s* of several leading medical colleges⟩ ⟨the ~ of the faculty of arts⟩ ⟨the student must obtain the approval of the appropriate ~*s* and the chairmen of the departments concerned⟩ **c** : an administrative officer at a college or secondary school who counsels students on academic matters (as choice of program, maintenance of academic standing, honors, or failure) and who in addition has some disciplinary authority pertaining to such matters as breach of dormitory rules, unexcused absences, cheating and plagiarism, suspension, or dismissal ⟨~ of men⟩ ⟨~ of women⟩ ⟨~ of freshmen⟩ ⟨~ of the senior class⟩ **4** : a high officer of the orders of the Thistle and of the Bath who is always a clergyman — compare CHAPLAIN **5** : the senior of a group of men : DOYEN 1a
[3]**dean** \"\ *vi* -ED/-ING/-S : to act as dean ⟨was asked to ~⟩
dea·ner *var of* DEENER
dean·ery \ˈdēn(ə)rē, -ri\ *n* -ES [ME *denerie,* fr. *deen, den* dean + *-erie* -ery] **1 a** : the office or position of a dean **b** : the residence of a dean **2** : the jurisdiction of a dean
deanery of christianity *usu cap C* : any of various British deaneries comprising certain city or town parishes (as Exeter or Lincoln)
dean·ess \-nəs\ *n* -ES : a nun who serves as dean in a convent
dean of a peculiar : a titular dean of the Church of England either without peculiar jurisdiction (as the dean of the Chapels Royal) or with jurisdiction but without a chapter
dean of christianity *usu cap C* : a holder of one of certain rural deaneries in England
dean of convocation : the president of a convocation in churches of the Anglican Communion
dean of guild **1** : the head of a guild (as in medieval and some existing European guilds) having the power to summon the members to meetings **2** : a magistrate of a Scottish burgh or town formerly having jurisdiction of mercantile causes within a burgh and still entrusted with the inspection of and control over the construction, alteration, or repair of buildings
dean of the arches *usu cap D&A* [fr. the Court of *Arches,* the court of appeal for the province of Canterbury] : a lay judge in an ecclesiastical court (as the chancery court of the province of York) : the official principal of the archbishop of Canterbury
deans *pl of* DEAN, *pres 3d sing of* DEAN
dean schedule \ˈdēn-\ *n, usu cap D&S* [after Albert F. *Dean* †1933 Am. actuary] : a system for measuring the relative fire hazard and determining fire insurance rates for a property by an analysis of location, structural features, occupancy, and exposure
dean's list *n* : a list of students receiving special recognition from the dean of a college because of superior scholarship
[1]**dear** \ˈdi(ə)r, -iə\ *adj* -ER/-EST [ME *dere* brave, bold, hard, severe, fr. OE *dēor;* prob. akin to OE *dēor* beast — more at DEER] : SEVERE, SORE ⟨our *dearest* need⟩ ⟨his *dearest* enemies⟩
[2]**dear** \"\ *adj* -ER/-EST [ME *dere,* fr. OE *dēore;* akin to OHG *tiuri* costly, ON *dýrr*] **1** *obs* : GLORIOUS, WORTHY, HONORABLE **2** : regarded very affectionately or fondly : highly valued or esteemed : BELOVED ⟨ran for ~ life⟩ ⟨his son was very ~ to him⟩ ⟨the cause of democracy . . . is so ~ to us —M.R. Cohen⟩ — often used formally or affectionately in address ⟨*Dear* Sir⟩ ⟨my ~ James⟩ ⟨Mother ~⟩ **3** : LOVING, AFFECTIONATE, FOND ⟨for the ~ love I bear him⟩ **4 a** *obs* : SCARCE **b** : high-priced or expensive either absolutely ⟨butter is cheap when it is plentiful and ~ when it is scarce —G.B.Shaw⟩ or relatively ⟨that wretched suit would be ~ at any price⟩ **5** *obs* : VALUABLE, IMPORTANT **6 a** : close to the heart : present in mind : engaging the attention ⟨my ~*est* wish is for your happiness⟩ **b** : HEARTFELT, EARNEST ⟨one whose ~*est* prayer has been granted—G.B.Shaw⟩ **syn** see COSTLY
[3]**dear** \"\ *adv* [ME *dere,* fr. OE *dēore,* fr. *dēore,* adj.] **1** : DEARLY ⟨the effort cost him ~⟩ **2** : FONDLY, AFFECTIONATELY
[4]**dear** \"\ *n* -s [ME *dere,* fr. *dere,* adj.] **1** : a dear one : DARLING, SWEETHEART ⟨that kiss I carried from thee ~ —Shak.⟩ **2** : a lovable person ⟨pretty little ~*s*⟩ : an endearing person or being ⟨carry this in for me, like a ~⟩
[5]**dear** \"\ *vt* -ED/-ING/-S [ME *deren,* fr. *dere,* adj.] **1** *obs* : to make dear : make high-priced **2 a** : to address as *dear* **b** *obs* : ENDEAR
[6]**dear** \"\ *interj* [[4]*dear*] — used typically to express annoyance or dismay
dear·born \ˈdi(ə)r,bȯrn, -bərn\ *n* -s *sometimes cap* [after Henry A. S. *Dearborn* †1851 Am. politician and writer who maintained such a carriage] : a light 4-wheeled carriage with curtained sides
dearling *obs var of* DARLING
dear·ly *adv* [ME *derely,* fr. OE *dēorlice,* fr. *dēore* dear + *-lice* -ly — more at DEAR] : in a dear manner: as **a** *obs* : PRECIOUSLY, WORTHILY, RICHLY **b** : with affection : FONDLY, AFFECTIONATELY ⟨to love one ~⟩ **c** : HEARTILY, EARNESTLY, DEEPLY, KEENLY ⟨the peace we so ~ seek —D.D.Eisenhower⟩ **d** : at a high rate or price ⟨the victory was ~ won⟩
dear·ness *n* -ES [ME *derenesse,* fr. *dere* dear + *-nesse* -ness] : the quality or state of being dear: as **a** : LOVABLENESS : endearing quality **b** : reciprocal affection : FONDNESS **c** : COSTLINESS
dearness allowance *n, India* : a bonus or pay increase to meet a rise in the cost of living
[1]**dearth** \ˈdərth, ˈdāth, ˈdəith\ *n* -s [ME *derthe,* fr. *dere* costly, dear + *-the* -th — more at DEAR] **1** *obs* : DEARNESS : highness of price **2** : scarcity that makes dear : WANT; *specif* : FAMINE ⟨there came a ~ over all the land of Egypt —Acts 7:11 (AV)⟩ **3** : lack of a present necessity : deficiency or inadequate supply of something (as news) or of some quality (as courage)
[2]**dearth** *vt* -ED/-ING/-S [ME *derthen,* fr. *derthe,* n.] *obs* : to make scarce, dear, or high-priced
deary *or* **dear·ie** \ˈdirē, -ri\ *n, pl* **dear·ies** [[4]*dear* + *-y, -ie*] : little dear : DARLING — often used as a term of address
deas \ˈdēs, -ā-,-e-\ *n* -ES [ME *deis, dees* raised table, raised platform — more at DAIS] *Scot* : BENCH, SETTLE; *esp* : one that can also be used as a table
de·ash \(ˈ)dē+\ *vt* [*de-* + *ash* (residue of combustion)] : to remove ash from
[1]**dea·sil** *also* **dei·seal** *or* **des·sil** \ˈdēzəl, ˈdes(h)əl\ *adv* [ScGael *deiseil;* akin to IrGael *deiseal* act of turning to the right, OIr *dess* right hand, south, ScGael *deas,* W *deheu, deau, de* right, southern, Bret *dehou* right, south, L *dexter* right — more at DEXTER] : RIGHT-HANDWISE, SUNWISE, CLOCKWISE — used esp. of the Masonic rite of circumambulation and also of Masonic floor work that is clockwise; compare WIDDERSHINS
[2]**deasil** \"\ *n* -s : a charm performed by going three times about an object in the direction of the sun and sometimes carrying fire in the right hand
de·aspirate \(ˈ)dē+\ *vt* [*de-* + *aspirate*] : to pronounce without aspiration
de·assimilation \ˌdē+\ *n* [*de-* + *assimilation*] : CATABOLISM
death \ˈdeth\ *n, pl* **deaths** \-ths *sometimes* -thz\ [ME *deeth, deth,* fr. OE *dēath;* akin to OHG *tōd* death, ON *dauthi,* Goth *dauthus;* derivative fr. the root of ON *deyja* to die — more at DIE] **1** : the ending of all vital functions without possibility of recovery either in animals or plants or any parts of them : the end of life : the act, process, or fact of dying **2 a** : the cause or occasion of loss of life ⟨drinking was the ~ of him⟩ : a deadly weapon or agency ⟨a cobra with ~ in its fangs⟩ **b** *archaic* : PLAGUE — see BLACK DEATH **3** *usu cap* : the bringer of death personified and conventionally represented as a skeleton with a scythe : the destroyer of life : GRIM REAPER **4 a** : the state of being no longer alive ⟨in ~ as in life⟩ **b** : a joyless dull tasteless existence : the state of being without full possession or enjoyment of the intellectual or physical faculties ⟨the ~ in life of long years spent in a hospital bed⟩ **c** : cessation or absence of spiritual life variously conceived as alienation from God, deadness to the appeals of spiritual ideals, annihilation of the spirit as a result of sin, or irredeemable damnation — called also *spiritual death* ⟨to be carnally minded is ~ —Rom 8:6 (AV)⟩ **5** : the passing or destruction of something inanimate ⟨the ~ of the rackety old Third Avenue El —*Newsweek*⟩ or intangible ⟨the ~ of all his hopes⟩ ⟨the ~ of vaudeville⟩ : the process of such passing ⟨the ~ of the empire⟩ : EXTINCTION ⟨the ~ of a species⟩ **6** : CIVIL DEATH **7** : lethal or murderous violence : HOMICIDE ⟨merchants of ~⟩ ⟨a man of ~ —Francis Bacon⟩ **8** *Christian Science* : the lie of life in matter : that which is unreal and untrue : ILLUSION — **at death's door** : close to death : critically ill : in real or apparent danger of dying — **be death on** **1** : to have marked talent for accomplishing or dealing with ⟨his approach shots are erratic but he *is death on* putts⟩ **2** : to dislike or oppose vigorously ⟨the boss *is death on* latecomers⟩ — **in at the death** : present at the conclusion of an event — **to death** *adv* : to the last extremity ⟨tired *to death*⟩ : beyond endurance : EXCESSIVELY ⟨that kind of plot has been done *to death*⟩ — **to the death** **1** : to death **2** : as long as life lasts : to the end : without wavering or compromise ⟨war *to the death*⟩ ⟨follow our leader *to the death*⟩ ⟨hunting a criminal *to the death*⟩
death adder *n* : a highly venomous elapid snake (*Acanthophis antarcticus*) of the Australian region having a stout body and a spine on the end of the tail; *also* : any of several other related venomous snakes of Australia and Tasmania
death alder *n* [so called fr. its poisonous effect on cattle] : a spindle tree (*Euonymus europaeus*)
[1]**death angel** *n* : AZRAEL
[2]**death angel** *n* : DEATH CUP 1
death apple *n* : MANCHINEEL
deathbed \ˈ=,=\ *n* [ME *deeth bed,* fr. *deeth* death + *bed*] : the bed in which a person dies : the last hours of life ⟨~ baptism⟩
deathbed deed *n, early Scots law* : a deed made after contracting a sickness that ended in death within 60 days after the date of granting and without such convalescence as is indicated by the grantor going unsupported to kirk or market
death bell *n* : PASSING BELL
death benefit *n* : money payable to the beneficiary or estate of a deceased under a policy of life or accident insurance or a pension plan
death bill *n* : an ecclesiastical list of dead to be prayed for
deathblow \ˈ=,=\ *n* : a mortal blow ⟨he received his ~ in his first battle⟩ : a stroke or event that kills, destroys, or puts an end to
death board *n* : a plank on which a corpse is laid for sea burial
death camas *n* : any of several plants of the genus *Zigadenus* (as *Z. venenosus* and *Z. glaucus*) that cause poisoning of grazing animals in the western U. S.
death candle *n* : CORPSE CANDLE
death cell *n* : a prison cell for one awaiting execution
death certificate *n* : a certificate in which various information (as age, race, occupation) relating to a dead person is given and in which a physician certifies the cause of death
death chamber *n* : a room in which a person is dying or lies dead; *specif* : a place of execution within a prison
death-come-quickly \ˌ=(ˌ)=ˈ=ˌ=\ *n, dial Eng* : HERB ROBERT
death cord *n* : a rope used for hanging a person — called also *death rope*
death cup *n* **1** *also* **death angel** : a very poisonous mushroom (*Amanita phalloides*) of wide distribution ranging in color from pure white (as usu. in the U.S.) to olive or yellow and having a prominent volva at the base **2** : the prominent cuplike enlargement at the base of the stipe in some fungi of the genus *Amanita* that is characteristic of poisonous forms though present also in some that are harmless
deathday \ˈ=,=\ *n* [ME *deethday,* fr. OE *dēathdæg,* fr. *dēath* death + *dæg* day — more at DAY] : the day of a person's death or its anniversary
death duty *n, chiefly Brit* : DEATH TAX
death fire *or* **death light** *n* : DEADLIGHT 3, CORPSE CANDLE
death·ful \ˈdethfəl\ *adj* [ME *deethful,* fr. *deeth* death + *-ful*] **1** *archaic* : full of or threatening death : DEADLY, MURDEROUS, DESTRUCTIVE, BLOODY **2** *archaic* : liable to undergo death : MORTAL **3** : like death : having the appearance of death : DEATHLY ⟨on his ~ face . . . a look of pain and baffled anger —Richard Hofstadter⟩ — **death·ful·ly** \-əlē\ *adv*
death herb *n* : BELLADONNA 1
death house *n* : the section of a prison for persons awaiting execution
death·in \ˈdethən\ *n* -s [prob. fr. *death* + *in*] **1** : a water hemlock (*Cicuta virosa*) of Europe **2** : a poisonous plant (*Oenanthe phellandrium*) closely related to the water hemlock
death instinct *n* : unconscious or biological tendencies toward self-destruction
death knell *n* **1** : PASSING BELL **2** : an action or event presaging death or destruction ⟨the coming of the power press was the *death knell* of the hand press⟩
death·less \ˈdethləs\ *adj* : not subject to death, destruction, or extinction : IMMORTAL, UNDYING, IMPERISHABLE ⟨~ fame⟩ ⟨~ poems⟩ — **death·less·ly** *adv* — **death·less·ness** *n* -ES
death·like \ˈ=,=\ *adj* : DEATHLY
death·li·ness \ˈdethlēnəs, -lin-\ *n* -ES : the quality or state of being deathly
death·ling \-liŋ\ *n* -s : one liable to death : MORTAL
[1]**death·ly** \ˈdethlē, -li\ *adj* [ME *dethlich* deadly, mortal, fr. OE *dēathlic* mortal, fr. *dēath* death + *-lic* -ly] **1** : DEADLY, FATAL, MORTAL, DESTRUCTIVE **2** : like or having the characteristics of death ⟨a ~ stillness⟩ **3** : of, relating to, or suggestive of death ⟨I marked each ~ change in him —Robert Browning⟩ **syn** see DEADLY
[2]**deathly** \"\ *adv* : in a way or to a degree resembling or approximating death ⟨~ sick⟩
death march *n* : a march (as of prisoners of war) in which those unable to go on are left to die as they fall
death mask *n* : a cast taken from the face of a dead person
death penny *n* **1** : a coin placed with a buried corpse as if to pay passage to the otherworld **2** : DEATH WEIGHT
death point *n* : a limit (as of degree of heat or cold) beyond which an organism or living protoplasm cannot survive
death rate *n* : the ratio between number of deaths and number of individuals in a specified population and period of time usu. expressed as number of deaths per hundred or per thousand population
death rattle *n* : a rattling or gurgling sound produced by air passing through mucus in the lungs and air passages of one dying
death rope *n* : DEATH CORD
death row *n* : a row of death cells
deaths *pl of* DEATH
death's-head \ˈdeths,hed\ *n* **1** : a human skull as the emblem of death : the head of Death **2** : a finger ring bearing the figure of a skull
death's-head moth *n* : a very large dark European hawkmoth (*Acherontia atropos*) with markings resembling a human skull on the back of the thorax
death's-herb *n, obs* : BELLADONNA 1
deaths·man \ˈdethsmən\ *n, pl* **deathsmen** *archaic* : a man who puts persons to death : EXECUTIONER

death–struck \'=,=\ *also* **death–stricken** \'=,==\ *adj* **:** mortally injured or sick

death tax *n* **:** a tax arising on the transmission of property (as an estate, inheritance, legacy, succession) after the owner's death

deathtrap \'=,=\ *n* **:** a structure or situation that is potentially very dangerous (as by fire) to life ⟨the boat was just seaworthy enough to be a ~ —Padraic Fallon⟩

death·ward \'dethwə(r)d\ *or* **death·wards** \-dz\ *adv* (*or adj*) [ME deethward, fr. *deeth* death + *-ward, -wards*] **:** toward death **:** approaching death

death warrant *n* **1 :** a warrant for the execution of a death sentence **2 :** something that puts an end to the existence or continuance of anything ⟨declared the new law the *death warrant* of unfettered competition⟩

[1]**deathwatch** \'=,=\ *n* [*death* + *watch* (timepiece); fr. the superstition that its ticking presages death] **:** any of several small insects that make a ticking sound: as **: a** *or* **death-watch beetle :** any of various small beetles of the family Anobiidae that are common in old houses where they bore in the woodwork and furniture making a clicking noise probably by knocking the head against the wood **b :** BOOK LOUSE

[2]**deathwatch** \'=¦=\ *n* [*death* + *watch* (vigil)] **1 :** a vigil kept with the dead or dying **2 a :** the guard set over a criminal before his execution **b :** a group of press reporters waiting for an expected announcement or break in a big story

deathweed \'=,=\ *n* **:** POVERTYWEED c

death weight *n* **:** a small weight (as a coin) laid on the eyelids of a corpse to keep them closed

death wish *n* **:** the conscious or unconscious desire for the death of another or of oneself

deathworm \'=,=\ *n* **:** a worm that feeds on a buried dead body

deathy \'dethē\ *adj* **:** DEATHLY, DEADLY

de·aurate \dē'ȯ,rāt\ *vt* -ED/-ING/-S [LL *deauratus*, past part. of *deaurare*, fr. L *de-* + *aurare* to cover with gold, gild, fr. *aurum* gold — more at ORIOLE] *archaic* **:** GILD — **de·aura·tion** \,dē,ȯ'rāshən\ *n* -S *archaic*

deau·ville sand \'dō,vil-, (')dō¦vēl-\ *n, often cap D* [fr. *Deauville*, Calvados dept., France] **:** a light grayish brown that is redder and paler than average fawn — called also *stucco*

deave \'dēv\ *vt* -ED/-ING/-S [ME *deven*, fr. OE *-dēafian* (as in *ādēafian* to become deaf), fr. *dēaf* deaf — more at DEAF] **1** *dial Brit* **:** to stun or stupefy with noise **:** DEAFEN **2** *dial Brit* **:** BOTHER, CONFUSE

deave·ly \-li\ *adj, often* -ER/-EST [prob. fr. [1]*deaf* + *-ly*] *dial Eng* **:** LONELY

deb \'deb\ *n* -S [by shortening] **:** DEBUTANTE

deb *abbr* debenture

de·babelization \(')dē+\ *n* -S [*de-* + *babelization*] **:** the removal of obstacles to verbal communication ⟨the question still remains whether ~ will be accomplished by the voluntary adoption of a national tongue —K.D.Burke⟩

de·ba·cle \dā'bäkəl, dā'-,dē'-, -ak-,-äk- *sometimes* dā'bäk(l[ə]) *or* dā'bák(l[ə])\ *n* -S [F *débâcle*, fr. *débâcler* to unbar, unbolt, fr. MF *desbacler*, fr. *des-* de- + *bacler* to bar, bolt, fr. OProv *baclar*, fr. (assumed) VL *bacculare*, fr. (assumed) VL *baculum* stick, staff, alter. of L *baculum* — more at BACTERIUM] **1 a** (1) **:** a breaking up of ice in a river (2) **:** the rush (as of water and ice) that follows such a breaking up **b :** a violent destructive flood **2 :** a sudden breaking up or breaking loose **:** a violent dispersion or disruption (as of an army or mob) **:** STAMPEDE, ROUT ⟨Custer's ~ on the Little Big Horn —Seth Agnew⟩ **3 :** a sudden breakdown **:** COLLAPSE ⟨the Wall Street ~ of 1929 —Isabel Leighton⟩

de·bag \(')dē+\ *vt* [*de-* + *bag* (trousers)] *Brit* **:** to remove the trousers from as a punishment or in hazing ⟨the new boy was *debagged* and thrown in the fountain⟩

de·bar \dē, də+\ *vt* [ME *debarren*, fr. MF *desbarrer* to remove the bars from a door, fr. OF, fr. *des-* de- + *barrer* to fasten with a bar — more at BAR] **1 :** to prevent from an action ⟨government contractors *debarred* from sitting in Parliament —J.H.Plumb⟩ **:** shut out **:** EXCLUDE ⟨custom ~*s* certain persons from marriage⟩ **:** bar from the possession, use, or enjoyment of something ⟨cities like New York . . . are *debarred* from a share of modern tax revenues —A.A.Berle⟩ **2 :** to set a barrier or prohibition against ⟨a gate ~*s* all passage⟩ **:** DEPRIVE ⟨they *debarred* him from the sacrament⟩ **3 :** to exclude from membership in a group or class ⟨the qualifications ~ most of the best applicants⟩ **syn** see EXCLUDE — **debar the tables :** to fence the tables

de·barbarize \(')dē+\ *vt* [*de-* + *barbarize*] **:** to free from barbarousness **:** make no longer barbarous

[1]**de·bark** \də'bärk,dē'-, -bák\ *vb* -ED/-ING/-S [MF *debarquer*, fr. *de-* + *barque* bark (sailing vessel) — more at BARK] **:** DISEMBARK

[2]**de·bark** \(')dē+\ *vt* -ED/-ING/-S [*de-* + *bark* (of a tree)] **:** to remove bark from

[3]**debark** \"\ *vt* -ED/-ING/-S [*de* + *bark* (sound made by a dog)] **:** to remove the vocal cords from (a dog) to check barking

de·bar·ka·tion \,dē,bär'kāshən, -bá'- *sometimes* də,- *or* ,dē,-\ *n* -S [[1]*debark* + *-ation*] **:** DISEMBARKATION

debarkation net *n* **:** a net that may be hung over the side of a ship to enable troops to climb down into small boats

de·bar·ment \dē'bärmənt, də'-, -bám-\ *n* -S **1 :** the act of debarring **2 :** the state of being debarred

de·bar·rance \-rən(t)s\ *also* **de·bar·ra·tion** \,dē,bä'rāshən, -bá-\ *n* -S **:** the act of fencing the tables in Scottish Presbyterian churches

de·bar·rass \də'barəs, dē'-\ *vt* -ED/-ING/-ES [F *débarrasser*, fr. MF *desbarrasser*, fr. *de-* + *embarrasser* to embarrass — more at EMBARRASS] **:** to disembarrass esp. by removing what impedes or encumbers ⟨~*ed* her of her coat and hat⟩

de·base \də'bās, dē'-\ *vt* -ED/-ING/-S [*de-* + *base* (low, vile); after *abase*] **1** *obs* **:** to lower in esteem by verbal attack **:** DISPARAGE, VILIFY **2 :** to lower in status or esteem ⟨~ himself by physical labor⟩ **:** put to a low or inferior use ⟨a style *debased* by many imitators⟩ **3 :** to lower the quality or character of **:** cause to deteriorate ⟨struggle with Hannibal had . . . *debased* the Roman temper —John Buchan⟩ **4 a :** to reduce the intrinsic value of (a coin) by increasing the base metal content **b :** to reduce the exchange value of (a monetary unit) **:** DEPRECIATE

syn VITIATE, DEPRAVE, CORRUPT, DEBAUCH, PERVERT: DEBASE indicates a drastic and regrettable lowering in worth, value, and dignity and a loss of fine or good qualities ⟨the human values cruelly and systematically *debased* by the Nazis—Vera M. Dean⟩ ⟨Strachey's attitude toward a respected historical figure and his new techniques were soon *debased* by a school of so-called debunking biographers —J.D.Hart⟩ VITIATE is applicable to the introduction or effect of something deleterious and the ensuing destruction of purity, impairment of validity, or enervation of effectiveness ⟨party jealousies *vitiated* the whole military organization —*Times Lit. Supp.*⟩ ⟨his endless muttering *vitiated* every effort I made to think out a line of action —H.G.Wells⟩ DEPRAVE indicates moral deterioration into the obscene and vicious ⟨the servants, wicked and *depraved*, corrupt and deprave the children; the children are bad, full of evil, to a sinister degree —Henry James †1916⟩ CORRUPT indicates bringing about a loss of soundness, purity, and integrity ⟨at sixteen the girl was further *corrupted* by a "perverse and wicked" young man —Edmund Wilson⟩ ⟨the ballot box, *corrupted*, no longer recorded the voice of the people —Oscar Handlin⟩ ⟨to *corrupt* their taste first and try to purify it afterwards —Bertrand Russell⟩ DEBAUCH usu. suggests corrupting and vulgarizing through sensual pleasure or other indulgence with loss of sense of morality, loyalty, duty, integrity, and resolution ⟨she takes them to an enchanted isle, where she *debauches* them with enervating delights and renders them oblivious to their duty —R.A.Hall b.1911⟩ ⟨readers *debauched* by sentimental and romantic liberalism and naturalism —Douglas Bush⟩ PERVERT suggests a debasing twisting or contorting into an untrue or abnormal condition ⟨those who *pervert* good words to careless misuse may be thought more often ludicrous than harmful —J.M.Barzun⟩ ⟨those who *pervert* honest criticism into falsification of fact —F.D.Roosevelt⟩ ⟨sexually *perverted* during his term in prison⟩

de·based·ness \-sədnəs, -s(t)n-\ *n* -ES **:** the quality or state of being debased

de·base·ment \-smənt\ *n* -S **1 :** the act or process of debasing ⟨the ~ of the coinage⟩ **2 :** the state of being debased **3 :** something that debases

de·bas·er \-sə(r)\ *n* -S **:** one that debases

de·bas·ing·ly *adv* **:** in a debasing manner

dé·bat \dā'bä, *F* dābà\ *n* -S [F, lit., debate, strife, altercation, fr. OF *debat*] **1 :** a type of literary composition popular esp. in medieval times in which two or more usu. allegorical characters discuss or debate some subject — compare TENSON **2 :** an extended discussion, debate, or philosophical argument between two characters in a work of literature

de·bat·able *also* **de·bate·able** \də'bād·əbəl, dē'-, -ātə-\ *adj* [ML *debatabilis*, fr. ME *debaten* to debate + L *-abilis* -able] **1 :** claimed by more than one country — used of land ⟨the governor . . . dispatched troops . . . into the ~ territory —H.E.Scudder⟩ **2 a :** open to question or dispute **:** DISPUTABLE, QUESTIONABLE, DOUBTFUL ⟨whether this report is accurate is a ~ question⟩ ⟨the ~ wisdom of your advice⟩ **b :** open to debate ⟨decisions are ~ in closed sessions but binding on members when a parliamentary vote is taken⟩ **:** capable of producing debate ⟨a list of ~ topics for classroom use⟩

[1]**de·bate** \-āt, *usu* -ād·+V\ *n* -S [ME *debat*, fr. OF, fr. *debatre*] **1 a** *obs* **:** a fight or fighting **:** CONTEST **b** *archaic* **:** QUARREL, DISSENSION, STRIFE **2 a :** a contention by means of words or arguments ⟨an evening's ~ among friends⟩ **:** strife in argument **:** CONTROVERSY; *specif* **:** the formal discussion, argumentation, and resolution of a motion before a legislative assembly or other public deliberative body according to the rules of parliamentary procedure **b :** consideration of or reflection upon a problem ⟨paused hesitantly, but after a moment of ~ she went forward⟩ **3 a :** an instance of debating ⟨we have just now engaged in a great ~ —F.D.Roosevelt⟩ **b** (1) **:** a regulated discussion of a proposition between two matched sides as a test of forensic ability (2) **:** a course of study of the methods and techniques of such discussion often taught in schools and colleges

[2]**debate** \"\ *vb* -ED/-ING/-S [ME *debaten*, fr. MF *debatre*, fr. OF, fr. *de-* + *batre* to beat, fr. L *battere*, alter. of *battuere* — more at BAT (stick)] *vi* **1** *obs* **:** to engage in combat or strife **:** FIGHT, CONTEND, QUARREL **2 a :** to contend in words **:** DISPUTE **b :** to discuss or examine a question by considering or stating different arguments ⟨Socrates *debated* on the subject of life and death⟩ **3 :** to participate in a debate or other public disputation or discussion **4 :** to reflect upon a question or problem ⟨~ with oneself before deciding to go⟩ **~** *vt* **1 a :** to argue about **:** DISCUSS ⟨the subject was hotly *debated*⟩; *esp* **:** to discuss (a matter of public concern) in a legislative assembly **b :** to engage in debate with (an opponent) ⟨Lincoln *debated* Douglas on this issue⟩ **2 :** to turn over (a matter) in one's mind **:** reflect upon ⟨I held her hand for a moment, *debating* a reply —L.C.Douglas⟩ **3** *archaic* **:** to engage in combat for **:** strive or fight for or over **:** CONTEST **syn** see DISCUSS

debatement *n* -S [MF, fr. *debatre* + *-ment*] *obs* **:** DEBATE, CONTROVERSY, CONFLICT

de·bat·er \də'bād·ə(r), dē-, -atə-\ *n* -S [ME, fr. *debaten* + *-er*] **:** one that debates

de·bat·ing·ly *adv* **:** in a debating manner

[1]**de·bauch** \də'bȯch, dē'-, -bäch\ *vb* -ED/-ING/-ES [MF *debaucher*, fr. OF *desbauchier* to scatter, separate, lit., to rough-hew (timber for a beam), fr. *des-* de- + *-bauchier* (fr. *bauch, bauc* beam, of Gmc origin; akin to OHG *balko* beam) — more at BALK] *vt* **1** *archaic* **a :** to lead away or seduce from one to whom duty or allegiance is owed **:** lead or seduce esp. to an evil party or action **b :** to seduce from duty or allegiance **:** make disloyal **:** DISAFFECT **2** *obs* **:** to disparage by unfavorable comment **3 a :** to lead astray from what is good or right ⟨a performance ~*ed* by an excess of vulgarity⟩ **:** win away from integrity ⟨corrupt the press and ~ the legislatures⟩ **:** corrupt in character or principle ⟨factory methods . . . ~*ed* Victorian design —*Country Life*⟩ **b :** to corrupt esp. by intemperance or sensuality **c :** to seduce from chastity **4** *obs* **:** to spend lavishly **:** SQUANDER **~** *vi* **:** to indulge excessively in sensual pleasure ⟨a man who never gambled or ~*ed*⟩ **syn** see DEBASE

[2]**debauch** \"\ *n* -ES [F *débauche*, fr. MF *debauche*, fr. *debaucher*] **1 a :** an act or occasion of debauchery ⟨a night's ~⟩ **b :** an act or occasion of indulging to excess esp. in a violent, emotional, or pleasurable activity ⟨I have had a vast ~ of reading —H.J.Laski⟩ ⟨a ~ of speculation on the stock exchange⟩ **2 :** excess in sensual pleasures **:** DEBAUCHERY ⟨tales of battle and ~ —Max Peacock⟩ **3** *obs* **:** DEBAUCHEE

de·bauched \-cht\ *adj* **:** DISSOLUTE, DEPRAVED ⟨old woman . . . with a ~ face —Liam O'Flaherty⟩ — **de·bauched·ly** \-chəd-lē, -chtlē\ *adv* — **de·bauched·ness** \-chədnəs, -ch(t)n-\ *n* -ES

de·bauch·ee \də'bȯ(,)chē, dē'-, -bä-, ,chi; də,bȯ'chē, (,)dē,-, -bä-; ¦debə¦shē, -bō,-, -e(,)bō¦-, -¦shā\ *n* -S [F *débauché*, fr. past part. of *débaucher* to debauch] **:** one given to sensual excesses (as intemperance) ⟨weird orgies . . . of jaded ~*s* —I.S.Cobb⟩

de·bauch·er \də'bȯchə(r), dē'-, -bäch-\ *n* -S **:** one that debauches; *esp* **:** one that seduces another from chastity

de·bauch·ery \-ch(ə)rē, -ri\ *n* -ES **1 a :** extreme indulgence in sensuality **:** INTEMPERANCE ⟨nights of riotous ~⟩; *esp* **:** excessive indulgence of sexual desire **b** **debaucheries** *pl* **:** ORGIES, CAROUSALS **2** *archaic* **:** corruption of fidelity **:** seduction from virtue, duty, or allegiance

debauchment *n* -S [F *débauchement*, fr. MF *debauchement*, fr. *debaucher* to debauch + *-ment*] **1** *obs* **:** the action of debauching **2** *obs* **:** the state of being debauched

de·beak \(')dē+\ *vt* [back-formation fr. *Debeaker*, a trademark] **:** to remove the tip of the upper mandible of (a bird) to prevent cannibalism and fighting

de·bel *or* **de·bell** \də'bel\ *vt* **debelled; debelling; debels** *or* **debells** [MF or L; MF *debeller*, fr. L *debellare*] **:** CONQUER, SUBDUE

debellate *vt* -ED/-ING/-S [L *debellatus*, past part. of *debellare*, fr. *de-* + *bellare* to wage war, fr. *bellum* war — more at DUEL] *obs* **:** DEBEL

de·bel·la·tio \,dābə'lād·ē,ō\ *n* -S [LL, fr. L *debellatus* + *-io* -ion] **:** complete subjugation of a belligerent nation usu. involving loss of sovereignty

deb·el·la·tion \,debə'lāshən\ *n* -S [LL *debellation-, debellatio*] **:** the action of debelling

de be·ne es·se \,dā,benē'esē\ *adv* [ML, lit., of well-being] **:** of sufficiency for the present **:** CONDITIONALLY, PROVISIONALLY — used of various things done subject to future exception or avoidance (as the taking of testimony before trial where it may be unavailable at the time of trial)

de·ben·ture \də'benchə(r), dē'-\ *n* -S [ME *debentur*, fr. L, they are due, 3d pers. pl. pres. pass. of *debēre* to owe — more at DEBT] **1 :** a writing or certificate signed by a public officer as evidence of a debt or of a right to demand or receive a sum of money: as **a :** a voucher from a government official certifying a sum of money to be due to a person (as for stores supplied to the ordnance department) **b :** a customhouse certificate entitling an exporter of imported goods to a drawback of duties paid on their importation **c :** an instrument issued as evidence of debt by a government on the security of the public assets or credit **2 a** *Brit* **:** a security issued by a company other than its shares **:** BOND **b** *or* **debenture bond :** a bond usu. secured by an indenture containing protective provisions but without a specific lien on any asset — now the usual U.S. use; distinguished from *mortgage bond;* compare [3]BOND 5b

debenture stock *n* **:** a corporate security issue common in Great Britain that usu. has no fixed maturity date for the principal but that has a fixed claim to interest payments which takes precedence over preferred and common stocks

de·benzylation \(')dē+\ *n* -S [*de-* + *benzyl* + *-ation*] **:** the removal of benzyl groups from a compound often by hydrogenation

deb·ile \'debəl, -,bīl, -(,)bil; 'dē,bīl\ *adj* [MF *debile*, fr. L *debilis* weak, feeble — more at DEBILITY] *archaic* **:** marked by debility **:** FEEBLE

de·bil·i·tate \də'bilə,tāt, dē'-, *usu* -ād·+V\ *vt* -ED/-ING/-S [L *debilitatus*, past part. of *debilitare* to weaken, fr. *debilis* weak] **:** to impair the strength of **:** WEAKEN, ENFEEBLE ⟨a body *debilitated* by disease⟩ ⟨war . . . left a *debilitated* economic plant —C.R.Decker⟩ **syn** see WEAKEN

de·bil·i·ta·tion \də,bilə'tāshən, (,)dē,-\ *n* -S [MF, fr. L *debilitation-, debilitatio*, fr. *debilitatus* + *-ion-, -io* -ion] **1 :** the act or process of debilitating **2 :** the state of being debilitated **:** WEAKNESS ⟨the greater the ~, the greater the need for protein replenishment —P.R.Cannon⟩

de·bil·i·ta·tive \də'bilə,tād·iv, dē'-, -,təd-\ *adj, archaic* **:** debilitating in its tendency **:** causing debility

de·bil·i·ty \-ləd·ē, -etē, -i\ *n* -ES [MF *débilité*, fr. L *debilitat-, debilitas*, fr. *debilis* weak (fr. *de* from, away + *-bilis* strength) + *-itat-, -itas* -ity; akin to Gk *belteros* better, OSlav *bolĭjĭ* larger, Skt *bala* strength — more at DE-] **:** the quality or state of being weak, feeble, or infirm; *esp* **:** physical weakness

[1]**deb·it** \'debət, *usu* -əd·+V\ *n* -S *often attrib* [L *debitum* debt — more at DEBT] **1 a :** an entry on the left-hand side of an account constituting an addition to an expense or asset account or a deduction from a revenue, net worth, or liability account **b :** any one of the items on the left-hand side of an account; *also* **:** the sum of these items — opposed to *credit;* abbr. *dr* **c :** a charge against a bank deposit account **2 :** something regarded as disadvantageous or unfavorable ⟨against these successes by the administration there are on the ~ side a number of serious failures⟩ **3 :** an area to which an insurance agent is assigned for the purpose of collecting premiums from the policyholders **syn** see DEBT

[2]**debit** \"\ *vt* -ED/-ING/-S **:** to enter upon the left-hand side of an account **:** charge to the debit of ⟨~ a creditor's account⟩ — opposed to *credit*

deb·it·able \'debəd·əbəl\ *adj* **:** that can or should be debited

de·bi·ta la·ico·rum \¦debəd·ə,lāə'kōrəm\ *n pl* [ML] **:** debts of the laity

deb·i·teuse \,debə¦tüz\ *n* -S [F *débiteuse*, fr. F *débiter* to discharge, yield, sell retail, cut up, (fr. MF *debiter* to cut wood, sell retail, fr. *de-* + *-biter*, of Scand origin; akin to ON *biti* beam, thwart) + *-euse* (fem. of *-eur* -or) — more at BOAT] **:** a rectangular clay block floating upon molten glass in a tank furnace and containing a long slot that shapes glass into a sheet as it is drawn through it

debit note *n* **:** a memorandum of goods returned and debited to a consignor by a consignee

debitor *n* -S [MF & L; MF *debiteur*, fr. L *debitor* — more at DEBTOR] *obs* **:** DEBTOR

de·bitter \(')dē+\ *vt* [*de-* + *bitter* (adj.)] **:** to remove the bitterness from (an edible substance)

de·bit·ter·ize \(')dē'bid·ə,rīz\ *vt* -ED/-ING/-S [*de-* + *bitter* (adj.) + *-ize*] **:** DEBITTER

debit ticket *n* **1 :** an order drawn by an employee of a bank at a depositor's request to pay out money against the depositor's account **2** *or* **debit memo :** a memorandum of a charge (as for service) made by a bank against a depositor's account **3 :** a slip indicating a transaction to be debited to an account or in the general ledger

deb·i·tum \'debəd·əm\ *n, pl* **debi·ta** \-d·ə\ [L — more at DEBT] **:** DEBT

debitum fun·di \-'fən,dī, -'fün,dē\ *n, pl* **debita fundi** [L, lit., debt of an estate] *Scots law* **:** a debt that is a lien on land

de·block \(')dē+\ *vt* [*de-* + *block*] **:** to relax or remove monetary restrictions on (as the transfer of bank funds or currency out of a country)

deboist *adj* [by alter.] *obs* **:** DEBAUCHED

deb·o·nair *also* **deb·o·naire** \¦debə¦na(a)(ə)r, -ne\, \|ə\ *adj* [ME *debonere*, fr. OF *debonaire*, fr. *de bon aire, de bonne aire* of good family, lineage, or nature] **1** *archaic* **:** kindly or gentle in disposition or manner **:** COURTEOUS, GRACIOUS ⟨~ and pleasing toward our lieges —Sir Walter Scott⟩ **2 a :** having grace, charm, or urbanity of manner and appearance **b :** LIGHTHEARTED, CAREFREE ⟨life that is gay, brisk, and ~ —H.M. Reynolds⟩ **:** NONCHALANT ⟨his ~ dismissal of serious difficulties —E.M.Earle⟩ — **deb·o·nair·ly** *adv*

deb·o·nair·ness *n* -ES [ME *debonerenesse*, fr. *debonere* + *-nesse* -ness] **:** the quality of being debonair **:** good humor **:** JAUNTINESS, LIGHTHEARTEDNESS

de·bone \(')dē+\ *vt* [*de-* + *bone* (n.)] **:** to remove (bone) from meat

de bo·nis as·por·ta·tis \,dā'bōnə,saspə(r)'täd·əs\ *n* [L, of goods carried away] **:** an action of trespass to recover money damages from one who has taken away or damaged property without right

de bonis non \(,)dā¦bōnə¦snän\ *or* **de bonis non ad·min·i·stra·tis** \dā'bōnə,snänəd,minə'sträd·əs\ [L, of the goods not (administered)] **:** concerning the goods of a deceased person not yet administered — used of an administrator or of letters of administration

de bonis pro·pri·is \(,)dā¦bō-nə'sprōprēəs\ [L, out of one's own goods] **:** out of his own pocket — used of a judgment against an administrator or executor to be satisfied out of his own funds

de·bord \də'bȯ(ə)rd, dē'-\ *vi* -ED/-ING/-S [F *déborder*, fr. MF *desborder*, fr. *des-* de- + *-border* (fr. *bord* shore, bank, edge, board of a ship, fr. OF *bort* edge, end, board of a ship) — more at BORDER] **1** *archaic* **:** to flow beyond its banks — used of a body of water **2** *obs* **:** to go beyond bounds **:** go to excess

de·boshed \-bäsht\ *adj* [by alter.] **:** DEBAUCHED

de·boss \(')dē+\ *vt* [*de-* + *boss* (protruding ornament)] **:** to depress (as a design on a book cover) below the surrounding surface esp. for decoration or lettering — opposed to *emboss*

de·bot effect \də'bō-\ *n, usu cap D* [after R. *Debot*, 20th cent. Belgian scientist] **:** a manifestation of the Herschel effect in which the internal latent image is converted into a surface latent image by the action of red or infrared radiation

de·bouch \də'büsh, dē-, -bauch\ *vb* -ED/-ING/-ES [F *déboucher*, fr. *dé-* de- (fr. OF *de-, des-*) + *bouche* mouth, opening, fr. OF *boche, bouche*, fr. L *bucca* puffed out cheek, mouth — more at POCK] *vi* **1 :** to march out (as from a wood or defile) into open ground ⟨the three regiments ~*ing* from three separate gorges —Rudyard Kipling⟩ **2 :** to emerge into a more open place **:** issue forth **:** pass out into ⟨the tributary ~*es* into the main stream⟩ **~** *vt* **:** to lead out into the open **:** cause to emerge **:** DISCHARGE ⟨motor coaches ~*ed* a crowd —William Sansom⟩

dé·bou·ché \,dā,bü¦shā\ *n* -S [F, fr. past part. of *déboucher*] **:** an opening or passage that can serve as an outlet (as for the debouching of troops)

de·bouch·ment \də'büshmənt, dē'-, -bauch-\ *n* -S [F *débouchement*, fr. *déboucher* + *-ment*] **1 :** the act or process of debouching **2 :** a mouth or outlet esp. of a river

de·bou·chure \-¦bü¦shü(ə)r\ *n* -S [F, fr. *déboucher* + *-ure*] **:** DEBOUCHMENT 2

de·bre·cen \'debrət,sen\ *adj, usu cap* [fr. *Debrecen*, Hungary] **:** of or from the city of Debrecen, Hungary **:** of the kind or style prevalent in Debrecen

de·bride \də'brēd, dā'-\ *vt* -ED/-ING/-S [F *débrider*, lit., to unbridle, fr. MF *desbrider*, fr. *des-* de- + *bride* bridle, fr. OF, fr. MHG *brīdel* — more at BRIDLE] **:** to cleanse by debridement

de·bride·ment \-d,mäⁿ, -dmənt\ *n* -S [F *débridement*, fr. *débrider* + *-ment*] **:** the surgical removal of lacerated, devitalized, or contaminated tissue

de·brief \də, dē+\ *vt* [*de-* + *brief*] **:** to interrogate (as a pilot returning from a mission or a government official returning from abroad) in order to obtain useful information or intelligence ⟨where photographs are examined and pilots are ~*ed* —Christopher Rand⟩

de·bris \də'brē *also* dā'b- *or* 'dā,b- *sometimes* de'b- *or* 'de,b-\ *n, pl* **debris** \-ēz\ [F *débris*, fr. MF *debris*, fr. *debriser* to break to pieces, fr. OF *debrisier*, fr. *de-* + *brisier* to break — more at BRISANCE] **:** the remains of something broken down or destroyed ⟨swaying buildings and crashing ~ —H.E. Rieseberg⟩ **:** RUINS ⟨the ~ of Alexander's empire —John Buchan⟩: as **a :** an accumulation of loose detached fragments of rock — compare DETRITUS **b :** waste sand and gravel produced by hydraulic mining operations **c :** organic waste from dead or damaged tissue **syn** see REFUSE

debris–avalanche \"+¦-\ *n* **:** a mass of rock fragments and soil that has moved rapidly down a steep mountain slope or hillside and because of its high water content has behaved like an avalanche of snow — compare DEBRIS-SLIDE

debris cone *n* **:** a mound of ice on a glacier protected by an isolated patch of fine rock debris from the more rapid melting that has lowered the surrounding surface

debris glacier *n* **:** a glacier composed of ice that has fallen in fragments from a larger and higher glacier

debris-slide \-ˌslīd\ *n* **:** a mass of predominantly unconsolidated and incoherent soil and rock fragments that has slid or rolled rapidly down a steep slope when comparatively dry to form an irregular hummocky deposit — compare DEBRIS AVALANCHE

de bro·glie equation \dəˈbrōˌglē-, dəˈbrōyə-\ *n, usu cap B* [after Prince Louis V. *de Broglie*] **:** an equation in physics: the de Broglie wavelength of a moving particle is equal to the Planck constant divided by the momentum of the particle

de broglie wave *n, usu cap B* [after Prince Louis V. *de Broglie* *b*1892 Fr. physicist] **:** the hypothetical wave train that in wave-mechanical theory corresponds to a moving elementary particle (as an electron or proton), moves with it, and gives the particle certain wave properties (as interference and diffraction)

de·bruise \dəˈbrüz, dēˈ-\ *vt* [ME *debrusen* to break to pieces, fr. OF *debruisier*, fr. *de-* + *bruisier* to break — more at BRUISE] **1** *of a heraldic ordinary* **:** to cross or partly cover (a coat of arms or charge) as if laid over **2** *of a person* **:** to assume or use a heraldic ordinary that crosses or partly covers (a coat of arms or a charge)

debs *pl of* DEB

¹debt \ˈdet, *usu* -ed·+V\ *n* -s [ME *debte*, alter. (influenced in spelling by MF *debte*, fr. OF, alter. — influenced in spelling by L *debitum* — of *dette, dete*) of *dette*, fr. OF *dette, dete*, fr. (assumed) VL *debita*, fr. L, pl. of *debitum* debt, fr. neut. of *debitus*, past part. of *debēre* to owe, fr. *de* from + *habēre* to have — more at DE-, HABIT] **1 :** a neglect or violation of duty **:** FAULT, SIN, TRESPASS ⟨forgive us our ~*s* —Mt 6:12 (RSV)⟩ **2 :** a state of owing ⟨hopelessly in ~⟩ **3 :** something (as money, goods, or services) owed by one person to another ⟨a mortgage ~⟩ **:** something that one person is bound to pay to another or perform for his benefit **:** something owed **:** OBLIGATION ⟨~ of gratitude⟩ **4 :** the common-law action for the recovery of a certain specified sum of money held to be due or of a sum that can be simply and certainly ascertained — called also *action of debt;* compare FORM OF ACTION

syn INDEBTEDNESS, OBLIGATION, LIABILITY, DEBIT, ARREAR, ARREARAGE: DEBT often applies to a single definite amount of money owed; in reference to things other than money it may indicate a definite service or favor equivalent to one rendered ⟨a *debt* of $200 to the store⟩ ⟨the immense *debt* the legal profession and the reading public owe to the publishers for their public spirit in producing these records —Norman Birkett⟩ INDEBTEDNESS in this sense refers to a total due ⟨in practically all states there is either a constitutional or a statutory limitation upon the amount of *indebtedness* that cities may incur —F.A.Ogg & P.O.Ray⟩ ⟨the Canadian government continued to make great progress in the reduction of its huge wartime *indebtedness* —*Collier's Yr. Bk.*⟩ OBLIGATION may suggest a formal expression of INDEBTEDNESS or a formal agreement to pay ⟨a contract is said to be 'performed' or 'discharged' when all the *obligations* have been fulfilled on both sides —Ronald Rubinstein⟩ ⟨to establish conditions under which justice and respect for the *obligations* arising from treaties and other sources of international law can be maintained —*U.N.Charter*⟩ LIABILITY is the term opposite in meaning to *asset* in the terminology of accountants; it applies to any item of indebtedness, as an account payable, tax due, interest payment pledged ⟨*liabilities* may be broadly classified as external and internal, external liabilities being accountabilities due to persons having no basic equity in the business, and internal being amounts due to the owners of the business and pertaining to their equities —*Jour. of Accountancy*⟩ DEBIT in accounting is the opposite of *credit* and designates a sum allotted for any outgo. ARREAR — more often ARREARS — and ARREARAGE refer to an unpaid balance on a debt or account ⟨*arrears* of rent are begun becoming a serious problem to local authorities —*New Statesman & Nation*⟩ ⟨*arrearages* piled up rapidly and Congress was forced to pass law after law for the relief of the settlers —D.E.Clark⟩

²debt \ˈ"\ *adj* [alter. of ME *dette*, fr. *dette*, n.] *obs* **:** DUE, OWED ⟨to pay ourselves what to ourselves is ~ —Shak.⟩

debt book *n, archaic* **:** an account book in which a record of debts is entered

debted *adj* [alter. of ME *detted*, fr. *dette*, n. + *-ed*] *obs* **:** INDEBTED, OBLIGED

debt·less \ˈdetləs\ *adj* [alter. of ME *detteles*, fr. *dette* + *-les* -less] **:** free from debt

debt monetization *n* **:** expansion of bank deposits through purchases of government securities by commercial banks

debt of honor : a debt (as one incurred by betting or gambling) which is not recoverable by law but which the debtor is conventionally considered in honor bound to pay

debt of record : JUDGMENT 2b(1)

debt·or \ˈdedə(r), -etə(r) *sometimes* -ed·ˌȯ(ə)r *or* -eˌtȯ- *or* -ȯ(ə) *esp in the Lord's Prayer*\ *n* -s [alter. of ME *dettour, detter*, fr. OF *detur, dettour*, fr. L *debitor*, fr. *debitum* debt + *-or* — more at DEBT] **1 :** one guilty of neglect or violation of duty **:** SINNER ⟨forgive us our debts as we also have forgiven our ~*s* —Mt 6:12 (RSV)⟩ **2 :** one indebted to another: **a :** one under obligation to another ⟨~*s* for our lives to you —Alfred Tennyson⟩ **b :** one owing money to another ⟨founded a colony for the relief of ~*s* —*Univ. of Ga. Press Books*⟩ — opposed to *creditor*

debtor nation *n* **:** a nation whose debts to other countries exceed its foreign investments — compare CREDITOR NATION

debt service *n* **:** the amount of interest and sinking fund payments due annually on long-term debt

de·bub·bliz·er \(ˈ)dēˈbəbəˌlīzə(r)\ *n* -s [*de-* + *bubble* + *-ize* + *-er*] **:** one that softens rods and tubes made of plastics and removes bubbles by heating the articles under pressure in an airtight tank of hot water and treating them with a coolant

de·bug \(ˈ)dē+\ *vt* [*de-* + *bug* (insect)] **1 :** to remove insects from ⟨~ squash vines⟩ **2 :** to detect and eliminate errors in or malfunctions of ⟨~ a new airplane before it is flown⟩

de·bunk \(ˈ)dē+\ *vt* [*de-* + *bunk* (bunkum)] **:** to take the bunk out of ⟨modern writers have ~*ed* the old myths —Bruce Marshall⟩: **a :** to expose the sham pretensions or exaggerated claims of ⟨the authorities were anxious that the natives gain enough literacy to ~ the witch doctors —Jerome Ellison⟩ **b :** to remove the false sentiments from ⟨our modern tendency to ~ traditional standards of honesty, patriotism, and morality —W.C.Nau⟩

de·bunk·er \-kə(r)\ *n* -s **:** one that debunks **:** CRITIC, ICONOCLAST

de·burr \(ˈ)dē+\ *vt* [*de-* + *burr* (rough edge)] **:** to remove the burrs from (a piece of machined work)

deburse *vt* -ED/-ING/-S [MF *desbourser* — more at DISBURSE] *obs* **:** DISBURSE

de·bus \dēˈbəs, (ˈ)dē'-\ *vi* [*de-* + *bus* (vehicle)] **:** to get off a bus ⟨when they *debussed*, each company had its piper at the head —Alaric Jacob⟩

¹de·but \ˈdāˌ(ˌ)byü, dāˈb-, dəˈb-, ˈde(ˌ)b-, deˈb-; dābēˈ\ *n* -s [F *début*, fr. *débuter* to make one's first appearance, play first, begin, fr. MF *desbuter* to play first, fr. *des-* de- + *-buter* (fr. *but* goal) — more at BUTT (end)] **1 :** a first public appearance (as of an actor or singer) ⟨the Hollywood ~ of an old Broadway favorite⟩ **2 :** a formal entrance into society ⟨had a daughter making her ~ —Hamilton Basso⟩

²debut \ˈ"\ *vb* -ED/-ING/-S [F *débuter*] *vi* **:** to make one's debut ⟨the choir ~*ed* the same evening —*Down Beat*⟩ ~ *vt* **:** to present to the public for the first time **:** INTRODUCE ⟨the band ~*s* a new song each week⟩

de·bu·tan·i·za·tion \(ˌ)dēˌbyütᵊnəˈzāshən\ *n* -s **:** the process of debutanizing

de·bu·tan·ize \(ˈ)dēˈbyütᵊnˌīz\ *vt* -ED/-ING/-S [*de-* + *butane* + *-ize*] **:** to remove by distillation butanes, butenes, and sometimes lighter fractions from (as cracked gasoline)

de·bu·tan·iz·er \-zə(r)\ *n* -s **:** one that debutanizes

deb·u·tant \ˈdebyüˌtänt, -yə,-, -tänt *also* ˈdāb- *or* -tant *or* -taa(ə)nt *or* -taint; ˌ==ˈ=\ *n* -s [F *débutant*, fr. pres. part. of *débuter*] **:** one making a debut; *specif* **:** one making his first public appearance or beginning his professional career ⟨one of last year's better ~*s* . . . produces another wholly unconventional and delightful detective story —Anthony Boucher⟩

deb·u·tante \ˈ"\ *n* -s [F *débutante*, fem. of *débutant*] **:** one making a debut; *specif* **:** a young woman making her formal entrance into society ⟨walked past flushed groups of ~*s* and their escorts —Raymond Chandler⟩

debutante pink *n* **:** LA FRANCE PINK

de·button \(ˈ)dē+\ *vt* [*de-* + *button* (n.)] **:** to remove the calyx and the end of the stem of (an orange) esp. to check disease in storage or shipment

de·bye-hück·el theory \dəˈbīˈhikəl-, -hæk-\ *n, usu cap D&H* [after Peter J. W. *Debye* *b*1884 Dutch physicist and E. *Hückel* *b*1896 Swiss physicist] **:** a theory in physical chemistry: the deviation of solutions of electrolytes from the laws of ideal solutions is due to electrical forces between ions

de·bye-scher·rer method \dəˈbīˈsherə(r)-\ *n, usu cap D&S* [after P. J. W. *Debye* and Paul *Scherrer* *b*1890 Swiss physicist] **:** a method of forming a diffraction pattern by directing a beam of X rays onto an aggregate of small crystals (as in the powdered form of a substance) and by photographing the pattern so formed to provide a means of identifying crystalline substances

debye temperature *n, usu cap D* [after P. J. W. *Debye*] **:** the temperature at which the atomic heat of a pure cubic crystal equals 5.67 calories per gram atom per degree — called also *characteristic temperature*

debye theory *n, usu cap D* [after P. J. W. *Debye*] **:** a theory in wave mechanics: the energy of thermal agitation in a crystal is distributed among the possible systems of standing waves that correspond to the normal modes of elastic vibration

debye unit *also* **debye** *n, usu cap D* [after P. J. W. *Debye*] **:** a unit of electric moment equal to 10^{-18} statcoulomb-centimeter

dec *abbr* **1** decade **2** decani **3** deceased **4** decimal **5** decimeter **6** declaration **7** declared **8** declension **9** declination **10** decorative **11** decrease **12** decrescendo

deca- *or* **dec-** *or* **deka-** *or* **dek-** *comb form* [ME, fr. L, fr. Gk *deka-, dek-*, fr. *deka* ten — more at TEN] **1 :** ten ⟨*decagon*⟩ **2** [F *déca-, déc-*, fr. L *deca-, dec-*] **:** ten times (a specified unit of measure) ⟨*decaliter*⟩ ⟨*decare*⟩ — used in terms belonging to the metric system

dec·a·canth \ˈdekəˌkan(t)th\ *n* -s [*deca-* + *-acanth* (fr. Gk *akantha* thorn) — more at ACANTH-] **:** a 10-hooked cestodarian larva — called also *lycophore;* compare HEXACANTH

dec·a·dal \ˈdekədᵊl\ *adj* [*decade* + *-al*] **:** of or belonging to a decade

dec·ade \ˈdeˌkād *also* deˈkād *or* dəˈkād *or* ˈdekəd; *the last is most frequent in the sense "division of a rosary" and many who first learned the word in this sense use this pronunciation for all senses; since d and t are identically pronounced in certain intervocalic environments by most U S speakers, some who first learn the word aurally in a context such as "decade of the rosary" originally apprehend the last consonant letter as t and pronounce the word in all its occurrences as if the last consonant letter were t, making the plural for instance* ˈdekəts\ *n* -s [ME, fr. MF *decade*, fr. LL *decad-, decas*, fr. Gk *dekad-, dekas*, fr. *deka*] **1 a :** a group or set of 10 ⟨his prisoners were divided into ~*s* —William Godwin⟩ ⟨a ~ of days⟩ ⟨a ~ of proposals⟩ ⟨the fourth ~ in a history⟩ **b :** a period of any 10 years ⟨to last for a ~⟩; *esp* **:** a 10-year period beginning with a year ending in 0 (as 1900–1909) ⟨the ~ of the twenties runs from Jan. 1, 1920 to Dec. 31, 1929⟩ **c :** one of the periods of a century divided in 10 calendric parts each beginning with a year ending in 1 (as 1901–10) ⟨the third ~ of the century runs from Jan. 1, 1921 to Dec. 31, 1930⟩ **d :** a division of the rosary usu. consisting of one Our Father and 10 Hail Marys followed by the minor doxology; *also* **:** one of the sets of rosary beads used to count these prayers and usu. consisting of one large bead and 10 small beads **2 a :** a ratio of 10 to 1 (as in the geometric progression 1, 10, 100, 1000 . . .) **b :** any one of the steps between sets of coils in a resistance box each coil of which has a resistance 10 times that of the corresponding coil in the preceding set

decade box *n* **:** an adjustable assembly of resistor or capacitor units in decimal steps facilitating selection by plug or switch of any multiple of the least unit up to the aggregate of all units

dec·a·dence \ˈdekədən(t)s, -kədᵊn- *also* dəˈkādᵊn- *or* dēˈkā-\ *n* -s [MF, fr. ML *decadentia*, fr. LL *decadent-, decadens* (pres. part. of *decadere* to fall, sink) + L *-ia* -y — more at DECAY] **1 :** the process of becoming decadent **:** the quality or state of being decadent **:** DETERIORATION ⟨escape the ~ that attends upon old age —G.L.Dickinson⟩ **2 :** the literary movement of the decadents or its animating spirit

dec·a·den·cy \-ənsē, -ᵊn-, -si\ *n* -ES [alter. (influenced by *-cy*) of *decadence*] **:** DECADENCE

¹dec·a·dent \-ənt, -ᵊnt\ *adj* [back-formation fr. *decadence*] **1 :** marked by decay or decline (as from an earlier condition of excellence or vitality): as **a :** characterized by self-indulgence ⟨a rich and ~ aristocracy⟩ **b :** tending to regress **:** becoming less prominent ⟨shell ornamentation ~⟩ — used chiefly in taxonomic diagnoses **2 a :** of, relating to, or having the qualities characteristic of the decadents **b :** of, relating to, or having the qualities characteristic of a period of decadence — **dec·a·dent·ly** *adv*

²decadent \ˈ"\ *n* -s **1 :** one that is decadent; *esp* **:** one characterized by or exhibiting the qualities of those who are degenerating to a lower type or of an age that is on the decline **2 :** one of a group of late 19th century French and English writers whose subjects often tended toward the artificial and abnormal and whose style was marked esp. by refinement and subtlety

dec·a·dent·ism \-ˌtizəm\ *n* -s [F *décadentisme*, fr. *décadent* decadent (back-formation fr. *décadence*) + *-isme* -ism] **:** DECADENCE 2

de·cad·ic \(ˈ)deˈkadik, dəˈk-\ *adj* [LGk *dekadikos* of the number ten, fr. Gk *dekad-, dekas* group of ten + *-ikos* -ic] **:** of or relating to the decimal system of counting

dec·a·drachm \ˈdekəˌdram\ *n* -s [*deca-* + *drachm*] **:** an ancient Greek silver coin worth 10 drachmas

de·caf·fein·ate \(ˈ)dēˈka(ˌ)fēˌnāt, -af(ē)əˌn-\ *vt* -ED/-ING/-S [*de-* + *caffeine* + *-ate*] **:** to remove caffeine from ⟨*decaffeinated* coffee⟩

de·caf·fein·ize \-ˌnīz\ *vt* -ED/-ING/-S [ISV *de-* + *caffeine* + *-ize*] **:** DECAFFEINATE

dec·a·gon \ˈdekəˌgän\ *n* -s [NL *decagonum*, fr. Gk *dekagōnon*, fr. *deka-* deca- + *-gōnon* -gon] **:** a plane polygon of 10 angles and 10 sides — **de·cag·o·nal** \(ˈ)deˈkagənᵊl, -kaig-\ *adj*

a regular decagon

deca·gram \ˈdekəˌgram, -aa(ə)m\ *n* -s [F *décagramme*, fr. *déca-* deca- + *gramme* gram] **:** a metric unit of mass and weight equal to 10 grams — see METRIC SYSTEM table

dec·a·he·dral \ˌdekəˈhēdrəl\ *adj* [*decahedron* + *-al*] **:** of or relating to a decahedron

dec·a·he·dron \-rən\ *n, pl* **decahedrons** \-rənz\ *or* **decahe·dra** \-rə\ [ISV *deca-* + *-hedron*] **:** a polyhedron of 10 faces

deca·hy·drate \ˌdekəˈhīdrət, -ˌdrāt\ *n* [ISV *deca-* + *hydrate*] **:** a compound with 10 molecules of water — **dec·a·hy·drat·ed** \-ˌād·əd\ *adj*

dec·a·hy·dro·naphthalene \ˌdekəˈhīdrō +\ *n* [ISV *deca-* + *hydr-* + *naphthalene*] **:** a colorless liquid hydrocarbon $C_{10}H_{18}$ obtained by hydrogenation of naphthalene and used as a solvent (as for paints, lacquers, and silicones)

de·caisn·ea \dəˈkānēə\ *n, cap* [NL, fr. Joseph *Decaisne* †1882 Fr. botanist] **:** a genus of Asiatic shrubs (family Lardizabalaceae) having compound leaves and greenish polygamous flowers in clusters

de·cal \ˈdēˌkal; dəˈkal, dēˈk-; ˈdekəl; *sometimes* ˈdeˌkōl\ *n* -s [by shortening] **:** DECALCOMANIA

de·ca·lage \ˌdekəˈläzh, ˌdāk-\ *n* -s [F *décalage* action of putting out of alignment, displacement, removal of a wedge, fr. *décaler* to put out of alignment, shift, remove a wedge from (fr. *dé-* de- — fr. OF *des-* — + *caler* to wedge, chock, fr. *cale* wedge, fr. G *keil*, fr. OHG *kīl*) + *-age* — more at CHINE] **:** the difference between the angles of incidence of the two wings of a biplane that is positive if the incidence of the upper wing is greater than that of the lower

de·calcification \(ˌ)dē +\ *n* [ISV *de-* + *calcification*] **:** the removal or loss of calcium or calcium compounds (as from bones or soil) ⟨~ of dental tissues by citrate ion is suggested —*Science*⟩

de·calcify \(ˈ)dē +\ *vt* [ISV *de-* + *calcify*] **:** to remove calcium or calcium compounds from

de·cal·co·ma·nia \(ˌ)dēˌkalkəˈmānēə\ *n* -s [F *décalcomanie*, fr. *décalco-* (fr. *décalquer* to copy by tracing, fr. *dé-* off — fr. OF *des-* off, do the opposite of — + *calquer* to trace) + *manie* mania, craze, fr. LL *mania* — more at DE-, CALQUE, MANIA] **1 :** the art or process of transferring pictures and designs typically from specially prepared paper to china, glass, or marble and permanently fixing them thereto **2 a :** a picture or design prepared for transfer by decalcomania **b :** a paper on which designs are printed for transfer printing

de·ca·les·cence \ˌdēkəˈlesᵊn(t)s, ˌdek-\ *n* -s [ISV *de-* + *-calescence* (as in *recalescence*)] **:** the decrease in temperature when the rate of heat absorption during transformation exceeds the rate of heat input while heating metal through a transformation range — compare RECALESCENCE

Dec·a·lin \ˈdekələn\ *trademark* — used for decahydronaphthalene

deca·li·ter \ˈdekə+ ˌ-\ *n* -s [F *décalitre*, fr. *déca-* deca- + *litre* liter] **:** a metric unit of capacity equal to 10 liters — see METRIC SYSTEM table

deca·lobate \ˌdekə+\ *adj* [prob. fr. (assumed) NL *decalobatus*, fr. NL *deca-* + *lobatus* lobate] **:** having 10 lobes

dec·a·logue *also* **dec·a·log** \ˈdekəˌlȯg *also* -ˌläg\ *n* -s [ME *decaloge*, fr. LL *decalogus*, fr. Gk *dekalogos*, fr. *deka* ten + *logos* speech, word — more at TEN, LEGEND] **:** a basic set of rules carrying binding authority (as the Ten Commandments found in Exod. 20: 2–17 and Deut. 5: 6–21 which in the biblical account were given by God to Moses on Mount Sinai)

de·cam·er·ous \dəˈkamərəs, (ˈ)deˈk-\ *adj* [*deca-* + *-merous*] **:** having 10 parts or divisions; *specif* **:** having the parts in tens — usu. used of a flower

¹de·cam·e·ter \dəˈkamədə(r), -deˈ-\ *n* [Gk *dekametron*, fr. *deka* ten + *metron* meter, measure — more at TEN, MEASURE] **:** a poetic line of 10 feet

²deca·me·ter \ˈdekəˌmēd·ə(r)\ *n* [F *décamètre*, fr. *déca-* deca- + *mètre* meter] **:** a metric unit of length equal to 10 meters — see METRIC SYSTEM table

dec·a·me·tho·ni·um \ˌdekəməˈthōnēəm\ *n* -s [*deca-* + *methonium*] **:** the bivalent substituted ammonium ion $[(CH_3)_3N(CH_2)_{10}NCCH_3)_3]^{++}$ derived by methylation of deca-methylene-diamine; *also* **:** any salt containing this ion (as the iodide or bromide used as a muscle relaxant)

de·camp \dē, də +\ *vi* [F *décamper*, fr. MF *descamper*, fr. *des-* de- + *camper* to camp — more at CAMP] **1 :** to break up a camp **:** move away from a camping ground **2 :** to depart suddenly **:** run away ⟨he ~*ed* with the stolen goods⟩ **syn** see ESCAPE

de·camp·ment \-pmənt\ *n* -s [F *décampement*, fr. *décamper* to decamp + *-ment*] **:** the act or process of decamping **:** departure from a camp

dec·an \ˈdekən\ *n* -s [LL *decanus*, lit., chief of ten — more at DEAN] **:** any of the three divisions of 10 degrees in each sign of the zodiac; *also* **:** the ruler of such a division

¹de·ca·nal \dəˈkānᵊl, ˈdekən-\ *adj* [ML *decanus* dean (fr. LL, chief of ten) + E *-al*] **1 :** of or relating to a dean or deanery ⟨~ duties⟩ **2 :** of or being the ecclesiastical south side of the choir of a cathedral or church — contrasted with *cantorial*

²dec·a·nal \ˈdekəˌnal\ *n* -s [ISV *decane* + *-al*] **:** a high-boiling liquid aldehyde $CH_3(CH_2)_8CHO$ found in essential oils (as oils of orrisroot and lemongrass) — called also *capraldehyde, capric aldehyde, decylaldehyde*

dec·ane \ˈdeˌkān\ *n* -s [ISV *deca-* + *-ane*] **:** any of several isomeric liquid paraffin hydrocarbons $C_{10}H_{22}$; *esp* **:** the normal hydrocarbon $CH_3(CH_2)_8CH_3$

de·ca·ni \dəˈkāˌnī\ *adj* [ML, of the dean, gen. of *decanus* dean] **:** DECANAL 2

dec·a·no·ic acid \ˌdekəˌnōik-\ *n* [ISV *decane* + *-oic*] **:** CAPRIC ACID — used in the system of nomenclature adopted by the International Union of Pure and Applied Chemistry

dec·a·nol \ˈdekəˌnȯl, -ōl\ *n* -s [*decane* + *-ol*] **:** any of the decyl alcohols derived from normal decane; *esp* **:** normal decyl alcohol

dec·a·no·yl \ˌdekəˈnōəl; deˈkanəˌwil, -ˌwēl\ *n* -s [ISV *decan-* (fr. *decanoic acid*) + *-oyl*] **:** CAPRYL 1

de·cant \dəˈkant, dēˈ-, -kaa(ə)nt\ *vt* -ED/-ING/-S [NL *decantare*, fr. L *de* from, away + NL *-cantare* (fr. ML *cantus* side, fr. L, iron ring round a carriage wheel) — more at DE-, CANT] **1 a :** to pour (as wine) from the original bottle into another container **b :** to pour (as wine) from one vessel into another **c :** to draw off (a liquid) without disturbing the underlying sediment or precipitate or the lower liquid layers **2 :** to pour out, transfer, or unload as if by pouring ⟨I was ~*ed* from the car —Ursula G. Bower⟩

de·cant·ate \-nˌtāt\ *n* -s [*decant* + *-ate*] **:** the liquid decanted

de·can·ta·tion \ˌdēˌkanˈtāshən\ *n* -s [NL *decantation-, decantatio*, fr. *decantatus* (past part. of *decantare*) + L *-ion-, -io* -ion] **:** the act or process of decanting ⟨the quality of the sand may be tested . . . for silt by ~ —C.M.Gay⟩

de·cant·er \dəˈkantə(r), dēˈ-, -aan-\ *n* -s **:** a vessel used to decant or to receive decanted liquids; *specif* **:** an ornamental glass bottle used esp. for serving wine

decanter

de·cap \(ˈ)dēˈkap\ *vt* **:** to remove the cap from; *esp* **:** to remove a priming cap from (a cartridge)

de·cap·i·tate \dəˈkapəˌtāt, dēˈ-, *usu* -ād· +V\ *vt* -ED/-ING/-S [LL *decapitatus*, past part. of *decapitare*, fr. L *de* from, away + LL *-capitare* (fr. *capit-, caput* head) — more at DE-, HEAD] **1 :** to cut off the head of **:** kill by beheading **:** BEHEAD **2 :** to remove summarily from office for political reasons ⟨the incoming administration *decapitated* many officeholders⟩ **3 :** to make ineffective **:** DESTROY ⟨a surprise attack on New York . . . could ~ a wide segment of American business —D.F.Cavers⟩

de·cap·i·ta·tion \dəˌkapəˈtāshən, (ˌ)dēˌ-\ *n* -s [ML *decapitation-, decapitatio*, fr. LL *decapitatus* + L *-ion-, -io* -ion] **:** the act or process of decapitating

de·cap·i·ta·tor \dəˈkapəˌtād·ə(r), dēˈ-, -ātə-\ *n* -s **:** one that decapitates

¹dec·a·pod \ˈdekəˌpäd\ *n* -s [NL *Decapoda*] **:** one of the Decapoda **:** a decapod mollusk or crustacean

²decapod \ˈ"\ *adj* **:** of or relating to the Decapoda

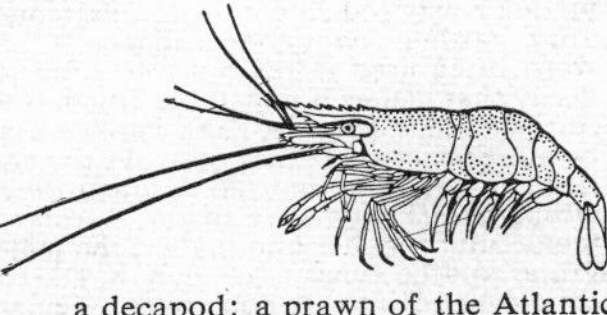

a decapod: a prawn of the Atlantic coast of America

de·cap·o·da \dəˈkapədə\ *n pl, cap* [NL, fr. *deca-* + *-poda*] **1 :** an order of Crustaceans (division Eucarida) including the most highly organized crustaceans (as shrimps, lobsters, crabs) having five pairs of thoracic appendages one or more of which are modified into pincers, a pair of movable stalked eyes, mouthparts consisting of a pair of mandibles, two pairs of maxillae, and three pairs of maxillipeds, and the head and thorax fused into a cephalothorax and covered by a carapace that encloses a gill chamber on each side — compare NATANTIA, REPTANTIA **2 :** an order of cephalopod mollusks (subclass Dibranchia) including the cuttlefishes, squids, and members of the genus *Spirula* that are distinguished from the Octopoda by the possession of 10 arms one pair of which is longer than the others and is enlarged at the end and of retractile, stalked suckers with horny rims that are sometimes armed with or replaced by hooks, and an internal horny or calcareous shell — **de·cap·o·dal** \-dᵊl\ *adj* — **de·cap·o·dan** \-dən\ *adj or n* — **de·cap·o·dous** \-dəs\ *adj*

dec·a·pod·i·form \ˌdekəˈpädəˌfȯrm\ *adj* [NL *Decapoda* + ISV *-iform*] **:** shaped like a decapod — used of the larvae of insects

de·cap·per \(ˈ)dēˈkapə(r)\ *n* **:** an instrument for removing a cap from a cartridge case

de·capsulate \(ˈ)dē +\ *vt* -ED/-ING/-S [*de-* + *capsule* + *-ate*] **:** to remove the capsule from ⟨~ a kidney⟩ ⟨~ a poppy head⟩ — **de·capsulation** \(ˌ)dē +\ *n*

de·carbonate \(ˈ)dē +\ *vt* [*de-* + *carbonate*] **:** to remove

carbon dioxide or carbonic acid from — **de·carbonation** \(ˈ)dē +\ *n*
de·carbonization \(ˈ)dē +\ *n* **:** the process of decarbonizing
de·carbonize \(ˈ)dē +\ *vt* [ISV *de-* + *carbonize*] **:** to remove carbon from (as an internal-combustion engine)
de·carboxylase \ˈdē +\ *n* [ISV *decarboxyl-* (fr. *decarboxylation*) + *-ase*] **:** any of a group of enzymes that accelerate decarboxylation esp. of alpha-amino acids — distinguished from *carboxylase;* see CODECARBOXYLASE
de·carboxylate \ˈdē +\ *vb* [*de-* + *carboxylate*] *vt* **:** to remove carboxyl from ~ *vi* **:** to lose carboxyl — **de·carboxylation** \ˈdē +\ *n*
de·carburation \(ˈ)dē +\ *n* [ISV *decarbur-* (fr. F *décarburer* to decarburize, fr. *dé-* de- — fr. OF *des-* — + *-carburer* — fr. *carbure* carbide) + *-ation* — more at CARBURANT] **:** DECARBURIZATION
de·carburization \(ˈ)dē +\ *n* **:** the process of decarburizing
de·carburize \(ˈ)dē +\ *vt* [*de-* + *carburize*] **:** to remove carbon from (as the surface of iron alloys)
dec·ar·chy *also* **dek·ar·chy** \ˈdeˌkärkē\ *n* -ES [Gk *dekarchia,* fr. *deka-* deca- + *-archia* -archy] **:** a governing body of 10
dec·are \ˈdeˌk+ˌ-\ *n* -S [F *décare,* fr. *déca-* deca- + *are*] **:** a metric unit of area equal to 10 ares, 1000 square meters, or 0.2471 acre
de·cartelization \(ˈ)dē +\ *n* **:** the act or process of decartelizing
de·cartelize \(ˈ)dē +\ *vt* [*de-* + *cartelize*] **:** to break up or dissolve (as a large industrial trust or monopoly)
deca·stere \ˈdekə +ˌ-\ *n* -S [F *décastère,* fr. *déca-* deca- + *stère* stere] **:** a metric unit of volume equal to 10 cubic meters — see METRIC SYSTEM table
dec·a·stich \ˈdekəˌstik\ *n* -S [*deca-* + *-stich*] **:** a poem or stanza of 10 lines
[1]**dec·a·style** \-ˌstīl\ *adj* [L *decastylos,* fr. Gk *dekastylos,* fr. *deka-* deca- + *-stylos* -style] **:** marked by columniation with 10 columns across the front — compare DISTYLE
[2]**decastyle** \"\ *n* -S **:** a temple or portico having 10 columns in front
de·ca·su·al·i·za·tion \(ˌ)dēˌkazh(əw)ələˈzāshən\ *n* -S **:** the act or process of decasualizing
de·ca·sual·ize \(ˈ)dēˈkazh(əw)əˌlīz\ *vt* -ED/-ING/-S [*de-* + *casual* + *-ize*] **:** to do away with the casual employment of (labor) ⟨the commission *decasualized* 3452 men during the year —Walter Hamshar⟩ **:** eliminate the casuals from ⟨industry will be . . . *decasualized* by making the employment relation more permanent —M.R.Cohen⟩
[1]**deca·syllabic** \ˈdekə +\ *adj* [prob. fr. F *décasyllabique,* fr. Gk *dekasyllabos* decasyllabic (fr. *deka-* deca- + *syllabē* syllable) + F *-ique* -ic — more at SYLLABLE] **:** having or composed of verses that have 10 syllables
[2]**decasyllabic** \"\ *n* -S **:** a line of 10 syllables
[1]**deca·syllable** \ˈdekə +\ *adj* [*deca-* + *syllable*] **:** [1]DECASYLLABIC
[2]**decasyllable** \"\ *n* -S **:** a word or verse having 10 syllables
de·cath·lon \dəˈkathlən, dēˈ-, -ˌlän\ *n* -S [F *décathlon,* fr. *déca-* deca- + Gk *athlon* contest — more at ATHLETE] **:** a 10-event athletic contest; *specif* **:** a composite contest that consists of the 100-meter, 400-meter, and 1500-meter runs, the 110-meter high hurdles, the javelin and discus throws, shot put, pole vault, high jump, and broad jump
dec·at·ing \ˈdekədˌiŋ\ *or* **dec·a·tiz·ing** \-kəˌtīziŋ\ *n* -S [*decating* fr. F *décatir* to steam, remove a stiff finish from (fr. *dé-* de- — fr. OF *des-* — + *catir* to press, fr. assumed VL *coactire* to press together, fr. L *coactus,* past part. of *cogere* to drive together, compel) + E *-ing; decatizing* fr. F *décatir* + E *-ize* + *-ing* — more at COGENT] **:** a textile process for adding luster to cloth (as woolen and worsted) and for setting the nap and size by winding it on perforated rollers and circulating hot water or steam through it
de·cau·date \(ˈ)dēˈkȯˌdāt\ *vt* -ED/-ING/-S [*de-* + L *cauda* tail + E *-ate* — more at COWARD] **:** to deprive of the tail — **de·cau·da·tion** \ˌdēˌkȯˈdāshən\ *n*
de·cau·ville \dəˈkōˌvil, -vēl, -kōˌvil\ *adj, usu cap* [after Paul *Decauville* †1922 French industrialist who invented equipment for such a railroad] **:** of, relating to, or being a narrow-gauge railroad whose track is mounted in sections upon transverse metal beams and is easily demountable and transportable
[1]**de·cay** \dəˈkā, dēˈ-\ *vb* -ED/-ING/-S [ME *decayen,* fr. ONF *decaïr,* fr. LL *decadere* to fall, sink, fr. L *de* down, away + *cadere* to fall — more at DE-, CHANCE] *vi* **1 a** *archaic* **:** to decline from a prosperous condition ⟨families . . . ~*ed* into the humble vale of life —Sir Walter Scott⟩ **b :** to pass gradually from a comparatively sound or perfect state to one of unsoundness, imperfection, or dissolution ⟨where wealth accumulates and men ~ —Oliver Goldsmith⟩ **2 :** to decrease in quantity, volume, activity, or force **:** dwindle away ⟨the voices . . . ~*ed* and died out upon her ear —Thomas Hardy⟩ **3 :** to fall into physical ruin ⟨the old house ~*ed* from lack of repairs⟩ **4 :** to decline in health, strength, vigor, or freshness ⟨a mind beginning to ~⟩ **5 :** to undergo decomposition **:** ROT ⟨fruit ~*s* in the sun⟩ ~ *vt* **1** *obs* **:** to cause to decay **:** IMPAIR ⟨infirmity that ~*s* the wise —Shak.⟩ **2 :** to destroy by decomposition **:** ROT ⟨rain and sun ~*ed* the building⟩
syn DECOMPOSE, ROT, PUTREFY, SPOIL, DISINTEGRATE, CRUMBLE: DECAY indicates deteriorating change, often gradual, from a sound condition or perfect state ⟨bruised apples *decaying* quickly⟩ ⟨*decaying* teeth⟩ ⟨with huge machines left to rust and *decay* —*Amer. Guide Series: Texas*⟩ ⟨the Aztec regime and culture collapsed and the native crafts and arts *decayed* —R.W.Murray⟩ DECOMPOSE implies breaking down into components or dissolution through corruption ⟨the strong odor of *decomposing* meat⟩ ⟨action of bacteria in *decomposing* the organic products —A.C.Morrison⟩ ⟨after slaying his colleague, he chemically *decomposed* the body —Leo Guild⟩ ROT, applied to animal or vegetable matter, indicates decaying with corruption, often with offensive foulness; otherwise it may indicate enervation or stagnation ⟨fruit *rotting* in the baskets⟩ ⟨the *rotting* corpses of the Americans and British whom the French allowed to be massacred at Fort William Henry —Cleveland Amory⟩ ⟨it was this garrison life. Half civilian, half military, with all the drawbacks of both. It *rotted* the soul, robbed a man of ambition, faith —Irwin Shaw⟩ PUTREFY may indicate noisome, extremely offensive, or nauseating rotting ⟨*putrefying* cadavers⟩ SPOIL is a less extreme word often used in reference to food to indicate a degree of decay that makes it uneatable ⟨the lettuce will *spoil* if it is not refrigerated⟩ DISINTEGRATE implies a separating of particles or a breaking apart that destroys the entity or integrity of the item in question ⟨mortar *disintegrating* in the old chimney⟩ ⟨icebergs *disintegrating* in the warm water⟩ ⟨if we raise the temperature higher and higher, the metal itself finally *disintegrates* and becomes a gas —K.K.Darrow⟩ ⟨[the] Whig party *disintegrated* into its component elements —H.S.Commager⟩ CRUMBLE implies a slow disintegration with a breaking and falling off of small particles ⟨winter rains had washed and washed against its narrow, faded old bricks until the plaster between them had *crumbled* —Margaret Deland⟩ ⟨still visible, although the stockade itself has long since *crumbled,* are the outlines of the ancient earthworks —*Amer. Guide Series: Mich.*⟩ ⟨Hood's army, *crumbled* in morale and depleted by wholesale desertion —*Amer. Guide Series: Tenn.*⟩
[2]**decay** \"\ *n* -S [ME, fr. *decayen*] **1 a :** the condition of a person or thing that has undergone a decline in strength, soundness, or prosperity or has been diminished in degree of excellence or perfection ⟨arts and letters had fallen into ~⟩ **b :** a progressive failure of strength, soundness, or prosperity **:** a diminishing in degree of excellence or perfection ⟨saw a rapid ~ of moral principles⟩ **2 a :** the material process of dilapidation **:** wasting or wearing away **:** the state of being wasted or worn away **:** RUIN ⟨ancient temples fallen into complete ~⟩ **b** *obs* **:** ruined remains **:** DEBRIS — usu. used in pl. **3** *obs* **:** DESTRUCTION, DEATH, RUIN ⟨sullen presage of your own ~ —Shak.⟩ **4** *obs* **:** a cause of decay ⟨my love was my ~ —Shak.⟩ **5 a :** ROT; *specif* **:** the aerobic decomposition of proteins chiefly by bacteria in which the products of putrefaction are completely oxidized to stable compounds having no foul odors **b :** the product of decay ⟨remove ~ from a tooth⟩ **6 a** *archaic* **:** a decline in health or vigor **b** *obs* **:** the manifestations of age or of decline in health — usu. used in pl. **c** *archaic* **:** a wasting disease; *esp* **:** CONSUMPTION **7 :** decrease in quantity, volume, activity, or force: as **a :** spontaneous decrease in the number of radioactive atoms in radioactive material (as uranium ore) **b :** spontaneous disintegration of an atom, an atomic nucleus, a neutron, or a meson
de·cay·able \-āəbəl\ *adj* **:** capable of or liable to decay
decay constant *n* **:** the constant ratio of the number of radioactive atoms disintegrating in any specified short unit interval of time to the total number of atoms of the same kind still intact at the beginning of that interval
de·cayed·ness \-ā(ə)dnəs\ *n* -ES **:** the quality or state of being decayed
de·cay·less \-ālə̇s\ *adj* **:** being without decay
dec·can \ˈdekən, -ˌkan\ *n* [*Deccan,* the whole peninsula of India south of the Narbada river] **1** *usu cap* **:** a breed of coarse-wooled sheep of southern India **2** -S *often cap* **:** a sheep of the Deccan breed
deccan hemp *n, often cap D* **:** KENAF
decd *abbr* **1** deceased **2** declared **3** decreased
[1]**de·cease** \də̇ˈsēs, dēˈ-\ *n* -S [ME *deces,* fr. MF, fr. L *decessus* departure, death, fr. *decessus,* past part. of *decedere* to depart, die, fr. *de* from, away + *cedere* to go — more at DE-, CEDE] **:** departure from life **:** DEATH
[2]**decease** \"\ *vi* -ED/-ING/-S [ME *decessen,* fr. *deces*] **:** to depart from life **:** DIE
[1]**deceased** *adj* [fr. past part. of [2]*decease*] **:** DEAD ⟨his ~ wife's sister⟩; *esp* **:** recently dead
[2]**deceased** *n, pl* **deceased :** a dead person ⟨the will of the ~⟩
de·ce·dent \də̇ˈsēdᵊnt, dēˈ-\ *n* -S [L *decedent-, decedens,* pres. part. of *decedere*] **:** a deceased person
de·ceit \də̇ˈsēt, dēˈ-, *usu* -ēd· +V\ *n* -S [ME *deceite,* fr. OF, fr. L *decepta,* fem. of *deceptus,* past part. of *decipere* to deceive] **1 :** the act or practice of deceiving (as by falsification, concealment, or cheating) **:** DECEPTION ⟨politics, being the art of ~, suits only little minds —*Encore*⟩ **2 a :** an attempt to deceive **:** a declaration, artifice, or practice designed to mislead another **:** wily device **:** TRICK, FRAUD **b :** any trick, collusion, contrivance, false representation, or underhand practice used to defraud another — see FRAUD **3 :** a disposition to deceive **:** DECEITFULNESS, STRATAGEM, WILE ⟨far from ~ or guile —John Milton⟩
syn DECEIT, DUPLICITY, DISSIMULATION, CUNNING, GUILE can mean, in common, the quality, act, or practice of imposing on credulity by dishonesty, fraud, or trickery. DECEIT implies the intent to mislead and can cover misrepresentation, falsification, fraud, or trickery of any kind ⟨believes that *deceit* and mistrust are the essence of human relationships —Bergen Evans⟩ ⟨they held that the basest trickery or *deceit* was not dishonorable if directed against a foe —*Amer. Guide Series: R.I.*⟩ ⟨there is an element of sham and *deceit* in every imitation —John Dewey⟩ DUPLICITY usually implies double-dealing, bad faith, or false pretense ⟨preaches honesty but practices *duplicity* —Leo Pfeffer⟩ ⟨so habitual was her *duplicity* that she would gaze softly at you, saying nothing when she was deceiving you —Ethel Wilson⟩ ⟨the cunning and *duplicity* they practiced —W.H.Hudson †1922⟩ DISSIMULATION implies deceit by concealing what one actually is or feels ⟨some in the household were convinced that her ravings and absurd actions were cunning *dissimulation* —E.J.Simmons⟩ ⟨she had revealed of late a chronic habit of *dissimulation,* and it was impossible to decide whether she was lying for diversion or speaking the truth from necessity —Ellen Glasgow⟩ CUNNING implies, in one use, deceit by trickery or strategem or, in another similar use, an extreme, often vicious shrewdness ⟨with such masterly *cunning* did they lay their measures for the avoidance of every possible chance of detection —George Meredith⟩ ⟨a third-rate, ungenerous person with a low mean *cunning* that is contemptible —H.J.Laski⟩ ⟨a people whose ruthlessness, tenacity, power, and *cunning* are . . . great —D.L.Cohn⟩ ⟨the bear is a favorite animal of the big-game hunter because of its *cunning* and agility —R.E.Trippensee⟩ GUILE stresses, more than *cunning,* a subtle concealment or lack of obviousness of the arts practiced or tricks used ⟨he had not the *guile,* patience, or ruthlessness to make a good Secret Service chief —Karl Robson⟩ ⟨*guile* and trickery —Willa Cather⟩ and occurring most commonly in certain stock phrases, usu. negative, the word has come to have a much weaker sense than *cunning,* implying only artfulness or the use of wiles ⟨his profound innocence, that thorough absence of *guile* —Harvey Breit⟩ ⟨her deceit and illusion were harmless, wholly without *guile* —William Beebe⟩ ⟨she cannot be honest in the legal sense when this minor honesty inhibits her purpose, but this is *guile* rather than dishonesty —Sidney Monas⟩ **syn** see in addition IMPOSTURE
de·ceit·ful \-tfəl\ *adj* [ME *desaitful,* fr. *desait, deceite* deceit + *-ful*] **1 :** having a tendency or disposition to deceive **:** given to deception **:** DISHONEST ⟨she was a ~ scheming little thing —Israel Zangwill⟩ **2 :** tending to deceive **:** DECEPTIVE, MISLEADING ⟨smooth, shining, and ~ as thin ice —S.T.Coleridge⟩
syn see DISHONEST
de·ceit·ful·ly \-fəlē, -li\ *adv* [ME *desaitfully,* fr. *desaitful* + *-ly*] **:** in a deceitful manner
de·ceit·ful·ness *n* -ES **:** the quality of being deceitful
de·ceiv·able \-sēvəbəl\ *adj* [ME, modif. (prob. influenced by *deceiven* to deceive) of MF *decevable,* fr. OF, fr. *deceivre, decevoir* + *-able*] **1** *archaic* **:** marked by deceit **:** DECEITFUL, DECEPTIVE **2** *archaic* **:** capable of being deceived **:** liable to be misled — **de·cei·va·bly** \-blē\ *adv, archaic*
de·ceive \də̇ˈsēv, dēˈ-\ *vb* -ED/-ING/-S [ME *deceiven,* fr. OF *deceivre, decevoir,* fr. L *decipere* to ensnare, deceive, cheat, fr. *de* down, away + *-cipere* (fr. *capere* to take) — more at DE-, HEAVE] *vt* **1** *archaic* **:** to take unawares esp. by craft or trickery **:** ENSNARE, MISLEAD ⟨it was whose guile . . . *deceived* the mother of mankind —John Milton⟩ **2 a** *obs* **:** to be false to **:** BETRAY ⟨you have *deceived* our trust —Shak.⟩ **b** *archaic* **:** to disappoint (as an expectation) ⟨nor are my hopes *deceived* —John Dryden⟩ **3** *obs* **:** to deprive esp. by fraud or stealth **:** CHEAT, DEFRAUD ⟨*deceived* me of a good sum of money —William Oldys⟩ **4 :** to cause to believe the false **:** DELUDE ⟨when we're young we can be very easily *deceived* —George Meredith⟩ **5** *archaic* **:** to while away (as time, care, or sorrow) **:** BEGUILE ⟨these occupations oftentimes *deceived* the listless hour —William Wordsworth⟩ ~ *vi* **:** to practice deceit **:** be deceitful ⟨his stunning technique that baffles and ~*s* —Eva M. Neumeyer⟩
syn MISLEAD, DELUDE, BEGUILE, BETRAY, DOUBLE-CROSS: DECEIVE indicates an inculcating of one so that he takes the false as true, the unreal as existent, the spurious as genuine ⟨it is a pity to make him the dupe of his more intelligent partner. If he is *deceived,* he has a way of getting his revenge —S.M.Crothers⟩ ⟨disguised Communists trying to *deceive* the ignorant natives —*Americas*⟩ MISLEAD indicates a causing to fall into error of some sort, intentionally or not ⟨I think it was Thrasyllus who tricked her into believing that she was meant. Thrasyllus never told lies but he loved *misleading* people —Robert Graves⟩ ⟨to *mislead* spies, Love and his squad pretended they were on their way to Los Angeles, but at night doubled back to the arroyo, where they surprised Murrieta and his gang —*Amer. Guide Series: Calif.*⟩ DELUDE implies a complete misleading or deceiving so that one remains a fool, dupe, or victim ⟨did he, did all the people who said they didn't mind things, know that they really did? Or were they indeed *deluded?* —Rose Macaulay⟩ ⟨scientists do little to discourage this view, and, indeed, many of them are quite as *deluded* as most laymen are about the subject —M.F.A.Montagu⟩ BEGUILE indicates deceiving or deluding one by subtle allure and wiling one into abandoning doubts or defenses ⟨marshlights to *beguile* mankind from tangible goods and immediate fruitions —Lewis Mumford⟩ ⟨the unique power by which Shakespeare compels 'faith in the emotions expressed' and *beguiles* Bradley and company into their absurdities —F.R.Leavis⟩ BETRAY indicates treacherously or deceitfully leading into enemy hands or into danger or difficulty ⟨the fact that he had *betrayed* his daughter into an ugly position gnawed at his consciousness —Sherwood Anderson⟩ DOUBLE-CROSS applies to deceiving or betraying a friend, partner, or accomplice ⟨De Valera charged that his own trusted negotiators had *double-crossed* him by signing an agreement to take the detested oath of loyalty to the British king without consulting him —Paul Blanshard⟩ ⟨they *double-crossed* the Pasha of Marrakesh, and ordered him to call off the revolt they had inspired —*New Statesman & Nation*⟩
de·ceiv·er \-və(r)\ *n* -S [ME, alter. (influenced by *-er, -ere* -er) of *deceivour,* modif. (influenced by *deceiven*) of MF *deceveur,* fr. OF *deceveor,* fr. OF *deceivre, decevoir* + *-eor* -or] **:** one that deceives
de·ceiv·ing·ly *adv* [ME, fr. *deceiving* (pres. part. of *deceiven*) + *-ly*] **:** in a deceiving manner
de·cel·er·ate \(ˈ)dēˈseləˌrāt, *usu* -ād· +V\ *vb* -ED/-ING/-S [*de-* + *accelerate*] *vt* **1 :** to cause to go progressively slower **:** lessen the speed of **:** slow down **:** RETARD ⟨~ a motor⟩ ⟨~ an automobile⟩ **2 :** to decrease the rate of progress of (as a process or development) ⟨~ erosion of the soil⟩ ⟨~ an educational program⟩ ~ *vi* **1 :** to move at a progressively slower speed **:** slow down ⟨the car *decelerated*⟩ **2 :** to cause something (as a vehicle) to move at a progressively slower speed ⟨the driver *decelerated* quickly⟩
de·cel·er·a·tion \(ˌ)dēˌseləˈrāshən\ *n* -S **1 :** the act or process of decelerating ⟨~ of a truck by braking⟩ ⟨~ of an aging process⟩ **2 :** the rate of decrease in velocity ⟨aeromedical research has shown man's ability to withstand high ~*s*⟩
deceleration lane *n* **:** a speed-change area or lane consisting of added pavement at the edge of through-traffic lanes to permit drivers to diverge from the through-traffic flow without reducing speed until after the diverging maneuver is completed — compare ACCELERATION LANE
de·cel·er·a·tor \(ˈ)dēˈseləˌrād·ə(r)\ *n* -S **:** one that decelerates
de·cel·er·om·e·ter \(ˌ)dēˌseləˈrämədˌə(r)\ *n* -S [*deceleration* + *-o-* + *-meter*] **:** an instrument for measuring the rate of change of speed of a moving vehicle during deceleration
de·cel·er·on \dēˈseləˌrän\ *n* -S [*decelerate* + *-on* (as in *aileron*)] **:** a split lateral control surface combining the functions of aileron and air brakes on an airplane
decem- *comb form* [MF or L; MF, fr. L, fr. *decem* ten] **:** ten ⟨*decem*costate⟩
de·cem·ber \də̇ˈsembə(r), (ˈ)dēˈs-\ *n* -S *usu cap* [ME *decembre,* fr. OF, fr. L *december* (tenth month), fr. *decem* ten — more at TEN] **:** the 12th month of the Gregorian calendar — abbr. *Dec.;* see MONTH table
de·cem·brist \-ˈbrə̇st\ *n* -S *usu cap* [*decembr-* (fr. *december*) + *-ist;* trans. of Russ *dekabrist;* fr. the fact that the uprising occurred in December 1825] **:** one of those who took part in the unsuccessful liberal uprising against the Russian emperor Nicholas I
de·cem·vir \də̇ˈsemvə(r)\ *n, pl* **decemvirs** \-və(r)z\ *also* **decem·vi·ri** \-vəˌrī\ [L, back-formation fr. *decemviri,* pl., fr. *decem viri* ten men, fr. *decem* ten + *viri,* pl. of *vir* man — more at VIRILE] **:** one of a commission, council, or ruling body of 10; *specif* **:** a member of either of two commissions made up of 10 men each who framed the Roman laws of the Twelve Tables and who had absolute power during their term of office
de·cem·vi·ral \-vərəl\ *adj* [L *decemviralis,* fr. *decemviri* + *-alis* -al] **:** of or relating to decemvirs or a decemvirate
de·cem·vi·rate \-vərə̇t, -əˌrāt\ *n* -S [L *decemviratus,* fr. *decemviri* + *-atus* -ate] **1 :** the office or government of decemvirs **2 :** a body of decemvirs
decence *n* -S [F *décence,* fr. L *decentia*] *obs* **:** appropriateness (as of action or deportment) **:** FITNESS
de·cen·cy \ˈdēsᵊnsē, -nsi\ *n* -ES [L *decentia,* fr. *decent-, decens* (pres. part. of *decēre* to be fitting) + *-ia* -y] **1** *archaic* **a :** suitability or fitness to circumstances ⟨his discourse on the scaffold was full of ~ and courage —David Hume †1776⟩ **b :** orderly condition of society **:** conformity to law ⟨no hundred-headed Riot here we meet, with *Decency* and Law beneath his feet —Robert Burns⟩ **2 :** the quality or state of being decent ⟨only doctors and nurses have the ~ to wear masks —Justina Hill⟩ **:** decent quality, behavior, dress, or deportment **:** DECORUM, PROPRIETY, MODESTY ⟨aid to the victims was simply a matter of common ~⟩ **:** conformity to standards of taste, propriety, or quality ⟨the first story of any real ~ that I ever wrote —Arnold Bennett⟩ **3 :** whatever is proper or becoming **:** standards of propriety ⟨the act was a gross violation of ~⟩ — usu. used in pl. ⟨the *decencies* of normal controversy . . . have been disregarded and men have been publicly criticized —Vannevar Bush⟩ **4 a :** conformity to the standard of living that becomes a person ⟨enabled a gentleman to afford the ~ of burning wood on his own hearth —Oscar Wilde⟩ **b decencies** *pl* **:** the external conditions of decent living ⟨did not provide her . . . children with the *decencies* justified by their inheritance —J.D.Wade⟩ **5 a :** literary decorum or its observance **b decencies** *pl* **:** the established conventions of literary decorum often with special reference to syntactical or grammatical propriety
[1]**de·cen·na·ry** \də̇ˈsenərē, dēˈ-\ *n* -ES [ML *decennarius* tithingman, fr. *decena, decenna* tithing (fr. L *decem* ten) + L *-arius* -ary] **:** [1]TITHING
[2]**decennary** \"\ *n* -ES [L *decennis* of 10 years + E *-ary*] **:** a period of 10 years
de·cen·ni·ad \-nēˌad\ *n* -S [L *decennium* + E *-ad*] **:** DECENNIUM
[1]**de·cen·ni·al** \-nēəl\ *adj* [L *decennium* + E *-al*] **1 :** consisting of or lasting for 10 years ⟨a ~ interval⟩ **2 :** occurring, appearing, or being made, done, or acted upon every 10 years ⟨~ games⟩ ⟨~ census⟩
[2]**decennial** \"\ *n* -S **:** a decennial anniversary or its celebration
de·cen·ni·al·ly \-nēəlē, -li\ *adv* **:** every 10 years
de·cen·ni·um \-nēəm\ *n, pl* **decenniums** \-ēəmz\ *or* **decennia** \-ēə\ [L, fr. *decennis* of 10 years, fr. *dec-* (fr. *decem* ten) + *-ennis* (fr. *annus* year) — more at ANNUAL] **:** a period of 10 years
de·cent \ˈdēsᵊnt\ *adj, sometimes* -ER/-EST [MF or L; MF, fr. L *decent-, decens,* pres. part. of *decēre* to be fitting, be proper; akin to L *decus* honor, ornament, *dignus* worthy, Gk *dokein* to seem good, seem, think, Skt *daśasyati* he worships, favors] **1** *archaic* **a :** appropriate to circumstances or to social status ⟨the funeral . . . was a ~ solemnity —John Evelyn⟩ **b :** having tasteful appearance or proportions **:** well-formed **:** SHAPELY ⟨her ~ hand —Alexander Pope⟩ **2 :** marked by acceptance as socially unobjectionable, proper, or suitable **:** not questionable or censurable **:** conforming to standards of propriety, etiquette, good taste, or morality ⟨forsake a ~ craft that he may pursue the gentilities of a profession —George Eliot⟩ ⟨his ~ reticence is branded as hypocrisy —W.S.Maugham⟩ **3 a :** free of anything improper or of suggestions of the immodest, lustful, or obscene **:** indicative or suggestive of virtue or propriety ⟨speech in this circle, if not always ~, never became lewd —George Santayana⟩ **b :** not nude **:** clothed with adequate modesty ⟨one of her shoulder straps slipped down, leaving her perfectly ~ by American standards —Santha Rama Rau⟩ **4 :** fairly good but not excellent **:** up to reasonable expectations **:** ADEQUATE, SUFFICIENT, SATISFACTORY ⟨in search of a ~ meal —Robert Shaplen⟩ ⟨vile insanitary barracks to serve as substitutes for ~ human shelter —Lewis Mumford⟩ **:** not poor, scant, questionable, or marginal ⟨only a single fortress put up a ~ resistance —Robert Graves⟩ **5 :** marked by a combination of goodwill, sincerity, tolerance, uprightness, generosity, or fairness **:** not cruel, repressive, or vindictive ⟨the ~ people, the people on the side of the angels, the kind, reasonable, fair-minded people —Gladys B. Stern⟩ **syn** see CHASTE, DECOROUS
de·cent·ly *adv* **:** in a decent manner
de·cent·ness *n* -ES **:** the quality or state of being decent
de·centralism \(ˈ)dē+\ *n* -S [fr. *decentralize,* after E *centralize: centralism*] **:** DECENTRALIZATION
de·centralist \(ˈ)dē+\ *n* -S [prob. fr. F *décentraliste,* fr. *décentraliser* to decentralize + *-iste* -ist] **:** one favoring decentralization, esp. urban decentralization
de·centralization \(ˈ)dē+\ *n* -S [prob. fr. F *décentralisation,* fr. *décentraliser* + *-ation*] **1 :** the dispersion or distribution of functions and powers from a central authority to regional and local governing bodies **2 :** the redistribution of population and industry from urban centers to suburban areas or outlying districts
de·centralize \(ˈ)dē+\ *vt* [prob. fr. F *décentraliser,* fr. *dé-* de- (fr. OF *des-*) + *centraliser* to centralize] **:** to deprive of centralization: as **a :** to disperse or distribute the functions or powers of (as a government) ⟨~ the administration of flood relief⟩ **b :** to cause to withdraw from the center or place of concentration ⟨~ downtown business areas —J.C.Ingraham⟩
de·cephalization \(ˈ)dē+\ *n* -S [*de-* + *cephalization*] **:** decrease or degeneration of organs and parts relating to the head or cephalic regions — opposed to *cephalization*

de·cep·tion \də'sepshən, dē'-\ *n* -s [ME *decepcioun*, fr. MF *deception*, fr. LL *deception-, deceptio*, fr. L *deceptus* (past part. of *decipere* to deceive) + *-ion-, -io* -ion — more at DECEIVE] **1 a :** the act of deceiving, cheating, hoodwinking, misleading, or deluding ⟨resort to falsehood and ~ in avoiding the tax⟩ **b :** the fact or condition of being deceived, fooled, or deluded ⟨the magician's ~ of the audience by clever tricks⟩ **2 :** a characteristic, arrangement, or situation that deceives or deludes with or without calculated intent **:** FRAUD, ARTIFICE, TRICK ⟨skilled in evasions, ~s, and ruses⟩

syn FRAUD, DOUBLE-DEALING, TRICKERY, CHICANE, CHICANERY, SUBTERFUGE: DECEPTION is a general term for any sort of deceiving, by whatever methods or for whatever motive ⟨the *deception* practiced by this corrupt and treacherous group⟩ ⟨the *deception* in this boxer's feints⟩ FRAUD, unless humorously or lightly used, indicates dishonest or even criminal deception, esp. misrepresentation or perversion of the truth in order to defraud ⟨he would sometimes "write in" for articles necessary for his education . . . in order to eke out his pocket money . . . these *frauds* were sometimes . . . in imminent danger of being discovered —Samuel Butler †1902⟩ DOUBLE-DEALING suggests performance of actions incompatible with or contradictory to an ostensible role; sometimes it indicates treachery by secretly aiding a party while professedly a member or ally of its enemy ⟨his *double-dealing* in collaborating secretly with the enemy occupation forces while belonging to the patriot resistance group⟩ TRICKERY indicates use or practice of tricks to deceive, of artful stratagems or crafty ingenuities, and usu. suggests sharp practice or actual dishonesty ⟨they held that the basest *trickery* or deceit was not dishonorable if directed against a foe —*Amer. Guide Series: R.I.*⟩ CHICANE and CHICANERY, the latter being now the more common form, suggest legalistic trickery, esp. trickery by misrepresenting, misleading, confusing, or other shyster devices ⟨the labyrinthine procedure that so delayed justice and helped *chicane* —*Times Lit. Supp.*⟩ ⟨a disintegrating society, rotten and fluid within . . . made . . . *chicane* indispensable to winning riches —Marvin Lowenthal⟩ SUBTERFUGE refers to any shady trick or artifice to conceal, escape, avoid, or evade ⟨whether notes issued by such a bank constituted a *subterfuge* by which the state in effect was emitting bills of credit in the sense forbidden by the Constitution —Harvey Pinney⟩ **syn** see in addition IMPOSTURE

de·cep·tious \-shəs\ *adj* [prob. fr. *deception*, after such pairs as E *faction: factious*] **:** tending to deceive — **de·cep·tious·ly** *adv*

de·cep·tive \-ptiv, -tēv *also* -təv\ *adj* [obs. F or LL; obs. F *déceptif*, fr. LL *deceptivus*, fr. L *deceptus* + *-ivus* -ive] **:** tending to deceive **:** having power to mislead ⟨a ~ appearance⟩ — **de·cep·tive·ly** \-təvlē, -li\ *adv* — **de·cep·tive·ness** \-tivnəs, -tēv- *also* -təv-\ *n* -es

deceptive cadence *n* **:** a cadence in which the full or final close is evaded by the use of an unexpected or foreign chord as the chord of resolution — called also *false cadence, interrupted cadence, suspended cadence;* see CADENCE illustration

de·cer·e·bel·late \¦dē,serə'belət\ *also* **de·cer·e·bel·lat·ed** \-,lād·əd\ *adj* [*decerebellate* fr. *de-* + *cerebell-* + *-ate*, adj. suffix; *decerebellated* fr. *de-* + *cerebell-* + *-ate*, vb. suffix + *-ed*] **:** deprived of the cerebellum — **de·cer·e·bel·la·tion** \(,)dē,serə(,)be'lāshən\ *n* -s

¹de·cerebrate \(')dē+\ *vt* -ED/-ING/-S [*de-* + *cerebr-* + *-ate*] **:** to remove the cerebrum from; *also* **:** to make incapable of cerebral activity — **de·cerebration** \(,)dē+\ *n* -s

²de·ce·re·brate \¦dē¦serəbrət, (')dē¦serəb-\ *adj* **1 :** DECEREBRATED **2 :** characteristic of decerebration ⟨~ rigidity⟩

de·cern \də'sərn\ *vb* -ED/-ING/-S [ME *decernen*, fr. MF *decerner*, fr. L *decernere* to decree, decide — more at DECREE] *Scots law* **:** to decree by judicial sentence

decerp *vt* -ED/-ING/-S [L *decerpere*, fr. *de* from, away + *-cerpere* (fr. *carpere* to pluck) — more at DE-, HARVEST] *obs* **:** PLUCK, GATHER

de·certification \(¦)dē+\ *n* [*de-* + *certification*] **:** the act or process of decertifying

de·certify \(')dē+\ *vt* [*de-* + *certify*] **:** to withdraw or revoke certification of (as a labor union acting as bargaining agent for a bargaining unit)

de·ces·sion \də'seshən\ *n* [L *decession-, decessio*, fr. *decessus* (past part. of *decedere* to depart, fr. *de* from, away + *cedere* to go) + *-ion-, -io* -ion — more at CEDE] *archaic* **:** WITHDRAWAL, DEPARTURE, DECREASE

dech·en·ite \'dekə,nīt\ *n* -s [G *dechenit*, fr. Heinrich von Dechen †1889 Ger. geologist + G *-it* -ite] **:** DESCLOIZITE

de·chlorinate \(')dē+'-\ *vt* [*de-* + *chlorinate*] **:** to remove chlorine from ⟨*dechlorinated* water⟩ — **de·chlorination** \(,)dē+\ *n*

de·christianization \(¦)dē+\ *n* [prob. fr. F *déchristianisation*, fr. *déchristianiser* + *-ation*] **:** the process of dechristianizing ⟨the last step in the gradual ~ of Europe —Nicolas Zernov⟩

de·christianize \(')dē+\ *vt* [prob. fr. F *déchristianiser*, fr. *dé-* (fr. OF *des-*) + *christianiser* to Christianize, fr. MF, fr. L *christianus* Christian + MF *-iser* -ize] **:** to cause to turn from Christianity **:** deprive of Christian characteristics

deci- *comb form* [F *déci-*, fr. L *decimus* tenth, fr. *decem* ten — more at TEN] **:** tenth part (of a specified unit of measure) ⟨*decigram*⟩ — chiefly in terms belonging to the metric system

de·cian \'dēsh(ē)ən\ *adj, usu cap* [Gaius Messius Quintus Trajanus *Decius* †A.D.251 Roman emperor + E *-an*] **:** of or relating to the Roman emperor Decius who persecuted the Christians ⟨the *Decian* persecution⟩

deci·are \'desē+,-\ *n* -s [F *déciare*, fr. *déci-* deci- + *are*] **:** a metric unit of area equal to 10 square meters or 11.96 square yards

dec·i·bel \'desə,bel, -,bəl\ *n* -s [ISV *deci-* + *bel*] **1** *in electronic communications* **a :** a unit for expressing the ratio of two amounts of electric or acoustic power equal to 10 times the common logarithm of the power ratio — abbr. *db* **b :** a unit for expressing the ratio of the magnitudes of two electric voltages or currents or analogous acoustic quantities (as sound pressure or particle velocity) equal to 20 times the common logarithm of the voltage or current ratio provided that the two voltages or currents are measured on equal resistances **2 :** a unit for measuring the relative loudness of sounds equal approximately to the smallest degree of difference of loudness ordinarily detectable by the human ear the range of which includes about 130 decibels on a scale beginning with 1 for the faintest audible sound

de·cid·able \də'sīdəbəl, dē'-\ *adj* **:** capable of being decided; *specif* **:** capable of being decided as following or not following from the axioms of a logical system — compare DECISION, PROBLEM

de·cide \də'sīd, dē'-\ *vb* -ED/-ING/-S [ME *deciden*, fr. MF *decider*, fr. L *decidere*, lit., to cut off, fr. *de* down, away + *-cidere* (fr. *caedere* to cut) — more at DE-, CONCISE] *vt* **:** to dispel doubt on: **a :** to arrive at a choice or solution concerning which ends uncertainty or contention ⟨~ what to order for breakfast⟩ **b :** to bring definitively and conclusively to an end esp. in matters relating to war ⟨the victory at San Jacinto *decided* the war⟩ **c :** to infer or conclude from available indications and evidence ⟨Washington *decided* . . . that the President could no longer avoid calling the Senator to account —*Economist*⟩ **d :** to choose or select as a future course of action ⟨she *decided* to buy a new hat⟩ ⟨*decided* to read a book instead⟩ **e :** to induce or force (as a person) to arrive at a choice, judgment, or decision ⟨this exordium . . . *decided* Mr. Cruncher —Charles Dickens⟩ ~ *vi* **:** to make a choice or decision esp. a binding or definitive one presumably after consideration **:** come to a conclusion ⟨some learned men, proud of their knowledge, only speak to ~ —Earl of Chesterfield⟩

syn RESOLVE, DETERMINE, RULE, SETTLE: DECIDE is less colorful and has less connotational range than others in this group; in this sense it simply means to come to a decision, presumably after some consideration, or to induce another to come to a decision ⟨the time for deliberation is then passed, he has *decided* —John Marshall⟩ ⟨had finally *decided* Amy to drop the mask of deference —Arnold Bennett⟩ RESOLVE in reference to a person's decisions about his own future actions may imply an earnest and strong-willed attitude ⟨suddenly he *resolved* to say something. He *resolved* to say it so firmly that he determined to say it even if Mr. Britling went on talking all the time —H.G.Wells⟩ but in reference to questions, problems, difficulties, and so on, it appears to stress clear analysis and consideration, with the implication of a final judgment ⟨the task is to *resolve* initial oppositions of interest into some moderate harmony by a process of mutual concessions —J.A.Hobson⟩ ⟨Mr. Fitzpatrick, who did not catch the point at issue very quickly, seemed unable to *resolve* the difficulty —James Joyce⟩ DETERMINE in reference to decisions on personal action implies about the same things as RESOLVE, although it may occas. be somewhat weaker and it may involve more consideration of limitation and choice ⟨she was *determined* that in her house Sophia should have all the freedoms and conveniences that she could have had in her own —Arnold Bennett⟩ ⟨he *resolved* to overcome the one-pawn disadvantage and *determined* on a scheme involving the quick and audacious use of his major pieces⟩ but in reference to less personal and more general matters the word may suggest bounds, limits, classes, or terms and may imply that considerations and judgments involved are decisive in a course, outcome, or judgment ⟨but every atom . . . is a miniature solar system, with electrons in numbers which *determine* the nature of the element —W.R. Inge⟩ ⟨but theories, intellectual systems, notions . . . may themselves create demands or *determine* their directions —Felix Frankfurter⟩ RULE stresses the act of deciding it; may imply a judicial, administrative, or otherwise authoritative positive attitude or procedure and a necessarily binding procedure or precedent set ⟨the procedure was *ruled* out as unparliamentary⟩ ⟨the president *ruled* that such matters should be taken care of in Mr. Smith's office⟩ SETTLE contains less implication than others in this series about procedure for arriving at a decision, more about the finality of the action ⟨the problem of the Pythagorean legend may be said to be *settled*. But the problem of the Socratic legend is still under consideration —Havelock Ellis⟩ ⟨the principle of law is too well *settled* to be disputed, that a court can give no judgment . . . where it has no jurisdiction —R.B.Taney⟩

de·cid·ed \-īdəd\ *adj* [fr. past part. of *decide*] **1 :** free from ambiguity **:** UNQUESTIONABLE, CLEAR-CUT ⟨a ~ advantage⟩ **2 :** free from doubt or wavering **:** DETERMINED, SETTLED ⟨a ~ way of talking and moving —S.H.Adams⟩ — **de·cid·ed·ly** *adv* — **de·cid·ed·ness** *n* -ES

de·cid·er \-də(r)\ *n* -s **:** one that decides

de·cid·ua \də'sijəwə, dē'-\ *n, pl* **decid·uae** \-,wē\ [NL, fr. L, fem. of *deciduus* deciduous] **1 :** the part of the mucous membrane lining the uterus that in higher placental mammals undergoes special modifications in preparation for and during pregnancy and is cast off at parturition, being made up in the human of (1) a part lining the uterus, (2) a part enveloping the embryo, and (3) a part participating with the chorion in the formation of the placenta — called also respectively (1) *decidua ve·ra* \-'virə\, (2) *decidua cap·su·lar·is* \-,kapsə'la(a)rəs\ or *decidua re·flexa* \-rə'fleksə\, and (3) *decidua ser·o·ti·na* \-,serə'tīnə, -tē-\ **2 :** the part of the mucous membrane of the uterus cast off in the ordinary process of menstruation — called also *decidua men·stru·al·is* \-,menztrə'waləs\

de·cid·u·al \-,wəl\ *adj* [NL *decidua* + E *-al*] **:** of or involving a decidua **:** having a decidua

decidual cell *n* **:** one of the large irregular cells formed in the decidua of pregnancy

de·cid·u·ary \-,werē\ *adj* [*deciduous* + *-ary*] **:** DECIDUOUS

de·cid·u·a·ta \•,••'wād·ə, -ād·ə\ *n pl, cap* [NL, fr. *decidua* + *-ata*] **:** the mammals having deciduate placentas

de·cid·u·ate \•'••,wət\ *adj* [NL *deciduatus*, fr. *decidua* + L *-atus* -ate] **1** *of a placenta* **:** having the fetal and maternal tissues firmly interlocked so that a layer of maternal tissue is torn away at parturition and forms a part of the afterbirth **2 :** DECIDUOUS

de·cid·u·ous \də'sijəwəs, dē'-\ *adj* [L *deciduus*, fr. *decidere* to fall off, fr. *de* down, away + *-cidere* (fr. *cadere* to fall) — more at DE-, CHANCE] **1 :** falling off or shed at the end of the growing period ⟨~ leaves⟩ ⟨~ fruit⟩, after anthesis ⟨~ flower petals⟩, at certain seasons ⟨the ~ hair of animals⟩ ⟨~ antlers of deer⟩, or at certain stages of development ⟨~ gills⟩ ⟨~ teeth⟩ — opposed to *persistent;* compare CADUCOUS, FUGACIOUS **2 :** having or made up of deciduous parts ⟨a ~ tree⟩ ⟨~ dentition⟩ — compare EVERGREEN **3 :** of passing interest or importance **:** EPHEMERAL, TRANSITORY ⟨there is nothing that is ~ in books —J.R.Lowell⟩ — **de·cid·u·ous·ly** *adv* — **de·cid·u·ous·ness** *n* -ES

deciduous cypress *n* **:** a bald cypress (*Taxodium distichum*)

deciduous holly *n* **:** BEARBERRY 3

deciduous tooth *n* **:** MILK TOOTH

deci·gram \'desə+,-\ *n* -s [F *décigramme*, fr. *déci-* deci- + *gramme* gram] **:** a metric unit of mass and weight equal to 1/10 gram — see METRIC SYSTEM table

¹dec·ile \'de,sīl, -,səl\ *n* -s [L *decem* ten + E *-ile* — more at TEN] **:** any one of nine numbers in a series dividing the distribution of the individuals in the series into 10 groups of equal frequency; *also* **:** any one of these 10 groups

²decile \"\ *adj* **:** relating to a decile or division into deciles

deci·liter \'desə+,-\ *n* -s [F *décilitre*, fr. *déci-* deci- + *litre* liter] **:** a metric unit of capacity equal to 1/10 liter — see METRIC SYSTEM table

de·cil·lion \də'silyən\ *n* -s *often attrib* [L *decem* + E *-illion* (as in *million*)] — see NUMBER table

¹dec·i·mal \'desəməl\ *adj* [fr. (assumed) NL *decimalis*, fr. ML, relating to tithes, fr. L *decima* tithe + *-alis* -al — more at DIME] **1 a :** numbered or proceeding by tens **:** based on the number 10 **b :** subdivided into 10th or 100th units ⟨~ coinage⟩ ⟨~ hour⟩ **c :** expressed in a decimal fraction ⟨a ~ equivalent⟩ **2** [ML *decimalis*] **:** of or relating to tithes

²decimal \"\ *n* -s **1 :** a number expressed in the scale of tens **2 :** DECIMAL FRACTION

decimal arithmetic *n* **1 :** the common arithmetic in which numeration proceeds by tens **2 :** calculation with decimals

decimal classification *n* **:** a system of classifying library books and other material whereby the main classes and subclasses are designated by a number composed of three digits and further subdivision is shown by numbers after a decimal point — called also *Dewey classification;* compare EXPANSIVE CLASSIFICATION, LIBRARY OF CONGRESS CLASSIFICATION

decimal fraction *n* **:** a proper fraction in which the denominator is some power of 10 usu. not expressed but signified by a point placed at the left of the numerator (as .2=2/10, .25=25/100, .025=25/1000)

dec·i·mal·ize \-,līz\ *vt* -ED/-ING/-S **:** to reduce to a decimal system ⟨~ the currency⟩

dec·i·mal·ly \-məlē, -li\ *adv* **:** by tens **:** by means of decimals

decimal measure *n* **:** a measure used in a decimal system

decimal notation *n* **:** the expression of numbers through powers of 10; *specif* **:** the common method employing nine digits and zero

decimal place *n* **:** a position of a digit as counted to the right or sometimes to the left of the decimal point in a decimal ⟨carried out to the fourth *decimal place*⟩

decimal point *n* **:** the dot at the left of a decimal fraction

dec·i·mate \'desə,māt, *usu* -ād·+V\ *vt* -ED/-ING/-S [L *decimatus*, past part. of *decimare*, fr. *decimus* tenth, fr. *decem* ten — more at TEN] **1 :** to select by lot and kill every tenth man of ⟨~ a regiment⟩ **2 a :** to take a tenth from **:** tax to the amount of one-tenth **b** (1) **:** to take in a definite part of (ore) by means of a sampling device (2) **:** to take every tenth one of ⟨~ carloads⟩ **3 :** to destroy a considerable part of **:** reduce to the point of almost complete extermination ⟨war, which . . . nearly *decimated* the Seminoles —R.F.Warner⟩ **:** decrease greatly ⟨inflation has *decimated* . . . buying power —*New Republic*⟩ **4 :** to rearrange (an alphabet or text) into another sequence by taking every *n*th item until all are taken (as, if *n* is 3 ABCDEFG becomes ADGCFBE if the counting applies to the complete original sequence but ADGECFB if the letters previously taken out are skipped in counting)

decimating factor *n* **:** any direct cause (as starvation or hunting) of reduction in population numbers

dec·i·ma·tion \,••'māshən\ *n* -s [LL *decimation-, decimatio*, fr. L *decimatus* (past part. of *decimare* to pay as a tithe, select by lot and kill every tenth man of) + *-ion-, -io* -ion] **1 a :** the taking of tithes or of a tax of one tenth **b :** the tithe or tax taken **2 :** a selection of every tenth person; *esp* **:** selection by lot for punishment with death **3 :** the destruction of a considerable part **:** reduction to the point of almost complete extermination ⟨~ of the forest Indians, brought about by disease —Farley Mowat⟩ **4 a :** the act of decimating cryptographically **b :** the new sequence resulting from decimating

dec·i·me·ter \'desə,mēd·ə(r)\ *n* -s [F *décimètre*, fr. *déci-* deci- + *mètre* meter] **:** a metric unit of length equal to 1/10 meter — see METRIC SYSTEM table

dec·i·mo·lar \-,mōlə(r)\ *adj* [*deci-* + *molar*] *chem* **:** tenth molar

dec·i·mole \-,mōl\ *n* -s [ISV *decim-* (fr. L *decimus* tenth) + *-ole*] **:** DECUPLET 2

dec·i·mo·sex·to \,desə(,)mō'sek(,)stō\ *n* -s [L *decimo sexto*, *sexto decimo*, abl. of *decimus sextus, sextus decimus* sixteenth, fr. *decimus* tenth + *sextus* sixth — more at SEXT] **:** SIXTEENMO

dec·i·normal \¦desə+\ *adj* [*deci-* + *normal*] *of a chemical solution* **:** having one tenth of the normal strength

¹de·cipher \də'sīfə(r), dē's-\ *vt* **deciphered; deciphered; deciphering** \-f(ə)riŋ\ **deciphers** [*de-* + ¹*cipher;* trans. of MF *deschiffrer*] **1 a** *obs* **:** to find out **:** DETECT, DISCOVER ⟨you are both ~*ed* . . . for villains —Shak.⟩ **b** *archaic* **:** to make known **:** INDICATE, REVEAL ⟨his favorite gesture . . . might ~ his whole character —Thomas Holcroft⟩ **2 :** to convert (a cryptic writing) into intelligible form: as **a :** to undo (an encipherment) by reversal of the enciphering procedure **b :** SOLVE ⟨~ a cipher⟩ **c** *obs* **:** to represent by oral description or pictorial art **:** DELINEATE, PORTRAY ⟨with her majesty's name ~*ed* in gold letters —Jonathan Swift⟩ **3 a :** to make out, read, or interpret despite obscuration or partial obliteration ⟨~*ing* the smudged postmark —Arnold Bennett⟩ **b :** to examine and find out or discover the meaning or explanation of (something difficult to understand) ⟨some philosophical message . . . that we fail to ~ —Henri Peyre⟩ **syn** see SOLVE

²decipher \"\ *n* -s **:** a secret message in deciphered form

de·ci·pher·able \də'sīf(ə)rəbəl, (')dē¦s-\ *adj* **:** capable of being deciphered — **de·ci·pher·ably** \-blē\ *adv*

de·ci·pher·er \də'sīfərə(r), dē's-\ *n* -s **:** one that deciphers

deciphering alphabet *n* [*deciphering* fr. gerund of ¹*decipher*] **:** a substitution alphabet with its cipher component in normal alphabetic order — see ALPHABET 1j, CONJUGATE ALPHABET

de·ci·pher·ment \-f(ə)rmənt\ *n* -s **1 :** the act or process of deciphering **2 :** the result of deciphering **:** PLAINTEXT

¹de·ci·sion \də'sizhən, dē'-\ *n* -s [MF, fr. L *decision-, decisio*, fr. *decisus* (past part. of *decidere* to decide) + *-ion-, -io* -ion — more at DECIDE] **1 a :** the act of deciding; *specif* **:** the act of settling or terminating (as a contest or controversy) by giving judgment **b :** a determination arrived at after consideration **:** SETTLEMENT, CONCLUSION — see JUDGMENT, PRECEDENT, STARE DECISIS **2 a :** an account or report of a conclusion, esp. of a legal adjudication or judicial determination of a question or cause ⟨a ~ of the Supreme Court⟩ **b :** an announcement (as of a judge) declaring the winner in a contest **3 :** the quality of being decided **:** prompt and fixed determination **:** FIRMNESS ⟨a man of unusual ~⟩ **4 a :** the act of forming an opinion or of deciding upon a course of action ⟨an exhausting ~⟩ **b :** an opinion formed or a course of action decided upon ⟨a favorable ~⟩ **5 :** WIN; *specif* **:** a victory in a boxing match decided on points instead of by a knockout

²decision \"\ *vt* **decisioned; decisioned; decisioning** \-zh(ə)niŋ\ **decisions :** to win a decision over (an opponent) ⟨the champion easily ~*ed* the challenger⟩

de·ci·sion·al \-zhən°l, -zhnəl\ *adj* **:** of, relating to, or involving a decision ⟨permeated with ~ . . . elements —Walter Cerf⟩

decisional law *n* **:** the law as determined by reference to the reported decisions of the courts — compare COMMON LAW

de·ci·sion·ism \-zhə,nizəm\ *n* -s **:** a system of legal philosophy based on the belief that right is what the legislature has determined it to be

decision problem *n* **:** the problem of finding an effective method for deciding whether a given formula is true within the framework of the calculus to which it belongs

de·ci·sive \də'sīsiv, dē's-, -ēv *also* -'sīz- *or* -əv\ *adj* [F *décisif*, fr. MF *decisif*, fr. L *decisus* + MF *-if* -ive] **1 :** having the power or quality of deciding **:** putting an end to ⟨a ~ controversy⟩ **:** CONCLUSIVE ⟨we shall win a complete and ~ victory over the forces of evil —Sir Winston Churchill⟩ **2 :** marked by or displaying decision **:** RESOLUTE, DETERMINED ⟨the clarity that comes from the ~ mind of the man of direct action —J.P.Wood⟩ **3 :** that is beyond doubt **:** UNMISTAKABLE, UNQUESTIONABLE ⟨a ~ superiority⟩ **syn** see CONCLUSIVE

de·ci·sive·ly \-əvlē, -li\ *adv* **:** in a decisive manner

de·ci·sive·ness \-əvnəs\ *n* -ES **:** the quality or state of being decisive **:** RESOLUTENESS

dec·i·stere \'desə,sti(ə)r\ *n* -s [F *décistère*, fr. *déci-* deci- + *stère* stere] **:** a metric unit of capacity equal to 1/10 cubic meter — see METRIC SYSTEM table

¹deck \'dek\ *n* -s [prob. modif. of (assumed) LG *verdeck* (whence G *verdeck*), fr. (assumed) MLG *vordeck* (trans. of OIt *coperta* or MF *couverte*, lit., cover), fr. MLG *vordecken* to cover, fr. MLG *vor-* (akin to OHG *fir-, fur-* for-) + *decken* to cover (akin to OHG *decken* to cover) — more at THATCH] **1 :** a platform in a ship extending within the hull from side to side and from stem to stern (as the main deck) or extending within or above the hull part of the width or the length (as the bridge deck) and serving as an important element in a ship's structural strength and forming the floor for its compartments **2 :** something resembling the deck of a ship: as **a :** a surface regarded as a floor to stand or move upon — used esp. in the U.S. Navy ⟨the third ~ of the barracks⟩ ⟨flying about 50 feet above the ~⟩ **b :** a story of a building **c :** a floor of a many-tiered stack in a library **d :** the roadway of a bridge **e :** the floor of a boxing ring **f :** a flat floored roofless area adjoining a house or built as a structural part of it and usu. being open on one or more sides **g :** the top of a mansard roof or curb roof when made nearly flat **h** (1) **:** the roof of a railroad passenger car (2) **:** a compartment for livestock in a freight car **i** (1) **:** the lid of the compartment at the rear of the body of an automobile (2) **:** the compartment covered by such a deck **j :** any one of the platforms of a large printing press **3 :** a group or packet usu. containing a specified number or amount: as **a :** PACK 3c **b :** a group or file of tabulation cards usu. punched **c :** a package of cigarettes **d :** a packet containing drugs **e :** a load of market lambs that fills a single-decked railroad shipping car **4 :** duty assignment of officer of the deck ⟨the lieutenant had the ~ that evening⟩ **5 a :** a platform for logs **b :** a pile of logs **6 :** a horizontal division of a newspaper or periodical headline **7 :** FEEDBOARD **8 :** the length of the short triangular deck piece in the bow of a racing shell ⟨led by a ~ to a half-length until there were three quarters of a mile to go —*N.Y. Times*⟩ — **below decks** *adv* **:** in or to a place under the main deck of a ship; *esp* **:** in or to the hold — **between decks** *adv* **:** in the space between the decks of a ship — **on deck** *adv (or adj)* **1 :** on the upper deck **2 a :** ready for duty **:** on hand ⟨every employee had to be *on deck* at nine o'clock⟩ **b :** next in line **:** next in turn ⟨in the fifth inning Jones was at bat and Smith *on deck*⟩

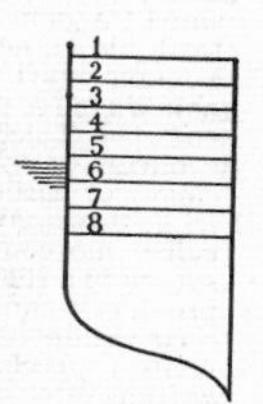

deck 1: decks of a typical merchant ship, amidships: *1* bridge; *2* boat; *3* promenade; *4* shelter, weather, or superstructure; *5* upper, or freeboard; *6* main, or second; *7* lower, or third; *8* orlop, or fourth

²deck \"\ *vt* -ED/-ING/-S [in senses 3, 4, and 5, fr. ¹*deck;* in senses 1 and 2, fr. D *dekken* to cover; akin to OHG *decken* to cover — more at THATCH] **1** *obs* **:** COVER, ARRAY ⟨~ with clouds the uncolored sky —John Milton⟩ **2 a :** DRESS, APPAREL ⟨the Chinese have ~*ed* themselves for festivity in red —James Cameron⟩ **b :** to clothe with more than ordinary elegance **:** ADORN, EMBELLISH — often used with *out* ⟨~*ed* out with festooned ribbons —Donn Byrne⟩ ⟨an airplane ~*ed* out with an ice-blue interior —*Saturday Rev.*⟩ **3 :** to furnish (as a ship) with or as if with a deck — often used with *in* or *over* **4 :** to load or pile up on a deck ⟨~ up logs⟩ **5 :** FLOOR, FLATTEN ⟨~*ed* every opponent he has fought —Lewis Eskin⟩ **syn** see ADORN

deck beam *n* **:** an athwartship beam supporting a deck

deck boy *n* **:** one who cleans decks and deck fittings of boats

deck bridge *n* **:** a bridge whose supporting elements (as trusses, girders, arches) are below the track or roadway — compare THROUGH BRIDGE

deck chair *n* **:** a folding chair often having an adjustable leg rest

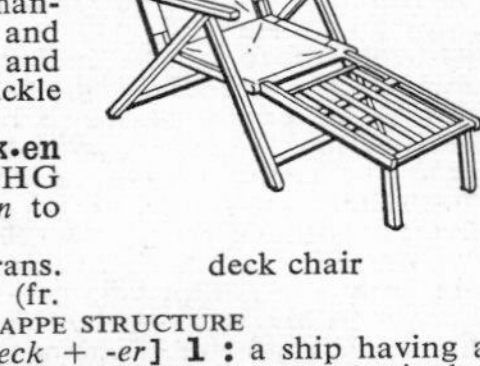
deck chair

deck curb *n* **:** a curb surrounding or edging a roof deck
deck department *n* **:** the department composed of those members of a ship's personnel whose duties involve the practical handling of the ship, of the lines, and of small boats and the use and maintenance of ground tackle and cargo-handling gear
decke \ˈdekə\ *n, pl* **deck·en** \-ən\ [G, lit., cover, fr. OHG *deckī*; akin to OHG *decken* to cover] **:** NAPPE
decken structure *n* [part trans. of G *deckenbau*, fr. *decken* (fr. *decke*) + *bau* structure] **:** NAPPE STRUCTURE
¹deck·er \ˈdekə(r)\ *n* -s [¹*deck* + -*er*] **1 :** a ship having a specified number of decks or amount of deck space ⟨a single=*decker*⟩ ⟨a half-*decker*⟩ **2 :** something constructed with a specified number of levels, floors, or layers ⟨a double-*decker* sandwich⟩ ⟨the single-*decker* country buses —Evelyn Waugh⟩ **3 :** TENEMENT, APARTMENT ⟨people who live in ~*s*⟩ **4** [²*deck* (to load) + -*er*] **:** one that decks logs **5** [prob. fr. the name *Decker*] **:** WET MACHINE **6 :** an opaque diaphragm having one or more openings and being used to limit the field of a microscope or the slit length of a spectroscope
²decker \ˈ"\ *vt* -ED/-ING/-S *papermaking* **:** to pass (pulp) over a wet machine
decker man *n, pl* **decker men :** a paper-mill worker who operates a wet machine — called also *filterman*
deck floor *n* **:** a floor that serves also as a roof
deckhand \ˈ=,=\ *n* **:** a sailor in the deck department who performs manual duties in connection with ship handling
deckhead \ˈ=,=\ *n* **:** the deck overhead **:** the ceiling of a compartment of a ship
deckhouse \ˈ=,=\ *n* **:** a superstructure (as a cabin) built on the upper deck of a ship but not extending to the sides
deck·ie \ˈdekē, -ki\ *n* -s [¹*deck* + -*ie*] *Brit* **:** DECKHAND
decking *n* -s [¹*deck* + -*ing*] **:** the surfacing material of a deck
deck key *n* **:** a key for the lock in the deck of an automobile
¹deck·le \ˈdekəl\ *n* -s [G *deckel*, lit., cover, fr. *decken* to cover, fr. OHG] **1 :** the detachable wooden frame around the outside edges of a papermaker's hand mold **2 a** *also* **deckle strap :** either of the endless rubber bands that run longitudinally upon the edges of the wire of a paper machine and thereby determine the width of the web **b :** the width of the web between deckles **3 :** DECKLE EDGE
²deckle \ˈ"\ *vt* **deckled; deckled; deckling** \-k(ə)liŋ\ **deckles 1 a :** to limit the width of (paper) by deckles **b :** to give a deckle edge to **2 :** to equip (as a papermaking machine or hand mold) with deckles
deckle edge *n* **:** the rough untrimmed edge of paper left by the deckle or produced artificially (as by sawing the edges of trimmed sheets)
deck light *n* **:** a glass-covered opening in a deck
deck log *n* **:** a written chronological record of the important data and events of a voyage usu. kept by the quartermaster and signed by the officer of the watch
deck·man \ˈdekmən, -,man\ *n, pl* **deckmen** [¹*deck*] **1 :** a worker who mixes ingredients for paper coatings **2 a :** DECKER 4 **b :** a sawmill worker who operates a bull wheel that pulls cars of logs from pond to mill **c :** a sawmill worker who rolls logs from deck to carriage and positions them for sawing — called also *tripper*
deck molding *n* **:** the molded finish of the edge of a deck (as of a mansard roof) making the junction with the lower elements
decko \ˈde(,)kō\ *var of* DEKKO
deck passage *n* **:** passage (as on a riverboat) without cabin accommodations
deck passenger *n* **:** one that has deck passage
deck pipe *n* **1 :** CHAIN PIPE **2** *or* **deck turret :** MONITOR 6
deck roof *n* **:** a nearly flat roof with no parapet walls
decks *pl of* DECK, *pres 3d sing of* DECK
deck sheet *n* **:** a sheet leading from the clew of a topmast studding sail to the deck forward of the yard
deck stopper *n* **:** a stopper fastened to the deck and used to hold the cable when the anchor is down
deck stringer *n* **:** a strake of plating secured to the deck beams along the outer edge of a ship's deck in order to connect the beams to the side of the ship and to each other
deck tennis *n* [so called fr. its being played on the deck of a ship] **:** a game consisting of tossing a ring or quoit back and forth over a net stretched across a small court that resembles a tennis court
deck watch *n* **:** the officer of the deck's watch
decl *abbr* **1** declaration **2** declension
de·claim \dəˈklām, dēˈ-\ *vb* -ED/-ING/-S [alter. (influenced by *claim*) of earlier *declame*, fr. ME *declamen*, fr. L *declamare*, fr. *de* down, away + *clamare* to cry out; akin to L *calare* to call — more at DE-, LOW (to moo)] *vi* **1 :** to speak or make a speech in a rhetorical manner **:** deliver an oration ⟨some of the province's most illustrious men visited the courthouse and ~*ed* within its four walls —Hazel Y. Grinnell⟩; *specif* **:** to recite a speech or poem as an exercise in elocution ⟨he took to writing verse and was chosen to ~ on occasions both public and private —Raymond Weaver⟩ **2 :** to speak for rhetorical effect or display **:** speak pompously, noisily, or theatrically **:** HARANGUE ⟨in presence of this historical fact it is foolish to ~ about natural rights —V.L.Parrington⟩ **:** INVEIGH ⟨~*ing* against the horrors of the place —C.D.Lewis⟩ **~** *vt* **:** to deliver (as an oration) in a rhetorical manner **:** utter rhetorically ⟨have forgotten the exact moment when he ~*ed* his quotation —Thomas Wood †1950⟩; *specif* **:** to recite as an exercise in elocution ⟨all these people ~*ing* selections from Shakespeare —Ellen Glasgow⟩ — **de·claim·er** \-mə(r)\ *n* -s
de·cla·man·do \,dāklä¦män(,)dō, ¦dekla¦man-\ *adv* (*or adj*) [It, declaiming, fr. L *declamandum*, gerund of *declamare*] **:** in declamatory style — used as a direction in music
dec·la·ma·tion \,dekləˈmāshən\ *n* -s [MF or L; MF, fr. L *declamation-, declamatio*, fr. *declamatus* (past part. of *declamare*) + -*ion-*, -*io* -ion] **1 :** the act or art of declaiming ⟨only in ~ was he unable to match his fellows —A.C.Cole⟩: **a :** the rhetorical delivery of an oration **b :** the recitation of a speech or poem as an exercise in elocution **2 a :** a rhetorical speech **:** HARANGUE ⟨they indulge in vague ~*s* against the existing social order —W.R.Inge⟩ **b :** a speech or poem suitable for recitation as an exercise in elocution **3 :** impassioned delivery or rhetorical style characteristic esp. of a declamation ⟨the impossible cannot be made reasonable even by ~ —W.L. Sullivan⟩ **4 a :** the rhetorical rendering of words in singing **b :** MELODRAMA **c :** ACCENTUATION
declamator *n* -s [ME, fr. L, fr. *declamatus* + -*or*] *obs* **:** one that declaims
de·clam·a·to·ry \dəˈklamə,tōrē, dēˈ-, -,tȯr-, -ri\ *adj* [L *declamatorius*, fr. *declamatus* + -*orius* -ory] **1 :** of, relating to, or having the characteristics of declamation ⟨~ American speech in the 1870's . . . was at both noble and pure —George Santayana⟩ ⟨~ exercises⟩ **2 :** marked by rhetorical effect or display **:** STILTED ⟨filled with long ~ speeches as artificial as the improbable plot —O.S.Coad⟩
de·clar·able \dəˈkla(a)rəbəl, dēˈ-, -ler-\ *adj* **:** capable of being declared **:** that must be declared
de·clar·ant \-rənt\ *n* -s [*declare* + -*ant*] **1 :** one that makes a declaration; *specif* **:** an alien who has declared his intention of becoming a citizen of the U.S. by signing the first papers required in the process of naturalization **2 :** DECLARER
dec·la·ra·tion \,dekləˈrāshən\ *n* -s [ME *declaracioun*, fr. MF *declaration*, fr. L *declaration-, declaratio*, fr. *declaratus* (past part. of *declarare* to declare, explain) + -*ion-*, -*io* -ion — more at DECLARE] **1 :** the act of declaring, proclaiming, or publicly announcing **:** explicit assertion **:** formal proclamation ⟨decided that it would be wiser if he left the place till after the ~ of the poll —John Buchan⟩ ⟨the ~ of an extra dividend⟩ **2 a :** the first pleading in a common-law action consisting of the plaintiff's statement in order and at large of his cause of complaint and demand for relief **:** the narration of the plaintiff's case containing a count or counts — compare ALLEGATION, BILL, COMPLAINT 1d, LIBEL **b :** a statement made or testimony given by a witness or by a party to a legal transaction usu. not under oath **c** *Scots law* **:** the voluntary statement made by the accused at his preliminary examination in criminal proceedings, taken in writing, and signed by the accused, the judge, and witnesses **3 a :** something that is declared, proclaimed, or publicly announced **:** formal statement **:** AVOWAL ⟨a ~ of love spiced with a few harsh words —*Atlantic*⟩ **b :** the document containing such a declaration: as (1) **:** a statement or document proclaiming the principles, aims, or policy of a public body ⟨the *Declaration* of Independence⟩ (2) **:** a statement listing property or goods liable to a tax or duty (3) **:** a statement forming part of an insurance policy and containing information regarding the insurance risk **4 a** *in card games* **:** the act of declaring — compare CALL, MELD **b** (1) **:** the make in bridge-whist (2) **:** the final bid in auction bridge (3) **:** the contract in contract bridge **c :** an announcement as to whether he will compete for high, low, or in some cases both high and low that each player in certain forms of high-low poker makes after the final call but before the showdown **5 :** a formal withdrawal of a horse from a race
declaration of rights : a formal declaration enumerating the rights of the citizen — compare BILL OF RIGHTS
declaration of trust *or* **declaration of use :** a usu. written acknowledgment by one holding or taking title to property that he holds the property in trust for or to the use of another
declaration of war : a formal announcement by a sovereign or state of the beginning of hostilities against another
de·clar·a·tive \dəˈkla(a)rəd·iv, dēˈ-, -ler-, -ətiv\ *adj* [MF or L; MF *declaratif*, fr. L *declarativus*, fr. *declaratus* (past part. of *declarare* to declare, explain) + -*ivus* -ive] **1** *obs* **a :** making clear or evident **:** ELUCIDATING **b :** declaring one's opinion **:** COMMUNICATIVE **2 :** having the characteristics of or making a declaration **:** ASSERTIVE ⟨a ~ law⟩ ⟨a letter ~ of his intentions⟩; *specif* **:** constituting a statement that can be either true or false ⟨*he has brown hair, I do not know him*, and Latin *adest* "he is here" are ~ statements⟩ ⟨~ clause⟩ ⟨~ sentence⟩ — **de·clar·a·tive·ly** \-əvlē, -li\ *adv*
de·clar·a·tor \-əd·ə(r)\ *n* -s [modif. of MF or ML; MF *declaratoire* declaratory, fr. ML *declaratorius*] **:** a legal declaration; *specif* **:** a legal action by which a judicial declaration of a fact is obtained
de·clar·a·to·ry \-ə,tōrē, -tȯrē, -ri\ *adj* [prob. fr. ML *declaratorius*, fr. L *declaratus* + -*orius* -ory] **1 :** serving to declare, set forth, or explain **:** being a manifestation of ⟨a philosophy of natural law which regards human law as ~ of divinely established fact —F.S.Cohen⟩ **2 a :** declaring what is the existing law — distinguished from *remedial* **b :** of, relating to, or being an action of declarator **c :** declaring a legal right or establishing a legal interpretation of an instrument ⟨a ~ judgment⟩
de·clare \dəˈkla(a)|(ə)r, dēˈ-, -le|, |ə\ *vb* -ED/-ING/-S [ME *declaren*, fr. MF *declarer*, fr. L *declarare*, fr. *de* from, away + *clarare* to make clear, fr. *clarus* clear, bright — more at DE-, CLEAR] *vt* **1** *obs* **:** to make clear **:** EXPLAIN, INTERPRET ⟨I told this unto the magicians but there was none that could ~ it to me —Gen 41:24 (AV)⟩ **2 :** to make known publicly, formally, or explicitly esp. by language ⟨reaffirm on this wider basis the truths which other writers . . . have already *declared* —Herbert Read⟩ **:** announce, proclaim, or publish esp. by a formal statement or official pronouncement ⟨we *declared* rubber a strategic and critical material —W.R.Langdon⟩ ⟨an armistice is called, peace is *declared* —Harrison Forman⟩ **:** communicate to others ⟨here the results of research are presented, here the progress of knowledge is *declared* —Bernard De Voto⟩ **3 :** to make evident or give evidence of **:** serve as a means of revealing **:** MANIFEST, SHOW ⟨a glimpse of his head in outline . . . *declared* his present state of mind —Osbert Sitwell⟩ **4 :** to make a formal acknowledgment of ⟨~ a trust⟩ **5 :** to state emphatically ⟨others ~ that the rains on the mountain sides . . . caused the disaster —C.L.Jones⟩ **:** AFFIRM, ASSERT ⟨happy the country that has no history, ~*s* the proverb —E.H.Collis⟩ **6 a :** to make a full statement of or about (property subject to tax or duty) **b :** to name (a taxable or dutiable item) as being in one's possession or ownership **7 :** SCRATCH 6d **8** *in card games* **a :** to make a bid or announcement naming (a trump suit or no-trump) **b :** to announce or show (scoring cards) **:** MELD **9** *of a cricket team* **:** to announce (its current unfinished innings) closed forthwith **10 :** to make payable esp. by vote of the directors of a corporation ⟨*declared* an extra dividend for the fourth quarter⟩ **~** *vi* **1 :** to make a declaration ⟨poetry . . . evokes rather than merely ~*s* —C.S.Kilby⟩: as **a** *in card games* (1) **:** CALL, BID (2) **:** MELD **b** *of a cricket team* **:** to declare its current unfinished innings closed forthwith **2 :** to make an open and explicit avowal (as of one's opinion or support) **:** announce or proclaim oneself — often used with *for* or *against* ⟨one of the first papers in New England to ~ for Jackson —H.K.Beale⟩ ⟨*declared* against the ancient languages as the staple of American education —Howard M. Jones⟩
syn ANNOUNCE, PUBLISH, ADVERTISE, PROCLAIM, PROMULGATE, BROADCAST: these seven verbs agree in signifying to make known openly or publicly. DECLARE, though often used as an equivalent of *say*, usu. suggests forthrightness or plainness, and often a certain formality, of manner or statement ⟨the visitor *declared* that it was his intention to leave early⟩ ⟨the court *declared* that the interim measures of protection . . . had ceased to operate —*Americana Annual*⟩ To ANNOUNCE is to declare for the first time, esp. something presumably of interest ⟨to *announce* one's arrival⟩ ⟨to *announce* an engagement⟩ ⟨to *announce* a new government economic policy⟩ To PUBLISH is to make public, now generally by means of printing ⟨they may only want to find the Monarchists in a thoroughly compromising position and *publish* it to the world —John Buchan⟩ ⟨if the national government resolves upon some drastic action at ten o'clock it *publishes* the decree at eleven —L.C.Douglas⟩ To ADVERTISE in its most general sense is to call public attention to by widely circulated statements, sometimes with unpleasant publicity or extravagance of statement ⟨deliberately *advertising* his willingness to make concessions —*Time*⟩ ⟨permanent residents also aided materially in *advertising* the territory —R.A.Billington⟩ ⟨to *advertise* one's products in newspapers, on the radio, and on television⟩ To PROCLAIM is to announce usu. orally and loudly and with conclusiveness in a public place or to people at large ⟨to *proclaim* the day a national holiday⟩ ⟨to *proclaim* the independence of the nation⟩ ⟨to *proclaim* one's innocence in the face of public disbelief⟩ To PROMULGATE is to make known to all concerned something that has binding force (as a dogma of the church) or something for which adherents are sought (as a theory or a doctrine) ⟨regulations *promulgated* by executive order —*Americana Annual*⟩ ⟨*promulgates* a brand of heaven=on-earth religion —John Kobler⟩ To BROADCAST is to make known in all directions over a large area, now commonly by radio or television ⟨the book he has written to *broadcast* this conviction —Gordon Harrison⟩ ⟨to *broadcast* the news every hour on the hour⟩ **syn** see in addition ASSERT
— **declare oneself 1 :** to make known one's opinion **:** announce one's position **2 :** to make known one's existence, identity, or true character **3 :** to make a declaration of love **4 :** to register as a member of a political party
de·clared \|(ə)rd, |(ə)d\ *adj* [fr. past part. of *declare*] **:** openly avowed or made known ⟨their ~ and their covert objectives⟩ — **de·clar·ed·ly** \|rədlē, -li\ *adv*
declared trump *n* **:** a trump suit announced in advance of the play in whist
declared value *n* **1 :** the value placed upon imported goods by the importer for clearance through the customhouse **2 :** the value per unit of a shipment as stated by the shipper upon delivery to a carrier usu. to obtain a released or lower rate
declare off *vi* **:** to withdraw esp. from a promise, engagement, or contest **:** back out ⟨no, I *declare off;* I'll fight no more —Oliver Goldsmith⟩
de·clar·er \|ra(r)\ *n* -s **:** one that declares; *specif* **:** the bridge player who plays both his own hand and that of the dummy
de·class \(ˈ)dē+\ *vt* [*de-* + *class* (n.); trans. of F *déclasser*] **:** to remove from a class **:** lower in one's class esp. socially ⟨the psychological effects of being ~*ed* —Francis Downing⟩
¹dé·clas·sé *or* **dé·clas·sée** \,dākləˈsā, -laˈ-, -läˈ-\ *n* -s [F, fr. *déclassé, déclassée*, adj.] **:** one that is déclassé ⟨the younger generation of ~*s* —Willi Frischauer⟩ ⟨treated as a ~, Austria found her credit seriously impaired —*Current History*⟩
²déclassé *or* **déclassée** \¦==¦=\ *adj* [F *déclassé* (masc.), *déclassée* (fem.), fr. *déclassé*, past part. of *déclasser* to declass, fr. *dé-* de- (fr. OF *des-*) + *classe* class — more at DE-, CLASS] **1 :** fallen or lowered in class, rank, or social position ⟨he was ~ enough to want to work with his hands —*Times Lit. Supp.*⟩ **2 :** of inferior status ⟨it's been a long time since dyed furs were considered ~ —Lois Long⟩
de·classicize \(ˈ)dē+\ *vt* [*de-* + *classicize*] **:** to make less classical ⟨went far toward *declassicizing* Latin prose —H.O. Taylor⟩
de·classification \(ˈ)dē+\ *n* -s **:** the act or process of declassifying
de·classify \(ˈ)dē+\ *vt* [*de-* + *classify*] **:** to remove or reduce the security classification of (as a document or weapon) ⟨admits that any policy-making official may . . . ~ any secret document —Bruce Bliven b.1889⟩
de clau·so frac·to \dā,klȯ(,)zō'frak(,)tō\ [NL, lit., of broken close] **:** of breach of close — used of the old legal action against a trespasser upon real property
de·clen·sion \dəˈklenchən, dēˈ-\ *n* -s [prob. alter. (influenced by -*ion*) of earlier *declenson*, modif. of MF *declinaison* grammatical declension, grammatical inflection, decline, fr. LL *declination-, declinatio* grammatical declension (fr. L, grammatical inflection) & L *declination-, declinatio* grammatical inflection, avoidance, turning aside, fr. L *declinatus* (past part. of *declinare* to inflect grammatically, turn aside) + -*ion-*, -*io* -ion — more at DECLINE] **1 a :** noun, adjective, or pronoun inflection **b :** a presentation in some prescribed order of the inflectional forms of a noun, adjective, or pronoun **c :** a class of nouns or adjectives having the same type of inflectional forms ⟨Latin nouns of the second ~ have their nominative singular in -*us* or -*um* and their genitive singular in -*ī*⟩ ⟨Latin adjectives of the third ~ such as *facilis*⟩ **2 :** a falling off or away esp. from a standard or a high point of development **:** DECLINE ⟨seems to mark a ~ in his career as an illustrator —F.J.Mather⟩ **:** DETERIORATION ⟨makes me wish to reflect, . . . to see if it is all loss, all ~ —A.C.Benson⟩ **3 :** a bending or sloping downward **:** DESCENT ⟨the ~ of the land from that place to the sea —Thomas Burnet⟩ **4 :** a courteous refusal **:** DECLINATION ⟨his ~ of the nomination⟩
de·clen·sion·al \-chənᵊl, -chnəl\ *adj* **:** of or belonging to grammatical declension — **de·clen·sion·al·ly** \-ᵊl|ē-əl|, |i\ *adv*
de·clin·able \dəˈklīnəbəl, dēˈ-\ *adj* [MF, fr. *decliner* to decline + -*able*] **:** capable of being grammatically declined
dec·li·nate \ˈdeklə,nāt, -,nət\ *adj* [L *declinatus*, past part. of *declinare* to turn aside] **:** bent or curved downward or aside
dec·li·na·tion \,==ˈnāshən\ *n* -s [ME *declinacioun*, fr. MF *declination*, fr. L *declination-, declinatio*, lit., turning aside] **1 :** latitude in the equator system of coordinates corresponding to terrestrial latitude; *specif* **:** angular distance from the celestial equator measured positively northward or negatively southward along a great circle passing through the celestial poles **2 :** a turning aside or swerving **:** DEVIATION ⟨makes his best virtue from the even line with fatal ~ swerve aside —Robert Southey⟩ **3 :** a decline (as from prosperity or vigor) **:** DETERIORATION ⟨something radically deficient in his makeup . . . brought on this moral ~ —Josephine T. Baker⟩ **4 :** a leaning or bending downward **:** INCLINATION ⟨a ~ of the antiquary's stiff backbone acknowledged the preference —Sir Walter Scott⟩ **5 a :** a formal refusal **:** NONACCEPTANCE ⟨~*s* of appointments and resignations had been frequent —G.W. Goble⟩ **6 :** the angle formed between a magnetic needle and the geographical meridian when the needle points east or west of true north ⟨east ~⟩ ⟨west ~⟩ — called also *variation*

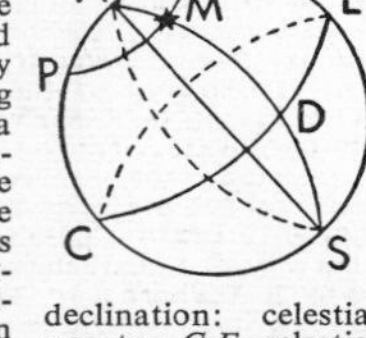

declination: celestial equator, *C E:* celestial poles, *N & S:* star, *M;* declination of star, *DM;* parallel of declination, *P M P'*

dec·li·na·tion·al \¦==¦=shənᵊl, -shnəl\ *adj* **:** of or relating to declination
declination axis *n* **:** the axis of rotation that is at right angles to the polar axis of an equatorial mounting and that permits pointing the telescope to celestial objects of different declinations
declination circle *n* **:** one of the setting circles of an equatorial mounting fastened to the declination axis to indicate the declination at which the telescope is pointing
declination compass *n* **:** DECLINOMETER
declination parallel *n* **:** PARALLEL OF DECLINATION
de·clin·a·to·ry \dəˈklīnə,tōrē, dēˈ-, -,tȯr-, -ri\ *adj* [ML *declinatorius* denying jurisdiction, fr. L *declinatus* + -*orius* -ory] **:** containing or involving a declination ⟨a ~ motion⟩
declinatory plea *n* [trans. of ML *declinatoria exceptio*] **:** a plea denying the court's jurisdiction; *esp* **:** the plea of benefit of clergy or of sanctuary
de·clin·a·ture \-nəchə(r)\ *n* -s [alter. (influenced by -*ure*) of earlier *declinatour*, fr. *declinatour*, adj., denying jurisdiction, fr. ME (Sc), modif. of ML *declinatorius*] **1** *Scots law* **:** a plea denying jurisdiction **2 :** DECLINATION 5
¹de·cline \dəˈklīn, dēˈ-\ *vb* -ED/-ING/-S [ME *declinen*, fr. MF *decliner* to inflect grammatically, turn aside, sink, fr. L *declinare* to inflect grammatically, turn aside, fr. *de* from, away + -*clinare* to incline — more at DE-, LEAN] *vi* **1 :** to turn aside **:** deviate from or as if from a straight course **:** STRAY ⟨walked in the ways of David his father and *declined* neither to the right hand nor to the left —2 Chron 34:2 (AV)⟩ **2 :** to take a downward direction: as **a :** to slope downward **:** DESCEND ⟨pipes used for the conveyance of gasoline shall ~ to tanks —*Fire Manual (Mass.)*⟩ ⟨the path ~*s* to the track⟩ **b :** to bend down **:** DROOP ⟨eyes . . . *declining* toward the ground —Henry Fielding⟩ **c :** to stoop or descend to what is unworthy ⟨the direful shameful state Adam *declined* into —Edward Taylor⟩ **3 a** *of a celestial body* **:** to sink toward setting ⟨the sun had begun to ~⟩ **b :** to draw toward a close ⟨as the day *declined* the place became insupportable —Ellen Glasgow⟩ **4 :** to tend toward an inferior state or weaker condition **:** become diminished or impaired **:** FAIL ⟨the powers of the mind and body begin with added years to ~ —C.W.Eliot⟩ **5** *obs* **:** INCLINE, TEND ⟨your weeping sister is no wife of mine . . . far more, far more to you do I ~ —Shak.⟩ **6 :** to withhold consent **:** REFUSE ⟨when I invited him he *declined*⟩ **~** *vt* **1 a :** to give in some prescribed order the various grammatical forms of **:** INFLECT — used formerly of any inflected word, now only of a noun, pronoun, or adjective ⟨~ the Latin adjective *bonus*⟩ **b** *obs* **:** to recite formally or in some prescribed order ⟨that you no harsh nor shallow rimes ~ —Michael Drayton⟩ **2** *obs* **a :** to cause to turn aside **:** AVERT ⟨evasions are sought to ~ the pressure of resistless arguments —Samuel Johnson⟩ **b :** to turn aside from **:** AVOID ⟨sinners . . . despairing to ~ their fate —Thomas Ken⟩ **3 :** to cause to bend, bow, or fall **:** bring or move down **:** bend downward ⟨the clover . . . ~*s* its blooms —W.C.Bryant⟩ **4 a :** to refuse to undertake, engage in, or comply with **:** REJECT ⟨sought out the English fleet but it *declined* battle —L.W.Dean⟩ **b :** to refuse courteously or politely **:** not to accept ⟨*declining* the unwanted manuscript —August Frugé⟩ **5 :** to refuse to accept (gambit) or pursue (a line of play) when an opponent in chess offers the opportunity
syn DECLINE, REFUSE, REJECT, REPUDIATE, and SPURN can all mean to turn away something or someone by not consenting to accept, receive, or consider it or him. DECLINE, the most courteous of the terms, is used chiefly in connection with invitations, offers of help, or services ⟨to *decline* an offer of a chairmanship⟩ ⟨to *decline* a formal invitation⟩ ⟨to *decline* to answer personal questions⟩ REFUSE is more positive, implying decisiveness, even ungraciousness ⟨to *refuse* an invitation and insult a friend thereby⟩ ⟨to *refuse* to answer personal questions⟩ ⟨to *refuse* all offers of marriage⟩ REJECT implies a refusal to have anything to do with a person or thing ⟨to *reject* an appeal for help⟩ ⟨*rejecting* with scorn all that can be called mysticism —W.R.Inge⟩ ⟨*rejected* by their mothers, shunted from one boarding home to another, these youngsters have lost faith in the kindliness of adults —Alice Lake⟩

REPUDIATE implies a disowning or rejecting with scorn as untrue, unauthorized, unworthy of acceptance, making false claim, and so on ⟨it is not so easy to *repudiate* one's heritage —A.J.Toynbee⟩ ⟨in permitting the husband to *repudiate* his wife at his own whim —Reuben Levy⟩ ⟨Bradburn had *repudiated* his promise —*Amer. Guide Series: Texas*⟩ SPURN implies even stronger disdain or contempt in rejection than REPUDIATE ⟨a devoted beau whom she had *spurned* for her lover —Joseph Schiffman⟩ ⟨neglected God for years and *spurned* His commandments —Bruce Marshall⟩ ⟨to *spurn* an offer of help⟩

²decline \" *sometimes* 'dē,-\ *n* -s [ME *declyn*, fr. MF *declin*, fr. *decliner* to sink] **1 :** the process of declining **:** a falling off ⟨the reading of books is suffering a ~ —J.D.Adams⟩: **a :** a change to a weaker condition **:** a gradual sinking and wasting away of the physical or mental faculties **b :** a change to an inferior or less favorable state ⟨the ~ of the aristocracy⟩ ⟨the ~ of the small nations⟩ **c** (1) **:** a downward movement or gradual fall (as in price or value) ⟨a late buying movement in these grains eliminated most early ~s —*Wall Street Jour.*⟩ **:** DIMINUTION ⟨a ~ in population⟩ (2) **:** a downward course (as of the blood pressure or of a fever) **:** DEFERVESCENCE **2 :** the period during which something is approaching its end or setting ⟨in the ~ of life⟩ **3 :** a downward slope **:** DECLIVITY ⟨constructed on a slight ~ away from the kennels to allow the water to drain away —*Smallholder Encyclopaedia*⟩ **4 a :** any wasting disease ⟨young men who work themselves into a ~ and are driven off in a hearse —R.L. Stevenson⟩; *esp* **:** pulmonary tuberculosis **b** *also* **decline disease :** any progressively deleterious disease or condition of plants — compare QUICK DECLINE

de·clin·er \-'nə(r)\ *n* -s **:** one that declines

dec·li·nom·e·ter \,deklə'nämədə(r)\ *n* [ISV *declino-* (fr. *declination*) + *-meter*] **:** an instrument for measuring magnetic declination

de·cli·vate \də'klī,vāt, dē'-, 'deklə,-, -,vət\ *adj* [L *declivis* + E *-ate*] **:** inclining downward **:** SLOPING

declive *adj* [F or L; F *déclive*, fr. L *declivis*] *obs* **:** sloping down

de·cli·vent \də'klīvənt, dē'-, 'deklәv-\ *adj* [L *declivis* + E *-ent*] **:** DECLIVOUS

de·cliv·i·tous \də'klivədəs, dē'-\ *adj* [*declivity* + *-ous*] **:** having a considerable downward slope **:** moderately steep — **de·cliv·i·tous·ly** *adv*

de·cliv·i·ty \-'klivədē, -ətē, -i\ *n* -ES [L *declivitat-, declivitas*, fr. *declivis* sloping down (fr. *de* down, away + *-clivis*, fr. *clivus* slope, hill) + *-tat-, -tas* -ty; akin to L *clinare* to incline — more at DE-, LEAN] **1 :** downward deviation from the horizontal **:** slope or gradient of a surface **:** INCLINATION ⟨streams of water in the larger valleys of gentler ~ —C.A.Cotton⟩ — opposed to *acclivity* **2 :** a descending slope (as of a hill) **:** a steep or overhanging slope (as of a cliff) ⟨a large village situated just on the ~ of the farther side of the hill —George Borrow⟩

de·cli·vous \-'klīvəs\ *adj* [L *declivis* + E *-ous*] **:** sloping downward — opposed to *acclivous*

de·clutch \(')dē+\ *vi* **:** to disengage a clutch ~ *vt* **:** to put out of action by releasing a clutch

de·coct \də'käkt, dē'-\ *vt* -ED/-ING/-S [L *decoctus*, past part. of *decoquere*, fr. *de* down, away + *coquere* to cook — more at COOK] **1 a :** to prepare by boiling **:** extract the flavor or active principle of by boiling **b :** to steep in hot water **2 a :** to boil down **:** concentrate by or as if by boiling ⟨here we have the thrice . . . ~*ed* essence of the critical study of generations —George Saintsbury⟩ **b** *obs* **:** DIMINISH **3** *obs* **:** KINDLE, EXCITE

de·coc·tion \-'käkshən\ *n* -s [ME *decoccioun*, fr. MF or LL; MF *decoction*, fr. LL *decoction-, decoctio*, fr. L *decoctus* (past part. of *decoquere*) + *-ion-, -io* -ion] **1 :** the act or process of boiling usu. in water so as to extract the flavor or active principle ⟨a substance obtained by ~⟩ — compare INFUSION **2 a :** an extract obtained by decocting **b :** a liquid preparation made by boiling a medicinal plant with water usu. in the proportion of 5 parts of the drug to 100 parts of water ⟨had slept the winter afternoon away, soothed by some ~ of medicinal herbs —Elinor Wylie⟩

decoction process *n* **:** a mashing process in which parts of the mash are removed, boiled, and returned to the main part thereby raising the whole to about 75°C — compare INFUSION PROCESS

de·coc·tive \-'käktiv\ *adj* [*decoct* + *-ive*] **:** relating to or suitable for decoction

de·coc·tum \-'käktəm\ *n, pl* **decoc·ta** \-ktə\ [L, fr. neut. of *decoctus*] **:** DECOCTION 2b

¹de·code \(')dē+\ *vb* [*de-* + ¹*code*] *vt* **1 :** to convert (a message in code) from code into ordinary language **2 :** DECRYPT **3 :** to identify the constituent significant elements of (a message in ordinary language) — compare ¹CODE 3 ~ *vi* **:** to convert a message in code from code into ordinary language

²decode \'dē+,-\ *n* -s **:** a secret message in decoded form

de·cod·er \(')dē+\ *n* -s **:** one that decodes; *specif* **:** CRYPTOGRAPHER

de·co·ic acid \də'kōik, (')dē'-\ *n* [*decane* + *-oic*] **:** any of the monocarboxylic acids $C_9H_{19}COOH$ (as capric acid) derived from the decanes

de·coke \(')dē+\ *vt* [*de-* + ¹*coke*] *Brit* **:** DECARBONIZE

¹de·col·late \də'kä,lāt, dē'-, 'dekə,-, -,lət\ *adj* [ME, fr. L *decollatus*, past part. of *decollare* to behead] *archaic* **:** BEHEADED

²de·col·late \-,lāt\ *vt* -ED/-ING/-S [L *decollatus*, past part. of *decollare*, fr. *de* from, away + *-collare* (fr. *collum* neck) — more at DE-, COLLAR] **:** to sever from the neck **:** BEHEAD, DECAPITATE

de·col·lat·ed \də'kä,lād·əd, (')dē'-, 'dekə,-\ *adj* [fr. past part. of ²*decollate*] **1 :** BEHEADED **2 :** having the apex broken or worn off **:** TRUNCATED — used esp of a spiral shell

de·col·la·tion \,dē,kä'lāshən\ *n* -s [ME *decollacioun*, fr. LL *decollation-, decollatio*, fr. L *decollatus* + *-ion-, -io* -ion] **:** DECAPITATION ⟨the feast of the ~ of St. John the Baptist is Aug. 29⟩

dé·col·le·tage *also* **de·col·le·tage** \(,)dā¦käl∂'täzh, (,)de¦-, -kōl-, -kōl-, -täzh, ¦≈≈≈'≈; deklə¦t-\ *n* -s [F, action of cutting a low neckline, wearing of a low-necked dress, fr. *décolleter* + *-age*] **1 :** the low-cut neckline of a woman's dress ⟨the square ~ . . . finished with a tiny border of oak leaves and acorns in gold —*N.Y. Times*⟩ **2 :** a décolleté dress ⟨a spectacular succession of off-the-shoulder ~s —*Newsweek*⟩

décolletage

¹dé·col·le·té *also* **de·col·le·te** \(,)dā¦kälə¦tā, (,)de¦-, -kōl-, -kōl-, ¦≈≈≈'≈; 'deklə¦tā\ *adj* [F *décolleté* (masc.), *décolletée* (fem.), past part. of *décolleter* to give a low neckline to, fr. *dé-* de- (fr. OF *des-*) + *collet* collar, fr. OF *colet*, fr. *col* collar, neck (fr. L *collum* neck) + *-et*] **1** *also* **dé·col·le·tée** \"\ **:** wearing a strapless or low-necked dress ⟨she came to the party ~⟩ **2 :** having a low-cut neckline or leaving the neck and shoulders uncovered ⟨a ~ dress⟩

²décolleté *also* **decollete** \"\ *n* -s [F *décolleté*, fr. past part. of *décolleter*] **:** DÉCOLLETAGE

de·color \(')dē+\ *vt* [*de-* + *color*] **:** DECOLORIZE

¹de·colorant \(')dē+\ *n* [*decolor* + *-ant*, n. suffix] **:** a substance that removes color

²decolorant \"\ *adj* [*decolor* + *-ant*, adj. suffix] **:** capable of removing color **:** BLEACHING

de·coloration \(,)dē+\ *n* [F *décoloration*, fr. L *decoloration-, decoloratio*, fr. *decoloratus* (past part. of *decolorare* to discolor, deprive of color, fr. *de* from, away + *colorare* to color, fr. *color*) + *-ion-, -io* -ion] **:** the removal of color **:** DECOLORIZATION

de·col·or·i·za·tion \(,)dē,kələrə'zāshən\ *n* **:** the process of decolorizing

de·col·or·ize \(')dē'kələ,rīz\ *vt* -ED/-ING/-S [*de-* + *color* + *-ize*] **:** to remove color from (as liquids by adsorption on activated carbon) — compare BLEACH

de·col·or·izer \-zə(r)\ *n* **:** one that decolorizes

de·commission \¦dē+\ *vt* [*de-* + *commission*] **:** to remove (as a ship) from service

de·compensate \(')dē+\ *vi* [prob. back-formation fr. *decompensation*] **:** to undergo decompensation

de·compensation \(,)dē+\ *n* [ISV *de-* + *compensation*] **:** loss of compensation; *esp* **:** loss of adequate functional power of a diseased heart after a period of compensation

de·com·pos·abil·i·ty \,dēkəm,pōzə'biləd·ē\ *n* -ES **:** the quality or state of being decomposable

de·com·pos·able \¦≈≈¦pōzəbəl\ *adj* **:** that can be decomposed

de·com·pose \,≈≈'pōz\ *vb* [F *décomposer*, fr. *dé-* de- (fr. OF *des-*) + *composer* to compose — more at COMPOSE] *vt* **1 a :** to separate or resolve into constituent parts or elements or into simpler compounds ⟨found that the water was *decomposed* into . . . hydrogen and oxygen —S.F.Mason⟩ **b :** to distinguish by analysis ⟨were I compelled to ~ the motives of my worthy friend —Sir Walter Scott⟩ **2 :** to cause chemical disintegration of (organic matter) **:** ROT ~ *vi* **:** to break up into constituent elements **:** undergo chemical change **:** DECAY, ROT, DISINTEGRATE **syn** see DECAY

decomposed *adj* [fr. past part. of *decompose*] **1 :** in a state of decomposition **2 :** not cohering **:** SEPARATED — used of the crest of birds when the feathers are divergent or of a feather when the barbs do not cohere

de·com·pos·er \-zə(r)\ *n* **:** one that decomposes

¹decomposite \(,)dē+\ *n* [LL *decompositus* derived from a compound word (trans. of Gk *parasynthetos*), fr. L *de* from, away + *compositus* composite, compound — more at DE-, COMPOSITE] **:** ¹DECOMPOUND

²decomposite \"\ *adj* [LL *decompositus*] **:** ³DECOMPOUND

¹decomposition *n* [prob. fr. ¹*decomposite*, after E *composite: composition*] *obs* **:** the combination of composites **:** repeated composition

²de·com·po·si·tion \(,)dē,kämpə'zishən\ *n* [prob. fr. F *décomposition*, fr. *décomposer*, after F *composer* to compose: *composition*] **:** the act or process of decomposing **:** the state of being decomposed: **a :** the separation or resolution (as of a substance) into constituent parts or elements or into simpler compounds ⟨~ of mercuric oxide into mercury and oxygen⟩ — compare DISSOCIATION 1a **b :** DISINTEGRATION ⟨~ by fission⟩ **c :** organic decay ⟨the ~ of a dead body⟩ **:** DISSOLUTION ⟨the complete ~ of the opposition⟩

decomposition potential *or* **decomposition voltage** *n* **:** the minimum electromotive force required to cause a steady electrolysis in any solution

¹de·compound \(')dē+\ *n* [*de-* + *compound*, n.; approximate trans. of LL *decompositus* derived from a compound word] **:** any compound that has a compound as one of its parts; *specif* **:** a word that has a compound as one of its immediate constituents (as *newspaperman, railroader*)

²de·compound \(,)dē+\ *vt* [in sense 1, fr. ¹*decompound*; in sense 2, fr. *de-* + *compound*, v.] **1** *obs* **:** to compound further **:** compound or mix with a compound **2 :** to reduce to constituent parts **:** DECOMPOSE

³decompound \"\ *adj* [¹*decompound*] **1 :** compounded of what is already compound **:** compounded again **2** *of a leaf* **:** having divisions that are themselves compound

de·compress \¦dē+\ *vb* [trans. of F *décomprimer*] *vt* **:** to subject to decompression ~ *vi* **:** to undergo decompression

de·compression \¦dē+\ *n* [prob. fr. F *décompression*, fr. *dé-* de- (fr. OF *des-*) + *compression*] **:** the act or process of releasing from pressure or compression: as **a :** reduction of pressure: (1) **:** the decrease of atmospheric pressure experienced by a workman in an air lock when he is returning to the outside air from a caisson under compression or by an aviator when he ascends to a great height (2) **:** the decrease of water pressure experienced by a diver when he ascends rapidly **b :** an operation or technique employed to relieve pressure upon an organ (as in fractures of skull or spine) or within a hollow organ (as in intestinal obstruction)

decompression chamber *n* **1 :** a chamber in which excessive pressure can be reduced gradually to atmospheric pressure **2 :** a chamber in which an individual can be gradually subjected to decreased atmospheric pressure (as in simulating conditions at high altitudes)

decompression sickness *n* **:** CAISSON DISEASE, AEROEMBOLISM

de·compressive \¦dē+\ *adj* **:** tending toward or for the purpose of decompression

de·concentrate \(')dē+\ *vt* **:** to reduce or abolish the concentration of **:** DECENTRALIZE

de·concentration \(,)dē+\ *n* **:** the act or process of deconcentrating **:** DECENTRALIZATION; *specif* **:** the devolution of power by a central government to local authorities

de·concentrator \(,)dē+\ *n* **:** a device for removing suspended or dissolved material from feedwater (as for a still or boiler)

de·condition \¦dē+\ *vt* **1 :** to cause to lose fitness ⟨prolonged inactivity ~*s* a person physically⟩ **2 :** to remove the effects of specialized training or unusual habits from **3 :** to cause extinction of (a conditioned response)

de·congest \¦dē+\ *vt* **:** to relieve the congestion of

de·con·ges·tant \,dēkən'jestənt\ *n* -s **:** an agent that relieves congestion (as of mucous membranes)

de·congestion \¦dē+\ *n* [*de-* + *congestion*] **:** the process of relieving congestion

de·congestive \¦dē+\ *adj* [*de-* + *congest* + *-ive*] **:** that relieves congestion ⟨a ~ agent⟩

de·consecrate \(')dē+\ *vt* [prob. trans. of F *déconsacrer*] **:** to remove the sacred character of ⟨the church building was *deconsecrated* and sold⟩ — **de·consecration** \(')dē+\ *n*

de·contaminate \¦dē+\ *vt* **:** to rid of contamination; *specif* **:** to make (as a building or area) harmless to unprotected personnel by the removal, destruction, or neutralization of chemical or biological warfare agents or radioactive material — **de·contamination** \¦dē+\ *n*

¹de·control \¦dē+\ *vt* [*de-* + *control*, n.] **:** to end the control of esp. by governmental agencies ⟨~ the coal industry⟩ **:** remove the controls on ⟨~ meat and dairy products⟩

²decontrol \"\ *n* **:** the abolition of controls, esp. of emergency government controls ⟨the gradual ~ of rents⟩

de·cor *or* **dé·cor** \dā'kō(ə)r, -kō(ə)r, -kō(ə), -kōə, '≈,≈ *sometimes* də'-\ *n* -s [F *décor*, fr. *décorer* to decorate, fr. L *decorare*] **1 :** ORNAMENTATION, DECORATION ⟨tweed made flashing by the adding of sequins and other incongruous ~ —Lois Long⟩ ⟨clothes with great ~ the stilted platitudes of present-day social thought —Max Lerner⟩ **2 :** stage scenery and furnishings **:** SETS ⟨has written plays in which the audience's chief interest is in the symbolic nature of the ~ —E.R.Bentley⟩ **3 :** pattern of decoration ⟨acquired enough old objects to enable you to establish an integrated ~ for your room —E.F. Robacker⟩ **:** ornamental disposition of accessories in interior decoration ⟨the ~ and the atmosphere of its three dining rooms are like those of a first-class restaurant —Joseph Wechsberg⟩ **4 :** the combination of features or elements that make up the background or milieu characteristic esp. of a place or a period in time ⟨jukeboxes, sports arenas, the couches of psychoanalysts, carnivals — these are the ~ —W.B.C.Watkins⟩ **:** ATMOSPHERE ⟨took . . . the appealing ~ of the Romantic school and fused with it his own kind of gentle and penetrating realism —T.G.Bergin⟩

dec·o·ra·ment \'dek(ə)rəmənt\ *n* -s [LL *decoramentum*, fr. L *decorare* + *-mentum* -ment] **:** ORNAMENT, DECORATION

¹dec·o·rate \'dek(ə)rət, -kə,rāt\ *adj* [ME, fr. L *decoratus*, past part. of *decorare*] *archaic* **:** DECORATED ⟨a fair hall and richly ~ —Sir Richard Burton⟩

²dec·o·rate \'dekə,rāt, *usu* -ād· + V\ *vt* -ED/-ING/-S [L *decoratus*, past part. of *decorare*, fr. *decor-, decus* ornament — more at DECENT] **1 :** to grace with what adorns or honors ⟨they dignified and *decorated* commerce with the splendid virtues of honor and loyalty —Geoffrey Household⟩ ⟨admiration and respect for the liberals who now ~ . . . the U.S. Senate —R.L.Neuberger⟩ **2 :** to furnish or adorn with something becoming, ornamental, or striking **:** EMBELLISH, DECK ⟨some of the farmhouses . . . are *decorated* with climbing roses —Tom Marvel⟩ ⟨the hospital train ghostly white and *decorated* with the red cross —Fred Majdalany⟩ ⟨the knife-edge remarks with which he ~*s* his conversation —Ian Bevan⟩ **3 :** to award a mark of honor (as a medal) to **:** honor with a decoration ⟨*decorated* for valor⟩ **syn** see ADORN

decorated *adj* [fr. past part. of *decorate*] **1 :** ORNAMENTED, ORNATE ⟨when a more ~ style was fashionable in many quarters, bombast and extravagance were common in the press —F.L.Mott⟩ **2** *often cap* **:** of, relating to, or resembling English Gothic architecture in its second phase; *specif* **:** characterized by geometrical bar tracery and floral decoration

dec·o·ra·tion \,dekə'rāshən\ *n* -s [MF or LL; MF, fr. LL *decoration-, decoratio*, fr. L *decoratus* + *-ion-, -io* -ion] **1 :** the act of adorning, embellishing, or honoring **:** ORNAMENTATION ⟨promote the intelligent care of public beauty spots and further ~ of the city with trees and plants —*Amer. Guide Series: Nev.*⟩ **2 :** something that adorns, enriches, or beautifies **:** EMBELLISHMENT, ORNAMENT ⟨a building of steel and stone with aluminum ~*s*⟩ **3 :** a badge of honor (as a medal or a cross); *specif* **:** a U.S. military award usu. of distinctive shape conferred for personal heroism or gallantry — compare SERVICE MEDAL **4 :** GARNITURE 2 **5 :** an arrangement in a work of art of purely sensory elements (as line, color, shape, texture) that stimulates pleasure without regard to meaning

decoration day *n, usu cap both Ds* **:** MEMORIAL DAY

dec·o·ra·tive \'dek(ə)rəd·iv, -rətiv; 'dekə,rād·iv, -ātiv, -ēv *also* -əv\ *adj* [*decorate* + *-ive*] **1 :** of or relating to decoration **:** serving to decorate: as **a :** having a purely ornamental function ⟨its buildings were utilitarian rather than ~ —Green Peyton⟩ **b** *of a work of art* **:** producing immediate sensory satisfaction without regard to meaning ⟨to demand that all art be ~ is . . . a limitation of the material of art —John Dewey⟩ **c :** suitable for decorating or embellishing **:** enhancing in attractiveness ⟨his delight in the use of ~ high-sounding words —Alvin Redman⟩ **2 a** *of a dahlia* **:** having flower heads much doubled with quilled rays **b** *of a chrysanthemum* **:** having loose open flower heads of quilled, flat, or fluted rays — **dec·o·ra·tive·ly** \-əvlē, -li\ *adv* — **dec·o·ra·tive·ness** \-ivnəs, -ēv- *also* -əv-\ *n* -ES

¹dec·o·ra·tor \'dekə,rād·ə(r), -ātə-\ *n* -s [*decorate* + *-or*] **:** one that decorates: as **a** (1) **:** one who plans, designs, and executes interiors and their furnishings (2) **:** one who paints and papers interior walls and paints woodwork and fixtures **b :** one who hand paints, stencils, or transfers decorations on glass, tile, wood, pottery, or such objects as jewelry, furniture, or stemware **c :** one who lays out, traces, or carves lettering or designs on building and monumental stone **d :** one who molds fancy ice cream or who frosts cakes or other confections **e :** one who arranges merchandise displays in retail stores

²decorator \"\ *adj* **:** contributing to a color scheme and style suitable for interior decoration ⟨a selection of ~ fabrics⟩ ⟨~ chair⟩ ⟨a plastic cover in a ~ color —Sylvia Wright⟩

decorator crab *n* **:** any of several spider crabs of the family Majidae that fasten bits of kelp or grasses to their shells; *esp* **:** a widely distributed crab (*Oregonia gracilis*) of the western coast of the U.S.

de·core \də'kō(ə)r, dē'-\ *vt* -ED/-ING/-S [MF *decorer*, fr. L *decorare*] *archaic* **:** DECORATE, BEAUTIFY

de·core·ment \-ōrmənt\ *n* -s [MF, prob. fr. LL *decoramentum*] *archaic* **:** DECORATION

dec·o·rist \'dek(ə)rəst, də'kōr-\ *n* -s [*decorum* + *-ist*] **:** one devoted to artistic decorum ⟨a man of taste and a ~ where *picturesque* effects were concerned —Norman Douglas⟩

dec·o·rous \'dekərəs *also* -krəs; də'kōr-, dē'k-, -'kōr-\ *adj* [L *decorus*, fr. *decor* beauty, grace; akin to L *decēre* to be fitting — more at DECENT] **:** marked by propriety and good taste esp. in conduct, manners, or appearance **:** characterized by conformity to accepted social standards and by unruffled staidness, correctness, or dignity ⟨when off the air are as ~ and restrained as they are volcanic while performing —G.S. Perry⟩ ⟨the ~ symbols of Victorian art —Ellen Glasgow⟩ ⟨a courtier's laugh, ~, brief, and not too hearty —J.H.Wheelwright⟩

syn DECENT, SEEMLY, PROPER, NICE, COMME IL FAUT, DEMURE: DECOROUS denotes an observance of all proprieties and sometimes connotes dignified or prim formality ⟨we, of course, maintained a most *decorous* exterior; and hence, by all the elderly people of the village, were doubtless regarded as pattern young men —Herman Melville⟩ ⟨the tête-à-tête had proved *decorous* in the extreme, and he had returned the willful maiden to her doorstep without so much as brushing her lips with his —Herman Wouk⟩ DECENT, as here considered detached from matters of sexual morality, suggests the fitting, appropriate, or accustomed, according to good taste or form ⟨the dead face on the pillow, which Dolly had smoothed with *decent* care —George Eliot⟩ ⟨nobody cares a straw for the internal administration of native states so long as oppression and crime are kept within *decent* limits —Rudyard Kipling⟩ SEEMLY stresses lack of discord with propriety and taste and may also suggest a pleasing appearance or manner ⟨for generations the Twyfords had drunk tea here at a *seemly* hour —Sinclair Lewis⟩ ⟨it was reckoned to him a major sin that he forgot his manners, for must not the Lord's work be carried on in *seemly* fashion, and the money changers be scourged from the temple politely? —V.L.Parrington⟩ PROPER stresses unquestioned conformity with social conventions, sometimes a stiff or prissy conformity ⟨Henchard's creed was that *proper* young girls wrote ladies' hand —Thomas Hardy⟩ ⟨but it is only *proper* that you first tell your husband distinctly that you are without any [money], and see what he will do —Thomas Hardy⟩ NICE in this sense suggests a complete and choice correctness in matters social ⟨the small provincial gentry of the West, as drawn by Miss Austen . . . are *nice* in their gentility almost to a fault —G.M.Trevelyan⟩ ⟨we've always been religious, Mother, and *nice* people in Queenborough go to church no matter what they believe —Ellen Glasgow⟩ COMME IL FAUT, more common in the 19th century than the 20th, implies complete correctness in polite society ⟨this remark, if the young lady had made it, would have been perfectly *comme il faut*; but, being made by the young gentleman, it was a most heinous and irremissible offense —T.L.Peacock⟩ DEMURE stresses a modest demeanor more than a staid propriety ⟨but lowering her glance unexpectedly till her dark eyelashes seemed to rest against her white cheeks she presented a perfectly *demure* aspect —Joseph Conrad⟩ ⟨Leora appeared as his assistant, very pretty and *demure* in a nurse's costume —Sinclair Lewis⟩

dec·o·rous·ly *adv* **:** in a decorous manner ⟨pretended to be pleased and applauded ~ —G.B.Shaw⟩

dec·o·rous·ness \-snəs\ *n* -ES **:** the quality or state of being decorous **:** DECORUM

decors *pl of* DECOR

¹de·cor·ti·cate \(')dē¦kō(r)d·ə,kāt, də'k-, -)tə,k-, *usu* -d·+V\ *vt* -ED/-ING/-S [L *decorticatus*, past part. of *decorticare* to remove the bark from, fr. *de* from, away + *-corticare* (fr. *cortic-, cortex* bark) — more at DE-, CORTEX] **1 :** to remove the bark, husk, or other outer covering from **:** HULL, PEEL, SKIN, STRIP ⟨*decorticated* rice⟩ ⟨~ a coconut⟩: as **a :** to remove all or part of the cortex from (as the brain) **b :** to remove the periostracum of (a mollusk) **c :** to separate (fiber) from the woody part of a fiber plant **2 :** FLAY 2 **syn** see SKIN

²de·cor·ti·cate \-ə,kāt, -ək∂t\ *adj* [L *decorticatus*] **:** without a cortical layer **:** DECORTICATED

de·cor·ti·ca·tion \(')≈¦≈≈'kāshən\ *n* -s [L *decortication-, decorticatio* removal of bark, fr. *decorticatus* + *-ion-, -io* -ion] **1 :** the act or process of decorticating ⟨the mechanical ~ of the dried black peppercorns —J.W.Parry⟩ **2 :** the medical operation of removing the cortex of an organ, an enveloping membrane, or a constrictive fibrinous covering ⟨the ~ of a lung⟩

de·cor·ti·ca·tor \-,kād·ə(r)\ *n* -s **:** one that decorticates; *specif* **:** a machine for decorticating fiber

de·cor·ti·co·sis \də,kō(r)d·ə'kōsəs\ *n* -ES [NL, fr. L *decorticare* + NL *-osis*] **:** SHELL BARK

de·co·rum \də'kōrəm, dē'k-, -kōr-\ *n* -s [L, fr. neut. of *decorus*] **1 :** literary and dramatic propriety esp. as formulated and practiced by the neoclassicists: **a :** a literary standard of appropriateness drawn from classical models and justified by nature, which was equated with social custom, and by reason, which was identified with good sense ⟨wishes to subject art and literature to an elaborate set of restrictions in the name of ~ —Irving Babbitt⟩ **b :** a dramatic standard requiring that a character be presented in a way congruous with his presumed type or social condition ⟨according to strict neoclassic ~ only the aristocracy had the right to appear in tragedy —Irving Babbitt⟩ **2 :** propriety and good taste esp. in conduct, manners, or appearance **:** CORRECTNESS ⟨most correct in her conduct, strict in her notions of ~, and with manners that were held a standard of good breeding —Jane Austen⟩ ⟨the whole performance was conducted with perfect ~ —Augustus John⟩ **3 :** the quality or state of being decorous **:** ORDERLINESS ⟨the organization's ~ has rarely been shaken —W.F.Longgood⟩ **4 a** *obs* **:** a fitting and appropriate act **b :** an observance or requirement of polite behavior **:** CONVENTION — usu. used in pl. ⟨their restoration to the established sobrieties and ~*s* of English life —H.G.Wells⟩ **5** *obs* **:** beauty deriving from fitness or congruousness **:** COMELINESS

de·cou·page *or* **dé·cou·page** \ˌdākü'päzh, -pȧzh, '≈≈,≈\ *n* -s [F *découpage* action of cutting up, action of cutting out, fr. MF *decoupage,* fr. *decouper* to cut up, cut out, fr. OF *decoper,* fr. *de-* (fr. L *de* from, away) + *coper, couper* to cut — more at DE-, COPE (to contend)] **1 :** the art of decorating surfaces with applied paper cutouts **2 :** work produced by decoupage ⟨would coil up on the frayed needlepoint of a rosewood sofa and spend her time making ~ —Leo Lerman⟩

¹de·coy \də'kȯi, dē'-, 'dē,-\ *n* -s *often attrib* [prob. fr. D *de kooi,* lit., the cage, fr. *de,* masc. def. article (fr. MD, akin to OE *thæt,* neut. def. article) + *kooi* cage, fr. MD *côie,* fr. L *cavea* — more at THAT, CAGE] **1 :** a pond or pool having net-covered channels into which wild fowl (as ducks) are lured for capture ⟨a vast game ~ used to provide sport for the local gentry —O.S.Nock⟩ **2 :** something intended to allure or entice esp. into a trap **:** LURE ⟨the commander of that sub . . . took us to be a ~ —H.A.Chippendale⟩; *specif* **:** an artificial bird used by hunters to attract live birds (as water fowl) within shot **3 :** a person used as a lure: **a :** one employed esp. by the police to induce a suspected person to commit an offense under circumstances that will lead to his detection **b :** one employed to lead another into a position where he may be swindled, robbed, or otherwise injured

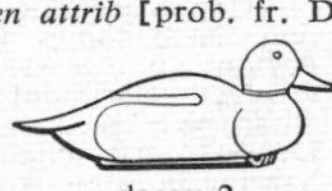
decoy 2

²de·coy \≈'≈ *sometimes* 'dē,-\ *vb* -ED/-ING/-S *vt* **:** to lure by or as if by a decoy **:** ALLURE, ENTICE, ENTRAP ⟨the female bird . . . practiced the same arts upon us to ~ us away —John Burroughs⟩ ⟨he had ~*ed* her . . . into holding him dearer than her own ambition —Victoria Sackville-West⟩ ~ *vi* **:** to become lured by or as if by a decoy **:** fall into a trap ⟨the wind was in the left front, so the old drake ~*ed* from the right rear —*Handbook on Shotgun Shooting*⟩ **syn** see LURE

de·cras·si·fy \(ˈ)dē¦krasə,fī\ *vt* -ED/-ING/-ES [*de-* + *crass* + *-i-* + *-fy*] **:** to free from what is crass

de·crat·er \(ˈ)dē¦krātə(r)\ *n* -s [*de-* + *crate* + *-er*] *Brit* **:** a machine for unloading bottles or cans from shipping cases — compare RECRATER

¹de·crease \(ˈ)dē¦krēs *also* də'-\ *vb* -ED/-ING/-S [ME *decreesen* fr. (assumed) AF *decreistre* (3d pers. pl. pres. indic. *decreissent*), fr. L *decrescere,* fr. *de* from, down, away + *crescere* to grow, increase — more at DE-, CRESCENT] *vi* **:** to grow less esp. gradually **:** become diminished (as in size, amount, or strength) **:** LESSEN, DWINDLE ⟨his stock *decreased* as the war went on⟩ ⟨his influence slowly *decreased*⟩ ~ *vt* **1 :** to cause to grow less esp. gradually **:** DIMINISH ⟨this medicine will ~ his pain⟩ ⟨it is necessary to ~ the amount of coal used⟩ **2 :** to remove (a stitch) by knitting two stitches together or by passing a slipped stitch over a knitted stitch

syn LESSEN, DIMINISH, REDUCE, ABATE, DWINDLE: DECREASE, frequently interchangeable with others in this set, may apply to any process of growing less ⟨the population of the area is *decreasing*⟩ ⟨a steadily *decreasing* income⟩ ⟨a rather even crest line, which *decreases* in elevation eastward —C.B.Hitchcock⟩ ⟨a *decreasing* chance for victory⟩ ⟨*decreasing* intensity⟩ ⟨belief in the evolution of man's body has *decreased* among paleontologists —R.W.Murray⟩ LESSEN, meaning simply to become less, is a close synonym for DECREASE except that it is usu. not used with stated numbers ⟨the valley widens, hills *lessen* in height —*Amer. Guide Series: Texas*⟩ ⟨*lessen* the pain of separation by a very frequent and most unreserved correspondence —Jane Austen⟩ ⟨I hoped to obtain your forgiveness, to *lessen* your ill-opinion —Jane Austen⟩ ⟨they find that in these quarters the Church is suspected of being an ally of 'capitalism,' and that their influence is *lessened* in consequence —W.R.Inge⟩ ⟨the fever is *lessened*⟩ but ⟨the fever *decreased* from 101° to 99°⟩ DIMINISH may add to the meaning of DECREASE the notion of loss, of subtraction, sometimes unfortunate ⟨with the retreat of the forest, the amount of variety of wild game inevitably *diminished* —*Amer. Guide Series: Minn.*⟩ ⟨with the advent of the railroad, trade *diminished* and the town gradually declined —*Amer. Guide Series: La.*⟩ ⟨he has shown that he is reluctant to use his prestige to such ends, and his continued refusal to use it *diminishes* his power to do so —R.H.Rovere⟩ REDUCE may heighten suggestion of the role of an agent or agency effecting a change; it may also implicate a lowering of status or significance ⟨devices adopted by the government to *reduce* unemployment —*Collier's Yr. Bk.*⟩ ⟨medical science has *reduced* the incidence of many communicable diseases virtually to zero —Gertrude Samuels⟩ ⟨the yeoman, it has been said, was being steadily *reduced* to a peasant —G.E. Fussell⟩ ABATE may be used to indicate the decrease in intensity, amount, force, or significance of something immoderate or excessive ⟨misfortune had *abated* the grandiosity of the Roman temper, and there was a widespread reaction towards simplicity —John Buchan⟩ ⟨the long tradition of mutual injury and revenge . . . had left animosities that took long to *abate* —G.M.Trevelyan⟩ ⟨physically weakened by a stomach disorder that will not *abate* —Hollis Alpert⟩ DWINDLE may apply to progressive lessening or weakening towards insignificance ⟨the last rays of daylight *dwindled* and disappeared —R.L. Stevenson⟩ ⟨the Zarafshan had already *dwindled* to an insignificant creek —Douglas Carruthers⟩ ⟨the great buffalo herds, once estimated at 60,000,000 head in Texas, have *dwindled* to a few animals —*Amer. Guide Series: Texas*⟩ ⟨the place *dwindled* in importance and at present is a small trading village —*Amer. Guide Series: Oregon*⟩

²de·crease \'dē,krēs *also* dē'- *or* də'-\ *n* -s [ME *decrees,* fr. (assumed) AF *decreis,* fr. (assumed) AF *decreistre,* v.] **1 :** the process of becoming less or the condition resulting from such a process **:** gradual diminution ⟨we shall be conscious of a certain ~ in scientific dogmatism —Irving Babbitt⟩ **2 :** the amount by which something decreases **:** DECLINE ⟨the ~ in exports for the year was 15 percent⟩ **3** *knitting* **a :** the act of decreasing **b :** the place where decreasing is done

decreasing *adj* [fr. pres. part. of *decrease*] **:** becoming less and less **:** DIMINISHING — **de·creas·ing·ly** *adv*

decreasing cost *n* **:** a decline in the cost per unit or on the average following a rise in the scale of production ⟨an industry showing *decreasing costs*⟩

decreasing function *n* **:** a function whose value decreases as the independent variable increases over a given range

¹de·cree \də'krē, dē'-\ *n* -s [ME, fr. MF *decré, decret,* fr. L *decretum,* fr. neut. of *decretus,* past part. of *decernere* to decide, fr. *de* from, away + *cernere* to sift, discern, decide — more at DE-, CERTAIN] **1 :** an order set forth by one having authority **:** authoritative decision **:** EDICT, LAW ⟨he needs to act by executive ~*s* . . . during the next two months —Frank Gorrell⟩ ⟨voluntarily entered into a ~ which cut the price of potash —T.W.Arnold⟩ **2 a** (1) **:** an ordinance enacted by council or titular head concerning religious doctrine or discipline ⟨a papal ~⟩ (2) **decrees** *pl* **:** a collection of such religious rules **b :** the will of the Deity ⟨God's ~⟩ **c :** something allotted by fate **3 :** a judicial decision: **a** *Roman law* (1) **:** a judicial decision of the emperor (2) **:** a command of the praetor enjoining some act or forbearance (3) **:** the judgment in a proceeding of praetorian cognizance **b** (1) **:** a decision or sentence given in a cause by a court of equity, admiralty, probate, or divorce (2) **:** JUDGMENT 2a(1) **c** *Scots law* **:** a final judgment of a civil court

²decree \"\ *vb* **decreed; decreed; decreeing; decrees** [ME *decreen,* fr. *decree,* n.] *vt* **1 :** to command or enjoin authoritatively **:** order or appoint by decree ⟨*decreed* that pecan shellers should be paid a minimum of twenty-five cents an hour —Hart Stilwell⟩ ⟨fashion used to be *decreed* by Paris —F.L. Allen⟩ **2 a :** to settle or decide (a legal cause) by a judgment **b :** to determine or order judicially by authority or by decree **:** ADJUDGE **3** *archaic* **:** to determine or decide mentally **:** RESOLVE ~ *vi* **:** to issue a decree **:** ORDAIN ⟨as my eternal purpose hath *decreed* —John Milton⟩ **syn** see DICTATE

decree arbitral *n* [alter. (influenced by E ¹*decree*) of earlier *decreet arbitral,* fr. ME (Sc) *decreite arbitral,* fr. ME *decreite, decret* decreet + *arbitrale, arbitral* arbitral] *Scots law* **:** a sentence proceeding on a submission to arbitration

decree dative *n* [alter. (influenced by E ¹*decree*) of earlier *decreet dative,* fr. *decreet* + *dative*] *Scots law* **:** a decree appointing an executor

decree–law \≈'≈,≈\ *n* [trans. of F *décret-loi,* It *decreto legge,* Sp *decreto ley,* & Pg *decreto lei;* It *decreto legge,* Sp *decreto ley,* & Pg *decreto lei* all prob. trans. of F *décret-loi*] **:** a decree of a ruler or ministry having the force of a law enacted by the legislature

decreement *n* -s *obs* **:** DECREE

decree ni·si \-'nī,sī, -'nē(,)sē\ *n* **:** the decree first made upon a petition for a divorce which is made absolute at such time thereafter as may be directed unless cause to the contrary is shown

decree of nullity : a declaration that a marriage has been void from its beginning

de·cre·er \də'krē̇ə(r), dē'-\ *n* -s **:** one that decrees

de·creet \də'krēt\ *n* -s [ME *decret* fr. MF or L; MF *decré, decret,* fr. L *decretum*] **:** DECREE 3c

dec·re·ment \'dekrəmənt\ *n* -s [L *decrementum,* fr. *decrescere* to decrease + *-mentum* -ment — more at DECREASE] **1 a :** the act or process of becoming gradually less **:** DECREASE, DIMINUTION ⟨a deer herd suffers no ~ if the legal hunting take is not permitted to exceed 20 percent of the total population —R.E. Trippensee⟩ **b :** the successive diminution of the layers of molecules applied to the faces of the primitive form of crystals by which the secondary forms were held to be produced **2 a :** the quantity lost by diminution or waste **b** *math* **:** a negative increment **c** *physics* **:** the ratio of the maximum amplitude of one oscillation to that of the next in an oscillating system subjected to damping

de·crem·e·ter \'dekrə,mēd·ə(r), də'kremədə-\ *n* [*decrement* + *-meter*] **:** an instrument for measuring the logarithmic decrement of electromagnetic waves

de·crep·it \də'krepət, dē'-, *usu* -əd+V\ *also* **de·crep·id** \-pəd\ *adj* [ME *decrepit,* fr. MF, fr. L *decrepitus,* prob. from *de* from, down, away + *crepitus,* past part. of *crepare* to crack, creak, break — more at DE-, RAVEN] **1 a :** wasted and weakened by or as if by the infirmities of old age **:** old and feeble ⟨the ~ manager who was too ancient and incompetent for more serious employment —Ellen Glasgow⟩ **b :** made useless or impaired by excessive wear or long use **:** WORN-OUT ⟨the bus is ~ and the seats and several of the windows are held together with friction tape —John Cheever⟩ **c :** in a state of ruin, dilapidation, or disrepair ⟨two or three ~ houses and a forlorn hotel —*Amer. Guide Series: Calif.*⟩ **2 :** lacking power (as for carrying sediment) — used of a stream in the last stage of an erosion cycle **syn** see WEAK

de·crep·i·tate \də'krepə,tāt, dē'-\ *vb* [prob. fr. (assumed) NL *decrepitatus,* past part. of *decrepitare,* fr. L *de* from, away + *crepitare* to crackle — more at DE-, CREPITATE] *vt* **:** to roast or calcine (as salt) so as to cause crackling or until crackling stops ~ *vi* **:** to undergo decrepitation

de·crep·i·ta·tion \≈,≈≈'tāshən\ *n* -s [prob. fr. (assumed) NL *decrepitation-, decrepitatio,* fr. (assumed) NL *decrepitatus* + L *-ion-, -io* -ion] **:** the breaking up or crackling of certain crystals upon heating

de·crep·it·ly *adv* **:** in a decrepit manner

de·crep·it·ness *n* -ES **:** the quality or state of being decrepit

de·crep·i·tude \də'krepə,t(y)üd, dē'-\ *n* -s [MF, irreg. fr. *decrepit* + *-tude*] **:** the quality or state of being decrepit: **a :** physical weakness **:** FEEBLENESS, INFIRMITY ⟨he had the physically strong man's impatience of ~ —S.H.Adams⟩ ⟨the humiliations of ~ and old age —L.P.Smith⟩ **b :** DECAY, DILAPIDATION ⟨carvings which turned out to be . . . atrocities in an advanced state of ~ —Mary Austin⟩ ⟨in its ghostly ~ the district looks like something out of a . . . cartoon —Gladwin Hill⟩

decrepity *n* -ES [MF & ML; MF *decrepité,* fr. ML *decrepitat-, decrepitas,* irreg. fr. L *decrepitus* + *-tat-, -tas* -ty] *obs* **:** DECREPITUDE

de·cres·cence \də'kresən(t)s, dē'-\ *n* -s [L *decrescentia,* fr. *decrescent-, decrescens* (pres. part. of *decrescere* to decrease) + *-ia* -y] **:** the act or process of decreasing; *specif* **:** DECREMENT 1b

¹de·crescendo \ˌdā +; *US also & Brit usu* ¦dē+\ *adj* (*or adv*) [It, lit., decreasing, fr. L *decrescendum,* gerund of *decrescere*] **:** diminishing in volume — used as a direction in music and often indicated by the abbr. *decresc.* or the sign >; compare CRESCENDO

²decrescendo \"\ *n* -s [It, fr. *decrescendo,* adj.] **1 :** a lessening in volume of sound **2 :** a decrescendo musical passage

¹de·crescent \(ˈ)dē, də +\ *adj* [alter. (influenced by E ²*crescent*) of earlier *decressant,* prob. fr. AF, pres. part. of *decresser* to decrease, prob. modif. of (assumed) AF *decreistre* (3d pers. pl. pres. indic. *decreissent*), fr. L *decrescere*] **1 :** becoming less by gradual diminution **:** DECREASING **2** *of the moon* **a :** WANING **b** *heraldry* **:** having the horns pointing to the sinister

²decrescent \"\ *n* -s [alter. (influenced by E ¹*crescent*) of earlier *decressant,* prob. fr. (assumed) AF *decressant* decrescent moon, fr. AF *decressant,* pres. part. of *decresser* to decrease] **:** a decrescent moon

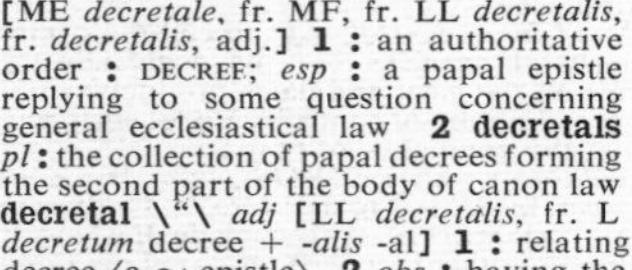
heraldic decrescent

¹de·cre·tal \də'krēd·ᵊl, dē'-, -ētᵊl\ *n* -s [ME *decretale,* fr. MF, fr. LL *decretalis,* fr. *decretalis,* adj.] **1 :** an authoritative order **:** DECREE; *esp* **:** a papal epistle replying to some question concerning general ecclesiastical law **2 decretals** *pl* **:** the collection of papal decrees forming the second part of the body of canon law

²decretal \"\ *adj* [LL *decretalis,* fr. L *decretum* decree + *-alis* -al] **1 :** relating to or containing a decree ⟨a ~ epistle⟩ **2** *obs* **:** having the binding effect of a decree **3** *obs* **:** DECISIVE, FINAL

de·cre·tal·ist \-ᵊləst\ *n* -s [¹*decretal* + *-ist*] **:** DECRETIST

de·cre·tist \-ēd·əst, -ētə-\ *n* -s [ME *decretiste,* fr. MF or ML; MF, fr. ML *decretista,* fr. L *decretum* decree + *-ista* -ist] **:** one specializing in the study of decretals **:** CANONIST

de·cre·tive \-əv\ *adj* [L *decretum* + E *-ive*] **:** having the force of a decree **:** DECRETORY ⟨the ~ will of God⟩

dec·re·to·ri·al \ˌdekrə¦tōrēəl, ¦dēk-, -¦tȯr-\ *adj* [*decretory* + *-al*] **:** DECRETORY

dec·re·to·ry \'dekrə,tōrē, -,tȯr-, -ri; də'krēd·ər-, dē'-, -ētə-\ *adj* [L *decretorius,* fr. *decretus* (past part. of *decernere* to decide) + *-orius* -ory — more at DECREE] **1** *archaic* **:** serving to determine **:** DECISIVE, CRITICAL ⟨when the ~ hour of death overtakes you —Cotton Mather⟩ **2** [L *decretum* + E *-ory*] **:** relating to or fixed by a decree, decision, or judgment ⟨the ~ rigors of a condemning sentence —Robert South⟩ **3** *obs* **:** POSITIVE, PEREMPTORY

de·cre·tum \də'krēd·əm, -ētəm, dē'-\ *n, pl* **decre·ta** \-ə\ [L — more at DECREE] **:** DECREE, ORDINANCE

de·cri·al \də'krī(ə)l, dē'-\ *n* -s [*decry* + *-al*] **:** DEPRECIATION

de·cri·er \-ī(ə)r\ *n* -s **:** one that decries ⟨an earnest ~ of entrenched privilege —*Time*⟩

de·crown \(ˈ)dē+\ *vt* **:** DISCROWN

de·crus·ta·tion \ˌdēkrə'stāshən\ *n* -s [LL *decrustatus* (past part. of *decrustare* to remove the crust of, fr. L *de* from, away + *crustare* to cover with a shell, cover with a crust, fr. *crusta* crust) + E *-ion* — more at DE-, CRUST] **:** the removal of a crust

de·cry \də'krī, dē'-\ *vt* [F *décrier,* fr. OF *descrier,* fr. *des- de-* + *crier* to cry — more at CRY] **1 :** to depreciate officially or publicly **:** reduce the value of esp. by public condemnation ⟨the king may at any time ~ . . . any coin of the kingdom —William Blackstone⟩ **2 :** to express strong disapproval of **:** criticize severely **:** DENOUNCE, DISPARAGE ⟨citizens of the more advanced democracies . . . ~ dictators and all their works —C.L. Jones⟩ ⟨in making his case for pure research . . . he was not ~*ing* applied research —Ritchie Calder⟩

syn DECRY, DEPRECIATE, DISPARAGE, DEROGATE, DEROGATE (*from*), DETRACT (*from*), BELITTLE, and MINIMIZE can mean, in common, to indicate one's low opinion of something. DECRY implies open condemnation with intent to discredit ⟨restraint of emotion was now *decried* in favor of strong expression of feeling —Gilbert Highet⟩ ⟨it would be a complete mistake to *decry* love of power altogether as a motive —Bertrand Russell⟩ ⟨county editors vying with each other to defend their champions and *decry* their foes —*Amer. Guide Series: Md.*⟩ DEPRECIATE implies a representing of something as of smaller value than it is usu. credited with ⟨the Renaissance . . . *depreciated* sculpture and gave the highest place to painting —Herbert Read⟩ ⟨the fashion in some quarters during the last few years to *depreciate* the entire scientific outlook —P.W. Bridgman⟩ DISPARAGE implies depreciation usu. by more subtle methods, as slighting or invidious comparison ⟨to *disparage* a train by comparing it with a stagecoach —G.B. Shaw⟩ ⟨he would sigh, shake his head, *disparage* his importance to anybody, even to himself —Marguerite Young⟩ ⟨the notion that Montaigne *disparaged* and sneered at the human race seems . . . absurd to us —L.P.Smith⟩ DEROGATE, often DEROGATE (*from*), and DETRACT (*from*) stress the idea of taking something away from the full or generally recognized quality of a person or thing, esp. quality of merit or reputation ⟨readers will inevitably . . . *derogate* what they cannot master —Edith R. Mirrielees⟩ ⟨I am not "blaming" the extraterritorial, specifically eastern, archaeologists nor attempting to *derogate* their contributions to southwestern archaeology —W.W. Taylor⟩ ⟨the right of the judiciary to review legislative and executive actions and nullify those measures which *derogate from* eternal principles of truth and justice as incarnated in the Constitution —J.P.Roche⟩ ⟨his underhanded actions *detract from* his reputation for honesty⟩ ⟨to say this in no way *detracts from* the distinguished qualities of the council itself —*Report: (Canadian) Royal Commission on Nat'l Development*⟩ ⟨a number of apologetic reservations which *detract from* the force of those forthright statements —Gleb Struve⟩ ⟨none of these moral imperfections appeared to *detract* an iota *from* the advantage of a face like an infant Aphrodite —Ellen Glasgow⟩ BELITTLE and MINIMIZE both imply depreciation, BELITTLE suggesting an effort to make contemptibly small in worth, MINIMIZE to make as small as possible ⟨Jack Dempsey was not one to underestimate. It was not his habit of mind to *belittle* an antagonist —Gene Tunney⟩ ⟨always delighted at a pretext for *belittling* a distinguished contemporary —Edmund Wilson⟩ ⟨I did not find anybody *minimizing* the tasks or inclined to exaggerate what had been done —E.P.Snow⟩ ⟨an evident tendency on the part of the writers to enlarge on the blessings of nature and to *minimize* her deficiencies —R.H.Brown⟩

de·crypt \(ˈ)dē¦kript *also* də'-\ *vt* -ED/-ING/-S [ISV *de-* + *-crypt* (fr. *cryptogram, cryptograph*); prob. orig. formed as It *decriptare*] **:** to decipher or decode esp. by cryptanalysis — **decrypt·ment** \-tmənt\ *n* -s

de·cryptograph \(ˈ)dē + *also* də +\ *vt* [*de-* + *cryptograph*] **:** to convert (a cryptogram) into plain language

-dec·tes \ˌdek(ˌ)tēz\ *n comb form* [NL, fr. Gk *dēktēs,* fr. *daknein* to bite — more at TONGS] **:** biter — in generic names of animals (Mixo*dectes*)

de·cu·bi·tal \də'kyübəd·ᵊl, dē'-, -ətᵊl\ *adj* [*decubitus* + *-al*] **1 :** relating to or resulting from lying down ⟨a ~ sore⟩ **2 :** relating to or resembling a decubitus

de·cu·bi·tus \-əd·əs, -ətəs\ *n, pl* **decubi·ti** \-əd·,ī, -ə,tī, -ē\ [NL, fr. L *decubitus,* past part. of *decumbere* to lie down, fr. *de* down, away + *-cumbere* to lie down (akin to *cubare* to lie down) — more at DE-, HIP] **1 :** a position assumed in lying down ⟨the dorsal ~⟩ **2 a :** ULCER **b** *or* **decubitus ulcer :** BEDSORE **3 :** prolonged lying down (as in bed)

de·cul·tur·ate \(ˈ)dē¦kəlchə,rāt *also* də'k-\ *vt* -ED/-ING/-S [*de-* + ¹*culture* + *-ate*] **:** to deprive of culture or cultural attainments ⟨some tribes are extinct, some *deculturated,* and some relatively undisturbed —*Man*⟩

de·cul·tur·a·tion \(ˈ)dē¦kəlchə¦rāshən *also* də¦k-\ *n* -s **:** the process of divesting a tribe or people of their indigenous traits ⟨for many native peoples brought involuntarily and reluctantly into contact with western civilization, acculturation is all too often ~ —David Bidney⟩

de·culture \(ˈ)dē+\ *vt* [*de-* + *culture*] **:** DECULTURATE

dec·u·man \'dekyəmən\ *adj* [L *decumanus, decimanus* of the tenth, large, fr. *decumus, decimus* tenth (fr. *decem* ten) + *-anus* -an — more at TEN] **1** *of a wave* **:** extremely large **:** HUGE ⟨that ~ wave that took us fore and aft —P.A.Motteux⟩ **2 :** of or relating to the tenth cohort — used esp. of the chief gate of a Roman camp

dec·u·mar·ia \ˌ≈≈'ma(a)rēə\ *n, cap* [NL, fr. L *decumus, decimus* tenth + NL *-aria;* fr. the decamerous flowers] **:** a small genus of woody vines (family Saxifragaceae)

dec·u·mary \'≈≈,merē\ *n* -ES [NL *Decumaria*] **:** a woody vine (*Decumaria barbata*) of the southeastern U.S. with white flowers in compound terminal clusters

de·cum·ben·cy \də'kəmbənsē, dē'-\ *also* **de·cum·bence** \-n(t)s\ *n, pl* **decumbencies** *also* **decumbences** [L *decumbere* + E *-ency, -ence*] **:** the act or position of lying down

de·cum·bent \-nt\ *adj* [L *decumbent-, decumbens,* pres. part. of *decumbere*] **1 :** lying down **:** RECUMBENT **2** *of a plant stem or shoot* **:** reclining on the ground but with ascending apex or extremity

de·cum·bi·ture \-bə,chü(ə)r, -bəchər\ *n* -s [L *decumbere* to lie down, lie ill + *-it-* (in *decubitus,* past part. of *decumbere*) + E *-ure*] **1** *obs* **:** confinement to a sickbed **2 a :** the time of taking to one's bed from sickness **b :** a horoscope of such a decumbiture

¹dec·u·ple \'dek(y)əpəl\ *n* -s [ME, prob. fr. MF, fr. *decuple,* adj.] **:** a sum 10 times as great as another **:** a tenfold amount **:** the tenth multiple

²decuple \"\ *adj* [F *décuple,* fr. MF *decuple,* fr. LL *decuplus,* fr. L *decem* ten + *-uplus* (as in *quadruplus* quadruple)] **1 :** consisting of 10 **:** being 10 times as great or as many **:** TENFOLD **2 :** taken by tens or in groups of 10

³decuple \"\ *vb* **decupled; decupled; decupling** \-p(ə)liŋ\ **decuples :** to make or become 10 times as much or as many

de·cu·plet \-plət\ *n* -s [²*decuple* + *-et*] **1 :** a combination of 10 of a kind **2 :** a group of 10 notes performed in the time of 8 or 4 of the same musical value — called also *decimole*

de·cu·ri·on \də'kyürēən, dē'-\ *n* -s [ME *decurioun,* fr. L *decurion-, decurio,* fr. *decuria* decury] **1 :** a Roman cavalry officer in command of 10 men **2 a :** a member of a municipal or colonial senate in ancient Rome **b :** a member of the great council in an Italian city or town

de·cu·ri·on·ate \-nət, -,nāt\ *n* -s [L *decurionatus,* fr. *decurion-, decurio* + *-atus* -ate] **:** the office of a decurion

de·cur·rence \də'kərən(t)s, dē'-\ *also* **de·cur·ren·cy** \-nsē\ *n, pl* **decurrences** *also* **decurrencies** [prob. fr. ML *decurrentia,* fr. L *decurrent-, decurrens* + *-ia* -y] **:** the act or state of running downward **:** downward flow or course

de·cur·rent \-nt\ *adj* [L *decurrent-, decurrens,* pres. part. of *decurrere* to run down, fr. *de* down, away + *currere* to run — more at DE-, CURRENT] **:** running or extending downward — used esp. of a leaf whose base extends downward from its point of insertion and often forms a wing or ridge along the stem — **de·cur·rent·ly** *adv*

decursion *n* -s [LL *decursion-, decursio,* fr. L, military maneuver, fr. *decursus* (past part. of *decurrere*) + *-ion-, -io* -ion] **1** *obs* **:** DECURRENCE **2** [L *decursion-, decursio*] *obs* **:** a military maneuver of classical antiquity; *specif* **:** a procession of armed troops around a funeral pile

de·cur·sive \də'kərsiv, dē'-\ *adj* [NL *decursivus,* fr. L *decursus* + *-ivus* -ive] **:** DECURRENT — **de·cur·sive·ly** \-sə̇vlē\ *adv*

decurt *vt* -ED/-ING/-S [L *decurtare,* fr. *de* from, away + *curtare* to shorten, fr. *curtus* short — more at DE-, CURT] *obs* **:** CURTAIL

¹decurtate *vt* -ED/-ING/-S [L *decurtatus,* past part. of *decurtare* to curtail] *obs* **:** SHORTEN

²de·cur·tate \də'kər,tāt, dē'-, -¸tət\ *adj* [L *decurtatus*] **:** CURTAILED, SHORTENED ⟨a ~ syllogism has one premise suppressed⟩

de·curved \də, (ˈ)dē+\ *adj* [part trans. of LL *decurvatus,* fr. L *de* down, away + *curvatus,* past part. of *curvare* to bend, curve — more at DE-] **:** curved downward **:** bent down ⟨the ~ bill of a curlew⟩

dec·u·ry \'dekyərē\ *n* -ES [L *decuria,* fr. *decem* ten] **:** a Roman division, company, or body of ten (as cavalrymen, senators, or judges)

¹dec·us·sate \'dekə,sāt, də'k-, dē'k-, *usu* -d·+V\ *vb* -ED/-ING/-S [L *decussatus,* past part. of *decussare,* fr. *decussis* number ten, numeral X, intersection of two lines, irreg. fr. *decem* ten + *ass-, as* copper coin — more at ACE] *vt* **:** to cross, cut, or divide in the form of an X : INTERSECT ~ *vi* : to cross each other in the form of an X : INTERSECT

2**dec·us·sate** \", -ˌsət\ *adj* [L *decussatus*, past part. of *decussare*] **1** : shaped like an X ⟨a ~ cross⟩ **2** *bot* : arranged in pairs each at right angles to the next pair above or below ⟨~ leaves⟩ — compare BRACHIATE — **dec·us·sate·ly** *adv*

decussated *adj* [fr. past part. of 1*decussate*] : DECUSSATE

dec·us·sa·tion \ˌdekəˈsāshən, ˌdēk-\ *n* -s [L *decussation-, decussatio*, fr. *decussatus* + *-ion-, -io* -ion] **1** : an intersection esp. in the form of an X ⟨the ~ of lines⟩ **2** *bot* : the quality or state of being decussate **3 a** : a band of nerve fibers that connects unlike centers of opposite sides of the central nervous system **b** : a crossed tract of nerve fibers passing between centers on opposite sides of the central nervous system : COMMISSURE

dec·yl \ˈdesəl *sometimes* ˈdēs-\ *n* -s [ISV *dec-* (fr. *decane*) + *-yl*] : any of numerous univalent radicals $C_{10}H_{21}$ derived from the decanes by removal of one hydrogen atom; *esp* : the normal radical $CH_3(CH_2)_8CH_2$–

decyl alcohol *n* [ISV *decyl* + *alcohol*] : a monohydroxy alcohol $C_{10}H_{21}OH$ derived from the decanes; *esp* : the colorless to light yellow liquid primary alcohol $CH_3(CH_2)_8CH_2OH$ derived from normal decane that is usu. made by reduction of coconut oil or the fatty acids from this oil and is used chiefly as an intermediate for surface-active agents and perfumes — called also *1-decanol, normal decyl alcohol*

decylaldehyde \ˌ==+\ *n* [ISV *decyl* + *aldehyde*] : DECANAL

dec·yl·ene \ˈ==ˌlēn\ *n* -s [ISV *decyl* + *-ene*] : any of numerous isomeric hydrocarbons $C_{10}H_{20}$ of the ethylene series

de·cyl·ic acid \dəˈsilik-, (ˈ)dē¦-\ *n* [ISV *decyl* + *-ic*] : DECOIC ACID

ded *abbr* dedicated; dedication

dedal *archaic var of* DAEDAL

dedalian *usu cap, archaic var of* DAEDALIAN

de·dans \dəˈdäⁿ\ *n, pl* **dedans** \"\ [F, lit., interior, fr. MF, fr. *dedans*, adv. & prep., within, in, fr. OF *dedenz*, fr. *de* of, from (fr. L, from, away) + *denz* within, in, fr. LL *deintus*, fr. L *de* from, away + *intus* within, in; akin to Gk *entos* within, in, Skt *antas*tya intestines; derivative fr. a prehistoric IE word represented by L *in* — more at DE-, IN] **1** : an open gallery that is one of the winning openings placed at the service end of the court in court tennis **2** : the spectators at a court-tennis match

de·den·dum \dəˈdendəm, dēˈ-\ *n* -s [L, neut. of *dedendus*, gerundive of *dedere* to give up, deliver, fr. *de* from, away + *-dere* (fr. *dare* to give); fr. the contrast with the addendum of a gear tooth — more at DE-, DATE] : the root of a gear tooth; *also* : the distance between the dedendum circle and pitch circle of a gear wheel or rack — compare ADDENDUM

dedendum circle *n* : the circle touching the bottom of the spaces between the teeth of a gear wheel

ded·i·cant \ˈdedəkənt\ *n* -s [*dedic*ate + *-ant*] : one that dedicates

1**ded·i·cate** \-ˌkāt, -ˌkət\ *adj* [ME, fr. L *dedicatus*, past part. of *dedicare* to affirm, dedicate fr. *de* from, away + *dicare* to proclaim, dedicate — more at DE-, DICTION] : DEDICATED — used chiefly of religious dedication ⟨~ mien of a clergyman⟩

2**ded·i·cate** \-dəˌkāt, -dēˌ-, *usu* -ād·+V\ *vt* -ED/-ING/-S [L *dedicatus*, past part. of *dedicare*] **1** : to devote exclusively to the service or worship of a divine being or to sacred uses : set apart with solemn rites **2 a** : to set apart or devote formally or seriously to a definite use, end, or service ⟨the playground was *dedicated* today⟩ ⟨a new nation . . . *dedicated* to the proposition that all men are created equal —Abraham Lincoln⟩ **b** : to commit to something as a constant goal or way of life ⟨we Americans are *dedicated* to improvement —Louis Kronenberger⟩ ⟨she has *dedicated* her life to her husband's comfort⟩ **3** : to inscribe, address, or name by way of compliment, honor, or commemoration ⟨~ a book to a patron⟩; *specif* : to commit (as a person, church, or society) to the protection and intercession of a patron saint **4** : to give, present, or surrender to public use ⟨obliged to ~ a road crossing his land⟩

dedicated *adj* [fr. past part. of 2DEDICATE] : devoted to a cause, ideal, or purpose : ZEALOUS ⟨a ~ ballet dancer⟩ ⟨a life of ~ patience⟩

ded·i·ca·tee \ˌdedəkəˈtē\ *n* -s [2*dedicate* + *-ee*] : one to whom a thing is dedicated

ded·i·ca·tion \ˌdedəˈkāshən, -dēˈ-\ *n* -s [ME *dedicacioun*, fr. L *dedication-, dedicatio*, fr. *dedicatus* + *-ion-, -io* -ion] **1 a** : act or rite of dedicating to a divine being or to a sacred use : solemn appropriation — often distinguished from *consecration* ⟨the ~ of Solomon's temple⟩ **b** : an annual commemoration of a dedication **2** : a devoting or setting aside for any particular purpose; *specif, law* : an appropriation or giving up of property to public use that precludes the owner or others claiming under him from asserting any right of ownership inconsistent with the use for which the property is dedicated **3** : a name and often a message prefixed to a literary, musical, or artistic production, formerly testifying respect to a patron and often recommending the work to his favor, now usu. expressing admiration or affection for a person or for a cause **4** : self-sacrificing devotion to or as if to an ideal or a cause : ZEAL, FAITHFULNESS, ENTHUSIASM ⟨a musical performance marked by technical skill and ~⟩ ⟨requirements for those in the public service should be ability, integrity, and ~⟩

ded·i·ca·tion·al \¦==¦=shənᵊl, -shnəl\ *adj* : of or relating to dedication

dedication copy *n* : the copy of a book presented by its author to the person to whom it is dedicated

ded·i·ca·tive \ˈ==ˌkād·|iv, -āt|, |ēv *also* |əv; -ˌkəd·iv, -ətiv\ *adj* [2*dedicate* + *-ive*] : DEDICATING, DEDICATORY

ded·i·ca·tor \-ˌkād·ə(r), -ātə-\ *n* -s [2*dedicate* + *-or*] : one that dedicates

ded·i·ca·to·ri·al \¦==kə¦tōrēəl, -tȯr-\ *adj* [*dedicatory* + *-al*] : DEDICATORY

ded·i·ca·tory \ˈ===ˌ=rē, -ri, *esp Brit* ˈdediˌkāt(ə)ri\ *adj* [2*dedicate* + *-ory*] : constituting or serving as a dedication — often used following the noun ⟨the epistle ~⟩

de die in di·em \(ˌ)dā¦dēˌā(ˌ)in¦dē(ˌ)em\ [L] : from day to day

de·differentiate \(ˈ)dē+\ *vi* [back-formation fr. *dedifferentiation*] : to undergo dedifferentiation : lose specialization of form or function

de·differentiation \(ˈ)dē+\ *n* [*de-* + *differentiation*] **1** *biol* **a** : reversion of specialized structures (as cells) to a more generalized or primitive condition often as a preliminary to major physiological or structural change **b** : return of plant cells to a meristematic state (as in the production of phellogen) **2** *biol* : disintegration of specialized habits and adaptations

de·di·mus \ˈdedēməs, ˈdād-\ *or* **dedimus po·tes·ta·tem** \-ˌpōd·əˈstäd·əm, -päd·əˈstäd·-\ *n* [*dedimus* fr. ME, fr. L, we have given, 1st pers. pl. perf. indic. of *dare* to give; *dedimus potestatem* fr. L, we have given the power; fr. the use of these words in the writ — more at DATE] : a writ to commission a private person to perform some act in place of a judge (as to examine a witness)

de·dit \dāˈdē\ *n* -s [F, fr. OF *desdit*, lit., contradiction, fr. *desdire* to deny, retract, contradict, fr. *des-* de- + *dire* to say, fr. L *dicere* — more at DICTION] *Canadian law* : a sum forfeited by one who has failed in an engagement

ded·i·ti·cian \ˌdedəˈtishən\ *n* -s [L *deditic*ius dedítician (fr. *deditus*, past part. of *dedere* to surrender, give up, deliver) + E *-an* — more at DEDENDUM] *Roman law* : a freedman not allowed full citizenship rights because of bad character or grave misconduct during slavery or because as a foreigner he had fought against Rome — **ded·i·ti·cian·cy** \-nsē\ *n* -ES

de·di·tion \dəˈdishən, dēˈ-\ *n* -s [L *dedition-, deditio*, fr. *deditus* (past part. of *dedere* to surrender) + *-ion-, -io* -ion] : act of yielding : SURRENDER

ded·o·lent \ˈdedᵊlənt\ *adj* [L *dedolent-, dedolens*, pres. part. of *dedolēre* to cease to grieve, fr. *de* from, away + *dolēre* to feel pain — more at CONDOLE] *archaic* : feeling no grief or compunction : CALLOUS

de do·lo \(ˈ)dā¦dō(ˌ)lō\ *adj* [L] *law* : of deceit or fraud ⟨an action *de dolo*⟩

de·duce \dəˈd(y)üs, dēˈ-\ *vt* -ED/-ING/-S [L *deducere*, lit., to lead away, fr. *de* from, away + *ducere* to lead — more at DE-, TOW (pull)] **1** : to trace the course or descent of ⟨~ the history of the wool trade⟩ ⟨~ their lineage⟩ **2** : to derive by logical process : INFER: as **a** : to draw (a conclusion) necessarily from given premises : CONSTRUCT ⟨~ a logical result⟩ **b** : to infer (something) about a particular case from a general principle that holds of all such cases **3** *archaic* **a** : BRING, CONDUCT, CONVEY ⟨~ blood to the tissues⟩ **b** : to lead or send out (a colony) **4** : to prove (title to property) by preparing and exhibiting the abstract of title **syn** see INFER

de·duce·ment \-smənt\ *n* -s *obs* : INFERENCE, DEDUCTION

de·duc·i·bil·i·ty \=ˌ=səˈbiləd·ē\ *n* -ES : the state or quality of being deducible

de·duc·i·ble \=ˈ=səbəl\ *adj* [*deduce* + *-able*] : capable of being deduced : derivable by reasoning as a result or logical consequence

1**de·duct** \dəˈdəkt, dēˈ-\ *vb* -ED/-ING/-S [L *deductus*, past part. of *deducere*, lit., to lead away] *vt* **1** : to take (an amount) away from a total : take off : REMOVE ⟨the tax is ~*ed* from the paycheck⟩ — compare SUBTRACT **2** : DEDUCE, INFER ~ *vi* : ABATE, DIMINISH, DETRACT — used with *from* ⟨the noisy street ~*s* from the value of the property⟩

2**de·duct** \(ˈ)dē¦-\ *n* -s : an amount deducted : DEDUCTION ⟨resentment of wage earners against the ~*s* —*Jour. Amer. Med. Assoc.*⟩ — not often in formal use

de·duct·ibil·i·ty \dəˌdəktəˈbiləd·ē, (ˌ)dē-, -ətē, -i\ *n* -ES : the state or quality of being deductible

1**de·duct·ible** \dəˈdəktəbəl, dēˈ-\ *adj* [*deduct* + *-able*] **1** : capable of being deducted : allowable as a deduction ⟨certain gifts are ~ from the taxable income⟩ **2** : DEDUCIBLE

2**deductible** \"\ *n* -s **1** : a clause in an insurance policy relieving the insurer of responsibility for an initial specified small loss of the kind insured against **2** : something that is the subject of a deductible (as a brief initial period of illness or damage to a car costing less than a specified amount to repair)

de·duc·tion \-kshən\ *n* -s [ME *deduccion*, fr. MF or L; MF *deduction*, fr. L *deduction-, deductio*, fr. *deductus* (past part. of *deducere*) + *-ion-, -io* -ion] **1** : an act or process of deducting or deducing: as **a** : an act of taking away : DIMINUTION, SUBTRACTION ⟨~ of all legitimate business expenses⟩ **b** : the deriving of a conclusion by reasoning : inference from evidence; *specif, logic* : inference in which the conclusion follows necessarily from the premises — contrasted with *induction;* compare TRANSFORMATION RULE **c** *archaic* : the leading or sending forth of a colony : establishment of a colony **2** : a product or result of deducting or deducing: as **a** : a conclusion reached by mental deduction : INFERENCE ⟨his behavior confirmed my ~*s* about his upbringing⟩ **b** : something that is or may be subtracted ⟨business expenses are proper ~*s* from one's taxable income⟩ : ABATEMENT **c** *archaic* : an orderly or chronological account

deduction new for old *n* : a subtraction made by a marine underwriter from the total cost of repairs in paying a claim under a hull-insurance policy to allow for the gain in excess of loss to the shipowner resulting from the new material installed during repairing

de·duc·tive \-ktiv, -tēv *also* -təv\ *adj* [1*deduct* + *-ive*] **1** : of or relating to deduction : employing deduction in reasoning **2** : capable of being deduced from premises : INFERENTIAL ⟨~ laws⟩ — **de·duc·tive·ly** \-təvlē, -li\ *adv*

deductive method *n* : a method of reasoning by which (1) concrete applications or consequences are deduced from general principles or (2) theorems are deduced from definitions and postulates — compare DEDUCTION 1b; INDUCTION 2

deductory *adj* [1*deduct* + *-ory*] *obs* : DEDUCTIVE

de·dust \(ˈ)dē +\ *vt* [*de-* + *dust*, n.] : to remove excessively fine particles of the same material or other material from ⟨~*ing* ground ore⟩

1**dee** \ˈdē\ *dial Brit var of* 1DIE

2**dee** *also* **de** \"\ *n* -s **1** : the letter *d* **2** : something having the shape of the letter D: as **a** : a metal ring for holding a saddle strap or belt **b** : either of two hollow semicylindrical metal electrodes in a cyclotron — called also *duant*

3**dee** \"\ *or* **deed** \ˈdēd\ *adj* [euphemistic pronunciation of *d—, d—d*] : DAMNED

deece *var of* DIX

1**deed** \ˈdēd\ *n* -s [ME *dede*, fr. OE *dǣd;* akin to OHG *tāt* deed, ON *dāth*, Goth ga*deths;* derivative fr. the root of E *do*] **1** : something that is done or effected by a responsible agent : ACT, ACTION ⟨what ~ is this that ye have done? —Gen 44:15 (AV)⟩ ⟨would serve his kind in ~ and word —Alfred Tennyson⟩ **2** : illustrious act : ACHIEVEMENT, EXPLOIT, FEAT ⟨whose ~*s* some nobler poem shall adorn —John Dryden⟩ **3** : PERFORMANCE, DOING ⟨take the will for the ~⟩ — often contrasted with *word* **4** *dial Eng* : DOINGS, ADO ⟨such ~ as never was⟩ **5** *law* : a signed and usu. sealed instrument in writing, duly executed and delivered, containing some transfer, bargain, or contract; *also* : such an instrument before it has been given effect by delivery — often used specifically of an instrument conveying a fee in land as distinguished from a lease, mortgage, or other instruments under seal; compare WILL 6

2**deed** \"\ *vt* -ED/-ING/-S : to convey or transfer by deed ⟨he ~*ed* all his estate to his son⟩

3**deed** \"\ *adv* [by shortening] : INDEED

deedbox \ˈ=ˌ=\ *n* : a strongbox for documents

deed·ful \ˈdēdfəl\ *adj, archaic* : full of deeds or exploits : ACTIVE, STIRRING

deed·i·ly \-dəlē, -li\ *adv* [*deedy* + *-ly*] *dial chiefly Eng* : ACTIVELY, INDUSTRIOUSLY, EARNESTLY

deed·less \-dləs\ *adj, archaic* : not performing or not having performed deeds or exploits : INACTIVE

deed of arrangement *English law* : ARRANGEMENT 6b(2)

deed of assumption *Scots law* : a deed by which a trustee assumes or appoints a new cotrustee

deed of trust *law* : a deed that serves as an evidence of and security for an indebtedness : MORTGAGE

deed poll *n, pl* **deeds poll** [*deed* + *poll* (polled); fr. its having the edge of the paper polled] : a deed made and executed by only one party

deedy \-di\ *adj* -ER/-EST *dial chiefly Eng* : INDUSTRIOUS, ACTIVE, EARNEST

deef \ˈdēf\ *dial var of* DEAF

dee·jay \ˈdē¦jā\ *n* -s [2*dee* + *jay* (letter); fr. the initials *D. J.*] : DISC JOCKEY

1**deem** \ˈdēm\ *vb* -ED/-ING/-S [ME *demen*, fr. OE *dēman;* akin to OHG *tuomen* to judge, ON *dœma*, Goth *domjan;* denominative fr. the root of E *doom*] *vt* **1 a** *obs* : to sit in judgment upon : DECIDE ⟨at the one side six judges were disposed to view and ~ the deeds of arms that day —Edmund Spenser⟩ **b** *archaic* : ADMINISTER ⟨the deemster was a hard judge and ~*ed* the laws in rigor —Hall Caine⟩ **2** : to come to view, judge, or classify after some reflection : HOLD, THINK ⟨essentially he ~*ed* himself a liberal —Robert Grant †1940⟩ ⟨this criticism I ~ to be without foundation —H.W.Dodds⟩ ⟨it is ~*ed* advisable to refrain from making definite statements until clinical . . . proof is available —H.G.Armstrong⟩ **3** *archaic* : EXPECT, HOPE ⟨a creature . . . whom she ~*ed* to render happy —Lord Byron⟩ ~ *vi* **1** : to form or have an opinion : BELIEVE, SUPPOSE — used with *of* ⟨I cannot ~ otherwise of them —J.P. Kennedy †1870⟩ **2** : to become aware : be cognizant — used with *of* ⟨something unearthly which they ~ not of —Lord Byron⟩ **syn** see CONSIDER

2**deem** \"\ *n* -s *obs* : JUDGMENT, SURMISE

3**deem** \"\ *n* -s [ME (Sc) *deme* lady, dame, mother, alter. of ME *dame*] *Scot* : GIRL; *specif* : a servant girl

de–emanate \(ˈ)dē +\ *vt* : to deprive of the property of giving off a radioactive emanation ⟨*de-emanate* thorium by heating⟩ — **de–emanation** \(ˈ)dē +\ *n* -s

de–emphasis \(ˈ)dē +\ *n* **1** : lessening of importance : removal from a position of prominence, favor, or special attention : a playing down ⟨a movement for the *de-emphasis* of football in college⟩ **2** : complete or partial suppression of unduly large amplitude components from the output of an oscillating system (as of harsh overtones from a loudspeaker)

de–emphasize \(ˈ)dē +\ *vt* : to reduce in importance esp. in relation to something else : play down : DEFLATE ⟨defense program, accenting science and air power, and *de-emphasizing* army and navy —*Time*⟩

deem·ster \ˈdēmztə(r), -m(p)st-\ *n* -s [ME *demestre* judge — more at DEMPSTER] : one of the two justices of the common-law courts of the Isle of Man — **deem·ster·ship** \ˈ==(r)ˌship\ *n* -s

de–emulsify *var of* DEMULSIFY

deen \ˈdēn\ *Scot var of* DONE

dee·ner \ˈdēnə(r)\ *n* -s [origin unknown] *slang Austral* : SHILLING

de–energize \(ˈ)dē +\ *vt* : to check the flow of current through (an electrical device)

1**deep** \ˈdēp\ *adj* -ER/-EST [ME *deep, dep*, fr. OE *dēop;* akin to OHG *tiof* deep, ON *djūpr*, Goth *diups* deep, OE *dyppan* to dip — more at DIP] **1** : extending far or comparatively far from some level, edge, surface, or area: as **a** : extending downward to a considerable degree ⟨a ~ well⟩ ⟨~ valleys between the ranges⟩ **b** : extending well inward from a surface accepted as outer ⟨a ~ gash in the side of the mountain⟩; *often* : not located superficially within the body ⟨~ pressure receptors in muscles and tendons⟩ **c** : extending well back from a surface accepted as front ⟨a ~ recess behind the organ⟩ ⟨fine ~ closets in every room⟩ **d** : extending far laterally from something expressed or implied that is regarded as central : wide and peripheral ⟨a ~ shrubbery about the house⟩ ⟨~ borders of ecru lace⟩ **e** *sports* : occurring relatively far from the center of activity : located near the outer limits of the playing area ⟨a hit to ~ right field⟩ ⟨the safety man took a ~ position⟩ **2** : having a specified extension in an implied direction usu. downward or toward the back — used postpositively ⟨a canyon a mile ~⟩ ⟨a shelf 20 inches ~⟩ or in combination ⟨cars parked three-*deep*⟩ ⟨knee-*deep* snow⟩ **3** : marked by complexity, intensity, or a high degree of development of pertinent qualities: as **a** : difficult to penetrate or comprehend : RECONDITE ⟨a ~ problem⟩ ⟨the ~*er* questions of the day⟩; *often* : MYSTERIOUS, OBSCURE, DEVIOUS ⟨a ~ dark secret⟩ ⟨~ and deadly plots against civilization⟩ **b** : grave in nature or effect : GRIEVOUS, SERIOUS ⟨a ~ wrong⟩ ⟨in ~*est* disgrace⟩ **c** : of penetrating intellect : WISE, SAGACIOUS ⟨a ~ thinker⟩ ⟨~ clerks she dumbs —Shak.⟩; *often* : CUNNING, SLY, CRAFTY ⟨ah, but he's a ~ one⟩ ⟨they're too ~ for me⟩ **d** : preoccupied with : ENGROSSED, ABSORBED, INVOLVED, ENTANGLED —used postpositively and followed by an explanatory *in* phrase ⟨a man ~ in debt⟩ ⟨~ in her book⟩ **e** : completely developed ⟨~ winter⟩ : UNMIXED, UNALLOYED, EXTREME ⟨~ grief⟩ ⟨~ darkness⟩ : HEAVY ⟨~ sleep⟩ **f** : characterized by close absorption or complete engagement ⟨~ study⟩ ⟨~ thought⟩ **g** : involving heavy liability or great self-indulgence : carried to excess — archaic except of drinking ⟨unable to resist the ~ drinking of his comrades⟩ **h** *of color* : high in saturation and low in lightness : vivid and dark ⟨fuchsia is a much ~*er* color than pink⟩ **i** *of tone* : not high or sharp : rich, full, and heavy ⟨the bass of heaven's ~ organ —John Milton⟩; *specif* : having a low musical pitch or pitch range — used esp. of the human voice ⟨a voice ~ and strong⟩ **4 a** : situated well within the boundaries of ⟨a lodge ~ in the forest⟩; *often* : remote in time or space : hidden away : SECLUDED — used postpositively and followed by *in* ⟨~ in the heart⟩ ⟨found ~ in rural England⟩ **b** : lying or being covered or protected by or as if by a deep layer of something — used postpositively ⟨lanes ~ in snow⟩ ⟨a country ~ in peace⟩ **c** (1) *archaic, of roads* : covered with uncompacted soil : MUDDY, SANDY, BOGGY (2) *of soils* : having a thick covering layer of topsoil ⟨~ sandy loams⟩ **d** : covered, enclosed, or filled to a specified degree — used postpositively, usu. in combination, and with an orienting phrase ⟨cows knee-*deep* in clover⟩ ⟨a box rim-*deep* with junk⟩ **5 a** : moving over or passing through a considerable distance downward ⟨a ~ dive⟩ ⟨a ~ drop from a cliff⟩ **b** (1) : coming from, reaching to, or acting on something (as a part or place) that is far down, back, or within : DEEP-SEATED ⟨a ~ breath⟩ ⟨a ~ strong taproot⟩ ⟨~ therapy⟩ (2) : originating or taking place below the surface of the body ⟨~ pain⟩ ⟨~ reflexes⟩; *often* : involving or operating on mental levels below the conscious ⟨~ neuroses⟩ **6** *now dial Eng* : advanced in time : LATE

syn PROFOUND, ABYSMAL: applied to physical things and situations DEEP is a simple antonym of *shallow* without especial connotation; applied to persons and to mental states, it may imply study, deliberation, penetration, subtlety, or craft ⟨a *deep* thinker⟩ ⟨*deep* scholarship⟩ ⟨a careful editing after a *deep* study of the inner meaning of the work must be undertaken —Warwick Braithwaite⟩ PROFOUND in its occasional use in reference to physical things is likely to indicate great depth, perhaps awe-inspiring ⟨canyons more *profound* than our deepest mountain gorges —Willa Cather⟩ and in its more common use in reference to persons and mental processes to imply thorough penetration into and resolution of weighty and complicated matters and evolving well thought out, just, and correct solutions ⟨a *profound* philosophy⟩ ⟨a *profound* search for truth⟩ ⟨a *profound* lawyer, peculiarly fitted for that high judicial office —Marie B. Owen⟩ ⟨the executive puts on a *profound* air, purses up his lips, looks at the ceiling with penetrating gaze, then trains his ponderous face on the subordinate —H.A.Overstreet⟩ ABYSMAL may describe things of infinite depth or mental conditions or processes showing infinite want, lack, demerit, or fault ⟨*abysmal* ignorance⟩ ⟨Schmaltz is arrogant and assertive; his *abysmal* ignorance is matched only by his conviction of his own influence —M.D.Geismar⟩ ⟨not much happens to starlight in its long passage through the *abysmal* depths of interstellar space —P.W.Merrill⟩ **syn** see in addition BROAD

— **in deep water** : in difficulty : in distress : in a situation with obscure and menacing possibilities

2**deep** \"\ *adv* -ER/-EST [ME *depe*, fr. OE *dēope;* akin to OHG *tiufo* deeply; derivative fr. the root of E 1*deep*] **1** : to a great depth : with depth : far down : PROFOUNDLY, DEEPLY ⟨drink ~⟩ ⟨cut ~⟩ ⟨*deep*-set⟩ ⟨*deep*-versed in books, and shallow in himself —John Milton⟩ **2** : far on (in time) : LATE ⟨~ in the night⟩

3**deep** \"\ *n* -s [ME *deep, depe*, fr. OE *dēop* deep water (fr. *dēop*, adj., deep) & OE *dȳpe* depth, sea; akin to OHG *tiufī* depth, Goth *diupei;* derivative fr. the root of E 1*deep*] **1 a** *now dial Eng* : measurable depth **b** : any of the fathom points on a sounding line that is not a mark : an unmarked estimated fathom measure — see SOUNDING LINE illustration **2** : something that is deep: **a** : a vast or immeasurable extent : ABYSS ⟨the ~ of space⟩ **b** : the extent of surrounding space or time : FIRMAMENT ⟨the azure ~⟩ : OCEAN ⟨the briny ~⟩ **c** : the world of the dead **3** : the middle part : the most intense or characteristic part ⟨~ of winter⟩ ⟨the forest ~*s*⟩ **4** : a profound or not easily fathomed recess (as of thought or feeling) ⟨thy judgments are a great ~ —Ps 36:6 (AV)⟩ **5 a** : one of the deep portions of any body of water; *specif* : a generally long and narrow area in the ocean where the depth exceeds 3000 fathoms ⟨the Aldrich *Deep* in the south Pacific⟩ **b** : a deep channel in a strait or estuary

deep brunswick green *n, often cap B* : a green that is yellower and darker than bottle green, bluer and duller than forest green (sense 1), and yellower, darker, and slightly stronger than evergreen — distinguished from *light Brunswick green* and *middle Brunswick green*

deep buff *n* : a layer of leather found immediately below the top grain layer, produced by splitting off the grain layer, and used chiefly as upholstery leather

deep chrome green *n* : a green that is yellower and duller than holly green (sense 1) or golf green, yellower and less strong than average hunter green — distinguished from *light chrome green* and *medium chrome green;* called also *cinnabar green, Milori green, silk green, zinc green*

deep chrome orange *n* : CHROME SCARLET

deep chrome yellow *n* : a moderate orange yellow that is redder and lighter than yellow ocher — called also *cavalry, chrome yellow orange, medium chrome yellow, middle chrome yellow*

deep culture *n* : a culture produced by a deep inoculation into a solid medium (as gelatin or agar) that is used esp. for the growth of anaerobic bacteria

deep–dish pie *n* : a pie baked in a deep dish and usu. having a fruit filling and no bottom crust

deep–draw \ˈ=¦=\ *vt* : to form (sheet metal) into cup-shaped, box-shaped, or cone-shaped articles or shells by forcing into a die (as with a punch press or drop hammer)

deep–dyed \ˈ=¦=\ *adj* : THOROUGH, UNRELIEVED, INGRAINED ⟨a *deep-dyed* villain⟩ ⟨a *deep-dyed* Tory⟩

deep·en \ˈdēpən, -pᵊm\ *vb* **deepened** \-pənd, -pᵊmd\ **deepened** \"\ **deepening** \-p(ə)niŋ\ **deepens** \-pənz, -pᵊmz\

vt : to make deep or deeper: as **a** : to increase the depth of ⟨~ a well⟩ ⟨~ a channel⟩ **b** : to make more intense ⟨the incident *~ed* the gloom⟩ or more profound ⟨*~ed* the meaning of his life⟩ **c** : to increase in degree ⟨~ sorrow⟩ **d** : to make lower in tone or range of pitch ⟨~ a pipe organ⟩ ~ *vi* : to become deeper ⟨the water *~ed* at every step⟩ : grow more profound or obscure ⟨with every day the mystery *~s*⟩

deepening *n* -s [fr. gerund of *deepen*] : decrease in the central pressure of a cyclone during an interval of time

deep·en·ing·ly *adv* : in a deepening manner

deeper *comparative of* DEEP

deepest *superlative of* DEEP

deep etch *n* : the etching of an offset printing plate to such a degree that the printing area becomes slightly recessed and thereby productive of sharper definition and longer runs

¹deep–etch \ˈ=ˌ=\ *adj* [*deep etch*] : involving the use of plates made by deep etch ⟨printing by *deep-etch* offset⟩

²deep–etch \"\ *vt* [*deep etch*] : to produce (a plate) by deep etch

deep fascia *n* : a firm fascia that ensheathes and binds together muscles and other internal structures — compare SUPERFICIAL FASCIA

deep fat *n* : hot fat deep enough in a cooking utensil to cover the food to be fried ⟨onion rings fried in *deep fat*⟩

deep field *n* : LONG FIELD

deep–focus \ˈ=ˌ=\ *adj, of an earthquake* : originating at a depth greater than 250 kilometers below the earth's surface

deep freeze *n* : a condition of being held in abeyance : COLD STORAGE 2 ⟨bill presently in *deep freeze* awaiting a new congress —*Newsweek*⟩

deep–freeze \ˈ=ˌ=\ *vt* **1** : QUICK-FREEZE **2** : CHILL, REFRIGERATE

Deepfreeze \"\ *trademark* — used for a freezer for the quick-freezing and storage of food

deep freezer *n* : FREEZER 1d(2)

deep fry *vt* : to cook by immersing in hot fat — distinguished from *sauté*

deep fryer *n* : a utensil suitable for deep frying usu. deep and often with a mesh or perforated compartment in which the food is exposed to the fat

deepgoing \ˈ=ˌ=\ *adj* : reaching or penetrating to the heart : SERIOUS ⟨~ differences of opinion⟩ : FUNDAMENTAL ⟨a ~ theory⟩

deep–grown \ˈ=ˌ=\ *adj, of wool* : having a long strong staple

deep·ing \ˈdēpiŋ\ *n* -s [fr. gerund of obs. *deep*, v., to deepen, immerse deeply, fr. ME *depen* to make deep, immerse deeply, fr. OE *dȳpan* to make deep; akin to Goth *gadiupjan* to make deep; causative-denominative fr. the root of E ¹*deep*] *Brit* : one of the usu. 6 foot wide sections of which a hand-netted drift net is made ⟨several *~s* are laced side to side to give the required depth to the net⟩

deep·ish \-pish, -pēsh\ *adj* : somewhat deep ⟨the theater was a complete little affair with a ~ stage —Ngaio Marsh⟩

deep kiss *n* : a kiss involving extensive or intensive contact of the inner lips, tongue, and teeth esp. with prolonged or rhythmic tongue-to-tongue contact

deep·ly *adv* [ME *deepliche*, fr. OE *dēoplīce*, fr. *dēoplīc* deep, fr. *dēop* deep + *-līc* -ly] **1** : at or to a great depth : far below the surface : far down : far in ⟨sink ~ into mud⟩ **2** : PROFOUNDLY, THOROUGHLY ⟨~ versed in nuclear theory⟩ : not superficially : in a high degree ⟨~ hurt by his remark⟩ **3** : with a tendency to richness and intensity of color ⟨~ tanned face⟩ **4** : with low or deep tone : SONOROUSLY ⟨hounds baying ~⟩ **5** : with profound skill : with cunning ⟨~ laid plot⟩ **6** : GRAVELY, SERIOUSLY ⟨~ compromised⟩ ⟨~ involved in a scandal⟩

deep·most \-p,mōst, *esp Brit also* -pməst\ *adj, archaic* : DEEPEST ⟨from her ~ glen —Sir Walter Scott⟩

deep mourning *n* : mourning clothes in which the garments are not only all black but also made of lusterless materials

deepmouthed \ˈ=ˌ=\ *adj* : having a deep sonorous voice ⟨~ dogs⟩

deep·ness \-pnəs\ *n* -ES [ME *depnesse*, fr. OE *dēopnes*, fr. *dēop* deep + *-nes* -ness] : the quality or state of being deep

deep psychology *n* : PSYCHOANALYSIS

deep–rooted \ˈ=ˌ==\ *adj* : marked by or having deep roots : deeply implanted, embedded, or established and difficult or impossible to alter, decrease, or eliminate ⟨these problems are *deep-rooted* and stubborn —H.S.Truman⟩ ⟨a *deep-rooted* loyalty⟩ **syn** see INVETERATE

deep–root·ed·ness \ˈ=ˈ==nəs\ *n* -ES : the quality or state of being deep-rooted

deeps *pl of* DEEP

deep–sea \ˈ=ˌ=\ *adj* [¹*deep* + *sea*] **1** : of, relating to, occurring in, or for use in the deeper parts of the ocean ⟨*deep-sea* currents⟩ ⟨*deep-sea* fishes⟩ ⟨a *deep-sea* line⟩ **2** : acting (as by sailing or fishing) or for use in parts of the oceans far from land ⟨*deep-sea* fishermen⟩ ⟨a *deep-sea* tug⟩ — sometimes distinguished from *coastal, longshore*

deep sea *n* [¹*deep* + *sea*] : those parts of the oceans in which the water is very deep; *specif* : areas in which it has a depth of 1000 fathoms or more — compare ³DEEP 5

deep–sea lead *n* : a lead used for sounding in deep water; *specif* : the heaviest of sounding leads used in water exceeding 100 fathoms in depth

deep–sea red crab *n* : a large light-colored crab (*Geryon quinquedens*) from deep water of the eastern coast of No. and So. America

deep–sea tangle *n* **1** : DRIFTWEED **2** : DEADMAN'S HAND 1c

deep–seated \ˈ=ˌ==\ *adj* **1** : situated, originating, or operating far below the surface : not susceptible to surface examination, analysis, or treatment ⟨the inflammation was *deep-seated*⟩ **2 a** : marked by establishment through long habitual practice or usage : unlikely to be changed, lessened, or eliminated ⟨easier to overturn the form of government than to uproot a *deep-seated* tradition —A.T.Mahan⟩ **b** : deeply ingrained : genuine and lasting as a characteristic : essential or as though essential to a character ⟨*deep-seated* preferences cannot be argued about —O.W.Holmes †1935⟩ **3** *of a rock, structure, movement, or process* : originating or occurring at depths of more than a few thousand feet below the earth's surface ⟨the origin of *deep-seated* quartzo-feldspathic rocks —*Jour. of Geol.*⟩ **syn** see INVETERATE

deep–sea tube *n* : a long tube that reaches to the sea bottom and that is so equipped mechanically that a man within it may perform work on objects outside (as for salvaging purposes)

deep six *n* [perh. so called fr. the idea of submersion under six fathoms of water] **1** *slang* : burial at sea ⟨it was not in keeping with the traditions of the navy . . . to give this lad a *deep six* in the darkness of midnight —H.M.Forgy⟩ **2** *slang* : DISCARD, OBLIVION — used esp. in the phrase *give it the deep six*

deep–six \ˈ=ˌ=\ *vt* -ED/-ING/-ES [*deep six*] *slang* : to discard or throw overboard

deep south *n, often cap D, usu cap S* : the southeasterly portion of the U.S. usu. including all states bordering on the Gulf of Mexico and some adjacent regions

deep space *n* : the effect esp. in painting of an uninterrupted view into great distance — compare STAGE SPACE

deep stone *n* : a light olive brown that is redder, stronger, and slightly lighter than drab, average mustard tan, or sponge —called also *tinsel*

deep tank *n* : a portion of a ship's hold bulkheaded off to hold water

deep–waisted \ˈ=ˌ==\ *adj, of a ship* : having a low waist ⟨*deep-waisted* with poop and forecastle high above the deck⟩

deepwater \ˈ=ˌ==\ *adj* [¹*deep* + *water*] : of, relating to, or characterized by water of considerable depth ⟨a ~ channel⟩; *often* : DEEP-SEA, OFFSHORE ⟨~ navigation⟩ ⟨~ sailors⟩

deep water *n* [¹*deep* + *water*] : difficulty esp. when serious : TROUBLE ⟨he'll find himself in *deep water* if he tries to keep up with the neighbors⟩ : PERPLEXITY — often used in pl. and usu. with *in* ⟨I was in *deep waters* before his explanation was well begun⟩

deep waterline *n* : the line on a ship's hull to which the water reaches when the ship is loaded to maximum safe capacity

deep·wa·ter·man \ˈ=ˌ==mən\ *n, pl* **deepwatermen** : a ship for navigating deep waters : a seagoing ship

deep well *n* : a well in which the water level is at a depth exceeding 22 feet beyond which the ordinary suction pump does not operate satisfactorily

deer \ˈdi(ə)r, ˈdiə\ *n, pl* **deer** *also* **deers** [ME, deer, animal, fr. OE *dēor* beast; akin to OHG *tior* wild animal, ON *dȳr*, Goth *dius* wild animal, Lith *dvėsti* to breathe, expire, Skt *dhvaṁsati* he falls to dust, perishes — more at DUST] **1** *obs* : ANIMAL; *esp* : a quadruped mammal ⟨rats and mice and such small ~ —Shak.⟩ **2 a** : any of numerous ruminant mammals that constitute the family Cervidae, that have two large and two small hoofs on each foot and antlers borne by the males of nearly all and by the females of a few forms, that are represented by numerous species and individuals in most regions except most of Africa and Australia, and that constitute an important source of food in many places for man and the larger carnivorous animals — see CARIBOU, ELK, MOOSE, MUSK DEER, REINDEER; VENISON **b** : any of the small or medium-sized members of the family as distinguished from certain esp. large forms (as elk, moose, or caribou) **3** : DEERSKIN **4** : a grayish yellowish brown that is lighter and slightly yellower than olive wood and lighter than acorn — called also *bobolink, camel's hair*

fallow deer

deerberry \ˈ=- — *see* BERRY\ *n* **1** : any of several fruits reputedly eaten by deer; *esp* : the extremely acid greenish or yellowish fruit of a rather small branching blueberry (*Vaccinium stamineum*) common in marshy areas in the eastern U.S. **2** : a plant bearing deerberries

deer brush *n* : any of several shrubby plants (as members of the genus *Ceanothus*) that are regularly browsed by deer; *esp* : a rapid-growing much-branched semi-evergreen shrub (*C. integerrimus*) that grows in dry upland areas of the western and southwestern U.S. and is a staple browse for mule deer and an important honey plant

deer cabbage *n* : a blue-flowered prostrate or decumbent evergreen lupine (*Lupinus diffusus*) of the southern U.S. with unifoliolate leaves

deer dance *n* : a mimetic dance widespread among American Indian tribes and performed to appease the deer spirit and thereby effect success in the hunt or cure diseases held to be caused by this spirit

deerdrive \ˈ=ˌ=\ *n* : a shoot in which deer are driven past the sportsmen

deer fern *n* : a fern (*Blechnum spicant*) of Europe and western No. America that is often cultivated for deer browse and has erect fronds of which the sterile are foliaceous and the fertile are contracted

deerfly \ˈ=ˌ=\ *n* : any of numerous small horseflies of *Chrysops* or related genera that usu. have wing markings and include serious bloodsucking pests of deer, man, and livestock some of which are vectors of tularemia

deer–fly fever *n* : TULAREMIA

deerfood \ˈ=ˌ=\ *n* : WATER SHIELD 1

deer–foot \ˈ=ˌ=\ *n, pl* **deer–foots** [prob. so called fr. the shape of the leaf] : WILD VANILLA

deer forest *n* : an open or forested but extensive and unenclosed tract set aside for the keeping and hunting of deer

deer grass *n* **1** : a bunch grass (*Epicampes rigens*) used for forage in the southwestern U.S. **2** : a plant of the genus *Rhexia* **3** : DEERHAIR

deerhair *also* **deer's–hair** \ˈ=ˌ=\ *or* **deerhair–bulrush** \ˈ=ˌ=ˈ==\ *n* [so called fr. the appearance of its stem] : a small club rush (*Scirpus caespitosus*) of Europe, Asia, and No. America with filiform stems

deerherd \ˈ=ˌ=\ *n* [*deer* + *herd* (herdsman)] : a keeper of deer

deerhorn \ˈ=ˌ=\ *n* **1** : the horny material making up the antlers of deer **2** : a large rough elongated freshwater mussel (*Tritigonia verrucosa*) found in the Mississippi drainage and used for making buttons

deerhorn cactus *n* : a night-blooming cereus (*Cereus greggii*) with spiny edible scarlet fruits

deerhound \ˈ=ˌ=\ *n* : a large tall dog of a breed developed in Scotland that was formerly much used in hunting deer and has the general conformation of a greyhound but is larger and taller with a rough usu. blue-gray coat

deerkill \ˈ=ˌ=\ *n* [by alter.] : KILLDEER

deer laurel *n* : BIG LAUREL

deer·let \ˈlət\ *n* -s **1** : a small deer **2** : CHEVROTAIN

deer mouse *n* [so called fr. its agility] : WHITE-FOOTED MOUSE

deer oak *n* : a small shrubby oak (*Quercus sadleriana*) of dry uplands of western U.S. that produces abundant acorns relished by deer, bear, and cattle

deers *pl of* DEER

deer's–ear \ˈ=ˌ=\ *n, pl* **deer's–ear** *or* **deer's–ears** : any of several tall-growing biennial or short-lived perennial herbs (as American columbo) that constitute a genus *Frasera* of the family Gentianaceae and are widely distributed in No. America esp. in warm dry upland areas of the Pacific states — compare DEER'S-TONGUE

deerskin \ˈ=ˌ=\ *n* [ME *deriskyn*, fr. *deri, der, deer* deer + *skyn, skin* skin] : leather made from the skin of a deer; *also* : a garment of such leather

deerstalker \ˈ=ˌ==\ *n* [so called fr. its suitability to be worn by a person stalking deer] : a close-fitting cap with a visor at the front and the back and with earflaps that may be tied up or down

deer's–tongue \ˈ=ˌ=\ *n, pl* **deer's–tongues** **1** : WILD VANILLA — used chiefly commercially **2** : a tall-growing perennial herb (*Frasera speciosa*) of the Pacific coast of the U.S. with long panicles of greenish white purple-spotted flowers — compare DEER'S-EAR

deer tiger *n* : COUGAR

deertongue \ˈ=ˌ=\ *n* **1** : WILD VANILLA — used chiefly commercially **2** : a narrow shovel blade for a cultivator

deervetch \ˈ=ˌ=\ *n* : a plant of the genus *Lotus*

deer vine *n* : TWINFLOWER b

deerweed \ˈ=ˌ=\ *n* : any of several bushy herbs of the genus *Lotus* (as *L. scoparius* and *L. purshianus*) occurring in southern California, having trifoliolate leaves and yellow flowers, and being a useful forage plant for arid regions

deerwood \ˈ=ˌ=\ *n* : HOP HORNBEAM

deerwort boneset \ˈ=ˌ=-\ *n* : WHITE SNAKEROOT

deeryard \ˈ=ˌ=\ *n* : a place where deer herd in winter

dees *pl of* DEE

de·e·sis \dēˈēsəs\ *n, pl* **dee·ses** \-(ˌ)sēz\ *usu cap* [Gk *deēsis* entreaty, prayer, fr. *dein* to lack, miss, *deisthai* to beg — more at DEUTER-] : a tripartite icon of the Eastern Orthodox Church showing Christ usu. enthroned between the Virgin Mary and St. John the Baptist

de–esterification \(ˈ)dē+\ *n* [*de-* + *esterification*] : the process of de-esterifying

de–esterify \(ˈ)dē+\ *vt* [*de-* + *esterify*] : to remove ester groups from (as pectin)

de–eth·a·nize \(ˈ)dēˈethəˌnīz\ *vt* -ED/-ING/-S [*de-* + *ethane* + *-ize*] : to remove ethane and sometimes lighter fractions from (as cracked gasoline) by distillation — **de–eth·a·niz·er** \-zə(r)\ *n* -s

de–ethicize \(ˈ)dē+\ *vt* [*de-* + *ethicize*] : to divest of ethical standards : dissociate (as religion) from ethics

deeve \ˈdēv\ *var of* DEAVE

dee·vil \ˈdēvəl\ *Scot var of* DEVIL

dee·vil·ick \-vlək\ *n* -s [Sc *deevil* + *-ick* (dim. suffix)] *Scot* : a little devil

de ex·com·mu·ni·ca·to ca·pi·en·do \(ˌ)dā,ekskə,münēˈkädˌ(ˌ)tō,käpēˈen(ˌ)dō\ *n* [NL, lit., of seizing an excommunicated person] : an ancient writ ordering the imprisonment of an excommunicated person until he submitted to the church

def *abbr* **1** defendant; defense **2** deferred **3** deficit **4** defined; definite; definition

de·face \dəˈfās, dēˈ-\ *vt* -ED/-ING/-S [ME *defacen* to disfigure, efface, fr. MF *desfacier, deffacier*, fr. OF, fr. *des-* de- + *-facier* (fr. *face*) — more at FACE] **1** : to destroy or mar the face or external appearance of : DISFIGURE : injure, spoil, or mar by effacing important features or portions of ⟨~ an inscription⟩ ⟨~ a bond⟩ **2** : to impair in value, influence, or effect **3** *obs* : DESTROY, EFFACE, ERASE **4** *obs* **a** : DEFAME, DISCREDIT **b** : to face down : OUTSHINE ⟨this holy tide of Christmas all others doth ~ — *God Rest You Merry, Gentlemen*⟩

de·face·ment \-smənt\ *n* -s : the act of defacing or state of being defaced : injury to surface or outward appearance

de·fac·er \-sə(r)\ *n* -s : one that defaces

de fac·to \(ˈ)dēˈfak,tō, (ˈ)dāˈ-; (ˈ)dāˈfäk,-\ *adv (or adj)* [L] **1** : ACTUALLY : in fact : in reality **2 a** : exercising the powers and demanding the privileges of a regularly and legally constituted authority often with a color of right ⟨a *de facto* court⟩ **b** : existing as the controlling power — used of a government actually functioning as a result of a revolution or rebellion but not yet permanently established or recognized **c** : existing in fact and in opposition to an assumed or fictitious state of affairs ⟨a *de facto* state of war⟩ — distinguished from *de jure*

def·ae·cate *Brit var of* DEFECATE

defailance *or* **defaillance** *n* -s [F *défaillance*, fr. OF *defaillance*, fr. *defaillir* to fail, be lacking + *-ance* — more at DEFAULT] *obs* : LACK, OMISSION : FAILURE

de·fal·cate \dəˈfal,kāt, dēˈ-, -fōl-, ˈdefəl-; ˈdefəl-; *usu* -ād-+V\ *vb* -ED/-ING/-S [ML *defalcatus*, past part. of *defalcare*, fr. L *de-* + *falc-, falx* sickle] *vt* **1** *archaic* : to cut off : lop off **2** *archaic* : to reduce by taking away a part : CURTAIL ~ *vi* : to take money committed to one's charge : EMBEZZLE

de·fal·ca·tion \(ˌ)dē,falˈkāshən, də-, -fōl-, ˌdefəl-\ *n* -s [ML *defalcation-, defalcatio*, fr. *defalcatus* + L *-ion-, -io* -ion] **1** *archaic* : a lopping off : CURTAILMENT ⟨sadly puzzled at the ~ of more than one-third of my income —Charles Lamb⟩ **2** *obs* : something lopped off : DEDUCTION **3 a** : misappropriation of money in one's keeping **b** : a sum of money so misappropriated **4** : a falling away : DEFECTION : a failure to meet a promise or an expectation

de·fal·ca·tor *pronunc at* DEFALCATE + ə(r)\ *n* -s : one guilty of breach of trust esp. in money matters : DEFAULTER

de·falk \dəˈfōk, dēˈ-\ *vt* -ED/-ING/-S [ME *defalken*, fr. MF *defalquer*, fr. ML *defalcare* — more at DEFALCATE] *archaic* : DEFALCATE

def·a·ma·tion \ˌdefəˈmāshən, -fəˈmā- *sometimes* ˌdēf-\ *n* -s [alter. (influenced by ¹*defame*) of earlier *diffamation*, fr. ME *diffamacioun*, fr. MF or ML; MF *diffamation*, fr. ML *diffamation-, diffamatio*, fr. L *diffamatus* (past part. of *diffamare*) + *-ion-, -io* -ion] **1** *obs* : a bringing into disrepute : DISHONOR, DISGRACE **2** : the act of defaming another or injuring another's reputation by any slanderous communication : DETRACTION, CALUMNY, ASPERSION — compare LIBEL, SLANDER

de·fam·a·to·ry \dəˈfamə,tōrē, dēˈ-, -ȯr-, -ri\ *adj* [alter. (influenced by ¹*defame*) of earlier *diffamatory*, fr. ML *diffamatorius*, fr. L *diffamatus* + *-orius* -ory] : containing defamation : injurious to reputation : CALUMNIOUS

¹de·fame \dəˈfām, dēˈ-\ *vt* -ED/-ING/-S [ME *diffamen, defamen*, fr. MF & L; ME *diffamen* fr. MF *diffamer*, fr. OF, fr. L *diffamare*, fr. *dif-* (fr. *dis-*) + *fama* reputation, fame; ME *defamen* fr. MF *defamer*, fr. OF, fr. L *defamare*, alter. (influenced by *de-*) of *diffamare* — more at FAME] **1** *archaic* : to harm or destroy the good fame of : make infamous : bring into disgrace ⟨my guilt thy growing virtues did ~ —John Dryden⟩ **2** : to harm the reputation or good name of by uttering injurious charges : LIBEL, SLANDER **3** *archaic* : ACCUSE, CHARGE ⟨Rebecca . . . is . . . *defamed* of sorcery —Sir Walter Scott⟩ **syn** see MALIGN

²defame *n* -s [ME, fr. MF *defame, diffame*, fr. OF *diffame*, fr. *diffamer*, v.] **1** *obs* : DISHONOR, INFAMY **2** *obs* : DEFAMATION, SLANDER

defamed *adj* **1** *obs* : DISHONORED : of bad repute **2** : SLANDERED, LIBELED

de·fam·er \-mə(r)\ *n* -s : one that defames

de·fam·ing·ly *adv* : so as to defame

de·fang \(ˈ)dē+\ *vt* [*de-* + *fang* (n.)] : to remove the fangs from (as a poisonous snake)

de·fas·sa \dəˈfasə\ *n, pl* **defassa** [NL (specific epithet of *Kobus defassa*), fr. L, *defassa, defessa*, fem. of *defassus, defessus*, past part. of *defatisci, defetisci* to become tired, weak, fr. *de-* + *fatisci* to become weak, tired; akin to L *fatigare* to weary, fatigue — more at FATIGUE] : a large gray African antelope (*Kobus defassa*) having a shaggy coat and spreading ringed horns — called also *waterbuck*

de–fat \(ˈ)dē+\ *vt* [*de-* + *fat* (n.)] : to remove fat from — used chiefly as a participle ⟨*de-fatted* milk powder⟩

¹de·fault \dəˈfȯlt, dēˈ- *sometimes* ˈdē,f-\ *n* -s [ME *defaulte*, alter. (influenced by AF *defaulte*, alter. — prob. influenced by OF *defaillir* to be lacking, fail, fr. assumed VL *defallire* — of OF *defaute*) of *defaute*, fr. OF, fr. (assumed) VL *defallita*, fr. fem. of *defallitus*, past part. of (assumed) VL *defallire* to be lacking, fail, fr. L *de-* + (assumed) VL *fallire* to deceive, fail — more at FAIL] **1** *obs* : the absence of something needed : LACK, WANT **2** : failure to do something required by duty or law : NEGLIGENCE, NEGLECT ⟨a position of advantage lost by mere ~⟩ **3** *archaic* : FAULT: as **a** : WRONGDOING, OFFENSE, MISDEED ⟨pardon our *~s*⟩ **b** : ERROR, IMPERFECTION, FLAW, BLEMISH **4** : a failure to pay financial debts ⟨salesmen sometimes oversell their prospects thereby laying the ground for later *~s* —H.E.Hoagland⟩ ⟨~ of his loan terms⟩ **5** : the failure of a defendant or plaintiff to appear at the required time to defend or prosecute an action or proceeding as a result of which a plaintiff may be nonsuited or a defendant may have judgment rendered against him — often used with *in* ⟨the defendant has made no appearance in the case, and is in ~⟩ — see JUDGMENT BY DEFAULT **6** : failure to compete in or to finish an appointed contest ⟨lose a race by ~⟩ **syn** see FAILURE — **in default of** *prep* : in case of failure or lack of : in the absence of ⟨*in default of* evidence there was no trial⟩

²default \"\ *vb* -ED/-ING/-S [alter. (influenced by ¹*default*) of ME *defauten*, fr. *defaute*, n.] *vi* : to fail to fulfill a contract or agreement, to accept a responsibility, or to perform a duty: as **a** : to fail to meet a financial obligation **b** : to fail to appear in court : let a case go by default **c** : to fail to compete in or to finish an appointed contest, esp. an athletic contest; *also* : to forfeit a contest by such failure ~ *vt* **1** : to fail to perform, pay, or make good ⟨~ a loan⟩ : OMIT ⟨~ a dividend⟩ **2** : to call (a defendant or other person whose duty it is to be present in court) and make entry of default for failure to appear : enter a default against **3 a** : to fail to compete in or to finish (an appointed contest) **b** : to forfeit (a contest) by such failure **c** : to exclude (a player or team) from a contest by default

de·fault·er \-tə(r)\ *n* -s : one that makes or commits a default : DELINQUENT: as **a** : one who fails to appear in court when summoned **b** : one who fails to account for money or property entrusted to his care : DEFALCATOR, EMBEZZLER **c** : one who fails to pay a debt **d** *Brit* : a soldier guilty of a military offense **e** *Brit* : a member of the stock exchange who has been publicly declared unable to meet his contracts

de·fau·nate \(ˈ)dēˈfȯ,nāt\ *vt* -ED/-ING/-S [*de-* + NL *fauna* + E *-ate*] : to remove a fauna from : remove the intestinal protozoans of (termites) — **de·fau·na·tion** \ˌdē,fȯˈnāshən\ *n* -s

de·fea·sance \dəˈfēzᵊn(t)s, dēˈ-\ *n* -s [ME *defesance*, fr. AF, fr. OF *desfesant, desfesant*, pres. part. of *desfaire, deffaire* to destroy, undo — more at DEFEAT] **1 a** : a rendering null or void **b** (1) : the ending of a property interest in accordance with conditions stipulated in the terms of a deed; *also* : a collateral deed or instrument stating such a condition of termination (2) : the ending of a property interest through a power of termination or an executory limitation **2** : DEFEAT, OVERTHROW, UNDOING

de·fea·si·ble \-zəbəl\ *adj* [AF, fr. OF *desfais-, deffais-* (stem of *desfaire, deffaire*) + *-ible*] : capable of being or liable to being voided, annulled, or undone : subject to defeasance esp. by being cut off through the exercise of a power or the happening of an event ⟨a claim to an estate may be ~ so long as the claimant is under 21 and unmarried⟩

1de·feat \də'fēt, dē'-, *usu* -fēd·+V\ *vt* -ED/-ING/-S [ME *deffeten*, fr. MF *desfait, deffait*, past part. of *desfaire, deffaire* to destroy, fr. OF, fr. ML *disfacere*, fr. L *dis-* + *facere* to do — more at DO] **1** *archaic* **:** UNDO, DESTROY ⟨his unkindness may ~ my life —Shak.⟩ **2** *obs* **:** to mar the looks of **:** DISFIGURE **3 :** to render null and void (as a title to property, a legal claim) **:** NULLIFY, FRUSTRATE ⟨~*ed* hopes⟩ **4 :** to win victory over, check the progress of, or destroy the power of **:** OVERCOME, OVERTHROW ⟨~ an army in battle⟩ ⟨~*ed* the opposing candidate by a large margin⟩ ⟨~*ed* in all his purposes⟩ ⟨the bill was ~*ed* in the senate⟩ **5 :** to decrease the ability of (as a stream) to erode or to maintain a course ⟨a stream ~*ed* by crustal movement⟩ **syn** see CONQUER

2defeat \"\ *n* -S **1** *archaic* **:** UNDOING **:** DESTRUCTION — often used with *on* ⟨upon whose property and most dear life a damned ~ was made —Shak.⟩ **2 :** frustration by rendering null and void or by prevention of success ⟨the ~ of a plan⟩ **3 :** an overthrow esp. of an army in battle **:** loss of a contest **:** REPULSE, DISCOMFITURE — opposed to *victory*

de·feat·ism \-fēd·,izəm, -ē,tiz-\ *n* -S [F *défaitisme*, fr. *défaite* defeat (fr. MF *deffaite, desfaite*, fr. fem. of *deffait, desfait*, past part.) + *-isme* -ism] **1 :** disbelief in the desirability of victory for one's own side under certain circumstances **2 :** the attitude, policy, or practice of accepting or of being resigned to defeat without any attempt to prevent or forestall it ⟨a mood of ~ overwhelmed them⟩ ⟨~ weakened the nation's ability to resist the enemy⟩

1de·feat·ist \-fēdəst, -ētə-\ *n* -S [F *défaitiste*, fr. *défaite* defeat + *-iste* -ist] **:** one who believes in, advocates, or is affected with defeatism **:** one who concedes defeat too readily

2defeatist \"\ *adj* **:** characterized by defeatism ⟨there was a ~ attitude about the proposal⟩ ⟨such talk is plainly ~⟩

defeatment *n* -S *obs* **:** DEFEAT

1de·fea·ture \də, dē+\ *n* -S [in sense 1, prob. fr. *de-* + *feature*; in sense 2, fr. *1defeat* + *-ure*] **1** *archaic* **:** DISFIGUREMENT ⟨careful hours . . . have written strange ~*s* on my face —Shak.⟩ **2** *obs* **:** DEFEAT

2defeature \"\ *vt* -ED/-ING/-S **:** DISFIGURE, DEFACE

1defecate *adj* [ME *deficate*, fr. L *defaecatus*, past part. of *defaecare*, fr. *de-* + *faec-, faex* dregs, lees] *obs* **:** freed from dregs or impurities **:** REFINED, PURIFIED

2def·e·cate \'defə,kāt, -fē,-, *esp Brit* 'dēf-; *usu* ād·+V\ *vb* -ED/-ING/-S [L *defaecatus*] *vt* **1 :** to free from impurities **:** CLARIFY, PURIFY, REFINE; *esp* **:** to clarify (juice for sugar production) by treating with a reagent (as lime), heating, and separating from scum and sediment **2 :** to free from that which is foreign, nonessential, or corrupting **:** PURGE ⟨~ religion of superstition⟩ **3 :** to discharge through the anus ⟨the seeds were *defecated* undigested⟩ ~ *vi* **:** to discharge feces from the bowels

def·e·ca·tion \,==ˈkāshən\ *n* -S [LL *defaecation-, defaecatio*, fr. L *defaecatus* + *-ion-, -io* -ion] **:** the act or process of defecating: as **a :** separation from impurities (as lees or dregs) **:** purification esp. of sugar **b :** discharge of feces

def·e·ca·tor \'==,kād·ə(r), -ātə-\ *n* -S **:** a tank in which cane juice is defecated **:** CLARIFIER

1de·fect \'dē,fekt *also* də'f- *or* dē'f-\ *n* -S [ME *defaicte* shortcoming, fr. MF *defect*, fr. L *defectus* lack, fr. *defectus* past part. of *deficere* to desert, fail, be wanting, fr. *de-* + *-ficere* (fr. *facere* to make, do) — more at DO] **1 :** an irregularity in a surface or a structure that spoils the appearance or causes weakness or failure **:** FAULT, FLAW ⟨carefully examine a piece of timber for ~*s*⟩ **:** SHORTCOMING ⟨a moral ~ in his nature⟩ ⟨several ~*s* can be found in this argument⟩ **2** [L *defectus*] **:** want or absence of something necessary for completeness, perfection, or adequacy in form or function **:** DEFICIENCY, WEAKNESS — opposed to *excess* ⟨laziness may be caused by a ~ of health⟩ ⟨a ~ in his hearing⟩ **syn** see ABSENCE, BLEMISH

2de·fect \də'fekt, dē'- *sometimes* 'dē,f-\ *vi* -ED/-ING/-S [L *defectus*, past part.] **1** *obs* **:** to become deficient **:** FAIL **2 :** to forsake or fall away from a cause or party esp. in order to embrace another **:** DESERT ⟨he ~*ed* to the West⟩

de·fec·ti·bil·i·ty \də,fektə'biləd·ē, (,)dē,-\ *n* -ES **:** inherent defectiveness **:** tendency to fall short of perfection

defectible *adj, obs* **:** liable to defect, failure, or error

de·fec·tion \də'fekshən, dē'-\ *n* -S [L *defection-, defectio*, fr. *defectus* (past part. of *deficere* to desert, fail, be wanting) + *-ion-, -io* -ion — more at DEFECT] **1 :** FAILING, FAILURE, LOSS ⟨fell into a ~ of spirit⟩ **2** *obs* **:** IMPERFECTION, DEFECT **3 :** the act of abandoning a person, cause, or doctrine to whom or to which one is bound by some tie (as of allegiance or duty) **:** DESERTION, APOSTASY

1de·fec·tive \-ktiv, -tēv *also* 'dē,f- *or* -təv\ *adj* [ME, fr. MF *defectif*, fr. OF, fr. LL *defectivus*, fr. L *defectus* + *-ivus* -ive] **1** *obs* **:** in error **:** at fault **2 :** wanting in something essential **:** falling below an accepted standard in regularity and soundness of form or structure ⟨a ~ imprint⟩ ⟨a ~ pane of glass⟩ or in adequacy of function ⟨a ~ mechanism⟩ ⟨~ eyesight⟩ **:** FAULTY, DEFICIENT, INSUFFICIENT ⟨~ method⟩ **3 a :** lacking one or more of the usual forms of grammatical inflection ⟨the ~ verb *quoth*⟩ **b** *of writing in a Semitic alphabet* **:** lacking a vowel letter to indicate a vowel sound — compare SCRIPTIO DEFECTIVA — **de·fec·tive·ly** \-tivlē, -li\ *adv*

2defective \"\ *n* -S **1 :** a word that lacks one or more of the usual forms of grammatical inflection ⟨the verb *ought* is a ~⟩ **2 :** a person who is subnormal physically or mentally; *specif* **:** one with marked stigmata or physical defects

defective delinquent *n* **:** an individual of abnormal intelligence who has manifested criminal or esp. psychopathic tendencies

de·fec·tive·ness \-tivnəs, -tēv- *also* -təv-\ *n* -ES **:** the quality or state of being defective

defective number *n* **:** DEFICIENT NUMBER

defective year *n* **:** a common year of 353 days or a leap year of 383 days in the Jewish calendar — see YEAR table

de·fect·less \'dē,fektləs *also* də'f- *or* dē'f-\ *adj* **:** being without a defect

defect of sex : disqualification for service (as jury duty) by reason of being a woman

de·fec·tor \də'fektə(r), dē'-, 'dē,f-\ *n* -S [L, fr. *defectus* (past part. of *deficere* to desert) + *-or* — more at DEFECT] **:** one that defects (as from a party or a doctrine)

de·fec·to·scope \də'fektə,skōp, dē'-\ *n* -S [*1defect* + *-o-* + *-scope*] **:** an instrument for detecting structural defects (as in a railroad rail)

defectuous *adj* [ML *defectuosus*, fr. L *defectus* defect + *-osus* -ous — more at DEFECT] *obs* **:** DEFECTIVE

def·e·da·tion \,defə'dāshən\ *n* -S [MF, fr. LL *defoedatus* (past part. of *defoedare* to pollute, fr. L *de-* + *foedare* to make ugly or filthy, fr. *foedus* ugly, filthy) + MF *-ion* — more at BEBUNG] *archaic* **:** POLLUTION, DEFILING

de·feminization \(ˌ)dē+\ *n* -S **:** loss of feminine qualities

de·feminize \(ˈ)dē+\ *vt* -ED/-ING/-S [*de-* + *feminine* + *-ize*] **:** to divest of feminine qualities or physical characteristics **:** MASCULINIZE

defence *chiefly Brit var of* DEFENSE

de·fend \də'fend, dē'-\ *vb* -ED/-ING/-S [ME *defenden*, fr. OF *defendre*, fr. L *defendere*, fr. *de-* + *-fendere* to strike; akin to OE *gūth* battle, war, OHG *gund-*, ON *gunnr* battle, war, Gk *theinein* to strike, Skt *hanti* he strikes, kills] *vt* **1** *archaic* **:** to ward or fend off **:** drive back or away **:** REPEL **2** *archaic* **:** PREVENT, FORBID, PROHIBIT ⟨which God ~ that I should wring from him —Shak.⟩ **3 :** to drive danger or attack away from **:** secure against attack **:** maintain against force **:** PROTECT, GUARD ⟨men ~*ing* their homes⟩ ⟨~ our shores⟩ — often used with *from* ⟨a floor . . . to the old woman's bones from the dampness —Ellen Glasgow⟩ **4 :** to maintain against argument or hostile criticism **:** UPHOLD, JUSTIFY ⟨~ a theory⟩ ⟨~*ed* his friend's behavior⟩; *specif* **:** to prove valid (as a doctoral thesis) by answering extempore questions asked by experts in an oral examination **5 :** to act as attorney for (an accused person) in criminal proceedings **6 :** to deny or oppose the right of a plaintiff in regard to (a suit or a wrong charged) **:** CONTROVERT **:** OPPOSE, RESIST ⟨~ a claim at law⟩ **:** CONTEST ⟨~ a suit⟩ ~ *vi* **1 :** to take action against attack or challenge ⟨the ~*ing* champion⟩ ⟨he preferred ~*ing* to attacking⟩; *specif* **:** to enter or make a defense in a legal action or suit **2** *in card games* **a :** to play against the high bidder **b :** to bid for the purpose of preventing an opponent from reaching an esp. advantageous bid

syn PROTECT, SHIELD, GUARD, SAFEGUARD: DEFEND may imply warding off what actually threatens or repelling what actually attacks or securing against attack ⟨to *defend* the settlers from the Indians⟩ ⟨the antitrust laws must constantly *defend* the ideal of industrial democracy against all sorts of pressures —T.W.Arnold⟩ PROTECT is somewhat wider and may imply shielding or guarding, sometimes as with a cover, from anything that might injure or destroy ⟨cherished and nurtured to strength by his mother, he may then *protect* and cherish another woman in his turn —Weston La Barre⟩ ⟨a refuge for deer, bear, and wildcats. It is *protected* by a private game warden —*Amer. Guide Series: N.C.*⟩ ⟨the ledge-lined harbor rimmed with well-kept estates affords a *protected* anchorage for a large yachting fleet —*Amer. Guide Series: Conn.*⟩ SHIELD suggests interposition of or as of a shield, screen, or other protective intervention against attack somewhat more imminent and specific than that suggested by PROTECT ⟨who *shielded* himself from importunate callers by an impassable barrage of clerks and secretaries —W.F.Hambly⟩ ⟨innocent, confessing to the crime to *shield* the real murderer, a close friend or relative who had a wife and many children —*Amer. Guide Series: Ariz.*⟩ GUARD implies protecting with vigilance, force, and strength ⟨to *guard* the pass against attack⟩ ⟨secret service men *guarding* the president⟩ ⟨the accumulation of private wealth in Boston, thriftily *guarded* by the canny Whigs —Van Wyck Brooks⟩ SAFEGUARD applies to any strong and careful protective measures against potential dangers and threats ⟨the proletariat, scared by the famine and the floods of the Tiber, looked to him to *safeguard* their precarious livelihood and their scanty pleasures —John Buchan⟩ ⟨tax reforms which will bring the most revenue to the government while *safeguarding* the best interests of our economy and the nation's investors —G.K.Funston⟩ ⟨Marge *safeguards* the reputation of the arresting policeman by riding with him when he takes the girl to the county clink —G.S. Perry⟩ **syn** see in addition MAINTAIN

de·fend·able \-dəbəl\ *adj* **:** DEFENSIBLE

1de·fend·ant \də'fendənt, dē'-\ *n* -S [ME *defendaunt*, fr. MF *defendant*, pres. part. of *defendre*, fr. OF] **1** *obs* **:** DEFENDER **2 :** a person required to make answer in an action or suit in law or equity or in a criminal action — opposed to *plaintiff*; see DEFEND 6

2defendant \", 'dē,f-\ *adj* [MF] **1 :** DEFENDING **:** being on the defensive **2** *obs* **:** DEFENSIVE

de·fend·er \də'fendə(r), dē'-\ *n* -S [ME *defendour, defender*, fr. OF *defendeor*, fr. *defendre* + *-eor* -or] **1 :** one that defends **:** PROTECTOR, ADVOCATE, CHAMPION, VINDICATOR, UPHOLDER **2** *Scots law* **a :** a party defendant in a legal proceeding — opposed to *pursuer* **b :** the lawyer acting for a party defendant in a legal proceeding

defender office *n* **:** a staff of lawyers whose duty is to defend poor persons charged with crime; *often* **:** such a staff holding public office

defender of the bond *or* **defender of the marriage tie** [translation of NL *defensor vinculi matrimonii*] *Roman Catholicism* **:** a diocesan official charged with defending the validity of the marriage bond in suits for annulment

defendress *n* -ES [*defender* + *-ess*] *obs* **:** a female defender

de·fen·es·tra·tion \(ˌ)dē,fenə'strāshən\ *n* -S [*de-* + L *fenestra* window + E *-tion* — more at FENESTRA] **:** a throwing of a person or thing out of a window ⟨the Thirty Years' War followed the ~ of deputies at Prague⟩

1de·fense \də'fen(t)s, dē'-, 'dē,f-\ *n* -S [ME *defens, defense*, fr. OF; OF *defens*, fr. ML *defensum*, fr. L, neut. of *defensus*, past part. of *defendere* to defend; OF *defense* fr. (assumed) VL *defensa*, fr. L, fem. of *defensus* — more at DEFEND] **1 a :** the act of defending ⟨the ~ of Moscow⟩ ⟨to die in ~ of liberty⟩ — opposed to *attack* **b :** a defendant's denial, answer, or plea **:** an opposing or denial of the truth or validity of the plaintiff's or prosecutor's case — compare ANSWER 2c **2 :** capability of resisting attack ⟨a football team weak in ~⟩ **:** practice or manner of self-protection ⟨the body's ~*s* against disease are weakened by hunger⟩ — usu. used in pl. **3 a :** means or method of defending ⟨weapons of ~⟩ **:** defensive plan, policy, or structure ⟨the inadequate ~*s* of the capital were easily penetrated by the enemy troops⟩ — usu. used in pl. **b :** the method and collected facts adopted by a defendant to protect himself against a plaintiff's action **c :** a sequence of moves available in chess to the second player in the opening; *also* **:** any opening having certain characteristic moves for the second player **d :** an argument prepared or advanced to defend an action, policy, or thesis **:** JUSTIFICATION **4 a :** defenders or the positions taken up by them ⟨ran through the ~ for a touchdown⟩ ⟨falsecarding to mislead the ~⟩ **b :** a cricket team's batting power or batsmen — contrasted with *attack* **5 :** a prohibitory ordinance **:** prohibition esp. of fishing or hunting ⟨the ~ months when fish are spawning⟩ — used chiefly in *in defense* ⟨trout streams were put *in defense*⟩

2defense \"\ *vt* -ED/-ING/-S [ME *defensen*, fr. MF *defenser*, fr. L *defensare*, fr. *defensus*, past part. of *defendere* to defend — more at DEFEND] **1** *obs* **:** to furnish with defenses **:** FORTIFY **2 a :** to impede the progress of (the football player or team in possession of the ball) ⟨he was thoroughly *defensed*⟩ **b :** to break up or defend against (a particular play) ⟨~ the single wing running pass⟩

defense in depth 1 : a tactical system of mutually supporting positions that are each capable of all-round defense and that have sufficient depth to prevent the enemy from achieving freedom of maneuver before his attack is broken up and absorbed **2 :** a strategic succession of defended areas which will permit continuation of a war after forward areas have been lost

de·fense·less \-ləs\ *adj* **:** being without defense **:** helpless against attack — **de·fense·less·ly** *adv* — **de·fense·less·ness** *n* -ES

defenseless mennonite *n, usu cap D&M* **:** a member of a conservative middlewestern religious group of Mennonites

de·fense·man \də'fen(t)smən, dē'-, -,man\ *n, pl* **defensemen :** a player in an athletic sport (as hockey) assigned to a defensive zone or position

defense mechanism *also* **defense reaction** *n* **1 :** a reaction whereby an organism defends itself (as against disease germs) **2 :** MECHANISM OF DEFENSE

de·fen·si·bil·i·ty \də,fen(t)sə'biləd·ē, (,)dē,-, -ətē, -i\ *n* -ES **:** the quality or state of being defensible

de·fen·si·ble \də'fen(t)səbəl, dē'-\ *adj* [ME, alter. (influenced by LL *defensibilis*, fr. L *defensus* — past part. of *defendere* to defend — + *-ibilis* -ible) of *defensable*, fr. OF, fr. LL *defensabilis*, fr. *defensare* to defend + *-abilis* -able — more at DEFEND, DEFENSE] **1 :** capable of being defended ⟨a ~ city⟩ **:** EXCUSABLE ⟨his action was ~ under those circumstances⟩ **2** *obs* **:** capable of offering defense — **de·fen·si·bly** \-blē, -li\ *adv*

1de·fen·sive \də'fen(t)siv, dē'-, 'dē,f-, -sēv *also* -səv\ *adj* [ME, fr. MF *defensif*, fr. ML *defensivus*, fr. L *defensus* (past part. of *defendere* to defend) + *-ivus* -ive] **1 :** serving to defend or protect **:** proper for defense **:** PROTECTIVE, SHIELDING ⟨a moat ~ to a house —Shak.⟩ **2 a :** devoted to resisting or preventing aggression or attack ⟨a ~ alliance⟩ ⟨~ strategy⟩ ⟨~ behavior⟩ — opposed to *offensive* **b** *cricket* **:** concerned with defense of the wicket rather than the scoring of runs — used of a batsman or his play **3** *obs* **:** DEFENSIBLE **4** *bridge* **a :** valuable in defensive play — used of a card that can be expected to win a trick against opponent's contract **b** *of a bid* **:** designed to keep opponent from being the highest bidder — **de·fen·sive·ly** \-sivlē, -li\ *adv* — **de·fen·sive·ness** \-sivnəs, -sēv- *also* -səv-\ *n* -ES

2defensive \"\ *n* -S [ME, fr. MF *defensif*, fr. *defensif*, adj.] **1** *obs* **:** something that defends **2 :** a defensive position — **on the defensive :** in a state or posture of defense or resistance **:** in opposition to an actual or expected aggression or attack

defensive allegation *n* **:** a pleading in English ecclesiastical law in which defendant does not deny plaintiff's allegations but avers special circumstances and facts constituting a matter thereby requiring plaintiff to answer upon oath the matter set up in defense

defensive gland *n* **:** REPUGNATORIAL GLAND

de·fen·sor \də'fen(t)sər, dē'-, -n,sȯ(ə)r\ *n* -S [ME *defensour*, fr. L *defensor*, fr. *defensus* (past part. of *defendere* to defend) + *-or* — more at DEFEND] **1** *obs* **:** DEFENDER **2 a** *Roman law* **:** one who voluntarily undertook the defense of a case and gave security to satisfy the judgment **b :** an advocate conducting the defense of a case in court **3** [LL, fr. L] **:** an advocate in the later Roman Empire: **a :** a municipal officer appointed to protect the people from oppression **b :** a layman or member of the clergy appointed to defend the rights and property of the church **4** [LL, fr. L] **:** the patron of a church **:** an officer having charge of the temporal affairs of a church

de·fen·sor·ship \-n(t)sər,ship\ *n* -S **:** the office of defensor

de·fen·so·ry \-n(t)s(ə)rē, -ri\ *adj* [LL *defensorius*, fr. L *defensus* + *-orius* -ory] **:** DEFENSIVE

1de·fer \də'fər, dē'-, +V -'fər·; -'fə, +V -'fər· *or* -'fə(r\ *vb* **deferred; deferred; deferring; defers** [ME *deferren, differren*, fr. MF *differer*, fr. L *differre* to postpone, be different — more at DIFFER] *vt* **1 :** DELAY ⟨God . . . will not long ~ to vindicate . . . His name —John Milton⟩: as **a :** to put off (a matter or person to be dealt with) deliberately to a future time ⟨*deferred* payment of a debt⟩ ⟨*deferred* talking with the boy⟩ **b :** to postpone induction of (a person) into military service **2** *obs* **:** to waste (time) by delay **:** PROLONG ~ *vi* **:** to delay to act **:** WAIT, PROCRASTINATE ⟨able to ~ and temporize at leisure —J.A.Symonds⟩

syn POSTPONE, INTERMIT, SUSPEND, STAY: DEFER indicates a delaying or putting off till a later time, often in recognition of developments that prevent proceeding ⟨reluctantly, he made up his mind to *defer* the more exacting examinations until another time —A.J.Cronin⟩ ⟨not more than three or four men could be found to continue the work, and its completion was long *deferred* —*Amer. Guide Series: Mich.*⟩ POSTPONE indicates a deferring, often until some set future time, although to *postpone* indefinitely means to cancel ⟨I think that we had better *postpone* our look round the church until after lunch —Compton Mackenzie⟩ ⟨let us *postpone* a final evaluation of Valla's treatise until after we have considered the handling of the selfsame problem by the English scholastic, Reginald Pecock —G.C.Selery⟩ INTERMIT suggests halting or delaying for a relatively short interval, usu. with the implication of a quick resumption ⟨seven centuries of hardly *intermitted* war created the Spanish people and they, the most medieval people in western Europe, created the Kingdom of Spain —Bernard DeVoto⟩ SUSPEND indicates a stopping or rendering inoperative for a time, usu. for a reason explicit or implicit in the context ⟨newspaper publication *suspended* during a strike⟩ ⟨shall I *suspend* final decision until I have further evidence? —M.R.Cohen⟩ ⟨had his driving license *suspended* for a month. Too many tickets —Raymond Chandler⟩ STAY suggests stopping activity or progress by or as if by interposing some obstacle ⟨an order *staying* the execution⟩ ⟨in September the injunction was *stayed* and on October 5 set aside by the Supreme Court —*Current Biog.*⟩ ⟨believing that by remaining neutral she could *stay* the forces of war —E.M.Coulter⟩

2defer \"\ *vb* **deferred; deferred; deferring; defers** [ME *deferen, differren*, fr. MF *deferer, deferer*, fr. LL *deferre*, fr. L, to bring down, bring, fr. *de-* + *ferre* to carry — more at BEAR (to carry)] *vt* **1 :** to refer or submit for determination or decision ⟨he could ~ his job to no one . . . if he did judge wrong, carnage on the carrier deck could be fearful —J.A. Michener⟩ ⟨the court ~*s* its own opinion to that of congress —C.P.Curtis⟩ **2 :** PROFFER, OFFER, TENDER ~ *vi* **:** to submit or yield through authority, respect, force, awe, propriety — used with *to* ⟨he assumed authority . . . everybody *deferred* to him —Ellen Glasgow⟩ **syn** see YIELD

def·er·ence \'def(ə)rən(t)s *also* -fərn-\ *n* -S [F *déférence*, fr. MF *deference*, fr. *deferer* to defer + *-ence*] **:** the act or attitude of deferring **:** a yielding of judgment or preference out of respect for the position, wish, or known opinion of another **:** courteous, complacent, or ingratiating regard for another's wishes ⟨the conquered population should be treated with extreme ~ —N.J.G.Pounds⟩ **syn** see HONOR — **in deference to** *prep* **:** in consideration of **:** in view of ⟨a shorter campaign . . . *in deference to* the belief . . . that television is *the* political weapon —Walter Goodman⟩

1def·er·ent \-f(ə)rənt\ *n* -S [ME *different*, fr. ML *deferent-, deferens*, fr. L, pres. part. of *deferre* to bring down, bring — more at DEFER] **:** an imaginary circle surrounding the earth in whose periphery, according to Ptolemy, either the celestial body or the center of its epicycle is supposed to move

2deferent \"\ *adj* [L *deferent-, deferens*, pres. part. of *deferre*] **1 :** serving to carry down or out ⟨a ~ conduit⟩ **2 :** of, relating to, or supplying the vas deferens ⟨~ arteries⟩ **3** [back-formation fr. *deference*] **:** 1DEFERENTIAL

1def·er·en·tial \,defə'renchəl\ *adj* [fr. *deference*, after such pairs as E *prudence: prudential*] **1 :** showing or expressing deference ⟨listened with ~ attention⟩ ⟨a ~ bow⟩ **2 :** given to deference ⟨the ~ nature of society —J.G.Pearson⟩ — **def·er·en·tial·ly** \-ch(ə)lē, -li\ *adv*

2deferential \"\ *adj* [2*deferent* + *-ial*] **:** 2DEFERENT 2

def·er·en·ti·al·i·ty \,defə,renchē'aləd·ē\ *n* -ES **:** the quality or state of being deferential

de·fer·ment \də'fərmənt, dē'-, -'fəm-\ *n* -S [1*defer* + *-ment*] **:** the act of delaying **:** POSTPONEMENT; *specif* **:** official postponement of induction into military service

1de·fer·ra·ble *also* **de·fer·able** \-'fərəbəl *also* -'fərə-\ *adj* [1*defer* + *-able*] **:** capable of or suitable for being deferred ⟨much ~ construction⟩ **:** eligible for deferment or such as renders one eligible for deferment esp. from compulsory military service

2deferrable \"\ *n* -S **:** one that is eligible for deferment

de·fer·ral \-'fərəl *also* -'fərəl\ *n* -S [1*defer* + *-al*] **:** DEFERMENT

deferred *adj* [fr. past part. of 1*defer*] **1 :** put off **:** ALLAYED, POSTPONED ⟨a ~ legal right⟩ **:** withheld for or until a stated time ⟨a ~ payment⟩ **2 :** charged in cases of delayed handling ⟨a ~ rate⟩; *also* **:** handled at a deferred rate ⟨~ telegram⟩

deferred annuity *n* **:** an annuity providing for the first payment to be made to the annuitant at some date later than the end of the first year following purchase

deferred bond *n* **1 :** a bond on which the payment of interest is postponed until some condition has been satisfied **2** *Brit* **:** a bond bearing interest at an increasing rate until a maximum is attained

deferred charge *or* **deferred asset** *n* **:** an expense (as a prepaid insurance premium or an inventory of supplies) that is incurred prior to the fiscal period to which it applies, temporarily carried on the books as an asset, and subsequently charged to expense at the appropriate time — called also *prepaid expense*

deferred credit *or* **deferred income** *or* **deferred liability** *n* **:** income received but not yet earned

deferred delivery *n* **:** delivery specified as deferred for some specified time — used of stocks and bonds ⟨sold, *deferred delivery* ten days⟩

deferred dividend *n* **:** an insurance dividend payable from the surplus accumulated during a given period to those policyholders only who are alive at its expiry and whose policies are then in force

deferred maintenance *n* **:** an amount needed but not yet expended for repairs, restoration, or rehabilitation of an asset

deferred shoot *n* **:** a shoot (as a water sprout) arising from a bud dormant for some time

deferred stock *n, chiefly Brit* **:** stock on which no dividend is payable until the happening of some contingent event (as the paying of a dividend on preferred stock)

de·fer·rer *R* də'fərər, dē'-, *-R* -'fər·ə(r *also* -'fərə(r\ *n* -S **:** one that defers

deferring *pres part of* DEFER

de·fer·ri·za·tion \(ˌ)dē,ferə'zāshən\ *n* -S [*de-* + L *ferrum* iron + E *-ization* — more at FARRIER] **:** removal of iron (as from water for industry)

defers *pres 3d sing of* DEFER

de·fer·vesce \ˌdē(ˌ)fər'ves, ˌdefər-\ *vi* -ED/-ING/-S [back-formation fr. *defervescence*] **:** to undergo defervescence

de·fer·ves·cence \ˌ=(ˌ)=ˈves³n(t)s\ *n* -S [G *deferveszenz*, fr. L *defervescent-, defervescens*, pres. part. of *defervescere* to stop boiling, cool down, fr. *de-* + *fervescere* to begin to boil, seethe — more at EFFERVESCE] **:** the subsidence of a fever

de·fer·ves·cent \ˌ=(ˌ)=ˈes³nt\ *adj* [back-formation fr. *defervescence*] **:** relating to, characterized by, or causing defervescence

de·fi \(')dā¦fē\ *n* -s [F *défi*, fr. MF *defi*, *desfi* — more at DEFY] : CHALLENGE, DEFIANCE

de·fi·al \də'fī(ə)l, dē'-\ *n* -s [¹*defy* + *-al*] *archaic* : DEFIANCE

de·fi·ance \də'fīən(t)s, dē'-\ *n* -s [ME *defyaunce*, fr. OF *desfiance*, *defiance*, fr. *desfier*, *defier* to defy + *-ance* — more at DEFY] **1** *obs* : a renunciation of allegiance or friendship **2** : act of defying, putting in opposition, or provoking to combat : CHALLENGE : a declaration of hostilities **3** : a state of opposition : willingness to fight : disposition to resist : contempt of opposition ⟨he breathed ~ to my ears —Shak.⟩ — **in defiance of** *prep* : in spite of : contrary to ⟨*in defiance of* the laws of physics⟩

de·fi·ant \-nt\ *adj* [F *défiant*, fr. OF *desfiant*, *defiant*, pres. part. of *desfier*, *defier* to defy] : full of defiance : BOLD, INSOLENT, UNAFRAID — **de·fi·ant·ly** *adv*

de·fiber \(')dē+\ *or* **de·fi·ber·ize** \(')dē'fībə,rīz\ *vt* -ED/-ING/-S [*defiber* fr. *de-* + *fiber* (n.); *defiberize* fr. *de-* + *fiber* + *-ize*] : DEFIBRATE

de·fi·brate \(')dē'fī,brāt\ *vt* -ED/-ING/-S [*de-* + L *fibra* fiber + E *-ate* — more at FIBER] : to separate (as a pulp sheet, waste paper, partly cooked wood) into its fibrous constituents — **de·fi·bra·tion** \,dē,fī'brāshən\ *n* -s

de·fi·bra·tor \(')dē'fī,brād·ə(r)\ *n* -s : a machine that defibrates

de·fi·bri·nate \(')dē+\ *vt* -ED/-ING/-S [*de-* + *fibrin* + *-ate*] : to remove fibrin from (blood) — **de·fi·bri·na·tion** \¦dē+\ *n* -s

deficience *n* -s [LL *deficientia*] *obs* : DEFICIENCY

de·fi·cien·cy \də'fishənsē, dē'-, -si\ *n* -ES [LL *deficientia*, fr. L *deficient-*, *deficiens* (pres. part. of *deficere* to be lacking) + *-ia* -y] **1** : the quality or state of being deficient : DEFECT, INADEQUACY ⟨so miserably ignorant that his *deficiencies* made him the ridicule of his contemporaries —H.T.Buckle⟩ **2** : inadequate amount : SHORTAGE: as **a** : a shortage of substances (as vitamins) necessary to health **b** : absence of one or more genes from a chromosome

deficiency account *n* : an account supplementing the balance sheet of a financially weak enterprise showing estimated realization values of assets and their insufficiency to meet creditors' claims and occas. indicating the causes of the difficulty

deficiency bill *n* **1** *Brit* : an advance made to the government by the Bank of England to meet a deficiency **2** : a legislative bill appropriating supplementary funds to meet a deficiency

deficiency disease *n* : a disease caused by a lack of one or more basic nutrients (as amino acids, minerals, or vitamins)

deficiency judgment *n* : a judgment for the balance of a debt after the security has been realized and the proceeds applied to payment; *esp* : such a judgment following foreclosure of a mortgage

¹de·fi·cient \də'fishənt, dē'-\ *adj* [L *deficient-*, *deficiens*, pres. part. of *deficere* to be lacking, fr. *de-* + *-ficere* (fr. *facere* to make, do) — more at DO] **1** : lacking in some quality, faculty, or characteristic necessary for completeness ⟨~ in judgment⟩ : not up to a normal standard : DEFECTIVE ⟨~ strength⟩ : needed to make up completeness ⟨by about one quarter of the whole amount⟩ **2** : having, relating to, or characterized by a gene deficiency — **de·fi·cient·ly** *adv*

²deficient \"\ *n* -s : one that is deficient ⟨percent of mental ~s institutionalized⟩

deficient number *n* : an imperfect number (as 8) that is greater than the sum of its divisors

def·i·cit \'defəsət, *rapid* -fsət, *usu* -əd·+V\ *n* -s [F *déficit*, fr. L *deficit* it is lacking, 3d pers. sing. pres. indic. of *deficere* to be lacking — more at DEFICIENT] **1** : deficiency in amount or quality ⟨a ~ in yearly rainfall⟩ : impairment of capital : a falling short esp. of income ⟨a ~ in revenue⟩ — opposed to *surplus* **2 a** : an excess of debit over credit items ⟨a ~ in a nation's balance of international payments⟩ **b** : a loss in business operations ⟨the year's operating ~⟩

deficit financing *n* : the financing of government expenditures by borrowing rather than by taxation

deficit spending *n* : the spending of public funds raised by borrowing rather than by taxation

de fi·de \(')dā'fē,dā\ *adj* [NL, fr. L, from faith] : held as an obligatory article of faith ⟨this doctrine of the Assumption is not *de fide* —John Dryden⟩

defied *past of* DEFY

de·fi·er \də'fī(ə)r, -īə\ *n* -s [*defy* + *-er*] : one that defies

defies *pl of* DEFY, *pres 3d sing of* DEFY

defiguration *n* -s [MF *defigurer*, *desfigurer* to disfigure + E *-ation* — more at DISFIGURE] *obs* : DISFIGURATION

¹def·i·lade \'defə,lād, -äd, -ād, ,≈≈'≈\ *vt* -ED/-ING/-S [prob. *de-* + *-filade* (as in *enfilade* (v.))] **1** : to arrange (fortifications) so as to protect the lines from frontal or enfilading fire and the interior of the works from plunging or reverse fire **2** : to protect by a natural or artificial mask against fire or observation from a given point

²defilade \"\ *n* -s [*de-* + *-filade* (as in *enfilade*, n.)] **1** : the act or process of defilading **2** : protection from observation or fire from the ground (as by a ridge, embankment, ravine)

¹de·file \də'fīl, dē'-, *esp before pause or consonant* -īəl\ *vt* -ED/-ING/-S [ME *defilen*, alter. (influenced by ME *filen* to defile) of *defoulen* to trample on, violate sexually, defile, fr. OF *defoler*, *defouler* to trample on, mistreat, fr. *de-* + *foler*, *fouler* to trample on, lit., to full (as cloth) — more at FULL (to thicken), FILE (to defile)] **1** : to make filthy : DIRTY, BEFOUL ⟨they that touch pitch will be *defiled* —Shak.⟩ **2** : to corrupt the purity or perfection of : DEBASE ⟨not even a tent *defiling* the primeval splendor —R.L.Neuberger⟩ **3** : to rob of chastity : RAVISH, VIOLATE **4** : to make ceremonially unclean : POLLUTE ⟨~ the temple⟩ **5** : TARNISH, DISHONOR ⟨*defiled* his memory with slander⟩ **syn** see CONTAMINATE

²defile \", 'dē,f-\ *vi* -ED/-ING/-S [F *défiler*, fr. *dé-* de- (fr. OF *de-*, *des-*) + *filer* to move in a column or columns (as of troops), fr. OF, to spin, fr. LL *filare*, fr. L *filum* thread — more at FILE (row)] : to march off or pass along in a line : file off

³defile *like* ²DEFILE\ *n* -s [F *défilé*, fr. past part. of *défiler*] **1** : a narrow passage in which troops can march only in a file or with a narrow front **2** : a long narrow pass (as between hills, rocks, or cliffs)

de·file·ment \də'fīlmənt, dē'-\ *n* -s [¹*defile* + *-ment*] : the act of defiling or state of being defiled : POLLUTION; *also* : something that defiles

de·fil·er \də'fīlə(r), dē'-\ *n* -s : one that defiles

de·fil·ing·ly *adv* : in a defiling manner

de·fin·abil·i·ty \də,fīnə'biləd·ē, dē,-\ *n* -ES : the quality or state of being definable

de·fin·able \də'fīnəbəl, dē'-\ *adj* [*define* + *-able*] : capable of being defined, limited, or explained : DETERMINABLE ⟨~ limits⟩ ⟨~ terms⟩ ⟨~ rules⟩ — **de·fin·ably** \-blē, -li\ *adv*

de·fine \də'fīn, dē'-\ *vb* -ED/-ING/-S [ME *definen*, *diffinen*, fr. MF & L; MF *definer*, *diffiner* to determine, bring to an end, fr. L *definire* to determine, bring to an end, explain, fr. *de-* + *finire* to limit, finish, end, fr. *finis* boundary, end — more at FINAL] *vt* **1** *obs* : to bring to an end : CONCLUDE; *often* : SETTLE ⟨*defined* the controversy⟩ : DECIDE, DETERMINE **2** : to fix, decide, or prescribe, clearly and with authority ⟨~ the power of a court by statutory enactment⟩ **3** : to mark the limits of : determine with precision or exhibit clearly the boundaries of ⟨~ the extent of a kingdom⟩ **4** : to make distinct in outline or features : bring into relief ⟨a tree *defined* against the sky⟩ ⟨a well-*defined* impression of an event⟩ ⟨the *defining* power of a lens⟩ **5 a** : to discover and set forth the meaning of (as a word or term); *specif* : to formulate a definition of **b** : to determine the essential qualities of (as a concept or thing) **c** : to determine the precise signification of **d** : DESCRIBE, EXPOUND, INTERPRET, EXPLAIN **6 a** *math* : to specify the construction or interpretation of (a concept) ⟨~ a conic section by a Cartesian equation⟩ **b** : to set apart in a class by identifying marks : CHARACTERIZE, DISTINGUISH ⟨good manners ~ the gentleman⟩ **c** : to establish in the mind so as to orient one's social reactions toward : IDENTIFY ⟨~ a situation as hostile⟩ ⟨~ a person as one of the four hundred⟩ ~ *vi* **1** *obs* **a** : to act as a judge in deciding or determining **b** : to deliver a precise opinion **2** : to formulate one or more precise statements of meaning : make a definition **syn** see PRESCRIBE

defined *adj* : clearly outlined, characterized, or delimited; *specif*, *of a culture medium* : consisting wholly of chemically identified substances in precisely determined proportions

de·fine·ment \-nmənt\ *n* -s [*define* + *-ment*] : the act of defining : DEFINITION

de·fin·er \-nə(r)\ *n* -s : one that defines

de·fin·i·en·dum \də,finē'endəm, ,dē,-\ *n*, *pl* **definien·da** \-də\ [L, neut. of *definiendus*, gerundive of *definire* to determine, bring to an end, explain — more at DEFINE] : whatever is being defined : the expression that precedes in a nominal definition the symbol of definitional equality — contrasted with *definiens*

de·fin·i·ens \də'finē,enz, dē'-\ *n*, *pl* **definien·tia** \də,finē'ench(ē)ə, (,)dē,-\ [L, pres. part. of *definire*] : whatever serves to define : the expression that follows in a nominal definition the symbol of definitional equality — contrasted with *definiendum*

¹def·i·nite \'def(ə)nət, *usu* -əd·+V\ *adj* [L *definitus*, past part. of *definire* to limit, determine, bring to an end — more at DEFINE] **1** : having distinct or certain limits : determinate in extent or character : LIMITED, FIXED ⟨~ dimensions⟩ ⟨a ~ period⟩ **2** : marked by absence of the ambiguous, obscure, doubtful, or tentative and by certain clear statement or expression by means of flat positive assertion, careful statement of limitation, or accepted, finished form ⟨whatever qualification of counter doctrine there was in his grouped arguments, there was none in the conclusion; and the ~ conclusion was what men wanted —H.O.Taylor⟩ **3 a** *of a grammatical modifier* : typically designating an identified or immediately identifiable person or thing ⟨*this* in "this card", *that* in "that house", *my* in "my father", *Paul's* in "Paul's absence" are ~ modifiers⟩ ⟨the ~ article *the*⟩ **b** *of an adjective form or set of adjective forms* : WEAK 8b **c** [F *défini*, fr. L *definitus*] (1) *of a verb form or set of verb forms in French* : typically denoting simple occurrence of an action without reference to its completeness or incompleteness, duration, or repetition — usu. used in the phrase *past definite* ⟨*je vis* "I saw" contains a past ~ verb⟩ (2) *of a verb form or set of verb forms in English* : PROGRESSIVE 7 **4 a** *of floral organs* : constant in number usu. less than 20 and in multiples of the petal number ⟨stamens ~⟩ **b** : CYMOSE **5** : REAL, ACTUAL ⟨ambition, which had been formless and remote, became ~ —Ellen Glasgow⟩ : POSITIVE, COGENT ⟨it is a ~ instrument for maldistribution of the world's income —J.A.Hobson⟩ **syn** see EXPLICIT

²definite \"\ *n* -s : a definite verb form or set of verb forms in a language

definite failure of issue : the failure of issue determined at a specific time that is or can become certain under the terms of an instrument creating estates in property (as upon the death of a designated person)

definite host *n* : DEFINITIVE HOST

definite integral *n* : the number obtained by finding an antiderivative of a function, substituting for the variable the first of two given numbers, then the second, and subtracting the second result from the first

definite integration *n* : the process of finding the definite integral of a function

def·i·nite·ly *adv* : in a definite way or manner : DISTINCTLY, UNMISTAKABLY, POSITIVELY

def·i·nite·ness *n* -ES : the quality or state of being definite

definite quadratic form *n* : a quadratic form that is always positive or always negative for every set of values of the variables involved in it except when all the variables are zero in which case the form has the value zero

definite–time \¦≈(≈)≈¦≈\ *adj* : having a purposely delayed action, the periods of delay being substantially alike regardless of the magnitude of the operating forces — used esp. of relays

def·i·ni·tion \,defə'nishən\ *n* -s [ME *diffinicioun*, fr. MF *diffinition*, *definition*, fr. L *definition-*, *definitio*, fr. *definitus* (past part. of *definire* to determine, bring to an end, explain) + *-ion-*, *-io* -ion — more at DEFINE] **1** : an act of determining or settling: as **a** *Roman Catholicism* : an official ecclesiastical statement concerning a matter of faith or of morals as pertaining to faith **b** : a prescribed or official standard for a commercial product ⟨the ~ for oatmeal prescribes that the amount of nitrogen contained shall not be less than 2.24 percent —*Scientific Monthly*⟩ **c** : the fixing or determination of social character ⟨personal status is a matter of social ~⟩ ⟨society has changed its ~ of women's political rights⟩ **2** : a word or phrase expressing the essential nature of a person or thing or class of persons or of things : an answer to the question "what is x?" or "what is an x?" **3 a** : a statement of the meaning of a word or word group ⟨the ~s in a dictionary⟩ **b** : the action or process of stating the meaning of a word or word group **4 a** *in Aristotelianism* : a determination of the real nature of a species by indicating both the genus that includes it and the specific differences or distinguishing marks **b** *in symbolic logic* (1) : an equation between a single symbol and a combination of symbols for which it is an abbreviation (as 1 = Df0[1] reading "1 is the successor of zero" where the special sign of equality indicates that the symbol on the left is always replaceable by the expression on the right) — see RECURSIVE DEFINITION (2) : a statement of the meaning to be attached to some symbols of a calculus when that calculus is given some particular interpretation (as $Sxy = x$ is the immediate successor of *y*) — called also *correlative definition*, *semantic definition*; see NOMINAL DEFINITION, PERSUASIVE DEFINITION, REAL DEFINITION **5 a** : the action or the power of making definite and clear or of bringing into sharp relief ⟨an emotion beyond ~⟩ ⟨the ~ of a telescope⟩ **b** : distinctness of outline or detail (as in a photograph) : clarity esp. of musical sound in reproduction **c** : sharp demarcation of outlines or limits ⟨a problem of clear ~⟩

def·i·ni·tion·al \¦≈≈¦≈shən°l, -shnəl\ *adj* : relating to definition : constituting a definition : employed in defining — **def·i·ni·tion·al·ly** \-°lē, -əlē\ *adv*

¹de·fin·i·tive \də'finəd·|iv, dē'-, -ət|\ *adj* [ME *diffinityf*, fr. MF *diffinitif*, *definitif*, fr. L *definitivus*, fr. *definitus* + *-ivus* -ive] **1** : serving to supply a final answer, solution, or evaluation and to end an unsettled unresolved condition ⟨a ~ victory⟩ ⟨~ surgical treatment⟩ **2** *archaic* : fixed and unalterable in opinion or judgment **3** : most authoritative, reliable, and complete usu. with the implication of final and perfected completeness or precision — used of research, scholarship, or criticism esp. of a biographical or historical study or of a text or edition of a literary work or author ⟨~ studies⟩ ⟨it is the ~ book on the ghost or near-ghost towns of the Old West —Vardis Fisher⟩ ⟨~ complete works⟩ ⟨the ~ review of this book has already been written —T.P.Thornton⟩ **4** : serving to define or specify precisely ⟨~ laws⟩ : DISTINGUISHING ⟨the term *communist*, orig. merely ~, has become loosely condemnatory⟩ ⟨species names are often ~ of the species⟩ **5** : exact, express, and clearly defined; *broadly* : real, actual, and positive : DEFINITE ⟨the fears and ~ disappointments of the period —Edmund Wilson⟩ ⟨a settled and ~ world order —Aldous Huxley⟩ **6** *biol* : COMPLETE : fully developed : FINAL ⟨a ~ organ⟩ — opposed to *immature*, *primitive* **7** *of a postage stamp* : issued as a regular stamp for the country or territory in which it is to be used — contrasted with *provisional* **syn** see CONCLUSIVE

²definitive \"\ *n* -s **1** *archaic* : a final judgment or sentence **2** : a definitive postage stamp

definitive callus *n*, *bot* : callus found in a sieve tube when it becomes or has become functionless

definitive host *n* : that host in which the sexual reproduction of a parasite takes place — compare INTERMEDIATE HOST

de·fin·i·tive·ly \|əvlē, -li\ *adv* : in a definitive way : FINALLY, DECISIVELY, UNALTERABLY

de·fin·i·tive·ness \|ivnəs, |ēv- *also* |əv-\ *n* -ES : the quality or state of being definitive

def·i·ni·tize \'defənə,tīz; də'fin-, dē'-\ *vt* -ED/-ING/-S : to make definite

def·i·ni·tor \'defə,nīd·ə(r), ,≈≈'≈≈\ *n* -s [ML, fr. LL, teacher, fr. L *definitus* (past part. of *definire* to determine, bring to an end, explain) + *-or* —more at DEFINE] **1** : an official charged under canon law with the supervision of ecclesiastical property in one of the districts into which a deanery is divided and with aiding the dean **2 a** : a member of the general chapter in some religious orders **b** : a member of the governing council of some religious orders chosen to aid the superior in the government of the order

de·fin·i·tude \də'finə,tüd, dē'- -ə·,tyüd\ *n* -s [¹*definite* + *-ude*] : PRECISION, DEFINITENESS

defis *pl of* DEFI

defix *vt* [ME *defixen*, fr. L *defixus*, past part. of *defigere*, fr. *de-* + *figere* to fasten, thrust in — more at DIKE] *obs* : FIX, FASTEN, ESTABLISH

def·la·grate \'deflə,grāt\ *vb* -ED/-ING/-S [L *deflagratus*, past part. of *deflagrare* to burn down, burn up, fr. *de-* + *flagrare* to burn — more at BLACK] *vt* : to cause or initiate deflagration in or of ~ *vi* : to burn rapidly : undergo deflagration — distinguished from *detonate*

deflagrating spoon *or* **deflagration spoon** *n* : a spoon with a long vertical handle used in deflagration experiments

def·la·gra·tion \,deflə'grāshən\ *n* -s [L *deflagration-*, *deflagratio*, fr. *deflagratus* + *-ion-*, *-io* -ion] : the process of deflagrating; *specif* : a chemical reaction producing vigorous evolution of heat and sparks or flame and moving through the material (as black powder or smokeless powder) at a speed less than that of sound — distinguished from *detonation*

de·flate \də'flāt, (')dē'-, *usu* -ād·+V\ *vb* -ED/-ING/-S [*de-* + *-flate* (as in *inflate*)] *vt* **1** : to release air or gas from (as a balloon or a tire) — opposed to *inflate* **2** : to reduce in size or importance : PUNCTURE ⟨~ a reputation⟩ ⟨*deflated* hopes⟩ ⟨~ pomposity⟩ **3** : to reduce (a price level) or contract (a volume of credit) esp. from an abnormally high level ~ *vi* : to lose firmness through the escape of air or gas (as of a balloon) : COLLAPSE, SAG **syn** see CONTRACT

de·fla·tion \-āshən\ *n* -s [*de-* + *-flation* (as in *inflation*)] **1** : an act or instance of deflating : the state of being deflated **2** : a contraction in the volume of available money or credit resulting in a decline of the general price level — contrasted with *inflation* **3** [L *deflatus* (past part. of *deflare* to blow off, fr. *de-* + *flare* to blow) + E *-ion* — more at BLOW] : WIND EROSION

deflagrating spoon

de·fla·tion·ary \də'flāshə,nerē, dē'-, -ri\ *adj* : relating to or productive of deflation ⟨~ signs⟩ ⟨~ measures⟩

deflationary gap *n* : a deficit in total disposable income relative to the current value of goods produced that is sufficient to cause a decline in prices and a lowering of production — compare INFLATIONARY GAP

¹de·fla·tion·ist \-sh(ə)nəst\ *n* -s : an advocate of deflation

²deflationist \"\ *adj* : tending to deflate : favoring deflation : DEFLATIONARY

de·fla·tive \də'flād·iv, (')dē¦f-\ *adj* : DEFLATIONARY

de·fla·tor \-d·ə(r)\ *n* -s : one that deflates; *specif* : a ratio or percentage by which monetary quantities are reduced to eliminate the effect of higher prices

de·flea \(')dē¦flē\ *vt* **deflead** \-ēd\ **deflead; defleaing; defleas** [*de-* + *flea* (n.)] : to rid of fleas

de·flect \də'flekt, (')dē¦f\ *vb* -ED/-ING/-S [L *deflectere* to bend downward, turn aside, fr. *de-* + *flectere* to bend, turn] *vt* : to turn from a straight course or fixed direction: **a** : BEND ⟨~ rays passing through a lens⟩ **b** : to change away from an accustomed, preferred, or likely course, pattern, or way to a goal ⟨~*ed* the course of the stream⟩ ~ *vi* : to turn aside : deviate from a straight line or from a position, course, or direction ⟨~ from the line of truth and reason —William Warburton⟩ **syn** see TURN

deflected *adj* : curved or turned downward ⟨a ~ septum⟩ — see DEFLEXED

de·flec·tion \-kshən\ *n* -s [L *deflexion-*, *deflexio*, fr. *deflexus* (past part. of *deflectere*) + *-ion-*, *-io* -ion] **1 a** : a turning aside : the state of being turned aside : a turning from a straight line or given course : a bending esp. downward : deviation esp. of a shot from its true course **b** : a result of bending or turning away : CURVE, BEND, TURN, DEVIATION **2** : the bending of one curve away from another or from a straight line **3 a** : the deviation of the neutral axis (as of a beam or girder) under stress from its normal position **b** : the vertical distance between the points of suspension in a suspension bridge and the axis of the lowest part of the chain **4 a** : the horizontal angle between the line of sighting and the axis of the bore of a gun **b** : a setting on the scale of a gunsight such that when the line of sighting is on the aiming point the piece is correctly laid for direction **5 a** : the turning aside or bending of radiation from a straight course ⟨~ of light due to diffraction⟩ ⟨~ of an electron beam in a magnetic field⟩ — called also *deviation* **b** : the angular departure of an indicator or pointer from the zero reading on a scale ⟨~ of an ammeter⟩ **6** [*de-* + *inflection*] : the loss of grammatical inflections

deflection bracket *n* : BRACKET 5a(2)

deflection offset *n* : the distance by which a bomb deviates to right or left of the vertical projection of the airplane path above the ground

deflection shooting *n* : the aiming of one's fire in aerial gunnery beyond a moving airplane to compensate for its movement

de·flec·tive \də'flektiv, (')dē¦f-\ *adj* : tending to deflect

de·flec·tom·e·ter \də,flek'tämәd·ə(r), (,)dē,-\ *n* [*deflect* + *-o-* + *-meter*] : an instrument for measuring minute deformations in bodies under transverse stress — compare EXTENSOMETER 2

de·flec·tor \də'flektə(r), (')dē¦f-\ *n* -s : one that deflects; *esp* : a baffle (as in a furnace or ventilating system or on a conveyor) to turn to one side part or all of the forward-moving stream (as of heated air)

de·flexed \-kst\ *adj* [L *deflexus* (past part. of *deflectere* to bend downward, turn aside) + E *-ed* — more at DEFLECT] **1** : DEFLECTED **2** *biol* : turned abruptly downward

de·flex·ion *chiefly Brit var of* DEFLECTION

de·floc·cu·lant *or* **de·floc·cu·lent** \(')dē'fläkyələnt\ *n* -s [*deflocculate* + *-ant* or *-ent*] : an agent that causes deflocculation; *specif* : a chemical (as sodium carbonate) added to a clay slip to minimize settling out

de·floc·cu·late \-,lāt\ *vt* [*de-* + *flocculate*] : to reduce or break up from a flocculent state : convert into very fine particles : disperse or maintain in a dispersed state — **de·floc·cu·la·tion** \(,)dē,fläkyə'lāshən\ *n* -s

def·lo·rate \'deflə,rāt, də'flōr,ā-, dē'-, -lō,rā-\ *vt* -ED/-ING/-S [ME *defloraten*, fr. LL *defloratus*, past part. of *deflorare* — more at DEFLOWER] : DEFLOWER

def·lo·ra·tion \,deflə'rāshən; də,flōr'ā-, (,)dē,-, -lō'rā-\ *n* -s [ME *defloracioun*, fr. LL *defloration-*, *defloratio*, fr. *defloratus* (past part. of *deflorare* to deprive of virginity, to cull excerpts from) + *-ion-*, *-io* -ion — more at DEFLOWER] **1** *archaic* : a gathering or culling of choice literary passages; *also* : the resulting collection : EPITOME **2** [ME *defloracioun*, fr. MF or LL; MF *defloration*, fr. LL *defloration-*, *defloratio*] : rupture of the hymen (as by sexual intercourse)

def·lo·res·cence \,deflə'res°n(t)s, ,dē,flōr'e-, ,dē,flō're-\ *n* -s [L *deflorescere* to fade, wither (fr. *de-* + *florescere* to blossom) + E *-ence* — more at FLORESCENCE] : the fading or disappearance of the eruption in an exanthematous disease

de·flower \(')dē *also* də+'-\ *vt* [ME *deflouren*, *defloren*, fr. MF or LL; MF *deflorer* fr. LL *deflorare*, fr. L *de-* + *flor-*, *flos* flower — more at FLOWER] **1** : to deprive of virginity : VIOLATE, RAVISH **2** : to take away the prime beauty and grace of : rob of the choicest ornament : RAVAGE, DESPOIL ⟨notion that any artist who accepts employment is ~*ed* of . . . integrity —*Advertising Age*⟩ **3** [prob. fr. *de-* + *flower*] : to deprive or strip of flowers ⟨an earthquake . . . ~*ing* the gardens —Walter Montagu⟩

¹def·lu·ent \'de,flüənt, 'defləwənt\ *adj* [L *defluent-*, *defluens*, pres. part. of *defluere* to flow down, fr. *de-* + *fluere* to flow — more at FLUENT] : flowing down : DECURRENT

²defluent \"\ *n* -s : something that flows down (as from a lake or icecap)

de·fluorinate \(')dē+\ *vt* [*de-* + *fluorinate*] : to remove fluorine from ⟨*defluorinated* phosphate rock⟩ — **de·fluorina·tion** \(¦)dē+\ *n* -s

de·flu·vi·um \dē'flüvēəm\ *n* -s [NL, fr. L, alopecia, lit., action of flowing down, fr. *defluere* to flow down] : the pathological loss of a part — used of hair, nails, or tree bark

deflux *n* -ES [L *defluxus*, fr. *defluxus*, past part. of *defluere*] *obs* : DEFLUXION

de·flux·ion \də'fləkshən, dē-\ *n* -s [LL *defluxion-*, *defluxio*, fr. L *defluxus* + *-ion-*, *-io* -ion] **1** : DOWNFLOW **2** *obs* **a** : a flowing down of fluid matter (as a copious discharge from the nose in catarrh) **b** : INFLAMMATION **c** : sudden loss of hair

de·foam·er \(ˈ)dēˈfōmə(r)\ *n* -s [*defoam* "to remove the foam from" (fr. *de-* + *foam*, n.) + *-er*] : a defoaming agent
de·foam·ing \-miŋ\ *adj* [fr. pres. part. of *defoam*] : destroying or preventing the formation of foam ⟨a ~ agent⟩
defoedation *var of* DEFEDATION
de·fo·li·ant \(ˈ)dēˈfōlēənt\ *n* -s [*defoliate* + *-ant*] : a chemical spray or dust applied to crop plants (as cotton that is to be harvested with a stripper) to cause the leaves to drop off prematurely
¹de·fo·li·ate \(ˈ)dēˈfōlēˌāt\ *vt* [LL *defoliatus*, past part. of *defoliare*, fr. L *de-* + *folium* leaf — more at BLADE] : to strip of leaves : cause the leaves of to fall esp. prematurely — **de·fo·li·a·tion** \(ˌ)dēˌfōlēˈāshən\ *n* -s
²de·fo·li·ate \(ˈ)dēˈfōlēət, -ēˌāt\ *or* **de·fo·li·at·ed** \-ēˌād·əd\ *adj* [LL *defoliatus*] : deprived of leaves (as by their natural fall)
de·fo·li·a·tor \-ēˌād·ə(r)\ *n* -s : one that defoliates: as **a** : an insect that strips plants of their leaves **b** : DEFOLIANT
de·force \(ˈ)dē +\ *vt* [ME *deforcen*, fr. AF *deforcer*, fr. OF *deforcier*, fr. *de-* + *forcier* to force — more at FORCE] **1** : to keep by force from the rightful owner : withhold wrongfully (as the possession of lands or tenements) **2** : to eject (a person) from possession by force : forcibly withhold possession from : deprive wrongfully **3** *Scots law* : to oppose or resist (an officer) forcibly so as to prevent execution of the law — **de·force·ment** \-smənt\ *n* -s
de·force·or \-sə(r)\ *n* -s [AF *deforceor*, fr. *deforcer* + *-eor* -or] : one that deforces
de·for·ciant \dēˈfōrshənt, -fȯr-\ *n* -s [AF, fr. pres. part. of *deforcer*] *English law* : one who deforces the rightful owner of an estate
de·forest \(ˈ)dē +\ *vt* [*de-* + *forest* (n.)] : to clear of forests : remove trees from — **de·forestation** \(ˌ)dē +\ *n* -s — **de·forester** \(ˈ)dē +\ *n* -s
¹de·form \dəˈfȯ(ə)rm, dēˈ-, -ō(ə)m\ *adj* [ME *deforme*, fr. L *deformis*, fr. *de-* + *-formis* (fr. *forma* shape, form) — more at FORM] *archaic* : DEFORMED, MISSHAPEN, SHAPELESS, HIDEOUS
²deform \"\ *vb* -ED/-ING/-S [ME *deformen*, fr. MF or L; MF *deformer*, fr. L *deformare*, fr. *de-* + *formare* to shape, form — more at FORM] *vt* **1** : to spoil the form or shape of : MISSHAPE, DISTORT ⟨~ the groove walls of a phonograph record⟩ **2** : to spoil the looks of : DISFIGURE, DEFACE ⟨a face ~*ed* by hatred and bitterness⟩ : mar the excellence or perfection of ⟨the minor characters are . . . ~*ed* by conditions beyond their power to change —Malcolm Cowley⟩ : make offensive ⟨~*ed* by marriage, irritable, acerb —George Meredith⟩ **3** : to alter the form or shape of: **a** *obs* : to unsettle the order of (as ranks of battle) **b** : to change the shape of (a body) by the action of forces **c** : to fold, fracture, compress, or otherwise change the shape or attitude of (rocks) by stresses developed within the earth ~ *vi* : to become deformed : change in shape ⟨certain metals will ~ permanently without breaking⟩
syn DISTORT, CONTORT, WARP, GNARL: DEFORM, the least specific of this group, applies to any marring or spoiling esp. resulting in disfigurement or loss of some particular good or normal quality or attribute ⟨basaltic and granitic rocks are seen *deformed* side by side in deeply eroded parts of the earth's surface —W.H.Bucher⟩ ⟨he was really hideous, positively *deformed* with malice —Christopher Isherwood⟩ ⟨a dread that it should cramp and *deform* the free operations of his own mind —T.S.Eliot⟩ DISTORT strongly implies a twisting or wrenching away from or out of the natural, regular, or true or, in application to intangibles, an imbalance or lack of reasonable proportion ⟨under such a light the features of the subject are sometimes *distorted*, as in a passport photograph —Hallett Smith⟩ ⟨news was *distorted* in his favor —S.H.Adams⟩ ⟨*distorting* facts to suit theories —R.A.Hall b.1911⟩ CONTORT implies a more involved or intense twisting together or upon itself, suggesting a grotesque or painful result ⟨the boy whose face was *contorted* with fury and frustration —Jean Stafford⟩ ⟨*contorted* thickets of lodgepole pine —*Amer. Guide Series: Oregon*⟩ ⟨their shadows *contorted* themselves grotesquely —Israel Zangwill⟩ WARP is literally a twisting or bending out of a flat plane and figuratively a twisting or wrenching that gives bias, false significance, or abnormal direction ⟨boards *warped* by exposure to the sun and rain⟩ ⟨their lives and minds have been *warped*, twisted and soured —John Lardner⟩ ⟨it degrades the individual and *warps* the nation's moral fabric⟩ GNARL implies, in literal use, the twistings and contortions, knots and protuberances of the roots or branches of an old tree; in extended use it suggests a condition similar to this as in the hands or limbs of the very old, the arthritic, or those who have long done heavy physical work, especially exposed to all weathers ⟨in the old orchard the trees are *gnarled* and broken —Corey Ford⟩ ⟨he was slight, dark, *gnarled*, with a face on him like a knotty piece of old mahogany —Alan Villiers⟩ ⟨the battlefields, *gnarled* by trenches, barbed-wire entanglements, shell holes —H.S.Commager⟩
de·for·ma·tion \ˌdēˌfȯ(r)ˈmāshən, ˌdefə(r)-\ *n* -s [ME *deformacioun*, fr. MF or L; MF *deformation*, fr. L *deformation-, deformatio*, fr. *deformatus* (past part. of *deformare* to deform) + *-ion-, -io* -ion — more at DEFORM] **1** : the action of deforming or state of being deformed **2** : change for the worse — opposed in theological use to *reformation* **3 a** : the process whereby rocks are folded, faulted, sheared, or compressed by earth stresses (as in the growth of mountain ranges) — see DIASTROPHISM **b** : the result of the process **4** : change in either shape or size of a material body or of a geometrical figure — compare STRAIN 1d
de·for·ma·tion·al \ˌ;=(ˌ)=ˈmāshənᵊl, -shnəl\ *adj* : relating to or causing deformation
deformation band *n* : a band within an individual cold-worked metal crystal that differs variably from the matrix in orientation
de·for·ma·tive \dəˈfȯ(r)məd·iv, dēˈ-\ *adj* [*deformation* + *-ive*] : tending to deform
deformed *adj* [ME, fr. past part. of *deformen* to deform] **1** *obs* **a** : DISFIGURED **b** : FORMLESS, AMORPHOUS **2 a** : distorted or unshapely in form : misshapen esp. in body or limbs : MONSTROUS, LOATHSOME ⟨a ~ imagination⟩ **b** : subjected to deformation — **de·formed·ly** \-m(ə)dlē\ *adv* — **de·formed·ness** \-mədnəs, -m(d)n-\ *n* -ES
deformed bar *n* : a steel bar with surface projections that increase its bond strength when used in reinforced concrete
de·for·me·ter \-ˈfȯ(r),mēd·ə(r)\ *n* [blend of *deformation* and *-meter*] : an instrument for measuring small deformations (as of structural materials)
de·for·mi·ty \dəˈfȯ(r)məd·ē, dēˈ-, -ətē, -i\ *n* -ES [ME *deformite*, fr. MF *deformité*, fr. L *deformitat-, deformitas*, fr. *deformis* deformed + *-tat-, -tas* -ty — more at DEFORM] **1** : the state of being deformed **2** : a conspicuous departure from regularity in shape or appearance : DISFIGUREMENT ⟨acne . . . so pronounced as to amount to positive ~ —H.G.Armstrong⟩ : a physical blemish or distortion : MALFORMATION ⟨the dwarf's humpbacked ~⟩ **3 a** : the state or result of having deviated from what is accepted as right, proper, or beautiful esp. in art or in moral behavior : UGLINESS, DEPRAVITY ⟨all the perversities and *deformities* of humanity —Dudley Fitts⟩ **b** : FLAW, IMPROPRIETY, CORRUPTION ⟨if he attempted decoration, seldom produced any thing but *deformity* —T.B.Macaulay⟩ **4** : a deformed person or thing ⟨hardly men, mere walking *deformities*⟩
¹de·fraud \dəˈfrȯd, dēˈ-\ *vb* -ED/-ING/-S [ME *defrauden*, fr. MF *defrauder*, fr. L *defraudare*, fr. *de* + *fraudare* to cheat, fr. *fraud-, fraus* fraud, deceit — more at DREAM] *vt* : to take or withhold from (one) some possession, right, or interest by calculated misstatement or perversion of truth, trickery, or other deception ⟨~ the heirs of the bequests⟩ ⟨citizens ~*ed* of their voting rights⟩ ~ *vi* : to engage in fraud **syn** see CHEAT
²defraud \"\ *n* -s [ME, fr. *defrauden*, v.] *archaic* : DEFRAUDATION
de·frau·da·tion \(ˌ)dēˌfrȯˈdāshən, dəˌ-\ *n* -s [MF, fr. LL *defraudation-, defraudatio*, fr. L *defraudatus* (past part. of *defraudare* to defraud) + *-ion-, -io* -ion] : the act of defrauding : a taking by fraud or deceit
de·fraud·ment \dəˈfrȯdmənt, dēˈ-\ *n* -s : DEFRAUDATION
de·fray \dəˈfrā, dēˈ-\ *vt* -ED/-ING/-S [MF *deffrayer, desfrayer*, fr. *des-* de- + *frayer* to expend, fr. OF, fr. (assumed) OF *frai* expenditure (whence OF *fres*, pl., expenditures), lit., damage caused by breaking something, fr. L *fractum*, neut. of *fractus*, past part. of *frangere* to break — more at BREAK] **1** *obs* **a** : to expend (money) : DISBURSE **b** : to avert or appease (as anger, vengeance) by paying off : REQUITE, SATISFY **2** : to pay or to provide for the payment of in money or its equivalent ⟨~ the expenses of a trip⟩ **3** *archaic* **a** : to meet the charges for or expense of **b** : to bear the expenses of (a person) : entertain without charge : REIMBURSE
de·fray·al \-ā(ə)l\ *n* -s : the act of defraying : PAYMENT
de·fray·ment \-āmənt\ *n* -s [MF *deffrayement*, fr. *deffrayer* + *-ment*] : DEFRAYAL
de·frock \(ˈ)dē;fräk\ *vt* [*de-* + *frock* (n.)] : UNFROCK
de·frost \(ˈ)dē + ;-, də + ˈ-\ *vb* -ED/-ING/-S [*de-* + *frost* (n.)] *vt* **1** : to thaw out or release from a frozen state ⟨~*ed* the meat for supper⟩ ⟨~*ed* some projects they had been holding in reserve⟩ **2** : to free or keep free (as a refrigerating unit, a windshield) from ice ~ *vi* : to thaw out esp. from a deep-frozen state ⟨heavily sugared foods are the first to ~⟩
de·frost·er \-tə(r)\ *n* : one that defrosts; *esp* : a device for freeing a windshield from frost or ice
deft \ˈdeft\ *adj* -ER/-EST [ME *defte* — more at DAFT] **1** : characterized by light neat facility and sure quick skill in handling or execution ⟨a ~ waiter⟩ ⟨the ~ handling of suspense —T.S. Eliot⟩ **2** *dial Eng* : NEAT, SPRUCE, TRIM **syn** see DEXTEROUS
deft *abbr* defendant
def·ter·dar \ˌdeftərˈdär\ *n* -s [Turk, fr. Per *daftardār* finance officer — more at DAFTARDAR] : a Turkish government officer of finance; *specif* : the accountant general of a province
deft·ly \ˈdeftlē, -li\ *adv* [ME *defly*, fr. *defte* deft + *-ly*] : in a deft manner : SKILLFULLY, DEXTEROUSLY, NEATLY
deft·ness \-f(t)nəs\ *n* -ES : the quality of being deft : DEXTERITY, NEATNESS, QUICKNESS
¹de·funct \dəˈfəŋ(k)t, dēˈ-\ *n* -s [L *defunctus*, past part. of *defungi* to acquit oneself, die, fr. *de-* + *fungi* to perform, discharge — more at FUNCTION] : a dead person — usu. used with *the*
²defunct \dəˈfəŋ(k)t, (ˈ)dē;f-\ *adj* [L *defunctus*] : having finished the course of life or existence : DEAD, DECEASED, EXTINCT ⟨a ~ aunt's will⟩ ⟨a ~ journal⟩ ⟨~ economic theory⟩
de·func·tion \dəˈfəŋ(k)shən, dēˈ-\ *n* -s [LL *defunction-, defunctio*, fr. L *defunctus*] : DEATH, DECEASE
de·functionalize \(ˈ)dē +\ *vt* [*de-* + *functional* + *-ize*] : to deprive of function
de·func·tive \dəˈfəŋ(k)tiv, dēˈ-\ *adj* [L *defunctus* + E *-ive*] : FUNEREAL
¹defuse *obs var of* DIFFUSE
²de·fuse *also* **de·fuze** \(ˈ)dē +\ *vt* [*dē* + *fuse, fuze* (n.)] : to remove the fuse from (as a mine or bomb)
de·fusion \"+\ *n* [*de-* + *fusion*] : a reversal of the fusion between instincts that accompanies maturity
¹de·fy \dəˈfī, dēˈ-\ *vt* -ED/-ING/-ES [ME *defyen*, fr. OF *desfier, defier*, fr. *des-, de-* de- + *fier* to entrust, confide, fr. (assumed) VL *fidare*, alter. of L *fidere* to trust — more at BIDE] **1** *archaic* **a** : to renounce all bonds of faith or obligation with : REJECT, REPUDIATE **b** : to declare war against : challenge to combat **c** : DESPISE, DISDAIN **2** : to seek to provoke or goad (a person, agency, or power) into trying to perform, do, or achieve something typically with mocking certainty that the attempt will fail ⟨I ~ him to find the Gate, however well he may think he knows the City —Rudyard Kipling⟩ **3** : to confront (a person, agency, force) with or as if with a superior resisting force felt as certain to prevail, vanquish, or baffle : withstand or contravene (as treatment or influence) with assured power of resistance ⟨the tall erect figure, ~*ing* age, and the perfectly bald scalp ~*ing* the weather —Upton Sinclair⟩ ⟨every great novel has broken many conventions. The greatest of all novels *defies* every formula —Ellen Glasgow⟩ **syn** see FACE
²defy \", ˈdē,fī\ *n* -ES [MF *defi, desfi*, fr. *defier, desfier* to defy, fr. OF] : CHALLENGE, DEFIANCE ⟨observers took this to be a form of ~ —Jack Alexander⟩
de·fy·ing·ly *adv* : in a defying manner : with defiance : DEFIANTLY
deg \ˈdeg\ *vt* **degged**; **degged**; **degging**; **degs** [perh. of Scand origin; akin to ON *döggva* to bedew, *dagg-, dögg* dew — more at DEW] *dial Eng* : to sprinkle : DAMPEN
deg *abbr* degree
dé·ga·gé \ˌdā,gäˈzhā, -gȧ-\ *adj* [F, fr. past part. of *dégager* to redeem a pledge, disengage, free from, fr. OF *desgagier*, fr. *des-* de- + *gage* pledge, security — more at GAGE] **1** : free of mental engagement and constraint of manner : carefree and indifferent to decorum : EASYGOING ⟨I adopted a ~ pose on the arm of a Morris chair —S.J.Perelman⟩ ⟨rather ~ after the nervousness he had shown at dinner —Edmund Wilson⟩ **2** : marked by a free and easy show of unconcern for strict conventions ⟨the famous slouch hat with the nonchalant ~ air —A.J.Liebling⟩ ⟨a model of crushed pink velvet dipped low over one eye and soaring in a ~ movement on the opposite side —*Hats*⟩ **3** *of the leg* : extended with toe pointed in preparation for a ballet step
degame *var of* DAGAME
de·gas \(ˈ)dē +\ *vt* [*de-* + *gas* (n.)] : to free from gas : remove gas from ⟨~ an electronic tube⟩
de·gasification \(ˈ)dē +\ *n* -s : the process of degasifying
de·gasify \(ˈ)dē + ˈ-\ *vt* [*de-* + *gasify*] : DEGAS
de gaull·ism \dəˈgō,lizəm, dēˈ-, -gō,-\ *n*, *usu cap G* [F *de Gaullisme*, fr. Charles *de Gaulle* b1890 Fr. general & president + F *-isme* -ism] : GAULLISM
de gaull·ist \-ˌləst\ *n*, *usu cap G* [F *de Gaulliste*, fr. C. *de Gaulle* + F *-iste* -ist] : GAULLIST
de·gauss \(ˈ)dē +\ *vt* -ED/-ING/-ES [*de-* + *gauss*] : to make (a steel ship) effectively nonmagnetic by means of electrical coils carrying currents that neutralize the magnetism of the ship itself and thereby prevent the detonating of magnetic mines — compare DEPERM
de·gen·er·a·cy \dəˈjen(ə)rəsē, dēˈ-, -si\ *n* -ES [*degenerate* + *-cy*] **1 a** : the state of being degenerate : DEGRADATION, DEBASEMENT ⟨centuries of ~ and transition —H.O.Taylor⟩ ⟨would it have committed suicide in an isolated act of intellectual and moral ~ —H.J.Morgenthau⟩ **b** : a state or instance of deteriorated or disintegrated energy or control ⟨simplifications and even *degeneracies* —J.A.Thomson⟩ **2** : the process of becoming degenerate : a decline to inferior standards of behavior, morality, culture, or art ⟨our progress in ~ appears to me to be pretty rapid —Abraham Lincoln⟩ ⟨moral ~ followed intellectual degeneration⟩ ⟨how can we prevent the ~ of man in modern civilization —Alexis Carrel⟩ **3** : sexual perversion
¹de·gen·er·ate \-n(ə)rət, *usu* -əd· + V\ *adj* [ME *degenerat*, fr. L *degeneratus*, past part. of *degenerare* to degenerate, fr. *de-* + *gener-, genus* race, kind — more at KIN] **1** : having sunk to a lower class or standard or to a state below that normal to a type or to a thing: **a** (1) : having declined markedly (as in vigor and stability or in racial or cultural character) from one's ancestors, predecessors, or one's former self ⟨just as the last ~ member of a noble family may be unattractive and uninspiring —W.E.Swinton⟩ (2) : losing distinctive racial culture : RETROGRADE ⟨the Mayas were ~ but they were stubborn —*Time*⟩ **b** : having deteriorated from a former level : DEVITALIZED, CORRUPTED ⟨Savonarola's ecclesiastical superior officer . . . was a monster of perfidy and immorality; and a despairing and ~ world had sunk into servitude beneath him —W.L.Sullivan⟩ ⟨the modern and ~ society, which had rejected the governance of religion —J.C.Ransom⟩ **c** : degraded or debased by loss of moral stability, aesthetic concord, or political integrity ⟨the studies of notorious ~ families prove nothing very significant about the inheritance of degeneracy —R.M.Lindner⟩ ⟨preferred to prop up an effete and ~ dynasty rather than face a vigorous reformed China —G.F.Hudson⟩ ⟨the profession of painting . . . has esthetically, morally, and in certain quarters even politically become a thoroughly ~ one —Huntington Hartford⟩ **d** : having deteriorated progressively (as in the process of evolution) esp. through loss of structure or function — compare DEGENERATION 3b **2** : characterized by lowered standards ⟨the great wrought nails binding the clapboards are unknown in these ~ days —Herman Melville⟩ **3** : breaking up into a product of factors of lower degree — used of an algebraic curve or surface **4** *of a gas* : characterized by having atoms stripped of most if not all of their electrons as the result of extremely high pressure and temperature in the interior of a very dense star (as a white dwarf) and by being compressed to a density as high as a million times that of water so that the ordinary laws of a perfect gas do not apply **syn** see VICIOUS
²de·gen·er·ate \-nə,rāt, *usu* -ād· + V\ *vb* -ED/-ING/-S [L *degeneratus*] *vi* **1** *obs* **a** : to show a decline from ancestral or earlier character and quality **b** : to show variation from normal type **2** : to pass from a higher to a lower type or condition: **a** : to descend to a markedly worse condition in kind or degree : worsen conspicuously ⟨the road . . . *degenerated* to little more than a goat track —Michael Swan⟩ ⟨its fine houses one by one *degenerating* into rooming houses —Marcia Davenport⟩ ⟨her fixed mysterious smile *degenerated* into a fatuous stare —J.C.Powys⟩ **b** : to become unstable and sink to some discreditable, despicable, or disastrous state ⟨unfortunately, in practice, rotation in office *degenerated* into the spoils system —E.M.Eriksson⟩ ⟨debate was *degenerating* into partisan squabbling⟩ ⟨lest this international crisis ~ into world war⟩ **c** : to decline to an unworthy secondary status through impairment of essential quality or integrity ⟨the phrase which they have reiterated ad nauseam has *degenerated* into a ponderous platitude —W.F.Hambly⟩ ⟨has not lost its dignity or *degenerated* into mere prettiness —O. Elfrida Saunders⟩ ⟨religion is tending to ~ into a decent formula wherewith to embellish a comfortable life —A.N.Whitehead⟩ **3** : to decline intellectually or morally or from one's peculiar character or former standards usu. to a shameful or despicable level ⟨mentally and physically the Indians *degenerated* with the taking on of the white men's vices —*Amer. Guide Series: Mass.*⟩ ⟨of heroic stature but ultimately *degenerating* into a typical medieval dictator —R.A.Hall b.1911⟩ **4** : to decline from a former thriving state or from standards proper to a species or race : RETROGRADE ⟨dinosaurs *degenerated* and disappeared⟩ ⟨mallards are prone anyway to ~ into the barnyard type —W.L.McAtee⟩ ⟨all through the evolution of life many forms have *degenerated*, losing their relative autonomy and becoming dependent parasites upon other creatures —Curt Stern⟩ **5** : to decline in literary, aesthetic, or artistic quality and become altered to a debased substitute or poor imitation ⟨denunciation of the rampant charlatanism into which the surrealist movement has apparently *degenerated* —Bernard Smith⟩ ⟨their metaphor ~*s* into a series of isolated and barren conceits —C.D.Lewis⟩ **6** *biol* : to undergo progressive deterioration : become of a lower type — see DEGENERATION 3 ~ *vt* : to cause to degenerate ⟨the Etruscans were receptive to new ideas and applied them with energy, usually only to ~ them in the end —A.L.Kroeber⟩
³de·gen·er·ate *like* ¹DEGENERATE\ *n* -s [¹*degenerate*] : a person declining conspicuously from the normal character or the standard set by his kind in the normal course of development: as **a** : one who is degraded from the normal moral standard ⟨they had rotted in the last two centuries into mere drunkards and dandy ~*s* —G.K.Chesterton⟩ ⟨~*s* are usually about the same type as psychopathics, namely, individuals who intellectually and especially affectively react differently from the average —A.A.Brill⟩ **b** : one who is debased by a psychopathic tendency ⟨he has an urge to kill and destroy women . . . he may be considered a sexual psychopath and ~ —Fred Galvin⟩ **c** : a sexual pervert — not used technically **d** : one showing signs of reversion to an earlier culture stage ⟨it is possible that some of these are cultural ~*s*; most ethnologists, however, prefer to regard the majority as culturally retarded —R.W.Murray⟩
de·gen·er·ate·ly \-ətlē, -li\ *adv* : in a degenerate manner
de·gen·er·ate·ness \-ətnəs\ *n* -ES : DEGENERACY
de·gen·er·a·tion \dəˌjenəˈrāshən, (ˌ)dē,-\ *n* [F or LL; F *dégénération*, fr. LL *degeneration-, degeneratio*, fr. L *degeneratus* + *-ion-, -io* -ion] **1** : the process of passing from a higher to a lower type: **a** : a lowering of effective power, vitality, or essential quality to an enfeebled and worsened kind or state ⟨that ~ and enhancement were processes that went on side by side in the stream of oral transmission —Douglas Kennedy⟩ ⟨of all the dangers that confront a nation at war this ~ of national purpose . . . is the greatest —*New Republic*⟩ **b** : a sinking to a despicable issue or disintegration ⟨aimed to prevent ~ of interservice rivalries into open hostility⟩ **c** : modification to a lower or inferior cultural stage ⟨the dance as a spectacle is generally regarded as a product of ~, a secularized form of what is really a religious art —Susanne K. Langer⟩ ⟨thus by a process of ~ the original religious insight of primitive man was overpowered and contaminated by demonistic and polytheistic beliefs—David Bidney⟩ **2 a** : intellectual or moral decline tending toward dissolution of character or integrity : a progressive worsening of personal adjustment ⟨that Zola's best novels are studies in ~ and failure —C.C.Walcutt⟩ **b** : degenerate condition : DEGENERACY ⟨theories explaining artistic genius as rooted in ~⟩ **3 a** : progressive deterioration of physical characters from a level representing the norm of earlier generations or forms ⟨suggests that the small features of the modern Bushman may have resulted from a long process of physical ~ —R.W. Murray⟩ : secondary simplification of a part or organism in the course of generations often to the extent of loss of function or complete disappearance of constituent structures ⟨vestigial organs may be interpreted as the product of ~ following alteration of habits⟩ : regression of the morphology of a group or kind of organism toward a simpler less highly organized state ⟨the scouring rushes have undergone ~ from treelike Mesozoic ancestors⟩ ⟨parasitisms leads to ~⟩ **b** : deterioration of a tissue or an organ in which its vitality is diminished or its structure impaired; *esp* : deterioration in which specialized cells are replaced by less specialized cells (as in fibrosis or in malignancies) or in which cells are functionally impaired (as by deposition of abnormal matter in the tissue) — compare INFILTRATION **4** : marked decline in excellence of workmanship, originality, technical skill, or decorative quality ⟨~ of human figures used in Polynesian decorative art —*Jour. of the Polynesian Soc.*⟩ **5** : the process by which part of the power in the output circuit in an amplifying device is caused to act upon the input circuit so as to restrict the amplification, improve linearity, and reduce distortion : NEGATIVE FEEDBACK — compare REGENERATION
degeneration disease *n* : a virus disease of plants causing a progressive deterioration
de·gen·er·a·tive \dəˈjenə,rād·iv, dēˈ-, -n(ə)rə|, |tiv, -ēv\ *adj* **1** : undergoing degeneration : tending to degenerate ⟨~ conditions of the nervous system —Morris Fishbein⟩ **2** : having the character of or involving degeneration ⟨the ~ changes which occur in the blood vessels, such as a hardening of the arteries —Lionel Whitby⟩ **3** : causing or tending to cause degeneration ⟨the continual brutality around me was ~ in its effect —Jack London⟩
degenerative arthritis *n* : arthritis of middle age characterized by degenerative and sometimes hypertrophic changes in the bone and cartilage of one or more joints and a progressive wearing down of apposing joint surfaces with consequent distortion of joint position usu. without bony stiffening — compare RHEUMATOID ARTHRITIS
degenerative disease *n* : a disease characterized by progressive degenerative changes in tissue (as arteriosclerosis, diabetes mellitus, or hypertrophic arthritis)
de·gen·er·es·cence \dəˌjenəˈresᵊn(t)s, (ˌ)dē,-\ *n* -s [F *dégénérescence*, fr. *dégénérer* to degenerate (fr. L *degenerare*) + *-escence* — more at DEGENERATE] : the process of becoming degenerate
degenerous *adj* [L *degener* degenerate (prob. back-formation fr. *degenerare* to degenerate) + E *-ous*] *obs* : DEGENERATE
de·germ \(ˈ)dē +\ *vt* -ED/-ING/-S [*de-* + *germ* (n.)] **1** : to remove germs from (as the skin) **2** : to remove the germ from (a seed) ⟨~*ed* wheat products⟩
de·ger·ma·tion \ˌdē,jərˈmāshən\ *n* -s : the action or result of degerming the skin
de·germinate \(ˈ)dē + ˈ-\ *vt* [*de-* + *germinate*] : DEGERM 2
de·ger·mi·na·tor \(ˈ)dēˈjərmə,nād·ər\ *n* : a machine for breaking the kernels of grain or cacao beans and removing the germ
degged *past of* DEG
degging *pres part of* DEG
de·glaciation \(ˌ)dē +\ *n* : the inclusive process whereby a glacier or ice sheet shrinks to disappearance; *also* : the result of this process

de·glamorization \(ˌ)dē+\ *n* -s **:** the action of deglamorizing

de·glamorize \(ˈ)dē+\ *vt* [*de-* + *glamorize*] **:** to remove the glamor from; *esp* **:** to treat in a way to counteract an accustomed glorification or charm

de·glaze \(ˈ)dē+\ *vt* [*de-* + *glaze* (n.)] **:** to remove the glaze from (as pottery or porcelain) so as to give a dull finish — compare DEPOLISH

de·glorify \(ˈ)dē+ˈ-\ *vt* [*de-* + *glorify*] **:** to deprive of accustomed glorification

de·glutinate \(ˈ)dē+ˈ-\ *vt* [L *deglutinatus*, past part. of *deglutinare*, fr. *de-* + *glutinare* to glue, fr. *glutin-, gluten* glue; akin to L *glut-, glus* glue — more at CLAY] **1 :** UNGLUE **2** [influenced in meaning by NL *gluten* (substance in flour)] **:** to extract or remove gluten from (as wheat flour) — **de·glutination** \(ˌ)dē+\ *n*

de·glu·ti·tion \ˌdēˌglüˈtishən, ˌdeˌg-\ *n* -s [F *déglutition*, fr. MF *deglutition*, fr. L *deglutitus, deglutitus* (past part. of *deglutire, degluttire* to swallow down, fr. *de-* + *glutire, gluttire* to swallow) + MF *-ion* — more at GLUTTON] **:** the act or process of swallowing (as food) **:** the power of swallowing — **de·glu·ti·tious** \ˈ;==;shəs\ *adj*

de·glu·ti·to·ry \dəˈglüdə,tōrē\ *adj* [*deglutition* + *-ory*] **:** serving for or aiding in deglutition

deg·ra·da·tion \ˌdegrəˈdāshən\ *n* -s [MF or LL; MF, fr. LL *degradation-, degradatio*, fr. *degradatus* (past part. of *degradare* to degrade) + L *-ion-, -io* -ion — more at DEGRADE] **1 a :** a canonical punishment in the Roman Catholic Church by which a clergyman is perpetually deprived of all office, titles, benefices, and ecclesiastical rights and privileges **b :** a censure of a Church of England clergyman involving deprivation of office and usu. the exercise of holy orders **c :** reduction to a lower rank, position, or level ⟨stripped of his insignia of rank in an act of public ~ —*United Press*⟩ **d :** demotion or deposition from office ⟨venality eventually brought about the official's ~⟩ **e** *obs* **:** demotion by one or more steps on a college list of precedence imposed as a punishment **f :** lowering or descent in standing, worth, or serviceability ⟨the ~ of reasonable sympathy into sentimentalism —W.R.Inge⟩ ⟨indicative of the early twentieth century's mischievous ~ of the elevated and elevation of the degraded —H.F.Mooney⟩ ⟨two great and not easily reversible evils follow: a conformity-minded speech community . . . and a ~ of the language —I.A.Richards⟩ **2 a :** decline to an inferior state of shamed or shameful distortion, neglect, repudiation, or dissolution **:** abandonment to defeat or corruption ⟨even translation to the screen is not always, as such, a ~ —E.R.Bentley⟩ ⟨the primal emotions of victory and defeat, exaltation and ~ —Allan Nevins⟩ **b :** a despised state of coarsening destitution, inhumane suppression, or demoralized dejection ⟨two centuries of ~ hardly left the freedmen in a position to take up the responsibilities of citizenship —Oscar Handlin⟩ ⟨shocked by the hopeless ~ of the "poor whites" —Edith Wharton⟩ ⟨the last household where I could have found the reckless Ireland of a hundred years ago in final ~ —W.B.Yeats⟩ **3 :** moral or intellectual decadence **:** reduction to ignominy or defilement ⟨three attempts to escape and subsequent punishment educated him in the bestiality and ~ that war brings —Drew Middleton⟩ ⟨the historical principle of cultural development and cultural progress from savagery to civilization as against any theory of cultural retrogression or ~ —David Bidney⟩ ⟨the ~ of art and religion to menial and mountebank offices —Clive Bell⟩ **4** [F *dégradation*, fr. It *digradazione*, fr. LL *degradation-, degradatio*] **:** the lessening in size or diminishing in light or color of objects in a drawing or painting to give perspective **5 :** impairment in respect to some physical property: **a :** damage by weakening or loss of some property, quality, or capability ⟨present synthetic rubber tires when used for this purpose are susceptible to a heat buildup that leads to excessive ~ —Roger Adams⟩ **b :** degeneration or arrest of development of any organ or of the body as a whole **c :** transformation into simpler substances or waste **d :** reduction to small lumps or particles ⟨because the ore is loaded only once, ~ is minimized —*Newsweek*⟩ **e :** the weakening of a fabric that brings about a tendency to disintegrate ⟨sodium hydroxide of 10 percent concentration at 85°C for 16 hours caused no apparent ~ of nylon —W.E.Shinn⟩ **f :** change of a soil to a type that is more highly leached or that has sodium replaced by hydrogen **6 :** change of a chemical compound to a less complex compound **7 :** a wearing down by erosion ⟨modifications of the course of the river caused by gradual accretion on the one bank or ~ on the other bank —E.D.Dickinson⟩ — compare AGGRADATION

deg·ra·da·tion·al \ˈ;==;dāshənᵊl, -shnəl\ *adj* **:** produced by, showing, or relating to degradation from a more to a less complex form or stage ⟨the weathering processes commonly are followed but not always immediately by ~ processes —V.C. Finch & G.T.Trewartha⟩

degradation of energy *physics* **:** the process by which energy becomes less available for doing work — compare CONSERVATION OF ENERGY, DISSIPATION OF ENERGY

deg·ra·da·tive \ˈdegrəˌdād·iv\ *adj* [*degradation* + *-ive*] **:** tending to degradation; *also* **:** DEGRADATIONAL

¹de·grade \dəˈgrād, dē-; *in senses definable "to make or become lower in grade",* " *or* ˈdē¦g-\ *vb* [ME *degraden*, fr. MF *degrader, desgrader*, fr. LL *degradare*, fr. L *de-* + *gradus* step, pace — more at GRADE] *vt* **1 :** to lower in rank, grade, or status: **a :** to reduce from a higher to a lower rank or from a position of dignity or privilege **:** DEMOTE, DEPOSE ⟨the world is weary of statesmen whom democracy has *degraded* into politicians —Benjamin Disraeli⟩ **b :** to strip of rank or honors; *specif* **:** to deprive (a priest) of office, privileges and in the Roman Catholic Church of all that outwardly betokens priesthood **c :** to lower from a superior to an inferior level **:** deprive of standing, efficacy, true function, or exalted status **:** PERVERT ⟨the writer who ~*s* the press to a mere means of material livelihood —J.T.Farrell⟩ ⟨they will claim that the biosystematists are attempting to ~ and wreck the classical concept of the genus —W.H.Camp⟩ ⟨like the grandees of the Classical Renaissance they *degraded* art, which is a religion, to upholstery, a menial trade —Clive Bell⟩ **d :** to lower in grade **:** scale or step down or reduce (as a commercial product) in desirability or salability ⟨because of the exposed area and the formation of callus tissue on its edges it seriously ~*s* logs —*Ecology*⟩ ⟨good honey can easily be *degraded* in quality by unskilled handling and careless presentation —*Brit. Book News*⟩ ⟨turkeys not in prime condition are *degraded*⟩ **2 :** to bring to low esteem or disrepute **:** expose to shame, humiliation, or contempt ⟨he had *degraded* his office by shameless extortion —John Buchan⟩ ⟨a compelled confession demoralizes the confessor and ~*s* the confessed —*Saturday Rev.*⟩ ⟨eagerness of millions of voters to respond to an appeal that does not ~ them or pander to their worst instincts —Elmer Rice⟩ **3 :** to bring low or drag down in moral or intellectual character **:** reduce to dishonor, ignominy, depravity, or moral degeneracy **:** DEBASE, CORRUPT ⟨the Indians who consume peyote buttons do not seem to be physically or morally *degraded* by the habit —Aldous Huxley⟩ ⟨by the end of the 19th century love of country was being unusually *degraded* into contempt for foreigners —Herbert Agar⟩ ⟨an age of compromise, or moral skepticism, and of practiced art in *degrading* the highest of all values into the service of the lowest of all compliances —W.L.Sullivan⟩ **4 :** to lower or impair in respect to some physical property: **a :** to damage by weakening or removing some requisite property ⟨it is recognized that rubber is *degraded* to some extent by contact with copper —D.W. Gay⟩ **b :** to diminish (some pertinent quality or capability) with deteriorating effect ⟨they will, if they obey the physical law, hold that society does work by *degrading* its energies —Henry Adams⟩ **c :** to reduce the definition of (a photographic or projected picture) ⟨in an air photographic system haze and air turbulence ~ the image⟩ **d :** to break up (as coal or ore) into small lumps or into dust **e :** to reduce the strength of (a fabric or textile fiber) giving a tendency to deteriorate or disintegrate ⟨exposure to sunlight ~*s* nylon yarn⟩ **5 :** to wear or scour by erosion ⟨a stream in flood *degrading* its channel⟩ ⟨the surrounding country . . . which has been *degraded* by the processes of denudation —Walter Fitzgerald⟩ **6 :** to reduce the complexity of (a chemical compound) by splitting off one or more groups or larger component parts **:** DECOMPOSE, DEPOLYMERIZE ⟨~ hexose sugars to pentoses⟩ ⟨cellulose is *degraded* by the action of some bacteria⟩ ~ *vi* **1 :** to pass from a higher grade or class to a lower ⟨areas of the forest have *degraded* into scrub⟩ **2 :** to postpone entering the examination for a degree in honors at Cambridge University beyond the usual or required time **3** *biol* **:** DEGENERATE **4** *of a chemical compound* **:** to undergo degradation

²de·grade \ˈdē,grād\ *n* **:** lumber or a log found to be below grade in quality; *also* **:** a reduction in grade

¹de·grad·ed *pronunc at* ¹DEGRADE + əd\ *adj* [ME, fr. past part. of *degraden*] **1 :** reduced far below ordinary standards of civilized life and conduct: **a :** marked by poverty, helplessness, and apathy ⟨dirty, wild, and ~ as only the worst slaves of antiquity had been —Lewis Mumford⟩ **b :** marked by indulgence in vice or debauchery **:** DEBASED ⟨he so deplorably dissipated and ~, and they so bloomy and idyllic —E.V.Lucas⟩ **c :** fallen far below genuine quality **:** CONTAMINATED, DISTORTED, VULGARIZED ⟨the writer . . . who suffers from what he is bound to consider the ~ and irresponsible taste of his time —*New Yorker*⟩ **2 :** characterized by degeneration of structure or function **3** *of a color* **:** not saturated to the practical maximum — **de·grad·ed·ly** *adv* — **de·grad·ed·ness** *n* -ES

²degraded \"\ *adj* [*de-* + L *gradus* + E *-ed*] *heraldry* **:** standing on steps — used of a cross; compare DEGREE 1b

de·grade·ment \-ādmənt\ *n* -s [obs. F *dégradement*, fr. *dégrader* to degrade + *-ment*] *archaic* **:** DEGRADATION

de·grad·er \-ādə(r)\ *n* -s **:** one that degrades

degrading *adj* **:** that degrades; *esp* **:** that causes human character to become degraded or debased ⟨moralists have often exposed the selfish pursuit of personal gain as a ~ motive in the business life —J.A.Hobson⟩ ⟨war for the most part is ~ and hateful⟩ ⟨the tendency of existentialists to deal with the ~ aspects of human nature⟩ — **de·grad·ing·ly** *adv* — **de·grad·ing·ness** *n* -ES

¹de·grain \(ˈ)dē+\ *vt* [*de-* + *grain* (n.)] **:** to remove the grain from

²de·grain \ˈdē+,-\ *n* **:** a degrained leather

de·gras \dāˈgrä\ *n, pl* **degras** \-äz\ [F *dégras*, back-formation (influenced by *gras* fat, fr. L *crassus* thick, fat) fr. *dégraisser* to remove the fat from, fr. MF *desgresser*, fr. *des-, de-* + *gresse, graisse* fat, grease — more at CRASS, GREASE] **1 a :** a fatty substance obtained by pressing certain skins following the action of oxidized fish oil on them and used in dressing leather — called also *moellon;* see SOD OIL **b :** a mixture of this substance with other fats or fatty oils (as fish oils) or sometimes wool grease **2 :** WOOL GREASE

de gra·tia \dāˈgräd·ē,ä, dēˈgrāsh(ē)ə\ *adv (or adj)* [L] *law* **:** by favor

de·grease \(ˈ)dē¦grēs, -ēz\ *vt* [*de-* + *grease* (n.)] **:** to treat with an extractant for grease, oil, or fatty matter ⟨a taxidermist *degreasing* specimens for the museum⟩: as **a :** to remove grease and dirt from (wool) with chemicals **b :** to remove grease, oil, or fatty matter from (a metal) with fumes from a hot solvent **c :** to remove excess grease from (hides or skins) by tumbling in solvents in tanning

de·greas·er \"+ə(r)\ *n* **1 :** one employed at degreasing materials in an industrial process **2 :** a solvent or a machine using solvents for degreasing materials, parts, specimens

¹de·gree \dəˈgrē, dē-\ *n* -s *often attrib* [ME, fr. OF *degré*, fr. (assumed) VL *degradus*, fr. L *de-* + *gradus* step, pace — more at GRADE] **1 a** *obs* **:** one member of a flight of steps or stairs **b** *heraldry* **:** a step (as of a Calvary cross) in a series — called also *grece* **c** *archaic* **:** a steplike member of a series (as of parts of a structure) **:** TIER, BANK **2 a :** a step in a process, course, or classificatory order ⟨shall the shadow go forward ten ~*s* or go back ten ~*s* — 2 Kings 20:9 (AV)⟩ **b :** a stage or point of an advance or retrogression ⟨rising by successive ~*s* to become general manager⟩ **c :** a measure of damage to tissue caused by disease or other force ⟨third ~ burn⟩ — compare CLASS 3b, GRADE 1c(3) **3 a :** a grade or point observed in a measuring or estimating of an action, relation, state of being, or mental attitude ⟨at a microphone they are men who know the pecuniary value of words inflated to the right ~ —O.D.Duncan⟩ ⟨the ~ to which the total effect resembles nature —Michael Kitson⟩ **b :** the extent, measure, or scope of an action, condition, or relation ⟨all of our presidents in varying ~*s* have experienced an intoxicating exhilaration in manipulating the levers of power —V.L.Albjerg⟩ ⟨I considered my giddiness and inconstancy when in London as in a great ~ the cause of her unhappiness —Benjamin Franklin⟩ **c :** level in the range and stress or accentuation of an attribute **:** relative efficacy **:** measure or dimension of an essential or distinctive quality ⟨the mental powers of ants differ from those of men not so much in kind as in ~ —John Lubbock⟩ ⟨it is a question of ~ whether I have been negligent —B.N.Cardozo⟩ ⟨most of the distinctions of law are distinctions of ~ —O.W. Holmes †1935⟩ **d :** a grade or point marking the attainment or existence of more or less of a quality, acquirement, or aspect **:** relative intensity ⟨combined literary distinction with a high ~ of historical objectivity —R.W.Van Alstyne⟩ ⟨requiring a high ~ of mastery in the chosen field of study⟩ ⟨the precise ~ of probability⟩ **e :** a positive and unquestionable though undefined quantitative measure and qualitative elevation ⟨the duties owed by the trustee have a ~ of definition and are enforceable before a court of equity —G.B. Huff⟩ ⟨the religious zeal of the Quakers was always tempered by a ~ of tolerance —*Amer. Guide Series: Pa.*⟩ **f :** one of the forms or sets of forms used in the comparison of an adjective or adverb to denote a particular intensity or level of the quality, quantity, or relation expressed by the adjective or adverb — see COMPARATIVE 1, POSITIVE 2a, SUPERLATIVE 1 **g :** a legal measure of the culpability of one who commits any of certain crimes that depends on attendant circumstances defined by law ⟨an offense in the first ~ is usually the most serious; among the offenses classified in this manner are often found murder or robbery⟩ **h :** one of the legal classes of negligence (as gross, ordinary, or slight) graded according to the determined culpability of the tort-feasor **4 :** a rank or grade of official, ecclesiastical, or social position or advancement ⟨people of low ~ were banished from the capital —E.R. Embree⟩ ⟨clerical hats colored and tasselled according to their ~ —Iain Moncreiffe⟩ ⟨a certain well-to-do air about the man suggested that he was not poor for his ~ —Thomas Hardy⟩ **5 a** *archaic* **:** a particular level, standing, or relative condition esp. as to dignity, reputation, worth ⟨for they that have used the office of a deacon well purchase to themselves a good ~ —1 Tim 3:13 (AV)⟩ **b :** the civil condition or status of a person **6 :** a step in a direct line of descent or in the line of ascent to a common ancestor and thence in line of descent to relatives by consanguinity **7 a :** a grade or class of membership attained in a ritualistic order or society denoting a stage of proficiency often after a set ordeal or examination **b :** the formal ceremonies observed in the conferral of such a distinction **c :** a title conferred upon students by a college, university, or professional school upon completion of a unified program of study carrying a specified minimum of credits, passing of certain examinations, and often completion of a thesis or other independent research project — compare ³ASSOCIATE 4b **d :** an academic title conferred honorarily in recognition of outstanding individual achievement outside the conferring institution ⟨his writings brought him an award of the ~ of Doctor of Humane Letters⟩ **8** *archaic* **:** a position or space on the earth or in the heavens as measured by degrees of latitude **9 :** one of the divisions or intervals marked on a scale of a measuring instrument or a gauge ⟨the length of a ~ depends on the expansion of the thermometric substance used —A.H.Thiessen⟩ **10 :** a 360th part of the circumference of a circle **:** the principal unit of measure for arcs and angles **11 :** the greatest sum of the exponents of the variables, unknowns, or indeterminates of a term of a polynomial or polynomial equation ⟨a^2b^3c is a term of the sixth ~⟩ **:** the power of the highest ordered derivative in a differential equation after the equation has been rationalized and cleared of fractions with respect to the derivatives ⟨$\frac{d^2y}{dx^2}-2\left(\frac{dy}{dx}\right)^2-4=0$ is of the first ~⟩ **12** *music* **a :** a line or space of the staff — compare LEDGER LINE **b :** a step, note, or tone of a scale ⟨the mediant is the third ~ of the scale⟩ **13** *logic* **:** the rank of a predicate according to the number of terms related by it ⟨"before" is a predicate of the second, "between" of the third ~⟩ — **by degrees** *adv* **:** step by step **:** by relatively small stages **:** GRADUALLY ⟨measures raising the minimum of teachers' pay *by degrees*⟩ — **to a degree** *adv* **1 :** to a rather large or remarkable extent **:** in liberal measure **:** HIGHLY, DECIDEDLY, EXCEEDINGLY ⟨but in some things she must have been stupid *to a degree* —I.V. Morris⟩ ⟨a fine classical scholar, of gentlest temper and manners, but easygoing *to a degree* —A.T.Quiller-Couch⟩ **2 :** in a measure **:** in a small way **:** SOMEWHAT ⟨this necessarily involved a departure from strict realism — *to a degree* a denial of reality —G.C.Sellery⟩

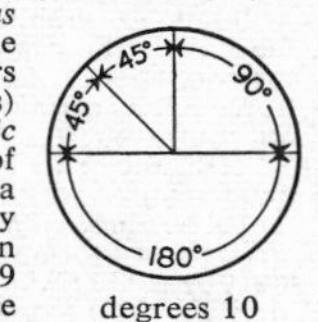

degrees 10

²degree \"\ *vt* **degreed; degreed; degreeing; degrees 1** *obs* **:** to advance by steps or degrees **2 :** to confer a degree upon

degree course *n* **:** a course of studies leading toward a degree **:** an academic subject accepted in partial fulfillment of the requirements for a degree

degree cut *n* **:** STEP CUT

de·greed \-ēd\ *adj* **:** ²DEGRADED

degree-day \-ˈ=,=\ *n* **:** a unit that represents one degree of declination from a given point (as 65°) in the mean outdoor temperature of one day and is often used in measuring fuel requirements of buildings

de·gree·less \-ēləs\ *adj* **1 :** not divisible into or measurable in degrees **2 :** having no academic degree

de·green \(ˈ)dē+\ *vt* [*de-* + *green* (adj.)] **:** to remove green color from (as citrus fruit) by subjection to a specific concentration of ethylene at a specific temperature and relative humidity

degree of curve : a measure of the sharpness of curvature, for U.S. railroads usu. being the angle subtended at the center of curvature by a chord 100 ft. long and for highways by an arc 100 ft. long

degree of freedom 1 : one of a limited number of ways in which a point or a body may move or in which a dynamic system may change, each way being expressed by an independent variable and all requiring to be specified if the physical state of the body or system is to be completely defined **2 :** a capability of variation possessed by a system by reason of the variability of one of its factors (as temperature, pressure, or concentration) ⟨the system water–water vapor has one *degree of freedom* because when either temperature or pressure is arbitrarily fixed the other is no longer variable⟩ — see PHASE RULE **3 :** the number of intervals in which the frequency may be arbitrarily assumed in a statistical distribution with equal intervals of the statistical variable

degree of frost *chiefly Brit* **:** the degree of temperature below the freezing point of water ⟨when the thermometer stands at 20° F there are twelve *degrees of frost*⟩

degree student *n* **:** a college or university student intending to take a degree

degree team *n* **:** a group of members of a ritualistic order who conduct the ceremonies and ritual connected with the working of an initiatory or other particular degree

degreewise \-ˈ=,=\ *adv* **:** by degrees esp. of the musical diatonic scale

de·gres·sion \dēˈgreshən\ *n* -s [ME *degressioun*, fr. ML *degression-, degressio*, fr. L *degressus* (past part. of *degredi* to go down, fr. *de-* + *-gredi*) to go, step + *-ion-, -io* -ion — more at CONGRESS] **1 :** a stepping or movement downward **:** DESCENT — used chiefly as a correlative of progression **2 :** the decrease in rate in degressive taxation

de·gres·sive \-esiv\ *adj* [*degression* + *-ive*] **:** tending to descend or decrease: **a :** based on a plan of taxation in which the rate decreases as the base increases, the rate structure containing some degree of progression in the lower brackets and then tapering off until all income over a certain figure is taxed at the same rate **b :** relating to or characterized by burning (as of solid grains of smokeless powder) in which the surface decreases as the burning advances — opposed to *progressive* — **de·gres·sive·ly** \-səvlē\ *adv*

dé·grin·go·lade \dāgraⁿgōˈläd\ *n* -s [F, lit., tumbling fall, fr. *dégringoler* to tumble (fr. *dé-* de- + *gringoler* to tumble, fr. MF) + *-ade*] **:** rapid decline or deterioration (as in strength, position, or condition) **:** DOWNFALL ⟨what a ~ from the period of that brilliant coterie —*Saturday Rev.*⟩ ⟨the ~ of a theater that once . . . occupied an important position —*Amer. Mercury*⟩

de·growth \ˈdē+,-\ *n* [*de-* + *growth*] *biol* **:** decrease in mass of an organism esp. at the end of a prolonged period of growth

degs *pres 3d sing of* DEG

de·gu \ˈdā(,)gü\ *n* -s [AmerSp] **:** any of several small hystricomorphic rodents (genus *Octodon*) of western So. America

de·gue·lia \dəˈgēlēə\ [NL, fr. Galibi *assa-ha-pagara undeguélé* derris plant + NL *-ia*] *syn of* DERRIS

de·guel·in \-lən\ *n* -s [NL *Deguelia* + E *-in*] **:** a crystalline ketone $C_{23}H_{22}O_6$ that is an active constituent of derris and roots of cube and is closely related to rotenone

de·gum \(ˈ)dē+\ *vt* [*de-* + *gum* (n.)] **:** to free from gum or gummy substance; *specif* **:** to free (silk fabric or yarn) from sericin by boiling in a soap solution

de·gust \dēˈgəst\ *also* **de·gus·tate** \-ˈgə,stāt\ *vt* -ED/-ING/-S [*degust* fr. L *degustare*, fr. *de-* + *gustare* to taste; *degustate* fr. L *degustatus*, past part. of *degustare* — more at CHOOSE] **:** TASTE; *esp* **:** to savor or relish as a connoisseur or tester ⟨observes and ~*s* the great world of London —E.K.Brown⟩ — **de·gus·ta·tion** \(ˌ)dē,gəˈstāshən\ *n*

de·gus·ta·tor \dēˈgə,stād·ə(r)\ *n* -s **:** one that tastes ⟨varieties of oranges rated by ~*s*⟩

de gus·ti·bus \dēˈgəstəbəs, dāˈgüstē,bùs\ [L *de gustibus (non est disputandum)* there is no disputing concerning tastes] **:** concerning taste ⟨I still detest the sound of him, but *de gustibus* —Jean Stafford⟩ — used elliptically for its full Latin original or its translation

de·hair \(ˈ)dē+\ *vt* [*de-* + *hair* (n.)] **:** to deprive of hair **:** UNHAIR; *specif* **:** to remove the hair or wool from (hides or skins)

de haut en bas \dəōtäⁿbä\ *adv (or adj)* [F, lit., from top to bottom] **:** with a superior or condescending air ⟨the landlady looked at him *de haut en bas* —D.H.Lawrence⟩

de·hep·a·tize \(ˈ)dēˈhepə,tīz\ *vt* [*de-* + *hepat-* + *-ize*] **:** to remove the liver from

de·hisce \dəˈhis, dēˈ-\ *vb* -ED/-ING/-S [L *dehiscere* to split open, gape, fr. *de-* + *hiscere* to gape; akin to *hiare* to yawn, gape — more at YAWN] *vi* **:** to discharge by dehiscence **:** GAPE ~ *vt* **:** to cause to gape

de·his·cence \-sᵊn(t)s\ *n* -s [NL *dehiscentia*, fr. L *dehiscent-, dehiscens* (pres. part. of *dehiscere*) + *-ia*] **:** a bursting open: as **a** (1) **:** the bursting open of a capsule, pod, or silique at maturity either between the carpels, through the middle of the carpels, or in some other manner — compare CIRCUMSCISSILE, LOCULICIDAL, SEPTICIDAL, SEPTIFRAGAL (2) **:** the opening of an anther for the discharge of pollen (as by longitudinal slits or pores) **b** *biol* **:** the opening of an organ along a suture or some other definite line for the purpose of discharging its contents **c :** the parting of the sutured lips of a surgical wound

de·his·cent \-sᵊnt, ˈdē,h-\ *adj* [L *dehiscent-, dehiscens*] **:** characterized by dehiscence **:** opening wide **:** GAPING — used esp. of ripe fruit or fungous fruiting bodies — see FRUIT illustration

deh·kan \ˈdā,kän\ *n, usu cap* **:** DEHWAR

dehn·stu·fe \ˈdān,shtüfə\ *n, pl* **dehnstu·fen** \-fən\ [G, fr. *dehnen* to stretch (fr. OHG *dennen*) + *stufe* step, fr. OHG *stuofa* — more at THIN, STEP] *in Indo-European ablaut* **:** a lengthened grade

de·horn \(ˈ)dē+\ *vt* [*de-* + *horn* (n.)] **1 :** to deprive of horns **:** prevent the growth of the horns of (cattle) esp. by destroying the undeveloped horn buds with heat or chemicals **2 :** to prune severely (as a fruit tree)

de·horn·er \"+ə(r)\ *n* -s **1 :** one that dehorns cattle **2 a :** a device for removing horns from cattle **b :** a device or chemical for checking the growth of horns in young cattle of horned breeds

de·hors \dəˈ(h)ō(ə)r\ *prep* [F, outside, fr. OF, fr. LL *deforis* from the outside, outside, fr. L *de* from + *foris* outside; akin to L *foris, fores* door — more at DE-, DOOR] *law* **:** out of (as an agreement, record, or will) **:** foreign to

de·hort \(ˈ)dēˈhō(ə)rt\ *vt* -ED/-ING/-S [L *dehortari*, fr. *de-*

+ *hortari* to urge, exhort — more at YEARN] *archaic* : to advise against (an action or policy) : DISSUADE — often used with *from*

de·hor·ta·tion \,dē,hȯr'tāshən\ *n* -s [LL *dehortation-, dehortatio*, fr. L *dehortatus* (past part. of *dehortari*) + *-ion-, -io* -ion] *archaic* : DISSUASION

deh·ra dun \'derə¦dün\ *adj, usu cap both Ds* [fr. *Dehra Dun*, India] : of or from the city of Dehra Dun, India : of the kind or style prevalent in Dehra Dun

dehrn·ite \'der,nīt\ *n* -s [*Dehrn*, village near Limburg, Germany, where it was discovered + E *-ite*] : a basic phosphate of calcium, sodium, and potassium $(Ca,Na,K)_5(PO_4)_3(OH)$

de·hull \(')dē+\ *vt* [*de-* + *hull* (n.)] : to remove the hulls from (seed)

de·humanization \(¦)dē+\ *n* -s : the act or process or an instance of dehumanizing

de·humanize \(')dē+\ *vt* [*de-* + *humanize*] : to divest of human qualities or personality : make machinelike ⟨*dehumanizing* the masses into unthinking conformity⟩ : make impersonal or unconcerned with human values ⟨an abstract, *dehumanized* art⟩

de·humidification \¦dē+\ *n* -s : the process of dehumidifying

de·humidifier \(')dē+\ *n* -s : a substance or apparatus for dehumidifying

de·humidify \(')dē+\ *vt* [*de-* + *humidify*] : to remove moisture from (as the air) : DRY

de·husk \(')dē+\ *vt* [*de-* + *husk* (n.)] : HUSK

deh·war \ dä,wär\ *n, pl* **dehwar** *or* **dehwars** *usu cap* [Per *dihwār*, fr. *dih* village (fr. MPer *dēh* land, fr. OPer *dahyu*-land, province) + *-wār* having, possessing (fr. Av *-baro* carrying, bringing); akin to Skt *bharati* he carries — more at DAS, BEAR] **1** : a Persian racial type recognizable in the population of Baluchistan **2** : a member of the Dehwar racial type usu. having the status of a laborer or slave

dehydr- *or* **dehydro-** *comb form* [ISV, fr. *de-* + *hydr-*] **1** : dehydrated ⟨*dehydro*mucic acid $C_4H_2O(COOH)_2$⟩ **2** : dehydrogenated ⟨*dehydro*abietic acid $C_{19}H_{27}COOH$⟩

de·hy·drant \dē'hīdrənt\ *n* -s [*dehydrate* + *-ant*] : a dehydrating substance

de·hy·drate \dē'hī,drāt, *usu* -ād.+V\ *vb* [*de-* + *hydrate*] *vt* **1 a** : to remove hydrogen and oxygen from (as a compound) in the proportion in which they form water ⟨*dehydrated* castor oil⟩ **b** : to remove chemically combined water or water of hydration from ⟨*dehydrated* alums⟩ **2** : to remove water or moisture from (as foods or air) : render free from water : dry completely : DESICCATE — compare DEHUMIDIFY **3** : to deprive of strength, meaning, or vitality ⟨creeps in like the desert wind and ~s the soul —James Jones⟩ : make flat, insipid, or uninspiring ⟨touches nothing that he does not ~ —*Economist*⟩ ~ *vi* : to lose water or the elements of water : become dehydrated **syn** see DRY

de·hy·dra·tion \(,)dē,hī'drāshən\ *n* [*de-* + *hydration*] **1** : the process of dehydrating; *esp* : an abnormal depletion of body fluids resulting from deprivation or loss (as in starvation, hemorrhage, or vomiting) **2** : the state of being dehydrated **3** : a procedure designed to reduce the fluid content of body tissues

de·hy·dra·tor *also* **de·hy·drat·er** \dē'hī,drād·ə(r),-ātə-\ *n* -s : one that dehydrates or operates dehydrating apparatus: as **a** : an operator of a still for removing water from lubricating oils **b** : an agent (as silica gel) for dehydrating **c** : a device or apparatus for dehydrating : DRYER

de·hy·dro \dē'hī(,)drō\ *adj* [*dehydr-*] **1** : chemically dehydrated **2** : DEHYDROGENATED

de·hy·dro·acetic acid \dē¦hīdrō+ . . . -\ *also* **de·hy·dracetic acid** \-dr+ . . . -\ *n* [ISV *dehydr-* + *acetic*] : a crystalline acid $C_8H_8O_4$ related to pyrone, obtained esp. by heating ethyl acetoacetate, and used as a fungicide, bactericide, and plasticizer

dehydroascorbic acid \"+ . . . -\ *n* [*dehydr-* + *ascorbic*] : a crystalline oxidation product $C_6H_6O_6$ of ascorbic acid occurring at times in some foodstuffs (as fruits, vegetables, and milk) that can be reduced to ascorbic acid and thus has potential vitamin C activity

de·hy·dro·cho·late \(,)dē,hīdrə'kō,lāt\ *n* -s [ISV *dehydrocholic* + *-ate*] : a salt of dehydrocholic acid

de·hy·dro·cholesterol \dē¦hīdrō+\ *n* [*dehydr-* + *cholesterol*] : a crystalline steroid alcohol $C_{27}H_{43}OH$ that occurs chiefly in higher animals and man (as in the skin), that is made synthetically from cholesterol, and that yields vitamin D_3 on irradiation with ultraviolet light — called also *7-dehydrocholesterol*

de·hy·dro·cholic acid \(¦)dē¦hīdrə+\ *n* [ISV *dehydr-* + *cholic*] : a colorless crystalline acid $C_{23}H_{33}O_3COOH$ made by the oxidation of cholic acid and used often in the form of its sodium salt as a choleretic and diuretic; 3,7,12-triketocholanic acid

de·hy·dro·corticosterone \(,)dē,hīdrō+\ *n* [ISV *dehydr-* + *corticosterone*] : a crystalline triketone $C_{21}H_{28}O_4$ extracted from the adrenal cortex and also made synthetically — called also *11-dehydrocorticosterone;* see CORTISONE

de·hy·dro·cyclization \dē¦hīdrō+\ *n* [*dehydr-* + *cyclization*] : cyclization involving dehydrogenation ⟨~ of heptane gives toluene⟩ — called also *cyclodehydrogenation*

de·hy·dro·freezing \"+\ *n* [*dehydr-* + *freezing*] : the process of preserving foods by partially dehydrating and then quick-freezing them

de·hy·dro·frozen \"+\ *adj* [*dehydr-* + *frozen*] : preserved by dehydrofreezing

de·hydrogenase \(¦)dē+\ *n* [ISV *de-* + *hydrogenase*] : any of various enzymes that accelerate the removal of hydrogen from metabolites and its transfer to other substances (as diphosphopyridine nucleotide) and thus play an important role in biological oxidation-reduction processes ⟨succinic ~⟩

de·hydrogenate \(¦)dē+\ *vt* [*de-* + *hydrogenate*] : to remove hydrogen from (a compound) ⟨~ butenes to butadiene⟩ — compare OXIDIZE 1b

de·hydrogenation \(¦)dē+\ *n* : the process of dehydrogenating

de·hydrogenize \(¦)dē+\ *vt* [*de-* + *hydrogenize*] : DEHYDROGENATE

de·hypnotize \(')dē+\ *vt* [*de-* + *hypnotize*] : to remove from a state of hypnosis

de·ice \(')dē+\ *vt* [*de-* + *ice* (n.)] : to keep free or rid of ice; *specif* : to keep (an airplane) free of ice by applying an antifreeze, by the use of electrical or exhaust-gas heating, or by alternately inflating and deflating air-filled bags overlying wing and tail surfaces — **de·ic·er** \"+ə(r)\ *n* -s

¹de·i·cide \'dēə,sīd\ *n* -s [prob. fr. F *déicide*, fr. MF *deicide*, fr. *dei-* (fr. L, fr. *deus* god) + *-cide* (killing)] : the act of killing a divine being or the symbolic substitute of such a being

²deicide \"\ *n* -s [LL *deicida*, fr. L *dei-* (fr. *deus* god) + *-cida* -cide (killer) — more at DEITY] : the killer or destroyer of a god : the officiator in certain religious ceremonies in which men or animals considered to be imbued with supernatural qualities are sacrificed

deic·tic \'dīktik\ *adj* [Gk *deiktikos*, fr. *deiktos* capable of proof (verbal of *deiknynai* to show) + *-ikos* -ic — more at DICTION] **1** : showing or pointing out directly ⟨pronouns differ from nouns in that they are essentially ~ —L.H.Gray⟩ **2** *logic* : proving directly : DIRECT — opposed to *elenctic*

deid \'dēd, 'dād\ *Scot var of* DEAD

de·if·ic \(')dē¦ifik\ *adj* [MF *deifique*, fr. LL *deificus* making divine, divine, holy, fr. L *dei-* (fr. *deus* god) + *-ficus* -fic — more at DEITY] : DIVINE, GODLIKE

de·i·fi·ca·tion \,dēəfə'kāshən\ *n* -s [ME *deificacioun*, fr. LL *deification-, deificatio*, fr. *deificatus* (past part. of *deificare* to deify, fr. *deificus*) + L *-ion-, -io* -ion] **1** : the act or an instance of deifying ⟨~ of natural phenomena⟩ : the state of being deified ⟨the emperor's ~ was proclaimed⟩ **2** : the process of becoming one with a deity : absorption (as of the soul) into deity — **de·if·i·ca·to·ry** \dē'ifəkə,tōrē\ *adj*

de·i·fi·er \'dēə,fī(ə)r\ *n* -s : one that deifies

de·i·form \-,fȯrm\ *adj* [ML *deiformis*, fr. L *deus* god + *-iformis* -iform — more at DEITY] : conforming to the nature of God : having the form of a god ⟨the universe shows no evidence of being ~ —R.W.Sellars⟩

de·i·fy \'dēə,fī\ *vb* -ED/-ING/-ES [ME *deifyen*, fr. MF *deifier*, fr. LL *deificare* — more at DEIFICATION] *vt* **1** : to make a god of : enroll among the national or tribal deities ⟨~*ing* their emperor became their link with the divine⟩ **2** : to make godlike in appearance or character : TRANSFIGURE **3** : to glorify or exalt as of supreme worth or excellence ⟨*deified* . . . the railroad builder, the gold-hungry miner —Leo Cherne⟩ ⟨*deifies* the political state⟩ ~ *vi* : to become divine : assume the status of a deity ⟨failed to completely ~ —Thornton Wilder⟩

deign \'dān\ *vb* -ED/-ING/-S [ME *deynen, deignen*, fr. OF *deignier* to consider worthy, deign, fr. L *dignare, dignari*, fr. *dignus* worthy — more at DECENT] *vi* : to think it appropriate to one's dignity : CONDESCEND ⟨did not even ~ to contradict —Louis Auchincloss⟩ ⟨~*ed* to cast an eye upon humble me —George Meredith⟩ ~ *vt* **1** *obs* : to condescend to receive or accept ⟨I fear my Julia will not ~ my lines —Shak.⟩ **2** : to condescend to give or offer ⟨never so much as ~*ing* a glance —George Meredith⟩

dei ju·di·ci·um \¦dā,ēyü'dikēəm\ *n, cap D* [ML, judgment of God] *law* : trial by ordeal

deil \'dē(ə)l\ *n* -s [ME *del*, alter. of *devel* — more at DEVIL] *Scot* : DEVIL

deil's buckie *n, Scot* : a mischievous person : imp of Satan

dein- *or* **deino-** — see DIN-

dei·no·ce·pha·lia \,dīnōsə'fālyə\ *n pl, cap* [NL, fr. *din-* + *cephal-* + *-ia*] : a suborder of Therapsida comprising reptiles known from Permian fossils of southern Africa and Russia that had massive skulls and heavy legs and included the largest of the reptiles foreshadowing mammals, some exceeding the modern rhinoceros in size — **dei·no·ce·pha·lian** \¦⸗⸗⸗¦fālyən\ *adj or n*

dei·no·don \'dīnə,dän\ *n, cap* [NL, fr. *din-* + *-odon*] : a genus of immense carnivorous saurischian dinosaurs of the upper Cretaceous of Alberta that with *Tyrannosaurus* and related genera constitutes a distinct family chiefly of No. America — **dei·no·dont** \-,dänt\ *adj or n*

de in·of·fi·ci·o·so tes·ta·men·to \¦dā,inə,fikē'ō(,)sō,testə'men,tō\ *adj* [L] *civil law* : concerning an inofficious or undutiful will — used of a form of action for setting aside such a will

dei·no·the·ri·an \¦dīnə¦thirēən\ *adj* [NL *Deinotherium* + E *-an*] : of or relating to the genus *Deinotherium*

dei·no·the·ri·um \,⸗⸗'ēəm\ *n, cap* [NL, fr. *din-* + *-therium*] : a genus (usu. coextensive with the family Deinotheriidae and suborder Deinotherioidea of the order Proboscidea) comprising Miocene and Pliocene mammals of Europe and Asia related to but often larger than the elephants and distinguished by a pair of tusks directed downward from the decurved apex of the lower jaw

De-ion \(')dē¦īən, (')dē'ī,än\ *trademark* — used for a circuit breaker that extinguishes the arc following the opening of a circuit by removing ions from the gap by means of an oil vapor produced by the arc

de·ionization \(¦)dē+\ *n* : the process of deionizing

de·ionize \(')dē+\ *vt* [*de-* + *ionize*] : to remove ions from (as water by ion exchange) : DEMINERALIZE, DESALT — **de·ion·iz·er** \-zə(r)\ *n* -s

deip·nos·o·phist \dīp'näsəfəst\ *n* -s [fr. the *Deipnosophists*, a work depicting a banquet where long discussions take place, written by Athenaus *fl* A.D. 200 Graeco-Egyptian writer, fr. Gk *Deipnosophistai*, lit., culinary experts, pl. of *deipnosophistēs*, fr. *deipnon* meal (prob. of non-IE origin) + *sophistēs* wise man, sophist — more at SOPHIST] : a person skilled in table talk

dei·rid \'dīrəd\ *n* -s [Gk *deirē, derē* neck, throat + E *-id* — more at DER-] : either of a pair of sensory papillae in the lateral cervical region of certain nematodes usu. considered tactile organs

deiseal *var of* DEASIL

de·ism \'dē,izəm\ *n* -s *sometimes cap* [F *déisme*, fr. L *deus* god + F *-isme* -ism — more at DEITY] : a rationalistic movement of the 17th and 18th centuries whose adherents generally subscribed to a natural religion based on human reason and morality, on the belief in one God who after creating the world and the laws governing it refrained from interfering with the operation of those laws, and on the rejection of every kind of supernatural intervention in human affairs

de·ist \'dēəst\ *n* -s *often cap* [F *déiste*, fr. L *deus* god + F *-iste* -ist] : an adherent of deism

de·is·tic \(')dē¦istik, -tēk\ *also* **de·is·ti·cal** \-təkəl, -tēk-\ *adj, sometimes cap* : relating to or characteristic of deists or deism : professing deism ⟨~ belief⟩ — **de·is·ti·cal·ly** \-tək(ə)lē, -tēk-, -li\ *adv*

dei·ters' cell \'dīd·ə(r)z-, -(r)s(əz)-\ *n, usu cap D* [after Otto F. K. *Deiters* †1863 Ger. physician] **1** : one of the modified supporting cells prolonged into a process ending in a terminal plate that are placed among and alternate with the outer hair cells of the organ of Corti **2** : a spider cell of the neuroglia

deiters' nucleus *n, usu cap D* [after O. F. K. *Deiters*] : a nucleus in the medulla oblongata on the inner side of the restiform body receiving fibers from the semicircular canals by way of the vestibular nerve and concerned in maintaining equilibrium and muscular tone and in conjugate movement of the eyes

deith \'dēth\ *Scot var of* DEATH

de·i·ty \'dēəd·ē, -ətē, -i *sometimes* 'dāə-\ *n* -ES [ME *deitee*, fr. MF *deité*, fr. LL *deitat-, deitas* (prob. trans. of Gk *theotēs*), fr. L *deus* god + *-itat-, -itas* -ity; akin to OE *Tīw*, god of war, OHG *Zīo*, ON *Tȳr*, god of war, Goth *sinteins* daily, L *divus* divine, god, *dies* day, *Juppiter*, god of the sky, Gk *dios* heavenly, *Zeus*, god of the sky, Skt *deva* god, *dyaus* sky, day; basic meaning: sky] **1 a** *often cap* : divine nature or rank : the essential nature of a god or of a supreme being : DIVINITY, GODHEAD, GODHOOD ⟨doctrines of the ~ of Christ⟩ **b** *cap* : SUPREME BEING, ²GOD ⟨entering into communion with the *Deity*⟩ **2** : a god or goddess ⟨the tutelary ~ of the village —J.G.Frazer⟩ **3 a** : a person or thing that is exalted or revered as supremely good or great ⟨such established American *deities* as Daniel Boone, Kit Carson —J.D.Hart⟩ ⟨a world in which power is the ~⟩ **b** : one that holds or wields supreme power or influence ⟨the *deities* of the banking world⟩

déjà vu *or* **déjà vue** \dāzhä'vü̅\ *n* [F, adj., already seen] : PARAMNESIA b

¹de·ject \də'jekt, dē'-\ *vt* -ED/-ING/-S [ME *dejecten*, fr. L *dejectus*, past part. of *dejicere* to throw down, fr. *de-* + *-jicere* (fr. *jacere* to throw) — more at JET] **1** *archaic* : to cast down : bend down : OVERTHROW **2 a** (1) *obs* : to lower esp. in rank or condition : ABASE, HUMBLE (2) *archaic* : to reduce esp. in force, degree, or quality : WEAKEN, LESSEN **b** : to make gloomy : DISPIRIT, DISHEARTEN ⟨nor think, to die ~s my lofty mind —Alexander Pope⟩ **syn** see DISCOURAGE

²deject \"\ *adj* [ME, fr. L *dejectus*] *archaic* : DEJECTED ⟨make livers pale and lustihood ~ —Shak.⟩

de·jec·ta \-ktə\ *n pl* [NL, fr. L, neut pl. of *dejectus*] : EXCREMENTS ⟨the ~ of the sick may be a source of infection⟩

dejected *adj* **1** : cast down in spirits : DEPRESSED, MOURNFUL ⟨grew timorous and ~ —William Bartram⟩ **2 a** *obs, of the eyes* : DOWNCAST ⟨her eyes ~ and her hair unbound —Alexander Pope⟩ **b** *archaic* : thrown down : PROSTRATE ⟨looking at her ~ pillar —Henry James †1916⟩ **3** *obs* : lowered in rank, estate, or condition : HUMBLED, ABASED ⟨the ~ state wherein he is —Shak.⟩ **syn** see DOWNCAST

de·ject·ed·ly *adv* : in a dejected manner : SADLY

de·ject·ed·ness *n* -ES : the quality or state of being dejected : DEJECTION

de·jec·tion \də'jekshən, dē'-\ *n* -s [ME *dejeccioun*, fr. LL & L; LL *dejection-, dejectio* act of lowering or pulling down, abject condition, humiliation, fr. L, purging, ejection, degradation, fr. *dejectus* + *-ion-, -io* -ion] **1** *obs* **a** : the act of lowering or the condition of being lowered in rank, estate, or circumstances : ABASEMENT, HUMILIATION **b** : a lowering of strength : diminution esp. of appetite **2** : lowness of spirits : DEPRESSION, MELANCHOLY ⟨slumped down on the wall, the picture of ~ —O.E.Rölvaag⟩ **3** [prob. fr. F, fr. MF, fr. L] **a** : DEFECATION **b** : FECES, EXCREMENT **syn** see SADNESS

dé·jeu·ner \'dāzhə,nā, F dāzhœnā\ *n* -s [F, fr. MF *desjeuner* fr. *desjeuner* to breakfast, fr. OF, fr. (assumed) VL *disjejunare* to break one's fast — more at DINE] **1** : breakfast or lunch **2** : a service for serving individual breakfasts on a tray

de ju·re \(')dē'jürē, (')dā'yü,rā; (')dā'yü,rā\ *adv (or adj)* [L] **1** : by right : of right : by a lawful title ⟨recognition extended *de jure* to the new government⟩ — distinguished from *de gratia* and *de facto* **2** : by law — distinguished from *de aequitate*

deka- *or* **dek-** — see DECA-

de·ka·brist \də'käbrəst, 'dekəb-\ *n* -s *usu cap* [Russ, fr. *dekabr'* December (fr. ORuss *dekębrĭ*, fr. MGk *dekembris, dekembrios*, fr. L *december*) + *-ist* (fr. F *-iste* & G *-ist*) — more at DECEMBER] : DECEMBRIST

dek·a·drachm \'dekə,dram\ *n* -s [Gk *deka-* deca- + E *drachm*] : DECADRACHM

dek·an \'dekən\ *n* -s [Gk *dekanos*, fr. *deka* ten; fr. the ten days of each subdivision — more at TEN] : one of 36 equal subdivisions of the equatorial belt of the celestial sphere including the ecliptic and the stars contained in it — used in ancient Egyptian astronomy — **dek·an·al** \'dekənᵊl\ *adj*

dek·ar \'dā'kär\ *n* -s [G, fr. F *décare* — more at DECARE] : DECARE

dekarchy *var of* DECARCHY

de·kay's snake \də'kāz-\ *n, usu cap D & 1st K* [after James E. *DeKay* †1851 Am. naturalist and writer] : a small brown harmless colubrid snake (*Storeria dekayi*) of No. America

de kho·tin·sky cement \¦dekə¦tinzkē-\ *n, sometimes cap D & usu cap K* [after Achilles *de Khotinsky* †1933 Am. industrial designer] : a thermoplastic cement resistant to water and most chemicals that is made by heating shellac and pine tar and used esp. in cementing glass, porcelain, metal, wood, and plastics

¹dek·ko \'de(,)kō\ *n* -s [Hindi *dekho* look!, imper. pl. of *dekhnā* to see, fr. Skt *dṛś* to see; akin to Skt *dṛṣṭi* seeing, sight, eye — more at DRAGON] *slang Brit* : LOOK, PEEP ⟨got out to have a ~ —J.B.Smyth⟩

²dekko \"\ *vt* -ED/-ING/-ES *slang Brit* : to look at ⟨~*ed* the front page —Richard Llewellyn⟩

del \'del\ *n* -s [short for *delta*; fr. its being symbolized by an inverted Greek delta] : an operator upon a function of three variables (as *x, y,* and *z*) interpreted as coordinates in a right-handed rectangular system for obtaining the partial derivatives of the function, for multiplying these derivatives by the unit vectors (as I, J, K) along the axes, and for adding the results ⟨the vector differential operator (read ~) is defined by $\nabla = I\frac{\delta}{\delta x} + J\frac{\delta}{\delta y} + K\frac{\delta}{\delta z}$ —Leigh Page⟩ — symbol ∇

del *abbr* **1** delegate **2** delete **3** [L *delineavit*] he drew **4** deliver

de·labialization \(¦)dē+\ *n* [*de-* + *labialization*] : the pronouncing of a sound without lip rounding

de·la·foss·ite \,delə'fȯ,sīt\ *n* -s [F, fr. Gabriel *Delafosse* †1878 Fr. mineralogist + F *-ite*] : a mineral $CuFeO_2$ consisting of an oxide of copper and iron formerly found in quantity at Bisbee, Arizona, and in small amounts elsewhere

de·laine \də'lān, dē'-\ *n* -s [F (*mousseline*) *de laine* muslin of wool] **1** : a lightweight dress fabric of wool or wool and cotton made in prints or solid colors **2** *usu cap* [by shortening] : DELAINE MERINO

delaine merino *n, pl* **delaine merinos** *usu cap D&M* : a sheep of an American strain of the Merino breed noted for its smooth body and long fine fleece

de·laminate \(')dē+\ *vb* [*de-* + *laminate*] *vi* **1**: to split into constituent layers **2** *of an embryo* : to undergo delamination ~ *vt* : to split (as a laminated plastic) along a plane of lamination

de·lamination \(¦)dē+\ *n* [*de-* + *lamination*] **1** : separation (as of plywood) into constituent layers **2** : gastrulation which is typical of meroblastic eggs with discoidal cleavage and in which the endoderm is split off as a layer from the inner surface of the blastoderm and the archenteron is represented by the space between this endoderm and the underlying yolk mass

de·lapse \də'laps, dē'-\ *vi* [L *delapsus*, past part. of *delabi* to descend, slip down, fr. *de-* + *labi* to slide — more at SLEEP] *archaic* : to slip down : DESCEND, LAPSE

de·late \-'lāt\ *vt* -ED/-ING/-S [L *delatus* (suppletive past part. of *deferre* to bring down, bring, report, indict, accuse), fr. *de-* + *latus*, suppletive past part. of *ferre* to bear — more at DEFER, TOLERATE] **1 a** *chiefly Scot* : to inform against : ACCUSE, DENOUNCE ⟨*delating* villagers suspected of witchcraft from the pulpit⟩ **b** *archaic* : to carry or spread abroad : make public : REPORT, RELATE **2 a** *medieval Roman law* : to offer or tender (as an inheritance) for acceptance **b** *archaic* : DELEGATE, REFER, TRANSFER

de·lateralization \(¦)dē+\ *n* [*de-* + *lateralization*] *phonetics* : replacement of a lateral by a nonlateral sound

de·la·tion \də'lāshən, dē'-\ *n* -s [L *delation-, delatio*, fr. *delatus* + *-ion-, -io* -ion] : an act or instance of delating; *usu* : ACCUSATION, DENOUNCEMENT

de·la·tive \-ād·iv\ *adj* [L *delatus* + E *-ive*] *of a grammatical case* : denoting motion down from

de·la·tor \-ād·ər *also* -ā,tō(ə)r\ *n* -s [L *delator*, fr. *delatus* + *-or*] : ACCUSER; *esp* : a professional informer — **del·a·to·ri·an** \¦delə¦tōrēən, -tȯr-\ *adj*

de·la·tyn·ite \də'latᵊn,īt\ *n* -s [G *delatynit*, fr. *Delatyn*, Ukraine + G *-it* -ite] : an amber high in carbon but lacking sulfur that is found at Delatyn in the Carpathian mountains of Galicia

¹del·a·ware \'delə,wa(a)(ə)r, -,we(ə)r, -,wə(r)\ *n, pl* **delaware** *or* **delawares** *usu cap* [fr. the *Delaware* river] **1 a** : an Indian people of New Jersey, New York, and parts of eastern Pennsylvania and northern Delaware **b** : a member of such people **2** : the Algonquian language of the Delaware people

²delaware \"\ *adj, usu cap* [fr. *Delaware*, middle Atlantic state of the U.S., fr. the *Delaware* river, after Thomas West, Lord *Delaware* (Baron De La Warr) †1618 colonial administrator in America] : of or from the state of Delaware : of the kind or style prevalent in Delaware

³delaware \"\ *n* -s *usu cap* [fr. *Delaware* state] : one of a breed of white dual-purpose fowls used esp. for broiler production that have faint black barring on hackles and tail and developed in Delaware from off-color sports produced in a cross between barred Plymouth Rock and New Hampshire fowls

¹del·a·war·e·an *or* **del·a·war·i·an** \¦⸗⸗¦wa(a)rēən, -wer-\ *adj, usu cap* [*Delaware* state + E *-an* or *-ian*] : of, relating to, or characteristic of Delaware or Delawareans

²delawarean *or* **delawarian** \"\ *n* -s *cap* : a native or resident of the state of Delaware

¹de·lay \də'lā, dē'-\ *n* -s [ME *delaye*, fr. OF *delaie*, fr. *delaier*] **1** : the act or practice of delaying : PROCRASTINATION, LINGERING ⟨~ in aircraft production⟩ ⟨~ and uncertainty could cripple our industries⟩ **2 a** : the state or an instance of being delayed : DETENTION ⟨the ~s incident to Latin diplomacy⟩ **b** : the time during which something is delayed ⟨a ~ of 30 minutes⟩

²delay \"\ *vb* -ED/-ING/-S [ME *delayen*, fr. OF *delaier*, fr. *de-* + *laier* to leave, alter. of *laissier*, fr. L *laxare* to slacken, loosen, untie, fr. *laxus* slack, loose — more at SLACK] *vt* **1** : to put off : prolong the time of or before : POSTPONE, DEFER ⟨we decided to ~ our departure until the weather improved⟩ **2 a** : to stop, detain, or hinder for a time : check the motion of, lessen the progress of, or slow the time of arrival of ⟨the mails were ~*ed* by heavy snows⟩ ⟨the upper house is ~*ing* the passage of important bills⟩ **b** : to cause to be slower or to occur more slowly than normal : RETARD — used esp. as a past participle ⟨~*ed* resolution in pneumonia⟩ ⟨a heavy child, ~*ed* in walking⟩ **3** *archaic* : to put (a person) off : make (a person) wait (as for a payment due) ~ *vi* : to move or act slowly, intermittently, or inconclusively

syn DELAY, RETARD, SLOW, SLACKEN, and DETAIN agree in meaning to make someone or something behind in schedule or usual rate of movement or progress. DELAY implies a holding back, as by interference, esp. from completion or arrival ⟨a storm *delayed* the ship for an hour⟩ ⟨the opening of the school year had been *delayed* by an epidemic —*Amer. Guide Series: Minn.*⟩ ⟨the symptoms of poisoning may be *delayed* for several days —H.G.Armstrong⟩ ⟨a criminal court jury on which I served *delayed* a verdict all afternoon —C.G.Jameson⟩ RETARD implies a reduction of speed or rate of motion often by interference ⟨snow *retarded* the car considerably⟩ ⟨shortages of labor continue to *retard* production —*Americana Annual*⟩ ⟨other factors *retarded* progress toward a stable economy —*Collier's Yr. Bk.*⟩ ⟨secrecy in research is bound to *retard* the growth of science as a whole —Hartley Shawcross⟩ SLOW, often with *down* or *up*, and SLACKEN also imply a reduction in speed or rate, SLOW often implying intention, SLACKEN stressing an easing up, letting up, or relaxation of effort ⟨as we turned into Compton Street together he *slowed* his step —G.W.Brace⟩ ⟨lack of coordination in the past has *slowed* extensive conservation of water resources —*Amer. Guide Series: Texas*⟩ ⟨perhaps existence was *slowing down* a trifle —Sylvia Berkman⟩ ⟨a bounty of $150 on every live Indian brought in somewhat *slowed up* the general shooting —Marjory S. Douglas⟩ ⟨their rate of growth *slackens* as they age —L.P.Schultz⟩ ⟨the river broadens, *slackening* its pace as it spreads out and turns —Ted Sumner⟩ ⟨economic expansion had *slackened* —Oscar Handlin⟩ DETAIN implies a holding back or being held back beyond an appointed or reasonable time, whether deliberate or not ⟨I slipped my arm around her slender body to *detain* her —W.H.Hudson †1922⟩ ⟨on the voyage thither they were *detained* in Honolulu —R.S.Kuykendall⟩ ⟨after being *detained* in England by the war then raging with Spain, White returned to Roanoke Island —*Amer. Guide Series: N.C.*⟩

syn DELAY, PROCRASTINATE, LAG, LOITER, DAWDLE, DALLY, and DILLYDALLY mean, in common, to move or act slowly so that expected progress is not made or prospective work is left undone or unfinished. DELAY suggests putting off ⟨do not *delay* in sending for your copies. Fill out the attached form today —*Current History*⟩ ⟨genuine success seemed as usual to *delay* and postpone itself —Arnold Bennett⟩ ⟨to *delay* foolishly until all opportunity is past⟩ PROCRASTINATE suggests blameworthy delay as from laziness, indifference, or habitual inertia ⟨to fumble, to vacillate, to *procrastinate* and so let war come creeping upon us almost unawares —W.A.White⟩ ⟨to *procrastinate* in letter writing and lose friends⟩ LAG implies a failure to maintain a required or desirable speed ⟨for half the race the one who finally won had *lagged* behind the others, conserving his strength⟩ ⟨work on the fort had *lagged* —*Amer. Guide Series: Ark.*⟩ ⟨confidence in the administration *lagged* until enemies of the regime were emboldened recently to attempt a revolution —P.P.Kennedy⟩ LOITER implies a delay while in progress, esp. walking, often suggesting a lingering about or an aimless sauntering ⟨a child *loitering* on the way to school⟩ ⟨after breakfasting he walked down the hill and *loitered* about the little streets —Willa Cather⟩ DAWDLE implies a slighter delay in progress than LOITER but connotes more strongly an aimlessness or a taking of more time than is necessary ⟨I did not hurry the rest of the way home; but neither did I *dawdle* —V.G.Heiser⟩ ⟨the sun *dawdles* intolerably on the threshold like a tedious guest —Jan Struther⟩ DALLY and, more strongly, DILLYDALLY suggest wasting time in trifling, pottering, or vacillation ⟨while the men *dallied*, the dogs set off briskly of their own accord —J.T.McNish⟩ ⟨they *dallied* to make mud pies or just to get themselves as muddy as time permitted —*English Digest*⟩ ⟨because the government had *dillydallied* with new export rules, trading in hides and skins had all but stopped —*Time*⟩ ⟨the protagonist is a maundering fellow who *dillydallies* too much in getting his murdering done —Margery Bailey⟩

³**delay** *vt* -ED/-ING/-S [MF *delayer*, fr. (assumed) VL *delicare*, for L *deliquare* to clarify, strain, decant, fr. *de-* + *liquare* to melt, strain — more at LIQUATE] *obs* : ALLAY: as **a** : MITIGATE, ASSUAGE **b** : WEAKEN, TEMPER, DILUTE

delayed–action *also* **delay–action** \ˌ=ˈ=ˌ==\ *adj* **1** : tending to act or become effective only after some usu. predetermined period of time **2** *of an explosive projectile* : detonating some time after it strikes the target

delayed action *n* [*delayed-action*] : a device for automatically releasing the shutter of a camera after a certain period of time to enable the photographer to appear in the picture

delayed dormant spray *n* : a pesticidal spray applied esp. to fruit trees after the green bud tips begin to show but before they are exposed ¼ to ½ inch

delayed subject *n* : a subject following its verb when an expletive or an anticipatory subject precedes (as *five people* in "there are five people here" or *to believe that* in "it is easy to believe that")

de·lay·er \də'lāə(r), dē'-\ *n* -S : one that delays

delaying *adj* : causing or involving delay — **de·lay·ing·ly** *adv*

delaying action *n* : a defensive military action in which advance of an enemy is delayed by fighting as long as possible without the defensive force becoming involved in decisive battle that would imperil its withdrawal

delay line *n, electronics* : a device put in series with a transmission line to introduce a time lag in signals traversing it

del cre·de·re \(ˈ)delˌkrādərē\ *adj* [It, of belief, of trust] *of a commission merchant or agent or an agency agreement* : relating to or guaranteeing performance or payment by third persons to the principal in connection with sales or transactions entered into by such merchant or agent for the principal usu. in return for higher commissions

deld *abbr* delivered

¹**de·le** \ˈdē(ˌ)lē, -ēli\ *vt* **deled; deled; deleing; deles** [L, imper. sing. of *delēre* to wipe out, destroy — more at DELETE] **1** : to remove (as a word or character) from typeset matter : ERASE **2** : to mark (as matter for deletion) with a dele

²**dele** \"\ *n* -S : a mark that is usu. made in a margin and that indicates something is to be deled

de·lead \(ˈ)dē+\ *vt* [*de-* + *lead* (n.)] : to remove lead from ⟨~ a chemical⟩

de·lec·ta·bil·i·ty \də̇ˌlektəˈbilədē, dēˌ-, -ətē, -i\ *n* -ES : delectable quality or condition

de·lec·ta·ble \=ˈ=təbəl\ *adj* [ME, fr. MF, fr. L *delectabilis*, fr. *delectare* to delight + *-abilis* -able — more at DELIGHT] **1** : highly pleasing : DELIGHTFUL **2** : deliciously flavored : SAVORY **syn** see DELIGHTFUL

de·lec·ta·ble·ness \-bəlnə̇s\ *n* -ES : the quality of being delectable

de·lec·ta·bly \-blē, -bli\ *adv* [ME, fr. *delectable* + *-ly*] : in a delectable manner

de·lec·tate \də̇ˈlekˌtāt, dēˈ-\ *vb* -ED/-ING/-S [L *delectatus*, past part. of *delectare* — more at DELIGHT] *vt* : DELIGHT, PLEASE, ENTERTAIN ~ *vi* : to obtain pleasure from or take pleasure in something

de·lec·ta·tion \ˌdē(ˌ)lekˈtāshən\ *n* -S [ME *delectacioun*, fr. MF or L; MF *delectation*, fr. L *delectation-*, *delectatio*, fr. *delectatus* + *-ion-*, *-io* -ion] **1** : DELIGHT **2** : PLEASURE, DIVERSION, ENJOYMENT **syn** see PLEASURE

de·lec·tus \də̇ˈlektəs\ *n* -ES [L, selection, fr. *delectus*, past part. of *deligere* to choose out, select, fr. *de-* + *-ligere* (fr. *legere* to gather) — more at LEGEND] : a book of selected passages esp. for learners of Latin or Greek

delectus per·so·nae \-pə(r)ˈsō(ˌ)nē, -ˌnī\ *n* [NL, choice of person] : the selection of a person satisfactory to oneself for a position involving trust and confidence in the other's character, capacities, or responsibility — used in the phrase *right of delectus personae*

de·lee·rit \də̇ˈlērə̇t\ *adj* [fr. past part. of Sc *deleer, delier*, prob. fr. F *délirer* to be delirious, fr. MF *delirer*, fr. L *delirare* to be crazy, be delirious, dote, rave — more at DELIRIUM] *Scot* : out of one's senses; *specif* : INTOXICATED

del·e·ga·ble \ˈdeləgəbəl, -lēg-\ *adj* [²*delegate* + *-able*] : that can be delegated ⟨~ responsibilities⟩

del·e·ga·cy \-gəsē, -si\ *n* -ES [¹*delegate* + *-cy*] **1 a** : the act of delegating or state of being delegated : appointment as delegate **b** : deputed power **2** : a body of delegates : DELEGATION; *specif* : a special permanent committee at Oxford University

de·legalize \(ˈ)dē+\ *vt* [*de-* + *legalize*] : to remove the status of statutory authorization from

del·e·gant \ˈdeləgənt, -lēg-\ *n* -S [L *delegant-*, *delegans*, pres. part. of *delegare* to delegate] : one that delegates

¹**del·e·gate** \ˈdeləgə̇t, -lēg-, -ˌgāt, *usu* -d·+V\ *n* -S [ME *delegat*, fr. ML *delegatus*, fr. L, past part. of *delegare* to delegate, fr. *de-* + *legare* to send — more at LEGATE] : a person sent and empowered to act for another : DEPUTY, REPRESENTATIVE, COMMISSIONER: as **a** : a representative to a convention or conference (as of a political party) **b** : a member of a committee for some branch of university business at Oxford University **c** : a representative of a U.S. territory in the House of Representatives who has the right to debate but not to vote **d** : a member of the lower house of the legislature of Maryland, Virginia, or West Virginia

²**del·e·gate** \-ˌgāt, *usu* -ād·+V\ *vt* -ED/-ING/-S [L *delegatus*, past part. of *delegare*] **1** : to entrust to another : TRANSFER, ASSIGN, COMMIT ⟨power *delegated* by the people to the legislature⟩ ⟨one may ~ one's authority to a competent assistant⟩ **2** : to send (someone) as one's representative or as a delegate : COMMISSION, DEPUTE ⟨*delegated* her to watch over the sleeping children⟩ ⟨the union will ~ three representatives to the convention⟩ **3** : to assign (a debtor of oneself) to a creditor as a debtor in place of oneself — compare DELEGATION

³**del·e·gate** \-gə̇t, -ˌgāt\ *adj* [L *delegatus*] *archaic* : DELEGATED

del·e·ga·tee \ˌdeləgəˈtē\ *n* -S : one to whom a debtor is delegated

del·e·ga·tion \ˌdeləˈgāshən, -lēˈ-\ *n* -S [L *delegation-*, *delegatio*, fr. *delegatus* + *-ion-*, *-io* -ion] **1** : the act of investing with authority to act for another : appointment of a delegate or delegates **2** : one or more persons appointed or chosen to represent others (as in a convention or congress) : a body of delegates : DEPUTATION **3** : LETTER OF DELEGATION; *also* : the transfer of a debt or credit by such a letter **4** *Roman & civil law* : a novation wherein a debtor extinguishes his debt by substituting a debt owed him for the one he owes his creditor

del·e·ga·tor \ˈ==ˌgād·ə(r)\ *n* -S : DELEGANT

del·e·ga·to·ry \ˈ==gəˌtōrē, -tȯr-, -ri\ *adj* [LL *delegatorius*, fr. L *delegatus* + *-orius* -ory] : of, relating to, or involving delegation of authority : conveying power or authority to one that has no independent right to it ⟨various ~ acts required to establish modern public-health services⟩

de le·ge fe·ren·da \(ˌ)dāˌlāˌjāfəˈrendə\ *adj (or adv)* [L, by means of a law to be made] : being on the basis of new law

deles *pres 3d sing of* DELE, *pl of* DELE

del·es·se·ria \ˌdeləˈsirēə\ *n, cap* [NL, fr. Benjamin *Delessert* †1847 Fr. banker and botanist + NL *-ia*] : a genus (the type of the family Delesseriaceae of the order Ceramiales) of red algae with flat thalli that often simulate the leaves of higher plants — **del·es·se·ri·a·ceous** \ˌ==ˌ=rēˈāshəs\ *adj*

de·lete \də̇ˈlēt, dēˈ-, *usu* -ēd·+V\ *vt* -ED/-ING/-S [L *deletus*, past part. of *delēre* to wipe out, destroy, fr. *de-* + *-lēre* (fr. the root of *linere* to smear) — more at LIME] : to reduce to nullity: as **a** *archaic* : DESTROY, ANNIHILATE **b** : to reject by physically obscuring (as by blotting out, scratching out, or cutting out) or by excluding or marking for exclusion during further processing (as retyping or printing) ⟨~ the third paragraph⟩ ⟨his name was *deleted* from the list⟩ : ERASE, EXPUNGE, DELE **c** : to eliminate as a factor or a matter for consideration ⟨new processes will probably ultimately ~ this crop from the economy⟩ ⟨it is impossible to ~ religious considerations and retain a clear view of colonial history⟩ **syn** see ERASE

del·e·te·ri·ous \ˌdeləˈtirēəs, -tēr- *sometimes* -ter-, *esp Brit* ˌdēl-\ *adj* [Gk *dēlētērios*, fr. *dēleisthai* to hurt; akin to L *dolare* to hew — more at CONDOLE] : HURTFUL, DESTRUCTIVE, NOXIOUS, PERNICIOUS ⟨~ plants⟩ ⟨~ effects of excessive drinking⟩ **syn** see PERNICIOUS

del·e·te·ri·ous·ly *adv* : in a deleterious manner

del·e·te·ri·ous·ness *n* -ES : the quality of being deleterious : HARMFULNESS ⟨arguments about the ~ of smoking⟩

¹**deletery** *adj* [Gk *dēlētērios*] *obs* : DELETERIOUS, POISONOUS

²**deletery** *n* -ES [ML or Gk; ML *deleterium*, fr. Gk *dēlētērion*, fr. neut. of *dēlētērios*] **1** *obs* : something deleterious or poisonous **2** *obs* : ANTIDOTE

de·le·thal·ize \(ˈ)dēˈlēthəˌlīz\ *vt* -ED/-ING/-S [*de-* + *lethal* + *-ize*] : to make nonlethal

de·le·tion \də̇ˈlēshən, dēˈ-\ *n* -S [L *deletion-*, *deletio*, fr. *deletus* (past part. of *delēre* to wipe out, destroy) + *-ion-*, *-io* -ion — more at DELETE] **1** : an act of deleting, blotting out, or erasing : DESTRUCTION, EXTINCTION **2 a** : something deleted esp. from written matter : a deleted passage : ERASURE ⟨~s by the censor⟩ **b** : DEFICIENCY 2b; *esp* : a large deficiency not including either end of a chromosome

de·leveling \(ˈ)dē+\ *n* [*de-* + *leveling*] : alteration of the elevation of a part of the earth's surface

delf \ˈdelf\ *also* **delft** \-lft\ *or* **delph** \-lf\ *n* -S [ME *delf*, fr. OE *gedelf*, fr. *delfan* to dig — more at DELVE] **1 a** *now dial Eng* : EXCAVATION; *usu* : MINE, QUARRY **b** : POND; *also* : DRAIN, DITCH **2** : a square heraldic bearing used as an abatement and supposed to represent a square sod

delft \ˈdelft\ *also* **delf** \-lf\ *or* **delph** \"\ *n* -S [short for *delftware, delphware*] **1 a** : DELFTWARE **b** : glazed pottery esp. when blue and white **2** *or* **delft blue** *also* **delf blue** : a variable color averaging a grayish purplish blue that is bluer, lighter, and stronger than regimental, redder, lighter, and stronger than average navy blue, and very slightly redder and darker than Wedgwood (sense 2b) — called also *Dutchware blue*

delftware *also* **delphware** \ˈ=ˌ=\ *n* [*Delft*, Netherlands, where it originated + E *ware*] **1** : a tin-glazed Dutch pottery; *esp* : a brown pottery covered with an opaque white glaze upon which the usu. predominantly blue decoration is painted **2** : common glazed English pottery for table and other uses **3** : any of various other glazed potteries

del·hi \ˈdelē, -li *sometimes* -lˌhī *or* -lˌhē\ *adj, usu cap* [fr. *Delhi*, India] : of or from the city of Delhi, India : of the kind or style prevalent in Delhi

delhi belly *n, usu cap D* [so called fr. its high incidence among Am. troops in the Delhi area during World War II] : DYSENTERY

delhi boil *n, usu cap D* [so called fr. its former high incidence among British troops in the Delhi area] : leishmaniasis of the skin

de·lia \ˈdēlēə, -lyə\ *n pl, usu cap* [Gk *Dēlia*, fr. neut. pl. of *Dēlios* of Delos] : a festival with games that was celebrated by the ancient Greeks every fourth year at Delos in honor of Apollo and was noted for musical contests

de·li·an \-ən\ *adj, usu cap* [L *Delius* of Delos (fr. Gk *Dēlios*, fr. *Dēlos*, island in the Aegean) + E *-an*] : of or relating to the island of Delos, held in antiquity to be the birthplace of Apollo and Artemis

delian problem *n, usu cap D* [so called fr. the problem posed by the judgment of the Delian oracle in ancient Greece that a plague in Athens could be brought to an end by doubling the size of a cubical altar to Apollo] : the problem of finding the edge of a cube the double in volume of a given cube

delibate *vt* -ED/-ING/-S [L *delibatus*, past part. of *delibare* to take away, decrease, taste, enjoy, fr. *de-* + *libare* to pour out, take out, taste — more at LIBATION] *obs* : to take a little of : dabble in : SIP — **delibation** *n* -S *obs*

de·lib·er·ant \də̇ˈlib(ə)rənt, dēˈ-\ *n* -S [²*deliberate* + *-ant*] : one who deliberates

¹**de·lib·er·ate** \də̇ˈlib(ə)rə̇t, dē-, *chiefly in substand speech* -bər|t; *usu* |d· + V\ *adj* [L *deliberatus*, past part. of *deliberare*, alter. (influenced by *liberare* to free) of (assumed) *delibrare*, fr. *de-* + *libra* scale, pound — more at LIBERATE] **1** : characterized by or resulting from unhurried, careful, thorough, and cool calculation and consideration of effects and consequences : not hasty, rash, or thoughtless ⟨a ~ judgement⟩ ⟨there is no ~ study of it; haphazard thoughts occupy the place of rational conclusions —Herbert Spencer⟩ **2** : characterized by presumed or real awareness of the implications or consequences of one's actions or sayings or by fully conscious often willful intent ⟨~ mischief⟩ ⟨a ~ lie⟩ ⟨it was no accidental meeting of fugitive glances . . . a ~ communication —*Joseph Conrad*⟩ **3** : slow, unhurried, and steady as though allowing time for decision on each individual action involved ⟨a ~ man, slow to anger but ruthless when aroused⟩ ⟨he had not heard her heavy ~ tread on the now uncarpeted stair —Willa Cather⟩ ⟨~ in speech⟩

syn CONSIDERED, ADVISED, PREMEDITATED, DESIGNED, STUDIED: DELIBERATE always indicates full awareness of what one is doing and, used precisely, implies careful and unhurried consideration of procedures or consequences ⟨before the U.S. could obtain an admission from Palmerston that the attack on the *Caroline* had been *deliberate* and official —S.E.Morison & H.S.Commager⟩ ⟨cautious, *deliberate*, methodical, he was in no danger, she felt, of plunging precipitately into marriage — Ellen Glasgow⟩ ⟨her methodicalness made her suicide more *deliberate*. Her self-possession was frightening —W.S. Maugham⟩ CONSIDERED, not usu. applied to questionable acts, suggests careful study and soundness and maturity of judgment ⟨in my *considered* opinion⟩ ⟨a fitting object to be called, by those who suspect all men of *considered* opinions and of wide systematized views, a dogmatist —*Contemporary Rev.*⟩ ADVISED, now used mostly with deprecatory modifying adverbs, means so well thought out that possible criticisms and objections can be readily answered and doubts resolved ⟨the very proper young man felt well *advised* to sound out the parents before proposing to the girl⟩ PREMEDITATED emphasizes previous planning and intent but does not necessarily indicate consideration of consequences ⟨both first and second degree murder (laying aside the exceptions which I thought it unnecessary to state) require an intent to kill, but in the one instance it is deliberate and *premeditated* intent and in the other it is not —B.N.Cardozo⟩ DESIGNED indicates intent and plan, perhaps despite appearances of spontaneity and naturalness ⟨perhaps the humor of this ruling was more unwitting than *designed* —B.N.Cardozo⟩ STUDIED connotes absence of spontaneity and presence of cool deliberateness, painstaking effort, or careful attention ⟨the student began to feel that the teacher's oppression of him was a *studied* effort⟩ ⟨the themes of these chaste exercises are often of a *studied* thinness. You may find that the author is disclaiming, almost anxiously, the idea of tarnishing the minute mirror of his sensibilities with any breath of thought —C.E.Montague⟩ **syn** see in addition SLOW, VOLUNTARY

²**de·lib·er·ate** \-ˈlibəˌrāt, *usu* -ād·+V\ *vb* -ED/-ING/-S [L *deliberatus*] *vt* : to ponder or think about with measured careful consideration and often with formal discussion before reaching a decision or conclusion ⟨he is *deliberating* what to do⟩ ⟨the committee *deliberated* the matter⟩ ~ *vi* : to ponder issues and decisions carefully often with the aid of counsel and formal consultation ⟨the jury *deliberated* throughout the night⟩ ⟨a club *deliberating* on what to do with the extra money in its treasury⟩ **syn** see THINK

de·lib·er·ate·ly \-ˈlibər(ə)tlē, -brət-, -li\ *adv* : in a deliberate manner : with deliberation

de·lib·er·ate·ness \-bər(ə)tnə̇s, -brət-\ *n* -ES : calm well-poised slowness (as of thought, speech, or bodily movement) ⟨shrewd Dutch ~⟩

de·lib·er·a·tion \də̇ˌlibəˈrāshən, dēˌ-\ *n* -S [ME *deliberacioun*, fr. MF or L; MF *deliberation*, fr. L *deliberation-*, *deliberatio*, fr. *deliberatus* + *-ion-*, *-io* -ion] **1** : the act of weighing and examining the reasons for and against a choice or measure : careful consideration : mature reflection ⟨after careful ~ he decided to study medicine rather than law⟩ **2** : a discussion and consideration by a number of persons of the reasons for and against a measure — often used in pl. ⟨the House concluded its ~s and its members hurried home to mend political fences⟩ **3** : the quality or state of being deliberate : DELIBERATENESS **4** *obs* : RESOLUTION, DECISION, DETERMINATION

de·lib·er·a·tive \=ˈ==ˌrād·|iv, -āt|, |ēv *also* |əv; -b(ə)rəd·|, -rət|\ *adj* [L *deliberativus*, fr. *deliberatus* + *-ivus* -ive] : of, relating to, or marked by deliberation : proceeding or acting by discussion and examination : engaged in or devoted to deliberation ⟨a ~ body⟩ — see DELIBERATIVE ASSEMBLY — **de·lib·er·a·tive·ly** \|əvlē, -li\ *adv* — **de·lib·er·a·tive·ness** \|əvnə̇s\ *n* -ES

²**deliberative** *n* -S *obs* : a deliberative discourse or topic

deliberative assembly *n* : a nonlegislative organization that conducts meetings according to parliamentary law

de·lib·er·a·tor \-bəˌrād·ə(r)\ *n* -S : one that deliberates

de·libidinize \ˌdē+\ *vt* [*de-* + *libidinize*] : to free of erotic significance

del·i·ble \ˈdeləbəl\ *adj* [alter. (influenced by *-ible*) of earlier *deleble*, fr. L *delebilis*, fr. *delēre* to wipe out, destroy + *-bilis* capable or worthy of (being acted upon) — more at DELETE] : capable of being deleted

del·i·ca·cy \ˈdeləkəsē, -lēk-, -si\ *n* -ES [ME *delicacie*, fr. *delicat* delicate + *-cie* -cy] **1** *obs* **a** : the quality or state of being pleasurable or agreeable **b** : addiction to sensuous pleasure or luxury : INDULGENCE; *also* : luxurious treatment or care **c** : PLEASURE, GRATIFICATION **2** : something that is dainty or delicate and gives uncommon pleasure; *esp* : something pleasing to eat that is accounted rare or luxurious ⟨fresh fruit in winter was once a ~ available only to the very rich⟩ **3 a** : fineness or daintiness of form, texture, or constitution ⟨the cobwebby ~ of fine lace⟩ ⟨the ~ of the long filament that the silkworm spins⟩ ⟨a slender figure of great ~⟩ **b** : want of vigor or robustness : susceptibility to ill-health or injury : FRAILTY, WEAKNESS, TENDERNESS ⟨an appearance of overrefinement and ~⟩ ⟨the ~ of the tea rose renders it useless for northern gardens⟩ **4** : nicety, fineness, or subtle expressiveness of manipulation or touch ⟨the ~ of a pianist's touch⟩ **5 a** : precise and refined perception and discrimination ⟨the ~ of his taste in art⟩ **b** : extreme sensitivity : capacity for reacting to minute changes or with great precision — used chiefly of devices and mechanisms ⟨a balance of such ~ that moisture from the breath would activate it⟩ ⟨the ~ of a fine watch movement⟩ **6 a** : nice sensibility esp. as to the decorous, honorable, modest, or kindly; *specif* : gentle consideration of the feelings of others **b** : excessive fastidiousness : SQUEAMISHNESS ⟨hunger knows no ~⟩ **7** : the quality or state of requiring careful, precise, or tactful procedure ⟨the ~ of the present international situation⟩

¹**del·i·cate** \-kə̇t, *usu* -ə̇d·+V\ *adj, sometimes* -ER/-EST [ME *delicat*, fr. L *delicatus* pleasing to the senses, voluptuous, pampered, dainty; akin to L *delicere* to allure — more at DELIGHT] **1** : gratifying to the senses : sensuously pleasing: **a** : generally agreeable or pleasant : DELIGHTFUL ⟨the most ~ air — Grecian air, pellucid —Richard Jefferies⟩ ⟨a ~ garden⟩ **b** : pleasing to the sense of taste or smell esp. without being heady, obtrusive, or intense ⟨a tea with a peculiarly ~ aroma⟩ ⟨a ~ blend of spices⟩ : subtly savory ⟨~ cookery⟩ ⟨~ dishes to tempt an invalid⟩ **c** : delightful to see esp. because of fine dainty charming color, lines, or proportions ⟨her face . . . was as ~ as porcelain —Ellen Glasgow⟩ **2** *obs* : characterized by or addicted to self-indulgence or ease : luxury-loving : VOLUPTUOUS; *also* : SLOTHFUL **3 a** : marked by or given to keen sensitivity of impression and analysis, fine discrimination, subtle distinction, nice appreciation; *also* : calling for observation and judgment with these qualities ⟨this ~ moralist, so sensitive to historical pathos —Cecil Sprigge⟩ ⟨a task so ~ as to exacts the scholar and philosopher —B.N. Cardozo⟩ **b** : marked by or given to fastidiousness esp. by exacting or squeamish tastes or prim interests and pursuits : likely to be repelled by the crude or gross; *also* : calling for fastidious treatment ⟨not a book for the ~ reader, but . . . not pornographic —Charles Lee⟩ **c** : strongly marked by or given to scruples, strict ethics, propriety, honor, punctilio, or finer feelings **4 a** : capable of or marked by precise or minute perception, detection, measure, discernment, or judgment **b** *of an instrument or device* : exhibiting great delicacy or extreme sensitivity : capable of reacting to or registering (as by deflection of a balance) a minute effect, force, or quantity ⟨an impulse so small as to be almost undetectable with even the . . . most ~ instruments —A.C.Morrison⟩ **c** : calling for or involving meticulously careful measurement, treatment, or calculation ⟨a ~ process⟩ ⟨~ tests for contamination⟩ : liable to being easily unsettled or mishandled; *sometimes* : precariously or very unevenly balanced ⟨the ~ interdependence of our credit-built finance and industry —Norman Angell⟩ **5 a** : marked by precise skillful meticulous technique or operation or by execution with adroit finesse in meeting uncommon difficulties or dangers; *also* : requiring such technique, operation, or execution ⟨a marvelously precise chart . . . the calculations were ~, minute, exquisitely clear —Sinclair Lewis⟩ **b** : marked by very fine structure, texture, finish, organization, or integration produced by or as if by immaculate or meticulous craftsmanship ⟨~ feminine handwriting —George Meredith⟩ ⟨a ~ celestial chain of sapphires —Elinor Wylie⟩ ⟨~ lace⟩ **c** : frail, fragile, or readily torn, bruised, damaged, or hurt ⟨a ~ butterfly wing⟩; *often* : lacking in physical strength and stamina : tending to suffer fatigue or illness from slight causes : WEAK, SICKLY **d** : marked by fine subtlety : having qualities perceived and appreciated only by the cultivated : not crude or obvious ⟨an irony so quiet, so ~, that many readers never notice it —J.B.Priestley⟩ **e** : marked by or given to elaborate tact, cautious judgment, and prudent discreetness to avoid offense, conflict, or difficulty ⟨~ semidiplomatic relationships with belligerent and neutral powers —W.B.Hesseltine⟩ ⟨he went off, ~ as always, so we could talk about it —Ernest Hemingway⟩; *also* : requiring such characteristics : SENSITIVE, UNCERTAIN, PRECARIOUS ⟨a ~ position, one requiring great tact —J.T.Farrell⟩

⟨one's spiritual concerns are rather ~ for a stranger to meddle with —Herman Melville⟩ **syn** see CHOICE

²delicate \"\ *n* -s [ME *delicat*, fr. L *delicatus* voluptuary, fr. *delicatus*, adj.] : one that is delicate: as **a** *obs* : a luxurious or fastidious person **b** *obs* : a delight esp. of the senses : LUXURY **c** *archaic* : a table delicacy

del·i·cate·ly *adv* [ME *delicatly*, fr. *delicat* + *-ly*] : in a delicate manner : with delicacy: as **a** : with fastidiousness ⟨picking ~ at the morsels on her plate⟩ **b** : with nice consideration ⟨words ~ chosen to avoid further offense⟩ **c** : gently and precisely ⟨stepping ~ from hummock to hummock⟩

del·i·cate·ness *n* -ES : the quality or state of being delicate : PRECARIOUSNESS, FRAGILITY, REFINEMENT, DELICACY

del·i·ca·tesse \,==kə'tes\ *n* -s [F *délicatesse*, fr. MF *delicatesse*, prob. fr. OIt *delicatezza*, fr. *delicato* delicate, dainty, tasty (fr. L *delicatus* pleasing to the senses, voluptuous) + *-ezza* -ess — more at DELICATE] : DELICACY, TACT

del·i·ca·tes·sen \-s°n\ *n pl* [G *delikatessen* (formerly spelled *delicatessen*), pl. of *delikatesse* delicacy, fr. F *délicatesse*] **1** : ready-to-eat food products (as cooked or processed meats, cheeses, prepared salads, canned foods, preserves, relishes) **2** *sing, pl* **delicatessens** [*delicatessen* (*store*)] : a store where delicatessen are sold either to be taken out or to be eaten on the premises (as in sandwiches)

de·lice \də'lēs\ *n* -s [ME, fr. OF, fr. L *delicium*, fr. *delicere* to allure — more at DELIGHT] *archaic* : something giving pleasure; *esp* : DELICACY

del·i·chon \'delə,kän\ *n, cap* [NL, anagram of *Chelidon*] : a genus of swallows with feathered feet that includes the European martin (*D. urbica*)

¹de·li·cious \də'lishəs, dē'-\ *adj* [ME, fr. OF, fr. LL *deliciosus*, fr. L *deliciae* delight (fr. *delicere* to allure) + *-osus* -ose — more at DELIGHT] **1 a** : affording great pleasure : DELIGHTFUL, ENCHANTING ⟨a stroll through the ~ spring landscape⟩ ⟨a ~ breeze cooled our heated foreheads⟩ **b** : appealing to one of the bodily senses : affording an enjoyable sensory reaction esp. involving the sense of taste or smell ⟨a ~ dessert⟩ ⟨a ~ mouth-watering smell drifted from the kitchen⟩ **c** : delightfully amusing ⟨her ~ impudence and enchanting grace held them spellbound⟩ **2** *obs* : characterized by or addicted to self-indulgent or sensuous pleasure : seeking voluptuous enjoyment : LUXURIOUS **syn** see DELIGHTFUL

²delicious \"\ *also* **delicious apple** *n, pl* **deliciouses** *or* **delicious** *often cap* : a largely red apple of American origin and superior form, aroma, and flavor that is much grown in warmer apple-producing sections; *broadly* : any of several apples having qualities in common with the delicious and possibly derived from it — usu. used in combination ⟨golden ~⟩ ⟨double-red ~⟩

de·li·cious·ly *adv* [ME, fr. *delicious* + *-ly*] : in a delicious manner ⟨~ flavored sauce⟩ : so as to produce delight ⟨a ~ exciting situation⟩

de·li·cious·ness *n* -ES [ME *deliciousnesse*, fr. *delicious* + *-nesse* -ness] : the quality or state of being delicious : DELIGHT

de·lict \də'likt, dē'- *also* 'dē,-\ *n* -s [L *delictum* fault, fr. neut. of *delictus*, past part. of *delinquere* to fail, offend — more at DELINQUENT] : a wrong or improper act : OFFENSE: as **a** : an offense or transgression against law — chiefly used in the civil and Scots law to designate civil wrongs corresponding closely to the torts of English law **b** : an act of a sovereign state that is considered under the law of nations to be an offense or injury against another state — **de·lic·tu·al** \=ˈlikchəwəl, (')dē;-\ *adj*

de·lic·tum \=ˈliktəm\ *n, pl* **delic·ta** \-tə\ [L] : DELICT

de·lie·ret \də'lērət\ *var of* DELEERIT

¹de·light \də'līt, dē'-, *usu* -īd·+V\ *n* -s [ME *delit*, fr. OF *delit*, *deleit*, fr. *delitier*, *deleitier*] **1** : a high degree of gratification of mind or sense : a high-wrought state of pleasurable feeling : lively pleasure : JOY ⟨filled with ~ at the thought of pleasant days ahead⟩; *also* : extreme satisfaction ⟨he took ~ in his new accomplishment⟩ **2** : something that gives great pleasure or gratification ⟨Heaven's last, best gift, my ever new ~ —John Milton⟩ ⟨the new car is a perfect ~⟩ **3** *archaic* : the power of affording pleasurable emotion or felicity ⟨of more ~ than hawks or horses be —Shak.⟩ **syn** see PLEASURE

²delight \"\ *vb* -ED/-ING/-S [ME *deliten*, fr. OF *delitier*, *deleitier*, fr. L *delectare*, fr. *delectus* past part. of *delicere* to allure, fr. *de-* + *-licere* (fr. *lacere* to allure); akin to OE *lǣl* switch, L *laqueus* snare] *vi* **1** : to have or take great satisfaction or pleasure : become greatly pleased or rejoiced—used with *in* or an infinitive ⟨love *delights* in praises —Shak.⟩ ⟨I *delight* to do thy will, O my God —Ps 40:8⟩ **2** : to give keen enjoyment or pleasure ~ *vt* **1** : to give joy or satisfaction to : affect very pleasurably : please highly : GRATIFY ⟨a beautiful scene ~*s* the eye⟩ ⟨their gifts ~*ed* the children⟩ **2** *obs* : to take delight in : ENJOY **syn** see PLEASE

delighted *adj* **1** *obs* : DELIGHTFUL **2** : highly pleased : GRATIFIED : JOYOUS — **de·light·ed·ly** *adv* — **de·light·ed·ness** *n* -ES

de·light·er \-īd·ə(r), -ītə-\ *n* -s : one that gives or takes delight

de·light·ful \-ītfəl\ *adj* **1** : highly pleasing : affording great pleasure and satisfaction ⟨a ~ day in the country⟩ **2** *obs* : experiencing delight

syn DELICIOUS, DELECTABLE, LUSCIOUS: DELIGHTFUL, very wide in its applications, may describe anything that gives keen lively pleasure to mind, heart, or senses ⟨this is the most charming and *delightful* book I have read in many a day —H.S.Canby⟩ ⟨he was a high-spirited ornamental youth with soft melting eyes, as good as he was beautiful, and so *delightful* to women that it was said they all longed to bite him —J.A. Froude⟩ ⟨for rest and recreation a warm, equable climate is doubtless most *delightful* —Ellsworth Huntington⟩ ⟨sex must be treated from the first as natural, *delightful* and decent —Bertrand Russell⟩ DELICIOUS commonly refers to that which is tasted, smelled, or otherwise savored with maximum pleasure and keenest appreciation ⟨the fish was *delicious*; the manner of cooking them in the ground preserving all the juices and rendering them exceeding sweet and tender —Herman Melville⟩ ⟨among the irises and roses and nodding tufts of lilac . . . snuffing in . . . the *delicious* scent —Virginia Woolf⟩ ⟨her gestures *delicious* in their modest and sensitive grace —Arnold Bennett⟩ DELECTABLE, a rather literary word, is close to DELICIOUS but may apply to what enraptures a refined or discriminating taste ⟨it was spicy sherry, and we drank out of the halves of fresh citron melons. *Delectable* goblets —Herman Melville⟩ ⟨the sweet cloister, with its walls of silver, surrounded by silvery herbage, all *delectable* beyond conception —H.O. Taylor⟩ ⟨its scoring is *delectable*, with the subtlest of balances, mixed colors and shifting sonorities —*Musical America*⟩ LUSCIOUS suggests a lush richness of taste, flavor, fragrance, or coloring ⟨the *luscious* figs, the grapes, oozy with southern juice —Nathaniel Hawthorne⟩ ⟨Renoir, whose appetizing La Source — an amply bosomed nude sitting beside a running fountain — showed the *luscious* tints and easy symbolism —*Time*⟩ ⟨the quatrains of wine and flowers translated for us in *luscious*, seductive rhyme —Donn Byrne⟩ LUSCIOUS may suggest overtones of excess or extravagance, as of coloring, fleshy ripeness, full-blown luxuriance, or voluptuousness ⟨others amuse themselves with *luscious* sonnets to Bessies and Jessies —*Publ's Mod. Lang. Assoc. of America*⟩ ⟨she was a blonde, who must once have been quite *luscious* and who was by no means even now undesirable — smooth and round, with a pink complexion that sometimes looked like strawberries and cream, sometimes a little blowsy —Edmund Wilson⟩ DELECTABLE and LUSCIOUS are more common in humorous and ironic uses than DELIGHTFUL and DELICIOUS ⟨one of the most *delectable* bees that ever buzzed in a bonnet —C.E.Montague⟩ ⟨a droll and *luscious* nasality —Thomas Wolfe⟩

de·light·ful·ly \-ītf(ə)lē, -li\ *adv* : in a delightful manner : in such a way or to such a degree as to be esp. pleasant ⟨~ gentle breezes⟩ ⟨a ~ restful season⟩

de·light·ful·ness \-fəlnəs\ *n* -ES : the quality of being delightful

de·light·ing *adj* : giving delight — **de·light·ing·ly** *adv*

de·light·less \-tləs\ *adj* : being without delight : JOYLESS

de·light·some \-ītsəm\ *adj* : very pleasing : DELIGHTFUL ⟨Elizabeth Barrett Browning found melancholy capable of being ~ —I.J.C.Brown⟩ — **de·light·some·ly** *adv*

de·lignification \(¦)dē+\ *n* [*de-* + *lignin* + *-fication*] : removal of lignin from woody tissue (as by natural enzymatic or industrial chemical processes) — **de·lignify** \(')dē+\ *vt*

de·lime \(')dē+\ *vt* [*de-* + *lime* (n.)] : to free from lime; *esp* : to remove lime previously used as a dehairing agent from hides or skins preparatory to tanning

de·limer \" + \ *n* -s : a tannery worker who removes from hides the lime that was used for dehairing

de·limit \(')dē, də+\ *vt* [F *délimiter*, fr. L *delimitare*, fr. *de-* + *limitare* to limit — more at LIMIT] **1** : to fix or determine the limits of ⟨the commission ~*ed* the frontier through the disputed region⟩ **2** : to serve as a boundary to or between ⟨a river ~*ing* the plain⟩ ⟨social custom ~*s* propriety and impropriety⟩

de·lim·i·tate \(')dē¦limə,tāt, də'-\ *vt* [L *delimitatus*, past part. of *delimitare* to delimit] : DELIMIT — **de·lim·i·ta·tion** \(,)dē,limə'tāshən\ *n* -s — **de·lim·i·ta·tive** \(')dē¦limə,tād·iv\ *adj*

de·limiter \(')dē, də+\ *n* -s : one that delimits

delineament *n* -s [L *delineamentum*, fr. *delineare* + *-mentum* -ment] *obs* : DELINEATION

¹de·lin·e·ate \də'linē,āt, dē'-, *usu* -ād·+V\ *vt* [L *delineatus*, past part. of *delineare*, fr. *de-* + *lineare* to draw a line, make straight, fr. *linea* line — more at LINE] **1 a** : to indicate by lines drawn in the form or figure of : represent by sketch, design, or diagram : sketch out : PORTRAY, PICTURE; *specif* : to represent in drawing and engraving by lines (as with pen, pencil, or graver) **b** : to represent with accuracy and minute attention to detail **2** : to describe in detail esp. with sharpness or vividness ⟨I do not intend to . . . ~ their wars, or describe their political backgrounds —W.H.Camp⟩ ⟨a good many nouns and adjectives have also been expended in *delineating* Abbott as a theater personality —Gilbert Millstein⟩ **syn** see REPRESENT

²de·lin·e·ate \-ēət\ *adj* [L *delineatus*] *archaic* : DELINEATED

de·lin·e·a·tion \=¦nē'āshən\ *n* -s [LL *delineation-*, *delineatio*, fr. L *delineatus* + *-ion-*, *-io* -ion] **1 a** : the act of representing, portraying, or describing (as by lines, diagrams, sketches) : a drawing in outline ⟨the ~ of a scene⟩; *esp* : representation in drawing and engraving by means of lines as distinguished from representation by means of tints and shades **b** : accurate and precise graphic representation as distinguished from that which is careless or sketchy as to details **2** : the act of delineating verbally ⟨the ~ of final metaphysical truth is no part of this lecture —A.N.Whitehead⟩ **3** : something (as a diagram, picture, description) made by delineating ⟨a photographic ~ of low life —T.S.Eliot⟩

de·lin·e·a·tive \=¦nē,ād·iv, -ēəd·-\ *adj* : serving or tending to delineate

de·lin·e·a·tor \-,ād·ə(r), -ātə-\ *n* -s **1** : one that delineates **2 a** : a surveying odometer that records distances and delineates a profile (as of a road) **b** : a person who makes perspective drawings from an architect's plans **c** : a row of light reflectors mounted on posts esp. on curves along the edge of a highway to guide traffic at night

de·lin·quence \də'liŋkwən(t)s, dē'-, -link-\ *archaic var of* DELINQUENCY

de·lin·quen·cy \-nsē, -nsi\ *n* -ES [LL *delinquentia*, fr. L *delinquent-*, *delinquens* (pres. part. of *delinquere*) + *-ia* -y] : the quality or state of being delinquent: as **a** : failure, omission, or violation of duty : transgression of law **b** : MISDEED, FAULT, OFFENSE : MISFEASANCE, MALFEASANCE, MISDEMEANOR; *often* : a tendency to commit such offenses — usu. distinguished from *crime* on the basis of an implied psychological rather than a judicial attitude toward the offender **c** : a debt on which payment of interest or principal is in arrears — used esp. of taxes and mortgage loans

¹de·lin·quent \-nt\ *n* -s [MF, fr. pres. part. of *delinquer* to do wrong, fail, fr. L *delinquere*] : a delinquent individual : a transgressor against duty or law esp. in a degree not constituting crime; *specif* : JUVENILE DELINQUENT **syn** see CRIMINAL

²delinquent \"\ *adj* [L *delinquent-*, *delinquens*, pres. part. of *delinquere* to fail, offend, fr. *de-* + *linquere* to *leave* — more at LOAN] **1 a** : failing in duty : offending by neglect or violation of duty or of law **b** (1) : in arrears in payment of debt or interest thereon ⟨~ debtor⟩ (2) : past due and unpaid ⟨~ taxes⟩ **2** : of or relating to a delinquent or delinquency — **de·lin·quent·ly** *adv*

de·lint \(')dē+\ *vt* -ED/-ING/-S [*de-* + *lint* (n.)] : to free (as cottonseed) from lint or linters — **de·linter** \(')dē+\ *n* -s

del·i·quesce \'delə'kwes\ *vi* [L *deliquescere*, fr. *de-* + *liquescere* to become fluid, melt, fr. *liquēre* to be fluid — more at LIQUID] **1** : to melt away : disappear as though by melting: **a** : dissolve gradually and become liquid by attracting and absorbing moisture from the air **b** : to become soft or liquid with age — used of certain plant structures (as some mushrooms) **2** : to divide repeatedly ending in fine divisions — used esp. of the veins of a leaf

del·i·ques·cence \-s°n(t)s\ *n* -s : the act or process of deliquescing; *also* : the resultant state or liquid product

del·i·ques·cent \¦==¦s°nt\ *adj* [L *deliquescent-*, *deliquescens*, pres. part. of *deliquescere* to become fluid, melt] : of, relating to, or exhibiting deliquescence : tending or liable to deliquesce

de·liq·ui·ate \də'likwē,āt, dē'-\ *vi* -ED/-ING/-S [alter. of earlier *deliquate*, fr. L *deliquatus*, past part. of *deliquare* to clarify, strain, fr. *de-* + *liquare* to melt, liquefy, strain; akin to L *liquēre* to be fluid — more at LIQUID] *archaic* : DELIQUESCE

de·liq·ui·um \-wēəm\ *n* -s [L, fr. *delinquere* to fail, offend — more at DELINQUENT] *archaic* : a failure of vitality : a fainting or sinking away

²deliquium \"\ *n* [LL, act of melting, fr. L *de-* + *-liquium* (fr. *liquēre* to be fluid) — more at LIQUID] *archaic* : DELIQUESCENCE

de·lir·a·ment \də'lirəmənt, dē'-\ *n* -s [ME, fr. L *deliramentum*, fr. *delirare* to be crazy + *-mentum* -ment — more at DELIRIUM] *archaic* : an insane fancy : CRAZE, DELUSION

del·i·ra·tion \,delə'rāshən\ *n* -s [L *deliration-*, *deliratio*, fr. *deliratus* (past part. of *delirare* to be crazy) + *-ion-*, *-io* -ion] *archaic* : abnormal state of mind : DELIRIUM; *often* : irrational action or speech

¹de·lir·i·ant \də'lirēənt, dē'-\ *adj* [*delirium* + *-ant*] : producing or tending to produce delirium

²deliriant \"\ *n* -s : a deliriant agent

de·lir·i·ous \də'lirēəs, dē'-\ *adj* [*delirium* + *-ous*] **1** : of, relating to, or characteristic of delirium ⟨~ mutterings⟩ **2** : affected with delirium ⟨the ~ children⟩ : wandering in mind esp. temporarily and as a result of physical disease ⟨he is ~ from fever⟩ **3** : tending to induce delirium esp. in the form of wild excitement or enthusiasm ⟨the ~ quality of her voice⟩ — **de·lir·i·ous·ly** *adv* — **de·lir·i·ous·ness** *n* -ES

de·lir·i·um \-rēəm\ *n, pl* **deliriums** \-mz\ *also* **delir·ia** \-rēə\ [L, fr. *delirare* to be crazy, fr. *de-* + *lira* furrow, track — more at LEARN] **1** : a transient mental disturbance that is characterized by confusion, disorientation, disordered speech, restlessness, excitement, and often delusions and hallucinations and sometimes occurs in the course of a mental illness but is usu. associated with high fever, toxemia, or injury **2** : frenzied excitement or wild enthusiasm ⟨the year was 1924, the great Florida land boom was just gathering ~ in the region of Sarasota —R.L.Taylor⟩; *also* : an instance or expression of it ⟨a veritable ~ of symbol hunting —Joseph Frank⟩ **syn** see MANIA

delirium tre·mens \=¦==ˈtrēmənz *also* -,menz *sometimes* -ˈtremənz\ *n* [NL, lit., trembling delirium] : a violent delirium induced by excessive and prolonged use of alcoholic liquors and characterized by terrifying hallucinations, mental confusion, restlessness, sweating, and tremor

de·list \(')dē+\ *vt* [*de-* + *list* (n.)] : to remove from a list (as from one indicative of approval); *often* : to remove (a security) from the list of securities that may be dealt in on a particular exchange

del·i·tes·cence \,delə'tesən(t)s\ *also* **del·i·tes·cen·cy** \-nsē\ *n, pl* **delitescenc·es** *also* **delitescen·cies** : delitescent state : OBFUSCATION, CONCEALMENT, OBSCURATION

del·i·tes·cent \¦==¦s°nt\ *adj* [L *delitescent-*, *delitescens*, pres. part. of *delitescere* to hide, be hidden, fr. *de-* + *litescere* (fr. *latescere* to hide, incho. of *latēre* to hide) — more at LATENT] : lying hidden : OBFUSCATED, LATENT

¹de·liv·er \də'livə(r), dē'-\ *vb* **delivered; delivered; delivering** \-v(ə)riŋ\ **delivers** [ME *deliveren*, fr. OF *delivrer*, fr. LL *deliberare*, fr. L *de-* + *liberare* to free — more at LIBERATE] *vt* **1** : to set free from restraint : set at liberty : release or liberate esp. from control : rescue from actual or feared evil : FREE, SAVE ⟨he that taketh warning shall ~ his soul —Ezek 33:5 (AV)⟩ — often used with *from* or *out of* ⟨~*ed* him from captivity⟩ **2** : GIVE, TRANSFER : yield possession or control of : make or hand over : make delivery of : COMMIT, SURRENDER, RESIGN — often used with *up* or *over*, *to* or *into* ⟨thou shalt ~ Pharaoh's cup into his hand —Gen 40:13 (AV)⟩ ⟨the constables have ~*ed* her over —Shak.⟩ **3 a** : to assist (a parturient female) in giving birth ⟨she was ~*ed* of a fine boy⟩ ⟨the doctor has ~*ed* several thousand women in his long career⟩; *also* : to aid in the birth of ⟨sometimes it is necessary to ~ a child with forceps⟩ **b** : to give birth to ⟨she ~*ed* a pair of healthy twins after a short labor⟩ **4 a** : to disburden (as oneself) in words : give forth in words : UTTER, SPEAK, ENUNCIATE ⟨he ~*ed* his speech effectively⟩ **b** : to make known to another : COMMUNICATE ⟨they ~*ed* their ultimatum to the enemy⟩ **5** : to send (something aimed or guided) to an intended destination ⟨~*ing* a short uppercut to the jaw⟩ ⟨the frigate ~*ed* a smashing broadside⟩ ⟨the pitcher ~*ed* a curve to the batter⟩ **6** *archaic* : to unload (as a ship) of cargo : EMPTY **7** : to bring (as votes) to the support of a particular candidate or cause ⟨couldn't ~ the votes of his ward⟩ ~ *vi* **1** : to set one free : DISBURDEN ⟨a deliverance which does not ~ —R.W.Emerson⟩ **2** : UTTER, DISCOURSE ⟨he ~*ed* beautifully but his speech had little real content⟩; *sometimes* : to express an opinion or judgment **3** : to give birth to offspring ⟨patients that repeatedly ~ prematurely present special problems⟩ **syn** see FREE, RESCUE — **deliver a jail** : to clear a jail by bringing all the prisoners to trial — **deliver the goods** : to give results that are promised, expected, or desired

²deliver \"\ *adj* [ME (also, free), fr. MF *delivre*, fr. *delivrer* to free] *archaic* : NIMBLE, SPRIGHTLY, ACTIVE

de·liv·er·abil·i·ty \=,=v(ə)rə'biləd·ē, -ətī, \i\ *n* -ES : ability to be delivered (as on demand)

de·liv·er·able \=ˈ=v(ə)rəbəl\ *adj* : suitable for, ready for, or in condition for delivery usu. immediately

de·liv·er·ance \-v(ə)rən(t)s, -vərn-\ *n* -s [ME *deliveraunce*, fr. OF *delivrance*, fr. *delivrer* to free, deliver + *-ance* — more at DELIVER] **1** : the act of delivering or state of being delivered: as **a** : the act of freeing or state of being freed (as from restraint, captivity, peril) : RESCUE, LIBERATION, RELEASE ⟨He hath sent me to heal the brokenhearted, to preach ~ to the captives —Lk 4:18 (AV)⟩ ⟨their ~ from the flood seemed a miracle⟩ **b** : the delivery of offspring **c** *archaic* : the act of speaking : UTTERANCE, DELIVERY **d** : the act of disburdening (as by uttering one's thoughts) **2** : something delivered or communicated: as **a** : an opinion or decision expressed publicly **b** (1) : a legal opinion, verdict, or decision expressed publicly (2) *Scots law* : an interlocutory order or decree

delivered *adj* : including the cost of delivery ⟨~ prices will vary somewhat⟩

delivered price *n* : a price for which a seller agrees to deliver merchandise to a purchaser at a designated place and which usu. includes the f.o.b. price at the shipping point plus lawful transportation charges actually incurred in delivery

de·liv·er·er \-v(ə)rə(r)\ *n* -s [ME *deliverere*, fr. MF, fr. *delivrer* + *-ere* -er] : one that delivers: as **a** : one that liberates or rescues : PRESERVER **b** : one that gives up or transfers (as letters or goods) **c** : one that utters or recites **d** : one that delivers something (as parcels or mail)

de·liv·er·ly \-və(r)lē\ *adv* [ME, fr. *²deliver* + *-ly*] *archaic* : ACTIVELY, NIMBLY, DEFTLY

de·liv·ery \-v(ə)rē, -ri\ *n* -ES [ME *deliverie*, fr. *deliveren* to deliver + *-ie* -y] **1** : a delivering from restraint : RESCUE, RELEASE, LIBERATION ⟨~ of a captive from a dungeon⟩ **2 a** : the act of delivering up or over : transfer of the body or substance of a thing : SURRENDER ⟨an agreement to make ~ of the bonds⟩ **b** : the physical and legal transfer of a shipment from consignor to carrier, between carriers, and from transport agency to consignee **c** : the act of putting property into the legal possession of another ⟨the ~ of a fort⟩ ⟨~ of hostages⟩ whether involving the actual transfer of the physical control of the object from one to the other or being constructively effected in various other ways (as by the handing over of something symbolical of the thing sought to be delivered) **d** : a part or instance of delivery ⟨we are prepared to make daily *deliveries*⟩ : something delivered at one time or in one unit ⟨each ~ will include five gross of assorted novelties⟩ **e** : a truck or other vehicle used for delivering merchandise esp. to retail customers **f** : an organization that engages to deliver goods (as retail parcels) within a local area **3 a** : the act of giving birth : the expulsion or extraction of a fetus and its membranes : PARTURITION **b** : the procedure of delivering the fetus and placenta by manual, instrumental, or surgical means **4** : utterance esp. of words : a delivering esp. of a speech; *often* : manner or style of uttering in speech or song : ENUNCIATION **5 a** : the act or manner of sending forth, discharging, or throwing (as a baseball) **b** : a pitched or bowled ball **6** *archaic* : the act of exerting one's strength or limbs : bodily poise : BEARING **7** *obs* : the act of communicating : STATEMENT, NARRATION, ACCOUNT **8** : the manner or form of output of a textile machine ⟨~ of the untwisted sliver⟩ **9** : a part of certain printing presses that receives and stacks the printed sheets

delivery boy *n* : a person employed by a retail store to deliver small orders to customers on call

delivery cylinder *n* : a cylinder (as in a rotary offset printing press) that conveys the printed paper to the delivery

delivery desk *n* : a desk in a library from which books are handed or sent to readers and borrowers upon request

de·liv·ery·man \-,man, -,maa(ə)n, -mən\ *n, pl* **deliverymen** : a person who delivers wholesale or retail goods to customers usu. over a regular local route

delivery room *n* **1** : a hospital room esp. equipped for the delivery of pregnant women **2** : the room or section of a library in which books are issued to and returned by borrowers

¹dell \'del\ *n* -s [ME *dele*, *delle*; akin to Fris, MD & MLG *delle* valley, MHG *telle* ravine, Goth *ibdalja* mountain slope, OE *dæl* valley — more at DALE] **1** : a small secluded natural hollow or valley usu. covered with trees or turf **2** *obs* : a deep pit in the ground

²dell \"\ *n* -s [D *del*, fr. MD *delle*, *dille* gossip, frivolous girl, fr. *dillen* to gossip, prattle] *archaic slang* : a young woman; *usu* : TRULL, DRAB, WENCH

¹del·la-crus·can \¦delə¦krəskən\ *adj*, *usu cap D&C* [Accademia *della Crusca*, Florentine academy founded 1582 for the cultivation of the Italian language and literature (fr. It, lit., academy of chaff) + E *-an*] **1 a** : of, relating to, or resembling the Accademia della Crusca or the literary style it championed **b** : of, relating to, or resembling the style of a school of chiefly expatriate English writers of affected rhetorically ornate poetry in the late 18th century **2** : affectedly pedantic — used of writings or literary style

²della-cruscan \"\ *n* -s *usu cap D&C* : a member of the Accademia della Crusca or the Della-Cruscan school

del·la rob·bia blue \¦delə¦rōbēə-, -rōb-\ *n*, *often cap R* [after *Della Robbia*, family of Ital. painters and sculptors of the 15th and 16th cents.] : a variable color averaging a light blue that is redder and deeper than average forget-me-not (sense 2a)

della robbia ware \"-\ *also* **della robbia** *n, usu cap D&R* [after Luca *della Robbia* †1482 Florentine sculptor who developed the process] : sculptured glazed and colored terra=cotta work produced in Florence by the workshop of Luca della Robbia and his nephews and followers

dells \'delz\ *n pl* [by folk etymology] : DALLES

del mar pine \'del,mär-\ *n*, *usu cap D&M* [fr. *Del Mar*, village near San Diego, Calif.] : TORREY PINE

del·mon·i·co potatoes \del'mänə,kō-\ *n pl*, *usu cap D* [fr. the *Delmonico* restaurants, New York City, after Lorenzo *Delmonico* †1881 Am. restaurateur] : hashed or sliced potatoes baked in cream sauce with butter and chives and with or without grated cheese

delmonico steak *also* **delmonico** *n* -s *usu cap D* [fr. the *Delmonico* restaurants] : CLUB STEAK

de·localization \(¦)dē+\ *n* -s : the state of being delocalized : the act of delocalizing

de·localize \(')dē+\ *vt* [*de-* + *localize*] **1** : to remove from its place **2** : to free from the limitations of locality or from connection with a particular place : free from provincialism or localism

de·lo·mor·phous \ˌdēlōˈmȯrfəs\ *or* **de·lo·mor·phic** \-fik\ *adj* [Gk *dēlo-* (fr. *dēlos* clear, visible, evident) + E *-morphous, -morphic* — more at ADEL-] **:** having a definite or fixed form ⟨the parietal cells of the cardiac glands are ~⟩

de·lo·nix \dəˈlōniks\ [NL] *syn of* POINCIANA

de·lo·ren·zite \ˌdēləˈrenˌzīt, ˌdel-\ *n* -s [It, fr. G. *De Lorenzo* *b*1871 It. geologist + It *-ite*] **:** a mineral approximately $(Y,U,Fe)(Ti,Sn)_3O_8$ consisting of an oxide chiefly of titanium, tin, yttrium, uranium, and iron

de·loul \dəˈlül\ *n* -s [F, fr. Ar *dhahūl* well-tamed] **:** a swift Arabian riding camel **:** DROMEDARY

de·louse \(ˈ)dē+\ *vt* -ED/-ING/-S [*de-* + *louse* (n.)] **1 :** to remove lice from **2 :** to free from something suggestive of lice in unpleasant or harmful character ⟨*delousing* a mine field⟩ ⟨comic book publishers will find it pays to ~ their own output⟩

1**delph** *var of* DELF

2**delph** *var of* DELFT

1**del·phi·an** \ˈdelfēən\ *or* **del·phic** \-fik,-fēk\ *adj, usu cap* [*Delphian* fr. *Delphi*, town in ancient Greece (fr. L, fr. Gk *Delphoi*) + E *-an; Delphic* fr. L *Delphicus*, fr. Gk *Delphikos*, fr. *Delphoi* + *-ikos* -ic] **1 :** of or relating to Delphi in ancient Greece or to the oracle located there **2 :** PROPHETIC, ORACULAR **3 :** characterized by obscurity or ambiguity ⟨*Delphian* pronouncements of certain government agencies⟩

2**delphian** \"\ *n* -s *usu cap* **:** a native or inhabitant of Delphi

del·phin \ˈdelfən\ *adj, cap* [fr. the *Delphin* classics; *Delphin* fr. ML *delphinus* dauphin, fr. MF *dalphin;* fr. the words *in usum Serenissimi Delphini* "for the use of the most serene Dauphin" inscribed on the title page — more at DAUPHIN] **:** of or relating to the Delphin classics, an edition of the Latin classics prepared in the reign of Louis XIV of France

del·phi·nap·ter·us \ˌ==ˈnaptərəs\ *n, cap* [NL, fr. L *delphinus* dolphin + Gk *apteros* wingless — more at APTEROUS] **:** the genus of cetaceans that consists solely of the beluga

del·phine \ˈdelˌfīn, -ˌfən\ *adj* [L *delphinus* dolphin — more at DOLPHIN] **:** of or relating to the dolphins

delphine blue B *n, usu cap D&B* **:** a mordant dye — see DYE table 1 (under *Mordant Blue 56*)

del·phin·i·dae \delˈfinəˌdē\ *n pl, cap* [NL, fr. *Delphinus*, type genus + *-idae*] **:** a family of moderate to small-sized toothed whales including the dolphins, grampuses, and usu. the porpoises — see PHOCAENIDAE — **del·phi·noid** \ˈ=fəˌnȯid\ *adj or n*

del·phin·i·din \delˈfinədən\ *n* -s [ISV, blend of *delphinin* and *-id*] **:** an anthocyanidin that occurs widely in plants in the form of glycosides (as delphinin) and is usu. obtained as the dark violet or brownish red crystalline chloride $C_{15}H_{11}ClO_7$ (as by hydrolysis of the glycosides or by synthesis from pyrogallol derivatives)

del·phi·nin \ˈ=fənən\ *n* -s [ISV *delphin-* (fr. NL *Delphinium*) + *-in*] **:** a violet crystalline anthocyanin pigment $C_{41}H_{38}O_{21}$ that is a glycoside of delphinidin found in larkspur

del·phi·nine \-ˌnēn, -ˌnən\ *n* -s [NL *Delphinium* (genus name of *Delphinium staphisagria*) + E *-ine*] **:** a poisonous crystalline alkaloid $C_{33}H_{45}NO_9$ obtained esp. from seeds of the stavesacre

del·phin·i·um \delˈfinēəm\ *n* [NL, fr. Gk *delphinion* larkspur, dim. of *delphin-*, *delphis* dolphin; fr. the shape of the nectary — more at DOLPHIN] **1** *cap* **:** a large genus of chiefly perennial erect branching herbs (family Ranunculaceae) that are widely distributed in temperate parts of the northern hemisphere, have palmately divided leaves and irregular flowers in showy spikes, and include several containing extremely poisonous substances **2** *pl* **delphiniums** \-mz\ *also* **delphin·ia** \-nēə\ **:** any plant of the genus *Delphinium; esp* **:** a cultivated perennial plant of this genus — compare LARKSPUR

delphinium blue *n* **:** a variable color averaging a brilliant blue

del·phi·nus \=ˈfīnəs\ *n, cap* [NL, fr. L, dolphin — more at DOLPHIN] **:** a genus of marine mammals that includes the common dolphin and is the type of the family Delphinidae

-del·phis \ˌdelfəs\ *n comb form* [NL, fr. Gk *delphis* — more at DOLPHIN] **:** dolphin — in generic names ⟨Cyrto*delphis*⟩

delphware *var of* DELFTWARE

dels *pl of* DEL

del·sar·ti·an \(ˈ)delˌsärd·ēən\ *adj, usu cap* [François A.N.C. *Delsarte* †1871 Fr. teacher of dramatic and musical expression who invented the system + E *-ian*] **:** of, relating to, or having the characteristics of a system or method of using body movements to express emotional concepts

delt \ˈdelt\ *vt* [origin unknown] *Scot* **:** PAMPER

delt *abbr* [L *delineavit*] he drew

1**del·ta** \ˈdeltə\ *n* -s [ME *deltha*, fr. Gk *delta*, of Sem origin; akin to Heb *dāleth* 4th letter of the Hebrew alphabet — more at DALETH] **1 :** the fourth letter of the Greek alphabet — symbol Δ or δ; see ALPHABET table **2 :** any of various things felt to resemble a capital Δ: as **a :** the alluvial deposit at the mouth of a river commonly forming a nearly flat fan-shaped plain of considerable area traversed by many separate branches in which the river distributes itself downstream and resulting from the accumulation of stream-borne sediment supplied more rapidly than it can be carried away by offshore and alongshore currents **b :** the closed figure produced by connecting three electrical coils or circuits successively end for end esp. in a three-phase system **c :** the triangular terminus of a pattern in a fingerprint formed either by bifurcation of a ridge or by divergence of two ridges that are parallel beyond it **3 :** an increment of a variable — symbol △

2**delta** \"\ *usu cap* — a communications code word for the letter *d*

3**delta** *or* δ- \"\ *adj* **1 :** of or relating to one of four or more closely related chemical substances ⟨δ-yohimbine⟩ — used somewhat arbitrarily to specify ordinal relationship or to specify a particular physical form, esp. an allotropic modification (as in δ-iron), or an isomeric or stereoisomeric form (as in δ-benzene hexachloride) **2 :** fourth in position in the structure of an organic molecule from a particular group or atom or having a structure characterized by such a position ⟨δ-hydroxy acids⟩ ⟨δ-lactones⟩ **3 :** fourth in order of brightness — used of a star in a constellation

delta connection *n* **:** a mesh connection for connecting electrical apparatus to a three-phase circuit, the three corners of the delta as represented being connected to the three wires of the supply circuit — compare OPEN-DELTA CONNECTION, STAR CONNECTION, T CONNECTION

delta fan *n* **:** FAN DELTA

del·ta·fi·ca·tion \ˌ==fəˈkāshən\ *n* -s [1*delta* + *-fication*] *geol* **:** the formation of a delta

del·ta·ic \(ˈ)delˌtāik\ *or* **del·tic** \ˈ=tik\ *adj* [1*delta* + *-ic*] **1 :** of, like, relating to, or typical of a delta ⟨~ deposits⟩ ⟨~ accumulation of silt⟩; *also* **:** constituting a delta ⟨a ~ area⟩ **2** *often cap* **:** arising or originating in the Nile delta ⟨early ~ civilization⟩ ⟨the *Deltaic* dynasties of ancient Egypt⟩

delta iron *n* **:** an iron that is stable between 1400°C and the melting point and is characterized by a body-centered cubic crystal structure — compare GAMMA IRON

del·ta·ite \ˈdeltəˌīt\ *n* -s *often cap* [1*delta* (Gk letter) + *-ite;* fr. the triangular appearance of the crystals in cross section] **:** a mineral $Ca_2Al_2(PO_4)_2(OH)_4.H_2O$ consisting of a basic hydrous phosphate of calcium and aluminum

delta lake *n* **:** a lake surrounded by deltaic deposits

delta plain *n* **:** the level or nearly level surface of a delta

delta plateau *n* **:** a raised delta plain

delta process *n, math* **:** the process of differentiation that employs deltas

delta ray *n* **:** an electron ejected by an ionizing particle (as an alpha particle) in its passage through matter

del·tar·i·um \delˈta(a)rēəm\ *n, pl* **deltar·ia** \-rēə\ [NL, fr. Gk *delta* + NL *-arium*] **:** DELTIDIUM 2

delta shoreline *n* **:** a shoreline produced by the building forward of a delta into a lake or sea

del·ta·tion \delˈtāshən\ *n* -s [1*delta* + *-ation*] **:** DELTAFICATION

delta wing *n* **:** a triangular swept-back airplane wing with straight trailing edge — **delta-winged** \ˈ==ˌ=\ *adj*

del·thy·ri·al \(ˈ)delˌthīrēəl\ *adj* [NL *delthyri*um + E *-al*] **:** of, relating to, or constituting a delthyrium

del·thy·ri·um \=ˈ=rēəm\ *n, pl* **delthy·ria** \-rēə\ [NL, prob. irreg. fr. Gk *dēlos* clear, visible, evident + *thyrion* little door, dim. of *thyra* door — more at ADEL-, DOOR] **:** the opening between the beak and the hinge through which the pedicle of certain brachiopods extends

del·tid·i·al \(ˈ)delˌtidēəl\ *adj* [NL *deltidi*um + E *-al*] **:** of, relating to, constituting, or functioning as a deltidium

del·tid·i·um \=ˈ=dēəm\ *n, pl* **deltid·ia** \-dēə\ [NL, fr. Gk *delta* + NL *-idium*] **1 :** a plate partly or wholly closing the delthyrium of certain brachiopods — called also *pseudodeltidium* **2 :** a pair of plates not homologous with the pseudodeltidium that performs the same function in other brachiopods — called also *deltidial plates*

del·ti·ol·o·gist \ˌdeltēˈäləjəst\ *n* -s **:** a person whose hobby is deltiology

del·ti·ol·o·gy \-əjē\ *n* -ES [Gk *deltion* small writing tablet (dim. of *deltos* writing tablet) + E *-logy;* akin to L *dolare* to hew — more at CONDOLE] **:** the hobby of collecting postcards

del·to·ceph·a·lus \ˌdeltəˈsefələs\ *n, cap* [NL, fr. *delto-* (fr. Gk *delta*) + *-cephalus*] **:** a large genus of leafhoppers containing one member (*D. dorsalis*) that is an important vector of rice dwarf

del·to·he·dron \-ˈhēdrən\ *n, pl* **deltohe·dra** \-drə\ [NL, fr. *delto-* + *-hedron*] **:** a solid (as a crystal) that is bounded by 12 quadrilateral faces and is a hemihedral form of the isometric system related to the tetrahedron — called also *deltoid dodecahedron, tetragonal tristetrahedron*

deltohedron

1**del·toid** \ˈdelˌtȯid\ *or* **del·toi·de·us** \=ˈ=dēəs\ *n, pl* **deltoids** \-dz\ *or* **deltoi·dei** \-dēˌī\ [*deltoid* fr. NL *deltoides*, fr. Gk *deltoeidēs* delta-shaped, fr. *delta* + *-oeidēs* -oid; *deltoideus*, NL, alter. of *deltoides*] **:** a large triangular muscle that covers the shoulder joint, serves to raise the arm laterally, arises from the upper anterior part of the outer third of the clavicle and from the acromion and spine of the scapula, and is inserted into the outer side of the middle of the shaft of the humerus

2**deltoid** \"\ *adj* [NL *deltoides*, fr. Gk *deltoeidēs*] **1 :** shaped like a capital delta **:** TRIANGULAR ⟨a ~ leaf⟩ ⟨the ~ muscle of the shoulder⟩ — see LEAF illustration **2 :** constituting or formed like a river delta

del·toi·dal \(ˈ)delˌtȯidᵊl\ *adj* **1 :** DELTOID **2 :** relating to or resembling a river delta

deltoid dodecahedron *n* **:** DELTOHEDRON

deltoid ligament *n* **:** a strong radiating ligament of the inner aspect of the ankle binding the base of the tibia to the bones of the foot

de·lude \dəˈlüd, dēˈ-\ *vt* -ED/-ING/-S [ME *deluden*, fr. L *deludere*, fr. *de-* + *ludere* to play — more at LUDICROUS] **1 :** to lead from truth or into error **:** mislead the mind or judgment of **:** impose on **:** DECEIVE, TRICK **:** make a fool of ⟨they *deluded* themselves with belief in their own superiority⟩ **2** *obs* **a :** to trifle with (one) as if acting seriously **:** MOCK **b :** to frustrate or disappoint **c :** EVADE, ELUDE **syn** see DECEIVE

de·lud·er \-də(r)\ *n* -s **:** one that deludes

de·lud·ing·ly *adv* **:** in a manner calculated to delude

1**del·uge** \ˈdel(ˌ)yü\|j *also* ˈde(ˌ)lü\| *or* ˈdelyəj *sometimes* ˈdāl(ˌ)yü\| *or* ˈdā(ˌ)lü\| *or* \|zh\ *n* -s [ME, fr. MF, fr. L *diluvium*, fr. *diluere* to wash away, fr. *di-* (fr. *dis-* apart) + *-luere* (fr. *lavere* to wash) — more at DIS-, LYE] **1 a :** an overflowing of the land by water **:** INUNDATION, FLOOD **b :** a drenching rain **:** DOWNPOUR **2 :** an irresistible rush of something (as in overwhelming numbers, quantity, or volume) ⟨a ~ of mail⟩ ⟨a ~ of offers⟩ **3 :** a forceful jet of water (as from a fire hose)

2**del·uge** \" *sometimes* dəˈlüj\ *vt* -ED/-ING/-S **1 :** to overflow with water **:** INUNDATE, FLOOD ⟨torrential rains *deluged* the region⟩; *sometimes* **:** DRENCH ⟨they were *deluged* before they could reach shelter⟩ **2 :** to overwhelm as if with a deluge **:** OVERRUN, SWAMP ⟨the empire was *deluged* with mercenaries⟩ ⟨he was *deluged* with letters⟩ ⟨I shall ~ the reader with examples, hundreds of them —Anna G. Hatcher⟩ **syn** see OVERPOWER

deluge set *n* **:** a large monitor nozzle used in fire fighting to produce a deluge

del·u·gi·nous \(ˈ)delˌyüjənəs, -eˌlü-\ *adj* **:** like a deluge

de lu·na·ti·co in·qui·ren·do \ˌdālüˌnäd·ē(ˌ)kō(ˌ)inkwēˌren(ˌ)dō\ *n* [LL, for inquiring concerning the lunatic] **:** a writ directing an inquiry as to whether a person named in the writ is insane

del·un·dung \ˈdelənˌdəŋ, dəˈl-\ *n* -s [Malay *dĕlundong*] **:** LINSANG

de·lu·sion \dəˈlüzhən, dēˈ-\ *n* -s [ME *delusioun*, fr. L *delusion-*, *delusio*, fr. *delusus* (past part. of *deludere* to delude) + *-ion-*, *-io* -ion — more at DELUDE] **1 :** act of deluding or state of being deluded; *often* **:** a misleading of the mind ⟨such pleasures end in ~⟩ **:** an abnormal mental state characterized by occurrence of delusions **2 :** something that is falsely or delusively believed or propagated **:** false belief or a persistent error of perception occasioned by false belief or mental derangement **:** customary or fixed misconception ⟨cling to a ~⟩: as **a :** a false conception and persistent belief unconquerable by reason in something that has no existence in fact **b :** a false belief regarding the self or persons or objects outside the self that persists despite the facts and is common in paranoia, schizophrenia, and psychotic depressed states ⟨~*s* of grandeur⟩

de·lu·sion·al \-zhənᵊl, -zhnəl\ *adj* **:** relating to, based on, or marked by delusions

de·lu·sion·ary \-zhəˌnerē\ *adj* **:** resulting in or marked by delusions ⟨~ hopes⟩ ⟨~ insanity⟩

de·lu·sion·ist \-zhənəst\ *n* -s **:** one given to deluding or to having delusions

de·lu·sive \dəˈlüs\|iv, dēˈ-, \|ēv *also* -üz\| *or* \|əv\ *adj* [*delus*ion + *-ive*] **1 :** apt or fitted to delude **:** DECEPTIVE, BEGUILING **2 :** constituting a delusion **:** DELUSIONAL — **de·lu·sive·ly** \\|əvlē, -li\ *adv* — **de·lu·sive·ness** \\|əvnəs\ *n* -ES

de·lu·so·ry \-üs(ə)rē, -üz(-, -ri\ *adj* [*delus*ion + *-ory*] **:** DECEPTIVE, DELUSIVE

de·luster \(ˈ)dē+\ *vt* [*de-* + *luster* (n.)] **:** to reduce the brightness of (as yarns or fabrics); *esp* **:** to add pigment to the spinning solution of (rayons)

de·lus·ter·ant \(ˈ)dēˌləst(ə)rənt, dəˈ-\ *also* **de·lus·trant** \-tr-\ *n* -s **:** a chemical agent for reducing the brightness of yarns and fabrics

de·lu·vi·al \dəˈlüvēəl, dēˈ-\ *adj* [by alter.] **:** DILUVIAL

de·lu·vi·um \-vēəm\ *n, pl* **deluviums** \-mz\ *also* **delu·via** \-vēə\ [NL, by alter.] **:** DILUVIUM

1**de·luxe** \dəˈlu̇ks, dēˈ-, -ləks, -lüks\ *adj* [F, lit., of luxury] **:** notably luxurious or elegant **:** sumptuous or elaborate (as in materials, style, or workmanship) ⟨a ~ edition of a book⟩ ⟨accommodations ~⟩ ⟨a ~ train⟩

2**deluxe** \"\ *adv* [F *de luxe*] **:** in a deluxe manner **:** LUXURIOUSLY, SUMPTUOUSLY ⟨traveling ~⟩

del·vaux·ite \delˈvȯkˌsīt, -vōkˌ-\ *n* -s [G *delvauxit*, modif. (influenced by G *-it* -ite) of F *delvauxine*, fr. J.S.P.J. *Delvaux de Feuffe* *b ab* 1782 Belgian chemist who first described it + F *-ine*] **:** a mineral approximately $Fe_4(PO_4)_2(OH)_6nH_2O$ consisting of an ill-defined hydrous phosphate of iron

1**delve** \ˈdelv\ *vb* -ED/-ING/-S [ME *delven*, fr. OE *delfan* to dig, bury; akin to OS bi*delban* to bury, OHG *telban* to dig, Lith *delba* crowbar, Russ *dolbit'* to chisel] *vt* **1** *archaic* **:** to make (as a ditch or hole) by digging **:** EXCAVATE **2 a** *now chiefly dial Brit* **:** SPADE ⟨~ a garden⟩ **b :** to dig into **:** explore by or as if by digging ⟨*delving* the garnered lore of centuries⟩ ~ *vi* **1 a :** to dig or labor with or as if with a spade; *often* **:** to labor as a drudge **b :** to seek laboriously (as in books or records) for information **2** *of a slope or sloping way* **:** to make a sudden descent **:** DIP **syn** see DIG

2**delve** \"\ *n* -s [partly fr. *delf*, partly fr. 1*delve*] **1 a** *archaic* **:** a place dug **:** PIT, DEN **b :** a surface depression **:** HOLLOW **2 :** an act of digging

delv·er \-və(r)\ *n* -s [ME, fr. OE *delfere*, fr. *delfan* to dig + *-ere* -er] **:** one that delves (as a device for clearing ditches)

delving *n* -s **:** careful and detailed investigation

dely *abbr* delivery

dem \ˈdem\ *chiefly Brit var of* DAMN

dem- *or* **demo-** *comb form* [*dem-* fr. L, fr. Gk *dēm-*, *dēmo-*, fr. *dēmos* deme, populace; *demo-* fr. MF, fr. LL, fr. Gk *dēm-*, *dēmo-;* akin to OIr *dām* retinue, company, Skt *dayate* he apportions — more at TIDE] **:** people **:** populace **:** population ⟨*demo*graphy⟩ ⟨*dem*oid⟩

dem *abbr* **1** demand **2** *often cap* democratic **3** demurrage **4** demy

-de·ma \ˌdəmə\ *n comb form* [NL, fr. Gk *demas* body, bodily build; akin to Gk *demein* to build — more at TIMBER] **:** one having (such) a body — in generic names of insects ⟨Dasy*dema*⟩

de·magnetization \(ˌ)dē+\ *n* **:** the process of demagnetizing or state of being demagnetized

de·magnetize \(ˈ)dē+\ *vt* [*de-* + *magnetize*] **:** to deprive of magnetic properties — **demagnetizer** *n*

dem·a·gog·ic \ˌdeməˌgäj\|ik, -gäg\|ik, \|ēk *also* -mēˌ- *or* -miˌ- *or* \|ək *sometimes* -gȯg\|\ *also* **dem·a·gog·i·cal** \\|əkəl, \|ēk-\ *adj* [Gk *dēmagōgikos*, fr. *dēmagōgos* + *-ikos* -ic, ical] **:** characteristic of or like a demagogue ⟨a ~ concept of Americanism⟩ ⟨took ~ advantage of a press interview⟩ ⟨the use of ~ terminology⟩ **:** tending or aiming to gain personal or partisan advantage by arousing or appealing to popular passions or prejudices esp. by making specious or extravagant claims, promises, or charges **:** RABBLE-ROUSING ⟨a ~ attack on the "plutocracy"⟩ ⟨a ~ manner of speech⟩ ⟨~ laws that he never meant to implement⟩ — **dem·a·gog·i·cal·ly** \\|ək(ə)lē, -li\ *adv*

dem·a·gog·ism *also* **dem·a·gogu·ism** \ˈ==ˌgäˌgizəm *also* ˌ==ˈ=ˌ== *sometimes* -gȯˌ-\ *n* -s **:** DEMAGOGUERY

1**dem·a·gogue** *or* **dem·a·gog** \ˈ==ˌgäg *sometimes* -gȯg\ *n* -s [Gk *dēmagōgos*, fr. *dēm-* dem- + *agōgos* leading, fr. *agein* to lead — more at AGENT] **1 :** a leader or orator in ancient times who championed the cause of the common people **:** a leader of the popular or plebeian party or faction in the state **2 :** one who employs demagogic methods; *esp* **:** a political leader who seeks to gain personal or partisan advantage by specious or extravagant claims, promises, or charges **:** RABBLE-ROUSER ⟨play statesman one moment and ~ the next —*Economist*⟩

2**demagogue** *or* **demagog** \"\ *vi* -ED/-ING/-S **:** to act the part of a demagogue **:** behave like a demagogue

dem·a·gogu·ery \ˈ==ˌgäg(ə)rē, -ri *also* ˌ==ˈ=(=)= *sometimes* -ˌgȯg-\ *n* -ES **:** the principles or practices of demagogues **:** demagogic character ⟨oversimplification and single-minded pursuit of an inflammatory issue are characteristics of modern ~ —*New Republic*⟩

dem·a·gogy \ˈ==ˌgäj\|ē, -gōj\|, -gäg\|, \|i *sometimes* -gȯg\|\ *n* -ES [Gk *dēmagōgia*, fr. *dēmagōgos* + *-ia* -y] **:** demagogic action or character **:** DEMAGOGUERY ⟨principles warped by ~⟩

demain *or* **demaine** *obs var of* DEMESNE

1**de·mand** \dəˈmand, dēˈ-, -maa(ə)nd, -mȧnd\ *n* -s [ME *demaunde*, fr. MF *demande*, fr. *demander*] **1 a :** the act of demanding or asking esp. with authority **:** a peremptory request ⟨wishes turned into ~*s* for obedience⟩ **b** (1) **:** the asking or seeking for what is due or claimed as due (2) **:** the right or title in virtue of which something may be claimed ⟨hold a ~ against a person⟩ (3) **:** a thing or amount claimed to be due **2** *archaic* **:** earnest inquiry **:** QUESTION, QUERY **3 a :** a manifested desire for ownership or use (as of a commodity) **:** a need or request for a commodity **b :** willingness and ability to purchase a commodity or service **c :** the quantities of goods or of a service that would be purchased at each of various possible prices at a given time **d :** the sum spent on or the quantity purchased of a commodity or service **4 a :** a seeking or state of being sought after esp. with authority or insistence ⟨his eloquence brought him into frequent ~ as an occasional speaker —Ella Lonn⟩ ⟨nickel is in great ~⟩ **b :** urgent need **:** REQUIREMENT ⟨increased ~*s* for manpower⟩ **5 :** something that is demanded esp. by right or as due **:** the substance of or matter presented in a claim ⟨~*s* that are justifiable and reasonable⟩ **6 :** the requirement of work or of the expenditure of some resource ⟨~*s* that overtax a piece of machinery⟩ ⟨equal to any ~*s* his old ship was likely to make on his competence —Joseph Conrad⟩ **7 :** a crude peremptory order to relinquish esp. without regard to legal right ⟨a kidnapper's ~*s* for money⟩ **8 :** the electricity load (as of an individual consumer or power plant) usu. indicated in kilowatts and averaged over a period of time **9 :** DEMAND BID — **on demand** *adv* **:** upon presentation and request for payment

2**demand** \"\ *vb* -ED/-ING/-S [ME *demaunden*, fr. MF *demander*, fr. LL *demandare* to demand, fr. L, to entrust, commit, fr. *de-* + *mandare* to commit to one's charge, order — more at MANDATE] *vi* **:** to make a demand **:** ASK, INQUIRE — used with *of* ~ *vt* **1** *obs* **:** to ask (a person) authoritatively or formally for information **2 :** to call for urgently and importunately or peremptorily and imperiously ⟨he no longer ~*ed* such recognition. Instead he prayed for it —Sherwood Anderson⟩ **3 a :** to ask or call for legally **:** make legal claim to as a rightful owner **b :** to claim as due, just, or fit ⟨the harpooner was ~*ing* the beam that he had paid for —H.A.Chippendale⟩ **c :** to ask or call for with force or authority and with expectation of compliance ⟨~ obedience to the rules⟩ **4 a :** to ask with authority or earnestness to be informed of ⟨~ the cause of her sorrow —Shak.⟩ **b :** to ask to see **:** bid (a person) to appear authoritatively or insistently ⟨the crowd ~*ed* the star⟩ **5 :** to call for as useful, necessary, or requisite **:** make imperative **:** NECESSITATE, REQUIRE ⟨the fire that the cool evenings of early spring ~*ed* —Mary Austin⟩ ⟨questions that ~ discussion of cultural conditions —John Dewey⟩ **6 :** to summon into court

syn REQUIRE, CLAIM, EXACT: DEMAND may suggest peremptory imperative communication or strongly necessitous indication ⟨Antonius tomorrow will *demand* your tribute —Alfred Tennyson⟩ ⟨the sun . . . *demanded* attention in a manner that would take no denial —C.S.Forester⟩ ⟨instincts which the conventions of good manners and the imperatives of morality *demand* that they should repress —Aldous Huxley⟩ REQUIRE is more likely to stress the fact of necessity or compulsiveness than the manner of communication or indication, and may seem less strident but more coolly insistent and exigent ⟨the duty of self-preservation *requires* us to be mentally as well equipped as the French, Germans, and Americans —W.R.Inge⟩ ⟨the government of the U.S. which in the administrations of Washington, Adams, and Jefferson *required* the services of slightly more than one thousand civilian employees —Alan Barth⟩ CLAIM may indicate a demand or request for due delivery or appropriate concession or recognition based on right, warrant, or sanction and calculated to overcome resistance or reluctance ⟨in Naples the beggars *claim* an alms noisily and as though by right —Aldous Huxley⟩ ⟨authoritarian methods now . . . come to us *claiming* to serve the ultimate ends of freedom and equity —John Dewey⟩ EXACT suggests not asking, claiming, or demanding but instead obtaining or forcing delivery, execution, or concession of what is sought ⟨the mistake of *exacting* reparation in money and then lending Germany money with which to pay —H.S. Truman⟩ ⟨kept a keen eye on her court and *exacted* prompt and willing obedience from king and archbishops —Henry Adams⟩

de·mand·able \-dəbəl\ *adj* **:** subject to being demanded

de·mand·ant \-dənt\ *n* -s [ME *demaundaunt*, fr. MF *demandant*, fr. pres. part. of *demander*] **1 :** the plaintiff in a real action at law; *also* **:** any plaintiff **2 :** one who makes a demand or claim **3 :** one who interrogates or asks questions ⟨refer his ~*s* to a history of the case⟩

demand bid *n* **:** a bridge bid obligating one's partner to certain responses (as an opening bid of two in a suit)

demand bill *or* **demand draft** *n* **:** SIGHT DRAFT

demand charge *n* **:** the part of a bill for electric power based on the amount of power that the customer requires to be kept available to him

demand curve *n* **:** a graphical presentation of the quantities of a good or service that will be purchased at each of various possible prices at a given time

demand deposit *n* **1 :** a bank deposit that is subject to payment by check and that may be withdrawn without notice **2 :** a bank deposit payable within 30 days

demand factor *n* **:** the ratio of the maximum demand during an assigned period upon an electric-power system to the load actually connected during that time expressed usu. in per cent

demanding *adj* **:** unremittingly severe or difficult in making demands **:** EXACTING, TAXING — **de·mand·ing·ly** *adv*

demand limiter *n* **:** CURRENT LIMITER

demand-load factor *n* **:** load factor at time of maximum electric-power demand

demand loan *n* **:** CALL LOAN

demand meter *n* **:** a meter used for measuring electric-power demand

demand note *n* **1 :** a note payable on demand **2 :** one of the notes composing the issues of paper money authorized by Congress in 1861–62

demand rate *n* **:** a rate (as of electric power) based on the maximum amount that a customer requires to be kept available to him

demands *pl of* DEMAND, *pres 3d sing of* DEMAND

demand schedule *n* **:** [1]DEMAND 3c

demand system *n* **:** an oxygen-dispensing system which automatically adjusts the rate of flow to the demand of a flyer's body as the altitude changes

de·manganize \(ˈ)dē+\ *vt* [*de-* + *manganize*] **:** to remove manganese or manganese compounds from

de·man·i·an system \dəˈmänēən-, -man-\ *also* **demanian vessel** *n* [after Johannes G. *de Man* †1930 Du. zoologist + E *-ian*] **:** a group of tubes near the anus of certain female nematodes that secrete a sticky substance which protects the eggs or functions during copulation

de·man·sia \dəˈman(t)sēə, dēˈ-\ *n, cap* [NL, irreg. fr. Anton van *Diemen* †1645 governor-general of Dutch East Indies + NL *-ia*] **:** a genus of snakes (family Elapidae) comprising the venomous Australian brown snake and related forms

de·man·toid \-ˈman,tȯid\ *n* -S [G, fr. obs. G *demant* diamond (fr. MHG *diemant*, fr. OF *diamant*) + *-oid* — more at DIAMOND] **:** a green variety of andradite that has a brilliant luster and is used as a gem

de·mar·cate \dəˈmär,kāt, dēˈ-, ˈdē(,)-, -mȧ,k-, *usu* -ād·+V\ *vt* -ED/-ING/-S [back-formation fr. *demarcation*] **1 :** to mark by bounds **:** determine the boundary of **:** DELIMIT ⟨the frontier with Yugoslavia had not yet been *demarcated* exactly —*Collier's Yr. Bk.*⟩ **2 :** to set apart clearly or distinctly as if by definite limits or boundaries **:** DISCRIMINATE ⟨the distinction between influence and imitation ~*s* equally the imaginatively creative from the merely cerebrally inventive writer —Elizabeth Bowen⟩ **syn** see DISTINGUISH

de·mar·ca·tion *also* **de·mar·ka·tion** \,dē(,)märˈkāshən, -mȧˈk-\ *n* -S [Sp *demarcación* & Pg *demarcação*, fr. *demarcar* to delimit (fr. *de-* — fr. L — + *marcar* to mark, fr. It *marcare*, of Gmc origin; akin to Goth *marka* boundary) + Sp *-ción*, Pg *-ção* -tion — more at MARK] **1 :** the act or process of demarcating **:** the act of ascertaining and setting a boundary or limit **:** DELIMITATION ⟨a distinct ~ between the clear and glacial waters⟩ **2 :** SEPARATION, DISTINCTION — often used in the phrase *line of demarcation* ⟨sharp lines of ~ between successive rock strata⟩

demarcative *adj* **:** serving to point out or draw attention to a significant dividing place ⟨language with ~ stress⟩

de·mar·ca·tor \dəˈmär,kād·ə(r), dēˈ-, (ˈ)dē(,)-, -mȧ,kād·ə(r), -ātə-\ *n* -S **:** one that demarcates

de·march \ˈdē,märk\ *n* -S [Gk *dēmarchos*, fr. *dēmos* deme, populace + *-archos* -arch — more at DEM-] **:** a ruler of a deme

dé·marche \dāˈmärsh, -mȧsh\ *n, pl* **démarches** \-shəz\ [F *démarche*, lit., walk, gait, fr. MF *demarche*, fr. *demarcher* to trample, march, fr. OF *demarchier*, fr. *de-* + *marchier* to trample, march — more at MARCH] **1 :** PROCEEDING, STEP **:** MOVE, COUNTERMOVE **:** course of action **:** MANEUVER ⟨she caught on to that ~ and . . . we always landed where we didn't want to go —Frederick Packard⟩ **2 :** a diplomatic move, countermove, or maneuver ⟨to visit an ambassador may be considered a ~, to visit his wife is merely an act of courtesy —G.H.Stuart⟩ ⟨began the necessary diplomatic ~*s* at Rome to secure their exclusive title —S.E.Morison⟩; *esp* **:** an oral or written diplomatic representation ⟨the two governments joined to present a vigorous ~ in their neighbor's capital⟩ ⟨made a solemn ~ insisting on withdrawal of all troops⟩ **3 a :** any formal or informal representation or statement of views to a public official ⟨opposition leaders made a ~ to the prime minister about police terror⟩ **b :** a verbal sally

dem·a·ree \ˈdemə,rē\ *vt* **demareed; demareed; demareeing; demarees** [after George W. *Demaree* †1915 Am. beekeeper who developed the method] **:** to remove the queen from the brood of (a strong colony of bees) to prevent swarming

de·mar·ga·rin·ate \(ˈ)dē¦märj(ə)rə,nāt *sometimes* -rg(-\ *vt* -ED/-ING/-S [*de-* + *margarin* + *-ate*] **:** DESTEARINATE

de·mark \dəˈmärk, dēˈ-, -mȧk, ˈdē,-\ *vt* [*de-* + *mark*] **:** DEMARCATE

de·mast \(ˈ)dē+\ *vt* [*de-* + *mast* (n.)] **:** to remove or strip masts from (a ship)

de·materialize \¦dē+\ *vb* [*de-* + *materialize*] *vt* **:** to make immaterial ~ *vi* **:** to become immaterial **:** VANISH

de·mat·i·a·ce·ae \də,mad·ēˈāsē,ē, (,)dē,-\ *n pl, cap* [NL, fr. *Dematium*, type genus (fr. Gk *dēmation* small cord, rope, dim. of *dema* band) + *-aceae*] **:** a family of imperfect fungi (order Moniliales) having hyphae, conidia, or both that are dark colored, brownish, or black — **de·mat·i·a·ceous** \-¦ˈāshəs\ *adj*

demd \ˈdemd\ *chiefly Brit var of* DAMNED

deme \ˈdēm\ *n* -S [Gk *dēmos* deme, populace — more at DEM-] **1 a :** a unit of local government in ancient Attica — compare PHRATRY, PHYLE **b :** a commune in modern Greece **2 a :** local population of closely related organisms — usu. used in combination ⟨gamodeme⟩ ⟨topodeme⟩

[1]de·mean \dəˈmēn, dēˈ-\ *vt* [ME *demenen*, fr. OF *demener* to conduct, guide, treat, fr. *de-* + *mener* to lead, drive, fr. L *minare* to drive (animals), fr. *minari* to threaten — more at MOUNT] **1** *obs* **:** MANAGE **:** carry on **:** deal with **2 :** to conduct or behave (oneself) ⟨he might have been observed to ~ himself as a person with nothing to do —Henry James †1916⟩ **3** *now dial* **:** MALTREAT **syn** see BEHAVE

[2]demean \"\ *n* -S [ME *demene*, fr. *demenen*, v.] **:** BEHAVIOR, MIEN

[3]demean *or* **demeane** *obs var of* DEMESNE

[4]de·mean \dəˈmēn, dēˈ-\ *vt* [*de-* + *mean* (adj.)] **:** to lower in status, condition, reputation, or character **:** DEGRADE, DEBASE ⟨her son would ~ himself by a marriage with an artist's daughter —W.M.Thackeray⟩ ⟨~*ed* his position by bullying and browbeating officers of the army —*N.Y.Times*⟩

de·mean·or \-nə(r)\ *n* -S *see -or in Explan Notes* [earlier *demeanure*, fr. [1]*demean* + *-ure*] **1 :** behavior toward others **:** outward manner **:** CONDUCT ⟨obsequious in speech and in ~ toward his superiors —D.C.Buchanan⟩ **2 :** BEARING, MIEN **:** facial appearance ⟨an ancient . . . ~ —R.L.Stevenson⟩

de me·di·e·ta·te lin·guae \dā,medēəˈtädāˈliŋ,gwī\ *adj* [L, (composed) of half of (one's own) tongue] *of a jury* **:** constituted half of aliens and half of citizens or subjects — referring to an arrangement that before 1870 might be claimed in an English civil or criminal case by one alien born or by a foreign merchant

de·me·gor·ic \¦dēmə¦gȯrik\ *adj* [Gk *dēmēgorikos*, fr. *dēmēgoros* popular orator (fr. *dēm-* dem- + *-ēgoros*, fr. *-agorein* to speak publicly) + *-ikos* -ic — more at CATEGORY] **:** of or relating to public speaking

de·mem·bra·tion \¦dē(,)memˈbrāshən\ *n* -S [ML *demembration-, demembratio*, fr. LL *demembratus* (past part. of *demembrare* to dismember, fr. *de-* of + *membrum* limb) + *-ion-, -io* -ion — more at MEMBER] *Scots law* **:** the crime of maliciously severing a limb from the body of a person

[1]de·ment \dəˈment, dēˈ-\ *vt* -ED/-ING/-S [LL *dementare*, fr. L *dement-, demens* out of one's mind, mad, fr. *de-* + *ment-, mens* mind — more at MIND] *archaic* **:** to deprive of reason

[2]dement \"\ *n* -S [MF, fr. L *dement-, demens*] **:** one who is demented

de·men·tate \-ˈ-,tāt\ *vt* -ED/-ING/-S [LL *dementatus*, past part. of *dementare*] *archaic* **:** DEMENT

de·men·ta·tion \,dē(,)menˈtāshən\ *n* -S [LL *dementation-, dementatio*, fr. *dementatus* + L *-ion-, -io* -ion] *archaic* **:** the process of dementing or state of being demented

de·ment·ed \dəˈmentəd, dēˈ-\ *adj* **1 :** having dementia **:** of unsound mind **:** DERANGED **2 :** marked by or arising from dementia ⟨~ screams⟩ ⟨~ conduct⟩ — **de·ment·ed·ly** *adv* — **de·ment·ed·ness** *n* -ES

dé·men·ti \,dāmäⁿˈtē, -(,)-\ *n* -S [F, contradiction, denial, fr. MF *dementi*, fr. *dementir* to contradict, fr. OF *desmentir*, fr. *des-* dis- + *mentir* to tell a lie, fr. LL *mentire*, fr. L *mentior*, fr. *ment-, mens* mind — more at MIND] **:** an official or formal denial of the truth of a report — used esp. in diplomacy

de·men·tia \dəˈmench(ē)ə, *also* |ēə\ *n* -S [L, fr. *dement-, demens* mad + *-ia* — more at DEMENT] **1 :** a condition of deteriorated mentality that is characterized by marked decline from the individual's former intellectual level and often by emotional apathy — contrasted with *amentia* **2 :** MADNESS ⟨the ~ of national hatreds —*Times Lit. Supp.*⟩ **syn** see INSANITY

de·men·tial \|(ē)əl\ *adj* **:** relating to or involving dementia

dementia par·a·lyt·i·ca \-,parəˈlid·əkə\ *n, pl* **dementi·ae paralyti·cae** \|ē,ē...,sē\ [NL, lit., paralytic dementia] **:** GENERAL PARESIS

dementia prae·cox *also* **dementia pre·cox** \-ˈprē,käks\ *n, pl* **dementiae prae·co·ces** \-ˈprēkə,sēz\ [NL, lit., premature dementia] **:** SCHIZOPHRENIA

dem·e·rara greenheart \¦deməˈra(a)rə-, -ˈrär-\ *n, cap D* [fr. *Demerara* county, British Guiana] **:** BEBEERU

demerara sugar *n, usu cap D* **:** a coarse light-brown raw sugar

[1]demerit *n* -S [ME *demerite*, fr. L *demeritum*, fr. neut. of *demeritus*, past part. of *demerēre* to deserve, fr. *de-* + *merēre* to deserve — more at MERIT] *obs* **:** MERIT, DESERT; *also* **:** a deserving or praiseworthy act

[2]demerit *vt* -ED/-ING/-S **1** *obs* **:** to be worthy of **:** DESERVE, MERIT **2** *obs* **:** to obtain by merit **:** EARN

[3]de·merit \(ˈ)dē + \ *n* -S [ME, fr. MF *demerite*, fr. *de-* dis- + *merite* merit — more at MERIT] **1** *obs* **:** an act that incurs blame or censure **:** OFFENSE — usu. used in pl. **2 a :** a quality or characteristic that deserves blame **:** CULPABILITY ⟨they see no merit or ~ in any man or any action —Edmund Burke⟩ **b :** lack of merit ⟨it was not wholly from ~, it was in part because of different merit, that he refused our exile —W.B.Yeats⟩ **3 :** FAULT, DEFECT, IMPERFECTION ⟨it has the merit of quickness, but the ~*s* of inaccuracy, ambiguity, and slackness —F.C.Avis⟩ ⟨if the work seems to have a conspicuous ~ at first hearing, it is the overindulgence of a passion for display work —Irving Kolodin⟩ **4 :** a mark usu. entailing a loss of privilege given to an offender by one in authority (as a teacher or an officer) ⟨~*s* for traffic violations⟩ ⟨a ~ system designed to ensure discipline⟩ **5** *Hinduism, Buddhism, & Jainism* **:** the accrual of evil consequences that determine the number and forms of an individual's future earthly reincarnations **:** bad karma

[4]demerit \"\ *vb* -ED/-ING/-S *vt* **1** *obs* **:** to divest of merit **:** DISPARAGE **2** *archaic* **:** to deserve not to have or to lose **:** fail to merit **3 :** to lower (a person) in rank or status ⟨an employee reprimanded or ~*ed* for continued tardiness⟩ ~ *vi*, *obs* **:** to deserve or incur guilt or blame

de·meritorious \(ˈ)dē + \ *adj* [*de-* + *meritorious*] **:** BLAMEWORTHY ⟨~ conduct⟩ — **de·meritoriously** \(ˈ)dē +\ *adv*

Dem·er·ol \ˈdemə,rȯl, -rōl\ *trademark* — used for meperidine

de·mer·sal \dəˈmərsəl, (ˈ)dē¦-\ *adj* [L *demersus* (past part. of *demergere* to sink, fr. *de-* + *mergere* to dip, sink, plunge) + E *-al* — more at MERGE] **:** bottom-dwelling — used of marine organisms (as fishes)

demes *pl of* DEME

de·mesmerize \(ˈ)dē + \ *vt* [*de-* + *mesmerize*] **:** to bring out of a hypnotic state

[1]de·mesne \dəˈmān, dēˈ-, -mēn\ *n* -S [ME, alter. (influenced by AF *demesne*, alter. of OF *demaine*) of *demeyne*, fr. OF *demaine* — more at DOMAIN] **1 a :** legal possession of land as one's own — used chiefly in the phrase *to hold in demesne* **b** *obs* **:** POSSESSION **:** POWER, SOVEREIGNTY **2** *Old English law* **:** an estate or land of which the owner was in possession including all an owner's land except that which was held by freehold tenants or sometimes only that actually occupied by the owner **3 a :** the land attached to a mansion or country house ⟨a celebrated ~ of 400 acres and a Georgian mansion⟩; *also* **:** the house and land together **b :** landed property **:** ESTATE ⟨the cattlemen's noble, unfenced ~ —John McCarten⟩ **c :** region in general **:** TERRITORY ⟨the vast ~ that lies to the west⟩ **4 :** realm, province, or range esp. of interests or activity ⟨through the exact ~*s* of grammar —W.S.Maugham⟩

[2]demesne \"\ *adj* **:** of or belonging to a demesne **:** DEMESNIAL ⟨a high ~ wall⟩

de·mesn·i·al \-nēəl\ *adj* **:** of or belonging to a demesne

de·methylate \(ˈ)dē +\ *vt* [*de-* + *methylate*] **:** to remove methyl from (a compound) — **de·methylation** \(¦)dē +\ *n*

demi- *in pronunciations below*, ¦-- = ¦demē *or (usu not before vowels)* ¦demə *sometimes* ¦de,mī\ *prefix* [ME, fr. *demi*, fr. MF, fr. LL *demedius*, alter. (influenced by L *medius*) of L *dimidius*, prob. back-formation fr. *dimidiare* to halve — more at DIMIDIATE] **:** half: as **a :** of less than full size ⟨*demi*cannon⟩ ⟨*demi*pike⟩ **:** shortened ⟨*demi*robe⟩ — compare SEMI- **b** *heraldry* **:** having only one half depicted, usu. the upper or foremost half but sometimes the dexter or the sinister half ⟨*demi*angel⟩ ⟨*demi*lion⟩ **c :** half in quantity or value ⟨*demi*barrel⟩ ⟨*demi*groat⟩ **d :** inferior in quality ⟨*demi*luster⟩ **e :** one that partly belongs to (a specified type or class) ⟨*demi*beast⟩ ⟨*demi*deity⟩ ⟨*demi*lawyer⟩ **f :** partial **:** incomplete ⟨*demi*nudity⟩ ⟨*demi*toilet⟩

demi·bastion \¦-- +\ *n* [*demi-* + *bastion*] **:** a half bastion consisting of one face and one flank

demi·brassard *or* **demi·brassart** \¦-- +\ *n* [*demi-* + *brassard, brassart*] **:** armor for the upper arm from shoulder to elbow — see BRASSARD

demi·cannon \¦-- +\ *n* [MF *demi canon*, fr. *demi* half + *canon* cannon — more at DEMI-, CANNON] **:** an obsolete cannon having a bore of about 6½ inches and carrying a ball weighing from 30 to 36 pounds

demi·canton \¦-- +\ *n* [F *demi-canton*, fr. *demi-* (fr. *demi* half) + *canton*] **:** one of the two divisions into which each of the three Swiss cantons Appenzell, Basel, and Unterwalden are separated

de·mi·ca·rac·tère \dəmēkȧrȧkteer, ¦demē,karəkˈte(ə)r\ *adj* [F, lit., half-character] **:** of, involving, or resembling a character dance that uses classical technique as a basis for interpretation

demi·circle \ˈ-- *at* DEMI- + ,-\ *n* [F *demi-cercle*, fr. MF *demi cercle*, fr. *demi* half + *cercle* circle — more at CIRCLE] *archaic* **:** SEMICIRCLE

demi·culverin \¦-- +\ *n* [MF *demie coulevrine*, fr. *demie* (fem. of *demi* half) + *coulevrine* culverin — more at CULVERIN] **:** a culverin of about 4½ inches bore for ball of 9 to 13 pounds

demies *pl of* DEMY

demi·glace \¦-- + ,-\ *n* [F, lit., half glaze, fr. *demi-* (fr. *demi* half) + *glace* glaze, ice — more at GLACE] **:** espagnole sauce simmered down, degreased, strained, and usu. seasoned with dry wine

demi·god \ˈ-- + ,-\ *n* [*demi-* + *god*; trans. of L *semideus*] **1 :** a mythological divine or semidivine being (as the offspring of a deity and a mortal) thought to possess less power than a god — compare HERO **2 :** one so preeminent in intellect, power, ability, beneficence, or appearance as to seem to approach the divine ⟨modern propaganda machines can quickly build even an inconspicuous character into a ~ —*Reporter*⟩

demi·goddess \ˈ-- + ,-\ *n* [*demi-* + *goddess*] **:** a female demigod

demi·john \ˈ-- + ,jän\ *n* [by folk etymology fr. F *dame-jeanne*, lit., Lady Jane] **:** a narrow-necked bottle of glass or stoneware holding from one to 10 gallons that is enclosed in wickerwork and has one or two wicker handles — compare CARBOY

demijohn

demi·lance \ˈ-- + ,-\ *n* [MF *demie lance*, fr. *demie* (fem. of *demi* half) + *lance*] **1 a :** a short light lance used chiefly in the 15th and 16th centuries **2 :** a light cavalryman carrying a demilance

demi·lancer \¦-- +\ *n* **:** DEMILANCE 2

de·militarization \(¦)dē, dē +\ *n* **:** the act, process, or result of demilitarizing

de·militarize \(¦)dē, dē +\ *vt*, *see -ize in Explan Notes* [*de-*+*militarize*] **1 :** to do away with the military organization and potential of ⟨*demilitarized* the vanquished country and its satellites⟩ **:** prohibit (as a zone or frontier area) from being used for any military purpose ⟨the treaty ~*s* a fifty-mile strip on either side of the border⟩ **2 :** to deprive of military characteristics or purposes ⟨~ atomic energy⟩

[1]demi·lune \¦-- *at* DEMI- + ,lün\ *or* **demilune of hei·den·hain** \-ˈhīdᵊn,hīn\ *or* **demilune of gia·nuz·zi** \-jəˈnüt-(,)sē\ *n, cap H&G* [*demilune* fr. F *demi-lune*, fr. *demi-* (fr. *demi* half) + *lune* moon, fr. L *luna*; *Heidenhain* after R.P.H. *Heidenhain* †1897 Ger. physiologist; *Gianuzzi* after Giuseppe *Gianuzzi* †1876 It. physiologist — more at DEMI-, LUNA] **:** one of the small crescentic groups of granular deeply staining zymogen-secreting cells lying between the clearer mucus-producing cells and the basement membrane in the alveoli of mixed salivary glands

[2]demilune \"\ *adj* [F *demi-lune*] **:** SEMILUNAR, CRESCENT

demi·metope \¦-- +\ *n* [*demi-* + *metope*] **:** an incomplete usu. one-half metope (as at the corner of a frieze)

de·mi·mon·dain \¦demē(,)mänˈdān, -(,)mōn¦-; dəmēmōⁿdaⁿ\ *adj* [F *demi-mondain*, fr. *demi-monde*] **:** of or belonging to the demimonde

demi·mon·daine \"; dəmēmōⁿden\ *n* -S [F *demi-mondaine*, fr. fem. of *demi-mondain*] **:** a woman of the demimonde **:** a kept woman

demi·monde \¦demē¦mänd, -mōnd; dəmēmōⁿd\ *n* -S [F *demi-monde*, fr. *demi-* (fr. *demi* half) + *monde* world, fr. L *mundus* — more at DEMI-, MUNDANE] **1 a :** a class of women on the fringes of respectable society characterized by liaisons with and economic dependence upon wealthy lovers but not engaged in open prostitution and usu. striving to present an appearance of respectability **b :** the class of prostitutes **:** COURTESANS ⟨the city's ~ grew during the war⟩ **2 :** a member of the demimonde **:** DEMIMONDAINE ⟨the richer ~*s* . . . joined London society in its glittering and fashionable parade —Hollis Alpert⟩ **3 a :** a group (as within a profession) characterized by dealings of doubtful legality or propriety or by cheap commercialism or hack work and often by conspicuous lack of financial success ⟨the ~ of letters⟩ ⟨the artistic ~⟩; *also* **:** the area in which such a group resides or is concentrated **b :** any group engaged in activity of doubtful or twilight legality or propriety ⟨the ~ of international fascism —Edmond Taylor⟩

de·mineralization \(ˈ)dē +\ *n* **1 :** the process of demineralizing **2 :** removal or loss of minerals (as salts of calcium) from the body esp. by disease

de·mineralize \(ˈ)dē +\ *vt* [*de-* + *mineralize*] **:** to remove the mineral matter from (as water) **:** DEIONIZE, DESALT

de·mineralizer \(ˈ)dē +\ *n* **:** an apparatus for demineralizing water

[1]demi·pique \ˈ-- *at* DEMI- + ,pēk\ *adj* [alter. (influenced by F *pique* pike) of *demipeak*, fr. *demi-* + *peak*] **:** having a peak of about half the height of that of an older style of saddle — used of an 18th century war saddle

[2]demipique \"\ *n* -S **:** a demipique saddle

de·mi-plié \dəmēplēā; ¦demē¦plēā, ¦---¦-\ *adj* [F, lit., half bent, fr. *demi-* + *plié*, past part. of *plier* to bend — more at PLY] **:** comprising a slight bending of the knee in ballet

de·mi-pointe \dəmēpwaⁿt, ¦demē¦pwant\ *n* [F, fr. *demi-* + *pointe* point, toe — more at POINT] **:** HALF-TOE

demi·rep \ˈdemē,rep\ *n* [*demi-* + *rep*] **:** DEMIMONDAINE

demi·rhumb \ˈ-- *at* DEMI- + ,-\ *n* [*demi-* + *rhumb*] **:** a halfway point between rhumbs on the compass card

demi·sang *also* **demi·sangue** \ˈ-- + ,saŋ\ *n* -S [AF *demy sangue*, fr. *demy* half (fr. MF *demi*) + *sangue* blood, fr. OF, fr. L *sanguen*, var. of *sanguin-, sanguis*] **1 :** HALF BLOOD **2 :** the offspring of full-blood parents of different races **:** HALF-BREED **3 :** a cross between a Thoroughbred stallion and a native English or French mare, esp. one of the heavier French mares **:** GRADE 5

[1]de·mise \dəˈmīz, dēˈ-\ *vb* -ED/-ING/-S [ME *demisen*, fr. MF *demis*, past part.] *vt* **1 :** to convey (as an estate) by will or by lease ⟨premises *demised* for a period of 10 years⟩ **2** *obs* **:** RELEASE **:** let go **3** *obs* **:** CONVEY, GIVE **4 :** to transmit (as a title or the sovereignty) by succession or inheritance ⟨declare the crown voluntarily *demised*⟩ ~ *vi* **1 :** to demise the sovereignty **2 :** DIE, DECEASE **3 :** to pass by descent or bequest ⟨the property *demised* to the king⟩

[2]demise \" *sometimes* dəˈmēz\ *n* -S [MF, fem. of *demis*, past part. of *demettre* to put away, dismiss, fr. L *demittere* to send down, lower, fr. *de-* from, down, away + *mittere* to send — more at DE-, SMITE] **1 :** the conveyance of an estate (as by lease for a number of years) **2 :** transference of the sovereignty to a successor (as by death or abdication) — used usu. in the phrase *demise of the crown* ⟨the appointment of a regent at the unexpected ~ of the crown⟩ **3 a :** DEATH ⟨the lady's ~ had been ascribed to apoplexy —Alan Hynd⟩ **b :** end of existence or being ⟨when the Roman Empire perished, neither contemporaries nor posterity acknowledged its ~ —A.J.Toynbee⟩ **:** discontinuance or cessation of activity or operation ⟨a paper . . . published daily until its recent unlamented journalistic ~ —Victor Riesel⟩

demise and re·de·mise \-ˈrēdə,mīz\ *n* **:** a conveyance by mutual leases made from one to another of the same land or of some profit or burden arising from the land

demi-sec \¦-- *at* DEMI- + ¦sek\ *adj* [F, fr. *demi-* (fr. *demi* half) + *sec* — more at DEMI-] *of champagne* **:** containing five to seven percent sugar by volume **:** drier than doux and sweeter than sec

demise charter *n* **:** a bareboat charter

demi·semiquaver \¦-- +\ *n* [*demi-* + *semiquaver*] **:** THIRTY-SECOND NOTE

demi·semitone \¦-- +\ *n* [*demi-* + *semitone*] **:** QUARTER TONE

demi·sphere \ˈdemə + ,-\ *n* [*demi-* + *sphere*] **:** HEMISPHERE

demiss *adj* [L *demissus*, past part. of *demittere* to send down, lower, drop — more at DEMISE] **1** *obs* **:** HUMBLE, SUBMISSIVE **2** *obs* **:** BASE, DEGRADED **3** *obs* **:** cast down **:** DEJECTED

[1]de·mis·sion \dəˈmishən, dēˈ-\ *n* [MF, fr. L *demission-, demissio*, act of sending down, lowering] **1 :** the act of resigning or giving up (as an office or dignity) **:** RELINQUISHMENT **2 :** a sending away **:** DISMISSAL, DISCHARGE ⟨a sudden and unexpected ~⟩

[2]demission \"\ *n* [L *demission-, demissio*, act of sending down, lowering, fr. *demissus* + *-ion-, -io* -ion] **1** *archaic* **:** ABASEMENT, DEGRADATION **2** *obs* **:** a lowering of the spirits **:** DEJECTION

[1]de·mit \dəˈmit, dēˈ-, *usu* -id·+V\ *vb* **demitted; demitted; demitting; demits** [MF *demettre* to put away, dismiss — more at DEMISE] *vt* **1** *archaic* **:** to let go **:** DISMISS **2 :** to give up (as an office) **:** RESIGN ~ *vi* **:** to relinquish office or membership usu. voluntarily **:** RESIGN, WITHDRAW

[2]de·mit \", ˈdē,-\ *or* **di·mit** \dəˈ-, ˈdi,-\ *n* -S **:** a letter or other document certifying that a person has honorably demitted (as from a Masonic lodge)

[3]de·mit \dəˈmit, dēˈ-, *usu* -id·+V\ *or* **di·mit** \dəˈ-\ *vt* **demitted** *or* **dimitted; demitted** *or* **dimitted; demitting** *or* **dimitting; demits** *or* **dimits** [L *demittere* to send down, lower — more at DEMISE] **1 :** to put or let down **:** send down **:** LOWER **2** *obs* **:** HUMBLE, ABASE

demi·tasse \ˈdemē,tas, -mə,-, -,täs,-,tȧs\ *n* -S [F *demi-tasse*, fr. *demi-* (fr. *demi* half) + *tasse* cup — more at DEMI-, TASS] **:** a small cup of coffee usu. taken black; *also* **:** the cup in which it is served

demi·tint \ˈ-- *at* DEMI- + ,-\ *n* [*demi-* + *tint*] **:** a tone intermediate between high light and deep shade **:** a medium tone; *also* **:** the part of a painting or engraving that exhibits such a tone — called also *half tint*

demi·toilet \¦--+\ *n* [*demi-* + *toilet*] **:** dress that is somewhat elaborate but less so than full dress

demi·tone \ˈ--+,-\ *n* [*demi-* + *tone*] **:** SEMITONE

demi·urge \ˈdemē,ərj, *esp Brit* ˈdē-\ *n* -S [LL *demiurgus*, fr. Gk *dēmiourgos*, lit., one who works for the people, fr. *dēmios* of the people (fr. *dēmos* people) + *-ourgos* worker (akin to *ergon* work) — more at DEM-, WORK] **1** *usu cap* **a** *in Platonism* **:** the subordinate god who fashions the sensible world in the light of eternal ideas **b** *in some Gnostic systems* **:** an inferior not absolutely intelligent deity who is the creator of the material world and is frequently identified with the creator God of the Old Testament **2 :** something (as an institution, idea, or individual) conceived as an autonomous creative force or decisive power ⟨that too was a gain in spiritual balance, provided the machine was not conceived as a ~ that ruled all other human needs —Lewis Mumford⟩

demi·ur·geous \¦--¦ərjəs\ *adj* **:** DEMIURGIC

demi·ur·gic \-jik\ *or* **demi·ur·gi·cal** \-jəkəl\ *adj* [Gk *dēmiourgikos*, fr. *dēmiourgos* + *-ikos* -ic, -ical] **:** relating to or having the characteristics of a demiurge **:** FORMATIVE, CREATIVE ⟨a demon of a man, a full-blooded exuberant Philistine, with a ~ brain and a bull's body —Van Wyck Brooks⟩ — **demi·ur·gi·cal·ly** \-jək(ə)lē\ *adv*

demi·ur·gism \ˈ--,ər,jizəm, ,--ˈ-,-\ *n* -S **:** belief in or the philosophy of a demiurge

de·mi-vierge \,demēvēˈeərzh, dəmēvyerzh\ *n* -S [F, lit., half virgin, fr. *demi-* (fr. *demi* half) + *vierge* virgin, fr. L *virgin-, virgo* — more at DEMI-, VIRGIN] **:** a girl or woman who engages in lewd or suggestive speech and usu. promiscuous petting but retains her virginity

demi·vol \'== *at* DEMI- + ,väl\ *n* [F *demi-vol*, fr. *demi-* + *vol*] *heraldry* **:** a single wing used as a bearing

demi·wolf \'==+,-\ *n* [*demi-* + *wolf*] **:** a mongrel dog; *specif* **:** the offspring of a dog and a wolf

demj *abbr* demijohn

dem·me \'demē, -mi\ *chiefly Brit var of* DAMME

dem·ni·tion \dem'nishən\ *n* -S [euphemism] **:** DAMNATION

demo \'de(,)mō\ *n* -S *usu cap* [by shortening] **:** DEMOCRAT

demo- — see DEM-

¹de·mob \(')dē'mäb, dē'-\ *vt* [by shortening] *chiefly Brit* **:** DEMOBILIZE ⟨when he was *demobbed* he decided to start at the beginning again —*Irish Digest*⟩

²demob \"\ *n* [by shortening] *chiefly Brit* **:** DEMOBILIZATION ⟨~ pay⟩

de·mobilization \(')dē, də +\ *n* **:** the act or process of demobilizing: as **a :** the reduction (as of forces, equipment, or resources) from a war basis to a peace basis ⟨the rapid ~ of factories⟩ **b :** the disarming of troops previously mobilized ⟨demonstrations against the slowness of ~ —*Current Biog.*⟩ **c :** release from the armed services ⟨upon ~ he entered local politics⟩

de·mobilize \(')dē, də +\ *vt* — *see -ize in Explan Notes* [*de-* + *mobilize*] **1 a :** to put on a peacetime footing or in a condition not prepared for war ⟨ships returning to port to be *demobilized*⟩ **b :** to disband or break up the organization of (as troops) ⟨the reserves were *demobilized* at once⟩ ⟨one of his best bands, *demobilized* a few years ago, was a powerhouse . . . outfit —Wilder Hobson⟩ **c :** to discharge from service with the armed forces ⟨he was *demobilized* in 1919 with the grade of captain —*Current Biog.*⟩ **2 :** to remove restrictions from **:** relax the governing rules and regulations of ⟨it allows us to mobilize and ~ our industrial combinations according to the actual necessities of the day —T.W.Arnold⟩ ⟨we shall never ~ the more highly integrated control that now exists over banking, credit, and the securities markets —*New Republic*⟩

de·moc·ra·cy \də'mäkrəsē, dē'-, -si\ *n* -ES [MF *democratie*, fr. LL *democratia*, fr. Gk *dēmokratia*, fr. *dēm-* dem- + *-kratia* -cracy] **1 a :** government by the people **:** rule of the majority **b** (1) **:** a form of government in which the supreme power is vested in the people and exercised by them directly (as in the ancient Greek city-states or the New England town meeting) — called also *direct democracy* (2) **:** a form of government in which the supreme power is vested in the people and exercised by them indirectly through a system of representation and delegated authority in which the people choose their officials and representatives at periodically held free elections — called also *representative democracy* **2 :** a community or state in which the government is controlled by the people; *specif* **:** a state in which the supreme power is held and exercised directly by the people rather than by their elected agents ⟨in a ~ the people meet and exercise their government in person; in a republic, they assemble and administer it by their representatives and agents —James Madison⟩ — compare REPUBLIC **3** *usu cap* **a :** the principles and policies of the Democratic party in the U.S. **b :** the Democratic party or its members **4 :** the common people esp. when regarded as the source of government **5 :** political, social, or economic equality **:** the absence or disavowal of hereditary or arbitrary class distinctions or privileges ⟨~ stands at a midway point, with personal freedom limited only by another concept — that of equality —Louis Wasserman⟩ **6 :** a state of society characterized by tolerance toward minorities, freedom of expression, and respect for the essential dignity and worth of the human individual with equal opportunity for each to develop freely to his fullest capacity in a cooperative community **7 :** control through representation by the rank and file esp. in industry — see INDUSTRIAL DEMOCRACY

dem·o·crat \'demə,krat, *usu* -ad·+V\ *n* -S [F *démocrate*, fr. *démocratie*, after such pairs as F *aristocratie* aristocracy: *aristocrate* aristocrat] **1 :** an adherent or advocate of democracy; *esp* **:** one who believes in or practices social equality **2** *usu cap* **:** a member of a political party advocating democracy; *esp* **:** a member of the Democratic party of the U.S. **3 :** DEMOCRAT WAGON

dem·o·crat·ic \¦==¦krad·|ik, -at|, |ēk *also* |ək\ *also* **dem·o·crat·i·cal** \|əkəl, |ēk-\ *adj* [*democratic* fr. MF *democratique*, fr. ML *democraticus*, fr. Gk *dēmokratikos*, fr. *dēm-* dem- + *-kratikos* -cratic; *democratical* fr. MF *democratique* + E *-al*] **1 a :** favoring, characterized by, or based upon the principles of democracy ⟨no church constitution has proved in practice so ~ as that of Scotland —J.R.Green⟩ **b :** of, relating to, or favoring a political system in which the supreme power is held and exercised by the people ⟨a ~ country⟩ — opposed to *authoritarian* **2** *often cap* **:** of or relating to one of the two major political parties in the U.S. evolving in the early 19th century from the anti-Federalists and the Democratic-Republican party and associated in modern times with policies of broad social reform and internationalism in foreign affairs — compare REPUBLICAN 2b **3 :** relating or appealing to or having the characteristics of the broad masses of the people ⟨a ~ art⟩ **4 :** favoring or disposed to favor social equality **:** disregarding or overcoming class distinctions **:** not snobbish or socially exclusive ⟨~ tastes⟩ ⟨bombs are completely ~. They are no respecters of persons, and do not distinguish between a hovel and a mansion —John Mason Brown⟩ **5 :** favoring the assessment of individuals upon their own merits and capacities **:** emphasizing the individual's potentiality for development ⟨promotion in industry along ~ lines⟩ — **dem·o·crat·i·cal·ly** \|ək(ə)lē, |ēk-, -li\ *adv*

democratic centralism *n* **:** a communist system or principle of hierarchic organization that seeks to combine democratic participation of the rank and file in the discussion of policy and the election of officers and of delegates to the next higher unit with strict obedience by the members and lower bodies to the decisions of the higher units and with absolute authority residing in fact at the apex of the hierarchic structure and their strict discipline being enforced

democratic–republican \¦==¦==¦===\ *adj, usu cap D & R* **:** of or relating to a major American political party of the early 19th century favoring a strict interpretation of the constitution to restrict the powers of the federal government and emphasizing states' rights

de·moc·ra·tism \də'mäkrə,tizəm, dē'-\ *n* -S [*democrat* + *-ism*] **:** the theory, system, or principles of democracy

de·moc·ra·ti·za·tion \=,==tə'zāshən, -,tī'-\ *n* -S **:** the act or process of making or becoming democratic ⟨this great ~ of music has been made possible, thanks to the radio and the phonograph —*Christian Science Monitor*⟩

de·moc·ra·tize \=¦==,tīz\ *vt* -ED/-ING/-S *see -ize in Explan Notes* [F *démocratiser*, fr. *démocrate* + *-iser* -ize] **:** to make democratic (as in character or principle) **:** give popularity to **:** make available to the masses ⟨efforts to ~ occupied territories since the war —E.O.Melby⟩ ⟨to recommend plans to ~ scientific research in that country —*Current Biog.*⟩ ⟨books and art and music are all to be *democratized* —E.C.Lindeman⟩

democrat wagon *n, sometimes cap D* **:** a light farm wagon or ranch wagon that has two or more seats and is usu. drawn by two horses

de·moc·ri·te·an \=¦==¦tēən\ *adj, usu cap* [*Democritus* †*ab*362 B.C. Gk. philosopher + E *-ean*] **:** of, relating to, or in the manner of Democritus or his materialist philosophy — compare ATOMISM

dé·mo·dé \¦dā(,)mō¦dā\ *adj* [F, fr. *dé-* (fr. OF *de-*, *des-* de-) + *mode* fashion + *-é* (past part. ending) — more at MODE] **:** no longer fashionable **:** OUT-OF-DATE, OUTMODED ⟨a short jacket of astrakhan, slightly ~ owing to its leg-of-mutton sleeves —Louis Bromfield⟩ ⟨classical formulas of exploitation are ~ —C.L.Sulzberger⟩

dem·o·dec·tic \¦demə¦dektik\ *adj* [irreg. fr. NL *Demodic-*, *Demodex* + E *-ic*] **1 :** of or relating to the genus *Demodex* **2 :** caused by mites of the genus *Demodex*

demodectic mange *n* **:** mange caused by mites of the genus *Demodex* that burrow in the hair follicles (as esp. of dogs) causing pustule formation and spreading bald patches — called also *red mange*

de·mod·ed \(')dē¦mōdəd, də'-\ *adj* [trans. of F *démodé*] **:** DÉMODÉ

dem·o·dex \'demə,deks, 'dēm-\ *n* [NL, fr. Gk *dēmos* fat + *dēx*, a wood worm] **1** *cap* **:** a genus (coextensive with a family Demodicidae) of minute elongated cylindrical mites with the legs greatly reduced that live in the hair follicles esp. about the face of man and various furred mammals and in the latter often cause follicular mange **2** -ES **:** any mite of the genus *Demodex* **:** FOLLICLE MITE

dem·o·di·co·sis \,==də'kōsəs\ *n, pl* **demodico·ses** \-,sēz\ [NL, irreg. fr. NL *Demodic-*, *Demodex* + *-osis*] **:** DEMODECTIC MANGE

de·modulate \(')dē, də +\ *vt* [*de-* + *modulate*] **1 :** to extract the intelligence from (a modulated radio signal) **2 :** DETECT 3c

de·modulation \(')dē, də +\ *n* **1 :** extraction of the intelligence from a modulated radio signal **2 :** DETECTION 2d

de·modulator \(')dē, də +\ *n* **1 :** a device for converting a modulated radio signal into the original modulating signal — called also *detector* **2 :** DETECTOR e(2), e(3)

de·mog·ra·pher \də'mägrəfə(r), dē'-\ *n* -S **:** one who specializes in demography

de·mo·graph·ic \,dēmə¦grafik, ¦dem-\ *adj* [F *démographique*, fr. *démographie* + *-ique* -ic] **:** of or relating to demography **:** relating to the dynamic balance of a population esp. with regard to density and capacity for expansion or decline ⟨~ pressures determining trends⟩ — **de·mo·graph·i·cal·ly** \-fək(ə)lē\ *adv*

de·mog·ra·phy \də'mägrəfē, dē'-\ *n* -ES [F *démographie*, fr. *démo-* dem- + *-graphie* -graphy] **:** the statistical study of the characteristics of human populations esp. with reference to size and density, growth, distribution, migration, and vital statistics and the effect of all these on social and economic conditions

de·moid \'dē,mȯid\ *adj* [*dem-* + *-oid*] **:** common or abundant esp. in a given geological formation — used of fossils

dem·oi·selle \,dem(w)ə'zel, '==,=\ *n* -S [F, fr. OF *dameisele*, *damoisele* — more at DAMSEL] **1 :** a young lady **:** DAMSEL **2 a :** a crane (*Anthropoides virgo*) of rather small size with long flowing secondaries and breast feathers and white plumes behind the eyes that is widely distributed in Asia, No. Africa, and southeast Europe **b :** LOUISIANA HERON **3 :** DAMSELFLY; *esp* **:** one of the genus *Agrion* **4 :** DAMSELFISH **5 :** EARTH PILLAR

de moi·vre's theorem \də'mȯivə(r)z-\ *n, cap D&M* [after Abraham *De Moivre* †1754 Fr. mathematician] **:** a theorem of complex numbers: the *n*th power of a complex number has for its absolute value and its argument respectively the *n*th power of the absolute value and *n* times the argument of the given complex number

de·mo·lay \,dēmə'lā\ *n* -S *usu cap D&M* [after Jacques B. *de Molay* †1314 Fr. grand master of the Knights Templar] **:** a member of the Order of DeMolay for Boys sponsored by Masonic orders as a secret society for boys aged 14 to 21

de·mol·ish \də'mälish, dē'-, -lēsh\ *vt* -ED/-ING/-ES [MF *demoliss-*, stem of *demolir* to demolish, fr. L *demoliri*, fr. *de-* + *moliri* to construct, set in motion, toil, fr. *moles* mass, massive structure — more at MOLE] **1 a :** to pull or tear down (as a building) **:** RAZE ⟨built in 1706 and ~*ed* in 1859 to make way for the present building —*Amer. Guide Series: N.J.*⟩ **b :** to break to pieces or apart usu. with force or violence **:** ruin completely **:** SHATTER, SMASH ⟨~*ing* the fortifications and the harbor⟩ **2 a :** to do away with **:** put an end to **:** DESTROY ⟨his research has been painstaking and he ~*es* a good many legends —Fletcher Pratt⟩ ⟨a filibuster which would effectively ~ the issue —*Current Biog.*⟩ **b :** to divest of any claim or pretense to merit, truth, credence, or acceptability ⟨I heard him on another occasion ~ a city financier of more wealth than probity —David Williamson⟩ **c :** to eat up ⟨they ~*ed* the roast⟩ **syn** see DESTROY

dem·o·li·tion \,demə'lishən, ,dēm-\ *n* -S [MF & L; MF, fr. L *demolition-*, *demolitio*, fr. *demolitus* (past part. of *demoliri* to demolish) + *-ion-*, *-io* -ion] **1 :** the act or process of demolishing or the state of being demolished **2 demolitions** *pl, obs* **:** RUINS, REMAINS **3 a :** destruction of structures, areas, or targets esp. in warfare by means of explosives ⟨~ of vital communication units⟩ ⟨~ experts⟩ **b demolitions** *pl* **:** the explosives used for such destruction

demolition bomb *n* **:** a bomb used against installations and materiel — used esp. of heavy bombs and bombs for which a lapse of time between impact and detonation is desirable

¹de·mon *also* **dae·mon** \'dēmən\ *n* -S [ME *demon*, fr. LL & L; LL *daemon*, *demon* evil spirit, fr. L *daemon* spirit, fr. Gk *daimōn* spirit, deity; prob. akin to Gk *daiesthai* to distribute — more at TIDE] **1 :** an attendant, ministering, or indwelling power or spirit **:** DAIMONION, GENIUS ⟨the only one of our five authors who writes because he has a ~ —*New Republic*⟩ **2 a :** an evil spirit **:** DEVIL ⟨a magical observance whose aim is to banish the ~*s* of pain, psychosis and bad luck —Paul Bowles⟩ **b :** an undesirable or evil emotion, trait, or state personified ⟨melancholy is a kind of ~ that haunts our island —Joseph Addison⟩ **3** *in late biblical Judaism and early Christianity* **a :** a pagan spirit **b :** an unclean spirit or evil superhuman being below a god but believed to be capable of inhabiting and actuating the bodies of men **4** *usu daemon* **:** a supernatural being in ancient Greek mythology whose nature is intermediate between that of a god and that of a man **:** an inferior divinity **5 :** one that possesses extraordinary drive, enthusiasm, or effectiveness in respect to some activity or function ⟨he is a positive ~ for work —William Ridsdale⟩

²demon \"\ *adj* **1 :** of, relating to, or involving demons ⟨~ worship⟩ ⟨the ~ herd⟩ **2 a :** being a demon **:** possessed of a demon ⟨a ~ lover⟩ **b :** having the characteristics of a demon ⟨the ~ driver of the village —Sinclair Lewis⟩

demon *abbr* **1** demonstration **2** demonstrative

de·monetization \(¦)dē+\ *n* [F *démonétisation*, fr. *démonétiser* to demonetize + *-ation*] **:** the process of demonetizing or the state of being demonetized ⟨the ~ of silver⟩

de·monetize \(')dē+\ *vt, see -ize in Explan Notes* [F *démonétiser*, fr. *dé-* de- (fr. OF *de-*, *des-*) + L *moneta* coin + F *-iser* -ize — more at MINT] **1 :** to abandon use of (a metal) as a monetary standard **2 :** to deprive (as a coin or stamp) of value for official payment

¹de·mo·ni·ac \də'mōnē,ak, dē'- *also* -'mān- *sometimes* ¦dēmə¦nī,ak *or* -īək\ *also* **de·mo·ni·a·cal** \¦dēmə¦nīəkəl\ *adj* [*demoniac* fr. ME *demoniak*, fr. LL *daemoniacus*, fr. Gk *daimoniakos*, fr. *daimonios* of a daimon, fr. *daimon-*, *daimōn* demon; *demoniacal* fr. LL *daemoniacus* + E *-al* — more at DEMON] **1 :** influenced or produced by a demon **:** possessed by an evil spirit ⟨through the ~ ambivalence of the passions, which make actions a pursuit of chimeras —Fritz Kaufmann⟩ ⟨a lunatic who is thinking of some ~ buffoonery in his muddled brain —Liam O'Flaherty⟩ **2 :** of, belonging to, or having the characteristics of a demon **:** FIENDISH, DEVILISH ⟨possessed with ~ energy⟩ — **de·mo·ni·a·cal·ly** \-k(ə)lē, -li\ *adv*

²demoniac \"\ *n* -S [ME *demoniak*, fr. LL *daemoniacus*, fr. *daemoniacus*, adj.] **:** one regarded as possessed by an evil spirit

de·mo·ni·an *or* **dae·mo·ni·an** \də'mōnēən, dē'-, -nyən\ *adj* [*demon* + *-ian*] **:** DEMONIAC 2

de·mon·ic *also* **dae·mon·ic** \-'mänik, -nēk *also* -nək *or* -mōn-\ *or* **de·mon·i·cal** \-nəkəl, -nēk-\ *adj* [*demonic*, *daemonic* fr. LL *daemonicus*, fr. Gk *daimonikos*, fr. *daimon-*, *daimōn* daimon + *-ikos* -ic; *demonical* fr. LL *daemonicus* + E *-al*] **1 :** DEMONIAC 2 ⟨~ energy⟩ ⟨a *daemonic* gift for blackmail and sabotage —*Economist*⟩ **2** *usu daemonic* **:** activating or compelling like an indwelling or ministering force **:** having extraordinary genius ⟨some physical rebellion . . . sets loose the pent-up *daemonic* powers —P.E.More⟩

de·mon·i·cal·ly \-nək(ə)lē, -nēk-, -li\ *adv* **:** in a demonic manner **:** DIABOLICALLY

de·mon·iza·tion \,dēmənə'zāshən\ *n* -S [ML *daemonizatus* (past part. of *daemonizare*) + E *-ion*] **:** the act of changing into or giving the characteristics of a demon ⟨their superstition is evident in the ~ of religion, faith, cult —Paul Tabori⟩

de·mon·ize \'==,nīz\ *vt* -ED/-ING/-S [ML *daemonizare*, fr. LL *daemon* + L *-izare* -ize — more at DEMON] **1 :** to convert into a demon **:** instill the principles, power, or fury of a demon into ⟨man *demonized* by war⟩ **2 :** to control or possess by a demon

de·mon·olog·ic \¦dēmənə¦läjik\ *or* **de·mon·olog·i·cal** \-jəkəl\ *adj* **:** of or relating to demonology — **de·mon·olog·i·cal·ly** \-jək(ə)lē\ *adv*

de·mon·ol·o·gist \,==¦nälәjəst\ *n* -S **:** one who specializes in demonology

de·mon·ol·o·gy *also* **dae·mon·ol·o·gy** \-jē\ *n* -ES [*demon*, *daemon* + *-o-* + *-logy*] **1 :** a branch of learning that deals with demons or with popular beliefs in or superstitions about demons or evil spirits; *also* **:** a treatise on demons or on beliefs in demons **2 :** belief in demons; *specif* **:** a systematized religious doctrine of evil spirits

de·mon·o·ma·nia \,dēmənə'mānēə\ *n* [*demon* + *-o-* + *mania*] **:** a delusion of being possessed by evil spirits

demon stinger *n* **:** a variably colored scorpaenid fish (*Inimicus japonicus*) of coral reefs of the tropical Pacific having long venomous dorsal spines

de·mon·stra·bil·i·ty \də,mänstrə'biləd·|ē, dē,-, -lət|, |i; ,demən-\ *n* -ES **:** the quality of being demonstrable

de·mon·stra·ble \də'mänstrəbəl, dē'-; 'demən-\ *adj* [ME, fr. L *demonstrabilis*, fr. *demonstrare* to demonstrate + *-abilis* -able] **1 :** capable of being demonstrated ⟨~ and systematically classifiable truths —Havelock Ellis⟩ **2 :** APPARENT, EVIDENT, PALPABLE ⟨uttering ~ nonsense —Aldous Huxley⟩ — **de·mon·stra·ble·ness** *n* -ES — **de·mon·stra·bly** *adv*

demonstrance *n* -S [ME *demonstraunce*, fr. MF *demonstrance*, *demonstrance*, fr. *demonstrer*, *demostrer* to demonstrate (fr. L *demonstrare*) + *-ance*] *obs* **:** DEMONSTRATION

de·mon·strant \-strənt\ *n* -S [*demonstrate* + *-ant*] **:** one making or participating in a public demonstration

dem·on·strat·able \¦demən¦strād·əbəl\ *adj* **:** DEMONSTRABLE ⟨easily ~ aural and visual proof —R.D.Darrell⟩

dem·on·strate \'demən,strāt *sometimes* də'män,- *or* dē'män,-, *usu* -ād·+V\ *vb* -ED/-ING/-S [L *demonstratus*, past part. of *demonstrare*, fr. *de-* + *monstrare* to show — more at MUSTER] *vt* **1 a** *obs* **:** INDICATE **:** point out **b :** to manifest clearly, certainly, or unmistakably **:** show clearly the existence of ⟨even if both sides ~ a will to agree —*New Republic*⟩ **2 a :** to make evident or reveal as true by reasoning processes, concrete facts and evidence, experimentation, operation, or repeated examples ⟨*demonstrated* that the geologic agencies are not explosive and cataclysmal but steady and patient —C.W. Eliot⟩ **b :** to illustrate or explain in an orderly and detailed way esp. with many examples, specimens, and particulars ⟨~ the essentials of the theistic position —W.R.Inge⟩ **3 :** to show or prove to a prospective customer (as by actual operation) the special value or merits of (an article or product) ~ *vi* **1 :** to make a demonstration; *specif* **:** to make a public display of sentiment for or against a person or cause ⟨students *demonstrating* for the ouster of the dictator⟩ **2 :** to teach or explain by demonstration **syn** see PROVE, SHOW

dem·on·stra·tion \,demən'strāshən\ *n* -S [ME *demonstracioun*, fr. MF or L; MF *demonstration*, fr. L *demonstration-*, *demonstratio*, fr. *demonstratus* + *-ion-*, *-io* -ion] **1 :** the act of making known or evident by visible or tangible means: as **a** *obs* **:** INDICATION, SIGN **b :** an expression or display (as of feelings) **:** SHOW, MANIFESTATION ⟨no one was called upon to make any great ~ of gratitude on receiving a gift —Havelock Ellis⟩ **2 :** the act, process, or means of demonstrating to the intelligence: as **a :** conclusive evidence ⟨seek for a ~ of his guilt⟩ **b :** a proof by experiment ⟨a lecture ~ of the neutralization of an acid by a base⟩ **c :** exhibition of methods of manufacture by means of specimens, examples, or specific instances ⟨~*s* in shingle making and other frontier crafts —*Amer. Guide Series: Texas*⟩ **d :** illustration of the practical application of theories or methods ⟨an early ~ of satisfactory housing within the limitations of the average city block —*Amer. Guide Series: N.Y. City*⟩ ⟨a ~ school for student teachers to observe approved teaching practices⟩ **3 :** an exhibition of armed force or a movement indicating an attack to show readiness for combat or to divert attention from the real point of attack ⟨tying down the main enemy forces with ~*s*, feints, or limited attacks —*Military Engineer*⟩ **4 :** a public display of group feeling (as of approval, sympathy, or antagonism) esp. towards a person, cause, or action of public interest ⟨while the delegates are howling and conducting their ~*s*, the leaders may be quietly engaged in the highest statesmanship —D.D.McKean⟩ **5 :** a logical proof; *specif* **:** one in which the conclusion is the immediate sequence of reasoning from axiomatic or established premises **6** *Roman law* **:** the first of the four principal parts of the formula or order of reference to a magistrate in which the general background and subject matter of a case in litigation was set forth — compare INTENTION 1c(1) **7 :** a showing to a prospective buyer or buyers (as by actual operation) of the merits of an article or product

dem·on·stra·tion·al \¦==¦shən³l, -shnəl\ *adj* **:** relating to or based on demonstration ⟨~ methods in farming⟩

¹de·mon·stra·tive \də'mänstrəd·|iv, dē'-, |t| *sometimes* 'demən,strā|\ *adj* [ME, fr. MF or L; MF *demonstratif*, fr. L *demonstrativus*, fr. *demonstratus* + *-ivus* -ive] **1 a :** demonstrating or manifesting as real and true **:** making evident **:** exhibiting conclusively ⟨the oath of office . . . is completely ~ of the legislative opinion on this subject —John Marshall⟩ **b :** characterized by, established by, or employing demonstration ⟨scientific honesty, however, makes us admit that where ~ knowledge ends only guessing begins —M.R.Cohen⟩ **2** *of a word or morpheme* **:** pointing out the person or thing that is directly or indirectly referred to and distinguishing it from others of the same class (as *this* in "who's this?", *that* in "that dog", *here* meaning "in this place") ⟨~ pronoun⟩ ⟨~ adjective⟩ ⟨~ adverb⟩ **3 :** EPIDEICTIC **4 a :** given to or characterized by a display of sentiment or feeling **:** expressed openly ⟨the reception of the young aviator in the capital of France was cordial and ~ —Kenneth Colegrove⟩ **b :** EFFUSIVE, EXUBERANT — **de·mon·stra·tive·ly** \|əvlē, -li\ *adv* — **de·mon·stra·tive·ness** \|əvnəs\ *n* -ES

²demonstrative \"\ *n* -S **:** a demonstrative word or morpheme

demonstrative legacy *n* **:** a legacy made payable out of a designated fund or asset

dem·on·stra·tor *pronunc at* DEMONSTRATE + ə(r)\ *n* -S [F or L; F *démonstrateur*, fr. L *demonstrator*, fr. *demonstratus* + *-or*] **:** one that demonstrates or makes a demonstration: as **a :** a teacher or teacher's assistant in a professional school or a science department who demonstrates the principles and theories studied (as by means of experiments, dissections, physical and chemical preparations) **b :** one that demonstrates an article or product to a prospective buyer; *also* **:** an article or product (as an automobile or vacuum cleaner) used in a demonstration **c :** one engaged in a public demonstration ⟨~*s* protesting the pact⟩

de·moralization \də, (¦)dē +\ *n* **:** the act or process of demoralizing **:** a demoralized state ⟨the ~ of peace was more difficult to combat than the madness of war —Ellen Glasgow⟩

de·moralize \də, (')dē +\ *vt* [*de-* + *moral* + *-ize*] **1 :** to corrupt or undermine in morals or moral principle **:** PERVERT, DEPRAVE **2 a :** to destroy the morals or morale of **:** deprive of self-reliance **:** weaken in courage, fortitude, or spirit **:** render untrustworthy in efficiency and discipline ⟨the prisoners carried on an endless war of nerves against their captors, taunting them, *demoralizing* them in dozens of different ways —Peter Blake⟩ ⟨the objective of a given campaign is to ~ enemy troops so that they will surrender or desert —L.W. Doob⟩ **b :** to upset or destroy the working order, proper functioning, or normal activity of ⟨powerful earth currents are induced that sometimes ~ the telegraph service —Waldemar Kaempffert⟩ ⟨foreclosures were further *demoralizing* an already desperate real-estate market —F.D.Roosevelt⟩ **3 :** to cast into disorder or confusion **:** BEWILDER, PERPLEX ⟨do many art critics deliberately set out to deceive and confuse and ~ the public? —Huntington Hartford⟩ ⟨the declarer was so *demoralized* that he discarded spades from both hands —*London Times*⟩

de mor·gan's theorem \də'mȯrgənz-, dē'-\ *n, usu cap D&M* [after Augustus *De Morgan* †1871 Eng. mathematician] **:** one of a pair of theorems in logic: the denial of a conjunction is equivalent to the alternation of the denials and the denial of an alternation is equivalent to the conjunction of the denials

¹de·mos \'dē,mäs\ *n* -ES [Gk *dēmos* deme, populace — more at DEM-] **1 :** the people of an ancient Greek state usu. democratic state **b** *sometimes cap* **:** the common people **:** POPULACE ⟨~ ruled in the age of the common man⟩ **2 :** the people of a nation considered as a political unit as distinguished from a tribe or kinship group — compare ETHNOS

²demos *pl of* DEMO

de·mo·spon·gea *or* **de·mo·spon·gia** \,dēmə'spänjēə\ *syn of* DEMOSPONGIAE

de·mo·spon·gi·ae \-jē,ē\ *n pl, cap* [NL, alter. of *Desmospongiae*] **:** a large class of Porifera comprising the majority of living sponges and being characterized by complex structure with a skeleton of tetraxial or simple siliceous spicules or of fibers of spongin or of both

de·mos·the·ne·an \dȧ'mästhə'nēən, (')dē'-\ *or* **de·mos·the·ni·an** \ˌdēməs'thēn-, ˌdem-\ *adj, usu cap* [*Demosthenes* †322B.C. Greek orator + E *-ean, -ian*] : DEMOSTHENIC ⟨a species of *Demosthenean* eloquence⟩

de·mos·then·ic \ˌdēməs'thenik, ˌdem-\ *adj, usu cap* [L *Demosthenicus*, fr. Gk *Dēmosthenikos* of Demosthenes, fr. *Dēmosthenes* + Gk *-ikos* -ic] : of or relating to the Athenian orator Demosthenes : resembling or suggesting his oratorical style or effectiveness; *esp* : oratorically impassioned and moving ⟨*Demosthenic* passages occur in Pitt's speeches —Gilbert Highet⟩

de·mote \dȧ, dē+'mōt, *usu* -ōd·+V\ *vt* -ED/-ING/-S [*de-* + *-mote* (as in *promote*)] : to reduce to a lower grade or rank ⟨~ a pupil⟩ ⟨a soldier *demoted* from sergeant to corporal⟩ : relegate to a subordinate or less important position — opposed to *promote* — **de·mo·tion** \-ōshən\ *n* -S

[1]**de·mot·ic** \dȧ'mäd·|ik, dē'-, -ät|\ *adj* [Gk *dēmotikos*, fr. *dēmotēs* commoner (fr. *dēmos* deme, populace) + *-ikos* -ic — more at DEM-] **1** : of or relating to the people : POPULAR, COMMON — used esp. of language ⟨the attempt to create beauty out of city life and style out of the ~ English which is spoken therein —Cyril Connolly⟩ **2 a** : written in, constituting, or belonging to a simplified form of the ancient Egyptian hieratic writing used at first chiefly for business and social purposes but later also for religious and literary works : ENCHORIAL, EPISTOLOGRAPHIC **b** : written in, constituting, or belonging to a relatively simple rapidly written cursive form of any of various systems of writing **3** : of, belonging to, or connected with the form of Modern Greek that is based on colloquial use and is characterized by free acceptance of loanwords and simplification of inflections — compare KATHAREVUSA

[2]**demotic** \"\ *n* -S : the demotic form of Modern Greek

demotic egyptian *n, cap E* : the stage of the Egyptian language that immediately preceded Coptic and that is known from writings in demotic characters dating approximately from the 8th century B.C. to the 3d century A.D.

de·mot·ist \'əst\ *n* -S [*demotic* (*Egyptian*) + *-ist*] : a student of demotic writings

de·mount \(')dē'maůnt\ *vt* [*de-* + *mount* (to assemble)] **1** : to remove from a mounted position ⟨~*ed* the tire from the wheel⟩ **2** : to take apart or to pieces esp. carefully or systematically with the purpose of reassembly : DISASSEMBLE ⟨~ an airplane motor⟩ ⟨~ a watch⟩

[1]**de·mount·able** \-təbəl\ *adj* [*demount* + *-able*] **1** : capable of being demounted ⟨~ wheel⟩ ⟨a planetarium with a ~ sky⟩ **2** : designed to allow disassembly with minimum damage to component parts ⟨a ~ house⟩

[2]**demountable** \"\ *n* : a demountable building

demp·ster \'demztər, -m(p)st-\ *n* -S [ME *dempster, demestre* judge, fr. *demen* to judge + *-ster* — more at DEEM] *old Scots law* : an officer whose duty it was to pronounce the doom of the court

[1]**de·mul·cent** \dȧ'məlsənt, dē'-\ *adj* [L *demulcent-, demulcens*, pres. part. of *demulcēre* to caress, soothe, fr. *de-* + *mulcēre* to caress, soothe] : SOOTHING, SOFTENING ⟨~ expectorants which give a protective coating to the throat —*Therapeutic Notes*⟩

[2]**demulcent** \"\ *n* -S : a substance (as tragacanth, acacia, or flaxseed) usu. of a mucilaginous or oily character capable of soothing an inflamed or abraded mucous membrane or protecting it from irritation

de·mul·si·bil·i·ty \dȧˌməlsə'biləd·ē, dēˌ-\ *n* -ES [*demulsify* + *-ibility*] : the ability to be demulsified being sometimes expressed as the rate at which a liquid (as an oil) separates from an emulsion

de·mul·si·fi·ca·tion \-səfȧ'kāshən\ *n* -S : the process of demulsifying

de·mul·si·fy \dȧ'məlsəˌfī, dē'-\ *also* **de–emulsify** \ˌdē+\ *vt* -ED/-ING/-ES [*de-* + *emulsify*] : to convert into a form that resists emulsification : BREAK *vt* 9e

[1]**de·mur** *R* dȧ'mər, dē'-, +V-mər·; *-R* -mə̄, + *suffixal vowel* -mər· *also* -mər, +V *in a following word* -mər· *or* -mə̄ *also* -mə̄r\ *vb* **demurred; demurred; demurring; demurs** [ME *demeoren, demeren* to linger, wait, fr. OF *demorer* (3d pers. pl. pres. indic. *demeurent*), fr. L *demorari* to linger, retard, fr. *de-* + *morari* to linger, retard, fr. *mora* delay — more at MEMORY] *vi* **1** *law* : to interpose a demurrer **2** : to object or have scruples : take exception — often used with *to* or *at* ⟨it would seem hazardous to ~ to a proposition which is so widely accepted —Samuel Alexander⟩ **3** *archaic* : to suspend proceedings or judgment in view of a doubt or difficulty : put off the determination or conclusion of an affair : DELAY, HESITATE ~ *vt* **1** *obs* : to cause delay to : put off **2** *obs* : to doubt or hesitate about **3** *archaic* : to object to

syn SCRUPLE, BALK, JIB or GIB, SHY, BOGGLE, STICK, STICKLE, STRAIN: DEMUR indicates delaying through personal doubt, uncertainty, objection, or exception ⟨we are bound to challenge many of our colleagues in the university who *demur* on academic grounds to the inclusion of theology —Walter Moberly⟩ ⟨they had been seated about the middle room with *demurring* and unwillingness to take seats, for politeness —Pearl Buck⟩ SCRUPLE implies reluctance to assent or proceed because of doubts about rightness, morality, propriety, or wisdom ⟨he does not *scruple* to ask the most abominable things of you —George Meredith⟩ ⟨Greece and in particular Athens was overrun by philosophers, who . . . did not *scruple* to question the foundations of social and moral obligation —G.L.Dickinson⟩ BALK indicates an obstinate stopping short, as though some sort of limit had been reached or check encountered ⟨one of the Marauder mules *balked* at the bottom of every rugged Burma hill —Dave Richardson⟩ ⟨minds can be pushed just so far and so fast, then they *balk* —Russell Lord⟩ JIB (GIB) may suggest balking and drawing back or away ⟨his soldiers, many of whom had served with Antony, *jibbed* at the attack on their old leader —John Buchan⟩ SHY implies starting or recoiling away in fright, like a frightened horse, or in wary suspicion or squeamish distaste ⟨she *shied* away from him like a startled Thoroughbred⟩ ⟨even the hardiest pioneer is likely to *shy* at the Valley of Death and put off going there to the very end —W.P.Webb⟩ BOGGLE may indicate shying away from in sudden alarm or with fussy scruple ⟨Lord Cardigan *boggled* at the incredible order, then squared his shoulders and took the Brigade to destruction —Anthony West⟩ ⟨when a native begins perjury he perjures himself thoroughly. He does not *boggle* over details —Rudyard Kipling⟩ ⟨but I do *boggle* at putting my tongue in my cheek and teaching what I know to be nonsense —Paul Roberts⟩ STICK indicates demurring because of conscientious scruples ⟨to *stick* at nothing in accomplishing his ends⟩ STICKLE involves refusing to accept because of something felt to be offensive or contrary to principles ⟨presumably that is his method — so the reader, eager to get good things where he can, will not *stickle* at it —K.D.Burke⟩ STRAIN in this sense indicates demurring at the unacceptable; it is often used in situations involving standards and tastes sharply varied by whimsical caprice ⟨to *strain* at a gnat and swallow a camel⟩

[2]**demur** \"\ *n* -S [ME *demure, demere* delay, abode, fr. OF *demore*, fr. *demorer*] **1** : difficulty in making up one's mind : IRRESOLUTION, INDECISION, UNCERTAINTY ⟨after some delay and ~, the door grudgingly turned on its hinges —Charles Dickens⟩ **2** : the act of objecting or taking exception : PROTEST ⟨to accept without ~⟩ ⟨rather than be brought into court he will pay without ~ —G.B.Shaw⟩ **syn** see SCRUPLE

[1]**de·mure** \dȧ'myů(ə)r, dē'-, -ůə\ *adj* -ER/-EST [ME, perh. fr. MF *demorer, demourer* to linger, wait] **1** : marked by quiet modesty, sedate reserve, restraint, or sobriety : not demanding attention : RETIRING, SHY ⟨by hustling male assistants very energetic and rapid, instead of by ~ anemic virgins —Arnold Bennett⟩ ⟨the recurring flash of mischief in its ~ and marvelously dainty humor —*Times Lit. Supp.*⟩ **2** : affectedly modest, reserved, or serious : PRIM, COY ⟨had a knack of adopting a ~ ingenue air —W.M.Thackeray⟩ ⟨linen, nonchalant and swank and cut with ~ and deceitful simplicity —Lois Long⟩ **syn** see DECOROUS

[2]**demure** *vi, obs* : to look demurely

de·mure·ly *adv* [ME, fr. *demure* + *-ly*] : in a demure manner : with affected or coy gravity or meekness : MODESTLY, PRIMLY ⟨pale fair hair that she ~ parted in the middle —Edmund Wilson⟩

de·mure·ness *n* -ES : the quality of being demure

de·mur·i·ty \dȧ'myůrəd·ē, dē'-\ *n* -ES [[1]*demure* + *-ity*] : DEMURENESS

de·mur·ra·ble \dȧ'mər·əbəl, dē'- *also* -mə̄rə-\ *adj* [[1]*demur* + *-able*] : susceptible of being demurred to (as in a legal action)

de·mur·rage \-'mər·|ij, -mə·r|, |ēj *also* -mə̄r|\ *n* -S [[1]*demur* (to delay) + *-age*] **1 a** : the detention of a ship by the freighter beyond the time allowed in her charter party for loading, unloading, or sailing — compare LAY DAY **b** : a charge assessed for detaining a freight car, truck, or other vehicle beyond the free time stipulated for loading or unloading **2** : a storage charge on goods in transit not called for within a reasonable or set time; *also* : the delay in collecting such goods

de·mur·ral \-'mər·əl *also* -mə̄rəl\ *n* -S [[1]*demur* + *-al*] : the act or an instance of demurring : OBJECTION, PROTEST, DISSENT

de·mur·rant \-'mər·ənt *also* -mə̄rə-\ *n* -S [[1]*demur* + *-ant*] : one that interposes a demurrer

demurred *past of* DEMUR

[1]**de·mur·rer** \-'mər·ə(r), -mə·rə(r) *also* -mə̄rə(r\ *n* -S [MF *demorer* to delay, linger, wait — more at DEMUR] **1** : a pleading by a party to a legal action that assumes the truth of the matter alleged by the opposite party and sets up that it is insufficient in law to sustain his claim or that there is some other defect on the face of the pleadings constituting a legal reason why the opposing party should not be allowed to proceed further **2** : an objection or exception : DEMUR 2 ⟨the only ~ one might register . . . would be in relation to the dangerous generalizations of the author's last chapter —J.J.Sweeney⟩

[2]**de·mur·rer** \-'mər·ə(r) *also* -mə̄rə(r\ *n* -S [[1]*demur* + *-er*] : one that demurs

demurring *pres part of* DEMUR

demurs *pres 3d sing of* DEMUR, *pl of* DEMUR

demy \dȧ'mī\ *n* -ES [ME, fr. *demi* half — more at DEMI-] **1 a** : a 15th century gold coin of Scotland weighing from 50 to 53 grains **b** : a unit of value equivalent to one demy coin ⟨a gold half-*demy* was issued⟩ **2** : a scholar on the foundation at Magdalen college, Oxford, orig. receiving half the allowance of a fellow **3** : a size of paper commonly 16 × 21, 15½ × 20, or 17½ × 22½ inches

de·my·e·li·nate \(')dē'mīələˌnāt, dȧ'-\ *vt* [*de-* + *myelin* + *-ate*] : to remove myelin from or destroy the myelin of ⟨a disease that ~*s* the cranial nerves⟩

de·my·e·li·na·tion \(ˌ)dēˌmīələ'nāshən, dȧˌ-\ *n* : the state of being demyelinated

de·my·e·lin·i·za·tion \(ˌ)dēˌmīələnə'zāshən, dȧˌ-\ *n* -S : DEMYELINATION

de·my·ship \dȧ'mīˌship\ *n* [*demy* + *-ship*] : a scholarship at Magdalen college, Oxford

de·mythologize \(ˌ)dē+\ *vb* [*de-* + *mythologize*] *vt* : to divest (a writing) of mythological forms in order to uncover the meaning underlying such forms ~ *vi* : to separate the meaning of a writing from the mythological forms in which it is expressed — **de·mythologization** \(ˌ)dē+\ *n* -S

[1]**den** \'den\ *n* -S [ME, fr. OE *denn;* akin to OE *denu* valley, OHG *tenni* threshing floor, Gk *thenar* palm of the hand, Skt *dhanu* sandy shore] **1** : the lair of a wild animal, esp. of a beast of prey ⟨a fox ~⟩ **2** : a cavern or hollow used esp. as a place of concealment or refuge ⟨a robber's ~ in the side of a mountain⟩ **3** *dial Brit* : a narrow glen or ravine : DINGLE **4** : a comfortable usu. secluded room provided in a dwelling for study, reading, or leisure ⟨every home that could afford one had a ~, with leather armchair, pennants on the wall —*Time*⟩ **5** : a place that is usu. small and dimly lit and that serves as or resembles a hideout or a center of secret activity ⟨the ~*s* where the gangs lived —S.H.Adams⟩ ⟨the amusement ~*s* of New York and Hollywood —R.L.Taylor⟩ ⟨gambling ~*s*⟩ ⟨a ~ of iniquity⟩ ⟨an opium ~⟩ **6** : the home, base, or goal in certain games **7** : a subdivision of a cub-scout pack of the Boy Scouts of America made up of two or more cub scouts and corresponding to a boy-scout patrol — see DEN MOTHER

[2]**den** \"\ *vb* **denned; denned; denning; dens** [ME *dennen*, fr. *den* lair] *vi* **1** : to live in or as if in a den ⟨there were hill folk who *denned* in log cabins with dirt floors and no windows —Vance Randolph & G.P.Wilson⟩ **2** : to retire to a den (as for hibernating) — often used with *up* ⟨the young bears ~ up together during the second winter —R.E.Trippensee⟩ ~ *vt* : to drive or pursue (an animal) into a den ⟨cold weather had *denned* up the coons for good —Hugh Fosburgh⟩ ⟨his dogs drove hard and long and never quit until the fox was killed or *denned* —*Red Ranger*⟩

den *abbr* denotation; denotative

denar *var of* DINAR

de·nar·i·us \dȧ'na(a)rēəs, dē-, -'när-\ *n, pl* **denar·ii** \-rēˌī, -rē(ˌ)ē\ [ME, fr. L — more at DENIER] **1** : a small silver coin of ancient Rome orig., under the Republic, equivalent to 10 bronze asses but later debased until by the late Empire its silver content became only a wash on copper **2** : a gold coin of the Roman Empire equivalent to 25 denarii **3** : [3]DENIER 1

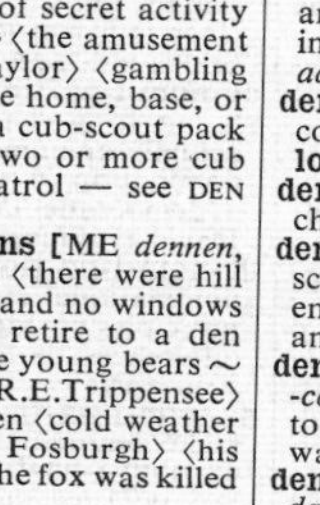

denarius of Julius Caesar, 44 B.C.

denarius dei \-'dēˌī, 'dā(ˌ)ē\ *n, pl* **denarii dei** *sometimes cap 2d D* [NL] : GOD'S PENNY

[1]**denary** *n* -ES [L *denarius*, fr. *denarius* adj.] *obs* : the number ten : a group of ten

[2]**de·na·ry** \'dēnərē, 'den-\ *adj* [L *denarius* — more at DENIER] : containing ten : based on or proceeding by tens : TENFOLD

de·nasalization \(ˌ)dē, dȧ+\ *n* : the act or an instance of denasalizing

de·nasalize \(')dē, dȧ+\ *vt* [*de-* + *nasalize*] : to eliminate nasality from ⟨in a choked *denasalized* voice —Natacha Stewart⟩

de·nationalization \(ˌ)dē, dȧ+\ *n* : the act of denationalizing or the state of being denationalized

de·nationalize \(')dē, dȧ+\ *vt, see -ize in Explan Notes* [*de-* + *nationalize*] **1** : to divest or deprive (as a people) of national character or rights **2** : to free from ownership or domination by the national government ⟨the coal industry was *denationalized*⟩ : free from obligation to serve the interests of any particular nation in preference to the universal good

de·naturalization \(ˌ)dē, dȧ+\ *n* : the act of denaturalizing or the state of being denaturalized

de·naturalize \(')dē, dȧ+\ *vt* [*de-* + *naturalize*] **1** : to make unnatural : take away or alter the true or proper nature of : alienate from nature ⟨it was landscape *denaturalized* . . . and with all that was left adapted to a decorative purpose —*N.Y. Herald Tribune*⟩ **2** [F *dénaturaliser*, fr. *dé-* de- (fr. OF *de-, des-*) + *naturaliser* to naturalize] : to deprive of the rights and duties of a subject or citizen — opposed to *naturalize*

de·na·tur·ant \dȧ'nāchərənt, dē'-\ *n* -S [*denature* + *-ant*] : a denaturing agent

de·na·tur·a·tion \dȧˌnāchə'rāshən, (ˌ)dēˌ-\ *n* -S : the process of denaturing — used esp. of proteins ⟨~ of egg white by heat leads to coagulation⟩

de·nature \(')dē, dȧ+\ *vb* -ED/-ING/-S [*de-* + *nature* (n.)] *vt* **1** : to deprive of natural qualities or characteristics : change the nature of ⟨a simplified but not *denatured* form of one of the world's existing major languages —I.A.Richards⟩ **2** : to so modify (a native protein) esp. by heat, acid, alkali, or ultraviolet radiation that some of the original properties (as solubility and specific activity) no longer are present or present in the same degree owing to a change in molecular structure **3** : to add nonfissionable material to (fissionable material) so as to render unsuitable for use in an atomic bomb without processing but not to affect value as a source of atomic power ~ *vi* : to become denatured — used esp. of proteins

denatured alcohol *n* : ethyl alcohol made unfit for drinking but still suitable for industrial or domestic purposes and freed from internal revenue tax in many countries (as the U. S.): as **a** : alcohol to which have been added sufficient malodorous and obnoxious substances (as products from the destructive distillation of wood or from petroleum) to prevent completely its use or recovery for beverage purposes but not for many industrial uses (as for an antifreeze) — called also *completely denatured alcohol* **b** : alcohol to which have been added small amounts of substances (as methanol, benzene, or acetaldehyde) that do not prevent its use in industry and the arts for specialized purposes (as for solvents) — called also *specially denatured alcohol;* compare METHYLATED SPIRIT

de·na·tur·ize \(')dē'nāchəˌrīz, dȧ'n-\ *vt* -ED/-ING/-S *see -ize in Explan Notes* [ISV *de-* + *nature* + *-ize*] : DENATURE

de·na·zi·fi·ca·tion \(ˌ)dēˌnätsəfȧ'kāshən, -nat- *sometimes* -näzȧ- *or* -nazȧ-\ *n* -S : the process of denazifying or the state of being denazified

de·na·zi·fy \(')dē'nätsȧˌfī, -nat- *sometimes* -näzȧˌ- *or* -nazȧˌ-\ *vt* -ED/-ING/-ES [*de-* + *nazify*] : to rid of nazism and its influence : free or pronounce free of the charge of nazism

den·bigh·shire \'denbȧˌshi(ə)r, -iə, -ˌshə(r)\ *or* **den·bigh** \-bē, -bi\ *adj, usu cap* [fr. *Denbighshire* or *Denbigh*, county of Wales] : of or from the county of Denbigh, Wales : of the kind or style prevalent in Denbigh

den chief *n* : a boy scout who cooperates with a den mother in supervising a cub-scout den of the Boy Scouts of America

den dad *n* : a male adult leader of a cub-scout den of the Boy Scouts of America

dendr- *or* **dendro-** *comb form* [NL *dendr-*, fr. Gk *dendr-, dendro-* tree, fr. *dendron;* akin to Gk *drys* tree — more at TREE] : tree ⟨*dendro*philous⟩ : resembling a tree ⟨*dendr*axon⟩

den·drag·a·pus \den'dragəpəs\ *n, cap* [NL] : a genus of grouses (family Tetraonidae) comprising the blue grouses

den·dras·pis \-'draspȧs\ *n, cap* [NL, fr. *dendr-* + L *aspis* asp — more at ASP] : a genus of African elapid snakes comprising the mambas

den·dri·form \'dendrəˌfȯrm\ *adj* [*dendr-* + *-iform*] : resembling a tree in structure ⟨~ sponge⟩

den·drite \'denˌdrīt\ *n* -S [*dendr-* + *-ite*] **1** : a branching figure resembling a tree produced on or in a mineral or stone (as in the moss agate) by an oxide of manganese or other foreign mineral; *also* : the mineral or stone so marked **2** : a crystallized arborescent form (as of gold or silver) **3** : any of the protoplasmic processes of a nerve cell that conduct impulses toward the cell body and that are usu. branched and comparatively short : an afferent fiber of a neuron — compare AXON

den·drit·ic \(')den'drid·ik\ *also* **den·drit·i·cal** \-d·ȧkəl\ *adj* : resembling a dendrite : branching like a tree : ARBORESCENT ⟨~ snow crystals⟩ ⟨~ pigment-bearing cells in the skin⟩ ⟨a ~ drainage system⟩ — **den·drit·i·cal·ly** \-d·ȧk(ə)lē\ *adv*

den·drob·a·tes \den'dräbəd·ˌēz\ *n, cap* [NL, fr. *dendr-* + *-bates;* prob. influenced by Gk *dendrobatein* to climb trees] : a genus of toothless mostly small brightly colored tropical American frogs of the family Ranidae having a poisonous skin secretion that has been used by certain Central American Indians as an arrow poison

den·drobe \'denˌdrōb\ *n* -S [NL *Dendrobium*] : an orchid of the genus *Dendrobium*

den·dro·bi·um \den'drōbēəm\ *n* [NL, fr. *dendr-* + *-bium*] **1** *cap* : a genus of epiphytic orchids that are chiefly native to tropical and subtropical Asia and have stems resembling canes and racemose flowers in which the labellum is connate with or articulate to the base of the column **2** -S : any plant of the genus *Dendrobium*

den·dro·calamus \ˌden(ˌ)drō+\ *n, cap* [NL, fr. *dendr-* + L *calamus* reed — more at CALAMUS] : a small genus of large Asiatic bamboos with long panicles of globular clusters of flowers succeeded by small fruits with thick hard walls

den·dro·chi·ro·ta \ˌdendrōˌkī'rōd·ə\ *n pl, cap* [NL, fr. *dendr-* + *-chirota* (fr. LGk *chirōtos* furnished with hands, fr. Gk *cheir* hand) — more at CHIR-] : an order of holothurians having tube feet and tentacles which branch like a small tree and occurring in shallow water thoughout the world but esp. in temperate and cold regions — **den·dro·chi·rote** \-'kīˌrōt\ *adj or n*

dend·ro·chronological \ˌden(ˌ)drō+\ *adj* : relating to or concerned with dendrochronology — **den·dro·chronologically** \ˌ=(ˌ)=+\ *adv*

den·dro·chronologist \ˌ=(ˌ)=+\ *n* : a specialist in dendrochronology

den·dro·chronology \ˌ=(ˌ)=+\ *n* [*dendr-* + *chronology*] : the science of dating events, intervals of time, and variations in environment in former periods by study of the sequence of and differences between rings of growth in trees and aged wood

den·dro·coe·lum \ˌdendrō'sēləm\ *n, cap* [NL, fr. *dendr-* + *-coelum*] : a common genus of Old World triclad turbellarians to which the common white planarian (*Procotyla fluviatilis*) was formerly assigned

den·dro·co·lap·tid \ˌ=(ˌ)=kə'laptȧd\ *n* -S [NL *Dendrocolaptidae*] : a bird of the family Dendrocolaptidae

den·dro·co·lap·ti·dae \ˌ=(ˌ)=kə'laptəˌdē\ *n pl, cap* [NL, fr. *Dendrocolaptes*, type genus (fr. *dendr-* + *-colaptes* (fr. Gk *kolaptein* to peck) + NL *-idae*] : a large family of tropical American birds (suborder Tyranni) that are closely related to the ovenbirds, are of climbing habit, and creep over trees from which they dig out insects — see WOODHEWER — **den·dro·co·lap·tine** \ˌ=(ˌ)=kə'lapˌtīn, -ˌtȧn\ *adj*

den·droc·o·pos \den'dräkəpəs\ *n, cap* [NL, fr. Gk *dendrokopos* woodcutter, fr. *dendr-* + *-kopos* (fr. the stem of *koptein* to smite, cut off) — more at CAPON] : a large genus of woodpeckers that are widely distributed in temperate parts of the northern hemisphere, and are all black or blackish brown with white markings and more or less red about the head

den·droc·to·nus \-'dräktənəs\ *n, cap* [NL, fr. *dendr-* + Gk *ktonos* murder; fr. their destructiveness] : a genus of small bark beetles that are esp. destructive to mature coniferous trees and that have a large prothorax, short clubbed elbowed antennae, serrated tibiae, and spiny elytra

den·dro·cyg·na \ˌdendrō'signə\ *n, cap* [NL, fr. *dendr-* + *-cygna* (fr. L *cygnus, cycnus* swan) — more at CYGNET] : a genus of long-legged ducks comprising the tree ducks and having long strong claws used in perching and a peculiar whistling call

den·dro·date \'dendrə+ˌ-\ *n* [*dendr-* + *date*] : a date (as of an archaeological site) obtained by dendrochronology

den·dro·gae·an *or* **den·dro·ge·an** \ˌdendrō'jēən\ *adj, usu cap* [NL *Dendrogaea, Dendrogea*, a biogeographic realm (fr. *dendr-* + *-gaea, -gea*) + E *-an*] : of, relating to, or being a biogeographic realm or region that includes all of the Neotropical region except temperate So. America

den·dro·gram \'dendrəˌgram\ *n* -S [*dendr-* + *-gram*] : a branching diagrammatic representation of the interrelations of a group of items sharing some common factors (as of natural groups connected by a common ancestral form)

den·dro·graph \'==ˌgraf\ *n* -S [*dendr-* + *-graph*] : an instrument for the automatic recording of changes in tree diameter

den·dro·graph·ic \ˌ=='grafik\ *adj* : of or relating to dendrography

den·drog·ra·phy \den'drägrəfē\ *n* -ES [*dendr-* + *-graphy*] : the recording of tree growth by a dendrograph

den·dro·hyrax \ˌdendrō+\ [NL, fr. *dendr-* + Gk *hyrax* mouse, shrew mouse — more at SOREX] *syn of* PROCAVIA

den·droi·ca \den'drȯikə\ *n, cap* [NL, fr. *dendr-* + *-oica* (fr. Gk *oikos* house, dwelling place) — more at VICINITY] : a genus of brightly colored No. American warblers (family Parulidae) including the Blackburnian, yellow, and magnolia warblers

den·droid \'denˌdrȯid\ *also* **den·droid·al** \(')='=dᵊl\ *adj* [*dendroeidēs*, fr. *dendr-* tree + *-oeidēs* -oid, -oidal] **1** : resembling a tree in form : ARBORESCENT **2** *of graptolites* : forming many-branched colonies

den·drol·a·gus \den'dräləgəs\ *n, cap* [NL, fr. *dendr-* + Gk *lagōs* hare] : the genus consisting of the tree wallabies

den·dro·log·ic \ˌdendrə'läjik\ *or* **den·dro·log·i·cal** \-jȧkəl\ *adj* : relating to dendrology

den·drol·o·gist \den'dräləjȧst\ *n* -S : a specialist in dendrology

den·drol·o·gy \-jē\ *n* -ES [*dendr-* + *-logy*] **1** : the study of trees **2** : a treatise on trees

den·drom·e·ter \den'drämәd·ə(r)\ *n* -S [*dendr-* + *-meter*] : any of several devices for measuring trees *esp* : one for measuring diameters and heights indirectly utilizing principles based on the relation of the sides of similar triangles — compare DENDROGRAPH

den·dron \'dendrən, -ˌdrän\ *n, pl* **dendrons** \-nz\ *also* **den·dra** \-ˌdrə\ [NL, fr. Gk, tree — more at DENDR-] : DENDRITE

-den·dron \ˌdendrən, -ˌdrän\ *n comb form, pl* **-dendrons**

\-nz\ also **-den·dra** \-,drə\ [L, fr. Gk, fr. *dendron* — more at DENDR-] **1 :** tree — esp. in generic names of plants ⟨*Liriodendron*⟩ ⟨*Trochodendron*⟩ **2 :** treelike formation ⟨*neurodendron*⟩ **3 :** stem : part of a stem ⟨*Schizodendron*⟩

den·droph·a·gous \(ˈ)denˈdräfəgəs\ *adj* [*dendr-* + *-phagous*] **:** feeding on trees — used of insects

den·droph·i·lous \-fələs\ *adj* [*dendr-* + *-philous*] **:** tree-loving **:** living in or on trees ⟨~ plants⟩

den·droph·y·sis \denˈdräfəsə̇s\ *n, pl* **dendrophy·ses** \-,sēz\ [NL, fr. *dendr-* + *-physis* (as in *paraphysis*)] **:** an arboreally branched hyphal thread in certain fungi that resembles a paraphysis

¹dene \ˈdēn\ *n* -s [ME *dene*, fr. OE *denu* valley; akin to OE *denn* den — more at DEN] **1** *dial Brit* **:** VALLEY — often used in place names **2** *dial Brit* **:** a deep wooded valley; *esp* **:** one with a stream flowing through it

²dene \"\ *n* -s [ME *den, denne;* prob. akin to OE *dūn* down (hill) — more at DOWN] *Brit* **:** a sandy tract or low sand hill by the sea

³dé·né \dāˈnā\ *n, pl* **déné** *or* **dénés** *usu cap* [F, fr. Déné] **1 a :** an Athapaskan people occupying most of the interior of Alaska and northwestern Canada **b :** a member of such people — compare PACIFIC ATHAPASKAN **2 :** the language of the Déné people — called also *Northern Athapaskan*

den·e·ga·tion \,denəˈgāshən\ *n* -s [ME *denegacioun*, fr. MF or L; MF *denegation*, fr. L *denegation-, denegatio*, fr. *denegatus* (past part. of *denegare* to deny) + *-ion-, -io* -ion — more at DENY] **:** DENIAL, REFUSAL

denehole \ˈ=,=\ *n* [prob. fr. ¹*dene* + *hole*] **:** an ancient excavation found chiefly in Essex and Kent in England and in the valley of the Somme in France consisting of a shaft sunk to the Chalk formation and enlarged into a room or rooms

de·ner·vate \dēˈnər,vāt, də̇ˈ-\ *vt* -ED/-ING/-S [*de-* + *nerve* + *-ate*] **:** to deprive of nerve supply (as by cutting a nerve)

de·ner·va·tion \,dēnərˈvāshən\ *n* **:** the act of denervating or the state of being denervated

den·gue \ˈdeŋ(,)gē, -(,)gā, -ŋgi *also* -ŋē *or* -ŋi; *S often* -ŋ-(,)gyü\ *also* **dengue fever** *n* -s [Sp *dengue*, prob. of African origin; akin to Swahili *kidinga* (*popo*) dengue, Giryama *kidhinghidhyo* fever, Rabai *dengeleka* go around, be dizzy] **:** an acute infectious disease characterized by sudden onset, headache, racking joint pain, and a rash and caused by a virus transmitted by mosquitoes of the genus *Aedes* chiefly in tropical and semitropical regions — called also *breakbone fever*

de·ni·able \də̇ˈnīəbəl, dēˈ-\ *adj* [*deny* + *-able*] **:** capable of being denied

de·ni·al \-ˈnī(ə)l\ *n* -s [*deny* + *-al*] **1 :** refusal to grant, assent to, or sanction **:** rejection of something requested, claimed, or felt to be due ⟨~ of his visiting privileges⟩ ⟨~ of passports to undesirables⟩ **2 a :** refusal to admit the truth of a statement, charge, or imputation **:** assertion that something alleged is untrue ⟨his ~ that he took the money⟩ ⟨her ~ that her son was involved⟩ **b :** refusal to accept or acknowledge the reality or validity of a thing or idea ⟨his ~ of the divine right of kings⟩ **3 :** refusal to acknowledge a person or thing as standing in a certain relationship or as having a certain character **:** DISAVOWAL, REPUDIATION ⟨a renegade's ~ of his leader⟩ ⟨the baron's ~ of his weakling son⟩ **4 :** the opposing by the defendant of an allegation of the opposite party in a law suit **5** *dial Eng* **:** HINDRANCE, HANDICAP, DISADVANTAGE ⟨his lame hand was a great ~ to him⟩ **6 :** a restriction or limitation upon one's own activity or desires **:** SELF-DENIAL ⟨the three thousand which he had hoarded at the price of sacrifice and ~ —William Faulkner⟩ **7 :** a bridge bid indicating inability to raise or support a partner's bid **8** *logic* **:** NEGATION

denial of the antecedent : the logical fallacy of inferring the negation of the consequent of an implication from the negation of the antecedent (as in "if it rains then the game is canceled but it has not rained therefore the game is not canceled") — compare AFFIRMATION OF THE CONSEQUENT

de·nicotinize *also* **de·nicotine** \(ˈ)dē, də + \ *vt* -ED/-ING/-S [*denicotinize* fr. *de-* + *nicotine* + *-ize; denicotine* fr. *de-* + *nicotine* (n.)] **:** to remove part of the nicotine from (tobacco)

denied *past of* DENY

¹de·ni·er \də̇ˈnī(ə)r, -īə\ *n* -s [ME, fr. *denyen* to deny + *-er*] **:** one that denies

²denier *n* -s [MF *denier* to deny — more at DENY] *obs* **:** DENIAL 4

³de·nier \də̇ˈni(ə)r, -niə; dənˈyā *also* ˈdenyə(r) *or* -enēə(r); *in sense 2 usu* ˈdenyə(r) *or* -enēə(r) *also* -en,yā *or* -enē,ā\ *n* -s [ME *denere*, fr. MF *denier*, fr. L *denarius*, Roman silver coin originally equivalent to ten asses, fr. *denarius* containing ten, fr. *deni* ten by ten (fr. the base of *decem* ten) + *-arius* -ary — more at TEN] **1 :** a small coin of France and western Europe from the time of Pepin the Short to the French Revolution, orig. of silver, later of billon, and finally of copper; *also* **:** a unit of value equal to one denier **2 a :** a unit of fineness for silk, rayon, or nylon yarn equal to the fineness of a yarn weighing 0.05 gram for each 450 meters of length or one gram for each 9000 meters ⟨9000 meters of a 15-*denier* yarn weigh 15 grams⟩ ⟨15-*denier* yarn is finer than 30-*denier* yarn⟩ **b :** the fineness of a silk, rayon, or nylon yarn or fabric

de·nier à dieu \dənyāädyœ\ *n, pl* **deniers à dieu** \"\ *sometimes cap 2d D* [F] **:** GOD'S PENNY

denies *pres 3d sing of* DENY

den·i·grate \ˈdenə,grāt, -nē,- *sometimes* ˈdēn-; *also* də̇ˈnī,g- *or* dēˈ- *sometimes* -ˈni,g-; *usu* -ād· + V\ *vt* -ED/-ING/-S [L *denigratus*, past part. of *denigrare*, fr. *de-* + *nigrare* to blacken, fr. *nigr-, niger* black] **1 :** to cast aspersion on the character or reputation of **:** belittle maliciously **:** DEFAME, SULLY ⟨*denigrating* his efforts and subjecting him to scorn —Manfred Nathan⟩ ⟨~ the values of living —Stephen Spender⟩ **2 :** to make black **:** DARKEN ⟨fog *denigrated* with factory smoke⟩

den·i·gra·tion \,denəˈgrāshən, -nēˈ- *sometimes* ,dēn-; *also* ,dē,nīˈ-\ *n* -s **1** *obs* **:** the act of denigrating **2 :** a sullying of reputation or character **:** DEFAMATION, DEGRADATION ⟨the ~ of man to his former animal level —G.L.Steibel⟩

den·i·gra·tor *pronunciation at* DENIGRATE + ə(r)\ *n* -s **:** one that denigrates

den·i·gra·to·ry \ˈdenə̇grə,tōre, -,tȯr-, -ri; də̇ˈnīg-, -ˈnig-\ *adj* **:** DEFAMATORY

den·im \ˈdenə̇m\ *n* -s [F (*serge*) *de Nîmes* serge of Nîmes, France] **1 :** a firm durable twilled usu. cotton fabric woven with colored warp and white filling threads; *also* **:** such a fabric woven in colored stripes **2 denims** *pl* **:** overalls or trousers usu. of dark blue denim for work or rough use

den·i·so·nia \,denəˈsōnēə\ *n, cap* [NL, fr. Sir William T. *Denison* †1871 Australian statesman and governor of New South Wales + NL *-ia*] **:** a genus of venomous Australian snakes (family Elapidae) including the copperhead

de·nitrate \(ˈ)dē + \ *vt* [*de-* + *nitrate* (n.)] **:** to remove nitric acid, nitrates, the nitro group, or nitrogen oxides from — **de·nitration** \ˌdē + \ *n*

de·nitrator \(ˈ)dē + \ *n* **:** one that denitrates: as **a :** an apparatus in which denitration is conducted **b :** one who operates denitrator towers for the recovery of nitric acid in the manufacture of trinitrotoluene

de·nitrification \(ˌ)dē + \ *n* **:** the act or process of denitrifying; *specif* **:** a process by which nitrates or nitrites are reduced with the formation of nitrites, nitrogen oxides, ammonia, or free nitrogen and which is commonly brought about (as in the soil or in sewage) by denitrifying bacteria usu. resulting in the escape of nitrogen into the air

de·nitrifier \(ˈ)dē + \ *n* **:** a denitrifying agent (as a denitrifying bacterium)

de·nitrify \(ˈ)dē + \ *vt* [*de-* + *nitrify*] **:** to deprive of or free from nitrogen or its compounds; *also* **:** to convert (nitrates or nitrites) into compounds of lower oxidation states **:** subject to denitrification

denitrifying bacteria *n pl* **:** various bacteria that bring about denitrification — used esp. of forms that reduce nitrates to nitrites or nitrites to nitrogen gas (as many common putrefactive organisms of manure and soil); see ACHROMOBACTER

de·nitrogenate \(ˌ)dē + \ *vt* [*de-* + *nitrogenate*] **:** to reduce the stored nitrogen in the body of by forced breathing of pure oxygen for a period of time esp. as a measure designed to prevent development of aeroembolism — **de·nitrogenation** \(ˌ)dē + \ *n*

de·nitrogenize \(ˌ)dē + \ *vt* [*de-* + *nitrogenize*] **:** DENITROGENATE

den·i·za·tion \,denəˈzāshən\ *n* -s **:** the act of making one a denizen **:** the process of being made a denizen

denize *vt* -ED/-ING/-S [prob. by alter. (influence of *-ize*)] *obs* **:** DENIZEN

¹den·izen \ˈdenəzən *also* -əsən\ *n* -s [ME *deynseen, denysen*, fr. MF *denzein*, fr. OF, inner, fr. *denz* in, within (fr. LL *deintus* within, from within, fr. L *de* from, away + *intus* within, fr. *in*) + *-ein* -an (fr. L *-anus*) — more at DE-, IN] **1 :** a dweller in a certain place or region **:** INHABITANT, RESIDENT ⟨~s of the village⟩ ⟨the ~s of the bayous love a holiday —R.M.Hodesh⟩ **2 :** one admitted to residence in a foreign country; *esp* **:** an alien admitted by favor to all or a part of the rights of citizenship **3 :** one that has been naturalized — used esp. of a word, animal, or plant **4 a :** one that remains in a place temporarily or for a period of time **b :** one that occupies or goes to a place frequently **:** HABITUÉ ⟨~s of out-of-town theaters⟩

²denizen \"\ *vt* -ED/-ING/-S **:** to make (one) a denizen **:** admit to residence with certain rights and privileges

den·mark \ˈden,märk, -,mäk\ *adj, usu cap* [fr. *Denmark*, kingdom in northwestern Europe] **:** of or from Denmark **:** of the kind or style prevalent in Denmark

den mother *n* **:** a female adult leader of a cub-scout den of the Boy Scouts of America

denned *past of* DEN

¹den·ner \ˈdenə(r)\ *Scot var of* DINNER

²den·ner \ˈdenə(r)\ *n* -s [¹*den* + *-er*] **:** a boy who serves as leader of a cub-scout den of the Boy Scouts of America

den·net \ˈdenə̇t\ *n* -s [prob. fr. the name *Dennet*] **:** a light open 2-wheeled carriage with the body suspended on leather braces that is drawn by one horse — compare WHISKEY

denning *pres part of* DEN

denn·staedt·ia \denˈsted·ēə, -tād-·\ *n, cap* [NL, fr. August W. *Dennstaedt*, 19th cent. Ger. botanist + NL *-ia*] **:** a genus of chiefly tropical ferns (family Polypodiaceae) having tripinnate fronds and globular sori with sporangia in elevated receptacles and with cup-shaped indusia — **denn·staedt·i·oid** \(ˈ)=ˈ=ē,ȯid\ *adj*

de·nom·i·nal \də̇ˈnämənᵊl, dēˈ-\ *adj* [*de-* + *nominal*] **:** DENOMINATIVE 3

¹de·nom·i·nate \-ˈnämə,nāt, *usu* -ād· + V\ *vt* [L *denominatus*, past part. of *denominare*, fr. *de-* + *nominare* to name — more at NOMINATE] **1 :** to give a name to **:** call by a name **:** DESIGNATE, CALL ⟨a fact is a fact and all evidence so *denominated* has the prestige of science —R.M.Weaver⟩ **2 :** to serve to distinguish **:** INDICATE, DENOTE ⟨anger ~s a state of mind —W.F.Hambly⟩ **3 :** to express or designate in some denomination ⟨exchange certificates *denominated* in dollars or pounds —R.F.Mikesell⟩

²de·nom·i·nate \-,nə̇t, -,nāt\ *adj* [L *denominatus*] **1** *archaic* **:** DENOMINATED, CALLED **2 :** having a specific name or denomination **:** specified in the concrete as opposed to the abstract ⟨*7 feet* is a ~ quantity, while 7 is an abstract quantity or number⟩

de·nom·i·na·tion \də̇,näməˈnāshən, dē,-\ *n* -s [ME *denominacioun*, fr. MF or LL; MF *denomination*, fr. LL *denomination-, denominatio*, fr. L, metonymy, fr. *denominatus* + *-ion-, -io* -ion] **1 :** the act of denominating or naming **2 :** that by which something is denominated or styled **:** APPELLATION, NAME, DESIGNATION, TITLE; *esp* **:** a general name for a class of like individuals **:** CATEGORY ⟨a sort of tribute under the ~ of presents —Tobias Smollett⟩ **3 :** a class or society of individuals called by the same name; *esp* **:** a religious group or a community of believers called by the same name ⟨Presbyterians form one ~ of Christians⟩ **4 :** a value or size naming one of a particular series of values or sizes (as of monetary issues, stamps, units of weight or measure) ⟨bills in $5 and $10 ~s⟩ ⟨liter is a metric ~⟩ **5 :** the suit or no-trump named in a bridge bid **syn** see CLASS, RELIGION

de·nom·i·na·tion·al \=ˌ==ˈ=shənᵊl, -shnəl\ *adj* **1 :** of or relating to a denomination **:** supported in part and either actually or nominally controlled by a particular religious denomination ⟨a ~ school⟩ **2 :** PARTISAN, SECTARIAN ⟨building a democratic labor movement free from ~ limitations —David Dubinsky⟩ — **de·nom·i·na·tion·al·ly** *adv*

de·nom·i·na·tion·al·ism \-nᵊl,izəm, -nə,liz-\ *n* -s **1 :** denominational spirit or policy **:** devotion to denominational principles or interests **2 :** the emphasizing of denominational differences to the point of being narrowly exclusive **:** SECTARIANISM

de·nom·i·na·tion·al·ize \-nᵊl,īz, -nə,līz\ *vt* -ED/-ING/-S **:** to make denominational

¹de·nom·i·na·tive \də̇ˈnämə,nā|d·|iv, dēˈ-, -,nə|, |t|, |ēv *also* |əv\ *adj* [*denominate* + *-ive*] **1 :** conferring a denomination or name **2** *of a word or term* **:** characterized by or referring to certain marks or qualities which determine the naming of the subject possessing them ⟨connotative names have hence been also called ~ because the subject which they denote is denominated by, or receives a name from, the attribute which they connote —J.S.Mill⟩ **3** [*de-* + L *nomin-, nomen* name, noun + E *-ative*] **:** derived from a noun or an adjective ⟨the ~ verbs *lengthen* and *sweeten* come from *length* and *sweet*⟩ — **de·nom·i·na·tive·ly** \|əvlē, -li\ *adv*

²denominative \"\ *n* [*de-* + L *nomin-, nomen* name, noun + E *-ative*] **:** a word derived from a noun or an adjective

de·nom·i·na·tor \-ˈnämə,nād·ə(r), -ātə-\ *n* -s **1 :** the part of a fraction that is below the horizontal or slanting line signifying division and that in fractions with numerator 1 indicates into how many parts the unit is supposed to be divided **:** DIVISOR **2** *archaic* **:** one that denominates **3 :** a common trait ⟨only a single ~ do they share —Osbert Sitwell⟩ **:** the average level (as of taste or opinion) **:** STANDARD ⟨manufacturers catering to a safely low ~ of public taste —*Time*⟩ — see COMMON DENOMINATOR

de·not·able \də̇ˈnōd·əbəl, dēˈ-, -ōtə-\ *adj* [*denote* + *-able*] **:** capable of being denoted

denotate *vt* [L *denotatus*, past part. of *denotare* — more at DENOTE] *obs* **:** DENOTE

de·no·ta·tion \,dēnōˈtāshən\ *n* -s [L *denotation-, denotatio*, fr. *denotatus* + *-ion-, -io* -ion] **1 a :** the act or process of signifying ⟨the ~ of plural forms by adding *-s*⟩ **b :** demarcation and explanation ⟨the ~ of the methods used⟩ **2 :** MEANING ⟨the ~ of an expression⟩; *esp* **:** direct specific meaning as distinct from additional suggestion — compare CONNOTATION 1 **3 a :** a term specifying or denoting a thing **:** NAME ⟨*mind* is the ~ for a faculty, *brain* for an organ⟩ **b :** SIGN, INDICATION ⟨visible ~s of divine wrath⟩ **4 :** the totality of things to which a term in logic is applicable — called also *extension;* contrasted with *connotation*

de·no·ta·tive \ˈdēnō,tā|d·|iv, |t|, |ēv *also* |əv; də̇ˈnōd·ə|, dēˈ-, -ōtə|\ *adj* **1 :** having the power of denoting **:** marking off **:** DESIGNATING **2** *logic* **:** bearing a denotation — **de·no·ta·tive·ly** \|əvlē, -li\ *adv* — **de·no·ta·tive·ness** \|əvnə̇s\ *n* -ES

denotative definition *n* **:** OSTENSIVE DEFINITION

de·no·ta·tum \,dēnōˈtād·əm\ *n, pl* **denota·ta** \-ād·ə\ [NL, fr. L, neut. of *denotatus*] **:** an actually existing object referred to by a word, sign, or linguistic expression — compare *designatum*

de·note \də̇ˈnōt, dēˈ-, *usu* -ōd· + V\ *vt* -ED/-ING/-S [MF *denoter*, fr. L *denotare*, fr. *de-* + *notare* to mark, note — more at NOTE] **1 :** to serve as indication of **:** show by signs the presence or existence of **:** BETOKEN ⟨symptoms that ~ tuberculosis⟩ ⟨thickets of aspen, willow, and cottonwood ~ underlying water —*Amer. Guide Series: Wash.*⟩ **2 :** to serve as an arbitrary mark for **:** designate as a sign **:** MARK ⟨red flares *denoting* danger⟩ ⟨the slanting strokes at the bottom ~ the number —Edward Clodd⟩ ⟨a flag flown upside down to ~ distress⟩ **3** *obs* **:** write down **:** DESCRIBE **4 :** to make known **:** ANNOUNCE ⟨*denoting* his feelings clearly⟩ **5 a :** serve as linguistic expression of the notion of **:** MEAN ⟨*mono-* may ~ "one" or "single"⟩ **b :** to designate by an indicated symbol ⟨let me ~ by T the lapse of time —K.K.Darrow⟩ **c** *logic* **:** to stand for **:** signify by way of denotation **:** NAME ⟨the name . . . is said to signify the subjects *directly*, the attributes *indirectly;* it ~s the subjects and . . . *connotes* the attributes —J.S.Mill⟩ **syn** see MEAN

de·note·ment \-tmənt\ *n* -s **:** the act or means of denoting

de·no·tive \də̇ˈnōd·iv, dēˈ-\ *adj* **:** serving to denote **:** DENOTATIVE

de·noue·ment \,dāˌnüˈmäⁿ, ˌ=ˌ=ˈ= *also* ˈ==,= *sometimes* dəˈnümənt *or* -,mänt; dānümäⁿ\ *n* -s [F *dénouement*, lit., action of untying, fr. MF *desnouement*, fr. *desnouer* to untie (fr. OF *desnoer*, fr. *des-* de- + *noer* to tie, knot, fr. L *nodare*, fr. *nodus* knot) + *-ment* — more at NET] **1 :** the final outcome, result, or unraveling of the main dramatic complication in a play or other work of literature ⟨many of the better stories are written round, rather than towards, their ~s —*Times Lit. Supp.*⟩ ⟨in the ~ the girl commits suicide⟩ **2 :** the outcome or result of any complex situation or sequence of events ⟨the whole devious development of Soviet-German relations until the final dramatic ~ of the treaty —*Economist*⟩

de·nounce \də̇ˈnaün(t)s, dēˈ-\ *vt* -ED/-ING/-S [ME *denouncen, denounsen*, fr. OF *denoncier* to proclaim, pronounce, announce, fr. L *denuntiare*, fr. *de-* + *nuntiare* to report, announce, fr. *nuntius* messenger] **1 :** to pronounce (as a person, idea, course of conduct, poiltical philosophy) to be blameworthy or evil **:** stigmatize or charge esp. publicly, unequivocally, and indignantly **:** inveigh against publicly ⟨*denounced* this perversion of his teaching with justifiable indignation —W.R.Inge⟩ ⟨~ the menaced proprietors as enemies of mankind —G.B.Shaw⟩ **2** *archaic* **:** to announce publicly and formally or solemnly; *sometimes* **:** to declare or publish (something calamitous) **3 :** to inform against **:** declare or make known (as a culprit) to authorities ⟨*denounced* the conspirators to the authorities⟩ **4 a** *obs* **:** to indicate by or as if by omen **:** PORTEND, AUGUR **b** *archaic* **:** to announce (as punishment, judgment, or other impending evil) in a warning or threatening manner **5 :** to proclaim formally and publicly the termination of (as a treaty, truce, pact) ⟨*denounced* the arrangement with their former ally⟩ **6** [Sp *denunciar*, lit., to proclaim, announce, fr. L *denuntiare*] *Mexican law* **:** to offer for record legal notice of a claim for a mining concession covering (a described area of land the mining rights for which are held by the government) **syn** see CRITICIZE

de·nounce·ment \-smənt\ *n* -s [MF *denoncement*, fr. *denoncier* + *-ment*] **1 :** the act of denouncing: **a** *obs* **:** DECLARATION, ANNOUNCEMENT **b :** DENUNCIATION **c :** public accusation **2** *Mexican law* **a :** the act of denouncing a mining claim; *also* **:** the record or documentary proof of such action **b :** the claim so denounced

de·nounc·er \-sə(r)\ *n* -s **:** one that denounces

de no·vo \dēˈnō(,)vō, (ˈ)dēˈ-, (ˈ)dāˈ-\ *adv* [L] **:** ANEW, AFRESH **:** over again ⟨a case tried *de novo*⟩ ⟨think out, almost *de novo*, the bases of such a synthesis —*Survey Graphic*⟩

¹dens *pl of* DEN, *pres 3d sing of* DEN

²dens \ˈdenz\ *n, pl* **den·tes** \-n,tēz\ [L — more at ¹TOOTH] *zool* **:** a tooth or part resembling a tooth

densate *vt* -ED/-ING/-S [L *densatus*, past part. of *densare* to thicken, fr. *densus*] *obs* **:** CONDENSE — **densation** *n, obs*

dense \ˈden(t)s\ *adj* -ER/-EST [L *densus;* akin to Gk *dasys* thick with hair or leaves, Hitt *dassuš* strong] **1 a :** marked by an arrangement of parts or units so crowded or massed together as to defy penetration **:** notably lacking empty spaces or unfilled intervals ⟨the backs of the pinafores were ~ with buttons —Natacha Stewart⟩ ⟨if I went into ~ jungle, by the time I was out of sight I was also lost —Agnes N. Keith⟩ **b :** crowded very close together **:** massed together with little or no intervening space and consequently obstructing easy penetration through **:** concentrated in large numbers in a limited space ⟨every balcony, every housetop was crammed with a ~ mass of spectators —J.G.Frazer⟩ ⟨~ hardwood hammocks alternate with vast swamps —*Amer. Guide Series: Fla.*⟩ ⟨the ~ print of the directory —Jean Stafford⟩ **2** *biol* **:** COMPACT ⟨a ~ flower spike⟩ **3 a :** insensible or dull ⟨human error's ~ and purblind faith —P.B.Shelley⟩ **b :** mentally dull **:** SLOW-WITTED, THICK-HEADED **c :** EXTREME, INTENSE ⟨~ stupidity⟩ **4 a :** marked by solidly interwoven texture, by texture permitting thick matting, by deep dark color, by opaqueness or other obstruction to passage of light, or by massive concentration ⟨a ~ fabric⟩ ⟨lost in a ~ fog⟩ ⟨the heart is a ~ organ for X-ray purposes⟩ ⟨her pallor made her dark hair seem *denser* —Edith Wharton⟩ **b :** marked by presentation without lighter or less significant passages and demanding concentration to follow or comprehend ⟨her prose . . . so ~ . . . that it is all but impenetrable —*New Yorker*⟩ **5** *math* **:** having between any two elements at least one element and hence an infinity of elements ⟨a set of proper fractions arranged in order of size is ~⟩ **6 :** possessing relatively great retarding power upon light waves and consequently relatively great refractive power — used esp. of optical glass **7 :** having high or relatively high density — used of a photographic negative or a positive transparency **syn** see CLOSE, STUPID

dense·ly *adv* **:** in a dense manner

dens·en \-sən\ *vb* **densened; densened; densening** \-s(ə)niŋ\ **densens** *vt* **:** to make dense ~ *vi* **:** to become dense

dense·ness \-snə̇s\ *n* -ES **:** the quality or state of being dense **:** DENSITY

den·si·fi·ca·tion \,den(t)səfəˈkāshən\ *n* -s **:** the act or the process of making dense

den·si·fi·er \ˈ==,fī(ə)r\ *n* -s **:** a densifying agent ⟨concrete ~⟩

den·si·fy \-,fī\ *vt* -ED/-ING/-ES **:** to make dense or denser; *specif* **:** to increase the natural density of (wood) by application of pressure and usu. impregnation with a resin or other material

den·sim·e·ter \denˈsimәd·ə(r)\ *n* -s [ISV *densi-* (fr. L *densus* dense) + *-meter*] **:** an instrument for determining density or specific gravity — **den·si·met·ric** \ˌden(t)səˈme·trik\ *adj* — **den·si·met·ri·cal·ly** \-k(ə)lē\ *adv*

den·si·tom·e·ter \,den(t)səˈtäməd·ə(r)\ *n* -s [*density* + *-o-* + *-meter*] **1 :** DENSIMETER **2 :** an instrument for measuring optical density; *specif* **:** an instrument usu. photoelectric or visual for measuring photographic density by means of the light transmitted or the light reflected — **den·si·to·met·ric** \ˌ=səd·əˈme·trik\ *adj* — **den·si·tom·e·try** \ˌ=səˈtä·mə·trē\ *n* -ES

den·si·ty \ˈden(t)səd·ē, -ətē, -i\ *n* -ES [F or L; F *densité*, fr. L *densitat-, densitas*, fr. *densus* + *-itat-, -itas* -ity] **1 :** the quality or state of being dense **:** closeness of texture or consistency **:** a crowded condition ⟨a fog of great ~⟩ ⟨the great ~ of growth in the jungle⟩ ⟨made difficult by the ~ of his style⟩ **2 a :** the mass of a substance per unit volume **b :** the distribution of a quantity (as mass, electricity, or energy) per unit usu. of space (as area, length, or volume) — see ENERGY DENSITY, FLUX DENSITY, SURFACE DENSITY **c :** the average number of individuals or units per space unit ⟨a ~ of population of about 100 per square mile⟩ **3 :** extreme stupidity **4** *of an inflorescence* **:** COMPACTNESS **5 a :** the degree of opacity of any translucent medium **:** the common logarithm of the opacity **b :** the degree of darkening of a photographic film or positive transparency approximately proportional to the mass of metallic silver or dye per unit area

density altitude *n* **:** the altitude that corresponds to a given air density in a standard atmosphere

density of freight traffic *or* **density of passenger traffic :** the amount of traffic carried over a certain transport route in a given unit of time usu. computed by dividing total ton-miles or passenger-miles by the length of route

density rule *n* **:** a set of specifications for grading lumber based on the width of annual rings

¹dent \ˈdent\ *n* -s [ME, stroke, blow, alter. of *dint* — more at DINT] **1** *now dial Eng* **:** STROKE, BLOW **2 :** a depression or hollow such as is made by a blow or by pressure **:** INDENTATION ⟨a ~ in a fender⟩ ⟨the touch of his finger made a ~ in the swollen flesh⟩ **3 :** DENT CORN **4 a :** an impression or effect often having a minimizing or weakening influence ⟨a sizable ~ in the literary consciousness of the American reading public —John Barkham⟩ ⟨a ~ in the weekly budget⟩ ⟨the Texas drought made no appreciable ~ on total production —*Reporter*⟩ **b :** HEADWAY, PROGRESS ⟨nor has any really effective ~ been made into the problem of shortages —F.M.Hechinger⟩

²dent \"\ *vb* -ED/-ING/-S [ME *denten*, alter. of *dinten* — more at DINT] *vt* **1 :** to make a dent in or on **:** INDENT ⟨the car hood was ~*ed* in⟩ ⟨~*ed* his fender in the collision⟩ **2 :** to make an impression or have an effect upon esp. with a weakening result ⟨such actions ~*ed* his political influence⟩ ~ *vi* **:** to form a dent by sinking inward **:** show dents **:** become dented ⟨tin ~s easily⟩

³dent \"\ *n* -s [MF, tooth, fr. L *dent-, dens* — more at TOOTH] **1 :** an indentation or notch **2 a** *in machinery* **:** a tooth esp. of a card or gear wheel or in a lock **b :** one of the fine flat wires which compose a reed in a loom and between which the warp threads pass; *also* **:** the space between two such wires by which

the number of practicable warp ends is determined **3** [F, fr. MF] **:** a mountain peak that resembles a tooth in shape
dent- *or* **denti-** *or* **dento-** *comb form* [ME *denti-*, fr. L *dent-*, *denti-*, fr. *dent-*, *dens*] **1 :** tooth **:** teeth ⟨*dent*algia⟩ ⟨*denti*form⟩ **2 :** dental and ⟨*denti*lingual⟩ ⟨*dento*surgical⟩
dent *abbr* dental; dentist; dentistry
¹den·tal \'dent³l\ *adj* [L *dentalis*, fr. *dent-*, *dens* tooth + *-alis* -al] **1 :** of or relating to the teeth or dentistry ⟨~ formula⟩ ⟨~ student⟩ **:** used for the care of the teeth or in dentistry ⟨~ paste⟩ ⟨~ file⟩ **2** *of a speech sound* **a :** articulated with the tip or blade of the tongue against or near the upper front teeth ⟨English \th\ and \th\ and French \t\ and \d\ are ~ sounds⟩ **b :** articulated either thus or alveolarly ⟨English \t\ and \d\ and\s\ and\z\ are ~ sounds⟩ — compare INTERDENTAL, LABIODENTAL
²dental \"\ *n* -s **1 :** DENTIL **2 :** a dental consonant **3 :** TOOTH — not often in formal use **4 :** a part (as a nerve or artery) supplying the teeth or the adjoining parts of the head
dental arch *n* **:** the curve of the row of teeth in each jaw
dental artery *n* **:** any of the several small arteries derived from the internal maxillary artery that supply the teeth and adjacent parts
den·ta·le \den'ta(,)lē, -tā-,-tä-\ *n, pl* **denta·lia** \-.lēə\ [NL, fr. neut. of L *dentalis* dental] **:** DENTARY
dental engine *n* **:** a dentist's drilling machine for rotating drills, burs, or other instruments at high speed
dental floss *n* **:** a flat waxed thread used to clean between the teeth
dental formula *n* **:** an abridged expression of number and kind of teeth of mammals, the kind of teeth being represented by *i* (incisor), *c* (canine), *pm* (premolar) or *b* (bicuspid), and *m* (molar) and the number in each jaw written like a fraction, the figures above the horizontal line showing the number in the upper jaw, and those below the number in the lower jaw, a dash separating the figures representing the teeth of each side of the jaw ⟨the *dental formula* of adult man is $i\,\frac{2-2}{2-2}$, $c\,\frac{1-1}{1-1}$, b or $pm\,\frac{2-2}{2-2}$, $m\,\frac{3-3}{3-3} = 32$⟩
dental hygienist *n* **:** one who assists a dentist in his professional duties; *esp* **:** one who cleanses teeth and performs other routine care on the patient
den·ta·li·i·dae \,dent³l'īə,dē\ *n pl, cap* [NL, fr. *Dentalium*, type genus + *-idae*] **:** a family of tooth shells that have the foot trilobate — see DENTALIUM
dental index *n, anthrop* **:** a measure of the relative size of teeth obtained as a ratio of the dental length to the distance from the nasion to the basion multiplied by 100
den·tal·i·ty \den'taləd·ē\ *n* -ES *phonetics* **:** dental quality
den·ta·li·um \-'tālēəm\ *n* [NL, fr. L *dentalis* dental + *-ium*] **1** *cap* **:** the type genus of Dentaliidae comprising a number of widely distributed tooth shells **2** *pl* **dentaliums** \-mz\ *or* **denta·lia** \-lēə\ **:** any mollusk or shell of the genus *Dentalium*; *broadly* **:** TOOTH SHELL, SCAPHOPOD
den·tal·i·za·tion \,dent³lə'zāshən\ *n* -s **:** the act of dentalizing
den·tal·ize \'dent³l,īz\ *vt* -ED/-ING/-S **:** to make (a speech sound) dental **:** change (a speech sound) into a dental
dental length *n* **:** the distance from the anterior surface of the first premolar tooth to the posterior surface of the last molar
dental·ly \-³lē\ *adv* **:** in a dental manner
dental nerve *n* **:** any of the nerves arising from the superior and inferior maxillary nerves that supply the teeth and adjacent parts
dental pad *n* **:** a firm ridge replacing the incisors in the upper jaw of cud-chewing herbivores
dental papilla *n* **:** the mass of mesenchyme that occupies the cavity of each enamel organ and gives rise to the dentin and the pulp of the tooth
dental plate *n* **1 :** any of various flattened often sharp-edged plates replacing teeth (as in certain worms) or representing fused teeth (as in parrot fishes and related forms) **2 :** DENTURE
dental preterit *n* **:** a past tense formed by the addition of a suffix containing a dental or alveolar consonant — used esp. of Germanic weak verbs
dental pulp *n* **:** the highly vascular sensitive tissue occupying the central cavity of a tooth
dental ridge *or* **dental lamina** *n* **:** a linear zone of epithelial cells of the covering of each embryonic jaw that grows down into the developing gums and gives rise to the enamel organs of the teeth
dental sac *n* **:** the mesenchymal investment of the developing tooth and enamel organ that differentiates into cementoblasts about the dentin and forms a connective tissue sheath about the enamel organ
dental star *n* **:** a marking on the incisor teeth of horses used in judging their age that appears in the lower central incisors at about eight years
dental surgeon *n* **:** DENTIST; *esp* **:** one engaging in oral surgery
dental technician *n* **:** one that engages in the construction of dental replacements or appliances (as bridges, inlays, dentures) from impressions taken by the dentist
den·tar·ia \den'ta(a)rēə\ *n* [NL, fr. L *dent-*, *dens* tooth + NL *-aria* — more at TOOTH] **1** *cap* **:** a small genus of herbs (family Cruciferae) with pungent scaly or toothed roots **2** -s **:** any plant of the genus *Dentaria* — compare CORALWORT CRINKLEROOT
den·ta·ry \'dentərē\ *n* -ES [*dent-* + *-ary*] **:** either of a pair of membrane bones of the lower jaw of most vertebrates, in lower forms being restricted to the distal area but in recent higher mammals forming the body of the mandible
den·tate \'den,tāt\ *or* **den·tat·ed** \-,tād·əd\ *adj* [L *dentatus*, fr. *dent-*, *dens* tooth + *-atus* -ate, -ated] **:** having teeth or pointed conical projections ⟨a ~ leaf margin⟩ — **den·tate·ly** \-ātlē\ *adv*
-den·tate \'den,tā|t, -,tə|, *usu* |d· + V\ *adj comb form* [NL *-dentatus*, fr. L *dentatus*] **:** having (such or so many) toothlike projections **:** -toothed ⟨multi*dentate*⟩ ⟨quadri*dentate*⟩
dentate fissure *or* **dentate sulcus** *n* **:** a fissure of the mesial surface of each cerebral hemisphere extending from behind the posterior end of the corpus callosum forward and downward to the recurved part of the hippocampal convolution — called also *hippocampal fissure*
dentate nucleus *n* **:** a large laminar nucleus of gray matter forming an incomplete capsule within the white matter of each cerebellar hemisphere
den·ta·tion \den'tāshən\ *n* -s **1 :** the quality or state of being dentate **2 :** an angular projection like a tooth
dent corn *n* ['dent] **1 :** an Indian corn forming a distinct variety (*Zea mays indentata*) and having kernels that contain both hard and soft starch and become indented at maturity — compare FLINT CORN **2 :** the kernels of dent corn
dented *past of* DENT
den·tel \'dent³l\ *n* -s [F *dentelle*, lit., small tooth, fr. OF — more at DENTELLE] **:** DENTIL
den·te·lat·ed *or* **den·tel·lat·ed** \'dent³l,ād·əd\ *adj* [modif. (influenced by E *-ate* & *-ed*) of F *dentelé*, fr. *dentelle*] **:** having fine serrations or serrated markings **:** DENTICULATE
den·telle \den'tel, dän'-\ *n* -s [F, fr. MF, lit., small tooth, fr. OF, dim. of *dent* tooth, fr. L *dent-*, *dens* — more at TOOTH] **1 a :** LACE **b :** LACEWORK **2 :** a lacy style of book-cover decoration featuring angular or toothed outlines around fine detail
dentes *pl of* DENS
den·tex \'den,teks\ *n* -ES [NL, fr. L *dentex*, *dentix*, a kind of marine fish] **:** a European marine sparid fish (*Dentex dentex*) or a related fish
denti- — see DENT-
den·ti·cle \'dentəkəl\ *n* -s [ME, fr. L *denticulus*, dim. of *dent-*, *dens* tooth — more at TOOTH] **1 :** a small tooth or other conical pointed projection ⟨the ~s of sharkskin⟩ **2 :** DENTIL
den·tic·u·lar \(')den¦tikyəl·ə(r)\ *adj* [L *denticulus* + E *-ar*] **:** like a denticle **:** DENTICULATE
den·tic·u·late \-,lāt, -,lət\ *or* **den·tic·u·lat·ed** \-,lād·əd\ *adj* [L *denticulatus*, fr. *denticulus* + *-atus* -ate] **1 :** having small teeth **:** covered with small pointed projections ⟨a ~ shell⟩; *sometimes* **:** repeatedly notched **:** SERRATE ⟨margin of propodium ~⟩ **2 :** cut into dentils ⟨*denticulated* Doric cornice⟩ **3 :** finely dentate ⟨a ~ leaf⟩ — **den·tic·u·late·ly** *adv*
den·tic·u·la·tion \(,)den,tikyə'lāshən\ *n* -s **1 :** the state of being denticulate **2 :** a diminutive tooth or denticle
den·ti·cule \'dentə,kyül\ *n* -s [MF, fr. L *denticulus* small tooth] **:** the member in which dentils are cut
den·ti·fi·ca·tion \,===fə'kāshən\ *n* -s [ISV *dent-* + *-fication*] **:** formation of or conversion into dental structure
den·ti·form \'dentə,fȯrm\ *adj* [*dent-* + *-form*] **:** having the form of a tooth or of teeth
den·ti·frice \'dentəfrəs\ *n* -s [MF, fr. L *dentifricium*, fr. *dent-* + *-fricium* (fr. *fricare* to rub) — more at BRINE] **:** a powder, paste, or liquid used in cleaning the teeth
den·tig·er·ous \(')den¦tijərəs\ *adj* [*dent-* + *-gerous*] **:** bearing teeth or structures resembling teeth
dentigerous cyst *n* **:** an epithelial cyst containing fluid and one or more imperfect teeth usu. thought to result from defects in the enamel-forming structures
den·til \'dent³l, -n,til\ *n* -s [obs. F *dentille*, fr. MF, dim. of *dent* tooth — more at DENT] **:** a small rectangular block in a series projecting like teeth (as under the corona of a cornice esp. in the Ionic, Corinthian, and composite orders)

dentils

den·ti·labial \,dentə+\ *adj or n* [*dent-* + *labial*] **:** LABIODENTAL
dentil band *n* **:** a molding in the bed molding of a cornice resembling a row of dentils with the interdentils filled up solid; *also* **:** one of diminished projection as if the dentils had been stripped away
¹den·ti·lingual \,dentə +\ *adj* [*dent-* + *lingual*] *of a speech sound* **:** articulated with tongue and teeth; *specif* **:** INTERDENTAL
²dentilingual \"\ *n* **:** a dentilingual consonant
den·tin \'dent³n, -tən\ *or* **den·tine** \'den-,tēn, =¦=\ *n* -s [*dent-* + *-in*, *-ine*] **:** a calcareous material similar to bone but harder and denser that composes the principal mass of a tooth, is formed by the odontoblasts of the surface of the dental papilla, and consists of a matrix containing minute parallel tubules which open into the pulp cavity and during life contain processes of the cells of the pulp — compare CEMENTUM, ENAMEL; see TOOTH illustration
den·ti·nal \(')den¦tēn³l, 'dent³nəl\ *adj* **:** of or relating to dentin
dentinal fiber *n* **:** one of the minute processes of the dental pulp that project into the dentinal tubules
dentinal papilla *n* **:** DENTAL PAPILLA
dentinal sac *n* **:** DENTAL SAC
dentinal tubule *n* **:** one of the minute parallel tubules of the dentin of a tooth that communicate with the dental pulp — see DENTINAL FIBER
¹den·ti·nasal \,dentə +\ *adj* [*dent-* + *nasal*] **:** both dental and nasal — used of the sound \n\
²dentinasal \"\ *n* **:** the sound \n\
denting *pres part of* DENT
den·tin·o·blast \den'tēnə,blast, -nō,-\ *n* [*dentin* + *-o-* + *-blast*] **:** a mesenchymal cell that forms dentin
den·tin·o·genesis \=¦==+,-\ *n* [NL, fr. *dentino-* (fr. ISV *dentin*) + *-genesis*] **:** the formation of dentin
den·tin·o·gen·ic \(')=¦==¦jenik\ *adj* [*dentin* + *-o-* + *-genic*] **:** forming dentin
den·ti·noid \den'tē,nȯid\ *n* -s [*dentin* + *-oid*] **:** the immature still uncalcified matrix of dentin
den·ti·no·ma \,dentə'nōmə\ *n, pl* **dentinomas** \-məz\ *also* **dentinoma·ta** \-məd·ə\ [NL, fr. ISV *dentin* + NL *-oma*] **:** an odontoma containing dentin
den·ti·ros·tral \,dentə¦rästrəl\ *or* **den·ti·ros·trate** \-,strāt, -,strət\ *adj* [*dent-* + *-rostral*, *rostrate*] **1 :** having a toothed or notched bill **2** [NL *Dentirostres* + E *-al* or *-ate*] **:** of or relating to the Dentirostres
den·ti·ros·tres \,===¦rä,strēz\ *n pl, cap* [NL, fr. *dent-* + *-rostres* (fr. L *rostrum* beak) — more at ROSTRUM] *in former classifications* **:** a group of passerine birds to which various limits have been assigned
den·tist \'dentəst\ *n* -s [F *dentiste*, fr. *dent* tooth + *-iste* -ist — more at DENT] **:** one whose profession it is to treat diseases of the teeth and associated tissues and to make and insert replacements for lost or damaged parts — called also *dental surgeon*; compare EXODONTIST, ORTHODONTIST
den·tis·try \-təstrē, -ri\ *n* -ES **1 :** the art or profession of a dentist **:** dental science and practice **2 :** something that is made by or under the supervision of a dentist (as inlays or dentures) **:** work done by a dentist
den·ti·tion \den'tishən\ *n* -s [L *dentition-*, *dentitio*, fr. *dentitus* (past part. of *dentire* to cut teeth, fr. *dent-*, *dens* tooth) + *-ion-*, *-io* -ion — more at TOOTH] **1 :** the development and cutting of teeth **:** TEETHING **2 :** the character of the teeth as determined by their form and arrangement ⟨carnivorous ~⟩ **3 :** the number, kind, and arrangement of teeth of an individual; *collectively* **:** TEETH

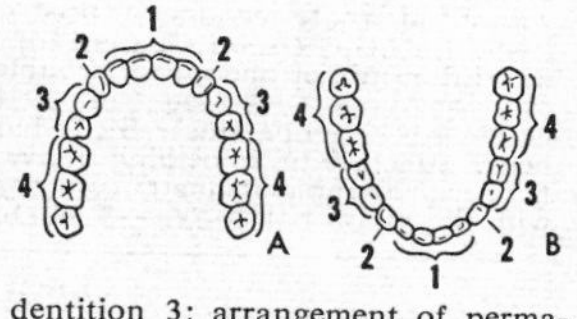

dentition 3: arrangement of permanent teeth of a human being: upper, *A;* lower, *B; 1* incisors, *2* canines, *3* bicuspids, *4* molars

dento- — see DENT-
den·to·facial \,dentə +\ *adj* [*dent-* + *facial*] **:** of or relating to the dentition and face
den·toid \'den,tȯid\ *adj* [*dent-* + *-oid*] **:** like or resembling a tooth
dents *pl of* DENT, *pres 3d sing of* DENT
den·tu·lous \'denchələs\ *adj* [back-formation fr. *edentulous*] **:** having teeth — opposed to *edentulous*
den·ture \'denchə(r)\ *n* -s [F, fr. MF, fr. *dent* tooth + *-ure*] **1 :** a set of teeth **2 :** an artificial replacement of one, several, or all of the natural teeth; *esp* **:** one not permanently anchored in the mouth — compare BRIDGE 4e
den·ty \'denti\ *chiefly Scot var of* DAINTY
¹de·nu·dant \də'n(y)üd³nt, dē'-\ *adj* [*denude* + *-ant*] **:** DENUDING
²denudant \"\ *n* -s **:** an agency that denudes
¹de·nu·date \'dē(,)n(y)ü,dāt, 'denyə,-, də'n(y)ü,-, dē'-, *usu* -d·+V\ *vt* -ED/-ING/-S [L *denudatus*, past part. of *denudare* — more at DENUDE] **:** to lay bare **:** DENUDE
²de·nu·date \", -,dət\ *adj* [L *denudatus*] **:** DENUDED, BARE
de·nu·da·tion \,dē(,)n(y)ü'dāshən, ,denyə'-\ *n* -s [LL *denudation-*, *denudatio*, fr. L *denudatus* + *-ion-*, *-io* -ion] **1 :** the act of denuding or the state of being denuded **:** EXPOSURE, DIVESTITURE **2 :** the laying bare of rocks or a formation through the removal of overlying material by erosion; *also* **:** the entire process of erosion whereby the land is worn down **3 :** complete destruction of trees and humus in a forest **:** BURNOUT
de·nu·da·tion·al \¦==¦shən³l, -shnəl\ *adj* **:** of or relating to denudation
de·nu·da·tive \'dē(,)n(y)ü,dā|d·|iv, 'denyə,-; də'n(y)üdə|t|, dē'-\ *adj* **:** causing denudation
de·nude \də'n(y)üd, dē'-\ *vt* -ED/-ING/-S [L *denudare*, fr. *de-* + *nudus* bare — more at NAKED] **1 a :** to divest of all covering **:** make bare or naked **:** STRIP, DEPRIVE ⟨~ him of clothing⟩ ⟨a room *denuded* of pictures⟩ **b :** to lay bare by erosion; *also* **:** ERODE ⟨rolling hills are soon marred by *denuded* banks —*Amer. Guides Series: Minn.*⟩ **c :** to divest or strip (land) of forests (as by lumbering or by fire) **2 :** to divest entirely or partially (as of an attribute, right, purpose, possession) **:** make useless **:** WEAKEN ⟨the world *denuded* by ceaseless activity —Harold Rosenberg⟩ **syn** see STRIP
de·nud·er \-d·ə(r)\ *n* -s **:** one that denudes
de·numerable \də, dē +\ *adj* [*de-* + *numerable*] **:** countable even though infinite — used of any class whose elements may be numbered successively (as the system of cardinal numbers) — **de·nu·mer·a·bly** \-blē\ *adv*
de·nun·ci·ate \də'nənsē,āt, dē'- *sometimes* -nchē,-, *usu* -ād·+V\ *vb* -ED/-ING/-S [L *denuntiatus*, past part. of *denuntiare* — more at DENOUNCE] **:** DENOUNCE
de·nun·ci·a·tion \=,==¦āshən\ *n* -s [L *denuntiation-*, *denuntiatio*, fr. *denuntiatus* + *-ion-*, *-io* -ion] **1 :** the act of denouncing **:** the utterance with which something is denounced **2 a** *archaic* **:** official announcement **:** PROCLAMATION **b** *archaic* **:** solemnly pronounced warnings of punishments or imminent evils **c** *Scots law* **:** the act of denouncing publicly as a rebel (as by blowing blasts on a horn) preliminary to enforcing the judgment of a court **d :** the act of formally giving information to a public prosecutor that another has committed a crime **e :** the act of inveighing against something or someone as evil ⟨praise of a glorious past that is dead, and ~s of a decadent present —G.L.Dickinson⟩ **f :** the action of giving formal notice of the termination of a treaty **g :** the furnishing of information in an ecclesiastical court by one other than the accuser
de·nun·ci·a·tive \də'nənsē,ā|d·iv, dē'-, -ēə|, |tiv *sometimes* -nchē-\ *adj* [LL *denuntiativus*, fr. L *denuntiatus*, + *-ivus* -ive] **:** DENUNCIATORY — **de·nun·ci·a·tive·ly** \|əvlē, -li\ *adv*
de·nun·ci·a·tor \-ē,ād·ə(r), -,ātə-\ *n* -s [MF *denonciateur*, fr. L *denuntiator* police officer, fr. *denuntiatus* + *-or*] **:** one that denounces, publishes, or proclaims: **a :** one that proclaims intended or coming evil **b :** one that threatens or accuses
de·nun·ci·a·to·ry \-ēə,tōrē, -,tȯr-, -ri\ *adj* **:** marked by or given to denunciation ⟨all his plays are contemptuous of people and ~ of human existence —*Times Lit. Supp.*⟩ **:** ACCUSING, THREATENING ⟨~ language⟩
¹den·ver \'denvə(r)\ *adj, usu cap* [fr. *Denver*, Colorado] **:** of or from Denver, the capital of Colorado **:** of the kind or style prevalent in Denver
²denver \"\ *n* -s *often cap* **:** BATTLESHIP GRAY
den·ver·ite \'denvə,rīt\ *n* -s *cap* [*Denver*, Colorado + E *-ite*] **:** a native or resident of Denver, Colorado
denver sandwich *n, usu cap D* **:** WESTERN SANDWICH
de·ny \də'nī, dē'-\ *vt* -ED/-ING/-ES [ME *denyen*, fr. OF *denier*, *denoier*, fr. L *denegare*, fr. *de-* + *negare* to say no, deny — more at NEGATION] **1 a :** to declare untrue **:** assert to be untenable **:** CONTRADICT ⟨the suspect *denied* the charge⟩ ⟨~*ing* that the explanation was true⟩ **b** *logic* **:** to assert the negative or contradictory of **2 :** to refuse to recognize or acknowledge **:** withhold acknowledgment from **:** disclaim connection with, allegiance to, or responsibility to or for **:** DISAVOW, RENOUNCE ⟨an apostate ~*ing* his faith⟩ **3 a :** to turn down or give a negative answer to (a person) ⟨hard to ~ an eager child⟩ ⟨~*ing* the petitioners⟩ **b :** to refuse to grant **:** WITHHOLD ⟨the king *denied* his vassal's plea⟩ ⟨the leave was *denied* to him⟩ ⟨*denied* the child the candy⟩ **c :** to restrain (oneself) from gratification of wishes or desires **:** restrain (oneself) from self-indulgence ⟨~*ing* herself any fun in life⟩ **4** *archaic* **a :** DECLINE — used with an infinitive **b :** to refuse or withhold permission to **:** preclude occasion for or occurrence of **5 a** *obs* **:** to withhold acceptance of **b** *obs* **:** to withhold admittance to, greeting to, or acknowledgment of **c :** to withhold acknowledging presence of to a caller ⟨the doctor did not wish to see the woman and told the nurse to ~ him⟩ **6 :** to refuse to accept the existence, truth, or validity of ⟨~*ing* the appearances of gods⟩ ⟨~*ing* witchcraft as an effective force⟩ **7 :** to make a bridge bid in no-trump or a suit bid different from (that bid by one's partner) in order to show inability to raise or support the partner's bid ⟨~*ing* his partner's spades⟩
syn GAINSAY, CONTRADICT, NEGATIVE, TRAVERSE, IMPUGN, CONTRAVENE: DENY implies a refusal, usu. outspoken, to accept as true, to grant or concede, or to acknowledge the existence or the claims of ⟨*deny* an accusation⟩ ⟨*deny* the possibility of peaceful coexistence⟩ ⟨history cannot be *denied* —James King⟩ GAINSAY, not now common in speech, implies opposition by a disputing of what someone else has said ⟨it cannot be *gainsaid* that cormorants are fish-eaters —C.L. Barrett⟩ ⟨no one would *gainsay* the right of anyone, the royal American right, to protest —W.A.White⟩ CONTRADICT, implying a flatter denial of the truth of an assertion, or a fact that lends itself to assertion, than does GAINSAY, commonly suggests that the contrary of an assertion is true or that the assertion is totally untrue ⟨nobody would have *contradicted* an assertion that it really was so —Thomas Hardy⟩ ⟨sales of that sort *contradicted* the spirit of the Homestead Act —R.A. Billington⟩ NEGATIVE is variable in its force but is often a mild term implying a refusal to assent ⟨it was not due to the banks that their request for loans was *negatived* —L.W.Mints⟩ ⟨he emphatically *negatived* the movement to nominate him as vice-president —Jonas Viles⟩ TRAVERSE, chiefly a legal term in this sense, implies a formal denial, as of the truth of an allegation or the justice of an indictment ⟨to *traverse* the decision of the House in rejecting a reasoned amendment on the second reading of the bill —T.E.May⟩ ⟨it *traverses* the theory of the Court in the Belmont and Pink cases —E.S.Corwin⟩ IMPUGN implies very strongly a direct, commonly insulting, disputing, questioning, or contradicting ⟨did not hesitate to challenge when he considered his honor *impugned* —J.A. Robertson⟩ ⟨his accuracy had often been *impugned*, his authority challenged —Osbert Sitwell⟩ ⟨to *impugn* the reality of the world as known to science —W.R.Inge⟩ CONTRAVENE implies strongly a coming into conflict but implies less strongly than the other terms an intentional opposition, suggesting rather some inherent incompatibility ⟨he could not strike out in any direction without wounding his wife or his friends, without *contravening* some loyalty that had become sacred to him —Van Wyck Brooks⟩ ⟨the power to abrogate actions of the constituent republics which *contravene* laws or decrees of the central government —F.A.Ogg & Harold Zink⟩
de·ny·ing·ly *adv* **:** in a denying manner
de·o·dand \'dēə,dand\ *n* -s [AF *deodande*, fr. ML *deodandum*, fr. L *Deo dandum* that must be given to God] **:** a thing that by English law before 1846 was forfeited to the crown and thence to pious uses because it had been the immediate cause of the death of a person
de·o·dar \'dēə,där\ *or* **deodar cedar** *or* **de·o·da·ra** \,dēə'därə\ *n* -s [Hindi *deodār*, fr. Skt *devadāru*, lit., timber of the gods, fr. *deva* god + *dāru* wood — more at DEVA, TREE] **:** an East Indian cedar (*Cedrus deodara*) highly valued for its size and appearance as well as for its timber
¹de·odor·ant \dē'ōdərənt\ *adj* [*de-* + *odor* + *-ant*] **:** destroying or masking offensive odors
²deodorant \"\ *n* -s **:** any of various preparations or solutions (as a soap or disinfectant) that destroy or mask unpleasant odors; *esp* **:** a cosmetic that neutralizes perspiration odors
de·odor·i·za·tion \(,)dē,ōdərə'zāshən, -,rī'z-\ *n* -s **:** the act or process of deodorizing or the state of being deodorized
de·odor·ize \dē'ōdə,rīz\ *vt* [*de-* + *odor* + *-ize*] **1 :** to eliminate or neutralize the offensive odor of ⟨he extracts the solvents from the dry-cleaned garments and . . . dries and *deodorizes* the extracted garments —*Opportunity & a Future*⟩; *specif* **:** to apply to or treat with a deodorant **2 :** to make (a reprehensible act or fact) more acceptable or palatable by placing in a pleasant light esp. by misrepresenting, glossing over, or evading ⟨their buccaneering was *deodorized* by the fact that their victims were Madagascar pirates —*N.Y. Herald Tribune Bk. Rev.*⟩ ⟨~ the unpleasant fact that in laboratories all over the world devices to rip out the heart and soul of man are being systematically . . . developed —Norman Cousins⟩
de·odor·iz·er \-zə(r)\ *n* -s **:** DEODORANT
de·on·tic \dē'äntik\ *adj* [Gk *deont-*, *deon* that which is obligatory, fr. neut. of pres. part. of *dein* to lack, be needful — more at DEUTER-] **:** of or relating to obligation ⟨~ propositions⟩
de·on·to·log·i·cal \(¦)dē¦äntə¦läjəkəl, -t³l¦ä-\ *adj* **1 :** of, relating to, or based on deontology **:** DEONTIC **2 :** that considers moral obligations to be knowable by intuition and without reference to conceptions of the good ⟨a ~ ethical theory⟩ — contrasted with *axiological*
de·on·tol·o·gist \(,)dē,än'täləjəst\ *n* **1 :** a specialist in deontology **2 :** a philosopher advocating a deontological theory of ethics — contrasted with *axiologist*
de·on·tol·o·gy \-jē\ *n* [Gk *deont-*, *deon* + E *-logy*] **:** the theory or study of duty or moral obligation **:** the ethics of duty
¹de·operculate \¦dē +\ *adj* [*de-* + *operculate*] **1 :** lacking an operculum — used of the capsule of a moss or hepatic after the lid has fallen **2 :** having an operculum that does not separate from the capsule — used of mosses
²de·oper·cu·late \,dēō'pərkyə,lāt\ *vi* -ED/-ING/-S [*de-* + NL *operculum* + E *-ate*] **:** to shed or cast off the operculum — used of mosses and liverworts
de·ordination \(¦)dē +\ *n* [LL *deordination-*, *deordinatio*, fr. L *de-* + *ordination-*, *ordinatio* order — more at ORDINATION] **:** departure from a natural or normal order **:** DISORDER
deo vo·len·te \¦dā(,)ōvō'len,tā, ¦dē(,)ōvə'lentē\ *usu cap D* [L] **:** God being willing **:** with God's sanction — abbr. *DV*
de·oxidant \(')dē +\ *n* -s [*deoxidate* + *-ant*] **:** DEOXIDIZER

de·oxidate \(')dē +\ *vt* [*de-* + *oxidate*] *archaic* : DEOXIDIZE

de·oxidation *also* **de·oxidization** \(ˌ)dē +\ *n* : the process of deoxidizing or state of being deoxidized

de·oxidize \(')dē +\ *vt* [*de-* + *oxidize*] : to remove oxygen from (as molten metals) : reduce from the state of an oxide — **de·ox·i·diz·er** \-zə(r)\ *n*

de·oxy \(')dēˈäksē\ *or* **des·oxy** \(')deˈzäksē,-eˈsä-\ *adj* [*deoxy-*] : containing less oxygen in the molecule than the compound to which it is closely related ⟨~ sugars⟩

deoxy- *or* **desoxy-** *comb form* [ISV, fr. *de-* or *des-* + *oxy-*] : containing less oxygen in the molecule than the compound to which it is closely related; *esp* : derivable from another compound by the removal of one oxygen atom ⟨*deoxy*nucleotide⟩ ⟨*desoxy*benzoin $C_{14}H_{12}O$⟩

de·oxy·cholate \dēˌäksē +\ *n* [*deoxy-* + *cholate*] : a salt or ester of deoxycholic acid

de·oxy·cholic acid \(ˌ)dēˈäksē +. . .-\ *n* [*deoxy-* + *cholic*] : a crystalline acid $C_{23}H_{37}(OH)_2COOH$ found esp. in bile and used as a choleretic and digestant and in the synthesis of adrenocortical hormones (as cortisone); 3,12-dihydroxy-cholanic acid

de·oxy·corticosterone \(ˌ)dēˈäksē +\ *n* [ISV *deoxy-* + *corticosterone;* orig. formed as G *desoxykortikosteron*] : a colorless crystalline steroid hormone $C_{21}H_{30}O_3$ occurring in the adrenal cortex that can be prepared synthetically and is used in the form of its acetate in the treatment of adrenal cortical insufficiency — called also *cortexone, deoxycortone*

de·oxy·cor·tone \(ˌ)dēˌäksēˈkȯrˌtōn\ *n* -S [by shortening] : DEOXYCORTICOSTERONE

de·oxy·ephedrine \(ˌ)dēˈäksē +\ *n* [*deoxy-* + *ephedrine*] : METHAMPHETAMINE

de·oxygenate \(ˌ)dē +\ *vt* [*de-* + *oxygenate*] : to remove oxygen (as free or loosely combined oxygen) from (as water, sewage, or blood) — **de·oxygenation** \"+\ *n* -S

deoxygenated *adj, of blood* : having the hemoglobin in the reduced state : VENOUS

de·oxy·pentose \(ˌ)dēˈäksē +\ *n* [*deoxy-* + *pentose*] : an aldose $C_4H_9O_3CHO$ having one less alcohol-type oxygen atom in the molecule than a pentose

deoxypentose nucleic acid *n* : any of various nucleic acids yielding a deoxypentose on hydrolysis; *esp* : DEOXYRIBONUCLEIC ACID

de·oxy·ribonuclease \(ˌ)dēˈäksē +\ *n* [*deoxy-* + *ribonuclease*] : a crystalline enzyme found esp. in the pancreas that hydrolyzes deoxyribonucleic acid to nucleotides

de·oxy·ribonucleic acid \"+ . . . -\ *n* [*deoxyribo*se + *nucleic acid*] : any of various nucleic acids that yield deoxyribose as one product of hydrolysis, are found in cell nuclei and esp. genes, and are associated with the transmission of genetic information — abbr. *DNA;* called also *thymonucleic acid;* compare RIBONUCLEIC ACID

de·oxy·ri·bo·nu·cleo·protein \(ˌ)dēˈäksēˌrī(ˌ)bōˈn(y)üklē(ˌ)ō +\ *n* [*deoxyribonucle*ic + *-o-* + *protein*] : a nucleoprotein that yields a deoxyribonucleic acid on hydrolysis

de·oxy·ribose \(ˌ)dēˈäksē +\ *n* [ISV *deoxy-* + *ribose*] : any of several sugars $C_5H_{10}O_4$ having one of the alcoholic hydroxyl groups of ribose replaced by hydrogen; *esp* : a sugar $HOCH_2(CHOH)_2CH_2CHO$ that is a constituent of nucleic acids

de·ozonize \(')dē +\ *vt* [*de-* + *ozonize*] : to remove ozone from — **de·ozon·iz·er** \-zə(r)\ *n*

dep *abbr* **1** depart; departure **2** department **3** deponent **4** deposed **5** deposit **6** depot **7** deputy

de pa·ce et pla·gis \(ˌ)dāˈpäˌkā(ˌ)etˈpläˌgēs\ *n* [ML, of peace and wounds] : an ancient appeal available in cases of breach of the peace and of assault

de·paint \dəˈpānt\ *vt* [ME *depeinten, depainten,* fr. OF *depeint,* past part. of *depeindre* to paint, fr. L *depingere* to paint, depict] **1** *archaic* : to delineate in colors or words **2** *obs* : to adorn with color or painted figures

de·palatalization \(ˌ)dē +\ *n* [*de-* + *palatalization*] *phonetics* : the loss of palatalization : the failure to palatalize

de·pancreatize \(')dē +\ *vt* [*de-* + *pancreat-* + *-ize*] : to deprive of the pancreas and thereby induce inability to utilize glucose and impair the digestion of fats — compare INSULIN

de·paraffinize \(')dē +\ *also* **de·paraffin** \(')dē +\ *vt* [*de-* + *paraffinize* or *paraffin* (n.)] : to remove paraffin from (a section of tissue prior to microscopic examination)

[1]**de·part** \dəˈpär|t, dēˈ-, -pȧ|, *usu* |d·+V\ *vb* -ED/-ING/-S [ME *departen* to divide, go away, fr. OF *departir,* fr. *de-* + *partir* to divide, go away, fr. L *partire, partiri* to divide, fr. *part-, pars* part — more at PART] *vi* **1 a** : to go forth or away : set forth : LEAVE ⟨the train ~*ed* from the station⟩ **b** *obs* : to leave and go — used with *into* **c** : to pass away : DIE, PERISH **2 a** : to turn aside : DEVIATE ⟨the river ~*ed* from its original course a few miles downstream⟩ ⟨his second account markedly ~*ed* from the first⟩ ⟨a homogeneous population that ~*s* reluctantly from long-accepted institutions —*Amer. Guide Series: Pa.*⟩ **b** *obs* : DESIST **3** *law* : to make a departure in pleading ~ *vt* **1** *obs* **a** : DIVIDE, SEPARATE, SUNDER **b** : deal out : DISTRIBUTE **c** : SHARE **2** : to go away from or out of : LEAVE ⟨~ the city for a summer cottage⟩ ⟨ships . . . ~ the land-locked harbor at the rate of one an hour —Franc Shor⟩ **syn** see GO, SWERVE — **depart with** *archaic* : to give up : SURRENDER ⟨willingly *departed with* a part —Shak.⟩

[2]**depart** \"\ *n* [ME, fr. MF, fr. *departir*] **1** *archaic* **a** : DEPARTURE **b** : DEATH **2** *old chem* : the separation of one metal (as gold) in an alloy from another

departed *n, pl* **departed** [fr. past part. of [1]*depart*] : one who has died ⟨the likeness of the ~ preserved on stone —*Amer. Guide Series: Fla.*⟩ ⟨the graves of the ~⟩

dé·par·te·ment \dāpȧrtəmäⁿ\ *n, pl* **départements** \-äⁿ(z)\ [F] : DEPARTMENT 2a(1)

de·part·ment \dəˈpärtmənt, dēˈ-, -pȧt-\ *n* -S [F *département,* fr. MF *departement,* fr. *departir* to divide + *-ment* — more at DEPART] **1** : appointed sphere or province (as of activity or thought) ⟨Pope's own peculiar ~ of literature —T.B.Macaulay⟩ **2 a** : a discrete territorial or functional division or section of a larger organized or systematized whole ⟨good taste . . . goes into every ~ of life —Elspeth Betjeman⟩: as (1) : the largest administrative subdivision in France and some of the French colonies presided over by a prefect (2) [AmerSp *departamento,* fr. F *département*] : a similar territorial division in some Central and So. American countries **b** : an administrative division or branch of a national or municipal government ⟨the welfare ~⟩ **c** : a discrete branch of instruction or study in a school or college ⟨the English ~⟩ ⟨the ~ of modern languages⟩ **d** (1) : a division of a business concern handling a major function ⟨the accounting ~⟩ (2) : a division of a store handling a distinct class of merchandise ⟨the furniture ~⟩ ⟨dry goods ~⟩ **e** (1) : a territorial subdivision for the administration, training, and tactical control of military units stationed within its limits (2) *usu cap* : such a former subdivision of the possessions of the United States outside the continental limits **3** : a regular column or feature devoted to a particular subject in a publication or radio program

de·part·men·tal \dəˌpärtˈmentᵊl, -pȧt-, ˌdēˌ-, ˌdēˌp-\ *adj* : of or relating to a department — **de·part·men·tal·ly** \-ntᵊlē, -li\ *adv*

de·part·men·tal·ism \dəˌ=ˈ==ˌizəm, (ˌ)dēˌ-\ *n* -S : strong emphasis upon or partiality for division into departments esp. at the expense of the whole (as in an educational institution) ⟨exaggerated ~ which splits the university into sections —*Report: (Canadian) Royal Commission on Nat'l Development*⟩

de·part·men·tal·i·za·tion \dəˌ=ˌ==ˌəˈzāshən, (ˌ)dēˌ-, -ˌīˈz-\ *n* -S : the process of departmentalizing or of being departmentalized ⟨the importance of ~ of your store cannot be overemphasized —*Jewelers' Circular-Keystone*⟩ ⟨breaks away from the ~ of knowledge —*School & Society*⟩

de·part·men·tal·ize \dəˌ=ˈ==ˌīz, (ˌ)dēˌ-\ *vt* -ED/-ING/-S : to divide or form into departments ⟨a highly *departmentalized* school organization⟩ : handle according to departmental divisions ⟨*departmentalizing* the costs⟩

departmental store *n, Brit* : DEPARTMENT STORE

de·part·men·ta·tion \dəˌpärtmən·ˈtāshən, (ˌ)dēˌ-, -pȧt-\ *n* -S : the process of departmentalizing an enterprise for gaining efficiency and coordination : the grouping of tasks into departments and subdepartments and delegating of authority for accomplishment of the tasks

de·part·ment·ize \=ˈ=mənˌtīz\ *vt* -ED/-ING/-S : DEPARTMENTALIZE ⟨department stores have taught all other types of retailers the value of *departmentizing* the business —J.B.Swinney⟩

department stamp *or* **departmental stamp** *n* : an official postage stamp issued for use in a particular government department, as one of a series issued in the U.S. 1873–79

department store *n* : a store that carries several lines of merchandise and that is organized into separate departments for the purpose of promotion, service, accounting, and control

departs *pres 3d sing of* DEPART, *pl of* DEPART

de·par·ture \dəˈpärchər, dēˈ-, -pȧchə(r\ *n* -S [[1]*depart* + *-ure*] **1** *obs* : DIVISION, SEPARATION **2 a** : removal from a place : the act of going away ⟨postpone ~ of its troops from Italy —*Collier's Yr. Bk.*⟩ **b** (1) : a setting out (as on a journey or a course of action or thought) ⟨anticipate his ~ for England⟩ ⟨we need a fairly definite point of ~ for intelligent discourse —Robert Humphrey⟩ (2) : a beginning of a new course of thought or action ⟨the purchase by the state of property for purely esthetic purposes was a new ~ —*Amer. Guide Series: N.Y.*⟩ **c** : a ship's position in latitude and longitude at the beginning of a voyage as a point from which to begin dead reckoning usu. ascertained by taking cross bearings of landmarks **3** *archaic* : removal from life : DEATH ⟨the time of my ~ has come —2 Tim 4:6 (RSV)⟩ **4** : the distance due east or west made by a ship in its course reckoned in plane sailing as the product of the distance sailed and the sine of the angle made by the course with the meridian — compare DEAD RECKONING **5 a** : deviation or divergence esp. from a rule, course of action, plan, or purpose ⟨a ~ from official procedure⟩; *also* : something that has deviated or diverged ⟨in nature most ~*s* from normal cannot survive long —W.F.Hollander⟩ **b** *law* : the desertion by a party to any pleading of the ground taken by him in his last antecedent pleading and the adoption of another **6** *surveying* : the projection on the east-west axis of a course in a plane survey, being equal to the length of the course multiplied by the sine of its bearing

departure track *or* **departure yard** *n* : a track or group of tracks where outgoing freight cars are made ready for movement in trains

de·pasturage \də, dē+\ *n* : pasturing or right of pasture of grazing animals

de·pasture \"+\ *vb* [*de-* + *pasture*] *vi, now chiefly Austral* : to feed on pasture : GRAZE ~ *vt* **1** *archaic* : to denude of pasture by too constant grazing **2** *now chiefly Austral* : put to graze : PASTURE **3** *archaic* : to use for pasture

[1]**de·pau·per·ate** \dəˈpȯp(ə)rət, dēˈ-\ *adj* [ME *depauperat,* fr. ML *depauperatus,* past part. of *depauperare,* fr. L *de-* + *pauperare* to impoverish, fr. *pauper* poor — more at POOR] **1** : IMPOVERISHED **2** *biol* : falling short of natural development or size: **a** : inferior in growth or differentiation as compared with the norm of a strain or group ⟨~ maize⟩ **b** : including few kinds of organisms — used of local floras and faunas ⟨a ~ island avifauna⟩

[2]**de·pau·per·ate** \-ȯpəˌrāt\ *vt* [ML *depauperatus*] : to make poor — **de·pau·per·a·tion** \dəˌpȯpəˈrāshən, (ˌ)dēˌpȯ-\ *n* -S

de·pauperization \də, dē+\ *n* : the process of becoming depauperate or the quality or state of being depauperate

de·pauperize \"+\ *vt* [*de-* + *pauperize*] : to make depauperate

dé·pay·sé \ˌdā(ˌ)pāˈzā\ *adj* [F, fr. past part. of *dépayser* to remove (a person) from his element, fr. OF *despaisier* to exile, fr. *des-* de- + *pais* region, country, fr. ML *pagensis* of a region, fr. L *pagus* region, district, village + *-ensis* -ese — more at PAGAN] : situated in unfamiliar surroundings : being out of one's element : DISPLACED : ASTRAY ⟨lived in hope of being instructed to drive me to Biarritz, where among the other hired-car chauffeurs . . . he would feel less ~ —A.J.Liebling⟩

de·pend \dəˈpend, dēˈ-\ *vi* -ED/-ING/-S [ME *dependen,* fr. MF *dependre* to hang down, be contingent or conditioned, modif. of L *dependēre,* fr. *de-* + *pendēre* to hang — more at PENDANT] **1** : to be contingent: **a** : to require something as a necessary condition — used with *on* or *upon* ⟨we ~ on food to keep us alive⟩ ⟨his life ~*s* on his undergoing an operation⟩ ⟨the merit of his piece ~*ed* on the brilliant things which arose under his pen as he went along —Matthew Arnold⟩ **b** : to become conditioned or based (as by subjection or relatedness) — used with *on* or *upon* ⟨sciences ~ on one another⟩ ⟨prices ~ upon supply and demand⟩ **2 a** : to hang in suspense : be pending or undecided ⟨matters of greatest moment were ~*ing* —John Milton⟩ **b** *obs* : to wait in suspense **c** *obs* : to be imminent : IMPEND **3** : to have a connection or relationship as a subordinate part or appurtenance — used with *on* or *upon* **4 a** : to trust, rely, or place belief or hope often without alternate recourse — used with *on* or *upon* ⟨~ on a friend for help⟩ ⟨~ on a parent for funds⟩ ⟨~ on your skill or wisdom to get one out of trouble⟩ **b** : to be dependent esp. for support — used with *on* or *upon* ⟨small children necessarily ~ on parents⟩ **5** : to hang down : be held up by being attached to something above ⟨a star was ~*ing* from his neck —Arnold Bennett⟩ ⟨crimson plush curtains intricate with tiny plush balls ~*ing* —T.W.Duncan⟩

syn HANG, HINGE, TURN: DEPEND is the general term to indicate a contingent relationship involving existence, nature, or characteristics ⟨the future of the American university *depends* primarily on keeping a proper balance between these four traditional elements of strength —J.B.Conant⟩ ⟨the conviction that winning the best satisfactions of later life will *depend* on possessing this power to think —C.W.Eliot⟩ HANG may refresh the now faded metaphor explicit in the etymology of DEPEND ⟨a good deal . . . *hangs* on the meaning, if any, of this short word *full* —T.S.Eliot⟩ ⟨the Crewe of today — a borough whose life no longer *hangs* on railway prosperity —*Times Lit. Supp.*⟩ HINGE may suggest resting on a cardinal or pivotal point, with a decisive swing in one direction or another as imminent ⟨on the outcome of the motion to dismiss the indictment . . . *hinge* issues of fundamental importance —*Nation*⟩ TURN may be less vivid in suggesting a cardinal point ⟨our continued backing of Chiang Kai-shek, and therefore his future, *turn* on the reactions of the conference committee —*New Republic*⟩ These words are completely interchangeable except in the few sentences in which unusual attention is paid to the implications of the metaphors involved. **syn** see in addition RELY

de·pend·abil·i·ty \dəˌpendəˈbiləd·ē, (ˌ)dēˌ-, -ətē, -i\ *n* -ES : the quality or state of being dependable

de·pend·able \dəˈpendəbəl, dēˈ-\ *adj* : worthy or capable of being depended upon : TRUSTWORTHY **syn** see RELIABLE

de·pend·able·ness *n* -ES : DEPENDABILITY

de·pend·ably \-blē, -li\ *adv* : in a dependable manner

de·pen·dence *or* **de·pen·dance** \-endən(t)s\ *n* -S [MF *dependance,* fr. *dependre* + *-ance*] **1** *archaic* : the quality or state of being undecided or undetermined **2 a** : the quality or state of depending upon or being dependent upon something else **b** : the quality or state of being influenced, conditional upon, or necessitated by something else ⟨scarcely a single incident which has any necessary ~ upon any one other —E.A.Poe⟩ ⟨the relation of a logical consequent to its antecedent or of an effect to its cause is one of ~⟩ **c** : the quality or state of being subject or subservient to or needful of the use, activity, assistance, direction, or approval of another or others — used with *on* or *upon* ⟨the nation's ~ upon its self-sacrificing men⟩ ⟨the modern age's ~ upon luxury goods⟩; *specif* : inability to provide for oneself ⟨a child's ~ upon its parents⟩ **3** : RELIANCE, TRUST ⟨place ~ upon old and trusted friends⟩ ⟨for a knowledge of Celtic law . . . ~ must be placed mainly on the written records —John MacNeill⟩ **4** : something on which one relies : the object of one's trust ⟨he was her sole ~⟩ ⟨cotton was the earliest crop . . . but ultimately rice became the chief ~ —R.H.Brown⟩ **syn** see TRUST

de·pen·den·cy \-dənsē, -si\ *n* -ES [MF *dependance* + E *-y*] **1 a** : DEPENDENCE 2 ⟨their ~ on the crown of England —Francis Bacon⟩ ⟨~ in the infant increases in evolutionary sequence —Weston La Barre⟩ **b** : the condition of receiving assistance from the community for the necessities of life : the condition of being on relief **2** : something that is dependent or in dependence upon something else: as **a** : something necessarily consequent upon something else **b** : a geographically separate territorial unit under the jurisdiction of but not formally annexed by a nation — compare COLONY 1b, MANDATE 4b **3** : a building (as a stable or a kennel) appurtenant to a main dwelling ⟨a double driveway leads to the palace and its *dependencies* —*Amer. Guide Series: Va.*⟩ **4** : the state of having dependents ⟨deferred from army service because of his ~⟩

[1]**de·pen·dent** \dəˈpendənt, (')dēˈp-\ *adj* [ME *dependant,* fr. MF, pres. part. of *dependre* to depend] **1** : hanging down ⟨a ~ bough⟩ ⟨lamps ~ from the ceiling⟩ **2 a** : determined or conditioned by something else : CONTINGENT ⟨a conclusion that is ~ on a premise⟩ **b** : unable to exist, sustain oneself, or act suitably or normally without the assistance or direction of another or others ⟨smelting operations were ~ on charcoal —Desmond Sprague⟩ ⟨a girl who remained excessively ~ on her parents even after marriage —Ruth & Edward Brecher⟩ ⟨the maple sugar and syrup crop, so ~ on weather conditions —*Amer. Guide Series: N.H.*⟩ ⟨traffic . . . has been ~ on ferries to cross five rivers —*Americana Annual*⟩ ⟨a child is pretty ~ on companionship⟩ **c** : connected in a subordinate relationship : subject to the jurisdiction of another ⟨~ territories⟩ **d** : lacking the necessary means of support and receiving aid from others (as from persons outside the immediate family or from a private or public welfare agency) ⟨a program of assistance for ~ children⟩ **e** *of a clause* : SUBORDINATE 2b **f** *of a compound* : belonging to the tatpurusha class **3** *obs* : IMPENDING **4** *phonetics* : COMBINATIVE — used of sound change — **de·pen·dent·ly** *adv*

[2]**de·pen·dent** *also* **de·pen·dant** \dəˈpendənt, dēˈ-\ *n* -S [MF *dependant,* fr. *dependant,* pres. part.] **1** *archaic, usu dependant* : something attached to something else : APPURTENANCE, DEPENDENCY **2** : one that depends or is dependent; *esp* : one relying on another for support ⟨a man taxed according to

EXECUTIVE DEPARTMENTS OF THE UNITED STATES*

DEPARTMENT	TITLE OF CHIEF	DATE OF CREATION	FUNCTIONS
Department of State	Secretary of State	July 27, 1789, as Dept. of Foreign Affairs; Sept. 15, 1789, under present name	conduct of foreign relations
Department of the Treasury	Secretary of the Treasury	Sept. 2, 1789	administration of national fiscal policies
*Department of Defense	Secretary of Defense	July 26, 1947, as National Military Establishment; Aug. 10, 1949, under present name	responsibility for national defense and security
Department of Justice	Attorney General (office created Sept. 24, 1789)	June 22, 1870	enforcement of federal laws; provision of legal counsel in federal cases; interpretation of laws for other departments
Post Office Department	Postmaster General (office created Sept. 22, 1789, became cabinet member 1829)	June 8, 1872, became executive department; its details of organization had been provided for by Act of Feb. 20, 1792	delivery of the mails; supervision of postal affairs
Department of the Interior	Secretary of the Interior	March 3, 1849	conservation and development of natural resources of U.S. and territories; guardianship of Indians
Department of Agriculture	Secretary of Agriculture	May 15, 1862; made executive department Feb. 9, 1889	acquisition and diffusion of useful information on agricultural subjects; supervision of national forests; administration of price support programs
Department of Commerce	Secretary of Commerce	Feb. 14, 1903, as the Dept. of Commerce and Labor; reorganized Mar. 4, 1913, under present name	promotion and development of foreign and domestic commerce
Department of Labor	Secretary of Labor	Mar. 4, 1913	administration and enforcement of statutes designed to promote welfare of wage earners
Department of Health, Education, and Welfare	Secretary of Health, Education, and Welfare	April 11, 1953	administration of agencies promoting general welfare in fields of health, education, and social security
Department of Housing and Urban Development	Secretary of Housing and Urban Development	Sept. 9, 1965	supervision and coordination of federal programs relating to housing and urban renewal
Department of Transportation	Secretary of Transportation	Oct. 15, 1966	administration and coordination of federal agencies and programs dealing with transportation

*The Department of the Army, created Aug. 7, 1789, as the Department of War and the Department of the Navy, created April 30, 1789, lost executive status July 26, 1947, on merger under their present names in the newly created National Military Establishment. The Department of the Air Force was created Sept. 18, 1947, as a third subordinate department of the National Military Establishment.

the number of ~s he has) ⟨~s were defined as those persons unable to care for themselves —J.F.Cuber⟩
dependent covenant *or* **dependent contract** *n* **:** a contract not enforceable until a connecting stipulation is performed
dependent differentiation *n* **:** differentiation of a tissue or structure in response to factors outside itself (as differentiation of ectoderm into a lens in the presence of an optic cup)
dependent variable *n* **:** the variable for which an equation that contains more than one variable is solved
de·pend·ing·ly *adv* **:** in a depending manner
de·per·di·tion \\,dē(,)pər'dishən\\ *n* [F *déperdition*, fr. LL *deperdition-, deperditio* loss, fr. L *deperditus* (past part. of *deperdere* to destroy, lose, fr. *de-* + *perdere* to lose) + *-ion-, -io* -ion — more at PERDITION] *archaic* **:** LOSS, DESTRUCTION
de·pé·ret's law \\də'pā,rāz-\\ *n, usu cap D* [after Charles J.*Depéret* †1929 Fr. geologist] **:** a principle in zoology: body size tends to increase within a natural group with increasing evolutionary development
dep·er·i·tion \\,depə'rishən\\ *n* -s [ML *deperitus* (past part. of *deperire* to perish, fr. L *de-* + *perire* to perish) + E *-ion* — more at PERISH] *archaic* **:** destructive process **:** waste and wear
de·perm \\(')dē¦pərm\\ *vt* -ED/-ING/-S [*de-* + *permanent* magnetism] **:** to demagnetize partly (a ship's steel hull) as a precaution against magnetic mines by surrounding in dry dock with a large coil through which is sent an alternating current very strong at first but gradually diminishing in intensity — compare DEGAUSS
de·personalization \\(¦)dē+\\ *n* **1 :** the act or process of depersonalizing or the quality or state of being depersonalized **2 :** loss of the sense of personal identity or of recognition of self
de·personalize \\(')dē+\\ *vt, see -ize in Explan Notes* [*de-* + *personalize*] **1 :** to deprive of personality ⟨our complex society necessarily ~s people —H.W.Dodds⟩ ⟨a *depersonalized* production system⟩ **2 :** to make impersonal ⟨an attempt to ~ his feeling in order to write about it more clearly⟩
depeter *var of* DEPRETER
de·phleg·mate \\(')dē'fleg,māt\\ *vt* -ED/-ING/-S [*de-* + *phlegm* + *-ate*] **1** *archaic* **:** to deprive (a spirit or an acid) of phlegm (sense 3) **:** free from an excess of water esp. by distillation **2 :** to rectify (a liquid) by distillation — **de·phleg·ma·tion** \\,dē,fleg'māshən\\ *n* -s
de·phleg·ma·tor \\(')dē'fleg,mād·ə(r)\\ *n* -s **:** an apparatus used in fractional distillation as a partial condenser to cool the mixed vapors and thus condense the higher-boiling portions
de·phlogisticate \\¦dē+\\ *vt* [*de-* + *phlogisticate*] **:** to remove phlogiston from
de·phosphorization \\(¦)dē+\\ *n* -s **:** the process of dephosphorizing or the state of being dephosphorized
de·phosphorize \\(')dē+\\ *vt* [*de-* + *phosphorize*] **:** to remove phosphorus from (as steel)
de·phos·pho·ryl·ate \\(')dē'fäsfərə,lāt\\ *vt* -ED/-ING/-S [*de-* + *phosphoryl* + *-ate*] **:** to remove the phosphate portion of (an organic compound of phosphoric acid) by hydrolysis (as with the aid of a phosphatase)
de·phosphorylation \\(¦)dē+\\ *n* **:** the process of dephosphorylating or the state of being dephosphorylated
de·pict \\də'pikt, dē'-\\ *vt* -ED/-ING/-S [L *depictus*, past part. of *depingere* to paint, depict, fr. *de-* + *pingere* to paint — more at PAINT] **1 a :** to form a likeness of by drawing or painting **b :** to represent, portray, or delineate in other ways than in drawing or painting ⟨elaborate carvings ~*ing* the history of the pioneer period —*Amer. Guide Series: Oregon*⟩ ⟨five 16th century tapestries ~*ing* the story of Vulcan and the loves of Venus and Mars —*Amer. Guide Series: N.C.*⟩ ⟨the quiet, unspectacular work of the United Nations . . . is ~*ed* in dozens of on the spot films —*Dun's Rev.*⟩ ⟨the countryside . . . has always been ~*ed* to us through art and photography as blazing with clear color —Virgil Thomson⟩ ⟨an annual pageant . . . ~*s* the Mormon migration to Utah —*Amer. Guide Series: Texas*⟩ ⟨bronze grillwork over the entrance ~*s* the evolution of mail transportation —*Amer. Guide Series: La.*⟩; *specif* **:** to portray in words **:** DESCRIBE ⟨a magazine article ~*ed* his beloved father, then deceased, as a mean, hard-fisted miser —Beverly Smith⟩ ⟨the neuroses which they have ~*ed* with relentless misanthropy —Harrison Smith⟩ **2 :** to represent by mapping **syn** see REPRESENT
de·pic·tion \\-kshən\\ *n* -s [LL *depiction-, depictio*, fr. L *depictus* + *-ion-, -io* -ion] **:** REPRESENTATION, DELINEATION, PORTRAYAL, DESCRIPTION
de·pig·ment \\(')dē¦pigmənt, -'pig,ment\\ *vt* [*de-* + *pigment* (n.)] **:** to cause to undergo depigmentation **:** deprive of pigment
de·pigmentation \\(¦)dē+\\ *n* [*de-* + *pigmentation*] **:** loss of normal pigmentation (as from skin or feathers)
dep·i·late \\'depə,lāt\\ *vt* -ED/-ING/-S [L *depilatus*, past part. of *depilare*, fr. *de-* + *pilus* hair — more at PILE] **:** to remove hair from
dep·i·la·tion \\,depə'lāshən\\ *n* -s [MF or ML; MF, fr. ML *depilation-, depilatio*, fr. L *depilatus* + *-ion-, -io* -ion] **:** the act or process of depilating or the state of being depilated; *specif* **:** the removal of the hair, wool, or bristles from an animal skin by chemical or mechanical methods in the processing of leather
¹de·pil·a·to·ry \\də'pilə,tōrē, dē'-, -ōr-, -ri\\ *adj* [prob. fr. F *dépilatoire*, fr. MF *depilatoire*, fr. L *depilatus* + MF *-oire* -ory] **:** having the power to remove hair
²depilatory \\"\\ *n* -ES **1 :** a cosmetic for the temporary removal of undesired hair **2 :** a chemical preparation usu. of sulfide used to remove hair, wool, or bristles from hides
de·pil·i·tant \\-lətənt\\ *n* -s [irreg. (influence of such words as *excitant, irritant*) fr. *depilate* + *-ant*] **:** an agent used in leather making to loosen hair before depilating
dep·i·lous \\'depələs\\ *adj* [L *depilis* (fr. *de-* + *-pilis*, fr. *pilus* hair) + E *-ous* — more at PILE] **:** HAIRLESS
de·plane \\(')dē+\\ *vb* [*de-* + *plane* (airplane)] *vi* **:** to descend from a plane after a flight ~ *vt* **:** to remove from or cause to descend from a plane after a flight
de plano \\dā'plä(,)nō\\ *adv* [L] **:** beyond argument **:** MANIFESTLY; *also* **:** in a summary way **:** as a matter of course — usu. used in legal documents
de·plasmolysis \\¦dē+\\ *n* [NL, fr. *de-* + *plasmolysis*] **:** swelling of the cytoplasm of a plasmolyzed cell **:** reversal of plasmolysis
de·plenish \\də+'-, (')dē¦-'\\ *vt* [*de-* + *plenish*] **:** to deprive of furniture, stock, or other contents ⟨a ~*ed* house⟩ ⟨a ~*ed* purse⟩
de·plet·able \\də'plēd·əbəl, dē'-, -lētə-\\ *adj* **:** capable of becoming depleted or exhausted ⟨~ assets⟩ ⟨~ resources⟩
de·plete \\də'plēt, dē'-, *usu* -lēd.+V\\ *vt* -ED/-ING/-S [L *depletus*, past part. of *deplēre*, fr. *de-* + *plēre* to fill — more at FULL] **1 :** to empty (as the blood vessels) of a principal substance ⟨a body *depleted* by excessive blood loss⟩ ⟨tissues *depleted* of vitamins⟩ **2 :** to lessen in number, quantity, significant content, or force or in vital power or value as a result of such lessening **:** exhaust (as a mine) of its valuable content or (a country) of its strength or resources ⟨army, crumbled in morale and *depleted* by wholesale desertion —*Amer. Guide Series: Tenn.*⟩ ⟨the house whose air was lifeless and *depleted* —Ethel Wilson⟩ ⟨sick and *depleted* children —Robert Payne⟩ ⟨leaves *depleted* of starch —*Experiment Station Record*⟩
syn DEPLETE, DRAIN, EXHAUST, IMPOVERISH, and BANKRUPT can mean, in common, to deprive a thing in whole or in part of what is essential to its existence or total functioning or power. DEPLETE can signify merely a lessening in number, quantity, or force, but generally stresses a consequent loss, or potential loss, in effective functioning from such a lessening ⟨cattle herds *depleted* by the heavy slaughter last year —*Time*⟩ ⟨under conditions of sustained or repeated injury the body may be so *depleted* that it no longer can withstand infection and new stresses —W.K.Livingston⟩ ⟨has not the soil been *depleted* of its riches? —G.R.Stewart⟩ DRAIN implies a gradual depletion and ultimate deprivation in force, or vigor, or in elements that provide it ⟨the summer had *drained* the last reserve of her strength —Ellen Glasgow⟩ ⟨a burden of arms *draining* the wealth and the labor of all peoples —D.D.Eisenhower⟩ ⟨excesses *drained* the last element of decency from him⟩ EXHAUST stresses the total loss of force or vigor or of elements that provide it ⟨cultivated ground is *exhausted* after only two or three harvests and a new plot must then be cleared —C.D. Forde⟩ ⟨evidently the old ideas had been *exhausted* and the time was ripe for new ideologies and a new order —R.W.Murray⟩ ⟨a person *exhausted* by constant worry⟩ IMPOVERISH implies a depletion or a draining of what is essential to richness or productiveness ⟨alleging that mechanization helps to *impoverish* the soil and thus to reduce the output of crops or animal products —*Farmer's Weekly (So. Africa)*⟩ ⟨ignorance of the Bible, of mythology, and of ancient literature in general *impoverishes* our understanding of much of the poetry of the past —C.S.Kilby⟩ ⟨an *impoverished* imagination⟩ BANKRUPT implies total impoverishment or total loss of effectiveness ⟨astronomical sums of time are so great that they *bankrupt* the imagination —D.C.Peattie⟩ ⟨*bankrupt* a creative power by constant hack work⟩
de·ple·tion \\-ēshən\\ *n* -s [LL *depletion-, depletio* bloodletting, fr. L *depletus* + *-ion-, -io* -ion] **:** the act or process of depleting or the state of being depleted: as **a** (1) **:** the reduction or loss of blood, body fluids, chemical constituents, or stored materials from the body (as by hemorrhage or malnutrition) (2) **:** a debilitated state caused by excessive loss of body fluids or other constituents **b** (1) **:** the reduction in capital value that results from the consumption or diminution of an asset (as an oil well or a mine) (2) **:** the measure or amount of exhaustion of such an asset — distinguished from *amortization* and *depreciation* (3) **:** the utilization of a natural resource (as a water reservoir, a stand of timber) at a rate greater than the rate of replenishment
depletion ration *n* **:** a basic experimental ration designed to exhaust the body reserve of a specific nutrient while maintaining other dietary requirements in balance
de·ple·tive \\-ēd·iv\\ *adj* [L *depletus* + E *-ive*] **:** tending to deplete
de·plor·abil·i·ty \\də,plōrə'biləd·ē, dē,-, -ōr-, ətē, -i\\ *n* -ES **:** the quality or state of being deplorable
de·plor·able \\ə'ʹ==bəl\\ *adj* [F *déplorable*, fr. MF *deplorable*, fr. *deplorer* to deplore + *-able*] **:** fit to be deplored **:** LAMENTABLE ⟨a ~ lack of tact⟩ ⟨a ~ intellectual confusion —C.I. Glicksberg⟩ ⟨uniforms of the servants were sleazy and often dirty and the service ~ —Virginia A. Oakes⟩ **:** WRETCHED, UNFORTUNATE ⟨in a truly ~ condition, only less filthy than the prison itself —C.B.Nordhoff & J.N.Hall⟩ **:** ABOMINABLE ⟨the food is ~ for a healthy man —John Buchan⟩ — **de·plor·able·ness** \\-ləbəlnəs\\ *n* -ES — **de·plor·ably** \\-blē, -li\\ *adv*
dep·lo·ra·tion \\,deplə'rāshən; ,dē,plōr'ā-, -ōr'rā-\\ *n* -s [L *deploration-, deploratio*, fr. *deploratus* (past part. of *deplorare*) + *-ion-, -io* -ion] **:** the act of deploring **:** LAMENTATION
de·plore \\də'plō(ə)r, -ō(ə)r, -ōə, -ō(ə)\\ *vt* -ED/-ING/-S [MF or L; MF *deplorer*, fr. L *deplorare*, fr. *de-* + *plorare* to wail, lament, prob. of imit. origin] **1** *obs* **:** to regard or abandon as hopeless **2 a :** to feel or express deep grief for **:** sorrow over ⟨~ the death of a close friend⟩ **b :** to regret strongly ⟨I ~ that I cannot conform to that practice —Tor Ulving⟩ **c :** to consider as very unfortunate or to be strongly lamented ⟨they ~ the fifteen years of slow whittling away of basic liberties —E.A.Mowrer⟩ ⟨their zeal to ~ the inferior position to which men have shoved women —Paul Engle⟩ **3** *obs* **:** to tell of or recount with sorrow
syn DEPLORE, LAMENT, BEWAIL, and BEMOAN agree in signifying to show grief or sorrow for something. DEPLORE usu. implies keen and profound regret for, but as commonly implies strong grieving objection to, esp. the irreparable, calamitous, or unavoidable ⟨helping the process of moral decay which he *deplores* —*New Republic*⟩ ⟨he *deplores* the fact that there is dissension within the Church —Robert Corkey⟩ ⟨how profoundly a man, holding that view, must *deplore* the whole course of academical literary study —A.T.Quiller-Couch⟩ ⟨purists *deplore* slang —*Quarterly Jour. of Speech*⟩ LAMENT implies a vehement demonstration of sorrow suggesting mourning but without tears or similar manifestation, usu., however, implying passionate utterance ⟨his yelling rose into an indignant *lament* as he waved his arms more wildly —Paul Bowles⟩ ⟨jails where the members were given ample time to *lament* their errors —R.A.Billington⟩ ⟨we need not gloat or *lament* about the limitations of finite minds —A.G.N.Flew⟩ BEWAIL and BEMOAN imply intense sorrow finding an outlet in words or cries, BEWAIL usu. suggesting a loud and BEMOAN a lugubrious expression of grief or, in popular use, grievance or complaint ⟨valet *bewailing* the loss of his wages —Samuel Alexander⟩ ⟨the large number who *bewail* the materialistic tendencies of modern life —*Times Lit. Supp.*⟩ ⟨he *bemoaned* their fate, his mood steadily growing gloomier and gloomier —O.E.Rölvaag⟩ ⟨as ready as any tycoon to *bemoan* the woes of being wealthy —*Time*⟩
de·plor·er \\-ōrə(r), -ōrə-\\ *n* -s **:** one that deplores something
de·plor·ing·ly *adv* **:** in a deploring manner
¹de·ploy \\də'plȯi, dē'p- *also* 'dē,p-\\ *vb* -ED/-ING/-S [F *déployer*, fr. L *displicare* to scatter — more at DISPLAY] *vt* **1 a :** to extend (a military or naval unit) in width or in both width and depth ⟨he ~*ed* his squad on both sides of the road⟩ **b :** to place or arrange (armed forces) in battle disposition or formation or in locations appropriate for their future employment ⟨~ forces to check aggressions⟩ **2 :** to extend or place as if deploying troops ⟨~*ing* the editors . . . in various phases of political reporting —*Newsweek*⟩ ⟨harried roadmasters ~ equipment and work gangs along the grade in military fashion —R.L.Neuberger⟩ ~ *vi* **:** to move in or as if in deployment ⟨the squad ~*ed* and made a dash for the hill —Hanama Tasaki⟩ ⟨the staff ~*ed* to their phones —*Time*⟩
²deploy \\ə'= *or* 'dē,p-\\ *n* -s **:** the power to use esp. in deployment ⟨two other weapons in the ~ of the Soviet block . . . propaganda and internal revolution —D.W.Mitchell⟩
de·ploy·ment \\ə'=mənt\\ *n* -s [F *déploiement*, fr. MF *deploiement*, fr. *deployer* + *-ment*] **:** the act or movement of deploying or the state of being deployed
de·plu·mate \\(')dē¦plü,māt, -mət\\ *or* **de·plu·mat·ed** \\-,mād·əd\\ *adj* [*deplumate* fr. ML *deplumatus*, past part. of *deplumare*; *deplumated* fr. ML *deplumatus* + E *-ed*] **:** destitute of feathers
de·plu·ma·tion \\,dē,plü'māshən\\ *n* -s [ML *deplumatus* + E *-ion*] **:** the stripping or falling off of feathers
de·plume \\(')dē+\\ *vt* [ME *deplumen*, fr. MF *deplumer*, fr. ML *deplumare*, fr. L, fr. *de-* + *pluma* feather — more at FLEECE] **1 :** to pluck off the feathers of **:** deprive of plumage **2 :** to strip of possessions, honors, or attributes
depluming mite *n* **:** an itch mite (*Knemidokoptes gallinae*) that attacks poultry feeding about the bases of the feathers and causing a mangy condition
de·polarization \\(¦)dē+\\ *n* **1 :** the process of depolarizing **2 :** the state of being depolarized
de·polarize \\(')dē+\\ *vt* [*de-* + *polarize*] **1 :** to cause (polarized radiation) to become partially or wholly unpolarized (as by scattering) **2 :** to prevent, decrease, or remove polarization of (as a dry cell) esp. by adding a substance that prevents accumulation of reaction products **3 :** DEMAGNETIZE
de·polarizer \\(')dē+\\ *n* **:** something that depolarizes; *specif* **:** a substance that reacts with the products accumulating at one of the electrodes of a cell and thus prevents polarization
de·polish \\(')dē+\\ *vt* [*de-* + *polish* (n.)] **:** to remove or destroy the smoothness, gloss, or polish of (as by sand blasting, acid, or grinding) **:** ROUGHEN
de·po·lym·er·ase \\,dēpə'limə,rās, -āz\\ *n* -s [*depolymerize* + *-ase*] **:** any of various enzymes (as nucleases) that bring about depolymerization
de·polymerization \\(¦)dē+\\ *n* **:** the process of depolymerizing
de·polymerize \\"+\\ *vt* [ISV *de-* + *polymerize*] **:** to decompose (macromolecular compounds) by various means (as by hydrolysis) into relatively simple compounds (as monomers) — opposed to *polymerize* ⟨starch and gelatin are easily *depolymerized*⟩ ⟨*depolymerized* nucleic acids⟩
de·pone \\də'pōn, dē'-\\ *vb* -ED/-ING/-S [ML *deponere*, fr. L, to put down, fr. *de-* + *ponere* to put — more at POSITION] **:** to assert under oath **:** TESTIFY **syn** see SWEAR
¹de·po·nent \\də'pōnənt, (')dē¦p-\\ *adj* [LL *deponent-, deponens*, fr. pres. part. of L *deponere* to put down; trans. of Gk *apothetikos*] *of a verb* **:** occurring with passive or middle voice forms but with active voice meaning ⟨the ~ verbs in Latin and Greek⟩
²deponent \\"\\ *n* -s [in sense 1, fr. LL *deponent-, deponens*, trans. of Gk *apothetion*; in sense 2, fr. ML *deponent-, deponens*, pres. part. of *deponere*] **1 :** a deponent verb **2 :** one who depones **:** one who gives evidence esp. in writing
de·po·nen·tial \\¦depə¦nenchəl\\ *adj* **:** of, relating to, or characteristic of a deponent verb ⟨a ~ ending⟩ **:** DEPONENT
de·popularize \\(')dē+\\ *vt* [*de-* + *popularize*] **:** to cause to be no longer popular
¹de·populate \\(')dē+\\ *vb* [L *depopulatus*, past part. of *depopulari, depopulare*, fr. *de-* + *populari, populare* to ravage, perh. fr. *populus* people — more at PEOPLE] *vt* **1** *obs* **:** to lay waste **:** DEVASTATE, RAVAGE **2 :** to deprive wholly or partly of inhabitants (as by war or pestilence) **:** reduce the population of ⟨the Black Death . . . *depopulated* parts of Europe in the 15th century —V.M.Ehlers & E.W.Steel⟩ ⟨the cities almost *depopulated* of Spaniards gone to seek the greater riches of Mexico —Marjory S. Douglas⟩ ~ *vi* **:** to become less populous
²de·pop·u·late \\(')dē¦päpyələt\\ *adj* [L *depopulatus*] *archaic* **:** DEPOPULATED
de·population \\(¦)dē+\\ *n* [ME *depopulacioun* devastation, fr. L *depopulation-, depopulatio*, fr. *depopulatus* + *-ion-, -io* -ion] **:** the act of depopulating or the state of being depopulated: **a** *archaic* **:** DEVASTATION ⟨the Danes . . . infested those parts with wide ~ —John Milton⟩ **b :** reduction of population ⟨the causes of ~ are physical, political, and economic —G.B. Longstaff⟩
de·populator \\(')dē+\\ *n* [ME, devastator, fr. L *depopulator*, fr. *depopulatus* + *-or*] **:** one that depopulates
¹de·port \\də'pō(ə)r¦t, dē'-, -ō(ə)r¦,-ōə¦,-ō(ə)¦, *usu* ¦d·+V\\ *vt* -ED/-ING/-S [MF *deporter* to behave, support, spare, fr. L *deportare* to carry away, exile, fr. *de-* + *portare* to carry — more at PORT (to carry)] **1 :** CARRY, DEMEAN, CONDUCT ⟨teaching the child how to ~ himself in public⟩ **2** [L *deportare*] **a :** to carry away or off **:** TRANSPORT ⟨200 miners . . . were forcibly ~*ed* from their homes —Zechariah Chafee⟩ **b :** to send out of the country **:** sentence to legal deportation ⟨~*ing* criminals⟩ ⟨in Moscow whither he had been ~*ed* —Louis Bromfield⟩ **syn** see BANISH, BEHAVE
²deport *n* -s [MF, fr. *deporter*] *obs* **:** BEARING, DEPORTMENT
de·port·abil·i·ty \\də,pōr¦d·ə'biləd·ē, (,)dē¦p-, -pō(r)¦,-pōə¦, ¦tə-, -ətē, -i\\ *n* -ES **:** the state of being liable to deportation
de·port·able \\də'pōr¦d·əbəl, (')dē¦p-, -pō(r)¦,-ōə¦, ¦tə-\\ *adj* **1 :** subject to deportation ⟨any alien who fails to give the required notices . . . is also ~ —*Harvard Law Rev.*⟩ **2 :** carrying the punishment of deportation ⟨cases of illegal entry, criminality . . . and other ~ offenses —F.A.Ogg & P.O.Ray⟩
de·por·ta·tion \\,dē,pōr'tāshən, -ō(r)'-,-ōə'- *also* -,pə(r)'-\\ *n* -s [MF & L; MF, fr. L *deportation-, deportatio*, fr. *deportatus* + *-ion-, -io* -ion] **:** the act or an instance of deporting or the state of being deported: as **a** *Roman law* **:** permanent banishment of a condemned criminal esp. to an island with resultant loss of citizenship and forfeiture of property — compare EXILE, RELEGATION **b :** the removal from a country of an alien whose presence in the country is unlawful or is held to be prejudicial to the public welfare — compare EXTRADITION, TRANSPORTATION
de·port·ee \\də¦pōr¦¦tē, dē¦-, ¦dē,pōr¦¦tē, -ōr¦,-ōə¦,-ō(ə)¦, ¦d·ē; ¦dēpə(r)¦tē\\ *n* -s **:** one who has been deported, is about to be deported, or is under sentence of deportation
de·port·ment \\də'pōrtmənt, -ōrt-,-ōət-,-ō(ə)t-\\ *n* -s [F *déportement*, fr. MF *deportement*, fr. *deporter* to behave + *-ment* — more at DEPORT] **:** the manner in which one deports himself **:** CARRIAGE, BEHAVIOR, CONDUCT ⟨a stranger clad in black, and of a clerical ~ —Owen Wister⟩ ⟨all the thousand and one artificialities which go to make up feminine ~ —Max Peacock⟩ ⟨he placed his feet, one before the other, with the care of a young woman practicing ~ —Fred Majdalany⟩ ⟨their teacher had trained them in ~ and manners —Gladys Skelley⟩
de·pos·able \\də'pōzəbəl, dē'-\\ *adj* [*depose* + *-able*] **:** capable of being deposed ⟨a czar of high finance as ~ as any other dictator⟩
de·pos·al \\-ōzəl\\ *n* -s [ME, prob. fr. *deposen* + *-al*] **:** the act of deposing or the process of being deposed esp. from a throne ⟨the ~ of James II and the ascension of William of Orange —Frank Thilly⟩
de·pose \\də'pōz, dē'-\\ *vb* -ED/-ING/-S [ME *deposen*, fr. OF *deposer*, modif. (influenced by *poser* to put, place) of LL & L *deponere* (perfect stem *depos-*); LL *deponere* to remove from office or authority, fr. L, to lay aside, put down — more at DEPONE] *vt* **1 :** to remove from a throne or other high position **:** divest or deprive of office or rank **:** DETHRONE ⟨striving to ~ the king in favor of his brother⟩ ⟨*deposed* from his post as prime minister —*Time*⟩ ⟨they *deposed* Philip Carteret as governor —*Amer. Guide Series: N.J.*⟩ ⟨*deposed* as unfit to hold office⟩ **2** *obs* **a :** to take away **:** REMOVE **b :** DIVEST, DISPOSSESS **c :** to lay aside **:** divest oneself of **3 :** to let fall **:** put down **:** DEPOSIT ⟨she carelessly *deposed* costly trinkets on the table —Arnold Bennett⟩ ⟨the practice . . . of *deposing* the sacrament in a carved recess —Francis Berry⟩ **4 a** [ME *deposen*, fr. ML *depos-*, perfect stem of *deponere* to assert under oath, fr. L, to put down] **:** to say under oath **:** TESTIFY; *esp* **:** to give witness of by an affidavit or other sworn statement in writing ⟨~ before the court that he had seen the man in the act of murder⟩ **b :** AFFIRM, ASSERT ⟨a fat grocer was *deposing* that he thought it was I who had stolen five feet of pork sausages from him —Carolyn Hannay⟩ **c** *obs* **:** to put under oath **:** call upon as witness ~ *vi* [ME *deposen*, fr. ML *depos-*, perfect stem of *deponere* to assert under oath] **:** to bear witness **:** make a deposition **:** TESTIFY ⟨he was a bit shaky when it came his turn to ~⟩ **syn** see SWEAR
de·pos·er \\-zə(r)\\ *n* -s **:** one who deposes; *esp* **:** one that testifies
¹de·pos·it \\də'päzət, dē'-, *usu* -əd·+V\\ *vb* **deposited** \\-zəd·əd, -z(ə)təd\\ **deposited** \\"\\ **depositing** \\-zəd·iŋ, -z(ə)tiŋ\\ **deposits** \\-zəts\\ [L *depositus*, past part. of *deponere* to put down, lay aside — more at DEPONE] *vt* **1 a :** to place, cache, or entrust esp. seriously and carefully (as for safekeeping, pledging or guaranteeing performance, or recording) ⟨until the last voter ~*ed* his ballot —R.M.Lovett⟩ **b :** to place in deposit in a bank or similar institution **c :** to set down or place esp. carefully or safely or in care or custody ⟨the maid had . . . ~*ed* a huge decanter on the table —A.N.Whitehead⟩ ⟨the adventurous gentlemen . . . were safely ~*ed* at their inn in London —T.B.Macaulay⟩ ⟨~*ed* in a clean hospital bed —Allen Churchill⟩ ⟨a giant wave lifted the tiny craft completely over the beached ship and ~*ed* it still intact, on the other side —*All Hands*⟩ **2** *archaic* **:** to lay aside or give up **:** rid oneself of **3 :** to lay down or let fall or drop by a natural process **:** foster the accretion or accumulation of as a natural deposit ⟨the intervening seasons had ~*ed* a thick layer of refuse over the vacant lot⟩ ⟨the wind ~*ed* a film of dust over the furniture⟩ ⟨in . . . hogs fed on copra . . . the cocoanut oil globules had been ~*ed* by nature in the tissues —V.G. Heiser⟩ ~ *vi* **1 :** to become precipitated **:** SETTLE **2 :** to make a deposit; *also* **:** to become deposited ⟨the zirconium metal . . . ~*s* on the filament —Samuel Glasstone⟩ **syn** see SET
²deposit \\"\\ *n* -s [L *depositum*, fr. neut. of *depositus*, past part.] **1 a :** the state of being deposited in trust or safekeeping **b :** the state of being deposited to one's credit in a bank **2 :** something placed (as in a bank or in someone's hands) for safekeeping: as **a :** money that is deposited in a bank or with a banker, that is subject to order, and that creates the relationship of creditor and debtor **b :** something given as a pledge or security (as a forfeit) ⟨post a ~ of money as evidence of his good faith —*Canadian Citizenship Series*⟩ ⟨~*s* which some librarians require from borrowers . . . returnable when the depositor ceases to use the library —W.C.B.Sayers⟩ ⟨a five-cent ~ on a soda bottle⟩ **c** *Roman & civil law* **:** a bailment of goods to be kept gratuitously for the bailor and without any benefit to the bailee or depositary — see IRREGULAR DEPOSIT, NECESSARY DEPOSIT, QUASI DEPOSIT, SEQUESTRATION, VOLUNTARY DEPOSIT **d :** a partial and first payment on account of the purchase price of property **3** [ML *depositum*] **:** a place of deposit **:** DEPOSITORY **4 :** the act of depositing ⟨is to come into force upon the ~ of ratifications with the government —Vera M.Dean⟩ ⟨ritual is . . . a slow ~, as it were, of people's imaginative insight into life —Susanne K.Langer⟩ **5 a :** something laid, placed, or thrown down; *esp* **:** matter deposited by some natural process ⟨the muddy and sandy ~*s* at the river's mouth⟩ ⟨the walls of the house are . . . less discolored by the ~ of carbon than usual in most towns —Richard Jefferies⟩ **b :** a natural accumulation (as of iron ore, coal, or gas) ⟨~*s* of phosphates suitable for agricultural fertilizer were discovered near Oruro —*Americana Annual*⟩
deposit account *n* **1** *Brit* **:** a bank account requiring advance notice of withdrawals and earning interest **:** SAVINGS ACCOUNT **2 :** the bank account of any depositor
deposit administration *n* **:** a plan for retaining retirement contributions made by employers in a special fund held by

the ensurer to be applied toward the purchase of annuities as employees reach retirement

¹de·pos·i·tary \-zə,terē, -ri\ *n* -ES [LL *depositarius*, fr. L *depositus* + *-arius* -ary] **1 :** one that receives a deposit **:** one with whom a depositor makes his deposit; *specif* **:** a bailee in a deposit **2 :** DEPOSITORY

²depositary \"\ *adj* **:** being or acting as a depositary ⟨a ~ bank⟩ ⟨a ~ agent⟩

de·pos·i·ta·tion \də,päzə'tāshən, (')dē,-\ *n* -S [¹*deposit* + *-ation*] **1 :** the act of depositing **:** DEPOSIT **2** *Scots law* **:** an agreement by which an owner of personal property gives possession of it to another for safekeeping to be restored upon demand

deposit banking *n* **:** banking in which bank credit is in the form of deposits instead of the issue of notes

deposit copy *n* **:** a copy of a publication deposited by legal requirement in any of certain specified libraries

deposit currency *n* **:** checks and other credit instruments drawn on deposits in banks and used as a medium of exchange

deposited *past of* DEPOSIT

depositing *pres part of* DEPOSIT

dep·o·si·tion \,depə'zishən *also* ,dēp-\ *n* -S [ME & LL; ME *deposicioun* dismissal, testimony, fr. LL *deposition-, depositio* act of putting down, laying away, dismissal, testimony, burial, fr. LL & L *depositus* (past part. of LL *deponere* to remove from office or authority & L, to lay aside, put down) + L *-ion-, -io* -ion — more at DEPONE] **1 :** the act of deposing or the process of being deposed (as a sovereign from a throne) **:** deprivation of authority ⟨the forceful ~ of the vice-regent⟩; *specif* **:** the depriving of a clergyman from the ministry **2 a :** an alleging or a giving of testimony **:** a testifying esp. before a court **b :** an opinion asserted **:** a statement made **:** something alleged **:** DECLARATION, TESTIMONY, ALLEGATION; *specif* **:** testimony taken down in writing under oath or affirmation in reply to interrogatories before a competent officer to replace the viva voce testimony of the witness or to supply necessary information for pretrial procedure — compare AFFIDAVIT **3** [L *depositus* + E *-ion*] **:** DEPOSITION FROM THE CROSS **4 :** the act or process of depositing or the state of being deposited: as **a** *obs* **:** a putting down or laying aside (as of a burden) **b :** a giving over or committing for safekeeping ⟨~ of the valuables into the hands of police⟩ **c :** a placing or a laying or throwing down often by a natural process ⟨glaciers caused denudation . . . more widely than ~ —Samuel Van Valkenberg & Ellsworth Huntington⟩ ⟨pneumoconiosis involves the ~ of foreign particles in the substance of the lungs⟩ **d :** PRECIPITATION ⟨the . . . ~ of metals on cotton from salt solutions —R.S.Horsfall & L.G.Lawrie⟩ ⟨sedimentary rocks . . . formed by the ~ of solids from the waters —S.F. Mason⟩ **5 :** BURIAL **:** interment (as of a saint's body) in a new place; *also* **:** a festival commemorating a burial **6** [¹*deposit* + *-ion*] **:** something deposited **:** DEPOSIT, SEDIMENT ⟨excavation revealed more than one type of ~ in the dry river bed⟩

dep·o·si·tion·al \¦==¦zishənᵊl, -shnəl\ *adj* **:** of, relating to, or made by, deposition ⟨the present erosional and ~ topography of semiarid regions —P.G.Worcester⟩

deposition from the cross : a work of art representing Christ's descent from the cross

deposit money *n* **:** bank demand deposits which can be used as money through drawing checks

deposit of faith [trans. of ML *depositum fidei*] **:** the body of revealed truth in the Scriptures and tradition proposed by the Roman Catholic Church for the belief of the faithful

de·pos·i·tor \də'päzəd·ə(r), -z(ə)tə-\ *n* -S [LL, fr. L *depositus* + *-or*] **:** one that deposits; *esp* **:** one that makes a bank deposit or has money in deposit at a bank

¹de·pos·i·to·ry \-zə,tōrē, -ȯr-, -ri\ *n* -ES [¹*deposit* + *-ory*] **1 :** a person or group with which something and esp. something nonmaterial is deposited for preservation or safekeeping ⟨a ~ of ancient tradition⟩ **2** [LL *depositorium*, fr. L *depositus* + *-orium* -ory] **a :** a place where something is deposited or stored (as for safekeeping or convenience) ⟨an official ~ for U.S. government publications —*Bull. of Bates Coll.*⟩ ⟨the original furniture is stored away in hidden *depositories* of the château —Arnold Bennett⟩ ⟨Congress officially became the ~ of Burma's gift to America —Cecil Hobbs⟩; *specif* **:** a bank chosen for the depositing of government funds — compare DEPOSITORY LIBRARY **b :** a device consisting of a bank vault and a mechanism on the outside wall of the bank building through which deposits may be inserted into the vault during the hours the bank is closed

²depository \"\ *adj* **:** of or relating to a depository

depository bond *n* **:** a bond that is often required from a bank for deposits of state and municipal governments and that guarantees the amount of the deposit in the event of the bank's insolvency

depository library *n* **1 :** a library legally designated to receive at no cost except postage all or a selected list of U.S. government publications **2 :** a library designated by the United Nations to receive all or a selected list of its publications

deposit premium company *or* **deposit premium mutual** *n* **:** a mutual insurance company issuing policies at a stated premium often with provision for assessment

deposits *pres 3d sing of* DEPOSIT, *pl of* DEPOSIT

deposit slip *n* **:** a slip accompanying a bank deposit and containing a list of checks or cash deposited, the date, and depositor's signature

deposit station *n* **:** a place (as a school, firehouse, or store) at which a public library maintains a small collection of books; *also* **:** the collection of books maintained there

de·pos·i·tum \-zəd·əm\ *n* -S [in sense 1, fr. L; in sense 2, fr. ML, fr. L — more at DEPOSIT] **1 :** DEPOSIT 2, 3 **2 :** the faith and doctrine committed to the Christian church — archaic except in law and theology

de·po·si·tum mi·se·ra·bi·le \",mizə'rabə(,)lē\ *or* **depositum ne·ces·sa·ri·um** \-,nesə'sa(a)rēəm\ *n, pl* **deposi·ta misera·bi·lia** \-zəd·ə,mizərə'bilēə\ *or* **deposita necessa·ria** \-rēə\ [L] **:** NECESSARY DEPOSIT

¹de·pot *in senses 1 & 2* 'de(,)pō *also* 'dē-; *in sense 3* 'dē-*sometimes* 'de-; *in all senses: archaic* 'dā(,)pō,\ *n* -S [F *dépôt*, fr. L *depositum* deposit] **1 :** a place organized for the reception, classification, storage, issue, or maintenance of military or naval supplies or equipment or for the reception, classification, detention, or forwarding of military or naval replacements **2 a :** a place at which things may be stored, collected, deposited, or cached or from which they may be conveniently distributed ⟨archiving is . . . the accumulation of material in a convenient ~ —M.B.Emeneau⟩ ⟨turning their house into a mere ~ for dilapidated objects —F.M.Ford⟩ ⟨a gasoline ~⟩ ⟨an auto-parts distribution ~ —*Newsweek*⟩ **b :** STORE, COLLECTION, DEPOSIT, CACHE ⟨we had the ship's stores and there was a food ~ on the north side of the island —H.A.Chippendale⟩ **3 a :** RAILROAD STATION **b :** a bus station **c :** an air terminal

²depot \"\ *vt* -ED/-ING/-S **:** to place (supplies) in a depot **:** CACHE ⟨that spring the first need was to ~ additional supplies for the dog-sledging parties —G.deQ.Robin⟩

³depot \"\ *adj, physiol* **:** STORED, REPOSITORY; *also* **:** adapted for prolonged action ⟨~ fat⟩ ⟨~ penicillin⟩ ⟨~ insulin⟩

depot ship *n* **:** a supply and repair ship in a flotilla of small naval vessels (as destroyers or submarines)

depr *abbr* depreciation

dep·ra·va·tion \,deprə'vāshən\ *n* -S [MF, fr. L *depravation-, depravatio* perversion, fr. *depravatus* + *-ion-, -io* -ion] **1** *obs* **:** DEFAMATION, CALUMNY **2 :** the act or process of depraving or the state of being depraved **:** CORRUPTION, PERVERSION, DEGENERACY, DEPRAVITY; *also* **:** an instance of this

de·prave \də'prāv, dē'-\ *vt* -ED/-ING/-S [ME *depraven*, fr. MF *depraver* to calumniate, pervert, fr. L *depravare* to pervert, distort, fr. *de-* + *-pravare* (fr. *pravus* crooked, wrong, bad) — more at PRAIRIE] **1 :** to speak ill of **:** DEPRECIATE, MALIGN **2 :** to make bad **:** ⟨things that would ~ the judgment rather than make it more discriminating⟩: as **a** *obs* **:** to pervert the meaning of by misconstruing **b** *archaic* **:** to make (a word or a text) corrupt **c :** to bring about the moral debasement of **d** *obs* **:** to reduce (coinage) in value **3** [by alter.] *obs* **:** DEPRIVE **syn** see DEBASE

de·praved \-vd\ *adj* **:** marked by debasement, corruption, perversion, or deterioration ⟨asserted that the present evils of society are the consequence of vicious institutions rather than of ~ human nature —V.L.Parrington⟩ ⟨scavenger birds with ~ habits⟩ — **de·praved·ly** \-v(ə)dlē\ *adv* — **de·praved·ness** \-v(ə)dnəs\ *n* -ES

depraved appetite *n* **:** PICA 2

de·prave·ment \-vmənt\ *n* -S **:** DEPRAVATION

de·prav·er \-və(r)\ *n* -S **:** one that depraves

de·prav·i·ty \-ravəd·ē, -ətē, -i\ *n* -ES **1 :** the quality or state of being depraved; *specif* **:** the state of sinfulness natural to unregenerate man according to certain religions **2 :** a corrupt act or practice

dep·re·cate \'deprə,kāt, -rē,-, *usu* -ād·+V\ *vt* -ED/-ING/-S [L *deprecatus*, past part. of *deprecari* to avert by prayer, intercede for fr. *de-* + *precari* to pray — more at PRAY] **1** *obs* **:** SUPPLICATE, BESEECH **2 a** *archaic* **:** to pray against (as an evil) **b :** to seek to avert (as by supplication) ⟨smilingly placed himself opposite him, with the look of one who ~*s* an expected reproof —J.C.Powys⟩ ⟨it would bring about the war we all dread and ~ —A.L.Guérard⟩ **3 :** to disapprove of often with mildness ⟨a man who advocates aesthetic effort and ~*s* social effort —Thomas Hardy⟩ ⟨shook her head, *deprecating* such wit —Arnold Bennett⟩ **4** [influenced in meaning by *depreciate*] **:** DEPRECIATE ⟨a shy self-*deprecating* manner⟩ ⟨insisted that he was merely a private citizen and *deprecated* any public honors paid to him —Robert Graves⟩ **syn** see DISAPPROVE

deprecating *adj* **:** depreciating or tending to depreciate; *esp* **:** APOLOGETIC ⟨he managed a ~ smile at the compliment⟩ — **dep·re·cat·ing·ly** *adv*

dep·re·ca·tion \,==''kāshən\ *n* -S [MF & L; MF, prayer, fr. L *deprecation-, deprecatio* prayer, act of averting by prayer, fr. *deprecatus* + *-ion-, -io* -ion] **1 :** a prayer that an evil may be removed or prevented **2 :** an act of deprecating: **a :** an often mild expression of disapproval **b :** deprecation esp. of oneself

dep·re·ca·tive \'==,kā¦d·¦iv, -,kə|, |t|, |ēv *also* |əv\ *adj* [LL *deprecativus*, fr. *deprecatus* + *-ivus* -ive] **:** DEPRECATORY — **dep·re·ca·tive·ly** \¦əvlē, -li\ *adv*

dep·re·ca·to·ry \-,kə,tōrē, -ȯr-, -ri\ *adj* [LL *deprecatorius*, fr. L *deprecatus* + *-orius* -ory] **:** DEPRECATING

de·pre·cia·ble \də'prēsh(ē)əbəl, (')dē¦p-\ *adj* **:** that can or may depreciate in valuation

de·pre·ci·ate \də'prēshē,āt, dē'-, *usu* -ād·+V\ *vb* -ED/-ING/-S [LL *depretiare* (often spelled *depreciare* in later MSS), fr. *de-* + *pretium* price — more at PRICE] *vt* **1 :** to lessen in price or estimated value **:** lower the worth of ⟨the owner's right to ~ such property —*Jour. of Accountancy*⟩ — opposed to *appreciate* **2 :** to represent as of little value or claim to esteem **:** UNDERVALUE, DISPARAGE, BELITTLE ⟨objected to scholars *depreciating* the craftsmen —S.F.Mason⟩ **~** *vi* **:** to become depreciated **:** fall in value or esteem ⟨perishable goods ~ rapidly⟩ ⟨a *depreciating* currency⟩ **syn** see DECRY

de·pre·ci·at·ing·ly *adv* **:** in a way that depreciates

de·pre·ci·a·tion \də,prēshē'āshən, (,)dē,-\ *n* -S [*depreciate* + *-ion*] **:** the act or process of depreciating or the state of being depreciated **:** loss of value ⟨the rapid ~ of currency⟩ ⟨made some bitter remarks in ~ of his enemies⟩ ⟨estimated the degree of ~ in a car after a year's use⟩

depreciation accounting *n* **:** a branch of accounting that deals with systematically distributing or allocating the cost or other basic value of a fixed asset over its estimated useful life by periodic charges to expense or against revenue

depreciation charge *n* **:** an amount in accounting that is commonly a fixed percentage of the original cost of a property and that is periodically charged off to expense or against revenue in order to compensate for the depreciation of the property

depreciation insurance *n* **:** insurance that is added to a fire insurance policy by endorsement and that covers the difference between the actual cash value and the replacement cost of the insured property

de·pre·cia·tive \də'prēshē,ād·iv, dē'-, -sh(ē)əd-\ *adj* **:** DEPRECIATING, DISPARAGING — **de·pre·cia·tive·ly** \-d·əvlē\ *adv*

de·pre·ci·a·tor \-shē,ād·ə(r)\ *n* -S [LL *depretiator* (often spelled *depreciator* in later MSS), fr. *depretiatus* + L *-or*] **:** one that depreciates

de·pre·ci·a·to·ry \-sh(ē)ə,tōrē\ *adj* **:** DEPRECIATING, DISPARAGING

dep·re·date \'deprə,dāt\ *vb* -ED/-ING/-S [LL *depraedatus*, past part. of *depraedari*, fr. L *de-* + *praedari* to plunder — more at PREY] *vt* **:** to lay waste **:** prey upon **:** PLUNDER, PILLAGE, DESPOIL ⟨*depredating* the surrounding countryside⟩ **~** *vi* **:** to make depredations **:** PLUNDER ⟨if you ~ in that country, we'll have to clash —J.E.Haley⟩

dep·re·da·tion \,deprə'dāshən\ *n* -S [ME *depredacioun*, fr. MF or LL; MF *depredation*, fr. LL *depraedation-, depraedatio*, fr. *depraedatus* + L *-ion-, -io* -ion] **1 a :** the act of depredating or the state of being depredated **:** an act of plundering, despoiling, or making inroads **b depredations** *pl* **:** RAVAGES ⟨trying to ease the ~*s* of the disease⟩ **2** *Scots law* **:** the forcible driving away of cattle in large numbers

dep·re·da·tor \'deprə,dād·ə(r)\ *n* -S [LL *depraedator*, fr. *depraedatus* + L *-or*] **:** one that plunders or despoils **:** PILLAGER

dep·re·da·to·ry \'deprəda,tōrē; də'predə-, dē'-; 'deprə,dād·ərē\ *adj* **:** tending to depredate **:** characterized by depredation **:** PLUNDERING

deprehend *vt* [L *deprehendere*, fr. *de-* + *prehendere* to lay hold of, seize — more at PREHENSILE] **1** *obs* **:** SEIZE, CAPTURE **2** *obs* **:** to take by surprise **3** *obs* **:** PERCEIVE, DETECT — **deprehension** *n* -S *obs*

de·press \də'pres, dē'-\ *vt* -ED/-ING/-ES [ME *depressen*, fr. MF *depresser*, fr. L *depressus*, past part. of *deprimere* to press down, fr. *de-* + *-primere* (fr. *premere* to press) — more at PRESS] **1 :** to put down or overcome forcibly **:** CRUSH, SUBJUGATE **2 :** to press down ⟨~ a typewriter key⟩ **:** LOWER: as **a :** to cause to sink, fall, or assume a lower level, position, point, situation, or attitude ⟨~*ed* the mounted gun⟩ ⟨~*ed* areas below sea level⟩ ⟨where the highway goes through cities you will find, perhaps, a ~*ed* express street . . . a bridge overhead —William Carter⟩ ⟨raise or ~ the roadbed at the crossing of a highway —B.N.Cardozo⟩ **b :** to lessen, diminish, impoverish, or depreciate the activity, strength, level, yield, or significance of ⟨confederates in Canada supplied cash for buying gold, shipping it to England and selling it in order to ~ Federal currency values —C.H.Coleman⟩ ⟨it has tended to ~ the culture of the minority below the point at which a full understanding of poetry becomes possible —C.D.Lewis⟩ ⟨able to ~ irritability of the heart muscle by the use of such a drug as procaine⟩ ⟨any number of factors can ~ germination in plants⟩ ⟨an injection to ~ the excretion⟩ **c :** to lower in spirit or mood **:** press down into dejection **:** make sad or downcast **:** DISCOURAGE, DISPIRIT ⟨the mere volume of work was enough to crush the most diligent of rulers and ~ the most vital —John Buchan⟩ **d :** to lessen or lower in value, esp. market value; *also* **:** to lower in marketability **e** *math* **:** to lower (as an equation) in degree **3 :** to cause (certain ore or gangue minerals) to sink while other minerals float — compare FLOTATION 3

syn OPPRESS, WEIGH (*down*), WEIGH (*on*), or WEIGH (*upon*): DEPRESS may stress the fact of lowering but does not stress the cause or agency involved. In reference to persons and their feelings it stresses dejection and discouragement ⟨she had been *depressed* by the failing trade of the shop —Arnold Bennett⟩ ⟨war had blighted his past, *depressed* his present and clouded his future with grave doubts —E.T.Weir⟩ OPPRESS stresses the fact of a weight or burden calculated to lower but does not stress the effect ⟨the butler, *oppressed* by the heat of the weather —G.B.Shaw⟩ ⟨the dismaying sense of it [the compulsion of a war period] . . . *oppressed* the mind —J.G. Cozzens⟩ WEIGH (*down*), WEIGH (*on*), and WEIGH (*upon*) are used to cover in-between situations; they suggest continuing concern with an urgent oppressive matter calculated to depress ⟨I know too well my own inefficiency; it has *weighed on* me from youth —Havelock Ellis⟩ ⟨Walter's mind had cleared itself of the depression which had *weighed on* him so heavily —T.B.Costain⟩

¹de·pres·sant \-sᵊnt\ *adj* **:** causing depression **:** tending to depress: as **a :** making unhappy **:** DISPIRITING ⟨a fatal accident always has a ~ effect on a crowd —Ken Purdy⟩ **b :** creating economic depression ⟨other government policies were ~ —R.C.Leffingwell⟩ **c :** lowering or tending to lower functional or vital activity ⟨a drug with a ~ effect on heart rate⟩

²depressant \"\ *n* -S **:** something that depresses: as **a :** a reagent (as cyanide) that depresses in ore flotation **b :** an agent that causes the lessening or depressing of some specified property ⟨pour-point ~⟩ ⟨foam ~⟩ ⟨perspiration ~⟩ **c :** an agent that reduces exaggerated functional activity (as irritability or spasm) of tissues ⟨a ~ of intestinal spasm⟩

depressed *adj* **1 a :** DEJECTED, DISPIRITED **b :** DEPRESSIVE **2 a :** vertically flattened ⟨a ~ cactus⟩ **b :** having the central portion lower than the margin ⟨a ~ pustule⟩ **c :** lying flat or prostrate ⟨~ herb⟩ **d :** dorsoventrally flattened **3 a :** being in, suffering from, or caused by a state or period of economic depression ⟨a ~ industry⟩ ⟨~ areas⟩ ⟨~ conditions⟩ **b :** economically or socially below standard, oppressed, or underprivileged ⟨peasants are deserting the villages and streaming into the towns to form the kind of ~ proletariat that existed in England during the industrial revolution —George Woodcock⟩ ⟨the ~ peoples of the ghetto⟩; *esp* **:** constituting or belonging to the lowest social and economic class usu. characterized by unsatisfactory living and working conditions ⟨the most notable of the ~ classes in India is the class of untouchables⟩ **syn** see DOWNCAST

depressed arch *n* **:** DROP ARCH

depressed center car *or* **depressed well car :** a railroad flatcar constructed with a low center section and used to handle oversized loads which otherwise would not clear tunnels or other way structures

depressed fracture *n* **:** a fracture esp. of the skull in which the fragment is depressed below the normal surface

de·press·ibil·i·ty \də,presə'biləd·ē, (,)dē,-, -ətē, -i\ *n* -ES **:** the quality or state of being depressed **:** susceptibility to being depressed

de·press·ible \də'presəbəl, dē'-\ *adj* **:** capable of being depressed

depressing *adj* **:** that depresses **:** causing esp. emotional depression ⟨hot weather is enervating and severe cold although temporarily stimulating is permanently ~ —C.C.Furnas⟩ ⟨a ~ sense of all the stupidity —Floyd Dell⟩ ⟨this a ~ book⟩ — **de·press·ing·ly** *adv* — **de·press·ing·ness** *n* -ES

de·pres·sion \-eshən\ *n* -S [in sense 1, fr. ME *depressioun*, fr. ML *depression-, depressio*, fr. LL, act of pressing down, fr. L *depressus* (past part. of *deprimere* to press down) + *-ion-, -io* -ion; in other senses, partly fr. MF & LL; MF *depression* act of pressing down, lowering, fr. LL *depression-, depressio*; partly fr. *depress* + *-ion* — more at DEPRESS] **1 a :** the angular distance of a celestial object below the horizon **b** (1) **:** the angular distance of an object beneath the horizontal plane that passes through the observer (2) *med* **:** a displacement downward or inward **2 :** the act of depressing or the quality or state of being depressed: as **a** *archaic* **:** ABASEMENT, HUMBLING, DEGRADATION ⟨the ~ of a haughty nobleman⟩ **b :** a pressing down **:** LOWERING, SINKING ⟨a quick ~ of the typewriter key⟩ ⟨recommend a ~ of the roadway where it goes under the bridge⟩ ⟨a rapid ~ of the mercury in the thermometer⟩ **c :** the state of feeling depressed **:** DISPIRITEDNESS, DEJECTION ⟨a chronic ~ of mind⟩ ⟨a physical reaction marked by ~ and languor⟩ **d** (1) **:** reduction, diminution, impoverishment, or depreciation in activity, strength, amount, quality, force, yield, value, or significance ⟨a ~ in trade⟩ ⟨a series of confiscations which completed the ~ of the English interest in the south —F.M.Stenton⟩ ⟨~ in Indian arts which may result in their disappearance —*Report: (Canadian) Royal Commission on Nat'l Development*⟩ ⟨as a surface mulch sawdust causes a ~ of nitrates⟩ (2) **:** a lowering of vitality or functional activity **:** the state of being below normal in physical or mental vitality **3 :** an instance of depression: as **a :** a region of low barometric pressure surrounded by higher pressures **:** LOW **b** (1) **:** a place or part that is depressed ⟨a slight ~ at the base of my left forefinger —Sidney Lovett⟩ (2) **:** ³HOLLOW 1 ⟨an open-air auditorium located in a natural ~ encircled by magnolias, oaks and sweet gum —*Amer. Guide Series: La.*⟩ **c :** a period of low general economic activity marked by mass unemployment, deflation, a decreasing use of resources, and a low level of investment **4 :** a mental disorder of psychoneurotic or psychotic proportions characterized by sadness, retardation of motor and certain vegetative processes, feelings of inadequacy and self-depreciation, and often by suicidal attempts — compare MANIC-DEPRESSIVE PSYCHOSIS **syn** see SADNESS

de·pres·sion·al \-shənᵊl,-shnəl\ *adj* **:** of or relating to depression or a depression

de·pres·sion·ary \-shə,nerē\ *adj* **:** DEPRESSIONAL ⟨such unemployment . . . will tend to cause a ~ movement in the whole economy —Gabriel Kolko⟩

depression of the dew point : the number of degrees that the dew point is lower than the temperature

depression slide *n* **:** a glass slide that has a concavity in one surface over which a cover glass can be placed and that is used in biology for hanging-drop cultures and for the microscopic study of small specimens

depression spring *n* **:** a spring where the earth's surface is coincident with the water table

¹de·pres·sive \də'presiv, dē'-, -sēv *also* -səv\ *adj* [*depress* + *-ive*] **:** tending to depress **:** involving, marked by, or affected with depression **:** DEPRESSING — **de·pres·sive·ly** \-səvlē, -li\ *adv*

²depressive \"\ *n* -S **:** one who is depressed; *specif* **:** one afflicted with manic-depressive psychosis in its depressive phase

de·pres·sor \-sə(r)\ *n* -S [LL, fr. L *depressus* + *-or*] **:** something that depresses: as **a :** a muscle that depresses or draws down a part — compare LEVATOR **b :** a device or appliance that depresses a part ⟨a tongue ~⟩ **c :** a nerve or nerve fiber that decreases the activity or the tone of an organ **d :** DEPRESSANT **e :** a substance (as a drug) that lowers blood pressure **f :** a substance that retards or prevents a chemical reaction or process

depressor nerve *n* **:** a nerve whose stimulation tends to decrease the activity or tone of the part or organ that it innervates

depressure *n* [*depress* + *-ure*] *obs* **:** DEPRESSION

dep·re·ter \'deprəd·ə(r)\ *or* **dep·e·ter** \-pəd-\ *n* -S [origin unknown] **:** a finish for a plastered wall made by pressing small stones in the soft plaster

de·priv·able \də'prīvəbəl, dē'-\ *adj* **:** subject to or capable of being deprived

de·priv·al \-vəl\ *n* -S **:** the act of depriving or the state of being deprived **:** DEPRIVATION ⟨assigns to them no punishment but the ~ of the Beatific Vision —G.G.Coulton⟩

dep·ri·va·tion \,deprə'vāshən *also* ,dē,prī- *sometimes* ,dēprə'-\ *n* -S [NL *deprivation, deprivatio*, fr. ML *deprivatus* (past part. of *deprivare* to deprive) + L *-ion-, -io* -ion] **1 a :** the act of depriving or the state of being deprived ⟨evidence that had been produced regarding the ~ of civil liberties in the area —*Collier's Yr. Bk.*⟩; *specif* **:** removal from an office, dignity, or benefice ⟨several months had been allowed him before he incurred suspension, several months more before he incurred ~ —T.B.Macaulay⟩ **b :** an act of depriving or an instance of being deprived ⟨the treatment of these slave laborers was stated in general terms not difficult to translate into concrete ~*s* —R.H.Jackson⟩ **2 :** the process of losing or the condition of having lost essentials vital to the body ⟨oxygen ~⟩ ⟨vitamin ~⟩

de·prive \də'prīv, dē'-\ *vt* -ED/-ING/-S [ME *depriven*, fr. ML *deprivare*, fr. L *de-* + *privare* to deprive — more at PRIVATE] **1** *obs* **:** to take away **:** REMOVE, DESTROY ⟨'tis honor to ~ dishonored life —Shak.⟩ **2 a :** to take something away from **:** DIVEST, BEREAVE ⟨last year's farm law that ~*s* farmers of soil conservation payments —*Wall Street Jour.*⟩ ⟨the proposed boundary settlement would permanently ~ that country of Silesia and East Prussia —Marshall Knappen⟩ **b :** to take an office, dignity, or benefice from **:** remove from office ⟨the Archbishop, accused of incontinence, would be *deprived* and sent to the Tower —Edith Sitwell⟩ **3 :** to keep from the possession, enjoyment, or use of something ⟨threatened to ~ American citizens of rights guaranteed them under the federal constitution —F.L.Mott⟩

syn DEPRIVE, DISPOSSESS, DISINHERIT, and BEREAVE can mean, in common, to prevent one from possessing. DEPRIVE, the most comprehensive of these words, usu. implies a taking away of what one has, owns, or has a right to ⟨to *deprive* a person of a week's wages⟩ ⟨I had *deprived* myself of rest and health —Mary W.Shelley⟩ ⟨the feeling that the system under which we live *deprives* the majority of the chance of a decent life —C.D. Lewis⟩ DISPOSSESS usu. applies to a removing or dislodging of a person in usu. illegitimate possession, less often implies a depriving of possessions, sometimes implies a deprivation of rights, qualities, or properties ⟨the family was *dispossessed* of their apartment and their furniture piled in the street⟩ ⟨he would at least try to *dispossess* her of the pistol —E.M. Lustgarten⟩ ⟨an attempt to *dispossess* nonproperty owners of voting rights⟩ DISINHERIT suggests an heir being deprived of the right to inherit an estate; in extension it often implies a robbing or divesting of a right, prerogative, or privilege, esp. acquired by birth ⟨*disinherited* by an angry father on his death-bed⟩ ⟨*disinherited* of all rights to citizenship or a decent livelihood⟩ BEREAVE means to deprive of something as by robbery, stripping, or seizing, usu. implying suddenness or surprise and now tending to occur in the form *bereaved* when loss by death is implied, in the form *bereft* when such things as hope, peace, friends, or intelligence are implied ⟨*bereaved* of both her parents and without a home of her own —Gabrielle Long⟩ ⟨the comedians full of jokes and *bereft* of humor —Bernard Kalb⟩ ⟨*bereft* of all hope of recovery⟩ ⟨to feel extremely *bereaved* after the death of a loved one⟩

deprived *adj* **:** marked by deprivations esp. of the necessities of life or of healthful environmental influences ⟨a childhood that was unhappy and ~, the family living a good deal off charity⟩ ⟨boys from a ~ environment, wherein the family life reveals a pattern of neglect, personality distortion, moral degradation and disregard for law —J.P.Murphy⟩

de·prive·ment \-vmənt\ *n* -s **:** DEPRIVATION

de·priv·er \-və(r)\ *n* -s [ME *deprivere*, fr. *depriven* + *-ere* -er] **:** one that deprives

de pro·fun·dis \ˌdāprōˈfu̇ndəs, -prə'-, -ˈfən-; ˌdē...ˈfən-; *sometimes* -ün,dēs\ *n* -ES [fr. *de profundis* 130th Psalm, fr. ME, fr. LL, out of the depths, the first 2 words of the psalm (Ps 129 in the Vulgate)] **:** a profound and esp. agonized expression of despair or misery ⟨if this ill-fated woman . . . could be enabled to write her confession, this *de profundis* would be different and would perhaps disclose agonies of soul never known before —*N.Y. Times*⟩

de·pro·pa·ni·za·tion \(ˌ)dē,prōpənə'zāshən\ *n* -s **:** the process of depropanizing

de·pro·pa·nize \(ˈ)dē'prōpə,nīz\ *vt* -ED/-ING/-S [*de-* + *propane* + *-ize*] **:** to remove propane and sometimes lighter fractions from (as cracked gasoline) by distillation — **de·pro·pa·niz·er** \-zə(r)\ *n* -s

de·pro·tein·i·za·tion \(ˌ)dē,prō,tēnə'zāshən, -ōd·ēənə'-\ *n* -s **:** the process of deproteinizing

de·pro·tein·ize \(ˈ)dē'prō,tē,nīz, -ōd·ēə,n-\ *vt* -ED/-ING/-S [*de-* + *protein* + *-ize*] **:** to remove protein from ⟨*deproteinized* blood⟩ ⟨*deproteinized* rubber⟩

dep·side \ˈdep,sīd, -sə̇d\ *n* -s [ISV *deps-* (fr. Gk *depsein* to knead) + *-ide* — more at DIPHTHERIA] **:** any of a class of esters formed by the condensation of two or more molecules of phenolic carboxylic acids

dep·si·done \-psə,dōn\ *n* -s [ISV *depside* + *-one*] **:** any of a class of chemical compounds that are esters like depsides and are also cyclic ethers

dept *abbr* **1** department **2** deponent **3** deputy

dept·ford \ˈdetfə(r)d\ *adj, usu cap* [origin unknown] **:** of or relating to a No. American Indian culture of coastal Georgia and northwestern Florida of about A.D. 700–900 characterized by slender cooking pots that have conical bases and are decorated by check stamping

deptford pink *n, usu cap D* [fr. *Deptford*, England] **:** a European wild pink (*Dianthus armeria*) that is naturalized in America and that has small bright pink flowers

depth \ˈdepth\ *n, pl* **depths** \-ps *also* -pt(h)s\ [ME, prob. fr. *dep* deep + *-th* — more at DEEP] **1 a :** something that is deep **:** a deep place **:** a deep part of something; *esp* **:** the deepest part — often used in pl. ⟨treasures in the ~*s* of the ocean⟩ **b :** a profound or intense or often the most profound or intense state (as of thought or feeling) — often used in pl. ⟨in the ~*s* of misery⟩ ⟨the ~*s* of reflection⟩; *also* **:** a reprehensibly low social, moral, or intellectual condition — often used in pl. ⟨criticism . . . having fallen to such ~*s*, it is hardly surprising that our standards of literature and the arts have fallen with it —Huntington Hartford⟩ **c :** the inner esp. midmost or more or less remote or unfathomable part — often used in pl. ⟨the ~*s* of the forest⟩ ⟨disappeared in the ~ of the crowd⟩ **d :** the part marked by the greatest, the most intense, or the severest degree (as of cold) — often used in pl. ⟨in the ~*s* of winter⟩ ⟨the ~*s* of the night⟩ ⟨in the lowest ~*s* of servility and superstition —T.L.Peacock⟩; *also* **:** the worst part — often used in pl. ⟨the ~*s* of the slums⟩ ⟨the ~ of the depression⟩ **2 a :** the perpendicular measurement downward from a surface ⟨the ~ of the river⟩ **:** the extent or measurement from the top downward ⟨the ~ of a mine shaft⟩ **b** (1) *of a square sail* **:** the extent from the headrope to the footrope (2) *of a staysail or boom sail* **:** the length of the after leech — compare ¹DROP 2b(2) ²HOIST 3b **c :** the distance between upper and lower or between dorsal and ventral points of a body **d :** the direct linear measurement from the point of viewing, from the usual position of an observer, or toward the back from a position usu. considered the front ⟨wishing he could measure the ~ of the sky⟩ ⟨the house lot was 200 ft. in ~⟩ ⟨the ~ of the crowd was considerable⟩; *specif* **:** the space from front to rear occupied by a military formation or position including front and rear elements **e :** a great distance into something immeasurable conceived of as extending from the observer — often used in pl. ⟨the ~*s* of space⟩ **3 a :** the quality of being deep or of having considerable extension downward or inward **b :** the quality of being profound (as in insight) or full (as of knowledge) **:** ACUTENESS, PENETRATION ⟨a certain ripeness of wisdom, a certain pertinency and ~ of meaning —P.E.More⟩ ⟨says much for the ~ of the impression he had received —Richard Garnett †1906⟩ ⟨Shakespeare gives the greatest width of human passion; Dante the greatest altitude and greatest ~ —T.S.Eliot⟩ **c :** the quality of being abstruse ⟨the great ~ of such thought left the ordinary brain tired and confused⟩ **d :** the quality of being intense or complete (as in moral quality or state of feeling) ⟨the ~ of a man's unrighteousness⟩ ⟨impossible to share another's ~ of grief⟩ ⟨no one knew the ~ of his guilt⟩ **e :** the quality of being low in pitch usu. with fullness of tone ⟨the vitality and ~ of the sound that reached the ear —Jack Gould⟩ **f :** physical intensity ⟨a great ~ of stillness in the woods⟩; *specif* **:** the degree of departure from colorlessness that is characteristic of the concentration or efficiency of a bulky color produced by increasing from zero the thickness of its layers or from white of a surface color **4** *archaic* **:** the number of attributes that an abstract conception or notion includes **:** CONNOTATION **5 :** the degree of engagement between a wheel and a pinion in a clock or watch — **beyond one's depth** *or* **out of one's depth 1 :** in water that is deeper than one's height **2 :** beyond the limit of one's mental capability — **in depth 1 :** extending over or for a considerable distance into an area **2** *of military defense* **:** extended for some distance forward from a primary combat zone and usu. supported by successive lines of defenders and materiel ⟨organize defense *in depth* —J.H.Plumb⟩ **3 :** in marked thoroughness **:** covering a great number and often a maximum of elements, considerations, or relevant matters ⟨here *in depth* is a portrait of Spain as it was and is —*NY Times Book Rev.*⟩ ⟨making a study *in depth* of the effects of the broadcast —Gilbert Seldes⟩

depth charge *or* **depth bomb** *n* **:** a projectile to be exploded underwater against submarines or other underwater targets

depth–charge *or* **depth–bomb** \ˈ=,=\ *vt* [*depth charge* or *depth bomb*] **:** to attack, damage, or destroy with a depth charge

depth gauge *n* **:** a gauge for measuring the depth of holes, grooves, or concavities

depth·ing tool \ˈdepthiŋ,-\ *n* **:** a tool for arranging a wheel and pinion of a watch at their proper working depth

depth interview *n* **:** an interview designed to probe attitudes, feelings, or motives not usu. tapped by the asking of standard or prepared questions

depth·less \-pt(h)lə̇s\ *adj* **1 :** immeasurable in depth **:** deep or profound beyond description ⟨new insight into the ~ nature of her loneliness —Ethel Waters⟩ ⟨the ~ misery and heroism of the people they served —*Time*⟩ **2 :** lacking significant depth **:** SHALLOW **:** SUPERFICIAL ⟨it promises to make life impersonal, mechanized and ~ —*Time*⟩

depth of compensation : the depth below the earth's surface at which the topographic inequalities are compensated by variations in rock density so that all columns of rock or of rock and water above that depth have approximately equal weights

depth of definition : DEPTH OF FOCUS 1

depth of engagement : the depth of thread contact measured radially of the mating parts of an external and an internal thread

depth of field : the range of distances of the object in front of a camera lens or other image-forming device measured along the axis of the device throughout which the image has acceptable sharpness

depth of focus 1 : the range of distances of the image behind a camera lens or other image-forming device measured along the axis of the device throughout which the image has acceptable sharpness **2 :** DEPTH OF FIELD — not used technically

depth of hold : the distance from the underside of the tonnage deck plank amidships to the ceiling of the hold of a ship

depth of thread : the distance between the crest and the base of a screw thread measured radially

depth·om·e·ter \depˈthämədˌə(r)\ *n* [*depth* + *-o-* + *-meter*] **:** an instrument for measuring the depth of water

depth perception *n* **:** the ability to judge more or less accurately the distance of objects away from the observer and the spatial relationship of objects at different distances and angles away from the observer

depth psychology *n* **:** PSYCHOANALYSIS

depths *pl of* DEPTH

depth–sounder \ˈ=,==\ *n* **:** an instrument (as a bathymeter or fathometer) for measuring mechanically the depth of water beneath a ship

depth table *n* **:** a table used in the appraisal of real estate that shows in percentages the variations of land value attributable to differences in the depth of lots

dep·u·rant \ˈdepyərənt, də̇ˈpyu̇r-\ *n* -s [ML *depurant-, depurans*, pres. part. of *depurare*] **:** an agent or means used to effect purification

dep·u·rate \ˈdepyə,rāt\ *vt* -ED/-ING/-S [ML *depuratus*, past part. of *depurare*, fr. L *de-* + *purare* to purify, fr. *purus* clean, pure — more at PURE] **:** to free from impurities or heterogeneous matter **:** PURIFY, CLEANSE — **dep·u·ra·tion** \ˌdepyəˈrāshən\ *n* -s

dep·u·ra·tor \ˈdepyə,rād·ə(r)\ *n* -s **:** one that purifies

de·purge \(ˈ)dē+\ *vt* [*de-* + *purge*] **:** to restore previous social and political status (as eligibility for public office) to (a formerly purged person)

depurse *vt* [*de-* + *purse* (n.)] *obs* **:** DISBURSE — **depursement** *n* -s

dep·u·ta·tion \ˌdepyəˈtāshən\ *n* -s [ME *deputacioun*, fr. ML *deputation-, deputatio*, fr. LL, delegation, fr. L *deputatus* + L *-ion-, io* -ion] **1 a** *obs* **:** appointment or ordination esp. to an office **b** *obs* **:** COMMISSION 1a, WARRANT 2c **c :** an appointment as gamekeeper on an English estate often made as a way of giving hunting privileges **2 a :** the act of deputing **:** the act of appointing a deputy or representative **b :** the office of deputy or delegate **3 a :** a person or group deputed to act on one's behalf ⟨the larger nations sent ~*s* to the peace conference⟩ **b :** a group acting as a unit ⟨waved to a halt by ~*s* of rugged, villainous-looking men —Mollie Panter-Downes⟩ ⟨a ~ of season-ticket holders protested to the management —O.S. Nock⟩ — **dep·u·ta·tion·al** \ˌdepyəˈtāshən°l, -shnəl\ *adj*

dep·u·ta·tive \ˈ==,tād·iv\ *adj* [*deputation* + *-ive*] **:** of, relating to, or having the character or authority of a deputy

¹**de·pute** \də̇ˈpyüt\ *n* -s [ME, fr. MF, past part. of *deputer*] *now Scot* **:** DEPUTY

²**de·pute** \də̇ˈpyüt, dē'-, *usu* -üd·+V\ *vt* -ED/-ING/-S [ME *deputen*, fr. MF *deputer* to appoint, fr. LL *deputare* to allot, destine, fr. L, to esteem, consider, lit., to cut off, fr. *de-* + *putare* to prune, esteem, consider, think — more at PAVE] **1** *obs* **:** APPOINT, DEVOTE **2 :** DELEGATE ⟨the duty of keeping in touch with the constituencies . . . was *deputed* to the party agents —H.J.Hanham⟩ ⟨he had been *deputed* to meet us and had forgotten —John Masters⟩ ⟨a body of men *deputed* to report the invasion of Europe —Richard Dimbleby⟩

dep·u·tize \ˈdepyə,tīz *also* ÷ -pə-\ *vb* -ED/-ING/-S *see -ize in Explan Notes* [*deputy* + *-ize*] *vt* **1 :** to appoint as deputy **:** make into a deputy esp. by an official swearing in **2 :** to entrust to a deputy ⟨friends would like to see him ~ part of his mountainous work to lieutenants —Li Shu-Fan⟩ ~ *vi* **1 :** to act as deputy ⟨a dearth of princes who could ~ for the sovereign —*Times Lit. Supp.*⟩ **2 :** to act or function as a substitute in another's place ⟨if photography was ever allowed to ~ for art . . . in the end it would either supplant or completely corrupt art —Douglas Cooper⟩

dep·u·ty \ˈdepyəd·ē, -ətē, -i *also* ÷ -pə-\ *n* -ES *often attrib* [ME, fr. MF *deputé, depute*, past part. of *deputer* to appoint — more at DEPUTE] **1 :** a person appointed, nominated, or elected as the substitute of another and empowered to act for him, in his name, or in his behalf **:** DELEGATE, REPRESENTATIVE ⟨the hostess left for awhile but picked a ~ hostess to take care of things in her absence⟩ ⟨each alderman has a ~ in the common council of London⟩; *specif* **:** a member of the lower house of certain legislative assemblies — compare GENERAL DEPUTY, LORD LIEUTENANT, SPECIAL DEPUTY, VICEROY **2 a :** a second in command or an assistant who usu. takes charge when his superior is absent ⟨a ~ supervisor⟩ ⟨a ~ editor⟩ ⟨a ~ marshal⟩ **b :** DEPUTY CHIEF **c :** DEPUTY SHERIFF **3 :** one who supervises such matters as shoring and bratticing in an English coal mine

deputy chief *n* **1 :** an official in a police or fire department usu. second in command **2 :** the rank of a deputy chief

deputy sheriff *n* **:** an assistant appointed to receive and serve writs and sometimes to act in place of the sheriff

deputy surveyor *n* **:** MINERAL SURVEYOR

de·queen \(ˈ)dē+\ *vt* [*de-* + *queen* (n.)] **:** to remove the queen from (a hive of bees) — compare SUPERSEDURE

der- *or* **dero-** *comb form* [NL, fr. Gk *der-*, fr. *derē, deirē*; akin to OSlav *griva* mane, Skt *grīvā* neck, L *vorare* to devour — more at VORACIOUS] **:** neck **:** throat ⟨*deradenitis*⟩ ⟨*Derotremata*⟩

der *abbr* derivation; derivative; derived

de·racialization \(ˌ)dē, də̇ +\ *n* **:** the act or process of deracializing

de·racialize \(ˈ)dē, də̇ +\ *vt* [*de-* + *racial* + *-ize*] **1 :** to attenuate or eliminate distinctive racial qualities of ⟨may ultimately ~ themselves through education and interbreeding⟩ **2 :** to free from appeal to race ⟨until local authorities ~ their outlook, the segregation problem won't be solved⟩

de·rac·i·nate \də̇ˈrasᵊn,āt, dē'-\ *vt* -ED/-ING/-S [F *déraciner* (fr. MF *desraciner*, fr. *des-* + *racine* root, fr. LL *radicina*, fr. *radic-, radix* root + *-ina*, fem. of *-inus* -ine) + E *-ate* — more at WORT] **:** to pull out by the roots **:** EXTIRPATE **:** separate from one's environment **syn** see EXTERMINATE

deracinated *adj* **:** physically, mentally, or emotionally separated from one's racial, social, or intellectual group **:** free from racial characteristics or influence ⟨as ~ as migrants from another country⟩

de·rac·i·na·tion \də̇,rasᵊnˈāshən, (ˌ)dē,-\ *n* -s **1 :** the act or process of deracinating **2 :** detachment from one's background ⟨as from homeland, customs, traditions⟩

¹**deraign** *vt* -ED/-ING/-S [ME *dereynen, deraynen*, fr. OF *deraisnier* to defend, champion, fr. *de-* + *raisnier* to speak, plead, fr. (assumed) VL *rationare*, fr. L *ration-, ratio* reckoning, calculation, reason — more at REASON] *obs* **:** to defend or prove (a claim) or settle (a dispute) esp. in personal combat

²**deraign** *vt* -ED/-ING/-S [ME *desrengier* to get out of place, disarrange — more at DERANGE] *obs* **:** to discharge from a religious order — **deraignment** *n* -s *obs*

¹**de·rail** \də̇ˈrāl, (ˈ)dē'-, *esp before pause or consonant* -āəl\ *vb* -ED/-ING/-S [F *dérailler*, fr. *dé* (fr. OF *des-, de-* de-) + *rail*, fr. E — more at RAIL] *vt* **1 :** to cause (a railroad engine or car) to run off the rails of the track **2 :** to throw off course (as a plan or project) **:** INTERRUPT **:** DIVERT ⟨new trade barriers could ~ British planning —*Atlantic*⟩ ⟨addiction to alcohol, which ~*ed* his career —Val Adams⟩ ~ *vi* **:** to leave the rails

²**de·rail** \ˈdē,r-,də'r-,dē'r-\ *also* **de·rail·er** \də̇ˈrālə(r), dē'-\ *n* **:** a device for guiding railway cars or locomotives off the rails at selected points when in danger of collision or other accident

de·rail·ment \də̇ˈrā(ə)lmənt, dē'-\ *n* -s [F *déraillement*, fr. *dérailler* + *-ment*] **:** an act or instance of derailing or being derailed **:** derailed state

de·range \də̇ˈrānj, dē'-\ *vt* -ED/-ING/-S [F *déranger*, fr. OF *desrengier* to get out of place, disarrange, fr. *des-* de- + *reng, renc* line, place, row — more at RANK] **1 a :** to put out of place or order **:** DISARRANGE ⟨war *deranged* the lines of communication and transportation⟩ ⟨hatless, with tie *deranged* —G.W.Stonier⟩ ⟨excessive erosion tends to ~ the continental water system —Russell Lord⟩ **b :** to throw into disorder or confusion **:** UPSET ⟨the arrival of guests *deranged* all his plans⟩ ⟨the music brought back memories and *deranged* her poise⟩ **2 :** to disturb the operation or functioning of ⟨even slight damage to the hearing mechanism may ~ it⟩ **3 :** to break in upon **:** INTERRUPT, DISTURB **syn** see DISORDER

de·range·able \-jəbəl\ *adj* **:** capable of being deranged

deranged *adj* **:** DISARRANGED, DISORDERED, UNBALANCED; *esp* **:** CRAZY, INSANE

de·range·ment \-jmənt\ *n* -s [F *dérangement*, fr. *déranger* + *-ment*] **:** the state of being deranged **:** DISARRANGEMENT, CONFUSION, DISORDER; *esp* **:** INSANITY

de·rat \(ˈ)dē +\ *vt* [*de-* + *rat* (n.)] **:** to rid of rats

de·rate \(ˈ)dē +\ *vt* [*de-* + *rate*] **1 :** to reduce or eliminate rates on ⟨the Local Government Act of 1929 *derated* British agricultural holdings⟩ **2 :** to lower the rated capability of (electrical apparatus) because of deterioration, inadequacy, age, or obsolescence

de·ration \(ˈ)dē +\ *vt* [*de-* + *ration*] **:** to cease to ration (as a commodity)

derationing *n* **:** a stopping or cancellation of rationing

de·rat·i·za·tion \(ˌ)dē,rad·əˈzāshən\ *n* -s **:** the ridding of rats

de·ray \di'rā\ *n* -s [ME, fr. OF *desrei*, fr. *desreer*, to disturb, put in disorder, prob. alter. of *desareer* — more at DISARRAY] *now dial Brit* **:** DISORDER, DISTURBANCE, CONFUSION; *specif* **:** disorderly merriment

der·bied *pronunc at* ¹DERBY +d\ *adj* **:** wearing a derby

derbies *see* ¹DERBY\ *var of* DARBIES

¹**der·by** \ˈdərbē, -əb-,-əib-, -bi, *in Brit speech usu* ˈdäb-; *in the US* ˈdärb- & ˈdäb- *are seriously used by many for Brit places, persons, or things having "derby" or "Derby" as or in their name*\ *n* -ES [fr. the *Derby*, famous horse race run at Epsom Downs, England; after Edward Stanley †1834, 12th earl of *Derby*, who founded it in 1780] **1 a** *usu cap* **:** any of certain traditionally prominent horse races held annually and usu. restricted to three-year-olds **b :** a race or contest open to all comers or all who fall within some specified category (as boys under a certain age or size) and offering prizes to winners ⟨a salmon ~⟩ ⟨bicycle *derbies*⟩ **c :** a field contest or trial for hounds or bird dogs classified as two-year-olds; *often* **:** a dog eligible to compete in such a derby **2 a** *or* **derby hat** *sometimes cap D* **:** a stiff felt hat with a dome-shaped crown and a rather narrow somewhat rolled brim — called also *bowler* **b :** a woman's hat (as of stiff straw or fabric) more or less resembling the felt derby **c :** a mute for trumpet or trombone in the shape of a derby used by jazz players **3** [*derby (vamp)*] **a** *often cap* **:** a low-heeled short-vamped usu. buckled sport shoe for men **b** *Brit* **:** BLUCHER ⟨a *derby*-front shoe⟩

derby 2a

²**derby** *see* ¹DERBY\ *adj, usu cap* [in sense 1, fr. *Derby*, county borough in England; in sense 2, fr. *Derby* county, England] **1 :** of or from the county borough of Derby, England **:** of the kind or style prevalent in Derby **2 :** DERBYSHIRE

³**derby** *see* ¹DERBY\ *or* **derby cheese** *n* -ES *often cap D* **:** a hard-pressed mild-flavored English cheese that is prepared from whole sweet cow's milk and resembles but is moister and flakier than cheddar

derby blue *n, often cap D* [so called fr. the characteristic color of Derby china] **:** a dark violet that is bluer, lighter, and stronger than plum purple (sense 2) and bluer and stronger than average blue plum — called also *elderberry*

derby china *also* **derby** *n, usu cap D* [²*Derby*] **:** a fine often highly ornamented china made at Derby, England — see CROWN DERBY

derby flycatcher *n, usu cap D* [after Edward S. Stanley, 13th earl of *Derby* †1851 Eng. zoologist] **:** a large conspicuously marked tyrant flycatcher (*Pitangus sulphuratus*) found in tropical America and northward to southern Texas

der·by·lite \ˈdərbē,līt\ *n* -s [Orville A. *Derby* †1915 Am. geologist + E *-lite*] **:** a mineral probably $Fe_6Ti_6Sb_2O_{23}$ consisting of an iron antimonate and titanate in black prismatic orthorhombic crystals (sp. gr. 4.53)

derby red *n, often cap D* [prob. fr. *Derby (china)*] **1 :** vermilion or a color resembling it **2 :** CHROME RED 1

¹**der·by·shire** \ˈ==,shi(ə)r, -iə, -,shə(r) — *see* ¹DERBY\ *adj, usu cap* [fr. *Derbyshire*, England] **:** of or from the county of Derby **:** of the kind or style prevalent in the county of Derby

²**derbyshire** \"\ *or* **derbyshire cheese** *n, usu cap D* **:** ³DERBY

derbyshire chair *n, usu cap D* **:** an English country chair of Jacobean style with arched top rail and open back

de·realization \(ˌ)dē, də̇+\ *n* [*de-* + *realization*] **:** loss of a sense of the reality of one's environment

de·re·cha·zo \ˌderəˈchä(ˌ)sō\ *n* -s [Sp, fr. *derecho* right hand (fr. *derecho*, adj., right, fr. L *directus* straight, direct) + *-azo*, suffix used to denote a blow of a (specified) nature — more at DIRECT] **:** a close pass in bullfighting done with the muleta in the right hand — compare NATURAL

de·re·ism \ˈdērē,izəm, ˈdāˈrā,-\ *n* -s [L *de re* away from reality + E *-ism*] **:** thinking directed away from reality and not following ordinary rules of logic — compare AUTISM

de·re·is·tic \ˌ;=ˈistik\ *adj* **:** characterized by or involving dereism — **de·re·is·ti·cal·ly** \-tə̇k(ə)lē\ *adv*

¹**der·e·lict** \ˈderə,likt\ *adj* [L *derelictus*, past part. of *derelinquere* to forsake wholly, abandon, fr. *de-* + *relinquere* to leave — more at RELINQUISH] **1 :** abandoned esp. by the owner or occupant **:** FORGOTTEN, UNUSED, RUN-DOWN ⟨a ~ hill farm⟩ ⟨books that lie ~ on the top shelf⟩ ⟨a house now ~ beyond redemption —*Country Life*⟩ **2 :** lacking in a sense of duty **:** REMISS, NEGLECTFUL ⟨school boards that were ~ in opening and maintaining public schools —C.S.Stine⟩ ⟨voters who feel that they would somehow be ~ in their civic duty . . . if they did not vote selectively —R.H.Rovere⟩ ⟨~ behavior toward racial minorities —H.L.Ickes⟩

²**derelict** \"\ *n* -s **1 a :** a thing voluntarily abandoned or willfully cast away by its owner with the intention of not retaking it and rightly claimed by the first person who takes possession of it; *specif* **:** a boat abandoned on the high seas **b :** a tract of land left dry by the sea or other body of water receding from its former bed **2 :** a person abandoned or forgotten **:** one that is not a responsible or acceptable member of society ⟨chronic ne'er-do-wells, useless ~*s* of society, seldom hired and then not for long —F.L.Allen⟩

der·e·lic·tion \ˌderəˈlikshən\ *n* -s [L *dereliction-, derelictio*, fr. *derelictus* + *-ion-, -io* -ion] **1 a :** an intentional abandonment ⟨~ of sins —Jeremy Taylor⟩ — now used chiefly in law **b :** the state of being abandoned **2** *obs* **:** failure esp. of physical or mental powers **3 :** a recession of water (as of the sea) so that land above high-water mark is left dry **4 a :** intentional or conscious neglect (as of principles) ⟨~ of duty⟩ **:** deviation esp. from conventional conduct **:** DELINQUENCY **b :** FAULT, SHORTCOMING **syn** see FAILURE

de·requisition \də̇, dē +\ *vt* [*de-* + *requisition*] **:** to release from requisition; *specif* **:** to release from government control

de·res·i·nate \(ˈ)dē'rezᵊn,āt\ *vt* [*de-* + *resinate*] **:** to remove resin from — **de·res·i·na·tion** \(ˌ)dē,rezᵊnˈāshən\ *n* -s

de·restrict \(ˌ)dē + \ *vt* [*de-* + *restrict*] **:** to remove restrictions from ⟨trading in Canadian dollar securities was ~*ed*⟩; *specif* **:** to remove a speed limit from (a road)

derf \ˈdərf\ *adj* [ME, of Scand origin; akin to ON *djarfr* bold; akin to OE *deorfan* to labor, perish, OS *derbi* strong, OFris *derve* bold, Arm *derbuk* rough, stiff, Lith *dirbti* to work; basic meaning: to work] *Scot* **:** BOLD, DARING

derham *var of* DIRHEM

de·ride \dəˈrīd, dēˈ-\ *vt* -ED/-ING/-S [L *deridēre*, fr. *de-* + *ridēre* to laugh — more at RIDICULOUS] **:** to laugh at with contempt **:** turn to ridicule or make sport of **:** MOCK ⟨sardonic wisecracks in which supposedly lofty ideals are mercilessly *derided* —*Times Lit. Supp.*⟩ **syn** see RIDICULE

de·rid·ing·ly *adv* **:** in a deriding manner

de ri·gueur \də(ˌ)rēˈgər, -ˌri-, +V -ər-; -gə̄, +V -ər-,-ə̄(r\ *adj* [F] **:** prescribed or required by fashion, etiquette, or custom **:** PROPER ⟨instructions as to when and where a silk hat is *de rigueur* —André Maurois⟩ ⟨the *de rigueur* luggage of a salesman —Bernard Kalb⟩ ⟨a type of architecture that became *de rigueur* for suburban homes⟩ ⟨at which it is *de rigueur* to drink as much champagne as possible —Robert Shaplen⟩

deringer *var of* DERRINGER

de·rip·ia \dəˈripēə\ [NL] *syn of* JUGULARES

de·ris·i·ble \dəˈrizəbəl, dēˈ-\ *adj* [*derision* + *-ible*] **:** worthy of derision or scorn

de·ri·sion \-izhən\ *n* -S [ME *derisioun*, fr. MF *derision*, fr. LL *derision-, derisio*, fr. L *derisus* (past part. of *deridēre* to deride) + *-ion-, -io* -ion — more at DERIDE] **1 a :** a laughing at what seems ridiculous or contemptible **:** the use of ridicule, mockery, or scorn to belittle or to show contempt **b :** a state of being derided ⟨a social life which . . . wins its way from ~ to acceptance —Samuel Alexander⟩ **2 :** an object of derision or scorn **:** LAUGHINGSTOCK ⟨I was a ~ to all my people —Lam 3:14 (AV)⟩

de·ri·sive \dəˈrīs|iv, dēˈ-, |ēv *also* |əv *sometimes* -riz| *or* -rīz| *or* -ris|\ *adj* [*derision* + *-ive*] **1 :** expressing or characterized by derision **:** JEERING ⟨~ taunts —Alexander Pope⟩ **2 :** causing derision **:** RIDICULOUS — **de·ri·sive·ness** *n* -ES

de·ri·sive·ly \|əvlē, -li\ *adv* **:** in a derisive manner **:** with derision

de·ri·so·ry \-rīs(ə)rē, -rīz(-,-riz(-, -ri\ *adj* [LL *derisorius*, fr. L *derisus* + *-orius* -ory] **1 :** expressive of derision **:** DERISIVE ⟨scornful ~ smiles —Katherine A. Porter⟩ **2 :** worthy of derision **:** RIDICULOUS ⟨~ sales of contemporary verse —Cyril Connolly⟩ ⟨a ~ excuse for an automobile —A.J.Liebling⟩

de·riv·abil·i·ty \dəˌrīvəˈbiləd·ē, dē,-\ *n* **:** the quality or state of being derivable

de·riv·able \ə'=vəbəl\ *adj* **1** *obs* **:** TRANSMISSIBLE **2 :** that can be derived **:** OBTAINABLE ⟨pleasure ~ from home life⟩; *specif* **:** capable of being known by inference (as from premises or data) **:** DEDUCIBLE **3 :** capable of being traced (as from a source) — **de·riv·ably** \-blē\ *adv*

[1]**der·i·vate** \ˈderəvət, -ˌvāt\ *adj* [L *derivatus*, past part. of *derivare* to draw off, derive — more at DERIVE] **:** DERIVED, DERIVATIVE — **der·i·vate·ly** *adv*

[2]**derivate** \"\ *n* -S **:** something derived (as a thing, word, idea) **:** DERIVATIVE ⟨faith in the possibility of science . . . is an unconscious ~ from medieval theology —A.N.Whitehead⟩

der·i·va·tion \ˌderəˈvāshən\ *n* -S [MF & L; MF, fr. L *derivation-, derivatio*, fr. *derivatus* + *-ion-, -io* -ion] **1 a** *historical linguistics* (1) **:** the formation of a word from an earlier word or base usu. by the addition of an affix usu. noninflectional (as in *rebuild* from *build* or *boyish* from *boy*), functional change (as in *picnic*, vb., from *picnic*, n.), or back-formation (as in *peddle* from *peddler*) (2) **:** an act of ascertaining or stating the derivation of a word (3) **:** ETYMOLOGY 1a **b** *descriptive linguistics* (1) **:** the relation of a word to its base as expressed usu. in terms of presence of an affix (as in *peddler*, base *peddle*, or *teaches*, base *teach*), vowel alternation (as in *rode*, base *ride*, or *song*, base *sing*), consonant alternation (as in *spent*, base *spend*, or German *halb* \hälp\ "half", base *halb-* \hälb\), difference of accent (as in *convict* \kənˈvikt\, base *convict* \ˈkänˌvikt\), absence of one or more sounds (as in French *gris* \grē\, masc., "gray", base *grise* \grēz\, fem.), suppletion (as in *better*, base *good*), or zero difference (as in *sheep*, pl., base *sheep*, sing.) (2) **:** the relation of a word to its base when the two do not belong to the same inflectional paradigm (as in *peddler*, base *peddle*, *song*, base *sing*, *convict* \kənˈvikt\, base *convict* \ˈkänˌvikt\) **2** *obs* **:** a handing on or transmission from a source **3 a :** the source from which a thing is derived **:** ORIGIN ⟨a style of writing which has long forgotten its ~ —Maurice Edelman⟩ ⟨hats of French ~⟩ **b :** ORIGINATION, DESCENT ⟨distinguished by ~ from royal ancestors⟩ **4** *obs* **a :** a drawing off of water from its main channel (as for irrigation) **b :** the drawing of inflammation or fluid out of or away from a diseased part of the body **5 :** something that is derived **:** DERIVATIVE, DEDUCTION ⟨the painting seems more like a copy than a ~⟩ ⟨a belief that proved to be an entirely false ~⟩ **6 a :** the act or process of deriving from or as if from an original source ⟨the rational ~ of human law from the law of nature —G.H.Sabine⟩ **b :** an instance or result of being derived ⟨Martha's Vineyard . . . was granted by ~ from the crown of England to Thomas Mayhew —L.C.M.Hare⟩ **7 :** a sequence of statements (as in logic or mathematics) showing that a certain result (as a formula) is a necessary consequence of previously accepted statements

der·i·va·tion·al \ˌderəˈvāshən°l, -shnəl\ *adj* **1 :** relating to derivation **2** *linguistics* **:** of, relating to, used in, or characterized by derivation — distinguished from *inflectional*

der·i·va·tion·ist \ˌderəˈvāsh(ə)nəst\ *also* **de·riv·a·tist** \dəˈrivəd·əst, dēˈ-\ *n* -S *archaic* **:** EVOLUTIONIST

[1]**de·riv·a·tive** \dəˈrivəd·|iv, dēˈ-, -vət|\ *adj* [LL *derivativus*, fr. L *derivatus* + *-ivus* -ive] **1** *linguistics* **:** formed by derivation **2 :** made up of or marked by elements or qualities derived from something else (as from an ultimate source) **:** arising from, obtained by, used in, or consisting of derivation **:** lacking originality ⟨~ ecclesiastical structures with which the landscape . . . was dotted in a time when people did not know how to build —G.N.Shuster⟩ ⟨~ presentation of already available data rather than an original contribution —*English Language Teaching*⟩ ⟨artists who spend most of their time with other artists . . . their work thins out, becomes ~, lacks the individual contour —Sidney Alexander⟩ **3 :** SECONDARY, DERIVATIONAL ⟨not only in their direct success but in the ~ benefits that would flow from them —Elmer Davis⟩

[2]**derivative** \"\ *n* -S **1 :** a word formed by derivation **2 :** something that derives from, grows out of, or results from an earlier or fundamental state or condition ⟨the sonata form (itself a ~ of opera) —Kingsley Martin⟩ ⟨nostalgia is a fine ~ from any book —Lewis Nichols⟩ **3 :** DERIVATIVE OF A FUNCTION **4 a :** a chemical substance that is so related structurally to another substance as to be theoretically derivable from it even when not so obtainable in practice ⟨the methoxy ~ of naphthalene⟩ **b :** a substance that can be made from another substance in one or more steps ⟨nitration of benzene to the *meta*-dinitro ~⟩ **5 :** one that holds derivative citizenship

derivative action *or* **derivative suit** *n* **:** a suit by a shareholder to enforce a corporate cause of action based upon a right of the corporation

derivative citizenship *n* **:** citizenship derived from that of another (as from a person who holds citizenship by virtue of naturalization)

derivative deposit *n* **:** a bank deposit consisting of the proceeds of a loan credited to the depositor's account — compare PRIMARY DEPOSIT

derivative hybrid *n*, *bot* **:** the progeny of a cross between a hybrid and either one of its parent species

de·riv·a·tive·ly \|əvlē, -li\ *adv* **:** by derivation

de·riv·a·tive·ness \|əvnəs\ *n* -ES **:** the quality or state of being derivative

derivative of a function : the limit if it exists of the quotient of an increment of a dependent variable to the corresponding increment of an associated independent variable as the latter increment tends to zero without being zero

de·riv·a·ti·za·tion \-ˌrivəd·əˈzāshən\ *n* -S **:** the process of derivatizing

de·riv·a·tize \-ˈrivəˌtīz\ *vt* -ED/-ING/-S [*derivative* + *-ize*] **:** to convert (a chemical compound) into a derivative usu. for the purpose of identification

de·rive \dəˈrīv, dēˈ-\ *vb* -ED/-ING/-S [ME *deriven* to come (as from a source), receive (as from a source), divert (as water) into a different channel, fr. MF *deriver*, fr. L *derivare* to divert (as water) into a different channel, derive (one word from another), fr. *de-* + *-rivare* (fr. *rivus* stream, brook) — more at RISE] *vt* **1 a :** to take or receive esp. from a source ⟨an English loanword *derived* from German⟩ ⟨the river ~s its name from an Indian chief⟩ ⟨the mills ~ their power from the falls⟩ ⟨he ~s much of his income from investments⟩ **b :** to obtain or gain through heredity or by transmission from environment or circumstance ⟨he *derived* his enthusiasm for the theater from his father⟩ ⟨*deriving* certain dignity from battles fought and won —Richard Llewellyn⟩ ⟨the word *girl* is *derived* from Middle English *girle*⟩ **c :** to acquire, get, or draw (as something pleasant or beneficial) ⟨the satisfaction *derived* from a sense of sharing in creative activities —John Dewey⟩ ⟨the mutual benefits that nations can ~ from trading which flows in both directions —*Lamp*⟩ **d :** ADAPT ⟨a movie *derived* from a novel⟩ **e :** to obtain (a substance) actually or theoretically from a parent substance (as by substitution or hydrolysis) — compare [2]DERIVATIVE 4 **2** *archaic* **:** to divert (as water) from its source or normal course **3 :** to gather or arrive at (as a conclusion) by reasoning and observation: **a :** to obtain inductively ⟨ideas *derived* from nature⟩ **:** INFER **b :** DEDUCE ⟨propositions *derived* from axioms⟩ **4** *archaic* **:** to pass along **:** TRANSMIT **5** *archaic* **:** to cause to come ⟨inconvenience that will be *derived* to them from stopping all imports —Thomas Jefferson⟩ **6 :** to trace the origin, descent, or derivation of ⟨we can ~ English *chauffeur* from French⟩ ⟨~ *toaster* from *toast*⟩ ⟨an early theory *derived* speech from involuntary cries⟩ **7 :** to be descended or formed from ⟨all were probably *derived* from the same ancestral stock —M.F.A. Montagu⟩ **:** be a derivative of ⟨the plural is normally *derived* from the singular⟩ ~ *vi* **1** *archaic* **:** DESCEND **2 :** to have or take origin **:** ORIGINATE **:** STEM, EMANATE **:** come as a derivative — usu. used with *from* ⟨all knowledge ~s from sensations —J.H.Randall⟩ ⟨half of his income ~s from wheat⟩ ⟨the social stratum from which he *derived* —Carl Van Doren⟩ ⟨stories *deriving* from his experiences in Africa⟩ **syn** see SPRING

derived *adj* **1 :** formed or developed out of something else **:** DERIVATIVE **:** reflected or secondary in character **:** not original or primary ⟨the belief that individuals are alone real, that classes and organizations are secondary and *derived* —John Dewey⟩ **2 :** brought from elsewhere **:** not native ⟨*derived* fossils⟩

derived curve *n* **:** the graph of the derivative of a function of one variable whose graph is the given curve — called also *first derived curve*

derived function *n*, *math* **:** the derivative of a given function — called also *first derived function*

derk \ˈderk\ *chiefly Scot var of* DARK

derm \ˈdərm, -ə̄m,-əim\ *n* -S [NL *derma* & *dermis*] **1 :** DERMIS **2 :** SKIN 2a **3 :** CUTICLE 1a

derm- *or* **derma-** *or* **dermo-** *comb form* [NL, fr. Gk *derm-*, *dermo-*, fr. *derma*, fr. *derein* to skin — more at TEAR] **1 :** skin ⟨*derm*algia⟩ ⟨*derma*hemia⟩ ⟨*dermo*skeleton⟩ **2 :** dermal and ⟨*dermo*humeral⟩

-derm \ˌdərm, -ə̄m,-əim\ *n comb form* -S [prob. fr. F *-derme*, fr. Gk *derma*] **:** skin **:** covering **:** integument ⟨blasto*derm*⟩

[1]**der·ma** \ˈdərmə, -ə̄mə,-əimə\ *n* -S [NL, fr. Gk *derma* skin — more at DERM-] **1 :** DERMIS 1 **2 :** the inner part of the skin of which leather is made, the fat cells and tissues determining the character of leather that can be produced

[2]**der·ma** \"\ *n pl but often sing in constr* [Yiddish *derme*, pl. of *darm* intestine, gut, fr. MHG, fr. OHG *darm, daram*; akin to OE *thearm* gut, OFris *therm*, ON *tharmr* gut, Gk *tormos* hole — more at TERM] **:** beef casing — see KISHKE

-der·ma \ˈdərmə, -ə̄mə,-əimə\ *n comb form*, *pl* **-dermas** \-məz\ *or* **-derma·ta** \-məd·ə,-mətə\ [NL, fr. Gk *dermat-*, *derma*] **1 :** skin **:** covering **:** integument ⟨sarco*derma*⟩ **2 :** skin or skin ailment of a (specified) type ⟨sclero*derma*⟩ **3 :** one having a (specified) type of skin — in generic names ⟨Helo*derma*⟩

der·ma·cen·tor \ˈdərməˌsentər, ˌ=='==\ *n*, *cap* [NL, fr. *derm-* + Gk *kentōr* goader, fr. *kentein* to sting, prick, goad] **:** a large widely distributed genus of ornate eyed ticks (family Ixodidae) including a number that attack man and other mammals and several that are vectors of important diseases (as anaplasmosis of cattle, piroplasmosis of dogs, and Rocky Mountain spotted fever of man)

der·mal \ˈdərməl\ *adj* [*derm-* + *-al*] **1 :** of or relating to skin, esp. to the dermis **:** CUTANEOUS **2 :** EPIDERMAL

dermal ossicle *n* **:** a small bone or concretion lying within the skin (as in various reptiles or the extinct ground sloths)

dermal pore *n* **:** one of the minute openings in the surface of a sponge that give access to the incurrent canals **:** OSTIUM

der·ma·nys·sid \ˌdərməˈnisəd\ *adj* [NL *Dermanyssidae*] **:** of or relating to the Dermanyssidae

der·ma·nys·si·dae \ˌ=='nisəˌdē\ *n pl*, *cap* [NL, fr. *Dermanyssus*, type genus + *-idae*] **:** a family of parasitic mites having the chelicerae adapted for piercing and including several economically important forms (as the chicken mite and the tropical rat mite)

der·ma·nys·sus \-ˈnisəs\ *n*, *cap* [NL, fr. *derm-* + *-nyssus* (fr. Gk *nyssein* to prick)] **:** the type genus of Dermanyssidae comprising a number of blood-sucking mites that are parasitic on birds — see CHICKEN MITE

der·map·tera \(ˌ)dərˈmaptərə\ *n pl*, *cap* [NL, fr. *derm-* + *-ptera*] **:** an order of insects consisting of the earwigs and usu. a few related forms parasitic on bats or rats — **der·map·ter·an** \(ˈ)=ˈ=tərən\ *adj or n* — **der·map·ter·ous** \-tərəs\ *adj*

dermasurgery \ˈ==(=)=\ *n* [*derm-* + *surgery*] **:** a branch of embalming that deals with the restoration of mutilated or destroyed features or members

dermat- *or* **dermato-** *comb form* [Gk, fr. *dermat-*, *derma*] **:** skin **:** hide ⟨*dermat*odynia⟩ ⟨*dermato*logy⟩

-der·ma·ta \ˈdərməd·ə, -ə̄m-,-əim-, -ətə\ *n pl comb form* [NL, fr. Gk *dermat-*, *derma*] **:** ones having a (specified) type of skin — in names of taxonomic categories of animals larger than a genus ⟨Sclero*dermata*⟩

der·ma·tit·ic \ˌdərməˈtid·ik, ˌdə̄m-,ˌdəim-, -titik\ *adj* [NL *dermatitis* + E *-ic*] **:** relating to dermatitis

der·ma·ti·tis \ˌ=='tīd·əs, -ītəs\ *n*, *pl* **dermatiti·ses** \-səz\ *or* **dermatit·i·des** \-ˈtid·əˌdēz\ [NL, fr. *dermat-* + *-itis*] **:** inflammation of the skin typically marked by reddening, swelling, oozing, crusting, or scaling

der·ma·to·bia \-ˈtōbēə\ *n*, *cap* [NL, fr. *dermat-* + *-bia*] **:** a genus of botflies whose larvae live under the skin of domestic mammals and sometimes of man in tropical America

der·mat·o·cranium \(ˌ)dərˌmad·ə, ˌdərməd·ə +\ *n* [NL, fr. *dermat-* + *cranium*] **:** the part of the skull that develops in the form of membrane bone — compare CHONDROCRANIUM

der·mat·o·gen \(ˌ)dərˈmad·əjən, -ˌjen, ˈdərməd·ə-\ *n* -S [ISV *dermat-* + *-gen*] **1 :** the outer primary meristem of a plant or plant part that according to the histogen theory gives rise to epidermis **2 :** the outer apical meristem of a root tip — called also PROTODERM

der·mato·glyph·ic \(ˌ)dərˌmad·əˈglifik, ˌdərməd·ə-\ *adj* [back-formation fr. *dermatoglyphics*] **:** of or relating to dermatoglyphics

der·mato·glyph·ics \-ks\ *n pl but sing or pl in constr* [*dermat-* + Gk *glyphein* to carve + E *-ics* — more at CLEAVE] **1 :** skin patterns; *specif* **:** patterns of the specialized skin of the inferior surfaces of the hands and feet **2 :** the science of the study of skin patterns

der·mat·o·graph \(ˌ)dərˈmad·əˌgraf, ˈdərməd·ə-\ *n* [*dermat-* + *-graph*] **:** an instrument for producing markings on the skin: as **a :** a crayon used by surgeons to outline internal organs on the body surface ⟨sketch the outline of the liver with a ~ on the abdominal skin⟩ **b :** a crayon used to test for allergies

der·mat·o·graph·ia \(ˌ)dərˌmad·əˈgrafēə, ˌdərməd·ə'-\ *or* **der·ma·tog·ra·phism** \ˌdərməˈtägrəˌfizəm\ *n* -S [*dermatographia*, NL, fr. *dermat-* + *-graphia* -graphy; *dermatographism* fr. *dermat-* + *-graph* + *-ism*] **:** DERMOGRAPHIA

der·ma·tog·ra·phy \ˌdərməˈtägrəfē\ *n* -ES [ISV *dermat-* + *-graphy*] **:** anatomical description of the skin

der·mat·o·histology \(ˌ)dərˌmad·ə, ˌdərməd·ō +\ *n* [*dermat-* + *histology*] **:** histology of the skin

der·ma·toid \ˈdərməˌtȯid\ *adj* [ISV *dermat-* + *-oid*] **:** resembling skin

der·mat·o·log·ic \(ˌ)dərˌməd·əˈläjik, ˌdərməd·ə'-\ *or* **der·mat·o·log·i·cal** \-jəkəl\ *adj* **:** of or relating to dermatology

der·ma·tol·o·gist \ˌdərməˈtäləjəst\ *n* -S **:** a specialist in dermatology; *usu* **:** a physician practicing in the field of dermatology

der·ma·tol·o·gy \-jē\ *n* -ES [*dermat-* + *-logy*] **:** a branch of science that is concerned with the skin, its structure, functions, and diseases

der·ma·tome \ˈdərməˌtōm\ *n* -S [ISV *derm-* + *-tome*] **1 :** an instrument for cutting skin for use in grafting **2 a :** the lateral wall of a somite from which the dermis is produced **b :** a segmental skin area delimited by nerve supply

der·mat·o·mere \(ˌ)dərˈmad·əˌmi(ə)r, ˈdərməd·ə,-\ *n* -S [ISV *dermat-* + *-mere*] **:** DERMATOME 2

der·ma·tom·ic \ˌdərməˈtämik\ *also* **der·ma·to·mal** \-ˈtōməl\ *or* **der·mat·o·mat·ic** \(ˌ)dərˌmad·əˈmad·ik, ˌdərməd·əˈ-\ *adj* **:** of or relating to a dermatome

der·mat·o·my·ces \(ˌ)dərˌmad·əˈmīˌsēz, ˌdərməd·əˈ-\ *n*, *pl* **dermatomyce·tes** \-ˌmīˈsēd·ēz\ [NL, fr. *dermat-* + *-myces*] **:** DERMATOPHYTE

der·mat·o·my·co·sis \-ˌmīˈkōsəs\ *n*, *pl* **dermatomyco·ses** \-ˌsēz\ [NL, fr. *dermat-* + *mycosis*] **:** a disease of the skin caused by infection with a fungus

der·mat·o·my·o·si·tis \-ˌmīəˈsīd·əs\ *n* [NL, fr. *dermat-* + *myositis*] **:** a chronic inflammation of the skin, subcutaneous tissue, and skeletal muscles of unknown cause

der·ma·to·path·ia \-ˈpathēə\ *also* **der·ma·top·a·thy** \ˌdərməˈtäpəthē\ *n*, *pl* **dermatopathias** *also* **dermatopathies** [NL *dermatopathia*, fr. *dermat-* + *-pathia* -pathy] **:** disease of the skin — **der·mat·o·path·ic** \(ˌ)dərˌmad·əˈpathik, ˌdərməd·əˈ-\ *adj*

der·mat·o·phyte \(ˌ)dərˈmad·əˌfīt, ˈdərməd·ə,-\ *n* -S [ISV *dermat-* + *-phyte*] **:** a fungus parasitic upon the skin or skin derivatives (as hair or nails) of man or lower animals — compare DERMATOMYCOSIS — **der·mat·o·phyt·ic** \(ˌ)dərˌmad·əˈfid·ik, ˌdərməd·əˈ-\ *adj* — **der·mat·o·phy·to·sis** \-ˌfīˈtōsəs\ *n*

der·mat·o·phy·tid \ˌdərˌmad·əˈfīd·əd, ˌdərməd·əˈ-\ *n* -S **:** a skin eruption associated with a fungus infection; *esp* **:** one considered to be due to allergic reaction

der·ma·top·sy \ˈdərməˌtäpsē\ *n* -ES [ISV *dermat-* + *-opsy*] **:** sensitiveness of the skin to light (as in some worms) — **der·ma·top·tic** \ˌ=='täptik\ *adj*

der·ma·to·sclerosis \(ˌ)dərˌmad·ə, ˌdərməd·ə+\ *n*, *pl* **dermatoscleroses** [NL, fr. *dermat-* + *sclerosis*] **:** SCLERODERMA

der·ma·to·sis \ˌdərməˈtōsəs\ *n*, *pl* **dermato·ses** \-ˌsēz\ [NL, fr. *dermat-* + *-osis*] **:** a disease of the skin

der·mat·o·some \(ˌ)dərˈmad·əˌsōm, ˈdərməd·ə,-\ *n* -S [ISV *dermat-* + *-some*; orig. formed as G *dermatosom*] **:** one of the ranked particulate elements joined by cytoplasm that in one theory of cell-wall structure are held to make up the plant cell wall; *broadly* **:** a structural unit of cellulose in a plant cell wall

der·mat·o·tome \-ˌtōm\ *n* -S [*dermat-* + *-tome*] **:** DERMATOME 2

dermatotropic *var of* DERMOTROPIC

-der·ma·tous \ˈdərməd·əs, -ə̄m-,-əim-, -mətəs\ *adj comb form* [NL *-dermata* + E *-ous*] **:** having a (specified) type of skin ⟨sclero*dermatous*⟩

der·mes·tes \dərˈmeˌstēz\ *n*, *cap* [NL, fr. Gk *dermēstēs* worm that eats skin or leather, fr. *derm-* + *-ēstēs* (fr. *esthiein* to eat); akin to Gk *edmenai* to eat — more at EAT] **:** the type genus of Dermestidae — see LARDER BEETLE, MUSEUM BEETLE

[1]**der·mes·tid** \dərˈmestəd\ *adj* [NL *Dermestidae*, fr. *Dermestes*, type genus + *-idae*] **:** of or relating to the Dermestidae

[2]**dermestid** \"\ *n* -S **:** a beetle of the family Dermestidae

der·mes·ti·dae \-təˌdē\ *n pl*, *cap* [NL, fr. *Dermestes*, type genus + *-idae*] **:** a family of small beetles that have clubbed antennae and are very destructive both as larvae and adults to organic material of animal origin (as dried meats, fur, wool, or insect collections)

-der·mia \ˈdərmēə, -ə̄m-,-əim-\ *n comb form* -S [NL, fr. Gk *derma* skin + NL *-ia* — more at DERM-] **:** skin or skin ailment of a (specified) type ⟨pachy*dermia*⟩

der·mic \ˈdərmik\ *adj* [*derm-* + *-ic*] **:** DERMAL

der·mis \ˈdərməs, -ə̄m-,-əim-\ *n* -ES [*-dermis*] **1 :** the sensitive vascular inner mesodermic layer of the skin made up chiefly of white fibrous connective tissue with some smooth muscle and elastic tissue and numerous nerves and sensory receptors — called also *corium*, *cutis* **2 :** the uppermost layer of the thallus of many lichens that consists of one or more layers of irregular flattened hyphal cells with somewhat gelatinous walls

-der·mis \ˌ==\ *n comb form* -ES [LL, fr. Gk, fr. *derma* skin] **:** layer of skin or tissue ⟨endo*dermis*⟩

dermo- — see DERM-

der·mo·blast \ˈdərməˌblast\ *n* -S [ISV *derm-* + *-blast*] **:** dermatomes (sense 2a) as a group

der·mo·branchia *or* **der·mo·branchiata** \ˌdərmə+\ [NL, fr. *derm-* + *branchia*, *-branchiata*] *syn of* NUDIBRANCHIA

der·mo·branchiate \ˌ==+\ *adj* [NL *Dermobranchia* + E *-ate*] **:** NUDIBRANCHIATE

der·moch·e·lys \dərˈmäkələs\ *n*, *cap* [NL, fr. *derm-* + Gk *chelys* tortoise — more at CHELYS] **:** a genus (the type of the family Dermochelidae) of large marine turtles including only the leatherback

der·mo·dermaptera \ˌdərmə+\ [NL, fr. *derm-* + *Dermaptera*] *syn of* DIPLOGLOSSATA

der·mog·e·nys \(ˌ)dərˈmäjənəs\ *n*, *cap* [NL, fr. *derm-* + Gk *genys* jaw, cheek — more at CHIN] **:** a genus of Siamese halfbeaks including one (*D. pusillus*) sometimes kept in a tropical aquarium

der·mo·graph·ia \ˌdərməˈgrafēə\ *or* **der·mog·ra·phism** \(ˌ)dərˈmägrəˌfizəm\ *n* -S [*dermographia*, NL, fr. *derm-* + *-graphia* -graphy; *dermographism* fr. *derm-* + *-graph* + *-ism*] **:** a condition in which pressure or friction on the skin gives rise to a transient raised usu. reddish mark so that a word traced on the skin becomes visible — **der·mo·graph·ic** \ˌdərməˈgrafik\ *adj*

der·moid \ˈdərˌmȯid\ *also* **der·moi·dal** \(ˈ)=ˈ=d°l\ *adj* [*derm-* + *-oid*, *-oidal*] **:** made up of cutaneous elements esp. of ectodermal derivatives ⟨a ~ tumor⟩ **:** resembling skin

dermoid cyst *also* **dermoid** *n* -S **:** a frequently ovarian cystic tumor containing skin and skin derivatives (as hair or teeth)

der·mo·muscular \ˌdərmə+\ *adj* [*derm-* + *muscular*] **1 :** of or relating to both skin and musculature **2 :** combining the function of skin and muscle ⟨certain cells in the body wall of lower invertebrate animals are ~⟩

der·mop·tera \dərˈmäpt(ə)rə\ *n pl*, *cap* [NL, fr. *derm-* + *-ptera*] **:** a small order of eutherian mammals comprising the flying lemurs — **der·mop·ter·an** \(ˈ)=ˈ=t(ə)rən\ *adj or n* — **der·mop·ter·ous** \-t(ə)rəs\ *adj*

der·mo·skeleton \ˌdərmə+\ *n* [*derm-* + *skeleton*] **1 :** EXOSKELETON **2 :** the portion of the vertebrate skeleton that develops as membrane bone

der·mo·tactile \ˌ==+\ *adj* [*derm-* + *tactile*] **:** of or relating to the tactile sensitivity of the skin

der·mo·trop·ic \ˌdərməˈträpik\ *also* **der·mat·o·trop·ic** \(ˌ)dərˈmad·əˌträpik, ˌdərməd·ə,-\ *adj* [*derm-* or *dermato-* + *-tropic*] **:** attracted to, localizing in, or entering by way of the skin ⟨~ viruses⟩ — compare NEUROTROPIC

derms *pl of* DERM

-derms *pl of* -DERM

[1]**dern** \ˈdern, ˈdərn\ *adj* [ME *derne*, fr. OE *dyrne*, *dierne*; akin to OS *derni* secret, OHG *tarni*, L *firmus* firm — more at FIRM] **1** *now chiefly dial* **a :** HIDDEN, SECRET **b :** CRAFTY, UNDERHANDED **2** *now chiefly dial* **:** DREAR, DARK, SOMBER, DIRE **3** *dial Eng* **:** EARNEST, DETERMINED

[2]**dern** \"\ *vb* -ED/-ING/-S [ME *dernen*, fr. OE *dyrnan*; akin to OHG *ternen*, *tarnen* to hide, conceal, OS *dernian*; denominatives fr. the root of OE *dyrne* secret, hidden] *now chiefly Scot* **:** HIDE, CONCEAL

[3]**dern** \ˈdərn, -ə̄n,-əin\ *dial var of* DARN

[1]**der·nier** \ˈdərnēər, (ˈ)dernˈyā\ *adj* [F, fr. OF *derrenier*, fr. *darrain*, *derrein* — more at DARREIN] *archaic* **:** LAST, FINAL

[2]**der·nier** \(ˈ)dernˈyā\ *n* -S [F, fr. *dernier* last] **:** the third of the three columns on a roulette layout on which one may bet and which embraces the numbers 25 to 36 inclusive

der·nier cri \ˌdernˌyāˈkrē\ *n* [F, lit., last cry] **:** the latest or most authoritative thing **:** the last word; *specif* **:** the newest fashion ⟨strapless gowns were the *dernier cri*⟩ **syn** see FASHION

dernier res·sort *or* **dernier re·sort** \-ərāˈzō(ə)r, -rəˈsō-\ *n* [F *dernier ressort*] **:** a last resort or expedient

dero \ˈde(ˌ)rō\ *n*, *cap* [NL] **:** a genus of small aquatic oligochaete worms (family Naididae) having an expanded anal hood from which project two pairs of cylindrical ciliated gills

dero- — see DER-

[1]**der·o·gate** \ˈderəˌgāt, *usu* -ād·+V\ *vb* -ED/-ING/-S [L

derogatus, past part. of *derogare,* fr. *de-* + *rogare* to ask, ask the people about a law — more at RIGHT] *vt* **1** *obs* **:** to annul or repeal in part (as a law or sentence) **:** restrict the force of (a law) **2 :** to make to seem inferior **:** lower in esteem **:** DISPARAGE, DECRY ⟨it is the aim of this paper to ~ a somewhat condescending attitude toward Oriental philosophy that is prevalent among a number of western thinkers —Jack Kaminsky⟩ **3** *archaic* **:** to take away (a part or quality of something) so as to do injury to the whole — used with *from* ~ *vi* **1 :** to place something at a disadvantage or in disesteem esp. by taking part of it away **:** DETRACT — used with *from* ⟨increase the authority of each dominion and not ~ from it —R.G.Menzies⟩ ⟨some are trying to ~ from his reputation as a leader⟩ **2 :** to deviate or go astray (as from a principle or standard) — used with *from* **syn** see DECRY

²der·o·gate \-gət,-ˌgāt\ *adj* [L *derogatus*] *archaic* **:** INFERIOR, DEBASED

derogately *adv, obs* **:** DEROGATORILY

der·o·ga·tion \ˌderəˈgāshən\ *n* -s [ME *derogacioun,* fr. MF or L; MF *derogation,* fr. L *derogation-, derogatio,* fr. *derogatus* + *-ion-, -io* -ion] **1 :** partial repeal (as of a law, contract, treaty) — used with *of* or *to* **2 a :** a taking away, lessening, or detraction esp. of power, reputation, value — used with *of* or *from* ⟨a serious ~ of his influence and prestige⟩ ⟨it is no necessary ~ from his book that the humor is about the humor of alumni magazines and college reunions —Howard M. Jones⟩ **b :** DISPARAGEMENT, DETRIMENT ⟨without ~ to his high rank⟩

de·rog·a·tive \dəˈrägəd·iv *also* ˈderəˌgād·-\ *adj* [ME, fr. MF or LL; MF *derogatif,* fr. LL *derogativus,* fr. L *derogatus* + *-ivus* -ive] **:** tending to derogate — used with *to* or *of*

derogator *n* -s [LL, fr. L *derogatus* + *-or*] *obs* **:** DETRACTOR

de·rog·a·to·ri·ly \dəˌrägəˈtōrəlē, dē¦-, -ór-, -li\ *adv* **:** in a derogatory manner

de·rog·a·to·ri·ness *pronunc at* DEROGATORY + nə̇s\ *n* -ES **:** the quality of being derogatory

de·rog·a·to·ry \də̇ˈrägəˌtōrē, dē-, -ór-, -ri\ *adj* [LL *derogatorius,* fr. L *derogatus* + *-orius* -ory] **1 :** characterized by or tending toward derogation **:** DISPARAGING, DETRACTING, DEGRADING, DEPRECIATORY — used with *to, from,* or *of* ⟨the crude fact of money-making was still regarded as ~ —Edith Wharton⟩ ⟨express his feelings on the tender or emotional side without feeling it ~ to his manhood —Bram Stoker⟩ **2 :** expressive of low estimation or reproach **:** DISDAINFUL ⟨trying to discredit the speaker by making ~ remarks about his appearance⟩ ⟨a child hostile and ~ toward everyone⟩ ⟨few of the Normans who received large estates in England deserve to be called adventurers, in the ~ sense of the word —F.M.Stenton⟩

derogatory clause *n* **:** a clause in a legal document (as a will) making any future altering or canceling document invalid except upon the recital of the clause word for word and its formal revocation

der·o·trem·a·ta \ˌderəˈtremədə, -rēm-\ *n pl, cap* [NL, fr. *der-* + *-tremata*] *in some esp former classifications* **:** a division of tailed amphibians typically retaining gill slits but not external gills when adult and comprising the Cryptobranchidae and Amphiumidae — **der·o·trem·ate** \¦==¦=māt, -ˌmāt\ *or* **der·o·trem·a·tous** \-mədəs\ *adj* — **der·o·treme** \ˈderəˌtrēm\ *n* -s

¹de·rout \(ˈ)dē, də̇+\ *vt* [obs. F *dérouter,* fr. OF *desroter, desrouter,* fr. *des-* de- + *rote, route* troop, band, defeat — more at ROUT (troop)] **:** to rout completely

²derout \"\ *n* [F *déroute,* fr. OF *desrote, desroute,* fr. *desroter, desrouter*] **:** utter defeat **:** ROUT

der·ren·ga·de·ra \(ˌ)deˌreŋgəˈderə\ *n* -s [AmerSp, fr. Sp *derrengar* to injure the back or kidneys, fr. (assumed) VL *derenicare,* fr. L *de-* + *ren* kidney] **:** MAL DE CADERAS

¹der·rick \ˈderik, -rēk\ *n* -s [after *Derick* (first name unknown) *fl* ab1600 hangman at Tyburn, England] **1** *obs* **a :** HANGMAN **b :** GALLOWS **2 :** any of various hoisting apparatus employing a tackle rigged at the end of a beam: as **a** *obs* **:** a tackle rigged at the outer quarter of a mizzen yard **b :** a spar standing on end and carrying at the upper end a hoisting tackle, the upper end being also secured by guys sometimes in such a manner as to permit adjustments of the angle of the spar to the horizontal **c :** a crane consisting of a pivoting mast having fastened to its lower end a boom carrying at its outer end a hoisting tackle, the outer end also being secured by a tackle to the head of the mast so as to permit raising and lowering of the end of the boom **d :** a fixed arm or bracket projecting from a wall with a hoisting tackle at its end (as over a warehouse door) **3 a :** the framework or tower over a deep drill hole (as that of an oil well) for supporting the tackle for boring or for hoisting and lowering **b :** a tall three-legged staging erected to support a hoisting crane (as in building construction)

derrick 3a

²derrick \", *esp in pres part* -rək\ *vt* -ED/-ING/-S **:** to hoist, convey, or load by means of a derrick

derricking *adj* **:** operating like a derrick in the raising and lowering of the jib ⟨a ~ crane⟩

der·rick·man \-mən, -ˌman\ *n, pl* **derrickmen 1 :** a worker who operates a derrick **2 :** a member of a crew that rigs oil-well derricks and assists with the drilling of wells

derrick post *n* **:** KING POST 2

der·ri·en·gue \ˌderēˈeŋˌgā\ *n* -s [MexSp] **:** a highly fatal paralytic disease of cattle and sometimes other livestock that occurs in the Pacific coast states of Mexico and is caused by a virus related to or identical with that of rabies and prob. transmitted by the bite of vampire bats

¹der·rière \¦derē¦e(ə)r, (ˈ)der¦ye-, -eə\ *adj* [F, fr. OF *deriere,* fr. L *de retro* from the back] **:** BACK, BEHIND — used in ballet of a movement, the execution of a step, or motion of arms or legs

²der·riere *or* **der·rière** \"\ *n* -s [F, fr. *derrière,* adj.] **:** BUTTOCKS, RUMP ⟨a wide tuck starts three inches below the pocket flaps and dips well below the ~ —Lois Long⟩ ⟨you should pull up with your chest, in with your diaphragm, and down with your ~ —Maribel Y. Vinson⟩

der·ring-do \ˌderiŋˈdü, -rēŋ-\ *n, pl* **derrings-do** [alter. of ME *dorring don, durring don* daring to do (taken as a n.), fr. pres. part. of *dorren, durren* to dare + *don* to do — more at DARE, DO] **1 :** daring action **:** DARING, COURAGE, BRAVERY ⟨the first airmail flight — a deed of *derring-do* by an army pilot —*Time*⟩ **2 :** BRAVADO ⟨the days of *derring-do* when swords flashed in rescue of beautiful highborn maidens —J.D. Hart⟩

der·rin·ger \ˈderənjə(r)\ *n* -s [after Henry *Deringer,* 19th cent. Am. inventor] **:** a short-barreled pocket pistol

der·ris \ˈderəs\ *n* [NL, fr. Gk, leather covering, skin, fr. *derein* to skin — more at TEAR] **1** *cap* **:** a large genus of tropical Old World shrubs and woody vines (family Leguminosae) including several that are used as sources of native fish poisons and arrow poisons and commercially as sources of rotenone and related insecticidal substances **2** -ES **:** any plant of the genus *Derris* (esp. *D. elliptica*) **3** -ES **:** a preparation of derris roots and stems that contains rotenone and rotenoids and is esp. important as an insecticide

¹der·ry \ˈderē, -ri\ *adj, usu cap* [by shortening] **:** LONDONDERRY

²derry \"\ *n* -ES [origin unknown] *Austral* **:** DISLIKE, AVERSION — usu. used with *on* ⟨her father had an unaccountable ~ on the family⟩

de·ru·ta \dəˈrüdə\ *n, usu cap* [fr. *Deruta,* village in Perugia province, Italy, where it is produced] **:** an Italian majolica ware

der·vish \ˈdərvish, -əv-,-əiv-, -vēsh *sometimes* ˈderv- *or* ˈdeəv-\ *n* -ES [Turk *derviş,* lit., beggar, fr. Per *darvēsh*] **1 :** a member of any Muslim religious fraternity of monks or mendicants noted for its forms of devotional exercises (as group repetition of religious formulas or concerted bodily movements often leading to a kind of trance or ecstasy) — often used with a qualifier such as *howling, whirling, dancing;* compare FAKIR **2 :** something that whirls or dances with or as if with the abandon of a dervish ⟨the most blinding of the snow ~*es* that whirled across him —W.V.T.Clark⟩ ⟨a very ~ dance of fury —Brendan Behan⟩

der·vish·hood \-sh,hu̇d\ *n* -s **:** the status of or the condition of being a dervish

der·vish·ism \-sh,izəm\ *n* -s **:** the principles or practices of the dervishes

des *pl of* DE

des- *prefix* [F *dés-,* fr. OF *des-* — more at DE-] **1 :** DE- 1 — esp. before vowels ⟨*des*amidate⟩ **2 :** DE- 6 — esp. before vowels ⟨*des*iodo-⟩ ⟨*des*oxy-⟩

des *abbr* **1** deserted; deserter; desertion **2** design; designed **3** desired

desa *also* **des·sa** \ˈdesə\ *n* -s [Jav *désa,* fr. Skt *deśa* place, country] **:** a village community in Java, Bali, or Madura formerly relatively independent

de·sa·cral·i·za·tion \(ˌ)dēˌsakrələ̇ˈzāshən\ *n* -s **:** the act of desacralizing or state of being desacralized

de·sa·cral·ize \(ˈ)dē¦sakrəˌlīz\ *vt* -ED/-ING/-S [*de-* + *sacral* + *-ize*] **:** to divest ceremonially of supernatural qualities or a taboo and render nonsacred

de·salinization *also* **de·salination** \(ˈ)dē+\ *n* -s [*de-* + *salinization* or *salination*] **:** removal of salt (as from water) **:** reduction of the salt content (as of soil by leaching)

de·salt \(ˈ)dē+\ *vt* [*de-* + *salt* (n.)] **:** to remove salt from (as sea water) **:** DEIONIZE, DEMINERALIZE — **de·salter** \"+\ *n* -s

desamidate *var of* DEAMIDATE

desamination *var of* DEAMINATION

de·sanctify \(ˈ)dē+\ *vt* [*de-* + *sanctify*] **:** to divest of sanctification

de·sand \(ˈ)dē+\ *vt* [*de-* + *sand* (n.)] **:** to remove sand from

de·sargues's theorem \dāˈzärgz-\ *n, usu cap D* [after Gérard *Desargues* †1662 Fr. mathematician] **:** a theorem in geometry: if the junction lines of corresponding vertices of two triangles are concurrent the junction points of the corresponding sides lie on the same straight line, the converse also being true

de·saturate \(ˈ)dē+\ *vb* [*de-* + *saturate*] *vt* **:** to cause to become unsaturated ⟨the polarizer helps remove scattered light that ~*s* color in the picture —*Eastman Kodak Monthly Abstract Bull.*⟩ ~ *vi* **:** to become unsaturated — **de·saturation** \"+\ *n*

desc *abbr* descendant

de·scale \(ˈ)dē+\ *vt* [*de-* + *scale* (n.)] **:** to free from scale

des·ca·mi·sa·do \ˌdeˌskaməˈsä(ˌ)dō\ *n* -s [Sp, fr. *descamisado* poor, fr. *des-* dis- (fr. L *dis-*) + *camisa* shirt + *-ado* -ate (fr. L *-atus*) — more at CAMISA] **1 a :** an extreme liberal of the Spanish revolution of 1820–23 **b :** a violent revolutionist **2** [AmerSp, fr. Sp] **:** an Argentine worker esp. when poor and underprivileged

¹des·cant \ˈdeˌskant, -kaa(ə)nt\ *or* **dis·cant** \ˈdiˌ-\ *n* -s [ME *dyscant,* fr. ONF & ML; ONF *descant,* fr. ML *discantus,* fr. L *¹dis-* + *cantus* song — more at CHANT] **1 a :** a melody or counterpoint sung above the plainsong of the tenor **b :** the art of composing or improvising contrapuntal part music; *also* **:** the music so composed or improvised **c :** the upper voice (as soprano, treble) in part music **d :** a superimposed counterpoint to a hymn tune or other simple melody sung typically by some or all of the sopranos **2 :** a song or strain of melody ⟨the birds in vain their amorous ~ join —Thomas Gray⟩ **3 a :** a musical prelude in which a theme is varied **b :** discourse or comment on a theme felt to resemble variations on a musical air **:** OBSERVATION, REMARK ⟨provides a noble ~ on the theme of our human mystery —*Times Lit. Supp.*⟩ **4** *obs* **a :** variation from what is customary or an instance of it **b :** carping criticism **5 :** an extended and often warmly enthusiastic expression of one's convictions or interests

²des·cant \ˈdeˌskant, də̇sˈ-,deˈs-, -kaa(ə)nt\ *vi* -ED/-ING/-S **1 a :** to sing or play a descant **b :** SING, WARBLE **2 :** to discuss discerningly and at considerable length on a subject evoking one's keen interest ⟨on that favorite poet of mine, Sir Thomas Wyat, I ~*ed* in a former lecture —A.T.Quiller-Couch⟩ ⟨~*ing* on her love of flowers, a passion that was among her prettiest originalities —Edith Sitwell⟩ ⟨the temptation to ~ in detail on tidbits —R.T.House⟩ **:** DILATE — used with *on* or *upon* **syn** see DISCOURSE

des·cant·er *pronunc at* ²DESCANT +ə(r)\ *n* -s **:** one that descants

des·cant·ist *pronunc at* ¹DESCANT +ə̇st\ *n* -s **:** one proficient in descant

descant recorder *n, chiefly Brit* **:** SOPRANO RECORDER

descant viol *n* **1 :** TREBLE VIOL **2 :** PARDESSUS DE VIOLE

des·cartes's rule of signs \(ˈ)dā¦kärts-, -kàts-\ *usu cap D* [after René *Descartes* †1650 Fr. philosopher and mathematician] **:** a rule of algebra: in an algebraic equation with real coefficients, $F(x) = 0$, arranged according to powers of x, the number of positive roots cannot exceed the number of variations in the signs of the coefficients of the various powers and the difference between the number of positive roots and the number of variations in the signs of the coefficients is even

des·cart·ian \(ˈ)dā¦kärd·ēən\ *adj, usu cap* [R. *Descartes* + E *-ian*] **:** CARTESIAN

des·ce·met's membrane \(ˈ)deˈsmə¦āz, ¦desə¦m\ *n, usu cap D* [after Jean *Descemet* †1810 Fr. anatomist] **:** a transparent highly elastic apparently structureless membrane lined with endothelium and covering the inner surface of the cornea

de·scend \də̇ˈsend, dēˈ-\ *vb* -ED/-ING/-S [ME *descenden,* fr. OF *descendre,* fr. L *descendere,* fr. *de-* + *-scendere* (fr. *scandere* to climb) — more at SCAN] *vi* **1 :** to go or come down: **a :** to pass from a higher place or spatial level to a lower one **:** move downward ⟨these fish winter up the river . . . and ~ to the sea . . . in the spring —*Biol. Abstracts*⟩ ⟨the river ~*s* 18 feet in one mile⟩ ⟨the paper ~*s* from one roller onto another⟩ **b :** to appear or enter from above or from a spiritual realm ⟨to her it seemed that a god had ~*ed* from the blue sky personally to aid her —Charles Beadle⟩ ⟨he felt a great being ~*ing* into him and strengthening him —W.B.Yeats⟩; *specif* **:** to settle down like a blanket or curtain ⟨the sound that irresistibly you make when death is about to ~ —F.M.Ford⟩ **c** *archaic* **:** to withdraw or retreat from social intercourse and seclude oneself in personal or mental absorption **d** *of the testes of a mammal* **:** to pass from the abdominal cavity into the scrotum **2 :** to pass in discussion from what in logical order precedes or from what is the more comprehensive or universal ⟨ascend to causes, ~ to consequences⟩ ⟨the writer ~*s* from the general to the particular —*Times Lit. Supp.*⟩ **3 a :** to come down or spring from a stock or source **:** ORIGINATE, DERIVE ⟨the family ~*ed* from Scotch-Irish immigrants who came to America in the 18th century⟩ ⟨historians report that he ~*ed* from an ancient family of noble lineage⟩ **b :** to pass by inheritance ⟨that kingship was divinely ordained to ~ according to strict hereditary principles —J.H.Plumb⟩ ⟨heirlooms which have ~*ed* in families since the original Pennsylvania Dutch immigrants arrived —V.R.Tortora⟩ **c :** to pass by transmission **:** take origin or pattern or acquire character from a precursor ⟨songs ~*ed* from early ballads⟩ ⟨if, as some scholars believe, Greek liturgical music ~*s* from the hymns to the Olympian gods —*N.Y.Times*⟩ **4 :** to incline, lead, or extend downward **:** form or follow a downgrade ⟨the coastal mountains ~*ed* precipitously to the very edge of the Pacific —R.A.Billington⟩ ⟨the road ~*s* to the flatland⟩ **5 a :** to swoop or pounce down or make a sudden attack — usu. used with *on* or *upon* ⟨the plague ~*ed* upon them⟩ ⟨if the enemy ~*ed* on his country⟩ **b :** to converge or materialize as if from above with disconcerting abruptness or in formidable array — used with *on* or *upon* ⟨one evening the police ~*ed* quietly, without warning, on a dozen or so drive-in taverns —Green Peyton⟩ ⟨over a hundred newspaper reporters from all over America ~*ed* upon this amazed little southern town to cover the trial —R.W.Murray⟩; *also* **:** to make a startling or exciting visitation ⟨the most famous visitors, licit or otherwise, to ~ on the island —Horace Sutton⟩ **c :** to pour down or in with beneficent effect — used with *on* or *upon* ⟨then fame and royalties ~*ed* upon him —E.A. Weeks⟩ **6 :** to proceed in a sequence or gradation from higher to lower or from more remote to nearer or more recent ⟨this list is arranged in ~*ing* order of the reliability of the information —R.N.Denney⟩ ⟨we shall expect to find the curves of art and spiritual fervor ascending and ~*ing* together —Clive Bell⟩ **7 a :** to sink in status or dignity **:** demean or degrade oneself by indulgence in pettiness or unworthy behavior **:** STOOP ⟨ashamed of myself for having ~*ed* to a kind of wheedling —Kenneth Roberts⟩ ⟨his successor, after failing to dominate, ~*ed* to reckless abuse —Raymond Moley⟩ **b :** to worsen and sink in condition or estimation **:** become degraded **:** DEGENERATE ⟨the family ~*ed* from comparative prosperity to poverty⟩ ⟨her autobiography ~*s* to a dragging pedestrianism⟩ ⟨his attacks ~ to a level almost indistinguishable from personal character assassination —Martin Gardner⟩ **c :** to pass from higher to lower musical notes or tones ~ *vt* **1** *obs* **:** to cause to descend **:** bring down ⟨power to raise some and ~ others⟩ **2 a :** to pass, move, or climb down or down along ⟨~*ed* the steps with senile deliberation —Arnold Bennett⟩ **b :** to journey downstream along (a stream) or toward the foot of (a lake) **3 :** to extend down along ⟨a raw scar ~*s* the side of the mountain showing the course of a slide⟩ ⟨vertical tucks ~*ing* the bodice —Lois Long⟩

syn DISMOUNT, ALIGHT: these have in common a sense of getting or coming down from a height. One DESCENDS when one goes or climbs down a slope or incline, as of a mountain, hill, ladder, stair, tree, and so on. One DISMOUNTS by getting off (the back of a horse or other ridable animal, a bicycle, motorcycle, or similar vehicle). One ALIGHTS when one dismounts with a certain springing lightness or grace or when one gets down from a carriage, gets out of a car or off a plane.

de·scend·ance *also* **de·scend·ence** \-ndən(t)s\ *n* -s [MF *descendance,* fr. OF, fr. *descendre* + *-ance*] **1 :** descent from a particular ancestor **2 :** derivation from predecessors

de·scend·an·cy *or* **de·scend·en·cy** \-dənsē, -si\ *n* -ES [F *descendance* (fr. OF) + E *-y*] *archaic* **:** lineal descent

¹de·scend·ant *also* **de·scend·ent** \-dənt\ *adj* [MF & L; MF *descendant,* fr. L *descendent-, descendens,* pres. part. of *descendere*] **1 :** DESCENDING 1 **2 :** proceeding from an ancestor or source ⟨eighth in the ~ line from the original immigrant⟩

²descendant *also* **descendent** \"\ *n* -s [F & L; *descendant,* fr. L *descendent-, descendens,* fr. *descendent-, descendens,* pres. part.] **1 a :** one that is descended from another or from a common stock ⟨the ~*s* of King David⟩ ⟨the several cultivated ~*s* of the native persimmon⟩ — distinguished from *ancestor, ascendant* **b :** a lineal or collateral blood relative usu. of a later generation — compare ISSUE **2 :** something that derives its character directly from a precursor or prototype ⟨the vertebral column is the altered ~ of the notochord⟩; *esp* **:** an offshoot from an antecedent practice or idea ⟨the modern signet ring is a ~ of the scarab ring—Elizabeth W. King⟩ ⟨the maypole dance is said to be a ~ of an ancient fertility dance⟩ **3 :** a follower or disciple who shows close adherence to the principles and methods of an earlier master in some literary, learned, or artistic specialty ⟨though not all the ~*s* of Kant agree —J.G.Gray⟩ — **in the descendant** *also* **on the descendant :** DECLINING, WANING

de·scen·den·tal \¦dēˌsen¦dentᵊl\ *adj* [¹*descendent* + *-al* (as in *transcendental*)] **:** EMPIRICAL, POSITIVISTIC — opposed to *transcendental* — **de·scen·den·tal·ism** \¦=¦=¦==ˌizəm\ *n* -s — **de·scen·den·tal·ist** \-ə̇st\ *n* -s — **de·scen·den·tal·is·tic** \¦=¦=¦==¦istik\ *adj*

¹descender *n* -s [ME, fr. MF *descendre* to descend — more at DESCEND] *law, obs* **:** DESCENT **:** title of descent

²de·scend·er \də̇ˈsendə(r), dēˈ-\ *n* -s [*descend* + *-er*] **1 :** one that descends ⟨the solitary ~ from the train —James Schuyler⟩ **2 a :** the part of a lowercase letter (as q, p, y, *f*) that is lower than the lowest part of an x-height letter (as o, a, e); *also* **:** a corresponding short tail to a letter whose lower limit does not exceed or markedly exceed the lower limit of an x-height letter **b :** a descending letter or character (as g and ;); *also* **:** the descending part of a descending character

de·scend·ibil·i·ty \=ˌ=dəˈbilədē\ *n* -ES **:** the property or condition of being descendible

de·scend·ible \=ˈ=dəbəl\ *adj* [ME *descendable,* fr. MF, fr. *descendre* to descend + *-able*] **1 :** descending or being capable of descending from an ancestor to an heir **:** DEVISABLE **2 :** admitting descent ⟨a downgrade safely ~ only with tire chains⟩

de·scend·ing \ˈdēˌsendiŋ, də̇sˈs-\ *adj* **1 :** that descends **:** moving or directed downward ⟨following are the amounts contributed by classes in ~ order⟩ ⟨does not distinguish ascending and ~ lineal relatives —G.M.Foster⟩ ⟨~ infection from the kidney —*Therapeutic Notes*⟩ ⟨the ~ interval of the minor third occurs with special prominence and frequency —*Amer. Guide Series: Minn.*⟩ **2 :** having a descender ⟨a ~ letter⟩ **3** *heraldry* **:** in a head-downward position ⟨a dolphin ~⟩

descending aorta *n* **:** the part of the aorta from the arch to its bifurcation that passes downward in the thoracic and abdominal cavities

descending diphthong *n* **:** FALLING DIPHTHONG

descending line *n* **:** the portion of a line of direct descent that represents descendants of a given individual — compare CONSANGUINITY 1

de·scend·ing·ly *adv* **:** in a downward direction; *specif* **:** southward in the sky

descending node *n* **:** the node passed as an astronomical body goes south

descending raceme *n* **:** a scorpioid cyme

descending rhythm *n* **:** FALLING RHYTHM

descends *pres 3d sing of* DESCEND

de·scen·sion \də̇ˈsenchən, dēˈ-\ *n* -s [ME *descensioun,* fr. MF *descension,* fr. L *descension-, descensio,* fr. *descensus* (past part. of *descendere* to descend) + *-ion-, -io* -ion — more at DESCEND] **1** *archaic* **:** downward motion or direction **2 :** the part of the zodiac in which in astrology a planet's influence is thought to be least — opposed to *exaltation* **3** *obs* **:** descent from an ancestor **4 :** descent from rank, station, or prosperity **:** ABASEMENT, CONDESCENSION

de·scen·sion·al \-chənᵊl,-chnəl\ *adj* **1 :** relating to descension **:** moving or directed downward **2 :** involving or produced by processes of disintegration of rock and aggregation of particles in beds ⟨sand produced by the disintegration of granite is a ~ deposit⟩

de·scen·sion·ist \-ch(ə)nə̇st\ *n* -s **:** one who holds the descension theory

descension theory *n* **:** the theory that ore deposits have been formed of material carried down in solution from above

de·scen·sive \-n(t)siv\ *adj* [*descension* + *-ive*] **:** tending to descend

de·scen·sus \-n(t)səs\ *n* -ES [NL, fr. L, *descent,* fr. *descensus,* past part. of *descendere*] *med* **:** DESCENT, PROLAPSE

¹de·scent \də̇ˈsent, dēˈ-\ *n* -s [ME, fr. MF *descente,* fr. *descendre* to descend — more at DESCEND] **1 :** the act or process of descending from a higher to a lower level, rank, or state ⟨a parachute ~⟩ ⟨during their ~ of the ski run⟩ ⟨some thirty-two separate rapids and cataracts in its final furious ~ —Tom Marvel⟩ ⟨~ by chromatic intervals⟩ ⟨ascent and ~ between the physical and spiritual worlds —*Times Lit. Supp.*⟩ **2 a :** a decline or comedown in station, respectability, or living conditions ⟨the ~ to being junior partners of the newcomer to world power —D.W.Brogan⟩ ⟨~ of the family to actual shabbiness⟩ **b :** a stepping down or stooping to an inferior level (as of intellectual elevation, dignity, self-respect) ⟨look around among my books for a further ~ from philosophy to literature —O.W.Holmes †1935⟩ ⟨~ from self-justification to self-deception⟩ ⟨a sudden ~ . . . from the sublimity of his highfalutin critical terminology —*Times Lit. Supp.*⟩ **c** *logic* **:** passage from the more general to the more particular **3 a :** derivation from an ancestor **:** BIRTH ⟨only three alternatives are known, namely, patrilineal, matrilineal, or bilateral ~, and every culture incorporates one of these rules or some combination thereof —G.P.Murdock⟩; *usu* **:** the established connection between an individual and his progenitors or the stock from which he is descended **:** EXTRACTION, LINEAGE ⟨of Pilgrim stock, eighth in ~ through his mother from a governor of the colony⟩ ⟨people of Polish ~⟩ **b** *obs* **:** DESCENDANT ⟨our ~ . . . born to certain woe, devoured by death —John Milton⟩ **c :** transmission or devolution of an estate by inheritance usu. but not necessarily in the descending line **d :** the fact or process of originating by generation from an ancestral stock (as a species or genus) **e :** the shaping or development in nature and character by transmission from a source **:** DERIVATION, ORIGINATION ⟨the home of an active legal science which could trace a faint but sure ~ from Roman law —R.W.Southern⟩ ⟨there was a line of ~ from these ideas to the Fascist movement —Cecil Sprigge⟩ ⟨native American voices tracing their ~ from the Know-Nothings of yesterday —T.H.White b.1915⟩ **4 a :** an inclination downward **:** an inclined or sloping surface : DECLIVITY ⟨it appears that the water is broken nowhere by striking against the rocks, and that therefore the ~ is perpendicular —Anthony Trollope⟩ **b :** a descending way (as a downgrade or stairway) **c** *obs* **:** the lowest part ⟨from the extremest upward of thy head to the ~ and dust below thy foot —Shak.⟩ **5 a :** a sudden disconcerting appearance (as for a visit) ⟨unprepared for the ~ of his in-laws⟩ **b :** a hostile raid or predatory assault ⟨the ~ of the Assyrians upon Israel⟩ ⟨~ of the locusts⟩ **6 :** a step downward in a scale of gradation; *specif* **:** one generation in an ancestral line or genealogical scale ⟨his pedigree shows 11 ~*s*⟩ **7 :** a former method of distillation in which the material was heated in a vessel having its outlet underneath so that the vapors produced were forced to descend

²de·scent \(')dē¦sent\ *vt* [*de-* + *scent* (n.)] **:** to rid of scent

descent cast *n, English law* **:** the descent of an estate to an heir by the death of one who held it adversely to the real owner which prior to 1833 barred the latter's right of entry so that he could recover only by suing — compare ADVERSE POSSESSION

des·champ·sia \də'shampsēə\ *n, cap* [NL, fr. Jean L. A. Loiseleur-*Deslongchamps* †1849 Fr. botanist + NL *-ia*] **:** a genus of perennial grasses of cold and temperate regions having loose or compact panicles with 2-flowered spikelets

des·cha·pelles coup \¦dāshə¦pel(z)-\ *n* [after Guillaume *Deschapelles* †1847 Fr. authority on whist] **:** the lead of a high card (as a king) in whist or bridge in the hope that an opponent will win it and make the next-higher card good for an entry in one's partner's hand

des·cloi·zite \dā'klōi,zīt, də'-\ *n* -s [F *descloizite*, fr. A.L.O.L. *Des Cloizeaux* †1897 Fr. mineralogist + F *-ite*] **:** a mineral (ZnCu)Pb(VO₄)(OH) consisting of a basic vanadate chiefly of lead and zinc and varying in color from cherry red to brown and black (hardness 3.5, sp. gr. 5.9–6.2)

des·cort \de'skȯ(ə)r\ *n* -s [F, fr. OF, lit., discord — more at DISCORD] **1 :** a medieval French lyric in which the stanzas are unlike **2 :** a poem in old Provençal literature with stanzas in different languages

des·cri·able \də'skrīəbəl, dē'-\ *adj* [*descry* + *-able*] **:** capable of being descried

des·cri·al \-ī(ə)l\ *n* -s [*descry* + *-al*] **:** the act or process of descrying; *esp* **:** discovery or disclosure of something recondite or to be held secret

de·scrib·abil·i·ty \də,skrībə'biləd·ē, dē,-, -ətē, -i\ *n* -ES **:** capability of being described

de·scrib·able \=ˈ=bəbəl\ *adj* **:** capable of being described — **de·scrib·ably** \-bəblē, -li\ *adv*

de·scribe \də'skrīb, dē'-\ *vt* -ED/-ING/-S [L *describere*, fr. *de-* + *scribere* to write — more at SCRIBE] **1 :** to represent by words written or spoken for the knowledge or understanding of others: **a :** to communicate verbally from the results of personal observation an account of salient identifying features of (something existing in space) ⟨unable to find words to ~ the mountain scene⟩ ⟨in 1886 a Boston surgeon . . . *described* the condition now called appendicitis —Morris Fishbein⟩; *specif* **:** to observe and narrate simultaneously with the action (as for radio or television) ⟨*describing* a football game to an unseeing audience⟩ **b :** to transmit a mental image, an impression, or an understanding of the nature and characteristics of (something immaterial) **:** present distinctly by means of properties and qualities ⟨the unique character of the artistic quality of a work . . . cannot be defined or even *described* —T.M. Greene⟩ ⟨there were so many things he wanted to ~ —James Joyce⟩ ⟨like Mark Twain he exhibits rather than ~*s* his characters: their speech is a portrait —Marvin Lowenthal⟩ **c :** to make clear by expounding esp. in a minute way ⟨had traveled in the principal countries of the world and *described* what it was like to live in a police state —Victor Boesen⟩ ⟨~ the life of the past from the various scraps of the fossil forms —W.E.Swinton⟩ **d :** to distinguish by a definitive label or other designation or by an individualizing phrase or similitude — used with *as* and a complement ⟨few doctors would ~ themselves as scientists⟩ ⟨the State is often rightly *described* as a machine: its total effect is inhuman —Herbert Read⟩ **e :** to convey an image or notion of **:** EXPRESS, SIGNIFY, DENOTE ⟨we have indicated that jealousy ~*s* a state of tension among various interests of the personality —Abram Kardiner⟩ ⟨while the natural sciences grow more modest in admitting that their laws ~ only probabilities —Reinhold Niebuhr⟩ **2** *obs* **:** to write down **:** INSCRIBE, TRANSCRIBE **3 :** to represent by a drawing, figure, model, or picture **:** PORTRAY, DELINEATE ⟨and when the curves thus brilliantly drawn ~ vividly some object in life toward which we have pleasing associations we get a complex pleasure —Roger Fry⟩ **4 :** to mark out **:** trace or traverse the outline of ⟨each planet ~*s* an ellipse with the sun in one focus —S.F.Mason⟩ ⟨while he *described* a big smooth arc with the muleta —Barnaby Conrad⟩ ⟨butted amidships he *described* a somersault backward⟩ **5** *obs* **:** to portion out **:** DISTRIBUTE ⟨ye shall therefore ~ the land into seven parts —Josh 18:6 (AV)⟩ **6** *archaic* **:** to discover by observation **:** ESPY, PERCEIVE **syn** see RELATE

de·scrib·er \-bə(r)\ *n* -s **1 :** one that describes **2** *Brit* **:** an instrument giving details about trains moving or scheduled to move between given points

descried *past of* DESCRY

des·cri·er \də'skrī(ə)r, dē'-, -īə\ *n* -s **:** one that descries

descries *pres 3d sing of* DESCRY

de·script \də'skript, (')dē¦s-\ *adj* [L *descriptus*, past part. of *describere*] **1** *archaic* **:** DESCRIBED **2** *archaic* **:** INSCRIBED

descripta *pl of* DESCRIPTUM

de·scrip·tion \də'skripshən, dē'-\ *n* -s [ME *descripcioun*, fr. MF or L; MF *description*, fr. L *description-, descriptio*, fr. *descriptus* + *-ion-, -io* -ion] **1 :** the act or an instance of describing: as **a :** a describing or a representation produced by a describing of something material or immaterial ⟨~ of things is a mode of classification which in turn furnishes material for a more general classification —V.F.Lenzen⟩ ⟨the meticulous ~*s* of the rocks of each of the Paleozoic systems —*Amer. Jour. of Science*⟩ ⟨reading a ~ of a murderer and looking at his picture both enable one to say "so that's what he's like" —J.M.Shorter⟩; *specif* **:** composition intended primarily to present to the mind or imagination graphically and in detail a unit of objective or subjective experience (as a scene, person, sensation, emotion) — used in textbooks in distinguishing a separate literary genre; compare EXPOSITION ⟨it is the purpose of such ~*s* that explains why their typical merits and demerits are what they are — namely: exactness, minuteness, accuracy, detail, fullness, sketchiness, misleadingness —S.E.Toulmin & K. Baier⟩ **b :** a statement of the properties of a thing or its relations to other things serving to identify it **:** a univocal designation of an object by means of a phrase beginning with *the* or *a* (as "the present king of the Belgians" or "a house next to my office") **c :** a descriptive statement or account — often contrasted with *analysis* and *valuation* **d :** an individualizing or identifying designation (as a name, label, epithet) ⟨the ~ "wax" is a misnomer since the substance is a fat —J.N.Goldsmith⟩ **2** *obs* **a :** INSCRIPTION **b :** ENROLLMENT **3 :** kind or character esp. as determined by salient features ⟨each state may still confer them upon an alien, or . . . upon any class or of persons —R.B.Taney⟩ ⟨opposed to any tax of any radical a ~⟩ **4** *obs* **:** pictorial representation **5 a :** a tracing out of a geometrical figure **b :** a traversing of a course ⟨the rocket's ~ of a high arching curve⟩ **6 :** a specification of the boundaries of a piece of land with sufficient accuracy for legal purposes (as in preparing a deed of transfer) **syn** see TYPE

de·scrip·tion·ist \-sh(ə)nəst\ *n* -s **1 :** one proficient in description **2 :** DESCRIPTIVIST

de·scrip·tion·less \-shənləs\ *adj* **:** being without description

de·scrip·tio per·so·nae \də'skripshē,ōpə(r)'sō(,)nē\ *n* [NL, description of the person] **:** matter merely descriptive of the persons of the parties and not essential to the validity of a legal document — compare DESIGNATIO PERSONAE

¹de·scrip·tive \də'skriptiv, dē'-, -tēv *also* -təv\ *adj* [LL *descriptivus*, fr. L *descriptus* + *-ivus* -ive] **1 :** serving to describe **:** characterized by description **:** representational through presentation of observed facts ⟨a minute anatomical and generally ~ account of the large fulvous orangutan —E.A.Poe⟩ ⟨outjutting formations have been given ~ names: the Devil's Chair is 80 feet high —*Amer. Guide Series: Minn.*⟩ ⟨purely ~ poetry —Yvor Winters⟩ — distinguished from *critical, evaluative,* and *theoretical* **2 a :** referring to, constituting, or concerned with empirical things or events or with their parts, characteristics, or functions ⟨~ expressions⟩ ⟨~ disciplines⟩ **b :** factually grounded or informative rather than normative, prescriptive, emotive, aprioristic, or analytical ⟨~ judgments⟩ ⟨~ theories⟩ ⟨that this meaning shall be called "~" when the responses evoked are cognitions and shall be called "emotive" when the responses evoked are attitudes —Asher Moore⟩ **3 a** *of a modifying word* **:** expressing the quality, kind, or condition of what is denoted by the modified term ⟨*hot* in "hot water" and *sick* in "a sick man" are ~ adjectives⟩ — distinguished from *limiting* **b** *of a modifier, esp a clause* **:** NONRESTRICTIVE **c** *of a compound* **:** belonging to the karmadharaya class **4 :** characterized by or connected with description of the structure of a language at a particular time usu. with rigorous exclusion of historical and comparative judgments ⟨~ linguistics⟩ ⟨~ grammar⟩ ⟨a ~ study⟩ — compare COMPARATIVE 4a **5 :** characterized by kinship name classes that apply in part only to lineal relatives (as grandfather, father, son, grandchild) and in part only to collateral relatives (as uncle, cousin, nephew) regardless of the sex of the connecting relatives ⟨regarded most European systems as ~ and those of primitive peoples as classificatory —R.H.Lowie⟩ — compare CLASSIFICATORY — **de·scrip·tive·ly** \-təvlē, -li\ *adv* — **de·scrip·tive·ness** \-təvnəs\ *n* -ES

²descriptive \"\ *n* -s **:** a distinctive word, phrase, or sentence applied to a particular product in advertising

descriptive anatomy *n* **:** anatomy dealing with the character, form, size, and position of organs and parts

descriptive bibliography *n* **:** a bibliographical record in complete detail of the physical characteristics and publishing history of the books of a related series properly including an account of internal printing variants requisite for textual criticism

descriptive botany *n* **:** a branch of botany dealing with the systematic description or diagnostic characters of plants

descriptive cataloging *n* **:** a library procedure by which a book or other item is identified and described by recording such items as author, title, imprint, and collation — contrasted with *subject cataloging*

descriptive geometry *n* **:** the theory of geometry treated by means of projections; *specif* **:** the theory of projecting an exactly defined body so as to deduce both projective and metrical properties from its projections, the projections usu. being made on two planes at right angles to each other

de·scrip·tiv·ism \-tə,vizəm\ *n* -s **1 :** a theory of ethics according to which only descriptive or empirical statements are meaningful **2 :** advocacy or use of the methods of descriptive linguistics

de·scrip·tiv·ist \-,vəst\ *n* -s **1 :** an advocate of descriptivism **2 :** a specialist in descriptive linguistics

de·scrip·tiv·is·tic \=¦==¦vistik\ *adj* **:** of, relating to, or based on descriptivism — **de·scrip·tiv·is·ti·cal·ly** \-tək(ə)lē\ *adv*

de·scrip·tor \də'skriptə(r) *also* -,tȯ(ə)r *or* -ō(ə)\ *n* -s [LL, describer, fr. L *descriptus* + *-or*] **:** an identifying sign or symbol

de·scrip·to·ry \-t(ə)rē\ *n* -ES [L *descriptus* + E *-ory*] **:** DESCRIPTIVE

de·scrip·tum \də'skriptəm, dē'-\ *n, pl* **descrip·ta** \-tə\ [L, fr. neut. of *descriptus*, past part. of *describere* to describe — more at DESCRIBE] *philos* **:** something that is described

de·scrive \də'skrīv, -rēv\ *vt* -ED/-ING/-S [ME *descriven*, fr. OF *descrivre*, fr. L *describere*] *Scot* **:** DESCRIBE ⟨let me fair Nature's face ~ —Robert Burns⟩

¹des·cry \də'skrī, dē'-\ *vt* -ED/-ING/-S [ME *descrien*, fr. OF *descrier* to proclaim, decry — more at DECRY] **1 a :** to spy out or come to see esp. with watchful attention and careful observation of the distant, uncertain, or obscure ⟨the grass was high in the meadow, and there was no ~*ing* her —George Eliot⟩ **b :** to attain to the realization or understanding of **:** DISCOVER ⟨examine the legend in a more critical spirit and ~ the reasons for Toscanini's preeminence —*Times Lit. Supp.*⟩ **2** *obs* **a :** to make known (as one's name) **:** DECLARE **b :** BETRAY **3** *obs* **:** CHALLENGE **4** *obs* **:** DECRY **syn** see SEE

²descry *n* -ES *obs* **:** discovery or view from afar

de·scum \(')dē+\ *vt* [*de-* + *scum* (n.)] **:** to rid of scum

des·cu·rain·ia \,deskə'rānēə, ,dāk-\ *n, cap* [NL, fr. François *Déscourain* †1740 Fr. botanist + NL *-ia*] **:** a genus of annual or biennial herbs (family Cruciferae) of America and Europe differing from members of the genus *Sisymbrium* in having a pubescence of stellate or forked hairs and comprising the tansy mustards — see TANSY MUSTARD

de·seam \(')dē+\ *vt* [*de-* + *seam* (n.)] **:** to chip out or flame-cut seams or other similar surface defects from (semifinished metal)

de·sea·son·al·ize \dē'sēz(ə)nə,līz, dē'-\ *vt* [*de-* + *seasonal* + *-ize*] **:** to adjust (as an industry) to continuous rather than seasonal operation

¹des·e·crate \'desə,krāt, -sē,-, *usu* -ād·+V\ *vt* -ED/-ING/-S [*de-* + *-secrate* (as in *consecrate*, v.)] **1 a :** to violate the sanctity of by diverting from sacred purpose, by contaminating, or by defiling ⟨they *desecrated* the shrine outright — bargaining with the Moslem merchants —*Time*⟩ ⟨it would ~ the Lincoln Memorial to have an obviously false voice speak from the statue there —*N.Y. Times Mag.*⟩ ⟨the quivering host whose house has been profaned and whose religion *desecrated* —W.L.Sullivan⟩ **b :** to divest of sacred character or treat as unhallowed ⟨many cemeteries were *desecrated*⟩ **2** *archaic* **:** to dedicate (someone or something) to false gods **:** condemn to an evil fate **3 :** to treat (an object of veneration, reverent devotion, or admiration) irreverently or contemptuously often in a way to provoke outrage on the part of others ⟨[his] great memory . . . has been *desecrated*. . . . —Margery Allingham⟩ ⟨Americans love the scenic outdoors, and they do not want to see it *desecrated* —R.L.Neuberger⟩ **4 :** to make desolate ⟨churned up lawns and drives, and *desecrated* houses with their broken windows —S.P.B.Mais⟩

²des·e·crate \-,krət, -krāt\ *adj* [*de-* + *-secrate* (as in *consecrate*, adj.)] **:** DESECRATED

des·e·crat·er *or* **des·e·cra·tor** \-,krād·ə(r)\ *n* -s **:** one that desecrates

des·e·cra·tion \,=='krāshən\ *n* -s **1 :** the act or an instance of desecrating ⟨I have heard this chorus sung in a uniform fortissimo right from the beginning. What a ~ —Warwick Braithwaite⟩ ⟨the United Nations Flag of Authority may be subject to ~*s* —*World Flag Encyc.*⟩ **2 :** the condition of being desecrated **syn** see PROFANATION

de·seed \(')dē+\ *vt* [*de-* + *seed* (n.)] **:** to remove the seed from

de·segmentation \(¦)dē+\ *n* [*de-* + *segmentation*] *zool* **:** coalescence of distinct segments **:** loss of segmentation

de·segregate \(')dē+\ *vb* [*de-* + *segregate*] *vt* **:** to rid of segregation **:** to end the practice of segregation in ⟨two more counties . . . *desegregated* their schools —*New Republic*⟩ ⟨impetus to ~ this swimming pool came from a court order —*Jour. of Social Issues*⟩ **~** *vi* **:** to effect or implement desegregation ⟨few Southern universities . . . *desegregated* without being required to do so —K.B.Clark⟩

de·segregation \(¦)dē+\ *n* **:** the act of desegregating **:** the process of effecting an end to the practice of segregation ⟨urbanization . . . may make ~ easier —J.B.Martin⟩ ⟨the process of ~ has been going forward steadily . . . in school districts throughout the country —J.W.Waring⟩ — compare INTEGRATION

de·se·mer \'dāzəmə(r)\ *n* -s [G, fr. LG, alter. of MLG *bisemer, besemer*, of Baltic origin; akin to Lith *bezmēnas*, of Slav origin; akin to ORuss *bezmĕnŭ* desemer, small weight, Pol *bezmian, przezmian* balance without pans, perh. of Turkic origin; akin to Turk *batman* small weight] **:** an ancient balance **:** STEELYARD

de·sensitization \(¦)dē, dē+\ *n* **:** the process of desensitizing ⟨~ consists in the gradual specific neutralizing of the sensitizing antibody —A.F.Coca⟩

de·sensitize \(')dē, dē+\ *vb* [*de-* + *sensitize*] *vt* **1 :** to render (a sensitized or hypersensitive individual) insensitive or nonreactive to a sensitizing agent ⟨*desensitized* to an allergenic pollen by repeated injections of an extract of that pollen⟩ **2 :** to render (a photographic material) less sensitive or completely insensitive to radiation **3 :** to make portions of (an offset plate) repellent to ink **4 :** to render insensible to some sensation or emotion or insensitive or callous to inhumanity, injustice, degradation ⟨they have been so successfully *desensitized* that they are unable to recognize the most obvious facts —Alfred Kantorowicz⟩ **5 :** to free (as by psychotherapy) of the emotional charge investing a complex

de·sensitizer \"+\ *n* **:** a desensitizing agent: as **a :** a drug that reduces sensitivity to pain ⟨a ~ which makes it possible to drill and fill teeth painlessly —*Industrial & Engineering Chemistry*⟩ **b :** a chemical (as a dye) that reduces the sensitivity of a photographic material to radiation

des·er·et \¦dezə¦ret, *usu* -ed·+V\ *adj, usu cap* [fr. *Deseret*, nickname for the state of Utah and from 1849–1850 official Mormon name for the Utah territory, fr. *deseret* honeybee, coined in the *Book of Mormon* (Ether 2:3)] **:** of or from Utah territory or the state of Utah

¹des·ert \'dezə(r)t, *usu* |d·+V\ *n* -s [ME, fr. OF, fr. LL *desertum*, fr. L, neut. of *desertus*, past part. of *deserere* to desert, fr. *de-* + *serere* to join together — more at SERIES] **1 a** *archaic* **:** a wild uninhabited and uncultivated tract **:** a desolate unoccupied plain or coast or pathless woodland **:** WILDERNESS, WASTE **b :** any of the formerly unsettled regions of the U.S. between the Mississippi river and the Rocky mountains thought to be arid and uninhabitable **2 a :** a region in which the vegetation is so scanty as to be incapable of supporting any considerable population (as a region perpetually cold or covered with snow or ice or a region located in the interior of a continent and characterized by scanty rainfall esp. of less than 10 inches annually) **b :** a more or less barren tract incapable of supporting any considerable population without an artificial water supply **c :** an area of an ocean believed to be devoid of marine life **3 :** a secluded place for secret worship by the Huguenots during the years 1715–1802 when Protestantism was under proscription in France **4 :** a desolating or forbidding prospect (as from pathless emptiness, bleak unrelieved changelessness or monotony, futility of effort, or destitution of mental or spiritual animation or stimulation) ⟨tiny figures lost in an immense ~ of darkness —Beverley Nichols⟩ ⟨lost in a ~ of doubt⟩ ⟨eagles still soar between the summit of Parnassus and the Corinthian gulf, but they look down upon a ~ of human history —Mark Van Doren⟩

²des·ert \", *in sense 1 usu like* ³DESERT\ *adj* [ME, fr. OF, fr. L *desertus*] **1** *archaic* **:** DESERTED ⟨the boat deck was utterly ~ —Waldo Frank⟩ **2 a :** desolate and sparsely occupied or unoccupied **:** INHOSPITABLE ⟨so ~ a country as the Highlands of Scotland —Adam Smith⟩ **b :** uncultivated and uninhabited **:** barren like a desert ⟨one could scarcely find a more ~ tract for a settler⟩ **3 :** having its habitat in a desert ⟨~ flora and fauna⟩ **4 :** peculiar to or adapted to life in a desert ⟨sturdy ~ boots⟩

³de·sert \də'zər|t, dē'-, -zə̄|, -zəi|, *usu* |d·+V\ *n* -s [ME *deserte*, fr. OF, fr. fem. of *desert* (past part. of *deservir* to deserve), fr. L *deservitus*, past part. of *deservire* to serve zealously — more at DESERVE] **1 a :** the quality or fact of being worthy of or deserving of rewards or recompense or of requital or punishment ⟨the concept of ~ is essentially indefinable except in terms of existing practices and ideas —G.H.Sabine⟩ **b :** a complex of actions calling for such returns ⟨in the midst is seated Justice to award to each according to his ~ —Carleton Brown⟩ **2 a :** reward or punishment deserved or earned by one's qualities or acts ⟨not weighing our ~*s* but pardoning our offenses —*Missale Romanum*⟩ ⟨by dint of much caballing and much dwelling upon his own ~*s* he triumphed over his enemies —Virginia Woolf⟩ **b deserts** *pl* **:** awards due for superior or inferior qualities of art or workmanship ⟨book reviewers . . . frequently praise the first venture of a writer beyond its just ~*s* —Harrison Smith⟩ **3 :** worthiness or excellence of character as adduced by a good course of conduct ⟨he won the appointment on grounds of ~ rather than through family prestige⟩ **syn** see DUE

⁴desert \"\ *vb* -ED/-ING/-S [F *déserter*, fr. LL *desertare*, fr. L *desertus*, past part. of *deserere* to desert — more at ¹DESERT] *vt* **1 :** to withdraw from or leave permanently or less often temporarily (as a place) **:** QUIT ⟨farmers continue to ~ the land to take up factory work⟩ ⟨the smile ~*ing* his broad face —T.B.Costain⟩ ⟨phrases which never ~ the memory —T.S. Eliot⟩ **2 a :** to turn away from (what has previously engaged one) esp. by withdrawing support or disrupting bonds of attachment or duty **:** reject in order to take up something else **:** ABANDON ⟨who, 30 years before, upon being ~*ed* by her lover had taken to her bed —Margaret Deland⟩ ⟨coming at last to ~ the Prohibition party⟩ ⟨he ~*ed* prose for the compensating rhythms of poetry —Tyrus Hillway⟩ **b :** to leave behind or give up (as a person) — used with *to* ⟨forced to ~ the rest of the miners to their fate⟩ **c :** to renounce marital relations by quitting the company of (one's spouse) **3 a :** to break away from or break off association with (some matter involving legal or moral obligation or some object of loyalty) **:** BETRAY ⟨not propose to ~ the 100-year-old Monroe Doctrine —A.H.Vandenberg †1951⟩ ⟨would be a calamity if these sciences ~*ed* the ideal of accurate and verifiable systematic knowledge for its own sake —M.R.Cohen⟩ **b :** to abandon (military service) without leave **:** forsake in violation of duty ⟨guilty of ~*ing* his fellow soldiers⟩ **4 :** to drop away or escape from (a person) usu. causing a distinct sense of loss or discomfiture **:** leave in the lurch **:** FORSAKE ⟨all sense of courtly etiquette ~*ing* him —T.B.Costain⟩ **~** *vi* **1 :** to quit one's post, leader, or service without leave ⟨the native guides quietly ~*ed* during the night⟩ ⟨the more liberal members of the party began ~*ing*⟩ **2 :** to change one's allegiance ⟨he gave fear of a return of Nazism as the reason for his ~*ing* to the Communists⟩ **3 a :** to quit military service without right (determined to ~) **:** absent oneself without leave from proper post, station, or duty with the intent to remain away permanently **b :** to leave one's proper place to avoid hazardous duty or to shirk important service **:** accept appointment or enlist in the same or another armed service without first being regularly separated **:** enter a foreign armed service without authorization by the U.S. **c** *of an officer* **:** to quit one's post without leave and with intent to remain away permanently after tendering one's resignation but before due notice of acceptance of it has been received

desert armor *n* **:** a concentration of pebbles and boulders on the surface of the ground in a desert resulting from removal of sand and dust particles by the wind and protecting the underlying material from further wind erosion

desert bat *n* **:** PALLID BAT

desert candle *n* **:** a plant of the genus *Eremurus*

desert cat *n* **:** any of several small wildcats of arid regions: as **a :** a widely distributed Asiatic wildcat (*Felis bieti*) **b :** KAFFIR CAT **c :** a pale sandy-colored bay lynx of desert parts of western No. America

desert date *n* **:** BITO

deserted *adj* **:** left without the accustomed occupants, company, or support **:** ABANDONED, FORSAKEN ⟨found shelter in a ~ shack⟩ ⟨stood there, motionless, without desire, like a ship at sea, ~ of all winds —L.P.Smith⟩ — **de·sert·ed·ly** *adv* — **de·sert·ed·ness** *n* -ES

de·sert·er *pronunc at* ³DESERT + ə(r)\ *n* -s [F & L; F *déserteur*, fr. L *desertor*, fr. *desertus* + *-or*] **:** one who forsakes a duty, a cause, or anyone to whom he owes service; *esp* **:** a member of a military force who deserts

desert fever *or* **desert rheumatism** *n* **:** a mild form of coccidioidomycosis resembling influenza

desert fox *n* **1 :** a fox (*Vulpes leucopus*) of the western deserts of Asia **2 :** the kit fox (*Vulpes macrotis*) of the southwestern U.S.

desert gum *n* **:** any of several trees of the genus *Eucalyptus* (esp. *E. rudis*)

desert holly *n* **:** a low saltbush (*Atriplex hymenelytra*) of arid regions of the southwestern U.S. and Mexico with smooth bluish green or silvery prickly-edged foliage that is often used for Christmas decoration

de·ser·tic \də'zərd·ik, de'-\ *adj* **:** belonging or peculiar to or having the distinctive character of a desert ⟨the red ~ hills dotted with juniper —D.C.Peattie⟩ **:** found in a desert ⟨a ~ soil may be rich in nutrients⟩ ⟨a ~ climate⟩

des·er·tic·o·lous \¦dezə(r)¦tikələs\ *adj* [¹*desert* + *-i-* + *-colous*] **:** dwelling in a desert

de·ser·tion \də'zershən, dē'-, -zə̄|, -zəi|\ *n* -s [MF or LL; MF, fr. LL *desertion-, desertio*, fr. L *desertus* + *-ion-, -io* -ion] **1 :** the act or an instance of deserting: **a :** abandonment of a person to whom one is obligated or bound by agreement ⟨we resolved to make the dash for the summit in spite of their ~⟩ **:** abandonment of that to which a degree of loyalty is considered due (as a post of duty, employment engaged for, a cause, a political party) **:** DEFECTION **b :** a deserting from the military or naval service **c :** the intentional and substantial abandonment permanently or for a period of time stated by law without legal excuse and without consent of one's duties arising out of a status (as that of husband and wife or parent and child) **2 :** a state of being deserted or forsaken **:** DESOLATION **3 :** one who deserts ⟨all the ~s gave themselves up⟩

desert ironwood *n* **1 :** a small leguminous tree (*Olneya tesota*) of the southwestern U.S. and Mexico with odd-pinnate leaves and purplish white flowers in short racemes — called also *Sonora ironwood* **2 :** the hard wood of the desert ironwood

desert lark *n* **:** any of several larks (as of the genus *Ammomanes*) inhabiting the deserts of Asia and Africa

desert lemon *n* **:** an Australian tree (*Eremocitrus glauca*) of the family Rutaceae bearing a small acid fruit

de·sert·less \dəˈzərtləs\ *adj* [³*desert* + *-less*] **1 :** UNDESERVING **2** *obs* **:** UNDESERVED — **de·sert·less·ly** *adv*

desert lily *n* **:** a bulbous herb (*Hesperocallis undulata*) of the family Liliaceae of the southwestern U.S. with narrow sword-shaped leaves and showy racemose flowers

desert locust *n* **:** a destructive migratory locust (*Schistocerca gregaria*) of southwestern Asia and parts of northern Africa

desert lynx *n* **:** CARACAL

desert mahogany *n* **:** a widely distributed mountain mahogany (*Cercocarpus ledifolius*) that grows as a large shrub or small tree on dry gravelly uplands of the western U.S. and is an important browse for deer

desert milkweed *n* **:** any of several plants of the genus *Asclepias* that grow in the dry regions of southwestern U.S. (esp. *A. subulata* and *A. erosa*)

desert mouse *n* **:** a small brown mouse (*Pseudomys hermannsburgensis*) of the central desert of Australia

des·ert·ness \ˈdezə(r)tnəs\ *n* -ES [ME *desertnes*, fr. ²*desert* + *-nes* -ness] **:** the condition of being like a desert ⟨that air of spellbound ~ which so significantly invests the isles —Herman Melville⟩

desert palm *n* **:** WASHINGTON PALM

desert pavement *n* **:** a natural mosaic of closely-packed pebbles, cobblestones, and boulders commonly found in a desert where the wind has swept away all smaller particles

desert pea *n* **:** STURT'S DESERT PEA

desert peach *n* **:** a thorny thicket-forming large shrub or small tree (*Prunus andersonii*) of dry uplands of the Pacific and Intermountain states that is locally important as browse for sheep and goats

desert plant *n* **:** a plant suited to the environment of arid regions of little rainfall that often stores water in its tissues or hollow center and reduces transpiration by total or seasonal leaflessness or by a densely hairy, waxy, varnished, or otherwise modified leaf **:** a xerophilous plant

desert plume *n* **:** a perennial herb (*Stanleya pinnata*) of the family Cruciferae of the southwestern U.S. with pinnatifid leaves, spirally coiled anthers, and long stalked seedpods — called also *prince's-plume*

desert rat *n* **1 :** any of several pale-coated active rodents found in deserts (as the American kangaroo rat or certain southern African rodents) **2** *West* **:** one who has lived much on the desert esp. as a prospector

desert rod *n* **:** any of several herbs of the genus *Eremostachys* (family Labiatae) found in arid regions of western and central Asia

deserts *pl of* DESERT, *pres 3d sing of* DESERT

desertscape \ˈ==,=\ *n* [¹*desert* + *-scape*] **1 :** a scenic view of a desert **2 :** a pictorial representation of a scenic view of a desert

desert soil *n* **:** any of a group of zonal soils that develop under sparse shrub vegetation in warm to cool arid climates and have a light-colored surface soil usu. underlain by calcareous material and a hardpan layer

desert sore *n* **:** an ulcer of unknown cause affecting chiefly the extremities and occurring in desert regions of the tropics

desert sparrow *n* **:** a black-throated sparrow (*Amphispiza bilineata*) of arid parts of southwestern No. America

desert sweet *n* **:** FERN-BUSH

desert·thorn \ˈ==,=\ *n* [¹*desert* + *thorn*] **:** MATRIMONY VINE

desert tortoise *n* **:** a large burrowing turtle (*Gopherus agassizii*) of arid regions of the western U.S. — compare TESTUDINIDAE

desert trumpet *n* **:** a tall perennial plant (*Eriogonum inflatum*) of arid uplands of the western U.S. with silvery leaves and the upper part of the nodes inflated

desert trumpet flower *n* **:** a perennial herb (*Datura meteloides*) of the southwestern U.S. with erect showy tubular rose-white flowers and spiny fruit

desert varnish *or* **desert polish** *n* **:** a dark coating or polish found on rocks and pebbles after long exposure in desert regions

¹**des·ert·ward** \ˈdezə(r)t·wə(r)d\ *adv* [¹*desert* + *-ward*] **:** toward a desert

²**desertward** \ˈ"\ *adj* **:** sloping toward a desert **:** lying near to a desert

desert willow *n* **:** a shrub or low tree (*Chilopsis linearis*) of the family Bignoniaceae resembling a willow, having showy purplish flowers and long seed pods, and occurring in dry regions of southwestern No. America — called also *flowering willow*

desertworthy \ˈ==,==\ *adj* **:** capable of functioning competently in a desert

de·serve \dəˈzərv, dēˈ-, -zəv,-zəiv\ *vb* -ED/-ING/-S [ME *deserven*, fr. OF *deservir*, fr. L *deservire* to serve zealously, fr. *de-* + *servire* to serve — more at SERVE] *vt* **1 a :** to come to be rightfully worthy of, to be fairly entitled to, or to be able to claim rightfully by virtue of actions done or qualities displayed ⟨we have the poetry we ~, just as we have the painting we ~ —Herbert Read⟩ ⟨rebels ~ no consideration —Kenneth Roberts⟩ ⟨a people indifferent to their civil liberties do not ~ to keep them —W.O.Douglas⟩; *also* **:** to be so circumstanced as to undergo as one's just due **:** have due as requital ⟨a drunken driver ~s to have his driving license suspended⟩ ⟨he ~s to lose because of his unsportsmanlike tactics⟩ **b :** to be rightfully qualified (as by excellence, utility, wrongness, or other special character) to have or receive **:** qualify for on the basis of right or justice ⟨a laboratory that hardly *deserved* the name⟩ ⟨the question ~s dispassionate consideration —Vera M. Dean⟩ ⟨what crimes ~ the death penalty?⟩ ⟨that his country's new society *deserved* all his energies —Jay Leyda⟩ ⟨acute and liberating observations which ~ to be widely disseminated —M.R.Cohen⟩ **2** *obs* **:** to be or prove of service to **:** BENEFIT **3 :** to win by reason of worthy performance or earn by reason of untoward performance ⟨they cannot command prosperity or continuing employment, but they are certainly doing their best to ~ them —Sam Pollock⟩ ⟨I do not know how he had *deserved* our disrespect —Mary Austin⟩ **4** *obs* **:** to give in return ~ *vi* **1 :** to be worthy, fit, suitable for some reward or requital **:** have acted in a worthy way ⟨that the Tudor translators have become recognized as they ~ —T.S.Eliot⟩ ⟨as one who had *deserved* well of his country —G.L.Dickinson⟩ **2** *obs* **:** to be of service

syn EARN, MERIT, RATE: DESERVE may suggest one's being rightfully entitled to reward for actions done or qualities exhibited in particular situations calling for special notice or evaluation ⟨if he [Dr. Johnson] inserts the poems of some who can hardly be said to *deserve* such an honor —William Cowper⟩ ⟨liberty is easier to win than to *deserve*, and if it is treated as either a license or a vacuum, the police will come or the walls will fall in —Curtis Bok⟩ ⟨a second point *deserves* renewed emphasis —Zechariah Chafee⟩ EARN may suggest a due reward or recompense according to a systematic or regulated plan of evaluation ⟨since he has not missed any hours of work I suppose that he has *earned* his salary, but from the caliber of his work I do not think that he deserves it⟩ ⟨advanced work . . . by men already graduates of theological schools *earns* the degree of Master or Doctor of Theology —*Official Register of Harvard Univ.*⟩ More certainly than the others in this set EARN suggests previous sustained expenditure of energy, effort, and time ⟨we had *earned* that right . . . no group of men can grant other men rights of any kind; they are achieved —H.D. Skidmore⟩ MERIT may be used in reference to lasting traits, rather than sustained action, more readily than EARN ⟨the idle politicos of the country do not *merit* our trust, but her zealous partisans have earned it⟩ MERIT highly stresses the fact of worthiness fit for reward or consideration but implies less about the fact of being rewarded than the others of this group ⟨a boost which in a sense it does *merit* —T.S.Eliot⟩ ⟨if hope's familiar whispers *merit* faith —William Wordsworth⟩ RATE in this sense may stress the idea of being fit or suited for some special reward or consideration in addition to what is officially earned and paid or conferred through rank, status, or connection ⟨important statesmen in the United States have usually *rated* eulogistic titles —E.C.Smith⟩ ⟨not that I *rated* the governor's suite on my own —Bennett Cerf⟩

de·served \-vd\ *adj* **:** such as one deserves ⟨a ~ reputation⟩ ⟨a ~ rebuke⟩ — **de·serv·ed·ly** \-vədlē, -li\ *adv* — **de·serv·ed·ness** \-vədnəs\ *n* -ES

de·serv·er \-və(r)\ *n* -s **:** one who deserves

¹**deserving** *n* -s [ME, fr. gerund of *deserven*] **:** DESERT, MERIT

²**deserving** *adj* [fr. pres. part. of *deserve*] **:** MERITORIOUS, WORTHY ⟨rewarding ~ workers⟩ ⟨the causes most ~ of help⟩ ⟨a charlatan ~ of the severest penalty⟩; *specif* **:** meriting financial assistance ⟨scholarship aid for needy and ~ students⟩ — **de·serv·ing·ly** *adv* — **de·serv·ing·ness** *n* -ES

-deses *pl of* -DESIS

de·sex \(ˈ)dē, də+\ *vt* [*de-* + *sex* (n.)] **1 :** to castrate or spay **2 :** to de-emphasize or minimize appeals to sexual interest in

de·sexualization \(ˌ)dē, də+\ *n* **:** the act or an instance of desexualizing ⟨the view that this ~ necessarily results in the choice of a higher, more socially acceptable channel of expression —G.S.Blum⟩

de·sexualize \(ˈ)dē, də+\ *vt* [*de-* + *sexualize*] **1 :** to deprive of sexual characters or power **:** UNSEX, CASTRATE **2** *psychoanalysis* **a :** to divest of sexual quality by diverting the libido to other goals (as in sublimation) **b :** to withdraw (sexual libido) from the genital to other areas of the body (as in perversions)

deshabille *var of* DISHABILLE

¹**de·si** \ˈdāsē, ˈdesē\ *adj* [Bengali *desī*, fr. Skt *deśīya*, fr. *deśa* point, country, district, fr. *diśati* he points out — more at DICTION] *India* **:** INDIGENOUS ⟨~ fowl⟩ ⟨~ goat⟩

²**desi** \ˈ"\ *also* **dai·see** \ˈdāsē\ *or* **daisee jute** *n* -s [Bengali *desī* indigenous] **:** an Indian jute obtained from Jew's mallow

desiatin *var of* DESSIATINE

¹**des·ic·cant** \ˈdesəkənt, -sek-\ *adj* [L *desiccant-, desiccans*, pres. part. of *desiccare* to dry up] **:** DRYING, DESICCATIVE

²**desiccant** \ˈ"\ *n* -s **:** a drying agent (as sulfuric acid, silica gel)

¹**des·ic·cate** \-kə̇t, -ˌkāt, *usu* \d·+V\ *adj* [ME, fr. L *desiccatus*] **:** DESICCATED ⟨a ~ romance —Allen Tate⟩

²**des·ic·cate** \ˈdesə̇ˌkāt, -sēˌ-, *usu* -ād·+V\ *vb* -ED/-ING/-S [L *desiccatus*, past part. of *desiccare* to dry up, fr. *de-* + *siccare* to dry, fr. *siccus* dry — more at SACK] *vt* **1 :** to dry up or cause to dry up **:** deprive or exhaust of moisture; *esp* **:** dry thoroughly ⟨artificial *desiccating* of timber in an oven with a current of hot air⟩ ⟨the surgeon removed a suspect mole by electrodesiccation and thoroughly *desiccated* the immediately adjoining tissue with a needle electrode⟩ ⟨requiring a *desiccated* hermetically sealed container⟩ **2 :** to preserve (a food) by drying **:** DEHYDRATE ⟨one cup of *desiccated* coconut⟩ **3 a :** to drain of vitality; *esp* **:** to divest of vigor, spirit, passion, or a capability of evoking mental or emotional excitement ⟨a charming little romance . . . not *desiccated* and compressed within the pages of a book —Elinor Wylie⟩ ⟨Mr. Copland's musical style — a deft fusion of ingredients assembled from Debussy and Satie and of *desiccated* elements of American folk music —Winthrop Sargeant⟩ **b :** to divest of spontaneity, animating or interesting properties, or stimulating capacity ⟨a secret-police system first unsettles, then ~s, then calcifies a free society —E.B. White⟩ ⟨the lopsidedly historical approach to literature which dominated and *desiccated* American academic studies for many years —G.H.Genzmer⟩ ⟨the thoughts and behavior of Londoners whose lives were *desiccated* by war —James Stern⟩ **c :** to divest of or divorce from aesthetic sensitivity and human sensibilities and abandon to intellectual aridity ⟨the typical scholar filled with such learning has been caricatured as an absent-minded and *desiccated* personality —C.F.Richards⟩ ~ *vi* **:** to become dried up **:** undergo a desiccating or divesting process ⟨some very small poikilotherms ~ and encapsulate for protection —Samuel Brody⟩ ⟨English philosophy, lost in the aridities of logical positivism and semantics, has tended to become pedantically *desiccated* —*Times Lit. Supp.*⟩ **syn** see DRY

³**desiccate** *like* ¹DESICCATE\ *n* -s **:** a product or residue from desiccation

desiccated *adj* **1 :** dried up **:** ANHYDROUS ⟨each gram of *desiccated* liver contains the equivalent of not less than 0.05 mg of riboflavin⟩ ⟨half-filled boxes of ~ Spanish cigars —Janet Flanner⟩ **2 :** lacking vitality, spirit, spontaneity, or emotional vigor ⟨a prissy and emotionless creature . . . settles into a mold of ~ snobbery —C.J.Rolo⟩

des·ic·ca·tion \ˌ==ˈkāshən\ *n* -s [L *desiccation-, desiccatio*, fr. L *desiccatus* + *-ion-, -io* -ion] **1 :** the act or process of desiccating or the state of being or becoming desiccated: **a :** a complete or nearly complete deprivation of moisture or of water not chemically combined (as by vaporization or evaporation) **:** DEHYDRATION ⟨attributed to some preconsolidation in the soils, particularly the clays, due to compaction by ~ —Mason Lockwood⟩ ⟨partial ~ of landlocked seas at many stages of geological history has given rise to extensive deposits of gypsum and rock salt —W.G.Fearnsides⟩ ⟨for industrial purposes enzymes are rarely purified beyond the stage of simple extraction and ~ of the extract —A.K.Balls⟩ ⟨from the long-wave diathermy machine two distinct currents are obtained which produce ~ and electrocoagulation respectively —W.H.Schmidt⟩ **b :** destitution of vitality from having been or having become desiccated; *esp* **:** deterioration through deprivation or loss of animating, stimulating, or inspiring qualities ⟨the prevalent ~ of the study of philosophy in universities —T.S.Eliot⟩ ⟨research, which alone preserves science from ~ and death —A.L.Guérard⟩ **2 :** a bit of desiccated matter ⟨ringed glasses, clotted tub drains, ~s of paste on toothbrushes —Philip Wylie⟩

desiccation crack *n* **:** MUD CRACK

desiccation polygon *n* **:** a structure bounded by mud cracks found in sedimentary rocks and mud flats

¹**des·ic·ca·tive** \ˈ==ˌkā|d·|iv, -kə|, də̇ˈsikə|, dēˈs-, |t|, |ēv *also* |əv\ *adj* [LL *desiccativus*, fr. L *desiccatus* + *-ivus* -ive] **:** drying up or tending to dry up ⟨intense ~ characteristics⟩

²**desiccative** \ˈ"\ *n* -s *archaic* **:** a desiccative agent

des·ic·ca·tor \ˈdesə̇ˌkād·ə(r), -sēˌ-, -ātə-\ *n* -s **1 :** a container (as a glass jar) fitted with an airtight cover and containing at the bottom some desiccating agent (as calcium chloride) ⟨when a substance to be dried would be decomposed by high temperature it is dried in a ~⟩ **2 :** a machine or apparatus for desiccating fruit, milk, or other food usu. by the aid of heat and sometimes in a vacuum

one form of glass desiccator

des·ic·ca·to·ry \ˈ==kəˌtōrē, də̇ˈsi-, dəˈsi-, ˈsē-, -ōr-, -ri\ *adj* **:** DESICCATIVE

desiderable *adj* [ME, fr. L *desiderabilis*, fr. *desiderare* to long for, miss, desire + *-abilis* -able — more at DESIRE] *obs* **:** PLEASING, DESIRABLE

de·sid·er·ant \də̇ˈsidərənt, dēˈ-, -ˈzi-\ *adj* [L *desiderant-, desiderans*, pres. part. of *desiderare*] *archaic* **:** DESIROUS

¹**desiderate** *n* -s [L *desideratum*, neut. of *desideratus*, past part. of *desiderare*] *obs* **:** a thing desired

²**de·sid·er·ate** \də̇ˈsidəˌrāt, dēˈ- *also* -ˈzi-; *usu* -ād·+V\ *vt* -ED/-ING/-S [L *desideratus*, past part. of *desiderare*] **1 :** to seek or advocate earnestly or call for as essential ⟨the author's practice may not achieve the scope he ~s for the complete "historiography of ideas" —J.L.Adams⟩ ⟨just what and how, for instance, the monastic teaching orders he ~s would teach —F.R.Leavis⟩ **2 :** to entertain or express a longing for or a wish to have or attain ⟨to think these two might negotiate peaceably is to ~ an impossibility⟩

de·sid·er·a·tion \ˌ=ˌ=dəˈrāshən\ *n* -s [L *desideration-, desideratio*, fr. *desideratus* + *-ion-, -io* -ion] **1 :** the act or an instance of desiderating **2 :** DESIDERATUM

¹**de·sid·er·a·tive** \=ˈ=dəˌrā|d·iv, -d(ə)rə|\ *adj* [LL *desiderativus*, fr. L *desideratus* + *-ivus* -ive] **1 :** relating to or denoting desire, esp. a wish to do ⟨the intellect does not include the emotional and immediately ~ elements of human nature —H.O.Taylor⟩ **2 a** *of a verb or verb form* **:** derived from or belonging to the inflectional paradigm of a verb and expressing a desire to perform the action denoted by that verb ⟨the ~ Latin verb *esurire* "to be hungry" is from *edere* "to eat"⟩ **b :** of or relating to a desiderative verb or verb form ⟨a ~ suffix⟩

²**desiderative** \ˈ"\ *n* -s **:** a desiderative verb or verb form

de·sid·er·a·tum \=ˌ=dəˈrä|d·əm, -ˈrā-, -rä|, |təm\ *n, pl* **desiderata** \|d·ə,|tə\ [L, neut. of *desideratus*, past part. of *desiderare* to desire — more at DESIRE] **:** something desired as essential or needed **:** something that is sought for or aimed at ⟨the correct reverberation is not, of course, the whole ~ behind concert-hall acoustics —E.G.Richardson⟩ ⟨detached individuality does not seem to be a ~ of the Vedantic mind —Robert Bierstedt⟩ ⟨the concept that peace of mind is the great ~ —Warren Weaver⟩

des·i·de·ri·um \ˌdesəˈdirēəm, -ezə-\ *n, pl* **desideria** \-ēə\ [L, fr. *desiderare* to desire] **:** an ardent desire or longing; *esp* **:** a feeling of loss or grief for something lost

de·sight \ˈdē+ ,-\ *n* [*de-* + *sight*] **:** an unsightly object **:** EYESORE

¹**de·sign** \də̇ˈzīn, dēˈ-\ *vb* -ED/-ING/-S [MF *designer*, fr. L *designare*, lit., to mark out, fr. *de-* + *signare* to mark — more at SIGN] *vt* **1 a :** to conceive and plan out in the mind ⟨a savage on seeing a watch would at once conclude that it was ~*ed* —Samuel Butler †1902⟩ **b :** DEVOTE, CONSIGN, DESTINE ⟨a city ~*ed* to destruction⟩ ⟨grants ~*ed* in his will for making amends⟩ **c :** to make up one's mind to set apart **:** settle in mind to reserve ⟨mementos of his travels that he had ~*ed* for friends⟩ **d :** to plan or have in mind as a purpose **:** INTEND, PURPOSE, CONTEMPLATE ⟨he was sociable by disposition, and I believe he ~*ed* particularly to shine in the world of talk and manners —Osbert Sitwell⟩ ⟨when some other foreign power ~*ed* division or seizure —Roger Burlingame⟩ **e** *archaic* **:** to have in mind or include as a matter of consideration **f :** to devise or propose for a specific function ⟨a book ~*ed* primarily as a college textbook⟩ ⟨a program obviously ~*ed* as a first approach to this problem⟩ **g :** to create, plan, or calculate for serving a predetermined end **:** prepare or lay out deliberately ⟨the challenging problem of ~*ing* a college curriculum for young women⟩ ⟨a little group of members which is ~*ed* for study, propaganda, and energetic canvassing —R.M.Dawson⟩ ⟨~*ed* to form a frame for what was to come after —E.M.Lustgarten⟩ **2 a** *obs* **:** to indicate with a distinctive mark or sign **b** *archaic* **:** to indicate by name or distinctive phrase **c :** to designate for office or function ⟨~*ing* a friend to act as substitute⟩ ⟨the other parties named and ~*ed* in the summons⟩ **d** *archaic* **:** ASSIGN, GRANT **3** [MF *desseigner*, fr. It *disegnare*, fr. L *designare*] **a** *archaic* **:** to make a drawing or sketch of (an object or scene) **b :** to outline or sketch in proportion for creating a work of art or to serve as a pattern in the practical arts ⟨she has ~*ed* the dances for several Broadway hits⟩ ⟨a curious woman whose dresses always looked as if they had been ~*ed* in a rage —Oscar Wilde⟩ **c :** to plan and plot out the shape and disposition of the parts of and the structural constituents of **:** draw the plans for ⟨the ~*ed* many buildings and bridges⟩ **d :** to create, fashion, execute, or construct according to plan ⟨he was also a clever artist and ~*ed* scenes with a flair for color —Winifred Bambrick⟩ ⟨buildings of the institution are so ~*ed* that each patient's room opens upon a porch —*Amer. Guide Series: Mich.*⟩ **e :** to originate, draft, and work out, set up, or set forth **:** DEVISE, CONTRIVE ⟨a landscaping authority to ~ the city's park system⟩ ⟨can start to ~ and execute a foreign policy without fear —H.W.Barber⟩ ⟨like most Communist propaganda it was very cleverly ~*ed* —Patrick McMahon⟩ ⟨knows how to ~ a part so that it develops and acquires momentum in performance —Brooks Atkinson⟩ **f :** to plan or produce with special intentional adaptation to a specific end — used in passive or participial form ⟨statutes are ~*ed* to meet the fugitive exigencies of the hour —B.N.Cardozo⟩ ⟨slogans are normally ~*ed* to get action without reflection —A.E.Stevenson b.1900⟩ ⟨marriage was a social institution ~*ed* to fit instinct into a legal framework —Bertrand Russell⟩ ⟨would do it for $5000, a price . . . ~*ed* to discourage offers —Elsa Maxwell⟩ ~ *vi* **1 :** to conceive a plan for making something **2 :** to draw, lay out, or otherwise prepare a design or designs ⟨those who ~ for the home⟩ ⟨in ~*ing* for motion pictures there is also the problem of geography —Cedric Gibbons⟩: **a :** to draw a preliminary figure, outline, or sketch (as for a machine, structure, or work of art) **b :** to fashion a work of art **c :** to fashion a decorative figure or pattern **3 :** to plan or intend to start out on a trip or course ⟨this ship ~s for Guam⟩ ⟨the young man ~s for law⟩ **syn** see INTEND, ¹PLAN

²**design** \ˈ"\ *n* -s [MF *dessein*, fr. It *disegno*, fr. *disegnare* to mark out] **1 :** a mental project or scheme in which means to an end are laid down **:** PLAN ⟨morality also, like religion, is a product of human ~ —Benjamin Farrington⟩ ⟨had no rivals among the secular rulers of Europe for largeness of ~s —R.W.Southern⟩ **2 a :** a particular purpose held in view by an individual or group **:** a planned intention ⟨my ~ in writing this preface is to forestall certain critics⟩ ⟨he has ambitious ~s for his son⟩ **b :** deliberate purposive planning ⟨what superficially may appear to be a masterpiece of ~ was likely to have been just an empirical policy of muddling through —*Times Lit. Supp.*⟩ ⟨his clumsiness is due to inattention rather than ~⟩ ⟨battle was joined apparently more by accident than ~ —John Buchan⟩; *also* **:** direction toward an ultimate end ⟨the teleological, which shows the marks of ~ in nature, and from them argues to a great designer —*Encyc. Americana*⟩ — opposed to *accident* **3 a :** a deliberate undercover project or scheme entertained with discreditable or hostile and often dishonest, treacherous, sinister, or seductive intent ⟨each camp accusing the other of imperialist ~s⟩ ⟨eager to ferret out any subversive ~⟩ ⟨a declaration of a ~ upon his life —John Locke⟩ **b designs** *pl* **:** such a scheme contemplating some rapacious or disruptive aggression or some illicit encroachment — used with *on* or *against* ⟨the United States has no . . . ~s against any of its neighbors anywhere —A.H.Vandenberg †1951⟩ ⟨has ~s on the money⟩ **4 :** a preliminary sketch or outline (as a drawing on paper or a modeling in clay) showing the main features of something to be executed **:** DELINEATION ⟨a textile ~ and its specifications constitute the complete working plan for the manufacture of a fabric —Alfred Higgins & R. L. La Vault⟩ **5 a :** a painter or sculptor's preliminary drawing or model ⟨he made two or three charming and blasphemous ~s —W.B.Yeats⟩ **b :** a scheme for the construction, finish, and ornamentation of a building as embodied in the plans, elevations, and other architectural drawings pertaining to it **c :** a conceptual outline or sketch according to which the elements of a literary or dramatic composition or series are disposed ⟨his sense of structure, both in the general ~ of *Paradise Lost* and *Samson*, and in his syntax —T.S.Eliot⟩ ⟨it is now widely agreed that such compositions as *Moby Dick* and *Billy Budd* are complete ~s —Nathalia Wright⟩ ⟨the main ~s of the poem, an imaginative control of dispersed material —*Times Lit. Supp.*⟩ **d :** a settled coherent program followed or imposed; *usu* **:** an underlying scheme that governs functioning, developing, or unfolding **:** PATTERN, MOTIF ⟨his ad-libbing . . . is not unfortified by ~ because he is far too fine a professional ever to trust entirely to chance —John Mason Brown⟩ ⟨whether or not there be a ~, . . . in nature, a man's biography frequently discloses haunting glimpses of a pattern —Perry Miller⟩ **6 a :** the arrangement of elements that make up a work of art, a machine, or other man-made object ⟨systematic art instruction begins with the study of ~, which includes little except the perception and creation of formal relations —Hunter Mead⟩ ⟨made her decide to introduce choreographic ~ into her free skating —*Current Biog.*⟩ **b :** the process of selecting the means and contriving the elements, steps, and procedures for producing what will adequately satisfy some need ⟨industrial ~⟩ ⟨included in ~ are the arrangement of the basic text page, choice of typeface, title page, and special pages —Joseph Blumenthal⟩; *specif* **:** the drawing up of specifications as to structure, forms, positions, materials, texture, accessories, decorations in the form of a layout for setting up, building, or

fabrication ⟨the ~ of the ship's bridge⟩ ⟨his experiments were noted for their simple ~⟩ ⟨the problems of stability were corrected by better ~ in duplicating equipment —R.O.Jordan⟩ **c :** structural constitution or fundamental framework of a musical composition ⟨unacceptable to our sense of melodic ~ —P.H.Lang⟩ ⟨inflated music with ambitious and mystical programmatic ~*s* —Nicolas Slonimsky⟩ **7 a :** a visual arrangement or disposition of lines, parts, figures, details usu. unified by an implicit key or clue of signification or an artistic motif (as in engravings, medals, textiles, metalwork) ⟨linoleum in a great number of ~*s*⟩ ⟨the ~*s* on the reverse of our coins⟩ ⟨an iron balustrade with a ~ of bows and arrows that rises from the eaves of the house —*Amer. Guide Series: Maine*⟩ **b :** a pattern or figuration applied to a surface (as of a vase) **:** DECORATION ⟨porcelain with carved or engraved floral ~*s*⟩ ⟨a gold-tooled ~ impressed on bookbindings⟩ **syn** see INTENTION, PLAN

[3]design \"\ *adj* **:** used as a basis for anticipating practical problems and solving them at the engineering stage — used chiefly in highway designing ⟨the ~ speed of a highway⟩

des·ig·na·ble \'dez|ignəbəl, |ēg *sometimes* -es|\ *adj* [L *designare* to mark out + E *-able*] **:** DISTINGUISHABLE, IDENTIFIABLE ⟨the probability that two parts of the same tree might be designated or ~ by the same term —J.T.Krumpelmann⟩

de·sig·na·do \ˌdesig'nä(ˌ)dō, -ezi-\ *n* -s [Sp. fr. *designado*, past part. of *designar* to designate, fr. L *designare*] **:** one legally appointed or elected in some Spanish-American countries to succeed the president

designata *pl of* DESIGNATUM

des·ig·nat·able \'dez|igˌnād·əbəl, -ēg-, -ātə- *sometimes* -es|\ *adj* **:** capable of being designated

[1]des·ig·nate \-ˌnā|t, -ˌnə|, *usu* |d·+V\ *adj* [L *designatus*, past part. of *designare*] **:** chosen for an office but not yet installed — used after the noun ⟨called president-elect or president-*designate*⟩ ⟨the pledges of the governor ~⟩

[2]des·ig·nate \-ˌnāt, *usu* -ād·+V\ *vt* -ED/-ING/-S [L *designatus*, past part. of *designare*, lit., to mark out — more at DESIGN] **1 a :** to point out the location of ⟨a marker *designating* the crest of the flood waters⟩ **b :** to make known directly as if by sign **:** SIGNIFY, INDICATE ⟨any reasonable task *designated* by the employer⟩ **c :** to distinguish as to class **:** DENOMINATE, IDENTIFY, LABEL ⟨the area we ~ as that of spiritual values —J.B.Conant⟩ **d :** SPECIFY, STIPULATE ⟨sending food packages to *designated* recipients in Europe⟩ ⟨a gift *designated* by the donor to be used for faculty compensation⟩ **2 a :** to call by a distinctive title, term, or expression ⟨a particle having approximately the mass of a proton but having no charge and so *designated* as a neutron —W.V.Houston⟩ ⟨the four parts were *designated A, B, C*, and *D* in the diagram⟩ **b :** to declare to be **:** CHARACTERIZE ⟨areas *designated* as strategic⟩ **3 :** to name esp. to a post or function **4 a :** to decide upon **:** NOMINATE, DELEGATE, APPOINT; *esp* **:** to assign officially by executive or military authority ⟨the operating agency last *designated* by the president⟩ ⟨the tanks had been *designated* to exploit a breakthrough of the enemy's defenses —R.D.Gardner⟩ **b :** to induct in a rank or position ⟨the supreme council is *designated* as the highest organ of state power⟩ ⟨the duke had been *designated* as king of a puppet state⟩ **c :** to choose and set apart (as by public will or in the process of government administration) ⟨a successful *designating* petition places the name of the candidate on the primary ballot —*Bk. of Civic Definitions*⟩ ⟨control dams *designated* for construction⟩ ⟨finally Queen Victoria was asked to ~ a site—B.K.Sandwell⟩ **5 :** to serve as a name of **:** stand for **:** DENOTE ⟨associate . . . the names with the persons they ~ —Weldon Kees⟩ ⟨names are now given bacteria as a sort of shorthand to ~ a whole series of complicated reactions —Justina Hill⟩ **6** *logic* **:** to refer to (an abstract or a concrete entity) — used of a sign, word, or linguistic expression

syn NAME, NOMINATE, ELECT, APPOINT: DESIGNATE may apply to choosing or detailing a person or group for a certain post by a person or group having power or right to choose ⟨the following deputies were *designated* by the three ministers to carry on the council's work —*Americana Annual*⟩ ⟨the vice-chairman is elected from among the commissioners, and the president *designates* the chairman —*Current Biog.*⟩ NAME differs little from DESIGNATE except that it may more strongly imply public announcement and less strongly suggest official action ⟨the president-elect has not yet *named* his secretary of state⟩ ⟨*named* to the position of general manager⟩ ⟨a council of the realm to advise him and to *name* his successor in the event of his death —*Current Biog.*⟩ NOMINATE today often indicates presentation of a candidate for the approval of or rejection by those who make final decisions ⟨the parties *nominate* their presidential candidates during the summer⟩ ⟨President Truman *nominated* him for promotion to full admiral, an advancement confirmed by the Senate —*Current Biog.*⟩ ELECT may apply to definitive selection by a qualified group from among persons nominated or offering themselves as candidates ⟨*elected* by a large majority of the voters⟩ ⟨*elected* to membership in a general meeting of the club⟩ APPOINT indicates selection without election by a qualified person or group, with or without confirmation by another instrumentality ⟨the president *appoints* postal officials⟩ ⟨by constitutional provision the chief executive *appoints*, not independently (except in a few instances as indicated above), but "by and with the advice and consent of the senate"; to speak with complete accuracy, he nominates, the Senate confirms (by a majority vote of the members present), and he thereupon *appoints* —F.A.Ogg & P.O.Ray⟩

des·ig·na·tion \ˌ==ˈnāshən\ *n* -s [ME *desygnacion*, fr. L *designation-*, *designatio*, fr. *designatus* + *-ion-*, *-io*, -ion] **1 :** the act of indicating or identifying by a mark, letter, or sign or by classification or specification ⟨contriving new characters for the ~ of sounds alien to the language⟩ ⟨anciently the law was that the mere repetition of a slander was not actionable if the repetition was accompanied by a ~ of the author —B.N.Cardozo⟩ **2 a :** a distinguishing name **:** a title earned or awarded ⟨for years the county seat had no proper ~⟩ ⟨as a writer of light verse; but this ~ isn't good enough —Charles Jackson⟩ **b :** NAMING ⟨perhaps the honor that touched him most deeply was the ~ during his last years of the new laboratory —C.H.Herty⟩ ⟨the ~ of degrees for women graduates puzzled the more liberal educators —*Amer. Guide Series: Texas*⟩ **3 a :** appointment or assignment to a post ⟨his next ~ was a second secretaryship at Panama City⟩; *also* **:** nomination for a political office ⟨seeking to win the Republican primary ~⟩ **b :** delegation, engagement, or allocation for a service ⟨his ~ by Chile and Argentina as umpire of a commission⟩ ⟨the revision of the rest of Matthew and of Genesis and all of Exodus by the ~ of different sections to various members of the committee —I.M.Price⟩ **c** *archaic* **:** a natural leaning that contributes to one's fitness **4** *obs* **:** end in view **5 :** an allotment of bottom for planting oysters; *also* **:** the space so allotted **6** *logic* **:** the relation between a sign, word, or linguistic expression and the object referred to; *also* **:** MEANING, CONNOTATION

des·ig·na·tio per·so·nae \ˌdezigˈnāshēˌōpə(r)ˈsō(ˌ)nē\ *n* [L, designation of the person] **:** matter designating the persons who are parties to and essential to the validity of a document — compare DESCRIPTIO PERSONAE

[1]des·ig·na·tive \'dez|igˌnā|d·|iv, |ēg-, -ˌnə|, |t|, |ēv *also* |əv *sometimes* 'des|\ *adj* [LL *designativus*, fr. L *designatus* + *-ivus* -ive] **:** serving to designate or indicate

[2]designative \"\ *n* -s **:** something designative

des·ig·na·tor \-ˌnād·ə(r), -ātə-\ *n* -s [LL, fr. L *designatus* + *-or*] **:** one that designates; *esp* **:** a designative sign in semantics

des·ig·na·to·ry \-ˌnəˌtōrē, -ȯr-, -ri\ *adj* **:** DESIGNATIVE

des·ig·na·tum \ˌdezigˈnād·əm\ *n, pl* **designa·ta** \-d·ə\ [L, neut. of *designatus*, past part. of *designare* to designate, design, lit., to mark out — more at DESIGN] **:** something that is referred to by a word, sign, or linguistic expression whether actually existing or not **:** the class of objects referred to by a sign, including the null class — contrasted with *denotatum*

design bedding *n* **:** an arrangement of herbaceous plants in a definite pattern of contrasting foliage or blossom ⟨the atrocities of *design bedding* still persist in some public gardens as geometric figures or stylized objects stiffly painted in varied colors of leaf and flowers⟩ — distinguished from *carpet bedding*

de·signed \dəˈzīnd, dēˈ-\ *adj* **:** done, performed, or made with purpose and intent often despite an appearance of being accidental, spontaneous, or natural ⟨style . . . is more than the deliberate and ~ creation —Havelock Ellis⟩ **syn** see DELIBERATE

de·sign·ed·ly \-nədlē, -li\ *adv* **:** with definite purpose **:** PURPOSIVELY, DELIBERATELY

des·ig·nee \ˌdezigˈnē *sometimes* -esi-\ *n* -s [*designate* + *-ee*] **:** one who is designated or delegated ⟨the favorite-son ~ of the New York delegation⟩ ⟨one of the plant supervisors is a union ~⟩

de·sign·er \dəˈzīnə(r), dēˈ-\ *n* -s **1 :** one who conceives plans (as large-scale plans or those for public or social projects) ⟨the ~*s* of the Fourth Republic provided what France wanted —*Time*⟩ ⟨it is strange that resistance to this proposition seems strongest among some of the most audacious social ~*s* —Curt Stern⟩ ⟨the planners and ~*s*, the inciters and leaders without whose evil architecture the world would not have been so long scourged —R.H.Jackson⟩ **2 :** one whose work is creating or laying out designs or reproducing designs made by others for products of mechanical, industrial, or practical arts or for architectural structures ⟨a famous industrial ~⟩ ⟨better planners, urban ~*s*, and landscape artists in our schools —J.L.Sert⟩ **3 a :** one who plans, produces, or creates utilitarian or aesthetic objects ⟨ceramic ~*s*⟩ ⟨an outstanding book ~ planned the format⟩ ⟨dress ~⟩ **b :** one who plans and directs the fashioning of theatrical stage settings, costumes, and ballet settings

de·sign·er·ship \-)ˌship\ *n* -s **:** the office or function of a designer **:** accomplishment as designer

de·sign·ful \-nfəl\ *adj* **:** full of design **:** INTENTIONAL — **de·sign·ful·ly** \-f(ə)lē\ *adv*

[1]designing *n* [fr. gerund of [1]*design*] **:** the art of making designs or sketches ⟨studied ~ under experts⟩

[2]designing *adj* [fr. pres. part. of [1]*design*] **1 :** practicing forethought **2 :** concealing under a complaisant manner crafty or evil designs esp. for advancing one's own interests **:** SCHEMING ⟨~ woman⟩ ⟨a selfish and ~ nation, obsessed with the dark schemes of European intrigue —Sir Winston Churchill⟩ ⟨a ~ Providence⟩ — **de·sign·ing·ly** *adv*

de·sign·less \-nləs\ *adj* **:** being without a design — **de·sign·less·ness** *n* -ES

design patent *n* **:** a patent granted to one who has invented any new, original, and ornamental design for an article of manufacture ⟨under a *design patent* the appearance of the article rather than its mechanical function receives protection —*Harvard Law Rev.*⟩

designs *pres 3d sing of* DESIGN, *pl of* DESIGN

de·silicate \(ˈ)dē+\ *vt* [*de-* + *silicate*] **:** to remove silica or silicate from; *esp* **:** to cause to undergo desilication

de·silication \(ˌˈ)dē+\ *n* -s **:** removal of silica from a magma esp. by interaction with limestone and its transfer to the enveloping wall rock where it is fixed in the form of various silicates

de·silt \(ˈ)dē+\ *vt* [*de-* + *silt* (n.)] **:** to remove suspended silt from (the water of a stream) ⟨a basin for ~*ing* water⟩

de·silverization \(ˌˈ)dē+\ *n* -s **:** the act or a process of desilverizing

de·silverize *also* **de·silver** \"+\ *vt* [*desilverize* fr. *de-* + *silver* + *-ize; desilver* fr. *de-* + *silver*] **:** to remove the silver from **:** free from silver ⟨*desilverizing* lead ores⟩ — **de·silverizer** \"+\ *n* -s

des·i·nence \'dezənən(t)s, -esə-\ *n* -s [MF, fr. ML *desinentia*, fr. L *desinent-*, *desinens* + *-ia*] **:** TERMINATION ⟨the ~ of a verse⟩; *often* **:** ENDING c (1) ⟨any Russian inflectional form comprehends a stem and a ~ —Roman Jakobson⟩

des·i·nent \-nənt\ *adj* [L *desinent-*, *desinens*, pres. part. of *desinere* to leave off, cease, fr. *de-* + *sinere* to leave — more at SITE] **:** TERMINAL

des·i·nen·tial \ˌ==ˈnenchəl\ *adj* **1 :** TERMINAL **2 :** of, relating to, or being an inflectional ending

de·sip·i·ence \dəˈsipēən(t)s, dēˈ-\ *also* **de·sip·i·en·cy** \-nsē\ *n, pl* **desipiences** *also* **desipiencies** [L *desipientia*, fr. *desipient-*, *desipiens* + *-ia*] **:** relaxed dallying in enjoyment of foolish trifles

de·sip·i·ent \-pēənt\ *adj* [L *desipient-*, *desipiens*, pres. past. of *desipere* to be foolish, fr. *de-* + *-sipere* (fr. *sapere* to have taste, be wise) — more at SAGE] **:** indulging in desipience ⟨and smiled to see ~ Horace play —Timothy Dwight⟩

de·sir·abil·i·ty \dəˌzīrəˈbiləd·ē, dēˌ-, -ətē, -i\ *n* -ES **1 :** the quality, fact, or degree of being desirable or of having worth ⟨they considered the chances and ~ of revolution⟩ **2 desirabilities** *pl* **:** a desirable condition ⟨we had understood and studied certain *desirabilities* in a truly integrated staff —D.D. Eisenhower⟩

[1]de·sir·able \-ˈzīrəbəl\ *adj* [ME, fr. MF, fr. *desirer* + *-able*] **1 :** capable of arousing desire: **a :** having the power to attract or bring into demand **:** of such properties or qualities as to be wished for or sought ⟨one of the city's most ~ neighborhoods⟩ ⟨a plant species that may prove to be commercially ~⟩; *often* **:** so valuable or excellent as to assure being desired or selected **b :** such as to awake urgent or passionate longing or craving ⟨there are circumstances in which a scoop of dirty water can be supremely ~⟩; *esp* **:** exciting erotic longing ⟨she was never more ~ than at this moment⟩ **2 a :** worth seeking or doing as advantageous, beneficial, or wise **:** ADVISABLE, EXPEDIENT ⟨having the footnotes at the back of the book is not nearly so ~⟩ ⟨even if the highest education were ~ for all, which I doubt —Bertrand Russell⟩ ⟨~ freedom and individual responsibility of the elective system —*Official Register of Harvard Univ.*⟩ **b :** suited to the purposes and objectives of normal society ⟨however ~ a common language for all the world may be —I.A.Richards⟩ ⟨the personal opinion of the judge as to what is ~ or undesirable legislation —M.R.Cohen⟩

[2]desirable \"\ *n* -s **:** one that is desirable ⟨a balanced diet and adequate rest are basic ~*s* for any convalescent⟩ **:** a person or thing that merits or attracts desire or favorable attention and consideration ⟨fostering the ~*s* and weeding out the undesirables⟩; *often* **:** a person regarded as of high social standing and eligibility ⟨moving always in a small circle of ~*s* he scarcely knew the lower world of clubs and theaters and balls existed⟩

de·sir·able·ness \-bəlnəs\ *n* -ES **:** the fact or quality of being desirable **:** DESIRABILITY ⟨I am quite ready to accept the ~ of government liability —O.W.Holmes †1935⟩

de·sir·ably \-blē, -bli\ *adv* **:** in a desirable place or manner **:** to a desirable extent or degree **:** in accordance with what is considered desirable ⟨land ~ situated in a sheltered river valley⟩

[1]de·sire \dəˈzī(ə)r, dēˈ-\ *vb* -ED/-ING/-S [ME *desiren*, fr. OF *desirer*, fr. L *desiderare* to long for, miss, desire, fr. *de-* + *-siderare* (fr. *sider-*, *sidus* star, constellation) — more at SIDEREAL] *vt* **1 :** to long or hope for **:** wish for earnestly **:** exhibit or feel desire for **:** COVET ⟨men who ~ success must be prepared to work⟩ ⟨he *desired* her approval above all things⟩ ⟨*desiring* only a peaceful haven⟩ **2 a :** to ask or call for (something) **:** express a wish for **:** REQUEST ⟨maid services available if *desired*⟩ ⟨they ~ an immediate answer⟩ **b :** to express a wish to (someone) **:** ASK, REQUEST, ENTREAT ⟨~ him to come in⟩ ⟨they *desired* the conference to reconsider its decision⟩ **3** *obs* **:** INVITE **4** *archaic* **:** to feel the loss of ~ *vi* **:** to desire something or the fulfillment of some aim ⟨he can be, if he so ~*s*, the complete master of his own cabinet —H.J.Laski⟩

syn WISH, WANT, CRAVE, COVET: DESIRE, WISH, and WANT are often used with identical intent though in such situations, usu. everyday ones where the degree of intensity of longing or need is not at issue, DESIRE and WISH occur more frequently than WANT as seeming to confer more dignity on the subject or implying more respectfulness ⟨we can definitely order anything you *wish*⟩ ⟨a position *desired* by young lady —*advt*⟩ DESIRE in more general use, however, emphasizes the strength or ardor of feeling and often implies strong intention or aim ⟨more than any other thing on earth he *desired* to fight for his country —W.A.White⟩ ⟨unions which *desired* to avail themselves of the benefits of the law —*Collier's Yr. Bk.*⟩ ⟨the waitress should not ask if wine is *desired*⟩ WISH is less strong, often suggesting a not usu. intense longing for an object unattained, unattainable, or questionably attainable ⟨Newton's law of gravitation could not be *wished* into existence —H.A.Overstreet⟩ ⟨not to have property, if one *wished* it, was almost a certain sign of shiftlessness —Van Wyck Brooks⟩ WANT is a less formal term than WISH and so is often interchangeable with it in situations where dignity of the subject or respectfulness is not at issue, though generally WANT implies a need or lack ⟨those who *wanted* to live long —Morris Fishbein⟩ ⟨the French *wanted* European unity —*N.Y. Times*⟩ CRAVE implies strongly the force of physical or mental appetite or need (as of hunger, thirst, love, or ambition) ⟨to *crave* peace and security after war⟩ ⟨that eternal *craving* for amusement —Donn Byrne⟩ ⟨what he *craved* was books of poetry and chivalry —E.A.Weeks⟩ COVET implies a strong, eager desire, often inordinate and envious and often for what belongs to another ⟨where water is the most *coveted* and essential resource because its supply is limited —*Amer. Guide Series: Texas*⟩ ⟨we hate no people, and *covet* no people's land —Wendell Willkie⟩

[2]desire \"\ *n* -s [ME, fr. MF *desir*, fr. *desirer*] **1 :** conscious impulse toward an object or experience that promises enjoyment or satisfaction in its attainment ⟨with Freud all human behavior seems to be the outcome of ~ — that is, of the search for pleasure —H.M.Parshley⟩ ⟨in all Indian thought since Buddhism, the original sin has been ~, which ensnares the spirit in material incarnation —Weston La Barre⟩ **2 a :** an enduring and passionate longing or intense yearning **:** an urgently impelling motive toward attainment **:** CRAVING, APPETENCY ⟨a ~ of serfs to get rid of the feudalism that has held them in a vise from time out of mind —W.O.Douglas⟩ ⟨the ~ for adventure⟩ ⟨if a plebiscite confirms the people's ~ for independence —Vera M. Dean⟩ ⟨humility is the most difficult of all virtues to achieve; nothing dies harder than the ~ to think well of oneself —T.S.Eliot⟩ **b** (1) **:** a strong physical inclination (2) **:** erotic urge **:** sexual attraction or appetite ⟨the full lips thrust out and taut like the flesh of animals distended by fear or ~ —Willa Cather⟩ ⟨~ is the natural consequence of the sexual instinct —W.S.Maugham⟩ **c :** a striving after in intent **:** a deliberate choice or preference ⟨the conductor's ~ to follow the composer's instructions to the letter⟩ ⟨he expressed a ~ to avoid compulsory measures⟩ **3 :** an asking or formal request for some action **:** PETITION ⟨the yeas and nays of the members of either house on any question shall, at the ~ of one fifth of those present, be entered on the journal —*U.S. Constitution*⟩ **4 :** something that is desired **:** an object of longing ⟨then the leaders got hold of it, took it to pieces and remolded it closer to the heart's ~ —S.H.Adams⟩

syn APPETITE, APPETENCY *or* APPETENCE, CONCUPISCENCE, LUST, PASSION, URGE: DESIRE is a general term applicable to any wish or longing of any sort ⟨the *desire* for change, for novelty, for a relief from the monotony of every day —Aldous Huxley⟩ ⟨a *desire* for admiration in general —Herbert Spencer⟩ ⟨the geisha is only what she has been made in answer to foolish human *desire* for the illusion of love mixed with youth and grace, but without regrets or responsibilities —Lafcadio Hearn⟩ APPETITE applies to a desire strongly calling for satisfaction; it may be wide in its application ⟨it gave men a familiarity with the method and outline of Aristotle's logic, and whetted their *appetite* for more —R.W.Southern⟩ ⟨young Nathaniel Bowditch, the future navigator, first fed his *appetite* for mathematical science —S.E.Morison & H.S.Commager⟩ It is likely to be used in reference to sensual desires and needs ⟨he collected guns and women, and his sexual *appetite* was awesome —E.D.Radin⟩ ⟨*appetites* for expensive clothes and jewelry, good food, strong liquor and weak women —Alan Hynd⟩ APPETENCY and APPETENCE may suggest appetite marked by strong craving ⟨the liquid shine of the workmen's eyes, like the eyes of drinking men when they smell liquor, bright with *appetence* —Mary Austin⟩ ⟨that gnawing dissatisfaction which his purely physical *appetencies* create in him again and again —R.W.Stallman⟩ CONCUPISCENCE may apply to any strong craving but commonly applies to strong or inordinate sexual desire ⟨the principle of sin was designated by the Schoolmen as "*concupiscence*", which included inordinate desires in general, the sexual passion being the prominent element —G.P.Fisher⟩ LUST may apply to any exigent desire but commonly is used in reference to crass craving for something unsanctioned, esp. illicit or inordinate sex ⟨no greed for the land or wealth of any other people, no vulgar ambition, no morbid *lust* for material gain at the expense of others —Sir Winston Churchill⟩ ⟨he had the *lust* for money as Martinez had for women —Willa Cather⟩ ⟨in his morning litany he could pray to be kept from lasciviousness, but when night came *lust* might come with it —Carl Van Doren⟩ PASSION indicates compelling, intense emotion or desire or its ardent fulfillment, often in matters sexual ⟨this consuming *passion* for law made him govern himself, keep in restraint the fierce wrath which leaped up within him —H.E.Scudder⟩ ⟨the *passion* of Giovanni and Annabella is not shown as an affinity of temperament due to identity of blood; it hardly rises above the purely carnal infatuation —T.S.Eliot⟩ ⟨and she loved him with a full, happy *passion* that responded frankly and generously to his —Rose Macaulay⟩ URGE is used of a persistent desire or inclination seeking satisfaction ⟨the *urge* of "backward" peoples to move rapidly from feudalism to industrialism, to acquire modern and expensive technology in a hurry and thus drastically raise their living standards —W.G.Carleton⟩ ⟨the *urges* of dishonest hired girls, prostitutes who didn't want to be reformed, or shiftless husbands —Barbara Klaw⟩

desired *adj* [ME, fr. past part. of *desiren*] **1 :** that is longed or hoped for **2 :** predetermined to be suitable or satisfactory **:** prescribed as requisite **:** RIGHT ⟨once the ~ level is obtained, the helicopter is in a standstill or hovering attitude —S.A. Constantino⟩ ⟨sawed to the ~ width⟩ — **de·sired·ness** \-ī(ə)rdnəs, -īəd-, -īrəd-\ *n* -ES

de·sire·ful \-ī(ə)rfəl, -īəf-\ *adj* [ME, fr. *desire* + *-ful*] **1** *archaic* **:** DESIRABLE **2** *archaic* **:** filled with desire **:** EAGER

de·sire·less \-ī(ə)rləs, -īəl-\ *adj* **:** being without desire

de·sir·er \-īrə(r)\ *n* -s [ME, fr. *desiren* + *-er*] **:** one that desires

desires *pres 3d sing of* DESIRE, *pl of* DESIRE

desiring *pres part of* DESIRE

de·sir·ing·ly *adv* **:** LONGINGLY, YEARNINGLY

de·sir·ous \-ī(ə)rəs\ *adj* [ME, fr. OF *desireus*, *desirous*, fr. *desir* + *-eus*, *-ous* -ous] **1 a :** impelled or governed by desire **:** eagerly wishing **:** SOLICITOUS ⟨the committee is ~ you should select a suitable speaker⟩ ⟨~ of many things⟩ ⟨~ to ask his help⟩ **b :** eager to obtain **:** COVETOUS **2** *obs* **:** expressive of desire **3** *obs* **:** eager and spirited esp. in combat **4** *archaic* **:** DESIRABLE, DELECTABLE — **de·sir·ous·ly** *adv* — **de·sir·ous·ness** *n* -ES

desis *pl of* DESI

-de·sis \ˌdəsəs\ *n comb form, pl* **-de·ses** \ˌdəˌsēz\ [NL, fr. Gk *desis*, fr. *dein* to bind + *-sis* — more at DIADEM] **:** binding ⟨arthro*desis*⟩

de·sist \dəˈzist, dēˈ-, -ˈsi-\ *vb* -ED/-ING/-S [MF *desister*, fr. L *desistere*, fr. *de-* + *sistere* to stand, stop, fr. *stare* to stand — more at STAND] *vi* **:** to give over or leave off **:** refrain from or forbear continuing an action, activity, or endeavor under way — often used with *from* or *in* ⟨he had made two attempts to shave but his hand had been so unsteady that he had been obliged to ~ —James Joyce⟩ ⟨~*ed* in his effort to press love upon her —Sherwood Anderson⟩ ⟨the city has been ordered to ~ from further levies⟩ — compare CEASE AND DESIST ORDER ~ *vt, obs* **:** to cease from **:** DISCONTINUE **syn** see STOP

de·sis·tance *also* **de·sis·tence** \-tən(t)s\ *n* -s **:** the act of desisting **:** cessation of action ⟨pending ~ from violence⟩

de·si·tion \-ˈzishən, -ˈsi-\ *n* -s [ML *desition-*, *desitio*, fr. L *desitus* (past part. of *desinere* to leave off, cease) + *-ion-*, *-io* -ion — more at DESINENT] *archaic* **:** a cessation of being

des·i·tive \'dezəd·iv, -esə-\ *adj* [L *desitus* + E *-ive*] **:** concluding or expressing a conclusion ⟨a ~ proposition⟩

de·size \(ˈ)dē, də+\ *vt* [*de-* + *size* (n.)] **:** to remove size or sizing from (cloth)

[1]desk \'desk\ *n* -s [ME *deske*, fr. ML *desca*, modif. of It *desco* board, table, fr. L *discus* dish, disk, quoit — more at DISH] **1 a :** a table, frame, or case that has a sloping or horizontal surface esp. for writing and reading and is often provided with drawers, compartments, and pigeonholes **b** *obs* **:** BOOKCASE, BOOKSHELF **c :** a reading table or lectern to support the book from which the liturgical service is read that differs from the pulpit from which the sermon is preached **d :** a table, counter, stand, or booth at which a person (as an editor, a police sergeant, a clerk) performs his duties ⟨speeding — at least for first offenders — can be settled for a set fine at the violations ~ —J. C. Ingraham⟩ ⟨leave your key at the ~ when you are out of the hotel⟩ **e :** a music stand **2 a** *Scot* **:** a pew or seat in a church **b :** a seating position according to rank in an orchestra ⟨a first-*desk* violinist⟩ **3 a :** a division of a complex organization that specializes in and is responsible for a particular phase of that organization's activity ⟨the city ~ of a metropolitan newspaper⟩ ⟨the head of the State Department's Northeast Asian ~⟩ **b :** a person officiating at or heading such a desk

2**desk** \"\ *adj* **1 :** engaged at or suitable for use at a desk ⟨no mere ~ executive⟩ ⟨a ~ dictionary⟩ ⟨a ~ chair⟩ ⟨he was a ~ colonel⟩ **2 :** given to theorizing without technical knowledge or experience of field conditions ⟨~ strategists⟩

deskbound \'=,=\ *adj* **:** tied down to work at a desk ⟨an officer ~ in Washington by a heart condition⟩

de·skill \(')dē+\ *vt* [*de-* + *skill* (n.)] **:** to mechanize or break down (as an operation) so that performance may require little or no skill

desk jobber *n* **:** DROP SHIPPER

desk·man \'desk,man, -,mən\ *n, pl* **deskmen 1 :** a supervisor or director of operations performing his duties at a desk: **a :** an official in charge of a desk in a government department **b :** a police sergeant on duty at the desk in a police station **c :** a hotel room clerk **2 :** a newsman who works primarily at a desk processing news and preparing copy

desk pad *n* **:** a pad for use on the writing surface of a desk

desk room *n* **:** rented desk space in a business office

desk shoe *n* **:** a cushioning rubber cap to be slipped on each foot of a metal desk

desk work *n* **:** work usu. performed at a desk

de·slime \(')dē+\ *vt* -ED/-ING/-S [*de-* + *slime* (n.)] **:** to remove slime from ⟨*desliming* of fine coal⟩

desm- *or* **desmo-** *comb form* [NL, fr. Gk, band, bond, fr. *desmos*, fr. *dein* to bind] **:** bond **:** ligament ⟨*desm*algia⟩ ⟨*desmo*graphy⟩

des·ma \'dezmə\ *n, pl* **desma·ta** \-məd·ə,-mətə\ [NL, fr. Gk, bond, fr. *dein* to bind — more at DIADEM] **:** an irregularly branched sponge spicule

des·ma·chyme \'dezmə,kīm\ *n* -S [NL *desma* + Gk *chymos* juice — more at CHYME] **:** connective tissue of sponges

des·ma·cyte \-,sīt\ *n* -S [NL *desma* + E *-cyte*] **:** one of the long fusiform cells forming a fibrous network in sponge cortex

des·man \'dezmən\ *n* -S [short for Sw *desmansråtta*, fr. *desman* musk (fr. MLG *desem*, *dessmer*) + *råtta* rat; akin to OE *disma* musk, OS *desemo*, MHG *tiseme*, *tesem*, all fr. a prehistoric WGmc word borrowed fr. ML *bisamum* musk, of Sem origin; akin to Heb *beśem* pleasant aroma] **1 a :** an aquatic insectivorous mammal (*Desmana moschata*) of Russia that resembles a mole **b :** a related animal (*Galemys pyrenaicus*) of the Pyrenees **2 :** the fur or pelt of a desman

des·man·thus \dez'man(t)thəs\ *n, cap* [NL, fr. Gk *desmē* bundle (fr. *dein* to bind) + NL *-anthus* — more at DIADEM] **:** a genus of American herbs or shrubs (family Leguminosae) with sensitive bipinnate leaves and small whitish flowers

des·ma·res·tia \,demə'restēə, ,dām-, -sch(ē)ə\ *n, cap* [NL, fr. A. G. *Desmarest* †1838 Fr. naturalist + NL *-ia*] **:** a genus of small feathery and usu. lithophytic brown algae (order Desmarestiales) that occur commonly in colder seas of both hemispheres esp. on rocky shores — **des·ma·res·ti·a·ceous** \¦==¦=tē¦āshəs, -chē¦-\ *adj*

des·ma·res·ti·a·les \,demə,restē'ā(,)lēz, ,dām-, -schē'ā-\ *n pl, cap* [NL, fr. *Desmarestia* + *-ales*] **:** an order of much-branched brown algae (class Heterogeneratae) with a single growing apex to each filament and complex pseudo-parenchymatous specialization of the basal part of the thallus — see DESMARESTIA

des·mid \'dezmәd\ *n* -S [NL *Desmidium*, *Desmidiaceae* & *Desmidiales*] **:** any of numerous unicellular or colonial green algae that belong to the order Zygnematales esp. to the family Desmidiaceae or to this together with the Mesotaeniaceae, and that lack asexual means of spore formation, have platelike green chromatophores, and differ from diatoms mainly in lacking a siliceous skeleton

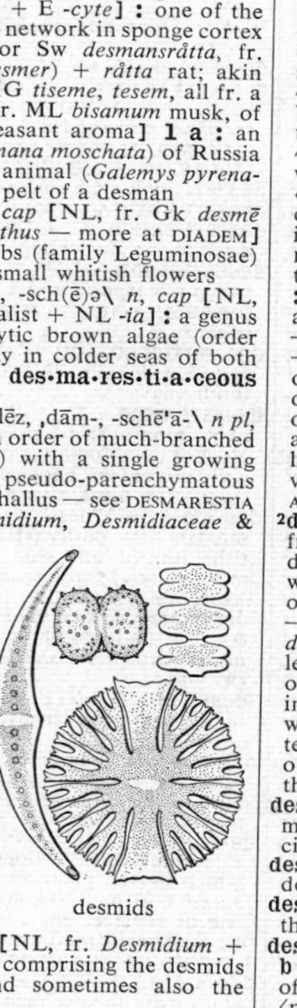

desmids

des·mid·i·a·ce·ae \(,)dez,midē'āsē,ē\ *n pl, cap* [NL, fr. *Desmidium*, type genus (fr. *desm-* + *-idium*) + *-aceae*] **:** a family of unicellular or colonial algae (order Zygnematales) comprising the placoderm desmids — compare MESOTAENIACEAE — **des·mid·i·a·ceous** \(¦)=¦==¦āshəs\ *adj*

des·mid·i·a·les \-'ā(,)lēz\ *n pl, cap* [NL, fr. *Desmidium* + *-ales*] *in some classifications* **:** an order comprising the desmids and including the Desmidiaceae and sometimes also the Mesotaeniaceae

des·mid·i·ol·o·gy \-dē'äləjē\ *n* -ES [NL *Desmidium* + E *-o-* + *-logy*] **:** a branch of botany that deals with desmids

des·mine \'dez,mēn, -,mәn\ *n* -S [Gk *desmē* bundle + E *-ine*] **:** STILBITE

desmo- — see DESM-

des·mo·cranium \,dezmə+\ *n* [NL, fr. *desm-* + *cranium*] **:** the earliest mesenchymal precursor of the chondrocranium

des·mo·cyte \'==,sīt\ *n* -S [*desm-* + *-cyte*] **:** any of certain elongated interstitial cells (as a fibroblast)

des·mo·di·um \dez'mōdēəm\ *n* [NL, prob. irreg. fr. Gk *desmos* band, bond + NL *-ium* — more at DESM-] **1** *cap* **:** a large genus of coarse chiefly tropical and perennial leguminous herbs comprising the tick trefoils and having stipulate pinnate leaves, racemose flowers, and indehiscent fruits that separate into one-seeded segments and often stick to anything touching them — see BEGGARWEED, TELEGRAPH PLANT **2** -S **:** a plant of the genus *Desmodium*

1**des·mo·dont** \'dezmə,dänt\ *adj* [NL *Desmodontidae*] **:** of or belonging to the family Desmodontidae

2**desmodont** \"\ *n* -S **:** a bat of the family Desmodontidae **:** VAMPIRE BAT

des·mo·don·ta \,=='däntə\ *n pl, cap* [NL, fr. *desm-* + *-odonta*] *in some classifications* **:** an order of Lamellibranchia comprising bivalve mollusks having no lateral teeth on the shell and the cardinal teeth often reduced or absent

des·mo·don·ti·dae \-tə,dē\ *n pl, cap* [NL, fr. *Desmodont-*, *Desmodus*, type genus + *-idae*] **:** a small family of bats (suborder Microchiroptera) comprising the true vampire bats

des·mo·dus \'dezmədəs\ *n, cap* [NL, fr. *desm-* + *-odus*] **:** the type genus of Desmodontidae comprising a number of common So. Amer. bloodsucking bats — see VAMPIRE

des·mo·gen \'dezməjәn, -,jen\ *n* -S [*desm-* + *-gen*] **:** vascular meristematic tissue

des·mog·na·thae \dez'mägnə,thē\ *n pl, cap* [NL, fr. *desm-* + *-gnathae*] *in former classifications* **:** a primary division of birds having the maxillopalatines united directly or by ossifications in the nasal septum and including the ducks, geese, herons, storks, totipalmate birds, birds of prey, parrots, and most picarian birds — **desmognathism** \-,thizəm\ *n* -S — **des·mog·na·thous** \(')=¦==,thəs\ *adj*

des·mog·na·thus \-nəthəs\ *n, cap* [NL, fr. *desm-* + *-gnathus*] **:** a genus of small dark salamanders (family Plethodontidae) common and widely distributed in the eastern U.S. — see DUSKY SALAMANDER

des moines \dē'mȯin, dә'-, *chiefly by outsiders* -nz\ *adj, usu cap D & M* [fr. *Des Moines*, Iowa] **:** of or from Des Moines, Iowa **:** of the kind or style prevalent in Des Moines

des·moines·ian \-n(z)ēən\ *adj, usu cap* [*Des Moines*, Iowa + E *-ian*] **:** of, relating to, or constituting a subdivision of the Pennsylvanian — see GEOLOGIC TIME table

des moines squash *n, usu cap D & M* **:** ACORN SQUASH

des·mo·kon·tae \,dezmə'kän(,)tē\ *n pl, cap* [NL, fr. *desm-* + *-kontae* (fr. Gk *kontos* pole)] **:** a class of chiefly solitary and motile algae (division Pyrrophyta) that have the cell wall divided vertically into two valves which are not in turn divided into plates like those of members of the class Dinophyceae

des·mo·lase \'dezmə,lās, -āz\ *n* -S [NL *desmolysis* + E *-ase*] **:** an enzyme (as aldolase) capable of breaking or forming a carbon-to-carbon bond in a molecule and playing a role in respiration and fermentation — often distinguished from *hydrolase*

des·mol·y·sis \dez'mäləsәs\ *n, pl* **desmoly·ses** \-,sēz\ [NL, fr. *desm-* + *-lysis*] **:** a chemical reaction in which a carbon-to-carbon double bond is broken (as by the action of a desmolase) — **des·mo·lyt·ic** \¦dezmə¦lid·ik\ *adj*

des·mon·cus \dez'mäŋkəs\ *n, cap* [NL, fr. *desm-* + Gk *onkos* barbed hook — more at ANGLE] **:** a genus of pinnate-leaved prickly climbing palms found from Mexico to Brazil — see JACITARA PALM

des·mo·neme \'dezmə,nēm\ *n* -S [*desm-* + *-neme*] **:** a nematocyst having a long coiled tube that wraps about projecting parts of the prey when extruded

des·mo·sco·lex \,dezmə'skō,leks\ *n, cap* [NL, fr. *desm-* + *-scolex*] **:** a genus (the type of the family Desmoscolecidae) that comprises minute marine worms having a globular head with four movable setae and a ringed pseudosegmented body and being usu. considered highly specialized nematodes

des·mose \'dez,mōs *also* -,mōz\ *n* -S [ISV *desm-* + *-ose*] **:** any fibril connecting the division centers in mitosis esp. in protozoans — see CENTRODESMOSE, PARADESMOSE

des·mo·spon·gia \,dezmə'spənjēə, -pän-\ *or* **des·mo·spon·gi·ae** \-jē,ē\ [NL, fr. *desm-* + *-spongia*, *-spongiae*] *syn of* DEMOSPONGIAE

des·mo·trope \'dezmə·,trōp\ *n* -S [*desm-* + *-trope*] **:** a form of a chemical element related to another by desmotropism

des·mo·trop·ic \¦==·¦träpik\ *adj* [*desm-* + *-tropic*] **:** of, relating to, or exhibiting desmotropism

des·mot·ro·pism \dez'mä·trə,pizəm\ *or* **des·mot·ro·py** \-rəpē\ *n, pl* **desmotropisms** *or* **desmotropies** [*desm-* + *-tropism*, *-tropy*] **:** tautomerism in which both tautomeric forms have been isolated

de·socialization \(¦)dē, dә+\ *n* -S **:** deprivation of the capacity for social intercourse

de·socialize \(')dē, dә+\ *vt* [*de-* + *socialize*] **:** to deprive of sociality ⟨industrialization tends to ~ man⟩

de·soil \(')dē+\ *vt* [*de-* + *soil* (n.)] **:** to free from dirt

1**des·o·late** \'des|əlәt *also* -ez| *sometimes* |lәt; *usu* -әd·+V\ *adj* [ME *desolat*, fr. L *desolatus*, past part. of *desolare* to abandon, desert, fr. *de* from, away + *-solare* (fr. *solus* alone) — more at DE-, SOLE] **1 :** devoid of inhabitants and visitors **:** DESERTED, ABANDONED ⟨a ~ ghost town⟩ **2** *obs* **a :** DESTITUTE **b :** lacking goodness **:** DISSOLUTE **3 a :** bereaved, forsaken, or abandoned esp. of or by one very dear and consequently inconsolable and crushed by grief ⟨this lady leaning at her window ~, pouring out her abandoned heart —George Meredith⟩ **b :** joyless, disconsolate, and sorrowful through or as if through some separation, destitution, or grief ⟨depressed and ~ of soul . . . and filled with anxious fear —William Wordsworth⟩ **c :** expressing or arising from such grief or sorrow ⟨a low ~ wail which made the terrible scream seem only the quick expression of an endless grief —Bram Stoker⟩ **4 a :** showing the effects of abandonment and neglect **:** RUINED, DILAPIDATED ⟨a ~ old house with sagging floors and broken shutters⟩ **b :** devoid of anything suggesting or furthering life **:** LIFELESS, BARREN, STARK ⟨passing through a ~ once-wooded area that had been ravaged by fire⟩ ⟨~ with crags and alkali —*Amer. Guide Series: Calif.*⟩ ⟨the empty, ~, endless waste —O.E.Rölvaag⟩ **c :** devoid of anything cheering, comforting, or suggesting warmth, comfort, pleasant human relations, or hope **:** DISHEARTENING, CHEERLESS ⟨the stormy howling of the wind in that avenue of great trees at night was wild and ~ —Thomas Wolfe⟩ ⟨a ~ memory of the sterile idle life I had lived —Edmund Wilson⟩ ⟨this wild, ~ lake . . . a very picture of unbroken solitude —John Burroughs⟩ **syn** see ALONE, DISMAL

2**des·o·late** \|ə,lāt, *usu* -ād·+V\ *vt* -ED/-ING/-S [ME *desolaten*, fr. L *desolatus* deserted, past part. of *desolare* to abandon, desert] **:** to make desolate: **a :** to deprive partially or wholly of inhabitants **:** DEPOPULATE ⟨the mines never again operated, and three townships in the vicinity were *desolated* —*Amer. Guide Series: Vt.*⟩ **b :** to lay waste **:** RAVAGE ⟨Hitler *desolated* British cities with bombs —F.L.Allen⟩; *also* **:** to leave in a ruinous or barren state ⟨boulders left by mining operations ~ the valley⟩ **c :** to forsake or leave alone — used in the past participial form ⟨the bulletin board listing casualties was haunted by *desolated* wives⟩ **d :** to rob of joy and contentment; *esp* **:** to leave grief-stricken and wretched ⟨so obsessed with gambling that they ruin their own lives, ~ their families, and alienate their friends —C.B.Davis⟩

des·o·late·ly \|əlәtlē, -tli\ *adv* **:** in desolate state, manner, or mood **:** in grief-stricken loneliness **:** without comforting circumstance or prospect **:** CHEERLESSLY, DISCONSOLATELY

des·o·late·ness \|əlәtnәs\ *n* -ES **:** the quality or state of being desolate **:** LONELINESS, BLEAKNESS

des·o·lat·er *or* **des·o·la·tor** \|ə,lād·ə(r), -ātə-\ *n* -S **:** one that brings desolation

desolating *adj* **:** that desolates: **a :** SADDENING ⟨a ~ letter⟩ **b :** DEJECTING, DISPIRITING, DEPRESSING ⟨the most ~ spectacle of human indiscipline it is possible to conceive —H.G.Wells⟩ ⟨people like myself who frequent the movies testify to their ~ romantic morality —G.B.Shaw⟩ — **des·o·lat·ing·ly** *adv*

des·o·la·tion \,desə'lāshən *also* -ezə-\ *n* -S [LL *desolation-*, *desolatio*, fr. *desolatus* + L *-ion-*, *-io* -ion] **1 :** the action of desolating ⟨Europe was living in a state of anarchy . . . until it erupted into the pitiful ~ and slaughter of World War I —D.F.Fleming⟩ **2 a :** the condition of being desolated **:** a state of ruin, dilapidation, devastation ⟨the Indians fled into the Great Smoky mountains, leaving ruin and ~ behind —*Amer. Guide Series: N.C.*⟩ **b :** a condition of shocking abandonment to confusion and disintegration or of forbidding natural barrenness and bleakness ⟨an appearance of ~ . . . dead cypress masts rise above thick gray underbrush; in others the boggy surface is littered with charred logs and stumps —*Amer. Guide Series: N.C.*⟩ ⟨little to distract the eye from the awful surrounding dreariness and ~ except the bleaching skeletons of horses —*Amer. Guide Series: Ariz.*⟩ **3 a :** gloomy lifeless barren wasteland ⟨bleak, gray, God-forsaken, the empty ~ stretched on every hand —O.E.Rölvaag⟩ **b :** a stark area repellent by reason of wild empty barrenness ⟨nothing was visible but an opaque mist veiling an immense, sun-brown ~ —James Hilton⟩ **c :** an area seeming empty and often repellent because of lacking the presence of man or evidence of his handiwork ⟨the unconquerable ~ of the Yorkshire moors —Ellen Glasgow⟩ **4 a :** disconsolate sorrow from bereavement, abandonment, or loss ⟨he put his trembling hands to his head and gave a ringing scream, the cry of ~ —George Eliot⟩ **b :** dejection **:** dreary sadness ⟨thoughts that climb from ~ toward the genial prime —William Wordsworth⟩

de·sonation \¦dē+\ *n* -S [*de-* + *son*ant + *-ation*] **:** DEVOICING

de son tort \dəsōⁿtȯȯr\ *adj* [F] **:** as a result of his own wrong act — used of persons assuming a responsibility (as of trusteeship) without rightful authority ⟨executor *de son tort*⟩

de·sophisticate \¦dē+\ *vt* [*de-* + *sophisticate*] **:** to divest of sophistication ⟨Joyce . . . is said to have *desophisticated* language —F.R.Leavis⟩ — **de·sophistication** \"+\ *n* -S

de·sorb \(')dē+\ *vt* [*de-* + *sorb*] **:** to free from a sorbed state **:** remove (a sorbed substance) by the reverse of adsorption or absorption — **de·sorb·able** \-əbəl\ *adj*

de·sorption \(')dē+\ *n* -S [fr. *desorb*, after E *absorb: absorption*] **:** the process of desorbing

de·sor's larva \də'zȯrz|-\ *or* **de·sor larva** \-r|-\ *n, usu cap D* [after Édouard *Desor* †1882 Fr. geologist and archeologist] **:** LARVA OF DESOR

desoxy *var of* DEOXY

desoxy- — see DEOXY-

desp *abbr* despatch

1**de·spair** \dә'spa(a)|(ə)r, dē'-, -pe|, |ə\ *vb* -ED/-ING/-S [ME *despeiren*, fr. MF *desperer* (assumed AF 3d pers. pl. pres. indic. *despeirent*), fr. L *desperare*, fr. *de-* + *sperare* to hope; akin to L *spes* hope and prob. to OE *spēd* success — more at SPEED] *vi* **1 :** to lose hope utterly ⟨sailors are too sanguine to ~, even at the last moment —Frederick Marryat⟩ ⟨to resign or ~ you must first of all have an aim that you cannot attain —Stefan Schimanski⟩; *also* **:** to give up all expectation — used with *of* ⟨I should ~, however, of any successful analysis of problems at once so large and so difficult within the limits of this paper —B.N.Cardozo⟩ ⟨we *~ed* of mastering the idiomatic niceties of the language⟩ **2 :** to give up hope for or belief in the success, progress, or achievement — used with *of* ⟨*~ed* of man —Karl Meyer⟩ ⟨~ of people who do not like poetry⟩ **~** *vt, obs* **:** to lose hope for

2**despair** \"\ *n* -S [ME *despeir*, fr. (assumed) AF *despeir*, fr. (assumed) OF *despeir* (whence OF *despoir*), fr. *desperer*, v. (3d pers. pl. pres. indic. *despeirent*)] **1 :** utter loss of hope **:** complete domination by feelings of hopelessness, futility, or defeat, wildly and bitterly expressed or quietly and pervasively dominant **:** complete loss of expectation of something wished for ⟨his ~, which may find expression in . . . suicide —Rudyard Kipling⟩ ⟨subject to alternating moods of elation and ~⟩ ⟨with the apathy of entire ~ he simply assented to whatever measures they suggested —Sheridan Le Fanu⟩; *often* **:** a fit of despair — usu. used in pl. ⟨the hopes, the *~s* that accompanied our labors⟩ **2 a :** something that constitutes a cause for despair ⟨an incorrigible child is the ~ of his parents⟩ **b :** something that causes bafflement and loss of hope that it can be successfully emulated, comprehended, or otherwise acted upon in the desired way ⟨his nondescript features are the ~ of caricaturists⟩ ⟨play on words is the translator's ~ —J.C.Swaim⟩ ⟨the theory of induction is the ~ of philosophy —A.N.Whitehead⟩

despaired *adj* [ME *despeired*, fr. past part. of *despeiren*] **:** no longer hoped for **:** UNHOPED — often used with *of*

de·spair·ful \|rfəl, |əf-\ *adj* **:** full of despair **:** HOPELESS — **de·spair·ful·ly** \-əlē, -li\ *adv*

despairing *adj* **:** given to, arising from, or marked by despair, vanished hope, vain wild hopes ⟨tauntingly repelling the last ~ claim of a condemned culprit —H.T.Cockburn⟩ **syn** see DESPONDENT

de·spair·ing·ly *adv* **:** in a despairing manner

de·spair·ing·ness *n* -ES **:** the quality or state of being despairing

despatch *var of* DISPATCH

de·specialization \(¦)dē+\ *n* **:** the act of despecializing

de·specialize \(')dē+\ *vb* [*de-* + *specialize*] *vi* **:** to reverse or reduce specialization **~** *vt* **:** to divest of specialization

de·spe·ci·ate \(')dē¦spēs(h)ē,āt\ *vt* -ED/-ING/-S [*de-* + *species* + *-ate*] **:** to remove the characteristic antigenicity of (a foreign protein) by chemical or other treatment — **de·spe·ci·a·tion** \(¦)dē,spēs(h)ē¦āshən\ *n* -S

de·specificate \(¦)dē+\ *vt* [*de-* + *specificate*] **:** to divest of specific signification — **de·specification** \"+\ *n*

de·spect \dә'spekt\ *n* -S [L *despectus*, fr. *despectus* past part. of *despicere* to look down upon, despise — more at DESPISE] *archaic* **:** CONTEMPT

desperacy *n* -ES [*desperate* + *-cy*] *obs* **:** DESPERATION

des·per·a·do \,despə'rä|(,)dō, -rā|, -rå|\ *n, pl* **desperadoes** *also* **desperados** [prob. alter. (influenced by Sp *-ado*, as in *renegado*) of 2*desperate*] **1** *obs* **:** one in despair or in desperate straits **2 :** a bold or violent criminal; *typically* **:** a bandit of the western frontier ⟨bands of *desperadoes* lay in wait every few miles along the highway —Green Peyton⟩

des·per·a·do·ism \-ō,izəm\ *n* -S **:** a wave or period of unusual activity by desperadoes

1**des·per·ate** \'desp(ə)rә|t, -pər|t, *usu* |d·+V\ *adj* [L *desperatus*, past part. of *desperare* to despair — more at DESPAIR] **1 :** having lost hope **:** yielding to despair ⟨he seemed, somehow, helpless and ~, as if he had come to the end of his tether —Rose Macaulay⟩ **:** giving no ground for hope ⟨the prospect was not only grim, it was ~. Britain stood alone; Dunkirk, for all its heroism, had been a disaster —H.S.Commager⟩ **2 a :** moved by despair ⟨there is reason to believe that they jumped overboard of their own will, made ~ at the sight of the sacrifice of a brother —B.N.Cardozo⟩ **:** likely to seize at wild vain hopes ⟨act with the folly and extravagance of ~ men —Adam Smith⟩ **:** involving the adoption of grim, rash, or otherwise extreme measures to escape defeat or frustration ⟨they have gradually lost faith in their own traditional ways and are ready for any ~ attempt to catch up with modern civilization —M.H.Trytten⟩ **b :** arising from or indicative of extreme need or pressure of circumstance ⟨those artists whom the presage of an early death stimulates to a ~ activity —Roger Fry⟩ ⟨had conceived the ~ idea of seeking the family fortune in the United States —Helen B. Woodward⟩ **c :** facing the worst with resolution and disregard of the cost ⟨it found her despairing **:** it left her ~ —two different states —Charlotte Brontë⟩; *esp* **:** exerting one's last ounce of energy in a do-or-die effort ⟨the ~ gallantry of our naval task forces marked the turning point in the Pacific —G.C.Marshall⟩ ⟨there is such a thing as a ~ pursuit of Truth; a pursuit fierce, relentless, absorbing —J.C.Powys⟩ **d :** suffering extreme need or anxiety ⟨the old lady was ~ for money —Mary R. Rinehart⟩ ⟨~ for something to do —F.L.Keefe⟩ ⟨in sudden terror at his tone, ~ to please him —B.A.Williams⟩ **3 a** (1) **:** devoid of any reasonable hope of betterment, solution, success, or salvation ⟨that *A* is in affluent circumstances while *B* is in ~ straits, with heavy responsibilities —W.M. Sibley⟩ ⟨for many institutions, the financial stringency which had been ~ during the war —T.L.Hungate⟩ (2) **:** practically irretrievable **:** UNCOLLECTIBLE ⟨a ~ debt⟩ **b :** fraught with extreme danger or impending disaster **:** CRUCIAL ⟨on all the fighting fronts the Allies were in a ~ situation due to lack of adequate materiel —G.C.Marshall⟩ ⟨the question of defense has been ~ for Israel from the day it became a state in 1948 —Claire Sterling⟩ **c :** suited to or incited by an all but hopeless situation ⟨the bitter, ~ striving unto death of the oppressed race —Rose Macaulay⟩ ⟨iron plates which Renwick had a ~ time getting because of the war —James Dugan⟩ **4 :** of extreme intensity **:** OVERPOWERING, OVERMASTERING, VEHEMENT ⟨I take ~ likes and dislikes —John Buchan⟩ ⟨a ~ languor descended heavily upon her, and she slept —Elinor Wylie⟩ ⟨two archrivals may be seen avoiding each other with ~ zeal —R.D.Altick⟩ **5 :** SHOCKING, OUTRAGEOUS ⟨everywhere there was a ~ grime and greasiness —William McFee⟩ ⟨sentimentality is a ~ word to hurl at an artist of any kind —Herbert Read⟩ **syn** see DESPONDENT

2**desperate** \"\ *n* -S **1** *archaic* **:** a person in desperate condition or circumstances **2** *obs* **:** a desperate character **:** DESPERADO 2

3**desperate** \"\ *adv, dial* **:** DESPERATELY

4**des·per·ate** \-pə,rāt\ *vt* -ED/-ING/-S **:** to render desperate

des·per·ate·ly \-pərtlē, -p(ə)rәt-, -li\ *adv* **1 :** in a desperate manner: **a :** so as to leave little hope (as of recovery or escape) **:** DANGEROUSLY ⟨became ~ ill with pneumonia⟩ ⟨the old fixation, the result of 14 years together, still ~ influences her mind and body —Leslie Rees⟩ **b :** with an intensified or all-out last-ditch effort in refusal to give up a struggle or purpose ⟨~ fighting asthma⟩ ⟨figures struggling ~ among the countless corpses that floated in the heavy seas —H.E. Rieseberg⟩ ⟨grasping ~ at any straw to stave off starvation⟩ **c :** in utter indifference to consequences or danger **:** with reckless abandon ⟨the tough cruel but ~ brave Arab slavers —Rodney Gilbert⟩ **d :** with a degree of obligation or pressure of necessity not to be denied or delayed **:** URGENTLY, INDISPENSABLY, COMPELLINGLY ⟨I emphasize the religious element in our national inheritance because I believe it is the one which ~ needs to be reexamined and recovered —Ruth Suckow⟩ ⟨~ needed potash in the soil⟩; *also* **:** with unyielding insistence ⟨~ ambitious to make up for lost time —Gerald Priestland⟩ ⟨I wanted ~ to be popular⟩ **2 a :** to such a degree or such a degree of intensity as to bring dismay or distress close to despair **:** APPALLINGLY, FRIGHTFULLY, SHOCKINGLY ⟨~ poor, they lived mostly on fat pork and cornbread⟩ ⟨all houses and cellars were ~ overcrowded —J.H.Plumb⟩ **b :** to a superlative degree **:** EXTREMELY, INTENSELY ⟨one must get ~ tired of a climate which knows no winter or summer —Vernon Bartlett⟩ ⟨never was the need for the proper discharge of this task so ~ urgent —*Publ's Mod. Lang. Assoc. of Amer.*⟩ ⟨consistently entertaining, and at times it is, in fact, ~ funny —C.J.Rolo⟩ ⟨I'm ~ sorry, sir⟩ **c :** with undue complication of detail or protraction **:** TORTUOUSLY ⟨it darkens toward the end and winds up in a ~ contrived coincidence —*Time*⟩

des·per·ate·ness \-p(ə)rәtnәs, -pərt-\ *n* -ES **:** DESPERATION

des·per·a·tion \,despə'rāshən\ *n* -S [ME *desperacioun*, fr. MF or L; MF *desperation*, fr. L *desperation-*, *desperatio*, fr. *desperatus* + *-ion-*, *-io* -ion] **1 :** the quality or state of being desperate ⟨disillusionment and disgust may become ~ —*Times Lit. Supp.*⟩ **:** a loss or abandonment of hope and surrender to misery or dread ⟨he shivered with fear and with cold, and a ~ began to possess him —Farley Mowat⟩; *also* **:** a strong urgency ⟨the very ~ of this dire need for some glimpse into that darkness which is the future —F.L.Mott⟩ **2 :** adoption of a last resource : a seizing on any action or means that offer any hope of success regardless of consequences : extreme recklessness ⟨with all the ~ of a fox caught by wire netting in a fowl run —J.C.Powys⟩ ⟨she had had the courage of ~, and that had saved her from failure —Ellen Glasgow⟩

de·spic·a·bil·i·ty \dә̇,spikә'bilәd·ē, -әtē, -i *also* ,despә̇k- *or* 'de,spik-\ *n* -ES : DESPICABLENESS

de·spic·a·ble \dә̇'spikәbәl *also* 'despә̇k- *or* 'de,spik-\ *adj* [LL *despicabilis*, fr. L *despicari* to look down upon, despise + *-abilis* -able; akin to L *despicere* to despise — more at DESPISE] **1 :** deserving to be despised : meriting hatred, scorn, or loathing ⟨the immorality of James's court was hardly more ~ than the imbecility of his government —J.R.Green⟩ **2** *obs* : CONTEMPTUOUS **syn** see CONTEMPTIBLE

de·spic·a·ble·ness *n* -ES : the quality or state of being despicable

de·spic·a·bly \-blē, -li\ *adv* : in a despicable manner : with contempt

despiciency *n* -ES [L *despicientia*, fr. *despicient-*, *despiciens* (pres. part. of *despicere* to look down upon, despise) + *-ia* — more at DESPISE] *obs* : a looking down upon : CONTEMPT

de·spiralization \(ˌ)dē, dә̇+\ *n* [*de-* + *spiralization*] *biol* : the uncoiling of the helical chromonema that is esp. evident toward the end of the meiotic prophase — **de·spiralize** \(')dē, dә̇+\ *vi*

de·spiritualization \(ˌ)dē+\ *n* : the process of despiritualizing

de·spiritualize \(')dē+\ *vt* [*de-* + *spiritualize*] : to deprive of spiritual character or influence ⟨~ education and you devitalize life —W.L.Sullivan⟩

de·spis·able \dә̇'spīzәbәl, dē'-\ *adj* [ME, fr. MF, fr. *despis-* (stem of *despire*) + *-able*] : DESPICABLE

de·spis·al \-zәl\ *n* -S : intense dislike : CONTEMPT, DESPISING ⟨this modern ~ of the pun —Clemence Dane⟩

de·spise \dә̇'spīz, dē'-\ *vt* -ED/-ING/-S [ME *despisen*, fr. OF *despis-*, stem of *despire*, fr. L *despicere*, fr. *de-* + *spicere*, *specere* to look — more at SPY] **1 a :** to look down on : think of (a person) as objectionable, reprehensible, discreditable, disgraceful : hold oneself above : regard as an inferior ⟨that the young are in full revolt against them, and that the child born now may grow up to ~ them —*Times Lit. Supp.*⟩ **b :** to feel disrespect or aversion toward or disgust of : DISDAIN, DETEST ⟨despised the poor whites as creatures distinctly inferior to Negroes —H.L.Mencken⟩ **2 a :** to regard (something) as negligible, worthless, distasteful, a nuisance, a disgrace ⟨health comes first and good looks are not to be *despised* —J.M.Barzun⟩ ⟨submariners have always *despised* the need to evade in order to survive —S.D.Cutter⟩ ⟨they ~ all forms of organized religion, yet luxuriate in theology historically considered —*N.Y.Herald Tribune Bk. Rev.*⟩ : think of or look on with shame, repugnance, disgust : LOATHE ⟨that the spirit of Charity which neither ~*s* nor fears the nations of another creed and color —J.L.Cranmer-Byng⟩ **b :** to ignore or scorn as not worth taking steps to avoid or counter : SPURN ⟨he was in a state to ~ consequences —Arnold Bennett⟩ **3** *now dial* : DISLIKE, SCORN ⟨~ to vote for a party controlled from the outside —R.B.Vance⟩

syn CONTEMN, SCORN, DISDAIN, SCOUT: DESPISE, implying any emotional reaction from strong disfavor to loathing, stresses the judging of a thing as mean, petty, worthless, or repulsive, and a consequent, often derisive, looking down upon it ⟨when the inferior creature appreciates us, we cease to *despise* her —George Meredith⟩ ⟨an enemy . . . he loathed and hated, never *despised* —Laura Krey⟩ ⟨to *despise* certain foods⟩ CONTEMN suggests a somewhat harsher though more intellectual judgment and condemnation than DESPISE ⟨his own early drawings of moss roses and picturesque castles — things that he now mercilessly *contemned* —Arnold Bennett⟩ ⟨the human need of entertainment as a counterbalance in modern life is *contemned* by the serious novelists as "escapism" —A.C. Ward⟩ SCORN implies quick, indignant or profound contempt, esp. vocal or visible ⟨they *scorn* decorative chrome on the body, and remove it ruthlessly to reduce the car to its cleanest lines —*Lamp*⟩ ⟨the Welshmen so *scorned* the Saxons that they refused to extend to them the blessings of Christianity in the third century —O.S.J.Gogarty⟩ DISDAIN suggests a supercilious and visible contempt for or aversion to something regarded as unworthy ⟨the psychiatric patient is *disdained* and ridiculed by his fellow inmates —R.S.Banay⟩ ⟨despised by those superior persons who *disdain* her as old-fashioned —M.R.Cohen⟩ SCOUT stresses the rejection or dismissal with ridicule of anything (as a person or idea) one considers unworthy of consideration ⟨his Majesty will be most provoked if his ideas are *scouted* —C.S.Forester⟩ ⟨we scorned presentiments and *scouted* occult influences —F.W.Crofts⟩

de·spised·ness \-zә̇dnә̇s, -z(d)n-\ *n* -ES : the quality or state of being despised

de·spise·ment \-zmәnt\ *n* -S : DESPISAL

de·spis·er \-zә(r)\ *n* -S [ME, fr. *despisen* + *-er*] : one that despises

de·spis·ing·ly *adv* : in a despising manner : SCORNFULLY

1**de·spite** \dә̇'spīt, dē'-, *usu* -īd·+V\ *n* -S [ME, fr. OF *despit*, fr. L *despectus* — more at DESPECT] **1 :** the feeling or attitude of despising : CONTEMPT ⟨the ~ in which cunners are held is a convention —*Yale Rev.*⟩ **2 :** ill will, aversion, or indignation toward another esp. accompanied with a desire to vex or harm : MALICE, GRUDGE, SPITE ⟨the whites mingle freely with these redskins, bearing them no such ~ —Horace Kephart⟩ **3 :** an act showing contempt or defiance ⟨to say that these habitually coincide is surely doing ~ to our judgment —T.S.Omond⟩ : HARM ⟨I know of no government which stands to its obligations, even in its own ~, more solidly —Sir Winston Churchill⟩ ⟨when, in ~ of American opinion and interests, things go awry —D.W.Brogan⟩ **syn** see MALICE

2**despite** \"\ *vb* -ED/-ING/-S [ME *despiten*, fr. MF *despitier*, fr. L *despectare*, fr. *despectus*] *vt* **1** *archaic* : to treat with contempt **2** *obs* : to vex or injure spitefully ~ *vi*, *obs* : to show despite or contempt

3**despite** \"\ *prep* [(*in*) *despite* (*of*)] : without deterrence or prevention by : NOTWITHSTANDING : without being blocked, balked, or thwarted by : in spite of ⟨he managed to hold his position until retirement ~ failing health⟩ ⟨privateers were fitted out in American ports ~ official opposition —D.G. Munro⟩ ⟨generous ~ their own economic troubles —Arthur Rucker⟩

de·spite·ful \-ītfәl\ *adj* [ME *dispitful*, fr. *despit* + *-ful*] **1** *obs* : CONTEMPTUOUS : INSOLENT ⟨backbiters, haters of God, ~, proud, boasters —Rom 1:30 (AV)⟩ **2 :** expressing malice or contemptuous hate : MALEVOLENT ⟨a ~ fiend⟩

de·spite·ful·ly \-әlē, -li\ *adv* [ME *despitfully*, fr. *despitful* + *-ly*] **1** *obs* : CONTEMPTUOUSLY **2 :** MALICIOUSLY, MALEVOLENTLY, ABUSIVELY ⟨bless them that curse you, pray for them that ~ use you —Lk 6:28 (AV)⟩

de·spite·ful·ness *n* -ES : MALICE, CRUELTY

de·spit·e·ous \dә̇'spid·ēәs, (')de¦s-\ *adj* [ME, alter. of *despitous*, fr. MF *despiteus*, fr. *despit* + *-eus* -ous] *archaic* : full of or moved by ill will : CONTEMPTUOUS, DESPITEFUL; *broadly* : MALICIOUS, CRUEL, PITILESS

de·spit·e·ous·ly *adv* [ME, fr. *despiteous* + *-ly*] *archaic* : DESPITEFULLY

1**de·spoil** \dә̇'spȯil, dē'-, *esp before pause or consonant* -ȯiәl\ *vt* -ED/-ING/-S [ME *despoylen*, fr. OF *despoillier*, fr. L *despoliare*, fr. *de-* + *spoliare* to strip, rob, plunder — more at SPOIL] **1 :** to strip of belongings or possessions : PLUNDER, PILLAGE ⟨the English buccaneers . . . fell upon their cities and ~*ed* them —F.J.Haskin⟩ ⟨the great northern war involving Sweden, Denmark, and Russia completely ~*ed* Poland —J.S.Davenport⟩ **2** *obs* : to strip of garments or armor : DISROBE **3 :** to deprive or divest coercively or wantonly — used with *of* ⟨monasteries were occasionally ~*ed* of their land and revenues —Owen & Eleanor Lattimore⟩ ⟨that Colombia had been ~*ed* of the Isthmus of Panama⟩ ⟨only the Etruscans ~*ed* the Sirens of all birdlike attributes —Norman Douglas⟩ **4 :** to strip of what is of value : DENUDE ⟨the ~*ing* of the land by their primitive methods of subsistence farming —Jean Fortt⟩; *also* : to strip away ⟨magnificent stands of pine ~*ed* by loggers⟩ **5 :** to wrest away, blast, or wreck as if by predatory raid ⟨her maternal instincts, stimulated and then ~*ed*, were increased, and when she loved it was always with an anxious and protective love —Susan Ertz⟩ ⟨you have disagreed and argued without calling each other liars and thieves, without ~*ing* our best traditions —A.E.Stevenson b. 1900⟩ **syn** see RAVAGE

2**despoil** \"\ *n* -S [MF *despoille*, fr. *despoillier*] **1** *archaic* : DESPOILING **2** *obs* : BOOTY

de·spoil·er \-ȯilә(r)\ *n* -S [ME *despoyler*, fr. *despoylen* + *-er*] : one that despoils ⟨no criminal was thought to be worse than a ~ of tombs⟩ ⟨warning against Communism as the No. 1 ~ of the democratic ideal —*Time*⟩

de·spoil·ment \-ȯi(ә)lmәnt\ *n* -S : DESPOLIATION ⟨the ~ of colored women by white men is likewise held in the spotlight —H.M.Gloster⟩ ⟨the ~ and division of Poland⟩

de·spoliation \dә̇, dē +\ *n* -S [LL *despoliation-*, *despoliatio*, fr. L *despoliatus* (past part. of *despoliare*) + *-ion-*, *-io* -ion] : a stripping or plundering : condition of being despoiled : SPOLIATION ⟨residents fear ~ of their charming community⟩

1**de·spond** \dә̇'spänd, dē'-\ *vi* -ED/-ING/-S [L *despondēre*, to promise, betroth, despair, fr. *de-* + *spondēre* to promise solemnly — more at SPOUSE] : to feel utter discouragement : undergo deep depression of spirits at vanishing hope, courage, or confidence

2**despond** \" *sometimes* 'de,spänd\ *n* -S : DESPONDENCY

de·spon·dence \-dәn(t)s\ *n* -S **1 :** DESPONDING ⟨his sudden ~ surprised us⟩ **2 :** DESPONDENCY ⟨often the prey of doubt and fear, of bleak ~, stark anxiety —Walter de la Mare⟩

de·spon·den·cy \-dәnsē, -si\ *n* -ES **1 :** condition of being despondent : discouragement and dejection inducing apathetic inertia ⟨I found him in a state, if not of ~, of dejection —O.S.J.Gogarty⟩ **2 :** an instance or cause of a despondent condition ⟨those nearest him noticed a ~ and indecision in his bearing —S.H.Adams⟩

1**de·spon·dent** \-dәnt\ *adj* [L *despondent-*, *despondens*, pres. part. of *despondēre*] : feeling extreme discouragement, dejection, or depression : experiencing or expressing an all but complete loss of hope or sense of defeat ⟨~ about his health, he killed himself⟩

syn FORLORN, HOPELESS, DESPAIRING, DESPERATE: DESPONDENT indicates utter discouragement and suggests either mournful or sullen dejection ⟨something dark and cold had settled over her thoughts. She could not shake it off though she told herself that it was unreasonable for her to feel so *despondent* —Ellen Glasgow⟩ ⟨Twain was filled with a *despondent* desire, a momentary purpose even, to stop writing altogether —Van Wyck Brooks⟩ FORLORN connotes pitiful, hopeless dejection, often resulting from a betrayal, calamity, or bereavement ⟨poor Columbine, *forlorn* and betrayed and dying, out in the cold at midnight — sinking down to hell, perhaps — was making her last frantic appeal —George du Maurier⟩ ⟨suggested by the portrait of Beatrice Cenci; and, in fact, there was a look somewhat similar to poor Beatrice's *forlorn* gaze out of the dreary isolation and remoteness, in which a terrible doom had involved a tender soul —Nathaniel Hawthorne⟩ Applied to actions or situations, it suggests a pathetic inadequacy certain of frustration or defeat ⟨spoke . . . with a *forlorn* effort at dignity —Sinclair Lewis⟩ HOPELESS suggests ending of hope and struggle and may imply dejection or resignation ⟨the little *hopeless* community of beaten men and yellow defeated women —Sherwood Anderson⟩ ⟨realizing now that pleading was useless, the men quieted down, and we resigned ourselves to the situation in that mood of *hopeless* apathy that comes over men powerless to help themselves —C.B.Nordhoff & J.N.Hall⟩ Of actions, it indicates impossibility of success and makes no implication about the spirit of the actors ⟨no body of men would stand against them, so *hopeless* was the enterprise —H.G.Wells⟩ DESPAIRING may suggest a situation in which a last, wild, vain hope is harbored ⟨tauntingly repelling the last *despairing* claim of a condemned culprit —H.T.Cockburn⟩ ⟨the author of 'Friendship's Garland' ended with a *despairing* appeal to the democracy, when his jeremiads evoked no response from the upper class, whom he called barbarians, or from the middle class, whom he regarded as incurably vulgar —W.R.Inge⟩ Applied to people, DESPERATE describes conditions in which reasonable hope is gone, or reckless action is considered ⟨now inhabited by a band of brigands, outlawed by government, strong in discipline, furious from penury, reckless by habit, *desperate* in circumstance — a crew which feared not God nor man nor devil —J.L.Motley⟩ ⟨driven from their cabins and little holdings, their crops and cattle taken from them, they were everywhere around *desperate* with poverty, and discontented equally with their own landlords and the restraints put upon them by the government —Anthony Trollope⟩ ⟨he felt *desperate*. He was ready to pay any price —Arnold Bennett⟩ Used with situations, it indicates wild crucial importunateness and exigency ⟨he is in a more *desperate* way financially than ever. He can borrow no more, and his debtors are clamoring —Gertrude Atherton⟩ ⟨when a country is in *desperate* straits, and everything hangs on the issue of a single battle —W.H.Mallock⟩ Of actions, it indicates motivation by despair ⟨the king's *desperate* efforts could hardly save his army from utter rout —J.R.Green⟩ ⟨such cries of terror and consternation on the part of the bird, tacking to the right and left, and making the most *desperate* efforts to escape —John Burroughs⟩

2**despondent** \"\ *n* -S : one who desponds

de·spond·ent·ly *adv* : in a despondent mood, manner, or tone

desponding *adj* **1 :** DESPONDENT ⟨I feel quite ~ about the election tonight —Emily Eden⟩ **2 :** causing despondency — **de·spond·ing·ly** *adv*

desponsories *n pl* [modif. (influenced by L *desponsare*) of Sp *desposorios*, fr. *desposar* to marry, betroth, fr. L *desponsare* to betroth, fr. *de-* + *sponsa* spouse — more at SPOUSE] **1** *obs* : BETROTHAL **2** *obs* : a writing formally announcing a betrothal

des·pot \'despә|t, -,spä|, *usu* |d· + V\ *n* -S [MF *despot*, *despote*, fr. Gk *despotēs* master, lord, despot; akin to Skt *dampati* lord of the house; both from a prehistoric compound whose first and second constituents are akin respectively to L *domus* house and to L *potis* able — more at TIMBER, POTENT] **1 a :** a Byzantine emperor or a prince of his imperial house : a vassal prince — used as a title of honor or address **b :** a bishop or patriarch of the Eastern Orthodox Church **c :** a petty Christian ruler tributary to the Turks after the Turkish conquest of Constantinople ⟨the ~ of Morea⟩ **d :** an Italian hereditary prince or military leader during the Renaissance **2 a :** a ruler with absolute or virtually absolute power and authority : AUTOCRAT ⟨Lord Curzon, the most enigmatic and greatest of those benevolent ~*s* —W.B.Willcox⟩ **b :** a ruler exercising absolute power abusively, oppressively, or tyrannously : TYRANT ⟨as a ~ he ruled by the force of arms⟩ **3 a :** a person having recognized and complete governance or authority and usu. domineering or oppressive ⟨affection by itself can turn an old nurse into a cranky ~ —Joyce Cary⟩ **b :** an animal or thing that seems to hold dominance and strict control ⟨it is not necessarily the strongest bird which becomes ~ —E.A.Armstrong⟩ ⟨the tireless machine is the ~ of our age —Waldemar Kaempffert⟩

des·po·tate \-pә,tāt\ *also* **des·po·tat** \-tat\ *n* -S [F *despotat*, fr. *despote* + *-at* -ate] : a state or principality ruled by a despot

des·pot·ic \dә̇'späd·|ik, (')de¦s-, -ät|, |ēk\ *also* **des·pot·i·cal** \|ә̇kәl\ *adj* [F *despotique*, fr. Gk *despotikos*, fr. *despotēs* + *-ikos* -ic, -ical] **1 :** belonging to or having the character of an absolute ruler ⟨God's universal law gave to the man ~ power over his female —John Milton⟩ ⟨the introduction of European civilization was forced from above by ~ rulers chiefly for military and political reasons —M.R.Cohen⟩ **2 :** ruling as or ruled by a despot ⟨the government of China was based upon natural law and was that of a ~ emperor —A.E.Nuquist⟩ ⟨moved from a feudal to a ~ order —K.A.Wittfogel⟩; *esp* : exhibiting imperious and usu. oppressive exercise of absolute power ⟨his administration remained arrogant and ~⟩ **3 :** generally domineering and arbitrary ⟨as ~ as an old-time schoolmaster⟩ **syn** see ABSOLUTE

des·pot·i·cal·ly \|ә̇k(ә)lē, |ēk-, -li\ *adv* : in a despotic manner : as a despot ⟨the company town implies a hierarchy ~, if benevolently, guiding the lives of those beneath —W.H. Whyte⟩ ⟨ruling his kingdom ~⟩

des·po·tism \'despә,tizәm *also* -pәd·,iz-\ *n* -S [F *despotisme*, fr. *despote* despot + *-isme* -ism] **1 a :** rule by a despot : TYRANNY ⟨~ is a perversion of sovereignty in which the interests of a governing class usurp the place belonging to the general interest —G.H.Sabine⟩ ⟨an excess of law is ~, from which free men revolt —S.B.Pettengill⟩ **b :** arbitrary or despotic exercise of power : any harsh or oppressive arbitrary domination ⟨under the parental ~ of the Confucian code of ethics —*Times Lit. Supp.*⟩ ⟨warnings against educational ~⟩ ⟨that ~ is one of the major biological principles; that whenever two birds are together invariably one is despot —W.C.Allee⟩ ⟨game fads sweep film circles, achieve a social ~ which lasts for weeks —Leo Rosten⟩ **2 a :** a system of government in which the ruler has unlimited power : ABSOLUTISM, AUTOCRACY ⟨the conception of government by naked, overwhelming power alone — power itself ungoverned by anything beyond the whims of its possessors . . . is of course the conception of tyranny or ~ —J.T.Dunlop⟩ ⟨the old ~ of the czars⟩ **b :** a despotic state ⟨that Communism is the surest way yet found to continue the old Asian ~*s* in modern times —*New Yorker*⟩ ⟨under the ~ of Cromwell —Hilaire Belloc⟩

des·pot·ist \-pәd·ә̇st, -pәtә̇-\ *n* -S : an advocate or supporter of despotism

des·po·tize \-pә,tīz, -pәd·,īz\ *vi* -ED/-ING/-S [F *despotiser*, fr. *despote* + *-iser* -ize] : to act the despot

des·pu·mate \'despyü,māt, dә̇'s-\ *vb* -ED/-ING/-S [L *despumatus*, past part. of *despumare* to skim off, fr. *de-* + *spuma* froth — more at SPUME] *vt*, *archaic* : to clarify (as wine or honey) by removing a surface scum : SKIM ~ *vi*, *archaic* : to cast off a scum : work off impurities in foam or scum

des·pu·ma·tion \,despyü'māshәn\ *n* -S [LL *despumation-*, *despumatio*, fr. L *despumatus* + *-ion-*, *-io* -ion] *archaic* : the act of discharging impurities from the body fluids; *sometimes* : matter so discharged

des·qua·mate \'deskwә,māt\ *vi* -ED/-ING/-S [L *desquamatus*, past part. of *desquamare*, fr. *de-* + *squama* scale — more at SQUAMA] : to peel off in the form of scales : scale off ⟨he came down with scarlet fever and did not finish *desquamating* until . . . Christmas —Frank Sullivan⟩ ⟨thus a particular skin patch may redden and ~ each time a barbiturate is taken —R.W.Gerard⟩ — **des·qua·ma·tion** \,deskwә'māshәn\ *n* -S

des·qua·ma·tive \'deskwә,mād·iv, dә̇'skwamәd·-\ *adj* : attended by or causing desquamation

des·qua·ma·to·ry \'deskwәmә,tōrē, dә̇'skwamә,-\ *adj* : characterized by or used for desquamation

1**dess** \'des\ *n* -ES [prob. of Celt origin; akin to OIr *dais* heap] **1** *dial Brit* : LEDGE, SHELF **2** *dial Brit* : PILE, STACK ⟨a ~ of hay⟩

2**dess** \"\ *vt* -ED/-ING/-ES *dial Brit* : to arrange or pile up in layers

des·sa \'desә\ *var of* DESA

des·sert \dә̇'zәr|t, -zә̄|,-zәi|, *usu* |d· + V\ *n* -S *often attrib* [MF, fr. *desservir* to clear the table, fr. *des-* de- + *servir* to serve, fr. L *servire* — more at SERVE] **1 :** a course of fruit, pastry, pudding, ice cream, or cheese served at the close of a meal — compare SAVORY, SWEET **2** *Brit* : a fresh fruit served after a sweet

dessert fork *n* : a fork slightly smaller than a dinner fork

dessert knife *n* : a knife slightly smaller than a dinner knife

dessert raisin *n* : a selected usu. light-colored raisin that is dried in the cluster esp. for eating out of hand

dessertspoon \=ˈ=,=\ *n* **1 :** a spoon intermediate in size between a teaspoon and a tablespoon used in eating dessert and sometimes soup or cereals **2 :** DESSERTSPOONFUL ⟨add a ~ of sugar⟩

des·sert·spoon·ful \=ˈ=¦=,=, =,=ˈ=,=\ *n* **1 :** as much as a dessertspoon will hold **2 :** a unit of measure equal to about 2½ fluidrams

dessert wine *n* : a still usu. sweet straw-colored to red wine containing over 14 percent and frequently 20 to 21 percent alcohol by volume (as port, tokay, and muscatel) often served with dessert or between meals — compare APPETIZER WINE, SPARKLING WINE, TABLE WINE

des·sia·tine \¦des(h)yә¦tēn\ *or* **des·sa·tine** \-sә¦-\ *or* **de·sia·tin** *also* **de·sya·tin** \-s(h)yә¦tin\ *n* -S [Russ *desyatina* tithe, unit of land area, fr. *desyat'* ten; akin to L *decem* ten — more at TEN] : a Russian unit of land area equal to 2.7 acres

dessil *var of* DEASIL

1**des·sous** \dә'sü\ *n*, *pl* **dessous** \-ü(z)\ [F, fr. *dessous*, adv. & prep., underneath, below, fr. OF *desoz*, fr. *de-* + *soz* below, underneath, fr. L *subtus*, fr. *sub* under — more at SUB-] : UNDERWEAR

2**dessous** \"\ *adj* [F, adv., underneath] *ballet* : UNDER — used of the movement in which the working leg passes behind the supporting leg

des·sus \dә'sǖ\ *adj* [F, adv., above, fr. OF *desus*, fr. *de-* + *sus* under, fr. L *susum*, *sursum* — more at SURSUM-] *ballet* : OVER — used of the movement in which the working leg passes in front of the supporting leg

de·stabilize \(')dē +\ *vt* [*de-* + *stabilize*] : to make unstable : cause or allow to fluctuate ⟨booms and depressions, both of which ~ the position of labor today —Eduard Heimann⟩; *specif* : to tend to increase economic fluctuations in ⟨that the use of replacement cost depreciation for tax purposes would be a *destabilizing* influence —J.F.Due⟩

1**destain** *var of* DISTAIN

2**de·stain** \(')dē +\ *vt* [*de-* + *stain* (n.)] : to selectively remove stain from (a specimen for microscopic study)

de·sta·lin·ize \(')dē'stälә̇,nīz, -tal- *also* -tȯl- *or* -tál- *sometimes* -lyә̇,- *or* -l(,)(y)ē,- *or* ¦dē(,)stä'lē,- *or* ¦dē(,)sta'lē,- *or* ¦dē(,)stá'lē,-\ *vb* -ED/-ING/-S [*de-* + Joseph *Stalin* (Dzhugashvili) †1953 Russ. political leader + E *-ize*] *vi* : to deflate the influence of Stalin as a Soviet leader of heroic stature by revelations of disastrous state policies and ruthless self-aggrandizement ~ *vt* : to offset and reverse the influence of Stalin on (as sports)

de·ste·a·rin·ate \(')dē¦stēәrә̇,nāt, -stir-\ *vt* -ED/-ING/-S [*de-* + *stearin* + *-ate*] : to remove the lower melting-point components from (a fatty oil)

de·sterilize \(')dē +\ *vt* [*de-* + *sterilize*] : to release (gold) from an insulated condition in the treasury to useful service (as in forming the base for further credit expansion through deposit in a central bank)

des·thio·biotin \,dez,thīә +\ *n* [*des-* + *thi-* + *biotin*] : a crystalline acid $C_{10}H_{18}N_2O_3$ obtained from biotin by removal of sulfur and held to be a precursor of biotin in some organisms (as many yeasts and bacteria)

de·stigmatize \(')dē +\ *vt* [*de-* + *stigmatize*] : to clear of a stigma

de stijl \dә'stī(ә)l, -tā(ә)l\ *n*, *usu cap S* [D *De Stijl*, lit., the style, a magazine published by members of the school] : a school of art founded in Holland in 1917 producing work that typically used rectangular forms, the primary colors plus black and white, and asymmetric balance and that had wide application in architecture and practical design

1**des·ti·nate** \'destәnә̇t, -,nāt\ *adj* [ME, fr. L *destinatus*, past part. of *destinare*] **1** *archaic* : ordained by fate **2 :** set apart for : INTENDED

2**des·ti·nate** \-,nāt\ *vt* -ED/-ING/-S [L *destinatus*, past part.] **1** *archaic* **a :** DESIGNATE **b :** DOOM **2** *archaic* : to predetermine as an act of fate or by divine decree **3** *archaic* : to design or intend

des·ti·na·tion \,destә'nāshәn\ *n* -S [LL & L; LL *destination-*, *destinatio* goal, from L, act of establishing, determination, purpose, fr. *destinatus* + *-ion-*, *-io* -ion] **1 a :** the act of appointing, setting aside to a purpose, or predetermining ⟨the clubs discuss the probable ~ of offices with that air of secret knowledge —H.J.Laski⟩ **b** *archaic* : the fact of being designated **2 :** purpose for which something is destined : predetermined end, object, or use ⟨to find the mainstream of one's period and its source of flow, dominant direction, and presumable ~ —Louis Kronenberger⟩ **3 :** a place which is set for the end of a journey or to which something is sent : place or point aimed at ⟨when buying your plane tickets always buy through to your farthest ~ —Richard Joseph⟩ **4** *Scots law* **a :** the nomination of successors to movable or heritable property in a certain order made by the will of a decedent **b :** the series of heirs so succeeding **5 :** the purpose to which property or money is intended to be applied **6 :** one that receives in a form recognizably like its original form a message transmitted through any medium and by any set of signals

des·tine \'destә̇n\ *vt* -ED/-ING/-S [ME *destinen*, fr. OF *destiner*, fr. L *destinare* to make fast, determine, destine, fr. *de-* + *-stinare* (akin to *stare* to stand) — more at STAND] **1 a :** to fix or decree beforehand : PREORDAIN — used orig. of a divine foreordaining or a decreeing by fate ⟨he was not *destined* to attain the throne⟩ **b :** to direct and impel inescapably on a fixed course : PREDETERMINE — used of an inevitable ordering in human eventualities, usu. followed by *to* and an infinitive, sometimes by *for* ⟨whose star in the Navy was bright and *destined* to grow brighter still —Burke Wilkinson⟩ ⟨*destined* to occupy a niche of some importance in the history of American music —Virgil Thomson⟩ ⟨he foretold the telescope and the microscope — inventions which were *destined* not to occur until centuries after his death —R.D.Altick⟩ ⟨the now somnolent villages which in the past seemed *destined* for an active commercial development —*Amer. Guide Series: Maine*⟩ **2 :** to determine the future condition, use, or action of: **a :** to designate, assign, or dedicate in advance ⟨where forces *destined* to invade Normandy would eventually be gathered —J.P.Baxter⟩ ⟨the librarianship, with its meagre income, to which I had been originally *destined* —L.P.Smith⟩ ⟨funds *destined* for scholarship endowments⟩ ⟨*destined* by his parents for the ministry⟩; *broadly* **:** INTEND ⟨a scheme of decoration however appropriate to its *destined* setting —C.W.H.Johnson⟩ **b :** to direct, devise, or set aside for a specific purpose or end ⟨boats were ordered made ready at Fort Pitt for an expedition *destined* for the Illinois posts —P.M.Angle⟩ ⟨freight *destined* for Israeli ports⟩

des·ti·nez·ite \ˌdestəˈnāˌzīt\ *n* -s [F *destinezite*, fr. Pierre *Destinez*, 19th cent. Belgian mineralogist + F *-ite*] **:** DIADOCHITE

des·ti·ny \ˈdestənē, -ni\ *n* -ES [ME *destinee*, fr. MF, fr. OF, fr. fem. of *destiné* (past part. of *destiner*), fr. L *destinatus*] **1 :** that to which any person or thing is destined: as **a :** predetermined state **:** condition foreordained by divine will or by human will **:** unavoidable lot **:** FATE, DOOM ⟨reconciled to one's ~⟩ **b :** culminating condition or end indicated as probable, inevitable, or having been reached **:** FORTUNE, GOAL ⟨manifest ~⟩ ⟨unhappy ~⟩ **2 a :** the predetermined course of events often conceived as a resistless power or agency **:** the foreordained future whether in general or of an individual ⟨pursued by ~⟩ ⟨turn aside ~⟩ **b :** continuing activity and functional behavior that tend to determine eventual status esp. as to progress or decadence — usu. used in pl. ⟨we could not tolerate control by a European power over the ~ of the former Spanish possessions⟩ ⟨that a man should manage the *destinies* of a corporation while owning only a minute fraction of its stock —F.L.Allen⟩ **3 :** a real or imaginary power or agency conceived as predetermining the course of events and choice of alternatives ⟨our helplessness, at least with respect to those events over which *Destiny* presides —Lucius Garvin⟩ ⟨the leader is simply the man whom ~ . . . has placed in such a position that he alone can assume the supreme leadership —Barbara & Robert North⟩ ⟨a flash of Free Will, pure and simple, which instantly gives place . . . to the dominion of what we call *Destiny* —Joseph Furphy⟩ **syn** see FATE

[1]**des·ti·tute** \ˈdestəˌtüt, -stəˌtyül, *usu* \|d· + V\ *adj* [ME *destitut*, fr. L *destitutus*, past part. of *destituere* to set away, leave alone, forsake, fr. *de-* + *-stituere* (fr. *statuere* to set) — more at STATUTE] **1** *obs* **:** ABANDONED **2 :** bereft or divested ⟨a city street ~ of trees⟩ ⟨no danger of our becoming ~ of facts —S.C.Pepper⟩ **:** bare or empty ⟨a lake ~ of fish⟩ **:** lacking any provision or showing a want ⟨a new religion of authority singularly ~ of safeguards against self-deception —W.R. Inge⟩ **:** subject to a lack or deficiency ⟨of all men alive he is possibly the most completely ~ of the mystical sense —W.L. Sullivan⟩ ⟨~ of all sense of personal dignity⟩ **:** possessing or showing no vestige ⟨as ~ of conscience as a snake —W.L. Sullivan⟩ — used with *of* **3 :** lacking possessions and resources; *esp* **:** lacking the necessaries of life **:** suffering extreme want ⟨the death of a ~ widow from starvation —Julian Maclaren-Ross⟩ ⟨homes for the ~⟩ ⟨the result was impoverished villages in India, hideous and ~ towns in England —Lewis Mumford⟩ ⟨in a ~ condition for clothes⟩ **syn** see POOR

[2]**destitute** \"\ *vt* -ED/-ING/-S [L *destitutus*] **1** *obs* **:** FORSAKE **2 a :** to deprive or divest — used with *of* ⟨the accident will ~ us of all our liquid assets⟩ **b** *archaic* **:** to deprive of office **:** DEPOSE **3** *archaic* **:** to lay waste **:** DEVASTATE **4** *obs* **:** to make void **:** FRUSTRATE

des·ti·tute·ly *adv* **:** in a destitute condition

des·ti·tute·ness *n* -ES **:** the state of being destitute

des·ti·tu·tion \ˌdestəˈtüshən, -stəˈtyü-\ *n* -S [ME *destitucioun*, fr. MF or L; MF *destitution*, fr. L *destitution-*, *destitutio*, fr. *destitutus* + *-ion-*, *-io* -ion] **1 :** state of being deprived of or lacking something **:** destitute condition ⟨many historic dwellings remain, sinking stage by stage from indigence to squalor, from squalor to grimy ~ —Lewis Mumford⟩ ⟨and what ~ of the spirit did he owe to his harsh memories of his father —Charles Lee⟩; *usu* **:** deprivation of the necessaries of life **:** poverty esp. when extreme ⟨forgotten men and women living at or below the ~ level —R.H.S.Crossman⟩ **2** *archaic* **:** dismissal from office

destn *abbr* destination

de·stock \(ˈ)dē +\ *vb* [*de-* + *stock*] *vt* **1** *Africa* **:** to remove livestock from ⟨~ an overgrazed range⟩ **2** *Africa* **:** to reduce the number of (livestock) on a range ~ *vi*, *Africa* **:** to remove stock from a range or pasture

de·stoner \(ˈ)dē +\ *n* -S [*de-* + *stone* + *-er*] **:** a worker who operates machines that remove hard particles from vegetables prior to freezing

de·stool \(ˈ)dē +\ *vt* [*de-* + *stool* (n.)] **:** to depose from office (a West African chief) — contrasted with *enstool* — **de·stool·ment** \" + . . . mənt\ *n* -S

des·trier \ˈdestrēər, (ˈ)dəˈstri(ə)r\ *n* -S [ME, fr. OF, fr. *destre* right hand, fr. L *dextera*, *dextra*, fr. *dexter* right; fr. the fact that the knight's horse was led by the squire with his right hand — more at DEXTER] **:** a large powerful horse used as a war-horse by a medieval knight

de·stroy \dəˈstrȯi, dēˈ-\ *vb* -ED/-ING/-S [ME *destroyen*, *destruyen*, fr. OF *destruire*, fr. (assumed) VL *destrugere*, alter. (influenced by L *destructus*, past part. of *destruere*) of L *destruere* to tear down, destroy, fr. *de-* + *struere* to pile up, build; akin to L *sternere* to spread out, scatter — more at STREW] *vt* **1 :** to ruin the structure, organic existence, or condition of: as **a :** to pull or tear down **:** RAZE, DEMOLISH ⟨~*ed* the altars of the gods⟩ **b** *obs* **:** to lay waste **:** DESOLATE **c :** to ruin completely or injure or mutilate beyond possibility of use (as by tearing, breaking, burning, or erosion) ⟨priceless art ~*ed* by fire⟩ ⟨water may undermine and ~ the riverbank⟩ **d :** to ruin as if by ripping to shreds ⟨~*ed* a goodly number of existing reputations —H.J.Laski⟩ **e :** to deprive of position, prestige, and reputation and of the power to oppose or offer resistance **:** reduce to political, financial, or professional impotence or ruin **:** defeat and discredit fully ⟨an author can weather the most damning criticisms but he is ~*ed* when he is ignored completely —Bennett Cerf⟩ **2 :** to bring to naught by putting out of existence: **a :** to take the life of **:** put to death **:** KILL ⟨the plague ~*ed* men by the thousands⟩ **b :** to cause to vanish **:** ABOLISH ⟨~ one's love⟩ **c :** COUNTERACT, NULLIFY, NEUTRALIZE ⟨the moon ~*s* the light of the stars⟩ **d :** to subject to a crushing defeat **:** wipe out **:** ANNIHILATE ⟨building a war machine capable of ~*ing* the enemy⟩ **3** *Irish* **:** DISTRESS, DEPRESS, PLAGUE ⟨and you ~*ed* with the grief has come on you —Mary Deasy⟩ ~ *vi* **1 :** to have the effect of destroying something or someone ⟨it is proverbially easier to ~ than to construct —T.S.Eliot⟩ **2 :** to become destroyed ⟨wear nothing that ~*s* easily⟩

syn DEMOLISH, RAZE, RUIN, UNDO, WRECK, WRACK, DILAPIDATE: DESTROY implies any force that smashes, tears down or apart, kills, or annihilates ⟨*destroy* a house⟩ ⟨*destroy* a document by burning it⟩ ⟨*destroy* a friendship by deceit⟩ ⟨*destroy* a bridge by blowing it up⟩ ⟨*destroy* a mood⟩ DEMOLISH implies more a pulling or smashing to pieces; in its frequent application to the smashing or tearing down of buildings or other structures it implies complete wreckage to the point of a heap of ruins ⟨a building *demolished* by a bomb⟩ ⟨a car *demolished* by a train at a railroad crossing⟩ RAZE implies a leveling whether by sudden destruction or an orderly process ⟨the governor formulated a plan to *raze* the old State prison and transfer the inmates to other institutions —*Current Biog.*⟩ ⟨in 1865 a Gulf hurricane *razed* the town —*Amer. Guide Series: Texas*⟩ ⟨the hotel was *razed*, and its colonial pillars were sent to Grand Rapids —*Amer. Guide Series: Mich.*⟩ RUIN usu. suggests a usu. total bringing to an end of the wholeness, value, beauty, well-being, or opportunities of someone or something as by fire, collision, or misuse, or by the loss of something essential to happiness or success ⟨*ruin* a car by neglect⟩ ⟨beauty *ruined* by dissipation⟩ ⟨big planters *ruined* by the failure of the Bank of Tallahassee —Marjory S. Douglas⟩ ⟨it is he who decides how loud or soft the music will be at any given moment, and therefore it is he who can make or *ruin* everything by the merest touch of the dials —Aaron Copland⟩ ⟨because of the destruction of the plantation system the Civil War *ruined* the town —*Amer. Guide Series: Texas*⟩ UNDO, in this comparison, is a more neutral synonym for RUIN ⟨an inordinate impulsion to *undo* his rivals —H.O.Taylor⟩ ⟨the cost of reequipping his many theaters proved one of the causes of his financial *undoing* —*Americana Annual*⟩ ⟨the battle left him untouched; it was the peace that *undid* him —Virginia Woolf⟩ ⟨to *undo* a lifetime of effort⟩ WRECK suggests a ruining as by a crash or by being shattered; in figurative use, it implies an injuring past all hope of repair or reconstruction ⟨the collision *wrecked* the car beyond repair⟩ ⟨she . . . *wrecked* several saloons with stones and iron bars —C.M.Thomas⟩ ⟨warned that if private educational institutions were *wrecked* it would be a disaster to the country —A.J.Schaefer⟩ ⟨attempting to degrade and *wreck* the classical concept of the genus —W.H.Camp⟩ ⟨*wreck* plans for a new school⟩ WRACK, now infrequent in this connection and even then archaic or largely in poetic use, suggests an overwhelming catastrophe or widespread ruin ⟨the seas . . . *wracking* whole fleets in pride like river toys —F.T.Palgrave⟩ ⟨a civilization *wracked* by its own evil ways⟩ DILAPIDATE, in earlier use implying ruin by wastefulness as well as neglect, now generally implies ruin, esp. of a building, mainly through neglect, suggesting a run-down, tumbledown condition ⟨they tax the country according to their pleasure, and *dilapidate* the estates of the King's friends —Sir Walter Scott⟩ ⟨a *dilapidated* old shack of a house⟩ ⟨its cities were *dilapidated*, its public buildings run down and dirty —Carleton Beals⟩ ⟨an old and *dilapidated*-looking car —Francis Stuart⟩

de·stroy·able \-ōiəbəl\ *adj* **:** capable of being destroyed

de·stroy·er \-ȯi(ə)r,-ōiə\ *n* -S [ME *destroyer*, *destruyer*, fr. *destroyen*, *destruyen* to destroy + *-er*] **1 :** a destroying agent or agency **2 :** a small fast warship armed with usu. 5-inch guns, depth charges, torpedoes, mines, and sometimes guided missiles — called also *can*, *tin can*

destroyer escort *n* **:** an antisubmarine warship similar to a destroyer but smaller and not as fast

destroyer leader *n* **:** a large destroyer — compare FRIGATE

destroying angel *n*, *often cap D&A* **1 :** a variably colored extremely poisonous mushroom (*Amanita phalloides*) that grows esp. in open woodlands and along field margins and in its white form is sometimes mistaken for the common edible agarics; *also* **:** a related poisonous mushroom (*A. verna*) **2 :** DANITE 2

de·stroy·ing·ly *adv* **1 :** in the role of destroyer **2 :** with destructive effect

de·struct \dəˈstrəkt, dēˈ-\ *vb* -ED/-ING/-S [back-formation fr. *destruction*] **:** DESTROY

de·struc·ti·bil·i·ty \-ˌstrəktəˈbilədē, -ətē, -i\ *n* -ES **:** the quality of being destructible

de·struc·ti·ble \-ˈstrəktəbəl\ *adj* [*destruction* + *-ible*] **:** capable of being destroyed **:** liable to destruction

de·struc·tion \-kshən\ *n* -S [ME *destruccioun*, fr. MF *destruction*, fr. L *destruction-*, *destructio*, fr. *destructus* (past part. of *destruere* to tear down) + *-ion-*, *-io* -ion — more at DESTROY] **1 :** the action or process of destroying a material or immaterial object: **a :** demolition or complete ruin ⟨~ of dead files by a government department⟩ ⟨bombers accomplished ~ of the city⟩ **b :** killing or annihilation ⟨~ of sheep by dogs and wild animals⟩ ⟨inflicted ~ on enemy units⟩ **c :** a bringing to an end **:** ELIMINATION, ERADICATION ⟨measures toward ~ of the dictatorship⟩ ⟨was his real purpose in creating this painting the ~ of religion rather than the furtherance of it —Huntington Hartford⟩ **d :** IMPAIRMENT, DISRUPTION, DISINTEGRATION ⟨~ of the universities by the Nazi regime⟩ ⟨the ~ of European civilization through internal strife⟩ **e :** INVALIDATION ⟨any act aimed at the ~ of any of the rights and freedoms set forth herein —*U.N. Declaration of Human Rights*⟩ **2 a :** the fact or experience of or subjection to being destroyed ⟨Albania . . . suffered whole or partial ~ of 1600 of its villages —*Current Biog.*⟩ ⟨Macbeth seemed eager for his own ~⟩ ⟨a study of communistic ideology and prospects of its gradual ~⟩ ⟨voluntary muscular movements become sluggish and finally tissue ~ and death may occur at temperatures of −25°F to −50°F —H.G.Armstrong⟩ **b :** loss of prestige and reputation **:** descent into a state of ignominy and degradation ⟨resolved on the teacher's personal ~ because of his stand on civil rights⟩ **c :** a condition of having been destroyed ⟨coffee planting on steep slopes has resulted in serious land ~ —P.E.James⟩ ⟨with economic and social ~ as the penalty for dissent —Archibald MacLeish⟩ ⟨the ~ resulting from the hurricane⟩ **3 :** a destroying agency **:** a cause of ruin ⟨alcohol is likely to be his ~⟩

de·struc·tion·al \-shənᵊl,-shnəl\ *adj* **:** resulting from destructive agencies ⟨~ erosion⟩

de·struc·tion·ism \-shəˌnizəm\ *n* -S **:** advocacy or a policy of destroying an institution or regime

de·struc·tion·ist \-sh(ə)nəst\ *n* -S **1 :** one who delights in destroying **2 :** an advocate of destroying existing institutions

[1]**de·struc·tive** \dəˈstrəktiv, dēˈ-, -ktēv *also* -təv\ *adj* [MF *destructif*, fr. LL *destructivus*, fr. L *destructus* + *-ivus* -ive] **1 :** having the capability, property, or effect of destroying **:** causing destruction: **a :** tending to bring about demolition or devastation ⟨~ storms are rare in Maine⟩ ⟨insects ~ of many trees⟩ ⟨abuse of mankind's scientific genius for ~ ends —Vera M. Dean⟩ **b :** tending to take life or promote death **:** dangerously injurious to a living being **:** DEADLY, ANNIHILATIVE ⟨a cavalry that checked to fire exposed itself to a ~ volley —Tom Wintringham⟩ ⟨an exceedingly ~ type of joint lesion known as a Charcot joint —G.A.Bennett⟩ ⟨otters are very ~ of salmon and trout —F.D.Smith & Barbara Wilcox⟩; *specif* **:** prompting one to destroy another or oneself ⟨passionate feeling is desirable, provided it is not ~ —Bertrand Russell⟩ ⟨harbors aggressive and ~ instincts to kill⟩ ⟨self-*destructive* human behavior⟩ **c :** tending to impair, damage, or wreck **:** productive of evil results **:** DELETERIOUS ⟨sharp or persistent inflations, deep and dragging depressions, are not corrective but ~ —*Defense Against Recession*⟩ **2 :** designed or tending to destroy, clear away, eliminate, or invalidate ⟨~ of firmly established ideas⟩ ⟨a ~ standard⟩ — opposed to *constructive* **3** *logic* **:** retroactively negating (as when the denial of a consequent invalidates the antecedent: if A is B, then C is D; but C is not D; hence A is not B) — **de·struc·tive·ly** \-ktəvlē, -li\ *adv*

[2]**destructive** \"\ *n* -S **1 :** a destructive agent or force **2 :** one destructive of an accepted norm

destructive distillation *n* **:** distillation involving decomposition of a substance (as wood, coal, or a hydrocarbon oil) by heat in a closed container (as a retort) and collection of the volatile products produced **:** CARBONIZATION — compare CRACKING, PYROLYSIS

de·struc·tive·ness \-ktəvnəs\ *n* -ES **:** the quality of being destructive **:** capacity for destruction ⟨the awesome ~ of the atom bomb⟩

destructive sorites *n* **:** a process of reasoning that involves the denial of the first of a series of dependent propositions as a consequence of the denial of the last

de·struc·tiv·i·ty \ˌdēˌstrəkˈtivədē, dəˌ-, -ətē, -i\ *n* -ES **:** capacity for destruction

de·struc·tor \dəˈstrəktə(r), dēˈ-\ *n* -S [LL *destructor* destroyer, fr. L *destructus* + *-or*] **1 :** a furnace or oven for the burning of refuse **:** INCINERATOR **2 a :** a device for destroying a missile or a part thereof at a desired time in its flight **b :** an explosive device for enabling quick destruction of matériel to prevent its falling into the hands of the enemy

de·stru·do \-ˈstrü(ˌ)dō\ *n* -S [NL, fr. L *destruere* to destroy — more at DESTROY] **:** DEATH WISH

de·sublimate \(ˈ)dē+\ *vt* [*de-* + *sublimate*] **:** to undo a sublimation of — **de·sublimation** \(ˌ)dē+\ *n*

de·substantival \(ˌ)dē+\ *adj* [*de-* + *substantival*] **:** derived from a substantive ⟨*bookish* from *book* is a ~ adjective⟩ ⟨*methodize* is a ~ verb⟩

des·ue·tude \ˈdeswēˌtüd, -swəˌ, \|·ˌtyüd *also* deˈsüə\| *sometimes* ˈdezw- *or* ˈdeˌsü- *or* ˈdesˌyü-\ *n* -S [F or L; F *désuétude*, fr. L *desuetudo*, fr. *desuetus*, past part. of *desuescere* to become unaccustomed, fr. *de-* + *suescere* to become accustomed; akin to L *suus* one's own — more at SUICIDE] **1 :** discontinuance from use, practice, exercise, or functioning ⟨as to the Scottish statute it is presumably abrogated by ~ —Frederick Pollock⟩ ⟨vexing myself today over the gradual ~ of our correspondence —A.T.Quiller-Couch⟩ ⟨figureheads . . . are being used again after long years of ~ —John Woodyatt⟩ ⟨there are those who foresee total ~ for our society with the profit motive thus wantonly eliminated —Irwin Edman⟩ **2 :** a state of protracted suspension or of apparent abandonment ⟨an ancient custom that has fallen into ~⟩ ⟨we all have this profound unconscious, but it falls into atrophy and ~ because most of us do not utilize it —L.K.Anspacher⟩ **:** a state of disuse or neglect attended by deterioration ⟨what energy and vision may do for an old school fast falling into ~ —J.P.Marquand⟩ **:** outmoded or discarded status ⟨the purely speculative and seemingly impractical things should have fallen into disfavor and disrepute, if not positive ~ —F.X.Meehan⟩

de·sugar *also* **de·sugarize** \(ˈ)dē+\ *vt* [*desugar* fr. *de-* + *sugar*, n.; *desugarize* fr. *de-* + *sugar*, n. + *-ize*] **:** to remove sugar from

de·sulfonate \(ˈ)dē+\ *vt* [*de-* + *sulfonate*] **:** to remove sulfonic groups from (a sulfonated substance) — **de·sulfonation** \(ˌ)dē+\ *n*

de·sul·fo·vibrio \(ˌ)dēˌsəlfō+\ *n*, *cap* [NL, fr. *de-* + *sulfo-* + *vibrio*] **:** a genus of curved motile anaerobic bacterial rods (family Spirillaceae) that reduce sulfates to hydrogen sulfide and include at least one form (*D. halohydrocarbonoclasticus*) capable of increasing the flow of oil wells by raising the gas pressure and enlarging the flow channels in the rock

de·sulfurization *also* **de·sulfuration** \(ˌ)dē, dō+\ *n* **:** the process of desulfurizing

de·sulfurize *also* **de·sulfur** \(ˈ)dē, dō+\ *vt* [*de-* + *sulfurize* or *sulfur* (n.)] **:** to remove sulfur or sulfur compounds from (as molten metals or petroleum oils) by suitable agents — compare SWEETEN — **de·sulfurizer** \"+\ *n*

de·sul·tor \dəˈsəltə(r), dēˈ-\ *n*, *pl* **desultors** \-(r)z\ *or* **desulto·res** \ˌdesəlˈtōrˌēz\ [L, fr. *desultus* + *-or*] **:** a rider trained to leap from one horse to another (as in the circensian games)

des·ul·to·ri·ly \ˌ\|desəl\|tōrəlē, -tȯr-, -li *also* -ezə-\ *adv* **:** in a desultory manner ⟨for another six years he ~ attended lectures in arts as well as canon law —G.C.Sellery⟩ ⟨a trollop of soldiery oozed ~ across the square, out of step —Bruce Marshall⟩

des·ul·to·ri·ness *n* -ES **:** the quality of being desultory

des·ul·to·ri·ous \-rēəs\ *adj* [L *desultorius*] *archaic* **:** DESULTORY

des·ul·to·ry \ˈdesəlˌtōrē, -tȯr-, -ri *also* -ezə-\ *adj* [L *desultorius*, fr. *desultus* (past part. of *desilire* to leap down, fr. *de-* + *-silire*, fr. *salire* to leap) + *-orius* -ory — more at SALLY] **1 :** lacking steadiness, fixity, regularity, or continuity **:** ERRATIC, WAVERING, SHIFTING ⟨whistling of trains —Edmund Wilson⟩ ⟨their one small cannon boomed a ~ fire to distract the attention of the Mexicans —Green Peyton⟩ ⟨lived for some time in regular contact with each other and in ~ contact with the surrounding larger American community —Ethel Albert⟩ **2 :** marked by lack of definite plan or method, sustained purpose, or regular persistent logical procedure or continuity **:** showing unsteadiness, inconsistency, or incoherence ⟨make reading have a purpose instead of being ~ —Bertrand Russell⟩ ⟨already they appeared to be strangers to each other and their last conversations grew more and more ~ —Ngaio Marsh⟩ **3 :** not connected with the main subject **:** not cogently relevant **:** DIGRESSIVE ⟨certain comments of a more or less ~ character seem to need making here —Samuel Alexander⟩ **syn** see RANDOM

de·superheat \(ˈ)dē, dō+\ *vb* [*de-* + *superheat*] *vt* **:** to lower the temperature of (superheated steam or other vapor) ~ *vi* **:** to desuperheat steam

de·superheater \(ˌ)dē, dō+\ *n* **:** a coil, wire-mesh baffle, spray nozzle, or other device to cool superheated steam

de·surface \(ˈ)dē, dō+\ *vt* [*de-* + *surface* (n.)] **:** to remove a surface layer from; *esp* **:** to strip of topsoil

de·swell \(ˈ)dē+\ *vb* [*de-* + *swell*] *vt* **:** to reduce swelling of (as the fiber of a textile) usu. by abstraction of water ~ *vi* **:** to become contracted — used esp. of colloids

desyatin *var of* DESSIATINE

des·yl \ˈdezəl, -esəl\ *n* -S [*des*oxybenzoin + *-yl*] **:** a univalent radical $C_6H_5COCH(C_6H_5)$— derived from desoxybenzoin by removal of one hydrogen atom from the methylene group; alpha-phenyl-phenacyl

de·synapsis \ˌdē+\ *n* [NL, fr. *de-* + *synapsis*] **:** failure of synapsis due to separation of homologous chromosomes after initial pairing in meiosis — compare ASYNAPSIS — **de·synaptic** \"+\ *adj*

de·synonymize \"+\ *vt* [*de-* + *synonymize*] **:** to deprive of synonymous character **:** differentiate meanings of (words often used as close synonyms or as interchangeable, as *semantics* and *semasiology*)

det *abbr* **1** detached; detachment **2** detail **3** detective **4** determine; determiner

de·tach \dəˈtach, dēˈ-\ *vt* -ED/-ING/-ES [F *détacher*, fr. OF *destachier*, fr. *des-* de- + *-tachier* (as in *atachier* to attach) — more at ATTACH] **1 :** to separate esp. from a larger mass and usu. without violence or damage ⟨~ a stamp from a sheet⟩ — opposed to *attach* **2 :** DISENGAGE, WITHDRAW ⟨~*ed* himself from the embrace⟩ **3 :** to separate from a parent organization for a special object or use ⟨~ a ship from a fleet⟩

syn DISENGAGE, ABSTRACT, PRESCIND: DETACH stresses the fact of separation, parting, removal, or isolation; it is unlikely to suggest forcible action ⟨I rose, and *detaching* the silver ornament from my cloak presented it to him —W.H.Hudson †1922⟩ ⟨I brought my face close and aroused no sign of life. Then I reached up and slowly *detached* the butterfly from its resting place —William Beebe⟩ DISENGAGE suggests an extricating or freeing of something involved, enmeshed, or entangled, literally or figuratively ⟨gently *disengaging* himself from her enfolding arms —Charles Dickens⟩ ⟨the taxi *disengaged* itself from the traffic —Dan Wickenden⟩ ⟨psychology, also, was beginning to *disengage* itself from its dependence on general philosophy —A.N.Whitehead⟩ ABSTRACT indicates a withdrawing, gathering, or separating out from a mass or body; it is used more often of intangibles than tangibles ⟨I suspect that some of these early chapters will be *abstracted* from the autobiography and be reprinted again and again —*Book-of-the-Month Club News*⟩ ⟨the Church of England, which might be supposed able to *abstract* the question from its worldly confusions, is of two minds also —Virginia Woolf⟩ PRESCIND indicates a separating or detaching mentally for purposes of consideration or philosophic analysis ⟨can anyone forget the great and gentle Buddha who, *prescinding* from any belief in soul or self, gave to thousands of millions of people a code of conduct? —*Times Lit. Supp.*⟩

de·tach·abil·i·ty \=ˌ=əˈbilədē, -ətē, -i\ *n* -ES **:** the quality or state of being detachable

de·tach·able \=ˈ=əbəl\ *adj* **:** capable of being or designed to be detached **:** capable of being separated or withdrawn without loss or damage — **de·tach·ably** \-blē, -li\ *adv*

dé·ta·ché \ˌdāˌta\|shā, dāˈta,shā\ *adv* (*or adj*) [F, lit., detached, fr. past part. of *détacher*] **:** NONLEGATO — used as a direction to players of bowed instruments

detached \dəˈtacht, dēˈ-\ *adj* [fr. past part. of *detach*] **1 :** standing by itself **:** SEPARATE, UNCONNECTED, ISOLATED; *specif* **:** not sharing any wall with another building ⟨a ~ house⟩ **2 :** UNBIASED, ALOOF ⟨a ~ view of the affair⟩ ⟨a ~ mood⟩ **3 :** DÉTACHÉ **syn** see INDIFFERENT

detached core *n* **:** the part of a compressed anticlinal or synclinal fold of rock that may be separated or pinched off from the main body of the strata

de·tached·ly \-chədlē, -chtlē, -li\ *adv* **:** in a detached manner

detached meristem *n*, *bot* **:** a meristematic region that originates directly from an apical meristem but because of the differentiation of intervening tissue becomes discontinuous with it

de·tach·ed·ness \-chədnəs, -ch(t)n-\ *n* -ES **:** the quality or state of being detached

detached service *n* **:** military service away from one's assigned organization ⟨during the course of their study the men are on *detached service* from their units —*Technical Education News*⟩ — compare TEMPORARY DUTY

de·tach·ment \-chmənt\ *n* -S [F *détachement*, fr. *détacher* + *-ment*] **1 :** the act or fact of detaching **:** SEPARATION ⟨~ of a leaf from a twig⟩ **2 a :** the dispatch of a body of troops or part of a fleet from the main body for a special mission or service **b :** the portion so dispatched **c :** a permanently organized separate unit usu. smaller than a platoon and different in composition from normal units ⟨a medical ~⟩ **3 :** indifference to worldly concerns or partisan opinion **:** absence of emotional bias **:** neutrality of feeling **:** UNWORLDLINESS ⟨saintly ~⟩ ⟨the ~ necessary to a historian⟩

¹de·tail \dəˈtāl, dēˈ-, ˈdē,-, *esp before pause or consonant* -āəl\ *n* -s [F *détail*, fr. OF *detail* piece cut off, small quantity, fr. *detaillier* to cut in pieces, fr. *de-* (fr. L *dis-* apart, to pieces) + *taillier* to cut — more at DIS-, TAILOR] **1 a :** extended treatment of or attention to particular items ⟨careful attention to ~⟩ ⟨give the argument without going into ~⟩ **b** *archaic* **:** a narrative that relates minute points **:** a particularized account **2 :** a part of a whole: as **a :** a small and subordinate part **:** PARTICULAR, ITEM, CIRCUMSTANCE ⟨this is only a ~⟩ ⟨ask for the ~s of a scheme⟩ **b :** a portion considered independently of the parts considered together ⟨reproduce a ~ of a painting⟩ ⟨elaborate in ~⟩ **c :** a minor part (as the cornice, caps of the buttresses, capitals of the columns of a building) **3 :** DETAIL DRAWING **4 a :** a written list of military duties for the day either for the entire command or for any portion; *also* **:** the distribution of the daily orders to the officers **b :** selection for a particular task of a person or a body of persons; *also* **:** the person or body selected or the task to be performed **5 :** the small elements of a photographic image corresponding to the small elements of the original subject ⟨strong lighting to achieve clarity of ~⟩ **syn** see ITEM, PART

²detail \"\ *vb* -ED/-ING/-S [F *détailler*, lit., to cut in pieces, fr. OF *detaillier*] *vt* **1 :** to relate in particulars **:** report minutely and distinctly ⟨~ a new drug⟩ **2 :** ENUMERATE, SPECIFY ⟨~ all the facts in a case⟩ **3 :** to assign (a person, a military unit) to a particular task ⟨the first sergeant will ~ the platoons for fatigue duty⟩ ⟨an infantry officer ~*ed* to an air-force unit during maneuvers⟩ **4 :** to furnish with detailing ⟨beautifully ~*ed* hats⟩ ⟨trimmings that ~ slips and petticoats⟩ ~ *vi* **:** to make detail drawings

detail drawing *n* **:** a separate large-scale drawing of a small part of a machine or structure; *esp* **:** WORKING DRAWING

detailed *adj* [¹*detail* + *-ed*] **:** marked by abundant detail or by thoroughness in treating small items or parts ⟨the ~ study of history should be supplemented by brilliant outlines —Bertrand Russell⟩ **syn** see CIRCUMSTANTIAL

de·tailed·ly \-l(ə)dlē, -li\ *adv* **:** in a detailed manner **:** item by item **:** THOROUGHLY

de·tailed·ness \-l(ə)dnəs\ *n* -ES **:** the quality or state of being detailed **:** PARTICULARITY

de·tail·er \-lə(r)\ *n* -s [²*detail* + *-er*] **1 :** one that makes detail drawings **:** one that elaborates general outlines (as of a building design) into specifics **2 :** one that details (as prescription drugs)

detail fracture *n* **:** a rail fracture from external cause that begins at or near the top surface of the rail and progresses crosswise

detailing *n* -s [fr. gerund of ²*detail*] **:** the smaller elements of design and finish (as on garments or building interiors)

detail man *n* **:** a representative of a drug manufacturer who introduces new drugs to professional users (as physicians or pharmacists)

de·tain \dəˈtān, dēˈ-\ *vt* -ED/-ING/-S [ME *deteynen*, fr. MF *detenir*, fr. OF, fr. L *detinēre*, fr. *de* from, away + *-tinēre* (fr. *tenēre* to hold) — more at DE-, THIN] **1 :** to hold or keep in or as if in custody ⟨~*ed* by the police for questioning⟩ **2** *obs* **:** to keep back (as something that is due) **:** WITHHOLD **3 :** to restrain esp. from proceeding **:** hold back **:** STOP, DELAY ⟨~*ed* by an accident⟩ **4 :** to hold the attention of ⟨the introduction . . . will ~ the reader as effectively as many of the selected passages that follow —*Brit. Book News*⟩ **syn** see DELAY, KEEP

de·tain·ee \də¦tā¦nē, dē¦-; ¦dē,t-\ *n* -s **:** a person (as an enemy alien) held in custody for political reasons

de·tain·er \dəˈtānə(r), dēˈ-\ *n* -s [modif. (influenced by E *detain*) of AF *detener* (inf. used as n.), fr. *detener, detenir* to detain, fr. L *detinēre*] **1 :** a keeping in one's possession; *specif* **:** the withholding from the owner of something which is rightfully his but which through lawful circumstances has come into the possession of the holder **2 :** detention in custody **3 :** a writ authorizing the keeper of a prison to continue to keep a person in custody

de·tain·ing·ly *adv* [*detaining* (pres. part. of *detain*) + *-ly*] **:** in a detaining manner

de·tain·ment \nmənt\ *n* -s **:** DETENTION

de·tassel \(ˈ)dē+\ *vt* **:** to remove the tassels that bear the staminate flowers of (corn) thereby preventing self-pollination

de·tect \dəˈtekt, dēˈ-\ *vt* -ED/-ING/-S [ME *detecten*, fr. L *detectus*, past part. of *detegere* to uncover, detect, fr. *de* from, away + *tegere* to cover — more at THATCH] **1 :** to discover the true esp. hidden or disguised character of (a person) ⟨~ a hypocrite⟩ ⟨potential crack-ups who should have been ~*ed* at the induction center —S.L.A.Marshall⟩ **2 :** to discover or determine the existence, presence, or fact of ⟨~ the presence of alcohol in blood⟩ ⟨radar devices to ~ enemy planes⟩ ⟨his keen eyes ~*ed* a slight movement in the bushes⟩ **3** *radio* **a :** to determine the presence of (a signal) **b :** RECTIFY **c :** to convert (a modulated wave or current) into the original modulating wave or current **:** DEMODULATE **syn** see DISCOVER

de·tect·able \-əbəl\ *adj* **:** capable of being detected

de·tec·ta·phone \-ktə,fōn\ *n* -s [*detect* + connective *-a-* + *-phone*] **:** a telephonic apparatus with an attached microphone transmitter used esp. for listening secretly

de·tect·er \-ktə(r) *also* ˈdē,t-\ *n* -s [by alter. (influenced by E *-er*)] **:** DETECTOR

de·tec·tion \dəˈtekshən, dēˈ-\ *n* -s [ME *deteccyon*, fr. LL *detection-, detectio* act of revealing, fr. L *detectus* (past part. of *detegere* + *-ion-, -io* -ion] **1 :** the act of detecting **:** the laying open of what was concealed or hidden or of what tends to elude observation **:** DISCOVERY ⟨~ of a thief⟩ ⟨the ~ of fraud⟩ ⟨techniques of crime ~⟩ **2** *radio* **a :** determination of the presence of a signal **b :** RECTIFICATION **c :** extraction of the intelligence from a signal **d :** conversion of a modulated wave or current into the original modulating wave or current — called also *demodulation*

¹de·tec·tive \dəˈtektiv, dēˈ-, -ktēv, *also* -ktəv\ *adj* [*detect* + *-ive*] **:** fitted for, employed for, or concerned with detection ⟨~ ability⟩ ⟨~ fiction⟩

²detective \"\ *n* -s **:** one employed or engaged in detecting lawbreakers or getting information that is not readily or publicly accessible **:** an investigator of private esp. illicit or criminal affairs **:** a plainclothes police officer

de·tec·tor \-ktə(r)\ *n* -s [LL, revealer, fr. L *detectus* + *-or*] **:** one that detects: as **a :** an arrangement in a lock designed to prevent forcing and to indicate any tampering **b :** an indicator showing the depth of the water in a boiler **c :** a device for indicating improper functioning or condition of a facility (as a railroad switch or signal) or to assure proper functioning **d :** a device for detecting the presence of electric waves or of radioactivity **e** *radio* (1) **:** a device for determining the presence of a signal (2) **:** a rectifier of high-frequency current (as a cat whisker and crystal or a vacuum tube) (3) **:** a device for extracting the intelligence from a signal (4) **:** DEMODULATOR 1

detector bar *n* **:** a device used to keep a railroad switch locked in position while a train is passing over it

detector car *n* **:** a self-propelled car equipped with a special mechanism for detecting flaws in rails and marking the rail for replacement

de·temporize *or* **de·temporalize** \(ˈ)dē+\-\ *vt* [*detemporize* fr. *de-* + L *tempor-, tempus* time + E *-ize*; *detemporalize* fr. *de-* + *temporalize* — more at TEMPORAL] **:** to dissociate from a particular historical time **:** make timeless ⟨war fiction that tries to disengage itself from its own historical background, to ~ and depersonalize its time-bound characters —Robert Pick⟩

de·tent \dəˈtent, (ˈ)dē¦t-\ *n* -s [F *détente*, fr. MF *destente*, fr. *destendre* to slacken, release, fr. OF, fr. *des-* de- + *tendre* to stretch, fr. L *tendere* — more at THIN] **:** a part of a mechanism (as a catch, pawl, dog, or click) that locks or unlocks a movement: as **a :** the part of a watch or clock that detains a wheel or a lever when moved in one direction but releases it on its return excursion **b :** the set lever in a stem-set watch **c :** the hook that locks and unlocks the striking mechanism in a clock

dé·tente \(ˈ)dā¦tä(ⁿ)nt, dāˈtäⁿt\ *n* -s [F, détente, detent] **1 :** a slackening or relaxing; *esp* **:** an easing or relaxation of strained relations and political tensions between nations **2** *phonetics* **:** OFF-GLIDE, RELEASE

de·ten·tion \dəˈtenchən, dēˈ-\ *n* -s [MF or LL; MF, fr. LL *detention-, detentio* retention, fr. L *detentus* (past part. of *detinēre* to detain) + *-ion-, -io* -ion — more at DETAIN] **1 :** the act or fact of detaining: **a :** a holding in custody ⟨~ of a tardy pupil after school hours⟩ **b :** a holding back ⟨the ~ of a motorist by a traffic officer⟩ **2 :** the state of being detained ⟨~ in jail⟩ **:** enforced delay ⟨accidental ~ on a journey⟩; *esp* **:** a period of temporary custody prior to disposition by a court ⟨the ~ of juvenile delinquents⟩ **3** *civil law* **:** a bare physical control without the mental element of intention required for possession

detention home *n* **:** a house of detention for juvenile delinquents usu. under supervision of the local juvenile court

de·ten·tive \-entiv\ *adj* [fr. *detention*, after E *retention: retentive*] **:** having the function of detaining

dé·te·nu *or* **dé·te·nue** \¦dātᵊn¦(y)ü, *F* dātnüe\ *n* -s [F *détenu* (masc.), *détenue* (fem.), fr. *détenu*, past part. of *détenir* to detain, fr. OF *detenir* — more at DETAIN] **:** a detained person; *esp* **:** a political prisoner in India

de·ter \dəˈtər, dēˈ-, +V -ər-; -ˈtə, +V -ər- *or* -ə(r\ *vt* **deterred; deterred; deterring; deters** [L *deterrēre*, fr. *de* from, away + *terrēre* to frighten — more at DE-, TERROR] **1 :** to turn aside, discourage, or prevent from acting by fear or consideration of dangerous, difficult, or unpleasant attendant circumstances or consequences **2 :** INHIBIT ⟨painting to ~ rust⟩ **syn** see DISSUADE

de·terge \dəˈtərj, dēˈ-, -əj,-əij\ *vt* -ED/-ING/-S [F or L; F *déterger* to cleanse, fr. L *detergēre* to wipe off, cleanse, fr. *de* from, away + *tergēre* to rub off, wipe off — more at TERSE] **:** to wash off **:** CLEANSE

de·ter·gency \-jənsē, -si\ *n* -ES [*detergent*, adj. + *-cy*] **:** cleansing quality or power

¹de·ter·gent \-jənt\ *adj* [F or L; F *détergent*, fr. L *detergent-, detergens*, pres. part. of *detergēre*] **:** CLEANSING

²detergent \"\ *n* -s **:** a cleansing agent: as **a :** SOAP **b :** an inorganic alkali, an alkaline salt (as a sodium phosphate or a sodium silicate), or a mixture of such compounds for use esp. in cleaning metals (as in dairy equipment) — called also *alkaline detergent* **c :** any of a large number of synthetic water-soluble or liquid organic surface-active agents for use in washing that resemble soaps in the ability to emulsify oils and hold dirt in suspension but differ in other respects (as in nonprecipitation of calcium and magnesium salts from hard water and in chemical composition) — called also *synthetic detergent;* see ANIONIC DETERGENT, CATIONIC DETERGENT, NONIONIC DETERGENT; compare WETTING AGENT **d :** an oil-soluble substance that holds insoluble foreign matter in suspension and is used in lubricating oils and dry-cleaning solvents

de·te·ri·o·ra·ble \dəˈtirēərəbəl, dēˈ-\ *adj* [*deteriorate* + *-able*] **:** liable to deteriorate

de·te·ri·o·rate \dəˈtirēə,rāt, dēˈ-, *chiefly in substand speech* -irē,āt *sometimes* -irə,rāt; *usu* -ād·+V\ *vb* -ED/-ING/-S [LL *deterioratus*, past part. of *deteriorare*, fr. L *deterior* worse, fr. *de* down, away + *-ter* (suffix as in L *uter* which of two) + *-ior* (comparative suffix) — more at DE-, WHETHER, -ER] *vt* **:** to make inferior in quality or value **:** IMPAIR ⟨laxity ~s discipline⟩ ~ *vi* **:** to grow worse ⟨the weather had *deteriorated* during the night —Nevil Shute⟩ **:** become impaired in quality, state, or condition **:** DEGENERATE ⟨idle houses ~⟩

de·te·ri·o·ra·tion \də,tirēəˈrāshən, dē,- *chiefly in substand speech* -irēˈā- *sometimes* -irəˈrā-\ *n* -s [LL *deterioration-, deterioratio*, fr. *deterioratus* + L *-ion-, -io* -ion] **:** the action or process of deteriorating or state of having deteriorated **:** gradual impairment

de·te·ri·o·ra·tion·ist \-sh(ə)nəst\ *n* -s **:** one who holds that the world and mankind are deteriorating

de·te·ri·o·ra·tive \-ˈtirēə,rād·|iv, -,rə|, |t|, |ēv *also* |əv\ *adj* **:** tending to deteriorate **:** DETERIORATING

de·te·ri·o·ra·tor \-,rād·ə(r), -ātə-\ *n* -s **:** one that deteriorates

de·te·ri·o·rism \-,rizəm\ *n* -s [L *deterior* worse + E *-ism*] **:** the belief in universal deterioration — compare MELIORISM

de·ter·ma \dəˈtərmə\ *n* -s [native name in Guiana] **:** a Central American tree (*Ocotea rubra*) valued for its light strong wood

de·ter·ment \dəˈtərmənt, dēˈ-, -tōm-\ *n* -s [*deter* + *-ment*] **1 :** the action of deterring **2 :** DETERRENT

de·ter·min·abil·i·ty \də,tərmənəˈbiləd·ē, (,)dē,t-, -tōm-, -təim-, -ətē, -i *also* -mn-\ *n* -ES **:** the quality or state of being determinable or determinate

¹de·ter·min·able \dəˈtərmənəbəl, dēˈ-, -tōm-,-təim- *also* -mn-\ *adj* [ME, fr. *determinen* to determine + *-able*] **1 :** capable of being determined, definitely ascertained, or decided upon **:** JUDICABLE **2 :** liable to be terminated **:** TERMINABLE — **de·ter·min·able·ness** *n* -ES — **de·ter·min·ably** \-blē, -li\ *adv*

²determinable \"\ *n* -s **:** a logical attribute or the name of a logical attribute (as color) of which certain more specific characters or their names are determinates (as red)

determinable fee *n* **:** a fee so qualified that it terminates upon the happening of a contingency or failure of a qualification

de·ter·mi·na·cy \-mənəsē, -si\ *n* -ES [*determinate* + *-cy*] **1 :** the quality or state of being determinate **2 a :** the condition of being definitely and unequivocally characterized **:** EXACTNESS ⟨the ~ of a logical statement⟩ **b :** the condition of being determined or necessitated ⟨the conflict between freedom of the will and universal ~⟩

¹de·ter·mi·nant \-nənt\ *adj* [L *determinant-, determinans*, pres. part. of *determinare* to limit, determine] **:** serving to determine **:** DETERMINATIVE

²determinant \"\ *n* -s **1 :** a fact, circumstance, or situation which identifies, aids diagnosis, or determines the nature of something or which fixes, determines, or conditions an outcome or issue **:** FACTOR ⟨there is no eternal ~ of obscenity, lasciviousness, indecency . . . the meanings of these terms change with the times —J.T.Farrell⟩ ⟨a semiconsciousness that education is the most important function of the state and the chief ~ of its way of life —Stephen Duggan⟩ **2 :** a determining bachelor of arts **3 :** a square array of numbers with which is associated a value that is the algebraic sum of all of the different products that can be formed by taking as factors an element from each column in succession, each one from a different row, the signs of the products being positive or negative depending upon whether the number of interchanges in the row indices necessary to restore them to natural order is even or odd **4** *logic* **:** a qualifying adjective or phrase **:** a mark or attribute distinguishing some class which falls under a more general concept **:** DIFFERENTIA **5 a :** a hypothetical aggregate of biophores conceived as comparable to the gene of more recent biological theory **b :** GENE; *broadly* **:** a comparable but subordinate agent (as a plasmagene or plastogene) **6 :** RADICAL 2c **7 :** ²DETERMINATIVE 3 **8** *archeol* **:** a trait or complex that is diagnostic of a cultural unit (as a component, aspect, phase) **9 :** one of the chemical groupings that together determine the specific reactivity of an antigen or antibody **syn** see CAUSE

de·ter·mi·nan·tal \=ˌ==¦nantᵊl\ *adj* **:** relating to, consisting of, or expressed in determinants

¹de·ter·mi·nate \dəˈtərmənət, dēˈ-, -|tōm-,-təim-, *usu* -nəd·+V\ *adj* [ME *determinat*, fr. L *determinatus*, past part. of *determinare* to limit, determine] **1 :** having defined limits **:** not uncertain **:** fixed by a rule or by some specific and constant cause **:** ESTABLISHED, DEFINITE ⟨~ variations in animals⟩ **2 :** definitely settled **:** fixed by authority or consent **:** INVARIABLE, ARBITRARY ⟨a ~ order of precedence⟩ **3 :** determined by resolving, deciding, or coming to a conclusion about **:** DEFINITIVE ⟨a ~ answer to the problem⟩ **4** *of a number* **:** having a fixed value — opposed to *indeterminate* **5 :** CYMOSE **6** *embryol* **:** undergoing determinate cleavage — **de·ter·mi·nate·ly** *adv* — **de·ter·mi·nate·ness** *n* -ES

²de·ter·mi·nate \-,nāt, *usu* -ād·+V\ *vt* -ED/-ING/-S [L *determinatus*, past part. of *determinare*] **1** *obs* **a :** to fix the boundaries or limits of **b :** to bring to an end **2** *obs* **:** to decide or settle (an issue) **3** *obs* **:** to guide or determine the course or end of **4 :** to find out for certain **:** ASCERTAIN **5 :** to fix the identity of **:** IDENTIFY

³determinate *like* ¹DETERMINATE\ *n* -s [¹*determinate*] **:** a logical character that is a further determination of some more general attribute — see ²DETERMINABLE

determinate cleavage *n* **:** cleavage (sense 4a) in which each cell division irreversibly separates portions of the zygote with specific and distinct potencies for further development — compare INDETERMINATE CLEAVAGE, MOSAICISM

determinate evolution *or* **determinate variation** *n* **:** ORTHOGENESIS 1

determinate growth *n* **1 :** growth in which the axis being limited by the development of the terminal flower bud or other reproductive structure does not continue to elongate indefinitely (as in a cymose inflorescence and in certain mosses) — compare INDETERMINATE GROWTH **2 :** growth that proceeds only during part of the vegetative season and then ceases

de·ter·mi·na·tion \də,tərməˈnāshən, dē,-, -tōm-,-təim-\ *n* -s [ME *determinacioun*, fr. ML *determination-, determinatio*, fr. L, boundary, end, fr. *determinatus* + *-ion-, -io* -ion] **1 :** the settling and ending of a controversy esp. by judicial decision **:** CONCLUSION, DECISION ⟨the contending parties came to a ~⟩ **2 :** the resolving of a question by argument or reasoning; *specif* **:** a disputation in English universities formerly held by those just made bachelors of arts as a condition of proceeding toward the master's degree **3** *archaic* **:** a bringing or coming to an end **:** TERMINATION **4 a :** the act of deciding definitely and firmly esp. regarding a course of action; *also* **:** the result of such an act of decision **:** fixed resolution **:** PURPOSE **b :** the power or habit of deciding definitely and firmly **:** ability to persist against opposition or attempts to dissuade or discourage **:** RESOLUTENESS ⟨men of great courage and ~⟩ **5 :** a fixing of the position, magnitude, or character of something: as **a :** the act, process, or result of an accurate measurement (as of weight, volume, intensity) ⟨a ~ of the salt in sea water⟩ ⟨a ~ of the orbit of a planet⟩ **b :** an identification of the taxonomic position of a plant or animal **6** *logic* **a :** the act of defining a concept or notion by giving its essential constituents **b :** the addition of a differentia to a concept or notion, thus limiting its extent **c :** a differentia added **7 :** direction or tendency to a certain end **:** IMPULSION ⟨a ~ of capital toward investment in transport industries⟩ **8 :** the fixation of the destiny of undifferentiated embryonic tissue **:** field formation

¹de·ter·mi·na·tive \=ˈ==,nā|d·|iv, -,nə|, |t|, |ēv *also* |əv\ *adj* [prob. fr. ML *determinativus* definite, fr. LL, relating to the crisis of a disease, fr. L *determinatus* + *-ivus* -ive] **1 :** having power or tendency to determine **:** LIMITING, SHAPING, DIRECTING, CONCLUSIVE **2 :** fixing or tending to determine the specific character **3** *of a compound word* **:** belonging either to the karmadharaya class or to the tatpurusha class **syn** see CONCLUSIVE

²determinative \"\ *n* -s **1 :** one that serves to determine **2 :** a sign attached to a word in any of various forms of writing (as hieroglyphic and cuneiform) to indicate its class, number, or other feature, thereby often serving to distinguish the word from its homographs — compare RADICAL 2c **3 :** a usu. suffixal sound or sequence of sounds added to a root and producing a longer root or base sometimes with perceptibly modified meaning to which derivational affixes or inflectional endings may be added (as *d* in reconstructed Indo-European *gheud-* "to pour", represented by Latin *fudi* "I have poured" and Gothic *giutan* "to pour", contrasted with reconstructed Indo-European *gheu-* "to pour", represented by Sanskrit *homa* "sacrifice", Greek *cheein* "to pour", *chylos* "juice") **4 :** a word belonging to any of several classes differently constituted by different grammarians but typically either consisting of certain uses of the definite article and of demonstrative adjectives and pronouns or including the definite article, demonstrative adjectives, demonstrative pronouns, and some limiting adjectives other than demonstratives **5 :** a determinative compound **6 :** CLASSIFIER 2

determinative judgment *n* [trans. of G *bestimmende urteilskraft*] *in Kantianism* **:** a judgment that proceeds from a general concept or universal principle and designates the particulars which are to be subsumed under the general — contrasted with *reflective judgment*

de·ter·mi·na·tive·ly \|əvlē, -li\ *adv* **:** in a determinative manner

de·ter·mi·na·tor \-,nād·ə(r), -ātə-\ *n* -s [MF & LL; MF *determinateur*, fr. LL *determinator*, fr. L *determinatus* + *-or*] **:** DETERMINER

de·ter·mine \dəˈtərmən, dēˈ-, -tōm-,-təim-\ *vb* **determined; determined; determining** \-m(ə)niŋ\ **determines** [ME *determinen*, fr. MF *determiner*, fr. L *determinare* to limit, determine, fr. *de* from, away + *terminare* to limit, fr. *terminus* limit, boundary — more at DE-, TERM] *vt* **1 a :** to fix conclusively or authoritatively ⟨a council was set up to ~ national policy⟩ **b :** to settle a question or controversy about **:** decide by judicial sentence ⟨the court heard and *determined* the plea⟩ **c :** to come to a decision concerning as the result of investigation or reasoning ⟨an attempt to ~ the date of his death⟩ **d :** to settle or decide by choice of alternatives or possibilities ⟨~ the list of guests to be invited⟩ **e :** to set up as a goal or purpose **:** resolve upon ⟨when did Thoreau ~ to become a man of letters —H.S.Canby⟩ **2 a :** to fix the form or character of beforehand **:** ORDAIN, FOREORDAIN **b :** to establish causally **:** bring about as a result **:** REGULATE ⟨demand ~s the price⟩ **3 :** to set bounds or limits to: as **a :** to fix the boundaries of **b :** to limit in extent or scope **c :** to put or set an end to **:** bring to a close **:** TERMINATE ⟨~ an estate⟩ **d** *logic* **:** to define or limit by adding a differentia **4 :** to direct or control the end or course of: as **a :** to turn to a definite resolution or intention **:** cause to come to a decision ⟨opposition only *determined* her further⟩ **b :** to give a definite direction, impetus, or bias to ⟨what we notice ~s what we do —William James⟩ **5 a :** to obtain definite and firsthand knowledge of as to character, location, magnitude, or quantity ⟨~ the salt in sea water⟩ **b :** to discover the taxonomic position of (a plant or animal) **:** ascertain the generic and specific names of **6** *embryol* **:** to cause or elicit determination of ~ *vi* **1 :** to come to a decision **:** RESOLVE ⟨the boy *determined* on becoming a painter⟩ **2 :** to come to an end **:** expire or become void **:** END, TERMINATE ⟨membership in the order ~s with the death of the sovereign⟩ **3 :** to dispute a question or maintain a thesis as formerly required at some European universities of those completing the assumption of a bachelor's degree **4** *obs* **:** to have a course (as toward an end) **:** TEND **syn** see DECIDE, DISCOVER

de·ter·mined \-mənd\ *adj* [fr. past part. of *determine*] **:** DECIDED, RESOLUTE ⟨even the most ~ realist has more than a streak in him of romanticist —John Galsworthy⟩ **:** BENT ⟨~ to get a rich husband⟩ — **de·ter·mined·ly** \-n(ə)dlē, -li\ *adv* — **de·ter·mined·ness** \-n(d)nəs\ *n* -ES

de·ter·min·er \-mənə(r)\ *n* -s **:** one that determines: as **a :** an inheritance factor **:** GENE, DETERMINANT **b :** a word belonging to a group of limiting noun modifiers that in English consists of *a, an, any, each, either, every, neither, no, one, some, the, that, those, this, these, what, whatever, which, whichever*, possessive adjectives (as *my*), and possessive-case forms (as *Joe's*) and is characterized by occurrence before descriptive adjectives modifying the same noun (as *that* in "that big yellow house" or *his* in "his new car")

de·ter·mi·nism \-mə,nizəm\ *n* -s [ISV *determine* + *-ism*] **1 a :** the doctrine that all acts of the will result from causes which determine them either in such a manner that man has no alternative modes of action or that the will is still free in the sense of being uncompelled — called also *ethical determinism;* compare INDETERMINISM **b :** the theory that all occurrences in nature are determined by antecedent causes or take place in accordance with natural laws — called also *cosmological determinism* **c :** a belief in predestination — called also *theological determinism;* compare FATALISM **2 :** a theory that regards a certain order of phenomena (as economic, geographical, or social factors) as the primary or determining causes for cultural change, social evolution, or the appearance of certain culture traits — compare ECONOMIC INTERPRETATION OF HISTORY **3 :** the quality or state of being determined: **a :** a natural process wherein all events are determined **b :** the determination of mental processes

de·ter·mi·nist \-,nəst\ *n* -s [ISV *determine* + *-ist*] **:** an adherent of determinism

de·ter·mi·nis·tic \ˌ=ˌ==ˈnistik\ *adj* **:** relating to or implying determinism — **de·ter·mi·nis·ti·cal·ly** \-tək(ə)lē\ *adv*

deterred *past of* DETER

de·ter·rence \dəˈtərən(t)s, dēˈ-, -tə·rə- *also* -tərə- *or* -tərə-; *esp in emphatic positions* -tərn- *or* -tern-\ *n* -s [*deter* + *-ence*] **:** the act or process of deterring; *esp* **:** the restraint and discouragement of crime by fear (as by the exemplary punishment of convicted offenders)

¹de·ter·rent \-nt\ *adj* [L *deterrent-, deterrens*, pres. part. of *deterrēre* to deter] **1 :** serving to deter ⟨the ~ effect of high prices on buying⟩ **2 :** relating to deterrence ⟨a ~ view of punishment⟩ — **de·ter·rent·ly** *adv*

²deterrent \"\ *n* -s **:** something that deters ⟨many . . . people feel that corporal punishment . . . does act as a ~ to potential offenders —W.T.McGrath⟩ ⟨U.S. superiority in atomic weapons seemed a ~ to all-out war —*New Statesman & Nation*⟩

deterring *pres part of* DETER

deters *pres 3d sing of* DETER

¹de·ter·sive \dəˈtərsiv *also* -rziv\ *adj* [MF *detersif*, fr. L *detersus* (past part. of *detergēre* to wipe off, cleanse) + MF *-if* -ive — more at DETERGE] *obs* **:** CLEANSING, DETERGENT

²detersive \"\ *n* -s **:** a cleansing agent **:** DETERGENT

de·test \dəˈtest, dēˈ-\ *vt* -ED/-ING/-S [ME *detesten*, fr. L *detestari*, lit., to curse while calling a deity to witness, fr. *de* from, down, away + *testari* to be a witness, testify, invoke as a witness, fr. *testis* witness — more at DE-, TESTIS] **1 :** to dislike intensely **:** ABHOR, LOATHE, HATE ⟨she delights in wrangles, noises, drafts, and almost everything that older people ~ —E.K. Brown⟩ **2** *obs* **:** CURSE, DENOUNCE, CONDEMN **syn** see HATE

de·test·able \-stəbəl, *archaically with stress on first syllable*\ *adj* [ME, fr. MF, fr. L *detestabilis*, fr. *detestari* + *-abilis* -able] **:** worthy of being detested **:** very odious **:** deserving abhorrence **:** ABOMINABLE ⟨~ vices⟩ — **de·test·able·ness** *n* -ES — **de·test·ably** \-blē, -li\ *adv*

de·tes·ta·tion \ˌdē,teˈstāshən *sometimes* də-, *or* ˌde,-\ *n* -s [ME *detestacion*, fr. MF & L; MF *detestation*, fr. L *detestation-, detestatio*, fr. *detestatus* (past part. of *detestari*) + *-ion-, -io* -ion] **1** *obs* **:** public or formal denunciation **2 :** the act or feeling of detesting **:** extreme hatred or dislike **:** ABHORRENCE, LOATHING ⟨~ of civil war⟩ **3 :** an object of hatred or contempt ⟨the ~ of all honest men⟩

de·throne \dēˈthrōn, dēˈ-\ *vt* **:** to remove or drive from a throne **:** divest of royal or supreme authority and dignity **:** DEPOSE — **de·throne·ment** \-mənt\ *n* -s

de·tin \(ˈ)dē + \ *vt* **:** to remove or recover tin from

det·i·net \ˈdetᵊn,et\ *n* -s [L, he detains, 3d pers. sing. pres. indic. act. of *detinēre* to detain — more at DETAIN] **:** a common-law action alleging merely that the defendant is withholding the money or chattels demanded — compare DETINUIT

det·i·nue \-tᵊn,(y)ü\ *n* -s [ME *detenewe*, fr. MF *detenue* detention, fr. fem. of *detenu*, past part. of *detenir* to detain — more at DETAIN] **1 :** detention of something due; *esp* **:** the unlawful detention of a personal chattel from another **2 :** a common-law action for the recovery of a personal chattel or its value wrongfully detained; *also* **:** the writ used for this action — compare TROVER

de·tin·u·it \dəˈtinyəwət\ *n* -s [L, he has detained, 3d pers. sing. perf. indic. act. of *detinēre*] **:** an action for replevin where the plaintiff already has the goods sued for — compare DETINET

detn *abbr* **1** detention **2** determination

det·o·na·bil·i·ty *n* -ES \ˌdetᵊnəˈbiləd·ē, -ed·ən-,-etən- *sometimes* ˌdē-\ **:** the quality or state of being detonable

det·o·na·ble \ˈdetᵊnəbəl, -ed·ən-,-etən- *sometimes* ˈdē-\ *adj* [*detonate* + *-able*] **:** capable of being detonated

det·o·nat·abil·i·ty \ˌ==,ād·əˈbiləd·ē, ˌ==,nā-\ *n* -ES **:** DETONABILITY

det·o·nat·able \ˈ==ˌ==bəl, ˌ==ˈ===\ *adj* **:** DETONABLE

det·o·nate \ˈ==,āt, ˈ==,nāt, *usu* -ād·+V\ *vb* -ED/-ING/-S [L *detonatus*, past part. of *detonare* to thunder down, fr. *de* down, away + *tonare* to thunder — more at DE-, THUNDER] *vi* **:** to explode almost instantaneously **:** undergo detonation — distinguished from *deflagrate* ~ *vt* **:** to cause to detonate ⟨~ TNT⟩ ⟨~ an atom bomb⟩

det·o·na·tion \ˌ=ˈ=ˈāshən, ˌ==ˈnā-\ *n* -s [F *détonation*, fr. ML *detonation-, detonatio*, fr. L *detonatus* + *-ion-, -io* -ion] **1 a :** the action or process of detonating; *specif* **:** a chemical reaction producing vigorous evolution of heat and sparks or flame and moving through the material detonated (as a high explosive such as dynamite or TNT) at a speed greater than that of sound — distinguished from *deflagration* **b :** a violent explosion **2 :** abnormally rapid combustion in an internal-combustion engine that replaces or occurs simultaneously with normal combustion and is manifested by loss of power, overheating, rough operation, and a characteristic knock

det·o·na·tive \ˈ==,ād|iv, ˈ==,nā|, ˈ==ə|, ˈ==nə|, |t|, |ēv *also* |əv\ *adj* **:** having the property of detonating or characterized by detonation **:** EXPLOSIVE

det·o·na·tor \ˈ==,ād·ə(r), ˈ==,nād·ə(r), -ātə-\ *n* -s **:** one that detonates: as **a :** a device (as a blasting cap) used for detonating a high-explosive charge **b** *Brit* **:** TORPEDO 4d **c :** an explosive (as mercury fulminate) that is more sensitive to heat or shock than the common high explosives and is used in small quantity to detonate another explosive

de·torsion \(ˈ)dē + \ *n* [*de-* + *torsion*] **:** the removal of torsion; *specif* **:** correction of abnormal twist (as of the intestine)

de·tort \dəˈtȯ(ə)rt\ *vt* -ED/-ING/-S [L *detortus*, past part. of *detorquēre*, fr. *de* from, away + *torquēre* to twist — more at DE-, TORTURE] *archaic* **:** TWIST, DISTORT, PERVERT — **de·tor·tion** \-ȯrshən\ *n* -s *archaic*

¹de·tour \ˈdē,tu̇(ə)r, dēˈt-, dəˈt-, -ùə\ *n* -s [F *détour*, fr. OF *destor*, fr. *destorner, destourner* to divert, turn aside, fr. *des-* de- + *torner, tourner* to turn — more at TURN] **:** a turning aside **:** a circuitous route **:** a deviation from a direct course or the usual procedure ⟨the ~s of the Mississippi⟩; *specif* **:** a roundabout way temporarily replacing part of a route

²detour \"\ *vb* -ED/-ING/-S *vi* **:** to proceed by a detour ⟨pits intervened and obliged the party to ~ around them⟩ ~ *vt* **1 :** to send by a circuitous route **:** deflect from a straight course ⟨heavy trucks were ~*ed* to avoid the bridge⟩ **2 :** to avoid by going around **:** BYPASS ⟨either flying above or ~*ing* storms⟩

de·toxicant \(ˈ)dē + ˈ-\ *n* -s [*detoxicate* + *-ant*] **:** a detoxicating agent

de·tox·i·cate \(ˈ)dēˈtäksə,kāt\ *vt* -ED/-ING/-S [*de-* + L *toxicum* poison + E *-ate* — more at TOXIC] **:** DETOXIFY — **de·tox·i·ca·tion** \(,)dē,täksəˈkāshən\ *n* -s — **de·tox·i·ca·tor** \(ˈ)dēˈtäksə,kād·ə(r)\ *n* -s

de·tox·i·fi·ca·tion \(,)dē,täksəfəˈkāshən\ *n* -s [alter. (influenced by E *-fication*) of *detoxication*] **:** the act of detoxifying or the state of being detoxified

de·tox·i·fi·er \(ˈ)dēˈtäksə,fī(ə)r\ *n* -s [*detoxify* + *-er*] **:** DETOXICANT

de·tox·i·fy \-,fī\ *vt* -ED/-ING/-ES [fr. *detoxification*, after such pairs as E *magnification: magnify*] **:** to remove the poison or effect of poison from

de·tract \dəˈtrakt, dēˈ-\ *vb* -ED/-ING/-S [ME *detracten*, fr. L *detractus*, past part. of *detrahere* to take away, withdraw, disparage, fr. *de* from, away + *trahere* to pull — more at DE-, DRAW] *vt* **1** *archaic* **:** to speak ill of **:** DISPARAGE, BELITTLE **2** *archaic* **:** to take away (a part) from something so as to lessen its value or importance **3 :** DIVERT, DRAW ⟨these exaggerated reports tend to ~ attention from the real issue —John Scott⟩ ~ *vi* **:** to diminish in importance or value or praiseworthiness **:** become reduced in effect **:** DEROGATE, BELITTLE ⟨far above our poor power to add or to ~ —Abraham Lincoln⟩ — often used with *from* ⟨any attempt to give a rational proof of the mysteries of religion really ~*s* from faith —Frank Thilly⟩ **syn** see DECRY

de·tract·er \-ktə(r)\ *n* -s [by alter.] **:** DETRACTOR

de·tract·ing·ly *adv* **:** in a detracting manner

de·trac·tion \dəˈtrakshən, dēˈ-\ *n* -s [ME *detraccioun*, fr. MF *detraction*, fr. LL *detraction-, detractio*, fr. L, withdrawal, fr. *detractus* (past part. of *detrahere*) + *-ion-, -io* -ion] **1 :** a lessening of reputation or esteem **:** defamation esp. by malicious misrepresentation or false charges **:** DISPARAGEMENT **2 :** a taking away **:** SUBTRACTION ⟨a ~ from the dignity of the legislature⟩

syn SLANDER, BACKBITING, CALUMNY, SCANDAL: DETRACTION, the least colorful of this group, is likely to stress the fact of damage to reputation, esteem, or credit and to leave unstressed motives for or kinds of malicious utterance ⟨I have no thought to paint the failings of our law in lurid colors of *detraction*. I have little doubt that its body is for the most part sound and pure —B.N.Cardozo⟩ ⟨no momentary happiness to have one enclosure where the voice that speaks in envy or *detraction* is not heard; which malice may not enter —William Wordsworth⟩ SLANDER, often legal or legalistic in suggestion, likewise connotes actual definite harm to the victim and suggests oral utterance of damaging statements, either quite maliciously and with full realization of their effect or quite carelessly and without consideration ⟨a *slander*, with which envy prompts the malignity of persons in their senses to asperse wittier than themselves —William Cowper⟩ ⟨this charge cannot be excused as a reckless *slander*. It was a deliberate falsehood, a lie —*New Republic*⟩ Sometimes SLANDER may involve statements true in fact but usu. not uttered and hence having the nature of the defamatory when uttered ⟨it is not hypocrisy to conceal the desires or imaginings which one would never act upon. To tell these is not true disclosure of oneself, but *slander* —H.O. Taylor⟩ BACKBITING suggests continued mean criticism, belittling, and unfair attacks on an absent friend, colleague, or associate by one from whom loyalty and fairness could be expected ⟨jealousy and intrigue and *backbiting*, producing a poisonous atmosphere of underground competition —Bertrand Russell⟩ CALUMNY may stress the purposive malice of the agent and the fact of his deliberate use of falsehood or misrepresentation ⟨these *calumnies*, indeed, could find credit only with the undiscerning multitude; but with these *calumnies* were mingled accusations much better founded —T.B.Macaulay⟩ ⟨a fellow . . . telling people that I was a consummate hypocrite. He could know nothing of it . . . I had given him no ground for that particular *calumny* —Joseph Conrad⟩ SCANDAL suggests gossipy repetition of and emphasis on discreditable details, esp. lurid ones, that defame ⟨I saw him coming out of the brush with that oldest girl of Trinidad's, only Sunday night. The reappearance of the priest upon the scene cut short further *scandal* —Willa Cather⟩ ⟨she was reconciled to the facts, but when she knew or suspected that they might be a subject of *scandal* among people who would be "sorry for her", she felt the situation intolerable —Havelock Ellis⟩

de·trac·tive \-ktiv, -tēv *also* -təv\ *adj* [MF *detractif*, fr. L *detractus* + MF *-if* -ive] **1 :** tending to detract **:** given to detraction ⟨~ influences on the volume of foreign investment⟩ **2 :** DEFAMATORY, CALUMNIOUS — **de·trac·tive·ly** \-təvlē\ *adv*

de·trac·tor \-ktə(r)\ *n* -s [ME *detractour*, fr. MF & L; MF *detracteur*, fr. L *detractor*, fr. *detractus* + *-or*] **:** one that detracts esp. habitually **:** DEROGATOR, DEFAMER, CALUMNIATOR

de·trac·to·ry \-kt(ə)rē, -ri\ *adj* [LL *detractorius*, fr. L *detractus* + *-orius* -ory] **:** DETRACTIVE

¹de·train \(ˈ)dēˈtrān\ *vb* -ED/-ING/-S [*de-* + *train*, n.] *vi* **:** to get off a railroad train ⟨the tourists ~*ed* wearily⟩ ~ *vt* **:** to remove from a railroad train ⟨~*ed* the troops and supplies as near the front as possible⟩ — **de·train·ment** \-mənt\ *n* -s

²detrain *vt* [*de-* + *train* (v.)] **:** DECONDITION 2

dé·tra·qué \ˌdā,träˈkā\ *adj* [F, past part. of *détraquer* to cause to stop functioning properly, fr. MF *detraquer* to divert from one's course, fr. *de-* (fr. OF *des-*) + *-traquer* (fr. *trac* track) — more at TRACK] **:** DERANGED, PSYCHOPATHIC

de·trash \(ˈ)dē + \ *vt* -ED/-ING/-ES [*de-* + *trash*, n.] **:** to remove the leaves and tops from (sugarcane stalks) before crushing

detrect *vt* [L *detrectare, detractare*, fr. *de* from, away + *tractare* to pull violently — more at DE-, TREAT] *obs* **:** to draw back from **:** REFUSE

de·trib·al·i·za·tion \(ˌ)dē,trībələˈzāshən\ *n* -s **:** the breaking down of a tribal organization esp. through culture contact

de·trib·al·ize \(ˈ)dēˈtrībə,līz\ *vt* -ED/-ING/-S [*de-* + *tribal* + *-ize*] **:** to cause to relinquish tribal customs **:** estrange or alienate from a tribe **:** ACCULTURATE ⟨*detribalized* natives working in mines⟩

det·ri·ment \ˈdetrəmənt\ *n* -s [ME, fr. MF or L; MF, fr. L *detrimentum*, fr. *detri-* (fr. *deterere* to wear out, impair, fr. *de* from, away + *terere* to rub) + *-mentum* -ment — more at DE-, THROW] **:** injury or damage or something that causes it **:** MISCHIEF, HURT ⟨study without ~ to one's health⟩

¹de·tri·men·tal \ˌ==ˈmentᵊl\ *adj* **:** causing detriment **:** HARMFUL, DAMAGING ⟨~ effects of a drug⟩ ⟨reports ~ to a reputation⟩ **syn** see PERNICIOUS

²detrimental \"\ *n* -s **1 :** a detrimental person or thing **2** *slang* **:** an ineligible suitor

de·tri·men·tal·ly \-ᵊlē, -ᵊli\ *adv* **:** in a detrimental manner

det·ri·men·tal·ness *n* -ES **:** detrimental quality

de·tri·tal \dəˈtrīdᵊl, dēˈ-, -ītl\ *adj* [*detritus* + *-al*] **:** of, relating to, or resulting from detritus

detrital rock *n* **:** rock composed mostly of constituents of clastic origin

de·trit·ed \|əd\ *adj* [L *detritus* worn down (past part. of *deterere* to wear down, wear out) + E *-ed*] **1 :** worn down ⟨a ~ coin⟩ **2 :** resulting from disintegration **:** DETRITAL

de·tri·tion \-rishən\ *n* -s [ML *detrition-, detritio*, fr. L *detritus* (past part. of *deterere*) + *-ion-, -io* -ion] **:** a wearing off or away by or as if by rubbing or by disintegration ⟨~ of sea cliffs⟩

de·tri·tus \-rīd·əs, -ītəs\ *n, pl* **detritus** [F *détritus*, fr. L *detritus*, past part. of *deterere*] **1 :** loose material that results directly from rock disintegration or abrasion esp. when composed of rock fragments **2 :** a product of disintegration or wearing away **:** fragment or fragmentary material ⟨the ~ of a conflagration⟩ ⟨ballads formed from the ~ of an old epic poem⟩ ⟨a ~ of broken-down bodily tissue⟩

detritus tank *n* **:** a chamber for removing the large heavy suspended matter from sewage

de·triv·o·rous \-rivərəs\ *adj* [*detritus* + *-vorous*] **:** feeding on animal wastes ⟨certain protozoans living on the skin of fishes and feeding on the mucous secretion are ~⟩

de·troit \dēˈtrȯit, də-ˈ-, *usu* -ȯid·+V\ *adj, usu cap* [*Detroit*, city in Michigan] **:** of or from the city of Detroit, Michigan **:** of the kind or style prevalent in Detroit

de·troit·er \-ȯid·ə(r), -ȯitə(r)\ *n* -s *cap* **:** a native or resident of Detroit, Michigan

de trop \dəˈtrō\ *adj* [F] **:** too much or too many **:** in the way **:** SUPERFLUOUS, UNWANTED ⟨a topcoat was *de trop* with the thermometer standing at 72 degrees —Irving Kolodin⟩

de·truck \(ˈ)dē + \ *vb* [*de-* + *truck*, n.] *vi* **:** to get down from a truck ~ *vt* **:** to unload (as troops) from a truck

de·trude \dəˈtrüd, dēˈ-\ *vt* -ED/-ING/-S [L *detrudere*, fr. *de* from, down, away + *trudere* to thrust, push — more at DE-, THREAT] **:** to thrust or force down, out, or away

de·truncate \də-, dē- + \ *vt* [L *detruncatus*, past part. of *detruncare*, fr. *de* from, away + *truncare* to cut off, mutilate — more at DE-, TRUNCATE] **:** TRUNCATE — **de·trun·ca·tion** \ˌdē + \ *n*

de·tru·sion \-üzhən\ *n* -s [LL *detrusion-, detrusio*, fr. L *detrusus* (past part. of *detrudere*) + *-ion-, -io* -ion] **:** the action of thrusting outward or downward

de·tru·sive \-üsiv *also* -üziv\ *adj* [fr. *detrusion*, after such pairs as E *intrusion: intrusive*] **:** tending to thrust out or down

de·tru·sor \-üzə(r), -üsə-\ *or* **detrusor muscle** *n* -s [NL, fr. L *detrusus* + *-or*] **:** the outer largely longitudinally arranged musculature of the bladder wall

de·tu·ba·tion \ˌdē,t(y)üˈbāshən\ *n* -s [*de-* + *tube* + *-ation*] **:** EXTUBATION

de·tumescence \ˌdēt\ *n* -s [L *detumescere* to cease swelling (fr. *de* down, away + *tumescere* to swell up) + E *-ence* — more at DE-, TUMESCENT] **:** diminution of swelling **:** subsidence of anything swollen

de·tune \(ˈ)dē + \ *vt* **:** to put (a radio receiver) out of tune or resonance (as by varying capacity or inductance)

de·tur \ˈdē,tər, -tù(ə)r\ *n* -s [L, let there be given, 3d pers. sing. pres. subj. pass. of *dare* to give — more at DATE] **:** a specially bound book awarded to a student for meritorious work

deturb *vt* -ED/-ING/-S [L *deturbare* to throw down, beat down, fr. *de* down, away + *turbare* to disturb — more at DE-, TURBID] *obs* **:** to throw down or out

de·turgescence \ˌdēt + \ *n* [*de-* + *turgescence*] **:** DETUMESCENCE

deturn *vt* [ME *deturnen*, fr. MF *detourner, destourner*, fr. OF *destorner, destourner* — more at DETOUR] *obs* **:** to turn aside **:** DIVERT

deturpate *vb* -ED/-ING/-S [L *deturpatus*, past part. of *deturpare* to disfigure, fr. *de* from, away + *turpare* to disfigure, defile, fr. *turpis* ugly, foul, shameful — more at DE-, TURPITUDE] *vt, obs* **:** DEBASE, DEFILE ~ *vi, obs* **:** to become vile or debased

¹deuce \ˈd(y)üs\ *n* -s [MF *deus* two, fr. OF, fr. L *duos*, accus. masc. of *duo* two — more at TWO] **1 a** (1) **:** the face of a die that bears two spots (2) **:** a playing card bearing an index number 2 or having two pips **:** TWOSPOT **b** (1) **:** a cast of dice yielding a point of two (2) **deuces** *pl* **:** a pair of deuces in a poker hand **2** [so called fr. the two successive points or games that must be won] **:** a tie in tennis in points toward a game or in games toward a set immediately below the minimum score needed for one side to win (as at 40 points or 5 games in lawn tennis) requiring scoring of two consecutive points by one side to win the game or set; *also* **:** a subsequent tie in a game in which deuce has occurred — compare ADVANTAGE **3** [prob. fr. *deuce* two at dice (as the lowest throw)] **a** *obs* **:** bad luck **:** PLAGUE — used chiefly as a mild oath **b :** DEVIL, DICKENS, HELL — used chiefly as a mild oath ⟨the ~ you say⟩ ⟨what the ~ is he up to now⟩ and as an intensive with *in* ⟨where in the ~ is he⟩ **c :** something notable of its kind — used quasi adverbially ⟨a ~ of a lovely day⟩ ⟨we had one ~ of a time getting there on schedule⟩ **4 :** any of various things of which the number two forms an important identification (as a two-dollar bill, a 2000-watt spotlight, or a score of two strokes on a hole at golf)

deuces 1a (2)

²deuce \"\ *vt* -ED/-ING/-S **:** to bring the score of (a tennis game or set) to deuce

deuce–ace \ˈ=ˈ=\ *n* -s [MF *deus as*, fr. OF, fr. *deus* two, deuce + *as* ace] **1 :** a throw of dice of two and one **2** *archaic* **:** bad luck **:** low condition

¹deuced \ˈd(y)üsəd, -st\ *adj* [*deuce* (devil) + *-ed*] **:** DARNED, CONFOUNDED, DEVILISH ⟨you're in a ~ fix now⟩

²deuced \"\ *or* **deuc·ed·ly** \-sədlē, -li\ *adv* **:** DAMNABLY, DEVILISHLY; *often* **:** VERY, REMARKABLY, EXTREMELY ⟨a ~ clever girl⟩ ⟨he was *deucedly* well-fixed⟩

deuces wild *n* **:** a variety of poker and certain other card games in which each deuce may be made to represent any other card designated by the holder of the deuce

deuk \ˈdyük\ *n* -s [ME (Sc) *duke*, fr. OE *dūce* — more at DUCK] *Scot* **:** ¹DUCK 1

de·us ex ma·chi·na \ˌdāəs,ekˈsmakənə, ˌdēə-; ˌdā,ü,sek-ˈsmäkənə; ÷ -ˌsməˈshēnə\ *n* [NL, a god from a machine, trans. of Gk *theos ek mēchanēs*] **:** a person or thing that appears or is introduced (as into a story) suddenly and unexpectedly and provides an artificial or contrived solution to an apparently insoluble difficulty

deut- *or* **deuto-** *comb form* [ISV, short for *deuter-*] **1 :** second in a regular series of chemical compounds ⟨*deut*oxide⟩ **2 :** second ⟨*deuto*mala⟩ **:** secondary ⟨*deuto*plasm⟩ — esp. in biological terms

¹deuter- *or* **deutero-** *comb form* [alter. (influenced by LL *deutero-*) of earlier *deutro-*, fr. ME, modif. of LL *deutero-*, fr. Gk *deuter-, deutero-*, fr. *deuteros* second; prob. akin to L *dudum* formerly, Gk *dein* to lack, miss, Gk (Homeric) *deuesthai* to be in need of, Skt *dūra* far] **1 :** second **:** secondary ⟨*deuter*agonist⟩ ⟨*deutero*plasm⟩ **2 :** belonging to any of various classes of chemical substances regarded as secondary products of decomposition ⟨*deutero*porphyrin⟩ ⟨*deutero*proteose⟩

²deuter- *or* **deutero-** *comb form* [ISV fr. *deuterium*] **:** DEUTERI- ⟨*deuter*ide⟩ ⟨*deutero*chloroform⟩

deu·ter·ag·o·nist \ˌd(y)üd·əˈragənəst, -raig-\ *n* -s [Gk *deuteragōnistēs*, fr. *deuter-* ¹deuter- + *agōnistēs* combatant, actor — more at AGONIST] **1 :** the actor taking the part of second importance in a classical Greek drama **2 :** a person who serves as a foil for another

deu·ter·anomalous \ˌd(y)üd·ər + \ *adj* [NL *deuteranomal*ia + E *-ous*] **:** exhibiting deuteranomaly

deu·ter·anomaly \" + \ *n* -ES [NL *deuteranomalia*, fr. ¹*deuter-* + L *anomalia* anomaly] **:** trichromatism in which an abnormally large proportion of green is required to match the spectrum — compare PROTANOMALY, TRICHROMAT

deu·ter·an·ope \ˈd(y)üd·ərə,nōp\ *n* -s [ISV, back-formation fr. *deuteranopia*] **:** an individual affected with deuteranopia

deu·ter·an·o·pia \ˌ===ˈnōpēə\ *n* -s [NL, fr. ¹*deuter-* + ²*a-* + *-opia*] **:** red-green blindness believed due to a defect in the optic nerve that interferes with normal transmission of red and green sensations and marked by confusion of purplish red and green — compare PROTANOPIA

deu·ter·an·op·ic \ˌ===ˈnäpik, -nōp-\ *adj* [*deuteranop*ia + *-ic*] **:** characterized by or affected by deuteranopia ⟨~ vision⟩ ⟨a ~ person⟩

deu·ter·at·ed \ˈd(y)üd·ə,rād·əd\ *also* **deu·ter·ized** \-,rīzd\ *adj* [*deuterated* fr. ²*deuter-* + *-ate* + *-ed*; *deuterized* fr. ²*deuter-* + *-ize* + *-ed*] **:** containing deuterium esp. as a constituent of a chemical compound

deu·ter·a·tion \ˌd(y)üd·əˈrāshən\ *or* **deu·ter·i·za·tion** \ˌd(y)üd·ərəˈzāshən\ *n* -s [*deuteration* fr. ²*deuter-* + *-ation*; *deuterization* fr. ²*deuter-* + *-ize* + *-ation*] **:** the introduction of deuterium esp. into a chemical compound

deuteri- *or* **deuterio-** *comb form* [ISV, fr. *deuterium*] **:** deuterium **:** containing deuterium — in names of chemical compounds ⟨*deuterio*ammonia⟩

deu·ter·ic \(ˈ)d(y)üˈterik\ *adj* [¹*deuter-* + *-ic*] **:** PAULOPOST — **deu·ter·i·cal·ly** \-rək(ə)lē\ *adv*

deu·ter·ide \ˈd(y)üd·ə,rīd\ *n* -s [²*deuter-* + *-ide*] **:** a binary compound of deuterium with a more electropositive element or radical analogous to a hydride

deu·te·ri·um \d(y)üˈtirēəm\ *n* -s [¹*deuter-* + *-ium*] **:** the isotope of hydrogen that has atoms of twice the mass of ordinary light hydrogen atoms, that occurs naturally in very small amounts in water, and that is used in nuclear reactions and as a tracer in chemical and biological investigations — called also *heavy hydrogen*; symbol D, H^2, or ^2H

deuterium oxide *n* **:** heavy water D_2O composed only of deuterium and oxygen

deu·tero·canonical \ˌd(y)üd·ə(,)rō + \ *adj* [NL *deuterocanonicus* deuterocanonical (fr. ¹*deuter-* + LL *canonicus* belonging to the canon of Scripture) + E *-al* — more at CANONIC] **:** of, belonging to, or constituting a second or later canon — used esp. by Roman Catholics (1) of those scriptural books in the canon fixed by the Council of Trent that are found only in the Septuagint and not in the Hebrew and constitute the Apocrypha of most Protestants and (2) of the following portions of the New Testament: Mark 16:9–20, Luke 22:43, 44, John 7:53–8:11, Hebrews, James, 2 Peter, 2 and 3 John, Jude, and Revelation

deu·ter·o·cone \ˈd(y)üd·ərə,kōn\ *n* [¹*deuter-* + *cone*] **:** the cusp of a mammalian premolar corresponding in position to the protocone of a true molar

deu·ter·o·co·nid \ˌ===ˈkōnəd\ *n* -s [*deuterocone* + *-id*] **:** the cusp of a mammalian premolar corresponding in position to the protoconid

deu·ter·og·a·my \ˌd(y)üd·əˈrägəmē\ *n* -ES [LGk *deuterogamia*, fr. Gk *deuter-* ¹deuter- + *-gamia* -gamy] **1 :** DIGAMY **2 :** secondary pairing of sexual cells or nuclei that replaces direct copulation in many fungi, algae, and higher plants

deu·tero·genesis \ˌd(y)üd·ə(,)rō + \ *n* [¹*deuter-* + *genesis*] **:** the appearance of a new adaptive character late in life — compare CENOGENESIS

deu·tero–malay \" + \ *n* -s *cap M* [¹*deuter-* + *Malay*] **:** a Malaysian whose physical appearance distinguishes him from the proto-Malay and from Veddoid or negritoid types but who is often described as having southern Mongoloid characteristics — called also *malayan, malaysian* — **deu·tero-malayan** *or* **deu·tero–malaysian** \" + \ *adj, usu cap M*

deu·ter·o·my·ce·tes \ˌd(y)üd·ə(,)rō,mīˈsēd·ēz\ [NL, fr. ¹*deuter-* + *-mycetes*] *syn of* FUNGI IMPERFECTI

deu·ter·on \ˈd(y)üd·ə,rän\ *also* **deu·ton** \ˈd(y)ü,tän\ *n* -s [*deuteron* fr. *deuterium* + *-on*; *deuton* fr. *deuterium* + *-on*] **:** the nucleus of the deuterium atom that consists of one proton and one neutron and is used as a projectile in nuclear bombardments (as with a cyclotron) — symbol *d*

deu·ter·o·nom·ic \ˌd(y)üd·ərəˈnämik\ *adj, usu cap* [*Deuteronomy*, the fifth book of the Old Testament (alter. — influenced by LL *Deuteronomium* — of earlier *Deutronome*, fr. ME *Deutronomie*, modif. of LL *Deuteronomium*, fr. Gk *Deuteronomion*, fr. *deuter-* ¹deuter- + *-nomion* — fr. *nomos* law) + E *-ic* — more at NIMBLE] **:** of, relating to, or in the style of the biblical book of Deuteronomy

deu·ter·on·o·mist \ˌd(y)üd·əˈränəmə̇st\ *n* -s *usu cap* [*Deuteronomy* + E *-ist*] **:** a writer or editor of the book of Deuteronomy, one of its versions, or Deuteronomic portions of the Old Testament of the Bible

deu·ter·os·co·py \-ˈräskəpē\ *n* -ES [¹*deuter-* + *-scopy*] **1** *obs* **:** something seen or perceived only at a second view **2** *archaic* **:** CLAIRVOYANCE

deu·ter·o·sto·ma·ta \ˌd(y)üd·ərəˈstōməd·ə\ [NL, fr. ¹*deuter-* + *-stomata*] *syn of* DEUTEROSTOMIA

¹deu·ter·o·stome \ˈ≡≡≡ˌstōm\ *adj* [NL *Deuterostomia*] **:** of or relating to Deuterostomia

²deuterostome \"\ *n* -s **:** an animal belonging to the group Deuterostomia

deu·ter·o·sto·mia \ˌ≡≡≡ˈstōmēə\ *n pl, cap* [NL, fr. ¹*deuter-* + *-stomia*] *in many classifications* **:** a major division of the animal kingdom comprising all bilateral animals (as the chordates) that lack ectomesoderm and have indeterminate cleavage and a mouth that does not arise from the blastopore

deu·ter·ot·o·kous \ˌd(y)üd·əˈräd·əkəs\ *adj* [¹*deuter-* + *-tokous*] **:** exhibiting deuterotoky **:** producing both male and female offspring parthenogenetically

deu·ter·ot·o·ky \ˌ≡≡ˈ≡≡kē\ *n* -ES [¹*deuter-* + *-toky*] **:** the parthenogenetic production of both males and females — compare ARRHENOTOKY, THELYTOKY

deu·ter·o·tonic \ˌd(y)üd·ərə+\ *adj* [¹*deuter-* + *tonic*] **:** characterized by accent on the second syllable — contrasted with *prototonic*

deu·ter·o·zooid \"+\ *n* [¹*deuter-* + *zooid*] **:** a zooid produced by budding or fission from a primary zooid

deuto- — see DEUT-

deu·to·cerebral \ˌd(y)üd·(ˌ)ō+\ *adj* [*deutocerebrum* + *-al*] **:** of or relating to the deutocerebrum

deu·to·cerebrum \"+\ *n* [NL, fr. *deut-* + *cerebrum*] **:** the midsection of the brain of most arthropods formed by the paired ganglia of the second true segment and consisting of paired antennary and olfactory lobes; *esp* **:** the median lobes of the insect brain that innervate the antennal segment

deu·to·ma·la \"+ˌmālə\ *n, pl* **deutoma·lae** \-ˌlē\ [NL, fr. *deut-* + *mala*] **:** either member of the second pair of mouthparts of a diplopod — **deu·to·ma·lal** \-ālal\ *or* **deu·to·ma·lar** \-ālə(r)\ *adj*

deu·tom·er·ite \d(y)üˈtämə̇ˌrīt\ *n* -s [ISV *deut-* + *mer-* (fr. Gk *meros* part) + *-ite* — more at MERIT] **:** the posterior segment of the trophozoite of certain gregarines

deuton *var of* DEUTERON

deu·to·nymph \ˈd(y)üd·ō+\ *n* [*deut-* + *nymph*] **:** a second larval form occurring in the development of most mites — compare PROTONYMPH, TRITONYMPH — **deu·to·nymphal** \ˌ≡≡+\ *adj*

deu·to·plasm \ˈ≡≡+\ *n* -s [ISV *deut-* + *-plasm*; orig. formed as F *deutoplasme*] **:** the nutritive inclusions of protoplasm; *esp* **:** the yolk reserves of an egg — **deu·to·plas·mic** \ˌ≡≡ˈplazmik\ *adj*

deu·to·plasmolysis \ˌd(y)üd·(ˌ)ō+\ *n* [*deutoplasm* + *-o-* + *-lysis*] **:** elimination of part of the yolk content of an egg following fertilization or during cleavage

deut·ovum \d(y)üd·ˈōvəm, -üˈtō-\ *n* [NL, fr. *deut-* + *ovum*] **:** the inactive incompletely developed larva of a mite after the rupture of the outer eggshell

deut·sche mark \ˈdȯichəˌmärk\ *also* **deutsch·mark** \ˈdȯichˌm-\ *n* -s [G *deutsche mark*, lit., German mark] **1 :** the German mark as established in 1948 by the German Federal Republic — see MONEY table **2 :** a coin representing one deutsche mark

deut·zia \ˈd(y)ütsēə, ˈdȯit-\ *n* [NL, fr. Jean *Deutz* †1784? Dutch patron of botanical researches + NL *-ia*] **1** *cap* **:** a genus of ornamental shrubs (family Saxifragaceae) that are native to Asia and Central America but widespread in cultivation and that have short-stalked toothed opposite leaves, usu. shreddy bark, and white or sometimes pink flowers mostly in panicles or cymes **2** -s **:** any shrub of the genus *Deutzia*

¹dev *var of* ¹DEVA

²dev *var of* DAEVA

dev *abbr* **1** developed; developer **2** deviation

¹de·va \ˈdāvə\ *or* **dev** \ˈdev\ *n* -s [Skt *deva* — more at DEITY] **:** a divine being or god in Hinduism and Buddhism

²deva *var of* DAEVA

de·va·chan \ˈdāˈvächən\ *n* -s [perh. irreg. fr. Skt *devāc* directed toward the gods, fr. *deva*] *theosophy* **:** a state intermediate between two earth lives into which the ego enters after leaving kamarupa — **de·va·cha·nic** \ˌdāvəˈchanik\ *adj*

de·va·da·si \ˌdāvəˈdäsē\ *n* -s [Skt *devadāsī* female servant of a god, fr. *deva* + *dāsī* dasi] **:** a dancing girl and courtesan of a Hindu temple

¹de·val \dəˈväl, -vōl\ *vi* -ED/-ING/-S [ME *devalen* to descend, sink, fr. MF *devaler*, fr. (assumed) VL *devallare* (fr. L *de* down, away + (assumed) VL *-vallare* (fr. L *valles, vallis* valley) — more at DE-, VALE] *chiefly Scot* **:** to leave off **:** CEASE ⟨it rained the whole day and never ∼*ed*⟩

²deval \"\ *n* -s *Scot* **:** CESSATION, PAUSE

de·va·lo·ka \ˌdāvəˈlōkə\ *n* -s [Skt, fr. *deva* + *loka* world — more at LEA] *Hinduism & Buddhism* **:** a world of gods **:** HEAVEN

de·valorize \(ˈ)dē+\ *vt* -ED/-ING/-S [F *dévaloriser*, fr. *dé-* de- (fr. OF *des-*) + *valor-* (alter. — influenced by ML *valor* — of *valeur* value, fr. ML *valor*) + *-iser* -ize — more at VALOR] **:** to diminish the value of **:** DEVALUE

de·valuate \(ˈ)dē+\ *vb* [*de-* + *value*, n. + *-ate*] **:** DEVALUE

de·valuation \(ˌ)dē+\ *n* -s [*devaluate* + *-ion*] **1 :** an official reduction in the exchange value of a currency by a lowering of its gold equivalency **2 :** a lessening esp. of status or stature **:** a reduction or minimizing esp. of importance **:** DECLINE

de·value \(ˈ)dē+\ *vb* [*de-* + *value*, n.] *vt* **1 :** to institute the devaluation of (money) **2 :** to cause or be responsible for a devaluation of (as a person or a literary work); *sometimes* **:** to divest of value or esteem ∼ *vi* **:** to institute devaluation

de·va·na·ga·ri \ˌdāvəˈnägərē\ *n*, *usu cap* [Skt *devanāgarī*, fr. *deva* + *nāgarī* Nagari] **:** the alphabet having as a characteristic feature long horizontal strokes on the tops of most of the characters that is usu. employed for Sanskrit and is also used as a literary hand for various modern languages of central, western, and northern India — see ALPHABET table; NAGARI

de·vance \də̇ˈvan(t)s\ *vt* -ED/-ING/-S [MF *devancer*, fr. OF *devancier, davancier*, fr. *devant, davant* in front, forward, after OF *avant* before: *avancier* to advance] *archaic* **:** FORESTALL, ANTICIPATE, OUTSTRIP

de·vant \də̇ˈväⁿ\ *adv* [F, fr. OF *devant, davant*, fr. *de* from (fr. L *de*) + *avant* before, fr. L *abante* — more at DE-, ADVANCE] **:** in front **:** FORWARD — used in ballet of the execution of a step or of the movement of an arm or leg in front of the body

de·vast \də̇ˈvast\ *vt* -ED/-ING/-S [MF or L; MF *devaster*, fr. L *devastare* to devastate] **:** DEVASTATE

dev·as·tate \ˈdevəˌstāt, *usu* -ād·+V\ *vt* -ED/-ING/-S [L *devastatus*, past part. of *devastare*, fr. *de* from, away + *vastare* to lay waste, fr. *vastus* empty, waste — more at WASTE] **1 :** to lay waste **:** RAVAGE ⟨whole countries *devastated* by storm and cold⟩ ⟨man has stripped the hills, *devastated* the valleys⟩ **2 :** OVERPOWER, OVERCOME, OVERWHELM ⟨he was *devastated* by grief⟩ ⟨her constant mischief *devastated* the classroom⟩ **syn** see RAVAGE

devastating *adj* [fr. pres. part. of *devastate*] **:** serving, tending, or having the power to devastate; *broadly* **:** highly effective ⟨a ∼ portrait of human folly⟩ — **dev·as·tat·ing·ly** *adv*

dev·as·ta·tion \ˌdevəˈstāshən\ *n* -s [LL *devastation-, devastatio*, fr. L *devastatus* + *-ion-, -io* -ion] **1 :** the action of devastating or state of being devastated **:** a laying waste **:** DESOLATION ⟨the ∼*s* of war⟩ **2 :** DEVASTAVIT 1

dev·as·ta·tive \ˈdevəˌstād·iv\ *adj* **:** tending to cause devastation **:** DESTRUCTIVE

dev·as·ta·tor \-d·ə(r)\ *n* -s [It & LL; It *devastatore*, fr. LL *devastator*, fr. L *devastatus* + *-or*] **:** one that devastates

dev·as·ta·vit \ˌdevəˈstāvə̇t, -iv-\ *n* -s [L, he has laid waste, 3d pers. sing. perf. indic. act. of *devastare*] **1 :** mismanagement or waste of the goods of a deceased person by his executor who may thereby be liable **2 :** a writ whereby a remedy for devastavit is sought

deve *var of* DEAVE

de·vein \(ˈ)dē+\ *vt* [*de-* + *vein*, n.] **:** to remove the dark dorsal vein from (shrimp)

¹de·vel \ˈdāvəl\ *n* -s [origin unknown] *Scot* **:** a severe blow

²devel \"\ *vt, Scot* **:** to strike forcibly

develin *var of* DEVILING

de·vel·op *also* **de·vel·ope** \də̇ˈveləp, dēˈ-\ *vb* -ED/-ING/-S [F *développer*, fr. OF *desveloper, desvoleper, desvoloper*, fr. *des-* de- + *veloper, voleper, voloper* to wrap up] *vt* **1 a :** UNFOLD, UNFURL — used only as a past participle and now only of flags **b :** to change the form of (a surface) by applying point by point to a specified surface; *specif* **:** to unroll (a developable surface) on a plane in this way without stretching any element **c :** to lay out (as a representation) in or evolve (as an idea) into a clear, full, and explicit presentation (as in a drawing or specification); *specif* **:** to determine (as by calculating or drafting) the precise size and shape of (a sheet metal blank from which an article is to be formed) **2 :** to make clear by or as if by unfolding some enclosing, enveloping, or obscuring cover **3 a :** EXPOUND, EXPLAIN ⟨∼*ing* the thesis with great skill⟩ **b :** to make visible or manifest **c :** to treat (as a dye intermediate applied to a fiber) with an agent to cause the appearance of color **:** subject (as a fiber impregnated with dye intermediate) to the action of an agent to produce color; *also* **:** to produce (color or color-producing dye) by such a method **d :** to cause (writing in secret ink) to become visible (as by the action of heat or chemicals) **e :** to subject (exposed photograph material) to a usu. chemical treatment designed to produce a visible deposit in matter previously modified by radiation; *also* **:** to render (a photographic image) visible by such a method **f** *obs* **:** DISCLOSE, REVEAL; *also* **:** DETECT, DISCOVER **g :** to express (as a mathematical equation or a formula) in expanded form **h :** to elaborate (a piece of music) by means of development **4 :** to open up **:** cause to become more completely unfolded so as to reveal hidden or unexpected qualities or potentialities **5 a :** to make (something latent) active **:** cause to increase or improve **:** promote the growth of ⟨he ∼*ed* his muscles by exercise, his mind by reading and study⟩ **b :** to make actually available or usable (something previously only potentially available or usable) ⟨an engine that ∼*s* 100 horsepower⟩ ⟨∼*ing* the natural resources of the region⟩: as (1) **:** to convert (as raw land) into an area suitable for residential or business purposes ⟨they ∼*ed* several large tracts on the edge of town⟩; *also* **:** to alter raw land into (an area suitable for building) ⟨the subdivisions that they ∼*ed* were soon built up⟩ (2) **:** to prepare (a mineral-bearing deposit) for the extraction of ore (as by driving mine workings and passageways and providing power, ventilation, and other equipment) **c :** to move (a chess piece) from the original position to one providing more opportunity for effective use ⟨∼*ed* the rook as soon as possible⟩ **6 a :** to cause to unfold gradually **:** conduct through a succession of states or changes each of which is preparatory for the next ⟨he ∼*ed* his argument point by point⟩ **b :** to expand by a process of growth ⟨a precocious child that ∼*ed* mature breasts when 8 years old⟩ ⟨they ∼*ed* a strong militant organization⟩ **c :** to cause to grow and differentiate along lines natural to its kind ⟨warm rains and summer suns ∼ the grain⟩ ⟨the zygote is gradually ∼*ed* into the adult plant or animal⟩ **7 :** to acquire usu. gradually ⟨∼*ing* a taste for dry wines⟩ ⟨he ∼*ed* a strong dislike for his mother-in-law⟩; *often* **:** to have (something) unfold or differentiate within one — used esp. of diseases and abnormalities ⟨too many children ∼*ed* tuberculosis⟩ ∼ *vi* **1 a :** to go through a process of natural growth, differentiation, or evolution by successive changes from a less perfect to a more perfect or more highly organized state **:** advance from a simpler form or state of existence to one more complex either in structure or function ⟨a blossom ∼*s* from a bud⟩ ⟨the fever ∼*s* normally⟩ ⟨the embryo ∼*s* into a well-formed animal⟩ **b :** to acquire secondary sex characters ⟨she is ∼*ing* rapidly for a girl of 12⟩ **c :** EVOLVE, DIFFERENTIATE; *broadly* **:** GROW **2 a :** to become gradually visible or manifest ⟨as the photographic negative ∼*s*⟩ ⟨his interest ∼*ed* as he watched her⟩ **b :** to become apparent **:** come to light ⟨it ∼*s* that neither one paid the bill⟩ ⟨they waited to see what would ∼ next⟩ **3 :** to develop one's pieces in chess **syn** see MATURE, UNFOLD

de·vel·op·abil·i·ty \ˌ≡ˌ≡ləpəˈbilə̇d·ē\ *n* **:** capacity or suitability for development

de·vel·op·able \ˈ≡ˈ≡ləpəbəl\ *adj* **:** capable of being developed

developable surface *n* [trans. of F *surface développable*] **:** a surface that may be imagined flattened out upon a plane without stretching any element

developed black BH *n, often cap D& 1st B* [*developed* fr. past part. of *develop*] **:** DIAMINE BLACK BH

developed dye *n* **:** any of a group of direct azo dyes that after application to the fiber can be further diazotized and coupled on the fiber to form shades faster to washing — called also *diazo dye*; compare AZOIC DYE

de·vel·oped·ness \-p(t)nə̇s, -pə̇dn-\ *n* -ES **:** the quality or state of being developed

de·vel·op·er \-pə(r)\ *n* -s **1 :** a person who develops something esp. habitually or as an occupation: as **a :** a worker who develops photographic materials (as films and prints) **b :** a person who develops real estate; *often* **:** one that improves and subdivides land and builds and sells residential structures thereon **2 :** something that develops or is used in developing: as **a :** a chemical agent used to produce a dye by reaction with a dye or dye intermediate on the fiber — see DYE table I **b :** a chemical bath or reagent used in developing exposed photographic materials

developing dye *n* [*developing* fr. pres. part. of *develop*] **:** a dye produced on the fiber; *esp* **:** DEVELOPED DYE

developing-out paper \ˌ≡ˌ≡≡ˈ≡ˌ≡\ *n* **:** a photographic paper coated with silver halide gelatin emulsion on which the image is invisible until developed

de·vel·op·ment *also* **de·vel·ope·ment** \də̇ˈveləpmənt, dēˈ-\ *n* -s **1 :** the act, process, or result of developing **:** the state of being developed **:** a gradual unfolding by which something (as a plan or method, an image upon a photographic plate, a living body) is developed ⟨a new ∼ in poetry⟩ **:** gradual advance or growth through progressive changes **:** EVOLUTION ⟨a stage of ∼⟩ **:** a making usable or available ⟨well worth ∼⟩ **2 a :** the whole process of growth and differentiation by which the potentialities of a zygote, spore, or embryo are realized; *broadly* **:** ONTOGENY **b :** the gradual differentiation of an ecological community or a natural group; *sometimes* **:** PHYLOGENY **3 :** the process of or position attained in developing chess pieces **4** *logic* **:** an expansion by means of which all the elements contained in a given expression are made explicit **5 :** work done in developing a mine **6 a :** the elaboration of a musical theme, subject, or idea by rhythmic, melodic, tonal, or harmonic modifications **b** *or* **development section :** the section of a musical movement where this elaboration occurs (as in the sonata form) **7 :** a method of reducing grade in railroading by increasing the length of a line between two predetermined points that differ much in elevation **8 :** a developed tract of land; *esp* **:** a subdivision having necessary utilities (as water, gas, electricity, sewers)

de·vel·op·men·tal \də̇ˌveləpˈmentᵊl, dēˌ-\ *adj* **1 :** of, relating to, or constituting development ⟨∼ processes⟩ ⟨∼ stages⟩ ⟨∼ questions⟩ **:** serving to develop ⟨∼ concessions for the region⟩ ⟨a long-range ∼ program⟩ ⟨∼ aid for backward areas⟩; *broadly* **:** EXPERIMENTAL ⟨a ∼ series of tests⟩ ⟨the ∼ stages of military aviation⟩ **2 :** designed to further growth (as of a child) or to bring about improvement (as of a skill) by gradual training adapted to the learner's physical and mental development ⟨∼ reading⟩ — **de·vel·op·men·tal·ly** \-ᵊlē, ˌli\ *adv*

developmental anatomy *n* **:** the anatomy of the embryo or fetus

de·vel·op·men·tal·ist \ˌ≡ˌ≡≡ˈ≡ᵊlə̇st\ *also* **de·vel·op·ment·ist** \ˈ≡≡ˌmәntə̇st\ *n* -s **:** EVOLUTIONIST; *usu* **:** an exponent of or specialist in any school of philosophic evolution

developmental pueblo *adj, usu cap D&P* **:** of, relating to, or constituting the early Pueblo stages of the 8th to 11th centuries A.D. during which the architecture was developing toward the complexity of the Great Pueblo period

developmental quotient *n* **:** a number expressing the development of a child determined by dividing his maturity age by his chronological age and multiplying by 100 — abbr. *DQ*

development area *n, Brit* **:** any of certain areas in which the government encourages the establishment of new industries particularly in order to increase industrial diversification and stability

de·vel·op·pé \dəˌveləˈpā, ˌdāv(ə)(ˌ)lōˈpā\ *n* -s [F, fr. past part. of *développer* to develop] *ballet* **:** an unfolding of the free leg into the air

develops *pres 3d sing of* DEVELOP

devels *pl of* DEVEL, *pres 3d sing of* DEVEL

de·verb·al \(ˈ)dē+\ *adj* [*de-* + *verb* + *-al*] **:** DEVERBATIVE

¹de·verb·a·tive \(ˈ)dēˈvərbəd·iv\ *adj* [*de-* + *verb* + *-ative*] **:** derived from a verb ⟨the ∼ noun *developer* is derived from *develop*⟩ **:** used in derivation from a verb ⟨the ∼ suffix *-er* in *developer*⟩

²deverbative \"\ *n* -s **:** a deverbative word

de·vertebrated \(ˈ)dē+\ *adj* [*de-* + *vertebrated*, past part. of *vertebrate*] **:** lacking stamina — **de·vertebration** \(ˌ)dē+\ *n* -s

de·vest \də̇ˈvest, (ˈ)dēˈ-\ *vb* [MF *desvestir, devestir*, fr. ML *disvestire*, fr. L *dis-* + *vestire* to dress, fr. *vestis* garment — more at WEAR] *vt* **1 a** *obs* **:** UNCLOTHE **b** *law* **:** to take away (as property, an authority, or title) **:** ALIENATE, DIVEST **c :** to deprive or dispossess (as a person) of a vested right — now used only in law **2** *obs* **:** to cast off **:** DISCARD, ABANDON ∼ *vi, of a title or estate* **:** to become devested

de·vi \ˈdā(ˌ)vē\ *n* -s [Skt *devī*, fem. of *deva* — more at DEVA] *Hinduism* **:** GODDESS — used in India as a title following the personal name of a married woman

de·vi·a·ble \ˈdēvēəbəl\ *adj* [*deviate* + *-able*] **:** capable of deviating or of being deflected

de·vi·ance \ˈdēvēən(t)s\ *n* -s [*deviate* + *-ance*] **:** deviant quality or state **:** DEVIANCY, DEVIATION

de·vi·an·cy \-ənsē\ *n* -ES [*deviant* + *-cy*] **:** the character or behavior of a deviant

¹de·vi·ant \-ənt\ *adj* [LL *deviant-, devians*, pres. part. of *deviare* to deviate] **:** deviating esp. from some accepted norm ⟨seriously ∼ conduct⟩ **:** characterized by deviation (as from a standard of conduct) ⟨∼ children⟩

²deviant \"\ *n* -s **:** something that deviates from a norm; *esp* **:** a person who differs markedly (as in intelligence, social adjustment, or sexual behavior) from what is considered normal or acceptable in the group of which he is a member

¹de·vi·ate \ˈdēvēˌāt, *usu* -ād·+V\ *vb* -ED/-ING/-S [LL *deviatus*, past part. of *deviare*, fr. L *de* from, away + LL *-viare* (fr. L *via* way, road) — more at DE-, VIA] *vi* **:** to diverge or turn aside **:** veer esp. from an established way or toward a new direction ⟨he *deviated* from the path⟩ ⟨*deviating* to the south⟩ **:** stray esp. from a standard, principle, or topic ⟨she never *deviated* from her first account⟩ ⟨*deviating* sharply from the traditional approach⟩ **:** turn aside from a previous, usual, normal, or acceptable course (as of conduct) ⟨party principles permit no one to ∼⟩ ⟨whenever I *deviated* I felt guilty⟩ ∼ *vt* **:** to turn (something) out of a previous course **:** cause to deviate ⟨he would ∼ rivers, turn the scorched plains of Lombardy into fertile pastures —F.M.Godfrey⟩ ⟨a deep iron keel will tend to ∼ the compass during heeling over⟩ **syn** see SWERVE

²de·vi·ate \-vēə̇t, -ēˌāt, *usu* |d·+V\ *n* -s [LL *deviatus*, past part. of *deviare*] **:** something that differs noticeably from the average or normal range of its kind: as **a :** a person that is a deviant; *esp* **:** SEXUAL PERVERT **b :** any item of a statistical distribution that differs significantly from the norm

³deviate \"\ *also* **de·vi·at·ed** \-ēˌād·ə̇d, -ˌātəd\ *adj* [*deviate* fr. LL *deviatus*; *deviated* fr. LL *deviatus* + E *-ed*] **:** characterized by or given to significant departure from the behavioral norms of a particular society

de·vi·a·tion \ˌdēvēˈāshən\ *n* -s [LL *deviation-, deviatio*, fr. *deviatus* + L *-ion-, -io* -ion] **:** an act or instance of deviating **:** DEFLECTION, VEERING, DIVERGENCE: as **a :** deflection of the needle of a compass caused by magnetic influences within the ship or airplane in which it is mounted **b** *in the old Ptolemaic system* **:** a motion of the deferent toward and from the ecliptic **c** (1) **:** the divergence laterally unless otherwise stated of a projectile from the plane of departure caused by extraneous factors (as drift, wind) (2) **:** the divergence of a projectile from the mean direction of a number of shots fired at the same target — called also *deviation from the center of impact* (3) **:** the angular measurement between a burst and a target as measured from an observation post **d :** voluntary and unnecessary departure of a ship from the regular and usual course of a specific voyage, such departure releasing underwriters of insurance on the ship from further responsibility **e :** DEFLECTION 5a **f :** the algebraic difference found by subtracting some fixed number (as the arithmetic mean of a series of statistical data) from any item of the series **g :** evolutionary differentiation involving interpolation of new stages in the ancestral pattern of morphogenesis — compare ANABOLY, ARCHALLAXIS **h :** departure from an established body of principles, a system of beliefs, an ideology, or a party line; *specif* **:** departure from strict Marxist doctrine ⟨he was expelled from the Communist party for ∼⟩ **i :** noticeable or marked departure from accepted societal norms of behavior

de·vi·a·tion·al \ˌ≡ˈ≡shənᵊl, -shnəl\ *adj* **:** involving or tending toward deviation esp. from political party principles — **de·vi·a·tion·al·ism** \ˌ≡ˈ≡shəˌnizəm, -shnəˌli-\ *n* -s

de·vi·a·tion·ism \ˌ≡ˈ≡shəˌnizəm\ *n* -s **:** defection or divergence from a party line esp. of the Communist party

¹de·vi·a·tion·ist \-sh(ə)nə̇st\ *n* -s **:** one who departs from the principles of an organization (as a political party) with which he is affiliated ⟨∼*s* in Communist countries⟩

²deviationist *adj* **:** of or relating to deviationism or deviationists

deviation warranty *n* **:** an implied warranty underlying all contracts of ocean marine insurance that a ship will not depart from the customary route between the ports for which insurance is granted

de·vi·a·tive \ˈdēvēˌād·iv, -vēəd·iv\ *adj* **:** tending to deviate

de·vi·a·tor \-ˌād·ə(r)\ *n* -s [*deviate* + *-or*] **:** something that deviates or causes to deviate; *sometimes* **:** DEVIATIONIST

de·vice \də̇ˈvīs, dēˈ-\ *n* -s [ME *devis, devise*, fr. OF *devis* will, intention & OF *devise* dividing line, difference, wish, fr. *deviser* to divide, regulate, tell — more at DEVISE] **1 :** something that is formed or formulated by design and usu. with consideration of possible alternatives, experiment, and testing **:** something devised or contrived **:** CONTRIVANCE, INVENTION, PROJECT, SCHEME: as **a :** a scheme to deceive or overreach **:** ARTIFICE, STRATAGEM **b :** something fanciful, elaborate, or intricate in design (as a trinket or a musical motive) **c :** something in a literary work designed to achieve a particular artistic effect (as a figure of speech, a special method of narration, or use of words or word sounds) **d** *archaic* **:** MASQUE, SPECTACLE **e :** a piece of equipment or a mechanism designed to serve a special purpose or perform a special function ⟨a ∼ for measuring heat release⟩ ⟨an improved steering ∼⟩ **2 :** WILL, DESIRE, INCLINATION, PURPOSE — now used only in pl. ⟨left to his own ∼*s*⟩ **3 a :** an emblematic design typically of one or more figures with a motto that is used esp. as a heraldic bearing denoting the historical situation, the ambition, or the desire of the person adopting it; *sometimes* **:** MOTTO **b :** an emblematic figure that is used to identify usu. an organization (as a publisher or navigation line) **4** *archaic* **:** INVENTION, DEVISING **5** *obs* **:** CONVERSATION, CHAT

de·vice·ful \-sfəl\ *adj* **:** full of devices; INGENIOUS — **de·vice·ful·ly** \-fəlē\ *adv*

¹dev·il \ˈdevəl *sometimes* -(ˌ)vil, *dial or as a mild imprecation* ˈdivəl\ *n* -s *often attrib* [ME *devel*, fr. OE *dēofol*, fr. LL *diabolus*, fr. Gk *diabolos*, lit., slanderer, fr. *diaballein* to throw across, discredit, slander, fr. *dia* through, across + *ballein* to throw; akin to OE *collen-* bold, OHG *quellan* to well, gush, Skt *galati* it drips — more at DIA-] **1** *sometimes cap* **:** the personal supreme spirit of evil and unrighteousness in Jewish and Christian theology **:** the tempter and spiritual enemy of mankind who is the adversary of God although subordinate to him and able to act only by his sufferance and is represented as frequently as the leader or prince of all apostate angels and as ruler of hell — called also *Apollyon, Beelzebub, Lucifer, Satan*; usu. used with *the* and often used as a mild imprecation or expression of surprise, vexation, or emphasis ⟨the ∼ you say⟩ ⟨the ∼ take it⟩ **2 :** one of the superhuman followers of the devil **:** a lesser evil or malignant spiritual being: as **a :** a heathen god or idol — used chiefly in scriptural and Christian clerical writings **b** *in the Bible* **:** a malignant spirit possessing and responsible for the state of a demoniac **3 a :** an extremely and malignantly wicked person **:** a human fiend; *often* **:** a person cantankerously self-centered and without regard for the rights of others **b** *archaic* **:** a great evil ⟨the ~ drunkenness —Shak.⟩ **4 a :** a person of notable energy, recklessness, and dashing spirit ⟨all those young ~*s* that followed Prince Charlie⟩ **b :** a person thought of as misconducting himself more from youthful folly and exuberance of spirits than from real wickedness ⟨both my cousins were perfect ~*s* as boys⟩ **c :** a person exhibiting marked intensity in some line of conduct **:** one excessively addicted or attracted to ⟨a ~ for gambling⟩ ⟨a ~ with the ladies⟩; *often* **:** one regarded as atypical ⟨a gentleman but a queer ~ all the same⟩ **5 a :** a wretched fellow **:** a person in a pitiable or markedly inferior position or condition — usu. used with *poor* ⟨poor ~*s* sleeping on park benches and in subways⟩ ⟨my uncle, poor ~, lost his wife in a wreck only weeks after their marriage⟩ ⟨poor ~*s* who make life sweeter for the rest by sweeping the streets, collecting the garbage, cleaning the sewers⟩ **b :** PRINTER'S DEVIL **c :** a junior legal counsel working usu. without pay **6 a :** an ill-tempered, vicious, or ugly creature ⟨a big bay stallion that was a perfect ~⟩ — often used in vernacular names of animals; see TASMANIAN DEVIL **b :** a firecracker or similar firework **c :** something very provoking, difficult, or trying ⟨most game birds are ~*s* to bring down without a good dog⟩ **:** a perturbed, disordered, or distressing state ⟨they found themselves in a ~ of a mess⟩ ⟨there was a ~ of a high sea running that day⟩ **7 :** a mood, passion, or quality that possesses, incites, or disturbs ⟨the victim of a moody ~ within his own heart⟩ — compare BLUE DEVIL 1 **8 :** a highly seasoned dish esp. of broiled or fried meat (as chops or meaty bones) **:** a grill with cayenne pepper **9 :** any of various machines, appliances, or devices: as **a :** a machine for tearing or shredding something or for grinding material into bits (as stock for papermaking, woolen for shoddy, or fur for felt) **b :** an iron fire basket or grate for open-air use **c :** a machine for making wooden screws **d :** a drag for clearing plowed ground **10 :** a seam in a ship's hull on or below the waterline **11** *India & Africa* **:** DUST DEVIL **12 :** POWER, EFFICACY, STING — used esp. of cricket bowling or a bowled ball ⟨you will never take wickets unless you put more ~ in your bowling⟩ **13** *Christian Science* **:** the opposite of Truth **:** a belief in sin, sickness, and death **:** EVIL, ERROR — **between the devil and the deep sea** *or* **between the devil and the deep blue sea :** between two equally objectionable or hazardous alternatives **:** between two comparable evils — **devil and all :** everything right or wrong; *esp* **:** everything bad — **devil of it :** a vexatious or mischief-making feature **:** something to be regretted or deplored — used with *the* ⟨the *devil of it* was that we could easily have come early⟩ ⟨they only did it for the *devil of it*⟩ — **devil's own time :** a very bad experience **:** a painful drawn-out struggle — used with *the* ⟨had the *devil's own time* with yellow fever⟩ — **devil to pay :** serious trouble **:** grave mischance or mischief — used with *the* ⟨there'll be the *devil to pay* when her father finds out⟩ — **in the devil :** EVER — used as an intensive ⟨where *in the devil* did he go⟩

²devil \"\ *vb* **deviled** *or* **devilled; deviled** *or* **devilled; deviling** *or* **devilling** \-v(ə)liŋ, -vil-\ **devils** *vt* **1 :** TEASE, ANNOY, TORMENT, HAZE; *esp* **:** to pester with importunities ⟨~*ing* her mother for a new dress⟩ **2 :** to chop (food) fine and mix with hot seasoning or sauce usu. after cooking — now usu. used as a past participle ⟨a tasty ~*ed* crab⟩ ⟨~*ed* eggs⟩ **3 :** to treat in a devil **:** tear to pieces ⟨~ rags⟩ ~ *vi* **:** to serve or function as a devil (as in a printshop or to a lawyer)

devil among the tailors : a firework that emits sparks, stars, and finally whirling imps

devil and the tailors *n* **:** FOX AND GEESE 1b

devil bolt *n* **:** a sham or faulty bolt sometimes used in contract shipbuilding

devil chaser *n* **:** a ranting moral reformer

devil-club *var of* DEVIL'S CLUB

devil dance *n* **1 :** a grotesque and often obscene impersonation of an evil spirit usu. with the aid of a mask that is important in Asiatic curative rites and stage dramas and popular in European carnivals as a remnant of medieval miracle plays **2 :** APACHE DEVIL DANCE

devil-dancer \ˈ==,==\ *n* **:** a performer of devil dances; *esp* **:** a professional performer of such dances

devil-devil \ˈ==,==\ *n* **:** CHARM, SPELL **:** magical incantation — used chiefly in pidgin English

devil-diver \ˈ==,==\ *n* **:** a dabchick or other small grebe

devil-dodger \ˈ==,==\ *n, slang* **:** PREACHER; *esp* **:** a military chaplain

devil dog *n* **:** MARINE

dev·il·dom \ˈdevəldəm\ *n* -S **:** the realm, rule, or power of the devil **:** diabolic influence or condition

devil drum *n* **:** a drum used in ceremonies (as of propitiation) of various primitive societies

devil duster *n* **:** DUST DEVIL

dev·il·er *also* **dev·il·ler** \ˈdev(ə)lə(r)\ *n* -S **:** one that devils or operates a devil

devil-fire \ˈ==,=\ *n* **1 :** WILL-O'-THE WISP **2 :** SAINT ELMO'S FIRE

devilfish \ˈ==,=\ *n* **1 :** any of several extremely large rays of the genera *Manta* and *Mobula* (family Mobulidae) that are widely distributed in warm seas; *esp* **:** a ray (*Manta birostris*) that is common in the Gulf of Mexico and along the southern coasts of the U.S. though probably cosmopolitan in warm seas, that may be 15 to 20 feet wide and several feet thick with a weight considerably in excess of one ton, that has a pair of movable cephalic lobes used in guiding small fishes into the nearly toothless mouth, and that reproduces viviparously usu. producing a single young at a birth **2 :** OCTOPUS; *broadly* **:** any large cephalopod

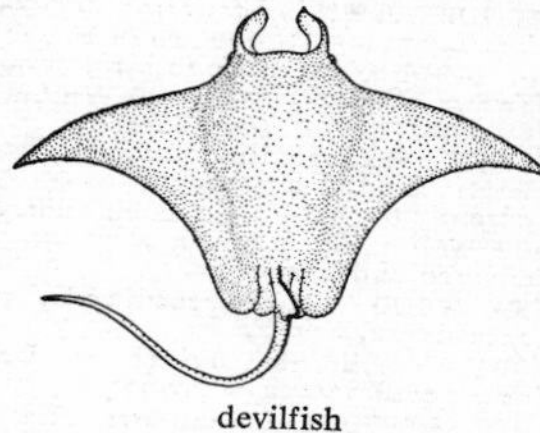

devilfish

devil-god \ˈ==,=\ *n* **1 :** a devil worshiped as a god **2 :** a heathen deity — used chiefly in Christian clerical writings

devil grass *n* **:** BERMUDA GRASS

devil horse *var of* DEVIL'S HORSE

devil-in-a-bush *or* **devil-in-the-bush** \ˈ====ˈ=\ *n* **1 :** LOVE-IN-A-MIST 1 **2 :** HERB PARIS

devil-in-a-mist \ˈ====ˈ=\ *n* **:** LOVE-IN-A-MIST 1

¹dev·il·ing \ˈdevəliŋ\ *n* -S [¹*devil* + *-ling*] **1 :** a young devil **:** IMP **2** *also* **dev·e·lin** *or* **dev·i·lin** \-v(ə)lən\ [*develin, devilin*, alter. of *deviling*] *dial Eng* **:** the common European swift (*Apus apus*)

²dev·il·ing \ˈdev(ə)liŋ\ *adj* [fr. *deviling, devilling*, pres. part. of ²*devil*] **:** TEASING, PESKY, IMPORTUNATE

dev·il·ish \ˈdev(ə)lish, -lēsh\ *adj* **1 :** resembling, typical of, or relating to the devil **:** DIABOLICAL ⟨~ tricks and stratagems⟩ **2 :** like or like that of a devil esp. in daring and rakishness or in arrogant disregard for the rights of others ⟨sheer ~ courage⟩ ⟨a ~ gang of young roughs⟩; *often* **:** EVIL, VICIOUS ⟨their ~ program⟩ ⟨their ~ practices⟩ **3 :** EXTREME, EXCESSIVE ⟨he was in a ~ hurry⟩ — **dev·il·ish·ly** *adv* — **dev·il·ish·ness** *n* -ES

²devilish \"\ *adv* **:** EXCESSIVELY, DEVILISHLY ⟨he's tough, sir, — tough, and ~ sly —Charles Dickens⟩

dev·il·ism \-və,lizəm\ *n* -S **:** devilish practice, doctrine, or quality

devil ivy *n* **:** IVY-ARUM

dev·il·ize \ˈdevə,līz\ *vt* -ED/-ING/-S **:** to make a devil of **:** cause to become devilish

dev·il·kin \-vəlkən\ *n* -S **:** a little devil **:** IMP

deviller *var of* DEVILER

de·vil·lite \dəˈvi,līt, -vi,-\ *n* -S [F *devilline* devillite (fr. Henri Étienne Sainte-Claire *Deville* †1881 Fr. chemist + F *-ine*) + E *-ite*] **:** a mineral $Cu_4Ca(SO_4)_2(OH)_6.3H_2O$ consisting of a hydrous basic sulfate of copper and calcium found in Cornwall and elsewhere in dark green 6-sided platy crystals

devil lore *n* **:** DEMONOLOGY; *often* **:** a body of folk belief and custom concerning evil spirits or devils

devil·man \ˈ==,man, -,mən\ *n, pl* **devilmen :** DEVILER

devil-may-care \ˈ===ˈ=\ *adj* **1 :** RECKLESS, ROISTERING, ROLLICKING **:** careless of authority ⟨a crew of *devil-may-care* swashbucklers⟩ ⟨an arrogant *devil-may-care* attitude⟩ **2 :** RAKISH, INFORMAL, CASUAL ⟨hat worn at a *devil-may-care* angle⟩

dev·il·ment \ˈdevəlmənt *sometimes* -,ment\ *n* -S **:** devilish conduct; *often* **:** reckless mischief **:** TEASING

devil ray *n* **:** DEVILFISH 1

dev·il·ry \ˈdevəlrē, -ri\ *or* **dev·il·try** \-l·tr-\ *n* -ES [ME *devilrie, develrie*, fr. *devil, devel* devil + *-rie* -ry] **1 a :** WITCHCRAFT **:** action performed with the help of the devil **:** diabolic art **b :** works of the devil **:** behavior typical of the devil ⟨fighting on the side of God against all the ~ of hell⟩ **c :** behavior felt to be suitable to a devil **:** extreme wickedness **:** gross or malignant cruelty ⟨the determined ~ of fanatics⟩ **d :** reckless unrestrained raffish conduct **:** irregular behavior that is mischievous, teasing, and unconsidered rather than vicious or dictated by evil intent **2 :** an act of devilry; *usu* **:** an act of studied malignancy or cruelty

devils *pl of* DEVIL, *pres 3d sing of* DEVIL

devil's advocate *n* [trans. of NL *advocatus diaboli*] **1** *Roman Catholicism* **:** an official of the Congregation of Rites whose duty is to point out defects in the evidence upon which a demand for beatification or canonization rests or in the character of the person for whom the honor is sought — called also *promoter of the faith;* compare POSTULATOR **2 :** a critic who picks flaws to evoke controversy or to bring out the whole truth **3 :** a champion of the worse cause for the sake of argument

devil's-apple \ˈ==ˈ==\ *n, pl* **devil's-apples 1 :** JIMSONWEED **2 :** MANDRAKE 1 **3 :** MAYAPPLE

devil's-apron \ˈ==ˈ==\ *n, pl* **devil's-aprons :** a kelp of the genus *Laminaria* (esp. *L. saccharina* of the Atlantic ocean) having a large flat leathery thallus shaped somewhat like an apron

devil's bit *n* [ME *develesbite* (trans. of ML *morsus diaboli*), fr. *develes* (gen. of *devel* devil) + *bite, bitt* bit, bite — more at BIT] **:** any of various plants with premorse rootstocks: **a** *also* **devil's bit scabious :** SCABIOUS 1; *esp* **:** a common purple or white flowered scabious (*Scabiosa succisa* or *Succisa pratensis*) that is native to Europe but naturalized in eastern No. America and that yields a blue dye from the leaves — compare WOAD **b :** any of several New World blazing stars (as *Chamaelirium luteum, Liatris spicata*, or *Aletris farinosa*) — compare BUTTON SNAKEROOT, COLICROOT

devil's-bite \ˈ==ˈ=\ *n, pl* **devil's-bites :** AMERICAN HELLEBORE 1

devil's-bones \ˈ==ˈ=\ *n pl* **1** *slang* **:** DICE **2** *sing or pl in constr* **:** a wild yam (*Dioscorea paniculata*)

devil's book *n* **:** DEVIL'S PICTURE BOOK

devil's buckie *n* **:** DEIL'S BUCKIE

devil's-claw \ˈ==ˈ=\ *n, pl* **devil's-claws 1 a :** UNICORN PLANT **b :** a cat's-claw (*Acacia greggii*) **2 :** a strong split hook used on a ship to grasp a link of a chain cable and act as a stopper; *also* **:** any of several hooked devices (as a grapnel or ice anchor)

devil's club *or* **devil-club** *n* **:** a spiny shrub (*Oplopanax horridus*) of the family Araliaceae with large simple petiolate lobed leaves and crowded terminal umbels of flowers

devil's coachhorse *n, chiefly Brit* **:** any of several rove beetles

devil's corkscrew *n* **:** any of certain large spiral fossils from Nebraska previously reported as fossil plants or animals but now usu. regarded as sediment-filled burrows of extinct rodents, possibly beavers

devil's-cotton \ˈ==ˈ==\ *n, pl* **devil's-cottons :** a shrub or small tree (*Abroma augusta*) of the East Indies that yields fiber used for cordage

devil's darning needle *n* **1 a :** DRAGONFLY **b :** DAMSELFLY **2 :** the common American virgin's bower (*Clematis virginiana*) **3 devil's darning needles** *pl* **:** any of certain grasses of the genus *Stipa; esp* **:** ESPARTO

devil's dozen *n, dial* **:** THIRTEEN

devil's dung *n* [trans. of G *teufelsdreck*] **:** ASAFETIDA

devil's dyke *n, usu cap both Ds* **:** any of several prehistoric British earthworks

devil's-fig \ˈ==ˈ=\ *n, pl* **devil's-figs 1 :** PRICKLY POPPY **2 :** PRICKLY PEAR

devil's-finger \ˈ==ˈ==\ *n, pl* **devil's-fingers :** BELEMNITE

devil's-flax \ˈ==ˈ=\ *n, pl* **devil's-flaxes :** a toadflax (*Linaria vulgaris*)

devil's food cake *also* **devil's food** *n* [so called fr. the contrast in color with angel food cake] **:** a rich dark chocolate cake

devil's-grandmother \ˈ==ˈ===\ *n, pl* **devil's-grandmothers :** a woolly herb (*Elephantopus tomentosus*) with bluish flowers — called also *elephant's-foot, tobaccoweed*

devil's-grass \ˈ==ˈ=\ *n, pl* **devil's-grasses 1 :** COUCH GRASS 1a **2 :** JOINT GRASS 1 **3 :** BERMUDA GRASS

devil's-grip \ˈ==ˈ=\ *n, pl* **devil's-grips 1 :** CARPETWEED **2 :** a malformation of sheep that consists of an indentation near the withers and down behind the shoulder as if a string had been put round that part of the sheep and tightened **3 :** EPIDEMIC PLEURODYNIA

devil's-gut *n, pl* **devil's-guts** \ˈ==ˈ=\ **:** DODDER; *broadly* **:** any of several weedy or destructive creeping plants (as dodder laurel or a bindweed) — usu. used in pl. but often sing. in constr.

devil's-hair \ˈ==ˈ=\ *n, pl* **devil's-hairs :** the common American virgin's bower (*Clematis virginiana*)

devil's-hand \ˈ==ˈ=\ *n, pl* **devil's-hands :** an ornamental Mexican tree (*Chiranthodendron pentadactylon*) of the family Sterculiaceae having bright red flowers with five stamens arranged like the fingers of a hand

devil's-head-in-a-bush \ˈ==,===ˈ=\ *n* **:** FLOWER-OF-AN-HOUR

devil's-horn \ˈ==ˈ=\ *n, pl* **devil's-horns 1** *dial Eng* **:** STINKHORN **2 :** UNICORN PLANT

devil's horse *n, South & Midland* **:** PRAYING MANTIS

devil's ironweed *n* **:** any of several American plants of the genus *Lactuca*

devil's ivy *n* **:** any of several climbing tender perennial plants of the family Aracaceae (as some members of the genus *Philodendron*) that are grown as ornamental foliage plants

devil's-knitting-needle \ˈ==ˈ===\ *n, pl* **devil's-knitting-needles :** ESPARTO 1

devil's mark *n* **:** a spot on the body of a person held guilty of witchcraft that was supposed to be insensible because the devil had touched it in sealing his bargain with the witch

devil's mass *n* **:** indiscriminate cursing

devil's milk *n* [trans. of G *teufelsmilch* or D *duivelsmelk*] **1 :** any of several plants having acrid milky juice (as the spurges *Euphorbia peplus* and *E. helioscopia* or the celandine) **2 :** the juice of a devil's milk plant usu. having reputed curative power (as on warts) or other remarkable attributes in folklore

devils on horseback [so called fr. the similarity to angels on horseback] **:** a dish consisting of oysters or pieces of chicken liver seasoned, wrapped in bacon, and broiled or fried **:** PIGS IN BLANKETS

devil's paintbrush *n* **:** ORANGE HAWKWEED; *broadly* **:** any of certain hawkweeds that are naturalized as weeds in the eastern U.S.

devil's paternoster *n* **1 :** the Lord's Prayer recited backward (as in late medieval witchcraft) **2 :** a muttering or grumbling of curses

devil's picture book *n* **:** playing cards — called also *devil's book;* formerly usu. used in pl.

devil's-pitchforks \ˈ==ˈ=,=\ *n pl but sing or pl in constr* [so called fr. the shape of the fruit] **:** BEGGAR-TICKS

devil's-plague \ˈ==ˈ=\ *n, pl* **devil's-plagues :** WILD CARROT

devil's-rattlebox \ˈ==ˈ==,=\ *n, pl* **devil's-rattleboxes** [so called fr. the rattling of the ripe seeds in the pod] **:** a bladder campion (*Silene latifolia*)

devil's-root \ˈ==ˈ=\ *n, pl* **devil's-roots :** CLOVER BROOMRAPE

devil's shoestring *n* **1 :** CATGUT 3a **2 devil's shoestrings** *pl* **:** the dried leaves and stems of the catgut formerly used as an anthelmintic — called also *turkey pea*

devil's slide *n* **:** the path of an avalanche down a steep slope **:** a long narrow mass of scree or talus descending a precipitous mountainside

devil's-snuffbox \ˈ==ˈ=,=\ *n, pl* **devil's-snuffboxes** *dial* **:** a fungus (as a puffball or corn smut) that releases clouds of minute spores when jarred or broken

devil's tattoo *n* **:** a drumming with or as if with fingers or feet

devil's toenail *n* **1 :** BELEMNITE **2 :** STYLOLITE

devil's-tongue \ˈ==ˈ=\ *n, pl* **devil's-tongues 1 :** a prickly pear (*Opuntia compressa*) **2 :** a foul-smelling somewhat fleshy tropical bulbous herb (*Hydrosme rivieri* or *Amorphophallus rivieri*) of the family Aracaceae that is sometimes grown in the greenhouse for its large leaves and showy dark red spathe surrounding a long spadix — called also *snake palm*

devil's trumpet *n* **:** JIMSONWEED

devil's-walking-stick \ˈ==ˈ==,=\ *n, pl* **devil's-walking-sticks :** HERCULES'-CLUB 3

devil's-weed \ˈ==ˈ=\ *n, pl* **devil's-weeds :** KING DEVIL

devil theory *n* **:** a theory in history and political economy: wars and other crises result not from objective causes but from the vicious conduct of individuals in power

deviltry *var of* DEVILRY

dev·il·ward \ˈdevəlwə(r)d\ *adv* (*or adj*) **:** toward the devil

devilwood \ˈ==,=\ *n* [prob. so called fr. the fact that it is very hard to cut or split] **:** a small tree (*Osmanthus americanus*) of the southern U.S. that is related to the olive and has whitish bark and panicles of dull white flowers which are succeeded by dark purple fruits — called also *American olive*

de·vi·ous \ˈdēvēəs *also* -vyəs\ *adj* [L *devius*, fr. *de* from, away + *-vius* (fr. *via* way, road) — more at DE-, VIA] **1 :** located off the highroad **:** OUT-OF-THE-WAY, REMOTE, RETIRED ⟨shipwrecks upon ~ coasts⟩ **2 a :** deviating from a straight line **:** WINDING, ROUNDABOUT, CIRCUITOUS ⟨a ~ path along the ridge⟩ **b :** moving without a fixed course **:** ERRANT, ROVING ⟨~ breezes⟩ **3 a :** deviating from a right, accepted, or common course **:** ASTRAY, ERRING ⟨~ arguments⟩ ⟨a ~ conscience⟩; *often* **:** seeking or advancing toward a right, accepted, or common end by roundabout means ⟨the ways of the Lord are ~⟩ **b :** hard to pin down or bring to agreement ⟨a ~ man⟩; *often* **:** SHIFTY, TRICKY, UNSCRUPULOUS, UNFAIR ⟨his ~ treatment of the allies⟩ ⟨a ~ attack on his character⟩ — **de·vi·ous·ly** *adv* — **de·vi·ous·ness** *n* -ES

de·vir·gin·ate \(ˈ)dēˈvərjə,nāt\ *also* **de·vir·gin·ize** \-,nīz\ *vt* -ED/-ING/-S [L *devirginatus*, past part. of *devirginare* to deflower, fr. *de* from, away + *-virginare* (fr. *virgin-, virgo* girl, virgin) — more at VIRGIN] **:** to deprive of virginity or of virginal quality — **de·vir·gi·na·tion** \(ˌ)dē,vərjəˈnāshən\ *n* -S — **de·vir·gi·na·tor** \(ˈ)dēˈvərjə,nād·ə(r)\ *n* -S

devis *pl of* DEVI

de·vis·abil·i·ty \də,vīzəˈbiləd·ē, dē,-\ *n* -ES **:** the quality or state of being devisable

de·vis·able \=ˈ=zəbəl\ *adj* [AF, fr. OF *deviser* to distribute, divide, regulate + *-able*] **1 :** capable of being devised or bequeathed ⟨lands, tenements and hereditaments, be not ~ by testament —*Act 27 Henry VIII*⟩ **2 :** capable of being devised, contrived, or invented

de·vis·al \=ˈ=zəl\ *n* -S **:** DEVISING

dev·i·sat vel non \ˈdevə,sat,velˈnän\ *n* [NL, he bequeaths or not] **:** a written document that sets forth the questions of fact pertinent to the validity of an alleged will and is sent from a court of probate or chancery having jurisdiction to allow or disallow a will to a court of common law having a jury so that the answers of the jury after trial will be recorded thereon and returned to the original court for the proper judgment as to the validity of the will

¹de·vise \dəˈvīz, dēˈ-\ *vb* -ED/-ING/-S [ME *devisen*, fr. OF *deviser* to divide, regulate, tell, modif. of (assumed) VL *divisare*, fr. L *divisus*, past part. of *dividere* to divide — more at DIVIDE] *vt* **1 a :** to form in the mind by new combinations of ideas, new applications of principles, or new arrangement of parts **:** formulate by thought **:** CONTRIVE, INVENT, PLAN, SCHEME ⟨~ an engine⟩ ⟨*devising* a new style in hats⟩ **b** *archaic* **:** SUPPOSE, IMAGINE, GUESS **c :** to plan to obtain or bring about **:** scheme for **:** PLOT — used esp. of objectives felt to be evil or unworthy ⟨the traitors *devised* the death of the king⟩ ⟨*devising* a plot to overthrow the government⟩ **2** *obs* **:** to describe fully **:** relate in detail **:** RECOUNT **3 :** to give by will — now used esp. of real estate; compare BEQUEATH 1a **4** *obs* **:** DRAW, DESIGN, DELINEATE ⟨that dear cross upon your shield *devised* —Edmund Spenser⟩ ~ *vi* **1 :** to form a scheme **:** develop a plan or intent **:** DESIGN, CONTRIVE, DETERMINE — now used chiefly as a present participle ⟨the *devising* spirit, the scheming brain⟩ **2** *obs* **:** to talk together **:** CONVERSE **syn** see CONTRIVE, WILL

²devise \"\ *n* -S [MF, fr. OF, division, deliberation, wish, will, testament, fr. *deviser* to divide, regulate] **1 :** the act of giving or disposing of property by will — now used technically only of real property but formerly used as well of the bequest of personal estate **2 :** a will or clause of a will disposing of real property **3 :** property given by will

³de·vi·se \dāˈvēzə\ *n, pl* **devi·sen** \-zᵊn\ *sometimes cap* [G, fr. F, motto, fr. MF, heraldic device, fr. OF, dividing line — more at DEVICE] **:** foreign exchange in readily available form

dev·i·see \,devəˈzē; də,vīˈzē, dē,-\ *n* -S [¹*devise* + *-ee*] **:** one to whom a devise of property is made — compare DEVISOR

de·vis·er \dəˈvīzə(r), dēˈ-\ *n* -S [ME *diviser*, alter. (influenced by ME *-er, -ere* -er) of *devysour*, fr. MF *deviseur*, fr. OF *deviseor*, fr. *deviser* to divide, regulate + *-eor* -or] **:** one that devises (as by planning, inventing, designing, or preparing) — compare DEVISOR

dev·i·sor \,devəˈzȯ(ə)r; dəˈvīzər, dēˈ-, -ˌvīˈzȯ(ə)r\ *n* -S [AF, fr. OF *deviser* to distribute, divide + *-or, -our* -or] **:** a person who devises property in a will — compare DEVISEE

de·vitalization \(ˌ)dē+\ *n* **:** an act of devitalizing or the condition of being devitalized ⟨~ of two affected teeth was necessary⟩ ⟨insect attack may cause ~ and leaf drop⟩

de·vitalize \(ˈ)dē+\ *vt* [*de-* + *vitalize*] **:** to deprive of life or vitality: as **a :** to deprive of force or effectiveness ⟨catchy tunes are often *devitalized* by constant repetition⟩ ⟨his clumsy presentation ~*s* his argument⟩ **b :** to refine (as foodstuffs) to the point that essential or desirable constituents are lost ⟨the processor that ~*s* our food and then restores a part of what he has thrown away⟩ **c :** to destroy the pulp of and usu. remove the pulp from (as a tooth)

de·vitaminize \(ˈ)dē+\ *vt* [*de-* + *vitamin* + *-ize*] **:** to deprive (as food) of vitamins esp. by cooking or hulling

de·vitrification \(ˌ)dē+\ *n* [F *dévitrification*, fr. *dévitrifier*] **:** the action or process of devitrifying or state of being devitrified; *specif* **:** the conversion of glassy matter into crystalline (as by slow cooling or by pressure, action of water, or chemical changes)

de·vitrify \(ˈ)dē+\ *vb* [F *dévitrifier*, fr. *dé-* de- (fr. OF *des-*) + *vitrifier* to vitrify] *vt* **:** to deprive of glassy luster and transparency; *esp* **:** to change (as a glass, glassy rock, or enamel) from a vitreous to a crystalline condition ~ *vi* **:** to change from a vitreous to a crystalline condition usu. with loss of transparency and luster

devize *obs var of* DEVISE

de·vocalize \(ˈ)dē+\ *vt* [*de-* + *vocalize*] **:** DEVOICE

de·voice \(ˈ)dē+\ *vt* [*de-* + *voice*, v.] **:** to pronounce without vibration of the vocal cords ⟨a sound that is voiced in certain other positions or was formerly voiced⟩

devoid \dəˈvȯid, dēˈ-\ *adj* [ME, prob. short for *devoided*, past part. of *devoiden* to get rid of, depart from, fr. MF *desvuidier* to empty, fr. OF, fr. *des-* dis- + *vuidier* to empty — more at VOID] **1** *obs* **:** VOID, EMPTY, VACANT ⟨when I awoke, and found her place ~ —Edmund Spenser⟩ **2 a :** not having or using **:** LACKING — used with *of* ⟨desert sand . . . ~ of humus —W.B.Fisher⟩ ⟨her somewhat sallow face ~ of makeup —Erle Stanley Gardner⟩ ⟨absolutely ~ of any ambition —L.P.Smith⟩ ⟨echoing phrases ~ of substance —W.L. Sullivan⟩ ⟨~ of teeth —R.W.Murray⟩ **b :** free from **:** unimpaired by — used with *of* ⟨love is never quite ~ of sentimentality —W.S.Maugham⟩ ⟨a conscience ~ of offense — Acts 24:16 (AV)⟩ ⟨a dignity of manner ~ of all stiffness —Anthony Trollope⟩

de·voir \dəvˈwär, -wȯ(ə)r, ˈdev,w-; dəˈvȯ(i)(ə)r\ *n* -S [ME, alter. (influenced by MF *devoir*, fr. OF *devoir, deveir*) of *dever*, fr. OF *devoir, deveir*, fr. *devoir, deveir*, v., to owe, be obliged, be supposed, fr. L *debēre* — more at DEBT] **1 a :** an act or conduct that may be required or expected of one **:** assigned task **:** DUTY ⟨I'm a part-time detective. My ~ is to study . . . people —Christopher Morley⟩ **b** *obs* **:** utmost effort **:** best endeavor **c :** an act of civility or respect ⟨a birthday ~ to the founder⟩; *often* **:** a formal act of greeting or leave-taking **:** RESPECTS — now usu. used in pl. ⟨he paid his ~*s* to his hostess and hurried down the steps⟩ **2 devoirs** *pl, obs* **:** money due for payment of duties or customs

dev·o·lute \'devə,lüt *also* -vəl,yüt\ *vt* -ED/-ING/-S [L *devolutus*, past part. of *devolvere*] : DEVOLVE

dev·o·lu·tion \,devə'lüshən *also* -vəl'yü-\ *n* -S [ML *devolution-, devolutio*, fr. LL, corruption, fr. L *devolutus* (past part. of *devolvere*) + *-ion-, -io* -ion] **1** : transference from one individual to another: as **a** : a passing or devolving (as of property, qualities, power, or rights) upon a successor ⟨the ~ of the crown⟩ **b** : delegation or conferral (as of authority, responsibility, or tasks) esp. to a subordinate ⟨~ of functions in industry⟩ **c** *in ecclesiastical law* : transfer of power and privilege in a particular case because of nonfeasance or misfeasance (as when the filling of a vacant benefice passes to the church because the patron failed to nominate or presented an unworthy candidate) **d** : the delegation or surrender of powers formerly held by a central government to regional or local authorities — compare DECENTRALIZATION **e** *Scots law* (1) : the reference of a matter to an umpire by arbiters who disagree (2) : the devolving of a purchase at auction upon the next highest bidder when the highest bidder fails to make good his bid **2 a** : descent or passage through a series (as of stages in development) **b** : retrograde evolution : DEGENERATION — **dev·o·lu·tion·ary** \-shə,nerē\ *adj*

dev·o·lu·tion·ist \-sh(ə)nəst\ *n* -S : an advocate or practicer of devolution esp. in government : a person favoring a high degree of autonomy in local government

de·volve \də'välv, dē'-, -vȯlv *also* -vä(u)v *or* -vȯv\ *vb* -ED/-ING/-S [ME *devolven* to roll down, fr. L *devolvere*, fr. *de* down, away + *volvere* to roll — more at DE-, VOLUBLE] *vt* **1** *archaic* : to roll onward or downward **2** *obs* : to cause to pass down, descend, be transferred, or changed (as by the course of events or operation of law) **3** : to transfer from one person to another : hand down — usu. used with *upon*, sometimes with *to* or *into* ⟨The God-Father . . . having *devolved* his potency upon men —Weston La Barre⟩ ⟨the risk of . . . *devolving* a measure of authority to people who are poor and politically immature —A.C.Jones⟩ ~ *vi* **1** : to pass by transmission or succession ⟨his estate *devolved* on a distant cousin⟩ : fall or be passed usu. as an obligation or responsibility ⟨after the general fell, command *devolved* upon the colonel⟩ ⟨the chairmanship shall ~ in strict order of seniority⟩ **2 a** : to flow or roll from a situation viewed as higher to one that is lower ⟨streams *devolving* from the mountains⟩ **b** *archaic* : to proceed from one point or condition into another as if by flowing or unrolling

¹dev·on \'devən\ *usu cap, var of* DEVONSHIRE

²devon \"\ *n* [*Devon*, county in England where it originated] **1** *usu cap* : a breed of vigorous red dual-purpose cattle that is commonly divided into (1) a predominantly beef type variety which produces meat of fine quality and (2) a strictly dual-purpose variety which has satisfactory meat conformation and produces moderate quantities of rich milk — called also (1) *North Devon*, (2) *South Devon* **2** -S *often cap* : any animal of the Devon breed

¹de·vo·ni·an \də'vōnēən, dē'-,-nyən\ *adj, usu cap* [*Devon*, county in England + E *-ian*] **1** : of or relating to Devonshire or Devon in England **2** : of or relating to the period of the Paleozoic that follows the Silurian and is next below the Mississippian or the system of rocks formed during this period which are commonly separable into marine and nonmarine facies and are characterized by abundant preservation of fossils including ferns, lycopods, horsetails, and a few gymnosperms as plants and abundant lower fishes and some air-breathing invertebrates — see GEOLOGIC TIME table

²devonian \"\ *n* -S *usu cap* **1** : a native or inhabitant of Devonshire **2** : the Devonian period or system of rocks

dev·on·shire \'devən,shi(ə)r, -iə, -,shə(r)\ *or* **dev·on** \'devən\ *adj, usu cap* [fr. *Devonshire, Devon*, county in England] : of or from the county of Devon, England : of the kind or style prevalent in Devon

devonshire cream *n, usu cap D* : cream allowed to rise on milk, set by heating and then cooling, and skimmed from the underlying skim milk

devon wrestling *also* **devonshire wrestling** *n, usu cap D* : a system of wrestling in which catching hold the opponent's strong loose linen jacket or any part of his body above the waist is permitted, in which two shoulders and one hip or two hips and one shoulder must touch ground simultaneously to constitute a fall, and in which contestants get up on their feet and the bout recommences if a man is thrown other than on his back

dé·vot \dā'vō, -vȯ\ *n* -S [F, fr. *dévot* devout, fr. OF *devot* — more at DEVOUT] : a man who is a devotee

¹de·vote \də'vōt, dē'-, *usu* -ōd·+V\ *adj* [partly fr. ME *devot* devout; partly fr. L *devotus* devoted, past part. of *devovēre* — more at DEVOUT] *archaic* : DEVOTED, DEVOUT

²devote \"\ *vt* -ED/-ING/-S [L *devotus*, past part. of *devovēre*, fr. *de* from, away + *vovēre* to vow — more at DE-, VOW] **1 a** : to set apart by a solemn act of appropriation : dedicate or consecrate esp. formally ⟨she vowed to ~ her child to God's service⟩ **b** : to provide (something) for use ⟨a chapel was *devoted* to the worship of each sect⟩ **2 a** : to give up (as time, money, thought, effort) to the cause, for the benefit, or to the advancement of something regarded as deserving support, improvement, or aid ⟨she *devoted* large sums to the care of the poor⟩ ⟨*devoting* all their thoughts to planning an escape⟩ **b** : to attach the attention or center the activities of (oneself) wholly or chiefly on a specified object, field, or objective : attach (oneself) to : set (oneself) on ⟨she *devoted* herself to her invalid sister⟩ **3 a** : to consign to the powers of evil : give over to destruction : DAMN, DOOM **b** *obs* : EXECRATE, CURSE **syn** see DIRECT

³devote *n* -S [prob. fr. ¹*devote*] *obs* : DEVOTEE

⁴dé·vote \dā'vōt\ *n* -S [F, fr. fem. of *dévot* devout] : a woman that is a devotee

devoted *adj* [fr. past part. of ²*devote*] : consecrated to a purpose; *broadly* : ARDENT, ZEALOUS, DEVOUT — **de·vot·ed·ly** *adv* — **de·vot·ed·ness** *n* -ES

dev·o·tee \,devə¦tē, -vō¦-, *also* -¦tā *sometimes* də¦vō¦tē *or* dē-¦vō¦tē *or* ¦dē,vō¦tē\ *n* -S [²*devote* + *-ee*] **1** : a person preoccupied with religious duties and ceremonies; *often* : one vowed, consecrated, or given over to esp. zealous and vigorous practice of his religion **2** : an ardent or zealous follower, supporter, or enthusiast (as of a cause, an art, a sport) : VOTARY

de·vote·ment \də'vōtmənt, dē'-\ *n* -S : the act of devoting or state of being set apart by or as if by a vow : DEDICATION

de·vo·tion \-ōshən\ *n* -S [ME *devocioun*, fr. OF *devotion*, fr. LL *devotion-, devotio*, fr. L, devotement, fr. *devotus* (past part. of *devovēre*) + *-ion-, -io* -ion] **1 a** : earnestness and zeal in the performance of religious duties and observations : religious fervor : REVERENCE, PIETY **b** : an act evincing religious devotion; *usu* : an act of prayer or supplication — now usu. used in pl. ⟨spent half the night at her ~s⟩ **c devotions** *pl* : prayers or service of worship usu. intended for private nonliturgical services ⟨a book of daily ~s⟩ **d** *obs* : an offering (as of money) devoted in worship : OBLATION; *often* : alms given from religious motives **2** : the act of devoting or quality of being devoted ⟨~ of such talents to the public service⟩ ⟨his ~ to the cause of justice is well known⟩ : ardent love or affection ⟨their ~ was beautiful to behold⟩ : strong attachment : ZEAL, ARDOR, ENTHUSIASM **3** *archaic* **a** : devoted service **b** : disposal or power of disposal : beck and call ⟨the . . . rabble were wholly at the ~ of those incendiaries —Edmund Burke⟩ **4** *obs* : something (as a cause) to which a person or thing is devoted : PURPOSE, MISSION **syn** see FIDELITY

¹de·vo·tion·al \-shənᵊl, -shnəl\ *adj* : relating to, suited to, used in, or characterized by devotion (as religious devotion) ⟨dedicated to the ~ life⟩ ⟨a ~ exercise⟩ ⟨the priest considered it more ~ to hear than to say mass⟩ — **de·vo·tion·al·ly** \-ᵊlē, -əlē, -li\ *adv*

²devotional \"\ *n* -S : a short worship service esp. when preceding or incorporated into a meeting (as of a club or discussion group) that is not predominantly religious

de·vo·tion·al·ism \-ᵊl,izəm, -ə,li-\ *n* -S : the quality or state of one markedly characterized by religious devotion

de·vo·tion·al·ist \-ᵊləst, -ələst\ *n* -S : one that is characterized by marked religious devotion

de·vo·tion·ary \-shə,nerē\ *archaic var of* DEVOTIONAL

devoto *n* -ES [It, fr. *devoto* devout, fr. LL *devotus*] *obs* : DEVOTEE

de·vour \də'vau(ə)r, dē'-, -auə, *chiefly S* -auwə(r\ *vt* -ED/-ING/-S [ME *devouren*, fr. MF *devourer*, fr. L *devorare*, fr. *de* down, away + *vorare* to eat greedily, swallow up — more at DE-, VORACIOUS] **1** : to eat up with greediness : consume ravenously : feast upon like a wild beast or a glutton ⟨~*ed* everything on his plate⟩ **2** : to seize upon and destroy or appropriate greedily, selfishly, or wantonly : swallow up : use up ⟨forests ~*ed* by fire⟩ : CONSUME, ENGULF, WASTE, ANNIHILATE ⟨the raging water ~*ed* the riverbank⟩ **3** : to prey upon : ABSORB — usu. used passively ⟨a man ~*ed* by remorse⟩ **4** : to enjoy with avidity; *often* : to take in eagerly by the senses or mind ⟨~ing the book⟩ ⟨~*ed* that graceful figure as though engraving it permanently on his mind⟩ **syn** see EAT

de·vour·er \-aùrə(r)\ *n* -S [ME, fr. *devouren* + *-er*] : one that devours: as **a** : a gluttonous eater **b** : a destructive agent : DESTROYER **c** : an avid reader

devouring *adj* [ME, fr. pres. part. of *devouren*] : GREEDY, AVID, CONSUMING ⟨fierce ~ affection⟩ — **de·vour·ing·ly** *adv* — **de·vour·ing·ness** *n* -ES

de·vour·ment \-aù(ə)rmənt, -aùəm-\ *n* -S : an act of devouring

de·vout \də'vaùt,dē'-, *usu* -aùd·+V\ *adj* [ME *devout, devot*, fr. OF *devot*, fr. LL *devotus*, fr. L, devoted, past part. of *devovēre* to devote — more at DEVOTE] **1** : devoted to religion or to religious feelings, duties, or exercises : given to devotion : PIOUS, REVERENT, RELIGIOUS ⟨a ~ man, and one that feared God —Acts 10: 2 (AV)⟩ **2** : expressing devotion or piety ⟨a ~ posture⟩ **3** : warmly devoted : HEARTY, SINCERE ⟨~ wishes for continued prosperity⟩

syn PIOUS, RELIGIOUS, PIETISTIC, SANCTIMONIOUS: DEVOUT stresses a genuine feeling, a mental or emotional attitude about religion leading to solemn reverence and fitting observance of rites and practices ⟨I was often *devout*, my eyes filling with tears at the thought of God and for my sins —W.B.Yeats⟩ ⟨a *devout* man, with a childlike trust in God —C.B. Nordhoff & J.N.Hall⟩ PIOUS may suggest faithful and fervent performance of the duties of one's religion rather than inner, genuine feelings or attitudes; it may also be used in connection with hypocrisy ⟨happy, as a *pious* man is happy when, after a long illness, he goes once more to church —Robert Hichens⟩ ⟨were *pious* Christians, taking their faith devoutly. But such religious emotion as was theirs, was reflected rather than spontaneous —H.O.Taylor⟩ ⟨a hypocrite — a thing all *pious* words and uncharitable deeds —Charles Reade⟩ RELIGIOUS may suggest genuine faith and adherence to a way of life consonant with religion ⟨he was a *religious* soul rather than a speculative intellect, and he measured all things by the principles of primitive Christianity —V.L.Parrington⟩ ⟨but Henry was a simple man, and a *religious*. On his knees before his confessor, he had learned that God was his friend —Francis Hackett⟩ ⟨they are not *religious*: they are only pew renters —G.B.Shaw⟩ Commonly derogatory, PIETISTIC stresses the emotional or ritualistic rather than the intellectual attitudes on religion and similar matters ⟨an emotional person with *pietistic* inclinations that nearly carried him over at different times to the Plymouth Brethren, to the Wesleyan Methodists, and to the Countess of Huntingdon's connection —H.G.Wells⟩ ⟨his kneeling on a stage, in front of a crowded house, as was recorded in the press, to receive the blessing of a visiting cardinal, was, to Sean, a humiliating thing for the head of a republican state to do. The *pietistic* Spaniard in him, Sean thought —Sean O'Casey⟩ SANCTIMONIOUS now always implies pretension to or appearance of exaltedness, or some other hypocrisy ⟨better in appearance anyway than that *sanctimonious* fellow, the missionary, who had passed straight from world service to one of the more exclusive tribes in the Congo —Ellen Glasgow⟩ ⟨if it only takes some of the *sanctimonious* conceit out of one of those pious scalawags —Robert Frost⟩

de·vout·ly *adv* [ME, fr. *devout* + *-ly*] : in a devout manner : REVERENTLY, SINCERELY, EARNESTLY, DEEPLY

de·vout·ness *n* -ES [ME *devoutnes*, fr. *devout* + *-nes* -ness] : a devout quality or state; *esp* : religious devotion

de·vove \də'vōv\ *vt* -ED/-ING/-S [L *devovēre*] *archaic* : DEVOTE, DEDICATE

devow *vt* -ED/-ING/-S [MF *devouer*, fr. *de-* (as in *devot* devout) + *vouer* to vow — more at VOW, v.] **1** \də'vaù\ *obs* : to dedicate esp. by a vow : DEVOTE **2** \(')dē¦v-\ [*de-* + *vow*, v.] **a** *obs* : RENOUNCE, DISAVOW **b** : to release from a vow

de·vulcanize \(')dē+\ *vt* [*de-* + *vulcanize*] : to treat (vulcanized scrap rubber) for recovery of original plastic properties even though vulcanizing agents are not removed — compare RECLAIMED RUBBER

de·vulcanizer \"+\ *n* : one that devulcanizes

¹dew \'d(y)ü\ *n* -S [ME, fr. OE *dēaw*; akin to OHG *tou* dew, ON *dögg* dew, Gk *thein* to run, Skt *dhavate* it flows] **1** : moisture condensed upon the surfaces of cool bodies esp. at night ⟨~ glistening in the early morning light⟩ ⟨the ~s of night⟩; *broadly* : small deposits of water that are produced by condensation of water vapor in the free atmosphere, by condensation of vapor directly from the ground, or less often by exudation of water through the leaf pores of a plant particularly at night upon the surfaces of cool bodies and in calm weather under an unclouded sky and more rapidly upon surfaces freely radiating heat and that remain as fluid water or frost according to the temperature **2** : something felt to resemble dew as in purity, freshness, or power to refresh ⟨the golden ~ of sleep —Shak.⟩ ⟨a lad in the ~ of his youth⟩ ⟨the ~ of God's grace lay over them⟩ **3** : moisture esp. when appearing in minute droplets: as **a** : TEARS **b** : SWEAT, PERSPIRATION **c** : a distilled liquor; *broadly* : an alcoholic beverage — usu. used with a qualifying term **d** : droplets of water produced by a plant in transpiration

²dew \"\ *vb* -ED/-ING/-S [ME *dewen*, fr. *dew*, n.] *vt* : to wet with or as if with dew : BEDEW ⟨every sense in slumber ~*ing* —Sir Walter Scott⟩; *esp* : to apply a fine spray of water to (woolen or worsted cloth) ~ *vi, archaic* : to fall or form as dew

³dew *past of* DAW

de·wa·li *or* **di·va·li** *or* **di·wa·li** \də'wälē, -'vä-\ *n* -S *usu cap* [Hindi *divālī*, fr. Skt *dīpālī, dīpāvalī*, lit., row of lights, fr. *dīpa* light, lamp + *ālī, āvalī* row; akin to Skt *dīdeti* he shines — more at ADEL-] : a Hindu festival of lights held late in October

de·wan \də'wän\ *n* -S [Hindi *dīwān*, fr. Per, account book — more at DIVAN] *India* : a chief officer: as **a** : a minister of finance under the former Muslim rule **b** : the prime minister of an Indian state

de·wa·nee *or* **de·wan·ny** *or* **di·wa·ni** \-nē\ *n, pl* **dewanees** *or* **dewannies** *or* **diwanis** [Hindi *dīwānī*, fr. *dīwān*] : the office or jurisdiction of a dewan; *specif* : the right to collect the revenues of Bengal, Bihar, and Orissa that was acquired by the East India Company in 1765

dew·ar \'d(y)üə(r), -üə-\ *or* **dewar flask** *or* **dewar vessel** *n* -S *usu cap D* [after Sir James *Dewar* †1923 Scot. chemist and physicist who invented it] : a usu. glass or metal container with at least two walls that has the space between the walls evacuated so as to prevent the transfer of heat, often has a coating (as silvering) on the inside to reduce radiation, and is used esp. for storing liquefied gases (as liquid air) or for investigations at low temperatures — compare VACUUM BOTTLE

Dewar flasks

de·water \(')dē+\ *vt* [*de-* + *water*, n.] : to remove water from (as by draining, pressing, pumping)

de·wax \(')dē¦waks\ *vt* [*de-* + *wax*, n.] : to remove wax from; *specif* : to remove paraffin wax from (oil) usu. by chilling, pressing, or treating with a solvent — **de·wax·able** \-səbəl\ *adj*

dewbeam \'⸗,⸗\ *n* : a ray of light reflected from dew

dew-beater \'⸗,⸗⸗\ *n, dial Eng* : a large thick-soled shoe

dew·ber·ry \'d(y)ü- — *see* BERRY\ *n* **1** : any of several sweet edible berries related to and resembling blackberries and including several distinct horticultural forms developed in cultivation **2** : a trailing or decumbent bramble of the genus *Rubus* (as the European *R. caesius* or the American *R. hispidis, R. flagellaris*, and *R. trivialis*) that bears dewberries

dew bit *n, dial Eng* : a snack before breakfast

dew bow \-bō\ *n* : a rainbow seen in dewdrops

dew·cap \'⸗,⸗\ *n* : a tube extending beyond the objective of a telescope to retard the deposition of dew on the object glass and to prevent entrance of light from the side

dewclaw \'⸗,⸗\ *n* : a vestigial digit not reaching to the ground on the foot of a mammal or a claw or hoof terminating such a digit (as on the inner aspect of a dog's foot or the false hoof of a deer, pig, or other hoofed mammal) — **dew·clawed** \-ód\ *adj*

1 dewclaw

dewcup \'⸗,⸗\ *n* : LADY'S-MANTLE

dew-drink *also* **dew-cup** \'⸗,⸗\ *n, dial Brit* : an early morning allowance of beer to harvesters taken before they begin work

dewdrop \'⸗,⸗\ *n* **1** : a drop of dew **2** : a low unarmed perennial herb (*Dalibarda repens*) of the family Rosaceae having entire leaves, 5-petalled white flowers like those of the strawberry, and fruits of several dry achenes enclosed in the enlarged calyx **3** : a small decorative bit of material suggesting a dewdrop (as a glass bead or button or a drop-shaped rhinestone) **4** : a drinking vessel for small animals that releases water by drops

dewdrop grass *n* : a small creeping perennial herb (*Dichondra repens*) that is related to the morning-glory, is cosmopolitan in warm regions esp. in low moist areas, and has been used in lawns as a substitute for grass

dewed *past of* DEW

dew·er \'d(y)üə(r), -üə-\ *n* -S : an operator of a textile machine that brushes or sprays water on woolen or worsted cloth during the finishing process

dew·ey·an \'d(y)üēən\ *adj, usu cap* [John *Dewey* †1952 Am. philosopher and educator + E *-an*] : of or relating to John Dewey, his followers, or his philosophy, esp. his pragmatism and instrumentalism

dew·ey classification \'d(y)üē-, -üi-\ *or* **dewey decimal classification** *n, usu cap 1st D* [after Melvil *Dewey* †1931 Am. librarian] : DECIMAL CLASSIFICATION

dew·ey·lite \-,līt\ *n* -S [Chester *Dewey* †1867 Am. clergyman and scientist + E *-lite*] : a mineral $Mg_3Si_2O_5(OH)_4$ occurring as a hydrous amorphous resinous magnesium silicate (hardness 2–3.5, sp. gr. 2.0–2.2)

dewfall \'⸗,⸗\ *n* [so called fr. the erroneous belief that dew comes down like rain] **1** : formation of dew; *also* : the time when dew begins to deposit **2** : the amount of moisture deposited during one period of dewfall ⟨a very heavy ~⟩

dewflower \'⸗,⸗\ *n* : any of several dayflowers; *esp* : COMMELINA 2

dew·i·ly \'d(y)üəlē, -li\ *adv* [*dewy* + *-ly*] : in a dewy manner ⟨gazed ~ into his eyes⟩

de·windt·ite \də'wint,īt\ *n* -S [F, fr. Jean *Dewindt*, 20th cent. Belg. geologist + F *-ite*] : a mineral $Pb_3(UO_2)_5(PO_4)_4(OH)_4 \cdot 10H_2O$ consisting of a hydrous basic phosphate of lead and uranium

dew·i·ness \'d(y)üēnəs, -üin-\ *n* -ES [*dewy* + *-ness*] : the quality or state of being dewy

dewing *pres part of* DEW

de·witt \də'wit\ *vt* -ED/-ING/-S *usu cap D & often cap W* [after Jan and Cornelis *De Witt* †1672 Dutch statesmen murdered by a mob] *archaic* : LYNCH

¹dew·lap \'d(y)ü,lap\ *n* -S [ME *dewlappe*, fr. ¹*dew* + *lappe* lap — more at LAP (loose part)] **1 a** : a pendulous fold of skin under the neck of bovine animals **b** : a corresponding fold on various other animals — see DOG illustration, GOOSE illustration **c** : a strip of hide cut to hang free from the neck or brisket of cattle as an identification mark **2** : a flaccid fold of fat or flesh on the human throat **3** : one of the two triangular or squarish areas just above the ligule that form the hinge of the blade joint in the sugarcane leaf

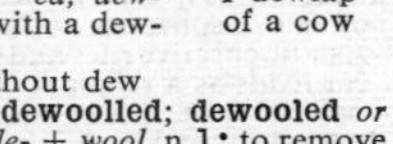

1 dewlap of a cow

²dewlap \"\ *vt* : to mark (cattle) with a dewlap

dew·lapped \-pt\ *also* **dew·lap·py** \-pē\ *adj* [*dewlapped* fr. ME, fr. *dewlappe* + *-ed*; *dewlappy* fr. ¹*dewlap* + *-y*] : furnished with a dewlap

dew·less \'d(y)üləs\ *adj* : being without dew

de·wool \(')dē+\ *vt* **dewooled** *or* **dewoolled**; **dewooled** *or* **dewoolled**; **dewooling**; **dewools** [*de-* + *wool*, n.] : to remove the wool from

de·worm \"+\ *vt* [*de-* + *worm*, n.] : to free from worms

dew plant *n* **1** : ¹ICE PLANT **2** : a sundew (*Drosera rotundifolia*) that has rounded leaves and white or rarely pink flowers and is widely distributed in the northern hemisphere

dew point *n* : the temperature at which a vapor begins to condense — used esp. of water vapor in the atmosphere

dew-point hygrometer *n* : a hygrometer for determining the dew point usu. by measuring the temperature of a liquid being cooled in a highly polished silver vessel at the moment when drops of moisture condense on the outer wall of the vessel

dew poison *n, Midland* : a cutaneous rash (as ringworm, athlete's foot, or a rash caused by penetration of hookworms) attributed to the toxic action of dew on the bare skin

dew pond *n* : a shallow artificial pond on the English downs filled and kept up chiefly by the condensation of dew and mist and used to provide water for cattle

dewret *also* **dewrot** \'⸗,⸗\ *vt* **dewretted**; **dewretted**; **dewretting**; **dewrets** [*dewret* fr. ¹*dew* + *ret* (to soak); *dewrot* by folk etymology (influence of *rot*, v.) fr. *dewret*] : to ret (flax or hemp) by exposure to rain, dew, and sun

dews *pl of* DEW, *pres 3d sing of* DEW

dew snail *n, dial Eng* : SLUG

dewtry *n* -ES [Marathi *dhutrā*, fr. Skt *dhattūra*] **1** *obs* : JIMSONWEED **2** *obs* : stramonium or an extract of stramonium apparently formerly used as an aphrodisiac

dew web *n, dial* : SPIDER WEB; *usu* : one found outdoors and covered with dew

dew worm *n* : an earthworm suitable for use as bait : NIGHT CRAWLER

dewy \'d(y)üē, -üi\ *adj* -ER/-EST [¹*dew* + *-y*] **1** : moist with dew : BEDEWED ⟨a ~ lawn⟩ **2** : accompanied or modified by dew ⟨a ~ light⟩ ⟨~ coolness of evening⟩ **3** : resembling or suggestive of dew (as in moistness, freshness, or purity) ⟨~ tears⟩ ⟨~ sleep⟩ ⟨a ~ maiden⟩

dewy-eyed \'⸗,⸗\ *adj* : naïvely credulous : exhibiting childlike innocence and trust; *sometimes* : artfully presenting an effect of innocence, trust, and credulity

dex·i·id \'deksēəd\ *adj* [NL *Dexiidae*] : of or relating to the family Dexiidae

dex·i·idae \dek'sīə,dē\ *n pl, cap* [NL, fr. *Dexia*, type genus (perh. fr. Gk *dexia* right hand, fr. fem. of *dexios*) + *-idae*] : a family of muscoid flies that are closely related to the tachina fly and have larvae which are parasitic in insects and other small arthropods

dex·io·trop·ic \¦deksēō¦träpik\ *or* **dex·i·ot·ro·pous** \¦deksē¦ä·trəpəs\ *also* **dex·tro·trop·ic** \¦dekstrō¦träpik\ *or* **dex·trot·ro·pous** \dek'strä·trəpəs\ *adj* [*dexiotropic* fr. *dexio-* (fr. Gk *dexios*) fr. *-tropic*; *dexiotropous* fr. *dexio-* + *-tropous*; *dextrotropic* fr. *dextr-* + *-tropic*; *dextrotropous* fr. *dextr-* + *-tropous*] : turning to the right : DEXTRAL — used esp. of certain shells, of spiral cleavage patterns, or of the movement of volvox colonies

¹dex·ter \'dekstə(r)\ *adj* [L; akin to OHG *zeso* relating to or situated on the right, Goth *taihswa*, Gk *dexiteros, dexios*, Skt *dakṣiṇa* relating to or situated on the right, L *decēre* to be fitting — more at DECENT] **1** : relating to or situated on the right ⟨the ~ wing of a fowl⟩ **2** : being or relating to the side of a heraldic shield or escutcheon at the right of the person wearing it **3** : appearing or facing toward the right and considered of good omen : AUSPICIOUS, FORTUNATE ⟨on sounding wings a ~ eagle flew —Alexander Pope⟩

²dexter \"\ *adv* : on the right side

³dexter \"\ *n* [prob. after Mr. *Dexter*, 19th cent. Irish stockbreeder who originated it] **1** *usu cap* : a breed of small short-legged hardy cattle originating from the Kerry breed of Ireland, being usu. chiefly black or sometimes red, and carrying in heterozygous condition the gene that when homozygous causes the bulldog calf — compare ACHONDROPLASIA **2** -S *often cap* : any animal of the Dexter breed

dexter base point *n* : the lower dexter part of the field of an escutcheon — see POINT illustration

dexter chief point *n* : the upper dexter part of the field of an escutcheon — see POINT illustration

dex·ter·i·ty \dek'sterəd·ē, -ətē, -i\ *n* -ES [MF or L; MF *dexterité*, fr. L *dexteritat-, dexteritas*, fr. *dexter* skillful, relating to or situated on the right + -*itat-, -itas* -ity] **1 :** readiness and grace in physical activity **:** skill and ease in using the hands **:** expertness in manual acts ⟨~ with the chisel⟩ ⟨it seemed impossible that the clarinetists could be doing more than improvisations, playing as they did with such reckless ~ —J.S.Bowman⟩ **2 :** readiness in the use or control of the mental powers **:** quickness and skill in managing any complicated or difficult affair **:** ADROITNESS ⟨~ in argument⟩ **3 :** RIGHT-HANDEDNESS

dex·ter·ous \'dekst(ə)rəs\ *or* **dex·trous** \-trəs\ *adj* [L *dexter* skillful, relating to or situated on the right + E *-ous*] **1 :** DEXTRAL **2 a :** skillful and active with the hands **:** deft and skillful in manipulation ⟨a ~ hand⟩; *broadly* **:** adroit and competent in the use of the limbs and body esp. in the performance of a task ⟨a ~ worker⟩ **b** *of a tool or machine* **:** designed for easy efficient operation; *often* **:** operated with sure expertness **3 a :** mentally adroit and skillful **:** quick at inventing expedients **:** EXPERT, CLEVER ⟨a ~ manager⟩ **b** *obs* **:** FOXY, CRAFTY, UNSCRUPULOUS **4 :** done with dexterity **:** SKILLFUL, ARTFUL ⟨~ management⟩ ⟨~ intrigue⟩ ⟨a ~ résumé of the play⟩
syn ADROIT, DEFT, FEAT, HANDY: these adjectives signify in common having or showing readiness or skill in the use of one's hands, limbs, or body. DEXTEROUS (or DEXTROUS) may imply expertness, cunning, and knowledge, with accompanying facility or agility ⟨one of the most *dexterous* novelists now writing, with an enviable command of styles —Saul Bellow⟩ ⟨by force or by *dexterous* diplomacy —Walter Moberly⟩ ⟨seized one corner of the blanket, and with a *dexterous* twist and throw unrolled it —C.G.D.Roberts⟩ ADROIT stresses artfulness, often a deceptive artfulness, in one's dexterity, and may indicate ability to cope well with likely situations ⟨an exceptionally *adroit* pianist —Douglas Watt⟩ ⟨a visionary and an idealist, he was at the same time the most thoroughly realistic and *adroit* political leader since Lincoln —Allan Nevins & H.S.Commager⟩ DEFT stresses lightness, neatness, and sureness of touch ⟨Angus seemed appallingly at home, and he waltzed off with the prettiest girl, sliding, swinging, *deft* —Sinclair Lewis⟩ ⟨there was a shifting of gears, and with . . . *deft* manipulations he reversed the car in the narrow road —W.H.Wright⟩ ⟨the lore of all men he knew, and was *deft* in every cunning, save the dealings of the sword —William Morris⟩ FEAT, archaic except in dialect, suggests deftness and grace in movement or execution of a task ⟨the *featest* fellow at the dance⟩ HANDY suggests a degree of skill, even though a lack of training, in performance of a wide variety of tasks, generally involving such activities as carpentry, plumbing, or general repairing ⟨to be *handy* around the house when the plumbing goes bad or the roof leaks⟩ ⟨as men become more *handy* at manipulating labels and symbols —Clive Bell⟩ ⟨*handy* at playing bridge, writing a sonnet, or cleaning the cellar⟩

dex·ter·ous·ly *adv* **:** in a dexterous manner **:** with dexterity

dex·ter·ous·ness *n* -ES **:** the quality or state of being dexterous

dextr- *or* **dextro-** *comb form* [LL, fr. L *dextr-, dexter*] **1 a :** right ⟨*dextr*ad⟩ **:** on or toward the right ⟨*dextro*rotatory⟩ **b :** dextral and ⟨*dextro*sinistral⟩ **2** *usu* **dextro-**, *usu ital* **:** dextrorotatory — in names of chemical compounds ⟨*dextr*ose⟩ ⟨*dextro*-tartaric acid⟩; symbol (+)- ⟨(+)-tartaric acid⟩; compare D-

dex·trad \'dek,strad\ *adv* [*dextr-* + *-ad*] **:** toward the right side **:** DEXTRALLY

¹dex·tral \'dekstrəl\ *adj* [ML *dextralis* southern, on the right, fr. L *dextr-, dexter* + *-alis* -al] **:** of or relating to the right **:** inclined to the right: as **a :** RIGHT-HANDED **b** *of certain flatfishes* **:** having the right side turned uppermost **c** *of a gastropod shell* **:** having the whorls turning from the left toward the right as viewed with the apex toward the observer or having the aperture open toward the observer to the right of the axis when held with the spire uppermost

²dextral \"\ *n* -S **:** a person exhibiting dominance of the right hand and eye **:** a typical right-handed individual

dex·tral·i·ty \dek'stralәd·ē\ *n* -ES **1 :** the quality or state of having the right side or certain of its parts (as the hand or eye) different from and usu. more efficient than the left or its corresponding parts; *also* **:** RIGHT-HANDEDNESS **2 :** the condition of being dextral ⟨in some snails ~ appears to be a simple Mendelian dominant⟩

dex·tral·ly \'dekstrəlē, -li\ *adv* **:** toward the right ⟨a ~ coiled shell⟩ ⟨the hands of a watch viewed from in front rotate ~⟩ — compare CLOCKWISE

dextral shell *n* **:** a spiral gastropod shell the whorls of which turn from left to right

dex·tran \'dek,stran, -strən\ *n* -S [ISV *dextr-* + *-an*] **:** any of numerous polysaccharides $(C_6H_{10}O_5)_n$ that yield only glucose on hydrolysis but differ otherwise from starch and glycogen (as in molecular structure): as **a :** any such polysaccharide of very high molecular weight usu. obtained by fermentation of sugar with bacteria of the genus *Leuconostoc* (as *L. mesenteroides*) — called also *native dextran* **b :** any such polysaccharide of reduced molecular weight obtained by controlled acid hydrolysis of native dextran as a white amorphous powder and used esp. in physiological saline as a plasma substitute — called also *clinical dextran*

dex·trin \'dekstrən\ *also* **dex·trine** \-,strēn, -strən\ *n* -S [F *dextrine*, fr. *dextr-* + *-ine* -in, -ine] **:** any of various water-soluble dextrorotatory gummy polysaccharides obtained from starch by the action of heat, acids, or enzymes as a yellow or white powder or granules, capable of yielding maltose or glucose by further hydrolysis, and used as adhesives, as sizes for paper and textiles, as gum substitutes, and in making syrups and beer — called also *British gum*

dex·trin·ate \'dekstrə,nāt\ *vt* -ED/-ING/-S **:** to convert into or impregnate with dextrin ⟨a *dextrinated* mash⟩

dex·trin·i·za·tion \,dekstrənə'zāshən\ *n* -S **:** an act or process of dextrinizing

dex·trin·ize \'dekstrə,nīz\ *vt* -ED/-ING/-S **:** to convert (starch) into dextrins

dex·trino·gen·ic \¦dekstrənō¦jenik\ *adj* [*dextrin* + *-o-* + *-genic*] **:** producing dextrins ⟨~ activity of α-amylase⟩

dextrinogenic enzyme *n* **:** AMYLASE 2a

dex·tro \'dek(,)strō\ *adj* [*dextr-*] **:** DEXTROROTATORY

dex·tro·amphetamine \¦dek(,)strō + \ *n* [*dextr-* + *amphetamine*] **:** the dextrorotatory isomer of amphetamine used in the form of the sulfate or hydrochloride as a central nervous system stimulant

dex·tro·car·dia \,dekstrō'kärdēə\ *n* -S [NL, fr. *dextr-* + *-cardia*] **:** an abnormal condition in which the heart is situated on the right side and the great blood vessels of the right and left sides are reversed — **dex·tro·car·di·al** \¦≈≈¦≈dēəl\ *adj*

dex·troc·u·lar \(')dek¦sträkyələ(r)\ *adj* [*dextr-* + *ocular*] **:** using the right eye habitually or more effectively than the left — **dex·troc·u·lar·i·ty** \(,)≈,≈≈'larəd·ē\ *n* -ES

dex·tro–glucose \¦dekstrō + \ *n* [*dextr-* + *glucose*] **:** DEXTROSE

dex·tro·gyrate \" + \ *or* **dex·tro·gyre** \'dekstrō,jī(ə)r\ *also* **dex·tro·gyratory** \¦dekstrō + \ *or* **dex·tro·gy·rous** \¦dekstrō¦jīrəs\ *adj* [*dextrogyrate* fr. *dextr-* + *gyrate*, adj.; *dextrogyre* ISV *dextr-* + *-gyre* (fr. L *gyrus* gyre); *dextrogyratory* fr. *dextr-* + *gyratory*; *dextrogyrous* fr. *dextr-* + *-gyrous* (fr. *gyre* + *-ous*)] **:** DEXTROROTATORY

dex·tro·pimaric acid \¦dekstrō + ...-\ *n* [ISV *dextr-* + *pimaric*] **:** a crystalline resin acid $C_{19}H_{29}COOH$ found esp. in oleoresins from pine trees

dex·tro·position \" + \ *n* -S [NL *dextroposition-, dextropositio*, fr. *dextr-* + L *position-, positio* position] **:** displacement to the right — used chiefly of the aorta

dex·tro·rotation \" + \ *n* [*dextr-* + *rotation*] **:** right-handed or clockwise rotation — used chiefly of the plane of polarization of light; opposed to *levorotation*; compare OPTICAL ROTATION

dex·tro·rotatory *also* **dex·tro·rotary** \" + \ *adj* [*dextr-* + *rotatory* or *rotary*] **:** turning toward the right hand or clockwise; *esp* **:** rotating the plane of polarization of light toward the right hand ⟨~ crystals⟩ ⟨~ sugar solutions⟩ — abbr. *dextro-, d-;* opposed to *levorotatory*; compare OPTICALLY ACTIVE

dex·trorse \'dek,strȯrs\ *also* **dex·tror·sal** \(')dek¦strȯrsəl\ *adj* [*dextrorse* fr. NL *dextrorsus*, fr. L *dextrorsum, dextrorsus* toward the right side, fr. *dexter* relating to or situated on the right + *versus*, past part. of *vertere* to turn; *dextrorsal* fr. NL *dextrorsus* + E *-al* — more at DEXTER, WORTH] **1 :** *of a plant or its parts* **:** twining spirally upward around an axis from left to right: **a :** twining clockwise (as in the hop) when the observer's point of view is felt to be within or above the spiral **b :** twining counterclockwise (as in the morning glory) when the observer's point of view is felt to be outside the spiral — compare SINISTRORSE **2 :** DEXTRAL c — **dex·trorse·ly** *adv*

dex·trose \'dek,strōs *also* -ōz\ *n* -S [ISV *dextr-* + *-ose*] **:** dextrorotatory glucose obtained usu. by acid hydrolysis of starch as sweet crystals of the anhydrous compound or of the monohydrate $C_6H_{12}O_6.H_2O$ and used chiefly in foods and beverages, in making caramel, and in intravenous feeding — called also *corn sugar, grape sugar*

dex·tro·sinistral \¦dek(,)strō + \ *adj* [*dextr-* + *sinistral*] **1 :** extending from the right toward the left ⟨a ~ line⟩ **2 :** naturally left-handed but trained to use the right hand in writing — **dextrosinistrally** *adv*

dextrotropic *or* **dextrotropous** *var of* DEXIOTROPIC

dextrous *var of* DEXTEROUS

dex·tro·version \'dekstrō + \ *n* -S [*dextr-* + ML *version-, versio* action of turning — more at VERSION] **:** movement or turning to the right (as of the eyes)

¹dey *or* **deye** \'dī\ *n, pl* **deyes** [ME *deye*, fr. OE *dǣge* kneader of bread — more at DAIRY] *now chiefly Scot* **:** DAIRYMAID

²dey \'dā\ *n* -S [F, fr. Turk *dayı*, lit., maternal uncle] **:** a ruling official of the Ottoman empire in northern Africa; *esp* **:** a governor of Algiers before the French conquest in 1830

deywoman \'≈,≈≈\ *n, pl* **deywomen** [¹*dey* + *woman*] *now chiefly dial* **:** DAIRYMAID

de·zinc \(')dē + \ *vt* [*de-* + *zinc*, n.] **:** DEZINCIFY

de·zincification \(,)dē + \ *n* [*de-* + *zinc*, n. + *-i-* + *-fication*] **:** the action or process of dezincifying

de·zincify *also* **de·zinkify** \(')dē + \ *vt* [back-formation fr. *dezincification*] **:** to remove zinc from **:** free from zinc

DF *abbr* **1** damage free **2** dead freight **3** [ML *Defensor Fidei*] Defender of the Faith **4** direction finder; direction finding

DFDT \,dē,ef,dē'tē\ *n* -S [*difluoro-diphenyl-trichloro-ethane*] **:** a white solid compound $(FC_6H_4)_2CHCCl_3$ that is a partial fluorine analogue of DDT and is held to be less toxic to animals and fish than DDT and more toxic to flying insects

d flat \'≈'≈\ *n, usu cap D* **1 :** the keynote of D-flat major **2 :** the tone a half step below D

d–flat major \'≈,≈'≈≈\ *n, usu cap D* **:** the major musical key having a signature of five flats

DFP \¦dē,ef'pē\ *abbr or n* -S diisopropyl fluorophosphate

dft *abbr* **1** defendant **2** draft

dftg *abbr* drafting

dg *abbr* decigram

DG *abbr* **1** degaussing **2** [LL *Dei gratia*] by the grace of God **3** [LL *Deo gratias*] thanks to God **4** directional gyro **5** director general

dghai·sa \'dīsə\ *n* -S [Maltese *dghajsa*] **:** a small boat resembling a gondola that is common in Malta

dgt *abbr* daughter

dhai \'dä,ē, 'dī\ *n* -S [Hindi *dhāī*, fr. (assumed) Skt *dhātrkā*, fr. *dhayati* he sucks — more at FEMININE] *India* **:** WET NURSE; *also* **:** MIDWIFE

dhaincha *var of* DAINCHA

dhak *also* **dak** \'däk, 'dōk\ *n* -S [Hindi *dhāk*] **:** an East Indian tree (*Butea frondosa*) whose flowers yield a yellow dye

dhal \'däl\ *n* -S [Hindi *dāl*] *India & East Indies* **:** PIGEON PEA

dha·man \'dämən\ *n* -S [Hindi *dhaman*, fr. Skt *dharmaṇa*] **:** an Indian tree (*Grewia tiliaefolia*) with reddish brown strong flexible wood used for wheel axles and spokes and for athletic equipment

dhan \'dən\ *n* -S [Hindi, fr. Skt *dhana*, fr. *dadhāti* he puts, places — more at DO] *India* **:** property or wealth; *specif* **:** the village cattle

dha·ra·na \'dӓrənə\ *n* -S [Skt *dhāraṇa*, lit., act of holding, fr. *dharayati*] *Hinduism, Buddhism, Jainism* **:** fixed attention; *esp* **:** a state of mental concentration on an object without wavering

dha·ra·ni \'dӓrə(,)nē\ *n, pl* **dharanis** *or* **dharani** [Skt *dhāraṇī*, lit., act of holding, remembering, fr. *dhārayati* he holds — more at FIRM] *Hinduism & Mahayana Buddhism* **:** MANTRA

dhar·ma \'dərmə\ *n* -S [Skt, lit., that which is established, fr. *dhārayati* he holds — more at FIRM] **1** *Hinduism* **a** (1) **:** social custom regarded as one's duty ⟨some ~ such as not eating beef and respecting Brahmans is common to all Hindus —Talcott Parsons⟩ (2) **:** caste custom; *esp* **:** the religious custom of the castes having a sacrament of spiritual regeneration **b :** civil and criminal law **c :** the body of cosmic principles by which all things exist **:** NATURE: (1) **:** essential function ⟨it is the ~ . . . of a stone to be hard, of fire to burn, of a tiger to be fierce, just as it is the ~ of a king to punish and to protect, of a Brahman to study and pray —Seymour Vesey-Fitzgerald⟩ (2) **:** NATURAL LAW (3) **:** MORAL LAW, JUSTICE ⟨the ruler so inaugurated was regarded not as a temporal autocrat but as the instrument of ~ —D.M.Brown⟩ **d :** conduct appropriate to one's essential nature, establishing the morally sound life that is one of man's four ends **:** RIGHTEOUSNESS, RELIGION — opposed to *adharma* **2** *Buddhism* **a :** ideal truth esp. as taught by Buddha **b** *Hinayana* **:** an element of existence **:** one of the minute brief appearances of which any experienced object is made up **3** *Jainism* **:** the uncreated and eternal substance that is the necessary condition of movement for souls and matter **:** the ontological principle of movement ⟨~ is compared to water, through which and by which fish are able to move —Heinrich Zimmer⟩ — compare ADHARMA

dhar·ma·ka·ya \,dərmə'käyə\ *n* -S [Skt *dharmakāya*, fr. *dharma* + *kāya* body; akin to Skt *cinoti* he gathers, heaps up — more at POET] **:** the ideal body or the essence of the Absolute in the Buddhist doctrine of trikaya

dhar·ma·shas·tra \-'shästrə\ *or* **dhar·ma·sas·tra** \-'sästrə\ *n* -S [Skt *dharmaśāstra*, fr. *dharma* + *śāstra* shastra — more at SHASTRA] **:** a Brahmanical collection of rules of life often in the form of a metrical law book

dhar·ma·su·tra \-'sü·trə\ *n* -S [Skt *dharmasūtra*, fr. *dharma* + *sūtra* sutra — more at SUTRA] **:** any of the early lawbooks of Brahmanism

dharm·sa·la \(,)dərm'sä(,)lə\ *or* **dharm·sha·la** \-'shä-\ *n* -S [Hindi *dharmsālā*, fr. Skt *dharmaśālā*, fr. *dharma* + *śālā* hall, house — more at HALL] *India* **:** a building devoted to a religious or charitable purpose; *esp* **:** a shelter for travelers

dhar·na *also* **dhur·na** \'dərnə\ *n* -S [Hindi *dharnā*] *India* **:** a method of appealing for justice by fasting even to the point of death while seated at the door of the offender

dhau·ra \'dòrə\ *n* -S [Marathi *dhāvḍā* dhauri] **:** DHAWA

dhau·ri \'dòrē\ *n* -S [Hindi *dhārī*] **1 :** DHAWA **2 :** an East Indian red-flowered shrub (*Woodfordia floribunda*) of the family Lythraceae that yields a gum resembling tragacanth

dha·wa *or* **dha·va** \'dävə\ *n* -S [Hindi *dhāvā*, fr. Skt *dhava*] **:** an East Indian tree (*Anogeissus latifolia*) of the family Combretaceae that is used for timber and tanning and is a source of gum ghatti

dhe·gi·ha \'dāgē,hä\ *n, pl* **dhegiha** *or* **dhegihas** *usu cap* **1 :** a Siouan language of the Omaha, Ponca, Osage, Kansa, and Quapaw peoples **2 a :** the peoples speaking Dhegiha **b :** a member of any of such peoples

dhikr \'dikər\ *n, pl* **dhikrs** *or* **dhikr** [Ar, mention, recitation, remembrance] **1 :** the ritual formula of a Sufi brotherhood recited devotionally in praise of Allah and as a means of attaining ecstatic experience **2 :** the recitation of the dhikr; *also* **:** the period of such recitation

dhim·mi \'dimē\ *n, pl* **dhimmis** *or* **dhimmi** [Ar *dhimmīy*] **:** a person living in a region overrun by Muslim conquest who was accorded a protected status and allowed to retain his original faith

dho·bi *also* **dho·bie** \'dōbē\ *n* -S [Hindi *dhobī*; akin to Skt *dhāvaka* dhobi, *dhāvati* he washes, *dhavala* white, Gk *thoos* bright, shining] **:** a member of a low caste of India employed as washermen **:** WASHERMAN

dhobie itch *n* [so called fr. the belief that the disease is transmitted by newly washed clothes] **:** ringworm attacking moist parts of the body (as the groin)

dhole \'dōl\ *n, pl* **dholes** *also* **dhole** [perh. fr. Kanarese *tōḷa* wolf] **:** a fierce wild dog (*Cuon dukhunensis*) of India that hunts in packs and may attack even large and fierce animals (as the tiger)

dholl \'däl\ *var of* DHAL

dho·luo \dō'lü(,)ō\ *n, usu cap* **:** LUO 2

dho·ni *also* **do·ni** \'dōnē\ *n* -S [Hindi *ḍonī*, Marathi *ḍonī*, Kanarese *dōni, ḍōni*, & Telugu *dōne*, fr. Skt *droṇī* trough, tub, fr. *dru* wood, tree — more at TREE] **:** a fishing or coastwise trading boat of India

dhoo·ly \'dülē\ *var of* DOOLY

dhoon \'dün\ *n* -S [Hindi *dūn*] *India* **:** VALLEY; *esp* **:** a valley in the Siwalik hills

d–horizon \'dē,≈≈\ *n, usu cap D* **:** a soil layer that sometimes occurs beneath the B-horizon or the C-horizon if present, that has not been subjected to weathering, and that may consist of the unmodified mineral matter from which the more superficial layers developed or of a different complex of mineral matter

dho·ti \'dōtē\ *or* **dhoo·tie** *or* **dhu·ti** \'dütē\ *n* -S [Hindi *dhotī*] **1 :** a long loincloth worn by Hindu men **2 :** a fabric used for dhotis

dhow *also* **dow** \'dau̇\ *n* -S [Ar *dāwa, dau*, prob. of Indic origin; akin to Marathi *dāw* dhow] **:** an Arab lateen-rigged boat of the Indian ocean usu. having a long overhang forward, a high poop, and an open waist

dhow

dhu'l–hij·ja \dül'hi(,)jä\ *n, usu cap D&H* [Ar *dhū-l-ḥijjah*, lit., the one of the pilgrimage] **:** the 12th month of the Muhammadan year — see MONTH table

dhu'l–qa·'dah \-'kä-(,)dä\ *n, usu cap 1st D&Q* [Ar *dhū-l-qa'dah*, lit., the one of the sitting] **:** the 11th month of the Muhammadan year — see MONTH table

dhurra *var of* DURRA

dhur·rie \'dərē\ *n* -S [Hindi *darī*] **:** a thick cotton cloth or carpet made in India

dhur·rin *also* **dur·rin** \'dùrən\ *n* -S [*dhurra* + *-in*] **:** a crystalline cyanogenetic glucoside $C_{14}H_{17}NO_7$ found in durra at a certain stage in its growth

dhya·na \dē'änə, 'dyä-\ *n* -S [Skt *dhyāna*, fr. *dhyāti* he thinks — more at SEMANTICS] **1** *Hinduism, Buddhism, Jainism* **:** MEDITATION; ESP **:** an uninterrupted state of mental concentration upon a single object **:** higher contemplation **2** *usu cap* **:** a Mahayana school of Buddhism relying on meditation as a method of enlightenment — compare CH'AN

di- *comb form* [ME, fr. MF, fr. L, fr. Gk; akin to OE *twi-* — more at TWI-] **1 :** twice **:** twofold **:** double ⟨*di*chromatic⟩ **2 :** containing two atoms, radicals, or groups (of a specified kind) ⟨*di*chloride⟩ **3 :** being a Greek coin or unit of value worth two specified units ⟨*di*stater⟩ ⟨*di*drachma⟩

DI *abbr* drill instructor

Di *symbol* didymium

dia- *also* **di-** *prefix* [ME, fr. OF, fr. L, fr. Gk, *dia*; akin to L *dis-* — more at DIS-] **1 :** through **:** during ⟨*dia*chronic⟩ **:** across ⟨*dia*ctinic⟩ **2 :** made of **:** consisting of — in names of compounded medicines ⟨*dia*codion⟩

dia *abbr* diameter

di·a·ban·tite \,dīə'ban,tīt\ *n* -S [modif. (influenced by *-ite*) of G *diabantachronnyn*, irreg. fr. G *diabase* + Gk *chrōnnyein* to stain] **:** a mineral approximately $(Mg,Fe,Al)_3(SiAl)_2O_5(OH)_4$ consisting of a basic silicate of magnesium, iron, and aluminum

di·a·base \'dīə,bās\ *n* [F, fr. Gk *diabasis* act of crossing over, fr. *diabainein* to cross over, fr. *dia-* + *bainein* to go — more at COME] **1** *archaic* **:** DIORITE **2** *chiefly Brit* **:** an altered basalt **3 :** a hypabyssal rock of the composition of gabbro but with an ophitic texture consisting of labradorite laths involved in a matrix of augite with magnetite a common accessory

di·a·bas·ic \¦dīə¦bāsik\ *adj* **:** consisting of or resembling diabase **:** OPHITIC

di·a·bat·ic \¦dīə¦bad·ik\ *adj* [Gk *diabatos* passable (fr. *diabainein* to cross over) + E *-ic*] *physics* **:** involving the transfer of heat ⟨~ flow of air⟩ — opposed to *adiabatic*

di·a·be·tes \,dīə'bēd·|ēz, -ēt|, |əs, |iz *sometimes* -bēd·,ēz *or* -bē,tēz\ *n, pl* **diabetes** [L, fr. Gk *diabētēs* compass, siphon, diabetes, fr. *diabainein* to walk or stand with legs wide apart, to cross over] **:** any of certain abnormal conditions characterized by the secretion and excretion of excessive amounts of urine ⟨bronze ~⟩; *esp* **:** DIABETES MELLITUS — see DIABETES INSIPIDUS

diabetes in·sip·i·dus \-in'sipədəs\ *n* [NL, lit., insipid diabetes] **:** a disorder of the pituitary gland characterized by intense thirst and the excretion of great amounts of dilute urine

diabetes mel·li·tus \-'meləd·əs, -'melətəs\ *n* [NL, lit., honey-sweet diabetes] **:** a familial constitutional disorder of carbohydrate metabolism involving inadequate secretion or utilization of insulin, characterized by hyperglycemia, glycosuria, polyuria, and marked by thirst, hunger, itching, weakness, loss of weight, and even severe acidosis and coma

¹di·a·bet·ic \¦dīə¦bed|ik, |t|, |ēk *sometimes* -bē|\ *adj* [prob. fr. F *diabétique*, fr. *diabète* diabetes (fr. L *diabetes*) + *-ique* -ic] **:** of, relating to, or concerning diabetes or diabetics: as **a :** afflicted with diabetes **b :** indicating, occurring in, caused by, or resulting from diabetes ⟨~ gangrene⟩ ⟨~ sugar⟩ ⟨~ coma⟩ **c :** suitable for diabetics ⟨~ food⟩

²diabetic \"\ *n* -S **:** a person having diabetes

di·a·be·to·gen·ic \,dīə¦bēd·ə¦jenik, -ētə-\ *adj* [*diabetes* + *-o* + *-genic*] **:** producing diabetes

dia·ble·rie \dē'äblə(,)rē, -'ab-, ≈,≈≈'≈, ≈'≈≈,ri\ *n* -S [F, fr. OF *diablerie, deablerie*, fr. *diable, deable* devil (fr. LL *diabolus*) + *-erie* -ery — more at DEVIL] **1 a :** actions or behavior of devils ⟨~ of a satyr⟩ **:** dealings with the devil or devils **:** black magic **:** WITCHCRAFT, SORCERY, DEVILRY ⟨practicing witchcraft and ~⟩ **b :** a quality or air of black magic or of dealings with the devil ⟨~ of gothic romance⟩ **2 a :** an infernal scene esp. as represented in words or painting **:** representation of devils ⟨a collection of ~s⟩ **b :** demon lore ⟨stories of ~⟩ **3 a :** mischievous conduct or manner **:** lighthearted and ingenious mischievousness **:** ⟨full of wit and ~⟩ **b :** WICKEDNESS ⟨house-burnings, assassinations, and other pieces of ~⟩

dia·blo \'dyäblō, 'thy-\ *n* -S [Sp, fr. LL *diabolus*] **:** DEVIL

dia·blo·tin \dē¦äblō¦taⁿ\ *n* -S [F, lit., imp, dim. of *diable*] **1** *West Indies* **:** BLACK-CAPPED PETREL **2 :** any of various dainties (as croutons, frozen custards, chocolate bonbons in paper) — usu. used in pl.

diabol- *or* **diabolo-** *comb form* [ME *deabol-*, fr. MF *diabol-*, fr. LL, fr. Gk, fr. *diabolos* — more at DEVIL] **:** devil ⟨*diabol*ism⟩ ⟨*diabolo*cracy⟩

dia·boleite \¦dīə + \ *n* [*dia-* + *boleite*] **:** a mineral $Pb_2CuCl_2(OH)_4$ consisting of a basic chloride of lead and copper

di·a·bol·ic \¦dīə¦bälik, -lēk\ *or* **di·a·bol·i·cal** \-ləkəl, -lēk-\ *adj* [*diabolic* fr. ME *deabolik*, fr. MF *diabolique*, fr. LL *diabolicus*, fr. *diabolus* devil + L *-icus* -ic; *diabolical* fr. MF *diabolique* + E *-al* — more at DEVIL] **1 :** of or relating to the devil or devils ⟨Lucifer is . . . forced to reassume his ~ shape —*Modern Language Rev.*⟩ ⟨~ lore⟩ **:** derived from the devil ⟨~ arts⟩ ⟨difference between the angelic and the ~ temperament —G.B.Shaw⟩ **:** being under the influence of devils ⟨*diabolical* sorcerers —Herman Melville⟩ **:** resembling a devil ⟨a ~ figure⟩ **:** being a devil ⟨a ~ visitor⟩ **:** suggestive of devils or hell ⟨fires lit up a truly ~ scene⟩ **2 :** resembling that of devils **:** befitting or characteristic of a devil typically in having or showing cunning, ingenuity, cruelty, or wickedness **:** DEVILISH, FIENDISH ⟨the cold calculation and the ~ art of these statesmen⟩ ⟨his expression changing to something *diabolical* —Rudyard Kipling⟩ — **di·a·bol·i·cal·ly** \-lək(ə)lē, -lēk-, -li\ *adv* — **di·a·bol·i·cal·ness** *n* -ES

di·ab·o·lism \dī'abə,lizəm\ *n* -S [*diabol-* + *-ism*] **1 a :** dealings with the devil **:** demonic possession **:** SORCERY ⟨conducting experiments in ~⟩ **b :** action or practice instigated or aided by the devil ⟨~ was rampant in the universe —Carl Van Doren⟩ **c :** evil conduct or intent **:** EVIL ⟨deeds of black misunderstanding rather than ~ —*Newsweek*⟩ **2 :** belief in or doctrine concerning devils; *esp* **:** a religious doctrine or a perversion of religious doctrine involving the worship of devils

di·ab·o·list \-ˌləst\ *n* -s [*diabol-* + *-ist*] **:** one who teaches or practices diabolism **:** one who worships the devil

di·ab·o·lize \-ˌlīz\ *vt* -ED/-ING/-S [*diabol-* + *-ize*] **1 :** to make diabolical **:** subject to diabolical influence ⟨his associations degrade and ~ him⟩ **2 :** to represent as diabolical ⟨newspapers *diabolized* the enemy soldiers⟩

di·ab·o·lo \dīˈabəˌlō, dēˈ-\ *n* -s [fr. *Diabolo*, a trademark] **:** a game in which an hourglass-shaped top is balanced and spun on a string stretched between the tips of two sticks; *also* **:** the top used in this game

di·a·bol·o·gy \ˌdīəˈbäləjē\ *or* **di·a·bo·lol·o·gy** \ˌdīəbəˈläl-, (ˌ)dīˌabəˈläl-\ *n* -ES [*diabology* blend of *diabol-* and *-logy; diabolology* fr. *diabol-* + *-logy*] **1 :** the study of the devil or of belief in devils **2 :** the theory or doctrine of devils **:** devil lore

1**di·a·bo·lo·nian** \ˌdiəbəˈlōnyən, (ˌ)dīˌabə-\ *n* -s [*diabol-* + *-onian* (as in *Babylonian*)] **:** a follower of the devil

2**di·a·bo·lo·nian** \ˌdīəbəˌl-, (ˌ)dīˌabə-\ *adj* **:** DEVILISH, DIABOLIC

di·a·brot·i·ca \ˌdīəˈbräd·əkə\ *n, cap* [NL, fr. Gk *diabrōtikē*, fem. of *diabrōtikos* corrosive, fr. (assumed) *diabrōtos* (verbal of *diabibrōskein* to consume, corrode, fr. *dia-* + *bibrōskein* to devour) + *-ikos* -ic — more at VORACIOUS] **:** a genus of small destructive leaf-eating beetles (family Galerucidae) that are usu. greenish yellow with spots or stripes — compare CUCUMBER BEETLE

1**dia·caus·tic** \ˌdīəˌkȯstik\ *adj* [prob. fr. F *diacaustique*, fr. *dia-* + *caustique* caustic, fr. L *causticus* — more at CAUSTIC] **:** relating to a caustic curve or caustic surface formed by refraction — compare CATACAUSTIC

2**diacaustic** \"\ *n* -s **:** a diacaustic curve or surface

di·acetate \(ˈ)dī+\ *n* [*di-* + *acetate*] **1 :** a salt, ester, or acylal containing two acetate groups ⟨ethylene ~⟩ **2 :** ACETOACETATE

di·acetic acid \ˌdī+-\ *n* [*di-* + *acetic*] **:** ACETOACETIC ACID

di·acetin \(ˈ)dī+\ *n* [ISV *di-* + *acetin*] **:** ACETIN b

diacetone alcohol *also* **di·acetone** \"+\ *n* [*di-* + *acetone*] **:** a liquid keto alcohol $CH_3COCH_2C(OH)(CH_3)_2$ made usu. by alkaline condensation of acetone and used chiefly as a solvent (as in lacquer formulations) and in hydraulic brake fluids

1**di·acetyl** \(ˌ)dī+\ *adj* [ISV *di-* + *acetyl*] **:** containing two acetyl groups

2**di·acetyl** \"+\ *n* -s **:** BIACETYL

diacetylmorphine *pronunc for* DIACETYL +\ *n* [ISV *diacetyl* + *morphine*] **:** HEROIN

dia·chronic \ˌdīəˌkränik\ *or* **dia·chro·nis·tic** \ˌdīəkrəˌnistik, -(ˌ)kräˌn-; (ˌ)dīˌakrəˌn-\ *or* **di·ach·ro·nous** \(ˈ)dīˌakrənəs\ *adj* [*diachronic*, ISV *dia-* + *chronic;* orig. formed as F *diachronique; diachronistic* fr. *dia-* + *-chronistic* (as in *synchronistic*); *diachronous* fr. *dia-* + *-chronous*] **:** considering or embracing phenomena (as the sounds of a language) as they occur, change, or develop over a period of time — contrasted with *synchronic* ⟨~ descriptions of a language are properly built up by a comparison of synchronic descriptions of the same language at different historical periods —D.W. Reed⟩ — **dia·chron·i·cal·ly** \ˌdīəˌkränək(ə)lē\ *adv* — **di·ach·ro·nous·ly** \(ˈ)dīˌakrənəslē\ *adv*

di·ach·ro·ny \dīˈakrənē\ *n* -ES [ISV *dia-* + *-chrony* (as in *synchrony*); prob. orig. formed as F *diachronie*] **1 :** diachronic analysis or point of view **:** diachronic arrangement or treatment — contrasted with *synchrony* **2 :** change extending through time

di·ach·y·lon \dīˈakəˌlän, -ələn\ *also* **di·ach·y·lum** \-ələm\ *n, pl* **diachylons** *also* **diachy·la** \-ələ\ [*diachylon* fr. ME *diaquilon*, fr. ML, fr. LL *diachylon*, a kind of medicine, fr. Gk, neut. of *diachylos* juicy, fr. *dia-* + *chylos* juice; *diachylum*, NL, alter. of ML *diaquilon* — more at CHYLE] **:** a plaster that is made of litharge and either olive oil or olive oil and lard and hence consists essentially of lead oleate and small amounts of glycerin and oleic acid and that is used for excoriated surfaces and wounds and as an adhesive

1**di·acid** \(ˈ)dī+\ *or* **di·acid·ic** \ˌdīəˌsidik\ *adj* [1*di-* + *acid* (adj.)] **1 :** able to react with two molecules of a monobasic acid or one of a dibasic acid to form a salt or ester — used esp. of bases **2 :** containing two hydrogen atoms replaceable by basic atoms or radicals — used esp. of acid salts

2**di·acid** \(ˈ)dī+\ *n* [ISV *di-* + *acid* (n.)] **:** an acid (as sulfuric acid or oxalic acid) having two acid hydrogen atoms

di·a·clase \ˈdīəˌklās, -āz\ *n* -s [ISV *dia-* + *-clase* (fr. Gk *klasis* breaking); orig. formed in F — more at -CLASIA] *geol* **:** JOINT, FRACTURE — **di·a·clas·tic** \ˌdīəˌklastik\ *adj*

di·a·cle \ˈdī(ə)kəl\ *n* -s [ME (Sc dial.), prob. alter. (influenced by *-cle*, as in *receptacle*) of *dyal* dial — more at DIAL] *chiefly Scot* **:** a pocket compass

dia·cli·nal \ˌdīəˌklīnᵊl\ *adj* [*dia-* + *-clinal*] *geol* **:** crossing a fold ⟨a ~ river⟩

di·a·co·di·um \ˌdīəˈkōdēəm\ *n* -s [NL, fr. L *diacodion*, fr. Gk *dia kōdeiōn* out of poppyheads, fr. *dia* through, out of + *kōdeiōn*, gen. pl. of *kōdeia* poppyhead — more at DIA-, CODEINE] **:** a syrup of poppies formerly used as a narcotic

di·a·coele \ˈdīəˌsēl\ *n* -s [*dia-* + *-coele*] **:** the third ventricle of the brain

di·ac·o·nal \(ˈ)dīˌakənᵊl *also* dēˈa-\ *adj* [LL *diaconalis*, fr. *diaconus* deacon + L *-alis* -al — more at DEACON] **:** of or relating to a deacon ⟨an astute showman lurks behind that ~ exterior —G.P.Meyer⟩

di·ac·o·nate \dīˈakənət, dēˈ-, -ˌnāt\ *n* -s [LL *diaconatus*, fr. *diaconus* deacon + L *-atus* -ate] **:** the office or period of office of a deacon **:** DEACONSHIP; *also* **:** a body or board of deacons

di·a·con·i·con \ˌdīəˈkänəˌkän, -əkən\ *also* **di·a·con·i·cum** \-əkəm\ *n, pl* **diaconi·ca** \-əkə\ [LL & LGk; LL *diaconicum*, fr. LGk *diakonikon*, fr. neut. of *diakonikos* of a deacon, fr. Gk, serviceable, fr. *diakonos* deacon, servant + *-ikos* -ic — more at DEACON] *Eastern Church* **:** the sacristy at the right or north side of the bema opposite to the prothesis

di·a·cran·te·ri·an \ˌdīəˌkranˌtirēən\ *also* **di·a·cran·ter·ic** \-ˌterik\ *adj* [*dia-* + Gk *krantēres* wisdom teeth + E *-ian* or *-ic*] **:** having the back teeth separated by an interval from the front ones ⟨the hognose snake is ~⟩ — opposed to *syncranterian*

1**di·a·crit·ic** \ˌdīəˌkrid·|ik, -it|, |ēk\ *or* **di·a·crit·i·cal** \|əkəl, |ēk-\ *adj* [*diacritic* fr. Gk *diakritikos* separative, able to distinguish, fr. *diakritos* separated (verbal of *diakrinein* to separate, distinguish, fr. *dia-* + *krinein* to separate) + *-ikos* -ic; *diacritical* fr. Gk *diakritikos* + E *-al* — more at CERTAIN] **1 :** serving as a diacritic **2 a :** serving to separate or distinguish **:** DISTINCTIVE ⟨the ~ elements in culture —S.F.Nadel⟩ **b :** capable of distinguishing or discerning ⟨students of superior ~ powers⟩

2**diacritic** \"\ *n* -s **:** a modifying mark or sign over, under, after, or through an orthographic or phonetic character or combination of characters indicating a phonetic or semantic value different from that given the unmarked or otherwise marked character — compare ACCENT 5a

di·acromyodi \(ˌ)dī+\ *n pl, cap* [NL, fr. *di-* + *Acromyodi*] *in some classifications* **:** a group of passerine birds having the intrinsic syringeal muscles attached to both ends of the bronchial half rings — **di·acromyodian** \"+\ *adj* — **di·acromyodous** \"+\ *adj*

di·ac·ti·nal \(ˈ)dīˌaktənəl, ˌdīˌakˌtīnᵊl\ *also* **di·ac·tine** \(ˈ)dīˌakˌtīn, -ˌtən\ *adj* [*di-* + *-actinal, -actine*] *zool* **:** having two rays **:** pointed at both ends

di·ac·tine \(ˈ)dīˈakˌtīn, -ˌtən\ *or* **di·act** \ˈdīˌakt\ *also* **di·ac·tin** \(ˈ)dīˈaktən\ *n* -s [*di-* + Gk *aktin-*, *aktis* ray — more at ACTIN-] **:** a sponge spicule having two pointed arms

di·ac·tin·ic \ˌdīˌakˌtinik, -īək-\ *adj* [*dia-* + Gk *aktin-*, *aktis* + E *-ic*] **:** capable of transmitting actinic rays

di·ac·tin·ism \(ˈ)dīˈaktəˌnizəm\ *n* -s **:** the property of transmitting actinic rays

1**di·ad** \ˈdīˌad, -īəd\ *var of* DYAD

2**diad** *also* **dy·ad** \"\ *adj* [1*diad*] *crystallog* **:** having symmetry that results in repetition after every 180° rotation ⟨a ~ axis⟩

di·a·dac·tic \ˌdīəˌdaktik\ *adj* [1*diad* + *-actic* (as in *syntactic*)] *geol* **:** having reference to a bedding sequence in sediments or sedimentary rocks that is characterized by the repetition of a pair of unlike laminae ⟨the ~ structure of varved clay⟩

di·a·del·phous \ˌdīəˌdelfəs\ *adj* [*di-* + *-adelphous*] *of stamens* **:** united by the filaments into two fascicles (as in Dutchman's-breeches and most legumes) — compare MONADELPHOUS, POLYADELPHOUS

1**di·a·dem** \ˈdīəˌdem, -ədəm\ *n* -s [ME *diademe*, fr. OF, fr. L *diadema*, fr. Gk *diadēma*, fr. *diadein* to bind on both sides, bind around, fr. *dia* through, across + *dein* to bind; akin to Alb *duai* sheaf, Skt *dāman* rope — more at DIA-] **1 :** CROWN; *specif* **:** an ornamental headband worn (as by Eastern monarchs) as a badge of royalty ⟨the regal ~ —John Milton⟩ **2 :** an emblem of regal power or dignity **:** SOVEREIGNTY, EMPIRE

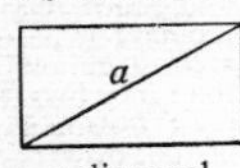

diadem 1

2**diadem** \"\ *vt* -ED/ING/-S **:** to adorn with a diadem **:** CROWN

di·a·de·ma \ˌdīəˈdēmə\ [NL, fr. L, diadem] *syn of* CENTRECHINUS

di·a·de·ma·toi·da \ˌdīəˌdēməˈtȯidə\ [NL, *Diademat-, Diadema* + *-oida*] *syn of* CENTRECHINOIDA

diadem monkey *n* **:** PLUTO MONKEY

diadem spider *n* [so called fr. its crown-shaped markings] **:** a European garden spider (*Aranea diadema*)

dia·derm \ˈdīəˌdərm\ *n* -s [*dia-* + *-derm*] **:** a blastoderm in the stage in which only ectoderm and endoderm are present

dia·dermal \ˌdīə+\ *or* **dia·dermatic** \"+\ *or* **dia·dermic** \"+\ *adj* [*dia-* + *dermal* or *dermatic* or *dermic*] **:** acting through the skin ⟨~ allergy⟩ ⟨a ~ ointment⟩

diadic *var of* DYADIC

di·ad·o·chite \dīˈadəˌkīt\ *n* -s [G *diadochit*, fr. Gk *diadochos* succeeding, relieving (fr. *diadechesthai* to succeed, relieve, fr. *dia-* + *dechesthai* to take, receive) + G *-it* -ite; akin to L *decēre* to be fitting, proper — more at DECENT] **:** a mineral $Fe_2(PO_4)(SO_4)(OH).5H_2O$ consisting of a basic hydrous ferric phosphate and sulfate that is brown or yellowish in color

di·ad·o·cho·kinesia \dīˌadəˌkō, ˌdīəˌdōkō+\ *or* **di·ad·o·ko·kinesia** \"+\ *n* -s [*diadochokinesia* fr. NL, fr. Gk *diadochos* + NL *-kinesia; diadokokinesia* fr. NL, alter. of *diadochokinesia*] **:** the normal power of alternating diametrically opposite muscular actions (as flexion and extension of a limb) — **di·ad·o·cho·kinetic** \"+\ *adj*

di·ad·o·cho·kinesis \"+\ *n* -ES [NL, fr. Gk *diadochos* + NL *-kinesis*] **:** DIADOCHOKINESIA

di·ad·ro·mous \(ˈ)dīˌadrəməs\ *adj* [*dia-* + *-dromous*] **1 :** migratory between salt and fresh waters — used of a fish; compare ANADROMOUS, CATADROMOUS **2 :** having venation that radiates like the spokes of a fan ⟨the ~ leaf of a gingko⟩

di·aene \ˈdīˌēn\ *n* -s [*di-* + tri*aene*] **:** a triaene with one ray reduced or absent

di·aer·e·sis \dīˈerəsəs, *esp Brit* -ˈi(ə)r-\ *also* **di·er·e·sis** \-ˈer-\ *n, pl* **diaere·ses** *also* **diere·ses** \-əˌsēz\ [LL *diaeresis*, fr. Gk *diairesis*, fr. *diairein* to divide (fr. *dia-* + *hairein* to take) + *-sis* — more at HERESY] **1 :** the resolution of one syllable into two esp. by separating the vowel elements of a diphthong or by resolving a *w* or *y* sound into a vowel — opposed to *syneresis* **2 :** the mark ¨ placed over a vowel (as over the second of two adjacent vowels) to indicate that the vowel is pronounced in a separate syllable (as in *naïve, Boëthius, Brontë*) — compare UMLAUT **3** *prosody* **:** the break caused by the coincidence of the end of a foot with the end of a word — distinguished from *caesura* **4 :** DIVISION 15

di·ae·ret·ic *also* **di·eret·ic** \ˌdīəˌred·ik\ *adj* [Gk *diairetikos*, fr. *diairetos* divided (verbal of *diairein* to divide) + *-ikos* -ic] **:** of or relating to diaeresis or division

diag *abbr* **1** diagonal **2** diagram

di·a·gen·e·sis \ˌdīəˈjenəsəs\ *n, pl* **diagene·ses** \-əˌsēz\ [NL, fr. *dia-* + L *genesis*] **1** *mineralogy* **:** recombination or rearrangement resulting in a new product (as in the formation of larger crystalline grains from smaller ones) **2 :** the reconstructive process by which changes are produced in sedimentary rocks during or immediately after their deposition and which is caused by such forces as the weight of overlying strata or hot waters

di·a·ge·net·ic \ˌdīəjəˌned·ik\ *adj* [*dia-* + *-genetic*] **:** caused by or relating to diagenesis ⟨~ changes that are taking place in these sediments —V.T.Allen⟩

dia·geotropic \ˌdīə+\ *adj* [*dia-* + *geotropic*] **:** characterized by diageotropism

dia·geotropism *or* **dia·geotropy** \"+\ *n, pl* **diageotropisms** *or* **diageotropies** [*dia-* + *geotropism* or *geotropy*] **:** the tropistic tendency of growing organs (as branches, rhizomes, or roots) to assume a position with the axis at right angles with the line of gravity

di·a·glyph \ˈdīəˌglif\ *n* -s [Gk *diaglyphos* hollowed out, fr. *diaglyphein* to scoop out, fr. *dia-* + *glyphein* to carve — more at CLEAVE] **:** INTAGLIO

di·a·glyph·ic \ˌdīəˌglifik\ *also* **di·a·glyp·tic** \-ˌgliptik\ *adj* [Gk *diaglyphos* & *diaglyptos* hollowed out + E *-ic*] **:** of or relating to sculpture or engraving formed by depressions in the general surface — opposed to *anaglyphic*

di·ag·nos·able *or* **di·ag·nose·able** \ˈdīəgˌnōsəbəl, -īēg- *also* -ōzə- *or* ˌ==ˈ===\ *adj* **:** capable of being diagnosed

di·ag·nose \ˈdīəgˌnōs, -īēg- *also* -ōz *or* ˌ==ˈ=\ *vb* -ED/-ING/-S [back-formation fr. *diagnosis*] *vt* **1 :** to identify (as a disease or condition) by symptoms or distinguishing characteristics **2 :** to determine the causes of or the nature of by diagnosis ⟨the teacher *diagnosed* and corrected the boy's reading difficulties⟩ ⟨roots of the change may not easily be *diagnosed* —Max De Schauensee⟩ ⟨an attempt to explain or ~ . . . the concrete historical situation of literary criticism at the present time —F.A. Pottle⟩ ~ *vi* **:** to make a diagnosis

di·ag·no·sis \ˌ==ˈnōsəs\ *n, pl* **diagno·ses** \-ōˌsēz\ [NL, fr. Gk *diagnōsis*, fr. *diagignōskein* to distinguish, fr. *dia-* + *gignōskein* to know — more at KNOW] **1 :** the art or act of identifying a disease from its signs and symptoms; *also* **:** the decision reached ⟨a ~ of pneumonia⟩ — see DIFFERENTIAL DIAGNOSIS **2 :** a concise technical description of a taxonomic entity giving its distinguishing characters **3 :** investigation or analysis of the cause or nature of a condition, situation, or problem ⟨heat-flow measurements in the earth can aid in our ~ of the earth's condition —A.E.Benfield⟩ **:** a statement or conclusion about the nature or cause of a phenomenon ⟨Arnold's ~ of the national characteristics —Herbert Read⟩

1**di·ag·nos·tic** \ˌ==ˌnästik, -tēk\ *adj* [Gk *diagnōstikos*, fr. *diagnōstos* to be distinguished (fr. *diagignōskein* to distinguish) + *-ikos* -ic] **1 :** adapted to or used for the furthering of diagnosis **:** employing or marked by the methods of diagnosis **:** concerned with diagnosis ⟨~ reading tests⟩ ⟨a ~ clinic⟩ ⟨~ social work⟩ ⟨~ information⟩ **2 :** serving to distinguish, identify, or determine **:** DISTINCTIVE: as **a :** characteristic of or indicating the presence of a particular disease ⟨a ~ sign of yellow fever —*Amer. Guide Series: La.*⟩ **b :** distinctive of the species or other group to which an animal or plant belongs ⟨a ~ character⟩ **c :** serving to identify a mineral or fossil ⟨colored by impurities so that the property is not ~ —W.J. Miller⟩ **:** indicative of the conditions of origin or the geologic age of a formation ⟨some minerals are ~ of certain source rocks —F.J.Pettijohn⟩

2**diagnostic** \"\ *n* -s **1 a :** the art or practice of diagnosis — often used in pl. ⟨his rare skill in ~*s* —T.B.Macaulay⟩ **b :** a diagnostic conclusion, opinion, or explanation ⟨a false ~⟩ **2 :** a distinguishing mark ⟨the true ~ of modern gentility is parasitism —G.B.Shaw⟩

di·ag·nos·ti·cal·ly \-tək(ə)lē, -tēk-, -li\ *adv* **:** by means of diagnosis **:** in a diagnostic manner

di·ag·nos·ti·cate \ˌ==ˈ=stəˌkāt\ *vb* -ED/-ING/-S **:** DIAGNOSE

di·ag·nos·ti·cian \-ˌnäˈstishən *sometimes* -ˌnōˈ-\ *n* -s **:** one that makes diagnoses; *esp* **:** a specialist in medical diagnostics

1**di·ag·o·nal** \(ˈ)dīˌagənᵊl, -aig-\ *adj* [L *diagonalis*, fr. Gk *diagōnios* from angle to angle (fr. *dia-* + *-gōnios*, fr. *gōnia* angle) + L *-alis* -al; akin to Gk *gony* knee — more at KNEE] **1 a :** joining two nonadjacent vertices of a rectilinear or polyhedral figure **:** running across from corner to corner **b :** passing through two nonadjacent edges of a polyhedron ⟨a ~ plane⟩ **2 a :** having a position, direction, or extension inclined from the vertical usu. at approximately 45 degrees ⟨a map with a number of ~ lines⟩ ⟨a ~ white cross on a blue ground⟩ **b :** having diagonal markings or parts ⟨a ~ weave⟩ ⟨wood with a ~ grain⟩ **3** *crystallog* **a :** having reference to certain axes of the isometric system which are the intersections between the principal and the secondary planes of symmetry **b :** having reference to the directions bisecting the angles between lateral axes in the tetragonal and hexagonal systems — **di·ag·o·nal·ly** \-gənᵊl|ē, -gnəl|, |i\ *adv*

2**diagonal** \"\ *n* -s **1 :** a straight line joining any two nonadjacent vertices of a polygon or any two vertices of a polyhedron not in the same face **2 a :** a diagonal direction **:** a diagonal row, arrangement, or pattern ⟨water bugs skated hither and thither in apparently purposeless ~*s* —S.E.White⟩ ⟨neckties with colorful ~*s*⟩ **b :** a twill weave **:** a twilled fabric esp. of wool **c :** a line of squares running obliquely across a chessboard or checkerboard ⟨one bishop moves along white ~*s*⟩ **d :** something lying in a diagonal positon (as in an inclined plane) ⟨its gable wall rises from the falling ~ of the ground —*Amer. Guide Series: Md.*⟩ **3 :** the secondary mirror in a Newtonian reflecting telescope that is used to bring the focus to the side of the tube and is usu. a flat mirror but sometimes a totally reflecting 45 degrees prism **4 :** the symbol / used esp. to denote "or" (as in *and/or*), "and or" (as in *straggler/deserter form*), "per" (as in *feet/second*), "in" or "of" (as in *U. S. Embassy/Paris*), "shilling" (as in 6/8*d*), to indicate division (as in *birth/death ratio*) or the end of a line of verse or of a display line when quoted in running text, to separate terms of quantity (as in 5 *tons*/7 *cwts*/57 *lbs*) or the figures of a date (as in 1/9/56), or to enclose phonemic rather than phonetic symbols — called also *oblique, scratch comma, separatrix, slant, solidus, virgule* **5 :** an inclined member of a truss or bracing system excepting the end post of a truss and the top chord of a roof truss whose top chords are inclined

a diagonal

diagonal biped *n* **:** a foreleg and the opposite hind leg of a quadruped — called also *diagonals*

diagonal bond *n* **:** a masonry bond in which the headers are laid diagonally

diagonal bracing *n* **:** a member of a wooden case or crate placed at an angle to adjacent members to add strength

diagonal bridging *n* **:** CROSS BRIDGING

diagonal eyepiece *n* **:** ZENITH EYEPIECE

diagonal fraction *n* **:** a fraction in which numerator and denominator are separated by a diagonal (as 1/7)

diagonal pitch *n* **:** the distance between the center of a rivet in one row and that of the nearest rivet in the next row in riveted joints having two or more rows of staggered rivets

diagonal rib *n* **:** one of the ribs in a groined arch springing from the corners in a diagonal direction

diagonal stratification *n* **:** CROSS-BEDDING

diagonial *adj or n* [Gk *diagōni*os + E *-al*] *obs* **:** DIAGONAL, OPPOSITE

1**di·a·gram** \ˈdīəˌgram, -raa(ə)m\ *n* -s [Gk *diagramma*, fr. *diagraphein* to mark out by lines, fr. *dia-* + *graphein* to write — more at CARVE] **1 :** a line drawing made for mathematical or scientific purposes **:** a mechanical drawing or geometrical figure **2 :** a graphic design that explains rather than represents **:** a drawing that shows arrangement and relations (as of parts to a whole, relative values, origins and development, chronological fluctuations, distribution) **:** CHART, GRAPH ⟨a ~ of the nervous system⟩ — see BLOCK DIAGRAM

2**diagram** \"\ *vt* **diagramed** *or* **diagrammed; diagramed** *or* **diagrammed; diagraming** *or* **diagramming; diagrams :** to represent by or put into the form of a diagram ⟨he *diagrammed* his route on the tablecloth —Willa Cather⟩

diagram factor *n, engin* **:** a numerical coefficient by which the area of an ideal indicator diagram or its mean effective pressure must be multiplied to approximate that of the probable actual indicator diagram or the probable actual mean effective pressure

di·a·gram·mat·ic \ˌdīəgrəˌmad·|ik, -mat|, |ēk\ *also* **di·a·gram·mat·i·cal** \|əkəl, |ēk-\ *adj* [*diagram* + *-atic, -atical* (as in *epigrammatic, epigrammatical*)] **:** being or relating to a diagram **:** showing by diagram **:** GRAPHIC — **di·a·gram·mat·i·cal·ly** \|ək(ə)lē, |ēk-, -li\ *adv*

di·a·gram·ma·tize \ˌdīəˈgraməˌtīz\ *vt* -ED/-ING/-S **:** to make a diagram of **:** DIAGRAM

di·a·gram·me·ter \ˈdīəˌgramˌmēd·ə(r)\ *n* -s [*diagram* + *-meter*] **:** an instrument for measuring diagrams; *esp* **:** one for measuring the ordinates of indicator diagrams

di·a·graph \ˈdīəˌgraf\ *n* -s [F *diagraphe*, fr. Gk *diagraphein* to mark out by lines — more at DIAGRAM] **:** a drawing instrument combining a protractor and scale — **di·a·graph·ic** \ˌ==ˌgrafik\ *adj*

di·a·gui·ta \ˌdēəˈgēd·ə\ *n, pl* **diaguita** *or* **diaguitas** *usu cap* [Sp, of AmerInd origin] **:** CALCHAQUI

di·a·gui·te \-d·ē\ *adj, usu cap* [*Diaguita*] **:** of or relating to the Calchaqui people

dia·heliotropism \ˌdīə+\ *n* [*dia-* + *heliotropism*] **:** diaphototropism in response to sunlight

dia·ki·ne·sis \ˌdīəkəˈnēsəs, -ˌkīˈ-\ *n, pl* **diakine·ses** \-ēˌsēz\ [NL, fr. *dia-* + *-kinesis*] **:** the final stage of the meiotic prophase immediately preceding formation of the metaphase plate and distinguished by marked contraction of the bivalents — **dia·ki·net·ic** \ˌ==(ˌ)=ˌned·ik\ *adj*

1**di·al** \ˈdī(ə)l\ *n* -s [ME *dyal*, fr. L *dies* day + ME *-al* — more at DEITY] **1 :** the face of a sundial whether horizontal, vertical, or inclined **2 a** *obs* **:** any of various timepieces (as a clock or watch) **b** *obs* **:** a mariner's compass **3 a :** the graduated face of a timepiece on which the time in hours and minutes and sometimes seconds is shown usu. by pointers or hands **b** *slang Brit* **:** the human face **4 a :** a face (as of a measuring instrument) upon which some measurement (as of force, pressure, speed) or other number is registered usu. by means of graduations and a pointer ⟨the hand of the ~ points to 50 pounds pressure⟩ **b :** a disk usu. with a knob or slot that may be turned to make electrical connections or to regulate the operation of a machine and typically with a series of markings around its border to serve as a guide for the operation ⟨increase the volume by turning the left-hand ~⟩ — see DIAL TELEPHONE **5 :** a lapidary's instrument for cutting a range of facets on a gem having a rod which holds the gem and is turnable on a ball-and-socket joint and a graduated dial and index at the other end for gauging the inclination between facets

dial 3a

2**dial** \"\ *vb* **dialed** *or* **dialled; dialed** *or* **dialled; dialing** *or* **dialling; dials** *vt* **1 :** to measure with or as if with a dial *specif* **:** to survey with a dial or circumferentor **2 a :** to manipulate a telephone dial so as to place a call to (a telephone number or subscriber) ⟨for a weather forecast one may ~ ST 1-0100⟩ ⟨~ the newspaper office⟩ **b :** to manipulate a dial so as to operate, regulate, or select ⟨~ a radio⟩ ⟨~ your favorite program⟩ ~ *vi* **1 a :** to manipulate a dial (as of a telephone or a television set) **b :** to make a call on a dial telephone **2 :** to tune, control, or regulate a radio or other apparatus by means of a dial ⟨many a radio owner, having ~*ed* into this discourse . . . ~*ed* out again —*Time*⟩

Dial \", ˈdīˌal\ *trademark* — used for diallylbarbituric acid

-di·al \-ˈdīˌal\ *n suffix* -s [ISV, fr. *di-* + *-al*] **:** containing two aldehyde groups replacing two methyl groups at the ends of an aliphatic hydrocarbon chain ⟨heptane*dial* $OCH(CH_2)_5CHO$⟩

dial *abbr* **1** dialect; dialectal **2** dialectic; dialectical; dialectics **3** dialogue

di·al·able \ˈdī(ə)ləbəl\ *adj* **:** capable of being dialed

di·al bird \ˈdī(ə)l-\ *n* [by folk etymology fr. Hindi *dahiyāl*] **:** any of several songbirds of India (as the magpie robin) related to the European robin

di·al·de·hyde \(ˈ)dī+\ *n* [*di-* + *aldehyde*] **:** a chemical compound containing two aldehyde groups

1**dialect** *n* -s [Gk *dialektos* debate, conversation, variety of language distinguished from other varieties of common origin] *obs* **:** 1DIALECTIC 1

2**di·a·lect** \ˈdīəˌlekt\ *n* -s *often attrib* [MF *dialecte*, fr. L *dialectus*, fr. Gk *dialektos*, fr. *dialegesthai* to converse — more at DIALOGUE] **1 :** a variety of language that is used by one group of persons and has features of vocabulary, grammar, or pronunciation distinguishing it from other varieties used by other groups: as **a :** a local or regional variety of language

distinguished by features of vocabulary, grammar, and pronunciation from other local or regional varieties and constituting together with them a single language of which no one variety is standard ⟨the Attic, Ionic, Aeolic, and Doric ~*s* of ancient Greek⟩ ⟨the Bavarian, Alemannic, and Franconian ~*s* of Old High German⟩ **b :** one of two or more cognate languages ⟨French and Italian are Romance ~*s*⟩ ⟨Russian and Bulgarian are Slavic ~*s*⟩ ⟨English and Sanskrit are Indo-European ~*s*⟩ **c :** a local or regional variety of a language chiefly oral and orally transmitted and differing distinctively in vocabulary, grammar, and pronunciation from other local or regional varieties and from the standard language ⟨the Lancashire ~ of English⟩ ⟨the Neapolitan ~ of Italian⟩ ⟨he knows the ~ of the southern mountains well⟩ — see MIDLAND DIALECT, NORTHERN, SOUTHERN; compare IDIOLECT
☞ In this dictionary the label *dial* is *dialect* sense 1c and is affixed to words and senses to indicate, when in combination with a specific regional label, a specific regional pattern of use and, when unqualified, a regional pattern too complex for summary, usu. including several regional varieties of American or of American and British English
d : a variety of a language that is used by the members of an occupational group in speech or writing directly concerned with their occupation and that differs from other varieties of the same language chiefly or solely in containing technical terminology ⟨the ~ of the atomic physicist⟩ **e :** a variety of a language ordinarily and habitually used by a group of persons whose identity is fixed by some factor other than geography (as social class ⟨peasant ~⟩, educational level ⟨he speaks and writes the standard ~ of his language⟩, or first language ⟨Italian-American ~⟩) **2 :** manner or means of expressing oneself esp. in language or in one of the fine arts **:** PHRASEOLOGY, STYLE ⟨this book is writ in such a ~ as may the minds of listless men affect —John Bunyan⟩ ⟨no composer of the first rank has been able to say all he wanted to without remolding the current musical language into at least a distinct ~ of his own to say it in —Gerald Abraham⟩ **3 :** the features of vocabulary, grammar, and pronunciation that distinguish a dialect (sense 1c or 1e) from the standard language ⟨some playwrights use more ~ than others⟩
syn PATOIS, CREOLE, JARGON, LINGO, SLANG, ARGOT, CANT, VERNACULAR, PATTER, along with DIALECT, are used in different meanings with varying degrees of exactness and with dissimilar value judgments involved. DIALECT is often used to designate the regional forms of a language ⟨Yorkshire *dialect*⟩ ⟨the *dialects* of Texas⟩ ⟨the following outline of Anglo-Saxon grammar is restricted to the West Saxon *dialect* —J.W.Bright⟩ This word may or may not connote marked difference from a received standard language or marked preference for that received standard language. PATOIS is likely to suggest a regional dialect, esp. one used by the unlettered ⟨the *patois* of the peasantry around Carcassonne⟩ The word is of French origin and its use is likely to be more common in Romance language areas than elsewhere. CREOLE is used mainly in reference to languages that come into existence when a politically or economically subordinate group adopts the language of a dominant group, usu. with very considerable modification ⟨the *creole* of Haiti⟩ JARGON may apply to a quickly evolved mixed linguistic form for simple communication between speakers of different languages, like Bêche-de-Mer or Pidgin English. JARGON may also signify a phase of language containing an undue number of words unfamiliar to the average speaker ⟨the technical *jargons* of sport —C.E. Montague⟩ ⟨the proper meaning of *jargon* is writing that employs technical words not commonly intelligible —Ernest Gowers⟩ LINGO, a word more common in preceding centuries than now, is often derogatory and stresses the incomprehensibility of a strange language or unfamiliar phase of one's own language ⟨a *lingo* that few people understand or care about —C.C.Furnas⟩ SLANG is likely to indicate a complex of words and constructions preferred within a limited group, esp. an informal one, to the standard language, and often more or less forceful or novel in their suggestion. ARGOT sometimes refers specif. to the forms of speech used in criminal groups ⟨the professional criminal speaks one or more *argots* in addition to colloquial English —D.W.Maurer⟩ CANT, which usu. has derogatory implications, may be applied to the language of thieves and their companions, or to the special languages of artisans or even of learned or professional groups, esp. if one wishes to ridicule, although JARGON is perhaps more common in designating the language of the latter. ⟨the pseudoscientific *cant* which is talked about the "Baconian philosophy" —T.H. Huxley⟩ VERNACULAR, with less suggestion of the derogatory than the others in this group, denotes the simple, colloquial, everyday speech of the commoner in contrast to more bookish and erudite speech ⟨his gumption, to use the *vernacular* word —William James⟩ PATTER may suggest fast, glib, voluble speech, ostensibly spontaneous, to lull or deceive ⟨the dispute resembles a conjuror's *patter* — its primary purpose is to divert attention from what is going on elsewhere —*Economist*⟩ ⟨the *patter* of a professional guide —H.S.Canby⟩ **syn** see in addition LANGUAGE

di·a·lec·tal \ˌdīəˈlektᵊl\ *adj* **:** of, belonging to, or characteristic of a dialect ⟨the ~ structure of the Eastern States —Hans Kurath⟩ — **di·a·lec·tal·ly** \-tᵊlē, -li\ *adv*

di·a·lec·tal·ism \ˌ==ˈlektəˌlizəm\ *n* -s **:** a characteristic feature of a dialect ⟨beginning to impose Castilian ~*s* on eastern León —W.J.Entwistle⟩

dialect atlas *n* **:** LINGUISTIC ATLAS

dialect geographer *n* **:** LINGUISTIC GEOGRAPHER

dialect geography *n* **:** LINGUISTIC GEOGRAPHY

di·a·lec·tic \ˌdīəˈlektik, -tēk\ *n* -s [alter. (influenced by L *dialectica*) of ME *dialetik*, fr. MF *dialetique*, fr. L *dialectica*, fr. Gk *dialektikē*, fr. fem. of *dialektikos*, adj.] **1 :** the theory and practice of weighing and reconciling juxtaposed or contradictory arguments for the purpose of arriving at truth esp. through discussion and debate: **a** *in the pre-Socratics* (1) **:** argument by critical examination of logical consequences (as the contradictory consequences of antinomies) (2) **:** sophistic reasoning **:** ERISTIC **b** *in Socrates* **:** discussion and reasoning by dialogue as a method of intellectual investigation **c** *in Plato* (1) **:** logical analysis or division of things into genera and species (2) **:** the discipline that investigates the eternal ideas esp. in their relation to those of the good, the true, and the beautiful **d** *in Aristotle* **:** a method of arguing with probability on any given problem as an art intermediate between rhetoric and strict demonstration **e** *in Stoicism* **:** formal logic as contrasted with rhetoric and grammar **2 a** *in Kantianism* **:** the logic of appearances and of illusions dealing with paralogisms, antinomies, and transcendental ideas as these arise through logical fallacies, perceptual errors, or the endeavor to use the principles of the understanding applicable only within experience for determination of such transcendental objects as the soul, the world, and God **b** *in Hegelianism* **:** a logical development progressing from less to more comprehensive levels that on its subjective side is the passage of thought from a thesis through an antithesis to a synthesis that in turn becomes a thesis for further progressions ultimately culminating in the absolute idea and on its objective side is an analogous development in the process of history and the cosmos **3** *usu* **dialectics** *pl but often sing in constr, in Marxism* **a :** the process of self-development or unfolding (as of an action, event, idea, ideology, movement, or institution) through the stages of thesis, antithesis, and synthesis in accordance with the laws of dialectical materialism **b :** a method that regards change in nature and history as taking place in this way **4** *usu* **dialectics** *pl but often sing in constr* **:** any systematic reasoning, exposition, or argument esp. in literature that juxtaposes opposed or contradictory ideas and usu. seeks to resolve their conflict ⟨the brilliant *dialectics* and irony of this comedy⟩ **:** play of ideas **:** cunning or hairsplitting disputation ⟨subtlety was foreign and *dialectics* distasteful to his character —S.H. Adams⟩ **:** argumentative skill ⟨his speech was a remarkable display of *dialectics*⟩ **5 :** the dialectical tension or opposition between two interacting forces or elements ⟨establishes a ~ between basic personality structure and institutions —Ralph Linton⟩ ⟨the ~ between Nature and Spirit —Joseph Frank⟩

di·a·lec·ti·cal \ˌdīəˈlektəkəl, -tēk-\ *also* **di·a·lec·tic** \-tik, -tēk\ *adj* [MF & L; MF *dialectique, dialetique*, fr. L *dialecticus*, fr. Gk *dialektikos*, fr. *dialektos* debate, conversation + *-ikos* -ic, -ical — more at DIALECT] **1 a :** of or relating to dialectic ⟨the ~ method⟩ ⟨the ~ process in history⟩ **:** marked by a dynamic inner tension, conflict, and interconnectedness of its parts or elements ⟨all educational situations are ~ at the core —G.E.Mueller⟩ **:** MUTUAL, RECIPROCAL ⟨a . . . fruitful ~ interplay between literary history and literary criticism —C.I.Glicksberg⟩ **b :** practicing, devoted to, or employing dialectic ⟨a ~ philosopher⟩ **:** regarding or interpreting from the point of view of dialectic ⟨a ~ approach to the problems of cultural change⟩ ⟨his thought . . . became to some extent ~; he began to conceive of life . . . as a whole which depends upon the conflict of the parts —*New Republic*⟩ **c :** of or relating to logical or systematic disputation or debate ⟨displayed great forensic and ~ skill⟩ ⟨an argument used as a ~ weapon in campaign oratory⟩ **2 :** DIALECTAL

di·a·lec·ti·cal·ly \-tək(ə)lē, -tēk-, -li\ *adv* **1 :** in a dialectical manner **:** in accordance with or on the basis of dialectic ⟨views the problem ~, in all its many-sided complexity⟩ ⟨Marxists believe that culture and economics are ~ interactive and interdependent —Melvin Rader⟩ **2 :** as regards argumentative or reasoning skill **:** LOGICALLY ⟨very agile ~, as shown by his persuasive speeches⟩

dialectical materialism *n* **1 :** the theory of reality advanced by Karl Marx and Friedrich Engels and adopted as the official Soviet philosophy combining elements of traditional materialism with the method of Hegel's dialectic and maintaining the independent objective reality of matter and its priority both in time and logical importance over mind **2 :** HISTORICAL MATERIALISM

dialectical theology *n* **:** neoorthodoxy esp. as holding against rationalism that man's attempts to know God by his own reasoning reach contradictory conclusions and must give way to a faith that awaits God's word

di·a·lec·ti·cian \ˌdīəˌlekˈtishən *sometimes* -ˌlək-\ *n* -s [MF *dialecticien*, fr. L *dialectica* + MF *-ien* -ian] **1 :** one who is skilled in or practices dialectic **:** LOGICIAN, REASONER **2 :** DIALECTOLOGIST

di·a·lec·to·log·i·cal \ˌdīəˌlektəˈläjəkəl\ *adj* **:** of or belonging to dialectology — **di·a·lec·to·log·i·cal·ly** \-jək(ə)lē\ *adv*

di·a·lec·tol·o·gist \ˌdīəˌlekˈtäləjəst *sometimes* -ˌlək-\ *n* -s **:** a specialist in dialectology

di·a·lec·tol·o·gy \-jē\ *n* -ES [ISV *dialect* + *-o-* + *-logy*] **1 :** the systematic study of dialect **2 :** the body of data available for use in the systematic study of a dialect or group of related dialects

dialects *pl of* DIALECT

dialed \ˈdī(ə)ld\ *adj* [¹*dial* + *-ed*] **:** provided with a dial ⟨a radium-*dialed* watch⟩

dial feed *n* **:** a circular conveyor that carries successive workpieces into position for action of a punch press or some other machine tool

dial gauge *or* **dial indicator** *n* **:** a gauge consisting of a circular graduated dial and a pointer actuated by a member that contacts with the part being calibrated

dialing *also* **dialling** *n* -s [fr. gerund of ²*dial*] **1 :** the art of constructing sundials **2 :** the measurement of time by sundials

di·a·lis·ter \ˌdīəˈlistə(r)\ *n, cap* [NL, fr. Gk *dia* through + *hylistēr* filter, fr. *hylazein* to filter, fr. *hylē* mud, dregs; akin to Gk *hyein* to rain — more at DIA-, SUCK] **:** a genus of minute gram-negative parasitic strictly anaerobic bacteria (family Bacterioidaceae) growing only in fresh sterile tissue or ascitic fluid, the cells occurring singly, in pairs, or in short chains

¹di·alkyl \(ˈ)dī+\ *n* [*di-* + *alkyl*] **:** a compound of two alkyl radicals with a metal ⟨zinc ~*s*⟩

²dialkyl \"\ *adj* [*di-* + *alkyl*] **:** containing two alkyl groups in the molecule

di·alkylamine \(ˌ)dī+\ *n* [*di-* + *alkylamine*] **:** an amine (as dimethylamine) containing two alkyl groups attached to amino nitrogen

di·al·lage \ˈdīəlij\ *n* -s [F, fr. Gk *diallagē* change, fr. *diallag-*, aorist stem of *diallassein* to interchange, exchange, change, fr. *dia-* + *allassein* to change, fr. *allos* other — more at ELSE] **:** a dark green or bronze-colored laminated pyroxene common in certain igneous rocks (hardness 4, sp. gr. 3.2–3.35) — **di·al·lag·ic** \ˌdīəˈlajik\ *adj*

dialled *past of* DIAL

di·al·lel \ˈdīəˌlel\ *adj* [Gk *diallēlos* reciprocating, confused, in a circle, fr. *di' allēlōn* through one another, fr. *dia* through + *allēlōn* of one another — more at PARALLEL] **:** mating according to a system in which each female is bred to each of two or more males in order to determine the relative importance of sire and dam in the transmission of certain qualities to the offspring

di·al·le·lon \ˌdīəˈlēˌlän\ *n, pl* **dialle·la** \-lə\ [Gk *diallēlon*, neut. of *diallēlos*] *logic* **:** definition in a circle

di·al·le·lus \-ləs\ *n, pl* **dialle·li** \-ˌlī\ [NL, fr. Gk *diallēlos*] **:** a reasoning in a circle

dial lock *n* **:** COMBINATION LOCK

di·al·lyl \(ˈ)dīˈalᵊl\ *adj* [ISV *di-* + *allyl*] **:** containing two allyl groups

di·al·lyl·barbituric acid \"+ . . . -\ *n* [*diallyl* + *barbituric*] **:** a white crystalline compound $C_{10}H_{12}N_2O_3$ used as a sedative and hypnotic

dialog *var of* DIALOGUE

di·a·log·ic \ˌdīəˈläjik, ǀēk *sometimes* -lōg ǀ *or* -läg ǀ\ *or* **di·a·log·i·cal** \ǀəkəl, ǀēk-\ *adj* [LL *dialogicus*, fr. Gk *dialogikos* of discourse, fr. *dialogos* debate, discourse + *-ikos* -ic, -ical — more at DIALOGUE] **1 :** having reference to or characterized by dialogue **:** consisting of dialogue or a dialogue ⟨~ writing⟩ ⟨the ~ form preferred by philosophers⟩ **2 :** taking part in dialogue — **di·a·log·i·cal·ly** \ǀək(ə)lē, ǀēk-, -li\ *adv*

di·al·o·gism \dīˈaləˌjizəm *sometimes* ˈdīəˌlōˌgi- *or* -ˌläˌg-\ *in sense 1* \ *n* -s [LL *dialogismos*, fr. Gk, fr. *dialogos* + *-ismos* -ism] **1** *archaic* **a :** the expression of an author's ideas by means of a dialogue between two or more characters **b :** DIALOGUE 2 **2 :** a disjunctive conclusion inferred from a single premise (as in "gravitation may act without contact; therefore, either some force may act without contact or gravitation is not a force")

di·al·o·gist \dīˈaləjəst *also* ˈdīəˌlōgə- *or* ˈdīəˌlägə-\ *n* -s [LL *dialogista*, fr. L *dialogus*] **1 :** one who participates in a dialogue **2 :** a writer of dialogues

di·a·lo·gis·tic \ˌdīəlōˈjistik *also* -(ˌ)lōˈgis-\ *or* **di·a·lo·gis·ti·cal** \-təkəl\ *adj* [Gk *dialogistikos*, fr. (assumed) *dialogistos* (verbal of *dialogizesthai* to debate, argue, fr. *dialogos* + *-izesthai* -ize) + *-ikos* -ic] **:** DIALOGIC

di·al·o·gite \dīˈaləˌjīt\ *n* -s [G *dialogit*, fr. Gk *dialogē* enumeration, estimate (fr. *dialegein* to pick out, fr. *dia-* + *legein* to speak) + G *-it* -ite] **:** RHODOCHROSITE

di·al·o·gize \dīˈaləˌjīz *also* -dīəˌlōˌgīz *or* ˈdīəˌläˌg-\ *vi* -ED/-ING/-S [Gk *dialogizesthai*] **:** DIALOGUE

¹di·a·logue \ˈdīəˌlōg *also* -läg\ *also* **di·a·log** \"\ *n* -s [ME *dialoge, dialogue*, fr. OF, fr. L *dialogus*, fr. Gk *dialogos*, fr. *dialegesthai* to converse, fr. *dia-* + *legesthai*, pres. middle infin. of *legein* to speak — more at LEGEND] **1 :** a written composition in which two or more characters are represented as conversing or reasoning on some topic ⟨the essay . . . is in the form of a ~ between two philosophers —*Times Lit. Supp.*⟩ **2 a :** a conversation between two or more persons ⟨he had just come from an angry ~ with his quarrelsome neighbor⟩ **:** CONVERSATION ⟨passed the time in ~⟩ **b :** an exchange of ideas and opinions; *esp* **:** a serious colloquy conducted or presented to entertain or instruct ⟨should be useful . . . in providing a genuine ~ between the English and the American intelligentsia —Stephen Spender⟩ — see DUOLOGUE; compare MONOLOGUE **3 :** the conversational element of literary or dramatic composition ⟨~ in which each phrase fits and reveals a character perfectly —Stanislaus Joyce⟩ **4 a** *obs* **:** a musical composition for two or more alternating voices typically in question and answer form **b :** any musical arrangement suggestive of a conversation ⟨the first movement, with its lovely initial ~ between wind and strings —Cecil Gray⟩

²dialogue \"\ *vb* -ED/-ING/-S *vi* **:** to take part in a dialogue ~ *vt* **:** to express in dialogue ⟨and *dialogued* for him what he would say —Shak.⟩

dialogue mass *n, often cap D & M, Roman Catholicism* **:** a low mass in which the congregation recites aloud the responses that are usu. given by the server

dial press *n* **:** a punch press with a dial-feed motion

dials *pl of* DIAL, *pres 3d sing of* DIAL

-dials *pl of* -DIAL

dial telegraph *n* **:** a telegraph in which letters and numbers or other symbols are placed upon the border of a circular dial plate at each station, the apparatus being so arranged that the needle or index of the dial at the receiving station copies the movements of that at the transmitting station

dial telephone *n* **:** a telephone from which connections may be automatically completed without the aid of an exchange operator by revolving a dial marked with numbers and letters into positions corresponding to the units of the desired telephone number

dial tone *n* **:** a characteristic tone emitted by a dial telephone as a signal that the system is ready for dialing

di·a·lu·ric acid \ˌdīəǀlu̇rik-\ *n* [ISV *di-* + *alloxan* + *uric*] **:** crystalline heterocyclic acid $C_4H_4N_2O_4$ formed by the reduction of alloxan or the oxidation of uric acid; 5-hydroxybarbituric acid

dialy- *comb form* [NL, fr. Gk *dialyein* to separate] **:** separated ⟨*dialy*carpic⟩ ⟨*dialy*petalous⟩

di·a·ly·pet·a·lae \ˌdīəlēˈpedᵊlˌē\ *n pl* [NL, fr. *dialy-* + *-petalae*] *syn of* CHORIPETALAE

di·a·ly·pet·a·lous \ǀ===ǀpedᵊləs\ *adj* [*dialy-* + *-petalous*] **:** CHORIPETALOUS

di·a·lyse \ˈdīəˌlīz\ *chiefly Brit var of* DIALYZE

di·al·y·sis \dīˈaləsəs\ *n, pl* **dialy·ses** \-əˌsēz\ [NL, fr. Gk, separation, dissolution, fr. *dialyein* to break apart, dissolve (fr. *dia-* + *lyein* to loosen) + *-sis* — more at LOSE] **1 :** the separation of substances in solution by means of semipermeable membranes (as of parchment, cellophane, or living cells) through which the smaller molecules and ions diffuse readily whereas the larger molecules and colloidal particles diffuse very slowly or not at all, such separations being important in nature (as in living organisms and in soils) and having many applications (as in blood fractionation or in the recovery of sodium hydroxide in the manufacture of viscose) — used esp. of the separation of noncolloids from colloids (as proteins); see ELECTRODIALYSIS; compare OSMOSIS, ULTRAFILTRATION **2** *bot* **:** the separation of parts which are normally united esp. in the same floral whorl

di·a·lyt·ic \ˌdīəǀlid·ik\ *adj* [Gk *dialytikos* able to sever, destructive, fr. *dialytos* capable of dissolution (fr. *dialyein* to dissolve) + *-ikos* -ic] **:** being or manifesting dialysis

di·a·lyz·able \ˈdīəˌlīzəbəl\ *adj* **:** capable of being dialyzed or of dialyzing; *esp* **:** capable of diffusing through a dialyzing membrane

di·al·y·zate \dīˈaləˌzāt\ *or* **di·al·y·sate** \-əˌsāt\ *n* -s [ISV *dialyze, dialyse* + *-ate*] **:** a product of dialysis — used either of the material that has failed to diffuse through the membrane or of the diffusate

di·a·lyze \ˈdīəˌlīz\ *vb* -ED/-ING/-S [fr. NL *dialysis*, after such pairs as NL *analysis* **:** E *analyze*] *vt* **:** to subject to dialysis **:** separate or obtain by dialysis ~ *vi* **:** to undergo dialysis **:** diffuse through a suitable membrane

di·a·lyz·er \-zə(r)\ *n* -s **:** an apparatus in which dialysis is carried out consisting essentially of one or more containers for liquids separated into compartments by membranes in any of various forms (as a sheet, bag, or tube)

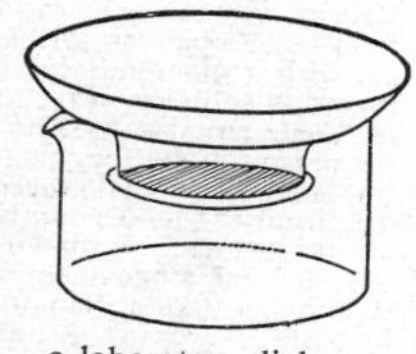
a laboratory dialyzer

diam *abbr* diameter

dia·magnet \ˈdīə+\ *n* -s [back-formation fr. ¹*diamagnetic*] **:** a substance that exhibits diamagnetism

¹dia·magnetic \"+\ *adj* [*dia-* + *magnetic*] **:** having a magnetic permeability less than that of a vacuum **:** having negative magnetic susceptibility ⟨~ bodies are feebly repelled by a strong magnet⟩ — compare PARAMAGNETIC — **dia·magnetically** \"+\ *adv*

²dia·magnetic \"+\ *n* -s **:** DIAMAGNET

dia·magnetism \"+\ *n* [*dia-* + *magnetism*] **:** the property of being diamagnetic **:** the characteristic phenomena exhibited by diamagnetic bodies

¹di·a·man·té \ˌdēəˌmänˈtā\ *adj* [F, fr. past part. of *diamanter* to set with diamonds or paste brilliants, fr. *diamant* diamond — more at DIAMOND] **:** decorated with diamanté

²diamanté \"\ *n* -s **:** sparkling decoration consisting usu. of paste brilliants or glass used esp. on evening gowns; *also* **:** a fabric so decorated

di·a·man·tif·er·ous \ˌdī(ə)mənˈtif(ə)rəs, ˌdēəm-\ *adj* [F *diamantifère*, fr. *diamant* diamond + *-i-* + *-fère* -ferous] **:** DIAMONDIFEROUS

di·a·man·tine \ˌdīəˈmanˌtīn, -tēn, -antᵊn\ *adj* [F *diamantin*, fr. *diamant* diamond + *-in* -ine] **:** consisting of or resembling diamond

di·a·mat \ˈdīəˌmat\ *n* -s [*dia*lectical *mat*erialism] **:** DIALECTICAL MATERIALISM

di·amb \ˈdīˌam *also* -mb\ *or* **di·iamb** \(ˈ)dīˌīˌa-\ *n, pl* **diambs** *or* **diiambs** \-mz\ *n* -s [LL *diiambus*, fr. Gk *diiambos*, fr. *di-* + *iambos* iamb] **:** a metrical foot consisting of two iambs **:** an iambic dipody reckoned as a single compound foot **:** a double iamb — **di·am·bic** \(ˈ)dīˈambik\ *or* **di·iam·bic** \ˌdīˌīˌa-\ *adj*

di·am·e·ter \dīˈaməd·ə(r), -mətə-\ *n* -s [ME *diametre*, fr. MF, fr. L *diametros*, fr. Gk *diametros*, fr. *dia-* + *-metros* (fr. *metron* measure) — more at MEASURE] **1 a :** a chord passing through the center of a figure or body (as a circle, conic section, sphere, cube) **b :** a line that bisects each of a system of parallel chords of a curve **c :** a unit of magnification of microscopic and telescopic observations equal to the number of times the linear dimensions of the object are increased ⟨a magnification of eight ~*s* means the dimensions are increased in the ratio of 8:1⟩ **2 a :** the length of a straight line through the center of an object **:** THICKNESS ⟨a tree two feet in ~ at the base of the trunk⟩ ⟨a rope one inch in ~ measured at its greatest dimension⟩ **b :** the distance through a column at its base used in architecture as a standard measure for all parts of an order — see MODULE **c :** one of the maximal breadths of a part of the body

diameter tape *n* **:** a measuring tape so scaled that when it encircles a tree trunk the diameter is read directly

di·am·e·tral \(ˈ)dīˈamə·trəl\ *adj* [MF, fr. *diametre* + *-al*] **1 :** of or relating to a diameter **:** located at the diameter **:** constituting a diameter ⟨the ~ plane⟩ **2** *obs* **:** DIAMETRIC 2

diametral curve *or* **diametral surface** *n* **:** any line or surface that bisects a system of parallel chords of a curve or surface

diametral pitch *n* **:** a ratio equal to the pitch diameter of a gear in inches divided by the number of teeth in the gear

diametral plane *n* **1 :** a plane bisecting a system of parallel chords of a quadric surface; *specif* **:** any plane through the center of a sphere **2** *of a linear complex* **:** a plane conjugate to a point at infinity

di·a·met·ric \ˌdīəǀme·trik, -rēk\ *or* **di·a·met·ri·cal** \-rəkəl, -rēk-\ *adj* [Gk *diametrikos*, fr. *diametros* + *-ikos* -ic, -ical] **1 :** DIAMETRAL 1 **2 :** completely opposed or opposite as if at the opposite end of a diameter ⟨in ~ contradiction to his claims⟩

di·a·met·ri·cal·ly \-rək(ə)lē, -rēk-, -li\ *adv* **1 :** as if at opposite ends of a diameter ⟨differing ~ from the earlier conception⟩ **:** COMPLETELY, UTTERLY ⟨ideas ~ opposite to his own⟩ **2 :** at or along the diameter **:** in the direction of the diameter

di·amide \(ˈ)dī+\ *n* [ISV *di-* + *amide*] **1 :** any compound containing two amido groups **2 :** HYDRAZINE

di·amidine \"+\ *n* [*di-* + *amidine*] **:** any compound containing two amidino groups (as stilbamidine)

diamido- *comb form* [ISV, fr. *di-* + *amid-*] **:** containing two amido groups — esp. in names of inorganic acids ⟨*diamido*phosphoric acid $HPO_2(NH_2)_2$⟩

di·amine \(ˈ)dī+\ *n* [ISV *di-* + *amine*] **:** any compound containing two amino groups

diamine black BH *n, often cap D&B* **:** a direct blue disazo dye that can be converted into a navy blue or black developed dye on the fiber — called also *developed black BH;* see DYE table I (under *Direct Blue 2*)

diamine dye *n, often cap 1st D* **:** any of numerous direct dyes — see DYE table I
diamine oxidase *n* **:** HISTAMINASE
diamino- *comb form* [ISV *di-* + *amin-*] **:** containing two amino groups — used in names of organic compounds ⟨2, 6-*diamino*purine⟩
di·ami·no \ˌdīə¦mē(ˌ)nō, (ˈ)dī¦amə,nō\ *adj* [*diamino-*] **:** relating to or containing two amino or substituted amino groups
di·ami·no·diphenyl sulfone \"+ . . . -\ *n* [ISV *diamino-* + *diphenyl*] **:** a crystalline compound $(NH_2C_6H_4)_2SO_2$ that like certain of its derivatives is used in the treatment of leprosy; 4, 4′-sulfonyl-di-aniline
Di·a·mi·no·gen \ˌdīə¦mēnəjən, -ˌjen\ *trademark* — used for a direct dye; see DYE table I (under *Direct Blue 126*)
di·ammonium \ˌdī+\ *adj* [*di-* + *ammonium*] **:** containing two ammonium radicals
diammonium phosphate *n* **:** AMMONIUM PHOSPHATE
¹di·a·mond \ˈdī(ə)mənd\ *n* -s [ME *diamaunt, diamaunde,* fr. MF *diamant, diamande,* fr. LL *diamant-, diamas,* alter. of (assumed) VL *adimant-, adimas* hardest iron or steel, diamond, fr. Gk *adamant-, adamas*] **1 a :** native carbon crystallized in the isometric system often in the form of octahedrons with rounded edges and usu. nearly colorless that when transparent and more or less free from flaws is highly valued as a precious stone because having high refractive and dispersive powers it shows when faceted a remarkable brilliance and play of prismatic colors and that when off-color or flawed is invaluable for industrial purposes (as for use in wire dies, abrasive powder, rock drills, and turning tools) because it is the hardest substance known (hardness 10, sp. gr. 3.52) — see WATER 7a; BRILLIANT 1, ROSE, TABLE DIAMOND; BORT **b :** a piece of this material **c :** a crystalline mineral that is like diamond in brilliance — used with a qualifying name; see ALENÇON DIAMOND **d :** crystallized carbon similar to the native but produced by artificial means **2** *obs* **:** a very hard substance **:** ADAMANT **3 a :** something that resembles a diamond (as in value, rarity, or brilliance) **b :** a person possessing very high character or other fine qualities **4 :** a square or rhombus-shaped configuration usu. having a distinctive orientation (as by having a diagonal perpendicular to the horizontal) **5 :** something shaped like a diamond; *specif* **:** any of the small diamond-shaped marks at regular intervals on the cushions of an American billiard table to aid the player in calculating the angles of his shots **6 a :** a red lozenge impressed on a playing card; *also* **:** a card marked with such lozenges **b diamonds** *pl but sing or pl in constr* **:** the suit comprising cards so marked **c** *bridge* **:** an odd trick won or contracted for with diamonds trumps ⟨four ~*s* bid and made⟩ **7 :** a tool holding a diamond; *specif* **:** any of several instruments varying in shape, size, and surfaces featuring diamond bonded on a metallic base and used typically in dental work and for cutting glass **8 :** an old size of printing type (approximately 4½ point) between brilliant and pearl — compare POINT SYSTEM **9 a :** the area of a baseball or softball field enclosed in a square with a base at each corner — called also *infield* **b :** the entire playing field in baseball or softball **10 :** something ornamented or set with a diamond; *specif* **:** an engagement ring set with a diamond solitaire **11 :** RERAILER **12 diamonds** *pl but sing in constr* **:** DIAMOND-SKIN DISEASE — **diamond in the rough :** a person of sterling character or other exceptional qualities but lacking in social graces or refinement of manner

diamond 4

²diamond \"\ *adj* **1 :** consisting or made of diamond **2 :** BRIGHT, SPARKLING ⟨the ~ dawn of a golden winter day —L.C. Stevens⟩ **3 :** ornamented or set with a diamond ⟨~ tiara⟩ **4 :** shaped like a diamond **:** having diamond-shaped figures or parts ⟨~ weave⟩ **5 :** of, relating to, or marking a 60th or a 75th anniversary
³diamond \"\ *vt* -ED/-ING/-S **:** to adorn with or as if with diamonds ⟨the grass is ~*ed* with cobwebs of dew —Stuart Kinzie⟩
di·a·mond albumin test \ˈdī(ə)mənd-\ *n, usu cap D* [after Louis S. *Diamond* b1920 Am. parasitologist] **:** a test for blocking antibodies (as in the Rh system) by use of red blood cells suspended in concentrated serum albumin — compare RH FACTOR
diamond anniversary *n* **:** a 60th or 75th anniversary
¹diamondback \ˈ=(=)=,=\ *n* **1 :** DIAMONDBACK RATTLESNAKE **2 :** DIAMONDBACK TERRAPIN **3 :** DIAMONDBACK MOTH
²diamondback \ˈ=(=)=,=\ *also* **diamond–backed** \ˈ=(=)=¦=\ *adj* **:** having marks like diamonds or lozenges on the back
diamondback moth *n* **:** a nearly cosmopolitan moth (*Plutella xylostella*) of European origin whose larva is a pest on cruciferous crops — called also *cabbage moth*
diamondback rattlesnake *n* **:** the largest and most deadly snake (*Crotalus adamanteus*) of No. America inhabiting the southern U.S. and sometimes attaining a length of eight feet
diamondback terrapin *n* **:** any of several terrapins constituting a genus *Malaclemys* and formerly widely distributed in salt marshes along the Atlantic and Gulf coasts from Buzzards Bay southward but now exterminated from much of the northern part of their range — see TERRAPIN illustration
diamondback water snake *n* **:** a harmless water snake (*Natrix rhombifera*) of southern No. America having a series of dark diamond-shaped marks along the back
diamond ball *n* **:** SOFTBALL
diamond bird *n* **1 :** any of several Australian flower-peckers (genus *Pardalotus*) sometimes kept as cage birds — called also *diamond sparrow, pardalote* **2 :** DIAMOND SPARROW 1
diamond bracket *n* **:** BRACKET 4b
diamond canker *n* **:** a virus disease of stone-fruit trees characterized esp. by corky roughening and thickening of the bark and by progressive weakening of the tree
diamond cement *n* **:** a cement used for setting diamonds (as a solution of mastic and isinglass in alcohol)
diamond chip *n* **:** CHIP 1e(2)
diamond crossing *n* **:** a railroad crossing in which the rails cross obliquely forming a diamond-shaped center
diamond dash *n* **:** a graphic character —◆— sometimes used to mark page or column divisions in printed matter — called also *swell dash*
diamond die *n* **:** a wiredrawing die made of diamond for drawing fine wire of hard metals (as tungsten)
diamond dove *n* **:** a small Australian dove (*Geopelia cuneata*) often kept as a cage or aviary bird that is largely gray and brown with the wings dotted with white
diamond dresser *n* **:** a tool carrying industrial diamond for dressing or truing the surface of a grinding wheel
diamond drill *n* **:** a usu. annular drill faced with bort diamonds and used for rock boring
diamond dust *n* **:** powdered or crushed diamond used as an abrasive — called also *diamond powder*
diamond dye *n, often cap 1st D* **:** any of several mordant or acid dyes — see DYE table I
di·a·mond·ed \ˈdī(ə)məndəd\ *adj* **1 :** ²DIAMOND 4 ⟨the windows had ~ panes —Edith Sitwell⟩ **2 :** adorned with or as if with diamonds ⟨he went ever gold-laced, highly powdered, scented, and ~ —Charles Reade⟩ **:** DIAMONDIZED
diamond–fish \ˈ=(=)=,=\ *n, Austral* **:** DEVILFISH 1
diamond flounder *n* **:** a large mottled brown flatfish (*Hypsopsetta guttulata*) of the coast of California — called also *diamond turbot*
diamond flower *n* **:** a low-growing tufted Portuguese annual herb (*Ionopsidium acaule*) of the family Cruciferae with rounded leaves and light violet flowers
diamond hitch *n* **:** a knot used in tying a pack on an animal so that the interlacing ropes form a diamond on the top of the pack
di·a·mon·dif·er·ous \ˌdī(ə)mən¦dif(ə)rəs\ *adj* [*diamond* + *-i-* + *-ferous*] **:** yielding diamonds ⟨~ earth⟩
diamond indentor *or* **diamond indenter** *n* **:** an instrument for measuring hardness by the depth of the indentation made by a pyramidal diamond point under a given load
diamonding *n* -s [¹*diamond* + *-ing*] **:** a distortion in wood usu. occurring during drying and resulting in a change in cross section from rectangular to diamond shape
di·a·mond·ize \ˈdī(ə)mən,dīz\ *vt* -ED/-ING/-S **1 :** to set with diamonds **:** ADORN, ENRICH **2 :** to change into diamond

diamond jubilee *n* **:** a diamond anniversary or its celebration
diamond knot *n* **:** a diamond-shaped knot tied in the strands of a rope used esp. to provide a foothold on a footrope
diamond–leaf laurel *n* **:** an Australian tree (*Pittosporum rhombifolium*) resembling a laurel of pyramidal habit
diamond mortar *n* **:** a small steel mortar used for pulverizing hard substances
diamond paste *n* **:** diamond dust in a jelly or oil used as an abrasive
diamond pencil *n* **:** a tool tipped with diamond (as for ruling gratings on metal)
diamond plate *n* **1 :** a steel plate spread with diamond dust and oil for rubbing down gems **2 :** a diamond-shaped plate or strap in a ship forming a connection and brace for the flanges of two frames or where they cross

diamond knot

diamond point *n* **1 :** an instrument (as a stylus or cutting tool) with a diamond tip **2 a :** a diamond-shaped figure formed by intersecting rails at a railroad diamond crossing **b :** one of the acute angles formed at this crossing
diamond–point \ˈ=(=)=,=\ *or* **diamond–pointed** \¦=(=)=¦==\ *adj* **:** having a point that is diamond-shaped or rhombus-shaped ⟨~ tool⟩
diamond–point chisel *n* **:** a cold chisel having a diamond-shaped cutting face for cutting V grooves or sharp internal corners
diamond powder *n* **:** DIAMOND DUST
diamond rattlesnake *n* **:** DIAMONDBACK RATTLESNAKE
diamonds *pl of* DIAMOND, *pres 3d sing of* DIAMOND
diamond saw *n* **:** a circular disk in the edge of which diamond dust or carbon diamonds are set to form a saw suitable for cutting hard material (as stone)
Di·a·mond·scope \ˈ=(=)=,skōp\ *trademark* — used for a low-power microscope fitted with a special illuminator for use in examining diamonds
diamond–skin disease *also* **diamond skin** *n* **:** a mild urticarial form of swine erysipelas characterized by 4-angled red patches on the skin
diamond snake *n* **1 :** a snake of a variety of the carpet snake restricted to parts of the east coast of Australia and distinguished by smaller size, darker color, and reduction of the pattern to diamond-shaped clusters of spots **2** *in Tasmania* **:** COPPERHEAD 1b
diamond sparrow *n* **1 :** an Australian weaverbird (*Zonaeginthus guttatus*) having white-spotted sides and a bright red tail base — called also *firetail* **2 :** DIAMOND BIRD 1
diamond stack *n* **:** a smokestack with a diamond-shaped top used on early steam locomotives
diamond tooth *n* **:** a compound tooth for crosscut saws
diamond truer *n* **:** a grinding wheel truer consisting usu. of a short steel rod inserted in a wooden handle and having in its free end a carbon diamond **:** DIAMOND DRESSER
diamond turbot *n* **:** DIAMOND FLOUNDER
diamond wedding *n* **:** a diamond anniversary of a wedding
diamond wheel *n* **:** a grinding wheel for very hard materials (as gems or tungsten carbide) using diamond dust as abrasive
diamondwork \ˈ=(=)=,=\ *n* **:** masonry in which pieces are set so as to form diamond-shaped patterns on the surface
dia·morphine \ˌdīə+\ *n* [*diacetyl* + *morphine*] **:** HEROIN
di·ana \dīˈanə\ *n* -s *often cap* [fr. the name *Diana*] **:** SQUILL BLUE
di·ana butterfly \(ˈ)dī¦anə-\ *n, usu cap D* [NL *diana* (specific epithet of *Speyeria diana*), fr. L *Diana*, Roman goddess of the moon, moon; fr. the silvery crescents on the wings] **:** a large butterfly (*Speyeria diana*) mainly of the southern Appalachian region, the male being brown above with a fulvous border and the female bluish black with blue spots
diana monkey *n, usu cap D* [NL *diana* (specific epithet of *Cercopithecus diana*), fr. L *Diana;* fr. the white crescent on the forehead] **:** a white-bearded monkey (*Cercopithecus diana*) of western Africa
di·an·drous \(ˈ)dī¦andrəs\ *adj* [*di-* + *-androus*] **1 :** having two stamens **2** *of a moss* **:** having two antheridia associated with each bract
di·ane pigment \(ˈ)dī¦an-\ *n, usu cap D* [prob. fr. the name *Diane*] **:** either of two organic pigments — see DYE table I (under *Pigment Blue 25* and *Pigment Orange 16*)
di·anisidine \ˌdī+\ *n* [ISV *di-* + *anisidine*] **:** BIANISIDINE — used chiefly commercially ⟨~ blue⟩
di·a·nite \ˈdīə,nīt\ *n* -s [G *dianit*, fr. NL *dianium* new metal held to be contained in dianite (fr. L *Diana* + *-ium*) + G *-it* -ite] **:** a variety of columbite
di·no·et·ic \ˌdīənō¦edˌik\ *adj* [Gk *dianoētikos*, fr. *dianoētos* (verbal of *dianoeisthai* to think) + *-ikos* -ic] **:** of or relating to dianoia **:** INTELLECTUAL
dianoetic virtue *n, Aristotelianism* **:** INTELLECTUAL VIRTUE
di·a·noia \ˌdīəˈnȯiə *also* -ōiyə\ *n* -s [Gk, fr. *dianoeisthai* to have in mind, think, fr. *dia-* + *nous* mind] **1 :** the capacity for, process of, or result of discursive thinking **2 :** OPINION 6 — contrasted with *noesis*
di·an·the·ra \dīˈan(t)thərə\ [NL, fr. *di-* + *-anthera*] *syn of* JUSTICIA
di·an·thus \dīˈan(t)thəs\ *n* [Gk *dios* heavenly + NL *-anthus* — more at DEITY] **1** *cap* **:** a very large and horticulturally important Old World genus of herbs (family Caryophyllaceae) including the pinks and carnations and distinguished by the cylindrical many-veined calyx with bracts at its base **2** -ES **:** any plant or flower of the genus *Dianthus* **3** -ES **:** a grayish to moderate red that is yellower and darker than Cambridge red
di·a·pasm \ˈdīə,pazəm\ *n* -s [L *diapasma*, fr. Gk *diapasma*, fr. *diapassein* to sprinkle, fr. *dia-* + *passein* to sprinkle — more at QUASH] *archaic* **:** a perfume of powdered aromatic herbs sometimes made into little balls and strung together
di·a·pa·son \ˌdīəˈpāzᵊn, -āsᵊn, *attrib* ¦==¦=\ *n* -s [ME *dyapason*, fr. L *diapason*, fr. Gk (*hē*) *dia pasōn* (*chordōn symphōnia*) the concord through all the notes, fr. *dia* through + *pasōn*, gen. pl. fem. of *pas* all — more at DIA-, PAN-] **1 a** (1) **:** the interval or consonance of the octave in Greek music (2) **:** a part in music sounding such a consonance (3) *obs* **:** complete accord, harmony, or agreement **b** (1) **:** a burst of harmonious sound **:** MELODY, STRAIN ⟨the sweet ~ of their girlish voices⟩ (2) **:** any full deep outburst of sound ⟨ugly, deep-throated sounds wove themselves together in a ~ of protest —Hodding Carter⟩ ⟨the foghorn sent deep ~*s* of sound rolling through the fog⟩ **c :** one of the two principal foundation stops in the organ extending through the complete scale of the instrument **d** (1) **:** the entire compass of musical tones (2) **:** the entire compass, scope, or range (as of an activity or other phenomenon) ⟨the vast ~ of his poetic talent⟩ ⟨the unchanging ~ of life in a small country town⟩ **2 a :** TUNING FORK **b :** a measure for determining the construction (as of flutes, oboes, organ pipes) so that the correct pitches may be produced **c :** a standard of pitch — see DIAPASON NORMAL
di·a·pa·son·al \ˌdīə¦pāzᵊnᵊl, -ās|, |nəl\ *adj* **:** relating to or like a diapason
diapason normal *n* [F, lit., normal diapason] **:** the standard pitch adopted by the French government in 1859 establishing A above middle C as 435 vibrations per second — called also *French pitch, international pitch, low pitch*
¹di·a·pause \ˈdīə,pȯz\ *n* [Gk *diapausis* pause, fr. *diapauein* to conclude, pause (fr. *dia-* + *pauein* to stop) + *-sis* — more at PAUSE] **:** a period of spontaneous dormancy independent of environmental conditions interrupting developmental activity in an embryo, larva, or pupa or arresting reproductive activity in an adult insect and usu. occurring during hibernation or aestivation; *sometimes* **:** a comparable period of dormancy intervening between two periods of activity in other forms (as in certain mammalian embryos) ⟨after the ~ of winter —P.H.Holloway⟩
²diapause \"\ *vi* **:** to undergo diapause — used chiefly as the present participle ⟨*diapausing* larvae⟩
di·a·pe·de·sis \ˌdīəpəˈdēsəs\ *n, pl* **diapede·ses** \-ē,sēz\ [NL, fr. Gk *diapēdēsis* act of leaping through, oozing through, fr. *diapēdan* to leap through, ooze through (fr. *dia-* + *pēdan* to leap) + *-sis* — more at PEDESIS] **1 :** the passage of blood cells through capillary walls into the tissues; *esp* **:** active amoeboid passage of leukocytes between the enclosing endothelial cells **2 :** loss of blood (as through a mucous membrane) without detectable gross lesions — **di·a·pe·det·ic** \¦===¦ded·ik\ *adj*

di·a·pen·sia \ˌdīəˈpensēə\ *n* [NL, perh. irreg. fr. Gk *dia pente* by fives + NL *-ia;* fr. the five-leaved calyx] **1** *cap* **:** a genus (the type of the family Diapensiaceae) of boreal dwarf evergreen plants with small crowded coriaceous leaves and flowers on short peduncles **2** -s **:** any plant of the genus *Diapensia*
di·a·pen·si·a·ce·ae \ˌdīə,pensēˈāsē,ē\ *n pl, cap* [NL, fr. *Diapensia*, type genus + *-aceae*] **:** a family (coextensive with the order Diapensiales or included in Ericales) of chiefly north temperate low evergreen plants having pentamerous flowers and epipetalous stamens and the ovary trilocular — compare GALAX, PYXIDANTHERA — **di·a·pen·si·aceous** \ˌ==¦==¦āshəs\ *adj*
di·a·pen·si·a·les \ˌdīə,pensēˈā(ˌ)lēz\ *n pl, cap* [NL, fr. *Diapensia* + *-ales*] *in some classifications* **:** an order of low evergreen plants distinguished from those of the order Ericales by a tricarpellate ovary and stamens in two whorls of which one is reduced to staminodia — see DIAPENSIACEAE
di·a·pen·te \ˌdīəˈpentē, -en·,tē\ *n* -s [ME, fr. L, fr. Gk (*hē*) *dia pente* (*chordōn symphōnia*) the concord through five notes, fr. *dia* through + *pente* five — more at DIA-, FIVE] **:** the interval or consonance of the fifth in ancient music
¹di·a·per \ˈdī(ə)pə(r)\ *n* -s [ME *diapre*, fr. *MF diapre, diaspre*, fr. ML *diasprum*, prob. fr. neut. of *diasprus* made of diaper, fr. MGk *diaspros* pure white, fr. Gk *dia* through, throughout + MGk *aspros* white — more at DIA-, ASPER] **1 :** a fabric with a distinctive pattern: **a :** a rich silk fabric **b** *also* **diaper cloth :** a soft usu. white linen or cotton fabric used for tablecloths, towels, and now chiefly for infants' wear **2 a** *archaic* **:** a towel or napkin **b :** a basic garment for infants consisting usu. of a piece of folded cloth or other absorbent material drawn up between the legs and fastened about the waist **3 :** an allover pattern consisting of one or more small repeated units of design (as geometric figures) connecting with one another or growing out of one another with continuously flowing or straight lines

examples of diaper pattern

²diaper \"\ *vb* **diapered; diapered; diapering** \-p(ə)riŋ\ **diapers** [ME *diapren*, fr. MF *diaprer, diasprer*, fr. *diapre, diaspre*] *vt* **1 :** to ornament with diaper designs **:** weave (cloth) in diaper patterns **:** make (a figure) in diaper pattern **2 :** to put on or change the diaper of (an infant) ~ *vi* **:** to draw diaper patterns (as on cloth)
diapered *adj* [ME *diapred*, fr. past part. of *diapren*] **:** having a design of or resembling a diaper pattern
diapering *n* -s **:** the act of ornamenting with diaper; *also* **:** the work or ornamentation
diaper rash *n* **:** an inflammation of the buttocks of infants; *esp* **:** the condition caused by exposure to excessive urinary ammonia
diaper service *n* **1 :** a business concern that supplies and launders diapers **2 :** the supplying and laundering of diapers carried out by a diaper service
diaphan- *or* **diaphano-** *comb form* [ME *diaphan-*, fr. MF, fr. *diaphane*] **:** transparent ⟨*diaphano*scopy⟩ **:** transparency ⟨*diaphano*meter⟩
¹di·a·phane \ˈdīə,fān\ *adj* [MF, fr. ML *diaphanus*] *archaic* **:** DIAPHANOUS
²diaphane \"\ *n* -s **1 :** a diaphanous substance **2 :** a complex resinous medium for microscopic mounts having a rather low refractive index and comparatively slight tendency to react with stains
di·aph·a·ne·i·ty \(ˌ)dī,afəˈnēəd·ē, ˌdīəfə-\ *n* -ES [F *diaphanéité*, fr. *diaphane* diaphanous + *-ité* -ity] **:** the quality or state of being diaphanous; *specif* **:** the ability of a mineral to transmit light
di·aph·a·nie \dīˈafənē\ *n* -s [F, fr. *diaphane* + *-ie* -y] **:** the art of imitating stained glass with translucent paper
di·aph·a·nom·e·ter \dī,afəˈnäməd·ə(r)\ *n* -s [*diaphan-* + *-meter*] **:** an instrument for measuring transparency (as of air or liquids) — **di·aph·a·no·met·ric** \=¦==nō¦me·trik\ *adj*
di·aph·a·no·scope \dīˈafənō,skōp\ *n* -s [ISV *diaphan-* + *-scope*] **:** a device for examining the accessory nasal sinuses of domestic animals — **di·aph·a·nos·co·py** \=,==ˈnäskəpē\ *n* -ES
di·aph·a·nous \(ˈ)dīˈafənəs\ *adj* [ML *diaphanus*, fr. Gk *diaphanēs*, fr. *diaphainein* to show through, fr. *dia-* + *phainein* to show — more at FANCY] **1 :** characterized by such fineness and delicacy of texture as to permit seeing through usu. with a high degree of clarity ⟨~ gowns of chiffon, lace, or net⟩ ⟨~ water through which fish may be clearly seen⟩ **2 :** composed or arranged to permit ready perception or comprehension of an inner or veiled essence or substance ⟨I like ~ illusions, with the shapes of things as they are showing not too faintly through them —L.P.Smith⟩ **3 :** characterized by extreme delicacy of form **:** ETHEREAL ⟨poetic and ~ landscapes —Wolfgang Born⟩ ⟨the fantastic, the ~, airy scherzo, nimble-footed and delicate, like a fairy's dance —Hugo Leichtentritt⟩ **4 :** INSUBSTANTIAL, VAGUE ⟨the ~ possibility, becoming each day more amorphous —Donn Byrne⟩ **syn** see CLEAR
di·aph·a·nous·ly *adv* **:** in a diaphanous manner
di·aph·a·nous·ness *n* -ES **:** the quality or state of being diaphanous
di·a·phone \ˈdīə,fōn\ *n* -s [*dia-* + *-phone*] **1 :** all the variants of a phoneme that occur in all utterances of all speakers of a language ⟨in French the tongue-trilled *r* used by some speakers and the uvula-trilled *r* used by other speakers belong to the same ~⟩ **2 :** a fog signal similar to a siren **3 :** a powerful pipe-organ stop of peculiar construction of 8-foot, 16-foot, or 32-foot pitch
di·a·pho·neme \ˌdīəˈfō,nēm, ˈdīə(ˌ)fō,n-\ *n* [*dia-* + *phoneme*] **:** a category or a member of a category consisting of the entire range of dialectal variants of an allophone — **di·a·pho·ne·mic** \ˌdīəfō¦nēmik\ *adj*
¹di·a·phon·ic \ˌdīə¦fänik\ *adj* [*diaphony* + *-ic*] **:** of or relating to diaphony
²diaphonic \"\ *adj* [*diaphone* + *-ic*] **1 :** of or relating to a diaphone **2 :** using a single symbol for an entire diaphone ⟨a ~ transcription⟩
di·aph·o·ny \dīˈafənē\ *also* **di·a·pho·nia** \ˌdīəˈfōnēə\ *n, pl* **diaphonies** *also* **diaphonias** [ML *diaphonia*, fr. Gk *diaphōnia*, fr. *diaphōnos* dissonant, (fr. *dia-* + *-phōnos*, fr. *phōnē* sound) + *-ia* — more at BAN] **1** *Greek music* **:** DISSONANCE — opposed to *symphony* **2** *medieval music* **:** ORGANUM 2b
di·aph·o·rase \dīˈafə,rās, -āz\ *n* -s [Gk *diaphoros* different + E *-ase*] **:** a flavoprotein enzyme capable of oxidizing the reduced form of diphosphopyridine nucleotide or of triphosphopyridine nucleotide at the expense of some nonphysiological electron acceptor (as the dye methylene blue)
di·a·pho·re·sis \ˌdīəfəˈrēsəs\ *n, pl* **diaphore·ses** \-ē,sēz\ [LL, fr. Gk *diaphorēsis*, fr. *diaphorein* to dissipate by perspiration, fr. *dia-* + *phorein* to carry, fr. *pherein* to carry) + *-sis* — more at BEAR] **:** PERSPIRATION; *esp* **:** profuse perspiration artificially induced
¹di·a·pho·ret·ic \¦===¦red·ik\ *adj* [LL *diaphoreticus*, fr. Gk *diaphorētikos*, fr. *diaphorētos* (verbal of *diaphorein*) + *-ikos* -ic] **:** having the power to increase perspiration
²diaphoretic \"\ *n* -s **:** an agent inducing sweating
di·aph·o·rite \dīˈafə,rīt\ *n* -s [G *diaphorit*, fr. Gk *diaphoros* different + G *-it* -ite] **:** a mineral $Pb_2Ag_3Sb_3S_8$ consisting of sulfide of lead, silver, and antimony in orthorhombic crystals
dia·phototropism \ˌdīə+\ *n* [*dia-* + *phototropism*] **:** the tropistic tendency of leaves to turn their upper surfaces to face a source of illumination
¹di·a·phragm \ˈdīə,fram, -raa(ə)m\ *n* -s [ME *diafragma*, fr. LL *diaphragma*, fr. Gk, partition, diaphragm, fr. *diaphrassein, diaphrattein* to barricade, fr. *dia-* + *phrassein, phrattein* to enclose, fence in — more at FARCE] **1 :** a body

partition of muscle and connective tissue; *specif* **:** the partition separating the chest and abdominal cavities in mammals that by its contraction and relaxation varies the relative size and the internal pressure of these cavities and thereby plays an important role in such activities as breathing, defecation, and parturition and that in man has the form of an obliquely placed domed sheet, higher in front than behind, attached to the xiphoid cartilage, the six or seven lower ribs and their cartilages, and the lumbar vertebrae — see HICCUP **2 :** a dividing membrane or thin partition esp. in a tube **3 :** any of various more or less rigid partitions in the bodies or shells of invertebrate animals: as **a :** the membrane separating the heart from the rest of the body of an insect **b :** a calcareous partition extending into the cavity of the shell of a slipper limpet **c :** a chitinous shelf extending from the hydrotheca about the base of a hydranth **d :** a partition dividing the zooecia of some bryozoans into two chambers **4 a :** the constriction in the neck of the nucule in the stoneworts **b :** a transverse septum in a stem (as at the nodes of a scouring rush or in the pith of some woody stems) **5 :** a device (as a perforated plate) that limits the aperture of a lens or optical system **:** STOP — see IRIS DIAPHRAGM **6 :** a thin flexible often metallic disk that vibrates when struck by sound waves (as in a microphone) or that vibrates to produce sound waves (as in a telephone receiver or loudspeaker) **7 :** a thin plate or partition between parallel parts of a structural steel member (as of a bridge) used to give rigidity to the member **8 :** a molded cap usu. of thin rubber fitted over the uterine cervix to act as a mechanical contraceptive barrier **9 :** a moving grid of lead strips used for producing sharper X-ray images by eliminating the oblique rays that pass through them before reaching the film

²diaphragm \"\ *vt* -ED/-ING/-S **1 :** to equip with a diaphragm **:** fit a diaphragm to **2 :** to cut down the aperture of (a lens or mirror) by means of a diaphragm

di·a·phrag·mat·ic \ˌdīəˌfragˌmad·ik, -fraig-, -at|, |ēk *also* -ˌfrə|m- *sometimes* -ˌfrəg|m-\ *adj* [F *diaphragmatique*, fr. MF, fr. Gk *diaphragmat-, diaphragma* + MF *-ique* -ic] **:** of, involving, or resembling a diaphragm — **diaphragmatically** \|ək(ə)lē, |ēk-, -li\ *adv*

diaphragmatic respiration *n* **:** inspiration and expiration produced chiefly by movements of the diaphragm — distinguished from *costal respiration*

diaphragm horn *n* **:** a foghorn that produces a loud signal by the vibration of a disk diaphragm

diaphragm pump *n* **:** a pump having a flexible diaphragm in place of a piston

diaphragm shutter *n* **:** a camera shutter that opens from and closes to the center

diaphragm valve *n* **:** a valve opened or closed by pressure of or against a diaphragm

di·aph·y·se·al \ˌdīˌafəˈsēəl, -ˌzē- *also* ˌdīəˈfizēəl\ *or* **di·a·phys·i·al** \ˌdīəˈfizēəl\ *adj* [*diaphyseal* alter. of *diaphysial*; *diaphysial* fr. NL *diaphysis* + E *-al*] **:** of, relating to, or involving a diaphysis

di·aph·y·sis \dīˈafəsəs\ *n, pl* **diaphy·ses** \-əˌsēz\ [NL, fr. Gk, ridge on the shaft of the tibia, fr. *diaphyesthai* to grow between, be connected with (fr. *dia-* + *phyesthai*, mid. of *phyein* to bring forth) + *-sis* — more at BE] **:** the shaft of a long bone — distinguished from *epiphysis*

di·a·pir \ˈdīəˌpi(ə)r\ *n* -S [irreg. fr. Gk *diapeirein* to drive through, pierce, fr. *dia-* + *peirein* to pierce; akin to Gk *poreuein* to convey — more at FARE] **:** an anticlinal fold in which a mobile core has broken through the more brittle overlying rocks — **di·a·pir·ic** \ˌdīəˈpirik\ *adj*

diapophysis \ˌdī+\ *n, pl* **diapophyses** [NL, fr. *dia-* + *apophysis*] **:** a transverse process of a vertebra in higher vertebrates that is an outgrowth of the neural arch and often articulates with the tubercle of a rib; *esp* **:** one of the dorsal pair of transverse processes when two or more pairs of transverse processes are present

di·a·por·tha·ce·ae \ˌdīəˌpȯrˈthāsēˌē\ [NL, fr. *Diaporthe*, type genus + *-aceae*] *syn of* VALSACEAE

di·a·por·the \ˌdīəˈpȯrthē\ *n, cap* [NL, fr. Gk *diaporthein* to destroy completely, fr. *dia-* + *porthein* to destroy] **:** a genus of ascomycetous fungi (family Valsaceae) having fusoid or ellipsoid hyaline 2-celled ascospores borne in perithecia that are embedded in diffuse or isolated stromata

dia·positive \ˌdīə+\ *n* [*dia-* + *positive*] **:** a photographic positive made on a transparent support (as a lantern slide or a small transparency of an aerial photograph used in the preparation of contour maps)

¹di·ap·sid \(ˈ)dīˈapsəd\ *adj* [NL *Diapsida*] **:** of or relating to the Diapsida

²diapsid \"\ *n* -S **:** any reptile of the subclass Diapsida

di·ap·si·da \dīˈapsədə\ *n pl, cap* [NL, fr. *di-* + *-apsida* (fr. Gk *hapsid-, hapsis* arch, loop) — more at APSIS] *in some classifications* **:** a subclass of reptiles having two pairs of temporal openings in the skull and including the extinct dinosaurs and pterosaurs, the crocodiles and rhynchocephalians, and usu. the lizards and snakes — compare PARAPSIDA — **di·ap·si·dan** \(ˈ)dīˈapsədᵊn\ *adj or n*

di·ap·to·mid \dīˈaptəməd\ *n* -S [NL *Diaptomidae*, family of copepods, fr. *Diaptomus*, type genus + -idae] **:** a copepod of the genus *Diaptomus* or the family Diaptomidae

di·ap·to·mus \-məs\ *n, cap* [NL, perh. fr. *di-* + Gk *haptein* to grasp, fasten + *ōmos* shoulder — more at APSIS, HUMERUS] **:** a genus (the type of the family Diaptomidae) of widely distributed freshwater copepods

di·ap·to·sauria \dīˌaptəˈsȯrēə\ [NL, fr. *di-* + *-apto-* (fr. Gk *haptein* to fasten) + *-sauria*] *syn of* ARCHOSAURIA

di·arch \ˈdīˌärk\ *adj* [*di-* + Gk *archē* beginning, origin — more at ARCHI-] **:** having two xylem groups

diarchy *var of* DYARCHY

di·ar·i·al \(ˈ)dīˈa(a)rēəl\ *adj* [*diary* + *-al*] **:** of or resembling a diary

di·a·rist \ˈdīərəst\ *n* -S **:** one who keeps a diary

di·a·ris·tic \ˌdīəˈristik\ *adj* **:** in the style of a diary ⟨~ account⟩ **:** like that of a diarist ⟨~ talent⟩

di·a·rize \ˈdīəˌrīz\ *vb* -ED/-ING/-S *see -ize in Explan Notes* [*diary* + *-ize*] *vi* **:** to keep or write in a diary ⟨~ for an hour each evening⟩ ~ *vt* **:** to record in a diary ⟨~ the affairs of the hour⟩

di·ar·rhea *or* **di·ar·rhoea** \ˌdīəˈrēə\ *n* -S [ME *diaria*, fr. LL *diarrhoea*, fr. Gk *diarrhoia*, lit., act of flowing through, fr. *diarrhein* to flow through, fr. *dia-* + *rhein* to flow — more at STREAM] **:** an abnormal frequency of discharge of more or less fluid intestinal evacuations due to infectious, fermentative, or toxic causes or physiologic disturbances — **di·ar·rhe·al** *or* **di·ar·rhoe·al** \ˌdīəˈrēəl\ *or* **di·ar·rhe·ic** *or* **di·ar·rhoe·ic** \-ēik\ *also* **di·ar·rhet·ic** *or* **di·ar·rhoet·ic** \-red·ik\ *adj*

di·ar·rhee \ˌdīəˈrē, (ˈ)dīˈrē\ *n* -S [by shortening] *dial* **:** DIARRHEA

di·arsenide \(ˈ)dī+\ *n* [*di-* + *arsenide*] **:** an arsenide containing two atoms of arsenic

di·ar·thro·di·al \ˌdīˌärˈthrōdēəl\ *adj* [*di-* + *arthrodial*] **:** of, relating to, or exhibiting diarthrosis

di·arthrosis \ˌdī+\ *n, pl* **diarthroses** [NL, fr. Gk *diarthrōsis*, fr. *diarthroun* to joint, articulate (fr. *dia-* + *arthroun* to fasten by a joint, fr. *arthron* joint) + *-sis* — more at ARTHR-] **:** a form of articulation that permits considerable change in position and spatial relationship between the articulated parts **:** a freely movable joint (as the arthrodia, the ginglymus, the pivot joint, the condyloid joint, the enarthrosis)

di·articular \ˌdī+\ *adj* [*di-* + *articular*] **:** of or involving two joints

¹di·a·ry \ˈdī(ə)rē, -ri\ *n* -ES [L *diarium*, fr. *dies* day + *-arium* -ary — more at DEITY] **1 :** a register or record of events, transactions, or observations kept daily or at frequent intervals **:** JOURNAL; *esp* **:** a daily record of personal activities, reflections, or feelings **2 :** a book intended or used for a diary

²diary \"\ *adj* [L *dies* day + E *-ary*] **:** lasting one day ⟨~ fever⟩

di·aryl \(ˈ)dī+\ *adj* [*di-* + *aryl*] **:** containing two aryl groups esp. in place of hydrogen

di·arylamine \ˌdī+\ *n* -S [*di-* + *aryl* + *amine*] **:** an amine (as diphenylamine) containing two aryl groups attached to amino nitrogen

di·as·chi·sis \dīˈaskəsəs\ *n, pl* **diaschi·ses** \-əˌsēz\ [NL, fr. Gk, division, fr. *diaschizein* to sever (fr. *dia-* + *schizein* to split) + *-sis* — more at SHED] **:** the breaking up of a pattern of brain activity by a localized injury that temporarily throws the whole activity out of function though destroying only part of a structure

di·a·schis·ma \ˌdīəˈskizmə\ *n* -S [NL, fr. Gk *diaschisma*, fr. *diaschizein* to sever] **1 :** one of several minute intervals in ancient Greek music **2 :** a small musical interval (as that between C and D double flat in pure intonation) that together with the schisma comprises the syntonic comma

dia·schistic \ˌdīə+\ *adj* [*dia-* + *schistic*] **1** *of chromosomes* **:** apparently separating longitudinally in one division but transversely in another during atypical meiosis — compare ANASCHISTIC **2** *of rock* **:** DIFFERENTIATED — opposed to *aschistic*

di·as·cia \dīˈash(ē)ə\ *n, cap* [NL, fr. *di-* + Gk *askos* wineskin, bladder, belly + NL *-ia*; fr. the two sacs that grow on the corolla — more at ASCUS] **:** a genus of chiefly annual southern African herbs (family Scrophulariaceae) having 2-lipped flowers with the lower lip 2-spurred

di·a·scope \ˈdīəˌskōp\ *n* -S [ISV *dia-* + *-scope*] **:** a plate of glass pressed against the skin so as to expel the blood from a part and show anatomical changes — **di·a·scop·ic** \ˌdīəˈskäpik\ *adj* — **di·as·co·py** \dīˈaskəpē\ *n* -ES

di·a·scor·di·um \ˌdīəˈskȯrdēəm\ *n, pl* **diascor·dia** \-ēə\ [NL, fr. Gk *dia* through, by means of + Gk *skordion* garlic germander, fr. *skordon* garlic; akin to Alb *hurdhë, hudhrë* garlic, OE *scort* short — more at DIA-, SHORT] **:** a stomachic and astringent electuary made from the dried leaves of the water germander or other herbs

di·a·skeu·ast *also* **di·a·sceu·ast** \ˌdīəˈskyüˌast, -ˌəst\ *n* -S [Gk *diaskeuastēs*, fr. *diaskeuazein* to make ready, revise, edit, fr. *dia-* + *skeuazein* to make ready, fr. *skeuos* vessel, implement — more at SKEUOMORPH] **:** one who makes a revision **:** EDITOR

Di·a·sone \ˈdīəˌsōn\ *trademark* — used for sulfoxone sodium

di·as·pid \dīˈaspəd\ *adj* [NL *Diaspididae*] **:** of or relating to the Diaspididae

di·as·pi·di·dae \dīˌaspəˈdī(ˌ)dē\ *n pl, cap* [NL, fr. *Diaspid-, Diaspis*, type genus (fr. *dia-* + *-aspid-, -aspis*) + *-idae*] **:** a family of scales that have a one-jointed beak and a female which secretes a firm scaly covering over herself and her eggs and that comprise the armored scales

di·as·pine \dīˈaˌspīn, -ˌspən\ *adj* [NL *Diaspinae* subfamily of scales, fr. *Diaspis*, type genus + *-inae*] **:** DIASPID

di·as·po·ra \dīˈasp(ə)rə, -ˈaas-\ *n* -S [Gk, dispersion, scattering, fr. *diaspeirein* to scatter, spread about, fr. *dia-* + *speirein* to sow, scatter — more at SPORE] **1** *usu cap* **a :** the settling of scattered colonies of Jews outside Palestine after the Babylonian exile **b :** the area outside Palestine settled by Jews ⟨in Israel or in the *Diaspora*⟩ **c :** the Jews living outside Palestine or modern Israel **d :** the state of the Jews living scattered in the Gentile world **2 :** a dispersion (as of people of a common national origin or of common beliefs) **:** spread (as of a national culture) **:** EXILE, SCATTERING, MIGRATION **3 :** the people of one country dispersed into other countries ⟨certain sections of the Armenian ~ scattered over the world could be attracted —Walter Kolarz⟩ **4 :** the dispersion of Christians isolated from their own communion

di·a·spore \ˈdīəˌspō(ə)r\ *n* -S [Gk *diaspora* dispersion, scattering] **1 :** a mineral consisting of aluminum hydrogen oxide $HAlO_2$ and occurring in white lamellar masses with pearly luster or in prismatic orthorhombic crystals **2 :** DISSEMINULE; *esp* **:** one specialized for dispersal

diaspore clay *n* **:** a rock consisting of diaspore bonded by fireclay

di·a·stase \ˈdīəˌstās\ *n* -S [F, fr. Gk *diastasis* separation, fr. *diistanai* to separate, fr. *dia-* through, apart + *histanai* to set, cause to stand — more at DIA-, STAND] **1 :** AMYLASE; *esp* **:** a mixture of amylases obtained usu. as a yellowish white amorphous powder from malt and used chiefly in desizing textiles and converting starch to maltose **2 :** ENZYME

di·a·sta·sic \ˌdīəˈstāsik\ *adj* [ISV *diastase* + *-ic*] **:** DIASTATIC

di·as·ta·sis \dīˈastəsəs, -ˈaas-\ *n, pl* **diasta·ses** \-əˌsēz\ [NL, fr. Gk, separation] **1** *med* **:** an abnormal separation of parts normally joined together **2** *physiol* **:** the rest phase of cardiac diastole occurring between filling of the ventricle and the start of auricular contraction

-diastasis \"\ *n comb form, pl* **-diastases** [NL, fr. Gk *diastasis* separation] **1 :** disintegration ⟨myelo*diastasis*⟩ **2 :** displacement ⟨adeno*diastasis*⟩

di·a·stat·ic \ˌdīəˈstad·ik\ *adj* [irreg. (influence of Gk *diastatikos* disintegrating) fr. *diastase* + *-ic*] **:** relating to or having the properties of diastase **:** AMYLOLYTIC ⟨~ activity of flour⟩ — **di·a·stat·i·cal·ly** \-ək(ə)lē\ *adv*

di·a·stem \ˈdīəˌstem\ *n* -S [LL *diastema*, fr. Gk *diastēma* interval, fr. *diistanai* to separate — more at DIASTASE] **1 :** an interval in ancient Greek music **2 :** DIASTEMA 1 **3 :** a minor interruption in sedimentation with little or no erosion before deposition is resumed — compare DISCONFORMITY, UNCONFORMITY — **di·a·stem·ic** \ˌdīəˈstemik\ *adj*

di·a·ste·ma \ˌdīəˈstēmə\ *n, pl* **di·a·ste·ma·ta** \-tēməd·ə, -tem-\ [NL, fr. LL, interval] **1 :** the modified cytoplasm in the equatorial plane during mitosis that indicates the division plane of the cell **2 :** a space between teeth in a jaw — **di·a·ste·mat·ic** \ˌdīəstəˈmad·ik\ *adj*

di·aster \(ˈ)dī+\ *n* -S [ISV *di-* + *-aster*] **:** a stage in mitotic cell division when the chromosomes, having split and separated, group themselves near the poles of the spindle preparatory to forming the new nuclei — **di·astral** \"+\ *adj*

dia·stereoisomer \ˌdīə+\ *or* **dia·ster·e·o·mer** \ˌdīəˈstereōmə(r), -tir-\ *n* -S [*dia-* + *stereoisomer*] **:** an isomer exhibiting diastereoisomerism — distinguished from *enantiomorph*

dia·stereoisomeric \ˌdīə+\ *or* **dia·ster·e·o·mer·ic** \ˌdīəˌstereōˈmerik, -tir-\ *adj* **:** of, relating to, or exhibiting diastereoisomerism

dia·stereoisomerism \ˌdīə+\ *n* -S **:** optical isomerism of compounds whose molecules contain more than one asymmetric atom and do not exhibit mirror-image relationship (as glucose and galactose or *meso*-tartaric acid and *dextro*-tartaric acid) — distinguished from *enantiomorphism*; compare ASYMMETRIC CARBON ATOM

di·a·stim·e·ter \ˌdīəˈstiməd·ə(r)\ *n* -S [ISV *diasti-* (fr. Gk *diastasis* interval, separation) + *-meter* — more at DIASTASE] **:** an instrument for measuring distances

di·as·to·le \dīˈastə(ˌ)lē, -ˈaas-, -ˌli\ *n* -S [Gk *diastolē* dilatation, fr. *diastellein* to expand, be dilated, fr. *dia-* + *stellein* to make ready, start out, send — more at STALL] **1 a :** the passive rhythmical expansion or dilatation of the cavities of the heart during which they fill with blood — compare SYSTOLE **b :** the rhythmical expansion of a pulsating vacuole **2** *prosody* **:** a lengthening of a short quantity or syllable **3 :** EXPANSION

di·a·stol·ic \ˌdīəˈstälik, -lēk\ *adj* **:** of, relating to, or occurring during diastole

diastolic pressure *n* **:** the lowest arterial blood pressure of a cardiac cycle occurring during diastole of the heart — compare SYSTOLIC PRESSURE

dia·stomatic \ˌdīəstōˈmad·ik\ *adj* [*dia-* + *stomatic*] **:** STOMATAL

di·as·tro·phe \dīˈastrəfē\ *n* -S [Gk *diastrophē* twisting, distortion, fr. *diastrephein* to twist about, distort, fr. *dia-* + *strephein* to turn, twist — more at STROPHE] **:** a deformation of the earth's crust

di·a·stroph·ic \ˌdīəˈsträfik\ *adj* **:** of, having reference to, or caused by diastrophism

di·as·tro·phism \dīˈastrəˌfizəm\ *n* -S **:** the process of deformation that produces in the earth's crust its continents and ocean basins, plateaus and mountains, folds of strata, and faults — compare EPEIROGENY, OROGENY

di·a·style \ˈdīəˌstīl\ *n* -S [L *diastylos* having a space of three diameters between columns, fr. Gk, fr. *dia-* through, apart + *stylos* column — more at DIA-, STYLE] **:** intercolumniation of three diameters — see INTERCOLUMNIATION illustration

di·a·tes·sa·ron \ˌdīəˈtesəˌrän, -rən\ *n* -S [ME *dyatessaron*, fr. L *diatessaron*, fr. Gk (*hē*) *dia tessarōn* (*chordōn symphōnia*) the concord through four notes, fr. *dia* through + *tessarōn*, gen. of *tessares, tettares* four — more at FOUR] **1 :** the interval of a fourth in ancient Greek music **2** *obs* **:** an electuary compounded of four medicines **3 :** a harmony of the four Gospels edited and arranged into a single connected narrative

di·a·ther·mal \ˌdīəˈthərməl\ *adj* [*dia-* + *thermal*] **:** DIATHERMIC

di·a·ther·man·cy \ˌdīəˈthərmənsē\ *or* **di·a·ther·ma·cy** \-məsē\ *n* -ES [*diathermancy* fr. F *diathermansie*, fr. Gk *dia-* + *thermansis* heating, fr. *thermainein* to heat, fr. *thermos* hot; *diathermacy* fr. F *diathermasie*, fr. Gk *diathermasia* heating effect, fr. *diathermainein* to heat through, fr. *dia-* + *thermainein* — more at WARM] **:** the ability to transmit infrared radiation — compare ATHERMANCY

di·a·ther·ma·nous \ˌdīəˈthərmənəs\ *adj* [F *diathermane*, irreg. (influence of *diaphane* diaphanous) fr. Gk *diathermainein*] **:** transmitting infrared radiation — compare ATHERMANOUS

di·a·ther·mic \ˌdīəˈthərmik, -ēm-, -əim-, -mēk\ *adj* [F *diathermique*, fr. *dia-* + *thermique* thermic] **1 :** DIATHERMANOUS **2 :** of or relating to diathermy ⟨~ treatment⟩

di·a·ther·my \ˈ==ˌ=mē, -mi\ *n* -ES [ISV *dia-* + *-thermy*] **:** the generation of heat in tissue for medical or surgical purposes by the application of high-frequency electric currents of various wavelengths by means of electrodes and other instruments — see ELECTROCOAGULATION, SHORTWAVE THERAPY

di·ath·e·sis \dīˈathəsəs\ *n, pl* **diathe·ses** \-əˌsēz\ [NL, fr. Gk, lit., arrangement, disposition, fr. *diatithenai* to arrange, dispose, fr. *dia-* + *tithenai* to set, put, place — more at DO] **1 :** a bodily tendency or constitutional predisposition toward some abnormality or disease ⟨hemorrhagic ~⟩ ⟨tubercular ~⟩ **2 :** an innate disposition toward or aptitude for some particular mental development **3** *of a verb* **:** VOICE 7

di·a·thet·ic \ˌdīəˈthed·ik\ *adj* [fr. NL *diathesis*, after such pairs as LL *antithesis*: E *antithetic*] **:** of or relating to a diathesis; *specif* **:** of or belonging to the voice of a verb

di·a·tom \ˈdīəˌtäm *sometimes* -əd·əm *or* -ətəm\ *n* -S [NL *Diatoma*] **:** any of the unicellular or colonial algae constituting a class (Bacillariophyceae), having a silicified cell wall that persists as a skeleton after death and forms diatomite, and forming a large part of the plankton of both fresh and salt water — see FRUSTULE, GIRDLE e(1), VALVE

di·at·o·ma \dīˈad·əmə\ *n, cap* [NL, fr. Gk *diatomē*, fem. of *diatomos* cut in half, fr. *diatemnein* to cut through, fr. *dia-* + *temnein* to cut — more at TOME] **:** a genus of freshwater diatoms (family Diatomaceae) that sometimes cause aromatic or disagreeable odors in water

¹di·a·to·ma·ce·ae \ˌdīəd·əˈmāsēˌē, (ˌ)dīˌad·ə-\ [NL, fr. *Diatoma*, type genus + *-aceae*] *syn of* BACILLARIACEAE

²diatomaceae \"\ *n pl, cap* [NL, fr. *Diatoma*, type genus + *-aceae*] **:** a family of rectangular diatoms

di·a·to·ma·ceous \ˌdīəd·əˈmāshəs, (ˌ)dīˌad·ə-\ *adj* [NL *¹Diatomaceae* + E *-ous*] **1 :** BACILLARIACEOUS **2 :** consisting of or abounding in diatoms or their siliceous remains ⟨~ silica⟩

diatomaceous earth *n* **:** DIATOMITE

di·a·to·ma·les \ˌdīəd·əˈmā(ˌ)lēz, (ˌ)dīˌad·ə-\ *n pl, cap* [NL, fr. *Diatoma* + *-ales*] *in some classifications* **:** an order coextensive with the class Bacillariophyceae

di·a·to·me·ae \ˌdīəˈtōmēˌē\ [NL, fr. *Diatoma* + *-eae*] *syn of* BACILLARIOPHYCEAE

di·atomic \ˌdī+\ *adj* [ISV *di-* + *atomic*] **1 :** consisting of two atoms **:** having two atoms in the molecule **2 :** having two replaceable atoms or radicals

di·at·o·min \dīˈad·əmən\ *n* -S [*diatom* + *-in*] **:** a yellow or yellowish brown pigment found in certain algae and diatoms — called also *phycoxanthin*

di·a·tom·ist \ˈdīəˌtäməst, dīˈad·əm- *sometimes* ˈdīəd·əm-\ *n* -S [*diatom* + *-ist*] **:** one who studies diatoms

di·at·o·mite \dīˈad·əˌmīt\ *n* -S [ISV *diatom* + *-ite*] **:** a light friable siliceous material resembling chalk that is derived chiefly from the remains of diatoms and is used as a filter aid, adsorbent, filler (as for paints and plastics), and abrasive, and for thermal insulation — called also *diatomaceous earth*; compare KIESELGUHR, TRIPOLI

diatom ooze *n* **:** deep-sea deposits rich in diatoms

di·a·ton·ic \ˌdīəˈtänik, -nēk\ *adj* [LL *diatonicus*, fr. Gk *diatonikos*, fr. *diatonos* stretching, extending (fr. *diateinein* to stretch out, extend, fr. *dia-* + *teinein* to stretch) + *-ikos* -ic — more at THIN] **1** *of a Greek tetrachord* **:** comprising two steps and a half step — distinguished from *chromatic* and *enharmonic* **2 :** relating to a standard major or minor scale of eight tones to the octave without chromatic deviation — **di·a·ton·i·cal·ly** \-nək(ə)lē, -nēk-, -li\ *adv*

di·a·ton·i·cism \ˌdīəˈtänəˌsizəm\ *also* **di·a·ton·ism** \ˈdīəˌtäˌnizəm, dīˈad·əˌn-\ *n* -S **1 :** the quality or state of being diatonic **2 :** the use of diatonic harmony — contrasted with *chromaticism*

di·a·tor·ic \ˌdīəˈtȯrik\ *adj* [G *diatoros* pierced (fr. *diateirein* to pierce, fr. *dia-* + *teirein* to bore, turn) + E *-ic* — more at THROW] **:** having a recess in its base for attachment to the dental plate — used of an artificial tooth

di·a·traea \ˌdīəˈtrēə\ *n, cap* [NL, irreg. fr. Gk *diateirein*] **:** a genus of moderate-sized dull-colored moths (family Pyralididae) producing boring larvae that are serious pests in a number of crop plants esp. in warm regions — see SOUTHERN CORNSTALK BORER

di·a·treme \ˈdīəˌtrēm\ *n* -S [*dia-* + Gk *trēma* hole — more at THROW] **:** a small generally circular volcanic vent produced by gaseous explosion usu. preceded by deep-seated rock fusion by hot gases

di·a·tribe \ˈdīəˌtrīb\ *n* -S [L *diatriba*, fr. Gk *diatribē* pastime, study, discourse, fr. *diatribein* to spend (time), wear away, fr. *dia-* + *tribein* to rub — more at THROW] **1** *archaic* **:** a prolonged discourse or discussion **2** [F, fr. MF, prolonged discourse, fr. L *diatriba*] **a :** a bitter, abusive, and usu. lengthy speech or piece of writing ⟨the melancholy ~*s* of the old prophets —Richard Chase⟩ ⟨a ~ against Nero —Berthe M. Marti⟩ **b :** bitter and abusive speech or writing ⟨to be irritated or offended by such ~ —*Time*⟩ **3 :** ironical or satirical criticism

di·a·trop·ic \ˌdīəˈträpik\ *adj* **:** characterized by diatropism

di·at·ro·pism \dīˈa·trəˌpizəm\ *n* -S [ISV *dia-* + *-tropism*] **:** the tropistic tendency of certain plant organs to place themselves transversely to the line of action of a stimulus — compare DIAGEOTROPISM, DIAPHOTOTROPISM

di·a·try·ma \ˌdīəˈtrīmə\ *n, cap* [NL, fr. *dia-* + Gk *tryma, trymē* hole] **:** a genus of large flightless Eocene birds from Wyoming and New Mexico having much reduced wings, large head and powerful beak, and long massive legs and constituting with extinct related forms (as *Gastornis*) an order of birds probably most nearly related to the surviving cariamas and bustards

di·au·los \dēˈaùˌläs, dēˈōˌl-\ *n, pl* **diau·li** \-aùˌlē, -ōˌlī\ [Gk, fr. *di-* + *aulos* pipe, reed instrument like an oboe, racecourse — more at ALVEOLUS] **:** the double course for footraces in ancient Greece in which the contestants ran down one side of the stadium, turned round a goal, and returned to the starting point

di·axon \(ˈ)dī+\ *also* **di·axone** \"+\ *n* -S [*di-* + *axon, axone*] **:** a nerve cell with two axons — **di·ax·on·ic** \ˌdīˌakˈsänik\ *adj*

diaz- *or* **diazo-** *comb form* [ISV, fr. *di-* + *az-*] **1** *usu diazo-* **:** containing the group N_2 united to carbon in one organic radical ⟨*diazo*acetic ester $N_2CHCOOC_2H_5$⟩ **2** *diazo-* **:** containing diazonium ⟨*diazo*benzenesulfonic acid $^+N_2C_6H_4SO_3^-$⟩

di·a·zine \ˈdīəˌzēn, dīˈaz-, -zən\ *n* -S [ISV *di-* + *az-* + *-ine*] **1 :** any of three parent compounds $C_4H_4N_2$ containing a ring composed of four carbon atoms and two nitrogen atoms and distinguished by indication of the positions of the nitrogen atoms or by trivial names: **a :** PYRIDAZINE **b :** PYRIMIDINE **c :** PYRAZINE **2 :** any of a large class of derivatives of the three parent diazines

¹di·azo \(ˈ)dīˈa(ˌ)zō, -ˈā-\ *adj* [*diaz-*] **1 :** relating to or containing the group N_2 united to carbon in one organic radical — distinguished from *disazo*; compare AZO **2 :** relating to or containing diazonium **3 :** of or relating to a diazotype ⟨~ paper⟩

²diazo \"\ *n* -S **:** any diazo compound — usu. used commercially

di·azo·amino \"+\ *adj* [*diazoamino-*] **:** containing the group $-N{=}N{-}NH{-}$

diazoamino- *comb form* [ISV *diaz-* + *amin-*] **:** containing the group $-N{=}N{-}NH{-}$ united to organic radicals ⟨*diazoamino*benzene $C_6H_5N{=}N{-}NHC_6H_5$⟩

di·az·o·ate \dīˈazōˌāt, -ˈāz-, -ōət\ *or* **di·az·o·tate** \-ˌtāt\

n -s [*diazoate* fr. *diaz-* + *-ate; diazotate* fr. *di-* + *azote* + *-ate*] **:** a salt of a diazoic acid

di·azo·dinitrophenol \(ˈ)dī¦a(ˌ)zō, -ā(ˌ)zō+\ *n* -s [*diaz-* + *dinitrophenol*] **:** a yellow solid diazo oxide $(NO_2)_2C_6H_2N_2O$ made by diazotization of picramic acid and used as an initiating explosive in mixtures

diazo dye *or* **diazo color** *also* **diazo** *n* **:** DEVELOPED DYE — see DYE table I (under *Direct*)

diazo fast yellow GG *n, usu cap D&F&Y* **:** a fluorescent brightener — see DYE table I (under *Fluorescent Brightener 5*)

di·a·zo·ic acid \¦dīə¦zōik-\ *n* [ISV *diaz-* + *-ic*] **:** any of a class of acids containing a diazo group united with hydroxyl; *esp* **:** an aromatic acid of the general formula ArN=NOH (as benzene-diazoic acid C_6H_5N=NOH) obtained in the form of salts by treating a diazonium chloride with alkali

di·azo·imide \(ˈ)dī¦a(ˌ)zō, -ā(ˌ)zō+\ *n* -s [ISV *diaz-* + *imide*] **:** AZIDE; *esp* **:** an aromatic azide

di·a·zole \ˈdīəˌzōl, dīˈaz-\ *n* -s [ISV *diaz-* + *-ole*] **1 :** either of two parent compounds $C_3H_4N_2$ containing a ring composed of three carbon atoms and two nitrogen atoms: **a :** PYRAZOLE **b :** IMIDAZOLE **2 :** a derivative of either parent diazole

di·a·zo·ma \ˌdīəˈzōmə\ *n, pl* **di·a·zo·ma·ta** \-məd·ə\ [L, fr. Gk *diazōma*, lit., girdle, fr. *dia-* + *zōma* girdle — more at ZONE] **:** a passage in the auditorium of an ancient Greek theater dividing the lower from the upper rows of seats for convenience of access — see THEATER illustration

di·azo·methane \(ˈ)dī¦a(ˌ)zō, -ā(ˌ)zō+\ *n* [ISV *diaz-* + *methane*] **:** a yellow odorless poisonous explosive gaseous compound CH_2N_2 used chiefly as a methylating agent (as for converting organic acids into their methyl esters) and in converting organic acids into the next higher homologues

di·a·zo·ni·um \ˌdīəˈzōnēəm\ *n* -s [ISV *diaz-* + *-onium*] **:** the univalent cation $-N_2^+$ composed of two nitrogen atoms united to carbon in one organic radical; *esp* **:** a cation ArN_2^+ (as benzenediazonium) obtained in the form of salts by diazotizing an arylamine and used chiefly in the manufacture of azo dyes — compare DIAZ-

diazo oxide *n* **:** any of a class of compounds (as diazodinitrophenol) that contain a diazo group and an oxygen atom attached to ortho positions of an aromatic nucleus and are formed by the action of nitrous acid on *ortho*-aminophenols with loss of water, a few of these compounds finding use as initiating explosives and in diazotypes — called also *diazophenol*

di·azo·phenol \(ˈ)dī¦a(ˌ)zō, -ā(ˌ)zō+\ *n* -s [ISV *diaz-* + *phenol*] **:** DIAZO OXIDE

diazo process *n* **:** the process of making diazotypes

diazo reaction *n* **:** a reaction in which a diazo compound is made or used; *specif* **:** a reaction in various diseases (as typhoid fever) consisting of a red discoloration of the urine on addition of diazobenzenesulfonic acid

di·azo·sulfonate \(ˈ)dī¦a(ˌ)zō, -ā(ˌ)zō+\ *n* -s [*diaz-* + *sulfonate*] **:** a salt of a diazosulfonic acid

di·azo·sulfonic acid \"+ . . . -\ *n* [*diaz-* + *sulfonic*] **:** any of a class of aromatic acids that contain a diazo group united with a sulfonic acid group, have the general formula ArN=NSO$_3$H, and are obtained in the form of salts by treating a diazonium salt with a sulfite

di·az·o·tiz·able \dīˈazəˌtīzəbəl\ *adj* **:** capable of being diazotized

di·az·o·ti·za·tion \dīˌazətəˈzāshən\ *n* -s **:** the process of diazotizing

di·az·o·tize \dīˈazəˌtīz\ *vt* -ED/-ING/-S [*di-* + *azote* + *-ize*] **:** to convert (a chemical compound) into a diazo compound; *esp* **:** to convert (an arylamine) into a diazonium salt by the action of nitrous acid in acid solution

di·az·o·type \-ˌtīp\ *n* [*diaz-* + *-type*] **:** a photograph or photocopy produced on a surface (as paper) by coating with a solution containing a diazo compound that is decomposed on exposure to light, the compound in the unexposed parts being then converted to a colored image formed by an azo dye by developing esp. with an alkaline solution or gaseous ammonia

[1]**dib** \ˈdib\ *vi* **dibbed; dibbed; dibbing; dibs** [perh. fr. obs. *dib* to dab, pat, prob. alter. of *dab*] **:** to fish by letting the bait bob and dip lightly

[2]**dib** \"\ *n* -s [short for *dibstone*] **1** *Brit* **a dibs** *pl but sing in constr* **:** the game of jacks **b :** a knucklebone or jack used in playing jacks — usu. used in pl. **2 dibs** *pl, slang* **:** money esp. in small amounts **3 dibs** *pl* **:** CLAIM, RESERVATION, RIGHTS — used with *on* ⟨I have ~s on that piece of cake⟩

[3]**dib** \"\ *var of* [3]DUB

di·basic \(ˈ)dī+\ *adj* [*di-* + *basic*] **1 :** having two hydrogen atoms capable of replacement by basic atoms or radicals — used of acids (as oxalic or sulfuric acid) **2 :** containing two atoms of a univalent metal or their equivalent ⟨~ sodium phosphate Na_2HPO_4⟩ **3 :** having two basic hydroxyl groups **:** able to react with two molecules of a monobasic acid — used of bases and basic salts — **di·basicity** \(ˌ)dī+\ *n* -ES

dib·a·tag \ˈdibəˌtag\ *n* -s [Somali *dabatag, dibtag*] **:** a small gazelle (*Ammodorcas clarkei*) of northeastern Africa having a long neck and tail and in the male short ringed recurved horns — called also *Clarke's gazelle*

dib·ber \ˈdibə(r)\ *n* -s [by alter.] **:** DIBBLE

[1]**dib·ble** \ˈdibəl\ *n* -s [ME *debylle*] **:** a small hand implement used to make holes in the ground for plants, seeds, or bulbs

[2]**dib·ble** \"\ *vb* **dibbled; dibbled; dibbling** \-b(ə)liŋ\ **dibbles** *vt* **:** to plant with a dibble **:** make holes in (soil) with or as if with a dibble (as for planting) **~** *vi* **:** to work with a dibble (as in planting)

[3]**dibble** \"\ *vi* -ED/-ING/-S [freq. of obs. *dib* to dab — more at DIB] **1 :** DABBLE 1b **2 :** [1]DIB

dibble

dib·bler \ˈdib(ə)lə(r)\ *n* -s **:** one that dibbles; *esp* **:** a machine having two wheels with long rounded projections on their rims that make spaced holes in a row for transplants

dibbuk *var of* DYBBUK

dibenz- *or* **dibenzo-** *comb form* [ISV, fr. *di-* + *benz-*] **:** containing two benzene rings — in names of organic compounds ⟨*dibenz*acridine⟩ ⟨*dibenzo*furan⟩

di·benz·anthracene \¦dī(ˌ)benz+\ *n* [*dibenz-* + *anthracene*] **:** an orange-brown crystalline actively carcinogenic cyclic hydrocarbon $C_{22}H_{14}$ found in trace amounts in coal tar — called also *1,2:5,6-dibenzanthracene, dibenz[a,h]anthracene*

dibhole \ˈ==,=\ *n* [[3]*dib* + *hole*] *Brit* **:** a drainage hole at the bottom of a mine shaft

di·borane \(ˈ)dī+\ *n* [*di-* + *borane*] **:** a gaseous compound B_2H_6 of boron and hydrogen that has a repulsive odor, is formed by reaction between a metal hydride and a boron halide usu. in ether solution, and decomposes rapidly in water to boric acid and hydrogen — called also *diborane(6)*

di·bothriocephalus \(ˌ)dī+\ [NL, fr. *di-* + *bothri-* + *-cephalus*] *syn of* DIPHYLLOBOTHRIUM

di·bot·ry·on \dīˈbä·trēˌän, -ˌən\ *n, cap* [NL, fr. *di-* + Gk *botryon* cluster of berries] **:** a genus of parasitic fungi (family Dothideaceae) having hyaline 2-celled spores borne in perithecia formed in dark stromata — see BLACK KNOT

di·brach \ˈdīˌbrak\ *n* -s [LL *dibrachys*, adj., fr. Gk, fr. *di-* + *brachys* short — more at BRIEF] **:** PYRRHIC

di·branch \ˈdīˌbraŋk\ *n* -s [NL *Dibranchia*] **:** one of the Dibranchia

di·bran·chia \dīˈbraŋkēə\ *n pl, cap* [NL, fr. *di-* + Gk *branchia* gills — more at BRANCHIA] **:** a subclass or order of Cephalopoda including the squids and octopuses, being characterized by 2 gills, 2 auricles, 2 nephridia, an apparatus for emitting an inky fluid, and either 8 or 10 cephalic arms bearing suckers or hooks, and comprising all living cephalopods except those of the genus *Nautilus* — **di·bran·chi·ate** \(ˈ)=¦=kēət, -ēˌāt\ *adj or n*

di·bran·chi·a·ta \(ˌ)=¦=kēˈäd·ə, -ˈād·ə\ [NL, fr. *di-* + *branchi-* + *-ata*] *syn of* DIBRANCHIA

dibrom- *or* **dibromo-** *comb form* [ISV, fr. *di-* + *brom-*] **:** containing two atoms of bromine — in names of chemical compounds ⟨*dibromo*acetic acid⟩; compare BROM-

di·bromide \(ˈ)dī+\ *n* [*di* + *bromide*] **:** a binary compound containing two atoms of bromine combined with an element or radical

[1]**dibs** *pres 3d sing of* DIB, *pl of* DIB

[2]**dibs** \ˈdibz\ *n pl but sing in constr* [Ar] **:** a sweet syrup made from grape juice or from dates and used in the East

dibstone \ˈ=,=\ *n* [[1]*dib* + *stone*] **1 :** DIB 1b **2 dibstones** *pl but sing in constr, archaic* **:** the game of jacks

di·bu·caine \(ˈ)dī¦byüˌkān\ *n* -s [*di-* + *butoxy-* + *-caine*] **:** a local anesthetic $C_{20}H_{29}N_3O_2$ that is administered parenterally as the bitter crystalline hydrochloride

di·butyl \(ˈ)dī+\ *adj* [*di-* + *butyl*] **:** containing two butyl groups in the molecule

dibutyl phthalate *n* **:** a colorless oily ester $C_6H_4(COOC_4H_9)_2$ used chiefly as a solvent and plasticizer

di·cac·i·ty \dīˈkasəd·ē\ *n* -ES [L *dicacitas*, fr. *dicac-, dicax* satirical, sarcastic, witty (fr. *dicere* to say) + *-itas* -ity — more at DICTION] *archaic* **:** RAILLERY **:** biting wit

di·cae·i·dae \dīˈsēəˌdē\ *n pl, cap* [NL *Dicaeum*, type genus + *-idae*] **:** a family of passerine birds containing the flowerpeckers

di·calcium \(ˈ)dī+\ *adj* [*di-* + *calcium*] **:** containing two atoms or equivalents of calcium in the molecule

dicalcium phosphate *n* **:** CALCIUM PHOSPHATE 1a(2)

di·camp·to·don \dīˈkamptəˌdän\ *n, cap* [NL, fr. *di-* + *campto-* + *-odon*] **:** a genus of large salamanders (family Ambystomidae) of the Pacific coast of No. America

di·carbocyanine \"+ *or* **dicarbocyanine dye** *n* [*di-* + *carb-* + *cyanine*] **:** any of certain cyanine dyes in whose structure the two heterocyclic rings are joined by a five-carbon chain (as =CH—CH=CH—CH=CH—); *specif* **:** such a dye containing two quinoline rings — called also *pentamethine*

di·carboxylic \(ˌ)dī+\ *adj* [*di-* + *carboxylic*] **:** containing two carboxyl groups in the molecule

dicaryon *var of* DIKARYON

dicaryophase *var of* DIKARYOPHASE

dicaryophyte *var of* DIKARYOPHYTE

dicaryotic *var of* DIKARYOTIC

di·cast *or* **di·kast** \ˈdīˌkast, ˈdiˌ-\ *n* -s [Gk *dikastēs* judge, juror, fr. *dikazein* to judge, fr. *dikē* right, judgment — more at DICTION] **:** a member of the highest court of law of ancient Athens who performed the functions of both judge and jury — **di·cas·tic** *or* **di·kas·tic** \(ˈ)dī¦kastik, diˈk-\ *adj*

di·cas·tery *or* **di·kas·tery** \dīˈkast(ə)rē, ˈdīˌk-, diˈk-\ *n* -ES [Gk *dikastērion* court of law, fr. *dikastēs*] **:** the court composed of the dicasts; *also* **:** the place where the court sat

[1]**di·catalectic** \(ˌ)dī+\ *adj* [*di-* + *catalectic*] *prosody* **:** composed of two catalectic members

[2]**dicatalectic** \"\ *n* **:** a dicatalectic verse

di·catalexis \(ˌ)dī+\ *n* [*di-* + *catalexis*] *prosody* **:** catalexis occurring twice within a line

[1]**dice** \ˈdīs\ *n, pl* **dice** *usu pl in constr, often attrib* [fr. pl. of [2]*die*] **:** [2]DIE — **no dice :** of no avail **:** no use **:** FUTILE ⟨falls in love with her . . . but it is *no dice* —Philip Hamburger⟩

[2]**dice** \"\ *vb* -ED/-ING/-S [ME *dycen*, fr. *dyce, dees*, pl. of *dee* die — more at DIE] *vt* **1 a :** to cut into dice ⟨~ bread⟩ ⟨*diced* potatoes⟩ **b :** to ornament with square markings or make in a pattern of small squares **:** CHECKER ⟨*diced* leather⟩ ⟨*diced* stockings⟩ **2 a :** to bring into some usu. unfavorable condition by playing dice games ⟨~ himself into debt⟩ **b :** to lose by dicing **:** throw away **c** *Austral* **:** to cast aside **:** REJECT ⟨*diced* by her sweetheart⟩ **3** *mil* **a :** to map (an area) by taking aerial photographs **b :** to fly as low as possible over to obtain detailed photographs of (a territory or objective) ⟨~ a target⟩ **~** *vi* **1 a :** to play games with dice **:** GAMBLE ⟨you may not even ~ for drinks in the bar —Malcolm Lowry⟩ **b :** to take a chance ⟨the temptation to ~ with death —*Newsweek*⟩ **2** *of glass* **:** to break into small pieces **:** SHATTER

dice board *n* **:** a board on which dice are thrown

dicebox \ˈ=,=\ *n* **:** a box from which dice are thrown

dice cup *n* **:** a small cup or box in which dice are shaken by hand and from which they are then thrown

dice girl *n* **:** a girl who acts as dealer at various dice games

di·cen·tra \dīˈsen·trə\ *n* [NL, fr. *di-* + *-centra* (fr. Gk *kentron* sharp point) — more at CENTER] **1** *cap* **:** a genus of No. American and Asiatic herbs (family Fumariaceae) with dissected leaves and irregular flowers — see BLEEDING HEART, DUTCHMAN'S-BREECHES **2** -s **:** any plant of the genus *Dicentra* (esp. *D. spectabilis*)

di·centric \(ˈ)dī+\ *adj* [*di-* + *-centric*] *biol* **:** having two centromeres

di·ceph·a·lus \(ˈ)dī¦sefələs\ *n, pl* **dicepha·li** \-ˌlī\ [NL, fr. *di-* + *-cephalus*] **:** a fetal anomaly having two distinct heads

dic·er \ˈdīsə(r)\ *n* -s [ME *dycer*, fr. *dycen* to dice + *-er*] **1 :** one who gambles at dice games **2** *slang* **:** a man's hat; *esp* **:** DERBY **3 a :** a machine that dices food (as fruits and vegetables) **b :** one that operates such a machine **4 :** GRAINER 1d

di·cer·as \ˈdisərəs, dīˈserəs\ *n, cap* [NL, fr. *di-* + *-ceras*] **:** a genus (the type of the family Diceratidae) of Jurassic lamellibranchs with the umbones of both valves produced and spirally curved and the hinges thick and bearing prominent teeth

dicerion *var of* DIKERION

dic·er·ous \ˈdisərəs, (ˈ)dī¦serəs\ *adj* [Gk *dikerōs* having two horns, fr. *di-* + *-kerōs* (fr. *keras* horn) — more at HORN] **:** having two tentacles or antennae

dich- *or* **dicho-** *comb form* [LL *dicho-*, fr. Gk *dich-, dicho-*, fr. *dicha*; akin to Gk *di-* — more at DI-] **:** in two **:** apart **:** asunder ⟨*dich*optic⟩ ⟨*dicho*gamy⟩

di·cha·pet·a·lum \ˌdīkəˈped·ᵊləm\ *n, cap* [NL, fr. Gk *dicha* in two + Gk *petalon* leaf — more at PETAL] **:** a genus (the type of the family Dichapetalaceae) of African and Malagasy shrubs that have coriaceous leaves and small regular flowers borne in compound cymes or in umbels

di·cha·si·al \(ˈ)dī¦kāzh(ē)əl\ *adj* [NL *dichasium* + E *-al*] **:** of, relating to, or of the nature of a dichasium

di·cha·si·um \dīˈkāzh(ē)əm\ *n, pl* **dicha·sia** \-(ē)ə\ [NL, irreg. fr. Gk *dichasis* division, halving, fr. *dichazein* to divide in half (fr. *dicha* in two) + *-sis*] **:** a cymose inflorescence that produces two main axes (as in a dichotomous cyme) — compare MONOCHASIUM, POLYCHASIUM

di·chel·y·ma \dīˈkeləmə\ *n, cap* [NL] **:** a genus of aquatic mosses (family Fontinalaceae) resembling those of the genus *Fontinalis* but distinguished by a midrib in the leaves and including one (*D. capillaceum*) that is common on stems of shrubs in swamps

di·chlamydeous \¦dī+\ *adj* [*di-* + *chlamyd-* + *-eous*] **:** having both calyx and corolla (as a rose)

di·chlone \ˈdīˌklōn\ *n* -s [*dichloro-* naphthoquin*one*] **:** a yellow crystalline compound $C_{10}H_4Cl_2O_2$ used as a fungicide and algicide; 2,3-dichloro-1,4-naphthoquinone

dichlor- *or* **dichloro-** *comb form* [ISV *di-* + *chlor-*] **:** containing two atoms of chlorine — in names of chemical compounds ⟨*dichloro*ethylene⟩; compare CHLOR-

di·chloramine \(ˈ)dī+\ *n* [ISV *di-* + *chloramine*] **1 :** an unstable compound $NHCl_2$ formed from ammonia by chlorination but not known in the pure state — called also *chlorimide* **2 :** any chloramine (sense 1) or chloramide (sense 1) having two chlorine atoms attached to the nitrogen atom; *esp* **:** DICHLORAMINE-T

dichloramine-T *n* **:** a yellow crystalline compound $CH_3C_6H_4SO_2NCl_2$ used esp. formerly as an antiseptic; *para*-toluenesulfon-dichlor-amide — called also *dichloramine;* compare CHLORAMINE-T

di·chloride \(ˈ)dī+\ *n* [*di-* + *chloride*] **:** a binary compound containing two atoms of chlorine combined with an element or radical

di·chlo·ro·acetic acid \(ˌ)dī¦klōrō+ . . . -\ *n* [ISV *dichlor-* + *acetic*] **:** a strong high-boiling liquid acid $CHCl_2COOH$ obtained esp. by chlorination of acetic acid

di·chlo·ro·benzene \"+\ *n* [ISV *dichlor-* + *benzene*] **:** any of three isomeric compounds $C_6H_4Cl_2$ made by chlorinating benzene: as **a :** ORTHODICHLOROBENZENE **b :** PARADICHLOROBENZENE

di·chlo·ro·butane \"+\ *n* [*dichlor-* + *butane*] **:** a liquid compound $Cl(CH_2)_4Cl$ made usu. from tetrahydrofuran and used chiefly in making adiponitrile for the manufacture of nylon — called also *1,4-dichlorobutane*

di·chlo·ro·diethyl ether \"+ . . . -\ *n* [*dichlor-* + *diethyl*] **:** DICHLOROETHYL ETHER

di·chlo·ro·di·flu·o·ro·methane \(ˌ)dī¦klōrōˌdīˌflü(ə)rō+\ *n* [*dichlor-* + *difluor-* + *methane*] **:** a nontoxic nonflammable easily liquefiable gas CCl_2F_2 made from carbon tetrachloride by reaction with antimony trifluoride and used as a refrigerant in refrigerators and air-conditioning units and as a propellant in aerosols

di·chlo·ro·ethyl ether \(ˌ)dī¦klōrō+ . . . -\ *also* **di·chlor·ethyl ether** \¦dīklōr+ . . . -\ *n* [*dichlor-* + *ethyl*] **:** a liquid ether $(ClCH_2CH_2)_2O$ that has an odor like chloroform, is made usu. by dehydration of ethylene chlorohydrin, and is used chiefly as a solvent and as a fumigant for insects; bis(2-chloroethyl) ether — called also *beta, beta'-dichlorodiethyl ether*

dichloroethyl sulfide \"+ . . . -\ *also* **di·chlor·ethyl sulfide** \¦dīklōr+ . . . -\ *n* **:** MUSTARD GAS

di·chlo·ro·hydrin \(ˌ)dī¦klōrō+\ *or* **di·chlor·hydrin** \¦dīklōr+\ *n* [ISV *dichlor-* + *-hydrin*] **:** either of two liquid compounds $C_3H_6Cl_2O$ made by the action of hydrochloric acid on glycerol or of hypochlorous acid on allyl chloride, distinguished as alpha- or alpha-gamma-dichlorohydrin $CH_2ClCHOHCH_2Cl$ and beta- or alpha-beta dichlorohydrin $CH_2ClCH_2ClCH_2OH$, and used chiefly in organic synthesis and as solvents

di·chlo·ro·phenarsine \(ˌ)dī¦klōrō+\ *n* [*dichlor-* + *phen-* + *arsine*] **:** an arsenical used in the form of its white powdery hydrochloride $HOC_6H_3(AsCl_2)NH_2.HCl$ in the treatment of syphilis esp. as an adjuvant to penicillin

di·chlo·ro·phenoxyacetic acid \"+ . . . -\ *n* [*dichlor-* + *phenoxyacetic*] **:** a white crystalline compound $Cl_2C_6H_3OCH_2COOH$ made from 2,4-dichloro-phenol and chloroacetic acid that is a growth regulator for plants and is used esp. in the form of salts and esters as a weed killer — usu. used with initial numbers ⟨2,4-*dichlorophenoxyacetic acid*⟩; called also *2,4-D*

dicho- — see DICH-

di·chog·a·mous \(ˈ)dī¦kägəməs\ *or* **di·cho·gam·ic** \¦dīkō¦gamik\ *adj* [*dich-* + *-gamous, -gamic*] **:** characterized by or relating to dichogamy

di·chog·a·my \dīˈkägəmē\ *n* -ES [G *dichogamie*, fr. *dich-* + *-gamie* -gamy] **:** production of male and female reproductive elements of hermaphroditic plants or animals at different times ensuring cross-fertilization

di·chon·dra \dīˈkändrə\ *n* [NL, fr. *di-* + *-chondra* (fr. Gk *chondros* grain)] **1** *cap* **:** a genus of chiefly tropical perennial herbs (family Convolvulaceae) having slender creeping stems, cordate-orbicular to reniform entire leaves, and very small obscure greenish yellow to white flowers borne in the leaf axils and including some (esp. *D. repens* or its varieties) that are naturalized or used as a ground cover and substitute for lawn grasses in parts of the southern U.S. **2** -s **:** any plant of the genus *Dichondra*

di·choph·y·sis \dīˈkäfəsəs\ *n* -ES [NL, fr. *dich-* + Gk *physis* nature — more at PHYSIC] **:** a regularly and dichotomously branching sterile hyphal end in the hymenium of certain fungi

dich·optic \(ˈ)dī¦käptik, (ˈ)di¦-\ *adj* [*dich-* + *optic*] *zoo* **:** having the borders of the compound eyes separate — compare HOLOPTIC

di·cho·ree \(ˈ)dī¦kōrˌē, ˌdīkəˈrē\ *n* -s [F *dichorée*, fr. L *dichoreus*, fr. *di-* + *choreus* trochee — more at CHOREUS] **:** DITROCHEE

di·chorial \(ˈ)dī+\ *adj* [*di-* + *chorial*] **:** having two chorions and two placentas — used esp. of human fraternal twins

di·cho·ri·san·dra \(ˌ)dīkōrəˈsandrə\ *n, cap* [NL, fr. *di-* + Gk *chōris* of a different kind + NL *-andra*] **:** a genus of tropical American herbs (family Commelinaceae) with sheathing leaves and blue or purple racemose or paniculate flowers

di·chot·o·mal \(ˈ)dī¦käd·əməl, -ätə- *sometimes* də'k-\ *adj* **:** of, relating to, or situated in a dichotomy — used esp. of the central flower in a dichasium

di·cho·tom·ic \¦dīkə¦tämik *sometimes* ¦dik-\ *adj* **:** of, relating to, or involving dichotomy — **di·cho·tom·i·cal·ly** \-mək(ə)lē\ *adv*

di·chot·o·mist \dīˈkäd·əməst, -ätə- *sometimes* dəˈk-\ *n* -s [Gk *dichotomia* dichotomy + E *-ist*] **:** one that dichotomizes **:** DUALIST

di·chot·o·mi·za·tion \(ˌ)dīˌkäd·əməˈzāshən, -ätə-, -ˌmīˈz- *sometimes* də,-\ *n* -s **:** the act or action of dichotomizing **:** the condition of being dichotomized

di·chot·o·mize \=ˈ==ˌmīz\ *vb* -ED/-ING/-S [LL *dichotomos* + E *-ize*] *vt* **1 :** to divide into two parts, classes, or groups ⟨~ all answers into those right and those wrong⟩ ⟨~ the animal world into vertebrate and invertebrate⟩ **2 :** to separate into several parts **~** *vi* **1 :** to become readily dichotomized **:** split readily into two groups or classes **2 :** to form or grow into a dichotomy

di·chot·o·mo·siphon \(ˌ)=ˌ==(ˌ)mō+\ *n, cap* [NL, fr. Gk *dichotomos* + *siphōn* tube, pipe, siphon — more at SIPHON] **:** a monotypic genus of erect tough fibrous coenocytic aquatic green algae (family Vaucheriaceae) that cause clogging of screens at water-pumping stations in some areas

di·chot·o·mous \(ˈ)dī¦käd·əməs, -ätə- *sometimes* dəˈk-\ *adj* [LL *dichotomos*, fr. Gk, fr. *dich-* + *-tomos* (fr. *temnein* to cut) — more at TOME] **1 :** dividing into two parts or groups **:** readily susceptible to dichotomy **:** readily dividing into pairs successively **:** showing a dual arrangement **2 :** relating to, involving, or proceeding from dichotomy ⟨a ~ division⟩ — **di·chot·o·mous·ly** *adv*

dichotomous key *n, biol* **:** a key to classification based on a choice between two alternative characters

di·chot·o·my \=ˈ==mē, -mi\ *n* -ES [Gk *dichotomia*, fr. *dichotomein* to cut in half (fr. *dichotomos*) + *-ia* -y] **1 a :** division into two parts, classes, or groups esp. into two groups mutually exclusive or opposed by contradiction ⟨a ~ into the good and the evil⟩ **b :** division into two **:** a splitting into two parts or groups **:** differentiation into two contrasted or sharply opposed groups ⟨~ between practice and theory⟩ ⟨a ~ between written and spoken evidence⟩ **2 :** the phase of the moon or an inferior planet in which just half its disk appears illuminated **3 a :** FORKING, BIFURCATION; *esp* **:** repeated bifurcation (as of the stem of a plant or a vein of the body) **b :** a system of branching in which the main axis forks repeatedly into two branches (as in the thallus of the seaweed *Dictyota dichotoma* and in many liverworts) forming a helicoid axis when the corresponding member of each pair is suppressed or a scorpioid axis when alternate members of adjacent pairs are suppressed — see FALSE DICHOTOMY, SYMPODIUM **c :** branching of an ancestral line into two more or less equal diverging branches **4 :** fee splitting by doctors

di·cho·triaene \¦dīkō+\ *n* -s [*dich-* + *triaene*] **:** a sponge spicule with dichotomously branched rays

di·chro·ic \(ˈ)dī¦krōik\ *also* **di·chro·it·ic** \¦=ˌ=¦id·ik\ *adj* [Gk *dichroos* two-colored (fr. *di-* + *-chroos* -chroous) + E *-ic, -itic*] **1 :** having the property of dichroism ⟨a ~ crystal⟩ ⟨a ~ mirror⟩ **2 :** DICHROMATIC

dichroic fog *n, photog* **:** a clouded effect or stain that is greenish by reflected light and reddish by transmitted light and is due to the deposition of very finely divided silver usu. on the surface of a film or plate during processing

di·chro·ism \ˈdīkrōˌizəm\ *n* -s [Gk *dichroos* + E *-ism*] **1 :** pleochroism in which the colors are unlike when a crystal is viewed in the direction of two different axes **2 a :** the property of some bodies of differing in color with the thickness of the transmitting layer or of some liquids of differing in color with the degree of concentration of the solution **b :** the property of some surfaces of reflecting light of one color and transmitting light of other colors **3 :** DICHROMATISM

di·chro·ite \-ōˌīt\ *n* -s [F, fr. Gk *dichroos* + F *-ite*] **:** CORDIERITE

di·chro·mat \ˈdīkrōˌmat\ *n* -s [back-formation fr. *dichromatic*] **:** one that requires only two primary colors to be mixed in order to match the spectrum as he sees it **:** one affected with dichromatism — compare MONOCHROMAT, TRICHROMAT

di·chromate \(ˈ)dī+\ *n* [ISV *di-* + *chromate*] **:** a salt of dichromic acid — called also *bichromate*

di·chro·mat·ic \¦dī+\ *adj* [*di-* + *chromatic*] **1 :** having or exhibiting two colors **2 :** having two color varieties or color phases independently of age or sex ⟨a ~ bird⟩ ⟨a ~ insect⟩ **3 a :** relating to or exhibiting dichromatism **b :** characteristic of a dichromat

di·chro·ma·tism \dīˈkrōməˌtizəm\ *n* -s [*dichromatic* + *-ism*] **1 :** the state or condition of being dichromatic **2 :** partial color blindness in which only two of the fundamental colors or two colors and their combinations are perceptible

di·chro·ma·top·sia \(ˌ)dī,krōmə'täpsēə\ *n* -s [NL, fr. *di-* + *chromat-* + *-opsia*] : DICHROMATISM 2

di·chromic \(ˈ)dī+\ *adj* [*di-* + *chromic*] : containing two atoms of chromium or their equivalents in the molecule

dichromic acid *n* : an acid $H_2Cr_2O_7$ known only in solution and esp. in the form of its salts (as potassium dichromate) most of which are orange or red

di·chro·nous \'dīkrənəs\ *adj* [LL *dichronus, dichronos*, fr. Gk *dichronos*, fr. *di-* + *-chronos* -chronous] *prosody* **1** : consisting of or lasting through two morae : DISEMIC **2** : COMMON 9c

di·chro·scope \'dīkrə,skōp\ *also* **di·chro·i·scope** *or* **di·chro·o·scope** \dī'krōə,-\ *n* -s [*dichro-, dichroi-, dichroo-* (fr. *dichroism*) + *-scope*] : an instrument for examining crystals (as gems) for pleochroism — **di·chro·scop·ic** \ˌ==ˈskäpik\ *adj*

dicht \'dikt\ *Scot var of* ²DIGHT

dicing *n* -s [ME *dycing*, fr. gerund of *dycen* to dice — more at DICE] **1** : the throwing of dice esp. in a gambling game **2** : ornamentation or an ornamenting in squares or cubes

dicing board *n* : DICE BOARD

¹dick \'dik\ *n* -s [fr. the nickname *Dick*, by shortening & alter. fr. *Richard*] **1** *chiefly Brit* : FELLOW, MAN, CHAP ⟨he's a queer ~, for sure⟩ **2** *dial Eng* : a leather apron and bib **3** : PENIS — usu. considered vulgar **4** [by shortening & alter.] : DETECTIVE ⟨a house ~ in one of the busiest hotels⟩

²dick \"\ *n* -s [ME *dick, dike* — more at DIKE] **1** *dial Brit* : DIKE **2** *dial Brit* : DITCH

³dick \"\ *n* -s [by shortening & alter.] *slang Brit* : DECLARATION ⟨I'll take my ~ he's wrong⟩ : a declared standard (as of value) ⟨a shipment not up to ~⟩

dick·cis·sel \dik'sisəl, 'ˌ=ˌ==\ *n* -s [imit.] : a common migratory finch (*Spiza americana*) that breeds throughout the central U.S., is brownish streaked with black and gray above with black throat, white chin, and yellowish breast, and feeds chiefly on weed seeds and grasshoppers

dick·ens \'dikənz\ *n* -ES [prob. fr. the name *Dickens*, euphemism for *devil*] **1 a** : DEVIL, DEUCE — used as a more or less meaningless intensive; often used interjectionally; usu. used with *the* ⟨I cannot tell what the ~ his name is —Shak.⟩ ⟨very mad and swearing like the ~⟩ **b** : worst disadvantage or difficulty : most serious part ⟨the ~ of it was that we had no money⟩ **2** : CHILD; *esp* : an exceptionally active and mischievous child

¹dick·en·si·an \di'ken(t)sēən, -kenzē-\ *adj, usu cap* [Charles J. H. *Dickens* †1870 Eng. novelist + E *-ian*] : characteristic of or having the qualities of the writings of Charles Dickens with respect to humor and pathos in the portrayal of odd often extravagant and picturesque character types usu. from the lower economic strata of 19th century English society ⟨the novel verges on the *Dickensian*: there is pathos, there is humor, and, above all, there is excellent characterization, with a tendency to noble caricature —John Cournos⟩ ⟨the *Dickensian* squalor of London's slums —*Time*⟩

²dickensian \"\ *n* -s *usu cap* : an ardent admirer or student of the works of Charles Dickens

¹dick·er \'dikə(r)\ *n* -s [ME *dyker*; akin to MLG *dēker* quantity of ten (hides), MHG *techer, decher*; all fr. a prehistoric WGmc word borrowed fr. L *decuria* quantity of ten, fr. *decem* ten — more at TEN] **1** : the number or quantity of 10 esp. of hides or skins **2** *obs* : a large quantity : LOT

²dicker \"\ *vi* **dickered; dickered; dickering** \-k(ə)riŋ\ **dickers** [origin unknown] : to seek to arrive at a workable arrangement by bargaining : discuss negotiations and arrangements : HAGGLE, BARGAIN ⟨a trapper ~*ing* for a higher price for his furs⟩ ⟨~*ing* with members of the opposition for their support⟩ ⟨~*ing* in connection with the merger between the companies⟩

³dicker \"\ *n* -s **1** : BARTER; *often* : goods bartered **2** : a swap made after haggling and bargaining : an act or session of haggling or bargaining : a political deal : negotiation with concessions offered and discussed ⟨a ~ for his saddle⟩ ⟨~*s* being argued in the lobbies outside the assembly room⟩

¹dick·ey *also* **dicky** \'dikē, -ki\ *n, pl* **dickeys** *also* **dickies** [fr. the nickname *Dicky*, dim. of *Dick*] **1** : any of various articles of clothing: as **a** *dial Eng* : PETTICOAT **b** : a man's separate or detachable shirtfront usu. worn under a jacket in place of a shirt and sometimes in addition to a shirt esp. with clerical garments **c** *chiefly New Eng* : a detachable shirt collar **d** : a small fabric insert that is worn to fill in the neckline of a dress, jacket, or other garment and give the appearance of a blouse **2** : one of various animals: as **a** *dial Brit* : a male donkey : JACK **b** (1) *also* **dickeybird** *or* **dickybird** \'==,=\ : a small bird (as a sparrow or a canary) (2) *dial Eng* : HEDGE SPARROW **3** *chiefly Brit* **a** *also* **dickey box** : the seat for the driver at the front of a carriage **b** : a seat at the back of a carriage or automobile : RUMBLE SEAT **4** : a supplementary device used in textile manufacturing; *esp* : an additional roll used to keep the working rolls clear in textile manufacturing

dickey 1d

²dickey *or* **dicky** \"\ *adj* [origin unknown] : of poor quality : being in bad condition : SHAKY, WEAK ⟨a ~ leg⟩ ⟨communications that are in a ~ state⟩

dick·in·son·ite \'dikənsə,nīt\ *n* -s [William *Dickinson*, 19th cent. Am. clergyman and mineralogist + E *-ite*] : a green mineral $H_2Na_6(Mn,Fe,Ca,Mg)_{14}(PO_4)_{12}.H_2O$ consisting of foliated hydrous acid phosphate chiefly of manganese, iron, and sodium (sp. gr. 3.34)

dick·ite \'di,kīt\ *n* -s [Allan B. *Dick* †1926 Eng. mineralogist + E *-ite*] : a mineral $Al_2Si_2O_5(OH)_4$ consisting of a basic silicate of aluminum found relatively well crystallized in clays : a polymorph of kaolinite

dicks *pl of* DICK

dick·so·nia \dik'sōnēə\ *n, cap* [NL, fr. James *Dickson* †1822 Eng. botanist + NL *-ia*] : a large genus of tropical tree ferns (family Cyatheaceae) having bipinnatifid or tripinnatifid fronds and marginal or submarginal sori with a surrounding membranous cup-shaped indusium and including one species (*D. antarctica*) that is often cultivated — **dick·so·ni·oid** \-nē,ȯid\ *adj*

dick test \'dik-\ *n, usu cap D* [after George F. *Dick* *b*1881 and Gladys H. *Dick* *b*1881 Am. physicians] : a test to determine susceptibility or immunity to scarlet fever made by injecting scarlet fever toxin into the skin

dick toxin *n, usu cap D* [after George F. and Gladys H. *Dick*] : the erythrogenic toxin of the scarlatinal streptococcus

dicky *var of* DICTY

dicky rice weevil \'dikē-\ *n* [prob. fr. the nickname *Dicky*] : a weevil (*Maleuterpes spinipes*) common in Australia and New Zealand whose adults feed on foliage and whose larvae feed on the roots of citrus and other fruit trees

di·cli·nism \(ˈ)dī'klī,nizəm\ *or* **di·cli·ny** \'dī,klīnē\ *n, pl* **diclinisms** *or* **diclinies** [*di-* + *-clinism, -cliny*] : the condition of being diclinous

di·cli·nous \(ˈ)dī¦klīnəs\ *adj* [*di-* + *-clinous*] : having the stamens and pistils in separate flowers — compare MONOCLINOUS, DIOECIOUS, MONOECIOUS

di·coc·cous \(ˈ)dī¦käkəs\ *adj* [*di-* + *-coccous* (fr. Gk *kokkos* grain, seed)] : composed of two coherent one-seeded carpels ⟨a ~ capsule⟩

di·co·lic \(ˈ)dī¦kōlik\ *adj* [Gk *dikōlos* (fr. *di-* + *-kōlos*, fr. *kōlon* limb, colon) + E *-ic* — more at COLON] : of, relating to, or having two cola ⟨~ verse⟩

di·colon \(ˈ)dī+\ *n, pl* **dicola** [*di-* + ²*colon*] : a verse or rhythmic period having two cola

di·con·dyl·i·an \ˌdī(ˌ)kän¦dilēən\ *adj* [*di-* + *condyle* + *-ian*] : having two occipital condyles

di·con·dyl·ic \-lik\ *adj* [*di-* + *condyle* + *-ic*] : having two articulatory condyles — used chiefly of joints between segments of the limbs of insects

di·co·phane \'dīkə,fān\ *n* -s [*dichloro-diphenyl-ethane*] : DDT

di·cot \'dī,kät\ *or* **di·cot·yl** \'dī,käd·ᵊl, dī'k-, -ät·ᵊl\ *n* -s [by shortening] : DICOTYLEDON

di·cotyledon \(ˌ)dī+\ *n* [NL *dicotyledones*] : a plant having two cotyledons : a member of the subclass Dicotyledoneae — compare MONOCOTYLEDON

di·cot·y·le·do·ne·ae \(ˌ)dī,käd·ᵊlə'dōnē,ē\ *n pl, cap* [NL, alter. of *Dicotyledones*, fr. *di-* + *cotyledones*, pl. of *cotyledon*] : a subclass of Angiospermae comprising seed plants (as cactuses and oaks) that produce an embryo with two cotyledons and have net-veined leaves, stems with secondary thickening resulting in annual ring formation in woody perennials, and floral organs usu. arranged in cycles of four or five, including most of the deciduous woody plants of temperate climates and the majority of herbaceous flowering plants, and commonly being divided into Archichlamydeae and Metachlamydeae — compare MONOCOTYLEDONEAE

di·cot·y·le·do·nes \(ˌ)dī,käd·ᵊl'ēdᵊn,ēz\ *n pl, cap* [NL] *in some classifications* : DICOTYLEDONEAE

di·cotyledonous *also* **di·cotyledonary** \(ˌ)dī+\ *adj* [*dicotyledon* + *-ous* or *-ary*] : of, relating to, or characteristic of the subclass Dicotyledoneae; *often* : having paired cotyledons — contrasted with *monocotyledonous*; compare POLYCOTYLEDONOUS

di·cot·y·les \dī'käd·ᵊl,ēz\ [NL, fr. *di-* + *-cotyles* (fr. Gk *kotylos* cup, anything hollow)] *syn of* TAYASSU

di·co·tyl·i·dae \,dīkə'tilə,dē\ [NL, fr. *Dicotyles*, type genus + *-idae*] *syn of* TAYASSUIDAE

di·cot·y·lous \(ˈ)dī¦käd·ᵊləs\ *adj* [by contr.] : DICOTYLEDONOUS

di·cou·ma·rol \dī'k(y)ümə,rōl, -ōl\ *or* **di·cou·ma·rin** \-,rən\ *n* -s [*dicoumarol* fr. *Dicumarol*, a trademark; *dicoumarin* fr. *di-* + *coumarin*] : a white crystalline compound $C_{19}H_{12}O_6$ that is obtained from spoiled sweet clover hay or made synthetically, is the actual pathogenic agent in sweet clover disease, and is used as an anticoagulant (as in the treatment of embolism); 3,3′-methylene-bis(4-hydroxy-coumarin) — called also *bishydroxycoumarin*

di·cra·na·les \,dīkrə'nā(,)lēz\ *n pl, cap* [NL, fr. *Dicranum* + *-ales*] : a widely distributed order of Musci comprising mosses with erect gametophores, a usu. acrocarpous sporophyte, and a capsule with 16 peristome teeth — see DICRANUM

di·cra·num \dī'krānəm\ *n, cap* [NL, fr. Gk *dikranon*, neut. of *dikranos* two-headed, fr. *di-* + *-kranos* (fr. *kranion* skull, head) — more at CRANIUM] : a large genus (the type of the family Dicranaceae) comprising mosses of the order Dicranales that have costate leaves, a cleft or bifid peristome, and long-stalked capsules

¹di·cro·coe·lid \,dīkrə¦sēləd\ *adj* [NL *Dicrocoeliidae*] : of or relating to the Dicrocoeliidae

²dicrocoelid \"\ *n* -s : a worm of the family Dicrocoeliidae

di·cro·coe·li·i·dae \,dīkrəsə'līə,dē\ *n pl, cap* [NL *Dicrocoelium*, type genus + *-idae*] : a family of small to medium-sized, flattened or more or less cylindrical digenetic trematode worms that as adults parasitize the biliary ducts or occas. other viscera of vertebrates

di·cro·coe·li·um \,==ˈsēlēəm\ *n, cap* [NL, fr. Gk *dikroos, dikrous, dikros* forked, cloven + NL *-coelium* (fr. Gk *koilia* cavity, fr. *koilos* hollow) — more at CAVE] : a widely distributed genus comprising small lanceolate digenetic trematodes of the livers of ruminants or occas. other mammals including man and being the type of the family Dicrocoeliidae

di·cros·to·nyx \dī'krästə(,)niks\ *n, cap* [NL, irreg. fr. Gk *dikroos, dikrous, dikros* + NL *-onyx*] : a genus consisting of the pied lemmings

di·crot·ic \(ˈ)dī¦kräd·ik\ *also* **di·cro·tal** \-rōd·ᵊl, -räd·-\ *or* **di·cro·tous** \'dīkrəd·əs\ *adj* [Gk *dikrotos* (fr. *di-* + *-krotos*, fr. *krotein* to beat, knock, rattle) + E *-ic* or *-al* or *-ous* — more at CROTALUS] **1** *of the pulse* : having a double beat (as in certain febrile states in which the heart is overactive and the arterial walls lacking in tone) — compare MONOCROTIC **2** : being or relating to the second expansion of the artery that occurs during the diastole of the heart — **di·cro·tism** \'dīkrə,tizəm\ *n* -s

di·cru·ri·dae \dī'krürə,dē\ *n pl, cap* [NL, fr. *Dicrurus*, type genus (fr. Gk *dikroos, dikrous, dikros* + NL *-urus*) + *-idae*] : a family of Old World passerine birds that are usu. black with rather large hooked bills, short metatarsi and small toes, long wings, and a tail with 10 rectrices and usu. a deep fork — see DRONGO

dict *abbr* **1** dictaphone **2** dictation **3** dictator **4** dictionary

dicta *pl of* DICTUM

dic·ta·men \dik'tāmən\ *n, pl* **dic·tam·i·na** \-tamənə\ [LL, fr. L *dictare* to pronounce, assert, dictate — more at DICTATE] : RULE, PRONOUNCEMENT ⟨the ~ of reason⟩ ⟨the *dictamina* of a master⟩

Dic·ta·phone \'diktə,fōn\ *trademark* — used for a phonographic instrument combining a recorder and reproducer for use in dictating

dic·ta·phon·ic \ˌ==ˈfänik, -ˈfōn-\ *adj, of speech* : reproduced with extreme accuracy ⟨the dialogue in the play is a little less ~ than it was in the book —John Mason Brown⟩

¹dic·tate \'dik,tāt *also* =ˈ=; *usu* -ād·+V\ *vb* -ED/-ING/-S [L *dictatus*, past part. of *dictare* to pronounce, assert, dictate, freq. of *dicere* to say — more at DICTION] *vi* **1** : to speak, recite, or read off for a person to write down or transcribe or for a machine to record for later transcription ⟨*dictating* too fast for the secretary to transcribe⟩ ⟨*dictating* into the machine⟩ **2** : to speak or act commandingly or domineeringly, imposing orders, injunctions, and terms authoritatively or autocratically ⟨a stern father and husband always *dictating* to his family⟩ : PRESCRIBE, COMMAND ⟨to act spontaneously as the heart ~*s* —Bertrand Russell⟩ ⟨as the situation ~*s*⟩ ~ *vt* **1** : to speak, recite, or read off (something) for a person to write down or transcribe or for a machine to record ⟨*dictating* a letter to the secretary⟩ ⟨*dictating* test questions to a class⟩ ⟨*dictating* a statement to the reporters⟩; *sometimes* : to compose while speaking **2 a** : to issue as an order usu. peremptorily ⟨the duke *dictating* what part each should take⟩ **b** : to command or impose authoritatively : PRESCRIBE, ENJOIN : direct forcefully or irresistibly ⟨*dictating* peace terms to the vanquished⟩ **c** : to require or determine necessarily ⟨the weight of the floor ~*s* use of heavy supports⟩ ⟨an arrangement *dictated* by the situation⟩ **d** : to bring into being, form, determine, or influence commandingly ⟨patroness who has set herself up to ~ public taste —Lillian de la Torre⟩ **e** : to designate authoritatively, overriding possible opposition ⟨a president strong enough to ~ his successor⟩

syn PRESCRIBE, ORDAIN, DECREE, IMPOSE: DICTATE implies an authoritative direction, usually peremptory, or intended as not to be questioned ⟨groups trying to *dictate* who shall and who shall not be retained on the faculties of the colleges and universities of the nation —W.T.Gossett⟩ ⟨he continued . . . to *dictate* the lives of the parishioners —Willa Cather⟩ ⟨the avarice which *dictated* every detail of their lives —Marcia Davenport⟩ PRESCRIBE implies a formulated rule, law, or order and an authoritative pronouncement ⟨my teachers should have *prescribed* to me, 1st, sincerity; 2d, sincerity; 3d, sincerity —H.D.Thoreau⟩ ⟨the terms *prescribed* by law —John Marshall⟩ ⟨driven to describe paths round the sun by exactly the same forces as *prescribed* the orderly motions of the planets —James Jeans⟩ ORDAIN implies enactment or institution by a supreme and unquestioned authority or power, usually suggesting the authoritatively definitive settlement of a question ⟨in this same period Parliament . . . *ordained* that everyone who died should be buried in English cloth —G.M. Trevelyan⟩ ⟨nature inexorably *ordains* that the human race shall perish of famine if it stops working —G.B.Shaw⟩ ⟨a code of rigid and inflexible rules, arbitrarily *ordained*, and to be blindly obeyed —Havelock Ellis⟩ DECREE implies a formal pronouncement by an authoritative power usu. ecclesiastic, civil, or judicial ⟨against the *decree* of fate there is no appeal —Aldous Huxley⟩ ⟨enforcement of order in court and obedience to its *decrees* —O.W.Holmes †1935⟩ ⟨one *decree* of the Egyptian government permitted the internment of any person suspected of antigovernmental activity —*Collier's Yr. Bk.*⟩ IMPOSE implies a subjecting to what must be borne, endured, or submitted to, or a dictatorial forcing of something upon someone or a compelling prescription of something ⟨to *impose* impossible taxes on a poverty-stricken people⟩ ⟨to *impose* limitations on hours of work —*Amer. Guide Series: N.H.*⟩ ⟨we are willing therefore to believe that destiny is *imposed* upon us —Archibald MacLeish⟩

²dic·tate \'=ˌ=; *sometimes* =ˈ=\ *n* -s [L *dictatum*, fr. neut. of *dictatus*] **1 a** : an authoritative rule : a prescription or injunction authoritatively pronounced (as in scripture or law) : a directive given cogency by conscience, reason, virtue, or other ruling principle ⟨the ~*s* of good taste⟩ ⟨~*s* of common sense⟩ **b** : a command by one in authority ⟨the ruler's ~*s*⟩ **2** *archaic* : material uttered for another's transcription **3** *obs* : DICTUM, MAXIM, PRECEPT **4** : DIKTAT

dic·tat·ing·ly *adv* [*dictating* (pres. part. of *dictate*) + *-ly*] : in a dictating manner

dictating machine *n* : a usu. electronic machine used esp. for the recording (as on a wax cylinder, a disc, or a tape) of dictated matter to be transcribed later in typed form

dic·ta·tion \dik'tāshən\ *n* -s [LL *dictation-, dictatio*, fr. L *dictatus* + *-ion-, -io* -ion] **1** : the act of uttering authoritatively : PRESCRIPTION : arbitrary command : necessitous injunction or requirement : forceful formation or shaping ⟨they would tolerate no outside ~ in matters concerning their own parishes —V.L.Parrington⟩ ⟨duty's stern ~ —W.S.Gilbert⟩ **2 a** : the act of uttering words to be written by another; *also* : manner of dictating **b** : the playing or singing of music so that it may be reproduced either orally or in written notation usu. by a student for the purpose of training the hearing to accurate appreciation of musical tones **3** : matter (as words or music) that has been presented by dictation ⟨the secretary took ~ all morning long⟩

dic·ta·tive \'dik,tād·iv, =ˈ==\ *adj* : DICTATORIAL

dic·ta·tor \'dik,tād·ə(r), -ātə- *also* =ˈ==\ *n* -s [L, fr. *dictatus* + *-or*] **1 a** : a chief magistrate appointed in emergencies and given absolute authority by the senate of ancient Rome **b** : a person granted absolute emergency power in a later republic ⟨making the general ~ of the state during the invasion⟩ ⟨when ~*s* resist the temptation to become despots —F.L.Schuman⟩ **c** : one enjoying complete autocratic control or leadership ⟨the secretary was actually the ~ of the party⟩ ⟨making him ~⟩; *often* : a supreme sometimes autocratic arbiter ⟨a ~ in the world of British art —DeLancey Ferguson⟩ **d** : one ruling absolutely, typically with brutality, oppression, and ruthless suppression of opposition ⟨political ~*s* who attempt to accomplish by calculated brutality and aggression what they lack the intelligence and magnanimity to consummate —Lewis Mumford⟩ **2** : one that dictates (as to a secretary or a recording machine)

dic·ta·to·ri·al \ˌdiktə¦tōrēəl, -tȯr-\ *adj* [L *dictatorius* (fr. *dictatus* + *-orius* -ory) + E *-al*] **1** : befitting or belonging to a dictator ⟨given ~ power but using it sparingly⟩ : ruled by a dictator ⟨a ~ government⟩ **2** : characteristic of an autocratic dictator : oppressive to or contemptuous of others ⟨imperious and ~, he knew how to command but not to obey —V.L.Parrington⟩ ⟨began a ~ rule that lasted for the duration of the war —*Amer. Guide Series: La.*⟩ — **dic·ta·to·ri·al·ly** \-ēəlē, -li\ *adv* — **dic·ta·to·ri·al·ness** *n* -ES

dictatorian *adj* [L *dictatorias* E *-an*] : DICTATORIAL 1

dic·ta·tor·ship \dik'tād·ə(r),ship, -ātə- *also* 'ˌ===ˌ=\ *n* -s **1** : the office or term of office of a dictator **2** : absolute authority or power ⟨there should not be a ~, that is, social choice conforming only to the will of one man —H.M.Somers⟩ ⟨the exploitation of labor by industrial ~ —Roger Burlingame⟩ **3** : a form of government in which a dictator or small clique has absolute power without effective constitutional limitations ⟨after the revolution the country became a ~ under a former army officer⟩ : a despotic state ⟨a war between a democracy and a ~⟩

dictatorship of the proletariat : the assumption of political power by the proletariat with concomitant repression of previously controlling or governing classes that in Marxist philosophy is considered an essential preliminary to establishment of the classless state

dic·ta·to·ry \'diktə,tōrē, -tȯr-, -ri\ *adj* [L *dictatorius*] : DICTATORIAL

dic·ta·tress \'dik,tā·trəs, =ˈ==\ *n* -ES [*dictator* + *-ess*] : a female dictator

dic·ta·trix \dik'tā·triks\ *n, pl* **dictatri·ces** \-ā·trə,sēz, ,diktə·'trī(,)sēz\ [L, fem. of *dictator*] : DICTATRESS

dic·ta·ture \dik'tāchər, 'diktə,chů(ə)r\ *n* -s [L *dictatura*, fr. *dictatus* + *-ura* -ure] : office of a dictator : DICTATORSHIP; *also* : a body of dictators

dictier *comparative of* DICTY

dictiest *superlative of* DICTY

dic·tion \'dikshən\ *n* -s [L & L; LL *diction-, dictio* word, fr. L, delivery in public speaking, fr. *dictus* (past part. of *dicere* to say) + *-ion-, -io* -ion; akin to OE *tēon* to accuse, OHG *zīhan* to accuse, ON *tjā* to show, Goth *gateihan* to tell, L *dicare* to dedicate, Gk *deiknynai* to show, *dikē* right, judgment, Skt *diśati* he shows] **1** *obs* **a** : WORD, PHRASE **b** : verbal expression or description **2** : choice of words esp. with regard to correctness, clearness, or effectiveness : wording used ⟨very careless ~ in the essay⟩ ⟨a new ~ for poetry⟩ ⟨trite ~ is so common in these pages —H.N.Fairchild⟩ **3 a** : vocal expression : ENUNCIATION; *esp* : clear, accurate, and pleasing delivery in public speaking **b** : pronunciation and enunciation of words in singing

dic·tio·nary \'dikshə,nerē, -ri\ *n* -ES *often attrib* [ML *dictionarium*, fr. LL *diction-, dictio* word + L *-arium* -ary] **1** : a reference book containing words usu. alphabetically arranged along with information about their forms, pronunciations, functions, etymologies, meanings, and syntactical and idiomatic uses ⟨a general ~ of the English language⟩ ⟨a monolingual ~⟩ — compare VOCABULARY ENTRY **2 a** : a reference book listing terms or names important to a particular subject or activity along with discussion of their meanings and applications ⟨a law ~⟩ ⟨a ~ of sports⟩; *broadly* : an encyclopedic listing ⟨a ~ of dates⟩ **b** : a reference book giving for words of one language equivalents in another ⟨an English-French ~⟩ ⟨a bilingual ~⟩ **c** : a reference book listing terms as commonly spelled together with their equivalents in some specialized system (as of orthography or symbols) ⟨a ~ of shorthand⟩ ⟨a pronouncing ~⟩ **3 a** : a general comprehensive list, collection, or repository ⟨a ~ of biography⟩ ⟨a usage ~⟩ **b** : vocabulary in use (as in a special field) : TERMINOLOGY ⟨the ~ of literary criticism⟩ **c** : a vocabulary of accepted terms ⟨in the ~ of the French Academy⟩ **d** : a vocabulary of the written words used by one author ⟨systematic *dictionaries* of individual authors —Hillis Miller⟩ **e** : LEXICON 4

dictionary catalog *n* : a catalog having its entries (as author, title, or subject) arranged in a single alphabet

dictionary definition *n* : a definition reporting established meanings or uses of words or symbols — compare STIPULATIVE DEFINITION

Dic·to·graph \'diktə,graf\ *trademark* — used for a telephonic instrument for picking up sounds in one room and transmitting them to another or recording them

dic·tum \'diktəm\ *n, pl* **dic·ta** \-tə\ *also* **dictums** \-təmz\ [L, fr. neut. of *dictus*, past part. of *dicere* to say — more at DICTION] **1** : SAYING, STATEMENT: **a** : an authoritative pronouncement often formal and definitive ⟨awaiting the king's ~ on the case⟩ : a statement in summation uttered with the intent or hope of acceptance as definitive ⟨a critic's *dicta* about art⟩ **b** : a formal statement of a principle or proposition ⟨a philosopher's ~ on the nature of good⟩ **c** : an opinionative statement uttered as though authoritatively and objectively ⟨the subjectivity and authoritarianism of many of his *dicta* —Thomas Pyles⟩ : MAXIM ⟨a would-be professor must heed the ~ "Publish or perish" —M.M.Hunt⟩ **2** : an opinion expressed by a judge on a point not necessarily arising or involved in a case in question or necessary for determining the rights of parties involved — see OBITER DICTUM; compare PRECEDENT, STARE DECISIS

dic·tum de om·ni et nul·lo \ˌdiktəmdā¦ȯmnē,et'nů(,)lō\ [L, maxim of all and none] : an axiom in logic: whatever may be affirmed or denied of a class may be affirmed or denied of every member of it

dic·ty *or* **dick·ty** \'diktē\ *adj* -ER/-EST [origin unknown] *slang* : HIGH-TONED, SNOBBISH; *often* : very good : very pleasing

dicty- *or* **dictyo-** *comb form* [NL, fr. Gk *dikty-, diktyo-*, fr. *diktyon*, fr. *dikein* to throw] : net ⟨*dictyosome*⟩

dic·tyn·i·dae \dik'tinə,dē\ *n pl, cap* [NL, fr. *Dictyna*, type genus (irreg. fr. Gk *diktyon* net) + *-idae*] : a family of spiders that spin irregular webs composed partly of threads curled by means of the calamistrum

dic·ty·o·cau·lus \,diktēə'kȯləs\ *n, cap* [NL, fr. *dicty-* + Gk *kaulos* stem, penis — more at HOLE] : a genus of small slender lungworms (family Metastrongylidae) infesting mammals (as ruminants) and often causing severe bronchial symptoms or even pneumonia in young animals

dic·ty·o·gen \'diktēə,jen, -,jən\ *n* -s [NL *dicty-* + E *-gen*]

: a monocotyledonous plant having net-veined leaves (as *Smilax rotundifolia*) — **dic·ty·og·e·nous** \¦==¦äjənəs\ *adj*
dic·ty·o·kinesis \ˌdiktē(ˌ)ō+\ *n* [NL, fr. *dicty-* + *kinesis*] : fission of the Golgi apparatus as a normal reproductive process
dic·ty·o·ne·ma \ˌ=tēə'nēmə\ *n, cap* [NL, fr. *dicty-* + *-nema*] : a genus of graptolites common in Ordovician and Silurian formations
dic·ty·o·ni·na \-ə'nīnə\ *n pl, cap* [NL, fr. Gk *diktyon* net + NL *-ina* — more at DICTY-] *in some classifications* : an order of Hyalospongiae comprising those members of the Hexasterophora with hexactine spicules fused into a rigid network — **dic·ty·o·nine** \'==əˌnīn\ *adj or n*
dic·ty·oph·o·ra \ˌdiktē'äf(ə)rə\ *n, cap* [NL, fr. *dicty-* + *-phora*] : a genus of stinkhorn fungi closely related to those of the genus *Phallus* but distinguished by an indusium that hangs like a skirt from below the pileus
dic·ty·o·siphon \ˌdiktēə+\ *n, cap* [NL, fr. *dicty-* + Gk *siphōn* tube, pipe, siphon — more at SIPHON] : a genus (the type of the family Dictyosiphonaceae) of brown algae (order Dictyosiphonales) having filiform fronds that taper to acute points — **dic·ty·o·siphonaceous** \"+\ *adj*
dic·ty·o·siphonales \ˌdiktēə+\ *n pl, cap* [NL, fr. *Dictyosiphon* + *-ales*] : an order of brown algae having a profusely branched cylindrical sporophyte which at maturity is differentiated internally into two or three regions
dic·ty·o·some \'diktēəˌsōm\ *n* -s [ISV *dicty-* + *-some*; orig. formed as It *dictiosoma*] : GOLGI BODY
dic·ty·o·sper·mum scale \ˌ===='spərməm-\ *n* [NL *dictyospermum*, alter. of *dictyospermi*, specific epithet of *Chrysomphalus dictyospermi*, fr. *dicty-* + *-spermi* (gen. of *-spermum*)] : a widely distributed rounded armored scale (*Chrysomphalus dictyospermi*) that is particularly destructive to citrus
dic·ty·o·spore \'diktēə+ˌ\ *n* [*dicty-* + *spore*] : a multicellular spore of certain fungi that has both longitudinal walls and cross septa — **dic·ty·o·spor·ous** \¦==ə¦spōrəs, ¦==ˌäspərəs\ *adj*
dic·ty·o·stele \'diktēəˌstēl *also* ¦===¦stēlē\ *n* -s [*dicty-* + *stele*] : a stele in which the vascular cylinder is broken up by leaf gaps into a longitudinal series or network of vascular strands around a central pith (as in many ferns) — **dic·ty·o·ste·lic** \¦===¦stēlik\ *adj* — **dic·ty·o·ste·ly** \'===ˌstēlē\ *n* -ES
dic·ty·o·ta \ˌdiktē'ōd·ə\ *n, cap* [NL, fr. Gk *diktyōtē*, fem. of *diktyōtos* latticed, made like a net, fr. *diktyon* net — more at DICTY-] : the type genus of Dictyotaceae comprising brown algae with the thallus dichotomously branched
dic·ty·o·ta·ce·ae \ˌdiktēə'tāsēˌē\ *n pl, cap* [NL, fr. *Dictyota*, type genus + *-aceae*] : a family of brown algae (order Dictyotales) that have an erect flattened parenchymatous thallus, oogamous sexual reproduction, and asexual reproduction by nonmotile spores — **dic·ty·o·ta·ceous** \¦===¦tāshəs\ *adj*
dic·ty·o·ta·les \ˌdiktēə'tā(ˌ)lēz\ *n pl, cap* [NL, fr. *Dictyota* + *-ales*] : an order of dichotomously branched parenchymatous brown algae (class Isogeneratae) that grow from apical cells
dic·ty·ox·y·lon \ˌdiktē'äksəˌlän, -ˌlən\ *n, cap* [NL, fr. *dicty-* + *-xylon*] : a form genus represented by Paleozoic fossil stems exhibiting radiating wedges of wood
di·cy·an·diamide \ˌdīˌsīˌan+\ *also* **di·cy·an·o·diamide** \(ˌ)dīˌsīə(ˌ)nō+\ *n* -s [ISV *di-* + *cyan-* + *diamide*] : a colorless crystalline water-soluble compound $H_2NC(=NH)NHCN$ formed by polymerization of cyanamide and used chiefly in making melamine and guanidine — called also *cyanoguanidine*
di·cyanide \(ˈ)dī+\ *n* [*di-* + *cyanide*] : a chemical compound containing two cyano groups combined with an element or radical
di·cyanine \"+\ *n* [*di-* + *cyanine*] : any of various blue cyanine dyes derived from quinoline
di·cyanogen \ˌdī+\ *n* [*di-* + *cyanogen*] : CYANOGEN 2
di·cy·cle \'dīˌsikəl, -ˌsək-, -ˌsek- *sometimes* -ˌsīk-\ *n* [*di-* + *cycle*] : a velocipede having the two wheels parallel instead of in the same line
di·cy·clic \(ˈ)dī¦sīklik, -¦sik-\ *adj* [*di-* + *cyclic*] **1 a** : having two whorls **b** : BIENNIAL 2 **2** : BICYCLIC 2 **3** : having two maxima of population each year — used chiefly of planktonic organisms — **di·cy·cly** \'dīˌsīklē\ *n* -ES
di·cyc·li·ca \(ˈ)dī'siklәkə, -ˌsīk-\ *n pl, cap* [NL, fr. *di-* + L *cyclica*, neut. pl. of *cyclicus* cyclic — more at CYCLIC] *in some classifications* : a division of Crinoidea comprising forms in which the cup of the calyx has a basal and an infrabasal series of ossicles
di·cyclopentadiene \(ˌ)dī+\ *n* [*di-* + *cycl-* + *pentadiene*] : a liquid tricyclic hydrocarbon $C_{10}H_{12}$ formed from cyclopentadiene on standing and yielding cyclopentadiene on boiling
di·cy·e·ma·ta \ˌdīˌsī'ēməd·ə\ [NL, fr. *Dicyema*, genus of Mesozoa + *-ata*] *syn of* DICYEMIDA
¹di·cy·e·mid \ˌdīˌsī'ēməd\ *adj* [NL *Dicyemida*] : of or relating to the Dicyemida
²dicyemid \"\ *n* -s : one of the Dicyemida
di·cy·e·mi·da \ˌ=ˌ='ēmədə\ *n pl, cap* [NL, fr. *Dicyema*, genus of Mesozoa (fr. *di-* + Gk *kyēma* embryo; fr. the 2 types of larvae produced at different stages) + *-ida*] : an order or other division of Mesozoa comprising minute ciliated vermiform internal parasites of cephalopod mollusks and occurring in a nematogen phase in the young host and in a rhombogen phase in the sexually mature host — compare ORTHONECTIDA
di·cyn·o·don \(ˈ)dī¦sinəˌdän, -¦sīn-\ *n, cap* [NL, fr. *di-* + *cyn-* + *-odon*] : a genus of heavily built small to moderately large Permian reptiles (order Therapsida) that were presumably herbivorous and semiaquatic or marsh-dwelling forms and that had the teeth reduced to a pair of large canines in the male only and the jaws covered by a horny beak
¹di·cyn·o·dont \-ˌdänt\ *adj* [NL *Dicynodont-*, *Dicynodon* & *Dicynodontia*] : of or relating to the Dicynodontia
²dicynodont \"\ *n* -s : a reptile of the suborder Dicynodontia
di·cyn·o·don·tia \(ˌ)=ˌ==='dänch(ē)ə\ *n pl, cap* [NL, fr. *Dicynodont-*, *Dicynodon* + *-ia*] : a suborder of Therapsida including a widely distributed group of apparently herbivorous Permian and Triassic reptiles with reduced dentition — compare DICYNODON
did [ME *did*, *dide*, fr. OE *dyde*] *past of* DO
di·dact \'dīˌdakt\ *n* -s [back-formation fr. ²*didactic*] : a didactic person
¹di·dac·tic \dī'daktik, -tēk, *Brit usu & US sometimes* də'd-\ *n* -s [Gk *didaktikos* apt at teaching] **1** *archaic* **a** : a didactic treatise **b** : a didactic writer **2 didactics** *pl but sing or pl in constr* : systematic instruction : PEDAGOGY; *sometimes* : TEACHINGS
²di·dac·tic \(ˈ)dī¦d-, *Brit usu & US sometimes* də'd-\ *also* **di·dac·ti·cal** \-tәkәl, -tēk-\ *adj* [Gk *didaktikos* apt at teaching, fr. *didaktos* taught, able to be taught (fr. *didaskein* to teach) + *-ikos* -ic — more at DOCILE] **1** : fitted or intended to teach : concerned with or functioning in the conveyance of instruction: as **a** : teaching some moral lesson ⟨the ~ aspect of the Mysteries is often overlooked⟩ **b** *of literature or other art* : intended to convey instruction and information as well as pleasure and entertainment ⟨~ poetry⟩ ⟨a fine piece of ~ writing⟩; *often* : overburdened with instructive or factual matter to the exclusion of graceful and pleasing detail : DRY : pompously dull and erudite ⟨his writing became increasingly arid and ~ as he withdrew from normal social life⟩ ⟨to write a ~ play is to suppose . . . the public in need of your advice —E.R.Bentley⟩ **c** : involving lecture and textbook instruction rather than demonstration and laboratory study ⟨a purely ~ course⟩ ⟨both ~ and laboratory instruction are used⟩ **d** *of grammar* : NORMATIVE **2** : making moral observations : urging the acceptance of moral conclusions : MORALISTIC — **di·dac·ti·cal·ly** \-tәk(ə)lē, -tēk-, -li\ *adv*
didactic analysis *n* : the psychoanalysis of one who will himself employ psychoanalysis in treatment or research
di·dac·ti·cism \=ˈ=təˌsizəm\ *n* -s : didactic method or quality; *often* : PEDANTRY
di·dac·tive \(ˈ)dī¦daktiv, də'd-\ *adj* [Gk *didaktos* + E *-ive*] *archaic* : DIDACTIC
di·dac·tyl *or* **di·dac·tyle** \(ˈ)dī¦daktəl\ *also* **di·dac·ty·lous** \-tələs\ *adj* [*di-* + *-dactyl*, *-dactyle*, *-dactylous* (fr. Gk *daktylos* finger)] : having only two digits on each extremity — **di·dac·ty·lism** \=ˈ=təˌlizəm\ *n* -s
di·dac·ty·la \-tələ\ *n pl, cap* [NL, fr. *di-* + *-dactyla* (fr. Gk *daktylos* finger)] *in some classifications* : a primary division of Marsupialia comprising forms in which the 2d and 3d pedal digits are bound together — compare POLYPROTODONTIA
di·dap·per \'dīˌdapə(r)\ *n* -s [ME *dydoppar*, prob. alter. of OE *dūfedoppa* pelican, fr. *dūfan* to dive + *-doppa* diver — more at DIVE, DOP] : a dabchick or other small grebe
di·das·cal·ic \ˌdīˌda¦skalik, -ˌidә¦-, ¦didә¦-\ *adj* [LL *didascalicus*, fr. Gk *didaskalikos*, fr. *didaskalos* teacher (fr. *didaskein* to teach) + *-ikos* -ic — more at DOCILE] **1** *archaic* : intended to teach (as a moral lesson) : MORALISTIC, DIDACTIC **2** : of, relating to, or contained in a didascaly
di·das·ca·ly \dī'daskəlē, də'-\ *n* -ES [Gk *didaskalia*, lit., teaching, instruction, fr. *didaskalos* + *-ia* -y] : any of various catalogs of Greek drama with names of authors and dates in the form of the original inscriptions or as later published by Alexandrian scholars
did·der \'didə(r)\ *vi* -ED/-ING/-S [ME *didderen*] *dial Brit* : QUIVER, SHAKE, TREMBLE
did·dle \'didᵊl\ *vb* **diddled; diddled; diddling** \-id(ᵊ)liŋ\ **diddles** [origin unknown] *vi* **1 a** *chiefly Scot* : to move rapidly back and forth : JIGGLE ⟨the fiddler's elbow *diddled* madly during the jig⟩ **b** *dial Brit* : to dance with a bouncing bobbing movement **2** : COPULATE — usu. considered vulgar **3** : to waste time : LOAF : DAWDLE ~ *vt* **1** *chiefly dial* : to move with short rapid motions **2** *chiefly dial* : DANDLE *vt* 1 **3** : to copulate with — usu. considered vulgar **4 a** : SWINDLE, CHEAT ⟨he will not ~ his employers⟩ **b** : HOAX, DELUDE ⟨when he forgot his part he *diddled* the audience into believing another actor had slipped⟩
diddle away *vt* : to waste (as time) in trifling : potter away ⟨they *diddled away* the afternoon and had nothing to show for it⟩
¹did·dle-dad·dle \¦didᵊl¦dadᵊl\ *n* -s [origin unknown] : FUSSING, TRIFLING, FIDDLE-FADDLE
²diddle-daddle \"\ *vi* **diddle-daddled; diddle-daddled; diddle-daddling** \-ad(ᵊ)liŋ\ **diddle-daddles** : DAWDLE, TRIFLE
did·dle-dee \¦didᵊl¦dē\ *n* -s [origin unknown] *Falkland islands* : RED CROWBERRY
did·dle·dees \-ēz\ *n pl* [origin unknown] *NewEng* : fallen pine needles
did·dler \'did(ᵊ)lə(r)\ *n* -s : one that diddles; *specif* : CHEAT
did·dy \'didi\ *n* -ES [alter. of *titty*] *dial Eng* : TEAT
diddy box *var of* DITTY BOX
di·del·phia \dī'delfēə\ *or* **didel·phes** \-ˌfēz\ [NL, fr. *di-* + Gk *delphys* womb + NL *-ia*, *-es* — more at DOLPHIN] *syn of* MARSUPIALIA
¹di·del·phi·an \(ˈ)=¦=fēən\ *adj* [NL *Didelphia* + E *-an*] : MARSUPIAL
²didelphian \"\ *or* **di·delph** \'dīˌdelf\ *n* -s : MARSUPIAL
di·del·phic \(ˈ)dī¦delfik\ *adj* [*di-* + Gk *delphys* womb + E *-ic*] **1 a** : having or relating to a double uterus **b** : having the female genital tract completely doubled (as certain worms) **2** [NL *Didelphia* + *-ic*] : MARSUPIAL
¹di·del·phid \(ˈ)dī¦delfәd\ *adj* [NL *Didelphidae*] : of or relating to Didelphidae or to *Didelphis* or to members of this family or genus
²didelphid \"\ *n* -s : a marsupial of the family Didelphidae or genus *Didelphis* : OPOSSUM
di·del·phi·dae \dī'delfəˌdē\ *n pl, cap* [NL, fr. *Didelphis*, type genus + *-idae*] : a family of marsupial mammals comprising the New World opossums
di·del·phine \(ˈ)dī¦delfən\ *adj* [NL *Didelphia* + E *-ine*] : of or relating to the Didelphidae or the Marsupialia
di·del·phis \=ˈ=fəs\ *n, cap* [NL, irreg. fr. *di-* + Gk *delphys* womb] : the type genus of Didelphidae which includes the Virginia opossum and a few related marsupials of tropical America
di·del·phy·i·dae \ˌdīˌdel'fīəˌdē\ [NL, fr. *Didelphys*, type genus + *-idae*] *syn of* DIDELPHIDAE
di·del·phys \=ˈ=fəs\ [NL, alter. of *Didelphis*] *syn of* DIDELPHIS
did·ger·i·doo *or* **did·jer·i·doo** \¦dijərē¦dü\ *n* -s [imit.] : a large bamboo musical pipe of the Australian aborigines
di·di·dae \'dīdəˌdē\ [NL, fr. *Didus*, type genus + *-idae*] *syn of* RAPHIDAE
didie *var of* DIDY
di·din·i·um \dī'dinēəm\ *n* [NL, fr. *di-* + Gk *deinos* terrible + NL *-ium* — more at DIN-] **1** *cap* : a genus of carnivorous protozoans (order Holotricha) that feed on paramecia **2** *pl* **didiniums** \-mz\ *or* **didin·ia** \-nēə\ : any protozoan of the genus *Didinium*
di·dip·lis \dī'dipləs\ [NL] *syn of* PEPLIS
di·diploid \ˌdī+\ *n* [*di-* + *diploid*] *biol* : an amphidiploid or autotetraploid
did·na \'didnə\ [by shortening & alter.] *chiefly Scot* : did not
didn't \'didᵊn(t), *chiefly substand* (ˈ)dint\ [by contr.] : did not
di·do \'dī(ˌ)dō\ *n, pl* **didoes** *or* **didos** [origin unknown] **1** : an absurd, foolish, or mischievous act : TRICK, PRANK, CAPER — usu. used in pl. and often in the phrase *cut didoes* ⟨such sums were too vast, and the economic *didoes* too complex, for comprehension —Michael Scully⟩ ⟨the sun had cut no *didoes* sufficiently serious to interrupt continent-to-continent radio broadcasting —*Newsweek*⟩ ⟨his harmless *didoes* that once scared me to death —Bennett Cerf⟩ **2 a** : an article of little worth : TRINKET **b** : a frivolous article of dress : FRILL, FURBELOW
di·dodecahedron \ˌdī+\ *n* [*di-* + *dodecahedron*] : DIPLOID 1
di·dot \dē¦dō\ *adj, usu cap* [after François-Ambroise *Didot* †1804 Fr. printer and publisher who devised it] : of or relating to a typographical point system commonly used in Europe
di·drachm \'dī+ˌ-\ *or* **di·drach·ma** \(ˈ)dī+\ *n* -s [LL & Gk; LL *didrachmon*, *didrachma*, fr. Gk *didrachmon*, fr. *di-* + *-drachmon* (fr. *drachmē* drachm) — more at DRAM] : an ancient Greek silver coin worth two drachmas — **di·drachmal** \(ˈ)dī+\ *adj*
did·ric \'didrik\ *or* **di·dric cuckoo** *or* **die·drik cuckoo** \'dē|-\ *n* -s [Afrik *diedrik*, of imit. origin] : a small African cuckoo (*Chrysococcyx caprius*) lustrous emerald green above and largely white below
didst *archaic past 2d sing of* DO
diduce *vt* -ED/-ING/-S [L *diducere*, fr. *di-* (fr. *dis-* ¹dis) + *ducere* to lead, draw — more at TOW] **1** *obs* : to draw apart **2** *obs* : EXPAND, ENLARGE
diduction *n* -s [L *diduction-*, *diductio*, fr. *diductus* (past part. of *diducere*) + *-ion-*, *-io* -ion] **1** *obs* : a drawing apart : SEPARATION **2** *obs* : DILATATION
di·duc·tor \(ˈ)dī¦dәktə(r)\ *n* -s *often attrib* [L *diductus* + E *-or*] : a divaricator muscle in arthropomatous brachiopods
di·dus \'dīdəs\ [NL, prob. modif. of E *dodo*] *syn of* RAPHUS
di·dy *or* **di·die** \'dīdē, -īdi\ *n, pl* **didies** [baby-talk alter. of *diaper*] : DIAPER 2b
didym- *or* **didymo-** *comb form* [Gk, fr. *didymos*, fr. *dyo* two — more at TWO] **1** : twin ⟨*didymolite*⟩ **2** : testicle ⟨*didymitis*⟩
di·dym·i·um \dī'dimēəm\ *n* -s [NL, fr. *didym-* + *-ium*] : a mixture of rare-earth elements that is freed from cerium, contains chiefly neodymium and praseodymium usu. associated with lanthanum, was once regarded as an element (symbol *Di*), and is used in coloring glass for optical filters
did·y·mo·lite \'didəməˌlīt\ *n* -s [*didym-* + *-lite*] : a mineral consisting of a calcium aluminum silicate $Ca_2Al_6Si_9O_{29}$ occurring in dark gray monoclinic twinned crystals
did·y·mous \'didəməs\ *also* **did·y·moid** \-ˌmȯid\ *or* **did·y·mate** \-ˌmāt, -mət\ *adj* [*didymous* fr. Gk *didymos*; *didymoid*, *didymate* fr. *didym-* + *-oid* or *-ate*] *biol* : growing in pairs : TWIN, TWOFOLD
di·dy·na·mia \ˌdidə'nāmēə\ *n pl, cap* [NL, fr. *di-* + Gk *dynamis* power + NL *-ia* — more at DYNAMIC] *in former classifications* : a class of plants including those having flowers with four stamens disposed in pairs of unequal length — **di·dy·na·mi·an** \¦==¦nāmēən\ *or* **di·dy·nam·ic** \-¦namik\ *adj*
di·dyn·a·mous \(ˈ)dī¦dinəməs\ *adj* [NL *Didynamia* + E *-ous*] : having four stamens disposed in pairs of unequal length — used esp. of plants of the families Scrophulariaceae and Labiatae — **di·dyn·a·my** \-mē\ *n* -ES
¹die \'dī\ *vb* **died; died; dy·ing** \'dīiŋ\ **dies** [ME *dien*, *deyen*, fr. or akin to ON *deyja* to die; akin to OS *dōian* to die, OHG *touwen* to die, Goth *diwans* mortal, OIr *duine* human being, Arm *di* corpse] *vi* **1** : to pass from physical life : suffer total and irreversible loss of the bodily attributes and functions that constitute life : EXPIRE, PERISH ⟨*died* in a fire⟩ ⟨may yet ~ at his brother's hand⟩ ⟨*dying* of old age⟩ ⟨likely to ~ from lack of care⟩ **2 a** : to pass out of existence : come to an end : become lost or extinct : become extinguished : CEASE ⟨his secret *died* with him⟩ ⟨their anger *died* at these words⟩ ⟨the bill *died* in committee⟩ **b** : to pass gradually out of existence : become imperceptible or extinct in the course of an appreciable period : recede and grow fainter : disappear or subside gradually — often used with *out*, *down*, or *away* ⟨in the course of millennia the dinosaurs *died out*⟩ ⟨the wind often ~s down at sunset⟩ ⟨childish voices *dying* away in the distance⟩ **c** : to disappear gradually in another surface — used esp. of moldings that become incorporated in a sloped or curved face (as of a building) **3** : to suffer spiritual death : become spiritually lost : become damned ⟨whosoever lives and believes in me shall never ~ —Jn 11:26 (RSV)⟩ **4 a** : to suffer or face the pains of death ⟨the martyr in spirit is ready to ~ every day for his faith⟩ **b** : to be brought to or as if to the point of death by intensity of emotion (as desire, envy, shame, embarrassment) **c** : to lose vitality : grow faint ⟨their hearts *died* at that uncanny cry⟩ **d** : to languish esp. from weakness, discouragement, or boredom ⟨simply *dying* from fatigue⟩ **e** : to long keenly or desperately : want exceedingly — usu. used with *for* or an infinitive ⟨*dying* for a smoke⟩ ⟨*dying* to go⟩ **5** : to become indifferent : cease to be subject ⟨~ to worldly things⟩ ⟨let them ~ unto sin⟩ **6** : to pass into an inferior state or situation: as **a** : to become flat : lose characteristic desired qualities (as of sparkle, bouquet, or fluid) — used chiefly of beverages ⟨the more delicate wines tend to ~ early⟩ **b** : to cease from functioning : STOP ⟨the motor *died* on the hill⟩ **c** *of a baseball player* : to be on base at the end of an inning ~ *vt* : to suffer in dying : come to death by — used with a cognate object ⟨*dying* a natural death⟩ ⟨*died* a shameful death⟩ — **die game 1** : to die while courageously struggling **2** : to persist valiantly to the end in behalf of a lost cause — **die hard 1** : to be long in dying as if struggling against death or destruction ⟨such rumors *die hard*⟩ **2** : to fight a hopeless fight : continue resistance against hopeless odds ⟨hard-shell conservatism *dies hard*⟩ — **die in bed** *or* **die in one's bed** : to die of disease or old age — **die in harness** : to die while still actively engaged in one's work or duty — **die in one's boots** *or* **die with one's boots on** *also* **die in one's shoes** *or* **die with one's shoes on** : to die otherwise than from disease or old age; *esp* : to die as a result of the violent act of another — **die laughing** : to laugh without restraint, immoderately, or to the point of physical distress — **die on the vine** : to fail to be productive of a planned or desired result esp. because of lack of concerted effort or popular enthusiasm ⟨he had sound ideas but they usually *died on the vine*⟩ ⟨the plan to draft the mayor as a candidate for governor *died on the vine*⟩
²die \"\ *n, pl* **dice** \-īs\ *or* **dies** \-īz\ [ME *dee*, fr. MF *dé*, perh. fr. Ar *dad* game] **1 a** *pl* **dice** : a small cube (as of ivory, bone, or plastic) marked distinctively on each face with one to six spots and used in pairs in various games and in gambling by being shaken and thrown to come to rest at random on a flat surface ⟨made a killing with loaded *dice*⟩ **b** *dice pl* : any of various games played with dice; *esp* : a gambling game so played **2** *pl* **dice** : a small cubical piece (as of food) — usu. used in pl. ⟨cut the meat into *dice*⟩ **3** *pl usu* **dice** : something determined by or as if by a cast of dice : CHANCE, FORTUNE, FATE ⟨there is no turning back now; the ~ is cast⟩ ⟨the *dice* appear to be loaded against a victory this year⟩ **4** *pl* **dies**, *Scot* : PLAYTHING, TOY **5** *pl* **dies** : DADO 1a **6** *pl* **dies** : any of various tools or devices for imparting a desired shape, form, or finish to a material: as **a** (1) : one of a pair of cutting or shaping tools that when moved toward each other produce a certain desired form in or impress a desired device on an object by pressure or by a blow, this tool being the larger of the pair or the part into which the punch enters — called also *matrix* (2) : a device composed of a pair of such tools (3) : a set of dies (as a set of triple-action dies including the matrices, punches, springs) that make up the complete tool **b** : a hollow internally threaded screw-cutting tool made in one piece or composed of several cutting parts, often adjustable as to distance, and used for forming screw threads (as on bolts) — compare DIE HEAD, DIESTOCK, SPRING DIE **c** : a knife or cutter used to cut out blanks (as for soles in shoemaking) **d** : the mold in which a die casting, a powdered-metal casting, or a drop forging is made **e** : a block of hard metal or precious stone with a perforation of definite shape that is used in making wire and rod by drawing or extrusion **f** : a perforated block through which plastic material is forced to make it assume a desired shape: as (1) : such a block through which clay is forced in molding bricks (2) : the metal end of a cookie press or cake decorator that is pierced with various designs through which dough or frosting can be forced out into fancy shapes **g** : a heavy iron ring or block on which ore is crushed (as in an edge mill or a stamp mill) **h** (1) : a metal block with a design in intaglio into which a matching counterpart forces material (as paper or board) to be die-stamped or embossed — compare COUNTER, PLATE (2) **2** : a comparable device used to stamp, emboss, or mold a seal (as on paper or wax) **i** : a rigid assembly of steel cutting and creasing rules with which flat sheets of paperboard are stamped out before being folded into cartons **7** *pl* **dies** : a block of metal on which the design of a postage stamp is engraved and which is used in making the repeated impressions that form the printing plate

dice

³die \"\ *vt* **died; died; dieing; dies** : to cut or shape with a die — often used with *out* ⟨~*ing* out leather for wallets⟩
die away *vi* : FAINT, SWOON ⟨I could have *died away* with embarrassment⟩
¹die-away \'=ˌ=\ *adj* [*die away*] : having a languid air : LANGUISHING ⟨a *die-away* glance⟩ ⟨*die-away* airs and graces⟩
²die-away \"\ *n* -s [*die away*] : a gradual fading out (as of a sound)
dieb \'dēb\ *n* -s [Ar *dhī'b*, *dhīb* wolf, jackal] : a jackal (*Canis anthus*) of No. Africa
die back *vi, of a plant or plant part* : to die from the top toward the base — used esp. of woody plants and of only part of their aboveground structure
dieback \'=ˌ=\ *n* -s [*die back*] **1** : a diseased condition in woody plants in which peripheral parts are killed either by parasites or by other agencies (as winter injury) **2** : EXANTHEMA 2
die break *also* **die crack** *n* : a defect or blemish on a coin or medal caused by a crack in the die
diecase \'=ˌ=\ *n* : MATRIX CASE
¹die-cast \'=ˌ=\ *vt* [²*die* + *cast*] : to make by forcing molten metal (as a zinc, tin, lead, or aluminum alloy) into a die
²die-cast \"\ *adj* : made by die-casting ⟨a *die-cast* seal⟩
die casting *n* : a part made by die-casting
die chaser *n* : a threading die or one of the cutters of a composite die or a die head
dieck·mann reaction *or* **dieckmann condensation** \'dēkmən-, -ˌmän-\ *n, usu cap D* [after Walter *Dieckmann* †1925 Ger. chemist] : a base-catalyzed condensation of an open-chain dicarboxylic ester to form a cyclic keto ester (as 2-keto-cyclopentane-carboxylic ester)
di·ec·ta·sis \dī'ektəsəs\ *n* -ES [LGk *diektasis*, fr. Gk *diekteinein* to stretch out, fr. *dia-* + *ekteinein* to stretch — more at ECTASIS] *prosody* : lengthening by an interpolated syllable
die-cut \'=ˌ=\ *vt* : to cut with dies
died *past of* DIE
die down *vi, of a plant* : to undergo death of the aboveground portions — used chiefly of a normal seasonal behavior of herbaceous perennials, less often of winterkilling of semihardy woody plants ⟨the spring bulbs ripen their foliage and *die down* soon after blooming⟩ ⟨buddleias *die down* each winter in the north but bloom from new wood the next season⟩
diedric cuckoo *or* **diedrik cuckoo** *var of* DIDRIC
dief·fen·bach·ia \ˌdēfən'bakēə, ¦==ˌ===\ *n* [NL, fr. Ernst *Dieffenbach* †1855 Ger. naturalist & NL *-ia*] **1** *cap* : a small genus of tropical American erect plants (family Araceae) with long sheathing or clasping petioles and united stamens **2** -s : any plant of the genus *Dieffenbachia*
die-forge \'=ˌ=\ *vt* : DROP-FORGE
di·e·gue·ño \ˌdēə'gān(ˌ)yō\ *n, pl* **diegueño** *or* **diegueños** *usu*

cap [Sp, fr. San *Diego*, Cal. + Sp *-eño* (suffix denoting an inhabitant)] **1 a :** an Indian people of southern California **b :** a member of such people **2 :** a Yuman language of the Diegueño people

diehard \ˈ=,=\ *n* -s [¹*die* + *hard*] **:** one that dies hard: as **a :** an irreconcilable opponent of a measure, situation, or condition ordinarily accepted as tolerable, normal, or desirable; *esp* **:** an extreme conservative who resists to the last any alteration in the political system **b :** SCOTTISH TERRIER

die–hard \"\ *adj* [¹*die* + *hard*] **:** offering extreme resistance to change ⟨*die-hard* optimism⟩ **:** completely and determinedly fixed ⟨*die-hard* conservatives⟩ ⟨a few *die-hard* colonists continued to farm⟩ **syn** see CONSERVATIVE

die–hard·ism \" + ,izəm\ *n* -s **:** the principles or attitudes of a political diehard

die head *also* **die holder** *n* **:** a device that holds a threading die when chasing threads on work revolving in a machine or that itself revolves and chases threads on work held stationary in a machine

di·el \ˈdīəl, ˈdēəl\ *adj* [irreg. fr. L *dies* day + E *-al* — more at DEITY] **:** involving a 24-hour period that usu. includes a day and the adjoining night — used chiefly in ecology ⟨fluctuating ~ light cycles⟩ ⟨a mild ~ periodicity⟩

diel·drin \ˈdēldrən\ *n* -s [*Diels*-Alder reaction + *-in*] **:** a white crystalline insecticide consisting chiefly or entirely of the epoxide $C_{12}H_8Cl_6O$ obtained by oxidation of aldrin

¹di·electric \ˌdī + \ *n* -s [*dia-* + *electric*] **1 :** a nonconductor of direct electric current **2 :** a substance in which a steady electric field can be set up with a negligible flow of current

²dielectric \"\ *adj* [*dia-* + *electric*] **:** relating to or having the properties of a dielectric ⟨~ material⟩ — **di·electrically** \ˌdī + \ *adv*

dielectric absorption *n* **:** ABSORPTION 3

dielectric constant *n* **:** a measure of the ability of a dielectric material to store electrical potential energy under the influence of an electric field, measured by the ratio of the capacitance of a condenser with the material as dielectric to its capacitance with vacuum as dielectric

dielectric heating *n* **:** the rapid and uniform heating throughout a nonconducting material by means of a high frequency electromagnetic field, the heat resulting from the dissipation of energy in the rapid reversal of the polarization of the molecules — compare INDUCTION HEATING

dielectric loss *n* **:** energy loss in a dielectric due to an alternating electric field

dielectric strength *n* **:** the maximum intensity of electric field that a given dielectric can sustain without disruptive discharge, usu. expressed in kilovolts per millimeter

diels–al·der reaction \ˈdēlˈsäldə(r)-\ *n, usu cap D&A* [after Otto *Diels* †1954 & Kurt *Alder* †1958 Ger. chemists] **:** an addition reaction in which a diene unites with the double or triple bond of an unsaturated compound to form a 6-membered ring (as in tetrahydro-phthalic anhydride)

diemaker \ˈ=,==\ *n* **:** a worker who makes cutting and shaping dies — called also *diesinker*

die·me·nia \dēˈmēnēə\ [NL, fr. Anton Van *Diemen* †1645 Dutch governor of Batavia who sent out the expedition that discovered Tasmania + NL *-ia*] *syn of* DEMANSIA

di·encephalic \(ˌ)dī + \ *adj* [NL *diencephalon* + E *-ic*] **:** of, relating to, or involving the diencephalon

di·encephalon \ˌdī + \ *n* -s [NL, fr. *dia-* + *encephalon*] **:** the posterior subdivision of the forebrain — called also *betweenbrain, thalamencephalon*

di·ene \ˈdī,ēn, =ˈ=\ *n* -s [ISV, fr. *-diene*] **:** a chemical compound containing two double bonds; *esp* **:** DIOLEFIN ⟨conjugated ~*s* like 1,3-butadiene⟩

-diene \ˌdī,ēn, ,=ˈ=\ *n suffix* -s [ISV, fr. *di-* + *-ene*] **:** chemical compound containing two double bonds ⟨hexa*diene*⟩

die·ner \ˈdēnə(r)\ *n* -s [G, servant, fr. MHG *dienære*, fr. *dienen* to serve (fr. OHG *thionōn*) + *-ære* -er — more at THEOW] **:** a laboratory helper esp. in a medical school

di·en·es·trol *also* **di·en·oes·trol** \ˌdīəˈneˌstrōl, -rōl\ *n* -s [*diphenol* + *estrogen, oestrogen* + *-ol*] **:** a white crystalline estrogenic diphenol $[HOC_6H_4C(=CHCH_3)-]_2$ containing two hydrogen atoms fewer than diethylstilbestrol

diene synthesis *n* **:** DIELS-ALDER REACTION

diene value *n* **:** a numerical measure of the conjugated double bonds in a fatty acid or fat (as a drying oil) that is calculated from the amount of maleic anhydride capable of reacting with a known weight of the acid or fat

di·eno·phile \dīˈēnə,fīl, ˈ=,==,=\ *n* -s [*diene* + *-o-* + *-phile*] **:** the olefinic or acetylenic component (as maleic anhydride) that is seeking a diene in the Diels-Alder reaction

di·entamoeba \(ˌ)dī + \ *n, cap* [NL, fr. *di-* + *Entamoeba*] **:** a genus of commensal amoebas of the human intestine distinguished by the presence of two nuclei in the trophozoite

die off *vi* **:** to be removed severally or in numbers by death ⟨her few remaining kinfolk *died off* one by one⟩

die–off \ˈ=,=\ *n* -s [*die off*] **:** a sudden sharp decline of a population (as of rabbits or game birds) not directly due to hunting or other human activity

die proof *n* **:** proof of a postage stamp made directly from a die

di·er \ˈdī(ə)r, -īə\ *n* -s **:** one that dies

dieresis *var of* DIAERESIS

die·ri \ˈdirē\ *n, pl* **dieri** *or* **dieris** *usu cap* **1 a :** a primitive people near Lake Eyre, Australia, having marriage customs in which a woman is pledged a husband at birth and in which the custom of pirraura exists **b :** a member of such people **2 :** the language of the Dieri people

dier·vil·la \dirˈvilə\ *n, cap* [NL, after M. *Dierville*, 18th cent. Fr. surgeon] **:** a genus of shrubs (family Caprifoliaceae) comprising the bush honeysuckles and having 2-lipped flowers and long-beaked capsular fruits

dies *pres 3d sing of* DIE, *pl of* DIE

di·es co·mi·ti·a·lis \ˌdē,äskə,mid·ēˈälės\ *n, pl* **dies comitiales** \-ä,lās\ [L, lit., comitial day] **:** any of the 190 days of each year on which the people under the Roman republic could meet for legislation or election

¹die·sel \ˈdēzəl, -ēsəl\ *adj, sometimes cap* [after Rudolf *Diesel* †1913 Ger. mechanical engineer and inventor] **1 :** relating to the diesel cycle or engine **2 :** equipped with or driven by a diesel engine ⟨a ~ truck⟩

²diesel \"\ *n, sometimes cap* **1 :** DIESEL ENGINE **2 :** a vehicle (as a truck, locomotive, or ship) driven by a diesel engine

diesel cycle *n, sometimes cap D* **:** an ideal-engine cycle during which the working substance successively undergoes adiabatic compression, constant-pressure heating, adiabatic expansion, and constant-volume cooling — compare DIESEL ENGINE, OTTO CYCLE

diesel–electric \ˌ===ˈ==\ *adj, sometimes cap D* **:** of, relating to, or employing the combination of a diesel engine driving an electric generator

diesel–electric locomotive *also* **diesel–electric** *or* **diesel locomotive** *n, sometimes cap D* **:** an electric locomotive having electric generators powered by diesel engines for the production of its own electric power

diesel engine *n, sometimes cap D* **:** an internal-combustion engine in which air is compressed to a temperature sufficiently high to ignite fuel injected directly into the cylinder where the combustion and expansion actuate a piston

diesel–engined \ˌ==ˈ==\ *adj, sometimes cap D* **:** driven by a diesel engine

die·sel·i·za·tion \ˌdēzələˈzāshən, -ēsə-, -ˌlīˈz-\ *n* -s *sometimes cap* **:** the act of dieselizing

die·sel·ize \ˈ==,līz\ *vt* -ED/-ING/-S *sometimes cap* **:** to equip with a diesel engine or with diesel-electric locomotives

diesel oil *also* **diesel fuel** *n, sometimes cap D* **:** a heavy mineral oil used as fuel in diesel engines

die set *n* **1 :** a set of cutting, shaping, or combination dies **2 :** a punch-press accessory for maintaining proper alignment between punch and die block

di·es fas·tus \ˌdē,äsˈfästəs\ *n, pl* **dies fas·ti** \-,stē\ [L, lit., court day] **1 :** a day on which Roman religious law permitted secular activities or an auspicious day for such activities **2 :** any of the 40 days of each year on which the praetors under the Roman republic could exercise their general powers in holding court; *broadly* **:** DIES COMITIALIS

die shoe *n* **:** a metal block inserted between the lower half of a cutting or shaping die and the bed of a press to spread the blow and avoid wear

die·sinker \ˈ=,==\ *n* **1 :** DIEMAKER **2 :** a vertical milling machine used in diesinking

die·sinking \ˈ=,==\ *n* **:** the art or process of forming cutting and shaping dies

di·e·sis \ˈdīəsəs\ *n, pl* **die·ses** \-ə,sēz\ [L, fr. Gk, fr. *diienai*, to drive through, let go through (fr. *dia-* + *hienai* to let go, send, throw) + *-sis* — more at JET] **1 a** *in ancient Greek music* **:** LIMMA **b :** ENHARMONIC DIESIS **c :** ⁴SHARP c(1), c(2) **2 :** DOUBLE DAGGER — compare REFERENCE MARK

di·es ju·ri·di·cus \ˌdē,äsyüˈridəkəs\ *n, pl* **dies juridi·ci** \-ə,kē\ [L] **:** COURT DAY — compare DIES NON

dies ne·fas·tus \-äsneˈfästəs\ *n, pl* **dies nefas·ti** \-,stē\ [L, lit., noncourt day] **:** a day on which secular activities were forbidden in ancient Rome; *specif* **:** a day on which the courts were closed and it was illegal (as for the praetors) to transact public judicial affairs

di·es non \ˌdē,äˈsnōn, ˌdī,ēzˈnän\ *also* **di·es non ju·ri·di·cus** \ˌdē,ä,snōnyüˈridəkəs\ *n, pl* **dies nons** \-nz\ *also* **dies non juridi·ci** \-də,kē\ [L *dies non juridicus* nonjuridical day] **1 :** a day on which the courts do not ordinarily sit or carry on business **2 :** a day on which general business may not lawfully be transacted

die–stamp \ˈ=,=\ *vt* **:** to form or cut out esp. from sheet stock or to emboss by means of a die

die stamper *n* **:** a worker who performs die-stamping (as of metal or stationery)

di·ester \ˈdī+,-\ *n* [ISV *di-* + *ester*] **:** a compound containing two ester groupings

die·stock \ˈ=,=\ *n* **:** a stock to hold dies used for cutting threads (as on screws or pipe)

di·estrous *or* **di·estrual** *also* **di·oestrous** *or* **di·oestrual** \(ˈ)dī+\ *adj* [NL *diestrus, dioestrus* + E *-ous* or *-al*] **:** of, relating to, or exhibiting diestrus

diestock: *1* diestock; *2* die

di·estrus *or* **di·estrum** *also* **di·oestrus** *or* **di·oestrum** \(ˈ)dī+\ *n* [NL, fr. *dia-* + *estrus, oestrus* or *estrum, oestrum*] **:** a period of sexual quiescence intervening between two periods of estrus

¹di·et \ˈdīət, *usu* -əd·+V\ *n* -s [ME *diete*, fr. OF, fr. L *diaeta* prescribed dietary regimen, fr. Gk *diaita*, lit., manner of living, fr. *diaitan* to arbitrate, govern, lead one's life, fr. *dia-* + *-aitan* (akin to Gk *aisa* destiny, share) — more at ETIOLOGY] **1 a :** food and drink regularly provided or consumed ⟨a ~ of simple country dishes⟩ ⟨the rough ~ of the ox⟩ ⟨an occasional change of ~⟩ **b :** habitual course of feeding ⟨a predominantly meat ~ is rich in protein⟩ **c :** a prescribed course or allowance of food esp. when restricted in kind or quantity as a health or punitive measure ⟨the monotonous prison ~⟩ ⟨a low-calory ~⟩ ⟨you must stick to your ~⟩ **d** *archaic* **:** an allowance for board **:** BOARD **2 a** *obs* **:** habitual course of life; *often* **:** way of thinking **:** cast of mind **b :** anything provided esp. habitually for use, consideration, or enjoyment ⟨we had that summer an unforgettable ~ of classic music⟩ ⟨too steady a ~ of swimming, tennis, and other sports was both tiring and boring⟩ **3** *archaic* **:** money allowed (as to officials) for living expenses **4 :** a sample of metal cut or scraped from plate for assay at the British mint

²diet \"\ *vb* -ED/-ING/-S [ME *dieten*, fr. MF *dieter*, fr. *diete*] *vt* **1 :** to cause to take food **:** FEED **:** provide for consumption **2 :** to cause to eat and drink according to prescribed rules **:** regulate the food of; *often* **:** to cause to eat sparingly **3** *archaic* **:** to provide with meals **:** BOARD ~ *vi* **:** to eat according to prescribed rules; *often* **:** to eat sparingly ⟨she said she ~*ed* but she didn't lose a pound⟩ ⟨the Lenten fast is often an occasion for many to ~ seriously⟩

³diet \"\ *n* -s [ME *dyet*, fr. ML *dieta*, fr. L *dies* day — more at DEITY] **1** *archaic, chiefly Scot* **a :** a day's journey **b :** the itinerary of a journey **:** JOURNEY **2** *Scot* **a :** a day set for an event (as a meeting); *specif* **:** the day on which a person is cited to appear in court **b :** a session or sitting of a court or assembly **3 a** *archaic* **:** a formal conference of notables meeting to attend to affairs of the realm **b** (1) **:** a formal public assembly esp. of the estates or governing body of a realm or of a confederation; *specif* **:** one of the great formal assemblies of councillors of the Holy Roman Empire ⟨the *Diet* of Worms condemned Luther as a heretic⟩ ⟨the *Diet* of Augsburg of 1530⟩ (2) **:** the estates or members participating in such a diet **c :** a legislative assembly **:** the national parliament or provincial legislature of a state (as Denmark, Germany, Japan, Paraguay)

¹di·e·tary \ˈdīə,terē, -ri\ *n* -ES [ME *dietarie*, fr. *diete* + *-arie* -ary (n. suffix)] **1** *obs* **:** a rule of diet; *also* **:** a treatise or discourse on such rules **2 :** an allowance or quantity of food provided or eaten by an individual, group, or population in accord with medical or other orders, availability, or social and economic controls ⟨the American ~⟩ ⟨the ~ changes according to need and age⟩

²dietary \"\ *adj* [¹*diet* + *-ary* (adj. suffix)] **:** of or related to a diet or to the rules of diet ⟨~ foods⟩ ⟨~ habits⟩ ⟨a ~ disease⟩ ⟨~ cuisine⟩

dietary law *n* **:** any of the laws relating to the fitness for consumption of various foods and to the prohibition of various combinations and contacts (as that of milk with meat) that are observed by orthodox Jews

dietary standard *n* **:** the food in the diet usu. expressed in terms of digestible nutrients supposed to be best adapted for man under different conditions

di·et·er \ˈdīəd·ə(r), -ītə-\ *n* -s **1** *obs* **:** a person who supervises and prescribes a diet or dietary **2 :** one that diets; *esp* **:** a person that consumes a reduced allowance of food in order to lose weight ⟨one of the food preparations most demanded by ~*s* —Vance Packard⟩

di·e·tet·ic \ˌdīəˈted·ik, -et|, |ēk\ *also* **di·e·tet·i·cal** \|əkəl, |ēk-\ *adj* [LL *diaeteticus*, fr. Gk *diaitētikos*, fr. *diaita* diet + *-ētikos* -etic, -etical — more at DIET] **1 :** of or relating to diet or the kind and quantity of food to be eaten ⟨~ rules⟩ **:** belonging to dietetics ⟨~ studies⟩ **2 :** adapted (as by elimination of sugar or salt) for use in special diets ⟨~ sweets⟩ ⟨a ~ canned tuna⟩

di·e·tet·i·cal·ly \|ək(ə)lē, |ēk-, -li\ *adv, archaic* **1 :** in the diet **2 :** in respect to or from the point of view of dietetics ⟨~ adequate meals⟩

di·e·tet·ics \ˌ==ˈted·|iks, -et|, |ēks\ *n pl but sing or pl in constr* [Gk *diaitētikē*, fr. fem. of *diaitētikos*] **:** the science or art of applying the principles of nutrition to the feeding of individuals or groups under different economic conditions or for hygienic or therapeutic purposes

di·ethanolamine \(ˌ)dī+\ *n* [*di-* + *ethanolamine*] **:** a colorless deliquescent crystalline or liquid amino alcohol $(HOCH_2CH_2)_2NH$ used similarly to ethanolamine (sense 1); bis(2-hydroxyethyl)-amine

di·ether \(ˈ)dī+\ *n* [*di-* + *ether*] **:** a chemical compound containing two atoms of oxygen with ether linkages

di·ethyl \(ˈ)dī+\ *adj* [ISV *di-* + *ethyl*] **:** containing two ethyl groups in the molecule

di·ethylamine \(ˌ)dī+\ *n* [ISV *diethyl* + *amine*] **:** a colorless flammable volatile liquid base $(C_2H_5)_2NH$ having a fishy odor and used chiefly in synthesis (as of accelerators for vulcanization)

di·eth·yl·car·bam·a·zine \ˌdī,ethəl,kärˈbamə,zēn, -,zōn\ *n* **:** an anthelmintic derived from piperazine and administered in the form of its crystalline citrate $C_{10}H_{21}N_3O.C_6H_8O_7$

di·ethylene glycol \(ˈ)dī+ . . . -\ *n* [*di-* + *ethylene*] **:** a sweet toxic hygroscopic syrupy compound $O(CH_2CH_2OH)_2$ made from ethylene oxide (as by reaction with ethylene glycol) and used chiefly as solvent, humectant, and plasticizer and in the production of polyester resins — called also *diglycol*

diethyl ether *n* **1 :** ETHER 3a **2 :** an ether containing two ethoxy groups ⟨the *diethyl ether* $C_6H_4(OC_2H_5)_2$ of pyrocatechol⟩

diethyl ketone *n* **:** PENTANONE b

diethyl phthalate *n* **:** a colorless liquid ester $C_6H_4(COOC_2H_5)_2$ used chiefly as a solvent and plasticizer

diethyl·stilbestrol *also* **diethyl·stilboestrol** \(ˌ)ˈ=+=\ *n* [ISV *diethyl-* + *stilbestrol, stilboestrol*] **:** a colorless crystalline diphenol $[HOC_6H_4C(C_2H_5)=]_2$ derived from stilbene and used as a potent estrogen in medicine and in livestock and poultry feed — called also *stilbestrol*

diethyl sulfate *n* **:** the ethyl sulfate $(C_2H_5)_2SO_4$

di·et·ic \(ˈ)dīˈed·ik\ *adj, archaic* **:** of or relating to diet

di·e·tine \ˌdīəˈtēn, ˌdēə-\ *n* -s [F *diètine*, fr. *diète* diet (fr. ML *dieta*) + -ine — more at DIET] **:** a subordinate or local assembly or diet; *specif* **:** a onetime local assembly of Polish nobles that elected deputies to the national diet

dieting *pres part of* DIET

di·e·ti·tian *also* **di·e·ti·cian** \ˌdīəˈtishən\ *n* -s [*dietitian* irreg. fr. ¹*diet* + *-ician*; *dietician* alter. (influenced by *-ician*) of *dietitian*] **:** a person qualified in or practicing dietetics usu. after technical training ⟨a hospital ~⟩

diet kitchen *n* **:** a kitchen in which special diets are prepared (as in a hospital) or where outpatients are instructed concerning diets and their preparation

diet list *n* **:** a list of foods and beverages permitted to a person on a diet usu. giving the absolute or relative quantities of different items that may be taken

diet loaf *n, Scot* **:** SPONGE CAKE

die·tl's crisis \ˈdēd·ᵊlz-\ *n, usu cap D* [after Joseph *Dietl* †1874 Pol. physician] **:** an attack of violent pain in the kidney region accompanied by chills, nausea, vomiting, and collapse that is caused by kinking of the ureter and is usu. associated with floating kidney

di·e·to·therapy \ˌdīəd·ō+\ *n* [¹*diet-* + *-o-* + *therapy*] **:** a branch of dietetics concerned with therapeutic uses of food and diet

die·trich·ite \ˈdē-tri,kīt\ *n* -s *usu cap* [G *dietrichit*, fr. Dr. *Dietrich* 19th cent. Austrian scientist who analyzed it + G *-it* -ite] **:** a mineral $(Zn,Fe,Mn)Al_2(SO_4)_4.22H_2O$ consisting of a hydrous sulfate of aluminum and one or more of the metals zinc, iron, and manganese

diets *pl of* DIET, *pres 3d sing of* DIET

diet·ze·ite \ˈdētsə,īt\ *n* -s [G *dietzeit*, fr. August *Dietze* †*ab*1893 Ger. chemist + G *-it* -ite] **:** a yellow mineral $Ca_2(IO_3)_2(CrO_4)$ commonly in fibrous or columnar form (hardness 3–4, sp. gr. 3.70)

die–up \ˈ=,=\ *n* -s [fr. *die up*, v.] *West* **:** a widespread destruction of range livestock caused usu. by some untoward natural phenomenon (as drought or blizzard); *sometimes* **:** an animal dead in a die-up ⟨salvaging the hides of *die-ups*⟩

diewise \ˈ=,=\ *adv* **:** in the shape of a die **:** with perfectly square corners **:** CUBICALLY

diff *abbr* **1** difference **2** different **3** differential

dif·fa \ˈdifə\ *n* -s [Ar *ḍiyāfāh* hospitality] **:** an Arabic reception or banquet

dif·far·re·a·tion \(ˌ)di,farēˈāshən\ *n* -s [L *diffarreation-, diffarreatio*, fr. *dif-* (fr. *dis-*) + *-farreation-, -farreatio* (as in *confarreation-, confarreatio* confarreation) — more at CONFARREATION] **:** the Roman ceremony of divorce performed by a pontiff who dissolves a marriage that had been celebrated by confarreation

¹dif·fer \ˈdifə(r)\ *vb* **differed; differed; differing** \-f(ə)riŋ\ **differs** [ME *differen*, fr. MF or L; MF *differer* to postpone, be different, fr. L *differre*, fr. *dif-* (fr. *dis-*) + *ferre* to carry — more at BEAR] *vi* **1 a :** to be unlike or distinct in one or more respects or characteristics ⟨the engines ~ greatly in power and endurance⟩ **:** be unlike in nature or form ⟨details of the two statements ~⟩ — often used with *from* ⟨the law of one state ~*s* from that of another⟩ **b :** to display variety or exist in variety **:** change from time to time or from one instance or occasion to another **:** VARY ⟨though ingredients ~, the basic process of manufacture remains the same⟩ **2 :** to be of unlike or opposite opinion **:** disagree in sentiment ⟨persecution of men who ~ on religious matters⟩ — used with *with* ⟨~*s* with the army on the use of air power⟩ or sometimes with *from* ⟨I ~ from him concerning an essential part . . . of religion —W.E.Gladstone⟩ **3** *archaic* **:** DISPUTE, QUARREL ~ *vt* **:** to make different or unlike **:** DIFFERENTIATE ⟨something it is that ~*s* thee and me —Abraham Cowley⟩

syn VARY, DISAGREE, DISSENT: DIFFER stresses the fact of unlikeness in kind or nature or in opinion, but conveys no implication of degree of difference ⟨the houses *differ* only in minor details⟩ ⟨day *differs* from day in respect of the importance of the public events they bring forth —C.E.Montague⟩ ⟨all business men and economists admit that there are grave defects in the present working of our economic system. But they *differ* widely in their diagnosis —J.A.Hobson⟩ VARY, often interchangeable with DIFFER, may call attention to readily apparent differences and may suggest some range among them ⟨tasks may be *varied* slightly, as when a worker in a cigarette factory is shifted from the job of packing and weighing —Aldous Huxley⟩ ⟨the form of political control *varied* widely from country to country, and depended both on the traditions of the different states and on their position with respect to the new balance of power —C.E.Black & E.C. Helmreich⟩ ⟨the strength and direction of sea currents *vary* considerably at different times of the year —W.H.Dowdeswell⟩ DISAGREE stresses lack of agreement and may call up notions of incompatibility, unfitness, or disharmony ⟨one can *disagree* with his views, but one can't refute them —Henry Miller⟩ ⟨the authorities *disagree* about the procedure to be followed in initiating inquiry —F.S.C.Northrop⟩ DISSENT applies to difference of opinion between persons ranging from withholding of assent to strong or formal expression ⟨we may all agree that a world auxiliary language would help. The cynical opinion, which *dissents* and says that the less we understand one another the better, will not be considered here —I.A. Richards⟩ ⟨he *dissented* vigorously from and refused to sign the award —*Americana Annual*⟩

²differ \"\ *n* -s [by shortening] *dial* **:** DIFFERENCE

¹dif·fer·ence \ˈdifərn(t)s, -f(ə)rən-, *-R sometimes* -fən-\ *n* -s [ME, fr. MF, fr. L *differentia*, fr. *different-, differens* + *-ia*] **1 a :** the quality or state of being different ⟨great ~ between the two ideas⟩ **b :** an instance of differing in nature, form, or quality ⟨~*s* in the manufacturing process result in a wide variety of flavors⟩ **:** a property or characteristic in which things or persons differ ⟨~*s* in color and texture between the two fabrics⟩ **c** *archaic* **:** a characteristic that distinguishes one person or thing from another or from the general ⟨an absolute gentleman full of the most excellent ~*s* —Shak.⟩ **d :** DIFFERENTIA 1 **e :** the element or factor that separates or distinguishes two contrasting situations or events ⟨water is the ~ between profit and loss to these farmers⟩ **2 :** distinction or discrimination in preference or choice ⟨the law should make no ~ between the rich and the poor⟩ **3 :** disagreement in opinion **:** DISSENSION, CONTROVERSY ⟨there has never been any ~ between the two men⟩ **:** an instance of disagreement or a point upon which there is disagreement ⟨nationalists have always used force to settle their ~*s* —H.S.Fowler⟩ **4 a :** the degree or amount by which things differ in quantity or measure ⟨10 cents ~ in price⟩; *specif* **:** the result obtained by subtracting one magnitude, number, or function from another of the same kind **b :** the amount payable to or by a seller on the occasion of the sale of securities or commodities orig. purchased by him as a speculation without intention to take physical possession and representing the change in price **c :** the amount paid or allowed for the delivery of a quality of produce better or poorer than that on which the contract price is based **5 :** an addition to or change in a coat of arms to distinguish the bearings of two persons which would otherwise be the same — compare AUGMENTATION 6, CADENCY MARK **6 :** a significant change in a situation **:** a significant effect on a situation ⟨what's the ~ whether I go or not⟩ ⟨streamlining did not make much ~⟩ **syn** see DISSIMILARITY

²difference \"\ *vt* -ED/-ING/-S [ME *differencen*, fr. *difference*, n.] **1 a :** to make different **:** differentiate or distinguish in nature or character ⟨every individual has something that ~*s* it from another —John Locke⟩ **b :** to make a distinction between (as in the mind) **:** DISCRIMINATE, DIFFERENTIATE ⟨~ gods from men —George Chapman⟩ **2 :** to make a heraldic difference in (a coat of arms)

difference limen *or* **difference threshold** *n* **:** JUST-NOTICEABLE DIFFERENCE

difference table *n* **:** an auxiliary table to facilitate interpolation between the numbers of the principal table giving approximate differences in values of the tabulated function corresponding to certain submultiples (as tenths) of the constant smallest increment of the independent variable in the table

difference tone *n* **:** a combination tone whose frequency is equal to the difference between the frequencies of the two tones generating it

dif·fer·en·cy \-nsē\ *n* -ES [L *differentia*] *archaic* : DIFFERENCE

¹dif·fer·ent \ˈdifərnt, -f(ə)rənt, -*R sometimes* -fənt\ *adj* [MF, fr. L *different-, differens*, pres. part. of *differre* to carry apart, be different, fr. *dif-* (fr. *dis-*) + *ferre* to carry — more at BEAR] **1** : partly or totally unlike in nature, form, or quality ⟨two men could hardly be more ~⟩ : having at least one property not possessed by another (of a specified pair or larger group) ⟨no thing is ~ from itself⟩ — used with *from* ⟨small, neat hand, very ~ from the captain's tottery characters —R.L.Stevenson⟩ or with *than* ⟨~ than any other piece we've done lately —*Harper's*⟩ ⟨vastly ~ in size than it was twenty-five years ago —N.M. Pusey⟩ or chiefly Brit. with *to* ⟨a very ~ situation to the . . . one under which we live —Sir Winston Churchill⟩ **2** : not the same : distinct or separate (from another or from others in a group) ⟨studying the behavior of males in ~ age groups⟩ : VARIOUS, SEVERAL ⟨~ members of your group could then tell . . . stories about these heroes —L.J.Davidson⟩ : ANOTHER ⟨not liking the first book, he tried a ~ one⟩ **3** : being out of the ordinary : UNUSUAL, SPECIAL ⟨advertising that strives continually to be ~⟩

syn DIFFERENT, DIVERSE, DIVERGENT, DISPARATE, and VARIOUS agree when they modify plural nouns and mean unlike in kind or character. DIFFERENT sometimes implies little more than separateness and sometimes implies contrast ⟨many *different* kinds of food⟩ ⟨*different* points of view⟩ DIVERSE implies marked difference and decided contrast ⟨*diverse* tendencies among the arts have given rise to opposed theories —John Dewey⟩ ⟨the important problems which arise when two different groups having *diverse* languages and cultures meet —T.A.Sebeok⟩ ⟨a curious fusion of *diverse* elements —Carl Van Vechten⟩ DIVERGENT, often used in the sense of markedly different, implies a movement away from sameness or similarity, usu. implying impossibility of again coming together as for close association, agreement, or reconciliation ⟨he recognized that labor and capital have *divergent* interests —M.R. Cohen⟩ ⟨a great part of the quarrel between science and religion arises from *divergent* opinions not about the world as it is, but about what it will be —W.R.Inge⟩ ⟨either the concepts of the great Powers coincide and they are in agreement, or their concepts are *divergent* and they therefore cannot agree among themselves as to . . . action —M.S.Fairchild⟩ DISPARATE usu. implies an unequivocal difference, usu. as between incongruous or incompatible things ⟨a nation believing in free speech can't federate with a nation believing in kept speech, and nobody should even consider raising a federal roof over two such *disparate* ideas —*New Yorker*⟩ ⟨the *disparate* elements of the medieval personality were as yet unblended —H.O.Taylor⟩ VARIOUS commonly lays stress on the number of kinds or the variety within one whole ⟨*various* people dropped in for tea⟩ ⟨a personality that is *various* and interesting⟩

²different \"\ *adv* : DIFFERENTLY ⟨they do things ~ here⟩

dif·fer·en·tia \ˌdifəˈrench(ē)ə\ *n, pl* **differenti·ae** \-chēˌē\ [L, difference — more at DIFFERENCE] **1** : the property or mark distinguishing a species from other species of the same genus : the determinant that added to the essence of the genus gives the essence of the species **2** : the element, feature, or factor that distinguishes one entity, state, or class from another ⟨the chief *differentiae* between man and the brute creation —Arthur Quiller-Couch⟩ **3** : a trope in medieval music

dif·fer·en·tia·bil·i·ty \ˌdifəˌrench(ē)əˈbiləd-ē\ *n* -ES : the property or quality of being differentiable ⟨the results of assuming ~ —E.G.Phillips⟩

dif·fer·en·tia·ble \ˌdifəˈrench(ē)əbəl\ *adj* [*differentiate* + *-able*] **1** : capable of being differentiated **2** : possessing a differential coefficient or derivative

¹dif·fer·en·tial \ˌdifəˈrenchəl\ *adj* [prob. fr. F *différentiel*, fr. MF *differentiel*, fr. *different* + *-iel* -ial] **1 a** : of, relating to, or constituting a difference or distinction : DISTINGUISHING : making a difference or distinction between individuals or classes ⟨~ legislation such as income tax laws⟩ **b** : based upon or resulting from a differential ⟨~ freight charges⟩ **c** : functioning or proceeding differently or at a different rate (as among members of a group or parts of a whole) ⟨~ melting results in an occasional sunken pool in the surface of the glacier⟩; *specif* : resulting from crustal movements whereby one part of the earth's crust is displaced in relation to other parts **2** : relating to or involving a differential or differentiation **3** : relating to quantitative differences (as of motion, area, pressure, or leverage) : producing effects by reason of such differences

²differential \"\ *n* -S **1 a** : an arbitrary increment of an independent variable **b** : the product of the derivative of a function of one variable by the increment of the independent variable **c** : the sum of the products of each partial derivative of several variables by the arbitrary increment of the corresponding variable **2 a** : a difference between transportation rates over two routes to the same point or over routes to different points competing for the same traffic often allowed to one or more of a number of carriers in order to insure equality in the distribution of traffic among competing lines — compare DIFFERENTIAL ROUTE **b** : an amount added to or deducted from a basic transportation rate, fare, or charge — compare PORT DIFFERENTIAL **3 a** : a difference in wage rate for similar work of comparable quality and quantity granted or imposed as a reflection of varying circumstances (as in location or time of work) or of varying status (as of race or sex) ⟨a shift ~ consisting of additional pay for night work⟩ **b** : a difference in wage reflecting difference in job duties, complexity of tasks, volume or quality of production, level of skill required **4** : the price difference between the basic grade and a superior or inferior grade of a commodity deliverable on a contract **5 a** : DIFFERENTIAL GEAR **b** : PLANET DIFFERENTIAL **6** : the amount or degree by which comparable individuals or classes of individuals differ in some particular respect ⟨wide ~*s* in living standards between the two countries⟩ : a difference between comparable things ⟨price ~ between regular and high-test gasoline⟩ **7** : DIFFERENTIAL BLOOD COUNT

differential analyzer *n* : an analogue computer for the mechanical solution of complicated nonlinear differential equations

differential association *n* : abnormal distribution of personal associations; *specif* : a theory in sociology: continuous contact with criminals is chiefly responsible for the development of criminal behavior in an individual

differential blood count *or* **differential count** *n* : an enumeration of the number of each kind of white blood cell in 100 cells counted — called also *differential white count*

differential brake *n* : a band brake acting on the difference of two motions or tensions and tending to be self-tightening when the rotating part turns in the normal direction

differential calculus *n* : a branch of mathematics dealing fundamentally with the rate of change of functions with respect to the variables on which they depend

differential chain block *or* **differential block** *n* : a chain-operated differential pulley

differential diagnosis *n* : the distinguishing of a disease or condition from others presenting similar symptoms

differential duties *n pl* : duties imposed unequally on the same products according to the sources of or methods of getting these products

differential equation *n* : an equation containing differentials or derivatives of functions

differential fertility *n* : variation in fertility of different groups or classes in the population ⟨relation of economic status to *differential fertility*⟩

differential gear *or* **differential gearing** *n* **1** : an arrangement of gears forming an epicyclic train for connecting two shafts or axles in the same line, dividing the driving force equally between them, and permitting one shaft to revolve faster than the other when required (as by the driving wheels of an automobile that is moving in a curve), the speed of the main driving member being always equal to the algebraic mean of the speeds of the two shafts **2** : PLANETARY GEAR

differential geometry *n* : geometry that involves the calculus in its development

differential grasshopper *also* **differential locust** *n* : a destructive grasshopper (*Melanoplus differentialis*) common in the western U.S.

differential indexing *n* : a method used on a dividing engine for dividing a circle into subdivisions otherwise unobtainable by utilizing the difference between simultaneous movements of index plate and index crank

dif·fer·en·tial·ly \ˌdifəˈrenchəlē, -li\ *adv* : in a differential manner : so as to constitute or create a differential : so as to make distinction between different individuals or types

differential motion *n* : a mechanism (as a differential screw or a differential chain block) having two driving elements so arranged that the net motion of the follower is the difference between the two motions that it would have if either driver acted alone

differential operator *n, math* : a prescribed combination or sequence of operations involving differentiation

differential piece-rate system *n* : a method of wage payment whereby after tests have set a standard time for a task the worker receives a high piece rate for doing the job in task time and a lower piece rate if he takes longer than task time

differential psychology *n* : the study of differences between human beings either as individuals or in groups esp. through the use of tests

differential pulley *n* : a tackle consisting of a fixed upper double block with pulleys of different diameters fixed together on the same axis, a movable single lower pulley that carries the load, and an endless cable or chain that passes around all the pulleys and hangs in a loop for operating the mechanism which is used to achieve a very high mechanical advantage

differential rate *n* : a transportation rate obtained by deducting a differential from or adding it to a standard rate

differential refraction *n, astron* : the change of the apparent place of one object relative to a second object near it due to atmospheric refraction; *also* : the correction necessary to fix the two places accurately

differential route *n* : a carrier (as a railroad or steamship line) allowed to give a lower rate than some of its competitors in order to equalize a competitive disadvantage

differential screw *n* : a screw having two parts of slightly different pitch cut on the same barrel each working in a nut so that when the screw is turned the nuts have a very slow relative motion

differential thermometer *n* : a thermometer for indicating difference in temperature

differential threshold *n* : JUST-NOTICEABLE DIFFERENCE

differential white count *n* : DIFFERENTIAL BLOOD COUNT

differential windlass *n* : a windlass that has a barrel with two parts of different diameters, a hoisting rope that winds upon one part as it unwinds from the other, and a pulley that sustains the weight to be lifted hanging in the bight of the hoisting rope — called also *Chinese windlass*

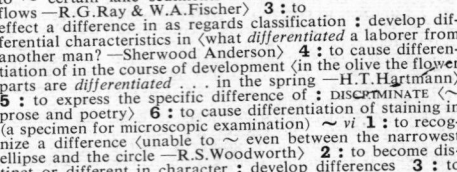

differential windlass: *A*, *B* drums; *C* pulley

¹dif·fer·en·ti·ate \ˌdifəˈrenchēˌāt *sometimes* -n(t)sē-; *usu* -ād.+V\ *vb* -ED/-ING/-S [prob. fr. (assumed) NL *differentiatus*, past part. of (assumed) NL *differentiare*, fr. L *differentia* difference — more at DIFFERENCE] *vt* **1** : to form the derivative of **2** : to make different : mark or show a difference in ⟨possible to ~ lava flows of similar color but of different ages and to ~ certain lake sediments from lava flows —R.G.Ray & W.A.Fischer⟩ **3** : to effect a difference in as regards classification : develop differential characteristics in ⟨what *differentiated* a laborer from another man? —Sherwood Anderson⟩ **4** : to cause differentiation of in the course of development ⟨in the olive the flower parts are *differentiated* . . . in the spring —H.T.Hartmann⟩ **5** : to express the specific difference of : DISCRIMINATE ⟨~ prose and poetry⟩ **6** : to cause differentiation of staining in (a specimen for microscopic examination) ~ *vi* **1** : to recognize a difference ⟨unable to ~ even between the narrowest ellipse and the circle —R.S.Woodworth⟩ **2** : to become distinct or different in character : develop differences **3** : to undergo differentiation **syn** see DISTINGUISH

²dif·fer·en·ti·ate \-ēət\ *n* -S : a differentiation rock

dif·fer·en·ti·a·tion \ˌ==ˌ==ˈāshən\ *n* -S [prob. fr. (assumed) NL *differentiation-, differentiatio*, fr. (assumed) NL *differentiatus* + L *-ion-, -io* -ion] **1** : the act or process or result of differentiating: as **a** : the process or result of forming the derivative of a function **b** : the act of distinguishing or describing a thing by giving its differentia or specific difference **c** : the enhancement of microscopically visible differences between tissue or cell parts by partial selective decolorization or removal of excess stain (as in regressive staining) **d** : the development of a discriminating conditioned response with a positive response to one stimulus and absence of the response on the application of similar but discriminably different stimuli **2** : development from the one to the many, the simple to the complex, or from the homogeneous to the heterogeneous ⟨~ of Latin into vernaculars⟩ **3 a** : modification of different parts of the body for performance of particular functions; *also* : specialization of parts or organs in the course of evolution **b** : RACIATION **c** : the sum of the processes whereby apparently indifferent cells, tissues, and structures attain their adult form and function — compare DETERMINATION **4** : the total of processes by which various rock types are produced from a common magma; *also* : a result of such processes **5** : the process whereby a social organization or culture or any of its parts becomes more complex through the growth of distinct societal functions, the development of privileged roles appropriate to individual capacity, the separation of social groups into class strata, and the establishment of political and religious structures; *also* : the result of such process

dif·fer·en·ti·a·tor \ˌ==ˈ==ˌād·ə(r), -ātə-\ *n* -S : one that differentiates

dif·fer·ent·ly *pronunc at* DIFFERENT +lē *or* li\ *adv* [ME, fr. *different* + *-ly*] **1** : in a different way or manner — often used with *from* or chiefly Brit. with *to* followed by a substantive ⟨~ from us⟩ ⟨~ to us⟩ or with *than* followed by a substantive or a clause ⟨~ than we do⟩ **2** : OTHERWISE ⟨very soon you will know ~⟩

dif·fer·ent·ness *n* -ES : the quality or state of being different

differing *pres part of* DIFFER

dif·fer·ing·ly *adv* : in a differing manner

differs *pres 3d sing of* DIFFER, *pl of* DIFFER

dif·fi·cile \ˈdifəˌsē(ə)l, ˌdif-, *archaic* dəˈfisəl\ *adj* [MF, fr. L *difficilis* difficult, fr. *dif-* (fr. *dis-*) + *-ficilis* (fr. *facilis* easy) — more at FACILE] **1** : hard to do or manage : DIFFICULT **2** : hard to deal with : PERVERSE, STUBBORN, UNREASONABLE

¹dif·fi·cult \ˈdifə(ˌ)kəlt *sometimes* -fēl *or* -fil\ *adj* [back-formation fr. *difficulty*] **1** : hard to do, make, or carry out : attended with or requiring effort, trouble, or painstaking : not easy : ARDUOUS ⟨a ~ climb⟩ ⟨a ~ task⟩ ⟨such a situation is ~ to imagine⟩ ⟨nesting places very ~ of access⟩ **2** : hard to deal with, manage or overcome : involving difficulties ⟨~ days lie ahead⟩: **a** : hard to understand : PUZZLING, OBSCURE ⟨~ reading⟩ ⟨a ~ text⟩ **b** : hard to approach : PERVERSE, STUBBORN ⟨a ~ child⟩ ⟨a ~ disposition⟩ ⟨~ music⟩ **c** : hard to obtain or produce ⟨getting a ~ living on worn-out lands⟩ **d** : HAMPERING, AWKWARD ⟨a fine performance under ~ circumstances⟩ **e** : causing pain or embarrassment ⟨the family had a ~ time after the father's death⟩ **syn** see HARD

²difficult \"\ *vt* -ED/-ING/-S **1** *obs* : to render difficult : IMPEDE **2** *chiefly Scot* : to place in difficulties : PERPLEX

dif·fi·cult·ly *adv* : with difficulty — usu. used before adjectives in *-able* and *-ible* ⟨a ~ soluble salt⟩

dif·fi·cult·ness *n* -ES : the quality or state of being difficult

dif·fi·cul·ty \-ˌkəltē, -ti *also* -ˌkə-\ *n* -ES [ME *difficulte*, fr. L *difficultas*, irreg. (influence of L *facultas* skill, ability) fr. *difficilis* difficult — more at DIFFICILE, FACULTY] **1 a** : the quality or state of being difficult or hard to do or to overcome : ARDUOUSNESS ⟨the ~ of a task⟩ **b** : unusual or laborious effort ⟨the ~ of climbing those steep stairs⟩ **2** : a thing hard to do or to overcome : something that causes labor or perplexity and requires skill and perseverance in mastering, solving, or achieving : a hard enterprise : OBSTACLE, IMPEDIMENT ⟨the *difficulties* of a science⟩ **3** : a show of reluctance : OBJECTION, CAVIL, DEMUR ⟨he made no ~ in granting the request⟩ **4** : embarrassment of affairs ⟨in days of ~ and pressure —Alfred Tennyson⟩: as **a** *usu pl* : embarrassment in financial affairs ⟨he is in *difficulties*⟩ **b** : CONTROVERSY : a falling out : DISAGREEMENT ⟨labor *difficulties* grew⟩

syn DIFFICULTY, HARDSHIP, RIGOR, and VICISSITUDE can mean in common something obstructing one's goal and demanding effort or endurance to overcome. DIFFICULTY, the most widely applicable of the terms, applies to any condition, situation, experience, or task which presents a problem hard to solve ⟨we ventured, however, over all these *difficulties*, and I took her to wife September 1st, 1730 —Benjamin Franklin⟩ ⟨*difficulties* occur and have to be surmounted —T.D.Weldon⟩ ⟨Galileo's *difficulties* with the church had nothing to do with his experiments —M.R.Cohen⟩ ⟨there are always *difficulties* between a man's dream and its achievement⟩ HARDSHIP stresses suffering, toil, or privation that is unusual or hard to bear, esp. in the pursuit of a goal ⟨the first decade in the history of Minnesota's newspapers brought them great *hardships* —*Amer. Guide Series: Minn.*⟩ ⟨they face the *hardships* of their comfortless lives with stolid indifference —P.E.James⟩ ⟨she insisted on sharing the *hardships* on equal terms with soldiers —*Current Biog.*⟩ RIGOR usu. applies to a hardship imposed upon one, as by ambition, a religion, a tyrannical government, or a trying climate ⟨anything which might soften the *rigor* of his prison —J.H.Wheelwright⟩ ⟨the *rigor* of parental authority —Abram Kardiner⟩ ⟨the *rigors* of the weather —Alexis Carrel⟩ ⟨a European custom which nowhere survived the *rigors* of the frontier —W.P.Webb⟩ VICISSITUDE, in this connection, applies to a difficulty or hardship incident to life or a career or course of action ⟨the dwarfing *vicissitudes* of poverty —Francis Hackett⟩ ⟨the *vicissitudes* of living, such as faulty diets, infections, intoxications, traumata, emotional stresses, overwork, laziness —A.J.Carlson & E.J.Stieglitz⟩ ⟨the *vicissitudes* of political persecution and exile —*Times Lit. Supp.*⟩

dif·fi·da·tion \ˌdifəˈdāshən\ *n* -S [ML *diffidation-, diffidatio*, fr. *diffidatus* (past part. of *diffidare* to renounce one's vassalage, renounce friendship, fr. L *dif-* — fr. *dis-* — + *fides* faith) + L *-ion-, -io* -ion — more at FAITH] *archaic* : a renunciation of faith or allegiance : formal severing of peaceful relations

diffide *vb* -ED/-ING/-S [L *diffidere* — more at DIFFIDENT] *vi*, *obs* : to lack faith : DISTRUST ~ *vt, obs* : to have no faith in : DOUBT, DISTRUST

dif·fi·dence \ˈdifədən(t)s *also* -dᵊn- *or* -ˌden-\ *n* -S [L *diffidentia*, fr. *diffident-, diffidens* + *-ia*] : the quality or state of being diffident: **a** *archaic* : DISTRUST : want of confidence : doubt of the power or disposition of others ⟨that affliction . . . weighed me down even to a ~ of God's mercy —John Donne⟩ **b** : distrust of oneself or one's own powers : lack of self-reliance : MODESTY : modest reserve : BASHFULNESS ⟨it is good to speak on such questions with ~ —T.B.Macaulay⟩

diffidency *n* -ES [L *diffidentia*] *obs* : DIFFIDENCE

dif·fi·dent \ˈdifədənt *also* -dᵊnt *or* -ˌdent\ *adj* [L *diffident-, diffidens*, pres. part. of *diffidere* to mistrust, fr. *dif-* (fr. *dis-*) + *fidere* to trust — more at BIDE] **1** *archaic* : lacking trust : DOUBTFUL, DISTRUSTFUL **2** : lacking confidence in oneself : distrustful of one's own powers : TIMID **3** : characterized by modest reserve ⟨one should feel ~ . . . when offering to comment on any Hindu myth —Heinrich Zimmer⟩ **syn** see SHY

dif·fi·dent·ly *adv* : in a diffident manner

dif·fi·dent·ness *n* -ES : the quality or state of being diffident

dif·flu·ence *also* **dif·lu·ence** \ˈdiˌflüən(t)s, -ˌfləwən-\ *n* -S **1** : a flowing off or away ⟨~ of glaciers into new channels⟩ **2** : DISSOLUTION

dif·flu·ent \-nt\ *adj* [L *diffluent-, diffluens*, pres. part. of *diffluere* to flow away or apart, dissolve, fr. *dif-* (fr. *dis-*) + *fluere* to flow — more at FLUENT] **1** : flowing away or off ⟨~ rivers⟩ — opposed to *confluent* **2** : readily dissolving : DELIQUESCENT

dif·flu·gia \dəˈflüjēə\ *n* [NL, irreg. fr. L *diffluere* + NL *-ia*] **1** *cap* : a genus of protozoans related to *Amoeba* but having an ovoid shell of cemented sand grains **2** -S : any protozoan of the genus *Difflugia*

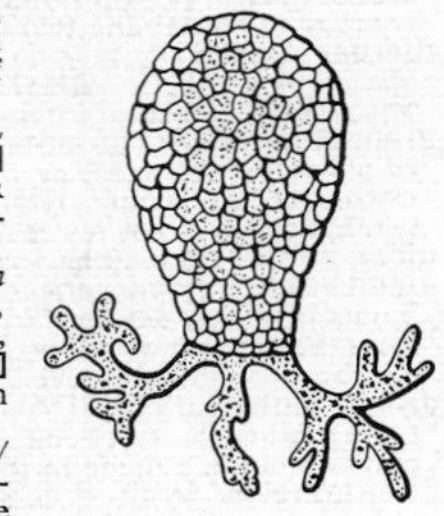

difflugia 2

dif·form *adj* [ML *difformis*, fr. L *dif-* (fr. *dis-*) + *-formis* -form] **1** *obs* : UNLIKE, DISSIMILAR **2** : irregular in form : ANOMALOUS

dif·for·mi·ty \(ˈ)diˈfȯrmədˌē\ *n* -ES [MF or ML; MF *difformité*, fr. ML *difformitat-, difformitas*, fr. L *difformis* + L *-itat-, -itas* -ity] : irregularity or diversity of form : lack of conformity

dif·fract \dəˈfrakt\ *vb* -ED/-ING/-S [back-formation fr. *diffraction*] *vt* : to break or separate into parts; *specif* : to cause to undergo diffraction ~ *vi* : to undergo diffraction

dif·frac·tion \-kshən\ *n* -S [NL *diffraction-, diffractio*, fr. L *diffractus* (past part. of *diffringere* to break to pieces, fr. *dif-* — fr. *dis-* apart — + *-fringere*, fr. *frangere* to break) + *-ion-, -io* -ion — more at DIS-, BREAK] : a modification which light undergoes in passing by the edges of opaque bodies or through narrow slits or in being reflected from ruled surfaces and in which the rays appear to be deflected and produce fringes of parallel light and dark or colored bands; *also* : a similar modification of other waves (as sound waves and electromagnetic waves) that occurs whenever the full wave front is not brought to a focus or utilized and that results in the curvature of waves around objects in their path — see ELECTRON DIFFRACTION

diffraction disk *n* : SPURIOUS DISK

diffraction grating *n* : GRATING 3

diffraction pattern *n* : an often photographic pattern produced by diffraction (as of light, X rays, or electrons) — compare LAUE PATTERN

dif·frac·tom·e·ter \ˌdiˌfrakˈtäməd·ə(r)\ *n* [*diffraction* + *-o-* + *-meter*] : an instrument for measuring the diameters of small particles in a microscope field by means of the diffraction rings which appear to surround them — **dif·frac·to·met·ric** \diˌfraktəˈme·trik\ *adj* — **dif·frac·to·met·ri·cal·ly** \-trək(ə)lē\ *adv*

dif·fu·sate \dəˈfyüˌzāt\ *n* -S [ISV *diffuse* + *-ate*] : a product of diffusion: as **a** : the material that passes through the membrane in dialysis; *also* : the liquid into which such material diffuses — sometimes called also *dialyzate* **b** : the material that passes through a suitable barrier in gaseous diffusion (as for the separation of isotopes of volatile uranium compounds)

¹dif·fuse \dəˈfyüs\ *adj* [ME, fr. MF or L; MF *difus* scattered, spread out, fr. L *diffusus*, past part. of *diffundere* to spread out, pour out, scatter, fr. *dif-* (fr. *dis-*) + *fundere* to pour — more at FOUND] **1** *obs* **a** : CONFUSED **b** : hard to understand : DIFFICULT **2** : poured or spread out : WIDESPREAD : not concentrated or restrained : COPIOUS, FULL **3** : VERBOSE, PROLIX ⟨a ~ writer⟩ **4** : spreading widely or loosely ⟨~ branches⟩ **5** : not localized : SCATTERED ⟨~ sclerosis⟩ **6** : moving in many directions ⟨~ radiation⟩ **7** : having the whole chorionic surface studded with villi ⟨whales and horses have ~ placentas⟩ **syn** see WORDY

²dif·fuse \dəˈfyüz *sometimes* dī-\ *vb* -ED/-ING/-S [MF or L; MF *diffuser*, fr. L *diffusus*, past part.] *vt* **1 a** : to pour out and permit or cause to spread freely (as a fluid out of a container) ⟨a drop of dye *diffused* through water⟩ ⟨gas being *diffused* through the air⟩ : spread out : permit to spread over a wide area or through a large space ⟨the all-pervasive spirit of sweetness and light *diffused* through the universe —V.L. Parrington⟩ **b** : to make widely perceptible, known, or familiar : send out : EXTEND, SCATTER, BROADCAST ⟨in place of the present chaos universities must again ~ a definite culture —Walter Moberly⟩ **c** : to spread out into many areas, spheres, agencies, and activities often with consequent reduced concentration or effectiveness ⟨a state in which power is concentrated will . . . be more bellicose than one in which power is *diffused* —Bertrand Russell⟩ ⟨it is like dynamite exploded in the open. Its force is *diffused* by going in all directions —*Saturday Rev.*⟩ **2** : to subject (as a light beam) to diffusion : treat by diffusion **3** : to break up and distribute (incident light) by reflection (as from a rough surface) ~ *vi* **1** : to spread out : pass or become transmitted often with slow tingeing or permeation ⟨culture traits are able to

~ apart from the migration of peoples —Brewton Berry⟩ **2 :** to undergo diffusion ⟨a gas in solution ~*s* from a region of greater to one of less concentration⟩ **syn** see SPREAD

dif·fused \-zd\ *adj* **:** spread out or abroad **:** DISPERSED, DIFFUSE ⟨a widely ~ opinion⟩ — **dif·fus·ed·ly** \-zədlē, -li\ *adv* — **dif·fus·ed·ness** \-zədnəs\ *n* -ES

dif·fuse·ly \dəˈfyüslē, -li\ *adv* [ME, fr. *diffuse* + *-ly*] **:** in a diffuse manner

diffuse nebula *n* **:** any of the numerous luminous or dark formations or irregularly distributed dust and gas seen within the Milky Way galaxy and in other spiral galaxies but not including the planetary nebulae

dif·fuse·ness \-üsnəs\ *n* -ES **:** the quality or state of being diffuse

diffuse placenta *also* **diffused placenta** *n* **:** a placenta made up of villi diffusely scattered over almost the whole surface of the chorion (as in whales, swine, and horses)

diffuse–porous \=ˌ=ˈ==\ *adj* **:** having vessels distributed more or less uniformly thoughout an annual ring and not varying greatly in size — used of certain woody stems and roots (as those of maples and birches); compare RING-POROUS

dif·fus·er \dəˈfyüzə(r) *sometimes* dīˈ-\ *n* -S **:** one that diffuses: as **a :** a chamber surrounding a turbine wheel commonly provided with stationary vanes into which the fluid is discharged **b :** a device (as a reflector placed above an electric lamp or a vaned shield placed below) to distribute the light from a concentrated source uniformly **c :** a device through which air or other gas is admitted in minute bubbles into sewage or water undergoing treatment **d :** a device for diffusing spray or vapor (as in a carburetor) **e :** a device for reducing the velocity and increasing the static pressure of a fluid passing through a system, usu. made in the form of a chamber having an effective cross section which increases in the direction of flow **f :** a screen (as of cloth or frosted glass) used to soften lighting (as in a motion-picture or television studio) **g :** a device (as a louver with slats at different angles) for deflecting air in various directions from an outlet to effect mixture with room air (as for heating or cooling a room)

dif·fus·ibil·i·ty \də,fyüzəˈbiləd·ē *sometimes* (ˌ)dī,-\ *n* -ES **:** the capability of being diffused

dif·fus·ible \dəˈfyüzəbəl *sometimes* dīˈ-\ *adj* **:** capable of diffusing or of being diffused — **dif·fus·ibly** \-blē, -li\ *adv*

dif·fu·sion \dəˈfyüzhən *sometimes* dīˈ-\ *n* -S [LL *diffusion-, diffusio*, fr. L *diffusus* + *-ion-, -io* -ion] **1 :** the action of diffusing or the state of being diffused **:** SPREADING, DISPERSION ⟨the ~ of knowledge⟩ **2 :** DIFFUSENESS, PROLIXITY **3 a :** the process whereby particles (as molecules and ions) of liquids, gases, or solids intermingle as the result of their spontaneous movement caused by thermal agitation and in dissolved substances move from a region of higher concentration to one of lower concentration — see GASEOUS DIFFUSION **b :** reflection of light by a rough reflecting surface **:** transmission of light through a translucent material **:** SCATTERING **4 :** the spread of linguistic or cultural elements from one area, tribe, or people to others through contact ⟨the ~ of tobacco from the New World to the Old World⟩ **5 a :** the process of slightly scattering a portion of the image-forming light to give a pleasing artistic softness to a photograph **b :** IRRADIATION 1c(3) **6 :** a radio broadcast — **dif·fu·sion·al** \-zhənᵊl,-zhnəl\ *adj*

diffusion coefficient *or* **diffusion constant** *n* **:** the quantity of a substance that in diffusing from one region to another passes through each unit of cross section per unit of time when the volume-concentration gradient is unity — called also *diffusivity*

diffusion disk *also* **diffusing disk** *n* **:** a piece of transparent material having special markings or embossings used with a photographic lens to give a soft focus or diffused effect to the image

dif·fu·sion·ism \-zhə,nizəm\ *n* **:** a theory in anthropology: widely separated cultural similarities are evidence of historical contact

dif·fu·sion·ist \-zhənəst\ *n* **:** one who emphasizes the role of diffusion in the history of culture: **a :** an advocate of diffusionism — contrasted with *evolutionist* **b :** a student of diffusion within a circumscribed geographical area esp. in America

diffusion pressure deficit *n* **:** the algebraic sum of all the forces tending to cause water to move into a plant cell

diffusion pump *n* **:** a vacuum pump for producing extremely high vacuums by diffusing gas into a jet of vapor of mercury or some heavy oil by which the gas is carried off and which is separated from the gas by condensation

diffusion–transfer process *n* **:** any of several document-copying photographic processes in which a facsimile of the original document is produced by development of a photographic image, by transfer by diffusion of the silver salts in the undeveloped areas to a receiving paper, and by development of the transferred image

dif·fu·sive \-üs|iv, -üz|, |ēv *also* |əv\ *adj* **1 :** having the quality of diffusing **:** tending to diffuse **:** characterized by diffusion **2** *obs, of a people or group* **:** acting as a mass of individuals having authority diffused throughout the entire membership — **dif·fu·sive·ly** \|əvlē, -li\ *adv* — **dif·fu·sive·ness** \|ivnəs, |ēv-\ *n* -ES

dif·fu·siv·i·ty \də,fyüˈsivəd·ē, -ˈzi- *sometimes* (ˌ)dē,-\ *n* -ES **1 :** DIFFUSION COEFFICIENT **2 :** the quantity of heat passing normally through a unit area per unit time divided by the product of specific heat, density, and temperature gradient

dif·fu·sor \dəˈfyüzə(r) *sometimes* dīˈ-\ *n* -S **:** DIFFUSER

difluence *var of* DIFFLUENCE

difluor- *or* **difluoro-** *comb form* [ISV *di-* + *fluor-*] **:** containing two atoms of fluorine — in names of chemical compounds ⟨1,1-*difluoro*ethane⟩; compare FLUOR-

di·fluoride \(ˈ)dī+\ *n* [*di-* + *fluoride*] **:** a compound containing two atoms of fluorine combined with an element or radical

[1]**dig** \ˈdig\ *vb* **dug** \ˈdəg\ *or archaic* **digged** \ˈdigd\ **dug** *or archaic* **digged**; **digging**; **digs** [ME *diggen*, perh. of imit. origin] *vi* **1 :** to turn up, loosen, or remove earth **:** DELVE ⟨~ for buried treasure⟩ ⟨*digging* in the garden⟩ **2 :** to work hard or laboriously **:** DRUDGE ⟨*digging* away at his geometry lessons⟩ **3 a :** to penetrate below the surface in search of something hidden or buried **:** pierce deeply — used with *into* ⟨~ into the facts of a case⟩ ⟨*digging* into the history of mankind⟩ **b :** to advance or progress by or as if by removing or pushing aside material **:** BURROW ⟨if we ~ down through the strata of English historical writing —B.R.Redman⟩ **4** *slang* **:** LODGE, DWELL ⟨this is the inn where I ~ —John Galsworthy⟩ **5** *of a tool* **:** to cut deeply into material being worked on because of some fault (as being ill-set or held at a wrong angle) **6 :** to run hard ⟨the runner on first base ~*s* for second with the first pitch⟩ ~ *vt* **1 :** to break up (earth) with a hard implement (as a spade, hoe, mattock) **:** pierce, loosen, or turn over (the soil) ⟨~ a field for planting⟩ **2 a :** to bring to the surface or get by digging **:** UNEARTH ⟨~ potatoes⟩ **b :** to bring to light or out of hiding — often used with *out* or *up* ⟨~ up facts⟩ **3 :** to hollow out (as a well) **:** form (as a ditch) by removing earth **:** EXCAVATE ⟨~ a trench⟩ ⟨~ a foundation⟩ **4 :** to drive down so as to penetrate **:** THRUST ⟨*dug* his fingers into the soft earth⟩ **5 :** POKE, PROD ⟨he *dug* me in the ribs with his sharp little elbow⟩ **6** *slang* **a :** to listen to or look at **:** pay attention to ⟨~ that fancy hat⟩ **b :** UNDERSTAND, APPRECIATE ⟨what I don't ~ over there is the British money —Jimmy Durante⟩ **c :** LIKE, ADMIRE ⟨a very corny gag, but people seem to ~ it —*Down Beat*⟩ — **dig into** *vt* **:** to take a substantial part from (a supply) **:** eat into **:** DEPLETE ⟨forced to *dig into* savings to pay current debts⟩

syn DIG, DELVE, SPADE, GRUB, EXCAVATE, EXHUME, and DISINTER mean, in common, to use a spade or similar implement in breaking up the ground to a point below the surface and turning or removing the earth or bringing to the surface anything below it. DIG, the commonest of the terms, implies a loosening of earth around or under something so as to bring it to the surface or any disturbing of earth to penetrate it in some way ⟨*dig* worms⟩ ⟨*dig* for gold⟩ ⟨*dig* a bone up⟩ ⟨*dig* into a cliff⟩ DELVE implies more commonly the use of a spade or efforts comparable to the use of one and suggests strongly a laborious digging around in or in among something ⟨lab scientists *delve* into the secrets of nature —*Investor's Reader*⟩ ⟨to *delve* into the mysteries of prehistoric man —E.J. Sawyer⟩ ⟨*delve* beneath these superficialities —William Petersen⟩ ⟨*delve* among the old records in the city archives —F.L. Pattee⟩ SPADE may apply to the manual preparation of soil for planting, to turning over and loosening the ground ⟨*spade* the garden early⟩ ⟨*spade* in the fertilizer⟩ GRUB usu. does not imply deep digging but rather suggests laborious dirty digging around in surface soil or dirt, or any dirty, groveling work resembling it ⟨scorning to *grub* the soil, they live off the produce of their herds —Jean & Franc Shor⟩ ⟨a group of ragpickers haphazardly *grubbing* about among a pile of human refuse —*Times Lit. Supp.*⟩ ⟨*grubbing* around Etruscan cemeteries —Robert Graves⟩ ⟨he *grubs* for the answers in the memory heap of five decades —*Time*⟩ EXCAVATE implies making a hollow in, into, or through something, usu. by spade, shovel or machine ⟨the powerful stream . . . *excavated* a new channel —*Amer. Guide Series: Wash.*⟩ ⟨an expedition of the Witte Memorial Museum of San Antonio *excavated* caves, the contents of which revealed the culture of a sedentary people —*Amer. Guide Series: Texas*⟩ ⟨*excavate* a cliff⟩ EXHUME implies the removal of something buried ⟨the ungrateful task of *exhuming* antiquities —*Americas*⟩ ⟨trees buried by the gray unweathered outwash gravels and *exhumed* through erosion of the valley train by the Rio Ameghino —R.L.Nichols & M.M.Miller⟩ DISINTER implies the exhuming of something buried by human hands ⟨the urns *disinterred* at Walsingham —A.T.Quiller-Couch⟩ ⟨bodies were *disinterred* from battlefields —*Amer. Guide Series: N.C.*⟩

[2]**dig** \"\ *n* -S **1 a :** THRUST, POKE ⟨gave the horse a good ~ in the side⟩ **b :** a verbal thrust **:** a cutting remark esp. containing a veiled allusion ⟨why all the small ungracious ~*s* and hedging of good report with evil suspicion —Philip Burnham⟩ **2 a :** a plodding and laborious student **:** GRIND **3** *dial Eng* **:** a tool for digging **4** [by shortening] **:** DIGGER 4 **5 digs** *pl, Brit* **:** DIGGINGS 3b **6 :** a site at which an archaeological excavation is made; *also* **:** the excavation itself and the conduct of the project as a whole ⟨on their return from some fruitful ~ in the Nile valley —David Garnett⟩ **7 :** a push of the ball of the foot against the floor in dancing

[3]**dig** \"\ *n* -S [ME *digge*] *now dial Eng* **:** DUCK

dig *abbr* digest

di·gallic acid \(ˈ)dī+ . . .-\ *n* [ISV *di-* + *gallic*] **1 :** a crystalline phenolic ester acid $C_{14}H_{10}O_9$ obtained as a decomposition product of tannins or made synthetically and yielding two molecules of gallic acid on hydrolysis — called also *meta-digallic acid* **2 :** GALLOTANNIN — used chiefly in pharmacy

di·gam·ba·ra \diˈgəmbərə\ *n* -S *cap* [Skt, lit., sky-clad, naked] **:** a member of a major Jain sect formed in the 3d century B.C. and distinguished by its original abandonment of all worldly possessions including clothes and by its denial that women can attain salvation

digametic \ˌdī+\ *adj* [*di-* + *gametic*] **:** forming two kinds of germ cells (as one with and one without the X chromosome) **:** heterozygous for sex

di·gam·ma \dīˈgamə, ˈdī,g-\ *n* [L, fr. Gk, fr. *di-* + *gamma*; fr. its resemblance to two capital gammas placed on top of each other] **1 :** a letter of the original Greek alphabet representing a sound approximately that of English *w* which early fell into disuse except in writing the western dialects and in numerical notation where it represented the number 6 — called also *vau*; symbol F, ϝ **2 :** the sound represented by the letter ϝ

di·gam·mat·ed \dīˈga,mād·əd\ *adj* **1 :** having the Greek letter digamma **2 :** inferred to have had a *w*-sound of which actual orthographic evidence does not survive — used of a Greek word or root or of the vowel following the inferred sound ⟨the number of ~ roots in Homer —R.C.Jebb⟩ **3 :** printed with digamma inserted where its sound is believed orig. to have been employed ⟨a ~ edition of Homer⟩

dig·a·my \ˈdigəmē\ *n* -ES [LL *digamia*, fr. LGk, fr. *digamos* married twice (fr. Gk, adulterous, fr. *di-* + *-gamos* -gamous) + Gk *-ia* -y] **:** a legal second marriage after the termination of a first marriage (as by death or divorce of the spouse) — called also *deuterogamy*; distinguished from *bigamy*

[1]**di·gastric** \(ˈ)dī+\ *n* -S [NL *digastricus*, fr. *di-* + *gastricus* gastric — more at GASTRIC] **:** either of a pair of digastric muscles that extend from the anterior inferior margin of the mandible to the temporal bone and serve to open the jaw

[2]**digastric** \"\ *adj* [NL *digastricus*, fr. *digastricus*, adj.] **1** *of a muscle* **:** having two bellies separated by a median tendon **2 :** of or relating to a digastric

dig–dig *var of* DIK-DIK

dig down *vi* **:** to pay money out of one's own pocket ⟨the customers will not *dig down* for such entertainment⟩

di·ge·nea \dīˈjēnēə\ *n pl, cap* [NL, fr. *di-* + Gk *genea* race, descent — more at KIN] **:** a subclass of Trematoda commonly divided into the orders Gasterostomata and Prosostomata, comprising forms with a complex life cycle involving alternation of sexual reproduction as an internal parasite of a vertebrate with asexual reproduction in a mollusk, and often including developmental stages in still other hosts — compare ASPIDOGASTREA I, MONOGENEA — **di·ge·ne·ous** \(ˈ)dīˈjēnēəs\ *adj*

di·genesis \(ˈ)dī+\ *n* [NL, fr. *di-* + *genesis*] **:** successive reproduction by sexual and asexual methods

di·genetic \ˌdī+\ *adj* [in sense 1, fr. *di-* + *genetic*; in sense 2, fr. NL *Digenetica*] **1 :** of or relating to digenesis **2 :** of or relating to the Digenea

di·ge·net·i·ca \ˌdījəˈned·əkə\ *syn of* DIGENEA

di·genic \(ˈ)dī+\ *adj* [*di-* + *-genic*] *biol* **:** induced by two genes — used of phenotypic effects manifested only when two nonallelic controlling genes interact

dig·e·nite \ˈdijə,nīt\ *n* -S [G *digenit*, fr. *di-* + L *genus* kind + G *-it* -ite — more at KIN] **:** a mineral $Cu_{2-x}S$ consisting of an isometric copper sulfide having a variable deficiency in copper

[1]**di·gest** \ˈdī,jest *sometimes* -,jəst\ *n* -S [ME *Digest* compilation of Roman laws ordered by Justinian, fr. LL *Digesta*, pl., fr. L, collection of writings arranged under various headings, fr. neut. pl. of *digestus*, past part. of *digerere* to divide, distribute, arrange, digest, fr. *di-* (fr. *dis-* apart) + *gerere* to bear, carry — more at DIS-, CAST] **1 :** a short summation of or the compressed kernel of a body of information: as **a :** a compilation of legal rules, statutes, or decisions systematically arranged **b :** a literary condensation or abridgment **c :** a periodical usu. of small format that characteristically prints condensed versions of articles previously published elsewhere ⟨on the shelves were ~*s* and pulp magazines⟩ **2 :** a product of digestion; *specif* **:** a mixture of breakdown products of a complex organic substance (as meat) resulting from the controlled action of one or more enzymes — see DIGEST MEDIUM **syn** see COMPENDIUM

[2]**di·gest** \(ˈ)dīˈjest *also* dəˈj-\ *vb* -ED/-ING/-S [ME *digesten*, fr. L *digestus*, past part.] *vt* **1** *obs* **:** SEPARATE, DISTRIBUTE **:** dispose separately or in parts or groups **2 :** to distribute or arrange systematically **:** work over and classify **:** reduce to portions for ready use or application; *specif* **:** CODIFY ⟨~ the laws⟩ **3 :** to think over and arrange systematically in the mind **:** receive in the mind and consider **:** COMPREHEND **4 a :** to subject to or transform by digestion **:** convert (food) into absorbable form **b :** to cause or aid the digestion of (food) ⟨pancreatic enzymes ~ most of the protein⟩ **c :** to break down in vitro in a manner similar to digestion in vivo ⟨sugars are ~*ed* by yeasts⟩ **5 :** to appropriate or assimilate mentally ⟨read, mark, learn, and inwardly ~ them —*Bk. of Com. Prayer*⟩ **6 :** to bear patiently **:** be reconciled to **:** BROOK ⟨~ many insults⟩ **7** *obs* **:** to cause to generate pus **8 :** to change the nature of (a substance) by various means: as **a :** to soften or decompose by heat and moisture or chemicals often under pressure **:** COOK **b :** to extract soluble ingredients from (as plant or animal materials) by warming with a liquid — compare MACERATE 3a **c :** to decompose by chemicals (as acids) without heating **9 :** to compress (a piece of literature or a body of information) into a short summary form containing the essential core of the matter ~ *vi* **1 a :** to digest food ⟨don't bother me; I'm resting and ~*ing*⟩ **b :** to become digested **:** undergo digestion ⟨soft-boiled eggs ~ easily⟩ **2** *obs* **:** to generate pus **:** SUPPURATE

di·ges·ta \dəˈjestə, dīˈ-\ *n pl* [NL, fr. neut. pl. of L *digestus*] **:** something undergoing digestion (as food in the stomach)

di·ges·tant \dəˈjestənt, dīˈ-\ *n* -S **:** DIGESTIVE 1

di·gest·er \-tə(r)\ *n* -S **1 :** one that digests or makes a digest **2 :** a medicine or an article of food that aids digestion **3 a** *also* **di·ges·tor** \"\ **:** a vessel or apparatus for digesting **:** COOKER, AUTOCLAVE **b :** a vessel in which cellulosic pulp is produced usu. from wood chips by cooking with chemicals under pressure **c :** a covered tank in which digestion of sewage sludge is carried out **4 :** RECOVERER

digester tankage *or* **digester meal tankage** *n* **:** tankage for feeding livestock

di·gest·ibil·i·ty \də,jestəˈbiləd·ē, (ˌ)dī,-, -ətē, -i\ *n* -ES **:** the fitness of a foodstuff or nutrient for digestion; *often* **:** the percentage of a foodstuff taken into the digestive tract that is absorbed into the body

di·gest·ible \dəˈjestəbəl, (ˈ)dīˈj-\ *adj* [ME, fr. MF or LL; MF, fr. LL *digestibilis*, fr. L *digestus* + *-ibilis* -ible] **:** capable of being digested — **di·gest·ible·ness** *n* -ES — **di·gest·ibly** \-blē,-bli\ *adv*

digestible nutrient *n* **:** any of the three basic classes of foodstuffs carbohydrate, fat, or protein; *esp* **:** the part of a protein that has actually undergone digestion and assimilation as distinguished from the part rejected in feces

di·ges·tion \dəˈjes(h)chən, dīˈ-\ *n* -S [ME *digestioun*, fr. MF *digestion*, fr. L *digestion-, digestio*, fr. *digestus* + *-ion-, -io* -ion] **1 :** the action or process of digesting; *also* **:** the power of digesting **2** *obs* **:** the generation of pus **:** SUPPURATION **3 :** the process of making food absorbable by dissolving it and breaking it down into simpler chemical compounds that occurs in the living body chiefly through the action of secretions containing enzymes (as the saliva and the gastric, pancreatic, and intestinal juices in the alimentary canal of higher animals) **4 :** the process in sewage treatment by which organic matter in sludge is decomposed by anaerobic bacteria with the release of a burnable mixture of gases (as methane with carbon dioxide) **5 :** partial or complete solution of rock in magma — **di·ges·tion·al** \dəˈjes(h)chənᵊl, (ˈ)dīˈj-\ *adj* — **digestionally** *adv*

diagrammatic figure of digestive organs of man, as seen from the front: *a* esophagus; *b* cardiac end of stomach; *c* pyloric end of stomach; *d* duodenum; *e, f* convolutions of small intestine; *g* cecum; *g′* vermiform appendix; *h* ascending colon; *i* transverse colon; *k* descending colon; *l* sigmoid flexure; *m* rectum; *n* anus; *o, o* lobes of liver, raised and turned back; *p* hepatic duct; *q* cystic duct; *r* gallbladder; *s* common bile duct; *t* pancreas; *u* pancreatic duct, entering the duodenum with the common bile duct

digestion coefficient *also* **digestibility coefficient** *n* **:** the proportion of a nutrient taken into the digestive tract that is actually digested — compare BIOLOGICAL VALUE

[1]**di·ges·tive** \dəˈjestiv, -tēv *also* dīˈ- *or* -təv\ *n* -S [ME, fr. MF *digestif*, fr. *digestif*, adj.] **1 a :** something (as a food or drug) that aids digestion **:** DIGESTER **b** *Brit* **:** a thin slightly sweet biscuit or wafer **2** *obs* **:** a substance that promotes suppuration

[2]**di·ges·tive** \dəˈj- *also* (ˈ)dīˈj-\ *adj* [MF or L; MF *digestif*, fr. L *digestivus*, fr. *digestus* (past part. of *digerere* to divide, distribute, arrange, digest) + *-ivus* -ive — more at DIGEST] **:** relating to digestion **:** having the power to cause or promote digestion ⟨~ ferments⟩ — **di·ges·tive·ly** \-təvlē, -li\ *adv* — **di·ges·tive·ness** \-tivnəs, -tēv- *also* -təv-\ *n* -ES

digestive gland *n* **:** a gland in an animal or plant that secretes digestive enzymes

digest medium *n* **:** a biological culture medium prepared from or containing a digest

digestor *var of* DIGESTER

digests *pl of* DIGEST, *pres 3d sing of* DIGEST

digesture *n* -S [[2]*digest* + *-ure*] *obs* **:** DIGESTION

digged *archaic past of* DIG

dig·ger \ˈdigə(r)\ *n* -S [ME, fr. *diggen* to dig + *-er*] **1 :** one that digs in the ground: as **a :** MINER **b :** a tool for digging **c :** a machine for digging ⟨trench ~⟩ ⟨posthole ~⟩ **d :** a plow used in England with a short high abruptly curved moldboard for turning and breaking up the furrow slice of soil **2** *usu cap* **:** a member of a short-lived equalitarian group that began in 1649 to cultivate certain English common lands as a protest against private property **3** *or* **digger indian** *usu cap D & I* **a :** BANNOCK **b :** PAIUTE 1 **4** [fr. earlier *digger* gold miner (i.e. a typical Australian)] **a :** AUSTRALIAN; *esp* **:** an Australian or New Zealand soldier of World War I **b** *Austral* **:** PAL, BUDDY **5** *slang* **:** one that buys theater tickets for speculative brokers

digger pine *n, usu cap D* **:** a California pine (*Pinus sabiniana*) with sparse foliage and nuts formerly used as food by the Digger Indians — called also *bull pine, gray pine*

digger wasp *n* **:** a burrowing wasp; *specif* **:** any of numerous usu. solitary wasps chiefly of the superfamily Sphecoidea that dig nest burrows in the soil and provision them with living insects or spiders which they paralyze by stinging

dig·ging \ˈdigiŋ, -gēŋ\ *n* -S [fr. gerund of *dig*] **1 diggings** *pl* **:** material taken out of an excavation **2** *usu* **diggings** *pl but sing or pl in constr* **:** a place of excavating **:** a place where ore, metals, or precious stones are got by digging (as by placer mining) **3 diggings** *pl* **a :** PLACE, PREMISES ⟨he hasn't been seen around these ~*s* lately⟩ **b** *chiefly Brit* **:** quarters or lodgings esp. for a student or other single person

digging stick *n* **:** a primitive agricultural implement consisting of a pointed stick sometimes weighted with a perforated stone or equipped with a crossbar upon which the digger steps

[1]**dight** \ˈdīt, *Scot* ˈdikt *or* ˈdī(k)t\ *vt* **dighted** *or* **dight; dighted** *or* **dight; dighting; dights** [ME *dighten*, fr. OE *dihtan* to arrange, dictate, compose (verse or prose); akin to OFris *dichta* to arrange; both fr. a prehistoric Anglo-Frisian word borrowed fr. L *dictare* to dictate, compose (verse or prose) — more at DICTATE] **1** *obs* **:** APPOINT, ORDER, ASSIGN **2** *archaic* **:** DRESS, ADORN **3** *chiefly Scot* **a :** to put in order **:** REPAIR **b :** to wipe clean **c :** SWEEP **d :** WINNOW

[2]**dight** \"\ *n* -S *chiefly Scot* **:** WIPE, RUB

[3]**dight** *var of* DITE

dig·i·lan·ide \ˌdijəˈla,nīd, -ˌnəd\ *or* **dig·i·lan·id** \-ˌnəd\ *n* -S [fr. *Digilanid*, a trademark] **:** LANATOSIDE; *also* **:** a mixture of the lanatosides

dig in *vt* **:** to cover by digging **:** BURY ⟨*dig in* fertilizer⟩ ~ *vi* **1 :** to prepare a defensive position by digging trenches ⟨the troops had no time to *dig in* before the attack came⟩ **2 :** to hold stubbornly to a position **3 a :** to go resolutely to work **b :** to begin eating **:** fall to **4 :** to run hard

dig·it \ˈdijət, *usu* -əd·+V\ *n* -S [ME, fr. L *digitus* finger, toe — more at TOE] **1 a :** any one of the whole numbers from one through nine **b :** one of the 10 arabic numerals by which all numbers may be expressed; *often* **:** any of the arabic numerals with the exception of the cipher **2 :** a unit of length based on the breadth of a finger and equal in English measure to ¾ inch **3 :** one of the divisions in which the limbs of amphibians and all higher vertebrates terminate numbering typically five on each limb but often reduced (as in the horse where the whole foot consists of an enormously developed middle digit) and having typically a series of bony phalanges which in most mammals do not exceed three in number and usu. bearing a horny nail at the tip which may be modified into a claw or hoof : a finger or toe **syn** see NUMBER

1**dig·i·tal** \'dijəd·ᵊl, -ətᵊl\ *adj* [L *digitalis*, fr. *digitus* + *-alis* -al] **1 :** of or relating to the fingers ⟨~ technique of a pianist⟩ ⟨~ grasp⟩ or toes **:** DIGITATE **2 :** performed with a finger ⟨~ examination⟩ **3 :** of or relating to calculation by numerical methods or by discrete units — distinguished from *analogical* — **dig·i·tal·ly** \-ᵊlē,-ᵊli\ *adv*

2**digital** \"\ *n* -s **1 :** FINGER **2 :** a key (as of an organ) to be played by the finger **3 :** the terminal joint of the pedipalpus of a spider

digital computer *n* **:** a computer that operates with numbers expressed directly as digits in a decimal, binary, or other system

dig·i·tal·in \,dijə'talən *sometimes* -tāl- *or* -täl- *or* -tål-\ *n* -s [NL *digitalis* + E *-in*] **1 :** a white crystalline steroid glycoside $C_{36}H_{56}O_{14}$ obtained from seeds of the purple foxglove **2 :** a mixture of the glycosides of digitalis varying in composition according to the method of preparation from the leaves or seeds

dig·i·tal·is \-ləs\ *n* [NL, fr. L, adj.] **1** *cap* **:** a genus of Eurasian herbs of the family Scrophulariaceae that have alternate leaves and racemes of showy bell-shaped flowers **2** -ES **:** the dried leaf of the purple foxglove containing the active principles digitoxin and gitoxin and constituting a powerful cardiac stimulant and a diuretic used principally in diseases of the heart to correct lost compensation

dig·i·tal·i·za·tion \,dijə,talə'zāshən\ *n* -s **:** the administration (as in heart disease) of digitalis until the desired physiologic adjustment is attained; *also* **:** the bodily state so produced

dig·i·ta·lize \'dijəd·ᵊl,īz, ,dijə'ta,līz\ *vt* -ED/-ING/-S [NL *digitalis* + E *-ize*] **:** to subject (a person) to digitalization

dig·i·tal·ose \,dijə'ta,lōs *also* -ōz\ *n* -s [ISV *digitalin* + *-ose*] **:** a sugar $C_7H_{14}O_5$ obtained esp. from digitalin by hydrolysis; the 3-methyl derivative of D-fucose

dig·i·tar·ia \,dijə'ta(a)rēə\ *n, cap* [NL, fr. L *digitus* finger + NL *-aria* — more at TOE] **:** a genus of grasses found in warm regions and having one-flowered spikelets in one-sided digitately arranged racemes — see CRABGRASS

dig·i·tate \'dijə,tāt\ *also* **dig·i·tat·ed** \-ād·əd\ *adj* [*digit* + *-ate, -ated*] **1 :** having digits **2 :** resembling a finger; *specif* **:** having divisions arranged like fingers of a hand — used esp. of compound leaves (as those of lupine or horse chestnut) having lobes that extend to the point of insertion of the petiole — **dig·i·tate·ly** *adv*

dig·i·ta·tion \,dijə'tāshən\ *n* -s **1 :** the state of being digitate **:** a division into fingers or digitiform processes **2 :** a process that resembles a finger

digiti *pl of* DIGITUS

digiti- *comb form* [F, fr. L *digitus* finger, toe — more at TOE] **1 :** digit **:** finger or toe ⟨*digiti*grade⟩ **2 :** finger ⟨*digiti*form⟩ **3 :** digitately ⟨*digiti*pinnate⟩

dig·i·ti·gra·da \,dijəd·ə'grādə\ *n pl, cap* [NL, fr. *digiti-* + *-grada* (neut. pl. of *-gradus* -grade)] *in former classifications* **:** a group consisting of the digitigrade Carnivora

1**dig·i·ti·grade** \'dijəd·ə,grād\ *adj* [F, fr. *digiti-* (fr. L *digitus* finger, toe) + *-grade* — more at TOE] *of an animal* **:** walking upon the digits with the posterior part of the foot more or less raised — opposed to *plantigrade*

2**digitigrade** \"\ *n* **:** a digitigrade animal

dig·i·ti·nervate *also* **dig·i·ti·nerved** \,dijəd·ə+\ *adj* [*digiti-* + *nervate* or *nerved*] **:** having veins that emerge from the petiole and spread out like fingers **:** straight-veined ⟨a ~ leaf⟩

dig·i·ti·pinnate \"+\ *adj* [*digiti-* + *pinnate*] **:** having digitate leaves of which the leaflets are pinnate **:** digitately pinnate

dig·i·tize \'dijə,tīz\ *vt* -ED/-ING/-S **:** to put (data) into digital notation (as for use in a digital computer) — **dig·i·tiz·er** \-zə(r)\ *n* -s

dig·i·to·gen·in \,dijəd·ə'jenən, ,==tājən-\ *n* -s [blend of *digitonin* and *-gen*] **:** a crystalline steroid sapogenin $C_{27}H_{44}O_5$ obtained by hydrolysis of digitonin

dig·i·to·nide \,dijə'tō,nīd\ *n* -s [*digitonin* + *-ide*] **:** a sparingly soluble complex of digitonin and some other compound ⟨cholesterol ~⟩

dig·i·to·nin \-'tōnən\ *n* -s [ISV *digit-* (fr. NL *Digitalis*) + *-onin* (as in *saponin*)] **:** a crystalline steroid saponin $C_{56}H_{92}O_{29}$ occurring in the leaves and seeds of purple foxglove

dig·i·to·plantar \,dijəd·ə+\ *adj* [*digito-* (fr. L *digitus* finger, toe) + *plantar*] **:** of or relating to the toes and the plantar surface of the foot

dig·i·tox·i·gen·in \,dijə,täksə'jenən, ,==,='sijən-\ *n* -s [ISV, blend of *digitoxin* and *-gen*] **:** a crystalline steroid lactone $C_{23}H_{34}O_4$ obtained esp. by hydrolysis of digitoxin

dig·i·tox·in \,=='täksən\ *n* [ISV *digi-* (fr. NL *Digitalis*) + *toxin*] **:** a poisonous crystalline steroid glycoside $C_{41}H_{64}O_{13}$ occurring as the most active principle of digitalis and used similarly to digitalis; *also* **:** a mixture of cardiotonic glycosides obtained from digitalis and consisting chiefly of digitoxin — see LANATOSIDE a

dig·i·tox·ose \-'täk,sōs *also* -ōz\ *n* -s [ISV *digitoxin* + *-ose*] **:** a sugar $CH_3(CHOH)_3CH_2CHO$ obtained by the hydrolysis of several glycosides of digitalis (as digitoxin or gitoxin); 2,6-di-deoxy-D-allose

digits *pl of* DIGIT

dig·i·tus \'dijəd·əs\ *n, pl* **digi·ti** \-jə,tī\ [NL, fr. L, finger, toe — more at TOE] **:** any of various small processes on insects; *esp* **:** the claw-bearing terminal segment of the tarsus

di·glos·sia \dī'gläsēə\ *n* [NL, fr. *di-* + *-glossia*] **:** the condition of having the tongue bifid

1**di·glot** \'dī,glät\ *adj* [Gk *diglōttos*, fr. *di-* + *-glōttos* -glot] **:** BILINGUAL 1

2**diglot** \"\ *n* -s **:** a bilingual publication

di·glucoside \(')dī+\ *n* [*di-* + *glucoside*] **:** a compound with two molecules of glucose

di·glyceride \"+\ *n* [ISV *di-* + *glyceride*] **:** a diester of glycerol

di·glycerol *or* **di·glycerin** \"+\ *n* [*di-* + *glycerol* or *glycerin*] **:** a viscous hygroscopic liquid polyhydroxy ether $O(CH_2CHOHCH_2OH)_2$ made by dehydration of glycerol and used esp. in making rosin esters for varnishes

di·glycol \"+\ *n* [ISV *di-* + *glycol*] **:** DIETHYLENE GLYCOL

di·glycolic acid *or* **di·glycollic acid** \(,)dī+ . . . -\ *n* [ISV *di-* + *glycolic, glycollic*] **:** a crystalline dicarboxylic acid $O(CH_2COOH)_2$ regarded as the ether of glycolic acid, formed from a salt of chloroacetic acid by reaction with calcium hydroxide, and used in the manufacture of plasticizers and resins

di·glyph \'dī,glif\ *n* -s [Gk *diglyphos* doubly indented, fr. *di-* + *-glyphos* (fr. *glyphein* to carve or hollow out) — more at CLEAVE (split)] **:** a projecting ornamental face like the triglyph but having only two grooves

di·glyphic \(')dī+\ *adj* [*di-* + *glyphic*] **:** having two siphonoglyphs ⟨~ polyps⟩

dignation *n* -s [ME *dignacion*, fr. MF or L; MF *dignation*, fr. L *dignation-, dignatio*, fr. *dignatus* (past part. of *dignare, dignari* to consider worthy, deign) + *-ion-, -io* -ion — more at DEIGN] *obs* **:** the act of showing esteem esp. to an inferior **:** CONDESCENSION

dig·ni·fi·cation \,dignəfə'kāshən\ *n* -s [MF, fr. LL *dignificatus* (past part. of *dignificare*) + MF *-ion*] **:** a dignifying or being dignified

dig·ni·fied \'dignə,fīd\ *adj* **:** showing or expressive of dignity in appearance, manner, or language ⟨his appearance was anything but ~; he was short and very fat, and had little or no appearance of neck —Anthony Trollope⟩ — **dig·ni·fied·ly** \-ī(ə)dlē, -li\ *adv* — **dig·ni·fied·ness** \-ī(ə)dnəs\ *n* -ES

dig·ni·fy \-ī\ *vt* -ED/-ING/-ES [MF *dignefier, dignifier*, fr. LL *dignificare*, fr. L *dignus* worthy + *-ficare* -fy — more at DECENT] **1 :** to invest with dignity or honor **:** make illustrious **:** give distinction to **:** EXALT, ENNOBLE ⟨your worth will ~ our feast —Ben Jonson⟩ **2 :** to confer dignity upon by changing name, appearance, or character ⟨~ a style with imagery⟩ ⟨~ thievery by calling it kleptomania⟩

dig·ni·tar·i·al \,dignə'terēəl\ *adj* **:** of or belonging to a dignitary

1**dig·ni·tary** \'dignə,terē, -ri\ *n* -ES [*dignity* + *-ary*] **:** one who possesses exalted rank or holds a position of dignity or honor ⟨a diplomatic ~⟩

2**dignitary** \"\ *adj* **:** of, belonging to, or having a dignity ⟨a ~ title⟩

dig·ni·ty \'dignəd·ē, -ətē, -i\ *n* -ES [ME *dignete, dignite*, fr. OF *digneté, dignité*, fr. L *dignitat-, dignitas*, fr. *dignus* worthy + *-itat-, -itas* -ity — more at DECENT] **1 :** the quality or state of being worthy **:** intrinsic worth **:** EXCELLENCE ⟨the ~ of this act was worth the audience of kings —Shak.⟩ ⟨all human beings are born free and equal in ~ and rights —*U.N. Declaration of Human Rights*⟩ **2 :** the quality or state of being honored or esteemed **:** degree of esteem **:** HONOR ⟨rose to the ~ of a judgeship⟩ **3 a :** high rank, office, or position ⟨aspir'd to ~ —Edmund Spenser⟩ **b** *archaic* **:** RANK, DEGREE ⟨clay and clay differs in ~, whose dust is both alike —Shak.⟩ **c :** a particular office, rank, or title of honor ⟨Napoleon persuaded the Archduke Maximilian . . . to accept the Mexican imperial ~ —*Times Lit. Supp.*⟩ **d** *Eng law* **:** a title of honor that is an incorporeal hereditament or real property **4** *archaic* **a :** one holding high rank **:** DIGNITARY ⟨in spite of pope or *dignities* of church —Shak.⟩ **b :** persons of high rank as a body **5 :** formal reserve of manner, appearance, behavior, or language **:** behavior that accords with self-respect or with regard for the seriousness of occasion or purpose **:** GRAVITY, POISE ⟨watched him kindly but with ~, as well-treated animals who have an assured position always do —Mary Webb⟩

di·go·nal \(')dī'gōnᵊl\ *adj* [*di-* + Gk *gōnia* angle + E *-al*] *of an axis of symmetry of a crystal* **:** TWOFOLD, DIAD

di·go·neu·tic \,dīgə'n(y)üd·ik\ *adj* [*di-* + (assumed) Gk *goneutos* (verbal of *goneuein* to produce, generate) + E *-ic*; akin to Gk *gignesthai* to be born — more at KIN] **:** having two broods in one year **:** BIVOLTINE — **di·go·neu·tism** \,dīgə'n(y)üd·,izəm\ *n* -s

di·gonial \(')dī+\ *adj* [*di-* + *gonial*] **:** BIGONIAL

di·go·nop·o·rous \,dīgə'näpərəs, -,gä'-\ *adj* [*di-* + *gon-* + *-porous* (fr. Gk *poros* passage) — more at FARE] **:** having separate orifices for the male and female reproductive organs ⟨~ hermaphroditic gastropods⟩

dig out *vt* **1 :** to make hollow by digging ⟨*dig out* a mud-filled spring⟩ **2 :** to get by searching or rummaging **:** bring out of storage ⟨*dig* a book *out* of the attic⟩ ~ *vi* **:** to set out or go at full speed ⟨the rabbit *dug out* for the woods⟩ **:** depart hastily ⟨he didn't say where he was going, just *dug out*⟩

di·gox·i·gen·in \(,)dī,gäksə'jenən, -'sijən-\ *n* -s [ISV, blend of *digoxin* and *-gen*] **:** a crystalline steroid lactone $C_{23}H_{34}O_5$ obtained by hydrolysis of digoxin

di·gox·in \dī'gäksən\ *n* -s [ISV *dig-* (fr. NL *Digitalis*) + *toxin*] **:** a poisonous bitter crystalline cardiotonic steroid glycoside $C_{41}H_{64}O_{14}$ obtained from the leaves of a foxglove (*Digitalis lanata*) and used similarly to digitalis — see LANATOSIDE C

di·gram \'dī,gram, -aa(ə)m\ *n* [*di-* + *-gram*] **:** a group of two successive letters or other symbols

di·graph \'dī,graf, -aa(ə)f,-aif,-åf\ *n* [*di-* + *-graph*] **1 :** a group of two successive letters whose phonetic value is a single sound (as *ea* in *bread*, *ng* in *thing*) or whose value is not the sum of a value borne by each in other occurrences (as *ch* in *chin*, where the value is \t\+\sh\) **2 :** any group of two successive letters

di·graphic \(')dī+\ *adj* **1 :** of or belonging to a digraph **2** *cryptology* **:** taking two letters at a time — see PLAYFAIR CIPHER — **di·graphically** \"+\ *adv*

di·gress \(')dī'gres *also* də'g-\ *vi* -ED/-ING/-ES [L *digressus*, past part. of *digredi*, lit., to go apart, fr. *di-* (fr. *dis-* apart) + *-gredi* to step, go (fr. *gradi*) — more at DIS-, GRADE] **1** *archaic* **:** to step or turn aside **:** DEVIATE, DIVERGE, SWERVE **2 :** to turn aside from the main subject of attention or course of argument in writing or speaking ⟨I shall not pursue these points further for fear of ~*ing* too far from my main theme —R.J.Spilsbury⟩ **3** *obs* **:** TRANSGRESS **syn** see SWERVE

di·gres·sion \dī'greshən *also* də'-\ *n* -s [ME *disgressioun*, fr. MF *digression, disgression*, fr. L *digression-, digressio*, fr. *digressus* + *-ion-, -io* -ion] **1** *archaic* **:** an act or instance of digressing **:** a going aside **2 a :** the act of digressing in a discourse or other usu. organized literary work ⟨other flights and ~*s* I find yet more doubtful than the humorous —B.N. Cardozo⟩ **b :** the portion of the discourse in which such a digression is made ⟨a lengthy ~ on the subject of free trade interrupted the main point of the speech⟩ **3** *obs* **:** TRANSGRESSION — **di·gres·sion·al** \-shənᵊl\ *adj*

di·gres·sive \(')dī'gresiv, də'g-, -sēv *also* -səv\ *adj* [L *digressivus*, fr. *digressus* + *-ivus* -ive] **1 :** of the nature of a digression ⟨a ~ chapter on a subject entirely different from that of the bulk of the book⟩ **2 :** characterized by digressions ⟨the book is amusingly ~: there are satirical thrusts at women's fashions and some neatly turned couplets —E.H.Dewey⟩ — **di·gres·sive·ly** \-səvlē, -li\ *adv* — **di·gres·sive·ness** \='=sivnəs, -sēv- *also* -səv-\ *n* -ES

digs *pres 3d sing of* DIG, *pl of* DIG

digue \'dēg\ *n* -s [MF *digue, dike*, fr. MD *dijc*; akin to OE *dīc* dike, ditch — more at DIKE] **:** EMBANKMENT, DIKE

dig up *vt* **:** to find or obtain or bring to light esp. with difficulty ⟨I'll *dig up* the money somehow⟩ ⟨*dig up* evidence in support of a case⟩ ~ *vi* **:** to make a money contribution ⟨taxpayers had to *dig up* to keep [the unemployed] on . . . relief —T.W. Arnold⟩

di·gyn·ia \dī'jinēə, -'gi-\ *n pl, cap* [NL, fr. *di-* + *-gynia*] **:** *in former classifications* **:** an order of plants including those having flowers with two pistils — **di·gyn·ian** \(')=';==ən\ *adj* — **di·gy·nous** \(')=';jīnəs, -';gī-\ *adj*

dihal- *or* **dihalo-** *comb form* [ISV *di-* + *hal-*] **:** containing two atoms of a halogen — in names of chemical compounds ⟨*dihalo*hydrin⟩

di·halide \(')dī+\ *n* [*di-* + *halide*] **:** a compound containing two atoms of halogen combined with an element or radical

1**di·he·dral** \(')dī'hēdrəl\ *adj* [*di-* + *-hedral*] **1 :** having or formed by two plane faces ⟨a ~ angle⟩ **2 a** *of a kite or an airplane* **:** having wings that make with one another a dihedral angle esp. when the angle between the upper sides is less than 180° **b** *of airplane wing pairs* **:** inclined at a dihedral angle to each other

2**dihedral** \"\ *n* -s **1 :** a mathematical figure formed by two intersecting planes **2 :** the angle between an aircraft supporting surface and a horizontal transverse line; *esp* **:** the angle between (1) an upwardly inclined wing or (2) a downwardly inclined wing and such a line — called also respectively (1) *positive dihedral* or (2) *negative dihedral*

dihedral angle *n* **1 :** the angle between two intersecting planes **2 :** 2DIHEDRAL 2

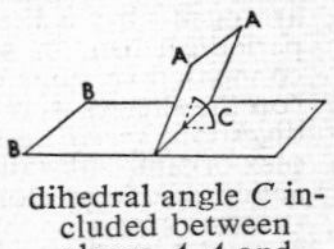

dihedral angle *C* included between planes *A A* and *B B*

di·hexagonal \,dī+\ *adj* [ISV *di-* + *hexagonal*] *crystallog* **:** being or relating to a symmetrical 12-sided figure the alternate angles of which are equal — used esp. in naming forms of the hexagonal system

dihexagonal-dipyramidal *adj* **:** of or characterized by the symmetry of the class of crystals in the hexagonal system having a vertical hexad axis, six horizontal diad axes, six vertical planes, and a horizontal plane of symmetry

dihexagonal prism *n* **:** a prism any horizontal section of which is dihexagonal

dihexagonal pyramid *n* **:** a pyramid any horizontal section of which is dihexagonal

di·hexa·he·dral \(,)dī'heksə'hēdrəl\ *adj* [*di-* + *hexahedral*] **:** of or relating to a dihexahedron

di·hexa·he·dron \-drən\ *n* -s [ISV *di-* + *hexahedron*] **:** a form of crystal having 12 faces (as a double 6-sided pyramid)

1**di·hybrid** \(')dī+\ *n* [ISV *di-* + *hybrid*] **:** an individual or strain that is heterozygous for two factors (as recessive genes)

2**dihybrid** \"\ *adj* **:** of, relating to, or being a dihybrid

dihydr- *or* **dihydro-** *comb form* [ISV *di-* + *hydr-*] **:** combined with two atoms of hydrogen — in names of chemical compounds ⟨*dihydro*naphthalene⟩

di·hydrate \(')dī+\ *n* [ISV *di-* + *hydrate*] **:** a chemical compound with two molecules of water ⟨calcium sulfate ~ $CaSO_4.2H_2O$⟩

di·hydrated \(')dī+\ *adj* [*di-* + *hydrated*] **:** combined with two molecules of water

di·hydrazone \(')dī+\ *n* [*di-* + *hydrazone*] **:** a compound containing two hydrazone groupings =NNHR — compare OSAZONE

di·hydric \(')dī+\ *adj* [ISV *di-* + *-hydric*] **1** *archaic* **:** containing two atoms of acid hydrogen **2 :** DIHYDROXY — used esp. of alcohols and phenols

di·hy·drite \dī'hī,drīt\ *n* -s [G *dihydrit*, fr. *di-* + *hydr-* + *-it* -ite] **:** PSEUDOMALACHITE

di·hy·dro \(')dī'hī(,)drō\ *adj* [*dihydr-*] **:** combined with two atoms of hydrogen

di·hydrochloride \(,)dī+\ *n* [*di-* + *hydrochloride*] **:** a chemical compound with two molecules of hydrochloric acid ⟨quinine ~ $C_{20}H_{24}N_2O_2.2HCl$⟩

di·hy·dro·co·de·inone \(,)dī,hīdrōkō'dēə,nōn\ *n* -s [*dihydr-* + *codeine* + *-one*] **:** a crystalline habit-forming compound $C_{18}H_{21}NO_3$ derived from codeine and used as an analgesic and cough sedative

di·hy·dro·er·go·cor·nine \dī'hīdrō,ərgō'kȯr,nēn, -,nən\ *n* [ISV *dihydr-* + *ergocornine* alkaloid from ergot (*ergo-* + *corn-* — fr. G *korn* grain, fr. OHG — + *-ine*) — more at CORN] **:** a hydrogenated derivative $C_{31}H_{41}N_5O_5$ of an alkaloid from ergot that is used in the treatment of peripheral vascular diseases and hypertension

di·hy·dro·ergotamine \,dī,h|īdrō, dī'h|+\ *n* [ISV *dihydr-* + *ergotamine*] **:** a crystalline compound $C_{33}H_{37}N_5O_5$ made by hydrogenating ergotamine and used in the treatment of migraine headaches

di·hydrogen \(')dī+\ *adj* [*di-* + *hydrogen*] **:** containing two atoms of hydrogen in the molecule

di·hy·dro·mor·phi·none \(,)dī,hīdrō'mȯrfə,nōn\ *n* -s [*dihydr-* + *morphine* + *-one*] **:** a crystalline ketone $C_{17}H_{19}NO_3$ derived from morphine that is about five times as active biologically as morphine

di·hy·dro·streptomycin \,dī,h|īdrō, dī'h|+\ *n* [ISV *dihydr-* + *streptomycin*] **:** an antibiotic $C_{21}H_{41}N_7O_{12}$ made by hydrogenating streptomycin and considered by some authorities to be less toxic than streptomycin with which it is often administered chiefly in the treatment of tuberculosis, tularemia, and infections caused by gram-negative organisms

di·hy·dro·tachysterol \"+\ *n* [*dihydr-* + *tachysterol*] **:** a crystalline alcohol $C_{28}H_{45}OH$ used in the treatment of hypocalcemia (as in hypoparathyroidism)

di·hy·droxy \,dī,hī'dräksē\ *adj* [*dihydroxy-*] **:** containing two hydroxyl groups in the molecule

dihydroxy- *comb form* [ISV *di-* + *hydroxy-*] **:** containing two hydroxyl groups — in names of chemical compounds ⟨*dihydroxy*succinic acid⟩

diiamb [LL *diiambus*, fr. Gk *diiambos*, fr. *di-* + *iambos* iamb] *var of* DIAMB

di·iam·bus \,dī,ī'ambəs\ *n, pl* **diiam·bi** \-,bī\ [LL] **:** DIIAMB

diiod- *or* **diiodo-** *comb form* [ISV *di-* + *iod-*] **:** containing two atoms of iodine — in names of chemical compounds ⟨*diiodo*fluorescein⟩; compare IOD-

di·iodide \(')dī+\ *n* [*di-* + *iodide*] **:** a compound containing two atoms of iodine combined with an element or radical

di·io·do·hy·droxy·quinoline \dī'īə,dō,hī'dräksē+\ *or* **di·io·do·hy·droxy·quin** \-,hī'dräksēkwən\ *n* [*diiodohydroxyquinoline* fr. *diiod-* + *hydroxyquinoline; diiodohydroxyquin* short for *diiodohydroxyquinoline*] **:** a colorless to tan crystalline compound $C_9H_5I_2NO$ used esp. in the treatment of amebic dysentery

di·io·do·methane \(,)dī'īə,dō+\ *n* [ISV *diiod-* + *methane*] **:** METHYLENE IODIDE

di·io·do·tyrosine \"+\ *n* [ISV *diiod-* + *tyrosine*] **:** a crystalline amino acid $HOC_6H_2I_2CH_2CH(NH_2)COOH$ obtained by hydrolysis of thyroglobulin and of proteins from corals and sponges and held to be a precursor of triiodothyronine and thyroxine in the thyroid gland — called also *3,5-diiodotyrosine, iodogorgoic acid*

di·isobutylene \(,)dī+\ *n* [*di-* + *isobutylene*] **:** a liquid mixture containing the two octylenes 2,4,4-trimethyl-1-pentene and 2,4,4-trimethyl-2-pentene obtained from isobutylene by reaction with acid catalysts and used as an intermediate (as for plastics)

di·isocyanate \"+\ *n* [ISV *di-* + *isocyanate*] **:** a compound containing two isocyanate groups in the molecule and sometimes used in making resins and plastics ⟨tolylene ~ $CH_3C_6H_4(NCO)_2$⟩

di·isopropyl \"+\ *adj* [ISV *di-* + *isopropyl*] **:** containing two isopropyl groups in the molecule

diisopropyl fluorophosphate *n* [ISV *diisopropyl* + *fluorophosphate*] **:** a volatile irritating liquid ester $[(CH_3)_2CH]_2PO_3F$ that acts as a nerve gas by inhibiting cholinesterases and as a myotic and that is used chiefly in treating glaucoma — called also *DFP, isoflurophate*

di·jon \(')dē'zhōⁿ\ *adj, usu cap* [fr. *Dijon*, city in France] **:** of or from the city of Dijon, France **:** of the kind or style prevalent in Dijon

di·judicate \(')dī+\ *vb* -ED/-ING/-S [L *dijudicatus*, past part. of *dijudicare* to decide, fr. *di-* (fr. *dis-* apart) + *judicare* to judge — more at DIS-, JUDGE] *vi* **:** to make a judicial decision **:** DECIDE, DETERMINE ~ *vt* **:** to judge between **:** decide on

di·judication \(,)dī+\ *n* -s [L *dijudication-, dijudicatio*, fr. *dijudicatus* + *-ion-, -io* -ion] **:** the act or action of dijudicating

di·ka \'dēkə\ *n* -s [Mpongwe *odika*, a condiment, prob. dika bread] **1 :** WILD MANGO **2 a** *also* **dika nut :** the fruit or seed of the African wild mango **b :** DIKA BREAD

dika bread *n* **:** a somewhat acid and astringent paste that is prepared by grinding and heating the seeds of the African wild mango usu. together with pepper and other spices and that is a staple food of some African peoples

dik·age *also* **dyk·age** \'dīkij\ *n* -s [*dike*, v. + *-age*] **:** the digging of dikes

di·karyon *also* **di·caryon** \(')dī+\ *n* [ISV *di-* + *karyon*] **1 :** a pair of associated but unfused haploid nuclei brought together in a cell by the union of plus and minus hyphae (as in the rust fungi) and capable of carrying on conjugate division prior to their ultimate fusion **2 :** a cell having or a mycelium made up of cells each having a dikaryon — compare HOMOKARYON

di·kary·ophase *also* **di·cary·ophase** \dī'karēə,fāz\ *n* [*di-* + *kary-* + *phase*] **:** the phase of the life cycle of a fungus (as the rusts) characterized by the dikaryotic condition — **di·kary·opha·sic** \(,)dī,karēə'fāzik\ *adj*

di·kary·ophyte *also* **di·cary·ophyte** \dī'karēə,fīt\ *n* -s [*di-* + *kary-* + *-phyte*] **:** the dikaryotic mycelium as a whole in fungi (as the rusts) — used esp. to distinguish such a mycelium from that having a single diploid nucleus in each cell — **di·cary·ophyt·ic** \(,)dī,karēə'fid·ik\ *adj*

di·kary·ot·ic *also* **di·cary·ot·ic** \dī,karē'äd·ik\ *adj* [*di-* + *kary-* + *-otic*] **:** of or relating to the dikaryon

dikast *var of* DICAST

dik-dik \'dik,dik\ *or* **dig-dig** \'dig,dig\ *n* -s [native name in East Africa] **:** any of several small East African antelopes (genera *Madoqua, Rhynchotragus*) of the size of a large rabbit

1**dike** *or* **dyke** \'dīk\ *n* -s [ME, fr. OE *dīc* ditch, dike; akin to MHG *tīch* pond, dike, ON *dīki* swamp, ditch, L *figere* to fasten, pierce, Lith *diegti* to prick] **1 a :** an artificial watercourse (as for drainage) **b** *now dial Brit* **:** any natural or artificial watercourse ⟨Thames, the king of ~*s* —Alexander Pope⟩ **c :** POOL, POND **2 a** *dial Brit* **:** a wall or fence of turf or stone **b :** a bank usu. of earth constructed to control or confine water **:** LEVEE ⟨the ~*s* of Holland prevent the sea from flooding the land⟩ **c :** a barrier preventing passage esp. protecting against or excluding something undesirable ⟨the legions were a ~ against the barbarian hordes⟩ **3 a** *dial Brit* **:** a bank of earth thrown up from a ditch **b :** a raised causeway **c** [so called fr. its standing up like a wall in places where the material that once surrounded it has been eroded away] **:** a tabular body of igneous rock that has been injected while molten into a fissure — see COMPOSITE DIKE

2**dike** *or* **dyke** \"\ *vb* -ED/-ING/-S [ME *diken*, fr. *dike*, n.] *vt* **:** to surround or protect with a dike; *also* **:** to drain by a dike or ditch ~ *vi* **:** to work as a ditcher **:** DIG **:** work at making a dike

3**dike** \"\ *vt* -ED/-ING/-S [perh. alter. of 2*deck*] *chiefly Midland* **:** to dress in fine clothes — usu. used with *out* or *up* ⟨all *diked* out for the party⟩

dike·grave \'dīk,grāv\ *n* -s [modif. of D *dijkgraaf*, fr. MD *dijcgrāve*, fr. *dijc* dike + *grāve* overseer; akin to OE *dīc* ditch, dike — more at BURGRAVE] **:** an officer in Holland in charge of dikes

dike·let \'dīklət\ *n* -s *geol* **:** a small dike approximately an inch in width

dike-loup·er \'dī,klau̇pə(r), -lōp-,-lüp-\ *n* -s [¹*dike* + E dial. *louper* leaper, fr. E dial. *loup* to leap + E *-er* — more at LOUP] *dial Brit* : one that jumps fences

dik·er *also* **dyk·er** \'dīkə(r)\ *n* -s [ME *dikere*, fr. *diken* to dike + *-ere* -er] : one that makes or works upon dikes

dike-reeve *also* **dyke-reeve** \'dī,krēv\ *n* -s [perh. alter. (influenced by E *reeve*) of *dikegrave* — more at REEVE (official)] : an English official in charge of the drains, sluices, and sea walls in a district of fen or marshy land

dike ridge *n* **1** *geol* : a hogback in which the formation resistant to erosion is a dike **2** *geol* : a small wall-like ridge on a glacier resulting from differences in the rate of melting **3** *geol* : any small wall-like ridge (as one along a shore) resulting from differences in the rate of erosion

di·ke·ri·on \thē'kēryōn\ *or* **di·ce·ri·on** \dī'sirē,än\ *n, pl* **dike·ria** \-yä\ *or* **dice·ria** \-ēə\ [NGk *dikērion*, fr. Gk *di-* + LGk *kērion* wax candle, fr. Gk, honeycomb, fr. *kēros* wax — more at CEREUS] *Eastern Orthodox Church* : a two-branched candlestick symbolizing the divine and human natures in Christ used by the bishop for blessing during the service — compare TRIKERION

di·ketene \(')dī+\ *n* [*di-* + *ketene*] : an unsaturated pungent liquid lactone $C_4H_4O_2$ made by spontaneous dimerization of ketene in solution and used chiefly in making derivatives of acetoacetic acid

diketo- *comb form* [ISV *di-* + *ket-*] : containing two ketone groups — in names of chemical compounds ⟨*diketo*adipic acid⟩; compare KET-

di·ketone \(')dī+\ *n* [ISV *di-* + *ketone*] : a chemical compound containing two ketonic carbonyl groups

di·ke·to·piperazine \'dī,k|ēd·(,)ō, dī¦k|+\ *n* [ISV *diketo-* + *piperazine*] **1** : a crystalline compound $C_4H_6N_2O_2$ that is obtainable from two molecules of glycine by dehydration and may be regarded as a cyclic dipeptide; 2,5-piperazine-dione **2** : any of various cyclic compounds formed similarly to diketopiperazine from alpha-amino acids other than glycine or obtained by partial hydrolysis of proteins

dik·kop \'di,käp\ *n* -s [Afrik, fr. *dik* thick (fr. D, fr. MD *dicke*) + *kop* head, fr. D, fr. MD *cop, coppe* drinking vessel, skull; akin to OHG *dicki* thick — more at THICK, CUP] *Africa* : STONE CURLEW

dik·tat \dik'tät\ *n* -s *sometimes cap* [G, lit., something dictated, fr. NL *dictatum*, fr. L, neut. of *dictatus*, past part. of *dictare* to dictate — more at DICTATE] : a harsh decision or settlement unilaterally imposed esp. on a defeated or subject people or nation ⟨the treaty was regarded by the vanquished as a ~⟩

dil *abbr* dilute; dilution

di·lacerate \(')dī, də+\ *vt* [L *dilaceratus*, past part. of *dilacerare*, fr. *di-* (fr. *dis-* apart) + *lacerare* to tear — more at DIS-, LACERATE] : to tear apart or in pieces

di·laceration \(')dī, də+\ *n* [LL *dilaceration-, dilaceratio*, fr. L *dilaceratus* + *-ion-, -io* -ion] **1** : the action of dilacerating or the state of being dilacerated **2** : injury (as partial fracture) of a developing tooth resulting in a curve in the long axis as development continues

di·lactone \(')dī + \ *n* [*di-* + *lactone*] : a chemical compound containing two lactone groupings

di·lamb·do·dont \(')dī¦lamdə,dänt\ *adj* [NL *Dilambdodonta*, category of insectivorous mammals recognized in some classifications, fr. *di-* + Gk *lambda* (Λ) + NL *-odonta*] : having two Λ-shaped transverse ridges on the molar teeth

Di·lan·tin \dī'lant³n, də'-, -tən\ *trademark* — used for diphenylhydantoin

di·lap·i·date \də'lapə,dāt, *usu* -ād.+V\ *vb* -ED/-ING/-S [L *dilapidatus*, past part. of *dilapidare* to throw away, squander, destroy, fr. *di-* (fr. *dis-* apart) + *lapidare* to throw stones, fr. *lapid-, lapis* stone — more at DIS-, LAPIDARY] *vt* **1** : to bring (as a building) into a condition of decay or partial ruin ⟨a ruined house *dilapidated* by marauders⟩ ⟨furniture is *dilapidated* by use —Janet Flanner⟩ — now usu. used in the past participle **2** *archaic* : to impair or ruin (as a fortune or estate) by waste or abuse : SQUANDER ~ *vi* : to become dilapidated ⟨the house was neglectfully allowed to ~⟩ **syn** see DESTROY

dilapidated *adj* [fr. past part. of *dilapidate*] : decayed, deteriorated, injured, or fallen into partial ruin esp. because of neglect or misuse ⟨the old house still had an air of ~ grandeur⟩ ⟨a ghost town of ~ buildings —*Amer. Guide Series: Calif.*⟩ ⟨a ~ notice that the place was for sale —Bram Stoker⟩

di·lap·i·da·tion \-,lapə'dāshən\ *n* -s [ME *dilapidacion*, fr. LL *dilapidation-, dilapidatio* action of squandering, fr. L *dilapidatus* + *-ion-, -io* -ion] **1** : the act of dilapidating or the state of being dilapidated ⟨the wreck of a ship in the last stages of ~ —R.L.Stevenson⟩ **2** *Eng law* **a** : ecclesiastical waste whether permissive or voluntary : waste of a building (as a parsonage) committed to the charge of ecclesiastical persons **b** : the charge for repairing such waste **3** : the natural disintegration and breaking away of rock from a cliff or mountainside; *also* : the resulting debris

di·lap·i·da·tor \-ˌ=,dād·ə(r), -ātə-\ *n* -s [*dilapidate* + *-or*] : one that causes or permits dilapidation

di·lat·abil·i·ty \(,)dī,lād·ə'bilǝd·ē, də,-\ *n* -ES : the property of being dilatable

di·lat·able \(')dī¦lād·əbəl, də'l-\ *adj* : capable of being dilated; *esp* : EXPANDABLE

di·la·tan·cy \dī'lāt³nsē, də'-, -si\ *n* -ES [*dilatant* + *-cy*] : the property of being dilatant

di·la·tant \-āt³nt\ *adj* [L *dilatant-, dilatans* dilating, pres. part. of *dilatare* to dilate] **1** : having the property of increasing in volume when changed in shape because of an increase of the space between the particles **2** : increasing in viscosity and setting to a solid as a result of deformation by expansion, pressure, or agitation — opposed to *thixotropic* ⟨~ quicksands⟩

dil·a·ta·tion \,dilə'tāshən, ,dīl-\ *n* -s [ME *dilatacioun*, fr. MF *dilatation* enlargement, fr. LL *dilatation-, dilatatio*, fr. L *dilatatus* (past part. of *dilatare* to dilate) + *-ion-, -io* -ion] **1** : amplification in writing or speech esp. by the addition of discussion, illustration, or detail **2 a** : the condition of being stretched beyond normal dimensions esp. as a result of overwork or disease ⟨~ of the heart⟩ or of abnormal relaxation ⟨~ of the stomach⟩ **b** : DILATION 2 **3** : the act of expanding or the state of being expanded : enlarging or spreading **4 a** : a dilated part or formation **5 a** : a change in volume of a rock body under confining pressure ⟨an increase in volume is positive ~ and a decrease is negative ~⟩ **b** : the strain produced by such pressure change — **dil·a·ta·tion·al** \¦==¦=shən³l, -shnəl\ *adj*

di·la·ta·tive \(')dī¦lād·əd·iv, də'l-; 'dilə,tā-, 'dilə-\ *adj* [L *dilatatus* + E *-ive*] : DILATIVE

dil·a·ta·tor \'dilə,tād·ə(r), 'dīl-\ *n* -s [prob. fr. F *dilatateur*, fr. *dilater* to dilate + *-ateur* -ator (fr. OF *-atour*)] : ²DILATOR b

¹di·late \(')dī¦lāt, də'l-, ÷ ¦dīə¦l-; *usu* -ād.+V\ *vb* -ED/-ING/-S [ME *dilaten*, fr. MF *dilater* to enlarge, comment at length, fr. L *dilatare* to enlarge, spread out, fr. *di-* (fr. *dis-* apart) + *-latare* (fr. *latus* wide) — more at DIS-, LATITUDE] *vt* **1** *archaic* : to describe or set forth lengthily or in detail ⟨~ at full what hath befallen of them and thee till now —Shak.⟩ **2** *obs* : to extend or diffuse through a wide space **3 a** : to enlarge or expand in bulk or extent ⟨matter is *dilated* by heat⟩ : WIDEN, EXTEND ⟨enrich and ~ our cultural heritage⟩ **b** : to widen or cause to be stretched (a contracted duct or part) ~ *vi* **1** : to comment at length : expand discussion : DISCOURSE — usu. used with *on* or *upon* ⟨he ~s on themes of love and death⟩ **2** : to expand or become wide : SWELL ⟨the pupil of the eye is able to ~ and contract⟩ **syn** see DISCOURSE, EXPAND

²dilate \"\ *adj* [ME *dilat*, fr. *dilaten*, v., after such pairs as ME *desolaten* to desolate: *desolat* desolate] : DILATED : EXPANDED

dilated *adj* [fr. past part. of ¹*dilate*] : expanded laterally : FLATTENED; *specif, of parts of insects* : having a broad expanded border — **di·lat·ed·ly** *adv* — **di·lat·ed·ness** *n* -ES

di·la·tion \dī'lāshən, də'-, ÷,dīə'l-\ *n* -s [¹*dilate* + *-ion*] **1** : the act of dilating or the state of being dilated : EXPANSION, DILATATION **2** : the action of stretching or enlarging an organ or part of the body ⟨~ of the cervix⟩ ⟨~ of the pupil by atropine⟩

di·la·tive \(')dī¦lād·iv, də'l-, ÷¦dīə¦l-\ *adj* : causing dilation : tending to dilate ⟨the ~ factor is a disadvantage in acute glaucoma —*Americana Annual*⟩

dil·a·tom·e·ter \,dilə'tämǝd·ǝr, ,dīl-\ *n* [ISV *dilate* + *-o-* + *-meter*] : an instrument for measuring thermal dilatation or expansion esp. in determining coefficients of expansion of liquids or solids — **dil·a·to·met·ric** \¦dilətə¦me·trik\ *adj* — **dil·a·to·met·ri·cal·ly** \-trə-k(ə)lē\ *adv* — **dil·a·tom·e·try** \,dilə'tämə·trē\ *n* -ES

dilatometer

¹di·la·tor \'dīləd·ə(r)\ *n* -s [ME *dilatour*, modif. of MF *dilatoire* delay, fr. OF, fr. *dilatoire*, adj., causing delay, fr. LL *dilatorius*] **1** *archaic* : a legal delay **2** *archaic* : DILATORY DEFENSE

²di·la·tor *also* **di·lat·er** \(')dī¦lād·ə(r), də'l-, -ātə-\ *n* -s [¹*dilate* + *-or* or *-er*] : one that dilates: as **a** : an instrument for expanding a tube, duct, or cavity ⟨a urethral ~⟩ **b** : a muscle that dilates a part **c** : a drug (as a vasodilator) causing dilation

dil·a·to·ri·ly \¦dilə¦tōrəlē, -tȯr-, -li\ *adv* : in a dilatory manner

dil·a·to·ri·ness \'dilə,tōrēnəs, -tȯr-, -rin-\ *n* -ES : the quality or state of being dilatory

dil·a·to·ry \'dilə,tōrē, -tȯr-, -ri, *chiefly dial* -,ter-\ *adj* [LL *dilatorius* causing delay, fr. L *dilatus* (suppletive past part. of *differre* to postpone, delay) (fr. *di-* — fr. *dis-* apart — + *latus* carried, suppletive past part. of *ferre* to carry) + *-orius* -ory — more at DIS-, TOLERATE] **1** : tending or having the intent to cause delay ⟨obstructive and ~ tactics⟩ **2** : characterized by procrastination or delay : TARDY : SLOW ⟨he is ~ in answering letters⟩ ⟨~ payment of bills⟩ **syn** see SLOW

dilatory defense *or* **dilatory plea** *n* : a defense or plea which is intended to defeat the pending action or proceeding without involving any decision on the merits of the case

dilatory motion *n* : a motion made for the purpose of evading or superseding a question before a legislative body

Di·lau·did \dī'lȯdəd, də'l-\ *trademark* — used for dihydromorphinone

dil·do \'dil(,)dō\ *n* -s [origin unknown] **1 a** : PHALLUS **b** *usu* **dil·doe** \"\ : an object serving as a penis substitute for vaginal insertion **2** *obs* — used as refrain syllables in a song **3** *obs* : a weak or effeminate man **4** : a cylindrical curl usu. of a wig or peruke **5** [prob. so called fr. its shape] : a West Indian spiny cactus (*Lemaireocereus hystrix*) with columnar joints and pink flowers

¹di·lem·ma \də'lemə *sometimes* dī'-\ *n* -s [LL, fr. LGk *dilēmmat-, dilēmma*, prob. back-formation fr. Gk *dilēmmatos* involving two assumptions, fr. *di-* + *-lēmmatos* (fr. *lēmmat-, lēmma* assumption) — more at LEMMA] **1** : an argument that offers an opponent a choice between two or more alternatives but that is equally conclusive against him no matter which alternative he chooses **2 a** : a choice or a situation involving choice between equally unsatisfactory alternatives ⟨the ~ was whether to lower prices or to accept fewer sales⟩ **b** : a difficult problem : a problem seemingly incapable of a satisfactory solution ⟨the modern ~; what to do to spend all this time —Peggy Bennett⟩ **3** : an argument that contains a premise consisting of the conjunctive affirmation of two hypothetical propositions and a disjunctive premise **syn** see PREDICAMENT

²dilemma \"\ *vt* -ED/-ING/-S *archaic* : to place in a dilemma

dil·em·mat·ic \¦dilə¦mad·ik *sometimes* ¦dīl-\ *also* **dil·em·mat·i·cal** \-d·ə̇kəl\ *or* **di·lem·mic** \də'lemik *sometimes* (')dī¦l-\ *adj* [*dilemmatic* fr. LGk *dilēmmat-, dilēmma* + E *-ic*; *dilemmatical* fr. LGk *dilēmmat-, dilēmma* + E *-ical*; *dilemmic* fr. *dilemma* + *-ic*] : of or containing a dilemma

dil·e·pid·i·dae \,dilə'pidə,dē\ *n pl, cap* [NL, fr. *Dilepid-, Dilepis*, type genus (fr. *di-* + *-lepis*) + *-idae*] : a family of cyclophyllidean tapeworms having a hooked rostellum and unarmed suckers and including a number of common parasites of birds and mammals

¹dil·et·tante \,dilə'täntē, -'tan-,-'taan-,-'tän-, -nti *sometimes* -lē- or -n·tā; ¦==¦tänt, -¦tant, -¦taa(ə)nt, -¦tȧnt\ *also* **dil·et·tant** *three syllables*\ *or* **dil·le·tante** *like* DILETTANTE\ *n, pl* **dilet·tantes** \-ntēz, -ntiz, -n(t)s *sometimes* -n·,tāz\ *or* **dilet·tan·ti** \-n(·)tē,-nti\ *also* **dil·et·tants** \-n(t)s\ *or* **dille·tantes** *like* DILETTANTES\ *or* **dille·tan·ti** \-n(·)tē,-nti\ [It *dilettante*, fr. pres. part. of *dilettare* to delight, fr. L *delectare* — more at DELIGHT] **1 a** : an admirer or lover of the arts **b** : a person who has discrimination or taste esp. in aesthetic matters : CONNOISSEUR **2 a** : a person who cultivates an art or branch of knowledge as a pastime without pursuing it professionally **b** : a person who pursues an art or branch of knowledge sporadically, superficially, or frivolously

²dilettante \¦==¦=, ¦==¦=\ *adj* : of or characteristic of a dilettante : AMATEURISH

dil·et·tant·ish \¦==¦t . . . ntish, -ntēsh\ *also* **dil·et·tan·te·ish** \¦==¦t . . . ntēish, -nti·ish\ *adj* : of, characteristic of, or like a dilettante

dil·et·tant·ism \,==¦t . . . n,tizəm\ *also* **dil·et·tan·te·ism** \-ntē,izəm, -nti,iz-\ *n* -s : the quality or procedure characteristic of dilettantes

dil·et·tant·ist \,==¦t . . . ntəst\ *adj* : DILETTANTISH

¹dil·i·gence \'diləjən(t)s\ *n* -s [MF, care, persevering application, haste, fr. L *diligentia* care, persevering application, fr. *diligent-, diligens* + *-ia* -y] **1 a** *obs* : caution or care **b** : persevering application : devoted and painstaking application to accomplish an undertaking : ASSIDUITY ⟨the proverbial ~ of the bee⟩ **c** *obs* : an act of labor or exertion **d** *obs* : speed or haste ⟨go hence with ~! —Shak.⟩ **e** *obs* : persistent effort to please **2 a** *Scot law* (1) : a process or warrant of the court to attach the person or property of a defendant to secure a judgment (2) : a process or warrant to enforce the appearance in court of a party or witness or to compel the production of a document (3) : the process of execution to enforce a judgment already entered **b** : the attention and care required of a person (as of a party to a contract) ⟨~ that may be required of a bailee⟩ — opposed to *negligence*

²di·li·gence \dēlē'zhäⁿs, ¦dēl-, 'diləjən(t)s\ *n, pl* **dili·gences** \-äⁿs(əz),-ən(t)səz\ [F, lit., haste] : a large closed public horse-drawn carriage formerly used esp. for long journeys

dil·i·gen·cia \,dilə'jen(t)sēə, -nchə, *or as Sp*\ *n* -s [Sp, trans. of F *diligence*] : ²DILIGENCE

dil·i·gen·cy \'diləjənsē, -si\ *n* -ES [L *diligentia*] : ¹DILIGENCE

dil·i·gent \-nt\ *adj* [ME, fr. MF, fr. L *diligent-, diligens*, pres. part. of *diligere* to esteem highly, love, fr. *di-* (fr. *dis-* apart) + *-ligere* (fr. *legere* to choose, gather) — more at DIS-, LEGEND] **1** : characterized by steady, earnest, attentive, and energetic application and effort in a pursuit, vocation, or study : not lackadaisical ⟨a ~ investigator⟩ ⟨a ~ search⟩ **2** *archaic* : CAREFUL, OBSERVANT, HEEDFUL ⟨be you watchful, and let us be ~ —J.A.Froude⟩ **syn** see BUSY

dil·i·gent·ly *adv* [ME, fr. *diligent* + *-ly*] : in a diligent manner : CAREFULLY, ASSIDUOUSLY, INDUSTRIOUSLY

dil·i·gent·ness *n* -ES : DILIGENCE

¹dill \'dil\ *n* -s [ME *dile*, fr. OE; akin to OS *dilli* dill, OHG *tilli*, Dan *dild*] **1** : any of several plants of the family Umbelliferae; *esp* : a European herb (*Anethum graveolens*) with aromatic foliage and seeds both of which are used in flavoring pickles and other foods **2** : DILL PICKLE

²dill \"\ *vt* -ED/-ING/-S [ME *dillen*, prob. fr. *dul* dull, adj.] *dial Brit* : CALM, SOOTHE

dill apiole *n* : APIOLE 1b

dil·le·nia \də'lēnēə\ *n, cap* [NL, fr. Johann J. *Dillen* †1747 Ger. botanist in England + NL *-ia*] : a genus of East Indian trees and shrubs (family Dilleniaceae) having panicles of large showy white or yellow flowers with numerous stamens

dil·le·ni·a·ce·ae \də,lēnē'āsē,ē\ *n pl, cap* [NL, fr. *Dillenia*, type genus + *-aceae*] : a family of chiefly tropical shrubs, trees, and climbers (order Parietales) with leathery leaves sometimes replaced by phyllodes and cymose inflorescences — **dil·le·ni·a·ceous** \¦=¦==¦āshəs\ *adj*

dil·le·ni·ad \də'lēnē,ad\ *n* -s [NL *Dillenia* + E *-ad*] : a dilleniaceous plant

dilletante *var of* DILETTANTE

dil·ling \'dilən\ *n* -s [origin unknown] **1** *now dial Eng* : the youngest child of a family — often used as a term of endearment **2** *dial Eng* : the smallest and weakest pig of a litter

dil·lisk *or* **dil·lesk** \'diləsk\ *n* -s [IrGael *duileasg*] *Irish* : DULSE

dill oil *n* : either of two essential oils derived from the common dill: **a** *or* **dillseed oil** : a colorless or pale yellow oil having a sweetish acrid taste that is obtained from the dried ripe fruits of the dill and is used as an aromatic carminative and as a flavoring agent **b** *or* **dillweed oil** : a similar oil obtained from the whole dill plant and used as a flavoring agent

dill pickle *n* : a large pickle seasoned with fresh dill or dill juice

dillseed \'=,=\ *n* : the seed of the dill plant used for flavoring pickles

dil·ue \də'lü\ *vt* -ED/-ING/-S [Corn *dyllo* to discharge, set free] *dial Eng* : to separate (tin ore) by washing in a hand sieve

dill water *n* : a distilled aqueous solution of the volatile constituents of dill — called also *gripe water*

dillweed \'=,=\ *n* [¹*dill*] **1** : MAYWEED 1 **2** : DILL

¹dil·ly \'dilē, -li\ *n* -ES [by shortening & alter.] **1** *obs* : ²DILIGENCE **2** *now dial Eng* : any of various horse-drawn vehicles (as a light wagon or cart) **3** : a haulage system on a short incline in a mine

²dilly \"\ *n* -ES [origin unknown] *dial Eng* : DUCK

³dilly \"\ *n* -ES [short for *daffadilly*] : DAFFODIL

⁴dilly \"\ *n* -ES [by shortening & alter.] **1** : SAPODILLA 1 **2** : a small tree (*Mimusops emarginata*) of Florida and the West Indies having hard dark brown wood susceptible of a fine polish and small edible fruits — called also *wild dilly, wild sapodilla*

⁵dilly \"\ *adj* [perh. blend of *dippy* and *silly*] *slang chiefly Austral* : SILLY, FOOLISH

⁶dilly \"\ *n* -ES [obs. slang *dilly*, adj., delightful, irreg. fr. E *del-* (fr. *delightful*) + *-y*] : one that is remarkably good or successful or strikingly different : something spectacular or extraordinary ⟨a ~ of a trial novel —Donald Gordon⟩ ⟨a ~ of a doll who, off screen, looks younger, is even prettier, and is just as witty —Helen Colton⟩ ⟨I have a long-standing and legitimate interest in middle names having been christened with a ~ myself —Alfred Gilliland Miller⟩ ⟨another joker was the Veterans of Future Wars — some guys in Princeton cooked that ~ up —Martin Dibner⟩ — not often in formal use

⁷dilly \"\ *vi* -ED/-ING/-ES [by shortening] : DILLYDALLY

dilly bag *n* [Australian *dhilla* hair] *Austral* : a mesh bag of native fibers used for carrying various articles and usu. having a drawstring

dil·ly·dal·li·er *pronunc at* DILLYDALLY +ə(r)\ *n* -s : one that dillydallies

dil·ly·dal·ly \¦dilē¦dalē, -ili¦dali\ *vi* -ED/-ING/-ES [redupl. of *dally*] : to act with unusual or improper slowness : waste time by loitering or delay ⟨for a month the governor had *dillydallied* over the choice of a successor⟩ **syn** see DELAY

dil·ly·man \'dilēmən, -lim-\ *also* **dilly boy** *n, pl* **dil·ly·men** [¹*dilly*] : a mineworker who starts and brakes the movement of cars on a dilly — called also *incline man*

di·lo \'dē(,)lō\ *n* -s [Fijian] : POON

dilse \'dils\ *Scot var of* DULSE

dilucidate *vt* -ED/-ING/-S [LL *dilucidatus*, past part. of *dilucidare*, fr. L *di-* (fr. *dis-* apart) + LL *lucidare* to make clear, fr. L *lucidus* clear, shining — more at DIS-, LUCID] *obs* : to make clear : ELUCIDATE — **dilucidation** *n* -s

dil·u·en·do \,dil(y)ə'wen(,)dō\ *adj* (*or adv*) [It, lit., diluting, fr. L *diluendum*, gerund of *diluere* to dilute] : dying away — used as a direction in music

¹dil·u·ent \'dilyəwənt\ *n* -s [L *diluent-, diluens*, pres. part. of *diluere* to wash away, dilute] : a diluting agent: as **a** : a volatile liquid (as toluene) used along with solvents in coating materials (as cellulose lacquers) esp. for reducing the cost — compare THINNER b **b** : an inert substance (as powdered talc) added to a mixture esp. for reducing the concentration of active ingredients (as in an insecticidal dust) — compare EXTENDER 1, FILLER 1a(1)

²diluent \"\ *adj* [L *diluent-, diluens*, pres. part. of *diluere*] : making thinner or less concentrated by admixture : DILUTING

di·lu·tant \dī'lüt³nt, də| *also* |l'yü-\ *n* -s : DILUENT

¹di·lute \(')dī¦lüt, də¦'l- *also* |l¦yü- *or* |l'yü-; *usu* -üd.+V\ *vb* -ED/-ING/-S [L *dilutus*, past part. of *diluere* to wash away, dilute, dissolve, partly fr. *di-* (fr. *dis-* apart) + *-luere* (fr. *lavere* to wash) and partly fr. *di-* (fr. *dis-* apart) + *luere* to atone for (akin to Gk *lyein* to unbind, release) — more at DIS-, LYE, LOSE] *vt* **1** : to make inferior or reduce (as in power or effect) ⟨the quality of the novel is *diluted* by the bad writing⟩ : make inferior (as in quantity or quality) : DEBASE ⟨~ the purity of a theory —H.W.Spiegel⟩ **2 a** (1) : to make thinner or more liquid by admixture (as with water) (2) : to make less concentrated : diminish the strength, activity, or flavor of (as by thinning or introducing an inert substance) ⟨~ wine⟩ ⟨~ combustible gases with carbon dioxide⟩ **b** : to change (something immaterial) by mixture with extraneous or foreign elements esp. with a resulting debasement ⟨Christianity . . . generously *diluted* with pagan beliefs —C.L.Jones⟩ ~ *vi* : to become diluted ⟨the iced coffee *diluted* rapidly⟩ **syn** see THIN

²dilute \"\ *adj* [L *dilutus*, past part. of *diluere*] **1** : deprived of its natural or proper force or quality : WEAK, ENFEEBLED ⟨a ~ form of democracy⟩ **2** : DILUTED, THIN : of relatively low strength or concentration — usu. contrasted with *concentrated* ⟨a ~ solution⟩ **3** : characterized genetically by reduced pigmentation — **di·lute·ly** *adv* — **di·lute·ness** *n* -ES

³di·lute \", 'dil,yü-\ *n* -s : an individual exhibiting reduced pigmentation

di·lut·ed \(')dī¦lüd·əd, də¦'l- *also* |l¦yü- *or* |l'yü-, -ütəd *also* ¦l¦yü- *or* ¦l'yü-\ *adj* [fr. past part. of ¹*dilute*] : reduced in strength, concentration, quality, or purity ⟨~ alcohol⟩ : THIN, WEAK, ATTENUATED ⟨a ~, doubtful, questioning faith⟩ — **di·lut·ed·ly** *adv* — **di·lut·ed·ness** *n*

dil·u·tee \,dilyə¦tē; dī¦lü¦tē, ¦dī¦(,)lü-, də¦lü- *also* |l¦yü- *or* |l(,)yü-\ *n* -s : an unskilled worker performing a task previously a part or process of a skilled operation — compare DILUTION 2

di·lut·er *or* **di·lu·tor** *like* ¹DILUTE +ə(r)\ *n* -s : one that dilutes

di·lu·tion \dī'lüshən, də| *also* |l'yü-\ *n* -s [¹*dilute* + *-ion*] **1 a** : the act of diluting or the state of being diluted ⟨the ~ of paint with thinner⟩ ⟨the sermon was a weak ~ of familiar ideas⟩ **b** : one that is diluted : a diluted substance ⟨lower ~s of serum showing no agglutination⟩ **2** : the breakdown of skilled jobs or operations into separate processes requiring little or no skill to perform **3** : the process of disposing of sewage by allowing it to mix with a large volume of water **4** : a reduction in value of a corporation's shares occurring when new shares are issued without the receipt of full consideration

di·lu·vial \də'lüvēəl, (')dī¦lü-, -vyəl *also* |l'yü- *or* |l¦yü-\ *adj* [LL *diluvialis*, fr. L *diluvium* flood + *-alis* -al] **1 a** : of, concerning, or relating to a flood or deluge, esp. the deluge described in the Bible **b** : resembling a flood : FLOODING **2** : effected or produced by a flood or deluge of water : of or characterized by diluvium **3** *usu cap* : of or belonging to the epoch during which man has existed

di·lu·vial·ist \-ləst\ *n* -s : a believer in diluvianism

di·lu·vian \-ēən,-yən\ *adj* [L *diluvium* + E *-an*] : DILUVIAL

di·lu·vian·ism \-,nizəm\ *n* -s : a theory in geology: many geological phenomena can be explained by a former universal deluge

di·lu·vion \-vēən,-vyən\ *n* -s [LL *diluvion-, diluvio* flood, fr. L *diluere* to wash away + *-ion-, -io* -ion — more at DELUGE] : DILUVIUM

di·lu·vi·um \-vēəm\ *n, pl* **diluviums** \-ēəmz\ *also* **dilu·via** \-ēə\ [L, flood — more at DELUGE] **1** : DRIFT 2g **2** *archaic* : any geological deposit produced by a flood of more than ordinary power

¹dim \'dim\ *adj* **dimmer; dimmest** [ME, fr. OE; akin to OHG *timber* dark, ON *dimmr* dark, gloomy, MIr *dem* black, dark, Gk *themeröpis* grave-looking, Skt *dhamati* he blows] **1 a** : not bright : emitting a limited or insufficient amount of light ⟨the moon is ~ on a cloudy night⟩ **b** : of a dull or subdued shade or tint : lacking brightness or clarity ⟨the iris was of a peculiar soft or ~ and tender red —W.H.Hudson †1922⟩ **c** : lacking pronounced, clear-cut, or vigorous quality or character ⟨~ affairs with women in which he flirts in a scared way —Anthony West⟩ **d** *slang* : BORING, DULL ⟨a pretty ~ celebration⟩ **2 a** : seen indistinctly : without clear outlines or details : scarcely visible ⟨the ~ distances of his own Mississippi river country —Sherwood Anderson⟩ **b** : indistinctly or faintly perceived by the senses : of low volume or strength ⟨the ~ strumming of a guitar⟩ ⟨strawberry leaves sent up their sweet ~ smell —Edith Sitwell⟩ **c** : perceived by the mind indistinctly or with difficulty ⟨a ~ awareness of his environment⟩ : indistinctly known or remembered ⟨the ~ centuries of the later empire —Roger Fry⟩ : sensed or perceived weakly in an emotional or intuitional manner ⟨led . . . early man to a ~ feeling for symbolism —Edward Sapir⟩ : of a hazy or indefinite nature ⟨claimed some ~ relationship with Houdini —R.G.G. Price⟩ **d** : having little prospect of favorable result or outcome ⟨a ~ future⟩ : unlikely to be fulfilled or realized ⟨the ~ expectancy that he might return —Ann Ryan⟩ **e** : characterized by an unfavorable, skeptical, pessimistic, disapproving, or unenthusiastic attitude — usu. used in the phrase *take a dim view of* ⟨he takes a ~ view of human nature⟩ ⟨the villagers take a ~ view of people who try to impress them⟩ **3 a** : not perceiving clearly and distinctly with one of the senses (as sight) ⟨eyes grown ~ with age⟩ **b** : dull and weak in understanding or comprehension ⟨big and overdeveloped and ~ in her wits —Louis Bromfield⟩ **syn** see DARK

²dim \"\ *vb* **dimmed; dimmed; dimming; dims** [ME *dimmen*, fr. *dim*, adj.] *vt* **1** : to make dim ⟨~ the theater lights⟩ ⟨the years could not ~ his early love⟩ ⟨the incident *dimmed* the prospects for peace⟩ **2** : to reduce the light from (headlights) by switching to the low beam ~ *vi* : to become dim ⟨her fame and beauty *dimmed* rapidly⟩ ⟨the way the lights ~ in a farmhouse during a storm —John Cheever⟩ **syn** see OBSCURE

³dim \"\ *n* -s **1** *archaic* : DIMNESS, DUSK **2 a** : PARKING LIGHT ⟨put his lights on the ~ and pulled into the curb —Erle Stanley Gardner⟩ **b** : LOW BEAM

dim *abbr* **1** dimension **2** [L *dimidium*] half **3** diminished **4** diminuendo **5** diminutive

dim·ble \ˈdim(b)əl\ *n* -s [perh. alter. of *dingle*] *dial Eng* : a ravine with a watercourse : DINGLE

dime \ˈdīm\ *n* -s [ME, fr. MF *dime, disme*, fr. L *decima*, fr. fem. of *decimus* tenth (adj.), fr. *decem* ten — more at TEN] **1** *archaic* : a tenth or tithe **2 a** : a coin of the U.S. first issued in 1796 and worth ¹⁄₁₀ dollar **b** : the sum of ten cents ⟨the price of admission was only a ~⟩ **c dimes** *pl, archaic* : money or financial gain ⟨no matter about her temper — has she got the ~*s* —Mary J. Holmes⟩ **d** : a petty sum of money ⟨they made hardly a ~⟩ ⟨they hadn't lost a ~ on the deal —Nelson Algren⟩ **3** : a Canadian ten-cent piece — **a dime a dozen** : plentiful or commonplace to the point of having little value ⟨heroes were *a dime a dozen* that day —*Infantry Jour.*⟩ — **on a dime** *adv* : in a very small area ⟨this car can turn *on a dime*⟩ : INSTANTLY ⟨stopped *on a dime*⟩

di·me·don \ˈdīmə‚dän\ *or* **di·me·done** \-‚dōn\ *n* -s [ISV *dime-* (fr. *dimethyl*) + *d-* (fr. *dihydr-*) + *-one*] : a crystalline diketone $C_8H_{12}O_2$ made by reaction of mesityl oxide and ethyl malonate and used in the analysis of aldehydes with which it forms insoluble derivatives; 5,5-dimethyl-1,3-cyclohexanedione

dime museum *n* : a collection of often lurid and sensational curiosities, monstrosities, and freaks exhibited for a low price of admission

di·men·hy·dri·nate \‚dī‚menˈhīdrə‚nāt\ *n* -s [*dime-* (fr. *dimethyl*) + *-n-* (fr. *amine*) + *-hydrin-* (fr. *diphenhydramine*) + *-ate*] : a crystalline compound $C_{17}H_{22}NO.C_7H_6ClN_4O_2$ made by reaction of diphenhydramine with 8-chloro-theophylline and used in the prevention or treatment of motion sickness and postoperative nausea

dime novel *n* **1** : an inexpensive paper-bound melodramatic novel of adventure popular in the U.S. from about 1860 to World War I — compare ³DREADFUL **2** : a cheap sensational and often lurid novel

¹di·men·sion \dəˈmenchən *sometimes* dīˈ-\ *n* -s *often attrib* [ME *dimensioun*, fr. MF *dimension*, fr. L *dimension-, dimensio*, fr. *dimensus* (past part. of *dimetiri* to measure out, fr. *di-* — fr. *dis-* apart — + *metiri* to measure) + *-ion-, -io* -ion — more at DIS-, MEASURE] **1 a** : measure in a single line (as length, breadth, height, thickness, or circumference) : one of the three coordinates of position; *specif* : the physical characteristic of length, breadth, or thickness ⟨a line has one ~ (length), a plane has two ~*s* (length and breadth), and a cube has three ~*s* (length, breadth, and thickness)⟩ — usu. used in pl. **b** : the quality of spatial extension ⟨~ is a common trait of all matter⟩ : MAGNITUDE, SIZE ⟨the town's modest ~*s* and leisurely ways —Jane Shellhase⟩ **c** (1) : the range over which or the degree to which something extends : EXTENT, SCOPE, PROPORTIONS ⟨the vast ~*s* of the disaster⟩ ⟨music grown to the ~*s* of a great art⟩ — usu. used in pl. (2) : the quality, character, or moral or intellectual stature proper to or belonging to a person ⟨reduced to his own natural ~*s* —J.G.Lockhart⟩ — usu. used in pl. (3) *chiefly in literature and art* : lifelike or realistic quality ⟨a portrayal from which the character of Hamlet emerges bloodless, without ~⟩ : largeness of vision or thought ⟨reasoned convictions give his work a ~ lacking in the plays of lesser men⟩ **d** (1) : the particular set of circumstances or environmental factors within which someone or something exists or with reference to which something is viewed ⟨for a social novelist . . . time is the ~ in which his materials exist —Granville Hicks⟩ (2) : one of the elements or factors making up a complete personality or entity ⟨no other character in the book has more than one ~⟩ : one of the planes of organization or one of the aspects of a cultural phenomenon ⟨every human situation has environmental, organic, and social ~*s*⟩ ⟨preoccupation with geography at the expense of other ~*s* of dialectal diversity —Glenna R. Pickford⟩ : an independent variable or a combination of variables ⟨a psychological test measuring ~*s* of personality⟩ : QUALITY, ASPECT, TRAIT **2** *archaic* : the act or an instance of measuring : MEASUREMENT **3** *obs* : bodily form or proportions ⟨hath not a Jew hands, organs, ~*s*? —Shak.⟩ **4** : one of a set of coordinates containing the number of coordinates necessary and sufficient to distinguish any one of the elements of a magnitude or aggregate from all others : one of the three coordinates of momentum **5** : one of the fundamental units or powers thereof that enter into the makeup of a derived unit ⟨the gram, the square of the centimeter, and the −2 power of the second are the ~*s* of the erg⟩ **6** : wood or stone cut to pieces of specified size: as **a** : yard lumber usu. over two inches and under five inches thick and of any width **b** : hardwood in small squares of varying length and thickness for the use esp. of manufacturers of furniture **c** : blocks or slabs of natural stone used chiefly for the construction of masonry walls and memorials **syn** see SIZE

²dimension \"\ *vt* **dimensioned; dimensioned; dimensioning** \-ch(ə)niŋ\ **dimensions 1** : to make or form (as by cutting or planing) to the required dimensions ⟨the shaft is ~*ed* to fit any wheel⟩ **2** : to figure with dimensions and sometimes also with tolerances (as an architectural plan or a working drawing) : indicate the dimensions on (a drawing)

di·men·sion·al \-chənᵊl, -chnəl\ *adj* **1** : of or relating to dimension ⟨the ~ stability of properly set nylon fabrics precludes trouble due to shrinkage —H.R.Mauersberger⟩ **2 a** : having dimension ⟨never matures as a ~ character; he is pasty, bland, faceless —Norman Cousins⟩ **b** : having a specified number of dimensions

dimensional analysis *n* : a method of analysis in which physical quantities are expressed in terms of their fundamental dimensions that is often used when there is not enough information to set up precise equations

di·men·sion·al·i·ty \=‚=ˈnaləd·ē\ *n* -ES : the quality or state of having dimension : SIZE, MAGNITUDE ⟨~ is the common attribute of all matter⟩

di·men·sion·al·ly \=ˈmenchənᵊlē, -chnəlē, -li\ *adv* : with respect to dimension ⟨glass is a ~ stable material⟩

di·men·sioned \-chənd\ *adj* [¹*dimension* + *-ed*] : having dimension : having a specified number of dimensions ⟨three-*dimensioned*⟩

di·men·sion·less \-nləs\ *adj* : having no dimensions

di·men·sive \-n(t)siv\ *adj* [L *dimensus* (past part. of *dimetiri* to measure out) + E *-ive* — more at ¹DIMENSION] *archaic* : DIMENSIONAL

di·mer \ˈdīmə(r)\ *n* -s [ISV *di-* + *-mer*] : a compound formed by the union of two molecules of a simpler compound : a polymer formed from two molecules of a monomer ⟨diisobutylene is the ~ of isobutylene⟩

di·mer·cap·rol \‚dī(‚)mərˈka‚prȯl, -rōl\ *n* -s [irreg. fr. *di-mercapto-propanol*] : a colorless viscous oily compound $CH_2(SH)CH(SH)CH_2OH$ with an offensive odor developed as an antidote to lewisite but now used in treating poisoning by compounds of arsenic and heavy metals (as mercury and gold); 2,3-di-mercapto-1-propanol — called also *BAL, British anti-lewisite*

di·mer·ic \(ˈ)dīˈmerik\ *adj* [*dimerous* + *-ic*] **1** *biol* **a** : consisting of two parts : DIMEROUS ⟨a ~ chromosome⟩ **b** : involving or mediated by two factors ⟨~ inheritance⟩ ⟨a ~ character⟩ **2** [*dimer* + *-ic*] : of or relating to a dimer

di·me·ride \ˈdīmə‚rīd, -rəd\ *n* -s [*dimer* + *-ide*] : DIMER

dim·er·ism \ˈdimə‚rizəm\ *n* -s [ISV *dimerous* + *-ism*] : the quality or state of being dimerous

di·mer·i·za·tion \‚dīmərəˈzāshən\ *n* -s [ISV *dimer* + *-ization*] : the process of dimerizing or the state of being dimerized

di·mer·ize \ˈdīmə‚rīz\ *vb* -ED/-ING/-S [back-formation fr. *dimerization*] : to polymerize to a dimer

dim·er·ous \ˈdimərəs\ *adj* [NL *dimerus*, fr. L *di-* + NL *-merus* -merous] : consisting of two parts: as **a** *of certain insects* : having the tarsi two-jointed **b** *of flowers* : having two members in each whorl

dimes *pl of* DIME

dime store *n* : FIVE-AND-TEN

dim·e·ter \ˈdimәd·ә(r)\ *n* [LL *dimeter, dimetrus*, n., dimeter, *dimeter, dimetrus*, adj., being a dimeter, fr. Gk *dimetros* being a dimeter, fr. *di-* + *-metros* (fr. *metron* meter, measure) — more at MEASURE] : a line consisting of two metrical feet or of two dipodies

di·me·thoxy- \‚dīmәˈthäksē, -me¦-\ *comb form* [ISV *di-* + *methoxy-*] : containing two methoxy groups ⟨*dimethoxy*benzene $C_6H_4(OCH_3)_2$⟩

di·methyl \(ˈ)dī+\ *adj* [ISV *di-* + *methyl*] : containing two methyl groups in the molecule

dimethyl·acetylene \(‚)dī‚methәl+\ *n* [ISV *dimethyl* + *acetylene*] : BUTYNE b

di·meth·yl·amine \(‚)dī‚methәlәˈmēn, -thәˈlamәn\ *n* [ISV *dimethyl* + *amine*] : an easily condensable gaseous compound $(CH_3)_2NH$ having a strong ammoniacal odor made by catalytic reaction of methanol with ammonia or methylamine and used chiefly in organic syntheses (as of vulcanization accelerators for rubber)

dimethylamino- *comb form* [ISV *dimethyl* + *amin-*] : containing the univalent group $(CH_3)_2N-$ derived from dimethylamine ⟨*p-dimethylamino*benzaldehyde⟩

di·meth·yl·aniline \(‚)dī‚methәl+\ *n* [ISV *dimethyl* + *aniline*] : a yellowish to brownish oily liquid compound $C_6H_5N(CH_3)_2$ made by methylating aniline and used chiefly as an intermediate (as in dye manufacture)

di·meth·yl·benzene \"+\ *n* [ISV *dimethyl* + *benzene*] : XYLENE 1

dimethyl ether *n* [ISV *dimethyl* + *ether*] **1** : METHYL ETHER 1 **2** : an ether containing two methoxy groups

di·meth·yl·formamide \(‚)dī‚methәl+\ *n* [*dimethyl* + *formamide*] : a liquid compound $HCON(CH_3)_2$ used esp. at elevated temperatures as solvent for certain polymeric materials in producing synthetic fibers

di·meth·yl·glyoxime \"+\ *n* [ISV *dimethyl* + *glyoxime*] : a crystalline compound $CH_3C(NOH)C(NOH)CH_3$ used as an analytical reagent esp. for precipitating nickel and palladium

dimethyl ketone *n* [ISV *dimethyl* + *ketone*] : ACETONE

di·meth·yl·ol·urea \dī‚methә‚lōlyūˈrēә, -lōl-\ *n* [*dimethyl* + *-ol* + *urea*] : a crystalline compound $CO(NHCH_2OH)_2$ formed as the first stage in making urea-formaldehyde resins and used chiefly in making adhesives and in treating textiles and wood

dimethyl phthalate *n* : a colorless liquid ester $C_6H_4(COOCH_3)_2$ used chiefly as a plasticizer and insect repellent

dimethyl sulfate *n* [ISV *dimethyl* + *sulfate*] : the methyl sulfate $(CH_3)_2SO_4$

di·meth·yl·tubocurarine \(‚)dī‚methәl+\ *n* : the dimethyl ether of tubocurarine used in the form of a salt (as the chloride $C_{40}H_{48}Cl_2N_2O_6$) as a skeletal muscle relaxant

dimetient *adj* [L *dimetient-, dimetiens*, pres. part. of *dimetiri* to measure out — more at DIMENSION] *obs* : DIAMETRAL

di·metric \(ˈ)dī+\ *adj* [*di-* + Gk *metron* measure + E *-ic*] : tetragonal or hexagonal — compare CRYSTAL SYSTEM

dimetric projection *n* : an axonometric projection in which only two faces are equally inclined to the plane of projection

di·met·ro·don \dīˈme·trә‚dän\ *n, cap* [NL, fr. *di-* + *metr-* (fr. Gk *metron* measure) + *-odon*] : a genus of No. American Lower Permian synapsid reptiles comprising terrestrial carnivores of moderate size distinguished by a curious crest or dorsal sail supported by greatly elongated neural spines of the vertebrae

dim·i·ca·tion \‚dimәˈkāshәn\ *n* -s [L *dimication-, dimicatio*, fr. *dimicatus* (past part. of *dimicare* to fight, fr. *di-* — fr. *dis-* apart — + *micare* to flash) + *-ion-, -io* -ion; akin to W *dirmygu* to despise, Per *miža, muža* eyelash, Gk *omichlē* mist — more at DIS-, MIST] *archaic* : CONTEST, STRIFE

¹di·mid·i·ate \dәˈmidē‚āt\ *vt* -ED/-ING/-S [L *dimidiatus*, past part. of *dimidiare*, fr. *di-* (fr. *dis-* apart) + *-midiare* (fr. *medius* mid) — more at DIS-, MID] **1** *archaic* : to halve or reduce to the half **2** *heraldry* : to represent the half of : cut in two : HALVE

²di·mid·i·ate \-ēәt\ *adj* [L *dimidiatus*, past part. of *dimidiare*] **1** : divided into two equal parts : HALVED **2** *biol* : consisting of only one half of the normal : seeming to lack one half or to have one part smaller than the other ⟨~ elytra that cover only half the abdomen are common among certain families of beetles⟩

di·mid·i·a·tion \-‚midēˈāshәn\ *n* -s [LL *dimidiation-, dimidiatio* action of halving, fr. L *dimidiatus* + *-ion-, -io* -ion] : a formation of marshaling by joining the dexter half of one heraldic shield with the sinister half of another divided per pale or sometimes per bend

di·min·ish \dәˈminish, -nēsh, *esp in pres part* -nәsh\ *vb* -ED/-ING/-ES [ME *deminishen*, alter. (influenced by ME *menusen, minishen* to lessen) of *diminuen*, fr. MF *diminuer*, fr. L *diminuere*, fr. *di-* (fr. *dis-* apart) + *minuere* to lessen — more at DIS-, MINISH, MINOR] *vt* **1** : to make less or cause to appear less : reduce in size, number, or degree ⟨losses and desertions sharply ~*ed* the forces at Washington's disposal⟩ ⟨a tiny figure, rather stooped and ~*ed* by constant ill health —May Sarton⟩ ⟨the passing years did not ~ their friendship⟩ **2** *obs* : to take away or subtract **3** : to lessen the authority, dignity, importance, or reputation of ⟨his society destroyed, his country defeated, his emperor ~*ed* —W.M.Hitzig⟩ : detract from : DISPARAGE, BELITTLE ⟨began to ~ the skill of the local skaters —S.H.Adams⟩ **4** *archit* : to cause to taper ⟨a ~*ed* column⟩ ~ *vi* **1** : to become less : DWINDLE ⟨his form . . . ~*ed* to a speck on the road —Thomas Hardy⟩ ⟨his interest in the subject had steadily ~*ed*⟩ **2** *archit* : TAPER ⟨a curious tower ~*ing* in five stages to an octagonal cupola⟩ **syn** see DECREASE

di·min·ish·able \-shәbәl\ *adj* : capable of being diminished

diminished *adj* [fr. past part. of *diminish*] **1** : made less or decreased **2** *of a musical interval* : made one half step less than perfect or minor ⟨a ~ fifth⟩

diminished arch *n* : an arch having less height than half its width (as a segmental or three-centered arch) — compare DROP ARCH

diminished seventh *n* **1** : a chord comprised of three superimposed minor thirds — see SEVENTH CHORD illustration **2** : an interval less by one half step than the minor seventh

diminished shaft *n* : the shaft of a tapering column

diminished triad *or* **diminished chord** *n* : a triad consisting of a minor third and diminished fifth — see TRIAD illustration

di·min·ish·ing·ly *adv* [*diminishing* (pres. part. of *diminish*) + *-ly*] : in a diminishing manner : DECREASINGLY ⟨the rain continued, but ~, all that night⟩

diminishing returns *n pl* : a rate of yield that at a certain point fails to increase in proportion to additional investments of labor or capital — see LAW OF DIMINISHING RETURNS

diminishing rule *n* : a template for contouring a shaft

diminishing stile *n* : a stile that is narrower in one part than in another (as in many glazed doors)

di·min·ish·ment \-shmәnt\ *n* -s : DIMINUTION

¹di·min·u·en·do \dә‚min(y)әˈwen(‚)dō\ *adv (or adj)* [It, lit., diminishing, fr. L *diminuendum*, gerund of *diminuere*] : with gradually diminishing volume or intensity : DECRESCENDO — used as a direction in music; abbr. *dim.* or *dimin.*

²diminuendo \"\ *n, pl* **diminuendos** *or* **diminuendoes** [It, fr. *diminuendo*, adj.] **1** : a gradual decrease in volume or intensity esp. of sound **2** : a musical passage, phrase, or note played with diminishing volume or force

diminute *adj* [ME *diminut*, fr. L *diminutus*, past part. of *diminuere*] *obs* : DIMINISHED, DIMINUTIVE — **diminutely** *adv, obs*

dim·i·nu·tion \‚dimәˈn(y)üshәn, ÷ -myәˈnish-\ *n* -s [ME *diminucioun*, fr. MF *diminution*, fr. L *diminution-, diminutio*, alter. (influenced by L *diminuere* to diminish) of *deminution-, deminutio*, fr. *deminutus* (past part. of *deminuere* to diminish, fr. *de* from, away + *minuere* to lessen) + *-ion-, -io* -ion — more at DE-, MINOR] **1** : the act, process, or an instance of diminishing : DECREASE ⟨experienced no ~ of his physical powers⟩ **2** *archaic* : a lowering in estimation : DEGRADATION, DEPRECIATION **3** : the reduction to smaller note values of the repetition of, imitation of, or answer to a musical subject or phrase — opposed to *augmentation* **4 a** : the defacing of part of a heraldic shield **b** : DIFFERENCE 5 **5** : omission or incompleteness in a record sent up by a lower court in proceedings for review **6** : the tapering or diminishing of a column or some other part of a building; *also* : the amount of such diminishing

di·min·u·ti·val \dә¦minyә¦tīvәl\ *adj* [*diminutive*, n. + *-al*] : ²DIMINUTIVE 1

¹di·min·u·tive \dәˈminyәd·|iv, -yәt|\ *n* -s [ME *diminutif*, fr. LL *diminutivum*, alter. (influenced by L *diminuere*) of *deminutivum*, fr. *deminutivus*, adj., fr. L *deminutus* + *-ivus* -ive] **1** : a diminutive word or affix ⟨*Jeanie* is a ~ of *Jean*⟩ **2** *heraldry* : any of several ordinaries corresponding in characteristic shape and position in the shield with other ordinaries which are greater in width ⟨the bendlet is a ~ of the bend, being one half its width⟩ **3** : a diminutive object or individual : a small variety or replica ⟨such water flies, ~*s* of nature —Shak.⟩

²diminutive \"\ *adj* [MF *diminutif*, fr. LL *diminutivus*, alter. (influenced by L *diminuere*) of *deminutivus*] **1** : indicating small size and sometimes the quality or condition of being loved, lovable, pitiable, or contemptible — used of affixes (as *-ette, -ie, -kin, -let, -ling, -y*) and of words formed with them (as in *kitchenette, Jeanie, lambkin, streamlet, witling, sonny*); contrasted with *augmentative* **2** : small esp. in size : TINY ⟨all was on a ~ scale, like a doll's house⟩ ⟨~ in stature⟩ **3** *archaic* : diminishing or tending to diminish; *also* : DISPARAGING **syn** see SMALL

di·min·u·tive·ly \|әvlē, -li\ *adv* **1** : in a diminutive manner : in a way expressing diminution **2** : to a very small degree : by a very little

di·min·u·tive·ness \|ivnәs\ *n* -ES : extreme smallness or littleness

di·mis·sion \dәˈmishәn, dīˈ-\ *n* -s [ME, conveyance by lease, fr. ML *dimission-, dimissio*, fr. L, dismissal, discharge, fr. *dimissus* (past part. of *dimittere* to dismiss) + *-ion-, -io* -ion] : dismissal or discharge ⟨a letter of ~⟩

dim·is·so·ri·al \¦dimә¦sōrēәl, -sȯr-\ *n* -s [NL *dimissorialis* dimissory and commendatory, fr. ML *dimissorius* dimissory and commendatory + L *-alis* -al] : a letter from a pope, bishop, abbot, or other high ecclesiastical official authorizing the ordination of the bearer — called also *dimissory letter*

dim·is·so·ry \ˈdimә‚sōrē, -sȯr-, -ri *sometimes* dәˈmisәr- *or* dīˈm-\ *adj* [ML *dimissorius* dimissory and commendatory, fr. LL, submitting a matter to a higher court, fr. L *dimissus* (past part. of *dimittere* to dismiss) + *-orius* -ory] : dismissing or granting leave to depart

dimissory letter *n* [trans. of ML *dimissoriae litterae*] **1** : a letter given by a bishop dismissing a clergyman to another diocese and recommending him for reception there **2** : DIMISSORIAL

¹di·mit \dәˈmit\ *vt* **dimitted; dimitted; dimitting; dimits** [ME *dimitten* to convey by lease, fr. ML *dimittere*, fr. L, to dismiss, renounce — more at DISMISS] : ¹DEMIT

²dimit *var of* DEMIT

dim·i·ty \ˈdimәd·ē, -әtē, -i\ *n* -ES [alter. of ME *demyt*, prob. fr. MGk *dimitos* of double thread, fr. LGk, fr. Gk *di-* + *mitos* thread of the warp; perh. akin to Gk *mitra* headband — more at MITER] : a sheer cotton fabric of plain weave that is usu. checked or striped by corded effects which are made by weaving two or more threads as one and that is used for clothing and curtains and in a heavier weight for bedspreads

dim·ly *adv* [ME, fr. ¹*dim* + *-ly*] : in a dim manner : FAINTLY, INDISTINCTLY, UNCLEARLY ⟨foghorns sounding ~ in the distance⟩ ⟨crooked little side streets, ~ lit by gas lamps —John Durant⟩ : VAGUELY, HAZILY, OBSCURELY ⟨only ~ aware of the meaning of these large events⟩

dimmed *past of* DIM

dimmed·ness \ˈdimәdnәs, -m(d)n-\ *n* -ES [*dimmed* (past part. of *dim*) + *-ness*] : the quality or state of being dimmed

¹dimmer *comparative of* DIM

²dim·mer \ˈdimә(r)\ *n* -s **1** : a device for causing an electric light to burn less brightly (as during a stage play); *esp* : a choke coil, rheostat, or transformer connected to the light **2 dimmers** *pl* **a** : PARKING LIGHTS **b** : headlights on low beam

dimmest *superlative of* DIM

dim·met *or* **dim·mit** \ˈdimәt\ *n* -s [irreg. fr. ¹*dim*] *dial Eng* : TWILIGHT, DUSK

dimming *pres part of* DIM

dim·mish \ˈdimish\ *adj* : somewhat dim

dim·ness *n* -ES [ME *dimnesse* darkness, obscurity, fr. OE *dimnes*, fr. *dim* dim, dark + *-nes* -ness] **1** : the quality or state of being dim **2** : something that is dim

di·molecular \¦dī+\ *adj* : BIMOLECULAR

di mol·to \dәˈmōl(‚)tō, dēˈ-\ *adv* [It] : very much — used as a direction in music

di·mo·ric \(ˈ)dīˈmōrik, -mȯr-,-mär-\ *adj* [*di-* + *mora* + *-ic*] : DISEMIC

di·morph \ˈdī‚mȯrf\ *n* -s [prob. back-formation fr. *dimorphism, dimorphous*] : either of the two crystalline forms of a dimorphous substance ⟨calcite and aragonite are ~*s*⟩

¹di·mor·phic \(ˈ)dī¦mȯrfik\ *adj* [*dimorphous* + *-ic*] **1 a** : DIMORPHOUS 1 **b** : occurring in two distinct forms ⟨~ leaves of emergent plants⟩ ⟨a sexually ~ butterfly⟩ **2** : combining qualities of two kinds of individuals in one — used chiefly by breeders of fancy-colored canaries

²dimorphic \"\ *n* -s : a dimorphic individual

di·mor·phism \(ˈ)dīˈmȯr‚fizәm\ *n* -s [ISV *dimorph-* (fr. Gk *dimorphos*) + *-ism*] : the condition or property of being dimorphic or dimorphous: as **a** : difference (as of form, color, size) between two individuals or kinds of individuals that might be expected to be similar or identical ⟨the floating and submerged leaves of aquatic plants may exhibit considerable ~⟩ ⟨in certain marine invertebrates sexual ~ is so extreme that the male is reduced to a minute parasite in the kidney of the female⟩ — compare POLYMORPHISM **b** : crystallization in two different forms

di·mor·phite \-‚fīt\ *n* -s [obs. E *dimorphine* dimorphite (fr. It *dimorfina*, fr. *dimorf-* — fr. Gk *dimorphos* — + *-ina* -ine) + E *-ite*] : a mineral As_4S_3 consisting of arsenic sulfide originally thought to be one of two dimorphous substances

di·mor·pho·the·ca \(‚)dī‚mȯrfәˈthēkә\ *n* [NL, fr. *dimorpho-* (fr. Gk *dimorphos*) + *-theca*] **1** *cap* : a genus of southern African herbs or subshrubs (family Compositae) with terminal solitary white, purple, orange, or yellow flower heads similar to those of plants of the genus *Calendula* and with conspicuously toothed leaves **2** -s : any plant of the genus *Dimorphotheca* — called also *African daisy, cape marigold, star of the veldt*

di·mor·phous \(ˈ)dī¦mȯrfәs\ *adj* [Gk *dimorphos* having two forms, fr. *di-* + *-morphos* -morphous] **1** : crystallizing in two different forms **2** : DIMORPHIC 1b — **di·mor·phous·ly** *adv*

dim out *vt* : to darken (as a city) by imposition of a dimout

dimout \ˈ=‚=\ *n* -s [*dim out*] : a restriction limiting the use of lighting or the showing of lights at night esp. during the threat of an air raid; *also* : a condition of partial darkness produced by such restriction ⟨the continuing crisis gradually imposes a ~ on the sources and channels of public information —H.D. Lasswell⟩ — compare BLACKOUT

¹dim·ple \ˈdimpәl\ *n* -s [ME *dympull*; akin to OHG *tumphilo* whirlpool, OE *dyppan* to dip — more at DIP] **1** : a slight natural indentation or hollow in the surface of some part of the human body (as on a cheek or the chin) **2** : a depression or indentation on any surface ⟨the pool's dark surface breaks into ~s —William Wordsworth⟩; *specif* **:** such a depression in a building material (as for the recessing of nailheads) **3 :** a slight mound in a building material (as for the holding of metal lath away from the flat surface to which it is applied in plastering)

²dimple \"\ *vb* **dimpled; dimpled; dimpling** \-p(ə)liŋ\ **dimples** *vt* **1 :** to produce dimples in **:** mark with dimples ⟨large, heavy drops that *dimpled* the smooth stream —Marguerite Steen⟩ **2 :** to form a conical depression around (a rivet hole in sheet metal) in order to countersink the rivet head ~ *vi* **:** to exhibit or form dimples esp. in the cheeks in the act of smiling ⟨she *dimpled* up at them, shyly —Mary McCarthy⟩ **:** ripple or break into ripples ⟨a little stream that ran *dimpling* all the way⟩

dim·ply \-p(ə)lē, -li\ *adj, often* -ER/-EST [¹*dimple* + -*y*] **:** having dimples **:** DIMPLED ⟨her face grew ~ with joy⟩

dimps \'dim(p)s\ *n* -ES [irreg. fr. ¹*dim*] *dial Brit* **:** DUSK, TWILIGHT

¹dimpsy \-sē\ *n* -ES [*dimps* + -*y*, n. suffix] *dial Eng* **:** DUSK

²dimpsy \"\ *adj* [*dimps* + -*y*, adj. suffix] *dial Eng* **:** DIM, DARK

dims *pres 3d sing of* DIM, *pl of* DIM

dim–sighted \'ₑ'ₑₑ\ *adj* **:** having dim sight **:** lacking perception — **dim–sight·ed·ness** *n* -ES

dimwit \'ₑ,ₑ\ *n* -S **:** a stupid or very undiscerning person **:** FOOL, BLOCKHEAD

dim–witted \'ₑ'ₑₑ\ *adj* **:** having little or no discernment **:** not mentally bright **:** STUPID ⟨a *dim-witted* remark⟩ ⟨the poor *dim-witted* girl —Louis Bromfield⟩ — **dim–wit·ted·ly** *adv* — **dim–wit·ted·ness** *n*

di·mya \dī'mīə\ [NL, fr. *di-* + -*mya*] *syn of* DIMYARIA

di·my·ar·ia \,dī,mī'a(a)rēə\ *n pl, cap* [NL, fr. *di-* + -*myaria*] *in some classifications* **:** a division of Lamellibranchia comprising the bivalve mollusks with both anterior and posterior adductor muscles, sometimes used synonymously with Isomyaria but commonly including also Heteromyaria — compare MONOMYARIA — **di·my·ar·i·an** \¦dī,mī¦a(a)rēən\ *adj or n* — **di·my·ar·ic** \-ī¦arik\ *adj*

¹din \'din\ *n* -S [ME, fr. OE *dyne*; akin to OHG *tuni* din, ON *dynr*, Skt *dhvanati* it roars] **:** a loud noise; *esp* **:** a welter of confused or discordant sounds **:** CLAMOR, UPROAR ⟨a ~ of whistles, catcalls . . . and trumpets —Whitney Balliett⟩

syn DIN, UPROAR, PANDEMONIUM, HULLABALOO, BABEL, HUBBUB, and RACKET mean, in common, a disturbingly loud or confusing sound or mélange of sounds. DIN stresses an extreme, usu. painful and prolonged, extremely distracting loudness, sometimes, however, applying to a noise or mélange of noises which, though not necessarily painful, totally or almost totally occupies the consciousness ⟨it made a *din* like all the boiler factories in the world and all the backfiring motors in creation trying to drown each other's noise out —W.F.Jenkins⟩ ⟨the general had forbidden the tolling of funeral bells so that the incessant mournful *din* might not pound perpetually at our ears —Kenneth Roberts⟩ ⟨the air was full of the usual tropic *din:* mosquitoes humming, cicadas trilling, bullfrogs twanging like guitars —R.A.W.Hughes⟩ UPROAR and PANDEMONIUM both imply tumult or the wildest disorder, usu. among persons but often among animals or the elements. UPROAR usu. implies disordered shouting or the clamor of an arguing, fighting, or protesting crowd ⟨it is the tenants of this upper gallery who, for their shilling, make all the noise and *uproar* for which the English playhouses are so famous —Eugene Burr⟩ ⟨two thousand choristers from 70 choral societies . . . beefed, brayed, and bellowed . . . the only listeners to the enormous *uproar* were sundry critics —*Sydney (Australia) Bulletin*⟩ ⟨often throw the parliamentary debates into an *uproar* —Paul Blanshard⟩ PANDEMONIUM is stronger than UPROAR, stressing a complete disorder and implying the noisy boisterousness of a crowd breaking bounds and running riot ⟨by this time the mob had its blood up, and *pandemonium* broke loose —Bertrand Russell⟩ ⟨their temple for the next hundred years was a *pandemonium* of contending priests —*Times Lit. Supp.*⟩ ⟨the result of his inflammatory speech was *pandemonium* in the hall⟩ HULLABALOO, often interchangeable with DIN or UPROAR, seldom suggests earsplitting noise or turmoil, but suggests rather noise attendant upon great excitement, esp. that disturbing peace and quiet, often applying to a quick storm of protest, a torrent of sudden sensational gossip, or an outburst of noisy passion ⟨the current political *hullabaloo* —*New Republic*⟩ ⟨the building was planned for nine stories, but the residents of the St.-Germain quarter raised such a *hullabaloo* against its towering bulk that one story was left off —Janet Flanner⟩ ⟨the music stopped and the familiar *hullabaloo* was reestablished in the room —Jean Stafford⟩ BABEL signifies a confusion esp. of mixed languages or vocal qualities, usu. strongly stressing the total meaninglessness or purposelessness of the noise ⟨young and old, fat and thin, all laughed and shouted in a *babel* of tongues —Winifred Bambrick⟩ ⟨among the *babel* of contradictory claims —Ruth Benedict⟩ ⟨must we fall into the jabber and *babel* of discord while victory is still unattained? —Sir Winston Churchill⟩ HUBBUB suggests the noisy and incessant movement of a busy bustling market place, seldom implying painful or disturbing noise or turmoil ⟨the *hubbub* about national politics —Leon Halden⟩ ⟨listening far into the night to the *hubbub* of voices —Howard Troyer⟩ ⟨further *hubbub* in the Beverly Hills sector was occasioned when headlines featured a well-known literary figure's suicide gesture —Bennett Cerf⟩ RACKET stresses the psychological effects of a noise more than its character, implying annoyance or disturbance and applying to any noise that strikes one as excessive or inordinate ⟨he could hear the *racket* in the street — loud now, the cries, the honkings, the vendors, the rattle of carriage wheels over cobbles, the harsh clang of the extra streetcars —Barnaby Conrad⟩ ⟨the children had police whistles and cap pistols and made a terrible *racket* in the street⟩

²din \"\ *vb* **dinned; dinned; dinning; dins** *vt* **1 :** to assail or deafen with loud noise or outcry ⟨*dinned* his ears with shrill reproaches and complaints⟩ **2 :** to utter or sound with great insistence **:** impress by or as if by insistent repetition — often used with *into* ⟨*dinned* the official doctrines into their minds⟩ ⟨*dinned* horns into their ears⟩ ~ *vi* **:** to make a loud noise **:** make a din **:** RESOUND ⟨a hundred horns *dinned* in protest as traffic ground to a stop⟩ ⟨the jukebox was *dinning* —Ralph Ellison⟩

din– *or* **dino–** *also* **dein–** *or* **deino–** *comb form* [NL, fr. Gk *dein-, deino-*, fr. *deinos* — more at DIRE] **:** terrible **:** mighty ⟨*Deinodon*⟩ ⟨*Deinotherium*⟩ ⟨*Dinornis*⟩ ⟨*dinosaur*⟩

din *abbr* dinar

di·nan·de·rie \də'nandərē, ,dē,nan'drē\ *n* -S [F, fr. MF, fr. *dinandier* coppersmith (fr. OF, fr. *Dinand* — now *Dinant* — town in Belgium + OF -*ier* -er) + -*ie* -y] **:** decorative objects of brass, copper, or bronze chiefly for ecclesiastical or domestic use such as were made in the 13th to 15th centuries

di·nan·tian \də'nanchən\ *adj, usu cap* [ISV *dinant-* (fr. *Dinant*, town in Belgium) + -*ian*] **:** of or relating to a division of the Carboniferous of Europe — see GEOLOGIC TIME table

dinaphth– *or* **dinaphtho–** *also* **dinaphtha–** *comb form* [ISV *di-* + *naphth-* or *naphtho-* (fr. *naphthalene*)] **:** containing two naphthalene nuclei ⟨*dinaphth*azine⟩ ⟨*dinaphtho*thiophene⟩ — compare NAPHTH- 2

di·naphthyl \(')dī+\ *adj* [ISV *di-* + *naphthyl*] **:** containing two naphthyl groups in the molecule

di·nar *also* **de·nar** \də'när, dē'-, -nö(ə)r, 'dē,n-\ *n* -S [Ar *dīnār*, fr. Gk *dēnarion* denarius, modif. of L *denarius*] **1 :** a gold coin first struck in the late 7th century A.D. which was for several centuries the basic monetary unit in territories under Muslim control **2 a :** any one of several monetary units: as (1) **:** a subsidiary unit in Iran (2) **:** the basic unit in Iraq, Jordan, Kuwait, Tunisia, and Yugoslavia — see MONEY table **b :** a coin or a note representing one dinar

di·nar·ic \də'narik\ *adj, usu cap* [L *dinaricus*] **:** of or belonging to the mountainous region in Yugoslavia lying east of the Adriatic

di·nas brick \'dēnəs-\ *n, usu cap D* [after *Craig-y-Dinas*, Wales] **:** a refractory silica brick made from an impure sandstone containing lime and clay and formerly used in furnace crowns

dinas clay *n, usu cap D* [after *Craig-y-Dinas*, crag near Neath river, south Wales, where it is found] **:** a disintegrated sandstone formerly used for making refractory brick

din·der \'dində(r)\ *n* -S [alter. of ³*denier*] **:** a small ancient coin found on the site of a Roman settlement in England — usu. used in pl.

¹din·dle \'din(d)ᵊl\ *vi* -ED/-ING/-S [ME *dindlen*, of imit. origin] *dial Brit* **:** VIBRATE

²dindle \"\ *n* -S *Scot* **:** VIBRATION, TREMOR

³dindle \"\ *n* -S [perh. alter. of *dandelion*] **1** *dial Eng* **:** SOW THISTLE **2** *dial Eng* **:** HAWKWEED **3** *dial Eng* **:** DANDELION 1

¹dine \'dīn\ *vb* -ED/-ING/-S [ME *dinen*, fr. OF *disner, diner* to dine, breakfast, fr. (assumed) VL *disjejunare* to break one's fast, fr. L *dis-* + LL *jejunare* to fast, fr. L *jejunus* fasting, hungry] *vi* **:** to eat a meal, esp. the principal meal of the day **:** take dinner — often used with *on* or *upon* ⟨*dined* elegantly on truffled goose livers⟩ or *off* ⟨*dining* off a hamburger . . . washed down with two cups of coffee —Hamilton Basso⟩ ~ *vt* **:** to give a dinner to **:** FEED ⟨often *dined* a dozen guests at his table⟩ **:** provide a feast for ⟨he was wined and *dined* at every stage of his triumphal tour⟩

²dine \"\ *n* -S [ME, fr. *dinen*, v.] **:** DINNER

³di·né \də'nā\ *n, pl* **diné** *or* **dinés** *usu cap* [Navaho, lit., people] **:** NAVAHO

dine out *vi* **:** to eat a meal away from home esp. in a restaurant

din·er \'dīnə(r)\ *n* -S **1 :** one that dines **2 a :** a railroad dining car **b :** a roadside short-order restaurant that has a long counter and usu. booths and that often resembles a dining car

din·er·gate \dī'nərgāt\ *n* -S [*din-* + -*ergate*] **:** the soldier form of ants with polymorphic castes that is distinguished by a greatly enlarged head

di·ner·ic \(')dī¦nerik, də'n-\ *adj* [*di-* + LGk *nēron, nēros* water + E -*ic*; akin to Gk *naein* to flow — more at NOURISH] **:** of or relating to the interface between two mutually immiscible liquids (as oil and water) contained in the same vessel

di·nero \də'ne(,)rō\ *n* -S [Sp, fr. L *denarius* Roman silver coin originally equivalent to ten asses — more at ³DENIER] *slang* **:** MONEY ⟨Man! You should have that old gal's ~ —Martin Dibner⟩

di·nette \(')dī¦net, *usu* -ed·+V\ *n* -S [¹*dine* + -*ette*] **:** a small space usu. off a kitchen or pantry and often containing a built-in table and seats that is used for informal dining; *also* **:** a set of furniture consisting of a small-sized table and chairs suitable for use in such a space

di·neutron \(')dī+\ *n* [*di-* + *neutron*] **:** a neutral particle of twice the neutron's mass that is produced by collision of tritons and that is very unstable and quickly disintegrates into two neutrons

¹ding \'diŋ\ *vb* **dinged** \-ŋd\ *or dial* **dang** \'daŋ\ **dinged** *or dial* **dang; dinging; dings** [ME *dingen*, fr. (assumed) OE *dingan* (whence OE *dencgan* to beat); akin to OHG *tangal* hammer, OSw *diunga* to beat, OE *dynt* blow — more at DINT] *vt* **1 :** to strike or beat **:** THRASH ⟨threatened to ~ him on the head⟩ **2 :** to throw violently **:** DASH, FLING, DRIVE ⟨the horse reared violently, ~*ing* off its rider⟩ **3 :** to overcome or surpass **:** get the better of **:** excel or beat ⟨this rating ~*s* all⟩ **4 :** DAMN *vt* 5 ⟨~ my buttons if she ain't more Southern than any of our own gals —A.W.Tourgee⟩ ~ *vi, obs* **1 :** to throw or fling oneself violently about **:** BOUNCE **2** *Scot, of rain* **:** to fall heavily — usu. used with *on* ⟨the rain *dang* on all night⟩

²ding \"\ *n* -S *dial* **:** a blow or stroke ⟨gave him a ~ that made his head buzz⟩

³ding \"\ *vb* -ED/-ING/-S [prob. imit.] *vt* **:** to talk, urge, or impress with tiresome repetition — often used in the phrase *to ding into the ears;* compare DIN *vt* 2 ~ *vi* **:** to make a ringing sound **:** CLANG ⟨the bell ~*ing* and the engine giving off quiet chuffs like a giant breathing —Helen Eustis⟩

⁴ding \"\ *n* -S **:** the sound of dinging — often used as part of a song refrain and often reduplicated ⟨when birds do sing, hey *ding a ding, ding* —Shak.⟩

din·gaan's day \'diŋ,gänz-\ *n, cap both Ds* [after *Dingaan* *fl*1838 Zulu chieftain defeated by the Afrikaners on Dec. 16, 1838] **:** DAY OF THE COVENANT

ding–a–ling *n* -S [imit.] **:** TING-A-LING

ding an sich \¦diŋ(,)än'zik\ *n, pl* **dinge an sich** \¦diŋə(-\ [G] **:** THING-IN-ITSELF

ding·bat \'diŋ,bat, *usu* -ad·+V\ *n* [origin unknown] **:** a typographical ornament (as a bullet or star) used typically to call attention to an opening sentence or to make a break between two paragraphs

¹ding·dong \'diŋ,dȯŋ, -,däŋ\ *n* [imit.] **1 :** the ringing sound produced by or as if by repeated strokes on a bell or some other metallic object — often used in oral imitation of such a sound ⟨hark! now I hear them, ~ bell —Shak.⟩ ⟨the bell goes ~⟩ **2 :** a bell or other metallic object (as a steel triangle) that makes a ringing sound ⟨every Monday mawnin', when the ~ sounds—*Midnight Special*⟩ **3 :** a verse or poem having a singsong monotonous character **:** JINGLE ⟨who would hold the order of the almanac so fast but for the ~, "thirty days hath September, etc." —R.W.Emerson⟩

²dingdong \'ₑ¦ₑ\ *adv* **:** with zeal **:** earnestly or heartily ⟨fell to work ~⟩

³dingdong \'ₑ,ₑ\ *vi* **1 :** to make a dingdong sound ⟨heard the whistle wail mournfully, heard the bell ~*ing* —A.W. Somerville⟩ **2 a :** to repeat an action with monotonous or mechanical regularity ⟨a good engineer . . . , but not adjusted to ~*ing* up and down the river at all —Richard Bissell⟩ **b :** to talk, urge, or scold tediously or insistently **:** DIN ⟨kept on ~*ing* in my ears —W.H.Hudson †1922⟩

⁴dingdong \'ₑ,ₑ\ *adj* **1 :** of, belonging to, or resembling the ringing sound made by a bell or other metallic object ⟨the ~ chime of cathedral bells⟩ **2 :** marked by a rapid exchange or alternation (as of blows) ⟨six weeks of ~ fighting with heavy tank and infantry losses —Arthur Davies⟩ — often used of a close contest or competition ⟨a ~ struggle in which both players were reaching great heights —*Sydney (Australia) Morning Herald*⟩

dingdong theory *n* **:** a theory that language originated out of a natural correspondence between objects of sense perception and the vocal noises which were a part of early men's reaction to them — compare BOWWOW THEORY, POOH-POOH THEORY

¹dinge \'dinj\ *n* -S [origin unknown] **:** a dent made by a blow **:** a surface depression **:** DINT ⟨the vertical frown had left an ineradicable ~ between her eyebrows —Gladys Schmitt⟩

²dinge \"\ *vt* **dinged; dinged; dingeing; dinges** *dial Brit* **:** to make a dinge or depression in **:** BATTER ⟨one of the gentlemen . . . held a *dinged* silk hat in his hand —James Joyce⟩

³dinge \"\ *vt* **dinged; dinged; dingeing; dinges** [back-formation fr. *dingy*, adj.] **:** to make dingy

⁴dinge \"\ *n* -S [back-formation fr. *dingy*, adj.] **:** DINGINESS ⟨the ~ and dust of these crumbling halls⟩ **:** DEPRESSION ⟨his mood threw a ~ even over the children —John Galsworthy⟩

⁵dinge \"\ *n* -S [back-formation fr. *dingy*, adj.] *slang* **:** NEGRO — usu. used disparagingly

¹ding·er \'diŋə(r)\ *n* -S [prob. fr. ¹*ding* + -*er*] *slang* **:** HUMDINGER

²ding·er \"\ *n* -S [prob. fr. ³*ding* + -*er*] *railroad slang* **:** a yardmaster or one who performs the duties of a yardmaster

ding·ey *like* DINGHY\ *archaic var of* DINGHY

dinghy \'diŋ(g)ē, 'diŋkl, 'diŋgl, ¦i\ *n* -ES [Bengali *ḍiṅgi* & Hindi *ḍiṅgī*, dim. of *ḍiṅgā* boat; perh. akin to Skt *droṇī* trough, tub — more at DHONI] **1 :** a rowboat or sailboat used to carry passengers or cargo on the coasts of India esp. in sheltered waters around the peninsula **2 :** any of various small boats propelled by oars, sails, or motors: as **a :** a man-of-war's or merchant ship's small boat **b :** a rowboat used as a tender and lifeboat in a yacht **c :** a sailboat or yacht used in racing **d :** an inflatable rubber life raft used by fliers forced to parachute into the sea

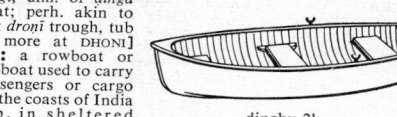

dinghy 2b

dingier *comparative of* DINGY

dingiest *superlative of* DINGY

din·gi·ly \'dinjəlē, -li\ *adv* **:** in a dingy manner

din·gi·ness \-jēnəs, -jin-\ *n* -ES **:** the condition of being dingy ⟨he was appalled by the ~ of the house⟩

dinging *pres part of* DING

dinging hammer *n* [*dinging* prob. fr. gerund of ¹*ding*] **:** BUMPING HAMMER

¹din·gle \'diŋgəl\ *n* -S [ME, abyss] **1 :** a narrow dale or dell **2 :** a small secluded well-wooded ravine or valley

²dingle \"\ *n* -S [origin unknown] **1** *North* **:** a storm door or protecting weather shed at the entrance of a camp or house **2** *North* **:** a roofed-over passageway between the cooking and sleeping areas of a logging camp often used as storeroom

din·gle·ber·ry \'diŋgəl— *see* BERRY\ *n* [*dingle-* (of unknown origin) + *berry*] **1 :** a shrub (*Vaccinium erythrocarpus*) of the southeastern U.S. **2 :** the globose dark red edible berry of the dingleberry

din·gle·bird \'diŋgəl,ₑ\ *n* [*dingle-* (of imit. origin) + *bird*] *Austral* **:** BELLBIRD

dingle stick *n* [by alter.] **:** DANGLE STICK

ding·man \'diŋmən\ *n, pl* **dingmen** [prob. fr. ¹*ding* + *man*] **:** ⁴BUMPER 1d(1)

din·go \'diŋ(,)gō\ *n* -ES [native name in Australia] **:** a wild dog (*Canis dingo*) of Australia with a wolfish face, bushy tail, and usu. a reddish brown color supposed to have been introduced by man at a very early period

ding–on \'diŋ,än\ *n* [Sc *ding on*, v., to continue raining heavily, fr. *ding* + *on*] *Scot* **:** a heavy rainstorm

dings *pres 3d sing of* DING, *pl of* DING

ding–toed \'diŋ¦tōd\ *adj* [*ding-* (of unknown origin) + *toed*] *NewEng* **:** PIGEON-TOED

din·gus \'diŋ(g)əs\ *n* -ES [D or G; D *dinges*, prob. fr. G *dings*, fr. gen. of *ding* thing, fr. OHG — more at THING] **1 :** something (as a gadget) whose common name is unknown or forgotten ⟨various slides and clips that replaced the tiepin of yesteryear are in turn being replaced . . . by a new sort of ~ adapted from army insignia —*New Yorker*⟩ ⟨the bell-shaped ~ on the end of an old electric-light cord —G.C.Furnas⟩ **2 :** PENIS — often considered vulgar

¹dingy *like* DINGHY\ *archaic var of* DINGHY

²din·gy \'dinjē, -ji\ *adj, usu* -ER/-EST [origin unknown] **:** DIRTY, SOILED, DISCOLORED ⟨~ white doors fastened with long iron bars —Rudyard Kipling⟩ ⟨shabby in attire, ~ of linen —W.M. Thackeray⟩ **:** dark, dull, or drab in color or appearance ⟨a nasty, ~ night⟩ **:** SHABBY, MEAN, SQUALID ⟨flashed from ~ obscurity into splendor —H.G.Wells⟩ ⟨the ~ loneliness of his life —*Punch*⟩ ⟨had no record of ~ conspiracy —T.E.M. McKitterick⟩ ⟨to make mean treaties and . . . accept the *dingiest* peace —Francis Hackett⟩

¹din·ich·thy·id \(')dī¦nikthēəd\ *adj* [NL *Dinichthys* + E -*id*] **:** of or relating to the genus *Dinichthys*

²dinichthyid \"\ *n* -S **:** a fish or fossil of the genus *Dinichthys*

din·ich·thys \dī'nikthəs\ *n, cap* [NL, fr. *din-* + -*ichthys*] **:** a genus of large Devonian fishes (subclass Arthrodira) known from both Europe and America and esp. abundant in parts of Ohio attaining a length of 30 feet and having the anterior bony armor reduced

dining *pres part of* DINE

dining alcove *n* [*dining* fr. gerund of ¹*dine*] **:** a recess usu. off a living room used as a dining area — compare DINETTE

dining car *n* **:** a railroad car which contains tables or counters and seats and usu. a kitchen and in which meals are served

dining hall *n* **1 :** a large dining room (as in a college) **2 :** a building containing a dining hall

dining room *n* **:** a room used for the taking of meals

dining table *n* **:** a table at which meals are taken

di·nitrate \(')dī+\ *n* **:** a chemical compound containing two nitrate groups

di·nitrile \(,)dī+\ *n* [ISV *di-* + *nitrile*] **:** an organic chemical compound (as adiponitrile) containing two cyano groups

dinitro– *comb form* [ISV *di-* + *nitr-*] **:** containing two nitro groups

di·ni·tro·benzene \(,)dī¦nī·trō+\ *n* [ISV *dinitro-* + *benzene*] **:** any of three isomeric toxic crystalline compounds $C_6H_4(NO_2)_2$ formed by nitration of benzene or nitrobenzene; *esp* **:** the yellow meta isomer used chiefly as a dye intermediate

di·ni·tro–or·tho–cresol \(,)dī,nī·trō,ȯrthō+\ *n* [ISV *dinitro-* + *orth-* + *cresol*] **:** a yellow crystalline compound $(NO_2)_2$-$C_6H_2(CH_3)OH$ used esp. as an insecticide and herbicide; 4,6-dinitro-*o*-cresol — called also *DNOC*

di·ni·tro·phenol \(,)dī¦nī·trō+\ *n* [ISV *dinitro-* + *phenol*] **:** any of six isomeric crystalline compounds $(NO_2)_2C_6H_3OH$ formed by nitration of phenol or nitrophenols: as **a :** the yellowish isomer formed as an intermediate step in making picric acid and used chiefly as an intermediate (as for sulfur dyes and photographic developers) — called also *2,4-dinitrophenol* **b :** a yellow commercial mixture usu. of three of the isomers

di·ni·tro·toluene \"+\ *n* [ISV *dinitro-* + *toluene*] **:** any of six isomeric toxic crystalline compounds $CH_3C_6H_3(NO_2)_2$ formed by nitration of nitrotoluenes: as **a :** the yellow isomer obtained as the sole first product from *para*-nitrotoluene and used chiefly in making dyes and explosives — called also *2,4-dinitrotoluene* **b :** a commercial mixture of two or more of the isomers

¹dink \'diŋk\ *adj* [origin unknown] *Scot* **:** TRIM, NEAT — used esp. of dress

²dink \"\ *vt* -ED/-ING/-S *Scot* **:** to dress elegantly **:** ADORN

³dink \"\ *n* -S [by shortening & alter. fr. *dinghy*] **:** a small boat; *esp* **:** one used in duck shooting

⁴dink \"\ *vt* -ED/-ING/-S [origin unknown] **:** to cut out with a die — see DINKING DIE

⁵dink \"\ *n* -S [prob. back-formation fr. *dinky*] *slang* **:** a small round close-fitting skullcap with a button on top often traditionally worn by freshmen during their first term at school or college **:** BEANIE

⁶dink \"\ *vt* -ED/-ING/-S [prob. imit.] **:** to hit (a tennis ball) into an opponent's court close to the net with so little force that he cannot reach it before it bounces twice

⁷dink \"\ *n* -S **:** a drop shot in tennis which falls close to the net

⁸dink \"\ *n* -S [prob. alter. of *dick*] **:** PENIS — usu. considered vulgar

din·ka \'diŋkə\ *n, pl* **dinka** *or* **dinkas** *usu cap* [modif. of Dinka *jieng* people] **1 a :** a numerous and powerful Negro people of the Nile valley inhabiting the country to the south of Khartoum and noted for their herds of humped cattle, goats, and sheep **b :** a member of such people **2 :** the language of the Dinka people

dink·er \'diŋkə(r)\ *n* -S [⁴*dink* + -*er*] **:** one that cuts various shapes from cloth, leather, or other material by means of a dinking die

dink·ey *or* **dinky** \'diŋkē, -ki\ *n, pl* **dink·eys** *or* **dink·ies** [prob. fr. *dinky*] **:** a small locomotive used esp. for hauling freight, logging, and shunting

dinking die *n* [*dinking* fr. gerund of ⁴*dink*] **:** a cutting punch either hand or machine operated used without a matrix to cut out various shapes (as from leather, cloth, paper)

¹din·kum \'diŋkəm\ *adj* [prob. fr. E dial. *dinkum*, n., work] **1** *Austral* **:** AUTHENTIC, GENUINE **2** *Austral* **:** fair and square

²dinkum \"\ *adv, Austral* **:** TRULY, HONESTLY

dinkum oil *n, slang Austral* **:** the truth

dinky \'diŋkē, -ki\ *adj, usu* -ER/-EST [¹*dink* + -*y*] **1** *chiefly Brit* **:** NEAT, SMART, SPRUCE **:** CUTE, PRETTY ⟨exemplified ~ femininity, with stylish cut and gay colors —Sam Pollock⟩ **2 :** SMALL, INSIGNIFICANT ⟨the ~ little engine switched loaded cars —John Faulkner⟩

din·ky–di \¦diŋkē¦dī\ *adj* [alter. of *dinkum*] **1** *Austral* **:** LOYAL, TRUE **2** *Austral* **:** DINKUM

din·le *Scot var of* DINDLE

din·mont \'din,mänt\ *n* -S [ME *dynmont*] *Scot* **:** a wether between one and two years old or between the first and second shearing

din·na \'dinə\ [Sc *din-* (fr. *dae*) + *na*] *Scot* **:** do not

dinned *past of* DIN

din·ner \'dinə(r)\ *n* -S *often attrib* [ME *diner*, fr. OF *disner, diner* to dine — more at ¹DINE] **1 :** the principal meal of the day eaten about midday or in the evening; *also* **:** a formal feast or banquet in honor of some person or event **2 :** TABLE D'HÔTE 2

dinner cloth *n* **:** a tablecloth esp. of fine fabric or lace for an elaborate or formal dinner

dinner clothes *n pl* **:** conventional attire for formal or semiformal dinners or social occasions — compare EVENING DRESS

dinner fork *n* **:** a large fork with 3 or 4 tines

dinner jacket *or* **dinner coat** *n* **1 :** TUXEDO 1a **2 :** a usu. light-colored shawl-collared jacket esp. for formal or semiformal summer or tropical wear worn with dark trousers and black tie
dinner knife *n* **:** a large table knife usu. with a steel or silver blade and a handle of any of a number of materials
dinner pail *or* **dinner bucket** *n* **:** a pail in which a worker carries his lunch or dinner
dinner plate *n* **:** a large plate usu. 10 inches in diameter used for the main course of a meal
dinner ring *n* **:** a usu. large and elaborate woman's ring with one large stone or a cluster of stones worn for afternoon and evening occasions

dinner jacket 2

dinner table *n* **:** DINING TABLE
dinnertime \ˈ⸗⸗,⸗\ *n* **:** the time at which it is customary to eat dinner
dinner wagon *n* **:** a small wheeled table with shelves that is used for the service of a dining room — see TEA CART
dinnerware \ˈ⸗⸗,⸗\ *n* **:** china, glassware, or tableware (as flatware and hollow ware) used in table service
dinning *pres part of* DIN
¹dino- — see DIN-
²dino- *comb form* [NL, fr. Gk *dinos* rotation, whirling, whirlpool; perh. akin to OIr *dian* rapid, Skt *diyati* he soars] **1 :** whirling ⟨*Dinobryon*⟩ **2 :** whirlpool **:** eddy ⟨*Dinocapsales*⟩ ⟨*Dinophilus*⟩
di·nob·ry·on \dīˈnäbrēən, -ē,än\ *n, cap* [NL, fr. ²*dino-* + L *bryon* moss, fr. Gk — more at BRY-] **:** a genus of plantlike flagellates (order Chrysomonadina) having delicate cuplike tests and sometimes fouling water supplies
di·no·cap·sa·les \,dīnō,kapˈsā(,)lēz\ *n pl, cap* [NL, fr. ²*dino-* + L *capsa* box, case + NL *-ales* — more at CASE] **:** an order of yellow-green or greenish brown algae (class Dinophyceae) having a temporary naked motile stage but otherwise forming irregular colonies within a common envelope
di·no·cap·sin·e·ae \-pˈsinē,ē\ *n pl, cap* [NL, fr. ²*dino-* + L *capsa* + NL *-ineae*] *in some classifications* **:** a subclass of yellow-green algae equivalent to the order Dinocapsales
di·no·ce·pha·lia \-ōsəˈfālyə\ *syn of* DEINOCEPHALIA
di·noc·er·as \dīˈnäsərəs\ [NL, fr. *din-* + *-ceras*] *syn of* UINTATHERIUM
di·no·cer·a·ta \,dīnōˈserəd·ə\ *n pl, cap* [NL, fr. *Dinocerat-, Dinoceras*] **:** a small order of primitive ungulate mammals of the Paleocene and Eocene — compare UINTATHERIUM — **di·noc·er·ate** \(ˈ)dīˈnäsərət, dəˈn-\ *adj or n*
di·no·coc·ca·les \,dīnō(,)käˈkā(,)lēz\ *n pl, cap* [NL, fr. ²*dino-* + L *coccum* berry + NL *-ales* — more at COCC-] **:** an order of unicellular yellow-green algae (class Dinophyceae) lacking vegetative cell divisions and forming new cells by the production of motile or nonmotile spores similar to the parent cells
di·nod·er·us \dīˈnädərəs\ *n, cap* [NL, prob. fr. *din-* + Gk *deros* skin; akin to Gk *derma* skin — more at DERM-] **:** a genus of chiefly tropical small cylindrical beetles (family Bostrychidae) that have the dorsal surface covered with short dense erect hairs and that live as borers in woody plants (as bamboos)
di·no·flagellata \ˌdīnō+\ *n pl, cap* [NL, fr. *dino-* + *flagellum* + *-ata*] **:** an order of chiefly marine usu. solitary plantlike flagellates that are typically enclosed in a cellulose envelope which may be simple and smooth or variously sculptured and divided into plates, that have one transverse flagellum running in a groove about the body, one posterior flagellum extending out from a similar median groove, usu. a single nucleus, and yellow, brown, or occas. green chromoplasts, and that constitute a significant element in marine plankton, including certain brilliantly luminescent forms (as noctilucas), important elements of marine food chains (as many peridinians), and most of the flagellates that cause red tide (as members of the genus *Gymnodinium*) — see DINOPHYCEAE — **di·no·flagellate** \"+\ *adj or n*
di·no·flagellatae \"\ [NL, fr. *dino-* + *flagellum* + *-atae* (fr. L, fem. pl. of *-atus* -ate)] *syn of* DINOFLAGELLATA
di·no·fla·gel·li·da \,dīnōflǝˈjelədə\ [NL, fr. *dino-* + *flagellum* + *-ida*] *syn of* DINOFLAGELLATA
di·no·hy·us _ōˈhīəs\ *n, cap* [NL, fr. *din-* + *-hyus* (fr. Gk *hys* hog, swine) — more at SOW (female hog)] **:** a genus of extinct giant pigs (family Entelodontidae) of the Lower Miocene of Nebraska some of which exceed the modern bison in size
¹di·no·my·id \ˌdīnōˈmīəd\ *adj* [NL *Dinomys* + E *-id*] **:** of or relating to the genus *Dinomys* or family Dinomyidae
²dinomyid \"\ *n* -s **:** a dinomyid rodent
di·no·mys \ˈdīnō,mis\ *n, cap* [NL, fr. *din-* + *-mys*] **:** a genus of Peruvian hystericomorph rodents (the type of the family Dinomyidae) resembling the pacas
di·no·phil·ea \,dīnōˈfilēə\ *n pl, cap* [NL, fr. *Dinophilus*, genus coextensive with the group Dinophilea, prob. fr. *dino-* + *-philus*] **:** a small group of minute vermiform invertebrate animals inhabiting salt water or brackish water, constituting a single genus, and being considered of uncertain systematic position or included as a class in Trochelminthes
di·no·phy·ce·ae \-ˈfīsē,ē, -fis-\ *n pl, cap* [NL, fr. *dino-* + *-phyceae*] **:** a class of the division Pyrrophyta coextensive with the order Dinoflagellata
di·no·phys·i·da·les \-,fizəˈdā(,)lēz\ *n pl, cap* [NL, prob. irreg. fr. *Dinophysis*, genus belonging to the order Dinophysidales (fr. *dino-* + Gk *physis* nature) + *-ales* — more at PHYSIC] **:** an order of algae (class Dinophyceae) having the cell wall made up of a definite number of plates arranged in a fixed pattern and vertically divided into two similar halves or valves — compare DESMOKONTAE
di·no·pi·the·cus \-,pəˈthēkəs, -ˈpithəkəs\ *n, cap* [NL, fr. *din-* + *-pithecus*] **:** a genus of extinct Pleistocene African baboons that were nearly the size of gorillas
din·or·nis \dīˈnórnəs\ *n, cap* [NL, fr. *din-* + *-ornis*] **:** the type genus of Dinornithidae comprising the largest of the moas
din·or·ni·thid \(ˈ)dīˈnórnəthəd\ *or* **din·or·nith·ic** \ˌ⸗ˌ⸗ˈnithik\ *adj* [*dinornithid* fr. NL *Dinornithidae; dinornithic* fr. NL *Dinornith-, Dinornis* + E *-ic*] **:** of or relating to the Dinornithidae
din·or·nith·i·dae \,dī,nórˈnithə,dē\ *n pl, cap* [NL, fr. *Dinornith-, Dinornis*, type genus + *-idae*] **:** a family of extinct ratite birds that are related to the emus and cassowaries though usu. placed in a distinct order — see DINORNIS, MOA
di·no·saur \ˈdīnə,sò(ə)r, -ō(ə)\ *n* -s [NL *Dinosauria*] **1 :** one

restored skeleton of a dinosaur

of the Dinosauria **2 :** any of various large extinct reptiles
di·no·sau·ria \,dīnəˈsòrēə\ *n pl, cap* [NL, fr. *din-* + *-sauria*] **:** a group of extinct reptiles widely distributed from the Triassic to the Mesozoic initially differing little from the generalized long-tailed quadrupedal common ancestors of modern birds and crocodilians but later becoming specialized for chiefly terrestrial carnivorous or herbivorous modes of life into distinct bipedal and quadrupedal groups, the latter including the largest known land animals — compare BRONTOSAURUS, DIPLODOCUS, ORNITHISCIA, SAURISCHIA, THECODONTIA
¹di·no·sau·ri·an \-ēən\ *n* -s [NL *Dinosauria* + E *-an*] **:** DINOSAUR
²dinosaurian \ˌ⸗⸗ˈ⸗⸗⸗\ *adj* [NL *Dinosauria* + E *-an*] **:** of, relating to, or like the Dinosauria
di·no·sau·ric \,dīnəˈsòrik\ *adj* [*dinosaur* + *-ic*] **:** of the size or nature of a dinosaur **:** HUGE, ENORMOUS
di·no·there \ˈdīnə,thi(ə)r\ *n* -s [NL *Dinotherium*] **:** one of the Deinotherioidea — compare DEINOTHERIUM
di·no·the·ri·um \,dīnəˈthirēəm\ *syn of* DEINOTHERIUM
di·no·tri·cha·les \,dīnōtrəˈkā(,)lēz\ *n pl, cap* [NL, fr. *Dinotrich-, Dinothrix*, genus belonging to the order Dinotrichales (fr. *dino-* + *-thrix*) + *-ales*] **:** an order of yellow-green algae (class Dinophyceae) that are immobile and form a branching system of nearly cylindrical cells
dins *pl of* DIN, *pres 3d sing of* DIN

din·some \ˈdin(t)səm\ *adj* [¹*din* + *-some*] *chiefly Scot* **:** NOISY
DIN system \ˌdēˌīˈen-\ *n* [*DIN* fr. G, abbr. of *Deutsche Industrie-Normen* (lit., German industry standards), standards for industrial products established by the Deutscher Normenausschuss, a German organization for the establishment and registration of standards in all branches of industry] **:** a system for determining the speed of photographic materials in terms of the logarithm of the reciprocal of the exposure required to obtain a density of 0.1 above fog density
¹dint \ˈdint\ *n* -s [ME, fr. OE *dynt;* akin to ON *dyttr* blow, *detta* to fall, Alb *gdhent* I chop wood] **1** *archaic* **:** BLOW, STROKE ⟨sharp-smitten with the ~ of armed heels —Alfred Tennyson⟩ **:** a clap of thunder **2 :** FORCE, POWER ⟨the ~ of pity —Shak.⟩ — now used chiefly in the phrase *by dint of* ⟨by ~ of patience and hard work . . . he gained the top of the mountain —S.E.White⟩ **3 :** a mark left by a blow or pressure **:** DENT, NOTCH ⟨produced a deep ~ in the car fender⟩ **:** a small hollow or indentation **:** IMPRESSION, IMPRINT ⟨does not make any deep ~ in their minds —Walter Moberly⟩ **4** *dial Brit* **:** a jarring blow **:** ATTACK **5** *Scot* **:** a momentary chance
²dint \"\ *vt* -ED/-ING/-S [ME *dinten*, fr. ¹*dint*] **1** *obs* **:** STRIKE, BEAT **2 :** to make a mark or cavity on or in by a blow or by pressure ⟨a financial nut not even a sledge hammer would ~ —J.H.Gray⟩ **3 :** to impress or drive in with force ⟨~*ed* the pointed nails into his own finger tips —Clemence Dane⟩ **:** IMPRINT
di·nucleotide \(ˈ)dī+\ *n* [ISV *di-* + *nucleotide*] **:** a nucleotide consisting of two mononucleotides in combination
di nuo·vo \dēnˈwò(,)vō, ,dēnəˈw-\ *adv* [It] **:** ANEW — used as a direction in music
¹di·oc·e·san \(ˈ)dīˈäsəsən *also* -əzən *sometimes* dəˈä- *or* dēˈä-\ *adj* [ME, fr. ML *diocesanus*, alter. of LL *dioecesanus*, fr. *dioecesis* + L *-anus* -an] **1 a :** belonging to a diocese and subject to the bishop of the diocese ⟨priests are divided into two categories, ~ and religious —P.H.Furfey⟩ **b :** restricted or devoted to a diocese ⟨he has never been able to be contentedly ~ or even insular —*Times Lit. Supp.*⟩ ⟨a book authorized for ~ use⟩ **c :** formed of dioceses ⟨advocating a ~ system⟩ **d :** being the seat of the bishop of a diocese ⟨a ~ city⟩ **2 a :** governing a diocese ⟨powers possessed by virtue of his position as ~ bishop⟩ **b :** entrusted with ecclesiastical enactments or discipline, administrative business, or missions of a diocese ⟨canons enacted at a ~ convention⟩ ⟨the bishop convokes a ~ synod⟩ **3 :** maintained by or serving a diocese ⟨attended ~ schools⟩ ⟨~ visitor to religious communities⟩
²diocesan \"\ *n* -s [ME, fr. ML *diocesanus*, fr. *diocesanus*, adj.] **1 :** a bishop having jurisdiction over a diocese **2** *archaic* **:** one of the clergy or the people of a diocese ⟨humble ~*s* of the old bishop⟩
diocesan conference *n* **:** a body in the Anglican communion that consists of all the clergy of a diocese and of elected representatives of the laity and that under the presidency of the bishop transacts certain diocesan business — called also *diocesan convention*
diocesan court *n* **:** CONSISTORY 6
diocesan curate *n* **1 :** a clergyman of the Church of Ireland at the disposal of the bishop to give help in emergencies to parish clergy **2 :** an assistant priest to a pastor appointed by the bishop of a diocese
di·o·cese \ˈdīəsəs *also* -ə,sēz *or* -ə,sēs *sometimes* -ə,sis\ *n, pl* **dioces·es** \-əsəsəz, -ə,sēzəz, -ə,sēsəz, ÷ -ə,sēz *sometimes* -ə,sisəz *or* ÷ dīˈäsəsēz\ [ME *diocise*, fr. MF *diocese, diocise*, fr. LL *diocesis*, alter. of *dioecesis*, fr. L, administrative division of a country, fr. Gk *dioikēsis* administrative division of a country, administration, fr. *dioikein* to keep house, administer, govern (fr. *dia* through + *oikein* to have one's dwelling place, keep house, fr. *oikos* house) + *-sis* — more at DIA-, VICINITY] **1 a :** the circuit or extent of a bishop's jurisdiction **:** the district in which a bishop has ecclesiastical authority — compare EPARCHY **b :** sphere of authority **2 :** an administrative division of a country; *esp* **:** a division of a prefecture of the Roman Empire
diocesian *obs var of* DIOCESAN
diocess *obs var of* DIOCESE
di·o·coel \ˈdīə,sēl\ *n* -s [prob. alter. of *diacoele*] **:** the cavity of the developing diencephalon that later gives rise to the third ventricle of the brain
di·octahedral \(ˌ)dī+\ *adj* [*di-* + *octahedral*] **1 :** having 16 faces; *esp* **:** octahedral with tetrahedral summits **2 :** having two of the three available octahedrally coordinated positions occupied ⟨a ~ mica⟩
di·oc·to·phy·ma \(,)dī,äktəˈfīmə\ *n* [NL, fr. *diocto-* (irreg. fr. Gk *dionkoun* to distend) + *-phyma* (fr. Gk *phyma* tumor)] *syn of* DIOCTOPHYME
di·oc·to·phy·ma·ti·na \-,fīməˈtīnə\ *n pl, cap* [NL, fr. *Dioctophymat-, Dioctophyma* + *-ina*] **:** a suborder of Enoplida (being sometimes considered a separate order and including solely the kidney parasite (*Dioctophyme renale*) distinguished from related nematodes by the absence of both setae and buccal stylet — compare DORYLAIMINA, ENOPLINA
di·oc·to·phy·me \-ˈfī(,)mē\ *n, cap* [NL, fr. *diocto-* (irreg. fr. Gk *dionkoun* to distend, fr. *dia-* + *onkoun* to raise, distend, fr. *onkos* bulk, mass) + *-phyme* (fr. Gk *phyma* tumor, fr. Gk *phyein* to bring forth, grow); akin to Gk *enenkein* to carry — more at ENOUGH, BE] **:** a genus (coextensive with a family Dioctophymidae) of nematode worms including a single form (*D. renale*) which is a destructive parasite of the kidney of dogs, other mammals, and occas. man — see DIOCTOPHYMATINA
di·octyl \(ˈ)dī+\ *adj* [ISV *di-* + *octyl*] **:** containing two octyl groups in the molecule
dioctyl phthalate *n* **:** an oily liquid ester $C_6H_4(COOC_8H_{17})_2$ used chiefly as a plasticizer; bis-(2-ethyl-hexyl) phthalate
di·ode \ˈdī,ōd\ *n* -s [ISV *di-* + *-ode*] **1 :** an electron tube having two electrodes, a cathode and an anode **2 :** an electrical rectifier that consists of a semiconducting crystal (as of germanium or silicon) with two terminals and that is analogous in use to an electron tube diode — called also *crystal diode*
di·o·dia \dīˈōdēə\ *n, cap* [NL, fr. Gk *diodos* thoroughfare (fr. *dia-* + *hodos* way) + NL *-ia;* fr. the frequent growth of these plants by the wayside — more at CEDE] **:** a genus of mostly American weedy herbs of the family Rubiaceae with opposite leaves and small tubular solitary axillary flowers — see BUTTONWEED 1
di·odon \ˈdīə,dän\ *n, cap* [NL, fr. *di-* + *-odon*] **:** the type genus of Diodontidae comprising the typical porcupine fishes — **di·odont** \-,dänt\ *adj or n*
di·o·done \-,dōn\ *n* -s [irreg. fr. *diiod-* + *pyridone*] **:** IODOPYRACET
di·odon·ti·dae \,⸗⸗ˈdäntə,dē\ *n pl, cap* [NL, fr. *Diodont-, Diodon*, type genus + *-idae*] **:** a family of blocky to nearly spherical plectognath fishes that live in warm shallow seas and have the body covered with spines and the teeth fused into a cutting plate in each jaw —see PORCUPINE FISH
Di·o·do·quin \ˈdīˈōdəkwən\ *trademark* — used for diiodohydroxyquinoline
di·o·do·re·an \,dīə,dōrēən, -dōr-\ *adj, usu cap* [*Diodorus* Cronus, 4th cent. B.C. Greek philosopher (Megarian school) + E *-ean*] **:** of or relating to the Megarian philosopher Diodorus Cronus or his contributions to modal logic
Di·o·drast \ˈdīə,drast\ *trademark* — used for iodopyracet
di·oe·cia \dīˈēsh(ē)ə\ *n, pl, cap* [NL, fr. *di-* + *-oecia*] *in former classifications* **:** a class of plants including those having staminate and pistillate flowers on different individuals
di·oe·cian \(ˈ)dīˈēshən\ *adj* [NL *Dioecia* + E *-an*] **:** DIOECIOUS
dioecio- *comb form* [*dioecious*] **:** dioeciously ⟨*dioeciodimorphous*⟩ ⟨*dioeciopolygamous*⟩
di·oe·cious \(ˈ)dīˈēshəs\ *adj* [NL *Dioecia* + E *-ous*] **1 :** having the male reproductive organs in one individual and the female in another — compare DICLINOUS **2** *of a seed plant* **:** having staminate and pistillate flowers borne on different individuals — **di·oe·cious·ly** *adv*
di·oe·cism \dīˈē,sizəm\ *n* -s [ISV *dioec-* (fr. NL *Dioecia*) + *-ism*] **:** the condition of being dioecious
di·oe·cy \dīˈēsē\ *n* -ES [ISV *dioec-* (fr. NL *Dioecia*) + *-y*] **:** DIOECISM
dioestrous *or* **dioestrual** *var of* DIESTROUS
dioestrus *or* **dioestrum** *var of* DIESTRUS
di·og·e·ne·an \(ˌ)dīˌäjəˈnēən\ *or* **di·o·gen·ic** \ˌdīəˈjenik\ *adj, usu cap* [*Diogenes* †323 B.C. Greek philosopher + E *-ean* or *-ic*] **:** characteristic of, attributed to, or associated with the philosopher Diogenes
di·og·e·nes crab \dīˈäjə(,)nēz-\ *n, usu cap D* [so called fr. its habit of living in an empty shell as Diogenes is reputed to have lived in a tub] **:** a terrestrial hermit crab (*Cenobita diogenes*) abundant in the West Indies and destructive to crops
di·og·e·nite \-,nīt\ *n* -s [G *diogenit*, fr. Gk *diogenēs* born of or descended from Zeus (fr. *Di-*, *Zeus* Zeus, god of the sky + *-genēs* born) + G *-it* -ite — more at DEITY, -GEN] **:** an achondritic meteorite composed essentially of orthopyroxene
-di·o·ic \ˌdīˈōik, -ōek\ *adj suffix* [ISV *di-* + *-oic*] **:** containing two carboxyl groups in place of two methyl groups ⟨hexane*dioic* acid $HOOC(CH_2)_4COOH$⟩
di·oi·cous \(ˈ)dīˈóikəs\ *adj* [NL *dioicus*, fr. *di-* + *-oicus* (fr. Gk *oikos* house) — more at VICINITY] **:** having archegonia and antheridia on separate plants — compare DIOECIOUS, HETEROICOUS, MONOICOUS, PAROICOUS, SYNOICOUS
di·ol \ˈdī,ól, -ōl\ *n* -s [ISV *-diol*] **:** a chemical compound (as a glycol) containing two hydroxyl groups
-di·ol \"\ *n suffix* -s [ISV *di-* + *-ol* (alcohol)] **:** chemical compound containing two hydroxyl groups ⟨1,5-pentane*diol*⟩
di·olefin *also* **di·olefine** \(ˈ)dī+\ *n* -s [ISV *di-* + *olefin*] **:** any of a series of aliphatic hydrocarbons C_nH_{2n-2} (as allene, butadiene, isoprene) containing two double bonds — called also *alkadiene, diene* — **di·olefinic** \(ˌ)dī+\ *adj*
di·o·ma·te \,dēəˈmäd·ē\ *n* -s [AmerSp] **:** GATEADO
di·o·me·dea \,dīəˈmēdēə\ *n, cap* [NL, prob. fr. L, fem. of *diomedeus* of Diomedes, fr. *Diomedes* (fr. Gk *Diomēdēs*), mythical or legendary Greek warrior; prob. fr. the story that Diomedes' companions were turned into birds in Italy after his return from the Trojan War] **:** a genus of albatrosses
di·o·me·de·idae \,dīəməˈdīə,dē, -ˈmēdē-\ *n pl, cap* [NL, fr. *Diomedea*, type genus + *-idae*] **:** a family of large sea birds (order Procellariiformes) comprising the albatrosses
-di·one \ˈdī,ōn\ *n suffix* -s [ISV *di-* + *-one*] **:** chemical compound containing two carbonyl groups — in names of diketones or di-oxo compounds that are not true diketones ⟨butane*dione*⟩ ⟨2,6-piperidine-*dione*⟩
di·o·nin \ˈdīənən\ *or* **di·o·nine** \-,nēn, -,nən\ *n* -s [G *dionin*, a former trademark] **:** ethylmorphine or its hydrochloride
dionise *n* -s [ME *diones*, fr. MF *dionise*, fr. L *dionysias*, fr. Gk, fr. *Dionysus*, fr. *Dionysos* Dionysus] *obs* **:** a precious stone dark with red streaks reputed when dissolved in water to prevent drunkenness
di·o·ny·sia \,dīəˈnizh(ē)ə, -nish(ē)ə, -nisēə\ *n pl, usu cap* [L, fr. Gk, fr. neut. pl. of *dionysios* of Dionysus, fr. *Dionysos* Dionysus, god of an orgiastic religion and of wine] **:** any of the Greek religious festivals held in honor of Dionysus esp. in Attica: as **a :** the lesser festival which was held in the autumn and from which the Greek drama is said to have originated **b :** the great festival which was held in the spring and at which plays were regularly given from the time of Pisistratus — compare BACCHANALIA 1
di·o·nys·i·ac \,dīəˈnisē,ak *also* -nī| *or* |zē-\ *also* **di·o·ny·si·a·cal** \-nəˈsīəkəl, -,nīˈ-; ,dīəˈnisēˈakəl, -nī|, |zē-\ *or* **di·o·ny·sic** \,dīəˈnisik, -nis-\ *adj* [*dionysiac* fr. LL *dionysiacus*, fr. Gk *dionysiakos*, fr. *Dionysia; dionysiacal* fr. LL *dionysiacus* + E *-al; dionysic* fr. L *Dionysus* (fr. Gk *Dionysos*) + E *-ic*] **1** *usu cap* **:** relating to the Greek mythical god Dionysus or the Dionysia ⟨in the cruder of *Dionysiac* mysteries the devotees drank of the fruit of the vine —K.S.Latourette⟩ **2** *often cap* **:** DIONYSIAN 2b ⟨the ~ rapture, . . . gives place to Apolline serenity —Hunter Mead⟩ ⟨the ~ character of hot jazz —R.L. Shayon⟩ — **di·o·ny·si·a·cal·ly** \ˌdīənəˈsīək(ə)lē, -,nīˈ-; ,dīəˈnisēˈakəlē, -nī|, |zē-\ *adv, often cap*
di·o·nys·i·an *in sense 1* \ˌdīəˈnisēən, *in sense 2* -nizhən *or* -nishən *or* -nīsēən\ *adj* [in sense 1, fr. *Dionysius* (personal name) + E *-an;* in sense 2, fr. L *Dionysia* + E *-an*] **1** *usu cap* **a** [*Dionysius* the Elder †367 B.C. Greek tyrant and his son *Dionysius* the Younger *fl* 345 B.C. Greek tyrant] **:** of or relating to the elder or the younger Dionysius ⟨*Dionysian* cruelty⟩ **b** [*Dionysius* Exiguus, 6th cent. Roman monk and scholar born in Scythia who introduced the method of reckoning the Christian era from the supposed date of the birth of Christ] **:** of or relating to Dionysius Exiguus ⟨the ~ period of 532 years after which the moon's changes recur on the same days of the week and month⟩ **c** [*Dionysius* the Areopagite *fl* A.D. 500 Greek author of *The Celestial Hierarchy* and other Neoplatonic Christian works that greatly influenced medieval thought] **:** of or relating to Dionysius the Areopagite **2 a** *usu cap* **:** devoted to the worship of the god Dionysus or connected with the Dionysia **:** DIONYSIAC 1 ⟨the Eleusinian, the *Dionysian*, and the Orphic rites were the most important mystery religions of Greece —G.E.Mylonas⟩ ⟨the most radical departure from the rationalistic interpretation of life and history is to be found in the *Dionysian* religious tradition —Reinhold Niebuhr⟩ **b** *usu cap* [trans. of G *dionysisch*] **:** of a character symbolized by the god Dionysus or the cult of his myth and worship: (1) **:** of a sensuous, frenzied, orgiastic, or Bacchic character **:** unbounded, lawless, or irrational in nature — contrasted with *Apollonian* ⟨Nietzsche had used the terms *Dionysian* and Apollonian to separate the creative-passionate from the critical-rational —J.M.Barzun⟩ ⟨the *Dionysian* experience, our ecstatic participation in the divine life —Sheldon Cheney⟩ (2) **:** pregnant with strength **:** creatively striving **:** PASSIONATE **:** FAUSTIAN ⟨the unleashed fury of *Dionysian* dynamics, —C.H.Cardinal⟩
di·oön \ˈdīˈō,än\ *n, cap* [NL, fr. *di-* + *-oön* (fr. Gk *ōion* egg) — more at EGG] **:** a genus of plants (family Cycadaceae) having a somewhat conical trunk crowned by a large tuft of pinnate leaves with spine-tipped pinnae
di·o·phan·tine \,dīəˈfantən, -an-,tīn\ *adj, usu cap* [*Diophantus*, 3d cent. A.D. Greek mathematician of Alexandria + E *-ine*] **:** of or relating to Diophantus
diophantine equation *n, usu cap D* **:** a polynomial equation for which the unknowns are to be rational numbers
di·op·side \dīˈäp,sīd, -,səd\ *n* -s [F, irreg. fr. *di-* + Gk *opsis* appearance, sight — more at OPTIC] **:** a pyroxene $CaMgSi_2O_6$ that contains calcium and magnesium but little or no aluminum, that varies in color from white to green, and that when transparent is sometimes used in jewelry — **di·op·sid·ic** \ˌdī,äpˈsidik\ *adj*
di·op·sis \dīˈäpsəs\ *n, cap* [NL, fr. *di-* + *-opsis*] **:** a genus of two-winged flies (group Acalyptrata) of the Old World tropics having the head produced into long lateral club-shaped projections bearing the antennae and eyes
di·op·tase \dīˈäp,tās, -āz\ *n* -s [F, prob. fr. LGk *dioptos* transparent (fr. Gk *dia-* + *optos* visible, fr. *opsesthai* to be going to see) + F *-ase* (as in *euclase*) — more at OPTIC] **:** a mineral $CuSiO_2(OH)_2$ consisting of hydrous copper silicate and occurring in emerald-green crystals and massive (hardness 5, sp. gr. 3.47)
di·op·ter \dīˈäptər, ˈdī,ä-\ *n* -s [MF & L; MF *dioptre*, fr. L *dioptra*, fr. Gk, fr. *dia-* + *-optra* (akin to *opsesthai* to be going to see)] **1** *obs* **:** an optical instrument invented by Hipparchus for taking altitudes and leveling **2** *archaic* **:** a stand or disk revolving about a vertical axis and carrying a lens or prism, leveling sights, or the index arm of a circle according to the kind of instrument to which it was applied **:** ALIDADE **3** *also* **di·op·tre** \"\ **:** a unit of measurement of the refractive power of a lens equal to the reciprocal of the focal length in meters **4 :** an instrument used in craniometry for making projections of the skull
di·op·tom·e·ter \,dī,äpˈtämәd·ə(r)\ *n* -s [*dia-* + *opto-* + *-meter*] **:** an instrument used in measuring the accommodation and refraction of the eye — **di·op·tom·e·try** \-mə·trē\ *n* -ES
di·op·tral \(ˈ)dīˈäptrəl\ *adj* [L *dioptra* + E *-al*] **:** relating to a diopter or to focal power in diopters
di·op·trate \dīˈäp,trāt, -,trət\ *adj* [*dia-* + *optr-* (irreg. fr. Gk *opsesthai* to be going to see) + *-ate*] **:** divided by a transverse line or septum — used of the compound eyes of certain insects (as water beetles) and of ocelli on the wings of certain moths and butterflies
dioptre *var of* DIOPTER
¹di·op·tric \(ˈ)dīˈäptrik\ *also* **di·op·tri·cal** \-rəkəl\ *adj* [*dioptric* fr. Gk *dioptrikos* of an optical instrument used for taking altitudes, fr. *dioptra* + *-ikos* -ic; *dioptrical* fr. Gk *dioptrikos* + E *-al*] **1 a :** that effects or serves in refraction of a beam of light **:** REFRACTIVE; *specif* **:** that assists vision by refracting

and focalizing light ⟨a ~ apparatus formed of ~ prisms⟩ ⟨the ~ mechanism of an insect's eye⟩ ⟨the ~ power of a lens⟩ **b :** produced by means of refraction ⟨the ~ images of objects in space that are formed on the retinas of the two eyes —Otto Glasser⟩ **2** *archaic* **:** TRANSPARENT ⟨discrepancy between the ~ certainty of the understanding and the immediate insight of the conscience —James Martineau⟩ — **di·op·tri·cal·ly** \-rə̇k(ə)lē\ *adv*

²dioptric \"\ *n* -s **:** DIOPTER 1, 3

di·op·trics \dī'äptriks\ *n pl but sing in constr* [trans. of Gk *dioptrika*, neut. pl. of *dioptrikos*] *archaic* **:** a branch of optics dealing with the refraction of light esp. by lenses

di·op·try \'dī,äptrē\ *n* -ES [ISV *dioptr-* (fr. *diopter*) + *-y*] **:** focal power expressed in diopters

di·o·rama \ dīə'ramə, -rämə,-rȧmə\ *n* -s [F, fr. *dia-* + *-orama* (as in *panorama*, fr. E)] **1 a :** a scenic representation in which a partly translucent painting is seen from a distance through an opening, the light shining through the painting being varied to achieve varying effects (as of changes in weather) **b :** a building used for an exhibition of such representations **2 a :** a scenic representation (as of a theatrical stage) in which sculptured figures and lifelike details are displayed usu. in miniature so as to blend indistinguishably with a realistic painted background **b** *chiefly Brit* **:** an imagined succession of brilliant scenes or episodes imperceptibly merging one into another like a pageant in miniature ⟨the style of Macaulay . . . is a ~ of political pictures —Walter Bagehot⟩ **3 a :** a scale model usu. under glass exhibiting with precise detail some phenomenon of nature or the layout of some engineering project ⟨a ~ indicating how a dam and powerhouse will look on completion⟩ **b :** a life-size exhibit of a wildlife specimen or scene mounted in the midst of realistically reproduced natural surroundings merging into a painted background ⟨recessed ~*s* of Colorado wildlife —Catherine L. Barker⟩ **c :** a miniature set used in television to represent a location that cannot be constructed in its actual size in the studio

di·o·ram·ic \¦dīə¦ramik\ *adj* **:** peculiar to or suggesting a diorama

di·ordinal \(')dī+\ *adj* [*di-* + *ordinal*] **:** of or relating to two orders

dioristic *adj* [Gk *dioristikos* capable of distinguishing, fr. *diorizein* to distinguish, delimit, fr. *dia-* + *horizein* to separate, bound, define — more at HORIZON] *obs* **:** serving to distinguish

di·o·rite \'dīə,rīt\ *n* -s [F, irreg. fr. Gk *diorizein* to distinguish + F *-ite*] **:** a granular crystalline igneous rock commonly of acid plagioclase and hornblende, pyroxene, or biotite — **di·o·rit·ic** \¦dīə¦rid·ik\ *adj*

di·or·tho·sis \,dī,ȯr'thōsə̇s\ *n, pl* **diortho·ses** \-ō,sēz\ [NL, fr. Gk *diorthōsis* correction, making straight, fr. *diorthoun* to correct, make straight, fr. *dia-* + *orthoun* to set straight, set upright, fr. *orthos* straight — more at ORTH-] *archaic* **:** a correcting or revision esp. of a text

di·or·thot·ic \¦dī ȯr¦thäd·ik\ *adj* [Gk *diorthōtikos*, fr. *diorthoun*] *archaic* **:** CORRECTIVE

di·os·co·rea \,dīə'skōrēə\ *n* [NL, irreg. fr. Pedanius *Dioscorides*, 1st cent. A.D. Greek physician] **1** *cap* **:** a genus of mostly tropical twining herbs (family Dioscoreaceae) including the yams and having net-veined leaves and small dioecious flowers **2** -s **:** the dried rhizome of a wild yam (*Dioscorea paniculata*) formerly used in hepatic disorders and rheumatism

di·os·co·re·a·ce·ae \,dīə,skōrē'āsē,ē\ *n pl, cap* [NL, fr. *Dioscorea*, type genus + *-aceae*] **:** a family of twining herbs and shrubs (order Liliales) comprising the yams and related plants — see TAMUS

di·os·cu·ric \¦dīə¦skyu̇rik\ *adj* [Gk *Dioskouroi* sons of Zeus, namely the twin heroes or demigods of Greek mythology known in Latin as Castor and Pollux and in Greek as Castor and Polydeuces, sons of Zeus and Leda (fr. *Dios*, gen. of *Zeus* Zeus, god of the sky + *kouroi*, pl. of *kouros*, *koros* boy, son) + E *-ic*; akin to L *crescere* to grow — more at DEITY, CRESCENT] **:** like Castor and Pollux of classical mythology **:** TWIN

di·ose \'dī,ōs *also* -ōz\ *n* -s [*di-* + *-ose*] **:** any of a class of monosaccharides containing two carbon atoms, glycolaldehyde being the only member — called also *biose*

di·os·gen·in \,dī,äz'jenən, dī'äzjən-\ *n* -s [*dios-* (fr. NL *Dioscorea*) + *-genin*] **:** a crystalline steroid sapogenin $C_{27}H_{42}O_3$ obtained chiefly in Mexico from locally available yams and used as a starting material for the synthesis of steroid hormones (as cortisone)

di·os·ma \dī'äzmə\ *n* [NL, irreg. fr. Gk *dios* heavenly + NL *-osma* — more at DEITY] **1** *cap* **:** a small genus of southern African heathlike shrubs of the family Rutaceae with fragrant foliage and small white or pinkish flowers **2** -s **:** any plant of the genus *Diosma* **3** -s **:** BUCHU

di·os·phenol \¦dī,äs+\ *n* -s [ISV *dios-* (fr. *diosma*) + *phenol*; prob. orig. formed in G] **:** a crystalline hydroxy terpenoid ketone $C_{10}H_{16}O_2$ obtained from the essential oil of buchu — called also *buchu camphor*

di·os·py·ros \,dīə'spīrəs\ *n, cap* [NL, fr. L, a plant, prob. gromwell, fr. Gk, fr. *Dios* (gen. of *Zeus*) + *pyros* wheat — more at FURZE] **:** a genus of trees and shrubs (family Ebenaceae) found throughout the warmer parts of the world that have beautiful and valuable wood, leaves alternate and leathery, and fruit a 1- to 10-seeded berry — see EBONY, PERSIMMON

di·otic \(')dī+\ *adj* [*di-* + *-otic*] **:** affecting or relating to the two ears **:** BINAURAL

di·oto·car·dia \(,)dī,ōd·ə'kärdēə\ [NL, fr. *di-* + *oto-* (fr. Gk *ōt-*, *ous* ear, auricle of the heart) + *-cardia* — more at EAR] *syn of* ASPIDOBRANCHIA

di·ovular \(')dī+\ *adj* [*di-* + *ovular*] **:** BIOVULAR

di·ox·ane \dī'äk,sān\ *also* **di·ox·an** \-,san, -sən\ *n* -s [ISV *di-* + *ox-* + *-ane*] **:** a flammable irritating water-soluble liquid cyclic diether $C_4H_8O_2$ obtainable from ethylene glycol and used chiefly as a solvent and dispersing agent — called also *para-dioxane*, *1,4-dioxane*

di·ox·ide \dī'äk,sīd, -sə̇d\ *n* [ISV *di-* + *oxide*] **:** an oxide containing two atoms of oxygen in the molecule — usu. distinguished from *peroxide* ⟨carbon ~⟩ ⟨manganese ~⟩

di·ox·o·lane \dī'äksə,lān\ *n* -s [*dioxol* chemical compound having the formula $C_3H_4O_2$ (ISV *di-* + *ox-* + *-ol*) + *-ane*] **1 :** a water-soluble liquid cyclic acetal $C_3H_6O_2$ made usu. from formaldehyde and ethylene glycol that is capable of polymerizing to poly-acetal resins having essentially the open-chain structure $(-OCH_2OCH_2CH_2-)_x$ — called also *1,3-dioxolane* **2 :** a derivative of dioxolane made usu. by reaction of an aldehyde or ketone with formaldehyde, many such derivatives being capable of polymerizing to useful products (as supports for photographic emulsions)

dioxy- *comb form* [ISV *di-* + *oxy-*] **:** containing two oxy groups

¹dip \'dip\ *vb* **dipped** *also archaic* **dipt**; **dipped** *also archaic* **dipt**; **dipping**; **dips** [ME *dippen*, fr. OE *dyppan*; akin to LG *düppen* to wash, OHG *tupfen* to wash, OIr *domain* deep, Lith *dubus* deep, hollow] *vt* **1 a :** to thrust, plunge, or slip momentarily or partially under the surface of a liquid or an adhesive substance so as to moisten, drench, cool, color, or coat **:** IMMERSE, SOUSE, DUCK ⟨ate clams *dipping* each in melted butter⟩ ⟨*dipped* my arms and face in the water trough⟩ ⟨the small parts are *dipped* in a primer paint —John Kobler⟩ **b :** to alter or move in a way to suggest immersion or the effect of immersion in a liquid ⟨you have constantly to ~ your hand in your pocket⟩ **2 a** *archaic* **:** to immerse in baptizing **b** *obs* **:** to wet as if by immersing ⟨a cold shuddering dew ~*s* me all over —John Milton⟩ **3 a :** to color by dipping (as in a dye) **b :** to make (a candle) by repeated immersion of a wick in melted fat or wax **c :** to immerse (as a sheep or hog) in an antiseptic or parasiticidal solution (as for the cure of the itch) **d :** to rub (snuff) on the teeth and gums with a brush or stick **e :** to immerse (candies) for the purpose of coating **4 :** to lift a portion of by reaching below the surface with an open utensil or something shaped to hold liquid **:** LADLE ⟨the cook *dipped* our soup from the kettle⟩ ⟨men who ~ ore out of freighters with an electric shovel⟩ **5** *Brit* **a** *archaic* **:** INVOLVE, IMPLICATE ⟨*dipt* in the rebellion —John Dryden⟩ **b :** MORTGAGE **c :** to involve in financial difficulty ⟨she was *dipped* as badly as her father —John Galsworthy⟩ **6 a :** to lower and then raise again ⟨put the helm alee and ~ the sail⟩ **b :** to haul (an ensign) part way down and then raise again in salute ⟨merchant ships salute each other by *dipping* the flag⟩ **c :** to swing (a signal flag) from vertical to somewhat below horizontal and then back to vertical **d :** to lower or cause to drop down somewhat and usu. temporarily ⟨he had to ~ his head to enter the cave⟩ ⟨*dipping* his chin into his muffler⟩ **e** *chiefly Brit* **:** to dim or lower the beam of (automobile headlights) ~ *vi* **1 a :** to immerse oneself **:** plunge into a liquid and quickly emerge ⟨the ship's bow *dipped* gently into the wave⟩ ⟨the sound of oars *dipping* rhythmically⟩ ⟨after the rain the ruts *dipped* in and out of the puddles —Helen B. Woodward⟩ ⟨the whale *dipped* playfully under the waves⟩ **b :** to immerse something into a processing liquid or finishing material ⟨waterproofing the surface of bisque ware is done in the *dipping* house⟩ **2 a :** to descend rather sharply **:** drop a slight distance ⟨the sun *dipped* at that moment below the horizon⟩ ⟨in Michigan three small tornadoes *dipped* to the ground, leveling barns —Seth King⟩ ⟨I saw purple martins pairing, *dipping*, and swooping —E.A. Weeks⟩ ⟨that the familiar prose ~*s* into the ordinary —E.T. Williams⟩ **b :** to make an abrupt slight downward movement ⟨we would one day enter to look round, ~ over the hill, and push the gate to the locked garden —G.W.Stonier⟩ ⟨fine brows *dipping* down with annoyance —Harriet La Barre⟩: *also* **:** to bring about a lowering of something ⟨salutes of the ensign are made by *dipping* —H.A.Calahan⟩ **c** (1) *of an ensign* **:** to become dipped ⟨regimental colors do ~ in salute —Elbridge Colby⟩ (2) *of a ship* **:** to dip its ensign **d :** to extend downward or below the surface ⟨branches that ~ in the water⟩ **e** *of a plane* **:** to drop suddenly before climbing **f :** to veer sharply ⟨the road follows the irregular shoreline and ~*s* back occasionally into the wooded hill country —*Amer. Guide Series: Minn.*⟩ **g :** to perform a dip in dancing **h :** to perform the gymnastic exercise constituting a dip **i :** to decline moderately and usu. temporarily ⟨prices *dipped* to a lower level before recovering⟩ ⟨commodity markets *dipped* but losses were not extensive —*Wall Street Jour.*⟩ **3 a :** to reach down inside or below a surface esp. for the purpose of withdrawing a part of the contents ⟨he *dipped* into the pocket and drew out a mixed collection —Dorothy Sayers⟩ ⟨one crane *dipped* five decks deep into No. 2 hold where the cars were carried —Vernon Pizer⟩ **b :** to appropriate a portion of some intangible ⟨that she had *dipped* in the wells of blissful oblivion —George Meredith⟩ ⟨not aware that in unjust suspicion a man ~*s* into himself for the colors he is painting —Francis Hackett⟩ **c :** to make an inroad for funds — used with *into* ⟨temptation of *dipping* into the public treasury to please constituents —Herbert Koshetz⟩ **d :** to dip snuff **4 a :** to make a slight or cursory subjective excursion **:** delve casually, aimlessly, or tentatively here and there — usu. used with *into* ⟨having *dipped* into the past we turn to the present⟩ ⟨the novel digressing here ~*s* into a bit of maudlin sentimentality⟩ ⟨I *dipped* into philosophy⟩ **b :** to read by sampling random disconnected passages or in the manner of browsing ⟨an ideal volume for *dipping* —B.R.Redman⟩ — usu. used with *into*; distinguished from *skim* ⟨it is a better book to ~ into than to read from cover to cover —Jane G. Mahler⟩ **c :** to explore or sample briefly or tentatively ⟨warily *dipping* into the possibilities of clairvoyance and telepathy⟩ **5 :** to incline downward **:** have a downward slant ⟨his landing lights *dipped* into the blackness and then *dipped* more steeply —Ira Wolfert⟩: **a :** to tilt or slope downward from the horizontal ⟨at this point in the trail land began to ~ the other way⟩ ⟨a forested cliff ~*s* steeply to the shore⟩ **b** *geol* **:** to incline downward from the plane of the horizon ⟨underlying the area are sedimentary rocks *dipping* gently eastward —M.A.Clement⟩ ⟨frequently, however, coal seams ~ steeply —H.R.Cox⟩ **c :** to tip downward ⟨the magnetic needle ~*s* in the direction of the earth's magnetism⟩ **d :** to take a course downgrade **:** have a downward pitch ⟨the narrow highway ~*s* and ascends like a crazy roller coaster —*Amer. Guide Series: Conn.*⟩ **6 :** to engage in reaching down and lifting out something from a liquid ⟨the whey that separates from the curd before *dipping*⟩ ⟨*dipping* on the turpentine plantation begins about April first⟩ **7** *archaic* **:** DIB

syn DIP, IMMERSE, SUBMERGE, DUCK, SOUSE, and DUNK may mean to plunge a thing into water or other liquid or may apply to any figurative action suggesting this. DIP implies a momentary or partial plunging or a cursory or short-lived looking or entering into (as into a subject) ⟨*dip* a finger in water⟩ ⟨*dip* a collar in starch⟩ ⟨*dip* into archaeology⟩ ⟨to *dip* into a doorway for a moment⟩ IMMERSE implies a total covering with liquid or an total engrossing or engaging (as in a study) ⟨*immerse* the clothes in a solution of dye⟩ ⟨become *immersed* in the study of history⟩ SUBMERGE implies total and often prolonged immersion or a sinking to a low level, grade, or status ⟨a barren, low-lying plain often partially *submerged* by the Mississippi —*Amer. Guide Series: Minn.*⟩ ⟨a boat *submerged* in four feet of water⟩ ⟨personality has been *submerged* by organization on all sides —W.P.Webb⟩ ⟨the older agrarian simplicity of New England was being *submerged* by the industrial revolution —V.L.Parrington⟩ ⟨the *submerged* lower classes⟩ DUCK implies a sudden plunging and withdrawal ⟨*duck* your head under water⟩ ⟨while he *ducks* into the doctor's office and back out again —*Advertising Age*⟩ ⟨*duck* under a low doorway⟩ SOUSE stresses a thorough soaking or can apply, figuratively, to any kind of saturating and, popularly, to intoxication ⟨she *soused* her hands in disinfectant before she touched him —*New Yorker*⟩ ⟨after being *soused* in the Atlantic ocean —T.B.Aldrich⟩ ⟨they ought to have *soused* the conscience in repentance or good resolutions —*Times Lit. Supp.*⟩ ⟨he hurries to *souse* himself in cheap red wine —*Time*⟩ DUNK applies to the dipping and soaking of something (as a doughnut) in a beverage; in extension, it is similar to DIP, DUCK, or IMMERSE ⟨*dunk* toast in her tea⟩ ⟨men dangling from lines, being *dunked* in the cold sea as the ship rolled —P.B.Cronk⟩

— **dip one's fingers into :** to obtrude oneself into participation in

²dip \"\ *n* -s **1 :** an act of dipping: as **a :** a brief immersion ⟨gaining a little with every ~ of the oars⟩ ⟨an earthenware cup ready for a ~ in the glaze tub⟩; *specif* **:** a plunge into the water for sport or exercise ⟨guests lingered on the beach, gossiping . . . and taking ~*s* —Alec Waugh⟩ ⟨either take ~*s* in little side eddies or hug the banks and wade in timidly —John Mason Brown⟩ **b :** a casual or experimental delving into a book or subject ⟨~*s* into heraldry⟩; *also* **:** a transient experimental or tentative excursion ⟨his early ~ into politics⟩ ⟨it is a Victorian-type novel, loosely constructed, with ~*s* into sentimentality —Ruth Suckow⟩ **c** *archaic* **:** CURTSY **d :** a reaching down into for withdrawing a portion ⟨a ~ in the punch bowl⟩ ⟨a ~ into the president's emergency fund⟩ **e :** a lowering in position ⟨a flag salute is one ~ of the ensign —C.D.Lane⟩ ⟨a ~ of a wigwag signal flag to the right indicates a dot⟩ **f :** a moderate decrease ⟨a 3 percent ~ in the claims for unemployment compensation⟩ ⟨how to account for ~*s* in his popularity⟩ ⟨tonight's forecast is for a ~ to 33°⟩; *specif* **:** a moderate and usu. temporary decline (as in prices or revenue) ⟨predictions of a business ~⟩ ⟨a sharper-than-seasonal production ~⟩ **g :** a gymnastics exercise on the end of the parallel bars in which the performer, resting on his hands, lets his arms bend until his chin is level with the bars and then raises himself by straightening his arms **h** (1) **:** a ballroom step in which the dancer bends one knee slightly and extends the other leg forward or backward (2) **:** a square-dance step in which the dancer bends forward and passes under an arch **2 :** inclination downward: **a :** downward slope, turn, or sag **:** divergence downward from the horizontal **:** PITCH ⟨the ~ of the lines from ship to pier⟩; *also* **:** decline from a level (as of performance) ⟨her graph of accomplishment was destined for a downward ~ —*Saturday Rev.*⟩ **b :** a sharp downward course or tilting ⟨a sudden ~ and rise out of a dingle —*Amer. Guide Series: Conn.*⟩ ⟨plotting the ~ of the indicator of a pressure gauge⟩ **c :** the angle that a stratum, sheet, vein, fissure, fault, or similar geological feature makes with a horizontal plane as measured in a plane normal to the strike **d :** position of an ensign hoisted part way to the yardarm or other point of hoist ⟨on the order "fox at the dip" the code flag for the letter *f* was hoisted two thirds of the way⟩ **e :** an abrupt but curved lowering of the belly of an archery bow on each side of the handle **3 a :** the vertical angle contained between the sensible horizon and a line to the visible horizon at sea, the latter because of the convexity of the earth's surface and the elevation of the observer being below the former **b :** the angle formed with the horizon by a magnetic needle free to rotate in the vertical plane of the magnetic meridian that is 0° at the magnetic equator and 90° at the magnetic poles — called also *inclination* **4 :** depth of submergence (as of a ship, oar, paddle wheel) **5 a :** a low spot with rather steeply sloping sides; *esp* **:** a hollow among hills or a gap in a ridge **b :** a pronounced depression in a surface or path ⟨the ~ that was destined to be the bed of Lake Superior —*Amer. Guide Series: Minn.*⟩; *specif* **:** a sharp depression in a highway at the point of crossing of a dry stream bed found chiefly in the western states **6 :** something obtained by or used in dipping: **a :** a candle made by repeated dippings of a wick in a fat or wax **b :** a stick or frayed twig dampened and used for dipping tobacco snuff ⟨with a snuff ~ in her mouth⟩ **c :** a portion dipped at one time ⟨writing steadily, one ~ of ink after another⟩ ⟨a double ~ of ice cream⟩; *specif* **:** as much snuff as clings to a dip at one dipping **d :** the viscid exudation constituting crude turpentine dipped from incisions in certain pine trees — compare SCRAPE 5 **7 :** a liquid or semiliquid flavoring or savory sauce into which solid food is dipped or which is served esp. on a dessert or on pie ⟨whip up chive cream cheese into a ~ for potato chips⟩ ⟨a ~ of sweetened cream on cobbler⟩ **8 a :** a liquid preparation into which objects may be dipped or immersed (as for cleansing, coloring, staining, or coating) ⟨a varnish ~ serves to bind the whole unit together —*Purchasing News*⟩; *specif* **:** an insecticide or parasiticide for use in a dipping tank **b :** a vat or tank in which such a dip is used ⟨a U-shaped sheep ~ with a 30-foot swim⟩ **c :** a moistening and flavoring solution through which some tobaccos are drawn **9** *slang* **:** PICKPOCKET **10 :** DIPHEAD **11** *slang* **:** a man's hat **12 :** a receptacle from which the contents may be dipped ⟨individual salt ~*s*⟩ **13** *Brit* **:** a small opening covered by a hinged flap in the floorboards of a theatrical stage for plugging leads into electric cables underneath

di·par·tite \(')dī¦pär,tīt, -pȧ| *also* |d·,īt; *usu* -īd· +V\ *adj* [*di-* + L *partitus*, past part. of *partire*, *partiri* to divide — more at PART] **:** separated into parts **:** DIVIDED — **di·partition** \¦dī + \ *n* -s

dip circle *n* **1 :** an inclinometer (sense 1) whose indications depend on a magnetized needle **2 :** DIP NEEDLE 2

¹dipcoat \'⸗,⸗\ *n* [²*dip* + *coat*, n.] **:** a vaporproof and waterproof coating applied over a wrapped container or item by dipping in molten wax

²dipcoat \"\ *vt* [²*dip* + *coat*, v.] **:** to coat by complete immersion in a proofing or finishing material

dip–dye \'⸗,⸗\ *vt* **1 :** to dye (knit goods) after knitting **2 :** to dye (furs) by completely immersing in the dye bath — compare TIP

di·pentene \(')dī+\ *n* [ISV *di-* + *pentene*] **:** a liquid terpene hydrocarbon $C_{10}H_{16}$ found in many essential oils (as Levant wormseed oil), usu. obtained along with other terpenoids from certain turpentines, and used chiefly as a solvent and dispersing agent (as for resins and varnishes); *dl*-limonene — called also *cajeputene*

di·pep·ti·dase \dī'peptə,dās, -āz\ *n* -s [ISV *dipeptide* + *-ase*] **:** any of various enzymes (as in yeast, kidney, and malt) that hydrolyze dipeptides but not polypeptides

di·peptide \(')dī+\ *n* [ISV *di-* + *peptide*; prob. orig. formed as G *dipeptid*] **:** a peptide that yields two molecules of amino acid on hydrolysis

di·pet·a·lo·ne·ma \(,)dī,ped·ᵊlō'nēmə\ *n, cap* [NL, fr. *di-* + *petal-* + *-nema*] **:** a genus of tropical filarial worms whose adults occur in connective tissue and skin of man and apes and monkeys and whose microfilariae occur in their blood — see DIPETALONEMATIDAE

di·pet·a·lo·ne·mat·i·dae \-ᵊl(,)ōnə'mad·ə,dē\ *n pl, cap* [NL, fr. *Dipetalonemat-*, *Dipetalonema*, type genus + *-idae*] **:** a family of filarial worms distinguished from Filariidae by possession of slender larvae with no anterior spines and including most filarial worms parasitic in man and domestic animals

di·pet·al·ous \(')dī¦ped·ᵊləs\ *adj* [NL *dipetalus*, fr. *di-* + *-petalus* -petalous] **:** having two petals

di pet·to \dē'ped·(,)ō\ *adv* (*or adj*) [It] **:** from the chest — used of the natural singing voice; compare FALSETTO

dip fault *n* **:** a geologic fault whose trend is at right angles to the strike

dip–grained \'⸗¦⸗\ *adj*, *of wood* **:** having undulations in the fibers such as occur around knots

di·phase \'dī + ,-\ *adj* **1 :** having two phases **2 :** TWO-PHASE

di·phasic \(')dī+\ *adj* [ISV *di-* + *phase* + *-ic*] **:** DIPHASE

diphead \'⸗,⸗\ *also* **dipheading** \'⸗,⸗⸗\ *n* **:** a drift inclined along the dip of a coal seam

di·phen·an \dī'fenən\ *n* -s [*di-* + *phen-* + *-an*] **:** a crystalline ester $C_6H_5CH_2C_6H_4OOCNH_2$ administered in the treatment of pinworms; *para*-benzyl-phenyl carbamate

di·phen·hydramine \¦dī,fen+\ *n* [*di-* + *phen-* + *hydr-* + *amine*] **:** a white crystalline amine $(C_6H_5)_2CHOCH_2CH_2N(CH_3)_2$ used in the form of its hydrochloride to treat allergy symptoms

di·phenol \(')dī+\ *n* [ISV *di-* + *phenol*] **:** a chemical compound containing two phenolic hydroxyl groups (as pyrocatechol and resorcinol)

¹di·phenyl \(')dī+\ *adj* [ISV *di-* + *phenyl*] **:** containing two phenyl groups in the molecule

²diphenyl \"\ *n* **:** BIPHENYL — used chiefly commercially

diphenylamine \(¦)⸗¦⸗⸗ + *pronunc at* AMINE\ *n* [ISV *diphenyl*, adj. + *amine*] **:** a crystalline pleasant-smelling compound $(C_6H_5)_2NH$ made usu. by heating aniline with aniline hydrochloride and used chiefly in the manufacture of dyes and in stabilizing explosives

di·phen·yl·amine·chlor·ar·sine \"+,klōr'är,sēn, -sən\ *n* [*diphenylamine* + *chlor-* + *arsine*] **:** ADAMSITE

diphenyl black base *n*, *often cap D & both Bs* **:** a crystalline diamine $C_6H_5NHC_6H_4NH_2$ — see DYE table I (under *Oxidation Base 2*)

di·phen·yl·chlo·ro·ar·sine \(¦)⸗¦⸗⸗+,klōrō'är,sēn, -sən\ *also* **di·phen·yl·chlor·ar·sine** \+,klōr'är-\ *n* [*diphenyl* + *chlor-* + *arsine*] **:** a colorless crystalline arsenical $(C_6H_5)_2AsCl$ used during World War I esp. by the Germans for producing a toxic smoke causing sneezing and vomiting

diphenyl dye *n*, *often cap 1st D* **:** any of numerous direct dyes — see DYE table I

di·phen·yl·en·im·ine \(,)dī,fenᵊl,ē'nimən\ *n* **:** CARBAZOLE

diphenyl ether *n* **1 :** PHENYL ETHER **2 :** an ether containing two phenoxy groups

di·phen·yl·guanidine \(,)⸗,⸗⸗+\ *n* [*diphenyl* + *guanidine*] **:** a crystalline compound $(C_6H_5NH)_2C{=}NH$ made by reaction of aniline and cyanogen chloride and used as an accelerator of vulcanization — called also *1,3-diphenylguanidine*

di·phen·yl·hydantoin \"+\ *n* [*diphenyl* + *hydantoin*] **:** a crystalline compound $C_{15}H_{12}N_2O_2$ used in the form of its sodium salt in the treatment of grand mal epilepsy

diphenyl ketone *n* [ISV *diphenyl* + *ketone*] **:** BENZOPHENONE

di·phen·yl·methane \(,)⸗,⸗⸗+\ *n* [ISV *diphenyl* + *methane*] **:** a crystalline hydrocarbon $(C_6H_5)_2CH_2$ that has an odor suggesting geranium, that is made usu. from benzene (as by reaction with benzyl chloride), that is used chiefly as a perfume in soaps, and that is the parent of some synthetic dyes

diphenyl oxide *n* **:** PHENYL ETHER — used chiefly commercially

di·phen·yl·thio·carbazone \(,)⸗,⸗⸗+,thīō+\ *n* [ISV *diphenyl* + *thi-* + *carb-* + *az-* + *-one*] **:** DITHIZONE

di·phen·yl·thiourea \(,)⸗,⸗⸗+\ *n* [*diphenyl* + *thiourea*] **:** THIOCARBANILIDE

di·phosgene \(')dī+\ *n* [ISV *di-* + *phosgene*] **:** a liquid compound $ClCOOCCl_3$ made by chlorinating methyl formate and used in World War I as a poison gas; trichloro-methyl chloroformate

di·phosphate \(')dī+\ *n* [ISV *di-* + *phosphate*] **1 :** PYROPHOSPHATE **2 :** a salt containing two phosphate radicals

di·phos·pho·pyr·i·dine nucleotide \(,)dī,fäsfō'pirə,dēn-\ *n* [*diphosphopyridine* fr. *di-* + *phosph-* + *pyridine*] **:** a coenzyme $C_{21}H_{27}N_7O_{14}P_2$ of numerous dehydrogenases that occurs in most cells and plays an important role in all phases of intermediary metabolism as an oxidizing agent or when in the reduced form as a reducing agent for various metabolites — called also *codehydrogenase I*, *coenzyme I*, *cozymase*, *DPN*; compare PYRIDINE NUCLEOTIDE

di·phos·phor·ic acid \¦dī+. . .-\ *n* [*di-* + *phosphoric*] **:** PYROPHOSPHORIC ACID

di·phos·pho·thiamine *also* **di·phos·pho·thiamin** \(,)dī-,fäsfō +\ *n* [*di-* + *phosph-* + *thiamine*] **:** COCARBOXYLASE

diph·the·ria \dif'thirēə, ÷dip'-, -thėr-\ *n* -s [NL, fr. F *diphthérie*, fr. Gk *diphthera* piece of leather (prob. fr. *depsein* to knead) + F -le -ia (fr. L -ia); fr. the toughness of the false membrane; akin to Gk dial. (Argos) *dephidastai* (pl.) fullers, Arm *top'el* to beat] **1 :** an acute highly contagious disease chiefly of young children that is marked by the formation of a false membrane upon any mucous surface esp. of the throat where it causes swelling and obstruction and possibly suffocation and that is caused by a bacterium (*Corynebacterium diphtheriae*) which produces a toxin causing inflammation of internal organs, esp. the heart and nervous system **2 :** any of several diseases of animals characterized by the formation of false membranes (as fowl pox and calf diphtheria) — **diph·the·ri·al** \(')=¦rēəl\ *or* **diph·the·ri·an** \-ēən\ *adj*

¹diph·ther·ic \(')=¦therik, -thir-\ *adj* [*diphtheria* + *-ic*] **:** DIPHTHERITIC

²diphtheric \"\ *n* -s **:** one suffering from diphtheria

diph·the·rit·ic \¦=thə¦rid·ik -rit¦, ¦ēk\ *adj* [obs. E *diphtheritis* diphtheria (fr. NL, fr. F *diphthérite*, fr. Gk *diphthera* + F *-ite* -itis) + E *-ic*] **:** typical of, attendant on, or produced by infection with diphtheria ⟨a ~ membrane⟩ **:** resembling diphtheria esp. in the formation of a false membrane ⟨~ dysentery⟩ **:** affected with diphtheria ⟨a ~ child⟩

¹diph·the·roid \'=thə,rȯid\ *adj* [*diphtheria* + *-oid*] **:** resembling diphtheria

²diphtheroid \"\ *n* -s **:** a bacterium that resembles the bacterium of diphtheria but does not produce diphtheria toxin

¹diph·thong \'dif,thȯŋ, ÷'dip,- *also* -thäŋ\ *n* -s [alter. (influenced by Gk *diphthongos*) of ME *diptonge*, fr. MF *diptongue*, fr. LL *dipthongus*, fr. Gk *diphthongos*, fr. *di-* + *phthongos* voice, sound] **1 :** a gliding monosyllabic speech item that starts at or near the articulatory position for one vowel and moves to or toward the position for another (as the vowel combination that forms the last part of *toy*) and that is usu. indicated in phonetic transcription by two symbols representing often only approximately the beginning and ending limits of the glide (as kaů or kaů or kaw or kåw for *cow*, tȯi or tȯy for *toy*, yät for *yacht*, wīz for *wise*) **2 :** DIGRAPH **3** [so called fr. their pronunciation as diphthongs in classical Latin] **:** a form of the ligature æ or œ — a printer's term

²diphthong \"\ *vb* -ED/-ING/-S **:** DIPHTHONGIZE

diph·thong·al \(')=¦=(g)əl\ *adj* **:** of or relating to a diphthong **:** having the character of a diphthong — **diph·thong·al·ly** \-(g)əlē, -li\ *adv*

diph·thong·ic \-(g)ik\ *adj* **:** DIPHTHONGAL

diph·thong·iza·tion \,=,=(g)ə'zāshən, -,(g)ī'z-\ *n* -s **:** the act of diphthongizing or the state of being diphthongized

diph·thong·ize \'=,=(g)īz\ *vb* -ED/-ING/-S *vi, of a simple vowel* **:** to change into a diphthong ~ *vt* **:** to pronounce as a diphthong

diphy- *or* **diphyo-** *comb form* [NL, fr. Gk *diphy-*, fr. *diphyēs*, fr. *di-* + *-phyēs* (fr. *phyein* to bring forth, produce) — more at BE] **:** twofold **:** double **:** bipartite ⟨*diphyodont*⟩ ⟨*diphyozooid*⟩

diphy·cercal \¦difē, -fə+\ *adj* [*diphy-* + *-cercal*] **1** *of a tail fin* **:** having the upper and lower portions alike or nearly so and the vertebral column extending to the tip without any upturning ⟨in lungfish and crossopterygians this symmetry is attained by the evolution of a ~ tail —A.S.Romer⟩ **2 :** having a diphycercal tail fin

diphy·cer·cy \'==,sərsē, -rkē\ *n* -ES [*diphy-* + *-cercy*] **:** the state of being diphycercal

diph·y·es \'difē,ēz\ *n, cap* [NL, fr. Gk *diphyēs* double] **:** a genus of oceanic hydrozoans of the order Siphonophora having two large swimming bells at the upper end of a stock that bears the polyps

diphy·genic \¦difē¦jenik, -fə¦-\ *adj* [*diphy-* + *-genic*] **:** following either of two alternate courses of embryonic development

di·phyletic \¦dī+\ *adj* [*di-* + *phyletic*] **:** derived from two lines of descent **:** marked by or based on duality as to source ⟨calling for reconsideration of the ~ origin of the dinosaurs⟩

di·phyl·la \dī'filə\ *n, cap* [NL, fr. *di-* + *-phylla* (fr. Gk *phyllon* leaf); fr. the bifoliate nose leaf — more at BLOW (to blossom)] **:** a genus of bloodsucking bats of the family Desmodontidae — see VAMPIRE 3

di·phyl·leia \,dīfə'līə, -lē(y)ə\ *n, cap* [NL, fr. *di-* + *-phylleia* (fr. Gk *phyllon* leaf)] **:** a small genus of perennial herbs (family Berberidaceae) with a single basal peltate leaf and two cauline leaves all deeply 2-cleft, 6-petaled white flowers, and globose or oblong berries

di·phyl·lid·ea \,dīfə'lidēə\ *n pl, cap* [NL, fr. *di-* + *phyll-* + *-idea*] **:** an order of Cestoda comprising tapeworms with two bothria on the scolex and dorsal and ventral rostellar hooks and including only a few parasites of elasmobranch fishes

di·phyl·lo·both·ri·a·sis \(,)dī,filō(,)bä'thrīəsəs\ *n* -ES [NL, fr. *Diphyllobothrium* + *-iasis*] **:** infestation with or disease caused by the fish tapeworm (*Diphyllobothrium latum*)

di·phyl·lo·both·ri·i·dae \-ə,dē\ *n pl, cap* [NL, fr. *Diphyllobothrium*, type genus + *-idae*] **:** a family of pseudophyllidean tapeworms (type genus *Diphyllobothrium*) having a complex life history with more than one intermediate host and the scolex of the adult usu. grooved and lacking suckers or hooks

di·phyl·lo·both·ri·um \-'bäthrēəm\ *n, cap* [NL, fr. *di-* + *phyll-* + *bothrium*] **:** a large genus of pseudophyllidean tapeworms comprising a number of parasites of fish-eating birds and mammals and including the common fish tapeworm (*D. latum*) of man

di·phyllous \(')dī¦filəs\ *adj* [NL *diphyllus*, fr. *di-* + *-phyllus* -phyllous] **:** having two leaves

¹di·phy·odont \(')dī¦fīə,dänt\ *adj* [ISV *diphy-* + *-odont*] **:** having deciduous and permanent sets of teeth successively ⟨a ~ mammal⟩; *also* **:** marked by the development of two such sets ⟨~ dentition⟩ — opposed to *monophyodont*

²diphyodont \"\ *n* -s **:** a diphyodont animal ⟨most mammals are ~s⟩

diphyo·zooid \¦difēō+\ *n* -s [*diphy-* + *zooid*] **:** one of the free-swimming sexual zooids of siphonophores

di·pic·ryl·amine \dī¦pikrəl¦əmēn\ *n* [ISV *di-* + *picryl* + *amine*] **:** HEXANITRODIPHENYLAMINE

dip-iron \'=,=(=)\ *n* **:** an implement used in removing resin from cups attached to trees tapped for resin production

dip joint *n* **:** a joint running in the same direction as the dip of the strata

dipl- *or* **diplo-** *comb form* [Gk, fr. *diploos* — more at DOUBLE] **1 :** double **:** twofold ⟨*diplococcus*⟩ ⟨*diplopia*⟩ **2 :** diploid ⟨*diplosome*⟩

dipl *abbr* **1** diplomat **2** diplomatic

dip·la·can·thi·dae \,diplə'kan(t)thə,dē\ *n pl, cap* [NL, fr. *Diplacanthus*, type genus + *-idae*] **:** a family of primitive placoderm fishes (subclass Acanthodii) having two dorsal fins — see DIPLACANTHUS

dip·la·can·thus \-thəs\ *n, cap* [NL, fr. *dipl-* + *-acanthus*] **:** the type genus of Diplacanthidae comprising small Devonian fishes with two strong spines between the pectoral fins

dip·la·cu·sis \,diplə'kyüsəs\ *n, pl* **diplacu·ses** \-ü,sēz\ [NL, fr. *dipl-* + Gk *akousis* hearing, fr. *akouein* to hear + *-sis* — more at HEAR] **:** the hearing of a single tone as if it were two tones of different pitch

dip·la·de·nia \,diplə'dēnēə\ *n, cap* [NL, fr. *dipl-* + Gk *aden-*, *adēn* gland + NL *-ia*; fr. the pair of nectar glands — more at ADEN-] **:** a genus of tropical So. American woody vines (family Apocynaceae) having large varicolored racemose flowers

di·pla·net·ic \¦dīplə¦ned·ik\ *adj* [*di-* + Gk *planētikos* migratory, fr. *planēt-*, *planēs* wanderer (fr. *planan* to cause to wander, *planasthai* to wander) + *-ikos* -ic — more at FLOOR] *of a fungus* **:** having two swarming periods each with a different form of zoospore and separated by an encysted stage (as in the Saprolegniales) — compare MONOPLANETIC — **di·plan·e·tism** \dī'planə,tizəm\ *n* -s

dip·lar·throus \(')di¦plärthrəs\ *adj* [*dipl-* + *arthr-* + *-ous*] **:** having each or most of the tarsal or carpal bones of one row articulating with more than one bone of the other row — used esp. of certain ungulate mammals; opposed to *taxeopodous*

di·pla·sic \(')dī¦plā¦zik, -la¦, ¦sik\ *adj* [Gk *diplasios* twofold (fr. *di-* + *-plasios* -fold) + E *-ic* — more at FOLD] *in classical prosody* **:** two to one in proportion **:** having a thesis twice the length of the arsis

di·pla·sio·coe·la \(,)dī,plāzēō'sēlə\ *n pl, cap* [NL, fr. *diplasio-* (fr. Gk *diplasios*) + *-coela* (fr. Gk *koilos* hollow) — more at CAVE] **:** a suborder of Salientia including the families Ranidae, Polypedatidae, and Brevicipitidae and having the anterior surface of the first seven vertebrae concave and the eighth vertebra biconcave, a firm median fusion of the shoulder girdle, and no ribs — **di·pla·sio·coe·lid** \=¦=|==¦lə̇d\ *adj or n* — **di·pla·sio·coe·lous** \-ləs\ *adj*

di·plec·trum \dī'plektrəm\ *n, cap* [NL, fr. *di-* + *plectrum*] **:** a genus of small marine and brackish-water fishes (family Serranidae) widely distributed along the warmer parts of both coasts of the Americas — compare SANDFISH

di·ple·gia \dī'plēj(ē)ə\ *n* -s [NL, fr. *di-* + *-plegia*] **:** paralysis of corresponding parts (as the legs) on both sides of the body

di·pleu·ru·la \dī'plu̇r(y)ələ\ *n, pl* **dipleurulas** \-ləz\ *or* **dipleuru·lae** \-,lē\ [NL, fr. *dipleura* bilaterally symmetrical organisms (fr. *di-* + *-pleura*) + *-ula*] **1 :** a hypothetical bilaterally symmetrical echinoderm larva sometimes regarded as a common ancestor of echinoderms and chordates **2 :** a larval echinoderm (as a bipinnaria or an echinopluteus) — not used technically

¹di·plex \'dī,pleks\ *adj* [alter. (influenced by *di-*) of *duplex*] **:** allowing telecommunication of two independent signals simultaneously by a single station or antenna or on a single carrier frequency without mutual interference ⟨~ radio and television transmission⟩ ⟨~ reception⟩ — distinguished from *duplex*

²diplex \"\ *vt* -ED/-ING/-ES **:** to effect diplex transmission or reception of

di·plex·er \-sə(r)\ *n* -s **:** a combining network (as an impedance bridge or a filter circuit) allowing operation of diplex transmission (as of a radar and a communication transmitter) ⟨a simple ~ may be used to feed the picture signal and the sound signal into the same antenna —*Radio Corp. of Amer. Rev.*⟩

dip·lo·bacillus \¦diplō+\ *n, pl* **diplobacilli** [NL, fr. *dipl-* + *bacillus*] **:** any of certain small aerobic gram-negative rod-shaped bacilli that are related to the genus *Hemophilus* and are parasitic on mucous membranes

dip·lo·bi·ont \¦diplō¦bī,änt, də̇'plōbē,änt\ *n* -s [*dipl-* + *-biont*] **:** an organism in which a haploid generation alternates with a usu. morphologically dissimilar diploid generation — compare DIPLOHAPLONT — **dip·lo·bi·on·tic** \¦diplō,bī¦äntik, də̇¦plōbē¦äntik\ *adj*

dip·lo·blas·tic \¦diplō¦blastik\ *adj* [*dipl-* + *-blastic*] **:** having two germ layers — used of embryos and of lower invertebrates (sponges and coelenterates) that lack a true mesoderm

dip·lo·car·dia \,diplō'kärdēə\ *n, cap* [NL, fr. *dipl-* + *-cardia*] **:** a common American genus of earthworms (family Megascolecidae) often abundant in moist forest soil

dip·lo·car·di·ac \¦diplō¦kärdē,ak\ *adj* [*dipl-* + *-cardiac* (fr. Gk *kardia*) — more at HEART] **:** having the heart completely divided so that one side is systemic and the other is pulmonary

dip·lo·car·pon \,diplō'kär,pän\ *n, cap* [NL, fr. *dipl-* + *-carpon* (fr. Gk *-karpon*, neut. of *-karpos* -carpous)] **:** a genus of fungi (family Microthyriaceae) with shield-shaped perithecia and unequally two-celled hyaline ascospores — see BLACK SPOT

dip·lo·caulescent \¦diplō+\ *adj* [*dipl-* + *caulescent*] **:** having axes of the second order — used of a plant that cannot reproduce until after the production of secondary axes; compare HAPLOCAULESCENT, TRIPLOCAULESCENT

dip·lo·chlamydeous \¦diplō+\ *adj* [*dipl-* + *chlamydeous*] **:** DICHLAMYDEOUS

dip·lo·chromosome \"+\ *n* [*dipl-* + *chromosome*] **:** a chromosome with four chromatids

dip·lo·coc·cal \¦diplō¦käkəl\ *or* **dip·lo·coc·cic** \-'äksik\ *adj* [*diplococcus* + *-al* or *-ic*] **:** of, or relating to diplococci or the genus *Diplococcus* **:** caused by diplococci

dip·lo·coc·coid \-¦kä,kȯid\ *adj* [*diplococcus* + *-oid*] **:** resembling a diplococcus

dip·lo·coc·cus \¦diplō'käkəs\ *n* [NL, fr. *dipl-* + *-coccus*] **1** *pl* **diplococ·ci** \-ä,kī, -äkē, -äk,sī, -äksē\ **:** a pair of adherent cocci (sense 2) **2** *cap* **:** a genus of gram-positive somewhat elongated encapsulated bacteria (family Lactobacillaceae) that occur usu. in pairs and sometimes in chains, are parasitic growing best in the animal body but poorly in artificial media, and include serious pathogens, as the pneumococcus (*D. pneumoniae*) **3** *pl* **diplococci :** any bacterium of the genus *Diplococcus*

di·plo·dia \də̇'plōdēə\ *n, cap* [NL, irreg. fr. *diploos* double; fr. the 2-celled spores] **:** a large form genus of imperfect fungi (of the family Sphaeropsidaceae, order Sphaeropsidales) having carbonous pycnidia and brown 2-celled spores — see DRY ROT 2b

di·plod·o·cus \də̇'pläd̮əkəs\ *n* [NL, fr. *dipl-* + *-docus* (fr. Gk *dokos* beam, bar, fr. *dekesthai*, *dechesthai* to take, receive); akin to L *decēre* to be fitting, be proper — more at DECENT] **1** *cap* **:** a genus of very large herbivorous saurischian dinosaurs (suborder Sauropoda) from the Upper Jurassic of Colorado and Wyoming **2** -ES **:** any animal of the genus *Diplodocus*

dip·lo·dus \'dipləd̮əs\ *n, cap* [NL, fr. *dipl-* + *-odus*] **:** a genus of deep-bodied fishes (family Sparidae) including a number of typical sargos

dip·loe \'diplə,wē\ *n* -s [NL, fr. Gk *diploē*, fr. *diploos* double] **:** the cancellous bony tissue between the tables of the skull

dip·lo·et·ic \¦diplə¦wed·ik\ *adj* [*diploe* + connective *-t-* + *-ic*] **:** DIPLOIC

dip·lo·gangliate \¦diplō+\ *adj* [*dipl-* + *gangliate*] **:** having the ganglia arranged in pairs

dip·lo·genesis \¦diplō+\ *n* [NL, fr. *dipl-* + *genesis*] **:** a hypothetical production of changes in the germ plasm corresponding to acquired modification of somatic structure — compare LAMARCKISM — **dip·lo·genetic** \"+\ *adj*

dip·lo·gen·ic \¦diplō¦jenik\ *adj* [*dipl-* + Gk *genos* race, kin + E *-ic* — more at KIN] **:** partaking of the nature of two bodies

dip·lo·glos·sa·ta \,diplō(,)glä'säd·ə, -säd·ə\ *n pl, cap* [NL, fr. *dipl-* + Gk *glōssa* tongue + NL *-ata* — more at GLOSS (interpretation)] **:** a suborder of Dermaptera including the single genus *Hemimerus* of ectoparasites on African rats

dip·lo·glossate \¦diplō+\ *adj* [*dipl-* + Gk *glōssa* tongue + E *-ate*] *of certain lizards* **:** having the end of the tongue retractile into the basal portion

dip·lo·haplont \¦diplō+\ *n* [ISV *dipl-* + *haplont*] **:** an organism in which a haploid generation alternates with a usu. morphologically similar diploid generation — compare DIPLOBIONT — **dip·lo·hap·lon·tic** \¦diplō¦ha¦pläntik\ *adj*

dip·lo·he·dral \¦diplō¦hēdrəl\ *adj* [*diplohedron* + *-al*] **:** of or relating to a diplohedron

dip·lo·he·dron \-ən\ *n* -s [ISV *dipl-* + *-hedron*] **:** DIPLOID 1

di·plo·ic \də'plōik, (')di¦p-\ *adj* [ISV *diploe* + *-ic*] **:** of or relating to the diploe

¹dip·loid \'di,plȯid\ *n* -s [*dipl-* + *-oid*] **1 :** an isometric crystalline form that has 24 similar quadrilateral faces arranged in pairs and that is a hemihedral form of the hexoctahedron — called also *diplohedron* **2** [²*diploid*] **a :** a diploid cell **b :** an individual or generation characterized by the diploid chromosome number

diploid 1

²diploid \"\ *adj* [ISV *dipl-* + *-oid*; prob. orig. formed in G] **:** double or twofold in appearance or arrangement **:** having the basic chromosome number doubled ⟨typical ~ somatic cells⟩ **:** comprising twice the number of chromosomes present in typical gametes ⟨the chromosome complement is ~ before reduction⟩ — compare HAPLOID, POLYPLOID

dip·loi·dal \də'plȯidᵊl, (')di¦p-\ *adj* [¹*diploid* + *-al*] **:** belonging to or characterized by the symmetry of the class of isometric crystals having diad axes parallel to the crystallographic axes, triad axes in the directions of the cube body diagonal, and axial mirror-image planes of symmetry

dip·lo·id·i·on \,diplō'idē,än, -ēən\ *n* -s [Gk *diploïdion*, dim. of *diploïd-*, *diploïs* double cloak, fr. *diploos* double] **:** an ancient Greek chiton for women having the part above the waist double and the outer fold hanging loose

dip·loid·i·za·tion \,di,plȯidə'zāshən\ *n* -s **:** the act or process of diploidizing or the state of being diploidized

dip·loid·ize \'di,plȯi,dīz\ *vb* -ED/-ING/-S *vt* **:** to make diploid (as by hyphal fusions in certain fungi) ~ *vi* **:** to become diploid

dip·loi·dy \'di,plȯidē\ *n* -ES [ISV *diploid* + *-y*] **:** the condition of being diploid

dip·lo·karyon \¦diplō+\ *n* [ISV *dipl-* + *karyon*; orig. formed in G] **:** a nucleus possessing twice the diploid number of chromosomes **:** a tetraploid nucleus — **dip·lo·kar·y·ot·ic** \¦diplō¦karē¦äd·ik\ *adj*

¹di·plo·ma \də̇'plōmə\ *n, pl* **diplo·mas** \-məz\ [L, passport, document conferring an honor or privilege, fr. Gk *diplōma* passport, folded paper, something doubled, fr. *diploun* to double, fr. *diploos* double] **1** *pl also* **diploma·ta** \-məd·ə, -mətə\ **:** an historical or state document **:** CHARTER ⟨in a ~ of Hlothhere, king of Kent — the first English charter of which a contemporary text has survived —F.M.Stenton⟩ **2 :** a letter or writing usu. under seal conferring some honor or privilege ⟨the council's peace prize was handed to him and along with it a ~⟩ **3 :** a document bearing record of graduation from or of a degree conferred by an educational institution

²diploma \"\ *vt* -ED/-ING/-S **:** to furnish with a diploma ⟨too many ~*ed* illiterates⟩

di·plo·ma·cy \də̇'plōməsē, -si\ *n* -ES [F *diplomatie*, fr. *diplomatique* diplomatic, after F *aristocratique* aristocratic: *aristocratie* aristocracy] **1 a :** the art and practice of conducting negotiations between nations for the attainment of mutually satisfactory terms ⟨the technique of direct ~, whereby responsible members of governments deal with each other face to face instead of through ambassadors or other intermediaries —N.F.Busch⟩ ⟨secondly, there is the other kind of ~ . . . : the search for agreement between friends on policies and tactics and timing —Lester Pearson⟩ — compare DIPLOMATIC AGENT **b :** the procedures, methods, and forms employed in conducting such negotiations ⟨colleges having specific courses in ~⟩ ⟨forget that ~ is itself a skilled profession — Llewellyn Woodward⟩ ⟨resolved to make a career of ~⟩ **c :** the skillful or successful settlement of differences between peoples ⟨~ is the peaceful resolution of disputes between autonomous groups —M.J.Herskovits⟩ **d :** a statesman's or nation's policies and strategies in conducting foreign relations ⟨when the ~ of certain aggressive statesmen was employed to isolate a particular enemy so as to facilitate his defeat —C.J. Friedrich⟩ **2 :** adroitness or artfulness in securing advantages without arousing hostility **:** address or tact in conduct of affairs ⟨he is a kind man, but simpleminded in the extreme; he has no gift for ~ —Elinor Wylie⟩ **3 :** the diplomatic corps ⟨members of UN ~⟩

diploma mill *n* **:** an institution of higher education operating without supervision of a state or professional agency and granting diplomas which are either fraudulent or because of the lack of proper standards worthless

diploma piece *n* **1 :** a finished piece of work by a new member of an academy or society of art and presented by him to the organization upon election to membership **2 :** an academic project (as a thesis or dissertation) undertaken for the purpose of obtaining a diploma rather than from interest in the subject

dip·lo·mat \'diplə,mat, *usu* -ad.+V\ *n* -s [F *diplomate*, back-formation fr. *diplomatique* diplomatic] **1 :** one employed or skilled in diplomacy ⟨the modern ~ will look upon himself as a liaison officer who will promote cooperation and understanding on all sides —C.J.Friedrich⟩ **2 :** DIPLOMATIST 2

¹diplomate *vt* -ED/-ING/-S [¹*diploma* + *-ate*, v. suffix] *obs* **:** to give a title, a degree, or a privilege to by means of a diploma

²dip·lo·mate \'diplə,māt\ *n* -s [¹*diploma* + *-ate*, n. suffix (one acted upon)] **:** one who holds a diploma; *esp* **:** a physician certified as qualified generally or as a specialist by an agency recognized as professionally competent to grant such certification ⟨a ~ of the American Board of Anesthesiology⟩

¹dip·lo·mat·ic \¦diplə¦mad·ik, -at¦, ¦ēk\ *adj* [in sense 1, fr. NL *diplomaticus*, fr. L *diplomat-*, *diploma* document conferring an honor or privilege + *-icus* -ic; in other senses, fr. F *diplomatique* connected with the documents that regulate international relations, fr. NL *diplomaticus*] **1 :** relating to the deciphering, age, authenticity, signatures, or textual emendations of writings of former times **:** PALEOGRAPHIC; *esp* **:** exactly reproducing the original — used of a copy or edition of a text or document ⟨their own translation is based on the critical, ~ text of Henri Lestienne (Paris, 1907), which provides all of Leibnitz's own alterations —Nicholas Rescher⟩ **2 a :** concerned or connected with international relations ⟨a ~ assignment in So. America⟩ ⟨~ techniques for preventing war⟩ **:** engaged or skilled in international relations ⟨a ~ expert⟩ ⟨sent over a ~ group to Europe⟩ **b :** belonging to or proper to the personnel responsible for the conduct of international relations ⟨~ secretaries and consuls⟩ ⟨~ privileges and immunities⟩ ⟨a breach of ~ etiquette⟩ ⟨the right of ~ sanctuary⟩ **:** composed of such personnel ⟨a ~ group⟩ **3 :** employing tact and conciliation ⟨tried a ~ approach before using strong-arm methods⟩ ⟨a ~ way of dealing with a touchy personal relationship⟩ **syn** see SUAVE

²diplomatic \"\ *n* -s **1** *archaic* **:** a diplomatic agent **:** DIPLOMATIST **2** *also* **dip·lo·mat·ics** \-ks\ *pl but sing in constr*, *archaic* **:** the art of international diplomacy **3 diplomatics** *pl but sing in constr* **:** critical study of official documents of history (as ancient registers, decrees, charters, treaties, judicial records) esp. of medieval times

diplomatic agent *n* **:** an agent employed by a state in its diplomatic service or in its intercourse or negotiation with other states

dip·lo·mat·i·cal·ly \-¦ək(ə)lē, ¦ēk, -li\ *adv* **1 :** according to the rules of diplomacy **2 :** in a diplomatic manner ⟨and ~ allowed a prince to beat him at chess —Elinor Wylie⟩ **:** TACTFULLY

diplomatic corps *n* [trans. of F *corps diplomatique*] **:** the whole body of diplomatic agents attached to a foreign legation at the seat of government including ambassadors, envoys, ministers, and their attachés and secretaries

diplomatic immunity *n* **:** freedom from arrest, taxation, payment of customs charges, and submission to police regulations usu. accorded by international law to diplomatic agents, their families, and servants

diplomatic pouch *n* **:** a mail pouch that is sealed shut in transit and is used for carrying communications between a legation and its home office

diplomatic service *n* **:** a branch of the foreign service that employs diplomatic agents and is concerned with foreign legations

di·plo·ma·tist \də̇'plōməd·əst, -mətəst\ *n* -s [fr. ¹*diplomatic*, after such pairs as E *dramatic: dramatist*] **1 :** DIPLOMAT ⟨churchmen were the natural intermediaries in this business, and a good clerical ~ might reasonably expect a bishopric — F.M.Stenton⟩ ⟨the greatest of the German professional ~s of the interwar period —H.J.Morgenthau⟩ **2 :** one who is dexterous, tactful, or artful in meeting situations (as in managing men) without arousing antagonism

di·plo·ma·tize \-mə,tīz\ *vb* -ED/-ING/-S [in sense 1 (transitive), fr. L *diplomat-*, *diploma* + E *-ize*; in other senses, fr. ¹*diplomatic*, after such pairs as E *dramatic: dramatize*] *vt* **1** *archaic* **:** to confer a diploma upon **2 :** to treat or manage with diplomacy **:** aid in the manner of a diplomatist ~ *vi* **:** to act like a diplomat or diplomatist **:** practice diplomacy

dip·lo·nephridia \¦diplō+\ *n pl* [NL, fr. *dipl-* + *nephridia* (pl. of *nephridium*)] **:** nephridia in whose formation both the ectoderm and mesoderm take part

dip·lo·neural \"+\ *adj* [*dipl-* + *neural*] **:** supplied by two different nerves

dip·lont \'di,plänt\ *n* -s [ISV *dipl-* + *-ont*] **:** an organism with somatic cells having the diploid chromosome number, only the gametes being haploid — compare HAPLONT, SPOROPHYTE — **di·plon·tic** \(')di¦pläntik\ *adj*

dip·lo·parthenogenesis \¦diplō+\ *n* [NL, fr. *dipl-* + *parthenogenesis*] **:** parthenogenesis characterized by the production of diploid offspring from unreduced primordial cells

dip·lo·phase \'diplō,fāz\ *n* [*dipl-* + *phase*] **:** the diploid phase (as the sporophyte) in the life cycle of certain organisms

di·plo·pia \də̇'plōpēə\ *n* -s [NL, fr. *dipl-* + *-opia*] **:** a disorder of vision in which two images of a single object are seen owing to unequal action of the eye muscles

di·plop·ic \də̇'pläpik, (')di¦p-, -lōp-\ *adj* [*diplopia* + *-ic*] **:** relating to or affected with diplopia

dip·lo·pod \'diplə,päd\ *n* -s [NL *Diplopoda*] **:** one of the Diplopoda **:** MILLIPEDE

²diplopod \"\ *adj* **:** of or relating to the Diplopoda

di·plop·o·da \də̇'pläpədə\ *n pl, cap* [NL, fr. *dipl-* + *-poda*] **:** a class of arthropods comprising the millipedes — **dip·lo·pod·ic** \¦diplə¦pädik\ *adj* — **di·plop·o·dous** \də̇'pläpədəs, (')di¦p-\ *adj*

di·plo·sis \də̇'plōsə̇s\ *n, pl* **diplo·ses** \-ō,sēz\ [NL, fr. Gk *diplōsis* action of doubling, fr. *diploun* to double (fr. *diploos* double) + -*sis* — more at DOUBLE] **1 :** the alchemical process of increasing the amount of a precious metal by transmutation **2 :** restoration of the somatic chromosome number by fusion of two gametes in fertilization — compare HAPLOSIS

dip·lo·some \ˈdiplə,sōm\ *n* -s [*dipl-* + *-some*] **:** a double centriole

dip·lo·somite \ˌdiplō+\ *n* [*dipl-* + *somite*] **:** one of the typical structural units of a diplopod, each bearing two pairs of appendages and representing two fused true segments

dip·lo·sphene \ˈdiplō,sfēn\ *n* -s [*dipl-* + Gk *sphēn* wedge — more at SPHEN-] **:** HYPOSPHENE

dip·lo·spon·dy·li \ˌdiplō'spändə,lī\ [NL, fr. *dipl-* + *-spondyli*] *syn of* NOTIDANI

dip·lo·spondylic \ˌdiplō+\ *also* **dip·lo·spondylous** \"+\ *adj* [*dipl-* + *spondylic, spondylous*] **:** EMBOLOMEROUS

dip·lo·spor·ous \ˌdiplə'spōrəs, də'pläspərəs\ *adj* [*dipl-* + *-sporous*] **:** being or belonging to diplospory

dip·lo·spory \ˈdiplə,spōrē, də'pläspərē\ *n* -ES [*dipl-* + *-spory*] **:** reproduction by means of unreduced spores

dip·lo·ste·mo·nous \ˌdiplō'stēmənəs, -tem-\ *adj* [prob. fr. (assumed) NL *diplostemonus*, fr. NL *dipl-* + (assumed) NL *-stemonus* -stemonous] **:** having the stamens in two whorls each of which has the same number as the petals and usu. an inner stamen opposite each petal and an outer one opposite each sepal — compare OBDIPLOSTEMONOUS

dip·lo·stom·u·lum \ˌdiplō'stämyələm\ *n, pl* **diplostomu·la** \-lə\ [NL, fr. *dipl-* + Gk *stoma* mouth + NL *-ulum* — more at STOMACH] **:** a modified metacercaria occurring unencysted esp. in the lens of the eye of fishes

dip·lo·tax·is \ˌ==ˈtaksəs\ *n, cap* [NL, fr. *dipl-* + *-taxis*] **:** a genus of Old World weedy herbs (family Cruciferae) with alternate pinnatifid leaves and yellow racemose flowers — see WALL ROCKET

dip·lo·te·gia \ˌdiplō'tējēə\ *n* -s [NL, fr. *dipl-* + *-tegia* (fr. Gk *tegos* roof) — more at THATCH] **:** a capsule developed in seed plants from an inferior ovary (as in iris)

dip·lo·tene \ˈdiplō,tēn\ *n* -s [ISV *dipl-* + *-tene;* orig. formed as F *diplotène*] **:** the stage of the meiotic prophase immediately following pachytene during which the homologous chromosomes tend to repel one another

dip·lo·zo·ic \ˌdiplə'zōik\ *adj* [*dipl-* + *-zoic*] *of an animal* **:** combining a double set of vital structures in one unit

dip·lo·zo·on \ˌdiplə'zō,än\ *n, cap* [NL, fr. *dipl-* + *-zoon*] **:** a genus of monogenetic trematode worms parasitic upon the gills of fishes (as minnows) and unique among animals in that two larvae fuse together permanently at the middle of their bodies forming an individual shaped like an X and only double individuals thus formed are capable of becoming sexually mature

di·plu·ra \də'plu̇rə\ *n pl, cap* [NL, fr. *dipl-* + *-ura*] **:** ENTOTROPHI — **di·plu·ran** \-rən\ *n* -s

dipmeter \ˈ=,==\ *n* **:** an instrument designed for determining the direction and angle of dip of geological formations

dip mold *n* **:** an open-top one-piece mold used in pattern molding in glassmaking

dip needle *n* **1** *or* **dipping needle :** a magnetic needle pivoted to rotate in the vertical plane of the magnetic meridian with its rotation axis through its center of gravity so that it points in the direction of the earth's magnetic intensity **2 :** an instrument similar to a dip needle but with a counterweight so adjusted as to give the needle maximum sensitivity to changes in the magnetic dip

dip needle 1

dip net *n* **:** a small bag net usu. with a rigid support about the mouth and a long handle used to scoop small fishes and other aquatic life from the water

dipnetter *n* **:** one who fishes with a dip net

dipnetting *n* **:** fishing by means of a dip net

¹dip·neu·mo·na \dī'n(y)ümənə, dip'n-\ *n pl, cap* [NL, fr. neut. pl. of *dipneumonus* dipneumonous] **1** *in some classifications* **:** a group of lungfishes including the genera *Protopterus* and *Lepidosiren* in which the lung is double and the lateral rays of the archipterygium are vestigial or absent **2** *in some classifications* **:** a division of holothurians having two branching respiratory organs

²dipneumona \"\ [NL, fr. neut. pl. of *dipneumonus*] *syn of* DIPNEUMONES

di·pneu·mone \(ˈ)dī'n(y)ü,mōn, (ˈ)dip'n-\ *adj* [NL *Dipneumones*] *of a spider* **:** having one pair of book lungs **:** DIPNEUMONOMORPH

di·pneu·mo·nes \dī'n(y)ümə,nēz, dip'n-\ *n pl, cap* [NL, fr. *di-* + *-pneumones* (fr. Gk *pneumones*, pl. of *pneumōn*, *pneumōn* lung) — more at PNEUMONIA] *in some classifications* **:** a division of spiders comprising those with a single pair of lungs

di·pneu·mo·no·morph \-mənō,mȯrf\ *adj* [NL *Dipneumonomorphae*] **:** of or relating to the Dipneumonomorphae

di·pneu·mo·no·mor·phae \(ˌ)=,===ˈmȯr,fē\ *n pl, cap* [NL, fr. *di-* + *pneumon-* + *-morphae*] **:** a suborder of Araneida comprising spiders that have a single pair of book lungs

di·pneu·mo·nous \(ˈ)=ˈ=mənəs\ *adj* [NL *dipneumonus*, fr. *di-* + *-pneumonus* (fr. Gk *pneumon-*, *pneumōn* lung)] **1 :** having two respiratory organs **2 :** belonging to or characteristic of the Dipneumona

dip·neust \ˈdip,n(y)üst\ *n* -s [NL *Dipneusti*] **:** a fish of the order Dipneusti

dip·neus·tal \(ˈ)dip'n(y)üstᵊl\ *adj* [NL *Dipneusti* + E *-al*] **:** of or relating to the Dipneusti

dip·neus·ti \dip'n(y)ü,stī\ *n pl, cap* [NL, fr. *di-* + *-pneusti* (irreg. fr. Gk *pneustikos* of breathing, fr. *pnein* to breathe) — more at PNEUMATIC] **:** an order of Choanichthyes coextensive with Dipnoi — see LUNGFISH

dip·neus·tid \-təd\ *adj* **:** DIPNEUSTAL

¹dip·no·an \ˈdipnəwən\ *adj* [NL *dipnoi* + E *-an*, adj. suffix] **:** belonging to the Dipnoi

²dipnoan \"\ *n* -s [NL *Dipnoi* + E *-an*, n. suffix] **:** one of the Dipnoi

dip·noi \ˈdip,nȯi, -pnə,wī\ *n pl, cap* [NL, fr. masc. pl. of *dipnous* having two apertures for breathing] **:** an order or other division of Choanichthyes including a number of fossil fishes known from the Devonian and later formations and three surviving genera, *Neoceratodus*, *Protopterus*, and *Lepidosiren*, comprising aberrant fishes that have overlapping cycloid scales and dermal fin rays, a largely cartilaginous skeleton with a persistent notochord, an autostylic skull, paired fins of the archipterygial type, gills covered by an operculum, and in addition a lung or pair of lungs communicating with the ventral side of the esophagus by a short tube

dip·noid \ˈdip,nȯid\ *adj or n* [NL *Dipnoi* + E *-oid*] **:** DIPNOAN

dip·no·ous \ˈdipnəwəs\ *adj* [NL *dipnous* having two apertures for breathing, fr. Gk *dipnoos*, fr. *di-* + *-pnoos* (fr. *pnoē* breath, fr. *pnein* to breathe)] **1 :** having both lungs and gills **2 :** DIPNOAN

di·pode \ˈdī,pōd\ *adj* [Gk *dipod-*, *dipous*] **:** BIPED

di·pod·ic \(ˈ)dī'pädik\ *adj* [*dipody* + *-ic*] **:** of, relating to, or composed of a dipody or dipodies ⟨a ~ verse⟩ ⟨poem . . . with ~ instead of short feet —Evelyn H. Scholl⟩

¹dip·o·did \ˈdipədəd\ *n* -s [NL *Dipodidae*] **:** a rodent of the family Dipodidae

²dipodid \"\ *adj* **:** of or relating to the Dipodidae

di·pod·i·dae \dī'pädə,dē\ *n pl, cap* [NL, fr. *Dipod-*, *Dipus*, type genus + *-idae* — more at DIPUS] **:** a family of myomorph rodents comprising the Old World jerboas and sometimes related forms

di·pod·o·mys \-də,mis\ *n, cap* [NL, fr. *dipodo-* (fr. Gk *dipod-*, *dipous* having two feet, fr. *di-* + *pod-*, *pous* foot) + *-mys* — more at FOOT] **:** a genus of sciuromorph rodents consisting of the No. American kangaroo rats

dip·o·dy \ˈdipədē\ *n* -ES [LL *dipodia*, fr. Gk, lit., condition of having two feet, fr. *dipod-*, *dipous* + *-ia* -y] **:** a prosodic unit or measure of two feet; *esp* **:** one in an accentual meter in which the stress or arsis of one of the feet is notably stronger than that of the other

di·po·lar \ˈdī,pōlə(r)\ *adj* [*di-* + *polar*] **:** of, relating to, or having a dipole

dipolar ion *n* **:** an ion charged both positively and negatively (as that of an amino acid in solution) **:** an amphoteric ion ⟨the *dipolar ion* $^{+}H_3NCH_2COO^{-}$ of glycine⟩ — called also *zwitterion;* compare BETAINE 1a, INNER SALT

di·pole \ˈdī,pōl\ *n* [ISV *di-* + *pole*] **1 a :** a pair of equal and opposite electric charges or magnetic poles of opposite sign separated esp. by a small distance **b :** a body or system (as a molecule) having such charges **2 :** a radio or television antenna consisting of two equal horizontal metal rods in line with each other and with their slightly separated adjacent ends connected to the input terminals of the transmitter or receiving set — see FOLDED DIPOLE

dipole moment *n* [ISV *dipole* + *moment*] **:** the electric moment of an electric dipole or the magnetic moment of a magnetic dipole

di·potassium \ˌdī+\ *adj* [*di-* + *potassium*] **:** containing two atoms of potassium in the molecule

dipped *adj* [fr. past part. of ¹*dip*] *of a horse's back* **:** excessively sloped between withers and croup

dip·pel's oil \ˈdipəlz-\ *n, usu cap D* [after Johann K. *Dippel* †1734 Ger. theologian and alchemist who prepared it] **:** BONE OIL 1

dip·per \ˈdipə(r)\ *n* -s [ME *dippere*, a diving bird, fr. *dippen* to dip + *-ere* -er — more at ¹DIP] **1 :** one that dips: **a** *usu cap* **:** a member of a religious sect that practices baptism by immersion **:** BAPTIST, ANABAPTIST, DUNKER **b :** a worker who dips articles into a processing solution (as cleaner, bleach, dye) or into a finishing solution (as color, glaze, paint); *also* **:** a worker who immerses animals in a dip **c :** a worker who builds up articles (as candles, candies, rubber gloves, match tips) by successive dipping into the forming solution **d :** one who only dips into a book ⟨few bona fide readers but many ~*s*⟩ **e :** one who dips snuff **f :** one who dips from cups the gum exuded from pine trees in the making of turpentine **g** *slang* **:** PICKPOCKET **2 :** any of several birds notable for their skill in diving: as **a :** WATER OUZEL **b** *or* **dipper duck :** BUFFLEHEAD **3 :** something that is used for dipping: **a :** a cup with a long handle for dipping liquids (as drinking water) **b :** the holder for immersing the collodionized glass plate in the silver bath in photoengraving **c :** a receptacle attachable to a palette for holding varnish or other medium **d :** the grab, bucket, or scoop of any of several kinds of excavating machines; *also* **:** the machine itself **4** *Brit* **:** a switch for dimming automobile headlights

dipper 3a

dipper clam *n* [prob. so called fr. the spoon-shaped receptacle near the umbones] **:** a surf clam (*Spisula solidissima*)

dipper dredge *also* **dipper shovel** *n* **:** a floating dredging machine with a single machine-operated bucket working on an arm

dip·per·ful \-(r),fu̇l\ *n* -s **:** the full quantity a dipper holds

dipper gourd *n* **1 :** a gourd shaped like a dipper; *esp* **:** such a fruit borne by the bottle gourd **2 :** a plant that bears dipper gourds

dipper stick *n* **1 :** a revolving dipper shovel **2 :** the shaft that connects the dipper to the boom in an excavating machine

dip·pi·ness \ˈdipēnəs\ *n* -ES *slang* **:** dippy behavior, appearance, or effect

dipping *n* -s [ME *dippinge*, fr. *dippen* to dip + *-inge* -ing — more at ¹DIP] **:** the liquid preparation in which a thing is dipped

dipping frame *n* **:** a frame used for dipping (as in dipping tallow candles and in dyeing)

dipping lug *n* **:** a lugsail in which the tack is made fast to the deck forward of the mast and the yardarm must be dipped and hoisted again on the other side of the mast in tacking — see LUGSAIL illustration

dip·ping·ly *adv* [*dipping* (pres. part. of ¹*dip*) + *-ly*] **:** with dipping movements

dipping needle *var of* DIP NEEDLE

dipping rod *n* **:** DIVINING ROD

dipping stick *n* **:** DIP 6b

dipping tank *n* **:** a tank or race arranged for complete immersion of an animal in an insecticide

dip pipe *n* **:** a pipe that conveys hot coal gas from retorts in gas manufacturing and discharges through its turned-down upper end into a water seal or into a hydraulic main for removing solubles or condensable impurities

dip·py \ˈdipē\ *adj* -ER/-EST [origin unknown] **1** *slang* **:** mildly insane **:** slightly out of one's mind **:** MAD ⟨a girl feeling ~ about the boy next door⟩ **2** *slang* **:** FOOLISH ⟨a ~ scheme for making money⟩ **:** ODD, QUEER ⟨wearing a very ~ hat on the top of a bun⟩

dip·ri·on·i·dae \ˌdiprē'änə,dē\ *n pl, cap* [NL, fr. *Diprion*, type genus (fr. *di-* + *-prion*) + *-idae*] **:** a small family of sawflies that have many-jointed antennae serrate in the female and pectinate in the male and that include various serious pests of coniferous trees

di·prismatic \ˌdī+(ˌ)=ˈ==\ *adj* [*di-* + *prismatic*] **:** doubly prismatic

dip rope *n* **:** a seaman's rope tailed with chain for clearing hawse or for mooring

di·propellant \ˌdī+\ *n* [*di-* + *propellant*] **:** BIPROPELLANT

di·propyl \(ˈ)dī+\ *adj* [ISV *di-* + *propyl*] **:** containing two propyl groups in the molecule

dipropyl ketone *n* **:** BUTYRONE

di·pro·so·pus \ˌdīprə'sōpəs\ *n* -ES [NL, fr. Gk *diprosōpos* having two faces, fr. *di-* + *-prosōpos* -prosopous] **:** a fetal anomaly with two faces

di·pro·to·don \dī'prōdə,dän\ *n, cap* [NL, fr. *di-* + *prot-* + *-odon*] **1** *cap* **:** a monotypic genus of Australian Pleistocene herbivorous marsupials related to the kangaroos, resembling a rhinoceros in size, and walking on four legs — see DIPROTODONTIA **2** -s **:** any animal or fossil of the genus *Diprotodon*

¹di·pro·to·dont \(ˈ)dī,prōd·ə,dänt\ *adj* [NL *Diprotodont-*, *Diprotodon*] **:** belonging to Diprotodontia

²diprotodont \"\ *n* -s [NL *Diprotodont-*, *Diprotodon*] **:** a diprotodont mammal

di·pro·to·don·tia \(ˌ)dī,prōd·ə'dänch(ē)ə\ *n pl, cap* [NL, fr. *Diprotodont-*, *Diprotodon* + *-ia*] *in many classifications* **:** a suborder of Marsupialia comprising the kangaroos, phalangers, koala, wombats, the extinct giants of the genus *Diprotodon*, and other marsupials that are all almost exclusively herbivorous, have only one well-developed pair of lower incisors, but usu. have three pairs of upper incisors — compare POLYPROTODONTIA

dips *pl of* DIP, *pres 3d sing of* DIP

dip·sa·ca·ce·ae \ˌdipsə'kāsē,ē\ *n pl, cap* [NL, fr. *Dipsacus*, type genus + *-aceae*] **:** a family of chiefly southern European herbs (order Rubiales) having the flowers in heads as in the Compositae but with the stamens separate — **dip·sa·ca·ceous** \ˌ==ˈkāshəs\ *adj*

dip·sa·ce·ae \dip'sāsē,ē\ [NL, prob. alter. of *Dipsacaceae*] *syn of* DIPSACACEAE

dip·sa·ceous \(ˈ)dip'sāshəs\ *adj* [NL *Dipsaceae* + E *-ous*] **:** DIPSACACEOUS

dip·sa·cus \ˈdipsəkəs\ *n, cap* [NL, fr. Gk *dipsakos* teasel, diabetes, fr. *dipsa* thirst] **:** a genus (the type of the family Dipsacaceae) of Old World prickly herbs comprising the teasels

dip·sad·i·dae \dip'sadə,dē\ [NL, fr. *Dipsad-*, *Dipsas*, genus of snakes (fr. L *dipsad-*, *dipsas* dipsas) + *-idae*] *syn of* AMBLYCEPHALIDAE

dip·sa·do·mor·phi·dae \ˌdipsə(ˌ)dō'mȯrfə,dē\ [NL, fr. *Dipsadomorphus*, genus of snakes (fr. *dipsado-* — fr. L *dipsad-*, *dipsas* dipsas — + *-morphus* — fr. Gk *-morphos* -morphous) + *-idae*] *syn of* BOIGIDAE

dip·sas \ˈdipsəs\ *n, pl* **dip·sa·des** \-sə,dēz\ [ME *dipsas*, fr. L *dipsad-*, *dipsas*, fr. Gk, fr. *dipsa* thirst] **:** a serpent with a bite anciently supposed to produce intense thirst

¹dip·sey *or* **dip·sie** *or* **dip·sy** \ˈdipsē, -si\ *adj* [by alter.] **:** DEEP-SEA ⟨a ~ line⟩

²dipsey *or* **dipsie** *or* **dipsy** \"\ *n, pl* **dipseys** *or* **dipsies** **1 :** DEEP-SEA LEAD **2 :** a sinker attached to a fishing line

dip shift *n* **:** the component of the shift parallel with the dip of a fault

dip slip *n* **:** the part of a fault displacement that is recorded by the separation of originally continuous beds or veins measured straight down the dip and in the plane of the fault

dip–slip fault *n* **:** a geologic fault the displacement of which is predominantly a dip slip

dip slope *n* **:** a land surface inclined in the same direction and at the same angle as the dip of the underlying rocks

dip·so \ˈdip(ˌ)sō\ *n* -s [by shortening] **:** DIPSOMANIAC

dip·so·ma·nia \ˌdipsə'mānēə, -sō'-, -nyə\ *n* -s [NL, fr. *dipso-* (fr. Gk *dipsa* thirst) + *mania*] **:** an uncontrollable often periodic craving for alcoholic liquors; *also* **:** ALCOHOLISM — compare CHRONIC ALCOHOLISM

dip·so·ma·ni·ac \-nē,ak\ *n* -s [fr. NL *dipsomania*, after E *mania: maniac*] **:** one affected with dipsomania — **dip·so·ma·ni·a·cal** \ˌ==,mə'nīəkəl\ *adj*

dip·so·sau·rus \ˌdipsō'sȯrəs\ *n, cap* [NL, fr. *dipso-* (fr. Gk *dipsa* thirst) + *-saurus*] **:** a genus of small iguanid lizards including one form (*D. dorsalis*) that inhabits the desert regions of the southwestern U. S. and feeds on buds and flowers

dipstick \ˈ=,=\ *n* -s **1 :** DIP 6b **2 :** a graduated wooden stick or metal rod for indicating depth (as of oil in a crankcase or gasoline in a tank)

dip stream *n* **:** a stream flowing in the direction of the geologic dip of the rocks it traverses

dip switch *n, Brit* **:** a switch for dimming or lowering automobile headlight beams

dip·sy doo·dle \ˌdipsē'düdᵊl\ *also* **dipsy doo** \-dü\ *n* -s *often attrib* [origin unknown] **1** *slang* **:** a bewildering plunge and lag by turns ⟨the *dipsy doodle* price of rice shows how unsound the country's economy is⟩ **2** *slang* **:** artfully deceptive or shady manipulation ⟨not theorists, not the advocates of any alien philosophies or political *dipsy doo* —Joseph W. Martin⟩ **3 :** a very slow curve on a pitched ball in baseball

dipt *archaic past of* DIP

dip tank *n* **1 :** DIPPING TANK **2 :** a tank (as of paint) into which objects are dipped for finishing

dip·ter \ˈdiptə(r)\ *n* -s [NL *Diptera*] **:** DIPTERON

dipter- *or* **diptero-** *comb form* [NL, fr. Gk *dipteros*] **1 :** two-winged **:** dipterous ⟨*dipteral*⟩ **2 :** Diptera ⟨*dipterology*⟩

dip·tera \ˈdipt(ə)rə\ *n pl, cap* [NL, fr. Gk, neut. pl. of *dipteros* having two wings, fr. *di-* + *-pteros* -pterous] **:** a large order of winged or rarely wingless insects including the true flies (as the housefly), mosquitoes, midges, gnats, and related forms and a few specialized parasitic forms with the anterior wings usu. functional and the posterior pair reduced to small club-shaped structures, mouthparts adapted for sucking, lapping, or piercing or vestigial, and cylindrical or spindle-shaped segmented often headless, eyeless, and legless larvae that pass through a complex metamorphosis — see BRACHYCERA, HALTER, NEMATOCERA — **dip·ter·an** \-rən\ *n or adj*

dip·ter·al \-t(ə)rəl\ *adj* [L *dipteros* dipteral (fr. Gk *dipteros* having two wings) + E *-al*] **:** marked by columniation consisting of a completely surrounding double row of free columns ⟨a ~ Greek temple⟩ — see PSEUDODIPTERAL; COLUMNIATION illustration

dip·ter·ist \-t(ə)rəst\ *n* -s [NL *Diptera* + E *-ist*] **:** a specialist in the study of Diptera

dip·ter·o·carp \ˈdiptərō,kärp\ *n* -s [NL *Dipterocarpus*] **:** a plant of the genus *Dipterocarpus* or of the family Dipterocarpaceae

dip·ter·o·car·pa·ce·ae \ˌ==(ˌ)=ˌkär'pāsē,ē\ *n pl, cap* [NL, fr. *Dipterocarpus*, type genus + *-aceae*] **:** a family of trees (order Parietales) chiefly of tropical Asia yielding valuable wood and aromatic oils and resins and distinguished by having 2-winged fruit — **dip·ter·o·car·pa·ceous** \ˌ==(ˌ)=ˌ=ˈpāshəs\ *adj*

dip·ter·o·car·pous \ˌ===ˈkärpəs\ *adj* [*dipterocarp* + *-ous*] **:** of or relating to the genus *Dipterocarpus* or to the family Dipterocarpaceae

dip·ter·o·car·pus \ˌ===ˈ==\ *n, cap* [NL, fr. *dipter-* + *-carpus*] **:** a large genus (the type of the family Dipterocarpaceae) of tall trees ranging from India to the Philippines where they are important as timber — see GURJUN BALSAM

dip·tero·cecidium \ˌdiptə(ˌ)rō+\ *n* [NL, fr. *dipter-* + *cecidium*] **:** a gall caused by an insect of the order Diptera

dip·ter·ol·o·gy \ˌdiptə'räləjē\ *n* -ES [ISV *dipter-* + *-logy*] **:** a branch of entomology which relates to Diptera

dip·ter·on \ˈdiptə,rän\ *n, pl* **dip·tera** \-t(ə)rə\ [Gk, neut. of *dipteros* having two wings] **:** one of the Diptera

dip·ter·os \-tə,räs\ *n, pl* **dipter·oi** \-,rȯi\ [L, dipteral, fr. Gk, having two wings] **:** a dipteral building

dip·ter·ous \ˈdipt(ə)rəs\ *adj* [NL *dipterus*, fr. Gk *dipteros* having two wings] **1 :** having two wings or winglike appendages **2 :** of or relating to the Diptera

dip·ter·us \"\ *n, cap* [NL, fr. Gk *dipteros* having two wings] **:** a genus of Devonian dipnoan fishes of Scotland and America having ganoid scales, two short dorsal fins, and a heterocercal tail

dip·ter·yx \ˈdiptə(,)riks\ *n, cap* [NL, fr. *di-* + *-pteryx;* fr. the wing-shaped lobes of the calyx] **:** a small genus of tropical American trees (family Leguminosae) having opposite pinnate leaves and the calyx with the two upper petaloid lobes like wings — see TONKA BEAN

dip toast *n* **:** toast drenched with milk, cream, or melted butter

dip·tote \ˈdip,tōt\ *n, pl* **dip·totes** \-ōts\ *or* **dip·to·ta** \dip'tōd·ə\ [LL *diptoton* noun with only two cases, fr. Gk *diptōton*, neut. of *diptōtos* having one form for two cases, fr. *di-* + *-ptōtos* (fr. *piptein* to fall, influenced in meaning by Gk *ptōsis* case) — more at SYMPTOM] **:** a noun or adjective with only two cases

dip tube *n* **:** a glass or plastic device used for removing debris from the bottom of an aquarium

dip·tych \ˈdip(,)tik, -,tēk\ *n* -s [LL *diptycha*, pl., fr. Gk, fr. neut. pl. of *diptychos* folded, doubled, fr. *di-* + *-ptychos* (akin to Gk *ptychē* fold, layer)] **1 :** a 2-leaved hinged tablet folding together to protect writing on its waxed surfaces used by the ancient Romans for everyday writing **2** *usu pl* [ML *diptychum* list of the dead for whom prayers were said at mass, fr. LL *diptycha*, pl., 2-leaved tablet] **a :** a 2-leaved tablet containing in one part the names of living and in the other those of dead persons commemorated in eucharistic services **b :** the catalog or list of such persons **c :** the intercession in the course of which the commemoration was made **3 :** a picture or series of pictures (as an altarpiece) painted on two tablets connected by hinges — compare TRIPTYCH **4 a :** a literary work consisting of two contrasting parts (as a narrative telling the same story from two opposing points of view) ⟨a ~, a pastoral in which the author narrates the birth of Christ . . . first as it has impressed the rich countryman Asveer, then as it has been seen by the skeptic Nicodemus —François Closset⟩ **b :** any work made up of two matching parts treating complementary or contrasting pictorial phases of one general topic ⟨the first volume of a ~ *Vegetation and Flora of the Sonoran Desert* —F.E.Egler⟩

dip tube

di·pus \ˈdīpəs\ *n, cap* [NL, fr. Gk *dipous* jerboa, fr. *dipous* having two feet, fr. *di-* + *pous* foot — more at FOOT] **:** the type genus of Dipodidae comprising the typical jerboas with but three toes on each hind foot

dipware \ˈ=,=\ *n* **:** pottery decorated by being dipped in slip

di·py·lid·i·um \ˌdī,pī'lidēəm, ˌdīpə'l-\ *n, cap* [NL, fr. *di-* + Gk *pylid-*, *pylis* little gate (dim. of *pylē* gate) + NL *-ium*] **:** a genus of taenioid tapeworms including the common double-pored tapeworm (*D. caninum*) that is a cosmopolitan parasite of dogs, cats, and other carnivores and occas. infests man

dip·y·lon \ˈdipə,län\ *adj, often cap* [*Dipylon*, gateway on the west side of ancient Athens, near which pottery in this style has been found] **:** distinctive of an elaborate stage of ancient Greek pottery making and decorating in the geometric style marked by pictures of funerals

di·pyramid \(ˈ)dī+\ *n* [*di-* + *pyramid*] **:** a crystal consisting of two pyramids base to base, the one geometrically a mirror image of the other with respect to the horizontal plane of symmetry ⟨~*s* occur in the tetragonal, hexagonal, and orthorhombic systems and may have corresponding orthorhombic, tetragonal, ditetragonal, hexagonal, or dihexagonal symmetry⟩

di·pyramidal \(ˌ)dī+\ *adj* [*dipyramid* + *-al*] **1 :** having the shape of a dipyramid **2 :** having symmetry such that the general form is a dipyramid — used of certain of the 32 classes of symmetry

di·pyre \ˈdī,pī(ə)r\ *n* -s [F, fr. *di-* + Gk *pyr* fire; fr. the double effect of fire in fusing it and making it phosphorescent — more at FIRE] : MIZZONITE; *specif* : a variety of scapolite with the components marialite and meionite in a ratio of about 3:2

dir *abbr* **1** direction; directional **2** director

di·radical \(ˈ)dī+\ *n* -S [*di-* + *radical*] : BIRADICAL

dir·ca \ˈdərkə\ *n* [NL, fr. L *Dirce*, a fountain near Thebes in Boeotia, fr. Gk *Dirkē*] **1** *cap* : a genus of shrubs (family Thymelaeaceae) having tough fibrous bark and clusters of yellow flowers — see LEATHERWOOD 1a **2** -S : any plant of the genus *Dirca*

¹dird \ˈdird\ *n* -S [prob. short for *dirdum*] *Scot* : a powerful blow or stroke

²dird \ˈ"\ *vb*, *Scot* : BUMP, BOUNCE, JOLT

dir·dum \ˈdirdəm\ *n* -S [ME (northern dial.) *durdan*, fr. ScGael, grumbling, hum, dim. of *durd* hum, word, sound; akin to IrGael *dordan* hum, buzz, *dord* humming, buzzing] **1** *Scot* : UPROAR, FUSS **2** *Scot* **a** : REBUKE, SCOLDING **b** : BLAME, PUNISHMENT **3** *Scot* : a piece of bad luck : MISFORTUNE

dire \ˈdī(ə)r, -īə\ *adj* -ER/-EST [L *dirus*; akin to Gk *dediénai* to fear, *deos* fear, *deinos* terrible, Av *dvaēthā* threat, Skt *dveṣṭi* he hates] **1 a** : exciting horror or terror esp. because of the great suffering or loss or devastating ruin actually caused or only threatened ⟨the ~ days of bombing raids⟩ ⟨if South America were to seek her imports elsewhere, it would be a ~ blow to us —Gustave Weigel⟩ ⟨the ~ fate which the Lord had seen fit to visit upon her sinful employers —W.H.Wright⟩ **b** : inducing mental suffering or depression by reason of concern with a dreaded eventuality or a grievous circumstance : AFFLICTIVE, PAINFUL ⟨palsied by the ~ news of the president's death⟩ **c** : oppressive to the feelings or spirit : DISMAL, CHEERLESS ⟨the heavy drag of winter is then at its most ~ —F.M.Ford⟩ ⟨despite its ~ point of view, the book jests and jostles with life —*Time*⟩ **2** : warning of disaster to come : OMINOUS, SINISTER ⟨in the fight against foot-and-mouth disease proposals to substitute vaccination for eradication evoked ~ forecasts⟩ **3 a** : demanding immediate action to fend off disastrous consequences : EXIGENT, URGENT ⟨spokesmen talked about the ~ need for school buildings, which had been at least equally ~ during the previous two years —W.L.Miller⟩ ⟨this was due to ~ necessities elsewhere and not to direct intent or indifference —Herbert Feis⟩ **b** : close to the utmost limit of sufferance : most acute : EXTREME, DESPERATE ⟨scope is left for instantaneous action, but only in the *direst* emergency —A.P.Ryan⟩ ⟨while their means were always modest there was no trace of ~ poverty —J.T.Ellis⟩ ⟨left his family in ~ financial straits⟩ **syn** see FEARFUL

¹di·rect \də'rekt *also* dī'r- *sometimes* ˈdī,r- — *compare* ²DIRECT\ *vb* -ED/-ING/-S [ME *directen*, fr. L *directus*, past part. of *dirigere* to set straight, direct, guide — more at DRESS] *vt* **1 a** *obs* : to dedicate to a person **b** *obs* : to write to a person **c** : to mark or label the outer surface of (a message or package to be delivered) with the name and residence or place of business of the intended recipient : SUPERSCRIBE **d** : to supply with a heading, statement, or other indication of a specific addressee or desired recipient ⟨the auditors' certificate ~*ed* to the stockholders⟩ **e** : to impart orally ⟨the speaker ~*ed* a side remark to the gallery⟩ **f** : to adapt and arrange in expression so as to have particular applicability or appeal : ANGLE — used with *to* or *at* ⟨a lawyer who ~*s* his appeals to intelligence and character⟩ **2** : to cause to turn, move, or point undeviatingly or to follow a straight course with a particular destination or object in view: **a** : to dispatch, aim, or guide usu. along a fixed path ⟨X rays are ~*ed* through a portion of the body⟩ ⟨wavelengths ~*ed* to southeast Asia⟩ ⟨sensitivity to humor ~*ed* toward himself⟩ ⟨to Peru was ~*ed* one of the main currents of Spanish colonial conquest —P.E.James⟩ ⟨that Locke's influence upon his successors was primarily to ~ them to empiricism —J.W.Yolton⟩; *also* : ASSIGN, ALLOT ⟨many industries ~ part of their earnings to academic scholarship funds⟩ **b** : to devote with concentration — used usu. with *to* or *toward* ⟨has he found that he must have someone else toward whom he can ~ his mind and in whom he can expand himself —H.A.Overstreet⟩ ⟨~*ing* their whole attention toward the international conflict⟩ **c** : to aim fixedly : concern or involve oneself primarily or totally with — used with *to* or *toward* ⟨ecclesiastical policy was ~*ed* primarily toward the liberation of the church from the fetters of secular interest and state expediency —H.D.Hazeltine⟩ ⟨applied research may be defined as research ~*ed* to the end of reducing the degree of empiricism in a practical art —J.B.Conant⟩ **d** : to point, extend, or project esp. upward or downward ⟨in these mammoths the tusks are vertically ~*ed* at their bases —A.S.Romer⟩ **e** : to engage in or launch hostilely : FOCUS — used with *against* or *at* ⟨our policy is not ~*ed* against any country or doctrine but against hunger, poverty, desperation, and chaos —G.C. Marshall⟩ ⟨if atomic or biological warfare should be ~*ed* against us⟩; *also* : to institute for possible launching or application ⟨binding agreements of a much more specific character ~*ed* at a potential aggressor —Vera M. Dean⟩ **3** : to show or point out the way for ⟨a guide ~*s* tourists to the marine museum⟩ ⟨the map ~*s* us to the left⟩ **4** : to regulate the activities or course of: **a** : to guide and supervise ⟨~*ed* the floor strategy in the House of Representatives⟩ ⟨the archaeologist ~*ing* the excavations⟩; *specif* : to carry out the organizing, energizing, and supervising of esp. in an authoritative capacity ⟨~*ed* the building and arming of an underground network⟩ ⟨not only public propaganda, but also cultural infiltration, is ~*ed* from the same source —A.T.Bouscaren⟩ **b** : ADMINISTER, CONDUCT ⟨ably ~*ed* music and language departments⟩ ⟨while in office he ~*ed* vigorous prosecutions of racketeers⟩ **c** : to dominate and determine the course of ⟨will not find it preposterous that the past should be altered by the present as much as the present is ~*ed* by the past —T.S.Eliot⟩ **d** : to assist by giving advice, instruction, and supervision ⟨the major professor ~*s* graduate students' thesis research⟩; *specif* : to lend a refining, cultivating, or inspiring influence to ⟨~ American taste and mold the genius of the young republic —Van Wyck Brooks⟩ **e** : to train and lead performances of (a musical or dramatic aggregation); *also* : to lead a group in presenting (a ballet, opera, concert, play, or motion picture) **5 a** : to request or enjoin esp. with authority ⟨the judge ~*ed* the clerk to pass him the paper⟩ ⟨the resolution ~*ed* the commission to prepare proposals⟩ ⟨I ~ my executors to present my library intact to my alma mater⟩; *also* : to issue an order to ⟨Lee ~*ed* Jackson to make a wide march to the southwest —T.R.Hay⟩ **b** : to prescribe esp. by formal or mandatory instruction or legal enactment ⟨a court order ~*ing* that the person be brought to a court hearing⟩ ⟨postal inspectors ~*ed* destruction of the obscene matter⟩ ~ *vi* **1** : to point out, prescribe, or determine a course or procedure ⟨however chance shall ~⟩ ⟨the ~*ing* agencies of society — the family, the city, the church, the school, the workshop, and above all the state —J.M.Cameron⟩ ⟨the old theological notion that there is in the universe besides ourselves some ~*ing* power that means well by us —J.W.Beach⟩ **2** : to direct an orchestra or chorus or a dramatic group or performance ⟨equally clever at composing and ~*ing*⟩

syn ADDRESS, DEVOTE, APPLY: these four verbs have in common a reflexive use signifying to turn or bend one's attention, energies, or efforts to something. DIRECT and ADDRESS are not significantly different; one can *direct* or *address* oneself to a task, to one's work, or to the study of something; one can *direct* or *address* one's attention, one's remarks, one's writings to something or someone. DIRECT may possibly stress more an aim or intent, ADDRESS more an appeal to or claim upon attention or interest ⟨asked myself to what purpose I should *direct* my energies —M.R.Cohen⟩ ⟨to *direct* my endeavors . . . toward the object of my search —Mary W. Shelley⟩ ⟨speakers *addressed* themselves to a common question —H.W.Sams⟩ ⟨a story *addressed* not only to one's sense of excitement and the exotic but also to his sense of honor and humanity —Charles Lee⟩ DEVOTE often adds the implication of persistence or of personal dedication ⟨at Cornell he *devoted* himself primarily to his studies and to athletics —*Current Biog.*⟩ ⟨*devoted* himself chiefly to the affairs of this school for the next eight or ten years of his life —S.P.Chase & R.E.Ham⟩ APPLY stresses often an intentional turning of the attention or energies, often a concentration or concentrated application; one APPLIES oneself to a task when, after consideration, he determines upon doing the task, or when he directs his whole attention to it, esp. for some time ⟨he cannot *apply* himself to study —Charles Clairmont⟩ ⟨after having received a careful education . . . he *applied* his attention to practical military subjects —*Encyc. Americana*⟩ **syn** see in addition COMMAND, CONDUCT

²di·rect \də'rekt *also* (ˈ)dī¦r-, *rapid* ˈdre-; *after a monosyllabic prefix* -dī- *occurs less often than in other environments, pronunciations like* dī¦rektə'nində,rekt ("*direct and indirect*") *being frequent*\ *adj sometimes* -ER/-EST [ME, fr. L *directus* straight, direct, fr. past part. of *dirigere*] **1 a** : proceeding from one point to another in time or space without deviation or interruption : not crooked, oblique, reflected, refracted, or circuitous ⟨~ blows of the gavel⟩ ⟨disintegrated by the ~ heat⟩ ⟨exposed to the ~ force of the hurricane⟩ **b** : leading by the short or shortest way to a point or end ⟨a ~ route⟩ ⟨~ means⟩ ⟨~ rays⟩ ⟨~ and speedy passenger service to the coast⟩ **c** *obs* : moving or extending at a right angle to a surface ⟨a ship needs a ~ wind to enter⟩ **d** : transmitted back and forth without an intermediary ⟨engaged in a ~ exchange of recriminations⟩ ⟨no ~ communication with the flooded area⟩ **e** : assigned in the postal service for separate delivery to a particular addressee rather than routed according to street address ⟨a letter deposited in a ~ pouch⟩ **f** : capable of being allocated to a particular portion or process of an undertaking and so treated in cost accounts; *specif* : chargeable to a particular job — compare DIRECT COST, DIRECT LABOR **2 a** : operating or guided without digression or obstruction ⟨while he gives his more ~ attention to something nearer at hand —Nathaniel Hawthorne⟩ ⟨her letters . . . are a ~ reflection of her personality —R.A.Hall b. 1911⟩ ⟨~ expansion of consumption is of utmost urgency —*New Republic*⟩ **b** : stemming immediately from a source ⟨having no ~ authority over factory employment policies⟩ **c** : being or passing in a straight line of descent from parent to offspring : LINEAL ⟨only a collateral relative, not his ~ ancestor⟩ ⟨the examiner should not overvalue the influence of ~ heredity —H.G.Armstrong⟩ **d** : clear-cut and distinctive : having no compromising or impairing element : GENUINE, OUT-AND-OUT ⟨an undertaking having a ~ social purpose⟩ ⟨the soldier's pleasures are simple and ~ —Fred Majdalany⟩ ⟨hoping to avoid ~ involvement in the war⟩ **e** : blunt and unqualified : delivered point-blank : CATEGORICAL ⟨his petition for a salary increase was met with a ~ rebuff⟩ ⟨get back to your post. That's a ~ order —Irwin Shaw⟩ ⟨evidence from original documents of the dark ages often give the lie ~ to sentimental novelists⟩ **f** *cryptanalysis, of alphabetic sequences* : arranged or employed in traditional order : not reversed **3 a** : characterized by or giving evidence of a close esp. logical, causal, or consequential relationship ⟨there is a ~ personal tie which assures the beginning of real understanding between individuals —D.J.Shank⟩ ⟨most scientific discoveries now have a ~ bearing on security⟩ ⟨for 20 years in ~ association with the library⟩ ⟨a hundred different complications in which we shall have a ~ interest —F.D. Roosevelt⟩ **b** : INEVITABLE, UNEQUIVOCAL ⟨one ~ result of improving the living conditions was a rise in the birthrate⟩ **c** : serving to get to the point : EFFECTIVE ⟨raising funds would be a ~*er* way of helping the cause⟩ **d** : communicating explicitly often with brusqueness : going straight to the point ⟨before any inquiry so ~ as to demand a positive answer was addressed to her —Jane Austen⟩ ⟨keeps the play ~, uncluttered, and so brisk that the long and familiar story does not make martyrs of its audience —Henry Hewes⟩ ⟨her choreography is ~, nowhere obscured by extraneous devices⟩ **e** : frank, natural, and positive : STRAIGHTFORWARD ⟨a charming, lively person who had a ~ mind, said what he thought and believed others did the same —*Times Lit. Supp.*⟩ ⟨that one's relations with others should be ~ and not diplomatic —A.C.Benson⟩ ⟨it often told you a great deal that was both too ~ and too elusive for words —Willa Cather⟩ **f** *of the object of a verb* : being the one that is the primary goal of an action ⟨*him* in "I saw him" and *me* in "he hit me" are ~ objects⟩ or that results from an action ⟨*a house* in "we built a house" is the ~ object⟩ **4** : marked by absence of an intervening agency, instrumentality, or influence : IMMEDIATE: **a** : made, carried on, or effected without any intruding factor or intervening step ⟨~ loans⟩ ⟨relying less and less on ~ observation of nature —Eric Newton⟩ ⟨some ~ borrowing of Anglo-Norman into English⟩ ⟨until the breaking off of ~ negotiations⟩ **b** : effected by the votes of the people or the electorate and not by representatives ⟨elected for 7 years by ~ suffrage —*Statesman's Yr. Bk.*⟩ ⟨institutions of ~ democracy — popular initiative, the referendum, and the recall —C.A.M.Ewing⟩ ⟨the ~ election of senators —E.P.Herring⟩ **c** : unhampered by divergent, intervening, or separative forces ⟨he had more ~ access to the governor than the legislators⟩ ⟨prefer the more ~ American approach to human problems —David Daiches⟩ **d** : effected by one object or substance in contact with another with no insulating or obstructing element between ⟨~ contact with another metal must be avoided⟩ ⟨there is no ~ connection between the apartments⟩ **e** : consisting of or reproducing the exact words of a real or supposed original speaker ⟨the words in quotation marks in the sentence *He said, "I can come"* are ~ quotation⟩ ⟨~ discourse⟩ **f** (1) : being without intermediate logical steps ⟨~ proofs⟩ (2) : independent of intermediate representations, percepts, images, or sense data ⟨~ knowledge of things⟩ **g** : not requiring an intermediate host for completion : MONOXENOUS — used of the life cycle or development of a parasitic organism **h** : capable of dyeing without the aid of a mordant : SUBSTANTIVE — see DIRECT DYE **5 a** : experienced personally without associative effort of anyone else ⟨his account of the battle contains much ~ evidence⟩ ⟨whereas to conceal ~ pain was a virtue, to conceal vicarious pain was a sin —Jan Struther⟩; *specif* : FIRSTHAND ⟨from ~ experience with youngsters at camp⟩ **b** : active, personal, and responsible ⟨taking ~ charge of the distribution of relief funds⟩ ⟨the ordinary worker has a ~ part in the production process⟩; *specif* : not deputed or to be deputed ⟨few were willing to assume ~ responsibility⟩ **6 a** *of a celestial body* : moving in the general planetary direction from west to east : not retrograde **b** *of a binary star* : following the direction of increasing position angle : COUNTERCLOCKWISE **7** *of a sundial* : having a vertical face and facing squarely toward one of the cardinal points of the compass

³di·rect \də'rekt *also* dī'-, *rapid* ˈdre-\ *adv* [ME, fr. *direct*, adj.] : in a direct way: **a** : from point to point without deviation : by the short or shortest way ⟨by helicopter it is now possible to go ~ from port to airport in forty minutes —Ivor Jones⟩ ⟨despatching individual books ~ to individual teachers —James Britton⟩ **b** : from the source or the original without interruption or diversion ⟨broadcast ~ from ringside⟩ ⟨the writer must take his material ~ from life —Douglas Stewart⟩ **c** : mechanically joined or in mesh : mechanically or electrically in contact ⟨*direct*-controlled by the helmsman⟩ **d** (1) : without any intervening agency or step : without any intruding or diverting factor ⟨some enter a career ~ from college⟩ ⟨refusal to negotiate ~ with the puppet regime⟩; *specif* : without use of a broker or other middleman ⟨butter that is sold ~ without going through the exchanges —Geoffrey Shepherd⟩ (2) : EXPLICITLY, UNEQUIVOCALLY ⟨the right information ~ from his office⟩ ⟨in reporting news the television camera brings the event and the personalities ~ to the public —*Collier's Yr. Bk.*⟩ (3) : VERBATIM ⟨translated ~ from the Russian text⟩

⁴direct \ˈ"\ *n* -S [²*direct*] **1** : a character sometimes put at the end of a musical staff or page of music on a line or space corresponding to the position of the first note of the next staff as a warning to the performer — called also *custos* **2** : a direct package of postal matter

di·rect·able \də'rektəbəl *also* dī'-, *rapid* ˈdre-\ *adj* : capable of being directed

direct-acting \¦≈¦≈≈, ¦≈≈¦≈≈\ *adj* : involving direct action without the intervention of other working parts ⟨*direct-acting* engine⟩ ⟨*direct-acting* pump⟩

direct action *n* : action that seeks to achieve an end directly and by the most immediately effective means as opposed to the use of diplomatic exchange or negotiation; *specif* : action by organized labor to obtain ends by means of boycott, sabotage, or striking — contrasted with *political action*

direct bearing *n* : direct vertical support for any structural element in a construction

direct black *n* : any of various direct dyes that dye cotton black — see DYE table I

direct cell division *n* : AMITOSIS

direct cerebellar tract *n* : a tract of fibers in the posterior lateral part of the spinal cord that is external to the crossed pyramidal tract, that arises from the cells of the nucleus dorsalis, and that passes through the restiform body of the medulla to the cerebellum

direct-connected \¦≈¦≈≈, ¦≈≈¦≈≈\ *adj, of machines* : being on a common shaft : DIRECT-COUPLED

direct contempt *n* : a contempt occurring in the presence of a court in session or so near as to interfere with the administration of justice or in the presence of a judge acting in a judicial capacity; *also* : a contempt directly obstructing a legislative body in the actual exercise of its lawful legislative powers — compare CONSTRUCTIVE CONTEMPT

direct control *n* : a control that is directly imposed upon the manufacturing, pricing, and distribution of specific goods in contrast with an indirect or general control (as a credit and fiscal policy) that affects the economy in its entirety and specific goods only indirectly

direct cost *also* **direct charge** *n* : a cost that may be computed and identified directly with a product, function, or activity and that usu. involves expenditures for raw materials and direct labor and sometimes specific and identifiable items of overhead — contrasted with *indirect cost*

direct-coupled \¦≈¦≈≈, ¦≈≈¦≈≈\ *adj* **1** *of belting or gearing* : coupled without intermediate connections **2** *of an electric circuit* : having conductive rather than inductive or capacitive coupling

direct current *n* : an electric current flowing in one direction only and substantially constant in value — abbr. *D.C.*; compare ALTERNATING CURRENT

direct deep black EW *n, usu cap both Ds&B* : a trisazo dye derived from benzidine and used esp. for dyeing cotton and leather and as a biological stain — called also *chlorazol black E, direct black EW*; see DYE table I (*under Direct Black 38*)

direct democracy *n* : DEMOCRACY 1b(1)

direct development *n* : development without a metamorphosis

direct distance dialing *n* : the dialing of a telephone number outside the local calling area by using initial code numbers to make a direct connection — abbr. *DDD*

direct drive *n* : a drive whose driving and driven parts are direct-connected

direct-driven \¦≈¦≈≈, ¦≈≈¦≈≈\ *adj* : driven by another machine to which it is direct-connected

direct dye *n* : a water-soluble dye usu. of the azo class that is used in alkaline or neutral solution esp. for dyeing cellulosic material (as cotton or paper) directly — see DYE table I

directed *adj* [fr. past part. of ¹*direct*] **1** : having a positive or negative sense — used of a line segment or vector **2** : subject to regulation by a guiding and supervising agency ⟨a ~ economy that would permit an increased volume of capital investments on the part of the state —C.A.L.Rich⟩ ⟨a ~ study program for gifted children⟩

di·rect·ed·ly *adv* : under guidance and supervision

di·rect·ed·ness *n* -ES : subjection to a guiding or motivating influence ⟨the interplay within the individual of these two ~*es* —Adam Curle⟩

directed number *n* : a number preceded by a plus or minus sign

directed verdict *n* : a verdict that the jury is instructed by the court to find when the facts proved do not admit in the court's opinion of any reasonable doubt

di·rect·ee \də,rek¦tē, dī,r-, ¦dī,rek¦-\ *n* -S [¹*direct* + *-ee*] : one who receives direction

directer *comparative of* DIRECT

directest *superlative of* DIRECT

direct evidence *n* : evidence that if true immediately establishes the fact to be proved by it

direct examination *n* : the first examination of a witness in the orderly course by the party calling him and upon the merits

direct exchange *n* : FIXED EXCHANGE

direct finder *n* : DIRECT VIEWFINDER

direct fire *n* [³*direct* + *fire*, v.] : gunfire by direct aiming on a visible target

direct-fire \¦≈¦≈, ¦≈≈¦≈\ *vt* : to fire without provision for preheating the air or gas ⟨some furnaces are *direct-fired*⟩

direct-geared \ˈ"\ *adj* : connected for power transmission by a gear on the power shaft of one machine meshing with a gear on the driving or following shaft of another machine

direct grant school *n, in England & Wales* : a private secondary school that receives a direct grant from the ministry of education and in return binds itself to obey certain conditions with reference to admission of pupils

directing *pres part of* DIRECT

directing piece *n* : BASE PIECE

direct initiative *n* : the legislative initiative where a proposed measure is submitted directly to the voters — distinguished from *indirect initiative*; compare INITIATIVE 3b

direct investment *n* : investment of capital in physical assets or in ownership of a whole enterprise — contrasted with *portfolio investment*

¹di·rec·tion \də'rekshən *also* dī'-, *rapid* ˈdre-\ *n* -S [MF & L; MF, fr. L *direction-, directio*, fr. *directus* (past part. of *dirigere* to direct, guide) + *-ion-, -io* -ion — more at DRESS] **1 a** : guidance or supervision of action, conduct, or operation ⟨the whole system of life had its culmination in the church; and parson and squire presided over its ~ —C.E.Raven⟩ ⟨under whose ~ this paper was written⟩ ⟨the doctrine that government should move forward toward ~ of the economy⟩; *specif* : chief executive function ⟨he was put in charge and given overall ~ of the program⟩ **b** : the art and technique of directing a stage play, a motion picture, or a television program consisting of the selection of the effects to be produced, the means to produce these effects, and the management and training of the cast **c** : the art and technique of directing the performance of an orchestra, opera, or concert or of a chorus or other musical group ⟨the musicianly ~ . . . helped illumine the score —Miles Kastendieck⟩ **d** : a word or phrase usu. in Italian or a sign indicating the appropriate tempo, mood, or intensity of a passage or movement in a musical score **2** *archaic* : the address placed on the outside of a letter or package to be delivered : SUPERSCRIPTION ⟨pray send me Grandmamma's ~. I must write to her —W.M.Thackeray⟩ **3 a** : something that is imposed as authoritative instruction or bidding ⟨the senate had been voting according to ~ for so long that they seemed to have lost the power of independent decision —Robert Graves⟩ ⟨he gave orders all round and men quickly obeyed—relieved at ~ —Harris Downey⟩ **b** : an explicit instruction : ORDER, COMMAND ⟨a report prepared at the ~ of the president⟩ — often used in pl. ⟨the author's stage ~*s* to actors and cameramen⟩ ⟨~*s* appear on the package⟩ **c** : the charge or instruction given on a point of law by a judge to a jury **4** *obs* : administrative capacity **5 a** : the property of space by which given two positions others may be generated or determined in the same dimension and relation, the aspect of progression being usu. implicit **b** : the line or course on which something is moving or is aimed to move or along which something is pointing or facing ⟨the ~ of a current is that toward which the water moves, which is the reverse of the way winds are named —G.W.Mixter⟩ ⟨follow the ~ of the arrow⟩ **c** : a line or course extending away from a given point through space and often designated by the point of the compass toward which it extends ⟨from the tower sweeping views in all ~*s*⟩ ⟨below the falls the river meanders in a southeasterly ~⟩ **d** : the shortest path toward the vicinity or source — used in the expression *in the direction of* ⟨throwing grenades in the ~ of the voices⟩ **e** : a position on a line extending through space toward a point of the compass ⟨from what ~ will the attack come⟩ ⟨protests poured in from all ~*s*⟩; *also* : a point of view or an angle from which something may be considered ⟨the three authors attack the same subject from three different ~*s*⟩ **f** : the angle between a true north-south line passing through the position of the observer and a great circle passing through both this position and a given point on the surface of the earth : BEARING **g** : the path of either the longest straight line that can be drawn along a sheet or band of paper or a straight line crossing this at right angles from edge to edge **6 a** : a channel or direct course of thought or action ⟨the outbreak of war gave another ~ to his activities⟩ ⟨the ~*s* in which voters can express their will are limited⟩ ⟨with business expanding in all ~*s*⟩ **b** : a course of progress, development, or evolution showing a distinct tendency or trend ⟨his latest title indicates the ~ his historical studies have taken〉 〈the existence of the censorship deters men . . . from essaying new ~s in drama —A.B.Walkley〉 〈it is because culture molds the specific ~ and activities of the personality —Abram Kardiner〉; *also* **:** tenor of a saying or writing 〈I had felt and written to him in the same general ~ —O.W.Holmes †1935〉 **c :** a path or course esp. of thought or effort marked by a specific aim or design 〈the introduction of printing in Italy in 1462 gave a new ~ to scholarship —R.A.Hall b. 1911〉 〈ideals are not meant to be reached; they merely indicate the ~ of movement —Edward Sapir〉 〈even those who do not accept the letter of his dogma are in accord with the ~ taken by his thought —W.L.Sperry〉; *also* **:** a pointing of thought or effort on a predetermined path or course 〈his ~ toward a life of asceticism and contemplation was already clear —W.P.Clancy〉 〈there the boy began to give ~ to the instinct for arranging nature that later was translated into a delightful profession —José Gómez-Sicre〉 〈a deep uncertainty about goals and obligations pervades all classes and all levels of culture. Our society has lost ~ —Walter Moberly〉 **d :** an onward path determined through inclination or guidance pointing toward some attainment 〈the conspiracy gained momentum and ~ —R.C.Doty〉 〈slow to make up his mind what his ~ as a writer ought to be〉 〈stood about idly on the street corners without purpose or ~ in their lives —Oscar Handlin〉 **e :** determinative guiding or governing design 〈cultivate the historical sense and a sense of ~, and read some good books on the history of law; at least, the law has ~ —Caroline Slade〉 **7 :** the way of advancement, furtherance, or cultivation **:** AIM, PURPOSE, OBJECTIVE — used in the expression *in the direction of* 〈gains made in the ~ of integration〉 〈a significant step in the ~ of cooperation between the executive and congress in treaty making —Vera M. Dean〉 〈advocate of reforms particularly in the ~ of equalizing the legal status of men and women —H.W.H.Knott〉 **8 :** an indicated sphere or role in which something may be regarded **:** a particular respect 〈a few pencil portraits do exist which show that he had great talent in this ~ —Herbert Read〉 〈much of the literature (geographical, historical, and economic) on Czechoslovakia is biased in one ~ or another —*Geog. Jour.*〉 **9** *archaic* **:** DIRECTORATE 1 **10 :** a calculation by reference to a horoscope of the times when events will happen **11** *in equity practice* **:** the part of a bill containing the address to the court **12 :** the lateral pointing of an artillery piece — compare ELEVATION **13 :** one of the cardinal points which among some peoples include the zenith, nadir, and center and intermediate points of the compass

²di·rec·tion \"\ *vt* **directioned**; **directioned**; **directioning** \-sh(ə)niŋ\ **directions :** to give a direction to **:** direct along a line 〈strangely ~*ed* water —D.L.Morgan〉

di·rec·tion·al \-shənᵊl, -shnəl\ *adj* **1 :** relating to direction in space: **a :** moving, aiming, or leading in some particular direction 〈a strictly ~ flight on a great circle〉 〈~ lines showing winds and ocean currents〉 **b :** suitable or used for detecting the direction in which or from which signals are received 〈plot position by ~ radio〉 〈flying on the beam of a ~ radio range〉 **c :** so designed that performance depends on direction or is restricted in direction **:** more effective in some directions than others 〈a polarized ~ electromagnet controls the position and shape of the tail flame —J.K.Elderkin〉 〈the use of ~ broadcasting techniques had made it possible to increase the number of radio stations —F.L.Mott〉; *specif* **:** narrowly selective as to direction in the emission or reception of signals 〈a highly ~ microphone picks up sounds coming from a single direction〉 〈that a Geiger-Müller tube cannot be made ~ enough and still retain any measure of workable sensitivity —*Surgical Forum*〉 **d** *of sound* **:** controlled for giving depth and realism in motion pictures by the use of several sound tracks recorded at different parts of the set or location **e :** indicating the direction in which something lies or the direction to take or about to be taken 〈a ~ airway marker〉 〈~ arrows for facilitating movement of traffic〉 〈flashing ~ signals for motorcars and trucks〉 **2 :** relating to direction (as of thought, effort, or culture): **a :** aimed or moving in the direction of one or another object, objective, or condition 〈the picture presented is frankly chaotic; it is hard to recognize in it any unifying pattern, any ~ trends —V.G.Childe〉 〈the ~ quality of cultural change〉 **b :** constitutive of purpose or motivation **3 a :** consisting of or imposing direction or guidance 〈the ~ role that profits play under capitalism〉 **b :** suitable or contributory to the direction of dramatic performance 〈good plays and even good ~ ideas frequently take on a distressingly ragged aspect in performance —H.E.Clurman〉 **c** *of an oil-well drilling* **:** made at an angle with the vertical

directional filter *n* **:** an electric filter designed to divide the band of frequencies available for carrier currents about midway using one portion of the band for east-to-west transmission and the other portion for west-to-east transmission

directional gyro *n* **:** an air-driven free gyroscope with rotor spinning on a horizontal axis that when manually set to some one direction maintains that fixed direction despite maneuvers of its conveyor and thereby indicates any deviation from the course

di·rec·tion·al·i·ty \də,reksha'naləd.ē, (,)dī,-\ *n* -ES **1 :** the property of directional selectivity or precision 〈a scintillation counter was devised in such a fashion as to give a ~ of fifteen degrees and adequate sensitivity —*Surgical Forum*〉 **2 :** maintenance of direction 〈among these properties is that of ~ —C.K.Kluckhohn〉

di·rec·tion·al·ize \də'reksh(ə)nə,līz, dī'-\ *vt* -ED/-ING/-S **:** to guide or govern as to direction

di·rec·tion·al·ly \-nəlē, -li\ *adv* **:** as to or with reference to direction

direction angle *n* **:** an angle made by a given line with an axis of reference; *specif* **:** one of the three angles made by a straight line with the three axes of a rectangular coordinate system

direction cosine *n* **:** one of the cosines of the three angles between a directed line in space and the positive directions of the axes of a rectangular Cartesian coordinate system — usu. used in pl.

direction finder *n* **:** a radio receiving device permitting determination of the direction from which received radio waves come to it, typically consisting of a coil antenna mounted on a vertical axis so that it can be rotated freely

direction finding *n* **:** the finding of the azimuth of a distant transmitter by the use of a direction finder

direction indicator *n* **:** a compass that assists an airplane pilot in flying a predetermined course by direct reading and comparison of two indicators one of which is set for the desired heading while the other shows the actual heading so that when the two indicators point alike the airplane is flying the desired course

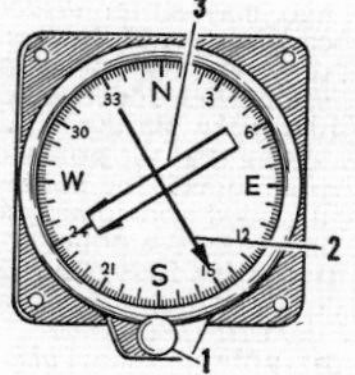

direction indicator: *1* index setting knob, *2* pointer, *3* reference index

di·rec·tion·ize \-shə,nīz\ *vt* -ED/-ING/-S **:** to impel in a particular direction

di·rec·tion·less \-ənləs\ *adj* **1 :** having no discernible direction **2 :** having no guiding purpose

direction post *n, Brit* **:** GUIDEPOST

directions *pl of* DIRECTION, *pres 3d sing of* DIRECTION

direction test *n* **:** a psychological test measuring an individual's success in following simple or complex directions

direction word *n* **:** CATCHWORD 1a

¹di·rec·tive \də'rektiv, -tēv *also* dī'- *or* -təv\ *adj* [MF & ML; MF *directif*, fr. ML *directivus*, fr. L *directus* (past part. of *dirigere* to direct, guide) + *-ivus* -ive — more at DRESS] **1 :** serving or qualified to lead, guide, or govern thought or action usu. by prompting and impelling rather than by dominating 〈the ~ power of conscience〉 〈experimenting to find which is superior, the permissive or the ~ method of teaching〉 〈every manager who has at least one subordinate engages in the ~ function —Harold Koontz & Cyril O'Donnell〉 **2 :** serving to point direction 〈the ~ power of a magnetized needle〉 〈the ~ function of a compass〉; *specif* **:** DIRECTIONAL 1c 〈a more ~ aerial〉 **3 :** pointing the way **:** concentrating or focusing on an objective **:** selective as to tendency or trend 〈like the realities of the external environment they exercise a ~ influence on the development of behavior patterns —Ralph Linton〉 **4 :** of or relating to psychotherapy or counseling in which the counselor introduces information, content, or attitudes not previously expressed by the client

²directive \"\ *n* -S **1 :** something that serves to direct, guide, and usu. impel toward an action, attainment, or goal: **a :** a pronouncement urging or banning some action or conduct **:** BIDDING 〈leaders became too fond of passing down ~s to the members instead of calling for a vote〉; *also* **:** a sharp or peremptory word of command 〈"keep your head down!" . . . and a heavy hand on top of his head added persuasion to the ~ —Helen Nielsen〉 **b :** an assignment, instruction, or injunction by a superior 〈the verdict of the people in the recent election constituted a ~ —B.C.Reece〉 **c :** an advisory instruction or set of directions 〈progress has been hampered by inadequate coordination, lack of clear ~s —*Economist*〉 〈dependent on the ~s of the guidebook and the hotel porter〉 **d :** an ideological, traditional, cultural, or moral influence or principle **:** EXEMPLAR 〈folk wisdom preserves many ~s —L.J.Davidson〉 〈they were not trained in a school of science which accepts Marxism-Leninism as the supreme ~ —C.P.Fitzgerald〉 **e :** a communication that initiates or governs action, conduct, or procedure **f :** an authoritative instrument that promulgates a program or regulation or directs or prohibits certain acts and that is issued by a high-level official body or competent official as a broad policy statement to be developed by technicians or as an explicit instruction with details; *usu* **:** such an instrument of a national regime or international body esp. of a head of a government or an administrative bureau whose decrees have the force of an executive order 〈a relatively new administrative device called the "~" . . . was frequently used by the president and other high officials to explain, modify, or amplify an order —C.O.Johnson〉 〈he issued a stream of ~s that in their entirety imposed a far-reaching social revolution upon Japan —Allan Taylor〉 〈~s which actually have the force of law —H.W. Sumners〉 **2 :** DIRECTIVE MESENTERY

directive antenna *n* **:** an antenna that radiates or receives better in some directions than in others

di·rec·tive·ly \-tə̇vlē, -li\ *adv* **:** so as to guide **:** with directive methods 〈taught a psychology class ~〉

directive mesentery *n* **:** either member of one or more pairs of mesenteries in actinians that differ from other mesenteries in the arrangement of the muscles and serve to determine the longitudinal plane of the body

di·rec·tive·ness \-tivnə̇s, -tēv- *also* -təv-\ *n* -ES **:** the quality of being directive; *specif* **:** the character of being determined in direction of development (as toward definitely organized structure) 〈impressed by the apparent ~ of evolution —*Brit. Book News*〉

di·rec·tiv·i·ty \də̇,rek'tivəd.ē, (,)dī,-\ *n* -ES **1 :** DIRECTIVENESS **2 :** the property of being directional or a measure of that property (as the front-to-back ratio of microphone response) **:** ORIENTATION; *specif* **:** a measure of the property in an antenna, loudspeaker, microphone, or other transducer used for sound transmission or reception by which its performance in one direction is better than that in another

direct labor *n* **1 :** labor (as machine operators) applied directly to a product in the manufacturing process so that the cost is computable, identifiable, and chargeable directly to the specific product — called also *productive labor;* compare INDIRECT LABOR **2 :** the wages paid to workers classed as direct labor

direct laying *n* **:** the laying of an artillery piece with the line of sighting directly upon the target

direct lighting *n* **:** lighting in which the greater part of the luminous flux goes directly from the fixture toward the area to be illuminated

direct loss by fire : loss traceable to fire as the proximate cause **:** loss that is caused by smoke or by water used in extinguishing a fire

¹di·rect·ly \də̇'rek(t)lē *or* -li *or* (*rapid in senses other than 6*) 'dre- *or* (*esp in senses other than 6*) (ˈ)dī¦re-; *in sense 6 often* 'drekl- *in both the US & England and chiefly substand South* tə'rekl-\ *adv* [ME, fr. ²*direct* + *-ly*] **1 a :** without any intervening space or time **:** next in order **:** SQUARELY, EXACTLY 〈~ opposite the city hall〉 〈~ in the center of the room〉 〈during the decade ~ before his birth〉 〈he holds a position ~ below that of the president〉 **b :** in a straight line **:** without deviation of course 〈the turnpike here runs ~ east and west〉 〈a dredged channel allows boats to get in and out ~〉 **:** by the shortest way 〈we headed ~ into the mountain country〉 **2 a :** straight on along a definite course of action without deflection or slackening 〈proceeds to go ~ to a children's hospital〉 〈the problem being ~ attacked〉 〈~ or by the most circuitous routes the fountain of happiness is what all living entities fumble and grope toward —J.C.Powys〉 **b :** purposefully or decidedly and straight to the mark 〈~ engaged in replacing muscle power with machine power〉 **:** in a straightforward manner without hesitation, circumlocution, or equivocation **:** plainly and not by implication 〈he ~ criticizes contemporary society〉 **:** in unmistakable terms **:** UNQUALIFIEDLY 〈deals ~ with the stated purpose of the book —Stanley Newman〉 **c :** without divergence from the source or the original 〈that the only valid method of painting was to paint ~ from nature and to imitate nature as closely as possible —Michael Kitson〉 **d :** simultaneously and exactly or equally 〈that certain types of costs are neither ~ variable with output nor entirely fixed —Harold Koontz & Cyril O'Donnell〉 **3 :** in close relational proximity 〈increased interest in art may be ~ traceable to present easy and lucrative employment〉 〈new evidence bearing ~ on the question of guilt〉 〈~ concerned in the founding of the university〉 **4 a :** without any intervening agency or instrumentality or determining influence **:** without any intermediate step 〈writes ~ in Spanish〉 〈paints ~ on canvas〉 〈take part in the government either ~ or through freely chosen representatives〉 **b :** in the exact words of the original **:** VERBATIM 〈permitted to take notes but enjoined not to quote anything ~〉 **5 a :** in independent action without any sharing of authority or responsibility 〈the initial steps in the process of demilitarization and democratization were handled ~ by the American occupying forces —C.E.Black & E.C.Helmreich〉 **b :** FACE-TO-FACE **:** in person 〈dealing ~ with the strikers〉 **6 a :** without a moment's delay **:** at once **:** IMMEDIATELY 〈get a doctor ~〉 **b :** after a little **:** in a little while **:** SHORTLY, PRESENTLY 〈we'll discuss that ~; first we must act on this motion〉

²directly *like sense 6 of* ¹DIRECTLY\ *conj, chiefly Brit* **:** immediately after **:** as soon as 〈apparently written ~ their agreement was made —K.J.Fielding〉 〈~ we enter it we breast some new wave of emotion —Virginia Woolf〉

direct mail *n* **:** printed matter prepared to solicit trade or contributions and sent directly through the mails to individuals (as letters, cards, circulars, catalogs, house periodicals)

direct material *n* **:** material used in manufacturing processes which becomes an integral part of the product and the cost of which is identifiable and chargeable directly to it — compare INDIRECT MATERIAL

direct method *n* **:** a teaching method that seeks to dispense with theoretical discussion and historical considerations in favor of concrete observation and practical experience; *specif* **:** a method of teaching a language through conversation, discussion, and reading in the language itself without translation and without the study of formal grammar

di·rect·ness *n* -ES **1 a :** the character of being true in course toward a target or goal 〈rivaling a hawk in ~ of aim〉 〈stared at her youngest niece with concentrated ~ —J.C.Snaith〉 **b :** strict pertinence or distinct forthrightness **:** straightforwardness often with a degree of abruptness or brusqueness 〈his sledgehammer ~ had often served him better than nice legal knowledge —Thomas Hardy〉 **2 :** closeness to actual experience and consequent vividness or incisiveness 〈described Ireland's troubles with a searing ~ that has rarely been equalled —*Time*〉 **3 :** open frankness and naturalness **:** freedom from barriers of pretense and pretension and from adornment and prettiness 〈created an atmosphere of ~ between herself and all men and women —Eden Phillpotts〉 〈what people take for rudeness is really ~ —Ian Bevan〉

di·rec·toire \də̇¦rek¦twär, dē¦r-, ¦dē,r-\ *adj, usu cap* [F, fr. *Directoire*, the body of five men that held executive power in France from 1795–1799, fr. *directoire* directory (book — influenced in meaning by *directeur* director), fr. MF, fr. ML *directorium* — more at DIRECTORY] **:** of, relating to, or imitative of the kind or style prevalent in France during the French Revolution: as **a** *of women's clothes* **:** imitative of classic dress and marked by a picturesque hat with a flaring brim and a décolleté gown usu. with short sleeves and a skirt hanging straight down like a tube from a waistline just under the bust **b** *of furniture* **:** transitional between the Louis Seize style and the Empire style and not sharply distinguishable from the latter

di·rec·tor \də̇'rektə(r) *also* (ˈ)dī¦r-, *rapid* 'dre-\ *n* -S [LL, fr. L *directus* (past part. of *dirigere* to direct) + *-or* — more at DRESS] **1 :** one that directs: as **a :** the head or chief of an organized occupational group (as a bureau, foundation, institute, school) 〈the ~ of the budget〉 〈orientation of new school ~s is the responsibility of the county superintendent〉 〈thousands of ~s of religious education now at work —J.O. Nelson〉 〈a department of public relations headed by a ~ —R.F.Harlow & M.M.Black〉 **b :** one of a group of persons entrusted by the shareholders of a corporation with the final overall control and direction of the corporate enterprise 〈final authority in a corporation of this sort lies with a board of ~s —P.M.Sweezy〉 **c :** one that supervises the production of a show (as for stage, screen, or radio transmission) with responsibility for action, lighting, music, rehearsals and generally for giving substance to the conception of the author — compare PRODUCER 4a **d :** CONDUCTOR 6 **e :** a college teacher that directs students individually in the choice of a program and in special projects (as research for a thesis or practice teaching) — compare ADVISER **f :** the head judge in a fencing match **2** [trans. of F *directeur*, fr. MF *directeur* director, fr. LL *director*] **:** a member of the French Directory of 1795–99 **3 :** an instrument grooved to guide and limit the motion of a surgical knife **4 :** a computing machine for controlling gunfire that automatically and continuously predicts the future position of the target and computes the ballistically correct firing data **5** *Brit* **:** a device to hold in position an unattended fire hose emitting a jet of water

di·rec·tor·al \-t(ə)rəl\ *adj* **:** DIRECTORIAL

di·rec·tor·ate \də̇'rekt(ə)rə̇t *also* dī'-, *rapid* 'dre-, *usu* -əd.+V\ *n* -S [F *directorat*, fr. LL *director* + F *-at* -ate] **1 :** the office or occupancy of the office of director (as of an agency) 〈served during the ~ of his predecessor〉 **2 :** ²DIRECTORY 2a 〈a perpetuating ~ which subordinates the making of laws and the processes of the courts to the orders of the executive —F.D. Roosevelt〉 **3 a :** a board of directors of a corporation 〈two subsidiary funds, each with its own ~ and administrative staff —Craig Thompson〉 **b :** membership on a board of directors 〈was required to resign his ~s before accepting the appointment〉 **4 :** an executive staff in charge of a program, bureau, department, or major subdivision 〈astronautics ~〉 〈four main ~s deal with the various aspects of local government —Brian Chapman〉 〈a 4-man aircraft ~ created to speed up production〉

director general *n, pl* **directors general** *also* **director generals :** a chief executive or administrator placed in overall charge of a bureau, department, or agency esp. in a national government or organization with international orientation

di·rec·to·ri·al \də̇¦rek¦tōrēəl, ¦dī,r-, -tór-\ *adj* [LL *directorius* + E *-al* — more at DIRECTORY] **1 :** serving to direct **:** DIRECTIVE, DIRECTORY 〈reading ~ books in preparation for citizenship〉 〈how far the council shall go in exercising these ~ powers —J.E.Pate〉 **2 a :** belonging to or having the function or qualities of a director 〈his earlier ~ assignments〉 〈employed in a ~ position at a large automobile plant —Paul Moor〉 **b :** adapted to or connected with the direction or directorship of dramatic or theatrical production 〈a new ~ genius〉 〈richly fulfilling his high ~ promise〉 **:** characteristic of a skilled director 〈an ambitious melodrama bristling with fine ~ touches —*Time*〉 **3** [F, fr. LL *directorius* (influenced in meaning by F *Directoire*, 18th cent. executive body) + F *-al* — more at DIRECTOIRE] **:** belonging to a directory or body of directors **:** done, constituted, or administered by a directory 〈during the period France was under ~ government〉

di·rec·to·ri·al·ly \-ēəlē, -li\ *adv* **:** in a directorial function or manner

di·rec·to·ri·um \də̇,rek'tōrēəm, (,)dī,r-, -tór-\ *n, pl* **directo·ria** \-ēə\ [ML, directory, guidebook] **:** ORDO

di·rec·tor·ship *pronunc at* DIRECTOR + ,ship\ *n* **1 :** the office of director **2 :** a position as a director esp. on a board of directors

¹di·rec·to·ry \də̇'rekt(ə)rē, -ri *also* dī'-, *rapid* 'dre-\ *adj* [ME, fr. LL *directorius*, fr. L *directus* (past part. of *dirigere* to direct) + *-orius* -ory — more at DRESS] **1 :** serving to direct **:** DIRECTIVE; *specif* **:** providing guidance that is advisory and authoritative but not compulsory **2** *of a law* **a :** directing what is to be done **b :** directing how a thing shall be done rather than what shall be done — opposed to *mandatory* **3** *usu cap* [trans. of F *Directoire*] **:** DIRECTOIRE

²directory \"\ *n* -ES **1** [ML *directorium* guidebook, fr. neut. of LL *directorius*] **:** a compilation, index, or treatise serving to direct or guide: **a :** a collection of directions, rules, or ordinances **b :** a book of directions for the conduct of worship; *specif, usu cap* **:** a Presbyterian book of rules for public worship used in the Church of Scotland and certain Presbyterian and Congregational churches elsewhere **c :** ORDO **d :** an alphabetical or classified list containing the names and addresses of the inhabitants or organizations of a locality or the names, location, and identifying data of persons or organizations connected with a particular profession or occupation or that are subscribers of a particular service 〈a city ~ is usually an annual or biennial publication〉 〈a ~ of manufacturers —*Eastman Kodak Monthly Abstract Bull.*〉 〈an annual ~ of "who is who" among the publishers, reviewers, publications, and organizations interested in literary material —Anne J. Richter〉 **e :** a tablet or sectional strips on the wall of the entry of a building bearing the names of occupants with indication of the floor level and room numbers of each **2** [fr. *Directory*, French executive body, trans. of F *Directoire* — more at DIRECTOIRE] **a :** a small governing body with executive power often unconstitutional and of a military character 〈the French ~ of the First Republic〉 〈to make sure that the cabinet did what it was supposed to do, they set up a ~, or shadow cabinet, behind it —Leigh White〉 **b :** a body of directors **:** DIRECTORATE

direct package *n* **:** a package of sorted mail containing matter to be distributed from a single post office

direct positive *n* **:** a positive in photography that is made directly by exposure to light and by development without the use of a negative

direct primary *n* **:** a preliminary election at which direct nominations of candidates for office are made usu. by a plurality vote by the qualified voters under the same procedures as used in final elections

direct printing *n* **:** the process of printing textiles by passing them between a succession of rollers having different colors and different parts of the pattern

direct process *n* **:** a process that yields metal by a single working from the ore — compare INDIRECT PROCESS

direct product *n* **:** SCALAR PRODUCT

direct proportion *n* **:** a proportion of two variable quantities when the ratio of the two quantities is constant

direct pyramidal tract *n* **:** a tract of descending fibers in the upper half of the spinal cord that is traceable from the cerebral cortex of the same side and that is situated next to the anterior median fissure

direct reduction *n* **:** a reduction of a syllogistic argument to the first figure by converting or obverting one or more of its propositions or by converting or obverting and interchanging the premises — contrasted with *indirect reduction*

direct rein *n* **:** the use of a rein in such a way as to place tension on the bit and move a horse's head toward the direction in which it is required to move — compare INDIRECT REIN

di·rec·tress \də̇'rektrə̇s, dī'-\ *n* -ES [*director* + *-ess*] **:** a female director 〈the social ~ said hopefully, "You're a bridge player" —Walter Hackett〉

di·rec·trice \də̇¦rek¦trēs\ *n* -S [F, fr. ML *directric-*, *directrix*] **:** DIRECTRESS 〈had been the ~ of wardrobe of a ballet company〉 〈could let its managing ~ draw a lavish stipend —Leslie Charteris〉

di·rec·trix \dəˈrektriks, dī'-\ *n, pl* **directrixes** \-ksəz\ *also* **directri·ces** \dəˈrektrəˌsēz, dī'-; dəˌrekˈtrī(ˌ)sēz, (ˌ)dī-\ [ML, fem. of LL *director* — more at DIRECTOR] **1** *archaic* **:** DIRECTRESS **2 :** a line the distance to which from any point of a conic section is in fixed ratio to the distance from the same point to a focus **3 :** the center line of the field of fire of an artillery piece

directs *pres 3d sing of* DIRECT, *pl of* DIRECT

direct salesman *n* **:** a house-to-house peddler or canvasser

direct selling *n* **:** the selling by a manufacturer or other producer or his agent to any other than a jobber or middleman **:** selling directly to a consumer

direct service *n, of social workers* **:** active service on cases and work with patients as distinguished from staff functions

direct syllogism *n* **:** a syllogism proceeding from a rule and the subsumption of a case under that rule to the result of the rule in that case

direct take *n* **:** an instant replacement of one picture with another in television transmission with no interval

direct tax *n* **:** a tax exacted directly from the person on whom the ultimate burden of the tax is expected to fall ⟨property, income, gift, inheritance, and poll taxes are generally included under *direct taxes*⟩

direct tide *n* **:** high tide at any given place on one side of the earth accompanied by high tide on the opposite side

direct viewfinder *n* **:** a finder in which the subject is viewed directly through a lens or sight

direct-vision spectroscope *n* **:** a spectroscope utilizing an Amici prism so that the observer looks in the direction of the light source

direct white 2GT *n, usu cap D&W* **:** a fluorescent brightener — see DYE table I (under *Fluorescent Brightener 34*)

direct-writing company *n* **1 :** an insurance company with which a policyholder directly insures his property — called also *originating company;* distinguished from *reinsurance company* **2 :** an insurance company that solicits and services business directly with the public through its own employees rather than through local agents

dire·ful \ˈdī(ə)rfəl, -īəf-\ *adj* **1 a :** exciting horror or terror **:** DREADFUL, FRIGHTFUL, DIRE ⟨entered upon a career of vengeance so ~ that London was shocked —G.W.Johnson⟩ **b :** oppressive to feelings or spirit **:** DISMAL ⟨the ~ sound of air-raid sirens⟩ **2 :** warning of disaster to come **:** OMINOUS ⟨seeing himself trapped, he filled the air with ~ cries⟩ — **dire·ful·ly** \-f(ə)lē, -li\ *adv* — **dire·ful·ness** \-fəlnəs\ *n* -ES

dire·ly \ˈdī(ə)rlē, -īəl-, -li\ *adv* **:** in a dire manner: **a :** DREADFULLY, FRIGHTFULLY **b :** DISMALLY **c :** FOREBODINGLY, OMINOUSLY

di·remp·tion \dəˈrem(p)shən\ *n* -S [L *diremption-, diremptio,* fr. *diremptus* (past part. of *dirimere* to take apart, separate, fr. *dir-* — fr. *dis-* apart — + *-imere,* fr. *emere* to take, buy) + *-ion-, -io* -ion — more at DIS-, REDEEM] **:** SEPARATION, DISJUNCTION **:** division into two ⟨because it does make that vast ~ of our world into a One and a Many —H.B.Alexander⟩

dire·ness \ˈdī(ə)rnəs, -īən-\ *n* -ES **:** the quality of being dire or of being dreadful to look upon or contemplate or of presaging coming disaster

di·rep·tion \dəˈrepshən\ *n* -S [MF or L; MF, fr. L *direption-, direptio,* fr. *direptus* (past part. of *diripere* to tear apart, plunder, fr. *di-* — fr. *dis-* apart — + *-ripere,* fr. *rapere* to seize and carry off) + *-ion-, -io* -ion — more at DIS-, RAPID] **1** *obs* **:** a tearing apart or away **2** *archaic* **:** DESPOLIATION

direr *comparative of* DIRE

direst *superlative of* DIRE

dire wolf *n* **:** a large lupine mammal (*Canis dirus* or *Aenocyon dirus*) found in Pleistocene deposits of No. America

[1]**dirge** \ˈdərj, -ōj, -əij\ *n* -S [ME *dirige, derge,* fr. L *dirige* (sing. pres. imper. act. of *dirigere* to direct, make straight), the first word of an antiphon adapted from Ps 5:9 (Vulgate) that opens the first nocturn in the Office of the Dead — more at DRESS] **1** *archaic* **:** the Office of the Dead in the Roman Catholic Church **2 a :** a psalm sung for a departed soul in the Roman Catholic Church; *also* **:** a requiem mass **b :** a song or hymn expressing grief or a solemn sense of loss esp. to accompany funeral or memorial rites **c :** any slow solemn and mournful piece of music **3 a :** a piece of writing resembling a dirge in being expressive of deep and solemn grief or sense of loss; *esp* **:** a poem of this kind **b :** any sorrowful or lugubrious literary expression

[2]**dirge** \"\ *vb* -ED/-ING/-S *vt* **1** *archaic* **:** to sing a dirge for **2** *archaic* **:** to sing as if a dirge ~ *vi* **:** to give forth a dirge or a sound like or having the effect of a dirge

dirge·ful \-jfəl\ *adj* **:** full of lamentation **:** FUNEREAL, MOURNFUL

dir·gie \ˈdirjē\ *n* -S [ME *derge, dirige* — more at DIRGE] **1** *Scot* **:** DIRGE 2 **2** *Scot* **:** a funeral feast

dir·hem \dərˈ(h)em\ *also* **dir·ham** *or* **der·ham** \-am\ *n* -S [Ar *dirham,* fr. L *drachma* drachma — more at DRAM] **1 :** a Muslim unit of weight orig. established in Arabia as equal to two thirds of the Attic drachma or nearly 45 grains, later used with varying values in Persia, Turkey, and No. Africa, but by the 1930s found as a chief unit only in Egypt, there being equal to about 41 grains **2 a :** a silver coin of Muslim countries the first issues of which in the 8th century weighed one dirhem **b :** a unit of value equivalent to the value of a dirhem coin orig. $\frac{1}{10}$ of a dinar **c :** the silver 50-fils piece of Iraq

di·rhin·ic \(ˈ)dīˈrinik, -rīn-\ *adj* [*di-* + *rhin-* + *-ic*] **:** affecting both nostrils alike

di·riá \ˌdirēˈä\ *n, pl* **diriá** *or* **diriás** *usu cap* [Sp *diriá, dirián, diriano,* of AmerInd origin] **1 :** an Indian people of southwestern Nicaragua **2** *also* **di·ri·an** \-ˈän\ **:** a member of the Diriá people

dir·i·ge \ˈdirəˌjē\ *n* -S [ME — more at DIRGE] *archaic* **:** DIRGE 1

dir·i·gi·bil·i·ty \ˌdirəjəˈbilәd·ē, də,rij-\ *n* -ES **1 :** the property of being dirigible **2 :** susceptibility to control ⟨usurpation is a crime to which men are tempted by human ~ —H.G.Wells⟩

[1]**dir·i·gi·ble** \ˈdirəjəbəl, dəˈrij-\ *adj* [L *dirigere* to direct, make straight + E *-ible* — more at DRESS] **:** that can be directed **:** STEERABLE ⟨a ~ balloon⟩ ⟨a ~ torpedo⟩

[2]**dirigible** \"\ *n* -S [*dirigible* (*balloon*)] **:** AIRSHIP

di·ri·gisme \dērēzhēs|m(ᵊ), -ēz-, |mə\ *n* -S [F, fr. *diriger* to direct (fr. L *dirigere*) + *-isme* -ism — more at DRESS] **:** economic planning and control by the state ⟨a middle course between ~ and laissez-faire⟩

dir·i·ment impediment \ˈdirəmənt-\ *n* [L *diriment-, dirimens,* pres. part. of *dirimere* to take apart, interrupt, destroy — more at DIREMPTION] **:** a disability that makes void a marriage contracted even with the required legal solemnities

[1]**dirk** \ˈdərk, -ōk, -əik\ *n* -S [alter. of Sc *durk*] **1 :** a long straight-bladed dagger formerly carried esp. by the Scottish Highlanders **2 :** a short sword formerly worn by British junior naval officers

[2]**dirk** \"\ *vt* -ED/-ING/-S **:** to stab with a dirk

dirk dance *n* **:** a leaping dance over and around a dirk or dagger done esp. by Manxmen

dirk knife *n* **:** a clasp knife having a large blade like that of a dirk

[1]**dirl** \ˈdirl\ *vb* -ED/-ING/-S [prob. alter. of *thirl*] *vt, Scot* **:** to pierce with pain or emotion ~ *vi* **1** *Scot* **:** to emit a rattling or ringing sound esp. when struck **2** *Scot* **:** to tremble or quiver esp. with pain or emotion

[2]**dirl** \"\ *n* -S **1** *Scot* **:** a powerful blow **:** JOLT **2** *Scot* **:** a vibration of sound or motion ⟨put your ear to the ground and you'll hear the ~ of their feet —J.M.Barrie⟩

dirndl \ˈdərndᵊl\ *also* ˈdir-\ *n* -S [short for G *dirndlkleid,* fr. G dial. (Bavarian) *dirndl* girl (dim. of *dirne,* fr. OHG *thiorna* maid, virgin) + *kleid* dress; akin to OS *thiorna* maid, MD *dierne* maid, maidservant, ON *therna* maidservant, OE *thegn* servant, thane — more at THANE] **1 :** a dress style marked by a tight bodice, short sleeves, low neck, and gathered skirt and copied from Alpine peasant costume **2** *also* **dirndl skirt :** a full skirt gathered or pleated on a tight waistband

di·ro·filaria \ˌdī(ˌ)rō+\ *n, cap* [NL, fr. *diro-* (fr. L *dirus* ominous, dreadful) + *Filaria* — more at DIRE] **:** a genus of filarial worms (family Dipetalonematidae) — see HEARTWORM

[1]**dirt** \ˈdər|t, ˈdō|, ˈdəi|, *usu* |d·+V\ *n* -S *often attrib* [alter. of ME *drit,* fr. ON, excrement; akin to OE *drītan* to defecate, OHG *trīzan,* ON *drīta* to defecate, L *foria* diarrhea, Serb *driskati* to have diarrhea, Lith *derkti* to defecate] **1 a :** EXCREMENT ⟨warm steamy knobbles of sheep ~ getting crushed between my toes —Janet Frame⟩ **b :** mud or waste matter mixed with water ⟨in summer there is dust, and in winter there is ~ —Jane Austen⟩ **c :** a foul or filthy substance that by adhering to a thing makes it unclean or foul ⟨the crew gutted the catch and hosed the ~ through the scuppers⟩; *esp* **:** an accumulation of dust, grit, refuse, waste, or litter ⟨how to remove . . . ~ consisting of dust, pollen, and sooty particles —*Pliotron*⟩ ⟨under its accumulated rust and ~ of five centuries —G.G.Coulton⟩ **d :** grime, spot, or stain resulting from travel, work, a fall, or other ordinary experience or from use ⟨a chance to wash the ~ off his face⟩ ⟨guaranteed to remove ~ from upholstery⟩ **e** *archaic* **:** something worthless ⟨is yellow ~ the passion of thy life? —Alexander Pope⟩ **f :** a person to be treated with contempt ⟨he's got beautiful manners. Doesn't chuck the stuff at you as if you were ~ like young Willis —Dorothy Sayers⟩ **g :** visible foreign matter that disfigures finished paper **2 a** (1) **:** EARTH, GROUND **:** loose or packed soil or sand ⟨tons of rock and ~ slid into the canal⟩ ⟨replacing ~ roads with macadam⟩ (2) **:** the surface of the ground ⟨alarmed at the first sound we hit the ~⟩ **b :** land as property ⟨a rare good little farm; a sound bit of ~ that is, sir —Adrian Bell⟩ **c :** a substance that is dug or comes from the earth ⟨mining gold by means of ~ washing⟩ **d** (1) **:** alluvial earth, gravel, and similar material in placer mining (2) **:** broken ore and in coal mines slate and other foreign matter **e** *dial Eng* **:** foul or flammable mine air **3 a :** an abject or filthy state **:** SQUALOR ⟨ignorance and ~ are not necessary concomitants of poverty⟩ **b :** moral obliquity **:** CORRUPTION, CHICANERY ⟨the ~ of jealousy⟩ ⟨there's more ~ to be uncovered at the capital⟩ **c :** moral uncleanness; *esp* **:** licentiousness of language or theme ⟨this leaves a rather amorphous concept of what obscenity is . . . Its one essential quality is ~ for ~'s sake —Curtis Bok⟩ ⟨a quite mistaken belief that to make his reader smell ~ is realism —H.J.Laski⟩ **d :** common scandalous gossip about discreditable personal behavior; *esp* **:** malicious or slanderous gossip ⟨a writer as much interested in writing ~ as in reporting the news⟩ **e :** suppressed information whose disclosure would be highly damaging ⟨he thought . . . investigations should be started only after the most careful consideration and when there was real prospect of turning up ~ —Vance Johnson⟩ **f :** an underhanded or despicable trick — used as the object of *do* ⟨wanting to do him ~, she sent his wife a poison-pen letter⟩ **4 :** dirty weather

[2]**dirt** \"\ *vt* -ED/-ING/-S **1** *archaic* **:** to make foul **:** DIRTY ⟨don't dog's-ear nor ~ them —R.H.Barham⟩ **2 :** to cover with dirt; *esp* **:** to draw soil up around the base of

dirt band *n* **:** a dark-colored layer or zone in a glacier representing a former surface where dust or other debris accumulated

dirt bed *n* **:** a buried soil often containing leaves and stems in a state of partial decay and sometimes occurring between sheets of glacial drift (as in some parts of the Mississippi basin)

dirtbird \ˈ=,=\ *n* [[1]*dirt* (weather); fr. its habit of chirping before rain] **:** GREEN WOODPECKER

dirtboard \ˈ=,=\ *n* **:** a guard placed on a carriage so as to keep dirt from the axle arm

[1]**dirt cheap** *adj* **:** exceedingly cheap

[2]**dirt cheap** *adv* **:** at an exceedingly low price

dirt dauber *or* **dirtdobber** \ˈ=,==\ *n, chiefly South & Midland* **:** MUD DAUBER

dirt·en \ˈdərtᵊn\ *adj* [in sense 1, alter. of ME *driten,* fr. OE, past part. of *drītan* to defecate — more at DIRT; in sense 2, fr. [1]*dirt* + *-en* (as in *earthen*)] **1** *dial Eng* **:** DIRTY, FILTHY **2** *dial Eng* **:** made of dirt

dirt farmer *n* **:** a farmer who works on the soil

dirt·i·ly \ˈdərd·ᵊ|ē, ˈdōl, ˈdəi|, |t|, |əlē,|ᵊli,|əli\ *adv* **1 a :** in a dirty or filthy manner ⟨a ~ robed camel driver⟩ **b :** with a dirty color or a sprinkling of dirt ⟨ill-modeled from some ~ glossy substance of a livid color —Ngaio Marsh⟩ **2 :** in a disgraceful, dishonest, or base manner **:** SORDIDLY, DESPICABLY ⟨as ~ drunk as usual —John Steinbeck⟩

dirt·i·ness \|d·ēnəs, |t|, |in-\ *n* -ES **:** the quality or state of being dirty **:** FOULNESS: as **a :** obscenity or licentiousness of language **b :** moral obliquity **:** SORDIDNESS

dirt line *n* **:** a layer appearing as a line in the front of a glacier and made up of earth that settled and was covered by a snowfall

dirtplate \ˈ=,=\ *n* **:** DIRTBOARD

dirt poor *adj* **:** lacking practically all the essentials of life or the resources for supporting life **:** DESTITUTE ⟨Rembrandt's last, *dirt poor* years —*Time*⟩ ⟨Greece had been *dirt poor* for centuries —Claire Sterling⟩

dirts *pl of* DIRT, *pres 3d sing of* DIRT

[1]**dirty** \ˈdər|d·ē, ˈdō|, ˈdəi|, |t|, |i\ *adj* -ER/-EST [[1]*dirt* + *-y*] **1 :** characterized by the presence of dirt or impurities: **a :** not clean or pure **:** soiled, defiled, or begrimed with dirt **:** overlaid or intermixed with dirt, impurities, or foreign matter ⟨the stage roustabouts' dungarees were convincingly ~⟩ **b :** likely to befoul, defile, or begrime with dirt ⟨put them on the *dirtiest* job in the camp⟩; *specif* **:** that befouls the hold of a transport ship ⟨a tanker carrying such ~ cargo as crude oil, diesel oil, or asphalt is not subjected to this high rate of corrosion⟩ **c** *of work* **:** consisting of drudgery that is tedious, disagreeable, and unrecognized or thankless and usu. makes the course easy for someone else ⟨she did, as always, quietly, complacently, the ~ work while her sisters fussed over their wardrobes⟩ **d :** requiring onerous or repulsive action that is most sordid, least rewarded, and most risky of the assignments made by the principal in an undertaking ⟨a male accomplice was sitting out there playing it safe, sending the girl in to do the ~ work —Erle Stanley Gardner⟩ ⟨determined that the bourgeois liberals should not use them for the ~ work at the barricades and then shove them . . . aside —Stringfellow Barr⟩ **e :** contaminated with infecting organisms ⟨~ wounds⟩ **2 :** characterized by unfairness, baseness, or evil **:** LOW, CONTEMPTIBLE, HATEFUL: **a :** repugnant to a sense of decency ⟨a mob . . . may lynch a Negro . . . and apparently enjoy the ~ business —C.C.Furnas⟩ **b** (1) **:** marked or characterized by dishonorable, unscrupulous, or treacherous dealing ⟨her father was a kind of ~ dog . . . he married a rich woman and left this kid to get along as best she could —Susan Ertz⟩ (2) **:** obtained through dishonest, corrupt, or inhumane dealing ⟨refused to legally name the higher-ups who got the millions in ~ money —Mike Stern⟩ **c :** marked by moral corruption or by criminality ⟨those who regard politics as a ~ business would do well to remember that war is a *dirtier* business —John Lodge⟩ ⟨called wire tapping a ~ business —*Newsweek*⟩ **d :** given to or characterized by covert attempts to harass or disable opposing players in violation of the rules of the sport or game **:** UNSPORTSMANLIKE ⟨a ~ hockey player⟩ ⟨overemphasis on winning is liable to produce ~ football⟩ **e :** violating ordinary standards of fair play in deadly combat ⟨a teacher of jujitsu and ~ fighting to recruits⟩ **f :** highly regrettable, distressing, or grievous ⟨it's a ~ shame you weren't given a fair chance⟩ **3 a :** characterized by expressed or suggested obscenity or indecency **:** BAWDY, SMUTTY ⟨anecdotes of a type that can be called earthy but not ~ —Sidney Lovett⟩ ⟨Shakespeare was the *dirtiest* of English authors if you knew the vocabulary —D.W.Brogan⟩ ⟨sniggering at ~ postcards —John Masters⟩ **b :** offensive and to be shunned or applied only with repugnance by reason of an implicit offensive idea ⟨but discipline? Ah, that's a ~ word and used only to describe the old Prussian army —*Time*⟩ ⟨for years in the entertainment business "documentary" has been a ~ word —Marya Mannes⟩ **4 :** rough and murky on sea or land or in the air; *esp* **:** stormy with squally winds and low visibility ⟨it developed into a ~ night. Fog shut down, reducing visibility to zero, and an unusually heavy tide was running —C.C.Hanks⟩ **5 a** *of color or light* **:** CLOUDED, SULLIED **:** DULLISH, DINGY **:** not clear and bright ⟨he was not ~ white, as I had often found whales of the smaller size to be, but pure white —H.A.Chippendale⟩ **b :** characterized typically by a husky, rasping, or raw tonal quality — usu. used of jazz or of the singing or playing of musical tones that are slightly off-key **6 a :** conveying ill-natured resentment ⟨the two girls give me a ~ look like it was my fault or something —Ring Lardner⟩ ⟨this is not meant as a ~ crack at the American railroads —Richard Joseph⟩ **b :** expressive of contempt **:** intended to affront, humiliate, or insult **:** SCURRILOUS, ABUSIVE ⟨quick to strike back at being called a ~ name⟩ ⟨some of the ~ epithets applied to immigrants from foreign countries⟩ **7** *printing* **a** *of copy* **:** difficult to follow because heavily emended or marked or poorly written **b** *of typesetting or a proof* **:** full of errors or heavily marked with corrections of errors — opposed to *clean;* compare FOUL 8 **c** *of a type case* **:** FOUL 13 **8** *of an atom bomb or hydrogen bomb* **:** having considerable fallout

syn FILTHY, FOUL, NASTY, SQUALID: DIRTY is a general term applicable to anything sullied or defiled ⟨the window so *dirty* you could hardly see the new houses opposite —George du Maurier⟩ ⟨he was *dirty* and bloodstained and his clothes were bedaubed with mud and weeds as though he had been in the river —Dorothy Sayers⟩ FILTHY intensifies the offensive suggestions of DIRTY ⟨tenements — rickety wooden structures five or six stories high, dark, ill-ventilated, and *filthy,* breeders of disease and nurseries of vice —Allan Nevins & H.S.Commager⟩ ⟨he was constantly drunk, *filthy* beyond all powers of decent expression . . . as disreputable an old wretch as was at that time to be found in New York —Leslie Stephen⟩ FOUL, the strongest term in this group, suggests revolting loathsomeness ⟨the stagnant water looked uninviting. Over its face lay a thick mantle of green slime, from which swelled curious bladder islands of floating fatty pink. The Arabs explained that the Turks had thrown dead camels into the pool to make the water *foul* —T.E.Lawrence⟩ ⟨Van Gogh knew the paleotechnic city in its most complete gloom, the *foul* bedraggled gaslighted London of the seventies —Lewis Mumford⟩ NASTY may imply highly repugnant qualities, esp. those repugnant to a fastidious person ⟨the *nasty* stench of the place turned me sick; if ever a man smelled fever and dysentery, it was in that abominable anchorage —R.L.Stevenson⟩ ⟨I wonder why he really did hide himself like that. Something *nasty,* I suppose; was he a leper? —G.K. Chesterton⟩ ⟨would they, pray, explain why instead of sharing their beds with decent women of their own class . . . they squandered all their virile energy on greasy slave girls and *nasty* Asiatic-Greek prostitutes? —Robert Graves⟩ SQUALID adds to DIRTY the suggestions of slovenliness or neglect ⟨magnified hovels, piled story upon story, and *squalid* with the grime that successive ages have left behind them —Nathaniel Hawthorne⟩ All these terms may describe things reprehensible morally ⟨public office in this country has become a *dirty* and *nasty* thing. Its attainment in most cases implies chicanery and deceit —M.L.Ernst⟩ ⟨I oughtn't to sell Max out like that. It would be utterly *filthy* —Dashiell Hammett⟩ ⟨secret murder was their object — black, *foul,* midnight murder —Anthony Trollope⟩ ⟨he has treated such malice with the stony contempt the utterances of *squalid* politicians and journalists deserve —*New Republic*⟩ All these terms but SQUALID apply often to unpleasant weather.

[2]**dirty** \"\ *adv* -ER/-EST **:** DIRTILY, BASELY

[3]**dirty** \"\ *vb* -ED/-ING/-ES *vt* **1 :** to make filthy **:** FOUL, SOIL ⟨he *dirtied* his clothes in the coal cellar⟩ **2 a :** to stain with dishonor **:** SULLY, TARNISH ⟨but with Jackson the common man poured into the White House and *dirtied* more than the carpets . . . theft on a great scale appeared for the first time —*Times Lit. Supp.*⟩ **b :** to debase or degrade by distorting the real nature of ⟨their religion took most of the rural whites' pleasures away from them, ~*ing* sex and the human body until it was a nasty thing —Lillian Smith⟩ ~ *vi* **:** to become soiled ⟨soft cloths ~ easily⟩ — **dirty one's hands :** to sully one's moral uprightness or good reputation ⟨a man who had never *dirtied his hands* with political intrigue —Bruce Marshall⟩

dirty al·lan \-ˈalən\ *n, sometimes cap D & A* [origin of *allan* unknown; called dirty fr. its habit of eating the excrement of smaller gulls] **:** PARASITIC JAEGER

dirty linen *n* **:** private or domestic matters whose exposure in public would bring shame or embarrassment — compare WASH ONE'S DIRTY LINEN IN PUBLIC

dis *var of* DIX

[1]**dis-** *prefix* [ME *dis-, des-,* fr. OF & L; OF *des-, dis-,* fr. L *dis-,* lit., apart, to pieces; akin to OE *te-* apart, to pieces, OHG *zi-, ze-,* Goth *dis-* apart, Gk *dia* through, Alb *tsh-* apart, L *duo* two — more at TWO] **1 a :** do the opposite of **:** reverse (a specified action) ⟨*dis*join⟩ ⟨*dis*establish⟩ ⟨*dis*own⟩ ⟨*dis*qualify⟩ **b :** deprive of (a specified character, quality, or rank) ⟨*dis*able⟩ ⟨*dis*prince⟩ **:** deprive of (a specified object) ⟨*dis*frock⟩ **c :** exclude or expel from ⟨*dis*bar⟩ ⟨*dis*castle⟩ **2 :** opposite of **:** contrary of **:** absence of ⟨*dis*union⟩ ⟨*dis*affection⟩ **3 :** not ⟨*dis*honest⟩ ⟨*dis*loyal⟩ **4 :** completely ⟨*dis*annul⟩ **5** [by folk etymology] **:** DYS- ⟨*dis*function⟩ ⟨*dis*trophy⟩

[2]**dis-** *prefix* [MF, fr. ML, alter. (influenced by Gk *dis-* twice, double, fr. *dis* twice) of L *di-,* fr. Gk — more at BIS, TWI-] **1 :** DI- 1 **2 :** DI- 2 ⟨*dis*azo⟩

dis *abbr* **1** discharge; discharged **2** disciple **3** discipline **4** disconnect **5** discontinued **6** discount **7** distance **8** distribute

di·sa \ˈdīsə\ *n* [NL] **1** *cap* **:** a genus of showy tropical African terrestrial orchids with tuberous rootstocks and dark green leaves **2** -S **:** any plant of the genus *Disa*

dis·ability \ˌdis *sometimes* -iz+\ *n* [[1]*dis-* + *ability*] **1 a** *archaic* **:** inability to do something **b** (1) **:** the condition of being disabled **:** deprivation or lack esp. of physical, intellectual, or emotional capacity or fitness; *also* **:** an instance of such a condition **:** a particular weakness or inadequacy ⟨he appeared sullen, melancholy, tongue-tied — a ~ stemming in part from a speech defect —H.M.Ledig-Rowohlt⟩ ⟨concluded that his *disabilities* were his best defense —M.W.Straight⟩ (2) **:** the inability to pursue an occupation or perform services for wages because of physical or mental impairment ⟨suffering from total ~⟩ ⟨receives a ~ pension⟩ (3) **:** the period of duration of such a condition ⟨receives monthly payments during his ~⟩ (4) **:** a physical or mental illness, injury, or condition that incapacitates in any way ⟨as a result of a personal accident . . . he lost his right arm, but he overcame this ~ —O.S.Nock⟩ (5) **:** a material object or condition that hinders, impedes, or incapacitates **:** HANDICAP ⟨the placement of the elevators is not so serious a ~ on the upper floors —Lewis Mumford⟩ **2 a :** lack of legal qualification to do a thing **:** legal incapacity, incompetence, or disqualification ⟨~ of infancy⟩ ⟨a law placing severe *disabilities* upon Catholics and Jews⟩; *also* **:** an instance or cause of such incapacity **b** (1) **:** a nonlegal disqualification, restriction, or discrimination ⟨nominally free, but actually subject to numerous social and economic *disabilities*⟩ ⟨a person with even the most tenuous Communist affiliation from years ago may suffer *disabilities* that could ruin his entire future career —A.H.Sulzberger⟩ (2) **:** DISADVANTAGE ⟨discussed the benefits and *disabilities* of price controls⟩ ⟨the special *disabilities* under which the industry operates⟩

disability clause *n* **:** a clause in a life-insurance contract providing that the policy continue in full force without payment of premiums if the policyholder becomes totally and permanently disabled and sometimes providing also for fixed monthly payments to the policyholder during the period of disability

disability insurance *n* **:** insurance against loss of income due to partial or total disability — compare ACCIDENT INSURANCE, HEALTH INSURANCE

dis·able \dəˈsābəl *also* -ˈzā-\ *vt* **disabled; disabled; disabling** \-b(ə)liŋ\ **disables** [ME *disablen,* fr. [1]*dis-* + *able* (adj.)] **1 :** to deprive of legal right or qualification **:** make legally incapable or incompetent **:** DISQUALIFY **2 :** to make incapable or ineffective **:** INCAPACITATE ⟨heavy financial losses *disabling* him from the execution of his plans⟩ ⟨~ a bomb⟩; *esp* **:** to deprive of physical, moral, or intellectual strength ⟨an English winter . . . *disabled* my mother like a mortal sickness —Sylvia T. Warner⟩ ⟨~*s* the rich as completely as the poor —G.B.Shaw⟩ **3** *obs* **a :** to deprive of what gives value **:** impair in worth ⟨I have *disabled* mine estate —Shak.⟩ **b :** to declare incompetent or invalid **:** DISPARAGE ⟨he *disabled* my judgment —Shak.⟩ **syn** see WEAKEN

disabled *adj* [fr. past part. of *disable*] **:** incapacitated by or as if by illness, injury, or wounds **:** CRIPPLED ⟨~ war veterans⟩; *also* **:** broken down ⟨~ cars⟩

dis·able·ment \-bəlmənt\ *n* -S [ME, fr. *disablen* + *-ment*] **1 :** deprivation of legal right or qualification **:** INCAPACITY **2 :** the act of disabling or becoming disabled or the state of being disabled ⟨the temporary ~ of most of her reasoning faculties —Elinor Wylie⟩

dis·abler \-b(ə)lə(r)\ *n* -s **:** one that disables ⟨heart disease is a major ~⟩

dis·abuse \ˌdisə'byüz\ *vt* [F *désabuser*, fr. *dés-* ¹dis- + *abuser* to abuse — more at ABUSE] **:** to set free from mistakes (as in reasoning or judgment) **:** UNDECEIVE **:** set right ⟨*disabused* us of the old belief that the universe revolved about the home of man —P.E.More⟩ ⟨he couldn't however ~ his mind of the idea —F.M.Ford⟩ **syn** see RID

di·saccharide *also* **di·saccharose** \(ˈ)dī+\ *n* [*di-* + *saccharide, saccharose*] **:** any of a class of sugars (as sucrose, lactose, or maltose) that yield on hydrolysis two monosaccharide molecules

disaccommodate *vt* [¹*dis-* + *accommodate*] *archaic* **:** DISCOMMODE

¹**dis·accord** \ˌdis+\ *vi* [ME *disacorden*, fr. MF *desacorder*, fr. *desacort* disagreement, lack of harmony, fr. *des-* ¹dis- + *acort* agreement — more at ACCORD] **:** to fail to be in accord or harmony **:** DISAGREE

²**disaccord** \"\ *n* **:** DISAGREEMENT **:** lack of harmony ⟨the economic and political systems of the country are in complete ~⟩

dis·accredit \ˌdis+\ *vt* [¹*dis-* + *accredit*] **:** to deprive of accreditation — **dis·accreditation** \"+\ *n*

dis·accustom \ˌdis +\ *vt* [MF *desaccoustumer*, fr. OF *desacostumer*, fr. *des-* ¹dis- + *acostumer* to accustom — more at ACCUSTOM] **1** *archaic* **:** to abandon as a custom **2 :** to free from a habit

disaccustomed *adj* **:** UNACCUSTOMED

dis·acidify \ˌdis +\ *vt* [¹*dis-* + *acidify*] **:** to free from acid

dis·acknowledge \ˌdis+\ *vt* [¹*dis-* + *acknowledge*] **:** to refuse to acknowledge **:** DENY, DISOWN **syn** see DISCLAIM

dis·acknowledgment \"+\ *n* **:** the refusal to acknowledge **:** DISCLAIMING, DISOWNING, DENIAL

dis·acquaintance \ˌdis+\ *n* [fr. obs. *disacquaint* to make unfamiliar, estrange (fr. ¹*dis-* + *acquaint*) + *-ance*] **:** loss of acquaintance or association ⟨long ~ with army life⟩

disadvance *vt* [alter. (influenced by *ad-*) of ME *disavauncen*, fr. MF *desavancer*, fr. OF *desavancier*, fr. *des-* ¹dis- + *avancier* to move forward, advance — more at ADVANCE] *obs* **:** to cause to draw back **:** STOP, CHECK

¹**dis·advantage** \ˌdis+\ *n* [alter. (influenced by *ad-*) of ME *disavauntage*, fr. MF *desavantage* unfavorable condition, fr. OF, fr. *des-* ¹dis- + *avantage* advantage — more at ADVANTAGE] **1 :** loss or damage esp. to reputation, credit, or finances **:** PREJUDICE, DETRIMENT ⟨his attempts to reach his enemy's face were greatly to the ~ of his own —G.B.Shaw⟩ ⟨spread reports to the ~ of the candidate⟩ **2 a :** the state or fact of being without advantage **:** an unfavorable, inferior, or prejudicial condition ⟨found himself at a ~ among his polished, cultivated friends⟩ **b :** an unfavorable or prejudicial quality or circumstance **:** HANDICAP ⟨the machine has two serious ~*s*⟩ ⟨the work has the ~ of being written in a tedious style⟩

²**disadvantage** \"\ *vt* **:** to place at a disadvantage **:** affect unfavorably **:** HARM ⟨their commercial interests were *disadvantaged* by the colonial relationship⟩ ⟨seriously *disadvantaged* by the general fall of raw material prices⟩

disadvantaged *adj* **:** lacking in the basic resources or conditions (as standard housing, medical and educational facilities, civil rights) believed to be necessary for an equal position in society ⟨a ~ class or section of the populace⟩ — compare UNDERPRIVILEGED

dis·advantageous \(ˈ)dis+, *also* ˌdisəd,v-\ *adj* [¹*dis-* + *advantageous*] **1 :** constituting a disadvantage **:** UNFAVORABLE, PREJUDICIAL ⟨a ~ trait⟩ ⟨found the terms of sale ~⟩ **2 :** tending to diminish esteem **:** DISPARAGING, DEROGATORY ⟨his action was viewed in a ~ light by many⟩ — **disadvantageously** *adv* — **disadvantageousness** *n* -ES

disadventure *n* [alter. (influenced by *ad-*) of ME *disaventure*, fr. MF *desaventure*, fr. OF, fr. *des-* ¹dis- + *aventure* chance, adventure — more at ADVENTURE] *obs* **:** MISHAP

disadventurous *adj* [¹*dis-* + *adventurous*] *obs* **:** DISASTROUS, UNFORTUNATE

dis·advise \ˌdis+\ *vt* [¹*dis-* + *advise*] **1 :** to advise against ⟨~ a long journey⟩ **2 :** to dissuade (a person)

¹**dis·affect** \ˌdis +\ *vt* [¹*dis-* + *affect* (have affection for)] **1** *archaic* **:** to lack affection for **:** be alienated from **:** DISLIKE **2 :** to alienate or diminish the affection or loyalty of **:** fill with discontent and unrest ⟨all hands were ~*ed* by the example of the ringleaders —R.L.Stevenson⟩ **syn** see ESTRANGE

²**disaffect** *vt* [¹*dis-* + *affect* (act upon)] *obs* **:** DERANGE, DISORDER

disaffected *adj* [fr. past part. of ¹*disaffect*] **:** filled with discontent and a sense of grievance esp. against those in authority **:** MUTINOUS, REBELLIOUS, DISLOYAL ⟨I . . . did my best to rally the ~ villains to a sense of their duty —C.B.Nordhoff & J.N.Hall⟩ ⟨in an age of ballistic warfare a ~ territory is . . . a liability —*Newsweek*⟩ — **dis·af·fect·ed·ly** *adv* — **dis·af·fect·ed·ness** *n* -ES

dis·affection \ˌdis+\ *n* [¹*dis-* + *affection* (feeling)] **1 :** the state of being disaffected **:** alienation of loyalty or affection **:** ESTRANGEMENT ⟨the problem that is created by the ~ of the intellectual . . . from the popular culture —J.L.Blaw⟩; *esp* **:** the state of being disaffected toward those in authority ⟨the order caused much ~ among the troops⟩ **2 :** lack of affection **:** DISLIKE, HOSTILITY, DISCONTENT ⟨except for a few expressions of ~, the British people were pleased with the engagement —*Current Biog.*⟩

dis·affiliate \ˌdis+\ *vb* [¹*dis-* + *affiliate*] *vt* **:** DISASSOCIATE, DETACH ⟨*disaffiliated* himself from the gangster-ridden organization⟩ ~ *vi* **:** to terminate an affiliation ⟨six rebel locals *disaffiliated* from the international union⟩

dis·affiliation \"+\ *n* **:** the act or an instance of disaffiliating

dis·affinity \ˌdis+\ *n* [¹*dis-* + *affinity*] **:** absence of affinity **:** OPPOSITION ⟨the ~ between the teachings of Plato and Aristotle⟩

dis·affirm \ˌdis+\ *vt* [¹*dis-* + *affirm*] **1 :** to assert the contrary of **:** CONTRADICT, DENY — used of something asserted **2** *law* **:** to refuse to confirm **:** REPUDIATE, ANNUL, REVERSE ⟨~ a judicial decision⟩ — opposed to *affirm*

dis·affirmance \"+\ *n* **:** the act of disaffirming **:** DENIAL, NEGATION, REPUDIATION, ANNULMENT, REVERSAL

dis·affirmation \(ˌ)dis+\ *n* **:** DISAFFIRMANCE

dis·afforest \ˌdis+\ *vt* [ML *disafforestare*, fr. L *dis-* ¹dis- + ML *afforestare* to afforest — more at AFFOREST] *Eng law* **:** to reduce from the privileges of a forest to the state of ordinary land **:** exempt from forest laws

dis·aggregate \(ˈ)dis+\ *vt* [¹*dis-* + *aggregate*] **:** to destroy the aggregation of **:** separate into component parts ⟨an easily *disaggregated* sandstone⟩

dis·aggregation \(ˌ)dis +\ *n* **1 :** the separation of an aggregate into its component parts **2 :** DISSOCIATION 1b(1)

dis·agio \(ˈ)dis+\ *n* [¹*dis-* + *agio*] **:** AGIO; *esp* **:** the agio charged for exchange of depreciated or foreign currency

dis·agree \ˌdis+\ *vi* [ME *disagreen*, fr. MF *desagreer*, fr. *des-* ¹dis- + *agreer* to agree — more at AGREE] **1 :** to fail to agree **:** lack harmony **:** be unlike or at variance ⟨the two accounts ~ with each other⟩ **2 a :** to differ in opinion **:** hold discordant views ⟨~*ing* on virtually every topic⟩ **b :** to refuse to agree **:** DISSENT ⟨by an overwhelming vote the Senate *disagreed* with the House motion⟩ **3 :** to be unsuitable **:** be harmful because of incompatibility ⟨fried foods ~ with me⟩ ⟨the damp climate seriously *disagreed* with her⟩ **syn** see DIFFER

dis·agreeability \"+\ *n* **:** the quality or state of being disagreeable **:** UNPLEASANTNESS

dis·agreeable \"+\ *adj* [ME *disagreable*, fr. ¹*dis-* + *agreable* agreeable] **1** *obs* **:** DISAGREEING **:** not conformable **:** INCONGRUOUS **2 :** causing discomfort, displeasure, or repugnance **:** UNPLEASANT, OFFENSIVE ⟨had a most ~ journey home⟩ ⟨a ~ odor⟩ ⟨a ~ predicament⟩ **3 :** marked by ill temper or irritability **:** PEEVISH ⟨a most ~ old man⟩ — **disagreeableness** *n* -ES

disagreeables \-bəlz\ *n pl* **:** disagreeable things ⟨in spite of my anxiety about Laurence's illness and the ~ resulting from it —Richard Aldington⟩ ⟨ready to put up with a host of ~ for the sake of having at her house the original Dr. Johnson —Virginia Woolf⟩

dis·agreeably \ˌdis+\ *adv* **:** in a disagreeable manner **:** UNPLEASANTLY, OFFENSIVELY ⟨~ surprised by the visit of the police⟩

dis·agreement \"+\ *n* [ME, fr. *disagreen* + *-ment*] **1 :** the act or an instance of disagreeing ⟨his verbal ~ provoked a duel of words⟩ ⟨rumors of these ~*s* soon reached the public⟩ **2 a :** the state of being at variance **:** DISPARITY, INCONGRUITY ⟨the clear ~ between the testimony of the two sides⟩ **b :** difference of opinion ⟨~ in matters of religion⟩

dis·allow \ˌdis+\ *vb* [ME *disallowen*, partly fr. MF *desallouer* to refuse praise, reprimand (fr. *des-* ¹dis- + *allouer* to approve) partly fr. ME ¹*dis-* + *allowen* to allow — more at ALLOW] *vt* **1** *archaic* **:** to refuse to commend or approve **:** disapprove of **2 :** to deny the force, truth, or validity of ⟨~*ing* the philosophical concept of free will⟩ ⟨tax officials ~*ed* the company's claim⟩ **3 :** to refuse to allow **:** REJECT ⟨~*ed* his timid request to take the afternoon off⟩ **4** [AF *desallower*, fr. MF *des-* ¹dis- + *allouer* to approve] **:** VETO ⟨~*ing* the charter⟩ — used chiefly of British parliamentary practice ⟨the king in council ~*ed* colonial statutes harmful to the British interest⟩ ⟨the Canadian federal government has not ~*ed* the Quebec statute⟩ ~ *vi*, *obs* **:** to refuse approval or sanction — used with *of* **syn** see DISCLAIM

dis·allowance \"+\ *n* **:** the act of disallowing **:** refusal to admit or permit **:** REJECTION ⟨the taxpayer was notified of the ~ of his claim for refund⟩

dis·ally \(ˌ)dis+\ *vt* [¹*dis-* + *ally*] *archaic* **:** to free from an alliance **:** SEVER

dis·amenity \ˌdis+\ *n* [¹*dis-* + *amenity*] **:** DISADVANTAGE, UNPLEASANTNESS ⟨a reasonable division of *disamenities* seems eminently fair —Christopher Hollis⟩

dis·anchor \(ˈ)dis+\ *vb* [ME *disancren*, fr. MF *desancrer*, fr. OF, fr. *des-* ¹dis- + *ancrer* to anchor, fr. *ancre* anchor, fr. L *ancora* — more at ANCHOR] *vt*, *archaic* **:** to loosen from anchorage ~ *vi*, *archaic* **:** to weigh anchor

dis·animate \ˌdis+\ *vt* [¹*dis-* + *animate*] **1** *archaic* **:** to deprive of life **2** *archaic* **:** to deprive of spirit **:** DISHEARTEN

dis·annex \(ˌ)dis+\ *vt* [ME *disannexen*, fr. ¹*dis-* + *annexen* to annex — more at ANNEX] **:** to undo the annexation of

dis·annul \ˌdis+\ *vt* [¹*dis-* + *annul*] **1 :** to annul completely **:** make void or of no effect **:** CANCEL, DESTROY ⟨*disannulled* the reforms conceded by earlier rulers⟩ **2** *obs* **:** to deprive esp. by an annulment of title

dis·anoint \ˌdis+\ *vt* [¹*dis-* + *anoint*] **:** to invalidate the consecration of ⟨~ a king⟩

dis·ap·pear \ˌdisə'pi(ə)r, -iə\ *vi* [¹*dis-* + *appear*] **1 :** to cease to appear or to be perceived **:** pass from view either suddenly or gradually ⟨the fantastic vision appeared and as swiftly ~*ed*⟩ ⟨the moon ~*ed* behind a cloud⟩ **2 :** to cease to be ⟨ancient evils have ~*ed*⟩ **:** become lost ⟨the book I left on this table has ~*ed*⟩ **:** cease to be known ⟨he ~*ed* without a trace two years ago⟩ **syn** *see* VANISH

dis·ap·pear·ance \ˌ=='pirən(t)s\ *n* **1 :** the act or an instance of disappearing **:** removal from sight **:** VANISHING ⟨the ~ of his name from the list of players⟩ ⟨the ~ of stately old mansions⟩ ⟨made a sudden ~ from the party⟩ **2 :** the depletion or diminution of world or national stocks or supplies (as of cotton, wheat) ⟨with the present rate of ~ the national marketing quota for the new crop of cotton would be 10 million bales⟩; *also* **:** the amount of such depletion ⟨the total annual ~ of wheat averaged 721 million bushels⟩

disappearing bed *n* **:** a bed that can be concealed (as in a recess or closet) when not in use

disappearing carriage *n* **:** a carriage for heavy coast guns on which the gun is raised above the parapet for firing and upon discharge is lowered automatically behind the parapet for protection

disappearing stair *n* **:** a stair built to swing upward and be concealed in a space in the ceiling

dis·ap·point \ˌdisə'pȯint\ *vb* [MF *desapointier*, fr. *des-* ¹dis- + *apointier* to arrange, settle — more at APPOINT] *vt* **1** *archaic* **:** to remove from office **2 :** to thwart or defeat the expectation or hope of ⟨expected a profitable year, but was badly ~*ed*⟩ ⟨I was much ~*ed* in him⟩ **:** FRUSTRATE, BALK ⟨~*ed* their best hopes⟩ **3** *obs* **:** UNDO, NULLIFY, DESTROY ~ *vi* **:** to cause disappointment ⟨somewhere, life had ~*ed* —Mollie Panter-Downes⟩

disappointed *adj* **1 :** defeated in expectation or hope **:** BALKED, THWARTED ⟨a ~ hope⟩ **2** *obs* **:** not adequately appointed or prepared **:** UNEQUIPPED — **dis·ap·point·ed·ly** *adv*

disappointing *adj* **:** failing to come up to expectations — **dis·ap·point·ing·ly** *adv*

dis·ap·point·ment \ˌdisə'pȯintmənt\ *n* **1 :** the act or an instance of disappointing **:** the state or condition of being disappointed **:** failure of expectation or hope **:** FRUSTRATION **2 :** one that disappoints ⟨he is a ~ to his parents⟩ ⟨the party was a great ~⟩

dis·approbation \(ˌ)dis+\ *n* [¹*dis-* + *approbation*] **:** the act or state of disapproving or the state of being disapproved **:** CONDEMNATION, DISAPPROVAL

dis·approbative \(ˌ)dis+\ *adj* [¹*dis-* + *approbative*] **:** DISAPPROBATORY

dis·approbatory \"+\ *adj* [¹*dis-* + *approbatory*] **:** containing or expressing disapprobation **:** DISAPPROVING ⟨cast a ~ glance at the boy⟩

dis·approval \ˌdis+\ *n* **:** DISAPPROBATION, CENSURE

dis·approve \"+\ *vb* [¹*dis-* + ¹*approve*] *vt* **1** *obs* **:** DISPROVE **2 :** to pass unfavorable judgment upon **:** regard as wrong **:** CONDEMN ⟨I ~ his conduct⟩ **3 :** to refuse approval to **:** decline to sanction **:** REJECT ⟨the treaty was *disapproved* by the senate⟩ ~ *vi* **:** to feel or express disapproval — often used with *of* ⟨*disapproved* of his attitude⟩

syn DISAPPROVE and DEPRECATE mean in common to feel or express an objection to or condemnation of (something or someone). DISAPPROVE implies an attitude of dislike or distaste and an unwillingness to accept though not necessarily connoting an expression of condemnation ⟨*disapprove* of a friend's actions⟩ ⟨*disapprove* of a fashion in dresses⟩ ⟨Lawrence *disapproved* of too much knowledge, on the score that it diminished men's sense of wonder —Aldous Huxley⟩ DEPRECATE, as here compared, usu. strongly implies regret, profound, diffident, or apologetic, often carrying also the idea of belittling ⟨it is customary to *deprecate* the literary achievement of the past decade —James Laughlin⟩ ⟨he *deprecates* the kind of criticism which is out to destroy long-established reputations —Daniel George⟩ ⟨I not only *deprecate*, I deplore, monkeyshines in Congress —H.L.Ickes⟩ ⟨the man who knows he too has been successful but can't help *deprecating* his position as an artist —Taliaferro Boatwright⟩

dis·ap·prov·ing·ly *adv* **:** in a disapproving way **:** CENSORIOUSLY ⟨eyed him ~⟩ ⟨spoke ~ of his methods⟩

dis·arm \dəs, (ˈ)dis+, *also* dəz *or* (ˈ)diz +\ *vb* [ME *desarmen*, fr. MF *desarmer*, fr. OF, fr. *des-* ¹dis- + *armer* to arm — more at ARM] *vt* **1 a :** to divest of arms ⟨methodically ~*ing* the captured troops⟩ **b :** to deprive of a means of attack or defense ⟨~ a city by razing its walls⟩ ⟨~ a ship⟩ **c :** to deprive of the capacity or means of inflicting material injury **d :** to make harmless (as a mine or bomb) by removing a fuse or other actuating device **2 a :** to make powerless **:** deprive of means or disposition to harm, criticize, or be hostile ⟨~*ed* the administration's foes by a series of reform laws⟩ ⟨~*ed* criticism by frank avowal of his errors⟩ **b :** to win over by persuasive words or acts ⟨~ her angry father with winning smiles and caresses⟩ ~ *vi* **1 :** to lay aside arms **2 :** to reduce materially or to a peace footing the military establishment of a country (as at the close of a war)

dis·armament \"+\ *n* [modif. (influenced by *armament*) of F *désarmement*, fr. *désarmer* + *-ment*] **:** the laying aside or depriving of arms; *esp* **:** the reduction of a military establishment to some minimum set by some specified authority ⟨the ~ of the defeated aggressor nation must be complete⟩

disarming *adj* **:** tending to allay or remove a critical or hostile attitude **:** INGRATIATING ⟨a ~ smile⟩ ⟨~ frankness⟩ ⟨dressed with the ~ simplicity that made her so noticeable —Morley Callaghan⟩ — **dis·arm·ing·ly** *adv*

dis·arrange \ˌdis+\ *vt* [¹*dis-* + *arrange*] **:** to unsettle or disturb the order or due arrangement of **:** to throw out of order ⟨sufficient to disturb and ~ her whole inner life —Ellen Glasgow⟩ ⟨her clothing was ripped and violently *disarranged* —J.P.Brown⟩ **syn** see DISORDER

dis·arrangement \"+\ *n* [¹*dis-* + *arrangement*] **:** the act of disarranging or the state of being disarranged **:** CONFUSION, DISORDER

¹**dis·array** \ˌdis+\ *n* -s [ME *disaray*, fr. MF *desarroi*, fr. OF fr. *desareer*] **1 :** a lack of order or sequence ⟨those dark and noisome hulks anchored in forlorn ~ —Kenneth Roberts⟩ **2 :** a confused state in which orderly disposition has been broken or lost **:** DISARRANGEMENT ⟨the ~ into which society had been thrown by this deplorable affair —Edith Wharton⟩ **3 :** incomplete or disorderly dress **syn** see CONFUSION

²**disarray** \"\ *vt* [ME *disarayen*, fr. MF *desarroyer*, fr. OF *desareer*, fr. *des-* ¹dis- + *areer* to prepare, provide, put in order — more at ARRAY] **1 :** to throw into disorder **:** put out of array ⟨the child had ~*ed* the bedcovers⟩ **2 :** to take off the dress of **:** UNROBE ⟨called to ~ the queen⟩ **3** *archaic* **:** DESPOIL, STRIP — used with *of*

dis·articulate \ˌdis +, *also* ˌdisə(r)ˌt-\ *vb* [¹*dis-* + *articulate*] *vi* **:** to become disjointed or severed **:** become separated joint from joint ~ *vt* **:** DISJOINT, SEVER, SUNDER

dis·articulation \ˌdis +, *also* ˌdisə(r),t-\ *n* [¹*dis-* + *articulation*] **1 :** the act of disarticulating; *specif* **:** amputation or separation of a body part at a joint **2 :** a condition of lack of unity or integration **:** DISJOINTEDNESS ⟨the ~ of society⟩

dis·assemble \ˌdis+\ *vb* [¹*dis-* + *assemble*] *vt* **:** to take apart **:** separate into constituent parts ⟨~ a watch⟩ ~ *vi* **:** to come apart ⟨automobile sections ~⟩

dis·assembly \"+\ *n* [¹*dis-* + *assembly*] **1 :** the state or condition of being disassembled **2 :** the act or process of disassembling or taking apart ⟨the careful ~ of a lens⟩

disassembly line *n* **:** a grouping of slaughtering equipment and workers so that carcasses for dismemberment are passed from worker to worker until completely dismembered

dis·assimilate \ˌdis +\ *vt* [¹*dis-* + *assimilate*] **:** to subject to catabolism — **dis·assimilation** \"+\ *n* — **dis·assimilative** \"+\ *adj*

dis·associate \ˌdis +\ *vb* [¹*dis-* + *associate*] *vt* **:** to detach from association **:** DISSOCIATE ⟨*disassociated* himself from the business⟩ ~ *vi* **:** to terminate an association ⟨deliberately *disassociated* from the circle of his old friends⟩

dis·association \"+\ *n* **:** the act, process, or an instance of disassociating **:** the state of being disassociated **:** DISSOCIATION ⟨the false ~ of the individual and the social —R.M.MacIver⟩

¹**di·sas·ter** \də'zastə(r), \aas-,\ais-,\äs *also* dä's-; -'s- *is less frequent in "disastrous" than in "disaster", probably because three identical sounds (here, S-sounds) within as many syllables cause a stronger tendency to dissimilation than do two*\ *n* -s *often attrib* [MF & OIt; MF *desastre*, fr. OIt *disastro*, fr. *dis-* ¹dis- (fr. L) + *astro* star, fr. L *astrum*, fr. Gk *astron* — more at STAR] **1** *obs* **a :** an unpropitious or baleful aspect of a planet or star **b :** PORTENT **:** malevolent influence of a heavenly body **2 a :** a sudden calamitous event producing great material damage, loss, and distress ⟨a flood ~⟩ ⟨a mine ~⟩ ⟨such a war would be the final and supreme ~ to the world —Archibald MacLeish⟩ **b :** a sudden or great misfortune **:** CALAMITY ⟨the loss of his wife was the culminating ~ of the trip⟩ **c :** a complete failure **:** FIASCO ⟨only his skillful direction saved the play from being an unqualified ~⟩

syn CALAMITY, CATASTROPHE, CATACLYSM: these words refer to events of great misfortune, duress, and loss, and they are often interchangeable. DISASTER may connote the sudden and unexpected, with attendant notions of lack of foresight ⟨accidents to various ships thwarted this attempt, and brought about a battle *disastrous* to him —A.T.Mahan⟩ The misfortunes of a disaster may be measurable ⟨taking the atom bomb out of the realms of unimaginable horror and showing it as a measurable *disaster* —*Economist*⟩ CALAMITY may heighten suggestions of lasting emotion, affliction, grief at loss ⟨a disaster, for me a *calamity* —John Galsworthy⟩ ⟨revolving this last chapter of *calamity* suddenly opened where happiness had promised —George Meredith⟩ CATASTROPHE is often stronger than DISASTER or CALAMITY ⟨which spell discomfort when one cycle, distress when two, *catastrophe* when all cycles are in the depression phase —E.R.Dewey & E.F.Dakin⟩ It may suggest finality ⟨has Europe been engulfed at last by irrevocable tragedy? Has the fair continent . . . been overtaken at last by irremediable *catastrophe* —T.R.Ybarra⟩ CATACLYSM suggests an upheaval that overwhelms, shatters, and submerges an established order; it usu. applies to the general or universal rather than to the limited or personal ⟨it is not clear whether the Norman Conquest and the Russian Revolution are *cataclysms* or forms of political activity —J.C.Rees⟩ ⟨the impact of war and defeat on the South was immediate and *cataclysmic* —Allan Nevins & H.S.Commager⟩ All of these words and their derivatives are used less precisely in milder situations ⟨a considerable incident. Almost a *disaster* —Joseph Conrad⟩ ⟨live down its small *calamities* —Frederic Morton⟩ ⟨to save the city from the *catastrophic* mismanagement of its own officials —T.E.Dewey⟩ ⟨the *cataclysmic* race, with two real chariots, each drawn by four Arabian horses —*Time*⟩

²**disaster** *vt* -ED/-ING/-S *obs* **:** to bring harm upon **:** INJURE, RUIN

disaster area *n* **:** an area officially declared to be the scene of an emergency created by a disaster and therefore qualified to receive certain types of governmental aid (as emergency loans and relief supplies)

di·sas·trous \-trəs *sometimes* -tərəs\ *adj* [MF & OIt; MF *desastreux*, fr. OIt *disastroso*, fr. *disastro* disaster + *-oso* (fr. L *-osus* -ous)] **1** *archaic* **:** subject to or affected by disaster **:** UNLUCKY, ILL-FATED **2** *archaic* **:** full of unfavorable stellar influences **:** UNPROPITIOUS, ILL-BODING **3 :** attended by or productive of suffering or disaster **:** very unfortunate **:** CALAMITOUS ⟨a ~ day⟩ ⟨a ~ termination⟩ **syn** see UNLUCKY

di·sas·trous·ly *adv* **:** in a disastrous manner **:** CALAMITOUSLY, UNLUCKILY ⟨the battle ended ~ for the enemy⟩

di·sas·trous·ness *n* -ES **:** the quality or state of being disastrous

dis·au·xiny \di'sȯksənē\ *n* -ES [¹*dis-* + *auxin* + *-y*] **:** a disturbance in auxin relations of plants sometimes associated with disease

dis·avouch \ˌdis+\ *vt* [¹*dis-* + *avouch*] *archaic* **:** DISAVOW

dis·avow \ˌdis+\ *vt* [ME *desavowen*, fr. MF *desavouer*, fr. OF, fr. *des-* ¹dis- + *avouer* to avow — more at AVOW] **1 :** to refuse to own or acknowledge **:** deny responsibility for, approbation of, or validity of **:** DISCLAIM, REPUDIATE, DISOWN ⟨~*ed* the actions of his subordinates⟩ ⟨~*ed* any desire for independence⟩ **2** *obs* **:** REFUSE, DECLINE **syn** see DISCLAIM

dis·avowal \"+\ *n* **:** the act or an instance of disavowing **:** REPUDIATION ⟨the official ~ of the minister's actions⟩ ⟨his ~ of responsibility for the incident⟩

dis·azo \(ˈ)diˌsa(ˌ)zō\ *adj* [*disazo-*, fr. ²*dis-* + *azo-*] **:** containing two azo groups in the molecule — distinguished from *diazo* ⟨~ dyes⟩

dis·balance \dəˌs'balən(t)s, (ˈ)diˌs,ba-, \ˌspa-,\ˌspa-\ *n* [¹*dis-* + *balance*] **:** lack of balance **:** IMBALANCE ⟨the ~ of power between the great and small states⟩ ⟨traumatic experiences which threw his personality into ~ —Wenzell Brown⟩

dis·band \dəˌs'bänd, (ˈ)diˌs,b\, \ˌsp\,\ˌsp\, \aand\ *vb* [MF *desbander*, fr. *des-* ¹dis- + *bande* troop — more at BAND] *vt* **1 :** to break up the organization of **:** DISSOLVE ⟨the dance group was ~*ed* after a farewell concert⟩; *esp* **:** to dismiss as a body from military service ⟨~ an army⟩ **2** *obs* **:** to release from a band or army **:** DISCHARGE **3** *obs* **:** to send away **:** DISMISS, DIVORCE ~ *vi* **:** to break up an organization ⟨the company gave its last performances in 1943 and has since ~*ed* —Anatole Chujoy⟩ **:** break ranks **:** DISPERSE, SCATTER ⟨the troops ~*ed* in the greatest disorder⟩

dis·band·ment \-n(d)mənt\ *n* -s **:** the act of disbanding or the state of being disbanded ⟨the symphony orchestra faced the prospect of ~⟩

¹**dis·bar** \dəˌs'bär, (ˈ)diˌs\b\, \ˌsp\,\ˌsp\, \ä(r\ *vt* [¹*dis-* + *bar* (v.)] **:** to exclude from a place or condition **:** DISQUALIFY, DEBAR ⟨his age and poor health *disbarred* him from further service in the senate⟩ ⟨automatically ~*s* it from strict classification as a sonata —A.E.Wier⟩ **syn** see EXCLUDE

²**disbar** \"\ *vt* [¹*dis-* + *bar* (court)] **:** to expel from the bar or the legal profession **:** deprive (an attorney) of legal status and privileges

disbark *vb* -ED/-ING/-S [prob. fr. MF *desbarquer*, *debarquer* — more at DEBARK] *obs* **:** DISEMBARK

dis·bar·ment \-ärmənt, -äm-\ *n* -s [²*disbar* + *-ment*] **:** the act or an instance of disbarring **:** the state of being disbarred

dis·be·lief \ˌdisbə'lēf, -spə-\ *n* [¹*dis-* + *belief*] **:** the act of disbelieving **:** mental refusal to accept (as a statement or proposition) as true ⟨listened to him with shocked ~⟩

dis·be·lieve \-ēv\ *vb* [¹*dis-* + *believe*] *vt* **:** to hold not to be true or real **:** reject or withhold belief in ⟨~ his professions of sincerity⟩ ⟨~ the existence of ghosts⟩ ~ *vi* **:** to withhold or reject belief — used with *in* ⟨~*s* in the sanctity of the status quo —W.C.Brownell⟩

dis·be·liev·er \-və(r)\ *n* **:** one that disbelieves **:** an unbeliever esp. in the doctrines of a religion

disbelieving *adj* **:** refusing to believe **:** withholding belief **:** UNBELIEVING — **dis·be·liev·ing·ly** *adv*

dis·bod·ied \dəs'bädēd, (')dis¦bä-, ¦'spä-,¦spä-\ *adj* [fr. past part. of obs. *disbody* to disembody, fr. ¹*dis-* + *body* (n.)] **:** DISEMBODIED ⟨while we rode we were ~, unconscious of flesh or feeling —T.E.Lawrence⟩

dis·bow·el \dəs'bau̇(ə)l, (')dis¦bau̇-, ¦'spau̇-,¦spau̇-\ *vt* **dis·bowelled; disbowelled; disbowelling; disbowels** [ME *disbowelen*, fr. ¹*dis-* + *bowel* (n.)] *archaic* **:** DISEMBOWEL

dis·branch \dəs'bra̲nch, (')dis¦br-, ¦'spr-,¦spr-, |aa(ə)n-, |ain-,|än-\ *vt* [MF *desbrancher*, fr. *des-* ¹*dis-* + *branche* branch — more at BRANCH] **:** to divest of a branch **:** tear off (as a branch)

dis·bud \dəs'bəd, (')dis¦bəd, ¦'spəd,¦spəd\ *vt* **disbudded; disbudded; disbudding; disbuds** [¹*dis-* + *bud* (n.)] **1 :** to deprive of buds or shoots for the purpose of training **:** thin out flower buds to improve the quality of bloom of **2 :** to dehorn (cattle) by destroying the undeveloped horn bud

dis·bur·den \dəs'bərdᵊn, (')dis¦b-, ¦'sp-,¦sp-, |əd-,|əid-\ *vb* [¹*dis-* + *burden* (n.)] *vt* **1 a :** to rid of a burden or load **:** DISENCUMBER ⟨~ a pack animal⟩ **b :** to relieve of something burdensome or oppressive to the mind ⟨enabled to ~ himself of some of his anxieties —R.J.B.Sellar⟩ ⟨~ your conscience by confession⟩ **2 :** to get rid of (a burden) **:** UNLOAD ⟨~*ed* their merchandise in the city square⟩ ~ *vi* **:** to get rid of a burden or load **:** DISCHARGE, UNLOAD ⟨vessels ~*ing* at a dock⟩

dis·burs·al \dəs'bərsəl, dəs'p-, |əs-,|əis-\ *n* -s **:** the act or an instance of disbursing **:** DISBURSEMENT ⟨made large ~*s* of money daily⟩

¹**dis·burse** \-s\ *vt* -ED/-ING/-S [MF *desbourser*, fr. OF *desborser*, fr. *des-* ¹*dis-* + *borser* to get money, fr. *borse* purse, fr. LL *bursa* oxhide — more at PURSE] **1 a :** to expend esp. from a public fund **:** pay out ⟨*disbursed* over $5,000,000 for roads and other improvements⟩ ⟨party bosses *disbursed* money freely in strategic election districts⟩ **b :** to pay in settlement of **:** DEFRAY ⟨his father's readiness to ~ such a thumping bill of —George Meredith⟩ **2 :** DISTRIBUTE ⟨his will *disbursed* property to the value of approximately $35,000,000 —R.S. Boardman⟩ ⟨the hundred kilograms of uranium . . . was to be *disbursed* under strictly bilateral agreement —John Lear⟩ **syn** see SPEND

²**disburse** \"\ *n* -s *archaic* **:** DISBURSEMENT

dis·burse·ment \-smənt\ *n* -s [MF *desboursement*, fr. *desbourser* + *-ment*] **:** the act of disbursing ⟨~ of the loan has been completed⟩; *also* **:** something that is disbursed **:** funds paid out ⟨made large ~*s* for research and development⟩

dis·burs·er \-sə(r)\ *n* -s **:** one that disburses ⟨foundations and other ~*s* of research money should deal directly with universities —S.E.Harris⟩

disc *var of* DISK

disc- *or* **disci-** *or* **disco-** *comb form* [L *disc-*, *disco-* & ML *disci-*, fr. Gk *disk-*, *disko-*, fr. *diskos* quoit — more at DISH] **1 :** disk ⟨*Discina*⟩ ⟨*discigerous*⟩ ⟨*discomycete*⟩ **2 :** phonograph record **:** recording ⟨*discography*⟩ ⟨*discophile*⟩

disc *abbr* **1** discharged **2** disconnect **3** discount **4** discovered

dis·cal \'diskəl\ *adj* **:** like or relating to a disk

dis·cal·ce·ate \(')di¦skalsēət\ *adj* [L *discalceatus*, fr. *dis-* ¹*dis-* + *calceatus*, past part. of *calceare* to furnish with shoes, shoe, fr. *calceus* shoe, half boot, fr. *calc-*, *calx* heel — more at CALK] **:** DISCALCED

dis·calced \(')di¦skalst\ *adj* [part trans. of L *discalceatus*] **:** UNSHOD, BAREFOOTED ⟨~ friars⟩ — compare CALCED

discal cell *n* **1 :** a large cell near the base of the wing of a butterfly or moth **2 :** a cell between the branches of the media in the two-winged fly

discamp *vb* [MF *descamper* — more at DECAMP] *vt*, *obs* **:** to drive from a camp ~ *vi*, *obs* **:** DECAMP

discandy *vi* [¹*dis-* + *candy*] *obs* **:** MELT, DISSOLVE

discant *var of* DESCANT

dis·can·tus \dəs'kantəs\ *n*, *pl* **discantus** [ML — more at DESCANT] **:** DESCANT

¹**dis·card** \dəs'kärd, 'di,s-, -kȧd\ *vb* -ED/-ING/-S [¹*dis-* + *card* (n.)] *vt* **1 a :** to remove (a playing card) from one's hand to prepare for drawing or to reduce the hand to the number specified **b :** to play (any card except a trump) from a suit different from the one led **2 :** to drop, dismiss, let go, or get rid of as no longer useful, valuable, or pleasurable ⟨a butterfly who has ~*ed* his chrysalis —A.T.Quiller-Couch⟩ ⟨on reaching Vancouver he had . . . ~*ed* his lightweight suits —V.G.Heiser⟩ ⟨the painful process of ~*ing* cherished illusions —Laurence Binyon⟩ ~ *vi* **:** to discard a playing card

syn SHED, SLOUGH, CAST, MOLT, SCRAP, JUNK: DISCARD indicates dispensing with, letting go of, getting rid of, as not immediately useful; it is not a forceful word and may connote only the mild action of getting rid of a playing card from one's hand ⟨he sorted and re-sorted his cargo, always finding a more necessary article for which a less necessary had to be *discarded* —Willa Cather⟩ ⟨the song appeared in a draft of the play's first act, and was later *discarded* from the revised versions —H.V.Gregory⟩ ⟨modern research, which *discards* obsolete hypotheses —W.R.Inge⟩ SHED, SLOUGH, CAST, and MOLT may all suggest an animal's discarding an old skin or integument. SHED suggests divesting oneself or letting go of something outworn, rough or callow, or burdensome ⟨some words *shedding* old meanings and acquiring new ones —*Times Lit. Supp.*⟩ ⟨as he mellowed, he *shed* such vulgarity —*Times Lit. Supp.*⟩ ⟨though statesmen may try to *shed* their responsibility —J.A.Hobson⟩ SLOUGH suggests the throwing off of the deleterious, objectionable, or disadvantageous ⟨in the face of death Sonya seemed transformed, *sloughing* off all earthly dross —E.J.Simmons⟩ ⟨as though her gaunt and worldly air had been only a mockery she began to *slough* it off —Louis Bromfield⟩ CAST may be more forceful in its suggestion and imply rejection and repudiation ⟨an Englishman like the Ethiopian cannot change his skin any more than a leopard can *cast* off his spots —Stuart Cloete⟩ ⟨the Mexican Revolution of 1820 *cast* off the shackles of Spanish mercantilism —R.A.Billington⟩ MOLT may imply casting off of feathers, skin, or other covering, esp. during a period of difficulty or transition ⟨the belief that social change can be effected without revolution or unpleasantness, that society can *molt* its outer covering and become new in shape and spirit —J.D.Hart⟩ SCRAP and JUNK suggest discarding as worthless in existent form or operation, as an automobile or a ship is scrapped or junked. SCRAP is milder and less summary and final in its suggestion ⟨most modern literary theory would be inclined to *scrap* the prose-poetry distinction —René Wellek & Austin Warren⟩ ⟨the idea of *scrapping* our two military academies or drastically altering them —C.T.Lanham⟩ JUNK is a more forthright term, more drastic in indicating a demonstrated lack of serviceability, validity, or worth ⟨the South has never been able to understand how the North, in its astonishing quest for perfection, can *junk* an entire system of ideas almost overnight —Donald Davidson⟩

²**dis·card** \'=,= *sometimes* =ˈ=\ *n* **1** *card games* **:** the act of discarding; *also* **:** the card or cards discarded **2 :** a person or thing cast off: as **a :** a person that is cast off or rejected by society **:** one that is economically or socially degraded or abased ⟨the West had been the land of new hope . . . for the ~*s* of industrialism —F.L.Allen⟩ ⟨finds his characteristic hero and characteristic story among the ~*s* of society —R.P.Warren⟩ **b :** the rejected top portion of an ingot **c :** a book or other publication officially withdrawn from a library collection as unfit for further use or as no longer needed — **into the discard** *adv* **:** into disuse or oblivion **:** out of consideration or existence ⟨sword and spear and battle-ax have gone *into the discard* of time —Tom Wintringham⟩

dis·car·nate \dəs'kärnət, -,nāt\ *adj* [¹*dis-* + *-carnate* (as in *incarnate*)] **:** having no physical body **:** INCORPOREAL ⟨~ intelligence thinking in self-sufficient silence on first and last things —Irwin Edman⟩ ⟨believe in the existence of ~ spirits⟩

dis·case \dəs, (')dis+\ *vb* [¹*dis-* + *case* (n.)] **:** UNDRESS

disc cultivator *n* **:** a cultivator consisting of discs that are grouped in sets and paired so that the discs of each pair incline in opposite directions

disced *past of* DISC

dis·cept \də'sept\ *vi* -ED/-ING/-S [L *disceptare* to separate, decide between, debate, fr. *dis-* apart + *-ceptare* fr. *captare* to chase, strive to seize) — more at DIS-, CATCH] **:** DEBATE, DISCUSS, DISAGREE ⟨as he ~*s* and distinguishes, classifies his kinds of tragedy, his orders of comedy —*Times Lit. Supp.*⟩

dis·cep·ta·tion \,di,sep'tāshən\ *n* -s [ME *deceptacioun*, fr. L *disceptation-*, *disceptatio*, fr. *disceptatus* (past part. of *disceptare*) + *-ion-*, *-io* -ion] *archaic* **:** CONTROVERSY, DISPUTATION, DISCUSSION

dis·cern \də'sərn, |ən,|əin *also* -'z|\ *vb* -ED/-ING/-S [ME *discernen*, fr. MF *discerner*, fr. L *discernere* to separate, distinguish between, fr. *dis-* apart + *cernere* to sift — more at DIS-, CERTAIN] *vt* **1 a :** to make out with the eyes (as something obscure or distant) **:** DETECT, DESCRY ⟨could ~ a narrow path winding up the mountainside⟩ ⟨a convoy of 30 vessels was ~*ed* this morning by our forces —Sir Winston Churchill⟩ **b :** to detect or discover with other senses than vision ⟨~*ed* a strange unfamiliar odor in the room⟩ ⟨~*ed* the muffled sobbing of a child⟩ **2 :** to sense or come to know or recognize mentally esp. something that is hidden or obscure ⟨the inductive apprehension of a truth imperfectly ~*ed* —B.N.Cardozo⟩ ⟨the ability to ~ and analyze the essentials of complicated questions —K.C.Wheare⟩ **3 :** DISTINGUISH: as **a** *obs* **:** to mark as separate and distinct **:** put a distinguishing mark upon **b :** to recognize or identify as separate and distinct **:** DIFFERENTIATE, DISCRIMINATE ⟨~ right from wrong⟩ ⟨~ the false from the genuine⟩ ~ *vi* **:** to see or understand the difference **:** make distinction ⟨~ between good and evil⟩ **syn** see SEE

dis·cern·er \-nə(r)\ *n* -s **:** one that discerns

dis·cern·ible *or* **dis·cern·able** \-nəbəl\ *adj* [*discernible* alter. (influenced by LL *discernibilis*, fr. L *discernere* + *-ibilis* -ible) of *discernable*; *discernable* fr. MF, fr. *discerner* + *-able*] **:** capable of being discerned by the senses or the understanding **:** DISTINGUISHABLE ⟨a ~ trend⟩ ⟨there was ~ the outline of an old trunk —Floyd Dell⟩ — **dis·cern·ible·ness** \-bəlnəs\ *or* **dis·cern·able·ness** *n* -ES

dis·cern·ibly *or* **dis·cern·ably** \-blē, -li\ *adv* **:** in a discernible manner

discerning *adj* **:** revealing insight and understanding **:** DISCRIMINATING ⟨a ~ critic⟩ ⟨~ criticism⟩ — **dis·cern·ing·ly** *adv*

dis·cern·ment \-nmənt\ *n* -s [MF *discernement*, fr. *discerner* + *-ment*] **1 :** the act of discerning ⟨his quick ~ of his opponent's weaknesses⟩ **2 :** the quality of skill in discerning esp. that which is hidden or obscure **:** readiness and accuracy in discriminating **:** keenness of insight ⟨a novel of depth and ~⟩ ⟨displayed ~ and courage⟩

dis·cerp \də'sərp, -'zərp\ *vt* -ED/-ING/-S [ME *discerpen*, fr. L *discerpere*, fr. *dis-* apart + *-cerpere* (fr. *carpere* to pick, pluck) — more at DIS-, HARVEST] **1 :** to tear apart **:** DISMEMBER **2** *archaic* **:** to tear off **:** sever from a whole

dis·cerp·ible \-pəbəl\ *adj*, *archaic* **:** DISCERPTIBLE

dis·cerp·ti·ble \-ptəbəl\ *adj* [L *discerptus* (past part. of *discerpere*) + E *-ible*] **:** capable of being torn to pieces or pulled apart **:** separable into parts ⟨cannot be told by poetry or by music . . . — nor ~ in logic —Robert Bridges †1930⟩

dis·cerp·tion \-pshən\ *n* -s [LL *discerption-*, *discerptio*, fr. L *discerptus* + *-ion-*, *-io* -ion] **:** the act of discerping **:** a pulling to pieces; *also* **:** something that is severed or separated

disc furrower *n* **:** a land furrower in which the customary shoe is replaced by a pair of concave discs set at an angle to the line of draft

disc go-devil *n* **:** RIDGE BUSTER

¹**dis·charge** \dəs(h)'chärj, 'dis(h),ch-, -chȧj\ *vb* -ED/-ING/-S [ME *dischargen*, fr. MF *descharger*, fr. OF *deschargier*, fr. LL *discarricare*, fr. L *dis-* ¹*dis-* + LL *carricare* to load — more at CHARGE] *vt* **1 :** to relieve of a charge, load, or burden: **a :** to empty of a cargo **:** UNLOAD ⟨~ a ship⟩ **b** *archaic* **:** to rid or deprive esp. of something that burdens **c :** to free from something that burdens **:** EXEMPT **:** release from an obligation ⟨*discharged* from further payment of taxes⟩ **d** *obs* **:** to clear of an accusation or charge **:** ACQUIT, EXONERATE **e :** to project the missile of **:** FIRE ⟨~ a gun⟩ **f :** to relieve the electrical tension or release the energy of by withdrawal or emission of that which charges ⟨~ a Leyden jar⟩ ⟨~ a storage battery⟩ **2 a :** to let go **:** clear out **:** REMOVE ⟨~ a cargo⟩ ⟨the train ~*s* passengers⟩ **b :** to send forth (as a projectile) **:** SHOOT **:** let fly **:** FIRE ⟨~ an arrow⟩ **c :** to set at liberty **:** release from confinement, custody, or care ⟨~ a prisoner⟩ ⟨*discharged* from parole⟩ ⟨~ a patient from the hospital⟩ **d** (1) **:** to give outlet to **:** pour forth **:** EMIT ⟨the river ~*s* its waters into the bay⟩ ⟨a motor ~*s* a certain amount of fumes⟩ ⟨a boil *discharging* pus⟩ (2) **:** to release or give vent to (as a pent-up emotion or repressed impulse) ⟨sometimes impossible . . . to ~ our emotions upon their proper objects —T.V.Smith⟩ ⟨into her diary she *discharged* her fury and brooding loneliness⟩ (3) **:** UTTER, PRONOUNCE ⟨he *discharged* a string of oaths⟩ ⟨*discharging* abuse on all his critics⟩ **3 a** (1) **:** to dismiss from employment **:** terminate the employment of ⟨a rich man can ~ anyone in his employment who displeases him —G.B.Shaw⟩ (2) **:** to end formally the service of **:** release from duty ⟨~ a soldier⟩ ⟨~ a jury⟩ ⟨~ a committee with thanks to its members⟩ **b** (1) **:** to get rid of (as a debt or duty) by paying or performing ⟨he *discharged* his liabilities⟩ **:** FULFILL, EXECUTE ⟨~ one's duties effectively⟩ (2) *obs* **:** to act the part of ⟨not a man in all Athens able to ~ Pyramus but he —Shak.⟩ **c** *obs* **:** to get rid of (as an office or obligation) by doing away with **d** (1) *obs* **:** to make a settlement with (as a creditor) ⟨the present money to ~ the Jew —Shak.⟩ (2) *archaic* **:** to pay for **:** PAY **e :** to set aside **:** dismiss legally **:** ANNUL ⟨~ a court order⟩ **f :** to release (a legislative committee) from further consideration of a bill in order to bring it before the house for action ⟨they moved to ~ the committee⟩ **4** *now chiefly Scot* **:** PROHIBIT, FORBID **5 a :** to receive and distribute (as the weight of a wall above an opening) **b :** to relieve (as an opening or the lintel spanning an opening) from the weight of a wall **6 a :** to bleach out or to remove (color or dye) in dyeing and printing textiles usu. by a chemical process ⟨~ the blue color from a dyed fabric⟩ **b :** to remove the color from (a dyed fabric) in this manner **7 :** to cancel the record of the loan of (a library book) upon its return ~ *vi* **1 :** to throw off or deliver a load, charge, or burden **:** UNLOAD **2 a :** to go off (as of a gun) **b :** RUN ⟨some dyes ~⟩ **c :** to emit or give vent to fluid or other contents ⟨the water pipe ~*s* freely⟩ **syn** see DISMISS, FREE, PERFORM

²**discharge** \'dis(h),ch-, dəs(h)'ch-\ *n* -s [ME, fr. MF *descharge*, fr. OF, fr. *deschargier*] **1 a :** the act of relieving of something that oppresses (as an obligation, accusation, penalty) ⟨ask for the ~ of a penalty⟩ **:** ACQUITTANCE, DISMISSAL, RELEASE ⟨ask for the ~ of a debtor⟩ **b :** something that discharges or releases (as from imprisonment, an obligation, or a liability); *esp* **:** a certification of release or payment ⟨produced his ~ as evidence⟩ **2 :** the state or fact of being discharged or relieved (as of a debt, obstacle, or accusation) **:** ACQUITTAL, EXONERATION ⟨received a full ~ from responsibility for the incident⟩ **3 :** the act of discharging **:** removal of a load **:** UNLOADING ⟨the ~ of a ship⟩ ⟨the ~ of a cargo⟩ **4 :** legal release from confinement **:** LIBERATION ⟨ordering a conditional ~ of the alien on habeas corpus —*Harvard Law Rev.*⟩ **5 :** a firing off **:** expulsion of a charge **:** EXPLOSION ⟨a ~ of arrows⟩ ⟨an artillery ~⟩ **6 a :** a flowing or issuing out; *also* **:** a rate of flow **:** EMISSION, VENT ⟨a rapid ~ of water from a pipe⟩ ⟨a ~ of spores from a fungus⟩ **b :** something that is emitted or evacuated ⟨a purulent ~ from a wound⟩ ⟨profuse intestinal ~*s*⟩ **7 :** the act of removing or getting rid of an obligation or liability (as by the payment of a debtor the performance of a trust or duty) **:** FULFILLMENT, ACCOMPLISHMENT ⟨active in the ~ of his professional functions⟩ **8 a :** release or dismissal esp. from an office or employment ⟨the ~ of a worker⟩ **b** (1) **:** the dismissal of a court's mandate (2) **:** the release of a bankrupt as a result of bankruptcy proceedings and after his estate has been settled **c :** complete separation from the military service; *also* **:** the certificate verifying the service performed and the separation **9 a :** a composition used for removing color from a dyed fabric **:** discharging agent **b :** the removal of color from a dyed fabric ⟨acid ~ of Turkey red⟩ **c :** the effect produced on a dyed fabric by discharging ⟨a white ~ is obtained⟩ **10 a :** the equalization of a difference of electric potential by a transfer of electricity, the character of the equalization being determined by the medium through which it occurs, by the amount of difference of potential, and by the form of the terminal conductors on which the difference exists — see BRUSH DISCHARGE, DISRUPTIVE DISCHARGE, GLOW DISCHARGE, OSCILLATORY DISCHARGE **b :** the converting of the chemical energy of a voltaic cell or battery into electrical energy **11 :** the transfer of an impulse from nerve fiber to effector

³**discharge** \"\ *adj* **:** of, relating to, or produced by the process of discharging in dyeing and printing textiles

dis·charge·able \-jəbəl\ *adj* **:** capable of being discharged

dischargeable weight *n* **:** all weight that can be consumed or discharged and still leave an airship in safe operating condition with a specified reserve of fuel, oil, water ballast, and provisions and with normal crew

discharge coefficient *n* **:** COEFFICIENT OF DISCHARGE

discharged *past of* DISCHARGE

dis·charg·ee \¦dis(h)chär¦jē, dəs(h)¦ch-, -chȧ¦-\ *n* -s [¹*discharge* + *-ee*] **:** one who has been discharged

discharge lamp *n* **:** an electric lamp in which discharge of electricity between electrodes causes luminosity of the enclosed metallic vapor (as sodium or mercury) or gas (as neon) or in which the luminosity of the enclosed gas is enhanced by phosphors (as in the fluorescent lamp)

discharge printing *n* **:** a process of printing textiles already dyed a solid color by bleaching out a pattern usu. producing a white or light-colored design on a dark background — compare ¹DISCHARGE 6

dis·charg·er *pronunc at* ¹DISCHARGE +ə(r)\ *n* -s **:** one that discharges: as **a :** an instrument for discharging a Leyden jar or electrical battery by making a connection between the two surfaces **b :** SPARK GAP 2 **c :** a device for discharging the tied bundles of grain from a binder

discharges *pres 3d sing of* DISCHARGE, *pl of* DISCHARGE

discharge tube *n* **:** an electron tube which contains gas or vapor at low pressure and through which conduction takes place when a high voltage is applied

discharging *pres part of* DISCHARGE

discharging arch *n* **:** RELIEVING ARCH

disc harrow *n* **:** a harrow that breaks up plowed or rough land by means of discs arranged at an angle with the line of draft

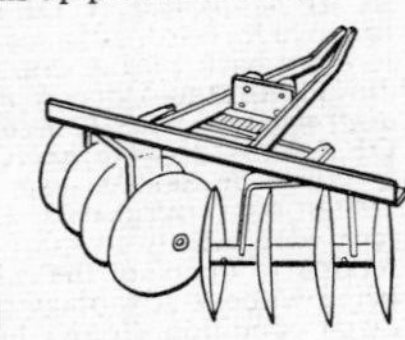
disc harrow

disc hiller *n* **:** a cultivator attachment having two series of discs arranged to throw topsoil around the roots of crops

disci *pl of* DISCUS

disci- — see DISC-

dis·ci·flo·ral \¦dis(k)ə¦flōrəl, -lȯr-\ *also* **dis·ci·flo·rous** \-rəs\ *adj* [*disc-* + *floral* or *-florous*] **:** having flowers with the receptacle enlarged into a conspicuous disc (as in the Rutaceae and other families of dicotyledons)

dis·ci·form \'dis(k)ə,fȯrm\ *adj* [*disc-* + *-form*] **:** of round or oval shape ⟨a ~ skin lesion⟩ **:** DISCOID

dis·cig·er·ous \(')di¦s(k)ijərəs\ *adj* [*disc-* + *-gerous*] **:** having a disk ⟨~ woody tissue of conifers⟩

dis·ci·na \də's(k)īnə\ *n*, *cap* [NL, fr. *disc-* + *-ina*] **:** a genus of recent African inarticulate brachiopods having a disk-shaped shell whose ventral valve is perforated by the pedicle — **dis·ci·noid** \'dis(k)ə,nȯid\ *adj*

dis·cinct \də'siŋ(k)t\ *adj* [L *discinctus*, fr. past part. of *discingere* to ungird, fr. *dis-* ¹*dis-* + *cingere* to gird — more at CINCTURE] **:** loosely dressed; *also* **:** LOOSE, NEGLIGENT

discing *pres part of* DISC

¹**dis·ci·ple** \də'sīpəl\ *n* -s [ME, fr. OE *discipul* & OF *deciple*, *desciple*, fr. LL *discipulus* personal follower of Jesus Christ in his lifetime (fr. L) & L *discipulus* pupil, perh. fr. (assumed) L *discipere* to grasp, comprehend, fr. L *dis-* ¹*dis-* + *-cipere* (fr. *capere* to seize) — more at HEAVE] **1 :** one who receives instruction from another **:** one who accepts the doctrines of another and assists in spreading or implementing them **:** FOLLOWER: as **a :** a professed follower of Christ in his lifetime; *esp* **:** one of the twelve apostles **b :** a convinced adherent of a school (as in philosophy, art, or politics) ⟨a ~ of Kant⟩ ⟨a ~ of Rubens⟩ ⟨a ~ of Jefferson⟩ **2** *usu cap* **:** a member of the Disciples of Christ who reject human creeds and sectarian names, hold the Bible alone to be the rule of faith and practice, celebrate the Lord's Supper every Sunday, baptize believers by immersion only and regard baptism after faith and repentance as essential to salvation, employ a congregational polity, and have been closely associated with the Churches of Christ

²**disciple** \"\ *vt* -ED/-ING/-S **1** *obs* **:** TEACH, TRAIN **2** *obs* **:** PUNISH, DISCIPLINE **3** *archaic* **:** to make a disciple of **:** CONVERT

dis·ci·plin·able \¦disə¦plinəbəl, 'disəplən-, 'displən-, də'siplən-\ *adj* [MF, fr. LL *disciplinabilis*, fr. L *disciplina* teaching, instruction + *-abilis* -able — more at DISCIPLINE] **1 :** capable of being disciplined or instructed **:** TEACHABLE **2 :** liable or deserving to be disciplined **:** subject to disciplinary punishment ⟨a ~ offense⟩

dis·ci·plin·al \'disəplənᵊl, -,plin-, 'displən-, də'siplən-\ *adj* **:** of or relating to discipline **:** constituting discipline **:** DISCIPLINARY ⟨~ measures⟩

dis·ci·plin·ant \'disəplənənt, -,plinənt, 'displən-, də'siplən-\ *n* -s [Sp & It; Sp *disciplinante*, fr. It, fr. ML *disciplinant-*, *disciplinans*, pres. part. of *disciplinare* to discipline — more at DISCIPLINE] **:** FLAGELLANT; *esp* **:** a member of a Spanish order noted for its severe discipline

¹**dis·ci·pli·nar·i·an** \,disəplə'nerēən, -na(ə)r-,-nār- *also* ,disp-\ *n* -s [¹*discipline* + *-arian*] **1** *usu cap* **:** an early English Puritan with Calvinistic leanings **2 :** one who disciplines **:** one who enforces order ⟨a strict ~ in school⟩

²**disciplinarian** \¦=(=)=¦===\ *adj* **1** *usu cap* **:** of or relating to the Disciplinarians **2 :** of or relating to discipline

dis·ci·pli·nary \'disəplə,nerē, -ri *also* -sp- *sometimes* də'sip-\ *adj* [¹*discipline* + *-ary*] **1** *obs* **:** of or relating to ecclesiastical discipline or legislation **2 :** of or relating to discipline ⟨in a certain classroom ~ problems were frequent —A.A.Hanson⟩ **:** strict in enforcing discipline ⟨if the mother is a cold, unforgiving, stern, and ~ one —Carl Binger⟩ **:** designed to correct or punish breaches of discipline ⟨took ~ action against three inspectors charged with taking bribes⟩ ⟨set up a committee to consider ~ measures against the senator⟩ **3** *archaic* **:** of, relating to, or serving the ends of teaching **4 :** of or relating to a discipline **:** regarded as a particular field of study ⟨political science in a formal ~ sense is of very recent origin in Japan —R.E.Ward⟩ **5 :** marked by discipline **:** DISCIPLINED, ORDERED ⟨Rousseau's view of life is above all emotional, that of Plato's supremely ~ —Irving Babbitt⟩

disciplinary barracks *n pl but usu sing in constr* **:** a military prison organized with a system of suspension of sentences, paroles, and restoration to duty

dis·ci·plin·a·to·ry \'dis(ə)plənə,tōrē, ¦disə¦plin-, də'siplən-\ *adj* [LL *disciplinatorius*, fr. *disciplinatus* disciplined (past part. of *disciplinare* to discipline) + L *-orius* -ory — more at DISCIPLINE] **:** DISCIPLINARY

¹**dis·ci·pline** \'disəplən, -,plin *sometimes* -splən\ *n* -s [ME, fr. MF & L; MF *discipline*, *descepline*, fr. L *disciplina*, lit., teaching, instruction, alter. of *discipulina*, fr. *discipulus* pupil — more at DISCIPLE] **1** *obs* **:** TEACHING, INSTRUCTION, TUTORING **2 :** a subject that is taught **:** a branch of learning **:** field of study ⟨such traditional ~*s* as history, literature, political science —W.R.Steckel⟩ **3 :** training or experience that corrects, molds, strengthens, or perfects esp. the mental faculties or moral character ⟨will submit willingly to severe ~ in order to acquire some coveted knowledge or skill —Bertrand Russell⟩ ⟨the valuable intellectual ~ of close research into a limited topic⟩ ⟨needs the ~ of hard work and early rising⟩ ⟨to learn to dance is the most austere of ~*s* —Havelock Ellis⟩ **4 :** PUNISHMENT: as **a :** chastisement self-inflicted as mortification or imposed as a penance or as a penalty **b :** an instrument of chastisement; *specif* **:** WHIP, SCOURGE **c :** punishment by one in authority esp. with a view to correction or training ⟨schoolboys kept in line by floggings and other severe ~⟩ **5 a :** control gained by enforcing obedience or order (as in a school or army) **:** strict government to the end of effective action ⟨maintained the strictest ~ in the barracks and the field⟩ **b :** behavior in accordance with the rules (as of an organization) **:** prompt and willing obedience to the orders of superiors **:** systematic, willing, and purposeful attention to the performance of assigned tasks **:** orderly conduct ⟨commended

the ~ of these veteran troops⟩ ⟨lack of ~ was made plain by the students' listless, apathetic recitation⟩; *also* **:** behavior (as of students or soldiers) regarded in terms of its conformity with an ideal or actual code or set of rules ⟨poor ~⟩ ⟨good ~⟩ **c :** conduct in accordance with a self-imposed rule or set of rules **:** SELF-CONTROL, SELF-RESTRAINT ⟨with a remarkable ~ she avoided all reference to this incident in the pages of her diary⟩ ⟨the sixty-six-pound free luggage allowance . . . forces me into a ~ in selecting what to take along —Richard Joseph⟩ **6 :** a rule or system of rules governing conduct or action **:** system of regulation ⟨in these revolutions the ~s, such as food rationing, either collapsed or near-collapsed —Herbert Hoover⟩: as **a :** a body of laws relating to conduct and church government **:** practical rules as distinguished from dogmatic formulations ⟨to introduce the Presbyterian polity and ~⟩ **b :** a body of purely ecclesiastical laws or practices that may be altered to meet new conditions ⟨changes in the Roman Catholic ~ relating to fasting⟩ **7 a :** an orderly or regular pattern of behavior ⟨watching the ~ of the tides, with their evident rhythm —Clare Leighton⟩ **b :** METHOD, APPROACH ⟨argued that the ~ of science differs from that of the humanities⟩

²discipline \"\ *vt* -ED/-ING/-S [ME *disciplinen*, fr. MF & LL; MF *discipliner*, fr. LL *disciplinare*, fr. *disciplina*] **1 :** to inflict suffering on or to penalize for the sake of discipline, regularity, order, or rule. as **a :** to whip or punish corporally in order to subjugate, mortify, or inflict penance on ⟨saw a dozen wretched creatures *disciplining* themselves with whips⟩ **b :** to punish or penalize in any way often by infliction of extra tasks or by loss of privileges ⟨cadets *disciplined* by confinement to quarters⟩ **c :** to inflict ecclesiastical censures and penalties upon **2 :** to train by instruction or exercise (as for the performance of some task) ⟨attention which modern education does not ~ the majority of our citizens to give —R.M. Weaver⟩ ⟨endless practice . . . had *disciplined* his muscles and nerves into beautiful coordination —P.B.Sears⟩ **:** train (the mental faculties) in habits of order, sobriety, and precision ⟨a *disciplined* mind⟩ ⟨a *disciplined* imagination⟩ **:** make effective by restraint ⟨so ~s his writing as to make every word count —Coleman Rosenberger⟩ **3 a :** to bring (a group) under control **:** govern strictly **:** train to habits of order **:** DRILL ⟨poorly armed and *disciplined* troops⟩ **b :** to impose order or measure upon **:** bring into order ⟨the enormous, confused, and unruly material has . . . been *disciplined* into a single coherent narrative —Walter Millis⟩ **syn** see PUNISH, TEACH

dis·ci·plin·er \-nə(r)\ *n* -S **1 :** one that disciplines **2** *cap* **:** DISCIPLINARIAN 1

dis·cip·u·lar \də'sipyələ(r)\ *adj* [L *discipulus* pupil + E *-ar* — more at DISCIPLE] **:** of, relating to, or befitting a disciple ⟨his ~ patience —Henry Morley⟩

dis·cis·sion \də'sishən\ *n* -S [LL *discission-, discissio* act of cutting apart, fr. L *discissus* (past part. of *discindere* to cut apart, fr. *di-* — fr. *dis-* apart — + *scindere* to cut, split) + *-ion-, -io* -ion — more at DIS-, SHED] **:** an incision of the capsule of the lens of the eye (as in treating cataract)

disc jockey *or* **disk jockey** *n* **:** a person who conducts and announces a radio or television program of musical recordings often with interspersed comments not relating to music

¹dis·claim \də'sklām\ *n* [ME *disclaime*, fr. AF, fr. *disclaimer, desclamer*] *archaic* **:** DISCLAMATION

²disclaim \"\ *vb* [AF *disclaimer, desclamer*, fr. *des-* ¹dis- + *claimer, clamer*, fr. OF *clamer* to cry out, complain, claim — more at CLAIM] *vi* **1 :** to renounce or repudiate a legal claim **:** make a disclaimer **2 a** *obs* **:** to disavow all part or share **:** make public denunciation or dissent **b :** to utter denial ⟨Catherine colored, and ~*ed* again —Jane Austen⟩ **3** *obs* **:** to cry out or declaim ~ *vt* **1 :** to renounce a legal claim to **:** deny or repudiate any interest in or connection with **2 :** to deny or disavow (as a connection with or responsibility for) ⟨~*ed* any knowledge of the contents of the letter⟩ **:** REPUDIATE, DISOWN ⟨~*ed* the libelous pamphlet⟩ ⟨~*ing* any ill will toward him⟩ **3 :** to deny or reject the right, validity, or authority of ⟨~*ed* the charge that he received financial backing from oil interests⟩ **:** DENY, DISPUTE ⟨accords wisdom to his hands . . . but ~s the wisdom of the heart —Ernest Ansermet⟩ **:** RENOUNCE, REPUDIATE ⟨~*ed* the authority of the supreme pontiff⟩ **4** *archaic* **:** to deny (as a claim) **:** REFUSE **5 a** *of a herald* **:** to denounce or make infamous (as one bearing arms without right or one usurping the title of esquire or gentleman) by proclamation **b :** to disown any claim to (as a right to bear arms) **:** DISAVOW, RENOUNCE

syn DISCLAIM, DISAVOW, REPUDIATE, DISOWN, DISACKNOWLEDGE, and DISALLOW can mean, in common, to refuse to admit, accept, or approve. DISCLAIM implies a refusal to admit or accept a claim, esp. anything claimed or likely to be claimed in one's favor or against him ⟨*disclaim* any responsibility for a crime⟩ ⟨the ordinary qualifications of the novelist, all pretension to which he entirely *disclaims* —Richard Garnett⟩ ⟨responded with characteristic modesty, *disclaiming* any right to special honor —D.G.Mandelbaum⟩ ⟨*disclaim* any intention of leaving⟩ DISAVOW is close to DISCLAIM but usu. applies to denial of responsibility for something besides refusal to accept or approve ⟨this Court always had *disavowed* the right to intrude its judgment upon questions of policy or morals —O.W.Holmes †1935⟩ ⟨the error of . . . putting forth in a permanent form work that I might subsequently wish to *disavow* —Havelock Ellis⟩ ⟨*disavow* the harsh materialism of mines and factories —*Time*⟩ REPUDIATE is usu. to disclaim responsibility for what one has previously or implicitly acknowledged or accepted ⟨a wise graduate student . . . accepted the degree for what it ostensibly stood for, and straightway *repudiated* everything it actually stood for —Bruce Dearing⟩ ⟨a law which everyone recognizes in fact, though everyone *repudiates* it in theory —G.L.Dickinson⟩ DISOWN implies repudiation of something with which one has previously stood in close relationship, often implying disinheritance or abjuration ⟨Keith and his followers were *disowned* by the orthodox Quakers —*Amer. Guide Series: Pa.*⟩ ⟨*disown* an erring son⟩ ⟨*disown* earlier obligations contracted in his name by friends⟩ DISACKNOWLEDGE is milder than disown, usu. applying to repudiation of something by denying any knowledge of it ⟨*disacknowledge* any responsibility to the community⟩ ⟨*disacknowledge* a signature on a note⟩ DISALLOW implies the withholding or taking away of sanction or approval, sometimes implying rejection or condemnation ⟨its duty of *disallowing* any proceedings which would infringe the rules of financial procedure —T.E.May⟩ ⟨if he is going to drive while intoxicated . . . his right to a driving license must be *disallowed* —Lucius Garvin⟩

dis·claim·ant \-mənt\ *n* **:** one who makes a disclaimer

dis·claim·er \-mə(r)\ *n* -S [AF *disclaimer* to disclaim] **1 a :** a denial or disavowal of legal claim (as in pleading where a defendant denies any interest in or claim to the subject of the action) **:** renunciation of a title, claim, interest, estate, or trust **:** relinquishment, waiver of, or formal refusal to accept an interest or estate **b** (1) **:** a writing by which a patentee that has by inadvertence, accident, or mistake claimed more than he had a right to claim as new disclaims such parts as he chooses not to claim or hold under the patent (2) **:** a clause in an original or reissue application referring to matter to which the disclaimant does not choose to claim title **:** a writing made to avoid the continuation of an interference **2 a :** a disavowal (as of pretensions, claims, or opinions) **:** DENIAL ⟨his first defense was a ~ of the authorship —S.H.Adams⟩ ⟨frowned in grave ~ of responsibility —Marguerite Steen⟩ **b :** REPUDIATION, DISOWNMENT ⟨his contemptuous ~ of stuff he did not keep —George Meredith⟩ **3** *heraldry* **a :** a proclamation by a herald of the illegitimacy of a person's right to bear arms or to be known by the title of esquire or gentleman **b :** a disavowal of any claim to such a right or title

dis·cla·ma·tion \,disklə'māshən\ *n* -S [ML *disclamatus* (past part. of *disclamare* to disclaim, prob. fr. AF *disclaimer, desclamer*) + E *-ion*] **1** *Scots law* **:** the act of a tenant or vassal who disclaims **2 :** DISAVOWAL, RENUNCIATION, DISCLAIMER

dis·clam·a·to·ry \də'sklamə,tōrē\ *adj* [ML *disclamatus* + E *-ory*] **:** having the character of a disclaimer ⟨his lordship waved a ~ hand —Max Peacock⟩ ⟨a shocked and most ~ tone —Charles Reade⟩

dis·climax \(')dis, dəs+\ *n* [¹*dis-* + *climax*] **:** a relatively stable ecological community that often includes kinds of organisms (as species) foreign to the region and that has displaced the climax because of disturbance esp. by man or domesticated animals — compare SUBCLIMAX

discloak *vt* [¹*dis-* + *cloak* (*n.*)] *obs* **:** UNCLOAK

¹dis·close \də'sklōz\ *vb* [ME *disclosen, desclosen*, fr. MF *desclor-*, stem of OF *desclore*, fr. ML *disclaudere* to open, fr. L *dis-* ¹dis- + *claudere* to close — more at CLOSE (adj.)] *vt* **1** *obs* **:** to open up **:** UNCLOSE **2 a :** to expose to view ⟨the curtain rises to ~ once again the lobby —J.T.Winterich⟩ **:** lay open or uncover (something hidden from view) ⟨excavations *disclosed* many artifacts⟩ **b :** to make known **:** open up to general knowledge ⟨her appearance *disclosed* an amazing vocal and acting talent⟩ ⟨a complete review of the literature fails to ~ a single comprehensive treatise on the subject —H.G.Armstrong⟩; *esp* **:** to reveal in words (something that is secret or not generally known) **:** DIVULGE ⟨the adventurer did not ~ his true objective⟩ ⟨*disclosed* that an exchange of views had taken place between the two governments⟩ **syn** see REVEAL

²disclose *n*, *obs* **:** DISCLOSURE

dis·clo·sure \də'sklōzhə(r)\ *n* **1 :** the act or an instance of opening up to view, knowledge, or comprehension **:** EXPOSURE ⟨a bill to require fuller ~ of stockholder groups in proxy contests —*Wall Street Jour.*⟩ ⟨his self-respect required a public ~ of his motives and actions⟩ **2 :** something that is disclosed **:** REVELATION, DIVULGATION ⟨these lurid ~s produced a scandal and led to the arrest of City Hall officials⟩ **3 :** a statement or description of an invention and its method of operation in a patent application

discloud *vt* [¹*dis-* + *cloud* (n.)] *obs* **:** UNCLOUD

disco- — see DISC-

dis·co·blas·tic \,diskō'blastik\ *adj* [*disc-* + *-blastic*] **:** MEROBLASTIC

dis·co·blastula \,diskō+\ *n* [NL, fr. *disc-* + *blastula*] **:** BLASTODERM

dis·cob·o·lus *also* **dis·cob·o·los** \də'skäbələs\ *n*, *pl* **dis·cobo·li** \-,lī, -,lē\ *also* **discobo·loi** \-,lȯi\ [L & Gk; L *discobolus*, fr. Gk *diskobolos*, fr. *diskos* quoit + *-bolos* (fr. *ballein* to throw) — more at DISH, DEVIL] **:** a discus thrower

dis·co·carp \'diskə,kärp\ *n* -S [NL *discocarpium*, fr. *disc-* + *-carpium*] **:** APOTHECIUM

dis·co·ceph·a·li \,diskō'sefə,lī\ *n pl*, *cap* [NL, fr. *disc-* + *-cephali*] **:** a small order of spiny-finned fishes comprising the remoras and having the dorsal fin modified into a flat sucking disk on top of the head used for adhering to the bodies of other fishes (as sharks and swordfishes)

dis·co·ceph·a·lous \;==;fələs\ *adj* [*disc-* + *-cephalous*] **:** having a sucker on the head — compare DISCOCEPHALI

dis·co·dac·ty·lous \;==;daktələs\ *adj* [*disc-* + *-dactylous*] **:** having sucking disks on the toes (as the tree frogs)

dis·co·dri·lid \,diskō'drīləd\ *n or adj* [NL *Discodrilidae* family of annelid worms, fr. *disc-* + Gk *drilos* earthworm + NL *-idae*] **:** BRANCHIOBDELLID

dis·co·gastrula \,diskō+\ *n* [NL, fr. *disc-* + *gastrula*] **:** a gastrula derived from a blastoderm

¹dis·co·glos·sid \,diskō'gläsəd\ *adj* [NL *Discoglossidae*] **:** of or relating to the Discoglossidae or to toads of this family

²discoglossid \"\ *n* -S **:** one of the Discoglossidae

dis·co·glos·si·dae \,==='gläsə,dē\ *n pl*, *cap* [NL, fr. *Discoglossus*, type genus (fr. *disc-* + *-glossus*, fr. Gk *glōssa* tongue) + *-idae* — more at GLOSS] **:** a family of Old World toads characterized by a fixed disklike tongue and having as well-known representatives the obstetrical toad and the fire-bellied toad — **dis·co·glos·soid** \;==;glä,sȯid\ *adj*

dis·cog·ra·pher \də'skägrəfə(r)\ *n* -S **:** one that compiles discographies **:** a specialist in discography

dis·co·graph·i·cal \,diskə'grafəkəl\ *also* **dis·co·graph·ic** \-fik\ *adj* **:** of or relating to discography

dis·cog·ra·phy \də'skägrəfē\ *n* -ES [F *discographie*, fr. *disc-* + *-graphie* -graphy] **1 :** a descriptive compilation of phonograph records by classes; *also* **:** a list of recordings of one composer or by one performer **2 :** the history or description of recorded music

¹dis·coid \'dis,kȯid\ *adj* [LL *discoides* quoit-shaped, fr. Gk *diskoeidēs*, fr. *disk-* disc- + *-oeidēs* -oid] **1 :** like a disk or discus **:** flat and circular ⟨a ~ body⟩ **2 :** relating to or having a disk: as **a** *of a composite floret* **:** situated in the floral disk **:** being a disk floret **b** *of a composite flower head* **:** having only tubular florets

²discoid \"\ *n* -S **1 :** something shaped like a discus or disk ⟨the concept of the galactic system as a stellar ~ . . . was soon abandoned —Harlow Shapley⟩ **2 :** DISCOIDAL

¹dis·coi·dal \də'skȯidᵊl, 'di,s-\ *adj* [LL *discoides* + E *-al*] **:** of, like, or producing a disk ⟨~ cleavage⟩ ⟨a ~ sponge⟩: as **a** *of a gastropod shell* **:** having the whorls form a flat coil ⟨snails of the genus *Planorbis* are ~⟩ **b :** having the villi restricted to one or more disklike areas ⟨most insectivores, bats, rodents, and primates have ~ placentas⟩ — see META-DISCOIDAL

²discoidal \"\ *n* -S **:** a disk-shaped stone artifact found in No. America that was probably used by the Indians in games

discoidal cleavage *n* **:** meroblastic cleavage in which a disk of cells is produced at the animal pole of the zygote (as in bird eggs) — compare SUPERFICIAL CLEAVAGE

dis·coi·dea \də'skȯidēə\ [NL, fr. *disc-* + *-oidea*] *syn of* DISCOPLACENTALIA

dis·co·lichen \,diskō+\ *n* [NL *Discolichenes*] **:** a member of the Discolichenes — compare BASIDIOLICHEN

dis·co·lichenes \"+\ *n pl*, *cap* [NL, fr. *disc-* + *Lichenes*] **:** a subgroup of ascolichens having an open rather flat and rounded or cup-shaped spore fruit — compare PYRENOLICHENES

dis·co·lith \'diskə,lith\ *n* -S [*disc-* + *-lith*] **:** a discoidal coccolith — compare TREMALITH

¹dis·color \dəs, (')dis+\ *vb* [ME *discolouren*, fr. MF *descolourer, descolorer*, fr. LL *discolorari* to change color, fr. L *discolor* of another color, fr. *dis-* ¹dis- + *color* — more at COLOR] *vt* **1 :** to alter the hue or color of **:** TARNISH ⟨a long row of ~*ed* frame houses⟩ **:** change to a different color **:** STAIN, TINGE ⟨~*ed* the water, changing it to a dull red⟩ **2 :** to change the intellectual or moral complexion or appearance of esp. for the worse ⟨~*ing* the luster of a glorious name⟩ **3 :** to deprive of color or coloring **:** DULL, FADE, STREAK ⟨a dress ~*ed* by the sun⟩ ~ *vi* **:** to change color **:** STAIN, FADE ⟨it will not ~ or stain if given reasonable care⟩

²discolor \"\ *n* [ME *discolour*, fr. *discolouren*, v.] *archaic* **:** change of color esp. for the worse **:** STAIN

³discolor \"\ *adj* [L, of another color, variegated] **:** of two or more colors **:** VARIEGATED

dis·coloration \dəs, ¦dis+\ *n* **1 :** the act of discoloring or state of being discolored **:** change of hue or appearance **2 :** a discolored spot or formation **:** STAIN ⟨a small ~ on the finger⟩ ⟨~s caused by microscopic marine organisms⟩

discolored *adj* [ME *discoloured*, fr. past part. of *discolouren* to discolor — more at DISCOLOR] **1 :** changed in color **:** STAINED, FADED ⟨~ teeth⟩ ⟨~ walls⟩ **2** *obs* **:** of different colors **:** VARIEGATED — **dis·col·ored·ness** *n* -ES

dis·col·or·ment \də'skələ(r)mənt, 'di,s-\ *n* -S **:** DISCOLORATION

dis·com·bob·u·late \,diskəm'bäb(y)ə,lāt\ *vt* -ED/-ING/-S [prob. alter. of *discompose* or *discomfit*] **:** UPSET, CONFUSE, DISCONCERT ⟨the offensive had *discombobulated* all the German defensive arrangements —A.J.Liebling⟩

dis·co·medusae \,diskō+\ *n pl*, *cap* [NL, pl., fr. *disc-* + *medusae*, pl. of *medusa*] *in some classifications* **:** a large order of Scyphozoa equivalent to the modern orders Rhizostomae and Semaeostomeae, or more broadly, nearly equivalent to Scyphozoa — **dis·co·medusan** \"+\ *adj or n* — **dis·co·medusoid** \"+\ *adj*

¹dis·com·fit \də'skəmfə̇t, *in dial speech in the southern US & the Brit Isles* ¦diskəm¦fi|; *usu* |d·+V\ *vt* -ED/-ING/-S [ME *discomfiten, discomfiten*, fr. OF *desconfit*, past part. of *desconfire* to destroy, defeat, fr. *des-* ¹dis- + *confire* to prepare — more at COMFIT] **1 a** *archaic* **:** to defeat in battle **:** put to rout **:** OVERTHROW ⟨~*ed* the pagans in two great battles⟩ ⟨pictured the ground . . . as strewn with the ~*ed* —Stephen Crane⟩ **b :** to defeat or rout (an opponent) in any way ⟨in the ensuing debate he utterly ~*ed* his less agile adversary⟩ ⟨~*ed* all her rivals in the race for colonies⟩ **:** frustrate the plans of **:** THWART, FOIL ⟨completely ~*ed*, the would-be robbers fled the scene⟩ **2 :** to cause perplexity or embarrassment to **:** DISCONCERT, UPSET ⟨completely ~*ed* by the unexpected question⟩ **:** ABASH ⟨hung his head in shame and looked quite ~*ed*⟩ **syn** see EMBARRASS

²dis·com·fit \də'skəmfə̇t\ *n* -S [ME *discomfite*, fr. *discomfiten*, v.] *archaic* **:** ROUT, OVERTHROW, DISCOMFITURE

dis·com·fi·ture \də'skəmfə,chu̇(ə)r, -ü(ə), -,chə(r)\ *n* -S [ME *discomfiture, desconfiture*, fr. MF *desconfiture*, fr. OF, fr. *desconfit* + *-ure*] **1 a :** defeat in battle **:** ROUT, OVERTHROW ⟨might well have been the scene of the ~ of the pursuing Egyptian chariotry —G.W.Murray⟩ **b :** defeat or rout of any kind ⟨the defeated candidate attributed his ~ to the disloyalty of party lieutenants⟩ ⟨the champion picked himself up from the floor, grinning wryly at his own ~⟩ **:** FRUSTRATION, DISAPPOINTMENT ⟨great hopes destined to end in ~⟩ **2 :** the state of being disconcerted or abashed **:** CONFUSION, EMBARRASSMENT ⟨blushed and lowered her eyes in evident ~⟩ ⟨smiling blandly at my ~⟩ **3 :** DISARRAY, DAMAGE, INJURY, INCONVENIENCE ⟨plunged through countless . . . hedges and ditches, without apparent ~ to her muslin —George Meredith⟩ ⟨the Waterside Workers' Federation has repeatedly demonstrated its strength, often to the ~ of the entire commonwealth —E.P.Hohman⟩

¹dis·comfort \dəs+\ *vt* [ME *discomforten*, fr. MF *desconforter*, fr. OF, fr. *des-* ¹dis- + *conforter* to comfort — more at COMFORT] **1** *archaic* **:** DISCOURAGE, DEJECT, GRIEVE, DISMAY ⟨his funerals shall not be in our camp, lest it ~ us —Shak.⟩ **2 :** to cause bodily or mental discomfort to **:** make uncomfortable or uneasy ⟨the tart rejoinder did not ~ him⟩

²discomfort \"\ *n* [ME, fr. MF *desconfort*, fr. OF, fr. *desconforter*] **1** *archaic* **a :** DISTRESS **b :** something that causes sorrow or distress **:** GRIEF, TROUBLE, MISFORTUNE ⟨'tis no ~ in the world to fall —Robert Herrick †1674⟩ **2 :** lack of comfort **:** uncomfortable condition **:** mental or physical uneasiness less intense and less localized than pain **:** EMBARRASSMENT, ANNOYANCE ⟨the ~ of a bad cold⟩ ⟨reducing to an acceptable range the ~s incident to business cycles —Clark Warburton⟩ ⟨he gave every sign of intense ~⟩

dis·comfortable \dəs+\ *adj* [ME, fr. MF *desconfortable*, fr. *desconforter* + *-able*] **1** *archaic* **:** causing mental discomfort or discouragement **:** affording no comfort **2** *archaic* **:** lacking in physical comfort **:** causing physical discomfort or inconvenience **3** *archaic* **:** feeling discomfort **:** UNCOMFORTABLE ⟨some among us . . . seemed most ~ because of the skimpiness of the rags they wore —Kenneth Roberts⟩

dis·comfortably \"+\ *adv* **:** in a discomfortable manner

discomforting *adj* [ME, fr. pres. part. of *discomforten*] **:** causing discomfort ⟨a thoroughly ~, disturbing book⟩ — **dis·com·fort·ing·ly** *adv*

dis·commend \,dis+\ *vt* [ME *discommenden*, fr. ¹*dis-* + *commenden* to commend — more at COMMEND] **1 :** to mention with disapproval **:** DISAPPROVE ⟨seldom ~ anything . . . or do it but moderately —Isaac Newton⟩ ⟨I shall . . . commend and ~ this book —*John o'London's Weekly*⟩ **:** DISPRAISE — opposed to *commend* **2 :** to speak of as not meriting consideration, adoption, or favor ⟨the book is ~*ed* to students⟩ **:** cause to be viewed unfavorably ⟨an act that ~s him to all honest men⟩ — opposed to *recommend*

dis·commendable \,dis+\ *adj*, *archaic* **:** deserving disapproval, blame, or unfavorable comment

dis·commendation \(¦)dis, dəs+\ *n*, *archaic* **:** BLAME, CENSURE, REPROACH, DISPRAISE

dis·com·mode \,diskə'mōd\ *vt* -ED/-ING/-S [MF *discommoder*, fr. *dis-* ¹dis- + *commode* convenient — more at COMMODE] **:** to cause inconvenience to **:** INCONVENIENCE, TROUBLE ⟨I don't think the war has *discommoded* him too seriously —L.C. Douglas⟩

dis·commodious \,dis+\ *adj* [¹*dis-* + *commodious*] **:** INCONVENIENT, TROUBLESOME ⟨a very ~, untimely accident⟩ — **dis·commodiously** *adv* — **discommodiousness** *n* -ES

dis·commodity \"+\ *n* [¹*dis-* + *commodity*] **1** *archaic* **a :** INCONVENIENCE, DISADVANTAGEOUSNESS ⟨you go about, in rain or fine, at all hours, without ~ —Charles Lamb⟩ **b :** something that is inconvenient **:** DISADVANTAGE, TROUBLE ⟨*discommodities* visited upon a stiff-necked disobedient people⟩ **2 :** a substance or action having no utility — opposed to *commodity*

dis·common \dəs, (')dis+\ *vt* [ME *discomenen*, fr. ¹*dis-* + *comen, commun* common (n.) — more at COMMON] **1** *obs* **:** to exclude or banish from a community of interest; *specif* **:** to deprive of citizenship or of church fellowship **2** *at Oxford and Cambridge Universities* **:** to forbid (a tradesman) to deal with undergraduates **3 a :** to deprive of the right of common (as of pasture) **b :** to deprive of commonable quality (as land by enclosing it)

dis·commons \"+\ *vt* -ED/-ING/-ES [¹*dis-* + *commons*] **:** to deprive of the right to commons in an English college ⟨could not dine in hall, as he was ~*ed* for persistent absence from lectures —Thomas Hughes⟩

discommune *vt* [¹*dis-* + *commune*] *obs* **:** to exclude from community or association of interests

dis·compose \,dis+\ *vt* [¹*dis-* + *compose*] **1 :** to destroy the composure or serenity of **:** deprive of equanimity or stability **:** AGITATE, DISCONCERT ⟨do not be *discomposed* by the opinions of inept persons —Norman Douglas⟩ ⟨he was still *discomposed* by the girl's bitter and sudden retort —James Joyce⟩ **2 :** to disturb the order of **:** DISARRANGE, DISARRAY ⟨the wind ruffled her hair, *discomposed* her dress⟩ **3** *obs* **:** to discharge from service **:** DISPLACE; *also* **:** to derange the health of

syn DISQUIET, DISTURB, PERTURB, AGITATE, UPSET, FLUSTER, FLURRY: DISCOMPOSE indicates a causing loss of self-control, self-confidence, or poise ⟨her look so *discomposed* him that he stopped, wandered, and began anew —Charles Dickens⟩ ⟨the even temperament of his mind was never *discomposed*, and at each moment he was able always to decide, and to do, what the moment required —J.A.Froude⟩ DISQUIET denotes a making uneasy, a causing loss of security and peace of mind ⟨Roylance drove a motorcar well but audaciously, so that he *disquieted* the nerves of those who accompanied him —John Buchan⟩ ⟨he was indubitably . . . restless and *disquieted*, his disquietude sometimes amounting to agony —Matthew Arnold⟩ DISTURB now applies to the effect of care, strain, conflict, worry, or disappointment in interfering with or confusing accustomed mental and nervous processes ⟨nothing is more *disturbing* than the upsetting of a preconceived idea —Joseph Conrad⟩ ⟨I slept, indeed, but I was *disturbed* by the wildest dreams —Mary W. Shelley⟩ ⟨a very badly *disturbed* child, one whom it would take a long, tough struggle to straighten out —J.N.Bell⟩ PERTURB applies to the worrisome or disturbing results of uncertainty, disappointment, or danger ⟨in this *perturbed* state of mind, with thoughts that could rest on nothing, she walked on —Jane Austen⟩ ⟨and a presence of mind which no emergency can *perturb* —C.W.Eliot⟩ AGITATE suggests show of obvious signs of nervous excitation and loss of self-control and calm ⟨she was too *agitated* to sit down. She lit a cigarette but her lips trembled and she could not smoke it —Audrey Barker⟩ ⟨Clara was so *agitated* that she was incoherent —Margaret Deland⟩ ⟨an infernal spirit which *agitates* them and makes them tremble —J.G.Frazer⟩ UPSET applies to any nervous unsettling, slight or serious ⟨what *upset* me in the . . . trial was not the conviction, but the methods of the defense —H.J. Laski⟩ ⟨Prospero, *upset* by a plot to murder him, philosophizing on the insubstantial quality of life —C.S.Kilby⟩ FLUSTER suggests confused or bewildered agitation in which one cannot act decisively or entirely rationally ⟨the Sognings were a people of even temperament, not easily *flustered*; they bore the affliction with remarkable calmness and fortitude —O.E.Rölvaag⟩ FLURRY suggests natural agitation, excitement, or confusion induced by haste, rush, and concern ⟨thoughts, with their attendant visions, which occupied and *flurried* her too much to leave her any power of observation —Jane Austen⟩ ⟨he recognized her and sat down immediately, *flurried* and confused by his display of excitement —Liam O'Flaherty⟩

discomposed \-zd\ *adj* **:** DISORDERED, DISTURBED, DISQUIETED ⟨looked about with a wandering and ~ countenance⟩ — **dis·com·pos·ed·ly** \-zədlē, -li\ *adv*

dis·composure \,dis+\ *n* **1 :** DISORDER, DISARRANGEMENT ⟨his royal robe covered his wounds, there was no stain nor ~ —Robinson Jeffers⟩ **2 :** the state of being disturbed or upset in feelings : AGITATION, PERTURBATION ⟨his trembling voice and flushed cheeks revealed his profound ~⟩ **3** *obs* : derangement of health

dis·co·my·cete \ˌdiskō'mīˌsēt, -ˌmī'sēt\ *n, pl* **discomyce·tes** \ˌ==ˌmī'sēd·ēz\ [NL *Discomycetes*] : a fungus of the group Discomycetes

discomycetes *n pl, cap* [NL, fr. *disc-* + *-mycetes*] *in some classifications* : a group of fungi of the class Ascomycetes in which the fruiting body is disklike or cup-shaped (as in Pezizales) — **dis·co·my·ce·tous** \ˌ==ˌmī'sēd·əs, ˌ== mī'sēd·əs\ *adj*

dis·co·nan·thae \ˌdiskə'nanˌthē\ *n pl, cap* [NL, fr. *disc-* + connective *-n-* + *-anthae* (fr. Gk *anthos* flower) — more at ANTHOLOGY] *in some classifications* : a division of Siphonophora comprising jellyfishes with a round flat many-chambered float (as members of the genera *Veletta* and *Porpita*) — **dis·co·nan·thous** \ˌdiskə'nan(t)thəs\ *adj*

¹dis·con·cert \də'skän(t)sə(r)|t, -n,sər|, -n,sə̄|, -n,səi|; 'dis,+ kän(t)sə(r)|; *usu* |d·+V\ *n* [¹*dis-* + *concert*] : lack of concert : the state of being disconcerted ⟨there was a brief ~ of the whole gay company —E.A.Poe⟩

²dis·con·cert \ˌdiskən'sər|t, -'sə̄|, -'səi|, *usu* |d·+V\ *vt* -ED/-ING/-S [obs. F *disconcerter*, alter. (influenced by L *dis-* ¹dis-) of MF *desconcerter*, fr. *des-* ¹dis- + *concerter* to concert — more at CONCERT] **1** : to break up the concert or arrangement of : throw into confusion : DISARRAY, UPSET, FRUSTRATE, DISTURB ⟨~*ing* enemy plans by a sudden offensive⟩ ⟨confessed that the eerie howls ~*ed* his slumbers —Rex Ingamells⟩ **2** : to disturb the composure or shake the complacency of : RUFFLE, EMBARRASS ⟨~*ed* his academic cronies by confessing that inspiration was most often induced in him by a pint of beer —Herbert Read⟩ ⟨in an interview with Washington, he succeeded chiefly in ~*ing* that most just of men —A.L.Kroeber⟩ **syn** see EMBARRASS

disconcerted *adj* : marked by loss of self-possession or composure : PERTURBED, EMBARRASSED ⟨look at each other dumbly, quite ~ —G.B.Shaw⟩ ⟨was somewhat ~ to learn that her daughter was a suffragist —Margaret A. Barnes⟩ : put out ⟨was a little ~ not to find the missing book⟩ — **disconcertedly** *adv* — **disconcertedness** *n* -ES

disconcerting *adj* : causing loss of composure or self-possession : DISTURBING, EMBARRASSING ⟨this ~ stare often caused people to falter nervously in their speech —Jean Stafford⟩ ⟨a ~ habit of greeting friends ferociously and strangers charmingly —Herb Caen⟩ — **dis·con·cert·ing·ly** *adv* — **disconcertingness** *n* -ES

dis·con·cer·tion \ˌdiskən'sərshən, -sə̄sh-, -səish-\ *n* -S : the action of disconcerting or state of being disconcerted : DISCOMPOSURE, PERTURBATION

dis·con·cert·ment \-'sərtmənt, -sə̄t-, -səit-\ *n* -S : DISCONCERTION

dis·confirm \ˌdis+\ *vt* [¹*dis-* + *confirm*] : to establish as untrue or invalid : DISPROVE ⟨~ a philosophical assertion by appeal to sense experience⟩ — opposed to *confirm*

dis·confirmation \ˌdis, dəs+\ *n* : the act, process, or an instance of disconfirming

dis·con·form \ˌdiskən'fȯ(ə)rm\ *adj* [¹*dis-* + *conform*] : not conformable — usu. used with *to*

dis·conformable \ˌdis+\ *adj* [¹*dis-* + *conformable*] **1** *archaic* : not conformable : DISAGREEING — used with *from* or *to* **2** : of or relating to a disconformity ⟨~ contact of Middle Devonian on Middle Silurian limestones —C.O.Dunbar⟩

dis·conformity \ˌdis+\ *n* [¹*dis-* + *conformity*] **1** *archaic* : lack of conformity or correspondence : NONCONFORMITY — used with *to* or *with* **2** : a break in a sequence of sedimentary rocks all of which have approximately the same dip indicating an interruption in sedimentation generally by an interval of erosion — compare DIASTEM 3, UNCONFORMITY

dis·congruity \ˌdis+\ *n* [¹*dis-* + *congruity*] : INCONGRUITY

¹dis·connect \ˌdis+\ *vb* [¹*dis-* + *connect*] *vt* : to sever the connection of or between : DETACH ⟨~ the fuse from a bomb⟩ : SEPARATE, DISUNITE ⟨~ church and state⟩ ~ *vi* : to terminate a connection

²disconnect \"\ *n* -S [by shortening] : DISCONNECTING SWITCH

disconnected *adj* : not connected : DISUNITED ⟨Congress . . . gives the impression of . . . a confusing sum of ~ local forces —Samuel Lubell⟩ : lacking logical or organic connection : DISJOINTED ⟨throwing down her pen after having written a few ~ lines —H.A.Overstreet⟩ — **disconnectedly** *adv* — **disconnectedness** *n*

disconnecting switch *n* : a switch that isolates a circuit or one or more pieces of electrical apparatus after the current has been interrupted by other means

dis·connection \ˌdis+\ *n* [¹*dis-* + *connection*] : the act of disconnecting or state of being disconnected : SEPARATION, DETACHMENT ⟨a curious feeling of loneliness or ~ from the busy crowds about him⟩

dis·con·nec·tor \"+\ *n* : DISCONNECTING SWITCH

dis·consider \ˌdis+\ *vt* [¹*dis-* + *consider*] : to deprive of consideration or esteem ⟨it was the sort of exploit that ~*ed* a young man for good with the more serious classes —R.L. Stevenson⟩ : view without regard or respect ⟨when humanity is ~*ed* the public is not protected, nor is the professional code honored —*Spectator*⟩

¹dis·con·so·late \də'skän(t)s(ə)lət, 'diˌs-, *usu* -əd·+V\ *adj* [ME *disconsolat*, fr. ML *disconsolatus*, fr. L *dis-* ¹dis- + *consolatus*, past part. of *consolari* to console — more at CONSOLE] **1** : lacking consolation : deeply dejected and dispirited : hopelessly sad : being beyond consolation ⟨a ~ parent⟩ **2** : inspiring dejection : SADDENING, CHEERLESS ⟨set up a wall . . . to shut off the ~ hills and the monotonous sea —M.R.Cohen⟩ : indicating or suggestive of dejection ⟨retired . . . with a ~ step —T.L.Peacock⟩ **syn** see DOWNCAST

²disconsolate *vt* -ED/-ING/-S *obs* : to make disconsolate

dis·con·so·late·ly *adj* : in a disconsolate manner ⟨gazed ~ at the smoking ruins of his house⟩ ⟨rows of cypresses standing ~ beside the brooding river⟩

dis·con·so·late·ness *n* -ES : the quality or state of being disconsolate : DEJECTION, DISPIRITEDNESS

dis·con·so·la·tion \dəˌskän(t)sə'lāshən, ˌdiˌ-\ *n* [¹*dis-* + *consolation*] : the state of being disconsolate

dis·consonant \dəs, (')dis+\ *adj* [¹*dis-* + *consonant*] : not agreeing : DISCORDANT, DISSIMILAR

¹dis·content \ˌdis+\ *adj* [¹*dis-* + *content* (adj.)] : DISCONTENTED — usu. used with *with* ⟨~ with his prospects and station in life⟩

²discontent \"\ *n* : one who is discontented : one who has a grievance : MALCONTENT ⟨his following had diminished to less than a dozen ~*s*⟩

³discontent \"\ *vt* [¹*dis-* + *content* (v.)] : to inspire feelings of grievance or dissatisfaction in : make discontented : DISPLEASE ⟨inflation . . . corrupted the civil service . . . , ~*ed* and disheartened the soldiers —C.P.Fitzgerald⟩

⁴discontent \"\ *n* [¹*dis-* + *content* (n.)] : lack of contentment : a sense of grievance or thwarted aspirations or desires : DISSATISFACTION ⟨abolitionists encouraged agitators to come south and stir up ~ —Helen B. Woodward⟩ ⟨unless such aid reaches down to the masses . . . , it will not be effective in preventing social ~*s* —Dexter Perkins⟩ : restless yearning or aspiration for improvement or perfection : inquietude of mind ⟨though yet young, he had sunk into a groove extremely deep, and had apparently lost all divine ~ —Arnold Bennett⟩

discontented *adj* : DISSATISFIED, UNSATISFIED, MALCONTENT : uneasy in mind ⟨hardly a ~ face to be seen —Thomas Gray⟩ ⟨~ with his position⟩ — **discontentedly** *adv* — **discontentedness** *n* -ES

discontenting *adj* **1** : causing discontent : DISSATISFYING, DISPLEASING ⟨a most ~ kind of activity⟩ **2** *obs* : DISCONTENTED

dis·contentment \ˌdis+\ *n* : DISCONTENT

dis·continuance \ˌdis+\ *n* [ME *discontinuance*, fr. ¹*dis-* + *continuance* continuance — more at CONTINUANCE] **1** : the act or an instance of discontinuing the use or practice of ⟨there were no automobiles to cause a ~ of walking —Morris Fishbein⟩ ⟨an appeal for the ~ of the electoral college⟩ : the state of being discontinued ⟨~ of dueling had changed the pattern of German university life⟩ : CESSATION, SHUTDOWN, CLOSURE ⟨a ~ of bus service between the two towns⟩ ⟨the site of the state fair until its recent ~⟩ ⟨almost 40 percent of small business ~*s* involve simply a change of ownership —*Nation's Business*⟩ : INTERRUPTION ⟨an intercourse renewed after many years' ~ —Jane Austen⟩ **2** *obs* : temporary absence **3** [ME *discontinuaunce*, fr. AF, fr. MF *dis-*, *des-* ¹dis- + *continuance* — more at CONTINUANCE] **a** : a breaking off or interruption of an estate upon an alienation made esp. by a tenant in tail of a larger estate than he was entitled to **b** : the termination of an action by the failure of the plaintiff to properly continue it or by the entry of a discontinuing order on his motion — compare DISMISS *vt* 4b **c** : the interruption of the proceedings in an action that follows where a party does not answer all the material allegations of the previous pleading and the opposite party fails to take judgment for the part unanswered

dis·continuation \"+\ *n* [MF, fr. ML *discontinuation-*, *discontinuatio*, fr. *discontinuatus* (past part. of *discontinuare*) + L *-ion-*, *-io* -ion] : DISCONTINUANCE

dis·continue \"+\ *vb* [ME *discontinuen*, fr. MF *discontinuer*, fr. ML *discontinuare*, fr. L *dis-* ¹dis- + *continuare* to continue — more at CONTINUE] *vt* **1** **a** : to break off : give up : TERMINATE ⟨found it necessary to ~ her course in Spanish⟩ ⟨*discontinued* bus service between the two points⟩ : end the operations or existence of ⟨the school was *discontinued* after a sharp drop in enrollments⟩ ⟨*discontinued* the business after the death of his partner⟩ : cease to use ⟨*discontinued* the pattern after it proved unsatisfactory⟩ **b** *obs* : to cease to attend, frequent, or occupy **c** : to break the continuity of : SEVER ⟨in regard to the mountains it was contended that a gap does not ~ the general line of the range —*Encyc. Americana*⟩ **d** (1) : to cease to publish ⟨~ an unprofitable journal⟩ (2) : to cease to subscribe to ⟨~ the morning newspaper⟩ **2** : to abandon or terminate by a discontinuance or by other legal action ~ *vi* : to cease to continue : come to an end; *specif* : to cease to be published ⟨the magazine will ~ after the next issue⟩ **syn** see STOP

dis·continuity \dəs, ˌdis+\ *n* [ML *discontinuitas*, fr. *discontinuus* + L *-itas* -ity] **1** : lack of continuity or cohesion : disunion of parts ⟨from chapter to chapter . . . there is a sense of ~, of failure on the author's part to "follow through" —Carlos Lynes⟩ **2** : a break in continuity : GAP ⟨microscopic *discontinuities* in the foil —N.A.Cooke⟩ ⟨conceived of the organic species as a hierarchy of creatures with comparatively large *discontinuities* between their ranks —S.F.Mason⟩ **3** *math* : a point or value of the argument at which a function is not continuous **4** : the boundary between two layers within the earth which display different physical properties made known by analysis of earthquake records **5** : a rapid change in meteorological elements in a short distance or a short time

dis·continuous \ˌdis+\ *adj* [ML *discontinuus*, fr. L *dis-* ¹dis- + *continuus* continuous — more at CONTINUOUS] **1** *obs* : causing discontinuity : GAPING ⟨with ~ wound —John Milton⟩ **2 a** : not continuous : marked by breaks or gaps ⟨a ~ mosaic of better watered and settled territory, embedded . . . in wide expanses of arid or semiarid land —*Geog. Jour.*⟩ ⟨the boy received a very jumbled and ~ schooling —Louis Kronenberger⟩ : not continued : DISCRETE, SEPARATE ⟨here and there were conspicuous elevations . . . but they were ~ features, not useful as regional boundaries —R.H.Brown⟩ : lacking logical or organic sequence or coherence ⟨a series of ~ events⟩ ⟨the tone poem is gay and always entertaining, but a trifle ~⟩ **b** *math* : having one or more discontinuities — used of a variable or a function **c** *of a linguistic form* : consisting of parts that are separated by other linguistic units of the same order or by parts of such units (as French *ne . . . pas* "not" in *je ne sais pas* "I do not know") ⟨~ morphemes⟩ ⟨~ phonemes⟩ — **discontinuously** *adv* — **discontinuousness** *n* -ES

discontinuous easement *n* : an easement or servitude that requires an act of man for its exercise or enjoyment (as a right of way or right to draw water) — compare CONTINUOUS EASEMENT

discontinuous phase *n* : DISPERSED PHASE

discontinuous variation *n, biol* : abrupt variation in which there are few or no intermediate forms

¹dis·convenience \ˌdis+\ *n* [ME, fr. LL *disconvenientia* fr. L *disconvenient-*, *disconveniens* (pres. part. of *disconvenire* to disagree, be inconsistent, fr. *dis-* ¹dis- + *convenire* to come together, agree) + *-ia* -y — more at CONVENE] *dial* : INCONVENIENCE

²disconvenience \"\ *vt, dial* : INCONVENIENCE

dis·convenient \ˌdis+\ *adj* [¹*dis-* + *convenient*] *now dial* : INCONVENIENT

dis·co·phile \'diskəˌfīl\ *n* -S [*disc-* + *-phile*] : one who is devoted to the study and collecting of phonograph records

dis·coph·o·ra \də'skäf(ə)rə\ *or* **dis·coph·o·rae** \-fəˌrē\ *n pl, cap* [NL, fr. *disc-* + *-phora*, *-phorae*] *in some classifications* : a group of jellyfishes: **a** : a group coextensive with Scyphozoa **b** : a group coextensive with Discomedusae

dis·coph·o·rous \də'skäf(ə)rəs, (')di¦s-\ *adj* [in sense 1, fr. *disc-* + *-phorous*; in sense 2, fr. NL *Discophora* + E *-ous*] **1** *zool* : bearing a disk or disklike structure **2** : of or relating to the Discophora

dis·co·placenta \ˌdiskō+\ *n* [NL, fr. *disc-* + *placenta*] : a discoidal placenta — **dis·co·placental** \"+\ *adj* — **dis·co·placentalian** \"+\ *adj*

dis·co·placentalia \"+\ *n pl, cap* [NL, fr. *disc-* + *Placentalia*] : mammals having discoidal placentas

dis·cop·o·dous \də'skäpədəs, (')di¦s-\ *adj* [*disc-* + *-podous*] *zool* : having the foot disk-shaped

¹dis·cord \'diˌskȯrd, -ȯ(ə)d\ *n* -S [ME *descord*, *discorde*, partly fr. OF *descort* (fr. *descorder*); partly fr. OF *descorde*, fr. L *discordia*, fr. *discord-*, *discors* discordant + *-ia* -y] **1 a** (1) : lack of harmony or agreement between persons : DISUNITY, DISAGREEMENT, DISSENSION ⟨must we fall into the jabber and babel of ~ while victory is still unattained —Sir Winston Churchill⟩ (2) : CONFLICT, STRIFE ⟨~ among the barons of the border country reached the point of daily raids, ambushes, and kidnappings⟩ **b** : lack of harmony or agreement between things or ideas : CONTRAST, DIFFERENCE, OPPOSITION ⟨the glaring ~ between the architecture of the two buildings⟩ ⟨the ~ between the idealist and materialist philosophies⟩ **2 a** : a combination of musical sounds which strike the ear harshly due either to an unprepared dissonance or to an effect of false intonation or tuning **b** : the interval between two discordant notes; *also* : a discordant note **c** : DISSONANCE **3** : any harsh or unpleasant sound ⟨the braying of automobile horns and other daily ~*s* of city life⟩

syn STRIFE, CONFLICT, CONTENTION, DISSENSION, VARIANCE: DISCORD may indicate sustained inharmonious disagreement marked by quarreling, factiousness, antagonism ⟨the meeting broke up in *discord*⟩ ⟨the *discord* among the brawling barons⟩ ⟨the controversies arising from this situation are bitter, and the *discord* is ominously apparent —H.A.Wagner⟩ DISCORD indicates the fact of existent disharmony, perhaps pointless; STRIFE may designate competition in a hectic struggle for victory or supremacy ⟨all must live together in harmony as good neighbors or in *strife* as bad neighbors —*Saturday Rev.*⟩ ⟨as the war drew to its end he, like Lincoln, sought to heal the wounds caused by internecine *strife* —H.A.Bridgman⟩ CONFLICT indicates existence of opposition or rivalry with desire or impetus to victory or mastery but not necessarily with the surging activity associated with STRIFE ⟨the medieval *conflicts* between England and France⟩ ⟨the age-old *conflict* between city and village —A.R.Williams⟩ ⟨the *conflict* of passion, temper, or appetite with the external duties —T.S.Eliot⟩ ⟨the union and *conflict* of two very different human impulses, the one urging men towards mysticism, the other urging them towards science —Bertrand Russell⟩ CONTENTION may suggest bickering quarrelsome altercation in words; it usu. does not apply to physically active strife ⟨*contention* about the new zoning laws⟩ ⟨*contention* between free trade and tariff groups⟩ ⟨the *contentions* and turmoils preceding Kentucky's admission into the Union —E.M.Coulter⟩ DISSENSION is likely to stress the existence of disharmony and noisy truculent antipathy between groups, with or without strife ⟨the party was split by internal *dissension* on religious, racial, and intellectual questions —*Amer. Guide Series: N. Y.*⟩ ⟨reports of internal *dissension* in Venezuela: a "moderate" group in the Venezuelan army threatened to revolt against the Gallegos government —*Current Biog.*⟩ VARIANCE may indicate a clash of opinion, temperament, or character that make for strife, discord, or cold hostility ⟨sectarian *variances* in the town had delayed the erection of a house of worship —*Amer. Guide Series: Vt.*⟩ ⟨the unwillingness of young men interested in the ministry to accept the required strict orthodoxy at *variance* with twentieth century viewpoints —*Current Biog.*⟩

²dis·cord \", də'skȯ(ə)rd, -'skȯ(ə)d\ *vi* -ED/-ING/-S [ME *discorden*, fr. OF *descorder*, *discorder*, fr. L *discordare*, fr. *discord-*, *discors* discordant, at odds, fr. *dis-* ¹dis- + *cord-*, *cor* heart — more at HEART] : to be at variance : DISAGREE, DIFFER ⟨several of his disclosures ~ strongly with my personal knowledge —E.J.Wayland⟩

dis·cor·dance \də'skȯrdᵊn(t)s, 'diˌs-, -ȯ(ə)d-\ *n* -S [ME *discordaunce*, fr. MF *descordance*, fr. OF, fr. *descorder* + *-ance*] **1** : the state or an instance of being discordant : lack of harmony : DISAGREEMENT ⟨the still unsolved ~ between Spaniard and Indians —P.E.James⟩ : lack of internal harmony : INCONGRUITY ⟨the violence and ~ of his imagery —C.D. Lewis⟩ **2** : discord of sounds : DISSONANCE **3** *geol* **a** : angular unconformity **b** : a discordant junction (as of valleys)

dis·cor·dan·cy \də'skȯ(r)dᵊnsē, -si\ *n* -ES : DISCORDANCE, DISPARITY ⟨the maze of apparent *discordancies* in the text —R.H.Popkin⟩

dis·cor·dant \də'skȯrdᵊnt, (')di¦s-, -ȯ(ə)d-\ *adj* [ME, fr. MF, fr. OF *discordant*, *descordant*, fr. L *discordant-*, *discordans*, pres. part. of *discordare* to discord — more at DISCORD] **1 a** : being at variance : DISAGREEING ⟨views ~ with present-day ideas⟩ : being at variance with each other : INHARMONIOUS, ANTAGONISTIC ⟨the various dissevered and ~ elements of feudal society —W.J.Shepard⟩ : not conforming with : INCONGRUOUS ⟨the ~ element in the picture was his face, which belied his garb —John Buchan⟩ **b** : marked by lack of inner harmony or agreement of its parts ⟨a poetry that . . . is not only confused and ~ but negative in its emphasis —C.I.Glicksberg⟩ **c** : marked by inner discord ⟨a ~ family⟩ : QUARRELSOME ⟨a ~, savage people⟩ **2** : relating to a discord : DISSONANT ⟨~ tones⟩ : HARSH, JARRING ⟨I heard a horrid ~ cry, something between a bray and a yell —George Borrow⟩ : making inharmonious sounds ⟨a ~ crowd . . . shouting and laughing —Hugh Walpole⟩ **3** : lacking conformity or parallelism of bedding or structure — used of geologic strata **4** *of twins* : dissimilar in respect to one or more particular characters — compare CONCORDANT — **dis·cor·dant·ly** *adv* — **dis·cor·dant·ness** *n* -ES

discording *adj* [ME, fr. pres. part. of *discorden* to discord] : DISCORDANT

¹dis·count \'diˌskau̇nt\ *n* -S [modif. (influenced by ¹*dis-* & ¹*count*) of F *décompte*, fr. OF *descont*, fr. *desconter*] **1** : an abatement or reduction made from the gross amount or value of anything: as **a** (1) : a reduction from a price made to a specific customer or class of customers — see TRADE DISCOUNT (2) : a proportionate deduction from an account as debt usu. made for cash or prompt payment — see CASH DISCOUNT **b** : a deduction made for interest in advancing money upon or purchasing a bill or note not due : payment in advance of interest upon money **2** : the rate of interest charged in discounting **3** : the act or an instance of discounting ⟨to employ bank funds in the ~ of bills of exchange⟩ **4** : a deduction in billiards of one point from the score of one player for every point made by his opponent **5** : a deduction taken or allowance made (as for the specious element in a story or something that qualifies the truth of an assertion) ⟨we may . . . have to make very heavy ~, or even sometimes to reject our author's conclusions altogether —G.G.Coulton⟩ ⟨after all the ~*s* are taken, timeliness remains a chief quality of good reporting —F.L.Mott⟩; *also* : an objectionable feature : DRAWBACK, HINDRANCE ⟨he does . . . mention smells and some other ~*s* to a pleasant day —*Times Lit. Supp.*⟩ — **at a discount** **1** : below par : below the nominal value ⟨the bond sold *at a discount*⟩ **2** : out of favor : poorly or lightly esteemed ⟨utopias and visionaries were *at a discount* in this sober workaday world⟩ : with reservations ⟨his continual complaints . . . must be taken . . . *at a discount* —Hilaire Belloc⟩

²dis·count \"*also* də's-\ *vb* -ED/-ING/-S [modif. of F *décompter*, fr. OF *desconter*, fr. ML *discomputare*, fr. L *dis-* ¹dis- + *computare* to reckon, compute — more at COUNT] *vt* **1 a** : to deduct esp. from an account, debt, or charge : make an abatement of ⟨~ a bill for early payment⟩ **b** : to offer for sale at a discount : sell at a discount ⟨dealers were heavily ~*ing* last year's unsold models⟩ **2** : to lend money upon, deducting the discount or allowance for interest ⟨banks ~ negotiable paper⟩ **3 a** : to leave out of account : DISREGARD, OMIT ⟨the influence of Hawaii on the American house is minute, ~*ing* the spectacle . . . of flapping shirttails printed with gaudy flora —T.H.Robsjohn-Gibbings⟩ **b** : to make a deduction in evaluating the significance or worth of : view as unimportant : MINIMIZE, DISPARAGE, DEPRECIATE, UNDERRATE ⟨~*ing* his offense as a pardonable action under the circumstances⟩ ⟨his mature judgment and long experience were ~*ed* by his juniors⟩ ⟨never ~ the fellow's cunning and ingenuity⟩ : DIMINISH, LESSEN ⟨the value of his criticism was ~*ed* by his ignorance of the subject⟩ **c** (1) : to make a deduction in evaluating the truth or validity of : make allowance (as for bias or exaggeration) in ⟨he ~*ed* seventy-five percent of all stable gossip —Gerald Beaumont⟩ ⟨~ some of the more enthusiastic claims made for the new drug⟩ (2) : to view with doubt or skepticism : DISBELIEVE ⟨I ~ the story that the brave bull gored Miss McCormick . . . because . . . she was an author —C.V.Little⟩ **d** : to anticipate or take into account (as a future event) in present calculations or planning ⟨mail came chiefly from those organized groups whose opposition had already been ~*ed* —*Time*⟩ ⟨businessmen had already ~*ed* the inflationary effects of the price increase⟩ **4** : to give a discount to in billiards ~ *vi* : **1** : to lend or make a practice of lending money, abating the discount ⟨banks ~ for 60 or 90 days⟩ **2** : to make allowance ⟨~*ing* for Richard's modesty —S.E.Hyman⟩

dis·count·able \'=,==bəl *or* ='===\ *adj* : capable of being discounted ⟨a ~ note⟩ ⟨the evident bias of the book is ~⟩ : set apart for discounting ⟨within the ~ period⟩

discount broker *n* : one who makes a business of discounting commercial paper usu. as an agent

discount company *n* : a company that discounts commercial accounts receivable : COMMERCIAL CREDIT COMPANY

discount day *n* : the weekday when a bank discounts bills

¹dis·countenance \dəs, (')dis+\ *vt* [¹*dis-* + *countenance* (n.)] **1** : to put out of countenance : put to shame : ABASH, DISCONCERT ⟨the republic soon confirmed the doubters and *discountenanced* its few friends —C.P.Fitzgerald⟩ **2** : to refuse to look with favor upon : use one's influence against : discourage by evidence of disapproval ⟨the intrenched interests *discountenanced* the teaching of reading and writing to the working classes —Helen Sullivan⟩

²discountenance \"\ *n* [¹*dis-* + *countenance*] : the act of discountenancing ⟨American actions gave discouragement and ~ to the Bolshevik and anarchist elements —Ward Moore⟩

dis·count·er \'diˌskau̇ntə(r) *also* də's-\ *n* -S : one that discounts; *specif* : the operator of a discount house

discount house *n* **1** : a firm selling branded goods (as consumer durables) at a discount from list prices **2** *Brit* : BILL BROKER

discount market *n* : an open market in which negotiable instruments (as acceptances, bills, and notes) are discounted — compare BANK DISCOUNT

discount rate *n* : the interest on an annual basis deducted in advance for a bank or other loan; *also* : the charge levied by central banks for advances and rediscounts

discounts *pl of* DISCOUNT, *pres 3d sing of* DISCOUNT

dis·cour·age \də'skər·ij, -kə·r|, |ēj, *esp in pres part* |əj\ *vb* -ED/-ING/-S [MF *descorager*, *descourager*, fr. OF *descoragier*, fr. *des-* ¹dis- + *corage* courage — more at COURAGE] *vt* **1** : to deprive of courage or confidence : DISHEARTEN, DEJECT ⟨loss of the bastion greatly *discouraged* the besieged garrison⟩ ⟨a succession of failures *discouraged* the young inventor⟩ **2 a** : to seek to check, hinder, or deter by disfavoring ⟨~ gambling by legislative enactment⟩ : DETER, HINDER ⟨a condition of feudal anarchy *discouraged* the growth of trade⟩ ⟨the aridity of the soil *discouraged* agriculture⟩ **b** : to attempt to dissuade from some action : dampen or lessen the boldness or zeal of for some action ⟨*discouraged* his son from pursuing a literary career⟩ ⟨a table-high platform . . . with a rail around it to ~ souvenir snatchers —Green Peyton⟩ ~ *vi* : to lose courage or heart ⟨I don't ~ easily⟩

syn DISCOURAGE, DISHEARTEN, DISPIRIT, DEJECT: DISCOURAGE implies loss of courage, confidence, and resolution, along with the sapping effect of fear and doubt and inability to muster up further hope and determination ⟨these accidents did great damage, and *discouraged* the French mariners to such a degree, that they became more afraid of their own guns than of those of the English —Tobias Smollett⟩ DISHEARTEN is a close synonym of DISCOURAGE; it may indicate temporary loss of heart or courage ⟨the days came, but not the visitor, though Lucetta repeated her dressing with scrupulous care. She was *disheartened* —Thomas Hardy⟩ ⟨a difficult undertaking that might have *disheartened* one less buoyant —Vera M. Dean⟩ DISPIRIT may indicate enervation, depriving of all cheer, and surrender to gloom ⟨in quelling a local Armenian revolt he was badly wounded. Sick and *dispirited*, he gave up his Arabian plan —John Buchan⟩ ⟨the shabby, *dispiriting* spectacle of Versailles, with its base greeds and timidities —C.E.Montague⟩ DEJECT implies a general casting down of spirits and a driving away of hope and cheer ⟨I pitied poor Miss Read's unfortunate situation. She was generally *dejected*, seldom cheerful, and avoided company —Benjamin Franklin⟩ ⟨the *dejected* appearance that is usually found only in the faces of old men who have been disappointed in life —Liam O'Flaherty⟩ **syn** see in addition DISSUADE

dis·cour·aged·ly *adv* **:** in a discouraged manner **:** with feelings of discouragement **:** DEJECTEDLY

dis·cour·age·ment \-jmənt\ *n* -S [MF *descouragement*, fr. OF *descoragement*, fr. *descoragier* + *-ment*] **1 :** the act of discouraging ⟨the encouragement of free enterprise and ~ of monopolies —*Current Biog.*⟩ **:** the state of being discouraged **:** DEPRESSION ⟨there are moments of ~ in us all —William James⟩ **2 :** something that discourages **:** something that tends to deter **:** DETERRENT ⟨rather an incentive than a ~ to vice —Rose Macaulay⟩

discouraging *adj* **:** lessening courage **:** DISHEARTENING ⟨gave a ~ picture of local economic conditions⟩ **:** DETERRING, HINDERING ⟨repeated accidental applications were found to have a ~ effect on warts —Ben Riker⟩ — **dis·cour·ag·ing·ly** *adv* — **dis·cour·ag·ing·ness** *n* -ES

discouraging card *n* **:** one's lowest card of a suit in bridge when played or discarded as a signal to one's partner not to lead that suit

1dis·course \ˈdi͵skō(ə)rs, -ȯ(ə)rs,-ōəs,-ȯ(ə)s *also* dəˈs-\ *n* -S [ME *discours*, modif. (influenced by *cours* course) of ML & LL *discursus;* ML, argument, course, fr. LL, conversation, fr. L, act of running about, fr. *discursus*, past part. of *discurrere* to run about, fr. *dis-* about, apart + *currere* to run — more at DIS-, CURRENT] **1** *archaic* **a :** the act, power, or faculty of thinking consecutively and logically **:** the process of proceeding from one judgment to another in logical sequence **:** the reasoning faculty **:** RATIONALITY ⟨he that made us with such large ~ —Shak.⟩ **b :** the capacity of proceeding in an orderly and necessary sequence — used chiefly in the phrase *discourse of reason* ⟨a beast that wants ~ of reason —Shak.⟩ **2** *obs* **:** progression or course esp. of events **:** course of arms **:** COMBAT **3 a :** verbal interchange of ideas ⟨we need to have a fairly definite point of departure for intelligent ~ —Robert Humphrey⟩; *often* **:** CONVERSATION ⟨let your ~ with men of business be short and comprehensive —George Washington⟩ **b :** an instance of such interchange ⟨his ~*s* with his puritan colleagues —Sidney Lovett⟩ **4 a :** the expression of ideas; *esp* **:** formal and orderly expression in speech or writing ⟨what seemed sapient ~ . . . is rather puerile chatter now —G.W.Johnson⟩ ⟨the forms of ~⟩ **b :** a talk or piece of writing in which a subject is treated at some length usu. in an orderly fashion ⟨the lecture . . . is an acute and suggestive ~ upon a subject that has always occupied his attention —Bliss Perry⟩ ⟨the preacher, who would interrupt his ~ to denounce a dormant worshiper —*Amer. Guide Series: Mich.*⟩ **5** *obs* **a :** power of conversing **:** conversational ability **b :** ACCOUNT, NARRATIVE, TALE **c :** social familiarity; *also* **:** familiarity with a subject **6** *linguistics* **:** connected speech or writing consisting of more than one sentence

syn TREATISE, TRACTATE, DISQUISITION, DISSERTATION, THESIS, MONOGRAPH: DISCOURSE is applicable to well formulated or coherently arranged serious and systematic treatment of a subject in writing or speaking ⟨the sermon was a *discourse* on the apostle's thoughts⟩ ⟨a learned *discourse* on the effect of the tariff⟩ TREATISE is likely to refer to a formal methodical written exposition, often more detailed but less pointed and persuasive than a discourse ⟨a scholarly and comprehensive *treatise*⟩ ⟨there are several excellent *treatises* on Thoreau's literary sources —H.S.Canby⟩ TRACTATE, now not much used, means and implies about the same things as TREATISE, but may be somewhat contentious ⟨the fabulists were right, he reflected, when they took beasts to illustrate their *tractates* of human morality —Aldous Huxley⟩ DISQUISITION may apply to a discussion more exploratory and investigative than definitive ⟨many of Burke's reflections on the theme of history are of a purely empirical character, being *disquisitions* about the direction human affairs are likely to follow if certain conditions are (or are not) fulfilled —*Times Lit. Supp.*⟩ DISSERTATION is likely to imply examination, usu. academic, of a subject, and discussion at length; often the word applies to treatises written to attest fitness for higher university degrees ⟨a tradition has developed that a *dissertation* in economics must be a sizable tome —H.R.Bowen⟩ ⟨the reason, perhaps, why scholarly *dissertations* upon literature are so often merely scholastic enumerations of minutiae —John Dewey⟩ THESIS may designate the statement, explanation, and defense of a proposition ⟨Miss L———'s extremely suggestive *thesis* is that the transition from Elizabethan-Jacobean to later Caroline comedy is primarily economic —T.S.Eliot⟩ It is often used in reference to essays written by candidates for the master's degree. MONOGRAPH may refer to a learned treatise on a limited subject ⟨a *monograph* on the earliest Roman coins⟩ ⟨a *monograph* on this subspecies⟩

2discourse \=ˈ=, ˈ=͵=\ *vb* -ED/-ING/-S *vi* **1 a :** to express oneself in esp. oral discourse **:** talk in a continuous or formal manner ⟨we talk in the bosom of our family in a way different from that in which we ~ on state occasions —J.L.Lowes⟩ **b :** TALK, CONVERSE ⟨let us ~ beneath this knotty carob tree —Norman Douglas⟩ **2** *obs* **:** REASON **~** *vt* **1** *archaic* **:** to expose or set forth in speech or writing **:** treat of **:** NARRATE, TELL, DISCUSS **2 :** PLAY, PERFORM ⟨an orchestra *discoursed* soft, seductive music —A.W.O'Neil⟩ ⟨eloquently *discoursed* and invested with the necessary virtuosity —*Current Biog.*⟩ **3** *obs* **:** to talk to **:** confer with **:** converse with

syn DISCOURSE, EXPATIATE, DILATE, and DESCANT can mean, in common, to talk more or less formally and at length upon a subject. DISCOURSE implies the manner of a lecturer, suggesting also detailed, ordered discussion ⟨to *discourse* knowledgeably about the laws of nature today requires a formidable apparatus of mathematics —*Times Lit. Supp.*⟩ ⟨*discourses* in his usual manner on the technique and value of mystical contemplation —Gerald Bullett⟩ EXPATIATE implies ranging over a subject, often without restraint and sometimes at will, connoting more copiousness in the product than does DISCOURSE ⟨was forever *expatiating* on the close resemblance between the methods of art, as shown especially in painting, and the methods of moral action —Havelock Ellis⟩ ⟨in another lecture I shall *expatiate* on the idea —William James⟩ ⟨he *expatiated* on the theme that organization produces the great thinker —H.J.Laski⟩ DILATE implies an enlarging upon the details of a subject of discourse ⟨as it is not right to damp a native enthusiasm, Redworth let him *dilate* on his theme —George Meredith⟩ ⟨he reverted to his conversation of the night before, and *dilated* upon the same subject with an easy mastery of his theme —Elinor Wylie⟩ DESCANT stresses free comment, often connoting a delight in the expression of one's views ⟨*descanted* again and again on the virtues of silence —Max Herzberg⟩ ⟨loves to *descant* on personalities—princes, statesmen, poets —G.K.Anderson⟩

discourse analysis *n* **:** structural analysis of texts larger than one sentence

dis·cours·er \=ˈ=ə(r), ˈ==-\ *n* -S **:** one that discourses ⟨Switzerland's brilliant Protestant ~ on religious and ethical problems —*Time*⟩

discourses *pl of* DISCOURSE, *pres 3d sing of* DISCOURSE

dis·cour·sive \=ˈ=siv, -sēv *also* -səv\ *adj* **1 a** *obs* **:** characterized by reason or reasoning **:** RATIONAL **b :** ARGUMENTATIVE, EXPOSITORY ⟨material quoted for critical, satirical, ~, . . . and scholarly purposes —Margaret Nicholson⟩ **2** *obs* **:** constituting or containing dialogue or discourse **:** CONVERSATIONAL — **dis·cour·sive·ly** \-sə̇vlē, -li\ *adv* — **dis·cour·sive·ness** \-sivnə̇s, -sēv- *also* -səv-\ *n* -ES

dis·courteous \dəs, (ˈ)dis+\ *adj* [1*dis-* + *courteous*] **:** lacking courtesy or good manners **:** UNCIVIL, RUDE ⟨distant and at times ~ to his associates⟩ **syn** see RUDE

discourteously *adv* **:** in a discourteous manner

discourteousness *n* -ES **:** the quality or state of being discourteous **:** RUDENESS

dis·courtesy \dəs, (ˈ)dis+\ *n* [1*dis-* + *courtesy*] **:** rudeness of behavior or language **:** ill manners **:** INCIVILITY ⟨complained of inattention and ~ on the part of her students⟩; *also* **:** a rude act ⟨committed the grave ~ of not first removing my spurs —R.H.Davis⟩

dis·cous \ˈdiskəs\ *adj* [*disc-* + *-ous*] **:** DISCOID 2

dis·cover \də̇ˈskəvə(r)\ *vb* **discovered**; **discovered**; **discovering** \-v(ə)riŋ\ **discovers** [ME *discoveren, discuren*, fr. OF *descovrir*, fr. LL *discooperire*, fr. L *dis-* 1dis- + *cooperire* to cover — more at COVER] *vt* **1 a :** to make known (something secret, hidden, unknown, or previously unnoticed) **:** EXPOSE, DISCLOSE ⟨~*ed* to his friend the sad state of his fortunes⟩ ⟨the novelist Emily Brontë had to ~ these absurdities to the girl Emily —Mark Schorer⟩ **b :** to reveal the identity of ⟨God, when he ~*ed* himself to the Israelites in Egypt —G.G.Coulton⟩ ⟨~*ing* himself to the lovely culprit as her adoring and magnanimous lover —T.L.Peacock⟩ **c** *archaic* **:** to make manifest (as a characteristic or attribute) **:** EXHIBIT, DISPLAY, MANIFEST ⟨the very attempt towards pleasing everybody ~*s* a temper . . . often false and insincere —Edmund Burke⟩ **d :** to disclose to view (something hidden, covered, or previously unseen); *specif* **:** to reveal on a theater stage when the curtain rises or when flats are parted or raised — used only in the past participial form ⟨at curtain wife and mother-in-law are ~*ed* packing fragile articles into a barrel —Saul Bellow⟩ **e** *archaic* **:** to disclose unwittingly (as by one's actions) **2 :** to remove or lift a covering from **:** UNCOVER **3 a :** to obtain for the first time sight or knowledge of ⟨~*ed* a large bay that now bears his name⟩ ⟨~*ed* the circulation of the blood⟩ ⟨~*ed* a number of writers who afterward gained wide recognition —*Current Biog.*⟩ **b :** to detect the presence of **:** FIND, DISCERN ⟨~*ed* arsenic in the patient's sleeping potion⟩ ⟨~ slights in the most innocent remarks —Joyce Cary⟩ **c :** to find out **:** ASCERTAIN ⟨~*ed* he had lost his purse⟩ **d** *archaic* **:** to get sight of **:** SIGHT, ESPY **e** *archaic* **:** EXPLORE, RECONNOITER **~** *vi* **1 :** to make a discovery ⟨the rumor is false, as far as I can ~⟩ **2** *obs* **a :** EXPLORE, RECONNOITER **b :** LOOK, DISCERN **c :** to make admission **:** CONFESS

syn ASCERTAIN, DETERMINE, DETECT, UNEARTH, LEARN: DISCOVER means to come to know something not previously known, either by purposive search and investigation or by accident ⟨a careful search at last *discovered* a small whirlpool —O.S.Nock⟩ ⟨we shall never know who first *discovered* how to pound up metal-bearing rock and heat it in the fire —Tom Wintringham⟩ ASCERTAIN usu. indicates purposively directed study and investigation to find the truth or discover the facts ⟨scientific experiment has *ascertained* how many trials are needed by a rat to grasp the idea that by taking a particular turn or giving a special push he can penetrate from one chamber of his prison house to a more desirable one —C.H.Grandgent⟩ ⟨it has been *ascertained* by test borings that salt extends for 2200 feet below the surface —*Amer. Guide Series: La.*⟩ DETERMINE may stress intent to decide or establish the truth definitively ⟨the executor must assemble all available records to *determine* the decedent's assets and liabilities —Richard Gehman⟩ ⟨his duties for the next seven years included inspecting ships, including nearly all the largest vessels in the world, to *determine* seaworthiness and compliance with laws —*Current Biog.*⟩ DETECT may apply to discovering something well hidden, masked, or present only in trace quantities ⟨it was he who first *detected* the small variations in hundreds of stars closely packed into the globular clusters —Leon Campbell⟩ ⟨the shadowy passages, often hard to *detect* —J.W. Schaefer⟩ ⟨still feebler is the final sonant, as in *bid, bed, bad*. So weak is it that few hearers would *detect* its complete omission —C.H.Grandgent⟩ UNEARTH indicates bringing to light something lost, hidden, or otherwise very hard to trace, often after intensive investigation ⟨and the Index of Design division of the project has *unearthed* and reproduced many valuable examples of early American design —*Amer. Guide Series: Wash.*⟩ ⟨when a legislative committee began an investigation of the activities of the previous session, the Yazoo land fraud was *unearthed* —Sidney Warren⟩ LEARN in this sense may indicate a being told or otherwise acquiring knowledge with little effort or intention ⟨go at once to your father, and *learn* where you stand —L.C.Douglas⟩ ⟨it is said that the young lieutenant who directed the bombardment was a staunch Episcopalian and that he was horrified when he *learned* that he had shelled his own church —*Amer. Guide Series: La.*⟩ **syn** see in addition REVEAL

—**discover check** *chess* **:** to produce a check by moving an intervening man

dis·cov·er·able \-v(ə)rəbəl\ *adj* **:** capable of being discovered, found out, or perceived **:** ASCERTAINABLE

discovered check *n* **:** a position in chess in which check has been discovered

dis·cov·er·er \-v(ə)rə(r)\ *n* -S [ME *discoverer, discurer*, fr. OF *descovreur*, fr. *descovrir* + *-eur* -or] **1** *obs* **a :** INFORMER **b :** SCOUT, SPY **2 :** one who first finds out the existence or truth of something hitherto unknown (as by exploration, experiment, research, reasoning) **3 :** one that discovers a vein or lode and makes the first location thereon — compare FREE MINER, LOCATOR

dis·covert \dəs, (ˈ)dis+\ *adj* [1*dis-* + *covert*] *law* **:** not covert **:** not under coverture

dis·coverture \də̇s+\ *n* -S **:** the state of being discovert

dis·cov·ery \də̇ˈskəv(ə)rē, -ri\ *n* -ES [*discover* + *-y* (as in *recovery*)] **1 a :** the act, process, or an instance of gaining knowledge of or ascertaining the existence of something previously unknown or unrecognized ⟨the ~ of a new chemical element⟩ ⟨his ~ of a strange tribe of pygmies⟩ **b** (1) *archaic* **:** the act of making known **:** REVELATION, DISCLOSURE (2) *obs* **:** display or manifestation esp. of a quality or attribute **c** *drama* **:** RECOGNITION **d :** the act or an instance of finding or finding out (as something that was lost or hidden) ⟨police announced ~ of the missing money⟩ ⟨for fear of ~ he changed his lodgings every night⟩ **e** *obs* **:** EXPLORATION, RECONNAISSANCE, INVESTIGATION ⟨to make a more perfect ~ of the island —Daniel Defoe⟩ **f :** the act of exposing the opponent's king to check by moving an intervening piece **2 :** something that is discovered (as by being brought to light, disclosed, or ascertained) ⟨brought home valuable *discoveries* including a large plant of exotic coloring and foliage⟩ **3 :** the disclosure in practice or in pretrial procedures by a party to an action or proceeding of facts or documents which will afford material evidence in determining the rights of the party asking it **4 :** the original finding of part of a vein or lode that is a prime requisite in the valid location of a mining claim

discovery bond *n* **:** a fidelity bond covering losses discovered during the term of the bond regardless of when any dishonest act is committed

discovery day *n, usu cap both Ds* **:** COLUMBUS DAY

discovery well *n* **:** the first well to produce oil in a new field

disc plow *n* **:** a plow adapted esp. for work in sticky or hard dry soils by replacement of the moldboard plow bottom with one or more concave steel discs

dis·create \(ˌ)dis, dəs+\ *vt* [1*dis-* + *create*] **:** to reduce to chaos **:** ANNIHILATE

1dis·credit \də̇s+\ *vt* [1*dis-* + *credit* (v.)] **1 :** to refuse to accept as true **:** DISBELIEVE ⟨contradicts the oath of witnesses whom we have no reason to ~ —Irving Bacheller⟩ **2 :** to deprive of credibility **:** destroy confidence or trust in **:** cause disbelief in the accuracy or authority of ⟨his careful researches ~*ed* the claims of his predecessors⟩ **:** designate as inaccurate or unreliable **3 :** to deprive of good repute **:** bring into discredit **:** make less reputable **:** DISGRACE ⟨the decadent and tyrannical past that they are so energetically trying to ~ —James Cameron⟩ ⟨thoroughly ~*ed* by his role in the recent police scandals⟩

2discredit \"\ *n* [1*dis-* + *credit* (n.)] **1 :** loss of credit or reputation **:** DISESTEEM, REPROACH ⟨I knew stories to the ~ of England —W.B.Yeats⟩ **2 :** lack or loss of belief or confidence **:** DISBELIEF, DOUBT ⟨contradictions cast ~ on his testimony⟩

dis·creditable \də̇s+\ *adj* **:** not creditable **:** injurious to reputation **:** DISGRACEFUL, DISREPUTABLE ⟨war is enormously ~ to those who order it to be waged —Aldous Huxley⟩ ⟨his marks . . . were not at all ~ —J.P.Marquand⟩

dis·creditably \"+\ *adv* **:** in a discreditable manner

discredited *adj* **:** having had its credit taken away **:** deprived of credit ⟨a ~ theory⟩ **:** brought into disrepute ⟨a ~ politician⟩; *also* **:** lacking in credit or repute **:** UNRESPECTED ⟨in Honduras a night attack is a ~ maneuver —R.H.Davis⟩

dis·creet \də̇ˈskrēt, *usu* -ēd·+V\ *adj, sometimes* -ER/-EST [ME *discreet, discret*, fr. MF *discret*, fr. OF, fr. ML *discretus*, fr. L, past part. of *discernere* to separate, distinguish between — more at DISCERN] **1 :** possessed of or displaying discernment or good judgment in conduct and esp. in speech **:** PRUDENT, CIRCUMSPECT, TACTFUL; *esp* **:** capable of preserving prudent silence (as with respect to confidences or delicate matters) ⟨his trusted ~ aide⟩ **2 a :** marked by, reflecting, or suggesting prudence, circumspection, or reticence **:** CAUTIOUS, UNOBTRUSIVE ⟨a ~ silence⟩ ⟨~ inquiries⟩ ⟨followed her at a ~ distance⟩ **b :** not showy **:** UNPRETENTIOUS, MODEST ⟨the warmth and ~ elegance of a civilized home —Joseph Wechsberg⟩ **:** RESTRAINED, MUTED ⟨her playing yesterday was extremely ~ in the sense of sonority and tonal impact —Olin Downes⟩ **:** not offensively vivid or strong ⟨perfumes became more "massive" and less ~ —T.F.Brady⟩ **3** *Scot* **:** observant of decencies **:** CIVIL, POLITE — **dis·creet·ness** *n* -ES

dis·creet·ly *adv* [ME *discretly*, fr. *discret, discreet* + *-ly*] **:** in a discreet manner: as **a :** TACTFULLY, PRUDENTLY ⟨his utterances never gave offense, being ~ academic⟩ **b :** with restraint **:** JUDICIOUSLY, CAREFULLY, UNOBTRUSIVELY ⟨rouge ~ applied to the cheek —Edward Sapir⟩ ⟨do not let a canary's claws grow too long . . . but trim them ~ —Emily Holt⟩

dis·crep·ance \də̇ˈskrepən(t)s\ *n* -S [ME *discrepaunce*, fr. MF *discrepance*, fr. L *discrepantia*, fr. *discrepant-, discrepans* (pres. part. of *discrepare*) + *-ia* -y] **:** DISCREPANCY

dis·crep·an·cy \-nsē, -si\ *n* -ES [L *discrepantia*] **1 :** the quality or state of being discrepant **:** DIFFERENCE, DISAGREEMENT ⟨its inveterate tendency to seek out areas of ~ rather than of agreement —Harriet de Onís⟩ **2 :** an instance of being discrepant **:** DIFFERENCE, VARIATION, INCONSISTENCY ⟨wide *discrepancies* of income⟩ ⟨discovered certain *discrepancies* in his financial reports⟩

dis·crep·ant \-nt\ *adj* [L *discrepant-, discrepans*, pres. part. of *discrepare* to sound differently or discordantly, disagree, fr. *dis-* 1dis- + *crepare* to rattle, crack, creak — more at RAVEN] **:** at variance **:** DISCORDANT, DISAGREEING, CONTRARY, DIFFERENT ⟨widely ~ statements⟩ — **dis·crep·ant·ly** *adv*

dis·cre·pate \ˈdiskrə͵pāt\ *vb* -ED/-ING/-S [L *discrepatus*, past part. of *discrepare*] **:** DISCRIMINATE, DISTINGUISH

dis·crete \dəˈskrēt, (ˈ)di͵s-, *usu* -ēd·+V\ *adj* [ME, fr. L *discretus* — more at DISCREET] **1 a :** possessed of definite identity or individuality **:** constituting a separate entity **:** DETACHED, SEPARATE ⟨the conclusion that gases are made of ~ units (molecules) —Lancelot Hogben⟩ **:** having no organic or reciprocal relationship with others of its kind ⟨human traits and abilities are not ~, like sticks in a bundle, but interact with each other in highly complex ways —*Educational Research Bull.*⟩ **:** concerned with distinct or disconnected parts **b :** characterized by discrete lesions ⟨~ smallpox⟩ — compare CONFLUENT 2b **2 :** consisting of distinct, unconnected, or unrelated parts **:** NONCONTINUOUS ⟨regarded society as a ~ mass of individuals guided by blind egotism⟩ **3** *logic* **a :** containing a clause that expresses exception or opposition by means of particles like *but, though, yet* ⟨"I resign my life but not my honor" is a ~ statement⟩ **b :** individually distinct but not generically different **c :** having no content in common **:** not overlapping — used specif. of individuals **4** *math* **:** capable of assuming, containing, or involving only a finite or countably infinite number of values, items, or objects **:** COUNTABLE **syn** see DISTINCT

dis·crete·ly *adv* **:** in a discrete manner **:** SEPARATELY **:** in an unrelated manner ⟨the events occur ~, as they would to someone who, though situated within this society, did not have any ongoing, extended relationship with it —Isaac Rosenfeld⟩

dis·crete·ness *n* -ES **:** the quality of being discrete: as **a :** SEPARATENESS ⟨the simple sentence tends to emphasize the ~ of phenomena within the structural unity —R.M.Weaver⟩ **b :** the quality of consisting of a number of individual parts ⟨in order to cast lots, the dice must have some quality of ~ in the form of two or more "sides" —C.J.Erasmus⟩

dis·cre·tion \də̇ˈskreshən *sometimes* ÷ -rēsh-\ *n* -S [ME *discrecioun*, fr. MF & LL; MF *discretion*, fr. LL *discretion-, discretio*, fr. L *discretus* (past part. of *discernere* to separate, distinguish between) + *-ion-, -io* -ion — more at DISCERN] **1 :** the quality of being discreet **:** PRUDENCE, CIRCUMSPECTION TACT, WARINESS ⟨use care and ~ in your choice of a cleaner —Richard Joseph⟩ **:** RESTRAINT, MODERATION, DELICACY ⟨plays with ~, even with beauty, but gives no impression of being a complicated person —E.R.Bentley⟩; *esp* **:** cautious reserve esp. in speech ⟨a manservant who exuded ~ from every pore —Basil Thompson⟩ **:** ability to maintain a secret **:** SECRECY ⟨~ is a trait of primary importance in a public official⟩ ⟨promises of complete ~ have been exchanged only a few minutes before —Henri Bonnet⟩ **2** *archaic* **:** the act or faculty of discerning, discriminating, or judging **:** DISCERNMENT ⟨it is not in mortal ~ to fathom her craft —Charlotte Brontë⟩ **3 a :** power of decision **:** individual judgment ⟨it is a matter that I cannot leave to anyone's ~ —Upton Sinclair⟩ **b :** power of free decision or choice within certain legal bounds ⟨for students of constitutional law the royal ~ in Australia has an illuminating history —Alexander Brady⟩ ⟨subject to the president's ~⟩; *specif* **:** the latitude of decision within which a court or judge decides questions arising in a particular case not expressly controlled by fixed rules of law according to the circumstances and according to the judgment of the court or judge (as in suspension of a sentence or the amount of a fine) **:** ability to make decisions which represent a responsible choice and for which an understanding of what is lawful, right, or wise may be presupposed — see AGE OF DISCRETION **4 a** *obs* **:** the act of separating or distinguishing **b** *archaic* **:** the quality or state of being separate and distinct **:** DISCRETENESS **5** *Scot* **:** POLITENESS, CIVILITY **syn** see PRUDENCE — **at discretion** *adv* **1 :** according to one's judgment or pleasure **:** at will ⟨allowing students to come and go *at discretion*⟩ **2 :** at the mercy of an antagonist ⟨forced to surrender *at discretion*⟩

dis·cre·tion·al \-shənᵊl, -shnəl\ *adj* **:** DISCRETIONARY — **dis·cre·tion·al·ly** \-ᵊlē,-əlē, -li\ *adv*

dis·cre·tion·ar·i·ly \=ˌ=shəˌnerəlē, -li\ *adv* **:** in a discretionary manner **:** according to one's discretion

dis·cre·tion·ary \=ˈ=shə͵nerē, -ri\ *adj* **1 :** left to discretion or individual judgment **:** exercised at one's own discretion ⟨an ambassador with ~ powers⟩ **2** *archaic* **:** characterized by discretion **:** DISCREET

1dis·cre·tive \də̇ˈskrēd·iv, ˈdiskrəd·-\ *adj* [LL *discretivus*, fr. L *discretus* (past part. of *discernere* to separate, distinguish between) + *-ivus* -ive — more at DISCERN] **1 :** DISCRETE 3 **2** *archaic* **:** marking distinction **:** DISCRIMINATIVE, DISTINGUISHING — **dis·cre·tive·ly** *adv*

2discretive *n* -S *obs* **:** a discretive proposition or conjunction

disc ridge buster *n* **:** RIDGE BUSTER

dis·crim·i·na·bil·i·ty \də̇͵skrim(ə)nəˈbiləd·ē\ *n* -ES **1 :** the quality of being discriminable ⟨the ~ of the various senses of a word⟩ **2 :** ability to discriminate ⟨pressure receptivity and ~ are very high in the lips and parts of the hands and feet where there are no hairs —F.A.Geldard⟩

dis·crim·i·na·ble \də̇ˈskrim(ə)nəbəl\ *adj* [2*discriminate* + *-able*] **:** capable of being discriminated ⟨treated as ~ aspects of institutional life within cultures —J.L.Blau⟩

dis·crim·i·na·bly \-blē, -li\ *adv* **:** in a discriminable manner

1dis·crim·i·nant \-m(ə)nənt\ *adj* [L *discriminant-, discriminans*, pres. part. of *discriminare*] **:** DISCRIMINATING

2discriminant \"\ *n* -S **:** a mathematical expression that provides a criterion for the behavior of another more complicated expression, relation, or set of relations — **dis·crim·i·nan·tal** \də̇ˌskriməˌnantᵊl\ *adj*

1dis·crim·i·nate \də̇ˈskrim(ə)nə̇t, *usu* -ə̇d·+V\ *adj* [L *discriminatus*] **1** *archaic* **:** having the difference marked **:** distinguished by certain tokens **:** DISTINCT **2 :** marked by discrimination **:** carefully distinguishing ⟨~ travelers who demand only the finest⟩ — **dis·crim·i·nate·ly** *adv* — **dis·crim·i·nate·ness** *n* -ES

²**dis·crim·i·nate** \-mə,nāt, *usu* -ād.+V\ *vb* -ED/-ING/-S [L *discriminatus*, past part. of *discriminare* to divide, distinguish, fr. *discrimin-, discrimen* division, distinction, decision, fr. *discernere* to separate, distinguish between — more at DISCERN] *vt* **1 a :** to mark or perceive the distinguishing or peculiar features of **:** recognize as being different from others ⟨depth perception may be defined as the ability to appreciate or ~ the third dimension —H.G.Armstrong⟩ **:** distinguish between or among ⟨whenever you have learned to ~ the birds, or the plants, . . . it is as if new and keener eyes were added —John Burroughs⟩ **b :** to serve to distinguish **:** DISTINGUISH, DIFFERENTIATE ⟨these curious markings ~ the bird from all related species⟩ **c :** to make out **:** ANALYZE, DISCERN, DEMARCATE ⟨he can very well ~ what the word means to him —Bernard Pares⟩ ⟨he is able to ~ eight stages in the poet's philosophical development⟩ **2 :** to distinguish (as objects, ideas, or qualities) by discerning or exposing their differences ⟨a warped mind that cannot ~ good from evil ways⟩; *esp* **:** to distinguish (one like object) from another by discerning or exposing the minute differences ⟨a dictionary of *discriminated* synonyms⟩ ~ *vi* **1 a :** to make a distinction **:** distinguish accurately ⟨~ between fact and fancy⟩ ⟨a climber must learn to ~ as to when compass bearings are necessary and when they are not —K.A. Henderson⟩ **b :** to use discernment or good judgment ⟨to expect that children should . . . ~ without experience, and save themselves by their own wits —R.A.W.Hughes⟩ **2 :** to make a difference in treatment or favor on a class or categorical basis in disregard of individual merit ⟨~ in favor of your friends⟩ ⟨habitually ~ against a certain nationality⟩ **syn** see DISTINGUISH

discriminating *adj* **1 a :** constituting a distinctive trait **:** DISTINGUISHING ⟨the ~ mark of this species is its varicolored plumage⟩ **b :** making a distinction **:** separating into constituent parts **:** ANALYTICAL ⟨there is a unifying as well as a ~ phase of judgment —John Dewey⟩ **2 :** capable of making fine discriminations (as in respect to quality) **:** careful or fastidious in selection **:** DISCERNING, JUDICIOUS ⟨a ~ and severe critic of the output of younger poets⟩ ⟨~ buyers⟩ ⟨~ taste⟩ — **dis·crim·i·nat·ing·ly** *adv*

discriminating duties *n pl* **:** DIFFERENTIAL DUTIES

dis·crim·i·na·tion \də̇,skrimə'nāshən\ *n* -S [LL *discrimination-, discriminatio* act of contrasting opposite thoughts, separation, distribution, fr. L *discriminatus* + *-ion-, -io* -ion] **1 a :** the act or an instance of discriminating: as (1) **:** the making or perceiving of a distinction or difference ⟨incapable of ~ between the imaginary and the real⟩ ⟨the same name was applied to both instruments with little ~⟩ (2) **:** recognition, perception, or identification esp. of differences ⟨the eye is capable of much finer ~ of detail —Otto Glasser⟩ **:** critical evaluation or judgment ⟨the public would need to be educated in the ~ of cider —*English Digest*⟩ **b** *psychol* **:** the process by which two stimuli differing in some aspect are responded to differently **:** DIFFERENTIATION **2** *archaic* **:** something that discriminates **:** a distinguishing mark **3 :** the quality of being discriminating **:** the power of finely distinguishing (as in respect to quality) **:** good or refined taste **:** DISCERNMENT ⟨nobody should reproach them for reading indiscriminately . . . only by so doing can they learn ~ —*Times Lit. Supp.*⟩ **4 :** the act, practice, or an instance of discriminating categorically rather than individually ⟨waged a lifelong campaign to end ~ against women⟩ ⟨relieved the working class of economic and political ~s found in other countries —T.S. Barclay⟩: as **a :** the according of differential treatment to persons of an alien race or religion (as by formal or informal restrictions imposed in regard to housing, employment, or use of public community facilities) **b :** the act or practice on the part of a common carrier of discriminating (as in the imposition of tariffs) between persons, localities, or commodities in respect to substantially the same service — **dis·crim·i·na·tion·al** \=ˌ==ˈnāshən³l, -shnəl\ *adj*

discrimination box *n* **:** a laboratory apparatus in which the experimental subject responds discriminatively to cues in order to gain a reward or avoid a punishment

discrimination time *n* **:** REACTION TIME

dis·crim·i·na·tive \də̇'skrimə,nād·|iv, -m(ə)nə|, |t|, |ēv *also* |əv\ *adj* [L *discriminatus* + E *-ive*] **1** *archaic* **:** DISTINGUISHING, DISTINCTIVE **2 :** making or observing distinctions **:** DISCERNING, DISCRIMINATING ⟨the eye . . . is the . . . subtlest, the supplest, the most ~, and the most docile of our organs —I.A. Richards⟩ **3 :** DISCRIMINATORY, DIFFERENTIAL ⟨it permitted tariffs which were grossly ~ —Mabel R. Gillis⟩ — **dis·crim·i·na·tive·ly** \|əvlē, -li\ *adv*

dis·crim·i·na·tor \-mə,nād·ə(r), -ātə-\ *n* -S [LL, fr. L *discriminatus* + *-or*] **:** one that discriminates; *specif* **:** a circuit that can be adjusted to accept or reject signals of different characteristics (as amplitude, frequency) — often used to describe a circuit in an FM receiver in which the FM signal is converted to an AM signal

dis·crim·i·na·to·ri·ly \də̇'skrim(ə)nə'tōrəlē, -tȯr-, -li\ *adv* **:** in a discriminatory manner

dis·crim·i·na·to·ry \də̇'skrim(ə)nə,tōrē, -tȯr-, -ri\ *adj* **:** DISCRIMINATIVE; *esp* **:** applying or favoring discrimination in treatment ⟨a ~ tax⟩ ⟨~ attitudes toward minority groups⟩

dis·crown \dəs, (ˈ)dis+\ *vt* [¹*dis-* + *crown* (n.)] **:** to deprive of a crown; *specif* **:** DEPOSE

discs *pl of* DISC, *pres 3d sing of* DISC

disct *abbr* discount

dis·cul·pate \ˈdi(,)skəl,pāt, də̇ˈs-\ *vt* -ED/-ING/-S [ML *disculpatus*, past part. of *disculpare*, fr. L *dis-* ¹dis- + *culpare* to blame, fr. *culpa* fault — more at CULPA] **:** EXCULPATE

dis·cum·ber \dəs, (ˈ)dis+\ *vt* [prob. by alter.] **:** DISENCUMBER

dis·cur·sion \də̇ˈskərzhən *sometimes* -rsh-\ *n* -S [MF (also, act of running about), fr. LL *discursion-, discursio* act of running about, motion, course, fr. L *discursus* (past part. of *discurrere* to run about) + *-ion-, -io* -ion — more at DISCOURSE] **1 :** discursive reasoning **2 :** a turning away from the main subject **:** ROVING, ROAMING, DIGRESSION ⟨each chapter returns there after a ~ into Asia, Africa or America —Gerald Sykes⟩

dis·cur·sive \də̇ˈskər|siv, -kə̄|, -kəi|, |ēv *also* |z| *or* |əv\ *adj* [ML *discursivus*, fr. L *discursus* + *-ivus* -ive] **1 a :** passing from one topic to another **:** ranging over a wide field **:** RAMBLING, DIGRESSIVE, DESULTORY, CHATTY ⟨a sprawling book, ~ and prolix —Brendan Gill⟩ **b :** proceeding logically or coherently from topic to topic ⟨no flaming into meaning but a steady ~ commentary in the course of which the meaning is eloquently conveyed —David Daiches⟩ **2 :** reasoning from premises to conclusions or proceeding from particulars to generalizations **:** utilizing or based upon analytical reasoning — contrasted with *intuitive* **3 :** passing from one place to another **:** ROAMING, ROVING ⟨entered into a life eternally ~ in search of superior grazing lands —J.B.Cabell & A.J.Hanna⟩ — **dis·cur·sive·ly** \|əvlē, -li\ *adv* — **dis·cur·sive·ness** \|ivnə̇s, |ēv- *also* |əv-\ *n* -ES

discursive reason *n* **:** the faculty of drawing inferences

dis·curtain \dəs, (ˈ)dis+\ *vt* [¹*dis-* + *curtain* (n.)] *archaic* **:** to divest of a curtain or cover **:** UNVEIL

dis·cus \ˈdiskəs\ *n, pl* **discuses** \-skəsə̇z\ *also* **dis·ci** \ˈdi-,s(k)ī\ [L — more at DISH] **1 a :** a disk of metal and wood, thicker in the center than at the perimeter and used for hurling for distance **b :** a field event in which a discus of about 4½ pounds is hurled for distance from a circle about 8 feet in diameter **2 :** DISK 2, 3, 4

discus 1a

-discus \"\ *n comb form* [NL, fr. L *discus*] **:** organism with a (specified) form of disk — in generic names ⟨Cephalo*discus*⟩

discus pro·lig·er·us \-prōˈlijərəs\ *n* [NL, lit., offspring-bearing disk] **:** CUMULUS 3

¹**dis·cuss** \də̇ˈskəs\ *vb* -ED/-ING/-ES [ME *discussen*, fr. LL & L *discussus*; LL, past part. of *discutere* to examine, investigate, fr. L, to dash to pieces, scatter, fr. *dis-* apart + *-cutere* (fr. *quatere* to shake, strike) — more at DIS-, QUASH (crush)] *vt* **1** *obs* **:** to clear away by breaking up or scattering **:** DISPEL, DISSIPATE **2 a** *obs* **:** to examine and pass upon judicially **:** TRY **b** (1) **:** to investigate (as a question) by reasoning or argument **:** argue by presenting the various sides of **:** DEBATE ⟨a committee of pilots and geographers ~*ed* the project but reached no conclusion⟩ ⟨the cabinet met in emergency session to ~ the draft law⟩ (2) **:** to discourse about **:** present in detail **:** EXPOUND ⟨a book that ~*es* the transmission of acquired characteristics⟩ ⟨in his afterword, Eban ~*ed* his views on Zionism and on the cures for anti-Semitism —*Current Biog.*⟩ (3) **:** to converse or talk about **:** exchange views or information about ⟨~*ing* what we'd do after graduation⟩ **3** *obs* **:** to make clear or open **:** EXPLAIN **:** disclose in speech **:** DECLARE ⟨~ the same in French unto him —Shak.⟩ **4 :** to consume (food or drink) with zest ⟨we settled down to ~ a plentiful supper of roast and boiled beef and mutton —W.H.Hudson⟩ **5 :** EXCUSS 3 ~ *vi* **:** to hold discussion **:** ARGUE, CONVERSE ⟨he would be squatting in the grass ~*ing* with someone —Helen Rich⟩

syn ARGUE, DEBATE, DISPUTE, AGITATE: these verbs all mean to discourse about something in order to arrive at the truth or to convince others. DISCUSS implies a reasoned conversational examining, esp. by considering pros and cons, in an attempt to clarify or settle ⟨*discuss* plans for a party⟩ ⟨*discuss* terms of a peace treaty⟩ ⟨they *discussed* the best way of raising money⟩ ARGUE usu. implies conviction and the often heated adducing of evidence or reasons in support of one's cause or opinion ⟨pros and cons of "mercy killing" are no longer very seriously *argued* in medical circles —W.T.Fitts & Barbara Fitts⟩ ⟨deep-seated preferences cannot be *argued* about — you cannot *argue* a man into liking a glass of beer —O.W.Holmes †1935⟩ DEBATE stresses formal or, often, public argument between opposing parties, although it can apply to a deliberation in one's own mind ⟨the . . . question was hotly *debated* in the spring parliamentary election campaign —*Collier's Yr. Bk.*⟩ ⟨the 82d Congress took many actions affecting social welfare and hotly *debated* a number of further measures —*Americana Annual*⟩ ⟨I held her hand for a moment, *debating* a reply —L.C.Douglas⟩ DISPUTE (in its older use signifying to debate) is to argue or to argue about, usu. contentiously ⟨the students *disputed* forensically this day a twofold question —Noah Webster⟩ ⟨Scotchmen and Irishmen anxious for distinction, who in previous centuries would probably have *disputed* about the classics or theology —E.L.Anderson⟩ AGITATE stresses vigorous argument toward a practical objective, an active propaganda in the interests of a change of some kind ⟨what Doc was *agitating* for . . . was recognition of battle exhaustion as an illness —Fred Majdalany⟩ ⟨the nine million refugees and expellees . . . are discontented with their economic plight and *agitate* for the recovery of their old homes —S.B. Fay⟩ ⟨the Senate was *agitating* an investigation of the department —E.M.Coulter⟩

²**discuss** *n* -ES *obs* **:** DISCUSSION, DEBATE

dis·cus·sant \-sᵊnt\ *n* -S **:** one who discusses; *esp* **:** one who takes part in a formal or prearranged discussion (as a symposium) ⟨the implicit expectation that a ~ should look for weaknesses or shortcomings in the paper on which he has been asked to comment —J.J.Honigmann⟩

dis·cuss·er \-sə(r)\ *n* -S **:** one that discusses

dis·cuss·ible \-səbəl\ *adj* **:** capable of being discussed

dis·cus·sion \də̇ˈskəshən\ *n* -S [ME *discussioun*, fr. MF & LL; MF *discussion*, fr. LL *discussion-, discussio* examination, investigation, fr. L, act of shaking, fr. *discussus* + *-ion-, -io* -ion] **1 a :** consideration of a question in open usu. informal debate **:** argument for the sake of arriving at truth or clearing up difficulties ⟨nothing promotes intellect like intellectual ~ —Walter Bagehot⟩ **b :** a formal or orderly treatment of a topic in speech or writing **:** EXPOSITION, DISCOURSE ⟨a recognized scholar . . . whose ~ . . . embodies the finest fruits of contemporary opinions and research —E.H.Swift⟩ **2** *obs* **:** dissipation or resolution esp. of a tumor **3 :** the exhaustion of legal remedies against a principal debtor or his property before recourse is had to the surety

dis·cus·sion·al \-shənᵊl, -shnəl\ *adj* **:** of or relating to discussion

discussion of heirs *Scots law* **:** the exhaustion of remedies against heirs for debts due by a deceased person in the order of their legal liability

dis·cus·sive \də̇ˈskəsiv\ *adj, archaic* **:** relating to debate or discussion

disc weeder *n* **1 :** an edged disc attachment to a cultivator that cuts off weeds and pulverizes surface soil **2 :** a cultivator with discs for use on intertilled row crops

¹**dis·dain** \də̇sˈdān, də̇ˈst| *sometimes* də̇zˈd|\ *n* -S [ME *dedeyn, disdeigne*, fr. OF *desdain, desdeing*, fr. *desdeignier*] **1 :** a feeling of contempt and aversion for something regarded as unworthy of or beneath one **:** haughty indifference or insolence **:** SCORN, CONTEMPT ⟨~ and scorn ride sparkling in her eyes —Shak.⟩ **2** *obs* **:** keen resentment due to injured pride **:** INDIGNATION **3** *obs* **:** something that provokes contempt

²**disdain** \"\ *vb* -ED/-ING/-S [ME *desdeynen*, fr. MF *desdeignier*, fr. (assumed) VL *disdignare*, fr. L *dis-* ¹dis- + *dignare* to consider worthy — more at DEIGN] *vi* **1 :** to experience disdain ⟨let us in America not ~ —D.M.Friedenberg⟩ **2** *obs* **:** to take offense **:** feel indignation or distaste ~ *vt* **1 a :** to look with scorn on ⟨did not ~ that rich rolling land⟩ ⟨~*ed* him for the coward he was⟩ **b :** to be unwilling because of disdain — used with a following infinitive ⟨he ~*ed* to cheat her⟩ ⟨we might well ~ to have any part in this affair⟩ **c :** to treat with contempt as being of little worth or consequence or as unworthy of oneself ⟨~*ed* shooting the unarmed fleeing men —*Time*⟩ ⟨~*ing* snakes, insects, and other hazards of the trip⟩ **2** *archaic* **:** to incite to scorn or anger **:** OFFEND **syn** see DESPISE

disdained *adj* [¹*disdain* + *-ed*] *obs* **:** DISDAINFUL

dis·dain·er \-nə(r)\ *n* -S **:** one that disdains

dis·dain·ful \-nfəl\ *adj* **:** full of or expressing disdain **:** haughtily indifferent **:** SCORNFUL, CONTEMPTUOUS **syn** see PROUD

dis·dain·ful·ly \-fəlē, -li\ *adv* **:** in a disdainful manner **:** with disdain

dis·dain·ful·ness \-fəlnə̇s\ *n* -ES **:** the quality or state of being disdainful

dis·diapason \dəs, (ˌ)dis+\ *n* -S [L, fr. Gk *dis dia pasōn* twice through all — more at DIAPASON] **:** FIFTEENTH 4b

¹**dis·ease** \də̇ˈzēz, *in sense 1a* də̇ˈs| *or* (ˈ)diˈs|\ *n* -S *often attrib* [ME *disese*, fr. MF *desaise*, fr. *des-* ¹dis- + *aise* ease — more at EASE] **1 a** *obs* **:** lack of ease **:** DISCOMFORT, UNEASINESS, TROUBLE, DISTRESS **b** (1) **:** an impairment of the normal state of the living animal or plant body or of any of its components that interrupts or modifies the performance of the vital functions, being a response to environmental factors (as malnutrition, industrial hazards, or climate), to specific infective agents (as worms, bacteria, or viruses), to inherent defects of the organism (as various genetic anomalies), or to combinations of these factors **:** SICKNESS, ILLNESS (2) **:** a particular instance or kind of such impairment ⟨baby-pig ~⟩ ⟨hampered by her ~⟩ **:** MALADY, AILMENT — compare HEALTH **c :** disorder or derangement (as of the mind, moral character, public institutions, or the state) **d :** an alteration that impairs the quality of a product usu. caused by the action of microorganisms ⟨the ~s of wine⟩ **2 a** *obs* **:** a cause of discomfort or harm **b :** an organism that causes disease — used chiefly in plant pathology

²**disease** \"\ *vt* -ED/-ING/-S [ME *disesen*, fr. MF *desaisier*, fr. *desaise*, n.] **1** *obs* **:** to deprive of ease **:** make uncomfortable **:** DISTRESS **2 :** to affect or infect with disease **:** DERANGE, DISORDER

diseased *adj* [ME *disesed*, fr. past part. of *disesen*] **:** affected with or as if with a disease **:** lacking health or soundness **:** SICKLY, FEVERED, DISORDERED ⟨hopelessly ~ lungs⟩ ⟨your trade requires you to read a mass of abominable stuff that it would be ~ to enjoy —Bernard De Voto⟩ ⟨a world ~ and decadent⟩ ⟨the evil imaginings of ~ minds⟩ **syn** see UNWHOLESOME

dis·eas·ed·ly \-ēz(ə̇)dlē\ *adv* **:** in a diseased manner **:** as though affected by disease

dis·eas·ed·ness \-ēzə̇dnə̇s, -ēz(d)n-\ *n* -ES **:** diseased condition **:** disordered state **:** SICKNESS

dis·ease·ful \-ēzfəl\ *adj* [ME *diseseful*, fr. *disese* + *-ful*] **1** *obs* **:** causing uneasiness, discomfort, or trouble **2 :** DISEASED, UNHEALTHY

disease germ *n* **:** a minute organism (as a bacterium or virus) that causes disease

disease rating *n* **:** a numerical expression of relative severity or incidence of a plant disease usu. based on comparison of conditions observed with certain arbitrary standards (as sizes and frequency of lesions) of severity or incidence

dis·economy \ˌdis+\ *n* [¹*dis-* + *economy*] **:** lack of economy **:** increase in costs or any factor responsible for such increase

dis·edge \dəs, (ˈ)dis+\ *vt* [¹*dis-* + *edge* (n.)] **:** to deprive of an edge **:** BLUNT, DULL

dis·edification \dəs, (ˌ)dis+\ *n* **:** an act or instance of disedifying; *also* **:** disedified state

dis·edify \dəs, (ˈ)dis+\ *vt* [¹*dis-* + *edify*] **:** to injure the piety or morals of **:** shock the higher sensibilities or religious feelings of — used chiefly as a participle

di·selenide \(ˈ)dī+\ *n* [*di-* + *selenide*] **:** a compound containing two atoms of selenium combined with an element or radical

di·sem·a·tism \dīˈsemə,tizəm\ *n* -S [*di-* + Gk *sēmat-, sēma* sign + E *-ism* — more at SEMANTICS] **:** the use in conjunction of two systems of writing (as the ideographic and the phonetic)

dis·embalm \ˌdis+\ *vt* [¹*dis-* + *embalm*] **:** to bring from obscurity to prominence or from disuse into use **:** DISINTER

dis·embark \ˌdis+\ *vb* [MF *desembarquer*, fr. *des-* ¹dis- + *embarquer* to embark — more at EMBARK] *vt* **:** to remove (as cargo) to shore from on board a ship **:** LAND, DEBARK ⟨~*ed* the troops during the night⟩ ~ *vi* **:** to go ashore out of a ship or boat **:** leave a ship; *broadly* **:** to get out of any vehicle

— **dis·embarkation** \dəs, (ˌ)dis+\ *or* **dis·embarkment** \ˌdis+\ *n*

dis·embarrass \ˌdis+\ *vt* [¹*dis-* + *embarrass*] **:** to free from embarrassment, impediment, or superfluity **:** CLEAR, EXTRICATE, RELIEVE ⟨~*ing* ourselves of preconceptions⟩ ⟨working for the balance of eighteenth-century rhythms and he soon learns how to ~ these of . . . pomposity —Edmund Wilson⟩ **syn** see EXTRICATE

dis·embarrassment \"+\ *n* **:** a disembarrassed state **:** a freeing from impeding or superfluous matter

dis·embellish \ˌdis+\ *vt* [*dis-* + *embellish*] **:** to deprive of adornment

dis·embodied \ˌdis+\ *adj* **:** lacking substance, solidity, or reality that would normally be expected to be present ⟨~ beliefs and ideals⟩ ⟨a life in which people are trained to hide their passions and act generally in a ~ way —David Riesman⟩

dis·embodiment \"+\ *n* **:** an act or instance of disembodying or the state of being disembodied

dis·embody \"+\ *vt* [¹*dis-* + *embody*] **1 :** to divest of the body, corporeal existence, or reality **2** *archaic* **:** to discharge (a body of troops) from military service

dis·em·bogue \ˌdisə̇mˈbōg, -,sem-\ *vb* **disembogued; disembogued; disemboguing; disembogues** [modif. of Sp *desembocar*, fr. *des-* (fr. L *dis-* ¹dis-) + *embocar* to put into the mouth, fr. *en* in (fr. L *in*) + *-bocar* (fr. *boca* mouth, fr. L *bucca* cheek, mouth) — more at IN, POCK] *vi* **1** *obs* **a :** to pass through a narrow channel (as a strait or the mouth of a river) into the open sea **b :** to come forth as if from a channel **:** EMERGE **2 a** *of a body of water* **:** to discharge water through an outlet or mouth; *often* **:** to flow to a specified place — used with *into* ⟨streams *disemboguing* into the sea⟩ **b :** to discharge contents as if they were flowing water ~ *vt* **1** *of a body of water* **:** to pour out (as waters) or discharge (itself) through an outlet or into another body of water ⟨a swift stream *disemboguing* its waters through a rocky outlet⟩ ⟨the river *disembogued* itself into the sea⟩ **2** *archaic* **:** to pour out (as contents) like water from a stream **:** empty (as oneself) by such pouring

dis·embosom \ˌdis+\ *vt* [¹*dis-* + *embosom*] **:** UNBOSOM, UNBURDEN

dis·embowel \ˌdis+\ *vt* [¹*dis-* + *embowel*] **1 :** to take out the bowels of **:** EVISCERATE; *also* **:** to tear, slash, or rip so that the bowels protrude **2 :** to exhaust of content **:** remove the substance of — **dis·embowelment** \"+\ *n* -S

dis·embroil \ˌdis+\ *vt* [¹*dis-* + *embroil*] **:** to bring out of a confused condition or situation **:** UNTANGLE, EXTRICATE

dis·emburden \ˌdis+\ *vb* -ED/-ING/-S [¹*dis-* + *emburden*] **:** DISBURDEN

di·seme \ˈdī,sēm\ *n* -S [back-formation fr. *disemic*] **:** a disemic syllable

di·se·mic \(ˈ)dīˈsēmik, -sem-\ *adj* [*di-* + *-semic*] *prosody* **:** equal to or having the length of two morae

dis·employ \ˌdis+\ *vt* [¹*dis-* + *employ*] **:** to dismiss from or put out of employment ⟨workers ~*ed* by the shift from a war to a peace economy —Leopold Lippman⟩ — **dis·employment** \"+\ *n*

dis·enable \ˌdis+\ *vt* [¹*dis-* + *enable*] **:** DISQUALIFY, INCAPACITATE — **dis·enablement** \"+\ *n* -S

dis·enchant \ˌdis+\ *vt* [MF *desenchanter*, fr. *des-* ¹dis- + *enchanter* to enchant — more at ENCHANT] **:** to free from enchantment **:** DISILLUSION

dis·enchanter \"+\ *n* **:** one that disenchants

dis·enchantingly \"+\ *adv* **:** so as to disenchant **:** tending to produce disenchantment

dis·enchantment \"+\ *n* **:** an act of disenchanting; *also* **:** the condition of one disenchanted **:** DISILLUSIONMENT

dis·encourage \ˌdis+\ *vt* [¹*dis-* + *encourage*] **:** DISCOURAGE — **dis·encouragement** \"+\ *n*

dis·encumber \ˌdis+\ *vt* [MF *desencombrer*, fr. *des-* ¹dis- + *encombrer* to encumber — more at ENCUMBER] **:** to free from encumbrance or from anything that clogs, impedes, or obstructs **:** DISBURDEN ⟨I have ~*ed* myself from rhyme —John Dryden⟩ ⟨~*ing* the mind of prejudices⟩ **syn** see EXTRICATE

dis·encumberment \"+\ *or* **dis·encumbrance** \"+\ *n* -S **:** an act of disencumbering or the state of being disencumbered

dis·endow \ˌdis+\ *vt* [¹*dis-* + *endow*] **:** to strip (as an established church) of endowment — **dis·endower** \"+\ *n* — **dis·endowment** \"+\ *n*

dis·enfranchise \ˌdis+\ *vt* [¹*dis-* + *enfranchise*] **:** DISFRANCHISE — **dis·enfranchisement** \"+\ *n*

¹**dis·engage** \ˌdis+\ *vb* [F *désengager*, fr. MF *desengager*, fr. *des-* ¹dis- + *engager* to engage — more at ENGAGE] *vt* **1 :** to release from anything that engages, engrosses, involves, or entangles **:** FREE, LIBERATE **2 a :** to free from a pledge or obligation — now used only as a past participle **b :** to extricate from something that entangles ⟨*disengaging* the rope from the gear⟩ **c :** to loosen or detach from something clung to ⟨gently *disengaged* the baby fingers wrapped about his thumb⟩ **d :** to remove (troops) from combat ⟨*disengaged* the first battalion⟩ ~ *vi* **1 :** to release or detach oneself **2 :** to shift one's blade from one side of an opponent's blade to the other in fencing **3 :** to withdraw from combat **syn** see DETACH

²**disengage** \"\ *n* -S **:** the act of disengaging in fencing

disengaged *adj* **:** not engaged **:** being at leisure **:** free from occupation or care

dis·engagement \"+\ *n* **1 :** the act of disengaging or state of being disengaged **:** DETACHMENT **2 :** freedom from ties, occupation, or constraint in mode of life or in manner **:** EASE **:** RELAXATION **3 :** the cancellation of an engagement of marriage

dis·enjoy \ˌdis+\ *vt* [¹*dis-* + *enjoy*] **:** to take no pleasure in (as an achievement); *sometimes* **:** to be bored with (as oneself) — **dis·enjoyment** \"+\ *n*

dis·enroll \ˌdis+\ *vt* [¹*dis-* + *enroll*] **:** to remove (as a name) from a roll; *broadly* **:** to release (an individual) from membership in an organization (as from a military reserve) — **dis·enrollment** \"+\ *n*

¹**dis·entail** \ˌdis+\ *vt* [¹*dis-* + *entail*] **:** to free (as property) from entail **:** break the entail of (an estate)

²**disentail** \"\ *or* **dis·entailment** \"+\ *n* **:** the act or process of disentailing

dis·entangle \ˌdis+\ *vb* [¹*dis-* + *entangle*] *vt* **:** to free from entanglement **:** straighten out **:** EXTRICATE, UNRAVEL ⟨~ a skein of yarn⟩ ⟨*disentangling* the threads of a plot⟩ ~ *vi* **:** to become disentangled ⟨shake your line free and let it ~ gradually⟩ **syn** see EXTRICATE

dis·entanglement \"+\ *n* **:** an act of disentangling or the state of being disentangled

dis·entangler \"+\ *n* **:** one that disentangles

dis·enthrall *also* **dis·enthral** \ˌdis+\ *vt* [¹*dis-* + *enthrall, enthral*] **:** to free from bondage

dis·enthrone \ˌdis+\ *vt* [¹*dis-* + *enthrone*] **:** DETHRONE, DEPOSE — **dis·enthronement** \"+\ *n*

dis·entitle \ˌdis+\ *vt* [¹*dis-* + *entitle*] **:** to deprive of title, claim, or right

dis·entomb \ˌdis+\ *vt* [¹*dis-* + *entomb*] **:** to take out from or as if from a tomb **:** bring to light **:** DISINTER — **dis·entombment** \"+\ *n*

dis·entrance \ˌdis+\ *vt* [¹*dis-* + *entrance* (to put into a trance)] **:** DISENCHANT

dis·entwine \¦dis+\ *vb* [¹*dis-* + *entwine*] : UNTWINE, DISENTANGLE

dis·envenom \¦dis+\ *vt* [¹*dis-* + *envenom*] : to free from venom

dis·equilibrate \(¦)dis, dəs+\ *vt* [¹*dis-* + *equilibrate*] : to put out of balance : cause disequilibrium in

dis·equilibration \"+\ *n* : the quality or state of being disequilibrated

dis·equilibrium \dəs, (¦)dis+\ *n* [¹*dis-* + *equilibrium*] : loss or lack of equilibrium : imbalanced state : INSTABILITY; *esp* : a condition of imbalance in economic affairs in which normally self-correcting forces are ineffective or inoperative

dis·establish \¦dis+\ *vt* [¹*dis-* + *establish*] : to alter the existent state of (as by ceasing to use or support or by withdrawing recognition from) ⟨daylight saving time was largely ~*ed* after the war⟩; *esp* : to deprive (a church) of the status and privileges of an established church

dis·establisher \"+\ *n* : an advocate of disestablishment

dis·establishment \"+\ *n* : the act or process of disestablishing or the state of being disestablished; *specif* : the act of a state in sundering the relationships between it and its established church

dis·establishmentarian \"+\ *n* : an advocate of disestablishment

dis·establishmentarianism \"+\ *n* : adherence to or advocacy of the principle of disestablishment

¹dis·esteem \¦dis+\ *vt* [¹*dis-* + *esteem* (v.)] : to consciously lack esteem for : regard with disfavor or slight contempt ⟨the healthy mind cannot help but ~ the abnormal⟩ ⟨~*ing* all his favors⟩

²disesteem \"\ *n* [¹*dis-* + *esteem* (n.)] : the act of disesteeming or the condition of being disesteemed : DISLIKE, DISFAVOR, DISREPUTE

dis·estimation \dəs, (¦)dis+\ *n* [¹*dis-* + *estimation*] : DISESTEEM

di·seur *R* dēˈzœr, diˈ-, +V -zər·; *–R* -zə̄, +V -zər· *or* -zə̄ *also* -zər\ *n, pl* **diseurs** \-ər(z), -ə̄(z)\ [F, fr. OF, fr. *dis-* (stem of *dire* to speak, say, fr. L *dicere*) + *-eur* -or — more at DICTION] : a skilled and usu. professional reciter (as of verse spoken to music)

di·seuse *R* -ˈzə̄|z, -ˈzœr|z, -ˈzə|z, *–R* -ˈzə̄|z\ *n, pl* **diseuses** \|z(əz)\ [F, fem. of *diseur*] : a skilled and usu. professional woman reciter (as a monologist); *usu* : a woman who recites verse or other text to music

dis·faith \dəs, (ˈ)dis+\ *n* [¹*dis-* + *faith*] : DISTRUST : lack of faith

dis·fashion \dəs, (ˈ)dis+\ *vt* [¹*dis-* + *fashion*] : DISFIGURE

¹dis·favor \dəs, (ˈ)dis+\ *n* [prob. fr. MF *desfaveur*, fr. *des-* ¹*dis-* + *faveur* favor — more at FAVOR] **1 a** : DISPLEASURE, DISAPPROVAL, DISLIKE ⟨he had nothing but ~ for his associates⟩ **b** *obs* : a disobliging act : UNKINDNESS **2** : the state or fact of not being favored or in favor: as **a** : absence of esteem : DISREPUTE, DISREGARD ⟨the poor . . . grown familiar with ~ —H.W.Longfellow⟩ **b** : the condition of being deprived of favor or under displeasure ⟨long in ~ at court⟩ **c** : absence or loss of that which favors one's standing or cause : DETRIMENT, DISADVANTAGE ⟨he acted to his own ~⟩ **syn** see DISLIKE

²disfavor \"\ *vt* [¹*dis-* + *favor* (v.)] : to withhold or withdraw favor from : regard with disesteem : DISCOUNTENANCE ⟨his system was ~*ed* by most people —*Encyc. Americana*⟩

dis·fea·ture \dəˈsfēchə(r), (ˈ)di¦s-\ *vt* [¹*dis-* + *feature* (n.)] : to mar the features of : DEFACE — **dis·fea·ture·ment** \-mənt\ *n* -s

¹dis·fellowship \dəs, (ˈ)dis+\ *n* [¹*dis-* + *fellowship*] : exclusion from or lack of fellowship

²disfellowship \"\ *vt* : to exclude from fellowship, esp. from religious communion

dis·figuration \dəs, (¦)dis+\ *n* : DISFIGUREMENT

dis·figure \dəs, (ˈ)dis+\ *vt* [ME *disfiguren*, fr. MF *desfigurer*, fr. *des-* ¹*dis-* + *figure* — more at FIGURE] **1** : to make less complete, perfect, or beautiful in appearance or character : DEFACE, DEFORM, MAR ⟨~ a landscape with billboards⟩ ⟨his face seamed and *disfigured* by time⟩ **2** *obs* : to disguise by changing the figure or appearance of **3** *archaic* : to carve (a peacock) at table

dis·fig·ure·ment \-mənt\ *n* -s **1** : the act of disfiguring or the state of being disfigured : DEFACEMENT **2** : something that disfigures : BLOT

dis·fig·ur·er \-ə(r)\ *n* : one that disfigures

dis·fig·ur·ing·ly *adv* : in a disfiguring manner

dis·forest \dəs, (ˈ)dis+\ *vt* [in sense 1, modif. (infl. by ME *forest*) of ML *disafforestare*; in sense 2, fr. ¹*dis-* + *forest* (n.) — more at DISAFFOREST] **1** : DISAFFOREST **2** : DEFOREST — **dis·forestation** \dəs, (¦)dis+\ *n*

dis·form \dəs, (ˈ)dis+\ *vb* [¹*dis-* + *form*] *vt* : *obs* : DEFORM ~ *vi* : to change or lose form or order

dis·franchise \dəs, (ˈ)dis+\ *vt* -ED/-ING/-S [ME *disfraunchisen*, fr. ¹*dis-* + *fraunchisen* to franchise — more at FRANCHISE] **1 a** : to deprive (as a corporation) of a franchise or of some privilege or immunity previously specifically granted ⟨the company will be *disfranchised* if it fails to maintain regular passenger service⟩ **b** : to deprive of a statutory or constitutional right; *esp* : to deprive (a person) of the right to vote **2** : to deprive (as a person) of a privilege, right, or pleasure ⟨any unconscious confusion of mate with mother tends to ~ him of enjoyment —Weston La Barre⟩ **3** : to remove (a person) from membership in a corporation — **dis·fran·chise·ment** \-mənt, -ˌchə̄zmənt *sometimes* -chə̄sm *or* də̇ˌsfra(a)nˈchī- *or* ˌdiˌsfra(a)nˈchī- *or* ˌdisfranˈchī\ *n* — **dis·franchiser** \dəs, (ˈ)dis+\ *n*

dis·frock \dəs, (ˈ)dis+\ *vt* [¹*dis-* + *frock* (n.)] : UNFROCK

disfunction *var of* DYSFUNCTION

dis·furnish \dəs, (ˈ)dis+\ *vt* [MF *desfourniss-*, stem of *desfournir*, fr. *des-* ¹*dis-* + *fournir* to furnish — more at FURNISH] **1** : to make (as a person) destitute of possessions : STRIP, DIVEST **2** *Midland* : DISCOMMODE, DEPRIVE, INCONVENIENCE — **dis·furnishment** \"+\ *n*

dis·garnish \dəs, (ˈ)dis+, *or* -sk- *instead of* -sg-\ *vt* [ME *disgarnysshen*, fr. MF *desgarniss-*, stem of *desgarnir*, fr. *des-* ¹*dis-* + *garnir* to furnish, garnish — more at GARNISH] *archaic* : to deprive of something that garnishes : DESPOIL

dis·garrison \dəs, (ˈ)dis+, *or* -sk- *instead of* -sg-\ *vt* [¹*dis-* + *garrison* (n.)] : to remove a garrison from

dis·gavel \dəs, (ˈ)dis+, *or* -sk- *instead of* -sg-\ *vt* [¹*dis-* + *gavel* (to subject to gavelkind)] : to deprive of or relieve from the tenure of gavelkind

dis·generic \¦dis+\ *adj* [¹*dis-* + *generic*] : belonging to different genera — opposed to *congeneric*

disgenic *var of* DYSGENIC

dis·gorge \dəs, (ˈ)dis+, *or* -sk- *instead of* -sg-\ *vb* [MF *desgorger*, fr. *des-* ¹*dis-* + *gorge* gorge, throat — more at GORGE] *vt* **1 a** : to discharge by the throat and mouth : VOMIT **b** : to discharge violently, confusedly, or as a result of force ⟨the volcano ~*s* lava⟩ ⟨day after day the tourist buses *disgorged* their multitudes —Mollie Panter-Downes⟩ **2** : to discharge the contents of (as the stomach) : EMPTY **3** : to remove sediment from (champagne) after secondary fermentation in the bottle is complete and before the addition of dosage ~ *vi* : to discharge contents; *esp* : to give up illicit or ill-gotten gains

dis·gorge·ment \-mənt\ *n* -s [MF *desgorgement*, fr. *desgorger* + *-ment*] : an act or instance of disgorging

dis·gorg·er \-ə(r)\ *n* : one that disgorges; *specif* : an implement for extracting a hook from a fish

¹dis·grace \də̇sˈg|rās, də̇ˈsk|\ *vt* -ED/-ING/-S [MF *disgracier*, fr. OIt *disgraziare*, fr. *disgrazia*] **1 a** *obs* : to spoil the appearance of : mar in outward seeming : DISFIGURE **b** *archaic* : to cause to seem inferior by comparison ⟨thy whiteness . . . shall ~ the swan —Robert Browning⟩ **2** : to bring as an accompaniment reproach or shame to : reflect discredit upon ⟨his behavior *disgraced* his family⟩ ⟨such manners are enough to ~ anyone⟩ **3** *obs* : to treat discourteously : UPBRAID, REVILE **4** : to put (as a person) to shame or out of favor : cast reproach upon : bring to dishonor ⟨seeking to ~ his enemies⟩; *specif* : to dismiss as discredited esp. from court

²disgrace \"\ *n* [MF, fr. OIt *disgrazia*, fr. *dis-* (fr. L *dis-* ¹dis-) + *grazia* grace, fr. L *gratia* — more at GRACE] **1 a** : loss of grace, favor, or honor : the condition of one fallen from grace or honor usu. through some indecorous, dishonest, or immoral action ⟨a courtier in ~⟩ ⟨the divorce suit ending in ~ for all⟩ **b** : the often widespread ill repute attendant on some fall from grace ⟨the colonel's ~ spread through the whole post⟩ **2** : something causing a fall from grace : a person, act, thing, or condition causing loss of grace ⟨the child's manners were a ~⟩ ⟨the mayor's conduct in office is a ~⟩ **3 a** *obs* : an action of degradation **b** *obs* : a specific action or instance indicating rebuke, degradation, downfall **c** : an expression or utterance condemning the indecorous, dishonest, or immoral **d** *obs* : disapproval or utterance of disapproval **e** : ill luck : MISFORTUNE **f** : the act of marring or disfiguring **g** : the condition of being unsightly **syn** see DISHONOR

dis·grace·ful \-āsfəl\ *adj* **1** *obs* : lacking grace or charm **2** : bringing or involving disgrace : causing shame : SHAMEFUL, DISHONORABLE, UNBECOMING — **dis·grace·ful·ly** \-fəlē, -li\ *adv* — **dis·grace·ful·ness** \-fəlnə̇s\ *n*

dis·grac·er \-āsə(r)\ *n* -s : one that disgraces

dis·gra·cious \dəsˈgrāshəs, (ˈ)di¦sg-, dəˈskr-, (ˈ)di¦skr-\ *adj* [MF *disgracieux*, fr. OIt *disgrazioso*, fr. *disgrazia* + *-oso* -ous] **1** *obs* : out of favor : in disgrace; *sometimes* : DISGRACEFUL **2** : lacking in consideration : UNGRACIOUS, INCONSIDERATE, UNKIND

dis·grade \dəsˈgrād, (ˈ)di¦sg-, dəˈskr-, (ˈ)di¦skr-\ *vt* [ME *disgraden*, fr. MF *desgrader*, *degrader* — more at DEGRADE] : DEGRADE

disgregate *vb* [LL *disgregatus*, past part. of *disgregare*, fr. L ¹*dis-* + *gregare* to collect, fr. *greg-*, *grex* flock — more at GREGARIOUS] : SEPARATE, DISINTEGRATE, SCATTER

dis·grun·tle \də̇sˈgrəntᵊl, də̇ˈskr-\ *vt* -ED/-ING/-S [¹*dis-* + *gruntle* (to grumble)] : to put in bad humor : arouse peevish dissatisfaction in — **dis·grun·tle·ment** \-mənt\ *n* -s

dis·grun·tled·ly \-ˈldlē, -li\ *adv* : in a disgruntled manner

dis·guis·able \də̇sˈgīzəbəl, də̇ˈskī- *sometimes* də̇zˈgī-\ *adj* : suitable for disguising : capable of being disguised

dis·guis·al \-īzəl\ *n* -s : DISGUISE

¹dis·guise \-īz\ *vt* -ED/-ING/-S [ME *disgisen*, fr. MF *desguiser*, fr. OF, fr. *des-* ¹*dis-*) + *-guiser* (fr. *guise* manner) — more at GUISE] **1** : to change the customary dress or appearance of : furnish with a false appearance or an assumed identity ⟨the noblemen *disguised* as hall porters look through you or past you —C.E.Montague⟩ **2** *obs* : to transform esp. for the worse : DEFORM, DISFIGURE **3** : to deny or obscure the existence, identity, or true state or character of : CONCEAL ⟨a *disguised* tax⟩ ⟨hate is *disguised* beneath all the fine phrases —Bertrand Russell⟩ ⟨I see no reason for *disguising* my settled conviction —G.G.Coulton⟩ **4** *archaic* : to affect or change by liquor : INTOXICATE

syn DISSEMBLE, CLOAK, MASK: DISGUISE, the most general of these four terms, stresses the fact of concealment of identity by usu. temporary alteration of appearance or by usu. temporarily presenting a false appearance as by assuming another's identity ⟨had not been able to *disguise* their disapproval —Archibald Marshall⟩ ⟨no judgment is so persuasive as when it is *disguised* as a statement of facts —R.P. Blackmur⟩ ⟨our author, *disguised* as Jonathan Oldstyle —Saxe Commins⟩ DISSEMBLE stresses more the intent to deceive, esp. as to one's own thoughts or feelings, usu. carrying a stronger implication of successful deception than does DISGUISE and often suggesting something censurable ⟨I account him faithful in the pulpit who *dissembles* nothing that he believes for fear of giving offense —William Cowper⟩ ⟨smiling in the face of misfortune in order to *dissemble* the truth to the world —Clare Sheridan⟩ ⟨a crafty child given to frequent *dissembling*⟩ CLOAK and MASK are often interchangeable with DISGUISE although both usu. carry the suggestion of only partial though deceptive concealment. CLOAK carries strongly the idea of covering something up usu. with the intent of misleading or in an attempt to make something unacceptable seem acceptable ⟨who *cloaks* the wisdom of her "uplift" talks in warm humanity —Muriel Segal⟩ ⟨intolerance and public irresponsibility cannot be *cloaked* in the shining armor of rectitude and righteousness —A.E.Stevenson b.1900⟩ MASK adds to CLOAK the idea of a certain obviousness in the covering and suggests even more strongly the unacceptableness of the thing masked, sometimes suggesting, correlatively, not only a neutral or even acceptable quality in the disguise as opposed to the thing masked but often a quality that positively ornaments or embellishes ⟨his pessimism . . . became an obvious pose, an attempt to *mask* his porky complacence —Granville Hicks⟩ ⟨the usual disorderly bustle which *masks* the deadly efficiency of the French people —Osbert Sitwell⟩ ⟨the windows were *masked* by long cretonne drapes⟩

²disguise \"\ *n* -s [ME *disgise*, fr. *disgisen*, v.] **1** : unfamiliar or uncharacteristic style of dress or apparel assumed to conceal one's identity ⟨a king in ~⟩; *often* : something used to conceal one's identity or counterfeit another's (as a masker's costume) ⟨grotesque ~*s* at carnival balls⟩ **2 a** : an outward form that misrepresents the true nature or identity of a person or thing : a deceptive appearance ⟨blessings in ~⟩ **b** : pretentious appearance : artifice or insincerity esp. in manners or speech : PRETENSE ⟨throw off all ~⟩ **c** : a misleading lack of correspondence between appearance and reality : DECEPTION, SPECIOUSNESS ⟨without fear of evil or ~ —P.B.Shelley⟩ **3** : the act of disguising : assumption of an appearance to hide the truth ⟨spoke with ~⟩ **4** *obs* : change of manner by drink : INTOXICATION **5** *obs* : MASQUERADE

dis·guised \-īzd\ *adj* [ME *disgised*, fr. past part. of *disgisen* to disguise — more at DISGUISE] **1** : altered by or for disguise : dressed in disguise : OBSCURED, COVERT **2** : INTOXICATED — **dis·guis·ed·ly** \-īzədlē, -li\ *adv*

dis·guise·less \-īzlə̇s\ *adj* : UNDISGUISED, UNOBSCURED, OPEN

dis·guise·ment \-īzmənt\ *n* -s [MF *desguisement*, fr. *desguiser* + *-ment*] **1** : a disguised state : the act of disguising **2** : something that disguises : DISGUISE; *sometimes* : added ornamentation or decoration that alters the appearance

dis·guis·er \-īzə(r)\ *n* -s [ME *disgiser*, fr. *disgisen* + *-er*] : one that disguises

disguising *n* -s [ME *disgising*, fr. gerund of *disgisen*] *archaic* : MASQUE, MASQUERADE

¹dis·gust \də̇sˈgəst, də̇ˈskə- *sometimes* də̇zˈgə-\ *n* -s [MF *desgoust*, fr. *desgouster*] **1 a** : marked aversion or repugnance toward food or toward a particular dish or kind of food : NAUSEA, SQUEAMISHNESS ⟨from that day to this he never smelled cooking beans without ~⟩ **b** : physical or emotional reaction comparable to nausea that is excited by exposure to something highly distasteful or loathsome ⟨their cruelty excited our ~⟩ ⟨impossible to see such wounds without ~⟩ **2** *archaic* **a** : a state or outbreak of mutual ill feeling or annoyance : QUARREL, DISAGREEMENT **b** : something that offends : a source of displeasure or repugnance : VEXATION, TRIAL, ANNOYANCE

²disgust \"\ *vb* -ED/-ING/-S [MF *desgouster*, fr. *des-* ¹*dis-* + *goust* taste, fr. L *gustus*; akin to L *gustare* to taste — more at CHOOSE] *vt* **1** *obs* : to experience intense dislike for **2 a** : to excite queasiness or strong physical distaste in : sicken the stomach of : NAUSEATE **b** : to provoke (one) to loathing, repugnance, or aversion : be offensive to the taste or sensibilities of ⟨your thoughtlessness ~*s* me⟩ ⟨~*ed* with her careless work⟩ ⟨he was ~*ed* at her answer⟩ ⟨everyone is ~*ed* by their behavior⟩ **3** : to cause or arouse effective aversion in : cause (one) to lose an interest or intention through exciting distaste ⟨his failures ~*ed* him against further efforts⟩ ~ *vi* : to cause disgust ⟨too rich food soon ~*s*⟩

syn DISGUST, SICKEN, and NAUSEATE agree in meaning to arouse extreme distaste for (a thing). DISGUST implies extremely offended sensibilities or a strong repugnance or aversion ⟨*disgusted* at what she thought of as the vulgarity of the men —Sherwood Anderson⟩ ⟨the majority of women that he meets offend him, repel him, *disgust* him —H.L.Mencken⟩ ⟨they were not *disgusted* at the torture of slaves —W.R.Inge⟩ SICKEN suggests a disgust so strong that one is affected physically, as by a turning of the stomach ⟨the national propaganda of all the belligerent nations *sickened* me —Bertrand Russell⟩ ⟨his unctuous morality, which *sickens* later ages —Roy Lewis & Angus Maude⟩ NAUSEATE is stronger still, suggesting a loathsomeness that provokes vomiting ⟨in letter after letter, she rinsed herself in the dirty tub-water of her miseries. It . . . *nauseated* one erstwhile friend —*Time*⟩ ⟨*nauseated* by a manifestly hypocritical saintliness⟩

disgusted *adj* : affected by disgust : disturbed physically or mentally by something distasteful — **dis·gust·ed·ly** *adv* — **dis·gust·ed·ness** *n* -ES

dis·gust·ful \-tfəl\ *adj* **1** : provoking disgust : DISGUSTING **2** : resulting from or accompanied by disgust ⟨~ curiosity —R.L.Stevenson⟩ — **dis·gust·ful·ly** \-fəlē\ *adv*

disgusting *adj* : causing disgust : SICKENING, REVOLTING, NAUSEATING, LOATHSOME — **dis·gust·ing·ly** *adv* — **dis·gust·ing·ness** *n* -ES

¹dish \ˈdish\ *n* -ES *often attrib* [ME, fr. OE *disc* plate; akin to OS *disk* table, OHG *tisc* dish, table; all fr. a prehistoric WGmc word borrowed fr. L *discus* dish, disk, quoit, fr. Gk *diskos*, fr. *dikein* to throw] **1 a** : a large shallow more or less concave vessel (as a platter) in which food is brought to the table for serving; *broadly* : any open vessel (as a tureen) similarly used ⟨a deep vegetable ~⟩ **b** *obs* : ALMS DISH 1 **c** *archaic* : a drinking vessel **d dishes** *pl* : table utensils — used esp. of those of pottery or china as distinguished from glass drinking vessels and metal implements but sometimes used inclusively ⟨I'll get out the ~*es* while you lay the silver⟩ ⟨you must wash the ~*es* before you go out⟩ **2 a** : food prepared for the table in a particular fashion ⟨a ~ of boiled potatoes⟩; *often* : food prepared according to a specified cuisine ⟨tasty Armenian ~*es*⟩ ⟨for those who like Chinese ~*es*⟩ — see MODE DISH **b** : something (as a literary work) felt to resemble a dish of food esp. in combining varied ingredients properly blended and seasoned ⟨the yeastiest ~ on TV this season —*Time*⟩ **c** : CUP OF TEA ⟨marriage was scarcely his ~⟩ **d** *slang* : an alluring young woman ⟨what a ~ my blind date turned out to be⟩ **3 a** : the contents of a dish; *usu* : food or drink served in a dish ⟨a ~ of strawberries⟩ **b** : the capacity of a dish : the quantity measured by a dish : DISHFUL **c** *dial Brit* : a trough about 28 inches long, 4 inches deep, and 6 inches wide in which ore is measured **d** *dial Brit* : the portion of a mine's product that is paid to the landowner or proprietor **e** *dial Brit* : a gallon of tin ore ready for the smelter **4 a** : any of various shallow concave vessels (as an evaporating dish) *broadly* : something that in shallow concavity is felt to resemble a dish (as a hollow in land or one between the eyes of certain mammals) **b** : the state of being concave or the degree of concavity present ⟨the ~ of a wheel⟩ **c** *slang* : HOME PLATE **d** : a microwave antenna that is often paraboloid in form and usu. highly directive in wave reflection

²dish \"\ *vb* -ED/-ING/-ES *vt* **1 a** : to put (as food for serving) into a dish or dishes — often used with *up* **b** : to make ready for acceptable presentation — usu. used with *up* ⟨~*ing* up the latest scandal⟩ **2 a** : to make concave like a dish ⟨a boiler with both ends ~*ed*⟩ — often used with *in* ⟨several car tops were ~*ed* in by the concussion⟩ **b** : HOLLOW ⟨~ a gutter⟩ — often used with *out* **3 a** *slang* : FRUSTRATE, CHEAT **b** : to get rid of : set aside : SHELVE ~ *vi* **1** : to become concave in the middle — used esp. of spoke wheels ⟨the rim hit a rock and the wheel ~*ed*⟩ **2** *of a horse* : to swing the forefeet sideways in trotting **3** *slang* : to talk casually : CHAT, CHATTER

dis·ha·bille \¦disə¦bē(ə)l, -is,(h)a¦-, -is,(h)ä¦-, ÷-ishə¦-, ÷-is,(h)ä¦-, ÷-ish,a¦-, ÷-ish,ä¦-, -¦bil, -¦bē\ *or* **des·ha·bille** *with* e *instead of* i *of the first syllable of, or with* -āz(,)- *instead of* -is- *or* -i(,)- *of the preceding pronunc; or as, or with approximation to, F* (F dāzȧbēyā)\ *n* -s [F *déshabillé*, fr. past part. of *déshabiller* to undress, fr. *dés-* ¹dis- + *habiller* to dress — more at HABILIMENT] **1 a** *archaic* : NEGLIGEE **b** : the state of being dressed in a loose or careless style **2** : disorder or dishevelment of body or mind

dis·hallow \dəs, (ˈ)dis+\ *vt* [¹*dis-* + *hallow*] : to violate the sanctity of ⟨~ the Sabbath with their conduct⟩ : PROFANE

dis·harmonic *or* **dis·harmonious** *also* **dis·harmonical** \¦dis+\ *adj* [¹*dis-* + *harmonic* or *harmonious* or *harmonical*] **1** : lacking in harmony : not harmonic or harmonious **2 a** : having a combination of bodily characters that results in an unusual form or appearance ⟨the ~ skeletal remains of certain European fossil hominids may result from interbreeding of separate distinct races⟩ **b** : ALLOMETRIC **c** : constituting a folded geologic structure in which the form of the fold in deeper beds differs from that in the overlying beds

dis·har·mo·nism \dəsˈhärmə,nizəm, (ˈ)dis¦-\ *n* -s : disharmonic state : DISHARMONY

dis·harmonize \dəs, (ˈ)dis+\ *vt* [¹*dis-* + *harmonize*] : to make disharmonic

dis·harmony \"+\ *n* [¹*dis-* + *harmony*] **1** : lack of harmony : DISCORD **2** : something incongruous : an instance of disharmonic condition or behavior

dishaunt *vt* [MF *deshanter*, fr. *des-* ¹*dis-* + *hanter* to frequent, dwell — more at HAUNT] *obs* : to absent oneself from

dish board *n* : DRAINBOARD

dishcloth \ˈ=,=\ *n* **1 a** : a cloth used for washing dishes **b** *Brit* : DISH TOWEL **2** : PURPLE TRILLIUM

dishcloth gourd *n* **1** : the fruit of any of several gourds of the genus *Luffa* (esp. *L. cylindrica*) distinguished by a fibrous interior that is dried and used like a sponge or cloth — called also *luffa*, *sponge gourd* **2** : a plant that bears dishcloth gourds

dishclout \ˈ=,=\ *n* **1** *Brit* : DISHCLOTH 1 **2** *chiefly Brit* : a weak or dull person

dish cross *n* : a low cross-shaped stand that is used for holding dishes at the table and that consists usu. of adjustable silver bars with a small lamp being placed beneath the center to keep the food hot

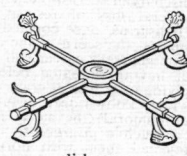

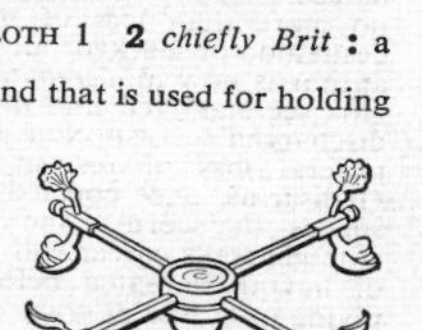

dish cross

dis·hearten \dəs, (ˈ)dis+\ *vt* [¹*dis-* + *hearten*] : to deprive of courage and hope : depress the spirits of : DEJECT, DISCOURAGE **syn** see DISCOURAGE

disheartening *adj* : inducing disheartenment, discouragement, or dejection — **dis·heart·en·ing·ly** *adv*

dis·heart·en·ment \-tᵊnmənt\ *n* -s : the state of being disheartened : DESPONDENCY

dished *adj* [fr. past part. of ²*dish*] **1 a** : depressed at or toward the center : CONCAVE ⟨a ~ face⟩ **b** *of a wheel* : having the hub inset in respect to the rim so that the joining structure (as spokes) forms a blunt cone with rim as base and hub as apex **2** *of vehicle wheels* : nearer together at the bottom than at the top

dished patch *n* : a piece of dished metal (as plate) used for patching usu. by welding

dished plate *n* : a concave metal plate shaped to allow for contraction (as after welding) and to increase resistance to force applied to the convex surface

¹dis·helm \dəs, (ˈ)dis+\ *vt* [¹*dis-* + *helm* (helmet)] : to deprive (as a person) of a helmet

²dishelm \"\ *vt* [¹*dis-* + *helm* (steering apparatus)] : to deprive (a ship or boat) of the rudder

dish·er \ˈdishə(r)\ *n* -s : one that dishes; *esp* : an ice-cream scoop

¹dis·her·i·son \(ˈ)disˈherəsən, -əzən\ *n* -s [ME *desertison*, *disheretison*, *disherison*, fr. OF *desheriteison*, *deseriteison*, fr. *desheriter*, *deseriter*] : the act of disinheriting

²disherison \"\ *vt* -ED/-ING/-S : DISINHERIT

dis·her·it \dəsˈherə̇t, (ˈ)dis¦h-\ *vt* -ED/-ING/-S [ME *deseriten*, *disheriten*, fr. OF *deseriter*, *desheriter*, fr. *des-* ¹*dis-* + *heriter* to inherit, fr. L *hereditare* to inherit — more at INHERIT] *archaic* : DISINHERIT

disheritor *n, obs* : a person who disinherits another

dishes *pl of* DISH, *pres 3d sing of* DISH

di·shev·el \də̇ˈshevəl\ *vt* **disheveled** *or* **dishevelled; disheveled** *or* **dishevelled; disheveling** *or* **dishevelling** \-v(ə)liŋ\ **dishevels** [back-formation fr. *disheveled*] : to loosen or let hang (as hair) : let fall in disorder (as clothing); *sometimes* : to cause disarray in (as a person) ⟨the wind tugged at and ~*ed* her⟩ ⟨like the fair flower ~*ed* in the wind —William Cowper⟩

disheveled *or* **dishevelled** *adj* [ME *discheveled*, part trans. of MF *deschevelé*, fr. OF, past part. of *descheveler* to disarrange the hair, fr. *des-* ¹*dis-* + *-cheveler* (fr. *chevel* hair of the head, fr. L *capillus*)] : being in loose disorder or disarray : DISARRANGED, RUFFLED ⟨~ hair⟩; *also* : marked by disarray or disorder : UNTIDY ⟨a ~ movie that charges futilely about —John McCarten⟩ **syn** see SLIPSHOD

di·shev·el·ment \-vəlmənt\ *n* -s **:** a disheveled state **:** DISORDER
dish-face \ˈ≠,≠\ *n* **:** a dish-faced animal
dish-faced \ˈ≠¦≠\ *adj* **:** having the face somewhat concave — used esp. of certain dogs, cattle, horses, and hogs
dish·ful \ˈdish,fu̇l\ *n, pl* **dishfuls** [ME, fr. *dish* + *-ful*] **:** the content of a dish **:** SERVING ⟨ate several heaping ~*s* of ice cream⟩
dish garden *n* **:** a miniature garden that is planted in a shallow dish
dish gravy *n* **:** meat juice usu. collected on the platter and served as gravy
dishing *pres part of* DISH
di·shiv·er \də+\ *vt* [¹*dis-* + *shiver*] *archaic* **:** SHIVER
dishmop \ˈ≠,≠\ *n* **:** a device for washing dishes consisting usu. of a head of fine soft cotton thread bound to a short wooden handle
dish mustard *n* [so called fr. the round flat pods] **:** PENNYCRESS
dis·hoard \dəs, (ˈ)dis+\ *vi* [¹*dis-* + *hoard*] **:** to put money or goods previously withheld into circulation — **dis·hoard·er** \-ə(r)\ *n*

dishmop

dish of tea : CUP OF TEA
dis·home \dəs, (ˈ)dis+\ *vt* [¹*dis-* + *home* (n.)] **:** to deprive of a home
¹**dishonest** *vt* [ME *dishonesten*, fr. MF *deshonester*, modif. (influenced by *deshoneste*) of L *dehonestare*, fr. *de-* + *honestare* to honor — more at HONEST] *obs* **:** to make dishonest **:** DEFAME, DISHONOR, DEFILE
²**dis·honest** \dəs, (ˈ)dis+\ *adj* [ME, fr. MF *deshoneste*, fr. *des-* ¹dis- + *honeste* honest — more at HONEST] **1** *obs* **a :** DISHONORABLE, SHAMEFUL **b :** INDECENT, UNCHASTE, LEWD **c :** DISFIGURED, REPULSIVE, UNSEEMLY **2 :** characterized by lack of truth, honesty, probity, or trustworthiness or by an inclination to mislead, lie, cheat, or defraud **:** FRAUDULENT ⟨~ politicians⟩ ⟨hoarding his ~ gains⟩ ⟨a ~ report on his earnings⟩
syn DECEITFUL, LYING, MENDACIOUS, UNTRUTHFUL: DISHONEST may apply to any breach of honesty or trust, as lying, deceiving, cheating, stealing, or defrauding ⟨a *dishonest* answer⟩ ⟨while it would be *dishonest* to gloss over this weakness, one must understand it in terms of the circumstances that conspired to produce it —Lewis Mumford⟩ ⟨a *dishonest* clerk fired for stealing⟩ DECEITFUL may imply an intent or inclination to mislead with the specious or spurious and conceal or distort truth or fact ⟨a *deceitful* schemer⟩ ⟨*deceitful* testimony⟩ ⟨educators, above all others, ought to be able to look behind the fine phrase and the fair words, to lift the hooded robe or tear away the *deceitful* mask, and to expose double-talk for what it is —B.G.Gallagher⟩ LYING describes a disposition to falsehood, a habit of telling lies ⟨a *lying* scoundrel⟩ ⟨silly newspapers and magazines for the circulation of *lying* advertisements —G.B.Shaw⟩ MENDACIOUS, a rather literary term, is a close synonym for LYING; it may have benign or bland overtones ⟨nothing would suit him but that they should go aboard the ships that caught his interest where the masters, hearing his quality, set out wine and told him *mendacious* tales of their trade —J.H.Wheelwright⟩ UNTRUTHFUL is milder than LYING and may center attention on the fact of discrepancy from truth or fact without suggestion of motive ⟨an *untruthful* explanation for the accident⟩ ⟨an *untruthful* account of the affair⟩
dis·honestly \"+\ *adv* [ME, fr. *dishonest* + *-ly*] **1** *obs* **:** DISHONORABLY, UNCHASTELY **2 :** in a deceptive or fraudulent manner **:** with dishonesty
dis·honesty \"+\ *n* [ME *deshonestee, dishonestee*, fr. MF *deshonesté*, fr. *des-* ¹dis- + *honesté* honesty — more at HONESTY] **1** *obs* **a :** DISHONOR, SHAME **b :** LEWDNESS, UNCHASTITY **2 :** lack of honesty, probity, or integrity in principle **:** lack of fairness and straightforwardness **:** disposition to defraud, deceive, or betray **:** FAITHLESSNESS **3 a :** a dishonest act **:** FRAUD **:** a deviation from probity
¹**dis·honor** \"+\ *n* [ME *dishonour*, fr. OF *deshonor, deshoneur*, fr. *des-* ¹dis- + *honor, honeur* honor — more at HONOR] **1 :** lack or loss of honor or a condition characterized by such lack or loss **2 a :** the state of one who has offended against honor **:** SHAME, DISGRACE, IGNOMINY ⟨a traitor to his kind, wrapped in ~ as in a cloak⟩ **b :** loss of prestige or place; *esp* **:** the obscure and disregarded state of one that has fallen from a position of prominence ⟨a courtier in ~⟩ **c :** strong speech in condemnation or other expressions of disapproval or scorn **:** INSULT ⟨exposed to ~ by every hack writer⟩ **3 :** a person, thing, or action bringing dishonor and sacrificing or endangering good repute ⟨the professor's conduct is a ~ to the university⟩ **4 :** the nonpayment or nonacceptance of commercial paper by the party on whom it is drawn
syn DISREPUTE, DISGRACE, SHAME, IGNOMINY, OBLOQUY, OPPROBRIUM, ODIUM, INFAMY: these words all involve loss of esteem and good repute and resulting denigration or hatred. DISREPUTE is the mildest in the group and means no more than loss of praise and popularity with ensuing desuetude or marked but not necessarily extreme dislike ⟨this author is now in *disrepute* and his works are no longer read⟩ ⟨the secretary fell into *disrepute* and was suspended but not discharged⟩ DISHONOR implies lost honor. It may imply general loss of respect and deference formerly accorded ⟨Belisarius, once courted, now exposed to *dishonor*⟩ It may suggest the scorn of the cowardly, corrupt, or untrustworthy ⟨the general's career will always be tarnished by the *dishonor* of having retreated before inferior forces⟩ DISGRACE, implying utter loss of grace or favor, is a strong term and implies widely known deep disfavor incurred by something improper or immoral ⟨the moral reputation of these Grandisons was . . . such a *disgrace* to the noble name they bore, that she rejected them with horror —George Meredith⟩ SHAME is central in this list; it is usable in various situations and with suggestions ranging from those of DISHONOR to those of INFAMY ⟨to soften the *shame* of this defeat in battle⟩ ⟨the lasting *shame* of a quisling or a Judas⟩ In this series SHAME is unusual in implying that inner feelings of guilt are likely to be experienced by the victim, along with scornful or hateful feelings of others ⟨*shame* is a reaction to other people's criticism. A man is shamed either by being openly ridiculed and rejected or by fantasying to himself that he has been made ridiculous —Ruth Benedict⟩ The extreme feelings attached to the following words blur their exact meanings and make comments on them difficult and inexact: IGNOMINY may imply something more intense than *scorn*, deeper than DISGRACE and may add notions of hatred and contempt ⟨he cast the pork solemnly upon the dunghill, with every attendant circumstance of *ignominy* —G.G.Coulton⟩ ⟨the *ignominy* [of being horsewhipped] he had been compelled to submit to —George Meredith⟩ OBLOQUY connotes strong widespread hatred and contempt for an important or well-known figure found guilty of something hateful, base, or shocking ⟨that unmerited *obloquy* had been brought on him by the violence of his minister —T.B.Macaulay⟩ ⟨all the *obloquy* which Weed's corruption had excited —H.S.Commager⟩ OPPROBRIUM may carry with it the suggestion of general condemnation for the fraudulent or the brutal, or a specific instance of them ⟨the name "educator", for many intelligent people, has become a term of *opprobrium* —C.H.Grandgent⟩ ⟨the *opprobrium* conveyed by the term headhunter —V.G.Heiser⟩ ODIUM is quite similar; it may occasionally suggest more lasting and less specific resentment, blame, and hatred ⟨whatever *odium* or loss her maneuvers incurred she [Queen Elizabeth] flung upon her counselors —J.R.Green⟩ INFAMY is perhaps the strongest of this group; it suggests long-lasting and extreme ill fame with attendant hatred, loathing, and contempt ⟨I have come, not from obscurity into the momentary notoriety of crime, but from a sort of fame to a sort of eternity of *infamy* —Oscar Wilde⟩ ⟨December 7, 1941, a date which will live in *infamy* —F.D.Roosevelt⟩ ⟨long remember the *infamy* of this kidnap-murder⟩
²**dishonor** \"\ *vt* [ME *deshonouren*, fr. MF *deshonorer, deshonerer*, fr. *des-* ¹dis- + *honorer, honerer* to honor — more at HONOR] **1 :** to deprive of honor **:** treat with indignity or as unworthy in the sight of others **:** stain the character or reputation of **2 :** to violate the chastity of **:** DEBAUCH, RAPE **3 :** to bring reproach or shame on **:** DISGRACE ⟨his behavior ~*ed* his family⟩ **4 :** to refuse to accept or pay (as a draft, bill, check, or note that is duly presented for acceptance or payment)
dis·honorable \"+\ *adj* [prob. fr. MF, fr. *des-* ¹dis- + *honorable*] **1 :** lacking honor **:** not honorable **:** bringing or deserving dishonor **:** SHAMEFUL, DISGRACEFUL ⟨the ~ conduct of trusted men⟩ ⟨a man ~ in thought and deed⟩ **2** *obs* **:** lacking esteem **:** DISESTEEMED, UNHONORED ⟨to find ourselves ~ graves —Shak.⟩
dishonorable discharge *n* **:** a discharge (as from employment or a position of trust or responsibility) without favorable recommendation; *specif* **:** a formal release without honor from military service given as a result of a sentence by a court-martial
dis·honorableness \dəs, (ˈ)dis+\ *n* -ES **:** the quality or state of being dishonorable
dis·honorably \dəs, (ˈ)dis +\ *adv* **:** in a dishonorable manner ⟨~ used his position for personal gain⟩
dis·honorer \"+\ *n* **:** one that dishonors
dis·horn \dəs, (ˈ)dis+\ *vt* [¹*dis-* + *horn* (n.)] **:** to remove the horns from
dis·horse \dəs, (ˈ)dis+\ *vb* [¹*dis-* + *horse* (n.)] **:** DISMOUNT
dis·house \dəsˈhau̇z, (ˈ)dis¦h-\ *vt* [¹*dis-* + *house* (n.)] **1 :** to deprive of a house **:** put out of a house **2 :** to clear (an area) of houses
dish out *vt* **1 :** to serve (food) from a dish **:** distribute in portions at table ⟨she *dished out* the chowder⟩ **2 a :** GIVE, PROVIDE, RELEASE ⟨*dishing out* important news releases⟩ ⟨those doctors who *dish out* opiates at the slightest provocation⟩ **b** *slang* **:** to present in glib, effusive, or exuberant outpourings ⟨that salesman could really *dish* it *out*⟩ ⟨you could *dish out* a memorized spiel —W.L.Gresham⟩
dishpan \ˈ≠,≠\ *n* **:** a large flat-bottomed orig. round or oval pan used for washing dishes; *broadly* **:** something (as a boat or a reflector) felt to resemble a dishpan
dishpan hands *n pl but sing or pl in constr* **:** a condition of dryness, redness, and scaling of the hands resulting typically from the constant exposure to, sensitivity to, or overuse of cleaning materials and other substances that are used in housework
dishrag \ˈ≠,≠\ *n* **1 :** DISHCLOTH **2** *or* **dishrag gourd :** DISHCLOTH GOURD **3 :** a pivoting of a dance couple under raised joined hands
dish ring *n* **:** a ring-shaped stand formerly used under dishes of hot food — called also *potato ring*
dish top *n* **:** a table top with a raised molded edge
dish towel *n* **:** a cloth for drying dishes
dish turner *n* **:** a worker who turns wooden dishes on a lathe
dish turning *n* **:** the process of turning wooden dishes on a lathe
¹**dishwash** \ˈ≠,≠\ *n* **1** *obs* **:** DISHWATER **2 :** NONSENSE
²**dishwash** \ˈ≠,≠\ *vi* **:** to cleanse dishes and other table and cookery utensils by washing esp. as a regular task or means of livelihood
dishwasher \ˈ≠,≠≠\ *n* **:** one that washes dishes: **a :** a worker employed to wash dishes (as in a restaurant) **b :** a contrivance or machine for washing dishes (as by means of jets of cleaning solution and water)
dishwater \ˈ≠,≠≠\ *n* **:** water in which dishes have been or are to be washed; *also* **:** any of various things felt to resemble dishwater (as in dullness, weakness, or uncleanness)
dishwatery \ˈ≠,≠≠≠\ *adj* **:** like dishwater esp. in weak or attenuated character ⟨~ speeches⟩
dis·identify \¦dis+\ *vt* [¹*dis-* + *identify*] **:** to rid of identity or characteristic qualities; *also* **:** DISSOCIATE
di·silane \(ˈ)dī+\ *n* -S [*di-* + *silane* or *silicane*] *also* **di·silicane** **:** a liquid compound Si_2H_6 of silicon and hydrogen that is spontaneously flammable in air
di·silicate \(ˈ)dī+\ *n* [*di-* + *silicate*] **:** a silicate containing two atoms of silicon in the molecule ⟨sodium ~⟩
di·silicide \(ˈ)dī+\ *n* [*di-* + *silicide*] **:** a compound containing two atoms of silicon combined with an element or radical
dis·illude \¦dis+\ *vt* -ED/-ING/-S [¹*dis-* + *illude*] **:** DISILLUSION
¹**dis·illusion** \¦dis+\ *n* [¹*dis-* + *illusion*] **1 :** the lack or loss of faith in illusions or in hopes previously held **:** DISENCHANTMENT ⟨facile ~ of our romantic intellectuals —*New Republic*⟩ **2 :** the state of having lost faith or illusions; *also* **:** an instance of this ⟨this romantic ~*s* and tangled, tragic problems —H.E. Salisbury⟩
²**disillusion** \"\ *also* **dis·il·lu·sion·ize** \,≠≠ˈ≠zhə,nīz\ *vt* **disillusioned** *also* **disillusionized; disillusioned** *also* **disillusionized; disillusioning** \-zh(ə)niŋ\ *also* **disillusionizing; disillusions** *also* **disillusionizes :** to free from or deprive of illusion **:** DISENCHANT ⟨~*ed* his fans by his sloppy play⟩ — **dis·il·lu·sion·ist** \,≠≠ˈzhənəst, -zhnəst\ *n* — **dis·il·lu·sion·iz·er** \-zhə,nīzə(r)\ *n* -S
dis·illusionary \¦dis+\ *or* **dis·illusive** \"+\ *adj* **:** constituting or tending to induce disillusion ⟨~ practices⟩
dis·il·lu·sion·ment \,disəˈlüzhənmənt *also* -səlˈyü-\ *n* -S **1 :** the state or process of being disillusioned ⟨the ~ of youth at the way the world was run —Agnes Repplier⟩ ⟨another novel about ~ with communism —Granville Hicks⟩ **2 :** an instance of being disillusioned ⟨a study of the ~*s* of the Australian radio world —Leslie Rees⟩
dis·imagine \¦dis+\ *vt* [¹*dis-* + *imagine*] **:** to dispel from existence in the imagination
dis·impassioned \¦dis+\ *adj* [¹*dis-* + *impassioned*] **:** divested of warmth of passion or feeling **:** CALM, COOL, DISPASSIONATE
dis·imprison \¦dis+\ *vt* [¹*dis-* + *imprison*] **:** to release from confinement — **dis·imprisonment** \"+\ *n*
dis·improve \¦dis+\ *vb* [¹*dis-* + *improve*] *vt* **:** to make worse ~ *vi* **:** to become worse — **dis·improvement** \"+\ *n*
dis·incarnate \¦dis+\ *or* **dis·incarnated** \"+\ *adj* [¹*dis-* + *incarnate, incarnated*] **:** free of or freed from the demands of the body **:** DISEMBODIED
dis·incarnation \dəs, (¦)dis+\ *n* [¹*dis* + *incarnation*] **:** the quality or state of being disincarnate
dis·incentive \¦dis+\ *n* [¹*dis-* + *incentive*] **:** something that stands in the way esp. of economic progress or production ⟨excessive taxes form a major ~ to industrial expansion in many states⟩
dis·inclination \dəs, (¦)dis+\ *n* [¹*dis-* + *inclination*] **:** a state of unwillingness **:** lack of inclination **:** DISTASTE, DISLIKE — usu. used with *to*, occas. with *for* ⟨a distinct ~ to stir from the hammock⟩ ⟨my ~ to reading arose early in life⟩
dis·incline \¦dis+\ *vt* [¹*dis-* + *incline*] **:** to turn away the inclination of **:** make unwilling or averse ⟨his background ~*s* him from needless disciplining of his subordinates⟩
disinclined *adj* **:** unwilling because of lack of inclination or through mild doubt or disapproval ⟨~ to go out⟩ ⟨~ to accept his story⟩ **:** lacking desire ⟨~ for conversation⟩
syn DISINCLINED, INDISPOSED, HESITANT, RELUCTANT, LOATH (or LOTH), and AVERSE can mean, in common, not having or not seeming to have the full will or desire to do, or have to do with, a thing indicated or implied. DISINCLINED implies a lack of taste or inclination ⟨*disinclined* to go to the movies⟩ ⟨the Italian, so affable as a rule, was rather preoccupied and *disinclined* for talk —Norman Douglas⟩ ⟨the various writers are *disinclined* to come to real grips with the vexed question of public control in industry —M.R.Cohen⟩ INDISPOSED implies an unfavorable, often hostile or unsympathetic attitude ⟨they were *indisposed* to put money into foolish enterprises⟩ HESITANT implies a holding back as through fear, uncertainty, or irresolution ⟨he smiled, in a *hesitant* way, as though not sure how Walter would take such familiarity on his part —T.B.Costain⟩ ⟨*hesitant* about spending the money required to build an experimental plant —Harold Griffin⟩ RELUCTANT implies a holding back through unwillingness ⟨he was *reluctant* to speak out, afraid to let his emotions seize upon his speech —V.L.Parrington⟩ ⟨worked only one shift, because workers were *reluctant* to change their accustomed hours —*Time*⟩ ⟨his passionate appeal to their loyalty wrested a *reluctant* assent to the prosecution of the war —J.R.Green⟩ LOATH connotes a prospective act incompatible with one's feelings, convictions, or makeup ⟨Frederick stood at the door, *loath* to go without some shred of victory to take with him —Irwin Shaw⟩ ⟨*loth* to perjure himself⟩ ⟨publishers have been *loath* to publish translations of anything except our surefire sex-and-mayhem fiction —W.H.Whyte⟩ AVERSE suggests a turning away from something distasteful or repugnant ⟨the adventurers, though not *averse* to courting, being unwilling to entangle themselves in a matrimonial alliance —Herman Melville⟩ ⟨not insensible to the power of female beauty, nor *averse* from excess in wine —T.B.Macaulay⟩ ⟨politicians . . . *averse* from political suicide —W.K.Hancock⟩ ⟨slow of speech, tenacious of opinion, and *averse* . . . to innovation of any sort —C.B.Nordhoff & J.N. Hall⟩
dis·incorporate \¦dis≠¦≠≠,rāt\ *vt* [¹*dis-* + *incorporate*] **:** to deprive of corporate powers, rights, or existence **:** divest of the condition of a corporate body
dis·incorporation \¦dis+\ *n* **:** the quality or state of being disincorporated
dis·infect \¦dis+\ *vt* [MF *desinfecter*, fr. *des-* ¹dis- + *infecter* to infect — more at INFECT] **:** to free from infection esp. by destroying harmful microorganisms; *broadly* **:** to relieve of some undesirable quality ⟨he must ~ his speech of emotional overtone —Irwin Edman⟩ **:** CLEANSE
¹**dis·in·fec·tant** \,disənˈfektənt\ *n* -S [F *désinfectant*, fr. pres. part. of *désinfecter* to disinfect] **:** an agent that frees from infection; *esp* **:** a chemical that destroys vegetative forms of harmful microorganisms but not ordinarily bacterial spores — used esp. of substances suitable for application to inanimate objects; compare GERMICIDE
²**disinfectant** \¦≠≠¦≠≠\ *adj* [F *désinfectant*, pres. part.] **:** serving or tending to disinfect **:** suitable for use in disinfecting
disinfecting candle *n* **:** a cylinder or cone of a combustible mixture usu. containing sulfur or formaldehyde that is burned for disinfecting purposes
dis·infection \¦dis+\ *n* **:** the act or process of disinfecting
dis·infective \"+\ *adj* **:** DISINFECTANT
dis·infector \"+\ *n* **:** one that disinfects; *esp* **:** an apparatus for applying disinfectants
dis·infest \¦dis+\ *vt* [¹*dis-* + *infest*] **:** to rid (as a house, a plant, or the intestine) of infestation **:** free from infesting insects, rodents, or other small animals — **dis·infestation** \(¦)dis+\ *n*
dis·in·fes·tant \,disənˈfestənt\ *n* -S **:** a disinfesting agent
dis·in·fes·tor \-tə(r)\ *n* -S **:** an agent or apparatus for disinfesting
dis·infeudation \dəs, (¦)dis+\ *n* [¹*dis-* + *infeudation*] **:** release from feudal tenure or obligation
dis·inflate \¦dis+\ *vb* [¹*dis-* + *inflate*] **:** DEFLATE
dis·inflation \"+\ *n* [*dis-* + *inflation*] **:** a reversal of inflationary pressures manifested by a leveling off or a moderate decline in prices **:** DEFLATION — **dis·inflationary** \"+\ *adj*
dis·ingenuity \dəs, (¦)dis+\ *n* [¹*dis-* + *ingenuity*] **:** disingenuous state, behavior, or act
dis·ingenuous \¦dis+\ *adj* [¹*dis-* + *ingenuous*] **:** not ingenuous **:** lacking in candor or frankness; *often* **:** unworthily or meanly artful **:** giving a false appearance of simple frankness — **dis·ingenuously** \"+\ *adv* — **dis·ingenuousness** \"+\ *n*
dis·inhabit \¦dis+\ *vt* [¹*dis-* + *inhabit*] *archaic* **:** DISPEOPLE
dis·in·her·i·son \,disənˈherəsən, -rəzən\ *n* -S [alter. (influenced by *disinherit*) of *disherison*] **:** DISHERISON
dis·inherit \¦dis+\ *vt* [ME *disinheriten*, fr. ¹*dis-* + *inheriten* to inherit — more at INHERIT] **1 :** to deprive (an heir apparent) of the right to inherit **:** prevent deliberately (as by making a will) from coming into possession of a property right or title that would otherwise devolve on the heir by law or custom in the course of descent **2 a :** to deprive of natural or human rights ⟨the ~*ed* millions behind the iron curtain⟩ **b :** to deprive of special privileges previously held ⟨as the peoples of Asia and Africa stir and gradually ~ the colonial powers⟩ **syn** see DEPRIVE
dis·inheritance \"+\ *also* **dis·in·her·i·ta·tion** \¦disən,herəˈtāshən\ *n* -S **:** an act of disinheriting or the state of being disinherited
dis·inhibition \dəs, (¦)dis+\ *n* [¹*dis-* + *inhibition*] **:** loss of a conditioned reflex (as by the action of interfering stimuli)
dis·inhibitory \¦dis+\ *adj* [¹*dis-* + *inhibitory*] **:** tending to overcome esp. psychological inhibition ⟨~ drugs⟩
dis·inhume \¦dis+\ *vt* [¹*dis-* + *inhume*] **:** DISINTER
dis·in·sec·ti·za·tion \,disən,sektəˈzāshən\ *n* -S [¹*dis-* + *insect* + *-ization*] **:** removal of insects (as from an aircraft) ⟨a ~ squad⟩
dis·integrable \dəs+\ *adj* [*disintegrate* + *-able*] **:** capable of being disintegrated
dis·integrate \dəs+\ *vb* [*dis-* + *integrate*] *vt* **1 :** to break or decompose (something) into constituent elements or into parts ⟨their attacks gradually *disintegrated* the government⟩ **2 a :** to reduce (rock) to particulate matter (as by weathering) **b :** to shatter (as a building) suddenly into bits (as by exploding) **c :** to cause disintegration of (an atomic nucleus) ~ *vi* **1 :** to break or separate into constituent elements or parts ⟨with the rise of nationalism, the colonial empires *disintegrated*⟩ **2 a** *of rock* **:** to become reduced to particulate matter usu. through the action of natural forces ⟨the older strata gradually ~⟩ **b** *of a structure* **:** to shatter suddenly **:** fly to bits ⟨the flaming building suddenly *disintegrated*⟩ ⟨the plane hit the ground and *disintegrated*⟩ **c :** to deteriorate by or as if by breaking into constituent parts ⟨asked if he thought theater was *disintegrating* —Louise Mace⟩ ⟨an actor long since *disintegrated* by the blacklist —Murray Kempton⟩ ⟨the *disintegrating* features of an aging woman —Philip Wylie⟩ **d :** to undergo disintegration — used of an atomic nucleus, a neutron, or a meson **syn** see DECAY
dis·integration \dəs, (,)dis+\ *n* **1 :** the act or process of disintegrating or state of being disintegrated ⟨~ of personality⟩; *specif* **:** a change in the composition of an atomic nucleus whether occurring spontaneously (as in the ejection of particles from the nucleus in radioactivity) or as a result of bombardment by particles (as by neutrons or protons) **2 :** the transformation of an elementary particle into others (as of a neutron into a proton and electron)
disintegration constant *n* **:** DECAY CONSTANT
dis·in·te·gra·tion·ist \-sh(ə)nəst\ *n* **:** a person who favors disintegration esp. of a social structure or order
dis·integrative \dəs+\ *adj* **:** tending to induce disintegration ⟨~ influences⟩
dis·integrator \dəs+\ *n* **:** one that disintegrates (as a machine for grinding or pulverizing); *specif* **:** a substance used in tablet formulations to cause the tablet to break up on contact with moisture and exert its medicinal action promptly
dis·in·te·grous \dəˈsintəgrəs, ¦disənˈtegrəs\ *adj* [*disintegrate* + *-ous*] **:** lacking cohesion
dis·inter \¦dis+\ *vt* [¹*dis-* + *inter*] **1 :** to take out of the grave or tomb **:** to dig up **:** EXHUME **2 :** to bring out of concealment **:** bring from obscurity into view **:** UNEARTH ⟨plays . . . remained unknown . . . until *disinterred* by a painstaking bibliophile —Saxe Commins⟩ **syn** see DIG
disinteress *vt* -ED/-ING/-ES [F *désintéresser*, fr. *dés-* ¹dis + *intéresser* to interest — more at INTEREST] *obs* **:** DISINTEREST
¹**dis·interest** \dəs, (ˈ)dis+\ *vt* [¹*dis-* + *interest* (v.)] **:** to divest of interest or interested motives ⟨criminal case histories, which usually have a way of ~*ing* theater audiences —G.J. Nathan⟩
²**disinterest** \"\ *n* [¹*dis-* + *interest* (n.)] **1 :** something contrary to interest **:** DISADVANTAGE ⟨to the ~ of the public⟩ **2 :** DISINTERESTEDNESS **:** lack of self-interest ⟨the highest honor ~ —James Martineau⟩ **3 :** lack of interest **:** APATHY, UNCONCERN ⟨two soldiers with slovenly ~ on their unlighted faces —Bruce Marshall⟩ ⟨the monumental ~ of the voters —Don Shoemaker⟩
disinterested *adj* **1 :** lacking or revealing lack of interest **:** INDIFFERENT, UNINTERESTED, APATHETIC, UNCONCERNED **2 :** not influenced by regard to personal advantage **:** free from selfish motive **:** not biased or prejudiced ⟨a ~ decision⟩ ⟨~ sacrifices⟩ **syn** see INDIFFERENT
dis·interestedly \dəs, (ˈ)dis+\ *adv* **:** in a disinterested manner; *usu* **:** without bias or selfish motive
dis·interestedness \"+\ *n* **:** disinterested state; *usu* **:** freedom from bias or selfish motives
disinteresting *adj* **:** not interesting
dis·interment \¦dis+\ *n* **1 :** the act of disinterring **:** EXHUMATION **2 :** something brought to light
dis·intoxication \¦dis+\ *n* [*dis-* + *intoxication*] **:** the freeing of an individual from an intoxicating agent (as an addict from a drug) stored in the body
dis·invest \¦dis+\ *vb* [¹*dis-* + *invest*] *vt* **:** to subject to disinvestment ~ *vi* **:** to engage in disinvestment (as by selling capital assets)

dis·investment \"+\ *n* **:** consumption of capital (as by uncompensated deterioration of assets or using up of stored inventory) ⟨~ in the economic sense occurs when national consumption exceeds national income —J.O.Kamm⟩; *sometimes* **:** withdrawal of capital from investment or from an investment

disinvite *vt* [*dis-* + *invite*] *obs* **:** to recall an invitation to

dis·in·vol·ture \,disǝn'välchə(r), -vōl-,-vōl-\ *n* -s [F *désinvolture*, fr. It *disinvoltura*, fr. *disinvolto* unconstrained, unembarrassed (fr. past part. of *disinvolgere* to unwrap, fr. *dis-* [1]dis- — fr. L *dis-* — + *involgere* to wrap) + *-ura* -ure; It *disinvolto*, trans. of Sp *desenvuelto*] **:** an unconstrained free and easy manner

dis·involve \¦dis+\ *vt* [[1]*dis-* + *involve*] **:** to relieve from involvement **:** DISENTANGLE

dis·jas·kit *also* **dis·jas·ked** \dǝs'jaskǝt\ *adj* [perh. alter. of *dejected*] **1** *Scot* **:** DEPRESSED, DEJECTED **2** *Scot* **:** BROKEN-DOWN, DILAPIDATED

dis·ject \dǝs'jekt\ *vt* -ED/-ING/-S [L *disjectus*, past part. of *disjicere*, fr. *dis-* apart + *-jicere* (fr. *jacere* to throw) — more at DIS-, JET] **:** to scatter about **:** DISPERSE

dis·jec·ta mem·bra \dǝs¦jektǝ'membrǝ\ *n pl* [L] **:** scattered parts; *usu* **:** literary fragments or disjointed quotations

dis·jec·tion \dǝs'jekshǝn\ *n* -s **:** the act of scattering or state of being scattered **:** DISPERSION

dis·join \dǝs, (')dis+\ *vb* [MF *desjoin-*, stem of *desjoindre*, fr. L *disjungere*, fr. *dis-* [1]dis- + *jungere* to join — more at YOKE] *vt* **:** to bring to an end the joining of **:** SEPARATE, DISUNITE, PART, SUNDER ⟨that marriage, therefore, God himself ~s —John Milton⟩ ⟨~s the physical cause from the final end —A.N.Whitehead⟩ ~ *vi* **:** to become detached **:** SEPARATE, PART ⟨the bivalents ~ normally —*Genetics*⟩

dis·join·able \-nǝbǝl\ *adj* **:** fit or suitable for disjoining

disjoined *adj*, *of a heraldic cross* **:** voided with the voiding extending through the ends of the four arms so as to leave only the sides of the arms outlined

[1]**dis·joint** \dǝs, (')dis+\ *adj* [ME *disjoynt*, fr. MF *desjoint*, past part. of *desjoindre* to disjoin — more at DISJOIN] **1** *obs* **:** DISJOINTED **2 :** having no members in common ⟨~ sets⟩

[2]**dis·joint** \dǝs, (')dis+\ *vb* [ME *disyointen*, fr. MF *desjoint*, past part.] *vt* **1 :** to separate the parts of **:** break up into divisions **:** disturb or undo the connections, order, or coherence of **:** DISLOCATE ⟨her work suffers from her reluctance to come to absolute grips with her subject, and this reluctance ~s her writing —*New Yorker*⟩ **2 :** to undo the joining of **:** DISUNITE ⟨Great Britain, ~ed from her colonies —Thomas Jefferson⟩ **3 :** to separate at junctures or joints **:** dissect, carve, or break into pieces at the joints ⟨~ a frying chicken⟩ ~ *vi* **:** to separate at the joints

disjointed *adj* **1 :** separated at or as if at the joint **:** DISLOCATED ⟨a ~ hip⟩ **2 :** DISCONNECTED, DISORDERED ⟨a ~ society⟩; *esp* **:** INCOHERENT ⟨~ words⟩ ⟨~ conversation⟩ — **dis·joint·ed·ly** *adv* — **dis·joint·ed·ness** *n*

dis·joint·ly \dǝs'jȯintlē, (')dis¦j-\ *adv* [[1]*disjoint* + *-ly*] **1 :** in a disjointed state **:** SEPARATELY — opposed to *conjointly* **2 :** DISCONNECTEDLY, INCOHERENTLY

dis·join·ture \dǝs, (')dis+\ *n* **:** absence of connection **:** SEPARATION

[1]**dis·junct** \dǝs'jǝŋ(k)t, (')dis¦j-\ *adj* [L *disjunctus*, past part. of *disjungere* to disjoin — more at DISJOIN] **1 :** marked by separation of or from usu. contiguous parts or individuals ⟨little isolated worlds, as abruptly ~ and unexpected ... as a palm-shaded well in the Sahara —*Scientific Monthly*⟩: as **a :** DISCONTINUOUS — now used almost entirely of distributions (as of statistical or natural populations) ⟨genera that are ~ between New and Old World xerophytic areas⟩ ⟨the ~ distribution of the king crabs⟩ **b :** relating to melodic progression by intervals larger than a major second — contrasted with *conjunct* **c** *of certain insects* **:** having head, thorax, and abdomen separated by deep constrictions

[2]**dis·junct** \'dis,jǝŋ(k)t\ *n* -s **:** any of the alternatives comprising a logical disjunction

dis·junction \dǝs, (')dis+\ *n* [ME *disjunccioun*, fr. L *disjunction-*, *disjunctio*, fr. *disjunctus* + *-ion-*, *-io* -ion] **1 :** the act of disjoining or state of being disjoined **:** DISUNION, SEPARATION, PARTING ⟨the ~ of soul and body⟩ **2 :** the relation of the terms or clauses of a logical proposition or judgment expressing alternatives; *also* **:** a statement of such a proposition usu. taking the form (1) *p* v *q* meaning *p* or *q* or both or (2) *p* + *q* meaning *p* or *q* but not both — called also respectively (1) *inclusive disjunction*, (2) *exclusive disjunction* **3 :** an area of discontinuity between areas in which populations of a specified organism are present

dis·junctional \"+\ *adj* **:** involving disjunction **:** by means of disjunction

[1]**dis·junctive** \dǝs'jǝŋ(k)tiv\ *n* -s [LL & L *disjunctivus*, adj.] **1 :** a disjunctive conjunction **2** *in Hebrew orthography* **:** a disjunctive accent **3 :** DISJUNCTION 2; *broadly* **:** a situation involving alternate choices

[2]**dis·junc·tive** \dǝs'==, (')dis¦==\ *adj* [L *disjunctivus*, fr. *disjunctus* + *-ivus* -ive] **1 a :** tending to disjoin **:** involving disjunction **:** SEPARATIVE **b** *of a vowel* **:** epenthesized in a cluster of consonants to facilitate pronunciation ⟨the parasitic vowel \ǝ\ in the pronunciation \'athǝ,lēt\ of *athlete* is ~⟩ **2** [LL *disjunctivus*, fr. L] **a** *of a conjunction* **:** expressing an alternative, contrast, or opposition between the meanings of the words or word groups that it connects ⟨the ~ conjunctions *or* in "peas or beans", *either ... or* in "either milk or cream", *but* in "small but important", and *though* in "they went on playing ball though it was raining"⟩ — contrasted with *copulative* **b :** pleading or marked by mutually exclusive alternatives joined by "or" ⟨the ~ statement *the defendant knew or ought to have known*⟩ ⟨~ pleading⟩ **3** *of a pronoun form* **:** stressed and not attached to the verb as an enclitic or proclitic (as French *moi*, *lui*, *toi*, *soi*) — contrasted with *conjunctive* **4** *in Hebrew orthography* **:** indicating that the word marked is separated to a greater or less degree rhythmically and grammatically from the word which follows it — used of an accent; opposed to *conjunctive* — **dis·junc·tive·ly** \-tǝvlē\ *adv*

disjunctive legacy *n*, *Roman law* **:** a legacy of the same thing given to two or more persons that is expressed in separate clauses with the latter gift or gifts apparently encroaching on the first gift

dis·junc·tiv·i·ty \(,)dis,jǝŋ(k)'tivǝd·ē, dǝs-\ *n* -ES **:** disjunctive state or quality

disjunct motion *n*, *music* **:** a succession of notes in a part progressing by intervals larger than a major second

dis·junc·tor \dǝs'jǝŋ(k)tǝ(r)\ *n* -s **1 :** a device for disconnecting an electrical circuit **2 :** a small cellulose body interposed between the conidia of certain fungi that ultimately breaks down and sets them free

disjunct species *n pl* **:** different logical species falling coordinately under a single genus

disjunct tetrachord *n* **:** either of two successive tetrachords in which the lowest tone of one is one step from the highest tone of the other

dis·juncture \dǝs, (')dis+\ *n* [ME, modif. (influenced by L *disjunctus*) of MF *desjointure*, fr. *desjoint* (past part. of *desjoindre* to disjoin) + *-ure* — more at DISJOIN] **:** DISJUNCTION

dis·june \dǝs'jün\ *n* -s [ME (Sc dial.) *disione*, fr. MF *desjun*, *desjeun*, fr. *desjuner* to breakfast, fr. (assumed) VL *disjejunare* to break one's fast] *Scot* **:** BREAKFAST

[1]**disk** *or* **disc** \'disk\ *n* -s *often attrib* [L *discus* dish, disk, quoit — more at DISH] **1** *archaic* **:** DISCUS 1 **2 :** the seemingly flat figure or image of a celestial body as it appears in the heavens **3 :** any of several more or less rounded and flattened plant structures: as **a :** the central portion of the flower head of a typical composite composed of closely packed tubular flowers — see DISCOID **b** *usu disc* **:** an enlargement of the torus surrounding, beneath, or above the pistil of some flowers **c :** the curved spore-bearing surface of an apothecium; *also* **:** the central upper portion of the pileus of a mushroom **d :** one of the adhesive circular enlargements at the ends of the tendrils in the Virginia creeper, Boston ivy, and similar plants by which they climb flat surfaces; *also* **:** any similar adhesive surface (as the base of a pollinium) **4 :** any of

head of chamomile, *d* disk, *r* rays

various rounded and flattened animal anatomical structures: as **a :** the flattened circumoral part of a coelenterate (as a sea anemone) **b** *usu disc* **:** the body of an echinoderm **c :** the area of modified plumage surrounding the eye of an owl **d :** a mammalian red blood cell **e :** OPTIC DISK **f :** INTERVERTEBRAL DISK **5 :** a thin circular object ⟨a metal ~⟩: as **a :** DISCOIDAL **b :** a round dish used in the Eastern Orthodox Church to hold the host **c :** a small tablet with glycerogelatin base used in eye medication; *also* **:** a small medicated mass of sugar and egg albumen used in homeopathic practice **d :** [3]PUCK 2a **e :** one of the circular wooden pieces used in shuffleboard **f** *usu disc* **:** a phonograph record **6 :** a rotating abrasive device used in dentistry **7 :** a circular symbol used by ancient Egyptians to represent the sun **8** *usu disc* **:** one of the concave circular hardened steel tools with sharpened edge that make up the working part of a disc harrow or plow; *often* **:** an implement employing such tools **:** DISC HARROW, DISC PLOW **9** *usu disc* **:** a small flat woman's hat of oval shape usu. worn forward on the head

[2]**disk** *or* **disc** \"\ *vt* -ED/-ING/-S **1 :** to cultivate with a disc harrow or disc cultivator **2** *usu disc* **:** to record on a phonograph disc

disk barrow *n* **:** a flat circular tumulus of the Bronze Age

disk bat *n* [so called fr. the appearance of the suckers] **:** any of several tropical American bats (family Thyropteridae) distinguished by the presence on the thumbs and on the soles of the hind feet of suckers by which they can hang from a smooth surface — called also *disk-wing bat*

disk bit *n* **:** a rotary drill bit consisting of sharp-edged disks set vertically

disk brake *n* **:** a friction brake in which the surfaces that rub together are in the form of disks

disk cipher *n*, *cryptology* **:** a cipher using the cipher disk

disk clutch *n* **:** a friction clutch in which the friction is between two parallel flat plates or sets of such plates

disk crank *n* **:** a balanced crank consisting of a disk revolving about its center and having a crankpin secured eccentrically in it

disk drill *n* **1 :** a primitive drill in which the spindle is weighted by a disk and which is operated by a strap or bow **2** *usu* **disc drill :** a drill for sowing grain or seeds using discs as furrow openers

di·skel·i·on \dī'skelēǝn, dǝ'-, -ē,än\ *n* -s [NL, fr. *di-* + *-skelion* (as in *triskelion*)] **:** a figure like the triskelion but with only two radiating members

disk engine *n* **:** any of various rotary engines in which the piston or its equivalent is a rotating or wobbling disk

disk·er \'diskǝ(r)\ *n* -s **:** a worker who readies automobile bodies for painting

disk·ery \-karē\ *n* -ES [[1]*disk* + *-ery*] *slang* **:** a phonograph-record manufacturer

disk flower *also* **disk floret** *n* **:** one of the tubular flowers in the disk of a composite plant — see COMPOSITE illustration

disk grinder *n* **:** a grinding machine equipped with one or more abrasive-coated disks that usu. revolve at high speed

diskindness *n* [[1]*dis-* + *kindness*] *obs* **:** UNKINDNESS

disk jockey *var of* DISC JOCKEY

disk·less \'disklǝs\ *adj* **:** lacking a disk

disklike *or* **disclike** \'=,=\ *adj* **:** circular and nearly flat ⟨a ~ acetabulum⟩

disk meter *n* **:** a meter for measuring fluids that has a disk that controls the alternate filling and emptying of the measuring chambers

disk of confusion : CIRCLE OF CONFUSION

dis·ko·gram \'diskǝ,gram\ *n* -s [[1]*disk* + *-o-* + *-gram*] **:** a roentgenogram of an intervertebral disk made after injection of a radiopaque substance — **dis·kog·ra·phy** \dǝ'skägrǝfē\ *n* -ES

disk pile *n* **:** a steel pile having a disk on its lower end to give increased supporting power

disk sander *n* **:** a machine having one or more flat circular disks faced with abrasive for smoothing wood surfaces (as floors)

disk-shaped \'=,=\ *adj* **:** flat and circular

disk signal *n* **:** an automatic block signal indicating train movements by the positions of colored disks

disk telegraph *n* **:** DIAL TELEGRAPH

disk-urchin \'=,==\ *n* **:** a flattened sea urchin (as a sand dollar or a keyhole urchin)

disk valve *n* **:** a valve opened or closed by a disk; *often* **:** a suction valve operated by a flexible disk (as of rubber or leather)

disk wheel *n* **1 :** a disk having a spiral on its flat face for engaging with a worm wheel **2 :** a wheel presenting a solid convex or concave surface from hub to rim

disk-wing bat *n* **:** DISK BAT

dis·leaf *or* **dis·leave** \dǝs, (')dis+\ *vt* **disleafed** *or* **disleaved; disleafing** *or* **disleaving; disleafs** *or* **disleaves** [[1]*dis-* + *leaf* (n.)] *archaic* **:** to remove the leaves from **:** strip of leaves ⟨the cankerworm that annually *disleaved* the elms —J.R.Lowell⟩

disleal *adj* [[1]*dis-* + *leal*] *obs* **:** DISLOYAL, PERFIDIOUS

dis·likable *or* **dis·likeable** \dǝs, (')dis+\ *adj* **:** such as to provoke dislike **:** UNLIKABLE

dis·likably *or* **dis·likeably** \"+\ *adv* **:** in a dislikable manner

[1]**dis·like** \dǝs, (')dis+\ *vt* [[1]*dis-* + *like* (v.)] **1** *archaic* **:** to awaken dislike in **:** DISPLEASE **2 :** to regard with dislike **:** feel aversion for **:** DISAPPROVE ⟨the two ... *disliked* each other by instinct —Henry Adams⟩ **3** *obs* **:** to show aversion to

[2]**dislike** \"\ *n* **1 :** a feeling of positive aversion (as to something unpleasant, uncongenial, or offensive) **:** DISAPPROBATION, REPUGNANCE, DISPLEASURE, DISFAVOR ⟨our determined ~ of hard work⟩ **2** *obs* **:** DISCORD, DISSENSION

syn DISLIKE, DISTASTE, AVERSION, and DISFAVOR agree in designating a state of mind or feeling marked by an inner shunning or avoiding of something or a finding of it unpleasant or positively repugnant. DISLIKE may, on the one hand, imply the mere finding of something unpleasant or, on the other, a reacting to it with detestation ⟨known ... for his *dislike* of large social functions —*Current Biog.*⟩ ⟨an aristocratic disdain and *dislike* of the bourgeoisie, whose virtues and shortcomings are alike displeasing to both the upper and the lower classes —W.R.Inge⟩ ⟨concerning phobias, care should be exercised in differentiating between mere aversion and *dislike* and morbid unreasonable fear or dread —H.G.Armstrong⟩ ⟨I don't mean *dislike*, or find distasteful, or have an aversion for; I mean hate —Hamilton Basso⟩ DISTASTE stresses a squeamishness or repugnance ⟨viewing liquor and tobacco with *distaste* —John Lawler⟩ ⟨a disdain amounting at times to a violent physical *distaste* for practically every human component of their lives —Florence Bullock⟩ ⟨the individual's *distaste* for his occupation —H.G.Armstrong⟩ AVERSION is stronger, stressing avoidance or a desire to evade or escape ⟨they stared at each other with instinctive repudiation, *aversion* almost —Margery Sharp⟩ ⟨the natural human *aversion* to cold, noise, vibration, high places, rapid ascents and descents, and the unfriendly and lonesome environment at high altitude —H.G. Armstrong⟩ DISFAVOR is the weakest of these four nouns, usu. suggesting no feeling stronger than disapproval though sometimes it may imply contempt or disdain as motives ⟨to look with *disfavor* upon frivolous conduct in public⟩ ⟨his father's *disfavor* prevented his asking for an allowance until more amicable relations should be established⟩

[3]**dislike** *adj* [[1]*dis-* + *like* (adj.)] *obs* **:** UNLIKE

dis·like·ful \dǝs'līkfǝl, (')dis¦l-\ *adj* **:** DISAGREEABLE

disliken *vt* [[3]*dislike* + *-en*] *obs* **:** to make unlike **:** DISGUISE

dis·liker \dǝs, (')dis+\ *n* **:** one that dislikes

disliking *n* [fr. gerund of [1]*dislike*] **:** DISLIKE, DISAPPROVAL

dis·limb \dǝs, (')dis+\ *vt* [[1]*dis-* + *limb* (n.)] **:** DISMEMBER

dis·limn \dǝs, (')dis+\ *vb* [[1]*dis-* + *limn*] **:** DIM ⟨the nocturnal pageant has ~*ed* and vanished —Thomas De Quincey⟩

dis·link \dǝs, (')dis+\ *vt* [[1]*dis-* + *link*] **:** DISUNITE, UNCOUPLE, UNLINK, SEPARATE

dis·load \dǝs, (')dis+\ *vb* [[1]*dis-* + *load*] **:** UNLOAD, DISBURDEN

dis·lo·ca·ble \'di(,)slōkǝbǝl *also* 'dislǝk- *or* ¦dǝ'slōk- *or* 'di'slōk-\ *adj* [*dislocate* + *-able*] **:** subject to dislocation

[1]**dis·lo·cate** \'dis(,)lō,kāt *also* 'dislǝ,k- dǝ'slō- *or* 'di'slō- *sometimes*, dislō'k- *or* ,dislǝ'k-; *usu* -ād·+V\ *vt* [ML *dislocatus*, past part. of *dislocare*, fr. L *dis-* [1]dis- + *locare* to place — more at LOCATE] **1 :** to put out of place: as **a :** to put (a body part) out of order by displacing a bone from its normal connections with another bone or other bones ⟨he slipped and *dislocated* his shoulder⟩; *also* **:** to displace (a bone) from normal connections with another bone or other bones ⟨the humerus was completely *dislocated* in the fall⟩ **b :** to displace from a former or proper place **:** move away from contiguous items **:** REMOVE ⟨*dislocating* whole sections in his revision⟩ **c :** to alter the position of in respect to contiguous items without removal to a distance **:** SHIFT ⟨major earth movements may occur without *dislocating* the strata locally⟩ **2 :** to cause confusion in **:** cause to deviate from a normal or predicted course, situation, or relationship **:** DISORDER, DISARRANGE, DISTURB ⟨economies *dislocated* by war⟩ ⟨revolution accomplished gradually by *dislocating* the internal structure of the empire⟩

[2]**dislocate** \"\ *adj*, *archaic* **:** DISLOCATED

[3]**dislocate** \"\ *n* -s **:** a stunt executed from a kip position on the flying rings in which the head is dropped backward, the body is straightened by arching the back and extending the hips, and the legs are made to describe an arc in the air

dislocated *adj* **1 :** put out of position **:** DISPLACED, DISARRANGED **2 :** put out of order **:** DISRUPTED

dis·lo·cat·ed·ly *adv* **:** in disorder **:** in or as if in the wrong place

dis·lo·cat·ed·ness *n* -ES **:** the quality or state of being dislocated

dis·lo·ca·tion \,di(,)slō'kāshǝn, ,dislǝ'k-\ *n* [ME *dislocacioun*, fr. MF *dislocation*, fr. ML *dislocatus* + MF *-ion*] **:** the act of dislocating or state of being dislocated: as **a :** displacement of one or more bones at a joint **:** LUXATION **b :** displacement of rocks by movement along a fracture **:** FAULT **c :** a discontinuity in the otherwise normal lattice structure of a crystal **d :** disruption of an established order (as in social, economic, or political affairs) ⟨postwar industrial ~s⟩

dis·lo·ca·tor *pronunc at* +ǝ(r)\ *n* **:** one that dislocates

dis·lo·ca·to·ry \'di(,)slōkǝ,tōrē, dǝ'slōk-, (')di'slōk- *also* 'dislǝk-, *chiefly Brit* 'dislǝ,kātǝri\ *adj* **:** causing or resulting from dislocation

dis·lodge \dǝs, (')dis+\ *vb* [ME *disloggen*, fr. MF *desloger*, fr. *des-* [1]dis- + *loger* to lodge — more at LODGE] *vt* **1 a :** to drive out of a dwelling place ⟨the wave of crisis that *dislodged* them from their native land —M.J.Clark⟩; *sometimes* **:** to drive (a wild animal) from a lair or hiding place **b :** to force to leave or give up an advantage or favorable position ⟨they gathered proxies and *dislodged* him at the next stockholders' meeting⟩ ⟨attempting to ~ the leftist faction in the union⟩ ⟨occupied the rugged mountains ... from which the Japanese never succeeded in *dislodging* them —*Current Biog.*⟩ **c :** to cause to shift from a fixed position esp. by exertion of physical effort on ⟨a sharp blow *dislodged* the lid⟩ ⟨*dislodging* a shower of pebbles as he slid down the hill⟩ **2** *obs* **:** to shift the quarters or station of (a military force) **:** move from one position to another ~ *vi* **:** to move from a place previously occupied **:** leave a lodging place ⟨the bone may ~ from his throat without surgery⟩

dis·lodgment *or* **dis·lodgement** \"+\ *n* **:** the act or process of dislodging or state of being dislodged

dislogistic *var of* DYSLOGISTIC

dis·loyal \dǝs, (')dis+\ *adj* [MF *desloial*, fr. OF *deslëal*, fr. *des-* [1]dis- + *lëal* loyal — more at LOYAL] **:** not loyal **:** marked by lack of adherence to a sovereign, leader, country, principle, or cause claiming allegiance or by lack of adherence to vows, obligations, or promises esp. in friendships or marriage ⟨great party people think ... openmindedness *disloyal* —G.B.Shaw⟩ **syn** see FAITHLESS

dis·loyalist \"+\ *n* **:** a person lacking in loyalty; *usu* **:** one supporting an enemy of the established government

dis·loyally \"+\ *adv* **:** in a disloyal manner **:** UNFAITHFULLY **:** with disregard to the dictates of loyalty

dis·loyalty \"+\ *n* [modif. (influenced by MF *desloial*) of MF *desloiauté*, fr. OF *deslëauté*, fr. *deslëal* + *-té* -ty] **1 :** lack of loyalty or fidelity **:** violation of allegiance **2 :** a disloyal act or thought

dis·luster \dǝs, (')dis+\ *vb* [[1]*dis-* + *luster*] *vt* **:** to deprive of luster ~ *vi* **:** to lose luster

dis·mail \dǝs, (')dis+\ *vt* [ME *dismailen*, fr. MF *desmaillier*, fr. *des-* [1]dis- + *maille* mail — more at MAIL] *archaic* **:** to divest of armor

[1]**dis·mal** \'dizmǝl\ *adj*, *often* -ER/-EST [ME, fr. *dismal*, n., set of 24 days (two in each month) identified as unlucky in medieval calendars, fr. AF, fr. ML *dies mali*, lit., evil days, fr. L *dies* (pl. of *dies* day) + *mali* (pl. of *malus* evil, bad) — more at DEITY, SMALL] **1 a** *obs*, *of a day* **:** UNLUCKY, ILL-OMENED, SINISTER **b** *obs* **:** bringing disaster or calamity **:** DREADFUL, OMINOUS **2 :** marked by, showing, or causing gloom, dejection, somberness, or depression of spirits **:** utterly wanting in anything cheering, gladdening, encouraging, or inspiring ⟨tones so ~ as to make woe itself more insupportable —William Cowper⟩ ⟨the ~ prison twilight —Charles Dickens⟩ **3 :** marked by weakness, ineptness, sparseness, impoverishment, or dullness **:** lacking interest or merit ⟨the tonal monotony, the ~ vocal ineffectiveness —E.T.Canby⟩

syn DREARY, CHEERLESS, DISPIRITING, BLEAK, DESOLATE: DISMAL and DREARY are often interchangeable. DISMAL may indicate extreme gloominess or somberness utterly depressing and dejecting ⟨*dismal* acres of weed-filled cellars and gaping foundations —Felix Morley⟩ ⟨rain dripped ... with a *dismal* insistence —T.B. Costain⟩ ⟨the most *dismal* prophets of calamity —J.W.Krutch⟩ DREARY may differ in indicating what discourages or enervates through sustained gloom, dullness, tiresomeness, or futility, and wants any cheering or enlivening characteristic ⟨the most *dreary* solitary desert waste I had ever beheld —William Bartram⟩ ⟨it was a hard *dreary* winter, and the old minister's heart was often heavy —Margaret Deland⟩ ⟨had the strength been there, the equipment was lacking. Harding's *dreary* appreciation of this was part of his tragedy —S.H.Adams⟩ CHEERLESS stresses absence of anything cheering and is less explicit than but as forceful as the others in suggesting a pervasive disheartening joylessness or hopelessness ⟨he would like to have done with life and its vanity altogether ... so *cheerless* and dreary the prospect seemed to him —W.M.Thackeray⟩ DISPIRITING refers to anything that disheartens or takes away morale or resolution of spirit ⟨it was such *dispiriting* effort. To throw one's whole strength and weight on the oars, and to feel the boat checked in its forward lunge —Jack London⟩ BLEAK is likely to suggest chill, dull, barren characteristics that dishearten and militate against any notions of cheer, shelter, warmth, comfort, brightness, or ease ⟨the *bleak* upland, still famous as a sheepwalk, though a scant herbage scarce veils the whinstone rock —J.R.Green⟩ ⟨the sawmill workers of the *bleak* mountain shack towns —*Amer. Guide Series: Calif.*⟩ ⟨the *bleak* years of the depression —J.D.Hicks⟩ DESOLATE applies to that which disheartens by being utterly barren, lifeless, uninhabitable or abandoned, and remote from anything cheering, comforting, or pleasant ⟨a semibarren, rather *desolate* region, whose long dry seasons stunted its vegetation —Tom Marvel⟩ ⟨some *desolate* polar region of the mind, where woman, even as an ideal, could not hope to survive —Ellen Glasgow⟩

[2]**dismal** \"\ *n* -s **1 dismals** *pl* **:** low spirits **:** extreme dejection **:** BLUES — used with *the* ⟨suffering from an attack of the ~s⟩ **2** *South* **:** SWAMP

dis·mal·i·ty \diz'malǝd·ē\ *n* -ES **:** the quality or state of being dismal **:** DISMALNESS; *also* **:** a dismal occurrence or feeling

dismal jim·my \-'jimi\ *or* **dismal jem·my** \-'jemi\ *n*, *usu cap J* [fr. *Jimmy*, *Jemmy*, nickname for *James*] *slang Brit* **:** a man noted for depressing pessimistic predictions and frame of mind

dis·mal·ly \'dizmǝlē, -li\ *adv* **:** in a dismal manner ⟨a frightened child crying ~ in a corner⟩ ⟨trying to make out with a ~ inadequate money intake —F.L.Allen⟩ ⟨~ wrong in some of his ... dogmas —W.H.Chamberlin⟩

dis·mal·ness \-mǝlnǝs\ *n* -ES **:** the quality or state of being dismal **:** GLOOMINESS

dismal science *n* **:** POLITICAL ECONOMY **:** ECONOMICS

dis·mantle \dǝs, (')dis+\ *vt* [MF *desmanteler*, lit., to deprive of a cloak, fr. *des-* [1]dis- + *mantel* cloak — more at MANTLE] **1 :** to strip or deprive of dress or covering **:** DIVEST, UNCLOAK **2 :** to strip of furniture and equipment or significant contents ⟨~ a house that is to be razed⟩ ⟨~ a ship before scrapping it⟩;

specif : to strip of guns, walls, and defenses ⟨~ a fort⟩ ⟨~ a town⟩ **3** : to wear down : do away with : RAZE, DESTROY; *also* : ANNUL, RESCIND ⟨~ price controls after the war⟩ **4** : to take to pieces : DISMOUNT **syn** see STRIP

dis·man·tle·ment \ᵊ'==mənt\ *n* -s : the act of dismantling or the state of being dismantled; *esp* : deprivation of defenses

dis·man·tler \də'smant(ᵊ)lə(r), -maan-\ *n* -s : one that dismantles; *esp* : one who disassembles

dis·mask \dəs, (ˈ)dis+\ *vb* [MF *desmasquer*, fr. *des-* ¹dis- + *masque* mask — more at MASK] *archaic* : UNMASK

dis·mast \dəs, (ˈ)dis+\ *vt* [¹*dis-* + *mast* (n.)] : to remove the mast from : carry away or break off the mast of ⟨a ship ~*ed* in the storm⟩ — **dis·mast·ment** \-mənt\ *n* -s

¹**dis·may** \də'smā *sometimes* dəz'\ *vb* -ED/-ING/-S [ME *dismayen*, fr. (assumed) OF *desmaiier* (whence Sp *desmayar* to dishearten, depress), fr. OF *des-* ¹dis- + *-maiier* (as in *esmaiier* to dismay, fr. — assumed — VL *exmagare*, fr. L *ex* out of, from + a word stem of Gmc origin; akin to OHG *magan* to be able) — more at EX-, MAY] *vt* **1 a** : to take away the courage or resolution of with alarm or fear : DAUNT ⟨shocked and ~*ed* . . . by the condescension and contempt to be found at every turn —H.J.Morgenthau⟩ **b** : to check suddenly the enthusiasm of : DISILLUSION, DISENCHANT ⟨the boy was ~*ed* to see his idol drunk and in disarray⟩ **c** : UPSET, PERTURB, ALARM ⟨the naïve scientific belief that the whole is nothing but its parts which so ~*ed* and irritated Goethe —Philip Toynbee⟩ **2** : to put to rout : SUBDUE ~ *vi, obs* : to become daunted, disheartened, or terrified

syn APPALL, HORRIFY, DAUNT: DISMAY indicates disconcerting, disabling, unnerving, or depriving of morale and initiative through blended fear, dread, perplexity, or discouragement ⟨who in one lifetime sees all causes lost, herself *dismayed* and helpless —Muriel Rukeyser⟩ ⟨an opponent that more than once puzzled Roosevelt, and in the end flatly *dismayed* him —H.L.Mencken⟩ APPALL suggests striking with overwhelming dread or with powerlessness before the monstrous, enormous, or shocking ⟨*appalled* by the magnitude of the tragedy —C.G.Bowers⟩ ⟨the ruffians were so utterly *appalled*, not only by the false powers of magic, but by veritable powers of majesty and eloquence, that they let her do what she would —Charles Kingsley⟩ ⟨the immense modern Cosmos in which we live — the great Creation of granite, planned in such immeasurable proportions, and moved by so pitiless a mechanism, that it sometimes *appalls* even its own creators —L.P.Smith⟩ HORRIFY indicates striking with horror at the ghastly or gruesome or revulsion at the hideously offensive; weakened, it is a synonym for *shock* ⟨to developed sensibilities the facts of war are revolting and *horrifying* —Aldous Huxley⟩ ⟨she *horrified* London society by pouring hot tea on a gentleman who displeased her —*Amer. Guide Series: Va.*⟩ ⟨Massachusetts owners, *horrified* by the loss of profits —*Amer. Guide Series: Mass.*⟩ DAUNT indicates a cowing, subduing, disheartening, or frightening in a venture requiring courage ⟨no adventure *daunted* her and risks stimulated her —Havelock Ellis⟩ ⟨the attempt to draw the future frontiers of Europe is a *daunting* and ticklish enterprise —*Times Lit. Supp.*⟩

²**dismay** \"\ *n* -s **1 a** : sudden loss of courage or resolution by reason of alarm or fear : CONSTERNATION ⟨facing with ~ a force too powerful to resist⟩ **b** : sudden loss of enthusiasm for something : DISILLUSIONMENT, DISENCHANTMENT **c** : PERTURBATION, ALARM ⟨views with ~ the fact that one of his sons may choose to become a composer —Huntington Hartford⟩ **2** *obs* : a condition or a result that dismays : DESTRUCTION, RUIN **syn** see FEAR

dis·mayed·ness \-ā(ə)dnəs\ *n* -ES : the quality or state of being dismayed : DISMAY

dis·may·ful \-āfəl\ *adj* : TERRIFYING, APPALLING, ALARMING — **dis·may·ful·ly** \-f(ə)lē\ *adv*

dis·may·ing·ly *adv* : in a dismaying manner ⟨since then . . . things had changed ~ for the worse —Joseph Wechsberg⟩

disme \'dīm\ *n* -s [fr. obs. E, tenth, fr. obs. F, fr. MF — more at DIME] : a U.S. ten-cent coin struck in 1792

dis·member \dəs, (ˈ)dis +\ *vt* -ED/-ING/-S [ME *dismembren*, fr. OF *desmembrer*, fr. *des-* ¹dis- + *membre* member, limb — more at MEMBER] **1 a** : to cut or tear off or disjoin the limbs, members, or parts of ⟨found a ~*ed* corpse in the rubbish heap⟩ ⟨piece by piece Mexico was being ~*ed* —R.A.Billington⟩ **b** : to tear into pieces : take apart roughly or divide (a whole) into sections or separate units ⟨~*ed* an old apple barrel —P.K.Thomajan⟩; *also* : MANGLE, MUTILATE ⟨amounts to ~*ing* the facts in order to make them fit a rather farfetched preconception —J.O.Nelson⟩ **c** : DISMANTLE ⟨~*ed* their wagons, loaded them upon rafts —*Amer. Guide Series: Oregon*⟩ **2** *obs* : LOP, SEVER **3** *archaic* : to deprive of membership **4** : to make (a tributary of a river) into an independent stream by a change of geologic conditions (as the submergence of the lower part of a valley)

dis·mem·ber·ment \də'smembə(r)mənt\ *n* -s : the act of dismembering or the state of being dismembered : division into separate parts or units : SEPARATION : MUTILATION ⟨the ~ of great estates —F.B.Millett⟩ ⟨the ~ of the Roman Empire —*Encyc. Americana*⟩ ⟨investigation revealed the ~ of the body after death⟩

¹**dis·miss** \də'smis\ *vb* -ED/-ING/-ES [modif. (influenced by *dis-*) of L *dimissus*, past part. of *dimittere*, fr. *di-* (fr. *dis-* apart) + *mittere* to send — more at DIS-, SMITE] *vt* **1 a** : to grant or furnish leave to depart : permit or cause to leave ⟨after instructing him, the master ~*ed* the servant⟩ **b** : to send away severally : DISBAND, DISPERSE ⟨~ one's retainers⟩; *specif* : to order (a military unit) to break ranks at the end of a formation **2 a** : to divorce (a wife) by sending away or repudiating **b** : REJECT ⟨forlorn as a ~*ed* suitor⟩ **3** : to send or remove from employment, enrollment, position, or office ⟨editors and journalists who express opinions in print that are opposed to the interests of the rich are ~*ed* —G.B.Shaw⟩ ⟨reserves the right to ~ a student at any time if his conduct is considered unsatisfactory —*Bull. of Meharry Med. Coll.*⟩; *specif* : to discharge (a military officer or cadet) without honor by reason of a sentence to dismissal by a general court-martial **4 a** : to put out of one's mind : cease further consideration of : refuse to consider seriously ⟨scarcely had the thought formed itself in my mind before I ~*ed* it as utterly incredible —W.H.Hudson †1922⟩ ⟨the older view . . . may now be ~*ed* as antiquated —Edward Sapir⟩ ⟨we may ~ these harmonizers as plainly ignorant of the history of religion —M.R.Cohen⟩ **b** : to put (a legal action or a party) out of judicial consideration : refuse to hear or hear further in court **5** : to put out (a batsman) in cricket ~ *vi* : to break ranks : DISPERSE ⟨when the drill was over the company ~*ed*⟩

syn DISCHARGE, CASHIER, DROP, SACK, FIRE, BOUNCE: DISMISS in the sense of letting go from employment, position, or service is more comprehensive in its use than any of its synonyms and less suggestive or rich in connotation ⟨spoke of the sovereign as receiving and holding all revenues, appointing and *dismissing* ministers, making treaties —F.A.Ogg & Harold Zink⟩ ⟨*dismissed* the night watchers from the room, and remained with her alone —George Meredith⟩ DISCHARGE is a more stringent term in reference to cessation of employment; it suggests a more positive and forceful termination, usu. permanent and often for cause ⟨you took workmen under pressure of the most extravagant assurances of competency, and found yourself next day involved in the necessity of *discharging* them for egregious ignorance of what they had been hired to do —Mary Austin⟩ ⟨although there was some evidence supporting the employer's claim that the employee was *discharged* for incompetence, the company has the obligation . . . to act in such a manner that there can be no doubt that they are *discharging* him and not merely laying him off —*Digest of Labor Relations Development*⟩ CASHIER is used in situations involving formal, decisive, summary dismissal with discredit from high position ⟨the few sentimental fanatics who . . . proceeded upon the assumption that academic freedom was yet inviolable, and so got themselves *cashiered*, and began posturing in radical circles as martyrs —H.L.Mencken⟩ ⟨it wasn't every decade that the republic fathered an Oriental proconsul or that a president *cashiered* him —Theodore Morrison⟩ DROP, SACK, FIRE and BOUNCE are all more or less informal. DROP is the mildest and is close to DISMISS in colorlessness ⟨he learned that he had been *dropped* from the army on May 31, 1834, for overstaying his leave of absence —W.J.Ghent⟩ SACK may indicate summary dismissal as contentious, incompetent, or no longer useful ⟨"If you insist on going beyond your authority—" "You can *sack* me" —Dorothy Sayers⟩ FIRE may indicate sudden, peremptory, and very decisive dismissal ⟨he was *fired* that afternoon when his drinking came to the boss's attention⟩ BOUNCE may imply being kicked out, that is, being dismissed abruptly and forcefully ⟨Wallace had to *bounce* him and 20 other AAA employees because too many people complained that the group was trying to change the world too fast —*Time*⟩ **syn** see in addition EJECT

²**dismiss** *n* -ES *obs* : DISMISSAL

dis·mis·sal \də'smisəl\ *n* -s **1** : the act of dismissing or the fact or state of being dismissed ⟨requesting the ~ of a new employee for incompetence⟩ ⟨Ross's robust ~ of Kant's theory of knowledge —*Times Lit. Supp.*⟩ **2** : the church rite of dismissing a congregation after a eucharistic service

dismissal wage *n* : a sum paid in addition to salary or wages to an employee discharged through no fault of his own : SEVERANCE PAY

dis·missed time \də'smist-, (ˈ)di'smis\ *n* : time provided in some communities for the religious education of students or for recreation one day a week by the early dismissal of schools

dis·miss·ing·ly \ᵊ'===\ *adv* : in a manner that dismisses ⟨they picked things up and shoved them ~ aside —Mary-Carter Roberts⟩

dis·mis·sion \də'smishən\ *n* -s [modif. (influenced by *dis-*) of L *dimission-, dimissio*, fr. *dimissus* + *-ion-, -io* -ion] **1** : the act of dismissing or of being dismissed **2** *archaic* : the document or the form of expression by which an act of dismissing is effected

dis·mis·sive \də'smisiv, (ˈ)di'smis-\ *adj* **1** : giving dismissal or serving to dismiss : REJECTING, REPUDIATING **2** : DISDAINFUL

dis·moded \də'smōdəd, (ˈ)di'smō-\ *adj* [¹*dis-* + *moded*] : OUTMODED

¹**dis·mount** \dəs, (ˈ)dis+\ *vb* [prob. modif. (influenced by *dis-* & *mount*) of MF *desmonter*, fr. *des-* ¹dis- + *monter* to mount — more at MOUNT] *vi* **1** *obs* : to come down : DESCEND **2** : to alight from or as if from a horse ⟨I preferred to ~ to ease the horse's burden —Ana Beker⟩ ⟨I took a taxi to within a third of a mile of the stadium, ~*ing* when my vehicle could no longer advance —A.J.Liebling⟩ ~ *vt* **1 a** : to remove often forcibly from a mount or a mounting or something felt to resemble one of these ⟨enabling the ~*ed* motorist to reach his urban destination by swift public transport —Lewis Mumford⟩; *esp* : UNHORSE ⟨I should like to ~ my men . . . and send the horses to the rear —Oliver La Farge⟩ **b** *obs* : to bring or force down from a height; *also* : to deprive of honor or authority : DEGRADE **2** *archaic* : to alight from (as a horse) **3** : to take down or apart from an assembled condition : DISASSEMBLE ⟨~ a revolver for cleaning⟩ **syn** see DESCEND

²**dismount** \"\ *n* : the act of dismounting; *specif* : movement to the floor from a position on a gymnastics apparatus

dis·mount·able \-əbəl\ *adj* : capable of being dismounted : removable from a carriage or mounting : easily disassembled

dis·mutation \ˌdis+\ *n* [¹*dis-* + *mutation*] : a process of simultaneous oxidation and reduction : DISPROPORTIONATION — used esp. of compounds taking part in biological processes ⟨~ of pyruvate to acetate and lactate⟩

dis·mutative \dəs, (ˈ)dis +\ *adj* : relating to or causing dismutation

dis·na \'diznə\ [by alter.] *chiefly Scot* : does not

dis·nature \dəs, (ˈ)dis +\ *vt* [ME *disnaturen*, fr. MF *desnaturer*, fr. *des-* ¹dis- + *nature* — more at NATURE] : to make unnatural : deprive of a natural quality or appearance

dis·ney·esque \ˌdiznē'esk\ *adj, usu cap* [Walter E. *Disney* b1901 American cartoonist and producer of animated motion-picture cartoons + E *-esque*] : resembling or having the character of an animated cartoon made by the Walt Disney studios ⟨the animals take part in circus acts of the most . . . *Disneyesque* nature —May L. Becker⟩ ⟨it has nothing in novelty on a *Disneyesque* railroad that runs 38 miles south of Myitkyina —*Newsweek*⟩

dis·obedience \ˌdis+\ *n* [ME, fr. MF *desobedience*, fr. *des-* ¹dis- + *obedience*] : refusal to obey or negligence in obeying a command : violation or disregard of a rule or prohibition ⟨the lads try to excel one another in mischief and ~ —Willa Cather⟩ ⟨that peculiar taint of barbarism which makes men prefer occasional ~ to systematic liberty —H.T.Buckle⟩

dis·obedient \"+\ *adj* [ME, fr. MF *desobedient*, fr. *des-* ¹dis- + *obedient*] **1 a** : refusing or neglecting to obey : disobeying an order or rule **b** : characterized by habitual disobedience : UNRULY ⟨a woman cursed with noisy and ~ boys⟩ **2** *archaic* : not yielding : INTRACTABLE — **dis·obediently** \"+\ *adv*

dis·obey \"+\ *vb* [ME *disobeyen*, fr. MF *desobeir*, fr. *des-* ¹dis- + *obeir* to obey — more at OBEY] *vt* : to refuse to obey : neglect to obey : transgress the commands, prohibitions, or rules of : violate the laws of ⟨a child prone to ~ a parent⟩ ⟨a driver who consistently ~*s* traffic regulations⟩ ⟨~*ing* one's conscience⟩ ~ *vi* : to be disobedient : refuse or fail to obey orders or to abide by rules or laws ⟨often punished for ~*ing*⟩

dis·obligation \dəs, (ˌ)dis+\ *n* [¹*dis-* + *obligation*] **1** *archaic* : an act that purposely inconveniences or offends : AFFRONT **2** *archaic* : the state or sensation of being disobliged : GRUDGE

dis·oblige \ˌdis+\ *vt* [F *désobliger*, fr. MF *desobliger*, fr. *des-* ¹dis- + *obliger* to oblige — more at OBLIGE] **1** : to go purposely counter to the wishes of : be unaccommodating to ⟨had promised to do a friend a favor but was finally forced to ~ him for lack of time⟩ **2 a** : to cause inconvenience to : put out : INCOMMODE ⟨the action was not offensive to him but proved somewhat *disobliging*⟩ **b** : AFFRONT, OFFEND ⟨not wishing to ~ a man who could be of so much help to him⟩ — **dis·oblig·er** \-ə(r)\ *n*

dis·oblig·ing·ly *adv* : in a manner that disobliges : UNACCOMMODATINGLY

dis·occupation \dəs, (ˌ)dis +\ *n* [¹*dis-* + *occupation*] : the state of being idle or unoccupied : INACTIVITY, LEISURE

di·sodium \(ˈ)dī +\ *adj* [*di-* + *sodium*] : containing two atoms of sodium in the molecule

disodium phosphate *or* **disodium hydrogen phosphate** *n* : SODIUM PHOSPHATE 1b

di·somatic \ˌdī +\ *adj* [*di-* + *somatic*] : characterized by disomaty

di·so·ma·ty \dī'sōməd-ē\ *n* -ES [*disomatic* + *-y*] : duplication in somatic cells of the chromosome number through a division of chromosomes without subsequent nuclear division

di·some \'dī,sōm\ *n* -s [F, fr. *di-* + *-some* (body)] : a chromosome set having members paired (as in a normal somatic cell)

di·so·mic \(ˈ)dī'sōmik\ *adj* [*di-* + *-somic*] **1** : having one or more chromosomes duplicated but not an entire genome duplicated **2** : of, relating to, or characterized by a disome

di·so·mus \dī'sōməs\ *n, pl* **diso·mi** \-,mī\ *or* **disomuses** [NL, fr. *di-* + *-somus*] : a 2-bodied monster

dis·operation \dəs, (ˌ)dis +\ *n* [¹*dis-* + *-operation* (as in *cooperation*)] : any harmful effect other than direct competition of the aggregation or crowding of two or more organisms or kinds of organism in a limited area that is manifested directly (as through accumulation of toxic wastes) or indirectly (as through alteration of the habitat by growth or feeding habits of one or more members of the population)

dis·operative \"+\ *adj* [¹*dis-* + *-operative* (as in *cooperative*)] : hostile to or hindering cooperation ⟨the balance between the cooperative, altruistic tendencies and those which are ~ and egoistic —M.F.A.Montagu⟩ ⟨working in ~ conditions⟩

disopinion *n* [¹*dis-* + *opinion*] *obs* : DISESTEEM

dis·orb \dəs, (ˈ)dis +\ *vt* -ED/-ING/-S [¹*dis-* + *orb* (orbit)] : to throw (as an asteroid or comet) out of its normal orbit

¹**dis·order** \dəs, (ˈ)dis +, *sometimes* dəz *or* (ˈ)diz +\ *vb* [¹*dis-* + *order* (v.)] *vt* **1 a** : to disturb the order of : DISARRANGE **b** : to disturb the regular or normal functions of (as the body or mind) : cause a disordered condition in ⟨eating enough to ~ his digestive system⟩ ⟨events shocking enough to ~ the mind⟩ **2** *archaic* : DISCONCERT : DISCOMPOSE ~ *vi* : to fall into disorder or confusion : become disordered

syn DISORDER, DISARRANGE, DERANGE, DISORGANIZE, UNSETTLE, and DISTURB can mean to undo the fixed or proper order of something. DISORDER implies the alteration to its marked detriment of a given, desirable, or proper order, applying commonly to what depends upon being properly ordered for its best functioning or effectiveness ⟨to *disorder* the carefully arranged contents of a drawer⟩ ⟨reasoning *disordered* by strong emotion⟩ ⟨a country *disordered* by war⟩ DISARRANGE implies merely the changing of a fixed, desirable, or neat order or arrangement ⟨*disarranged* his carefully brushed hair⟩ ⟨*disarrange* the normal functioning of the household⟩ DERANGE implies a marked throwing out of proper order of parts which exist in their best state or function best in a given order or interrelationship, differing from the previous words in implying a resulting confusion or a destruction of normal or healthy conditions ⟨within the power of man irreparably to *derange* the combinations of inorganic matter and organic life —Russell Lord⟩ ⟨the news of his cousin Anne's engagement . . . *deranged* his best plan of domestic happiness —Jane Austen⟩ ⟨[war] lays its blight on whole peoples, *deranges* their life —C.E. Montague⟩ DISORGANIZE implies the destruction of the order and functioning of an organization of interrelated things, suggesting, therefore, a disordering that runs through an entire system, breaking it up or seriously impeding its full operation or effectiveness ⟨world economy and national currencies in 1948 were highly *disorganized* and unbalanced —*Collier's Yr. Bk.*⟩ ⟨an expenditure which would *disorganize* his whole scheme of finance —John Buchan⟩ ⟨the normal metabolic activity of this organ is *disorganized* by infections —H.R. Litchfield & L.H.Dembo⟩ UNSETTLE suggests a disordering or disarrangement of a fixed or desirable order, or a calm attendant upon such an order, and a resulting instability and often turbulence ⟨learned enough of it to *unsettle* his religious beliefs —R.A.Hall b.1911⟩ ⟨war *unsettles* the institutions and practices of even the firmest culture⟩ ⟨*unsettle* the thoughts⟩ DISTURB implies a force that unsettles or disarranges; often it suggests an interruption that affects a settled order or condition ⟨the headlights also *disturbed* the slumbers of the night —Sherwood Anderson⟩ ⟨those emotions which *disturb* the reason —Virginia Woolf⟩ ⟨the warps and strains of civilized life, with its excessive industrialism and militarism, seem to *disturb* the wholesome balance of even the humblest elements of the possessive and aesthetic instincts —Havelock Ellis⟩ ⟨a noise that *disturbs* one's thoughts⟩

²**disorder** \"\ *n* [¹*dis-* + *order* (n.)] **1** : a condition marked by lack of order, system, regularity, predictability, or dependability : the act or fact of disturbing, neglecting, or breaking away from a due order ⟨the scientific view . . . regards ~ and inexplicable irregularity as a scandal —W.R.Inge⟩ ⟨those rooms are all in ~, there has been hurried packing —Charles Dickens⟩ **2 a** : breach of public order : disturbance of the peace of society **b** : MISCONDUCT, MISDEED, MISDEMEANOR ⟨she had been a sinner from her early youth and . . . continued her ~*s* even until an advanced age —Willa Cather⟩ **c** : an instance of such disorder or misconduct ⟨widespread lawlessness in the 1850's appeared . . . in lynchings of abolitionists and in the ~*s* in Kansas —H.E.Davis⟩ **3** : a derangement of function : an abnormal physical or mental condition : SICKNESS, AILMENT, MALADY ⟨an intestinal ~⟩ ⟨suffering from a nutritional ~ caused by lack of calcium and phosphorus —*Time*⟩ **syn** see CONFUSION

disordered *adj* **1** *obs* : morally reprehensible : UNRULY **2** : marked or characterized by disorder: as **a** : lacking a visible order or organization ⟨the country was ~ for years, but gradually white traders . . . began to establish a foothold in the region of the Lower Congo —Tom Marvel⟩ **b** : existing in turmoil : lacking a central organizing control ⟨a ~ country with a history of successive revolutions⟩ **c** (1) : not functioning in an organically normal orderly healthy way ⟨during hysterical conditions various functions of the human body are ~⟩ (2) : mentally unbalanced ⟨a ~ patient⟩ : not functioning in a sane manner ⟨a ~ mind⟩ — **dis·or·dered·ly** *adv* — **dis·or·dered·ness** *n*

dis·orderliness \"+\ *n* : the quality or state of being disorderly ⟨it gives a certain typical ~ to our behavior which baffles some foreign observers —Dean Acheson⟩

¹**dis·orderly** \"+\ *adv* [¹*dis-* + *orderly* (adv.)] *archaic* : in a disorderly manner : without law or order : IRREGULARLY, CONFUSEDLY, TURBULENTLY

²**disorderly** \"\ *adj* [¹*dis-* + *orderly* (adj.)] **1 a** : not complying with the restraints of law and order : UNRULY, TURBULENT ⟨a weak government and a ~ people⟩ **b** : constituting a public nuisance by reason of behavior that violates public order or is offensive to public decency; *esp, of a person* : guilty of disorderly conduct **2** : not in order : marked by disorder : DISARRANGED : lacking a reasonable or apparent system ⟨a ~ array of books⟩ ⟨romantic artists were rather expected to live ~ lives at odds with God, man, the Devil, and various mistresses —*New Yorker*⟩ ⟨help correct ~ market conditions —*Federal Reserve System*⟩ ⟨the usual ~ bustle that masks the deadly efficiency of the French people —Osbert Sitwell⟩

disorderly conduct *n, law* : one of a wide range of petty offenses chiefly against public order and decency that fall short of indictable misdemeanors, that are usu. provided for by municipal ordinances, and that are tried before a magistrate

disorderly house *n* : BROTHEL

disorders *pl of* DISORDER, *pres 3d sing of* DISORDER

dis·ordinate \dəs, (ˈ)dis+\ *adj* [ME *disordinat*, fr. ¹*dis-* + *ordinat* ordinate — more at ORDINATE] *archaic* : INORDINATE, IMMODERATE

dis·organization \dəs, (ˌ)dis +\ *n* [F *désorganisation*, fr. *désorganiser* + *-ation*] : the act of disorganizing or the quality or state of being disorganized ⟨accomplish the total ~ of the existing government⟩ ⟨suffering from a ~ of mind incident to mild hysteria⟩

dis·organize \dəs, (ˈ)dis +\ *vt* [F *désorganiser*, fr. *dés-* ¹dis- + *organiser* to organize, fr. ML *organizare* — more at ORGANIZE] : to destroy the organic structure or regular or systematic arrangement of : deprive of organization : throw into disorder or confusion : DISARRANGE ⟨an attempt to ~ the government failed⟩ ⟨I became so jumpy and *disorganized* that I am unable to concentrate on anything —John Willig⟩ **syn** see DISORDER

disorganized *adj* : lacking coherence, system, or central guiding principle or agency ⟨analyzing the needs of the country's ~ areas⟩ ⟨two thousand pages of ~, muddy prose —*Saturday Rev.*⟩

dis·organizer \dəs, (ˈ)dis +\ *n* : one that disorganizes or disrupts

dis·orient \dəs, (ˈ)dis +\ *vt* [F *désorienter*, fr. *dés-* ¹dis- + *orienter* to orient — more at ORIENT] **1 a** : to cause to lose bearings ⟨by the time he had made three turns, one to the right and two to the left, he was totally ~*ed* and had to seek directions⟩ **b** : to cause to lose identity **2** : to confuse (as in one's sense of what is right or proper) to the point of causing to act irrationally or of preventing from acting purposively or sensibly ⟨it has ~*ed* and confused the electorate —Daniel James⟩ **3** : to cause to deviate from correct or normal alignment ⟨~ magnetic domains by heat⟩

dis·orientate \dəs, (ˈ)dis +\ *vt* [¹*dis-* + *orient* + *-ate*] **1** : to turn from the east or from an eastward course **2** : DISORIENT

dis·orientation \dəs, (ˌ)dis+\ *n* **1** : the state of being disorientated ⟨takes for granted that we all recognize our homelessness, that we all believe the rootlessness and ~ of his hero to be typical —H.E.Clurman⟩ **2** : an often transient state of mental confusion esp. as to time, place, or identity resulting from a toxic condition caused by disease, drugs, or other agency — compare DELIRIUM

disoriented *adj* **1 a** : markedly displaced from a normal, usual, or accustomed relationship with others or with the world ⟨his fellow employees are all badly ~ . . . and include a homicidal pastrymaker, a sluttish salesgirl, and a former German petty functionary —*New Yorker*⟩ **b** : confused as to aim or purpose ⟨the present ~ condition of the world —*Yale Rev.*⟩ **2** : having no fixed or accustomed relationship with society or its more common ideologies : at sea ⟨a poet and intellectual of the most sophisticated and ~ type⟩ **3** : wandering in the mind : having no rational grasp of time, place, or one's own identity ⟨he was conscious but ~ and close to death —John Kobler⟩

disour *n* -s [ME, fr. OF *diseur* — more at DISEUR] *obs* : STORYTELLER, JESTER

dis·own \dəs, (ˈ)dis +\ *vt* [¹*dis-* + *own*] **1 a** : to refuse to acknowledge as belonging to oneself : REPUDIATE ⟨the man ~*ed* the gun when he found it had been used to kill⟩ ⟨faithlessly ~*ing* a friend if it profited him to do so⟩ **b** : to dismiss or expel from the Society of Friends **2 a** : DENY, DISCLAIM

⟨I cannot ~ that I should like to go⟩ ⟨the prime minister ~*ed* any intention of pursuing a policy of isolation —*Collier's Yr. Bk.*⟩ **b :** to refuse to acknowledge the validity of ⟨the Jacobites ~*ed* any king but James II or a descendant⟩ ⟨every president ~*s* and disparages the doctrine of the indispensable man —R.H.Rovere⟩ **syn** see DISCLAIM

dis·own·ment \-mənt\ *n* -s **:** the act of disowning or the state of being disowned

disp *abbr* **1** dispatch; dispatcher **2** dispensary; dispenser

dis·palatalization \dəs, (ˈ)dis + \ *n* [¹*dis-* + *palatalization*] *phonetics* **:** a depriving of palatal quality

dis·par·age \dəˈsparij, -rēj *also* -per-, *esp in pres part* -rəj\ *vt* -ED/-ING/-S [ME *disparagen*, fr. MF *desparagier*, fr. OF, fr. *des-* ¹dis- + *-paragier* (fr. *parage* extraction, lineage, high birth, fr. *per* peer + *-age*) — more at PEER (equal)] **1 a** *obs* **:** to lower or degrade esp. by marriage to one socially inferior **b :** to lower in esteem or reputation **:** diminish the respect for ⟨the Labor party, in turn, is being carried further to the left . . . in an effort to ~ the Tory party —*New Republic*⟩ **c :** DISCOURAGE, DISHEARTEN **2 a** *obs* **:** to discredit or bring reproach upon by comparing with something inferior **:** lower in rank by actions or words **b :** to speak slightingly of **:** run down **:** DEPRECIATE ⟨I get very hot under the collar when I hear this country *disparaged* —Victor Ross⟩ ⟨I do not wish to ~ the bouillabaisse, which is a dish for heroes —A.T.Quiller-Couch⟩ **syn** see DECRY

dis·par·age·ment \-jmənt\ *n* -s [MF *desparagement*, fr. *desparagier* + *-ment*] **1 a :** diminution of esteem or standing **:** INDIGNITY, DISGRACE **b** *archaic* **:** marriage to one of an inferior social position; *also* **:** dishonor by reason of such a marriage ⟨it was regarded as no ~ for the daughter of a duke . . . to espouse a distinguished commoner —T.B.Macaulay⟩ **2 a :** the expression of a low opinion of something **:** DETRACTION ⟨these comparisons are certainly not to be taken in any way as a ~ **:** rather as a compliment —Douglas Stewart⟩ **b :** low opinion **:** CONTEMPT ⟨every age seems to develop a certain ~ of its immediate predecessor —P.H.Muir⟩

dis·par·ag·er \-jə(r)\ *n* -s **:** one that disparages ⟨hater of war and ~ of nationalism —W.P.Hall⟩

dis·par·ag·ing·ly *adv* **:** in a manner that disparages ⟨these mythological figures are occasionally described almost ~ as belonging "only to a story" —F.G.Hawley⟩

¹**dis·par·ate** \dəˈsparət *also* -ˈsper- *or* ˈdisp(ə)r-; *usu* -əd.+V\ *n* -s [L *disparatum*, fr. neut. of *disparatus*] **:** something disparate **:** one of two or more things so unequal or unlike that they cannot be compared with each other — usu. used in pl.

²**disparate** \"\ *adj* [L *disparatus*, past part. of *disparare* to separate, fr. *dis-* ¹dis- + *parare* to make ready, prepare — more at PARE] **1 a :** distinct in quality or character **:** UNEQUAL, DISSIMILAR ⟨cast as a young lady who has three ~ personalities —John McCarten⟩ ⟨connecting ~ thoughts purely by means of resemblances in the words expressing them —S.T. Coleridge⟩ ⟨a series of ~ biological essays strung loosely within a historical framework —L.C.Eiseley⟩ ⟨such ~ attractions as grand opera and game fishing —M.A.Santin⟩ **b :** comprising markedly dissimilar and unequal elements **:** not homogeneous ⟨a ~ aggregate of creeds, prayers, and songs —Joseph Kerman⟩ ⟨this most ~ genius of the middle ages —H.O.Taylor⟩ ⟨a poet's mind . . . is constantly amalgamating ~ experience —T.S.Eliot⟩; *specif, of polygamy and polyandry* **:** characterized by inequality of the plural partners **2** *of two or more statements* **:** having no definitive relation in common **:** connected only by some notion of great generality or by some interest of extreme catholicity — opposed to *connex* **3 :** indicating or stimulating dissimilar points on the retina of each eye **syn** see DIFFERENT

dis·par·ate·ly *adv* **:** in a disparate manner ⟨taken ~, item by item —R.H.Pearce⟩

dis·par·ate·ness *n* -ES **:** the quality or state of being disparate

dis·pa·ra·tum \ˌdispəˈräd·əm, -rāl\ *n, pl* **dispara·ta** \|d·ə\ [L — more at DISPARATE] **:** a disparate term or concept in logic

dis·par·i·ty \dəˈsparəd·ē, -ətē, -i *also* -per-\ *n* -ES [MF *desparité*, fr. LL *disparitat-, disparitas*, fr. L *dis-* ¹dis- + LL *paritat-, paritas* parity — more at PARITY] **:** the state of being disparate **:** marked difference (as in age, rank, grade, condition, quantity, quality, or kind) **:** DISSIMILARITY, INEQUALITY ⟨shocking ~ between the rich and the poor —A.E.Stevenson b.1900⟩ ⟨the present ~ between the military resources and her [Poland's] will to fight —O.D.Tolischus⟩ ⟨the tragicomic ~ which exists between man's aspirations and his accomplishments, between his yearning and his attaining —B.R.Redman⟩

dis·park \dəs, (ˈ)dis + \ *vt* [¹*dis-* + *park* (n.)] **:** to throw open (a private park); *esp* **:** to convert (a park) to something else than a private park ⟨Henry VIII decided to ~ the Duchy parks and turn them more profitably into pasture —A.L. Rowse⟩

dis·part \dəs, (ˈ)dis + \ *vb* [It & L; It *dispartire* to divide, separate, fr. L *dispertire, dispartire* to distribute, divide, fr. *dis-* ¹dis- + *partire* to divide, distribute — more at PART] *vt* **1** *archaic* **:** to put or force apart **:** SEPARATE, DIVIDE ⟨what face is this . . . peering through the ~*ed* branches? —R.L.Stevenson⟩ **2** *obs* **:** to divide into parts or portions ~ *vi, archaic* **:** to open up **:** SEPARATE, DIVIDE

dis·passion \dəs, (ˈ)dis + \ *n* [¹*dis-* + *passion*] **:** freedom from or lack of strong feeling **:** CALMNESS, DISPASSIONATENESS ⟨his own experience . . . is a deeply horrifying one, but he presents it with a noble ~ —M.R.Ridley⟩

dis·passionate \"+ \ *adj* [¹*dis-* + *passionate*] **:** free from the influence of passion or strong feeling **:** **a :** equitable of disposition **:** CALM, COOL, COMPOSED ⟨it was his fate in life to have his equanimity mistaken for pluck, whereas it was actually something much more ~ and much less virile —James Hilton⟩ **b :** calm in judgment **:** uninfluenced by prejudice, favoritism, or partisanship **:** JUDICIAL ⟨plumes himself upon this spirit, even when he is sufficiently ~ to perceive the ruin it works —Charles Dickens⟩ **syn** see FAIR

dis·passionately \"+ \ *adv* **:** in a dispassionate manner ⟨a scientist . . . does not praise or censure; he ~ studies the forces at work —Irving Kristol⟩

dis·passionateness \"+ \ *n* **:** the quality or state of being dispassionate

dis·passioned \"+ \ *adj, obs* **:** free from passion **:** DISPASSIONATE

¹**dis·patch** \dəˈspach *sometimes* ˈdi,s-\ *or* **des·patch** \dəˈs-\ *vb* -ED/-ING/-ES [Sp *despachar* or It *dispacciare*, fr. Prov *despachar* to get rid of, fr. MF *despeechier* to set free, fr. OF, fr. *des-* ¹dis- + *-peechier* (as in *empeechier* to hinder) — more at IMPEACH] *vt* **1 a :** to send off or away (as to a special destination) with promptness or speed often as a matter of official business ⟨~ a letter to one's superior reporting on progress⟩ ⟨~ troops to the scene of conflict⟩ ⟨~ a messenger to the king requesting military assistance⟩ ⟨organized and ~*ed* a motorcade over the proposed route —*Amer. Guide Series: Fla.*⟩ **b :** to perform the job of dispatcher of ⟨employed to ~ buses at a terminal⟩ ⟨~ seamen in a hiring hall⟩ ⟨the starter is better equipped to ~ elevators to maintain an even flow of traffic —*Dun's Rev.*⟩ ⟨truck ~*ing* and maintenance, which he had learned as a motor transport officer in the army, being the only trade he knew —Oakley Hall⟩ **2 a :** to get rid of (as by sending away) **:** DISMISS, DISCHARGE ⟨with the heavyset girl ~*ed* amid gaiety —Harriet LaBarre⟩ **b :** to put to death **:** KILL ⟨promptly seized the trap and ~*ed* the bear with one blow on the head —*Amer. Guide Series: Vt.*⟩ **c** *obs* **:** to rid or free oneself of **d** *obs* **:** to do away with (life) **3 a :** to dispose of rapidly or efficiently (as a piece of business) **:** execute quickly ⟨anxious to ~ the matter at hand and get on to other business⟩ **b :** to eat with avid concentration **:** clean up by eating ⟨~ a seven-course dinner without effort or pause⟩ ⟨the salad and frozen pudding were ~*ed* as promptly as the roast had been —Willa Cather⟩ ~ *vi, archaic* **:** to make haste **:** HASTEN **syn** see KILL, SEND

²**dispatch** \"\ *or* **despatch** \"\ *n* -ES [Sp *despacho* or It *dispaccio*, resp. fr. Sp *despachar* & It *dispacciare*] **1 :** the act of dispatching: as **a** *obs* **:** DISMISSAL, DISCHARGE; *esp* **:** official dismissal **b :** the act of putting to death **:** KILLING ⟨her well-planned loathing of Scarpia, and her equally determined ~ of him once her plan of action was clear —*Saturday Rev.*⟩ **c** (1) **:** prompt settlement or disposal (as of an item of business) ⟨concerned more with grievances and their redress than with the ~ of the crown's business —T.E.May⟩ (2) **:** quick riddance **d :** a sending off esp. to a particular destination ⟨requested the ~ of two companies to the front⟩ ⟨the ~ of goods trains from important centers of traffic —O.S.Nock⟩ **:** SHIPMENT ⟨fine white clay being bagged for ~ to the potteries —L.D. Stamp⟩ **2 a :** a message dispatched or sent with speed; *esp* **:** an important official message often in cipher sent by an officer of the diplomatic, military, or naval service of a government ⟨his military record brought him three mentions in ~*es* —*Current Biog.*⟩ ⟨~ to the war department via the state department from . . . the consul at Tsingtao —J.D.Morris⟩ **b :** a news item sent with promptness or speed by a correspondent to a newspaper or news agency **3 :** promptness or exactness and efficiency ⟨the gallery stages its auctions with such ~ and charm that one might be attending a cunningly directed play —*New Yorker*⟩ **4** *Brit* **:** EXPRESS 1c **syn** see HASTE

dispatch boat *n* **:** an official boat for the conveying of dispatches

dispatch box *or* **dispatch case** *n* **1 :** an oblong box or case usu. with a lock for carrying dispatches or other papers **2** *chiefly Brit* **:** a stiff case (as of metal) in the style of a briefcase

dis·patch·er *also* **des·patch·er** \-chə(r)\ *n* -s **:** one that dispatches or expedites usu. as a vocation: as **a :** an employee of a transportation company who directs the departures of trains, planes, buses, trucks, boats, or other vehicles according to traveling conditions and in the best interests of efficient service **b :** one that assigns jobs to waiting seamen in a hiring hall **c :** one that expedites repair service or delivery of materials or goods within a plant or for customers **d :** a telephone local test deskman who directs the locating, testing, and clearing of trouble on subscriber lines **e :** one that upon receiving reports of forest fire from lookouts organizes men and equipment to combat it **f :** one that directs the departure of passenger elevators (as from the main floor of a large building) ⟨worked as ~ at a big hotel⟩ **g :** one that receives information about crimes and transmits it by radio to police patrols **h :** one that directs the movement of oil or gas into and through pipeline systems or the disposition of loads and generating capacity on an electric power system **i :** a telegraph worker who directs the flow of messages during times of wire shortage or emergency or who assigns additional personnel when needed **j :** MOTOR BOSS

dis·patch·ful \-chfəl\ *adj, archaic* **:** fitted to achieve or bent upon achieving an end with dispatch; *also* **:** HASTY

dis·patch·ment \-chmənt\ *n* -s **:** the act of dispatching ⟨the first ~ of workers to the U.S. —*Nassau (Bahamas) Guardian*⟩

dispatch money *n* **:** a money allowance given to a charterer of a ship by the owner of it for any shortening in the lay days stipulated in the contract between them

dispatch note *n* **:** a tag required on a parcel-post package in international mail giving facts (as weight, postage, names of sender and addressee, and sender's directions to the foreign post office if the parcel is undeliverable) that are essential to the handling of the package

dispatch rider *n* **:** a bearer of military dispatches traveling usu. by motorcycle

dis·pauper \dəs, (ˈ)dis + \ *vt* [¹*dis-* + *pauper* (n.)] **:** to deprive of the claim of a pauper to public support **:** deprive of the privilege of suing in forma pauperis

dis·pauperize \"+ \ *vt* [¹*dis-* + *pauperize*] **:** to free from pauperism or from paupers

dis·peace \dəs, (ˈ)dis + \ *n* [¹*dis-* + *peace*] **:** DISSENSION, STRIFE, TURMOIL ⟨~ between the two countries⟩ ⟨even marriage offered no lasting balm to his inner ~ —J.B.Noss⟩

dis·pel \dəˈspel\ *vt* **dispelled; dispelled; dispelling; dispels** [L *dispellere*, fr. *dis-* ¹dis- + *pellere* to push, drive, strike — more at PULSE] **:** to drive away by scattering **:** clear away **:** DISSIPATE ⟨~ a mist⟩ ⟨~ one's doubts by ascertaining the facts⟩ ⟨~ illusions⟩ **syn** see SCATTER

dis·pel·ler \-lə(r)\ *n* -s **:** one that dispels

dispend *vt* -ED/-ING/-S [ME *despenden*, fr. OF *despendre*, fr. L *dispendere* to weigh out — more at DISPENSE] **1** *obs* **:** SPEND, EXPEND **2** *obs* **:** DISTRIBUTE, DISPENSE

dis·pen·di·ous \dəˈspendēəs, (ˈ)di¦s-\ *adj* **:** EXPENSIVE, COSTLY; *also* **:** EXTRAVAGANT — **dis·pen·di·ous·ly** *adv*

dis·pens·abil·i·ty \dəˌspen(t)səˈbiləd·ē, (ˌ)di,-, -ətē, -i\ *n* -ES **:** the quality or state of being dispensable ⟨his ~ to his corporation and his corporation's indispensability to him are bound to remain the crux of his problem —John McDonald⟩

dis·pens·able \dəˈspen(t)səbəl, (ˈ)di¦s-\ *adj* [ML *dispensabilis*, fr. L *dispensare* + *-abilis* -able] **1** *obs* **a :** REMITTABLE **b :** PARDONABLE, ALLOWABLE **2 :** capable of being dispensed with **:** not essential ⟨the communications machines will render excess and ~ whole assembly lines and whole echelons of supervisory employees —Irwin Edman⟩ — **dis·pen·sa·ble·ness** *n* -ES — **dis·pen·sa·bly** *adv*

dis·pen·sa·ry \dəˈspen(t)s(ə)rē, -ri\ *n* -ES [ML *dispensaria* storeroom, pantry, fr. L *dispensare* to distribute + *-aria* -ary] **1 :** a place where medicines or medical or dental aid are dispensed to ambulant patients ⟨a ~ in an industrial plant⟩ **2 :** a liquor store in some southern states (as So. Carolina) where by the dispensary law intoxicating liquors are sold but not to be drunk on the premises

dis·pen·sa·tion \ˌdispənˈsāshən, ˌdiˌspen-\ *n* -s [ME *dispensacioun*, fr. ML, LL, & L; ML *dispensation-, dispensatio* exemption, pardon, fr. LL, arrangement, administration, fr. L, distribution, fr. *dispensatus* (past part. of *dispensare* to distribute) + *-ion-, -io* -ion — more at DISPENSE] **1 a** (1) **:** ORDERING, ADMINISTRATION, MANAGEMENT ⟨under the new ~ private distillers are first to be licensed and then gradually bought out —D.W.McConnell⟩; *specif* **:** a divine ordering and administration of worldly affairs (2) **:** a system of principles, promises, and rules divinely ordained and administered **:** the divine economy ⟨the Mosaic ~⟩ ⟨the Christian ~⟩ (3) **:** a period of history during which a particular divine revelation has predominated in the affairs of mankind (4) **:** any general state or ordering of things ⟨the triumph of the predatory dog-eat-dog ~ —John Gassner⟩ **b :** an arrangement or provision esp. of providence or nature; *also* **:** FAVOR ⟨the 400 merino sheep that he had purchased by special ~ from the Escurial royal flock of Spain —*Amer. Guide Series: Vt.*⟩ **2 :** a dispensing with or doing without something **:** remission of a sin **:** exemption from a rule of civil or ecclesiastical law or from an impediment, vow, or oath **3 a :** the act of dispensing **:** a dealing out **:** DISTRIBUTION ⟨a ship's pharmacist concerns himself with the ~ of medicines⟩ **b :** something dispensed or distributed ⟨one of the most remarkable cultural ~*s* in the country's history, the paperback book —T.E.Cooney⟩ **4 :** formal authorization by a fraternal organization (as for the purpose of forming a chapter) ⟨four other Freemasons met to petition the Grand Lodge of Louisiana for a ~ to organize a lodge at Brazoria —*Amer. Guide Series: Texas*⟩ — **dis·pen·sa·tion·al** \ˌ=(ˌ)=ˈsāshənᵊl, -shnəl\ *adj*

dis·pen·sa·tion·al·ism \ˌ=(ˌ)=ˈ=(=)=ˌizəm\ *n* -s **:** adherence to or advocacy of a system of interpreting history in terms of a series of God's dispensations

dispensative *adj* [ML *dispensativus*, fr. L *dispensatus* + *-ivus* -ive] **1** *obs* **:** ADMINISTRATIVE **2** *obs* **:** granting or serving to grant dispensation

dispensator *n* -s [ME *dispensatour*, fr. ML *dispensator*, fr. L, household manager, treasurer, fr. *dispensatus* + *-or*] **1** *obs* **:** DISPENSER **2** *obs* **:** one that manages or administers

¹**dis·pen·sa·to·ry** \dəˈspen(t)səˌtōrē, -tȯr-, -ri\ *n* -ES [ML *dispensatorium*, fr. L *dispensatus* + *-orium* -ory] **1 :** a book or medicinal formulary containing a systematic description of most of the drugs and preparations used in medicine — compare PHARMACOPOEIA **2 :** DISPENSARY

²**dispensatory** *adj* [ML *dispensatorius*, fr. L *dispensatus* + *-orius* -ory] *obs* **:** DISPENSATIVE

¹**dispense** *n* -s [ME, expense, expenditure, supplies, fr. MF *despense*, fr. ML *dispensa*, fr. fem. of L *dispensus*, past part. of *dispendere* to weigh out] *obs* **:** EXPENSE, EXPENDITURE

²**dis·pense** \dəˈspen(t)s\ *vb* -ED/-ING/-S [ME *dispensen*, fr. ML, LL, & L; ML *dispensare* to exempt, pardon, grant a dispensation, fr. LL, to administer, fr. L, to distribute, fr. *dispensus*, past part. of *dispendere* to weigh out, fr. *dis-* ¹dis- + *pendere* to weigh — more at SPAN] *vt* **1 a :** to deal out in portions **:** DISTRIBUTE, GIVE, PROVIDE ⟨*dispensing* alms among the poor⟩ ⟨~ goodwill with each kindness⟩ **b :** ADMINISTER ⟨~ the sacraments⟩ ⟨~ justice in his own special way⟩ **c :** to deal with **:** HANDLE ⟨the smaller roles were *dispensed* by equally capable actors⟩ **2 :** to give dispensation (as from a vow) **:** RELEASE, EXEMPT ⟨~ a friend from keeping a promise⟩ ⟨in exceptional circumstances the dean of the faculty may . . . ~ the candidate from the oral examination —*Durham Univ. Calendar*⟩ **3 a :** to put up (a prescription or medicine) **b :** to prepare and distribute (medicines) to the sick ~ *vi* **1 a** *archaic* **:** to grant permission by exempting one from a law or obligation or the penalty for its infringement or neglect **b** *obs* **:** PERMIT, ALLOW **2 a :** to grant or arrange for special exemption from a law or obligation — used with *with* ⟨asked the king to ~ with statutes that prevented immediate action against the enemy⟩ **b :** to set aside or disregard something — used with *with* **c :** to do without something — used with *with* ⟨made an analysis of production to see how many men and jobs could be *dispensed* with⟩ ⟨~ with all formalities and get to the business at hand⟩ **3 :** to be rid **:** do away — used with *with* ⟨trying to ~ with the futile necessity of eating three times a day⟩ ⟨the design reduced framing at least 25 percent and *dispensed* with foundation and wooden sills —*Monsanto Mag.*⟩ **4** *obs* **:** HANDLE, DEAL **syn** see DISTRIBUTE

³**dispense** *n* -s *obs* **:** DISPENSATION

dis·pens·er \dəˈspen(t)sə(r)\ *n* -s [ME *dispenser, dispensour*, fr. *dispensen* + *-er* & *-our* -or] **:** one that dispenses ⟨a ~ of favors⟩ ⟨a ~ of justice⟩: as **a** *archaic* **:** a steward or manager of a household **b :** PHARMACIST **c :** one in charge of a dispensary (sense 2) in one of certain southern states **d :** a container that extrudes, sprays, or feeds out in convenient units something (as facial tissues, tape, perfume, pills) usu. sold or acquired in multiple units or in bulk **e :** a usu. mechanical device for vending merchandise (as candy, gum, or postage stamps) ⟨a soft-drink ~⟩

dispensible *adj, obs* **:** DISPENSABLE

dispensing power *n* **:** the authority of a judge or an executive (or certain of his agents) to suspend the operation of a specific statute or rule of law where the interests of justice can be better served by such action

dis·people \dəs, (ˈ)dis + \ *vt* [¹*dis-* + *people* (n.)] **:** DEPOPULATE ⟨a plague that nearly ~*s* a country⟩ ⟨~ the woods of all game⟩

di·spermic \(ˈ)dī + \ *adj* [*di-* + *-spermic*] **:** of, relating to, or involving dispermy

di·spermous \"+ \ *adj* [*di-* + *-spermous*] **:** having or producing two seeds

di·sper·my \ˈdīˌspərmē\ *n* -ES [ISV *di-* + *-spermy*] **:** the entrance of two spermatozoa into one egg — compare MONOSPERMY, POLYSPERMY

dis·per·sal \dəˈspər|səl, -pə̄s|, -pəis| *sometimes* |zəl\ *n* -s **:** the act or result of dispersing **:** DISPERSION, DISTRIBUTION; *esp* **:** the process or result of spreading by active migration or of passive transfer of organisms from one place to another

dispersal area *n* **:** an area adjacent to an airfield runway connected to the runway by taxi strips and used for parking airplanes in widely separated positions to protect them from enemy air attacks

dispersal bay *or* **dispersal point** *n* **:** a dispersed parking place for an airplane in a combat area usu. protected from enemy air attack by earth or concrete revetments

dis·per·sant \|sᵊnt\ *n* -s **:** a dispersing agent; *esp* **:** a substance (as a polyphosphate) for promoting the formation and stabilization of a dispersion of one substance in another — compare EMULSIFIER, SURFACE-ACTIVE AGENT

¹**dis·perse** \dəˈspərs, -pə̄s, -pəis\ *vb* -ED/-ING/-S [ME *dyspersen*, fr. MF *disperser*, fr. L *dispersus*, past part. of *dispergere* to scatter, fr. *dis-* ¹dis- + *-spergere* (fr. *spargere* to strew, scatter) — more at SPARK] *vt* **1 a :** to cause to break up and go in different ways **:** send or drive into different places **:** SCATTER ⟨his command was *dispersed* by a bayonet charge —T.R.Hay⟩ **b :** to cause to become spread widely **:** DISTRIBUTE ⟨the party left the bus and *dispersed* themselves to various hotels⟩ ⟨*dispersing* barges and crews along the route as convenient —C.S.Forester⟩; *esp* **:** to separate and distribute (as troops or planes) over a large area to avoid offering the enemy a concentrated target **c :** DISSIPATE, DISPEL ⟨the sun *dispersing* the vapors of the night⟩ ⟨this explanation had at least *dispersed* the feeling of weirdness that had gripped the colony —O.E. Rölvaag⟩ **2 :** to spread or distribute from a fixed or constant source: as **a :** to spread abroad from a center of supply or control **:** DISSEMINATE ⟨~ news throughout the state⟩ ⟨80 percent of the discharge of this river at Baghdad is *dispersed* in these marshes —Wilfred Thesiger⟩ **b :** to cause to diverge **c :** to break up (light) into colors of the spectrum by refraction or diffraction **d :** to distribute (as finely divided particles) more or less evenly throughout a liquid, gaseous, or solid medium with the formation of a two-phase system ⟨~ a pigment in an oil by grinding⟩ ~ *vi* **1 a :** to break up and move or scatter to different places or go in different directions ⟨the crowd *dispersed* at the first shot⟩ ⟨his senses . . . seemed to be *dispersing* hopelessly and uncontrollably all about him —Hanama Tasaki⟩ **b :** to become dispersed ⟨the particles *dispersed* throughout the mixture⟩ **2 :** to dispel itself **:** DISSIPATE ⟨the fog *dispersed* toward morning⟩ **syn** see SCATTER

²**dis·perse** \dəˈs-, (ˈ)di¦s-\ *adj* [L *dispersus*] **:** widely distributed by dispersion **:** DISPERSED ⟨vitamin B is so ~ in rice polishings that ten tons of raw material yields only an ounce of vitamin —A.C.Morrison⟩

dispersed harmony \(ˈ)=¦=-\ *n* **:** OPEN HARMONY

dis·persed·ly \dəˈspər|sədlē, -pə̄|, -pəi|, |stlē, -li\ *adv* **:** in a dispersed manner

dis·persed·ness \|sədnəs, |s(t)n-\ *n* -ES **:** the state of being dispersed

dispersed phase *or* **disperse phase** *n* **:** the phase in a two-phase system that consists of finely divided particles (as colloidal particles), droplets, or bubbles of one substance distributed through another substance — called also *discontinuous phase, internal phase*

disperse dye *or* **dispersed dye** *n* **:** an insoluble dye used in the form of a dispersion (as in water) for dyeing acetate and other synthetic fibers — see DYE table I

dis·pers·er \dəˈspərsər, -pə̄sə(r, -pəisə(r\ *n* -s **:** one that disperses

disperse system *n* **:** a two-phase system consisting of a dispersion medium and a dispersed phase **:** COLLOID 1b **:** DISPERSION 4b

dis·pers·ibil·i·ty \dəˌspərsəˈbiləd·ē, (ˌ)di,s-, -pə̄s-,-pəis-, -lətē, -i\ *n* -ES **:** the quality or state of being dispersible

dis·pers·ible \-səbəl\ *adj* **:** capable of being dispersed

dis·per·sion \dəˈspər|zhən, -pə̄|, -pəi|, |shən\ *n* -s [ME *dispersioun*, fr. MF *dispersion*, fr. L *dispersion-, dispersio*, fr. *dispersus* + *-ion-, -io* -ion] **1** *usu cap* **:** DIASPORA 1a **2 :** the act or process of dispersing or the state of being dispersed: **a :** the scattering of the values of a frequency distribution from their average **b :** the spreading of troops, weapons, vehicles, or airplanes over a wide area to avoid offering the enemy a concentrated target **c :** the spreading of chemical agents in warfare by means of a bursting charge in a container **d :** the scattering of projectiles or bombs fired or released under apparently identical conditions **3 a :** the selective separation of a nonhomogeneous emission in accordance with some characteristic (as wavelength, particle mass, speed, or energy); *esp* **:** the separation of light into colors by refraction or diffraction with formation of a spectrum **b :** a measure of the degree of dispersion for any region of the spectrum commonly being the derivative of the separation with respect to the chosen characteristic (as wavelength) — compare DISPERSIVE POWER **4 a :** a dispersed substance **:** DISPERSED PHASE **b :** a system (as an emulsion or suspension) consisting of a dispersed substance and the medium in which it is dispersed **:** COLLOID 1b **:** DISPERSE SYSTEM

dispersion medium *n* **:** the liquid, gaseous, or solid phase in a two-phase system in which the particles of the dispersed phase are distributed — called also *continuous phase, external phase*

dis·per·si·ty \|səd·ē\ *n* -ES [²*disperse* + *-ity*] **:** the state or the degree of chemical dispersion

dis·per·sive \|siv, |ziv\ *adj* [¹*disperse* + *-ive*] **:** of or belonging to dispersion **:** tending to disperse ⟨the modern society and the modern economy have been ~ —E.S.Griffith⟩ — **dis·per·sive·ly** \|səvlē, |zə-\ *adv* — **dis·per·sive·ness** \|sivnəs, |zi-\ *n* -ES

dispersive power *n* **:** the power of a transparent medium to

separate different colors of light by refraction as measured by the difference in refractivity for two specified widely differing wavelengths divided by the refractivity at some specified intermediate wavelength
dis·per·soid \ˌsȯid\ *n* -s [²*disperse* + *-oid*] **1 :** matter in a form produced by dispersion **:** DISPERSE SYSTEM **:** COLLOID 1b **2 :** DISPERSED PHASE
dis·personify \ˌdis+\ *vt* [¹*dis-* + *personify*] **:** to consider or call impersonal
dis·petal \dəs, (ˈ)dis+\ *vt* [¹*dis-* + *petal* (n.)] **:** to remove petals from **:** deprive of petals
dis·pharynx \dəs+\ *n, cap* [NL, fr. ¹*dis-* + *pharynx*] **:** a genus of spiruroid nematodes including destructive parasites of the proventriculus and gizzard of gallinaceous birds and usu. having intermediate stages in sow bugs
di·sphenoid \(ˈ)dī+\ *n* [*di-* + *sphenoid*] **1 :** a wedge-shaped crystal form of the tetragonal or orthorhombic system having four like triangular faces that correspond in position to alternate faces of the tetragonal or orthorhombic dipyramid and being symmetrical about each of three mutually perpendicular diad axes of symmetry in all classes except the tetragonal-disphenoidal in which the form is generated by an inverse tetrad axis of symmetry **2 :** a form of crystal bounded by eight scalene triangles arranged in pairs **:** the tetragonal scalenohedron — **di·sphenoidal** \(ˈ)dī+\ *adj*
dis·phol·i·dus \dəˈsfäləd əs\ *n, cap* [NL, fr. ¹*dis-* + *-pholidus* (fr. Gk *pholid-, pholis* scale of a reptile) — more at PHOLID-] **:** a genus of boigid snakes that includes the boomslang
di·spireme *also* **di·spirem** \(ˈ)dī+\ *n* [*di-* + *spireme*] **:** a supposed late phase in mitotic division characterized by association of each set of daughter chromosomes into a spireme and now usu. considered an observational artifact
di·spirit \də, (ˈ)di+\ *also* **dis·spirit** \də, (ˈ)di(s)+\ *vt* [¹*dis-* + *spirit* (n.)] **1** *obs* **:** to take away the vigor or force from **2 :** to deprive of cheerful or sanguine spirits **:** DEPRESS, DISCOURAGE ⟨~*ed* by their futile efforts —C.H.Grandgent⟩ ⟨a sparsely settled community laid out on ~*ing* flat lands —*Amer. Guide Series: N.Y. City*⟩ **syn** see DISCOURAGE
dispirited *adj* **1 :** marked by gloom of spirit, by a sense of personal defeat, or by a pessimistic outlook **:** DISCOURAGED, DEPRESSED, DOWNCAST ⟨had never seen a more ~ man than he when he lost the election⟩ **2 a :** lacking independent vigor or forcefulness **:** flaccid in moral quality ⟨the weakness doesn't lie in the pessimism of the younger writers so much as it lies in their rather ~ correctness and conformity —Malcolm Cowley⟩ **b :** lacking an essential spirit **:** FLAT **:** LIFELESS ⟨the black gummy ~ air —R.P.Warren⟩ **syn** see DOWNCAST
di·spir·it·ed·ly *adv* **:** in a dispirited manner ⟨working ~ at a job he would never finish⟩
di·spir·it·ed·ness *n* **:** the quality or state of being dispirited **:** DEJECTION, DEPRESSION
dispiriting *adj* **:** acting to dispirit **:** DISCOURAGING, DISHEARTENING, CHEERLESS ⟨one person whose struggle for existence was more hopeless and ~ than his —Erskine Caldwell⟩ ⟨no ~ rows of tenements are to be seen —Ellery Sedgwick⟩ **syn** see DISMAL
di·spir·it·ing·ly *adv* **:** in a dispiriting manner
di·spir·it·ment \-mənt\ *n* -s **:** the state of being dispirited or disheartened **:** DISCOURAGEMENT
dis·pit·e·ous \dəˈspid·ēəs, (ˈ)di¦s-\ *adj* [alter. of *despiteous*] *archaic* **:** CRUEL, SPITEFUL, PITILESS — **dis·pit·e·ous·ly** *adv*
dis·place \dəs, (ˈ)dis+\ *vt* [prob. fr. MF *desplacer*, fr. des- ¹dis- + *place* — more at PLACE] **1 a :** to remove from the usual or proper place **:** put out of place; *specif* **:** to expel or force to flee from home or homeland ⟨the war has *displaced* thousands of people⟩ **b :** to remove from an office or position of dignity **:** DISCHARGE, DEPOSE **c** *obs* **:** to drive away **:** BANISH **d :** to shift or redirect from a previous or usual objective or form of outlet ⟨in every society there are hatreds and frustrations which the movement of events ~*s* on chosen victims —Max Lerner⟩ **2 :** to crowd out **:** take the place of esp. by force **:** move from place by occupying the space **:** SUPPLANT ⟨the Bishop's Bible that immediately *displaced* the Great Bible as the ecclesiastical version in use in the churches —I.M.Price⟩ ⟨today, when barns have been *displaced* by garages —*Amer. Guide Series: Minn.*⟩; *specif* **:** to set free from chemical combination by taking the place of ⟨zinc ~*s* the hydrogen of dilute acids⟩ **3 :** to put (an object) in place of another **:** substitute (one thing) for another ⟨an effort . . . to ~ the American shoe with the English boot —*Encyc. Americana*⟩ **4 :** to subject to percolation **syn** see REPLACE
dis·place·able \-əbəl\ *adj* **:** that can be displaced
displaced person *n* **:** a person expelled, deported, or impelled to flee from his country of nationality or habitual residence by the forces or consequences of war or oppression — abbr. *DP*
displaced speech *n* **:** the use of a word to refer to something that is not present
dis·place·ment \-mənt\ *n* **1 a :** the act or process of displacing or the state of being displaced ⟨sideward ~ of the foundation of a house by earth pressure⟩ ⟨the final ~ of an ancient and unjust law⟩ ⟨the uneven ~ of population and consequent disorganization of tribal village life —Tom Marvel⟩ **:** DEPOSITION ⟨the ultimate ~ of the autocratic ruler⟩ **:** DISLOCATION ⟨the ~ of a knee joint⟩ **b :** PERCOLATION 1d **2 :** the quantity in which or the degree to which something is displaced: as **a :** the volume or weight of a fluid (as water) displaced by a floating body (as a ship) of equal weight **b :** the difference between the initial position of a geologic body and its later position along a geologic fault **c :** the distance from a neutral or equilibrium point to any specified point of a path in vibratory motion **d :** PISTON DISPLACEMENT **3 a :** the electric intensity in a dielectric medium under electric influence multiplied by the dielectric constant of the medium **b :** the product of this multiplication divided by 4π **4 :** a vector drawn from an initial position of a material particle to any subsequent position **5 a :** transfer of libidinal energy from its original object to a person or idea that is more acceptable to the ego **b :** SUBLIMATION 1b
displacement angle *n* **:** angular phase change in the terminal voltage of an alternator when the orig. open external circuit is closed upon a load
displacement current *n* **:** a limited shifting of electric components that occurs within a dielectric when a voltage is applied to or removed from it (as in charging or discharging a capacitor) and that corresponds to the current in the circuit supplying the voltage
displacement law *n* **:** any of three statements in physics or chemistry: (1) WIEN'S DISPLACEMENT LAW or (2) the emission of an alpha particle by an atom reduces the atomic number by two while the emission of a beta particle increases it by one or (3) ionization of an element causes both its spectrum and its chemical properties to resemble those of the element whose atomic number is less by one, two, or more according as the ionization is single, double, or higher
displacement pump *n* **:** a pump (as an air lift or pulsometer) that raises or transfers a fluid by direct displacement with no transformation of the kinetic energy due to the fluid's motion into potential energy due to pressure
displacement theory *n* **:** WEGENER HYPOTHESIS
dis·pla·cen·cy \dəˈsplāsᵊnsē\ *n* -ES [ML *displacentia*, alter. of L *displicentia*, fr. *displicent-, displicens* (pres. part. of *displicēre* to displease) + *-ia* -y — more at DISPLEASE] *archaic* **:** DISLIKE, DISSATISFACTION, DISPLEASURE
dis·placer \dəˈsplāsə(r), (ˈ)di¦s-\ *n* **:** one that displaces; *specif* **:** PERCOLATOR b
dis·pla·cive \dəˈsplāsiv, (ˈ)di¦s-\ *adj, of a crystal* **:** affected by, resulting from, or causing displacement
displant *vt* [MF *desplanter*, fr. des- ¹dis- + *planter* to plant — more at PLANT] **1** *obs* **:** to take (a plant) out of the ground **:** UPROOT **2** *obs* **a :** to deprive (as a town or settlement) of inhabitants **:** destroy the essential character of (as a town or settlement) **b :** to remove from a place (as of habitation or a colony or a settlement) **:** root out **:** DISPLACE; *also* **:** SUPPLANT
¹dis·play \dəˈsplā *sometimes* ˈdi,s-\ *vb* -ED/-ING/-S [ME *displayen*, fr. AF *despleier*, fr. L *displicare* to scatter, fr. *dis-* ¹dis- + *plicare* to fold — more at PLY] *vt* **1 a :** to spread or stretch out or wide **:** UNFOLD ⟨~ a map on the table⟩ **b** *obs* **:** DEPLOY 1 **2 a :** to spread before the view **:** exhibit to the sight or mind **:** give evidence of **:** SHOW, MANIFEST, DISCLOSE ⟨~ a passion for accuracy⟩ ⟨~ one's appreciation⟩ ⟨~ criminal tendencies⟩; *specif* **:** to put on exhibition ⟨these reproductions have been ~*ed* throughout Canada —*Report: (Canadian) Royal Commission on Nat'l Development*⟩ ⟨two model houses were ~*ed* for a week⟩ **b :** to exhibit conspicuously ⟨~ a gift for ham acting⟩ **c :** to set forth (as in representation or narrative) **:** DESCRIBE, DEPICT ⟨the canvases ~*ed* shabby acrobats —*Time*⟩ **d :** to set in display in printing **3** *obs* **:** DISCOVER, DESCRY ~ *vi* **1 :** to make a display **:** act as one making a show or demonstration **2 :** to present or advertise by means of a display **syn** see SHOW
²display \"\ *n* -s *often attrib* **1** *obs* **:** a presentation by representation or narrative **:** DESCRIPTION **2 a :** an exhibiting or showing of something **:** an unfolding or opening out to view **:** EXHIBITION, MANIFESTATION ⟨want no ~ of emotion —Henry Adams⟩; *specif* **:** the means by which radar echoes or other information is given to an operator in visual form in communications **b :** ostentatious show **:** exhibition for effect ⟨the Church of the Brethren or the Mennonite Church, neither of which countenances worldly ~ —*Amer. Guide Series: Pa.*⟩ ⟨making a disgusting ~ in front of company⟩ **c :** composition designed to catch the eye (as by the use of lines of uneven length or different type sizes or styles) and typically used in title pages, advertising brochures, and magazine covers ⟨~ composition⟩ ⟨~ typefaces⟩; *also* **:** printed matter so composed ⟨the local press gave top ~ to the murder story⟩ **d :** an often artistic conspicuous eye-catching construction or assemblage by which something (as merchandise or collector's items) is exhibited or advertised ⟨his pictures are on ~ at the art gallery⟩; *also* **:** the use of such constructions or assemblages ⟨~ is the key to self-service sales —*Printers' Ink*⟩ **3 :** a stereotypic pattern of behavior exhibited esp. by male birds in the breeding season that serves to initiate specific responses in another individual (as a possible breeding partner or a potential territorial rival) ⟨the males congregate on a low knoll serving as a ~ ground —J.M.Flagler⟩
syn PARADE, ARRAY, POMP: DISPLAY may suggest a spectacular spreading out in or as if in exhibition to impress by extent, detail, beauty, number, or lavishness ⟨the *display* of political partisanship on the part of the Hamilton-Jefferson faction —J.C.Fitzpatrick⟩ ⟨fine editions that make an impressive *display* in an oilman's library —Green Peyton⟩ ⟨a fine *display* of camellias in bloom —*Amer. Guide Series: La.*⟩ ⟨an imitation of the jousts of the middle ages, providing *displays* of horsemanship —*Amer. Guide Series: N.C.*⟩ PARADE may indicate ostentatious flaunting, usu. sustained, to impress, dazzle, or awe another ⟨he does not make the least *parade* of his wealth or his gentility —J.C.Snaith⟩ ⟨in the ritornello, with its *parade* of themes, one immediately recognizes the orchestral opulence and virtuosity of the incomparable Toscanini —Abram Chasins⟩ ARRAY may suggest order and brilliancy in display of or as if of marshaled ranks of soldiers ⟨we look up at this facade and see a magnificent *array* of saints, all ordered in their appropriate niches; we recognize Homer, Dante, Shakespeare and several others —Herbert Read⟩ ⟨today's motorists come in all seasons to revel in such an *array* of splendors as few other roads of the state can offer —Maynard Leahey⟩ POMP, once often used of a ceremonial process or pageant, now suggests spectacular brilliance or splendid ostentation often accomplished with vain or lofty punctiliousness ⟨a *pomp* of flaming colors —F.D.Ommanney⟩ ⟨the *pomp* of nations that pretend to be sovereign —C.W.Ferguson⟩
display advertising *n* **:** advertising not classified headings in a newspaper or magazine; *esp* **:** advertising that utilizes various kinds of display techniques or devices (as large print, colorful makeup, or a large spread)
display artist *n* **:** one who prepares advertising displays for windows or interiors of business concerns
displayed *adj* [ME, fr. past part. of *displayen*] **:** having wings spread out — used of a heraldic representation of a bird of prey, esp. an eagle
display key *n* [*display (room)*] **:** a key generally used in hotel rooms to prevent any unwarranted entrance and that when used to operate a given lock of a master-keyed lock system prevents the lock from being opened by any other key except an emergency key
display line *n* **:** matter set in one line in nontext often ornamental type
dis·play·man \dəˈsplāmən, -ˌman\ *n, pl* **displaymen :** DISPLAY ARTIST
display pipe *n* **:** a pipe forming part of an organ case; *sometimes* **:** a dummy pipe
displays *pres 3d sing of* DISPLAY, *pl of* DISPLAY
display window *n* **:** a large window usu. in the front of a store for the display of merchandise
disple *vt* -ED/-ING/-S [ME *dissplyen*, alter. of *disciplinen*] *obs* **:** DISCIPLINE
displeasant *adj* [ME *displesaunt*, fr. MF *desplaisant*, pres. part. of *desplaire, desplaisir*] **1** *obs* **:** DISPLEASING **2** *obs* **:** DISPLEASED
dis·please \dəˈsplēz, (ˈ)di¦s-\ *vb* [ME *displesen*, fr. MF *desplais*, stem of *desplaisir, desplaire*, fr. (assumed) VL *displacēre*, alter. of L *displicēre*, fr. *dis-* ¹dis- + *-plicēre* (fr. *placēre* to please) — more at PLEASE] *vt* **1 :** to incur the disapproval of esp. as accompanied by annoyance, aversion, or dislike ⟨a rich man can discharge anyone in his employment who ~*s* him —G.B.Shaw⟩ ⟨the verdict *displeased* the judge⟩ **2 :** to arouse unpleasant feelings in **:** be offensive to ⟨the colors of the picture *displeased* her the most⟩ ~ *vi* **:** to give displeasure or offense ⟨it is best to avoid *displeasing* if it can be decently avoided⟩
dis·pleased·ly \-z(ə)dlē, -li\ *adv* **:** in a manner that shows one's displeasure
displeasing *adj* [ME *displesing*, fr. pres. part. of *displesen* to displease] **1 :** causing displeasure ⟨~ behavior⟩ **2 :** lacking in pleasing quality or effect ⟨~ voice⟩
dis·pleas·ing·ly *adv* **:** in a displeasing manner ⟨making ~ cutting remarks about one's friends⟩
dis·pleas·ing·ness *n* **:** the quality or state of being displeasing
¹dis·pleasure \dəs, (ˈ)dis+\ *n* [ME *displesure*, alter. (influenced by *plesure, plesire* pleasure) of *displesire*, fr. MF *desplaisir*, fr. *des-* ¹dis- + *plaisir* pleasure — more at PLEASURE] **1 :** the feeling of one that is displeased **:** DISAPPROVAL, DISLIKE, DISFAVOR, INDIGNATION ⟨not anxious to incur further government ~ —H.C.Atyeo⟩ **2 a :** DISCOMFORT, UNEASINESS **b :** PAIN, SORROW, UNHAPPINESS ⟨pleasure and ~ are intensive quantities —Lucius Garvin⟩ **3** *archaic* **:** something that displeases **:** a cause of irritation or annoyance **:** OFFENSE, INJURY
²displeasure \"\ *vt, archaic* **:** DISPLEASE
dis·plenish \dəs, (ˈ)dis+\ *vt* [*dis-* + *plenish*] *Scot* **:** to divest or strip (as a house or farm) of contents and equipment **:** DEPLENISH
displenishing sale *n, Scot* **:** a disposal sale esp. of farm or household goods
displicence *n* -s [L *displicentia*] *obs* **:** DISPLICENCY
dis·plic·en·cy \dəˈsplisᵊnsē, ˈdispləs-\ *n* -ES [L *displicentia* — more at DISPLACENCY] *archaic* **:** DISSATISFACTION, AVERSION, DISCONTENT
dis·plode \dəˈsplōd\ *vb* -ED/-ING/-S [L *displodere*, fr. *dis-* apart + *-plodere* (fr. *plaudere* to clap, beat, applaud) — more at DIS-] *archaic* **:** to discharge explosively **:** EXPLODE — **dis·plo·sion** \-ōzhən\ *n* -s
dis·plume \dəs, (ˈ)dis+\ *vt* [¹*dis-* + *plume* (n.)] **:** DEPLUME
dis·pone \dəˈspōn\ *vt* -ED/-ING/-S [ME *disponen* to set in order, arrange, dispose, fr. L *disponere* — more at DISPOSE] *Scots law* **:** to dispose of, grant, or transfer (real or personal property) legally — **dis·pon·er** \-nər\ *n* -s
dis·pon·ee \ˌdi(ˌ)spōˈnē, dəˌs-\ *n* -s [*dispone* + *-ee*] *Scots law* **:** one to whom property is disposed
dis·pon·ible \dəˈspōnəbəl\ *adj* **:** capable of being placed, arranged, or disposed of as one wishes **:** AVAILABLE
dis·pope \dəs, (ˈ)dis+\ *vt* -ED/-ING/-S [¹*dis-* + *pope* (n.)] **:** to depose from the office of pope
di·sporous \(ˈ)dī+\ *adj* [*di-* + *-sporous*] **:** having two spores
¹di·sport \dəˈ+\ *n* -s [ME, fr. MF *desport*, fr. *desporter*] **1 a :** PLAY, SPORT, DIVERSION **b :** a pastime or game **2** *archaic* **:** MIRTH, AMUSEMENT, DELIGHT **syn** see ²PLAY
²disport \"\ *vb* -ED/-ING/-S [ME *disporten*, fr. MF *desporter*, fr. *des-* ¹dis- + *porter* to carry — more at PORT (to carry)] *vt* **1 :** DIVERT, AMUSE, ENTERTAIN ⟨converted one of the stables . . . into a billiard room and here the youths ~*ed* themselves to their hearts' content —Thomas Wall⟩ ⟨sea lions bark and ~ themselves before a gallery of enthusiasts —*Amer. Guide Series: N.Y. City*⟩ **2 :** to make a fine display of ⟨the town ~*ed* three bright shiny new hacks with rumbling wheels —W.A.White⟩ ⟨gave the . . . critics an opportunity to ~ their innocence of Christian knowledge or culture —*Time*⟩ **3 :** to conduct or behave (oneself) **:** DEPORT ⟨~*ed* himself like the high-bred virtuoso he is —*Musical Digest*⟩ ⟨equip a man to ~ himself gracefully in the domain of American speech —*Saturday Rev.*⟩ ~ *vi* **:** to amuse or divert oneself esp. in a light, frolicsome, lively, or wanton way ⟨do you dig in the garden, ride horses, ~ at dude ranches, or amble around the countryside? —*Better Homes & Gardens*⟩ ⟨in this den he would ~ among books, radios, tape recorders —Murray Schumach⟩ **syn** see PLAY
di·sportive \dəˈ+\ *adj, archaic* **:** SPORTIVE
di·spo·rum \(ˈ)dī¦spōrəm, ˈdispər-\ *n* [NL, fr. *di-* + *-sporum* (fr. Gk *sporos* seed) — more at SPORE] **1** *cap* **:** a small genus of herbs of the family Liliaceae with leafy branching stems, small terminal greenish, yellow, or purplish flowers, and oval berries **2** *pl* **dispo·ra** \-rə\ *or* **disporums** \-rəmz\ **:** a plant of the genus *Disporum*
dis·pos·abil·i·ty \dəˌspōzəˈbiləd·ē, (ˌ)di,s-, -ətē, -i\ *n* -ES **:** the quality or state of being disposable ⟨the ~ of paper napkins is their great recommendation⟩
dis·pos·able \dəˈspōzəbəl\ *adj* [*dispose* + *-able*] **1 :** free to be used as occasion requires **:** not assigned to any special use ⟨needs all ~ air-combat units for the Mediterranean front —*New Republic*⟩ **2 :** capable of being disposed of easily; *esp* **:** designed to be thrown away after use with only negligible loss ⟨fabrics from which are made ~ napkins, towels, and diapers —S.B.Hunt⟩ — **dis·pos·able·ness** *n* -ES
disposable income *n* **:** the personal income that is left after the deduction of personal taxes and that is available for consumption and savings
disposable weight *n* **:** all weights on an aircraft other than the fixed weight
¹dispos·al \dəˈspōzəl\ *n* -s [*dispose* + *-al*] **1 :** the act or process of disposing: as **a :** orderly or systematic placement, distribution, or arrangement ⟨the ~ of troops along the ridge⟩ ⟨the pitching of the tent and the ~ of the gear under cover⟩ **b :** the regulation of the fate or condition of something **:** ADMINISTRATION, DISPENSATION **c :** the transference of something into new hands or to a new place **:** BESTOWAL ⟨the ~ of political offices by patronage⟩ ⟨worrying about the ultimate ~ of one's property⟩ **d :** a discarding or throwing away ⟨the ~ of the dirty paper napkins⟩ ⟨the ~ of all the rubbish on the desk⟩ **:** DESTRUCTION ⟨the ~ of all enemy aircraft by concentrated flak⟩; *esp* **:** the discarding or destroying of garbage or sewage or its transformation into something useful (as fertilizer) or innocuous (as by incineration) **2 :** the power or authority to dispose of or use at one's convenience **:** discretionary use, command, or control — used esp. in the phrase *at the disposal of* ⟨a plane was always at the ~ of the president⟩ ⟨Congress had at its ~ the means of alleviating the high cost of living —*Current Biog.*⟩ ⟨the shortness of the period at our ~ —D.C.Buchanan⟩ ⟨the effectiveness of the central organization depended in the last resort on the amount of money it had at its ~ —H.J.Hanham⟩
²disposal \"\ *or* **disposal unit** *n* -s [garbage-*disposal (unit)*] **:** DISPOSER c
disposal field *n* **:** an area of ground under whose surface the overflow from a septic tank is distributed in drain tile to be absorbed in the soil
¹dis·pose \dəˈspōz\ *vb* -ED/-ING/-S [ME *disposen*, fr. MF *disposer*, modif. (influenced by *poser* to put, place) of L *disponere* to set in order, arrange (perfect stem *dispos-*), fr. *dis-* ¹dis- + *ponere* to put, place — more at POSITION, POSE] *vt* **1 a :** to give a tendency to ⟨night air was thought to ~ one to sickness⟩ **:** put in a frame of mind or feeling that is favorable (as to an act or a condition) ⟨the remark *disposed* him to like the man immediately⟩ **b :** to put into a condition (as for a particular action) **:** make ready **:** PREPARE ⟨troops *disposed* for immediate withdrawal⟩ **2 a :** to put in place or order **:** distribute and arrange esp. for greatest effectiveness, economy, ease, or conformity to a pattern ⟨she carried an armful of books; these she *disposed* within reach —Elinor Wylie⟩ ⟨branches and leaves were *disposed*, not as combinations of color in mass, but as designs in line —Laurence Binyon⟩ ⟨the general who *disposed* his forces so as to counteract a greater force —W.E.Channing⟩ **b** *obs* **:** REGULATE, DETERMINE, ORDER, MANAGE **c** *archaic* **:** deal out **:** assign to a use **:** bestow for a purpose **:** dispose of **d** *obs* **:** to assign to a particular place or position ~ *vi* **1 :** to arrange or settle a matter finally or definitively **:** make disposition; *esp* **:** to regulate the fate or condition finally or definitively ⟨man proposes but God ~*s*⟩ **2** *obs* **:** BARGAIN **syn** see SET — **dispose of 1 a :** to place, distribute, or arrange esp. in an orderly or systematic way (as according to a pattern) ⟨the men *disposed of* the weapons in convenient quickly accessible places⟩ **b :** to apportion or allot (as to particular purposes) freely or as one sees fit ⟨she has been allowed to *dispose of* her time in the most idle and frivolous manner —Jane Austen⟩ **2 a :** to transfer into new hands or to the control of someone else (as by selling or bargaining away) **:** RELINQUISH, BESTOW ⟨*dispose of* some property to a man all too anxious to buy⟩ ⟨*dispose of* public offices to all his political friends⟩ **b** (1) **:** to get rid of **:** throw away **:** DISCARD ⟨*dispose of* a lot of old clothes by burning them⟩ ⟨*dispose of* the trash in several barrels⟩ (2) **:** to treat or handle (something) with the result of finishing or finishing with ⟨the article *disposed of* the matter in two paragraphs⟩ ⟨the ability of supervisors and employees to *dispose of* differences —*Annual Report Pa. Railroad*⟩ **:** COMPLETE, DISPATCH ⟨they had quickly *disposed of* the meal⟩ **c :** DESTROY ⟨*disposed of* three enemy planes in an afternoon⟩
²dispose *n* -s **1** *obs* **:** the disposal or the power or right of disposal **2** *obs* **:** DISPOSITION; *also* **:** DEMEANOR
dis·posed \-zd\ *adj* [ME, fr. past part. of *disposen*] **1 :** having a particular temperament, disposition, or tendency or being of a particular frame of mind or condition of bodily health ⟨a dog that is ~ to bite⟩ ⟨a man generally ~ to love his fellow men⟩ ⟨a man well ~ in all physical qualities⟩ ⟨a young boy already criminally ~⟩ ⟨those ~ to violate or evade the decrees of the sovereign —M.R.Cohen⟩ **2** *obs* **:** MERRY, JOLLY, MIRTHFUL, HAPPY
dis·pos·ed·ly \-zədlē, -li\ *adv* **:** in a dignified manner ⟨a stout man moving ~ along the promenade⟩
dis·pos·er \-zə(r)\ *n* -s **:** one that disposes: as **a** *archaic* **:** MANAGER, DIRECTOR **b** *archaic* **:** DISPENSER **c :** an electrical device that forms part of a sink drain and disposes of garbage by grinding it up to be flushed through the house drain pipes
dis·pos·ing·ly *adv* **:** in a disposing manner
dis·po·si·tio \ˌdispəˈzishē,ō, -zid·ē,ō\ *n* -s [L] **:** the rhetorical and logical arrangement of the matter or the discrete elements of a discourse esp. in classical and Renaissance rhetorical systems
dis·po·si·tion \ˌdispəˈzishən\ *n* -s [ME *disposicioun*, fr. MF *disposition*, fr. L *disposition-, dispositio*, fr. *dispositus* (past part. of *disponere* to set in order, arrange) + *-ion-, -io* -ion — more at DISPOSE] **1 :** the act or the power of disposing or disposing of or the state of being disposed or disposed of: as **a :** ADMINISTRATION, CONTROL, MANAGEMENT; *often* **:** divine dispensation ⟨received the law by the ~ of angels —Acts 7:53 (AV)⟩ **b :** a placing elsewhere, a giving over to the care or possession of another, or a relinquishing ⟨saw to the ~ of all surplus goods by shipment to needy countries⟩ ⟨the ~ of the garbage was always a problem⟩ **:** the power so of so placing, giving, ridding oneself of, relinquishing, or doing with as one wishes **:** discretionary control — used esp. in the phrase *at the disposition of; specif* **:** the transfer of property from one to another (as by gift, barter, or sale or by will) or the scheme or arrangement by which such transfer is effected **c :** an ordering or arranging or a state of being ordered or arranged usu. systematically or in an orderly way and esp. of the parts of a whole **:** orderly preparation or placing **:** ARRANGEMENT ⟨the ~ of the parts of his argument made his speech forceful and tidy⟩ ⟨the ~ of the artillery was shown on the map⟩ **2 a :** the prevailing tendency, aspect, mood, or inclination of one's spirits ⟨with large blue eyes that . . . showed her thoughts and ~*s* —Hugh Walpole⟩ ⟨woke up in a nasty ~⟩ **:** the complex of attitudes, proclivities, and responses conditioning conduct **:** PROPENSITY ⟨his ~ was to make the worst of bad for-

tune⟩ ⟨conservatism with them is not so much a program as a ~ or attitude or temper —Daniel Aaron⟩ **:** temperamental makeup ⟨a man of broad sympathies and a genial ~⟩ **b** (1) *obs* **:** physical condition **:** HEALTH (2) *archaic* **:** CONSTITUTION, NATURE **c :** the inclination, tendency, or power of anything to act in a certain manner under given circumstances ⟨the ~ of sugar to dissolve in water⟩ ⟨the ~ to war or to peace in human societies seems to be a matter of economic, political, social, and psychological structurings of the society itself —Weston LaBarre⟩ **3 :** the number and types of stops in an organ **:** the makeup of an organ **4 dispositions** *pl* **:** strategical or tactical military plans ⟨the general perfected his ~s for the campaign⟩ **5 :** the sentence given to or treatment prescribed for a juvenile offender ⟨boys 12 to 16 who were sent to his ward for routine observation pending ~ by the courts —Charles Grutzner⟩

syn COMPLEXION, TEMPERAMENT, PERSONALITY, INDIVIDUALITY, TEMPER, CHARACTER: DISPOSITION refers to one's accustomed attitudes and moods in reacting to life around one ⟨ages of fierceness have overlaid what is naturally kindly in the *dispositions* of ordinary men and women —Bertrand Russell⟩ ⟨the taint of his father's insanity perhaps appeared in his unbalanced *disposition* —E.S.Bates⟩ COMPLEXION blends together notions involving mood and attitude and ideas about ways of thinking ⟨the rationalist mind, radically taken, is of a doctrinaire and authoritative *complexion:* the phrase 'must be' is ever on its lips —William James⟩ ⟨great thinkers of various *complexion,* who differing in many fundamental points, all alike assert the relativity of truth —Havelock Ellis⟩ TEMPERAMENT may suggest individual proclivities, esp. as colored by feeling and emotion and esp. in matters social or creative ⟨the electric amenities that pass between artistic *temperaments* at different tensions still find free play —J.L.Lowes⟩ ⟨melancholy was the dominant note of his *temperament* . . . a melancholy tempered by recurrences of faith and resignation and simple joy —James Joyce⟩ PERSONALITY stresses those traits the composite of which tends to individualize one in his society, often those which attract, which give popularity, ready appeal, or decisive or compelling interest ⟨the *personality* of the brilliant secretary of the treasury is not clearly defined. The inner man . . . is unfortunately neglected —J.C.Miller⟩ ⟨by sheer *personality* he has so far propped up a somewhat artificial arrangement with the smaller parties —*Economist*⟩ INDIVIDUALITY stresses an individualizing and distinguishing composite of traits ⟨an *individuality,* a style of its own —Willa Cather⟩ ⟨detected for the first time, beneath the dehumanized drudge, the stirrings of a separate and perhaps capricious *individuality* —Arnold Bennett⟩ TEMPER may indicate the frame of mind with which one makes choices and decisions, faces difficulties or problems, or controls and governs himself ⟨a less dogmatic *temper* is becoming apparent among the scientists themselves —Irving Babbitt⟩ ⟨after four years of fighting, the *temper* of the victors was such that they were quite incapable of making a just settlement —Aldous Huxley⟩ CHARACTER may suggest the deep, fundamental, and established complex of moral traits, the genuine and lasting individualizing inner nature of a person ⟨that inexorable law of human souls that we prepare ourselves for sudden deeds by the reiterated choice of good or evil that determines *character* —George Eliot⟩ ⟨*character,* or what is fixed, hard, and resistant in human nature, cannot be expressed lyrically —*Times Lit. Supp.*⟩

dis·po·si·tion·al \ˌdispəˈzishənᵊl, -shnəl\ *adj* **:** of, belonging to, or characterizing the disposition ⟨~ statements, namely statements to the effect that a mentioned thing, beast, or person has a certain capacity, tendency or propensity, or is subject to a certain liability —Gilbert Ryle⟩

dis·po·si·tioned \ˌdispəˈzishənd\ *adj* **:** having a particular disposition ⟨a friendly-*dispositioned* person, anxious to help⟩

dispositions *pl of* DISPOSITION

dispositios *pl of* DISPOSITIO

dis·pos·i·tive \dəˈspäzəd·iv, -pōz-\ *adj* [L *dispositus* (past part. of *disponere* to set in order, arrange) + E *-ive* — more at DISPOSE] **1** *archaic* **:** having the capacity or quality of giving a tendency or inclination to something **2 :** disposing or belonging to the disposition or direction of something **:** of or belonging to disposal or control

dispositively *adv, obs* **:** as a possibility **:** in respect to a tendency or to a future eventuality

dis·pos·i·tor \dəˈspäzəd·ə(r)\ *n* -S [L, arranger, fr. *dispositus* + *-or*] **:** a planet which is in astrology lord of the sign where another planet is

dis·possess \ˌdis +\ *vt* [MF *despossesser,* fr. *des-* ¹dis- + *possesser* to possess — more at POSSESS] **1 a :** to put out of possession esp. of property or land — usu. used with *of* before the thing taken away ⟨~ a man of his goods and chattels⟩ **b :** to strip of possessions ⟨a depression in which many people found themselves ~*ed*⟩ **2 a :** to put out of occupancy **:** EJECT, OUST **b :** to drive out **:** BANISH ⟨~*ing* the French from the southern shores of the Mediterranean —Percy Winner⟩ **3** *archaic* **:** to free from possession by an evil spirit **syn** see DEPRIVE

dispossessed *adj* **:** deprived of physical or spiritual security (as by the loss of property, rank, faith, or patriotic ties) **:** physically or spiritually homeless ⟨made a living out of shepherding ~ people from one country to another —James Stern⟩ ⟨a ~ man in every sense, abandoned by a feckless wife, deprived of spiritual zest by isolation —*Time*⟩

dis·possession \ˌdis +\ *n* **:** the act of dispossessing or the state of being dispossessed ⟨Alexander proposed to himself nothing short of complete ~ of Darius in favor of himself as captain general of Hellas—*Encyc. Americana*⟩ ⟨waves of ~ that have marked American history — Indian driven out by pioneer, pioneer displaced by planter, planter superseded by speculator —Paul Pickrel⟩; *specif* **:** legal ouster

dispossess notice *n* **:** an official notice from an owner (as of a house or store) to one in possession to evacuate the premises within a certain time

dis·pos·ses·sor \"+\ *n* **:** one that dispossesses someone of something

dis·possessory warrant \ˌdis+...-\ *n* [*dispossess* + *-ory*] **:** a warrant giving authority to dispossess (as by eviction)

dis·post \dəˈspōst, (ˈ)diˈs-\ *vt* [¹*dis-* + *post* (position)] **:** to remove from a position

dis·po·sure \dəˈspōzhə(r)\ *n* -S [*dispose* + *-ure*] *archaic* **:** DISPOSAL, DISPOSITION

dis·prais·al \dəˈsprāzəl, (ˈ)diˈs-\ *n* -S **:** DISPRAISE

¹**dis·praise** \-āz\ *vt* [ME *dispraisen,* fr. OF *despreisier, desprisier,* fr. *des-* ¹dis- + *preisier, prisier* to praise — more at PRAISE] **:** to notice or comment on with disapprobation or some degree of censure **:** DISPARAGE, DEPRECIATE ⟨*dispraising* it in a few light easy sentences of condemnation —Arnold Bennett⟩ — **dis·prais·er** \-zə(r)\ *n*

²**dispraise** \"\ *n* **:** the act of dispraising **:** DISPARAGEMENT, DEPRECIATION ⟨her addiction to whining ~ and her parsimony when dispensing appreciation —C.J.Rolo⟩

dis·prais·ing·ly *adv* **:** in a dispraising manner **:** with dispraise ⟨he usually spoke ~ of anyone who disagreed with him⟩

di·spread *or* **dis·spread** \də +\ *vb* [¹*dis-* + *spread*] **:** to spread abroad or out **:** spread in different directions **:** open out **:** EXPAND ⟨the morning sun ~ his beams⟩ ⟨a peacock with tail ~⟩

dis·privilege \dəs, (ˈ)dis+\ *vt* [¹*dis-* + *privilege*] **:** to deprive of privilege, a privilege, or normal privileges ⟨members of *disprivileged* ethnic minorities —Jerome Himelhoch⟩

dis·prize \dəˈspriz, (ˈ)diˈs-\ *vt* [MF *despriser,* fr. OF *despreisier, desprisier* — more at DISPRAISE] **1** *obs* **:** UNDERVALUE, UNDERESTIMATE **2 :** to hold in contempt **:** DESPISE ⟨the pangs of *disprized* love —Shak.⟩

¹**dis·profit** \dəs, (ˈ)dis+\ *vt* [¹*dis-* + *profit* (v.)] *archaic* **:** to prove to be a loss or detriment to

²**disprofit** \"\ *n* [¹*dis-* + *profit* (n.)] *archaic* **:** DAMAGE, DETRIMENT, LOSS

dis·proof \dəs, (ˈ)dis +\ *n* [¹*dis-* + *proof*] **1 :** a proving that something is other than someone says or maintains **:** CONFUTATION, REFUTATION ⟨offering evidence in ~ of a claim⟩ **2 :** evidence that disproves or tends to disprove ⟨he would not believe even with the ~ before his eyes⟩

¹**dis·proportion** \ˌdis+\ *n* [¹*dis-* + *proportion*] **1 :** absence of proportion **:** lack of symmetry or proper relation ⟨~ between a maternal pelvis and a fetal head⟩ **:** DISPARITY ⟨a ~ between the large head and the average-size body⟩ **:** a relationship in which there is this absence or lack ⟨a supply in ~ with the demand⟩ **2 :** an instance of disproportion ⟨the paintings . . . abound in bad drawing and ~s —Aldous Huxley⟩

²**disproportion** \"\ *vt* **:** to make out of proportion **:** cause to be unsuitable in quantity, form, or fitness **:** MISMATCH

dis·proportionable \ˌdis +\ *adj, archaic* **:** DISPROPORTIONAL, DISPROPORTIONATE

dis·proportional \"+\ *adj* **:** DISPROPORTIONATE — **dis·proportionality** \"+\ *n* — **dis·proportionally** \"+\ *adv* — **dis·proportionalness** \"+\ *n*

¹**dis·proportionate** \"+\ *adj* [¹*dis-* + *proportionate*] **:** not properly or pleasingly proportioned **:** out of proportion **:** UNSYMMETRICAL ⟨making a case ~ to facts —J.B.May⟩ ⟨an influence quite ~ to their relatively small numbers —William Petersen⟩ — **dis·proportionately** \"+\ *adv* — **dis·proportionateness** \"+\ *n*

²**disproportionate** \"+\ *vt* **:** to subject to disproportionation ~ *vi* **:** to undergo disproportionation

disproportionated rosin *n* **:** a substance consisting essentially of dehydrogenated resin acids (as dehydro-abietic acid) together with hydrogenated resin acids (as dihydro-abietic acid) obtained by heating rosin or by treating it with acid and used chiefly in the form of a soap as an emulsifier in making GR-S-type rubber

dis·pro·por·tion·a·tion \ˌdisprəˌpōrshəˈnāshən, -pȯr-\ *n* **:** the transformation of a substance into two or more dissimilar substances usu. by a process involving simultaneous oxidation and reduction **:** DISMUTATION ⟨~ of hydrogen peroxide to water and molecular oxygen⟩

dis·provable \dəs, (ˈ)dis +\ *adj* **:** capable of being disproved ⟨making outrageous assertions that were manifestly and easily ~⟩

dis·prove \"+\ *vt* [ME *disproven,* fr. MF *desprover,* fr. *des-* ¹dis- + *prover* to prove — more at PROVE] **1 a :** to prove to be other than is claimed or maintained **:** show to be fake **:** REFUTE ⟨the defendant's claims were *disproved* by the evidence⟩ **b** *archaic* **:** to prove wrong a claim or assertion by (a person) **2** *obs* **:** to disapprove of **:** DISALLOW

syn REFUTE, CONFUTE, REBUT, CONTROVERT: DISPROVE is the most general of these terms in implying only the demonstration of the falsity, invalidity, or erroneousness of an argument or claim ⟨charges of this kind have the peculiar advantage that even when *disproved* or shown to be manifestly absurd, they leave a stain behind them —J.A.Froude⟩ ⟨the final values of life, the ultimate meanings of experience, are just those that no man can prove, and that no man can *disprove* either —George Hedley⟩ ⟨he argues . . . that scientific thinking proper can do nothing to *disprove* Christian doctrines —W.P.Alston⟩ ⟨the authenticity of this runic writing . . . is far from *disproved* —*Amer. Guide Series: Minn.*⟩ REFUTE usu. suggests disproof of an argument or claim by careful logical or legal method as by the presenting of evidence, authoritative opinion, testimony of witnesses, or closely reasoned argument, or disproof by a fact or method acceptable to logic or legal process ⟨to *refute* all claims against the man by convincing circumstantial evidence⟩ ⟨the president's power to see that the laws are faithfully executed *refutes* the idea that he is to be a lawmaker —*Current History*⟩ ⟨one can disagree with his views, but one can't *refute* them . . . every particle of him asseverates the truth which is in him —Henry Miller⟩ ⟨with respect to that other, more weighty accusation, of having injured Mr. Wickham, I can only *refute* it by laying before you the whole of his connection with my family —Jane Austen⟩ ⟨the universe *refutes* our closet rationalizations and our kitchen diagrams —W.L.Sullivan⟩ CONFUTE suggests more the attempt to overwhelm or the actual overwhelming of someone else's arguments by any method even though it may be legitimate refutation ⟨the dialectical arguments employed by the Sophists . . . were designed to *confute* their adversaries rather than to establish true knowledge —Frank Thilly⟩ ⟨hypotheses which may be *confuted* by experience —A.J.Ayer⟩ ⟨to *confute* the too-frequent misstatement that poor laws came in with the Reformation —G.G. Coulton⟩ ⟨ignorance of the law excuses no man . . . because it is an excuse every man will plead, and no man can tell how to *confute* him —Robert Just⟩ REBUT throws stress upon the act of opposing an argument or claim as well as suggesting a certain formality of method although not necessarily implying successful refutation ⟨the author carefully examined and *rebutted,* point by point, many of the arguments —M.F.A. Montagu⟩ ⟨this presumption could be *rebutted* only by clear and convincing evidence to the contrary —*U.S. Code*⟩ ⟨he *rebuts* the legend about the Italian not being a good fighter —*Times Lit. Supp.*⟩ CONTROVERT like REBUT stresses the act of opposing but suggests such opposition as in denial or contradiction as much as in refutation, suggesting often a certain valiant effort to refute, although like REBUT not necessarily implying success ⟨a number of character witnesses . . . testified . . . and the prosecution did not try to *controvert* what they said —St. Clair McKelway⟩ ⟨delivering her opinion on every subject in so decisive a manner as proved that she was not used to have her judgment *controverted* —Jane Austen⟩ ⟨the two series of experiments, one which favors their view, the other *controverting* it —*Annual Rev. of Med.*⟩ ⟨reasons of a new kind to *controvert* the dangerous arguments of their opponents —M.F.A.Montagu⟩ ⟨the thesis which is maintained by one school and *controverted* by another —A.J.Ayer⟩ ⟨a few *controvert* and reject it by reasoning —J.A.Hobson⟩

dis·provided \ˌdis+\ *adj* [¹*dis-* + *provided*] *archaic* **:** UNPROVIDED **:** UNSUPPLIED

¹**di·spunge** \dəˈspənj\ *vt* -ED/-ING/-S [¹*dis-* + *spunge,* obs. var. of *sponge*] *archaic* **:** to pour down upon

²**dispunge** *vt* -ED/-ING/-S [¹*dis-* + *-punge* (as in *expunge*)] *obs* **:** EXPUNGE

dis·punishable \dəs, (ˈ)dis+\ *adj* [AF, fr. ¹*dis-* (fr. OF *des-* ¹dis-) + *punishable,* fr. MF *punissable* — more at PUNISHABLE] *archaic* **:** not punishable

dis·put·abil·i·ty \dəˌspyüd·əˈbiləd·ē, |tə-, -əté, -i; ˌdispyəl, ˌdiˌspyül\ *n* -ES **:** the quality or state of being disputable

dis·put·able \dəˈspyüd·əbəl, |tə-; ˈdispyə|, ˈdiˌspyü\ *adj* [MF, fr. L *disputabilis,* fr. *disputare* to discuss, examine + *-abilis* -able — more at DISPUTE] **1 :** capable of being disputed or contested **:** liable to be called in question ⟨presenting many ~ claims to the committee⟩ ⟨a speech full of ~ statements⟩ **2** *obs* **:** ARGUMENTATIVE, CONTENTIOUS — **dis·put·able·ness** \-bəlnəs\ *n* -ES

dis·put·ably \-blē, -li\ *adv* **:** in a disputable manner

¹**dis·pu·tant** \dəˈspyütᵊnt; ˈdispyəd·ənt, -yətənt\ *n* -S [L *disputant-, disputans,* pres. part. of *disputare*] **:** one that disputes **:** one engaged in a dispute **:** CONTROVERSIALIST ⟨attempting to make peace between the ~s⟩ ⟨the ~s on both sides were ignorant of the matter they were disputing about —Havelock Ellis⟩

²**disputant** \"\ *adj* [L *disputant-, disputans,* pres. part.] **:** DISPUTING **:** engaged in controversy

dis·pu·ta·tio \ˌdispəˈtäd·ē,ō\ *n, pl* **disputati·o·nes** \-ˌtäd·ēˈō,nās\ [L] **:** disputation or a disputation esp. in medieval or Renaissance rhetorical principle or practice

dis·pu·ta·tion \ˌdispyəˈtāshən, -(ˌ)spyüˈ-\ *n* -S [ME *disputacioun,* fr. L *disputation-, disputatio,* fr. *disputatus* (past part. of *disputare*) + *-ion-, -io* -ion] **1 :** the act of disputing **:** CONTROVERSY, DEBATE ⟨there is a familiar ~ among painters and critics over the relative merits of modern and traditional art —*Atlantic*⟩ ⟨in a heated ~ with another driver who had dented his front fender⟩; *specif* **:** a formal rhetorical exercise in which somebody propounds and defends a thesis or in which two parties reason in opposition to each other **2** *obs* **:** interchange esp. conversational

dis·pu·ta·tious \ˌdispyəˈtāshəs, -(ˌ)spyüˈ-\ *adj* [*disputation* + *-ous*] **1 a :** inclined to dispute **:** apt to wrangle or cavil **:** ARGUMENTATIVE, CONTENTIOUS ⟨the wrangling of many ~ . . . councils of French churchmen —H.O.Taylor⟩ ⟨man by his nature is a ~ and fighting animal —Horace Sutton⟩ **b :** marked by disputation ⟨philosophers loll in their ~ ease —R.P.Warren⟩ ⟨had a ~ time at the meeting⟩ **2 :** CONTROVERSIAL ⟨a paper so concise, so lacking in ~ matter —D.C. Peattie⟩ — **dis·pu·ta·tious·ly** *adv* — **dis·pu·ta·tious·ness** *n* -ES

dis·pu·ta·tive \dəˈspyüd·əd·iv, -ütətiv\ *adj* [LL *disputativus,* fr. L *disputatus* + *-ivus* -ive] **1 :** DISPUTATIOUS ⟨the journalism of all pioneer communities has been abusive and ~ and personal —*Scribner's*⟩ **2 :** of or belonging to disputation — **dis·pu·ta·tive·ly** *adv* — **dis·pu·ta·tive·ness** *n* -ES

¹**dis·pute** \dəˈspyüt, *usu* -üd·+V\ *vb* -ED/-ING/-S [ME *disputen,* fr. OF *desputer,* fr. L *disputare* to examine, discuss, fr. *dis-* ¹dis- + *putare* to prune, esteem, consider, think — more at PAVE] *vi* **1 :** to contend in argument **:** argue for or against something asserted or maintained **:** engage in a disputation **:** DEBATE ⟨*disputing* with opposing firms over what constituted ethical trade practices⟩; *often* **:** to argue irritably or with irritating persistence **:** WRANGLE ⟨a bitter old man much given to *disputing* over any suggestion made by others⟩ **2** *obs* **:** to struggle against something **:** FIGHT ~ *vt* **1 a :** to make the subject of disputation **:** argue pro and con **:** DEBATE ⟨the charge of treason would be *disputed* before a government committee⟩ **b :** to call into question (as the validity or the existence of something) ⟨its right to issue authoritative orders for the settlement of a conflict is *disputed* —*Economist*⟩ ⟨the bravery of the people has never been *disputed* —H.T.Buckle⟩; *also* **:** to oppose by argument or assertion **:** CONTROVERT ⟨likely to ~ any propositions not to his liking⟩ **c** *obs* **:** to argue or contend in favor of **:** MAINTAIN **d** *obs* **:** to influence, persuade, or argue into or out of a belief or action by a process of disputation **2 a :** to struggle against **:** OPPOSE, RESIST ⟨trying to ~ the man's entry into the house⟩ **b :** to strive or contend about **:** CONTEST ⟨~ a former enemy's possession of land⟩ ⟨~ a victory⟩ ⟨during the Revolutionary War this territory was much *disputed* on both sides of the river —A.C.Flick⟩ ⟨the dogs were *disputing* ownership of a bone —T.B.Costain⟩ **syn** see DISCUSS

²**dis·pute** \" *also* ˈdiˌs-\ *n* -S **1 a :** verbal controversy **:** strife by opposing argument or expression of opposing views or claims **:** controversial discussion **:** DEBATE; *also* **:** an instance of such controversy ⟨was investigating the frontier ~s of Greece with the adjacent countries —*Current Biog.*⟩ **b :** a wrangling altercation **:** QUARREL **2** *obs* **:** physical combat **:** STRUGGLE, FIGHT — **in dispute :** in the process of being disputed

dis·put·er \dəˈspyüd·ə(r), -ütə-\ *n* -S [ME *disputar,* fr. *disputen* to dispute + *-ar* -er] **:** one that disputes esp. quarrelsomely

dis·qualification \dəs, (ˌ)dis+\ *n* [¹*dis-* + *qualification*] **1 :** the act of disqualifying or the state of being disqualified ⟨protesting his ~ from office under the new law⟩ **2 :** something that disqualifies or incapacitates ⟨a crime conviction is automatically a ~ for that public office⟩ ⟨his ~ for the team was a bad knee⟩

dis·qualify \dəs, (ˈ)dis+\ *vt* [¹*dis-* + *qualify*] **1 :** to deprive of the qualities, properties, or conditions necessary for a purpose **:** make unfit ⟨a bad back *disqualified* him from competition⟩ ⟨he remains . . . psychologically *disqualified* for appreciating the fears and despairs that today afflict so large a part of the world —H.S.Commager⟩ **2 :** to deprive of a power, right, or privilege **:** DISBAR ⟨a conviction of perjury *disqualified* him from being a witness⟩ ⟨he was *disqualified* for citizenship by certain controversial restrictions⟩ ⟨two infringements of the rules will ~ a player from further participation in the game⟩

dis·quantity \dəs, (ˈ)dis+\ *vt* -ED/-ING/-ES [¹*dis-* + *quantity* (n.)] **1** *obs* **:** to reduce in quantity **:** DIMINISH, LESSEN **2 :** to utter without accurate distinction of metrical quantity — used of syllables of quantitative verse

¹**dis·quiet** \dəs, (ˈ)dis+\ *vt* [¹*dis-* + *quiet* (v.)] **:** to take away the peace, rest, easy frame of mind, or normal relaxation of by disturbing, stirring up, making restless or uneasy, or alarming ⟨why should we ~ ourselves in vain in the attempt to direct our destiny —S.M.Crothers⟩ ⟨each day brought ~*ing* news of war threats⟩ ⟨felt a ~*ing* shame about the act⟩ ⟨all questions about the future of mankind are ~*ing*⟩ ⟨~*ing* symptoms of illness⟩ **syn** see DISCOMPOSE

²**disquiet** \"\ *n* [¹*dis-* + *quiet* (n.)] **1 :** the lack of quiet or of tranquillity in body or mind **:** UNEASINESS, RESTLESSNESS, ANXIETY ⟨instead of inspiring you, she filled you with ~ —R.H.Davis⟩ ⟨even in less . . . hostile hands, the capacity for a surprise attack with fusion weapons would be a source of ~ —H.A.Kissinger⟩ ⟨to spread suspicion and ~ —Evelyn G. Cruickshanks⟩ **2** *obs* **:** an instance of disquiet **:** DISTURBANCE

³**disquiet** \"\ *adj* [¹*dis-* + *quiet* (adj.)] *archaic* **:** DISQUIETED

disquieted *adj* **:** DISTURBED, UNEASY — **dis·qui·et·ed·ly** *adv* — **dis·qui·et·ed·ness** *n* -ES

dis·quieten \"+\ *vt* [¹*dis-* + *quieten*] **:** DISQUIET ⟨~*ing* rumors of war⟩

dis·qui·et·ing·ly *adv* **:** in a manner that disquiets ⟨the ~ close sounds of gunfire⟩

dis·qui·et·ly *adv* **:** in a turbulent manner **:** UNPEACEFULLY, RESTLESSLY ⟨all ruinous disorders follow us ~ to our graves —Shak.⟩

disquietment *n* -S *obs* **:** DISQUIET

dis·qui·et·ness \ˈ=ˈ===\ *n* **:** UNEASINESS

dis·quietude \dəs, (ˈ)dis+\ *n* [³*disquiet* + *-ude* (as in *quietude*)] **:** lack of peace or tranquillity **:** UNEASINESS, AGITATION, ANXIETY ⟨there was rest now, not ~, in the knowledge —Ellen Glasgow⟩ ⟨the initial mild ~ developed soon into outright fear⟩

dis·qui·si·tion \ˌdiskwəˈzishən\ *n* -S [L *disquisition-, disquisitio* inquiry, investigation, fr. *disquisitus* (past part. of *disquirere* to inquire diligently, to investigate, fr. *dis-* ¹dis- + *-quirere,* fr. *quaerere* to seek, inquire) + *-ion-, -io* -ion] **:** a formal or systematic inquiry into or discussion of a subject **:** an elaborate analytical or explanatory essay or discussion ⟨with long and profound ~s on questions of social economics —Carolyn Hannay⟩ ⟨pedantic ~s about the nature of his conservatism —H.A.Kissinger⟩ **syn** see DISCOURSE

dis·qui·si·tion·al \ˌ==ˈzishənᵊl, -shnəl\ *adj* **:** of, belonging to, resembling, or being a disquisition

dis·quis·i·tive \dəˈskwizəd·iv\ *adj* [L *disquisitus* + E *-ive*] **:** INQUIRING, INVESTIGATIVE ⟨a man with a ~ and discerning mind⟩

dis·quis·i·tor \-zəd·ə(r)\ *n* -S [L *disquisitus* + E *-or*] *archaic* **:** a writer of a disquisition **:** RESEARCHER

disrank *vt* [¹*dis-* + *rank* (n.)] *obs* **:** to throw into disorder

dis·rate \dəs, (ˈ)dis+\ *vt* [¹*dis-* + *rate* (n.)] **:** to reduce to a lower rating, rank, or class; *esp* **:** DEMOTE ⟨~ a noncommissioned officer⟩

¹**dis·regard** \ˌdis+\ *vt* [¹*dis-* + *regard* (v.)] **1 a :** to treat without fitting respect or attention ⟨flouting convention and ~*ing* his own clerical position —Oscar Handlin⟩ **b :** to treat as unworthy of regard or notice ⟨~ the rudeness of an associate⟩ ⟨~*ing* with broad tolerance the aberrations of the youthful mind⟩ **2 :** to give no thought to **:** pay no attention to ⟨the artistic merit . . . was ~*ed* in a storm of protest against the use of nude figures —*Amer. Guide Series: Pa.*⟩ ⟨~*ing* for a moment the practical aspects of the case in order to discover the principle at work⟩ **syn** see NEGLECT

²**disregard** \"\ *n* [¹*dis-* + *regard* (n.)] **:** the act of disregarding or the state of being disregarded; *esp* **:** intentional slight or neglect ⟨his flip ~ for the consequences of his actions —Arthur Knight⟩ ⟨they acted with complete ~ of danger —*Current Biog.*⟩ ⟨treated his former friend with withering ~⟩

dis·regardant \ˌdis+\ *adj* [*disregard* + *-ant* (as in *regardant*)] **:** DISREGARDFUL

dis·regardful \ˌdis+\ *adj* [¹*dis-* + *regardful*] **:** NEGLECTFUL, HEEDLESS ⟨a procedure ~ of the true issue at stake⟩ ⟨~ of one's responsibilities⟩ — **dis·regardfully** \"+\ *adv* — **dis·regardfulness** \"+\ *n*

dis·relate \ˌdis+\ *vt* [¹*dis-* + *relate*] **:** to break the relationship between or among **:** DISUNITE ⟨tends to ~ the components of immediate experience —D.S.Savage⟩

disrelated *adj* **:** UNRELATED ⟨trying to control the operations of corporations largely by means of negative and ~ rules —*World Social Economic Planning*⟩

dis·relation \"+\ *n* [¹*dis-* + *relation*] **:** lack of a fitting or proportionate connection or relationship ⟨the danger lies in the ~ between its newly acquired powers and its characteristic methods and techniques —E.C.Lindeman⟩; *also* **:** DISUNITY, DISSOCIATION ⟨lads, whose every gesture . . . bespoke a lethargic ~ with their surroundings —Adrian Bell⟩

¹**dis·relish** \dəs, (ˈ)dis+\ *vb* [¹*dis-* + *relish* (v.)] *vt* **1** *obs* **:** to take away the flavor of or give a bad flavor to **:** make distasteful **2 :** to find unpalatable or objectionable **:** DISLIKE

⟨murdered six persons he ~*ed* —John Sack⟩ ⟨however much our riper and sophisticated judgment may ~ the fact, it is the trick . . . in a story which assures it immortality —Marvin Lowenthal⟩ 3 *archaic* : DISGUST ~ *vi, obs* : to be distasteful or objectionable

2disrelish \"\ *n* [1*dis-* + *relish* (n.)] : lack of relish : DISTASTE ⟨a ~ for some kinds of food⟩ : DISLIKE ⟨~ of him as a human being does not prevent the author from recognizing his intellect —Leonidas Dodson⟩

dis·remember \ˌdis+\ *vt* [1*dis-* + *remember*] : FORGET ⟨I ~ what he was praying for at the time —Helen Eustis⟩ ⟨for a minute I ~*ed* where I was —Shelby Foote⟩

dis·remembrance \"+\ *n* [1*dis-* + *remembrance*] : DISREGARD, OBLIVION ⟨has fallen into ~ because he made so many enemies during his lifetime —Leon Edel⟩

dis·repair \ˌdis+\ *n* [1*dis-* + *repair*] : the quality or state of being in need of repair ⟨here were several crumbling stone buildings . . . and a mile or two distant a newer homestead also in ~ —George Farwell⟩ ⟨the human personality in states of hopeless, neurotic ~ —*Time*⟩ ⟨the house had fallen into ~⟩

dis·reputability \dəs, (ˌ)dis+\ *n* : the quality or state of being disreputable

1dis·reputable \dəs, (ˈ)dis+\ *adj* [1*dis-* + *reputable*] **1** : not reputable or decent : UNRESPECTABLE ⟨like a man who deals in something ~ — pornographic books or illegal operations —Graham Greene⟩ ⟨the penniless daughter of a woman too ~ to bring her up —Louis Auchincloss⟩ **2** : in bad condition : markedly worn, dirty, or tattered ⟨wearing an old ~ coat⟩ ⟨a very ~ armchair in the sitting room —*Current Biog.*⟩ — **dis·reputableness** \"+\ *n*

2disreputable \"\ *n* -s : a disreputable person

dis·reputably \"+\ *adv* : in a disreputable manner

dis·reputation \dəs, (ˌ)dis+\ *n* [1*dis-* + *reputation*] *archaic* : loss or lack of a good reputation or good name : DISHONOR, DISREPUTE, DISCREDIT

1disrepute *vt* [1*dis-* + *repute* (v.)] *obs* : to bring into discredit : DISESTEEM

2dis·repute \ˌdis+\ *n* [1*dis-* + *repute* (n.)] : a condition in which there is an absence or lack of esteem or good reputation : low estimation ⟨the habit of pub-crawling — so much the fashion when I was their age — seems to have happily fallen into ~ —M.P.O'Connor⟩ ⟨the viola has also been held in ~ from the fact that it is often played by inferior violinists —A.E.Wier⟩ ⟨these treaties gradually fell into ~ —Vera M. Dean⟩ **syn** see DISHONOR

1dis·respect \ˌdis+\ *vt* [1*dis-* + *respect* (v.)] : to have disrespect for : show disrespect to or for ⟨the man's remark gave us every reason for ~*ing* and profoundly disliking him⟩ ⟨~*ing* the law by violating it⟩

2disrespect \"\ *n* [1*dis-* + *respect* (n.)] **1 a** : lack of respect or reverence ⟨had an enormous ~ for party-line intelligentsia —*Newsweek*⟩ ⟨a ~ for authority⟩ **b** : an instance or act of disrespect : INCIVILITY, DISCOURTESY ⟨she regarded the remark as a ~⟩ **2** : an expression or sentiment of disrespect ⟨in the speech the mayor paid his extended ~*s* to his enemies⟩

dis·respectable \"+\ *adj* [1*dis-* + *respectable*] : not conforming to conventional standards of conduct : not respectable ⟨~ poems, straight off the street —Randall Jarrell⟩

dis·respectful \"+\ *adj* [1*dis-* + *respectful*] : lacking proper respect in speech or action : showing disesteem or contempt ⟨remarks that were ~ of the law⟩ ⟨~ of a man's rights⟩ : UNCIVIL, DISCOURTEOUS ⟨~ in the presence of elders⟩ — **disrespectfully** \"+\ *adv* — **dis·respectfulness** \"+\ *n*

disrespective *adj* [1*dis-* + *respective*] *obs* : DISRESPECTFUL

disrest *n* [1*dis-* + *rest*] *obs* : UNREST, DISQUIET

dis·robe \dəs, (ˈ)dis+\ *vb* [MF *desrober*, fr. OF, fr. *des-* 1*dis-* + *robe* robe, garment — more at ROBE] *vt* **1 a** : to divest of a robe **b** : to remove the clothing from : UNDRESS ⟨the medical officer requested that the patient ~ himself before the examination⟩ **2** : to divest or strip of (something that clothes, decorates, or dignifies) ⟨has given us a certain view of kings, queens, and princes, *disrobed* of their formalities —C.G. Bowers⟩ ~ *vi* **1** : to divest oneself of a robe **2** : to undress oneself ⟨on cold nights the children *disrobed* before the fire⟩ — **dis·rob·er** \-ə(r)\ *n*

dis·roof \dəs, (ˈ)dis+\ *vt* [1*dis-* + *roof* (n.)] : UNROOF

dis·root \dəs, (ˈ)dis+\ *vt* [1*dis-* + *root* (n.)] **1** : to tear up the roots of : tear up by the roots ⟨replanted the ~*ed* shrubbery⟩ **2** : to dislodge esp. from a fixed position

disrump *vb* [L *disrumpere*] *obs* : DISRUPT

1dis·rupt \dəsˈrəpt\ *adj* [L *disruptus*] DISRUPTED

2disrupt \"\ *vt* -ED/-ING/-S [L *disruptus, diruptus*, past part. of *disrumpere, dirumpere*, fr. *dis-* apart + *rumpere* to break — more at DIS-, REAVE] **1 a** : to break apart : RUPTURE ⟨the suction tube was left in to draw off gas lest he become distended and ~ his wound —*Time*⟩ ⟨three periods of faulting ~*ed* the rocks —*Univ. of Ariz. Record*⟩ ⟨many communications routes remained unsafe or ~*ed* —*Americana Annual*⟩ **b** : to throw into disorder or turmoil ⟨the speech totally ~*ed* the meeting⟩ ⟨India was not ~*ed* by the Japanese War —Christopher Rand⟩ ⟨she would hate to have the job, because it will ~ her domestic coziness —David Sylvester⟩ **c** : to destroy the unity or wholeness of ⟨the party was ~*ed* by the defection of a large group of radical members⟩ **2** : to interrupt to the extent of stopping, preventing normal continuance of, or destroying ⟨that experience ~*ed* my interest in the life about me —Jack McLaren⟩ ⟨she had ~*ed* a bridge game by permanently hiding up the ace of spades —Scott Fitzgerald⟩ ⟨traffic on the main railway lines was largely ~*ed* during the war —*Collier's Yr. Bk.*⟩

dis·rupt·er *also* **dis·rup·tor** \-tə(r)\ *n* -s : one that disrupts

dis·rup·tion \dəsˈrəpshən\ *n* -s [*disruption-, disruptio*, fr. *disruptus* + *-ion-, -io* -ion] : the act or process of disrupting : the state of being disrupted ⟨bandaged the leg tightly to prevent ~ of the partly healed wound⟩ ⟨he was . . . the center of intrigues framed against the royal power and directed toward the ~ of the state —Hilaire Belloc⟩ ⟨the sixteenth century of our era saw the ~ of western Christianity and the rise of modern science —A.N.Whitehead⟩ ⟨foresee the speedy ~ and eventual collapse of our entire society —Lewis Mumford⟩

dis·rup·tion·ist \-sh(ə)nəst\ *n* -s **1** : one who favors disruption (as among groups constituting a political party) **2** : DISRUPTER

1dis·rup·tive \-ptiv, -tēv *also* -təv\ *adj* [2*disrupt* + *-ive*] : causing or tending to cause disruption ⟨~ movements trying to go faster than the main body of the party wishes to go —Harry Walston⟩ ⟨pragmatically, religion is necessary to the average individual to overcome the shattering ~ anticipation of death, of disaster, and of destiny —B.K.Malinowski⟩ — **dis·rup·tive·ly** \-tə̇vlē, -li\ *adv* — **dis·rup·tive·ness** \-tivnə̇s, -tēv- *also* -təv-\ *n* -ES

2disruptive *n* -s : HIGH EXPLOSIVE

disruptive discharge *n* : a discharge through an insulating material subjected to an electrostatic stress with an accompanying breaking down or rupture of the material

dis·rupture \dəs, (ˈ)dis+\ *n* [2*disrupt* + *-ure* (as in *rupture*)] : DISRUPTION ⟨~ of telephone service⟩

dis·ruptured \"+\ *adj* : broken up : SPLIT, DIVIDED

diss \ˈdis\ *n* -ES [Ar *dīs*] : a reedy grass (*Ampelodesma tenax*) common in the Mediterranean region that is used in basketry and cordage making

diss- *or* **disso-** *comb form* [NL, fr. Gk, fr. *dissos, dittos;* akin to Gk *dyo* two — more at TWO] : double ⟨*diss*oconch⟩ ⟨*disso*phyte⟩

diss *abbr* dissertation

dis·satisfaction \də(s), (ˌ)di(s)+\ *n* [1*dis-* + *satisfaction*] **1** : the quality or state of being dissatisfied, unsatisfied, or discontented : uneasiness, disturbance, or distress resulting from a lack of gratification ⟨~ with the world in which we live and determination to realize one that shall be better —G.L.Dickinson⟩ ⟨had grown discouraged with his son-in-law but did not openly voice his ~ —Sherwood Anderson⟩ **2** : DISPLEASURE ⟨~ with inflation was not confined to organized labor —*Collier's Yr. Bk.*⟩

dis·satisfactory \"+\ *adj* [1*dis-* + *satisfactory*] : UNSATISFACTORY

dissatisfied *adj* : expressing or showing dissatisfaction ⟨a ~ scowl on his face⟩ ⟨a ~ complaint⟩ — **dis·satisfiedly** \"+\ *adv* — **dis·satisfiedness** \"+\ *n*

dis·satisfy \də(s), (ˈ)di(s)+\ *vt* [1*dis-* + *satisfy*] : to fail to satisfy : fail to provide with something desired, expected, or hoped for or to the extent desired, expected, or hoped for : frustrate wishes or expectations of ⟨a ~*ing* dinner⟩ ⟨we cannot prove that it is better to be a human being *dissatisfied* than a pig satisfied —H.J.Muller⟩ ⟨*dissatisfied* with the dollar a day he earned —*Current Biog.*⟩ ⟨a book that is one part superb and two parts stimulating yet ~*ing* —J.F.McComas⟩

dis·sa·va \dəˈsävə\ *n* -s [Sinhalese *disāwa*] : one of the district governors of Ceylon

dis·save \də(s), (ˈ)di(s)+\ *vi* [1*dis-* + *save*] : to engage in or practice dissaving — **dis·saver** \"+\ *n*

dissaving *n* : the use of past savings for current consumption : consumption in excess of income ⟨the savings of those still rich are offset by the ~*s* of the poorer ones —*Canadian Jour. of Economics & Political Science*⟩

dis·scepter \də(s), (ˈ)di(s)+\ *vt* [1*dis-* + *scepter* (n.)] *archaic* : to deprive of a scepter

dis·seat \də(s), (ˈ)di(s)+\ *vt* [1*dis-* + *seat*] *archaic* : UNSEAT

dis·sect \dəˈsekt *also* ÷(ˈ)dī¦s-\ *vb* -ED/-ING/-S [L *dissectus*, past part. of *dissecare* to cut apart, fr. *dis-* apart + *secare* to cut — more at DIS-, SAW] *vt* **1** : to divide or separate into parts **2 a** : to cut so as to separate into pieces or to expose the several parts and their locations and connections esp. with precision and deftness for scientific examination; *specif* : to separate or follow along natural lines of cleavage (as through connective tissue) ⟨~ out the regional lymph nodes⟩ ⟨a ~*ing* aneurysm⟩ **b** : to divide and separate into different phases, items, or parts and to examine, interpret, or evaluate minutely ⟨~*ing* the claims of John Quincy Adams to the support of abolitionists —William MacDonald⟩ ⟨those words which it is the business of criticism to ~ and reassemble —T.S.Eliot⟩ **c** : to cut or divide (land) into hills and ridges with valleys between — used esp. of a river **d** : to break up for colors in printing **3** : to separate out for special attention or different treatment or consideration : isolate out — used with *out* ⟨pupils . . . often could not ~ out the subject or object in a Miltonic sentence —H.R.Warfel⟩ ~ *vi* **1** : to make a medical dissection **2** : to analyze and evaluate something in great detail **syn** see ANALYZE

dissected *adj* **1** : cut into parts or sections ⟨a ~ map⟩ **2 a** *of a leaf* : cut deeply into many fine lobes or divisions **b** : divided into hills and ridges by valleys and gorges ⟨a ~ plateau⟩

dissecting room *n* : a room (as in a hospital or medical school) where anatomical dissecting is performed for instruction, research, or analysis

dis·sec·tion \-kshən\ *n* -s [prob. fr. F, fr. MF, fr. L *dissectus* + MF *-ion*] **1** : the act or process of dissecting or the state of being dissected ⟨sharpened the big carving knife, beamed at the turkey, and pretended to be absorbed in its ~ —Anne Green⟩ **2 a** : a detailed critical analysis of something (as of a type represented in a novel) ⟨although there were novels on a great variety of themes, the two characters most favored for ~ were American businessmen or young ladies uncertain of their identity —Harrison Hayford⟩ **b** (1) : the surgical removal along the natural lines of cleavage of tissues which are or might become diseased — compare BLOCK DISSECTION (2) : the digital separation of tissues (as in heart-valve operations) — compare FINGER FRACTURE **c** : the process of erosion whereby a land surface is cut by gullies, ravines, canyons, or other kinds of valleys **3 a** : something (as a part or the whole of an animal or plant) that has been dissected **b** : an anatomical specimen prepared in this way

dis·sec·tion·al \-kshənᵊl, -shnəl\ *adj* : DISSECTIVE ⟨in setting, personalities, and ~ treatment, this part is reminiscent of . . . novels of psychopathic provincial people —Dorothy Chamberlain⟩

dis·sec·tive \-ktiv\ *adj* : of or relating to dissection ⟨it is only ~ analysis and knowledge of history that reveal the compositeness of any culture —A.L.Kroeber⟩

dis·sec·tor \-tə(r)\ *n* -s [L *dissectus* + E *-or*] : one that dissects

Dissector \"\ *trademark* — used for an image dissector

dissed *past of* DIS

dis·seise *or* **dis·seize** \də(s)ˈsēz, (ˈ)di(s)¦s-\ *vt* -ED/-ING/-S [ME *disseisen*, fr. ML *disseisire* & AF *disseisir*, fr. OF *dessaisir* to dispossess, fr. *des-* 1*dis-* + *saisir* to put in possession of — more at SEIZE] : to deprive of seisin; *usu* : to wrongfully dispossess or oust (as one in freehold possession of land) — used with *of*, formerly with *from*

dis·seis·ee *or* **dis·seiz·ee** \də(s)¦sēˌzē, ˌdi(s),s-\ *n* -s [AF *disseisi*, fr. pres. part. of *disseisir*] : a person disseised — contrasted with *disseisor*

dis·seisin *or* **dis·seizin** \də(s), (ˈ)di(s)+\ *n* -s [ME *dysseysyne*, fr. ML *disaissina* & AF *disseisine*, fr. OF *dessaisine* dispossession, fr. *des-* 1*dis-* + *saisine* seisin — more at SEISIN] : the act of disseising or the state of being disseised

dis·sei·sor *or* **dis·sei·zor** \də(s)ˈsēˌzȯ(ə)r, ¦di(s)¦s-\ *n* -s [ME *disseiser*, fr. AF *disseisour*, fr. *disseisir* + *our* -or] : one that disseises another — contrasted with *disseisee*

dis·sel·boom \ˈdisəlˌbüm, -ˌbōm\ *n* -s [Afrik, fr. D, fr. *dissel* tongue or shaft of a wagon (fr. MD) + *boom* pole, tree, fr. MD; akin to OS *thīsla* tongue or shaft of a wagon, OE *thīxl*, OHG *dīhsala*, ON *thīsl* tongue or shaft of a wagon, OSlav *tęgnąti* to pull, and to OHG *boum* tree — more at BEAM] *Africa* : the pole of a horse-drawn wagon

1dis·semblance \dəˈsemblən(t)s\ *n* [ME, fr. MF *dessemblance*, fr. *dessembler* to be unlike (fr. *des-* 1*dis-* + *-sembler*, as in *resembler* to resemble) + *-ance* — more at RESEMBLE] : lack of resemblance : DISSIMILITUDE

2dissemblance \"\ *n* [*dissemble* + *-ance*] : the act or the art of dissembling : DISSIMULATION

dis·sem·ble \dəˈsembəl\ *vb* **dissembled; dissembled; dissembling** \-b(ə)liŋ\ **dissembles** [alter. (influenced by MF *dessembler* to be unlike) of *dissimule*] *vt* **1** : to hide under a false appearance : conceal with intent to deceive : FEIGN ⟨the propagandist . . . is a man so convinced of the truth of a certain proposition that he ~*s* the facts that tell against it —Katharine F. Gerould⟩ **2** *obs* : OVERLOOK, IGNORE **3** *archaic* : to put on the appearance of : make pretense of : SIMULATE ⟨the soon *dissembled* a sleep —*Tatler*⟩ ~ *vi* : to put on a false appearance : conceal facts, motives, intentions, or feelings under some pretense ⟨we are all brought up to have a strict regard for the truth, but in adult life we learn to ~⟩ **syn** see DISGUISE

dis·sem·bler \-b(ə)lə(r)\ *n* -s : one that dissembles ⟨we shall have to become ~*s* — saying one thing while knowing in our own minds that it is a lie —Asher Moore⟩

dis·sem·bling·ly \-b(ə)liŋlē\ *adv* : in a manner that dissembles

dissembly *n* -ES [by alter.] *obs* : ASSEMBLY

dis·sem·i·nate \dəˈseməˌnāt, *usu* -ād.+V\ *vb* -ED/-ING/-S [L *disseminatus*, past part. of *disseminare*, fr. *dis-* 1*dis-* + *seminare* to sow, fr. *semin-, semen* seed — more at SEMEN] *vt* **1 a** : to spread or send out freely or widely as though sowing or strewing seed : make widespread ⟨as citizens devoted to the use of books and as librarians and publishers responsible for *disseminating* them —*Amer. Library Assoc. Bull.*⟩ ⟨distrusting the great city twenty miles away that *disseminated* its virus through the outlying villages and farms —V.L.Parrington⟩ **b** : to foster general knowledge of : BROADCAST, PUBLICIZE ⟨unlicensed preachers went about the country *disseminating* heresies and notorious errors —G.G.Coulton⟩ ⟨*disseminating* information about the latest scientific discoveries⟩ ⟨~ the latest events, regardless of the inconclusive shape they are in —Harvey Breit⟩ **2 a** : to disperse throughout in small particles : distribute in every part : DIFFUSE, PERMEATE ⟨reported that copper was *disseminated* through the rock⟩ **b** : to spread out : extend widely : strew or scatter over a large area or into many places ⟨silt from the Amazon is *disseminated* for hundreds of miles⟩ ⟨*disseminated* multiple sclerosis⟩ ~ *vi* : to spread widely : become found widely ⟨seeds, wind-borne, ~ over quite a wide area from the parent plant⟩ **syn** see SPREAD

dis·sem·i·na·tion \dəˌseməˈnāshən\ *n* -s [L *disseminatio-, disseminatio*, fr. *disseminatus* + *-ion-, -io* -ion] : the action or process of disseminating : the state of being disseminated : DIFFUSION ⟨the ~ of ideas⟩ ⟨devoted himself to the ~ of a modified form of Darwinism —S.F.Mason⟩

dis·sem·i·na·tor \dəˈseməˌnād·ə(r), -ātə-\ *n* -s [LL, fr. L *disseminatus* + *-or*] : one that disseminates ⟨wild birds may also serve as ~*s* of infection —E.H.Barger & L.E.Card⟩ ⟨the newspaper . . . still the most important news ~ —R.E. Wolseley⟩

dis·sem·i·nule \-ˌnyül\ *n* -s [*disseminate* + *-ule*] : a part or organ of a plant that ensures propagation (as a seed or spore)

dis·sen·sion *also* **dis·sen·tion** \dəˈsenchən\ *n* -s [ME *dissensioun, dissencioun*, fr. MF *dissension*, fr. L *dissension-, dissensio*, fr. *dissensus* (past part. of *dissentire*) + *-ion-, -io* -ion] **1** : disagreement in opinion esp. partisan and contentious : breach of friendship : QUARRELING ⟨continued ~ in the ranks of the party —J.G.Colton⟩ ⟨one of the unions fraught with disharmony and ~ —Honor Tracy⟩ **2** *archaic* : dissent from religious doctrine or practice **syn** see DISCORD

1dis·sent \dəˈsent\ *vi* -ED/-ING/-S [ME *dissenten*, fr. L *dissentire*, fr. *dis-* 1*dis-* + *sentire* to feel — more at SENSE] **1** : to withhold assent : not to approve : OBJECT ⟨~*ing* to the most outrageous invasion of private right ever set forth as a decision of the court —J.P.Boyd⟩ **2 a** : to differ in opinion : DISAGREE ⟨~ from the prevailing opinion⟩ ⟨all who ~ from its orthodox doctrines are scoundrels —H.L.Mencken⟩ **b** *archaic* : to be in discord : QUARREL **c** : to differ from an established church in the matter of doctrines, rites, or government ⟨~*ing* from the Church of England⟩ **syn** see DIFFER

2dissent \"\ *n* -s **1 a** : difference of opinion : NONAGREEMENT, NONCONCURRENCE, DISAGREEMENT: as (1) : religious dissension or nonconformity (2) : a justice's statement with or without an accompanying opinion of nonconcurrence with a decision of the majority of the justices of a court **b** : an instance of such disagreement or nonconcurrence ⟨his major ~*s* have now become the law —Francis Biddle⟩ **2** *obs* : DISPARITY, DIVERSITY, DIFFERENCE

dis·sen·ta·ne·ous \ˌdisᵊn·¦tānēəs\ *adj* [L *dissentaneus*, fr. *dissentire* + *-aneus* (as in *subterraneus* subterranean) — more at SUBTERRANEAN] *archaic* : being at variance : DISCORDANT

dis·sent·er \dəˈsentə(r)\ *n* -s **1** : one that dissents ⟨always finds himself drawn to the ~, the rebel, the nonconformist —Sara H. Hay⟩; *esp* : a person who worships in a communion other than that of an established state church **2** *usu cap* : an English nonconformist

dis·sen·tience \dəˈsench(ē)ə|n(t)s\ *n* : the quality or state of being dissentient : DISAGREEMENT

1dis·sen·tient \|nt\ *n* -s [L *dissentient-, dissentiens*, pres. part. of *dissentire* to dissent — more at DISSENT] : one that dissents ⟨gained him a vote of confidence with only four ~*s* —E.A. Peers⟩

2dissentient \"\ *adj* [L *dissentient-, dissentiens*, pres. part.] : not concurring : DISSENTING, DISAGREEING ⟨such suppression does not carry with it the destruction of recalcitrant individuals but only of their powers of ~ action —Samuel Alexander⟩

dis·sent·ing·ly *adv* : in a manner that shows or expresses dissent

dis·sen·tious \dəˈsenchəs, (ˈ)di¦s-\ *adj* [irreg. fr. *dissension* + *-ous*] : marked by dissensions : FACTIOUS — **dis·sen·tious·ly** *adv*

dis·sen·tive \dəˈsentiv\ *adj* : marked by dissent : DISAGREEING ⟨an interest in reform and an occasional ~ attitude socially and religiously —Allan Holaday⟩

dis·sep·i·ment \dəˈsepəmənt\ *n* [L *dissaepimentum* partition, fr. *dissaepire, dissepire* to separate, divide (fr. *dis-* apart + *saepire, sepire* to fence in) + *-mentum* -ment — more at DIS-, SEPIMENT] : a separating tissue : PARTITION: as **a** : SEPTUM **b** : TRAMA **c** : one of the transverse calcareous partitions between the radiating septa of a coral **d** : a crossbar between branches of a lace bryozoan colony **e** : a similar support of a graptolite

dis·sep·i·men·tal \də¦sepə¦mentᵊl\ *adj* : of or relating to a dissepiment

dis·sert \dəˈsərt\ *vi* -ED/-ING/-S [L *dissertus*, past part. of *disserere*, fr. *dis-* 1*dis-* + *serere* to place, arrange, join together — more at SERIES] : to give a dissertation : speak at some length and in detail : DISCOURSE ⟨I am not going to ~ on Hood's humor; I am not a fair judge —John Ruskin⟩

dis·ser·tate \ˈdisə(r)ˌtāt\ *vi* -ED/-ING/-S [L *dissertatus*, past part. of *dissertare*, freq. of *disserere*] : DISSERT

dis·ser·ta·tion \ˌdisə(r)ˈtāshən\ *n* -s [L *dissertation-, dissertatio*, fr. *dissertatus* + *-ion-, -io* -ion] **1** *obs* : DISCUSSION, DEBATE **2** : an extended usu. systematic oral or written treatment of a subject : TREATISE, DISQUISITION; *specif* : a substantial paper that is submitted to the faculty of a university by a candidate for an advanced degree that is typically based on independent research and that if acceptable usu. gives evidence of the candidate's mastery both of his own subject and of scholarly method — see THESIS **syn** see DISCOURSE

dis·ser·ta·tion·al \ˌdisə(r)¦tāshənᵊl, -shnəl\ *adj* : of, relating to, or consisting of a dissertation

dis·ser·ta·tive \ˈdisə(r)ˌtād·iv\ *adj* : of, relating to, or consisting of a dissertation

dis·serve \də(s), (ˈ)di(s)+\ *vt* [1*dis-* + *serve*] : to serve ill or falsely or be of inadequate service to ⟨if I am not *disserved* by my memory . . . Mr. Hayes used to intersperse this cycle of spirituals with readings —J.M.Conly⟩ : INJURE, DAMAGE, HARM ⟨*disserving* the very democracy in which he ardently believes —*New Republic*⟩ ⟨has *disserved* his art by a self-conscious preachment —Parker Tyler⟩

dis·service \"+\ *n* [1*dis-* + *service*] : ill service : INJURY, HARM, MISCHIEF ⟨charts what is called "passenger *disservice*" — all the things which go to delay flights or otherwise incommode the passenger —R.P.Cooke⟩ ⟨there would be no greater ~ to the American people than to underestimate the gravity of the dangers —A.E.Stevenson⟩ ⟨it does a country great ~ to claim for it a perfection to which it cannot aspire —Richard Joseph⟩

dis·serviceable \"+\ *adj* : tending or calculated to do disservice : INJURIOUS, HARMFUL ⟨dismisses . . . all such checks as the referendum as ~ interventions of a crude electorate —*Contemporary Rev.*⟩

dis·serviceably \"+\ *adv* : in a disserviceable manner

disses *pres 3d sing of* DIS, *pl of* DISS

dissettle *vt* [1*dis-* + *settle*] *obs* : UNSETTLE

dis·sever \də̇+\ *vb* [ME *deseveren, disseveren*, fr. OF *dessevrer*, fr. LL *disseparare*, fr. L *dis-* 1*dis-* + *separare* to separate — more at SEPARATE] *vt* : SEVER, DISUNITE, SEPARATE, PART ⟨he loved knowledge; yet he would not ~ it from its value in the art of living —H.O.Taylor⟩ ⟨great wastes of empty land ~*ed* the single farm from the rest of the world —Oscar Handlin⟩ ⟨Henchard's wife was ~*ed* from him by death —Thomas Hardy⟩; *also* : to divide or cut into parts or separate units ⟨the ~*ed* carcass of the chicken⟩ ~ *vi* : to dissever two or more things ⟨deep beneath the surface of the legal system . . . are these attractions and repulsions, uniting and ~*ing* as in one unending paradox—B.N.Cardozo⟩

dis·severance \"+\ *n* [ME *deseveraunce, disseveraunce*, fr. MF *dessevrance*, fr. *dessevrer* + *-ance*] : the act of dissevering : the state of being dissevered : SEPARATION ⟨complete selfishness and ~ from anything that might cause her discomfort —Amy Loveman⟩

dis·severation \"+\ *n* -s [*dissever* + *-ation*] : DISSEVERANCE

dis·si·dence \ˈdisədən(t)s, -dᵊn-\ *n* -s [L *dissidentia*, fr. *dissident-, dissidens* + *-ia* -y] : DISSENT, DISAGREEMENT, CONTENTION ⟨arresting people for political ~ —Peggy Durdin⟩ ⟨confronted by religious revolts or ~ —G.C.Sellery⟩

1dis·si·dent \-ənt,-ᵊnt\ *adj* [L *dissident-, dissidens*, pres. part. of *dissidēre* to sit apart, disagree, fr. *dis-* apart + *-sidēre* (fr. *sedēre* to sit) — more at DIS-, SIT] **1 a** : not agreeing : DISSENTING : not concurring ⟨psychological theory, like economic theory, is in the hands of several ~ schools —J.S.Gambs⟩; *esp* : differing often contentiously with an established political or religious system or belief of a country or people ⟨~ elements within the Thai navy attempted to overthrow Pibul's regime —*Current Biog.*⟩ ⟨the aristocrats and ~ politicians demanded that the army demagogue be removed —D.M. Friedenberg⟩ **b** : QUARRELSOME, CONTENTIOUS ⟨what a united, aggressive minority can do to a ~, lethargic majority —*Time*⟩ **2** : clashingly unharmonious ⟨an aesthetic jungle of ~, competing buildings —Lewis Mumford⟩ — **dis·si·dent·ly** \-əntlē, -li\ *adv*

2dissident \"\ *n* -s : one that is dissident ⟨the Labor government . . . had been forced by a number of Labor ~*s* to announce a reduction in the period of national service

—Woodrow Wyatt⟩ ⟨had two ~s burned alive in 1575 —George Willison⟩ ⟨protect the constitutional rights of pacifists and other wartime ~s —Dwight MacDonald⟩

dis·sight \də(s), (ˌ)di(s)+\ *n* [[1]*dis-* + *sight*] **:** an unsightly object

dis·sil·ient \dəˈsilyənt, -lēənt\ *adj* [L *dissilient-*, *dissiliens*, pres. part. of *dissilire*, fr. *dis-* apart + *-silire* (fr. *salire* to leap) — more at DIS-, SALLY] **:** springing apart; *specif* **:** bursting open (as the ripe capsules of the balsam)

dis·similar \də(s), (ˈ)di(s)+\ *adj* [[1]*dis-* + *similar*] **:** not similar **:** UNLIKE ⟨Americans who had been reared in the most ~ places and born into the most ~ families —Oscar Handlin⟩ ⟨completely ~ cultures —K.E.Read⟩ ⟨the military requirements are not ~ from those for defense —Fletcher Pratt⟩ ⟨those pumps . . . were not ~ to those once familiar to everyone on a farm —J.B.Conant⟩ — **dis·similarly** \"+\ *adv*

dis·similarity \də(s), (ˈ)di(s)+\ *n* **:** the quality or state of being dissimilar **:** difference in appearance or nature **:** UNLIKENESS, HETEROGENEITY ⟨progress toward full union has remained stalled because of *dissimilarities* between the Belgian and the Netherlands economies —*Americana Annual*⟩

syn DISSIMILARITY, UNLIKENESS, DIFFERENCE, DIVERGENCE, DIVERGENCY, and DISTINCTION all mean lack of agreement or correspondence in appearance, quality, or nature, or an instance of this. DISSIMILARITY and UNLIKENESS, the most general terms in this group, are often interchangeable; DISSIMILARITY, however, often stresses the lack of agreement or correspondence more than UNLIKENESS which often applies more to a lack of resemblance as among things in the same species or in some other more or less uniform category ⟨there are often not mere *unlikenesses* but marked *dissimilarities* of belief between members of the same religious group⟩ ⟨what a *dissimilarity!* In the ground of the two lives, a likeness; in all their circumstance, what *unlikeness!* —Matthew Arnold⟩ ⟨a noticeable *unlikeness* between twins⟩ DIFFERENCE implies a quality or feature which marks one thing as apart from another — want of resemblance in one or more particulars, a want of identity, or a disagreement or cause of disagreement ⟨dwell with satisfaction upon the poet's *difference* from his predecessors —T.S.Eliot⟩ ⟨*differences* in the type of ware manufactured by the various crafts —H.E.Steele⟩ ⟨an obvious *difference* between the statesman and the politician⟩ ⟨settle the *differences* between hostile nations⟩ DIVERGENCE or DIVERGENCY usu. applies to things which have or have had much in common, implying strongly a cleavage or a purposeful separation in path or character ⟨one university system might show considerable *divergence* from another —J.B.Conant⟩ ⟨in the old days I demanded agreement; I am now amused by *divergence* —A.C.Benson⟩ ⟨his *divergence* from his sister in this sphere of religion was never so wide as she feared —Matthew Arnold⟩ ⟨increasing *divergencies* between British and French policies —Sumner Welles⟩ ⟨the *divergencies* between these three passages are obvious —A.P.d'Entrèves⟩ DISTINCTION implies a difference, usu. in a detail, brought out by close observation or analysis ⟨the natural *distinction* between literary and graphic art —John Ruskin⟩ ⟨he had lost all sense of the *distinction* between reality and illusion —Van Wyck Brooks⟩ ⟨these *distinctions* in national character are rooted in some quality of human nature —J.A.Hobson⟩

dis·sim·i·late \dəˈsiməˌlāt, (ˈ)di¦s-, *usu* -ād·+V\ *vb* -ED/-ING/-S [[1]*dis-* + *-similate* (as in *assimilate*)] **:** to make or become dissimilar **:** undergo or cause to undergo dissimilation

dis·sim·i·la·tion \dəˈsiməˈlāshən, (ˈ)diˌsimə¦l-\ *n* -S [[1]*dis-* + *-similation* (as in *assimilation*)] **:** the act of making or the process of becoming dissimilar: as **a :** CATABOLISM — contrasted with *assimilation* **b :** the development of dissimilarity between two identical or closely related sounds in a word; *also* **:** the loss or dropping of one of two such sounds (as in Vulgar Latin pe*l*eg*r*inus, from Latin pe*r*eg*r*inus or as in the pronunciation \ˈgəvənər\ instead of \ˈgəvərnər\ for *governor* by speakers of English who do not ordinarily "drop" their *r*'s) — compare ASSIMILATION 4

dis·similative \dəs, (ˈ)dis+\ *adj* **:** belonging to or causing dissimilation

dis·sim·i·la·to·ry \dəˈsimələˌtōrē, (ˈ)di¦s-, -tȯr-, -ri\ *adj* **:** of, relating to, or caused by dissimilation

dis·similitude \¦di(s)+\ *n* [L *dissimilitudo*, fr. *dissimilis* unlike (fr. *dis-* [1]dis- + *similis* like) + *-tudo* -tude — more at SAME] **:** lack of resemblance **:** DISSIMILARITY; *also* **:** an instance or example of dissimilarity

dis·simulate \də, (ˈ)di+\ *vb* [L *dissimulatus*, past part. of *dissimulare*, fr. *dis-* [1]dis- + *simulare* to simulate — more at SIMULATE] **:** to hide under a false appearance **:** DISSEMBLE ⟨during the first three centuries . . . the cross of Christ is invariably *dissimulated* under the form of an object which recalls its image —Eugene Goblet d'Alviella⟩ ⟨a man trained to conceal or ~ all strong feeling⟩ ⟨as a politician he was not good at *dissimulating*⟩

dis·simulation \də, (¦)di+\ *n* [ME *dissimulacioun*, fr. MF *dissimulation*, fr. L *dissimulation-*, *dissimulatio*, fr. *dissimulatus* + *-ion-*, *-io* -ion] **:** the act of dissembling or the fact of being dissembled ⟨some of these may recognize themselves in these pages . . . but I believe that I have been careful enough in ~ that they will not be recognized by others —J.A.Pike⟩ **:** false pretense ⟨try to keep my detachment from becoming so complete a lie that I myself am deceived by it . . . but one thing can be gained by ~, and that is an increment in dignity —Isaac Rosenfeld⟩ **syn** see DECEIT

dis·simulative \də, (ˈ)di+\ *adj* **:** belonging to, consisting of, or marked by dissimulation ⟨the ~ arts⟩

dis·simulator \"+\ *n* [L, fr. *dissimulatus* + *-or*] **:** DISSEMBLER

dissimule *vb* -ED/-ING/-S [ME *dissimulen*, fr. MF *dissimuler*, fr. L *dissimulare*] *obs* **:** DISSEMBLE

dissing *pres part of* DIS

dissipable *adj* [L *dissipabilis*, fr. *dissipare* + *-abilis* -able] *obs* **:** capable of being dissipated

[1]**dis·si·pate** \ˈdisəˌpāt, *usu* -ād·+V\ *vb* -ED/-ING/-S [L *dissipatus*, past part. of *dissipare*, fr. *dis-* [1]dis- + *-sipare* (fr. *supare* to throw); akin to OE *geswōpe* trash, ON *sōfl* broom, *svāf* spear, Skt *svapū* broom, OSlav *sypati* to shake; basic meaning: throwing, shaking] *vt* **1 a :** to break up and drive off (as a crowd) **:** SCATTER, DISPERSE ⟨~ the enemy forces by unremitting gunfire⟩ **b :** to cause to disappear esp. by dispersion or diffusion **:** cause to spread out or spread thin to the point of vanishing **:** DISPEL, DISSOLVE ⟨the morning sun *dissipated* the night mists⟩ ⟨if this absorbed heat is not *dissipated*, the surfaces of the combustion chambers would become red hot —Ernest Venk⟩ ⟨a bright light *dissipated* the darkness of the night —W.H.G.Kingston⟩ ⟨familiarity . . . *dissipated* the prejudice born of ignorance —Oscar Handlin⟩ ⟨the common bond which drew them together is *dissipated* by the divergent interests of adult life —Carmen Rosa⟩ **2 a :** to expend aimlessly or foolishly ⟨~ our energies in trivial occupations⟩ ⟨the union would be *dissipating* its bargaining power — using it wastefully instead of conserving it —S.H.Slichter⟩ **b :** to spend so as to have no further possession of ⟨had a small patrimony . . . but that he *dissipated* before he left college —George Meredith⟩; *also* **:** to lose by squandering ⟨*dissipated* the family fortune in only a few years of wild living⟩ ~ *vi* **1 a :** to separate into parts and scatter or disappear **:** DISPERSE, VANISH ⟨mist will usually ~ in the sun's rays⟩ ⟨the crowd lost interest and *dissipated*⟩ **b :** to spread out so that an original identity is lost ⟨the skirts flowed down to ~ . . . where they touched the floor —Elizabeth Bowen⟩ ⟨the river *dissipated* in several smaller streams⟩ **2 :** to be extravagant or dissolute in the pursuit of physical pleasure; *esp* **:** to drink alcoholic beverages excessively ⟨paying with a hangover for his extended *dissipating* of the night before⟩ **syn** see SCATTER, WASTE

[2]**dissipate** *adj* [L *dissipatus*] *obs* **:** thinly dispersed **:** SCATTERED

dissipated *adj* **1 :** given to dissipation and having a resultant deteriorated condition of physical health ⟨the young baronet was weak and ~ —Humphry Bullock⟩ ⟨so deplorably ~ and degraded —E.V.Lucas⟩ **2 :** marked by or fostering intemperance and dissipation ⟨a ~ society⟩ ⟨more than half the seamen remaining were more or less unwell from a long sojourn in a ~ port —Herman Melville⟩ — **dis·si·pat·ed·ly** *adv* — **dis·si·pat·ed·ness** *n* -ES

dis·si·pat·er \ˈdisəˌpād·ə(r), -ātə-\ *n* -S **:** one that dissipates

dis·si·pa·tion \ˌdisəˈpāshən\ *n* -S [L *dissipation-*, *dissipatio*, fr. *dissipatus* + *-ion-*, *-io* -ion] **1 :** the act of dissipating or the state of being dissipated: **a :** a scattering or spreading out or being scattered or spread out to the point of destroying an original identity **:** DISPERSION, DIFFUSION ⟨the ~ of the enemy's forces in battle⟩ ⟨the ~ of the mist⟩ ⟨the ~ of gloom⟩ ⟨the ~ of ignorance⟩ **b** *archaic* **:** DISINTEGRATION, DISSOLUTION **c :** wasteful expenditure ⟨the ~ of one's energies⟩ ⟨the quick ~ of his fortune in foolish investments⟩ **d :** dissolute or intemperate living ⟨passing one's life in a round of ~⟩; *esp* **:** excessive drinking **2 :** AMUSEMENT, DIVERSION ⟨my only ~ is an occasional Sunday concert —Havelock Ellis⟩ ⟨amidst the innumerable conflicting impulses and attractions and ~s of life —P.E.More⟩

dissipation of energy : a physical process (as the cooling of a body in the open air) by which energy becomes not only unavailable but irrecoverable in any form — compare CONSERVATION OF ENERGY, DEGRADATION OF ENERGY

dis·si·pa·tive \ˈdisəˌpād·iv\ *adj* **:** of or relating to dissipation **:** tending to dissipate ⟨the loss characteristics of the ~ material —*Technical News Bull.*⟩ **:** marked by dissipation esp. of energy ⟨aluminum consumed in various ~ uses —D.D. Blue⟩ ⟨a ~ system⟩ — **dis·si·pa·tiv·i·ty** \ˌdisəpəˈtivəd·ē\ *n* -ES

dis·si·pa·tor \ˈdisəˌpād·ə(r), -ātə-\ *n* -S **:** DISSIPATER; *specif* **:** a part of a glacier in which the loss by melting exceeds the gain by the accumulation of snow

dissite *adj* [L *dissitus*, fr. *dis-* apart + *situs* placed — more at DIS-, SITE] *obs* **:** lying apart **:** REMOTE

disso- — see DISS-

dis·sociability \də, (ˌ)di+ — *see* DISSOCIABLE\ *n* **:** the quality of being dissociable or being capable of dissociation

dis·so·cia·ble \ *in sense 1* dəˈsōshəbəl *or* (ˈ)di¦s-, *in sense 2* " *or* -ōs(h)ēəb-\ *adj* [in sense 1, fr. [1]*dis-* + *sociable;* in sense 2, fr. L *dissociabilis*, fr. *dissociare* + *-abilis* -able] **1 :** UNSOCIABLE **2 :** capable of being dissociated **:** SEPARABLE

dis·social \də(s), (ˈ)di(s)+\ *adj* [[1]*dis-* + *social*] **:** unfriendly to society **:** UNSOCIAL, SELFISH ⟨motivated by ~ feelings into ~ and aggressive behavior⟩

[1]**dis·so·ci·ant** \dəˈsōs(h)ēənt\ *adj* [L *dissociant-*, *dissocians*, pres. part. of *dissociare*] **:** producing or resulting from dissociation; *specif, of bacteria* **:** MUTANT

[2]**dissociant** \"\ *n* -S **:** a dissociant substance or individual

[1]**dis·so·ciate** \dəˈsōs(h)ēə̇|t, (ˈ)di¦sō-, -ōshə̇|, -ōs(h)ēˌā|, *usu* |d·+V\ *adj* [L *dissociatus*, past part.] **:** DISSOCIATED ⟨perched on the edge of the old sofa in the living room . . . she would appear oddly ~ from her surroundings —Frances G. Patton⟩

[2]**dis·so·ci·ate** \-ōs(h)ēˌāt, *usu* -ād·+V\ *vb* -ED/-ING/-S [L *dissociatus*, past part. of *dissociare* to separate from fellowship, disunite, estrange, fr. *dis-* [1]dis- + *sociare* to join, share, fr. *socius* companion — more at SOCIAL] *vt* **1 :** to cut off (as from society) **:** separate esp. from association or union with another **:** disconnect from association with another ⟨~s him from the company of cynics —Marya Mannes⟩ ⟨modern architecture cannot be *dissociated* from town or community planning —*Report: (Canadian) Royal Commission on Nat'l Development*⟩ ⟨*dissociated* themselves from the saloons and the distillers —M.R.Cohen⟩ ⟨never possible to ~ the meaning of words from the words themselves —Samuel Alexander⟩ **2 :** to separate into discrete units or parts **:** DISUNITE ⟨those two elements of feeling which Freud says have become *dissociated* in the life of modern man —Irving Howe⟩ ⟨nor are Joyce's characters merely the sum of the particles into which their experience has been *dissociated* —Edmund Wilson⟩; *specif* **:** to subject to chemical dissociation ~ *vi* **1 :** to undergo dissociation **2** *of bacteria* **:** to mutate esp. reversibly

dissociated *adj* **1 :** having nothing to do with **:** not connected **:** UNRELATED ⟨inflationary rises resulting from causes ~ from money —*Current Biog.*⟩ **2 :** giving evidence of or marked by psychological dissociation ⟨a ~ personality⟩ ⟨a ~ idea⟩

dis·so·ci·a·tion \dəˌsōsēˈāshən, (¦)diˌsō-, -ōshē- — *compare* ASSOCIATION\ *n* -S [L *dissociation-*, *dissociatio*, fr. *dissociatus* + *-ion-*, *-io* -ion] **1 :** the act or process of dissociating or the state of being dissociated **:** SEPARATION, SEPARATENESS, DISUNION: as **a :** the process by which a chemical combination breaks up into simpler constituents usu. capable of recombining under other conditions — used esp. of the action of heat or other forms of energy on gases and of solvents upon dissolved substances ⟨~ of ammonia at high temperatures⟩ ⟨electrolytic ~⟩; compare DECOMPOSITION a, IONIZATION **b** (1) **:** isolation, abstraction, or extraction from the total perceptual field of some element which is to be separately observed or analyzed (2) **:** the separation of an idea or activity from the main stream of consciousness or of behavior esp. as a mechanism of ego defense (3) **:** the decompensation of defense permitting fragmentation of the ego into disunited parts (as under hypnosis or in psychotic states) **2 :** the property inherent in certain biological stocks of differentiating into two or more distinct and relatively permanent strains (as the rough and smooth strains of certain bacteria); *also* **:** such a strain

dissociation constant *n* **:** a constant that depends upon the equilibrium between the dissociated and undissociated forms of a chemical combination; *esp* **:** IONIZATION CONSTANT — symbol *K*

dis·so·cia·tive \dəˈsōs(h)ēˌād·iv, (ˈ)di¦sō-, -ōshəd·iv, -ōs(h)ēəd·iv\ *adj* **:** of, relating to, or tending to produce dissociation ⟨a ~ chemical reaction⟩ ⟨the ~ phenomena associated with schizophrenia⟩; *specif* **:** tending to produce nonsocial or antisocial behavior ⟨~ emotions in the adolescent⟩

dis·so·conch \ˈdisə+ˌ-\ *n* [*diss-* + *conch*] **:** the larval shell of a bivalve mollusk in the veliger stage

dis·sog·e·ny \də̇ˈsäjənē\ *also* **dis·sog·o·ny** \-ägə-\ *n* -ES [ISV *diss-* + *-geny* or *-gony;* orig. formed as G *dissogonie*] **:** the occurrence of sexual maturity at two distinct periods in the life of an individual (as in the larva and again in the adult of certain ctenophores)

dis·sol·u·bil·i·ty \də̇ˌsälyəˈbiləd·ē, *archaic* ˌdisəly-\ *n* **:** the quality or state of being dissoluble ⟨the ~ of sugar⟩

dis·sol·u·ble \dəˈsälyəbəl, *archaic* ˈdisəly-\ *adj* [L *dissolubilis*, fr. *dissolvere* to dissolve + *-bilis* -able] **:** capable of being dissolved: **a :** capable of being disintegrated or decomposed ⟨matter is ~⟩ **b :** soluble in a liquid ⟨sugar is ~ in water⟩ **c :** capable of being disunited or disconnected ⟨a ~ bond between the two⟩ **d :** liable to be dispersed or terminated ⟨a ~ bank of mist⟩ ⟨a ~ contract⟩

dis·so·lute \ˈdisəˌlü|t, -sələ| *also* -səlˌyü|, *usu* |d·+V\ *adj* [L *dissolutus*, past part. of *dissolvere* to loosen, dissolve, relax, destroy — more at DISSOLVE] **1 a** *obs* **:** REMISS, NEGLIGENT, CARELESS **b** *archaic* **:** lacking energy, consistency, or firmness **:** LOOSE **2 :** lacking restraint **:** unrestrained or lawless in conduct ⟨the ~ condition of masterless men —Frank Thilly⟩; *esp* **:** loose in morals or conduct **:** WANTON, PROFLIGATE, LICENTIOUS ⟨the obscenity used in their books and the tendency to deal with the ~ and degrading aspects of human nature —Wallace Fowlie⟩ **3** *obs* **:** DISJOINED, DISCONNECTED, SEPARATE, DISSOLVED — **dis·so·lute·ly** *adv* — **dis·so·lute·ness** *n* -ES

dis·so·lu·tion \ˌdisəˈlüshən *also* -səlˈyü-\ *n* [ME *dissolucioun*, fr. MF & L; MF *dissolution*, fr. L *dissolution-*, *dissolutio*, fr. *dissolutus* + *-ion-*, *-io* -ion] **1 :** the act or the process of dissolving or breaking up: as **a :** separation into component parts ⟨the ~ of the phoneme into simultaneous distinctive features —John Lotz⟩ **b :** DISINTEGRATION, DECAY ⟨the old hostelry, then not many years from its final ~ —A.W.Long⟩; *esp* **:** the extinction of life in the human body **:** DECEASE, DEATH ⟨grew convinced of his friend's approaching ~ —Elinor Wylie⟩ **c :** termination or destruction by breaking down, disrupting, or dispersing ⟨the ~ of the republic⟩ ⟨the ~ of a treaty⟩ ⟨the ~ of American urban life —Richard Hofstadter⟩ ⟨he saw his lifework threatened with ~ through the political and shortsighted muddling —J.C.Fitzpatrick⟩ **d :** final dispersion (as of an organized group) ⟨the power of ~ of a legislature at will possessed by the colonial governor —O.P. Field⟩ **e :** LIQUEFACTION ⟨the ~ of ice⟩ **f :** SOLUTION 2a **g :** the final liquidation of a business **2 :** the process of becoming or the state of being relaxed or loosened or a becoming or being dissolute: as **a** *obs* **:** a becoming lax **:** ENFEEBLEMENT **b :** a loosening or a loss of restraint esp. in moral behavior **:** DISSOLUTENESS, PROFLIGACY **c :** the dissolving of a tie or connection ⟨the ~ of the partnership⟩ **3 :** an instance or product of dissolution or something dissolved or dissolute: as **a :** SOLUTION 2b **b** *obs* **:** a dissolute or profligate act **:** EXTRAVAGANCE, EXCESS **c :** an opening in rock produced by the solution of part of the rock

dis·sol·u·tive \də̇ˈsälyə|d·iv, ˈdisəˌlü| *also* ˈdisəlˌyü|\ *adj* [ME, fr. LL *dissolutivus*, fr. L *dissolutus* + *-ivus* -ive] **:** of or relating to dissolution

dis·solv·abil·i·ty \=ˌ=(*with sounds as in* DISSOLVE) + əˈbiləd·ē *or* -ətē *or* -i\ *n* **:** the quality of being dissolvable

dis·solv·able \=ˈ=+əbəl\ *adj* **:** capable of being dissolved esp. by liquefaction or of being broken up and dispersed ⟨a soap not easily ~ in cold water⟩ ⟨inclined to think marriage a too easily ~ union⟩ ⟨a committee ~ at the will of the president⟩

[1]**dis·solve** \də̇ˈz|älv, |ȯlv *also* |ä(ü)v *or* |ȯv *sometimes* də̇ˈs|\ *vb* [ME *dissolven*, fr. L *dissolvere*, fr. *dis-* [1]dis- + *solvere* to loosen, release, dissolve — more at SOLVE] *vt* **1 a :** to cause to disperse or disappear **:** get rid of **:** do away with **:** DESTROY ⟨a direct hit had *dissolved* one of the destroyers —R.L.Schwartz⟩ ⟨poetry ~s traditional preconception —Harold Rosenberg⟩ ⟨help to ~ some of the rancor —Edward Shils⟩ **b** *obs* **:** to cause the death of **:** KILL **c :** UNDO, END ⟨*dissolved* their alliance⟩ **:** break the continuity of **:** DISCONNECT, DISUNITE ⟨~ a marriage⟩ ⟨~ a bond⟩ **d :** to separate into component parts **:** DISINTEGRATE, DECOMPOSE ⟨the American Tobacco Company was *dissolved* into smaller units —*Amer. Guide Series: N.C.*⟩ ⟨this would ~ a vocabulary into an infinite number of nonce words —Weston La Barre⟩ **e :** to bring to an end by dispersal or by causing the dissociation of **:** TERMINATE ⟨the king's former power to ~ parliament⟩ ⟨he had *dissolved* army courts —*Farmer's Weekly (So. Africa)*⟩ ⟨~ a partnership⟩ **f :** to destroy the influence or effect of by counteracting **:** ANNUL, ABROGATE ⟨~ an injunction⟩ **2 a :** to cause to pass into solution ⟨the difference in content of *dissolved* gases in cold and warm waters —R.E.Coker⟩ **b :** MELT, LIQUEFY ⟨the heat *dissolved* the candles into opaque pools of wax⟩ **c :** to cause to be emotionally moved **:** melt emotionally ⟨the news *dissolved* her so completely she ran from the room weeping⟩; *also* **:** to unstring emotionally and totally — used esp. in the phrase *dissolved in tears* **d :** to totally occupy **:** IMMERSE ⟨his life was *dissolved* in a round of frivolities⟩ **e :** to fade out (a shot in a motion-picture or television sequence) in a dissolve **3** *archaic* **:** to set free **:** RELEASE, DETACH **4 :** to clear up **:** SOLVE ⟨~ the mystery⟩ ~ *vi* **1 a :** to waste away or become dissipated **:** become broken up or decomposed **:** VANISH, DISAPPEAR ⟨the mist . . . *dissolved* as it touched the valleys —Han Suyin⟩ ⟨she would simply have *dissolved* like a slug with salt poured on it —Jean Stafford⟩ ⟨our goals themselves were in flux and . . . we should only find them *dissolving* in our hands —Brand Blanshard⟩ **b :** to break up **:** DISPERSE ⟨the assembly *dissolved*⟩ ⟨orders . . . direct the soldiers to ~ before a stronger force —W.O.Douglas⟩ ⟨the interim committees *dissolved* as soon as the regular committees returned from vacation⟩ **c :** to fade away **:** fall to nothing **:** lose power ⟨his strength *dissolved* before her irresistible charm⟩ ⟨the solidity of the main characters seems almost to ~ —John Lehmann⟩ **2 a :** to become fluid **:** MELT, LIQUEFY ⟨ice cream *dissolving* in the sun⟩ **b :** to pass into solution ⟨sugar ~s in liquid⟩ **c :** to melt or be overcome emotionally ⟨the father *dissolved* in grief⟩; *also* **:** to become totally unstrung emotionally — used esp. in the phrase *dissolve into tears* **d :** to resolve itself as if by dissolution ⟨on closer inspection the street riot *dissolved* into a mob of students struggling to get into an empty store building to see an exhibition of books —Robert Payne⟩ — **dis·solv·er** \-və(r)\ *n*

[2]**dissolve** \"\ *n* -S **:** a superimposing of one motion-picture or television shot upon another on a screen in which the overlapped shot is gradually darkened as the emergent shot is brightened usu. to indicate a lapse of time or change of scene — called also *lap dissolve;* compare FADE, WIPE

dissolved bone *n* **:** a phosphatic fertilizer made by treating ground bone or bone meal with sulfuric acid

[1]**dis·sol·vent** \-vənt\ *n* [L *dissolvent-*, *dissolvens*, pres. part. of *dissolvere*] **:** something that is dissolvent ⟨a corrosive ~ upon traditional orthodoxy —F.H.A.Micklewright⟩ ⟨industrial democracy, itself a product of cultural dissolution, is a ~ of decadent cultures —Waldo Frank⟩

[2]**dissolvent** \"\ *adj* [L *dissolvent-*, *dissolvens*, pres. part.] **1 :** SOLVENT 2 **2 :** tending to dissipate or to destroy by slow degrees ⟨its respect for the rights of religious dissent has proved a ~ force both for bigotries and hostilities —Max Lerner⟩

dis·solv·ing·ly *adv* **:** in a dissolving manner

dissolving shutter *n* **:** a camera attachment used in motion pictures and television for producing dissolves

dis·so·nance \ˈdisənən(t)s\ *also* **dis·so·nan·cy** \-sənənsē, -si\ *n*, *pl* **dissonances** *also* **dissonancies** [MF or LL; MF, fr. LL *dissonantia*, fr. L *dissonant-*, *dissonans* + *-ia* -y] **1 :** a mingling of discordant sounds **:** DISCORD ⟨the ~ of the two bands playing different pieces too close to each other⟩; *specif* **:** a harsh or clashing musical interval or combination of notes ⟨varying the flow of harmonious progressions with occasional jarring ~⟩ — compare CONSONANCE **2 a :** lack of agreement **:** INCONGRUITY, DISCREPANCY **b :** DISSIDENCE, CONTENTION, STRIFE ⟨frustrations of the preceding hours, and . . . the occasional ~s that those could but produce between him and her —Elizabeth Bowen⟩ **c :** an instance or example of such incongruity or such dissidence ⟨the mingling of bitter comedy and stark tragedy produces sharp ~s —F.B. Millett⟩ **3 :** an unresolved musical note or chord; *specif* **:** an interval not included in a major or minor triad or its inversions — compare CONSONANCE 2b

dis·so·nant \-sənənt\ *adj* [MF or L; MF, fr. L *dissonant-*, *dissonans*, pres. part. of *dissonare* to disagree, be discordant, fr. *dis-* [1]dis- + *sonare* to sound — more at SOUND] **1 :** marked by dissonance **:** DISCORDANT ⟨clamor of voices ~ and loud —H.W.Longfellow⟩ ⟨on white grounds, at least two shades often ~ of blue are used together —*Women's Wear Daily*⟩ ⟨held the ~ factions together and patiently built it into a potent political machine —*Time*⟩ **2 :** INCONGRUOUS, DISSIDENT, DISCREPANT ⟨even his discussion of experimental science has touches of medievalism, which are peculiarly ~ —H.O.Taylor⟩ **3 :** disagreeable or unsatisfying in sound ⟨the ~ noises from the badly tuned piano⟩; *specif* **:** harmonically unresolved — contrasted with *consonant* — **dis·so·nant·ly** *adv*

disspirit *var of* DISPIRIT

disspread *var of* DISPREAD

dis·suad·able \də̇ˈswādəbəl\ *adj* **:** capable of being dissuaded

dis·suade \-ād\ *vt* -ED/-ING/-S [MF or L; MF *dissuader*, fr. L *dissuadēre*, fr. *dis* [1]dis- + *suadēre* to advise, urge — more at SUASION] **1 a** *archaic* **:** to advise or exhort against (an action) **b :** to advise (a person) against something — usu. used with *from* ⟨a faithful monitor persuading us to whatever in conduct is gentle, honorable, of good repute, and so silently *dissuading* us from base thoughts, low ends, ignoble gains —A.T.Quiller-Couch⟩ **2 :** to divert by advice or persuasion **:** turn from something by reasoning ⟨~ a friend from making a grave mistake⟩ ⟨could easily ~ immigrant labor from unionism —*Amer. Guide Series: N.J.*⟩ ⟨if humanity can be *dissuaded* from suicide —Sumner Welles⟩

syn DISSUADE, DETER, DISCOURAGE, and DIVERT can mean in common to turn (one) aside from a purpose or project. DISSUADE suggests the method of argument, advice, or exhortation, implying coaxing or wheedling rather than bullying or browbeating ⟨he wrote a book to *dissuade* people from the use of tobacco —H.E.Scudder⟩ ⟨were not easily *dissuaded* and sought to have their way several times —A.N.Dragnich⟩ DETER usu. suggests fear as the cause of the turning aside though it can apply to any influence or consideration that alters the purpose or plan ⟨not *deterred* by threat of retaliation⟩ ⟨lured by desire, and yet *deterred* by conscience or want of decision —Theodore Dreiser⟩ ⟨his pride . . . must *deter* him from such foul misconduct —Jane Austen⟩ DISCOURAGE implies a deterring by undermining spirit or enthusiasm or weakening the intent or sense of purpose in some way ⟨strict laws *discourage* if they do not prevent crime⟩ ⟨nothing in these standards that will prohibit or *discourage* bakers from making improvements in the nutritional or other qualities of their products —*Americana Annual*⟩ ⟨the public was exhorted to avoid and *discourage* panic —H.G.Wells⟩ DIVERT implies the turning aside of the interest toward a new object or the turning of the attention in a new direction ⟨*divert* a person by flattery from causing a scandal⟩ ⟨*divert* a child from mischief by a toy⟩

dis·suad·er \-də(r)\ *n* -s **:** one that dissuades from a course of action

dis·sua·sion \-āzhən\ *n* -s [MF or L; MF, fr. L *dissuasion-, dissuasio,* fr. *dissuasus* (past part. of *dissuadēre*) + *-ion-, -io* -ion] **:** the act of dissuading **:** exhortation against something ⟨the man was bent upon squandering his money and no ~ would prevent it⟩

[1]**dis·sua·sive** \-āsiv, -āz\ *adj* [*dissuasion* + *-ive*] **:** tending to or intended to dissuade **:** expostulating against some action ⟨~ advice⟩ ⟨she made slight ~ gestures with her . . . hands —Mary Norton⟩ — **dis·sua·sive·ly** \ivlē\ *adv* — **dis·sua·sive·ness** \ivnəs\ *n* -ES

[2]**dissuasive** \"\ *n* -s **:** a dissuasive argument, treatise, or exhortation

dis·sunder \dəs+\ *vt* [[1]*dis-* + *sunder*] *archaic* **:** SUNDER, SEVER, SEPARATE

dissyllable *var of* DISYLLABLE

dis·symmetrical *also* **dis·symmetric** \ˌdi(s)+\ *adj* **:** characterized by dissymmetry — **dis·symmetrically** \"+\ *adv*

dis·symmetry \də(s), (ˈ)di(s)+\ *n* [[1]*dis-* + *symmetry*] **1 :** the absence of or the lack of symmetry **:** ASYMMETRY; *specif* **:** ENANTIOMORPHISM **2 :** biradial symmetry

dist- *or* **disto-** *or* **disti-** *comb form* [*distant*] **:** distal ⟨*disto*occlusion⟩ — opposed to *proximo-*

dist *abbr* **1** distance **2** distilled **3** distinguished **4** district

dis·tad \ˈdiˌstad\ *adv* [*distant* + *-ad*] **:** DISTALLY

[1]**dis·taff** \ˈdiˌstaf, -taa(ə)f, -tai̇f, -tȧf\ *n, pl* **distaffs** \fs, vz\ [ME *distaf,* fr. OE *distæf,* fr. *dis-* bunch of flax (akin to MLG *dise* bunch of flax on a distaff) + *stæf* staff — more at DIZEN, STAFF] **1 a :** a staff for holding the bunch of flax, tow, or wool from which thread is drawn in spinning by hand or with the spinning wheel **b :** woman's work, authority, or domain ⟨a man fitter for the ~ than for war⟩ **2 a** *archaic* **:** WOMAN, FEMALE; *esp* **:** a female heir **b :** the mother's side of a family ⟨tracing their descent by ~⟩ — compare SWORD SIDE

distaff 1a

[2]**distaff** \"\ *adj* **:** of or relating to a woman **:** FEMALE ⟨cooking, sewing, and such ~ matters⟩ ⟨~ applicants must be high-school graduates—*Springfield (Mass.) Daily News*⟩ ⟨a golf swing that is the ~ counterpart of the male champion's⟩ ⟨the entries in the golf tournament were largely on the ~ side⟩; *esp* **:** consisting of, derived from, or related to the mother or female line ⟨the ~ side of the family⟩ ⟨the ~ branch of a family⟩ — compare SPEAR

dis·taff·er \fə(r)\ *n* -s *slang* **:** WOMAN

dis·tain \dəˈstān\ *vt* -ED/-ING/-S [ME *disteynen,* fr. MF *desteindre* to take away the color of, fr. OF, fr. *des-* [1]dis- + *teindre* to dye, color, fr. L *tingere* to wet, dye — more at TINGE] **1** *archaic* **:** to tinge with a color different from the natural and proper one **:** STAIN, DISCOLOR **2** *archaic* **:** DEFILE, DISHONOR, SULLY

dis·tal \ˈdistᵊl\ *adj* [*dist-* + *-al*] **1 :** remote from the point of attachment or origin, from a point conceived of as central, or from the point of view: as **a :** located away from the center of the body ⟨the ~ end of a bone⟩ — opposed to *proximal* **b :** located away from the mesial plane of the body — opposed to *mesial* **2 :** physical or social rather than sensory — opposed to *proximal*

distal convoluted tubule *n* **:** the convoluted portion of the vertebrate nephron that lies between the loop of Henle and the collecting tubule in intimate association with the afferent vessel, that resembles the proximal convoluted tubule in structure though lacking the striated border, and that is concerned esp. with concentration of the urine

dis·tale \dəˈsta(ˌ)lē, -ā(ˌ)lē, -ä(ˌ)lē\ *n, pl* **distal·ia** \-lēə\ [NL, fr. *dist-* + L *-ale* (neut. of *-alis* -al)] **:** any of the distal row of carpal or tarsal bones

dis·tal·ly \ˈdistəlē\ *adv* **:** toward or near a distal part or end

[1]**dis·tance** \ˈdistən(t)s\ *n* -s [ME *distaunce,* fr. OF *destance, distance,* fr. L *distantia,* fr. *distant-, distans* (pres. part. of *distare* to stand apart, be distant) + *-ia* -y — more at DISTANT] **1** *obs* **:** DISCORD, DISSENSION, QUARREL **2 a** (1) **:** a portion of time between two events or between an event and the present **:** INTERVAL ⟨the ~ between birth and death⟩ ⟨not sure he could endure the ~ to the time of his release from captivity⟩ (2) **:** separation in time ⟨it is impossible to judge, at this ~, whether most of these cases would pass for willful murder at the present day —G.G.Coulton⟩ **b :** the degree or amount of separation between two points, lines, surfaces, or objects in geometrical space measured along the shortest path joining them ⟨the ~ between the two houses was exactly one mile⟩ ⟨the ~ between the eyes varies with individuals⟩: (1) **:** the space between troops in ranks, vehicles, or units measured from front to rear — contrasted with *interval* (2) **:** the space between the foremasts of adjacent ships in column, line, or line of bearing (3) **:** the amount of space between the eye and an object of perception **c :** an extent of space measured linearly along a route **:** the length esp. of a surface or road traveled or to be traveled ⟨the Gambia river, navigable for ocean vessels for a ~ of 150 miles —*Americana Annual*⟩ ⟨he did not know the ~ he had walked⟩ ⟨whoever guided the Stevens Party in 1844 would have kept as close as possible to the point of this hill in order to save ~ —G.R.Stewart⟩ ⟨a considerable ~ of highway⟩ ⟨followed for a ~ by a stray dog⟩ **d :** an extent or degree of figurative advance or movement away or along from a point considered primary or original ⟨they carried Puritan severity quite a ~ —John Gould⟩ ⟨the firm is now quite a ~ from what it was when it was founded⟩ **e :** a portion (as of landscape) extended in breadth and depth esp. viewable all at once **:** EXPANSE ⟨a ~ of field, woods, and diluted November sky did indeed stretch without any other feature —Elizabeth Bowen⟩ ⟨a country of flat plains and great ~*s*⟩ **f** *in racing* (1) **:** COURSE, ROUTE ⟨was able to run the ~ in record time⟩ (2) **:** an extent or length of the track marked by a post or flag placed in the last part of a racecourse which a horse in a heat race must reach by the time the winner crosses the finish line or be disqualified for later heats **3 a :** the quality or state of being distant or spatially remote ⟨~ lends enchantment⟩ **b :** remoteness in nonspatial relationships **:** the quality or state of being distant or not near or not close in ways other than spatial ⟨the gradual elimination of the ~ between a character and a writer's sympathy for that character —J.B.Ludwig⟩: as (1) **:** personal and esp. emotional or moral separation or lack of involvement **:** absence of intimacy or familiarity ⟨the sensitive young hero, shiveringly conscious of his ~ from the school community around him —Anthony Quinton⟩; *also* **:** COLDNESS, RESERVE ⟨an unusual ~ between the two formerly inseparable friends⟩ (2) **:** the degree of separation from immediate succession or close blood relationship ⟨the ~ between the duke and the throne was not great⟩ ⟨a great ~ between the two cousins⟩ (3) **:** AESTHETIC DISTANCE ⟨trying to preserve the ~ between the play and the audience⟩ **c :** DIFFERENCE, DISPARITY ⟨the spiritual, economic, and social ~*s* between the city dweller and farmer —*Amer. Guide Series: Minn.*⟩ **4 a :** a distant point or region or its representation in drawing or painting **:** a point not near or close ⟨the house was at a ~ from his work⟩ ⟨I can see things from a great ~, and look back across a fairly wide gulf of years —Harold Nicolson⟩ **b :** the representation of distance or spatial separation in drawing or painting **:** PERSPECTIVE; *also* **:** the background of a distant view — often used in pl. ⟨shaded ~*s*⟩ — **go the distance** *or* **last the distance :** to complete a specified course or a succession of commitments **:** last out a series of events or a course of action — **keep one's distance** *or* **keep at a distance :** to stay aloof **:** maintain an attitude of reserve — **know one's distance :** to avoid undue familiarity

[2]**distance** \"\ *vt* -ED/-ING/-S **1 a :** to place or keep at a distance ⟨to one who contrives to ~ himself from contemporary emotional disputation —*Times Lit. Supp.*⟩ ⟨apartness in space is the most common factor in such *distancing* of the potential aesthetic object —Hunter Mead⟩ **b :** to cause to appear remote or as if at a distance **2 a :** to leave far behind **:** OUTSTRIP ⟨they both intended to take the road to Irkutsk, and being well mounted hoped to ~ the Emir's scouts —W.H.G.Kingston⟩; *specif* **:** to beat by a distance in racing **b :** to surpass greatly **3 :** to declare disqualified for later heats in racing because of losing one heat by a distance or more

[3]**distance** \"\ *adj* **:** intended for or designed to facilitate the clearer perception of things at a distance ⟨~ glasses⟩

distance flag *n* **:** a flag held at a distance pole in a racecourse

distance language *n* **:** a mode of communication (as by means of drums or horns) for use beyond the range of the articulate voice

dis·tance·less \-ləs\ *adj* **1 :** lacking the effect of distance ⟨in the clear atmosphere the mountains seemed ~⟩ **2 :** not allowing an extended view or visibility ⟨a foggy ~ day⟩

distance meter *n* **:** a photographic range finder

distance pole *n* **:** the pole that indicates the distance on a racecourse

distance rate *n* **:** a transportation rate or scale of rates (as most passenger rates) that increases with or is affected by the distance of transportation

distance receptor *n* **:** a receptor for physiological stimuli (as light or sound) produced by distant objects — compare CONTACT RECEPTOR

distance ring *n* **:** a ring (as one shrunk on a piston) to separate two other rings

distances *pl of* DISTANCE, *pres 3d sing of* DISTANCE

distance signal *n* **:** one of a system of signals in the shape of spheres, cones, or cylinders used for communication at sea (as when conditions of visibility will prevent use of signal flags)

dis·tant \ˈdistənt\ *adj* [ME, fr. MF, fr. L *distant-, distans,* pres. part. of *distare* to stand apart, be distant, fr. *dis-* apart + *stare* to stand — more at DIS-, STAND] **1 a :** separated away in space **:** situated at some distance ⟨set up a pole a mile ~ from the beginning mark⟩ ⟨the ridge of hills some miles ~ —*Amer. Guide Series: Mich.*⟩ ⟨traveling to a more ~ place⟩; *also* **:** at a great distance **:** FAR-OFF ⟨the ship was headed for ~ countries⟩ ⟨would like to escape to some ~ spot⟩ **b :** separated by intervals of greater or less regularity ⟨when he smiled he showed a row of ~ teeth⟩ ⟨a grove of ~ trees⟩; *also* **:** being far apart **:** separated by a great distance from each other ⟨communication was difficult between such ~ places⟩ **c :** separated in a relationship other than spatial (as that of time, blood, or character) ⟨heartbeats that were ~ and very feeble⟩ ⟨in those ~ years when scholars will be able to write the history of the Far East with access to all the sources —Robert Payne⟩ ⟨a ~ relative⟩ ⟨willful blindness to ~ consequences —A.L.Guérard⟩ **2 :** different in kind ⟨a play far ~ from the one he first wrote⟩ ⟨pieces by far ~ composers⟩ **3 :** reserved or aloof in personal relationship **:** not cordial **:** somewhat haughty **:** COLD ⟨treated all people with a ~ politeness⟩ ⟨a ~ manner⟩ **4 :** coming from or going to a distance ⟨~ voyages⟩; *also* **:** concerned with or directed toward things at a distance ⟨~ thoughts⟩ ⟨a ~ look in the eye⟩ — **dis·tant·ly** *adv* — **dis·tant·ness** *n* -ES

distant signal *or* **distant block signal** *n* **:** a railroad signal placed at a distance that will allow adequate advance warning of the setting of a home signal at which the train must stop — called also *approach signal*

[1]**dis·taste** \dəˈstāst, (ˈ)diˈs-\ *vb* [[1]*dis-* + *taste* (v.)] *vt* **1 a** *obs* **:** to dislike the taste of **:** DISRELISH **b** *archaic* **:** to feel repugnance for or aversion to **2 a** *obs* **:** to cause a physical distaste in **:** DISGUST, NAUSEATE **b** *archaic* **:** to cause aversion or repugnance in **:** OFFEND, DISPLEASE **3** *obs* **:** to deprive of taste or relish **:** make unsavory **~** *vi, obs* **:** to become distasteful **:** taste offensive

[2]**distaste** \"\ *n* [[1]*dis-* + *taste* (n.)] **1 a :** dislike of food or drink **:** DISRELISH **b :** DISINCLINATION, DISLIKE, AVERSION, REPUGNANCE ⟨~*s* are equally legitimate, including a distaste for music itself —Virgil Thomson⟩ ⟨a ~ for work⟩ ⟨a ~ for book and thought —A.C.Benson⟩ **c** *obs* **:** mutual aversion **:** ALIENATION, ESTRANGEMENT **2** *obs* **:** DISCOMFORT, UNEASINESS, DISTRESS **3** *obs* **:** a cause of offense **:** OFFENSE **syn** see DISLIKE

distasted *adj, now dial* **:** DISLIKED, DISAPPROVED

dis·taste·ful \-āstfəl\ *adj* **1 a :** unpleasant or disgusting to the taste **:** NAUSEOUS, LOATHSOME ⟨a ~ plate of cold and underdone food⟩ **b :** OFFENSIVE, DISAGREEABLE ⟨the truth proved ~⟩ ⟨a succession of ~ chores⟩ **2 :** showing distaste or aversion ⟨viewed the cold and greasy potatoes on his plate with a ~ expression on his face⟩ **syn** see HATEFUL

dis·taste·ful·ly \-fəlē, -li\ *adv* **:** in a distasteful manner

dis·taste·ful·ness \-fəlnəs\ *n* **:** the quality or state of being distasteful

dis·tel·fink \ˈdis(h)tᵊlˌfiŋk\ *n* -s [PaG *dischdelfink,* lit., goldfinch, fr. G *distelfink,* fr. *distel* thistle (fr. OHG *distila*) + *fink* finch, fr. OHG *finco, fincho* — more at THISTLE, FINCH] **:** a traditional Pennsylvania Dutch design motif in the form of a stylized bird

[1]**dis·temper** \dəs +\ *vt* [ME *distempren, destempren,* fr. LL *distemperare* (to mix badly), fr. L *dis-* [1]dis- + *temperare* to temper, mingle properly — more at TEMPER] **1 :** to throw out of order or proper or smoothly working adjustment **:** afflict with a distemper **:** DISORDER, DERANGE ⟨no sophism is too gross to delude minds ~*ed* by party spirit —T.B.Macaulay⟩ ⟨he has seldom been grievously ~*ed* by repressions, guilt, despondency, or philosophical doubt —C.J.Rolo⟩ **2** *archaic* **a :** to make unhealthy **:** SICKEN **b :** to derange the mind of **:** make insane **3** *archaic* **:** to deprive of even temper or moderation **:** make ill-humored

[2]**dis·temper** \" *sometimes* ˈdi+,-\ *n* [partly fr. [1]*distemper,* partly fr. [1]*dis-* + *temper*] **1 :** bad or ill humor **:** bad temper **:** ill feeling **2 :** a disordered or abnormal bodily state usu. of an animal: as **a :** a highly contagious virus disease of dogs, minks, wolves, and foxes that is marked by fever, skin eruptions, acute respiratory inflammation frequently passing into pneumonia and sometimes by symptoms referable to invasion and demyelination of nervous tissue; *also* **:** any of certain allied and ill-distinguished virus infections of dogs — compare HARD PAD **b :** STRANGLES **c :** PANLEUCOPENIA **d :** a severe frequently fatal infectious nasopharyngeal inflammation of rabbits **3** *obs* **:** INTOXICATION **4 a :** disorder or derangement esp. civil or political or a particular disorder, affliction, or derangement ⟨in the middle ages . . . resistance was an ordinary remedy for political ~*s* —T.B.Macaulay⟩ ⟨the ~*s* of monarchy were the great subjects of apprehension and distress —J.R.Newman⟩ **b** *archaic* **:** unpleasant or inclement condition (as of weather or climate)

[3]**dis·temper** \dəs +\ *vt* -ED/-ING/-S [ME *distemperen,* fr. MF *destemprer,* fr. ML *distemperare,* fr. L *dis-* [1]dis- + *temperare* to mingle properly] **1 a** *obs* **:** to dilute with or soak, steep, or dissolve in a liquid **b** *archaic* **:** to corrupt or impair by dilution or by a counteragent **2 a :** to mix (colors or ingredients) to produce distemper for painting **b :** to paint in or with distemper

[4]**dis·temper** \" *sometimes* ˈdi+,-\ *n* -s **1 :** a process of painting in which the pigments are mixed with an emulsion of egg yolk, with size, or with white of egg, or when distinguished from tempera with size only as a vehicle and usu. used for scene painting or the decoration of usu. plaster walls and ceilings **2 a :** the paint or the prepared ground used in the distemper process of painting **b :** a painting done in distemper **c :** a pigment used esp. for distemper paint **3 :** any of a number of paints or coloring materials using water as a vehicle (as whitewash, calcimine, or cement wash)

distemperate *adj* [ME *distemperat,* fr. ML *distemperatus,* past part. of *distemperare*] **1** *obs* **:** being out of order **:** not functioning normally **2** *obs* **:** INTEMPERATE, IMMODERATE

dis·temperature \dəs, (ˈ)dis+\ *n* **1 :** DISTEMPER **2** *archaic* **:** lack of moderation **:** EXCESS, INTEMPERATENESS

distempered *adj* [ME, fr. past part. of *distemperen*] **1 :** DISORDERED, UNHEALTHY ⟨a ~ national economy⟩ **2 :** suggesting disease (as in color or appearance) ⟨moldy ~ walls⟩ — **dis·tem·pered·ly** *adv* — **dis·tem·pered·ness** *n* -ES

distempering *n* -s **:** [4]DISTEMPER 2a

dis·tem·per·oid \dəˈstempəˌrȯid\ *adj* [[2]*distemper* + *-oid*] **:** resembling distemper; *specif* **:** of, relating to, or being a strain of canine distemper virus attenuated by passage through ferrets and used to develop immunity in dogs and other susceptible hosts to natural distemper infection

dis·tend \dəˈstend\ *vb* [ME *distenden,* fr. L *distendere,* fr. *dis-* apart + *tendere* to stretch — more at DIS-, THIN] *vt* **1** *archaic* **:** to extend in one direction **:** lengthen out **:** spread apart **2 a :** to stretch out or extend in more than one direction ⟨the main outlines of the land yet lay clearly ~*ed* before them —Norman Douglas⟩ **b :** to enlarge from internal pressure **:** SWELL, DILATE, BLOAT ⟨the bat's body was so ~*ed* that it appeared spherical —R.L.Ditmars & A.M.Greenhall⟩ ⟨a ~*ed* bladder⟩ ⟨~*ed* nostrils⟩ **c :** to make larger or increase beyond a due, expected, or reasonable proportion ⟨the ~*ed* profits of the enemy trade —F.L.Paxson⟩ ⟨a much-*distended* land power —W.G.East⟩ ⟨this simple drama as it has been ~*ed* into a spectacle to catch the eye of Broadway —John Mason Brown⟩ **:** unduly increase or magnify the importance of ⟨print headlines that attract the reader, even if the facts of the story have to be ~*ed* —Jean Hills⟩ **~** *vi* **:** to become larger, expanded, or inflated **:** SWELL, ENLARGE ⟨her eyes seemed to ~ with surprise⟩ **syn** see EXPAND

distended *adj* **:** greatly enlarged **:** SWOLLEN, BULGING, DILATED — **dis·tend·ed·ly** *adv* — **dis·tend·ed·ness** *n* -ES

dis·ten·si·bil·i·ty \dəˌsten(t)səˈbilədē, (ˌ)diˌs-\ *n* -ES **:** the quality or state of being distensible **:** the capacity of stretching

dis·ten·si·ble \dəˈsten(t)səbəl\ *adj* [LL *distensus* (past part. of L *distendere*) + E *-ible*] **:** capable of being distended, extended, or dilated **:** able to stretch or expand or to be stretched or expanded ⟨its stomach . . . is extraordinarily ~ —R.E. Coker⟩ ⟨the arterial walls are . . . not rigid but elastic and ~ —F.A.Faught⟩

dis·tensile \dəs+\ *adj* [LL *distensus* + E *-ile* (as in *tensile*)] **1 :** DISTENSIBLE **2 :** causing distension

dis·ten·sion *or* **dis·ten·tion** \dəˈstenchən\ *n* -s [L *distention-, distentio,* fr. *distentus* + *-ion-, -io* -ion] **:** the act of distending or the state of being distended esp. unduly or abnormally ⟨~ of the abdomen, vomiting, and localized pain and swelling —Morris Fishbein⟩

dis·ten·sive \-n(t)siv\ *adj* [*distension* + *-ive*] **:** DISTENSIBLE

[1]**distent** *adj* [L *distentus,* past part. of *distendere* to distend — more at DISTEND] *obs* **:** spread out **:** DISTENDED

[2]**dis·tent** \dəˈstent\ *n* -s [L *distentus,* fr. *distentus,* past part.] **:** BREADTH, DISTENSION

[1]**disterminate** *vt* [L *disterminatus,* past part. of *disterminare,* fr. *dis-* [1]dis- + *terminare* to bound, limit, terminate — more at TERMINATE] *obs* **:** to separate by forming a boundary

[2]**disterminate** *adj* [L *disterminatus*] *obs* **:** marked off **:** SEPARATED

dis·thene \ˈdisˌthēn, ˈdīs-\ *n* -s [F *disthène,* fr. *di-* + Gk *sthenos* force — more at STHENIC] **:** CYANITE

dis·throne \dəs, (ˈ)dis+\ *vt* [[1]*dis-* + *throne* (n.)] **:** DETHRONE ⟨a queen *disthroned*⟩

disthronize *vt* -ED/-ING/-S [[1]*dis-* + *throne* + *-ize*] *obs* **:** DETHRONE

disti- — see DIST-

dis·tich \ˈdi(ˌ)stik, -ˌstēk\ *n* -s [L *distichon,* fr. Gk, fr. neut. of *distichos* with two rows, of two verses, fr. *di-* + *stichos* row, line, verse; akin to Gk *steichein* to go — more at STAIR] **:** a strophic unit or unit of verse consisting of two lines and usu. comprising a sense unit

dis·ti·chal \ˈdistəkəl, -tēk-\ *adj* **:** of, relating to, or comprising a distich

dis·tich·lis \dəˈstikləs\ *n, cap* [NL, irreg. fr. Gk *distichos*] **:** a small genus of American grasses found along seashores and in alkaline regions and having creeping rhizomes, distichous leaves, and several-flowered spikes in small panicles — see SALT GRASS

dis·ti·chous \ˈdistəkəs\ *adj* [L *distichus* fr. Gk *distichos* with two rows] **1** *of plant or animal parts* **:** disposed in two vertical rows **:** two-ranked ⟨a grass with ~ leaves⟩ **2 :** divided into two distinct segments **:** BIPARTITE ⟨~ antennae⟩ — **dis·ti·chous·ly** *adv*

dis·till *also* **dis·til** \dəˈstil\ *vb* **distilled; distilled; distilling; distills** *also* **distils** [ME *distillen,* fr. MF *distiller,* fr. LL *distillare,* alter. of L *destillare,* fr. *de-* down + *stillare* to drip, trickle, fr. *stilla* drop; akin to G *stieren* to stare, ON *stira* to stare, L *stiria* icicle, Lith *stýrti* to stiffen, OE *stān* stone — more at DE-, STONE] *vt* **1 a :** to send or pour forth in small quantities **:** INFUSE ⟨snowy . . . blossoms that ~ their fragrance through the countryside —*Amer. Guide Series: Va.*⟩ **b :** to let fall or precipitate in drops or in a wet mist ⟨some caves are dry, others ~ water from invisible rifts or pendent beards —Norman Douglas⟩ **2 a :** to subject to or transform by distillation ⟨~ molasses into rum⟩ **b :** to get, extract, or make by distillation, by a process suggesting distillation, or as if by distillation ⟨a strong drink ~*ed* from grain⟩ ⟨~ gasoline from crude oil⟩ ⟨~ coal tar from coal⟩ ⟨basic truths must be discovered and ~*ed* out of the available mass of mental acrobatics, common sense, horse sense, and nonsense —P.M.Mazur⟩ ⟨they manage to ~ comedy out of the spiritual loneliness of the characters they are playing —Brooks Atkinson⟩ ⟨a 1500-page narrative ~*ed* from 168 bound volumes of his papers —A.S. Henning⟩ **c :** to obtain an extract from (as a plant) by infusion and distillation ⟨making medicines by ~*ing* herbs she had gathered⟩ **d :** to remove by distillation — usu. used with *out* or *off* ⟨~ impurities from the elixir⟩ ⟨~ off the impurities⟩ ⟨the heavy oil left after gasoline and light oils are ~*ed* off the crude —*Newsweek*⟩ **e :** to make concentrated by abridgment and purification or by the extraction of an essential or typical portion **:** CONCENTRATE, PURIFY ⟨~ the information before presenting it to the committee⟩ ⟨she ~*s* the lore of the ancients and the learning of modern specialists into a literary form palatable to a wide public —W.E.D.Allen⟩ ⟨a lyric poet works in a more ~*ed* medium than narrative prose —Cyril Connolly⟩ **3** *obs* **:** DISSOLVE, MELT **~** *vi* **1 a :** to fall or materialize in drops or in a fine moisture **:** DROP, TRICKLE ⟨water ~*ing* over the rocks from the moist undergrowth⟩ **b :** to fall, appear, or materialize slowly or in small quantities at a time as if by distillation ⟨spiritual values ~ slowly from the interaction of sensation, emotion, or thought —G.R.Harrison⟩ **2 :** to undergo distillation **:** condense or drop from a still after distillation ⟨a liquor that ~*s* easily⟩ **3 :** to perform distillation

dis·till·able \-ləbəl\ *adj* **:** capable of being distilled esp. without chemical change ⟨alcohol is ~⟩

dis·till·age \-lij\ *n* -s [*distill* + *-age*] **:** the product of distillation

dis·til·land \ˈdistəˌland\ *n* -s [L *distillandum,* neut. of *distillandus,* gerundive of *distillare*] **:** material to be or being distilled — compare DISTILLATE

dis·til·late \ˈdistəˌlāt, -ˌlət *also* dəˈstilə; *usu* ǀd.+V\ *n* -s [ISV *distill* + *-ate*] **1 :** the usu. liquid product that is condensed from vapor during distillation (as of petroleum) — compare DISTILLAND **2 :** something resembling a distillate in being a concentration, an abstract, or an essence ⟨the very ~ of idolatry —D.C.Williams⟩ ⟨this book is the clear sparkling ~ of the wide experience gained during a lifetime —A.C.Morrison⟩ ⟨this book is a ~ of facts —*N. Y. Times Book Rev.*⟩ ⟨put into their letters the ~ of their wisdom and nobility —G.W. Johnson⟩

dis·til·la·tion \ˌdistəˈlāshən\ *n* -s [ME *distillacioun,* fr. L *distillation-, distillatio,* fr. *distillatus* (past part. of *distillare* to distill) + *-ion-, -io* -ion] **1 :** the process of driving off gas or vapor from liquids or solids by heating (as in a still or retort) and condensing to liquid products, such processes being used esp. for purification, fractionation, or the formation of new substances by decomposition **:** RECTIFICATION — see AZEOTROPIC DISTILLATION, DESTRUCTIVE DISTILLATION, EXTRACTIVE DISTILLATION, MOLECULAR DISTILLATION; compare EVAPORATION, SUBLIMATION **2 :** DISTILLATE ⟨every paragraph is a ~ of wide reading, sound judgment, and unemotional reasoning —*Times Lit. Supp.*⟩ ⟨these translations . . . can be accepted as genuine ~*s* of the Orient —G.P.Meyer⟩

distilled green *n* **:** VERDIGRIS 4

distilled liquor *n* **:** an alcoholic liquor (as brandy, whiskey, gin, rum, or arrack) obtained by distillation from wine or other fermented fruit juice or plant juice or from a starchy material (as various grains) that has first been brewed — called also *hard liquor*

distilled water *n* **:** water that has been freed of dissolved or suspended solids and from organisms by distillation (as for medical or chemical purposes)

dis·till·er \dəˈstilə(r)\ *n* -s **:** one that distills: as **a :** one that distills alcoholic liquors **b :** a distilling apparatus **:** STILL

distillers' beer *n* **:** WASH 6b (1)

distillers' grains *n pl* **:** the residue from the manufacture of

alcohol or alcoholic beverages distilled from grains and used as livestock feed
distillers' solubles *n pl but often sing in constr* : the dissolved remains and fine particles left after the solid grains have been strained from the residue from alcoholic distillation; *esp* : such remains and particles when dehydrated and used as a source of vitamins and minerals in animal rations
dis·till·ery \də'stil(ə)rē, -ri\ *n* -ES [*distill* + *-ery*] **1** *archaic* : DISTILLATION **2** : the building and works where distilling (as of alcoholic liquors) is carried on
dis·till house \də'stil-\ *n, archaic* : a building used for distilling; *also* : DISTILLERY
distilling *n* -S [fr. gerund of *distill*] : the making of distilled liquors as a business
distilling flask *n* : a glass usu. round-bottomed flask for holding a substance to be distilled
dis·till·ment *or* **dis·til·ment** \də'stilmənt\ *n* -S *archaic* : DISTILLATION
distills *pres 3d sing of* DISTILL
distils *pres 3d sing of* DISTIL

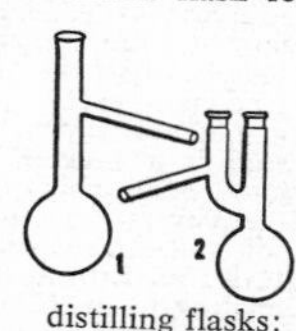

distilling flasks: *1* common type, *2* Claisen flask

dis·tinct \də'stiŋ(k)t\ *adj, often* -ER/-EST [ME, fr. MF, fr. L *distinctus*, past part. of *distinguere* to distinguish — more at DISTINGUISH] **1 a** *obs* : discriminated by a visible sign : marked out : DISTINGUISHED **b** : characterized by qualities individualizing or distinguishing as apart from, unlike, or not identical with another or others ⟨things similar in effect but wholly ~ in motive —Hilaire Belloc⟩ **2** : capable of being easily perceived: as **a** : capable of being readily seen, felt, or heard through sharp, clear, unmistakable impression : not blurred, obscured, or indefinite ⟨the slender and fragile tracery that must be preserved unventilated and ~ —B.N. Cardozo⟩ ⟨her last death shriek ~ among a thousand —William Wordsworth⟩ **b** : capable of being easily grasped or comprehended by the mind because of clear cogent appearance or presentation ⟨a promise that Mr. Nicholls should have a ~ refusal —Virginia Woolf⟩ ⟨left us with a clear and ~ idea of human nature —*Times Lit. Supp.*⟩ **3** *archaic* : notably marked or decorated **4 a** : NOTABLE, UNUSUAL ⟨so overrun with camera'ed foreigners that it is a ~ achievement to get an unencumbered photo —William Petersen⟩ **b** : UNEQUIVOCAL, UNQUESTIONABLE ⟨a ~ liberal⟩ ⟨hot, dry summers . . . with drought a ~ possibility —W.B.Johnston & I.Crkvencic⟩
syn SEPARATE, SEVERAL, DISCRETE: these words agree in referring to two or more things not the same or not blended or united. DISTINCT is likely to stress characteristics that distinguish or that indicate that the thing modified is apart from or different from others ⟨probably to Guido de Bres . . . the Dutch Reformed Church owed the beginning of its sturdy life, and that it did not become a mere limb of either the French Calvinistic, or German Reformed body, but grew as a "shield and blessing to both" with a *distinct* and rooted life of its own —J.L.Motley⟩ ⟨Mrs. Yeobright, who, possessing two *distinct* moods in close contiguity, a gentle mood and an angry, flew from one to the other without the least warning —Thomas Hardy⟩ Often interchangeable with DISTINCT, SEPARATE may stress lack of connection or difference in identity between two things ⟨a part of the citizens seceded from the main body, and formed a *separate* community on the neighboring marshes —W.H.Prescott⟩ ⟨this rupture of the supposed continuity of nature and the reestablishment of ethics and aesthetics as *separate* and autonomous realms —J. W.Krutch⟩ ⟨she had a command of hand, a nicety and force of touch, which is an endowment *separate* from pictorial genius, though indispensable to its exercise —Nathaniel Hawthorne⟩ In older, archaic, or formal English SEVERAL may also indicate distinctness, difference, or separation from similar items ⟨her knowledge of three *several* tongues —Elinor Wylie⟩ ⟨a network of concrete highways upon the *several* states —W.H.Hamilton⟩ DISCRETE forcefully stresses individuality and lack of connection despite apparent similarities ⟨*discrete* quantity consists of the separate and unjointed units. Continuous quantity resists and even defies description in terms of disjunct ultimate units —Josiah Royce⟩ ⟨the conclusion that gases are made up of *discrete* units (molecules) —Lancelot Hogben⟩ ⟨by confining his operations to those aspects of reality which had, so to say, market value, and by isolating and dismembering the corpus of experience, the physical scientist created a habit of mind favorable to *discrete* practical inventions —Lewis Mumford⟩ **syn** see in addition EVIDENT
dis·tinc·tio \də'stiŋ(k)t(s)ē,ō, -)shē,ō\ *also* **dis·tinc·tion** \-)shən\ *n, pl* **distincti·o·nes** \ˌ=ˌ=tsē'ō,nās, -shē'ō,nēz\ *also* **distinctions** \-shənz\ [ML *distinction-, distinctio* section, division, fr. L] : a phrase in a Gregorian melody indicated by markings in the text
dis·tinc·tion \də'stiŋ(k)shən\ *n* -S [ME *distinccioun*, fr. OF *distinction*, fr. L *distinction-, distinctio*, fr. *distinctus* (past part. of *distinguere* to distinguish) + *-ion-, -io* -ion — more at DISTINGUISH] **1 a** *archaic* : a part of a divided whole : CATEGORY, SECTION **b** *obs* : the act of separating into parts : PARTITION, DIVISION **c** : CLASS, GRADE, RANK ⟨Mr. Hemingway's . . . prose is of the first ~ —Edmund Wilson⟩ **2 a** : the act of distinguishing a difference : DISCRIMINATION, DIFFERENTIATION ⟨not interested in ~s between philosophic entities⟩ ⟨without ~ as to race, sex, language, or religion —Vera M. Dean⟩ **b** : the object or result of distinguishing or discriminating ⟨the ~s of degree had lost much of their rigidity —Douglas Bush⟩ ⟨the line of ~ between the citizen and the subject —R.B.Taney⟩ ⟨crooked crooks and honest crooks, a ~ which does represent a difference —Gerald Carson⟩ : CONTRAST ⟨he was pretty reasonable in ~ to the other men⟩ ⟨the classical economists in ~ to the modern price theorists —Paul Mattick⟩; *also* : special favor ⟨full commissions are payable to the galleries to the same extent as if sold to other bidders, without ~ or preference shown to such consignors or agents —*Parke-Bernet Galleries Catalog*⟩ **c** *archaic* : the faculty of distinguishing : DISCERNMENT **3** : something that distinguishes one thing from another : a distinguishing quality or mark : DIFFERENTIA ⟨the ~ between good and evil⟩ ⟨a ~ between the two men was their manner of treating inferiors⟩ **4** : the quality or state of being distinguishable or distinct: as **a** : DIFFERENCE, DISPARITY ⟨the ~ between the twins was great enough to eliminate the usual identification trouble⟩ **b** *obs* : CLEARNESS, DISTINCTNESS **5 a** : the quality or state of being distinguished or of having distinguished oneself ⟨the man's ~ was in his entire bearing⟩ **b** : EMINENCE, SIGNIFICANCE ⟨a politician of some ~ in the town⟩ ⟨looking for actions that would reveal his guilt, but found none of ~⟩ : special honor or regard ⟨graduated from college with ~⟩ ⟨grant him the ~ he deserves⟩ **c** : the mark or indication of special honor or regard ⟨has the ~ of being both rich and handsome⟩ **d** : worthiness or fitness for special or professional honor or recognition ⟨accomplished the difficult task with rare ~⟩ **6** : the act of giving special recognition (as by honoring) ⟨Urban received him with great ~—*Encyc. Americana*⟩ **syn** see DISSIMILARITY
dis·tinc·tion·less \-ləs\ *adj* : lacking distinctions
¹dis·tinc·tive \də'stiŋ(k)tiv, -tēv *also* -təv\ *adj* [ML *distinctivus*, fr. L *distinctus* + *-ivus* -ive] **1 a** : serving to distinguish : setting apart from others : INDIVIDUALIZING ⟨a ~ character of the type is a tendency to procrastinate⟩ **b** : CHARACTERISTIC, PECULIAR ⟨actions ~ of a brutal man⟩ ⟨a call that was almost ~ to the catbird⟩ ⟨the moist, salt air of the Cape is said to turn the shingles on roofs and walls to a ~ gray —Jackson Rivers⟩ : SPECIAL ⟨not only was homicide frequent but the tough hombres of the town added a ~ touch in their manner of disposing of the body —*Amer. Guide Series: Texas*⟩ **c** : having or giving style or distinction ⟨a woman with a talent for wearing consistently ~ clothes⟩ ⟨an old ~ residential quarter —*Amer. Guide Series: N.Y. City*⟩ **2** *archaic* : having the ability to distinguish : DISCRIMINATING **3** *phonetics, of a feature of speech* : capable of making a segment of utterance different in meaning as well as in sound from an otherwise identical utterance : that makes or helps to make a speech item a phoneme rather than an allophone **4** : DISJUNCTIVE 4 **syn** see CHARACTERISTIC
²distinctive \"\ *n* -S : DISJUNCTIVE 2
distinctive insignia *n* : the distinctive metal badges or other devices authorized for wear by members of a regiment or battalion of the U.S. Army
dis·tinc·tive·ly \-təvlē, -li\ *adv* : in a distinctive manner ⟨a bird with ~ mottled coloring⟩ ⟨a man ~ attired⟩
dis·tinc·tive·ness \-tivnəs, -tēv- *also* -təv-\ *n* -ES : the quality or state of being distinctive
dis·tinct·ly \də'stiŋ(k)tlē, -ŋklē, -li\ *adv* [ME, fr. *distinct* + *-ly*] : in a distinct manner: as **a** *obs* : SEPARATELY **b** : with distinctness : not confusedly : without a blending or merging of one thing with another ⟨the efforts of the writers to paint ~ and separately these six heads —Irving Babbitt⟩ ⟨that which is clearly and ~ conceived as the truth —C.W.Hendel⟩ **c** : CLEARLY, OBVIOUSLY, UNEQUIVOCALLY ⟨the end which Charles ~ proposed to himself —T.B.Macaulay⟩ ⟨the younger of the two boys is ~ the brighter⟩ : DECIDEDLY ⟨the boy was ~ angry when he lashed out with his fists⟩ **d** : DISTINCTIVELY ⟨his characters are ~ Irish —*Univ. of Arizona Record*⟩ ⟨the swamp forests are a ~ southern plant community —*Amer. Guide Series: N.C.*⟩
dis·tinct·ness \-ŋtnəs, -ŋkn-\ *n* -ES : the quality or state of being distinct
dis·tin·gué \ˌdē,staŋ'gā, ˌdi,s-, -taiŋ-, də'=ˌ=, dē'=ˌ=\ *adj* [F, fr. past part. of *distinguer*] **1** : distinguished in manner or bearing : marked by an appearance of distinction ⟨a rather ~ foreign diplomat with graying temples and a black homburg⟩ : giving distinction ⟨black is always ~ for evening wear⟩ **2** : special to a group laying claim to distinction : superior fashionably or culturally; *sometimes* : AFFECTED ⟨there is something rather ~ in being damned —George Orwell⟩
dis·tin·guish \də'stiŋgwish, -wēsh, *chiefly in pres part* -wəsh; ÷ -ŋw-\ *vb* -ED/-ING/-ES [MF *distinguer*, fr. L *distinguere*, fr. *dis-* ¹dis- + *-stinguere* (akin to L *instigare* to urge on, stimulate) — more at STICK] *vt* **1 a** : to perceive as being separate or different : recognize a difference in ⟨able to ~ normally confused sounds⟩ **b** *obs* : to draw fine distinctions in respect to **2 a** : to mark as separate or different (as one thing from another) : make a difference between : DISCRIMINATE ⟨the concept of culture . . . ties some phenomena and interpretations together; it dissimilates and ~es others —A.L.Kroeber⟩ ⟨he was slightly built, shy, deferential almost, with nothing in his dress to ~ him from his workmen —G.S. Gale⟩ ⟨the church was ~ed by the absence of a tower⟩ ⟨a man ~ed by a shock of wild white hair⟩; *also* : to make clearly visible ⟨street lamps and lighted windows ~ the hills and valleys that are obscured in the day by tenements and apartment houses —*Amer. Guide Series: N.Y. City*⟩ **b** : to separate into kinds, classes, or categories (as by logical division) ⟨unable to ~ the notes into anything more than high or low⟩ **c** : to set above or apart from others : make eminent : give prestige to ⟨he has ~ed himself by negotiating a number of international trade agreements —*Amer. Guide Series: Tenn.*⟩ ⟨the New Jersey Constitution is ~ed as one of the briefest in the country —*Amer. Guide Series: N.J.*⟩ ⟨men who had ~ed themselves in action in several significant battles⟩ **d** *obs* : to separate or divide into portions or sections : mark (parts) as separate **e** : to make identifiable or discernible as a separate entity : mark off : CHARACTERIZE ⟨once writers were a class apart, ~ed by ink-stained fingers, unkempt hair, and a predilection for drinking cheap wine in cellars —Edward Uhlan⟩ ⟨nothing ~es the taste of an age more clearly than the language which it admires —R.W.Southern⟩ **3 a** : to perceive, discern, or descry (something easily confused or blended with adjacent things) ⟨I glanced seaward . . . and ~ed nothing except a single green light, minute and far away, that might have been the end of a dock —Scott Fitzgerald⟩ ⟨unable to ~ road markings in the fog⟩ **b** : to pick out or single out ⟨the examiner must be careful to ~ the excitable individuals —H.G. Armstrong⟩ **4** *archaic* : to pay special attention to : note especially **5** *obs* : to argue subtly and speciously ~ *vi* : to perceive a difference : exercise discrimination ⟨a judge ~es between cases apparently similar⟩ — **distinguish of** *obs* : DISTINGUISH
syn DISTINGUISH, DIFFERENTIATE, DISCRIMINATE, and DEMARCATE, can mean, in common, to point out or mark the differences between things that are or seem to be very much and often confusingly alike. DISTINGUISH implies a reason for confusion as between two things having an extremely close relationship or connection ⟨nothing more profoundly *distinguishes* the Hellenic from the modern view of life than the estimate in which women were held by the Greeks —G.L.Dickinson⟩ ⟨he must be taught to *distinguish* between the truth and his imagination —Mary Austin⟩ ⟨a child under four will hardly *distinguish* between yesterday and a week ago —Bertrand Russell⟩ ⟨Dr. Dunham *distinguished* between the terms *public relations* and *publicity* —T.F.Reidy⟩ DIFFERENTIATE implies the possession of a distinguishing character or characters or the ascertainment of the differences between things easily confused ⟨his immaculate appearance *differentiates* him from his fellow workers⟩ ⟨classes small enough to enable the teacher to *differentiate* the strong and the willing from the sluggards —C.H.Grandgent⟩ ⟨he *differentiates* industrial, political, and moral activities —D.S.Robinson⟩ DISCRIMINATE can imply the possession of obvious distinguishing characteristics ⟨his gift of fine oratory *discriminates* him from other statesmen⟩ but usu. implies the power to discern differences, often slight, between similar things ⟨irritated by the wasp's inability to *discriminate* a house from a tree —E.K.Brown⟩ ⟨no dictionary *discriminates* perfectly among these finely shaded distinctions in trade vocabularies —Ben Riker⟩ DEMARCATE, implying the literal setting of boundaries, can be used to suggest a distinguishing between things as if by marking them off ⟨how shall we *demarcate* reproduction from growth —G.H. Lewes⟩
dis·tin·guish·abil·i·ty \ˌ=ˌ=ə'biləd·ē, -ətē, -i\ *n* -ES : the quality or state of being distinguishable
dis·tin·guish·able \-shəbəl\ *adj* **1** : capable of being distinguished : SEPARABLE, DIVISIBLE, DISCERNIBLE ⟨have maintained that dialectic and rhetoric are ~ stages of argumentation —R.M.Weaver⟩ ⟨an essay with a meaning that was not always ~⟩ ⟨a project ~ into four separate stages of progress⟩ **2** *obs* : DISTINGUISHED, DISTINCTIVE, EMINENT — **dis·tin·guish·able·ness** \-nəs\ *n* -ES
dis·tin·guish·ably \-blē, li\ *adv* : in a distinguishable manner
dis·tin·guished \-sht\ *adj* **1 a** : marked by eminence and distinction : noted for significant achievement or great dignity ⟨under the general's ~ leadership⟩ ⟨his name was placed on the roster of ~ statesmen⟩ ⟨a ~ figure in American architecture⟩ ⟨a ~ career as a mathematical logician —M.R.Cohen⟩ ⟨~ for his facility in languages⟩ **b** : marked by excellence in quality ⟨many facets of the mind and personality of the greatest scientist of our time presented in a ~ translation —I.B.Cohen⟩ ⟨it is not ~, but has the clarity of action and plot demanded by oral storytelling —*N.Y. Herald Tribune Bk. Rev.*⟩ ⟨a book ~ for its handling of an intricate period in history⟩ **2** : befitting an eminent person : conferring dignity ⟨blue eyes made bluer by dark hair with a ~ streak of gray —Eva Gabor⟩ ⟨wearing a ~ velvet-collared coat⟩ — **dis·tin·guished·ly** \-shtlē, -shədlē, -li\ *adv*
distinguishing *adj* : serving to separate or set apart from others in nature, character, or quality : marking off as different : DISTINCTIVE ⟨the really ~ feature of the directories is their great accuracy —*Report of Amer. Tel. & Tel. Co.*⟩ ⟨it was . . . a ~ characteristic of the Greek religion that it did not concern itself with the conscience at all —G.L. Dickinson⟩ — **dis·tin·guish·ing·ly** *adv*
distinguishing flag *n* **1** : any of certain flags flown to indicate the presence of an officer of high rank or of the holder of a high governmental office — used in the British navy and the U.S. Army; compare PERSONAL FLAG **2** : a flag flown to identify the headquarters of a major unit of the U.S. Army that does not have an organizational color or standard **3** : a flag indicative of the ownership of a vessel (as the house flag of a commercial ship or the private signal of a yacht)
distinguishing pennant *n* : any of a number of pennants that various naval officers are entitled to fly as an indication of their rank or command (as the broad pennant of a British commodore or a command pennant in the U.S. Navy)
dis·tin·guo \də'stiŋ(,)gwō\ *n* -S [L, I distinguish, 1st pers. sing. pres. indic. of *distinguere*] : a quibbling distinction
dis·ti·style \'distə,stīl\ *n* [*dist-* + *style*] : one of the blade-shaped accessory parts of the male genitalia of certain insects
distn *abbr* distillation
disto- — see DIST-
dis·to·clu·sion \ˌdistə'klüzhən\ *n* -S [*dist-* + *occlusion*] : malposition of a lower tooth or teeth distal to the upper when the jaws are closed
dis·toe·chu·rus \ˌdistə'kyürəs\ *n, cap* [NL, fr. Gk *distoichos* in two rows + NL *-urus*] : a genus of marsupial mammals consisting of the pen-tailed phalanger
dis·to·ma \'distəmə\ [NL, fr. *di-* + *-stoma*] *syn of* FASCIOLA
di·sto·ma·ta \dī'stōməd·ə\ *n pl, cap* [NL, fr. *di-* + *-stomata*] *in some classifications* : a large suborder of Prosostomata comprising flukes with oral and ventral suckers and with the reproductive organs mostly posterior to the ventral sucker — **di·sto·mate** \-ō,māt, -ōmət\ *adj* — **di·stome** \'dī,stōm\ *adj or n*
dis·to·mat·i·dae \ˌdistə'mad·ə,dē\ [NL, fr. *Distomat-*, *Distoma*, type genus + *-idae*] *syn of* FASCIOLIDAE
di·sto·ma·to·sis \ˌdī,stōmə'tōsəs\ *also* **di·sto·mi·a·sis** \ˌdīstō'mīəsəs\ *n, pl* **distomato·ses** \-ō,sēz\ *also* **distomia·ses** \-īə,sēz\ [NL, fr. *Distomata* + *-osis* or *-iasis*] : infestation with or disease caused by digenetic trematode worms; *specif* : LIVER ROT
di·stomatous \(')dī+\ *adj* [*di-* + *stomatous*] **1** : having two mouths or suckers **2** : of or relating to Distomata
dis·tom·i·dae \də'stämə,dē\ [NL, fr. *Distoma*, type genus + *-idae*] *syn of* FASCIOLIDAE
dis·to·mum \'distəməm\ [NL, fr. *di-* + *-stomum*] *syn of* FASCIOLA
dis·tort \də'stȯr|t, -stȯ(ə)|, *usu* |d·+V\ *vt* -ED/-ING/-S [L *distortus*, past part. of *distorquēre*, fr. *dis-* ¹dis- + *torquēre* to twist — more at TORTURE] **1** : to twist out of the true meaning : alter or pervert to give a false or unnatural picture or account ⟨his ~ed account of Mrs. Lincoln had become thoroughly embedded in Lincoln literature —Ruth P. Randall⟩ ⟨~ing the news to make it sensational⟩ ⟨do not ~ their writings in order to conform to the prejudices and values of any group —*New School for Social Research Bull.*⟩ **2 a** *obs* : to twist or wrench out of a straight position **b** : to twist out of a natural, normal, or original shape or condition : wrench into an unnatural shape or condition ⟨a car whose frame is ~ed by a collision⟩ ⟨in playing, he ~ed the music out of all recognition⟩ ⟨putting ideas on paper seems to ~ our perspectives —E.S.McCartney⟩ ⟨a judgment ~ed by strong feeling⟩ ⟨a face ~ed by pain⟩ **c** : to twist or make misshapen mentally or morally ⟨delusions of various kinds ~ed his outlook on life⟩ ⟨falling into a ~ed pattern of behavior⟩ **syn** see DEFORM
distorted *adj* : TWISTED, DEFORMED — **dis·tort·ed·ness** *n* -ES
dis·tort·ed·ly *adv* : in a distorted manner ⟨a ~ inadequate conception of self-interest —Edgar Johnson⟩
dis·tor·tion \|shən\ *n* -S [L *distortion-, distortio*, fr. *distortus* + *-ion-, -io* -ion] **1** : the act of distorting: as **a** : an altering or perverting that essentially falsifies true or accurate facts or true significance ⟨a gross ~ of the news for propaganda purposes⟩ **b** : a twisting or deforming out of a natural, normal, or original shape, form, or condition ⟨a ~ of the car chassis resulting from collision⟩ ⟨~ of the sort that later became so striking a feature of Cubist painting —Edgar Levy⟩ ⟨~ of the economic structure of the country⟩ **c** *psychoanalysis* : the censorship of unacceptable unconscious impulses so that they are unrecognizable to the ego in the manifest dream content **2** : the quality or state of being distorted or the product of distortion ⟨the pain showed in the ~ of the facial muscles⟩ ⟨most of the books about the Orinoco are spiced with enough ~ and fake adventure to nauseate anyone who knows the country —Marston Bates⟩ ⟨the economic ~ and confusion which will be an inevitable aftermath of the war —L.G. Melville⟩: as **a** : a distorted form or image ⟨a painter who paints not observed objects but colorful ~s of them⟩; *also* : distorted dream content **b** : a lack of proportionality between corresponding dimensions of an object or its optical image resulting from spherical aberration or other defects in the optical system **c** : the change in wave form of a composite wave train (as a signal over a telephone line or radio) due to unequal speed of transmission or nonproportional attenuation of different frequencies **3** : a sound or sound-producing current introduced into an electrical system that results in falsified reproduction of the original current or sound — **dis·tor·tion·al** \|shən°l, |shnəl\ *adj*
dis·tor·tion·ist \|sh(ə)nəst\ *n* -S : one that practices distortion esp. in painting
dis·tor·tion·less \|shənləs\ *adj* : free of distortion
dis·tor·tive \|d·iv\ *adj* : causing or marked by distortion ⟨what they offer as pure facts are actually descriptions with . . . ~ interpretation —S.C.Pepper⟩
distr *abbr* distribute; distribution; distributive; distributor
¹dis·tract \də'strakt, (')dis¦s-\ *adj* [ME, fr. L *distractus*, past part.] **1** *obs* : drawn apart or pulled to pieces; *also* : DIVERTED **2 a** *obs* : experiencing confusion of mind : DISTRAUGHT **b** *archaic* : INSANE, MAD
²dis·tract \də'strakt\ *vt* -ED/-ING/-S [ME *distracten*, fr. L *distractus*, past part. of *distrahere*, lit., to draw or pull apart, fr. *dis-* apart + *trahere* to draw, pull — more at DIS-, DRAW] **1 a** : to draw or cause to turn away (from an original position, goal, purpose, direction, association, or interest) ⟨the last thing he wanted was to be ~ed from his present high purpose —Archibald Marshall⟩ ⟨Roeder and his associates were not at once ~ed from the sawmill —*Amer. Guide Series: Wash.*⟩ **b** *obs* : to draw apart or away : DIVIDE, SEPARATE; *also* : DISPERSE **c** : to draw (the sight, mind, or attention) to a different object or compellingly and confusingly attract in divergent directions at once ⟨irritated and ~ed during the first part of the concert by the entrance of late concertgoers⟩ ⟨they have ~ed our eyes from the pastoral beauty of another Ireland —Sean O'Faolain⟩ **d** : to provide amusement or diversion for ⟨the excursion to the zoo served to ~ him for at least one afternoon⟩ **2 a** : to stir up or confuse with conflicting emotions or motives or unsettling worries : HARASS, CONFOUND ⟨she was ~ed by the uncertainty of her future⟩ **b** : to disrupt or cause dissension in by reason of divergent or conflicting desires, aims, or motives ⟨shifting governments and violent oppositions, whose component groups found advantage in forming connections with interests and groups within the ~ed company —*Times Lit. Supp.*⟩ ⟨the famous "Elizabethtown Controversy" which long ~ed the politics of New Jersey —E.P.Tanner⟩ ⟨the Christian Church . . . ~ed by an internecine conflict —W.R.Inge⟩ **3** : to unsettle the reason of : make insane : MADDEN ⟨for six weeks or more before his death he was ~ed, not childish but really raving —Thomas Gray⟩ **syn** see PUZZLE
distracted *adj* **1** : intensely worried : harassed or confused by conflicting feelings **2** : maddened or deranged esp. by grief or anxiety — **dis·tract·ed·ness** *n* -ES
dis·tract·ed·ly *adv* : in the manner of one that is distracted: as **a** : DISTRAUGHTLY ⟨the mother of the lost child could do nothing but pace ~ up and down the room until the child was found⟩ **b** : to the point of mental disorder ⟨felt it was foolish to love so ~ as the two young people did⟩
dis·tract·er *or* **dis·trac·tor** \-ktə(r)\ *n* -S : one that distracts
dis·tract·ibil·i·ty \də,straktə'biləd·ē, -ətē, -i\ *n* -ES : susceptibility to distraction
dis·tract·ible \də'straktəbəl\ *adj* : capable of being distracted : having one's attention readily diverted ⟨described by his teacher as lovable but extremely restless and ~ —Edwin Powers & Helen Witmer⟩
dis·tract·ing·ly *adv* : in a distracting manner ⟨she looked ~ provocative and she knew it —Winifred Bambrick⟩
dis·trac·tion \də'strakshən\ *n* -S [ME *distraccioun*, fr. L *distraction-, distractio*, fr. *distractus* (past part. of *distrahere* to distract) + *-ion-, -io* -ion — more at DISTRACT] **1** : the act of distracting or the state of being distracted: **a** : diversion of the attention ⟨where he felt he could live more cheaply and with fewer ~s from his scholarly labors —Kemp Malone⟩ **b** : DISORDER, DISSENSION ⟨a unified organization distracted by only minor ~s that were easily resolved⟩ **c** : mental derangement : MADNESS ⟨drove her adoring audiences to ~ and tears —Roma Lipsky⟩ ⟨goaded to ~⟩ **d** : agitation from violent usu. conflicting emotions : PERTURBATION ⟨an inward ~ drove

her to pacing the room like a mad woman〉; *also* **:** PERPLEXITY, CONFUSION 〈faced the problem with ~ showing in his uncertain words and troubled countenance〉 **e :** AMUSEMENT, ENTERTAINMENT, RECREATION 〈the need for relaxation and ~ was not forgotten —*Report: (Canadian) Royal Commission on Nat'l Development*〉 〈obsessed by the pursuit of pleasure, driven by the insatiable craving for ~ —A.J.Cronin〉 **2 :** something that distracts esp. by diverting or amusing 〈offering all kinds of ~*s* to the bored vacationer〉

dis·trac·tive \-ktiv\ *adj* **:** causing distraction

distracts *pres 3d sing of* DISTRACT

dis·train \də'strān\ *vb* -ED/-ING/-S [ME *distreynen*, fr. OF *destreign-, destrein-*, stem of *destreindre* to press, oppress, force, fr. ML *distringere* to compel, distrain, fr. L, to hinder, molest, fr. *dis-* [1]dis- + *stringere* to draw tight, press together — more at STRAIN] *vt* **1 a** (1) **:** to coerce or punish by levying a distress (2) **:** to levy a distress upon in order to obtain payment of a debt by sale of the goods taken **b :** to seize as a pledge or indemnification **:** take possession of as security (as on nonpayment of rent or the reparation of an injury done) **:** take by distress 〈~ goods for rent or an amercement〉 **c** *obs* **:** to seize by force **:** CONFISCATE **2** *obs* **a :** CONFINE, CONSTRICT, BIND **b :** DISTRESS, AFFLICT, TORMENT **3** *obs* **:** REND, TEAR ~ *vi* **:** to levy a distress — often used with *upon* or *on*

dis·train·able \-nəbəl\ *adj* [AF *distreignable*, fr. OF *destreign-* + *-able*] **:** subject to distraint; *also* **:** recoverable by distraint

dis·train·ee \ˌdi,strā'nē, də'ˌs-\ *n* -S [*distrain* + *-ee*] **:** one who is distrained

dis·train·er \də'strānər\ *or* **dis·trai·nor** \", ˌdi,strā'nȯ(ə)r, də'ˌstrā'nȯ(ə)r\ *n* -S [AF *destreinor*, fr. OF *destrein-* + *-or*] **:** one who distrains

dis·traint \də'strānt\ *n* -S [fr. *distrain*, after such pairs as E *constrain: constraint*] **:** the act or proceeding of distraining

dis·trait \də'strā, (')di¦s-, (')dē¦s-\ *adj* [F, fr. L *distractus*, past part. of *distrahere* to distract — more at DISTRACT] **1 :** INATTENTIVE, ABSTRACTED 〈Marcus Aurelius could sit for hours in the amphitheater, bored and ~, it is true, but with unmoved serenity —Agnes Repplier〉 **2 :** anxiously or apprehensively divided or withdrawn in attention **:** DISTRAUGHT, UPSET 〈so ~ he was unable to listen to the speaker for worrying what was going to happen if he lost his job〉 〈at the bad news the woman became so ~ she was incapable of answering simple questions coherently〉

dis·traite \-āt, *usu* -ād·+V\ *adj* [F, fem. of *distrait*] **:** DISTRAIT — used of a female 〈made her as ~ as a mother bird —Elizabeth Bowen〉

dis·traught \də'strȯt, *usu* -ȯd·+V\ *adj* [ME, modif. of L *distractus* — more at DISTRACT] **1 a :** beset with doubt or mental conflict **:** deeply troubled **:** DISTRACTED, FRANTIC 〈he must always be doing something, seeking relief in a factitious gaiety and nervous garrulity . . . a man beset and ~ —S.H. Adams〉 〈in his ~ state he allows himself to be hit by a truck —H.M.Jones〉 〈~ with grief for the dead queen —Edna S. V. Millay〉; *also* **:** thrown into confusion or disorder (as through indecision, dissension, or lack of clear direction) 〈the affairs of the U.N. itself are tangled and ~ —*Reporter*〉 〈the post-revolutionary period which was more excited with aspirations, and nearly as ~ with terrors as our present epoch —*Times Lit. Supp.*〉 **b :** mentally deranged **:** CRAZED 〈she waited, pacing back and forth, pale and almost ~ —P.I.Wellman〉 〈as if thou wert ~ and mad with terror —Shak.〉 **2** *obs* **:** torn apart **:** SEPARATED 〈his greedy throat . . . ~ —Edmund Spenser〉 — **dis·traught·ly** *adv*

[1]**dis·tress** \də'stres\ *n* -ES [ME *destresse*, fr. OF *destresse, destresce*, fr. (assumed) VL *districtia*, fr. L *districtus* (past part. of *distringere* to hinder, molest) + *-ia* -y — more at DISTRAIN] **1 a :** the act or remedy of distraining **:** the seizure and detention of the goods of another by way of pledge for the reparation of an injury or the performance of a duty or in order to obtain satisfaction of a claim (as for rent, taxes, or an injury) by the sale of the goods seized **b :** the thing taken by distraining **:** something that is seized to procure satisfaction **2** *obs* **:** the act or the condition of straining or forcing **:** STRESS, CONSTRAINT, COMPULSION **3 a :** an oppressed or distressed state **:** PAIN, SUFFERING **:** anguish of body or mind **:** TROUBLE, NEED 〈each side sees its own security and prosperity in the insecurity, destitution, and ~ of the other —Isaac Deutscher〉 〈in great ~ for money —*Encyc. Americana*〉 〈poetry, that immortal medium fallen into ~, if not disrepute or desuetude —Harvey Breit〉 〈these days when the world is in tension and ~ because of the conflict of two ideologies —R.D. Jacobs〉 **b :** a painful situation **:** MISFORTUNE, CALAMITY **:** great trouble **:** SUFFERING, AFFLICTION 〈suffered most severely in the interwar years from unemployment and economic ~ —L.D.Stamp〉 〈his attempts to succor the various ~*es* of these people invariably land Mike in trouble —*Saturday Rev.*〉 **4 a :** a state of danger or necessity 〈a ship in ~〉 〈respiratory ~〉; *also* **:** evidence of such a state **b :** an indication of weakness or incipient failure in a structure subjected to stress

syn SUFFERING, MISERY, AGONY, DOLOR, PASSION: these nouns designate in common the condition of one in great trouble or in mental or physical pain. DISTRESS commonly implies conditions or circumstances that cause physical or mental stress or strain, suggesting strongly the need of assistance; in application to a mental state, it implies the strain of fear, anxiety, shame, or the like 〈the *distress* of the underprivileged —Oscar Handlin〉 〈the personal *distress* of those who cannot emotionally readjust themselves to new views —M.R.Cohen〉 〈the spring and summer of 1842 brought severe *distress* to many in County Mayo in the form of famine —J.T.Ellis〉 SUFFERING applies esp. to human beings, implying an awareness of distress and often a conscious endurance 〈the losses and hardships and *sufferings* entailed by war —Bertrand Russell〉 〈the *suffering* of unhappy adolescence〉 MISERY stresses the unhappy or wretched conditions attending distress or suffering as well as the distress itself, often suggesting an unalleviated or chronic suffering 〈the stench and *misery* of poverty —Harrison Smith〉 〈anguish that wept aloud; *misery* that could find no voice; sorrow that was dumb —Oscar Wilde〉 AGONY suggests intense, usu. unbearable, pain or suffering 〈fell with a scream of mortal *agony* —F.V.W.Mason〉 〈she suffered *agonies* of mortification —Margaret Deland〉 〈the *agonies* of an impaled beetle —Rudyard Kipling〉 DOLOR, a literary word, applies chiefly to mental suffering involving sorrow, somber depression, or anxiety, often intense 〈heaviness is upon them, and *dolor* thickens the air they walk through —Waldo Frank〉 〈accept national and local calamities, such as invasions, droughts, famines . . . with a quiet *dolor* which suggests passivity and stoicism — *New Republic*〉 〈the "happy child" she was though underlaid by *dolor* —Louise Nicholl〉 PASSION is now rare in this sense except in application to the suffering of Christ before and during the crucifixion 〈the *passion* of Our Lord〉

[2]**distress** \"\ *vt* **distressed** *also archaic* **distrest; distressed** *also archaic* **distrest; distressing; distresses** [ME *destressen*, fr. MF *destresser, destrecer*, fr. *destresse, destrece*] **1 a :** to subject to great strain or difficulties; *esp* **:** to bring to dire and painful esp. economic straits 〈~*ed* companies would get technical advice, loans, government contracts and fast tax amortizations to help them diversify their products and find new markets —*Time*〉 〈public housing for ~*ed* families of veterans, servicemen, government employees —*Current Biog.*〉 〈relief shipments to Europe and other ~*ed* war areas —Harry Truman〉 **b :** to afflict or exhaust esp. with strain or discomfort **c :** to cause pain or suffering to **:** oppress with calamity **:** make miserable **:** PAIN, HARASS 〈wild speculation and unwholesome overexpansion . . . caused several bank failures and a ~*ing* public debt —*Amer. Guide Series: N.C.*〉 〈the sight of blood, in fact, always ~*ed* him —Charles Lee〉; *also* **:** to cause to worry or be troubled **:** UPSET, DISTURB 〈the bitter remarks ~*ed* the sensitive boy considerably〉 〈it ~*es* me somewhat to hiss at trolley-car conductors who . . . were my personal heroes some decades back —Horace Sutton〉 〈stories not involving military security occasionally ~*ed* Captain Lee to the point where he felt it necessary to call in an offending correspondent and explain to him that some stories were better left unprinted —E.L.Jones〉 **:** TROUBLE, BOTHER 〈the ~*ing* accumulation of down and dust —Emily Holt〉 **2 a :** to force or compel by or as if by inflicting pain or suffering 〈men who can neither be ~*ed* nor won into a sacrifice of duty —Alexander Hamilton〉 **b** *obs* **:** to rout in battle **:** OVERWHELM **3** *archaic* **:** to levy a distress upon **:** DISTRAIN

[3]**distress** \"\ *adj* [*distress*] **1** *of merchandise* **:** sold or offered for sale at a sacrifice **:** disposed of cheaply because of financial necessity 〈the weaker the market becomes, the more ~ merchandise comes on the market —E.B.Weiss〉 〈the resulting so-called ~ cargoes of spot gasoline, offered through brokers, often have a strong depressing effect on prices —Harold Fleming〉 **2 :** involving distress goods 〈a ~ sale〉

distress call *n* **:** SOS

dis·tressed \-est\ *adj* **1 :** afflicted with trouble, pain, or grief **2 :** purposely marred to give the appearance of great age — used of furniture or leather — **dis·tressed·ly** \-esədlē, -estlē, -li\ *adv* — **dis·tressed·ness** \-esədnəs, -es(t)n-\ *n* -ES

distresses *pl of* DISTRESS, *pres 3d sing of* DISTRESS

dis·tress·ful \-esfəl\ *adj* **:** causing distress 〈for four years lived in heroic if somewhat ~ isolation —*Amer. Guide Series: N.H.*〉 〈wandering into the past as a refuge from the ~ present —Rebecca West〉 — **dis·tress·ful·ly** \-fəlē, -li\ *adv* — **dis·tress·ful·ness** \-lnəs\ *n* -ES

distressing *pres part of* DISTRESS

dis·tress·ing·ly *adv* **:** in a manner that distresses 〈a ~ meager income for such a large family〉 〈the transition at times is ~ swift —B.N.Cardozo〉 〈she had grown ~ deaf —Osbert Sitwell〉

distress signal *n* **:** an emergency signal (as a flare, flag, or SOS) used by one in distress or in need of help

dis·trib·ut·able \də'stribyəd·əbəl, -yətə-\ *adj* **:** capable of being distributed 〈income ~ to a beneficiary —Benjamin Harrow〉

[1]**dis·trib·u·tary** \-yə,terē\ *adj* [*distribute* + *-ary*] **:** DISTRIBUTIVE; *esp* **:** of or relating to a distributary

[2]**distributary** \"\ *n* -ES **1 a :** a river branch flowing away from the main stream and not rejoining it — contrasted with *tributary* **b :** one of the channels of a braided stream **2 :** an irrigation canal or ditch leading away from the main canal; *esp* **:** one of the smaller conduits by which irrigation water is delivered directly to the consumer from the larger branches of the system

dis·trib·ute \də'stribyət, -i(,)byüt, *chiefly in substand speech* -,bət; *usu* -d·+V\ *vb* **distributed** \-yəd·əd,-yətəd\ **distributed** \"\ **distributing** \-yəd·iŋ,-yətiŋ\ **distributes** \-yəts,-yüts\ [ME *distributen*, fr. L *distributus*, past part. of *distribuere*, fr. *dis-* [1]dis- + *tribuere* to assign, give, allot — more at TRIBUTE] *vt* **1 a :** to divide among several or many **:** deal out **:** apportion esp. to members of a group or over a period of time **:** ALLOT 〈the American Relief Administration *distributed* nearly five million tons of foodstuffs —*Current Biog.*〉 〈the problem of how to ~ taxes equitably among the various economic groups —*Collier's Yr. Bk.*〉 〈precipitation is not ample, but is *distributed* throughout the year —G.G.Weigend〉 **b :** DISPENSE, ADMINISTER 〈~ justice〉 〈lamented that the great fields of private law, where justice is *distributed* between man and man, should be left without a caretaker —B.N.Cardozo〉 **2 a :** to spread out or scatter so as to cover a surface or a space 〈*distributing* the seed over the lawn〉 〈*distributing* the ink evenly over the print〉; *also* **:** to give out or deliver esp. to the members of a group 〈*distributing* magazines to subscribers〉 〈the U.N. secretariat, which *distributed* a 125-page questionnaire to member governments —*Current Biog.*〉 **b :** to place or position usu. so as to be properly apportioned over or throughout an area 〈the blood vessels *distributed* throughout the arm〉 〈he seems chunkier than the 175 pounds *distributed* over his five feet ten inches would indicate —W.B.Furlong〉 〈the various factories *distributed* throughout the city —*Amer. Guide Series: N.H.*〉 〈a widely *distributed* company —Marquis James〉 〈our Indians are not evenly *distributed* —Juan Comas〉 **c** *logic* **:** to use (a term) so as to convey information about every member of the class named 〈the proposition "all men are mortal" ~*s* a universal affirmative subject, here "man", but does not ~ the predicate〉 **3 a :** to divide or separate esp. into classes, orders, kinds, or species **:** CLASSIFY, ASSORT 〈spend a good deal of time *distributing* his specimens into their proper classes〉 **b** (1) **:** to separate the units of (as type-set matter or handset matrices) and return to the proper storage places (2) *of a keyboard slugcasting machine* **:** to return (matrices) automatically to the proper magazine channels **4 :** to market (a commodity) under a franchise in a particular area esp. at wholesale ~ *vi* **:** to make distribution **:** spread out

syn DISTRIBUTE, DISPENSE, DIVIDE, DEAL, and DOLE can agree in meaning to give out, usu. in shares, to each person or thing of a group of persons or things. DISTRIBUTE implies (1) an apportioning of something among many by separating it into parts, units, or amounts and assigning each part, etc., to its appropriate person or place or (2) a spreading or scattering of something more or less evenly over an area 〈*distribute* their possessions among their children〉 〈*distribute* profits among corporation members〉 〈*distribute* different size nails to their appropriate containers〉 〈*distribute* loam over a lawn〉 DISPENSE carries no strong implication, as does DISTRIBUTE, of the lessening of a whole by subdivision or scattering but suggests a giving of a carefully weighed and measured portion as a right or due, or in answer to a need 〈*dispense* drugs to plague victims〉 〈the host is *dispensing* drinks —Agnes M. Miall〉 〈he liberally *dispensed* hospitality to all . . . with whom he came into contact —E.H.Collis〉 〈*dispense* justice〉 〈*dispense* charity〉 DIVIDE stresses the separation of a whole into parts in order to dispense to or share among each of a group, equality of shares usu. being implied in default of other specification 〈*divide* a cake among 10 guests〉 〈*divide* profits evenly among themselves〉 〈*divide* the spoils of war〉 DEAL, usu. with *out*, stresses a giving out piece by piece or in suitable portions 〈*deal* out the day's ration of water〉 〈*deal* out paper plates to the picnickers〉 DOLE, frequently with *out*, still often implies a dispensing of alms to the needy but more commonly now suggests merely a dispensing in scanty, usu. niggardly, portions 〈mother collects the paychecks and *doles* out allowances to all hands —J.H.Fenton〉 〈there cannot be in this republic any class of human beings in practical subjection to another class, with power in the latter to *dole* out to the former just such privileges as they may choose to grant —O.K. Fraenkel〉 〈a prince *doling* out favors to a servile group of petitioners —Theodore Dreiser〉

dis·trib·ut·ed·ly *adv* **:** in a distributed manner

dis·trib·u·tee \də¦stribyə¦tē\ *n* -S [*distribute* + *-ee*] **:** one to whom something is or is to be distributed; *esp* **:** one sharing in or entitled to share in an estate

distributer *var of* DISTRIBUTOR

dis·tri·bu·tion \ˌdistrə'byüshən\ *n* -S [ME *distribucioun*, fr. L *distribution-, distributio*, fr. *distributus* + *-ion-, -io* -ion] **1 a :** the act or process of distributing or the condition of being distributed **:** APPORTIONMENT, ALLOTMENT 〈the ~ of money among creditors〉 〈the ~ of the cards to the players〉 〈a twice yearly ~ of the profits among the stockholders〉 **b :** the process of apportionment by which the value of a product is divided and imputed to the various factors of production as payment for their use **c :** the apportionment in a student's program (as required in some American universities) of a certain number of courses to widely different departments or fields of learning for breadth of training — compare CONCENTRATION 1d **d :** the apportionment by a court of the personal property of an intestate or its proceeds among those entitled to it according to the statutes of distribution **2 a :** a spreading out or scattering over an area or throughout a space 〈the ~ of the seed over the field〉 〈the ~ of the oil throughout the engine parts〉 **b :** the position, placement, or arrangement (as of a mass or the members of a group) over an area or throughout a space or unit of time **:** the frequency of occurrence **:** ARRANGEMENT 〈the ~ of iron ore in So. America〉 〈~ of eclipses over a thousand years〉 〈the ~ of the stars〉 〈the ~ of population〉 〈the ~ of the nation's wealth〉 **c :** the natural geographic range of a kind of organism (as a species) or category of organisms (as an order); *sometimes* **:** the range of such a kind or category in geologic time **d :** the occurrence of a linguistic item in terms of context or geography 〈the ~ of the allophones of /t/ in English〉 **e :** the disposition or arrangement in rational groups or classes **:** CLASSIFICATION 〈the accurate ~ of several rare zoological specimens〉 **f :** delivery or conveyance (as of newspapers or goods) to the members of a group 〈the ~ of telephone directories to customers〉 〈in charge of company sales and ~〉 **3 a :** something distributed 〈supported his family only with the help of charitable ~*s*〉 **b :** an array in statistics of the instances of a variable arranged by classes according to their value 〈the ~ showed the heights of all the men in the regiment given at one-inch intervals〉 **c :** PROBABILITY DENSITY FUNCTION **4 :** the status of a term in logic with respect to its being distributed or undistributed **5 :** a device, mechanism, or system by which something is distributed (as from a main source): as **a :** the operations regulating the passage of the working fluid (as steam) through an engine cylinder including admission, cutoff, release, exhaust, and compression **b :** the pattern of branching and termination of a nerve, artery, or other ramifying structure **c :** the part of an electric supply system between bulk power sources (as generating stations or transformation stations tapped from transmission lines) and the consumers' service switches **6 :** the marketing or merchandising of commodities 〈the mail-order ~ of books〉 〈keeping track of all ~ costs of a manufactured article for a year〉 **7 :** the manner in which the suits in a pack of playing cards are divided in one player's hand or in which one suit is divided among the hands of all the players 〈a hand with 4-3-3-3 ~ contains four cards in one suit and three cards in each of the other suits〉

dis·tri·bu·tion·al \ˌdistrə¦byüshənᵊl, -shnəl\ *adj* **1 :** of or relating to distribution **2 :** of or relating to the trick-winning value of long suits and trumps rather than high cards — **dis·tri·bu·tion·al·ly** \-ᵊlē,-əlē, ¦i\ *adv*

distribution board *n* **:** PANELBOARD 3

distribution box *n* **:** a contrivance used to equalize the flow of septic-tank effluent into the various tile lines of the disposal field

distribution coefficient *or* **distribution ratio** *n* **:** the ratio of the amounts of solute dissolved at equilibrium in two immiscible liquids

distribution cost *n* **1 :** cost incurred by a producer incident to activities connected with placing a finished product in the hands of a customer (as the expense of selling, advertising, shipping) **2 :** any cost incurred by a wholesaler, retailer, or distributor

distribution curve *n* **:** a graph of the frequencies of different values of a variable in a statistical distribution

distribution function *n* **:** the expression of a relationship between the values and the corresponding frequencies of a variable in a statistical distribution

dis·trib·u·tism \də'stribyə,tizəm\ *n* -S **:** the theory or practice of distributing private property (as land) to the maximum degree among individual owners **:** AGRARIANISM

dis·trib·u·tist \-yəd·əst\ *n* -S **:** an advocate of distributism

[1]**dis·trib·u·tive** \də'stribyəd·|iv, -yət|\ *adj* [ME, fr. MF *distributif*, fr. LL *distributivus*, fr. L *distributus* (past part. of *distribuere* to distribute) + *-ivus* -ive — more at DISTRIBUTE] **1 :** of or relating to distribution: as **a :** serving to divide and assign in portions **:** dealing a proper share to each of a group 〈serving both a collective and ~ function in the charity organization〉 **b :** spreading out, covering, diffusing, or scattering more or less evenly over an area or throughout a space 〈you may interpret the word "salvation" in any way you like, and make it as diffuse and ~, or as climacteric and integral a phenomenon as you please —William James〉 **c :** engaged in or concerned with distribution esp. of goods 〈the ~ and service trades〉 〈he had founded the Ceylonese cooperative movement, which was to become the major ~ agency for foodstuffs in the island —*Current Biog.*〉 **2** *of a word* **:** referring singly and without exception to the members of a group (*each, every, either, neither*, and *none* are ~); referring to a single member of a group (*which* in "which one of the men" is ~); expressing division of a group into smaller groups 〈the ~ Latin word *bini* "two by two"〉 or individuals 〈the ~ Latin word *singuli* "one by one"〉 **3 :** taken in its full extension — used of a term in logic **4** *logic* **:** operating upon the whole by operating upon each part — **dis·trib·u·tive·ness** \-nəs\ *n* -ES

[2]**distributive** \"\ *n* -S **:** a distributive word

distributive fault *n* **:** one of two or more closely associated parallel geologic faults — called also *step fault*

distributive function *n* **:** a function of the sum of two or more variables that is equal to a sum each term of which is the same function of one of the variables **:** any function F such that $F(u+v)=F(u)+F(v)$

distributive justice *n* **:** the justice that is concerned with the apportionment of privileges, duties, and goods in consonance with the merits of the individual and in the best interest of society

dis·trib·u·tive·ly \|əvlē, -li\ *adv* **1 :** in a distributive manner 〈not predicating something about the class as such but about its membership ~ —Jørgen Jørgensen〉 〈marine vertebrates . . . have their body weight supported ~ by water displacement, instead of having it concentrated on two or four columns of leg bone —Weston La Barre〉 **2 :** as individuals or separate units **:** INDIVIDUALLY, SEPARATELY 〈their potential rights, which, taken ~, are imperceptible, amount collectively to a most important interest —John Marshall〉

distributive operation *n* **:** a mathematical operation obeying a distributive principle

distributive principle *also* **distributive law** *n* **:** a mathematical principle expressed by a distributive formula (as $a(b+c+d)=ab+ac+ad$)

dis·trib·u·tiv·ism \|ə,vizəm\ *n* -S **:** DISTRIBUTISM

dis·trib·u·tiv·i·ty \də,stribyə'tivəd·ē\ *n* -ES **:** the quality of being distributive (sense 4)

dis·trib·u·tor *also* **dis·trib·ut·er** \də'stribyəd·|ə(r), -yət|\ *n* -S **1 :** one that distributes 〈bill ~*s* may cover the same territory, leaving circulars at the same houses —H.E.Agnew〉 〈if the lawn is large some type of seed ~ may well be used —C.E. Millar & L.M.Turk〉 **2 a :** one that markets a commodity; *esp* **:** WHOLESALER **b :** an apparatus for directing the secondary current from the induction coil to the various spark plugs of a multicylinder engine in their proper firing order — compare TIMER **c :** a device for spreading sewage over the surface of a filter **d :** CARRIER 2d

dis·trib·u·tor·ship \-,ship\ *n* -S **:** a franchise granted by a manufacturer or company to market its goods esp. at wholesale in a particular area; *also* **:** an office or business concern having such a franchise

[1]**district** *adj* [L *districtus*, fr. past part. of *distringere* to hinder, molest — more at DISTRAIN] *obs* **:** RIGOROUS, STRICT

[2]**dis·trict** \'di(,)strikt, -,strēkt\ *n* -S *often attrib* [F, fr. MF, fr. ML *districtus* coercive action, justice, jurisdiction, area of jurisdiction, district, fr. *districtus*, past part. of *distringere* to compel — more at DISTRAIN] **1** *obs* **:** the territory under a feudal lord's jurisdiction **2 :** a territorial division (as of a nation, state, county, or city) marked off or defined for administrative, electoral, judicial, or other purposes: as **a :** an administrative unit established as a quasi-municipal corporation for the performance of a special governmental function or functions 〈park ~〉 〈water supply ~〉 〈fire protection ~〉 〈a police ~〉 〈a postal ~〉 〈a ~ school〉 — see CONGRESSIONAL DISTRICT, DRAINAGE DISTRICT, ELECTION DISTRICT, MAGISTERIAL DISTRICT **b :** the most important administrative unit of a province or presidency in British India **c :** one of the subdivisions of the United States or of the individual states served by a particular federal or state court **d :** an ecclesiastical division of an English parish made under the Church Building Acts and having its own church and pastor **e :** an urban or rural subdivision of a British administrative county constituted by the Local Government Act of 1894 and having an urban or rural district council **f :** an area usu. comprising several subordinate territories that is demarcated by a commercial firm for convenience of sales promotion, assignment to sales representatives, or distribution 〈a ~ sales manager〉 〈a ~ representative〉 **3 :** an area, region, or tract or a portion of one of these usu. marked by a distinguishing quality, set of characteristics, devotion to a distinguishing purpose, or habitation by a more or less homogeneous group 〈a barren ~〉 〈a wooded ~〉 〈a shopping ~〉 〈a residential ~〉 〈the Italian ~〉 〈the theater ~〉 〈a fertile farming ~〉 〈a slum ~〉 **4 :** a subdivision of an embryonic field determined for the production of a specific definitive structure

[3]**district** \"\ *vt* -ED/-ING/-S **:** to divide or organize into

districts ⟨attending to a new ~*ing* of the city⟩ ⟨the area was ~*ed* according to population figures only⟩ ⟨interlocking problems of zoning and school ~*ing* —Merrill Folsom⟩

district attorney *n* **:** the prosecuting officer of a district who is appointed by the president in federal districts but generally elective in counties

district check *n* **1 a :** a plaid or a fabric design in checks that is peculiar to or presumed to be special to the dress of a Scottish district **b** an imitation or variation of such a design **2 :** a fabric with a district check

district council *n* **:** the local governing body of a rural or urban district in Great Britain and of certain administrative districts in Australia and parts of British Africa

district court *n* **:** a court of first instance having jurisdiction in certain cases within a judicial district; *esp* **:** the U.S. federal court of first instance

district heating *n* **:** the distribution of heat by steam or otherwise from a central plant to buildings more or less widely distributed — compare 1CENTRAL 4a

district judge *n* **:** the judge of a district court

district leader *n* **:** the party leader or boss of an American assembly district or ward

district manager *n* **:** one who supervises the sales activity in a district

district superintendent *n* **:** an official of the Methodist Church appointed by a bishop to have the oversight of the churches and the preachers in a district

district visitor *n* **:** a woman worker in a Church of England parish who gives voluntary assistance to the rector (as by visiting and reporting cases of sickness)

di·strin·gas \dəˈstriŋgəs, -ˌgas\ *n* -ES [ML, that you distrain 2d pers. sing. pres. subj. of *distringere*] **:** a writ commanding the sheriff to distrain a person by his goods or chattels

1**dis·trust** \dəˈstrəst, (ˈ)dis-\ *vb* [ME *distrusten* to suspect, fr. 1*dis-* + *trusten* to trust — more at TRUST] *vt* **1 :** to have no trust or confidence in **:** MISTRUST ⟨~ the sword as a cure for all ills —John Buchan⟩ ⟨he ~*ed* mathematics and the art of deductive logic that went with it —S.F.Mason⟩ **2 :** to suspect of evil consequences or designs **:** feel wary or suspicious of ⟨it would deprive him of the enormous personal satisfaction of ~*ing* what he doesn't know and despising what he has never seen —E.B.White⟩ ⟨the Cistercians disliked and ~*ed* Abelard —Henry Adams⟩ ⟨traditionally the American ~*s* ceremony and all its accouterments —W.L.Sperry⟩ ~ *vi, obs* **:** to have no trust or confidence

2**distrust** \"\ *n* [1*dis-* + *trust*] **:** the lack or absence of trust **:** SUSPICION, WARINESS ⟨the Swiss, with their traditional ~ of personal power —*Current Biog.*⟩ ⟨an atmosphere of ~ and suspicion has been allowed to permeate the government —Vannevar Bush⟩ ⟨his self-criticism, his ~ of his own ideas —Harold Callender⟩ ⟨growing ~ of the efficacy of parliamentary bodies —John Dewey⟩

dis·trust·ful \-fəl\ *adj* **1 :** having or showing distrust **:** SUSPICIOUS, WARY ⟨vigilant and ~ superintendence —Thomas Jefferson⟩ ⟨a man of ~ nature⟩ ⟨my experience as a judge in other fields of law has made me ~ of rules of thumb generally —B.N.Cardozo⟩ **2** *archaic* **:** causing or arousing distrust — **dis·trust·ful·ly** \-fəlē, -li\ *adv* — **dis·trust·ful·ness** \-lnəs\ *n* -ES

dis·trust·ing·ly *adv* **:** in a distrustful manner

dis·trust·less \-ləs\ *adj, archaic* **:** having no distrust or suspicion **:** UNSUSPECTING, INNOCENT

dis·tune \dəs, (ˈ)dis+\ *vt* [1*dis-* + *tune*] **:** to put out of tune

1**dis·turb** \dəˈstərb, -tə̄b, -təib\ *vb* -ED/-ING/-S [ME *disturben, destourben*, fr. OF & L; OF *destorber, destourber*, fr. L *disturbare*, fr. *dis-* 1*dis-* + *turbare* to throw into disorder, disturb, make turbid — more at TURBID] *vt* **1 a** *obs* **:** to turn or distract (a person) by disturbance **b :** to interfere with (as by hindering or causing to turn from a course or to stop) ⟨~ the sequence of events⟩ ⟨~ a man's reflections by shouting⟩ ⟨a synthetic plant hormone which ~*s* plant growth and eventually destroys it —*Collier's Yr. Bk.*⟩ ⟨he failed to ~ the dominant current of thought —A.N.Whitehead⟩ ⟨another factor was beginning to ~ the tenor of life in their curious household —T.B.Costain⟩; *specif* **:** to interfere with in the lawful enjoyment of a right **c** (1) **:** to break into the preoccupations of or command the attention of esp. annoyingly or disquietingly ⟨she had ~*ed* an antique god in his sylvan haunt —G.B.Shaw⟩ ⟨she sat outside his door, and none of us dared ~ her —George Meredith⟩ (2) **:** to alter the position or arrangement of **:** move from place **:** ⟨he found that the papers on his desk had been ~*ed*⟩ **:** cause to move, wave, bend, or otherwise change position ⟨the wind ~*ing* the grass⟩ ⟨the coal seams were later ~*ed* by the crushing of the valley —L.D.Stamp⟩ ⟨no bone was broken and no joint was ~*ed* —Arthur Morrison⟩ ⟨how is my relation to the environment ~*ed* —John Dewey⟩ (3) **:** to break up or damage (as by handling, shaking, or jarring) ⟨do not ~ the laboratory apparatus⟩ **2 a :** to destroy the rest, tranquillity, or settled state of **:** stir up **:** AGITATE, TROUBLE ⟨strikes and war talk ~*ing* the country⟩ ⟨that fact poisons me, ~*s* my serenity —John Reed⟩ ⟨the most calculated, among contemporary writings, to ~ the reader, to startle and excite him —Wallace Fowlie⟩ ⟨a few passages of verse . . . have still the power to ~ our hearts —Edward Sapir⟩ ⟨the ~*ed* state of the country —*Americana Annual*⟩ **b :** to upset the mental or emotional composure of **:** deprive of mental or emotional peace **:** DISQUIET ⟨his passion for his cause ~*ed* me —W.A.White⟩ ⟨the times are too upset and ~*ing* —Louis Bromfield⟩ **c :** to throw into confusion or disorder ⟨his incompetence ~*ed* the once smoothly running system⟩ **d :** to rouse esp. from thought or sleep ⟨~ a scholar in his study⟩ **:** ALARM ⟨afraid of ~*ing* the sleeping animal⟩ **e :** to put to inconvenience ⟨do not ~ yourself to get supper for us⟩ ~ *vi* **:** to cause disturbance

syn see DISCOMPOSE, DISORDER

2**disturb** *n* -S *obs* **:** DISTURBANCE

dis·tur·bance \dəˈstərbən(t)s, -tə̄b-, -təib-\ *n* -S [ME *destourbaunce, disturbaunce*, fr. OF *destorbance, destourbance*, fr. *destorber, destourber* + *-ance*] **1 :** the act or process of disturbing or the state of being disturbed **2 a :** an interruption of a state of peace or quiet **:** an agitating or agitation esp. of the mind or feelings ⟨understandable that the awkward age should be for the girl a period of painful ~ —H.M.Parshley⟩ **b :** the hindering or disquieting of a person in the lawful and peaceable enjoyment of his right ⟨the ~ of an easement⟩ **c :** an interference with a planned, ordered, or regular procedure, state, or habit **:** INTERRUPTION ⟨hated the ~ of his privacy⟩ ⟨the ~ of his routine always made him grouchy⟩ **:** a moving out of place ⟨the ~ of his papers⟩ **:** ALTERATION ⟨an obesity related to endocrine ~*s*⟩ ⟨some basic ~ of the body's chemistry —G.W.Gray⟩; *also* **:** COMMOTION ⟨put his head out of the window to see what the ~ was all about⟩ **:** DERANGEMENT ⟨a certain appalling ~ in the body politic⟩ ⟨market ~*s* to which the less integrated and smaller business enterprises frequently find it difficult or even impossible to adjust —A.D.H.Kaplan⟩ ⟨the large-scale and national ~*s* which so disrupted affairs —*Collier's Yr. Bk.*⟩ **d :** a movement of the earth's crust (as in crustal crumpling to form a mountain range) **:** DIASTROPHISM; *also* **:** the result of such movement **e :** a local variation from the average or normal wind conditions; *esp* **:** a cyclone or tornado **f :** abnormal variation from a mental or emotional norm ⟨the disturbed personality is not always aware of the ~⟩

dis·tur·bant \-bənt\ *adj* [L *disturbant-, disturbans*, pres. part. of *disturbare* to disturb — more at DISTURB] **:** DISTURBING ⟨pouring forth ~ and gusty heresies —V.L.Parrington⟩

dis·turbed \-bd\ *adj* **1 :** marked by a variable degree of pathological variation from a mental or emotional norm **:** showing symptoms of emotional illness or personality abnormality ⟨the handling of ~ children —George Edwards⟩ ⟨~ and backward children — aggressive, neurotic, recessive —Avima Dushkin⟩ **2 :** designed for or occupied by disturbed patients ⟨a ~ ward⟩

disturbed area *n* **:** the area within which an earthquake shock is appreciable by the unaided senses

dis·turbed·ly \-b(ə)dlē\ *adv* **:** in a disturbed manner

dis·turb·er \-bə(r)\ *n* -S [ME, fr. *disturben* to disturb + *-er*] **:** one that disturbs; *specif* **:** an English bishop who unlawfully refuses to examine and admit the patron's clerk to a benefice

dis·turb·ing·ly *adv* **:** in a disturbing manner **:** in a way that upsets or agitates emotionally or tends to throw into disorder ⟨a ~ long drought⟩ ⟨a ~ large incidence of petty thievery⟩

dis·turnpike \dəs, (ˈ)dis+\ *vt* [1*dis-* + *turnpike* (n.)] **:** to convert into a toll-free road

di·style \ˈdīˌstīl, ˈdiˌ-\ *adj* [*di-* + *-style*] **:** marked by columniation with two columns across the front — compare DECASTYLE, DODECASTYLE, ENNEASTYLE, HEPTASTYLE, HEXASTYLE, OCTASTYLE, PENTASTYLE, TETRASTYLE

distyle in an·tis \-ˈänˌtās, -ˌi'n-, -ˈan·ˌtēs\ *adj* [L *in antis* between antas] **:** having two columns between two antas

di·substituted \(ˈ)dī+\ *adj* [*di-* + *substituted*] **:** having two substituent atoms or groups in the molecule ⟨~ barbiturates⟩

di·sulfate \(ˈ)dī+\ *n* [*di-* + *sulfate*] **1 :** PYROSULFATE **2 :** BISULFATE **3 :** a compound containing two sulfate groups

di·sulfide \(ˈ)dī+\ *n* [*di-* + *sulfide*] **1 :** a compound containing two atoms of sulfur combined with an element or radical ⟨iron ~⟩ **2 :** an organic compound containing the bivalent group –SS– composed of two sulfur atoms united to carbon atoms ⟨diethyl ~⟩

di·sul·fi·ram \dīˈsəlfəˌram\ *n* -S [*disulf*ide + tetraethylthi*uram*] **:** TETRAETHYLTHIURAM DISULFIDE — used esp. of the drug

disulfo- *comb form* [ISV *di-* + *sulf-*] **1 :** containing two sulfonic acid groups esp. replacing hydrogen **2 :** DITHI-

di·sulfonate \(ˈ)dī+\ *n* [*di-* + *sulfonate*] **:** a compound containing two sulfonate groups

di·sulfonic acid \(ˌ)dī+. . .-\ *n* [*di-* + *sulfonic*] **:** a compound containing two sulfonic acid groups

di·sulfuric acid \(ˌ)dī+. . .-\ *n* [*di-* + *sulfuric*] **:** PYROSULFURIC ACID

dis·unification \dəs, (ˌ)dis+\ *n* **:** the act or process of disunifying or the state of being disunified **:** the destruction of concord or harmony among a group **:** the breaking up of a unified whole into separate often dissident parts

dis·uniform \dəs, (ˈ)dis+\ *adj* [1*dis-* + *uniform*] *archaic* **:** not uniform **:** lacking uniformity

dis·unify \"+\ *vt* [1*dis-* + *unify*] **:** to destroy the unity of **:** bring about a lack of concord or harmony in or among **:** break up (a unified whole) into separate often dissident parts ⟨set out deliberately to divide and ~ this nation —S.A. Mitchell⟩ ⟨humanity, already profoundly perplexed and *disunified* —J.D.Ratcliff⟩

dis·union \dəs, (ˈ)dis+\ *n* [1*dis-* + *union*] **1 :** the termination or destruction of union **:** DISJUNCTION, SEPARATION ⟨the ~ of the body and soul at death⟩ ⟨looking forward to the ~ of the two parts of the organization⟩; *esp* **:** the termination of political union ⟨the Southerners favoring ~ prior to the Civil War⟩ **2 a :** the quality or state of being disunified **:** DISUNITY ⟨some of the remaining 10 towns were held by Macedonian garrisons, some by local tyrants, a state of ~ equally gratifying to Macedonia and intolerable to Greek patriots —*Encyc. Americana*⟩ ⟨he thought political unity sufficient in spite of religious ~ to secure the monarchy —Hilaire Belloc⟩ **b :** ALIENATION, DISSENSION ⟨a group torn by ~⟩

dis·unionist \"+\ *n* **:** one who favors disunion; *specif* **:** an American secessionist

dis·unite \ˌdish + (y)ü..., ˌdis + yü...\ *vb* [1*dis-* + *unite*] *vt* **1 :** to destroy the unity of **:** DIVIDE, SEPARATE ⟨might we not ~ our war effort by trying prematurely to unite our peace effort —A.H.Vandenberg †1951⟩ ⟨a league of *disunited* nations —E.B.White⟩ ⟨the family was deeply *disunited*, and each member be unhappy for a different reason —George Santayana⟩ **2 :** to alienate in spirit **:** destroy the concord or harmony between or among ⟨attempted to ~ the members of the club by gossip⟩ ~ *vi* **:** to fall apart or separate into individual units **:** become disunified or disjoined

disunited *adj, of a horse or its gait* **:** using the legs in the wrong order when cantering or galloping

dis·unity \dəsh, (ˈ)dish + ˌ(y)ü...; dəs, (ˈ)dis + ˌyü...\ *n* [1*dis-* + *unity*] **:** the state of being disunified in spirit **:** lack of concord, harmony, or a cooperative spirit **:** ALIENATION, DISSENSION ⟨states . . . are destroyed by their folly, weakness, ~ —John Strachey⟩ ⟨the unpreparedness of the West, its woeful ~, and its pitiful mutual incriminations —Hans Kohn⟩ ⟨the much more difficult kind of ~ made by deep cleavages of race, religion, or culture —Margery Perham⟩

dis·usage \" + \ *n* [ME, fr. 1*dis-* + *usage*] **:** DISUSE

1**disuse** \" +\ *vt* [ME *disusen*, fr. 1*dis-* + *usen* to use — more at USE] **1** *archaic* **:** to make unaccustomed or unused **:** DISACCUSTOM **2 :** to discontinue the use or practice of **:** DISCARD, ABANDON — now used chiefly in the past participial form ⟨a golf course long *disused*⟩ ⟨a *disused* cigarette package⟩ ⟨the baroque scroll pediment had been *disused* on exteriors before the revolution —Fiske Kimball⟩

2**disuse** \"\ *n* [1*dis-* + *use*] **:** cessation of use, practice, or exercise **:** DESUETUDE ⟨intellectual vigor has been circumscribed by the ~ of the scholar's language —A.A.Hill⟩ ⟨the mine ultimately fell into ~⟩ ⟨combat intelligence had atrophied by ~ —Shipley Thomas⟩ ⟨we should die of idiocy through ~ of our mental faculties if we did not fill our heads with romantic nonsense out of illustrated newspapers and novels and plays and films —G.B.Shaw⟩

dis·utility \ˌdish + (y)ü..., ˌdis + yü...\ *n* [1*dis-* + *utility*] **:** the absence or lack of utility; *specif* **:** the quality of causing inconvenience, discomfort, or pain or of thwarting the satisfaction of desires

dis·valuable \dəs, (ˈ)dis+\ *adj* [1*dis-* + *valuable*] **:** characterized by disvalue

dis·valuation \dəs, (ˌ)dis+\ *n* [1*dis-* + *valuation*] **:** the action of losing value **:** DEPRECIATION ⟨they faced the problem of living in a world which was in process of ~ —R.M.Weaver⟩

1**dis·value** \dəs, (ˈ)dis+\ *vt* [1*dis-* + *value* (v.)] **1** *archaic* **:** UNDERVALUE, DEPRECIATE **2 :** to consider of little value **:** DISESTEEM ⟨in civilized man the variety of the valued and *disvalued* increases greatly —E.L.Thorndike⟩

2**disvalue** \"\ *n* [1*dis-* + *value* (n.)] **1 :** DISESTEEM, DISREGARD **2 :** a negative value; *specif* **:** one that is positively detrimental (as an evil) ⟨has chosen on the contrary to pair every value exactly with its corresponding ~ —P.B.Rice⟩ ⟨the artist, in projecting an individual experience, or his own interpretation of it, is indicating values to be salvaged, ~*s* to be avoided —*Jour. of Aesthetics*⟩

disweapon *vt* [1*dis-* + *weapon* (n.)] *obs* **:** DISARM

disworship *n* [ME, fr. 1*dis-* + *worship*] *obs* **:** a withholding or deprivation of honor **:** DISHONOR

di·syllabic *or* **dis·syllabic** \ˌdī, ˌdi +\ *adj* [F *dissyllabique*, fr. *dissyllabe* (fr. MF *dissilabe*) + *-ique* -ic] **:** consisting of or having two syllables only ⟨a ~ word⟩ ⟨an iambic foot is ~⟩

di·syllabify *or* **dis·syllabify** \"+\ *vt* [*disyllable, dissyllable* + *-i-* + *-fy*] **:** DISYLLABIZE

di·syl·la·bism *or* **dis·syl·la·bism** \dīˈsiləˌbizəm, dīˈ-\ *n* [F *dissyllabisme*, fr. *dissyllabe* + *-isme* -ism] **:** the quality or state of being disyllabic

di·syllabize *or* **dis·syllabize** \(ˈ)dī, (ˈ)di+\ *vt* [*disyllable, dissyllable* + *-ize*] **:** to make two syllables of

di·syllable *or* **dis·syllable** \(ˈ)dī, (ˈ)di+\ *n* [part trans. of MF *dissilabe*, fr. ML *dissyllabus* of two syllables, alter. (influenced by Gk *dis-* twice, double, fr. *dis* twice) of L *disyllabus*, fr. Gk *disyllabos*, fr. *di-* + *-syllabos* (fr. *syllabē* syllable) — more at BIS, TWI-] **:** a linguistic form consisting of two syllables (as *many, repeat*)

1**dit** *or* **ditt** \ˈdit\ *vt* **ditted; ditted; ditting; dits** *or* **ditts** [ME *ditten*, fr. OE *dyttan*; akin to Icel *dytta* to repair, stop up (as a crack) — more at DOT] *Scot* **:** to close up **:** obstruct the course of

2**dit** \"\ *n* -S [alter. (influenced by *ditty*) of ME *dite*, fr. MF *dit* word, speech, poem, song, fr. L *dictum* saying, dictum — more at DICTUM] *archaic* **:** DITTY, SONG

3**dit** \ˈdē\ *n, pl* **dits** \-ē(z)\ [F, fr. OF, word, speech, poem, song] **:** a short usu. didactic sometimes satirical poem in old French literature often dealing with homely subjects

4**dit** \ˈdit, *usu* -id·+V\ *n* -S [imit.] **:** a dot in radio or telegraphic code — used by operators as an oral representation of the transmitted sound; compare DAH

di·ta \ˈdēˈtä\ *n* -S [Tag *ditā*] **1 :** a forest tree (*Alstonia scholaris*) of eastern Asia and the Philippines the bark of which was formerly used as an antiperiodic **2 :** the bark of the dita tree **3 :** UPAS 1a

di·tal \ˈdēd·ᵊl, ˈdiˌ, ˈdīˌl\ *n* -S [It *dito* finger (fr. L *digitus*) + E *-al* (as in *pedal*) — more at TOE] **:** a key by which the pitch is raised a half step in a harp guitar

dital harp *n* **:** a harp guitar provided with a dital

di·ta·li \dēˈtälē\ *also* **di·ta·li·ni** \ˌdēd·ᵊlˈēnē\ *n pl* [*ditali* fr. It, pl. of *ditale*, lit., thimble, fingerstall; *ditalini* fr. It, pl. of *ditalino*, dim. of *ditale*] **:** elbow-shaped pieces of macaroni

1**ditch** \ˈdich\ *n* -ES *often attrib* [ME *dich*, fr. OE *dīc* dike, ditch — more at DIKE] **1 :** a long narrow excavation dug in the earth **2 a :** a trench for guarding or fencing enclosures **b :** a trench for conveying water for drainage or irrigation **c :** the area at either side of a road usu. consisting of a drainage trench ⟨a car headed for the ~⟩ **3** *chiefly Irish* **:** a bank of earth from an excavation **4 :** a natural or artificial usu. narrow watercourse or waterway **5 :** the ground bounding a bowling green sometimes consisting of a shallow trench **6 :** a borrow pit of a road **7 :** a trough for disposing of the drilling fluid in rotary drilling of an oil well

2**ditch** \"\ *vb* -ED/-ING/-ES [ME *dichen*, fr. *dich*, n.] *vt* **1 a :** to enclose with a ditch ⟨a pasture hedged and ~*ed*⟩ **b :** to dig a ditch in (as for drainage or irrigation) **2 :** to cause (a train) to derail **:** drive (a car) into the ditch **3 a :** to discard, dismiss, or abandon as no longer useful or desirable **:** get rid of ⟨~*ed* the old policy when it proved ineffective⟩ ⟨~ his fiancée⟩ **b** *slang* **:** to hide, put away, or put aside with the intent of recovery ⟨~ the stolen goods⟩ **c** *slang* **:** to get away from or avoid by artifice or stratagem ⟨~*ed* me by sneaking out the back door⟩ ⟨let's ~ school today⟩ **4 :** to crash-land (a landplane) on water ~ *vi* **1 :** to dig a ditch **2** *dial* **:** to clean or repair a ditch **3 :** to crash-land a landplane on water

ditch bank blade *n* **:** a weed and grass cutter comprising a hooked blade at the end of a long wooden handle

ditch boss *n* **:** an official in the western U.S. having the authority to apportion irrigation water

ditchbur \ˈ=,=\ *n* **:** COCKLEBUR

ditch check *n* **:** a small usu. wood or concrete dam placed at frequent intervals below the surface of a road ditch to prevent erosion

ditch crowfoot *n* **:** CURSED CROWFOOT

ditchdigger \ˈ=,==\ *n* **1 :** one that digs ditches **2 a :** one employed at menial and usu. hard physical labor **b :** DITCHER 2

ditchdigging \ˈ=,==\ *n* **:** the occupation of a ditchdigger

ditch·er \ˈdichə(r)\ *n* -S [ME *dicher*, fr. *dichen* to make a ditch + *-er* — more at DITCH] **1 :** a workman who digs or repairs ditches **2 :** a machine that digs ditches and usu. piles the dirt in a bank to the side (as by means of a conveyor belt)

ditch fern *n* [ME *diche fern*] **:** ROYAL FERN

ditch grass *n* **:** a slender branching marine aquatic plant (*Ruppia maritima*) with linear leaves like those of grasses

ditching car *n* **:** a railroad car equipped for excavation

ditch·less \ˈdichləs\ *adj* **:** lacking a ditch

ditch·man \ˈdichmən\ *n, pl* **ditchmen :** a ditcher in a mine

ditch millet *n* **:** a grass (*Paspalum scrobilatum*) grown esp. in India, Africa, and Australasia and said to poison the milk of cows that eat it

ditch moss *n* **:** WATERWEED a

ditch reed *n* **:** a tall reed (*Phragmites communis*) that has creeping rhizomes, broad flat leaves, and a large bushy panicle, is widely distributed in moist areas throughout most of No. America, and has been used for weaving mats, screens, and lattices and for making arrow shafts — called also *giant reed*

ditch rider *n* **:** a person who patrols and inspects irrigation systems and distributes water to farmers

ditch stonecrop *n* **:** a common American perennial weed (*Penthorum sedoides*) with united carpels, flowers in loose spikes, and scattered leaves

ditch sunflower *n* **:** TICKSEED SUNFLOWER

ditchwater \ˈ=,==\ *n* [ME *dich water*, fr. *dich* ditch + *water*] **1 :** foul stagnant water collected in a ditch **2 :** something regarded as typically dull and lifeless ⟨writing as dull as ~⟩

1**dite** *vt* -ED/-ING/-S [ME *diten*, fr. OF *ditier*, fr. L *dictare* to pronounce, assert, dictate — more at DICTATE] **1** *obs* **:** INDITE, COMPOSE **2** *obs* **:** INDICT

2**dite** \ˈdīt\ *n* -S [alter. of *doit*] *dial* **:** a small amount **:** MITE, BIT

di·ten·tion \(ˈ)dīˈtenchən\ *n* -S [*divided* at*tention*] **:** a mode of attention in which ideational reactions are distorted by the unconscious intrusion of elements of feeling and emotion — compare COTENTION

di·ten·tive \-entiv\ *adj* **:** of, relating to, or marked by ditention

di·terpene \(ˈ)dī+\ *n* [*di-* + *terpene*] **:** any of a class of terpenes $C_{20}H_{32}$ containing twice as many atoms in the molecule as monoterpenes; *also* **:** a derivative of such a terpene

1**di·terpenoid** \"+\ *adj* [*diterpene* + *-oid*] **:** resembling a diterpene in molecular structure

2**diterpenoid** \"\ *n* -S **:** a diterpene or diterpene derivative (as phytol or abietic acid)

di·tetragonal \ˌdī+=ˈ===\ *adj* [ISV *di-* + *tetragonal*] **1 :** relating to or being a prism in the tetragonal system that has eight similar faces whose alternate interfacial angles only are equal; *also* **:** relating to or being a pyramid corresponding to such a prism **2 :** relating to or being a type of symmetry that requires a ditetragonal pyramid or dipyramid

di·the·ism \ˈdīthēˌizəm, (ˈ)dīˈth-\ *n* -S [*di-* + *-theism*] **:** belief in or theory of the existence of two gods or of two original principles, one good and one evil (as in Manichaeism) — **di·the·is·tic** \ˌdīthēˈistik\ *or* **di·the·is·ti·cal** \-stəkəl\ *adj*

di·the·ist \ˈdī(ˌ)thēəst, (ˈ)dīˈth-\ *n* **:** an advocate or adherent of ditheism

di·thematic \ˌdī+\ *adj* [*di-* + *thematic*] **:** having or characterized by two themes ⟨a ~ chess problem⟩

1**dith·er** \ˈdith|ə(r) *sometimes* -th|\ *vi* **dithered; dithered; dithering** \|(ə)riŋ\ **dithers** [alter. of *didder*] **1 :** SHIVER, SHAKE, TREMBLE ⟨the ~*ing* of grass —Wallace Stevens⟩ **2 :** to act or move nervously, hesitantly, confusedly, or without clear purpose ⟨the stage manager was ~*ing* in the wings⟩ **:** act indecisively **:** VACILLATE, WAVER ⟨faced with unpleasant choices she merely ~*s*⟩ **3 :** BABBLE ⟨~*ing* on the phone⟩

2**dither** \"\ *n* -S **1** *dial Eng* **:** a trembling, shaking, or quivering esp. with cold **2 :** a state of strong excitement or agitation ⟨the outbreak of war threw all parties into a ~⟩ — **dith·ery** \|(ə)rē\ *adj*

dithered *adj* **:** being in a state of confusion or excitement **:** DAZED

dithi- *or* **dithio-** *comb form* [ISV *di-* + *thi-*] **:** containing two atoms of sulfur usu. in place of two oxygen atoms ⟨*dithi*ane⟩ ⟨*dithio*benzoic acid⟩

di·thio \dīˈthī(ˌ)ō\ *adj* [*dithi-*] **:** relating to or containing two atoms of sulfur usu. in place of two oxygen atoms ⟨~ acids⟩

di·thio·carbamate \ˌdīˌthīō+\ *n* [*dithiocarbamic* + *-ate*] **:** a salt of dithiocarbamic acid or of one of its organic derivatives

di·thio·carbamic acid \"+. . .-\ *n* [ISV *dithi-* + *carbamic*] **:** an unstable acid NH_2CSSH known best in the form of salts and disubstituted organic derivatives (as salts of the dimethyl derivative) that are made from carbon disulfide (as by reaction with ammonia or amines) and that in many cases are used as fungicides or accelerators of vulcanization

-di·thi·o·ic \ˌdīˌthīˈōik\ *adj comb form* [ISV *dithi-* + *-ic*] **:** containing two atoms of sulfur replacing two oxygen atoms in the molecule of an acid ⟨phosphoro*dithioic* acid $H_3PO_2S_2$⟩

-di·thi·ol \dīˈthīˌōl, -ōl\ *n comb form* -S [ISV *dithi-* + *-ol*] **:** containing two mercapto groups replacing hydrogen ⟨1,2-ethane*dithiol* CH_2SHCH_2SH⟩

di·thionate \(ˈ)dī+\ *n* -S [ISV *dithionic* + *-ate*] **:** a salt of dithionic acid

di·thionic acid \ˌdī+. . .-\ *n* [ISV *di-* + *thionic*] **:** a strong dibasic acid $H_2S_2O_6$ made by oxidizing sulfurous acid but known only in solution and in the form of salts

di·thi·o·nite \dīˈthīəˌnīt\ *n* -S [*di-* + *thion-* + *-ite*] **:** HYDROSULFITE

di·thi·o·nous acid \(ˈ)dīˈthīənəs-\ *n* [*di-* + *thion-* + *-ous*] **:** HYDROSULFUROUS ACID — used in the nomenclature adopted by the International Union of Pure and Applied Chemistry

di·thi·zone \dīˈthīˌzōn\ *n* -S [*diphenylthiocarbazone*] **:** a bluish black crystalline compound $C_6H_5N{=}NCSNHNHC_6H_5$ used for the colorimetric determination of heavy metals (as lead) — called also *diphenylthiocarbazone*

di·thra·nol \ˈdīthrəˌnōl, ˈdith-, -nōl\ *n* -S [*di*hydroxyan*thranol*] **:** ANTHRALIN

dith·y·ramb \ˈdith|əˌram, |ē,-, -raa(ə)m *sometimes* -ith|\ *n* -S

[Gk *dithyrambos*, prob. of non-IE origin] **1 :** a choric poem, chant, or hymn of ancient Greece sung by revelers at the festival in honor of the god Dionysus **2 :** a poem in an inspired wild irregular strain **3 :** a statement or piece of writing in an exalted impassioned style usu. in praise of something ⟨went into ~s over the beauty of the landscape⟩

¹dith·y·ram·bic \ˌ=ˌ=ˈrambik, -bēk\ *adj* [Gk *dithyrambikos*, fr. *dithyrambos* + *-ikos* -ic] **1 :** of or relating to dithyrambs **:** composing dithyrambs **2 :** like a dithyramb esp. in being impassioned and elevated ⟨he grew ~ in speaking of the candidate's merits⟩ — **dith·y·ram·bi·cal·ly** \-bək(ə)lē, -bēk-, -li\ *adv*

²dithyrambic \"\ *n* -s **:** DITHYRAMB

di·thy·rid·i·um \ˌdīˌthīˈridēəm, ˌdithəˈr-\ *n* -s [NL, fr. *di-* + Gk *thyridion*, dim. of *thyra* door — more at DOOR] **:** a larva of certain taenioid tapeworms consisting of a scolex invaginated into an elongated solid body

diting *pres part of* DITE

dition *n* -s [MF, fr. L *dicion-*, *dicio* word of command, command, dominion, fr. *dicere* to say + *-ion-*, *-io* -ion — more at DICTION] *obs* **:** DOMINION, RULE

dit·o·kous \ˈdidəkəs\ *adj* [Gk *ditokos* having borne two at one birth, fr. *di-* + *tokos* childbirth, offspring] **1 :** producing two eggs or young at a time ⟨pigeons are generally ~⟩ **2 :** producing two kinds of young ⟨~ worms⟩

di·tone \ˈdīˌtōn\ *n* [Gk *ditonon*, fr. neut. of *ditonos* having two tones, fr. *di-* + *tonos* tone — more at TONE] **:** the Greek musical interval of a major third comprehending two major steps, corresponding to the ratio 81:64, and being slightly larger than the modern major third — **di·ton·ic** \(ˈ)dīˈtänik\ *adj*

ditonic comma *n* [trans. of NL *comma ditonicum*] **:** the difference in pitch between two musical tones respectively twelve perfect fifths and seven octaves from the same tone and represented by the ratio of 531,441:524,288 — called also *Pythagorean comma*

di·trem·a·ta \dīˈtremədə\ [NL, fr. *di-* + *-tremata*] *syn of* THERIA

di·trem·a·tous \(ˈ)dīˈtremədəs\ *adj* [*di-* + Gk *trēmat-*, *trēma* hole + E *-ous* — more at THROW] **1 :** having the two genital openings separate — used of freshwater pulmonate snails **2 :** having the genital and anal openings separate — used of viviparous fishes

di·triglyph \(ˈ)dī+\ *n* [F *ditriglyphe*, fr. *di-* + *triglyphe* triglyph] **:** a horizontal division in the Doric architectural style assumed to contain two triglyphs: as **a :** a single metope with its limiting triglyphs **b :** two metopes with one whole and two half triglyphs, equaling an intercolumniation **c :** the wide middle intercolumniation found in some porticoes **d :** the space from the vertical axis of one metope to that of the next but one — **di·triglyphic** \ˌdī+ˌ=ˈ==\ *adj*

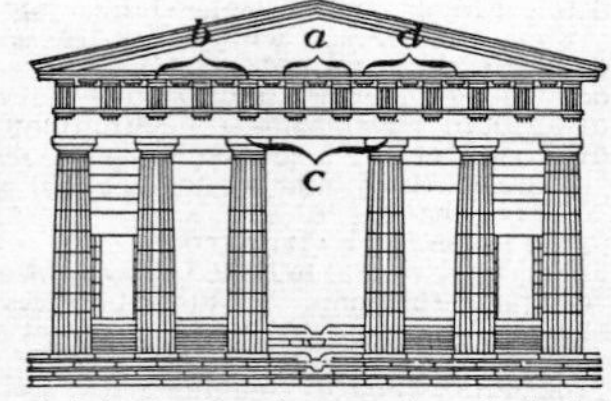

ditriglyph, showing portions included according to senses *a*, *b*, *c*, and *d*

di·trigonal \(ˈ)dī+\ *adj* [ISV *di-* + *trigonal*] *of a six-sided prism or pyramid* **:** having only the alternate interfacial angles equal — see SCALENOHEDRON illustration — **di·trigonally** \"+\ *adv*

di·tro·che·an \(ˈ)dīˌtrōkēən, ˌdī(ˌ)trōˈk-\ *adj* **:** of, containing, or consisting of a ditrochee

di·trochee \(ˈ)dī+\ *n* [LL & Gk; LL *ditrochaeus*, fr. Gk *ditrochaios*, fr. *di-* + *trochaios* trochee — more at TROCHEE] **:** a double trochee **:** a trochaic dipody reckoned as a single measure or compound foot

dits *pres 3d sing of* DIT, *pl of* DIT

ditt *var of* DIT

dit·tan·der \dəˈtandə(r), ˈditᵊn-\ *n* -s [AF *ditaundere*, alter. of OF *ditan*] **1 :** CRETAN DITTANY **2 :** a perennial European pepperwort (*Lepidium latifolium*) with sepals broadly white-margined from the base

dit·ta·ny \ˈditᵊnē\ *n* -ES [ME *diptannus*, *ditoyne*, fr. ML & MF; ML *diaptannus* & MF *ditan*, fr. L *dictamnus*, *dictamnum*, fr. Gk *diktamnon*, perh. fr. *Diktē*, mountain in Crete] **1 :** CRETAN DITTANY **2 :** FRAXINELLA **3 :** a small aromatic herb (*Cunila origanoides*) of the family Labiatae **4 :** BASTARD DITTANY

dit·tay \ˈdiˌtā, -ˌti\ *n* -s [ME (Sc dial.), fr. MF *dité*, *ditié*, past part. of *diter*, *ditier* to compose, indict — more at DITE] *Scots law* **:** the matter charged in an indictment; *also* **:** the indictment itself

ditted *past of* DIT

ditting *pres part of* DIT

¹dit·to \ˈdid·(ˌ)ō, -i(ˌ)ō\ *n, pl* **dittos** *also* **dittoes** [It *ditto*, *detto* (past part. of *dicere* to say), fr. L *dictus*, past part. of *dicere* to say — more at DICTION] **1 a :** a thing mentioned previously or above — used to avoid repeating a word ⟨mamma polar bears clutching infant ~s —Mollie Panter-Downes⟩; abbr. *do;* often symbolized by inverted commas, apostrophes, or other small marks **b :** a ditto mark **2** *dittoes pl, Brit* **:** clothes of one material or color throughout ⟨a dark-colored suit of ~*es*⟩ **3 :** a duplicate or close copy ⟨he is the ~ of his father⟩

²ditto \"\ *vb* -ED/-ING/-ES *vt* **:** to repeat the action or statement of ⟨the second speaker ~*ed* his argument⟩ ~ *vi* **:** to repeat an act or statement

³ditto \"\ *adv* **:** as before or aforesaid **:** in the same manner ⟨I shall act ~⟩

dit·to·graph \ˈdidōˌgraf, -itō-, -rȧf\ *n* -s [Gk *dittos*, *dissos* twofold + E *-graph*] **:** a letter or letters or words unintentionally repeated in copying or printing

dit·tog·ra·phy \diˈtägrəfē\ *n* -ES [Gk *dittographia*, *dissographia*, fr. *dittos*, *dissos* + *-graphia* -graphy] **:** the unintentional repetition of letters or words in copying or printing (as literatature for literature)

dit·tol·o·gy \-täləjē\ *n* -ES [Gk *dittologia*, *dissologia* repetition of a word, fr. *dittos*, *dissos* + *-logia* -logy] **:** a double reading or twofold interpretation (as of a biblical text)

¹dit·ty \ˈdid·ē, -it|, |i\ *n* -ES [ME *dite*, fr. OF *ditié* composition, poem, moral tract, fr. past part. of *ditier* to compose, indict — more at DITE] **1 :** a song or short poem intended to be sung; *esp* **:** one of a simple unaffected character ⟨a plaintive ~ sung by a Highland lass⟩ **2** *obs* **:** the words or subject of a song as distinguished from its tune

²ditty \"\ *vb* -ED/-ING/-ES *vi, obs* **:** SING ~ *vt, obs* **:** to celebrate in song **:** set to music **:** SING ⟨with his soft pipe, and smooth-*dittied* song —John Milton⟩

ditty bag *n* [origin unknown] **:** a small bag used esp. by sailors to hold thread, needles, tape, or other small articles of gear

ditty box \"-\ *also* **did·dy box** \-id|ē, |i\ *n* [origin unknown] **:** a box used for the same purpose as a ditty bag

dit·y·len·chus \ˌdidəˈleŋkəs\ *n, cap* [NL, fr. Gk *ditylos* having two humps (fr. *di-* + *tylos* callus, lump, penis) + *enchos* spear, lance] **:** a genus of small slender nematode worms (family Tylenchidae) including serious plant parasites (as the potato rot nematode and the bulb eelworm) as well as a number of harmless soil forms and commensals

di·um·vi·rate \dīˈəmvərət, -rāt\ *n* -s [by alter. (influence of *di-*)] **:** DUUMVIRATE

di·ure·sis \ˌdīyəˈrēsəs\ *n, pl* **diure·ses** \-ēˌsēz\ [NL, fr. LL *diureticus*, after Gk *ourētikos* uretic: *ourēsis* uresis — more at URETIC, URESIS] **:** an increased excretion of urine

¹di·uret·ic \ˌdīyəˈred·|ik, -et|, |ēk\ *adj* [ME, fr. MF or LL; MF *diuretique*, fr. LL *diureticus*, fr. Gk *diourētikos*, fr. (assumed) *diourētos* (verbal of *diourein* to urinate, have diuretic properties, fr. *dia-* + *ourein* to urinate) + *-ikos* -ic — more at URINE] **:** tending to increase the flow of urine — **di·uret·i·cal·ly** \|ək(ə)lē, |ēk-, -li\ *adv*

²diuretic \"\ *n* -s [ME, fr. *diuretic*, adj.] **:** an agent that increases the flow of urine

¹di·ur·nal \(ˈ)dīˈərnᵊl, -ˈən-, -ˈəin-\ *adj* [ME *diurnall*, fr. L *diurnalis* — more at JOURNAL] **1 a :** repeated or recurring every day **:** DAILY ⟨the ~ round of tasks and cares⟩ **b :** going through its changes in a day; *specif* **:** having a recurrent daily cycle of change ⟨~ rotation of the heavens —D.J.Price⟩ **2 a :** performed in or belonging to the daytime ⟨black bats, inverted in ~ slumber —P.M.Hubbard⟩ ⟨the city's ~ noises faded with the night⟩ **b :** chiefly active during the daytime ⟨hunting dogs are mainly ~ animals —James Stevenson-Hamilton⟩ — compare NOCTURNAL **3** *of a flower* **a :** opening during the day and closing at night **b :** lasting only a day **:** EPHEMERAL **4** *of a sign of the zodiac* **:** UNEVEN ⟨the 1st, 3d, and 5th are ~ signs⟩ — **di·ur·nal·ly** \-ᵊlē, -ᵊli\ *adv*

²diurnal \"\ *n* -s **1** *obs* **:** a small volume containing the services for the canonical hours which are said in the daytime **2** *archaic* **:** DAYBOOK, DIARY **3** *archaic* **:** a daily newspaper or journal

diurnal arc *n* **:** the portion of the diurnal circle of a celestial body that is above the observer's horizon ⟨the *diurnal arc* of the sun is its apparent path from sunrise to sunset⟩

diurnal circle *n* **:** the apparent circle or parallel of declination described by a celestial body in consequence of the earth's rotation

di·ur·nal·ist \=ˈ=nᵊləst\ *n* -s [²*diurnal* + *-ist*] *archaic* **:** JOURNALIST

diurnal motion *n* **:** the apparent westward motion of the celestial sphere and celestial bodies resulting from the rotation of the earth; *also* **:** the earth's rotation

diurnal parallax *n* **:** GEOCENTRIC PARALLAX

di·ur·na·tion \ˌdī(ˌ)ərˈnāshən\ *n* -s [L *diurn*us of the day, daily + E *-ation* (as in *hibernation*) — more at JOURNAL] **1 :** the habit of sleeping or being quiescent by day ⟨the ~ of bats⟩ **2 :** a daily recurrent fluctuation in an ecological community (as the vertical movement of plankton)

di·u·tur·nal \ˌdīyüˈtərnᵊl\ *adj* [L *diuturn*us (fr. *diu* lasting a long time, a long time ago) + E *-al*] **:** of long continuance **:** LASTING

di·u·tur·ni·ty \ˌ==ˈ=nəd·ē\ *n* -ES [ME *diuturnite*, fr. L *diuturnitat-*, *diuturnitas*, fr. *diuturnus* + *-itat-*, *-itas* -ity] **:** the quality or state of being continuous or lasting

¹div \ˈdiv\ *n* -s [Per *dēv* — more at DAEVA] **:** DAEVA

²div *substand past of* DIVE

div *abbr* **1** divergence **2** diversion **3** divide **4** dividend **5** divine; divinity **6** [It *divisi*] separate **7** division **8** divorce

di·va \ˈdēvə\ *n, pl* **divas** \-vəz\ *or* **di·ve** \-ˌvā\ [It, lit., goddess, fr. L, fem. of *divus* god — more at DEITY] **:** PRIMA DONNA 1

diva blue *n* **:** a moderate blue that is redder and duller than average copen and redder and deeper than azurite blue or Dresden blue

di·va·gate \ˈdīvəˌgāt, ˈdiv-\ *vi* -ED/-ING/-S [LL *divagatus*, past part. of *divagari*, fr. L *di-* (fr. *dis-* apart) + *vagari* to wander — more at DIS-, VAGARY] **1 :** to wander about or stray from one place or subject to another ⟨now he *divagated* into the field of literature⟩ **2 :** DIVERGE ⟨natural science *divagated* more and more from metaphysics —George Boas⟩

di·va·ga·tion \ˌ==ˈgāshən\ *n* -s [LL *divagation-*, *divagatio*, fr. *divagatus* + L *-ion-*, *-io* -ion] **:** the act or fact of divagating **:** DIGRESSION ⟨numerous ~s of the plot⟩ **:** DEVIATION, DIVERGENCE ⟨fashionable ~s from classic literary nouns⟩

di·valent \(ˈ)dī+\ *adj* [ISV *di-* + *valent*] **:** BIVALENT

divali *usu cap, var of* DEWALI

di·van *in sense 3* ˈdīˌvan *or* -vaa(ə)n *sometimes* dīˈv- *or* dəˈv- *or* ˈdīvən; *in other senses the preceding pronunciations having heavy stress in the last syllable, and* dəˈvän *or* dēˈ- *or* -ˈvȧn, *are frequent*\ *n* -s [Turk, fr. Per *dīwān* account book] **1** *or* **di·wan** \dēˈwän, də-, -ˈwȧn\ **a :** a Muslim council of state; *specif* **:** the Turkish privy council that was presided over by the sultan or grand vizier **b :** COUNCIL ⟨meet the family . . . in full ~ —Sir Walter Scott⟩ **2** *or* **diwan a :** a room or hall where a divan is held **b :** a Muslim court of justice **c :** SMOKING ROOM **3 a :** a large low couch with no back or ends **b :** SOFA, DAVENPORT **c :** a couch usu. without back or arms and often designed for use as a bed **4** *or* **diwan :** a collection of poems esp. in Persian or Arabic; *specif* **:** a series of poems by one author

di·variant \(ˈ)dī+\ *adj* [ISV *di-* + *variant*] **:** BIVARIANT

¹di·var·i·cate \dīˈvarəˌkāt, dəˈv-\ *vb* -ED/-ING/-S [L *divaricatus*, past part. of *divaricare*, fr. *di-* (fr. *dis-* apart) + *varicare* to straddle — more at DIS-, PREVARICATE] *vi* **1 :** to spread apart **:** diverge from each other ⟨at this spot the two roads ~⟩ **2 :** to divide or break up into distinct parts ~ *vt* **1** *obs* **:** to cause to divide into branches **2 :** to stretch or spread apart ⟨*divaricated* two fingers of his hand⟩ **syn** see BRANCH

²di·var·i·cate \(ˈ)dīˈvarəkət, dəˈv-\ *adj* [L *divaricatus*] **:** widely diverging or spreading apart — used esp. of branches and wings — **di·var·i·cate·ly** *adv*

di·var·i·ca·tion \(ˌ)dīˌvarəˈkāshən, də,-\ *n* -s [ML *divarication-*, *divaricatio*, fr. L *divaricatus* (past part. of *divaricare*) + *-ion-*, *-io* -ion] **1 :** the process or fact of separating into parts or branching out ⟨~ of dialects from a common tongue⟩; *also* **:** one of the branches or subdivisions made by such separation **2 :** a disagreement or divergence of opinion ⟨~ of philosophical systems⟩ **3 :** the action or an instance of stretching or spreading apart (as the legs)

di·var·i·ca·tor \=ˈ=rəˌkād·ə(r)\ *n* -s **:** one that divaricates; *esp* **:** a muscle that causes divergence or separation of parts (as one of those which open the shell of brachiopods)

divd *abbr* dividend

¹dive \ˈdīv\ *vb* **dived** \ˈdīvd\ *or* **dove** \ˈdōv, *substand* ˈdəv\ *or substand* **div** \ˈdiv\ **dived; diving; dives** [ME *diven*, *duven*, fr. OE *dȳfan* (vt) to dip & *dūfan* (vi) to dive; OE *dȳfan*, causative fr. the root of *dūfan*; akin to MLG be*düven* to be covered, ON *dȳfa* to dip, OHG *tobal* narrow valley, OSlav *dupina* cave, OE *dyppan* to dip — more at DIP] *vi* **1 a :** to plunge into water headfirst **:** thrust the body under or deeply into water or other fluid; *specif* **:** to execute a dive **b :** SUBMERGE ⟨the submarine *dived*⟩ **2 a :** to descend or fall precipitously ⟨the mercury *dived* to eight below zero⟩ **b :** to plunge one's hand into something ⟨*dived* into her pocketbook⟩ **c** *of a plane* **:** to descend in a dive — compare GLIDE **3 a :** to plunge into or explore some matter or subject ⟨~ into the heart of the matter⟩ **b :** to throw oneself into some activity **:** make a vigorous start ⟨*dived* into his food⟩ ⟨~ boldly into a strange new profession⟩ **c :** to plunge or dash (as for shelter) into some place or across some space ⟨bystanders *dived* for cover⟩ **:** lunge esp. with the intent of seizing something ⟨*dived* for his legs⟩ ~ *vt* **1 a** *archaic* **:** to plunge (a person or thing) into water **b :** to thrust (as the hand or anything held) into something ⟨~ his hand into the earth —Mollie Panter-Downes⟩ **2 :** to cause (as an airplane or submarine) to descend ⟨*dived* his plane through the sonic barrier⟩ **3** *archaic* **:** to penetrate or explore by or as if by diving ⟨he ~s the hollow, climbs the steeps —R.W.Emerson⟩ **syn** see PLUNGE

²dive \"\ *n* -s **1 :** the act or an instance of diving: as **a** (1) **:** a plunge into water executed in a prescribed manner and consisting of a takeoff (as from a springboard), an evolution in the air, and entry into the water either headfirst (as in a swan dive or jackknife) or feet first (as in a somersault or gainer) — called also *fancy dive* (2) **:** a submerging esp. of a submarine (3) *of an airplane* **:** a steep descent with or without power in which the airspeed attained is greater than the maximum speed in horizontal flight (4) **:** a headfirst leap in tumbling into the air from the mat or over a piece of apparatus followed immediately by a forward roll **b :** a plunge into or exploration of some matter or subject ⟨undismayed by his first ~ into calculus⟩ **c :** a plunge or dash (as for shelter) into some place or across some space ⟨made a ~ for the ditch⟩ **:** a lunge esp. with the intent of seizing something ⟨made a ~ for the gun⟩ **d :** a sharp decline (as of stocks or intangible values) ⟨morale took a ~ as the news spread⟩ **2 :** a disreputable resort for drinking or entertainment ⟨this is a respectable roadhouse; this is no ~ —Erskine Caldwell⟩ **3** *slang* **:** a pretended knockout resulting from collusion between two prizefighters ⟨took a ~ in the third round⟩

³dive *pl of* DIVA

dive-bomb \ˈ=ˌ=\ *vt* **:** to bomb by making a steep dive toward the target before releasing the bomb ~ *vi* **:** to engage in dive-bombing

dive bomber *n* **:** a bomber designed for dive-bombing

dive brake *n* **:** a retractable usu. hinged flap that may be extended into the airstream to increase the aerodynamic drag and thereby reduce the speed of a diving airplane

divekeeper \ˈ=ˌ==\ *n* **:** a keeper of a dive

di·vel \(ˈ)dīˌvel, dəˈv-\ *vt* **divelled; divelled; divelling; divels** [L *divellere*, fr. *di-* (fr. *dis-* apart) + *vellere* to pluck, pull — more at DIS-, VELLICATE] *archaic* **:** to tear asunder or draw apart

di·vel·lent \dīˈvelənt, dəˈ-\ *adj* [L *divellent-*, *divellens*, pres. part. of *divellere*] *archaic* **:** drawing or tending to draw apart

di·vel·li·cate \dīˈveləˌkāt, dəˈ-\ *vt* -ED/-ING/-S [L *di-* (fr. *dis-* apart) + *vellicatus*, past part. of *vellicare* to pluck, twitch, fr. *vellere* to pluck, pull] *archaic* **:** to tear apart **:** break off **:** DETACH

div·er \ˈdīvə(r)\ *n* -s **1 :** one that dives **2 a :** a person who stays under water (as in salvage work) for long periods by having air supplied from the surface **b :** a fancy diver — compare DIVE 1a(1) **c :** any of various birds skillful in diving (as the grebe, sea duck, auk or penguin); *specif* **:** LOON **d** *slang chiefly Brit* **:** PICKPOCKET

diverb *n* [prob. fr. L *di-* (fr. *dis-* apart) + E *-verb* (as in *proverb*)] *obs* **:** a proverbial expression **:** PROVERB

di·verge \dəˈvərj, (ˈ)dīˈv-, -vōj, -vəij\ *vb* -ED/-ING/-S [ML *divergere*, fr. L *di-* (fr. *dis-* apart) + *vergere* to bend, incline — more at DIS-, WRENCH] *vi* **1 a :** to move or extend in different directions from a common point **:** draw apart ⟨these two roads ~ like the branches of a Y⟩ — opposed to *converge* **b :** to become different in character or form **:** differ in opinion ⟨dialects of the same language have *diverged* so widely that their relationship is no longer apparent⟩ **2 a :** to turn aside or lead away from a particular route or direction ⟨*diverging* from his direct path —Thomas Hardy⟩ **b :** to turn aside or deviate from a particular policy, course of action, subject, or line of thought **:** DIGRESS ⟨~ to another topic⟩ **:** differ in form, character, or opinion ⟨the traditions recorded there ~ from those that my mother handed down —George Santayana⟩ ~ *vt* **:** to cause to take a different direction **:** DEFLECT ⟨~ a compass needle⟩ **syn** see SWERVE

di·verge·ment \=ˈ=mənt\ *n* -s *archaic* **:** DIVERGENCE

di·ver·gence \dəˈvərjən(t)s, dīˈ-, -vəj-, -vəij-\ *n* -s [ML *divergere* + E *-ence*] **1 a :** a drawing apart (as of lines extending from a common center) ⟨an angle is formed by the ~ of straight lines⟩ **b :** a difference or disagreement in form, character, opinion ⟨growing ~ of opinion between the two countries⟩ — opposed to *convergence* **c :** the acquisition of dissimilar characters by related organisms or strains under the influence of unlike environments **2 :** a turning aside or departure from a direction, course, policy **:** DEVIATION, DIGRESSION ⟨~ from a theoretical norm⟩ **3 :** dissemination of the effect of activity of a single nerve cell through multiple synoptic connections — compare CONVERGENCE **4 :** the depletion of air in a layer or region of the atmosphere due to outflowing winds **syn** see DISSIMILARITY

di·ver·gen·cy \-nsē, -si\ *n* -ES **:** DIVERGENCE

di·ver·gent \dīˈvərjənt, -vəj-, -vəij- *also* dəˈv- *or* ˈdīˌv-\ *adj* [ML *divergent-*, *divergens*, pres. part. of *divergere*] **1 a :** diverging from each other **:** radiating from a common center ⟨~ lines⟩ ⟨the ~ evolution of two species⟩ **:** SPREADING ⟨~ branches⟩ — opposed to *convergent* **b :** differing from each other or from a standard **:** DEVIATING, DEVIANT ⟨how to reconcile these ~ statements⟩ ⟨frowned on his ~ behavior⟩ **2** *math, of a series* **:** having the property that the sum of the first *n* terms does not approach a limit as *n* increases indefinitely **3 :** causing divergence of rays ⟨a ~ lens⟩ **syn** see DIFFERENT

di·ver·gent·ly *adv* **:** in a divergent manner

diverging lens *n* **:** a lens that causes divergence of rays and has a virtual focus for parallel rays — compare CONVERGING LENS

di·verg·ing·ly *adv* **:** in a diverging manner

diverging meniscus *n* **:** a meniscus lens that is thicker at the edge than in the center — see LENS illustration

¹di·vers \ˈdīvə(r)z *sometimes* -və(r)s *or* -ˌvərz *or* -ˌvōz *or* -ˌvəiz\ *adj* [ME *divers*, *diverse* — more at DIVERSE] **1** *obs* **:** different in kind or species **:** DIVERSE **2 :** more than one but indefinite in number **:** SEVERAL, VARIOUS, SUNDRY ⟨~ styles of musical expression —Virgil Thomson⟩

²divers \"\ *pron, pl in constr* [ME *divers*, *diverse*, fr. *divers*, *diverse*, adj.] **:** an indefinite number more than one (as of persons or objects) ⟨~ of the enemy were captured⟩

³divers *pl of* DIVER

di·verse \(ˈ)dīˈvərs, dəˈv-, -vōs,-vəis\ *adj* [ME *divers*, *diverse*, fr. OF & L; OF *divers*, fr. L *diversus*, fr. past part. of *divertere* to turn aside, go different ways, differ — more at DIVERT] **1 :** differing from one another **:** UNLIKE, DISTINCT ⟨offered ~ judgments on the matter⟩ ⟨a people of such ~ racial origins⟩ **2** *obs* **:** DIVERS 2 **3 :** having or capable of having various forms or qualities ⟨the exceedingly ~ nature of man⟩ **:** composed of unlike or distinct elements ⟨a most ~ group of politicians⟩ **syn** see DIFFERENT

di·verse·ly *adv* [ME, fr. *diverse* + *-ly*] **:** in a diverse manner **:** in different ways **:** VARIOUSLY ⟨treated the subject most ~⟩

di·verse·ness *n* -ES [ME *diversenes*, fr. *diverse* + *-nes* -ness] **:** DIVERSITY

diversi- *comb form* [ME, fr. MF, fr. L, fr. *diversus*] **:** different **:** diverse **:** diversely ⟨*diversi*form⟩ ⟨*diversi*foliate⟩

di·ver·si·fi·ca·tion \dəˌvərsəfəˈkāshən, -vōs-,-vəis- *also* (ˌ)dī,-\ *n* -s [ML *diversification-*, *diversificatio*, fr. *diversificatus* (past part. of *diversificare* to diversify) + L *-ion-*, *-io* -ion — more at DIVERSIFY] **1 :** the act or process of diversifying or becoming diversified **:** the state of being diversified ⟨~ of our population⟩ **2 a :** the practice of spreading investments among a variety of securities or classes of securities **b :** the act or policy of increasing the variety of products or manufactures (as of a manufacturing concern)

diversified *adj* **1 :** having variety of character, of form, or of the elements of composition ⟨~ musical program ranging from classical to modern⟩ ⟨~ scenery⟩ **2 a :** having investments distributed among a variety of securities **b :** producing a variety of crops or manufactures

di·ver·si·form \dəˈvərsəˌfȯrm, dīˈ-\ *adj* [*diversi-* + *-form*] **:** varied or differing in form

di·ver·si·fy \dəˈvərsəˌfī, -vōs-,-vəis- *also* dīˈ-\ *vb* -ED/-ING/-ES [ML *diversificare*, fr. LL *diversificus* varied, fr. L *diversi-* + *-ficus* -fic] *vt* **1 a :** to make diverse (as in character, form, quality) **:** give variety to **:** VARIEGATE ⟨~ the educational program by introducing new subjects⟩ ⟨skyscrapers which now ~ the skyline —P.E.James⟩ **b :** to distribute (as investments) among different kinds of securities **c :** to increase the variety of the products or manufactures of ⟨seeking manufacturing plants to ~ a predominantly agricultural economy —*Wall Street Jour.*⟩ **2** *obs* **:** to differentiate or distinguish (one) from another ~ *vi* **:** to produce variety **:** VARY; *specif* **:** to produce a variety of crops or of manufactures ⟨low wheat prices forced farmers to ~⟩

di·ver·sion \dəˈvər|zhən, dīˈ-, -vō|, -vəi|, *Brit often & US sometimes* |shən\ *n* -s [F, fr. MF, fr. LL *diversion-*, *diversio*, fr. L *diversus* (past part. of *divertere* to turn aside, go different ways, differ) + *-ion-*, *-io* -ion — more at DIVERT] **1 a :** the act or an instance of diverting from one course or use to another ⟨charged the board with ~ of public funds⟩ **b :** the act or an instance of diverting (as the mind or attention) from some activity or concern ⟨recommended ~ of his mind from business⟩ **c :** a turning aside of one's attention, course, or concern **:** DEVIATION, DIGRESSION ⟨a ~ from the main highway⟩ ⟨mars the story by a ~ into irrelevant material⟩ **2 a :** something that turns the mind from serious concerns or ordinary matters and relaxes or amuses **:** RELAXATION, AMUSEMENT, PASTIME ⟨hiking is a favorite ~⟩ **b :** the turning of the mind to pleasure **:** the act of receiving pleasure or amusement ⟨life consisted . . . entirely of ~ —V.G.Heiser⟩ ⟨a play performed for our ~⟩ **c :** VARIATION 5 **3 :** the act or an instance of drawing the attention and force of an enemy from the point of the principal operation (as by an attack or feint which diverts attention) **4 a :** the act or process of changing the route or destination of a shipment while in transit — compare RECONSIGNMENT **b** *Brit* **:** DETOUR **c :** a channel constructed to divert water from one course or body of water to another

di·ver·sion·al \-nᵊl\ *adj* **:** used for or tending to produce diversion or recreation ⟨~ activities for tuberculosis patients⟩

di·ver·sion·ary \-ˌnerē, -ri\ *adj* **1 :** tending to draw attention away from the principal or most important concern **2** *of a military operation* **:** intended to draw the enemy's forces away from the point of principal attack

di·ver·sion·ist \-nəst\ *n* -s **:** one that engages in irregular military action, sabotage, or subversive and disruptive activity behind enemy lines or that engages in such activity against his own government

di·ver·si·ty \də'vərsəd·ē, dī'-, -vəs-, -vəis-, -ətē, -i\ *n* -ES [ME *diversite*, fr. MF *diversité*, fr. L *diversitat-, diversitas*, fr. *diversus* + *-itat-, -itas* -ity] **1 :** the condition of being different or having differences **:** VARIETY ⟨much ~ in their choices⟩ ⟨~ of opinion⟩ **2 :** an instance of being different **:** a point of difference ⟨the climatic *diversities* result in a great variety of plant life⟩ **3** *archaic* **:** a variety, kind, or species esp. of plants or animals **4 :** diversity of state or national citizenship esp. in determining the jurisdiction of a court **syn** see VARIETY

diversity factor *n* **:** the ratio of the sum of the maximum power demands of the subdivisions of any electric power system to the maximum demand of the whole system measured at the point of supply

diversity reception *n* **:** a method of radio reception in which the best signal impulse is automatically selected from among those available (as those produced by several antennas in different locations)

di·vers·ly *pronunc at* ¹DIVERS + lē *or* li\ *adv* [ME, fr. *divers* + *-ly* — more at DIVERSE] **:** in divers ways **:** VARIOUSLY

diversory *n* -ES [L *diversorium*, alter. (influenced by *divertere*) of *deversorium*, fr. *deversus* (past part. of *devertere* to turn aside, go aside, turn in at an inn, lodge, fr. *de-* + *vertere* to turn) + *-orium* -ory — more at WORTH] *obs* **:** a place of shelter by the wayside

diver's palsy *or* **diver's paralysis** *n* **:** CAISSON DISEASE

¹di·vert \də'vər|t, dī'-, -və̄|, -vəi|, *usu* |d.+V\ *vb* -ED/-ING/-S [ME *diverten*, fr. MF & L; MF *divertir*, fr. L *divertere* (also *divortere*) to turn aside, go different ways, differ, fr. *di-* (fr. *dis-* away, apart) + *vertere* to turn — more at WORTH] *vi* **:** to turn aside from a course or purpose **:** DEVIATE ⟨traffic was forced to ~ to side streets⟩ ⟨was trained as a surgeon, but ~*ed* to diplomacy⟩ **:** DIGRESS ⟨~*ed* drearily to the figure he would cut —George Meredith⟩ ~ *vt* **1 a :** to turn from one course, direction, objective, or use to another ⟨~ a stream to a new channel⟩ ⟨~ tax money to his own pocket⟩ **:** turn aside **:** DEFLECT ⟨~ calamity from his own head⟩ **b :** to turn or draw (as the mind or the attention) from one occupation or concern to another **:** DISTRACT ⟨grief did not ~ him from his duty⟩ ⟨Bunker Hill . . . had ~*ed* General Gage's mind —Kenneth Roberts⟩ **2 a :** to give pleasure or amusement to **:** ENTERTAIN ⟨the people ~*ed* themselves with games⟩ **b :** to excite mirth in ⟨he was ~*ed*, though his face betrayed no sign of his amusement —C.B.Kelland⟩ **3** *archaic* **:** to while away (the time) **syn** see AMUSE, DISSUADE, TURN

²di·vert \di'vert\ *n* -S *Scot* **:** ENTERTAINMENT, DIVERSION

di·vert·ed·ly *adv* **:** with amusement **:** AMUSEDLY

di·vert·ible \də'vər|d·əbəl, dī'-, -və|, -vəi|, |təb-\ *adj* **:** capable of being diverted

di·ver·ti·cle \|d·əkəl, |tə-\ *n* -S [L *diverticulum* — more at DIVERTICULUM] *archaic* **:** BYWAY, BYPATH

di·ver·tic·u·lar \ˌdīvə(r)ˌtikyələ(r)\ *adj* [NL *diverticulum* + E *-ar*] **:** consisting of or resembling a diverticulum

di·ver·tic·u·late \-lət, *usu* -əd.+V\ *also* **di·ver·tic·u·lat·ed** \-ˌlād·əd, -ātəd\ *adj* [NL *diverticulum* + E *-ate, -ated*] **:** having a diverticulum

di·ver·tic·u·lec·to·my \ˌdīvə(r)ˌtikyə'lektəmē, -mi\ *n* -ES [ISV *diverticul-* (fr. NL *diverticulum*) + *-ectomy*] **:** the surgical removal of a diverticulum

di·ver·tic·u·li·tis \-'līd·əs, -ītəs\ *n* -ES [NL, fr. *diverticulum* + *-itis*] **:** inflammation of a diverticulum

di·ver·tic·u·lo·sis \-'lōsəs\ *n* -ES [NL, fr. *diverticulum* + *-osis*] **:** an intestinal disorder characterized by the presence of many diverticula

di·ver·tic·u·lum \ˌdīvə(r)'tikyələm\ *n*, *pl* **diverticu·la** \-lə\ [NL, fr. L, bypath, prob. alter. of *deverticulum*, fr. *devertere* to turn aside, go aside + *-i-* + *-culum* -cle — more at DIVERSORY] **1 :** a pocket or closed branch opening off a main passage **2 a :** an abnormal pouch or sac opening from a hollow organ (as the intestine or bladder) **b :** a blind tube or sac branching off from a cavity or canal of the body **3 :** one of the filaments arising from the fused cells of a fertilized procarp and giving rise to carpospores in certain red algae **4 :** a branch produced laterally on the mycelium of a fungus (as of the genus *Pythium*)

di·ver·ti·men·to \dəˌvərd·ə'men(ˌ)tō, -ver-, dēˌver-\ *n*, *pl* **divertimen·ti** \-n(ˌ)tē\ [It, lit., diversion, amusement, fr. *divertire* to divert, amuse (fr. F *divertir*) + *-mento* -ment — more at DIVERT] **1 :** an instrumental musical composition having from 4 to 10 movements that is written as a chamber work in the form of a dance suite or in the form and style of symphonic music **:** SERENADE **2 :** DIVERTISSEMENT 1

diverting *adj* **:** giving pleasure or causing mirth **:** AMUSING, ENTERTAINING ⟨a ~ story⟩ — **di·vert·ing·ly** *adv* — **di·vert·ing·ness** *n* -ES

divertise *vt* -ED/-ING/-S [F *divertiss-*, stem of *divertir* to divert — more at DIVERT] *obs* **:** DIVERT, ENTERTAIN

di·ver·tise·ment \də'vərd·əsmənt, -əzm-\ *n* -S [F *divertissement*, fr. MF, fr. *divertiss-* + *-ment*] **1 :** DIVERSION, AMUSEMENT, RECREATION ⟨jam sessions and nightclubbing, among other ~*s* —Bernard Kalb⟩ **2 :** DIVERTISSEMENT 1

di·ver·tisse·ment \də'vərd·əsmənt, -əzm-, *F* dēvertēsmäⁿ\ *n* -S [F, lit., diversion, amusement] **1 a :** a suite of ballet numbers used as an interlude in a full-length ballet, opera, or similar program **b :** a light diverting piece of music **c :** an episode in a fugue **d :** a potpourri of airs **2 :** DIVERTIMENTO 1 **3 a :** an activity or performance that gives pleasure and entertainment to participants or audience **:** DIVERSION, ENTERTAINMENT ⟨such ~*s* as horse racing, dog racing, and swimming⟩ **b :** an artistic or intellectual production of a light, informal, and entertaining character ⟨detective story . . . has an honorable history as an intellectual ~ —Anthony Boucher⟩

di·ver·tive \də'vərd·iv, dī-\ *adj*, *archaic* **:** tending to divert **:** AMUSING, INTERESTING

di·ver·tor *or* **di·vert·er** \-d·ə(r)\ *n* -S **:** a resistor used to divert part of an electric current (as one connected in shunt with the series winding or with the commutating-pole winding of a machine

diverts *pres 3d sing of* DIVERT, *pl of* DIVERT

¹di·ves \'dīˌvēz\ *n*, *pl* **di·ves·es** \-ēzəz\ *usu cap* [ME, fr. L, rich, rich man (often interpreted as a proper noun in Luke 16), prob. fr. *divus* divine, god (the gods being distributors of largess) — more at DEITY] **:** a rich man **:** a rich worldling

²dives *pres 3d sing of* DIVE, *pl of* DIVE

dives costs \"-\ *n pl*, *usu cap D* [L *dives* rich man] **:** ordinary costs allowed in English law to a successful plaintiff by a chancery court as distinguished from costs on a reduced scale allowed to one suing in forma pauperis

di·vest \dī'vest, də'-\ *vt* -ED/-ING/-S [alter (influenced by L *di-*, fr. *dis-* ¹dis-) of *devest*] **1 a :** to undress or strip esp. of clothing, ornament, or equipment ⟨~ him of his clothes⟩ ⟨trees ~*ed* of summer finery⟩ **b :** to dispossess or deprive esp. of possessions, qualities, rights ⟨compelled to ~ himself of his holdings⟩ **2 a** *archaic* **:** to lay aside **:** ABANDON **b :** to take away (possessions or vested rights) **:** DEVEST **syn** see STRIP

di·ves·ti·tive \-stəd·iv\ *adj* [*divestiture* + *-ive*] *law* **:** having the function or effect of divesting ⟨a ~ fact puts an end to a right altogether —T.E.Holland⟩

di·ves·ti·ture \-stəˌchu̇(ə)r, -ˌchər\ *n* -S [*divest* + *-iture* (as in *investiture*)] **1 :** the act of divesting or state of being divested **2 :** the compulsory transfer of title or disposal of interests (as stock in a corporation) upon government order

di·vest·ment \-s(t)mənt\ *n* -S **:** DIVESTITURE

di·vid·able \də'vīd·əbəl\ *adj* **:** DIVISIBLE

¹di·vide \də'vīd\ *vb* -ED/-ING/-S [ME *dividen*, fr. L *dividere*, fr. *di-* (fr. *dis-* apart) + *-videre* to separate — more at DIS-, WIDOW] *vt* **1 a :** to separate into two or more parts, areas, groups **:** split up ⟨~ the city into wards⟩ **b (1) :** to separate into classes, categories, or divisions **:** CLASSIFY ⟨~ the field of history into epochs⟩ **(2)** *logic* **:** to separate (classes or class terms) by abstraction or by restriction of denotation **:** DISTINGUISH **c :** to pass through **:** cleave in passage ⟨the swift ship *dividing* the waves⟩ **2 a :** to separate into parts or portions and give out in shares **:** DISTRIBUTE ⟨~ the profits among the several owners of the business⟩ — sometimes used with *up* ⟨they *divided* up the remaining food⟩ **b :** to possess, enjoy, or make use of in common **:** share in ⟨~ the blame with his companion⟩ **c :** to separate into parts or portions and assign to or set apart for various dispositions, concerns, or activities ⟨~ his time between the office and the golf course⟩ **3 a :** to cause to be separate, distinct, or apart from one another ⟨deep gulf which . . . ~*s* the living from the dead —W.R.Inge⟩ **:** keep apart by or as if by a partition ⟨stone walls ~ the fields⟩ **b :** to separate into opposing sides or parties **:** disunite in opinion or interest **:** set at variance **:** cause to disagree ⟨no controversy had ever so *divided* the country⟩ ⟨students were *divided* on the issue⟩ **c** *Brit* **:** to call (a parliamentary body) to a vote on a question or issue **4 a :** to mark divisions on **:** GRADUATE ⟨~ a sextant⟩ **b (1) :** to subject to mathematical division **(2) :** to locate one or more points on (a line or its extension) **c** *obs* **:** to play or sing in a florid style **:** perform divisions upon (as a melody) ~ *vi* **1** *archaic* **:** to make distinctions (as in logic) ⟨~ with reason between self-love and society —Francis Bacon⟩ **2 :** to perform mathematical division **3 a (1) :** to become separated into parts ⟨each of the four chromosomes ~*s* longitudinally —J.B.Grace⟩ **(2) :** to branch out **:** FORK, DIVERGE ⟨the railway ~*s* here into two lines⟩ **(3) :** to become separate from another part ⟨Collier county . . . *divided* from Lee county in 1923 —*Amer. Guide Series: Fla.*⟩ **b :** to become separated (as in opinion or interest) ⟨on these issues the court *divided*⟩ **:** become disunited ⟨the party *divided* into warring factions⟩ **c :** to vote by separating into two groups with those in favor in one group and those opposed in another ⟨the House again *divided*, and the bill was passed by 11 votes⟩ **4 a** *archaic* **:** to have a share **:** PARTAKE ⟨you shall in all ~ with us —Shak.⟩ **b :** to give out something in portions or shares ⟨having plenty, he ~*s* with others⟩ **syn** see DISTRIBUTE, SEPARATE

²divide \"\ *n* -S **1 :** a division or distribution esp. of spoils or assets **2 a :** a dividing ridge or section of high ground between two basins or areas of drainage **:** WATERSHED **b :** a point or line of division (as between differing situations or sets of circumstances) ⟨a period marking the ~ between two eras of American history⟩

divided *adj* **1 a (1) :** separated into parts or pieces ⟨finely ~ particles of steel⟩ **(2) :** consisting of distinct parts or divisions ⟨a book ~ into 30 chapters⟩ **b :** separated into distinct divisions, sections, classes, groups **c** *of a leaf* **:** cut into distinct parts by incisions extending to the base or to the midrib — compare CLEFT, PARTED **d :** subjected to logical division **e** *of a road* **:** having the stream of traffic moving in one direction separated (as by a strip of planted land) from that moving in the opposite direction **2 a :** separated into opposing sides or groups **:** at variance with each other **:** DISUNITED ⟨the allies were sharply ~ over this issue⟩ **b :** distributed among two or more specified objects or individuals ⟨the population is about equally ~ between Swedes and Norwegians⟩ **:** directed or moved (as by affection, inclination, duty) toward conflicting interests, states, or objects ⟨~ loyalties kept him aloof from the struggle⟩ **c :** DIVISI **3 :** separated by distance from another **:** kept apart ⟨familiar objects from which she had never dreamed of being ~ —James Joyce⟩ **4** *Hindu law* **:** separated or freed from the bond or obligation of the joint family ⟨a ~ brother⟩ — **di·vid·ed·ness** *n* -ES

divided highway *n* **:** a highway of four or more traffic lanes having two roadways with a median strip between them separating opposing traffic streams — called also *dual highway*

di·vid·ed·ly *adv* **:** in a divided manner **:** SEPARATELY, INDIVIDUALLY ⟨viewed the matter ~ from the standpoints of their several interests⟩

divided pitch *n* **:** the distance between corresponding points in two adjacent threads measured parallel to the axis in a multiple-threaded screw — compare PITCH, SCREW THREAD

divided skirt *n* **:** a woman's garment that gives the appearance of a flared skirt but is divided and seamed in the manner of trousers

divided skirt

divided stop *n* **:** an organ stop so arranged that the treble and bass registers may be drawn independently of one another

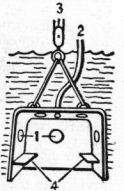

div·i·dend \'divəˌdend *sometimes* -ˌdənd *or* -dᵊnd\ *n* -S [ME *divident*, fr. L *dividendum* something to be divided, neut. of *dividendus*, gerundive of *dividere* to divide — more at DIVIDE] **1 a :** an individual share of something distributed among a number of recipients **b :** a share in a pro rata distribution (as of profits) to stockholders **c :** a share of surplus allocated to a policyholder in a participating insurance policy generally representing a return of a portion of the premium not needed to meet losses and expenses and a distribution of earnings from investment **d :** a bonus item given to a customer with each purchase of a set number of items ⟨a book ~ given with every four books purchased⟩ **e :** the return or reward resulting from an activity, effort, or undertaking ⟨better training was paying big ~*s* in increased efficiency⟩ **f :** something received unexpectedly or in addition to that which is usual or that which is expected or sought **:** BONUS ⟨three fine stories in the book, and, as a ~, all happen to be true⟩ **g :** a portion of a mixed iced drink remaining after the regular servings have been poured out ⟨there's a ~ here for someone before I mix another round⟩ **2** [AF *dividende*, fr. L *dividendum*] **a** *obs* **:** the act or an instance of dividing (as profits or spoils) among a number of individuals **b :** a pro-rata distribution of money, securities, or other property; *esp* **:** such a distribution to corporate shareholders or to creditors of a bankrupt estate — see STOCK DIVIDEND **3** *math* **:** a number or quantity to be divided **4** *archaic* **:** a body of land in one patent or survey — **dividend off :** EX DIVIDEND — **dividend on :** CUM DIVIDEND

dividend warrant *n* **:** an order (as a check payable to a shareholder) in which a dividend is paid

di·vid·er \də'vīd·ə(r)\ *n* -S **1 :** one that divides **2** *usu* **dividers** *pl* **:** an instrument for measuring or marking (as in dividing lines and transferring dimensions) **:** COMPASS **3 :** one of a series of transverse timbers in a mine shaft which help to resist lateral pressure on the wall plates and divide the shaft into compartments — called also *bunton* **4 :** a prow on the outer end of the cutter bar of a mower or harvester that parts off the crop to be cut **5 :** the second incisor tooth of a horse situated between the center and corner incisors on each side — compare NIPPER **6 :** a piece of material (as paperboard) placed between adjacent articles in a shipping case to prevent damage **7 :** a device that divides dough into equal portions (as for rolls); *also* **:** a bakery worker who operates such a device **8 :** a mechanical device used in knitting for equalizing the amount of yarn in each loop of a course **9 :** something serving as a partition between separate spaces within a larger area ⟨a low bookcase ~ between living room and dining area⟩

dividers

divides *pres 3d sing of* DIVIDE, *pl of* DIVIDE

dividing *adj* [fr. pres. part. of ¹*divide*] **:** serving to separate (as regions) ⟨the ~ line between two estates⟩ **:** serving to divide (as into parts) ⟨a ~ machine⟩ — **di·vid·ing·ly** *adv*

dividing engine *or* **dividing machine** *n* **:** a machine for graduating circles (as for surveying instruments) or bars (as for scales) or for spacing off and cutting teeth in wheels

dividing head *n* **:** INDEX HEAD

dividing network *n* **:** CROSSOVER NETWORK

dividing plate *n* **:** INDEX PLATE

divi-divi \ˌdivēˌdivē, ˌdēvēˌdēvē\ *n*, *pl* **divi-divi** *or* **divi-divis** [Sp *dividivi*, of Cariban origin; akin to Cumanagoto *diwidiwi* divi-divi] **1 :** a small tree (*Caesalpinia coriaria*) of tropical America **2 :** the twisted astringent pods of the divi-divi tree that yield a large proportion of tannin

di·vid·u·al \də'vijəwəl\ *adj* [L *dividuus* (fr. *dividere* to divide) + E *-al* — more at DIVIDE] **1** *archaic* **:** SEPARATE, DISTINCT **2** *archaic* **:** DIVISIBLE, DIVIDED **3** *archaic* **:** divided among or shared by a number ⟨the moon . . . her reign with thousand lesser lights ~ holds —John Milton⟩ — **di·vid·u·al·ly** *adv*, *archaic*

di·vid·u·ous \-wəs\ *adj* [L *dividuus*] *archaic* **:** DIVISIBLE, SEPARABLE, DIVIDED

div·il \'divəl\ *dial var of* DEVIL

div·i·na·tion \ˌdivə'nāshən\ *n* -S [ME *divinacioun*, fr. L *divination-, divinatio*, fr. *divinatus* (past part. of *divinare* to divine) + *-ion-, -io* -ion — more at DIVINE (v.)] **1 :** the art or practice that seeks to foresee or foretell future events or discover hidden knowledge usu. by means of augury or by making use of a psychical condition of the diviner in which supernatural powers are assumed to cooperate (as in the case of a spiritualistic medium or a crystal gazer); *also* **:** an instance of this practice **2 :** unusual insight or intuitive perception ⟨the brilliant ~*s* of the ancient Greeks in the field of atomic theory⟩

div·i·na·tor \'divəˌnād·ə(r)\ *n* -S [LL, fr. L *divinatus* + *-or*] **:** one that practices divination **:** DIVINER

di·vin·a·to·ry \də'vinəˌtōrē, -'vīn-; 'divən-; *chiefly Brit* 'divəˌnātəri\ *adj* [*divination* + *-ory*] **:** of or relating to divination **:** used in divination ⟨~ lots⟩ **:** using or depending upon intuition or perception ⟨mysterious and ~ healing powers —*Jour. Amer. Med. Assoc.*⟩

¹di·vine \də'vīn *sometimes* dē'-\ *adj*, *sometimes* -ER/-EST [ME *devin, divin*, fr. MF, fr. L *divinus*, fr. *divus* divine, god + *-inus* -ine — more at DEITY] **1 a :** of or relating to God **:** proceeding from God ⟨the ~ will⟩ ⟨~ judgment⟩ **b :** of or relating to a god **:** having the nature of a god ⟨the custom of killing the ~ king upon any serious failure of his . . . powers —J.G. Frazer⟩ **:** proceeding from a god ⟨the ~ strength of Achilles⟩ **:** like a god or like that of a god ⟨~ capacity for love⟩ **2 a :** devoted or addressed to God **:** RELIGIOUS, HOLY, SACRED ⟨summoned the people to ~ worship⟩ **b** *obs* **:** relating to divinity or theology **:** concerned with sacred things **3 a :** supremely good or admirable ⟨admired the writings of the ~ Shakespeare⟩ ⟨her pies were simply ~⟩ **b :** having a sublime or inspired character ⟨in her role as the mother, woman is regarded as ~ —R.N.Dandekar⟩

²divine \"\ *n* -S [ME *divine, devine*, fr. ML *divinus*, fr. L, soothsayer, fr. *divinus*, adj.] **1 a :** a minister of the gospel **:** PRIEST, CLERGYMAN ⟨a Puritan ~⟩ **2 :** one skilled in divinity **:** THEOLOGIAN ⟨great Protestant ~*s* such as Luther, Calvin, Melanchthon, and Zwingli⟩ **3 :** a priest, theologian, or spiritual guide of a non-Christian religion **4** *often cap* **:** something having the qualities and attributes of an ultimate reality that is regarded as sacred ⟨man's relation to the ~⟩

³divine \"\ *vb* -ED/-ING/-S [ME *devinen, divinen*, fr. MF & L; MF *deviner, diviner*, fr. L *divinare*, fr. *divinus* soothsayer] *vt* **1 a :** to discover or make known by divination ⟨she *divined* the fall of the city⟩ **b :** to discover or locate (as water) by means of a divining rod **2 a :** to perceive, make out, or discover intuitively or through keenness of insight ⟨*divined* her unhappiness before she had uttered a word⟩ ⟨no other critic has so well *divined* the poet's essential meaning⟩ **b** *archaic* **:** to be or give a sign or indication of (future events or something unknown) **:** PORTEND ⟨all things wait for and ~ him —R.W.Emerson⟩ ~ *vi* **1 a :** to prophesy with supernatural aid ⟨a Cassandra, *divining* of evils to come⟩ **b :** to use or practice divination ⟨*divined* in tent-shaking rites to discover the . . . cause of illness or death —*Amer. Anthropologist*⟩ **2 a :** CONJECTURE, SUPPOSE, INFER ⟨I either know them or ~ by the root —O.W.Holmes †1935⟩ **b :** to perceive, recognize, or acquire understanding concerning some fact or circumstance esp. by insight or intuition ⟨all the time only too well *divining* —John Galsworthy⟩ **syn** see FORESEE

divine decree *n* **:** DECREE 2b

divine healing *n* **:** healing attributed to the direct agency of God usu. in response to faith

divine liturgy *n*, *often cap D&L* **:** LITURGY 1

di·vine·ly *adv* **1 a :** in a divine or godlike manner **b :** to a supreme degree ⟨~ beautiful⟩ **:** supremely well **:** EXCELLENTLY ⟨she danced ~⟩ **2 :** by the agency or influence of God ⟨we are ~ endowed with certain rights⟩

di·vine·ness \-īnnəs\ *n* -ES **:** the quality or state of being divine **:** superhuman or supreme excellence **:** DIVINITY

divine office *n*, *often cap D&O* **:** the daily office for the canonical hours of prayer; *esp* **:** BREVIARY 2b

¹di·vin·er \də'vīnə(r)\ *n* -S [ME *devinour, divinour*, fr. MF *devineor*, fr. LL *divinator*, fr. L *divinatus* (past part. of *divinare* to divine) + *-or* — more at DIVINE (v.)] **:** one that practices divination **:** SOOTHSAYER, ORACLE; *specif* **:** one that seeks to discover the location of water or minerals underground with the aid of a divining rod

²diviner *comparative of* DIVINE

divine right *n* **1 :** the right of a king to rule as set forth by the theory of government that his right to govern came directly from God, that he could do no wrong, and that neither he nor his heirs could forfeit their right to the throne and to the obedience of the people **2 :** a right or claim (as to a certain privilege or possession) supposed to proceed from God

divine service *n* **:** the worship of God; *specif* **:** a public service for worship

divinest *superlative of* DIVINE

diving *adj* [fr. pres. part. of ¹*dive*] **:** that dives or is used for diving ⟨swam over to the ~ raft⟩

diving beetle *n* **:** a beetle of the family Dytiscidae habitually living under water and rising to the surface to obtain air

diving bell *n* **:** an early diving apparatus consisting of a steel cylinder or box open only at the bottom and supplied with compressed air by a hose

diving board *n* **:** SPRINGBOARD

diving boat *n* **:** a small boat specially fitted for tending deep-sea divers

diving buck *n* [trans. of Afrik *duikerbok*] **:** DUIKER 1

diving duck *n* **:** any of various ducks that frequent deep waters and obtain their food by diving — compare DABBLER

diving petrel *n* **:** any of several diving birds of the southern hemisphere that somewhat resemble auks in appearance and habits and constitute the family Pelecanoididae

diving plane *also* **diving rudder** *n* **:** a rudder or plane structure hung on a horizontal axis on a submarine for steering it in an upward or downward direction

diving suit *or* **diving dress** *n* **:** a waterproof suit used in diving; *esp* **:** one that has a helmet and that is supplied with air pumped through a tube to enable the diver to breathe under water

section of one form of diving bell: *1* windows, *2* air tube, *3* hoisting tackle, *4* seats

di·vin·i·fy \də'vinəˌfī\ *vt* -ED/-ING/-ES [L *divinus* divine + E *-ify* — more at DIVINE] **:** to make divine **:** DEIFY

divining *pres part of* DIVINE

divining rod *n* **:** a forked rod believed to divine the presence of water or minerals by dipping sharply downward when held over a vein

di·vin·i·ty \də'vinəd·ē, -ətē, -i\ *n* -ES [ME *devinite, divinite*, fr. MF *devinité, divinité*, fr. L *divinitat-, divinitas*, fr. *divinus* divine + *-itat-, -itas* -ity — more at DIVINE] **1 :** the quality or state of being divine **:** nature or essence of God **:** GODHEAD ⟨the ~ of Jesus⟩ **2 :** DEITY, GOD **:** ultimate reality ⟨there's a ~ that shapes our ends —Shak.⟩ **3 :** a celestial being inferior to the supreme God but superior to man ⟨one of the subservient *divinities*⟩ **4 :** the science of divine things **:** the science that deals with God, his laws and moral government, and the way of salvation **:** THEOLOGY **5 a** *also* **divinity fudge :** fudge made from whipped whites of eggs, white or brown sugar, and nuts **b :** a frosting made of whipped whites of eggs, corn syrup, sugar, and flavoring beaten until of the right consistency to spread

divinity calf *n* [so called fr. its use in the binding of theological books] **:** a style of bookbinding featuring calf stained dark brown and blind title and decoration

divinity circuit binding *n* **:** a style of bookbinding that is often used for Bibles and hymnbooks and that is characterized by rounded corners on both book and cover and by a flexible leather cover with projecting flaps bent over to protect the edges of the leaves — called also *circuit binding, yapp binding*

divinity school *n* **:** SEMINARY 2b(4)

di·vin·i·ty·ship \-ˌship\ *n* **:** the quality or state of being divine **:** the status of a divinity

div·i·ni·za·tion \ˌdivənəˈzāshən, -ˌnīˈ-\ *n* -s **:** the act, process, or an instance of investing with a divine character or of making into an object of worship **:** DEIFICATION, GLORIFICATION ⟨~ of the state is a feature of his political thought⟩
div·i·nize \ˈdivəˌnīz\ *vt* -ED/-ING/-S [F *diviniser*, fr. *divin* divine + *-iser* -ize — more at DIVINE] **:** to deify or clothe with a divine character **:** EXALT, GLORIFY ⟨the romantic poets *divinized* nature⟩
[1]**di·vinyl** \(ˈ)dī+\ *n* [ISV *di-* + *vinyl*] **:** BUTADIENE
[2]**divinyl** \"\ *adj* **:** containing two vinyl groups in the molecule
di·vi·nyl·acetylene \(ˌ)ˌ=ˌ==+\ *n* [[1]*divinyl* + *acetylene*] **:** a liquid hydrocarbon $CH_2{=}CHC{\equiv}CCH{=}CH_2$ formed by trimerization of acetylene and used in surface coatings since it polymerizes to a hard resin on contact with air
di·vi·nyl·benzene \"+\ *n* [[1]*divinyl* + *benzene*] **:** a liquid hydrocarbon $C_6H_4(CH{-}CH_2)_2$ obtained usu. as a mixture containing the ortho, meta, and para isomers and used in polymerization (as with styrene for making ion-exchange resins)
di·vi·sa \dəˈvēsə, -ēzə\ *n* -s [Sp, lit., emblem, heraldic device, fr. fem. of *diviso* (obs. past part. of *dividir* to divide), fr. L *divisus*] **:** colored ribbons denoting the breeder that are attached by a barb to a bull's withers as it enters the bullfighting arena
di·vi·si \dəˈvēzē\ *adj* [It, pl. of *diviso* (past part. of *dividere* to *divide*), fr. L *divisus* divided — more at DIVISION] **:** SEPARATE — used as a direction in music for orchestral players reading the same musical staff to divide into two or more voice parts; abbr. *div.*
di·vis·i·bil·i·ty \dəˌvizəˈbilədˌē, -ətē, -i\ *n* -ES **:** the quality or state of being divisible
di·vis·i·ble \dəˈvizəbəl\ *adj* [LL *divisibilis*, fr. L *divisus* + *-ibilis* -ible] **:** capable of being or liable to be divided or separated — **di·vis·i·ble·ness** \-nəs\ *n* -ES
divisible contract *n* **:** a contract containing agreements one of which can be separated from the other so that one part may be valid or enforceable although another is void or so that a right may accrue on one and not on another
divisible offense *n* **:** an offense the commission of which involves the commission of one of a lesser grade so that on the former there can be an acquittal and on the latter a conviction
divisible surplus *n* **:** the part of the annual surplus fund of an insurance company which is available for payment in the form of dividends to policyholders
di·vi·sion \dəˈvizhən\ *n* -s [ME *devisioun*, fr. MF *division*, fr. L *division-*, *divisio*, fr. *divisus* (past part. of *dividere* to divide) + *-ion-*, *-io* -ion — more at DIVIDE] **1 a :** the act, process, or an instance of dividing into parts or portions **:** PARTITION ⟨made a ~ of his empire⟩ ⟨~ of the day into hours, minutes, seconds⟩ **:** the state of being divided ⟨remarked on the peculiar geographic ~ of the state⟩ **b :** the act, process, or an instance of dividing or distributing among a number **:** DISTRIBUTION, APPORTIONMENT ⟨protested his method of ~ of the profits⟩ **c** *obs* **:** a method of arranging or disposing (as troops) ⟨nor the ~ of battle knows more than a spinster —Shak.⟩ **2 :** one of the parts, sections, or groupings into which a whole is divided **3 a :** the elementary organic unit of combined arms that is tactically and administratively a self-contained unit capable of independent action **b :** a military unit made up normally of five battle groups **c (1) :** one of the groups usu. of four ships into which a fleet or large squadron is divided **(2) :** the basic unit of men for administration aboard ship and ashore **d :** a tactical subdivision of a squadron of ships or aircraft **4** *obs* **:** a portion of land allotted to an individual settler or to a group of settlers **5 :** a definite portion of a nation, state, county, or other political unit marked off for administrative, judicial, or other purposes: as **a :** an election district in Great Britain **b :** a subdivision of a province or presidency in British India **6 :** a segment of a transportation system (as a railroad, truckline, pipeline, or airline) designated by management as a semi-independent or autonomous operating unit **7 :** a group of organisms forming part of some larger group; *specif* **:** a major primary category of the plant kingdom — compare PHYLUM 2 **8 a :** a subordinate administrative unit of the executive department of the U.S. government usu. ranking below a bureau **b :** a subordinate unit of state and local government **9 :** a competitive class or category (as in boxing and wrestling) based on age, weight, skill, or other standard of eligibility **10 :** a major administrative unit in an education institution of organization usu. embracing several departments ⟨the ~ of modern languages⟩ **11 :** a major administrative unit of an industrial enterprise comprising at least several departments or constituting a complete integrated unit for a specific purpose ⟨the radio ~ of an aviation corporation⟩ **12 a :** something that divides, separates, or marks off ⟨the ~s of the compass mark off its 32 points⟩ **:** a dividing line **b :** the act, process, or an instance of separating or keeping apart (two objects or individuals) ⟨used a screen to complete the ~ of the dining room from the kitchen⟩ **:** the state of being separated **:** SEPARATION ⟨the lovers mourned their hopeless ~⟩ **13 :** the condition or an instance of being divided in opinion or interest **:** DISAGREEMENT, DISUNITY ⟨attempted to exploit the ~s between the two countries⟩ **14 :** the process of finding how many times one number or quantity is contained in another **15 :** the separation of a genus into its constituent species — compare FALLACY OF DIVISION, TREE OF PORPHYRY **16 a :** a florid instrumental variation upon a given melody of 17th and 18th century England **b :** a melismatic song or phrase of the 17th and 18th centuries **17 :** a numerical determination of those members of a deliberative body that are for a motion and those who are against it either by a rising vote or by a physical separation into two groups ⟨a ~ was being taken⟩ ⟨the results of the ~⟩ ⟨the motion passed without a ~ —T.B.Macaulay⟩ **18 :** the practice or an instance of dividing words or word elements in writing or printing by the use of a hyphen **19 :** the apportionment of revenue among carrier participants sharing interline traffic **:** the distribution of revenue or expense among various parts of a system or organization **20 :** plant propagation by dividing parts (as of a crown or a clump of suckers or tubers) and planting segments capable of producing roots and shoots **syn** see PART
di·vi·sion·al \-zhənᵊl,-zhnəl\ *adj* **1 :** that divides **:** marking or noting a division ⟨the ~ line between two states⟩ **2 :** constituting a division or an aliquot part **:** FRACTIONAL ⟨American ~ coins include the dime and the nickel⟩ **3 :** of or relating to a division ⟨the ~ artillery⟩ — **di·vi·sion·al·ly** \-ᵊlˌē, -əl, |i\ *adv*
divisional title *n* **:** a title page immediately preceding a major division of a book — called also *part title*
di·vi·sion·ary \-zhəˌnerē\ *adj* **:** DIVISIONAL
division bar *n* **:** a structural or nonstructural element connecting or aligning two panels or pieces of glass
division bell *n* **:** a bell rung to summon members of a deliberative body when a vote is to be taken — compare DIVISION 17
division center *n, biol* **:** the structure at the center of the aster or central body **:** CENTRIOLE
division fence *n* **:** a fence separating adjacent areas of the same farm or ranch — distinguished from *line fence*
di·vi·sion·ism \-zhəˌnizəm\ *n* -s *often cap* **1** *painting* **:** the theory or practice of breaking color — compare NEO-IMPRESSIONISM **2 :** the neo-impressionist use of small strokes or dots of pure color juxtaposed on a canvas — compare POINTILLISM
[1]**di·vi·sion·ist** \-zh(ə)nəst\ *n* -s [*division* + *-ist*] **1 :** one that advocates division or disunion ⟨the ~s objected to the existing boundary line⟩ **2** *often cap* **:** an adherent or practitioner of divisionism **:** NEO-IMPRESSIONIST
[2]**divisionist** \"\ *adj, often cap* **:** of or relating to divisionism **:** NEO-IMPRESSIONIST
division of labor : the separation of labor into its components or into various distinct processes and their apportionment among different individuals, groups, or machines for the purpose of increasing productive efficiency: as **a :** the distribution of occupations or vocations among the members of society ⟨*division of labor* in this tribe is limited to the separation between hunters and farmers⟩ **b :** the breaking up of technical tasks (as in a modern factory) into their component parts or processes and their distribution to specific individuals, groups, or machines **c :** specialization in the production of a specific commodity or group of commodities by a particular region or country
division of powers 1 : SEPARATION OF POWERS **2 :** the principle that sovereignty should be divided between the federal government and the states esp. as expressed by the Constitution of the U.S.
division point *n* **:** the location of a railroad division headquarters
divisions *pl of* DIVISION
division viol *n, obs* **:** VIOLA DA GAMBA
division wall *n* **:** a wall subdividing a building into major portions — compare FIRE WALL, PARTY WALL
di·vi·sive \dəˈvīs|iv, |ēv *also* -vizǀ *or* -visǀ *or* |əv *sometimes* -vīz|\ *adj* [ML *divisivus*, fr. L *divisus* (past part. of *dividere* to divide) + *-ivus* -ive — more at DIVIDE] **1** *archaic* **:** having the quality of separating or distinguishing **:** DISTRIBUTIVE, ANALYTICAL **2 :** creating or tending to create disunity or dissension ⟨criticized his ~ activities in a time of peril⟩ — **di·vi·sive·ly** \|ivlē, -li\ *adv* — **di·vi·sive·ness** \|ivnəs, |ēv- *also* |əv-\ *n* -ES
di·vi·sor \-ˈvīzə(r)\ *n* -s [ME *diviser*, *divisor*, fr. L *divisor*, fr. *divisus* + *-or*] **1 :** the number by which the dividend is divided **2 :** any of various devices for apportioning the water in an irrigating ditch to the holders of water rights in the ditch
di·vi·so·ry \-īz(ə)rē, -ri\ *adj* [L *divisus* + E *-ory*] **1 :** of or relating to division or distribution ⟨~ actions in law relate to the partition of property⟩ **2 :** DIVISIVE 2 ⟨did not understand the ~ issues of the day —W.A.White⟩
di·vi·su·ral line \dəˈvizhərəl-\ *n* [L *divisura* division, fork of a tree (fr. *divisus* + *-ura* -ure) + E *-al*] *of a moss* **:** the median line along which the peristome teeth split
[1]**di·vorce** \dəˈvō(ə)rs, -ó(ə)rs,-ōəs,-ó(ə)s\ *n* -s *often attrib* [ME *devors*, *divors*, *divorse*, fr. MF *divorse*, *divorce*, fr. L *divortium*, fr. *divortere*, *divertere* to turn aside, go different ways, leave one's husband — more at DIVERT] **1 :** a legal dissolution in whole or in part of a marriage relation usu. by a court or other body having competent authority: **a :** an absolute dissolution of a valid marriage made by decree of court for lawful cause arising after the marriage — called also *divorce a vinculo matrimonii*; distinguished from *annulment* **b** *among some non-Christian peoples* **:** a formal separation of man and wife by the act of one party or by consent according to established custom — see TALAK **c :** DECREE OF NULLITY **d :** a divorce a mensa et thoro — compare JUDICIAL SEPARATION, SEPARATION 4a **2 :** disunion of things closely united ⟨the ~ between ownership and management in the corporate system —David Fellman⟩ **:** a complete or final separation ⟨demanded the ~ of the subsidiary from the parent firm⟩
[2]**divorce** \" *sometimes* dīˈ- *in vt sense 1*\ *vb* -ED/-ING/-S [MF *divorcer*, fr. *divorce*] *vt* **1 :** SEPARATE, DISUNITE ⟨proposed to ~ church and state⟩ ⟨*divorced* himself from the position taken by his colleagues⟩ ⟨when the second rocket ~s itself from the first spent rocket —William Stringer⟩ **2 :** to get rid of (one's spouse) by divorce **:** dissolve the marriage contract of either wholly or partly **:** separate by divorce **3** *archaic* **:** to put away **:** REMOVE, BANISH **~** *vi* **:** to obtain a divorce **syn** see SEPARATE
di·vorce·able \-səbəl\ *adj* **:** capable of or subject to being divorced
di·vor·cée *also* **di·vor·cee** \dəˌvōrˈsā, -vórˈ-, -vōəˈ-, -vó(ə)ˈ-, -sē\ *n* -s [F, fr. fem. of *divorcé*, past part. of *divorcer*] **:** a divorced woman
di·vorce·ment \dəˈvōrsmənt, -vórs-,-vōəs-,-vó(ə)s-; *sometimes* dīˈ- — *see* [2]DIVORCE\ *n* -s **1** *archaic* **:** the act or an instance of divorcing **:** dissolution of marriage ties **:** DIVORCE **2 :** the act, process, or an instance of separating things closely joined ⟨claimed the ~ of theory from practice had gone to extreme lengths⟩ **:** the state of being separated ⟨too long have art and the church lived in ~ from each other —J.F. Hayward⟩
divorce mill *n* **:** a jurisdiction in which divorce is allowed upon liberal grounds and in which the legal requirements (as residence within the jurisdiction) are easily met
di·vorc·er \-sə(r)\ *n* -s **:** one that divorces or produces a divorce
div·ot \ˈdivət, *usu* -əd·+V\ *n* -s [origin unknown] **1** *Scot* **a :** a square of turf or sod used in covering cottages **b :** a piece of peat used for fuel **2 :** a piece of turf dug from a golf fairway in making a stroke
di·vo·to \dəˈvō(ˌ)tō, dēˈ-, -vōd·(ˌ)ō\ *adv* (*or adj*) [It, devout, fr. LL *devotus* — more at DEVOUT] **:** with religious emotion — used as a direction in music
divs *pl of* DIV
di·vul·gate \dəˈvəlˌgāt, dīˈ-; ˈdivə-,ˈdīvə-\ *vt* -ED/-ING/-S [L *divulgatus*, past part. of *divulgare*] **1** *obs* **:** DIVULGE 1 **2** *archaic* **:** DISCLOSE, REVEAL
di·vul·ga·tion \(ˈ)dīˌvəlˈgāshən, dəˌvəl-, ˌdivəl-\ *n* -s [LL *divulgation-*, *divulgatio*, fr. L *divulgatus* + *-ion-*, *-io* -ion] **:** the act or an instance of divulging or spreading abroad **:** PUBLICATION, DISCLOSURE
di·vulge \dəˈvəlj *also* dīˈ-\ *vt* -ED/-ING/-S [ME *divulgen*, fr. L *divulgare*, fr. *di-* (fr. *dis-* [1]*dis-*) + *vulgare* to make known, publish — more at VULGATE] **1** *archaic* **:** to make public **:** spread abroad **2 :** to tell or make known (a secret or confidence or what had been previously unknown) ⟨knew of the conspiracy, yet did not ~ it⟩ ⟨*divulged* to me his dearest hopes⟩ **syn** see REVEAL
di·vulge·ment \-jmənt\ *n* -s **:** DIVULGENCE
di·vul·gence \-jən(t)s\ *n* -s **:** the act or an instance of divulging **:** REVELATION, DISCLOSURE ⟨forbids the ~ of classified information⟩
di·vulse \dīˈvəls, dəˈ-\ *vt* -ED/-ING/-S [L *divulsus*, past part. of *divellere* — more at DIVEL] **:** to pull or tear apart **:** REND — now used chiefly in surgery
di·vul·sion \-lshən\ *n* -s [L *divulsion-*, *divulsio*, fr. *divulsus* + *-ion-*, *-io* -ion] **:** the act or an instance of tearing or pulling apart or away from — now used chiefly in surgery
di·vul·sive \-lsiv\ *adj* [L *divulsus* + E *-ive*] **:** tending to divulse
di·vul·sor \-lsə(r)\ *n* -s **:** DILATOR
div·vers \ˈdivə(r)z\ *n pl but sing in constr* [*divinity* + *-er* (Oxford Univ. slang suffix) + *-s* (representing pl. *moderations*)] *slang Brit* **:** an examination in biblical literature and history required of every Oxford undergraduate up to 1932
[1]**div·vy** \ˈdivē, -vi\ *n* -ES [by shortening & alter. fr. *dividend*] *slang* **:** DIVISION, DISTRIBUTION ⟨a four-way ~ of the profits⟩
[2]**divvy** \"\ *vb* -ED/-ING/-ES *vt, slang* **:** DIVIDE, SHARE, DISTRIBUTE ⟨absent when the money was *divvied*⟩ — often used with *up* ⟨*divvied* up the loot and fled⟩ **~** *vi, slang* **:** to divide or distribute among a number — often used with *up*
diwali *usu cap, var of* DEWALI
[1]**diwan** *var of* DIVAN
[2]**di·wan** \dēˈwän, dəˈ-, -wän\ *var of* DEWAN
diwani *var of* DEWANEE
dix \ˈdēs\ *also* **dis** \"\ *or* **deece** \"\ *n, pl* **dixes** *also* **dises** *or* **deeces** \ˈdēsəz\ [F *dix* ten, fr. L *decem* — more at TEN] **:** the lowest trump (as the nine or seven) in some card games (as pinochle, bezique, klaberjass) that in certain circumstances is exchangeable for a higher trump and has a scoring value of ten
dix·e·nite \ˈdiksəˌnīt, dīˈzeˌn-\ *n* -s [*di-* + *xen-* + *-ite*] **:** a manganese arsenite and silicate $(MnOH)_2Mn_5SiO_3(AsO_3)_2$ occuring in black hexagonal scales
[1]**dix·ie** \ˈdiksē, -si\ *adj, usu cap* [fr. *Dixie*, nickname for the southern states of the U.S.] **:** of or related to the southern states of the U.S., ⟨a *Dixie* lullaby⟩
[2]**dix·ie** \"\ *or* **dixy** \"\ *n, pl* **dixies** [Hindi *degcī*, dim. of *degcā* kettle, pot] *Brit* **:** a mess tin or oval pot often used in camp for cooking or boiling (as tea); *specif* **:** a 12-gallon camp kettle
Dixie \"\ *trademark* — used for a paper cup used esp. for ice cream or beverages
dix·ie·crat \-ˌkrat\ *n* -s *usu cap, often attrib* [*Dixie* Democrat] **:** a member of a secessionist party of southern Democrats who bolted the Democratic party because of its advocacy of civil-rights legislation in the U.S. presidential campaign of 1948 — compare REPUBLOCRAT — **dix·ie·crat·ic** \ˌ==ˈkrad·ik\ *adj, usu cap*
dix·ie·land \-ˌland, -ˌlaa(ə)nd\ *also* **dixie** *n* -s *usu cap* [fr. *Dixieland*, *Dixie* the South, its origin (in New Orleans)] **:** jazz music characterized by two beats to the measure with strong afterbeats, a small combination of instruments in the band (as cornet, clarinet, trombone, piano, and drums), and a style of performance consisting of lyrical solo choruses, improvised solo choruses, and polyphonic improvisation by the entire group
di·zain \dēˈzaⁿ, dəˈzān\ *or* **di·zaine** \dəˈzān\ *n* -s [F *dizain*, fr. *dix* ten — more at DIX] **:** a poem or stanza of ten lines
[1]**di·zen** \ˈdīzᵊn, ˈdiz-\ *vt* -ED/-ING/-S [fr. earlier *disen* to dress a distaff with flax, fr. (assumed) ME, fr. MD, fr. or akin to MLG *dise* bunch of flax on a distaff] *archaic* **:** to dress gaudily or with finery **:** BEDIZEN ⟨'tis the vulgar great who come ~*ed* with gold and jewels —R.W.Emerson⟩
[2]**diz·en** *or* **diz·zen** \ˈdizᵊn\ *Scot var of* DOZEN
di·zo·ic \(ˈ)dīˈzōik\ *adj* [*di-* + *-zoic*] **:** having two young — used of a sporocyst containing two sporozoites
di·zygotic \ˌdī+\ *adj* [*di-* + *zygotic*] *of twins* **:** FRATERNAL
diz·zard \ˈdizə(r)d\ *n* -s [prob. alter. of *disour*] **1** *obs* **:** JESTER **2** *now dial* **:** BLOCKHEAD, NITWIT
diz·zi·ly \ˈdizəlē, -li\ *adv* [ME *disyly*, fr. *disy* + *-ly*] **:** in a dizzy manner **:** in such a way, manner, or degree as to cause dizziness or vertigo ⟨looked down from a ~ high bridge⟩ **:** with a sensation of giddiness ⟨~ tried to comprehend his terrible message⟩ **:** in an unsteady or uncertain way ⟨tottered ~ across the floor⟩
diz·zi·ness \-zēnəs, -zin-\ *n* -ES [ME *dysinesse* folly, vertigo, fr. OE *dysignes* folly, fr. *dysig* foolish + *-nes* -ness] **:** the condition of being dizzy; *esp* **:** a sensation of unsteadiness accompanied by a feeling of movement within the head **:** GIDDINESS — compare VERTIGO
[1]**diz·zy** \ˈdizē, -zi\ *adj* -ER/-EST [ME *disy*, fr. OE *dysig* foolish, stupid; akin to OHG *tusig* stupid, MLG *dūsich* stunned, dizzy, OE *dwǣs* stupid, foolish MLG *dwas* stupid, foolish, ON *dos* quiet, *dusa* to be quiet, L *furere* to rage, *fumus* smoke — more at FUME] **1 :** FOOLISH, SILLY, INANE, HEEDLESS — not often in formal use **2 a :** having a whirling sensation in the head with a tendency to fall **:** GIDDY ⟨round and round they danced until ~⟩ **b :** mentally confused or dazed **:** being in a whirl ⟨could juggle mathematical formulas in such a way as to make the ordinary man ~ —A.W.Long⟩ **3 a (1) :** causing or tending to cause dizziness or giddiness **:** VERTIGINOUS ⟨gazing down from those ~ heights⟩ **(2) :** confusing or tending to confuse mentally **:** making one's head swim ⟨~ and exuberant rhetoric⟩ **b :** caused by or associated with dizziness ⟨his fever rose enveloping him in a ~ mist⟩ **c :** whirling or moving with extreme rapidity ⟨drawn into the ~ vortex of the whirlpool⟩ **d :** exceeding normal or reasonable limits **:** EXTREME, IMMODERATE ⟨prices continued to rise at a ~ rate⟩
[2]**dizzy** \"\ *vt* -ED/-ING/-ES **1 :** to make dizzy or giddy **:** cause a swimming sensation in the head of **:** DAZE ⟨we were *dizzied* by the beating wind —T.E.Lawrence⟩ **2 :** to make unsteady in thought or mind **:** CONFUSE, STUPEFY, BEWILDER ⟨prospects so brilliant as to ~ the mind⟩ ⟨the disaster *dizzied* her brain and paralyzed her will⟩
dizzying *adj* **1 :** causing or tending to cause dizziness or giddiness **:** CONFUSING, BEWILDERING ⟨ten years of ~ reverses of policy⟩ **2 :** DAZZLING, BRILLIANT ⟨crowned a ~ career with this triumph⟩
diz·zy·ing·ly *adv* **:** in a dizzying manner ⟨watching the rows of waist-high corn curve ~ away from him as he passed them —Florette Henri⟩
DJ *abbr* **1** disc jockey **2** district judge **3** *often not cap* dust jacket
dja·kar·ta *or* **ja·kar·ta** \jəˈkärd·ə\ *adj, usu cap* [fr. *Djakarta*, Indonesia] **:** of or from Djakarta, the capital of Indonesia **:** of the kind or style prevalent in Djakarta
djal·ma·ite \ˈjalməˌīt\ *n* -s [Pg *djalmaita*, fr. *Djalma* Guimarães, 20th cent. Brazilian mineralogist + Pg *-ita* -ite] **:** an isometric oxide of uranium, tantalum, columbium, and other minerals closely related to betafite
dja·ti \ˈjäd·ē\ *n* -s [Malay *jati*] *in the Malay peninsula* **:** TEAK
djave *var of* NJAVE
dje·bel *or* **je·bel** \ˈjebəl\ *n* -s [Ar *jebel*] **:** a hill in northern Africa
djellaba *var of* JELLABA
djen·kol·ic acid \(ˈ)jen|ˈkälik-, -eŋ|-\ *n* [*djenkol* (*bean*) velvet bean (fr. Java *djenkol*) + *-ic*] **:** a crystalline amino acid $CH_2[SCH_2CH(NH_2)COOH]_2$ obtained esp. from the velvet bean
djerma *usu cap, var of* DYERMA
djibbah *var of* JIBBA
djig·ga \ˈjigə\ *n* -s [of African origin — more at CHIGGER] **:** CHIGOE 1
djin *or* **djinn** *or* **djinni** *var of* JINN
djok·ja·kar·ta \ˌjäkyəˈkärd·ə\ *or* **jog·ja·kar·ta** \ˌjägy-\ *or* **jok·ya·kar·ta** \ˌjäky-\ *adj, usu cap* [fr. *Djokjakarta*, Indonesia] **:** of or from the city of Djokjakarta, Indonesia **:** of the kind or style prevalent in Djokjakarta
dju·ka \ˈjükə\ *n, pl* **djuka** *or* **djukas** *usu cap* [D, of AmerInd origin] **1 :** a Bush Negro people of Dutch Guiana **2 :** a member of the Djuka people
dk *abbr* **1** dark **2** deca-; deka- **3** deck **4** dock **5** duck
dkg *abbr* decagram
dkl *abbr* decaliter
dkm *abbr* decameter
dks *abbr* decastere
dkt *abbr* docket
dl- \(ˈ)dēˈel\ *prefix* [ISV *d-* + *l-*] **1** *also* **d,l- :** consisting of equal amounts of the dextro and levo forms of a specified compound — usu. printed in italic ⟨*dl*-tartaric acid⟩; compare RACEMIC **2 :** consisting of equal amounts of the D- and L-forms of a specified compound — usu. printed as small capitals ⟨DL-fructose⟩; compare RACEMIC
dl *abbr* deciliter
DL *abbr* **1** day letter **2** demand loan **3** dominical letter
d layer *n, usu cap D* **1 :** a layer that may exist within the D region of the ionosphere; *also* **:** D REGION **2 :** D-HORIZON
dld *abbr* delivered
d line *n, usu cap D* **:** a yellow persistent first line of the principal series of the sodium spectrum constituting in the Fraunhofer lines a doublet whose nearly equal components have wavelengths 5895.93 and 5889.96 angstroms respectively
D Litt *abbr or n* -s [L *doctor litterarum*] **:** a doctor of letters
DLO *abbr* **1** dead letter office **2** dispatch loading only
dlvy *abbr* delivery
dly *abbr* **1** daily **2** delivery
dm *abbr* **1** decimeter **2** drum
DM *abbr* **1** [It *destra mano*] right hand **2** deutsche mark
d major *n, usu cap D* **:** the major musical key having a signature of two sharps
d-mark \ˈdēˌmärk\ *n, usu cap D* [G] **:** DEUTSCHE MARK
DMD *abbr or n* -s [NL *dentariae medicinae doctor*] **:** a doctor of dental medicine
DME *abbr or n* -s [*d*istance *m*easuring *e*quipment] **:** an electronic device that informs the pilot of an airplane of its distance from a particular ground station
d minor *n, usu cap D* **:** the minor musical key having a signature of one flat
dn *abbr* **1** down **2** dun
DN *abbr* debit note
DNA *abbr* deoxyribonucleic acid
dne·pro·dzer·zhinsk \ˌneprōdə(r)ˈzhinzk, -n(t)sk\ *adj, usu cap* [fr. *Dneprodzerzhinsk*, U.S.S.R.] **:** of or from the city of Dneprodzerzhinsk **:** of the kind or style prevalent in Dneprodzerzhinsk
dne·pro·pe·trovsk \-pəˈtrófsk\ *adj, usu cap* [fr. *Dnepropetrovsk*, U.S.S.R.] **:** of or from the city of Dnepropetrovsk **:** of the kind or style prevalent in Dnepropetrovsk
d net *n, cap D* **:** a net with an orifice shaped like the letter D used for collecting bottom plankton
DNOC \ˌdēˌen(ˌ)ōˈsē\ *abbr or n* -s dinitro-ortho-cresol
dnus *abbr* dominus
[1]**do** \(ˈ)dü, ˌdə *or* +V ˌdəw\ *vb, past 1st & 3d sing* **did** \(ˈ)did, ˌdəd\ *or substand* **done** \ˈdən\ *2d sing* **did** *or substand* **done** *or archaic* **didst** \(ˈ)di|dzt, ˌdə|, |dst,|tst\ *pl* **did** *or substand* **done**; *past part* **done**; *pres part* **do·ing** \ˈdüiŋ\ *pres 1st sing* **do**; *2d sing* **do** *or archaic* **do·est** \ˈdüəst\ *or archaic* **dost** \(ˈ)dəst\ *3d sing* **does** \(ˈ)dəz\ *or now chiefly substand* **do** *or archaic* **do·eth** \ˈdüəth\ *or archaic* **doth** \(ˈ)dəth\ *pl* **do** [ME

don, fr. OE *dōn*; akin to OFris *duā*, *duān* to do, OS *dūan*, OHG *tuon* to do, L *-dere* to put, *facere* to make, do, Gk *tithenai* to place, set, Skt *dadhāti* he puts, places, sets, OSlav *děti* to lay; basic meaning: setting, placing] *vt* **1** *archaic* **:** CAUSE, MAKE — used with an infinitive following the object ⟨~ me not before my time to die —Edmund Spenser⟩ **2 :** to bring to pass **:** carry out ⟨it is my earnest desire to know the will of Providence . . . and if I can learn what it is I will ~ it —Abraham Lincoln⟩ **3 :** PUT ⟨he *did* the diadem on —Philemon Holland⟩ — now usu. used in the phrase *do to death* ⟨had been hounded down and *done* to death as heretics —Stringfellow Barr⟩ **4 :** to perform (as an action) by oneself or before another **:** EXECUTE ⟨you're bound to ~ much more walking . . . than you're accustomed to —Richard Joseph⟩ ⟨watched the natives ~ a sacred dance⟩ **5 a :** to be the cause of **:** bring about as a result **:** EFFECT ⟨his vacation *did* him a great deal of good⟩ ⟨the portrait . . . *does* him great injustice —Mary R. Mitford⟩ **b :** to give freely **:** RENDER, PAY ⟨have not sought the honor you have *done* me —A.E.Stevenson b.1900⟩ ⟨pilgrims having *done* their homage to the tomb —Virginia Woolf⟩ **6 :** to bring to an end **:** COMPLETE, FINISH ⟨when she had *done* washing, it was a soft white silky fleece —Seumas O'Kelly⟩ ⟨work waiting for them back on the . . . prairies when the fun was *done* —F.B.Gipson⟩ **7 :** to put forth in achieving an end **:** EXERT ⟨treason has *done* his worst —Shak.⟩ ⟨he *did* his best to win the race⟩ ⟨a place where there are men ~*ing* thinking —Woodrow Wilson⟩ **8 :** to wear out esp. by physical exertion **:** EXHAUST, TIRE ⟨men and horses . . . were pretty well *done* by the time we got in —C.A.Murray⟩ **9 :** to bring (as a work of art) into existence esp. through the exercise of thought or imagination ⟨he's going to ~ an article on you —Barnaby Conrad⟩ ⟨the . . . paintings were *done* under the immediate influence of his academic masters —Herbert Read⟩ ⟨the commission to ~ a work for the . . . Music Festival —Ross Parmenter⟩ **10 a :** to play the part of (as a character in a play) ⟨*did* the leading lady in several comedies⟩ **b :** to act in or serve as producer of ⟨told one of the directors . . . that she would have *done* my play —Thomas Wolfe⟩ ⟨they were ~*ing* a purely musical program —Jack Gould⟩ **11 :** to take advantage of **:** treat unfairly ⟨a great bookseller who . . . charges very high prices, he has *done* me many a time —H.J. Laski⟩; *esp* **:** CHEAT ⟨had played the dirty trick on the farmer and *done* him out of his woodland —Dorothy C. Fisher⟩ ⟨they *did* him out of his share of the fortune⟩ **12 :** to convert from one language or literary form to another — usu. used with *into* ⟨~ a book from Latin into English⟩ ⟨a prose essay *done* into rhyming couplets⟩ **13 :** to treat or deal with in any way typically with the sense of preparation or with that of care or attention: as **a** (1) **:** to put in order **:** CLEAN ⟨was ~*ing* the parlor when the phone rang⟩ (2) **:** to make ready for use **:** WASH ⟨*did* the dishes right after supper⟩ **b** (1) **:** to make ready for cooking or serving ⟨~ the beets with vinegar⟩ (2) **:** COOK ⟨likes his steak well *done*⟩ **c :** SET, ARRANGE ⟨her hair is *done* in that ugly pompadour of the period —J.P. Marquand⟩ **d :** to apply cosmetics to ⟨she had *done* her face and fixed her . . . hair —Hamilton Basso⟩ **e :** DECORATE, FURBISH ⟨*did* the front bedroom in blue⟩ ⟨*did* the dining room over⟩ **14 a :** to be occupied with or employed in **:** work at esp. as a vocation ⟨wanted to go on ~*ing* chemistry all his life —J.B.S.Haldane⟩ ⟨hardly knows what he wants to ~ when he finishes college⟩ **b :** to prepare or work out esp. by studying ⟨*did* his lessons faithfully⟩ **15 a :** to pass over (as distance) **:** COVER, TRAVERSE ⟨*did* 300 miles on the second day of their trip⟩ ⟨the car *did* 18 miles to the gallon of gasoline⟩ **b :** to travel at a speed of ⟨two cars ~*ing* 80 on the turnpike⟩ **16 :** to visit and explore as or as if a sightseer **:** TOUR ⟨tried to ~ England in a month⟩ ⟨spent all afternoon ~*ing* one wing of the museum⟩ **17 :** to satisfy the needs of **:** SERVE, SUFFICE ⟨our coats would ~ us for the goalposts —Mary Purcell⟩ **18 :** to serve (as a term of imprisonment) under restraint **:** UNDERGO ⟨was ~*ing* five years for forgery⟩ **19 :** to approve esp. by custom, opinion, or propriety — usu. used in the passive voice and with a negative ⟨you oughtn't to say a thing like that . . . it's not *done* —Dorothy Sayers⟩ **20 :** to provide esp. for the physical comfort of — usu. used with *well* ⟨the largish restaurant was full of lunchers all ~*ing* themselves exceedingly well —Arnold Bennett⟩ **21** — used as a substitute verb to avoid repetition of a verb ⟨I . . . chose my wife as she *did* her wedding gown —Oliver Goldsmith⟩ often in a conclusion to a condition ⟨if you have anything more to say, ~ it now⟩ **~** *vi* **1 :** to conduct oneself **:** ACT, BEHAVE ⟨never knew him to ~ like this before —J.M.MacDonald⟩ ⟨~ as I say⟩ **2 a :** to get along **:** FARE ⟨men who wish to ~ well in the world —R.M.Weaver⟩ ⟨how are your crops ~*ing*?⟩ ⟨the airlines were ~*ing* pretty well —Richard Witkin⟩ **b :** to be as regards health **:** FEEL ⟨how do you ~⟩ **3 :** to take place **:** go on **:** HAPPEN ⟨should get to know more about . . . Africa and what's ~*ing* there —Emory Ross⟩ **4 :** to carry on business or affairs **:** MANAGE ⟨how shall we ~ for money for these wars —Shak.⟩ **5 :** to come to or make an end **:** FINISH ⟨worked busily for a few minutes and when he had *done*, the stretcher was a rectangle —Norman Mailer⟩ ⟨he had *done* with speech for that evening and gave us no reply —Arnold Bennett⟩ **6 :** to exert oneself **:** be active **:** WORK ⟨let us then be up and ~*ing* —H.W.Longfellow⟩ **7** *obs* **:** to continue with an action that one is already performing **:** proceed with an action that one has prepared to perform **:** go ahead — used in the imperative to express encouragement or incitement **8 a :** to be adequate or sufficient **:** answer the purpose **:** SERVE ⟨said this country would ~ for dairy farming —Ellen Glasgow⟩ ⟨an ordinary trout rod of about five ounces . . . will ~ nicely —Pete Barrett⟩ ⟨will not ~ as a translation —R.A.Fowkes⟩ **b :** to be fitting or appropriate **:** conform to custom or propriety ⟨it would never ~ to neglect official obligations —W. F. de Morgan⟩ **9** — used as a substitute verb to avoid repetition of a verb ⟨when beauty lived and died as flowers ~ now —Shak.⟩ often in a reply to a question ⟨did you go to the movies? I *did*⟩ **10** — used in the imperative after an imperative verb to add emphasis ⟨be quiet, ~⟩ **~** *verbal auxiliary* **1 a** *archaic* — used with the infinitive without *to* to form periphrastic present and past tenses virtually interchangeable with the corresponding simple tenses; now used in biblical or ecclesiastical language ⟨I ~ set my bow in the cloud —Gen 9:13(AV)⟩ or in legal or parliamentary language ⟨the motion for adjournment, in order to supersede a question, must be simply that the House ~ now adjourn —T.E.May⟩ or in poetry ⟨so offers he to give what she *did* crave —Shak.⟩ or in British dialect ⟨ye ~ be always with the hounds —Charles Lever⟩; not used with *be* in American English or in standard British English, nor with *have* in the literal sense of "possess" in standard British English **b** — used with the infinitive without *to* to form periphrastic present and past tenses now more generally current and acceptable than the corresponding simple tenses in declarative sentences with inverted word order ⟨fervently ~ we pray —Abraham Lincoln⟩ or in interrogative sentences ⟨*did* you hear that⟩ or in negative sentences ⟨we ~ not know⟩ ⟨*don't* you see⟩; not used with *be* in American English or in standard British English, nor with *have* in the literal sense of "possess" in standard British English **c** — used with full stress with the infinitive without *to* to form periphrastic present and past tenses expressing greater emphasis than the corresponding simple tenses ⟨just as I expected, you *did* forget my birthday⟩; not used with *be* in American English or in standard British English, nor with *have* in the literal sense of "possess" in standard British English **2 a** — used with full stress with the infinitive without *to* to form a periphrastic imperative expressing greater emphasis than the simple imperative ⟨~ be careful⟩ **b** — used with the infinitive without *to* to form a periphrastic imperative now used to the exclusion of the simple imperative in negative sentences ⟨please ~ not enter⟩ ⟨*don't* be foolish⟩ — **do by :** to deal with **:** TREAT ⟨publishers always *do* handsomely *by* the nursery set —Katharine T. Kinkead⟩ — **do one's block** *Austral* **:** to lose one's head **:** become flustered, excited, or angry — **do proud :** to give cause for pride or gratification ⟨looks magnificent, *does* you *proud* anywhere on earth —*N.Y. Times Mag.*⟩ — **do withal** *obs* **:** to help or prevent it ⟨they fell sick and died; I could not *do withal* —Shak.⟩ — **to do :** necessary to be done ⟨ten thousand times I've done my best and all's *to do* again —A.E.Housman⟩

²do \ˈdü\ *n, pl* **dos** *or* **do's** \ˈdüz\ **1** *now chiefly dial* **:** fuss and commotion **:** ADO ⟨a great deal of ~ and a great deal of trouble —Sir Walter Scott⟩ **2** *archaic* **:** DEED, DUTY — used esp. in the phrase *to do one's do* **3** *chiefly Brit* **a :** a festive get-together **:** AFFAIR, PARTY ⟨it is fashionable to support the public school system with an annual ~ —A.C.Spectorsky⟩ **b :** a military engagement **:** SHOW ⟨he was at Dieppe for the big ~ —Robert Trout⟩ **4 :** a command or entreaty to do something ⟨the basic ~*s* and don'ts of mental health —Peg Bradner⟩ **5** *Austral* **:** GO, SUCCESS ⟨looks a bit of a gamble to me but if you think you can make a ~ of it —Vance Palmer⟩

³do *also* **doh** \ˈdō\ *n, pl* **dos** *or* **do's** \ˈdōz\ [It *do*] **1 :** the first tone of the diatonic scale in solmization **:** TONIC **2 :** the tone *C* in the fixed-do system of solmization

⁴do \ˈ"\ *n* -s [Jap *dō*] **:** any of numerous regions or large districts each containing several provinces into which Japan was formerly divided

do *abbr* ditto

DO *abbr* **1** defense order **2** delivery order **3** district officer **4** duty officer

DOA *abbr* dead on arrival

do·ab \ˈdō,äb\ *n* -s [Per *doāb*, fr. *dō two* (fr. MPer) + *āb* water, fr. OPer *āpi-*; akin to Av *dvā-* two, Skt *dva*, and to Av *āp-* water — more at TWO] **:** a tract of land between two rivers **:** INTERFLUVE

do·able \ˈdüəbəl\ *adj* [ME, fr. *don* to do + *-able* — more at DO] **:** that can be done **:** PRACTICABLE ⟨likes to . . . get something done that is not considered ~ —Otis Ferguson⟩

do–all *n* -s *obs* **:** a general manager **:** FACTOTUM

doat *var of* DOTE

do away *vt, archaic* **:** to put an end to **:** DESTROY ⟨a dislike which not all his fortune and consequence might *do away* —Jane Austen⟩ — **do away with 1 :** to put an end to **:** ABOLISH, DISCONTINUE ⟨the motor did not *do away with* steam power —Roger Burlingame⟩ ⟨attempted to *do away with* the entire civic art program —Jules Langsner⟩ **2 :** to put to death **:** KILL ⟨thousands of persons have been *done away with* in this manner —*Manchester Guardian Weekly*⟩

¹dob \ˈdäb\ *var of* DAB

²dob \ˈ"\ *var of* DAUB

¹dob·ber \ˈdäbə(r)\ *n* -s [D, fr. MD, float; perh. akin to OE *dūfan* to dive — more at DIVE] *dial* **:** a float to a fishing line

²dobber \ˈ"\ *n* -s [¹*dob* + *-er*] **:** a dabchick or other small grebe

dob·bin \ˈdäbən\ *n* -s [fr. *Dobbin*, alter. of *Robin*, nickname for Robert] **:** a farm horse **:** a quiet plodding family horse ⟨he is no agile cow pony but is more like some comfortable ~ —G.R.Stewart⟩

dob·by *also* **dob·bie** \ˈdäbē, -bi\ *n* -ES [prob. fr. *Dobby*, nickname for *Robert*] **1** *dial Brit* **:** a silly person **:** DOLT **2** *dial Brit* **:** a brownie or sprite believed to possess powers of good and evil **3 a** (1) **:** a loom attachment resembling a jacquard for weaving small figures usu. about 12 to 16 threads and seldom more than 30 threads (2) **:** a loom having such an attachment **b :** a fabric or figured weave made with a dobby

do·be *or* **do·bie** *or* **do·by** \ˈdōbē, -bi\ *n, pl* **dobes** *or* **dobies** [by shortening & alter.] **:** ADOBE

do·bell's solution \(ˈ)dō¦belz-\ *n, usu cap D* [after Horace B. *Dobell* †1917 Eng. physician] **:** an aqueous solution of sodium borate, sodium bicarbonate, glycerin, and phenol used as a spray for the nose and throat

do·ber·man pin·scher \ˌdōbə(r)mən'pinchə(r), *rapid–R sometimes* -b(ə)m-\ *also* **doberman** *n* -s *usu cap D* [after Ludwig *Dobermann*, 19th cent. Ger. dog breeder] **:** a short-haired working dog of a breed of German origin characterized by medium size, long slender head with moderate stop, strong arched neck, deep chest and compact trunk with the back rather short and lower at rump than shoulder, long strong legs terminating in compact feet, and typically by a black coat with rusty brown markings

do·bie man \ˈdōbē-\ *n* [origin unknown] **:** one who blasts rock, coal, or ore from a quarry or mine

do·bla \ˈdōblə\ *n* -s [Sp — more at DOUBLOON] **:** an old Spanish gold coin

do·blon \dōˈblōn\ *n, pl* **doblons** \-ōnz\ *or* **doblo·nes** \-ˈōnēz, -ō,nās\ [Sp *doblón* — more at DOUBLOON] **:** an old gold coin of Spain and Spanish America worth two gold escudos

do·bos torte \ˈdō,bōs(h)-\ *also* **dobos** *n* -ES *usu cap D* [after Jozsef C. *Dobós* †1928 Hung. pastry chef] **:** a torte made of multiple thin layers of sponge cake often containing ground hazelnuts, put together with a mocha-chocolate filling, and topped with caramel glaze

do·bra \ˈdōbrə, ˈdōb-\ *n* -s [Pg, fr. fem. of obs. *dobro* (now *dobre*) double, fr. L *duplus* — more at DOUBLE] **1 :** any of various former Portuguese coins; *specif* **:** a gold coin of the 18th and early 19th centuries equivalent to 12,800 reis — compare JOHANNES **2 :** a unit of value equivalent to one dobra coin ⟨a *half-dobra* coin⟩

dob·son \ˈdäbsən\ *n* -s [prob. fr. the name *Dobson*] **:** HELLGRAMMITE

dobsonfly \ˈ⸗⸗,⸗\ *n* **:** a winged insect of the family Corydalidae distinguished by the very long slender mandibles of the male and the large carnivorous aquatic larvae — compare HELLGRAMMITE

do·bu·an \ˈdō,büən, dōˈb-\ *n, pl* **dobuan** *or* **dobuans** *usu cap* [*Dobu* island + E *-an*] **1 :** a member of a Melanesian people of Dobu island, Territory of Papua **2** *or* **do·bu** \ˈdō,bü\ **:** the language of the Dobuans

doc \ˈdäk\ *n* -s [by shortening] **1 :** DOCTOR — used chiefly as a familiar term of address **2** *slang* **:** DOCUMENT

doc·cia ware \ˈdōch(ē)ə-\ *n, usu cap D* [fr. *Doccia*, town near Florence, Italy + E *ware*] **:** fine porcelain ware produced in or of the kind produced in the Italian town of Doccia

¹do·cent \ˈdōsᵊnt\ *adj* [L *docent-*, *docens*, pres. part. of *docēre* to teach — more at DOCILE] **:** serving to instruct **:** TEACHING, INSTRUCTIVE

²do·cent \ˈdōsᵊnt *or, esp with reference to German institutions*, dō(t)ˈsent *or* də(t)ˈs-\ *n* -s [G *dozent* (formerly spelled *docent*), fr. L *docent-*, *docens*, pres. part.] **:** TEACHER, LECTURER: as **a :** a college or university teacher or lecturer holding a rank inferior to that of a professor **b :** a person who conducts guided groups through a museum or art gallery and discusses and comments on the exhibits — **do·cent·ship** \-,ship\ *n*

do·ce·tae \dōˈsē,tē\ *n pl, usu cap* [Gk *Dokētai*, fr. *dokein* to seem good, seem, think — more at DECENT] **:** an early Christian sect that adhered to the doctrine of Docetism

do·ce·tic \dōˈsēd·ik, \ed-\ *or* **do·ke·tic** \dōˈk|\ *also* **do·ce·tist** \dōˈsēd·əst\ *adj, often cap* **1 :** relating to, held by, or like the Docetists **2 :** of, espousing, or relating to Docetism — **do·ce·ti·cal·ly** \-d·ək(ə)lē\ *adv*

do·ce·tism \dōˈsēd·,izəm, ˈdōsə,ti-\ *n* -s *usu cap* **:** an early Christian doctrine advanced by the Docetae that Jesus Christ appeared to men in a spiritual body and that since he had no actual human body he only seemed to suffer and die on the cross

do·ce·tist \dōˈsēd·əst\ *also* **do·cete** \ˈdō,sēt\ *n* -s *usu cap* **:** a person adhering to or believing in some form of Docetism

doch–an–dor·rach *or* **doch–an–dor·ris** \ˌd(y)äkənˈdōrəs, -där-\ *n* [ScGael & IrGael *deoch an doruis*, lit., drink of the door] *Scot & Irish* **:** a parting drink **:** STIRRUP CUP

¹doch·mi·ac \ˈdäkmē,ak\ *adj* [Gk *dochmiakos*, fr. *dochmios*] **:** of, relating to, or composed of the dochmius

²dochmiac \ˈ"\ *n* -s **:** DOCHMIUS

doch·mi·a·cal \(ˈ)däkˈmīəkəl, ˌdäkmēˈak-\ *adj* [Gk *dochmiakos* + E *-al*] **:** of or relating to dochmiac verse

doch·mi·us \ˈdäkmēəs\ *n, pl* **doch·mii** \-ē,ī\ [L, fr. Gk *dochmios*, fr. *dochmos*, *dochmios* slanted, oblique; akin to Skt *jihma* slanted, oblique] *prosody* **:** a foot of five syllables typically having the first and fourth short and the rest long

doch·ter \ˈdōktər, ˈdäk-\ *n* -s [ME *doghter*, *doughter* — more at DAUGHTER] *Scot* **:** DAUGHTER

doc·i·bil·i·ty \ˌdäsəˈbiləd·ē, ˌdōs-\ *n* -ES [LL *docibilitas*, fr. *docibilis* + L *-itas* -ity] *archaic* **:** TEACHABLENESS, DOCILITY

doc·i·ble \ˈ⸗⸗bəl\ *adj* [LL *docibilis*, fr. L *docēre* to teach + *-ibilis* -ible] **:** easily taught or managed **:** TEACHABLE

doc·ile \ˈdäsəl *sometimes* ˈdä(,)sil *or* ˈdä,sīl, *Brit usu & US sometimes* ˈdō,sīl\ *adj* [L *docilis*, fr. *docēre* to teach (causative fr. the root of L *decēre* to be fitting) + *-ilis* -ile — more at DECENT] **1 :** TEACHABLE ⟨~ pupils looking for instruction —H.O.Taylor⟩ **2 :** TRACTABLE, OBEDIENT ⟨a good ~ lass ever ready to help her fellows⟩; *often* **:** lacking in independence **:** SUBMISSIVE ⟨the ~ masses of an enslaved nation⟩ **syn** see OBEDIENT

doc·ile·ly \-sə(l)lē, -,sīll|, -,sīll|, |i\ *adv* **:** in a docile manner **:** with docility

do·cil·i·ty \däˈsiləd·ē, dō'-,də'-, -əté, -i\ *n* -ES [MF or L; MF *docilité*, fr. L *docilitat-*, *docilitas*, fr. *docilis* + *-itat-*, *-itas* -ity] **:** the quality or state of being docile

doc·i·mas·tic \ˌdäsəˈmastik\ *also* **doc·i·mas·ti·cal** \-təkəl\ *adj* [Gk *dokimastikos* of or for scrutiny, fr. *dokimazein* to assay, test] *archaic* **:** of or relating to docimasy

doc·i·ma·sy \ˈdäsəməsē\ *or* **doc·i·ma·sia** \ˌdäsəˈmāzh(ē)ə\ *n, pl* **docimasies** *or* **docimasias** [NL *docimasia*, fr. Gk *dokimasia* examination, scrutiny, test, fr. *dokimazein* to assay, test, approve (fr. *dokimos* approved, tested, fr. *dekein* to seem good, seem, think) + *-ia* -y — more at DECENT] **1** *archaic* **:** the art or practice of assaying ores **2 :** determination as to whether a dead infant was stillborn by placing the body in water in which it sinks unless the infant has expanded the lungs in respiration

do·cious \ˈdōshəs\ *adj* [by alter.] *dial* **:** DOCILE

doc·i·ty \ˈdäsəd·ē\ *n* [prob. contr. of *docility*] *dial* **:** ability to comprehend quickly **:** mental energy or vigor **:** TEACHABLENESS

¹dock \ˈdäk\ *n* -s [ME *dock*, *docke*, fr. OE *docce*; akin to MD, MLG, & ODan *docke* dock, ScGael *dogha* burdock] **1 :** any of certain coarse weedy plants with long strong taproots that constitute the genus *Rumex*, that are sometimes used as table greens, and that have long been used in folk medicine — often used with a qualifying or descriptive adjective; see BITTER DOCK, SOUR DOCK **2 :** any of several usu. broad-leaved weedy plants (as members of the genera *Arctium*, *Petasites*, *Tussilago*, or *Malva*)

²dock \ˈ"\ *n* -s [ME *dok*, *docke* fr. OE *-docca* (as in *fingirdocca* finger muscle); akin to Fris *dok* bundle, ball, OHG *tocka* doll, ON *dokka* girl, bundle] **1 a :** the solid part of an animal's tail as distinguished from the hair **:** the part of a tail left after clipping the hair or cropping the end **b :** the part of the body of certain animals adjacent to the base of the tail: (1) **:** RUMP (2) **:** VULVA **2 a :** a docking esp. of wages; *also* **:** the amount docked

³dock \ˈ"\ *vt* -ED/-ING/-S [ME *docken*, fr. *dok*, *docke* (end of tail)] **1 a :** to cut off the end of some body part of; *specif* **:** to remove part of the tail of (a horse or lamb) ⟨~*ed* lambs are cleaner and command a premium on the market⟩ **b :** to cut (as a tail) short ⟨nobody'd ~ his cattle's ears that close —H.L.Davis⟩ ⟨the boxer's tail should be ~*ed* and ears cropped soon after birth⟩ **2 :** to cut short: as **a :** to take away a part of **:** ABRIDGE, LESSEN, REDUCE ⟨while it has been necessary . . . to ~ some [of the writings] . . . nothing of crucial import has been omitted —W.B.Scott⟩ ⟨if we grow absorbed in work . . . to the exclusion of . . . human elements, we ~ and maim our lives —A.C.Benson⟩ **b :** to bring (an entail) to an end **c :** to subject (as wages) to a deduction; *often* **:** to cheapen (market livestock) by assessing a deduction from weight or in price as a penalty for defects **3 :** to deprive (as a person) of some benefit ordinarily due esp. as a penalty for a fault ⟨he was ~*ed* $10 for repeated tardiness⟩ — often used with *of* ⟨~ him of the small pleasures of childhood —Samuel Butler †1902⟩

⁴dock \ˈ"\ *n* -s [prob. fr. MD *docke* dock, ditch, fr. L *ductio* act of conducting — more at DOUCHE] **1 a** *archaic* **:** natural or artificial inlet or hollow in which a ship can be received **:** MOORING, HARBOR **b :** a usu. artificial basin or enclosure in connection with a harbor or river for the reception of ships and equipped with means for controlling the water height — see DRY DOCK, FLOATING DOCK, WET DOCK **c :** the waterway extending between two piers or projecting wharves or cut into the land for the reception of ships **d :** a series of slips and adjoining wharves, offices, and other buildings — often used in pl. **2 :** a place for the loading or unloading of materials (as from ships or carts) or for their storage: as **a :** WHARF **b :** a raised platform used for loading or unloading wheeled freight carriers (as trucks or railway cars) **c :** an elevated platform where sawed lumber is stored at the sawmill until shipped; *also* **:** DOLLYWAY **d :** the space usu. under the floor of the stage in which scenery is stored in a theater **3 a :** scaffolding enclosing and giving access to exterior parts of an aircraft **b :** a place or building equipped for the inspection and repair of aircraft; *broadly* **:** HANGAR **syn** see WHARF

⁵dock \ˈ"\ *vb* -ED/-ING/-S *vt* **1 :** to haul or guide (as a ship) into a dock (as for repairing, cleaning, or loading) **2 :** to supply (as a port) with a dock **~** *vi* **:** to come or go into dock ⟨the ship ~*ed* here⟩

⁶dock \ˈ"\ *n* -s [Flem *docke*, *dok cage*] **:** the place in court where a prisoner stands or sits — **in the dock :** on trial ⟨it is the civilization that permits such acts that should be *in the dock*⟩ ⟨but you cannot put a dog *in the dock* —*Manchester Guardian Weekly*⟩

⁷dock \ˈ"\ *vt* -ED/-ING/-S [origin unknown] **:** to perforate (as a cracker) before baking

¹dock·age \-ij, -ēj\ *n* -s [⁴*dock* + *-age*] **1 :** a charge for the use of a dock **2 :** docking facilities **3 :** the docking of ships

²dockage \ˈ"\ *n* -s [³*dock* + *-age*] **1 :** a deduction (as from wages, a going price, or the recorded weight of a salable commodity) taken or withheld (as by an employer or purchaser) as compensation for some defect **2 :** the foreign material in market grain (as wheat) that is readily removable by ordinary cleaning devices

dockage period *n* [¹*dockage*] **:** the period during which water and current conditions allow a ship to enter or leave a dock (as in a particular harbor or port)

dockboard \ˈ⸗,⸗\ *n* [⁴*dock* + *board*] **:** a movable often metal plate for bridging the gap between a motor truck or freight car and a loading platform

dock boss *or* **docking boss** *n* [³*dock*] **:** a foreman who checks carloads of newly mined coal to estimate the amount of slate and other foreign matter that has been included in order to establish a rate of dockage — called also *gager*

dock brief *n* [⁶*dock*] *English law* **:** a brief from a prisoner in the dock who is unable to provide counsel for himself; *also* **:** the privilege granted such a prisoner at the discretion of the trial judge of selecting a barrister from among those present to represent him for a nominal fee

dock·en \ˈdäkən\ *n* -s [ME *doken* (pl. of *dock*, *docke*), fr. OE *doccan*, pl. of *docce* dock — more at DOCK] **1** *chiefly Scot* **:** ¹DOCK **2** *chiefly Scot* **:** something of small value ⟨I don't care a ~ —John Buchan⟩

¹dock·er \ˈdäkə(r)\ *n* -s [³*dock* + *-er*] **:** one that docks: as **a :** a worker that docks the tails of animals **b :** a device for docking tails esp. of lambs

²docker \ˈ"\ *n* -s [⁴*dock* + *-er*] **:** one connected with docks or wharves; *usu* **:** a dock laborer **:** LONGSHOREMAN

³docker \ˈ"\ *n* -s [⁷*dock* + *-er*] **:** a stamp for cutting out and perforating dough in making certain unleavened breads (as crackers)

¹dock·et \ˈdäkət, *usu* -əd·+V\ *n* -s [ME *doggette*] **1 :** a document containing the heads or a summary of a writing: as **a :** an abstract of a proposed letters patent of the throne of England **b :** an abridged entry of a judgement or proceeding in an action at law **c** *Brit* **:** a form accompanying merchandise and containing data relevant to its disposal (as owner's name or date, time, and place of delivery) **:** LABEL, TICKET; *also* **:** a British customhouse warrant certifying payment of duties or facts entitling the holder to a delivery order **d :** a memorandum or identifying statement about a document that is placed on its outer surface or cover **2 :** LIST: as **a** (1) **:** a list of dockets of a court or quasi-judicial body or a session of one of these (2) **:** a book of original entries kept by the clerk of a court or quasi-judicial body and containing a formal list of the names of parties and minutes of proceedings in each case in that court or body (3) **:** a record containing a list of causes waiting to be tried in a court or quasi-judicial body **b :** a calendar of matters to be acted on by any formally organized body (as a board of directors or a legislative assembly) **:** AGENDA **c :** a sequence of things to be presented, dealt with, or done whether formally listed or not ⟨on the Broadway ~ for early this season —J.P.Shanley⟩ ⟨anyone who has a tailor-made cloth coat on his or her Christmas ~ —*New Yorker*⟩ **3 :** the documents relating to a particular matter or topic ⟨the

~ of the case — a manila folder as big as the phone book, bulging with forms, applications, vouchers —Bernard Taper); *broadly* **:** a mass of documents

²**docket** \"\ *vt* -ED/-ING/-S **:** to inscribe (as a document or bill) with or in a docket **:** endorse with an abstract; *esp* **:** to make a brief abstract of (a legal matter) and inscribe it in a list

dockhand \ˈ=,=\ *n* [⁴*dock* + *hand*] **:** a freight handler **:** STEVEDORE, LONGSHOREMAN

dockhead \ˈ=,=\ *n* [⁴*dock* + *head*] **:** the foremost part of a dock

docking *pres part of* DOCK

docking block *n* [fr. gerund of ⁵*dock*] **:** one of the heavy timbers on which a ship rests when in dry dock

docking bridge *n* **:** a raised platform on a large ship near the stern

docking keel *n* **:** either of two keels placed near and parallel to the bilge keels of some ships and between them and the main keel and used for supporting the ship in dry dock

dock·i·za·tion \ˌdäkəˈzāshən\ *n* -S **:** conversion of an area (as of waterfront) into docks

dock·ize \ˈdäˌkīz\ *vt* -ED/-ING/-S [⁴*dock* + *-ize*] **:** to equip (a river) with docks or (a harbor) for docking

dock·land \ˈdäˌkland\ *n* [⁴*dock* + *land*] *Brit* **:** the part of a port occupied by docks; *often* **:** the blighted residential section adjacent to docks — **dock·land·er** \-də(r)\ *n*

dock·mack·ie \ˈdäkˌmakē\ *n* -S [prob. fr. D, fr. Lenape *dogekumak*] **:** a No. American shrub (*Viburnum acerifolium*) with white flowers succeeded by red berries — called also *arrowwood, mapleleaf viburnum*

dock·man \ˈdäkmən\ *n, pl* **dockmen** [⁴*dock* + *man*] **:** a worker at a dock: as **a :** one that helps to catch and cast off mooring lines **b :** DOCKER **c :** a person in charge of placing or assembling shipments on a dock

dockmaster \ˈ=,==\ *n* [⁴*dock* + *master*] **:** a person in charge of a dock; *esp* **:** one that supervises the actual docking of a ship

dock receipt *n* [⁴*dock*] **:** a receipt issued by a shipping company for cargo delivered at the pier and later exchanged for a bill of lading

docks *pl of* DOCK, *pres 3d sing of* DOCK

dockside \ˈ=,=\ *n, often attrib* [⁴*dock* + *side*] **:** the shore or area adjacent to a dock ⟨a destructive ~ fire⟩ ⟨the price was quoted as landed at ~⟩ ⟨planning improvements for the municipal ~⟩

dockside switcher *n* [⁴*dock*] **:** a small locomotive designed for switching work in close quarters around waterfront and industrial areas

dock spike *n* [⁴*dock*] **:** a spike usu. from 6 inches to 2 feet in length and from ½ inch to 1 inch square in section with a wedge-shaped point and often barbed like a rag bolt

dock-tailed \ˈ=,=\ *adj* [²*dock* + *tailed*] **:** having a docked tail ⟨*dock-tailed* lambs bring better prices⟩

dockwalloper \ˈ=,===\ *n* [⁴*dock*] **1 :** a loafer about docks who picks up casual employment **2 :** a freight handler on a dock

dockwalloping \ˈ=,===\ *n* -S **:** the work of a dockwalloper

dockyard \ˈ=,=\ *n* [⁴*dock* + *yard*] **1 :** a storage place for naval stores or timber for shipbuilding with facilities for building or repairing ships **2** *Brit* **:** NAVAL SHIPYARD — **dock·yard·man** \-mən\ *n, pl* **dockyardmen**

doc·o·glos·sa \ˌdäkəˈgläsə, -lȯsə\ *n pl, cap* [NL, fr. Gk *dokos* beam + NL *-glossa*] **:** a suborder of Aspidiobranchia comprising primitive marine gastropods having a conical shell, paired nephridia and osphradia, a long radula, and no operculum and including the true limpets and certain related mollusks — **doc·o·glos·san** \ˌ==ˈ=sən\ *adj* — **doc·o·glos·sate** \-sāt\ *adj*

doc·o·sane \ˈdäkəˌsān\ *n* -S [ISV *docos-* (fr. *do-* — as in *dodeca-* — + *-cos-* — fr. *eicosa-*) + *-ane*] **:** a paraffin hydrocarbon of the formula $C_{22}H_{46}$; *esp* **:** the crystalline normal isomer $CH_3(CH_2)_{20}CH_3$

doc·o·sa·no·ic acid \ˌdäkəsəˌnōik-\ *n* [*docosane* + *-o-* + *-ic*] **:** BEHENIC ACID

doc·quet *archaic var of* DOCKET

¹**doc·tor** \ˈdäktə(r)\ *n* -S [ME *doctour*, fr. MF & ML; MF *doctour, docteur*, fr. ML *doctor*, fr. L, teacher, fr. *doctus* (past part. of *docēre* to teach) + *-or* — more at DOCILE] **1 a :** a religious scholar who is eminent in theological learning and personal holiness and usu. an expounder and defender of established doctrine ⟨Christ disputed with the ~s⟩ ⟨St. Jerome was one of the great ~s of the church⟩ **b** *archaic* **:** a person competent by reason of skill and knowledge to teach or expound authoritatively a subject or field of knowledge; *broadly* **:** a person who teaches or expounds something — used with *of* **c :** a person who has earned one of the highest academic degrees (as a PhD) conferred by a university usu. by spending several years in advanced study of a specialized field, by writing an acceptable dissertation, and by passing numerous rigorous examinations **d :** a person awarded an honorary doctorate (as an LLD or LittD) by a college or university **2 :** one skilled or specializing in healing arts: **a :** a practitioner of medicine, dentistry, or veterinary medicine **b :** a person who has completed a course of study in one of these fields and been duly licensed to practice his profession **c :** PHYSICIAN — distinguished from *surgeon* **d :** a medicine man in a primitive culture; *broadly* **:** any practitioner (as a rainmaker or shaman) of mysterious or magic arts in such a culture **3** *archaic slang* **:** a loaded die **4 :** a recurrent cool breeze; *esp* **:** a tropical sea breeze **5 :** material added to produce a desired effect: **a :** something added to food or drink to improve its apparent quality (as acid to certain candies) **b :** DOCTOR SOLUTION **6 :** a mechanical contrivance or attachment for remedying a difficulty esp. when makeshift and used in an emergency: as **a** *or* **doctor blade :** a blade (as of metal, wood, or plastic) for spreading a coating (as of glue on layers of material being laminated) or for scraping a surface (as for removing ink from the nonprinting part of an intaglio printing surface or lint from a textile printing roll) **b :** a small engine for providing water for a boiler system **:** DONKEY ENGINE **c :** a tool used for electroplating surfaces that cannot conveniently be placed in a bath **d :** a soldering tool **e :** a knife for scraping up and incorporating rubber dough in a mixing machine **7 a** *slang* **:** a ship or camp cook **b :** a person who puts things in or restores things to order: as (1) **:** a repairer of broken or disordered items, esp. of mechanical apparatus or systems — used often with a qualifying attributive ⟨a first-rate loom ~⟩ (2) **:** PLAY DOCTOR **c :** a person in charge (as of a situation) **:** one responsible for decisions to be made — used chiefly in the phrase *you're the doctor* **8 :** any of several brightly colored artificial flies used by anglers

²**doctor** \"\ *vb* **doctored; doctored; doctoring** \-t(ə)riŋ\ **doctors** *vt* **1 a :** to confer a doctorate upon **:** make (someone) a doctor **b :** to address or refer to as "Doctor" ⟨a false humility that made him ~ all his associates⟩ **2 a :** to treat (a patient or ailment) as a physician **:** apply remedies to ⟨faithfully ~*ed* her old mother⟩ ⟨~*ed* his boil⟩ **b :** to restore to good condition **:** MEND, REPAIR ⟨he tinkered with the old clock until he finally ~*ed* its strike⟩ **3 a :** to adapt or modify for a desired end by alteration or special treatment ⟨~*ed* the play by tightening its whole structure and abridging the last act⟩ **b :** to conceal the real state or actual quality of by deceptive alteration (as with chemicals) ⟨~*ing* poor wine to get a better price⟩ ⟨hoping to ~ the election returns⟩ — often used with *up* ⟨you'll have to ~ up your plans if you hope to fool anybody⟩ ~ *vi* **1 :** to practice medicine ⟨my grandfather ~*ed* in the backwoods country for over 50 years⟩ **2** *dial* **:** to take medicine or medical treatment ⟨~*ing* for the asthma⟩ ⟨she ~*ed* with my nephew all that winter⟩

doc·tor·al \ˈdäkt(ə)rəl\ *also* **doc·to·ri·al** \(ˈ)däkˈtȯrēəl\ *adj* **:** of, relating to, or characteristic of a doctor or doctorate ⟨a ~ hood⟩ ⟨~ candidates⟩ — **doc·tor·al·ly** \-əlē, -li\ *adv*

doc·to·rand \ˌdäktəˈrand\ *also* **doc·to·ran·dus** \ˌdäktəˈrandəs\ *n, pl* **doctorands** \-n(d)z\ *also* **doctoran·di** \ˌ==ˈranˌdī\ [ML *doctorandus*, gerundive of *doctorare*] **:** a candidate for a doctorate

doc·tor·ate \ˈdäkt(ə)rə̇t, -ktəˌrāt, *usu* |d.+V\ *n* -S [ML *doctoratus*, fr. *doctoratus*, past part. of *doctorare* to become a doctor, fr. *doctor*] **:** the degree, title, or rank of a doctor

doctorbird \ˈ==,=\ *n* [prob. so called fr. the resemblance of the bill to a surgical needle] **1 :** GREEN TODY **2 :** a curve-billed hummingbird (*Sericotes holosericeus*) of the West Indies; *broadly* **:** any of various West Indian hummingbirds

doctor book *n* **:** a book intended to supplement the knowledge of the individual in matters of home medication usu. helping to identify common ailments and suggesting simple medication that can be undertaken without the supervision of a physician

doctorfish \ˈ==,=\ *n* [so called fr. the sharp spines on each side of the tail] **:** SURGEONFISH

doctor gum *n* **1 :** POISONWOOD 1 **2 :** a gum obtained from the doctor-gum tree and used locally for medicinal purposes

doc·tor·hood \ˈdäktə(r)ˌhu̇d\ *n* -S **:** doctoral position or rank

doc·tor·ize \-təˌrīz\ *vt* -ED/-ING/-S **:** to confer the degree of doctor on

doc·tor·ly \-tə(r)lē\ *adj* **:** like a doctor **:** befitting a doctor

doctors *pl of* DOCTOR, *pres 3d sing of* DOCTOR

doc·tor·ship \-tə(r)ˌship\ *n* **1 :** DOCTORATE **2** *archaic* **:** the position, function, or characteristics of a doctor; *sometimes* **:** LEARNING, SCHOLARSHIP

doctor solution *n* **:** a solution made by adding litharge to sodium hydroxide solution and used in sweetening petroleum distillates (as naphtha) by reaction with any malodorous sulfur compounds (as mercaptans) present

doctor test *n* **:** a test with doctor solution for detecting the presence of undesirable sulfur compounds in petroleum distillates (as naphtha)

doc·tress \ˈdäktrə̇s\ *also* **doc·tor·ess** \-t(ə)rə̇s\ *n* -ES [*doctor* + *-ess*] **:** a female medicine man or witch doctor

¹**doc·tri·naire** \ˌdäktrəˈna(a)(ə)r, -ne|, |ə\ *n* -S [F, fr. *doctrine* doctrine, teaching + *-aire* -ary (fr. L *-arius*)] **1 :** a member of a French political party that persisted from about 1815 to 1830, advocated a constitutional monarchy, and was opposed both to the ultraroyalists and to the revolutionists **2 :** one who attempts to put into effect some esp. political doctrine or theory with little or no regard for practical difficulties

²**doctrinaire** \"\ *adj* **:** relating to or characteristic of a doctrinaire **:** stubbornly devoted to some particular doctrine or theory without regard to practical considerations **:** DOGMATIC ⟨an atonal composition in the ~ sense —Winthrop Sargeant⟩

doc·tri·nair·ism \ˌ==ˈna(a)ˌrizəm, -ˈneˌr-\ *n* -S **:** the principles or practices of a doctrinaire **:** stubborn attachment to a doctrine or theory without regard to its practicality

¹**doc·tri·nal** \ˈdäktrən°l, *Brit often & US sometimes* däkˈtrīn°l\ *n* -S [ME, fr. MF, fr. *doctrinal*, adj.] **1** *obs* **:** a manual of instruction **2 doctrinals** *pl, archaic* **:** matters of doctrine or instruction

²**doc·tri·nal** \ˈdäktrən°l, *Brit often & US sometimes* (ˈ)däkˈtrīn°l\ *adj* [ME, fr. MF or LL; MF, fr. LL *doctrinalis*, fr. L *doctrina* teaching + *-alis* -al] **1 a :** of, relating to, or preoccupied with doctrine ⟨quibbling and hairsplitting over ~ minutiae⟩ ⟨Milton was a ~ poet —Douglas Bush⟩ **b :** containing or involving something taught and to be believed ⟨those who seek ~ support of spending now turn to the statistics of national income —H.L.Lutz⟩ **2** *obs* **:** relating to teaching **:** DIDACTIC — **doc·tri·nal·ly** \-°lē, -°li\ *adv*

doc·tri·nal·i·ty \ˌdäktrəˈnaləd·ē\ *n* -ES **:** doctrinal character

doc·tri·nar·i·an \ˌdäktrəˈna(a)rēən, -ner-\ *n* -S [modif. of F *doctrinaire* + E *-ian*] **:** DOCTRINAIRE

doc·tri·nar·i·ly \ˌdäktrəˈnerəlē, -na(a)r-\ *adv* **:** with respect to basic principles and outlook ⟨~ opposed to the present government⟩

doc·tri·nar·i·ty \ˌdäktrəˈnarəd·ē\ *n* -ES **:** DOCTRINALITY

doc·tri·nary \ˈdäktrəˌnerē\ *adj* [F *doctrinaire*] **:** of, relating to, or holding certain basic usu. abstract doctrines or theories

doc·trine \ˈdäktrən\ *n* -S [ME, fr. MF & L; MF, fr. L *doctrina*, fr. *doctor* teacher] **1** *archaic* **:** TEACHING, INSTRUCTION ⟨He . . . said unto them in his ~, Hearken —Mark 4:2(AV)⟩ **2 a :** something that is taught **:** something that is held, put forth as true, and supported by a teacher, a school, or a sect ⟨the ~ and lore of the early fathers⟩ **b :** a principle or position or the body of principles in any branch of knowledge **:** a principle of faith **:** TENET, DOGMA ⟨the ~ of atoms⟩ ⟨Christian ~⟩ **c :** a principle of law established through past decisions and interpretations ⟨the ~ of caveat emptor⟩ **d :** a formulation of the principles on which a government proposes to base its actions or policy in some matter esp. in the field of international relations ⟨the Truman ~⟩ ⟨the Monroe ~⟩ **3** *obs* **:** LEARNING, KNOWLEDGE

syn DOGMA, TENET: DOCTRINE may indicate a formulated theory supported or not controverted by evidence, backed or sanctioned by authority, and proposed for acceptance; it may refer to authoritative teaching accepted by a body of believers or adherents ⟨the *doctrine* of Einstein, which sweeps away axioms so familiar to us that they seem obvious truths, and substitutes others which seem absurd because they are unfamiliar —Havelock Ellis⟩ ⟨there was also a nascent theory of sound waves; and out of it there grew a tremendous mathematical *doctrine* of waves which nowadays has almost come to dominate the physics of these times —K.K.Darrow⟩ DOGMA applies to authoritative teaching or ruling laid down or promulgated as true and unquestionable ⟨those who rejected the Marxist *dogma* found it easy to accept the dogma of those racists who represented Hitler as a modern synthesis of Frederick the Great, Bismarck, Nietzsche, and Kaiser Wilhelm II —Quincy Howe⟩ ⟨he sees orthodox science, despite all its achievements, become now the most dangerous enemy of a true philosophy, because its *dogmas* are least often questioned —J.W.Krutch⟩ ⟨the *dogma* of the bodily assumption of the Virgin Mary⟩ TENET may apply to any principle or opinion generally believed, whether taught and actively maintained or not ⟨the other *tenet* of his materialism is that supernaturalism, though it may have a certain practical justification for the majority of men, has no rational basis —Vivian J. McGill⟩ ⟨sympathy for the afflicted, a Christian *tenet*, has done much to alleviate the sufferings of these unfortunate people —V.G. Heiser⟩

doctrine of correspondence : the theory in Swedenborgianism that natural objects correspond to or participate in transcendent archetypes — compare PARTICIPATION

doctrine of descent : a theory in biology: all animals and plants are direct descendants of previous animals or plants — opposed to *special creation*

doctrine of signatures : a theory in old natural philosophy: the outward appearance of a body signalizes its special properties (as of magic or healing virtue) and there is a relationship between the outward qualities of a medicinal object and the diseases against which it is effective

doc·trin·ism \-ˌnizəm\ *n* -S **:** devotion to or enunciation of doctrine — **doc·trin·ist** \-nə̇st\ *n* -S

¹**doc·u·ment** \ˈdäkyəmənt\ *n* -S [ME, fr. MF, fr. LL & L; LL *documentum* official paper, fr. L, lesson, example, fr. *docēre* to teach + *-mentum* -ment — more at DOCILE] **1** *obs* **:** something taught **:** TEACHING, INSTRUCTION **2 a** *archaic* **:** something (as a writing) that serves to demonstrate or prove something **:** PROOF, EVIDENCE **b :** an original or official paper relied upon as the basis, proof, or support of something **c documents** *pl* **:** the bill of lading and policy of insurance and sometimes other papers that evidence or effect the shipment of goods, their insurance, the transfer of title to the consignee, and other procedures and that are annexed to a documentary bill of exchange **d documents** *pl* **:** SHIP'S PAPERS **e :** a formal or official writing or personal identification **:** an identity card (as of a seaman) **f** (1) **:** a writing (as a book, report, or letter) conveying information (2) **:** a material substance (as a coin or stone) having on it a representation of the thoughts of men by means of some conventional mark or symbol **g :** DOCUMENTARY **h :** a publication of federal, state, or local government — chiefly in library usage **3** *archaic* **:** a piece of information **:** LESSON; *often* **:** a warning or admonition

²**doc·u·ment** \-ˌment, -mənt — *see* ²-MENT\ *vt* -ED/-ING/-S **1** *obs* **:** TEACH, SCHOOL, INSTRUCT **2 :** to evidence by documents **:** furnish documentary evidence of ⟨carefully ~*ing* his claims⟩ **3 :** to furnish with documents **4 a :** to furnish (a ship) with ship's papers as required by law for the manifesting of ownership and cargo **b :** to annex to (a bill of exchange) the shipment documents — see DOCUMENTARY BILL **5 a :** to provide with factual or substantial support for statements made or a hypothesis proposed; *esp* **:** to equip with exact references to authoritative supporting information (as by means of footnotes or other textual annotation) ⟨pointed out, and ~*ed* in his book, that great progress has been made in the professional study of world affairs —F.M.Hechinger⟩ ⟨~ a thesis⟩ **b :** to construct or produce (as a movie or novel) with a high proportion of details closely reproducing authentic situations or events ⟨my desire to compose a highly ~*ed* picture of the modern world —R.P.Warren⟩

doc·u·ment·able \ˌdäkyəˈmentəbəl\ *adj* **:** capable of demonstration by documentary evidence

doc·u·men·tal \-nt°l\ *adj* **:** DOCUMENTARY

doc·u·men·tal·ist \ˌ===ˈ=əst\ *n* -S **:** a specialist in documentation of recorded knowledge

doc·u·men·tar·i·an \ˌdäkyəmən·ˈterēən, -ˌmen-\ *n* -S **:** a person who employs or advocates the stressing of documentary presentation (as in photographic art or fiction)

doc·u·men·tar·i·ly \ˌ==(ˌ)=ˈterəlē\ *adv* **1 :** by means of documents ⟨a ~ verifiable incident in American history⟩ **2 :** in a documentary manner ⟨quiet ~ unhighlighted acting —H.E.Clurman⟩

doc·u·men·ta·rist \ˌdäkyəˈmentərə̇st\ *n* -S **:** a specialist in documentary presentation (as of theatrical or literary material)

¹**doc·u·men·ta·ry** \ˌdäkyəˈmentər|ē, |i *also* ˈ==ˌmen·tr| *or* ˈdäkyəmən·ˌter|\ *adj* [¹*document* + *-ary*] **1 :** being or consisting of documents **:** contained or certified in writing ⟨~ evidence⟩ **2 :** of, relating to, or employing documentation in literature or art ⟨~ annotations⟩ ⟨a careful ~ writer⟩; *broadly* **:** having or claiming the objective quality, authority, or force of documentation in the representation of a scene, place, or condition of life or of a social or political problem or cause **:** FACTUAL, OBJECTIVE, REPRESENTATIONAL — used of works of literature, the theater, art, photography, radio and TV programs

²**documentary** \"\ *n* -ES **:** a documentary presentation (as a film or novel)

documentary bill *or* **documentary draft** *also* **document bill** *n* **:** a bill of exchange drawn on a consignee of goods and having appended to it the shipment documents by way of collateral security for its payment

documentary stamp *n* **:** a revenue stamp issued for use on documents

doc·u·men·ta·tion \ˌdäkyəmən·ˈtāshən, -ˌmen-\ *n* -S **1** *archaic* **:** INSTRUCTION, ADMONITION **2 :** the act or an instance of furnishing or authenticating with documents **3 a :** the provision of ship's papers to a ship **b :** the provision of documents in substantiation; *also* **:** documentary evidence (as in a treatise) **c** (1) **:** the use of historical documents esp. in the writing of history or of works relying on the authenticity of historical information (2) **:** conformity to historical or objective facts (as in writing or painting) (3) **:** the provision of footnotes, appendices, or addenda referring to or containing documentary evidence in verification of facts or in support of theory in a piece of writing (as a biography or history) **4 :** the assembling, coding, and disseminating of recorded knowledge comprehensively treated as an integral procedure utilizing semantics, psychological and mechanical aids, and techniques of reproduction including microcopy for giving documentary information maximum accessibility and usability

document board *n* **:** smooth and flexible paperboard of a kind usable for protective folders for documents and letters

documentize *vt* -ED/-ING/-S *obs* **:** to furnish with evidence **:** TEACH, ADMONISH

document of title : a document affording evidence of title to property; *specif* **:** any document that is used in the ordinary course of business as proof of the possession or control of goods or that imparts authority in the possessor of the document to transfer or receive the goods in question

documents *pl of* DOCUMENT, *pres 3d sing of* DOCUMENT

¹**dod** *or* **dodd** \ˈdäd\ *vt* **dodded; dodded; dodding; dods** *or* **dodds** [ME *dodden*] **1** *dial Brit* **:** to lop or clip hair or wool from ⟨it is time to ~ the sheep⟩ **2** *dial Brit* **:** POLL

²**dod** \"\ *n* -S **1 :** a perforated metal plate through which clay is forced to mold it to a desired shape **2 :** an annular die for making drainpipe

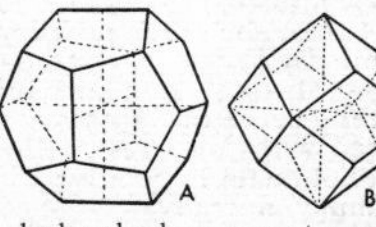
dod for pipe

³**dod** \"\ *interj* [euphemism for *God*] — used as a mild oath esp. as an intensive with a verb

do·da \ˈdōdə\ *n* -S [native name in India] **:** FOUR-HORNED ANTELOPE

dodad *var of* DOODAD

¹**dod·der** \ˈdädə(r)\ *n* -S [ME *doder;* akin to MLG *doder, dodder* dodder, MHG *toter* dodder, yolk, OHG *totoro* yolk, OS *dodro*, OE *dydring* yolk, Norw *dudra* to tremble, Gk *thyssetai* to tremble, *thysanos* tassel, Skt *dodhat-* shaking, raging, L *fumus* smoke — more at FUME] **:** any of certain plants comprising the genus *Cuscuta* with seeds that germinate and produce elongated seedlings which come in contact with stems of a suitable host plant and which obtain nourishment through haustoria — called also *love vine*

²**dodder** \"\ *vi* **doddered; doddered; doddering** \-d(ə)riŋ\ **dodders** [alter. of earlier *dadder*, fr. ME *dadiren*] **1 :** to tremble or shake (as from weakness or age) **:** become enfeebled ⟨we . . . have no excuse for ignoring a sick and ~*ing* church school —Iva Kilpatrick⟩ ⟨in the pulpit a ~*ing* priest was preaching —Bruce Marshall⟩ **2 :** to progress feebly and unsteadily ⟨an old man ~*ing* down the walk⟩

dod·dered \ˈdädə(r)d\ *adj* [prob. alter. of *dodded*] **1 :** deprived of branches through age or decay ⟨a ~ oak⟩ **2 :** SHATTERED, INFIRM **:** enfeebled esp. by age ⟨auld, feckless, ~ men —R.L.Stevenson⟩

dod·der·er \ˈdädərə(r)\ *n* -S **:** one that dodders; *esp* **:** a person enfeebled and doddering from weakness or age

doddering *adj* **:** feeble and dull esp. from age

dodder laurel *n* [¹*dodder*] **:** a parasitic plant of the genus *Cassytha* found commonly along tropical coasts — called also *devil's-guts, woevine*

dodder oil *n* **:** CAMELINE OIL

dodder seed *n* **:** the seed of the gold of pleasure that yields cameline oil

dod·dery \ˈdäd(ə)rē\ *adj* [²*dodder* + *-y*] **:** unsteady or trembling esp. by reason of age or weakness **:** DODDERING

dod·die *or* **dod·dy** \ˈdädē\ *n, pl* **doddies** [¹*dod* + *-ie, -y*] **1** *chiefly Scot* **:** a hornless cow or bull **2 :** ABERDEEN ANGUS

¹**dod·dle** \ˈdäd°l\ *adj or n* [¹*dod* + *-le*] **:** POLLARD

²**doddle** \"\ *vb* **doddled; doddled; doddling** \-d(°)liŋ\ **doddles** [prob. alter. of *dodder*] *vi, now dial* **:** DODDER, TODDLE ~ *vt, chiefly Midland* **:** to shake or nod (as the head)

dod·dy mitten \ˈdädē-\ *n* [prob. so called fr. the resemblance of a mitten to the head of a doddie] *Scot* **:** MITTEN 1

dod·dy·poll \ˈdädēˌpōl\ *n* [alter. (influenced by ¹*dod*) of ME *dotypolle, dotepol*, prob. fr. *dote* fool (fr. *doten* to dote) + *polle, pol* poll — more at DOTE, POLL] *now dial Eng* **:** BLOCKHEAD

dodeca- *or* **dodec-** *comb form* [L *dodeca-*, fr. Gk *dōdeka-, dōdek-*, fr. *dōdeka, dyōdeka*, fr. *dyō, dyo* two + *deka* ten — more at TWO, TEN] **:** twelve ⟨*dodeca*hedron⟩ ⟨*dodec*yl⟩

do·dec·a·gon \dōˈdekəˌgän\ *n* -S [Gk *dōdekagōnon*, fr. *dōdeka-* + *-gōnon* -gon] **:** a polygon of 12 sides — **do·de·cag·o·nal** \ˌdōdəˈkagən°l, ˌdōˌdeˈ-\ *adj*

do·deca·he·dral \(ˌ)dōˌdekəˈhēdrəl\ *adj* [*dodecahedron* + *-al*] **:** relating to or like a dodecahedron

dodecahedral cleavage *n* **:** cleavage in a mineral parallel to the faces of the rhombic dodecahedron

do·deca·he·dron \(ˌ)dōˌdekəˈhēdrən\ *n, pl* **dodecahedrons** \-nz\ *or* **dodecahe·dra** \-rə\ [Gk *dōdekaedron*, fr. *dōdeka-* dodeca- + *-edron* -hedron] **:** a solid having 12 plane faces and commonly in either of two forms: (1) with 12 equal regular pentagonal faces or (2) with 12 equal rhombic faces — called also respectively (1) *regular dodecahedron*, (2) *rhombic dodecahedron*

dodecahedrons: pentagonal, *A;* rhombic, *B*

do·deca·hydrate \(ˌ)dōˌdekə+\ *n* [*dodeca-* + *hydrate*] **:** a compound with 12 molecules of water

do·de·cam·er·ous \ˌdōdəˈkamərəs\ *adj* [*dodeca-* + *-merous*] **:** having the whorls of floral parts in twelves — often written 12-*merous*

do·de·cane \ˈdōdəˌkān\ *n* -S [ISV *dodeca-* + *-ane*] **:** any of the oily paraffin hydrocarbons having the formula $C_{12}H_{26}$; *esp* **:** the normal isomer $CH_3(CH_2)_{10}CH_3$ occurring in some petroleums

¹**do·dec·a·ne·sian** \(ˌ)dōˌdekəˈnēzhən, -ēsh-; ˌdōdəkə-\ *or*

do·dec·a·nese \-ēz,-ēs\ *also* **do·dec·a·ne·san** \-ēsᵊn,-ēzᵊn\ *adj, usu cap* [fr. *Dodecanese* islands] **:** of, relating to, or produced in the Dodecanese islands in the Aegean

²**dodecanesian** \"\ *or* **dodecanese** \"\ *n* -s *cap* **:** a native or inhabitant of the Dodecanese islands

do·dec·a·no·ic acid \(ˌ)dō¦dek¦ə¦nōik-, ¦dōdək¦-\ *n* [*dodecane* + *-o-* + *-ic*] **:** LAURIC ACID

do·dec·ant \ˈdō,dekənt, ˈdōdək-, dōˈdek-\ *n* -s [*dodeca-* + *-ant*] **:** any of the 12 parts into which the space about the center of a hexagonal crystal is divided by the four axial planes

do·deca·phon·ic \(ˌ)dō¦dekə¦fänik\ *adj* [*dodeca-* + *phon-* + *-ic*] **1 :** *of musical composition* **:** composed by using as a device the mechanical application of a particular numerical arrangement of the successive notes of the chromatic scale **2 :** of, relating to, or involved in the composition of dodecaphonic music ⟨a ~ technique⟩ ⟨the ~ tradition —Howard Taubman⟩

do·deca·pho·nism \dōˈdekə,fō,nizəm, -fä-; ,dōdəˈkafə,n-\ *n* -s **:** musical composition employing dodecaphonic techniques

do·deca·pho·nist \-,nəst\ *n* -s **:** an exponent of dodecaphonic techniques in musical composition; *esp* **:** a composer who uses these techniques

do·deca·pho·ny \dōˈdekə,fōnē, -,fänē; ,dōdəˈkafənē\ *n* -ES [*dodeca-* + *-phony*] **:** the practice of dodecaphonic composition

do·de·car·chy \ˈdōdə,kärkē\ *n* -ES [*dodeca-* + *-archy*] **:** a ruling body of 12

do·deca·se·mic \(ˌ)dō¦dekə¦sēmik\ *adj* [LL *dodecasemus* (fr. Gk *dōdekasēmos*, fr. *dōdeka-* dodeca- + *-sēmos*, fr. *sēma* sign) + E *-ic* — more at SEMANTICS] *prosody* **:** comprising 12 morae ⟨a dactylic tripody is ~⟩

¹**do·deca·style** \dōˈdekə,stīl\ *n* -s [Gk *dōdekastylos*, fr. *dōdeka-* dodeca- + *stylos* pillar — more at STOIC] **:** a dodecastyle structure (as a portico)

²**dodecastyle** \"\ *adj* **:** marked by columniation with 12 columns across the front — compare DISTYLE

do·deca·syllabic \(ˌ)dō¦dekə+\ *adj* [*dodeca-* + *syllabic*] **1 :** having or composed of 12 syllables **2 :** of or related to a dodecasyllable

do·deca·syllable \dōˈdekə+,-, (ˌ)dō,dekə+ˈ-\ *n* [*dodeca-* + *syllable*] **1 :** a line of 12 syllables **2 :** a word consisting of 12 syllables

do·de·cath·eon \,dōdəˈkathēən\ *n* [NL, fr. Gk *dōdekatheon* primrose, fr. neut. of *dōdekatheos* of twelve gods, fr. *dōdeka-* dodeca- + *theos* god — more at THEISM] **1** *cap* **:** a genus of No. American and Asiatic herbs (family Primulaceae) having basal leaves and scapose nodding flowers with reflexed corolla and monadelphous stamens **2** -s **:** any plant of the genus *Dodecatheon*

do·deca·tonal \(ˌ)dō¦dekə+\ *adj* [*dodeca-* + *tonal*] **:** DODECAPHONIC

do·dec·u·ple scale \(ˈ)dō¦dekyəpəl-\ *n* [*dodeca-* + *-uple* (as in *octuple*)] **:** the twelve-tone chromatic scale

do·dec·u·plet \dōˈdekyəplət, -,plet\ *n* -s [*dodeca-* + *-uplet* (as in *octuplet*)] **:** 12 musical notes performed in the time of the same value

do·de·cyl \ˈdōdə,sil\ *n* -s [ISV *dodeca-* + *-yl*] **1 :** an alkyl radical $C_{12}H_{25}$ derived from a dodecane by removal of one hydrogen atom; *esp* **:** the normal radical $CH_3(CH_2)_{10}CH_2$— **2 :** a mixture of branched-chain alkyl radicals averaging $C_{12}H_{25}$ in composition — used chiefly industrially ⟨benzene substituted by ~⟩

dodecyl alcohol *n* **:** LAURYL ALCOHOL 1

dod·gas·ted \ˈdäd,gastəd\ *adv* (*or adj*) [euphemism for *God blasted*] — used as a mild oath

¹**dodge** \ˈdäj\ *vb* -ED/-ING/-s [origin unknown] *vi* **1 a** *obs* **:** to behave evasively in speech or action **:** haggle over terms **:** PARLEY **b :** to evade responsibility or a duty esp. by trickery or deceit ⟨she *dodged* again, she lied again, and felt no guilt —Ethel Wilson⟩ **c :** to minimize a presentation (as of facts) **:** present something less harshly or forcefully than might be possible ⟨he never ~*s*, never seeks refuge in platitudinous generalities —*Saturday Rev.*⟩ **d :** to move to and fro or from place to place usu. in an irregular course ⟨had to ~ backward and forward between London, Scotland, and Ireland —*Times Lit. Supp.*⟩ ⟨*dodging* in and out among the crowd⟩ ⟨*dodged* in long zigzag leaps⟩; *often* **:** to make a sudden movement in a new direction (as to evade a blow) ⟨he *dodged* behind the door⟩ **2 :** to step backward in striking order — used of a bell in change ringing ~ *vt* **1 :** to evade (as a responsibility) usu. subtly and without positive repudiation ⟨that's *dodging* the question⟩ ⟨the fact that these deficiencies exist ought not to be *dodged* —Dexter Perkins⟩ ⟨those young men who ~ the draft⟩ **2 :** to evade by a sudden or by repeated shift of place or position ⟨*dodging* a hail of bullets⟩ **:** avoid an encounter with (as by suddenly turning aside) ⟨she *dodged* him in the crowd⟩ **3** *archaic* **:** to follow (as a person) stealthily concealing oneself from view **:** DOG **4 :** to reduce the intensity of (a portion of a photograph) by selectively shading or selectively masking by chemical means during printing — compare BURN IN

syn DODGE, PARRY, SIDESTEP, DUCK, SHIRK, FENCE, and MALINGER agree in meaning to avoid or evade by some maneuver or shift. DODGE implies quickness of movement or a sudden shift of position esp. in an unexpected direction (as in evading a blow or pursuit) ⟨I looked up just in time to *dodge* a window frame falling from a fourth-story apartment —T.P. Whitney⟩ ⟨the trouble has often been diagnosed, but it is always being *dodged* or minimized by the moralist —E.M. Forster⟩ ⟨he hides in a dream world, *dodging* all responsibility —Ruth Blodgett⟩ PARRY implies a warding off (as of a blow) by turning the object aside, extending commonly to any adroitness in defending oneself ⟨the Modoc bands *parried* thrust after thrust of the Federal troops —*Amer. Guide Series: Oregon*⟩ ⟨a new species of general, to *parry* a kind of enemy that was not described in the textbooks —*Time*⟩ ⟨developing some adroitness in *parrying* awkward questions from the press —Edmond Taylor⟩ SIDESTEP implies a refusal to face by suddenly or ingeniously moving out of the way (as of something that threatens) ⟨a man who *sidesteps* difficulties by quick thinking —Hazel Sullivan⟩ ⟨Thomas *sidestepped* the snare which besets the prose playwright —Kenneth Tynan⟩ ⟨he realized that every single speaker, with two courageous exceptions, had *sidestepped* the issue —H.A.Overstreet⟩ DUCK, close to SIDESTEP, implies avoidance or evasion by or as if by bobbing down the head or suddenly stooping out of the way, suggesting possibly more purposeful evasion than SIDESTEP ⟨the way for a reviewer to *duck* such a question —*Newsweek*⟩ ⟨on the whole the major studios have *ducked* controversy, seldom fighting censorship —*Saturday Night*⟩ ⟨certainly some ministers and teachers have *ducked* the facts of life —McGeorge Bundy⟩ SHIRK implies evasion by means that suggest laziness, cowardice, or sneakiness ⟨that is my duty and I shall not *shirk* it —H.S.Truman⟩ ⟨a war which must be fought out and not *shirked* —Walter Moberly⟩ ⟨the critic cannot forgo the attempt nor *shirk* the responsibility —C.I. Glicksberg⟩ ⟨does not *shirk* the horrors of his scene —W.E. Allen⟩ FENCE, usu. figurative, in this context suggests any dexterous purposeful maneuver to avoid an issue or to ward something off (as embarrassing questions) ⟨spent much time in *fencing* on the witness stand⟩ ⟨it is rather odd that, after successfully *fencing* with police, prosecutors, and other officials for weeks, she should have made a slip and mentioned Halloran's name —E.D.Radin⟩ ⟨the president showed a new capability for *fencing* with the press —*Time*⟩ MALINGER implies a shirking or delaying by pretense of illness, weakness, or incapacity ⟨a *malingering* old colonel . . . pleading dysentery —*Time*⟩ ⟨*malingering* was rare, however, if we adhere to the definition that it is an act or behavior in an otherwise normal individual for the purpose of evading military duty —W.C. Menninger⟩ ⟨tried to escape it for more than ten juvenile years of my life, often successfully by playing truant day after day, or by *malingering* —F.N.Souza⟩

²**dodge** \"\ *n* -s **1 :** an act or means of evading **2 a :** avoidance (as of contact) by sudden evasive bodily movement ⟨he made a sudden ~ aside as the door swung to⟩ **b :** an artful device to evade, deceive, or trick **:** a crafty or subtle evasion ⟨the surprising ~*s* used to escape taxation⟩ ⟨just another ~ to get out of working⟩ **c :** an expedient or scheme ⟨through the ~*s* and changes of Latin America's most dangerously significant revolution —Duncan Aikman⟩ ⟨penny-pinching ~*s*⟩; *often* **:** a method, technique, or way of life that tends to effect an end usu. with notable or increased effectiveness ⟨if you think the jingle ~ is easy —H.D.Quigg⟩ ⟨got into the cowboy ~ because it looked more promising than cotton picking —Martin Levin⟩ ⟨making use of a new market ~ to increase unit sales⟩ **3 :** a backward step or one of a series of zigzags taken by a bell in change ringing **syn** see TRICK — **on the dodge** *slang* **:** living without settled abode to escape arrest

dodge ball *n* **:** a game in which players formed around a circle try to hit opponents within the circle with a large ball and in which the player or team staying unhit longest is the winner

dodge chain *n* [fr. *Dodge Chain*, a trademark] **:** an accurately pitched cable chain in which detachable bearing blocks are inserted between the links

dodge chain

Dodg·'em \ˈdäjəm\ *trademark* — used for an amusement ride consisting of small electric cars which are steered about in an enclosure and may be frequently bumped into each other

dodg·er \ˈdäjə(r)\ *n* -s **1 :** one that dodges **:** HAGGLER; *usu* **:** one who plays fast and loose or uses tricky devices **2 :** a small handbill **:** CIRCULAR, THROWAWAY **3 a :** CORN DODGER **b** *slang Austral* **:** BREAD; *broadly* **:** FOOD **4 :** a device or chemical used for photographic dodging **5 :** a canvas or wood screen to protect lookouts on a ship from spray

dodg·ery \ˈdäj(ə)rē\ *n* -ES **:** TRICKERY, ARTIFICE, *also* **:** EXPEDIENT

dodgy \ˈdäjē\ *adj* -ER/-EST **:** full of dodges **:** EVASIVE, TRICKY

dod·kin \ˈdädkən\ *n* -s [AF *doydekyn*, fr. MD *duitkijn*, dim. of *duit* doit — more at DOIT] *archaic* **:** DOIT

dod·man \ˈdädmən\ *n* -s [origin unknown] *dial Eng* **:** SNAIL

do·do \ˈdō(,)dō\ *n, pl* **dodoes** *or* **dodos** [Pg *doudo*, fr. *doudo* silly, stupid] **1 a :** a large heavy flightless extinct bird (*Raphus cucullatus*, syn. *Didus ineptus*) related to the pigeons but larger than a turkey, that had dark ash-colored plumage with the breast and tail whitish, the rudimentary wings being yellowish white with black-tipped coverts, the bill blackish, and the legs yellow; that inhabited forests and laid a single large white egg in a nest of grass; and that was present in great numbers on the island of Mauritius prior to the arrival of European settlers but became extinct by 1681 **b :** a similar and apparently closely related bird of the neighboring island of Réunion that became extinct under similar circumstances at a slightly later date **2 a :** a person who is simplemindedly unaware of changing conditions and new ideas **:** a dull stupid person **b** *slang* **:** a flight cadet who has not yet soloed **3** *also* **dodo ball :** an illegally weighted bowling ball

dodo

do·do·naea \,dōdᵊnˈēə\ *n, cap* [NL, after Rembert *Dodoens* (*Dodonaeus*) †1585 Dutch botanist] **:** a genus of tropical shrubs or trees (family Sapindaceae) with alternate gummy leaves and reticulated capsules

do·do·nae·an \¦dōdᵊn¦ēən\ *or* **do·do·ne·an** \", dəˈdōnēən\ *also* **do·do·ni·an** \dəˈdōnēən\ *or* **do·do·nae·ic** \¦dōdᵊn¦ēik\ *adj* [L *Dodonaeus* (fr. Gk *Dōdōnaios*, fr. *Dōdōnē* Dodona, town and oracle in northwestern Greece) + E *-an*, *-ian* or *-ic*] **:** of or relating to the ancient oracle of Zeus at Dodona on Mount Tomarus in Epirus

dodo split *n* **:** a spare formation in bowling in which the headpin and either the 7 or 10 pin are left standing

do down *vt, Brit* **:** to get the better of (as by trickery) **:** OVERCOME ⟨if it's a game of skill you'll *do* me *down* —W.J.Locke⟩ ⟨hope you don't think I'm *doing* you *down* over selling the house —Clemence Dane⟩

do·drans \ˈdō,dranz\ *n, pl* **dodran·tes** \dōˈdran·,tēz\ [L, three quarters of an as, three quarters, alter. of (assumed) *dequadrans*, fr. *de* from + *quadrans* quarter of an as, quarter — more at DE, QUADRANT] **:** a unit of six syllables in Greek and Latin prosody of which either the last four or the first four form a choriambus and the other two are of indeterminate quantity — symbol (ᴗ ᴗ –ᴗᴗ– or –ᴗᴗ–ᴗ ᴗ)

dod-rot \(ˈ)däd¦rät\ *vt* [euphemism for *God rot*] **:** DAMN — used as a mild oath ⟨*dod-rot* their souls —P.E.Green⟩ ⟨that *dod-rotted* old lady —R.D.Saunders⟩

¹**dods** *pres 3d sing of* DOD, *pl of* DOD

²**dods** \ˈdädz\ *n pl* [ScGael *dod* + E *-s*] *Scot* **:** a grouchy mood **:** SULKS

do·dunk \ˈdō,dəŋk\ *n* -s [origin unknown] *NewEng* **:** a stupid person **:** DULLARD

doe \ˈdō\ *n, pl* **does** *or* **doe** [ME *do*, *doo*, fr. OE *dā*; akin to G dial. (Alemannic) *tē* doe and perh. to Skt *dhayati* he sucks — more at FEMININE] **1 a :** the adult female fallow deer **b :** the female esp. when adult of any of various mammals of which the male is called buck (as most deers, antelope, goat, rabbit, and rat) — compare COW, HIND **2 :** ALMOND 6a

doe·ling \ˈdōliŋ\ *n* -s [¹*doe* + *-ling*] **:** a young unbred female goat

do·er \ˈdüə(r), ˈdu̇(ə)r, ˈdu̇ə\ *n* -s [ME, fr. *don* to do + *-er* — more at DO] **1 :** one that does **:** one that performs or executes ⟨a thinker or a ~ —Sinclair Lewis⟩ **2 :** a domestic animal considered in terms of its capacity to respond to proper care and feeding — used with a qualifying adjective ⟨those steers are very poor ~*s*⟩ ⟨it doesn't pay to hold over any but your best ~*s*⟩ **3** *Austral* **:** ECCENTRIC

does *pres 3d sing of* DO

doeskin \ˈ=,=\ *n* [ME *doskin*, fr. *do* + *skin*] **1 :** the skin of does or leather made of it; *also* **:** soft glove leather tanned from sheep or lambskins by a formaldehyde and alum process **2 :** a compact coating and sportswear fabric napped and felted for a smooth surface and made in satin weave of wool or worsted or in twill weave of cotton or rayon

doeskin brown *n* **:** MONKEY SKIN

does·n't \ˈdəzᵊn(t), *rapid* ˈdəd|\ [by contr.] **:** does not

doest *archaic pres 2d sing of* DO

doeth *archaic pres 3d sing of* DO

DOF *abbr* delivery on field

¹**doff** \ˈdäf, ˈdȯf\ *vb* -ED/-ING/-s [ME *doffen*, fr. *don* to do + *offe*, *off* off] *vt* **1 a :** to divest oneself of (clothing) **:** take off (one's clothes); *esp* **:** to lift (the hat) **b :** to lay aside **:** rid oneself of ⟨retailers have ~*ed* their rose-colored glasses —Gene Boyo⟩ **2** *obs* **:** to put off (as an unwelcome petitioner) **:** turn away **3 :** to remove (material) from a textile-manufacturing machine ⟨~ full bobbins from a spinning frame⟩ ⟨~ cotton from a carding machine⟩ ~ *vi* **1** *obs* **:** to take off clothing **:** UNDRESS **2** *archaic* **:** to take off or raise the hat

²**doff** \"\ *n* -s **:** the act of removing material from a textile-manufacturing machine; *also* **:** material so removed

doff·er \-fə(r)\ *n* -s **1 a :** a small roller usu. covered with wire teeth used to strip material from another roller or cylinder on textile machinery; *esp* **:** a roller on a carding machine **b :** a machine or device for doffing bobbins **c :** a device for stripping cotton from the spindle of a mechanical cotton picker **2 :** a textile worker who removes full bobbins or cones from machines and puts in empty ones

doffing *adj* **:** relating to or used in the process of removing material from a doffer or carder ⟨~ comb⟩ ⟨~ cylinder⟩

do for \ˈdüfə(r), -,fȯ. . .\ *vt* **1 :** to attend to the wants and needs of **:** take care of; *esp* **:** to act as the domestic servant of ⟨during her illness she was *done for* by a neighbor⟩ **2 :** to bring about the death or ruin of **:** DESTROY, KILL ⟨a gash in the side of the helmet which would have *done for* a man of lesser breed —Richard Joseph⟩

do·fun·ny *or* **doo·fun·ny** \ˈdü,fənē\ *n* [¹*do* + *funny*] **:** DOODAD, GADGET

¹**dog** \ˈdȯg *sometimes* ˈdäg\ *n* -s [ME *dog*, *dogge*, fr. OE *docga*] **1 a :** a carnivorous mammal (*Canis familiaris*) of the family Canidae that has been kept in a domesticated state by man since prehistoric times, is undoubtedly descended from some unknown wild member of the genus *Canis* possibly the common wolf, varies in its artificially produced breeds far more than any other mammal (as in form, size, color, and length and character of coat), and is kept chiefly for sporting use or as a guard or companion or esp. formerly for light draft and other labor; *broadly* **:** any animal of the family Canidae **b :** a male dog — opposed to *bitch* **2 a :** a mean worthless fellow **:** CUR, WRETCH, RASCAL ⟨~ of an unbeliever —Sir Walter Scott⟩ **b :** a sportive or roguish fellow **:** BIRD, CHAP ⟨a gay old ~⟩ **c :** FELLOW — used with a qualifying adj. ⟨a lazy ~⟩ ⟨a very sad ~⟩ **3 :** any of various usu. simple mechanical devices for holding, gripping, or fastening something: as **a :** any of various devices consisting essentially of a spike, rod, or bar of metal with a ring, hook, claw, or lug at the end used in various ways (as by driving or embedding in an object or hooking to an object) **b :** either of the hooks of a pair of sling dogs **c :** an iron for holding wood in a fireplace **:** FIREDOG, ANDIRON **d :** a clamp in a lathe for gripping the piece of work and for communicating motion to it from the faceplate **e :** STOP, DETENT, CLICK **f :** a drag for the wheel of a vehicle **g :** a short heavy sharp-pointed steel hook with a ring at one end **h :** a steel projection on a log carriage or on an endless chain that conveys logs into a sawmill **i :** the hammer in a gunlock **4 a** (1) **:** DOGFISH (2) **:** DOG SALMON (3) **:** PRAIRIE DOG **b** (1) **:** SUN DOG (2) **:** WATER DOG 4 (3) **:** FOGBOW **c** (1) **:** DOGSHORE (2) **:** DOGWATCH **d :** HOT DOG **5 :** ostentatious display **:** affected stylishness or dignity ⟨there was a lot of ~ about the affair⟩; *often* **:** dress and behavior not characteristic of or suited to one's station — used esp. in the phrase *put on the dog* **6 :** dogskin used as fur **7 dogs** *pl, slang* **:** FEET **8 :** something inferior of its kind ⟨you call your agent but the only scripts available are real ~*s* —Paul Newman⟩ **9 dogs** *pl* **:** RUINATION, DESTRUCTION — used with *the* ⟨it's enough to drive anyone to the ~*s*⟩ ⟨everything is going to the ~*s* around here⟩ **10 :** PROMISSORY NOTE **11 a :** a poor investment; *usu* **:** a stock or bond not worth its price **b :** a domestic animal of inferior quality or performance **c :** a sluggish horse or a racehorse that does not do well in competition **d :** a low-grade beef animal **e :** a slow-moving or undesirable piece of merchandise — compare RUNNER **f :** a poor-quality motor vehicle **:** LEMON; *esp* **:** a badly worn used car **g** *slang* **:** a woman inferior in looks, character, or accomplishments; *sometimes* **:** PROSTITUTE **h** *slang* **:** a theatrical or musical flop **:** a poor, hackneyed, or outmoded presentation **12** *usu cap* **:** any of certain American Indian peoples: as **a :** CHEYENNE **b :** FOX **13 dogs** *pl* **:** dog racing **14 :** one of the wooden sawhorses placed on a racetrack near the rail when the track is soft to keep horses out of the mud during workouts

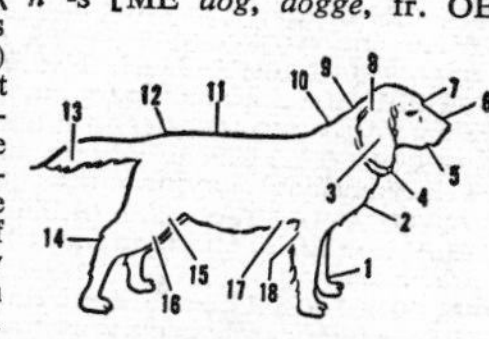

dog: *1* pastern, *2* chest, *3* leather, *4* dewlap, *5* flews, *6* muzzle, *7* stop, *8* occiput, *9* crest, *10* withers, *11* loin, *12* rump, *13* feather, *14* hock, *15* stifle, *16* knee, *17* brisket, *18* elbow

²**dog** \"\ *vb* **dogged** \-gd\ **dogged** \"\ **dogging; dogs** *vt* **1 a :** to hunt or track like a hound **:** follow insidiously or indefatigably ⟨she *dogged* him until he gave in and married her⟩ **b :** to chase with a dog **c :** to worry as if by dogs **:** HOUND ⟨he was *dogged* by financial worries⟩ **2 :** to fasten with a dog — sometimes used with *down* ⟨a sailor *dogged* down the hatch⟩ **3** *South & Midland* **:** DAMN, DARN ⟨well ~ my boot⟩ ⟨~ it all⟩ ~ *vi, archaic* **:** to follow slavishly or pertinaciously — **dog it 1** *slang* **:** to run away **2** *slang* **:** to fail to try one's best **:** loaf on the job **:** GOLDBRICK — **dog the watches :** to change the order of night watches by means of dogwatches

³**dog** \"\ *adv* **:** EXTREMELY, VERY, UTTERLY — often used in combination ⟨*dog-poor*⟩ ⟨*dog-tired*⟩ ⟨*dog-lame*⟩

⁴**dog** \"\ *adj* **1 :** of or for dogs ⟨~ diseases⟩ ⟨~ breeders⟩ ⟨a ~ collar⟩ **:** CANINE **2 :** MALE — used chiefly of carnivorous mammals ⟨a ~ otter⟩ **3 :** MONGREL, SPURIOUS, INFERIOR ⟨~ rhyme⟩; *esp* **:** unlike that used by native speakers or writers ⟨~ Latin⟩ ⟨~ French⟩

⁵**dog** \"\ *usu cap* — a communications code word for the letter *d*

dog alley *n, Midland* **:** DOGTROT

do·ga·na \dōˈgänə\ *n* -s [It, fr. Ar *dīwān*, fr. Per, account book] **:** an Italian customhouse

dog ape *n* **:** a baboon or related monkey

do·ga·res·sa \,dōgəˈresə\ *n* -s [It, fr. It dial. (Venice), fr. L *ducatrix* female leader, fem. of *duc-*, *dux* leader — more at DUKE] **:** the wife of a doge

dogbane *also* **dog's-bane** \ˈ=,=\ *n, pl* **dogbanes** *also* **dog's-banes 1 :** a plant of the genus *Apocynum* **2 :** WOLFSBANE 1

dogbane family *n* **:** APOCYNACEAE

dog bent *or* **dog's bent** *n* [so called fr. its being eaten by sick dogs, supposedly as an emetic] **:** a common grass (*Agrostis canina*) with slender culms, narrow leaves, and a long-awned lemma

¹**dog·ber·ry** \ˈdȯg,berē *sometimes* ˈdäg-\ *n, pl* **dogberrys** *usu cap* [fr. *Dogberry*, a foolish constable in Shakespeare's *Much Ado about Nothing*] **:** a blundering official; *often* **:** POLICEMAN, CONSTABLE

²**dogberry** \ˈ=— *see* BERRY\ *n* [¹*dog* + *berry*] **1 :** any of certain small fruits usu. considered inferior or unfit for human consumption (as the chokeberry, prickly wild gooseberry, certain rose hips, or the fruit of the mountain ash); *esp* **:** the fruit of the red dogwood **2 :** any plant (as certain dogwoods, mountain ash, or yellow clintonia) that bears dogberries

dogberry tree *n* **:** RED OSIER 2

dog biscuit *n* **:** a hard dry cracker for dogs containing cereal and other vegetable nutrients together with meat and bone meals and flavoring; *sometimes* **:** a hard coarse cracker (as hardtack) for human consumption

dogbit \ˈ=,=\ *adj, South & Midland* **:** bitten by a dog

dogbody \ˈ=,==\ *n* [so called fr. its square stern] **:** a square-sterned boat similar to a chebacco boat

¹**dog·bolt** \ˈ=,bōlt\ *n* [ME *doggebolde*, perh. fr. *dogge* dog + *bolde* bold — more at DOG, BOLD] *archaic* **:** wretched fellow **:** mean contemptible person

²**dogbolt** \"\ *n* [¹*dog* + *bolt*] **1 :** a long slim bolt for uniting two parts at right angles or for securing girders to a supporting post by being driven through one piece then bent and driven into the other **2 :** a bolt used to hold the work in machining

³**dogbolt** \"\ *vt* **:** to secure with a dogbolt

dog brier *n* [trans. of L *sentis canis*] **:** DOG ROSE

dog bur *n* **:** a hound's-tongue (*Cynoglossum officinale*); *also* **:** WILD COMFREY

dog button *n* [so called fr. its having been used to poison dogs] **:** NUX VOMICA

dog cabbage *or* **dog's cabbage** *n* **:** a fleshy southern European herb (*Cynocrambe prostrata*) often eaten as a potherb

dog camomile *n* **:** MAYWEED

dog carrier *n* **:** a ventilated crate with a handle on the top for transporting small or medium-sized dogs

dogcart \ˈ=,=\ *n* **1 :** a cart drawn by a dog or dogs **2 :** a light usu. one-horse carriage that is commonly two-wheeled and high with two transverse seats set back to back

dogcart 2

dogcatcher \ˈ=,==\ *n* **1 :** one that catches dogs; *specif* **:** a person employed or elected to catch and get rid of the stray dogs of a community **2** *slang* **:** a member of a train crew sent to relieve another who is temporarily prohibited by law from further train operation because of having worked 16 hours consecutively

dog-cheap \ˈ⸗ˌ⸗\ *adv (or adj)* **1 :** CHEAPLY **:** for a very low price ⟨he worked *dog-cheap*⟩ ⟨if you come across another *dog-cheap* house —Mark Twain⟩ **2** *archaic* **:** in little repute
dog clutch *n* **:** a machinery clutch in which projections of one element fit into recesses in the other
dog cockle *n* **:** any of certain marine bivalve mollusks (family Glycymeridae) having substantial rounded shells with dark velvety periostraca and prominent hinge teeth, a crescentic foot, and an open mantle and living chiefly on the bottom of warm seas
dog collar *n* **1 :** a collar for a dog **2 :** *slang* **:** CLERICAL COLLAR **2 :** a wide flexible necklace fitting the neck snugly that is often composed of multiple rows of gems or beads
dog daisy *n* **:** any of several composite plants having flower heads with white rays (as certain daisies, the mayweed, or the field chamomile)
dog dance *n* **:** a ceremonial dance among certain western No. American Indians; *esp* **:** one in which eating of dog meat was a feature
dog dandelion *n* **:** FALL DANDELION
dog day *n* [back-formation fr. *dog days,* trans. of LL *dies caniculares,* trans. of Gk *hēmerai kynades;* fr. their being reckoned in ancient times from the heliacal rising of the Dog Star (Sirius)] **1 a dog days** *pl* **:** the period between early July and early September when the hot sultry weather of summer usu. occurs **b :** a day in dog days **:** a hot sultry day **2 dog days** *pl* **:** a period marked by dull lack of progress ⟨the *dog days* following any major upheaval⟩
dog-day cicada *n* **:** any of several large American cicadas (genus *Tibicen*) having a prolonged trilling note that is heard esp. in late summer
dog disease *n* **:** DISTEMPER 2a
dog dollar *n* **:** a silver dollar of the Netherlands that circulated in New Jersey, Pennsylvania, and Maryland about 1700 and had on the obverse a lion rampant
dog·dom \ˈ⸗dəm\ *n* -s **:** the world of dogs or of dog fanciers
doge \ˈdōj, *It* ˈdȯjā\ *n, pl* **dog·es** \ˈdōjəz\ [It, fr. It dial. (Venice), fr. L *duc-, dux* leader — more at DUKE] **:** the chief magistrate in the former republics of Venice (697–1797) and Genoa (1339–1797 and 1802–5) — **doge·ship** \ˈdōj,ship\ *n*
¹dog-ear *also* **dog's-ear** \ˈ⸗ˌ⸗\ *vt* **:** to disfigure or damage with a dog-ear ⟨a book for me is something to be read . . . I want to *dog-ear* it, to underline it, to annotate it —John Mason Brown⟩
²dog-ear *also* **dog's-ear** \ˈ"\ *n, pl* **dog-ears** *also* **dog's-ears 1 :** the corner of a leaf esp. of a book turned down like the ear of a fox terrier **2 :** the small bight made in the leech rope of a sail in reefing
dog-eared *also* **dog's-eared** *adj* **1 :** having dog-ears ⟨a *dog-eared* book⟩ **2 :** WORN, SHABBY, DISFIGURED ⟨a somewhat *dog-eared* . . . duke, a bit run down —Clifton Fadiman⟩
¹dog-eat-dog \ˈ⸗ˌ⸗ˈ⸗\ *adj* **:** marked by ruthless self-interest ⟨a *dog-eat-dog* business from start to finish, with each side playing a fast and underhanded game —F.B.Gipson⟩
²dog-eat-dog *n* **:** ruthless self-interest ⟨a raw tough city where *dog-eat-dog* was the law —*New Republic*⟩
dogey *var of* DOGIE
dogface \ˈ⸗ˌ⸗\ *n* **:** an army soldier; *esp* **:** INFANTRYMAN
dog-faced ape \ˈ⸗ˌfāst-\ *or* **dog-faced baboon** *n* **:** BABOON
¹dogfall \ˈ⸗ˌ⸗\ *n* [¹*dog* + *fall*] **1 :** a falling in wrestling of both contestants in which neither is given an advantage **2 :** an inconclusive result to any kind of contest **:** DRAW, TIE **3 :** a throw of a steer resulting in a position with his feet still under him
²dogfall \ˈ"\ *vt* -ED/-ING/-S **:** to put (a steer) down by roping or bulldogging with his feet under him
dog fennel *n* **1 :** MAYWEED 1 **2 :** an annual weed (*Eupatorium capillifolium*) with dissected leaves and a lax elongate inflorescence
¹dogfight \ˈ⸗ˌ⸗\ *n* [¹*dog* + *fight*] **1 :** a fight between or as if between dogs **:** MELEE; *broadly* **:** a fiercely disputed contest ⟨political ~s and skulduggery⟩ **2 :** a fight in aerial warfare between two or more fighter planes usu. maneuvering at close quarters
²dogfight \ˈ"\ *vi* **:** to engage in an aerial dogfight ~ *vt* **:** to dogfight with
dogfish \ˈ⸗ˌ⸗\ *n* [ME *dokefyche,* fr. *doke, dogge* dog + *fyche, fissh* fish — more at DOG, FISH] **1 :** any of various small sharks (as of the families Squalidae, Carcharhinidae, and Scyliorhinidae) that often appear in schools near shore, that are destructive to fish and fishing gear, and that have livers valued for oil and flesh often made into fertilizer — see SMOOTH DOGFISH, SPINY DOGFISH **2 :** any of various other fishes: as **a :** BOWFIN **b :** the New World burbot **c :** BLACKFISH 1f **3 :** a mud puppy (*Necturus maculosus*)
dog flea *n* **:** a flea (*Ctenocephalides canis*) feeding chiefly on dogs and cats
dog flower *n* **1 :** DAISY 1b **2 :** PURPLE TRILLIUM
dog fly *n* **:** STABLE FLY 1
dogfoot \ˈ⸗ˌ⸗\ *n* [so called fr. the appearance of the flower panicles] **:** ORCHARD GRASS
dog·ged \ˈdȯgəd *sometimes* ˈdäg-\ *adj* [ME, fr. *dog, dogge* dog + *-ed* — more at DOG] **1** *obs* **:** DOGLIKE; *esp* **:** exhibiting unattractive qualities (as belligerence) sometimes attributed to dogs **2 :** obstinately determined **:** UNSHAKABLE, UNREMITTING ⟨~ determination⟩ ⟨resumed his ~ efforts⟩ **syn** see OBSTINATE
dog·ged·ly \-gədlē, -li\ *adv* [ME, fr. *dogged* + *-ly*] **:** in a dogged manner
dog·ged·ness \-gədnəs\ *n* -ES **:** the quality or state of being dogged **:** RESOLUTENESS
¹dog·ger \-gə(r)\ *n* -S [ME *doggere,* perh. fr. MD *dogge* fishing boat] **:** a broad-bowed two-masted fishing boat used esp. by the Dutch in the North sea
²dogger \ˈ"\ *n* -S [¹*dog* (contrivance) + *-er*] **:** a worker who attaches dogs (as to logs), moves articles mechanically by dogs, or fastens articles (as stock to be machined) into dogs that will hold them for further processing
³dogger \ˈ"\ *adj, usu cap* [fr. *dogger,* a kind of ironstone prevalent in strata of this period, of unknown origin] **:** of, relating to, or constituting a subdivision of the European Jurassic — see GEOLOGIC TIME table
¹dog·ger·el *also* **dog·grel** \ˈdȯg(ə)rəl, ˈdäg-\ *adj* [ME *dogerel*] **1** *of poetry* **:** quickly contrived, loose, and often irregular esp. if also burlesque or comic **2** *of poetry* **:** trivial or bad ⟨not poetry but mere ~ verse⟩
²doggerel *also* **doggrel** \ˈ"\ *n* -s **1 :** doggerel verse **2 :** a poem in doggerel
dog·gery \ˈdȯgərē, -ri *sometimes* ˈdäg-\ *n* -ES [¹*dog* + *-ery*] **1 :** doglike behavior; *usu* **:** mean or mischievous actions **2 a :** DOGS **b :** RABBLE, MOB **3** *archaic slang* **:** a low grogshop
dogging *pres part of* DOG
dog·gish \-gish, -gēsh\ *adj* [ME *doggissh,* fr. *dogge* dog + *-issh* -ish — more at DOG] **1 :** like a dog esp. in bad qualities **:** CURRISH, SNAPPISH, SULKY **2 :** stylish in a showy way **:** DASHING — **dog·gish·ly** *adv* — **dog·gish·ness** *n* -ES
dog·gle \ˈdägəl\ *n* -S [origin unknown] *Scot* **:** a child's marble
dog·go \ˈdȯ(ˌ)gō *sometimes* ˈdä(-\ *adv* [prob. fr. *dog* + *-o*] *slang* **:** quietly out of sight esp. in concealment — used chiefly in the phrase *to lie doggo*
¹dog·gone \ˈdägˈgän *also* ˈdȯgˈgȯn — *many who have* ȯ *in "dog" and/or "gone" have* ä *in both syllables of "doggone"*\ *vt* -ED/-ING/-S [euphemism for *God damn*] **:** ¹DAMN 5 ⟨~ him⟩ ⟨I'll be *doggoned* if I'll go⟩
²doggone \ˈ"\ *or* **dog·goned** \-n(d)\ *adj* -ER/-EST [euphemism for *God damn, God damned*] **:** DAMNED 2 ⟨go and use up all the towels, every ~ one of them —Sinclair Lewis⟩ ⟨one of the *doggonedest* quirks there is in human nature —W.J.Reilly⟩
³doggone \ˈ"\ *or* **doggoned** \ˈ"\ *adv* [euphemism for *God damn, God damned*] **:** DAMNED ⟨has been pretty ~ self-centered —James Kelly⟩ ⟨is not the country too *doggoned* big? —*New Republic*⟩
⁴doggone \ˈ"\ *n* -S [euphemism for *God damn*] **:** ²DAMN 2 ⟨doesn't give a ~ what happens⟩
dog grass *also* **dog's grass** *n* [so called fr. its being eaten by sick dogs] **1 :** DOG BENT **2 :** COUCH GRASS 1a **3 :** YARD GRASS
dog grate *n* **:** a movable metal frame or basket orig. supported on dogs or andirons that is used for burning logs or coal in a fireplace
doggrel *var of* DOGGEREL
¹dog·gy \ˈdȯgē, -gi *sometimes* ˈdäg-\ *adj* **doggier; doggiest** [ME, fr. *dogge* dog + *-y* (adj. ending) — more at DOG] **1 :** like or like that of a dog ⟨a ~ odor⟩ **2 a** *of wool* **:** straight, lustrous, and inferior in quality **:** like the hair of a dog **b** *of a bitch* **:** masculine in conformation **3 :** interested or specializing in or fond of dogs ⟨the country club and ~ sets⟩ ⟨a book of interest to all ~ experts⟩ **4 :** DASHING, STYLISH; *often* **:** pretentiously fashionable
²doggy \ˈ"\ *or* **doggie** \ˈ"\ *n, pl* **doggies** [¹*dog* + *-y, -ie* (dim. suffix)] **1 :** a small dog — used also as a pet name or calling name for any dog **2** *usu* **doggie :** DOGFACE
doghead \ˈ⸗ˌ⸗\ *n* **:** the hammer of a gunlock
dogheaded \ˈ⸗ˌ⸗ˌ⸗\ *adj* **:** having a head shaped like that of a dog ⟨~ bears⟩
dog hip *or* **dog hep** *n, dial Brit* **:** the fruit of the dog rose
dog hobble *n* [so called fr. its tough interlacing branches that obstruct the progress of dogs] **:** DOG LAUREL
doghole \ˈ⸗ˌ⸗\ *n* **1 :** a place fit only for dogs **2 :** a mean miserable abode **3 :** a small opening (as in a mine) **4** *West* **:** a small inlet on the coast where ships tie up in order to load lumber
dog hook *n* **:** any of various hooks used in logging
doghouse \ˈ⸗ˌ⸗\ *n* **1 :** a shelter for a dog **:** KENNEL **2 :** something felt to resemble a kennel esp. in form or compactness: as **a :** a shed for workmen to store and change clothes (as at a pithead or oil-well drilling); *also* **:** TOOLSHED **b :** the housing of a machine part **c :** a shelter over the cockpit or deck of a boat **d :** an entry chamber through which the batch is fed into a glass furnace **e** *slang* **:** CABOOSE 3 **f** *slang* **:** CIRCUMFLEX 1 ⟨ô is sometimes called ~ o⟩ — **in the doghouse** *adv (or adj)* **:** in a state of disfavor or repudiation ⟨put *in the doghouse* for getting drunk the other night⟩ ⟨has been *in the doghouse* with the administration for months⟩
dog hysteria *n* **:** CANINE HYSTERIA
do·gie *also* **do·gey** *or* **do·gy** \ˈdōgē, -gi\ *n* -S [origin unknown] *chiefly West* **:** a motherless calf in a range herd; *sometimes* **:** a poor or inferior adult animal
dogies *pl of* DOGY
dog in the manger [so called fr. the fable of the dog who would not allow a horse or ox to eat the hay in a manger, even though he did not want it himself] **:** a person who selfishly withholds from others something that he himself cannot use or does not need
dog iron *n* **1** *South & Midland* **:** ANDIRON **2 :** a short bar of iron having its ends bent at right angles for use as a cramp or joggle (as to hold together timbers or stones) **3 :** a short bar of iron with an eye at one end for driving or fitting into a timber or stone to hold it or lift it

dog iron 3

dog killer \ˈ⸗ˌ⸗⸗\ *n* **:** a person in charge of killing mad or unwanted dogs
dog laurel *n* **:** an evergreen shrub (*Leucothoe editorum*) of the southern U.S. with racemose white flowers
dog leech *n* **1** *archaic* **:** QUACK 1 **2** *archaic* **:** one that treats dogs' diseases
¹dogleg \ˈ⸗ˌ⸗\ *n* **1 :** tobacco of poor quality marketed in twists **2 :** something having an abrupt angle felt to resemble the hind leg of a dog: as **a** *or* **dogleg hole :** a golf hole having an angled fairway that offers the player a choice of following the fairway or risking a shot across the rough **b :** KINK ⟨a ~ in a cable⟩ ⟨a ~ in pipe⟩ **c :** a course (as of an airplane) involving movement first in one direction then in another; *also* **:** an abrupt change in course or direction
²dogleg \ˈ"\ *also* **doglegged** *US usu* -ˌlegəd, *Brit usu* -gd\ *or* **dog's-leg** *adj* **:** crooked or bent like a dog's hind leg; *specif, of stairs* **:** consisting of two or more flights connected by a platform or platforms and running in opposite directions without an intervening well
³dogleg \ˈ"\ *vi* [¹*dogleg* (course)] **:** to proceed along a dogleg course
dogleg fence *n* **:** WORM FENCE
dog letter *var of* DOG'S LETTER
dog lichen *n* **:** a common foliose lichen (*Peltigera canina*) that has the thallus brownish green above and whitish beneath and fruiting bodies resembling the teeth of a dog and that was formerly believed to cure hydrophobia
doglike \ˈ⸗ˌ⸗\ *adj* **:** felt to resemble a dog **:** characteristic of a dog esp. in dumb devotion ⟨a ~ affection⟩
dog lily *n* **:** SPATTERDOCK 1
dog louse *n* **:** either of two lice that infest dogs: **a :** a bird louse (*Trichodectes canis*) **b :** a sucking louse (*Linognathus setosus*)
dog·ly \ˈdȯglē *sometimes* ˈdäg-\ *adj* **:** CANINE
dog·ma \ˈdȯgmə *also* ˈdägmə\ *n, pl* **dogmas** \-məz\ *also* **dogma·ta** \-məd·ə, -mətə\ [L, fr. Gk, fr. *dokein* to seem good, seem, think — more at DECENT] **1 a :** something held as an established opinion; *esp* **:** one or more definite and authoritative tenets **b :** a code or systematized formulation of such tenets (as by a theoretician or a school of art or philosophy) ⟨pedagogical ~⟩ ⟨communist ~⟩ **c :** a point of view or alleged authoritative tenet put forth as dogma without adequate grounds **:** an arrogant or vehement expression of opinion **2 :** a doctrine or body of doctrines of theology and religion formally stated and authoritatively proclaimed by a church **syn** see DOCTRINE
dog·man \ˈdȯgmən *sometimes* ˈdäg-; *in sense "specialist"* -ˌman\ *n, pl* **dogmen 1 :** KENNELMAN **2 :** a dog fancier or specialist ⟨the best ~ among our local veterinarians⟩
¹dog·mat·ic \dȯgˈmad·|ik -at|, |ēk *also* däg-\ *n* -S [Gk *dogmatikos,* fr. *dogmatikos,* adj.] **1** *archaic* **:** DOGMATIST **2** *archaic* **:** DOGMATICS
²dogmatic \(ˈ)⸗ˈ⸗|⸗\ *also* **dog·mat·i·cal** \(ˈ)⸗ˈ⸗|əkəl, |ēk-\ *adj* [LL *dogmaticus,* fr. Gk *dogmatikos,* fr. *dogmat-, dogma* + *-ikos* -ic] **1 a :** characterized by or given to the use of dogmatism ⟨a ~ critic⟩ **:** asserting a matter of opinion as if it were fact **:** directly affirmed rather than qualified, debated, or discovered by induction ⟨a ~ statement⟩ **b :** excessively positive in manner or utterance **2 a :** based on or proceeding from a priori truths or assumptions rather than empirical evidence **:** DEDUCTIVE ⟨~ philosophy⟩ **b :** of or relating to a school using a dogmatic approach ⟨a ~ physician⟩ **3 :** of, relating to, or constituting established and authorized doctrine **:** DOCTRINAL ⟨~ writings of the early fathers⟩ — **dog·mat·i·cal·ly** \|ək(ə)lē, |ēk-, -li\ *adv* — **dog·mat·i·cal·ness** \-kəlnəs\ *n* -ES
dog·ma·ti·cian \ˌdȯgməˈtishən *also* ˌdäg-\ *n* -S **:** a specialist in dogmatics or dogmatism
dog·mat·i·cism \dȯgˈmad·|əˌsizəm, -at| *also* däg-\ *n* -S **:** DOGMATISM 1
dog·mat·ics \|iks,|ēks\ *n pl but sing or pl in constr* **:** a branch of theology dealing with religious doctrines **:** DOGMATIC THEOLOGY
dogmatic theology *n* **:** doctrinal theology that seeks to present the intellectual content of a religious faith and to explicate its meaning from the base of authoritative doctrines generally regarded as derived from revelation **:** DOGMATICS
dog·ma·tism \ˈdȯgməˌtizəm *also* ˈdäg-\ *n* -S [F *dogmatisme,* fr. MF, fr. L *dogmat-, dogma* + MF *-isme* -ism] **1 a :** positiveness in assertion in matters of opinion **:** statement of a view or belief as if it were an established fact; *often* **:** marked positiveness of statement when unwarranted or arrogant **b :** the use of dogmatic statement as a method of exposition ⟨the ~ of Emerson's writings⟩ **2 a :** a viewpoint or system of ideas based upon insufficiently examined premises **b :** a doctrine that insists upon the existence of certain truths and is opposed to skepticism **c :** philosophy grounded in principles preponderantly established by reason to the neglect of recourse to experience; *specif* **:** an epistemologically uncritical philosophical system
dog·ma·tist \-məd·əst, -mət-\ *n* -S [MF & ML; MF *dogmatiste,* fr. ML *dogmatista,* fr. Gk *dogmatistēs,* fr. *dogmatizein*] **1 :** a person who believes in or propounds dogmatism **:** a member of a dogmatic school (as of philosophy) **2** *archaic* **:** a propounder of new dogma **3 :** a person who dogmatizes or employs dogmatic methods of exposition; *sometimes* **:** a presumptuously dogmatic person
dog·ma·ti·za·tion \ˌ⸗məd·əˈzāshən, -mətə-, -məˌtīˈz-\ *n* -S **:** an act or instance of dogmatizing
dog·ma·tize \ˈ⸗məˌtīz\ *vb* -ED/-ING/-S [F *dogmatiser,* fr. LL *dogmatizare* to lay down an opinion, fr. Gk *dogmatizein,* fr. *dogmat-, dogma* + *-izein* -ize] *vi* **:** to speak or write dogmatically **:** make declarations or contend confidently or arrogantly about matters that are open to question ⟨had no wish to ~ concerning the best mode of living —V.L.Parrington⟩ ~ *vt* **:** to state as a dogma or dogmatically — **dog·ma·tiz·er** \-zə(r)\ *n* -S
dogmeat \ˈ⸗ˌ⸗\ *n* **1** *also* **dog's meat :** meat for or fit only for dogs; *sometimes* **:** OFFAL, CARRION **2 a :** dog flesh used as food **b :** inferior table meat; *broadly* **:** something disliked
dog mercury *var of* DOG'S MERCURY
dog mint *n* **:** WILD BASIL
dogmouth *var of* DOG'S-MOUTH
dog nail *n* **1 :** a nail with a head that fits flush in a countersink **2 :** a nail with a head projecting considerably on one side
dog nap *n* **:** a brief sleep
dog·nap \ˈdȯgˌnap *sometimes* ˈdäg-\ *vt* **dognapped; dognapped; dognapping; dognaps** [¹*dog* + *-nap* (as in *kidnap*)] **:** to steal or lure away (a dog) — **dog·nap·per** \-apə(r)\ *n* -S
dog nettle *n* **1 :** HEMP NETTLE **2 :** an annual dead nettle (*Lamium purpureum*) having deep green or purplish leaves, a hairy calyx, and a ring of hairs inside the slender corolla tube
do·gon \ˈdōˌgän\ *n, pl* **dogon** *or* **dogons** *usu cap* **1 :** a people located in the central bend of the Niger and noted for their woodcarving esp. of masks **2 :** a member of the Dogon people
do-good \ˈ⸗ˌ⸗\ *or* **do-good·ing** \ˈ⸗ˌ⸗iŋ\ *adj* **:** designed sometimes impracticably and overzealously toward bettering the conditions under which others live ⟨*do-good* schemes⟩ ⟨little patience with the *do-gooding* type of foreign aid —*Time*⟩ — **do-good·ism** \-ˌizəm\ *n* -S
do-good·er \ˈ⸗ˈ⸗ə(r)\ *n* -S **:** an earnest usu. impractical-minded humanitarian bent on promoting welfare work or reform — commonly used with a derogatory implication of naïveté or blundering ineffectualness
dog paddle \ˈ⸗ˌ⸗⸗\ *n* **:** an elementary form of swimming often learned by children in which the arms reach forward alternately in the water, the head remains above water, and the legs maintain a kicking motion
dog-paddle \ˈ"\ *vi* [*dog paddle*] **:** to swim clumsily esp. using the dog paddle
dog parsley *or* **dog's parsley** *n* **1 :** FOOL'S PARSLEY **2 :** WILD CHERVIL 1
dogplate \ˈ⸗ˌ⸗\ *n* **:** FACEPLATE
dog plum *n* **:** CAPE ASH
dog point *n* **:** the usu. blunted cylindrical thread-free point of a screw designed to clamp or hold
dog poison *n* **:** FOOL'S PARSLEY
do·gra \ˈdōgrə\ *n, pl* **dogra** *or* **dogras** *usu cap* **:** one of a group of hill dwellers in the Dogra district between Punjab and Kashmir
dog·rib \ˈdȯˌgrib *sometimes* ˈdä,-\ *n, pl* **dogrib** *or* **dogribs** *usu cap* [trans. of Déné *Thlingchadinne*] **1 a :** an Athapaskan people of the region between Great Slave Lake and Great Bear Lake, Canada **b :** a member of such people **2 :** a language of the Dogrib people
dog robber *n, slang* **:** an officer's orderly
dog rose *n* **:** a common European wild rose (*Rosa canina*) with stout hooked prickles, five to seven leaflets, and light pink single flowers that is often used as a grafting stock
dog run \ˈ⸗ˌ⸗\ *n* **:** DOGTROT 2
¹dogs *pl of* DOG, *pres 3d sing of* DOG
²dogs \ˈdȯgz *sometimes* ˈdägz\ *n, pl* **dogs** [by folk etymology fr. LaF *dos gris,* lit., gray back] *South* **:** SCAUP DUCK
dog's age *n* **:** a long time
dog salmon *n* **1 :** a salmon (*Oncorhynchus keta*) that occurs abundantly in streams of the American Pacific coast from the Sacramento northward and also on the Asiatic side and that is the common large salmon in Japan — called also *chum salmon* **2 :** any of various other salmons (as the king salmon, the silver salmon, or the humpback salmon)
dogs-and-cats \ˈ⸗⸗ˈ⸗\ *n pl but sing or pl in constr* **:** RABBIT-FOOT CLOVER
dog's-bane *var of* DOGBANE
dog's bent *var of* DOG BENT
dog's cabbage *var of* DOG CABBAGE
dog's camomile *n* **:** MAYWEED
dog's chance *n* **:** a bare chance in one's favor — usu. used negatively ⟨he didn't have a *dog's chance* of proving his innocence⟩
dog screw *n* **:** a screw with an eccentric head or with one side of its head removed that is used for attaching a watch in a case
dog's death *n* **:** a miserable end; *often* **:** a dishonorable or shameful death
dog's-ear *var of* DOG-EAR
dog's-eared *var of* DOG-EARED
dog's grass *var of* DOG GRASS
dog shark *n* **:** DOGFISH 1
dogshore \ˈ⸗ˌ⸗\ *n* **:** a short timber between a block bolted to the ground ways and a similar block on one of the bilge ways to hold a ship while the keelblocks and shores are removed before launching
dogskin \ˈ⸗ˌ⸗\ *n* **1 a :** the skin of the dog **b :** leather from it **2 :** leather (as from sheepskins or goatskins) resembling dogskin ⟨a pair of ~ gloves⟩
dogsled \ˈ⸗ˌ⸗\ *or* **dog sledge** *n* **:** a sled drawn by dogs
dogsleep \ˈ⸗ˌ⸗\ *n* **1** *obs* **:** pretended sleep **2 :** fitful sleep **:** DOZING
dog's-leg *var of* DOGLEG
dog's letter *also* **dog letter** *n* [trans. of L *littera canina;* fr. the fancied resemblance of the trilled *r* to the growl of a dog] **:** the letter *r*
dog's life *n* **:** a miserable drab existence
dog's meat *var of* DOGMEAT 1
dog's mercury *also* **dog mercury** *n* **:** a European perennial weedy plant (*Mercurialis perennis*) with greenish flowers
dog's-mouth *also* **dogmouth** \ˈ⸗ˌ⸗\ *n, pl* **dog's-mouths** *also* **dogmouths** \-ths,-t͟hz\ [so called fr. the appearance of the bearded palate that closes the throat of the corolla] **:** SNAPDRAGON 1a
dog snapper *n* **:** a brightly marked silvery or coppery snapper (*Lutjanus jocu*) common in the West Indies and on the Florida coast
dog's nose \ˈ⸗ˌ⸗\ *n, pl* **dog's noses :** a mixed drink of malt liquor and spirits; *esp* **:** a hot drink of spiced porter laced with gin or rum
dog soldier *n* [trans. of Cheyenne *Hotámitäniu*] **1 :** a member of one of the war societies of the Cheyenne **2 :** a U.S. cavalryman in the period of the Plains Indian wars **3** *slang* **:** SOLDIER, DOGFACE
dog's parsley *var of* DOG PARSLEY
dog spike *n* **:** a dog-nail railroad spike
dogstail \ˈ⸗ˌ⸗\ *or* **dogstail grass** *n* **1 :** a grass of the genus *Cynosurus; esp* **:** CRESTED DOGSTAIL **2 :** YARD GRASS
dog standard *or* **dog stander** *n, dial Eng* **:** TANSY RAGWORT
dog stinkhorn *n* **:** a basidiomycetous fungus (*Mutinus caninus*) of the order Phallales
dog's-tongue \ˈ⸗ˌ⸗\ *n, pl* **dog's-tongues 1 :** HOUND'S-TONGUE **2 :** WILD VANILLA
dog's tooth *n* **:** a string course in masonry with the bricks laid so that one corner projects
dog's-tooth bond *n* **:** a bond in masonry in which no through bonds are introduced and in which headers overlap one another from opposite sides
dog's-tooth grass *n* **1 :** COUCH GRASS 1a **2 :** BERMUDA GRASS
dog's-tooth violet *var of* DOGTOOTH VIOLET
dog-stopper \ˈ⸗ˌ⸗⸗\ *n* **:** an extra cable stopper for relieving the strain on a deck stopper of a ship
dog tag *n* **1 :** a metal disk or plate on a dog collar bearing a license registration number **2 :** a military identification tag — usu. used in pl.
dogtail \ˈ⸗ˌ⸗\ *or* **dogtail trowel** *n* **:** a molder's small usu. heart-shaped trowel with a curved handle
dog tapeworm *n* **:** a tapeworm (*Dipylidium caninum*) occurring in dogs and cats and occas. in man — called also *double-pored tapeworm*
dog tent *n, slang* **:** SHELTER TENT, PUP TENT
dog tick *n* **:** any of several ticks infesting dogs and commonly other animals: as **a :** AMERICAN DOG TICK **b :** LONE STAR

TICK **c :** a common European tick (*Ixodes ricinus*) that is a vector of canine piroplasmosis **d :** an Australian tick (*Ixodes holocyclus*) that chiefly infests native marsupials and that may cause respiratory paralysis in dogs or man by its bite **e :** BROWN DOG TICK

dog–toes \ˈ=,=\ *n pl but sing or pl in constr* **:** PUSSYTOES

[1]**dogtooth** \ˈ=,=\ *n, pl* **dogteeth** [ME *dogge toothe*, prob. trans. of L *dens caninus*] **1** *often* **dog tooth :** CANINE TOOTH, EYETOOTH **2 :** an architectural ornament common in early English Gothic that consisted usu. of four leaves radiating from a raised point at the center

dogtooth 2

[2]**dogtooth** \ˈ=,tüth, -th\ *vt* **:** to decorate with dogteeth

dogtooth spar *n* **:** a variety of calcite that occurs in acute crystals resembling the tooth of a dog

dogtooth tuna *n* **:** a medium-sized scaleless tuna (*Gymnosarda nuda*) of the Southwest Pacific ocean that is distinguished by a large mouth with prominent powerful teeth

dogtooth violet *also* **dog's–tooth violet** *or* **dogtooth** *n* **:** a plant of the genus *Erythronium:* as **a :** a European bulbous herb (*Erythronium denscanis*) with two mottled basal leaves and a solitary nodding purple flower appearing in early spring **b :** any of several related American spring-flowering plants: as (1) **:** a yellow-flowered low-growing woodland plant (*E. americanum*) (2) **:** a white-flowered or pinkish purple-flowered plant (*E. albidum*) of similar habit

dog town *n* **1 :** a community of prairie dogs **2** *slang* **:** a city commonly used for theatrical tryouts before a play receives metropolitan presentation

dogtown grass *n* **:** a needle grass (*Aristida longiseta*) of the western U.S.

dog tree *n* **:** any of several Old World trees and shrubs: as **a :** RED DOGWOOD 1 **b :** a spindle tree (*Euonymus europaeus*) **c :** an elder (*Sambucus nigra*) **d :** GUELDER ROSE **e :** a common alder (*Alnus glutinosa*)

dogtrick \ˈ=,=\ *n, archaic* **:** a scurvy knavish trick

[1]**dogtrot** \ˈ=,=\ *n* [[1]*dog* + *trot*] **1 :** a quick easy gait suggesting that of a dog **2** *South & Midland* **:** a roofed passage similar to a breezeway; *esp* **:** one connecting two parts of a cabin ⟨born in a ~ cabin in Kentucky⟩

[2]**dogtrot** \ˈ"\ *vi* **:** to move or progress at a dogtrot

dog tune *n, slang* **:** a poor song of little musical worth

dog typhus *n* **:** STUTTGART DISEASE

dogvane \ˈ=,=\ *n* **:** a small vane carried on the weather rail aboard ship to indicate the direction of the wind

dog violet *n* [trans. of NL *viola canina*] **1 :** a leafy-stemmed blue-flowered violet (*Viola canina*) found throughout the northern portions of the Old World **2 :** any of several closely related plants of the genus *Viola* (esp. *V. conspersa*)

dog wagon *n* [(*hot*) *dog*] **:** a small restaurant often specializing in short orders that occupies a converted vehicle (as a streetcar or bus) or that is built to suggest such a vehicle

dog warp *n* **:** a rope with a strong hook for moving logs

dogwatch \ˈ=,=\ *n* **1 :** either of two watches of two hours on shipboard that extend from 4 to 6 and from 6 to 8 p.m. and make an odd number of watches in a day so that crew members who work on a rotating watch system will not stand the same watches every day **2 a :** any of various night shifts; *esp* **:** the last shift of an organization which is on duty at all times (as a police department) **b :** LOBSTER SHIFT

dog wheel *n* **1 :** a wheel turned by dog power **2 :** RATCHET WHEEL

dog whelk *also* **dog winkle** *n* **:** any of certain thick-shelled marine snails: as **a :** BASKET SHELL 2 **b :** any of numerous members of the genus *Thais* that feed chiefly on other mollusks

dog whistle \ˈ=,=\ *n* **:** a whistle to call or direct a dog; *esp* **:** one sounding at a frequency inaudible to the human ear

dogwood \ˈ=,=\ *n* **1 a :** a tree or shrub of the genus *Cornus:* as (1) **:** FLOWERING DOGWOOD (2) **:** RED DOGWOOD 1 (3) **:** RED OSIER 2 **b :** the hard tough wood of any dogwood of the genus *Cornus* resembling boxwood in qualities and uses and including some woods that are also classed as boxwoods **2 :** any of various trees and shrubs felt to resemble those of the genus *Cornus:* as **a** *Brit* (1) **:** SPINDLE TREE (2) **:** GUELDER ROSE **b :** POISON SUMAC **c :** STRIPED MAPLE **d :** any of several Australian shrubs and trees: as (1) **:** a large leguminous shrub (*Jacksonia scoparia*) having leafless drooping branches and sweet-scented yellow or orange pealike flowers — called also *native broom, stinkwood* (2) **:** BOOBYALLA 2; *also* **:** any of several other trees or shrubs of the family Rubiaceae **e :** JAMAICA DOGWOOD **3 :** a light brown to moderate yellowish brown that is very slightly redder than Mosul

dogwood borer *n* **:** a larval clearwing moth (*Thamnosphecia scitula*) that tunnels in the cambium of flowering dogwood

dogwood family *n* **:** CORNACEAE

dogwood winter *n, South & Midland* **:** a brief spell of wintry weather in spring

dog wrench *n* **:** a wrench with a crank handle

[1]**do·gy** \ˈdōgē\ *n* -ES [by folk etymology fr. LaF *dos gris*, lit., gray back] *Midland* **:** SCAUP DUCK

[2]**dogy** *var of* DOGIE

doh *var of* DO

doig·té \dwäˈtā\ *n* -s [F, fr. *doigt* finger, fr. L *digitus* — more at TOE] **:** FINGERING

doiled \ˈdȯi(ə)ld\ *adj* [ME *dold*] *dial Brit* **:** CONFUSED, DAZED

doi·ly \ˈdȯilē, -li\ *n* -ES [fr. *Doily* or *Doyley fl*1712 London draper] **1** *obs* **:** a light woolen fabric **2 a** *archaic* **:** a small napkin (as one provided at table with a fruit course) **b :** a small often decorative piece (as of linen, lace, or paper) usu. serving as a mat beneath some object (as a vase) either for ornament or to protect an underlying surface **3** *slang* **:** TOUPEE 2

do in \(ˈ)düˈin\ *vt* **1 a :** to bring about the defeat or destruction of **:** inflict great injury upon **:** RUIN ⟨an agent sent to *do in* the current government —Herbert Gold⟩ ⟨the stock-market crash *did* him *in* —Thomas Whiteside⟩ **b :** to bring about the death of **:** KILL ⟨after twice trying to *do* him *in* with gas —Alexander Woollcott⟩ **c :** to bring almost to the point of exhaustion **:** wear out ⟨would see I was *done in* and tell me to stop working —Frank Sargeson⟩ **2 :** to take in **:** CHEAT ⟨one feels as though one has been somehow swindled and *done in* —Aldous Huxley⟩

doi·na \ˈdȯinə\ *n, pl* **doinas** \-nəz\ *also* **doi·ne** \-,ne\ [Romanian *doină*] **:** a Romanian folk song usu. in the form of a lament

doing *n* -s [ME, fr. gerund of *don* to do — more at DO] **1 a :** the act of performing or executing **:** ACTION ⟨art is primarily not a contemplation but a ~ —Havelock Ellis⟩ ⟨any such grandiose plan will take some ~ —Green Peyton⟩ **b :** the result of such an action ⟨the picture and the story I recognized as my father's ~ —Ben Riker⟩ **2 doings** *pl* **a :** things that are done or that occur **:** ACTS, DEEDS, EVENTS ⟨the daily ~*s* of the forge and field and market —H.O.Taylor⟩ **b** *dial* **:** social activities ⟨went to the ~*s* at the schoolhouse Saturday night⟩ **3 doings** *pl, dial* **:** materials for a dish or meal **:** food esp. when made up into a dish ⟨a breakfast of corn ~*s* and flapjacks⟩

[1]**doit** \ˈdȯit\ *n* -s [D *duit*, fr. MD *duit, doyt;* akin to ON *thveiti* small coin, *thveita* to hew — more at WHITTLE] **1 :** an old Dutch coin equal to ⅛ stiver or about ½ farthing **2 :** a small amount **:** TRIFLE, BIT, WHIT

[2]**doit** \ˈ"\ *vb* -ED/-ING/-s [prob. alter. of [1]*dote*] *vi, dial Brit* **:** DOTE 1 **~** *vt, Scot* **:** PERPLEX

doit·ed \-əd,-ət\ *adj* [ME (Sc dial.), prob. alter. of *doted*, past part. of *doten* to dote — more at DOTE] *chiefly Scot* **:** turned to dotage **:** CONFUSED

doit·kin \-kən\ *n* -s [AF *doydekyn* — more at DODKIN] **:** DOIT

doit·ri·fied \ˈdȯitrə,fēt\ *adj* [blend of *doited* and *petrified*] *Scot* **:** DAZED

do·jo \ˈdō(,)jō\ *n* -s [Jap *dojō*] **:** a speckled brownish loach (*Misgurnus anguillicaudata*) of eastern Asia that is sometimes kept as a scavenger in the tropical aquarium — compare WEATHERFISH

doke \ˈdōk\ *n* -s [prob. alter. of *dalk*, fr. ME, perh. dim. of ME *dale* — more at DALE] *dial Eng* **:** a depression or indentation; *esp* **:** DIMPLE

doketic *often cap, var of* DOCETIC

dol \ˈdōl\ *n* -s [L *dolor* pain — more at DOLOR] **:** a unit for the measurement of pain intensity usu. taken as one tenth of the range of increasing sensation from that produced by the least perceptible stimulus to that at which further increase in stimulation causes no further increase in sensation

dol *abbr* **1** [It *dolce*] soft; sweet **2** dollar

do·lab·rate \dōˈlabrət, ˈdälə,brāt\ *adj* [LL *dolabratus*, fr. L *dolabra* mattock, pickax + *-atus* -ate] **:** DOLABRIFORM

do·lab·ri·form \dōˈlabrə,fȯrm\ *adj* [L *dolabra* + E *-iform*] **:** shaped like the head of an ax or hatchet

do·lan·tal \dəˈlantᵊl\ *n* -s [alter. of *dolantin*] **:** meperidine hydrochloride

do·lan·tin \-tᵊn\ *n* -s [ISV *dol-* (fr. L *dolor* pain) + ˈ*anti-* + *-in* — more at DOLOR] **:** meperidine hydrochloride

dol·can \ˈdälkən\ *n* -s [alter. of *dulciana*] **:** an 8-foot pipe-organ stop similar to the dulciana

[1]**dol·ce** \ˈdōl(,)chā, -,chē\ *adj* (*or adv*) [It, lit., sweet, fr. L *dulcis* — more at DULCET] **:** SOFT, SMOOTH — used as a direction in music — **dol·ce·men·te** \,dōlchāˈmentē, -n·(,)tā\ *adv*

[2]**dolce** \ˈ"\ *n, pl* **dol·ci** \-(,)chē\ [It, fr. *dolce*, adj.] **1 :** a sweet dessert **2 :** a very soft flute pipe-organ stop of either 8-foot or 4-foot pitch

dolce cornet *n* **:** a pipe-organ mixture of soft singing quality of tone

dol·ce far nien·te \ˈdōlchē,fārnēˈentē, -(,)chā,-, -ärnˈye-, -en·(,)tā\ *n* -s [It, lit., sweet doing nothing] **:** delightful relaxation in carefree indolence

dol·ci·an \ˈdälsēən, ˈdōl-,ˈdōl-\ *or* **dul·ci·an** \ˈdəl-\ *also* **dol·ci·no** \dōlˈchē(,)nō\ *n* -s [*dolcian, dulcian* alter. of *dulciana*; *dolcino* fr. It, modif. of ML *dulciana* — more at DULCIANA] **1 :** a small musical instrument sounding like a bassoon and used in the 16th and 17th centuries **2** *also* **dul·zi·an** \ˈdəlzēən\ **:** a pipe-organ stop sounding like a bassoon

[1]**dol·cis·si·mo** \dōlˈchēsə,mō, -chis-\ *adj* (*or adv*) [It (superl. of *dolce* sweet), fr. L *dulcissimus*, superl. of *dulcis* sweet — more at DULCET] **:** very sweet or soft — used as a direction in music

[2]**dolcissimo** \ˈ"\ *n* -s [It, fr. *dolcissimo*, adj.] **:** an extremely soft pipe-organ stop of flute quality

dol·drum \ˈdōldrəm, ˈdäl- *sometimes* ˈdȯl-\ *n* -s [prob. akin to OE *dol* foolish, silly — more at DULL] **1 doldrums** *pl* **a :** a spell of listlessness or despondency **:** BLUES **b :** a state of bafflement **:** QUANDARY **2** *archaic* **:** a sluggish or slow-witted person **3 doldrums** *pl* **a :** a region over the ocean near the equator abounding in calms, squalls, and light baffling winds **b :** the calms met with in that region **4 doldrums** *pl* **:** a condition of inactivity, retardation, or stagnation: **a :** a downswing, slump, or slack period (as in business or industry) ⟨through the economic ~*s* of the late forties —Drew Middleton⟩ ⟨bring the antiques business out of the depression ~*s* —Alice Winchester⟩ **:** a period of sagging or falling off (as in sales or financial or political activity) **b :** a deterioration to a low ebb of vigor, creative power, or effectiveness ⟨that American fiction is at present in the ~*s* is borne out anew —Amy Loveman⟩

[1]**dole** \ˈdōl\ *n* -s [ME, fr. OE *dāl* division, separation, share, lot; akin to OE *dǣl* part, share, lot — more at DEAL] **1 a** *archaic* **:** one's allotted share or portion ⟨hath not our great Queen my ~ of beauty trebled —Alfred Tennyson⟩ **b** *archaic* **:** one's lot in life **:** one's destiny or fate ⟨happy man be his ~, say I; every man to his business —Shak.⟩ **c** *dial Eng* **:** an allotment of land in a common **2 a** (1) **:** a giving or distribution of food, money, or clothing to the needy ⟨the weekly ~ at a parish charity station⟩ (2) **:** a direct distribution of government funds made at regular intervals to the unemployed **:** UNEMPLOYMENT INSURANCE ⟨all his family was on the ~ —Margaret Kennedy⟩ ⟨it was as well to starve or live on the ~ in the Old World as the New —Oscar Handlin⟩ **b :** something distributed at intervals as charity **:** a ration for the needy ⟨people able and willing to work forced to accept ~*s*⟩ **c :** something portioned out and distributed in driblets or pittances **d** *obs* **:** a blow or some dire treatment administered ⟨dealing ~ among his foes —John Milton⟩ **e :** a gratuitous bestowal; *specif* **:** a distribution of sustaining or subsidizing contributions ⟨the country's industrial recovery is an illusion; it is living on an American ~⟩

[2]**dole** \ˈ"\ *vt* -ED/-ING/-s [ME *dolen*, fr. *dole*, n.] **1 :** to give or distribute as a charity — used often with *out* ⟨he gathered all the blankets, pillows, pieces of clothing, and other supplies . . . and *doled* them out to the distraught, homeless natives of the island —Clay Blair⟩ **2 :** to give or deliver in small portions (as in driblets) guardedly or calculatingly **:** PARCEL — used with *out* ⟨puts all my money in the bank and just ~*s* out a few dollars to me once in a while —Lucy M. Montgomery⟩ **3 :** to give or deliver in equal portions or according to a prescribed allotment — used with *out* ⟨stopped his scribbling long enough to ~ out sheets and mattress covers, shelter half and blankets, pack and all the rest of it —James Jones⟩ **syn** see DISTRIBUTE

[3]**dole** \ˈ"\ *n* -s [ME *dol, doel, del*, fr. OF, fr. LL *dolus* pain, grief, alter. (influenced by L *dolus* fraud, deceit) of L *dolor* — more at TALE, DOLOR] **1 a :** GRIEF, SORROW ⟨deep questioning, which probes to endless ~ —George Meredith⟩ **b :** bad luck **:** MISFORTUNE **2** *obs* **:** mourning clothes **syn** see SORROW

[4]**dole** \ˈ"\ *vi* -ED/-ING/-s [ME *dolen*, fr. MF *doloir*, fr. L *dolēre* to feel pain, grieve — more at CONDOLE] **:** LAMENT, MOURN

[5]**dole** \ˈ"\ *n* -s [in sense 1, fr. ME, prob. fr. MD *doel* trench used as a landmark; in sense 2, prob. fr. Fris *doel* goal, fr. OFris *dōl;* both akin to OHG *tuolla* small valley, ON *dæll* inhabitant of a valley, OE *dæl* valley — more at DALE] **1** *now dial Brit* **:** a landmark or boundary marker **2** *now dial Brit, in some children's games* **:** GOAL

[6]**dole** \ˈ"\ *n* -s [MF *dol*, fr. L *dolus* fraud, deceit — more at TALE] **1** *obs* **:** TRICKERY **2** *Scots law* **:** criminal intent **:** MALICE

dole chaser *n* [[1]*dole*] *Austral* **:** a vagrant living on food issued by dole stations

dole cupboard *n* [[1]*dole*] **:** an ecclesiastical cupboard to contain bread or other supplies for the poor of the parish

dole·ful \ˈdōlfəl\ *adj* **dolefuller; dolefullest** [ME *dolful, doelful, delful*, fr. *dol, doel, del* dole + *-ful* — more at DOLE (grief)] **1 a :** causing grief or affliction **:** WOEFUL, LAMENTABLE ⟨a head and heart full of ~ thoughts, anxieties, and fears —Nathaniel Hawthorne⟩ **b :** attended with or indicating grief or a morose or despairing attitude **:** CHEERLESS ⟨in the *dolefullest* dumps after flunking⟩ ⟨abandoning the argument, she gave a ~ shake of her head⟩ **c :** DISCONSOLATE ⟨the ~ one is obviously the defeated competitor⟩ **2 a :** expressing mourning or lamentation ⟨the body is carried around in front of the mourners, who are singing a very ~ dirge —W.H.Goodenough⟩ **b :** evoking sadness or gloom **:** inducing depression of spirits **:** LUGUBRIOUS ⟨he was constitutionally gloomy, a congenital pessimist who always saw the ~ side of any situation —W.A.White⟩ — **dole·ful·ly** \-fəlē, -li\ *adv* — **dole·ful·ness** \-lnəs\ *n* -ES

dole·fuls \-fəlz\ *n pl* **:** BLUES — used with *the*

do·lent \ˈdōlənt\ *adj* [ME, fr. MF, fr. L *dolent-, dolens*, pres. part. of *dolēre* to feel pain, grieve — more at CONDOLE] **:** SORROWFUL — **do·lent·ly** *adv*

do·len·te \dōˈlentē, -n·(,)tā\ *adj* (*or adv*) [It, fr. L *dolent-, dolens*] **:** SORROWFUL — used as a direction in music

do·len·tis·si·mo \,dō,len·ˈtisə,mō\ *adj* (*or adv*) [It, superl. of *dolente*] **:** most mournful — used as a direction in music

dol·er·ite \ˈdälə,rīt\ *n* -s [F *dolérite*, fr. Gk *doleros* deceitful (fr. *dolos* deceit) + *-ite;* fr. its being easily mistaken for diorite — more at TALE] **1 :** a coarse basalt **2** *Brit* **:** DIABASE 3 **3 :** a dark igneous rock whose constituents are not determinable megascopically — **dol·er·it·ic** \ˈdäləˈridik\ *adj*

dol·er·oph·a·nite \,däləˈräfə,nīt\ *also* **dol·er·o·phane** \ˈdälərə,fān, dəˈler-\ *n* -s [*dolerophanite* fr. *dolerophane* + *-ite; dolerophane* fr. It *dolerofano*, fr. Gk *doleros* deceitful + It *-fano* (fr. Gk *phainesthai* to appear)] **:** a basic copper sulfate $Cu_2(SO_4)O$ of volcanic origin occurring in brown monoclinic crystals

doles *pl of* DOLE, *pres 3d sing of* DOLE

doles·man \ˈdōlzmən\ *n, pl* **dolesmen :** one who receives a dole

dole·some \ˈdōlsəm\ *adj* [[3]*dole* + *-some*] **:** DOLEFUL ⟨the ~ realms of darkness and of death —Alexander Pope⟩ — **dole·some·ly** *adv*

do·less \ˈdüləs\ *adj* [[1]*do* + *-less*] *dial* **:** lacking energy or ambition **:** SHIFTLESS

dolia *pl of* DOLIUM

do·li ca·pax \ˈdō,līˈkā,paks\ *adj* [L, capable of deceit] **:** old enough or of sufficient intelligence and sane enough to be legally responsible for wrongful acts — opposed to *doli incapax*

dolich- *or* **dolicho-** *comb form* [NL, fr. Gk, fr. *dolichos* — more at INDULGE] **1 :** long ⟨*dolicho*cephalic⟩ **2 :** narrow ⟨*dolicho*hieric⟩

dol·i·cho·blond \ˈdälə(,)kō,-lē(-+\ *n* [*dolich-* + *blond*] **:** a longheaded blond person

dol·i·cho·ceph·al \ˈ=(,)=ˈsefəl\ *n, pl* **dolichocephals** \-əlz\ *also* **dolichocepha·li** \-ə,lī\ [NL *dolichocephalus*, fr. *dolich-* + *-cephalus*] **:** a dolichocephalic person

dol·i·cho·ce·phal·ic \ˈ=(,)=səˈfalik\ *also* **dol·i·cho·ceph·a·lous** \-ˈsefələs\ *adj* [*dolichocephalic* fr. NL *dolichocephalus* + E *-ic; dolichocephalous* fr. NL *dolichocephalus*] **:** having a relatively long head with a cephalic index of less than 75 — **dol·i·cho·ceph·a·lism** \,=(,)=ˈsefə,lizəm\ *n* -s — **dol·i·cho·ceph·a·ly** \-fəlē\ *n* -ES

dol·i·cho·cra·ni·al \ˈ=(,)=ˈkrānēəl\ *also* **dol·i·cho·cra·nic** \-nik\ *adj* [ISV *dolich-* + *cranial, cranic;* orig. formed as G *dolichokran*] **:** having a relatively long head with a cranial index of less than 75 — **dol·i·cho·cra·ny** \ˈ=(,)=,krānē\ *n* -ES

dol·i·cho·facial \ˈ=(,)=+\ *adj* [*dolich-* + *facial*] **:** LEPTOPROSOPIC

dol·i·cho·glos·sus \,=(,)=ˈgläsəs, -lȯs-\ *n, cap* [NL, fr. *dolich-* + *-glossus* (fr. Gk *glōssa* tongue) — more at GLOSS] **:** a genus of hemichordate worms differing from those of *Balanoglossus* in lacking liver sacs and in having a long proboscis with a single pore — compare ENTEROPNEUSTA

dol·i·cho·hi·er·ic \ˈ=(,)=,hīˈerik\ *adj* [*dolich-* + *-hieric*] **:** having a relatively long narrow sacrum with a sacral index of less than 100 — compare PLATYHIERIC, SUBPLATYHIERIC

dol·i·choid \ˈdälə,kȯid\ *adj* [*dolich-* + *-oid*] *anthrop* **:** tending to be long and narrow

dol·i·cho·mor·phic \ˈdäləkōˈmȯrfik, -lēk-\ *adj* [*dolich-* + *-morphic*] **:** ECTOMORPHIC, ASTHENIC — opposed to *brachymorphic* — **dol·i·cho·mor·phy** \ˈ=,=,mȯrfē\ *n* -ES

dol·i·cho·pel·ic \ˈ=(,)=ˈpelik\ *adj* [*dolich-* + *-pellic*] **:** having a pelvis relatively long dorsoventrally with a pelvic index of 95 or more — **dol·i·cho·pel·ly** \ˈ=(,)=,pelē\ *n* -ES

dol·i·chop·o·did \ˈdäləˈkäpədəd\ *adj* [NL *Dolichopodidae*] **:** of or relating to the Dolichopodidae

dol·i·cho·pod·i·dae \,däləkōˈpädə,dē, -lēk-\ *n pl, cap* [NL, fr. *Dolichopod-, Dolichopus*, type genus (fr. *dolich-* + *-pus*) + *-idae*] **:** a large family of small bristly usu. metallic green long-legged two-winged flies that feed on other insects and mites

dol·i·chop·o·dous \ˈdäləˈkäpədəs\ *adj* [*dolich-* + *-podous*] **:** having a relatively long foot

dol·i·cho·prosopic \ˈdälə(,)kō, -lē(-+\ *adj* [*dolich-* + *prosop-* + -IC] **:** LEPTOPROSOPIC

dol·i·cho·psyl·li·dae \,=,=_kōˈsilə,dē, -,käp's-\ *n pl, cap* [NL, fr. *Dolichopsylla*, type genus (fr. *dolich-* + Gk *psylla* flea) + *-idae*] **:** a family of fleas chiefly of temperate zones including many that attack rodents and act as vectors of plague among rodents — see CERATOPHYLLUS

dol·i·chos \ˈdälə,käs\ *n* [NL, fr. L, a leguminous plant, fr. Gk, lit., racecourse, fr. *dolichos* long — more at INDULGE] **1** *cap* **:** a genus of chiefly tropical vines (family Leguminosae) having a bearded style and the keel of the corolla coiled **2** -ES **:** any plant of the genus *Dolichos*

dol·i·cho·saur \ˈdäləkō,sȯ(ə)r, -lēk-\ *n* -s [NL *Dolichosaurus*] **:** a lizard of the genus *Dolichosaurus*

dol·i·cho·sau·rus \,=,=ˈsȯrəs\ *n, cap* [NL, fr. *dolich-* + *-saurus*] **:** a genus (the type of the family Dolichosauriidae) of small long-necked aquatic fossil lizards from the Upper Cretaceous of England closely related to the recent Varanidae

dol·i·cho·so·ma \-ˈsōmə\ *n, cap* [NL, fr. *dolich-* + *-soma*] **:** a genus of slender limbless extinct amphibians (order Aistopoda) from the Carboniferous and Permian of Europe

dol·i·cho·sty·lous \ˈ=(,)=ˈstīləs\ *adj* [*dolich-* + *-stylous*] **:** long-styled (as certain dimorphic or trimorphic flowers)

dol·i·chu·ran·ic \ˈdäləkyüˈranik\ *adj* [*dolich-* + *uran-* + *-ic*] **:** having an upper alveolar arch index of less than 110

dol·i·chu·ric \ˈdäləˈkyürik\ *adj* [NL *dolichurus* + E *-ic*] **:** having a redundant syllable ⟨~ hexameter⟩

dol·i·chu·rus \,däləˈkyürəs\ *n, pl* **dolichu·ri** \-ü,rī\ [NL, fr. Gk *dolichouros*, lit., long-tailed, fr. *dolich-* + *-ouros* -urous] **:** a dactylic hexameter with an actual or apparent redundant syllable in the last foot

do·li·idae \dəˈlīə,dē\ [NL, fr. *Dolium*, type genus + *-idae*] *syn of* TONNIDAE

do·li in·ca·pax \ˈdō,līˈinkə,paks, -iŋk-\ *adj* [L, incapable of deceit] **:** incapable of guilt — opposed to *doli capax*

do·li·ne *also* **do·li·na** \dəˈlēnə\ *n* -s [Russ *dolina* plain, valley, bottomland, fr. *dol* valley; akin to OSlav *dolŭ* pit, hole, valley — more at DALE] **:** SINK 5

doling *pres part of* DOLE

do·li·o·form \ˈdōlēə,fȯrm\ *adj* [L *dolium* large jar, cask + E *-o-* + *-form* — more at DOLIUM] **:** shaped like a barrel

do·li·o·li·dae \,dōlēˈäləˌdē\ *n pl, cap* [NL, fr. *Doliolum*, type genus + *-idae*] **:** a small family of oceanic tunicates coextensive with the suborder Cyclomyaria

do·li·o·lum \dəˈlīələm\ *n, cap* [NL, fr. L, small cask, dim. of *dolium*] **:** a genus of free-swimming oceanic tunicates developing with alternation of generations and having a cask-shaped transparent body surrounded by complete muscular rings

dolittle \ˈ=,=\ *n* -s [[1]*do* + *little*] **:** IDLER

[1]**do·li·um** \ˈdōlēəm\ *n, pl* **do·lia** \-ēə\ [L; akin to ORuss *delva, delvi* cask, L *dolare* to hew — more at CONDOLE] **:** an earthenware cask or jar of Roman antiquity sometimes large enough to hold a man — compare PITHOS

[2]**dolium** \ˈ"\ [NL, fr. L, large jar, cask] *syn of* TONNA

[3]**dolium** \ˈ"\ *n, pl* **dolium** *or* **doliums** [NL, fr. L, large jar, cask] **:** a mollusk of the genus *Tonna* **:** TUN SHELL

doll \ˈdäl, ˈdȯl\ *n* -s *often attrib* [prob. fr. *Doll*, nickname for *Dorothy*] **1 a :** a small-scale figure of a human being (as of a baby or child) used esp. as a child's plaything ⟨busy dressing and undressing her ~*s*⟩ ⟨~ clothes⟩ **b :** PUPPET **1a c :** a small carved or molded figure serving as a cult object or representing a nursery-story or cartoon character ⟨carrying a Mickey Mouse ~ for good luck⟩ **2 a :** a young woman with pretty babyish face and often frilly clothes that is sometimes featherbrained, frivolous, or giddy ⟨the most stuck-up ~ in the world —Willa Cather⟩ **b** *slang* **:** WOMAN ⟨a realm where men are guys, women are ~*s*, and gambling . . . is a profession —John Mason Brown⟩ **c** *slang* **:** PARAMOUR **d** *slang* **:** a male who is an object of female admiration ⟨he is tall, handsome, and muscular. In short, he's a ~ —Ethel Merman⟩ **e :** a sweet kind good-natured woman

dol·lar \ˈdälə(r)\ *n* -s *often attrib* [alter. of earlier *daler*, fr. D or LG, fr. G *taler*, short for *joachimstaler*, fr. Sankt *Joachimsthal* (Jáchymov), town in northwestern Bohemia, Czechoslovakia, where the first talers were made] **1 :** an old German taler coin **2 :** any one of a number of coins of various countries patterned after the taler: as **a :** a Spanish or Spanish-American peso or piece of eight **b :** any of several coins issued in the U.S. (as a silver coin issued 1794–1935, after 1837 weighing 412.5 grains or 26.730 grams of silver .900 fine, and a gold coin issued 1849–89, weighing 25.8 grains or 1.6718 grams of gold .900 fine) — see TRADE DOLLAR **c :** a silver coin of Canada issued since 1935 chiefly for commemorative purposes **d :** any of several British coins issued for use in certain territories of the Commonwealth (as a silver coin for Hong Kong issued 1866–68 and a silver coin issued at intervals between 1903 and 1926 for the Straits Settlements) — called also *British dollar* **3 a :** the basic monetary unit of the U.S. serving as a medium, standard, or basis of foreign exchange ⟨provided the ~*s* required as credit to finance reconstruction in war-devastated areas⟩ ⟨a loan to enable a country to pay in ~*s* for additional imports from the U.S.⟩ ⟨the area of American minor satellites and its accompanying ~ bloc would have to be indicated —O.S.Knauth⟩ **b :** any of various basic monetary units — see MONEY table **4 a :** a currency bill representing one dollar **b :** a token representing one dollar **5 :** PESO **6 :** YUAN **7** *slang Brit* **:** CROWN 8a (3) **8 :** the commercial interests of the U.S. in trade in foreign countries ⟨whether the flag will follow the ~⟩

dollar-and-cent *or* **dollars-and-cents** \ˌ===ˈ=\ *adj* **:** expressed or expressible in money **:** measurable in or calculated hardheadedly in terms of money value exclusively or in exact amount of money ⟨from the *dollars-and-cents* approach⟩
dollar area *n* **:** the area of the world where the U.S. dollar is used as a basis for exchange and currencies can be converted freely into dollars
dollar averaging *n* **:** a practice of investing a uniform sum in common stocks periodically regardless of the level of prices
dollar-a-year \ˌ===ˈ=\ *adj* **:** compensated by a token salary (as one dollar a year) usu. for government service ⟨a *dollar-a-year* man⟩
dollar bird *n* [so called fr. the light spot, about the size of a Straits dollar, on its open wing] **:** a roller (*Eurystomus orientalis*) found from Manchuria to Ceylon and Australia
dollar day *n* **:** a day on which the merchants of a locality make special offerings of goods and services for one dollar; *broadly* **:** a day on which bargain prices in many lines are offered
dol·lar·dee \ˈdälə(r)ˌdē\ *n* -s [origin unknown] **:** BLUEGILL
dollar diplomacy *n* **1 :** diplomacy used by a country to promote its financial or commercial interests abroad **2 :** diplomacy that seeks to strengthen the power of a country or effect its purposes in foreign relations by the use of its financial resources
dollarfish \ˈ==ˌ=\ *n* [so called fr. its shape and the silver color of the young] **1 :** a small marine butterfish (*Poronotus triacanthus*) of the family Stromateidae with a laterally compressed body common in summer on the Atlantic coast of the northern and middle U.S. — called also *harvest fish* **2 :** LOOKDOWN
dollar gap *also* **dollar shortage** *n* **:** the amount of additional dollar receipts required by a country to equal dollar payments that must be made for imports from dollar nations or to meet other obligations
dollarleaf \ˈ==ˌ=\ *n* **1 :** FALSE WINTERGREEN **2 :** a prostrate round-leafed tick trefoil (*Desmodium rotundifolium*)
dollar mark *or* **dollar sign** *n* **:** a mark $ or $ placed before a number to indicate that it stands for dollars
dollar of account : the U.S. dollar reckoned on the London stock exchange at four shillings (instead of actual exchange value) for facility of calculation
dollar spot *n* **:** a disease of golf-green and lawn grasses caused by a fungus (*Sclerotinia homeocarpa*) and characterized by areas in the turf about two inches in diameter that are first brownish but become bleached straw colored and finally coalesce to form large irregular patches — compare GREASE SPOT
dollarwise \ˈ==ˌ=\ *adv* [*dollar* + *-wise*] **:** in terms of dollars **:** so far as values are translatable into money equivalents
doll baby *n* **1 :** a child's doll **2 :** DOLL 2a **3 :** SWEETHEART — used chiefly as a pet name
doll carriage *also* **doll buggy** *n* **:** a child's small-scale baby carriage for play with a doll
doll cheeses *n pl* **:** CHEESE 4
doll·dom \ˈdäldəm, ˈdȯl-\ *n* -s **:** the realm of dolls
dollface \ˈ=ˌ=\ *n* **:** a person having a face with a smooth prettiness and childish expression suggestive of a doll
dollhouse \ˈ=ˌ=\ *n* **1 :** a child's small-scale toy house **2 :** a dwelling so small as to suggest resemblance to a house for dolls
dolli·er \ˈdälīə(r)\ *n* -s [²*dolly* + *-er*] *Brit* **:** a worker who scours or polishes with a dolly
doll·ish \ˈdälish, ˈdȯl-, -lēsh\ *adj* **:** like a doll; *specif* **:** pretty but rather empty-headed — **doll·ish·ly** \-ləshlē, -lēsh-, -shli\ *adv* — **doll·ish·ness** \-lishnə̇s, -lēsh-\ *n* -ES
¹**dol·lop** \ˈdäləp\ *also* **dal·lop** \ˈdal-\ *n* -s [origin unknown] **1** *obs* **:** a tuft or clump esp. of grass **2 a :** a lump or blob of a semiliquid, mushy, or plastic substance ⟨drop a ~ of ice cream or of whipped cream on a piece of pie⟩ ⟨a ~ of stew hit me on the back of the neck —Allan Ashbolt⟩ **b :** a dash or splash or a small portion of a liquid; *specif* **:** a small drink ⟨lingering over a few ~*s* of brandy⟩ **c :** a slight admixture or one of several interspersed bits ⟨the author has essayed a charming fantasy with a ~ of satire —Lee Rogow⟩ ⟨experimental novels . . . served up in ~*s* of bogus poetic prose —J.B.Priestley⟩ **3** *dial Brit* **:** SLUT, TROLLOP
²**dollop** \"\ *also* **dallop** \"\ *vb* -ED/-ING/-S *vt* **1** *chiefly Brit* **:** to serve in dollops **2** *chiefly Brit* **:** to admix with a dollop or intersperse with dollops ~ *vi* **:** PLOP ⟨salt water ~*ed* over the boat's side⟩
dol·lo's law \ˈdä(ˌ)lōz-\ *n, usu cap D* [after Louis *Dollo* †1931 Belgian paleontologist] **:** a generalization in biology: characters lost in the course of evolution are never regained in the original form
doll out *vt* **:** to doll up
doll post *n* **:** a railroad signal consisting of a short post mounted on a bracket
dolls *pl of* DOLL
doll's-eyes \ˈ=ˌ=\ *n pl* **:** the fruits of a white baneberry (*Actaea brachypoda*)
doll's head *n* **:** a projection of the top rib that fits into a corresponding hollow in the breech of a gun
doll up *vi* **:** to dress oneself in formal, elegant, or fancy attire and personal adornments ⟨insisted that he must *doll up* for this party⟩ ~ *vt* **1 :** to array in elegance, extravagance, or showy outfit ⟨all *dolled up* in top hat and tails, dancing attendance on a certain show girl —Polly Adler⟩ **2 :** to make more attractive with a freshening up and addition of decorative details ⟨a country schoolhouse all *dolled up* by the pupils for a Christmas party⟩
¹**dolly** *also* **doll·ey** *or* **doll·ie** \ˈdälē, ˈdȯl-, -li\ *n, pl* **dollies** *also* **dolleys** [*doll* + *-y*, *-ey*, *-ie*] **1 a** *dial Eng* **:** an untidy woman **b** *slang* **:** an attractive young woman **:** DOLL **c** *cricket* **:** SITTER **2 :** DOLL 1a — a child's term **3 a :** a hand-operated wooden-pronged instrument that washes clothes by turning and pounding them in a tub **b :** a contrivance turning on a vertical axis by a handle or winch used in mining operations to give a circular motion to the ore to be washed **:** STIRRER **c :** a large mortar and pestle for crushing ore **d :** a machine for scouring textiles (as woolens and worsteds) during manufacture **4 a :** a block put between the head of a pile and the ram of a pile driver **b :** a heavy steel bar with a cupped head for holding against the head of a rivet while the other end is being headed **c :** a shaped metal block used as an anvil in sheet-metal work (as in reshaping an automobile fender) **5 a :** an auxiliary car (as one attached to a cable and used to push a standard car up an incline) **b :** a compact narrow-gauge railroad locomotive used for moving construction trains and for switching **6 a :** a small cart or wheeled platform used to move freight in terminals or in loading and unloading **b :** a platform on a roller or on wheels or casters used for transporting heavy objects (as logs, girders, or machines) short distances or for supporting a person working under an automobile **c :** a small wheeled truck used to support the tail of an airplane when moving the latter on the ground **d :** a wheeled platform on which a motion-picture or television camera is mounted for ready movement about a set **e :** a standard that is swung down in position to support the forward part of a semitrailer when it is detached from a truck tractor

dolly 3a

²**dolly** \"\ *vb* -ED/-ING/-ES *vt* **1 :** to treat with a dolly: **a** *dial Eng* **:** to wash (clothes) with a dolly **b :** to crush (rock) with a dolly **2 :** to move (a camera) about on a dolly **3 :** to convey on a dolly ⟨movers *dollied* away the file cabinets⟩ ~ *vi* **:** to move the camera about on a dolly while shooting a scene for motion pictures or television ⟨we *dollied* in for a close-up of the two faces⟩ ⟨~ out for a long shot⟩; *also, of a camera* **:** to be moved on a dolly ⟨the camera can pan or ~ along with the subject⟩
³**dol·ly** \ˈdälē\ *n* -ES [Hindi *ḍālī*, lit., basket, tray] *India* **:** a present or offering (as of fruit, flowers, or confections)
dolly bar *n* **:** DOLLY 4b
dolly block *n* **:** DOLLY 4c
dollyhead \ˈ==ˌ=\ *n* [¹*dolly* + *head*] **:** an artificial model (as of papier-mâché) of a head made by a furrier for filling out the scalp of a skin
dol·ly·man \ˈ==mən\ *n, pl* **dollymen** [¹*dolly* + *man*] **:** one who works with a dolly **:** BUCKER
dolly-mop \ˈ==ˌ=\ *n* [¹*dolly* (woman)] *slang Brit* **:** STRUMPET, DRAB
dolly shot *n* [¹*dolly*] **:** a motion-picture or television shot taken while the dolly on which the camera is mounted is moving
dolly tub *n* [¹*dolly*] *dial Eng* **:** a washtub for washing with a dolly
dolly var·den \ˌdälēˈvärdᵊn, ˌdȯl-\ *n, cap D&V* [after *Dolly Varden*, gaily dressed coquette in *Barnaby Rudge* (1841), novel by Charles Dickens †1870 Eng. novelist] **1 :** a 19th century clothing style for women consisting of a print dress with a white fichu, tight bodice, and skirt with panniers, and a beflowered hat with a wide drooping brim **2 :** a large char (*Salvelinus malma*) that is olivaceous in color with round red or orange spots, attains a length of two or three feet and a weight of 20 pounds, is closely related to or possibly a variety of the eastern brook trout, and has an extensive range in streams west of the Cascade Range from the upper Sacramento northward, in the Columbia basin east to Montana, and in northern Japan as well as in coastal salt waters
dolly varden crab \ˌ==ˈ==-\ *n, usu cap D&V* **:** CALICO CRAB
dollyway \ˈ==ˌ=\ *n* [¹*dolly* + *way*] **:** an elevated runway from a sawmill to the drying yard over which lumber is moved
dol·ma \ˈdōlmə, -ˌmä\ *n* -s [Turk, lit., something stuffed, fr. *dolma* stuffed] **:** a vegetable shell (as of eggplant, green pepper, or zucchini) or a grape or cabbage leaf stuffed with a mixture of meat, rice, herbs, and seasonings and boiled
dol·man \ˈdōlmən, ˈdȯl-, ˈdäl-\ *n* -s [alter. of earlier *doliman*, fr. F, fr. Turk *dolama*, lit., act of winding, fr. *dolamak* to wind] **1 :** a long robe with sleeves worn by Turks **2 a :** a woman's wrap like a cape in vogue in the 19th century with wide sleeves cut in one piece with the body **b :** a woman's coat or jacket with similarly wide sleeves **3** [G, fr. Turk *dolama*] **:** a short jacket distinctive of many hussar uniforms usu. worn slung across one shoulder and fastened with a cord or chain
dolman sleeve *n* **:** a sleeve that is very wide at the armhole and tight at the wrist, is either set into a deep armhole or cut in one piece with the bodice, and is used in women's clothing

dolman sleeve

dol·men \ˈdōlmən, ˈdȯl-, ˈdäl-\ *n* -s [F, irreg. fr. Bret *tol*, *taol* table (fr. L *tabula* board, plank) + *maen*, *mēn* stone — more at TABLE, MENHIR] **:** a prehistoric monument consisting of two or more upright stones supporting a horizontal stone slab found esp. in Britain and France and thought to be a tomb
dol·o·me·des \ˌdäləˈmē(ˌ)dēz\ *n, cap* [NL, fr. Gk *dolomēdēs* crafty, wily] **:** a genus of large long-legged spiders (family Pisauridae) common in wet places and able to move freely over the surface of water
do·lo·mite \ˈdōləˌmīt, ˈdäl-, *usu* -īd.+V\ *n* -s [F, fr. Déodat de *Dolomieu* †1801 Fr. geologist & F *-ite*] **1 :** a mineral $CaMg(CO_3)_2$ consisting of a calcium magnesium carbonate found in rhombohedral crystals and in extensive beds as a compact limestone that is often crystalline granular and either white or clouded — called also *bitter spar* **2 :** a limestone or marble rich in magnesium carbonate
do·lo·mit·ic \ˌ==ˈmid·ik\ *adj* **1 :** containing dolomite **2 :** containing magnesium ⟨a pressure-hydrated ~ lime⟩
do·lo·mit·i·za·tion \ˌ==ˌmīd·əˈzāshən, -ˌməd-\ *n* -s **:** the process of converting into dolomite
do·lo·mit·ize \ˈ==ˌmīd·ˌīz, -ˌməˌtīz\ *vt* -ED/-ING/-S **:** to convert into dolomite
Dol·o·phine \ˈdäləˌfēn, -ˌfōn\ *trademark* — used for methadone
do·lor \ˈdōlə(r), *archaic* ˈdäl-\ *n* -s *see -or in Explan Notes* [ME *dolour*, fr. MF, fr. L *dolor*, fr. *dolēre* to feel pain, grieve — more at CONDOLE] **1** *obs* **:** physical pain — used in old medicine as one of five cardinal symptoms of inflammation **2 :** mental suffering or anguish **:** SORROW ⟨and yet nationally we go into the ~*s* whenever somebody remarks that we are weak in "preparation for citizenship" —W.W.Waymack⟩ **3** *obs* **:** LAMENTATION **syn** see DISTRESS
doloriferous *adj* [ML *doloriferus*, alter. of LL *dolorifer*, fr. L *dolor* + *-i-* + *-fer* -ferous] *obs* **:** producing pain
do·lo·rif·ic \ˌdōləˈrifik *sometimes* ˌdäl-\ *adj* [MF *dolorifique*, fr. ML *dolorificus*, fr. L *dolor* + *-i-* + *-ficus* -fic] **:** causing pain or grief
do·lor·i·fuge \dəˈlōrəˌfyüj\ *n* -s [*dolor* + *-i-* + *-fuge*] **:** something that banishes or mitigates grief
do·lo·ri·met·ric \ˌdōlərəˈme·trik, ˌdälərə-, dəˌlōrə-\ *adj* **:** using or obtained by dolorimetry — **do·lo·ri·met·ri·cal·ly** \-trə̇k(ə)lē\ *adv*
do·lo·rim·e·try \ˌdōləˈrimə·trē, ˌdäl-\ *n* -ES [*dolor* + *-i-* + *-metry*] **:** a method of measuring intensity of pain perception in degrees ranging from unpleasant to unbearable by using heat applied to the skin as a gauge
do·lo·ro·so \ˌdōləˈrō(ˌ)sō\ *adj (or adv)* [It, fr. LL *dolorosus*] **:** SORROWFUL, PLAINTIVE — used as a direction in music
do·lo·rous \ˈdōlərəs *sometimes* ˈdälər- *or* dəˈlōr- *or* dəˈlȯr-\ *adj* [ME, fr. MF *doleureus*, fr. LL *dolorosus*, fr. L *dolor* pain + *-osus* -ous] **1 :** occasioning pain ⟨washed down with wine of ~ acerbity —Nathaniel Hawthorne⟩ **2 a :** causing mental suffering or distress ⟨women and children howling and weeping — a most ~ sight —Dorothy Thompson⟩ **b :** highly regrettable **:** DEPLORABLE, LAMENTABLE ⟨the causes which have brought the world to its present ~ pass —P.E.More⟩ **3 :** marked by deep misery **:** WOEFUL ⟨during the ~ years of the depression —Amy Loveman⟩ **4 :** expressive of sorrow or affliction **:** DOLEFUL, LUGUBRIOUS ⟨that ~ aspect of human nature which in comedy is best portrayed by Molière —T.S. Eliot⟩ ⟨~ ballads of death and violence⟩ — **do·lo·rous·ly** *adv* — **do·lo·rous·ness** *n* -ES
dol·os \ˈdäˌläs\ *n, pl* **do·los·se** \dəˈläsə\ [Afrik] **:** a knucklebone of a sheep or goat used by Kafir witch doctors in divining — usu. used in pl.
do·lose \ˈdōˌlōs, dəˈl-\ *also* **do·lous** \ˈdōləs\ *adj* [L *dolosus* cunning, deceitful, fr. *dolus* fraud, deceit + *-osus* -ose, -ous — more at TALE] *Roman, civil, & Scots law* **:** characterized by criminal intent
¹**dol·phin** \ˈdälfən, ˈdȯl-\ *n* -s [ME, fr. MF *dophin*, *doffin*, *daufin*, fr. OF *dalfin*, fr. OProv, fr. ML *dalfinus*, alter. of L *delphinus*, fr. Gk *delphin-*, *delphis*, *delphin*; akin to Gk *delphys* womb; fr. its shape; akin to Skt *garbha* womb, Av *garəwa-*] **1 a :** any of various small toothed whales of the family Delphinidae that have the snout more or less elongated into a beak and the neck vertebrae partially fused — distinguished from *porpoise* **b :** PORPOISE 1 **2 :** either of two active pelagic spiny-finned fishes constituting the genus *Coryphaena* (family Coryphaenidae) which are widely distributed in tropical and temperate seas and the commoner of which (*C. hippurus*) usu. becomes about six feet long and is esteemed as food and noted for its brilliant colors when it is taken out of the water and is dying **3 :** one of the handles above the trunnions of an ancient cannon for lifting it **4 a :** a mass of iron or lead hung from the yardarm on ancient Greek ships of war to be dropped on the deck of an enemy's vessel **5 a** *archaic* **:** a wreath or strap of plaited cordage around a mast to aid in supporting the yard **b :** a mooring spar or buoy furnished with a ring to which boats may fasten their cables **c :** a mooring post on a wharf or beach — called also *bollard* **d :** a cluster of piles driven into the bottom of a harbor and bound firmly together for the mooring of boats **e :** a permanent fender around a heavy boat just below the gunwale **f :** SPLINE WEIGHT **6 :** a cluster of piles to which a boom is secured (as for protecting a bridge pier) **7 a** *or* **dolphin butterfly** *or* **dolphin fishtail :** BUTTERFLY 3g(2) **b :** a synchronized swimming stunt in which the body from a back floating position is arched and goes down headfirst to describe a complete circle back to the starting position
²**dolphin** \"\ *vi* -ED/-ING/-S **:** to swim in a series of plunges like a dolphin
³**dolphin** *obs var of* DAUPHIN
dolphinfish \ˈ==ˌ=\ *n* **:** DOLPHIN 2
dolphin flower *n* [so called fr. the shape of the nectary] **:** either of two larkspurs (*Delphinium consolida* and *D. ajacis*)
dolphin oil *n* **:** an unsaturated fatty oil obtained from the body, head, or jaw of a dolphin and used esp. as a fine lubricant — compare PORPOISE OIL
dolphin striker *n* **:** a vertical spar under the end of the bowsprit of a sailboat to extend and support the martingale — called also *martingale;* see SHIP illustration
dols *pl of* DOL
dolt \ˈdōlt\ *n* -s [prob. akin to OE *dol* foolish, silly — more at DULL] **:** a heavy stupid fellow **:** BLOCKHEAD, NUMSKULL
dolthead \ˈ=ˌ=\ *n* **:** BLOCKHEAD
dolt·ish \ˈdōltish, -tēsh\ *adj* **:** like a dolt **:** BLOCKISH, STUPID — **dolt·ish·ly** *adv* — **dolt·ish·ness** *n* -ES
do·lus \ˈdōləs\ *n* [L — more at TALE] **1** *Roman, civil, & Scots law* **:** the doing of anything that is contrary to good conscience **:** the use of a trick, stratagem, artifice, or device to deceive another **:** DECEIT **2** *Roman, civil, & Scots law* **:** evil or criminal intent similar to malice at the common law in the law of crimes **:** willful and wanton misconduct in the law of delicts **:** FRAUD, DECEPTION
dolus bo·nus \-ˈbōnəs\ *n* [L, good deceit] *Roman, civil, & Scots law* **:** simple cunning or sagacity in bargaining or in other transactions that is not actionable or punishable as fraud or misrepresentation or ground for rescinding the transaction induced by it
dolus ma·lus \-ˈmäləs, -ˈmāl-\ *n* [L, bad deceit] *Roman, civil, & Scots law* **:** fraud and misrepresentation that is actionable and punishable or is ground for rescinding the transaction resulting from it
¹**dom** \ˈdäm\ *n* -s [L *dominus* master — more at DAME] — often used as a title before the names of Benedictine and some other monks and canons regular
²**dom** \ˈdōm\ *n* -s *usu cap* [Hindi *ḍom*, fr. Skt *ḍoma*, *ḍomba* man of a low caste of musicians — more at ROMANY] **:** a member of a Hindu caste of untouchables that are like gypsies in their habits, engage in blacksmithing, tinsmithing, and basket-making, and cremate the dead
³**dom** \ˈdōm\ *n* -s [F *doum* — more at DOOM PALM] **:** DOOM PALM
-dom \dəm\ *n suffix* -s [ME, fr. OE *-dōm;* akin to OS *-dōm* -dom, OHG *-tuom*, ON *-dōmr;* all fr. a prehistoric Gmc noun represented by OE *dōm* judgment — more at DOOM] **1 a :** dignity **:** office ⟨duke*dom*⟩ **b :** realm **:** jurisdiction ⟨king*dom*⟩ ⟨Christen*dom*⟩ **c :** geographical area ⟨Anglo-Saxon*dom*⟩ **2 :** state, condition, or fact of being ⟨free*dom*⟩ ⟨martyr*dom*⟩ **3 :** those having a (specified) office, occupation, interest, or character ⟨official*dom*⟩ ⟨dog*dom*⟩ ⟨stamp*dom*⟩
dom *abbr* **1** domestic **2** dominion **3** dominus
DOM *abbr* [ML *Deo optimo maximo*] to God, the best and greatest
do·main \dōˈmān *also* dəˈ-\ *n* -s [MF *demaine*, *domaine*, fr. L *dominium*, fr. *dominus* master, owner — more at DAME] **1** *archaic* **:** landed property which one has in his own right **:** DEMESNE 2 **2 a :** the possessions of a sovereign, feudal lord, nation, or commonwealth ⟨built up the ~*s* of the Papal States—R.A.Hall b.1911⟩ ⟨the great Forest of Galtres . . . was a royal ~ —Edwin Benson⟩ ⟨the buffaloes and bears marched in single file, as did also the Indians when traveling beyond the ~ of their nation —S.C.Williams⟩ **b :** a territory possessed and governed of right or over which authority is exercised of right ⟨the Roman Church has had a far greater ~ and longevity than the Roman Empire —Weston La Barre⟩ ⟨where great cattle ~*s* stretched over seemingly endless miles —*Amer. Guide Series: Texas*⟩ **c :** field of control or range of governance ⟨our highways and roads have been in the ~ of state and local governments —T.H.White b. 1915⟩ ⟨poetical works belong to the ~ of our permanent passions —Matthew Arnold⟩ — see EMINENT DOMAIN, PUBLIC DOMAIN **d :** a region distinctively marked or wholly overspread or dominated by some physical feature ⟨a ~ of peaks, forests, and roaring rivers —R.L.Neuberger⟩ **3 a :** a distinctly delimited sphere of knowledge or of intellectual, institutional, or cultural activity (as a humanistic or scientific discipline, a form of artistic creation, a department of research) ⟨the ~ of biblical scholarship⟩ ⟨psychiatry seems unwilling merely to resist invasion of its ~ —Bernard DeVoto⟩ ⟨the ~ of ascertainable fact should be clearly distinguished from the ~ of personal opinion —Stuart Hampshire⟩ **b :** a circumscribed realm of human concern ⟨in the ~ of rural economy⟩ ⟨argot is really a dialect whose ~ is social instead of regional —A.L.Guérard⟩ **c :** one's peculiar and exclusive function or field of active cultivation and responsibility ⟨without intruding on the expert's ~ —S.L.A.Marshall⟩ ⟨problems which were formerly regarded as belonging exclusively to the ~ of philosophers —W.V.Houston⟩ ⟨intellectual qualities which liberal education has typically staked out for itself as its own special ~ —H.D.Gideonse⟩ **4 a :** a mathematical aggregate to which a variable is confined ⟨the ~ of real numbers⟩ ⟨the ~ of rational numbers⟩ **b :** an aggregate of elements each of which is a first element of an ordered pair **5 :** a small region of a ferromagnetic substance that contains many atoms all oriented in the same direction so that the group as a whole acts as a completely saturated magnet, the relative orientations of these regions determining the magnetization of the magnet **6** *logic* **a :** the realm of applicability of an idea or notion or the range of values within which a variable may govern **b** *for a relation R* **:** the class of things *x* for which there is at least one thing *y* such that *xRy* holds ⟨the ~ of *father of* is the class of male parents⟩ **7 :** the segment of speech throughout which a linguistic feature such as grammatical agreement or a pitch or stress contour extends **syn** see FIELD
do·main·al \-ᵊnᵊl\ *adj* **:** DOMANIAL
¹**do·mal** \ˈdōməl\ *adj* [in sense 1, fr. L *domus* house + E *-al;* in sense 2 & 3, fr. ¹*dome* + *-al*] **1** *archaic* **:** relating to a house **2 :** shaped like a dome ⟨a ~ arrangement of the strata far beneath the ocean floor —R.E.Hardwicke⟩ ⟨a ~ eruption⟩ **3 :** RETROFLEX — **do·mal·ly** \-əlē\ *adv*
²**domal** \"\ *n* -s **:** a domal speech sound
domal mountain *n* **:** DOME MOUNTAIN
do·ma·ni·al \dōˈmānēəl\ *adj* [ML *domanialis*, fr. L *dominium* domain + *-alis* -al — more at DOMAIN] **1 :** constituting or belonging to a domain or to a particular domain (as a manor) **:** held in one's own hands as possessor by free tenure — distinguished from *alodial* and *feudal* **2 :** having or belonging to a domain
do·mat·ic \(ˈ)dōˈmad·ik\ *adj* [ISV ¹*dome* + *-atic* (as in *prismatic*)] **:** belonging to a crystallographic class of symmetry of the monoclinic system that is characterized by a dome **:** CLINODOMATIC
do·ma·tium \dōˈmāsh(ē)əm\ *n, pl* **doma·tia** \-(ē)ə\ [NL, fr. Gk *dōmation* small house, bedroom, dim. of *dōma* house; akin to Gk *domos* house — more at TIMBER] **:** a portion of a plant (as on or in a leaf) modified to form a chamber or other form of shelter for insects, mites, or fungi
dom·beya \dämˈbāə, ˈdämbēə\ *n, cap* [NL, after Joseph *Dombey* †1794 Fr. botanist] **:** a genus of African shrubs or small trees (family Sterculiaceae) having palmately nerved leaves, showy flowers with five petals, and capsular fruit
dom·dan·iel \dämˈdanyəl\ *n* -s *usu cap* [fr. *Domdaniel*, fictitious submarine chamber in Arabic tales translated by Jacques Cazotte †1792 Fr. writer & Dom Denys Chavys, 18th cent. Fr. monk of Arabian origin] *archaic* **:** a den of iniquity
¹**dome** \ˈdōm\ *n* -s [F, It, & L; F *dôme* dome, cathedral, fr. It *duomo* cathedral, fr. ML *domus* church, fr. L, house — more at TIMBER] **1 a** *archaic* **:** a stately building **:** MANSION **b :** RESORT, RETREAT — used esp. with *pleasure* ⟨the pleasure ~*s* of Reno or Las Vegas —Jack Goodman⟩ **2 :** a vaulted circular roof or ceiling **3** *obs* **:** a cathedral church **4 :** a natural formation, a structure, or a projecting part arched and rounded that has some resemblance to a cupola or vaulted ceiling of a building: **a :** the upper part of a reverberatory furnace **b :** the roof of a vaulted cavern **c :** a rounded mountaintop or vast mound of ice **d :** an overhanging hemispherical space or area ⟨the sun seeming to hang in a coppery ~⟩ ⟨projected on the ~ of the planetarium⟩ **e :** the vertical chamber on the top of a steam boiler or of a tank car **f :** the hemispherical or cylindrical roof of an astronomical observatory providing for rotation of the observing slit to any part of the sky **g** (1) **:** a glass-enclosed compartment built into the roof of a railroad

dome 2

car to permit upper-deck passengers an unobstructed view in every direction ⟨adopted the ~ car as standard equipment⟩ (2) : ASTRODOME **h** : the arching periphery of the carcass of a pneumatic tire **i** : a concave approximately quarter-spherical usu. plaster structure backing and overhanging a theatrical stage **5** : the back inside cap or case of a jointed-case watch **6 a** : a form of crystal composed of planes parallel to a lateral axis which meet above in a horizontal edge like a roof — see BRACHYDOME, CLINODOME, MACRODOME, ORTHODOME **b** : a form of crystal composed of only two faces intersecting along and astride of a symmetry plane regardless of the orientation of the line of their intersection **7 a** : a doubly plunging anticline that is broad in comparison with its length and consequently approximately circular or elliptical in plan : a quaquaversal fold ⟨the Ozark ~ is many miles in diameter⟩ ⟨some small and steep-sided salt ~*s* in Louisiana⟩ ⟨at the top of a ~ oil and gas may have collected⟩ **b** : a rock mass in domical form ⟨the granite ~*s* of the Yosemite⟩ **c** : a rounded snow peak **d** : a broad gently sloping volcano — called also *shield volcano, volcanic dome* **8** : a rounded isolated elevation on the ocean bottom at depths greater than 100 fathoms **9** *chiefly slang* : a person's head **10** : a ball-shaped or mushroom-shaped clothing accessory: **a** : a raised button **b** : SNAP FASTENER **11** : a rounded-arch element in the wave tracing in an electroencephalogram

²dome \"\ *vb* -ED/-ING/-S *vt* **1** : to cover with or as if with a dome **2** : to press, bend, or thrust up into a dome ⟨upward pressure from underlying magma ~*s* the surface —*Jour. of Geology*⟩ ⟨shaping the cover with a *doming* mallet⟩ ~ *vi* **1** : to swell upward or outward like a dome **2** : to arch overhead in a dome (as of the sky)

dome bed *n* : a bed with a dome-shaped canopy

domed \-md\ *adj* **1** : having an arched and rounded shape like that of an approximately hemispherical dome ⟨his ~ forehead, great white moustache —John Galsworthy⟩ ⟨red and blue ~ precision-prism lenses⟩ **2** : constructed or roofed with a dome ⟨topped by a ~ belfry⟩

dome light *n* : a light in the ceiling (as of an automobile)

dome mountain *n* : a mountain range resulting from dissection of a structural dome (as the Black Hills in So. Dakota) — called also *domal mountain*

do·ment \ˈdüment, -ˌment\ *n* -S [¹*do* + *-ment*] *dial Eng* : CELEBRATION, ENTERTAINMENT, AFFAIR

dome of silence : a furniture caster consisting of a single large ball in a retainer

dom·er \ˈdōmə(r)\ *n* -S : an operator or a machine that shapes box tops

¹domes·day \ˈdümz,dā, ˈdōm-\ *archaic var of* DOOMSDAY

²domesday \"\ *adj* [fr. the 11th cent. *Domesday (Book)*] : of or relating to the 11th cent. Domesday Book or the time of its compilation

domesday book *n, usu cap D&B* [fr. the *Domesday Book*, a Latin census of English property compiled by order of William the Conqueror 1085–86] : a census compiled usu. from a comprehensive survey of a geographical sector ⟨a sort of *Domesday Book*, in which the merits and demerits of each individual were recorded —J.W.Waterhouse⟩

¹do·mes·tic \dəˈmestik, dōˈ-, -tēk\ *adj* [MF *domestique*, fr. L *domesticus*, fr. *domus* house — more at TIMBER] **1** *obs* : enjoying intimate status (as in a household) : being familiar as if at home **2 a** : relating to the household or the family : concerned with or employed in the management of a household or private place of residence — distinguished from *public* ⟨affects the house at large and the course of ~ affairs —Herbert Spencer⟩ ⟨the servant has risen in the world and become a ~ worker —Gabriel Ullstein⟩ **b** : connected with the supply, service, and activities of households and private residences — distinguished from *industrial* ⟨coke as a fuel for ~ heating plants⟩ ⟨sewing, interior decoration, and other ~ arts⟩ ⟨a scarcity of ~ help⟩ **c** : suited to the physical requirements and livability of a private dwelling ⟨the community, which possesses a ~ architecture of charm and distinction —*Amer. Guide Series: N.C.*⟩; *also* : engaged in designing private dwellings ⟨both an ecclesiastical and a ~ architect⟩ **d** : belonging to or incumbent on the family or members of the family ⟨~ status⟩ ⟨the ~ chastity required is recommended in effect to produce an equilibrium population —G.E.Hutchinson⟩ : participated in by or emanating from members of a family ⟨there seemed no place for myself in this ~ tableau —Christopher Isherwood⟩ ⟨under strict ~ orders not to sit out of doors —John Buchan⟩ **e** : peculiar to or affecting the intimate relations and amenities of a family group living together ⟨Diderot never achieved ~ happiness, either in his marriage or in his many affairs of the heart —J.S.Schapiro⟩ ⟨there are others beside Charles Lamb who are peculiarly sensitive to the charm of the ~ —John Dewey⟩; *also* : associated with family obligations and harmony ⟨her many ~ virtues⟩ ⟨weighed down with ~ worries⟩ **f** : dealing with the intimate life of a family group ⟨we have the ~ epic dealing with the details of modern life which pass daily under our eyes —Matthew Arnold⟩ ⟨~ drama of the sentimental kind⟩ **3** : relating and limited to one's own country or the country under consideration or its internal affairs and interests **4 a** : belonging or occurring within the sphere of authority or control or the fabric or boundaries of the indicated nation or sovereign state : INTERNAL ⟨charts of ~ as well as foreign waters⟩ ⟨once a state has assumed such an obligation the matter ceases to be within its ~ jurisdiction —Quincy Wright⟩; *specif* : involving activities of or within the national government ⟨a ~ power struggle between the president and the congress⟩ **b** : affecting the welfare of or experienced or participated in by the citizenry of the indicated country ⟨a depression that proved one of our worst ~ calamities⟩ ⟨evincing a major interest in ~ politics⟩ ⟨painting the ~ scene in somber colors⟩; *also* : living and occupied within one's own country ⟨the various forms of entertainment available to ~ vacationers⟩ ⟨all the critics, ~ and foreign —S.P.Sherman⟩ **c** : carried on, operating or serving, produced, or distributed within the bounds of the indicated country or region ⟨the ~ shipping industry declined after 1939⟩ ⟨the acknowledged power of a state to regulate its police, its ~ trade —John Marshall⟩ ⟨~ corporations, that is, those chartered by the state in which they do business —M.S.Kendrick⟩ ⟨short trip services by a ~ airline⟩ ⟨formerly scornful of the quality of our ~ wines⟩ ⟨caves used for the ripening of a ~ Roquefort-type cheese⟩ ⟨cats of various breeds, some ~, some imported⟩; *also* : applying only within these bounds ⟨~ airmail rates⟩ ⟨~ prices of oil products⟩ **d** : INDIGENOUS ⟨~ snails representing 12 species of the family Bulimidae⟩ **e** : domiciled in the home state of the regulatory authority concerned — used of an insurance company **5 a** : living near or about the habitations of man ⟨rats, roaches, and other ~ vermin⟩ **b** : DOMESTICATED, TAME **6** : devoted to home duties and pleasures ⟨author of blood-and-thunder novels, yet quite ~ in his tastes⟩

²domestic \"\ *n* -S **1** *obs* : HOUSEMATE **2** *obs* : a native citizen **3** : a household servant **4** : an article of domestic manufacture: as **a** : common cotton cloth (as sheeting) **b** : an American-made rug as distinguished from an Oriental rug **c domestics** *pl* : household linens and bedding

do·mes·ti·ca·ble \-təkəbəl, -tēk-\ *adj* [*domesticate* + *-able*] : capable of being domesticated

do·mes·ti·cal \-kəl\ *adj* [ME *domysticall*, fr. MF *domestique* + ME *-al* — more at DOMESTIC] *archaic* : DOMESTIC

do·mes·ti·cal·i·ty \dəˌmestəˈkaləd·ē, dō,-\ *n* -ES : DOMESTICITY

do·mes·ti·cal·ly \-ˈmestək(ə)lē, -tēk-, -li\ *adv* **1** : in a domestic or familiar way **2** : in domestic territory **3** : with respect to domestic affairs ⟨~ he proposed a conservative program⟩

domestic animal *n* : any of various animals (as the horse, ox, or sheep) which have been domesticated by man so as to live and breed in a tame condition — compare FERAE NATURAE

domestic architecture *n* : the architecture of single or multiple dwellings

¹do·mes·ti·cate \dəˈmestə,kāt, dōˈ- *usu* -ād.+V\ *vb* -ED/-ING/-S [¹*domestic* + *-ate*] *vt* **1 a** : to bring into domestic use : ADOPT, NATURALIZE ⟨a European custom *domesticated* here⟩ **b** : to bring into a degree of conformity and comfortable accommodation with one's home environment ⟨an alien philosophy difficult to ~ here⟩ **2** : to cause to be domestically engaged, inclined, or adapted ⟨offering home economics to ~ the female prisoners⟩ ⟨whether she could ~ her explorer husband⟩ **3 a** : to adapt (an animal or plant) to life in intimate association with and to the advantage of man or another species usu. by modifying growth and traits through provision of food, protection from enemies, and selective breeding during generations of living in association and often to the extent that the domesticated form loses the ability to survive in nature ⟨the fungi *domesticated* by certain ants produce special bromatia on which the ants feed⟩ ⟨man *domesticated* the dog⟩ **b** : to subject to the control and service of man ⟨settled communities were made possible by *domesticating* watercourses⟩ **4 a** : to bring to the level (as of understanding) of ordinary people : FAMILIARIZE ⟨he *domesticated* the fairy tale and gave it a townsman's home —Robert Lynd⟩ **b** : to force into a mold of accepted conduct or thought : make conform ⟨this deliberate attempt of the universities to ~ our poets, if not to tame them —Conrad Aiken⟩ ~ *vi* **1** *archaic* **a** : to live in the same household **b** : to settle in or become habituated to an ordered household **c** : to make one's home : SETTLE **2** : to obtain a charter of incorporation in a particular state ⟨an unlicensed foreign corporation doing business in the state without *domesticating*⟩

²domes·ti·cate \-stəkə̇t, -stə,kāt, *usu* ǀd.+V\ *n* -S : a domesticated animal or plant

domesticated *adj, Brit* : experienced in the duties of housekeeping and the details of household management

do·mes·ti·ca·tion \ˌ,mestəˈkāshən\ *n* -S : the action or process of domesticating or the state of being domesticated ⟨according to Hahn, ~ involves free breeding in captivity —R.H.Lowie⟩ ⟨the ant's ~ of the aphid⟩ ⟨carbon monoxide . . . has been a hazard to man since the ~ of fire —Berton Roueché⟩ ⟨what might be expected to result from the ~ in a free environment of the inchoate idealisms of English Puritanism —V.L.Parrington⟩

do·mes·ti·ca·tive \-ˈmestə,kād·iv, -təkəd-\ *adj* : tending to domesticate

do·mes·ti·ca·tor \-tə,kād·ə(r)\ *n* -S : one that domesticates

domestic bill *n* : INLAND BILL

domestic cat *n* : CAT 1a

domestic economy *n* : the theory and practice of household management

domestic factor *n* : a factor doing business in the same state or country as his principal — compare FOREIGN FACTOR

domestic fowl *n* **1** : POULTRY **2** : a bird of one of the breeds developed from the jungle fowl (*Gallus gallus*) including some specialized for meat production and others for egg laying, for fighting, or purely for ornament or show : CHICKEN — see BANTAM, BRAHMA, GAME FOWL, LEGHORN

do·mes·tic·i·ty \(ˌ)dō,meˈstisəd·ē, də,-, -atē, -i\ *n* -ES [¹*domestic* + *-ity*] **1** : the quality or state of being domestic or domesticated ⟨a royal family living in unpretentious ~⟩ ⟨the untidy ~ of pigeons —Lewis Mumford⟩ **2** : domestic activities or life ⟨making a hobby of ~⟩ **3 domesticities** *pl* : domestic affairs ⟨she bore the brunt of *domesticities* of which he was ever utterly impatient —M.A.D.Howe *b*1864⟩

do·mes·ti·cize \dəˈmestə,sīz, dōˈ-\ *vt* -ED/-ING/-S [*domestic* + *-ize*] : DOMESTICATE

domestic relations court *n* : COURT OF DOMESTIC RELATIONS

domestic science *n* : instruction and training in domestic management and the household arts (as cooking and sewing) — compare HOME ECONOMICS

domestic ship *n* : a ship whose owner is resident in the country considered as one's own

domestic system *n* : a system of manufacturing based upon work done at home on materials supplied by merchant employers — contrasted with *factory system;* compare COTTAGE INDUSTRY

do·met *or* **do·mett** \dōˈmet, ˈdämə̇t\ *n* -S [origin unknown] : a cotton or cotton and wool flannel similar to outing flannel

domey *var of* DOMY

do·mey·kite \dōˈmā,kīt\ *n* -S [G *domeykit*, fr. Ignacio *Domeyko* †1889 Polish mineralogist in Chile + G *-it* -ite] : a mineral Cu_3As (sp. gr., 7.2–7.75) of tin-white or steel-gray color consisting of copper arsenide

dom·ic \ˈdōmik, ˈdäm-\ *or* **dom·i·cal** \-məkəl\ *adj* [¹*dome* + *-ic, -ical*] : relating to, shaped like, or having a dome — **dom·i·cal·ly** \-mək(ə)lē\ *adv*

dom·i·cil·able \ˈdämə,sīləbəl, ˈdōm-, ,≈ˈ≈≈≈\ *adj* : eligible to be domiciled

¹dom·i·cile \ˈdämə,sīl, ˈdōmə,sīl, ˈdäməsəl, ˈdämə(,)sil\ *also* **dom·i·cil** \ˈdäməsəl, -(,)sil\ *n* -S [MF, fr. L *domicilium*, fr. *domus* house — more at TIMBER] **1** : the place of residence either of an individual or of a family : ABODE **2 a** : the place with which a person has a settled connection for important legal purposes (as determination of his civil status, jurisdiction to impose personal judgments or taxes on him, or determination of the succession to his personal property on his death) : the place of his permanent and principal home or of his last such home if he has not yet acquired a new one or the place assigned by law to him as his home if he has no legal capacity to choose his own (as in the case of a minor or insane person) **b** : an actual dwelling place that is one's permanent and principal home **c** : the state in which a corporation or business concern is created or incorporated : the principal place of doing business or maintaining an office of a corporation or business concern as registered in accordance with law

²domicile \"\ *vt* -ED/-ING/-S **1** : to settle in or provide with a domicile ⟨benefits extended to veterans *domiciled* in hospitals⟩ **2** : to make (a bill of exchange or promissory note) payable at a designated place other than that of the residence of the drawee

domiciled *adj* : having an established domicile

domicile of choice : a domicile that a person acquires by an exercise of his own will while he has legal capacity to change his domicile

domicile of origin : the domicile assigned to a person at his birth; *esp* : the domicile of a child's father at the time of the child's birth

¹dom·i·cil·iary \ˌdäməˈsilē,erē, ,dōm-, -lyərē, -ri\ *also* **dom·i·cil·i·ar** \-lēə(r), -ē,är, -ē,å(r)\ *adj* [F *domiciliaire*, fr. MF, fr. ML *domiciliarius*, fr. L *domicilium* domicile + *-arius* -ary — more at DOMICILE] : relating to a domicile: **a** : serving as a domicile ⟨~ mounds⟩ **b** : including or regarding the domicile of the person under consideration ⟨jeopardizing his ~ status⟩ **c** : provided or attended in the home rather than in an institution ⟨~ obstetrics⟩ **d** : providing, constituting, or provided by a rest home for chronically ill or permanently disabled war veterans requiring minimal medical attention ⟨~ care available⟩ ⟨state ~ facilities⟩

²domiciliary \"\ *n* -ES : a domiciliary establishment (as for disabled veterans) : BARRACKS

domiciliary visit *n* : a visit to a private dwelling (as for searching it) under authority

dom·i·cil·i·ate \-lē,āt\ *vb* -ED/-ING/-S [L *domicilium* domicile + E *-ate*] *vt* **1** : DOMICILE **2** : DOMESTICATE 3, 4 ~ *vi* : to establish residence : RESIDE — **dom·i·cil·i·a·tion** \ˌ≈≈,≈≈ˈāshən\ *n* -S

domify *vt* -ED/-ING/-ES [ME *domifyen*, fr. ML *domificare* to build a house, fr. *domi-* (fr. L *domus* house) + L *-ficare* -fy — more at TIMBER] **1** *obs* : to divide (the zodiac) into 12 houses **2** *obs* : to specify the position of (a planet) in one of the houses of the zodiac

domina *n, pl* **dominae** *often cap* [L, mistress, lady — more at DAME] *obs* : a woman of rank; *specif* : a woman holding a barony in her own right

do·mi·na li·tis \ˈdämənə ˈlēǀd·əs, -ˈlīǀ\ *n, pl* **domi·nae litis** \-,nīˈlē|, -,nēˈlī|\ [L, mistress of the suit] : a female client in a law case

dom·i·nance \ˈdämənən(t)s\ *n* -S **1** : dominant position in an order of forcefulness : ASCENDANCY ⟨the sexes in chimpanzees are about as different from each other dimorphously as human sexes are, but ~ in the band may be by either sex —Weston La Barre⟩ ⟨in total, it would create a situation ultimately favorable to Soviet ~ in the world —Dean Acheson⟩; *specif* : the relative position of an animal in the social hierarchy of its kind — compare PECK ORDER **2** : position or exercise of dominant authority, leadership, or influence ⟨the ~ of government in the field of labor relations⟩ ⟨even boards of directors, the theoretical representatives of the stockholders, have more and more come under managerial ~ —*Fortune*⟩ **3** : dominant position in space ⟨the ~ of the towers of the cathedral over the city⟩ **4** : highest or superior prevalence : PREPONDERANCE ⟨on a continent where the rural life is predominant, Argentina is notable for the ~ of its big cities —P.E. James⟩ ⟨the area provides a ~ of effusive igneous rocks⟩ **5 a** : the quality of one of a pair of alleles that suppresses the expression of the other member of the pair when both are present; *also* : the suppression so exerted **b** : the influence or control over ecological communities exhibited by dominants **c** : functional asymmetry between a pair of bodily structures ⟨~ of the right hand over the left in right-handedness⟩

¹dom·i·nant \-mənənt\ *adj* [MF or L; MF, fr. L *dominant-, dominans*, pres. part. of *dominari* to rule, govern — more at DOMINATE] **1 a** : commanding, controlling, or having supremacy or ascendancy over all others by reason of superior strength or power ⟨the emperors were the ~ members of the papal-imperial partnership which claimed universal rule over all Christendom —W.K.Ferguson⟩ ⟨considered as a subordinate and inferior class of beings, who had been subjugated by the ~ race —R.B.Taney⟩ ⟨in spite however of this rapid recovery of its strength by Mercia, Northumberland remained the ~ state in Britain —J.R.Green⟩ ⟨during the latter part of this period Islam was ~ over the greater part of India —Seymour Vesey-Fitzgerald⟩ **b** *astrology* : exercising chief influence ⟨having Saturn ~ in his horoscope⟩ **2 a** : superior to all others in guiding and directive influence : most determinative ⟨an archaistic movement running counter to the ~ historical movement —Bernard Smith⟩ ⟨I will not say that money has ceased to be the ~ force in American life —Max Lerner⟩ ⟨this society has been the ~ influence in the city's musical life⟩ **b** : having authority or prestige or compelling character such as to subordinate others ⟨during the middle ages, for example, the feudal family was ~ over business and frequently ignored government —Herbert Agar⟩ ⟨a ~ individuality refuses to be subdued to what it works in —J.L. Lowes⟩ ⟨he occupied a ~ position in the Republican party counsels —H.W.H.Knott⟩ **3 a** : overlooking and commanding from a superior elevation ⟨the dome of the state capitol ~ on the skyline⟩ ⟨the ~ hill⟩ **b** *of a forest tree* : sufficiently taller than surrounding trees as to have the crown exposed to sunlight from the sides as well as above **4** : prevailing over all others in number, frequency, or distribution or in productivity or fecundity : PREDOMINANT, PREPONDERANT, CHIEF ⟨the ~ industry⟩ ⟨the four principal eras of geological time may be identified by the names given to the ~ form of animal life in each —R.W.Murray⟩ ⟨cotton and corn are the ~ crops in the section⟩ **5 a** : prevailing over all others in extent and firmness of acceptance ⟨why a complex of beliefs is ~ at one time and subordinate at another —Irving Howe⟩ ⟨prolonged economic depression will invariably be accompanied by a loss of confidence in the ~ system —L.S.Feuer⟩ : surpassing or overshadowing others in prominence ⟨melancholy was the ~ note of his temperament —James Joyce⟩ ⟨the ~ hue of the glass should be sage green —H.G.Armstrong⟩ **b** : holding the foremost position or rank or the preeminence in fulfilling a function or role ⟨and certainly the least debatable fact in terms of American myth is that Abraham Lincoln became our ~ folk hero —E.H.Eby⟩ ⟨the ~ theme in the first book is the splendor of life —E.K.Brown⟩ **6** : having a right of servitude or easement attached or enjoying such a right ⟨a ~ estate⟩ ⟨a ~ owner⟩ **7** : relating to the dominant of the musical scale **8** : of or relating to an ecological dominant : exerting ecological dominance **9** : *of paired bodily structures* : being the one that is more effective or predominant in action ⟨~ eye⟩ ⟨~ hand⟩ ⟨~ hemisphere⟩ **10** *of an allele* : predominating over a contrasting allele in its manifestation — opposed to *recessive* ⟨tallness is ~, dwarfness recessive⟩ ⟨many apparently ~ characters are actually examples of multifactorial determination⟩; compare MENDEL'S LAW **11** : growing more vigorously than other parts of the same embryo and exerting a controlling influence on adjacent tissues

syn PREDOMINANT, PARAMOUNT, PREPONDERANT, PREPONDERATING, SOVEREIGN: DOMINANT connotes swaying, ruling, or commanding ⟨a *dominant* economic group which calls itself an aristocracy —V.L.Parrington⟩ ⟨the *dominant* tendency of thought in the nineteenth century as expressed by Darwin —H.J.Mackinder⟩ ⟨the emigration to America had fortunately taken place in a way which made the English language and English institutions everywhere *dominant* —Allan Nevins & H.S.Commager⟩ PREDOMINANT stresses commanding influence and occas. may suggest recent ascendancy ⟨the Catholic Church must prosper by the French energy and with the French Crown at least strong and independent; better yet, *predominant* —Hilaire Belloc⟩ ⟨the emotional elements (and they were the *predominant* and overwhelming) of the Christian *vita contemplativa* —H.O.Taylor⟩ PARAMOUNT indicates supremacy in power, rank, or importance ⟨Napoleon was master of the whole continent . . . . In the Europe of 1808 every State had been brought into a defined relation to the *paramount* power, by annexation, by vassalage, or by alliance on terms of submission —G.M.Trevelyan⟩ ⟨certainly all those who have framed written constitutions contemplate them as forming the fundamental and *paramount* law of the nation —John Marshall⟩ ⟨as the *paramount* question in the life of a bird is the question of food —John Burroughs⟩ PREPONDERANT and PREPONDERATING describe influence or power that outweighs everything else ⟨some contact of some human individuals must necessarily happen if anything cultural is to spread. But the contact need by no means be the migration of whole populations; and the evidence is *preponderant* that mostly it is not —A.L.Kroeber⟩ ⟨through its banking and financial affiliations it also exercises a *preponderating* control over the money and credit of the country —*Current History*⟩ Every other thing is clearly subordinate or inferior to that which is SOVEREIGN ⟨forced to defend their contention that Parliament, although *sovereign* in the empire, did not have control over the internal affairs of the colonies —S.E.Morison & H.S.Commager⟩ ⟨the older superstition of medieval medicine that bloodletting is the only and the *sovereign* remedy for all bodily ills —M.R.Cohen⟩

²dominant \"\ *n* -S **1** : something that is dominant ⟨elimination of undesirable ~*s* in color films⟩ ⟨the deeper-lying psychic elements are the least readily brought into consciousness, while they are the constant unrealized ~*s* of the mind —A.G. Tansley⟩ : one that is dominant ⟨to the urban ecologist the central business district is considered a ~, maintaining the control of certain environmental characteristics —*Social Forces*⟩ ⟨among the more traditional painters Dufy on the one hand and Van Gogh on the other seem to be the ~*s* —R.M. Coates⟩ **2 a** : the principal reciting note in the ecclesiastical modes usu. a fifth above the final in the authentic modes and a third above in the plagal **b** : the fifth note of the scale ⟨G is the ~ of the key of C⟩ **3** *biol* **a** : a dominant character or factor **b** : an organism possessing one or more dominant characters **4 a** : any of one or more kinds of organism (as a species or variety) in an ecological association that by reason of size, number, or habits exerts a controlling influence on the environment and thereby largely determines what other kinds of organisms share in the association **b** : any of one or more kinds of organism that constitutes the bulk or most conspicuous element of an ecological community **5** : a dominant forest tree

dom·i·nant·ly *adv* **1** : to a surpassing extent or degree : for the most part : PREVAILINGLY **2** : in a dominant position

dominant seventh chord *n* : a seventh chord comprising a major triad and a minor seventh and occurring on the dominant of a major or a minor scale — see SEVENTH CHORD illustration

dominant term *n* : the mathematical term greater in absolute value than any other (as in a set) or than the sum of the others

dominant wavelength *n* : wavelength of the spectrum light that when combined in suitable proportions with the specified achromatic light yields a match with the light being considered — see COLOR 1c

dom·i·nate \ˈdämə,nāt, *usu* -ād.+V\ *vb* -ED/-ING/-S [L *dominatus*, past part. of *dominari* to rule, govern, fr. *dominus* lord, master — more at DAME] *vt* **1 a** : to hold supremacy or mastery over by reason of superior power, strength, authority, or prowess ⟨it has been said that whoever ~*s* Germany controls

Europe⟩ ⟨regional blocs *dominated* by the great powers might well defy the decisions of the Security Council —Vera M. Dean⟩ ⟨the Cabinet ~*s* the government of a province in much the same way and to the same extent as the federal Cabinet ~*s* the government of Canada —R.M.Dawson⟩ ⟨the family financial houses that *dominated* prewar Japan's industry⟩ ⟨a racketeer-*dominated* union⟩ **b :** to hold in subjection through force of personality or other intangible force ⟨the emotions of the prima donna in the hour when she ~*s* her audience must be unique —Arnold Bennett⟩ ⟨the resentment of subordination and the tendency to ~ others are both grounded in fear —G.S.Blum⟩ ⟨the power to alter and so to ~ much of his environment —W.E.Swinton⟩ **2 a :** to determine decisively the course or aim or the direction of development of ⟨the Nile ~*s* all life in Egypt for good and for bad —Herbert Moller⟩ ⟨two other leaders ~ that dynamic age: Innocent III and Frederick II —Will Durant⟩ ⟨the highest efficiency cannot be produced in any human being unless his whole character and his whole activity be *dominated* by some sentiment or passion —C.W.Eliot⟩ **b :** to exert the supreme determining or guiding influence upon ⟨I have been criticized for "being *dominated*" by ideas rather than *dominating* them while composing —J.D.Cook⟩ ⟨painting, essentially a two-dimensional art, was for centuries *dominated* by the effort to achieve tridimensionality —Herbert Read⟩ ⟨Brown was well over 50 years of age before the idea of freeing the slaves by force *dominated* his mind⟩ **3 :** to overlook from a superior elevation or command because of superior height ⟨the once fiery volcano ~*s* the land for a hundred miles around —G.W. Long⟩ ⟨the Presidentials ~ the other mountain ranges —Bernard DeVoto⟩ ⟨a war-memorial tower ~*s* the campus⟩ ⟨the meetinghouse which ~*s* the square —R.M.Hodesh⟩ **4 a :** to overspread or permeate so as to push all else into the background : PREDOMINATE ⟨the cypress, gum, and white cedar which ~ this swamp forest⟩ ⟨Easterners early fixed the culture pattern *dominating* this section⟩ ⟨this dream pervades the life of a culture as the fantasies of night ~ the mind of a sleeper —Lewis Mumford⟩ ⟨the idea of inescapable illness and operations *dominated* his life some years before he died —R.T. Hopkins⟩ **b :** to occupy in respect to prevalence or prominence the foremost position in ⟨cotton manufacture ~*s* the city⟩ ⟨name brands ~ the market⟩ ⟨in Congress law ~*s* the professions⟩ ⟨national security expenditures continue to ~ the budget⟩ ⟨Egyptian art is *dominated* by religion⟩ **5 a :** to prevail or be paramount in by virtue of superior or significant quality ⟨he is one of those figures that ~ an age —Clive Bell⟩ ⟨collecting rather than creating man ~*s* the art scene at the moment —Emily Genauer⟩ ⟨his eyes were closed and no longer *dominated* his face with their fierce pride —T.B.Costain⟩ **b :** to hold a preeminence in or over esp. so as to submerge all else in obscurity ⟨in his interiors . . . color so ~*s* the canvas that the composition dissolves into a series of lights —Denys Sutton⟩ ⟨budgetary developments so drastic as to ~ the economic outlook —R.A.Musgrave⟩ ~ *vi* **1 :** to hold superiority or mastery in power or strength ⟨it was necessary for her to ~ and enslave, all her virtues — her strong lust to serve, to give, to nurse, to amuse — came from the imperative need for dominance over almost all she touched —Thomas Wolfe⟩ ⟨his lust for power, his craving to ~, his burning sense of a historical mission given to him by God —W.L.Shirer⟩ **2 :** to provide directive control : constitute governing or determining influence ⟨at times such material considerations as oil are allowed to ~ —Karl Baehr⟩ ⟨the application by the courts of the method of sociology . . . . Even when it does not seem to ~, it is always in reserve —B.N.Cardozo⟩ ⟨a *dominating* factor in industrial growth⟩ **3 :** to occupy a more elevated or superior position ⟨a village nestled under a *dominating* crag⟩ **4 :** to prevail over or exceed all others in number, proportion, or frequency ⟨flimsy temporary structures ~ —P.S.Fritz⟩ ⟨the *dominating* rocks are granitic⟩ ⟨the *dominating* winds are westerly⟩ **5 :** to surpass or overshadow all others in prominence, recognition, prestige ⟨let one color ~, using it in the largest areas —Betty Fisk⟩ ⟨the *dominating* theme in all this avant-garde fiction —G.A.Wagner⟩

dominating *adj* **1 :** having an air of command ⟨a great many women, brave in mannish clothes, ~ and active in manner —Louis Bromfield⟩ **2 :** given to exercising an autocratic or otherwise unwarranted ascendancy over another ⟨because the boy remains fixed in an outmoded dependency relationship with his ~ and overprotective mother and does not dare the rewards of a more dangerous manhood —Weston La Barre⟩

dom·i·nat·ing·ly *adv* : in a dominating manner

dom·i·nation \ˌdäməˈnāshən\ *n* -s [ME *dominacioun*, fr. MF *domination*, fr. L *domination-, dominatio*, fr. *dominatus*, + *-ion-, -io* -ion] **1 :** supremacy or ascendancy over another or others **2 a :** exercise of mastery or ruling power ⟨looking out for one's own today is rapidly taking the form of attempted global ~ —Norman Cousins⟩ ⟨the only alternative to complete ~ in Southeast Asia —Hugh Gaitskell⟩ **b :** DOMINION, SUZERAINTY ⟨named during the French and Spanish ~ of Louisiana⟩ **3 :** exercise of preponderant influence **4 a :** compelling political and economic influence ⟨with the empire going, the establishment of British ~ has to take a new direction: in the field of technology —Jean Hills⟩ **b :** governing or controlling influence ⟨the long period of Chinese ~ in Japanese art —Laurence Binyon⟩ ⟨perhaps not marry, for she was under the ~ of her creed which did not permit divorce —Donn Byrne⟩ ⟨what varies surprisingly little is the efficacy of his personal ~ of both orchestra and public —Virgil Thomson⟩ **c :** the dominating by an employer of a labor organization **5 dominations** *pl* : DOMINION 4

dom·i·na·tive \ˈdäməˌnād|iv, -ˌnət\ *adj* [ML *dominativus*, fr. L *dominatus* + *-ivus* -ive] : GOVERNING, DOMINATING, DETERMINING

dom·i·na·tor \-ˌnād·ə(r), -ātə-\ *n* -s [ME *dominatoure*, fr. MF *dominateur*, fr. L *dominator*, fr. *dominatus* (past part. of *dominari* to rule, govern) + *-or* — more at DOMINATE] **1 :** a dominating person or power : RULER, MASTER **2** *obs* **:** a planet or sign supposed in astrology to have a commanding influence **3 :** a brightness receptor in the retina of the eye that is supposedly a group of cones linked to the terminals of a single nerve fiber

do·mi·ne *like* DOMINIE\ *n* -s [L, voc. of *dominus* lord, master — more at DAME] **1** *obs* **:** MASTER — used as a title of respect **2** [D *dominee*, fr. L *domine*] *archaic* : DOMINIE 3

dom·i·neck \ˈdäməˌnek\ *or* **dom·i·neck·er** \-kə(r)\ *n* -s *often cap* [fr. *Dominique* (Dominica), one of the Windward islands, West Indies] : DOMINIQUE

¹**dom·i·neer** \ˌdäməˈni(ə)r, -iə\ *vb* -ED/-ING/-S [D *domineren*, fr. F *dominer*, fr. L *dominari* to rule — more at DOMINATE] *vi* **1 :** to exercise or to attain despotic mastery : rule with arbitrariness or with insolence **2** *obs* **a :** REVEL **b :** SWAGGER **3 :** to be prevalent ⟨tetanus is no longer a very ~*ing* menace —Berton Roueché⟩ **4 :** to tower dominantly ~ *vt* **1 :** to rule over with arbitrariness or with insolence : tyrannize over **2 :** to tower above

²**domineer** \"\ *n* -s : a domineering air ⟨one recognizes a ~ about him before he speaks⟩

domineering *adj* : disposed to exercise or to flaunt dictatorial authority in a way to override any protestation : OVERBEARING, TYRANNICAL ⟨then, and ever, she felt humbly about herself at heart, however arrogant and ~ she could be on the surface —Havelock Ellis⟩ ⟨like ~ mothers, the states refuse cities the right to run their own lives —T.C.Desmond⟩ ⟨the self-pride of the merchant that sustained him in his encounters with a ~ aristocracy —V.L.Parrington⟩ **syn** see MASTERFUL

dom·i·neer·ing·ly *adv* : in a domineering manner

dom·i·neer·ing·ness *n* -ES : the quality or state of being domineering

doming *pres part of* DOME

domini *pl of* DOMINUS

dom·i·ni·ca cedar \ˌdäməˈnēkə-, -ˈnikə-\ *n, usu cap D* [fr. *Dominica*, one of the Windward islands, West Indies] : a tropical American tree (*Tabebuia bahamensis*)

¹**do·min·i·cal** \dəˈminəkəl, -nēk-\ *adj* [in sense 1, fr. ML *dominicalis*, fr. L *dominicus* of a master or lord (fr. *dominus* master, lord + *-icus* -ic) + *-alis* -al; in sense 2, fr. LL *dominicalis*, fr. *dominicus (dies)* Sunday (fr. L *dominicus* of a master or lord) + L *-alis* -al — more at DAME] **1 :** given by or closely associated with Jesus Christ as Lord ⟨the ~ prayer⟩ ⟨the ~ supper⟩ **2 :** belonging or relating to the Lord's day

²**dominical** \"\ *n* -s **1 :** DOMINICAL LETTER **2** [by shortening] **:** one who observes Sunday but not as representing the Sabbath of the Old Testament — compare SABBATARIAN

dominical altar *n* : an ecclesiastical high altar

dominical letter *n* : the letter designating Sundays in a given year esp. for use in determining the date of Easter (as when the first seven letters of the alphabet are applied consecutively to the days of the year beginning with *A* on Jan. 1 and skipping the intercalary day in leap year) — called also *Sunday letter;* see EASTER table

¹**do·min·i·can** \dəˈminəkən, -nēk-\ *n* -s *cap* [after St. *Dominic* (Domingo de Guzmán) †1221 Span. Roman Catholic priest who founded it + E *-an*] : a member of an order of mendicant preaching friars founded in Languedoc in 1215 under the rule of St. Augustine with many borrowings from the Premonstratensian statutes — called also *friar preacher*

²**dominican** \"\ *adj, usu cap* **1 :** of or relating to St. Dominic **2 :** of or relating to the Dominicans

³**dominican** \"\ *adj, usu cap* [*Dominican* Republic, Hispaniola island, West Indies] : of or from the Dominican Republic : of the kind or style prevalent in the Dominican Republic

⁴**dominican** \"\ *n* -s *cap* : a native or inhabitant of the Dominican Republic

dom·i·ni·ca oak \ˌdäməˈnēkə-, -ˈnikə-\ *n, usu cap D* [*Dominica*, one of the Windward islands, West Indies] : a West Indian holly (*Ilex sideroxyloides*)

dominica rosewood *n, usu cap D* : SPANISH ELM

dom·i·nick \ˈdäməˌnik\ *or* **dom·i·nick·er** \-ˌnikə(r)\ *n* -s *often cap* [fr. *Dominque* (Dominica)] : DOMINIQUE

dom·i·nie \ˈdämənē, ˈdōm-, -ni *sometimes* -mn-; ˈdäm- *is more frequent in senses 1 & 2,* ˈdōm- *in sense 3*\ *n* -s [alter. of *domine*] **1** *chiefly Scot* : PEDAGOGUE, SCHOOLMASTER **2** *archaic* : the master of a boardinghouse for oppidans at Eton **3** [D *dominee* — more at DOMINE] **a :** a pastor of the Reformed Dutch Church **b** *dial* : MINISTER

do·min·i·gene \dəˈminəˌjēn, ˈdämən-\ *n* [*dominance* + *-i-* + *gene*] : a gene that modifies the dominance of another gene

do·min·ion \dəˈminyən\ *n* -s [ME *dominioun*, fr. MF *dominion* modif. of L *dominium* — more at DOMAIN] **1 a :** a supremacy in determining and directing the actions of others or in governing politically, socially, or personally : acknowledged ascendancy over human or nonhuman forces such as assures cogency in commanding or restraining and being obeyed : SOVEREIGNTY ⟨the federal government's claim of ~ over the resources of the marginal sea⟩ ⟨I became profoundly conscious of the ~ of unalterable law —John Buchan⟩ ⟨theorists who suggested that man had ~ over the environment through his intellect —S.F.Mason⟩ **b :** the exercise of such supremacy or ascendancy : RULE ⟨little people striving to free themselves from the ~ of their oppressors⟩ ⟨of the way young people should look, and of the things they should do, under the ~ of the passion —George Meredith⟩ **c :** preponderant or overriding influence : DOMINANCE ⟨the fact is that the free ~ of the mind and of art has never been achieved in capitalist democracy —J.T. Farrell⟩ ⟨neither in their lives nor their work were they able to escape the dream's ~ —Leo Marx⟩ ⟨he possessed, superlatively, that air of ~ by which it is possible to single out the stage favorite —Osbert Sitwell⟩ **2 :** something that is subject to sovereignty or control **3 a :** the estate or domain of a feudal lord **b :** a territory or country subject to a ruler or under the control of a particular government ⟨the ~*s* of a king⟩ **c :** the special realm of activity or influence of a particular branch of art or knowledge : DOMAIN **4 dominions** *pl* : an order of angels — see CELESTIAL HIERARCHY **5** *often cap* : one of the self-governing, autonomous states within the British Commonwealth equal in status with the United Kingdom and with each other ⟨as far as the world of states is concerned, *Dominion* status is tantamount to statehood —H.M.Clokie⟩ ⟨born in reaction against colonial inferiority, *Dominion* nationalism was promptly stimulated by the advances in autonomy and in turn furthered these advances —Alexander Brady⟩ **6 :** absolute ownership : DOMINIUM **syn** see POWER

dominion day *n, usu cap both Ds* **1 :** July 1 observed in Canada as a legal holiday commemorating the anniversary of the proclamation of dominion status in 1867 **2 :** Sept 26 observed in New Zealand as a statutory bank holiday celebrating the anniversary of the coming into dominion status in 1907

do·min·ion·hood \-ˌhu̇d\ *n* : status as a dominion

do·min·ion·ite \-yəˌnīt\ *n* -s *often cap* : an advocate of dominion status for his community

dom·i·nique \ˈdäməˌnik, -ˌnēk, ˌdäməˈnēk\ *n* [fr. *Dominique* (Dominica), one of the Windward islands, West Indies] **1** *usu cap* : an American breed of domestic fowls with rose combs, yellow legs, and barred plumage **2** -s : any bird of the Dominique breed; *sometimes* : any barred fowl

do·min·i·um \dəˈminēəm\ *n* -s [L — more at DOMAIN] **1** *Roman law* : absolute ownership of corporeal property by a person subject only to the power of the state and including the right to use and enjoy, the right to take profit therefrom, and the right of disposal **2** [ML, fr. L] *in medieval Europe & England* **a :** any of various property rights; *esp* : OWNERSHIP **b :** political power (as through lordship, sovereignty, suzerainty)

dominium di·rec·tum \-dəˈrektəm, -dīˈ-\ *n* [L, direct ownership] *Roman & feudal law* : the general ownership of property of one holding the title — called also *superiority;* contrasted with *dominium utile*

dominium uti·le \-ˈyüdᵊl(ˌ)ē\ *n* [L, ownership of use] *Roman & feudal law* : the right of one not having title (as a vassal) of using property (as for enjoyment, improvement, or profit) : beneficial tenancy or ownership — compare DOMINIUM DIRECTUM

¹**dom·i·no** \ˈdäməˌnō\ *n, pl* **dominoes** *or* **dominos** [F, prob. fr. L *domino* (in the prayer formula *benedicamus Domino* let us bless the Lord), dat. of *dominus* lord, master — more at DAME] **1 a :** a hood worn by cathedral canons : AMICE **b :** a hooded cape worn by members of certain religious sisterhoods **2 :** a long loose lightweight cloak with a hood usu. worn with a half mask as a masquerade costume **3 :** a half mask that is worn with a masquerade costume and formerly was used by women when traveling **4 :** a person wearing a domino **5** [F, fr. It, prob. fr. *domino* master, lord (exclamation of the winner), fr. L *dominus*] **a :** a flat rectangular block of bone, ivory, wood, or plastic the face of which is divided into two equal parts called ends which are blank or bear from one to usu. six dots arranged as on dice faces **b** *dominoes pl but usu sing in constr* : any of several games played with a set of usu. 28 pieces of dominoes and characterized generally by the matching of the end of a domino in the hand with an unmatched end of a domino already played **c** (1) **:** the matching by a player of the last domino in his hand ⟨the player who makes ~ wins the hand⟩ — often used interjectionally in the game (2) **:** an act or moment of completion or irrevocable finality ⟨I felt sure it was ~ for me and my prospects⟩

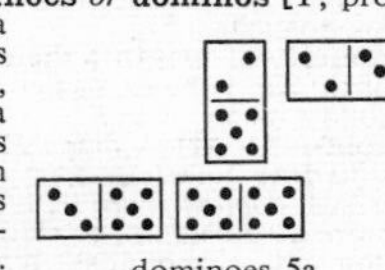

dominoes 5a

²**domino** \"\ *vi* -ED/-ING/-ES : to match the last domino in one's hand with one already played and thereby win the hand

domino bridge *n* : DRAWBRIDGE

dom·i·nule \ˈdäməˌnyül\ *n* -s [²*dominant* + *-ule*] : an ecological dominant in a microhabitat

dom·i·nus \ˈdämənəs\ *n, pl* **domi·ni** \-ˌnē, -ˌnī\ [L, lord, master — more at DAME] **1 :** an owner as distinguished from a user **2 :** a principal as distinguished from an agent

dominus di·rec·tus \-dəˈrektəs, -dīˈ-\ *n, pl* **domini direc·ti** \-məˌnēdəˈrekˌtē; -məˌnīdəˈrekˌtī, -dīˈ-\ [L, direct master] : the person having the dominium directum

dominus li·tis \-ˈlēd·əs, -ˈlīt\ *n, pl* **domini litis** \-ˌnēˈlē|, -ˌnīˈlī|\ [L, master of the suit] : a male client in a law case

dom·i·ta·ble \ˈdämədəbəl\ *adj* [L *domitare* to tame (freq. of *domare*) + E *-able* — more at TAME] : TAMABLE

do·mi·tae na·tu·rae \ˈdäməˌtīnəˈtu̇ˌrī, -məˌtēnəˈtu̇ˌrē\ *adj* [L, of a tamed nature] : DOMESTICATED

do·mi·tian \dəˈmishən, dōˈ- *sometimes* -shēən\ *or* **do·mi·ti·an·ic** \-ˌmishēˈanik\ *adj, usu cap* [after *Domitian* (Domitianus Augustus) †A.D.96 Roman emperor] : peculiar to or relating to the Roman emperor Domitian or his reign ⟨two documents emanating from the *Domitian* terror —M.H.Shepherd⟩

dom·nei \dämˈnā\ *n* [OProv, fr. *domna* lady, fr. L *domina* — more at DAME] : the Provençal ideal or cult of courtly love prevalent among the troubadours

dom nut \ˈdōm-\ *n* [³*dom*] : the ivory nut as produced under cultivation in eastern Africa usu. consisting of the seed plus the endocarp

dom palm \"-\ *n* [F *doum* — more at DOOM PALM] : DOOM PALM

¹**dom pe·dro** \dämˈpē(ˌ)drō\ *n, usu cap D&P* [prob. fr. Pg *dom* master, sir (as in *Dom Pedro* II †1891 emperor of Brazil) + E *pedro*] : pedro in which the 3, 5, and 9 of trumps are counted at face value and a joker is added which ranks as the lowest trump but counts 15 points when taken in a trick

²**dom pedro** \"\ *n* [after *Dom Pedro* II †1891] : a stout work shoe having one buckle and a bellows tongue.

dompt \ˈdäm(p)t\ *vt* **dompted; dompted; dompting; dompts** \-m(p)(t)s\ [F *dompter* to tame, fr. L *domitare*, fr. *domare* to tame — more at TAME] : to hold (as a lion) at bay

dom·ra \ˈdämrə, ˈdȯm-\ *n* -s [Russ *domra, dombra*, of Turkic origin; akin to Turk *tambura*, a kind of guitar, Kirghiz *dombra*] : a Russian instrument like a lute

doms *pl of* DOM

-doms *pl of* -DOM

dom·siek·te \ˈdämˌsēktə\ *n* -s [Afrik, lit., stupid disease, fr. *dom* stupid (fr. MD) + *siekte* disease, fr. MD *siecte*, fr. *siec* ill, sick; akin to OHG *tumb* inexperienced, foolish and OHG *sioh* sick, ill — more at DUMB, SICK] : a pregnancy disease of sheep in southern Africa

do·mus \ˈdōməs\ *n, pl* **domus** [L — more at TIMBER] : a dwelling of ancient Roman or medieval times

domy *or* **dom·ey** \ˈdōmē\ *adj* [¹*dome* + *-y*] **1 :** having a dome **2 :** like a dome

¹**don** \ˈdän\ *n* -s [Sp, fr. L *dominus*, master, lord — more at DAME] **1 a :** LORD, SIR — prefixed to the Christian name of a Spaniard of high rank **b** (1) : SENOR — used among Spanish-speaking people prefixed to the Christian name as a courtesy title (2) : MASTER — used as a form of address for an Italian priest **2** *often cap* : a Spaniard or man of Spanish descent ⟨he played on Jackson's obsession against the Spanish by promising to drive the ~*s* from America —C.G.Bowers⟩ **3 a** *archaic* : a great or famous person : a person of consequence : GRANDEE ⟨the great ~*s* of wit —John Dryden⟩ **b :** a head, tutor, or fellow in an English university ⟨she didn't want to be a ~*'s* wife and live in Oxford forever —Virginia Woolf⟩; *broadly* : a college or university teacher

²**don** \"\ *vt* **donned; donned; donning; dons** [contr. of *do* + *on*] **1 a :** to put on (an article of wear) : dress in ⟨*donned* the robes of his office⟩ **b :** to apply (as greasepaint) to the face or body **c :** to insert (a cone) in the holder in a textile machine **2 :** to clothe or envelop oneself in : ASSUME ⟨able to ~ the personality of another person⟩ ⟨perhaps the truest understanding would come from the *donning* of new and more tyrannous moralities —Edward Sapir⟩

¹**do·ña** \ˈdōnyə\ *n* -s [Sp, fr. L *domina* — more at DAME] : a Spanish or Spanish-American woman — used esp. as a title prefixed to the Christian name of a married woman of rank

²**do·na** \ˈdōnə\ *n* -s [Pg, fr. L *domina*] : a Portuguese or Brazilian woman — used esp. as a title prefixed to the Christian name of a married woman of rank

do·na·ble \ˈdōnəbəl\ *adj* [L *donabilis*, fr. *donare* to present, grant + *-abilis* -able — more at DONATION] : capable of being donated ⟨army surplus declared ~ to educational institutions⟩

do·nac·i·dae \dōˈnasəˌdē\ *n pl, cap* [NL, fr. *Donac-, Donax*, type genus + *-idae*] : a family of marine bivalve mollusks (suborder Tellinacea) comprising the wedge shells that are esp. abundant in warm shallow seas — see DONAX

do·nac·i·form \-səˌfȯrm\ *adj* [NL *Donac-, Donax* + E *-iform*] : shaped or formed like a mollusk of the genus *Donax*

donack *n* -s [by alter.] : ²DORNICK 1

do·nah \ˈdōnə\ *n* -s [perh. fr. It *donna* woman, wife, lady, fr. L *domina* lady — more at DAME] *slang Brit* : WOMAN; *esp* : SWEETHEART

do·na·ry \ˈdōnərē\ *n* -ES [L *donarium* place in a temple where an offering is made, offering, fr. *donum* gift + *-arium* -ary — more at DONATION] *archaic* : a gift to a sacred, charitable, or educational use

do·na·tary \ˈdōnəˌterē, ˈdän-\ *n* -ES [ML *donatarius*, fr. L *donatus* (past part. of *donare* to present, grant) + *-arius* -ary — more at DONATION] *Scots law* : the receiver of a donation; *specif* : the receiver of any right bestowed by the king after its forfeiture to the crown

do·nate \ˈdōˌnāt *also* dōˈn-; *usu* -ād·+V\ *vb* -ED/-ING/-S [back-formation fr. *donation*] *vt* **1 a :** to make a free gift of or a grant of : contribute esp. to a charitable cause or toward a public-service institution ⟨a retired manufacturer *donated* a site for a park⟩ ⟨city physicians ~ part-time services⟩ ⟨magazines *donated* space⟩ **b :** SUPPLY, LOAN ⟨*donated* property for the theatrical performance⟩ **2 :** EMIT, TRANSFER ⟨~ electrons⟩ ~ *vi* : to donate something

donated stock *n* : stock that is returned to a corporation by promoters or stockholders who have received it as fully-paid stock in exchange for property in order that it may be sold to provide capital

do·na·tee \ˌdōnəˈtē, -ˌnāˈ-\ *n* -s : a recipient of a free gift

do·na·tio \dōˈnäd·ē|ō, -nāshē|ō\ *n, pl* **donati·o·nes** \-ˌnäd·ēˈōˌnās, ˌnāshēˈōˌnēz\ [L] *law* : GIFT; *esp* : DONATION

donatio in·ter vi·vos \-ˌintərˈwēˌwōs, -ˈvīˌvōs\ [L, gift between living people] : a voluntary gratuitous alienation of property by one person to another not made in contemplation of death that constitutes in the civil law an executed gift that takes effect and becomes irrevocable on acceptance by the donee but in the common law requires delivery

donatio mor·tis cau·sa \-ˈmȯrd·əˈskau̇ˌsä, -ˈskȯzə\ [L, gift because of death] : a gift of personal property made by one believing himself near to death and to take effect only in case the giver dies, being valid if there is an actual delivery of the gift

do·na·tion \dōˈnāshən *sometimes* dəˈ-\ *n* -s [ME *donatyowne*, fr. L *donation-, donatio*, fr. *donatus* (past part. of *donare* to give as a gift, present, grant, fr. *donum* gift, fr. *dare* to give) + *-ion-, -io* -ion — more at DATE] **1** *archaic* : a formal grant of sovereignty or dominion **2 :** the action of making a gratuitous gift or free contribution esp. to a charity, humanitarian cause, or public institution or utility ⟨yearly ~ of prizes for scholastic and athletic achievement⟩ **3 :** voluntary alienation of property : gratuitous transfer of property from one to another **4 a :** assignment of public land on liberal terms under act of Congress to settlers **b :** a portion of land so assigned ⟨owner of the ~ land claim on which the town was built⟩ **5 :** a free contribution : GIFT ⟨the money value of ~*s* to needy applicants⟩

donation party *n* : a party at which some gift is brought to the host by each guest ⟨a *donation party* for the minister⟩

donatio prop·ter nup·ti·as \-ˌprōptərˈnu̇ptēˌäs, -ˌpräptər-ˈnəpshēəs\ [L, gift because of marriage] : a marriage gift or settlement required by law of the husband or his family early during the later Roman Empire and that was required by Justinian to be equal to the wife's dowry but permitted to be made after and used for expenses of the marriage — formerly called when made before the marriage *donatio ante nuptias*

don·a·tism \ˈdänəˌtizəm, ˈdōn-\ *n* -s *usu cap* [*Donatus* + E *-ism*] : the doctrines or beliefs peculiar to the Donatists

don·a·tist \-ˌtəst\ *n* -s *usu cap* [ML *Donatista*, fr. *Donatus*, 4th cent. bishop of Carthage + L *-ista* -ist] : a member of a schismatic party of Christians in No. Africa from 311 to the 7th century who held that the validity of the sacraments depends on the spiritual state of the minister, that sanctity is essential for church membership, and that all who joined their group should be rebaptized

don·a·tis·tic \ˌ==ˈtistik\ *adj, usu cap* : of or referring to Donatists or Donatism

¹**do·na·tive** \ˈdōnəd·iv, ˈdän-\ *n* -s [L *donativum*, fr. neut. of *donativus*, adj., fr. *donatus* (past part. of *donare* to give as a gift, present, grant) + *-ivus* -ive — more at DONATION] **1 :** a special compensation or donation : PREMIUM, BOUNTY ⟨the doles and ~*s* which kept the populace and the army in good temper —R.M.French⟩ **2 :** a donative benefice

[2]**donative** \"\ *adj* [L *donativus*] **1 :** having the character or object of or being subject to donation ⟨at the time of the transfer the deceased had full ~ capacity⟩ ⟨~ disposition of land⟩ **:** vested or vesting by donation ⟨a ~ advowson⟩ — opposed to *presentative* **2 :** conferred upon a bishop or priest of the Church of England by the founder or patron without either presentation or institution by the ordinary or induction by his orders ⟨~ benefices were abolished in 1898⟩ — **do·na·tive·ly** \-d.əvlē, -li\ *adv*

[1]**do·na·tor** \ˈdō,nād·ə(r), -ātə- *also* dō'n-\ *n* -S [L, fr. *donatus* + *-or*] **:** DONOR

[2]**do·na·tor** \ˈdōnətər, ˈdän-, -nə,tȯr\ *n* -S [ML *donatorius*, fr. L *donatus* + *-orius* -ory] *Scots law* **:** DONEE

do·nax \ˈdō,naks\ *n* [NL, fr. L, a shellfish, fr. Gk] **1** *cap* **:** a genus of small marine bivalve mollusks that is the type of the family Donacidae and that includes forms having long separate siphons, a well-developed foot, and an equivalve somewhat triangular shell **2** -ES **:** COQUINA 1

don·cel·la \dän'selə\ *n* -S [AmerSp, fr. Sp, girl, virgin, housemaid, fr. (assumed) VL *domnicilla*, dim. of L *domina* lady — more at DAME] **1 :** any of several brightly colored wrasses of the West Indies and Florida: **a :** the slippery dick and closely related fishes **b :** LADYFISH b **2 :** either of two West Indian timber trees (*Byrsonima spicata* and *B. cuneata*) valued for their hard wood — compare SURETTE

don·cy \ˈdän(t)sē\ *var of* DONSIE

don·dom \ˈdändəm\ *n* -S [[1]*don* + *-dom*] **:** the office or position of an academic don

[1]**done** [ME *doon, ydoon* (past part. of *don, doon* to do), fr. OE *gedōn*, past part. of *dōn* to do; akin to OHG *gitān* done — more at DO] *past part & substand past of* DO

[2]**done** \ˈdən\ *adj* [ME *doon, ydoon*, fr. *doon, ydoon*, past part.] **1 :** conformable to social convention or the proprieties of a sport, profession, or system of protocol **:** according with good breeding or the amenities **:** DECOROUS ⟨you know it isn't ~ to hold hands in public places —Louis Auchincloss⟩ ⟨at table there are cases where now it is the ~ thing to use the fingers⟩ **2 :** arrived at the finish or the very end of a course or of one's concern **:** having reached adequate accomplishment or the limit of one's need, use, or endurance **:** THROUGH ⟨just one more question and I'm ~⟩ ⟨certain to make history before he's ~⟩ ⟨will you never get ~ with that scraping⟩ **3 :** having strength or energy depleted **:** quite exhausted **:** suffering collapse **:** SPENT ⟨the camels were too ~ to carry our weight —T.E.Lawrence⟩ — often used with *up* ⟨are you ~ up, or would you like to take me up the ladder and show me the sights —Elmer Davis⟩ **4** *of time* **:** brought to an end **:** gone by ⟨he said the day of the circus big top is ~⟩ **5 :** doomed to failure, defeat, or death ⟨industry in this section is ~⟩ **6 :** cooked or roasted sufficiently (as for serving) ⟨the meat is ~⟩ **7 :** fitted out or dressed esp. in flawless or in elaborate fashion **:** given finishing touches ⟨his clothes in press, his shoes perfectly ~ —Emily Post⟩ — sometimes used with *up*

[3]**done** \"\ *adv* **1** *dial* **:** ALREADY **2** *dial* **:** ACTUALLY, EXCEEDINGLY

do·nee \(ˈ)dō¦nē\ *n* -S [*donor* + *-ee*] **1 :** a recipient of a gift **2 a :** one on whom a power to transfer property by will or deed is conferred for execution — called also *appointor* **b :** the recipient of a blood transfusion or of tissue or an organ for grafting

done for \ˈdən,fō(ə)r, -ō(ə)\ *adj* **1 :** irretrievably lost or mortally stricken **:** DOOMED ⟨when we saw the explosion we thought he was *done for*⟩ **2 :** left with no effective power and no capacity or opportunity for recovery **:** DOWN-AND-OUT ⟨defeat in this election would mean he was *done for*, his career at an end⟩ **3 :** sunk in defeat **:** WASHED-UP, BEATEN ⟨you know, it may come out any day, and then we're *done for* —George Meredith⟩ ⟨if this country ever runs out of people who don't like to be pushed around, we are *done for* —Elmer Davis⟩ **4 :** relegated to the discard ⟨the impression that the old, great, simple books are declassed, passé, dated, outmoded, *done for* —J.C.Powys⟩

don·e·gal \ˈdänē,gȯl, ˈdən-, -nə,-, ,==ˈ=\ *adj, usu cap* [fr. *Donegal* county, Ireland] **:** of or from County Donegal, Ireland **:** of the kind or style prevalent in County Donegal

donegal tweed *n, usu cap D* **:** a heavy woolen homespun of Irish origin characterized by colorful slubs in the weft yarn and a neutral color in the warp; *also* **:** a tweed of similar character woven plain or in twill from wool or other fibers

done in \,də'nin\ *adj* **:** physically exhausted

do·netsk \də'netsk\ *adj, usu cap* [fr. *Donetsk*, city in eastern Ukraine, U.S.S.R.] **:** of or from the city of Donetsk **:** of the kind or style prevalent in Donetsk

done with \ˈdən,wit͟h, -th\ *adj* **:** brought to an end **:** decisively abandoned or dismissed ⟨but killing was *done with* except for predators that molested him —Stuart Cloete⟩ ⟨in my craft a thing done is a thing *done with* —Katharine F. Gerould⟩ — **have done with :** to bring to an end **:** have no further concern with **:** ABANDON, DISMISS ⟨he was soon to *have done with* calendared time, and it had already ceased to count for him —Willa Cather⟩ ⟨let us *have done with* character assassination⟩

[1]**do·ney** \ˈdōni\ *n* -S [alter. of ME *donek, dunoke* — more at DUNNOCK] *dial Brit* **:** HEDGE SPARROW

[2]**doney** \"\ *n* -S [by alter.] **:** [2]DORNICK 1

[3]**doney** \"\ *n* -S [prob. alter. of *donah*] *chiefly Midland* **:** GIRL FRIEND, SWEETHEART

[1]**dong** \ˈdȯŋ, ˈdäŋ\ *vb* -ED/-ING/-S [imit.] *vi* **:** to give a deep-toned sound of or as if of a large bell ~ *vt, chiefly Austral* **:** HIT, STRIKE

[2]**dong** \"\ *n* -S **1 :** a sound of donging **2** *chiefly Austral* **:** a heavy blow (as with the fist) **3 :** PENIS — usu. considered vulgar

[3]**dong** \"\ *n, pl* **dong** [Annamese] **1 :** SAPEQUE **2 :** PIASTER 4

don·ga \ˈdäŋgə, ˈdȯŋ-\ *n* -S [Afrik, fr. Zulu] *chiefly Africa* **:** a narrow steep-sided ravine formed by water erosion but usu. dry except in the rainy season

don·go·la kid \ˈdäŋ¦gələ-, ˈdȯŋ¦-; ÷(ˈ)dän¦gōlə-, ÷(ˈ)dän¦-, ÷(ˈ)dȯŋ¦-\ *n, usu cap D* [fr. *Dongola*, region of Sudan] **:** a leather made by a process of tanning goatskin, calfskin, or sheepskin so that it resembles kid

don·go·lese \ˈdäŋgə¦lēz, ¦dȯŋ-, -ēs\ *n, pl* **dongolese** *cap* [*Dongola* + E *-ese*] **:** a native or inhabitant of Dongola

dong·on \ˈdȯŋ,ȯn\ *n* -S **:** DUNGON

dong-son \ˈdäŋ,sän, ˈdȯŋ-\ *adj, usu cap D&S* [fr. *Dong-Son*, site in northern Annam, Indochina, where artifacts were found] **:** of or relating to a culture of northern Indochina of not later than 300 B.C. characterized by bronze drums and weapons including the kris

doni *var of* DHONI

don·ick \ˈdänik\ *n* -S [by alter.] **:** [2]DORNICK 1

don·ick·er \ˈdänikə(r)\ *n* -S [E dial. *dunnekin, donnick* privy, open cesspool] *slang* **:** PRIVY, TOILET

don·jon \ˈdänjən, ˈdən-\ *n* -S [ME *donjon, dongeoun* — more at DUNGEON] **:** a massive chief tower in ancient castles — see CASTLE illustration

donjon keep *n* **:** DUNGEON

don juan \(ˈ)dän'(h)wän, dän'jüən, ,dänə'wän — *usu* -ˈjüən *with reference to Byron's poem, where such a pronunc is required by rhymes* \n, *pl* **don juans** *usu cap D&J* [after *Don Juan*, legendary Spanish nobleman featured in many works of literature, esp. *El Burlador de Sevilla* by Gabriel Tellez (Tirso de Molina) †1648 Span. dramatist, and *Don Juan*, by George Gordon, Lord Byron †1824 Eng. poet] **:** a man that pursues women **:** LIBERTINE

don·juan·esque \,dän,(h)wä¦nesk, (,)dän¦jüə¦n-, ¦dänə,wä¦n-\ *adj* **:** resembling a Don Juan **:** of or relating to a Don Juan

don juan·ism \-,nizəm\ *n, pl* **don juanisms** *usu cap D&J* **:** male sexual promiscuity attributable to feelings of impotence or inadequate masculinity

[1]**donk** \ˈdäŋk, -ə-, -ō-\ *n* -S [by shortening] **:** DONKEY 1

[2]**donk** \ˈdäŋk, ˈdəŋk\ *dial var of* DANK

don·key \ˈdäŋkē, -ki *also* ˈdəŋ- *or* ˈdȯŋ-\ *n* -S [perh. fr. *dun* + *-key* (as in *monkey*)] **1 :** the domestic ass **2 :** a stupid or obstinate person **3 :** a workbench fitted with a frame on which is mounted a fine saw for cutting marquetry veneers; *also* **:** a machine for this operation

donkeyback \ˈ==,=\ *adv* **:** on a donkey

donkey boiler *also* **donkey** *n* -S **:** an auxiliary boiler (as one carried aboard ship for use in port)

donkey boy *n* **1 :** a driver of donkeys **2 :** an operator of a donkey engine

donkey cart *n* **:** a cart with an underslung axle and two lengthwise seats — called also *pony cart, tub-cart;* compare GOVERNESS CART

donkey doctor *n* **:** a logging mechanic who maintains and repairs a donkey engine

donkey engine *also* **donkey** *n* -S **1 :** a small usu. portable auxiliary steam, diesel, compressed-air, or other engine; *esp* **:** one used to power a windlass on shipboard or in logging **2 :** a small locomotive used in switching

don·key·ish \-ish\ *adj* **:** showing the stupidity or obstinacy of a donkey **:** ASININE

don·key·ism \-,izəm\ *n* -S **:** ASININITY

donkey-lick \ˈ==,=\ *vt, Austral* **:** to beat so easily as to humiliate

don·key·man \-mən\ *n, pl* **donkeymen :** an operator of a donkey engine ⟨the second engineer and the ~ were firing up —Joseph Conrad⟩

donkey party *n* **:** a parlor game in which blindfolded players try to attach a tail to the right place on a picture of a donkey

donkey pump *also* **donkey** *n* -S **:** an auxiliary pump

donkey puncher *n* **:** a donkeyman in a logging camp

donkey's breakfast *n, slang* **:** a straw mattress

donkey sled *n* **:** a heavy foundation frame for a donkey engine

donkey stack *n* **:** an auxiliary smokestack on a steamship

donkey's years *n pl* **:** a very long time

donkeywork \ˈ==,=\ *n* **:** plodding and toilsome work **:** DRUDGERY ⟨electronic brains are taking over the ~ of mathematics —Edwin Colston Shepherd⟩; *also* **:** heavy work

dön·meh *or* **dun·meh** \ˈdən¦mā, (ˈ)dən¦-\ *n pl, usu cap* [Turk *dönme*, lit., convert, renegade] **:** crypto-Jewish descendants of the followers of the pseudo messiah Sabbatai Zebi (1626–1676) now centered chiefly in Salonika and professing Islam — compare SABBATIAN

don·na \ˈdänə, *It* ˈdȯnnä\ *n, pl* **don·ne** \ˈdä,nā, ˈdȯnnā\ [It, fr. L *domina* lady — more at DAME] **:** an Italian woman — used esp. as a title prefixed to the Christian name of a married woman of rank

don·nan equilibrium \ˈdänən-\ *n, usu cap D* [after Frederick G. Donnan †1956 Brit. chemist and physicist] **:** the ionic equilibrium reached in a solution of an electrolyte whose ions are diffusible through a semipermeable membrane but are distributed unequally on the two sides of the membrane because of the presence of a nondiffusible colloidal ion (as a protein ion) on one side of the membrane

don·né \(ˈ)dä¦nā, ¦dȯ-\ *n, pl* **donnés** \-ā(z)\ [F, fr. past part. of *donner* to give, fr. L *donare* to give as a present, present, grant — more at DONATION] **:** one who has dedicated himself to missionary work

don·ne·an *or* **don·ni·an** \ˈdänēən, ˈdän-\ *adj, usu cap* [John *Donne* †1631 Eng. poet + E *-an* or *-ian*] **:** of or relating to John Donne or his metaphysical poetry

donned *past of* DON

don·née \(ˈ)dō¦nā, ¦dȯ-\ *n, pl* **données** \-ā(z)\ [F, fr. fem. past part. of *donner*] **1 :** the main assumption or set of assumptions (as a social situation or set of personal relationships) upon which a work of literature or drama proceeds **2 :** a basic fact, condition, or notion offering the chief source of dependence in shaping an action at a particular moment or juncture

donne·ish \ˈdänish, ˈdän-\ *adj, usu cap* [John *Donne* + E *-ish*] **:** having characteristics of John Donne or his poetry

don·nered \ˈdänərd\ *also* **don·nert** \-rt\ *adj* [fr. past part. of Sc *donner, dunner* to stupefy, make a noise like thunder, perh. fr. D *donderen* to thunder, fr. *donder* thunder, fr. MD; akin to OHG *thonar* thunder — more at THUNDER] *chiefly Scot* **:** DAZED, STUPEFIED

don·nesque \ˈdä¦nesk, (ˈ)dä¦-\ *adj, usu cap* [John *Donne* + E *-esque*] **:** like or suggestive of John Donne's poetry esp. in manner or style

don·nick \ˈdänik\ *n* -S [by alter.] **:** [2]DORNICK 1

don·nick·er *var of* DONICKER

donning *pres part of* DON

don·nish \ˈdänish, -nēsh\ *adj* [[1]*don* + *-ish*] **:** relating to or characteristic of a university don **:** ACADEMIC, PEDANTIC ⟨a certain ~ carefulness of speech —L.P.Smith⟩ — **don·nish·ly** *adv* — **don·nish·ness** *n* -ES

don·nism \ˈdä,nizəm\ *n* -S [[1]*don* + *-ism*] **:** donnish attitude or manner

don·not \ˈdänət\ *n* -S [by alter.] *dial* **:** DONOUGHT

don·ny·brook \ˈdänē,brůk, -ni,-\ *also* **donnybrook fair** *n, often cap D* [fr. *Donnybrook Fair*, an annual event known for its brawls held in Donnybrook, suburb of Dublin, Ireland] **1 :** an uproarious brawl **:** FREE-FOR-ALL **2 :** a rowdy contention between rival forces carried on in public (as in legislative halls and public print)

do·nor \ˈdōnə(r) *also* ˈdō,nō(ə)r *or* ˈdō,nō(ə) *sometimes* ˈdänə(r) *or* dō'nō-\ *n* -S [MF *doneur*, fr. L *donator* — more at DONATOR] **1 :** one that gives, donates, or presents ⟨a ~ of funds to research foundations⟩ ⟨a list of paintings and the ~s⟩: **a :** one that confers a power for execution — opposed to *donee* **b :** one used as a source of biological material ⟨a ~ of blood for transfusion⟩ ⟨a ~ of a chromosome complex to a hybrid⟩ ⟨a ~ of a tissue for transplantation⟩ **2** *chem* **:** a substance capable of giving up part of itself (as an atom, radical, or elementary particle) for combination with another substance ⟨water may act as a hydrogen ~⟩ ⟨adenosine triphosphate is a phosphate ~⟩ ⟨an amine with its unshared electrons is an electron ~⟩ — compare ACCEPTOR 3 **3 :** an impurity that yields a limited supply of mobile electrons that contribute to the conductivity of a semiconducting material — compare ACCEPTOR 4c

do·nor·ship \-,ship\ *n* **:** presentation by or relation of a donor ⟨of unavowed ~⟩

[1]**do-nothing** \ˈ=,==\ *n* **:** a shiftless or habitually slothful person

[2]**do-nothing** \"\ *adj* **:** marked by slothful inactivity or minimal activity; *specif* **:** marked by lack of initiative, disinclination to disturb the status quo and attack problems, or failure to make positive progress esp. toward reform of public policy ⟨the alleged *do-nothing* record of that session of Congress⟩ ⟨an outcry from the progressives against the *do-nothing* policy of the administration⟩ — compare LAISSEZ-FAIRE — **do-noth·ing·ness** *n* -ES

do-noth·ing·ism \-,izəm\ *n* -S **:** commitment to a do-nothing policy

do-nought \ˈ=,=\ *n* [[1]*do* + *nought*] *archaic* **:** DO-NOTHING 1

don·o·van body \ˈdänəvən-, ˈdən-\ *n, usu cap D* [after Charles *Donovan* †1951 Brit. physician] **:** an organism of the genus *Calymmatobacterium* characterized by one or two opposite polar chromatin masses

don qui·xote \,dänkē'(h)ōd·|ē, -ānk-, -ōt|, |i, -ō,tā; *sometimes* dän'kwiksə|t *or* -,sō|t *or* (+V) |d·\ *n* -S *usu cap D&Q* [Sp (now spelled *Quijote*), after *Don Quixote*, foolishly idealistic and anachronistically chivalric hero of *Don Quijote de la Mancha* by Miguel de Cervantes Saavedra †1616 Span. writer] **:** an impractical idealist and quixotic enthusiast bent on righting wrongs

dons *pl of* DON, *pres 3d sing of* DON

don·ship \ˈdän,ship\ *n* [[1]*don* + *-ship*] **1 :** possession of the title or rank of a don **2 :** position as a university don

don·sie *or* **don·sy** \ˈdän(t)sē\ *adj* [perh. fr. ScGael *donas* evil, harm, hurt + E *-ie, -y*] **1** *dial Brit* **:** inclined to misfortune **:** UNLUCKY **2** *dial* **:** neat and tidy; *often* **:** FASTIDIOUS **3** *Scot* **a :** QUICK-TEMPERED, TESTY, UNMANAGEABLE **b :** SAUCY, PERT **4** *dial* **:** slightly ill **:** SICKLY, FEEBLE

[1]**don't** \(ˈ)dō|n(t), *before a pause* |nt; *before* p, b, m: |n(t) *or* |m(p) *or* (*before* m) (ˈ)dō; *before* k, g: |n(t) *or* |ŋ(k); *before* n: |n(t) *or* (ˈ)dō *or* (*in* "*don't know*") (,)də *or* ˌdᵊ\ [contr. of *do not*] **1 :** do not **2 :** does not — often used with a singular subject by cultivated speakers though the construction is sometimes objected to

[2]**don't** \ˈdōnt\ *n* -S **:** a command or entreaty not to do something **:** PROHIBITION ⟨a long list of ~s⟩

do·num \ˈdänəm, ˈdon-\ *n* -S [Turk *dönüm*, lit., turn] **:** a land measure used in regions included in the former Ottoman Empire and of varying size but usu. less than one acre

do·nut *n* [by alter.] **:** DOUGHNUT

don·zel \ˈdänzəl\ *n* -S [It *donzello*, fr. OIt, fr. OProv *donzel*, fr. (assumed) VL *domnicillus*, dim. of L *dominus* master — more at DAME] *archaic* **:** a young gentleman in training for knighthood **:** SQUIRE, PAGE

don·zel·la \dän'zelə, dōnt'selə\ *n* -S [It, fr. OIt, fr. OProv *donsela*, fr. (assumed) VL *domnicilla*, dim. of L *domina* lady — more at DAME] **:** DAMSEL

doo \ˈdü\ *n* -S [ME (Sc dial.) *dow*, var. of *douve, dove, doufe* — more at DOVE] *Scot* **:** DOVE

doob \düb\ *n* -S [Hindi *dūb*, fr. Skt *dūrvā* — more at TARE] *India* **:** BERMUDA GRASS

doo·cot \ˈdükət\ *n* -S [ME *dowcot, dowecote* — more at DOVECOT] *Scot* **:** DOVECOT

doo·dad *also* **do·dad** \ˈdü,dad, -aa(ə)d\ *or* **doo·dab** \-ab, -aa(ə)b\ *n* -S [origin unknown] **:** a small unrecognizable or nondescript article: as **a :** an accessory implement or device **:** GADGET, JIGGER, THINGUMBOB ⟨a newfangled ~ for peeling potatoes⟩ **b :** a fancy article for wear about the person **:** TRINKET ⟨from its crown sprang a number of wired ~s that tinkled like wind bells when they shook —Cornelia O. Skinner⟩ **c :** an ornamental attachment or decoration ⟨an angler catching nothing despite his array of pretty ~s⟩ ⟨a mantelpiece cluttered up with all kinds of ~s⟩ **d :** a fancy food item **e :** a decorative detail or design (as a printer's ornament) ⟨star, asterisk, or other ~ at the margin —M.J.Adler⟩

doo·dah \ˈdü,dä\ *n* -S [origin unknown] *Brit* **:** a state of tremulous excitement ⟨opening night — all of a ~ —J.B.Priestley⟩

doodeen *or* **doodheen** *var of* DUDEEN

doo·dia \ˈdüdēə\ *n* [NL, fr. Samuel *Doody* †1706 Eng. botanist + NL *-ia*] **1** *cap* **:** a small genus of Asiatic and Australasian ferns (family Polypodiaceae) with curved sori in rows between the margin and midrib of the frond segments **2** *pl* **doo·diae** \-ē,ē\ **:** any plant of the genus *Doodia*

[1]**doo·dle** \ˈdüdᵊl\ *n* -S [perh. fr. LG *dudeldopp*] **:** a foolish or frivolous person

[2]**doodle** \"\ *vt* -ED/-ING/-S *dial* **:** to make a fool of **:** CHEAT

[3]**doodle** \"\ *vt* -ED/-ING/-S [G *dudeln*, fr. *dudel* bagpipe, fr. Czech or Pol *dudy;* akin to Russ *dudá* fife, shawm, Lith *daudýtė* shawm] *dial Brit* **:** to play on (the bagpipe)

[4]**doodle** \"\ *n* -S [short for *haydoodle*, perh. fr. [2]*hay* + *doodle* (in *cock-a-doodle-do*), euphemism for *-cock* (associated with [1]*cock* penis)] *dial* **:** a small pile of hay in the field **:** HAYCOCK

[5]**doodle** \"\ *n* -S [by shortening] **:** DOODLEBUG 1

[6]**doodle** \"\ *vb* **doodled; doodled; doodling** \-üd(ᵊ)liŋ\ **doodles** [perh. fr. [2]*doodle*] *vi* **1 :** to make a doodle ⟨the chairman during the questioning continued to ~ with a red pencil⟩ **2 :** to engage in aimless, haphazard, or inconsequential activity **:** DAWDLE, TRIFLE, TOY ⟨acquired the habit of mental *doodling* that went through life with him —Florence B. Lennon⟩ ⟨for the last six years he has been *doodling* at an autobiography —J.K.Hutchens⟩ ~ *vt* **1 :** to mark or overspread with doodles **2 :** to expend in doodling ⟨he *doodled* the hours away⟩ **3 :** to trace in the manner of a doodle ⟨he reread the stack of invoices and *doodled* dollar signs on the blank edges —David Wagoner⟩

[7]**doodle** \"\ *n* -S **:** an aimless more or less automatic scribble, outline, design, or improvised sketch traced while one is mentally occupied with something else

[1]**doodlebug** \ˈ==,=\ *n* [prob. fr. [1]*doodle* + *bug*] **1 :** the larva of an ant lion; *broadly* **:** any of several other insects **2 :** one who does not stand up for his convictions **3 a** (1) **:** an unscientific device (as a divining rod) for locating underground gas, water, oil, or ores (2) *also* **doo·dle·bug·ger** \"+ə(r)\ **:** one professing skill with such a contrivance (3) **:** a seismograph, gravimeter, or other scientific device for the location of minerals **b :** a small tractor used in lumbering or farming **c** (1) **:** a rail motorcar used by railroad employees in construction and maintenance-of-way work (2) **:** a small local train **d** (1) **:** a small military tank (2) **:** an army utility truck **e :** ROBOT BOMB **f :** a magnetic detecting device; *specif* **:** an airborne magnetometer used for spotting submarines **g :** a midget racing automobile **h :** a very small airplane

[2]**doodlebug** \"\ *vi* **:** to use a doodlebug in a search

doo·dler \ˈdüd(ᵊ)lə(r)\ *n* -S [[6]*doodle* + *-er*] **1 :** one that practices doodling **2 :** one that dillydallies

doo·dle·sack \ˈdüdᵊl,sak\ *n* [G *dudelsack*, fr. *dudel* bagpipe + *sack* bag, fr. OHG *sac* — more at DOODLE, SACK] *dial Brit* **:** BAGPIPE

doodling *n* -S [fr. gerund of [6]*doodle*] **:** a doodle or a plot or sequence of doodles ⟨collected his random ~s from his wastebasket, inked over the penciled lines, submitted the pictures to the art editor —Russell Maloney⟩

doods·kop \ˈdüt,skäp\ *n* -S [Afrik, fr. *doods* (gen. of *dood* death, fr. MD *doot*) + *kop* head, fr. MD *cop, coppe* drinking vessel, skull, head; akin to OE *dēath* death — more at DEATH, CUP] **:** a southern African shallow-water edible chimaera (*Callorhynchus capensis*) having the snout prolonged into a fleshy lobe which is used in rooting up mollusks and crabs from sandy bottoms

doofunny *var of* DOFUNNY

doo·hick·ey \ˈdü,hikē, -ki\ *n* [prob. fr. *doodad* + *hickey*] **:** DINGUS, THINGUMBOB

[1]**dook** \ˈdük\ *Scot var of* DUCK

[2]**dook** \"\ *n* -S [prob. fr. [1]*dook*] **:** a haulage incline at a mine

dool \ˈdül\ *Scot var of* DOLE

dool·fu \ˈdülfə\ *chiefly Scot var of* DOLEFUL

doo·ly *or* **doo·lie** \ˈdülē\ *n, pl* **doolies** [Hindi *ḍolī*, fr. Skt *dolikā*, fr. *dola* swinging] *India* **:** a litter borne on men's shoulders **:** PALANQUIN

[1]**doom** \ˈdüm\ *n* -S [ME, fr. OE *dōm*; akin to OHG *tuom* condition, state, dignity, ON *dōmr* judgment, court, sentence, Goth *doms* sentence, fame; all fr. a prehistoric Gmc verb represented by OE *dōn* to do — more at DO] **1 a :** a law established by custom and judicial interpretation **b :** ORDINANCE, DECREE **2** *obs* **a :** rectitude and just dealing **b :** JUDGMENT, DISCRIMINATION ⟨with . . . unerring ~ he sees what is —John Dryden⟩ **3 a :** a judgment or decision pronounced ⟨whose ~ discording neighbors sought —Sir Walter Scott⟩ ⟨there are no such things as rules or principles: there are only isolated ~s —B.N.Cardozo⟩; *esp* **:** a condemnation or penal decree ⟨the inspired teaching of the ~ of men to excruciation in endlessness —George Meredith⟩ ⟨the guilty person who excessively fears death, anticipating it as a punishment and unconsciously acknowledging the justice of such a ~ can now be reassured —Weston La Barre⟩ **b :** God's final judgment of mankind **:** LAST JUDGMENT ⟨we thought the day of ~ had come⟩ **c** *obs* **:** the end of one's life **4** *archaic* **:** the process of judging **:** legal trial ⟨awaiting the opening of the ~⟩ **5 :** something that is inevitably destined to befall: **a :** a state or end to which one is inexorably bound to come; *esp* **:** a final unhappy or calamitous fate, destiny, or lot ⟨they were glad he was going West at once, to fulfill his ~ where they would not be onlookers —Willa Cather⟩ ⟨luminous organs for attracting other creatures to their ~ —J.L.B.Smith⟩ **b :** inevitable ending in frustration, desolation, or tragedy **:** predestined calamity or extinction ⟨feverish enterprise, as if everyone was aware of approaching ~ and was in a hurry to get somewhere before the thunderbolt fell —Harrison Smith⟩ ⟨the sense of ~ that infects many contemporary poets —C.I.Glicksberg⟩ **c :** inescapable penalty **:** unavoidably attendant or consequent ill fortune ⟨his proud spirit sank under the ~ of prison life —Thomas Barbour⟩ **syn** see FATE

[2]**doom** \"\ *vb* -ED/-ING/-S [ME *domen*, fr. *doom*, n.] *vt* **1** *archaic* **:** to weigh or assess and pass judgment on **2 :** to render judgment against **:** pronounce sentence on **:** CONDEMN ⟨absolves the just and ~s the guilty souls —John Dryden⟩ ⟨sometimes a ~*ed* book published in England reaches the Irish market in large quantities ahead of the censorship ban —Paul Blanshard⟩ **3** *archaic* **:** to ordain as penalty or sentence ⟨have I tongue to ~ my brother's death —Shak.⟩ **4 a :** to force irresistibly or inexorably, consign irrevocably, relegate irretrievably, or constrain inescapably **:** destine or predestine ineluctably — used with *to* ⟨some people will say that the world ~s itself to war because man is still aggressive at heart —J.B.Priestley⟩ ⟨pity for one inexorably ~*ed* to die for his people at the hands of a brutal mob —Alan Paton & Liston Pope⟩ ⟨I was of those ~*ed* to imperfect achievement —W.B. Yeats⟩ ⟨its vitality was ~*ed* to wane before the rivalry of the vernacular tongue —H.O.Taylor⟩ **b :** to render certain of failure, defeat, or nullification **:** set on a fixed course to elimination, destruction, or other disastrous conclusion **:** inflict impending ruin, disaster, or death upon ⟨if the blowoff comes it may forever ~ the efforts of Europe to undo peacefully the colonial harm she has done —Emory Ross⟩ ⟨life is a

risk and all individual plans precarious, all human achievements transient, and all individual lives ~*ed* —Irwin Edman⟩ ⟨once the horrors that lay in the background of Calvinism were disclosed to common view, the system was ~*ed* —V.L. Parrington⟩ ⟨experiments which were from the outset plainly ~*ed* —Osbert Sitwell⟩ **5** *archaic* **:** to assess a tax upon (one not making return of his taxable property) by estimate or at discretion ~ *vi, archaic* **:** to pronounce judgment ⟨who's to ~ when the judge himself is dragged to the bar —Herman Melville⟩

doom·age \-ij\ *n* -s **:** an assessing on default

doombook \ˈ=,=\ *n* [trans. of OE *dōmbōc*] **:** an ancient code of laws; *specif* **:** a code of laws of West Saxon kings

doom·er \-mə(r)\ *n* -s [²*doom* + *-er*] **1** *archaic* **:** one that pronounces sentence **2 :** a prognosticator of doom

doom·ful \-mfəl\ *adj* **1 :** presaging or betokening doom **:** FATEFUL, PORTENTOUS, OMINOUS ⟨the ~ drums of jungle tragedy —*Newsweek*⟩ **2** *obs* **:** appointed for pronouncing judgment — **doom·ful·ly** \-fəlē\ *adv*

doomlike \ˈ=,=\ *adj* **:** suggestive of impending doom **:** PORTENTOUS, FATEFUL

doom palm \ˈdüm-\ *n* [F *doum*, fr. Ar *dawm*] **:** a large African fan palm (*Hyphaene thebaica*) that is important as a soil stabilizer in desert areas and that has fibrous leafstalks used for ropes and a fruit with a gingerbread-flavored pulp and a rind which is used in making a beverage

doom ring *n* [trans. of ON *dōmhringr*, fr. *dōmr* court, judgment + *hringr* ring — more at DOOM, RING] **:** a stone circle of Norway marking the limits of an ancient Norse court of justice

¹**dooms** *pl of* DOOM, *pres 3d sing of* DOOM

²**dooms** \ˈdümz\ *adv (or adj)* [euphemism] *Scot* **:** DAMNED

doom·say·er \ˈdüm,sāər, -,se(ə)r\ *n* **:** one given to forebodings and predictions of impending calamity **:** a prophet of doom

dooms·day \ˈdümz,dā\ *n* [ME *domesday*, fr. OE *dōmes dæg*, fr. *dōmes* (gen. of *dōm* judgment) + *dæg* day — more at DOOM, DAY] **1 :** a day of final judgment ⟨from now until ~⟩ ⟨a profound sense of irony enables him to distill savage comedy and atrocious farce out of his ~ vision of the world —C.J. Rolo⟩ **2** *archaic* **a :** a day of judgment **b :** a day of death or dissolution

dooms·man \-_mən\ *n, pl* **doomsmen** [ME *domesman*, fr. *domes* (gen. of *doom* judgment) + *man* — more at DOOM] *archaic* **:** DOOMSTER

doom·ster \-mztə(r), -mst-\ *n* -s [alter. (influenced by ¹*doom*) of *dempster*] **:** one invested with authority as a judge

doom tree *n* **:** a tree used for hanging the condemned

¹**doon** \(ˈ)dün\ *Scot var of* DOWN

²**doon** \ˈdün\ *n* -s [Sinhalese *dun*-gaha doon tree] **:** a large tree (*Doona zeylanica*) of the family Dipterocarpaceae of Ceylon that yields a colorless varnish resin and wood that is very durable

doo·put·ty \dü'pəd-ē\ *var of* DOPATTA

door \ˈdō(ə)r, -ó(ə)r,-ōə,-ó(ə)\ *n* -s [ME *dor*, fr. OE, door, gate & ME *dure*, fr. OE *duru*; akin to OHG *tor* & *turi* door, gate, ON *dyrr*, Goth *daur*, L *fores*, Gk *thyra*, Skt *dvār*] **1 a :** a movable piece of firm material or a structure supported usu. along one side and swinging on pivots or hinges, sliding along a groove, rolling up and down, revolving as one of four leaves, or folding like an accordion by means of which an opening may be closed or kept open for passage into or out of a building, room, or other covered enclosure or a car, airplane, elevator, or other vehicle — see KALAMEIN DOOR, PANEL DOOR **b :** a similar part by which access is prevented or allowed to the contents of a repository, cabinet, vault, or refrigeration or combustion chamber **2 a :** an opening in a wall of a building, room, or a side or rear of a vehicle by which to go in or out **:** DOORWAY **b :** one of two openings 3½ ft. wide in the wall of a court-tennis court between the first and second gallery **3 a :** a means of access, admittance, participation, or enjoyment ⟨the opening of our ~s to all the distressed peoples of Asia —M.R.Cohen⟩ ⟨leaving the ~ open for a settlement⟩ ⟨opening with the magic of storytelling the ~s to the world's great treasure-house of literature —Nancy K. Hosking⟩ **b :** an opening or route that suggests or resembles a door in giving physical access, entrance, or exit ⟨this pass was the ~ through which the invaders poured into the doomed country⟩ ⟨slipped into Switzerland by almost the last remaining ~ out of France —Robert Payne⟩ **4 a :** one of the entranceways to buildings in a row; *esp* **:** one facing on a street ⟨he resides three ~s beyond the church⟩ ⟨living next ~ to you⟩ **b :** one's home and immediate family or one's personal knowledge and experience ⟨striving to keep scandal from his ~⟩ ⟨this fact was not left to Japanese research to discover: it was brought to their ~ —A.M.Young⟩ **5 :** a gateway at the threshold of some supernatural realm or giving escape from the normal human state ⟨the old statesman lingered for several weeks at death's ~⟩ **6 :** OTTER BOARD — **a foot in the door :** an assurance of a continuing chance of eventual accomplishment of one's purpose ⟨those connections . . . would at best enable him only to get his *foot in the door* —Hamilton Basso⟩ — **at door** *or* **at doors** *obs* **:** at the door — **at one's door 1 :** very close and accessible to one or to one's place of residence or business **:** in closest proximity **2 :** as a charge against one as being accountable **:** to one's responsibility ⟨it is hard to consider it aright and know *at whose door* to lay it —John Locke⟩ ⟨errors as well as omissions in it, which, however, he lays mainly *at the door* of the Constantinopolitan excerpter —Benjamin Farrington⟩ — **in doors :** inside, within, or into the house or any covered building **:** INDOORS — **next door 1 :** very close in position or relation **2 :** nearly equivalent **:** nearest thing ⟨*next door* to starving —Daniel Defoe⟩ ⟨it must be *next door* to impossible to rise to power in a democratic community unless you can catch the ears of the public —W.S.Maugham⟩ — **open the doors 1 :** to accept enrollments **2 :** to initiate business operations; *esp* **:** to begin to make sales — **out of doors 1 :** outside or out of the house or any covered building **:** in or into the open air **:** OUTDOORS **2** *obs* **:** out of consideration **:** beside the point — **within doors :** INDOORS — **without doors :** OUTDOORS

door 1a: *a* stile, *b* rail, *c* mullion

doora *var of* DURRA

door badge *n* **:** a floral spray hung at the door of a house as a sign that a death has occurred within

door bed *n* **:** a form of recess bed designed to be hung on a door

doorbell \ˈ=,=\ *n* **1 :** a bell, gong, or set of chimes to be rung usu. by a push button at an outer door **2 :** a push button connected with a doorbell **3 :** the sound of a ringing doorbell **4 :** a bell so connected to a door as to ring automatically when the door is opened

door bolt *n* **:** a sliding bolt for locking a door

doorboy \ˈ=,=\ *n* **:** a boy who tends a door esp. in a mine

door·brand \ˈ=,brand\ *n* [alter. of earlier *doorband*, fr. ME *dorband*, fr. *dor* door + *band*] **:** STRAP HINGE; *esp* **:** one securing the boards composing the door

door buck *n* **:** ¹BUCK 6b

door butt *n* **:** a door hinge

doorcase \ˈ=,=\ *n* **:** the visible frame of a door — compare CASING 1a, DOORFRAME

door chain *n* **:** a chain serving as an inside lock for preventing a door from opening more than a few inches until one end is withdrawn from a slide fitting

door check *or* **door closer** *n* **:** a device to check a door; *specif* **:** an attachment that is used to close a door and prevent its slamming

doorcheek \ˈ=,=\ *n, dial Brit* **:** the jamb or sidepiece of a door; *also* **:** DOOR, DOORWAY

do-or-die \ˌ==ˈ=\ *adj* **1 :** inflexibly, doggedly, or desperately determined to reach one's objective **:** unyielding and unwavering **:** INDOMITABLE ⟨*do-or-die* revolutionaries⟩ **2 :** presenting as the only alternatives complete success or complete ruin ⟨a *do-or-die* conflict⟩

doored \ˈdō(ə)rd, -ó(ə)rd,-ōəd,-ó(ə)d\ *adj* **:** having a door ⟨a dresser with ~ compartments⟩ ⟨a wide-*doored* entrance⟩

door face *n* **1** *also* **door facing :** DOORCASE **2 :** a papier-mâché mask for masqueraders

doorframe \ˈ=,=\ *n* **:** the jambs and upper transverse member enclosing the sides and top of a doorway and usu. supporting a door

door grass *n* **:** KNOTGRASS 1

door handle *n, chiefly Brit* **:** DOORKNOB

doorhead \ˈ=,=\ *n* **:** the upper transverse member of a doorframe; *esp* **:** one of ornamental woodwork often with ogive or pediment in 18th century style

door holder *n* **:** a device for holding a door open

doorjamb \ˈ=,=\ *n* **:** an upright piece forming the side of a door opening

doorkeeper \ˈ=,==\ *n* **1 a :** one that tends the door of an establishment and admits only those qualified to enter **b :** an officer of a legislative chamber who has charge of the furniture and equipment and enforces the rules regulating admission to the floor and galleries **2** *Roman Catholicism* **:** a member of the lowest of the minor orders — called also *ostiary, porter*

door-key child *n* **:** a child who because his parents are absent from home all day carries the door key of the home to school and goes home to an empty house or roams the streets

doorknob \ˈ=,=\ *n* **:** a knob that when turned releases a door latch

door·less \ˈ=ləs\ *adj* [ME *dorless*, fr. *dor* door + *-less*] **:** having no door

door·man \ˈ=,man, -mən, -,maa(ə)n\ *n, pl* **doormen 1 :** one that tends a door: as **a :** one that tends the door of a hotel, apartment house, or other building and assists people by calling taxis and helping in and out of cars — called also *footman* **b :** a theater barker or ticket taker **2 :** one that solicits business for tobacco-warehouse auctions, arranges display space for patrons, and attempts to attract the goodwill of customers **3** *Brit* **:** a farrier's assistant

doormat \ˈ=,=\ *n* **1 :** a mat placed before or just inside a door for wiping mud and dirt from the shoes **2 :** a constant and unprotesting sufferer from the impositions and ill-treatment of another **:** one that submits supinely or spinelessly to abuse or indignities ⟨becomes a despised ~ or an overworked drudge or both —Agnes M. Miall⟩ **3** *slang* **:** a team that usu. finishes hopelessly last

door money *n* **:** money collected for admission to an entertainment at the time of entering

doornail \ˈ=,=\ *n* [ME *dornail*, fr. *dor* door + *nail*] **:** a large-headed nail easily clinched for nailing doors through the battens — used chiefly in the phrase *dead as a doornail*

doorn·boom \ˈdu̇rn,büm\ *n* -s [obs. Afrik (now *doringboom*), fr. obs. Afrik *doorn* thorn (now *doring*) (fr. MD *dorn*) + Afrik *boom* tree, fr. MD; akin to OHG *dorn* thorn & to OHG *boum* tree — more at THORN, BEAM] **:** a southern African thorny shrub or small tree (*Acacia horrida*) whose bark is used in tanning

door opener *n* **1 :** a device to open a door: as **a :** a tool used by firemen to jimmy a locked door **b :** a release mechanism attached to a door lock and activated by a pushbutton or electric eye **2 :** an inexpensive gift or premium offered to a prospect by a door-to-door salesman in order to get inside the house and present his sales talk

doorplate \ˈ=,=\ *n* **1 :** a plate on a door of a house or apartment bearing the name of the occupant **2 :** FINGER PLATE

doorpost \ˈ=,=\ *n* **:** DOORJAMB

door prize *n* **:** a prize awarded to a holder of one of the winning coupons passed out at the door of an entertainment

door rock *n, archaic* **:** DOORSTONE

door roller *n* **:** a wheel or roller supporting a sliding door usu. running on a door track

doors *pl of* DOOR

doorsill \ˈ=,=\ *n* **:** ¹SILL c

doors·man \ˈdō(ə)zmən\ *Brit var of* DOORMAN

door starter *n* **:** a device for helping to start a door of a railroad boxcar to open

door·stead \ˈdōr,sted, ˈdu̇r-, -,stēd, -_stəd\ *n* [*door* + *stead* place] *now dial Eng* **:** DOORWAY

doorstep \ˈ=,=\ *n* **:** a step or one of several steps before an outer door — **at one's doorstep :** at one's door

doorstone \ˈ=,=\ *n* **:** a flat-topped stone used as a threshold or doorstep

doorstop \ˈ=,=\ *n* **1 :** a device for holding a door open to any degree or preventing it from opening beyond a particular point **2 :** a projection usu. covered with rubber used to prevent damaging contact between an opening door and a wall or piece of furniture

doorstops 2

door strap *n* **:** a metal part fastened to the top of a door (as of a garage or barn) and suspended from a hanger

door-to-door \ˌ=ˈ=\ *adj* **1 :** HOUSE-TO-HOUSE ⟨a *door-to-door* salesman⟩ **2 :** providing delivery to the specified house address ⟨direct *door-to-door* service⟩

door track *n* **:** a usu. overhead track for door rollers

door trap *n* **:** a trap with a closing door for taking birds or animals alive

door·ward \ˈ=wə(r)d\ *or* **door·wards** \-dz\ *adv* **:** toward a door

doorway \ˈ=,=\ *n* **1 :** the passageway or opening that a door closes **:** the entranceway into a building or a room **:** PORTAL **2 :** a means of gaining access to or enjoyment of (as some desirable condition) ⟨these studies brought the inquirer only to the ~ of a rich country of spiritual truth invisible to the superficial observer —R.W.Southern⟩ ⟨the Asians actually regard freedom and national independence as the ~ to international order — just as we do —A.E.Stevenson †1965⟩

doorweed \ˈ=,=\ *n* **:** KNOTGRASS 1

door window *n* **:** a casement window reaching to the floor and opening like a pair of folding doors

dooryard \ˈ=,=\ *n* **:** a yard about the door of a dwelling

dooryard grass *n* **:** KNOTGRASS 1

dooryard plantain *n* **:** BROAD-LEAVED PLANTAIN 1

doos *pl of* DOO

doot \ˈdüt\ *Scot var of* DOUBT

doot·ed \ˈdütəd\ *var of* DOTED

do-over \ˈ=,==\ *n* -s [fr. *do over*, v.] **1 :** a reprocessing or a product of reprocessing (as a garment returned by an inspector in a dry-cleaning establishment for recleaning or refinishing) **2 :** a beauty-shop transformation treatment for women

doo·zer \ˈdüzə(r)\ *or* **doo·zy** \-zē\ *n, pl* **doozers** *or* **doozies** [perh. alter. of *daisy*] *slang* **:** an extraordinary one of its kind **:** HUMDINGER ⟨it made one of those ~s that yank the long arm of probability right out of its socket —E.J.Abbott⟩

¹**dop** *vi* **dopped; dopped; dopping; dops** [ME *doppen;* akin to OE *dūfedoppa* pelican, *doppettan* to plunge in, immerse, MD *doppen* to dip into, *dop, doppe* shell, goblet, pot, MHG *topf* pot, OHG *topfo* dot, OE *dyppan* to dip — more at DIP] **1** *obs* **:** to sink abruptly beneath the surface of water **:** DIVE **2** *obs* **:** to duck the head or suddenly lower the body **:** CURTSY

²**dop** *n* -s *obs* **:** a dip esp. of head or body **:** CURTSY

³**dop** *also* **dopp** \ˈdäp\ *n* -s [D, fr. MD *dop, doppe* shell, goblet, pot — more at ¹DOP] **:** a device in which a diamond or other gemstone is held while being cut

⁴**dop** \"\ *vt* **dopped; dopped; dopping; dops :** to fasten (as a diamond) in a dop usu. with a cement

⁵**dop** \"\ *n* -s [Afrik, lit., husk, fr. MD *dop, doppe* husk, shell, goblet, pot — more at ¹DOP] **:** a brandy of southern Africa similar to French marc and made from the distilled residue of grapes after pressing

DOP *abbr* developing-out paper

do·pa \ˈdōpə\ *n* -s [*dihydroxyphenylalanine*] **:** a crystalline amino acid $(HO)_2C_6H_3CH_2CH(NH_2)COOH$ found in various fruits and vegetables and formed as an intermediate product in the oxidation of tyrosine by oxidases to dark pigments (as melanins); B-(3,4-dihydroxyphenyl)=alanine

do-pas-so \ˌdō,paˈsō\ *n* -s [blend of *do-si-do* and *pass*] **:** a square-dance variation of do-si-do for three or four couples in which the man with right arm around his partner's waist turns her around counterclockwise into starting position

do·pat·ta \dōˈpəd-ə\ *n* -s [Hindi *dopaṭṭā*] *India* **:** a scarf of silk or muslin often with gold or silver threads

dop·chick \ˈdäp+,-\ *archaic var of* DABCHICK

¹**dope** \ˈdōp\ *n* -s [D *doop* sauce, fr. *dopen* to dip, baptize, fr. MD *dōpen;* akin to OHG *toufen* to baptize, Goth *daupjan* to baptize, dip into, ON *deypa* to dive, OE *dyppan* to dip — more at DIP] **1 a :** any of various thick liquid or pasty preparations (as formerly of pan drippings or gravy and more recently of grease for use as a lubricant) ⟨pipe ~ should be applied to the male end in making up a screwed joint⟩ ⟨coated the water pipelines with a corrosive-resisting ~⟩ **b :** a lubricant for the bottoms of skis **c :** any of various cosmetic or medicinal preparations or insect repellents ⟨~ for dry skin⟩ **2 :** any of various additive substances or liquid preparations introduced into a substance or applied to a surface to contribute a desired quality: as **a :** a food adulterant **b :** a coating (as a cellulose lacquer) applied esp. to a fabric (as of airplanes to produce tautness and increase strength or of balloons to increase gastightness) **c** (1) **:** a syrupy liquid consisting chiefly of cellulose derivatives in solution from which the transparent support or backing of a sensitive film is made (2) **:** a liquid preparation or varnish used to facilitate retouching, to block out parts of a negative, or to reduce reflection from the surface of a print **d :** a material (as an antiknock agent) added in small quantities to an internal-combustion fuel (as gasoline) to improve engine performance — called also *fuel dope* **e :** a light varnish added to lithographic ink to reduce the tack **3 a :** absorbent or adsorbent material (as wood pulp or kieselguhr) used in certain manufacturing processes ⟨active ~ for dynamite⟩ — compare ¹BASE 2b(1) **b :** absorbent material used in packing to reduce the effects of friction or to provide lubrication (as the oil-soaked cotton waste packed in the journal boxes of freight cars) **4 a :** a preparation of opium or other narcotic or habit-forming drug (as cocaine, heroin, marihuana) esp. as used for a certain initially pleasurable stimulating or stupefying effect **b** *slang* **:** a preparation (as of opium) given to a horse to depress or stimulate it temporarily (as before a race) **c** *slang* **:** an opium or narcotic addict **d :** a dull-witted, obtuse, or stupid person **:** NITWIT **5** *slang* **a :** information, factual data, details, or comment concerning a particular subject esp. when purporting to come from an informed source ⟨the British Travel Association has a great deal of ~ on this subject —Richard Joseph⟩ **b :** information or prediction concerning the progress or outcome of a situation or coming event ⟨advance ~ on military purchasing policies⟩ **6** *South & Midland* **:** a cola beverage **7 :** a solution (as of cellulose acetate in acetone) for spinning synthetic fibers **:** a spinning bath — called also *spinning dope*

²**dope** \"\ *vb* -ED/-ING/-S *vt* **1 a :** to smear or lubricate with dope ⟨ready with snowshoes thoroughly *doped*⟩ **b :** to apply dope to (as the fabric of an airplane or balloon) **2 a :** to introduce an adulterant into (a food) or an additive into (a fluid) ⟨a compound for *doping* the fluid of a battery⟩ **b :** to treat or impregnate with a foreign substance to impart a desired appearance or property **:** DOCTOR ⟨prepare leather for tanning by *doping* it with fatty compounds⟩ ⟨ways of *doping* a used car to hide its faults⟩ ⟨samples of germanium *doped* with iron and cobalt⟩ **3 a :** to give a stupefying or exhilarating drug to **:** DRUG **b :** to put a stupefying drug into ⟨knocked out by *doped* wine⟩ **c :** to administer a drug to (a horse) to increase or decrease speed in a race **d :** to induce inaction, apathy, or submissiveness in by a mental diet designed to produce such qualities or attitudes ⟨keep them in submissive slavery by *doping* them with promises of bliss after death —G.B.Shaw⟩ **4** *slang* **:** to work out from one's interpretation of available information a forecast about the outcome of (a competition) or the performance or placing of (competitors) ⟨busy *doping* the day's horses⟩ ~ *vi* **:** to indulge in or be addicted to a narcotic

dope fiend *n, slang* **:** a habitual user of a narcotic

dopehead \ˈ=,=\ *n, slang* **:** an opium addict

dope off *vi, slang* **:** to drowse stupidly or doze as if under the effect of a narcotic ⟨the way you *doped off* on that ditchdigging detail yesterday —L.M.Uris⟩

dope out *vt* **1** *slang* **:** to figure out from one's interpretation of what information is available ⟨lists of football games around the country which he had been *doping out* —T.H.White b.1915⟩: **a :** to devise by system ⟨then some practical guy came along later and *doped out* how it could be sold —Theodore Morrison⟩ **b :** to puzzle out, solve, or discover by mental effort or ingenuity ⟨the specifications are there . . . could you *dope* them *out* and build the boat without blueprints —K.M.Dodson⟩ **c :** to reason or infer by guess ⟨anyone with half an eye could *dope out* from this that there's a big deal, that it's a back-door deal —Claud Cockburn⟩ **d :** to discern the identity and intentions of ⟨I could see him stare as he tried to *dope* us *out* —Saul Bellow⟩ **2** *slang* **:** to plan out or arrange in advance ⟨we are to *dope out* a full year's schedule of major and minor sports⟩

dop·er \ˈdōpə(r)\ *n* -s **:** one that dopes: as **a** *also* **dope puller :** a railroad employee who packs the journal boxes of freight cars with dope — called also *greaser* **b :** a worker who applies dope to airplane fabric **c** *also* **dope·man** \-p,man, -pmən\ *pl* **dopemen :** one that applies a protective dope (as to airplane fabric, pipelines, automobiles)

dope ring *n* **:** a gang conspiring to import or distribute opium or other narcotic

dopesheet \ˈ=,=\ *n* **1** *also* **dopebook** \ˈ=,=\ **:** a circular of information for bettors listing entries of racehorses and their past records **2 :** a circular of up-to-date information, reports, and analyses on any special activity or personnel ⟨reports on keys by locksmiths over the country are tabulated in a ~⟩ ⟨a stock exchange ~⟩ ⟨every district attorney comes to the task of jury selection with a special ~ on all members of the panel —H.M.Robinson⟩

dope·ster \ˈdōpstə(r)\ *n* -s [¹*dope* + *-ster*] **:** one that makes a practice of publicly forecasting the outcome of sports contests, political elections, or like events marked by a high degree of uncertainty

dope story *n* **:** a background story presenting explanatory, interpretative, and evaluative material designed to make more understandable some news event — compare THINK PIECE

dop·ey *also* **dopy** \ˈdōpē, -pi\ *adj* **dopier; dopiest** [¹*dope* + *-y*] **1 :** having the mind and senses dulled and responses slowed from the effects of alcohol or a narcotic **:** FUDDLED, BEMUSED **2 :** feeling and acting in a benumbed or dazed state **:** sluggish and listless ⟨I am still ~ from amazement —L.L.Rice⟩ **3 :** mentally dull **:** fatuous and rather ridiculous or contemptible ⟨its theme, I gather, is that men are all dopes, and the biggest of us would be just that much *dopier* if it weren't for the women in our lives —Richard Joseph⟩

dop·i·ness *also* **dop·ey·ness** \ˈdōpēnəs, -pin-\ *n* -ES **:** a dopey state ⟨prepare ourselves . . . to face courageously the rising curve of ~ —*Wall Street Jour.*⟩

dop·ing·ly *adv* **:** in such a manner as to lull one as does a narcotic ⟨when they have nothing to say their music ticks over ~ —Charles Reid⟩

doping rod *n* **:** a long steel rod used by dopers to pack freight car journal boxes with dope

dopp *var of* DOP

dopped *past of* DOP

dop·pel·flö·te \ˈdäpəl,flād-ə, -lōd-ə, *G* ˈdȯpəl,flœtə\ *n* -s *usu cap* [G, fr. *doppel-* double (fr. MHG *dobbel*, fr. OF *doble*) + *flöte* flute, fr. earlier *fleute*, fr. MHG *vloite, floute*, fr. MD *flûte, fleute, floyte*, fr. OF *flaute, fleute* — more at DOUBLE, FLUTE] **:** an 8-foot flute pipe-organ stop each pipe of which has two mouths

dop·pel·gäng·er *or* **dop·pel·gang·er** *also* **dop·pel·gaeng·er** \ˌdäpəlˈgaŋə(r), -geŋ-, ˈ==,==, *G* ˈdȯpəl,geŋər\ *n* -s [G *doppelgänger*, fr. *doppel-* double + *-gänger* goer, fr. MHG *gengære*, fr. OHG *-gengeri*, fr. *gangan* to go + *-eri, -ari* -er — more at GANG] **:** a ghostly counterpart and companion of a person; *esp* **:** a ghostly double of a live person that haunts him through life and is usu. visible only to himself

¹**dop·per** \ˈdäpə(r)\ *n* -s [ME, fr. *doppen* to dop, dive + *-er* — more at DOP] **:** any of certain diving birds (as a dabchick or bufflehead)

²**dopper** \"\ *n* -s *usu cap* [Afrik, fr. 16th cent. D, fr. *dop*, a kind of hat, lit., shell, pot (fr. MD *dop, doppe* shell, goblet, pot) + *-er* — more at DOP] **:** a member of a rigidly Calvinistic sect of Afrikaners

dop·pia \ˈdäpēə, ˈdȯp-,ˈdop-, It ˈdȯppyä\ *n* -s [It, fr. fem. of *doppio* double, fr. L *duplus* — more at DOUBLE] **:** any one of several old gold coins of Italian states constituting the double

of some unit (as the sequin or scudo); *also* **:** a unit of value equal to a doppia coin ⟨an 8-*doppia* coin⟩ ⟨¼-*doppia* coin⟩
dopping *pres part of* DOP
dop·pio \'däpē,ō, 'dōp-,'dōp-, *It* 'dòppyō\ *adj* (*or adv*) [It, fr. L *duplus* — more at DOUBLE] **:** DOUBLE, TWICE — used as a direction in music
doppio mo·vi·men·to \-,mōvə'men·(,)tō\ *adv* (*or adj*) [It, double movement] **:** twice as fast as the preceding — used as a direction in music
doppio pe·da·le \-pā'dä(,)lā\ *adv* (*or adj*) [It, double pedal] **:** using both feet simultaneously in parallel octaves or independent parts — used as a direction in organ music
doppio più lento \-,pyü'len·(,)tō, -,pē,ü-\ *adv* (*or adj*) [It *doppio più lento* twice as slow] **:** twice as slow as the preceding — used as a direction in music
dopp·ler broadening \'däplə(r)-\ *n, usu cap D* [after Christian J. *Doppler* †1853 Austrian physicist] **:** a lack of sharpness in the spectrum lines of gases due to the Doppler effect of the random thermal motion of the molecules
doppler effect *n, usu cap D* [after C. J. *Doppler*] **:** a change in the frequency with which waves (as sound, light, or radio waves) from a given source reach an observer, the frequency decreasing with the speed at which source and observer move away from each other and increasing with the speed at which they move toward each other so that the pitch of a sound is apparently raised or lowered as the source and the observer move toward or away from each other or the spectral lines of a star are shifted toward red or violet as the star recedes or approaches the earth
dopp·ler·ite \'däplə,rīt\ *n* -s [G *dopplerit*, fr. C. J. *Doppler* + G *-it* -ite] **:** a brownish black elastic acid substance occurring in peat beds that is composed of carbon, hydrogen, oxygen, and possibly calcium
doppler navigation *n, usu cap D* **:** navigation (as of an airplane) in which the change of frequency of reflected radar waves due to the Doppler effect is utilized by automatic devices to give information on velocity and position
doppler shift *n, usu cap D* [after C. J. *Doppler*] **1 :** a change in frequency of an electromagnetic radiation caused by the motions of the atoms, molecules, or nuclei in the line of sight **2 :** the slight displacement in the positions of the spectrum lines of light from a star or other celestial body due to the Doppler effect
dops *pres 3d sing of* DOP, *pl of* DOP
dop·ster \'däpstə(r)\ *n* -s [origin unknown] **:** a clerk who uses the measurer's notes to make out order tickets for custom-made clothing
dop stick *n* [³*dop*] **:** a short handle for a dop; *also* **:** the dop with its handle or stem or other means for holding or for fastening to a tang
¹dopy *var of* DOPEY
²dopy \'dōpē, -pi\ *n* -ES [¹*dopy*] *slang* **:** a narcotic addict
¹dor *or* **dorr** \'dȯ(ə)r, -ō(ə)\ *also* **dor bug** *n* -s [ME *dorre, dore*, fr. OE *dora* bumblebee; akin to MLG *dorte* drone, OE *drān* — more at *drone*] **:** any of various insects that fly with a buzzing noise — used often in combination ⟨~ fly⟩
²dor \"\ *also* **dorre** \"\ *n* -s [prob. of Scand origin; akin to ON *dār* mockery, fr. *dāra*] *archaic* **:** TRICK, DECEPTION **:** MOCKERY — **give one the dor** *archaic* **:** to make a fool of one
³dor \"\ *also* **dorre** \"\ *vt* **dorred; dorred; dorring; dors** *also* **dorres** [prob. of Scand origin; akin to ON *dāra* to mock, scoff, fr. MLG *bedōren* to make a fool of, fr. *dōre* fool, lunatic; akin to MD *dōr* fool, MHG *tōre* fool, lunatic, deaf person, *dōsen* to be quiet, doze, L *fumus* smoke — more at FUME] *obs* **:** to make a fool of **:** MOCK
⁴dor \"\ *n, pl* **dor** *or* **dors** *usu cap* **:** ¹BONGO
do·rab \'dōr,ab, də'rab\ *n* -s [origin unknown] **:** the common wolf herring (*Chirocentrus dorab*) of the tropical Indian and Pacific oceans
do·rad \'dōr,ad\ *n* -s [NL *Doradidae*] **:** a catfish of the family Doradidae
do·rad·i·dae \də'radə,dē\ *n pl, cap* [NL, fr. *Dorad-, Doras*, type genus + *-idae*] **:** a family of So. American armored catfishes (type genus *Doras*) having a series of bony plates along the sides that are reputed to journey overland in search of water during dry seasons
do·ra·do \də'rä(,)dō\ *n* -s [Sp *dorado*, fr. past part. of *dorar* to gild, fr. L *deaurare*, fr. *de-* + *-aurare* (fr. *aurum* gold) — more at ORIOLE] **1** *also* **dou·ra·de** \dō'rädə\ *or* **dou·ra·do** \-ä(,)dō\ **a :** DOLPHIN 2 **b** [AmerSp, fr. Sp] **:** a large golden characin (*Salminus maxillosus*) of the Rio Plata drainage of So. America and sometimes related species that resemble salmons and are outstanding sport and food fishes **2 :** a light yellowish brown that is redder, lighter, and stronger than khaki, lighter and stronger than walnut brown, and lighter, stronger, and slightly yellower than cinnamon — called also *cuir, honey beige*
do·ra·pho·bia \,dōrə'fōbēə\ *n* -s [NL, fr. Gk *dora* hide, skin + NL *-phobia*] **:** a dread of touching the skin or fur of an animal
do·ras \'dōrəs\ *n, cap* [NL] **:** the type genus of the family Doradidae
dorbeetle \'⸗,⸗⸗\ *n* [¹*dor* + *beetle*] **:** any of various beetles that fly with a buzzing sound; *specif* **:** a common European dung beetle (*Geotrupes stercorarius*)
dor·cas gazelle \'dȯrkəs-\ *n* [NL *dorcas* (specific epithet of *Gazella dorcas*), fr. L, gazelle, fr. Gk *dorkas, dorkos, dorx*, alter. of *zorkas, zorx* gazelle, deer; akin to W *iwrch* roebuck, Corn *yorch*, Bret *yourc'h*] **:** a common gazelle (*Gazella dorcas*) of northern Africa and parts of southwestern Asia
dor·cas·try \'dȯrkəstrē\ *n* -ES [*Dorcas*, Christian woman of Joppa celebrated in the early church for her good works (Acts 9:36) + E *-try* (as in *deviltry*)] **:** a church auxiliary organized to plan and execute benevolent work
dor·ca·the·ri·um \,dȯrkə'thirēəm\ *n, cap* [NL, fr. Gk *dorkas* gazelle, deer + NL *-therium*] **:** a genus of extinct chevrotains related to the water chevrotain
dor·cop·sis \dȯr'käpsəs\ *n, cap* [NL, fr. Gk *dorkas* + NL *-opsis*] **:** a genus of marsupials comprising the gazelle-faced wallabies of New Guinea
¹do·ré \də'rā, dō'-\ *n* -s [CanF, fr. F, past part. of *dorer*] *chiefly Canad* **:** WALLEYED PIKE
²do·ré \də'rā, (')dō¦rā\ *adj* [F, fr. past part. of *dorer* to gild, fr. L *deaurare* — more at DORADO] **1 :** golden in color **2 :** containing gold ⟨~ silver⟩
³doré *or* **doré bullion** *n* -s **:** unparted gold and silver in bars
doree *var of* ¹DORY
doré furnace *n* **:** a furnace in which doré bullion is refined
do-re-mi \¦dō,rā'mē\ *n* -s [fr. *do, re, mi*, the first three notes of the major musical scale, influenced in meaning by *dough* (money)] *slang* **:** MONEY
dorey *var of* ²DORY
dorhawk \'⸗,⸗\ *n* [¹*dor* + *hawk*; fr. its diet] **:** the common European nightjar (*Caprimulgus europaeus*)
do·ria \'dōrēə\ *n* -s [Hindi *ḍoriyā*, fr. *ḍor* line, cord] **:** a striped Indian muslin
¹do·ri·an \'dōrēən, 'dȯr-\ *adj, usu cap* [L *dorius* Dorian (fr. Gk *dōrios*, fr. *Dōris*, region in the central part of ancient Greece that included the cities of Sparta and Corinth) + E *-an*] **1 :** belonging to a racial and linguistic division of classical Greece ⟨the stark severity of *Dorian* shrines⟩ **2 :** peculiar to or having characteristics of the people of the Dorian division of Greece ⟨she was a *Dorian* girl . . . who had undergone a training as severe as a boy's —Van Wyck Brooks⟩ ⟨a *Dorian* festival in honor of Apollo⟩
²dorian \"\ *n, pl* **dorian** *or* **dorians** *usu cap* **:** one of a Hellenic race that about the 12th century B.C. completed the overthrowing of Mycenaean civilization and settled in Doris, Megaris, Argolis, Laconia, and Messenia, in Crete and other islands, and on the coast of Asia Minor
dorian mode *n, usu cap D* [trans. of Gk *dōria harmonia*] **1 :** a Greek mode consisting of two disjunct tetrachords represented on the white keys of the piano by a descending diatonic scale from E to E — see GREEK MODE illustration **2 :** an authentic ecclesiastical mode consisting of a pentachord and an upper conjunct tetrachord represented on the white keys of the piano by an ascending diatonic scale from D to D — see MODE illustration
dorian tetrachord *n, usu cap D, in Greek music* **:** a descending tetrachord consisting of two whole steps followed by a half step

¹dor·ic \'dȯrik, 'där-,'dōr-\ *adj, usu cap* [L *doricus*, fr. Gk *dōrikos*, fr. *Dōris*, region of ancient Greece + Gk *-ikos* -ic] **1 :** DORIAN 1 ⟨the *Doric* idiom⟩ **2 :** peculiar to the institutions and culture of the Dorians ⟨the *Doric* trend was martial⟩; *specif* **:** belonging to the oldest and simplest of the ancient Greek architectural orders characterized by a fluted column shaft with no base and with a capital consisting of an echinus separated from the shaft by one or more annulets and supporting a square unmolded abacus **3 :** having the characteristics of the Dorians (as boldness, rugged masculine strength) ⟨could be capable of a fierce baroque if not a *Doric* manner —Rolfe Humphries⟩ **4** *of a dialect of English* **:** UNCOUTH, UNREFINED, BROAD ⟨the *Doric* dialect of the lake district —*Athenaeum*⟩

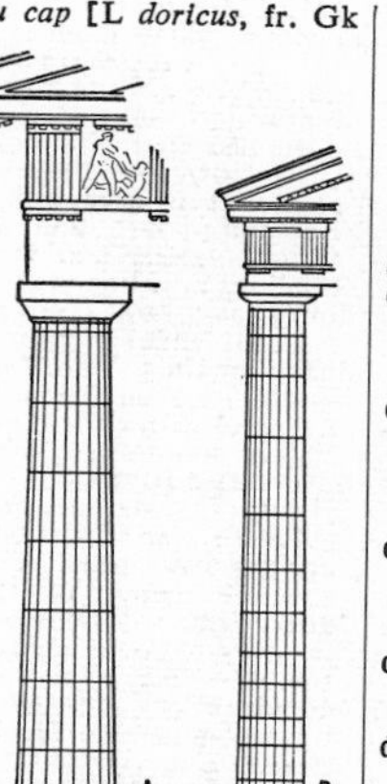

Doric order: Greek, *A;* Roman *B*

²doric \"\ *n* -s **1** *usu cap* **:** a dialect of ancient Greek spoken in southern and eastern Peloponnesus, the Isthmus of Corinth, some of the southernmost Aegean islands, Crete, Rhodes, the southwest coast of Asia Minor, and several colonial areas esp. in Sicily and southern Italy and used in literature esp. by the Greek poets Pindar †443 B.C. and Theocritus 3d cent. B.C. **2** *cap* **:** a rustic dialect of English ⟨her nervous northern *Doric* —Charlotte Brontë⟩ **3** *usu cap* **a :** SANS SERIF **b :** a boldface type with strokes of fairly even weight and rather wide set
dor·i·cism \-rə,sizəm\ *n* -s *usu cap* **:** a Doric phrase or idiom
doric mode *n, usu cap D* **:** DORIAN MODE
doric tetrachord *n, usu cap D* **:** DORIAN TETRACHORD
do·rid·i·dae \də'ridə,dē\ *n pl, cap* [NL, fr. *Dorid-, Doris*, type genus + *-idae*] **:** a large family of gastropods including the genus *Doris*
dories *pl of* DORY
do·rip·pid \də'ripəd\ *n* -s [NL *Dorippidae*] **:** a crab of the family Dorippidae
do·rip·pi·dae \-pə,dē\ *n pl, cap* [NL, fr. *Dorippe*, type genus (prob. fr. *Dorippa*, a L & Gk feminine name) + *-idae*] **:** a nearly cosmopolitan family (type genus *Dorippe*) of small deep-water oxystomatous crabs
dor·is \'dȯrəs\ *n, cap* [NL, fr. *Doris*, the daughter of Oceanus, fr. L, fr. Gk *Dōris*] **:** a cosmopolitan genus (the type of the family Dorididae) of the suborder Nudibranchia consisting of nudibranchs or sea slugs having a depressed body, two oral lobes, and a retractile tuft of pinnate branchiae around the anus
dor·ism \'dō,rizəm, 'dä,ri-, 'dōr,i-\ *n* -s *usu cap* [Gk *dōrismos*, fr. *dōrios* Dorian + *-ismos* -ism — more at DORIAN] **1 :** Dorian character, manners, or speech **2 :** a Doric phrase or idiom
dor·king \'dȯrkiŋ, -ō(ə)k-, -kēŋ\ *n* [fr. *Dorking*, Surrey, England] **1** *usu cap* **:** an English breed of large domestic fowls having five toes or the hind toe double **2** -s *often cap* **:** a bird of the Dorking breed that was developed as a general-purpose fowl, but is now largely a fancier's breed
dor·lach \'dȯrlək, -lək\ *n* -s [ScGael *dòrlach*, lit., handful] **1** *obs Scot* **:** a quiver for arrows **2** *Scot* **a :** BUNDLE, PACKAGE **b :** SUITCASE
¹dorm \'dȯ(ə)rm\ *vi* [prob. fr. MF *dormir* — more at DORMANT] *now dial Eng* **:** SLEEP, DOZE
²dorm \"\ *n* -s [by shortening] **:** DORMITORY
dor·man·cy \'dȯ(r)mənsē, -si\ *n* -ES **:** the quality or state of being dormant **:** QUIESCENCE, LATENCY, ABEYANCE ⟨~ in bacterial spores⟩ ⟨some volcanoes have eruptive cycles followed by stretches of ~⟩ ⟨Egypt is just awakening from centuries of ~; she and her neighbors are gradually adopting western techniques of farming and industry —Keith Wheelock⟩
dor·mant \'dȯrmənt, 'dȯ(ə)m-\ *adj* [ME *dormaunt*, fr. MF *dormant*, fr. pres. part. of *dormir* to sleep, fr. L *dormire*; akin to Gk *edrathon, erdathon* I slept, Skt *drāti, drāyati* he sleeps, OSlav *drĕmati* to doze, Arm *tartam* slow, sleepy] **1 a** *archaic* **:** fixed in position ⟨a ~ timber across a foundation⟩ **b :** relaxed or immobile ⟨one of the ancient's hoary eyebrows seemed to go up a few millimeters but otherwise his face remained ~ —Earle Birney⟩ **2 :** INACTIVE: **a** *heraldry* **:** lying down with the head resting on the forepaws — distinguished from *couchant* **b** (1) **:** sleeping or drowsing ⟨the preacher, who would interrupt his discourse to denounce a ~ worshiper —*Amer. Guide Series: Mich.*⟩ (2) **:** having the faculties suspended or as if suspended **:** SLUGGISH, LETHARGIC ⟨he lay there ~ with his eyes closed but waiting for a chance to escape⟩ **c :** having growth, development, or other biological activity suspended; *esp* **:** being in a state of suspended animation (as in hibernation) ⟨when the surrounding water gets too hot mollusks become ~⟩ **d** (1) **:** RESTING, INACTIVE — used of buds or other plant parts (2) **:** associated with, carried out, or applied during dormancy ⟨~ grafting⟩ ⟨a 5 percent ~ oil is used to control fruit-tree leaf roller⟩ **e** *of a volcano* **:** passing a considerable period in a state of repose yet still eruptive **3 a** *archaic* **:** written with name or particulars blank to be filled in when put to use **b :** of no effect or unevoked or unenforced during an interval of time ⟨reviving a long-*dormant* statute⟩ **c :** vacant or neglected by the rightful holder yet heritable ⟨a peerage said to be ~⟩ **4 :** temporarily devoid of discernible activity, energy, power, or effect: **a :** existing in latent form or in a minimum degree but capable of bursting into full activity ⟨it seemed to him that crime was a seed in the whole of humanity . . . it lay ~ everywhere —Ben Hecht⟩ ⟨that native musical talent lay ~ in the mountain folk⟩ ⟨feeling between the two girls which had for some time been reasonably ~ flared up again —Ernest Beaglehole⟩ ⟨thoughts lie ~ for ages; and then, almost suddenly as it were, mankind finds that they have embodied themselves in institutions —A.N.Whitehead⟩ **b :** waiting only to be called into play ⟨his imaginative powers will for the most part lie ~ —C.S. Kilby⟩ ⟨which power can never be exercised by the people themselves but must be placed in the hands of agents or lie ~ —John Marshall⟩ **c :** having natural or normal functions suspended yet capable of resumption ⟨the Church of England was, indeed, if anything more ~ than the Catholic Church in France —Stringfellow Barr⟩ ⟨a ~ corporation⟩ **d** (1) **:** marked by or giving an appearance of inactivity or stagnation **:** slow-moving **:** DROWSY ⟨the mouse-chewed papers of an old family in a ~ English hamlet —R.D.Altick⟩ (2) **:** tending to stagnate socially, intellectually, or artistically **:** failing to make strides **:** UNPROGRESSIVE ⟨where science had been ~ since the days of Kepler —S.F.Mason⟩ **5 :** neglected or allowed to lapse into disregard or obscurity yet revocable or revivable ⟨the controversy lay ~ through 1873 and 1874 and might have expired altogether —J.A.Cassidy⟩ **6 :** discarded or unused but of potential utility ⟨methods of salvaging ~ metals in the printing industry⟩ **7** *of stock* **:** moving imperceptibly in the market **8** *of a period of time* **:** marked by suspension of activity **:** covering the extent of dormancy ⟨war all over again after five ~ years —Robert Sherrod⟩ **syn** see LATENT, PRONE
dormant account *n* **:** a deposit account in which there has been no deposit or withdrawal for a number of years
dormant bolt *n* **:** a concealed door bolt movable only by a special contrivance (as a key or knob)
dormant lock *n* **:** a lock with no self-closing bolt
dormant partner *n* **:** SLEEPING PARTNER
dormant spray *n* **:** a spray applied to trees and shrubs when they are in an inactive state at any time between leaf fall and the beginning of bud swelling at the start of the next growing season
dormant table *n* [ME *table dormant, dormaunt table*, fr. MF *table dormant*] *archaic* **:** a table that is fixed to the floor or forms a stationary piece of furniture

dormant window *n, now dial* **:** DORMER WINDOW
dor·mer \'dȯrmər, 'dȯ(ə)mə(r\ *n* -s [F *dormoir*, fr. L *dormitorium* — more at DORMITORY] **1** *obs* **:** BEDROOM **2** *or* **dormer window a :** a usu. gabled extension of an attic room through a sloping roof to allow for a vertical window opening into the room **b :** the window in such an extension

dormer window

dormered \-mə(r)d\ *adj* **:** having dormers
dor·mette \(')dȯr¦met\ *n* -s [F *dormir* to sleep + E *-ette* (as in *roomette*) — more at DORMANT] **:** an adjustable airplane seat that can be made fully reclining
dor·meuse \(')dȯ(ə)¦mœz\ *n* -s [F, lit., female sleeper, fem. of *dormeur*, sleeper, fr. MF, fr. *dormir* + *-eur* -or] *Brit* **:** a private traveling carriage having a long forward boot carrying a mattress for extending the seat into a bed and providing leg room for a passenger reclining at full length
dor·mi·dera \,dȯrmə'derə\ *n* -s [Sp, short for *adormidera*, fr. *adormir* to put to sleep, fr. *a-* (fr. L *ad-*) + *dormir* to sleep, fr. L *dormire*; fr. the narcotic properties of the seeds — more at DORMANT] **:** CALIFORNIA POPPY
dor·mie *or* **dor·my** \'dȯr¦mē, -ō(ə)¦, ¦mi\ *adj* [origin unknown] *golf* **:** being up as many holes as remain to be played ⟨he stood ~8 — 8 up and 8 holes to play⟩ — used of a player or side
dormie house \"-\ *n* [*dormie* prob. short for *dormitory*] *Brit* **:** a building with dormitory accommodations operated by a golf club for lodging members and guests
dor·mi·ent \'dȯrmēənt\ *adj* [L *dormient-, dormiens*, pres. part. of *dormire* to sleep — more at DORMANT] *archaic* **:** SLEEPING
dor·mi·tion \dȯr'mishən\ *n* -s [MF, fr. LL *dormition-, dormitio*, fr. L, act of sleeping, fr. *dormitus* (past part. of *dormire* to sleep) + *-ion-, -io* -ion — more at DORMANT] **:** death resembling falling asleep
dor·mi·tive \'dȯrməd·iv\ *adj* [MF *dormitif*, fr. L *dormitus* + MF *-if* -ive] **:** inducing sleep
dor·mi·to·ry \'dȯ(r)mə,tōrē, -tȯr-, -ri\ *n* -ES *often attrib* [L *dormitorium*, fr. *dormitus* + *-orium* -ory] **1 :** a room intended primarily to be slept in; *esp* **:** a large room providing sleeping quarters for many persons and sometimes divided into cubicles **2 :** a residence hall providing separate rooms or suites for individuals or for groups of two, three, or four with common toilet and bathroom facilities but usu. without housekeeping facilities ⟨most of the students of the college live in *dormitories*⟩ ⟨reading in the ~ of the fire station⟩ — called also *hostel* **3** *archaic* **:** a retreat for taking rest **4** *obs* **:** a place for repose of the dead **5 :** a residential community consisting of homes for sleeping and personal activities from which the majority of the working population commute to places of employment, trade, and recreation ⟨brings the millions from their ~ suburbs to their benches and desks and takes them home again at night —Sam Pollock⟩
dormitory car *n* **:** a passenger-train car equipped with sleeping and toilet facilities for members of dining-car and other service crews
dormitory ship *n* **:** a ship equipped with dormitory accommodations (as for round-trip student tours)
dor·mouse \'dȯr,maůs\ *n, pl* **dor·mice** \-mīs\ [ME *dormowse*, perh. fr. F *dormir* to sleep + ME *mowse, mous* mouse; fr. its cold-weather torpidity — more at DORMANT, MOUSE] **:** any of numerous small Old World rodents of the family Gliridae that resemble small squirrels, live in trees, feed on nuts and acorns, become torpid in cold weather, and yield a velvety fur used in trimming — see LEROT, LOIR
dormouse opossum *or* **dormouse phalanger** *n* **:** any of several small phalangers (genus *Cercaertus* syn. *Dromicia*) that resemble mice with long nearly naked prehensile tails, that are chiefly nocturnal, and that feed on insects and fruit
dorms *pl of* DORM
¹dor·nick *also* **dor·neck** \'dȯrnik\ *or* **dar·nick** \'där-\ *n* -s [ME *dornewick*, fr. *Doornik* (Tournai), city in Belgium where such fabrics were first manufactured] **:** a coarse damask of wool and silk formerly used for hangings and vestments
²dor·nick \'dȯrnik, 'dän-\ *n* -s [prob. fr. IrGael *dornóg* handful, small stone, fr. *dorn* hand, fist] **1** *dial* **:** a roundish stone or chunk of rock usu. of a size suitable for throwing by hand **2 :** a boulder of iron ore found in limonite mines
do·ro·bo \də'rō(,)bō\ *n, pl* **dorobo** *or* **dorobos** *usu cap* **1 :** a people of southern and central Kenya that speak Nandi and that were formerly dependent on hunting **2 :** a member of the Dorobo people
do·ron \'dōr,än\ *n* -s *usu cap* [Brig. Gen. Georges F. *Doriot* b1899 Am. business executive army officer + E *-on* (as in *nylon*)] **:** a layered glass cloth impregnated with a hard plastic that is used for body armor
do·ron·i·cum \də'ränəkəm\ *n* [NL, fr. Ar *dorūnaj, darūnaj*] **1** *cap* **:** a genus of Eurasian perennial herbs (family Compositae) having alternate often clasping stem leaves and long peduncled yellow flower heads and comprising the leopard's-banes several of which are cultivated for their flowers **2** -s **:** any plant of the genus *Doronicum*
dor·o·so·ma \,dȯrə'sōmə\ *n, cap* [NL, fr. *doro-* (fr. Gk *dory* wood, trunk of a tree, spear) + *-soma* — more at TREE] **:** a genus (sometimes the type of the family Dorosomidae or Dorosomatidae) of fishes that includes the gizzard shad and is now usu. placed among the Clupeidae
dor·o·thy bag \'dȯr¦əthē-, 'där¦, -thi-\ *n, usu cap D* [fr. the name *Dorothy*] *Brit* **:** a woman's handbag hung from the wrist
dorothy dix \¦⸗⸗⸗'diks\ *n, pl* **dorothy dixes** *usu cap both Ds* [after *Dorothy Dix*, pseudonym of Elizabeth M. Gilmer †1951 Am. journalist and conductor of a syndicated advice-to-the-lovelorn column] **:** a counselor esp. of women on personal adjustment, etiquette, or other intimate matters
dorp \'dȯ(ə)rp\ *n* -s [D, fr. MD; akin to OHG *dorf* village — more at THORP] **1** *archaic* **:** a village esp. in the Netherlands **2** [Afrik, fr. MD] *Africa* **:** VILLAGE, TOWNSHIP
dor·per \'dȯrpər\ *n* [*Dor*set Horn + *Per*sian (sheep)] **1** *usu cap* **:** a breed of mutton-type sheep with white body and black face and a pelt of mingled wool and hair developed in So. Africa by crossing the blackhead Persian and the Dorset Horn breeds **2** -s *often cap* **:** any sheep of the Dorper breed
¹dorr *var of* DOR
²dorr \'dȯ(ə)r, 'dō(ə)\ *n* -s [fr. the name *Dorr*] **:** a glacial trough crossing a ridge or mountain range
dorre *var of* DOR
dorred *past of* DOR
dorring *pres part of* DOR
dors *pl of* DOR, *pres 3d sing of* DOR
dors- *or* **dorsi-** *or* **dorso-** *comb form* [LL *dors-* back, fr. L *dorsum*] **1 :** back ⟨*dors*al⟩ **:** dorsal ⟨*dorsi*flexion⟩ **:** dorsally ⟨*dorsi*fixed⟩ **2 :** dorsal and ⟨*dorso*lateral⟩
dorsa *pl of* DORSUM
dor·sad \'dȯr,sad\ *adv* [*dors-* + *-ad*] **:** toward the back **:** DORSALLY — used chiefly of anatomic relations
¹dor·sal \'dȯrsəl, 'dȯ(ə)s-\ *adj* [LL *dorsalis*, fr. L *dorsum* back + *-alis* -al] **1 a :** belonging to or situated near or on the back of an animal or of one of its parts — opposed to *ventral* **b** *chiefly Brit* **:** THORACIC **c** *of echinoderms and coelenterates* **:** ABORAL **d :** having or forming an elongated ridge suggestive of an animal's back **:** situated on such a part ⟨a ~ gun turret⟩ **e :** placed or worn on a human back **2** *bot* **a :** ABAXIAL **b :** belonging to the upper surface of a creeping dorsiventral structure (as a thallus) **3 :** articulated with a part of the tongue posterior to the tip; *specif* **:** articulated with a part of the tongue posterior to that employed in a palatal articulation
²dorsal \"\ *n* -s **1 :** a dorsally located part; *esp* **:** THORACIC VERTEBRA **2 :** a dorsal sound **3** [ML *dorsale*, fr. neut. of LL *dorsalis*, adj.] **:** DOSSAL
dorsal carpal ligament *n* **:** a broad flat ligament at the back of the wrist serving to hold in place the tendons of the extensor muscles
dorsal column *n* **:** a column lying dorsally in each lateral half of the spinal cord and receiving terminals from certain afferent fibers of the dorsal roots of the spinal nerves
dor·sa·le \dȯr'sa(,)lē, -sä-, -sā-\ *n* -s [ML] **:** DOSSAL
dorsal fin *n* **1 :** a median longitudinal vertical fin on the back of a fish or other aquatic vertebrate — see FISH illustration **2 :** a vertical fin on the upper side of the after end of an airplane fuselage to provide greater directional stability

dor·sa·lis \dȯr'sāləs, -sal-, -säl-\ *n, pl* **dorsa·les** \-a(ˌ)lēz, -ā(ˌ)lēz, -ä,lās\ [NL, fr. LL, adj., dorsal — more at DORSAL] **:** any of several arteries situated in and supplying the back of the parts with which they are associated
dorsal lamina *n* **:** a longitudinal membrane in tunicates that projects into the cavity of the branchial sac and is borne by the large median dorsal blood vessel; *also* **:** that vessel itself
dorsal lip *n* **:** the margin of the fold of blastula wall that delineates the dorsal limit of the blastopore in the gastrulating amphibian embryo or corresponds to this in other vertebrate embryos and that constitutes the primary organizer, is essential to the formation of neural tissue, and forms the point of origin of chordamesoderm
dor·sal·ly \'dȯ(r)səlē, -li\ *adv* **:** in a dorsal situation or direction
dor·sal·most \'=səl,mōst\ *adj* **:** most nearly dorsal
dorsal nerve *n* **:** THORACIC NERVE
dorsal pore *n* **:** an opening in the mid-dorsal part of nearly every segment in many earthworms by which the body cavity is placed in communication with the exterior and which is believed to permit moistening of the body surface with coelomic fluid for lubrication and to facilitate respiration
dorsal root *n* **:** the one of the two roots of a spinal nerve that passes dorsally to the spinal cord and consists of sensory fibers — compare VENTRAL ROOT
dorsal-root ganglion *n* **:** SPINAL GANGLION
dorsal suture *n* **:** the outer suture of a pod or other monocarpellary fruit that is the midrib of the carpellary leaf from which the fruit is formed
dorsal vertebra *n* **:** THORACIC VERTEBRA
dorsal vessel *n* **:** the elongated dorsally situated heart of insects and other arthropods
dor·sal·ward \'dȯ(r)səlwərd\ *or* **dor·sal·wards** \-dz\ *adv* **:** toward the dorsal surface **:** DORSAD
d'or·say \(ˈ)dȯr¦sā, -¦zā\ *or* **d'orsay pump** *n, often cap D&O* [after Count Alfred G.G. d'*Orsay* †1852 Fr. society leader and arbiter of fashion] **:** a pump-type shoe or slipper made with a circular vamp and a quarter that curves to meet the vamp at the shank line
dorse \'dȯ(ə)rs\ *n* -s [L *dorsum* back] *archaic* **:** the back of a book or folded document
dorser *var of* DOSSER

d'orsay

[1]**dor·set** \'dȯrsət, -ó(ə)s-, *usu* -əd.+V\ *n* -s *often cap* [fr. the county of *Dorset*, England, where it was first made] **:** BLUE VINNY
[2]**dorset** \"\ *n, usu cap* [fr. Cape *Dorset* near Baffin island, Franklin district, Northwest Territories, Canada] **:** an Eskimo culture of northeastern Canada and northern Greenland about A.D. 100-1000 characterized by the hunting of caribou and seals and by microlithic flake tools and harpoon heads having gouged rather than drilled holes
dorset down \¦==¦daùn\ *n* [fr. the county of *Dorset*, England, where it was originally bred] **1** *usu cap both Ds* **:** an English breed of short-wooled mutton-type sheep derived from the Hampshire Down **2** *pl* **dorset downs** *often cap both Ds* **:** a sheep of the Dorset Down breed
dorset horn \¦==¦=\ *also* **dorset** *n* [fr. the county of *Dorset*, England] **1** *usu cap D&H* **:** an English breed of sheep with very large and in the ram much-coiled horns that has a close-textured fleece of medium-length wool and that has been much used for hothouse lamb production because of the early breeding of the ewes and the high percentage of twin lambs **2** -s *often cap D&H* **:** a sheep of the Dorset Horn breed
dor·set·shire \'==,shi(ə)r, -iə, -,shə(r)\ *or* **dorset** *adj, usu cap* [fr. *Dorsetshire* or *Dorset*, England] **:** of or from the county of Dorset, England **:** of the kind or style prevalent in Dorset
dorsi- — see DORS-
dor·sian \'dȯrzhən, -rshən\ *n, usu cap* [blend of *Dorset* (*Horn*) and *Persian* (*sheep*)] **:** DORPER
dor·si·branchiate \¦dȯ(r)sə+\ *adj* [*dors-* + *branchiate*] **:** having branchiae along the back
dor·si·col·lar \¦dȯ(r)sə¦kälə(r)\ *adj* [*dors-* + L *collum* neck + E *-ar* — more at COLLAR] **:** belonging or relating to the back and neck
dor·si·duct \'dȯ(r)sə,dəkt\ *vt* -ED/-ING/-S [*dors-* + L *ductus*, past part. of *ducere* to lead — more at TOW] *physiol* **:** to turn or draw toward the back
dor·sif·er·ous \(ˈ)dȯ(r)¦sif(ə)rəs\ *adj* [*dors-* + *-ferous*] **1 :** bearing the sori on the back of the frond — used of various ferns **2 :** carrying the eggs or young upon the back
dor·si·fixed \'dȯ(r)sə,fikst\ *adj* [*dors-* + *fixed*] **:** attached by the back — used esp. of anthers
dor·si·flex \-,fleks\ *vb* [*dors-* + *flex*] *vi* **:** to flex in a dorsal direction ⟨the toe will ~⟩ ~ *vt* **:** to cause to flex in a dorsal direction ⟨various central lesions both ~ and supinate the foot⟩ — **dor·si·flex·ion** \¦==¦flekshən\ *n*
dor·si·flex·or \'==,fleksə(r)\ *n* [NL, fr. *dors-* + *flexor*] **:** a muscle causing flexion in a dorsal direction
dor·si·grade \'==,grād\ *adj* [*dors-* + *-grade*] **:** walking on the back of the toes ⟨~ armadillos⟩
dor·si·spinal \¦dȯ(r)sə+\ *adj* [*dors-* + *spinal*] **:** of or relating to the back and spine
dor·si·ventral \"+\ *adj* [*dors-* + *ventral*] **1 :** having distinct dorsal and ventral surfaces ⟨~ leaves⟩ **2 :** DORSOVENTRAL 1 — **dor·si·ven·tral·i·ty** \,dȯ(r)səven·'tralәd·ē\ *n* -ES — **dor·si·ventrally** \¦==+\ *adv*
dorso- — see DORS-
dor·so·caudad \¦dȯ(r)(ˌ)sō+\ *adv* [*dors-* + *caudad*] **:** to or toward the dorsal surface and caudal end of the body
dor·so·lateral \"+\ *also* **dor·si·lateral** \¦dȯ(r)sə+\ *adj* [*dors-* + *lateral*] **:** of, relating to, or involving both the back and sides
dor·so·lumbar \¦dȯ(r)(ˌ)sō+\ *also* **dor·si·lumbar** \¦dȯ(r)sə+\ *adj* [*dors-* + *lumbar*] **:** of or involving structures in the region occupied by the dorsal and lumbar vertebrae ⟨~ myelitis⟩
dorso·lumbar nerve *n* **:** a small nerve connecting the last thoracic nerve with the lumbar plexus
dor·so·medial \¦dȯ(r)(ˌ)sō+\ *or* **dor·so·median** \"+\ *also* **dor·si·median** \¦dȯ(r)sə+\ *adj* [*dors-* + *medial* or *median*] **:** located toward the back and near the midline
dor·so·posteriad \¦dȯ(r)(ˌ)sō+\ *adv* [*dors-* + *posteriad*] **:** to or toward the dorsal surface and posterior end of the body
dor·so·ulnar \"+\ *adj* [*dors-* + *ulnar*] **:** of or relating to the inner side of the back of the forearm or hand
dor·so·ventral \"+\ *adj* [ISV *dors-* + *ventral*] **1 :** extending from the dorsal toward the ventral side ⟨the ~ axis of an animal⟩ **2 :** DORSIVENTRAL 1 — **dor·so·ventrally** \"+\ *adv*
dor·ste·nia \dȯ(r)'stēnēə\ *n* [NL, fr. Theodor *Dorsten* †1552 Ger. botanist + NL *-ia*] **1** *cap* **:** a large genus of tropical herbs (family Moraceae) having basal leaves and small monoecious flowers crowded upon a fleshy receptacle at the end of a long naked peduncle — see CONTRAYERVA **2** *pl* **dorstenias** *also* **dor·steni·ae** \-ē,ē\ **:** any plant of the genus *Dorstenia*
dor·sum \'dȯrsəm, -ó(ə)s-\ *n, pl* **dor·sa** \-sə\ [L] **1 :** BACK; *esp* **:** the entire dorsal surface of an animal or the upper surface of an appendage or part (as of the nose, tongue, or foot) ⟨the ~ of a segment⟩ **2** [NL, fr. L] **:** the upper side of the tongue behind the tip; *specif* **:** the part opposite the velum when the tongue is at rest
dors·umbonal \(¦)dȯ(r)s+\ *adj* [*dors-* + *umbonal*] **:** dorsal and umbonal **:** being one of the accessory valves of mollusks of the family Pholadidae
dort \'dȯrt\ *vi* -ED/-ING/-S [origin unknown] *Scot* **:** to take offense **:** SULK
dor·ter *or* **dor·tour** \'dȯrd·ər\ *n* -s [ME, fr. OF *dortoir*, fr. L *dormitorium* — more at DORMITORY] **:** a dormitory esp. in a religious house
dort·mund \'dȯrt,mùnt, -nd, -,mənd\ *adj, usu cap* [fr. *Dortmund*, Germany] **:** of or from the city of Dortmund, Germany **:** of the kind or style prevalent in Dortmund
dorts \'dȯrts\ *n pl* [origin unknown] *chiefly Scot* **:** a mood of bad temper **:** SULKS
dorty \'dȯrtī\ *adj* [*dort* + *-y*] *Scot* **:** PEEVISH, SULKY
[1]**do·ry** *also* **do·ree** \'dōrē, 'dȯr-, -ri\ *n, pl* **dories** *also* **dorees** [ME *dorre, dorray*, fr. MF *dorée*, fr. fem. of *doré*, past part. of *dorer* to gild — more at DORÉ] **1 :** the John Dory or a related fish **2 :** WALLEYED PIKE
[2]**do·ry** \"\ *also* **do·rey** \"\ *n, pl* **dories** *also* **doreys** [Mosquito *dóri, dúri* dugout] **:** a flat-bottomed boat with high flaring sides, sharp bow, and deep V-shaped transom that is used esp. on the New England coast and by American fishing vessels and is noted for its qualities in riding seas

dory

dory- *comb form* [NL, fr. Gk *dory* — more at TREE] **:** spear ⟨*Dory*anthes⟩
dor·y·an·thes \,dōrē'an(ˌ)thēz\ *n, cap* [NL, fr. *dory-* + *-anthes*] **:** a small genus of Australian plants (family Amaryllidaceae) with a basal rosette of large leaves and a large long-stalked spike of red flowers — see SPEAR LILY
dor·y·lai·mi·na \,dȯrə'līmənə\ *n pl, cap* [NL, fr. *Dorylaimus*, genus of nematode worms (fr. *dory-* + Gk *laimos* throat, gullet) + *-ina*] **:** a suborder of Enoplida including free-living and parasitic nematodes lacking setae but having a buccal stylet — compare DIOCTOPHYMATINA, ENOPLINA
[1]**dor·y·line** \'dȯrə,līn\ *adj* [NL *Dorylinae*, subfamily of ants, fr. *Dorylus*, type genus (fr. Gk *dory* wood, trunk of a tree, spear) + *-inae* — more at TREE] **:** of or relating to dorylines
[2]**doryline** \"\ *n* **:** any of various large specialized migratory tropical ants that are blind except for the functional males **:** ARMY ANT
do·ry·man \'dōrēmən, 'dȯr-, -rim-\ *n, pl* **dorymen :** a fisherman working from or handling a dory
dor·y·mouse \'däri,maùs\ *n* [by alter.] *dial Eng* **:** DORMOUSE
dory trawler *n* [[2]*dory*] **:** a trawler with several dories working for her
[1]**dos** *or* **do's** *pl of* DO
[2]**dos** \'dōs, 'däs\ *n* -ES [L — more at DOWER] **1** *Roman law* **:** the property contributed by the wife or by someone else on her behalf to the husband for sustaining the burdens of matrimony, orig. becoming the husband's absolutely but by the time of Justinian required to be surrendered to the original donor on the termination of the marriage by death or divorce **2** *English law* **:** the property settled by a husband upon his wife at the time of the marriage
do-sa-do *or* **dos-a-dos** *var of* DO-SI-DO
[1]**dos-à-dos** \¦dōzə¦dō *or like* DO-SI-DO\ *adv* [F] *archaic* **:** back to back ⟨passing *dos-à-dos* in a quadrille⟩
[2]**dos-à-dos** \"\ *n, pl* **dos-à-dos** [F, fr. *dos-à-dos* back to back] **:** a dogcart having four wheels and seats set back to back
[3]**dos-à-dos** \"\ *adj* [F, lit., back to back] *of two books* **:** bound back to back with one common board between and the fore edge of one next to the backbone of the other ⟨a psalter and a New Testament in a *dos-à-dos* style⟩
dos·age \'dōsij, -sēj\ *n* -s **1 a :** the amount of medicine or other therapeutic agent (as X rays) prescribed or proper for a given patient or illness ⟨the ~ of the vitamins and of calcium received through the diet and in other ways will be determined by the doctor —Morris Fishbein⟩ **b :** the administration of such dosages by any means **c :** a dose of radiation encountered other than in medical treatment **2 a :** addition of some ingredient or application of or treatment with some agent in one or more measured doses ⟨yeast ~*s* of sewage⟩ ⟨the recommended spraying ~ for controlling codling moth⟩ ⟨even heavy ~*s* of antioxidant do not prolong the life of polyethylene to more than one or two years —B.S.Biggs⟩ **b :** a mixture of sweet syrup and aged wine added to bottle-fermented sparkling wines after secondary fermentation and disgorgement **c :** the presence and relative representation or strength of some factor or agent ⟨the effects of six rather than the usual three levels of gene ~ —*Genetics*⟩ **3 a :** regulation or determination of doses ⟨an old practitioner's expertness in ~⟩ ⟨research in radiation ~⟩ **b :** a dealing out of or an exposure to (some experience) in or as if in measured portions ⟨he had a nice sense of ~, spicy but not obtrusive, in dealing with the percussion section —Virgil Thomson⟩ ⟨minute portions of melodrama every day, a fragmentation of suspense into endless daily anxiety — with a special ~ on Friday to carry over the weekend —Gilbert Seldes⟩ ⟨education as the only antidote for a ~ of propaganda⟩ ⟨for dramatic sopranos and contraltos a moderate ~ of unhappiness is splendid forcing ground for the emotional side of their temperaments —*N.Y. Times*⟩
dosage meter *n* **:** DOSIMETER
dosage response *n* **:** the effect of a biologically active agent (as a chemical) upon a disease organism
[1]**dose** \'dōs\ *n* -s [F, fr. LL *dosis*, fr. Gk, lit., act of giving, gift, fr. *didonai* to give — more at DATE] **1 a :** the measured quantity of a medicine or other therapeutic agent to be taken at one time or in a period of time ⟨the same amount daily in divided ~*s* until the temperature remains normal⟩ **b :** the quantity of radiation administered to (as in radiotherapy) or absorbed accidentally by a given volume or mass of tissue at one time, measured in terms of the intensity of radiation, the distance from the source, and the length of exposure **2 :** a portion of an additive admitted during a process ⟨a faulty champagne can be hidden rather conveniently under a strong ~ of sugarcane —Barrett McGurn⟩ **3 a :** a measure or portion of some experience to which one is exposed or subjected ⟨schools where reluctant youths are being exposed to a heavy ~ of book learning unrelated to their interests and their ambitions —J.B.Conant⟩ ⟨so we gave him a large ~ of squash and track work —Harry Gordon⟩ ⟨I had a long ~ of Spinoza with far more admiration than previously —H.J. Laski⟩ ⟨after I saw my first burst damaged him I flew in closer and gave him a second ~⟩ ⟨taken in easy ~*s*, a chapter at a time because of its close-packed variety, this book is a treasure-house of marvelous reading —Hal Lehrman⟩ ⟨feeding them immense ~*s* of propaganda⟩ **b** *nonstand* **:** a gonorrheal infection **4 :** a standard increment of labor and capital conceived as being applied to land to measure changes in its productiveness at different intensities of cultivation
[2]**dose** \"\ *vb* -ED/-ING/-S *vt* **1 :** to proportion (a medicine or other therapeutic agent) properly with reference to the patient or illness **2 :** to give a dose to: **a :** to give medicine to **b :** to subject to an experience by way of correction or instruction ⟨*dosed* the jeering lads with a bucket of water⟩ ⟨*dosed* him with a stiff course of reading in the Greek and Latin⟩ **3 :** to treat with an application or agent ⟨a powerful ray that *dosed* the paint for a long period⟩ ⟨his dark mustache . . . was liberally *dosed* with bear grease —R.W.Thorp⟩ **4 :** to apply a dose of labor or capital to ~ *vi* **:** to take medicine ⟨he is forever *dosing*, but he gets worse⟩
dos gris \¦dō¦grē\ *n, pl* **dos gris** [LaF, fr. F, lit., gray back] *chiefly South* **:** SCAUP DUCK
do-si-do *or* **do-se-do** *also* **do-sa-do** *or* **dos-a-dos** \¦dō(ˌ)sē'dō *sometimes* -ōt(ˌ)sē'- *or* -ō,sī'- *or* -ō(ˌ)chē'- *or* -ōsə'- *or* -ōzə'-\ *n, pl* **do-si-dos** *or* **do-se-dos** ['dos-à-dos] **:** a square-dance figure in which the dancers passing by right shoulder circle each other back to back
do·sim·e·ter \dō'simәd·ə(r)\ *also* **dose·me·ter** \'dōs,mēd·ə(r)\ *n* [*dosimeter*, ISV *dosi-* (fr. L *dosis* dose) + *-meter*; *dosemeter* fr. [1]*dose* + *-meter* — more at DOSE] **:** an instrument or device for measuring doses of X rays or of radioactivity — **do·sim·e·try** \dō'simə·trē\ *n* -ES
do·si·met·ric \¦dōsə¦me·trik\ *adj* [ISV *dosimetry* + *-ic*] **:** devoted or relating to dosimetry
dosing tank *n* **:** a tank in which sewage is collected and later discharged at the rate required by subsequent treatment processes
do·sin·ia \dō'sinēə\ *n, cap* [NL, fr. *dosin*, native name in Senegal for a species of this genus + NL *-ia*] **:** a genus of bivalve mollusks (family Veneridae) having a flattened rounded shell, large foot, and united siphons
do·sith·e·an \dō'sithēən\ *n* -s *usu cap* [*Dositheus*, 1st cent. A.D. Jewish heretic + E *-an*] **:** a member of a Samaritan sect believing in the heretic Dositheus as the Messiah and stressing esp. the precepts of the law concerning the Sabbath
dos no·mi·na·ta \-,nämə'nād·ə, -nād·ə\ *n* [L, specified dower] *English law* **:** a dos consisting of certain specified lands
dos ra·ti·o·na·bi·lis \-,rād·ēō'näbələs, -,rashə'nab-\ *n* [L, reasonable dower] *English law* **:** a dos consisting of one third of the lands of which the husband is seised at the time of the espousals
[1]**doss** \'däs\ *vt* -ED/-ING/-ES [perh. alter. of *toss*] *dial Eng* **:** to toss with the horns
[2]**doss** \"\ *n* -ES [origin unknown] **1** *chiefly Brit* **:** a makeshift bed **2** *or* **doss house** *chiefly Brit* **:** a cheap rooming house **3** *chiefly Brit* **:** SLEEP
[3]**doss** \"\ *vi* -ED/-ING/-ES *chiefly Brit* **:** to sleep or bed down in any convenient place ⟨pea pickers sometimes ~*ed* under the straw stack —Thomas Wood †1950⟩ — often used with *down* ⟨never mind, we can ~ down in the car —Joyce Cary⟩
dos·sal *or* **dos·sel** \'däsəl\ *n* -s [ML *dossale, dorsale* — more at DORSAL] **1** *archaic* **:** an ornamental cloth for the back of a throne or chair **2 :** an ornamental cloth hung back of and above the altar or beside the chancel
dos·sen·nus \də'senəs\ *n* -ES [L *Dossennus, Dossenus*] **:** a stock character of Roman comedy representing a sharp-witted hunchback
[1]**dos·ser** \'däsər\ *also* **dor·ser** \'dȯrsər\ *n* -s [ME *dosser, dorser*, fr. MF & ML; MF *dossier*, fr. ML *dorsarium*, fr. L *dorsum* back + *-arium* -ary] **1** *archaic* **:** DOSSAL **2 :** a basket to be carried on a person's back or, in pairs, by a horse or other beast of burden **:** PANNIER
[2]**dos·ser** \'däsə(r)\ *n* -s [*doss* (*house*) + *-er*] *chiefly Brit* **:** one that frequents doss houses
dos·se·ret \¦däsə¦ret\ *n* -s [F, fr. MF, small dosser, dim. of *dossier*] **:** a clearly defined block resting on the capital of a column and serving as an extra impost in Byzantine and Romanesque architecture
dos·sier \'dȯs,yā *also* 'däs- *or* =¦=; 'däsē,ā *also* ,=s=¦=\ *n* -s [F, bundle of documents with a label on the back, dossier, fr. *dos* back (fr. L *dorsum*) + *-ier* -er] **1 :** an accumulation of records, reports, miscellaneous pertinent data, and documents bearing on a single subject of study or investigation **:** FILE ⟨a ~ of criminal acts of occupation troops⟩ ⟨a numbered ~ is kept on each patient containing a full history of his physical condition⟩ ⟨a year ahead of production of the film researchers began a ~ on the locale and period⟩ ⟨no censorship of written or spoken words, no tapping of telephones, opening of letters, compiling of ~*s* —*Horizon*⟩ ⟨methods of the police state that run the gamut from wire tapping to the maintenance of the ~ —G.B.Oxnam⟩ **2 :** an author's accumulation of notes toward the creation of a projected fictional character

dosseret

doss·i·ly \'däsəlē, -li\ *adv, chiefly Brit* **:** in a dossy manner
dossy \'däsē, -si\ *adj* -ER/-EST [Sc *dossie* sprucely dressed person, fr. *doss* neat (fr. *doss* to dress, fr. D *dossen*, fr. *dos* clothes, fr. MD, perh. fr. OF *dos* back, fr. L *dorsum*) + *-ie*] *chiefly Brit* **:** pretentiously fashionable
[1]**dost** *archaic pres 2d sing of* DO
[2]**dost** \'dōst\ *dial var of* DOSE
dos·to·ev·ski·an \¦dästə¦yefskēən, ¦dōs-, -stō¦ye-, -stē¦e-, -(ˌ)stō¦(y)e-, -evzk-, -evsk-, -kiən *sometimes* ¦dəs- *or* -stə¦e- *or* -stō¦e-\ *adj, usu cap* [Fedor *Dostoevski* †1881 Russ. novelist + E *-an*] **:** of, relating to, or typical of Fedor Dostoevski or his writings ⟨the *Dostoevskian* milieu seemed barbaric, lawless, Eastern, an enemy of the "sanity and method" he clung to —Irving Howe⟩
[1]**dot** \'dät, *usu* -äd·+V\ *n* -s [fr. (assumed) ME, fr. OE *dott* head of a boil; akin to OHG *tutta* nipple, D *dot* knot, tuft, Norw *dot* lump, small knot, OE *dyttan* to stop up] **1 :** a minute particle of a substance or liquid or a spot of color visible on a surface ⟨sori appear as ~*s* on a fertile fern frond⟩ ⟨the telltale ~*s* of measles⟩ ⟨watching the wagon as it grew smaller and smaller until it was only a ~ on the horizon —O.E.Rölvaag⟩ ⟨islands show as mere ~*s* on the ocean⟩ **2 :** a small round mark made on a surface with or as if with a pointed instrument ⟨the ~ on the chart represents the ship's position⟩ ⟨put a ~ before the name of each as he pays⟩: **a :** such a mark written or printed as a sign or part of a sign of orthography or punctuation: as (1) **:** PERIOD ⟨a colon consists of one ~ on the base line with another directly above⟩ ⟨a row of printed ~*s* denoting the omission of words⟩ ⟨*W.A.C.* written with ~*s* or without⟩ (2) **:** the topmost element of a lower-case letter *i* or *j* (3) **:** a centered period as a divider of syllables **b :** such a mark as an integral part of certain letters (as *ṁ* in Sanskrit) in various forms of the Roman alphabet or in phonetics used above, below, or after a symbol with any of various values **c** (1) **:** DECIMAL POINT (2) **:** a sign of multiplication **d :** one of the points used in braille or other raised-point system of writing for the blind **e** *in music notation* (1) **:** a point placed immediately after a note or rest indicating augmentation of its time value by one half (2) **:** a point placed over a note indicating a moderate staccato — compare DASH 3d **f :** one of the spots constituting the printing surface of a halftone **g** *logic* (1) **:** a sign for "and" — compare CONJUNCTION (2) **:** a sign used to indicate the beginning or end of a group of statements belonging together **3 :** something very small; *esp* **:** a very small portion or specimen ⟨a ~ of a child⟩ **4 :** a precise point in time or space; *esp* **:** a moment exactly appointed ⟨arriving and departing on the ~⟩ ⟨correct to a ~⟩ **5 a :** a striking of a pointed object or the sound of its striking on a hard surface ⟨we knew him far off by the ~ of his crutch⟩ **b :** a short click on a telegraph sounder forming a letter or part of a letter (as in the Morse code) — compare DASH 8a **c :** a flash of a beam from a momentary opening of the shutter of a signal light representing a letter or part of a letter in a communication system (as the Morse code) — compare DASH 8c **d :** a wave of a flag through an arc of 90 degrees to the right from vertical as an element of a code alphabet in flag signaling — compare WIGWAG **6 :** a small circle of solid color used as a design motif ⟨a broadcloth print with big coin ~*s*⟩ — compare POLKA DOT — **in the year dot** *Brit* **:** in the year one **:** as long ago as anyone can count ⟨says they have used this system *in the year dot* —*Motor*⟩ — **off one's dot** *slang Brit* **:** disordered in mind **:** DOTTY
[2]**dot** \"\ *vb* **dotted; dotted; dotting; dots** *vt* **1 a :** to mark with a dot ⟨a *dotted* 32d note⟩ **b :** to put a dot over (a letter *i* or *j*) **c :** JOT — used with *down* ⟨~ down these notes⟩ **2 a :** to mark or diversify with numerous dots or objects scattered at random **:** INTERSPERSE ⟨one of those enigmas that ~ the literary landscape in every period —J.G.Keller⟩ ⟨a curious type of formal English *dotted* with sudden colloquialisms —J.J.Espey⟩ ⟨*dotted* across the country are pressure groups which complain loudly that education has gotten away from the fundamentals —E.O.Melby⟩ ⟨pictures of animals which are *dotted* about in the text of the bestiaries —O. Elfrida Saunders⟩ **b** (1) **:** to cause a scattering of marks resembling dots to appear on ⟨a rising southeast wind that *dotted* the lake with whitecaps —Joseph Millard⟩ (2) **:** to make a dot or dots upon ⟨*dotted* the canvas with infinitely small specks of paint⟩ **3** *cookery* **:** to dab here and there with small bits of a soft substance (as butter) **:** scatter small bits of an ingredient over **4** *slang Brit* **:** HIT ~ *vi* **:** to make a dot ⟨a pen point that ~*s* without blotting⟩ — **dot and carry one 1** *archaic* **:** to set down, point, and carry the figures as in elementary arithmetic **2** *archaic* **:** DOT AND GO ONE — **dot and go one 1** *archaic* **:** to walk with a limp or with the aid of a crutch **2** *archaic* **:** to progress jerkily — **dot the i :** to fill in details **:** make explicit statement ⟨the chairman *dotted no i's* but everyone present knew the man he meant⟩ ⟨Henry James suggests the dissolute vulgarity of the malignant janitor without *dotting the i* as much as he might be expected to —Henry Hewes⟩
[3]**dot** \'dä¦t, 'dō¦, *usu* ¦d.+V\ *n* -s [F, fr. L *dot-, dos* dowry — more at DOWER] **:** a woman's marriage portion
dot·age \'dōd·¦ij, -ōt¦, ¦ēj\ *n* -s [ME, fr. *doten* to dote + *-age*] **1 a :** feebleness or impairment of understanding and reason **:** mental infirmity ⟨I may venture to assert, without exposing myself to the charge of ~ —William Cowper⟩ **b :** advanced age attended by enfeebled mentality and childishness — called also *second childhood* **2 :** an utterance or a work showing a writer's or artist's feebleness of mind or execution from old age ⟨more important than Galsworthy's increasingly desiccated social propaganda and the ~*s* of Bernard Shaw —F.B. Millett⟩ **3** *archaic* **a :** a weak and foolish or silly doting

: a blind fondness or affection **b :** the object of such fondness or affection

do·tal \'dōd·ᵊl\ *adj* [L *dotalis*, fr. *dot-*, *dos* dowry + *-alis* -al — more at DOWER] **:** relating to a woman's marriage portion

¹dot-and-dash \ˌ⸗⸗'⸗\ *or* **dot-dash** \'⸗'⸗\ *adj* **1 :** formed of or as if of alternating dots and dashes ⟨run a *dot-and-dash* line across the sheet⟩ **2 :** consisting of or using an alphabet made up of dots and dashes as signals for communicating ⟨secret conversations by means of long and short muscular movements in the Morse *dot-and-dash* system⟩

²dot-and-dash \"\ *or* **dot-dash** \"\ *vt* **1 :** to mark with a succession of dots and dashes **2 :** to convey by means of a dot-and-dash system

dotant *n* -s [¹*dote* + *-ant*] *obs* **:** DOTARD 1a

dot·ard \'dōd·ə(r)d, -ōtə-\ *n* -s [ME, fr. *doten* to dote + *-ard*] **1 a** *obs* **:** IMBECILE **b :** one in his dotage **2 :** HARBOR SEAL **3** *obs* **:** a tree stump that has lost its branches by decay

¹dote *also* **doat** \'dōt, *usu* -ōd·+V\ *vb* -ED/-ING/-S [ME *doten*; akin to MLG *dotten*, *dutten* to be foolish, MD *dutten* to be enraged, be mad, Icel *dotta* to nod from fatigue, Norw *dudra* to tremble — more at DODDER] *vi* **1 a** *archaic* **:** to be or become foolish or imbecilic or deranged ⟨a sword is upon the liars and they shall ~ —Jer 50:36 (AV)⟩ **b :** to be weak-minded or mentally deficient by reason of old age **2 :** to show strong, excessive, or fatuous fondness or affection — used with *on* or *upon* ⟨those who hate him seem to agree in certain respects with those who ~ on him⟩ ⟨I ~ on the serene pleasures of marvelous landscapes —Vance Locke⟩ ⟨here are two peoples both of whom love palaver and ~ on uproar —Elizabeth Monroe⟩ **3** *of a tree or lumber* **:** to begin to decay or to become partly decayed ⟨an old *doting* oak —O.W.Holmes †1894⟩ **~** *vt*, *obs* **:** to cause to dote **syn** see LIKE

²dote \"\ *n* -s [ME, fr. *doten*, v.] **1** *now dial* **:** IMBECILE, DOTARD **2 :** decay in timber **:** ROT

³dote *n* -s [MF or L; MF *dot* dowry, fr. L *dot-*, *dos* dowry, gift — more at DOWER] **1** *obs* **:** ³DOT **2 dotes** *pl* [L *dot-*, *dos*] **:** natural endowments

dot·ed *also* **doat·ed** \'dōtəd\ *adj* [ME *doted*, fr. past part. of *doten*] **1** *now Scot* **:** weak-minded from age **2** *obs* **:** extravagantly fond

do tell \'⸗'⸗\ *interj* — used esp. to express mild or polite surprise

dot·er *also* **doat·er** \'dōd·ə(r), -ōtə-\ *n* -s **1 :** a man whose understanding is enfeebled by age **:** DOTARD **2 :** one that is foolishly or excessively fond ⟨a ~ on fried clams⟩

dot etching *n* **:** a method in printing of correcting the color or tones of a halftone negative or positive usu. utilizing the chemical reduction of halftone dots

dot figure *n* **:** a collection of dots arranged regularly or irregularly that on being steadily examined seem to fall successively into different groupings

doth *archaic pres 3d sing of* DO

doth·er \'däthə(r)\ *dial Eng var of* DODDER

do·thid·e·ace·ae \(ˌ)dōˌthidē'āsēˌē\ *n pl*, *cap* [NL, fr. *Dothidea*, type genus (fr. Gk *dothiēn* small abscess, boil) + *-aceae*] **:** a family of saprophytic or parasitic fungi (order Dothideales) with a plurilocular stroma that is erumpent and superficial at maturity — **do·thid·e·aceous** \(ˌ)dōˌthidē'āshəs\ *adj*

do·thid·e·ales \-'ā(ˌ)lēz\ *n pl*, *cap* [NL, fr. *Dothidea* + *-ales*] **:** an order of ascomycetous fungi (subclass Euascomycetes) having the mycelium embedded in the substrate and a stroma with a hard dark rind and soft pale inner layer that is divided into cavities resembling perithecia within which asci are produced in tufts or hymenial layers

doth·i·del·la \ˌdäthə'delə, ˌdōth-\ *n*, *cap* [NL, fr. Gk *dothiēn* + NL *-ella*] **:** a genus of fungi (family Dothideaceae) having hyaline, unequally 2-celled ascospores, and including a fungus (*D. ulmi*) that attacks the leaves of elm

do·thid·i·a·ce·ae \(ˌ)dōˌthidē'āsēˌē\ *syn of* DOTHIDEACEAE

do·thid·i·a·les \-'ā(ˌ)lēz\ *syn of* DOTHIDEALES

do·thi·o·rel·la \ˌdōthēə'relə\ *n*, *cap* [NL, irreg. fr. Gk *dothiōn*, *dothiēn* small abscess, boil + NL *-ella*] **:** a form genus of imperfect fungi (family Sphaeriopsidaceae) characterized by single-celled hyaline spores (grouped in superficial stromata) of the pycnidia

dotier *comparative of* DOTY

dotiest *superlative of* DOTY

doting *also* **doating** *adj* [fr. pres. part. of ¹*dote*, *doat*] **1 :** IMBECILE, FOOLISH; *esp* **:** weak-minded from old age **2 :** excessively or foolishly fond **:** OVERINDULGENT ⟨deceiving her preoccupied and ~ husband with a young captain⟩ ⟨~ mothers end by ruining their children —Hallam Tennyson⟩ — **dot·ing·ly** *adv* — **dot·ing·ness** *n* -ES

dot·ish *also* **doat·ish** \'dōd·ish\ *adj* [²*dote* + *-ish*] *archaic* **:** IMBECILE

dotkin *var of* DODKIN

dot·let \'dätlət\ *n* -s [¹*dot* + *-let*] **:** a small dot

do·to \'dōd·(ˌ)ō\ *n*, *cap* [NL, fr. L *Doto*, a sea nymph, fr. Gk *Dōtō*] **:** a genus of nudibranch mollusks with tuberculated cerata

dot product *n* [¹*dot*; fr. its being commonly written *A·B*] **:** the scalar product of two vectors

do·tri·a·con·tane \ˌdōˌtriə'känˌtān\ *n* -s [ISV *dotriacont-* (fr. *do-* — as in *dodeca-* — + *triacont-* — fr. Gk *triakonta* thirty) + *-ane*] **:** a paraffin hydrocarbon of the formula $C_{32}H_{66}$; *esp* **:** the crystalline normal isomer $CH_3(CH_2)_{30}CH_3$

dots *pl of* DOT, *pres 3d sing of* DOT

dotted *adj* [fr. past part. of ²*dot*] **1 :** made of or executed with dots **:** STIPPLED ⟨~ leaders in the table of contents⟩ ⟨the ~ manner of engraving⟩ **2 :** marked or covered with dots or small spots ⟨the ~ scad called cigarfish⟩ **3 :** strewn with scattered objects resembling dots ⟨a vast plain ~ with infrequent settlements⟩ **4 :** relating to a musical note or rest increased in length by one half of its value by the addition of a dot

dotted line *n* **1 :** a row of dots on a paper indicating the place for a signature **2 :** a succession of dots as a guide for cutting or partial perforations resembling dots for easy detachment — **on the dotted line :** in full acceptance of a written statement or agreement; *esp* **:** in unquestioning acceptance of the binding terms of an engagement ⟨your signature *on the dotted line* guarantees freedom from worries about heat⟩

dotted manner *n* **:** MANIÈRE CRIBLÉE

dotted smartweed *n* **:** WATER SMARTWEED

dotted swiss *n* **:** a sheer muslin with open weave and crisp finish characterized by small evenly spaced dots woven in by the use of extra filling yarns and used esp. for clothing or curtains

¹dot·ter \'dätə(r)\ *vi* [ME *doteren*, perh. alter. of *toteren* to totter — more at TOTTER] *dial Brit* **:** to walk shakily **:** TOTTER

²dot·ter \'däd·ə(r), -ätə-\ *n* -s [²*dot* + *-er*] **1 :** one that makes dots **2 a :** a worker who by means of a centering machine locates the optical and focal centers, axis, and terminal points of ground lenses to guide workers who will cut, edge, trim, and mount the lenses — called also *spotter* **3 :** a device for training gun pointers without using ammunition consisting of a vertically oscillating paper target close to the gun's muzzle that is dotted by an electrically operated pencil at the point at which the sights are directed when the pointer presses the firing key

dot·ter·el *or* **dot·trel** \'däd·ərəl, -ätərəl, -ä·trəl\ *n* -s [ME *dotrelle*, fr. *doten* to dote + *-erelle* (as in *cokerelle* cockerel) — more at DOTE, COCKEREL] **1** *sometimes pl* **dotterel** *or* **dottrel :** a plover (*Charadrius morinellus*) of Europe and Asia formerly common in England; *also* **:** any of various congeners chiefly of eastern Asia, Australia, and So. America that are highly regarded as table birds **2** *Brit* **:** a stupid foolish person **:** DOTARD

dot·ti·ly \'däd·ᵊlē, -ätᵊl-, \ə̇lē, -i\ *adv* [²*dotty* + *-ly*] **1 :** with a feeble or unsteady gait **2 :** in a crazy manner

dot·ti·ness \|ēnə̇s, |in-\ *n* -ES [²*dotty* + *-ness*] **1 :** unsteadiness of gait **2 a :** FEEBLEMINDEDNESS, CRAZINESS ⟨was already showing such symptoms of future ~ as ... greeting oak trees as old friends —*Time*⟩ **b :** droll eccentricity

dotting *pres part of* DOT

¹dot·tle *also* **dot·tel** \'däd·ᵊl, -ätᵊl\ *n* -s [ME *dottel*, *dotelle*, fr. (assumed) ME *dot* lump, dot — more at DOT] **1** *obs* **:** PLUG **2 :** unburnt and partially burnt tobacco caked in the bowl of a pipe **:** HEEL

²dottle \"\ *adj* [Sc, fool, fr. ME *dotel*, fr. *doten* to dote — more at DOTE] *Scot* **:** FOOLISH, FEEBLEMINDED

³dottle \"\ *vt* -ED/-ING/-S [*dottle* (*pin*)] **:** to keep apart by dottle pins or by thimbles (as in glost firing)

dottle pin *n* [¹*dottle*] **:** a small plug or pin of burned fireclay used to separate articles during firing

dot·to·re \dō'tōrē, -ōr,ā\ *n*, *usu cap* [It, doctor, fr. L *doctor* teacher — more at DOCTOR] **:** a stock character in the commedia dell' arte represented as a windy pedantic jurist, philosopher, or physician ridiculed by the other characters

¹dot·ty \'däd·|ē, -ät|, |i\ *adj* -ER/-EST [¹*dot* + *-y*] **:** composed of or characterized by dots

²dotty \"\ *adj* -ER/-EST [alter. of ²*dottle*] **1 :** unsteady in gait **2 :** obsessed or infatuated with ⟨if your friend is so ~ about Judith, he'd better ask her to marry him —Edith Wharton⟩ **3 :** slightly unbalanced mentally **:** touched in the head **:** FEEBLEMINDED, ECCENTRIC ⟨her deliciously ~ Aunt Elinor, at the moment incarcerated in an expensive sanitarium —Florence Bullock⟩ **4 :** ABSURD, RIDICULOUS

doty \'dōd·|ē, -ōt|, |i\ *adj* -ER/-EST [¹*dote* + *-y*] **1** *of timber* **:** affected by incipient or partial decay often with discoloration **2** *South* **:** WEAK-MINDED; *esp* **:** having the mentality impaired in old age

douane \dwän\ *n*, *pl* **douanes** \-n(z)\ [F, fr. MF, fr. OIt *doana*, fr. Ar *dīwān*, fr. Per, account book — more at DIVAN] **:** CUSTOMHOUSE

doua·nier \dwänyā\ *n*, *pl* **douaniers** \-ā(z)\ [F, fr. MF, fr. *douane*] **:** a customs officer

dou·ar \dü'är, də'wär\ *n* -s [Ar *dawwār*] **:** an Arabian village consisting typically of a group of tents or huts that encircle an open space

¹dou·ble \'dəbəl\ *adj* [ME, fr. OF *doble*, *double*, fr. L *duplus*, fr. *du-* (fr. *duo* two) + *-plus* multiplied by; akin to OFris *twīfil* doubt, OHG *zwīval*, Goth *tweifls* doubt, MIr *dīabul* double, Gk *diploos* double, OE *fealdan* to fold — more at TWO, FOLD] **1 :** having a twofold relation or character **:** combining two often dissimilar things or qualities **:** DUAL ⟨the wonderful ~ gift of seeing and saying —Carlos Baker⟩ ⟨a discussion of verbs with ~ function . . . verbs used both transitively and intransitively —A.M.Sturtevant⟩ **2 :** consisting of two usu. combined members, things, or sets **:** having two parts joined together **:** forming a pair ⟨~ balconies running around three sides of a grassy courtyard —Tom Marvel⟩ ⟨an egg with a ~ yolk⟩ **3 :** being two times as great or as many **:** multiplied by two **:** TWOFOLD ⟨the college had ~ the number of expected applicants⟩ ⟨was produced in quantities ~ the prewar output⟩ **4 :** characterized by duplicity **:** acting two parts or in two ways, one usu. being praiseworthy and the other blameworthy **:** DECEITFUL, HYPOCRITICAL, INSINCERE ⟨never speaks with a ~ tongue —T.B.Costain⟩ ⟨a ~ agent . . . pretending to serve the Nazis while actually working for the British —*N. Y. Herald Tribune*⟩ **5 :** folded in two **:** DOUBLED ⟨letters written on ~ sheets of stationery⟩ **6 :** made, being, or having parts twice as large, strong, or valuable: as **a** *of a coin* **:** worth two of the specified unit ⟨~ ducat⟩ ⟨~ taler⟩ **b** *printing* **:** of twice or almost twice the belly-to-back size of — used only of pre-point-system type names ⟨~ great primer⟩ ⟨~ paragon⟩ ⟨~ pica⟩; compare TWO-LINE **c :** having the shorter dimension doubled — used of a paper size ⟨crown is 15 x 20 and ~ crown is 30 x 20⟩; compare QUAD **7 a :** of extra size, strength, or value ⟨a mighty mug of . . . ~ ale —Lord Byron⟩ **b :** having more than the normal number of floral leaves often at the expense of the sporophylls ⟨~ stamens⟩ — used esp. of cultivated plants **8** *music* **a :** DUPLE 2a **b :** sounding an octave lower than the single or normal instrument **9 a** *of meter* **:** DUPLE 2b **b** *of rhyme* **:** having two syllables **10** *of a card game* **:** played with two full packs of cards mixed together ⟨~ pinochle⟩

²double \"\ *n* -s [ME, fr. *double*, adj.] **1 :** something twice the ordinary size, strength, speed, quantity, or value: as **a** (1) **:** an old French billon coin worth about two deniers (2) **:** a copper or bronze coin of Guernsey worth about ⅛ English penny **b :** any of various feasts in the Roman Catholic church ranking above a simple in order of precedence **c :** a 16-foot organ stop **d doubles** *pl* **:** a game between two pairs of players ⟨played three sets of ~s⟩ ⟨his ~s partner⟩ **e :** a two-base hit in baseball ⟨led the league in ~s⟩ **f** *Brit* **:** a double count made with a single stroke in billiards (as by pocketing both cue ball and object ball) **g :** the catching of two fish on one line at the same cast **h :** DOUBLE TIME — usu. used with *on* or *at* ⟨marched back again on the ~ —Earle Birney⟩ ⟨began to march at the ~ —Francis Hackett⟩ **i doubles** *pl* **:** sheet metal having a thickness of approximately ¹⁄₃₂ inch **2 :** one that is the counterpart of another **:** COPY, DUPLICATE: as **a** (1) **:** a living person that closely resembles another living person ⟨thought I saw you on the street yesterday but it turned out to be your ~⟩ (2) **:** the apparition of a living person **:** WRAITH ⟨the appearance of a ~ or fetch has ever been held . . . to signify approaching death —R.A.Procter⟩ **b :** one who resembles an actor and who performs in his stead typically when the script requires special talent that the actor does not possess **c :** one (as an actor or singer) prepared to substitute for another in his absence **:** UNDERSTUDY **3 :** a twofold or repeated action: as **a** (1) **:** a sharp turn or reversal (as in running) (2) **:** an evasive shift (as in argument) **b** (1) **:** a 16th century court-dance step consisting of three steps and a close (2) **:** a folk-dance sequence of four running steps forward or backward **c** (1) **:** a musical variation (as in a classical suite) (2) **:** a repeated version of a movement of a musical composition (as a suite) with variation **d doubles** *pl* **:** the changes rung or capable of being rung on a set of five bells **e :** a twofold victory or defeat (as in two races on the same day or in a match and a return match) **4 :** something consisting of two paired members: as **a :** something doubled over or together **:** FOLD ⟨hit the horse with the ~ of his rope⟩ **b** *printing* (1) **:** DOUBLET (2) **:** a sheet inadvertently printed twice on one side **c :** DOUBLE STAR **d :** a letter occurring twice in succession in a word or in adjoining words of connected text **e :** a two-horse parlay **f :** DOUBLE JUMP 1 **g :** a double-barreled shotgun **h :** a domino with the same number of pips on each half **i :** two consecutive strikes in bowling **j :** two targets thrown simultaneously in skeet shooting **k :** a cricketer's feat of scoring 1000 runs and taking 100 wickets in one season **l doubles** *pl* **:** two fishing hooks fastened together at the shank so as to form a double hook **5 a** (1) **:** an act of doubling in card games (2) **:** the announcement by which a player in such games signifies that he doubles **b** (1) **:** a call in bridge that has the effect of increasing the points scored for odd tricks if the declarer fulfills his contract and for undertricks if he does not (2) **:** a hand strong enough to justify making such a call **c :** an act of doubling the stakes in backgammon

³double \"\ *vb* **doubled; doubled; doubling** \-b(ə)liŋ\ **doubles** [ME *doublen*, fr. OF *dobler*, *doubler*, fr. L *duplare*, fr. *duplus* double — more at ¹DOUBLE] *vt* **1 :** to increase by adding an equal quantity **:** multiply by two **:** make twice as great or as many ⟨his brother was *doubling* in this new will his posthumous provision for her —F.M.Ford⟩: as **a :** to be twice as great or as many as **:** amount to twice the number of ⟨births *doubled* deaths in the state last year⟩ **b** (1) **:** to line or cover (a wooden ship) with an additional layer of planking (2) **:** to line or trim (a garment) with additional material — now used chiefly in heraldry **c** (1) **:** to combine (as two slivers of yarn) by compressing or twisting into a single unit (2) *chiefly Brit* **:** PLY ⟨~ yarns⟩ **d** (1) **:** to add a note an octave above or below to (a specified note) (2) **:** to reinforce (a musical part) with an additional part having the same notes either at the same pitch or at the octave **e** (1) **:** to make a call in bridge that increases the value of odd tricks or undertricks at (an opponent's bid) (2) *Brit* **:** RAISE ⟨he *doubled* my poker bet⟩ **f** (1) **:** to advance (a base runner in baseball) by a two-base hit ⟨the batter walked and was *doubled* to third base⟩ (2) **:** to bring about the scoring of (a run in baseball) by a two-base hit ⟨*doubled* in two runs in the third inning⟩ **g :** to put out (a base runner in baseball) in completing a double play ⟨was *doubled* off second base when the batter lined to the shortstop⟩ ⟨forced the runner at second and was *doubled* at first base⟩ — sometimes used with *up* ⟨was *doubled* up at first⟩ **2 a :** to make of two thicknesses by turning or bending usu. in the middle **:** FOLD **b :** to close tightly (the hand or fist) **:** CLENCH ⟨he turned swiftly, *doubling* his fists —Hamilton Basso⟩ — often used with *up* **c :** to cause to stoop **:** BEND ⟨hit him in the stomach and *doubled* him over⟩ — often used with *up* ⟨*doubled* him up⟩ **3 a :** to avoid by doubling **:** ELUDE **b** *of a ship* **:** to sail around (as a cape) by reversing the direction of motion ⟨had *doubled* so many capes and run before the wind and brought back news of faraway men —Van Wyck Brooks⟩ **c** *Brit* **:** to cause (a billiard ball) to rebound **4** [trans. of F *doubler*] **a :** to replace in a dramatic role ⟨he was *doubling* the hero in a sword fight —Niven Busch⟩ **b :** to play (dramatic roles) by doubling ⟨~s the part of leader or squire with that of clown or entertainer —Douglas Kennedy⟩ **c :** to prepare (a talking part in a motion picture) for audiences speaking different languages **~** *vi* **1 :** to become increased to twice the ordinary size, strength, speed, quantity, or value **:** increase or grow to twice as much ⟨the population *doubled* in 10 years⟩: as **a :** to march at double time **b** (1) **:** to reread a line inadvertently ⟨lines sufficiently separated to prevent *doubling* —Stanley Morison⟩ (2) **:** to set a doublet **c** (1) **:** to double a bid (as in bridge) (2) **:** to propose that the stake be doubled (as in backgammon) **d :** to make a two-base hit in baseball ⟨*doubled* off the left-field fence⟩ **e :** to fire both rounds in a double-barreled shotgun with a single trigger pull **f :** to use an additional layer of planking on a wooden ship **2 a :** to turn sharply and suddenly in running; *esp* **:** to turn back on one's course — often used with *back* ⟨the rabbit *doubled* back on his tracks⟩ **b :** to follow a circuitous course ⟨a road . . . *doubled* round the hollow in a long sweep —H.E.Bates⟩ **c :** to enclose an enemy's fleet between two fires **d** *Brit* **:** REBOUND — used of a billiard ball **e** *archaic* **:** to make evasive shifts **:** act deceitfully ⟨if thy tongue ~s with me —Sir Walter Scott⟩ **3 :** to become bent or folded usu. in the middle **:** bend over — often used with *up* ⟨she *doubled* up with pain⟩ **4 a :** to serve an additional purpose or perform an additional duty ⟨a big gymnasium that ~s as an auditorium —C.B.Palmer b.1910⟩ ⟨court's switchboard operator was *doubling* as a receptionist —Katherine T. Kinkead⟩ **b :** to play an additional instrument — usu. used with *on* ⟨the guitarist *doubled* on piano⟩ **c :** to play two parts esp. in a dramatic production ⟨she *doubled* as the maid in the first act and the secretary in the third⟩ **d :** to play a dramatic role as a double ⟨*doubled* for the hero in the fencing match⟩ — **double in balk :** to leave the object ball and the cue ball in balk at the end of one's turn in billiards when the opponent's ball is not yet in play — **double in brass 1 :** to perform on a musical instrument other than one's regular instrument **2 :** to serve an additional purpose or perform an additional duty ⟨the jeep *doubled in brass* as a snowplow⟩ ⟨the announcer *doubled in brass* as the station's music librarian⟩ — **double the hill :** to cut a railroad train in half and take it over a hill in two sections because of the steep grade

⁴double \"\ *adv* [ME, fr. *double*, adj.] **1 a :** to twice the extent or amount **:** DOUBLY ⟨bright eyes were ~ bright —John Keats⟩ **b :** two together **:** in a pair ⟨some people sleep better ~ and some single —Morris Fishbein⟩ **2** *archaic* **:** with duplicity **:** DECEITFULLY ⟨if you should deal ~ with her —Shak.⟩ **3 :** downward and forward from the usual position ⟨he was bent ~ with pain⟩

⁵dou·blé \(')dü¦blā\ *adj* [F, past part. of *doubler* to line, fr. MF, to line, double — more at ³DOUBLE] *of a book cover* **:** made with a doublure

double account *n* **:** a system of accounting prescribed by British law for railway and public utility enterprises whereby permanent capital is offset against fixed assets purchased with monies contributed from permanent capital

double-acting \ˌ⸗⸗¦⸗⸗\ *adj* **:** acting or operating in two directions or with two motions ⟨a *double-acting* engine⟩ ⟨a *double-acting* pump⟩

double-action \ˌ⸗⸗¦⸗⸗\ *adj* **1 :** DOUBLE-ACTING **2** *of a firearm* **:** capable of being cocked and fired by a single pull of the trigger ⟨a fairly accurate *double-action* shot —Harry Reeves⟩

double-action harrow *n* **:** DOUBLE-DISC HARROW

double-and-twist \ˌ⸗⸗⸗¦⸗\ *n* **:** a two-ply yarn with contrasting colors

double appoggiatura *n* [trans. of It *appoggiatura doppia*] **1 :** two disjunct appoggiaturas above and below the principal note — see APPOGGIATURA illustration **2 :** two appoggiaturas occurring simultaneously in different voices or parts

double-aspect theory *n* **1 :** a philosophical theory that takes mind and body or the mental and the material to be related aspects of a single more ultimate reality — compare NEUTRAL MONISM **2 :** a philosophical theory that holds the conscious processes and the neural processes in the brain to be aspects of the same real series of events — compare INTERACTIONISM, PSYCHOPHYSICAL PARALLELISM

double assurance *n* [trans. of G *doppelte sicherung*] **:** dual control of differentiation resulting from synergistic interaction of a specific organizer and a competent embryonic tissue capable of self-differentiation in the absence of the organizer

double ax *n* **:** an ax with a 2-edged blade; *specif* **:** such an ax used as a sacred symbol in the art of prehistoric Crete and later associated with the worship of Zeus

double ballade *n* **:** a ballade having six stanzas and usu. an envoi

double-banked \ˌ⸗⸗¦baŋkt, -aiŋ-\ *adj* **1 a** *of a rowboat* **:** having two banks of rowers sitting side by side **b** *of an oar* **:** manned by two rowers **2 :** having two tiers ⟨the bireme was a *double-banked* galley⟩ ⟨a *double-banked* frigate⟩ ⟨a *double-banked* organ⟩

double bar *n* **:** two adjacent vertical lines or a heavy single line separating principal sections of a musical composition — see BAR illustration

double-barrel \ˌ⸗⸗¦⸗⸗\ *n* **:** a double-barreled gun

double-bar·reled *or* **double-bar·relled** \ˌ⸗⸗¦barəld *also* -ber-\ *adj* **1** *of a firearm* **:** having two barrels mounted side by side — compare OVER-AND-UNDER **2 :** TWOFOLD; *esp* **:** having a double purpose ⟨our *double-barreled* desire to make things profitable as well as attractive —Louis Kronenberger⟩

double-base powder *n* **:** an explosive powder or propellant that contains nitrocellulose and nitroglycerin as the essential components — compare SINGLE-BASE POWDER

double bass *n* [¹*double* + *bass*] **:** CONTRABASS

double bassoon *n* **:** CONTRABASSOON

double bed *n* **:** a bed designed for two persons

double-bed·ded \ˌ⸗⸗¦bedəd\ *adj* **1 :** having two beds **2 :** furnished with a double bed

double bill *n* **:** a bill (as at a theater) offering two principal features

double-bit ax *n* **:** an ax having a head with two cutting edges

double-bitt \ˌ⸗⸗'⸗\ *vt* [³*double* + *bitt*, v.] **:** to secure (a cable) by passing it around a pair of bitts

double-bit·ted \ˌ⸗⸗¦bid·əd\ *adj* **:** having two sharp edges ⟨a *double-bitted* ax⟩ — see AX illustration

double blossom *n* **:** a disease of dewberry and blackberry caused by a fungus (*Fusarium rubi*) and characterized by witches'-brooms and enlargement and malformation of the flowers

double boiler *n* **:** a cooking utensil consisting of two vessels, one fitting into the other, the contents of the upper being cooked by boiling water in the lower

double boiler

double bond *n* **:** a chemical bond consisting of two covalent bonds between two atoms in a molecule, usu. represented in chemical formulas by two lines, two dots, or four dots denoting two pairs of electrons (as in the formulas for ethylene $H_2C{=}CH_2$, $H_2C{:}CH_2$, or $H_2C{::}CH_2$) — compare TRIPLE BOND, UNSATURATED

double bottom *n* **1 :** the space in a ship between the inner bottom and the shell plating **2 :** a market decline on the stock exchange characterized by two successive low points and regarded by chart readers as a prelude to a recovery — compare DOUBLE TOP

double-breasted \ˌ⸗⸗¦⸗⸗\ *adj* **1** *of a coat or jacket* **:** having one half of the front lapped over the other and usu. a double row of buttons and a single row of buttonholes **2** *of a suit* **:** having a double-breasted coat

double brilliant *n* **:** a brilliant with 72 facets, 40 above and 32 below the girdle — called also *split brilliant*, *trap brilliant*

double-brood·ed \ˌ⸗⸗¦brüdəd\ *adj* **:** producing two broods each year **:** BIVOLTINE

double buggy *n* **:** a buggy having two seats

double cabin *n* **:** a log cabin consisting of two rooms connected by a roofed passage

double canon *n* **:** a musical canon with two subjects

double capital *n* **1 :** a capital so carved as to suffice for two shafts **2 :** a capital having a dosseret

double carom *n* **:** a shot in certain table games (as pool) in which the cue ball strikes each of three object balls

double centner *n* **:** METRIC CENTNER

double chair *n* **1 :** a light chaise having two seats **2 :** a chair for two persons with the back formed by two chair backs joined together

double chant *n* **:** an Anglican chant 14 measures long and covering 2 verses

double check *n* [1*double* + *check*] **1 :** a situation in chess in which the move of a checking piece discovers a check by another piece **2 :** a careful examination, investigation, or inspection designed esp. to determine accuracy, condition, or progress

double-check \¦⸗⸗¦⸗\ *vb* [*double check*] *vt* **:** to subject to a double check ⟨the final version was *double-checked* for accuracy —*Time*⟩ ~ *vi* **:** to make a double check ⟨send his accountant to a publisher's office to *double-check* against the possibility of error —*Saturday Rev.*⟩

double chin *n* **:** a fleshy or fatty fold under the chin — **double-chinned** \¦⸗⸗¦⸗\ *adj*

double chorus *n* **1 :** a musical composition for a divided choir **2 :** the two choirs singing a double chorus

double circulation *n* **:** a circulatory system in which the blood makes two distinct circuits — compare PULMONARY CIRCULATION, SYSTEMIC CIRCULATION

double-claw \ˈ⸗⸗ˌ⸗\ *n* **:** UNICORN PLANT

double cloth *n* **1 :** a compound cloth consisting of two distinct fabrics united at regular intervals by having a thread of warp or filling passing from one to the other and used esp. for coating, blankets, and upholstery **2 :** a backed cloth

double-clutch \¦⸗⸗¦⸗\ *vi* [1*double* + *clutch*, n.] **:** to shift gear in an automotive vehicle usu. to a lower speed by shifting first into neutral and then to the speed required with the clutch being released each time

double coat *n* **:** a pelt (as of various dogs) consisting of a dense soft or woolly undercoat and a long coarse outer coat

double-coat·ed \¦⸗⸗¦kōd·əd\ *adj, of paper* **:** having two coatings or a single heavy coating on one side

double coconut *n* **:** SEA COCONUT 1b

double column *n* **1 :** an advertisement covering the width of two columns (as of a newspaper) **2 :** a newspaper article having a headline and sometimes its body set two columns wide

double concerto *n* **:** a composition for two solo instruments with orchestra

double cone *n* **:** a complete cone formed by straight lines through the vertex, the straight lines being indefinitely extended in both directions — opposed to *half cone*

double consciousness *n* [prob. trans. of F *double conscience*] **:** the presence of two apparently unconnected streams of consciousness in one individual

double consonant *n* **1 :** a consonant letter occurring twice in succession in a word (as *nn* in *tunnel*) **2 a :** an acoustic impression apprehended or functioning as two consonants, produced by prolonging an articulation (as of \s\ in *bus seat*), by repeating an articulation (as of \r\ in Spanish *parra*, or by prolonging the interval between successive components of an articulation (as between the occlusion and the release of \t\ in *coattail*) **b :** a consonant produced by a simultaneous double articulation (as a \p\ pronounced with release of both lips and glottis) **c :** two different consonant sounds occurring in succession (as \mp\ in *stamp*)

double contraoctave *n* **:** SUBCONTRAOCTAVE

double contrast enema *n* **:** BARIUM ENEMA

double corner *n* **:** one of the two diagonally opposed corners of a checkerboard that have a light square flanked by two dark playing squares

double counterpoint *n* **:** 2-part counterpoint so constructed that either part may be above or below the other — called also *invertible counterpoint*

double couplers *n pl* **:** two coupling grabs united by a short chain or cable and used for fastening logs together

double-coursed \¦⸗⸗¦kō(ə)rst, -ȯ(ə)rst,-ōəst,-ȯ(ə)st\ *adj* **:** having building cover (as shingles) placed so that all areas are covered with no less than two thicknesses of material

double-crested cormorant \¦⸗⸗¦⸗⸗-\ *n* **:** a large long-tailed cormorant (*Phalacrocorax auritus*) with a tuft of feathers on each side of the head, present on both coasts of No. America and on inland waters north to Hudson Bay

double-crop \¦⸗⸗¦⸗\ *vb* [4*double* + *crop*, v.] *vi* **:** to grow two or more crops on the same land in the same season or at the same time ⟨the land is so fertile that most ranchers *double-crop* —*Time*⟩ ~ *vt* **:** to cultivate for double-cropping ⟨part of the land is *double-cropped* —Royall Brandis⟩

double cross *n* [1*double* + *cross*] **1 :** an act of treachery **:** BETRAYAL ⟨politics is too full of stories of *double crosses* and sellouts —D.D.McKean⟩ ⟨master of the art of the *double cross* —D.G.Haring⟩: **a :** an act of winning or trying to win a fight or match after agreeing to lose it **b :** an act of betraying a person with whom one is associated in an enterprise **2 :** a cross between first-generation hybrids of four separate inbred lines (as in the production of hybrid seed corn)

double-cross \¦⸗⸗¦⸗\ *vt* [*double cross*] **:** to deceive by double-dealing **:** BETRAY ⟨don't go out on a limb for a man who may *double-cross* you tomorrow —Stanley Walker⟩ **syn** see DECEIVE

double-crosser \ˌ⸗⸗ˈ⸗⸗\ *n* **:** one that double-crosses

Double-Crostic \ˌ⸗⸗ˈkrȯstik, -räs-, -tēk\ *trademark* — used for a puzzle whose object is to fill in with words guessed from definitions a column of numbered dashes and then copy each letter in the correspondingly numbered square of a diagram so that words in the diagram form a quotation and the initial letters of the words in the column spell the author and title from which the quotation is taken

double-current signaling *n* **:** a system of telegraphy using both direct and inverse electric currents

double-cut file *n* **:** a file with a surface cut into two series of parallel ridges crossing each other usu. at less than a right angle, both ridges being diagonal to the center line of the file

double-cut saw *n* **:** a saw having teeth that cut during both the pushing and pulling strokes

doubled *past of* DOUBLE

double dagger *n* **:** the character ‡ used commonly as the third in the series of reference marks — called also *diesis*

double dash *n* **:** a graphic character consisting of two long parallel horizontal dashes of which the top one is heavy and the bottom one light that is sometimes used to mark page or column divisions in printed matter — called also *oxford dash*

double date *n* [1*double* + *date*] **:** a date participated in by two couples

double-date \¦⸗⸗¦⸗\ *vi* [*double date*] **:** to participate in a double date

double daylight saving time *n* **:** daylight saving time that is two hours in advance of standard time

double-dealer \ˌ⸗⸗ˈ⸗⸗\ *n* **:** one who practices double-dealing

1**double-dealing** \ˌ⸗⸗ˈ⸗⸗\ *n* [1*double* + *dealing*, fr. gerund of *deal*] **:** deception by action contradictory to an attitude professed or a role assumed **:** DUPLICITY ⟨incompetence in many places, ignorance in others, and downright *double-dealing* in still others —F.V.W.Mason⟩ **syn** see DECEPTION

2**double-dealing** \¦⸗⸗¦⸗⸗\ *adj* [4*double* + *dealing*, fr. pres. part. of *deal*] **:** given to or marked by duplicity

double-deck \¦⸗⸗¦⸗\ *or* **double-decked** \¦⸗⸗¦dekt\ *adj* **:** having two stories, decks, or levels ⟨a *double-deck* bus⟩ ⟨a *double-deck* bed⟩

double-decker \ˌ⸗⸗ˈ⸗⸗\ *n* [*double deck* (fr. 1*double* + *deck*) + *-er*] **1 :** a ship with two decks above the waterline **2 :** a conveyance with one level over another level for additional passengers, stock, or freight (as a railway car, bus, or airplane) **3 :** a house or building (as a 2-family tenement) having two stories **4 :** BIPLANE **5 :** something having two horizontal layers like decks: as **a :** a large machine having upper and lower operating platforms (as a printing press) **b :** two single beds one above the other **c :** a sandwich made of three layers of bread and two of filling **d :** an outdoor advertising stand with one billboard built on top of another **6 :** a long novel in two volumes

double decomposition *n* **:** a chemical reaction between two compounds in which part of the first compound becomes united with part of the second and the remainder of the first compound becomes united with the remainder of the second (as in AB + CD → AD + BC) — called also *metathesis*

double descent *n* **:** descent through both the patrilineal and the matrilineal group with attendant rights and obligations

double detection *n* **:** superheterodyne reception

double diapason *n* **:** a large open organ pipe yielding characteristic diapason tone at 16-foot or 32-foot pitch

double-disc \¦⸗⸗¦⸗\ *vt* [4*double* + *disk*, v.] **:** to cultivate (soil) twice with a disc harrow either with a tandem disc or by lapping half of the width of a single disc on each round to provide a more even seedbed

double-disc harrow *n* [*double-disc* fr. 1*double* + *disk*, n.] **:** a harrow with two sets of discs so arranged that one set throws soil outward and the other throws it inward — called also *double-action harrow*

double-distilled \¦⸗⸗⸗¦⸗\ *adj* **:** being without any qualification or reservation **:** ABSOLUTE, THOROUGHGOING ⟨a *double-distilled* fool⟩

double-dog dare *vt, chiefly South & Midland* **:** to challenge defiantly

double-dome \ˈ⸗⸗ˌ⸗\ *n* **:** EGGHEAD ⟨had demonstrated his machine to scores of scientific *double-domes* —W.M.Swann⟩

double door *n* **:** an opening provided with two vertical doors which meet in the middle of the opening when closed — compare DUTCH DOOR

double dot *n* **:** two points placed immediately after a musical note or rest to indicate augmentation of its time value by three-quarters

double dribble *n* **:** a dribble made in violation of the rules by a basketball player who has already completed a legal dribble

double drift *n* **:** a method of determining the speed and direction of the wind by measuring the drift angle on each of two aircraft headings at a known airspeed

double drum *n* **:** KETTLEDRUM 1

double drummer *n, Austral* **:** any of several noisy cicadas; *esp* **:** a large red and black form (*Thopha saccata*)

double dummy *n* **:** bridge or whist played by two players, each having a dummy and from observation of the two exposed hands and his own knowing the exact location of every card

double dutch *n, usu cap 2d D* **:** something that is unintelligible; *esp* **:** unintelligible speech

double-duty \¦⸗⸗¦⸗⸗\ *adj* **:** designed for two purposes or performing two duties

double-dyed \¦⸗⸗¦⸗\ *adj* **1 :** dyed twice **:** thoroughly or intensely colored **2 :** confirmed esp. in habits or opinions **:** THOROUGHGOING ⟨a *double-dyed* villain⟩

double eagle *n* **1 :** a 20-dollar gold piece of the U.S. first issued in 1849 and last issued in 1933 — see EAGLE **2 :** a score of three under par made on a hole in golf

double edge *n* **:** FLAT 14b

double-edged \¦⸗⸗¦ejd\ *adj* **1 :** having two cutting edges ⟨a *double-edged* sword⟩ **2 a :** having a dual purpose or effect ⟨fighter-bombers often carried out *double-edged* missions —*Coast Artillery Jour.*⟩ **b :** capable of being understood or interpreted in two ways **:** AMBIGUOUS, EQUIVOCAL ⟨the old-timers gave the new arrival a *double-edged* welcome —*Time*⟩

double-end·ed \¦⸗⸗¦endəd\ *adj* **:** similar at both ends ⟨a *double-ended* bolt⟩

double-end·er \ˌ⸗⸗ˈendə(r)\ *n* [*double end* (fr. 1*double* + *end*) + *-er*] **1 a :** a ship with bow and stern of similar shape **b :** a self-propelled vehicle (as a streetcar) constructed and equipped to permit normal operation in either direction **2** *or* **double-ender file** \¦⸗⸗¦⸗⸗-\ **:** a file with teeth cut from both ends toward the middle

double englishman's knot *n, usu cap E* [1*double* + *englishman's knot*] **:** BARREL KNOT b

dou·ble en·ten·dre \ˌdübəˌlä^{n}(n·)ˈtä(ä)^{n}(n)\|dr(ᵊ), ˌdəbəˌlä-, ˌdüˌblä-, -län·ˈtän\|, \|d(rə)\ *n, pl* **double entendres** [obs. F, lit., double meaning] **1 :** ambiguity of meaning arising from language that lends itself to more than one interpretation ⟨rooted mainly in the basic humor of insult, malapropism, and *double entendre* —Wolcott Gibbs⟩ **2 :** a word or expression capable of two interpretations, one of them often having a risqué connotation ⟨a kind of old-fashioned bedroom farce with many of the *double entendres* that go with that form of entertainment —John McCarten⟩

double entry *n* **:** a method or system of bookkeeping that recognizes both the receiving and the giving sides of a business transaction by debiting the amount of the transaction to one account and crediting it to another account, the total debits in the system always equaling the total credits — compare SINGLE ENTRY

double envelopment *n* **:** simultaneous attack on both flanks of an enemy

double exposure *n* **:** two photographic exposures on the same sensitized surface

double-faced \¦⸗⸗¦⸗\ *adj* **1 :** having two faces or sides designed for use ⟨*double-faced* clocks⟩: as **a** *of cloth* **:** finished on both sides **:** REVERSIBLE **b** *of corrugated paperboard* **:** having liners attached on both sides **c** *of a disc record* **:** having a recording on each side **2 a :** having two aspects **:** AMBIGUOUS ⟨these facts, as facts so often do, prove *double-faced* —Virginia Woolf⟩ **b :** given to duplicity **:** HYPOCRITICAL, INSINCERE ⟨a *double-faced* infernal traitor and schemer —W.M.Thackeray⟩

double fault *n* **:** two consecutive faults made while serving in tennis and resulting in the loss of a point

double feature *n* **:** a movie program consisting of two main pictures

double fertilization *n* **:** fertilization that is characteristic of most seed plants and that involves a fusion between the egg nucleus and a sperm nucleus, which results in the production of the embryo, and a fusion between the second sperm nucleus and the two separate or fused polar nuclei, which gives rise to the endosperm — compare XENIA

double first *n* **1 :** first-class honors in two different subjects esp. at Cambridge and Oxford universities **2 :** a student who takes a double first

double fisherman's knot *n* [1*double* + *fisherman's knot*] **:** BARREL KNOT b

double flageolet *n* **:** a musical instrument of the flute family composed of two tubes connected to a single mouthpiece

double flaming *n* **:** the burning off of weeds with oil-burning equipment that throws flames on both sides of a row of plants

double flat *n* **:** a character ♭♭ placed after a note in musical notation that lowers its pitch by a whole step

double floor *n* **:** a floor in which binding joists support flooring joists above and ceiling joists below

double-fold \¦⸗⸗¦⸗\ *adj* [ME, fr. 1*double* + *-fold*] *archaic* **:** TWOFOLD

double foul *n* **:** two personal fouls in basketball committed by opponents against each other at the same time

double-framed floor \ˈ⸗⸗ˌ⸗-\ *n* **:** a double floor having girders into which the binding joists are framed

double fugue *n* **:** a musical fugue with two subjects

dou·ble·gang·er \ˌdəbəlˈgaŋə(r), ˈ⸗⸗ˌ⸗⸗\ *n* -S [part trans., part modif. of G *doppelgänger* — more at DOPPELGÄNGER] **:** DOPPELGÄNGER

double genitive *n* **:** DOUBLE POSSESSIVE

double glazing *n* **:** two layers of glass set in a window to reduce heat flow in either direction

double gown *n* **:** a heavy dressing gown usu. of reversible material

double-graft \¦⸗⸗¦⸗\ *vt* **:** DOUBLE-WORK

double gun *n* **:** a double-barreled gun

1**doublehanded** \¦⸗⸗¦⸗⸗\ *adj* [1*double* + *handed*] **1 :** adapted for use with both hands (as by having two handles) **2 :** capable of double use, interpretation, or action

2**doublehanded** \"\ *adv* [1*double* + *-handed* (as in *singlehanded*)] **:** with each of two persons helping the other ⟨captured an . . . admiral ~ —R.L.Taylor⟩

double-head \¦⸗⸗¦⸗\ *vb* [back-formation fr. *doubleheader*] *vi* **:** to run powered by two locomotives ⟨the train *double-headed* up the mountain⟩ ~ *vt* **:** to pull (a train) with two locomotives ⟨the heavy coal trains were *double-headed*⟩

double-headed \¦⸗⸗¦⸗⸗\ *adj* **1 :** having two heads ⟨a *double-headed* muscle⟩ **:** BICIPITAL **2** *of a railroad rail* **:** having a dumbbell-shaped cross section keyed into chairs spiked to the ties

dou·ble·head·er \ˌ⸗⸗ˈhedə(r)\ *n* [*double head* (fr. 1*double* + *head*) + *-er*] **1 :** a railroad train pulled by two locomotives **2 a :** two games (as of baseball) played consecutively on the same day by the same teams **b :** two games (as of basketball) played consecutively on the same day by two different pairs of teams

double header \"\ *n* [*doubleheader*] **:** a door or window lintel made from two pieces of lumber placed upright next to each other and usu. nailed or bolted together

doublehearted \¦⸗⸗¦⸗⸗\ *adj* **:** having a dissembling heart

double house *n* **1 :** a house with rooms on each side of an entrance hall **2 :** a house divided vertically by a party wall and designed for two families living side by side

double-hung \¦⸗⸗¦⸗\ *adj, of a window sash* **:** supported on each side by a counterweighted sash cord or a spring tension device for easy raising and lowering and holding position

double hyphen *n* **:** a punctuation mark ⸗ used in place of a hyphen at the end of a line to indicate that a word so divided is normally hyphenated

double indemnity *n* **:** a provision in a life-insurance or accident policy whereby the company agrees to pay twice the face of the contract in case of accidental death

double insurance *n* **:** several policies of insurance covering at least part of the same subject, having the same insurable interest, and subject to the same hazards

double jeopardy *n* **:** the putting of a person on trial for an offense for which he has previously been put on trial under a valid charge **:** two adjudications for one offense

double-jointed \¦⸗⸗¦⸗⸗\ *adj* **:** having joints that permit exceptional degrees of freedom of motion of the parts joined

double jump *n* **1 :** the action of capturing two checkers in successive jumps by the same man in one move **2 :** a double hurdle consisting typically of two fences set at such a distance that a horse must jump each in turn **3 :** a bid in bridge of two tricks more than necessary to overcall (as three spades over one club)

double-key cipher *n* **:** polyalphabetic substitution; *esp* **:** a Vigenère cipher with a key-word-mixed alphabet

double killing *n* **:** DOUBLE PLAY

doubleleaf \ˈ⸗⸗ˌ⸗\ *n, pl* **doubleleaves :** a plant of the genus *Listera; esp* **:** TWAYBLADE

double letter *n* **1 :** LIGATURE **2 :** a letter written on two sheets and requiring double postage

double liability *n* **:** the liability of the owner of stock (as of a bank) that is subject to assessment up to its face value although orig. full-paid

double-lock \¦⸗⸗¦⸗\ *vt* **:** to lock with two bolts or by two turns of the key **:** fasten doubly

double long *n* **:** LARGE 4

double-mate \¦⸗⸗¦⸗\ *vt* **:** to practice breeding from distinctive matings of (poultry) to produce males and females of exhibition type esp. when the standards adopted for color for the two sexes differ (as in barred Plymouth Rocks)

double meaning *n* **:** DOUBLE ENTENDRE ⟨the men and girls strained to anticipate the *double meanings* —Charles Jackson⟩

double-minded \¦⸗⸗¦⸗⸗\ *adj* **1 :** wavering in mind **:** UNDECIDED, VACILLATING ⟨a *double-minded* man unstable in all his ways —Jas 1:8 (RSV)⟩ **2 :** marked by hypocrisy **:** INSINCERE

double monastery *n* [trans. of ML *monasterium duplex*, trans. of LGk *diploun monastērion*] **:** a religious community of men and women living in adjacent establishments, using the same church, governed by one superior, and usu. obeying the same rule

double mordent *n* **:** a melodic ornamentation consisting of four grace notes or tones preceding a principal note or tone and executed by a rapid alternation of a principal tone with its lower auxiliary tone

double-name paper *n* **:** TWO-NAME PAPER

double negative *n* **1 :** a now substandard syntactic construction containing two negatives and having a negative meaning (as in *I didn't hear nothing* meaning "I didn't hear anything") **2 :** a reiterated denial that equals an affirmative — compare NEGATION

double nelson *n* **:** FULL NELSON

dou·ble·ness *n* -ES [ME *doublenesse*, fr. 1*double* + *-nesse* -ness] **:** the quality or state of being double or doubled

double-nose \ˈ⸗⸗ˌ⸗\ *or* **double-nosed** \¦⸗⸗¦nōzd\ *adj* **:** having more than one growing point and usu. producing more than one flower stalk — used of narcissus and various other bulbs

double note *n* **:** BREVE 4b

double numeration *n* **:** the numbering of the pages of a book with one or more sets of numbers in addition to or in place of page numbers so that the first number in one representative system denotes chapter or section and the second number denotes page or numbered paragraph

double-o \ˌ⸗⸗ˈ⸗\ *n* -S *often cap O* [so called fr. the two *O*'s in *once-over*] **:** a close examination or inspection ⟨gave the two strangers the well-known *double-o* —Walker Matheson⟩

double octave *n* **:** a musical interval of two octaves **:** FIFTEENTH

double or nothing *also* **double or quits** *of a bet or chance* **:** with the result being the cancellation or the doubling of a debt

double oxer *n* **:** an oxer with a guardrail on each side

double paddle *n* **:** a canoe paddle with a blade at each end used esp. with kayaks

double-page spread *n* **:** DOUBLE-SPREAD

double pair royal *n* **:** FOUR OF A KIND

double paper *n* **:** a paper composed of a thin surface layer and a thicker backing layer used in the printing of postage stamps esp. to prevent the removal of cancellation marks

double-park \¦⸗⸗¦⸗\ *vb* **:** to park in a street next to automobiles parked parallel to the curb

double pedal point *or* **double pedal** *n* **:** two pedal points sustained through a succession of musical harmonies (as tonic and dominant)

double pedro *n* **:** 3CINCH

double-pitch \¦⸗⸗¦⸗\ *adj* **:** pitched in two planes **:** sloping in two directions **:** GABLED ⟨a *double-pitch* roof⟩

double play *n* **:** a defensive play in baseball by which two players are put out ⟨grounded into a *double play* short to second to first⟩

double plea *n* **:** a plea in law alleging two or more distinct matters in answer to the declaration where either of such matters alone would be a sufficient bar to the action

double plow *n* **:** a plow with two different shares or discs: **a :** a two-way plow that turns the soil in one direction while moving in the opposite direction **b :** a deep tiller that turns soil at two depths simultaneously

double pneumonia *n* **:** pneumonia involving both lungs

double point *n* **:** a point on a curve at which there are two tangents

double-pole switch *n* **:** an electrical switch having two blades with their contacts for simultaneous opening or closing both sides of a circuit

double ponceau R *n, usu cap D&P* **:** an organic pigment — SEE DYE table I (under *Pigment Red 54*)

double-pored tapeworm \ˈ⸗⸗ˌ⸗-\ *n* **:** DOG TAPEWORM

double possessive *n* **:** a syntactic construction in English consisting of the preposition *of* followed by a noun in the possessive case (as *of Bill's* in *a friend of Bill's*) or by a possessive pronoun (as *of mine* in *this brain of mine*) and having the same meaning as if the idea of possession were expressed only once

double postal card *n* **:** a double-size postal card having two halves one of which is to be torn off and used for making reply to a communication on the other half with postage for the reply being paid by the original sender

double predestination *n* **:** the theological doctrine that God has chosen some to be saved and some to be lost — compare ELECTION, REPROBATION

double prime *n* **:** a symbol ″ suffixed to distinguish one character from a related character (as *a*″ from *a*′) or to indicate a relative unit (as a second of angle or an inch)

double-print \¦⸗⸗¦⸗\ *vt* **:** to produce two images from two negatives in a fixed position on (a photoengraving plate)

double procession *n* **:** the theological doctrine of the procession of the Holy Spirit from the Father and the Son

double quartet *n* **1 :** a musical composition for eight voices or instruments **2 :** eight musicians performing a double quartet

double quatrefoil *n* **:** an ornamental foliation with eight foils used as the cadency mark of a ninth son

double-queued \'=='kyüd\ *adj* [¹*double* + F *queue* tail + E *-ed* — more at QUEUE] **:** having a double tail — used of a lion in heraldry

¹double-quick \'==,=, ,==¦=\ *n* [⁴*double* + *quick*, adj.] **:** DOUBLE TIME

²double-quick \"\ *vi* **:** DOUBLE-TIME

double-quirked bead \'==,=-\ *n* **:** a bead set off by two quirks — see BEAD illustration

¹dou·bler \'dūblə(r)\ *n* -S [ME *dobler*, fr. MF *doblier, doublier*, fr. *doblier, doublier*, adj., double, fr. LL *duplarius*, fr. L *duplus* double + *-arius* -ary — more at DOUBLE] *dial Eng* **:** a large plate or bowl

²dou·bler \'dəb(ə)lə(r)\ *n* -S [³*double* + *-er*] **1 :** one that doubles: as **a :** a textile worker who doubles thread or folds cloth usu. by machine **b :** a textile machine for doubling yarn **2 a :** an instrument for so increasing a small initial quantity of electricity that it may be detected by the electroscope or the appearance of sparks **b :** an amplifier circuit whose output has twice the frequency of the input when the plate circuit is tuned to oscillate twice to each cycle of grid potential ⟨frequency ~⟩ **c :** a rectifier circuit in which each blocked half cycle of input voltage charges a capacitor so connected as to add its discharge to the next forward cycle and thus double the rectified output voltage ⟨voltage ~⟩ **3 :** a part of a distilling apparatus for intercepting the heavier fractions and returning them to be redistilled **4 :** either of a pair of mating crabs **5 :** a usu. fabric interlining that reinforces the lining of a shoe at vamp and tip

double raise *n* **:** a bid in bridge in the same suit as but two tricks higher than one's partner's bid and at least one trick more than is necessary to overcall any intervening bid

double reed *n* **:** two cane reeds bound together to form an air passage so that one can vibrate against the other and used as the mouthpiece of musical instruments of the oboe family

double-reef \'==¦=\ *vt* **:** to reduce the spread of (a sail) by taking in two reefs

double-refined iron \'===¦=-\ *n* **:** newly wrought iron made from iron rolled into bars that have been twice piled and rerolled

double refraction *n* **:** the refraction of light (as in most crystals) in two slightly different directions to form two rays — called also *birefraction, birefringence*

double rhyme *n* **:** end rhyme involving two syllables (as in *ceases* and *releases* or *inviting* and *exciting*) — compare FEMININE RHYME

double rhythm *n* **:** rhythm in which the thesis is twice as long as the arsis

double rifle *n* **:** a rifle having two barrels mounted side by side

double-ripper \,=='==\ *n*, *NewEng* **:** BOBSLED 2

double-rivet \,=='==\ *vt* **:** to rivet (a joint) in such a manner that all the rivets used are arranged in two rows if a lap joint or four rows if a butt joint

double root *n* **:** a root that appears twice in the solution of an algebraic equation

double rose *n* **:** a gem (as a diamond) cut so that it has 48 facets and the shape of two ordinary roses placed base to base

double round *n* **:** an archery round shot twice and the scores added

double rum *n* [¹*double* + *rum* (var. of *rummy*)] **:** COONCAN

double-runner \,=='==\ *n* **1** *NewEng* **:** BOBSLED 2 **2 :** a child's skate with two parallel blades

doubles *pl of* DOUBLE, *pres 3d sing of* DOUBLE

double salt *n* **1 :** a salt (as an alum) yielding on hydrolysis two different cations or anions **2 :** a salt regarded as a molecular combination of two distinct salts rather than as a coordination complex

double scull *vi, of a skater* **:** to move backward by weighting the inner edge of each skate and moving the feet alternately apart and together

double seamer *n* **:** a closing machine that rolls together the rims and lids of metal cans to make a hermetic seam

double-seater \,=='==\ *n* [*double seat* (fr. ¹*double* + *seat*) + *-er*] **:** TWO-SEATER

double series *n* **:** a mathematical series made up of terms each of which is itself a series

double-set trigger *n* **:** a set-trigger mechanism employing two triggers one in front of the other by means of which a very light trigger pull may be obtained

double sharp *n* **:** a character × or ※ placed after a note in musical notation that raises its pitch by a whole step

double shear *n* **:** simultaneous shear across two usu. parallel planes (as when a rivet passes through three thicknesses of metal)

double-shear steel *n* **:** shear steel that has been cut into shorter lengths, heated to a welding heat, piled, and rehammered into a single bar

double shuffle *n* **1 :** a clog dance characterized by fast syncopated taps of the feet **2 :** the characteristic step in the double shuffle

double-sided \'==¦==\ *adj* **:** having two sides or aspects ⟨every stage of the process has a *double-sided* result —J.H. Muirhead⟩

double-sighted \'==¦==\ *adj* **:** having double sight or two sights; *specif* **:** having unusual clearness of vision

double snipe *n* **:** GREAT SNIPE

double sole *n* **:** the foot of fine single-thread hosiery reinforced by knitting in an extra thread

double solitaire *n* **:** a card game for two in which each player plays his own game of Klondike or Canfield but can build upon his opponent's as well as his own aces, the winner being the one who has played the greater number of cards to the center

double-space \'==¦=\ *vt* **:** to type (copy) leaving alternate line spaces blank **~** *vi* **:** to type on every second line space

double spanish burton *n, usu cap S* **:** a tackle having one double block and two single blocks

double-spread \'==¦=\ *n* **:** an advertisement that covers two facing pages (as in a newspaper) — called also *double-page spread*

double spruce *n* **1 :** BLACK SPRUCE 1 **2 :** WHITE SPRUCE 1a **3 :** FRASER FIR

double square *n* **:** ADJUSTABLE SQUARE

double standard *n* **1 :** BIMETALLISM **2 :** a set of principles that applies differently and usu. more rigorously to one group of people or circumstances than to another; *specif* **:** a code of morals that applies different and more severe standards of sexual behavior to women than to men — compare SINGLE STANDARD

double star *n* **1 :** BINARY STAR **2 :** two stars in very nearly the same line of sight but seen as physically separate by means of a telescope — called also *optical double star*

double-starred \'==¦=\ *adj* **:** marked with a double star to indicate more than usual interest or excellence ⟨the places *double-starred* on my educational program —Hamlin Garland⟩

double steal *n* **:** a play in baseball in which each of two base runners steals a base

double stitch *n* **:** a stitch (as in a pamphlet) made by fastening two loops of a single thread in the center of the fold

¹double-stop \'==¦=\ *vt* **:** to produce two or more tones simultaneously on (a stringed instrument)

²double-stop \"\ *n* **:** an instance of double-stopping ⟨his famous silken tone, his equally famous *double-stops* —Virgil Thomson⟩

double-strength \'==¦=\ *adj, of glass* **:** having a thickness of 0.118 to 0.133 inch

double-struck \'==¦=\ *adj, of a coin* **:** bearing a double impression as a result of having shifted between the dies

double substitution *n* **:** DOUBLE-KEY CIPHER

double summer time *n, Brit* **:** daylight saving time two hours ahead of standard time — abbr. *DST*

double-surfaced \'==¦==\ *adj* **:** having two finished surfaces — used of airplane wings covered on both sides with fabric

double-swing door *n* **:** a door with hinges that permit it to swing either in or out

dou·blet \'dəblət, *usu* -əd+V\ *n* -S [ME, fr. MF, fr. OF, fr. *doble, double* double + *-et* — more at DOUBLE] **1 a :** a man's close-fitting garment for the upper body made with or without long sleeves and with or without short skirts, usu. padded, quilted, and decorated with slashes, embroidery, and jewels, and worn in western Europe esp. during the 16th and 17th centuries **b :** a quilted undergarment reinforced by rings of mail and worn under armor **2 :** something consisting of two identical or similar parts: as **a** (1) **:** a gem composed of two pieces of crystal or semiprecious stone sometimes with a layer of colored glass between them (2) **:** a piece of paste or glass covered by a veneer of real stone **b :** a lens consisting of two components (as for reducing aberration or increasing power); *specif* **:** a small magnifying hand lens consisting of two single lenses mounted in a metal cylinder and often with an attached metal carrying case **c :** a spectrum line having two close components **d :** a radio antenna of two wires pointing in opposite directions from the point where the power is supplied and usu. having dimensions that are small compared to the wavelength of the signal being used **e :** DOUBLE 4 h **3 :** a set of two identical or similar things **:** PAIR, COUPLE: as **a :** the result of a cast of two dice when each has the same number of spots on the face lying uppermost — usu. used in pl. **b :** two birds killed in the air at one time with a double-barreled gun **4 :** one of a pair **:** one of two identical or similar things: as **a :** one of two or more words in the same language derived by different routes of transmission from the same source (as English *dais* from Middle English *deis* from Old French *deis* from Latin *discus*, English *dish* from Middle English *dish* from Old English *disc* from Latin *discus*, and English *discus* from Latin *discus*) **b :** one or more characters or words typeset or typed twice by mistake — called also *double* **c :** material (as a news item) unintentionally repeated in an issue of a newspaper

doublet 1a

double take *n* **1 :** a delayed reaction to a surprising or significant situation after initial failure to recognize anything unusual — usu. used in the phrase *do a double take* ⟨we all did a *double take* at the sight of two housewives hanging out the family wash in a pouring rain —E.J.Moran⟩; *specif* **:** a technique of comic acting in which an actor at first reacts inappropriately (as if from absentmindedness) to a line of dialogue or to a situation and then quickly reacts appropriately **2 :** a second look ⟨bypassers sometimes gave the lawn a quick *double take* and went on —R.M.Yoder⟩

¹double-talk \'==,=\ *n* **1 :** language that appears to be earnest and meaningful but in fact is a mixture of sense and nonsense **:** GIBBERISH ⟨*double-talk* . . produces in the victim upon whom it is worked a strong suspicion that he is either hard of hearing or slowly going mad —*Life*⟩ **2 :** inflated, involved, and often deliberately ambiguous language **:** GOBBLEDYGOOK, JARGON ⟨lost in the miasma of *double-talk*, hypocrisy, and shortsightedness —R.E.Lauterbach⟩ ⟨writes the sort of *double-talk* which is all things to everybody —Max Lerner⟩

²double-talk \"\ *vi* **:** to use double-talk ⟨go on *double-talking* with him, always skirting the main subject but never touching it —Philip Barry⟩

double taxation *n* **:** the imposition by the same taxing body of two taxes on what is essentially the same thing (as in the case of taxing the income of corporations under the corporate income tax and taxing the part of corporate income distributed to stockholders as dividends under the personal income tax)

double-team \'==¦=\ *vi* **1 :** to use two teams in hauling ⟨a steep sandy hill up which the wagons must be got by *double-teaming* —D.L.Morgan⟩ **2 :** to bring double force to bear — used with *on* or *upon* ⟨we *double-teamed* on one section of his army —T.E.Watson⟩ **3 :** to use two players to block or guard an opponent (as in football) **~** *vt* **:** to block or guard (an opponent) with two players ⟨the center and left tackle *double-team* the guard —*Athletic Jour.*⟩

double ten *also* **double tenth** *n, usu cap D&T* [trans. of Chin *shuang¹ shih²*; fr. its being the tenth day of the tenth month] **:** October 10th celebrated by Nationalist China as the anniversary of the 1911 revolution against the Manchu dynasty

doublethink \'==,=\ *n* -S **:** the keeping of two contradictory ideas or opinions in one's mind at the same time and the conscious belief in both of them ⟨his mind slid away into the labyrinthine world of ~ —George Orwell⟩

double thread *n* **:** two parallel threads of equal dimensions on the same screw one of which is 180° ahead of the other

double-threaded \'==¦==\ *adj* **:** consisting of two threads twisted together **:** having or using two threads

double three *n* **:** a fancy skating figure resembling a cloverleaf and consisting of two threes executed in one circle

double-throw switch *n* **:** an electric switch having moving blades that may engage either of two different sets of fixed contacts

double time *n* [¹*double* + *time*] **1 :** a marching cadence of 180 36-inch steps per minute — called also *double-quick* **2 :** payment of a worker at twice his regular wage rate (as on holidays)

double-time \'==,=\ *vb* [*double time*] *vi* **:** to move at double time ⟨he reached the crest of the hill and *double-timed* over the top —A.C.Fields⟩ **~** *vt* **:** to cause to move at double time ⟨they could *double-time* him forever and work him till he dropped —James Jones⟩

dou·ble·ton \'dəbəltən, -t°n\ *n* -S [¹*double* + *-ton* (as in *singleton*)] **:** an original holding (as in bridge) of two cards in any suit — compare SINGLETON

doubletone \'==,=\ *n* **:** a printing ink producing the effect of one hue in the parts printed in full color and another hue in parts printed less solidly

¹double-tongue \'==,=\ *n* [¹*double* + *tongue*, n.; fr. the foliose bract that grows from the cladophyll] **:** a dwarf shrub (*Ruscus hypoglossum*) of southern Europe

²double-tongue \'==¦=\ *vi* [⁴*double* + *tongue*, v.] **:** to play a wind musical instrument by using the tongue in rapidly alternating articulations to produce enunciation of fast or repeated notes in groups of two

double-tongued \'==¦=\ *adj* [ME *double tonged*, fr. ¹*double* + *tonged* tongued] **:** characterized by hypocrisy **:** INSINCERE

double-tongue graft *n* **:** a graft similar to a whip graft except that two clefts instead of one are made in both stock and scion

double-tooth \'==,=\ *n* -S [prob. trans. of NL *Bidens*, genus name] **:** a bur marigold (*Bidens cernua*)

double top *n* **:** a market rise on the stock exchange characterized by two successive high points and regarded by chart readers as a prelude to a decline — compare DOUBLE BOTTOM

double topsails *n pl* **:** two sails used in square-rigged ships and made in the same width as but half the height of the old-fashioned topsail

double touch *n* **:** a mechanism in a pipe organ for causing one effect when keys or pistons are fully depressed and another when they are depressed only partly

double-track \'==¦=\ *vt* **:** to furnish (a railroad) with two parallel lines of track

double transfer *n* **:** a double impression on a lithographed postage stamp produced in the transfer of the design to the stone

double transposition *n* **:** encipherment by successive transpositions usu. with different keys

dou·ble·tree \'dəbəl·(,)trē,-l·tri\ *n* **:** an evener for use with a two-horse team

double-trip \'==¦=\ *vi* **:** to tie up to the shore some of the barges in a tow, proceed through a difficult stretch of river with the others, tie them up, and return to pick up the barges left behind

double-trouble \'==¦'==\ *n* **:** a step in a rustic dance originated by plantation Negroes

double truck *n* [prob. fr. ¹*double* + *truck* (vehicle)] **:** a 2-page editorial or advertising layout (as in a newspaper) made up as a single unit

doublets *pl of* DOUBLET

dou·blette \dü'blet, ,də'-\ *n* -S [F, fr. *double* + *-ette*] **1 :** a 2-foot stop in a French pipe organ **:** FIFTEENTH 4a **2 :** MIXTURE STOP

double-u *also* **double-you** *same pronunc as at* w\ *n, sometimes cap U* **:** the letter *w*

double up *vi* **1 :** to share accommodations typically designed for one person or family ⟨you wouldn't mind *doubling up* with your brother —Marcia Davenport⟩ **2 :** to bet double the amount of the previous bet **3 :** to increase the mooring lines of a ship by putting out bights on lines already run

double vision *n* **:** DIPLOPIA

double wall *n* **1 :** a composite paperboard of two corrugations and three attached liners **2 :** a bag of two separate plies used for packaging — called also *duplex bag*

double weighing *n* **:** a method of weighing in which the object is balanced first on one pan and then on the other in order to eliminate any possible error from inequality in the balance

double whip *n* **:** a purchase consisting of two single blocks and a standing part not secured to one of the blocks

double whole note *n* **:** BREVE 4b

double window *n* **:** a window having two sets of glazed sashes with an air space between them

double wingback formation *or* **double wing** *n* **:** an offensive football formation in which two halfbacks play approximately one yard outside the offensive ends and one yard behind the line of scrimmage

double-work \'==¦=\ *vt* **:** to propagate (a plant) by grafting or budding a scion to an intermediate piece of one variety grafted on a stock of another variety (as for overcoming incompatibility between scion and stock or for providing a superior trunk) — **double-working** *n*

double-woven \'==¦==\ *adj* **1** *of cloth* **:** woven as a double cloth **2** *of pile cloth* **:** woven face to face and later cut apart **3** *of a single cloth* **:** having two finished sides

double zero *n* **:** a compartment on roulette wheels used in the U.S. that is colored green, marked 00, and equal in effect to the zero

doubling *n* -S [ME *doublinge*, fr. *doublen* to double + *-inge* -ing] **1 :** the act or process of one that doubles: as **a :** a sudden unexpected turn (as in running) **b :** the process of redistilling spirits to improve the strength and flavor **c :** a process for the treatment of antimony sulfide or crude antimony containing the sulfide by fusing it with iron or other antimony containing iron so as to form an iron sulfide the removal of which eliminates both iron and sulfur **d** (1) **:** the process of combining by machine two or more laps, slivers, or rovings into one lap, sliver, roving, or yarn (2) **:** the process of plying two or more yarns **e :** a reduplication of chromosomes **2 :** something used to make a second layer or thickness: as **a :** the lining of a garment — used esp. in heraldry **b :** DOUBLURE 1 **c :** a second thickness of planks or plates in a ship **3 :** something that is doubled: as **a doublings** *pl* **:** redistilled liquor **b :** the doubled border of a sail **c :** the overlapping part of each of two masts esp. of a lower mast and topmast — see SHIP illustration

doubling cube *n* **:** a cube used in backgammon to indicate the current value of the stake as a result of doubling

dou·bloon \,də'blün\ *n* -S [Sp *doblón*, aug. of *dobla*, old Spanish gold coin, fr. L *dupla*, fem. of *duplus* double — more at DOUBLE] **1 :** an old gold coin of Spain and Spanish America worth 8 gold escudos or 16 pieces of eight **2 :** OCHER BROWN

dou·blure \,də'blü(ə)r, dü'-\ *n* -S [F, fr. MF, lining of a garment, fr. *doubler* to line, double + *-ure* — more at DOUBLE] **1 :** the lining of a book cover; *esp* **:** an ornamental lining (as of tooled leather, painted vellum, or rich brocade) **2 :** the reflexed margin of a trilobite's carapace

dou·bly \'dəb(ə)lē, -li\ *adv* [ME, fr. ¹*double* + *-ly*] **1 a :** to twice the degree **:** in twice the quantity ⟨this responsibility is ~ heavy —Hunter Mead⟩ ⟨would now be ~ certain to investigate —T.B.Costain⟩ **b :** in a twofold manner **:** in two degrees — used chiefly in botany ⟨~ crenate⟩ ⟨~ dentate⟩ **2** *obs* **:** in a deceitful manner **:** DISHONESTLY ⟨they lay a man under a necessity to deal ~ with them —Samuel Richardson⟩

doubly ruled surface *n, math* **:** a ruled surface with two systems of rulings or generators; *specif* **:** a quadric surface

¹doubt \'daut, *usu* -aud.+V\ *vb* -ED/-ING/-S [ME *douten* to fear, doubt, fr. OF *douter*, fr. L *dubitare* to doubt; akin to L *dubius* doubtful — more at DUBIOUS] *vt* **1** *archaic* **a :** to be afraid of **:** FEAR — used with an infinitive phrase or a clause as object ⟨I ~ I have been beguiled —Sir Walter Scott⟩ **b :** to be apprehensive of (something feared or not desired) ⟨fear nought — nay, that I need not say — but ~ not aught from mine array —Sir Walter Scott⟩ **2 :** to be in doubt about; *specif* **:** to be uncertain or undecided in opinion or belief in ⟨begins to ~ all the maxims he has hitherto accepted —Bertrand Russell⟩ **3 a :** to lack confidence in **:** DISTRUST, SUSPECT ⟨find myself ~*ing* him even when I know that he is honest —H.L.Mencken⟩ **b :** to be inclined not to believe or accept **:** consider unlikely or improbable ⟨I ~ that they would have helped me —George Santayana⟩ ⟨I ~ whether the facts bear him out —Adelaide Hahn⟩ ⟨I ~ if he ever wrote a single paragraph that was not carefully planned —Deems Taylor⟩ ⟨ready to fight anyone who dared to ~ its success —Sherwood Anderson⟩ **~** *vi* **1 :** to be in doubt; *specif* **:** to be uncertain or undecided in opinion or belief ⟨its obvious elements are willingness to hold belief in suspense, ability to ~ until evidence is obtained —John Dewey⟩ **2** *archaic* **:** HESITATE, SCRUPLE ⟨hath not ~*ed* to assert that you may see a spirit in open daylight —Henry Fielding⟩

²doubt \"\ *n* -S [ME *doute* fear, doubt, fr. OF, fr. *douter*] **1 a :** uncertainty of belief or opinion; *specif* **:** the subjective state of being uncertain of the truth of a statement or the reality of an event as a result of incomplete knowledge or evidence ⟨like one that prayed in sorrow, under some extremity of ~, for light that should guide him to the better choice —Thomas De Quincey⟩ **b :** a deliberate suspension of judgment or withholding of belief ⟨took his point of departure in something deeper than an abstract intellectual ~, namely, in a concrete personal despair —D.F.Swenson⟩ — compare CARTESIANISM, SKEPTICISM **c :** a systematic weighing of the reasons for holding a belief or opinion ⟨~ is the beginning and the end of our efforts to know —William Hamilton †1856⟩ **2 :** the condition of being objectively uncertain **:** a state of affairs giving rise to uncertainty, hesitation, or suspense ⟨there were four states whose votes were in ~ —Carol L. Thompson⟩ **3 :** a feeling of uncertainty ⟨had already fallen a prey to those ~*s* and misgivings which are ever the result of a lack of decision —Theodore Dreiser⟩ **4** *obs* **:** an uncertain or unsettled point or matter **:** DIFFICULTY ⟨and I have heard of thee, that thou canst make interpretations and dissolve ~*s* —Dan 5:16 (AV)⟩ **5 a :** a lack of confidence **:** DISTRUST, SUSPICION ⟨the ~ everyone felt concerning his past —Sherwood Anderson⟩ ⟨their mutual ~*s* and suspicions . . have been enhanced rather than alleviated by the war —Vera M. Dean⟩ **b :** an inclination not to believe or accept **:** QUESTION ⟨there can be little ~ that in matters of literary style the sovereign virtue . . . is clearness —B.N. Cardozo⟩ **syn** see UNCERTAINTY — **no doubt :** DOUBTLESS

doubt·able \'daud·əbəl, -autə-\ *adj* [ME *doutable*, fr. MF, causing doubt, doubting, fr. LL & L; LL *dubitabilis* doubting, fr. L, capable of being doubted, fr. *dubitare* to doubt + *-abilis* -able] **:** capable of being doubted **:** QUESTIONABLE

doubtedly *adv* [*doubted* (fr. past part. of ¹*doubt*) + *-ly*] *obs* **:** DOUBTFULLY, QUESTIONABLY

doubt·er \'daud·ə(r), -autə-\ *n* -S **:** one that doubts **:** SKEPTIC, UNBELIEVER

¹doubt·ful \'dautfəl\ *adj* [ME *douteful*, fr. *doute* doubt + *-ful*] **1 :** giving rise to doubt **:** open to question **:** not obvious, clear, or certain **:** not easily defined, classed, or named ⟨a method of investigation whose object is the establishment of truth about ~ propositions —R.M.Weaver⟩ ⟨it is ~ whether the captain had ever had so much fun —John Steinbeck⟩ **2** *archaic* **a :** giving rise to apprehension **:** PERILOUS ⟨reported the ~ and dangerous situation of the empire —Edward Gibbon⟩ **b :** full of apprehension **:** FEARFUL ⟨I hear things which make me ~ and anxious —Edmund Burke⟩ **3 a :** lacking settled opinion, conviction, or determination **:** unsure about beliefs, observations, or decisions : WAVERING, HESITATING ⟨even after they had been assured . . . they looked ~ —Harold Griffin⟩ ⟨some were ~ how the law would hold —Alfred Tennyson⟩ **b** : uncertain in outcome, issue, or result : UNDECIDED ⟨were fighting a ~ battle in which victory was not assured —D.W.Brogan⟩ **c** : not certain or easily predictable in regard to political preferences : likely to be carried by either political party ⟨concentrated on winning the electoral votes of the ~ states⟩ **4** : characterized by qualities that impugn and raise often well-founded doubts about worth, honesty, or validity : of uncertain worth or soundness : of equivocal character ⟨the only difference between themselves and others is that they are nice men and the others of very ~ repute —T.S.Eliot⟩ ⟨she wrote rather ~ grammar —W.M.Thackeray⟩

syn DUBIOUS, PROBLEMATICAL, PROBLEMATIC, QUESTIONABLE: DOUBTFUL and DUBIOUS indicate uncertainty and indecision in reference to persons or uncertainty, undeterminedness, or unpredictability in reference to events and situations. DOUBTFUL simply indicates lack of certainty or conviction; DUBIOUS stresses lack of these qualities to somewhat greater degree ⟨she takes me in, telling me there's nobody there. I'm *doubtful*, but she swears she's alone —Dashiell Hammett⟩ ⟨there is the defense of Egypt and the Canal, against greatly superior numbers of the enemy, which six months ago, at all events, looked rather a difficult affair, a *doubtful* affair —Sir Winston Churchill⟩ ⟨the president-elect had expressed the opinion that government, after all, was a pretty simple business. He is now to put that hopeful theory to the test. Friendly counselors thought the prospect more *dubious* —S.H.Adams⟩ In reference to value judgments, PROBLEMATICAL and PROBLEMATIC describe something of the nature of a problem or refer to a situation with a quite unpredictable outcome ⟨at present it is easy to make rash predictions. Publishing is now in a very *problematic* state —J.T.Farrell⟩ ⟨effect of the union endorsement on the labor vote is *problematical* —*New Republic*⟩ Often DOUBTFUL so strongly questions worth, honesty, or validity that it implies their absence or lack ⟨in very many interpretations where words play no recognizable part, introspection, unless excessively subtle and therefore of *doubtful* value as evidence, fails to show the imagery is present —C.K.Ogden & I.A.Richards⟩ ⟨the builder, on the other hand, who had spent a long life of constant industry, but *doubtful* honesty, in scraping up a decent fortune —Anthony Trollope⟩ Not so strong, DUBIOUS stresses suspicion or mistrust, perhaps well grounded ⟨all sorts of dogmatic standards have been set up by which to measure the degree of a people's civilization . . . Yet the more carefully we look into the nature of these standards the more *dubious* they become —Havelock Ellis⟩ ⟨millions were stolen outright, and additional millions . . . poured into *dubious* railroads and business ventures which rarely repaid ten cents on the dollar —Allan Nevins & H.S.Commager⟩ QUESTIONABLE may mean simply open to question ⟨the detailed study of history should be supplemented by brilliant outlines, even if they contained *questionable* generalizations —Bertrand Russell⟩ It often describes falsity, unsoundness, or immorality to such a degree that it may be commonly believed in but may be asserted only in guarded statements or hints ⟨the virtues that feed on suffering are very *questionable* virtues —G.B.Shaw⟩

²doubtful \"\ *n* -s : one that is doubtful

doubt·ful·ly \-fəlē, -li\ *adv* [ME *doutefully*, fr. *douteful* + *-ly*] : in a doubtful manner ⟨looking ~ at it two or three times as if to be sure that it was really there —Charles Dickens⟩

doubt·ful·ness \-fəlnəs\ *n* -ES : the quality or state of being doubtful : UNCERTAINTY

doubting *pres part of* DOUBT

doubt·ing·ly *adv* : in a manner that indicates doubt

doubting mania *n* [prob. trans. of F *folie du doute*] : compulsive doubt and indecision permeating the entire personality

doubt·ing·ness *n* -ES : the quality or state of one that doubts

doubting thom·as \-'täməs\ *n, usu cap T* [after *Thomas*, one of Jesus' twelve apostles, who according to Jn 20:24–29 doubted Jesus' resurrection until he had proof of it] : an incredulous or habitually doubtful person : DOUBTER ⟨even the *doubting Thomases* . . . were forced to admit the fertility of the black soil —R.H.Brown⟩

¹doubt·less \'dau̇tləs\ *adv* [ME *doutelees*, fr. *doute* doubt + *-lees* (adv. suffix), fr. *-lees* (adj. suffix) -less] **1** : without doubt : UNQUESTIONABLY ⟨was ~ the smartest girl in her class⟩ **2** : in all probability : PRESUMABLY

²doubtless \"\ *adj* [ME *doutelees*, fr. *doute* doubt + *-lees* -less] **1** : free from doubt : CERTAIN ⟨one of the ~ sources of many Shakespearean quotations —*Notes & Queries*⟩ **2** *obs* : free from fear or suspicion ⟨pretty child, sleep ~ and secure —Shak.⟩ — **doubt·less·ly** *adv*

doubt·less·ness *n* -ES : the quality or state of being doubtless

doubts *pres 3d sing of* DOUBT, *pl of* DOUBT

doubt·some \'dau̇tsəm, 'düt-\ *adj, dial Brit* : DOUBTFUL

douc \'dük\ *n* -s [native name in Cochin China] : a monkey (*Presbytis nemaea*) of Cochin China remarkable for its variegated colors

douce \'düs\ *adj* [ME, fr. MF, fr. OF, fem. of *douz*, fr. L *dulcis* — more at DULCET] **1** *obs* : SWEET, PLEASANT ⟨the ~ sound of harps —Patrick Forbes⟩ **2** *dial Brit* **a** : HOSPITABLE, GENIAL, CHEERFUL **b** : MODEST **c** : NEAT, TIDY **3** *chiefly Scot* : DECOROUS, RESPECTABLE, SEDATE ⟨the ~ faces of the mourners —L.J.A.Bell⟩ **4** [F (fem. of *doux* sweet), fr. OF, fem. of *douz*] : DOLCE — used as a direction in music — **douce·ly** *adv*

douce·pere \'düs(ə),pi(ə)r, -pe(-\ *n* -s [ME *doseper*, back-formation fr. *doseperes*, pl., the twelve peers of Charlemagne, fr. OF *doze pers, doze per*, lit., twelve peers] *archaic* : an illustrious noble; *specif* : one of the twelve peers of Charlemagne's guard of honor

doucets *var of* DOWSETS

dou·ceur \(')dü¦sər\ *n* -s [F, sweetness to the sense of taste, pleasantness, fr. LL *dulcor*, fr. L *dulcis* sweet] **1** *archaic* : gentleness and sweetness of manner : AMIABILITY ⟨answered with all his accustomed ~ and politeness —Fanny Burney⟩ **2** *archaic* : an amiable remark : COMPLIMENT ⟨such elaborate ~s . . . look too much like adulation —*Edinburgh Rev.*⟩ **3** : a conciliatory gift : GRATUITY, PRESENT ⟨would not give permission for the train to go out until he received a substantial ~ —*N.Y.Times*⟩

¹douche \'düsh\ *n* -s [F, fr. It *doccia*, fr. *docciare* to gush, pour, fr. *doccia* water pipe, prob. back-formation fr. *doccione* conduit pipe, fr. L *duction-, ductio* action of leading or conducting, fr. *ductus* (past part. of *ducere* to lead) + *-ion-, -io* -ion — more at TOW] **1 a** : a jet or current (as of water) directed against a part or into a cavity of the body **b** : a bath taken by means of a douche **2** : a device (as a syringe) for giving douches

²douche \"\ *vb* -ED/-ING/-S *vt* : to administer or apply a douche to : DRENCH ~ *vi* : to take a douche

dou·cine \(')dü¦sēn\ *n* -s [F, fr. MF *doulcine*, prob. fr. *doulz, doux* sweet, fr. OF *douz*] : a molding that is convex and concave in continuous curve : CYMA

doudle *var of* ³DOODLE

douf \'dau̇f\ *var of* DOWF

doug \'dau̇g\ *Scot var of* DOG

¹dough \'dō\ *n* -s [ME *dogh*, fr. OE *dāg*; akin to OHG *teic* dough, ON *deig*, Goth *daigs* dough, *digan* to mold, shape, L *fingere* to shape, Gk *teichos* wall, Skt *degdhi* he smears] **1** : a mixture of flour and other ingredients stiff enough to knead or roll — compare BATTER **2** : something resembling dough esp. in consistency: as **a** : a soft mass of rubber and other ingredients produced during the mixing and vulcanizing processes **b** : the material from which puppies used by bookbinders are made **3** : MONEY, CASH ⟨bright young graduate students who needed to pick up a little ~ on the side —Dwight Macdonald⟩ **4** : DOUGH STAGE ⟨grain in the ~⟩ **5** [short for *doughboy*] : INFANTRYMAN

²dough \"\ *vb* -ED/-ING/-S *vi* : to make dough : become dough or like dough ~ *vt* : to make (a mixture) into or like dough; *specif* : to mix (malt) with water to form mash — usu. used with *in*

dough–baked \'ˌ=ˌ=\ *adj* **1** *obs* : imperfectly baked : DOUGHY **2** *dial Eng* : HALF-WITTED, STUPID

doughball \'ˌ=ˌ=\ *n* **1** : a small lump of dough usu. cooked with meat or vegetables **2** : a small quantity of dough used as bait for fishing

doughbelly \'ˌ=ˌ=ˌ=\ *n, West* : a pail-fed calf

doughbird \'ˌ=ˌ=\ *n* : ESKIMO CURLEW

doughboy \'ˌ=ˌ=\ *n* **1 a** *chiefly Brit* : a flour dumpling **b** : a piece of bread dough fried in deep fat and served as a hot bread **2** [prob. so called fr. the large round brass buttons on the U.S. infantry uniform in the Civil War] : INFANTRYMAN **3** : a small flattish brightly colored edible scallop (*Mimachlamys asperrimus*) common off the southern coast of Australia and about Tasmania

dough·er·ty wagon \'dō|ərd·ē-, 'där|, 'dō|, 'däg|, 'dōg|; ÷'dōrəd·ē-, ÷'därəd·ē-\ *n, often cap D* [prob. fr. the name *Dougherty*] : a four-wheeled covered wagon with side doors, two or three transverse seats for passengers, and canvas side curtains

doughface \'ˌ=ˌ=\ *n* **1** : FALSE FACE, MASK **2 a** : a congressman from a northern state who did not oppose slavery **b** : a northerner sympathetic to the South during the Civil War

dough–faced \'ˌ=¦=\ *adj* : having the traits of a doughface

doughfoot \'ˌ=ˌ=\ *n, pl* **doughfeet** *or* **doughfoots** *slang* : INFANTRYMAN

dough god \'ˌ=ˌ=\ *n, North & West* : a fried biscuit

doughhead \'ˌ=ˌ=\ *n, slang* : BLOCKHEAD, FOOL

dough·i·ness \'dōēnəs, -ōin-\ *n* -ES : the quality or state of being doughy

doughlike \'ˌ=ˌ=\ *adj* : resembling dough

dough·nut \'dō(,)nət, *usu* -əd·+V\ *n* -s **1** : a small cake fried in deep fat: **a** : one typically ring-shaped made of rich dough leavened usu. with baking powder **b** : one shaped like a ring or a ball and made of yeast-leavened dough — called also *raised doughnut* **2** : something resembling a doughnut esp. in shape

doughnut tire *n* : a balloon tire extra large in annular section and requiring very low air pressure

dough stage *n* : a stage in the development of cereal grains when the interior of the kernel is of doughlike consistency

dought \'däkt\ [ME *doughte*, fr. OE *dohte*; akin to OHG *tohta* had worth — more at DOW] *chiefly Scot past of* ¹DOW

dough·ti·ly \'dau̇d·ᵊlē, -au̇t|, |ᵊlē, -li\ *adv* [ME, fr. *doughty* + *-ly*] : in a doughty manner

dough·ti·ness \|ēnəs, |in-\ *n* -ES [ME *doughtinesse*, fr. *doughty* + *-nesse* -ness] : the quality or state of being doughty

dough tray *or* **dough trough** *n* : a piece of kitchen furniture consisting of a trough for holding rising dough and a removable flat top on which the dough is kneaded — called also *kneading table*

dough·ty \|ē, |i\ *adj* -ER/-EST [ME, fr. OE *dohtig*, prob. alter. (influenced by *dohte* dought) of *dyhtig*; akin to MD *duchtich* strong, MHG *tühtec* good for something, OE *dēah, dēag* have worth, OHG *toug*, Goth *daug* have worth, Gk *teuchein* to make, build, Lith *daug* much, and perh. to Skt *dogdhi* he milks] : marked by fearless resolution and by stoutness in contest or struggle : ABLE, STRONG, VALIANT ⟨the ~ little man had not a hand's breadth on head or arm without its scar —Charles Kingsley⟩ ⟨he was a soldier's soldier — rough, tough, and ~ —Frederick Nebel⟩ **syn** see BRAVE

doughy \'dōē, -ōi\ *adj, usu* -ER/-EST [¹*dough* + *-y*] : having the characteristics of dough esp. in appearance or consistency: as **a** : not thoroughly baked ⟨~ bread⟩ **b** : unhealthily pale ⟨his face had gone a little ~ but his voice was almost normal —Dashiell Hammett⟩ **c** : heavy and formless ⟨the radio was still sending forth the ~ music of the organ —Irwin Shaw⟩ **d** : soft and lifeless ⟨all that ~, woolly, anodyne writing that exists merely to fill a gap of leisure —Aldous Huxley⟩

doug·las fir *also* **douglas spruce** *or* **douglas pine** *or* **douglas hemlock** \'dəgləs-\ *n, usu cap D* [after David *Douglas* †1834 Scot. botanist in America] : a tall evergreen timber tree (*Pseudotsuga menziesii* or *P. taxifolia*) of the western U. S. having thick bark, pitchy wood, and pendulous cones, with bracts that protrude conspicuously beyond the cone scales — called also *Oregon pine, red fir*

douglas–fir beetle *also* **douglas fir bark beetle** *n, usu cap D* : a bark beetle (*Dendroctonus pseudotsugae*) very destructive to Douglas fir and sometimes to western larch

douglas–fir tussock moth *n, usu cap D* : a dull-colored moth (*Hemerocampa pseudotsugata*) with a red-spotted hairy larva that feeds on and may seriously defoliate Douglas fir and sometimes other firs

doug·la·site \'dəglə,sīt, 'dúg-\ *n* -s [G *douglasit*, fr. *Douglashall*, near Stassfurt, Germany, its locality + G *-it* -ite] : a mineral $K_2[FeCl_4.2H_2O]$(?) consisting of a hydrated potassium iron chloride

douglas's cul–de–sac *or* **douglas's fossa** *or* **douglas's pouch** *n, usu cap D* [after James *Douglas* †1742 Scot. anatomist] : POUCH OF DOUGLAS

doug·las squirrel \'dəgləs-\ *n, usu cap D* [after David *Douglas* †1834] : a large ground squirrel (*Tamiasciurus douglasii*) of the western coastal area of No. America typically grizzled gray with a wedge-shaped black mark on the nape

dou·kho·bor *or* **du·kho·bor** \'dükə,bō(ə)r\ *n, pl* **doukhobors** *or* **dukhobors** \-rz\ *also* **dukho·bor·tsy** \,dükə'bȯrtsē\ *usu cap* [Russ *dukhobortsy*, fr. *dukho-* (fr. *dukh* spirit) + *borets* wrestler, fr. *borot'* to overcome; akin to Lith *dvasas* spirit breath and to L *ferire* to strike — more at DUST, BORE] : a member of a Russian sect originating in the 18th century that emphasizes the supreme authority of inner experience, that believes in the embodiment of the Spirit in different persons whom it follows as prophets and leaders, and that rejects all external ecclesiastical and civil authority (as by refusing to do military service or pay taxes)

doum \'düm, 'dau̇m\ *also* **doum palm** *n* -s [F *doum* — more at DOOM] : DOOM PALM

douma *var of* DUMA

doun·da·ké \'dün'däkē\ *or* **doundaké bark** *n* -s [Wolof *dundakè*, a creeper] : the bark of the country fig formerly used as an astringent and febrifuge

doup \'dau̇p, 'dəu̇p\ *n* -s [modif. of D *dop* eggshell, fr. MD; akin to MLG *dop* pot, MHG *topf*, and prob. to OE *dyppan* to dip — more at DIP] **1** *Scot* : the end or bottom of something: as **a** : the rounded end of an egg **b** : the end of a burned-down candle **c** : BUTTOCKS **2** : a special heddle used in leno weaving

do up *vt* **1 a** : to clean and make ready for use or wear : LAUNDER ⟨the only laundress left who knew how to *do up* damask —Josephine Pinckney⟩ **b** : to put in order : straighten up ⟨one of the girls was sick and I had to help to *do up* the rooms —Henry Lapham⟩ **c** : REPAIR, RENOVATE ⟨for years no one . . . had their houses *done up* —John Galsworthy⟩ **2 a** : to wrap up ⟨are now *done up* in neat bundles —Creighton Peet⟩ **b** : to put up : CAN ⟨*did up* two bushels of peaches⟩ **3 a** : to arrange and fasten (the hair) in place ⟨her golden hair was *done up* on the top of her head —John Steinbeck⟩ **b** : to deck out : CLOTHE ⟨the waitresses are *done up* in abbreviated bloomers and net stockings —Horace Sutton⟩ **4** : to wear out : EXHAUST ⟨this contact with righteousness has about *done me up* —Sinclair Lewis⟩ — **do up brown** : to make a thorough job of : do thoroughly ⟨set out to *do* the romantic historical novel *up brown* once and for all —*N.Y.Times*⟩

doup·er \-pər\ *n* -s : a textile worker who replaces broken doups

dou·pi·o·ni *or* **dou·pi·o·ni** *also* **du·pi·o·ni** \,düpē'ōnē\ *or* **dou·pi·on** *or* **du·pi·on** \'düpē,ōn\ *n* -s [F & It; F *doupion*, fr. It *doppione* (pl. *doppioni*) double cocoon made by two silkworms, aug. of *doppio* double, fr. L *duplus* — more at DOUBLE] **1** : a usu. large and uneven double silk thread reeled usu. from two united cocoons and used in various fabrics (as shantung and pongee) **2** : a fabric of douppioni yarn

dour \'du̇(ə)r, 'dau̇|, |ə, *Scot* 'dür\ *adj, usu* -ER/-EST [ME, prob. fr. L *durus* hard — more at DURE (hard)] **1** : marked by sternness or severity : HARSH, FORBIDDING ⟨a literary mode that had slowly percolated through the crust of Puritan provincialism and imparted a certain sprightliness to a ~ temper —V.L.Parrington⟩ ⟨an imposing composition, somewhat ~ and ascetic in character but full of theatrical thunder and loud declamation —Winthrop Sargeant⟩ **2** : marked by obstinacy or stubbornness : UNYIELDING, DOGGED ⟨an insistent hunger for learning and a ~ and often sacrificial determination to achieve it —Walter Moberly⟩ ⟨resisted change with a ~ persistence —Russell Kirk⟩ **3** : marked by gloomy silence or ill humor : SULLEN ⟨an independent individual, suspicious of strangers and frequently ~ in disposition —Pamela Gulliver & P.H.Gulliver⟩ ⟨in camp . . . he was silent, gloomy and ~, frequently irritable, unfriendly and hostile to everybody —C.W.M.Hart⟩ **4** *chiefly Scot* **a** *of weather* : bleak and gloomy **b** *of land* : barren and infertile **syn** see SULLEN

doura *or* **dourah** *var of* DURRA

dourade *or* **dourado** *var of* DORADO

dou·rine \'dü,rēn, 'dü,-, ˌ=ˈ=\ *n* -s [F, perh. fr. Ar *darin* filthy, scabby] : a contagious disease esp. of horses and asses that is caused by a trypanosome (*Trypanosoma equiperdum*) transmitted from host to host during copulation and that commonly assumes a chronic course marked by inflammation of the genitals, subcutaneous edematous plaques, low-grade fever, progressive paralysis, emaciation, and death

dour·lach \'du̇rlək, -lək\ *var of* DORLACH

dour·ly *adv* [ME, fr. *dour* + *-ly*] : in a dour manner

dour·ness *n* -ES [ME *dournes*, fr. *dour* + *-nes* -ness] : the quality or state of being dour

dou·rou·cou·li *also* **dou·ro·cou·li** *or* **du·ru·ku·li** \,du̇rə'külē\ *n* -s [native name in So. America] : any of certain small roundheaded stocky-bodied bushy-tailed nocturnal monkeys (genus *Aotes*) of tropical America distinguished by their very large eyes

¹douse \'düs, 'dau̇s\ *also* **dowse** \'dau̇s\ *n* -s [origin unknown] *Brit* : BLOW, STROKE

²douse *also* **dowse** \'dau̇s\ *vt* -ED/-ING/-S **1 a** : to take in : LOWER, STRIKE ⟨~ a sail⟩ ⟨~ a mast⟩ **b** : SLACKEN ⟨~ a rope⟩ **2** : to take off : DOFF

³douse *also* **dowse** \'dau̇s, 'dau̇z\ *vb* -ED/-ING/-S [prob. fr. ²*douse* (in obsolete sense "to smite"), after E *souse* to strike; *souse* to immerse] *vt* **1** : to plunge into water : IMMERSE ⟨begin your washing by *dousing* curtains in clear water to remove surface dust —Mary B. Picken⟩ **2 a** (1) : to throw water on : DRENCH ⟨she leaned over the basin and began to ~ her face with the cold water —W.V.T.Clark⟩ ⟨the monsoon . . . ~s the hillsides —Christopher Rand⟩ (2) : to cover with water or another liquid ⟨picking a little mess of red raspberries for her breakfast . . . she *doused* them good with cream —Jean Stafford⟩ **b** : THROW ⟨*doused* water at each other⟩ : SLOSH ⟨still use their native bathhouse . . . in which they ~ water on a heated rock fireplace —*Amer. Guide Series: Minn.*⟩ **3** : to put out (as a light or fire) : EXTINGUISH ⟨his wife *doused* the candle —S.H.Holbrook⟩ ~ *vi* **1** : to fall or become plunged into water ⟨no jesting trivial matter to swing in the air or ~ in water —Samuel Butler †1680⟩ **2** : to lie in water : BATHE ⟨I *doused* pleasantly in the cool fresh water for an hour or two every day —F.N.Souza⟩

⁴douse *also* **dowse** \"\ *n* -s : DOWNPOUR, DRENCHING ⟨his voice came to the crew like a ~ of ice water —T.O. Heggen⟩

dous·er *also* **dows·er** \-sə(r), -zə-\ *n* -s : one that douses; *specif* : a fireproof shutter that controls or intercepts the light reaching the film aperture of a motion-picture mechanism (as a projector) or of a stereopticon

dousing chock *or* **dowsing chock** *n* [*dousing* prob. fr. gerund of ²*douse*] : a piece of curved timber laid across the apron and secured to the knightheads at the upper deck of a ship

dous·ti·o·ni \,düstē'ōnē\ *n, pl* **doustioni** *or* **doustionis** *usu cap* [F, of AmerInd origin] **1** : a Caddo people of the Natchitoches confederacy **2** : a member of the Doustioni people

dout \'dau̇t, 'düt\ *vt* -ED/-ING/-S [¹*do* + *out*] *dial* : to put out : EXTINGUISH

do ut des \,dō,u̇t'dās\ *n* [NL, I give in order that you may give] : a commutative contract whereby something is given so that something may be received in return

dout·er \'dau̇tər, 'düt-\ *n* -s *now dial Eng* : EXTINGUISHER; *specif* : CANDLESNUFFER

do ut fa·ci·as \,dō,u̇t'fākē,äs\ [NL, I give in order that you may do] : a commutative contract whereby something is given so that something may be done in return

doux \'dü\ *adj* [F, lit., sweet, fr. OF *douz* — more at DOUCE] *of champagne* : containing at least seven percent sugar by volume : sweeter than demi-sec : very sweet

dou·zaine \(')dü¦zān\ *n* -s [F, lit., dozen, fr. OF *dozaine* — more at DOZEN] : a body of 12 men representing a Guernsey parish

dou·zai·nier \,dü,zān¦yā\ *n* -s [F, fr. *douzaine*] : a member of a douzaine

do·vap \'dō,vap\ *n* -s *usu DOVAP* [Doppler velocity and position] : a method of tracking long-range missiles that utilizes continuous radio waves and the Doppler effect

¹dove \'dəv\ *n* -s [ME *douve, dove, doufe*, fr. (assumed) OE *dūfe* (in *Dūfe*, fem. prop. name); akin to OHG *tūba* dove, ON *dūfa*, Goth hraiwadūbo turtledove, and prob. to OE *dēaf* deaf — more at DEAF] **1** : any of numerous birds of the family Columbidae: **a** : any of various smaller wild pigeons (as the turtledove or mourning dove) **b** : PIGEON **2** : a pure and gentle woman or child — used esp. as a term of endearment ⟨come little ~, don't be afraid⟩ **3 a** : PELICAN 4 **b** : DOVE GRAY

²dove *past of* DIVE

dove·cote \'dəv,kō|t *sometimes* -,kä| *or* -kə|; *usu* |d·+V\ *or* **dove·cot** \-,kä|t *sometimes* -,kə|\ *n* -s [ME *dowecote, doufecot*, fr. *douve, doufe* dove + *cote* or *cot* — more at COTE (coop), COT (cottage)] **1** : a small compartmented raised house or box for domestic pigeons **2** : a settled or harmonious group or organization ⟨his determined aggressiveness caused a real flutter in the ~⟩

dove dock *n* [¹*dove* + *dock* (plant)] : COLTSFOOT a

dove–eyed \'ˌ=¦=\ *adj* : having soft gentle eyes

doveflower \'ˌ=ˌ=\ *n* **1** : a tropical American orchid (*Peristeria elata*) having a tall scape with numerous fragrant white flowers and a column in the center of the flower suggesting a dove **2** : the blossom of the doveflower

dovefoot \'ˌ=ˌ=\ *n* -s [so called fr. the shape of the leaf] : SPOTTED CRANESBILL

dove gray *n* : a purplish gray that is redder, lighter, and stronger than crane, lighter than granite, slightly stronger than cinder, and redder and deeper than zinc

dovehouse \'ˌ=ˌ=\ *n* [ME *dowfhows*, fr. *dowf, douve* dove + *hows, hous* house] : DOVECOTE 1

dove·kie *also* **dove·key** \'dəvkē\ *n* -s [dim. of ¹*dove*] **1** : BLACK GUILLEMOT **2** : a small short-billed auk (*Plautus alle*) breeding on arctic coasts and ranging south in winter

dove·let \'dəvlət\ *n* -s [¹*dove* + *-let*] : a small or immature dove

dovelike \'ˌ=ˌ=\ *adj* : mild as a proverbial dove : pure and lovable : GENTLE ⟨our host introduced us to his two daughters, beautiful and ~ creatures⟩

dove pox *n* : PIGEON POX

do·ve prism \'dōvə-\ *n, usu cap D* [prob. after Heinrich W. *Dove* †1879 Ger. physicist] : a prism that reverts an image but does not produce deviation or displacement of the beam, the rotation of the prism about the axis of the beam rotating the beam at twice the rate of rotation of the prism

¹do·ver \'dōvər\ *vi* -ED/-ING/-S [freq. of (assumed) E dial. (16th cent. Sc) *dove* to be stupid, fr. (assumed) ME *doven*, fr. OE *dofian*; akin to OHG *tobōn, tobēn* to be insane, ON *dofinn* benumbed, OE *dēaf* deaf — more at DEAF] *Scot* : to doze off or lose consciousness for a moment — often used with *over*

²dover \"\ *n* -s **1** *chiefly Scot* : a drowsy state **2** *chiefly Scot* : NAP

³dover \'dōvə(r)\ *adj, usu cap* **1** [fr. *Dover*, England] : of or from Dover, England : of the kind or style prevalent in Dover **2** [fr. *Dover*, Delaware] : of or from Dover, the capital of Delaware ⟨a *Dover* merchant⟩ : of the kind or style prevalent in Dover

dover beater *n* [fr. *Dover*, a trademark] : ROTARY BEATER

dover catchfly *n, usu cap D* [perh. fr. *Dover*, port city in southeastern England] : NODDING CATCHFLY

dover gray *n, often cap D* [prob. fr. *Dover*, England] : a dark gray that is darker than pelican and lighter than fashion gray or Oxford gray

dover sole *n, often cap D* [prob. fr. *Dover*, England] **1** : a common European sole (*Solea solea* or *S. vulgaris*) that is

DOGS

DALMATIAN
BOXER
MINIATURE PINSCHER
BEAGLE
MINIATURE SCHNAUZER
IRISH SETTER
AFGHAN
COCKER SPANIEL
POMERANIAN
FOX TERRIER (WIRE-HAIRED)
STANDARD POODLE
COLLIE

highly esteemed as a food fish **2 :** a brownish blotched flatfish (*Microstomus pacificus*) of the Pacific coast of No. America that attains a length of about two feet and is becoming an important market fish in California

do·ver's powder \'dōvə(r)z,-\ *n, usu cap D* [after Thomas *Dover* †1742 Eng. physician] **:** a powder of ipecac and opium that is now compounded in the U.S. with lactose and in England with potassium sulfate and that is used as an anodyne and diaphoretic

doves *pl of* DOVE

dove's-foot \'ˌ=,=\ *n, pl* **dove's-foots** [so called fr. the shape of the leaf] **:** any of several chiefly European plants of the genus *Geranium* (esp. *G. molle*)

dove shell *n* [so called fr. the color of the shell] **:** any of numerous small marine gastropod mollusks (family Columbellidae) with oval to conical shells that have a high luster and brilliant coloring

¹**dovetail** \'=,=\ *n* -s **:** something (as a flaring tenon, tongue, or machine part) felt to resemble a dove's tail in shape ⟨cutting ~s in the end of a timber⟩; *esp* **:** DOVETAIL JOINT

²**dovetail** \"\ *vb* -ED/-ING/-S *vt* **1 a :** to join (as timbers) by means of dovetails **b :** to cut to a dovetail or into dovetails ⟨~ing the end of the board with a special device⟩ **2 a :** to fit, connect, or combine skillfully or exactly to form a continuous or harmonious whole **:** fit ingeniously or precisely ⟨the manner in which he ~s his investigations into their sociological framework is unique —*New Statesman & Nation*⟩ **b :** to fit together with **:** interlock with ⟨my discoveries ~ those made by others⟩ ~ *vi* **:** to fit together into a unified or coordinated whole ⟨the way the laws of chemistry and physics ~⟩ ⟨corn growing and hog raising ~ into a practical efficient enterprise in parts of the Middle West⟩

dovetail cramp *n* **:** a dovetailed cramp used to hold masonry

dovetailed \'=,tāld\ *adj* [¹*dovetail* + *-ed*] **1 :** having a tail like a dove's **2 :** joined with or as if with dovetails **:** having a dovetail or a dovetailed part ⟨carefully ~ air and land operations made the attack successful⟩ **3** *heraldry* **:** partitioned or bounded by a line broken into a series of dovetails ⟨per chevron ~ gules and argent⟩ ⟨gules a chevron ~ ermine⟩

dove·tail·er \'=,tālə(r)\ *n* -s **:** one that dovetails; *specif* **:** an operator of a machine for cutting dovetails in wood

dovetail hinge *n* **:** BUTTERFLY HINGE

dovetail joint *n* **:** a flaring tenon and a mortise into which it fits tightly making an interlocking joint between two pieces that resists pulling apart in all directions except one

dovetail joints

dovetail molding *n* **:** an architectural molding of any convex section that is zigzag like a series of dovetails

dovetail plane *n* **:** a woodworking plane specially adapted for forming the tongue and grooves of dovetail joints

dovetail saw *n* **:** a small backsaw with thin blade, fine teeth, and straight handle used for accurate work (as in cabinetmaking and patternmaking)

dove tree *n* [so called fr. the appearance of the flowers] **:** a Chinese deciduous tree (*Davidia involucrata*) of the family Cornaceae that has flower heads with two large unequal creamy-white bracts and alternate leaves which sometimes release a nauseous odor

doveweed \'=,=\ *n* **1 :** any of several New World plants of the genus *Croton* **2 :** TURKEY MULLEIN

¹**dow** \'daù, 'dō, *Scot* 'dəù\ *vi* -ED/-ING/-S [ME *dow, deih* have worth, am good for something (1st & 3d sing. pres. indic. of assumed *dowen*, pl. pres. *dowen*, past *doughte*), fr. OE *dēah, dēag* (infin. assumed *dugan*, pl. pres. *dugon*, past *dohte*); akin to OHG *toug* have worth (infin. assumed *tugan*, 3d pl. pres. *tugun*), Goth *daug* have worth (infin. assumed *dugan*, 3d pl. pres. assumed *dugun*), ON *duga* (infin.) to help — more at DOUGHTY] **1** *obs* **:** to have worth, value, validity, availability, or suitableness **2** *chiefly Scot* **:** to be able or capable **3** *dial Brit* **a :** to thrive and prosper **b :** to recover from illness **c :** to feel sufficiently concerned to take action — usu. used with a negative

²**dow** \'daù\ *vt* -ED/-ING/-S [ME *dowen*, fr. OF *doer, douer*, fr. L *dotare*, fr. *dot-, dos* gift, dower — more at DOWER] *archaic* **:** to endow or give as an endowment ⟨he . . . ~*ed* her with all the virtues in the Bible —Rudyard Kipling⟩

³**dow** \'dü\ *dial Brit var of* DOVE

⁴**dow** \'dəù\ *vi* [origin unknown] *chiefly Scot* **:** to fade away **:** become dull or withered

⁵**dow** *var of* DHOW

⁶**dow** \'daù\ *n* -s [Hindi *dāo*, fr. Skt *dātra* crooked knife, fr. *dāti* he cuts; akin to Skt *dayate* he apportions — more at TIDE] **:** ¹DAH

dow·able \'daùəbəl\ *adj* [AF, fr. OF *doer, douer* to endow + *-able*] **:** capable of being endowed; *esp* **:** legally entitled to dower

dow·a·ger \'daùəjə(r), 'daùēj-\ *n* -s *often attrib* [MF *douagiere*, fr. *douage* dower, fr. *douer* to endow (fr. OF *doer, douer*) + *-age*] **1 :** a widow in the enjoyment of some property or a title that has come to her from her deceased husband — often added to a title so enjoyed esp. when there is a wife of the new incumbent of the title of the deceased husband ⟨the empress's seal as ~⟩ ⟨the ~ duchess⟩ ⟨countess ~ of Rimrock⟩ **2 :** an elderly woman of imposing appearance or dominant personality; *often* **:** one of the elder women of assured position who tend to set the tone of an assembly, social group, or community ⟨the ~s shook their heads over the younger generation⟩ ⟨appealing to the ~ trade⟩

dowd \'daùd\ *n* -s [ME *doude*] **:** a dowdy person; *esp* **:** a dowdy woman

dowd·i·ly \'daùdᵊlē, -dəlē, -li\ *adv* **:** in a dowdy manner

dowd·i·ness \'daùdēnəs, -din-\ *n* -ES **:** dowdy state; *esp* **:** drab slovenly dress

¹**dowdy** \'daùdē, -di\ *n* -ES [*dowd* + *-y* (diminutive suffix)] **1 :** a dowdy woman **2 :** PANDOWDY

²**dowdy** \"\ *adj* -ER/-EST **1** *of feminine appearance or apparel* **:** lacking neatness and charm; *often* **:** slovenly or slatternly **:** untidily shabby ⟨an old woman bedraggled and ~⟩ ⟨a ~ gray dress⟩ **2 a :** lacking in smartness or taste ⟨a clean sunny but completely ~ room⟩ ⟨expensive ~ country tweeds⟩ **b :** not modern in style **:** OLD-FASHIONED **:** out of date ⟨two ~ meandering novelettes —*New Yorker*⟩ **syn** see SLATTERNLY

dowdy·ish \-dēish, -di-ish\ *adj* **:** somewhat dowdy

¹**dow·el** \'daù(ə)l\ *n* -s [ME *dowle*, prob. fr. MLG *dövel*; akin to OHG *tubili* plug, MLG *dövicke* plug, LGk *typhos* wedge] **1 a :** a headless smooth or barbed pin usu. of circular section fitting into corresponding holes in abutting pieces to act as a temporary fastening or to keep them permanently in their proper relative position; *also* **:** a round rod or stick used esp. for cutting up into dowels **2 :** a piece of wood driven into a wall so that other pieces may be nailed to it **3 :** DOVETAIL CRAMP

a dowels

²**dowel** \"\ *vt* **doweled** *or* **dowelled; doweled** *or* **dowelled; doweling** *or* **dowelling; dowels :** to fasten or locate (a part with reference to another part) by dowels **:** furnish with dowels

dow·el·er \'daù(ə)lə(r)\ *n* -s **1 :** a worker who inserts dowels by hand or by machine **2 :** an operator of a dowel-making machine

dowel jig *or* **doweling jig** *n* **:** a jig for holding material to be doweled

dowel screw *n* **:** a dowel threaded on both ends

¹**dow·er** \'daù(ə)r, 'daùə\ *or* **dow·ry** \'daù(ə)rē, -ri\ *n, pl* **dowers** *or* **dowries** [*dower* fr. ME *dowere, dowaire*, fr. MF *douaire, douaire*, modif. (influenced by OF *doer, douer* to endow, fr. L *dotare*, fr. *dot-, dos*) of ML *dotarium*, fr. L *dot-, dos* gift, dower + *-arium* -ary; *dowry* fr. ME *dowerie*, fr. AF, irreg. fr. ML *dotarium*; akin to Gk *dōs* gift, L *dare* to give — more at DATE] **1** *usu dower* **:** the portion of or interest in the real estate of a deceased husband that is given by law to his widow during her life **2 a** *usu dowry* **:** the money, goods, or estate that a woman brings to her husband in marriage **:** a bride's portion **:** DOT **b** *usu dowry* **:** a gift of property by a man to or for his bride ⟨ask me never so much *dowry* and gift, and I will give . . .; but give me the damsel to wife —Gen 34:12 (AV)⟩ **c :** a sum of money or its equivalent required of postulants by some religious communities (as of cloistered nuns) **3 :** gift of nature **:** TALENT, ENDOWMENT

²**dower** \"\ *vt* -ED/-ING/-S **:** to supply with a dower or dowry **:** ENDOW ⟨nature had so richly ~*ed* him —J.A.Symonds⟩

dower chest *n* **:** HOPE CHEST

dow·er·ess \'daù(ə)rəs\ *n* -ES *archaic* **:** a dowered widow **:** DOWAGER

dower house *n, Brit* **:** a residence forming part of the dower of or intended for the use of a widow and usu. being a less pretentious dwelling on the same grounds as the family residence

dow·er·less \'daù(ə)rləs, |əl-\ *or* **dow·ry·less** \|(ə)rēl-, -ril-\ *adj* **:** lacking a dower or dowry

dowf *also* **dowff** \'dəùf\ *adj* [perh. fr. ON *daufr* deaf — more at DEAF] **1** *chiefly Scot* **:** lacking in force and energy **:** LISTLESS, APATHETIC **2** *chiefly Scot* **:** dismal and gloomy **3** *chiefly Scot, of sound* **:** lacking resonance **:** HOLLOW

dowg \'dəùg\ *Scot var of* DOG

dow·ie *also* **dowy** \'dəùi\ *adj* [alter. of earlier *dolly*, fr. ME (Sc), perh. fr. ME *dol, dul* dull + *-y*, adj. suffix — more at DULL] **1** *chiefly Scot* **:** dreary and dispirited **:** DOLEFUL **2** *chiefly Scot* **:** dull and oppressive — **dow·i·ly** \'dəùəli\ *adv*

dow·ie·ism \'daùē,izəm\ *n, usu cap* [John A. *Dowie* †1907 + E *-ism*] **:** the principles and practices of Dowieites

dow·ie·ite \-ē,īt\ *n* -s *usu cap* [John A. *Dowie* †1907 Scot. religious leader in the U.S. + E *-ite*] **:** a member of the Christian Catholic Apostolic Church in Zion, a religious organization chiefly centered in Zion City near Chicago, Ill., formed in 1896 by John Alexander Dowie and devoted orig. to the practice of a religious communal life, faith healing, and abstinence

dowing *pres part of* DOW

dow·itch \'daùich\ *n* -ES [by shortening] *dial* **:** DOWITCHER

dow·itch·er \'daùəchə(r)\ *n, pl* **dowitchers** *also* **dowitcher** [of Iroquoian origin; akin to Mohawk & Cayuga *tawis* dowitcher, Onondaga *tawish*] **:** a long-billed snipe (*Limnodromus griseus*) that is intermediate in characters between the typical snipes (genus *Capella*) and the sandpipers and that breeds in northern No. America and winters largely in Central America or So. America — called also *brownback, grayback, red-breasted snipe*

do with \'=(,)=\ *vt* **1 :** to deal with **:** MANAGE ⟨I can't *do with* a man of his age who never speaks the truth —Archibald Marshall⟩ **2 :** to get along on **:** manage with ⟨have *done with* very little sleep throughout their lives —Geoffrey Jefferson⟩ **3 :** to make use of **:** profit from ⟨I could *do with* a cup of coffee —Frances P. Keyes⟩ ⟨they could *do with* some typographical improvement —J.E.Gloag⟩

do without \¦=='=\ *vt* **:** to dispense with **:** get along without ⟨limiting the production of goods that we could *do without* —M.R.Cohen⟩

dow-jones average *also* **dow-jones index** \'daù¦jōnz-\ *n, usu cap D&J* [after Charles H. *Dow* †1902 and Edward D. *Jones* †1920 Am. financial statisticians] **:** an index of the relative price of securities based on the daily average price of selected lists of industrial, railroad, and utility common stocks

dowl *or* **dowle** \'daù(ə)l\ *n* -s [ME *doule*] *now dial Eng* **:** feathery or woolly down **:** FILAMENT a (4)

dow·las \'daùləs\ *n* -ES [alter. (influenced by *Daoulas*) of ME *douglas*, by folk etymology (influence of name *Douglas*) fr. *Daoulas*, Brittany, France] **1 :** a coarse linen cloth used widely in the 16th and 17th centuries and manufactured orig. in Brittany but later esp. in northern England and Scotland **2 :** a cotton imitation of dowlas

dow·ly \'daùlē, 'dōlē\ *adj* [ME, dull, miserable, perh. fr. ON *daufligr* dull, lonely, fr. *daufr* deaf — more at DEAF] *dial* **:** DULL, LOWERING

¹**down** \'daùn\ *n* -s [ME *doun* hill, fr. OE *dūn*; akin to MD *dūne* dune, OIr *dūn* fortress, Skt *dhūnoti* he shakes — more at DOWN (feathers)] **1** *archaic* **:** HILL; *often* **:** a hillock of sand thrown up by the wind on or near a shore **:** DUNE **2 a :** an undulating generally treeless upland with sparse soil — usu. used in pl. **b downs** *pl, often cap* **:** treeless chalk uplands along the south and southeast coast of England **3** *often cap* **:** a sheep of any breed originating in the downs of southern England typically being of good mutton conformation and producing moderately fine wool of medium length — compare SOUTHDOWN

²**down** \"\ *adv* [ME *doun*, fr. OE *dūne*, short for *adūne, of dūne*, fr. *a-* (fr. *of*) or *of* off, from + *dūne*, dat. of *dūn* hill — more at OF] **1 a :** in the direction of gravity or toward the center of the earth ⟨~ beneath the solid crust of the earth⟩ **:** from a higher point to or toward the earth's surface ⟨the wind blew all the apples ~⟩ **:** to the ground or other base ⟨the house burned ~ during the night⟩ ⟨planning to tear ~ the old shed⟩ **b :** from a higher to a lower place or position ⟨pull ~ the blind⟩ ⟨then we turned ~ toward the valley⟩ ⟨looking ~ over the face of the cliff⟩ **c :** from an upright position to or toward a surface regarded as a base in respect to which something is normally oriented ⟨the roof sagging, the chimney tumbling ~⟩ or to or into a state more relaxed or more humble ⟨do sit ~⟩ ⟨let slaves bow ~ when freemen pass⟩ **d :** out of one's hands or charge ⟨put the cake ~ on the table⟩ ⟨lay ~ your book for a minute⟩; *often* **:** into such a position as to free or relieve one ⟨put ~ your load and rest⟩ ⟨laying ~ the burdens of state⟩ **e :** in or into a recumbent position ⟨lie ~ and go to sleep⟩ ⟨knocked his opponent ~ with a sudden blow⟩ **f :** toward or below the horizon ⟨the sun far ~ in the west⟩ ⟨the moon went ~ an hour ago⟩ **g :** to or toward the bottom of a body of water ⟨sank ~ before they could reach him⟩ **h :** from an upper to a lower floor in a building esp. to meet or join companions ⟨I'll come ~ in a minute⟩ ⟨all of us hurried ~ to dinner⟩ **i :** toward the bottom of a sheet or page of paper ⟨here your hand, guiding your rapid pen, moved up and ~ —Edna S.V.Millay⟩ — in most senses opposed to or contrasted with *up*; often used as a function word to intensify a modified verb esp. of action or motion; sometimes used with the force of a verb in command or exclamation ⟨~ before he sees who you are⟩ ⟨~ on your knees, ungrateful girl, and pray for forgiveness⟩ **2 a :** in a direction that is conventionally or temporarily the opposite of *up* **b :** from an outlying part to or toward a center of activity (as a business district, a metropolis, or a terminal point); *often* **:** to or toward the lower part of town **:** DOWNTOWN **c :** from a center of activity to or toward an outlying part or remote place ⟨going ~ to the country for a rest⟩; *often* **:** to a place other than one's regular or urban abode to which one has a right to issue invitations ⟨come ~ to our camp on the river anytime⟩ ⟨grandma would love to have you run ~ some weekend⟩ **d** *Brit* **:** away from a university or other seat of learning ⟨sent ~ for misconduct without his degree⟩ ⟨he got a job in advertising shortly after he came ~ and has stayed with the firm ever since⟩ **e :** in a southerly direction ⟨they went ~ to Florida for Christmas⟩ **f :** to a source or a place of concealment ⟨tracking ~ a wounded deer⟩ ⟨run ~ this vile rumor⟩ ⟨I'm not sure how you can track ~ that quotation⟩ **g :** in or into the stomach ⟨he eats but the food won't stay ~⟩ ⟨get your drink ~, we're late already⟩ **3 a :** to or into a lower or inferior state (as of humility, defeat, disgrace, or restraint) ⟨held ~ by his lack of education⟩ ⟨a man come ~ in life⟩ **b :** to a point of complete control, stoppage, or quiet ⟨tie ~ the load⟩ ⟨now calm ~, my dear⟩ ⟨they had to strap the patient ~⟩ ⟨shouting ~ the opposition⟩ **c :** to a great or the utmost degree **:** very heavily ⟨burdened ~ with the cares of a family⟩ **d :** to completion **:** FULLY **:** from top to bottom ⟨I dusted ~ the whole house⟩ ⟨wash ~ the car⟩ **e :** under a perennial crop ⟨it is sometimes profitable to leave land ~ to hay for several years⟩ **4 a :** with forcible or abrupt descent ⟨fell ~ and cut his lip⟩ **b :** ACTIVELY, SERIOUSLY, VIGOROUSLY ⟨finally settled ~ to work⟩ **5 :** from a past time **:** from remoter times or people ⟨tales handed ~ by word of mouth⟩ ⟨these spoons have passed ~ in our family since the 17th century⟩ **6 a :** from a greater to a lesser amount, bulk, or strength ⟨don't forget to water ~ the wine⟩ **b :** from a thinner to a thicker consistency ⟨boiled ~ the sap into syrup⟩ **:** from a larger dilute volume to a smaller more concentrated one ⟨finally got his report ~ to three pages⟩ **c :** from a higher to a lower value ⟨most stocks went ~ last week⟩ **d :** in descending order of rank — used of a series of plays or discards from the same suit in certain card games **7 :** in or into symbols (as written letters) that can be preserved for future reference ⟨write ~ everything she says⟩ ⟨put ~ the following figures⟩ **8 a :** in or into a position indicative of an intent to bet (as on a particular number) ⟨he put his money ~ on the red⟩ **:** at hazard ⟨the chips are ~, the result is in the hands of fate⟩ **b :** immediately in cash ⟨I can't pay more than $10 ~⟩ **9 :** into defeat — used chiefly in relation to the scoring of games ⟨we went ~ two tricks⟩ **10 a :** in lower case or with a lower-case initial letter **b :** on a verso page and with its head next to the binding edge — used of the facing of an illustration **11 :** to press or the pressroom — used of newspaper copy or an edition of a newspaper ⟨the edition has already gone ~⟩ **12 :** toward the front of a theatrical stage — compare DOWNSTAGE **13 :** in or into a perfected or thoroughly understood state ⟨had the subject ~ pat⟩ — **down to the ground :** COMPLETELY, EXCELLENTLY, PERFECTLY ⟨that suits me *down to the ground*⟩ — **down with** \'=(,)=\ **1 :** in the direction of gravity or toward the center of the earth **:** from a higher point to or toward the earth's surface — often used interjectionally to express a wish, exhortation, or command that someone or something should be moved in such a direction ⟨*down with* the flag that is flying yonder⟩ ⟨*down with* him into the pit⟩ **2 :** to or into a lower or inferior state (as of humility, defeat, disgrace, or restraint) — often used interjectionally to express a wish, exhortation, or command that someone or something should be brought into such a state ⟨*down with* the government!⟩

³**down** \(')daùn\ *prep* **1 a :** in a descending direction along ⟨swiftly rolling ~ the hill⟩ **b :** from a higher to a lower point upon or within ⟨sweat trickling ~ his neck⟩ **c :** at a lower level on or in ⟨we keep the butter ~ the well⟩ **2 a :** along the course of ⟨children running ~ the street⟩ **b :** from the source toward the mouth of ⟨a rapids three miles further ~ the stream⟩ **:** toward the outlet or southerly end of ⟨we wandered ~ the valley⟩ **c :** along the margin of ⟨steaming ~ the coast⟩ **d :** in the same course as **:** WITH ⟨clouds blowing ~ the wind⟩ **3** — used as a function word to indicate movement in the opposite direction to a direction arbitrarily designated *up* without regard to actual ascent or descent ⟨pacing up and ~ the room⟩ **4 :** down into the ⟨he went ~ town⟩ ⟨he went ~ cellar⟩ **:** down in the ⟨they had some canned goods ~ cellar⟩ — often used in combination with a following noun to form adverbs and adjectives ⟨the *down*river end of town⟩

⁴**down** \'daùn\ *adj* **1 a :** going or directed down **b :** declining from a previous or normal level ⟨new construction is sharply ~⟩ **c :** conveying or for conveying downward **d :** running vertically ⟨~ lines on a ledger page⟩ **2 a :** reduced temporarily to a state of inactivity, inoperativeness, or depression ⟨the wind is ~⟩ **b :** low in spirits **:** DOWNCAST ⟨I'm completely ~ and out of sorts today⟩; *also* **:** fallen from a better to a worse or from a higher to a lower state ⟨don't kick a man when he's ~⟩ **c :** suffering from ill health ⟨my wife is ~ with malaria⟩; *sometimes* **:** off the feet esp. because of illness ⟨always try to get a ~ horse on his feet⟩ ⟨half the herd was ~ before morning⟩ **d :** closed down (as for repairs, remodeling, reorganization) ⟨the shop will be ~ while the new machines are installed⟩ ⟨it's unlikely that most of the ~ watermills will reopen⟩ **e** *of an electric battery* **:** not adequately charged **f** *of a football* **:** not being in play because its progress is wholly stopped or the officials stop the play for any reason **3 :** occupying or returned to a low or a lower position or state ⟨the window is ~ from the top⟩ **:** on or toward the ground, floor, or any surface regarded as a base with respect to which something is oriented ⟨the shades are ~⟩ ⟨all the vines are ~⟩: as **a :** below the horizon ⟨the moon is ~⟩ **b :** lower in price or characterized by lower prices ⟨wheat is ~ over 10 per cent⟩ **c** *of grass* **:** fallen to the ground after being mowed **d** *of timber* **:** lying on the ground esp. as the result of being blown over or cut **e** *of a boxer* **:** having any part of the body other than the feet in contact with the floor; *also* **:** in a position of helplessness if so recognized by the referee **f** *of a team or contestant* **:** defeated or behind an opponent (as in points scored) ⟨he was ~ on all cards at the middle of the 10th round⟩ ⟨the honors broke badly and they were ~ two tricks⟩ **g :** retired from play **:** OUT — used chiefly in baseball **h** *of a cricket wicket* **:** broken so that a batsman is out **i :** written or printed with a lower-case letter or initial letter; *also* **:** partial to lower-case rather than capital initial letters ⟨a ~ style⟩ **4 a :** directed to or forming part of the traffic to a place (as a business section, metropolis, or terminal) conventionally regarded as lower ⟨you can take a ~ train at the local station⟩ ⟨~ traffic is heavy this morning⟩ **b :** of, relating to, or intended for the use of down traffic or transportation ⟨go to the ~ platform in the subway station⟩ **5** *of a payment* **:** being that part of a price that is paid at the time of purchase or delivery when the entire price is not then paid ⟨a ~ payment of $10⟩ **6 :** gone to press — used of an item of news copy or of an edition of a newspaper ⟨the paper was ~ in the late afternoon⟩ **7 :** FINISHED, CONSUMED, PROCESSED ⟨eight ~ and two to go⟩ — **down on** \'=,=\ **:** full of dislike for **:** with a grudge against

⁵**down** \'daùn\ *n* -s **1 a :** a descent, decline, depression, or dwindling — used esp. in the phrase *ups and downs* ⟨emotional ups and ~s⟩ ⟨the recurrent ups and ~s of the business cycle⟩ ⟨the erratic ups and ~s of livestock production⟩ **b :** a reverse in fortune; *often* **:** a period of depressed activity (as in business) ⟨certain industries are esp. subject to seasonal ~s⟩ **c :** an alteration in the quality of a speaker's voice (as in radio acting) designed to distinguish narration from dialogue in matter he is reciting **2 a :** an instance of putting down (as an opponent in wrestling) **b** (1) **:** the termination of an attempt to advance the ball in football occurring when the referee blows his whistle or declares the ball dead (2) **:** a complete play to advance the ball or its duration **c :** failure to score on a badminton serve — called also *handout* **3 :** a firm and persistent dislike **:** GRUDGE — used with the indefinite article and with *on* ⟨why should she have such a ~ on me?⟩

⁶**down** \"\ *vb* -ED/-ING/-S *vt* **:** to cause to come or go down: as **a :** SWALLOW ⟨quickly ~*ing* his drink⟩ **b :** to relegate to obscurity or forgetfulness **:** SUPPRESS ⟨he could not ~ his regrets⟩ **c :** to get the better of **:** DEFEAT ⟨the coalition ~*ed* the bill after a lengthy fight⟩ ⟨do our best to protect the one and ~ the other —John Buchan⟩ **d** (1) **:** to bring to a stop (as a game animal or an adversary) by a shot or blow ⟨market hunters ~*ing* geese by the hundreds⟩; *often* **:** KILL (2) **:** to bring to the ground (a football opponent) by tackling (3) **:** to shoot from the air (an aircraft) ⟨accidentally ~*ed* a British airliner⟩ **e** (1) **:** to put (the helm) down (2) **:** to lower (as a signal or sail) (3) **:** to decrease the rate or speed of (the revolutions of a propeller) **f :** to lay aside **:** put down ⟨he ~*ed* his ax and sat on a stump to rest⟩; *often* **:** to cease to employ or engage in — usu. used with a material object that may be taken as a symbol of an activity or occupation ⟨the boys ~*ed* their bats and fishing rods at vacation's end and went back to school⟩ ⟨the union will certainly ~ tools if no settlement is reached⟩ ~ *vi* **:** to go down or be put down: as **a :** to become swallowed; *sometimes* **:** to appeal to the taste ⟨a drink that really ~*s* on a wintry evening⟩ **b :** to become brought to nothing or suppressed ⟨his regret may never ~⟩

⁷**down** \"\ *n, pl* **down** *also* **downs** *often attrib* [ME *down*, fr. ON *dūnn*; akin to ON *daunn* odor, *dȳja* to shake, Goth *dauns* odor, L *suffire* to fumigate, Gk *thyein* to rage, Skt *dhūnoti* he shakes, L *fumus* smoke — more at FUME] **1 a :** a covering of soft fluffy feathers somewhat resembling fur that clothes young precocial birds before they acquire true feathers **b :** the small fluffy feathers that lie next to the body of adult birds, that are esp. prominent over the abdomen, and that are notably developed and fine in texture in ducks, geese, and other water birds from which they are often collected and used for stuffing (as in pillows, sleeping bags, or bedcovers) because of their light weight and good insulating quality ⟨a ~ comforter⟩ ⟨pluck the ~ from a hundred geese⟩ **c** *pl downs* **:** one of the feathers making up the down of a bird **2 :** something felt to resemble down esp. in soft fluffy quality: as **a :** the first growth of

beard on the human face ⟨a slender lad with just a trace of ~ on his cheeks⟩; *also* **:** fine soft hair elsewhere on the body ⟨tanned arms lightly covered with a silvery ~⟩ **b :** the pubescence of a plant ⟨wipe the ~ off the peaches⟩; *also* **:** a soft tuft (as a coma or pappus) on some plant part **c :** soft fur fiber usu. from the undercoat of an animal **d :** a fine powdery coating or surface ⟨a ~ of crystals⟩ — **in the down** *of a young bird* **:** covered with down

⁸down \"\ *vt* -ED/-ING/-S **:** to cover, ornament, line, or stuff with down **:** make downy ⟨a mouse ~*ed* in its winter coat —Herbert Gold⟩

⁹down \"\ *adj, usu cap* [fr. *Down*, county of Northern Ireland] **:** of or from County Down, Northern Ireland **:** of the kind or style prevalent in County Down

dow·na \ˈdau̇nə\ [¹*dow* + *na*] *chiefly Scot* **:** CANNOT

down-along \ˌ¦ˌ=\ *adv, dial* **:** down the length of something (as a coast or road) **:** to or at a point in the distance

¹down-and-out \ˌ==¦=\ *adj* [⁴*down* + *and* + *out*, adj.] **1 :** so weakened, disabled, or incapacitated as to be ineffective **:** broken in health **2 :** suffering irrecoverably from financial losses or deficiencies **3** *of a boxer* **:** so broken down by past beatings as to be incompetent as a pugilist

²down-and-out \"\ *n* -S [¹*down-and-out*] **1** *also* **down-and-out·er** \-ə(r)\ [*down-and-outer* fr. ¹*down-and-out* + *-er*] **:** a person who is down-and-out **2 :** the play or discard in bridge of a high card of a nontrump suit followed by a lower card of the same suit to indicate ability to trump if a third round of the suit is led

down-at-heel \ˌ==¦=\ *or* **down-at-the-heel** \ˌ===¦=\ *also* **down-at-heels** \ˌ==¦=\ *or* **down-at-the-heels** \ˌ===¦=\ *adj* **:** marked by a slovenly slipshod condition or having a threadbare faded appearance **:** SHABBY ⟨loneliness gnawed at the lives of all the guests in . . . a *down-at-the-heel* private hotel in an English seaside town —Pamela Taylor⟩ ⟨occurred to him that he was *down-at-heel*, dingy —Martha Gellhorn⟩ ⟨should have to pass the hat round or try (dressed like a *down-at-heels* corner boy) to get some sort of job —Nicholas Monsarrat⟩

downbear \(ˈ)=¦=\ *vt* [ME *dounberen*, fr. *doun* down + *beren* to bear, carry — more at DOWN, BEAR] *archaic* **:** to bear down **:** DEPRESS **:** press upon

¹downbeat \ˈ=ˌ=\ *n* **1 :** the downstroke of the conductor indicating the first stressed beat of a musical composition; *also* **:** any first beat **:** THESIS **2 :** an ictus or arsis **:** STRESS **3 :** a decline in activity or prosperity **:** depressed condition

²downbeat \"\ *adj* **:** PESSIMISTIC, GLOOMY, UNHAPPY ⟨a movie with a ~ ending⟩

down-beater \ˈ=ˌ==\ *n* [²*down* + *beater*] **:** a rotating device used on a combine to beat down the moving grain and help to feed it uniformly to the cylinder

downbend \ˈ=ˌ=\ *n* **:** a depression (as in the bed of the sea) due to downward bending of the earth's crust

downbent \ˈ=ˌ=\ *adj* **:** bowed or drawn downward ⟨~ trees marked the path of the storm⟩ ⟨a tired ~ old man⟩

downbound \ˈ=ˌ=\ *adj* **:** heading or leading in any direction that is conventionally down ⟨a ~ channel⟩ ⟨~ traffic⟩

down-bow \ˈ=ˌbō\ *n* **:** a stroke in playing a bowed instrument (as a violin) from the heel toward the point of the bow — contrasted with *up-bow*; symbol ∧ or ⊓

downbuckle \ˈ=ˌ==\ *n* **:** a generally long and relatively narrow portion of the earth's crust that has been bent sharply downward — **downbuckling** \ˈ=ˌ=(=)=\ *n*

down-budding \ˈ=ˌ==\ *n* **:** a method of budding in which the scion is inserted in an inverted position

downbye *also* **downby** \(ˈ)dün¦bī\ *adv* [²*down* + *by*, adv.] *Scot* **:** down that way **:** down below

down calver *n* [²*down* + *calve* + *-er*] *Brit* **:** a down-calving cow

down-calving \ˈ=ˌ==\ *adj* [²*down* + *calving*, fr. pres. part. of *calve*] *Brit* **:** nearly ready to calve

down card \ˈ=ˌ=\ *n* **1 :** a card dealt face down in any card game in which certain other cards are dealt face up **2 :** a card that is part of a player's hand but is left face down on the table while other of his cards are exposed **3 :** HOLE CARD

¹downcast \(ˈ)=¦=\ *vt* [ME *douncasten*, fr. *doun* down + *casten* to cast — more at DOWN, CAST] *archaic* **:** OVERTHROW, DEMOLISH; *also* **:** DEJECT

²downcast \ˈ=ˌ=\ *n* [ME *douncast*, fr. *douncasten*, v.] **1 :** a casting down **:** OVERTHROW **2 :** a downcast or melancholy glance or appearance **3 :** a ventilating shaft down which fresh air passes in circulating (as through a mine or the hold of a ship); *also* **:** the current of air through the shaft

³downcast \ˈ=ˌ=\ *adj* [fr. past part. of ¹*downcast*] **1 :** low in spirit **:** DEPRESSED, DISPIRITED, DEJECTED **2** *of looks* **:** cast downward **:** directed to the ground (as from bashfulness modesty, dejection, or guilt) **3 :** having a downward draft ⟨a ~ mine shaft⟩

syn DISPIRITED, DEJECTED, DEPRESSED, DISCONSOLATE, WOEBEGONE: DOWNCAST suggests utter lack of cheer, confidence, and hope, perhaps accompanied by shame, chagrin, or bashfulness ⟨their smiling faces became *downcast*, their eyes held a look of furtiveness and uneasiness —Francis Birtles⟩ DISPIRITED indicates low-spiritedness and discouragement, usu. after failure or disappointment ⟨they could make no impression, and fell back at daybreak beaten and *dispirited* —J.A.Froude⟩ ⟨a fragile, *dispirited* gentlewoman who appeared to find everything in the world immeasurably sad and who spoke mostly in the past tense —Jean Stafford⟩ DEJECTED may imply more utter lowering of spirits and remarkable loss of hope, courage, and strength ⟨timorous and *dejected*, apprehending themselves to be haunted and possessed with vengeful spirits —William Bartram⟩ DEPRESSED implies a sinking under heavy burdens, often economic ones; it may describe chronic underprivilege or indicate psychological incapacity for hope, gladness, or even purposive activity ⟨the *depressed* populations of the ghettos of the Middle East and North Africa —John Hersey⟩ ⟨*depressed* by his failures and contemplating suicide⟩ ⟨*depressed* and stolid after the manic phase⟩ DISCONSOLATE describes one so utterly dispirited that he cannot be consoled, comforted, or encouraged ⟨the Jews sat *disconsolate* on the poop; they complained much of the cold they had suffered —George Borrow⟩ ⟨the *disconsolate* frown of a hunter who has seen nothing but warblers all day —James Thurber⟩ WOEBEGONE describes the appearance of dejection and defeat, sometimes lugubrious ⟨officers, seamen, and prisoners alike, we were as gaunt and *woebegone* a crowd as had ever been cast ashore from a shipwrecked vessel —C.B.Nordhoff & J.N.Hall⟩

down·cast·ness *n* -ES **:** the quality or state of being downcast

down·come \ˈdau̇nˌkəm\ *n* -S [ME (Sc) *douncome*, fr. ME *doun* down + *come* action of coming, alter. (influenced by *comen* to come) of *kime*, fr. OE *cyme*, fr. *cuman* to come — more at DOWN, COME] **1** *archaic* **:** a coming down **:** DESCENT **:** sudden fall **:** DOWNFALL **:** OVERTHROW **2 :** DOWNCOMER a

downcomer \ˈ=ˌ==\ *n* [²*down* + *comer*] **:** a pipe to conduct something downward: as **a :** a pipe for leading the hot gases from the top of a blast furnace downward to the dust collectors and flue system — see BLAST FURNACE illustration **b :** a tube larger in diameter than the water tubes in some watertube boilers to conduct water from each top drum to a bottom drum under the influence of thermal circulation

downcountry \ˈ=¦==\ *adv* (*or adj*) [³*down* + *country*] **:** in, toward, or of the seaboard or peripheral regions of an area

downcourt \ˈ=¦=\ *adv* (*or adj*) **:** in or into the direction of the goal (as in basketball)

downcry \(ˈ)=¦=\ *vt* **:** to cry down **:** DISPARAGE

downcurved \ˈ=¦=\ *adj* **:** curved downward esp. at the end — used of projecting parts ⟨the long ~ bill of the curlew⟩

downcut \(ˈ)=¦=\ *vb* **:** to cut down or downward by or as if by erosion — used chiefly as a present participle and esp. in distinguishing between downward and lateral stream erosion

downdale \ˈ=¦=\ *adv* **:** DOWNHILL

downdraft \ˈ=ˌ=\ *n* -S *often attrib* **:** a downward current of air or other gas (as in a mine shaft, kiln, or carburetor or during a thunderstorm)

down east \ˈ=¦=\ *adv* (*or adj*), *often cap D&E* **:** in or into the northeast coastal section of the U. S. and parts of the Maritime Provinces of Canada; *specif* **:** in or into coastal Maine

down east·er \dau̇ˈnēstə(r)\ *n, often cap D&E* **1 :** one born or living down east **2 :** a ship built down east; *esp* **:** a sailing ship from Maine

downed *past of* DOWN

down·er \ˈdau̇nə(r)\ *n* -S [⁶*down* & ⁴*down* + *-er*] **:** one that downs or that takes, brings, gets, or puts down; *esp* **:** a weak, sick, or crippled animal in a shipping load that is down and unable to rise

downface \(ˈ)=¦=\ *vt* [²*down* + *face*, v.] **:** CONTRADICT

down-faced \ˈ=¦=\ *adj* **:** having a continuous slope from forehead top to end of muzzle or bill with little or no stop — used of domestic mammals and birds; compare DISH-FACED

downfall \ˈ=ˌ=\ *n* -S [ME *dounfal*, fr. *doun* down + *fal* fall — more at DOWN, FALL (noun)] **1 a :** a sudden fall from high estate, power, reputation, or happiness **:** DESTRUCTION, RUIN ⟨the ~ of the government⟩ **b :** a fall (as of snow or rain) esp. when sudden or heavy **:** DESCENT **2 a** *archaic* **:** a precipitous descent **:** ABYSS **b :** a trap having some device that falls and imprisons or injures the prey when the trap is sprung — compare DEADFALL **c :** something that causes a downfall (as of a person) ⟨drink was his ~⟩

downfallen \ˈ=¦==\ *adj* [²*down* + *fallen*] **:** FALLEN, RUINED

downfalling \ˈ=ˌ==\ *adj* [²*down* + *falling*, adj.] *archaic* **:** falling down **:** DECAYING

downfaulted \ˈ=ˌ==\ *adj* [²*down* + *faulted*, fr. past part. of *fault*] *of a geological formation* **:** lowered by faulting

downfield \ˈ=¦=\ *adv* (*or adj*) [³*down* + *field*] **:** in or into the part of a football field beyond the line of scrimmage toward the opposing team's goal ⟨a play should be planned to allow the ends to get ~ if needed⟩ ⟨effective ~ blocking⟩

downflow \ˈ=ˌ=\ *n* **:** a downward flow or something that flows down; *esp* **:** a downward flowing current of air

downflowing \ˈ=ˌ==\ *adj* **:** running or cascading down

downfold \ˈ=ˌ=\ *n* **:** SYNCLINE — **downfolded** \ˈ=¦==\ *adj*

down·gone \ˈdau̇nˌgȯn *also* -gän\ *adj* [prob. alter. (influenced by ²*down* and *gone*, past part. of go) of ²*doggone*] *dial* **:** in poor condition **:** DISTRESSED; *often* **:** DARNED, DOGGONE

¹downgrade \ˈ=ˌ=\ *n* [⁴*down* + *grade*, n.] **1 :** a downward grade (as of a road) **2 :** a descent toward an inferior state **:** DETERIORATION — used esp. in the phrase *on the downgrade*

²downgrade \ˈ=¦=\ *adv* (*or adj*) **:** DOWNHILL ⟨the road dips ~⟩ ⟨the crossing where the ~ freights hit so many buggies and teams —Wright Morris⟩

³downgrade \(ˈ)=¦=\ *vt* [²*down* + *grade*, v.] **1 :** to minimize or depreciate in grade ⟨the folly of *downgrading* Soviet technology⟩ ⟨those countries preparing to ~ their commitments to NATO⟩ **2 a :** to lower the market class of (as grain or produce) esp. because of impurities or defects ⟨several carlots of wheat were *downgraded* for excessive cockle⟩ **b :** to alter the status of (a workman or his job) so as to lower the rate of pay ⟨older workers may often be kept employed by *downgrading* them to jobs that they are still able to handle⟩ ⟨any major shift in production or methods is likely to require extensive *downgrading* of jobs⟩ **3 :** to assign (as a document) to a less restricted classification of security

downgrowth \ˈ=ˌ=\ *n* **:** the growing downward of a structure; *also* **:** the product of such growth

down-gyved *adj* [²*down* + *gyved*, fr. past part. of *gyve*] *obs* **:** hanging down like gyves

downhand \ˈ=ˌ=\ *adj* [prob. fr. ³*down* + *hand*, n.] *of welding* **:** performed from the upper side of the joint with the face of the weld approximately horizontal

downhaul \ˈ=ˌ=\ *n* [²*down* + *haul*, v.] **:** a rope or line for hauling down or holding down a sail or spar ⟨a staysail ~⟩

downhearted \ˈ=¦==\ *adj* **:** DEJECTED — **down·heart·ed·ly** \(ˈ)=¦===\ *adv*

down·heart·ed·ness *n* -ES **:** the quality or state of being downhearted

¹downhill \ˈ=ˌ=\ *n* [⁴*down* + *hill*] **1 a** *archaic* **:** the slope toward the bottom of a hill **:** DECLIVITY, DESCENT **b :** a descending gradient (as in circumstances or human existence) ⟨the tragic ~*s* that bring many promising careers to an end⟩ **2** [²*downhill*] **:** a competitive ski event consisting of skiing down a trail against time

²downhill \ˈ=¦=\ *adv* [³*down* + *hill*] **1 :** toward the bottom of a hill ⟨traveling ~ we really got up speed⟩ **2 :** toward a lower, poorer, or inferior state or level — used esp. in the phrase *go downhill* < the town has gone ~ since the mill closed⟩ ⟨after he retired he went ~ very rapidly⟩

³downhill \ˈ=ˌ=\ *adj* [²*downhill*] **1 :** sloping downhill **2** [¹*downhill* 2] **:** of, relating to, or designed for use in skiing downhill ⟨a leading ~ contestant⟩ ⟨attractive ~ trousers⟩

downhill turn *n* **:** any skiing turn down the slope from a traverse run

downhold \ˈ=ˌ=\ *n* **:** an act of minimizing (as of expenses) ⟨a stringent ~ on cable tolls⟩

down-house \ˈ=¦=\ *adv* [³*down* + *house*] *dial Brit* **:** DOWNSTAIRS

downier *comparative of* DOWNY

downiest *superlative of* DOWNY

down·i·ly \ˈdau̇nᵊlē, -nəlē\ *adv* **:** in a downy manner **:** ARTFULLY

down·i·ness \ˈdau̇nēnəs, -au̇nin-\ *n* -ES **:** the quality or state of being downy

downing *pres part of* DOWN

dow·nin·gia \dau̇ˈniŋ(g)ēə\ *n, cap* [NL, fr. Andrew J. *Downing* †1852 Am. horticulturist + NL *-ia*] **:** a small genus of annual dwarf American herbs (family Lobeliaceae) with alternate leaves and showy sessile flowers having an unsplit corolla tube

down-in-the-mouth \ˌ===¦=\ *adj* **:** DEPRESSED, DOLOROUS

down-land \ˈ=ˌland\ *n* **:** ¹DOWN 2

down-lead \ˈ=ˌlēd\ *n* **:** a radio lead-in

down·less \ˈ-ləs\ *adj* **:** having or growing no down ⟨a ~ chick⟩

downlight \ˈ=ˌ=\ *n* **:** a small spotlight set in the ceiling and directed downward

downline \ˈ=¦=\ *adv* [³*down* + *line*, n.] **:** down the railway line

down lock *n* **:** a device in an airplane that locks the landing gear in the down position after it has been lowered

down-looked \ˈ=ˌlu̇kt\ *adj* [⁴*down* + *look*, n. + *-ed*] *archaic* **:** downcast in countenance as or as if from guilt **:** SHEEPISH

downlying \ˈ=ˌ==\ *n* -S [²*down* + *lying*, fr. gerund of *lie*] **1** *now dial Eng* **:** the time or act of going to bed **:** time of repose **2** *also* **down·lig·ging** \ˈ=ˌligən, -giŋ\ [*downligging* fr. ²*down* + *ligging*, fr. gerund of *lig*] *chiefly Scot* **:** LYING-IN

down milling *n* [⁴*down* + *milling*] **:** CLIMB MILLING

down·most \ˈ=ˌmōst *sometimes chiefly Brit* -ˌməst\ *adv* (*or adj*) **:** farthest down

down·ness \ˈdau̇nnəs\ *n* -ES **:** the state or condition of being down

downpipe \ˈ=ˌ=\ *n, Brit* **:** DOWNSPOUT

downpour \ˈ=ˌ=\ *n* **:** a pouring or streaming downward (as of sunlight); *esp* **:** a heavy drenching

¹downright \ˈ=ˌ=\ *adv* (*or adj*) [ME *dounright*, fr. *doun* down + *right*, adv. — more at DOWN] **1** *archaic* **:** straight down **:** in a perpendicular course **2 :** OUT-AND-OUT, PLAIN, OUTRIGHT ⟨I was ~ ashamed of our party⟩ ⟨a ~ liar⟩; *sometimes* **:** VERY **:** to the utmost degree ⟨the sunset was ~ lovely⟩ **3 :** without ceremony **:** with plain blunt honesty **:** FORTHRIGHT ⟨a ~ answer⟩ ⟨so ~ a moralist⟩ ⟨he was kind but ~⟩ ⟨went ~ to his task⟩ — **down·right·ness** \ˈ=ˌ=nəs\ *n*

²downright \"\ *n* **:** an inferior short-staple wool — usu. used in pl.

down·right·ly \ˈ=ˌ=lē, -li\ *adv* [¹*downright* + *-ly*] **:** in a straightforward or forthright manner **:** without hesitation

downriver \ˈ=¦==\ *adv* (*or adj*) [³*down* + *river*] **:** from, toward, or at a point near the mouth of a river ⟨drifted ~ on a raft⟩ ⟨important ~ markets⟩

downs *pl of* DOWN, *pres 3d sing of* DOWN

down·set \ˈdünˌset\ *n* [²*down* + *set*, v.] *Scot* **:** a provision of money or an establishment; *specif* **:** MARRIAGE SETTLEMENT

down-sexed \ˈdau̇nˌsekst\ *adj* [²*down* + *sexed*] **:** having sex appeal minimized ⟨*down-sexed* illustrations⟩

¹downshift \ˈ=¦=\ *vi* [²*down* + *shift*, v.] **:** to shift an automotive vehicle into a lower gear ⟨~ into low or second gear⟩

²downshift \ˈ=ˌ=\ *n* **:** a shift into a lower automotive gear

downside \ˈ=ˌ=\ *n* **1 :** the under or lower side ⟨a gaily tilted hat with a decorative clasp on the ~⟩ **2 :** a trend downward (as of prices) — used chiefly in the phrase *on the downside*

downside up *adv* **:** TOPSY-TURVY

downsitting \ˈ=ˌ==, *Scot* ˈdün-\ *n* [²*down* + *sitting*, fr. gerund of *sit*] **1 :** the action of sitting down **:** REPOSE **2** *Scot* **:** DOWNSET

downslide \ˈ=ˌ=\ *n* **:** a decline to a lower level (as of prices or business)

¹downslope \ˈ=¦=\ *adv* [³*down* + *slope*] **:** in a downward direction **:** DOWNHILL ⟨khaki-clad figures . . . sliding ~ toward him —Walt Sheldon⟩

²downslope \"\ *adj* **:** DOWNHILL, DESCENDING ⟨~ winds⟩ ⟨~ movement of ice⟩

³downslope \ˈ=ˌ=\ *n* [⁴*down* + *slope*] **:** DOWNHILL ⟨he had only to remember to keep the ~ on his right —W.V.T.Clark⟩

downs·man \ˈdau̇nzmən\ *n, pl* **downsmen** [*downs* (pl. of ¹*down*) + *man*] **:** a dweller on the downs

down·some \ˈdau̇n(t)səm\ *adj* **:** DISPIRITED, DEPRESSED

down south \ˈ=¦=\ *adv, often cap S* **:** in or into a more southerly location ⟨learned about the ways of fish in Canadian waters before he came *down south* —*Sydney (Australia) Bull.*⟩; *esp* **:** in or into the southeastern part of the U.S.

downspout \ˈ=ˌ=\ *n* **:** a pipe leading downward; *esp* **:** a pipe to carry off rain water from a roof

down's syndrome \ˈdau̇nz-\ *n, cap D* [after J.L.H. *Down* †1896 Eng. physician, who first described it] **:** MONGOLISM

¹downstage \ˈ=¦=\ *adv* (*or adj*) [³*down* + *stage*, n.] **:** toward or at the front of a theatrical stage ⟨swept her train ~⟩ ⟨bent the ~ knee⟩ — compare UPSTAGE

²downstage \ˈ=ˌ=\ *n* **:** the front of a stage immediately behind the footlights

¹downstairs \(ˈ)=¦=\ *adv* [³*down* + *stairs*, pl. of *stair*] **1 :** down the stairs **:** on or to a lower floor **2** *aeronautics* **:** on, near, or to the ground

²downstairs *also* **downstair** \ˈ=¦=\ *adj* **1 :** situated on the main, lower, or ground floor of a building **2 :** placed at or occupying a lower level ⟨the ~ television channels⟩

³downstairs \(ˈ)=¦=\ *n pl but sing or pl in constr* **1 :** the part of the house belowstairs **:** the lower floor or floors **2 :** persons occupying the lower part of a building; *often* **:** the servants of a household ⟨~ were shocked at such goings on⟩

downstart \ˈ=ˌ=\ *n* [²*down* + *-start* (as in *upstart*)] **:** an Irishman of good birth and upbringing but with little fortune; *often* **:** a younger son of good family

¹downstate \ˈ=¦=\ *adv* (*or adj*) [³*down* + *state*, n.] **1 :** into or in a part of a state designated as downstate ⟨the voting was light ~⟩ **2 :** characteristic of a part of a state designated as downstate ⟨peculiarities of ~ pronunciation⟩

²downstate \"\ *n* **:** the more southerly part of a state of the U.S. as distinguished from a northerly part conventionally designated as *upstate* — **down·stat·er** \ˈ=ˈstād·ə(r)\ *n* -S

downstream \ˈ=¦=\ *adv* (*or adj*) [³*down* + *stream*, n.] **:** down a stream **:** in the direction of flow of a stream

downstreet \ˈ=¦=\ *adv* [³*down* + *street*, n.] **:** to, toward, or in the main retail business section of a town ⟨going ~ after supper⟩

downstroke \ˈ=ˌ=\ *n* **1 :** a stroke (as of a piston in a cylinder or of a conductor's baton) made in a downward direction **2 a :** a stroke (as of a handwritten cursive letter) commonly written in a downward direction and in some styles heavier than an upstroke **b :** a corresponding stroke of a printed letter

downsun \ˈ=¦=\ *adv* (*or adj*) [³*down* + *sun*, n.] **:** in a direction from or out of the sun ⟨a ~ attack by an aircraft⟩

downswing \ˈ=ˌ=\ *n* **1 :** a swing downward; *esp* **:** the forward and downward sweep of a golf club following the backswing **2 :** a downward or depressed trend ⟨the ~ in interest in politics⟩ ⟨in the ~ of a cyclic mania⟩; *esp* **:** the contraction phase of a business cycle

downtake \ˈ=ˌtāk\ *n* [²*down* + *-take* (as in *intake*)] **:** a pipe, duct, or flue (as for air, gas, or water) that leads downward

down-the-line \ˌ==¦=\ *adv* (*or adj*) **:** all the way **:** to the end ⟨supporting the party ticket right *down-the-line*⟩ ⟨a *down-the-line* union man⟩

down the river *n, often cap D&R* **:** SEVEN-CARD STUD

downthrow \ˈ=ˌ=\ *n* **1 :** the act or process of throwing down **:** state of being overthrown **:** OVERTHROW ⟨the sudden ~ of a reputation⟩ **2 :** the side of a geologic fault that moved downward relative to the other side — compare THROW

downthrown \ˈ=ˌ=\ *adj* [²*down* + *thrown*, fr. past part. of *throw*] **:** thrown down **:** DEPRESSED

downthrust \ˈ=ˌ=\ *n* **:** downward movement of an object under impact or steady pressure; *also* **:** an impact or pressure tending to cause downthrust

downtime \ˈ=ˌ=\ *n* [⁴*down* + *time*] **1 :** time during which a machine, department, or factory is inactive during normal operating hours (as for repairs or setting up or from lack of materials) **2 a :** a period during which an incentive worker is unable to produce because of plant factors beyond his control and therefore receives payment at an agreed base rate **b :** money paid a worker for downtime

down-to-date \ˌ==¦=\ *adj* **:** UP-TO-DATE

down-to-earth \ˌ==¦=\ *adj* **:** practical and straightforward **:** having no frills or foibles **:** REALISTIC

down·to·ni·an \(ˈ)dau̇nˈtōnēən\ *adj, usu cap* [*Downton*, town in Wiltshire, England + E *-ian*] **:** of, relating to, or constituting a subdivision of the European Silurian — see GEOLOGIC TIME table

¹downtown \ˈ=¦=\ *adv* (*or adj*) [³*down* + *town*] **1 :** to, toward, or in the lower part or business center of a city ⟨this bus goes ~⟩ ⟨delinquents roaming the ~ streets⟩ **2 :** relating to or characteristic of the business center of a city ⟨always patronizes the ~ stores⟩

²downtown \"\ *n* **:** the business center of a city ⟨the ~*s* of a hundred cities dressed and lighted for Christmas⟩ — **down·town·er** \ˈ=ˈtau̇nə(r)\ *n* -S

down tree *n* [⁷*down* + *tree*; fr. the thick cottony fibers surrounding the seeds] **:** BALSA 1

downtrend \ˈ=ˌ=\ *n* **:** a tendency downward esp. in economic matters ⟨a persistent ~ in sales⟩

downtrod *obs var of* DOWNTRODDEN

down·trod·den \(ˈ)=ˌträdᵊn\ *adj* [²*down* + *trodden*, fr. past part. of *tread*] **:** abused by superior power — **down·trod·den·ness** \-ᵊn(n)əs\ *n* -ES

downturn \ˈ=ˌ=\ *n* **1 :** an act or instance of turning down ⟨the ~ of an anticlinal fold —W.Y.Westervelt⟩; *also* **:** the state of being turned down ⟨the ~ of her mouth became a habit —Dorothy Parker⟩ **2 :** DECLINE, DECREASE ⟨a sharp ~ in new construction⟩; *usu* **:** a downward trend in economic matters ⟨the ~ of prices⟩ ⟨business began to show a ~⟩

down-twister \ˈ=ˌ==\ *n* **:** a textile manufacturing machine with downward feeds for plying yarn while adding some twist — compare UP-TWISTER

¹down under *adv* [²*down* + *under*, adv.; fr. the conception of the antipodes as being located beneath one's feet] **:** into or in Australia or New Zealand

²down under *n, sometimes cap D&U* **:** ANTIPODE 2

¹down·ward \ˈdau̇nwə(r)d\ *also* **down·wards** \-dz\ *adv* [*downward* fr. ME *dounward*, fr. *doun* down + *-ward*; *downwards* fr. ME *dounwardes*, fr. *dounward* + *-es* (adverbially functioning gen. sing. ending of nouns) — more at DOWN, -S] **1 :** from a higher place to a lower **:** in a descending course ⟨looking ~ to the grass⟩ ⟨the streams roll ~ to the sea⟩ **2 :** from a higher to a lower condition ⟨revised his estimate ~⟩ **:** toward misery, humility, disgrace, or ruin ⟨fell from grace and went ~ in life⟩ **3 :** from a remote or earlier time **:** from an ancestor or predecessor **:** from one to another in a descending line ⟨prophets from Elijah ~ who preached repentance⟩

²downward \"\ *adj* [ME *dounward*, fr. *dounward*, adv.] **1 :** moving or extending from a higher to a lower place **:** tending toward the earth or its center or toward a lower level ⟨the ~ pull of gravity⟩ **2 :** descending from a head, origin, or source ⟨a ~ line of descent⟩ ⟨the ~ course of a stream⟩ **3 a** *archaic* **:** tending to a lower state **:** DEJECTED **b :** directed toward or leading to ruin, destruction, or damnation ⟨a man on the ~ path⟩ ⟨took her ~ way⟩ **c :** DEBASING ⟨the scripture contains many ~ comparisons of man and his ways⟩ **4** *archaic* **:** being below **:** LOWER — **down·ward·ly** *adv* — **down·ward·ness** *n* -ES

¹downwarp \(ˈ)=¦=\ *vb* [²*down* + *warp*, v.] *vt* **:** to cause or produce a downwarp in ~ *vi* **:** to undergo downwarping

²downwarp \ˈ=ˌ=\ *n* **:** a broad generally shallow geological downfold

downwash \ˈ=ˌ=\ *n* **1 :** material washed downward (as from a mountainside) **2** *aeronautics* **:** the airstream which is deflected downward by an airfoil and the momentum of which gives rise by its reaction on the airfoil to the lift

1downwind \'=¦=\ *adv* (*or adj*) [3*down* + *wind*, n.] **:** in the direction that the wind is blowing **:** LEEWARD ⟨problems involved in making a safe ~ landing⟩ ⟨the smell of her cooking traveled ~ to where we were working⟩

2downwind \'=,=\ *n* [4*down* + *wind*, n.] **:** a wind blowing in or along one's course

down·with \'dün(,)=\ *adj* [ME (Sc) *dounwith*, fr. *dounwith* (adv.) downward, fr. ME *doun* down + *with* (adv.) together, fr. OE, fr. *with* (prep.) with, against — more at DOWN, WITH (prep.)] *Scot* **:** DOWNWARD

down wool *n* [1*down* + *wool*] **:** wool produced by Down sheep

1downy \'dau̇nē, -ni\ *adj* -ER/-EST [7*down* + -*y*] **1 :** like the down of a bird esp. in softness and fluffiness ⟨the ~ milkweed seeds⟩ **2 a :** having or covered with down, pubescence, or soft hairs ⟨a *downy*-cheeked lad⟩ ⟨the ~ surface of a ripe peach⟩ **b** *of a young bird* **:** not yet having developed feathers other than down **3 a :** made of down ⟨a ~ quilt⟩ **b :** soft or quiet **:** SOOTHING ⟨the ~ touch of her hand⟩ **4** [obs. E slang *down* in a state of awareness (fr. E 2*down*) + E -*y*] *slang* **:** CUNNING, WARY, KNOWING

2downy \"\ *adj* -ER/-EST [1*down* + -*y*] **:** being or characterized by downs ⟨a rolling ~ landscape⟩

downy ash *n* [1*downy*] **:** RED ASH 1

downy brome *or* **downy bromegrass** *or* **downy cheat** *or* **downy chess** *n* **:** an annual or winter annual grass (*Bromus tectorum*) with softly pubescent leaves and leaf sheaths

downy false foxglove *n* **:** a false foxglove (*Gerardia virginica*) with gray downy oak-shaped leaves

downy grape *n* **:** a wild grape (*Vitis cinerea*) of the central U.S. with downy foliage and black acid fruit

downy haw *also* **downy hawthorn** *n* **:** RED HAW

downy mildew *n* **1 :** a fungus of the family Peronosporaceae that is parasitic on higher plants (as grapes, potatoes, and various cucurbits) and that produces whitish masses of sporangiophores or conidiophores on the undersurface of the leaves of the host — called also *false mildew* **2 :** a plant disease caused by a downy mildew — compare POWDERY MILDEW

downy myrtle *n* **:** an evergreen shrub (*Rhodomyrtus tomentosa*) of the family Myrtaceae that is native to tropical Asia and the Philippines and is sometimes cultivated for its pink flowers and edible berrylike fruits

downy oat grass *n* **:** an erect grass (*Trisetum spicatum*) with a spikelike panicle that is a valuable forage grass in many alpine and northern parts of the northern hemisphere

downy poplar *n* **:** SWAMP COTTONWOOD

downy woodpecker *n* **:** a small black-and-white woodpecker (*Dendrocopos pubescens*) of No. America

downy yellow violet *n* **:** a spring-flowering violet (*Viola pubescens*) having clear yellow flowers with brown-purple veins near the base of the petals and softly pubescent leaves and stems

1dowp *var of* DOUP

2dowp \'dau̇p, 'dōp\ *n* -S [origin unknown] *dial Eng* **:** CARRION CROW

dowry *var of* DOWER

dows *pres 3d sing of* DOW, *pl of* DOW

dow·sa·bel \'dau̇sə,bel, -aüzə-\ *n* -S [*Dowsabel*, fem. proper name] *obs* **:** SWEETHEART

1dowse *var of* DOUSE

2dowse \'dau̇¦z *sometimes* |s\ *vb* -ED/-ING/-S [origin unknown] *vi* **1 :** to use the divining rod (as in search of water or ore) **2 :** to seek something with meticulous care esp. with the aid of a mechanical device ⟨electrical devices for use in *dowsing* for cable⟩ ~ *vt* **:** to find (as water) by dowsing

1dows·er \|zə(r) *sometimes* |sə(r)\ *n* -S [2*dowse* + -*er*] **:** a divining rod for dowsing; *also* **:** a person who uses it

2dowser *var of* DOUSER

dow·sets \'dau̇səts\ *n pl* [ME *doucette* (pl. *doucettes*), a sweet dish, fr. MF *doucette* (fem. of *doucet*), fr. OF *doucete*, fem. of *doucet* sweet, pleasant, fr. *douz* sweet, fr. L *dulcis* — more at DULCET] *archaic* **:** the testes of a deer

dowsing rod *n* [*dowsing* fr. gerund of 2*dowse*] **:** a dowser's divining rod

dowst \'deüst\ *dial Eng var of* DUST

dow·ter \'dōtə(r)\ *dial Eng var of* DAUGHTER

dow theory \'dau̇-\ *also* **dow's theory** \'dau̇z-\ *n*, *usu cap D* [after Charles H. *Dow* †1902 — more at DOW-JONES AVERAGE] **:** a system of stock-market forecasting based on the observed swings of the market itself

dowy *var of* DOWIE

dox·ic \'däksik\ *also* **dox·i·cal** \-sәkәl\ *adj* [Gk *doxa* opinion + E -*ic*, -*ical*] **:** of, relating to, or based on such intellectual processes as belief or opinion

dox·og·ra·pher \däk'sägrәfә(r)\ *n* -S [modif. (influenced by E -*grapher*) of NL *doxographus*, fr. *doxo*- (fr. Gk *doxa* opinion) + -*graphus* writer, fr. Gk -*graphos* — more at -GRAPH] **:** a collector and compiler of extracts from and commentator on ancient Greek philosophers — **dox·o·graph·i·cal** \,däksә¦grafәkәl\ *or* **dox·o·graph·ic** \-fik\ *adj* — **dox·og·ra·phy** \däk'sägrәfē\ *n* -ES

dox·o·log·i·cal \,däksә¦läjәkәl, -jēk-\ *adj* [*doxology* + -*ical*] **1 :** relating to doxology or a doxology **2 :** giving praise to God — **dox·o·log·i·cal·ly** \-jәk(ә)lē, -jēk-, -li\ *adv*

dox·ol·o·gize \däk'sälә,jīz\ *vb* -ED/-ING/-S [*doxology* + -*ize*] *vi* **:** to give glory to God (as in a doxology) ~ *vt* **:** to praise (God) with doxologies

dox·ol·o·gy \-ləjē, -ji\ *n* -ES [ML *doxologia*, fr. Gk, fr. *doxo*- (fr. *doxa* glory, opinion, fr. *dokein* to seem good, seem, think) + -*logia* -logy — more at DECENT] **1 a** *obs* **:** praise to the Deity **:** thanksgiving for divine protection **b :** an utterance expressing pleasure in or thanksgiving for some event or occurrence **2 :** a commonly short hymn or formula expressing praise to God and usu. designed to be sung, chanted, or said by the choir or the congregation; *esp* **:** one used in Christian worship

1doxy *also* **dox·ie** \'däksē, -si\ *n*, *pl* **doxies** [perh. modif. of obs. D *docke* doll, fr. MD; akin to OHG *tocka* doll — more at DOCK] **1 :** a loose wench **:** TROLLOP, PROSTITUTE; *sometimes* **:** MISTRESS 6a **2** *dial* **:** GIRL FRIEND, SWEETHEART, MISTRESS 6b

2doxy \"\ *n* -ES [by shortening fr. *orthodoxy* & *heterodoxy*] **:** OPINION, DOCTRINE; *esp* **:** religious opinion — compare ISM

dox·yl·a·mine \däk'silә,mēn, -mәn\ *n* [prob. fr. *d*- (fr. *dimethyl*) + *oxy*- + -*l* (fr. -*yl*) + *amine*] **:** an antihistamine $C_{17}H_{22}N_2O$ derived from pyridine and usu. administered in the form of its succinate

doyen \(')dȯi¦(y)en, 'dȯi(y)ən, -ȯ¦yen, -ȯyən; (')dwä¦yen, ¦yaⁿ(n), ¦yan, 'dwäyən, -wä; (')dwī¦en, 'dwīən\ *n* -S [F, fr. LL *decanus* chief of ten — more at DEAN] **1 a :** the senior male member of a body or group (as of a diplomatic corps) — called also *dean*; *esp* **:** one specifically or tacitly allowed to speak for the body or group ⟨the ambassador as ~ objected strenuously to the foreign office on behalf of his colleagues⟩ **b :** a person uniquely skilled by long experience in some field of endeavor ⟨rightly regarded as the ~ among English and American specialists on Japan —K.S.Latourette⟩ ⟨the ~ of the Arlberg ski instructors —Joseph Wechsberg⟩ **2 a :** the oldest example of some category ⟨the ~ of the country's papers⟩ **b :** something outstanding of its kind ⟨some fanciers think dried ant's eggs the ~ of fish food⟩ ⟨among the few virtues to which I lay vigorous claim, punctuality is the ~ —Jerome Weidman⟩

doyenne \(')dȯi¦(y)en, -ȯ¦yen; (')dwä¦yen, -wä¦-; (')dwī¦en\ *n* -S [F, fem. of *doyen*] **:** a female doyen

doy·ley *or* **d'oy·ley** *or* **doy·ly** \'dȯili\ *Brit var of* DOILY

doylt \'dȯilt\ *var of* DOILED

doz *abbr* dozen

1doze \'dōz\ *vb* -ED/-ING/-S [prob. of Scand origin; akin to ON *dūsa* to doze, *dūs* lull, calm; akin to MLG *dōre* fool, MHG *dōsen* to be quiet, doze — more at DOR] *vt* **1** *archaic* **:** to make dull **:** STUPEFY, MUDDLE, CONFUSE **2 :** to pass (as time) drowsily — usu. used with *away* ⟨*dozing* his life away⟩ ~ *vi* **1 a :** to sleep lightly or intermittently **b :** to fall into a light sleep **2 :** to be in a dull or stupefied condition as if half asleep **:** be drowsy **syn** see SLEEP

2doze \"\ *n* -S **1 :** a light sleep **:** DROWSE **2 :** decay in timber **:** DOTE

3doze \"\ *vt* -ED/-ING/-S [prob. back-formation fr. *dozer* (bulldozer)] **:** BULLDOZE 3

dozed \-zd\ *adj* [prob. fr. past part. of 1*doze*] *of timber* **:** unsound from decay

1doz·en \'dәzᵊn\ *n*, *pl* **dozens** *or* **dozen** *often attrib* [ME *dozeine*, fr. OF *dozaine*, fr. *doze* twelve, fr. L *duodecim*, fr. *duo* two + -*decim* (fr. *decem* ten) — more at TWO, TEN] **1 a :** a group of 12 ⟨oranges sold by the ~⟩ ⟨a ~ eggs⟩ ⟨three ~ of ale⟩ ⟨~*s* of people⟩ **b :** any of the three columns respectively representing the numbers 1 to 12, 13 to 24, and 25 to 36 on which one may bet at roulette **2 a :** a group containing an indefinite small number ⟨a ~ years ago⟩ ⟨scribbled a ~ words on a scrap of paper⟩ **b :** a larger number than one might expect — usu. used in pl. ⟨I've ~*s* of things to do⟩ ⟨she had ~*s* of chances to marry⟩ **3** *archaic* **:** coarse woolen cloth formerly made in England and commonly woven in approximately 12-yard lengths — usu. used in pl.

2dozen \"\ *vt* -ED/-ING/-S **:** to make up into lots of a dozen

do·zened \'dōzᵊnd, 'däz-\ *adj* [ME (Sc) *dosnyt*, *dosinnit*, perh. of Scand origin; akin to ON *dūsa* to doze] *chiefly Scot* **:** STUPEFIED ⟨~ with drink —R.L.Stevenson⟩

do·zent \dō'sent\ *n*, *pl* **dozen·ten** \-ntᵊn\ [G — more at DOCENT] **:** a docent in a German university

doz·enth \'dәzᵊn(t)th\ *adj* [*dozen* + -*th*] **1 :** TWELFTH **2 :** being about the twelfth ⟨I'm telling you for the ~ and last time⟩

1doz·er \'dōzә(r)\ *n* -S [1*doze* + -*er*] **:** one that dozes

2dozer \"\ *n* -S [by shortening] **:** HOPPERDOZER

3dozer \"\ *n* -S [by shortening] **:** BULLDOZER 3

dozy \'dōzē, -zi\ *adj* -ER/-EST [1*doze* + -*y*] **1 :** DROWSY **:** inclined to doze **:** SLEEPY, SLUGGISH ⟨a tired ~ child⟩ **2 :** in a state of decay **:** DOTY ⟨~ flawed wood⟩ **:** somewhat dozed ⟨a ~ post⟩

DP *abbr* **1** dew point **2** direct port **3** displaced person **4** documents against payment; documents for payment **5** double play **6** double pole **7** duty paid

DPB *abbr* deposit passbook

DPDT *abbr* double pole, double throw

DPH \,dē(,)pē'ăch\ *or* **DPhil** \'dē'fil\ *abbr or n* -S **:** a doctor of philosophy

dpl *abbr* diploma

DPN \,dē(,)pē'en\ *abbr or n* -S diphosphopyridine nucleotide

DPST *abbr* double pole, single throw

dpt *abbr* **1** department **2** deponent **3** depth

dpty *abbr* deputy

DQ *abbr* **1** development quotient **2** direct question

dr *abbr* **1** debit; debtor **2** *often cap* doctor **3** door **4** drachma **5** dram **6** drawer; drawing; drawn **7** drive **8** drum

DR *abbr* **1** dead reckoning **2** deposit receipt **3** differential rate **4** dining room **5** district registry **6** dock receipt

1drab \'drab, -aa(ә)b\ *n* -S [perh. of Celt origin; akin to ScGael *drabag* dirty woman, IrGael *drabog* slattern, slut, fr. & akin to IrGael *drab* spot, stain, dirt, fr. MIr, grape husks, dregs — more at DRAFF] **1 :** a slatternly woman **2 :** PROSTITUTE, HARLOT

2drab \"\ *vi* **drabbed; drabbed; drabbing; drabs :** to associate with strumpets **:** WENCH ⟨a waster, an idler; drinking and *drabbing* —Aldous Huxley⟩

3drab \"\ *n* -S [MF *drap* cloth, fr. LL *drappus*, prob. of Celt origin; akin to Celt personal names *Drappō*, *Drappus*; akin to Gk *drepein* to pluck, Skt *drāpi* mantle, garment, OE *teran* to tear — more at TEAR] **1 :** any of various cloths of a dull brown or gray color ⟨the carpet was an ancient ~ —Ethel Wilson⟩; *esp* **:** a thick woolen coating or a heavy cotton **2** [4*drab*] **a :** a light olive brown that is slightly less strong than sponge, less strong and slightly redder than average mustard tan, and darker than the color dust — called also *mode beige*, *rustic drab*, *sand dune* **b :** a dull, lifeless, or faded hue or appearance ⟨the silks with which the figures are embroidered have mostly faded to a general ~, but it is still possible to make out some red and green —O. Elfrida Saunders⟩ **3 :** the quality or state of being drab **:** DULLNESS ⟨for this slight relief from the intolerable ~ of his life story one may be grateful —V.L.Parrington⟩

4drab \"\ *adj* **drabber; drabbest 1 a :** of the dull brown color of drab cloth **b :** of the color drab **2 :** characterized by dullness and monotony **:** COLORLESS, CHEERLESS ⟨a ~ pile of masonry⟩ ⟨a usually ~ and lifeless subject —R.T.Hoober⟩ ⟨the writer's ~ vision of life⟩ — **drab·ly** *adv* — **drab·ness** *n* -ES

5drab \"\ *vt* **drabbed; drabbed; drabbing; drabs** [4*drab*] **:** to dull or tone down (color)

6drab \"\ *n* -S [prob. alter. of 2*drib*] **:** a petty sum — usu. used in the phrase *dribs and drabs* ⟨its only newspaper operates on the dribs and ~*s* of cash mailed in by the faithful —Mollie Panter-Downes⟩

7drab \"\ *n* -S [origin unknown] **:** a wooden box used in saltworks for holding the salt taken out of the pans used in boiling

dra·ba \'drābə, -ăbə\ *n* [NL, fr. Gk *drabē*, a kind of cress] **1** *cap* **:** a very large genus of low tufted herbs (family Cruciferae) of temperate and arctic regions with small flowers and oblong or linear siliques **2** -S **:** any plant of the genus *Draba* — compare WHITLOW GRASS

drab·bet \'drabət\ *n* -S [3*drab* + -*et*] *dial Eng* **:** a coarse unbleached linen fabric usu. in twill weave

drab·ble \'drabəl\ *vb* **drabbled; drabbled; drab·bling** \-b(ə)liŋ\ **drabbles** [ME *drabelen* — more at DRIVEL] *vt* **:** to wet and befoul by draggling **:** DRAGGLE ⟨~ a gown or cloak⟩ ~ *vi* **1 :** to be or become wet and muddy **:** dabble in or go through wet or miry places **2 :** to fish with a rod and a long line that is drawn along through the water ⟨~ for barbels⟩

drab·bler *or* **drab·ler** \'drablə(r)\ *n* -S **:** a piece of canvas laced to the bonnet of a sail to give it more drop

dra·bi \'dräbē\ *n* -S [fr. various languages of India, modif. of E *driver*] *India* **:** DRIVER

dra·cae·na \drə'sēnə\ *n* [NL, fr. LL, she-serpent, fr. Gk *drakaina*, fem. of *drakōn* serpent — more at DRAGON] **1** *cap* **:** a genus of shrubs or trees (family Liliaceae) native to the Old World tropics that have branches terminated by clusters of sword-shaped leaves, that bear panicles of small greenish white flowers, and that yield a dragon's blood — see DRAGON TREE **2** *or* **dracaena palm** *or* **dracena** -S **:** any plant of the genus *Dracaena* or of the related genus *Cordyline*

drachm \'dram, -aa(ə)m\ *n* -S [alter. (influenced by L *drachma*) of ME *dragme*, *drame* — more at DRAM] **1 :** DRACHMA **2 :** DRAM

drach·ma \'drakmə\ *n*, *pl* **drachmas** \-məz\ *also* **drach·mae** \-,mē, -,mī\ *or* **drach·mai** \-,mī\ [L, fr. Gk *drachmē* — more at DRAM] **1 a :** any of various ancient Greek units of weight; *specif* **:** the Attic unit equal to about 66.4 grains or 4.30 grams **b :** any of various modern units of weight: (1) **:** DRAM 1 (2) **:** a Greek unit equal to 15.432 grains or 1 gram **2 a :** an ancient Greek silver coin equivalent to 6 obols and according to the Attic standard weighing 4.37 grams or 67.5 grains; *also* **:** a unit of value equivalent to a drachma coin being the basic unit of the silver coinage **b :** the basic monetary unit of modern Greece; *also* **:** a coin representing this unit — see MONEY table

drach·mal \'drakməl, -a(a)ml\ *adj* **:** of or relating to a drachm

dra·co \'drā(,)kō\ *n* [in sense 1, fr. LL, fr. L, serpent; in sense 2, NL, fr. L, serpent — more at DRAGON] **1** *pl* **dra·co·nes** \drā'kō(,)nēz, drə'-\ **:** a flag in the form of a serpent-shaped or dragon-shaped bag made open at one end so as to be inflated by the wind when carried and used in the later imperial period of Rome as the standard of a cohort and in armies in medieval Europe **2** *cap* **:** a genus of agamid lizards — see DRAGON 7

dra·co·ceph·a·lum \,drākō'sefələm\ *n*, *cap* [NL, fr. L *draco* + NL -*cephalum* (neut. of *cephalus*); fr. the form of the corolla] **:** a genus of American mints comprising the dragonheads and having opposite serrate leaves and bracted bilabiate flowers

dra·co·ni·an \(')drā¦kōnēən, drə'k-\ *adj*, *often cap* [L *Dracon*-, *Draco fl* 621 B.C. Athenian lawgiver (fr. Gk *Drakōn*) + E -*ian*] **1 :** of, relating to, or suggestive of the lawgiver Draco or the severe code of laws that is said to have been framed by him as thesmothete **2 :** marked by extreme severity or cruelty **:** HARSH, RIGOROUS ⟨emancipation at the price of a ruinous war and a *Draconian* peace —G.W.Johnson⟩ ⟨by ~ labor laws . . . the regime makes life harder than it need be —F.C.Barghoorn⟩

1dra·con·ic \drə'känik\ *adj* [L *dracon*-, *draco* serpent + E -*ic*] **:** of, relating to, or like a dragon

2dra·con·ic \(')drā¦känik, drə'k-\ *adj* [L *Dracon*-, *Draco*, Athenian lawgiver + E -*ic*] *adj*, *sometimes cap* **:** DRACONIAN — **dra·con·i·cal·ly** \-nək(ə)lē\ *adv*

draconic period *n* [L *Dracon*-, *Draco*, a northern circumpolar constellation (fr. Gk *Drakōn*, fr. *drakōn* serpent) + E -*ic* — more at DRAGON] **:** NODICAL MONTH

drac·on·ti·a·sis \,dra,kän'tīəsəs\ *n* [NL, fr. Gk *drakontiasis*, fr. *drakontion* Guinea worm (dim. of *drakont*-, *drakōn* serpent) + -*iasis*] **:** DRACUNCULOSIS

dra·con·ti·um \drə'känchēəm\ *n*, *cap* [NL, fr. L, a kind of arum, fr. Gk *drakontion*, dim. of *drakont*-, *drakōn* serpent] **:** a genus of tropical American herbs (family Araceae) with compound leaves and hooded spathes

drac·u·la \'drakyələ\ *n* -S *usu cap* [after Count *Dracula*, a vampire depicted in the novel *Dracula* (1897) by Bram Stoker †1912 Brit. writer] **:** one who maintains a relationship like that of a vampire toward another by sapping his physical or emotional strength ⟨I wish I could find a truly cruel, fiendish woman, a sheer vicious *Dracula* —Calder Willingham⟩

dra·cun·cu·li·a·sis \drə,kəŋkyə'līəsəs\ *n* [NL, fr. 1*Dracunculus* + -*iasis*] **:** DRACUNCULOSIS

dra·cun·cu·lo·sis \-'lōsəs\ *n* [NL, fr. 1*Dracunculus* + -*osis*] **:** infestation with or disease caused by the Guinea worm

1dra·cun·cu·lus \drə'kəŋkyələs\ *n*, *cap* [NL (trans. of Gk *drakontion* Guinea worm), fr. L, small serpent, dim. of *draco* dragon — more at DRAGON] **:** a genus (the type of the family Dracunculidae) of greatly elongated nematode worms including the Guinea worm

2dracunculus *n* [NL, fr. L, tarragon, small serpent] **1** *cap* **:** a genus of herbs (family Araceae) with compound leaves — see GREEN DRAGON **2** *pl* **dracuncu·li** \-,lī\ **:** any plant of the genus *Dracunculus*

drae·ger·man \'drägə(r)mən\ *n*, *pl* **draegermen** [Alexander B. *Dräger* †1928 Ger. scientist and inventor of a combined gas mask and oxygen inhalator worn in underground rescue work + E *man*] **:** one of a crew of miners trained in underground emergency and rescue work

draff \'draf, -aa(ə)-,-ai-\ *n* -S [ME *draf* dregs, draff, fr. (assumed) OE *dræf* or ON *draf*; akin to OHG *trebir* grape husks, draff, MIr *drab* dregs, OE *deorc* dark — more at DARK] **:** the damp remains of malt after brewing often used as an appetizer or supplement in animal rations

draff·sack \'=,=\ *n* [ME *draf sak*, fr. *draf* draff + *sak* sack — more at SACK (bag)] **1** *Scot* **:** a sack for draff **2** *Scot* **:** a lazy glutton **3** *Scot* **:** PAUNCH ⟨celebrated his son's arrival by filling his ~ with ale —T.B.Costain⟩

draffy \-fē\ *adj*, *often* -ER/-EST **:** resembling draff **:** WORTHLESS

1draft *or* **draught** \'draft, -aa(ə)-, -ai-, -ȧ-\ *n* -S [ME *draht*, *draght*, *draught*; akin to OHG *traht*, *trahta* act of carrying, ON *dráttr* act of pulling; derivatives fr. the root of OE *dragan* to draw — more at DRAW] **1 :** the act of drawing a net **:** a sweeping of the water for fish; *also* **:** the quantity of fish taken at one drawing ⟨but not a single fish of all the ~ —S.T. Coleridge⟩ **2 a :** the act of moving loads by drawing or pulling **:** PULL, TRACTION ⟨these animals make poor beasts of ~ or burden⟩ **b :** the harness for work animals **c :** a team of animals together with what they draw **3 a :** the force required to pull a plow or other implement ⟨the effect on plow ~ of 5 factors was tested by means of a hydraulic dynamometer —*Biol. Abstracts*⟩ **b :** load or load-pulling capacity ⟨the ~ . . . of a typical draft horse working at about 2½ miles per hour has been given as the order of 150 lb. —F.D.Smith & Barbara Wilcox⟩ **4 a :** the act of drawing into the mouth and throat liquor, smoke, vapor, or air **:** the act or an instance of drinking or inhaling ⟨inhaled the smoke in long luxurious ~*s*⟩ ⟨swallowed the beer at one ~⟩; *also* **:** the portion or quantity that is drunk or inhaled at a single swallow or inhalation ⟨breathing in great ~*s* of invigorating . . . air —Hugh Walpole⟩ **b :** a portion of liquid (as medicine) poured out or mixed for drinking **:** DOSE, POTION ⟨thought himself well enough at night to omit the opium ~ —J.B.Holroyd⟩ ⟨a ~ whose ingredients included the juice of willow bark was esteemed . . . as an antipyretic —Berton Roueché⟩ **5 :** a portion of some particular kind of experience to which one is exposed or subjected ⟨the criminal of old was given copious ~*s* of exhortation and homily —B.N. Cardozo⟩ ⟨the officeholder is refreshed by periodic ~*s* of opposition —S.B.Chrimes⟩ **6 a :** a delineation or representation (as a drawing, painting, sculpture, map, plan, sketch); *specif* **:** the plan of something to be constructed ⟨it is usual . . . for any person before he begins to erect a building, to have designs or ~*s* made —Joseph Moxon⟩ **b :** SCHEME, DESIGN, PLOT **c :** a preliminary or tentative sketch, outline, or version (as of a document or picture) ⟨asked him to prepare a ~ of the proposed law⟩ ⟨carefully revised the first ~ of the poem⟩ **7** *archaic* **:** INCLINATION, ATTRACTION, TENDENCY **8 :** the act, result, or plan of drawing out or stretching: as **a :** the act in spinning of drawing or attenuating fiber webs, slivers, or rovings **b :** the amount of such attenuation expressed as a ratio between length of material produced and length of material fed in or as a ratio between surface speeds of rollers effecting that result **c :** the act in shoe manufacturing of stretching fabric or leather or the placing of paper to determine the pattern shape and contours of a last **d :** a plan of drawing the warp through the heddles to produce a desired pattern in weaving **9 a :** the act of drawing (liquid) from a cask, barrel, or other container **b :** a portion of liquid that is so drawn ⟨a ~ of ale⟩ **10 a :** a drawing down of the pan or platform of a balance or scale **b :** the material weighed at one time esp. when a quantity is ascertained in several weighings **c** *Brit* **:** any of a number of measures of weight of fish ⟨their cod brought only $1.80 a ~ (238 lbs.) —*Time*⟩ **d :** a slight deduction in weight to offset the amount by which something being weighed must overbalance the weights of a scale **e :** an allowance granted a buyer for loss in weight (as that due to drying or repacking); *specif* **:** an allowance of one pound per hundredweight deducted with the tare from the gross weight of any package of wool **11** *obs* **:** SINK, SEWER, DRAIN, PRIVY **12 :** the depth of water a ship draws esp. when loaded ⟨a ship of 12 feet ~⟩ ⟨found the fleet too deep of ~ to enter small rivers and inlets —S.E. Morison⟩ **13 a :** the detaching or selecting of an individual from a group or mass for some special purpose ⟨a ~ of cattle for branding⟩ **:** the condition of being so drafted ⟨the ex-governor accepted his ~ as candidate with misgivings⟩; *specif* **:** a selecting of persons for compulsory military service ⟨the ~ has affected some industries⟩ **b :** a group of individuals so selected ⟨in a normal year 25 lambs per acre are fattened, the first ~ being taken between February 20 and 25 —T.A.Sellwood⟩ **c :** a group of men drafted for compulsory military service ⟨discipline when our new ~*s* first hit the field left a lot to be desired —J.W.Bellah⟩ **d** *Brit* **:** a group of soldiers or sailors moved or assigned on a particular occasion as a body **14 a :** a drawing of money from a fund or stock: as (1) **:** a written order drawn by a creditor directing a debtor to pay a sum of money to a third party or to bearer — used chiefly of a domestic order or one directed to a person in the country of its origin; compare BILL OF EXCHANGE (2) **:** CHECK 10b **b :** the act or an instance of drawing from or making demands upon something **:** DEMAND, CLAIM ⟨a serious ~ on national resources⟩ **15 a :** a current of air in a closed-in space (as a room, ventilator, furnace, or chimney) **b :** the difference in pressure between the air outside (as of a furnace or chimney) and the gases inside that is responsible for a flow of air **c :** a contrivance for regulating the flow of air (as in a fireplace, stove, or furnace) **16 a** *chiefly Midland* **:** GULLY, GORGE **b** *Midland* **:** a small stream **:** CREEK **17 a :** the taper given to a pattern so that it can be easily withdrawn from a mold **b :** the taper given to a die so that the work can be easily withdrawn from it **c :** the slant that is given to the furrows of a millstone **18 :** a narrow border worked to a plane surface along the edge of a stone or across its face esp. as a guide to the stonecutter **19 :** 2DRAW 2f **20 :** a system whereby exclusive rights to selected new players are apportioned among teams of a professional baseball, football, or hockey league — **on draft** *adj, of a liquid* **:** ready to be drawn (as from a cask or other container) ⟨the little drugstore with cologne *on draft* like beer —Claudia Cassidy⟩ — **on draft** *adv* **:** from a cask ⟨beer or ale to be served *on draft* —*Brewing in Brief*⟩

²**draft** *or* **draught** \"\ *adj* [ME *draght*, fr. *draht, draght*, n.] **1 :** used for drawing loads ⟨~ animals⟩ — see DRAFT HORSE **2 :** SELECTED — used chiefly of animals selected from a herd or flock (as for branding or classification) **3 :** constituting a preliminary or tentative version, sketch, or outline (as of a literary composition or other document) ⟨Pope . . . proposed to write a history of English poetry, and the ~ scheme of that history has been preserved —A.T.Quiller-Couch⟩ ⟨a ~ treaty⟩ ⟨~ conventions submitted to member nations for their approval⟩ **4 :** on draft; *also* **:** DRAWN ⟨~ beer⟩ — distinguished from *bottled*

³**draft** *or* **draught** \"\ *vb* **drafted** *or* **draughted; drafted** *or* **draughted; drafting** *or* **draughting; drafts** *or* **draughts** [¹*draft, draught*] *vt* **1 a :** to detach or select (an individual) for some special purpose with or without the element of compulsion being present ⟨the convention ~*ed* and nominated the popular attorney general⟩ ⟨his friend . . . was ~*ed* to paint prepared areas —Robert Berkelman⟩ ⟨she had no call to the religious life but was ~*ed* into it by her family —Anthony West⟩ ⟨all able-bodied men were ~*ed* to work on the levee⟩; *specif* **:** to conscript (a person) for service in the armed forces ⟨~*ed* all able-bodied youths⟩ **b** *Austral* **:** to separate into flocks **:** select and detach (an animal) from a herd for a special purpose ⟨~ sheep and take them to sale⟩ **2 a :** to make a draft of **:** draw the preliminary sketch or plan of **:** OUTLINE ⟨~*ing* speeches to be polished and styled by his resourceful secretary⟩ **b :** to draw up **:** COMPOSE, PREPARE, FRAME ⟨at once ~*ed* a telegram, signing it with the code word which he employed in emergencies —John Buchan⟩ ⟨~*ing* plans to meet the anticipated emergency⟩ **3 :** to draw up, off, or away ⟨all pumpers should be capable of ~*ing* water where necessary —*Fire Manual (Mass.)*⟩ ⟨her rents had been ~*ed* to London —Henry Fielding⟩ **4 :** to reduce (fiber webs, slivers, or rovings) in bulk in the processes between loose fiber and spun yarn **5 :** to design (a pattern) in weaving for drawing in warp threads **6 :** to mark (as a stone) with a draft in masonry **7 :** to draw or stretch (leather) in the lasting of shoes ~ *vi* **:** to engage in drafting (as of documents) **:** practice draftsmanship ⟨if anyone thinks that he can ~ more simply . . ., I advise him to try his hand —Ernest Gowers⟩

draft·able \-təbəl\ *adj* **:** qualified for or subject to draft into the armed forces

draft allowance *n* **:** DRAFT 10d, 10e

draft chair *n* **:** WING CHAIR

draft·ee \(ˈ)drafˈtē, -raaf-,-raif-,-rȧf-\ *n* -s [³*draft* + *-ee*] **:** one that is drafted into the armed forces **:** CONSCRIPT

draft·er \ˈ=ˌtə(r)\ *n* -s **1 :** one that drafts **2 :** DRAFT HORSE

draft gear *n* **:** a mechanism for transmitting the pull from one railroad car to another

draft horse *n* **:** a horse adapted for or used in drawing heavy loads; *specif* **:** such a horse over 1600 pounds in weight and over 16 hands high — compare CARRIAGE HORSE, CART HORSE, CHUNK, SADDLE HORSE

draft·i·ly \ˈ=tə̇lē, -li\ *adv* **:** in the manner of a draft **:** in such a manner as to cause a draft ⟨a brakeman came ~ into the dirty plush coach —Thomas Wolfe⟩

draft·i·ness \ˈtēnə̇s, -tin-\ *n* -ES **1 :** the condition of being exposed to or abounding in drafts ⟨complained of the ~ of her room⟩ **2 :** the condition of being drafty esp. in conformation of body

drafting *pres part of* DRAFT

drafting board *n* **:** DRAWING BOARD

drafting machine *n* **:** a drafting instrument consisting of linked parts that perform the functions of the T square, triangle, linear scale, and protractor

drafting race *n, Austral* **:** a race used for dividing sheep into groups

drafting table *n* **:** DRAWING TABLE

drafting yard *n, Austral* **:** a yard divided into compartments where cattle may be separated into groups

draft·man \-f(t)mən\ *n, pl* **draftmen** [by alter.] **:** DRAFTSMAN — **draft·man·ship** \-ˌship\ *n* -s

draft mark *n* **:** one of various marks required by law to be painted at the bow and stern of a ship to show how much water she draws — compare PLIMSOLL MARK

draft net *n* **:** a hauling net **:** SEINE

draft off *vt* **:** ³DRAFT 1b

draft rein *n* **:** the long outer rein of a harness

draft rod *n* **:** a hooked rod attachment on a planter for raising and lowering the marker

drafts *pl of* DRAFT, *pres 3d sing of* DRAFT

drafts·man \-f(t)smən\ *n, pl* **draftsmen** [*drafts* (gen. of ¹*draft*) + *man*] **1 :** one who draws pleadings or other writings **2 :** one who makes drawings; *specif* **:** one who draws plans and sketches (as of machinery or structures) **3 :** an artist who excels in drawing ⟨his genius as a ~ has obscured his talent as a colorist⟩

drafts·man·ship \-ˌship\ *n* -s **:** the art or practice of drawing or drafting ⟨the forms of his earliest documents show that the clerks of his chapel included men trained in English conventions of ~ —F.M.Stenton⟩ ⟨though the subjects of these paintings are different . . ., they are similar in their free ~ and their decorative motifs —*Technical Studies*⟩

draft stop *n* **:** CURTAIN BOARD

draft tube *n* **:** an airtight pipe or channel extending downward into the tailrace from a turbine wheel located above it to make the whole fall available

drafty \-ftē, -ti\ *adj* -ER/-EST **1 :** relating to or exposed to a draft ⟨a ~ room⟩ **2 :** resembling or characteristic of a draft horse esp. in conformation

¹**drag** \ˈdrag, -aa(ə)g,-aig\ *n* -s *often attrib* [ME *dragge*, prob. fr. *draggen*, v.] **1 :** something that is dragged, pulled, or drawn along or over a surface: as **a :** HARROW 1 **b** *chiefly NewEng* **:** a sledge for conveying heavy bodies ⟨a stone ~⟩ **c :** a steel instrument for completing the dressing of soft stone **d :** an apparatus (as a wooden or metal frame) drawn over ground (as a road) to smooth it — see DRAG SCRAPER **e :** CONVEYANCE; *esp* **:** a private coach that has seats on its top and that is usu. drawn by four horses **f :** the bottom part of a foundry molding flask, mold, or pattern — called also *nowel* **g :** FLOAT 5d (1) **h :** a railroad car or set of cars moved usu. by a switching engine from one part of a yard to another or from one yard to another **i :** crushed and broken ore found in and along a fault zone **2 :** something that is used to drag with: as **a :** a device (as a wire, grapnel, net, or scoop) for dragging under water along the bottom or through the water below the surface to detect the presence of, dislodge, obtain, or recover objects **b :** the log carriage in a veneer sawmill **c** [by shortening] **:** DRAGROPE **a 3 a :** something that retards motion: as (1) *also* **drag anchor :** something towed in the water to retard a ship's progress or to keep her head up to the wind **:** SEA ANCHOR; *esp* **:** a canvas bag with a hooped mouth used in this manner — compare DRAG SAIL (2) **:** a skid for retarding the motion of a carriage wheel — called also *shoe, dragshoe, skidpan* (3) **:** any of several adjustable devices attached to a fishing reel to prevent the spool from spinning too freely (4) [by shortening] **:** DRAGBAR 1 (5) **:** the retarding force acting on a body (as an airfoil or airplane) moving through a fluid (as air) parallel and opposite to the direction of motion **:** the component of the total aerodynamic force on a body parallel to the relative wind (6) **:** friction esp. between engine parts; *also* **:** retardation due to friction **b :** something that hinders or obstructs nonphysical movement or progress ⟨material . . . unrelated to the running narrative and a considerable ~ on it —Bernard DeVoto⟩ ⟨considered them a ~ on humanity —L.G.Derisseau⟩ **:** STRAIN, DRAIN, BURDEN ⟨sustained the ~ and turmoil of an active career in the deserts and marshes of Hindustan —Humphrey Bullock⟩ ⟨counted on the continued ~ of occupation costs and manpower to bring the Western Powers around —*Collier's Yr.Bk.*⟩ **4 a** (1) **:** the scent left by a fox or by other game **:** TRAIL (2) **:** an object (as a bag of aniseed) drawn over the ground to leave a scented trail for hounds to follow (3) **:** the hunting with hounds upon an artificial scent **b** (1) **:** a log or other heavy object fastened to a trap as a clog to prevent the escape of the trapped animal (2) **:** a scented bait drawn over the area adjacent to a trap to attract a desired kind of animal to the trap **5 a :** the act or an instance of dragging or drawing: as (1) **:** a drawing along or over a surface with considerable effort or pressure ⟨the ~ of chalk on blackboard slate —Lee Anderson⟩ **:** PULL, TUG ⟨the beat and ~ of the wind⟩ (2) **:** motion effected with slowness or difficulty ⟨it was a long ~ up the hill⟩; *also* **:** the condition or appearance of painful slowness or impeded movement ⟨there was a ~ in his walk⟩ ⟨no torture was comparable with the ~ of that single hour after luncheon —Osbert Sitwell⟩ (3) **:** a draw on a pipe, cigarette, or cigar **:** PUFF ⟨the professor took a long, deliberate ~ on his five-cent cigar —O.W.Butz⟩; *also* **:** a draft of liquid **:** DRINK ⟨he took a ~ from the glass —R.P. Warren⟩ **b :** a movement, inclination, or retardation caused by or as if by dragging: as (1) *Brit* **:** backspin imparted to a cue ball by striking it somewhat below the center so as to cause it perceptibly to slide along the cloth and to stop dead or nearly so on striking the object ball; *also* **:** a shot so played (2) **:** an excess of draft at the stern of a ship as compared with the bow (3) **:** a downward portamento in lute playing (4) **:** a stroke used in playing the snare drum usu. consisting of 3 or 4 grace notes preceding the beat (5) **:** a bending of rock strata adjacent to a fault (6) **:** a drooping or sagging **:** INCLINATION, HANG ⟨an habitual ~ of the lips⟩ **c** (1) **:** pull exerted by the knife that causes a sliding movement of the lower sheets in a book or pile of sheets being cut typically in the direction of travel of the knife (2) **:** the resistance of cotton fibers to being pulled apart **d** *slang* **:** influence securing special favor or partiality **:** PULL ⟨he must have lots of ~⟩ **6 :** something characterized by slow retarded motion: as **a :** a slow freight train **b** *West* (1) **:** the rear section of a herd or flock; *also* **:** a weak or footsore animal in such a herd or flock (2) **:** the men assigned to trail the drag portion of a herd ⟨it was . . . hell for swing and flank and double hell for ~ —A.B.Guthrie⟩ **c** (1) **:** a popular dance in slow rhythm originating in New Orleans; *also* **:** the music for such a dance (2) *or* **dragging step :** a dance step involving the dragging of one foot after the other **7** *slang* **:** STREET, ROAD ⟨strolling up and down this bustling ~ —J.P.O'Donnell⟩ ⟨the main ~⟩ **8** *slang* **a :** woman's dress worn by a man ⟨the first to perform were three queer boys who were completely in ~, with wigs, false eyelashes, high-heeled pumps and beautiful evening gowns —Polly Adler⟩ **b :** a homosexuals' party **9** *slang* **:** a girl that one is escorting **:** GIRL FRIEND, DATE ⟨cadets strolling down the walk with their ~*s*⟩ **10** *or* **drag race** *slang* **:** an acceleration contest between automobiles, esp. hot rods

drag 1e

²**drag** \"\ *vb* **dragged** \-gd\ *or dial* **drug** \ˈdrəg\ **dragged** *or dial* **drug; dragging; drags** [ME *draggen*, fr. ON *draga* to drag, draw, pull or OE *dragan* to drag, draw — more at DRAW] *vt* **1 a** (1) **:** to pull along by main force **:** draw slowly or heavily **:** HAUL ⟨~ stone⟩ ⟨~ a net in fishing⟩ (2) **:** to move (as oneself) with painful slowness or difficulty ⟨the tired man *dragged* himself home⟩ ⟨~ one foot after the other⟩ ⟨the negotiations *dragged* their interminable length along⟩ **b :** to force (a person or group) by nonphysical means into or out of some situation, condition, or course of action ⟨*dragged* me into a fruitless discussion⟩ ⟨*dragging* his friends down to ruin with him⟩ ⟨his infectious humor *dragged* me out of my black musings⟩ ⟨did not want his country *dragged* into a useless war⟩ **c** (1) **:** to pass (a space of time) in lingering pain, tedium, or unhappiness — used chiefly with *out* ⟨*dragged* out his remaining years in bitter loneliness⟩ (2) **:** to protract (as a narrative or musical passage) unduly or tediously — often used with *out* ⟨*dragged* out his anecdote to an intolerable length⟩ ⟨*dragged* out the florid run to impress her audience⟩ **2 a** (1) **:** to pass a drag over (as a field or dirt road) (2) **:** to explore with a drag ⟨*dragged* the river for the drowned boy⟩ (3) **:** SEARCH **:** RANSACK ⟨even when she *dragged* her mind for an excuse or even an idea, she could not unearth one —Ellen Glasgow⟩ **b :** to catch with a dragnet or trawl **3 :** to smooth and pulverize (soil) by the use of a drag or harrow **4 :** to retard by or as if by a drag ⟨the singer continually *dragged* his tempi⟩ **5** *Midland* **:** RALLY, TEASE **6 :** to dress the surface of (a stone) with a drag **7 :** to apply (pigment) by drawing a loaded brush over a tacky surface so that the pigment adheres in irregular spots allowing the ground color to appear between them **8 :** to hit (a bunt) esp. by pulling the bat back at the moment of impact and without being squared around toward the pitcher **9 :** to fly low over (an area) for the purpose of observing the surface conditions esp. if an emergency landing is to be made ~ *vi* **1 :** to hang or lag behind ⟨suddenly noticed that one of the climbers was beginning to ~⟩; *specif* **:** to lag behind in singing or playing ⟨a singing comedienne, she has an effective way of *dragging* behind the beat —*New Yorker*⟩ **2 :** to fish or search with a drag **3 a :** to trail along on the ground ⟨her silken gown *dragged* behind her⟩ **b** (1) **:** to yield or give way along the ground or along the bottom of the sea (as of an anchor that does not hold) (2) *of a ship* **:** to drag anchor **4 a :** to move onward heavily, laboriously, or slowly **:** advance with weary effort ⟨a rheumy old man, crumpled together, bent at the shoulders, feet *dragging* —Elizabeth M. Roberts⟩ **:** go on lingeringly ⟨the negotiations *dragged*, without any prospect of an early solution⟩ **:** cause tedium esp. because of length or lack of interest ⟨the last act ~*s* terribly, and is enough to kill any play —Arnold Bennett⟩ — often used with *on* or *along* ⟨the ride homeward *dragged* on indefinitely —Sherwood Anderson⟩ **b** (1) **:** to move with friction over a surface ⟨the overturned car *dragged* along the street for some distance before stopping⟩ (2) *of brakes* **:** to fail to release **5 :** to make a plucking or pulling movement **:** TUG — used chiefly with *at* ⟨he plucked his thin linen trousers and *dragged* at his collar —Rudyard Kipling⟩ **6 :** DRAW ⟨~ on a cigarette⟩ **7** *slang* **:** to race with a drag ⟨anybody's got the bug to ~ can use the strip long as they have a driver's license —J.M.Flagler⟩ **syn** see PULL — **drag anchor :** to have the anchor fail to hold on the bottom — **drag one's feet** *or* **drag one's heels :** to fail to act with the necessary promptness or vigor **:** be deliberately slow, dilatory, or ineffective in action **:** do less than required or expected ⟨at times local organizations may knife the presidential candidate or at least *drag their feet* in the campaign —V.O.Key⟩

dra·gade \drəˈgäd\ *vt* -ED/-ING/-S [origin unknown] **:** to break up (glass) by pouring while melted into water

drag anchor *n* **:** DRAG 3a (1)

dragbar \ˈ=ˌ=\ *n* [¹*drag* + *bar*] **1 :** a hinged or pivoted bar or yoke attached to the back of a mine car on inclines to prevent its backing if the cable breaks — called also *drag* **2** *Brit* **:** DRAWBAR 2a

dragboat \ˈ=ˌ=\ *n* **:** DRAGGER

dragbolt \ˈ=ˌ=\ *n* **:** COUPLER 1a

drag bunt *n* **:** a slow bunt made by pulling the bat back at the moment of impact and without being squared around toward the pitcher

drag cart *n* **:** BUMMER 3

drag chain *n* **:** a chain that drags: as **a :** a chain for coupling freight cars **b :** a metal conveyor belt for removing the clinker from a cement kiln **c :** a chain that is attached to the chassis of a motor vehicle (as a gasoline tank truck) and drags on the roadway to ground the chassis and prevent accumulation of static electricity

drag chute *n* **:** DRAG PARACHUTE

drag coefficient *n* **:** a factor representing the ratio of the aerodynamic drag acting esp. on an airfoil to the product of the airspeed and the area of the airfoil

drag conveyor *n* **:** a conveyor consisting of wooden or steel plates attached to endless chains and running in a trough through which the material is dragged

drag down *vt* **1** *slang* **:** to earn as a wage or salary **:** bring in (a certain sum of money) ⟨two hundred dollars . . . means a lot when you're just *dragging down* an ensign's pay —Land Kaderli⟩ ⟨the super show . . . *dragged down* good money and continued to do so —F.B.Gipson⟩ **2 :** to remove part of (one's craps winnings) and leave the rest as one's next bet

dra·gée \(ˈ)draˈzhā\ *n* -s [F, fr. MF *dragie*, prob. fr. L *tragemata* sweetmeats, fruits eaten as dessert, fr. Gk *tragēmata*, fr. *trōgein* to gnaw, eat fruits; akin to OE *thurh* through — more at THROUGH] **1 a :** a sweetmeat in the form of a sugar-coated nut **b :** a small round usu. silvered confection often used for decorating cakes **2 :** a sugar-coated medicated confection

drag fold *n* **:** a minor geological fold produced in soft or thinly laminated beds lying between harder or more massive beds in the limbs of a major fold

dragged *past of* DRAG

drag·ger \ˈdragə(r), -raag-,-raig-\ *n* -s **:** one that drags; *specif* **:** a fishing boat operating a trawl or dragnet

dragger-down \ˈ=ˌ=ˈ=\ *n, pl* **draggers-down :** one who draws heated billets from furnaces

drag·ger·man \-mən\ *n, pl* **draggermen :** one that operates or works on a dragger

dragger net *n* **:** DRAGNET 1a

dragger-out \ˈ=ˌ=ˈ=\ *n, pl* **draggers-out :** one that drags out; *specif* **:** a worker who withdraws bars from a roughing furnace

dragging *adj* [fr. pres. part. of ²*drag*] **1 :** used in dragging, hauling, or dredging ⟨searched the bottom of the lake with a ~ rope⟩ **2 :** marked by a painfully slow, tired, or sluggish manner (as of movement or speech) ⟨it was a strange ~ approach, half a walk and half a slide —J.P.Marquand⟩ ⟨a soft and ~ voice —Carson McCullers⟩ **:** painfully or tediously protracted **:** LINGERING ⟨two years of ~, ruinous war and military control —Giorgio de Santillana⟩ **:** TEDIOUS ⟨do not . . . prevent the play from being a ~ riddle —Marya Mannes⟩ — **drag·ging·ly** *adv*

dragging beam *or* **dragging piece** *or* **dragging tie** *n* **:** DRAGON BEAM

dragging step *n* **:** DRAG 6c(2)

drag·gle \ˈdragəl, -raig-\ *vb* **draggled; draggled; draggling** \-g(ə)liŋ\ **draggles** [²*drag* + *-le*] *vt* **:** to make thoroughly wet **:** make limp and sodden by wetting **:** drag or trail (as through dirt or mire) **:** DRABBLE, BESMIRCH ⟨a bough of brier rose whose pale blossoms sweet were *draggled* in the dust —William Morris⟩ ~ *vi* **1 :** to trail on the ground **:** become wet or dirty by being dragged or trailed ⟨her long gown *draggling* on the ground⟩ **2 :** to straggle in the rear **:** trail along with a slovenly or dragging gait **:** SHUFFLE ⟨the girl ~*s* about in sneakers and a short cotton frock —Frank Swinnerton⟩ ⟨most of the actors ~ through their paces —*Time*⟩

draggled *adj* **1 :** thoroughly wet and limp **:** SOAKED, SODDEN ⟨the ~ ends of her hair⟩ ⟨gave him that bright-hued shirt she wore, sadly ~ and muddy now —B.A.Williams⟩ **2 :** soiled esp. by dragging through mud or dirt ⟨scarecrows in battered hats or ~ skirts —Israel Zangwill⟩ ⟨dresses . . . yet gorgeous in color . . . but ~, torn, and untidy —Osbert Sitwell⟩ ⟨grimy, haggard men and a few ~ women —Kenneth Roberts⟩ **:** DIRTY, UNKEMPT, UNTIDY

draggle-tail \ˈ=ˌ=ˌ=\ *n* **1 :** a woman who lets her skirt trail along the ground **2 :** SLATTERN

draggletailed \ˈ=ˌ=ˈ=\ *adj* **:** UNTIDY, SLUTTISH, SLATTERNLY — **drag·gle·tailed·ness** \ˈ=ˌ=ˈtālə̇dnə̇s, -l(d)n-\ *n* -ES

drag·gly \ˈdrag(ə)lē, -raig-\ *adj* -ER/-EST **:** DRAGGLED, UNTIDY ⟨wagging her old ~ tail —P.E.Green⟩

drag·gy \ˈdragē, -raag-,-raig-\ *adj* -ER/-EST **:** inclined to drag **:** SLUGGISH, DULL ⟨a bleak, ~ little picture —*Time*⟩ ⟨~ sales are attributed to a . . . psychology of caution —*Nation's Business*⟩

draghound \ˈ=ˌ=\ *n* **:** a hound trained to follow a scent made with a drag

drag hunt *or* **drag hunting :** DRAG 4a(3)

drag in *vt* **:** to bring in or inject esp. into an argument irrelevantly or inappropriately ⟨the speaker's references to his political opponent were only *dragged in* out of spite⟩ ⟨a ballet that, for once, isn't *dragged in*, that is a perfectly legitimate part of the scene —Deems Taylor⟩

drag iron *n* **:** an attachment for the bottom of a lister to steady the implement and keep a uniform depth

dragline \ˈ=ˌ=\ *n* **1 :** a line used in or for dragging **2 :** an excavating machine in which the bucket is attached only by cables and is drawn toward the machine during the filling operation — compare BACKHOE **3 :** a glacial stria formed on the lee side of older grooves

drag link *n* **1 :** a link joining the cranks of two shafts **2 :** a rod connecting the steering-gear lever to the steering knuckle in automotive vehicles

drag·man \ˈdragmən, -raag-,-raig-\ *n, pl* **dragmen :** a man who drags something: as **a :** a fisherman who uses a dragnet **b :** the man who trails the drag in hunting **c :** one who operates a drag conveyor to load metal ore into cars or chutes **d :** an operator of a system of drag chains that convey cement clinker from burning kiln to storage pile

dragnet \ˈ=ˌ=\ *n* **1 a :** a net that is specially designed to be drawn along the bottom of a body of water **:** TRAWL **b :** a similar net used on the ground (as to capture small game) **2 a :** a device for gathering objects usu. of a certain kind in the mass ⟨do not send out wholesale ~*s* to collect opinions and data —A.T.Weaver⟩ **b :** a network of measures for apprehension (as of criminals) ⟨suspects caught in the police ~⟩

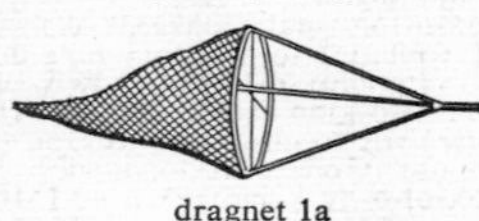
dragnet 1a

dragnet clause *n* **:** a clause in a tariff law that imposes a certain rate of duty on articles not enumerated as free from duty or as subject to any other duty

dra·go \ˈdrä(ˌ)gō\ *n* -s [MexSp, fr. Sp, dragon tree, fr. L *draco* dragon, serpent — more at DRAGON] **:** a Mexican tree (*Pterocarpus acapulcensis*) with large yellow flowers and a red juice that forms a resin similar to kino

drag·o·man \ˈdragəmən, -raig-\ *n, pl* **dragomans** \-mənz\ *or* **drago·men** \-mən\ [ME *drogman*, fr. MF *drogman, droguement, dragoman*, fr. OIt *dragomanno*, fr. MGk *dragomanos*, fr. Ar *tarjumān*, fr. Aram *tūrgĕmānā*] **:** an interpreter chiefly of Arabic, Turkish, or Persian employed as official interpreter by an embassy or consulate or as a guide by tourists

drag·on \ˈdragən, -raig-\ *n* -s [ME *dragun, dragoun*, fr. OF *dragon, dragon*, fr. L *dracon-, draco* serpent, dragon, fr. Gk *drakōn* serpent; akin to OE *torht* bright, splendid, noble, OHG *zoraht* bright, clear, Goth *gatarhjan* to mark, Gk *derkesthai* to see clearly, look at, *drakos* eye, MIr *derc* eye, Skt *darśayati* he causes to see; basic meaning: seeing] **1** *archaic* **:** a huge serpent **2 :** a fabulous animal generally represented as a monstrous winged and scaly serpent or saurian with a crested head and enormous claws **3 a :** the heraldic representation of a monster with a griffin's head, a scaly winged body with four legs and claws, and a long barbed tail and tongue borne as a charge or used as a supporter **b** *dial Brit* **:** a paper kite of dragon form **c :** a beneficent supernatural creature in Chinese mythology connected with rain and floods **4 :** a violent, combative, or very strict person; *esp* **:** a woman that watches fiercely and vigilantly over the welfare of her charges ⟨jealous and touchy, but a very faithful old ~ with the family —Ngaio Marsh⟩ **5 :** any of several arums popularly associated with dragons: as **a :** GREEN DRAGON **b :** JACK-IN-THE-PULPIT 1 **c :** WATER ARUM **d :** a plant of the genus *Dracontium* **6 a :** a short musket formerly carried hooked to a soldier's belt; *also* **:** a soldier carrying such a musket **b :** an armored tractor for artillery **7** [trans. of NL *Draco*] **a :** any of numerous small brilliantly colored arboreal agamid lizards (genus *Draco*) of the East Indies and southern Asia having five or six of the hind ribs on each side prolonged and covered with a web of skin forming a sort of wing and aiding them in making long gliding leaps from tree to tree — called also *flying dragon* **b :** any of certain other lizards of related genera: as (1) **:** JEW LIZARD (2) **:** WATER DRAGON 1

dragon 3a

dragon arum *n* **1 :** a plant of the genus *Arisaema* **2** *Brit* **:** GREEN DRAGON 1
dragon beam *or* **dragon piece** *n* **:** a beam in a hip roof that runs horizontally into the angle of the wall plate and is framed to the hip rafter above — called also *dragon tie*
dragon boat festival *n, usu cap D&B&F* **:** a Chinese festival held just before the summer solstice that has as its chief event a race among long narrow boats resembling dragons
dragon–bushes \ˈ=,==\ *n pl but sing or pl in constr, dial Eng* **:** a toadflax (*Linaria vulgaris*)
drag·on·et \ˈ=,=ˈet, ˈ== ət\ *n* -s [ME, fr. *dragon, dragoun* dragon + *-et*] **1 :** a little dragon **2** [trans. of NL *dracunculus*] **:** any of various small often brightly colored scaleless marine fishes having flattened heads, sharp spines on the gill covers, and marked sexual dimorphism, constituting the family Callionymidae, and including a well-known European fish (*Callionymus lyra*) sometimes used as food
dragonfish \ˈ==,=\ *n* **1 :** DRAGONET **2 :** a fish of the genus *Pegasus* **3 :** any of various elongated black deep-sea stomiatoid fishes constituting *Idiacanthus* and related genera, having luminous organs of the cheeks and in rows along the sides, and exhibiting strong sexual dimorphism with the males neotenic and greatly reduced in size
dragonfly \ˈ==,=\ *n* **1 :** any of numerous large predaceous insects constituting the order Odonata, having a large freely movable head with enormous compound eyes, minute antennae, long slender abdomen, four long narrow finely net-veined wings, strong jaws, and legs adapted for grasping their prey, being entirely harmless and among the most useful of insects, the adults feeding on insects which they capture on the wing and destroying vast numbers of flies, gnats, and mosquitoes, and the aquatic predaceous nymphs destroying mosquito larvae — compare DAMSELFLY **2 :** a strong greenish blue that is bluer and duller than grotto and greener and duller than cobalt blue

dragonfly

dragonhead *or* **dragon's–head** \ˈ==,=\ *n, pl* **dragonheads** *or* **dragon's–heads** [trans. of NL *Dracocephalum*] **:** a mint of the genus *Dracocephalum; esp* **:** a No. American plant (*D. parviflorum*)
drag·on·ish \ˈ==ish\ *adj* **:** being or resembling a dragon in character or temper ⟨it needs . . . ~ duennas to inflame desire to passion —Aldous Huxley⟩
dragon lizard *n* **:** an Indonesian monitor lizard (*Varanus komodoensis*) that is the largest of all known lizards and reaches 11 feet in length
dragon plant *n* **:** a tree or other plant of the genus *Dracaena*
dragonroot \ˈ==,=\ *n* **:** a jack-in-the-pulpit or green dragon
dragons *pl of* DRAGON
dragon's blood *n* **1 :** any of several resinous mostly dark red substances derived from various trees; *specif* **:** the resin from the fruit of several palms of the genus *Daemonorops* (esp. *D. draco*) that yields the true dragon's blood of commerce which is used for coloring varnish and in photoengraving for preventing undercutting of the printing surface during etching **2 :** the thickened juice of the dragon tree of the Canary islands or a related tree of Socotra **3 :** a synthetic powder used in photoengraving similarly to true dragon's blood **4** *or* **dragon's–blood red :** POMPEIAN RED
dragon's–claw *also* **dragon claw** \ˈ==,=\ *n, pl* **dragon's–claws** *also* **dragon claws :** either of two coralroots (*Corallorhiza odontorhiza* or *C. maculata*)
dragon's–mouth \ˈ==,=\ *n, pl* **dragon's–mouths 1 :** SNAPDRAGON 1a **2 :** an orchid (*Arethusa bulbosa*) with a wide-gaping corolla
dragon's teeth *n pl* **1** [so called fr. the story in Greek mythology that Cadmus, the founder of Thebes in Boeotia, sowed the teeth of a dragon that sprang into armed men who fought each other until only five survived] **:** seeds of mutual strife **2 :** wedge-shaped concrete antitank obstacles laid in multiple rows
dragon's–tongue \ˈ==,=\ *n, pl* **dragon's–tongues :** SPOTTED WINTERGREEN
dragon tie *n* **:** DRAGON BEAM
dragon tree *n* **:** a tree of the Canary islands (*Dracaena draco*) notable for reaching great age
dragon worm *n* **:** GUINEA WORM
¹dra·goon \drəˈgün, draˈ-,draiˈ-\ *n* -s [F *dragon* dragon, military standard, dragoon, fr. MF — more at DRAGON] **1 a :** a mounted infantryman of the 17th and 18th centuries; *esp* **:** one armed with a carbine **b :** CAVALRYMAN **2** *obs* **:** an ancient carbine **:** DRAGON **3 :** a variety of medium-sized blocky wattled domestic pigeons
²dragoon \"\ *vt* -ED/-ING/-S **1 :** to reduce to subjection by dragoons **:** persecute by the harsh use of troops **2 :** to compel or attempt to compel into submission by violent measures **:** HARASS, PERSECUTE ⟨they ~*ed* him into working⟩
dragoon bird *n* [so called fr. its crest that suggests the headdress of a dragoon] **:** a brightly colored Australian pitta (*Pitta versicolor*) that feeds on snails — called also *noisy pitta*
dragooner *n* -s [prob. fr. G *dragoner*, fr. F *dragon* — more at DRAGOON] *obs* **:** DRAGOON 1a
dragos *pl of* DRAGO
drag parachute *n* **:** a parachute released from the rear of an airplane to help slow it down during the ground run in landing
drag race *n* **:** DRAG 10
drag rake *n* **1 :** a heavy rake used for harvesting **2 :** a rake with curved teeth used for digging clams
dragrope \ˈ=,=\ *n* **:** a rope with which something is dragged or that drags from a thing: as **a :** a rope with a short chain and a hook that is attached to an artillery carriage and used in emergencies in dragging it or locking its wheels **b :** a rope dropped from an aerostat for use as a variable ballast, as a brake, or as a mooring line
drags *pl of* DRAG, *pres 3d sing of* DRAG
drag sail *or* **drag sheet** *n* **:** a sea anchor made from a sail or piece of canvas
dragsaw \ˈ=,=\ *n* **:** a saw with teeth that are slanted so as to cut on the pulling stroke; *specif.* **:** a large power-operated saw for sawing felled trees
drag scraper *n* **1 :** an earth-digging and transporting device consisting of a crescent-shaped bottomless bucket operated along the ground by a cable between a mast and an anchor **2 :** a bottomless tractor-towed earth scraper
drag seine *n* **:** BEACH SEINE
dragshoe \ˈ=,=\ *n* **:** DRAG 3a(2)
dragshovel \ˈ=,==\ *n* **:** BACKHOE
drags·man \ˈdragzmən, -raag-,-raig-\ *n, pl* **dragsmen** [*drags* (gen. of ¹*drag*) + *man*] **:** a driver of a drag; *also* **:** one who works with a drag
dragstaff \ˈ=,=\ *n* **:** a trailing pole pivoted on the rear of a vehicle to check any backward movement
drag·ster \-gztə(r), -gst-\ *n* -s [¹*drag* + road*ster*] **:** an automobile rebuilt or stripped down esp. for use in a drag race **:** HOT ROD
drag–stone mill *n* **:** a mill in which ores are ground by means of a heavy stone dragged around on a circular or annular stone bed
drag strip *n* **:** the site of a drag race
drag strut *n* **:** a fore-and-aft compression member of the internal bracing system of an airplane
drag through *vt* **:** to test the fit of (a probable word, a segment of key, or another message) everywhere throughout a cipher-text
drag tooth *n* **:** RAKER 1f
drag truss *n* **:** a horizontal truss between the wing spars for stiffening the structure and resisting the drag forces acting on the wing of an airplane
drag wire *n* **:** a member of a truss in the wing and also in the wing support of an airplane for sustaining the backward reaction due to the drag of the wing
draht·haar \ˈdrätˌhär\ *n* -s [G, lit., wire hair, fr. *draht* wire (fr. OHG *drāt* thread) + *haar* hair (fr. OHG *hār*) — more at THREAD, HAIR] **:** a dog of a German breed of wire-haired pointers

drai·gle \ˈdrāgəl\ *Scot var of* DRAGGLE
drai·gon \ˈdrāgən\ *Scot var of* DRAGON
¹drail \ˈdrāl, *esp before pause or consonant* -āəl\ *n* -s [fr. obs. E *drail* to drag or trail along, perh. alter. (influenced by *draw & drag*) of *trail*] **1 :** a hook with a lead-covered shank used in trolling for fish (as bluefish) **2 :** a perforated iron projecting from the beam of a plow to which the horses are hitched
²drail \"\ *vb* -ED/-ING/-S **:** to fish by trolling with a drail
¹drain \ˈdrān\ *vb* -ED/-ING/-S [ME *draynen*, fr. OE *drēahnian, drēhnian;* perh. akin to ON *drangr* dry log, Fris *drūgen* to strain, OE *drȳge* dry — more at DRY] *vt* **1** *obs* **:** to pass (liquid) through some permeable substance **:** FILTER **2 a :** to draw off (liquid) by degrees **:** cause to flow gradually out or off **:** draw off completely (as by means of a drain or trench) ⟨~ the water from a tank⟩ ⟨waterspouts to ~ off the rain⟩ **b** (1) **:** to cause the gradual disappearance or extinction of ⟨fright had ~*ed* all color from his face⟩ ⟨the urge to conform was slowly ~*ing* the boy's individuality⟩ **:** EXHAUST ⟨war had ~*ed* the country's treasure and best manhood⟩ (2) **:** VENT, DISCHARGE ⟨~ an undesirable emotion⟩ ⟨enabling the patient to ~ his deeply repressed anxieties⟩ (3) **:** to exhaust physically or emotionally ⟨~*ed* as he was by his session . . . , he did not feel up to it —Hamilton Basso⟩ ⟨matinee days are tough; two shows a day ~ a girl —Ethel Merman⟩ **3 a :** to exhaust of liquid contents by drawing them off **:** make gradually dry or empty ⟨~ a flooded mine⟩ ⟨~ a marsh⟩ **:** receive or carry away the surface water or discharge of ⟨~*ing* mountains of everlasting snow, the river twists for nineteen hundred miles —J.F.Dobie⟩ ⟨this lake ~*s* the numerous small streams of the area⟩ **b** (1) **:** EMPTY ⟨~ of wealth or resources⟩ ⟨~*ed* the country of its gold⟩ (2) **:** to drink (a liquid) to the last drops ⟨took the drink out of the drawer and ~*ed* it —Barnaby Conrad⟩ **:** empty (a glass or other container) by drinking ⟨allow you a respectable interlude in which to ~ your glass —Richard Joseph⟩ **~** *vi* **1 a :** to flow off gradually ⟨blood ~*ing* from a wound⟩ **b :** to disappear gradually **:** DWINDLE — often used with *away* ⟨his nervousness ~*ed* away, as it always did —H.A.Sinclair⟩ ⟨all his wealth had ~*ed* away⟩ **2 :** to become emptied or freed of liquid by its flowing or dropping ⟨put the umbrella on the porch to ~⟩ **3 :** to discharge surface or surplus water or streams in a given direction or to an outlet ⟨the middle western states ~ into the Gulf of Mexico⟩ **syn** see DEPLETE
²drain \"\ *n* -s *often attrib* **1 a :** an artificial channel by means of which liquid or other matter is drained or carried off **:** SEWER, SINK, TRENCH **b :** a watercourse esp. when narrow **2 a :** the act of draining or drawing off liquid **:** gradual outflow or withdrawal ⟨~ from a wound⟩ ⟨~ from a leaky faucet⟩ **b** (1) **:** a gradual outflow or withdrawal of something nonliquid **:** depletion or the amount of such depletion ⟨a ruinous ~ of dollars⟩ ⟨a net ~ from the East of five million souls —G.W.Pierson⟩ (2) **:** something that causes depletions (as of resources) **:** BURDEN, STRAIN ⟨indebtedness is apt to be one of the great ~*s* upon the income of peasant families —*Notes & Queries on Anthropology*⟩ ⟨the medical and social care of old people . . . constitutes a heavy ~ on the economic resources of society —M.A.Abrams⟩ ⟨the office worker emerged as a major ~ on business profits —Gabriel Kolko⟩ **3 drains** *pl* **a :** DREGS ⟨as though . . . I had emptied some dull opiate to the ~*s* —John Keats⟩ **b** *brewing, Brit* **:** the grain from the mash tun **4 a :** the liquid or other matter that is drained off or away ⟨the ~ had collected at the foot of the spout, forming a small pool⟩ **b :** a small remaining amount of liquid ⟨they still had a tiny ~ of petrol for the works car for station trips —Nevil Shute⟩ **c :** a drink esp. of some alcoholic beverage ⟨she thought a ~ of gin and peppermint . . . would do most good —William Heath⟩ ⟨his cigar going and a ~ of brandy . . . before him —A.J.Cronin⟩ **5 :** a tube or a cylinder usu. of absorbent material for drainage of a wound — compare CIGARETTE DRAIN
drain·age \-nij,-nēj\ *n* -s **1 a :** the act or an instance of draining ⟨by this ~ of colonial wealth the empire financed its costly wars⟩ ⟨~ of the marshy lands was completed in a short time⟩ **b :** DRAINING **:** a gradual flowing off or dropping down ⟨complained of ~ of rain water into the cellar⟩ ⟨gold ~ and gold hoarding . . . were feared —F.L.Paxson⟩; *also* **:** something that is drained off ⟨this lake receives the ~ of many mountain streams⟩ **c** *chiefly Brit* **:** SEWAGE; *also* **:** the sewage system of a building **2 :** the manner in which the waters of a country pass off (as by streams and rivers) ⟨subsurface ~⟩ **3 a :** the removal of excess water from land by means of surface or subsurface conduits; *also* **:** a system of such conduits **b :** AERIAL DRAINAGE **4 a :** area or district drained (as by a river) **b** *or* **drainage system :** the streams or other waterways by which a region is drained **5 :** the act, process, or means of drawing off fluids from a cavity or wound by means of suction or gravity **6 :** a process or means of release of internal conflicts or pent-up feelings (as hostility or guilt)
drainage basin *n* **:** BASIN 2d
drainage district *n* **:** a governmental corporation or quasi corporation created by a state for the drainage of a specified territory
drainage line *n* **:** the course of a major stream in a drainage system
drainageway \ˈ==,=\ *n* **:** a route or course along which water moves or may move to drain a region
drainboard \ˈ=,=\ *n* **:** a sloping shelf beside and draining into a sink
drained *adj* [fr. past part. of ¹*drain*] **1 :** emptied or freed of excess water or other liquid; *also* **:** drawn off (as by pouring or flowing) ⟨a ~ marsh⟩ **2 :** exhausted physically or emotionally **:** emptied of emotion **:** DULL ⟨leaving him ~ and apathetic, an old man . . . not caring any longer about anything —Angus Mowat⟩
drain·er \-nə(r)\ *n* -s **:** one that drains: as **a :** a worker who tends to the filling and emptying of vats of bleached wood pulp **b :** a kitchen device used in draining ⟨a wire mesh ~ for vegetables⟩ **c :** DRAINING VAT

dish drainer

drain·er·man \-mən\ *n, pl* **drainermen :** a worker who attends to draining vats in papermaking
draining *pres part of* DRAIN
draining board *n, Brit* **:** DRAINBOARD
draining vat *n* **:** a tank with a porous bottom through which water may drain that is used in papermaking
drain·less \ˈdrānləs\ *adj* **1 :** impossible to drain **:** INEXHAUSTIBLE ⟨a ~ fund of energy⟩ **2 :** not provided with drains ⟨tumbledown ~ hovels⟩
drainpipe \ˈ=,=\ *n* **:** a pipe for drainage; *esp* **:** DOWNSPOUT
drainpipe trousers *n pl* **:** tight-fitting trousers that taper to the ankles
drains *pres 3d sing of* DRAIN, *pl of* DRAIN
drai·sine \drāˈzēn, drāˈzēnə, drīˈzēnə\ *n* -s [F & G; F *draisine, draisienne*, fr. G *draisine*, fr. Baron Karl von *Drais* †1851 Ger. forester, its inventor + G *-ine* (as in *maschine* machine)] **:** DANDY HORSE
¹drake \ˈdrāk\ *n* -s [ME, fr. OE *draca;* akin to OHG *trahho* dragon, MLG & MD *drake*, ON *dreki;* all fr. a prehistoric WGmc-NGmc word borrowed fr. L *draco* dragon, serpent — more at DRAGON] **1** *archaic* **:** DRAGON **2 :** a small piece of artillery of the 17th and 18th centuries **3** [by shortening] **:** DRAKE FLY
²drake \"\ *n* -s [ME; akin to G dial. *drache, trech* drake, OHG an*trahho*, anu*trehho*, LG *drake*] **1 :** the male of a wild or domestic duck **2 a :** the flat stone used in the game of duck on a rock **b :** DRAKESTONE **3** *or* **drake green :** a dark greenish blue that is bluer and stronger than average teal, bluer, lighter, and stronger than average teal blue, and greener, lighter, and stronger than teal duck — called also *drake's-neck green*
drake fly *n* [ME *drake flye*, fr. ¹*drake* + *flye* fly — more at FLY] **:** MAYFLY
drake foot *n* [²*drake*] **:** a furniture foot carved with three lobes so as to suggest the contracted toes of a male duck — compare DUTCH FOOT; see FOOT illustration

drake·let \-lət\ *also* **drake·ling** \-liŋ\ *n* -s [²*drake* + *-let, -ling*] **:** a young drake
drake's–neck green *n* **:** ²DRAKE 3
drakestone \ˈ=,=\ *n* [²*drake* + *stone*] **:** a flat stone used for skipping in the game of ducks and drakes
¹dram \ˈdram, -aa(ə)m\ *n* -s [ME *drame, dragme*, fr. MF & LL; MF *drame, dragme* dram, drachma, fr. LL *dragma*, fr. L *drachma*, fr. Gk *drachmē*, lit., handful, fr. *drassesthai* to grasp — more at TARGET] **1 a :** either of two units of weight: (1) **:** an avoirdupois unit equal to 27.343 grains (2) **:** an apothecaries' unit equal to 60 grains — see MEASURE table **b :** FLUIDRAM **2 a :** a small portion of something to drink (as of distilled alcoholic liquor) ⟨a ~ of brandy⟩ **b :** a small amount **:** MITE ⟨a ~ of well-doing —John Milton⟩
²dram \"\ *vb* **drammed; drammed; dramming; drams** *vi, archaic* **:** to drink liquor **:** TIPPLE **~** *vt, archaic* **:** to give a drink of liquor to
dra·ma \ˈdrämə, -amə,-àmə\ *n* -s [LL, fr. Gk, deed, action on the stage, drama, fr. *dran* to do, act; akin to Gk *drainein* to be ready to do and prob. to Lith *daryti* to do, make, Latvian *darīt*] **1 :** a composition in verse or prose arranged for enactment (as by actors on a stage) and intended to portray life or character or to tell a story through the actions and usu. dialogue of the enactors **:** PLAY **2 :** dramatic art, literature, or affairs ⟨a person skilled in ~⟩ ⟨a devotee of the ~⟩ ⟨the highlights of English ~⟩ **3 a :** a condition, situation, or series of events involving interesting or intense conflict of forces suggesting that characteristic of a play ⟨whatever happens in the ~ of today, the future lies with freedom —J.T. Shotwell⟩ ⟨between fantasy and exact knowledge, between ~ and technology, there is an intermediate station: that of magic —Lewis Mumford⟩ **b :** dramatic state, effect, or quality ⟨the ~ of New York's skyline⟩ ⟨why not use candles sometimes for a bit of ~ at the family table⟩
dramage *var of* DRAMMAGE
dra·ma·logue \-,lȯg *also* -,läg\ *n* -s [*drama* + *-logue*] **:** a reading of a play to an audience
Dram·a·mine \ˈdramə,mēn\ *trademark* — used for dimenhydrinate
¹dra·mat·ic \drəˈmad·ik, -at|, |ēk\ *adj* [MF & LL; MF *dramatique*, fr. LL *dramaticus*, fr. Gk *dramatikos*, fr. *dramat-, drama* deed, drama + *-ikos* -ic — more at DRAMA] **1 a :** of or relating to or for the drama ⟨exquisitely staged ~ performances⟩ ⟨something is achieved by way of drama which we of the ~ stage could never attempt —*New Republic*⟩ **b :** of, relating to, devoted to, or concerned specifically or professionally with current drama or the contemporary theater ⟨a ~ critic⟩ ⟨one of the outstanding ~ events of the current theatrical season⟩ **2 a :** suitable to or characteristic of the drama esp. in being expressed with or as if with action ⟨a highly ~ appeal⟩ ⟨his ~ attempt to escape⟩ **b :** striking in appearance or effect ⟨continued after a ~ pause⟩ ⟨there could be no more ~ reminder of this fact than the contrast between the subsequent career of Sir Winston Churchill and his school record —F.C.James⟩ ⟨~ floral prints were popular⟩ **3** *of a singing voice* **:** having expressive power and a ringing quality and capable of a declamatory or theatrical style ⟨a ~ soprano⟩ ⟨a ~ tenor⟩ — compare LYRIC
²dramatic *n* -s *obs* **:** DRAMATIST
dra·mat·i·cal \drəˈmad·əkəl, -at|, |ēk-\ *adj, archaic* **:** DRAMATIC 1
dra·mat·i·cal·ly \-k(ə)lē, -li\ *adv* **:** in a dramatic manner **:** so as to have striking effect **:** VIVIDLY
dramatic irony *n* **:** irony produced by incongruity between a situation developed in a drama and accompanying or preceding words or actions whose inappropriateness it reveals
dra·mat·i·cism \|ə,sizəm\ *n* -s **:** dramatic character
dramatic monologue *n* **:** a literary work (as a poem) in which the character of a protagonist is vividly revealed in a monologue addressed to another person or a group of persons usu. with interplay of speaker and audience
dra·mat·i·co-musical \drəˈmad·|ə(,)kō, -at|, |ē(,)kō+\ *adj* [¹*dramatic* + *-o-* + *musical*] **:** consisting of drama and music ⟨*dramatico-musical* works⟩
dramatic overture *n* **:** the orchestral prelude to or as if to an opera
dramatic present *n* **:** HISTORICAL PRESENT
dramatic reading *n* **:** a public reading or recitation of a work of literature (as a poem or play) with an interpretative or dramatic use of the voice and often of gestures
dra·mat·ics \drəˈmad·iks, -at|, |ēks\ *n pl but sing or pl in constr* **1** *obs* **:** dramatic writings **2 a :** theatricals esp. as an extracurricular activity in school or college — usu. construed as pl. **b :** theatrical technique ⟨studied ~ under one of the best coaches in New York⟩ **3 :** dramatic behavior or expression ⟨I hoped she would go without any ~ —Hartley Howard⟩ ⟨a flair for ~ in his painting⟩
dra·mat·i·cule \|ə,kyül\ *n* -s [LL *dramat-; drama* drama + E *-i-* + *-cule* (fr. L *-culus*, dim. suffix)] **:** a little or insignificant drama
dramatic unities *n pl* **:** the unities of time, place, and action observed in classical drama
dram·a·tism \ˈdramə,tizəm, -räm-,-ram-\ *n* -s [LL *dramat-, drama* + E *-ism* — more at DRAMA] **1 :** dramatic manner or form (as of speech or writing) **2 :** a technique of analysis of language and thought as basically modes of action rather than as means of conveying information
dra·ma·tis per·so·nae \ˌdramədəspərˈsō(,)nē, -äm-, -,nī, ÷ drəˈmad·-\ *n pl* [NL, lit., people of a drama] **1 a :** the characters or actors in a drama or in a novel or poem **b :** a descriptive list of the characters in a drama; *esp* **:** one printed at the beginning of the text of a drama **2 :** the participants in an actual event or series of events
dram·a·tist \ˈdramədəst, -äm-,-ám-, -mətə-\ *n* -s [LL *dramat-, drama* + E *-ist*] **1 :** PLAYWRIGHT **2 :** one that dramatizes ⟨a man of moods . . . both a poet and a ~ of his instrument who gave to everything he played . . . a unique coloring —Duncan MacDougald⟩
dram·a·tis·tic \ˌ==ˈtistik\ *adj* **:** of, relating to, or by the methods of dramatism ⟨a ~ analysis of the poem⟩ — **dram·a·tis·ti·cal·ly** \-stək(ə)lē\ *adv*
dram·a·ti·za·tion \ˌdramədəˈzāshən, -ətəˈz-, -ə,tīˈz- *also* -äm- *or* -àm-\ *n* -s **1 :** an act, process, or product of dramatizing ⟨the ~ of ideas⟩ ⟨his conscious ~ of his troubles⟩ ⟨a ~ of a problem⟩; *esp* **:** a dramatized version (as of a novel) **2 :** the transformation which in psychoanalytic theory the underlying dream thoughts undergo into dramatic and pictorial form before they can take part in the actual dream
dram·a·tize \ˈ=mə,tīz\ *vb* -ED/-ING/-S *see -ize in Explan Notes* [LL *dramat-, drama* drama, play + E *-ize* — more at DRAMA] *vt* **1 a :** to rewrite (as a novel) or adapt (as an incident or account) for theatrical presentation ⟨several of his short stories were later *dramatized*⟩ ⟨one of the shows for which he *dramatized* episodes of colonial history⟩ **b :** to act out (material usu. read or presented in writing) ⟨*dramatizing* commercials on television⟩ **2 a :** to recount in a dramatic manner ⟨she often seems to be *dramatizing* her material according to the methods of painting rather than those of literature —*New Republic*⟩ ⟨a long epic that ~*s* the gradual dissolution of a family⟩ **b :** to present or represent in a dramatic manner: as (1) **:** to make a dramatic scene of ⟨she never fails to ~ her entries and exits⟩ (2) **:** to display (oneself or one's problems or motives) to advantage as if playing a part on a stage ⟨he lost votes because of his inability to ~ himself to his constituents⟩; *often* **:** to display outwardly and often flauntingly one's own conception of (oneself or one's virtues) ⟨compensating for lack of real ability by consciously *dramatizing* her appearance⟩ (3) **:** to exhibit graphically in such a manner as to show forth qualities, attributes, or aspects likely to be overlooked ⟨wartime shortages *dramatized* the importance of foreign trade⟩ ⟨the new vaccine ~*s* the need for continued medical research⟩ (4) **:** to make (as an article of apparel) strikingly attractive esp. by careful attention to detail ⟨a brocade wrap *dramatized* by huge sleeves⟩ **~** *vi* **1 :** to be suitable for dramatization ⟨the story would ~ well⟩ **2 :** to dramatize oneself **:** put on an act
dram·a·tiz·er \-zə(r)\ *n* -s **:** one that dramatizes
dram·a·turge \ˈdramə,tərj, -äm-,-ám-\ *n* -s [G *dramaturg* & F *dramaturge*, fr. Gk *dramatourgos* dramatist, fr. *dramat-, drama* deed, drama + *-ourgos* (fr. *ergon* work) — more at

DRAMA, WORK] **:** a person skilled in the writing or revision of plays; *also* **:** a functionary of certain European theaters who is responsible esp. for selecting and arranging the repertoire and often cooperates with and advises the producer in the course of rehearsal

dram·a·tur·gic \ˌ=ˌ=ˈtərjik\ *or* **dram·a·tur·gi·cal** \-jəkəl\ *adj* **1 :** relating to dramaturgy, esp. to the technical aspects of play construction ⟨~ theory⟩ ⟨modification of ~ techniques to the peculiar needs of the motion picture⟩ **2 :** DRAMATIC, THEATRICAL ⟨the ~ heights attained by some of the older Shakespearean actors⟩

dram·a·tur·gy \ˈ=ˌ=ˌjē\ *n* -ES [G *dramaturgie* (in *Die hamburgische Dramaturgie*, critical work by Gotthold E. Lessing †1781 Ger. dramatist and critic), fr. Gk *dramatourgia* dramatic composition, action of a play, fr. *dramatourgos* + *-ia* -y] **1 :** the art or technique of writing drama ⟨a professor of ~⟩ **2 :** the technical devices that are used in writing drama and that tend to distinguish it from other literary forms ⟨a play with sound ~ and excellent acting⟩ ⟨a first-rate clinical example of ~ but a second-rate "show" —G.J.Nathan⟩; *often* **:** use of or the product of the use of such technical devices ⟨reviewers . . . neglecting honest ~ for incandescent performing —*N.Y. Herald Tribune*⟩

drame \ˈdräm, -ȧm\ *n* -S [F (also, drama), fr. LL *drama* — more at DRAMA] **:** TRAGICOMEDY 1a

dram equivalent *n* **:** the weight of a smokeless shotgun powder that gives the same shot velocity and the same approximate gas pressure as a given weight in drams of black powder

dram·mage *or* **dram·age** \ˈdramij\ *n* -S **:** a measure of silk size based on the weight in drams of a 1000-yard skein

dram·ma per mu·si·ca \ˈdrämə,perˈmüzēkə\ *n* [It, lit., drama for music] **:** early lyric drama that was a precursor of opera

dram·ma·ti·co \drəˈmad·ē,kō\ *adv (or adj)* [It, dramatic, fr. LL *dramaticus* — more at DRAMATIC] **:** in a dramatic manner — used as a direction in music

drammed *past of* DRAM

dram·mer \ˈdramə(r), -aam-\ *n* -S **:** one that drinks **:** TIPPLER

dramming *pres part of* DRAM

dram·mock \ˈdramək\ *n* -S [ScGael *dramag* foul mixture, crowdy] **1** *chiefly Scot* **:** raw oatmeal mixed with cold water **2** *chiefly Scot* **:** an unpalatable mixture

dram pers *abbr* dramatis personae

drams *pl of* DRAM, *pres 3d sing of* DRAM

dramseller \ˈ=ˌ==\ *n, archaic* **:** a seller of distilled liquors by the drink

dramshop \ˈ=ˌ=\ *n, archaic* **:** BARROOM

drang \ˈdraŋ\ *var of* DRONG

drank *past of* DRINK

drant \ˈdrant, -ȧ-\ *vi* -ED/-ING/-S [Sc *drant, draunt* droning or drawling tone, modif. of ScGael *dranndan, draundan* hum, buzzing, complaint, growl; akin to IrGael *dranntan* hum, buzzing, growl] *chiefly Scot* **:** to speak in a tiresome whining drawl

¹drap \ˈdrȧ\ *n, pl* **draps** \ˈ"\ [F — more at DRAB (cloth)] **:** CLOTH

²drap \ˈdrap\ *dial var of* DROP

drap·able *also* **drape·able** \ˈdrāpəbəl\ *adj* **:** fit for draping **:** capable of being draped ⟨heavy ~ satins⟩

drap–de–ber·ry \ˌdrädə,beˈrē\ *n, usu cap B* [F, lit., cloth from Berry (region in France)] **:** a woolen cloth formerly made in Berry, France

drap d'é·té \ˌdrä(ˌ)dāˈtā\ *n* [F *drap d' été*, lit., summer cloth] **:** a thin woolen or blended fabric that has a twill weave and is used esp. for summer clothing

¹drape \ˈdrāp\ *vb* -ED/-ING/-S [ME *drapen*, fr. MF *draper*, fr. *drap* cloth — more at DRAB (cloth)] *vt* **1** *obs* **:** to make into cloth **:** WEAVE **2 :** to cover or adorn with or as if with or swathe in or as if in folds of cloth ⟨great cypress trees *draped* with Spanish moss⟩ ⟨*draping* the building fronts with bunting⟩: as **a :** to cover following the contours of ⟨dark chestnuts ~ the mountainside —F.L.Lucas⟩ **b :** ENFOLD ⟨the child was *draped* in expensive linens⟩ ⟨*draping* himself in abstruse thought⟩ **c :** to hang or put on (as a garment) casually or loosely **d :** to let (as oneself) sprawl ⟨*draping* garlands about the singer's neck⟩ ⟨*draped* her furs over her arm⟩ ⟨several of the regulars had *draped* themselves around the bar⟩ **e :** to shroud or enclose with surgical drapes ⟨~ a patient for operation⟩ **3 :** to arrange in flowing lines or folds or according to a pattern or design ⟨*draping* a satin dress to minimize heavy hips⟩ ⟨a cleverly *draped* suit⟩ **~** *vi* **1 :** to fall in or into folds, esp. into graceful folds ⟨this silk ~*s* beautifully⟩; *often* **:** to become arranged in decorative folds ⟨a full skirt that ~*s* to a huge bow⟩

²drape \ˈ"\ *n* -S [partly fr. F *drap* cloth; partly fr. ¹*drape*] **1** *archaic* **:** CLOTH, TEXTILES **2 a :** a drapery esp. for a window; *esp* **:** OVERDRAPE **b :** a sterile covering used in an operating room (as about the operative site or between the anesthetist and the surgical team) to decrease the chance of contamination — usu. used in pl. **3 a :** arrangement in or of folds ⟨the classic ~ of her gown⟩; *often* **:** decorative fold or folds in a garment or hanging ⟨a soft ~ in front flattered her flat chest⟩ **b :** the property of falling in graceful folds ⟨a silk with excellent ~⟩ **4 a :** the cut or hang of clothing (as of a man's double-breasted suit jacket) **b** *slang* (1) **:** a man's suit with jacket of unusual length and exaggerated cut sometimes popular with adolescents — compare ZOOT SUIT (2) **:** a wearer of a drape

¹drap·er \-pə(r)\ *n* -S [in sense 1, fr. ME, maker of cloth, fr. MF *drapier*, fr. OF, fr. *drap* cloth + *-ier* -er; in sense 2, fr. ¹*drape* + *-er*] **1** *Brit* **:** a dealer in cloth and sometimes also in clothing and dry goods **2 :** one that drapes (as cloth) or arranges draperies (as on a stage setting)

²dra·per \ˈ"\ *n* -S [origin unknown] **1 :** a machine for cleaning sugar-beet seed **2 :** the canvas conveyor of a header, binder, or combine

drap·er·ied \ˈdrāp(ə)rēd, -rid\ *adj* [¹*drapery* + *-ed*] **:** covered or supplied with drapery or draperies

draper's cap *n* **:** a strong brown wrapping paper that is glazed on one side

draper's teasel *n* [¹*draper*; fr. its being formerly used to raise a nap on cloth] **:** FULLER'S TEASEL

¹drap·ery \ˈdrāp(ə)rē, -ri\ *n* -ES [ME *draperie* (also, manufacture of cloth, dealing in cloth), fr. MF, fr. OF, fr. *drap* cloth + *-erie* -ery — more at DRAB (cloth)] **1** *Brit* **:** DRY GOODS **2** *Brit* **:** the occupation of a draper **3 :** a piece of material (as cloth, lace, or plastic) used for decorative purposes and usu. hung in loose folds arranged in a graceful design: as **a :** clothing or a piece of cloth arranged in graceful folds and worn or represented in art as worn on the human body **b :** CURTAIN 1a; *esp* **:** a curtain of heavy fabric often used over sheer curtains **c :** loose coverings for furniture; *also* **:** an arrangement of cloth for use in interior decoration esp. as a wall covering **:** HANGINGS **4 :** something that serves to cover, adorn, or conceal ⟨facts buried under the *draperies* of his turgid prose⟩ **5 :** the draping or arranging of materials or their representation ⟨great skill in ~⟩

²drapery \ˈ"\ *vt* -ED/-ING/-ES **:** to furnish or adorn with or as if with drapery — used chiefly as a past participle ⟨she was *draperied* in soft flowing velvet⟩

drapet *n* -S [It *drappetto*, dim. of *drappo* cloth, fr. LL *drappus* — more at DRAB (cloth)] *obs* **:** CLOTH, COVERING

drap·ey \ˈdrāpē, -pi\ *adj* **1 :** of, relating to, or characterized by drape ⟨a soft ~ fabric⟩ **2 :** depending on drape for effect ⟨a ~ lace dress⟩

drapped *past of* DRAP

drap·pie *or* **drap·py** \ˈdrapē, -pi\ *n, pl* **drappies** [²*drap* + *-ie, -y*] **1** *chiefly Scot* **:** a small amount of liquid **2** *chiefly Scot* **:** intoxicating drink ⟨was unco fond o' the ~ —James Ballantine⟩

drapping *pres part of* DRAP

draps *pl of* DRAP, *pres 3d sing of* DRAP

drash \ˈdrash\ *dial var of* THRASH

¹dras·tic \ˈdrastik, -aas-,-ais-, -tēk *sometimes* -ȧs-\ *adj* [Gk *drastikos*, fr. (assumed) *drastos* (verbal of *dran* to do, act) + *-ikos* -ic] **1 :** acting rapidly and violently — used chiefly of purgatives **2 a :** acting with violence or harshness **:** extreme or radical in effect **:** RIGOROUS ⟨~ measures⟩ ⟨~ repressive laws⟩ **b :** notably severe or vigorous ⟨~ alterations in the national economy⟩ ⟨a ~ wave of pain⟩ — **dras·ti·cal·ly** \-tək(ə)lē, -tēk-, -li\ *adv*

²drastic \ˈ"\ *n* -S **:** a powerful medicinal agent; *esp* **:** a strong purgative

drat \ˈdrat, *usu* -ad·+V\ *vb* **dratted; dratted; dratting; drats** [prob. euphemistic alter. of *God rot*] **:** DAMN — used as a mild oath ⟨~ their interference⟩

dratch·ell \ˈdrachəl\ *n* -S [origin unknown] *dial Eng* **:** a loose slatternly woman **:** SLUT

draught *var of* DRAFT

draughtboard \ˈ=ˌ=\ *n* [*draughts* + *board*] *Brit* **:** CHECKERBOARD

draught·house \ˈ=ˌ=\ *n* [¹*draft* (privy) + *house*] *archaic* **:** PRIVY

draughts \ˈdrafts\ *n pl but sing or pl in constr* [ME *draghtes*, fr. pl. of *draght, draught* act of moving, move in chess — more at DRAFT] *Brit* **:** the game of checkers

draughts·man \ˈdraf(t)smən\ *n, pl* **draughtsmen** [*draughts* + *man*] *Brit* **:** one of the pieces used in the game of draughts

draunt \ˈdrant, -a-\ *var of* DRANT

¹drave *archaic past of* DRIVE

²drave \ˈdrāv\ *n* -S [ME (northern dial.) *drave* act of driving, var. of *drove* — more at DROVE] **1** *Scot* **:** the season in which herring are fished **2** *Scot* **:** a herring fishing expedition

draves test \ˈdrāvz-\ *n, usu cap D* [after Carl Z. *Draves* b1894 Am. chemist, its deviser] **:** a test of the efficiency of a wetting agent based on the time required for a standard skein of cotton yarn carrying a standard weight to sink in a water solution of that wetting agent

dra·vi·da \ˈdrävədə\ *n, pl* **dravidas** *also* **dravida** *usu cap* [Skt *Drāvida, Draviḍa*, of Dravidian origin; akin to Tamil *tamiḻ* Tamil] **1 :** DRAVIDIAN 1 **2 :** any of several Dravidian languages **3 :** one of the basic styles of medieval Indian architecture

¹dra·vid·i·an \drəˈvidēən\ *n* -S *usu cap* [Skt *Drāvida, Draviḍa* + E *-ian*] **1 :** an individual of an ancient Australoid race in India that forms the bulk of the population of southern India except on the west coast which is occupied by Scytho-Dravidians **2 :** the speech of the Dravidians — see DRAVIDIAN LANGUAGE

²dravidian \ˈ"\ *also* **dra·vid·ic** \-dik\ *adj, usu cap* **:** of or relating to the Dravidians or their languages

dra·vid·i·an·ist \-dēənəst\ *n* -S *usu cap* **:** a specialist in Dravidian languages

dravidian language *n, usu cap D* **:** a language of a family of languages that are used in southern India, northern Ceylon, and in the isolated case of Brahui in West Pakistan, that have no established genetic relationship to any other family, and that are classified into a Dravida group comprising Tamil, Malayalam, Kanarese, Kurukh, and Malto, an Andhra group comprising Telugu, Gondi, and Khond, and a Brahui group containing only Brahui

dra·vite \ˈdrä,vīt\ *n* -S [G *dravit*, fr. the *Drave* or *Drava* river, Austria and Yugoslavia, its locality + G *-it* -ite] **:** a magnesium-containing tourmaline that is often brown in color

¹draw \ˈdrȯ\ *vb* **drew** \ˈdrü\ *also archaic or substand* **drawed** \ˈdrȯd\ **drawn** \ˈdrȯn\ **drawing** \ˈdrȯiŋ\ **draws** [ME *dragen, drawen*, fr. OE *dragan* to pull, draw, drag; akin to OHG *tragan* to carry, ON *draga* to pull, draw, Goth *gadragan* to accumulate, Russ *doroga* way, trip and perh. to L *trahere* to pull, draw, drag] *vt* **1 :** to cause to move toward or after a compelling force, forward or in another indicated or implied direction, or toward a surface **:** PULL, DRAG ⟨the horse *drew* us along at a smart pace⟩ ⟨we *drew* up our nets full of fishes⟩ ⟨using a poultice to ~ inflammation to a head⟩: as **a :** to haul (as a load) usu. in a cart or wagon ⟨he *drew* over 100 cords of wood that winter⟩ **b :** to drag (a criminal) to the place of execution (as at a horse's tail or on a hurdle) **c :** to cause (as a sail or drawbridge) to be raised **d :** to pull (as a curtain) over so as to cover or conceal or aside so as to uncover or reveal ⟨*drew* the bedcovers over her⟩ ⟨~ the blinds and light the lamps⟩ **e :** to bring out or cause to come out (as from a setting or receptacle) ⟨~ the cork gently and decant the wine⟩ ⟨the dentist *drew* the abscessed tooth⟩ ⟨the blow *drew* blood⟩ ⟨~ me a glass of ale⟩ **f :** to remove (a weapon) from a sheath ⟨now ~ your swords and fall to it⟩ **g :** to promote suppuration in (as a wound); *broadly* **:** to cause (an unwanted element) to depart (as from the body or a lesion) ⟨this will help ~ the poison⟩ **h :** to cause (a bow) to bend; *also* **:** to pull back (an arrow) on the bowstring **i :** to pull off (as a tablecloth after a meal); *also* **:** to remove a tablecloth from (a table) **j :** to remove (as coals) from a grate ⟨the furnaces are *drawn* during a strike⟩; *also* **:** to remove a fire from (a grate) **k :** to pull (warp threads) through the heddles in proper order to produce a desired pattern in weaving — often used with *in* ⟨~*ing* warps in by hand⟩ **l :** to cause (the ball or other mobile piece used in certain sports) to move in a particular direction or toward a particular objective usu. by applying a specialized stroke or imparting a specialized movement (as of spinning) — used in golf, billiards, bowls, cricket, and curling **m :** to remove (seedlings) from a plant bed preparatory to transplanting **2 a :** to cause (as a person) to move, proceed, or act (as by leading, conducting, or diverting) ⟨~*ing* his cousin to one side⟩ ⟨tried to ~ her thoughts from her troubles⟩ **b :** ATTRACT ⟨the accident *drew* a great crowd⟩ ⟨like iron filings *drawn* by a magnet⟩ **:** ENTICE, ALLURE ⟨~*ing* him with an unspoken promise in her eyes⟩ **c :** to influence toward or away from a particular course (as of action) ⟨kindness and understanding will often ~ a boy to unburden his conscience⟩; *often* **:** to influence to do something undesirable **:** SEDUCE ⟨he was *drawn* from his family and religion by selfish interests⟩ ⟨don't let me ~ you away from your work⟩ **d :** to force (a hunted animal) from cover ⟨using dogs to ~ the game⟩ **e :** to rouse (as a person) to action or response ⟨the final taunt *drew* him⟩ ⟨her insolence *drew* him to say things he knew he would regret⟩ **f :** to force the playing of (a particular card or suit) in a card game ⟨lead the king to ~ her opponent's ace⟩ ⟨won with the queen and then *drew* three rounds of spades⟩ **3 :** TAKE, GAIN; as **a :** to take (breath) into the lungs ⟨she *drew* a deep breath of clean pine-scented air⟩ **b :** to require (a specified depth) of a supporting medium in which to float ⟨a ship that ~*s* 12 feet of water⟩ **c** (1) **:** to take or accept at random (one from a number of things) esp. in order to decide something by chance ⟨let's ~ straws to see who gets dinner⟩ (2) **:** to receive (as a prize) from a lottery ⟨he *drew* one of the favored horses in the sweepstakes and sold his ticket profitably long before the race was run⟩ (3) **:** to obtain by luck or chance **:** gain by fortune **:** WIN ⟨a man who seemed to ~ money⟩ (4) **:** to select by the drawing of lots ⟨the jury panel was *drawn*⟩ (5) **:** to take or accept (a card) in a card game according to some arbitrary or randomizing system and usu. after an initial deal (as to improve a poker hand) (6) **:** to similarly take or accept (a piece) in various games **d :** to acquire in the course of events ⟨he *drew* the hardest job of all⟩ **e :** to separate (as sheep for fattening) from a larger group or number **:** select (as specimens) for a test or experiment **f :** to gain as a recompense or one's due (as for services, use of property, or misconduct) ⟨he ~*s* a good salary every week⟩ ⟨the speech *drew* a round of applause⟩ ⟨let your extra money stay in the bank and ~ interest⟩ ⟨if he keeps on chasing married women he's likely to ~ a punch in the jaw⟩ ⟨~ rations for three days⟩ **g :** EXTRACT, ELICIT, DERIVE ⟨you'll never ~ a compliment from her⟩ **h :** to infer from evidence or reasons **:** deduce from premises ⟨let the future ~ lessons from the past⟩ ⟨~ your own conclusions from what you have seen⟩ **i :** to take (as money) from a place of deposit ⟨*drew* several hundred dollars from the bank⟩ **4 :** to alter esp. in form or content: as **a :** to tear to pieces ⟨condemned to be *drawn* asunder by wild horses⟩ **b :** CONTRACT, PUCKER, WRINKLE ⟨persimmons ~ the mouth unless thoroughly ripened⟩ ⟨her face *drawn* with pain⟩; *also* **:** to cause to swell ⟨rubber soles ~ my feet⟩ **c** (1) **:** to extend in length or lengthwise **:** PROTRACT, STRETCH ⟨*drew* out her call interminably⟩ ⟨a rubber band *drawn* to its greatest length⟩ (2) *obs* **:** to build or cause to extend (as a ditch or wall) lengthwise from one place to another (3) **:** to cause (a plant) to become spindly and etiolated (as from lack of light) — used chiefly as a participial adjective **d :** to shave (stonework) to shape **e** (1) **:** to stretch, spread, or shape (metal) by hammering or by pulling it through dies or by stamping successively (as with a series of dies or by hammering); *specif* **:** to make a metal rod into (wire) by pulling it through a series of holes of diminishing size thus decreasing the sectional area and increasing the length at each stage (2) **:** to shape by stretching (as plastic) or by drawing (as plastic filaments) through dies (3) **:** to shape (as a shingle) or smooth (as a spoke) with a drawknife or comparable tool (4) **:** to shape (glass) by guiding molten glass from the furnace over a series of automatic rollers **f :** TEMPER *vt* 4a(1) **g :** to attenuate (textile slivers or rovings) by passing successively through rollers each pair of which revolves slightly faster than its predecessor thereby causing the fibers to be straightened **h** *of honeybees* **:** to build up (foundation) into comb — often used with *out* **i :** to make (candles) by passing a length of wick repeatedly through molten wax and successively larger circular holes **5 a** (1) **:** to produce by or as if by tracing a pen or other instrument of delineation over a surface ⟨~ a line⟩ ⟨~*ing* pictures in the sand⟩ (2) **:** to represent by lines drawn **:** make a picture of in this manner ⟨he ~*s* the scene from memory⟩ **b :** to represent by words: (1) **:** to write in due form **:** prepare a draft of **:** INDITE ⟨*drew* a memorial to the queen⟩ ⟨~ a check for the whole amount⟩ (2) **:** to express graphically in words **:** DELINEATE ⟨~*ing* acid pen-portraits of her neighbors⟩ ⟨the novelist *drew* his characters precisely and believably⟩ **c :** to set forth in due and proper form or formally **:** FORMULATE ⟨it is often necessary to ~ fine distinctions⟩ ⟨have a lawyer ~ up your will if your plans are at all complicated⟩ **6 :** to remove the contents of: as **a :** to remove the viscera of **:** EVISCERATE ⟨fowls come to market plucked and *drawn*⟩ **b :** to extract or drain the essence of ⟨that final climb seemed to ~ his strength away⟩ ⟨some people ~ their tea too long⟩ **c :** to force or draw something from (as a place of security) **:** drive game out of (as a covert) ⟨they *drew* the open fields with beaters, the rugged hills with dogs⟩ **:** fish by dragging a net through (as a pond) ⟨they *drew* the river above the weir⟩ **d :** to remove (as fired brick) from a kiln **7 :** to bring (an existing relation or situation) to an end: as **a** *archaic* **:** to withdraw (as a horse) from a race **b :** to finish (a contest) in a draw **:** bring (as a game) to a conclusion without having established the superiority (as in skill or scoring) of any contestant **~** *vi* **1 :** to come or go; MOVE **:** draw oneself — now used only with prepositions and adverbs of direction ⟨he *drew* away from the smoldering wall⟩ ⟨night ~*s* near⟩ ⟨as we *drew* toward the town⟩ **2** *obs* **:** to approach or tend esp. to a particular state **3 :** to perform the act of drawing something: as **a :** move something by pulling ⟨*drew* continuously without emptying the well⟩ ⟨there's nothing like a team of oxen for ~*ing* in really rugged country⟩ **b :** to exert an attractive force **:** act as an inducement or enticement ⟨the play is still ~*ing* well⟩ **c :** to pull back the string of a bow preparatory to releasing the arrow **d :** to perform the act or practice the art of delineation **:** form figures or pictures by tracing lines; *often* **:** SKETCH **e :** to make a written demand for payment of money deposited or due; *often* **:** to make demands (as on a person or a resource) — usu. used with *on* or *upon* ⟨he *drew* on his savings account for a down payment⟩ ⟨~ on me for any help you need⟩ ⟨~*ing* on his last reserve of energy⟩ **f :** to search for game; *often* **:** to track game by the scent — used chiefly of a sporting dog **g** (1) **:** to cause local congestion **:** induce blood or other body fluid to localize at a particular point **:** be effective as a blistering agent or counterirritant — used of a poultice and comparable means of medication (2) *of a lesion* **:** to become localized — used in the phrase *draw to a head* **h :** to leave a game or contest undecided **:** end a contest in a draw ⟨our team *drew* three times this year⟩ **i :** to draw one or more cards in a card game **4 :** to sink in water **:** require a depth for floating ⟨greater hulks ~ deep —Shak.⟩ **5 :** to alter in form or content: as **a :** to change shape by or as if by pulling **:** STRETCH, WRINKLE, CONTRACT ⟨she shivered and her skin seemed to ~ with the cold⟩ ⟨the spring *drew* longer and longer with the strain⟩ **b** *of a sail* **:** to swell out with the wind **c :** STEEP, INFUSE ⟨the tea may ~ a bit longer⟩ **d** *of curing tobacco* **:** to become uniformly moist — used of the hand of leaves after petuning **6 a :** to become subjected to drawing or suitable for being drawn ⟨the new cart ~*s* easily⟩ **b** *of liquid* **:** to drain away **c :** RISE **d :** to produce a draft whereby a current (as of hot gases) is drawn ⟨the chimney ~*s* well since it was cleaned⟩; *sometimes* **:** to pass in a current ⟨breezes *drew* through the room⟩ **e :** to pull a pattern from a mold in an indicated manner (as hard, easily, cleanly) **7 :** to obtain information, supplies, or other matters ⟨~*ing* from a common fund of knowledge⟩ ⟨*drew* heavily on their supply of food⟩ **8 :** to perform a draw in dancing **syn** see PULL — **draw a bead on :** to bring into line with the front sight and rear sight of a rifle **:** take aim at; *broadly* **:** use as a target ⟨always ready to *draw a bead on* an errant public official⟩ — **draw a blank** *also* **draw blank 1 :** to draw a loser **:** obtain something without value **2 :** to fail to find what one seeks — **draw a line** *or* **draw the line :** to fix an arbitrary boundary between things that tend to intermingle ⟨the courts must *draw a line* between the right of free speech and genuinely subversive utterance⟩; *often* **:** to fix a boundary excluding what one will not tolerate or engage in ⟨I'm not intolerant but one must *draw the line* somewhere⟩ — **draw a longbow** *or* **draw the longbow :** to exaggerate or overstate the truth — **draw blood :** to wound in body or spirit; *often* **:** to subject to distress and embarrassment ⟨he *drew blood* when he guyed us about our failure⟩ — **draw in one's horns :** to act more conservatively or cautiously than at some former time ⟨he'd better *draw in his horns* if he wants to keep out of trouble⟩ — **draw it fine :** to be very precise (as in making distinctions) — **draw it mild** [so called fr. its original use in reference to beer] *chiefly Brit* **:** to express or tell (something) without exaggerating — usu. used imperatively ⟨*draw it mild*, after all, we saw the whole thing happen⟩ — **draw lots :** to decide or assign by or as if by the drawing of lots — **draw on 1 :** to order (as a bank or business firm) to pay out money held to the credit of the drawer **2 :** to withdraw (money) from one's account ⟨*drew on* his savings for the whole amount⟩ **3** *or* **draw upon :** to use or depend on as a base or as source material **:** exploit the resources of ⟨she has *drawn on* her mother's old notebooks for some excellent recipes⟩ ⟨*drawing on* the Bible for authority⟩ — **draw one's time :** to quit a job esp. under pressure ⟨get to work or *draw your time* right now⟩ ⟨he *drew his time* and went south⟩ — **draw rein :** to check one's speed (as in riding) **:** stop short **:** STOP — **draw straws :** to draw lots using straws of uneven length for lots — **draw the fangs :** to render harmless or ineffective — used with *of* ⟨this forthright answer *drew the fangs* of his criticism⟩ — **draw the temper :** to reduce or impair the hardness of tempered steel by heating ⟨he tried to sharpen his ax on an emery wheel and completely *drew the temper*⟩ — **draw together 1 :** to draw into unity **:** render whole **:** UNITE, UNIFY ⟨I'll just *draw together* this snag in your cuff⟩ ⟨only hatred shared *drew* them *together*⟩ **2 :** to come to accord **:** UNITE ⟨sensible people will *draw together* to face a common danger⟩

²draw \ˈ"\ *n* -S *often attrib* **1 :** an act or process of drawing (as of metals, loads, lots, or a bow) **:** PULL: as **a :** one complete outward and inward run of a mule carriage in spinning **b :** DRAWING-IN **c :** a sucking pull on something (as a sipping straw or cigarette) held with the lips ⟨took a long ~ on his pipe before answering⟩; *sometimes* **:** a drawing (as of vapor or liquid) into the system **d** (1) **:** the removing of a revolver or automatic pistol from its holster ⟨a cross ~ with the left hand⟩; *esp* **:** near simultaneous drawing of such weapons by individuals proposing to shoot at one another — used with *the* ⟨the sheriff was quicker on the ~⟩ (2) **:** advantage esp. when gained by superior alertness or skill **:** EDGE — usu. used with *the* ⟨the senator's experience gives him the ~ on his opponents⟩ **e :** a stroke or play in certain games or sports involving drawing (as of a ball) **f :** a competition in which the pulling ability of draft animals is tested under standardized conditions ⟨the ox ~*s* at New England fairs⟩ **g** *or* **draw step :** a dance step in which one foot is drawn on the floor to meet the other **2 :** something that draws or serves as a means of drawing: as **a** [by shortening] *dial* **:** DRAWER 2 **b** *archaic* **:** something designed to draw out, entrap, or mislead **c** (1) *also* **drawspan :** the movable part of a drawbridge (2) **:** the opening through it **d :** a stroke or blow given in drawing metal **e :** a natural drainageway or gully generally shallower or more open than a ravine or gorge **:** a dry stream bed **:** COULEE 1a ⟨a small stream that cuts through a large ~ in which deer like to winter —Robert Crichton⟩ **f :** the angle given to the locking faces of the pallets in a lever-escapement watch that when acted upon by the force of the escape-wheel teeth draws the lever to the banking pins and ensures freedom of the roller **g :** an influence that draws attention or a crowd ⟨a dogfight has a powerful ~ for small boys⟩ : ATTRACTION; *often* : a theatrical event or personality that draws patronage **h** : the weaving pattern formed by drawing-in **3** : the product or state of drawing or of being drawn: as **a** : a lot or chance drawn **b** : a contest that ends without a clear-cut victory for either side ⟨the battle was a ~⟩: (1) : a sporting event (as a boxing or wrestling match) in which each contestant receives equal scores : TIE (2) : a sporting event or game in which there is no winner because some impasse precludes carrying the contest to a decisive end (as in a cricket match with the batting team behind and time expiring before the innings is complete) **c** : the essence or strength of tea **d** : a young shoot or sprout; *specif* : one of the young spring shoots of the sweet potato **e** : ANGLE, TAPER, DRAFT; *specif* : the taper of a leaf spring **f** : the distance from the string to the back of a drawn bow; *often* : the force required to draw a bow fully ⟨a bow with a 50-pound ~⟩ **g** : a list of contestants in a sports event arranged in an order obtained by drawing lots **4** : something that is or can be drawn: as **a** : DRAWER PULL **b** (1) : a card or piece drawn in certain games (as for replacement of one expended); *also* : the deal in draw poker to improve the hands after players have discarded (2) : DRAW POKER **c** : the distance that a camera bellows may be extended **d** : a number, allocation, or amount (as of money or goods) that is available at regular or particular intervals: (1) : DRAWING ACCOUNT 2 (2) : the part of a seaman's pay that he has a right to draw while in port in the course of a voyage (3) : the number of each issue of a periodical (as a magazine or newspaper) regularly consigned to a particular vendor

draw away *vt* : WITHDRAW, REMOVE ⟨*drew* his hand *away* from her touch⟩ ⟨*drawing* her *away* from the window⟩ ~ *vi* : to move away (as from one's opponent in a race) ⟨we started even but he soon *drew away* from me⟩

draw back *vt* **1** : to receive back (as duties paid on goods for exportation); *broadly* : to cause to return **2** : DISCOUNT, DEDUCT ~ *vi* : RETREAT, SHRINK, WITHDRAW — usu. used with *from* ⟨*drew back* from the scorching heat⟩ ⟨*drawing back* slowly⟩

drawback \ˈ=ˌ=\ *n* -S [*draw back*] **1** : money remitted after being collected : REFUND: as **a** : customs or other duties refunded on (1) an imported product subsequently exported, (2) an imported product used in the production of a product for export, or (3) on the part of an imported product (as tobacco) which becomes scrap in the manufacturing process **b** : a refund of excise or other tax on a product used for some favored purpose (as alcohol used for nonbeverage purposes) **c** : money refunded as compensation (as for damages) or as a special often secret favor or inducement — compare KICKBACK **2** : an objectionable feature : DEFECT, HINDRANCE ⟨the ~s of country living⟩ ⟨slow drying is the chief ~ of this paint⟩ **3** : a part of a mechanical device that can be drawn back: as **a** (1) : a part of a foundry mold that can be drawn back to permit the removal of a pattern from the mold (2) : a plate or comparable structure on which this part of the mold may be lifted out **b** : a door bolt that can be released by drawing back on a knob on the inside

drawback lock *n* **1** : a door lock that can be opened from the inside by a handle and from the outside by a key **2** : a lock that can ordinarily be opened by hand (as by turning a knob) except when locked with a key

drawband \ˈ=ˌ=\ *n* : a metal or woven fabric strip that connects the mainspring and carriage of a typewriter to provide motive power — called also *carriage band*

drawbar \ˈ=ˌ=\ *n* **1** : a removable bar in a fence **2 a** (1) : a bar that is used to connect a steam locomotive and tender and is secured in the drawhead of the locomotive by a pin (2) : a railroad coupler — not used technically **b** : a beam across the rear of a tractor to which implements are hitched **3** : a clay block submerged in molten glass in a tank furnace for controlling the position of sheet glass during drawing

drawbar pull *n* : the pulling power exerted at the drawbar (as by a locomotive or tractor)

drawbench \ˈ=ˌ=\ *n* : a machine for drawing strips of metal through dies; *esp* : one used in making wire

drawboard \ˈ=ˌ=\ *n* : a movable board or assembly of boards for bridging an open space (as between railroad cars and platforms or boats and docks)

drawbolt \ˈ=ˌ=\ *n* **1** : COUPLER 1a **2** : a bolt with washer and nut used to draw parts of an assembly tightly together **3** : BOLT 2a

¹drawbore \ˈ=ˌ=\ *n* [¹*draw* + *bore*] : a bore for a mortise pin placed so as to draw the tenon and thus make the joint tighter

²drawbore \"\ *vt* **1** : to make a drawbore in (as a tenon) **2** : to enlarge the bore of (a tube, as a gun barrel) by drawing through with the working tool instead of thrusting

drawbore

drawboy \ˈ=ˌ=\ *n* : a boy who operates the harness cords of a hand loom; *broadly* : a part of a power loom that performs the same task

drawbridge \ˈ=ˌ=\ *n* [ME *drawebrigge*, fr. *drawen* to draw + *brigge* bridge — more at DRAW, BRIDGE] : a bridge of which either the whole or a part is made to be raised up, let down, or drawn aside so as to permit or hinder passage

draw bridge *n* : a two-handed bridge game in which each player is dealt 13 cards and draws one of the undealt cards after each trick — called also *domino bridge, strip bridge*

drawbridge of a medieval castle

drawcard *var of* DRAWING CARD

draw cock *n* : PET COCK

drawcord \ˈ=ˌ=\ *n* : a cord so arranged as to draw draperies across or back from an opening in a single operation

draw curtain *n* **1** : a curtain in front of a stage that meets or overlaps in the middle and is drawn back on both sides when open **2** : one of a pair or set of domestic curtains usu. of rather substantial and more or less opaque material that may be drawn together or apart by a mechanical device (as a traverse rod)

drawcut \ˈ=ˌ=\ *n* : a cut toward the machine or operator (as in shaping a part)

drawcut shaper *n* : a shaper that cuts toward the column of the machine

draw down *vt* **1** : to be the cause of : ATTRACT ⟨their behavior *drew down* a storm of protest⟩ **2** : EARN, RECEIVE ⟨*drew down* full pay⟩ **3** : EXPEND, DEPLETE ⟨*drawing down* gold reserves⟩ ⟨*drew down* his balance in the checkbook⟩

drawdown \ˈ=ˌ=\ *n* -S [*draw down*] **1** : the distance by which the fluid surface level (as in a well or reservoir) is lowered (as by pumping or gate opening) **2** : the curving downward of the water surface near the edge of a weir notch

drawed *archaic or substand past of* DRAW

draw·ee \(ˈ)drȯ¦ē\ *n* -S [¹*draw* + *-ee*] : the person on whom an order or bill of exchange is drawn — contrasted with *drawer*

draw·er *R* ˈdrȯ(ə)r; *-R before pause or consonant* -ȯə *also in senses 2 & 3* -ȯ, *before vowel* " *or* -ȯ(ə)r\ *n* -S [ME, fr. *drawen* to draw + *-er* — more at DRAW] **1** : one that draws: as **a** : a person who draws liquor for guests in a place of public resort : a waiter in a taproom **b** : a person who delineates or depicts : DRAFTSMAN ⟨a clever ~ of animals⟩ **c** (1) : a textile worker who operates a drawing frame (2) : DRAWER-IN **d** : a worker who forms wire, rod, or tubing by drawing metal through a series of successively smaller dies **e** : a worker who assists in the removal of firebrick or other wares from kilns **f** (1) : an individual who draws or issues a bill of exchange or order for payment — contrasted with *drawee* (2) : the maker of a promissory note **2** : something that is drawn: as **a** (1) : a sliding box or receptacle (as one of a number enclosed in a case or frame) that is opened by pulling out and closed by pushing in ⟨a desk ~⟩ ⟨a bureau ~⟩; *sometimes* : a post-office box in the form of a drawer (2) **drawers** *pl* : a chest made up of several drawers with a suitable cabinet and base **b drawers** *pl* : an undergarment enclosing the lower trunk and having independent sheaths for all or part of each leg **3** : level of social or professional status, accomplishment, worth

drawer-down \ˈ=(=)¦=\ *n, pl* **drawers-down** : one that draws down; *esp* : a worker in a rolling mill who draws hot billets down to rolls

drawer-in \ˈ=(=)¦=\ *n, pl* **drawers-in** : a textile worker who does drawing-in

drawer-off \ˈ=(=)¦=\ *n, pl* **drawers-off** : one that draws something off esp. as an occupation ⟨got work as a *drawer-off* at the brewery⟩

drawer-out \ˈ=(=)¦=\ *n, pl* **drawers-out** : one that draws out; *esp* : a worker who draws metal bars or blooms from furnaces

drawer pull *n* : a handle for pulling open a drawer

drawfile \ˈ=ˌ=\ *vt* : to file by pushing the file held with its length transverse to the direction of its motion

draw frame *var of* DRAWING FRAME

draw game *n* : a domino game in which a player having no playable piece is forced to draw from the stock until he gets one

draw gang *n* : the group of workers that cuts and handles glass as it comes from the lehr

drawgear \ˈ=ˌ=\ *n, Brit* : a device used to connect adjoining railroad carriages or cars : COUPLER

drawhead \ˈ=ˌ=\ *n* : the socket or base on the ends of locomotives and cars to which the drawbar or other coupling device is secured

draw in *vt* **1** : to induce to participate or enter : ENTICE, INVEIGLE ⟨was asked to participate but he refused to be *drawn in*⟩ **2** : to draw roughly or as part of a whole : SKETCH ⟨*drew in* the background⟩ **3** : to shape (as the toe of a sock) so that the area of each succeeding section along a longitudinal axis will be smaller than that of the section preceding it ~ *vi* **1** : to draw quickly toward an end ⟨as day *drew in* and twilight deepened⟩ : shorten in a seasonally normal manner ⟨the evenings are *drawing in* and it will soon be winter⟩ **2** : to be or become more economical or conservative ⟨we've spent too much lately, we'll have to *draw in* for a while⟩ ⟨when I read him his own words he *drew in* and admitted he had gone too far⟩

draw-in bolt \ˈ=ˌ=-\ *n* : a bolt for tightening collets in the headstock of a lathe

drawing *n* -S *often attrib* [ME, fr. gerund of *drawen* to draw — more at DRAW] **1** : an act or instance of drawing; *specif* : an occasion when something is decided by a drawing of lots ⟨there being 607 applications for 81 parcels of land a ~ will be held to determine the recipient of each parcel⟩ **2 a** : the projection of an image or a series of points by the forming of lines on a surface (as by use of a pencil, pen, or etchers' point) ⟨neat careful ~⟩; *broadly* : formation of a representation in which delineation plays a determining part **b** : the art or technique of representing an object or outlining a figure, plan, or sketch by means of lines ⟨a professor of ~⟩ **3** : something that is drawn or subject to drawing: as **a** : money taken in (as by a business or for a particular purpose) **b** : a figure or representation formed by drawing : SKETCH, PLAN ⟨a ~ of his sister⟩ ⟨a magnificent scale ~⟩ **c** : a portion of tea for steeping — **in drawing** : correctly drawn or delineated — **out of drawing** : incorrectly drawn; *broadly* : INAPPROPRIATE : out of keeping (as with surrounding elements)

drawing account *n* **1** : CURRENT ACCOUNT **2** : an account showing usu. periodic cash payments to an employee in advance of actual earnings or for expenses to be incurred; *esp* : one showing advances to a salesman against commissions on future sales or for traveling expenses **3** : an account showing the withdrawals of a proprietor or partner from his business; *esp* : one showing withdrawals against current or anticipated profits — called also *personal account*

drawing awl *n* : an awl with an eye for pulling a thread through the hole bored

drawing block *n* **1** : a block of drawing paper **2** : ¹BLOCK 1h

drawing board *n* **1** : a board that has at least one straight edge against which a T square may be placed and that is used as a base for paper to be drawn on **2** : a heavy bond or bristol board with hard smooth surface that is used for drawing or lettering

drawing card \ˈ==ˌ=\ *also* **drawcard** \ˈ=ˌ=\ *n* : something (as a feature or performer) that attracts a great deal of attention or patronage

drawing chamber *n* [short for obs. E *withdrawing chamber*, fr. ME *withdrawyng chambre*] *archaic* : DRAWING ROOM

drawing cloth *n* : TRACING CLOTH

drawing die *n* : a die used to shape cuplike articles out of sheet metal that is pushed into it by a punch and prevented from wrinkling by a blank holder which holds the outer edge of the metal firm

drawing frame *or* **draw frame** *n* : a machine for combining and drawing slivers of a textile fiber (as of hemp for rope manufacture or cotton for spinning)

drawing-in \ˈ==¦=\ *n, pl* **drawings-in** : the action or operation of drawing warp yarns through the eyes of the heddles of a loom

drawing knife *var of* DRAWKNIFE

drawing paper *n* : a paper specially prepared for the use of drawers (as draftsmen or sketchers)

drawing pen *n* : a pen designed for use in drawing: as **a** : RULING PEN **b** : a freehand artist's pen that varies the width of strokes according to the pressure applied

drawing pin *n, Brit* : THUMBTACK

drawing pliers *n pl but sing or pl in constr* : DRAWTONGS

drawing point *n* : ANCHOR POINT

drawing power *n* : the capacity for drawing; *esp* : the ability to attract business or customers

drawing press *or* **draw press** *n* : a punch press that performs a drawing and cutting operation (as in forming hollow vessels from sheet metal)

drawing punch *n* : the punch that operates with a drawing die

drawing right *n* : a grant of credit from one nation to another that is a condition for the granting of funds or credit to the first nation from a third and is intended to stimulate and facilitate international trade

drawing room *n* [short for *withdrawing room*] **1 a** *archaic* : a room to which one may retire for privacy or rest : CLOSET; *esp* : one adjacent to public apartments **b** *obs* : a room or apartment forming a private part of the suite of a person (as a king) living in state and being often the setting of various informal activities or gatherings **c** : a more or less formal reception room (as in a home or hotel); *esp* : the room to which ladies withdraw from the dining room — compare PARLOR, SITTING ROOM **d** : a private room on a railroad passenger car with three berths and an enclosed toilet **2** : a formal or ceremonial reception; *esp* : one that is an official function of a royal court ⟨made her curtsy at the queen's last *drawing room*⟩ **3 a** : persons gathered in a drawing room ⟨disturbed the *drawing room* with his radical talk⟩ **b drawing rooms** *pl* : people of substance and position accustomed to formal living : polite society ⟨the report of her elopement shocked the *drawing rooms*⟩

drawing-room \ˈ==ˌ=\ *adj* [*drawing room*] **1** : of, relating to, characteristic of, or suitable for a drawing room ⟨*drawing-room* manners⟩ ⟨a new *drawing-room* rug⟩ **2** : dealing with or representing the drawing room; *esp* : concerned with life in polite society ⟨a *drawing-room* comedy⟩ **3** *of a railroad car* : equipped with drawing rooms

drawing string *var of* DRAWSTRING

drawing table *n* : a table with a surface adjustable for elevation and angle of incline

drawing table

draw into *vt* : to draw in

drawk \ˈdrȯk\ *vt* -ED/-ING/-S [ME (Sc dial.) *drawken*, perh. of Scand origin; akin to ON *drukna* to drown — more at DROWN] *dial Brit* : to saturate with moisture

drawknife \ˈ=ˌ=\ *also* **drawing knife** *n* : a woodworker's tool having a blade with a handle at each end used to shave off surfaces by drawing it toward one — called also *drawshave*

draw-knob \ˈ=ˌ=\ *n* : a knob in a pipe organ for admitting wind to a set of pipes or in a reed organ to a set of reeds

drawknot \ˈ=ˌ=\ *n* **1** : SLIPKNOT **2** : a half bowknot

¹drawl \ˈdrȯl\ *vb* -ED/-ING/-S [prob. freq. of ¹*draw*] *vi* **1** : to speak slowly esp. as a matter of habit with vowels greatly prolonged so that vowels monophthongal in other styles of speech are often diphthongized (as in *bin, web, bad, knob, talk, good*) **2** *archaic* : to move slowly : LOITER ~ *vt* **1** : to utter in a slow lengthened tone ⟨~*ed* out the hymn⟩ **2** *archaic* : to cause to pass or move sluggishly : drag out — **drawl·er** \-lə(r)\ *n* -S

drawknot

²drawl \"\ *n* -S : a drawling manner of speaking; *often* : something spoken in a drawling manner

¹drawl·ing \ˈdrȯliŋ, -lēŋ\ *adj* [fr. pres. part. of ¹*drawl*] **1** : slow-moving : LAGGING **2** *of speech* : uttered with a drawl — **drawl·ing·ly** *adv*

²draw·ling \"\ *n* -S [¹*draw* + *ling* (plant); prob. fr. the belief that sheep seize the plant and draw up a long underground part] : COTTON GRASS

drawlink \ˈ=ˌ=\ *n* [¹*draw* + *link*] : a drawbar on a railroad car

drawloom \ˈ=ˌ=\ *n* [¹*draw* + *loom*] : a hand loom formerly used for figure weaving and operated by a drawboy

drawly \ˈdrȯlē\ *adj* -ER/-EST [²*drawl* + *-y*] : characterized by drawling

draw·man \ˈdrȯmən\ *n, pl* **drawmen** : a worker who draws precut plastic materials to desired shapes in a hand or power press

draw-moss \ˈ=ˌ=\ *n* [so called fr. the fact that sheep pull out its leaf bases] : a cotton grass (esp. *Eriophorum vaginatum*)

drawn *past part of* DRAW

drawn bond *n* : a bond called for redemption before maturity

drawn butter *n* : melted butter often with chopped herbs or other seasoning

drawn edge *n* : COMB MARBLING

drawnet \ˈ=ˌ=\ *n* [¹*draw* + *net*] : a net formerly used for catching large wild birds

drawn glass *n* : glass (as window glass or fiber glass) that is made by continuous drawing of the molten glass by a series of rolls on automatic machinery

drawn grain *n* : a shrunken wrinkled condition of leather usu. due to improper handling of hides during tanning

drawn-out \ˈ=¦=\ *adj* : stretched to great or greater length ⟨the story of a simple-minded girl whose sweetness manages to survive *drawn-out* brutality —*Newsweek*⟩; *esp* : made to seem or be longer than desirable or normal (as by monotony) ⟨that lecture was long and *drawn-out*⟩

drawn teind *n, Scots law* : the part of a crop selected by the church as its tithe from the whole crop after reaping but before removal from the land

drawnwork \ˈ=ˌ=\ *n* **1** : decoration on fabric articles (as clothing and household linens) made by drawing out threads according to a pattern and usu. grouping and stitching the exposed threads in lacy designs **2** : plastering in which a brown coat is applied over the scratch coat before it is dry

draw off *vt* : to remove esp. from an environment or container : WITHDRAW, ABSTRACT; *often* : to extract by distillation ~ *vi* : to move away esp. to allow oneself room for action, regrouping, or reconsideration ⟨the enemies' losses forced them to *draw off*⟩ ⟨we *drew off* from that approach and reexamined the situation⟩

drawoff \ˈ=ˌ=\ *n* -S [*draw off*] **1** : something (as a liquid) that is drawn off **2** : a device (as a tap or valve) by which something is drawn off

draw on *vi* : APPROACH ⟨winter *draws on* apace⟩ — often used with *toward* ⟨*drawing on* toward destruction⟩ ~ *vt* **1** : to occasion as a consequence : bring on : CAUSE ⟨their folly *drew on* their disgrace⟩ **2** : to lead (one) on : INDUCE ⟨their encouragement *drew* him *on* to speak freely⟩ **3** : to pull or put on (as clothes) ⟨he *drew on* his boots⟩

draw out *vt* **1 a** : REMOVE, EXTRACT ⟨it might have been worthwhile to *draw out* these resemblances —W.R.Inge⟩ ⟨*drawing out* the fundamental meaning of his work⟩ **b** : to cause or lead (a person) to speak out freely ⟨your calm interest may serve to *draw* him *out*⟩ **c** : to call upon : demand the full expression of ⟨the new responsibilities *drew out* his latent talents⟩ **2** : to cause to become longer ⟨*drawing out* glass tubing⟩ : LENGTHEN, PROLONG ⟨he refused to *draw out* the interview⟩ ~ *vi* **1** : to become longer ⟨the days are *drawing out*⟩ **2** : to pull away : get ahead of companions or rivals ⟨at the head of the stretch the horse *drew out* from the field and won by six lengths⟩

drawout \ˈ=ˌ=\ *n* -S [*draw out*] : something that is drawn out; *esp* : a small portion of colored paste spread out in a thin layer on a sheet of white paper to show its color characteristics

draw pin *n* : a mortise pin used in a drawbore

drawplate \ˈ=ˌ=\ *n* **1** : a die with holes through which wires are drawn **2** : BAR PLATE

drawpoint \ˈ=ˌ=\ *n* : a pointed tempered steel tool used to scratch in transferred pencil lines or to stitch and pierce holes (as a mandrel for making small rings)

draw poker *n* : a game of poker in which each player is dealt five cards face down and after preliminary betting may discard unwanted cards and receive other cards to replace them prior to further betting

draw press *var of* DRAWING PRESS

drawrod \ˈ=ˌ=\ *n* : a rod that unites the drawgear at opposite ends of adjoining railroad cars in the European type of coupling

drawrope \ˈ=ˌ=\ *n* : a large heavy drawstring

draw runner *or* **draw slip** *n* : either of a pair of small pieces of wood that may be pulled out to support the drop front of certain desks or secretaries

draws *pres 3d sing of* DRAW, *pl of* DRAW

drawshave \ˈ=ˌ=\ *n* : DRAWKNIFE

drawsheet \ˈ=ˌ=\ *n* : a sheet drawn tight over a surface: as **a** : the outside or top sheet that holds the makeready on the platen or the impression cylinder of a printing press **b** : a narrow sheet used chiefly in hospitals and stretched across the bed lengthwise often over a rubber sheet underneath the patient's trunk

draw shot *n* : a pool stroke in which a player applies backspin to the cue ball to cause it to draw back from the object ball after hitting it — compare FOLLOW SHOT

drawspan \ˈ=ˌ=\ *n* : ²DRAW 2c(1)

drawspring \ˈ=ˌ=\ *n* : the spring to which a drawbar between railroad cars is attached in the European type of coupling

draw step *n* : ²DRAW 1g

drawstring \ˈ=ˌ=\ *also* **drawing string** *n* : a string, cord, or tape inserted into hems or casings or laced through eyelets for use in closing a bag or controlling fullness in garments or curtains

drawstroke \ˈ=ˌ=\ *n* : a canoeing stroke executed by reaching the paddle out to the side and pulling it toward the canoe with the blade flattened

draw table *n* : a table whose top is extendible by pulling out leaves from under each end

bag with drawstring

draw taper *n* : draft as given to a foundry pattern

drawtongs \ˈ=ˌ=\ *n pl but sing or pl in constr* : a tool for handling wire in wiredrawing

drawtube \ˈ=ˌ=\ *n* : a telescoping tube (as that containing the eyepiece of certain optical instruments)

drawtwister \ˈ=ˌ==\ *n* : a machine used to stretch synthetic textile yarns (as nylon) soon after extrusion

draw up *vt* **1** : to arrange (as a body of troops) in order **2** : to draft in due form: **a** : to formulate and produce ⟨*drew up* a plan for more equitable taxation⟩ **b** : to write out ⟨a list *drawn up* in a strange handwriting⟩ **3** : to straighten (oneself) to an erect posture esp. as an assertion of dignity or resentment ⟨she *drew* herself *up* indignantly⟩ **4** : to bring to a halt ⟨he *drew up* his horse and came in⟩ ~ *vi* : to come to a halt : STOP ⟨the car *drew up* at the door⟩

draw well *n* : a relatively deep well from which water is drawn (as by a bucket and chain) rather than dipped up with a container held in the hand

draw works *n pl but sing or pl in constr* : an oil-well drilling apparatus that consists of a countershaft and drum and that is used for supplying driving power and lifting heavy objects

1dray \ˈdrā\ *n* -s [ME *draye*, fr. OE *dræge* dragnet; akin to ON

dray 2

draga timber carried on horseback and trailing on the ground; derivative fr. the root of E *draw*] **1 :** any of several wheelless land vehicles used for haulage: as **a :** STONEBOAT **b :** TRAVOIS 1 **c :** a single bobsled used to support the forward end of a log in skidding on bare or rough ground — compare ALLIGATOR 6b **2 :** a strong low cart or wagon without permanent sides used for carrying heavy loads esp. locally and for hire; *broadly* **:** any vehicle (as a motortruck) that serves the purposes of a dray

2dray \"\ *vb* -ED/-ING/-S *vt* **1 :** to carry or transport on a dray **:** CART ~ *vi* **1 :** to drive a dray esp. for a livelihood **2 :** to haul goods usu. locally

3dray *var of* DREY

dray·age \ˈdrāij, -āēj\ *n* -s [1*dray* + *-age*] **1 :** the draying of goods **2 :** the charge or sum paid for draying (as of goods)

dray horse *n* **1 :** DRAFT HORSE; *esp* **:** one used for draying **2 :** DRUDGE

draying *n* -s [fr. gerund of 2*dray*] **:** the action or business of hauling with drays or hauling (as goods) locally ⟨engaged in ~ for over 20 years⟩

dray·man \-āmən\ *n, pl* **draymen :** a man who drives a dray or drays goods

DRE *abbr* director of religious education

1dread \ˈdred\ *vb* -ED/-ING/-S [ME *dreden*, fr. OE *drǣdan*; akin to OS *antdrādan* to fear, dread, OHG *intrātan*] *vt* **1 a :** to fear greatly **:** be in terror of ⟨a burned child ~s the fire⟩ **b** *archaic* **:** to stand in awe of **:** REVERENCE **2 :** to anticipate with fear of evil, pain, or trouble **:** look forward to with apprehensiveness **:** feel great anxiety about ⟨they ~ change, lest it should make matters worse —G.B.Shaw⟩ ~ *vi* **:** to be very apprehensive or fearful ⟨~ not, neither be afraid of them —Deut 1:29 (AV)⟩

2dread \"\ *n* -s [ME *drede, dred*, fr. *dreden*, v.] **1 a :** great fear esp. in the face of impending evil **:** fearful apprehension of danger **:** anticipatory terror ⟨looked forward with ~ to the night alone in the dark farmhouse —Sherwood Anderson⟩ ⟨~ of insecurity⟩ **b** *archaic* **:** reverential or respectful fear **:** AWE **2 :** a person or thing regarded with fear or awe ⟨the days of wooden ships and wooden homes, when fire was an omnipresent ~ —F.W.Saunders⟩ **3** [trans. of Dan & G *angst*] **:** ANXIETY 3 **syn** see FEAR

3dread \"\ *adj* [ME *dred*, fr. past part. of *dreden*, v.] **1 :** causing great fear or apprehensiveness **:** FRIGHTENING ⟨~ "secret" weapons which are evaluated solely by their capacity to kill —B.M.Baruch⟩ ⟨a ~ disease⟩ **2 :** inspiring reverential fear or awe ⟨most ~ lord⟩ — **dread·ly** *adv*

dreaddour *var of* DREDDOUR

1dread·ful \ˈdredfəl\ *adj* [ME *dredful*, fr. *drede, dred* + *-ful*] **1 a :** full of dread or terror **:** FEARFUL **b** *obs* **:** full of reverence or awe **2 a :** inspiring dread **:** causing great fear **:** FRIGHTENING ⟨a ~ storm⟩ ⟨that snake provided me with one of the most ~ experiences of my life —Jack McLaren⟩ **b :** inspiring awe or reverence ⟨out from the portico there gleamed a god, Apollon . . . all his shape one ~ beauty —Robert Browning⟩ **3 a :** exciting repugnance or loathing **:** REVOLTING, HORRIBLE ⟨no more ~ horror through the whole story than the bloody sack of Limoges —H.O.Taylor⟩ ⟨the ~ theory that if a teacher has studied education, he does not have to have a real mastery of the subject he is teaching —Oliver La Farge⟩ **b :** arousing great pity or sympathy **:** TRAGIC ⟨when she's alone and humiliated and broken it would be ~ if she had nowhere to go —W.S.Maugham⟩ **c :** arousing feelings of disapproval or dissatisfaction: as (1) **:** of poor quality ⟨a ~ road⟩ ⟨~ acoustics⟩ (2) **:** socially unacceptable **:** UNREFINED ⟨to prevent her marrying ~ people —Edith Wharton⟩ (3) **:** offensive to good taste ⟨~ furniture⟩ ⟨a ~ sight in her country clothes —R.H. Sampson⟩ **d :** unpleasant to experience, remember, or contemplate ⟨the ~ conclusion that the date 1869 . . . marks definitely the hour at which Latin . . . became a dead language —A.T.Quiller-Couch⟩ **4 :** EXTREME **:** very great ⟨a lady in a long skirt . . . was making ~ havoc with the standing grass —F.M.Ford⟩ ⟨boats and tackle were in ~ disrepair —Arthur Rucker⟩ **syn** see FEARFUL

2dreadful \"\ *adv, chiefly North* **:** VERY, EXTREMELY ⟨~ sick⟩ ⟨a ~ good man⟩

3dreadful \"\ *n* -s **:** a cheap and sensational story or periodical; *esp* **:** a story of crime or desperadoes such as was popular in late Victorian England ⟨a shilling ~⟩ — compare DIME NOVEL, SHOCKER

dread·ful·ly \-f(ə)lē, -li\ *adv* [ME *dredfully*, fr. *dredful* + *-ly*] **1 :** with dread ⟨he looked ~ over his shoulder to see if he were followed —Eric Linklater⟩ **2 :** in such a way as to cause dread **:** FRIGHTENINGLY ⟨the war whoop ripped ~ through the dewy greenness and freshness —Marjory S. Douglas⟩ **3 :** in such a manner or to such a degree as to excite repugnance, pity, disgust, dissatisfaction, or unpleasantness ⟨her response to all her varied experiences strikes the reader as ~ deficient in both thought and feeling —A.S.P.Woodhouse⟩ **4 :** EXTREMELY, EXCEEDINGLY ⟨I'm ~ tired, ~ stupid, nervy, worked up —Walter de la Mare⟩

dread·ful·ness \-fəlnəs\ *n* -ES [ME *dredfulnesse*, fr. *dredful* + *-nesse* -ness] **:** the quality or state of being dreadful

dread·ing·ly *adv* **:** in the manner of one that dreads ⟨approached the task fearfully, ~⟩

dread·less \-ləs\ *adj* [ME *dredelees*, fr. *drede, dred* + *-lees* -less] *archaic* **:** free from dread **:** INTREPID, DAUNTLESS — **dread·less·ly** *adv, archaic*

dreadnought *also* **dreadnaught** \ˈ=,=\ *n* -s **1 :** FEARNOUGHT 1 **2** [fr. *Dreadnought*, Brit. battleship finished 1907, the first of this type] **:** a battleship of the 20th century that has its main armament entirely of big guns all of one caliber

1dream \ˈdrēm\ *n* -s [ME *dreem*, fr. OE *drēam* noise, joy, music, prob. influenced in meaning by ON *draumr* dream; prob. akin to OHG *troum* dream, ON *draumr*, Gk *thrylos* noise, din, Latvian *duñduris* gadfly, wasp — more at DRONE] **1 a :** a series of thoughts, images, or emotions occurring during sleep **:** a semblance of reality or events occurring to one asleep **b** *psychoanalysis* **:** condensed, elaborated, symbolized, or otherwise distorted images of memories or of unconscious impulses experienced esp. during sleep but also during other lapses in attention the meaning of which is concealed from the ego; *also* **:** the verbal or written report of such images or experiences **2 :** an experience of waking life having the characteristics of a dream: as **a :** a visionary creation of the imagination **:** DAYDREAM ⟨the ~s of youth⟩ **b :** a state of mind marked by abstraction or release from the sense of reality **:** REVERIE ⟨lives in a ~, oblivious of all practical concerns⟩ **c :** an object seen in a dreamlike state **:** VISION ⟨if you be what I think you, some sweet ~ —Alfred Tennyson⟩ **3 :** something that is notable for its beauty, excellence, or enjoyable quality ⟨she wore a ~ of a dress⟩ ⟨it was a ~ of a trip⟩ ⟨the food is marvelous . . . and the setting is an absolute ~ —T.H. Fielding⟩ **4 :** a major aim, goal, or purpose the attainment of which is ardently desired or longed for **:** IDEAL ⟨the shore thou foundest verifies thy ~ —Walt Whitman⟩ ⟨the ~ of . . . an empire stretching to the Pacific —R.W.Van Alstyne⟩ ⟨achieved her ~ of becoming a professional writer —*Current Biog.*⟩ **syn** see FANCY

2dream \"\ *vb* **dreamed** \ˈdrem(p)t, -ēmd\ *or* **dreamt** \-em(p)t\ **dreamed** *or* **dreamt; dreaming** \-ēmiŋ\ **dreams** \-ēmz\ [ME *dremen*, fr. *dreem*, n.] *vi* **1 :** to have a dream **:** have ideas or images in the mind while asleep ⟨there are very normal people who ~ nightly —Otto Fenichel⟩ ⟨she ~*ed* of taking a trip and awoke with a feeling of excitement⟩ **2 :** to let the mind run on in idle reverie **:** give oneself over to effortless thought esp. of a fanciful nature ⟨the tendency of the population to ~ about their ancient glory rather than struggle with contemporary facts —Samuel Van Valkenburg & Ellsworth Huntington⟩ ⟨~*ing* of renown to come —Charles Kingsley⟩ **3 :** to wish for something ardently or yearningly **:** LONG **:** scheme, plan, or aspire for the attainment of some object — usu. used with *of* ⟨she ~*ed* of becoming a language teacher —Gertrude Samuels⟩ ⟨those powers who ~ of further aggrandizement in the East⟩ **4 :** to appear tranquil or dreamy **:** be suggestive of or give an impression of tranquility or dreaminess ⟨quaint historic villages where pre-Revolutionary houses ~ in leafy shadows —Gladys Taber⟩ ⟨the pale ~*ing* sky —Dorothy C. Fisher⟩ ~ *vt* **1 :** to have a dream of **:** imagine in sleep **:** think of or seem to have a sensory impression of while asleep ⟨your old men shall ~ dreams —Acts 2:17 (RSV)⟩ ⟨according to Descartes a dreamer supposes that what he ~s are real objects and incidents —Margaret Macdonald⟩ ⟨I *dreamt* that I dwelt in marble halls —Alfred Bunn⟩ **2 :** to consider as a possibility **:** conceive of **:** IMAGINE ⟨little ~*ing* that I could park my car, climb down the bank, set up my rod and catch big trout —Joseph Novick⟩ ⟨the great new country whose expanse they did not ~ —Meridel Le Sueur⟩ **3 :** to pass (time) in reverie or inaction — usu. used with *away* ⟨he ~*ed* his life away⟩ — **dream of :** to think of as possible, fitting, or proper **:** give serious consideration to ⟨inventions that our grandfathers never *dreamed of*⟩ ⟨they would never *dream of* building a cumbersome railway . . . when the cableway is so much less expensive to build and to operate —M.L.Hoffman⟩ ⟨only a madman would *dream of* attempting to drive at that speed in such places —Priscilla Hughes⟩

3dream \"\ *adj* [1*dream*] **1 :** of, relating to, involved in, or resembling a dream **2 :** experienced in a dream ⟨~ myths of the Mohave, that are sung by the person who has dreamt the myth —Edward Sapir⟩ **3 :** appropriate to a pleasant dream **:** marked by as desirable qualities as can be imagined **:** approaching perfection or the ideal ⟨win a ~ holiday in Europe⟩ ⟨he is the ~ competitor — the one in 10,000 who has the temperament to match the talent —*Time*⟩ ⟨a display of ~ cars⟩

dreamboat \ˈ=,=\ *n* **1** *slang* **:** the embodiment of what one imagines or thinks to be highly desirable ⟨the local college student who declared . . . he'd rather have a 1934 Ford than any other car has finally found his ~ —*Springfield (Mass.) Daily News*⟩ ⟨black Alaska seal, the new ~ for not only daytime but cocktails and evening —Lois Long⟩ **2** *slang* **a :** the person that most nearly fulfills one's idea of what a member of the opposite sex should be like ⟨brought to movie stardom a lady who, after 25 years, is still my ~ —S.J.Perelman⟩ **b :** SWEETHEART ⟨waiting for her ~ to finish his 21-month hitch in gaol —*Police Detective*⟩

dream book *n* **:** a book claiming to interpret the significance of dreams esp. as omens of the future

dream·er \ˈdrēmə(r)\ *n* -s [ME *dremere*, fr. *dremen* to dream + *-ere* -er] **1 :** one that dreams: as **a :** one who has ideas or images in the mind while asleep ⟨the ~ apparently moves about at will in the past, as in the present —Weston La Barre⟩ **b :** one that engages in daydreaming or idle reverie **:** one that builds castles in the air ⟨~s who yearned for things that are not . . . or things that have been —Norman Douglas⟩ **c :** one that conceives and usu. attempts to achieve a major objective (as of social change or scientific or geographic discovery) that is regarded by most of his contemporaries as impracticable or fanciful ⟨the great ~s, seers, and visionaries of history⟩ **2** *usu cap* **:** an adherent of a No. American Indian religious sect originated by the Wanapûm chief Smohalla about 1850–60 and extending to many of the Oregon, Washington, and Idaho tribes **3 :** one who claims to select lucky policy-game numbers or horse-race tips by occult means and sells them to bettors

dream·ery \ˈdrēmərē\ *n* -ES **:** impractical fancies

dream·ful \-mfəl\ *adj* **:** full of dreams **:** DREAMY ⟨awake after ~ sleep —Max Steele⟩ ⟨various peculiarities and faults of my writings are due to this mechanical and ~ way of composing them —George Santayana⟩ — **dream·ful·ly** \-fəlē\ *adv* — **dream·ful·ness** \-lnəs\ *n* -ES

dream·i·ly \-mǝlē, -li\ *adv* **:** as if in a dream **:** in a dreamy manner **:** VAGUELY

dream·i·ness \-mēnǝs, -min-\ *n* -ES **:** the quality or state of being dreamy

dream·ing·ly *adv* [*dreaming* (pres. part. of 2*dream*) + *-ly*] **:** as if dreaming **:** DREAMILY

dream·land \-m,land, -aa(ə)nd\ *n* **:** an unreal delightful country existing only in imagination or in dreams **:** NEVER-NEVER ⟨a charming fantasy set in a ~ filled with desirable girls and prime wine⟩

dream·less \-mləs\ *adj* **:** having no dreams ⟨a ~ sleep⟩ — **dream·less·ly** *adv* — **dream·less·ness** *n* -ES

dreamlike \ˈ=,=\ *adj* **:** like that seen or occurring in a dream ⟨the old castle stood there in all its ~ loveliness⟩ **:** resembling a dream (as in transitoriness or unreal quality) ⟨that fast furious ride across the moor he remembered only as a frightening ~ experience⟩ **:** VAGUE, NEBULOUS, SHADOWY ⟨night invested the quiet lake with a ~ charm⟩

dreams *pl of* DREAM, *pres 3d sing of* DREAM

dreamt *past of* DREAM

dreamtime \ˈ=,=\ *n* [prob. trans. of Australian *alchera, alcheringa*] **:** the aboriginal time of creation in the mythology of the Australian natives **:** the mythical beginning time when all things were created, including the first human ancestors, and to which myths are generally traceable ⟨a patriarchal or ~ father —Daisy Bates⟩

dream up *vt* **:** to invent, devise, or concoct esp. in an outburst of artistic improvisation or an unbridled flight of fancy ⟨the most fantastic rumors he could *dream up* —Joseph Millard⟩ ⟨all the magnificent plans they're *dreaming up* —Bennett Cerf⟩

dream vision *n* **1 :** a poetic framework esp. popular in medieval literature in which the poet pictures himself as falling asleep and envisioning in his dream a series of allegorical people and events **2 :** a poem utilizing the dream vision

dreamwork \ˈ=,=\ *n* [trans. of G *traumarbeit*] **:** the process of concealing the latent content of dreams from the conscious mind

dreamworld \ˈ=,=\ *n* **1 :** DREAMLAND; *also* **:** a world of illusion or fantasy ⟨his struggle to grow out of the ~ of childhood —J.W.Aldridge⟩ **2 :** a state of intense preoccupation with or absorption in intellectual or unworldly concerns ⟨musicians are pictured as tempestuous characters . . . lost in a ~ of creation —Gretchen Finletter⟩

dreamy \ˈdrēmē, -mi\ *adj* -ER/-EST [1*dream* + *-y*] **1 a :** VAGUE, IDLE, HAZY ⟨the drone of the greenfinch lulls me into ~ meditations —L.P.Smith⟩ **b :** given to dreaming or fantasy ⟨the child was ~ and introverted, playing with imaginary playmates and having visions⟩ ⟨you're frightfully ~ and unpractical and unbusinesslike —Christopher Isherwood⟩ **2 :** having the quality or characteristics of a dream **:** DREAMLIKE **3 a :** INDISTINCT ⟨the mountains growing softer in outline and ~ looking —John Muir †1914⟩ **b :** quiet and soothing ⟨~ waltzes⟩ **c :** DELIGHTFUL, PLEASING, IDEAL ⟨own and run a hotel and ski resort in a perfectly ~ spot in Utah —Carl Jonas⟩ ⟨he's so handsome . . . real ~ —Greg Foley⟩ **4 :** suggestive of a dream or a dreamlike state ⟨her eyes were ~ and great, as of one who looketh afar —William Morris⟩ ⟨she walked home that night in a ~ silence —Robert Fawcett⟩

drean \ˈdrēn\ *dial var of* DRAIN

1drear \ˈdri(ə)r, -iə\ *n* -s [back-formation fr. *dreary*] *archaic* **:** DREARINESS

2drear \"\ *adj* [short for *dreary*] **1 :** cheerless and depressing **:** uninteresting and dull **:** DREARY ⟨though the setting is ~ and circumstances oppressive, this is not a degrading story —E.A. Weeks⟩ ⟨a barren and ~ existence⟩ **2 :** SAD ⟨I had taken a hot whisky punch to the master, poor creature, he seemed so lone and ~ —James Reynolds⟩ — **drear·ly** *adv* — **drear·ness** *n* -ES

drear·i·head *pronunc at* DREARY +,hed\ *or* **drear·i·hood** \-,hu̇d\ *n* [*drearihead* fr. ME *drerihed*, fr. *drery* dreary + *-hed, -hede* (akin to ME *-hod* -hood); *drearihood* fr. *dreary* + *-hood*] *archaic* **:** DREARINESS

drear·i·ly \ˈdrirəlē, -rēr-, -li\ *adv* [ME *drerily*, fr. OE *drēorīglīce*, fr. *drēorig* sad, bloody + *-līce* -ly] **:** in a dreary way

drear·i·ment \-rēmənt, -rim-\ *n* -s **:** the quality or state of being dreary

drear·i·ness \-rēnǝs, -rin-\ *n* -ES [ME *drerinesse*, fr. OE *drēorignys*, fr. *drēorig* sad, bloody + *-nys, -nes* -ness] **1** *archaic* **:** SADNESS **2 a :** the quality or state of being dull and uninteresting **:** MONOTONY, GLOOMINESS ⟨the occasional ~ of being dutiful —Claudia Cassidy⟩ **b :** something that is dull, monotonous, and uninteresting ⟨the concert was one of those fragmentary ~*es* that people endure because they are fashionable —Mark Twain⟩

drear·i·some \-rēsəm, -ris-\ *adj, archaic* **:** characterized by dreariness

dreary \ˈdrir|ē, -rēr|, |i\ *adj* -ER/-EST [ME *drery*, fr. OE *drēorig* sad, bloody, fr. *drēor* gore, falling blood; akin to OE *drēosan* to fall, OHG *trūrēn* to be sad, MHG *trōr* dripping liquid, ON *dreyri* flowing blood, Goth *driusan* to fall, Gk *thrauein* to shatter] **1** *obs* **:** CRUEL, DIRE, GRIEVOUS **2 :** feeling, displaying, or reflecting a settled mood of listlessness or discouragement **:** without liveliness, cheer, joy, or hope ⟨she would fix her eyes on the distance in ~ contemplation, and her mind would follow her eyes in a vacant and wistful regard —G.D.Brown⟩ ⟨restore a crazy constitution and cheer a ~ mind —George Berkeley⟩ **3 :** not having anything likely to cheer, comfort, encourage, interest, or enliven **:** making for gloomy dullness **:** DEPRESSING, DISCOURAGING, ENERVATING ⟨~ sketches of people in breadlines —R.H.Rovere⟩ ⟨abandoned farms alone remained as ~ reminders of former prosperity —*Amer. Guide Series: Mass.*⟩ ⟨life in a perfectly sensible, utilitarian community would be intolerably ~ —Aldous Huxley⟩ **syn** see DISMAL

dreck \ˈdrek\ *n* -s [Yiddish *drek* & G *dreck*, fr. MHG *drec*; akin to OE *threax* rubbish, ON *threkkr* excrement, L *stercus* excrement, LGk *sterganos* privy, Gk *tryg-, tryx* dregs, and prob. to Russ *sterva* carrion] **1 :** FILTH, LITTER, TRASH, JUNK ⟨your food is ~, it is fit only for pigs —Michael Gold⟩ ⟨the ~ of the cities⟩ **2 :** a garment badly made or of inferior materials

dred·dour \ˈdredər\ *n* -s [ME (Sc) *dredour*, fr. ME *drede* dread + *-our* (as in *horrour* horror) — more at DREAD] *chiefly Scot* **:** DREAD, TERROR

1dredge \ˈdrej, ˈdrəj\ *n* -s [alter. of ME *dragge, draggeye*, fr. MF *dragie* mixture of grains grown as a forage crop, fr. (assumed) VL (of Gaul) *dravocata*, fr. Gaulish *dravoca* darnel; akin to ME *tare* vetch — more at TARE] *dial Brit* **:** mixed grains sown together; *esp* **:** a mixture of oats and barley grown together for making malt

2dredge \ˈdrej, *chiefly dial* ˈdrəj\ *n* -s *often attrib* [prob. alter. of Sc *dreg-* (in the compound *dregbot* dredge boat), fr. ME (Sc) *dreg-*, perh. irreg. fr. the root of OE *dragan* to pull — more at DRAW] **1 :** an implement or machine for scooping or digging objects or earth from the bed of a body of water: **a :** an oblong iron frame with a bag net attached or a similar apparatus for gathering fish, shellfish, or natural history specimens **b :** a machine for scooping up or removing earth (as in excavating or deepening stream or harbor channels, building levees, or digging ditches) usu. by a series of buckets on an endless chain, a pump or suction tube, or a single bucket or grab at the end of an arm — see DIPPER DREDGE, HYDRAULIC DREDGE; compare DRAGLINE 2 **2 :** a boat or barge used in dredging

3dredge \"\ *vb* -ED/-ING/-S *vt* **1 a :** to catch, gather, or pull out with a dredge — often used with *up* ⟨silt and old refuse were *dredged* up from the river bottom —Green Peyton⟩ **b :** to bring to light or gather by deep searching as if with a dredge — often used with *up* ⟨facts *dredged* from the records⟩ ⟨I tried to ~ up a little of that deep, involuntary wisdom that tells you what to do in a critical situation —Anne S. Mehdevi⟩ **c :** to make a search of or dig into deeply with or as if with a dredge ⟨the harbor still is being *dredged* for boats sunk —*Springfield (Mass.) Union*⟩ ⟨*dredging* his memories and finding them intolerable —*Time*⟩ **2 :** to deepen with a dredging machine **:** excavate with a dredge ⟨*dredged* a cutoff three blocks long . . . where the river swings eastward in a wide semicircle —Green Peyton⟩ ~ *vi* **:** to use a dredge **:** to search with or as if with a dredge ⟨*dredging* for oysters⟩ ⟨he *dredged* into himself for words —Oliver La Farge⟩

4dredge \"\ *vt* -ED/-ING/-S [obs. *dredge*, n., sweetmeat, fr. ME *drege*, alter. of *drage*, fr. MF *dragie, dragee*, modif. of L *tragemata* (pl.) sweetmeats, fr. Gk *tragēmata*, pl. of *tragēmat-, tragēma* sweetmeat, dried fruit] **:** to sprinkle with a powdered substance: as **a :** to coat (food) by sprinkling (as with flour or sugar) **b :** to dust (hot ware) with dry enamel powder in dry process enameling

5dredge \"\ *n* -s **:** a box or package attachment with holes for sprinkling or sifting the contents

dredge corn *n* [1*dredge*] **:** a mixed crop of oats and barley used in Great Britain for stock feed

dredge·man \-mən\ *n, pl* **dredgemen** [2*dredge*] **1 :** DREDGER 1 **2 :** one who is in charge of the operation of a dredge used to mine metal-bearing sands from the bottom of a body of water

1dredg·er \-jə(r)\ *n* -s [3*dredge* + *-er*] **:** one that dredges; *esp* **:** 2DREDGE

2dredger \"\ *n* -s [4*dredge* + *-er*] **1 :** a shaker for condiments used at the table **2 :** 5DREDGE

dredger master *n* **:** DREDGEMAN 2

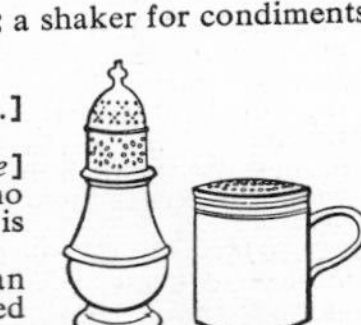

dredgers 1

dred·gie \ˈdrejē\ *n* -s [by alter.] **:** DIRGIE 2

dredging *n* -s [fr. gerund of 3*dredge*] **:** the act or operation of one who dredges; *also* **:** something that is dredged up

dredging bucket *n* **:** a bucket (as an orange-peel or clamshell bucket) used in dredging

1dree \ˈdrē\ *vb* **dreed; dreed; dreeing; drees** [ME *dreen, drien*, fr. OE *drēogan* to perform, endure — more at DRUDGE] *vt* **1** *chiefly Scot* **:** ENDURE, SUFFER ⟨the slighted maids my torments see and laugh at a' the pangs I ~ —Robert Burns⟩ **2** *archaic Scot* **:** to pass (time) or spend (one's life) usu. unhappily **3** *chiefly Scot* **:** DREAD, FEAR ~ *vi, dial Brit* **:** ENDURE — **dree one's weird** *chiefly Scot* **:** to endure one's fate

2dree \"\ *n* -s *chiefly Scot* **:** MISFORTUNE, SUFFERING

3dree \"\ *var of* DREICH

dreed \ˈdrēd\ *dial Brit var of* DREAD

dreel \ˈdrēl\ *Scot var of* DRILL

dreen \ˈdrēn\ *dial var of* DRAIN

dreep \ˈdrēp\ *dial Brit var of* DRIP

dreepy \-pi\ *adj* -ER/-EST [*dreep* + *-y*] *dial Brit* **:** spiritless and ineffective **:** DROOPY

dreg \ˈdreg\ *n* -s [ME, fr. ON *dregg*; akin to L *fraces* dregs of oil, Gk *tarattein, tarassein* to disturb, stir, Alb *dia* dregs of oil, OE *deorc* dark — more at DARK] **1 :** sediment contained in a liquid or precipitated from it **:** LEES — usu. used in pl. ⟨the night-porter took a tankard from a hook and emptied all the ~s from the glasses into it —George Bellairs⟩ **2 :** the poorest or most undesirable part of anything — usu. used in pl. ⟨the ~s of society⟩ **3 :** the last remaining part **:** VESTIGE ⟨with some ~s of timidity still in his soul —John Buchan⟩

dreg·gy \-gē\ *adj* -ER/-EST [ME, fr. *dreg* + *-y*] **:** full of dregs **:** MUDDY, FOUL

d region *n, usu cap D* **:** the lowest part of the ionosphere occurring between 25 and 40 miles above the surface of the earth and capable of reflecting radio waves of very low frequency but absorbing energy of radio waves of high frequencies that are reflected by higher ionosphere layers

dregs of wine : a dark red to deep reddish brown that is less strong than Malaga — called also *wine dregs, wine lees*

dreich *or* **dreigh** \ˈdrēk\ *adj* [ME *dregh, dreich*, of Scand origin; akin to ON *drjūgr* substantial, lasting; akin to OE *drēogan* to perform, endure — more at DRUDGE] **1** *chiefly Scot* **a :** long and drawn out **:** PROTRACTED ⟨a ~ job hoeing potatoes⟩ **b :** tedious and uninteresting **:** TIRESOME ⟨a ~ sermon⟩ **2** *chiefly Scot* **:** slow or tardy esp. in paying debts **3** *chiefly Scot* **:** dismal and gloomy **:** DREARY ⟨~ damp days —D.B. Forrester⟩

dreid \ˈdrēd\ *Scot var of* DREAD

drei·del *or* **drei·dl** \ˈdrādᵊl\ *n, pl* **dreidels** *or* **dreidels** [Yiddish *dreidl*, fr. *drehen* to turn, fr. MHG *dræjen, dræhen*, fr. OHG *drāen* — more at THROW] **1 :** a 4-sided die that revolves like a spinning top, that is marked on each side with a different Hebrew letter, and that is used as a toy esp. during the Hanukkah festival **2 :** a children's game of chance similar to put-and-take that is played with the dreidel

drei·kan·ter \ˈdrī,käntə(r), -kan-\ *n, pl* **dreikanters** *or* **dreikanter** [G, lit., one having three edges, fr. *drei* three (fr. OHG *drī*) + *kante* edge (fr. LG *kant, kante*, fr. MLG, fr. MD *cant*) + *-er* (fr. OHG *-āri*) — more at THREE, CANT, -ER] **:** a

3-faced pebble faceted by wind-blown sand; *broadly* **:** VENTIFACT

dreis·sen·sia \drī'sen(t)sēə, -nch(ē)ə\ *n, cap* [NL, irreg. fr. *Dreyssen*, 19th cent. Belg. physician + NL *-ia*] **:** a genus of Old World bivalve mollusks (suborder Tellinacea) somewhat resembling the true mussels

[1]drench \'drench\ *n* -ES [ME, fr. OE *drenc;* akin to OHG *trank* drink, Goth *dranc;* derivative fr. the root of OE *drincan* to drink — more at DRINK] **1 a :** DRINK, DRAFT **b :** a poisonous or medicinal drink; *specif* **:** a large dose of medicine mixed with liquid and put down the throat of an animal **2 a :** something that drenches ⟨this alternation of sun and ~ proliferates plant and beast —Waldo Frank⟩ **b :** a quantity sufficient to drench or saturate ⟨the heather of the bogs, the hill turf, and the gravel of the road had lost their color under a ~ of dew —John Buchan⟩ ⟨few men have subjected all their borrowings to so strong a ~ of personality —H.S.Canby⟩ **c :** a solution usu. of fermenting bran used for drenching hides

[2]drench \"\ *vb* -ED/-ING/-ES [ME *drenchen* to cause to drink, drown, fr. OE *drencan;* akin to OHG *trenken* to cause to drink, ON *drekkja* to drown, Goth *drankjan* to cause to drink; causative fr. the root of OE *drincan* to drink] *vt* **1 a** *archaic* **:** to force to drink **b :** to administer a drench to (an animal) **2** *obs* **a :** to submerge in water **b :** DROWN **3 :** to steep or saturate by immersion in liquid ⟨desserts ~*ed* in brandy —Dwight Macdonald⟩; *specif* **:** to soak (hides) in a weak acid bath to remove lime left by the liming process **4 :** to soak or cover thoroughly with liquid that falls or is precipitated ⟨within five minutes the daily downpour of tropical rain would ~ the jungle —William Beebe⟩ ⟨the sweat poured down his body until he was ~*ed* —Pearl Buck⟩ **5 :** to fill completely as if by soaking or precipitation **:** SATURATE, STEEP, PERVADE ⟨ominous iridescences ~ every paragraph —Frederic Morton⟩ ⟨familiar with the Hebrides and ~*ed* in Highland lore —J.W.Krutch⟩ ⟨klieg lights snapped on, ~*ing* rostrum and orchestra floor with hot light —F.L.Allen⟩ ⟨sun-*drenched* Italy —G.C. Sellery⟩ **~** *vi* **:** to fall heavily and cause saturation ⟨driving snow and sleet, which ~*ed* cruelly down on little townships that already . . . had had too much of water —Mollie Panter-Downes⟩

drench·er \-chə(r)\ *n* -S **:** one that drenches; *specif* **:** a delimer who uses bran drench

drench·ing·ly *adv* **:** in a manner that drenches

dreng *also* **drengh** \'dreŋ\ *n* -S [ME *dreng, dring*, fr. OE *dreng* warrior, fr. ON *drengr* young man, valiant man; akin to MIr *dringid* he steps, Russ *derzhat'* to hold, L *firmus* firm — more at FIRM] *old English law* **:** a free tenant esp. in ancient Northumbria who held under a partly military and partly servile form of tenure antedating the Norman conquest

dren·gage \'dreŋ(g)ij\ *n* -S [ML *drengagium*, fr. ME *dreng* + ML *-agium* -age (fr. OF *-age*)] *old English law* **:** the tenure or service of a dreng

drep·a·nas·pis \,drepə'naspə̇s\ *n, cap* [NL, fr. Gk *drepanē* sickle (fr. *drepein* to pluck) + NL *-aspis* — more at DRAB] **:** a genus of Devonian ostracoderms (class Heterostraci)

drep·a·ne \'drepə(,)nē\ *n* [NL, fr. Gk *drepanē* sickle; prob. fr. the shape of its pectoral fins] **1** *cap* **:** a genus (coextensive with a family Drepanidae) of compressed percoid food fishes comprising a single species (*D. punctata*) and having a protrusible mouth that when extended forms a tubular downward projection **2** -S **:** any fish of the genus *Drepane*

drep·a·nid \-,nə̇d\ *n* -S [irreg. fr. NL *Drepanididae*] **:** a bird of the family Drepanididae **:** a Hawaiian honeycreeper

dre·pan·i·dae \drə'panə,dē\ *n pl, cap* [NL, fr. *Drepana*, type genus (fr. Gk *drepanē* sickle) + *-idae*; fr. the shape of the forewings] **:** a family of small slender moths usu. having the tips of the forewings hooked — see HOOKTIPS

drep·a·nid·i·dae \,drepə'nidə,dē\ *n pl, cap* [NL, fr. *Drepanid-*, *Drepanis*, type genus (fr. L *drepanis*, a bird, perh. the swift, fr. Gk *drepanid-, drepanis*, fr. *drepanē* sickle) + *-idae*] **:** a family of Hawaiian passerine birds having the bill precisely adapted in curvature and length for the obtaining of nectar from various plants of the family Lobeliaceae — see MAMO

dre·pan·i·form \drə'panə,fȯrm, 'drepən-\ *adj* [Gk *drepanē* sickle + E *-iform*] *biol* **:** shaped like a sickle **:** FALCATE

drep·a·no·cy·to·sis \,drepə(,)nō,sī'tōsə̇s\ *n, pl* **drepanocytoses** \-ō,sēz\ [NL, fr. *drepano-* (fr. Gk *drepanē* sickle) + *cyt-* + *-osis*] **1 :** SICKLE-CELL ANEMIA **2 :** SICKLEMIA

drep·a·noid \'drepə,nȯid\ *adj* [Gk *drepanoeidēs*, fr. *drepan-* (fr. *drepanē, drepanon* sickle) + *-oeidēs* -oid] **:** shaped like a sickle

drep·a·no·phy·cus \,drepənō'fīkəs\ *n, cap* [NL, prob. fr. *drepano-* (fr. Gk *drepanē, drepanon* sickle) + *-phycus* (fr. Gk *phykos* seaweed) — more at FUCUS] **:** a genus of very large Devonian fossil plants resembling and prob. closely related to the psilophytons but distinguished by spiny verticellate or spiral appendages resembling leaves and sometimes having sporangia in their axils

[1]dres·den \'drezdən\ *adj, usu cap* [fr. *Dresden*, industrial city of Saxony, Germany] **:** of or from the city of Dresden, Germany **:** of the kind or style prevalent in Dresden

[2]dresden \"\ *n* -S *usu cap* **:** DRESDEN CHINA

dresden blue *n, often cap D* **:** a moderate blue that is greener and duller than average copen, redder, lighter, and stronger than azurite blue or pompadour, and greener and paler than bluebird

dresden brown *n, often cap D* **:** FOX 5

dresden china *or* **dresden ware** *n, usu cap D* [*Dresden*, Germany] **:** hard-paste porcelain (as Meissen) made in the vicinity of Dresden and typically characterized by daintiness of design and ornate decoration

dresden-china \ˌ=ˌ=ˈ=ˌ=\ *adj, usu cap D* [*Dresden china*] **:** having a delicate or insipid prettiness ⟨proud of his *Dresden-china* doll of a wife⟩

[1]dress \'dres\ *vb* -ED/-ING/-ES [ME *dressen*, fr. MF *dresser*, fr. OF *drecier*, fr. (assumed) VL *directiare*, fr. L *directus* direct, past part. of *dirigere* to direct, fr. *di-* (fr. *dis-* apart) + *-rigere* (fr. *regere* to rule) — more at DIS-, RIGHT] *vt* **1 :** to make or set straight **:** put in proper position: as **a** *now dial* **:** ERECT, PRICK ⟨the cat ~*ed* up her ears at the sound⟩ **b :** to arrange (troops, equipment) in a straight line and at proper intervals **:** ALIGN ⟨~ the ranks⟩ **c :** to place the actors on (a stage) so as to create a pleasing and well-balanced scene **2** *archaic* **:** to dress down **3 :** to put clothes on **:** provide with clothing **:** CLOTHE ⟨she ~*ed* the child in a snowsuit⟩ ⟨she ~*es* her family on a small budget⟩ **4 :** to cover with, array in, or add something that improves the appearance or heightens the effectiveness of **:** add decorative details or accessories to **:** EMBELLISH ⟨the ruins, which are ~*ed* by the moon in even more compelling mystery —P.E.Deutschman⟩ ⟨then I ~ my hair with the little chrysanthemums —Amy Lowell⟩ — often used with *up* ⟨she ~*ed* up her black dress with rhinestone clips⟩ ⟨cars ~*ed* up with chrome⟩ ⟨needlessly rebinding old manuscripts and incunabula in order to *dress* up books —Edith Diehl⟩ **5 a :** to provide with the suitable furnishings for a particular purpose or occasion **:** make ready **:** OUTFIT ⟨~*ed* the table for supper —George Meredith⟩ ⟨besides doubling and tripling as performers, everyone took a turn ~*ing* the ring for the other acts —Bill Ballantine⟩ — compare WINDOW DRESSING **b :** to cover (the hooped curd) with cloth in cheese making **6 a :** to apply dressings, bandages, or therapeutic materials to (as wounds) **b** (1) **:** to arrange (the hair) by combing, brushing, curling (2) **:** to groom and curry (an animal) **c :** to make ready or put in order for use or service: as (1) **:** to prepare (a fishhook) for fishing; *also* **:** prepare (flies or bait) for use on a hook (2) **:** to prepare (food animals) for market usu. by bleeding and cleaning — often used with *out* ⟨bleed and ~ out the animal so that no meat would be wasted —Frances Judge⟩ (3) **:** CULTIVATE, TEND ⟨~ a crop⟩ ⟨~ a field⟩; *specif* **:** to apply manure or fertilizer to — compare TOP-DRESS (4) *chiefly Brit* **:** PACK ⟨~ the impression cylinder of a printing press⟩; *also* **:** to attach the printing surface to (the plate cylinder of a press) **d** (1) **:** to free (as grain or ore) of impurities or irregularities; *specif* **:** to sift (flour) so as to remove bran flakes and insure even granulation (2) **:** to remove worn-out abrasive from (an abrasive wheel) **7 :** to put through a finishing operation or process: as **a :** to cure (fur skins) by softening, fleshing, oiling, and drumming; *sometimes* **:** TAN 1 **b :** to give a smooth or glossy finish to (as leather, textiles, pottery) **c :** to make trim and smooth (lumber, stone, a gem) **d :** to shape (as a tool) by grinding **e :** to impart a surface finish to (a race track) esp. by scraping **~** *vi* **1 a :** to put on clothing ⟨he ~*ed* quickly⟩ ⟨she ~*ed* warmly for skiing⟩ **b :** to put on or wear one's best clothes or formal clothes ⟨she is ~*ing* for the opera⟩ — often used with *up* ⟨he ~*es* up only when guests are coming⟩ **c :** to dress elaborately or bizarrely ⟨~*ing* up for a masquerade ball⟩ **d :** to wear clothes ⟨she always ~*es* in good taste⟩ **2** *of a food animal* **:** to weigh after being dressed ⟨the chicken ~*ed* four pounds⟩ — often used with *out* ⟨the steer ~*ed* out to 70 percent of his weight⟩ **3 :** to align oneself with the next soldier in a line to make the line straight — **dress one's droddum** *Scot* **:** to give a thrashing or beating — **dress ship 1 :** to ornament a ship while in port by hoisting national ensigns at the mastheads and running a line of signal flags and pennants from bow to stern by way of the mastheads in honor of a special occasion (as a national holiday) or as a courtesy to a foreign nation or a distinguished person **2 :** to ornament a ship in the U.S. Navy by hoisting national ensigns at the mastheads, the ship's largest ensign at the flagstaff, and the jack at the jackstaff

[2]dress \"\ *n* -ES **1** *obs* **:** the action of making right or setting straight **:** REDRESS **2 :** utilitarian or ornamental covering for the human body: as **a :** clothing and accessories suitable to a specific purpose or occasion ⟨a soldier in battle ~⟩ ⟨in pilgrimage ~ on his way to Mecca —R.C.Doty⟩ **b :** clothing characteristic of a particular period, geographic area, or nation ⟨18th century ~⟩ ⟨Oriental ~⟩ ⟨Arab ~⟩ **c :** style of clothing **:** manner of wearing clothes ⟨conservative in ~⟩ ⟨thoughtless about his ~⟩ **3 a :** an outer garment for females or small children usu. made in a one-piece style of bodice and skirt **b :** a two-piece garment consisting of blouse and skirt or jacket and skirt **4 :** covering, adornment, or appearance that is appropriate or peculiar to a particular time or season ⟨mountains, proud and glistening in full winter ~ —Marcia Davenport⟩: as **a :** a particular state of plumage of a bird ⟨breeding ~⟩ ⟨summer ~⟩ **b :** the style of makeup and typography of a newspaper or periodical **c :** the particular form under which something is presented ⟨routine love story in pioneer ~ —Joan S. Bishop⟩ ⟨the whole Bible appeared in English ~ —I.M. Price⟩ ⟨no one will object to ornateness if it is the proper ~ for your thoughts and feelings —A.T.Weaver⟩

[3]dress \"\ *adj* [[2]*dress*] **1 :** relating to or used for a dress ⟨~ material⟩ ⟨~ pattern⟩ ⟨~ buttons⟩ **2 a :** suitable for a ceremonial or formal occasion ⟨~ clothes⟩ ⟨~ shoes⟩ — compare DRESS SUIT, DRESS UNIFORM **b :** suitable for wear or use with ceremonial or formal clothing ⟨a ~ sword⟩ ⟨a ~ watch⟩ **3 :** requiring or permitting formal dress ⟨the graduation will be a ~ affair⟩ — compare DRESS PARADE, DRESS REHEARSAL

dres·sage \drə'säzh, dre'-, -säzh\ *n* -S [F, preparation, straightening, training, fr. *dresser* to prepare, make straight, train + *-age* — more at DRESS] **:** the execution by a horse of maneuvers involving changes of gait, pace, and airs in response to barely perceptible movements of a rider's hands, legs, and weight; *also* **:** the systematic training of a horse in obedience and deportment

dress cap *n* **:** a cap of a specified design to be worn with any of the dress uniforms of the military services

dress circle *n* [so called because dress clothes were once commonly worn there] **:** the first or lowest curved tier of seats in a theater or opera house; *also* **:** a corresponding section of seats in a motion-picture theater

dress coat *n* **1 :** TAILCOAT **2 :** the coat of a dress uniform

dress down *vt* **:** to reprove severely **:** REBUKE, REPRIMAND ⟨he is *dressed down* for violating the code of the regiment —E.A. Weeks⟩

dressed *adj* [fr. past part. of [1]*dress*] *of poultry* **:** killed, bled, and more or less completely prepared for cooking — compare FULL-DRESSED, NEW YORK DRESSED

dressed and matched *adj, of a board* **:** planed and shaped at the edges to make intimate joints (as by tongue and groove)

dressed masonry *n* **:** masonry faced and smoothed

dressed overall *adj, Brit* **:** FULL-DRESSED 2

[1]dress·er \'dresə(r)\ *n* -S [ME *dressore, dresser*, fr. MF *dresseur*, fr. OF *dreçor*, fr. *drecier* to arrange, make straight — more at [1]DRESS] **1** *obs* **:** a table or sideboard on which meat and other things were prepared for use or from which food was served **2 :** a cupboard or set of shelves to hold dishes and cooking utensils **3 :** a piece of bedroom furniture (as a chest of drawers or bureau) with a mirror

dresser 3

[2]dresser \"\ *n* -S [[1]*dress* + *-er*] **1 :** one that dresses commercial articles in preparation for their use: as **a :** one that finishes leather **b :** one that smooths and polishes pottery **c :** one that cleans fish **d :** one that sets up machinery (as well-drilling rigs) for operation **e :** one that takes care of growing plants (as fruit trees or fruiting vines) by performing operations (as cultivating, pruning, thinning) required to insure a crop — usu. used in combination ⟨a vine*dresser*⟩ **2 a :** one that assists another in dressing; *specif* **:** one that cares for the wardrobe of an actor and helps with costume changing **b** (1) **:** one that dresses in a particular way ⟨a careful ~⟩ ⟨a careless ~⟩ (2) **:** one that is noted for the use of careful or stylish dress ⟨look well enough for anybody, though he will never be much of a ~ —Thomas Hughes⟩ **3 :** one that serves as a doctor's assistant esp. in the dressing of wounds or other lesions **4 :** a tool or machine for dressing something: as **a :** a pick for shaping large coal **b :** a mallet for working sheet lead **c :** a machine for facing millstones **d :** a flour bolter **e :** a smith's tool which fits into the hardie hole and over which the work is finished to shape **f :** a device for removing worn-out abrasive from abrasive wheels **g :** a textile machine used in preparing warp (as of wool) for the loom

dres·ser coupling \'dresə(r)-\ *n, usu cap D* [after Solomon R. *Dresser* †1911 Am. congressman, its inventor] **:** a pipe coupling for unthreaded pipe

dresser set *n* [[1]*dresser*] **:** a set for use on a dresser or dressing table consisting of comb, hairbrush, and mirror and sometimes including such other personal items as manicure articles and cosmetics containers

dresser tray *n* **:** a tray (as of glass, ceramic, or plastic) for holding small objects on the top of a dresser

dresses *pres 3d sing of* DRESS, *pl of* DRESS

dress form *n* **:** a paper, cloth, or wire representation of a woman's figure from shoulder to thighs but minus arms that is mounted on a stand and used for fitting garments

dress goods *n pl but sometimes sing in constr* **:** fabrics suitable for lightweight clothing (as women's dresses)

dressier *comparative of* DRESSY

dressiest *superlative of* DRESSY

dress in *vt* **:** to outfit (a new prisoner) with prison clothes; *also* **:** to admit to prison

dress·i·ness \'dresēnə̇s, -sin-\ *n* -ES **:** the quality or state of being dressy

dressing *n* -S [ME *dressinge*, fr. *dressen* to dress + *-inge* -ing] **1 a :** the act or process of one who dresses **b :** an instance of such act or process **2 :** something added to a basically complete article or object to decorate, enhance, or lend character or interest: as **a :** a sauce or similar mixture (as mayonnaise) for adding to a certain dish (as a salad) **b :** a seasoned mixture (as of bread, potato, nuts, oysters) used as a stuffing for poultry, meat, or fish or baked separately **c :** an ornamental finish ⟨reconstructed in brick with stone ~*s* —Nikolaus Pevsner⟩ **3 :** something used as a cleaning or conditioning agent: as **a :** a material (as ointment, gauze) applied to cover a sore, wound, or other lesion — compare PRESSURE DRESSING **b :** manure, compost, or other material used as a fertilizer — see SIDE-DRESSING, TOPDRESSING **c :** sizing applied to yarns and fabrics usu. to make them smooth and firm during manufacturing processes or sometimes to improve their weight and appearance when finished **d :** a substance used to soften, clean, polish, or waterproof leather **4 :** DRESSING DOWN

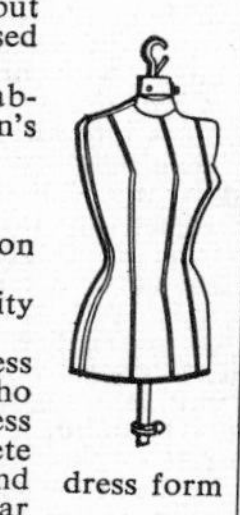

dress form

dressing case *n* **1 :** a small piece of hand luggage containing or fitted with makeup and toilet articles **2** *archaic* **:** BUREAU, DRESSER

dressing down *n, pl* **dressing downs** [fr. gerund of *dress down*] **:** a severe reprimand ⟨gave him a *dressing down* for lying⟩

dressing glass *n* **:** a small mirror set to swing in a standing frame for use on a dresser or chest

dressing gown *n* **:** an ankle-length or knee-length loose or tailored robe usu. of silk or other fine material that is worn informally (as at home) esp. while dressing or resting ⟨enveloped . . . in a man's *dressing gown* of silk brocade —C.G. Norris⟩ ⟨a thin *dressing gown* over her nightdress —*Scribner's*⟩

dressing line *n* **:** a line to which flags are attached for dressing ship

dressing room *n* **:** a room used primarily for dressing and making one's toilet; *esp* **:** a room backstage in a theater where a performer changes costumes and makeup

dressing sack *or* **dressing sacque** *n* **:** a woman's loose jacket worn while dressing or lounging

dressing station *n* **:** AID STATION

dressing table *n* **:** a low table often fitted with drawers and a mirror in front of which one sits while making a toilet — called also *vanity*

dressmake \'=,=\ *vi* [back-formation fr. *dressmaker*] **:** to make dresses

[1]dressmaker \'=,==\ *n* [[2]*dress* + *maker*] **:** one that does dressmaking; *sometimes* **:** COUTURIER

[2]dressmaker \"\ *adj, of women's clothes* **:** having softness, rounded lines, and intricate detailing in contrast with the straight-lined simplicity of tailored clothes ⟨a ~ suit⟩

dressmaking \'=,==\ *n* [[2]*dress* + *making*] **:** the process or occupation of making clothes, esp. dresses

dress parade *n* **:** a formal ceremonial parade in dress uniform

dress rehearsal *n* **:** a full rehearsal of a play in costume and with stage properties shortly before the first performance

dress shield *n* **:** SHIELD 2h

dress shirt *n* **:** a man's white shirt; *specif* **:** a white shirt with a starched or pleated front for wear with evening dress

dress suit *n* **:** a suit worn for full dress — compare EVENING DRESS

dress uniform *n* **1 :** a uniform for formal wear; *specif* **:** a blue uniform worn by U.S. Army personnel for formal occasions **2 :** a dark blue U.S. Navy uniform regularly worn in cool seasons or climates — compare FULL-DRESS UNIFORM, UNDRESS

dress up *vt* [[1]*dress* + *up*] **1 a :** to attire in best or formal clothes ⟨*dressed* the child *up* for the birthday party⟩ **b :** to attire in clothes suited to a particular role ⟨*dressed* him *up* for the part of Othello⟩ **2 :** to present or cause to appear in a certain light (as by distortion, exaggeration, or padding) **:** DISGUISE, CAMOUFLAGE ⟨some conservative newspapers have tried to *dress up* the delegation as treachery to democracy —*New Republic*⟩ ⟨accounting devices for *dressing up* the balance sheet —Albert Lepawsky⟩; *esp* **:** to embellish or enhance the interest of (an event or account) with supplementary usu. fanciful details ⟨a remarkable feat of bodily exertion, which . . . he should be able to *dress up* and magnify —George Eliot⟩

dress-up \'=,=\ *n* [*dress up*] **:** a situation or time requiring the wearing of good clothes ⟨a *dress-up* occasion⟩

dressy \'dresē, -si\ *adj* -ER/-EST [[2]*dress* + *-y*] **1 a :** habitually wearing or fond of wearing elaborate or formal dress ⟨his wife's friends were too ~ to suit him⟩ **b :** requiring or characterized by fancy or formal dress ⟨a ~ affair⟩ **2 :** having more or less fancy or formal details: as **a :** suitable for social or festive occasions ⟨a ~ handbag⟩ ⟨a ~ blouse⟩ **b :** ELABORATE, ORNATE ⟨she appeared in an outfit that was much too ~ for the occasion⟩ ⟨a ~ office⟩

drew *past of* DRAW

drey *or* **dray** \'drā\ *n* -S [origin unknown] **:** a squirrel's nest

drey·fu·sard \,drīfə'särd, ,drāf-, -f(y)ü'-, -'zä-\ *n* -S *usu cap* [F, fr. Alfred *Dreyfus* †1935 Fr. army officer + F *-ard*] **:** a defender or partisan of Captain Dreyfus

drg *abbr* drawing

dri·as \'drīəs\ *n* -ES [origin unknown] **:** DEADLY CARROT

[1]drib \'drib\ *vb* **dribbed; dribbed; dribbing; dribs** [prob. alter. of *drip*] *vi* **:** DRIBBLE ⟨a jokester's *dribbing* glass with inconspicuous holes near the top⟩ **~** *vt* **1** *obs* **:** to utter bit by bit **2** *obs* **:** to shoot (an arrow) aside from the mark

[2]drib \"\ *n* -S [prob. back-formation fr. *dribble & driblet*] *chiefly dial* **1 :** a drop of liquid ⟨as the tide draws away, the ~*s* and dregs of water left behind —Thomas Wood⟩ **2 :** a small amount **:** FRAGMENT ⟨various lesser ~*s* for my side endeavors —I.S.Cobb⟩ ⟨the word-by-word reader brings the thought from the printed page in ~*s* —P.D.Leedy⟩

[1]drib·ble \'dribəl\ *vb* **dribbled; dribbled; dribbling** \-b(ə)liŋ\ **dribbles** [freq. of [1]*drib*] *vi* **1 a :** to fall or flow in drops or in a quick succession of drops or in a thin intermittent stream **:** TRICKLE ⟨to prevent *dribbling* of fuel from an injection nozzle⟩ ⟨uncontrollable *dribbling* of urine⟩ **b :** to issue like a trickling liquid slowly and sporadically in a succession of tiny portions ⟨the *dribbling* sands of an hourglass⟩ ⟨allowing the seeds to ~ along the ground⟩ ⟨letting smoke ~ through his chiseled nostrils —John Galsworthy⟩ **2 :** to let saliva drip, trickle, or ooze from a corner of the mouth (as of a teething infant or an imbecile) **:** DROOL, DRIVEL ⟨picnickers *dribbling* in anticipation of the barbecue⟩ **3 :** to drift, sift, issue, or dwindle slowly, little by little, or one by one in a sluggish succession ⟨replies to the questionnaire are *dribbling* in⟩ ⟨words, like ideas, were *dribbling* back into her mind —Ellen Glasgow⟩ ⟨he saw the people *dribbling* out by twos and threes —Mary Austin⟩ ⟨the piano and the singing *dribbled* away —Berton Rouechè⟩ **4 a :** to dribble a ball or puck **b :** to proceed by dribbling ⟨the guard *dribbled* down the sideline⟩ **~** *vt* **1 :** to let or cause to fall in drops or slowly little by little ⟨the chief *dribbled* wine on the ground⟩ ⟨~ in the cereal and boil⟩ ⟨the young couple ~ rice from their clothes⟩ **2 a :** to dispense or disperse sporadically and in small bits ⟨*dribbled* out funds in small grants-in-aid to individual scientists —J.P.Baxter⟩ ⟨a very famous informer *dribbled* out his revelations over a period of ten years —John Steinbeck⟩ **b :** FRITTER — used with *away* ⟨why had they *dribbled* away (yes, and sold out) their gifts for such trifling gains —Samuel Yellen⟩ ⟨as they ~ away their days in futility, hoping vainly for a miracle —*Time*⟩ **c :** to daub or press (paint) straight from the tube onto canvas ⟨~ his paint instead of using brushes —R.M.Coates⟩ **3 :** to propel and maintain control of (a ball or puck) by successive slight taps or bounces with hand, foot, or stick

[2]dribble \"\ *n* -S **1 a** *archaic* **:** a small quantity of a liquid ⟨burghers husbanded their ~*s* of brandy —Sir Walter Scott⟩ **b :** liquid dripping in a small stream (as from the mouth or a leak) ⟨a brown ~ at the corner of his mouth⟩ **2 a :** a descent of liquid in drops or a thin stream: (1) **:** a drizzling shower (2) **:** a falling or leaking in drops ⟨need we call a plumber for these few ~*s*⟩ **b :** an inconsiderable and fitful flow **:** TRICKLE ⟨on the roads a monotonous ~ of gray army lorries, jeeps, motorcycles —Earle Birney⟩ ⟨the export of private capital is a ~, not a flow —R.R.Nathan⟩ **3 a :** a tiny or insignificant bit of something that appears sporadically ⟨they come in ~*s* from Shanghai —Han Suyin⟩ ⟨news material issued in ~*s*⟩ **b :** a trifling or insignificant sum of money ⟨until I can begin to send you a ~ now and then —Booth Tarkington⟩ **4 :** an act or instance of dribbling a ball or puck **5 :** dregs of molten glass remaining in the melting pot after pouring

drib·bler \-b(ə)lə(r)\ *n* -S **1 :** one that dribbles ⟨damned ~ . . . you need a bib —C.S.Barry⟩ ⟨a violation for a ~ to step on or outside a boundary line⟩ **2 :** a worker who removes dribble after molten glass has been poured

dribblet *obs var of* DRIBLET

drib·let \'driblə̇t\ *n* -S [[1]*drib* + *-let*] **1 :** a trifling sum ⟨do not like having money doled out to me in ~*s* —D.G.Gerahty⟩ **2 :** one of a succession of small or insignificant quantities, amounts, portions, or bits ⟨~*s* of information that drifted in⟩ ⟨withdrew his army in ~*s*⟩ **3 :** a falling drop **:** DRIBBLE 1b ⟨~*s* came through the bedroom ceiling⟩

driblet cone *n* **:** a miniature lava cone formed by the accretion of drops of lava projected from gas vents or blowholes and falling on one spot

dribs and drabs *n pl* **:** miserably small or paltry amounts, portions, or fragments usu. scattered over a period of time ⟨taxes collected in *dribs and drabs*⟩ ⟨set to *dribs and drabs* of Meyerbeer's music —Douglas Watt⟩

drid·der \ˈdridər\ *var of* DREDDOUR
drid·dle \ˈdridᵊl\ *vi* -ED/-ING/-S [origin unknown] **1** *chiefly Scot* **:** to proceed in an unsteady or feeble manner **2** *chiefly Scot* **:** to lag behind **:** DAWDLE
drie *obs var of* ¹DREE
driech *var of* DREICH
dried *past of* DRY
dried alum *n* **:** BURNT ALUM
dried beef *n* **:** beef preserved by being pickled in brine, dried, and smoked
dried–fruit beetle *n* **:** a very small broad brown beetle (*Carpophilus hemipterus*) with pale-spotted elytra which do not cover the abdomen that is a cosmopolitan pest on stored products and is esp. destructive to dried fruit and cereals
dried milk *n* **:** milk dehydrated to about 5 percent of moisture by evaporation — called also *milk powder, powdered milk;* compare EVAPORATED MILK
dried–up \ˈ=ˌ=\ *adj* [fr. past part. of *dry up*] **:** WIZENED
driegh *var of* DREICH
¹**dri·er** *also* **dry·er** \ˈdrī(ə)r, -īə\ *comparative of* DRY
²**drier** *also* **dryer** \"\ *n* -S [*dry*, v. + *-er*, n. suffix] **1 a :** something that extracts or absorbs moisture **b** *or* **dri·er·man** \-mən\ **:** a worker who attends to the drying of a material or a product in process of manufacture **c :** a piece of blotting paper used in drying herbarium specimens **2 :** a liquid or solid substance (as a metallic soap) that accelerates the drying of drying oils and of paints, varnishes, and printing inks containing such oils **3** *usu dryer* **:** a device for drying esp. by heat, forced ventilation, centrifugal action, or a vacuum or freezing process: as **a :** a furnace or revolving kiln for drying raw material (as ore, stone, sand) **b :** a rack on which laundry is hung to dry or a machine in which laundry is dried by a current of heated air **c :** a blower for drying hair **d :** any of the heated drums on which paper is dried on a papermaking machine

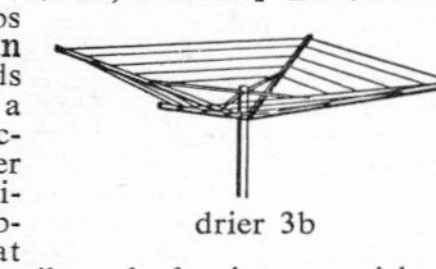
drier 3b

drier–down \ˈ=ˌ=ˈ=\ *n* -S **:** TAKER-DOWN
dries *pres 3d sing of* DRY, *pl of* DRY
driest *also* **dryest** *superlative of* DRY
¹**drift** \ˈdrift\ *n* -S *often attrib* [ME; akin to MD *drift* herd, ford, MHG *trift* driving, pasturage, ON *drift* snowdrift; derivative fr. the root of OE *drīfan* to drive — more at DRIVE] **1 :** the act of driving something along: as **a :** the driving together of the cattle in a forest to determine ownership — used in British forest law **b :** the horizontal thrust of an arch **c :** continued movement of a machine due to inertia after the shutoff of power **d :** a skid of a motor vehicle **:** SIDESLIP **e :** the flow or the velocity of the current of a river or ocean stream **2 :** something driven, propelled, or urged along or drawn together in a clump by or as if by a natural agency: as **a :** wind-driven snow, rain, cloud, dust, or smoke usu. at or near the ground surface ⟨watched the ~*s* of rain moving up the valley —E.L.Thomas⟩ **b** (1) **:** a mass of matter driven or forced onward together in a body or deposited together by or as if by wind or water ⟨scudding over ~*s* on skis⟩ ⟨harbor ~ collects in streaks⟩ (2) **:** a helter-skelter accumulation of something appearing as if windblown ⟨a ~ of newspapers around his feet⟩ (3) **:** something filmy or fleecy fluttering or undulating lightly in masses or folds as if afloat in a breeze or on water ⟨as the beach plums dapple our dunes and fields with snowy ~*s* —*Christian Science Monitor*⟩ ⟨putting away the ~*s* of muslin and curd-soft silk —Edith Sitwell⟩ **c** *dial* **:** DROVE, FLOCK ⟨a ~ of coyotes cried at moonrise⟩ ⟨a ~ of hogs⟩ ⟨a steady ~ of terns could be seen on a northeasterly course —Llewellyn Howland⟩; *also, West* **:** a casual assemblage or swarm of persons ⟨some of the newly arrived ~ were smooth-spoken gentry —Julian Dana⟩ **d :** a volley of arrows esp. when aimed high in air **e :** something (as driftwood or seaweed) that has been washed ashore by waves and tide and left stranded ⟨hauled himself out on a dry bit of ~ —Frederick Way⟩ ⟨strolling the sands . . . searching for ~ that he might turn to a profit —Morris Markey⟩ **f :** a set of fishnets; *also* **:** DRIFT NET **g** (1) **:** rock debris moved by natural agents from one place and deposited in another (2) **:** a deposit of clay, sand, gravel, and boulders transported by a glacier and deposited unstratified or more or less stratified by running water emanating from the glacier — compare ⁹TILL 2 **h :** something wafted by gentle air currents to be caught by the senses ⟨a ~ of woodsmoke curled up —Ellen Glasgow⟩ ⟨it submerged entirely the ~ of far-off band music —J.G.Cozzens⟩ ⟨a faint ~ of the clean, light scent that she had always used —Robert Murphy⟩ **3 :** observable course or direction taken toward an effect: as **a :** a general underlying and inferable design and intent (as of thought, policy, or program) ⟨we see the ~ of his thought in the manuscripts —R.I.Aaron⟩ ⟨the whole ~ of his social philosophy —W.L.Miller⟩ ⟨in agreement with the temper and main ~ of his naturalism —J.E.Smith⟩ **b :** tendency discernible in the past and present course ⟨until the time the upward ~ in the propensity to spend should level off⟩ ⟨in this survey of the ~ of 20th century poetry —Herbert Read⟩; *often* **:** development, progress, or evolution whose general course is assumed to be impersonally determined and continuous into the future ⟨while reasoning on this matter is somewhat a priori, the ~ of history and archaeology confirms it —A.L.Kroeber⟩ ⟨to combat disease, pestilence, prolong the span of life — all these mean a fight against the ~ of Nature —Mildred Gilman⟩ **c :** prevalent leaning or dominant inclination in the current thought and opinion **:** SLANT ⟨the ~ being on the whole away from the home toward the church —W.L.Sperry⟩ **d :** the meaning, import, or purport to be gathered from what is spoken or written ⟨made out the ~ of a conversation going on round me —A.W.Long⟩ ⟨maybe they understand you better in the town you come from, but I don't get your ~ —Maxwell Anderson⟩ **e :** trend (as of a rate) esp. when fluctuating ⟨the upward ~ of respiration in a germinating seed⟩ **4 :** something driven down upon or forced into a body: as **a :** a tool used for ramming down or driving something (as a metal wedge used in tightening hoops on a barrel) **b** *obs* **:** piles sunk in an interlocking row **c :** the difference between the size of a bolt and the hole into which it is driven or between the circumference of a hoop and that of a mast on which it is to be driven **d :** a place in an old-fashioned deep-waisted ship where the sheer was raised and the rail was cut off and usu. terminated by a scroll **e** *or* **driftpin** \ˈ=ˌ=\ **:** a broach or reamer of square section and with one or more cutting faces for cleaning out holes too small to be drilled and slotted — called also *cutting drift, square drift* **f :** a tool used in charging the case of a firework (as a rocket) **g** *or* **driftpin :** a smooth tapered pin resembling a punch for stretching rivet holes and bringing them into alignment — called also *smooth-taper drift* **h :** a punch with the point inclined to the shank for knocking out keys — called also *key drift* **5 :** the motion or action of drifting spatially usu. under external influence ⟨distal ~ of all lower teeth to the right of the lower central incisor —H.M.Lang⟩: as **a :** the deviation of a ship from its set course caused by currents; *also* **:** a voyage of a ship allowed to drift ⟨the icebreaker carried out its three regular annual ~*s*⟩ **b :** the length of a seaman's rope from a point where it is made fast whether stretching to another point of fastening, remaining loose or coiled as an extra length, or running from the fixed block to the movable block of a tackle **c :** one of the slower movements of oceanic circulation **:** a general tendency of surface water subject to diversion or reversal by the wind ⟨the easterly ~ of the North Pacific⟩ — see CURRENT table **d :** a deviation of a missile out of a rifled gun from the vertical plane of fire due to rotation and the resistance of the air **e :** the lateral motion of an airplane due to air currents; *also* **:** DRIFT ANGLE **f :** tendency to alter and esp. to decrease in weight during shipment; *also* **:** the amount by which the weight is altered **g :** CREEP 8b **h :** the distance cargo in the hold of a ship has to be dragged to a hatch **i :** an easy moderate more or less steady flow, sweep, or shifting along a spatial course ⟨aerial ~ of pollen⟩ ⟨the general ~ of population from country to city —H.C.Laxson⟩ ⟨the industrial ~ southward⟩ ⟨any ~ of our solar system in our galaxy —N.E.Nelson⟩ **j :** a slow onward, upward, or downward course (as an advance, transition, or withdrawal) proceeding usu. by inconspicuous steps **:** a gradual shift in attitude, opinion, or position not pronounced in process but unmistakable in direction ⟨a ~ to war⟩ ⟨the ~ toward centralization of power⟩ ⟨the gradual ~ of wealth from farm to industry —S.A.Spiller⟩ ⟨this steady ~ away from the conception of a divine Will that dwarfed the human will —V.L. Parrington⟩ ⟨signs he sees of a dangerous ~ in American life away from standards of excellence in politics —William Barrett⟩ **k :** an aimless directionless course; *often* **:** a foregoing of any attempt at direction or control letting events and developments take their own course **:** abdication of control to a blind flow of circumstances ⟨vigorous local action, moreover, can reverse the policy of ~ which has seen local government denuded of function after function, largely by default —R.V.Presthus⟩ ⟨to continue the policy of ~, of blind stumbling from crisis to crisis —*Time*⟩ **l :** a deviation or veering off from a true reproduction, representation, or reading ⟨frequency ~ is merely the inability of the set to remain exactly tuned to the frequency for which you have adjusted it —*Pilots' Radio Handbook*⟩ **6 :** a passage driven or for driving in a particular direction: as **a :** a nearly horizontal mine passageway driven on or parallel to the course of a vein or rock stratum — compare LEVEL 8 **b :** a small crosscut in a mine connecting two larger tunnels; *also* **:** an exploratory mine tunnel **c** [Afrik, fr. D, fr. MD] *Africa* **:** a ford in a river **7 :** a slow gradual change in character, aspect, or some attendant phenomenon: as **a :** an assumed trend toward a general change in the structure of a language over a period of time underlying or revealed by various specific changes ⟨the ~ toward loss of final syllables in the Germanic languages⟩ **b :** change in genotypes of small populations due to random loss or multiplication of certain gene groups **c :** a gradual change in the zero reading of an instrument or more generally in any quantitative characteristic of a given piece of equipment that is supposed to remain constant **d :** a gradual change in some aspect of culture deriving from an accumulated variation in behavior or belief and resulting in a new pattern or institutional form ⟨a cultural ~ away from spiritual values to materialistic ones⟩ **syn** see TENDENCY — **on the drift** *West* **:** roving about the country without or seeking employment ⟨restless unsettled youths *on the drift*⟩

drift 4g: driftpin for stretching rivet holes

²**drift** \"\ *vb* -ED/-ING/-S *vi* **1 a :** to become driven or carried along by a current of water, wind, or air ⟨can ~ in a canoe the 30 miles from the falls —*Amer. Guide Series: Minn.*⟩ ⟨with the tide at the ebb he was ~*ing* in those dark depths out through the Golden Gate —P.B.Kyne⟩ ⟨a wisp of smoke ~*ing* from the chimney⟩ ⟨rain fell at intervals from ~*ing* shreds of clouds —O.E.Rölvaag⟩ ⟨an evasive and delicate fragrance ~*ed* from her person —Agnes S. Turnbull⟩; *also* **:** to move gently and silently without propulsion often floating or gliding along through the air with slight quivering motions ⟨a solitary leaf ~*s* down⟩ **b :** to wander or stray lightly, gently, effortlessly offering no resistance as if suspended and floating in the air and usu. seeming to leave the choice of direction to the drift of the air ⟨let my eyes ~ around the room —R.Y.Thurman⟩ ⟨a very faint smile ~*ed* across his face —Raymond Chandler⟩ ⟨it is only by ~*ing* with the wind that I have found myself —John Reed⟩; *also* **:** to float through the air in mild and soothing or vibrant waves of sound ⟨the corporal's voice sounded deceptively kind ~*ing* in from away across the North Parade Ground —Earle Birney⟩ ⟨street noises that ~ through closed windows and doors⟩ **c :** to move smoothly and unhurriedly with little or no apparent effort or unobtrusively a few at a time in a manner suggestive of floating on water — usu. followed by a directional word ⟨strikers began to ~ back to work⟩ ⟨the orchestra stopped playing and dancers ~*ed* off the floor⟩ ⟨he'd ~ with the play and make the quarterback commit himself, then make the tackle either way —H.R.Sanders⟩; *also* **:** to migrate in a slow stream ⟨other roving soldiers . . . ~*ed* out to Colorado, Wyoming, Montana —Dixon Wecter⟩ **d :** to pass without contributory effort or serious resistance or become borne slowly by imperceptible degrees toward or away from an association or into or out of some state ⟨he ran with a gang and ~*ed* into petty crime —S.L.A.Marshall⟩ ⟨those dreamy spells of hers, the way she used to go ~*ing* off into space —Hamilton Basso⟩ ⟨the chances are that Asia will gradually ~ toward Communism —K.S.Latourette⟩ ⟨written and spoken languages tend to ~ ever further apart —Frank Denman⟩ **e :** to retain momentum for a further time after shutoff of power **2 a :** to wander without hurry and without clear purpose or goal esp. moving along the line of least resistance ⟨he ~*ed* around for eight years without a trace of his whereabouts —Liam O'Flaherty⟩ ⟨loved best to ~, elusive as a skeleton leaf, along the streets of Rome —Elinor Wylie⟩ **b** *West, of cattle* **:** to bunch up and wander from the home range in a storm **c :** to travel about in a random way as an itinerant workman or in search of work **d :** to become carried along subject to no guidance or control ⟨whether this conversation was ~*ing* or aimed, certain that it was out of his hands —Edmund Fuller⟩; *often* **:** to relinquish planning, decision, initiative, and conscious direction leaving control to chance or circumstances ⟨allowing students to ~ through four years without developing sufficient incentive or goal —*Bull. of Bates Coll.*⟩ **3 a :** to accumulate in a mass or be piled up in heaps by action of wind or water ⟨~*ing* snow banked in the side of the house up to the windowsills⟩ ⟨miles of fence had already been buried under ~*ed* dust —K.S.Davis⟩ ⟨an old hulk far out on the beach fast filling with ~*ing* sand at every high tide⟩ **b :** to become covered with a drift ⟨the streets ~*ed* level with the marquees of the buildings —William Fifield⟩ **4** *mining* **:** to make a drift **:** DRIVE **5 :** to fish with drift nets **6 a :** to vary or deviate from a set course or adjustment ⟨some television sets ~ during warmup and require retuning⟩ **b :** to vary sluggishly usu. without establishing a definite trend — used esp. of prices or income ⟨its freight revenues ~*ed* down more than 14 percent last year —R.E.Bedingfield⟩ ⟨the market has been ~*ing* the last few days, probably because of the approaching holidays⟩ ⟨grain futures ~*ed* in a narrow range⟩ **c :** SKID **7** *of a language* **:** to develop in the direction characteristic of its drift ~ *vt* **1 a :** to cause to be driven in a current ⟨the tide turning began ~*ing* back the ship helplessly seaward —Herman Melville⟩ ⟨a smudge ~*ing* smoke across their beds to keep insects away —B.A.Williams⟩ **b** *West* **:** to drive (livestock) slowly esp. to allow grazing ⟨leaving orders for the outfit to ~ the herd into it and water —Andy Adams⟩ **2 a :** to drive by the force of the wind and deposit in heaps ⟨heavy clay when granulated is readily ~*ed* —A.F.Gustafson⟩ **b :** to cover with drifts ⟨southwestern slopes were deeply ~*ed*⟩ **3 :** to use a drift in or upon (as for enlarging holes, forcing holes into alignment, driving out pins and keys) **4 :** to cant (as a pole) over at the top
drift·age \ˈdriftij, -tēj\ *n* -S [²*drift* + *-age*] **1 :** a drifting of some object esp. through action of wind or water **2 :** deviation from a set course (as from a ship's course due to leeway or currents) **3 :** something that is drifting or has drifted ⟨I sell them stuff: bait and lobsters, and sometimes an interesting bit of ~ —Erle Stanley Gardner⟩
drift alarm *n* **:** a device that indicates when the anchor of a ship is dragging
drift anchor *n* **:** SEA ANCHOR
drift angle *n* [prob. trans. of F *angle de dérive*] **1 :** the angle between the axis of a ship when turning and the tangent to the path on which it is turning **2 :** the horizontal angle between the longitudinal axis of an airplane and its path relative to the ground **:** the angle between the heading and the track — called also *leeway*
drift avalanche *n* **:** an avalanche composed of dry powdery snow initially set in motion by wind
drift boat *n* **:** DRIFTER 2b
driftbolt \ˈ=ˌ=\ *n* **1 :** a bolt for driving out other bolts or pins **2 :** a metal rod for securing timbers resembling a spike but with or without point or head
drift bottle *n* **:** a bottle containing a record of the time and place at which it was set adrift in the ocean for supplying when recovered data to aid in determining the circulation of surface waters in the ocean — called also *floater*
drift copper *n* **:** fragments of native copper carried from their source by glaciers
drift current *n* **:** a slowly moving current in a lake or ocean
drift dam *n* **:** a deposit of glacial drift that dams or has dammed a stream
drift·er \-tə(r)\ *n* -S **1 a :** a living being that travels or moves about aimlessly ⟨there were about 40 in the family and usu. a dozen ~*s* —W.D.Wyman⟩ ⟨these ~*s* vary in size from the bacteria and the minute yellowish microscopic plants . . . to copepods —R.E.Coker⟩ **b :** a worker who moves from job to job without remaining long at any one place of employment **c :** a person of passive spiritless character lacking aim, ambition, and initiative and given to roving from one diversion to another without any steady interest **:** TEMPORIZER **d :** a fierce and driving snowstorm (as in the far north) **2 a** *also* **drift·er·man** \-tə(r)mən\ *pl* **driftermen :** a person who fishes with a drift net — called also *drift netter* **b :** a boat equipped for and employed in drift-net fishing — called also *drift boat* **3 a :** an excavator of mine drifts **b :** a rock drill used for driving mine drifts and crosscuts **c :** an operator of a heavy drill for drilling through rock in tunnel construction, mining, or quarrying
drift fence *n, West* **:** a stretch of fence strung by ranchers across the open range for preventing grazing cattle from drifting from their home range
drift float *n* **:** a float dropped from an aircraft flying over water as a marker for determining the drift angle or the direction of surface wind
drift ice *n* **:** sea or lake ice broken apart by winds and currents **:** fragments of a floe
driftier *comparative of* DRIFTY
driftiest *superlative of* DRIFTY
drift indicator *or* **drift meter** *or* **drift sight** *n* **:** a flight instrument used for measuring the angle of drift of an aircraft and equipped with a hairline or sight wire that may be rotated until objects on the ground appear to travel parallel with it so that from the position of the wire the drift angle may then be read directly from a calibration chart
¹**drifting** *adj* [fr. pres. part. of ²*drift*] **1 :** disposed to drift or move aimlessly **:** PUSILLANIMOUS, AMBITIONLESS ⟨seemed gentle, affectionate, ~ —W.B.Yeats⟩ ⟨we see weak, neurotic, helpless, ~, unhappy people —J.C.Powys⟩ **2 :** constantly shifting or floating about ⟨a ~ double-dealer has appeared . . . and chiseled himself in as top man —Hoffman Birney⟩
²**drifting** *n* -S [fr. gerund of ²*drift*] **:** the act or motion of one that drifts; *specif* **:** the act of driving a mine drift
drift·ing·ly *adv* [¹*drifting* + *-ly*] **:** in an unguided or random manner
drift·land \ˈdrift,land\ *n* [¹*drift* + *land*] **:** DROFLAND
drift lead \-ˌled\ *n* **:** a heavy lead put overboard when a ship is at anchor with a line attached and left slack so that its tautening will indicate any drift or dragging
drift·less \ˈdriftləs\ *adj* [¹*drift* + *-less*] **1 :** having no aim or direction **:** being without purpose ⟨to the rookie, military directives seem ~⟩ **2 :** free from glacial drift ⟨a section ~ except for loess deposits⟩
driftless area *n* **:** an area (as in Wisconsin and parts of Minnesota, Illinois, and Iowa) that is free from glacial drift and seems not to have been covered by the Pleistocene ice
drift·less·ness *n* -ES **:** the quality or state of being driftless ⟨the ~ of the play's characters⟩
drift·man \ˈdriftmən\ *n, pl* **driftmen** [¹*drift* + *man*] **:** a worker who drives drifts in a coal mine
drift mine *n* [¹*drift* + *mine*] **:** a placer or gravel deposit worked by underground-mining methods
drift mining *n* **:** mining gold-bearing gravel deposits by shafts and drifts instead of by hydraulic methods
drift net *n* **:** a large net that is arranged to drift with the tide or current and that is either buoyed up by floats or attached to a drift boat
drift netter *n* [*drift net* + *-er*] **:** DRIFTER 2a
drift period *n, often cap D* **:** GLACIAL EPOCH
driftpiece \ˈ=ˌ=\ *n* **1 :** an upright or curved piece of timber connecting the plank sheer with the gunwale of a ship **2 :** a scroll terminating a rail at the drift — compare DRIFT 4d
driftpin *n* **:** ¹DRIFT 4e, 4g
drift plain *n* **:** a plain underlain with glacial drift
drift plug *n* [¹*drift* + *plug*] **:** a hardwood plug that is conical or has rounded ends to be driven into or through a lead pipe to flare it or to straighten a buckle
drift punch *n* **:** a blunt-ended punch of long taper used to align holes (as for bolts, pins, rivets)
drift sail *n* **:** DRAG SAIL
drift sheet *n* **:** a widespread deposit of glacial drift
drift slide *n* **:** a device on the rear sight of a gun to permit making compensation for the drift of the projectile
driftway \ˈ=ˌ=\ *n* [¹*drift* + *way;* so called fr. its use as a passage for herds or flocks] *dial* **:** a sometimes private lane or narrow country road **:** DRIVEWAY 1
driftweed \ˈ=ˌ=\ *n* **1 :** seaweed or other aquatic vegetation drifted ashore **2 :** any of various seaweeds (as members of the genus *Laminaria*) that tend to break free and drift ashore
driftwind \ˈ=ˌ=\ *n* **:** wind that drifts snow, sand, or other material
driftwood \ˈ=ˌ=\ *n* **1 :** wood drifted or floated by water **2 :** useless or worthless scraps cast off by a social or cultural activity ⟨that 12th century temperament which loved to gather ~ from the wreckage of the ancient world of thought —H.O. Taylor⟩; *specif* **:** social parasites or human idlers drifting along with the current of civilized life **:** FLOTSAM 2, WRECKAGE 3 ⟨the unemployed were the political ~ of the revolution —*Political Science Quarterly*⟩
drifty \ˈdriftē, -ti\ *adj* -ER/-EST [¹*drift* + *-y*] **1 :** full of drifts **:** tending to form drifts **2** [²*drift* + *-y*] **:** giving the effect of drifting or floating ⟨dress collection . . . has a ~ quality which immediately evokes resort backgrounds —*Women's Wear Daily*⟩
driki *var of* DRY-KI
¹**drill** \ˈdril\ *vt* -ED/-ING/-S [ME *drillen* to delay] **1** *now dial Brit* **a :** to waste (time) idly **:** DAWDLE **b :** to let (something) continue — used with *out* or *on* **2** *now dial Brit* **:** LURE, DRAW ⟨easily ~*ed* on to vote yea⟩ ⟨they soon ~*ed* him into the plot⟩
²**drill** \"\ *vi* -ED/-ING/-S [perh. alter. of *trill* — more at TRILL (to trickle)] *obs* **:** TRICKLE, DRIP
³**drill** \ˈdril\ *n* -S *archaic* **:** a small trickling stream **:** RILL
⁴**drill** \"\ *vb* -ED/-ING/-S [D *drillen*, fr. MD; akin to MHG *drillen* to turn, round off, OHG *drāen* to turn — more at THROW] *vt* **1 a :** to make (a rounded hole or cavity in a solid) by removing bits with a rotating drill — compare BORE 1 **b :** to make or excavate a hole in (a solid material) with a drill ⟨they ~*ed* boulders for inserting dynamite st[ic]ks⟩ ⟨bones ~*ed* for insertion of a pin⟩ ⟨~*ing* a tooth for a fi[lling]⟩ **c :** to drive a hole in, puncture, or perforate as if with a [dri]ll **:** pierce, penetrate, or drive deep into the interior of ⟨the lightning ~*ing* the hills to the east and upriver —Frederick Way⟩ **d :** to open or sink (a well) in the earth by striking a spot repeatedly with a sharp pointed instrument or by using a rotary drill **e :** to shoot through the head or body ⟨would haul out a gun and indiscriminately ~ them both —Marjorie Brace⟩; *also* **:** to penetrate or puncture like a bullet ⟨we are ~*ed* by about 100 cosmic rays every minute of our lives —Stuart Chase⟩ **2** *archaic* **:** to whirl or twirl like a drill ⟨~ a stick into a pit containing tinder to kindle fire⟩ **3 a :** to instruct thoroughly in the rudiments and methods of any skill or branch of knowledge **:** DISCIPLINE **b :** to impart or communicate (ideas) in this way ⟨~ knowledge or sense into a pupil⟩ ⟨trade secrets ~*ed* into a man's subconscious⟩ **c :** to train or exercise (as a soldier) in military evolutions and in servicing and using weapons and other equipment **4 :** to remove (a railroad car) from among others on the same track by switching ⟨the diner to be added to number 41 had already been ~*ed*⟩ ~ *vi* **1 a :** to pierce or sink a hole with a drill ⟨reaming, ~*ing*, and honing are also considered boring operations —H.D. Burghardt & Aaron Axelrod⟩ ⟨intending to ~ for oil⟩ ⟨painless dental ~*ing*⟩ **b :** to penetrate in a straight line as if driven with a drill ⟨he sensed that the eyes of the men were ~*ing* into the back of his neck —Fred Majdalany⟩ ⟨the violent daylight ~*ing* into the room —Brendan Gill⟩ **2 :** to practice an exercise **:** engage in a drill **3 :** to give forth a series of metallic percussive sounds or tones ⟨the sharp ~*ing* of the telephone had sounded from the hall —F.H.Ford⟩ **4** *of a motor vehicle* **:** SKID, SIDESLIP **syn** see PERFORATE, PRACTICE

5drill \"\ *n* -s [in sense 1, prob. fr. D *dril*, fr. MD, fr. *drillen* to drill; in other senses, fr. *4drill*] **1 a :** an instrument with an edged or pointed end used for making holes in hard substances; *specif* **:** a tool that cuts with its end by revolving (as in drilling metals) or by a succession of blows (as in drilling stone) — see CROSS BIT, TWIST DRILL; compare AUGER, 1BIT 3a **b :** a drill with the appliance or machine for operating it or the appliance or machine alone (as a drill press or a portable drill) **2 :** the act or exercise of training soldiers in the execution of evolutions and the using and servicing of weapons and other equipment; *specif* **:** a kind or method of military exercise ⟨infantry *drill*⟩ **3 a :** repetitive instruction and strictly supervised exercise in methods (as of business, sport, education) ⟨we build up habits by ~, but we build up intelligent capacities by training —Gilbert Ryle⟩ **b :** a physical or mental exercise aimed at perfecting facility and skill in a particular operation esp. by regular practice ⟨the methods were largely lecture and ~s for memory, with daily and monthly reviews —H.R.Douglass⟩ **c :** a formal exercise by a team of marchers consisting of strictly timed figures and evolutions as part of a ritual or as an exhibition of skill ⟨the competition will continue until each drum corps has completed its ~⟩ **d** *chiefly Brit* **:** the approved or correct procedure for accomplishing something efficiently ⟨two people who knew the ~ perfectly and could easily mount an expedition in the given time —L.J.Van Der Post⟩ **4 a :** a marine snail (*Urosalpinx cinerea*) that is very destructive to oysters on the Atlantic coast of the U.S. by boring through their shells and feeding on the soft parts **b :** any of several other mollusks of the family Muricidae (as *Thais floridana*) **5 :** sharp closely repeated taps or insistent moderately percussive tones ⟨tried to shut his ears against the sharp ~ of his voice —Hamilton Basso⟩ ⟨the prolonged ~ of cicadas⟩ ⟨counted the separate, muffled ~s on the wire —Kay Boyle⟩

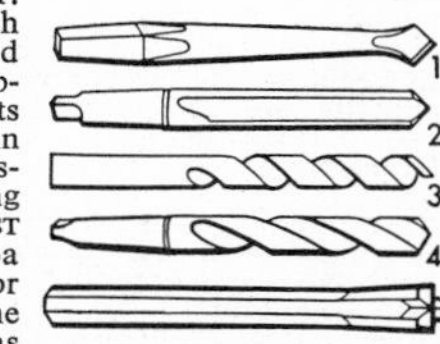

drills 1a: *1* flat, *2* straight-flute, *3* single-twist, *4* two-groove, *5* star

6drill \"\ *n* -s [prob. native name in West Africa] **:** a West African baboon (*Mandrillus leucophaeus*) closely related to the typical mandrills but smaller and lacking the bright facial coloring of the latter

7drill \"\ *n* -s [perh. fr. *3drill*] **1 a :** a shallow furrow or trench into which seed is sown **b :** a row of seed sown in such a furrow **2 :** a planting implement that makes holes or furrows, drops in the seed and sometimes fertilizer, and covers them with earth ⟨tractor-drawn ~s used to sow wheat⟩ ⟨a ~ adjusted to four rows at one time of forest-tree seeds⟩ — see HOE DRILL, PLOW DRILL, PRESS DRILL

8drill \"\ *vt* -ED/-ING/-S **1 :** to sow (seeds) by dropping along a shallow furrow ⟨he ~s soybeans in the same rows with corn to be cut together for silage⟩ **2 a :** to sow with seed or set with seedlings inserted in drills ⟨we've ~*ed* a whole hill with slash pine —Kathleen L. Sutton⟩ **b :** to distribute seed or fertilizer in by means of a drill ⟨compare the yields of a ~*ed* acre and a broadcast acre⟩

9drill \"\ *n* -s [back-formation fr. *drilling* — more at DRILLING (fabric)] **:** a strong durable cotton fabric in twill weave made in various weights for clothing, interior decoration, and industrial uses

drill·able \-ləbəl\ *adj* **:** capable of or fit for being drilled ⟨an alloy not readily ~⟩ ⟨recruits scarcely ~⟩ ⟨mixed fertilizers granulated in order to make a more ~ product⟩

drill barrow *n* **:** a wheeled machine for planting in drills

drill bit *n* **:** 5DRILL 1a

drill block *n* **:** a steel block containing one or more V-shaped grooves in which cylindrical pieces may be held while being drilled

drill bow *n* **:** a small bow used for turning a bow drill by giving the string a turn about the drill

drill chuck *n* **:** a chuck for holding a drill on a spindle usu. by means of adjustable jaws — see CHUCK illustration

drill corps *n* **:** DRILL TEAM

drill drift *n* **:** a wedge-shaped drift for knocking loose a drill or drill socket from a receiving member

drilled *past of* DRILL

drill·er \-lə(r)\ *n* -s **:** one that drills something, drills others, engages in drill, or is employed to carry out drilling operations

drill file *n* [*5drill*] **:** a small fine-toothed flat file having square or round edges and teeth on the edges only

drill hall *n* **:** a spacious hall suitable for drilling: as **a :** such a hall for drill by military or other drill teams (as in an armory) **b** *Brit* **:** a building containing such a hall

drill head *n* **:** DRILL CHUCK; *esp* **:** one that holds and drives two or more drills at once

drill in *vt* **:** to complete (an oil or gas well) by penetrating the producing formation

1drilling \ˈdriliŋ, -lēŋ\ *n* -s [fr. gerund of *4drill*] **:** material removed by a drill in making a hole — usu. used in pl. ⟨brushed aside the ~s from about the hole⟩

2dril·ling \"\ *n* -s [by folk etymology fr. G *drillich*, fr. MHG *drilich* fabric woven with a threefold thread, fr. *drilich* threefold, fr. OHG *drilīh* made up of three threads, by folk etymology (influence of OHG *drī-* — akin to OHG *drī* three — & OHG *-līh* -ly) fr. L *trilic-, trilix*, fr. *tri-* + *-lic-, -lix* (fr. *licium* thread); perh. akin to L *liquis* oblique — more at OBLIQUE, THREE, -LY (adj. suffix)] **:** 9DRILL

3drill·ing \"\ *adj* [fr. pres. part. of *4drill*] **1 :** appearing to see far into **:** PIERCING ⟨sharp ~ eyes —Olive H. Prouty⟩ **2 :** deeply penetrative **:** BITING ⟨~ sarcasm about money —Marcia Davenport⟩

drilling cable *n* [*drilling* fr. gerund of *4drill*] **:** a cordage product made of three ropes twisted together with a left lay, having the surface treated with lubricant to resist abrasion, heat, and water, and used as the line to which drilling tools are attached in well drilling and quarry drilling

drilling fluid *or* **drilling mud** *n* **:** a preparation of water, clays, and chemicals circulated in oil-well drilling for lubricating and cooling the bit, flushing the rock cuttings to the surface, and plastering the side of the well to prevent cave-ins

drilling hammer *n* **:** a stonecutter's hammer having a flat square face at each end of the head for striking rock drills

drilling machine *n* **:** a machine for drilling, reaming, counterboring, and tapping holes; *esp* **:** a power machine for drilling holes in metal (as a drill press or radial drill)

drill–like \ˈdril,līk\ *adj* **:** like a drill in form or action ⟨pointed *drill-like* shells⟩ ⟨an evolution *drill-like* in its precision⟩

drill·man \-ilmən, -,man\ *n, pl* **drillmen :** one who operates a drill or drilling machine

drillmaster \ˈ=,==\ *n* [trans. of G *drillmeister*] **:** one who teaches or coaches drill or by drilling: as **a :** an instructor in military drill or of an exhibition drill corps or lodge team **b :** a police officer who instructs, drills, and trains members of the force in military tactics, marksmanship, and discipline **c :** an instructor or director who maintains severe discipline stressing method, formalities, minutiae ⟨the expert ~s whose only concern was to see that I mastered the contents of textbooks —H.N.Fairchild⟩ ⟨marshals notes before us like a ~, making them execute intricate formations with almost incredible precision and high style —Edward Cushing⟩

drill pin *n* **:** the pin in a lock which enters the key stem

drill pipe *or* **drill rod** *n* **:** a pipe or rod that drives a rotary drill bit (as in drilling wells)

drill plow *n* **:** a combination of plow and drill

drill press *n* **:** an upright drilling machine the drill of which is pressed to the work by a hand lever or by power

drills *pres 3d sing of* DRILL, *pl of* DRILL

drill sergeant *n* **:** a noncommissioned officer who instructs soldiers in military exercises and evolutions

drill steel *or* **drill rod** *n* **:** steel usu. with 0.85 percent or more carbon content used for rock drills, pins, and dowels

drill stem *n* **:** the string of drill pipe that transmits power from the surface down to the drill bit in well drilling

drill–stem test *n* **:** a test for determining productivity of an oil or gas well by means of sampling the flow while the drill stem is still in the bore

drillstock \ˈ=,=\ *n* **:** a frame or head for holding a drill spindle or a drill

drill team *n* **:** an exhibition marching team for demonstrating precision in drill — called also *drill corps*

drill tower *n* **:** a structure resembling the side of a building used in fire-fighting drill, to practice ladder raising and jumping into life nets

dril·vis \ˈdril,fis\ *n* -ES [Afrik, fr. *dril* to shake, vibrate, drill (fr. D *drillen*) + *vis* fish; akin to OE *fisc* fish — more at DRILL, FISH] *Africa* **:** ELECTRIC RAY

drily *var of* DRYLY

dri·mys \ˈdrīməs\ *n* [NL, fr. Gk, sharp, acrid; fr. the taste of the bark; akin to Latvian *drisme* crack, split, Gk *derein* to skin — more at TEAR] **1** *cap* **:** a genus of chiefly Australian shrubs or trees (family Magnoliaceae) having evergreen aromatic foliage — see WINTER'S BARK **2** -ES **:** any plant of the genus *Drimys*

d ring *n, cap D* **:** a metal ring having the shape of a capital D through which straps or ropes are passed (as one to which the suspension ropes of a parachute are attached)

1drink \ˈdriŋk\ *vb* **drank** \ˈdraŋk, -aiŋk\ *or dial* **drunk** \ˈdrəŋk\ *or substand* **drinked** \ˈdriŋ(k)t\ **drunk** *or* **drank** *or substand* **drinked** *or archaic* **drunk·en** \ˈdrəŋkən *sometimes* -kᵊŋ\ **drinking; drinks** [ME *drinken*, fr. OE *drincan*; akin to OHG *trinkan* to drink, ON *drekka*, Goth *drinkan*] *vt* **1 a :** SWALLOW, IMBIBE ⟨~ liquid⟩ ⟨don't sip it . . . but ~ it like the divine draught it is —Margery Allingham⟩ ⟨other animals and birds stand by to ~ its blood —*Interpreter's Bible*⟩ ⟨not a drop left. Who *drank* it up⟩ ⟨hurry, child, ~ it down so that we can start⟩ ⟨ordered a Scotch and *drank* it off —Polly Adler⟩ **b :** to take in or suck up **:** ABSORB ⟨~ up moisture⟩ ⟨the hot surface of the porous rock *drank* water like a sponge⟩; *broadly* **:** to take in (something intangible) or cause to vanish in a way suggestive of a liquid being swallowed ⟨~*ing* the thin sharp air⟩ ⟨atmospheric pressure then pushes air in, and your lungs can ~ their fill —A.C.Fisher⟩ ⟨*drank* in eagerly the latest version of the news⟩ **c** *obs* **:** SMOKE ⟨~ tobacco⟩ **2 :** to salute and wish health and honor to (a person) or success to (some prospect or wish) or to give or join in (a toast) or give a toast to (another's health) by raising and then drinking from a vessel ⟨will you ~ our good luck⟩ **3 a :** to spend in or expend or waste on consumption of alcoholic beverages — often used with *away* ⟨they *drank* the hours away⟩ ⟨a son-in-law who'd hit her and take her pension off her and ~ it to the last penny —Ruth Park⟩ **b :** to bring to a specified state by taking drink ⟨don't ~ that fountain dry⟩ ⟨had *drunk* himself into the poorhouse or the grave —Ellen Glasgow⟩ ⟨how we love the unexpected turn, like ~*ing* the devil under the table —Coulton Waugh⟩ **4 :** to take into one's mind or consciousness pleasurably through one or more of the senses — usu. used with *in* ⟨I just wanted to ~ in all those monumental buildings, dynamic streets full of hurrying people —Dong Kingman⟩ ⟨while his ears *drank* in the wonderful story of the great mare —Gerald Beaumont⟩ ⟨young men passed his door, *drank* the enchantments of his conversation —Van Wyck Brooks⟩ ⟨as I walked along the river ~*ing* in its beauty my soul expanded —Alexander MacDonald⟩ **5** *archaic* **:** to accommodate with drink by way of refreshment **~** *vi* **1 a :** to take liquid into the mouth for swallowing ⟨we saw baby elephants ~*ing* from their mothers —Stuart Cloete⟩ **b :** to receive into one's mind or consciousness a portion of something refreshing or pleasurable ⟨a desire to seek this inspiration at its source and ~ from the living waters —V.L.Parrington⟩ ⟨Ben Franklin who *drank* deep from the stream in Europe and then democratized his knowledge —Roger Burlingame⟩ ⟨students can hardly be blamed for ~*ing* deep of the culture which surrounds them —L.R.Ward⟩ **2 :** to partake of alcoholic beverages esp. habitually ⟨he ~s but does not smoke⟩; *specif* **:** to indulge in alcoholic beverages with disagreeable effect ⟨to say that a man ~s means that he ~s too much —Joyce Cary⟩ ⟨began to ~ in childhood and was an alcoholic by the time he was 18 —*Times Lit. Supp.*⟩ ⟨obvious that he had been ~*ing* —Louis Auchincloss⟩ **3 :** to make or join in a toast ⟨~ to the prosperity of the newest state⟩ **4** *obs* **:** TASTE

2drink \"\ *n* -s [ME *drink, drinke*, fr. OE *drinc, drinca*, fr. *drincan*, v.] **1 a :** liquid suitable for swallowing by man or beast esp. to quench thirst or to provide nourishment or refreshment ⟨I was thirsty and you gave me ~ —Mt 25:35 (RSV)⟩ ⟨natives satisfied my demands for food and ~⟩ ⟨the only available ~ was the milk of coconuts⟩ ⟨for centuries before a very light beer was the common ~ —G.E.Fussell⟩ **b** *archaic* **:** liquid taken in or absorbed (as by a plant) **c :** a source of mental and emotional refreshment or stimulation ⟨it was meat and ~ to him to be the guardian of a secret —John Buchan⟩ **2 a :** any particular natural or prepared usu. agreeable liquid for swallowing **:** BEVERAGE, POTABLE, BREW, LIQUOR ⟨able to make a palatable ~ from seawater⟩ ⟨a fermented ~ made of water and honey⟩ ⟨my favorite among the carbonated soft ~s is ginger ale⟩ **b :** alcoholic liquor ⟨excessive indulgence in ~ and tobacco —A.A.Bogomolets⟩ ⟨a *drink*-sodden derelict⟩ ⟨we speak of ~ as if it were synonymous with alcoholic beverages and use such phrases as the ~ traffic —O.A.Mendelsohn⟩ **3 :** a draft or portion of liquid (as water or a prepared beverage) taken or to be taken by or served to an individual at one time ⟨taking a long ~ from the spring⟩ ⟨it requires a barium ~, fluoroscopic examination, and several radiographs — *X Rays & You*⟩ ⟨give the dog a ~ of water⟩ ⟨the plant needs a ~⟩ **4 a :** the consuming of or habit of consuming alcoholic beverages liberally or to excess ⟨that the old doctor is befuddled with ~ all the time —Ellen Glasgow⟩ ⟨~ will be his ruination⟩ ⟨he took to ~ when his business failed⟩ ⟨her didos will drive me to ~⟩ **b** *Brit* **:** a convivial get-together **:** DRUNK, SPREE **5 :** a sizable body of water or a broad stream ⟨slipped off the rock and into the ~⟩; *esp* **:** OCEAN ⟨my regiment embarked, leaving me on this side of the ~⟩ ⟨off West Palm Beach, Fla., an air force crash boat pulled a pilot from the ~ —*Time*⟩ ⟨burst into flames and went headlong into the ~ —J.S.Childers⟩ — **in drink :** DRUNK ⟨the poor monster's *in drink* —Shak.⟩

1drink·able \-kəbəl\ *adj* **:** suitable or safe for drinking **:** POTABLE ⟨a barely ~ substitute for coffee⟩ ⟨the sulfur gives the water an unpleasant flavor and odor but it is perfectly ~⟩ — **drink·ably** \-blē, -li\ *adv*

2drinkable \"\ *n* -s **:** a liquid suitable for drinking **:** POTABLE, BEVERAGE

drink·er \-kə(r)\ *n* -s [ME *drinkere*, fr. OE *drincere*, fr. *drincan* to drink + *-ere* -er] **1 a :** one that drinks ⟨all the ~s of the toast⟩ **b :** one that drinks alcoholic beverages ⟨a bar that stays open for the lone ~⟩ ⟨a problem ~⟩ **2** *or* **drinker moth** [so called fr. its long suctorial proboscis] **:** a large brownish European moth (*Cosmotriche potatoria*) with a larva that feeds on grasses **3 :** a vessel or device used to provide water for domestic animals or poultry

drink·ery \-kərē, -ri\ *n* -ES **:** BARROOM, SALOON

drink hail *n* [ME *drinkhayl*, fr. *drink* (imper. sing. of *drinken* to drink) + *hayl* healthy, being in good health, fr. ON *heill* healthy — more at WHOLE] *obs* **:** an early English bidding to drink to good health or good luck made in reply to a pledge of wassail

1drinking *n* -s [fr. gerund of *1drink*] **1 :** a drinking party **:** CAROUSAL **2** *dial Eng* **:** a light lunch eaten between meals

2drinking *adj* [fr. pres. part. of *1drink*] **1 :** addicted to or marked by immoderate consumption of alcoholic beverages ⟨traffic accidents caused by ~ drivers⟩ ⟨not a ~ woman⟩ **2 :** ABSORBENT, BIBULOUS — used of paper or other materials **3** [fr. *drinking*, gerund of *1drink*] **:** used or designed to be used in drinking ⟨a ~ room⟩; *esp* **:** used to contain an individual portion of beverage ⟨a ~ glass⟩

drinking fountain *n* **:** a fixture with nozzle delivering a stream or jet of water for drinking esp. one with an upward jet enabling one to drink directly without use of a cup — called also *bubbler*

drinking fountain

drinking song *n* **:** a song on a convivial theme composed usu. for singing in accompaniment to drinking

drink·less \ˈdriŋkləs\ *adj* [ME *drinkelees*, fr. *drinke* drink + *-lees* -less] **:** being without or deprived of drink ⟨with liquor flowing freely he forced himself to go ~⟩

drink money *n, archaic* **:** a gratuity orig. for drink **:** POURBOIRE

drink offering *n* **:** a libation of wine, milk, or oil often in biblical times made with other sacrifices and required with every public offering

drink·om·e·ter \driŋˈkämə|d·ə(r), ˈdriŋkə,mēl\ *n* [*2drink* + *-o-* + *-meter*] **:** an apparatus for recording fluid consumption (as of an experimental animal)

drinky \ˈdriŋkē\ *adj, sometimes* -ER/-EST [*2drink* + *-y*] **:** partially inebriated **:** DRINKING

drinn \ˈdrin\ *n* -s [Ar *darīn* dry herbage] **:** a coarse prickly weedy grass (*Aristida pungens*) of northern Africa; *broadly* **:** a stretch of country overgrown with this grass

1drip \ˈdrip\ *vb* **dripped** *or* **dript; dripped** *or* **dript; dripping; drips** [ME *drippen*, fr. OE *dryppan*; akin to MD *druppen* to drip, trickle, OE *dropa* drop — more at DROP] *vt* **1 a :** to let fall in drops ⟨the rain fell in a steady drizzle, and the air was so damp that [her] hair *dripped* moisture —Laura Krey⟩ ⟨*dripping* paint direct from the tube onto their canvases —W.C. Smith⟩ ⟨each word she said *dripped* acid on the Italian woman's heart —Donn Byrne⟩ **b :** to spill or emit (something likened to a copiously dropping liquid) in an overflow or enveloping shower ⟨the honey locusts ~ their golden scent —Mary A. Taylor⟩ ⟨their crimes have increased in violence and often ~ horror —*Time*⟩ ⟨*dripping* invective from every sentence⟩ **2 :** to provide (a pipe) with a cock for draining condensate **3 :** to prepare (the beverage coffee) by letting boiling water seep slowly through finely ground coffee **~** *vi* **1 a :** to let fall drops of moisture or liquid ⟨trees *dripping* after the rain⟩ ⟨icicles *dripping* on the roof⟩ ⟨allowing the paint to ~ evenly upon the ground color —H.A.Helverston⟩ **b :** to become so saturated as to overflow in drops ⟨toast *dripping* with butter⟩ **c :** to exude or become enveloped in a shower of something likened to a dropping liquid ⟨tunic *dripping* with gold braid and lace —Marcia Davenport⟩ ⟨she beamed, she seemed fairly to ~ with the milk of human kindness —P.B.Kyne⟩ ⟨the latest ballads *dripping* with sentiment —Carl Wittke⟩ **d** *obs, of weather* **:** DRIZZLE, MIST **2 a :** to fall in drops ⟨water ~s from the eaves⟩ **b :** to hang or appear to hang suspended like a drop about to fall ⟨a brown, handmade cigarette forever *dripped* from his lower lip —Harold Sinclair⟩ **c :** to seem to drift down or to overflow slowly and gently like drops of a light rain ⟨the music ~s from saxophones —Maxwell Anderson⟩ ⟨pale moonlight, *dripping* through the leaves, spilled down in splashes —Hamilton Basso⟩ ⟨the most abject sentimentality ~s from every page —Pamela Taylor⟩

2drip \"\ *n* -s **1 a :** a falling in drops ⟨the woods by day and by night were full of nothing but solitude . . . and ~ —John Collier b. 1884⟩ ⟨an overflow of the wax called guttering but more commonly known as ~ —W.W.Klenke⟩; *also* **:** a letting something fall in drops or blobs ⟨a water clock — a ~ affair on the order of an hourglass —A.L.Kroeber⟩ ⟨the first application of the ~ technique to painting —*Time*⟩ **b :** liquid that falls, leaks, overflows, or is extruded in drops ⟨the jungle was exuding its fog ~ —Norman Mailer⟩ ⟨a pan for catching the ~ from wet umbrellas —J.E.Gloag⟩ ⟨the ~ of frozen foods exuded during thawing⟩ ⟨gripping the ~ gutters of a car⟩ ⟨postnasal ~ into the trachea⟩ ⟨gobs here, ~s there, the palette knife always more active than the brush —R.M.Coates⟩ **c :** an accumulation formed by descending or extruded drops: (1) *Brit* **:** DRIPPING 2b ⟨bread and ~⟩ (2) **:** a collection of drops (as of paint or varnish) at the bottom edge of an article that has been coated by dipping **d :** a manner of hanging suggestive of something dripping wet or having been dripping wet ⟨a tricolor or two hung in a dry ~ from an occasional balcony —Bruce Marshall⟩ ⟨the long ~ of her straight hair —Edith Sitwell⟩ **2 :** the sound made by or as if by falling drops ⟨a faint ~ of oars⟩ ⟨the stiff, tinny ~ of the banjos on the lawn —Scott Fitzgerald⟩ **3** *also* **drip pipe :** a small pipe or outlet for draining condensate (as from a main or a heating-system radiator) **4 :** a part of a cornice, sill course, window head, or other horizontal architectural member that projects beyond the rest and is of such section as to throw off the rainwater; *also* **:** an overlapping lead or strip of tin or copper serving the same purpose **5 :** a device for the slow continued administration of a fluid at a steady rate esp. into a vein of the body; *also* **:** any material so administered ⟨a glucose ~⟩ **6** *slang* **:** a trickle or weak stream of senseless fatuous talk or writing **:** sloppy sentiment **:** DRIVEL ⟨the daily ~ I have to listen to —Thorne Smith⟩ ⟨just the sort of ~ one has come to expect from the author⟩ **7** *slang* **:** someone looked on as tiresome or annoyingly dull from lack of personality, animation, or social amenability; *also* **:** a rather simple or stupid person

drip cap *n* **:** a drip or head flashing installed over a window or door

drip coffee *n* **:** coffee made by letting boiling water drip slowly through finely ground coffee

drip culture *n* **:** a method of hydroponic plant culture in which a nutrient solution drips slowly onto sand or other inert medium in which the plants are growing — compare SLOP CULTURE

drip–drip \ˈ=,=\ *n* [redupl. of *2drip*] **:** a continued dripping

1drip–dry \ˈ=ˈ=\ *vi* **:** to dry with few or no wrinkles when hung dripping wet ⟨nylon *drip-dries* in seconds, takes little ironing —*advt*⟩

2drip–dry \ˈ=,=\ *adj* [*1drip-dry*] **:** made of a washable fabric that will drip-dry ⟨a *drip-dry* suit⟩

drip loop *n* **:** a downward loop (as in a wire entering a building to permit rainwater to drip off or in a pipe to collect water condensed in the pipe system)

drip mold *n* **:** a drip (as along an eaves) formed of wooden molding

drip oil *n* **:** a liquid by-product of the manufacture of illuminating gas that condenses from the gas stream and contains styrene, indene, and related compounds

drip·page \ˈdripij\ *n* -s **1 :** a dripping esp. of water from the eaves of a house **2 :** something accumulated by dripping ⟨had to clean the ~ from the sump pit⟩

drip pan *or* **dripping pan** *n* [*drip pan* fr. *2drip* + *pan*; *dripping pan* fr. ME *drepyngpanne*, fr. *drepyng* dripping + *panne* pan] **1** *usu* **drip pan :** a container for catching material that drips from above (as from the burners of a gas range or a piece of oily machinery) **2** *usu* **dripping pan :** a usu. shallow rectangular metal pan used for baking and roasting

drip·per \-ipə(r)\ *n* -s **:** one that drips **:** something from which a liquid is allowed to drip

1dripping *n* -s [ME *drippinge, drepyng*, fr. *drippen* to drip + *-inge, -ing* -ing] **1 :** the sound made by falling drops **2 a :** liquid waste that drips (as from machines) — often used in pl. **b :** fat and juices drawn from meat during cooking esp. when used as shortening or a spread — often used in pl.

2dripping *adv* [fr. pres. part. of *1drip*] **:** to a high degree **:** THOROUGHLY — usu. used in the phrase *dripping wet*

drip·ple \ˈdripəl\ *vi* **drippled; drippling** \-p(ə)liŋ\ **dripples** [prob. blend of *1drip* and *1dribble*] **1 :** to dribble briskly **2 :** to drip with wet

drip pot *n* **:** a pot for making drip coffee

drip primrose *n* **:** MISTASSINI

drip·py \ˈdripē\ *adj* -ER/-EST [*2drip* + *-y*] **1 :** characterized by dripping **:** RAINY, DRIZZLY ⟨a ~ climate⟩ **2 :** nauseatingly emotional **:** MAWKISH ⟨a lot of ~ endearments —H.L.Spinner⟩

drips *pres 3d sing of* DRIP, *pl of* DRIP

dripstone \ˈ=,=\ *n* **1 :** a drip (as along an eaves) made of stone **2 :** calcium carbonate in the form of stalactites or stalagmites

dript *past of* DRIP

dri·sheen \drəˈshēn\ *n* -s [IrGael *drisīn*] **:** a sausage prepared with sheep's blood, milk, and seasonings chiefly in the vicinity of Cork in Ireland

drisk \ˈdrisk\ *n* -s [origin unknown] *NewEng* **:** a drizzling mist

drite \ˈdrīt\ *vi* [ME *driten*, fr. OE *drītan* — more at DIRT] *Scot* **:** DEFECATE

driv·able *also* **drive·able** \ˈdrīvəbəl\ *adj* **:** capable of being driven ⟨as soon as the colt is ~⟩ ⟨the road is not ~ in winter⟩; *specif* **:** suitable for floating logs

driv·age \ˈdrīvij\ *n* -s **:** a driving of a mine passage

1drive \ˈdrīv\ *vb* **drove** \ˈdrōv\ *or archaic* **drave** \ˈdrāv\ *or dial* **driv** \ˈdriv\ *or* **druv** \ˈdrəv\ **driv·en** \ˈdrivən *also* -iᵇm\ *or* -ibᵊm\ *or archaic* **drove** *or dial* **driv** *or* **druv; driv·ing** \ˈdrīviŋ\ **drives** \ˈdrīvz\ [ME *driven*, fr. OE *drīfan*; akin to OHG *trīban* to drive, ON *drīfa* to dash (said of spray), Goth *dreiban* to drive, and perh. to Lith *dribti* to fall in mushy flakes (said of snow)] *vt* **1 :** to set and keep in motion or in action through application of some amount of force: **a :** to impart an onward or forward motion to by expenditure of physical force **:** PROPEL ⟨he slammed the door and *drove* the bolt home⟩ ⟨cheerily *drove* his pen afresh —George Meredith⟩ ⟨as white as the *driven* snow⟩ ⟨the trade winds ~ the equatorial currents⟩ ⟨*driving* his canoe onto the beach⟩ **b :** to impart violent motion or great impetus to **:** hurl, thrust, plunge, or press irresistibly — used with a following preposition or adverb indicating the direction ⟨a tackler should ~ his body so as to hit the ball-carrier just above the knees⟩ ⟨he *drove* the muzzle hard into the man's face —Max Peacock⟩; *specif* **:** VAPORIZE — used with *off* ⟨heat will ~ off the quicksilver⟩ **c :** to urge along (as cattle) guiding and often goading ⟨cowboys *drove* herds north⟩ ⟨prisoners were *driven* onto barges⟩ **d :** to cause to penetrate with force ⟨as a man would ~ a nail —J.G.Frazer⟩ **:** plunge forcibly ⟨I *drove* my sword through his heart —Padraic Colum⟩ **e :** to direct hostile force or a strong offensive movement against **:** exert strong effective pressure against — used with a separative expression ⟨many attempts to ~ the British out of Egypt⟩ ⟨the task of *driving* the invaders back across the border⟩ ⟨with the German eagle *driven* from the seas —R.W.Van Alstyne⟩ ⟨the noise would ~ you out of the place —Ellwood Kirby⟩ **f :** to constrain to go or to remove by reason of superior authority or influence or because of circumstantial pressure (as political or economic) ⟨engaged in a long attempt to ~ Burr from public life —Nathan Schachner⟩ ⟨this wetback competition annually ~*s* thousands of Texans as far north as Oregon in search of work —D.L.Graham⟩; *also* **:** to force the removal or banishment of ⟨radio has *driven* the newspaper extra from the streets⟩ **g :** to supply with motive power ⟨machines *driven* by clockwork⟩ ⟨whether it was being *driven* as a generator or was running as a motor —F.A.Annett⟩ **:** set or keep in operation ⟨*drove* their mills with water power⟩ **2 a :** to direct the motions and course of (a draft animal) **b :** NAVIGATE ⟨~ a watercraft⟩ **c :** to operate the controls of (a locomotive) or to operate the mechanism and controls and direct the course of (as a motor vehicle or speedboat) **d :** to convey in a vehicle ⟨he had to ~ his produce to market before daylight⟩ **e :** to guide a vehicle along or through ⟨*drove* the river road in all kinds of weather⟩ ⟨*drove* creek beds and side-hills to reach his backcountry patients⟩ **f :** to own and use (as an automobile of an indicated kind) ⟨he always *drove* a sedan⟩ **g :** to float (logs) down a stream **3 a :** to carry on or carry through energetically ⟨shipowners were *driving* a roaring trade in oriental ports⟩ **b :** to carry through to a conclusion or to completion in spite of hindrances ⟨they will not give up their bargaining advantage without *driving* a hard bargain politically —Cecil Hobbs⟩; *specif* **:** to lay out and construct by the methods of engineering ⟨superhighway being *driven* across the state⟩ **c :** to build (a highway, canal, railroad) along a projected course **4 :** to subject to effective pressure or compulsion to act in a certain way or to submit to a certain condition: as **a :** to exert inescapable or coercive pressure on (a person) **:** motivate or incite irresistibly **:** COERCE, CONSTRAIN, OBLIGE — used often with a following preposition or infinitive indicating the direction of constraint ⟨hunger *drove* him to steal⟩ ⟨to make us believe that his characters are fellow beings *driven* by their own passions and idiosyncracies —Virginia Woolf⟩ ⟨he used only persuasion, for he knew she could not be *driven*⟩ ⟨a wayward genius who is *driven* to incredible writing feats by pressure of debts —Leslie Rees⟩ ⟨economic insecurity that ~*s* young people into vocational training —A.W.Griswold⟩ **b :** to oblige to suffer or have recourse to a mood or mental state ⟨to what depths of bitterness she had been *driven* —Herbert Read⟩ ⟨continuing pressure of the unsolved problem ~*s* the society . . . to a precipitate and spurious defense mechanism —Weston La Barre⟩; *specif* **:** to compel to undergo or suffer a change of state ⟨*driven* desperate by the pressures of drab life —Evelyn Eaton⟩ ⟨a stupid cocotte who has begun by *driving* him mad with jealousy —Edmund Wilson⟩ **c :** to urge relentlessly to continuous exertion ⟨he ~*s* them hard with five-mile runs before breakfast —Harry Gordon⟩ ⟨I have been ruthlessly *driven* — hence this silence —H.J.Laski⟩ **:** press or spur to greater intensity of determined striving ⟨a tired spirit *driving* body and nerves to an effort they were crying to avoid —Fred Majdalany⟩ ⟨believed men were *driven* hardest by ambition —M.A.Kline⟩ ⟨he lacked the will that *drives* one to disregard human factors, to crush all who opposed him⟩ **d :** to press or force (something) inflexibly into a certain activity, course, direction, or state ⟨forces which had *driven* the tide of population across the Alleghenies —R.A. Billington⟩ ⟨discipline required to ~ the bill through congress⟩ ⟨advised against *driving* the party underground⟩; *specif* **:** to subject to pressure to bring about change either up or down ⟨going to try to ~ interest rates down which meant *driving* up the capital value of existing loans —Harold Wincott⟩ **e :** to project, inject, or impress incisively ⟨only a few are willing to ~ this doctrine straight through to its logical conclusion —Clinton Rossiter⟩ ⟨the basic point at last is *driven* solidly home in a 56-page booklet —R.D.Darrell⟩ ⟨the laconic or sententious phrase to ~ home and imbed what might otherwise be lost or scattered —B.N.Cardozo⟩ **f :** to cause (something intangible) to dissipate or vanish decisively through the pressure of some moving power or influence ⟨as the corroborative detail *drove* doubts from his mind —T.B.Costain⟩ ⟨a sad day for the U.S. if the tradition of dissent were *driven* out of the universities —J.B.Conant⟩; *specif* **:** to dispel and replace ⟨resolved that sound Latin . . . should ~ out, for literary purposes, the Italian vernaculars and medieval Latin —G.C. Sellery⟩ **5** *archaic* **:** BRING ⟨~ bad luck⟩ **:** CAST ⟨~ not the fault on him —Robert Bridges †1930⟩ **6 a** *obs* **:** to cause to pass ⟨~ the tedious hours away —John Dryden⟩ **b :** PROTRACT, DEFER ⟨~ bedtime⟩ **7** *obs* **:** to conclude from premises **:** DEDUCE **8 a** *obs* **:** to pursue (game) as a hunter **b :** to cause (as game animals) to move in a desired direction (as toward waiting hunters) ⟨beaters *drove* the birds toward the guns⟩; *also* **:** to drive game in (a particular place) ⟨we will ~ the small woods by the stream tomorrow⟩ — compare STALK, WALK UP **c** *obs* **:** to clear or strip (as a region) of animals or other property; *also* **:** to drive off **:** SEIZE ⟨~ animals⟩ **9 a :** to advance (as a tunnel or a horizontal or upwardly inclined mine passage) by cutting and excavating **b :** PRODUCE ⟨~ a well⟩ **10 :** to propel (an object of play) swiftly (as by a powerful stroke or throw): **a :** to strike (a bowled cricket ball) with the bat so as to propel in a forward direction **b :** to send (a croquet ball) to some desired position by striking another ball held in contact **c :** to play (a golf ball) from the tee esp. with a full stroke made with a driver **d :** to hit (a tennis ball) on the bounce with a below-shoulder-level swing and with top spin — distinguished from *chop, slice,* and *volley* **e :** to return (a shuttlecock) with a low hard shot parallel to the ground — compare SMASH **f :** to cause (a run or runner) to be scored in baseball esp. by making a hit — usu. used with *in* **g :** to force (a billiard ball) to strike one or more cushions and return to the desired position for the next shot ~ *vi* **1 a :** to dash, plunge, or press ahead rapidly or violently ⟨the halfback *drove* through the line⟩ ⟨he *drove* rudely past her into the room —E.F.McGuire⟩ **b :** to rush along thrusting or striking with force against any obstruction ⟨he crossed the river in the midst of *driving* ice⟩ ⟨a meteor *driving* toward the earth⟩ ⟨the slanting rain, which *drove* faster every minute —Ellen Glasgow⟩ **c :** to press a hostile attack ⟨the division *drove* some 400 miles⟩ **d :** to penetrate with force ⟨the harpoon *drove* deep⟩ **2 :** to move to leeward or with the tide out of control by rudder, sail, or engines; *also* **:** to carry excessive sail **3 :** to launch a blow or missile or discharge a bullet — often used with a following *at* and a preceding *let* ⟨just as a snarling Queen's Ranger *drove* at him —F.V.W.Mason⟩ ⟨he then seized the shotgun and let ~ with both barrels⟩ **4 a :** to strive determinedly on a course or toward an objective ⟨try to ~ toward a generalization and a hypothesis —Lionel Trilling⟩ ⟨*driving* through obstacles —*Time*⟩ ⟨the decision to ~ ahead with all speed for the manufacture of the hydrogen bomb —W.H. Chamberlin⟩; *also* **:** to make a strong effort ⟨the justices are *driving* hard to clean up pending cases —*Christian Science Monitor*⟩ **b :** to spur oneself or others to strenuous effort or to greater intensity of physical or mental exertion ⟨even after reaching the top he continues to ~⟩ **5 a :** to guide a horse-drawn vehicle **b :** to operate and steer a motor vehicle ⟨road signs warning motorists to ~ slow⟩ **c :** to have oneself carried in a vehicle ⟨I *drove* there with a friend and flew back by myself⟩ **6** *archaic* **:** to levy a distress to obtain satisfaction of a claim for rent **:** DISTRAIN **7 :** to drive a mine passage **8 :** to drive an object of play (as a golf ball) **9 :** to perform music with a strong rhythmic impulse **:** play with momentum **syn** see MOVE — **drive at :** to aim or intend to express ultimately often despite initial failure to achieve clarity or to reveal the full implications ⟨many of their statements are so qualified as to make it difficult to know what they are *driving at* —L.A.White⟩ — usu. used with the pronoun *what* as inverted object

²drive \"\ *n* -s **1 :** an act of driving: **a :** a short trip in a vehicle (as a carriage or automobile) wholly or partly under one's control as distinguished from a vehicle (as a train) under the control of another ⟨an afternoon ~ along the lakefront⟩ ⟨a 2-hour ~ to the next city⟩ **b :** an overland journey in a vehicle esp. along a highway for a long distance ⟨a cross-state ~⟩ ⟨the third day's ~ became wearisome⟩ **c :** an urging and gathering together of animals (as cattle or sheep) from a wide area; *also* **:** the animals gathered for capture, slaughter, or branding **d :** a driving of cattle or sheep overland ⟨the long ~ lingered only in the memories and imaginations of old cowhands — D.B.Davis⟩ **e :** a hunt or shoot in which the game is driven within range past the weapons of hunters; *also* **:** the mass of animals so driven **f :** the guiding of logs downstream to a mill; *also* **:** the floating logs amassed in a drive **g** (1) **:** the act or an instance of driving an object of play (as a ball) ⟨the ~ is called the basic scoring shot in cricket⟩ ⟨a low ~ that hit the net⟩ (2) **:** the flight of a hard-hit ball or shuttlecock ⟨his solid ~*s* range between 220 and 240 yards⟩ **h :** the forward thrust or propulsive force of a boat under way **i** *Brit* **:** a stately or ceremonious public procession **2 a :** a private road for vehicles affording access to a residence or other buildings ⟨the house stands at the end of a long ~ surrounded by spacious lawns and gardens —*Amer. Guide Series: Fla.*⟩ **:** DRIVEWAY 2 **b :** a road for leisure driving esp. in a park or along a scenic route ⟨the highway now skirts the lakeshore with all the fresh beauty of a seacoast ~ —*Amer. Guide Series: Vt.*⟩ **c :** an urban street or boulevard ⟨Morningside *Drive* overlooking the Hudson⟩ **3 :** a tract over which game is driven **:** the site of an organized hunt **4 :** an offensive, aggressive, or expansionist move ⟨in the path of the Soviet ~ toward the Adriatic —H.C.Wolfe⟩ ⟨both touchdowns capped long ~*s*⟩; *esp* **:** a strong military attack against enemy-held terrain ⟨a swift nine-month ~ from the Normandy bridgehead . . . across France and Germany and into Austria —*Current Biog.*⟩ **5 :** the state of being hurried and under pressure ⟨elude the ruthless ~ of work and worry —S.H.Adams⟩ ⟨I am in such a ~ that I can't expatiate —H.J.Laski⟩ **6 :** a driven mine passage or tunnel **7 :** STRIKE 14 **8 :** a systematic effort strenuously participated in by a group or organized by a group and insistently urged upon a community or a nation toward attainment of a certain objective or furtherance of some special design **:** an intensive campaign ⟨an annual ~ for membership in the league⟩ ⟨a propaganda ~ aimed at undermining our prestige abroad⟩ ⟨sparked ~*s* that raised many hundreds of thousands of dollars for veterans' hospitals and . . . relief —J.A.Morris b. 1904⟩ ⟨the ~ for national independence has had a long history in Indochina —Cecil Hobbs⟩ **9 :** a progressive game (as of whist or bridge) **10 :** inciting or impelling character or quality: **a :** an urgent basic or instinctual need pressing for satisfaction **:** a physiological tension, lack, or imbalance (as a state of hunger or thirst) impelling the organism to activity ⟨those sexual ~*s* which are such a fertile source of conflict among most vertebrates —Ralph Linton⟩ ⟨habits attached to the hunger ~⟩; *also* **:** a tendency or disposition to act following or as a result of a deprivation or need **b :** a powerfully impelling culturally acquired concern, interest, or longing that incites one to unremitting action ⟨possessed with a ~ for perfection —*Time*⟩ ⟨the integrating ~ or disposition that gives a life history its continuity or a personality its consistency and integrity —H.J.Muller⟩ ⟨a prisoner of the old national and imperialist ~*s* —*Partisan Rev.*⟩ ⟨"Asia for the Asians" . . . represents the ~ of millions upon millions of people —W.O.Douglas⟩ **c :** dynamic quality marked by initiative, promptness of decision, abundance of concentrated energy, and indomitable persistence in carrying through an undertaking toward accomplishment **:** vigorous enterprise **:** the amount of energy and persistence evidenced in a given activity **:** ÉLAN, PUSH ⟨his ~ and enthusiasm overcame all obstacles —*Times Lit. Supp.*⟩ ⟨a tremendous energy ~ that keeps him in a constant state of high gear —Martin Gardner⟩ ⟨the city had lost . . . the surging ~ that supposedly was so characteristically American —Harold Sinclair⟩ ⟨concerned with the dynamic core of a society, its central impulse and ~ —Charles Maughan⟩ **d :** a quality of sustained vitality and intensity of expression in intellectual or artistic composition or performance ⟨he developed irresistible ~ in the performance of plays —Sheldon Cheney⟩ ⟨a stronger ~ in the big climaxes —Irving Kolodin⟩ **e :** dramatic intensity and suspensiveness that captures attention **f :** a strong rhythmic impulse communicated in musical performance **11 a :** the means for giving motion to a machine or machine part ⟨belt ~⟩ ⟨electric ~⟩; *also* **:** a method of driving machines ⟨a group ~⟩ **b :** the means by which the propulsive power of an automobile is applied to the road ⟨front-wheel ~⟩ ⟨four-wheel ~⟩ **c :** the means by which the propulsion of an automotive vehicle is controlled and directed ⟨a left-hand ~⟩; *also* **:** the place where the operator sits to drive ⟨an enclosed ~⟩ **12 :** the pressure that causes oil or other fluid to enter a well from the surrounding rock strata ⟨water ~⟩ ⟨gas-cap ~⟩ **13 :** an offering of goods at a low price (as in reducing inventory) **syn** see VIGOR

³drive \"\ *adj* **:** used in or for driving **:** serving to drive **:** IMPELLING ⟨a ~ chain⟩

driveaway \ˈ⸗ˌ⸗⸗\ *n* -s [*drive away,* v., fr. ¹*drive* + *away*] **:** the delivery of an automobile by driving it under its own power from the factory to a purchaser or dealer ⟨organized a ~ service⟩ ⟨a ~ of 60 cars⟩

driveboat \ˈ⸗ˌ⸗\ *n* **:** a rowboat used in menhaden fishing to drive the fish into the nets

drivehead \ˈ⸗ˌ⸗\ *n* **:** a plug, ring, or cap for screwing into or fitting over the end of a mechanical part so that it can be driven with minimum deformation or bruising

drive-in \ˈdrīˌvin\ *n* -s *often attrib* [*drive in,* v., fr. ¹*drive* + *in*] **:** a place of business (as a motion-picture theater, bank, or refreshment stand) laid out and equipped so as to allow its patrons to be served or accommodated while remaining in their automobiles ⟨a new *drive-in* business⟩ ⟨the convenient *drive-in* window at the bank⟩ ⟨let's eat at the *drive-in* tonight⟩

¹driv·el \ˈdrivəl\ *vb* **driveled** *or* **drivelled; driv·eled; driveling** *or* **drivelling** \-v(ə)liŋ\ **drivels** [ME *drivelen,* alter. of *drevelen,* fr. OE *dreflian;* akin to ME *draf* draff — more at DRAFF] *vi* **1 :** to let saliva drip or run in a thin stream from the mouth or mucus from the nostrils (as of an infant or imbecile) **:** SLAVER ⟨the panting dog ~*ed* on my hand⟩ **2 :** to talk stupidly and carelessly without due thought, knowledge, or consideration **:** be silly in manner or content of speech ⟨while the idiots on the platform were ~*ing,* the people kept calling for Lincoln —Winston Churchill⟩ ⟨he ~*ed* on about his family, his influence, his properties⟩ **3** *archaic* **:** TRICKLE, DRIBBLE ⟨water ~*ing*⟩ ~ *vt* **1** *obs* **:** to let trickle like saliva from the mouth ⟨the wound is ~*ing* blood⟩ **2 :** to utter in an infantile or imbecilic way ⟨he ~*ed* a few words of apology then left at once⟩ **3 :** to waste or fritter in a childish fashion

²drivel \"\ *n* -s [ME *drivil, drevel,* fr. *drivelen, drevelen,* v.] **1** *archaic* **:** saliva trickling from the mouth **2 :** inarticulate or foolish utterance ⟨phrases which on the face of them may be platitudinous to a degree approaching ~ —C.E.Montague⟩ ⟨writes endless narcissistic ~ in a stream-of-consciousness and disorganized manner —Albert Deutsch⟩

driv·el·er *or* **driv·el·ler** \-v(ə)lə(r)\ *n* -s **:** one that drivels **:** one who talks in a silly, foolish, or babyish way

driveling *or* **drivelling** *adj* [ME *drivelinge* talking stupidly, fr. *drivelen* to let saliva drip from the mouth, talk stupidly + *-inge, -ing* -ing] **1 :** feeble like an infant in thought or action ⟨reduced to a ~ idiot⟩ **2 :** inane in an infantile or feeble-minded way ⟨a ~ and idiotic and superficial travesty of the Italian culture —Ezra Pound⟩ — **driv·el·ing·ly** *or* **driv·el·ling·ly** *adv*

¹driven *adj* [fr. past part. of ¹*drive*] **:** evidencing marked strenuousness of effort or a compelling sense of urgency ⟨even his Beethoven performances . . . were sometimes too ~ and sleek for my taste —Winthrop Sargeant⟩ ⟨then his own ~ sense of obligation would rear up —Norman Kelman⟩

²driven *n* -s **:** a gear wheel or pulley that takes its motion from another **:** FOLLOWER

driven note *n, obs* **:** DRIVING NOTE

drive nozzle *n* **:** a high-pressure spraying nozzle the stream from which breaks at about 30 feet in the air into a coarse mist for spraying tall trees

driven well *n* **:** a well made by driving a tube into the earth to a water-bearing stratum

drive out *vt* **:** to space (typeset matter) widely

drivepipe \ˈ⸗ˌ⸗\ *n* **:** a pipe with a sharp edge for driving short distances into the solid ground (as to reach a water-bearing stratum or to insert concrete piles)

driv·er \ˈdrīvə(r)\ *n* -s *often attrib* [ME *drivere,* fr. *driven* to drive + *-ere* -er] **1 :** one that drives something: as **a :** one that drives cattle, sheep, or beasts of burden **b :** a person in actual physical control of a vehicle (as an automobile) ⟨~ for the colonel⟩ ⟨hundreds of ~*s* parked their cars by the shore⟩ ⟨Sunday ~*s*⟩ — compare OPERATOR **c :** one that dispels or expels ⟨a pianist is my surest ~ away of worry⟩ ⟨a dedicated ~ out of superstition⟩ **d :** a beater, drover, or other individual engaged in driving animals toward a destination **e :** one competent to carry projects to execution or completion ⟨a ~ of bargains⟩ **f :** one skilled or adept at driving an object in flight, into desired shape, or so as to penetrate ⟨he proved the longest ~ in the tournament⟩ ⟨a ~ of rivets⟩ ⟨the steam driller was taking work from ~*s*⟩ **g :** an overseer of a gang of workers responsible for their working at a satisfactory pace; *broadly* **:** a harsh and exacting taskmaster **h :** a workman who guides logs being floated down a stream **i :** the operator or tender of a machine that drives ⟨a pile ~⟩ **j :** a member of a purse-seiner crew who goes out ahead in a small boat to determine the direction and size of schools of fish and helps to keep fish from escaping while the net is being set **k :** an individual with executive ability and the tense and rigorous disposition to spur others to maintain a high level of well-directed exertion — used often with an implication of pushing relentlessly and ruthlessly ⟨almost invariably he is a tense or intense person, enthusiastic, conscientious, more or less of a perfectionist, a go-getter, a real ~ —C.M.Jones⟩ ⟨a great man is a leader of men, not a ~ —S.McC.Crothers⟩ ⟨every steel company needs at least one hard-boiled ~ of men —*Current Biog.*⟩ **2 :** any of certain implements or tools used for driving: as **a :** MALLET **b :** a tamping iron **c :** a hammer for driving on barrel hoops **d :** any of various sporting implements (as a bat, racket, or club) esp. adapted for driving (as by shape); *esp* **:** a golf club with a wooden head and nearly straight face used in driving a ball from the tee — see WOOD illustration **e :** an electrical device (as an electron tube) that produces and sustains oscillations or pulses in a circuit **f :** the magnetic device that actuates a loudspeaker diaphragm to produce sound **3 a** *obs* **:** a square sail set on a yard at the end of a spanker boom with the wind aft **b :** SPANKER 2 **c :** the sixth mast on a many-masted schooner; *also* **:** the lower sail set on this mast **4 :** a piece for imparting motion to another piece either directly or indirectly: as **a :** the first of a train of wheels giving motion to the rest **b :** a locomotive driving wheel **c :** a dog in the faceplate of a lathe for driving a straight-tailed dog **d :** a crossbar on a grinding-mill spindle for driving the upper stone **5 :** DOWITCHER

driver ant *also* **driver** *n* **:** ARMY ANT; *specif* **:** any of various African and Asian ants of *Dorylus* and related genera that move in vast armies and devour insects and small animals

driver boom *n, obs* **:** SPANKER BOOM

driv·er·less \ˈdrīvə(r)ləs\ *adj* **:** having no driver

driver salesman *n* **:** a salesman (as of beverages, ice cream, cigars) who calls on customers along a regular route carrying samples of new products and combining sales activities with deliveries and collection of empties

driv·er·ship \-ˌship\ *n* -s **1 :** skill in driving vehicles **2 :** attitude and method in overseeing and supervising men at work or study; *esp* **:** hard driving and exacting method

driver's license *n* **:** a license issued under governmental authority that permits the holder to operate a motor vehicle

driver's seat *n* **1 :** the position of top authority and governing power ⟨whether a czar or a commissar sits in the *driver's seat* is immaterial —L.A.White⟩ **2 :** the position of dominance or of tight control (as of a situation) ⟨the feeling that the occupation authorities unwittingly assisted the Nazis back into the *driver's seat*⟩ ⟨with cars no longer scarce the buyer seemed firmly in the *driver's seat*⟩

drives *pres 3d sing of* DRIVE, *pl of* DRIVE

drivescrew \ˈ⸗ˌ⸗\ *n* **:** a screw that is driven home or nearly home with a hammer

drive shaft *n* **:** a shaft that transmits mechanical power — see JET ENGINE illustration

drive shoe *n* **:** the sharp edge of a drivepipe

drive-volley \ˈ⸗ˌ⸗⸗\ *n* **:** a tennis volley executed in the manner of a forehand drive

driveway \ˈ⸗ˌ⸗\ *n* **1 :** a road or way along which animals (as stock or game) are driven **2 :** a private road giving access from a public thoroughfare to a building or buildings on abutting grounds **3 :** a way leading to an upper level (as of a barn) for passage of vehicles

drivewell \ˈ⸗ˌ⸗\ *n* **:** DRIVEN WELL

drive wheel *n* **:** DRIVING WHEEL

drive-yourself \ˈ⸗⸗ˌ⸗\ *adj* [¹*drive*] **:** of or constituting a service providing automobiles for hire to be driven by the hirer

¹driving *adj* [fr. pres. part. of ¹*drive*] **1 :** acting with vigor **:** ENERGETIC ⟨responsibility turned the spoiled playboy into a ~ young executive⟩ **2 :** prone to urge or goad others (as subordinates or employees) to stepped-up or unreasonable exertion ⟨a ~ supervisor⟩ **3 :** being of such character as to produce or effect and sustain consistently directed, progressive, or constructive action ⟨the ~ force was not academic training but his innate enthusiasm for constructive and creative work —John Bradford⟩ ⟨the ~ energy required of an executive⟩ ⟨in the 1860s and 1870s the irresistible ~ power of the American trek westward —*Amer. Guide Series: Texas*⟩ **4 :** exercising an inescapable pressure or compulsive influence in inciting and stimulating thoughts or actions in mounting sequence **:** DYNAMIC ⟨little by little the pleasure of opiates gives way to the ~ necessity to take drugs in order to avoid withdrawal distress —D.W.Maurer & V.H.Vogel⟩ ⟨the stirring and ~ quality of all truly spiritual leaders who are in the world but not of it —M.R.Cohen⟩ ⟨the ~ concern of the book to expose actual conditions in the institution⟩ ⟨a ~ personal ambition⟩ **5 :** having a dramatic and suspensive quality stimulative to readers or hearers ⟨he gives us a quick and ~ narrative of a tired and indomitable and angry man —*Saturday Rev.*⟩

²driving *n* -s [fr. gerund of ¹*drive*] **:** management of an automobile or other vehicle on the road ⟨clever at ~ in heavy traffic⟩

driving axle *n* **:** the axle of a driving wheel (as of a locomotive)

driving box *n* **:** the journal box of a locomotive driving axle

driving clock *n* **1 :** a mechanism for turning an equatorial telescope or a coelostat around its polar axis at the proper rate to keep a celestial body in the field of view **2 :** a driving mechanism for a chronograph or other recording mechanism

driving face *n* **:** BLADE FACE

driving horse *n* **:** a light horse suitable for hauling a passenger vehicle

driving iron *n* **1 :** a sharp-pointed steel rod for driving holes (as for subsoil blasting, stump blasting, tree planting) **2 :** an iron golf club with little loft that is used sometimes in making the drive — called also *number one iron;* see IRON illustration

driv·ing·ly *adv* **:** with driving force or energy

driving mashie *n* **:** MASHIE IRON

driving note *n, obs* **:** a syncopated note in music

driving park *n* **:** an area with a racetrack for harness racing

driving range *n* **:** an area or field equipped with distance markers, clubs, balls, and tees for practicing the golf drive and iron shots

driving spring *n* **:** a supporting spring resting upon a locomotive driving box to minimize shock

driving wheel *n* **:** a wheel that communicates motion: as **a :** one of the large wheels of a locomotive to which the side rods are attached and which are driven by the engine connecting rods **:** DRIVER **b :** the main wheel of a watch or clock that transmits the driving power of the spring, weight, or electromagnetic impulse to the succeeding parts of the train

¹driz·zle \ˈdrizəl\ *vb* **drizzled; drizzled; drizzling** \-z(ə)liŋ\ **drizzles** [perh. alter. of ME *drysnen* to fall, fr. OE *-drysnian* to disappear; akin to OE *drēosan* to fall — more at DREARY] *vi* **1 :** to rain in very small drops ⟨a raw *drizzling* rain⟩ ⟨it *drizzled* off and on all day⟩; *sometimes* **:** to rain lightly **:** SPRINKLE ⟨come on, it's only *drizzling* now⟩ **2 :** to shed minute drops or particles like fine rain ⟨the *drizzling* eyes to eat her beauty —Robinson Jeffers⟩ ~ *vt* **1 :** to shed or let fall in minute drops or particles ⟨the aphids *drizzled* honeydew on our heads⟩ ⟨the air doth ~ dew —Shak.⟩ ⟨after four minutes turn roe and mushrooms . . . then slowly ~ on wine, sprinkle with parsley —*Ford Times*⟩ **2 :** to make wet with minute drops ⟨the dew on the branches disturbed by our passage *drizzled* our hair and shoulders⟩

²drizzle \"\ *n* -s **1 :** a fine misty rain; *specif* **:** a light rain of very small drops falling at a velocity of between 144 feet per hour and 2¼ feet per second — compare SHOWER **2 a :** a slow dribble or trickle of a liquid ⟨a lukewarm ~ from the faucet⟩ **b :** a slow steady issue of hints or bits (as of an idea or attitude) ⟨a ~ of sensationalism —Elizabeth Janeway⟩

driz·zle–droz·zle \ˈdrizəl,dräzəl\ *n* -s [redupl. of *²drizzle*] **:** a gentle continuous rainfall

driz·zling·ly *adv* [*drizzling* (fr. pres. part. of *¹drizzle*) + *-ly*] **:** in a drizzle ⟨it rained ~, disappointing the farmers in the drought area who were praying for a good hard rain⟩

driz·zly \-z(ə)lē, -li\ *adj* -ER/-EST [*²drizzle* + *-y*] **:** characterized by fine rain ⟨this section of the country is unpleasant and ~ in the winter⟩

drod·dum \ˈdrädəm\ *n* -s [origin unknown] *Scot* **:** BUTTOCKS

drof·land \ˈdrōflənd\ *also* **dryf·land** \ˈdrif-\ *n* [alter. of *¹drove* + *land*] **:** land held in early England by the service of driving the lord's cattle from place to place

drog \ˈdräg, ˈdrōg\ *n* [ME *drogge* — more at DRUG] *Scot* **:** DRUG

dro·gher \ˈdrōgə(r)\ *n* -s [D *droger* (formerly spelled *drogher*), lit., drier (i.e., of herring), fr. *drogen* to dry (fr. *droog* dry, fr. MD *drōge*) + *-er* — more at DRY] **1 :** a sailing barge used in the West Indian coastal trade esp. in the Gulf of Paria **2 :** a clumsy cargo boat esp. of coasting type ⟨a pulpwood ~ lumbering up the tide-torn river —S.W.Dean & Marguerite Marshall⟩ **3 :** CARRIER, PORTER ⟨one of our best and most reliable ~s had brought his woman along to carry rations and dunnage —P.A.Zahl⟩

drogue \ˈdrōg\ *n* -s [prob. alter of *¹drag*] **1 :** a device attached to the end of a harpoon line to retard or tire out a whale when running or sounding **2 a :** a sea anchor (as a canvas bag with a hooped mouth) used to reduce the speed of a boat and keep her head into the wind **b** (1) **:** a sea anchor trailed from the stern of a seaplane to reduce yawing (2) **:** a cylindrical cloth target towed by an airplane for air-to-air firing practice (3) **:** a towed aerodynamic drag device used to maintain tension in a refueling hose; *also* **:** a small parachute for deceleration or stabilization of something **3 :** a device shaped like a funnel or cone with a wide mouth which is attached to the end of a long flexible hose suspended from a tanker airplane in flight and into which the probe of another airplane in flight is fitted so as to receive fuel from the tanker airplane

droich \ˈdrȯik\ *n* -s [ScGael] *Scot* **:** DWARF

¹droil *or* **droile** *n* -s [origin unknown] *obs* **:** DRUDGE

²droil *or* **droile** *vi* **droiled; droiled; droiling; droils** *or* **droiles** *obs* **:** DRUDGE

droit \ˈdrȯit\ *n* -s [origin unknown] **:** a former moneyers' unit of weight equal to ¹⁄₂₄ mite or ¹⁄₄₈₀ grain

droit ad·mi·nis·tra·tif \drwäädmēnēstrátēf\ *n* [F] **1** *French law* **:** ADMINISTRATIVE LAW **2 :** the rules of continental European administrative law exempting governmental agents from liability in other than administrative tribunals

droit d'au·baine \drwädōban\ *n* [F, right of escheat] **:** the right formerly possessed by the crown or state in France of confiscating all the property, real and personal, of which a domiciled alien died possessed

droit du sei·gneur \drwädüsānʸœr\ *n* [F, right of the lord] **:** a supposed legal or customary right at the time of a marriage whereby a feudal lord had sexual relations with a vassal's bride on her wedding night

droits ci·vils \drwäsēvēl\ *n pl* [F] *French law* **:** private rights

droits of admiralty \ˈdrȯits-\ *usu cap A* [MF *droit* law, right, fr. ML *directum*, fr. neut. of LL *directus* just, fr. L, straight, direct — more at DRESS] *English law* **:** certain rights or perquisites (as the proceeds of enemies' ships seized in port or taken by uncommissioned captors or from wrecks and derelicts) that formerly belonged to the Court of Admiralty but are now allowed to the captor

droi·tu·ral \ˈdrȯichərəl\ *adj* [F *droiture* straightforwardness, honesty (fr. *droit* straight, upright — fr. L *directus* straight, direct — + -ure) + E *-al* — more at DRESS] **:** relating to right or title of property as distinguished from right of possession ⟨~ actions at law⟩

droke \ˈdrōk\ *n* -s [origin unknown] *Canad* **:** THICKET, COPSE ⟨put my camp in a ~ of spruce —J.G.Millais⟩

drokpa *usu cap, var of* DRUPA

drô·le·rie \ˌdrōlə¦rē, (ˌ)drōl¦rē\ *n* -s [F — more at DROLLERY] **:** DROLLERY

¹droll \ˈdrōl\ *adj, usu* -ER/-EST [F *drôle*, fr. *drôle* scamp, rascal, fr. MF *drolle*, fr. MD, imp, elf, sprite] **:** causing or capable of causing mirth or amusement by funny, whimsical, or odd speech or conduct ⟨a ~ little man⟩ **:** having a humorous, whimsical, or odd character ⟨says things so ~ I can't answer him for laughing —Kenneth Roberts⟩ ⟨a book of ~ stories for the invalid⟩ **syn** see LAUGHABLE

²droll \"\ *n* -s [F *drôle*] **1 a :** one that habitually amuses or diverts by droll speech or behavior **:** WAG, JESTER ⟨played the ~ with his quips and sallies⟩ **b :** an actor in comedy ⟨an out-of-work comedian, an old ~ of the halls —May L. Becker⟩ **2 a :** a short dramatic composition or stage presentation of a comic or farcical character **:** BURLESQUE ⟨incipient circuses, ~s, and puppet shows all had a share in clearing the way for the stage in New England —Katharine L. Bates⟩; *also* **:** PUPPET SHOW **b :** a farcical folktale — compare FABLIAU

³droll \"\ *vb* -ED/-ING/-S *vi* **1** *archaic* **:** to jest or sport **:** make fun — often used with *on, upon* or *at* ⟨~*ing* a little upon the corporal —Laurence Sterne⟩ **2 :** to speak monotonously **:** DRONE ⟨~*s* on plaintively about the *Last Rose of Summer* —*Belfast (Ireland) Telegraph*⟩ ~ *vt, archaic* **:** to decline or put away in a jesting manner **:** influence (a person) toward or away from some action or opinion by jesting or raillery

droll·ery \ˈdrōl(ə)rē, -ri\ *n* -ES [F *drôlerie*, fr. *drôle* droll + *-erie* -ery] **1 :** something that is droll: as **a :** a comic picture or drawing ⟨for thy walls, a pretty slight ~ —Shak.⟩ **b :** DROLL 2a **c :** an amusing story or manner **:** JEST ⟨could not keep his *drolleries* out of the pulpit —H.E.Starr⟩ **d :** an artistic or intellectual production of a light and humorous character ⟨the delightful *drolleries* of Gilbert and Sullivan⟩ ⟨produced some excellent verse, *drolleries*, and children's books —H.E. Starr⟩ **2 :** the act or an instance of making jest of or burlesquing ⟨a notable talent for ~⟩ **3 :** the quality of being droll **:** whimsical humor ⟨stories that amuse not by their wit but by their ~⟩

droll·ing·ly *adv* **:** in the manner of one that drolls

droll·ness *n* -ES **:** the quality or state of being droll ⟨the lecturer's ~ endeared him to his listeners⟩

drol·ly \ˈdrōl(l)ē, -)li\ *adv* [*¹droll* + *-ly*] **:** in a droll manner **:** HUMOROUSLY, QUIZZICALLY ⟨looked at me ~ as if only half believing what I said⟩ ⟨spoke ~ and cleverly⟩

drom- *or* **dromo-** *comb form* [Gk, fr. *dromos*] **1 :** course **:** racecourse **:** running ⟨*Dromornis*⟩ **2 :** speed ⟨*dromometer*⟩

drome \ˈdrōm\ *n* -s [short for *airdrome*] **:** AIRPORT

¹-drome \ˌdrōm\ *n comb form* -s [MF, fr. L *-dromos*, fr. Gk *dromos*; akin to Gk *dramein* to run] **1 :** racecourse ⟨*motordrome*⟩ **2 :** large specially prepared place ⟨*aerodrome*⟩ ⟨*picturedrome*⟩

²-drome \"\ *adj comb form* [Gk *-dromos*, fr. *dromos* course, racecourse, act of running] **:** running ⟨*homodrome*⟩

drom·e·dary \ˈdrämə,derē, -ri *sometimes* ˈdrəm-\ *n* -ES [ME *dromedarie*, fr. MF *dromedaire*, fr. LL *dromedarius* (*camelus*), fr. Gk *dromad-*, *dromas* running (as in *dromas kamēlos* dromedary, lit., running camel) + L *-arius* -ary; akin to Gk *dramein* to run, *dromos* racecourse, Skt *dramati* he runs, OE *treppan* to tread, trap — more at TRAP] **1 a :** a camel of unusual speed bred and trained esp. for riding **b :** the Arabian camel (*Camelus dromedarius*) as distinguished from the Bactrian camel **2** *obs* **:** a stupid or clumsy person **3 :** a trailer truck in which the tractor unit itself has a short freight compartment

dromedary

dro·mi·a·cea \ˌdrōmēˈāsh(ē)ə\ *n pl, cap* [NL, fr. *Dromia*, genus of crabs (fr. Gk *dromias* a kind of crab) + NL *-acea*] **:** a group of crabs (suborder Brachyura) in which the last pair of thoracic legs are modified, dorsal, and often chelate and are used for placing sponges, shells, and other objects on the carapace — **dro·mi·a·ceous** \¦==¦āshəs\ *adj*

drom·ic \ˈdrämik\ *also* **drom·i·cal** \-mək əl\ *adj* [*dromic* fr. Gk *dromikos*, fr. *dromos* course, racecourse, running + *-ikos* -ic; *dromical* fr. *dromic* + *-al*] **1 :** of, relating to, or in the form of a racecourse **2** [MGk *dromikos*, fr. Gk] *archit* **:** having a long and narrow ground plan

dro·mi·cia \drōˈmish(ē)ə\ [NL, fr. Gk *dromikos* swift (fr. *dromos* + *-ikos* -ic) + NL *-ia*] *syn of* CERCAERTUS

drom·o·ma·nia \ˌdräməˈmānēə\ *n* [NL, fr. *drom-* + *-mania*] **:** an exaggerated desire to wander

drom·ond \ˈdrämənd, ˈdrəm-\ *n* -s [ME *dromond*, *dromoun*, *dromon*, fr. MF *dromont*, *dromon*, fr. LL *dromon-*, *dromo*, fr. Gk *dromōn* light ship, fr. *dramein* to run] **:** a large medieval fast-sailing galley or cutter

dro·mor·nis \drəˈmȯrnəs\ *n, cap* [NL, fr. *drom-* + *-ornis*] **:** a genus of ratite birds of Queensland related to the cassowaries and emus

drom·os \ˈdrä,mäs, ˈdrō,-, -,məs\ *n, pl* **dromi** \-,mī, -,mē\ *or* **drom·oi** \-,mȯi\ [Gk *dromos*, racecourse, course, public walk — more at -DROME] **:** the passage to an ancient Egyptian or Mycenaean subterranean tomb

drom·o·trop·ic \ˌdräməˈträpik, -rōm-\ *adj* [*drom-* + *-tropic*] **:** affecting the conductivity of cardiac muscle — used of the influence of cardiac nerves

-dro·mous \ˌdrəməs\ *adj comb form* [NL *-dromus*, fr. Gk *-dromos* — more at -DROME] **:** running ⟨*catadromous*⟩

¹drone \ˈdrōn\ *n* -s *often attrib* [ME *drane*, *drone*, fr. OE *drān*, *drǣn*; akin to OS *dreno*, *dran* drone, OHG *treno*, MLG *drone* drone, ON *drynja* to roar, Goth *drunjus* sound, OE *drēam* joy, mirth, music, LGk *thrōnax* drone, Gk *thorybos* confused noise, Latvian *dul̃duris* wasp, Skt *dhraṇati* it sounds; basic meaning: buzzing, murmuring] **1 :** a male bee; *esp* **:** the male of the honeybee that develops from an unfertilized egg, is larger and stouter than the worker, lacks a sting, takes no part in honey gathering or care of the hive, and is of use to the colony only if a virgin queen requires insemination — see DRONE CELL **2 :** one that lives on the labors of others **:** IDLER, PARASITE ⟨a new Utopia in which robots . . . do all the work while human ~s recline in pneumatic bliss —John Diebold⟩ **3 a :** a pilotless airplane remote-controlled by radio signals (as from another airplane) **b :** a seagoing ship remote-controlled by radio

²drone \"\ *vb* -ED/-ING/-S *vi* **1 a :** to make a sustained deep murmuring, humming, or buzzing sound ⟨threshing machine was *droning* like a gigantic swarm of June beetles —Ellen Glasgow⟩ **b :** to talk in a persistently dull or monotonous tone ⟨eyes closed and heads nodded as he *droned* on and on⟩ **2 :** to live in idleness like a drone bee ⟨who would ~ when he might live by honest labor⟩ **:** be inactive; *also* **:** DROWSE ⟨found him *droning* by the fire —*Western Rev.*⟩ **3 :** to pass or proceed in a dull, drowsy, or uneventful manner ⟨the chill November days *droned* by —Earle Birney⟩ **:** act or perform in a drowsy, routine, or indifferent manner ⟨*droned* through Bryce's two fat volumes —H.J.Laski⟩ ~ *vt* **1 :** to utter or pronounce with a drone ⟨*droning* out dull papers on dull subjects⟩ **2 :** to pass or spend in idleness ⟨*droned* away the precious years of youth⟩ or in dull or monotonous activity ⟨*droned* away the years in the dust of musty libraries⟩

³drone \"\ *n* -s [*²drone*] **1 a :** BAGPIPE **b** (1) **:** one of the usu. three pipes on a bagpipe that sound fixed continuous tones as accompaniment to the melody played by the chanter (2) **:** one or more strings on a medieval bowed instrument playing a drone accompaniment to the melody **c :** the sound emitted by the drone of a bagpipe **2 :** any deep sustained or monotonous sound **:** HUM ⟨a sleepy ~ of well-wheels across the fields —Rudyard Kipling⟩ **:** a monotonous tone of voice ⟨the steady ~ of some tiresome old bore⟩ **3 a** *or* **drone bass :** an unvarying sustained bass note in a musical composition (as a pastoral) **:** PEDAL POINT **b :** one who speaks monotonously (as with a drawl)

drone bee *n* **:** ¹DRONE 1

drone cell *n* **:** one of the larger cells of a honeycomb in which the larvae of drones are reared

drone fly *n* **:** a nearly cosmopolitan two-winged fly (*Eristalis tenax*) of the family Syrphidae superficially resembling the drone bee — see RAT-TAILED LARVA

drone layer *n* **:** a queen bee capable only of producing drones

dron·er \ˈdrōnə(r)\ *n* -s **:** one that drones

drong \ˈdrăŋ\ *n* -s [prob. akin to OE *thringan* to press, compress — more at THRONG] *dial Eng* **:** a passageway or lane esp. between walls or hedges ⟨as if this homely ~ had been transformed to a royal path in some greenwood —Llewelyn Powys⟩

dron·go \ˈdrăŋ(,)gō\ *n* -s [native name in Madagascar] **1** *also* **drongo–shrike :** a bird of the family Dicruridae native to Asia, Africa, and Australia **2** *slang Austral* **:** ROOKIE, NOVICE

drongo cuckoo *n* **:** a cuckoo of India (*Surniculus lugubris*) resembling the black drongo

dron·ing·ly *adv* **:** in a droning manner

dron·ish \ˈdrōnish\ *adj* [*¹drone* + *-ish*] **:** like a drone **:** INDOLENT, SLOW

dronk·grass \ˈdrăŋk+,-\ *n* [Afrik *dronkgras*, lit., intoxication grass, fr. *dronk-* intoxication (fr. *dronken* drunk, fr. MD) + *gras* grass; akin to OHG *gras* — more at DRUNK, GRASS] **:** a southern African grass (*Melica decumbens*) the eating of which causes cattle to become semidelirious

drony \ˈdrōnē\ *adj, usu* -ER/-EST [*¹drone* + *-y*] **1 :** like a drone **:** SLUGGISH, LAZY **2 :** characterized by or producing a drone ⟨the drowsy ~ hum of bees⟩

drook \ˈdrük\ *var of* DROUK

¹drool \ˈdrül\ *vb* -ED/-ING/-S [perh. alter. of *drivel*] *vi* **1 a :** to secrete saliva in anticipation of food **:** water at the mouth ⟨three hungry men . . . ~*ed* at the thought of fresh chops —G.G.Carter⟩ **b :** to let saliva or some other substance flow from the mouth **:** SLAVER ⟨most babies begin to ~ at about four months —Louise Zabriskie⟩ **2 :** to make a profuse display of pleasure or delight **:** show enthusiasm ⟨a show for the ages, one that nature-lovers have ~*ed* over since 1925 —Alfred Stefferud⟩ **3 :** to talk nonsense **:** speak in a pointless manner **:** DRIVEL ⟨I won't keep on ~*ing* on this same old subject —E.A. Robinson⟩; *esp* **:** to fill up allotted time on a radio or television program with improvised and trivial talk or activity ~ *vt* **1 :** to let (saliva or some other substance) flow from the mouth ⟨~*ed* his food and displayed other senile traits⟩ **2 :** to utter or phrase unctuously or sentimentally ⟨political candidates ~*ing* reform measures and promises of a Utopian way of life⟩ **:** perform with cloying sentimentality ⟨every movie pianist ~*ed* out its saccharine phrases —Irving Lowens⟩

²drool \"\ *n* -s **1 :** saliva flowing from the mouth **2 :** NONSENSE, DRIVEL

drooly \-lē,-li\ *adj* -ER/-EST **:** that drools **:** tending to drool ⟨~ infants⟩

droon \ˈdrün\ *Scot var of* DROWN

¹droop \ˈdrüp\ *vb* -ED/-ING/-S [ME *drupen*, *droupen*, fr. ON *drūpa*; akin to OE *dropian* to drop, drip, MLG *drūpen* to drip, ON *drjūpa* — more at DROP] *vi* **1 :** to have or assume a slouched or bent posture (as from exhaustion or grief) **:** hang, bend, or incline downward ⟨a tree that ~*s* gracefully as if inviting to its shade —H.A.Overstreet⟩ ⟨his heavy eyelids ~*ed* —Kenneth Roberts⟩ **2 :** to fall, sink, or go down ⟨~*s* the soaring youth with slackened wing —S.T.Coleridge⟩ ⟨as night drew near the crimson sun ~*ed* slowly in the west⟩ **3 a :** to become depressed **:** decline in spirit or courage ⟨let not your spirits ~ too low when the decision is adverse —B.N. Cardozo⟩ **b** (1) **:** to lack strength or energy **:** pine away **:** LANGUISH ⟨who ~*s* far off on a sick bed —S.T.Coleridge⟩ (2) **:** to show signs of exhaustion **:** FLAG ⟨her thoughts ~*ed* with fatigue —Ellen Glasgow⟩ ~ *vt* **:** to let droop or sink ⟨the bird ~*ed* his wings⟩

syn WILT, FLAG, SAG: DROOP may indicate either a literal or a figurative hanging or bending downward through exhaustion after a period of thriving or flourishing ⟨he shrank, *drooped*, sank heavily into his chair, and once more his face folded into its lines of despair —G.W.Brace⟩ ⟨"He knows it", the trainer said to himself with a *drooping* of the heart —Donn Byrne⟩ WILT often applies to the loss of freshness and firmness of flowers and leaf or stalk vegetables deprived of water; it is often used of enervation, discouragement, and loss of spirit, force, and resolution ⟨flowers *wilting* in the sun⟩ ⟨I fear it's a feeble and sickly patriotism that *wilts* before such dreadful hardships —Kenneth Roberts⟩ FLAG indicates a dwindling into forcelessness or vacuity of interest or energy ⟨for a couple of hours he wrote with energy, and then his energy *flagged* —H.G. Wells⟩ ⟨these devices succeed, every time, in stimulating our interest afresh just at the moment when it was about to *flag* —T.S.Eliot⟩ ⟨to keep him up to his duties when he showed signs of *flagging*, he was made much of by his superiors and told what a fine fellow he was —Rudyard Kipling⟩ SAG may indicate a sinking out of line at one point; more figuratively it indicates a drooping or decline accompanying loss of strength, determination, spirit, resiliency, or power ⟨the *sagging* floor of the old house⟩ ⟨in places the rail level may *sag* out of true —O.S.Nock⟩ ⟨his heart *sagged* with disappointment —Van Wyck Mason⟩ ⟨stared out of the window, his face *sagging* once more —Gertrude Atherton⟩

²droop \"\ *n* -s **1 :** downward deflection ⟨the ~ of a gun⟩ **:** the condition or appearance of drooping ⟨her figure had a listless ~ —A.J.Cronin⟩ **2 :** a downward drift in the value of a variable quantity or in the indication of a measuring instrument

drooped ailerons *n pl* **:** hinged trailing-edge flag-type ailerons so rigged that both right and left ailerons have a positive downward deflection of 10 to 15 degrees with the control column in the neutral position

drooping *adj* **1 :** inclining downward **2 :** NODDING — used specif. of inflorescence — **droop·ing·ly** *adv* — **droop·ing·ness** *n* -ES

droopy \-pē,-pi\ *adj* -ER/-EST [ME *drupy*, fr. *drupen* to droop + *-y* — more at DROOP] **1 :** drooping or tending to droop ⟨a bent posture or a ~ position while at work —Morris Fishbein⟩ **2 :** GLOOMY, DEJECTED ⟨looking ~ and miserable⟩

¹drop \ˈdräp\ *n* -s *often attrib* [ME *drope*, *drop*, fr. OE *dropa*; akin to OS *dropo* drop, OHG *tropfo*, *troffo*, ON *dropi*, OIr *drucht* drop, OE *drēopan* to drip, OS *driopan*, OHG *triofan*, ON *drjūpa* to drip, Goth *driusan* to fall — more at DREARY] **1 a** (1) **:** the quantity of fluid which falls in one spherical or spheroidal mass **:** a liquid globule (2) **drops** *pl* **:** a medicine the dose of which is measured by drops; *specif* **:** a solution (as of atropine) for dilating the pupil of the eye **b** (1) **:** a minute quantity or degree of something nonmaterial or intangible ⟨wrings the last ~ of meaning from the word⟩ ⟨has not a ~ of kindness in him⟩ (2) *obs* **:** an old Scottish unit of weight equal to ¹⁄₁₆ oz. (3) **:** a small quantity or portion of drink esp. of an alcoholic beverage ⟨obviously had had a ~ too much⟩ (4) **:** the smallest practical unit of liquid measure varying in size according to the specific gravity and viscosity of the liquid and to the conditions under which the drop is formed — compare MINIM (5) **:** a minute quantity of some nonliquid substance ⟨a mere ~ of animated jelly —*Encyc. Americana*⟩ **c :** something that hangs like or resembles a liquid drop: as (1) **:** a pendent jewel or ornament attached to a piece of jewelry or jeweled decoration; *also* **:** an earring with such a pendant (2) **:** GUTTA (3) **:** PENDANT 2a (3) (4) **:** a small candy approximately globular in form ⟨chocolate ~*s*⟩ (5) **:** a small pear-shaped figure occas. borne as a heraldic charge but more often borne bestrewed in an indefinite number over the field — called also *goutte*; *see* GUTTÉE **2** [*²drop*] **a** (1) **:** the act or an instance of dropping **:** a fall or descent in space ⟨the slow ~ of idle tears⟩ (2) **:** a decline in quantity ⟨a relatively mild ~ in farm prices⟩ or quality ⟨his reputation took a sudden ~⟩ (3) **:** a curve in which a baseball breaks down and usu. away from a right-handed batter (4) [by shortening] **:** DROPKICK (5) **:** the act of giving birth to young; *also* **:** the young so born ⟨the entire ~ of lambs for the year⟩ (6) **:** a descent by parachute; *also* **:** the men or equipment dropped by parachute — compare AIRDROP (7) **:** a central point or depository to which something is brought for distribution or transmission; *specif, slang* **:** a place used for the deposit and distribution of stolen goods **b** (1) **:** the distance from a higher to a lower level ⟨a ~ of 2000 feet from mountain to sea⟩ **:** the distance through which something drops ⟨made a ~ of 15 feet⟩ **:** a slope or incline often steep or precipitous ⟨a steep ~ of 300 feet on the mountain face⟩ (2) **:** the depth of a course measured at mid-spread from headrope to foot — compare HOIST (3) **:** the fall in pressure of the steam in a compound steam engine between the high-pressure cylinder and the receiver, or between receiver and low-pressure cylinder (4) **:** a fall of electric potential due to resistance of the circuit or other causes (5) **:** the distance of the axis of a shaft in a mechanical device below the base of a hanger (6) **:** the space through which an unrestrained escape wheel moves while disengaged from the pallets (7) **:** the distance of the comb of the butt of a rifle or shotgun below the line of the top of the barrel (8) *music* **:** a fall or reduction in pitch ⟨the octave ~*s* are conspicuous⟩ **c :** a slot or other opening into which something is to be dropped ⟨mail ~⟩; *also* **:** the receptacle into which the dropped object falls **3** [*²drop*] **:** something that drops, hangs, or falls: as **a :** a movable plate serving to cover the keyhole of a lock **b :** an unframed piece of cloth scenery in a theater; *also* **:** DROP CURTAIN **c :** a hinged platform or trapdoor on a gallows on which a condemned person stands; *also* **:** the gallows itself **d :** an immature usu. unfertilized or diseased fallen fruit; *also* **:** a fallen but normal ripe fruit ⟨a peach ~⟩ **e :** a drop hammer or punch press **f :** a shutter in an electric annunciator that drops when the circuit is closed **g :** the group of wires used to extend a power circuit or telephone circuit from a pole to a building ⟨a telephone ~⟩ **h :** a structure built in an open drainage channel having excess grade that permits the water to go abruptly from one level to a lower level without injury to the channel **4 :** a destructive wilt and stem rot of various garden vegetables (as lettuce) caused by a fungus (*Sclerotinia sclerotiorum*) or a closely related fungus **5 :** the advantage of having an opponent covered with a firearm; *also* **:** any kind of advantage or superiority over an opponent — usu. used in the phrase *get the drop on* ⟨kept my eyes open for fear he'd get the ~ on me⟩ or *have the drop on* ⟨the nation enjoying industrial supremacy has the ~ on all the others⟩ — **at the drop of a hat :** as soon as the slightest occasion is given **:** readily or promptly ⟨he would blush *at the drop of a hat*⟩ — **drop in the bucket :** a part so small as to be negligible

²drop \"\ *vb* **dropped** *or archaic* **dropt; dropped** *or archaic* **dropt; dropping; drops** [ME *droppen*, fr. OE *dropian*; akin to OE *drēopan* to drip — more at ¹DROP] *vi* **1 a :** to fall in drops ⟨a gentle rain *dropped*⟩ **b** *archaic* **:** to let drops fall **:** be so wet that moisture falls in drops ⟨~ with sweat and blood⟩ **c** *of an animal* **:** DEFECATE **2 a** (1) **:** to fall in any manner ⟨the book *dropped* from his hand⟩ ⟨tunes . . . *dropped* into my mind unbidden —Noel Coward⟩ (2) **:** to descend from one line or level to another ⟨the river ~*s* some 850 feet to virtually sea level —Tom Marvel⟩ **:** incline downward ⟨the road ~*s* into the valley⟩ **b** (1) **:** to fall or sink to the ground ⟨under that withering fire men *dropped* like flies⟩ ⟨*dropped* dead from a heart attack⟩ **:** fall in a state of collapse (as from exhaustion) ⟨so tired she felt she would ~⟩ (2) **:** DIE — sometimes used with *off* ⟨*dropped* off peacefully in his sleep⟩ (3) **:** to let oneself down ⟨she *dropped* gratefully into the chair⟩ **:** let oneself fall ⟨*dropped* safely from a third-story window⟩ (4) **:** to alight or descend from a vehicle — used with *off* ⟨*dropped* off at the square and changed to a suburban bus⟩ (5) *of a card* **:** to become played by reason of the obligation to follow suit ⟨the king *dropped* under the ace⟩ ⟨all the trumps *dropped*⟩ (6) **:** to withdraw from participation in a poker pot by discarding one's hand or announcing refusal to call the preceding bet — often used with *out* **c** (1) **:** to move (as down a river) with a favoring wind or current — usu. used with *down* ⟨we *dropped* down the harbor and were soon steering south⟩ (2) **:** RETREAT, WITHDRAW — usu. used with *back* ⟨order the troops to ~ back⟩ (3) **:** to fail to maintain a proper or desired pace — usu. used with *behind* ⟨*dropped* behind in his work⟩ **d** *of a dog* **:** CROUCH **3 :** STOP *vi* 4d — used with *around, by, in, over, up* ⟨an old friend just *dropped* in⟩ **4 :** to enter as if without conscious effort of will into some state, condition, or activity ⟨*dropped* into a troubled sleep —Margaret A. Barnes⟩ ⟨*dropped* into reminiscence about old military campaigns⟩ **5 a :** to come to an end **:** cease to be of concern **:** CEASE, LAPSE ⟨resolved to let the matter ~⟩ **:** VANISH, DISAPPEAR **b** (1) **:** to become less, diminish, or decline in any way (as in force, degree, level, amount) ⟨world production of bauxite *dropped*⟩ ⟨her voice *dropped*⟩ — often used with *off* ⟨business ~*s* off in the stores⟩ (2) **:** FALL *vi* 3b(4) **c :** to withdraw from participation or membership **:** QUIT, LEAVE **:** pass or become lost (as from view or notice) ⟨one man *dropped* from the group⟩ — often used with *out* ⟨forced to ~ out of amateur athletics —Gilbert Millstein⟩ **~** *vt* **1 a :** to let fall or cause to fall in any way ⟨stumbled and *dropped* the vase⟩ ⟨pulled a lever and *dropped* the missile⟩ ⟨a few species of trees ~ their leaves in the dry season —P.E.James⟩ ⟨*dropped* anchor in a spacious harbor⟩ **b** (1) **:** to lower or cause to descend from one line or level to another ⟨the dress would look better if you ~ the hem two inches⟩ ⟨*dropped* the water level eight or nine feet⟩ (2) **:** to lower (wheels) in preparation for landing an airplane (3) **:** to cause to lessen or decrease ⟨*dropped* his speed by three knots⟩ **:** reduce in quality or degree (4) **:** to set down from a ship or vehicle ⟨asked him to ~ me at the hotel⟩ **:** UNLOAD, DEPOSIT ⟨*dropping* groceries and beer casks at the port of Louth —C.E.W.Bean⟩ ⟨new hotels to care for the 150 passengers that each jet will ~ at the big airports —P.J.C. Friedlander⟩; *also* **:** AIR-DROP (5) **:** to unhitch and drive away from (a trailer or trailing implement) ⟨~ the harrow before driving onto the highway⟩ (6) **:** to cause (the voice) to be less loud ⟨*dropped* his voice as he saw strangers approaching⟩ ⟨we ~ our voice at the end of a sentence⟩ **c :** CURTSY ⟨she learned . . . to ~ a graceful curtsy —Max Peacock⟩ **d** (1) **:** to bring down with a shot ⟨leaden slugs *dropped* his Indians as they worked —Julian Dana⟩; *also* **:** to knock down (as in boxing) **:** FLOOR ⟨as he had *dropped* the great champion —Donn Byrne⟩ (2) **:** to force another player to play (a high card) by leading a card to which he must follow suit ⟨he led the ace and *dropped* the king⟩ (3) *sports* **:** to cause (a ball) to fall into a hole or basket ⟨*dropped* a 3-foot putt⟩ ⟨raced down the floor to ~ a shot⟩ **2 a :** to pour or let fall in drops ⟨~ a tear⟩ **b** *archaic* **:** to cover with drops **:** BESPRINKLE ⟨their waved coats *dropped* with gold —John Milton⟩ **3 a :** to abandon or give up (as an activity, idea, or concern) **:** cease to hold, use, or concern oneself with ⟨advised him to ~ the matter⟩ ⟨permission to ~ the course⟩ **:** leave incomplete ⟨~ a sentence in the middle⟩ **:** not take into account ⟨~ the four poorest years in computing the average⟩ **b :** to break off an association or connection (as friendship, employment) with ⟨~ a failing student⟩ ⟨his clubs *dropped* him⟩ **:** DISMISS ⟨a number of stations and sponsors *dropped* him —Gilbert Seldes⟩ **c** (1) **:** to leave behind (as in sailing) **:** LEAVE ⟨that day they *dropped* the last of the islands⟩ (2) **:** to take leave of or dismiss (as a pilot or escort) after a mission is accomplished ⟨the submarine zone left behind, the convoy *dropped* her destroyer escorts⟩ **d :** to use a variant pronunciation that is less accurately represented by (a letter present in the standard orthography, esp. *g, h,* or *r*) than is another variant pronunciation: as (1) **:** to omit the sound of (as *r* in \ˈwȯ\ instead of \ˈwȯr\ for *war* or *h* in \ˈyüj\ instead of \ˈhyüj\ for *huge*) (2) **:** to substitute another sound for (as *r* in \ˈwȯə\ instead of \ˈwȯr\ for *war* or *ng* for \n\ instead of \ŋ\ in *going*) (3) **:** to omit and compensate for (as *r* in \ˈfäːm\ instead of \ˈfärm\ for *farm*, with compensatory lengthening of \ä\) **e :** to leave off (an ending) in inflecting a word ⟨a tendency to ~ the *-ly* of certain adverbs⟩ **f :** to leave out (as a letter, line, or paragraph) in writing ⟨~ a whole line in copying⟩ **4 a :** to utter or mention in a casual or offhand way ⟨a foreman ~*s* a suggestion⟩ or with pretended casualness ⟨obtained his release by *dropping* a word in the right quarter⟩ **b :** to send (as a letter or postcard) by mail — often used in the phrase *drop a line* ⟨expected he would ~ me a line by now⟩ **5** *of an animal* **:** to give birth to ⟨lambs *dropped* in June⟩ **6 :** to lose (money or a contest) ⟨he was *dropping* money every day at the track —Ernest Hemingway⟩ ⟨the team *dropped* five straight games⟩ **:** SPEND ⟨*dropped* $200 on her new spring outfit⟩ **7 :** SINK *vt* 13 **8 :** to draw from an external point (as from a point to a line or plane) ⟨~ a perpendicular⟩ **syn** see DISMISS, FALL — **drop a brick** *slang* **:** to do or say something indiscreet **:** make a blunder — **drop into :** to pitch into **:** SCOLD, REPROVE — **drop one's lines :** to forget or misquote one's lines in a play or other theatrical performance ⟨a state of confusion before curtain time caused the actor to *drop his lines*⟩

drop arch *n* **:** a two-centered blunt pointed arch drawn from centers within the span

drop ball *n* **:** a method of putting a soccer ball in play by dropping it between two players after a temporary suspension or when a free kick is not called for

drop band *also* **drop bunch** *n, West* **:** a group of ewes about ready to lamb

drop bar *n* **1 :** a bar or roller that guides a sheet into a printing press or folding machine — called also *drop roller* **2 :** any of the vertical bars in a suspension bridge connecting the roadway and the chain or cable

drop batter *n* **:** batter of such consistency as to drop from a bowl or spoon without running usu. made in a proportion of two parts flour to one part liquid — compare POUR BATTER

drop black *n* **:** any of several black pigments sometimes in the form of drops or pellets: as **a :** FRANKFORT BLACK **b :** bone black esp. when reclaimed after use as a decolorizing agent

drop bolt *n* **1 :** a bolt designed to drop into a socket **2 :** a bolt whose withdrawal releases the drop of a gallows

drop bottom *n* **:** a bottom opening downward ⟨a railroad freight car with a *drop bottom*⟩

drop-bottom bucket *n* **:** a bucket with a bottom that can be opened and used esp. in excavating earth and in placing concrete under water

drop bow *or* **drop compass** *n* **:** a bow compass that permits the center leg to remain stationary while the pen or pencil rotates around the center shaft and that is used esp. for drawing small circles

drop box *n* **:** a box on a loom containing two or more shuttles with filling yarns of different colors or types that can be brought into action as required by the weaving pattern

drop chalk *n* **:** PREPARED CHALK

drop cloth *n* **:** a sheet of cloth or paper used esp. by house painters and laid over floors, furniture, and fixtures to protect them during painting or decorating

drop cord *n* **:** an electric-light cord used to suspend a lamp usu. from an overhead outlet

drop crop *n* **:** PENDULOUS CROP

drop curtain *n* **:** a stage curtain that is lowered instead of drawn

drop ear *n* **:** BUTTON EAR — **drop-eared** \ˈ=ˌ=\ *adj*

drop elbow *n* **:** an elbow made with ears or lugs for attachment to a wall and used for joining pipes

drop fence *n* **:** a fence on one side of which the ground is lower than on the other side

drop flare *n* **:** a flare capable of being dropped from an airplane to illumine an area or target

drop fly *n* **:** DROPPER 1a

drop folio *n* **:** a page number at the bottom of a page

drop-forge \ˈ=ˌ=\ *vt* **:** to forge between dies by a drop hammer or punch press — **drop forger** *n*

drop forging *n* **:** a forging made by the force of a dropped weight (as in a drop hammer)

drop frame *n* **:** a machine for stamping sheets of candy and cutting them into pieces or figures

drop-frame \ˈ=ˌ=\ *adj* **:** having most or all of the floor at an unusually low level — used esp. of the chassis of a motor truck or a trailer

drop front *n* **:** a hinged cover on the front of a desk or secretary that may be lowered to form a writing table — **drop-front** \ˈ=ˌ=\ *adj*

drop front

drop glass *n* **:** DROPPER, PIPETTE

drop goal *var of* DROPPED GOAL

drop hammer *n* **1 :** a power hammer (as for forging or striking metal) that is raised and then released to drop on the metal resting on an anvil or die **2 :** PILE HAMMER — **drop hammerman** *n*

drop handle *n* **:** a pendent handle; *specif* **:** a door handle or drawer pull that hangs like a pendant when not in use

drop hanger *n* **:** an adjustable frame for attaching a shaft bearing to the ceiling; *also* **:** the frame and bearing combined

[1]**drophead** \ˈ=ˌ=\ *n* **1 :** a device for a desk or table that enables an attached typewriter or sewing machine to be swung or dropped down to leave a flat table top **2** [[2]*drophead*] *Brit* **:** a convertible automobile

[2]**drophead** \"\ *adj, Brit, of an automobile* **:** CONVERTIBLE

drop head *n* **:** a newspaper headline that accompanies but is subordinate to a banner head **:** DROPLINE

drop initial *n* **:** DROP LETTER 3

drop keel *n, Brit* **:** CENTERBOARD

dropkick \ˈ=ˌ=\ *n* **1 :** a kick made by dropping a football to the ground and kicking it at the moment it starts to rebound **2 :** an attempt to floor a wrestling opponent by diving at him feetfirst

drop-kick \ˈ=ˌ=\ *vb* [*dropkick*] *vi* **:** to make a dropkick **~** *vt* **:** to score (a goal) with a dropkick — **dropkicker** \ˈ=ˌ==\ *n*

drop kip *n* **:** a kip on the high or parallel bars in which the leg kick is executed as the body swings backward

drop leaf *n* **:** a table leaf hinged to the side or end of a table and folded down when not in use

drop·let \ˈdräplə̇t\ *n* -s **:** a tiny drop (as of water)

droplet infection *n* **:** infection by means of contact with airborne droplets of sputum containing infectious organisms

drop letter *n* **1 :** a letter mailed at a post office not having carrier service and addressed locally to someone who is to call for it at the same office **2** *Canad* **:** a letter mailed at or in the delivery area of the same post office from which it will be delivered **3 :** an initial letter (as at the beginning of a chapter in a book) that extends downward to a depth of two or more text lines

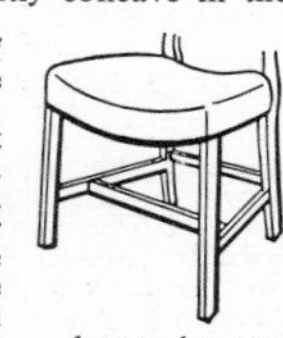

drop leaf

droplight \ˈ=ˌ=\ *n* **1 :** a gaslight brought down to a lower level (as over a table) from an outlet by means of a usu. flexible tube **2 :** an electric light suspended by a flexible cord from the ceiling or a wall bracket

drop line *n* **:** HANDLINE 1c

dropline \ˈ=ˌ=\ *n* **:** a newspaper headline employing lines of equal length with each lower line indented a consistent number of spaces more than the line above

drop lock *n* **:** the spot on the locking surface of a timepiece pallet upon which the escape tooth first makes contact after drop

drop manhole *n* **:** a shaft in which sewage is dropped from a higher to a lower level

drop off *vi* **:** to fall asleep

drop-off \ˈ=ˌ=\ *n* -s [fr. *drop off*, v.] **:** a very steep or perpendicular drop or descent ⟨shoals here at the *drop-off* are referred to as the outer reefs —P.A.Zahl⟩ ⟨a climb of many short turns and dizzy *drop-offs* —C.F.Saunders⟩

drop out *vi* **:** to make a dropout in rugby football **~** *vt* **:** to mask or etch away (the highlight dots of a halftone negative or plate) in order to increase the highlights

dropout \ˈ=ˌ=\ *n* -s [*drop out*] **1 :** a dropkick in rugby football made from within a defending player's 25-yard line after the ball has crossed a touch-in-goal line or has been touched down **2 a :** one who drops out before achieving his goal (as from school or a program of training) **b :** the act or an instance of dropping out **3 a :** a halftone having a dropped-out area; *also* **:** a print made from it — called also *highlight halftone* **b :** the dropped-out area of a dropout

drop-out voltage *n* **:** the voltage at which the contacts of an electromagnetic cutout open under normal conditions

drop·pa·ble \ˈdräpəbəl\ *adj* **:** capable of being dropped ⟨early hydrogen devices . . . became ~ bombs —*Time*⟩

drop·page \-pij\ *n* -s **1 :** a portion of a quantity of material that is dropped in the process of its use or application (as of mortar while laying brick) **2 :** a portion of a fruit crop that falls from the tree before it is ready for picking ⟨warm weather, which caused much tree ~ —*Wall Street Jour.*⟩

dropped *past of* DROP

dropped egg *n* **:** POACHED EGG

dropped goal *also* **drop goal** *n* **:** a goal scored in rugby by a dropkick that is not a free kick or penalty kick and that counts 3 points or formerly 4 points

dropped seat *n* **:** a chair seat made slightly concave in the center

dropped shoulder *n* **:** the shoulder line of a garment extended beyond the top of the upper arm

drop·per \ˈdräpə(r)\ *n* -s **1 :** one that drops: as **a :** a fly attached in fishing to a leader above the tail fly usu. by means of a snell **b** (1) **:** one that sows after a dibbler (2) **:** an attachment to a reaping machine for dropping the grain in gavels on the ground; *also* **:** a machine having such an attachment **c :** a dog (as a cross between a setter and a pointer) that drops at sight of game **d :** one that regulates the dropping of articles into receptacles in the process of manufacture **e :** a heavy vertical wire on the horizontal wires of a fence to maintain the vertical spacing **2 :** a branch vein in a mine which drops off from or leaves the main lode on the footwall side **3 :** a vegetative shoot that grows downward and develops a new bulb at its apex in certain bulbous plants (as the tulip) **4 a :** a short glass tube with one end constricted and the other fitted with a small rubber bulb used to measure liquids by drops — called also *eyedropper, medicine dropper* **b :** a similar tube having the external diameter of the outlet three millimeters and adjustable to deliver at 15°C 20 drops of distilled water weighing one gram — called also *normal dropper, standard dropper* **5 :** a mechanical attachment on a loom or warper for stopping the machine when a warp yarn breaks — called also *drop wire* **6 :** a worker who runs cars down the inclined haulageways of a mine by riding or pushing or lowering by cable — called also *car dropper, load dropper* **7** *Africa* **:** a fence post

dropped seat

dropper fly *n* **:** DROPPER 1a

dropping *n* -s [ME, fr. gerund of *droppen* to drop — more at DROP] **1 :** something dropped ⟨the ground was littered with ~*s* from the trees⟩ ⟨~*s* from a candle⟩ ⟨gulls screaming and diving after the galley ~*s* at the stern —Katherine Mansfield⟩ **2 :** the dung of animals — now usu. used in pl. **3 droppings** *pl* **:** wool or other fiber cast off from the different cylinders in carding **:** [2]FLY 7d **4 :** LETTING-OUT

dropping angle *n* **:** RANGE ANGLE

dropping board *also* **droppings board** *n* **:** a surface directly under the roost in a poultry house on which droppings accumulate

dropping bottle *n* **1 :** a small pitcher-shaped bottle with a curved or tapered neck used to supply liquids in small amounts (as to test tubes) — compare BURETTE **2 a :** a small bottle with a grooved glass stopper and neck permitting the contents to be poured out in drops **b :** a bottle furnished with a dropper or a glass rod applicator

dropping fire *n* **:** a continuous desultory discharge of firearms

dropping ground *n* **:** DROP ZONE

drop·ping·ly *adv* [ME, fr. *dropping* (pres. part. of *droppen* to drop) + *-ly* — more at DROP] **:** in the manner of something that drops **:** drop by drop **:** in drops

dropping plate *n* **:** an attachment to a hill planter (as for corn or cotton) regulating the dropping of seeds at intervals

dropping system *n* **:** a brewing process in which wort having passed through the first stage of fermentation is dropped or run down into a lower vessel for skimming off the yeast

drop pit *n* **:** a pit built crosswise of the tracks in an enginehouse; *esp* **:** one designed to give access for removing the wheels of a locomotive

drop pod *n* **:** a detachable part (as a fuel tank) of an airplane designed to be dropped in flight

drop press *n* **1 :** PUNCH PRESS **2 :** DROP HAMMER

drop roller *n* **1 :** DROP BAR 1 **2 :** a printing-press roller that drops at intervals to carry ink to the distributing table and rollers — called also *ductor*

drops *pl of* DROP, *pres 3d sing of* DROP

drop scene *n* **:** a drop curtain on which a scene is painted

drop scone *n, Brit* **:** GRIDDLE CAKE

drop seat *n* **1 :** a hinged seat (as in a vehicle) that may be dropped down **2 :** a seat (as in an undergarment) that falls down when unbuttoned

dropseed \ˈ=ˌ=\ *n* **:** a grass of the genus *Sporobolus*

drop shipment *n* **:** a shipment of goods made by a manufacturer directly to a retailer and not by the wholesaler who made the sale

drop shipper *n* **:** a wholesaler who deals in drop shipments — called also *desk jobber*

drop shot *n* **1 :** a delicately hit ball or shuttlecock that drops quickly after crossing the net or dies after hitting the front wall — used in racket games (as tennis, rackets, badminton) **2 :** shot made by dropping molten shot metal from a height

drop shutter *n* **:** an early form of camera shutter consisting of a plate which when released falls vertically and carries an aperture in its center past the opening of the lens

drop·si·cal \ˈdräpsə̇kəl, -sēk-\ *adj* [*dropsy* + *-ical*] **1 :** of, relating to, characterized by, or affected with dropsy **2 :** PUFFY, SWOLLEN ⟨her pretty face became ~ and red —Jean Stafford⟩ **:** excessively large **:** INFLATED, TURGID ⟨cast-off clothes that gave Sam a ~ look —Dixon Wecter⟩ — **drop·si·cal·ly** \-sə̇k(ə)lē, -sēk-, -li\ *adv* — **drop·si·cal·ness** \-kəlnə̇s\ *n* -ES

drop siding *n* **:** building siding with a tongue-and-groove edge joint or a rabbeted or shiplap joint — called also *matched siding, novelty siding*

drop·sied \ˈdräpsēd, -sid\ *adj* [*dropsy* + *-ed*] **:** DROPSICAL

drop·sonde \ˈdräpˌsänd\ *n* -s [*drop* + radio*sonde*] **:** a radiosonde dropped by parachute from a high-flying airplane to obtain pressure, temperature, and moisture measurements of the air below

drop stitch *n* **:** a pattern in machine knitting made by disengaging certain needles at regular intervals

dropstone *n* [[1]*drop* + *stone*] *obs* **:** a stalactite or stalagmite

drop strake *n* **:** a strake that terminates toward the stem or stern of a ship because of the hull's decreasing girth

drop·sy \ˈdräpsē, -si\ *n* -ES [ME *dropesie*, short for *ydropesie*, fr. OF *idropisie, ydropesie*, fr. L *hydropisis*, modif. of Gk *hydrōps*, fr. *hydōr* water — more at WATER] **1 :** EDEMA 1; *specif* **:** ANASARCA **2 :** EDEMA 2

dropsy plant *also* **dropsywort** \ˈ==ˌ=\ *n* [so called fr. its being reputed to cure dropsy] **:** LEMON BALM

dropt *archaic past of* DROP

drop table *n* **:** a hinged tabletop that folds against a wall when not in use

drop-tank \ˈ=ˌ=\ *n* **:** an auxiliary gas tank for airplanes that is usu. attached to the underside of the wing and can be jettisoned when empty

drop test *n* **:** an instance of drop-testing

drop-test \ˈ=ˌ=\ *vt* [*drop test*] **:** to test by dropping under trial conditions ⟨*drop-testing* parachutes with dummies⟩

drop the handkerchief *n* **:** a game in which one player runs behind the other players as they stand in a circle and drops a handkerchief behind one of them who then must pick up the handkerchief and run around the circle after the first player and try to tag, catch, or kiss him before he gets to the vacant place in the circle left by the second player

drop weight *n* **:** the weight of a drop of a liquid falling from a given opening used as a measure of the surface tension

drop window *n* **:** a window usu. double hung and with a single sash that is opened by lowering it into a concealed pocket or slot

drop wire *n* **:** DROPPER 5

dropwise \ˈ=ˌ=\ *adv* [[1]*drop* + *-wise*] **:** drop by drop ⟨add a 5 percent solution of the chemical ~⟩

dropwort \ˈ=ˌ=\ *n* [[1]*drop* + *wort*] **1 :** a Eurasian herb (*Filipendula hexapetala*) with pinnate incised leaves and panicles of white or reddish flowers **2 :** a plant of the genus *Oenanthe* — usu. used with an attributive ⟨hemlock ~⟩

drop zone *n* **:** the area on which troops, supplies, or equipment are to be air-dropped

dros·era \ˈdräsərə\ *n* [NL, fr. Gk, fem. of *droseros* dewy, watery, fr. *drosos* dew, water] **1** *cap* **:** the type genus of Droseraceae comprising numerous low perennial or biennial bog-inhabiting insectivorous plants generally with leaves in a basal tuft and flowers in a one-sided racemose inflorescence on a naked scape — see SUNDEW **2** -s **a :** any plant of the genus *Drosera* **b :** the air-dried flowering plant of either of two droseras (*D. rotundifolia* and *D. longifolia*) used in the medication of chest disorders

dros·er·a·ce·ae \ˌdräsəˈrāsēˌē\ *n pl, cap* [NL, fr. *Drosera*, type genus + *-aceae*] **:** a small family of insectivorous plants (order Sarraceniales) comprising the sundews and having flat to filiform circinate leaves with the blade covered by long glandular hairs — see DROSERA — **dros·er·a·ceous** \ˌdräsəˈrāshəs\ *adj*

drosh·ky \ˈdräshkē, -ki\ *also* **dros·ky** \-sk-\ *n* -ES [Russ *drozhki*, fr. *droga* pole of a wagon; akin to OE *dragan* to draw — more at DRAW] **:** a low 4-wheeled open carriage used esp. in Russia and consisting of a long bench on which the passengers ride sideways or astride as on a saddle with their feet on bars near the ground; *also* **:** any of various 2-wheeled or 4-wheeled public carriages used in Russia and other countries

dro·som·e·ter \drōˈsämədə(r)\ *n* [F *drosomètre*, fr. Gk *drosos* dew + F *-mètre* -meter] **:** an instrument for measuring the weight of dew deposited on a body

dro·soph·i·la \drōˈsäfələ\ *n* [NL, fr. Gk *drosos* + NL *-phila*] **1** *cap* **:** a genus (the type of the family Drosophilidae) of small two-winged flies that have been used extensively in breeding experiments to study basic mechanisms of inheritance **2** -s **:** any fly of the genus *Drosophila* (as fruit fly)

dro·soph·i·list \-ləst\ *n* -s [NL *Drosophila* + E *-ist*] **:** one who uses the vinegar fly (genus *Drosophila*) in the study of genetics

dros·o·phyl·lum \ˌdräsəˈfiləm\ *n* [NL, fr. Gk *drosos* + NL *-phyllum*] **1** *cap* **:** a genus of insectivorous plants (family Droseraceae) having narrow leaves arranged like those of plants of the genus *Drosera* and yellow flowers with 10 stamens — compare SUNDEW **2** *pl* **drosophyl·la** \-lə\ **:** any plant of the genus *Drosophyllum* — called also *flycatcher*

[1]**dross** \ˈdräs, ˈdrȯs\ *n* -ES [ME *dros, drosse*, fr. OE *drōs* filth, dregs, sediment; akin to OE *drōsna, drōsne* filth, dregs, sediment, OHG *truosana* dregs, lees, ON *dregg* dreg — more at DREG] **1 :** the solid scum that forms on the surface of a metal (as lead, antimony) when molten or melting largely as a result of oxidation but sometimes of the rising of dirt and impurities to the surface **2 :** waste or foreign matter mixed with a substance or left as a residue after that substance has been used or processed **:** IMPURITY ⟨every bushel of corn contains

a quantity of ~⟩ **3 :** something that is base, gross, or commonplace ⟨the riches of this world are mere ~⟩ **:** the base, unworthy, or trivial part or element in something that is otherwise good or admirable ⟨less ~ in *Hamlet* than in other Shakespeare plays —G.W.Stone⟩

2**dross** \"\ *vt* -ED/-ING/-ES **1 :** to make dross of (lead) **:** convert into massicot by calcining **2 :** to free from dross

dross·er \-sə(r)\ *n* -S **:** a furnaceman who makes red lead from litharge or who recovers spelter from dross

drossy \-sē,-si\ *adj* -ER/-EST [ME, fr. *dros, drosse* + *-y*] **:** of, relating to, or resembling dross **:** full of dross **:** WORTHLESS ⟨a wise man . . . can gather gold out of the *drossiest* volume —John Milton⟩

drost·dy \drȯ'stā, -ȯs'dā\ *n* -S [Afrik (now *drosdy*), fr. *drost* sheriff (fr. MD *drossāte*, fr. *dros-* retinue + *-sāte* commander) + *-y* (fr. MD *-ie*, fr. OF *-ie -y*); akin to OE *dryht* retinue and to OE *-sǣta* commander, OHG *-sazzo*, derivatives fr. the root of E *sit* — more at DRUDGE, SIT] *southern Africa* **1 :** the office or residence of a landdrost **2 :** the jurisdiction of a landdrost

drott-kvaett \'drōt,kfāt\ *n* -S [modif. of ON *drōttkvæthr*, *drōttkvæthi*, fr. *drōtt* retinue + *-kvæthr, kvæthi* poem, fr. *kvetha* to say, speak, recite — more at QUOTH] **:** an Old Icelandic verse consisting of a stanza of eight regular lines with a complex pattern of internal and terminal rhyme, alliteration, and esp. alternation of consonance with full rhyme at the ends of lines

drought *or* **drouth** \'drau̇|th, |t, *or* +V |d·; *sometimes* -rō|\ *n* -S [ME *drougth, drought, drouth*, fr. OE *drūgath, drūgoth*, fr. *drūgian* to dry up, wither, fr. the root of *drȳge* dry — more at DRY] **1** *archaic* **:** the condition or quality of being dry **:** DRYNESS **:** lack of moisture ⟨the ~ of the sun-baked ground⟩ ⟨crickets sing at the oven's mouth . . . the blither for their ~ —Shak.⟩ **2 :** a period of dryness esp. protracted and causing extensive damage to crops or preventing their successful growth **3** *now dial* **:** a thirst usu. for alcoholic drink ⟨there's a great ~ on me, and the night is young —J.M.Synge⟩ **4 :** a prolonged or chronic shortage or lack of something that is needed or desired ⟨behind the candy scarcity lies the sugar ~ — *Wall Street Jour.*⟩ ⟨suffering from a ~ of intellect and sensitivity⟩

drought·i·ness \-th|ēnəs, -d·|, -t|, -in-\ *n* -ES **:** the quality or state of being droughty **:** lack of rain **:** ARIDITY

drought spot *n* **:** an external physiological disorder of fruits caused by a boron deficiency

droughty *or* **drouthy** \|ē, |i\ *adj* -ER/-EST **1 :** DRY, ARID **:** lacking moisture ⟨the ~ desert —A.D.Carruthers⟩ **2 :** of, relating to, or afflicted by a prolonged drought ⟨we look into a ~ sky —I.R.Tannehill⟩ ⟨over most of the area ~ conditions still prevail⟩ **3 :** THIRSTY

drouk \'drük\ *vt* **drouk·it** *or* **drouk·et** \-kət\ **droukit** *or* **drouket**; **drouking**; **drouks** [perh. of Scand origin; akin to ON *drukna* to drown — more at DROWN] *dial Brit* **:** to wet through and through **:** SOAK, DRENCH

1**drove** \'drōv\ *n* -S [ME, fr. OE *drāf*, fr. *drīfan* to drive — more at DRIVE] **1** *dial Eng* **:** an unimproved road used mainly for driving cattle **2 a :** a crowd or group of people esp. when acting, following, or moving in concert or in a docile manner as if in a herd ⟨they repaid him by voting in ~*s* as he directed —Paul Blanshard⟩ **b :** a large group of animals esp. when moving or being driven in a body ⟨bees . . . flew in ~*s* about her head —Sherwood Anderson⟩; *also* **:** a group of things moving in this manner ⟨icebergs . . . often came in large ~*s* —Valter Schytt⟩ **3 :** a flock or herd of livestock esp. when being driven **4 a** *also* **drove chisel :** a stonecutter's chisel about two inches wide used in forming a grooved surface or a roughly shaped finish in preparation for the finer work to follow — called also *boaster* **b** *also* **drove work :** the grooved surface of stone finished by the drove chisel

2**drove** \"\ *vb* -ED/-ING/-S [prob. back-formation fr. *drover*] *vi, Brit* **:** to follow the occupation of a drover ⟨he learnt to ride while *droving* on the plains —A.B.Paterson⟩ ~ *vt* **1** *Brit* **:** to drive (as cattle or sheep) to pasture or to market **2** *Brit* **:** to finish (as stone) with a drove

3**drove** *past & archaic past part of* DRIVE

dro·ver \'drōvə(r)\ *n* -S [ME *drovare*, fr. *drove* + *-are* -er] **1 :** one that drives cattle or sheep to pasture or to market **:** a cattle herder; *specif* **:** a person in charge of taking a large number of cattle to market by rail **2** *archaic* **:** DRIFTER 2b

drove road *or* **drove way** *n* ['drove] *chiefly Scot* **:** a public cattle road not kept up for motor traffic

1**drow** \'drau̇\ *n* -S [origin unknown] *Scot* **:** a cold mist or drizzle

2**drow** \"\ *n* -S [origin unknown] *Scot* **:** a momentary illness; *esp* **:** a fainting spell

drown \'drau̇n\ *vb* **drowned** \-nd\ *or substand* **drownd·ed** \-ndəd\ **drowned** *or substand* **drownded**; **drown·ing** \-niŋ\ *or substand* **drownd·ing** \-ndiŋ\ **drowns** \-nz\ *or substand* **drownds** \-n(d)z\ [ME *drunen, drounen*, prob. alter. of *drunknen*, fr. OE *druncnian*; akin to ON *drukna* to drown; inchoatives fr. the root of E *drink* — more at DRINK] *vi* **1 a :** to suffocate in water or some other liquid ⟨fell in the water and ~*ed*⟩ **b :** to suffocate because of excessive body fluid that interferes with the passage of oxygen from the lung to the tissues (as in pulmonary edema) **2** *of things* **:** to sink in water or some other liquid and become submerged ⟨the boat ~*ed* but we were saved⟩ **:** become flooded **:** lie under water impounded by a dam ⟨many towns ~ —A.W.Baum⟩ **3 a :** to become overpowered by or come completely under the influence of something (as an emotion or idea) ⟨~*ing* in bliss—Ellen Glasgow⟩ ⟨~*ing* in self-condemnation —Marcia Davenport⟩ **b :** to swoon or have the senses reel (as under the influence of strong emotion) ⟨stare on beauty till his senses ~ —Edna S. V. Millay⟩ ⟨a passionate, knowing, ~*ing* experience —Irwin Shaw⟩ **c :** to experience extreme difficulty or perplexity ⟨~*ed* in extracurricular paperwork⟩ ⟨~*ing* in the intricacies of calculus⟩ ~ *vt* **1 a :** to suffocate by submersion in water or some other liquid ⟨~*ed* three kittens⟩ ⟨~*ed* himself in the river⟩ **b :** to submerge esp. by a rise of the water level or by a sinking of the land ⟨the river overflowed, ~*ing* whole villages⟩ ⟨a movement of the sea ~*ed* the lower ends of the valleys⟩ **c :** to sink (an object) in water or some other liquid **:** send to the bottom ⟨deeper than ever did plummet sound I'll ~ my book —Shak.⟩ **:** immerse in water ⟨~ the nitrated sheets in water at 40° C⟩ **d :** to wet thoroughly **:** cover with moisture **:** SOAK, DRENCH ⟨a heavy rain, soaking cartridges and ~*ing* powder horns⟩ ⟨~*ed* the fish in a rich sauce⟩ **2 :** to engage (oneself) deeply or strenuously ⟨~*ed* himself in work⟩ — used with *in* **3 :** to cause (a sound) not to be heard by making a loud noise —often used with *out* ⟨a clamor of denials ~*ed* out the landlord —T.B.Costain⟩ **4 a :** to drive out (as a sensation or an idea) **:** EXTINGUISH ⟨the smell of coffee ~*ed* the spruce smell and the sea smell —Willa Cather⟩ ⟨their system tends to ~ initiative —Andrew Buchanan⟩ **:** REPRESS ⟨try to ~ their fundamental instincts —Paul Blanshard⟩ **:** extinguish by merging in something else ⟨~*ed* the main issue in a general debate⟩ **b :** to tower over **:** OVERWHELM **:** reduce to insignificance ⟨a personality that ~*ed* all who stood beside him⟩ **:** STUN, DAZZLE ⟨vistas that ~ the imagination⟩ **c :** to drive from the memory or consciousness — often used in the phrase *drown one's sorrows* ⟨tried to ~ his sorrows in liquor⟩ — **drown the shamrock :** to drink on St. Patrick's day

drownd \'drau̇nd\ *substand var of* DROWN

drown out *vt* **:** to drive (a person or an animal) from home by flooding **:** force (as a mine) to shut down by inundation

1**drowse** \'drau̇z\ *vb* -ED/-ING/-S [prob. akin to OE *drūsan, drūsian* to sink, become low, inactive, *drēosan* to fall — more at DREARY] *vi* **1 :** to be half asleep **:** fall into a light slumber — often used with *off* ⟨*drowsed* off and awoke with a start⟩ **2 :** to be inactive or present an appearance of peaceful inactivity or isolation ⟨villages *drowsing* in the sun⟩ ~ *vt* **1 :** to make drowsy or inactive ⟨the spells that ~ my soul —S.T. Coleridge⟩ **2 :** to pass (time) drowsily or in drowsing — usu. used with *away* ⟨~ away the afternoon⟩ **syn** see SLEEP

2**drowse** \"\ *n* -S **:** the act or an instance of drowsing **:** a light slumber **:** DOZE ⟨nudged papa who was just falling into a ~ —J.T.Farrell⟩

drow·si·head \-zē,hed\ *also* **drow·si·hood** \-hu̇d\ *n* [*drowsy* + *-head* or *-hood*] *archaic* **:** DROWSINESS

drows·i·ly \'drau̇zəlē, -li\ *adv* **:** in a drowsy manner

drows·i·ness \-zēnəs, -zin-\ *n* -ES **1 :** the state of being drowsy ⟨an exquisite ~ had spread through him —Stephen Crane⟩ **2** *archaic* **:** LETHARGY, SLOTH

drowsy \-zē, -zi\ *adj* -ER/-EST ['drowse + *-y*] **1 a :** ready to fall asleep **:** SLEEPY ⟨made ~ by the long ride⟩ **b :** tending to induce sleep ⟨that ~ undertone with which men talk in the dark —Washington Irving⟩ **c :** INDOLENT, LETHARGIC ⟨his ~ slow-moving mode of life⟩ **2 :** giving the appearance or impression of peaceful inactivity ⟨a ~ village⟩ ⟨~ cornlands and solemn forests —John Buchan⟩

1**drub** \'drəb\ *vb* **drubbed**; **drubbed**; **drubbing**; **drubs** [perh. fr. Ar *daraba* to beat] *vt* **1 :** to beat severely (as with a cudgel or stick) **:** PUMMEL, THRASH **2 :** to drive as if by cudgeling or pummeling ⟨he *drubbed* those silly notions out of his son's head⟩ ⟨constantly *drubbed* the state legislature for money — *Time*⟩ **3 :** to abuse with words **:** BERATE, CENSURE ⟨the book was *drubbed* by every critic⟩ **4 :** to defeat decisively ⟨*drubbed* her opponent in the tennis match⟩ ⟨*drubbed* in the election by a heavy margin⟩ ~ *vi* **:** STAMP, TAP **:** DRUM, POUND ⟨*drubbing* with their heels —Thomas Hughes⟩ ⟨the blood *drubbed* in his old man's veins —Audrey Barker⟩

2**drub** \"\ *n, archaic* **:** a heavy blow (as with a cudgel) **:** THUMP

druck·en \'drükən, -rək-\ *chiefly Scot var of* DRUNKEN

1**drudge** \'drəj\ *vb* -ED/-ING/-S [ME *druggen*; prob. akin to OE *drēogan* to work, perform, endure, Goth *driugan* to do service as a soldier, OE *dryht* retinue, armed followers, OHG *trukt*, ON *drōtt* retinue, Goth *gadraubts* warrior, OSlav *drugŭ* companion, L *firmus* firm — more at FIRM] *vi* **:** to perform hard, menial, or monotonous work ⟨~ all day doing wasteful work badly —Bertrand Russell⟩ ⟨*drudging* over the translation of a Japanese history —K.C.Lamott⟩ ~ *vt* **:** to force to do hard and monotonous work ⟨wouldn't like to have a daughter of mine dragged and *drudged* all her life —Michael McLaverty⟩

2**drudge** \"\ *n* -S **1 :** one who is obliged to work at hard, unpleasant, or menial tasks **:** SLAVEY ⟨the lodging-house ~ bustled in and out —Oscar Wilde⟩ **2 :** a routine and boring task **:** GRIND ⟨reporters on a daily ~ through the Surrogate's Court —*Time*⟩ **3 :** one whose work is routine and boring; *also* **:** one who through lack of imagination allows his life to become centered around and limited by the physical tasks that he must perform **:** HACK ⟨men of originality and spirit became docile ~*s* —Virginia Woolf⟩

3**drudge** \"\ *dial var of* DREDGE

drudg·ery \-j(ə)rē, -ri\ *n* -ES **:** dull, fatiguing, and unrelieved work or expenditure of effort **:** work of an irksome or menial nature done through necessity ⟨day-in, day-out ~ —G.S.Perry⟩ ⟨the mechanical and uninspired ~ of a scrivener —Newton Arvin⟩ **syn** see WORK

drudging *adj* **:** marked by drudgery **:** MONOTONOUS, TIRING ⟨the waiting, ~ side of war —William Gilman⟩ ⟨a ~ but indispensable chore —A.C.Spaulding⟩

drudg·ing·ly *adv* **:** in the manner of one that drudges **:** with drudgery

1**drug** \'drəg\ *n* -S *often attrib* [ME *drogge*, perh. fr. MD *drōge* (*vat*) dry barrel — more at DRY] **1 a** *obs* **:** something used in dyeing or chemical operations **b :** a substance used as a medicine or in making medicines for internal or external use **c** *according to the Food, Drug, & Cosmetic Act* (1) **:** a substance recognized in an official pharmacopoeia or formulary (2) **:** a substance intended for use in the diagnosis, cure, mitigation, treatment, or prevention of disease in man or other animal (3) **:** a substance other than food intended to affect the structure or function of the body of man or other animal (4) **:** a substance intended for use as a component of a medicine but not a device or a component, part, or accessory of a device **2 :** a commodity that lies on hand or is not salable **:** something for which there is little or no demand — now used only in the phrase *drug on the market* or *drug in the market* **3 a :** a narcotic substance or preparation ⟨~ addict⟩ ⟨~ user⟩ **b :** something that is narcotic in its effect ⟨power is sweet; it is a ~, the desire for which increases with habit —Bertrand Russell⟩ ⟨with his ~ of study, in his closed-in, precarious world —Edmund Wilson⟩ **4 drugs** *pl* **:** stocks or bonds of drug companies

2**drug** \"\ *vb* **drugged**; **drugged**; **drugging**; **drugs** *vt* **1 :** to poison with or as if with a drug ⟨the very air was *drugged* with the long-festering animosity —L.C.Douglas⟩ **2 :** to administer a drug to ⟨his wife, *drugged* against pain —Victor Canning⟩ **3 :** to lull or stupefy as if with a drug ⟨the kind of overly familiar music that delights most audiences and ~*s* most critics —*Time*⟩ ⟨her mind was still *drugged* by the stupor of exhaustion —Ellen Glasgow⟩ ⟨the strong aromatic sunlight *drugged* him into cheerfulness —John Buchan⟩ ~ *vi* **:** to take drugs for narcotic effect ⟨he neither drinks nor ~*s*⟩ ⟨it wouldn't surprise me if they *drugged!* They've got a very queer look in their eyes —Osbert Sitwell⟩

3**drug** \", 'dru̇g\ *vt* **drugged**; **drugged**; **drugging**; **drugs** [prob. by alter.] *dial Brit* **:** DRAG

4**drug** \'drəg\ *n* -S **:** a low heavy horse-drawn truck used esp. in moving timber

5**drug** \"\ *dial past of* DRAG

drug-fast \'=,=\ *adj* **:** resistant to the action of a drug

drugger *n* -S ['drug + *-er*] *obs* **:** DRUGGIST

drug·gery \'drəgərē\ *n* -ES [MF *droguerie*, fr. *drogue* drug (fr. MD *drōge*) + *-erie* -ery — more at DRUG] **1** *obs* **:** DRUGS, MEDICINE **2 :** the practice of giving drugs

drug·get \'drəgət\ *n* -S [MF *droguet*, dim. of *drogue* trash, stuff, drug] **1 :** a fabric of wool or wool mixed with linen or silk formerly used for clothing **2 :** a coarse durable cloth usu. of wool mixed with linen, jute, or cotton used chiefly as a lining or protective covering for carpets **3 :** a rug having a cotton warp and a wool filling made from fleece of wire-haired sheep of India — called also *India drugget*

drug·gist \'drəgəst\ *n* -S [prob. fr. F *droguiste*, fr. *drogue* drug + *-iste* -ist] **1 :** one who sells drugs wholesale or retail **2 :** PHARMACIST — compare APOTHECARY **3 :** one who owns or manages a drugstore

drug·gist·er \'drəg(ə)stə(r), 'drüg-\ *n* [F *droguiste* + E *-er*] *dial Eng* **:** DRUGGIST

drug ice *n* [3drug] **:** soft ice that slows up the stone in curling

drug·less \'drəgləs\ *adj* **:** not using drugs ⟨~ therapy⟩

drugs \'drəgz\ *dial var of* DREGS

drugster *n* -S ['drug + *-ster*] *obs* **:** DRUGGIST

drugstore \'=,=\ *n* **1 :** PHARMACY 3; *also* **:** a retail shop where medicines and miscellaneous articles (as candy, magazines, cosmetics) and usu. refreshments (as at a soda fountain) are sold **2 :** a place in Europe where medicines are sold but no compounding or dispensing is done

drugstore beetle *or* **drugstore weevil** *n* **:** a small light-brown beetle (*Stegobium paniceum*) of the family Anobiidae that infests stored products (as tobacco and drugs) and old books

drugstore cowboy *n* **1 :** one who wears cowboy clothes but has had no experience as a cowboy **2 :** a loafer who loiters on street corners or in drugstores

drugstore fold *n* **:** a multiple folding over of the lapped parts of a hand-formed small packet or wrapper

dru·id \'drüəd\ *n* -S [L *druides, druidae*, pl., fr. Gaulish *druides*; akin to OIr *druī* (pl. *druid*) wizard, *daur* oak tree, W *derwen* oak tree, OE *trēow* tree — more at TREE] **1 a** *often cap* **:** a member of a priesthood in ancient Gaul, Britain, and Ireland who are said to have studied the natural sciences, prophesied through priestly sacrifices, and acted as judges and teachers but who later appeared in Irish and Welsh sagas and Christian legends as magicians and wizards **b :** BARD, PROPHET **2 :** an officer of the Welsh bardic assembly — compare GORSEDD

dru·id·ess \-dəs\ *n* -ES **:** a female druid

dru·id·i·cal \(')drü¦idəkəl, -dēk-\ *or* **dru·id·ic** \(')drü¦idik, -dēk\ *also* **druid** *adj* **1 :** of or relating to the druids **2 :** resembling a druid ⟨groves of ~ trees —J.M.Brinnin⟩

druidical bead *n* **:** ADDER STONE

druidical circle *n* **:** STONE CIRCLE

dru·id·ism \'drüə,dizəm\ *n* **:** the system of religion, philosophy, and instruction of the druids consisting of early Celtic and perhaps pre-Celtic beliefs and including belief in the immortality of the soul

druids' altar *n* **:** a dolmen or cromlech of Great Britain sometimes ascribed to the druids

druid stone *n* **:** one of the sarsen stones of Great Britain often found in ancient stone circles

drukpa *usu cap, var of* DRUPA

1**drum** \'drəm\ *n* -S *often attrib* [prob. fr. D *trom*, fr. MD *tromme*; akin to MLG & MHG *trumme*, prob. of imit. origin] **1 a :** a musical instrument of percussion usu. consisting of a hollow cylinder with a skin head stretched over each end which is beaten with a stick or pair of sticks in playing; *broadly* **:** a hollow instrument or device of any nonmetallic material beaten in any manner to produce a deep-toned rumbling or booming sound **b :** DRUMMER 1 **2 a :** TYMPANUM 1a(1) **b :** the timbal of a sound-producing insect **3 a :** the sound of a drum **b :** a repetitious action similar to the beating of a drum ⟨woodpeckers' ~*s*⟩; *also* **:** the sound made by such an action ⟨heard the swooping ~ of the racer's hooves —Eve Langley⟩ **4 :** something resembling a drum in shape: as **a** (1) **:** one of the cylindrical or nearly cylindrical blocks of which the shaft of a column is composed (2) **:** a vertical wall that is circular or polygonal and carries a cupola or dome **b :** a revolving cylinder in which hides are tumbled during processing into leather (as for washing, pickling, tanning, dyeing) or in which furs are cleaned (by tumbling with fine sawdust) **c :** a hollow revolving cylinder for containing something to be acted upon: as (1) **:** a cask in which the colors of fabrics are fixed by steaming (2) **:** a drum washer in paper making (3) **:** a perforated cylinder for sorting ore (4) *also* **drum barker :** a long open-ended cylinder in which logs are tumbled in water to loosen and remove the bark **d :** a hollow or solid revolving cylinder or barrel that acts or is acted upon by something exterior to itself: as (1) **:** the winding part of a capstan or hoisting machine (2) **:** a doffer in a carding machine (3) **:** the roller for an autographic record (4) **:** a long pulley for several belts (5) **:** BRAKE DRUM **e :** the barrel of a clock upon which the weight cord is wound **f :** the circular housing of a banjo-clock movement **g :** a straight-sided cylindrical shipping container of metal, plywood, or paperboard with flat or slightly bowed ends one of which may be removable; *specif* **:** a metal container for liquids having a capacity between 12 and 110 gallons or a fiber container with a capacity up to 10 cubic feet **h :** a small paper tube with a paper or transparent film covering one end ⟨face-powder ~⟩ **i :** a cylindrical or rounded attachment for hot water, steam, or gases (as for a radiator or a reservoir) **j :** any of several disk-shaped magazines for feeding ammunition to automatic arms **5 :** any of various fishes of the family Sciaenidae that are capable of making a drumming noise — compare CROAKER 2; see BLACK DRUM, CHANNEL BASS, FRESHWATER DRUM **6** *Austral* **:** a bundle of personal possessions carried by a swagman

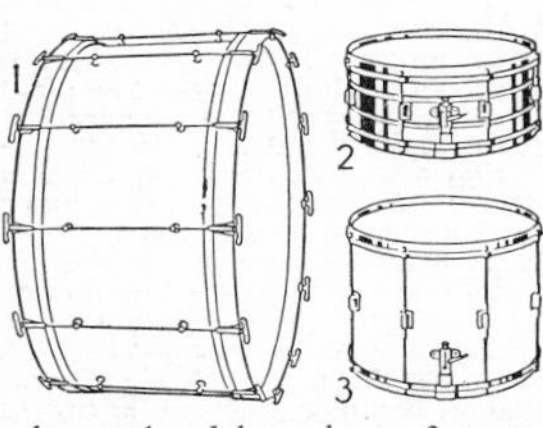

drums, 1a: *1* bass drum, *2* snare drum (for orchestra), *3* snare drum (for parades)

2**drum** \"\ *vb* **drummed**; **drummed**; **drumming**; **drums** *vi* **1 :** to beat a drum **2 :** to make a succession of strokes or vibrations that produce sounds like drumbeats ⟨his fingers *drummed* on the table⟩; *specif, of a bird* **:** to produce such vibrations esp. by beating the wings ⟨the male grouse *drumming* in the distance⟩ **3 :** to throb or sound rhythmically with or as if with drumbeats ⟨the spring freshet ~*s* in the narrow brooks —S.V.Benét⟩ ⟨a plane ~*s* in the sky overhead — Coulton Waugh⟩ **4 :** to stir up interest **:** SOLICIT, CANVASS ⟨gangsters who fear peace and ~ for war —*Newsweek*⟩ ⟨*drumming* for business⟩ ~ *vt* **1 a :** to summon, gather, or enlist by or as if by beating a drum ⟨to confound such time that ~*s* him from his sport —Shak.⟩ ⟨to make the detective appear a figure of power the police . . . are *drummed* into his service —W.O.Aydelotte⟩ ⟨*drumming* up talent —*New Republic*⟩ **b :** to arouse or further interest in by repeated promotional efforts ⟨cheered on by poets *drumming* the new struggle with Spartan despotism —E.R.May⟩ **2 :** to drive or dismiss ignominiously as if with accompaniment of drumbeats **:** EXPEL — now used with *out* ⟨a beggar being *drummed* out of town —J.H. Allen⟩ ⟨*drummed* out of military school —*Springfield (Mass.) Republican*⟩ **3 :** to drive or force by unremitting effort or reiteration ⟨~*s* into the girls two mottoes of her own —*Time*⟩ ⟨my father *drummed* the idea out of my head⟩ ⟨two issues almost daily *drummed* into the ears of Californians —M.F. A.Montagu⟩ **4 a :** to strike or tap repeatedly ⟨began to ~ her heels against the wall —T.B.Costain⟩ ⟨*drummed* the table with his fingers⟩ **b :** to produce (rhythmic sounds) by such action ⟨rain *drummed* an accompaniment to the words —Christine Weston⟩ **5 a :** to treat (a hide) in a drum **b :** to clean (a fur) by prolonged shaking with fine sawdust in a revolving drum **6 :** to put into a drum

3**drum** \"\ *n* -S [ScGael *druim* back ridge; akin to OIr *druimm* back ridge, W *trum*] **1** *chiefly Scot* **:** a long narrow hill or ridge **2 :** DRUMLIN

drum armature *n* **:** an armature having drum winding

drumbeat \'=,=\ *n* **:** a stroke on a drum or its sound; *also* **:** the measured beat of a percussion section of an orchestra

drumbeater \'=,==\ *n* **:** one that beats the drum for an idea, doctrine, or policy **:** a vociferous supporter of a cause ⟨~ for U.S. intervention in World War II —Ralph de Toledano⟩

drumbeating \'=,==\ *n* **:** vociferous advocacy of a cause

drum·ble-drone \'drəm(b)əl,drōn, 'drəm-\ *n* [*drumble* to buzz (of imit. origin) + *drone*] **1** *dial Eng* **:** a drone bee **2** *dial Eng* **:** a stupid or useless person

drum controller *n* **:** a rotary contactor mechanism for manual control of motors and electrically propelled vehicles

drumfire \'=,=\ *n* **1 :** artillery firing so continuous as to sound like a drum **2 :** something suggestive of drumfire in its disquieting continuance **:** BARRAGE ⟨conservative politicians kept up a ~ of warnings —Roy Lewis & Angus Maude⟩ ⟨an incessant ~ of lies and hatred —Barry Bingham⟩

drumfish \'=,=\ *n* **:** 1DRUM 5

drum gate *n* **:** a hinged gate at the top of a dam consisting of a horizontal cylindrical sector that can be raised from its compartment to increase the height of the spillway

1**drumhead** \'=,=\ *n* ['drum + *head*] **1 :** the skin stretched over either end of a drum **2 :** TYMPANIC MEMBRANE **3 :** the top of a capstan which is pierced with sockets for levers used in turning it **4** *also* **drumhead cabbage :** a cabbage having a rounded flattened head

2**drumhead** \"\ *adj* **:** taking place at or having the characteristics of a drumhead court-martial; *often* **:** taking place on the spot **:** SUMMARY ⟨~ judgment⟩ ⟨~ procedure⟩ ⟨~ trial⟩

drumhead court-martial *n* [fr. its having been held around a drumhead as table] **:** a court-martial to try offenses on the battlefield or the line of march

drumheads \'=,=\ *n pl but sing in constr* **:** a milkwort (*Polygala cruciata*) of the eastern U.S. with a thick cylindrical raceme of flowers

drum·lie *also* **drum·ly** \'drəmlē\ *adj* [alter. of ME *drubly*] **1** *chiefly Scot, of water* **:** turbid and muddy **2** *chiefly Scot, of weather* **:** dark and gloomy ⟨~ winter, dark and drear —Robert Burns⟩ **3 :** in a muddle **:** CONFUSED, TROUBLED

drumlike \'=,=\ *adj* **:** like the head of a drum **:** attached peripherally but free to vibrate centrally — used chiefly of various plant and animal membranes

drum·lin \'drəmlən\ *n* -S [IrGael *druim* ridge, back (fr. OIr) + E *-lin* (alter. of *-ling*) — more at DRUM] **:** an elongate or oval hill of glacial drift

drum major *n* **1** *archaic* **:** the first drummer of a regiment **2 :** the marching leader of a band or drum corps

drum majorette \,drəm,mājə'ret\ *n* [*drum major* + *-ette*] **:** a female baton twirler who accompanies a marching band or drum corps; *also* **:** a female drum major

drummed *past of* DRUM

drum·mer \'drəmə(r)\ *n* -S **1 :** one who plays a drum **2 a :** a large cockroach (*Blaberus giganteus*) of Central America, the West Indies, and tropical So. America that drums on woodwork as a sexual call; *also* **:** any of several related insects of similar habits **b :** any of various fishes that make a sound when caught: as (1) **:** WEAKFISH (2) **:** a member of the family Kyphosidae; *esp* **:** a common Australian fish (*Kyphosus syd-*

neyanus) little regarded for food or sport **3 :** SWAGMAN **4 :** TRAVELING SALESMAN **5 :** a workman who tends a drum

drumming *pres part of* DRUM

drum·mock \ˈdrəmək\ *var of* DRAMMOCK

drum·mond light \ˈdrəmənd-\ *n, usu cap D* [after Thomas *Drummond* †1840 Brit. engineer] **:** LIMELIGHT 1a, 1b

drum·mond's phlox \-mən(d)z-\ *n, usu cap D* [after James *Drummond* †1863 Brit. botanical collector] **:** a phlox (*Phlox drummondii*) native to Texas and widely cultivated in many varieties as an ornamental

drum printing *n* **:** a process for dyeing woolen yarns for tapestry and velvet carpets by winding the yarns on a large drum and applying the dye in horizontal bands of varying width

drums *pl of* DRUM, *pres 3d sing of* DRUM

drum sander *n* **:** a cylindrical wheel with abrasive (as sandpaper) mounted on its outer curved surface and used for sanding flat surfaces of decorative stones

drum saw *n* **:** BARREL SAW

drum scale *n* **:** CYLINDER SCALE

drum sieve *n* **:** a sieve in a box like a drum used for fine powders

drumskin \ˈ=,=\ *n* **:** TYMPANIC MEMBRANE

drumslade *n* -s [D *trommenslager, trommelslager,* fr. *tromme, trommel* drum + *slager* beater, fr. *slagen* to beat (fr. MD *slaen*) + *-er;* akin to OE *slēan* to beat, slay — more at DRUM, SLAY] *obs* **:** DRUMMER

drum slide *n* **:** a drawing of the backs of the fingers across the strings of a banjo to produce an arpeggio chord

drumstick \ˈ=,=\ *n* **1 :** a stick for beating a drum — see DRUM illustration **2 :** something resembling a drumstick in form; *specif* **:** the segment of a fowl's leg between the thigh and tarsus **3 :** a capsule of the horseradish tree

drumstick tree *n* [so called fr. the shape of the pods] **1 :** an East Indian tree (*Cassia fistula*) having pods whose pulp is used medicinally — called also *pudding-pipe tree, purging cassia;* see CASSIA FISTULA **2 :** HORSERADISH TREE 1

drum-stretch \ˈ=,=\ *vt, bookbinding* **1 :** to fasten (as fabric) to another material by drawing taut and securing at the edges **2 :** to flatten and dry out (pasted or wet materials) by fastening clamps or weights to the edges

drum stuffing *n* **:** a rapid method of stuffing a leather by rotating it in a heated drum until warm, adding liquid grease to the drum, and then rotating again for a short time

drum switch *n* **:** an electric switch in which the connecting parts are held by spring pressure against contact surfaces in a revolving cylinder or sector

drum table *n* **:** a round-topped table supported on a central pedestal with a deep apron often containing drawers

drum table

drum up *vt* **:** to arouse by persistent effort **:** SOLICIT ⟨tried to *drum up* sentiment against the commission —A.H.Raskin⟩ ⟨*drum up* trade⟩ ⟨*drum up* support⟩; *also* **:** ORIGINATE, INVENT ⟨when the campaign was over, he told himself, he was going to *drum up* some way of making liquor —Norman Mailer⟩

drum washer *n* **:** a drum for washing paper pulp

drum winding *n* **:** an armature winding in which the coils are arranged upon the outer surface of a cylinder with those under consecutive poles being united by end connections — distinguished from *ring winding*

drungar *n* -s [ML *drungarius,* fr. LL *drungus* body of soldiers (of Gmc origin; akin to OE *thrang* crowd, throng) + L *-arius* -ary, -ar — more at THRONG] *obs* **:** a military commander

¹drunk \ˈdrəŋk\ *adj* -ER/-EST [ME *drunke, dronke,* alter. of *drunken*] **1 :** being in a condition caused by alcoholic drink in which control of the faculties is impaired and inhibitions are broken and in later stages of which one tends toward or reaches insensibility ⟨he came home ~⟩ ⟨~ folks were never quiet —Truman Capote⟩ **2 :** dominated as if under the influence of alcohol by some feeling (as fanatic zeal, imperious pride, or passionate love) so that calm, judicious, realistic reflection is impossible ⟨if ~ with sight of power, we loose wild tongues —Rudyard Kipling⟩ ⟨he was ~, not with wine, but with joy —Maurice Samuel⟩ **3** *obs* **:** DRUNKEN 2 ⟨arrows ~ with blood —Deut 32:42 (RSV)⟩ **4 :** relating to, caused by, or attended by intoxication ⟨a ~ and fitful sleep⟩ ⟨convicted of ~ driving —*Time*⟩

syn DRUNKEN, INTOXICATED, INEBRIATED, TIPSY, TIGHT: DRUNK and DRUNKEN are plainspoken rather blunt words which do not imply either censure or apology and do not suggest exact degrees of intoxication. The former is generally postposed or predicative, the latter often preposed ⟨"you think I am *drunk?*" "I think you have been drinking" —Charles Dickens⟩ ⟨he had seen front yards littered with empty bottles, and three *drunken* boys sprawling on the grass after a dance at a club —Ellen Glasgow⟩ DRUNKEN may suggest habitual excessive use of alcohol ⟨a *drunken* sot⟩ INTOXICATED does not indicate an exact degree of drunkenness, but, since its suggestions are learned and polite, it may indicate relatively slighter effects ⟨and *intoxicated* as he was . . . he knew enough to charge the steward . . . with the present safety of the ship —Herman Melville⟩ INEBRIATED and the less common INEBRIATE suggest more noisy, hilarious, or roistering indulgence ⟨volunteering to sing a song (which he did in that maudlin high key peculiar to gentlemen in an *inebriated* state) —W.M.Thackeray⟩ All of these preceding words may be used to describe the effects of any dominating feelings, emotions, or thoughts ⟨England was *drunk* with her glory and with the hope of plunder —J.R.Green⟩ ⟨he was no longer conscious of his emotions. He had become demented, *drunk* with the fury of his hatred —Liam O'Flaherty⟩ ⟨*drunken* with blood and gold —P.B.Shelley⟩ ⟨I dream that at Naples, at Rome, I can be *intoxicated* with beauty —R.W.Emerson⟩ ⟨he drank in the natural influences of the scene, and was *intoxicated* as by an exhilarating wine —Nathaniel Hawthorne⟩ ⟨intellects *inebriate* with summer —Emily Dickinson⟩ TIPSY, mild and venial in suggestion, implies difficulty with muscular coordination and unsteadiness ⟨drinking steadily, until just manageably *tipsy,* he contrived to continue so —Herman Melville⟩ TIGHT implies rather pronounced intoxication almost to the point of loss of muscular control, discretion, or judgment ⟨He was *tight,* and, as was characteristic of him, he soon dropped any professional discretion that he might have been supposed to exercise —Edmund Wilson⟩

²drunk \"\ *n* -s **1 :** a period of excessive drinking **:** SPREE ⟨after a week's ~ and a week to sober himself —F.M.Ford⟩; *also* **:** a condition of drunkenness ⟨old men sleeping off ~s in the gutters —*Wisconsin Idea Theatre Quarterly*⟩ **2 :** a drunken person **:** DRUNKARD ⟨the great cost of jailing and hospitalizing ~s⟩

drunk·ard \-kə(r)d\ *n* -s [¹*drunk* + *-ard*] **1 :** one who habitually becomes drunk **:** one suffering from or subject to acute or chronic alcoholism **2 drunkards** *pl, NewEng* **:** CHECKERBERRY

drunkard's chair *n* **:** a wide upholstered armchair popular in 18th century England

¹drunk·en \-kən *sometimes* -kᵊŋ\ *adj* [ME, fr. OE *druncen,* fr. past part. of *drincan* to drink — more at DRINK] **1 :** DRUNK 1 ⟨when he was ~, he was vulgar and silly —Katherine A. Porter⟩ ⟨reeled like a ~ giant —H.G.Wells⟩ **2** *obs* **:** saturated with liquid or moisture **:** DRENCHED ⟨let the earth be ~ with our blood —Shak.⟩ **3 a :** given to habitual excessive use of alcoholic drinks ⟨we can not afford to have poor people anyhow, whether they be lazy or busy, ~ or sober —G.B.Shaw⟩ **b :** of, relating to, attended by, or characterized by intoxication ⟨they come from . . . broken homes, ~ homes —P.B. Gilliam⟩ ⟨a ~ cry⟩ ⟨not in a ~ triumph but with awe —S.T. Coleridge⟩ **c :** resulting from or as if from alcoholic intoxication ⟨~ stupor⟩ ⟨the diver is subject to wild, ~ delusions —Rachel L. Carson⟩ **4 :** unsteady or lurching as if from alcoholic intoxication ⟨insects which have walked on films of DDT soon begin to stagger in a ~ manner —*Atlantic Monthly*⟩ **5 :** DRUNK 2 ⟨still ~ with hope and despair —Eve Langley⟩ **6** *of a screw thread* **:** having inequalities of pitch **:** WOBBLY

syn see DRUNK

²drunken *vi* -ED/-ING/-S *obs* **:** to become drunk

drunk·en·ly *adv* **:** in a drunken manner

drunk·en·ness \-kən(n)əs\ *n* -ES [ME *drunkennesse,* fr. OE *druncenness,* fr. *druncen* + *-nesse* -ness] **1 :** the condition of being drunk with or as if with alcohol **:** INTOXICATION **2 :** ALCOHOLISM **3 :** mental or emotional extravagance suggestive of the disorders caused by alcohol ⟨the ~ of factious animosity —T.B.Macaulay⟩

drunken saw *n* **:** a circular saw fixed askew on its spindle so as to cut a groove whose width is determined by the angle of tilt of the saw — called also *wobble saw*

drunker *comparative of* DRUNK

drunk·ery \ˈdrəŋkərē\ *n* -ES *archaic* **:** a place for drinking liquor **:** SALOON

drunkest *superlative of* DRUNK

drunk·om·e·ter \,drəŋˈkäməd·ə(r), ˈdrəŋkə,mēd·\ *n* [¹*drunk* + *-o-* + *-meter*] **:** a device for measuring the alcohol content of the blood through a chemical analysis of the breath

dru·pa \ˈdrüpə\ *also* **drok·pa** \ˈdräkpə\ *or* **druk·pa** \-rük-\ *n, pl* **drupa** *or* **drupas** *usu cap* **1 :** a mountain-dwelling nomadic people of Tibet **2 :** a member of the Drupa people

dru·pa·ceous \(ˈ)drüˈpāshəs\ *adj* [*drupe* + *-aceous*] **:** of or relating to a drupe **:** bearing drupes ⟨~ fruits⟩ ⟨~ trees⟩

drupe \ˈdrüp\ *n* -s [NL *drupa,* fr. L *drupa, druppa* overripe olive, fr. Gk. *dryppa* olive] **:** a one-seeded indehiscent fruit having a hard bony endocarp, a usu. fleshy mesocarp, and a thin epicarp like a skin (as in the cherry, plum, and peach) or dry and almost leathery (as in the almond) — called also *stone fruit;* see DRUPELET

drupe of peach showing section of skin and flesh and surface of stone

drupe·let \-plət\ *also* **drup·el** \-pəl\ *n* -s [*drupelet* fr. *drupe* + *-let; drupel* fr. NL *drupella,* fr. *drupa* + *-ella*] **:** a small drupe; *specif* **:** one of the individual parts of an aggregate fruit (as the raspberry)

dru·pif·er·ous \(ˈ)drüˈpif(ə)rəs\ *adj* [*drupe* + *-i-* + *-ferous*] **:** bearing drupes

druse \ˈdrüz *also* -zə *esp in sense 3*\ *n* -s *see sense 3* [G, fr. OHG *druos* gland, bump] **1 a :** a mineral surface covered with small projecting crystals **b :** a cavity in a rock having its interior surface studded with crystals and sometimes filled with water **:** GEODE **2 :** a globose cluster of crystals occurring in plant cells — compare CRYSTAL **3** *pl* **dru·sen** \-zᵊn\ **:** one of the small hyaline usu. laminated bodies sometimes appearing behind the retina of the eye

dru·sy \-zē\ *adj, usu* -ER/-EST **:** covered with minute crystals **:** containing cavities lined with crystals ⟨a ~ surface⟩ ⟨a ~ vein⟩

druth·ers \ˈdrəthə(r)z\ *n pl but sing in constr* [*druther* (dial. alter. of *would rather*) + *-s*] *dial* **:** free choice **:** PREFERENCE ⟨if I had my ~ I'd go fishing⟩

druv *dial past of* DRIVE

druxy \ˈdrəksē\ *adj, usu* -ER/-EST [alter. of earlier *dricksie,* fr. obs. *drix* decayed part of timber + *-y*] *of timber* **:** having decayed spots in the heartwood

druze *or* **druse** \ˈdrüz\ *n* -s *cap* [Ar *Durūz,* pl., fr. Muḥammed ibn- Ismʿaīlal- *Daraziy* †1019 Muslim religious leader, one of the founders] **:** a member of a tightly organized independent religious sect dwelling chiefly in the mountains of Syria and Lebanon since the 11th century, whose founder advanced the claim that Hakim the sixth Fatimid caliph was the final incarnation of God, and whose other beliefs including the unity of God, the transmigration of souls, and final perfection are drawn from various religions (as Judaism, Christianity, and Islam) — **druz·ean** *or* **druz·ian** \-üzēən,-üzhən\ *adj, cap*

¹dry \ˈdrī\ *adj* **dri·er** *also* **dry·er** \-ī(ə)r, -īə\ **dri·est** *also* **dry·est** \-īəst\ [ME *drie, dry,* fr. OE *drȳge;* akin to OHG *truckan, truchan* dry, MLG *dröge, drēge,* MD *dröge* and perh. to ON *draugr* dry wood] **1 :** free or relatively free from water or liquid **:** not wet or moist: as **a** *obs* **:** naturally having no moisture — used in ancient and medieval sciences to describe one of the qualities of the four elements; opposed to *moist* **b** *of a sign of the zodiac* **:** having a dry complexion **2 :** characterized by loss of water or of life-giving moisture: as **a :** lacking or comparatively free from precipitation and humidity ⟨the path is dusty on a ~ day⟩ ⟨a ~ summer⟩ **b :** lacking freshness **:** WITHERED **c :** ANHYDROUS **3 a :** not being in or under water **:** beneficially not having undue moisture or water ⟨~ land⟩ ⟨~ clothes⟩ **b :** employing no liquid or as little as possible ⟨the ~ method of assaying gold⟩ ⟨portland cement may be manufactured by ~ process or wet process⟩ — compare WET 8 **c :** built or constructed without the use of any process that requires water: (1) **:** using no mortar ⟨~ masonry⟩ ⟨a ~ stone wall⟩ (2) **:** using prefabricated plaster board, composition board, or wood paneling rather than a construction involving plaster or mortar bonding ⟨a ~ wall⟩ ⟨~ wall construction⟩ **d** *of breadstuff* **:** served or eaten without butter or milk — now used chiefly of toast without butter **e** *of a foodstuff* **:** having the water removed by evaporation **:** DEHYDRATED; *often* **:** reduced to powder or flakes **f** *of natural gas* **:** containing little or no recoverable gasoline or other liquid hydrocarbon **g** *of a friction clutch* **:** intended to function without lubrication **4 a** (1) **:** harmfully devoid of water or lubricant ⟨the garden is ~ from lack of rain⟩ ⟨the machine automatically stops when it runs ~⟩ (2) **:** THIRSTY ⟨he felt ~ after his walk⟩ **b :** marked by the absence of or abstention from alcoholic beverages ⟨it was a ~ party but the food was good⟩ ⟨a man who had been ~ for a dozen years —*N.Y. Times Bk. Rev.*⟩ **c** (1) **:** containing no uncombined water — used esp. of a paint or pigment (2) **:** wholly solidified **:** no longer liquid or sticky — used esp. of a coating (as paint) or ink applied to a surface or of the surface so treated; opposed to *wet* **d :** exclusive of accessories and operating fluids (as lubricant and coolant) — used of the weight of an engine **5 :** characterized by exhaustion of a supply of water or other liquid: as **a** *of a container or receptacle* **:** depleted of liquid contents **:** EMPTY ⟨a ~ well⟩ ⟨the fountain pen ran ~ in the middle of a sentence⟩ **b :** devoid of running water ⟨a ~ ravine⟩ **6** *of an animal or its udder* **:** not giving milk **:** not lactating ⟨a ~ cow⟩ **7 a** (1) **:** not shedding tears ⟨hardly a ~ eye at the funeral⟩ (2) **:** not accompanied by tears ⟨a ~ sob⟩ **b :** continent of urine ⟨some children learn to stay ~ much earlier than others⟩ **c** (1) **:** marked by the absence or scantiness of secretions, effusions, or other forms of moisture ⟨a ~ pleurisy⟩ (2) *of a cough* **:** not accompanied by the raising of mucus or phlegm **8 a** *obs* **:** free from bloodshed **:** not causing or accompanied by an effusion of blood ⟨~ war⟩ ⟨~ death⟩ **b :** designed or executed in practice or planning for the future and lacking some essential (as live ammunition) of the situation being simulated **:** intended for practice only ⟨~ rehearsal⟩ ⟨~ firing⟩ **9 a :** solid as opposed to liquid ⟨~ groceries⟩ ⟨~ provisions⟩ ⟨~ cargo⟩ **b :** SLACK 6 **10 a :** not manifesting or communicating warmth, responsiveness, sympathy, enthusiasm, or tender feeling whether through natural indifference or studied unconcern **:** IMPASSIVE, UNEMOTIONAL, MATTER-OF-FACT ⟨under that peculiar sort of ~, blunt manner, I know you have the warmest heart —Jane Austen⟩ ⟨she sat there looking ~ and indifferent —Lionel Trilling⟩ **b** *fine art* **:** exhibiting a sharp frigid preciseness of execution **:** lacking delicate contour in form or easy transition in coloring **11 a :** not yielding what is expected or desired **:** not giving satisfaction **:** BARREN, STERILE, UNPRODUCTIVE ⟨a poet who is going through a ~ period which he finds frustrating —Rosemary Benét⟩ **b** *obs, of a person* **:** STINGY **c** *dial* **:** RESERVED, ALOOF **12 :** marked by a matter-of-fact manner of expression that seems unconscious or unintentional but is actually ironic, caustic, keen, shrewd, terse — used esp. of humor or the person expressing it ⟨his ~ humor which made him say the most amusing things and keep his face so absolutely solemn —Eleanor Roosevelt⟩ **13 :** having no personal inclination, bias, or emotional concern **:** having clear impartial perception or judgment ⟨ought . . . to have used the ~ light of reason in discussing matters of high morality, politics and religion —*Times Lit. Supp.*⟩ ⟨a certain ~ spirit of detachment and analysis —Aldous Huxley⟩ **14 :** dull because lacking in inherent interest and adornment **:** lacking elements that would lend attractiveness and appeal **:** UNINTERESTING, WEARISOME, INSIPID ⟨in the *dryest* passages of her historical summaries these delightful descriptions come running to the rescue —Robert Payne⟩ ⟨his ~ schoolmaster temperament, the hurdy-gurdy monotony of him —William James⟩ **15 a :** having nothing superfluous **:** lacking embellishment **:** consisting of essentials only **:** UNADORNED, PLAIN, BARE ⟨~ simplicity⟩ ⟨~ fact⟩ ⟨~ formality⟩ **b** *archaic* **:** paid in actual coin — used of money or fees **c** *of a dog* **:** having the skin close fitting esp. about the neck and mouth **16 a** (1) *of beverages* **:** lacking sweetness (2) *of wines and other fermented beverages* **:** having all or most sugar fermented to alcohol **:** SUGARLESS ⟨~ champagne⟩ ⟨~ sauterne⟩ — see SEC **b** *of mixed drinks* **:** containing only ingredients low or lacking in sugar content ⟨a ~ martini⟩ **c :** marked by a harsh, rasping, or jarring tone **:** lacking smooth or liquid sound qualities ⟨a ~ rasping voice⟩ ⟨a chipping sparrow gives a ~, unmusical trill —W.P.Smith⟩ ⟨the ~ whisper of winter leaves —Edith Sitwell⟩ ⟨this recording of the piano solo is ~ and harsh⟩ **17 :** relating to or favoring the prohibition or drastic regulation and limitation of the manufacture or distribution of alcoholic beverages ⟨~ law⟩ ⟨~ agent⟩ ⟨~ sentiment⟩ ⟨a ~ state⟩

syn ARID: ARID is usu. more extreme than DRY. DRY suggests freedom from moisture or deficiency of moisture, ARID destitution or deprivation of moisture and extreme dryness ⟨not a drop of water could we find, and the *arid* aspect of the valley as a whole showed only too plainly that the rainfall, on this side of the island at least, must be scant indeed —C.B. Nordhoff & J.N.Hall⟩ DRY suggests lack of qualities compelling interest, ARID absence of worthwhile, fruitful, or significant, as well as interesting, qualities ⟨a very *dry* book⟩ ⟨the frank elucidation of such a principle, with an aesthetic near to a moral obligation, might imply only bleak and *arid* results —Holbrook Jackson⟩ Applied to persons, their manner or sayings, DRY implies loss of warmth, responsiveness, enthusiasm, or emotion, ARID an absence of or incapacity for these ⟨this structural defect might have been overcome — and may still be overcome — if the intellectual leadership were less *arid* —Barbara Ward⟩ **syn** see in addition SOUR

— **not dry behind the ears :** IMMATURE, NAIVE

²dry \"\ *vb* **dried; dried; drying; dries** [ME *drien, dryen,* fr. OE *drȳgan,* fr. *drȳge,* adj.] *vt* **1 :** to make dry **:** to rid of moisture or liquid (as by wiping, rubbing, draining, squeezing) — often used with *up, out, off; specif* **:** to remove or reduce the moisture content of by exposure to heat or air **:** DESICCATE — compare DEHYDRATE, EVAPORATE **2 :** to take up (moisture or liquid) by absorption — usu. used with *up* ⟨the sun will ~ up the dew quickly⟩ **3 :** to cause (a female mammal) to stop giving milk — used with *off* or *up* ~ *vi* **1 :** to become dry **:** become free from wetness or moisture — often used with *off, out* ⟨nylon *dries* rapidly⟩ ⟨I *dried* at the electric blower —Saul Bellow⟩ **2 a** *of moisture or a liquid* **:** to evaporate, become absorbed, or drain away — often used with *up* ⟨the ~*ing* up during the summer of the shallow ponds —W.H.Dowdeswell⟩ **b :** to become hard, tough, and elastic as a result of oxidation and polymerization **:** SOLIDIFY — used esp. of various oils, paints, and varnishes applied as thin films **3** *of a female mammal* **:** to stop giving milk — used with *off* or *up*

syn DESICCATE, DEHYDRATE, BAKE, PARCH: DRY is a general term applicable to any process, natural or artificial, whereby moisture is extracted from something ⟨clothes *drying* on the line⟩ ⟨to *dry up* a swamp⟩ ⟨*drying* the dishes with a towel⟩ DESICCATE indicates a complete exhaustion of moisture, with resultant shriveling or withering; in reference to persons it indicates loss of animation, vitality, capacity to interest ⟨*desiccated* fish⟩ ⟨*desiccated* coconut meat⟩ ⟨the spur of an imagination not yet *desiccated* by a too strict adhesion to those so-called 'laws' —Eric Partridge⟩ ⟨achieves her dream of gentility by marrying a stockbroker and settles into a mold of *desiccated* snobbery —C.J.Rolo⟩ DEHYDRATE, like DESICCATE, indicates complete elimination of water but usu. lacks additional suggestion ⟨*dehydrated* fruits⟩ It may refer to a condition of the body resulting from loss or deprivation of fluids ⟨he may develop fever from becoming *dehydrated* —Benjamin Spock⟩ BAKE in the meaning here involved may indicate not only drying by heat or fire but also hardening, sometimes with resulting cracking ⟨clay tablets on which all three types were present — that is, tablets on which the wedges had been impressed while they were still soft and then *baked* in —Fletcher Pratt⟩ ⟨the sun-*baked* mud flats⟩ PARCH suggests drying by dry heat or drought; it may imply effects comparable to thirst and suggest that water will restore and refresh ⟨record heat waves which have *parched* mid-America's usually productive plains —*N.Y. Times Mag.*⟩ ⟨we had drunk all our water and so were *parched* and all done in when we finally espied a small, scattered Bedouin camp —*Nat'l Geographic*⟩

³dry \"\ *n* -ES *see sense 6* [ME *drie, dry,* fr. *drie, dry,* adj.] **1 :** the condition of being dry **:** DRYNESS **2 :** something dry: as **a** *chiefly Austral* (1) **:** the rainless season of the year (2) **:** a desert area **b :** a place that is dry (as a piece of dry land) **3** [by shortening] **:** DRYHOUSE **4 :** a natural seam constituting a flaw in stone **5 :** THIRST; *esp* **:** a craving for intoxicating liquor **6** *pl* **drys :** PROHIBITIONIST **7 :** the action of becoming dry ⟨speed of ~ of printing inks⟩

⁴dry \"\ *adv* [¹*dry*] **:** in a dry way ⟨"what a thrilling life you have!" "Yeah," I says, ~ —Bant Singer⟩

dry- *or* **dryo-** *comb form* [NL, fr. Gk, fr. *drys* tree, oak — more at TREE] **:** tree — in generic names ⟨*Dryo*pithecus⟩

dry·ad \ˈdrīəd, -ī,ad\ *n* -s [L *dryad-, dryas,* fr. Gk, fr. *drys*] **:** WOOD NYMPH 1

dry·as \ˈdrīəs\ *n* [NL, fr. L] **1** *cap* **:** a small genus of arctic and alpine tufted plants (family Rosaceae) with simple leaves and white or yellow solitary flowers **2** *pl* **dryas :** any plant of the genus *Dryas*

¹dryasdust \ˈ=‚=\ *n* -s *often cap* [after Dr. Jonas *Dryasdust,* fictitious person to whom Sir Walter Scott †1832 Scottish author dedicated some of his novels] **:** one that is uninteresting because of concentration upon minutiae **:** PEDANT ⟨the researches of a *Dryasdust* —C.E.Montague⟩

²dryasdust \"\ *adj* **:** marked by characteristics that bring about lack of interest or boredom **:** UNINSPIRED, PEDANTIC, PROSAIC ⟨~ presentation⟩ ⟨~ scholarship⟩ ⟨a ~ teacher⟩

dry-ash \ˈ=‚=\ *vt* **:** to convert (a sample) to ash in chemical analysis

dry band *or* **dry bunch** *n* **:** a flock of sheep not including gravid or lactating ewes

dry bark *n* **:** a phase of shell bark of citrus in which the outstanding symptoms are yellowing and some defoliation, loss of vigor, and death of tissues nearly down to the cambium of trunk and large branches with checking but little or no shelling of the bark

dry battery *n* **:** a battery of dry cells; *also* **:** DRY CELL

dry bible *or* **dry bible disease** *n* [¹*bible* (omasum)] *Austral* **:** botulism of cattle

dry bone *or* **dry-bone ore** *n* **:** SMITHSONITE

dry bridge *n, NewEng* **:** a bridge over a dry way (as a railroad)

drybrush \ˈ=‚=\ *n* **:** a method of ink or watercolor painting in which most of the pigment has been removed from the brush before application

dry budding *n* **1 :** PLATE BUDDING **2 :** CHIP BUDDING

dry-bulb temperature *n* **:** temperature indicated by a dry-bulb thermometer that is the actual temperature of the air — contrasted with *wet-bulb temperature;* compare PSYCHROMETER

dry-bulb thermometer *n* **:** an ordinary thermometer; *specif* **:** the thermometer with unmoistened bulb in a psychrometer

dry camp *n* **:** a camp made where there is no source of water

dry cell *n* **:** a voltaic cell whose contents are made nonspillable by the use of some absorbent (as sawdust or gelatin); *esp* **:** a cell of the Leclanché type in which a mixture of plaster of paris, flour, and sal ammoniac with water takes the place of the solution

dry-clean \ˈ=‚=\ *vt* [back-formation fr. *dry cleaning*] **:** to subject to dry cleaning

dry cleaner *n* **:** one whose business is the dry cleaning of textiles

dry cleaning *n* **:** the cleansing of fabrics with substantially nonaqueous organic solvents (as petroleum naphtha or chlorinated hydrocarbons) to which special detergents or soaps are often added — compare WET CLEANING

dry coal *n* **:** coal containing little volatile matter

dry color *n* **:** a pigment in powder form — compare FLUSH COLOR, PULP COLOR

dry course *n* **:** a starter course in roofing consisting of roofing felt or paper laid over insulation and not bedded in tar or asphalt

dry-cure \ˈ=‚=\ *vt* **:** to cure (as meat) by drying **:** DRY-SALT — compare PICKLE

dry dash *n* **:** ROCK DASH

dry·de·ni·an \(ˈ)drīˈdēnēən, -ˈden-\ *adj, cap* [John *Dryden* †1700 Eng. poet + E *-ian*] **:** of or in the manner of the poet Dryden
dry digging *n* **:** an alluvial mine in an arid region — usu. used in pl.; called also *dry placer*
dry-dip \ˈ=,=\ *n* **:** a tanning solution into which sole leather is dipped to increase firmness and restore color
dry-disk rectifier *n* **:** a rectifier cell of the barrier-layer type
dry distillation *n* **:** the distillation of substances in a dry condition; *esp* **:** DESTRUCTIVE DISTILLATION
dry dock *n* **:** a dock that can be kept dry for use during the construction or repairing of ships — see FLOATING DOCK, GRAVING DOCK; compare MARINE RAILWAY
dry-dock \ˈ=,=\ *vt* [*dry dock*] **:** to place in a dry dock
dry-dye \ˈ=,=\ *vt* **:** to dye (a fabric) by using a nonaqueous solvent (as petroleum naphtha)
dry end *n* **:** the section of a papermaking machine extending from the place where the wet web is first subjected to the drying process to the place where the finished paper is reeled — compare WET END
dryer *var of* DRIER
dryest *var of* DRIEST
dry face *n* **:** a chipped or tapped area on a turpentine tree that fails to produce a flow of oleoresin
dry farm *n* **:** a nonirrigated farm on dry land
dry-farm \ˈ=,=\ *vt* [*dry farm*] **:** to farm without irrigation — **dry farmer** *n*
dry farming *n* **:** production of crops on dry land without irrigation principally by tillage methods conserving soil moisture and by the use of drought-enduring or drought-evading crops — called also *dryland farming*
dry-fine \ˈ=,=\ *vt* **:** to repolish (metals) on a dry fine-grained wheel when an esp. smooth surface is required
dry finish *n* **:** a finish given to paper or board by calendering dry — compare WATER FINISH — **dry-finished** \ˈ=ˈ==\ *adj*
dryfist *n* [¹*dry* + *fist*] *obs* **:** NIGGARD, MISER
dryfland *var of* DROFLAND
dry fly *n* **:** an artificial fly designed to float upon the surface of the water
dry fog *n* **1 :** a haze caused by dust or smoke in the air **2 :** a fog occurring above the dew point and caused by some substance (as coal-tar vapor) that prevents evaporation of the water droplets
dryfoot \ˈ=,=\ *adv* [ME *drie foot*] **1 :** with dry feet **2** *obs* **:** by the scent of the foot
dry foot *n* **:** the bottom of a piece of pottery when unglazed
dry fruit *n* **:** a fruit (as a capsule or achene) in which the pericarp is not succulent or pulpy
dry gangrene *n* **:** gangrene that develops in the presence of pure arterial obstruction, is sharply localized (as in an extremity or an udder), and is characterized by dryness of the dead tissue which is of a dark brown or black color and sharply demarcated from adjacent tissue by a line of inflammation
dry goods \ˈ=,=\ *n pl but sometimes sing in constr* **:** textiles, ready-to-wear clothing, and notions as distinguished from hardware, jewelry, groceries, and wet goods
dry-grind \ˈ=,=\ *vt* **:** to grind without using liquid
dry grins *n pl* **:** smiling caused by a feeling of embarrassment
dry-gulch \ˈ=,=\ *vt* **:** to kill from ambush
dry-handed \ˈ=ˈ==\ *adj* **:** without weapons
dry hole *n* **1 :** a hole drilled (as through rock in a quarry) without using water **2 :** a well that does not yield oil or gas in commercial quantities — called also *dry well, duster*
dry hopping *n* **:** the addition of hops to beer in the cask
dryhouse \ˈ=,=\ *n* **1 :** CHANGE HOUSE **2 :** a drying room (as in a factory)
dry ice *n* **:** a substance that consists of solidified carbon dioxide usu. in the form of blocks, that at −78.5° C changes directly to a gas as it absorbs heat, and that is used chiefly as a refrigerant and coolant
drying *adj* [ME, fr. the pres. part. of *dryen, drien* to dry — more at DRY] **:** capable of rapidly becoming dry and hard by absorbing oxygen on exposure to air — see DRYING OIL
drying loft *n* **:** a loft in which paper is dried under carefully regulated atmospheric conditions
drying oil *n* **:** a natural or synthetic unsaturated fatty oil (as linseed oil or dehydrated castor oil) that changes readily to a hard, tough, elastic substance when exposed in a thin film to the air and may serve as a vehicle in paints, varnishes, and printing inks — compare BLOWN OIL, BODIED OIL, BOILED OIL
drying oven *n* **:** a heated chamber for drying; *specif* **:** one for drying clay ware or glazed ware before firing
dry·i·nid \ˈdrīənəd, -,nid\ *n* -S [NL *Dryinidae*] **:** one of the Dryinidae
dry·in·i·dae \drīˈinə,dē\ *n pl, cap* [NL, fr. *Dryinus*, type genus + *-idae*] **:** a family of small broad-headed wasps parasitic as larvae on the nymphs of leafhoppers and related insects
dry-ki *or* **dri·ki** \ˈ=,kī\ *n* -S [origin unknown] **:** standing or fallen weather-beaten timber (as of trees killed by flooding)
dry kiln *n* **:** a heated chamber for drying and seasoning cut lumber
dry labor *n* **:** childbirth characterized by premature escape of the amniotic fluid
dry lake *n* **:** a tract of salt-encrusted land in a region of slight rainfall which may occas. be covered by a temporary lake **:** PLAYA
dry land *n* **1** \ˈ=ˈ=\ **:** a region of low or inadequate rainfall **2** \ˈ=ˈ=\ **:** TERRA FIRMA ⟨eager to set foot on *dry land* again⟩
dry-land \ˈ=,=\ *adj* [*dry land*] **1 :** of, relating to, or found on terra firma ⟨where the toad is called a *dry-land* frog⟩ ⟨*dry-land* rice⟩ **2** *usu* **dryland :** of or relating to arid regions or to dry farming ⟨*dryland* wheat⟩ ⟨typical *dryland* genera⟩
dryland blueberry *n* **1 :** a low shrub (*Vaccinium pallidum*) of eastern No. America **2 :** the sweet blue berry borne by the dryland blueberry
dryland farming *n* **:** DRY FARMING
dry lodging *n, obs* **:** lodging without board
dry loft *n* **:** a tannery area where leather is hung to dry
drylot \ˈ=,=\ *n* **:** an enclosure of limited size that is usu. bare of all vegetation and is used for feeding and fattening livestock
dry·ly *or* **dri·ly** \ˈdrīlē, -li\ *adv* [ME *dryely*, fr. *drye, dry* + *-ly*] **:** in a dry manner: as **a :** without moisture **b :** with caustic or sardonic humor **:** SARCASTICALLY **c :** without emotion **:** INDIFFERENTLY, COLDLY ⟨freely, if ~, advised lady guests on the respective qualities of moire and surah —Margery Sharp⟩ **d :** in a plain unadorned style **:** in a dull uninteresting manner ⟨he is never ~ didactic —*Manchester Guardian Weekly*⟩; *also* **:** in a clear, forthright, and unbiased manner ⟨~ academic and methodical —*Nation*⟩
dry·man \ˈ=mən, -,man\ *n, pl* **drymen :** one in charge of a dryhouse
dry measure *n* **1 :** a series of units of capacity for dry commodities — see MEASURE table **2 :** a measure for dry commodities
dry milk *n* **:** whole or skim milk from which the water has been removed
dry milk solids *n pl* **:** the constituents of milk (as protein, lactose, minerals, vitamins, ash) remaining after the removal of water
dry mop *n* **:** a long-handled duster for use on floors — called also *dust mop*
dry mounting *n* **:** a method of attaching photographic prints to a support by means of a thermoplastic tissue treated with shellac and the application of heat and pressure
dry multure *n, Scots law* **:** a yearly tax payable in money or grain to a mill owner for the grinding of grain grown on land subject to thirlage or for the right to have that grain ground elsewhere

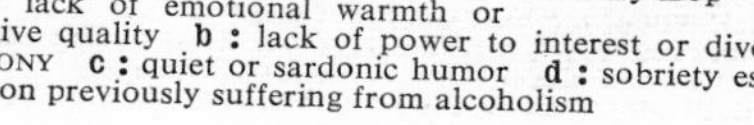

dry mop

dry·ness *n* -ES [ME *drynesse*, fr. OE *drȳgnes*, fr. *drȳge* dry + *-nes* -ness — more at DRY] **:** the quality or state of being dry: as **a :** lack of emotional warmth or imaginative quality **b :** lack of power to interest or divert **:** MONOTONY **c :** quiet or sardonic humor **d :** sobriety esp. in a person previously suffering from alcoholism

dry nurse *n* **1 :** a nurse who cares for but does not suckle an infant — compare WET NURSE **2 :** one who aids or instructs another usu. unnecessarily
dry-nurse \ˈ=,=\ *vt* [*dry nurse*] **:** to act as dry nurse to; *esp* **:** to give unnecessary supervision to ⟨I have gone round the world alone and do not need to be *dry-nursed* through a tour in Ireland —G.B.Shaw⟩
dryo- — see DRY-
dry·o·bal·a·nops \,drīōˈbalə,näps\ *n* [NL, fr. *dry-* + *balan-* + *-ops*] **1** *cap* **:** a small genus of resin-producing trees (family Dipterocarpaceae) having flowers with a cup-shaped calyx the limb of which is divided into leafy segments — see BORNEO CAMPHOR **2** -ES **:** any tree of the genus *Dryobalanops*
dry·o·ba·tes \drīˈäbə,tēz\ [NL, fr. *dry-* + *-bates*] *syn of* DENDROCOPOS
dry off *vt* **:** to develop dormancy in (a plant) by withholding water
dry offset *n* [so called fr. the fact that no water is used] **:** offset printing in which the inked impression from letterpress or relief is etched on a thin metal surface, then printed on an intermediate rubber surface (as a blanket), and then offset onto the paper
dry·o·phyl·lum \,drīōˈfiləm\ *n, cap* [NL, fr. *dry-* + *-phyllum*] *bot* **:** a genus of widely distributed Upper Cretaceous and Tertiary fossil trees (family Fagaceae) considered to be ancestors of modern oaks and beeches
dry·o·pi·the·cid \,drīōpəˈthēsəd, -ēkəd, -ˈpithə,sid, -ə,kid\ *n* -S [NL *Dryopithecus* + E *-id*] **:** an ape of the subfamily Dryopithecinae
dry·o·pith·e·ci·nae \-,pithəˈsī(,)nē, -ˈkī-\ *n pl, cap* [NL *Dryopithecus*, type genus + *-inae*] **:** a subfamily of Pongidae comprising Miocene and Pliocene Old World anthropoid apes regarded by some as common ancestors of man and modern anthropoids and including the genera *Dryopithecus, Proconsul, Sivapithecus*, and less-known related forms — **dry·o·pith·e·cine** \-ˈpithə,sīn, -,kīn\ *adj or n*
dry·o·pi·the·cus \,==pəˈthēkəs, -ˈpithəkəs\ *n, cap* [NL, fr. *dry-* + *-pithecus*] **:** a genus of generalized Miocene and Pliocene Old World apes sometimes regarded as common ancestral forms of the anthropoid apes and man
dry·op·te·ris \drīˈäptərəs\ *n, cap* [NL, fr. L, a kind of fern, fr. Gk, fr. *dry-* + *pteris*, a kind of fern, fr. *pteron* feather — more at FEATHER] **:** a large cosmopolitan genus of medium-sized ferns (family Polypodiaceae) having the indusium reniform or orbicular with a deep sinus and comprising the shield ferns
dry·op·te·roid \-ə,rȯid\ *adj* [NL *Dryopteris* + E *-oid*] **:** resembling or relating to the genus *Dryopteris*
dry ore *n* **:** an ore very valuable for gold or silver but containing little lead and much silica and so requiring additions of lead and fluxes for successful treatment
dry painting *n* **:** SAND PAINTING
dry pan *n* **:** a grinder for ceramic materials consisting of a rotating perforated metal pan containing revolving mullers
dry-pick \ˈ=,=\ *vt* **:** to remove the feathers from (fowl) without scalding
dry-pipe system *n* **:** a sprinkler system in which water is admitted to the system upon the release of air pressure that the pipes normally contain and which is used where there is danger of freezing
dry-pipe valve *also* **dry valve** *n* **:** a valve admitting water to a dry-pipe sprinkler system upon the release of air pressure in the system
dry placer *n* **:** DRY DIGGING
dry plate *n* **:** a photographic plate coated with a sensitized silver halide emulsion (as in gelatin) and dried before exposure — called also *plate*
dry pleurisy *n* **:** pleurisy in which the exudation is mainly fibrinous
drypoint \ˈ=,=\ *n* **1 :** an engraving made with a needle or other pointed instrument instead of a burin directly into the metal plate without the use of acid as in etching, the burr made by the point being retained to produce the characteristic soft line in the print **2 :** a print made from such an engraving
dry-press \ˈ=,=\ *vt* **:** to mold (clayware) by compressing moist powdered clay in metal dies
dry rendering *n* **:** a process of cooking animal tissues in the absence of water for extraction of the fat
dry rent *n, old English law* **:** RENT SECK
dry rice *n* [so called fr. its being grown without irrigation] **:** UPLAND RICE
dry rot *n* **1 :** a decay of seasoned timber caused by certain fungi (as the house fungi and some polypores) that consume the cellulose of wood leaving a mere soft skeleton that is readily reduced to powder **2 :** a rot of plant tissue in which the affected areas are not soft and wet but dry and often firmer than normal or more or less mummified: as **a :** decay of standing timber involving such rot and caused chiefly by polypores **b :** any of various fungous diseases of cultivated plants involving such rot esp. of roots, tubers, and fruits and caused usu. by fungi of the genera *Fusarium, Diaporthe, Diplodia*, or *Volutella* **3 :** a fungus causing dry rot **4 :** deterioration and decay from within caused by apathy or by resistance to new and vitalizing forces; *also* **:** the cause of such decay ⟨warned against the *dry rot* which infects art when it becomes more interested in itself than in what it is saying —*Saturday Rev.*⟩ ⟨in a representative democracy lack of strong conviction in the electorate is a form of *dry rot* capable of eventually destroying the whole fabric —G.W.Johnson⟩
dry-rot \ˈ=,=\ *vb* [*dry rot*] *vt* **:** to affect with dry rot **~** *vi* **:** to become affected with dry rot ⟨what counted inside you *dry-rotted* if you pretended it wasn't there —Hugh MacLennan⟩
dry rubble *n* **:** rubble masonry laid without mortar
dry run *n* **1 :** a practice exercise or rehearsal without ammunition (as of a military combat operation) **2 :** a practice exercise **:** REHEARSAL, TEST, TRIAL ⟨after 17 *dry runs*, using paid actors as the quizzees, the kinks were ironed out and the show went on the air —*Newsweek*⟩
drys *pl of* DRY
dry-salt \ˈ=,=\ *vt* **:** to treat with salt in the dry state **:** cure (as meat or hides) by salting and drying
drysalter \ˈ=,==\ *n* [¹*dry* + *salter*] *Brit* **:** a dealer in crude dry chemicals and dyes
drysaltery \ˈ=,===\ *n* **1** *Brit* **:** the articles kept by a drysalter **2** *Brit* **:** the business of a drysalter
dry sand *n* **1 :** foundry sand artificially dried after being made into a mold — distinguished from *greensand* **2 :** a sand not producing oil or gas
dry sausage *n* **:** SUMMER SAUSAGE
dry-shave \ˈ=,=\ *vt, slang* **:** DEFRAUD, CHEAT
dry-shod \ˈ=,=\ *adj* **:** having dry shoes on **:** not wetting the shoes or feet ⟨a land bridge over which men and animals could have crossed *dry-shod* —*Scientific American*⟩
dry shrinkage *n* **:** shrinkage occurring in kiln-dried lumber after removal of the surface crust (as by planing)
dry-sickness \ˈ=,==\ *n* **:** pine of sheep and cattle caused by cobalt deficiency
dry skin *n* **:** skin or hide preserved by air drying after slaughter
dry socket *n* **:** a tooth socket in which after tooth extraction a blood clot fails to form or disintegrates without undergoing organization; *also* **:** a condition that is marked by the occurrence of such a socket or sockets and that is usu. accompanied by neuralgic pain but without suppuration
dry spot *n* **:** GRAY SPECK
dry steam *n* **:** steam containing no free water particles — compare WET STEAM
dry storage *n* **:** cold storage (as for milk and cream) in which refrigeration is by a current of cooled air
dry stove *n* **:** a hothouse with low relative humidity for xerophytic plants
dry suit *n* **:** a close-fitting waterproof rubber suit used esp. by a skin diver
dryth \ˈdrīth\ *n* -S [¹*dry* + *-th* (as in *warmth*)] *now dial Eng* **:** DRYNESS, DROUGHT
dry trust *n* **:** PASSIVE TRUST
dry up *vt* **:** to end the existence of by or as if by cutting off at the source or exhausting the supply ⟨fear *dried up* the words —E.T.Thurston⟩ ⟨closure of the Mediterranean *dried up* commerce in Western Europe⟩ ⟨the finance-ministry project to *dry up* . . . their purchasing power by compulsory saving —George Axelsson⟩ **~** *vi* **1 :** to disappear as if by evaporation, absorption, or draining **:** become exhausted (as of a supply) **:** cease to exist because of the cutting off of a source of supply or of vital elements ⟨without intellectual enterprise, economic enterprise *dries up* —H.S.Commager⟩ ⟨they are filling the vacuum left by the virtual *drying up* of immigration from Europe —Hal Burton⟩ ⟨is not the only one whose power of expression *dries up* —*Times Lit. Supp.*⟩ **2 :** to wither or die through gradual loss of vitality ⟨the skin keeps the body from *drying up* through evaporation of fluid —Morris Fishbein⟩ ⟨under tyranny individual men *dry up* for lack of spiritual exercise —Lyman Bryson⟩ **3 a :** to stop talking **:** be at a loss for words ⟨he was so surprised and angry that he just *dried up*⟩ ⟨"*Dry up!*" advised the grizzled old-timer —S.E.White⟩ **b** *of an actor* **:** to forget one's lines
dry valve *var of* DRY-PIPE VALVE
dry wash *n* **1 :** laundry washed and dried but not ironed **2** *West* **:** WASH 3d
dry-waxed \ˈ=ˈ=\ *adj, of waxed paper* **:** so made that the wax is almost all driven into the paper — compare WET-WAXED
dry well *n* **1 :** DRY HOLE 2 **2 :** a hole excavated in porous ground and usu. covered and filled with loose gravel or rubble or walled (as with stone, brick, or cinder blocks) to receive water (as drainage from a roof) and allow it to percolate away
dry whiskey *n* [so called fr. the fact that eating the tops of the tubercles causes intoxication] **:** MESCAL BUTTON
dry-wood termite *n* **:** any of various termites (family Kalotermitidae) that live and feed in dry wood without a soil connection and include some which are destructive pests in domestic construction — see CRYPTOTERMES
ds *abbr* decistere
DS *abbr* **1** [It *dal segno*] from the sign **2** days after sight **3** day's sight **4** detached service **5** document signed **6** double stitch
d's *or* **ds** *pl of* D
DSc *abbr or n* -S **:** doctor of science
dsgn *abbr* design
d sharp \ˈ=ˈ=\ *n, usu cap D* **1 :** the keynote of D-sharp minor **2 :** the tone a half step above D
d-sharp minor \ˈ=,=ˈ==\ *n, usu cap D* **:** the minor musical key having a signature of six sharps
DSP *abbr* [L *decessit sine prole*] he died without issue
DST *abbr* **1** daylight saving time **2** double summer time
dstn *abbr* destination
dstspn *abbr* dessertspoon
DT *abbr* **1** daylight time **2** double throw **3** double time
dt's \ˈdēˈtēz\ *n pl, often cap D&T* [by abbr.] **:** DELIRIUM TREMENS
du *dial Brit var of* DO
du *abbr* **1** dual **2** duke
du·ad \ˈd(y)üˌad\ *n* -S [irreg. fr. Gk *dyad-, dyas* two (n.), pair — more at DYAD] **:** a union of two **:** PAIR
¹du·al \ˈd(y)üəl, ˈüəl *also* ˈül\ *adj* [L *dualis*, fr. *duo* two + *-alis* -al — more at TWO] **1** *of an inflectional form or grammatical number* **:** denoting reference to two ⟨Gothic *wit* "we two" is a first person ~ pronoun⟩ — compare PLURAL, QUADRUAL, SINGULAR, TRIAL **2 a :** consisting of two parts or elements **:** DOUBLE, TWOFOLD ⟨the ~ tones of an American toad's song —W.P.Smith⟩ ⟨that the work of a painter who looks important in England . . . has stood up to the ~ test of international competition and the Adriatic sun —David Sylvester⟩ **b :** having two aspects **:** having a double character or nature ⟨the man had a ~ nature, one half positive and passionate to yearning, one half negative, satirical, and really perverse —H.S.Canby⟩ ⟨immigrants, as a rule, retain a ~ patriotism —Bertrand Russell⟩ **c :** containing two or being one of two often identical parts **:** TWIN ⟨high-compression heads complete with a ~ exhaust system —Gregor Felsen⟩ **d :** consisting of or used on a pair of wheels (as automotive driving wheels) joined together side by side (as by bolting or welding) on a common axle ⟨~ tires⟩ **3 :** characterized by a division of controlling agents or factors: as **a :** consisting of two sets of authorities having mutually exclusive spheres of power ⟨a ~ federalism⟩ ⟨a ~ form of government⟩ **b :** fitted for operation by either or both of two agents ⟨driving lessons given on *dual*-control cars⟩ ⟨*dual*-fuel engines that run on oil or oil and gas⟩
²dual \"\ *n* -S **1 :** the dual number of a language or a form in it **2 :** the result obtained in consequence of interchanging conjunction and alteration throughout a formula in the propositional calculus **3 :** a chess problem for which two solutions exist **4 :** a pair of dual wheels or dual tires
du·a·la \düˈ(w)älə\ *n, pl* **duala** *or* **dualas** *usu cap* **1 a :** a Bantu-speaking people of the coastal area of Cameroun **b :** a member of such people **2 :** the Bantu language of the Duala people used as a language of trade and education in Cameroun
dual banking *n* **:** banking in which both state and national banks operate in the same state or community
dual citizenship *n* **1 :** the citizenship of a citizen of a state that is organized under a constitution with other states into a national state (as the U. S.) recognized as a nation by the family of nations **2 :** DUAL NATIONALITY
dual highway *n* **:** DIVIDED HIGHWAY
dual ignition *n* **:** automobile ignition by two independent currents from a battery and from a magneto
du·al·ism \ˈd(y)üə,lizəm, -üə-\ *n* -S [F *dualisme*, fr. L *dualis* + F *-isme* -ism] **1 :** a theory that divides the world or a given realm of phenomena or concepts into two mutually irreducible elements or classes of elements: as **a :** an ontological theory that divides reality into (1) subsistent forms and spatiotemporal objects or into (2) mind and matter ⟨Cartesian *dualism*⟩ — compare MONISM, PLURALISM **b :** an epistemological theory that objective reality is known by means of subjective ideas, representations, images, or sense data — contrasted with *monism* **2 :** the quality or state of being dual **:** twofold division ⟨all our policies . . . have been plagued by ~; we have too often tried to straddle the fence of expediency —H.W.Baldwin⟩ **3 a :** the doctrine that the universe is under the dominion of two opposing principles one of which is good and the other evil **b :** a view of man as constituted of two original and independent elements (as matter and spirit) **4 :** the theory originated by Lavoisier and developed by Berzelius that all definite chemical compounds are binary and consist of two distinct constituents, themselves simple or complex, and possess opposite electrical properties — compare UNITARY THEORY **5 :** a theory in hematology holding that the blood cells arise from two kinds of stem cells one of which yields lymphatic elements and the other myeloid elements — compare HEMATOPOIESIS
du·al·ist \-ləst\ *n* -S **:** an adherent or advocate of dualism or a dualism
du·al·is·tic \ˈ==ˈlistik\ *also* **du·al·ist** \ˈ== ləst\ *adj* **1 :** consisting of two **:** DUAL **2 :** characterized by dualism **:** having reference to dualism — **du·al·is·ti·cal·ly** \ˈ==ˈlistək(ə)lē\ *adv*
dualistic formula *n* **:** a chemical formula written in accordance with the theory of dualism ⟨$CaO.SO_3$ is the *dualistic formula* for calcium sulfate ($CaSO_4$)⟩ — called also *Berzelian formula*
du·al·i·ty \d(y)üˈalədē, -ətē, -i\ *n* -ES [ME *dualitie*, fr. MF *dualité*, fr. LL *dualitat-, dualitas*, fr. L *dualis* dual + *-itat-, -itas* -ity — more at DUAL] **:** the quality or state of being dual or of being made up of two elements or aspects **:** DOUBLENESS, DICHOTOMY ⟨he was amused by the eternal ~ of truth and fiction —John Fountain⟩ ⟨a deep ~ was introduced between morality and the life of impulse —Bertrand Russell⟩ — see PRINCIPLE OF DUALITY
du·al·ize \ˈd(y)üə,līz, -üə-\ *vt* -ED/-ING/-S **:** to make dual ⟨*dualized* into a four-lane highway —Richard Thruelsen⟩
du·al·ly \-əlē, -li\ *adv* **:** in a double capacity **:** in two ways
dual nationality *n* **:** the status of an individual when two or more nations each claim sole allegiance from him — called also *multiple nationality*; compare DUAL CITIZENSHIP
dual organization *n* **:** division (as of a tribe or society) into moieties
dual pay *n* **:** wages determined on that one of two alternative bases of computation which is more advantageous to the employee (as on a mileage or hourly basis in the transportation industry)
dual-purpose \ˈ==ˈ==\ *adj* **1 :** intended for or serving two

purposes **2 :** bred for two purposes (as to provide milk and meat or eggs and meat)

dual-rotation propeller *n* **:** an assembly of two airplane propellers mounted one behind the other on coaxial shafts and rotating in opposite directions

duals *pl of* DUAL

dual union *n* **:** a labor union claiming jurisdiction over workers organized by another union — **dual unionism** *n*

du·an \'düən, 'thü-\ *n* -s [ScGael] **:** a division of a Gaelic poem corresponding to a canto **:** POEM, SONG

du·ant \'d(y)üənt\ *n* -s [L *duo* two + E *-ant* — more at TWO] **:** DEE

du·ar \dü'är\ *n* -s [Hindi *duār, dvār,* lit., door, fr. Skt *dvār* — more at DOOR] *India* **:** a tract of land leading to a mountain pass

du·ar·chy \'d(y)ü,ärkē\ *n* -ES [irreg. fr. LGk *dyarchia,* fr. Gk *dy-* + *-archia* -archy] **:** a government by two rulers having equal power

1dub \'dəb\ *vb* **dubbed; dubbed; dubbing; dubs** [ME *dubben,* fr. OE *dubbian* to dub a knight; akin to ON *dubba* to dub a knight, EFris *dubben* to strike against, push, MLG *dobbel* die, MHG *toppel* die, Norw *dubb* peg, plug, OHG *tubili* plug — more at DOWEL] *vt* **1 a :** to confer knighthood upon by the ceremonial tapping of the shoulder with a sword ⟨the king *dubbed* his son a knight⟩ **b :** to dignify or give new character to by a name, title, or description ⟨a man of wealth is *dubbed* a man of worth —Alexander Pope⟩ ⟨*dubbed* him a "born actor" —*Time*⟩ ⟨a region *dubbed* the Switzerland of America⟩ **c :** to call by a descriptive name or epithet **:** NICKNAME ⟨people *dubbed* his enterprise a folly⟩ ⟨if a man persists in advancing views that are contradicted by all available evidence . . . he will rightfully be *dubbed* a crank by his colleagues —Martin Gardner⟩ **2** *Brit* **:** DRESS ⟨~ a line for fly fishing⟩ **3 :** to thrust or make a thrust at **4 a :** to trim or remove the comb and wattles of (as a cockerel) — compare CROP 1b (2) **b :** to trim or make smooth with an adz (as a timber) **5 :** to rub with grease (as in stuffing leather) **6 a :** to hit (a golf ball or a golf shot) poorly **b :** to execute poorly ⟨he *dubbed* his first attempt at a sale⟩ ⟨he *dubbed* the exam⟩ ~ *vi* **:** to thrust or make a thrust **:** POKE

2dub \"\ *n* -s **:** one who is unskillful (as at a game, a trade, politics) because of inexperience or lack of talent **:** a clumsy or stupid person **:** DUFFER

3dub \"\ *n* -s [ME (Sc dial.) *dubbe;* akin to MLG *dobbe* pool, puddle, Fris *dobbe* pit, hole] **1** *chiefly Scot* **:** a pool of water: as **a :** a water hole or stagnant pond **b :** a deep pool in a river **c :** a pool of rainwater **:** MUD PUDDLE **2** *Scot* **:** BOG, MIRE

4dub \"\ *n* -s [Telugu *ḍabbu* & Marathi *ḍhabbū*] **:** a small copper coin formerly current in parts of India

5dub \"\ *vt* **dubbed; dubbed; dubbing; dubs** [by shortening & alter. fr. *double*] **1 :** to provide (a motion-picture film) with a new sound track (as for substituting dialogue in a foreign language) **2 :** to add (sound effects) to a motion-picture film or to a radio or television production — usu. used with *in* **3 :** to transpose (sound already recorded) to a new record **:** RERECORD; *also* **:** to combine (two or more sources of sound at least one of which is a recording) into one record

6dub \"\ *n* -s **:** DUBBING

dub-a-dub \,dəbə'dəb\ *n* -s [imit.] **:** the sound of drum beating

1du bar·ry \d(y)ü'barē\ *n, often cap D&B* [prob. after Marie Jean Bécu, Comtesse *du Barry* †1793 mistress of King Louis XV of France] **:** BITTERSWEET PINK

2du barry \(')=¦==\ *adj, usu cap D&B* [after Comtesse *du Barry*] *of a soup or sauce* **:** made with cauliflower

du·bash \dü'bash\ *n* -ES [Hindi *dubhāṣiyā,* fr. *du-* two (fr. Skt *dvi*) + *-bhāṣiyā* (fr. Skt *bhāṣā* language); akin to Skt *bhāṣate* he talks — more at TWO, BELLOW] *India* **:** INTERPRETER

dub·bel·tje \'dəbəlchə\ *n* -s [D, fr. *dubbel* double (fr. MD *dubbel, dobbel,* fr. OF *doble*) + *-tje* (dim. suffix) — more at DOUBLE] **:** a former silver coin of the Netherlands equivalent to two stivers or 1/10 of a gulden

1dub·ber \'dəbə(r)\ *n* -s [1*dub* + *-er*] **:** one that dubs

2dubber \"\ *or* **dup·per** \'dəpə(r)\ *also* **dub·ba** \'dəbə\ *n* -s [Per *dabba*] **:** a large globular leather bottle used in India to hold ghee, oil, or other liquid

1dub·bin \'dəbən\ *also* **dub·bing** \", -biŋ\ *n* -s [fr. gerund of 1*dub* (to dress leather)] **:** a mixture of oil and tallow for dressing leather

2dubbin \"\ *vt* -ED/-ING/-S **:** to apply dubbin to

1dubbing *n* -s [fr. gerund of 1*dub* (to dress a fly)] **:** the materials tied to a fishhook in making the body of an artificial fly

2dubbing *n* -s [fr. gerund of 5*dub*] **:** a record made by dubbing

1dub·by \'dəbi\ *adj* -ER/-EST [1*dub* + *-y*] *dial Brit* **:** DULL, BLUNT

2dubby \"\ *adj* -ER/-EST [3*dub* + *-y*] *Scot* **:** MUDDY

du·ber·some \'d(y)übə(r)səm\ *adj* [alter. of *dubious* + *-some*] *dial* **:** DOUBTFUL

du·bi·e·ty \d(y)ü'bīəd·ē, -ətē, -i\ *n* -ES [LL *dubietas,* fr. L *dubius* + *-etas* (fr. *-itas* -ity)] **1 :** the quality or state of being doubtful or skeptical **:** DUBIOUSNESS, UNCERTAINTY ⟨there was ~ in his voice and a hint of uncertainty in his eye —John Buchan⟩ **2 :** a doubt or matter of doubt ⟨the problems and *dubieties* of an average individual⟩ **syn** see UNCERTAINTY

du·bi·os·i·ty \,d(y)übē'äsəd·ē, -ətē, -i\ *n* -ES [fr. *dubious,* after such pairs as E *curious: curiosity*] **:** DOUBT, UNCERTAINTY, DUBIETY **syn** see UNCERTAINTY

du·bi·ous \'d(y)übēəs\ *adj* [L *dubius,* fr. *dubare* to doubt, vacillate, fr. *duo* two — more at TWO] **1 :** occasioning doubt **:** EQUIVOCAL, UNCERTAIN, UNDETERMINED ⟨what one finds certain and indubitable in the situation, the other finds ~ or downright false —S.C.Pepper⟩ **2 a :** being in doubt **:** unsettled in opinion **:** DOUBTFUL, QUESTIONING, UNDECIDED ⟨he had never heard of me and was a little ~ about signing his name —Henry Miller⟩ ⟨she was nervous and ~ about the project⟩ **b :** expressive of doubt or uncertainty ⟨this loyalty . . . does not become shaky or ~ as the years pass —D.F. Miller⟩ **3 :** of doubtful promise or uncertain outcome **:** UNPROMISING, UNLIKELY ⟨seemed the most promising of all the ~ solutions presented⟩ ⟨a ~ and potentially dangerous gift —Vera M. Dean⟩ ⟨I was a ~ scholastic risk —Sidney Lovett⟩ **4 :** characterized by qualities that occasion suspicion, mistrust, disparaging suggestion, or hesitation **:** questionable as to value, quality, origin, or character **:** open to question ⟨spies, traitors, or others of ~ reliability and patriotism —R.E. Cushman⟩ ⟨rhetorically effective, but of ~ value scientifically —M.R.Cohen⟩ ⟨if not actually disreputable, was at best a ~ figure —S.H.Adams⟩ **syn** see DOUBTFUL

du·bi·ous·ly *adv* **:** in a manner expressive of doubt, hesitation, or suspicion **:** DOUBTFULLY, UNCERTAINLY

du·bi·ous·ness *n* -ES **:** the quality or state of being dubious

du·bi·ta·ble \'d(y)übəd·əbəl, |təb-\ *adj* [L *dubitabilis,* fr. *dubitare* to doubt + *-abilis* -able — more at DOUBT] **:** open to doubt or question ⟨on what grounds would my thesis be ~? —S.M.Brown⟩ ⟨it was more than ~ whether the friend was as influential as she thought —Karen Horney⟩

du·bi·tan·cy \|d·ənsē, |tən-\ *n* -ES [ML *dubitantia,* fr. L *dubitant-, dubitans* + *-ia* -y] **:** DOUBT, UNCERTAINTY

du·bi·tant \-nt\ *adj* [L *dubitant-, dubitans,* pres. part. of *dubitare* to doubt — more at DOUBT] **:** DOUBTING

1du·bi·tan·te \,d(y)übə'tän,tā\ *adj* [L, abl. sing. masc. of *dubitant-, dubitans*] **:** DOUBTING — used of a judge who expresses doubt about a decision reached by the court

2dubitante \"\ *n* -s **1 :** DOUBTER — used of a judge **2 :** the expression of doubt of a dubitante

du·bi·tate \'d(y)übə,tāt\ *vi* -ED/-ING/-S [L *dubitatus,* past part. of *dubitare* — more at DOUBT] *archaic* **:** DOUBT

du·bi·ta·tion \,d(y)übə'tāshən\ *n* -s [ME *dubytacion,* fr. MF *dubitation,* fr. L *dubitation-, dubitatio,* fr. *dubitatus* + *-ion-, -io* -ion] *archaic* **:** the quality or state of doubting **:** an instance of doubting **:** DOUBT ⟨I am in some ~ whether it ever existed at all —T.A.Guthrie⟩

du·bi·ta·tive \'d(y)übə,tād·iv\ *adj* [F *dubitatif,* fr. LL *dubitativus,* fr. L *dubitatus* + *-ivus* -ive] **1 :** tending or given to doubt **:** DOUBTING **2 :** expressing doubt ⟨the ~ mood of a verb⟩ — **du·bi·ta·tive·ly** \-d·ə̇vlē\ *adv*

dub·lin \'dəblən\ *adj, usu cap* [fr. *Dublin,* city & county in Ireland] **1 :** of or from Dublin, the capital of the Republic of Ireland **:** of the kind or style prevalent in the city of Dublin **2 :** of or from county Dublin, Ireland **:** of the kind or style prevalent in county Dublin

dub·lin·er \-nə(r)\ *n* -s *cap* [*Dublin,* Ireland + E *-er*] **:** a native or resident of Dublin, Ireland

du·boi·sia \d(y)ü'bȯizēə\ *n, cap* [NL, fr. F. N. *Dubois* †1824 Fr. botanist + NL *-ia*] **:** a genus of soft-wooded Australian shrubs or small trees (family Solanaceae) having white flowers in axillary clusters and yielding an alkaloid having an action similar to atropine

du bois-rey·mond's law \(')d(y)üb¦wä|rā'mōⁿz-, -ü¦bȯi|\ *or* **du bois-reymond principle** *n, usu cap D&B&R* [after Emil *du Bois-Reymond* †1896 Ger. physiologist] **:** a statement in physiology: a nerve is stimulated only by a change in electric current and not by a steady flow of electricity

du·bon·net \¦d(y)übə¦nā\ *n* -s [*Dubonnet*] **:** very dark purplish red

Dubonnet \"\ *trademark* — used for a sweet purplish red aromatized wine used as an aperitif or as a cocktail ingredient

dubonnet cocktail *n, cap D* **:** a cocktail consisting of approximately equal parts of Dubonnet wine and gin chilled and usu. garnished with a twist of lemon peel

1dubs *pres 3d sing of* DUB, *pl of* DUB

2dubs \'dəbz\ *interj* [short for *doubles*] — a call by a player in the game of marbles invoking a special privilege according to the rules of the game

du·cal \'d(y)ükəl\ *adj* [MF, fr. LL *ducalis* of a leader, fr. L *duc-, dux* leader + *-alis* -al — more at DUKE] **1 :** of, belonging to, or befitting a duke or dukedom ⟨a ~ palace⟩ **2 :** having the rank of a duke ⟨a mere ~ husband —*Time*⟩ — **du·cal·ly** \-əlē, -li\ *adv*

ducal coronet *n* **1** *heraldry* **:** a coronet ornamented with three strawberry leaves and often used as a crest coronet **2 :** DUKE'S CORONET

ducal crest coronet *n* **:** a ducal coronet borne as a crest coronet

du·cape \(')d(y)ü¦kāp\ *n* -s [origin unknown] **:** a heavy corded silk dress fabric popular chiefly in the 18th century

du·cat \'dəkət, *usu* -əd.+V\ *n* -s [ME *ducat, doket,* fr. MF *ducat,* fr. OIt *ducato* coin with a portrait of the doge on it, fr. *duca* doge, guide, fr. MGk *douk-, doux* leader, fr. LGk, fr. L *duc-, dux* — more at DUKE] **1 :** any one of a number of gold coins of European countries copied from a coin issued by Roger II of Sicily about 1150, 20th century issues of which include a coin of Austria issued 1901–15 and one of Czechoslovakia issued 1923–38 **2 :** a unit of value equivalent to the value of one gold ducat ⟨many fractional and multiple ~ pieces have been coined⟩ **3** *also* **duck·et** \"\ *slang* **:** TICKET

duc·a·toon \,dəkə'tün\ *or* **duc·a·ton** \-tän\ *n* -s [F *ducaton,* dim. of *ducat*] **:** a silver crown-sized coin of the Netherlands first struck in 1598; *also* **:** a similar coin of Italy

du·ce \'dü(,)chā\ *n* -s [after Il *Duce* (It, lit., the leader), title of Benito Mussolini †1945 Italian dictator] **:** DICTATOR

duces *pl of* DUX

duces tecum *n* -s **:** SUBPOENA DUCES TECUM

duchan *var of* DUKAN

du·ches·nea \d(y)ü'kānēə\ *n, cap* [NL, after Antoine N. *Duchesne* †1827 Fr. botanist] **:** a small genus of perennial Asiatic herbs (family Rosaceae) comprising two species of plants that resemble strawberries but have yellow flowers and spongy dry fruits — see INDIAN STRAWBERRY

duch·ess \'dəchə̇s\ *n* -ES [ME *duchesse,* fr. MF, fr. *duc* duke + *-esse* -ess — more at DUKE] **1 :** the wife of a duke **2 :** a woman who holds a ducal title in her own right

du·chesse \(')d(y)ü¦shes\ *n* -s [F, lit., duchess] **1 :** a chaise longue with arms that was popular in 18th century France **2** *also* **duchess :** a fine lustrous rayon or silk satin for clothing **3 :** a very small cream puff with sweet or savory filling used as dessert or served with cocktails

duchesse lace *also* **duchess lace** *n* [part trans. of F *dentelle duchesse*] **:** a fine bobbin lace of Flemish origin having delicate floral and foliage designs joined by bobbin-made brides

duchesse potato *n* [F *duchesse,* lit., duchess] **:** potato mashed and mixed with raw egg used as a garnish or made into patties and oven-browned

duchy \'dəchē, -chi\ *n* -ES [ME *duche, duchie,* fr. MF *duché,* fr. *duc* duke — more at DUKE] **:** the territory or dominions of a duke or duchess **:** DUKEDOM

1duck \'dək\ *n* -s *often attrib* [ME *doke,* fr. OE *dūce* — more at 2DUCK] **1** *or pl* **duck a :** any of various swimming birds of the family Anatidae which have the neck and legs short, the body more or less depressed, the bill often broad and flat, the tarsi scutellate in front, and the sexes almost always differing from each other in plumage and which are distinguished by these characteristics and by their comparatively small size from the swans and geese **b :** the flesh of any of these birds used as food **2 :** a female duck as distinguished from a male — compare DRAKE **3** *Brit* **a** *or* **ducks** *pl but sing in constr* **:** PET, DARLING — often used as a term of address **b :** something or someone attractive or charming ⟨a ~ of a car —*Everybody's Magazine*⟩ ⟨he was a nice old ~, and very fond of her —Margery Sharp⟩ **4 :** one that cannot act effectively because of disablement or other cause — compare DEAD DUCK, LAME DUCK, SITTING DUCK **5 :** DUCK ON A ROCK; *also* **:** one of the players' stones **6** *slang* **a :** a person with peculiar mental or physical characteristics ⟨a little old ~ with waxed mustache, you say, and a cane? —Frank King⟩ ⟨he's a queer ~⟩ **b :** RASCAL **7** *Brit* **:** a score of nothing **:** GOOSE EGG ⟨the batsman was bowled first ball for a ~⟩ **8 :** MIG **9** [so called fr. its shape] *slang* **:** URINAL

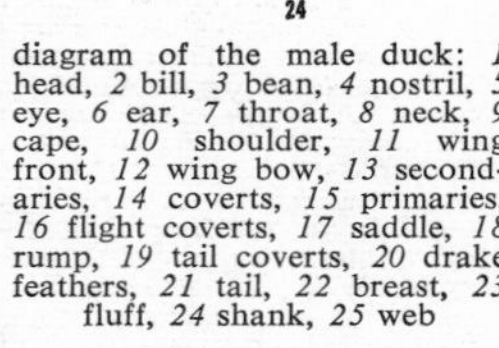

diagram of the male duck: *1* head, *2* bill, *3* bean, *4* nostril, *5* eye, *6* ear, *7* throat, *8* neck, *9* cape, *10* shoulder, *11* wing front, *12* wing bow, *13* secondaries, *14* coverts, *15* primaries, *16* flight coverts, *17* saddle, *18* rump, *19* tail coverts, *20* drake feathers, *21* tail, *22* breast, *23* fluff, *24* shank, *25* web

2duck \"\ *vb* -ED/-ING/-S [ME *douken, duken;* akin to OE *dūce* duck, MLG & MD *dūken* to dive, OHG *tūhhan*] *vt* **1 :** to plunge under water; *specif* **:** to plunge the head of (a person or animal) under water **2 :** to lower (as the head or body) quickly **:** BOW ⟨~*ed* her head to everyone on the platform, and ran down the steps —Hodding Carter⟩ ⟨~*ing* her head against the rain, hastened on —Pearl Puckett⟩ **3 :** AVOID, EVADE ⟨he tried to ~ the blame⟩ ⟨most of the Senate wanted to ~ the issue —T.R.Ybarra⟩ ⟨much evidence that administrators, faculties, and trustees ~ their separate responsibilities —Albert Lumley⟩ ~ *vi* **1 a :** to go quickly under the surface of water and reappear **b :** to descend suddenly **:** DIVE, DIP ⟨the trail ~*ed* into a narrow gulch —Wallace Stegner⟩ **2 a :** to lower the head or body suddenly ⟨the batteries he fired at promptly ceased their fire as the gunners ~*ed* behind cover —C.S.Forester⟩ ⟨she would ~ through the low entrance of her hut —Jacquetta & Christopher Hawkes⟩ **b :** BOW, BOB **3 :** to try to seize an apple with the teeth as it floats in a tub of water — used with *for;* compare BOB *vi* 1c **4 a :** to move quickly and often surreptitiously (as to escape danger or observation) **:** disappear suddenly **:** DODGE ⟨at sight of the officer he ~*ed* around the corner and into an alley⟩ — often used with *out* ⟨I ~*ed* out of the convention hall half a dozen times to watch the TV —E.D.Canham⟩ **b :** to avoid a duty, question, or responsibility **:** back out ⟨some grocery bills that a little hole-in-the-wall lunch counter was trying to *duck* out on —H.L. Davis⟩ **5 :** to play a low card rather than cover a card previously played or try to win a trick **syn** see DIP, DODGE

3duck \"\ *n* -s **:** a sudden lowering of the head or stooping of the body **:** a dip or quick plunge

4duck \"\ *n* -s [D *doek* cloth, linen, canvas, fr. MD *doec;* akin to OS *dōk* cloth, OHG *tuoh,* and perh. to Skt *dhvaja* flag, Av *dvazh-* to flutter] **1 :** a durable plain closely woven fabric now usu. of cotton made in various weights and used in the gray (as for sails, bags, belting) or with various finishes (as for tents, awnings, clothing) — compare CANVAS **2 ducks** *pl* **:** light clothes made of duck; *esp* **:** trousers made of such material

5duck \"\ *n* -s *sometimes cap* [alter. (influenced by 1*duck*) of *DUKW,* its code designation] **:** a 2½-ton 6-wheel-drive truck equipped with a propeller and watertight hull for ferrying, lighter service, or amphibious landing of troops

duck acorn *n* **:** WATER CHINQUAPIN

1duck and drake *var of* DUCKS AND DRAKES

2duck and drake *n* **:** DUCK ON A ROCK

1duckbill \'=,=\ *n* [1*duck* + *bill*] **1** *or* **duckbill platypus :** PLATYPUS **2** *or* **duckbill cat :** PADDLEFISH **3 :** DUCK-BILLED DINOSAUR **4 :** a metal flange welded to a tank tread for giving increased traction in muddy terrain **5 :** a power shovel with a flat round nose for loading coal in a mine

2duckbill \"\ *or* **duckbilled** \'=¦=\ *adj* **1 :** having a bill shaped like that of a duck **:** shaped like or terminating in something shaped like a duck's bill **2** *of a cap or hat* **:** having a visor in the shape of a duck's bill

duck-billed dinosaur *n* **:** any of numerous herbivorous ornithischian dinosaurs having flattened side teeth resembling blades, no incisors, and the fore part of the jaws covered by a horny birdlike bill and constituting *Trachodon* and related genera — see HADROSAUR

duckbill gar *n* **:** SHORTNOSE GAR

duck blue *n* **:** INDIGO CARMINE 2

duckboard \'=,=\ *n* **:** a boardwalk or slatted flooring laid on a wet, muddy, or cold surface for the ease and safety of people crossing or standing on it — usu. used in pl. ⟨the ~*s* are down for students to cross the muddy green —Corey Ford⟩; see TRENCHBOARD

duckboat \'=,=\ *n* **:** a low-lying flat-bottomed boat used by duck hunters

duck bumps *n pl, dial* **:** GOOSE PIMPLES

duck call *n* **:** a device like a whistle for imitating the calls of ducks

duck disease *n* **:** DUCK SICKNESS

ducked *past of* DUCK

duck egg *or* **duck's egg** *n, Brit* **:** GOOSE EGG, ZERO ⟨an opening batsman ignominiously dismissed for a ~⟩

duck·er \'dəkə(r)\ *n* -s [2*duck* + *-er*] **:** one that scalds carcasses in a slaughterhouse

ducket *var of* DUCAT

duck fit *n* **:** FIT 4

1duckfoot \'=,=\ *n, pl* **duckfoots** *or* **duckfeet** *see numbered senses* [1*duck* + *foot*] **1** *pl duckfeet* **:** DUTCH FOOT **2** *pl duckfoots* **:** a gastropod mollusk (*Aporrhais occidentalis*) of offshore waters of the western No. Atlantic that has a long vertical aperture and a much-expanded somewhat triangular outer lip — called also *duck's-foot shell* **3 :** a triangular cultivator blade or shovel used as an attachment to a cultivator

2duckfoot \"\ *vt* -ED/-ING/-S **:** to till land with a duckfoot cultivator

1duckfooted \'=¦==\ *adj* **:** having the hind toe directed more or less forward — used of domestic fowls

2duckfooted \"\ *adv* **:** with feet pointed outward **:** FLAT-FOOTED

duck grass *n* **1 :** a submerged aquatic plant (*Potamogeton pectinatus*) with filamentous leaves and hard bony fruits that are relished by ducks **2 :** FOWL MEADOW GRASS

duck green *n* **:** a dark bluish green that is greener and duller than average teal green and greener and slightly stronger than invisible green (sense 2) — called also *bluegrass, pine tree, vagabond*

duck hawk *n* **1 :** the American falcon that is a variety of the peregrine falcon **2** *Brit* **:** MARSH HARRIER

duckie *var of* DUCKY

duckier *comparative of* DUCKY

duckies *pl of* DUCKY

duckiest *superlative of* DUCKY

1duck·ing \'dəkiŋ, -kēŋ\ *n* -s [1*duck* + *-ing*] **:** the sport of hunting wild ducks ⟨a good gun for ~⟩

2ducking \"\ *n* -s [4*duck* + *-ing*] **:** 4DUCK

ducking stool *n* [fr. pres. part. of 2*duck*] **:** a seat attached to the end of a plank overhanging a pond used as a means of punishment in the 15th to 18th centuries the culprit being tied to the seat and plunged into the water — compare CUCKING STOOL

duck-legged *US usu* '=¦legəd, *Brit usu* -gd\ *adj* **:** having short legs — used of a person or animal

duck·let \'dəklə̇t\ *n* -s **:** DUCKLING 1

duck·ling \-liŋ, -lēŋ\ *n* -s [ME *dokelynge,* fr. *doke,* duck + *-lynge, -ling*] **1 :** a young duck **2 :** a dark greenish blue that is bluer and duller than average teal and darker and slightly bluer and stronger than average teal blue

duck malaria *n* **:** a destructive febrile disease of wild and domestic ducks caused by a blood protozoan (*Leucocytozoon anatis*) that is transmitted by a blackfly of the genus *Simulium*

duckmole \'=,=\ *n* **:** PLATYPUS

duck moss *n* **:** DUCK GRASS 1

duck oak *n* **:** WATER OAK 1

duck on a rock *or* **duck on the rock** *also* **duck on drake :** a game in which each player has a stone that he places on a rock for other players to try to knock off before retrieving their own stones without getting tagged by the first player

duck pass *n* **:** an aerial path used by wild waterfowl usu. over a narrow strip of land between two lakes

duckpin \'=,=\ *n* [so called fr. its short squat appearance] **1 :** a small bowling pin shorter than a tenpin but proportionately wider at mid-diameter **2 duckpins** *pl but sing in constr* **:** a bowling game using duckpins and differing from tenpins in that a smaller ball is used and three balls per frame are bowled

duck potato *n* **:** WAPATOO

duck river baptist *n, cap D&R&B* [fr. *Duck river,* Tenn.] **:** a member of a Baptist body founded in Tennessee in 1807 holding Calvinistic doctrines and observing the practices of close communion and foot washing

ducks *pl of* DUCK, *pres 3d sing of* DUCK

ducks and drakes *also* **duck and drake** *n* **:** the pastime of skimming flat stones or shells along the surface of calm water — **play ducks and drakes with** *also* **make ducks and drakes of :** to throw away heedlessly **:** SQUANDER

duck's bill brachiopod *n* **:** an elongated more or less oblong dorsoventrally flattened inarticulate brachiopod (genus *Lingula*) somewhat resembling the bill of a duck

duck's egg *var of* DUCK EGG

duck's-foot \'=,=\ *n, pl* **ducks'-foots** *or* **ducks'-feet :** MAYAPPLE

duck's-foot shell *n* **:** DUCKFOOT

duck shot *n* **:** a medium-heavy lead shot used in duck hunting

duck sickness *n* **:** a highly destructive form of botulism affecting esp. wild ducks in areas of the western U.S. in which drought has caused decay of aquatic vegetation thereby permitting excessive multiplication of botulinus bacteria (*Clostridium botulinum* type C) and spreading of their characteristic toxin in feeding areas — compare LIMBERNECK

duck's-meat \'=,=\ *n, pl* **duck's-meats :** DUCKWEED

duck soup *n* **:** something requiring little effort **:** something easy to do and often remunerative

duck stamp *n* **:** the federal migratory-bird hunting stamp first issued in 1934 that is required on the hunting licenses of wildfowl hunters over 16 years of age and that is sold to raise funds for the protection of migratory birds (as by the purchase of sanctuary areas)

duckstone \'=,=\ *n* **:** DUCK ON A ROCK; *also* **:** the stone on which the duck is placed

ducktail \'=,=\ *n, often attrib* **:** a teen-age boy's haircut in which the sides are kept long and brushed to meet at the back of the head

duckwalk \'=,=\ *n* **:** DUCKBOARD

duck walk *vi* **:** to walk with a waddle or with turned-out toes; *specif* **:** to walk as a hazing stunt while grasping the ankles with the hands

duckweed \'=,=\ *n* [ME *dockewede,* fr. *docke,* duck + *wede,* weed] **:** any small floating aquatic plant of the family Lemnaceae; *esp* **:** a plant of the genus *Lemna*

duckweed family *n* **:** LEMNACEAE

duck wheat *n* **:** TARTARIAN BUCKWHEAT

duckwing \'=,=\ *n* **:** Modern Game fowl having wing coverts that form a bluish black bar across the wing

1ducky *also* **duck·ie** \'dəkē, -ki\ *n, pl* **duckies** [1*duck* + *-y, -ie*

(n. suffix)] **1 :** a young duck **2** *chiefly Brit* **:** PET, DARLING — usu. used as a term of address

[2]**ducky** \ "\ *adj* -ER/-EST [[1]*duck* + *-y* (adj. suffix)] **1 :** very satisfactory **:** FINE, PLEASANT ⟨everything is just ~ for you to do, but all wrong for everybody else —Mark Reed⟩ ⟨everybody has a ~ time at a cost of about $300 per camper —*Reader's Digest*⟩ **2 :** DARLING, CUTE ⟨a ~ little restaurant⟩

[1]**duct** \'dəkt\ *n* -S [L *ductus* act of leading, shape (of a letter), fr. past part. of *ducere* to lead — more at TOW] **1** *obs* **a :** action of leading **:** GUIDANCE **b :** DIRECTION **c :** PASSAGE **d :** a stroke of a letter **2** [NL *ductus*, fr. ML, aqueduct, fr. L] *anat* **:** a tube or vessel — used esp. of those that carry off the secretion of a gland but used also of lymphatic vessels, certain blood vessels, and other canals ⟨thoracic ~⟩ ⟨acoustic ~⟩ **3 a :** a pipe, tube, or channel by which a substance (as water, gas, air) is conveyed **b :** a usu. underground pipe or tubular runway for carrying an electric power line, telephone cables, or other conductors **4** *bot* **a :** a continuous tube formed by a row of elongated cells which have lost their intervening end walls — compare TRACHEA, VESSEL **b :** an elongated cavity formed by disintegration or separation of cells (as a resin canal of a conifer) **5 :** INK FOUNTAIN **6 :** an atmospheric condition which usu. obtains when warm dry air is resting on cool moist air and by which radio waves are confined to the neighborhood of the earth's surface with resulting abnormally long transmission ranges

[2]**duct** \ "\ *vt* -ED/-ING/-S **:** to convey (as a gas) through a duct

duc·tal \-tᵊl\ *adj* **:** of or belonging to a duct **:** made up of ducts

duct·ed \-təd\ *adj* [[1]*duct* + *-ed*] **:** situated or operating in a duct ⟨a ~ fan⟩ ⟨a ~ rocket⟩

duc·ti·ble \-təbəl\ *adj* [ME, fr. MF, fr. ML *ductibilis*, fr. L *ductus* (past part.) + *-ibilis* -ible] *archaic* **:** DUCTILE

duc·tile \'dəktᵊl *also* -,tīl *or* -(,)til\ *adj* [MF & L; MF, fr. L *ductilis*, fr. *ductus* (past part. of *ducere* to lead) + *-ilis* -ile — more at TOW] **1 :** capable of being fashioned into a new form **2 a :** capable of being permanently drawn out without breaking ⟨a ~ metal⟩; *specif* **:** capable of being drawn out into wire or thread — compare MALLEABLE **b :** capable of being molded or worked **:** PLIANT, FLEXIBLE **3 :** capable of being conveyed in channels — used of water **4 :** easily led or influenced **:** TRACTABLE, COMPLIANT ⟨a vast portion of the public feels rather than thinks, a ~ multitude drawn easily by the arts of the demagogue —Amy Loveman⟩ **syn** see PLASTIC

duc·tile·ly \-ᵊl(l)ē, -īll, -il(l)|, |i\ *adv* **:** in a ductile manner

duc·til·i·ty \,dək'tiləd·ē, -ətē, -i\ *n* -ES **:** the quality or state of being ductile

duct·ing \'dəktiŋ\ *n* -S [[1]*duct* + *-ing*] **:** a system of ducts; *also* **:** the material composing a duct

duct·less \'dəktləs\ *adj* **:** being without a duct

ductless gland *n* **:** ENDOCRINE GLAND

duct of bo·tal·lus \-bō'taləs\ *usu cap B* [trans. of NL *ductus Botalli*, fr. *Botallus* (Leonardo Botallo), 16th cent. Ital. physician] **:** DUCTUS ARTERIOSUS

duct of cu·vier \-'k(y)üvē,ā, -kūēvyā\ *usu cap C* [after Baron Georges *Cuvier* †1832 Fr. naturalist] **:** either of a pair of large transverse venous sinuses that conduct blood from the cardinal veins to the sinus venosus of the vertebrate embryo — called also *common cardinal vein*

duct of gaert·ner \-'gertnər\ *usu cap G* [after Hermann T. *Gärtner* †1827 Dan. anatomist] **:** the remains in the female mammal of a part of the wolffian duct of the embryo

duct of mül·ler \-'myüla(r), -'mil-,-'mūl-,-'məl-\ *usu cap M* [after Johannes P. *Müller* †1858 Ger. anatomist] **:** MÜLLERIAN DUCT

duct of ri·vi·nus \-rə'vēnəs\ *usu cap R* [after Augustus Q. *Rivinus* †1723 Ger. physiologist] **:** any of several small inconstant efferent ducts of the sublingual gland

duct of san·to·ri·ni \-,santə'rēnē, -,sän-\ *usu cap S* [after Giovanni D. *Santorini* †1737? Ital. anatomist] **:** an accessory pancreatic duct branching from the duct of Wirsung and opening into the duodenum above the main duct

duct of steno *usu cap S* [after Nicolaus *Steno* (Niels Stensen) †1687 Dan. anatomist] **:** STENO'S DUCT

duct of wharton *usu cap W* [after Thomas *Wharton* †1673 Eng. anatomist] **:** WHARTON'S DUCT

duct of wir·sung \-'virzüŋ, -rzəŋ\ *usu cap W* [after Johann G. *Wirsung* †1643 Ger. anatomist] **:** the chief duct of the pancreas conducting its secretions to the duodenum — compare DUCT OF SANTORINI

duc·tor \'dəktə(r)\ *n* -S [L *ductor* leader (fr. *ducere* to lead + *-or*) — more at TOW] **:** DROP ROLLER 2

ductor blade *n* **:** DOCTOR 6a

ducts *pl of* DUCT, *pres 3d sing of* DUCT

duc·tule \'dək,t(y)ül\ *n* -S [[1]*duct* + *-ule*] **:** a small duct

duc·tus \'dəktəs\ *n, pl* **ductus** [in sense 1, NL; in sense 2, fr. L — more at DUCT] **1 :** DUCT 2 **2 :** HANDWRITING **:** the general shape of manuscript letters ⟨a bold monumental ~ formed of straight lines and circles —H.A.R.Gibb⟩

ductus ar·te·ri·o·sus \-(,)är,tirē'ōsəs\ *n* [NL, arterial duct] **:** a short broad vessel connecting the pulmonary artery and descending aorta of the fetus — called also *duct of Botallus, ductus Botalli*

ductus cho·le·do·chus \-kə'ledəkəs\ *n* [NL, choledoch duct] **:** COMMON BILE DUCT

ductus de·fer·ens \-'defə,renz, -,rənz\ *n* [NL, deferent duct] **:** VAS DEFERENS

ductus ve·no·sus \-və'nōsəs, -vē'-\ *n* [NL, venous duct] **:** a vein passing through the liver and connecting the left umbilical vein with the inferior vena cava of the fetus, losing its circulatory function after birth, and persisting as one of the supporting ligaments of the liver

ductwork \'=,=\ *n* **:** a system of ducts (as in hot-air heating or air conditioning)

ducu·la \'dəkyələ, 'd(y)ük-\ *n, cap* [NL] **:** a genus of large coppery brown or black and white Asiatic pigeons — see NUTMEG PIGEON

[1]**dud** \'dəd\ *n* -S [ME *dudde*] **1 :** an article of clothing — now usu. used in pl. ⟨another thing you can scratch off the vacation budget is a heavy outlay for resort ~*s* —*Christian Science Monitor*⟩ **2 duds** *pl, slang* **:** personal belongings ⟨pack up yer ~*s* an' get off'n my land —Hamlin Garland⟩ **3 duds** *pl, chiefly dial* **:** ragged or cast-off clothes **:** RAGS, TATTERS **4 a :** person or thing that proves to be ineffective **:** a flat failure ⟨the convention . . . is turning out to be a ~ as far as business is concerned —Lucille Eddinger⟩ **5 :** an explosive-filled missile that fails to explode when it should

[2]**dud** \ "\ *adj* **:** of little or no worth **:** INEFFECTIVE, FAKE, BAD ⟨garage proprietor who issued ~ checks and then committed suicide —James Agate⟩

du·daim \'d(y)ü,dīm, =ˈ=\ *n* -S [Heb *dūdhā'īm* mandrake] **1 :** MANDRAKE **2** *also* **dudaim melon :** a melon (*Cucumis melo dudaim*) probably orig. of central Asia with small fragrant fruit grown chiefly for ornament

dud·die *or* **dud·dy** \'dədē\ *adj* [[1]*dud* (rag) + *-ie, -y*] *Scot* **:** RAGGED, TATTERED

dude \'d(y)üd\ *n* -S [origin unknown] **1 :** a man who is overfastidious in dress and manner **:** an ultrafashionable man **:** FOP, DANDY **2 a :** a city man **:** TENDERFOOT; *esp* **:** an easterner touring or staying in the West **b :** a guest at a dude ranch

du·deen *also* **du·dheen** *or* **doo·deen** *or* **doo·dheen** \(')dü¦dēn\ *n* -S [IrGael *dūidīn*, dim. of *dūd* pipe] **:** a short tobacco pipe made of clay

du·del·sack \'düdᵊl,sak, *G* -,zäk\ *n* -S [G — more at DOODLESACK] **:** a German bagpipe

dude ranch *n* **:** a ranch or resort for vacationers offering primarily horseback riding and other activities typical of western ranches

dude up *vi, slang* **:** to dress up ⟨he *duded up* for the dance⟩

dude wrangler *n* **:** one who runs a dude ranch

dudgen *adj* [origin unknown] *obs* **:** HOMELY, RUDE, COARSE

[1]**dud·geon** \'dəjən\ *n* -S [ME *dogeon, dugion*, fr. AF *digeon*] **1** *obs* **:** a wood perhaps boxwood used esp. for the handles of daggers **2** *archaic* **:** a dagger or other implement having a handle of dudgeon **3** *obs* **:** a haft made of dudgeon

[2]**dudgeon** \ "\ *n* -S [origin unknown] **:** aggrieved or angered feeling **:** ILL HUMOR, RESENTMENT — usu. used with *in* and a qualifier ⟨fuming, he stalked off in high ~⟩ **syn** see OFFENSE

dud·ine \(')d(y)ü¦dēn\ *n* -S [*dude* + *-ine*] **:** a female dude

dud·ish \'d(y)üdish\ *adj* [*dude* + *-ish*] **:** having the appearance of a dude **:** like a dude — **dud·ish·ly** *adv*

dud·ism \-ü,dizəm\ *n* -S [*dude* + *-ism*] **:** the quality or state of being a dude

dud·ley \'dədlē\ *adj, usu cap* [prob. fr. the name *Dudley*] *of a dog's nose* **:** having a flesh or pink color undesirable in some breeds

dud·ley·ite \-,īt\ *n* -S [*Dudley*ville, Ala. + E *-ite*] **:** a variety of vermiculite

[1]**due** \'d(y)ü\ *adj* [ME *dewe, due*, fr. MF *deu* (past part. of *devoir* to owe), fr. L *debitus*, past part. of *debēre* to owe — more at DEBT] **1 :** owed or owing as a debt **2** *obs* **:** owed or owing as a necessity **:** FATED, INEVITABLE **3 a :** owed or owing in accordance with natural or moral right ⟨every character gets the reward or the punishment ~ to his wit and address or his lack of both —J.W.Krutch⟩ ⟨such awe is ~ to the high name of God —P.B.Shelley⟩ **b :** requisite or appropriate in accordance with accepted notions of what is right, reasonable, fitting, or necessary ⟨representatives . . . who have exhibited their full powers found to be in good and ~ form —*Charter of the United Nations*⟩ ⟨will exercise this right with ~ respect to their obligations —Gilbert Seldes⟩ ⟨he has written with care and skill, with ~ regard for beauty and suitability of style —L.R.McColvin⟩ **4 a :** satisfying or capable of satisfying a need, requirement, obligation, or duty **:** ADEQUATE, SUFFICIENT ⟨education for adults is receiving ~ attention⟩ ⟨walking all the while in ~ fear of the Lord —Guy McCrone⟩ ⟨seafaring activities which in ~ course came to be so vital a part of English life —Kemp Malone⟩ **b :** REGULAR, LAWFUL ⟨indemnity for loss will be paid subject to ~ proof of loss⟩ — see DUE PROCESS OF LAW **5 :** owing or attributable **:** ASCRIBABLE — used with *to* ⟨this advance is partly ~ to a few men of genius —A.N.Whitehead⟩ ⟨his success was ~ to his persistence⟩; compare DUE TO **6 :** having reached the date at which payment is required **:** PAYABLE — used esp. of a note or obligation in which the time for payment is specified **7 :** required or expected in the prescribed, normal, or logical course of events **:** SCHEDULED ⟨tax legislation that Congress is ~ to consider⟩ ⟨the train is ~ at noon⟩ ⟨he is ~ for a promotion⟩; *specif* **:** about to bring forth young

syn RIGHTFUL, CONDIGN: DUE applies to what is owing or obligatory in accordance with legal agreements, formal procedure, or sanctioned ways or with what is just, right, or reasonable ⟨driving fast but with *due* caution⟩ ⟨tried according to *due* processes of law⟩ ⟨with *due* religious rites⟩ ⟨the parishes sent their *due* contingent of armed men —J.R.Green⟩ ⟨the characteristically Greek love of moderation, proportion, harmony, and *due* measure —Lucius Garvin⟩ ⟨so painful a scandal may well be allowed to die out. With *due* discretion the incident itself may, however, be described —A.C.Doyle⟩ RIGHTFUL applies to what is right, just, equitable, fair, or fitting; it is commonly used in situations in which these characteristics have been, or are in danger of being, ignored, lost sight of, or flouted ⟨looked askance, jealous of an encroacher on his *rightful* domain —Nathaniel Hawthorne⟩ ⟨the disloyal subject who had fought against his *rightful* sovereign —T.B.Macaulay⟩ ⟨happy the man at such a period, who enjoys a bedroom which he can secure with a key — for without such precaution the *rightful* possessor is not at all unlikely, on entering his own premises, to find three or four somewhat rough-looking strangers —Anthony Trollope⟩ ⟨years of neglect followed, but it finally acquired its *rightful* place among the nation's hallowed relics —*Amer. Guide Series: Pa.*⟩ CONDIGN indicates what is exactly or fitly deserving or meriting; it now applies more frequently to punishments than to anything else ⟨trembled with rage as he lay, and he resolved on *condign* revenge —Arthur Morrison⟩ ⟨to defy those papal laws which protected clerical sinners from *condign* punishment —G.G.Coulton⟩

[2]**due** \ "\ *n* -S [ME *dewe, due*, fr. *dewe, due* adj.] **1 a :** something that is due or owed **:** something that rightfully belongs to a person or thing ⟨was denied the promotion which his scientific colleagues thought his ~ —Anthony Harris⟩ ⟨those advanced in culture and in wealth longed to have their ~ in social recognition —Oscar Handlin⟩ ⟨the southern talent for government has won the recognition which is its ~ —Adlai Stevenson b. 1900⟩ **b :** a payment or obligation required by custom, law, morality, ethics **:** DEBT ⟨a vast personal revenue . . . from the feudal ~*s* of his vassals and towns —Hilaire Belloc⟩ **c dues** *pl* **:** the fee or charge required for membership, affiliation, initiation, use, subscription ⟨the membership ~*s* are five dollars a year⟩ **2** *obs* **:** just title or claim **:** RIGHT **3 :** POSTAGE-DUE STAMP

syn DESERT, MERIT: DUE in this sense is likely to suggest a quite apt or fitting reward decided upon judiciously and with consideration ⟨giving each man his *due* . . . impartial as the rain from Heaven's face —Vachel Lindsay⟩ ⟨this qualified respect, the old man's *due*, is paid without reluctance —William Wordsworth⟩ DESERT is likely to suggest a reward rightly owed in view of ethics, fairness, moral right ⟨the manly desire to exercise the talents which are given us by Heaven and reap the prize of our *desert* —W.M.Thackeray⟩ ⟨but families of less illustrious fame whose chief distinction is their spotless name must shine by their true *desert* —William Cowper⟩ MERIT stresses the existence of qualities or actions worth consideration in connection with rewards or punishments rather than the fact of their being considered or judged ⟨had this latter part of the charge been true, no *merits* on the side of the question which I took could possibly excuse me —Edmund Burke⟩ ⟨but originality, as it is one of the highest, is also one of the rarest, of *merits* —E.A.Poe⟩

[3]**due** \ "\ *adv* [[1]*due*] **1** *obs* **:** DULY **2 :** DIRECTLY, EXACTLY ⟨the road runs ~ north⟩

[4]**due** *vt* [ME *duen*, fr. MF *douer*, fr. L *dotare*, fr. *dot-, dos* dower — more at DOWER] *obs* **:** ENDUE **:** ENDOW

due bill *n* **1 :** a written acknowledgment of a debt not made payable to order used esp. to make payment in services rather than cash (as by hotels for advertising) **2 :** a bill for the balance due where the first bill was insufficient

due care *n* **:** the care that an ordinarily reasonable and prudent person exercises under all circumstances for his own protection

due cor·de \¦dü(,)ā'kȯr,dā\ [It, two strings] — used as a direction in music (1) to play the same tone on two strings (as of the violin) simultaneously or (2) to release the una corda or soft pedal of the piano; compare TRE CORDE

due date *n* **:** the date on which a debt becomes payable **:** the maturity date of a bill, note, bond, or other evidence of debt

dueful *adj* [[2]*due* + *-ful*] *obs* **:** FIT, BECOMING

[1]**du·el** \'d(y)üəl, -ü|əl *also* -ü|l, *chiefly Brit* |(,)il\ *n* -S [ML *duellum* (influenced in meaning by folk etymological association with L *duo* two), fr. L, war (poetical variant of *bellum*), fr. OL; perh. akin to Gk *daiein* to ignite, burn up — more at TWO, TEEN] **1 :** a combat between two persons: **a** *obs* **:** personal combat to determine a trial by battle **b :** a prearranged formal combat with deadly weapons fought between two persons in the presence of witnesses usu. as a result of an injury done or an insult given by one to the other — compare [2]PRINCIPAL, [2]SECOND **2 :** a conflict between persons, ideas, or forces that are antagonistic ⟨when the long-drawn-out ~ . . . ended in a war —W.J.Hail⟩ ⟨artillery ~⟩ ⟨propaganda ~⟩ ⟨a ~ between the two emotions of repugnance and duty —Hilaire Belloc⟩

[2]**duel** \ "\ *vb* **dueled** *or* **duelled; dueled** *or* **duelled; dueling** *or* **duelling; duels :** to fight in or as if in a duel

dueling *or* **duelling** *n* -S **:** the fighting of duels

dueling pistol *n* **:** a long-barreled pistol designed esp. for dueling and usu. made in pairs

du·el·ist *or* **du·el·list** \'d(y)üələst, -üə-\ *n* -S **:** one who engages in duels

du·el·is·tic *or* **du·el·lis·tic** \¦==¦listik\ *adj* **:** having reference to dueling or a duelist

du·el·lo \d(y)ü'e(,)lō\ *n* -S [It, fr. ML *duellum* — more at DUEL] **1 :** DUELING **2 :** the rules of dueling **3 :** DUEL

due·ness *n* -ES **:** the quality or state of being due

du·en·na \d(y)ü'enə\ *n* -S [Sp *dueña*, fr. L *domina* lady — more at DAME] **1 :** an elderly woman serving as governess and companion to the younger ladies in a Spanish or a Portuguese family **2 :** GOVERNESS, CHAPERON

due process of law *or* **due course of law :** a course of proceedings at law or carried out through agency rules or other devices that is in accordance with the law of the land — called also *due process*

dues *pl of* DUE, *pres 3d sing of* DUE

duesseldorf *usu cap, var of* DÜSSELDORF

due stamp *n* **:** POSTAGE-DUE STAMP

[1]**du·et** \(')d(y)ü¦et, *usu* -ed·+V\ *n* -S [It *duetto*, dim. of *duo* duet — more at DUO] **1 a :** a musical composition or movement for two singers or two instrumentalists with or without accompaniment **b :** a performance of such a composition **c :** two musicians performing such a composition **2 :** a dance by two people **:** PAS DE DEUX **3 :** an action participated in by two parties ⟨the birds which continue ~*s* of "mouth opening" and other dual rites and mutual displays —E.A.Armstrong⟩

[2]**duet** \ "\ *vi* **duetted; duetted; duetting; duets :** to perform a duet

due to *prep* **:** because of ⟨the number and influence of investors are increasing, *due to* several causes —*Mag. of Wall Street*⟩ ⟨when German power was at its peak, *due to* the unpreparedness of her neighbors —Joseph Rosenfarb⟩ ⟨the event was canceled *due to* inclement weather⟩ ⟨he failed *due to* faulty training⟩ — compare [1]DUE 5

du·et·tist \d(y)ü'ed·əst, -etə-\ *n* -S **:** a participant in a duet

du·et·to \dü'ed·(,)ō\ *n, pl* **duet·tos** \-d·,ōz\ *or* **duet·ti** \-d·(,)ē\ [It] **:** DUET

due vol·te \¦dü(,)ā'vōl,tā\ *adv* [It] **:** two times — used as a direction in music to repeat a passage

[1]**duff** \'dəf\ *n* -S [E dial. *duff*, var of [1]*dough*] **1 :** a stiff flour pudding usu. containing raisins and currants and boiled in a bag or steamed ⟨plum ~⟩ — compare PLUM PUDDING **2 :** the partly decayed organic matter on the forest floor ⟨scratchings of dirt and twigs and forest ~ —Verne Athanas⟩ — compare HUMUS, LITTER, MOR **3 :** fine coal **:** SLACK

[2]**duff** \ "\ *vt* -ED/-ING/-S [back-formation fr. *duffer*] **1** *slang* **a :** to treat or manipulate so as to give a specious appearance to **:** FAKE **b :** CHEAT **2** *Austral* **:** to alter the brand on (stolen cattle or horses) **:** steal and alter the brand on (cattle or horses) **3** *Brit* **:** to misplay (a golf ball) esp. by striking the ground back of the ball before the club strikes the ball

[3]**duff** \ "\ *n* -S [origin unknown] *slang* **:** BUTTOCKS

duffadar *var of* DAFADAR

duf·fel *or* **duf·fle** \'dəfəl\ *n* -S [D *duffel*, fr. *Duffel*, town near Antwerp, Belgium] **1 :** a coarse heavy woolen blanketing or overcoating with a thick nap **2** *usu duffle* **:** transportable personal belongings, equipment, and supplies ⟨a car that bulged with people, suitcases, and assorted *duffle* —F.L.Allen⟩ ⟨soldiers stowing *duffle* and rifles into hard canvas bunks —K.M.Dodson⟩

duffel bag *n* **:** a large cylindrical canvas or rubberized fabric bag for transporting personal belongings ⟨with tents, a camping outfit, and *duffel bags* —Van Wyck Brooks⟩

duf·fer \'dəfə(r)\ *n* -S [origin unknown] **1** *slang* **a :** a peddler or hawker esp. of cheap flashy articles (as sham jewelry) **b :** something counterfeit or worthless **2 a :** a stupid, dense, or stubbornly unreasonable person **b :** one that is incompetent or clumsy (as at a game or a trade) ⟨horsemen, both skilled and ~*s* —Gladwin Hill⟩ **c :** an elderly and ineffectual man ⟨he was quite used to having people set him down as a harmless, worn-out old ~ —Dorothy C. Fisher⟩ **3** *Austral* **:** a cattle rustler **4** *Austral* **:** SHICER

duffle coat *or* **duffel coat** *n* **:** a heavy woolen coat usu. knee-length and hooded worn for protection against cold and stormy weather

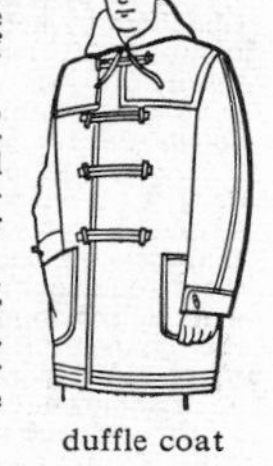
duffle coat

duf·fy antigen \'dəfē-\ *also* **duffy factor** *n, usu cap D* [after *Duffy*, the patient in whose blood it was first found] **:** an antigen of human red blood cells

du·fre·nite \d(y)ü'frā,nīt\ *n* -S [F *dufrénite*, fr. O.P.A. Petit-*Dufrénoy* †1857 Fr. mineralogist + F *-ite*] **:** a blackish green mineral $Fe_5(PO_4)_3(OH)_5.2H_2O$ consisting of hydrous iron phosphate commonly massive or in nodules

du·fre·noy·site \,d(y)üfrə'nȯi,zīt\ *n* -S [F *dufrénoysite*, irreg. fr. O.P.A. Petit-*Dufrénoy* + F *-ite*] **:** a lead-gray mineral $Pb_2As_2S_5$ consisting of a compound of lead arsenic sulfur occurring in orthorhombic crystals or massive

duf·ter \'dəftə(r)\ *var of* DAFTAR

dufterdar *var of* DAFTARDAR

duf·tery *or* **duf·try** \'dəft(ə)rē\ *n* -ES [Hindi *daftarī* record keeper, office keeper, fr. Per, fr. *daftar* book, record — more at DAFTAR] *India* **:** a servant in an office whose duty is to dust and bind records, rule paper, make envelopes **:** OFFICE BOY

duft·ite \'dəf,tīt\ *n* -S [G *duftit*, fr. G. *Duft*, 20th cent. director of mines at Tsumeb, South-West Africa + G *-it* -ite] **:** a mineral $PbCu(AsO_4)(OH)$ consisting of a basic arsenate of lead and copper

[1]**dug** \'dəg\ *past of* DIG

[2]**dug** \ "\ *n* -S [perh. of Scand origin; akin to OSw *dæggia* to suckle, Dan *dægge*; akin to Goth *daddjan* to suckle — more at FEMININE] **:** an udder or breast; *also* **:** a teat or nipple — usu. used of a suckling animal but vulgar when used of a woman

dug·dug \'dəg,dəg\ *n* -S [native name in Guam] **:** the fertile form of the breadfruit tree

du·ge·sia \d(y)ü'jēzh(ē)ə\ *n, cap* [NL, fr. Antoine-Louis *Dugès* †1838 Fr. physician and zoologist + NL *-ia*] **:** a genus of widespread No. American triclad flatworms including a common brown freshwater planarian (*D. tigrina*)

du·gong \'dü,gäŋ, -gȯŋ *also* 'dyü-\ *n* [NL modif. of Malay & Tag *duyong*] **1** *cap* **:** a monotypic genus (the type of a family Dugongidae) of aquatic herbivorous mammals that with the manatees constitute the order Sirenia, that are distinguished from the manatees by a bilobate tail resembling that of a whale, fewer molar teeth and less deeply cleft upper lip, and upper incisors which are altered into tusks in the male, and that commonly attain a length of 8 feet or more **2** *pl* **dugongs** *also* **dugong :** any mammal of the sole species (*Dugong dugon*) of the genus *Dugong* — called also *sea cow*

dugout \'=,=\ *n* -S **1 :** a canoe or boat made by hollowing out a large log **2 :** a shelter or primitive dwelling excavated in a hillside or dug in the ground and roofed with sod **:** ABRI; *specif* **:** a cave in the side of a trench for quarters, storage, or protection from gunfire **3 :** a low shelter facing the baseball diamond and containing the players' bench

dugway \'=,=\ *n* **1 :** a road constructed along a hillside by using for the fill on the downhill side material excavated immediately above it **2 :** an excavated road

dug well *n* **:** a well made by excavating with hand tools or power machinery instead of by drilling or driving

du·hat \'dü,hät\ *n* -S [Tag] *Philippines* **:** JAVA PLUM

dui·ker *also* **duy·ker** \'dīkə(r), 'dāk-\ *n, pl* **duikers** *also* **duiker** [Afrik *duiker* (formerly spelled *duyker*), lit., diver, fr. *duik* to dive (fr. MD *dūken*) + *-er* — more at DUCK] **1 :** any of several small African antelopes of *Cephalophus* and related genera having short straight horns and commonly regarded as forming a subfamily of the Bovidae — compare BLUE DUIKER **2** *Africa* **:** CORMORANT

dui·ker·bok \-(r),bäk\ *also* **dui·ker·buck** \-,bək\ *n, pl* **duikerbok** *or* **duikerboks** [Afrik, fr. *duiker* diver + *bok* male antelope; akin to OHG *boc* male goat — more at BUCK] **:** DUIKER 1

duis·burg-ham·born \¦düs,bərg'häm,bȯrn, -üz,-, -,bərg-, -,ham'bȯ(ə)rn, -häm-; *G* 'dūesbürkhäm'bȯrn *or* -ürk- *or* -'häm-,b-\ *adj, usu cap D&H* [fr. *Duisburg-Hamborn*, Germany] **:** of or from the city of Duisburg-Hamborn, Germany **:** of the kind or style prevalent in Duisburg-Hamborn

duit \'dȯit, 'dīt\ *n* -S [D — more at DOIT] **:** DOIT 1

du jour \də'zhü(ə)r, dü'-\ *adj* [F, of the day] **:** as cooked or prepared on a particular day ⟨potatoes *du jour*⟩ ⟨the soup *du jour* is onion⟩

du·kan *or* **du·chan** \dü'kän, -'k-, '=,=; 'dùkən\ *n* -S [Heb *dūkhān* platform] **1 :** the platform on which the priest of the Hebrew Temple stood to pronounce the benediction **2 :** PRIESTLY BLESSING

duk-duk \'dùk,dùk\ *n* -S [native name in New Britain] **1 :** a native secret society of islands of the Pacific ocean certain of whose members form a self-constituted judiciary and pose as sorcerers **2 :** a member of a duk-duk

duke \'d(y)ük\ *n* -S [ME *duc, duke*, fr. OF *duc*, fr. L *duc-, dux* leader, commander, fr. *ducere* to lead — more at TOW] **1** *obs* **:** LEADER, CHIEF **2 :** a sovereign prince or ruler of a duchy on the continent of Europe **3 a :** a nobleman of the highest hereditary rank in certain continental European countries **b** : a member of the first and highest grade of the peerage in Great Britain **4** *slang* **a** : FIST; *also* : HAND — usu. used in pl. **b** : the raised fist as a symbol of victory (as in a prizefight) ⟨the winner was given the ~ at the end of the fight⟩ **c** : a player's hand of cards **5** *also* **duke cherry** : any of several cultivated cherries that are intermediate in characteristics between sweet cherries and sour cherries and are usu. considered to have originated by hybridization of these — compare BIGARREAU CHERRY, HEART CHERRY

duke·dom \-kdəm\ *n* -s [ME *ducdom*, fr. *duc, duke* + *-dom*] **1** : the state or territory ruled by a duke or duchess : DUCHY **2** : the rank or dignity of a duke

duked up *adj* : dressed up ⟨chips . . . *duked up* with the master's initials or his whole name —*Mademoiselle*⟩

duke·ling \'d(y)üklįŋ\ *n* -s **1** *archaic* : the child of a duke **2** : a petty or insignificant duke

duke·ly \-lē\ *adj* : of or suitable to a duke

duke's coronet *n* : the coronet of a British or Irish duke having eight conventional strawberry leaves upon the rim of the circlet — compare DUCAL CORONET

duk·ey rider \'d(y)ükē,-, 'dùkē,-\ *n* [alter. of ²*dook* + *-ey* (var. of *-ie*)] : BRAKEMAN 1a(2)

dukhn \'dùkən\ *n* -s [Ar] *Sudan* : PEARL MILLET 1

dukhobor *usu cap, var of* DOUKHOBOR

du·ku \'dü(,)kü\ *n* -s [Malay] : a lanseh tree having nearly round dark-colored fruit

dukw *n* -s *sometimes cap* [fr. *DUKW*, its code designation] : ⁵DUCK

du·lat \'dü,lat\ *also* **du·lan** \-an\ *n* -s *usu cap* : one of the major divisions of the Great Horde

dul·bert \'dəlbə(r)t, 'dùl-\ *n* -s [prob. fr. ¹*dull* + *-bert* (fr. ¹*beard*)] *dial Brit* : BLOCKHEAD, DULLARD

dul·ca·ma·ra \,dəlkə'mărə, -ma(a)rə\ *n* -s [NL, fr. L *dulcis* sweet + *amara*, fem. sing. of *amarus* bitter — more at DULCET, AMARINE] **1** : BITTERSWEET 2a **2** : dried stems of dulcamara formerly used as a diuretic and sedative

¹**dulce** *adj* [L *dulcis*] *obs* : sweet to the taste : SOOTHING, AGREEABLE

²**dul·ce** \'dül(,)sā\ *n* -s [Sp, fr. *dulce*, adj., sweet, fr. L *dulcis*] **1** *Southwest* : SWEETMEAT, CANDY **2** : a sweet Spanish wine

³**dulce** *var of* DULSE

¹**dul·cet** \'dəlsət, *usu* -əd.+V\ *adj* [alter. (influenced by L *dulcis*) of ME *doucet*, fr. MF, fr. *douz* sweet (fr. L *dulcis*) + *-et* (dim. suffix); perh. akin to Gk *glykys* sweet] **1** *archaic* : sweet to the taste : LUSCIOUS **2** : sweet to the ear : MELODIOUS : agreeable, pleasant, or soothing to the eye, ear, or feelings **syn** see SWEET

²**dulcet** \"\ *n* -s : a pipe-organ stop like the dulciana but an octave higher

dul·cet·ly *adv* : in a dulcet manner

dulcian *var of* DOLCIAN

dul·ci·ana \,dəlsē'anə, -'änə\ *n* -s [NL, fr. ML, bassoon, fr. L *dulcis* + *-ana* (fem. sing. of *-anus* -an)] : a labial pipe-organ stop having metal pipes and a tone of soft sweet string quality of 8-foot pitch in the manual organ but 16-foot in the pedal organ

dul·ci·fy \'dəlsə,fī\ *vt* -ED/-ING/-ES [LL *dulcificare*, fr. L *dulcis* sweet + *-ficare* -fy — more at DULCET] : to make sweet or pleasant: as **a** : to free from saltness or acidity ⟨*dulcified* spirits of niter⟩ **b** : to make agreeable : MOLLIFY, APPEASE ⟨*dulcified* by her pipe of tobacco —Nathaniel Hawthorne⟩

dul·ci·mer \'dəlsəmə(r)\ *n* -s [alter. (influenced by L *dulcis* sweet) of ME *dowcemere*, fr. MF *doulcemer*, fr. OIt *dolcimelo*, fr. *dolce* sweet, fr. L *dulcis* — more at DULCET] **1** : a wire-stringed instrument of trapezoidal shape encompassing two to three octaves and played with light hammers held in the hands : CIMBALOM **2** : DULCIMORE

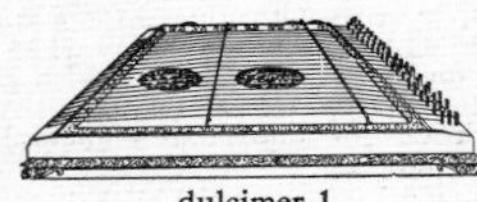
dulcimer 1

dul·ci·more \-,mō(ə)r\ *n* -s [alter. of *dulcimer*] : a folk instrument somewhat resembling the violin in shape and having two or three drone strings and a melody string which is plucked while sliding a cane along the string to alter pitch — compare ZITHER

Dul·cin \'dəlsən\ *trademark* — used for a sweet crystalline compound used as a sweetening agent

dul·ci·nea \,dəlsə'nēə, ,dəl'sinēə\ *n* -s [Sp. after *Dulcinea* del Toboso, the beloved of Don Quixote — more at DON QUIXOTE] : MISTRESS, SWEETHEART

dul·ci·tol \'dəlsə,tòl, -ōl\ *n* -s [obs. *dulcite* (fr. L *dulcis* sweet + E *-ite*) + *-ol* — more at DULCET] : a white faintly sweet crystalline hexahydric alcohol $HOCH_2(CHOH)_4CH_2OH$ occurring in various plants, obtained from a manna from Madagascar, and made from galactose by reduction

Dul·ci·tone \-tōn\ *trademark* — used for a keyboard instrument similar to the celesta in which hammers strike a set of tuning forks for sound production

dul·ci·tude \'dəlsə,tüd, -sə-,tyüd\ *n* -s [L *dulcitudo*, fr. *dulcis* + connective *-t-* + *-udo* -ude] *archaic* : SWEETNESS

dulcorate *vt* [L *dulcoratus*, fr. (assumed) *dulcor* sweetness (whence LL; fr. L *dulcis* + *-or*) + *-atus* -ate] *obs* : DULCIFY — **dulcoration** *n, obs*

dül·fer rappel \'dülfə(r)-, 'dùl\ *n, usu cap D* [after *Dülfer*, 20th cent. Ger. alpinist] : BODY RAPPEL

du·lia \d(y)ü'līə\ *n* -s [ML, fr. LGk *douleia* service, work done, business, fr. Gk, slavery, fr. *doulos* slave (prob. of non-IE origin) + *-eia* -y] *Roman Catholicism* : veneration or respect paid to the saints and angels as the servants and friends of God — compare LATRIA

¹**dull** \'dəl\ *adj* -ER/-EST [ME *dul, dulle;* akin to OE *dol* foolish, OHG *tol* foolish, ON *dul* concealment, conceit, Goth *dwals* foolish, OIr *dall* blind, Gk *tholeros* muddy, troubled, and prob. to L *fumus* smoke — more at FUME] **1** : mentally slow : somewhat lacking in intelligence : STUPID, DOLTISH, THICKHEADED ⟨although ~ at classical learning, at mathematics he was uncommonly quick —W.M.Thackeray⟩ ⟨be ~ and soulless, like a beast of the field — a brainless animal, with listless eye, unlighted by any ray of fancy, or of hope, or fear, or love, or life —J.K.Jerome⟩ **2 a** : slow or blunted in perception or sensibility : UNFEELING, INSENSIBLE ⟨she was worn out; so exhausted that she was ~ to what went on about her —Willa Cather⟩ **b** *dial Brit* : HARD-OF-HEARING **3** : lacking zest or vivacity : depressed in spirits : DISHEARTENED, LISTLESS, HOPELESS ⟨you must not fall back into any of your ~ moods —William Black⟩ ⟨~ apathy of despair —Oscar Wilde⟩ **4 a** : slow in action, motion, or response : SLUGGISH, INERT, LIFELESS, PONDEROUS ⟨the ~ heaviness in his heart —Agnes S. Turnbull⟩ ⟨his ~ brain⟩ **b** : marked by inactivity esp. in business ⟨talk of further curtailment by mills because of the ~ market in cotton goods —*Wall Street Jour.*⟩ ⟨lay off some of their staff in the ~ season —*Jour. of Accountancy*⟩ **5** : lacking sharpness of edge or point : BLUNT **6** : lacking brilliance or luster ⟨*dull*-finish aluminum⟩ : MUFFLED, MUTED : not clear : INDISTINCT, DIM : lacking in force or intensity ⟨the kerosene lamp gave a ~ light⟩ ⟨the ~ boom of the breaking waves —John Cooke⟩ ⟨~, rankling anger —Rudyard Kipling⟩ **7** *of a color* : low in saturation and low in lightness **8** *of the weather* : CLOUDY, OVERCAST, GLOOMY **9** *of paper or its finish* : smooth but relatively low in gloss **10** : furnishing little delight, spirit, or relative variety : TEDIOUS, UNINTERESTING ⟨eating ~ food and wearing shabby clothes —J.E.Evans⟩ ⟨I find the book long-winded, incredibly boring, heavy to the last degree, and deadly ~ —*John o' London's Weekly*⟩ ⟨a ~ speaker⟩

syn BLUNT, OBTUSE: DULL may refer to an edge or point that has lost its sharpness ⟨a *dull* knife⟩ It may apply to lack or loss of keenness, pungency, interest, poignancy, or intensity ⟨a *dull* pain⟩ ⟨a *dull* diet⟩ ⟨transferred from the *dull* pages of the textbook to the livelier writing of romance —T.C.Chubb⟩ ⟨compared with her, other women were heavy and *dull;* even the pretty ones seemed lifeless —Willa Cather⟩ BLUNT may refer to an edge or point not intended or designed to be sharp ⟨the *blunt* edge of a table knife⟩ BLUNT may indicate lack of keenness in perception, sensitivity, or discrimination ⟨*blunt* in perception and feeling and quite destitute of imagination —A.C.Bradley⟩ ⟨*blunt*, unemotional, completely lacking in subtlety, Mr. Strydom accepts and proclaims without question —James Gray⟩ OBTUSE may apply in technical or mathematical writing to an angle or convergence of more than 90 degrees. Otherwise OBTUSE suggests more-or-less stupid lack of perception or sensitivity ⟨carelessly egotistical as she was, she was not really *obtuse;* she had realized from the outset that she was being allowed to come on this expedition as a favor —Ann Bridge⟩ ⟨there was, one vaguely feels, something a little *obtuse* about Dr. Burney. The eager, kind, busy man, with his head full of music and his desk stuffed with notes, lacked discrimination —Virginia Woolf⟩ **syn** see in addition STUPID

²**dull** \"\ *vb* -ED/-ING/-S [ME *dullen*, fr. *dul, dulle*, adj.] *vt* : to make dull: **a** : to make less clear, distinct, or bright ⟨the painting's original warm colors have been greatly ~*ed* by age⟩ ⟨grime ~*ed* his brown skin—Audrey Barker⟩ **b** : to make less keen or acute : make less active or forceful : STUPEFY, DEVITALIZE ⟨fear ~*s* the sense of adventure —Mary E. Chase⟩ ⟨~*ed* by routine and sunk in apathy —John Dewey⟩ ⟨old age is ~*ing* my taste for books —O.W.Holmes †1935⟩ **c** : to deprive of sharpness (as of edge or point) : BLUNT ⟨~*ed* somewhat the cutting edge of popular resentment —Cabell Phillips⟩ ⟨believes tighter credit has done its job and ~*ed* the inflation threat —*Newsweek*⟩ **d** : to lessen the sensitivity of (as the physical senses) ⟨eyes and ears ~*ed* by age⟩ **e** : to reduce the luster of (as rayon) : DELUSTER, BLIND ~ *vi* : to be or become dull

¹**dul·lard** \'dələ(r)d\ *n* -s [MF *dullarde*, fr. *dul, dulle* + *-arde* -ard] : a stupid person

²**dullard** \"\ *adj* : characterized by dullness or insensitivity

dull emitter *n* : an electron tube in which the cathode is a filament which does not glow brightly

¹**duller** *comparative of* DULL

²**dull·er** \'dələ(r)\ *n* -s [²*dull* + *-er*] : one that produces a dull or clouded effect on furniture by a mildly abrasive rubbing of or action on the finish

dullest *superlative of* DULL

dull gold *n* : a light olive color that is redder and deeper than citrine or grape green and redder and slightly darker than old moss green

dullhead \'=,=\ *n* : BLOCKHEAD, DULLARD

dull·ish \'dəlish, -lēsh\ *adj* [ME *dullisshe*, fr. *dul, dulle* + *-isshe* -ish] : somewhat dull

dull·ness *or* **dul·ness** *n* -ES [ME *dulnesse*, fr. *dul, dulle* + *-nesse* -ness] **1** : the quality or state of being dull : STUPIDITY, APATHY, DROWSINESS, BLUNTNESS : a lack of luster, vividness, or brightness : MONOTONY ⟨the village street is well shaded by elms, with flower beds brightening the general ~ —*Amer. Guide Series: Vt.*⟩ ⟨exports . . . underwent a quick recovery after the seasonal ~ of the summer months —*Paper Trade Jour.*⟩ ⟨the men were getting freshened up from the day's monotonies and ~*es* —Mark Twain⟩ **2** : something that is dull ⟨checkbooks and columns of figures and rent bills and grocer's bills and light bills and telephone bills and other awful ~*es* —J.L.Street †1947⟩

¹**dull-normal** \'=ˈ==\ *adj* : having an intelligence level on the borderline between normal intelligence and mental deficiency

²**dull-normal** \"\ *n* [¹*dull-normal*] : one who is dull-normal

dul·ly \'dəl(l)ē, -lī\ *adv* : in a dull manner : STUPIDLY, SLOWLY, DIMLY, SLUGGISHLY : without life or spirit

du·long and pe·tit's law \,d(y)ü,lòŋənpə'tēz-, d(y)ü¦lȯ¦\ *n, usu cap D&P* [after Pierre L. *Dulong* †1838 and Alexis T. *Petit* †1820 Fr. physicists] : a law in physics and chemistry: the atomic heats of most solid elements are nearly the same averaging a little over 6 calories per degree C per gram atom

du·lo·sis \d(y)ü'lōsəs\ *n, pl* **dulo·ses** \-ō,sēz\ [NL, fr. Gk *doulōsis* slavery, fr. *douloun* to enslave (fr. *doulos* slave) + *-sis* — more at DULIA] : enslavement by an insect (as some ants of the genera *Formica* and *Polyergus*) that captures and rears the larvae or pupae of another species — **du·lot·ic** \(')d(y)ü¦läd·ik\ *adj*

dulse *also* **dulce** \'dəls *also* -lts\ *n* -s [ScGael & IrGael *duileasg;* akin to W *delysg* dulse] : any of several coarse red seaweeds (esp. *Rhodymenia palmata*) found principally in northern latitudes and used as a food condiment

dult \'dəlt\ *or* **dult·ie** \-tē\ *n* -s [*dult* alter. of *dolt; dultie* fr. *dult* + *-ie*] *Scot* : DOLT, DUNCE

du·luth \də'lüth\ *adj, usu cap* [fr. *Duluth*, Minn.] : of or from the city of Duluth, Minnesota : of the kind or style prevalent in Duluth : DULUTHIAN

¹**du·luth·ian** \-thēən\ *adj, usu cap* [*Duluth*, Minn. + E *-ian*] **1** : of, relating to, or characteristic of Duluth, Minnesota **2** : of, relating to, or characteristic of the people of Duluth

²**duluthian** \"\ *n* -s *cap* : a native or resident of Duluth

du·ly \'d(y)ülē, -li\ *adv* [ME *dueliche, duly*, fr. *dewe, due* + *-liche, -ly* — more at DUE] : in a due manner, time, or degree : as is right and fitting : PROPERLY, REGULARLY, SUFFICIENTLY ⟨any infringements must be clearly recognized and their authors ~ punished —J.S.Pictet⟩ ⟨~ authorized representatives⟩ ⟨all pertinent factors should be ~ considered⟩

dulzian *var of* DOLCIAN

dum *or* **dumb** \'dəm\ *adj (or adv)* [euphemism] : DAMN

du·ma *also* **dou·ma** \'dümə, -,mä\ *n* -s [Russ *duma*, of Gmc origin; akin to Goth *doms* judgment — more at DOOM] **1** : an elective council in Russia ⟨Catherine II introduced elective municipal ~*s* —F.A.Ogg & Harold Zink⟩ **2** *often cap* : a legislative assembly functioning primarily as a council of state in czarist Russia ⟨an unsatisfactory bill was presented by the government for the consideration of the Third *Duma* —Valentine Ughet & Eleanor Davis⟩

du·ma·gat \'dümə,gät\ *n, pl* **dumagat** *or* **dumagats** *usu cap* [Tag, fr. *dagat* sea] **1** : any of several Negroid pagan peoples inhabiting the eastern coast of central Luzon, Philippines **2** : a member of any of the Dumagat peoples

¹**dumb** \'dəm\ *adj* -ER/-EST [ME, fr. OE; akin to OHG *tumb* mute, inexperienced, stupid, ON *dumbr* mute, Goth *dumbs* mute, OE *dēaf* deaf — more at DEAF] **1** : destitute of the power of speech ⟨he must have been ~, for never a word did he utter —Herman Melville⟩ **2 a** : by nature incapable of speech like that of human beings ⟨~ animals⟩ **b** *of an animal* : having no capacity to make sounds : MUTE **c** : having no voice — used of inanimate things ⟨the great ~ trees —Anton Vogt⟩ **3** : temporarily unable to speak (as from astonishment, grief, shock) ⟨one pictures newspaper reporters going about, struck ~ with amazement at every smallest incident in this amazing life we lead —Rose Macaulay⟩ **4** : not expressed in uttered words : not communicated verbally : incapable of being expressed or communicated verbally — used of feelings, emotions, ideas ⟨how terrible is that ~ grief which has never learned to moan —John Galsworthy⟩ ⟨let the world wail! . . . my sorrow shall be ~! —Edna S. V. Millay⟩ ⟨the expression of loss and loneliness and ~ desire on his face —Irwin Shaw⟩ **5** : SILENT, QUIET: as **a** : saying little or nothing usu. through lack of desire to speak : TACITURN, UNCOMMUNICATIVE ⟨if they had nothing to say, they were capable of sitting for hours, ~ and unabashed, over their pipes or their plugs of tobacco —Ellen Glasgow⟩ ⟨I beg that you remain ~, that you write no more poems —Amy Lowell⟩ **b** : not having the usual accompaniment of speech or sound ⟨with frantic ~ play Anton signaled to Vincent —Basil Thomson⟩ ⟨legend and tradition demand that bells be ~ until they are blessed —P.D.Peery⟩ **6** : having little or no meaning : INEXPRESSIVE ⟨his work is infantile, ~ with botched detail, wooden scenes, and collapsed characterizations —J.S.Shrike⟩ **7** : lacking some usual attribute or concomitant; *esp, of a boat* : having no means of self-propulsion ⟨~ barge⟩ ⟨~ lighter⟩ **8** [influenced in meaning by D *dom* stupid, G & PaG *dumm*] : STUPID, FOOLISH: **a** *of a person* : lacking perception or understanding : UNRESPONSIVE ⟨too ~ to do things in the right way —W.J.Reilly⟩ ⟨blind to Galileo on his turret, ~ to Homer, ~ to Keats —Robert Browning⟩ **b** *of an action or thing* : resulting from or characterized by stupidity ⟨must learn to disregard the ~ advice . . . of relatives and friends —R.V.Seliger⟩ ⟨bad weather, youthful recklessness, carelessness, and plain ~ flying —*Time*⟩

syn MUTE, SPEECHLESS, INARTICULATE: DUMB and MUTE are often interchangeable, but some differences may be noted. In reference to animals, MUTE implies an inability to make sounds, DUMB an incapacity for speech ⟨must I live all my life as *mute* as a mackerel? —L.P.Smith⟩ ⟨yon *dumb* patient camel —Robert Browning⟩ In reference to persons, DUMB may imply some physical defect, MUTE an insensibility to speech brought about through deafness ⟨the other was a wretch from infancy made *dumb* by poison —P.B.Shelley⟩ ⟨like the *mute* dwarfs which wait upon a naked Indian queen —Robert Browning⟩ In reference to persons normally able to speak, DUMB may suggest a quite short deprivation of ability to utter sounds ⟨I was bewildered and *dumb* until Livilla gave me a good pinching, at which I burst into tears —Robert Graves⟩ ⟨he made despairing gestures with his hands, but still no words came from his mouth. He might have been struck *dumb* —W.S. Maugham⟩ MUTE may be used when an inner compulsion to stay silent is suggested ⟨but every man was *mute* for reverence —Alfred Tennyson⟩ ⟨as the conversation took fire, she hadn't so much as a chip to throw in. She sat *mute* —Sinclair Lewis⟩ SPEECHLESS, although it often has the same suggestions of DUMB or MUTE, commonly indicates momentary loss of power to speak ⟨overcome with *speechless* gratitude —William Wordsworth⟩ ⟨I can remember, across the years, standing there with that paper in my hand; dumb, *speechless* and probably tearful —W.A.White⟩ INARTICULATE implies either lack of satisfactory speech functions or an inability to speak coherently, clearly, or purposefully ⟨his jaws opened, and he muttered some *inarticulate* sounds —Mary W. Shelley⟩ ⟨but when Richard, *inarticulate* at first, in his haste, cried out: "My dear, dear father!" —George Meredith⟩ ⟨his rage was a madness. His lips were flecked with a soapy froth, and sometimes he choked and became *inarticulate* —Jack London⟩ ⟨as shyly *inarticulate* as a schoolgirl on this theme so vital to her —Rose Macaulay⟩ **syn** see in addition STUPID

²**dumb** \"\ *vb* -ED/-ING/-S *vi* : to become dumb or silent — used with *up* ~ *vt* : to make silent : DEADEN ⟨the sight of the great assembly that ~*ed* the words in his mouth —Donn Byrne⟩ ⟨would lie around, ~*ed* by the drugs —Norman Mailer⟩

dum·ba \'dəmbə, 'düm-\ *n* -s [Per, fr. *dumb* tail; akin to OHG *zumpho* penis, Ar *duma-* tail, OE *tæppa* tap — more at TAP] : a fat-tailed sheep of Bokhara and the Kirghiz steppe that furnishes astrakhan

dumb act *n* : an act (as in vaudeville) without dialogue

dumb ague *n* : malarial fever with no well-defined chill and with slight periodicity

dumbartonshire *or* **dumbarton** *usu cap, var of* DUNBARTONSHIRE

dumb barter *also* **dumb commerce** *n* : a primitive system of barter in which the parties avoiding personal contact leave goods at accepted locations in return for others

dumbbell \'=,=\ *n* **1** : an apparatus similar to that formerly used in ringing a church bell that is used in learning bell ringing or for bodily exercise **2** : a weight (as of wood or metal) that consists of two identical spheres connected by a short bar serving as a handle and that is used usu. in pairs for calisthenic exercise **3** : something shaped like a calisthenic dumbbell **4** : one that is dull and stupid : DUMMY ⟨if we don't give him a shove the poor ~ never will propose —Sinclair Lewis⟩ ⟨every time I opened the chicken-house door . . . the ~*s* would fly up in the air —Betty MacDonald⟩

dumbbell 2

dumbbell tenement *n* [so called fr. its resemblance in shape to a dumbbell] : a tenement building formerly common in New York City and having a long narrow plan characterized by two narrow air wells at each side

dumb bet·ty \-'bed·|ē, -et|, |i\ *n* [fr. the name *Betty*] *n* : a primitive mechanical household contrivance (as a washing machine or dumbwaiter) used to lighten the work of early American housewives

dumb bid *n* : the owner's undisclosed limit below which no bid shall avail as a purchase in an auction

dumb-bird \'=,=\ *n* : RUDDY DUCK

dumb cane *n* : a tropical American herb (*Dieffenbachia seguine*) that when chewed causes the tongue to swell — called also *mother-in-law plant*

dumb cluck *or* **dumb bunny** *n, slang* : DUMBBELL 4

dumb compass *n* [so called fr. its having no magnets or directive force] : PELORUS

dumb crambo *n* : a game in which one team chooses a word to be guessed and gives a rhyming word as a clue to the other team which then pantomimes its guess as to the original word

dumb do·ra \¦=ˈdōrə\ *n, usu cap 2d D* [fr. the name *Dora*] : a stupid and often naïve woman

dum be·ne se ges·se·rit \(,)dùm¦benē,sā'gesərət\ *adv* [L, while he behaved well] : during his good behavior — used of an appointment that is not for a period of time or at the pleasure of the appointer but that ends only at the appointee's death or misconduct

dumber *comparative of* DUMB

dumbest *superlative of* DUMB

dumbfish \'=,=\ *n* : DUNFISH

dumb·found *or* **dum·found** \¦dəm¦faùnd\ *vt* -ED/-ING/-S [¹*dumb* + *-found* (as in *confound*)] : to strike dumb : confuse with astonishment : AMAZE ⟨she was ~*ed* by the rebuke⟩ **syn** see PUZZLE

dumbfounded *or* **dumfounded** *adj* : CONFUSED, BEWILDERED, AMAZED — **dumb·found·ed·ly** *adv*

dumb·found·er *or* **dum·found·er** \-də(r)\ *vt* : DUMBFOUND ⟨she takes possession of it and by her action ~*s* and antagonizes the family and the countryside —*Spectator*⟩

dumbhead \'=,=\ *n, slang* : BLOCKHEAD

dumb iron *n* **1** : a caulking iron used to open up and straighten close seams prior to caulking esp. in new work **2** : a rigid connecting piece between the frame of an automotive vehicle and the spring shackle

dumb jockey *n* : a contrivance for bitting and training colts that consists of a saddle to the lower part of which sidechecks are fastened and two arms with elastic ends extending upward to which adjustable reins and crupper strap are fastened

dum·ble \'dəm(b)əl, 'düm-\ *var of* DIMBLE

dum·ble·dor *also* **dum·ble·dore** \'dəmbəl,dō(ə)r, -ó(ə)r\ *n* -s [*dumble* + *dor*] **1** *dial* : BUMBLEBEE **2** *dial* : COCKCHAFER

dumb·ly \'dəmlē, -li\ *adv* : in a dumb manner : VAGUELY

dumb·ness *n* -ES [ME *dumbnesse*, fr. *dumb* + *-nesse* -ness] **1** : the quality or state of being dumb : MUTENESS, SILENCE : inability to speak **2** : STUPIDITY, DULLNESS

dumb piano *n* : a portable keyboard for soundless piano practice and finger exercising

dumb rabies *n* : rabies marked by sluggishness and by early paralysis esp. of the muscles of jaw and throat — compare FURIOUS RABIES

dumbs *pres 3d sing of* DUMB

dumb sheave *n* : a block with a sheaveless hole or a groove in a spar for a rope to be rove through

dumb show *n* **1** : a part of a dramatic representation presented by actions unaccompanied by speech **2** : a presentation that communicates solely by signs and gestures : PANTOMIME ⟨the art of conveying a story by *dumb show* —W.P.Frith⟩ ⟨in fables that might be acted by puppets or in a *dumb show* and yet be tragical —W.P.Ker⟩

dumb struck *also* **dumb stricken** *adj* : struck dumb : made silent by astonishment : surprised and confused

dumbwaiter \'=ˈ==\ *n* **1** : a portable serving table or stand often with revolving shelves arranged in tiers **2** : a small elevator used for conveying food and dishes or small goods from one story of a building to another

dumb watches *n pl* [so called fr. the disk-shaped style] : PITCHER PLANT a

dum cas·ta \dùm'kästə\ *adv* [L] : while chaste — used as a proviso in limiting a bequest or devise to a widow or in conditioning the payment of alimony

dum·dum \'dəm,dəm\ *n* -s [fr. *Dum-Dum*, town near Calcutta, India, where dumdum bullets were once made] : a soft-nosed bullet or a standard bullet with vertical cuts made in its point so that it expands upon hitting an object

dumdum fever *n* [fr. *Dum-Dum*, India, where it was once prevalent] : KALA AZAR

dumbwaiter 1

dum·fries·shire \,dəm'frēs(h),shi(ə)r, -(h)shər *also* də-\ *or* **dum·fries** \-ēs\ *adj, usu cap* [fr. *Dumfriesshire* or *Dumfries* county, Scotland] : of or from the county of Dumfries, Scotland : of the kind or style prevalent in Dumfries

dum fu·it in·fra ae·ta·tem \dům'fü̇ət·ˌinfrə,ī'tād·əm\ *adv* [L, while he was under age] **:** while under age — used of an old writ for enabling a man after coming of age to recover lands he alienated while an infant
dum·ka \'dümkə, -üm-\ *n, pl* **dum·ky** \-kē\ [Czech, elegy, of Gmc origin; akin to Goth *dōms* judgment — more at DOOM] *music* **:** a slow movement of melancholy character
dum·mel \'dəməl, 'dům-\ *adj* [prob. fr. ¹*dumb* + *-el* (var. of *-le*)] **:** slow and stupid
dum·mi·ness \'dəmēnəs, -min-\ *n* -ES **:** the condition of being a dummy — used esp. of a horse
dumm·kopf \'dům,kȯf *also* 'dəm- *or* -ȯpf\ *n* -S [G, fr. *dumm* stupid (fr. OHG *tumb* mute, inexperienced, stupid) + *kopf* head, fr. OHG, drinking vessel — more at DUMB, CUP] *slang* **:** BLOCKHEAD
1dum·my \'dəmē, -mi\ *n* -ES [¹*dumb* + *-y*] **1 :** one that is dumb: as **a :** one that is incapable of speaking **b :** one that is habitually silent **c :** one that is stupid **:** DOLT, DUMBBELL **2 a :** the exposed hand in bridge played by declarer in addition to his own hand **b :** a player in bridge who lays his cards face up on the table to be so played by declarer **3 :** an imitation, copy, or likeness of something intended for use as a substitute **:** EFFIGY: as **a** (1) **:** a form representing part or all of the human figure used for displaying or fitting clothes — compare LAY FIGURE (2) **:** a stuffed figure representing the trunk and legs of a man and supported by a rope or frame that is used by football players for practice in tackling and blocking (3) **:** a large puppet usu. having movable head, jaws, and arms and held on the knees of a ventriloquist entertainer **b :** a sham package or one that does not contain what its exterior indicates; *esp* **:** an empty package used for display **c** *chiefly Brit* **:** a false nipple **:** PACIFIER **4 :** one (as a person, body of people, corporation) that although seeming to act for itself is in reality acting for another usu. with little or no freedom of action or with fraudulent intent ⟨the directors, being controlled by one man, are only *dummies*⟩ ⟨if a woman appears as the owner of a business, it should be ascertained that she is not a ~ for the real owner . . . who for legal or other reasons may not be able to hold property —A.F.Chapin⟩ **5 a :** a block (as of wood) put on a library shelf to replace a missing book and marked with title, call number, and indication of the book's whereabouts **b :** a card in a file or catalog indicating location of material filed elsewhere or temporarily missing from the file **6 :** something usu. mechanically operated that serves to replace or aid a human being in the performance of a task: as **a :** DUMBWAITER **b :** a glassblower's device operated by foot pedals for wetting, raising, opening, and shutting a paste mold **c :** a device having lights on four sides placed at a street intersection to control traffic **7 :** one that plays a part (as in a play) intended merely to fill in (as in a group or scene) or fulfill an expectation and having no essential significance **8 :** a piece that serves as a model in a profiling machine **9 :** DRIFT PLUG **10 a :** a pattern volume (as of a book, magazine, or newspaper) projected or in process with blank pages or pasted-in examples of type or illustrative material **b :** LAYOUT **11 a :** an early comparatively quiet locomotive made with condensing engines and no blast pipe and sometimes used in city transit service **b :** a switching locomotive having the boiler and running gear entirely housed **12 :** a horse lacking the ability to respond to ordinary stimuli because of cerebral damage esp. following encephalomyelitis
2dummy \"\ *adj* **1 :** marked by sham or deception: as **a :** having the appearance of being real but lacking capacity to function **:** ARTIFICIAL ⟨~ foods in the shop windows —*Times Lit. Supp.*⟩ ⟨~ hinges⟩ **b :** existing in name only **:** FICTITIOUS ⟨a specialist in secretly buying up the stock of companies under ~ names —*Newsweek*⟩ ⟨pack the ballot with ~ candidates to split the vote —*New Republic*⟩ **2 :** having the appearance of acting independently or for oneself while really acting at the instruction of another ⟨issued patents for sixty thousand acres to ~ holders, who deeded the land to him after he had retired from office —V.L.Parrington⟩
3dummy \"\ *vb* -ED/-ING/-ES *vt* **1** *Austral* **:** to take up (land) for another in one's own name **2 :** to make a dummy of (as a book or page of a publication) ⟨the book was *dummied* and ready to go to press⟩ — often used with *up* ⟨the editor is now *~ing* up the editorial page⟩ ~ *vi* **1** *Austral* **:** to dummy land **2** *slang* **:** to refuse to talk — used with *up* ⟨when I mentioned his name they *dummied* up⟩
dummy duck *n* **:** RUDDY DUCK
dummy index *n* **:** UMBRAL SYMBOL
dum·my·ism \-,izəm\ *n* -S *Austral* **:** the act or practice of dummying land
dummy share *or* **dummy stock** *n* **:** a share or stock issued to a person to qualify him for election or for a vote
dummy whist *n* **:** whist played by three players with a fourth hand that is dealt opposite the dealer, turned face up before play begins, and managed by the dealer
du·mont·ite \'d(y)ü,mänt,īt, ⸗'⸗,⸗\ *n* -S [F *dumontite*, fr. André *Dumont* †1857 Belgian geologist + F *-ite*] **:** a hydrated phosphate $Pb_2(UO_2)_3(PO_4)_2(OH)_4.3H_2O$ of uranium and lead occurring in yellow orthorhombic crystals
du·mont's blue \'d(y)ü,män(t)s-, ⸗'⸗-\ *n, often cap D* [fr. the name *Dumont*] **:** SMALT 2
du·mor·ti·er·ite \d(y)ü'mȯrd·ēə,rīt, ,d(y)ü(,)mȯr'ti,rīt\ *n* -S [F *dumortiérite*, fr. Eugène *Dumortier*, 19th cent. Fr. paleontologist + F *-ite*] **:** a bright blue or greenish blue mineral perhaps $Al_8BSi_3O_{19}OH$ consisting of basic aluminum borosilicate
1dump \'dəmp\ *n* -S [prob. fr. D *domp* exhalation, haze, fr. MD *damp*, *domp* — more at DAMP] **1** *obs* **:** a state of reverie or perplexity **2 :** a dull gloomy state of mind **:** low spirits **:** DESPONDENCY — now used in the pl. chiefly in the phrase *in the dumps* ⟨doleful *~s* the mind oppress —Shak.⟩ ⟨she will be there to cuddle him, praise him, help him out of his occasional *~s* —H.A.Overstreet⟩ ⟨she gets easily discouraged and down in the *~s*⟩ **3** *obs* **a :** a slow mournful melody or song **b :** a dance to such music **syn** see SADNESS
2dump \"\ *vb* -ED/-ING/-S *vi* **1** *obs* **:** MUSE **2** *obs* **:** to be downcast and sad ~ *vt, obs* **:** to cast into melancholy **:** GRIEVE, SADDEN
3dump \"\ *n* -S [perh. back-formation fr. *dumpling*] **1** *dial Brit* **:** something thick, ill-shaped, or shapeless ⟨*~s* of soft paper . . . to arrest bleeding —B.H.Chamberlain⟩; *specif* **:** a small leaden counter used in such games as chuck-farthing **2 a :** a coin that is small and very thick **b :** a small Australian silver coin bearing the words *fifteen pence* made from a piece cut from the center of a holey dollar **3** *archaic* **:** a short stout person
4dump \"\ *vb* -ED/-ING/-S [perh. fr. D *dompen* to immerse, tumble, topple; akin to MLG *dumpeln* to duck, OHG *tumpfilo* whirlpool, OE *dyppan* to dip — more at DIP] *vt* **1 a :** to let fall in a heap or mass **:** cast down or away ⟨had proceeded to the wharf and had *~ed* the first shipload of tea into the harbor —C.G.Bowers⟩ ⟨she *~ed* the contents of her purse onto the table⟩ ⟨uncork the bottle and ~ the stuff out —D.B. Chidsey⟩ ⟨a hydraulic hoist to tip the truck body and ~ the coal out⟩ ⟨the conveyor *~ed* the dirt into self-discharging barges —N.M.Clark⟩ **b :** to get rid of unceremoniously (as if by dumping) **:** dispose of somewhat irresponsibly **:** JETTISON ⟨France *~ed* her third government in a few months⟩ ⟨captains of industry speedily *~ed* labor from their payrolls, and the breadlines grew —Stringfellow Barr⟩ ⟨the indenture system offered huge profits to the masters of the vessels which *~ed* their human cargo on American shores —A.D.Graeff⟩ ⟨the biggest problem that was ever *~ed* into his lap⟩ **2** *slang* **:** to hit hard **:** knock down **:** BEAT ⟨*~ed* their attackers, who scrambled to their feet and fled⟩ **3** *Austral* **:** to compress and secure (wool) into bales **4 :** to sell (commodities or securities) in quantity at a very low price; *specif* **:** to sell (surplus goods) abroad at less than the market price at home ⟨some factory owners fear that the military will ~ surplus goods on the market at cut-rate prices —*N.Y.Times*⟩ ⟨the union complained that foreign residual oil, *~ed* into this country with low import taxes, had displaced more than 30 million tons of coal production —*Wall Street Jour.*⟩ **5 :** to transfer (typeset matter) from stick to galley or galley to form or (as slugs) to bank; *often* **:** to lay aside (dead matter) for distribution ~ *vi* **1 :** to fall abruptly **:** PLUNGE, DROP **2 :** to dump goods or refuse ⟨no *~ing* allowed⟩
5dump \"\ *n* -S *often attrib* **1 a :** an accumulation of refuse or other discarded materials ⟨the city ~ caught fire⟩ ⟨is now a resort town, but its former greatness shows in the tremendous *~s* and the sprawling buildings of the Argo mine —G.R. Stewart⟩ **b :** a place where such materials are dumped **2 a :** a quantity of supplies or reserve materials accumulated at one conveniently located but safe place ⟨we have laid out *~s* of food and petrol across the polar plateau —Edmund Hillary⟩ **b :** the place where such materials are stored: as (1) **:** a place for the temporary storage of military supplies in the field ⟨ammunition ~⟩ (2) **:** the place in a composing room where dead matter is placed before it is distributed **3 :** a disorderly, slovenly, or dilapidated place indoors or outdoors ⟨instead of working in such a ~ he could have been in his comfortable hotel room —Morley Callaghan⟩ **4 :** something that has been dumped or deposited in a pile ⟨fresh avalanche *~s* contain large quantities of snow and ice, with occasional rock inclusions —R.L.Ives⟩ **5 :** DUMP TRUCK **6 :** DEFECATION — often considered vulgar
dum palm \'düm-\ *n* [F *doum* — more at DOOM PALM] **:** DOOM PALM
dump body *n* **:** a motor-truck or trailer body that can be manipulated to discharge its contents by gravity
dump car *n* **:** a railroad car whose body can be tilted for the dumping out of its contents
dumpcart \'⸗,⸗\ *n* **:** a cart having a body that can be tilted or a bottom opening downward for emptying the contents without handling

dumpcart in position for dumping

dump·er \'dəmpə(r)\ *n* -S **1 :** one that dumps: as **a :** DUMPCART, DUMP TRUCK **b :** a device that is used for unloading freight cars by tilting or dumping **c :** a worker who tips up the body and releases the gates of loaded cars to dump the contents (as coal, ore, rock) — called also *dumpman, tipman, tipper* **d :** a worker who empties materials or products from the molds in which they are formed or the containers in which they are stored or transported **2 :** a textile worker who examines cloth before it is printed in order to cut out and reverse any pieces that have been sewed in face down
dump hook *n* **:** a chain grabhook with a lever attachment for releasing it (as in unhitching a team in loading logs)
dump·i·ly \'dəmpəlē, -li\ *adv* **:** in a dumpy manner **:** shortly and thickly **:** PUDGILY ⟨a girl rather ~ constructed⟩
dump·i·ness \'dəmpēnəs, -pin-\ *n* -ES **:** the quality or state of being dumpy
dumping *n* -S [fr. gerund of ⁴*dump*] **:** the selling of goods in quantity at below market price (as to dispose of a surplus or to break down competition) esp. in international trade
dumping duty *n* **:** a duty imposed by an antidumping law
dumping syndrome *n* **:** a condition characterized by weakness, dizziness, flushing and warmth, nausea, and palpitation immediately or shortly after eating and produced by abnormally rapid emptying of the stomach in persons who have had part of the stomach removed or in hypersensitive or neurotic individuals
dump·ish \'dəmpish, -pēsh\ *adj* [¹*dump* + *-ish*] **1** *obs* **:** DULL, STUPID **2 :** SAD, MELANCHOLY, DEJECTED — **dump·ish·ly** *adv*
dump·ler \-plə(r)\ *n* -S [D *dompelaar*, fr. *dompelen* to immerse (freq. of *dompen* to immerse, tumble, topple) + *-aar* -er — more at DUMP] *archaic* **:** DUNKER
dump·ling \'dəmpliŋ, -lēŋ\ *n* -S *often attrib* [perh. alter. of ¹*lump* + *-ling*] **1 a :** a small mass of leavened dough cooked by boiling or steaming (as with soup, stew, or fruit with which it is to be served) **b :** a dessert made by wrapping fruit (as a whole apple) in biscuit dough and baking **2 :** something that has a somewhat rounded shapelessness like a dumpling ⟨a large, evenly terraced red mass, topped by a ~ of buff sandstone, rises above symmetrical outlying buttes —*Amer. Guide Series: Ariz.*⟩; *specif* **:** a short fat person or animal **3 :** APPLEBERRY — usu. used in pl. **4 :** something precious **:** DARLING — used as a term of endearment ⟨a new doll for your ~ daughter —*Wall Street Jour.*⟩
dump·man \'⸗,man, -mən\ *n, pl* **dumpmen** [⁴*dump* + *man*] **1 :** BANKMAN **2 a :** DUMPER 1c **b :** one that operates cable machinery for drawing cars of raw materials to a crane for dumping in a cement storage yard
dump power *n* [⁵*dump*] **:** surplus electric power that is in excess of existing local load requirements and that is made available because of overabundance of stored water in a hydroelectric plant
dump rake *n* **:** a hay rake mounted on two wheels consisting of a set of long curved steel teeth and equipped with a device for raising the teeth to dump the hay
dumps *pl of* DUMP, *pres 3d sing of* DUMP
dump shot *n* **:** DUNK SHOT
dump trailer *n* **:** a truck trailer with a dump body
dump truck *n* **:** a motor or hand-propelled truck for transporting and dumping loose materials; *esp* **:** a motor-driven truck that has a dump body and is designed esp. for the transportation of heavy bulk material (as sand, rock, or coal)
dump valve *n* **:** a large emergency valve at the bottom of a container (as an airplane fuel tank) by which it may be emptied much more quickly than by the ordinary drain cock (as in emergency jettisoning of fuel)
dump wagon *n* **1 :** DUMPCART **2 :** DUMP TRUCK
1dumpy \'dəmpē, -pi\ *adj* -ER/-EST [¹*dump* + *-y*] **:** DUMPISH 2
2dumpy \"\ *adj* -ER/-EST [³*dump* + *-y*] **1** *also* **dump·ty** \-m(p)tē, -ti\ **:** lacking graceful height, length, or stature **:** being short and thick in body **:** SHAPELESS ⟨a *dumpy*-looking bunch of women . . . beefy and sturdy —Joseph Bennett⟩ ⟨fitting ~ concrete columns into the balustrade —Harold Brodkey⟩ **2** *of a coin* **:** small and thick **syn** see STOCKY
dumpy level *n* [²*dumpy*] **:** a surveyor's level with a short usu. inverting telescope that is rigidly fixed to a table and capable only of rotatory movement in a horizontal plane — called also *Troughton level*; compare Y LEVEL
dum so·la \dům'sōlə\ *adv* [L] **:** while unmarried — used of the status of a woman either maiden, widow, or divorced
1dun \'dən\ *adj, often* **dunner; dunnest** [ME, fr. OE *dunn* — more at DUSK] **1 a :** having a dun color **b** *of a horse* **:** exhibiting reduced hair pigmentation usu. accompanied by black points and dorsal stripe so that a basically black coat becomes pale grayish, a bay becomes yellowish, or a sorrel becomes pale and drab **2 :** marked by dullness and drabness **:** DARK, GLOOMY ⟨the ~ and dreary prairie —Laura Krey⟩ ⟨when ~ clouds flooded the naked plains with foul remorseless rains —Edmund Blunden⟩ ⟨the ~ professorial period of his life —V.L.Parrington⟩ — **dun·ness** \'dənnəs\ *n* -ES
2dun \"\ *vt* **dunned; dunned; dunning; duns** [ME *dunnen*, fr. OE *dunnian*, fr. *dunn*, adj.] **1 :** to make dun colored **:** DARKEN **2 :** to cure (as codfish) by the method formerly common in New England of salting, laying in a pile in a dark place, and covering (as with salt grass)
3dun \"\ *n* -S [ME, fr. *dun*, adj.] **1 :** a dun horse **2 :** a variable color averaging a nearly neutral slightly brownish dark gray and ranging from red to yellow in hue **3 a :** the subimago of a mayfly; *also* **:** an artificial fly tied to imitate such an insect **b :** CADDIS FLY
4dun \"\ *vt* **dunned; dunned; dunning; duns** [origin unknown] **1 :** to make persistent demands upon (as for money) **:** ask for repeatedly ⟨the grocer *dunned* that customer monthly by mail and by telephone for payment of his bill⟩ ⟨some organizations are always *dunning* their members for contributions⟩ **2 :** to plague or pester constantly ⟨*dunned* by troubles literary and monetary —*Irish Digest*⟩ ⟨hear her ~ him for a secret —Edith Sitwell⟩
5dun \"\ *n* -S **1 :** DUNNER 1 **2 :** an urgent request; *esp* **:** a demand for payment
6dun \'dün\ *n* -S [ScGael & IrGael. *dūn*, fr. OIr — more at DOWN] **:** a fortified residence in Scotland and Ireland surrounded by two or more concentric circular earthen mounds with a deep moat filled with water between them or a wall and a circular mound fortified with palisades
du·al \'d(y)ün³l\ *adj* [*dune* + *-al*] **:** of or relating to a dune
du·nam *also* **du·num** \'dünəm\ *n* -S [NHeb *dunam*, fr. Turk *dönüm*] **:** a unit of land area used esp. in the state of Israel equal to 1000 sq. meters or about ¼ acre
dun·bar·ton·shire \,dən'bärt³n,shi(ə)r, -,shər\ *or* **dun·bar·ton** \-t³n\ *also* **dum·bar·ton·shire** *or* **dum·bar·ton** \,dəm'-\ *adj, usu cap* [fr. *Dunbartonshire, Dumbartonshire* or *Dunbarton, Dumbarton* county, Scotland] **:** of or from the county of Dunbarton, Scotland **:** of the kind or style prevalent in Dunbarton
dunbird \'⸗,⸗\ *n* [¹*dun* + *bird*] **:** any of several ducks: as **a** *Brit* **:** POCHARD **b :** RUDDY DUCK
dun·can phyfe \,dəŋkən'fīf *sometimes* -k³ŋ'-\ *adj, usu cap D&P* [after *Duncan Phyfe* †1854 Scot.-Am. cabinetmaker] **1 :** of, relating to, being, or imitative of furniture designed and built by or in the style of Duncan Phyfe who used modified Hepplewhite, Sheraton, Directoire, and Empire forms characterized in chairs by turned and reeded legs, lyre-backs, and scrolled arms, in sofas by turned legs and back and arm rails carved in low relief and later by outward⸗sweeping cornucopia legs and rolled arms, in tables by turned or lyre-shaped pedestal bases with outflaring feet, and generally by decorative carvings of cornucopias, wheat sprays, plumes, and drapery swags **2 :** EMPIRE b

a Duncan Phyfe chair

dunce \'dən(t)s\ *n* -S *often attrib* [alter. of earlier *duns*, after John *Duns* Scotus †ab1308 Scot. scholastic theologian, whose once widely accepted writings were strongly ridiculed in the 16th cent.] **1** *obs* **a :** a copy of writings by Duns Scotus **b :** a textbook, comment, or gloss containing his teachings or written after his manner **2** *obs* **a :** SCOTIST **:** a sophist who cavils or splits hairs **b :** PEDANT **3 :** a dull-witted and stupid person **:** DUMBBELL, DULLARD
dunce cap *or* **dunce's cap** *n* **:** a conical cap sometimes marked with a D formerly used as a punishment for slow learners at school
dunc·ery \'dən(t)s(ə)rē\ *n* -ES **1** *obs* **:** something characteristic of a Scotist **2** *archaic* **:** intellectual dullness **:** STUPIDITY
1dunch \'dənch, 'dünch\ *vt* -ED/-ING/-ES [ME *dunchen*; prob. akin to Icel, Sw & Norw *dunka* to strike, ON *dynkr* noise, *dynr* din — more at DIN] *dial chiefly Brit* **:** to nudge or bump esp. with the elbow
2dunch \'dənch\ *n* -ES [ME *dunche*, fr. *dunchen*, v.] *chiefly Scot* **:** BLOW, PUSH
3dunch \'dənch, 'dünch\ *adj* [origin unknown] **1** *dial Eng* **:** HARD-OF-HEARING **2** *dial Eng* **:** slow in recognition or comprehension
dun·ci·cal \'dən(t)səkəl\ *adj* **1** *obs* **:** having the characteristics of a dunce **2 :** marked by the qualities of a dunce **:** STUPID, DUNCISH
dun·ci·fy \-sə,fī\ *vt* -ED/-ING/-ES **:** to cause to appear stupid **:** make a dunce of
dunc·ish \-sish\ *adj* **:** like a dunce — **dunc·ish·ly** *adv*
dun crow *n* **:** the European hooded crow
dun·das·ite \'dəndə,sīt, ,dən'da,s-\ *n* -S [*Dundas*, Tasmania + E *-ite*] **:** a mineral $PbAl_2(CO_3)_2(OH)_4.2H_2O$ consisting of a basic lead aluminum carbonate occurring in white spherical aggregates
dun·dathu pine \,dən'da(,)thü-\ *also* **dun·dath·ee pine** \-athē-\ *n* [native name in Queensland, Australia] **:** an Australian timber tree (*Agathis robusta*) resembling the kauri pine but having wood much lighter in weight and softer — called also *Queensland kauri*
dun·dee \ˌdən'dē\ *adj, usu cap* [fr. *Dundee*, Scotland] **:** of or from the city of Dundee, Scotland **:** of the kind or style prevalent in Dundee
1dun·der \'dən(d)ər\ *n* -S [perh. fr. D *donderen* to thunder — more at DONNERED] *chiefly Scot* **:** a noise like thunder **:** a noisy blow
2dun·der \'dəndə(r)\ *n* -S [origin unknown] **:** the lees of cane juice used to promote fermentation in the distillation of rum
dun·der·funk \'dəndə(r),fəŋk\ *n* -S [origin unknown] **:** broken sea biscuits or crackers mixed with molasses and baked
dun·der·head \-,hed\ *n* [perh. fr. D *donder* thunder (used as an intensifier in nominal compounds; fr. MD) + E *head*; akin to OHG *thonar* thunder — more at THUNDER] **:** DUNCE, NUMSKULL, BLOCKHEAD
dun·der·head·ed \ˌ⸗⸗'⸗əd\ *adj* **:** being a dunderhead — **dun·der·head·ed·ness** *n* -ES
dun·der·pate \-,pāt\ *n* [prob. fr. D *donder* + E *pate*] **:** DUNDERHEAD
dun diver *n* **:** a female or immature merganser
dun·drear·ies \,dən'drirēz\ *or* **dun·dreary whiskers** \(')dən-ˌdrirē-\ *n pl, often cap D* [after Lord *Dundreary*, character in the play *Our American Cousin* (1858), by Tom Taylor †1880 Eng. dramatist, as portrayed by Edward A. Sothern †1881 Eng. actor] **:** long flowing side whiskers
dune \'d(y)ün\ *n* -S *often attrib* [F, fr. OF, fr. MD *dune* — more at DOWN] **:** a hill or ridge of sand piled up by the wind commonly found along shores, along some river valleys, and generally where there is dry surface sand during some part of the year **2 :** TWINE 5
dun·edin \ˌdə'nēd³n, -dən\ *adj, usu cap* [fr. *Dunedin*, New Zealand] **:** of or from the city of Dunedin, New Zealand **:** of the kind or style prevalent in Dunedin
dune heath *n* **:** a treeless area of low heathlike vegetation found on sand dunes and sand plains
dune plant *n* **:** a plant (as beach heather, certain bayberries, and many grasses) adapted to growth on a sand dune esp. by its ability to resist drought
dunfish \'⸗,⸗\ *n* [²*dun* + *fish*] **:** fish cured by dunning
1dung \'dəŋ\ *n* -S [ME, fr. OE, dung, prison; akin to OE *dyncge* manure, manured land, OHG *tunga* manuring, *tung* cellar roofed with manure, ON *dyngja* manure pile, women's workroom, OIr *dingid* he suppresses, Lith *deñgti* to cover; basic meaning: pressing, covering] **1 :** MANURE **2 :** the excrement of an animal **3 :** something vile or loathsome
2dung \"\ *vb* -ED/-ING/-S [ME *dungen*, fr. *dung*, n.] *vt* **1 :** to fertilize or dress with dung **2 :** to immerse or steep (printed cloth) in a dung bath ~ *vi* **:** DEFECATE — used of an animal
dungan *usu cap, var of* TUNGAN
dun·ga·ree \ˌdəŋgə'rē, '⸗⸗,⸗\ *n* -S [Hindi *dūgrī*] **1 :** a heavy coarse durable cotton twill woven from colored yarns; *specif* **:** blue denim **2 dungarees** *pl* **:** heavy cotton work clothes (as pants or overalls) made usu. of blue dungaree
dun·ga·run·ga \ˌdəŋgə'rəŋgə\ *n* -S [native name in Australia] **:** a small Australian tree (*Notelaea ovata*) yielding a very hard wood used for tool handles — compare AXBREAKER
dung bath *n* **:** a bath orig. made with dung but now with chemicals for removing acid and thickening from printed cloth so that it will receive dye
dung beetle *also* **dung chafer** *n* **:** a scarabaeid beetle (as a dorbeetle or tumblebug) that rolls balls of dung in which the eggs are laid and on which the larvae feed
dun·ge·ness crab \ˌdənjə'nes-\ *n, usu cap D* [fr. *Dungeness*, village on Juan de Fuca strait, northwest Washington] **:** a large edible crab (*Cancer magister*) of the Pacific coast of No. America from Alaska to San Francisco that is the chief commercial crab of the region
1dun·geon \'dənjən\ *n* -S *often attrib* [ME *donjon, dongeoun, dungeon*, fr. MF *donjon*, fr. ML *dominion-, dominio*, fr. L *dominus* lord, master + *-ion-, -io* -ion — more at DAME] **1 :** DONJON **2 :** a close dark prison or vault commonly underground; *esp* **:** a lower room in the keep of a castle **3** *chiefly Scot* **:** a person having a notable talent or ability ⟨a ~ of wit⟩
2dungeon \"\ *vt* -ED/-ING/-S **:** to shut up in or as if in a dungeon ⟨*~ed* in the human breast doubtless secrets lie —Emily Dickinson⟩
dung·er \'dəŋə(r)\ *n* -S **:** an operator of a machine for chemically removing acetic acid and thickening from printed cloth so that it will receive mordant dye
dung fly *n* **:** any of numerous small two-winged flies (family Scatophagidae) that breed in dung and decaying vegetable matter; *broadly* **:** any fly of similar habits
dunghill \'⸗,⸗\ *n* [ME, fr. ¹*dung* + *hill*] **1 :** a heap of dung **2 :** a vile or degraded situation, condition, or thing ⟨He . . . lifteth up the beggar from the ~ —1 Sam 2:8 (AV)⟩ **3** *also* **dunghill fowl :** the common domestic fowl — opposed to *game fowl*

dung·on \ˈdüŋ,ȯn\ *n* -s [Tag] **1 :** a valuable Philippine timber tree (*Tarrietia sylvatica*) **2 :** the hard pale reddish wood of the dungon

dungs *pl of* DUNG, *pres 3d sing of* DUNG

dung worm *n* **1 :** any of certain earthworms living in dung heaps; *esp* **:** a common pink worm (*Eisenia foetida*) sometimes used as bait **2 :** an insect larva (as of a two-winged fly) that develops in dung

dungy \ˈdəŋē\ *adj* -ER/-EST [ME, fr. ¹*dung* + -*y*] **:** like dung **:** FILTHY

du·nic \ˈd(y)ünik\ *adj* **:** of, relating to, or resembling a dune

dunier *comparative of* DUNY

duniest *superlative of* DUNY

du·nie·was·sal \ˌdünēˌwäsəl\ *or* **dun·nie·was·sel** \ˌdən-\ *n* [ScGael *duine-uasal*, lit., noble man] **1** *Scot* **:** a Highland gentleman **2** *Scot* **:** a cadet of a family of rank

du·nite \ˈdü,nīt, ˈdə,-\ *n* -s [Mt. *Dun*, near Nelson, New Zealand, its locality + E -*ite*] **:** a granitoid igneous rock belonging to the peridotites and consisting chiefly of olivine with a little chromite or other spinel — **du·nit·ic** \(ˈ)düˌnid·ik, ˌdəˌ-\ *adj*

¹**dunk** \ˈdəŋk\ *vb* -ED/-ING/-S [PaG *dunke* to dip, fr. MHG *dunken, tunken*, fr. OHG *dunkōn, thunkōn* — more at TINGE] *vt* **1 :** to dip (as a piece of bread, cake, or doughnut) into liquid (as coffee, milk, or tea) while eating **2 :** to dip or submerge temporarily in liquid ⟨a varnish that can be ~*ed* in acid without ill effect⟩ ⟨the old man ~*ed* the two plates up and down in a bucket of water and wiped them —Shirley A. Grau⟩ ~ *vi* **:** to submerge oneself in water (as by swimming or falling in) ⟨an outdoor, glass-protected pool to ~ in —Horace Sutton⟩ ⟨aviators who had ~*ed* signaled for rescue —O.O.Jensen⟩ **syn** see DIP

²**dunk** \ˈ"\ *n* -s **:** DIP 7

dun·ka·doo \ˌdəŋkəˌdü\ *n* -s [imit.] *dial* **:** AMERICAN BITTERN

dun·ker \ˈdəŋkə(r)\ *or* **dun·kard** \-(r)d\ *also* **tun·ker** \ˈtəŋkə(r)\ *n* -s *usu cap* [*dunker* fr. PaG, fr. *dunke* to dip + -*er*; *dunkard, tunker* alter. of *dunker*] **:** a member of one of the denominations (as the Church of the Brethren) deriving from an orig. German Baptist group that practice trine immersion, love feasts, simplicity of life, and avoidance of oaths, lawsuits, and military service — called also *Dipper*

dunking *n* -s **:** IMMERSION ⟨shrinks after each ~ in hot water⟩

¹**dun·kirk** *also* **dun·kerque** \ˈdən,kərk *also* ,≈ˈ≈ *sometimes* -əŋ-\ *n* -s *usu cap* [fr. *Dunkirk* or *Dunkerque*, seaport in northern France, scene of the evacuation of allied troops in World War II after the fall of France, May 29–June 2, 1940] **1 :** a desperate evacuation under bombardment of remnants of a defeated army **2 :** a serious crisis demanding decisive action ⟨the immediate effect would plainly be a *Dunkirk* for U.S. foreign policy —*Time*⟩

²**dunkirk** \ˈ"\ *vt* -ED/-ING/-S **:** to force to execute a Dunkirk

dun·kirk·er \-kərkə(r)\ *n* -s *usu cap* [*Dunkirk*, France + E -*er*] **:** a 17th century privateer from Dunkirk; *also* **:** one of its crew

dunk shot *n* **:** a basketball shot made usu. by a tall player who jumps up and drops the ball over the rim and into the basket

dun·lin \ˈdənlən\ *n, pl* **dunlins** *or* **dunlin** [¹*dun* + -*lin* (alter. of -*ling*)] **:** RED-BACKED SANDPIPER

dun·lop \ˈdən,läp, *chiefly Scot* ,dənˈl-\ *or* **dunlop cheese** *n* -s *usu cap D* [fr. *Dunlop*, Ayr co., Scotland] **:** a rich white pressed Scotch cheese

dunmeh *usu cap, var of* DÖNMEH

¹**dun·nage** \ˈdənij\ *n* -s [origin unknown] **1 a :** mats, boughs, pieces of wood, or other loose materials placed under or among goods carried as cargo in the hold of a ship to keep them dry and to prevent their motion and chafing **b :** temporary blocking or bracing installed by the shipper in the hold of a ship, in a railroad car, or in a truck to protect freight during shipment **c :** cushioning or padding used in a shipping container to protect fragile articles against shock and breakage **2 :** baggage or personal effects ⟨mules would pack our ~ from this jump-off point to the various camps we would pitch along our route —D.R.Brower⟩ **3 :** lumber below the recognized merchantable grades

²**dunnage** \ˈ"\ *vt* -ED/-ING/-S **:** to stow or secure with dunnage

dunned *past of* DUN

¹**dunner** *comparative of* DUN

²**dun·ner** \ˈdənə(r)\ *n* -s [⁴*dun* + -*er*] **1 :** one that duns; *esp* **:** one that solicits payment of debts **2 :** ⁵DUN 2

³**dunner** \ˈ"\ *var of* ¹DUNDER

dunnest *superlative of* DUN

dunniewassel *var of* DUNIEWASSAL

dunning *pres part of* DUN

dunning draft *n* [fr. pres. part. of ⁴*dun*] **:** a draft drawn on a delinquent customer and deposited with a bank for payment

dun·nish \ˈdənish\ *adj* [¹*dun* + -*ish*] **:** somewhat dun

dun·nock \ˈdənək, ˈdùn-\ *n* -s [ME *donek, dunoke*, fr. ¹*dun* + -*ek*, -*oke* -ock] *dial Eng* **:** HEDGE SPARROW

¹**dunny** *adj* [¹*dun* + -*y*] *obs* **:** DUNNISH

²**dun·ny** \ˈdənī, ˈdùnī\ *adj* [origin unknown] *dial Brit* **:** slow to perceive **:** DULL

duns *pres 3d sing of* DUN, *pl of* DUN

dun·siek·te \ˈdən,sēktə\ *also* **dun·ziek·te** \-,zē-\ *n* -s [Afrik *dunsiekte* (formerly spelled *dunziekte*), fr. *dun* thin (fr. MD *dunne*) + *siekte* disease, fr. MD *siecte*, fr. *siec* ill; akin to OHG *dunni* thin and to OHG *sioh* sick, ill — more at THIN, SICK] **:** a serious intoxication of animals (as horses) of southern Africa that is caused by eating plants of the genus *Senecio* and is marked by emaciation, liver degeneration, and sometimes by nervous symptoms — compare WALKABOUT DISEASE

dunst \ˈdənzt, -n(t)st\ *n* -s [origin unknown] **:** the finest middlings usu. still containing some bran

dun·sta·ble \ˈdənztəbəl, -n(t)st-\ *adj* [fr. the *Dunstable* way, a road from London to the municipal borough of Dunstable, Bedfordshire, England, known for its straightness] *archaic* **:** PLAIN, DIRECT

¹**dunt** \ˈdənt\ *n* -s [ME *dount, dunt*, var. of *dint* — more at DINT] **1** *chiefly Scot* **:** a heavy blow or stroke **2** *chiefly Scot* **:** BRUISE, WOUND **3** *chiefly Scot* **:** a quickened beat of the heart **:** THROB **4** *Scot* **:** a sizable lump

²**dunt** \ˈ"\ *vb* -ED/-ING/-S *vt, chiefly Scot* **:** to strike heavily **:** BEAT ~ *vi* **1** *chiefly Scot* **:** to fall with a heavy sound **2** *chiefly Scot, of the heart* **:** THROB

³**dunt** \ˈ"\ *vi* -ED/-ING/-S [origin unknown] *ceramics* **:** to crack while firing or afterward by temperature change or by inversion of crystals to greater volume

dunum *var of* DUNAM

duny \ˈd(y)ünē\ *adj* -ER/-EST **:** having many dunes

duo \ˈd(y)ü(,)ō\ *n, pl* **du·os** \-ü,ōz\ [It, fr. L *duo* two — more at TWO] **1 :** DUET; *also* **:** the participants in a duet **2 :** a group of two **:** PAIR

duo- *comb form* [L *duo* — more at TWO] **:** two ⟨*duo*secant⟩ ⟨*duo*machy⟩

duo *abbr* duodecimo

du·o·decennial \ˌd(y)ü(,)ō+\ *adj* [LL *duodecennium* period of 12 years (fr. L *duodecim* twelve — fr. *duo* two + -*decim*, fr. *decem* ten — + -*ennium*, fr. *annus* year) + E -*al* — more at TWO, TEN, ANNUAL] **:** occurring once in 12 years

du·o·decillion \ˈ"+\ *n, often attrib* [L *duodecim* twelve + E -*illion* (as in *million*)] — see NUMBER table

¹**du·o·dec·i·mal** \ˌdüəˈdesəməl, -üō-\ *adj* [L *duodecim* twelve + E -*al*] **:** of or relating to twelve or twelfths **:** proceeding in computation by twelves **:** expressed in the scale of twelves — **du·o·dec·i·mal·i·ty** \ˌ≈≈ˌ≈≈ˈmaləd·ē\ *n* -ES — **du·o·dec·i·mal·ly** \ˌ≈≈ˈdesəmәlē\ *adv*

²**duodecimal** \ˈ"\ *n* -s **:** a twelfth part

du·o·dec·i·mo \ˌ≈≈ˈdesə,mō\ *n* -s [L, abl. of *duodecimus* twelfth, fr. *duodecim* twelve] **1 :** TWELVEMO — symbol *D*; see BOOK tables **2** [modif. of It *duodecima*, fr. fem. of *duodecimo* twelfth, fr. L *duodecimus*, fr. *duodecim* twelve] **:** the musical interval of a twelfth

du·o·dec·i·mole \ˌ≈≈ˈ≈≈,mōl\ *n* -s [It, fr. *duodecimo*] **:** DODECUPLET

duo·decyl \d(y)üə, -üō+\ *n* [*duo-* + *decyl*] **:** DODECYL

duoden- *or* **duodeno-** *comb form* [NL, fr. ML *duodenum*] **1 :** duodenum ⟨*duoden*itis⟩ ⟨*duodeno*gram⟩ **2 :** duodenal and ⟨*duodeno*jejunal⟩

du·o·de·nal \ˌd(y)üəˈdēnᵊl, (ˈ)d(y)üˈädᵊnəl\ *adj* [NL *duodenalis*, fr. ML *duodenum* + L -*alis* -al] **:** of or relating to the duodenum

duodenal gland *n* **:** BRUNNER'S GLAND

duodenal juice *n* **:** an alkaline protein-containing fluid of weak digestive power that is secreted by the duodenum, aids in neutralizing the acid chyme of the stomach, and contains invertase, maltase, lactase, erepsin, and enterokinase

duodenal tube *n* **:** a long flexible rubber tube that can be passed through the esophagus and stomach into the duodenum

duodenal ulcer *n* **:** a peptic ulcer situated in the duodenum

du·o·den·a·ry \ˌd(y)üəˈdenərē, -dēn-\ *adj* [L *duodenarius*, fr. *duodeni* twelve each (fr. *duodecim* twelve) + -*arius* -ary — more at DUODECENNIAL] **1 :** containing 12 ⟨a ~ cycle of years⟩ **2 :** based on the number 12 ⟨a ~ system of computation⟩

du·o·de·ni·tis \ˌd(y)üə,dēˈnīd·əs, (,)d(y)ü,ädᵊnˈī-\ *n* -ES [NL, fr. *duoden-* + -*itis*] **:** inflammation of the duodenum

du·o·de·num \ˌd(y)üəˈdēnəm, d(y)üˈädᵊn-\ *n, pl* **duode·na** \-ēnə, -ᵊnə\ *or* **duodenums** \-ēnəmz,-ᵊnəmz\ [ME, fr. ML, fr. L *duodeni* twelve each; fr. its length, about 12 fingers' breadth] **:** the first, shortest, and widest part of the small intestine that in man is about 10 inches long and that extends from the pylorus to the undersurface of the liver where it descends for a variable distance and receives the bile and pancreatic ducts and then bends to the left and finally upward to join the jejunum near the second lumbar vertebra — see DIGESTION illustration

duo·drama \ˈd(y)üə+,-\ *n* [*duo-* + *drama*] **:** a drama for two performers in which the dialogue is spoken with an instrumental accompaniment

duo·graph \ˈd(y)üə,graf, -räf\ *n* [*duo-* + -*graph*] **:** DUOTONE

du·o·logue \-,lȯg *also* -,läg\ *n* -s [*duo-* + -*logue*] **1 :** dialogue confined to two **2 :** a dramatic or musical piece for two participants

duo·mo \ˈdwȯ(,)mō\ *n* -s [It — more at DOME] **:** CATHEDRAL

duo-pianist \ˌd(y)ü(,)ō+\ *n* [*duo*] **:** one of two pianists that play duets each at a separate piano

du·op·o·ly \d(y)üˈäpəlē\ *n* -ES [*duo-* + mono*poly*] **:** a market situation in which two competing sellers hold the controlling power of determining the amount and price of a product or service offered to a large number of buyers — compare DUOPSONY, MONOPOLY, OLIGOPOLY

du·op·so·ny \-psənē\ *n* -ES [*duo-* + Gk *opsōnia* purchase of victuals, catering, fr. *opsōnein* to purchase victuals (fr. *opson* prepared food, relish) + -*ia* -*y*] **:** a market situation in which two rival buyers hold the controlling power of determining the demand for a product or service from a large number of sellers — compare MONOPSONY, OLIGOPSONY

duos *pl of* DUO

¹**duo·tone** \ˈd(y)üə,tōn\ *or* **duo·toned** \-nd\ *adj* [*duo-* + *tone* or -*toned*] **:** having or yielding two tones or colors

²**duotone** \ˈ"\ *n* -s **:** a process for making prints typically in two shades of the same color or in black and one tint by the use of two halftone plates made with the screen set at two different angles ⟨~ plates⟩ ⟨~ illustrations⟩; *also* **:** a print made by this process

duo·type -,tīp\ *n* [*duo-* + *type*] **:** a process for making prints in two colors by the use of two halftone plates made from the same negative but etched differently; *also* **:** a print made by this process

dup \ˈdəp\ *vt* [contr. of *do up*] *now dial Brit* **:** OPEN

dup *abbr* **1** duplex **2** duplicate

dup·able \ˈd(y)üpəbəl\ *adj* **:** that can be duped

¹**dupe** \ˈd(y)üp\ *n* -s [F, fr. MF *duppe*, prob. fr. a dial. word meaning "hoopoe", alter. (resulting fr. false word division of *de huppe*) of *huppe* hoopoe — more at HOOPOE] **1 :** one that is easily deceived (as by flattering promises) because lacking power to discriminate **:** FOOL **2 :** a puppet or tool esp. of a powerful person or idea **:** SLAVE ⟨he that hates truth shall be the ~ of lies —William Cowper⟩ ⟨with the same mental rigidity that made him a ~ to communism —Bradford Smith⟩

²**dupe** \ˈ"\ *vt* -ED/-ING/-S [F *duper*, fr. *dupe*] **:** to make a dupe of **:** mislead or trick by imposing on one's credulity **:** DECEIVE, FOOL ⟨refuses to be *duped* by his foiled lover's frenzies —Karl Polanyi⟩

syn DUPE, GULL, BEFOOL, TRICK, HOAX, HOODWINK, and BAMBOOZLE mean, in common, to delude by underhanded or deceptive means esp. for one's own ends. DUPE stresses the unwariness of the one deluded and his unsuspecting acceptance of the false as true, the worthless as genuine, and so on ⟨men in high positions are as gullible and as easily *duped* as the rest of us —*New Statesman & Nation*⟩ ⟨hunters bent on *duping* a wild turkey gobbler —Allen Rankin⟩ GULL implies the gre t credulousness of the one imposed upon and generally made a laughingstock of ⟨"good people" they call them, because they are easily *gulled* in the matter of weights and measures —Norman Douglas⟩ ⟨Barnum knew the American public loved to be *gulled*. It was a shame not to take the money. His genius consisted in knowing how to swindle them —W.L.Phelps⟩ ⟨could not tell . . . whether he was enlightened by fact or *gulled* by pretense —F.L.Paxson⟩ BEFOOL usu. stresses no weakness in the victim nor does it suggest very strongly an intent to delude on the part of the agent, stressing rather the victim's being made foolish ⟨innocent philosophic critics, too easily *befooled* by words —Havelock Ellis⟩ ⟨a world long *befooled* by false messiahs and enslaved by false loyalties —John Bright †1889⟩ ⟨pictures supplant one another so swiftly as to *befool* the eye with the illusion of continuity —S.H.Adams⟩ TRICK stresses an intent to delude or deceive, by strategem, ruse, wiles, or fraud, not necessarily implying a base end, suggesting strongly the use of craft or cunning ⟨it enables some lawyers to *trick* us into bringing in the wrong verdict —W.J.Reilly⟩ ⟨his accidental abandonment, which Sam never forgot, but which his recollection *tricked* him into placing at the earlier date of 1839, as if to heighten the pathos —Dixon Wecter⟩ ⟨never recommended it to my students because I knew they would suspect me of trying to *trick* them into reading it —A.W.Long⟩ HOAX in one sense implies the use of trickery for fun or as a demonstration of someone else's gullibility; in another it suggests a fraud, often on a large scale, intended to deceive even the most skeptical, usu. to one's own advantage ⟨he was flawed with impish faults. He *hoaxed* poor Rafinesque into solemn belief in the "red-headed swallow", concocted for his benefit, and even got him to accept drawings of imaginary fishes and publish them as new species —D.C.Peattie⟩ ⟨a get-rich-quick scheme intended to *hoax* the public⟩ HOODWINK often stresses a deliberate confusing of another so as to blind him to the truth, and often a self-delusion arising from an inability to distinguish false from true ⟨injures the interests of whatever nation is *hoodwinked* by the lie —Lucius Garvin⟩ ⟨since she'd *hoodwinked* your uncle, she thought she could pull the wool over my eyes, too —Kenneth Roberts⟩ ⟨*hoodwinked* by a simple political trick⟩ BAMBOOZLE usu. implies the use of out-and-out humbug or illusion or a transparent cajolery, though it may often be interchanged with TRICK, HOAX, or HOODWINK, being generally less fixed in its implications ⟨we circus people are scoundrels, we do all sorts of tricks to *bamboozle* the world —Eduard Bass⟩ ⟨is it not a technique for persuading people that they themselves have chosen what has been dexterously palmed off on them? And that is to add insult to injury; you not only manipulate people but also *bamboozle* them —Walter Moberly⟩

³**dupe** \ˈ"\ *n or vb* [by shortening] **:** DUPLICATE

dup·ery \-pərē\ *n* -ES [F *duperie*, fr. *dupe* + -*erie* -ery] **1 :** the act or practice of duping **:** DECEPTION ⟨when Maximilian's ~ could no longer be hidden —Francis Hackett⟩ **2 :** the condition of being duped ⟨the ~ and weakness of the sufferers —Adam Smith⟩

dupioni *or* **dupion** *var of* DOUPPIONI

du·pla·tion \d(y)üˈplāshən\ *n* -s [LL *duplation-, duplatio* act of doubling, fr. *duplatus* (past part. of *duplare* to double, fr. L *duplus* double) + -*ion-*, -*io* -ion] **:** multiplication by repeated doubling (as done formerly esp. in Egypt)

du·ple \ˈd(y)üpəl\ *adj* [L *duplus* — more at DOUBLE] **1 a :** consisting of two **:** TWOFOLD, DOUBLE **b :** taken by twos or in groups of two **2 a** *music* **:** having two or a multiple of two beats per measure ⟨~ time⟩ **b** *of meter* **:** consisting of feet of two syllables **c** *of rhythm* **:** consisting of cadences that rise and fall within a space of two syllables

du·plet \-plət\ *n* -s [*duple* + -*et*] **:** two musical notes played in the time of three of the same value — compare TRIPLET

¹**du·plex** \ˈd(y)ü,pleks\ *adj* [L, fr. *duo* two + -*plex* (akin to Gk *diplax* double) — more at TWO, SIMPLE] **1 :** having two parts or elements **:** DOUBLE, TWOFOLD: as **a** *of a machine tool or other device* **:** having two parts that operate at the same time or in the same way where the simpler form has but one **b** *of paper or paperboard*: (1) **:** consisting of two or more plies (2) **:** having two surfaces that differ in color, texture, or finish **c** *of an electric cable* **:** having two insulated conductors **2 :** having or distinguished by two homologous dominant genes — used chiefly of autotetraploids; compare SIMPLEX **3 :** allowing telecommunication in opposite directions simultaneously ⟨~ system⟩ ⟨~ telephony⟩ — distinguished from *diplex*

²**duplex** \ˈ"\ *n* -ES **:** something duplex: as **a :** DUPLEX APARTMENT **b :** TWO-FAMILY HOUSE

³**duplex** \ˈ"\ *vt* -ED/-ING/-ES **:** to make duplex: as **a :** to arrange (as a telegraph line) so that two messages may be transmitted simultaneously **b :** to use in dual combination in a specific metallurgic process (as two furnaces in a duplex process) **c :** BORROW 8

duplex apartment *n* **:** a suite in an apartment house that includes rooms on two floors

duplex bag *n* **:** DOUBLE WALL 2

duplex dahlia *n* **:** any of various dahlias having open centered flowers with only two rows of rays

du·plex·er \-sə(r)\ *n* -s **:** a switching device that utilizes two electron tubes to permit alternate transmission and reception with the same radar antenna

duplex house *n* **:** TWO-FAMILY HOUSE

duplex iron *n* **:** cast iron that has been heated in an electric furnace after being melted in the usual manner in a cupola

du·plex·ite \ˈd(y)ü,plek,sīt\ *n* -s [S. *Duplex*, 20th cent. Australian quarry manager who found it + E -*ite*] **:** a mineral perhaps $Be_4Ca_6Al_2Si_{14}O_{41}.2H_2O$ consisting of hydrous beryllium calcium aluminosilicate

du·plex·i·ty \d(y)üˈpleksəd·ē\ *n* -ES [¹*duplex* + -*ity*] **:** DUPLICITY 2

duplex lock *n* **:** a cylinder lock with two pin-tumbler cylinders acting independently on the same bolt, one for an ordinary key and the other for a master key

duplex process *n* **:** a process for making steel in which the material is partially treated in a furnace of one type, orig. a Bessemer, and then transferred without interruption to a furnace of another type, orig. an open-hearth furnace

duplex pump *n* **:** a pump with two cylinders; *esp* **:** one whose plungers are driven directly by the piston rods of a compound steam engine

duplex querela *n* [L, double complaint] **:** a complaint in the nature of an appeal from the ordinary to his immediate superior (as from a bishop to an archbishop)

duplex steel *n* **:** steel made by a duplex process

du·pli·ca·ble \ˈd(y)üpləkəbəl, -lēk-\ *or* **du·pli·cat·able** \ˈd(y)üplə,kād·əbəl, -ātə-, ,≈≈ˈ≈≈≈\ *adj* [*duplicate* + -*able*] **:** capable of being duplicated

du·pli·cand \ˌd(y)üpləˌkand\ *also* **du·pli·can·do** \-n(,)dō\ *n* -s [L *duplicando*, abl. of *duplicandum*, gerund of *duplicare*] *Scots law* **:** the doubling of a feu-duty; *also* **:** the double duty itself

¹**du·pli·cate** \ˈd(y)üpləkə|t, -lēk- *sometimes* -lə,kā|; *usu* |d·+V\ *adj* [ME, fr. L *duplicatus*, past part. of *duplicare* to double, fr. *duplic-, duplex* double, twofold — more at DUPLEX] **1 :** consisting of or existing in two corresponding or identical parts or examples ⟨the firm always made out ~ invoices, one for its own records and one for the customer⟩ **2 :** being exactly the same as one or more others of its kind ⟨in eleven years he has not made a ~ prayer —*N.Y.Times*⟩ ⟨make six ~ copies of the memo⟩ **3 :** of, relating to, or being a card game in which all players play identical hands in order to allow a comparison of scores — compare DUPLICATE BRIDGE

²**duplicate** \ˈ"\ *n* -s **1 :** either of two things that exactly resemble or correspond to each other — usu. used of a copy or transcript made at the same time or by the same pattern as its original **2 :** something that is like another thing in content or appearance but is not derived from the same source or made in the same manner **:** COUNTERPART ⟨doll carriages that are ~*s* of baby carriages⟩; *specif* **:** an additional copy of a book, periodical, or pamphlet already in a library **3 :** a duplicate game; *specif* **:** DUPLICATE BRIDGE **4** *law* **:** an original instrument repeated **:** a document the same as another in essential particulars and differing from a copy in that it is valid as an original **5 a :** a photographic negative prepared from another negative by printing first a master positive from which the later negative is printed **b :** a positive print either black and white or color that is made by reversal development of a print from a positive — **in duplicate** *adv* **:** with an original and one copy

³**du·pli·cate** \-lə,kāt, *usu* -ād·+V\ *vb* -ED/-ING/-S *vt* **1 :** to make double or twofold ⟨the walls should be *duplicated* . . . in order to have a second line of defense if the outer wall is breached —J.A.Steers⟩ **2 :** to be or make a duplicate, copy, or transcript of ⟨the furnishings ~ those used by Washington —*Amer. Guide Series: Pa.*⟩ ⟨we are totally unable, after decades of experiment, to ~ Attic glazed pottery —W.F. Albright⟩ ⟨small firms may ~ their own business forms⟩ ~ *vi* **:** to celebrate mass twice in a day

duplicate board *n* **:** BOARD 5 f(1)

duplicate bridge *n* **:** bridge (as contract bridge) in which each contestant, pair, or team of four players plays the same hands as other contestants and each deal of which is scored independently of each other deal with match-point or cumulative-point scoring — see BOARD 5 f(1)

duplicate factor *or* **duplicate gene** *n, biol* **:** any of two or more nonallelic factors having the same expression

duplicate stitch *n* **:** a hand-sewn stitch that imitates a knitted stitch and that is used for working patterns on finished knitted garments

duplicating machine *n* **1 :** a machine or attachment that shapes an exact copy of a given sample (as of a die or key) or shapes two or more identical parts at once **2 :** DUPLICATOR 1a

du·pli·ca·tion \ˌd(y)üpləˈkāshən\ *n* -s [ME *duplicacioun*, fr. MF *duplication*, fr. L *duplication-, duplicatio*, fr. *duplicatus* + -*ion-*, -*io* -ion] **1 :** the action or process of duplicating or doubling or the quality or state of being duplicated or doubled ⟨save time and money by avoiding ~ of effort⟩ ⟨after his initial success, the author's successive novels were marked mainly by ~⟩; **2 :** DUPLICATE, COPY, COUNTERPART **3 :** CHORISIS **4 :** celebration of mass by the same priest twice in a day **5** [L *duplication-, duplicatio*, lit., action of doubling] **:** a rebuttal pleading in Roman, canon, and civil law by which a party to litigation avoids the legal effect of matter just pleaded by his adversary

duplication of the cube : the mathematical problem of finding the edge of a cube having twice the volume of a given cube

du·pli·ca·tive \ˈd(y)üplə,kā|d·iv, -ləkə|, -lēkə|, |tiv\ *adj* **1 :** able to duplicate ⟨~ memory⟩ **2 :** marked by duplication ⟨the two agencies working in this area are not ~⟩

duplicato- *comb form* [prob. fr. NL, fr. L *duplicatus* duplicate — more at DUPLICATE] **:** doubly ⟨*duplicato*-dentate⟩

du·pli·ca·tor \ˈd(y)üplə,kād·ə(r), -ātə-\ *n* -s **1 :** one that duplicates: **a :** a machine for making one or more copies of typed, drawn, and often printed matter **b :** a device (as an attachment on a cash register or meter) for recording particular readings or for recording and duplicating the recording (as on a customer invoice or other separate slip) **2 :** LAYOUT MAN

duplicator 1a

du·pli·ca·ture \-ləkə,chů(ə)r, -ləkəchər, -lə,kāchər\ *n* -s [F, fr. MF, fr. L *duplicatus* + F -*ure*] **:** a doubling or fold esp. of a membrane

du·plici·den·ta·ta \d(y)ü,plisə,denˈtäd·ə, -äd·ə\ *n pl, cap* [NL, fr. L *duplic-, duplex* double, twofold + -*i-* + *dentata*, neut. pl. of *dentatus* toothed — more at DUPLEX, DENTATE] *in former classifications* **:** a suborder of Rodentia coextensive with the order Lagomorpha

du·plic·i·tous \(ˈ)d(y)üˈplisəd·əs, -sətəs\ *adj* **:** showing duplicity

du·plic·i·ty \d(y)ü'plisəd·ē, -ətē, -i\ *n* -ES [ME *duplicite*, fr. MF *duplicité*, fr. LL *duplicitat-, duplicitas*, fr. L *duplic-, duplex* + *-itat-, -itas* -ity] **1 :** doubleness of heart, thought, speech, or action **:** deception by pretending to entertain one set of feelings and acting under the influence of another **:** bad faith **:** DOUBLE-DEALING ⟨the simplicity and openness of their lives brought out for him the ~ that lay at the bottom of ours —Mary Austin⟩ **2 :** the quality or state of being double or twofold ⟨these double stars . . . show a doubling of the spectral lines that must be caused by a ~ in the source of light —*New Internat'l Encyc.*⟩ **3 a :** the use of two or more distinct allegations or answers where one is sufficient **:** pleading double **b :** the union of two incompatible offenses in an indictment **syn** see DECEIT

duplicity theory *or* **duplicity principle** *n* **:** a theory in physiology: the normal retina in man and other vertebrates contains a dual receptor mechanism consisting of (1) organs of achromatic low-intensity vision and (2) organs of chromatic high-intensity vision — compare CONE, ROD; PHOTOPIA, SCOTOPIA

du·ply \'dü'plī\ *n* -ES [ML *duplica*, fr. L *duplic-, duplex* double, twofold — more at DUPLEX] **:** a defendant's answer to a plaintiff's reply in Scots law

du·pon·di·us \d(y)ü'pändēəs\ *n, pl* **dupon·dii** \-ē,ī\ [L, fr. *duo* two + *-pondius* (fr. *pondus*, a weight) — more at POUND] **:** an ancient Roman bronze or under the Empire brass coin worth two asses

dupper *var of* DUBBER

dup·py \'dəpē\ *n* -ES [Bube *dupe* ghost] **:** a haunting spirit of the dead conceived in folklore of West Indian Negroes as a usu. malevolent shadow or immaterial body

du·puy·tren's contracture \də¦pwē·tra"z-, də'pwē·trənz-\ *n, usu cap D* [after Guillaume *Dupuytren* †1835 Fr. surgeon and anatomist] **:** a condition marked by fibrosis with shortening and thickening of the palmar fascia resulting in flexion contracture of the fingers into the palm of the hand

dur \'dù(ə)r\ *adj* [G, fr. MHG *bedūre*, fr. ML *b durum* b natural, fr. L *b* + *durum*, neut. of *durus* hard — more at DURE] **:** MAJOR ⟨C ~⟩

¹du·ra \'d(y)ùrə\ *n* -S [by shortening] **:** DURA MATER

²dura *var of* DURRA

du·ra·bil·i·ty \,d(y)ùrə'biləd·ē, -ətē, -i\ *n* -ES [ME *durabilite*, fr. MF *durabilité*, fr. LL *durabilitat-, durabilitas*, fr. L *durabilis* durable + *-itat-, -itas* -ity] **:** the quality or state of being durable

du·ra·ble \'d(y)ùrəbəl\ *adj* [ME, fr. MF, fr. L *durabilis*, fr. *durare* to last, endure + *-abilis* -able — more at DURE] **:** able to exist for a long time with retention of original qualities, abilities, or capabilities **:** LASTING, ENDURING, UNCHANGEABLE, STRONG ⟨traditional controversies between member nations . . . must be settled before there can be created the general goodwill that makes economic union ~ —Alan Valentine⟩ ⟨the ~ Michelangelo who lived to be 89 —*Time*⟩ ⟨the less ~ rocks were gradually worn away to form the valley⟩ ⟨the small body of ~ poetry written in our time —T.S.Eliot⟩ — compare PERDURABLE

du·ra·ble·ness *n* -ES **:** the quality or state of being durable **:** DURABILITY

durables *or* **durable goods** *n pl* **:** consumer goods or producer goods (as household appliances, automobiles, or machinery) whose usefulness continues for a number of years and is not consumed or destroyed in single usage — called also *hard goods;* sometimes used in sing. ⟨since television became a mass market *durable* —*Wall Street Jour.*⟩

du·ra·bly \-blē, -li\ *adv* **:** in a lasting manner **:** LASTINGLY, STRONGLY ⟨~ bound in buckram⟩

du·rain \'d(y)ù,rān\ *n* -S [L *durus* hard + *-ain* (as in *fusain*)] **:** one of two dull constituents of banded bituminous coal forming lenses or layers and composed of finely comminuted woody debris only partly decomposed — compare CLARAIN, FUSAIN, VITRAIN

¹du·ral \'d(y)ùrəl\ *adj* [¹*dura* + *-al*] **:** of or relating to the dura mater

²du·ral \'d(y)ù,ral\ *n* **:** a Duralumin alloy

Du·ral·u·min \d(y)ə'ralyəmən, d(y)ù'-; ,d(y)ùrəl'yü-\ *sometimes* ,d(y)ùrəl'yü-\ *trademark* — used for an alloy consisting of 95.5 parts of aluminum to 3 parts of copper, 1 of manganese, and 0.5 of magnesium that after age-hardening is comparable in strength and hardness to soft steel

du·ra ma·ter \'d(y)ùrə,mäd·ə(r), -ür-, -mä|, -mā|, |tə-, ,=¦=\ *also* **dura** *n* -S [ME, fr. ML, lit., hard mother] **:** the tough fibrous membrane lined with endothelium on the inner surface that envelops the brain and spinal cord external to the arachnoid and pia mater, in the cranium closely lining the bone and not dipping down between the convolutions though certain large supporting folds (as the falx cerebri and tentorium cerebelli) are derived from it and containing numerous blood vessels and venous sinuses and in the spinal canal being separated from the bone by a considerable space and containing no venous sinuses

du·ra·men \d(y)ə'rāmən, -)ù'-\ *n* -S [NL, fr. L, hardness, fr. *durare* to harden, fr. *durus* hard — more at DURE] **:** HEARTWOOD

du·rance \'d(y)ùrən(t)s, -ür-\ *n* -S [MF, fr. *durer* to last, endure + *-ance* — more at DURE] **1 a** *obs* **:** CONTINUANCE, DURATION **b** *archaic* **:** DURABILITY **c** *archaic* **:** ENDURANCE **2 :** restraint by or as if by physical force **:** CONFINEMENT, IMPRISONMENT ⟨he has not, certainly, been cramped . . . there has been no ~ within the four walls of the House of Commons —Max Beerbohm⟩ — often used in the phrase *durance vile* ⟨after ~ vile of ten days he was released —J.E.Davies⟩ **3 :** an obsolete strong felted cloth of woolen or worsted usu. made in imitation of buff leather

du·ran·gite \d(y)ə'raŋ,gīt, -)ù'-\ *n* -S [*Durango*, state in Mexico + E *-ite*] **:** an orange-red mineral $NaAlFAsO_4$ consisting of a fluoride and arsenate of sodium and aluminum

du·ran·go \-ŋ(,)gō\ *n* -S *often cap* [fr. *Durango*, Mexico] **:** CARTOUCHE 6

du·ra·ni \dü'ränē\ *n, pl* **durani** *or* **duranis** *usu cap* [Pashto] **1 :** a people of mixed Semitic and Iranian stock that comprise the most dominant group of Afghans **2 :** a member of the Durani people

dur·ant \'d(y)ùrənt\ *n* -S [by alter.] **:** DURANCE 3

du·ran·ta \d(y)ə'rantə, -)ù'-\ *n, cap* [NL, after C. *Durante* †1590 Ital. herbalist] **:** a genus of tropical American shrubs (family Verbenaceae) with terminal long racemes of small flowers

du·ran·te \-tē\ *prep* [L, abl. of *durant-, durans*, pres. part. of *durare* to last — more at DURE] *law* **:** DURING

durante ab·sen·tia \-(,)ab'sench(ē)ə, -,əb-\ *adv* [L] **:** during absence

durante be·ne·pla·ci·to \-,benə'plasə,tō, -nē'-\ *adv* [L] **:** during the pleasure or at the discretion (as of a king) — usu. used of a tenure of office

durante fu·ro·re \-fyə'rōrē, -yü'-\ *adv* [L] **:** during madness

durante mi·no·re ae·ta·te \-mə'nōrē,ī'täd·ē\ *adv* [L] **:** during minority

durante vi·du·i·ta·te \-,vijəwə'täd·ē\ *adv* [L] **:** during widowhood

durante vi·ta \-'vīd·ə; dü'rän,tä'wē,tä\ *adv* [L] **:** during life

duras *pl of* DURA

du·ra·tion \d(y)ə'rāshən, -)ù'-\ *n* -S [ML *duration-, duratio*, fr. L *duratus* (past part. of *durare* to last) + *-ion-, -io* -ion — more at DURE] **1 :** the quality or state of lasting for a period of time **:** continuation in time or existence **:** LASTINGNESS ⟨a play of short ~⟩ **2 :** a portion of time which is measurable or during which something exists, lasts, or is in progress ⟨gave up all worries for the ~ of the holiday⟩ ⟨the ~ of a meal⟩ ⟨the ~ of life⟩ ⟨the ~ of the world⟩ ⟨the ~ of the play⟩; *specif* **:** the period of time during which something that almost totally obstructs or prevents normal activities (as a war) or that engages virtually all one's efforts or attention is in progress — used with *the* ⟨universities had to be persuaded to scrap their scientific and educational responsibilities for the ~ and take on war work —J.B.Conant⟩ ⟨once you were in the theater, and the lights were dimmed, you were there for the ~ —Burns Mantle⟩ **3** *obs* **:** durableness or endurance in use — **du·ra·tion·al** \-shənᵊl, -shnəl\ *adj* — **du·ra·tion·al·ly** \-ē\ *adv*

¹du·ra·tive \'d(y)ùrəd·iv\ *sometimes* d(y)ə'rād-- *or* -)ù'-\ *adj* [ISV *durat-* (fr. L *duratus*, past part. of *durare* to last) + *-ive*] **1 a :** not completed **:** CONTINUING **b :** implying duration or continuance ⟨a ~ prefix⟩ **2 :** IMPERFECTIVE

²durative \"\ *n* -S [ISV, fr. *durative*, adj.] **1 :** CONTINUANT **a 2 :** the durative aspect in a language **:** a durative verb form

dur·azol blue 8G \'d(y)ùrə,zōl-, -,zōl-\ *n, usu cap D&B* [origin unknown] **:** a direct dye — see DYE table I (under *Direct Blue 86*)

¹dur·ban \'dùrbən\ *n* **:** DURBEN OIRAT

²dur·ban \'dərbən\ *adj, usu cap* [fr. *Durban*, Union of So. Africa] **:** of or from the city of Durban, Union of So. Africa **:** of the kind or style prevalent in Durban

dur·bar \'dər,bär, (,)dər'b-\ *n* -S [Hindi *darbār*, fr. Per, fr. *dar* door + *bār* door, admission, audience] **1 a :** court held by a native Indian prince **b :** a festive reception given by a maharajah for his subjects at which they pledge their fealty to him **c :** a formal reception of native Indian princes given by the British governor-general **2** *India* **:** an audience hall **3 :** the governing body of a native Indian state; *also* **:** a member of such a body

dur·ben oi·rat \,dùrbən'òirət\ *n, pl* **durben oirat** *or* **durben oirats** *usu cap D&O* **:** a Mongol people found in the western part of the Mongolian plateau and in the lake region of Tsinghai province in China

durch·kom·po·niert \¦dùrk,kòmpō¦ni(ə)rt\ *adj* [G, fr. past part. of *durchkomponieren* to create through-composed music, fr. *durch* through (fr. OHG *duruh*) + *komponieren* to compose, fr. L *componere* — more at THROUGH, COMPOSE] **:** THROUGH-COMPOSED

dur·dum \'dərdəm\ *var of* DIRDUM

¹dure \'d(y)ù(ə)r\ *vb* -ED/-ING/-S [ME *duren*, fr. OF *durer*, fr. L *durare* to last, endure, prob. fr. *durare* to harden, fr. *durus* hard] *vi, archaic* **:** ENDURE ~ *vt, obs* **:** SUSTAIN, ENDURE

²dure \"\ *adj* [ME, fr. MF *dur*, fr. L *durus* hard, rough; perh. akin to Skt *dāruṇa* hard, rough, *dāru* wood — more at TREE] *archaic* **:** HARD, SEVERE ⟨the winter is severe, and life is ~, and rude —W.H.Russell⟩

du·rene \'d(y)ù,rēn\ *n* -S [ISV *dur-* (fr. L *durus* hard) + *-ene*] **:** a colorless crystalline hydrocarbon $C_6H_2(CH_3)_4$ having an odor like camphor and occurring in coal tar and in petroleum; 1,2,4,5-tetramethyl-benzene

dü·rer·esque *or* **du·rer·esque** \¦d(y)ùrə¦resk, ¦dūrə¦-\ *adj, usu cap* [Albrecht *Dürer* †1528 German painter and engraver + E *-esque*] **:** resembling in style or manner the work of the artist Dürer noted for his accurate and delicate drawing and his delineation of character esp. in his engravings which are characterized by profuse and literal detail

du·ress \d(y)ə'res, -)ù'- *sometimes* 'd(y)ù,res *or*)ü,-\ *n* -ES [ME *duresse* hardness, severity, oppression, restraint, confinement, fr. MF *duresce, durece* hardness, hardheartedness, fr. L *duritia*, fr. *durus* hard — more at DURE] **1 :** restraint or check by force (as arrest or imprisonment) **:** DURANCE ⟨while the German army was still held in ~ by the Versailles treaty —S.L.A.Marshall⟩ **2 :** stringent compulsion by threat of danger, hardship, or retribution **:** distress arising from such compulsion **:** COERCION ⟨a population working under the ~ of dictatorship —*Science*⟩ ⟨ordinary clergymen subscribe them under ~ because they cannot otherwise obtain ordination —G.B.Shaw⟩ **3 :** compulsion or constraint by which a person is illegally forced to do or forbear some act by actual imprisonment or physical violence to the person or by threat of such violence, the violence or threat being such as to inspire a person of ordinary firmness with fear of serious injury to the person (as loss of liberty or of life or limb), reputation, or fortune **syn** see FORCE

du·rez·za \dü'retsə\ *n* -S [It, lit., hardness, fr. L *duritia*] *music* **:** HARSHNESS

dur·fee grass \'dərfē,-\ *n* [origin unknown] **:** COUCH GRASS 1a

dur·gan *or* **dur·gen** \'dərgən\ *n* -S [perh. fr. ME *dwerg* dwarf — more at DWARF] *dial Eng* **:** an undersized person or animal

¹dur·ham \'dər·əm, 'də·rəm, 'dùrəm\ *adj, usu cap* [fr. *Durham* county, England] **:** of or from the county of Durham, England **:** of the kind or style prevalent in Durham

²durham \"\ *n* -S *usu cap* **:** SHORTHORN

durham boat *n, usu cap D* [after Robert *Durham*, 18th cent. Am. boat builder] **:** a long narrow flat-bottomed boat used to transport freight on the rivers of No. America in the 18th and early 19th centuries

du·ri·an \'dùrēən, ¦dùrē¦än\ *also* **du·ri·on** \'dùrēən\ *n* -S [Malay *durian*, fr. *duri* thorn] **1 :** the large oval or globose fruit of a tree (*Durio zibethinus*) of the East Indian islands having a hard prickly rind, a soft cream-colored pulp, a most delicious flavor, an offensive odor, and seeds that are roasted and eaten like chestnuts **2 :** the tree that bears durians

du·ri·crust \'d(y)ùrə,krəst\ *n* [L *durus* hard + E *-i-* + *crust* — more at DURE] **:** a hard crust formed at or near the surface of the ground as a result of the upward migration and evaporation of mineral-bearing ground water — compare CALICHE

¹dur·ing \'d(y)ùriŋ, -ür-, -rēŋ\ *prep* [ME, fr. pres. part. of *duren* to last — more at DURE] **1 :** throughout the continuance or course of ⟨no attainder of treason shall work corruption of blood or forfeiture except ~ the life of the person attainted —*U.S.Constitution*⟩ **2 :** at some point in the course of ⟨been away for a couple of weeks ~ the summer —J.M.Barzun⟩

²during \"\ *adj* [ME, fr. pres. part. of *duren* to last] *archaic* **:** ENDURING, LASTING

du·rio \'d(y)ùrē,ō\ *n* [NL, fr. Malay *durian*] **1** *cap* **:** a small genus of tall Asiatic and Indian trees (family Bombacaceae) with tapering leaves and small greenish flowers **2** -S **:** any tree of the genus *Durio*

durity *n* -ES [L *duritas*, fr. *durus* hard + *-itas* -ity — more at DURE] *obs* **:** HARDNESS

durk \'dərk\ *Scot var of* DIRK

durk·hei·mi·an \(')d(y)ùr¦kemēən, -kām-,-kīm-\ *adj, usu cap* [Émile *Durkheim* †1917 Fr. sociologist + E *-ian*] **:** of or relating to Émile Durkheim or his sociological theory esp. that social science must be made an objective statistical study

dur·mast \'dər,mast\ *also* **durmast oak** *n* [perh. alter. of *dun mast*, fr. ¹*dun* + *mast* (acorns)] **:** a European oak (*Quercus sessiliflora* or *Q. petraea*) that is valued esp. for its dark heavy tough elastic wood

¹durn \'dərn\ *n* -S [ME *dyrne*, of Scand origin; akin to OSw *dyrni* doorpost, Norw *dyrn;* akin to ON *dyrr* door — more at DOOR] **1** *dial Eng* **:** GATEPOST, DOORPOST **2** *dial Eng* **:** the wooden framework of a door — usu. used in pl.

²durn *var of* DARN

durned *var of* DARNED

du·ro \'dù(,)rō\ *n* -S [Sp, short for *peso duro*, lit., hard peso] **:** a Spanish or Spanish American peso or silver dollar

du·roc \'d(y)ù,räk, -ü,-\ *n* [after *Duroc*, 19th cent. Am. stallion living on the farm where the Duroc breed of swine was developed] **1** *usu cap* **:** a breed of large vigorous red lard-type hogs of American origin **2** -S *often cap* **:** any animal of the Duroc breed

duroc-jersey \'=¦=¦=\ *n, usu cap D&J* **:** DUROC

du·rom·e·ter \d(y)ə'rämǝd·ə(r)\ *n* [ISV *duro-* (fr. L *durus* hard) + *-meter* — more at DURE] **:** an instrument for measuring hardness that consists essentially of a small drill or blunt indenter point working under pressure (as that exerted by a spring)

du·roy \d(y)ə'rȯi\ *n* -S [origin unknown] **:** a coarse woolen cloth made in England in the 18th century and used chiefly for men's wear

dur·ra *also* **du·ra** *or* **dhur·ra** *or* **doo·ra** *or* **dou·ra** *or* **dou·rah** \'dùrə\ *n* -S [Ar *dhurah*] **:** any of several grain sorghums that are of medium size with dry pithy stalks and narrow leaves and are widely grown in warm dry parts of southern Asia and northern Africa and to a limited extent in the southwestern U.S. — called also *guinea corn, Indian millet*

durrin *var of* DHURRIN

durst *archaic & dial past of* DARE

durukuli *var of* DOUROUCOULI

du·rum wheat \'d(y)ùr|əm-, -)ər|\ *also* **durum** *n* -S [NL *durum* (specific epithet of *Triticum durum*), fr. L, neut. of *durus* hard — more at DURE] **:** a wheat (*Triticum durum*) that occurs in several cultivated varieties, is grown esp. in southern Russia, No. Africa, and north central No. America as a spring wheat, has slender compact spikes with spikelets containing two to four very hard translucent white or red kernels, and yields a flour which is high in gluten-producing proteins and is chiefly used in making semolina, macaroni, and spaghetti

dur·wan \də(r)'wän, -wȯn\ *n* -S [Per *darwān*, fr. *dar* door (fr. MPer, fr. OPer *duvar-*) + Per *-wān* keeping, guarding, fr. MPer *-pān;* akin to Skt *dvār* door — more at DOOR] *India* **:** PORTER, DOORKEEPER

dur·yl \'d(y)ùrəl\ *n* -S [ISV *durene* + *-yl*] **:** a univalent radical $C_6H(CH_3)_4$ derived from durene; 2,3,5,6-tetramethyl-phenyl

dur·za·da \də(r)'zädə\ *n, pl* **durzada** *or* **durzadas** *usu cap* **1 :** a Persian people extending throughout Makran and similar to the Dehwar **2 :** a member of the Durzada people

dur·zee \dər'zē, '=,=\ *var of* DARZI

¹dusk \'dəsk\ *adj* [ME *dosk, duske*, alter. of OE *dox;* akin to OE *dunn* dun, OHG *tusin* yellow, OS *dosan* chestnut brown, ON *dunna*, a kind of duck, MIr *doun* dark, L *fuscus* dark brown, blackish, Skt *dhūsara* dust colored, L *fumus* smoke — more at FUME] **:** DUSKY ⟨the dim, ~ yard —Thomas Williams⟩ ⟨~ faces with white silken turbants wreathed —John Milton⟩ ⟨called the children in when it grew ~⟩ **syn** see DARK

²dusk \"\ *vb* -ED/-ING/-S [ME *dosken, dusken*, fr. *dosk, duske*, n.] *vi* **:** to become dusky or dark ⟨in the ~*ing* room —Walter Karig⟩ ~ *vt* **1 :** to make dark or dim ⟨a gray light ~*ed* the room —William Sansom⟩ **2 :** to darken in mood or spirit **:** cast gloom upon ⟨his national formality ~*ed* by the saturnine mood of ill health —Herman Melville⟩

³dusk \"\ *n* -S [¹*dusk*] **1 :** the darker part of twilight or of dawn **2 a :** darkness or semidarkness caused by the shutting out of light ⟨the cool ~ of ancient tombs⟩ ⟨the ~ of the great forest⟩ **b :** the condition of being dark or darkish in color ⟨ivory skin framed in the silken ~ of her tresses —Kay Rogers⟩ **3 a :** a variable color averaging a bluish gray that is redder and deeper than clair de lune, redder, lighter, and stronger than Medici blue, and redder and deeper than puritan gray **b :** a dark purplish gray that is bluer and duller than slate, redder, lighter, and slightly stronger than charcoal, and bluer and darker than pigeon

dusk blue *n* **:** a pale purplish blue to pale violet that is darker than average twilight blue

dusk dark *also* **dusky dark** *n, chiefly South & Midland* **:** TWILIGHT

dusk·i·ly \'dəskəlē, -li\ *adv* **:** in a dusky manner **:** OBSCURELY

dusk·i·ness \-kēnəs, -kin-\ *n* -ES **:** the quality or state of being dusky **:** DUSK

dusk·ish \-kish\ *adj* **:** rather dark or black **:** partially obscured — **dusk·ish·ly** *adv* — **dusk·ish·ness** *n* -ES

dusk·ly \-klē, -li\ *adv* [¹*dusk* + *-ly*] **:** DUSKILY

dusk·ness \-knəs\ *n* -ES **:** DUSKINESS

¹dusky \'dəskē, -ki\ *adj* -ER/-EST [¹*dusk* + *-y*] **1 :** somewhat dark in color **:** of low lightness **:** BLACKISH ⟨a ~ brown⟩ ⟨a ~ blush rose to her cheek —Edith Wharton⟩; *specif* **:** having dark skin — used of a colored person **2 :** characterized by slight or deficient light **:** somewhat dark **:** DIM ⟨the room was already ~ . . . and one of the boys switched on the light —Willa Cather⟩ ⟨in that ~ firelight —Ellen Glasgow⟩ **3 :** GLOOMY, DEPRESSING ⟨a ~ frown settled on his face⟩ **4 :** not clear **:** partially hidden **:** OBSCURE ⟨through all the winding corridors of literary history to the ~ regions of folklore —Newton Arvin⟩ ⟨the records of his life . . . are ~ and brief —Carl Van Doren⟩ **syn** see DARK

²dusky \"\ *n* -ES **:** a dusky color ⟨a white bird barred with ~⟩

dusky duck *n* **:** BLACK DUCK a

dusky-footed rat \'==,==-\ *n* **:** an Australian water rat (*Rattus lutreolus*)

dusky grouse *n* **:** a large grouse (*Dendragapus obscurus*) of the mountains of the western U.S.

dusky salamander *n* **1 :** a dark color phase of the red-backed

a dusky salamander 2

salamander **2 :** any of several common No. American plethodontid salamanders (genus *Desmognathus*) typically mottled or marked with dull browns or grayish black

dusky shark *n* **:** a shark (*Carcharias obscurus*) of the No. Atlantic similar to the cub shark but darker

dusky wing *n* **:** any of numerous skipper butterflies (genus *Erynnis*) having dark wings with inconspicuous patterns — compare SKIPPER

düs·sel·dorf *or* **dues·sel·dorf** *or* **dus·sel·dorf** \'düsəl,dȯrf, 'dyü-, G 'dʊs-\ *adj, usu cap* [fr. *Düsseldorf*, Germany] **:** of or from the city of Düsseldorf, Germany **:** of the kind or style prevalent in Düsseldorf

dusserah *usu cap, var of* DASEHRA

dus·sert·ite \'dəsə(r),tīt\ *n* -S [F, fr. D. *Dussert*, 20th cent. Fr. mining engineer + F *-ite*] **:** a mineral $BaFe_3(AsO_4)_2(OH)_5.H_2O$ consisting of hydrous basic arsenate of barium and iron

dus·su·mie·ri·idae \,dəsəmə'rīə,dē\ *n pl, cap* [NL, fr. *Dussumieria*, type genus (fr. the name *Dussumier* + NL *-ia*) + *-idae*] **:** a family of marine fishes (order Isospondyli) comprising the round herrings — see ETRUMEUS

¹dust \'dəst\ *n* -S *often attrib* [ME, fr. OE *dūst;* akin to OHG *tunst, tunist* storm, breath, Dan *dyst* flour dust, Norw *dysja* to drizzle, L *furere* to rage, Gk *thyein* to rage, seethe, sacrifice, *thymos* breath, life, spirit, soul, Lith *dvasas* spirit, breath, Skt *dhvaṁsati* he perishes, falls to dust, L *fumus* smoke — more at FUME] **1 :** fine dry pulverized particles of earth or other matter **:** something reduced to minute portions **:** fine powder ⟨the floors were deep in the ~ of spring sandstorms —Willa Cather⟩ ⟨a huge cloud of snow spray and snow ~ —Carl Jonas⟩: as **a :** VOLCANIC DUST **b :** meteoric dust **c :** GOLD DUST **d :** finely divided or ground food ⟨asparagus, dipped in egg and cracker ~ —H.H.Huff⟩ **e :** a material (as an insecticide or fungicide) used in a dry form resembling dust to control pests **2 a :** the particles into which a thing disintegrates **:** the earthy remains of a body (as a human corpse) once alive ⟨the repository of the ~ of many of those illustrious men —C.B.Fairbanks⟩ **b :** something that is left after the substance of a thing is gone ⟨stirring up the ~ of history —Richard Joseph⟩ **c :** something that beclouds or dulls ⟨yes, I know, . . . though he tried to throw ~ in my eyes —Kathleen Freeman⟩ ⟨society can do something for itself . . . by blowing out of the museums and galleries the ~ of erudition and the stale incense of hero worship —Clive Bell⟩ **3 :** the mortal body of a human being ⟨the troubles of our proud and angry ~ are from eternity, and shall not fail —A.E.Housman⟩ **4 a :** something worthless ⟨vile gold, dross, ~ —Shak.⟩ **b :** a state of humiliation ⟨her spirit is contrite to the ~ —Eden Phillpotts⟩ **5 a :** the earth esp. as a place of burial ⟨for now shall I sleep in the ~ — Job 7:21 (AV)⟩ **b :** the surface of the ground ⟨he railed at me and made to fight me, I took off my hat, and there I laid him in the ~ —Gilbert Parker⟩ — compare *bite the dust* at ¹BITE **6** *archaic* **:** MONEY **7 :** a small quantity (as of a fine or powdered substance) ⟨add a ~ of flour⟩ ⟨a cherry sundae with a ~ of nuts over the top —Hugh MacLennan⟩ **8 a :** a cloud of dust ⟨the wagon, with a thin ~ rising from the hooves, went on into the lazy afternoon —H.V.Morton⟩ **b :** CONFUSION, DISTURBANCE ⟨let us kick up what ~ we will over "Imperial ideals" —A.T.Quiller-Couch⟩ **c :** DUSTUP **9** *now dial* **:** a single particle (as of earth) ⟨to touch a ~ of England's ground —Shak.⟩ **10** *Brit* **:** sweepings or other refuse ready for collection **11 :** a light olive brown that is lighter than drab, paler than sponge, and paler and slightly redder than average mustard tan — called also *antelope* **12** *slang Austral* **:** FLOUR — **in dust and ashes 1 :** with dust and ashes put on the head as a sign of grief or humiliation **2 :** with repentance and sorrow **:** in sackcloth and ashes

²dust \"\ *vb* -ED/-ING/-S [ME *dustyn*, fr. *dust*, n.] *vt* **1 a :** to reduce to dust **b :** to reduce to a fine powder **:** LEVIGATE **2** *archaic* **:** to make dusty **:** soil with dust **3 a :** to make free of dust **:** brush, wipe, or sweep away dust from ⟨~ the table⟩ — often used with *off* **b :** to brush away like dust ⟨~*ed* the moths out of the furs —Meridel Le Sueur⟩ **c :** to prepare to use again **:** refurbish or renovate for use (something that has long been neglected or disused) — used with *off* ⟨standards are ~*ed* off again and reappraised, reassessed —L.H.Bristol⟩ **d :** to free (raw wool) of loose dirt by shaking in a machine **4 :** to sprinkle with or as if with dust, powder, or other fine particles ⟨whipped cream ~*ed* with cinnamon —S.H.Delaplane⟩ ⟨a face . . . covered with little freckles as if it had been ~*ed* over with gold motes of the light —Edith Sitwell⟩ ⟨~*ing* crops with insecticide⟩ ⟨~*ed* the table for fingerprints⟩; *specif* **:** to spread or distribute a coating of finely ground rock or shale dust in (coal-mine workings) in order to reduce the explosion hazard **5 :** to give a beating to **:** THRASH, WHIP ⟨I will ~ their backsides for them —T.B.Costain⟩ **6 a :** to strew or sprinkle in the form of dust **:** SIFT ⟨sulfur ~*ed* into shoes and clothes —*Girl Scout Handbook*⟩ ⟨airplanes ~ insecticides over the crops⟩ **b :** to sow (a crop) in dry soil — used with *in* ⟨*dusted*-in rye⟩ **7 :** to dupe or confuse as if by throwing dust in the eyes ~ *vi* **1 a :** to disintegrate into dust **b :** to give off or produce dust — used of a concrete floor **2** *slang* **:** HURRY; *esp* **:** to leave in a hurry **3** *of a bird* **:** to sprinkle itself with dust **4 :** to remove dust (as from furniture) ⟨I went in now and then to ~ and clean —B.A.Williams⟩ — **dust a dam :** to fill up the interstices between the planks in a splash-dam gate with earth or gravel — **dust one's jacket :** to give one a beating

dust bag *n* **:** the part of a vacuum sweeper in which dust and other sweepings are collected

dust ball *n* **:** a concretion composed of vegetable or mineral matter found in the intestines (as of the horse) and varying in size from a few ounces to several pounds — called also *intestinal calculus;* compare HAIR BALL

dustband *n* **:** a metal ring inserted between the upper and lower plates of a watch to exclude dust

dustbin \ˈ=,=\ *n* **1** *Brit* **a :** a usu. metal receptacle for rubbish **:** TRASH CAN **b :** a garbage can **2 :** a place of neglect or oblivion ⟨the ~ of public indifference⟩

dust·blu \ˈ=ˌblü\ *n* -s [ˡ*dust* + *blu,* alter. of *blue*] **:** a pale blue that is redder and darker than average powder blue, redder and duller than Sistine, and redder, stronger, and slightly darker than average cadet gray

dust board *also* **dust bottom** *n* **:** a horizontal board that separates one drawer from another (as in a chest of drawers)

dust bowl *n* **:** a region that suffers from prolonged droughts and dust storms

dust bowler *n* **:** an inhabitant of a dust bowl

dustbox \ˈ=,=\ *n* **1 :** a box used to hold or collect dust: as **a :** a box containing sand or powder (as for drying ink) **b :** DUSTBIN **c :** DUST CHAMBER **2 :** the part of a box strike that encloses the opening thus concealing the jamb

dust cap *n* **:** a protecting cover for the lens of a telescope sight

dust cart *n, Brit* **:** a vehicle used for rubbish collection

dust cell *n* **:** a pulmonary histiocyte that takes up and eliminates foreign particles introduced into the lung alveoli with inspired air

dust chamber *n* **:** a chamber through which gases are passed to permit them to deposit solid particles (as in connection with a lead or copper smelting furnace)

dustcloth \ˈ=,=\ *n* **1 :** a cloth for dusting **2 :** DUST COVER 1

dustcoat \ˈ=,=\ *n, chiefly Brit* **:** DUSTER 2

dust counter *n* **:** an instrument for determining the number of dust particles or condensation nuclei per unit volume of a sample of air

dust cover *n* **1 :** a piece of cloth (as sheeting) used to protect furniture and other articles when not in use from soil, fading, wear **2 :** JACKET 3f(1)

dust devil *n* **:** a whirlwind containing sand or dust seen esp. in arid and semiarid regions — called also *dust whirl, sand column*

dust disease *n* **:** PNEUMOCONIOSIS

dusted target *n* **:** a target in trapshooting that is struck by the shot but not broken and thus not scored as a hit

dust·er \ˈdəstə(r)\ *n* -s **1 :** one that removes dust and dirt: as **a :** a cloth or brush for dusting (as furniture) **b :** a machine typically employing a rotating wire-cloth cylinder for removing dust from raw material (as rags) prior to pulping — called also *willow* **c :** a machine for brushing and sifting the flour from bran or shorts **2 a :** a lightweight washable overgarment usu. made like a coat and worn to prevent clothing from becoming soiled **b :** a woman's lightweight dress-length housecoat **c :** a woman's loose-fitting unlined summer coat made of lightweight material **3 :** one that scatters dustlike material: as **a :** a container with a perforated lid for sifting or sprinkling ⟨a sugar ~⟩ **b :** an implement or machine for applying insecticidal or fungicidal dusts to crops **4 :** one whose work is removing dust or sprinkling with a dusting of some substance **5 :** a nonproductive oil well **6** *South & Midland* **:** DUST STORM **7** *slang Brit* **:** a ship's flag **8 a :** a baseball pitched at or near the batter

duster 3b

dust exhaust *n* **:** a device for drawing off dust (as that produced in dry grinding)

dust furrow *n* **:** a furrow or trench around a field used to check migrating insects (as chinch bugs)

dust gun *n* **:** a hand device used for applying dust to a surface (as an insecticide to crops or calcium cyanide in the burrows of rodents to destroy them by gas)

dustheap \ˈ=,=\ *n* **1 :** a pile of refuse **2 :** the status to which something unimportant, unwanted, or forgotten is relegated ⟨ferreting out from the ~ of time the half-obliterated data of circumstance and events —*Manchester Guardian Weekly*⟩

dust·i·ly \ˈdəstəlē, -li\ *adv* **:** in a dusty condition **:** with much dust

dust·i·ness \-tēnəs, -tin-\ *n* -ES **:** the quality or state of being dusty

dusting *n* -s [fr. gerund of ²*dust*] **1 :** a small quantity lightly applied to or sprinkled on or appearing as if sprinkled on a surface ⟨a ~ of powder over her distressing freckles —Elizabeth Goudge⟩ ⟨the wing is much overlaid with olivaceous ~ —A.B. Klots⟩ **2** *slang* **a :** BEATING **b** *of a boat* **:** a buffeting in stormy weather **3 :** the formation of dust by the wearing away of concrete floor surfaces under traffic

dusting brush *n* **:** a brush used for dusting

dusting powder *n* **:** a powder used esp. on the skin or on wounds (as for allaying irritation or absorbing moisture)

dust jacket *n* **:** JACKET 3f(1)

dust·less \ˈdəstləs\ *adj* **:** free from dust

dustlike \ˈ=,=\ *adj* **:** as fine and powdery as dust

dustman *n* **:** BOOK LOUSE

dust·man \ˈdəs(t)mən\ *n, pl* **dustmen 1** *Brit* **:** a trash collector or a garbage collector **2** *Brit* **:** SANDMAN

dust mop *n* **:** DRY MOP

dust mulch *n* **:** a fine loose dry layer of surface soil maintained by cultivation under the assumption that it will prevent evaporation of soil moisture

dust off *vt* **1 :** to intentionally pitch a baseball directly at or near (the batter) **2** *slang* **:** KILL

dus·toor *or* **dus·tour** \dəˈstü(ə)r\ *var of* DASTUR

dus·too·ree *or* **dus·too·ri** \-ürē\ *var of* DASTURI

dustpan \ˈ=,=\ *n* **:** a shovel-shaped pan usu. with a short handle for receiving and conveying away dirt swept from the floor

dust pearl *n* **:** a very small seed pearl

dust process *n* **:** the process of molding ceramic ware by dry pressing

dustproof *or* **dust-tight** \ˈ=ˈ=\ *adj* **:** impervious to dust **:** so tight as to exclude dust

dustrag \ˈ=,=\ *n* **:** DUST CLOTH 1

dust remover *n* **:** a filter for the air intake of an internal-combustion engine

dustpan

dust ruffle *n* **1 :** a ruffle on the lower edge of a woman's skirt; *esp* **:** one on the inside to keep the skirt clean **2 :** a decorative ruffle attached to the rails or springs of a bed and reaching the floor; *also* **:** a wide ruffle on the edge of a bedspread

dusts *pl of* DUST, *pres 3d sing of* DUST

dust sheet *n* **:** DUST COVER 1

dust shot *n* **:** the smallest size of shot

dust storm *n* **1 :** a violent dust-laden whirlwind that moves across an arid region and that is usu. associated with very hot excessively dry air and attended by high electrical tension **2 :** strong winds bearing clouds of dust

dus·tuck *or* **dus·tuk** \ˈdə(ˌ)stək\ *n* -s [Hindi *dastak,* fr. Per] *India* **:** a passport or customs permit

dustup \ˈ=,=\ *n* -s [fr. *dust up,* v.] **:** QUARREL, ROW, ARGUMENT ⟨another literary ~ . . . has been raging between publishers and authors —Mollie Panter-Downes⟩

dust well *n* **:** a pit in a glacier formed by the more rapid melting of the ice beneath a deposit of dust or earth

dust whirl *n* **:** DUST DEVIL

dust wrapper *n* **:** JACKET 3f(1)

dusty \ˈdəstē, -ti\ *adj* -ER/-EST [ME, fr. ¹*dust* + *-y*] **1 :** marked by the presence of dust **:** filled with dust **:** covered or clouded with dust ⟨the table is ~⟩ ⟨two thirsty travelers . . . came upon the lake after a ~ trek —*Amer. Guide Series: Calif.*⟩ **2 :** consisting of dust **:** POWDERY ⟨two acres of stony, ~ ground —Bernard Gutteridge⟩ **3 :** WORTHLESS, CONTEMPTIBLE, MISERABLE, SORDID ⟨he who is born on the steps of a throne and never ascends them has a ~ fate —*Times Lit. Supp.*⟩ **4 :** DIM, CLOUDED ⟨in the moonlight grows a smile mid its rays of ~ pearl —G.W.Russell⟩ ⟨your splendor is ~ —Max Beerbohm⟩ **5** *of the weather* **:** STORMY, BLOWY **6 :** dry and lifeless (as from age or disuse) **:** BARREN, UNPRODUCTIVE, STALE, UNSATISFYING; *also* **:** lacking in interest **:** DULL ⟨the old man will suck a little of her sweetness to prolong his ~ life —Elinor Wylie⟩ ⟨while the work of his contemporaries today seems ~ and dated, his drawings still retain their freshness and vigor —L.R.Sander⟩ ⟨ah, what a ~ answer gets the soul when hot for certainties in this our life —George Meredith⟩ — **not so dusty** *Brit* **:** pretty good **:** not bad

dusty aqua *n* **:** a pale blue that is greener and duller than average powder blue, greener and less strong than Sistine, and greener and slightly lighter than average cadet gray

dusty aqua blue *n* **:** a pale blue that is greener and duller than average powder blue and greener and less strong than Sistine

dusty aqua green *n* **:** a pale green that is bluer and deeper than celadon gray, bluer and stronger than bayberry gray, and bluer and darker than spray green

dusty blue *n* **:** a variable color averaging a pale blue that is redder and darker than average powder blue, redder and less strong than Sistine, and greener and stronger than average cadet gray — called also *mist blue, misty blue*

dusty cedar *n* **:** a variable color averaging a grayish red that is paler and very slightly bluer than bois de rose and yellower and paler than blush rose or appleblossom

dusty clover *n* **:** a bush clover (*Lespedeza capitata*) with silvery foliage

dusty copen blue *n* **:** a deep blue that is greener and much paler than Yale blue and greener and much paler than royal (sense 8b)

dusty coral *n* **:** a variable color averaging a dark pink that is yellower and paler than wild rose and yellower and lighter than average colonial rose

dustyfoot \ˈ=,=\ *n, pl* **dustyfeet** *or* **dustyfoots** [ME *dustiefute,* fr. *dustie, dusty* dusty + *fute, fot* foot; trans. of AF *piepowdrous*] *Scot* **:** a wayfaring peddler — compare COURT OF PIEPOUDRE

dusty green *n* **1 :** a variable color averaging a pale green that is yellower and deeper than spray green and bluer, stronger, and slightly darker than aloes green **2 :** a light grayish olive that is darker than Quaker gray and greener and less strong than hemp

dusty jade green *n* **:** a pale green that is bluer, lighter, and stronger than celadon gray or bayberry gray and bluer, lighter, and stronger than spray green

dusty lavender *n* **:** a pale violet that is deeper than old lavender (sense 1) and redder and deeper than dusty periwinkle blue

dusty lilac *n* **:** a grayish purple that is redder, lighter, and stronger than telegraph blue, bluer and stronger than mauve gray or average orchid gray, and bluer, lighter, and stronger than average rose mauve

dusty mauve *n* **:** a pale purple that is redder and duller than average lavender or wistaria (sense 2a) and redder and deeper than flossflower blue

dusty miller *n* **1 :** any of several plants having ashy-gray or white tomentose leaves: as **a :** a stiff perennial (*Senecio cineraria*) with very white woolly pinnatifid leaves **b :** SNOW-IN-SUMMER a **c :** MULLEIN PINK **d :** either of two plants of the genus *Centaurea* (*C. cineraria* and *C. gymnocarpa*) with white tomentose foliage **e :** BEACH WORMWOOD **2 :** MILLER 2a

dusty olive *n* **:** a variable color averaging a light olive that is greener and stronger than citrine, deeper and slightly redder than grape green, and stronger and slightly redder than old moss green

dusty orange *n* **:** a moderate orange that is yellower, darker, and slightly stronger than honeydew and yellower and duller than Persian orange

dusty orchid *n* **:** a variable color averaging a pale reddish purple that is bluer and duller than anemone

dusty peach *n* **:** a grayish to moderate yellowish pink

dusty periwinkle blue *n* **:** a pale violet that is bluer, lighter, and stronger than old lavender (sense 1) and bluer and paler than dusty lavender

dusty pink *n* **:** a moderate yellowish pink that is yellower and duller than coral pink, redder and duller than peach pink, and redder and duller than average peach

dusty rose *n* **:** a variable color averaging a light grayish purplish red

dusty turquoise *n* **:** a moderate greenish blue that is greener and paler than average peacock blue and greener and less strong than Brittany

dusty turquoise blue *n* **:** a variable color averaging a light greenish blue that is bluer and duller than average turquoise blue or average aqua and bluer, less strong, and very slightly lighter than average turquoise (sense 2a)

dusty turquoise green *n* **:** a variable color averaging a moderate bluish green that is bluer and paler than porcelain green or sea blue

dusty wing *n* **:** CONIOPTERYGID

dusty yellow *n* **:** a grayish greenish yellow that is redder, lighter, and stronger than yellow stone or hay and redder, lighter, and slightly stronger than absinthe yellow

du·sun \ˈdüsᵊn\ *n, pl* **dusun** *or* **dusuns** *usu cap* [Malay (*orang*) *dusun* country people] **1 :** a Dayak people in British North Borneo **2 :** a member of the Dusun people

¹**dutch** \ˈdəch\ *adj, usu cap* [ME *Duch, Duche,* fr. MD *duutsch, dūtsch,* fr. a prehistoric EGmc-WGmc compound (represented also by OE *thēodisc* gentile, OS *thiudisk,* OHG *thiutisc, diutisc* German, Goth *thiudisko* gentile) whose components are akin to OS *thioda* people and OE *-isk* -ish; akin to OE *thēod* people, retainers, gentiles, OHG *diot* people, Goth *thiuda,* ON *thjōth,* OIr *tuath* people, Oscan *touto* city, OPruss *tauto* land, Latvian *tauta* people] **1 a** *archaic* **:** of or relating to the Germanic peoples of Germany, Austria, Switzerland, and the Low Countries **b :** of or relating to the Netherlands or its inhabitants **c** [influenced in meaning by G *deutsch,* fr. OHG *thiutisc, diutisc*] *slang* **:** GERMAN 1b **2 a** *archaic* (1) **:** of, relating to, or in any of the Germanic languages of Germany, Austria, Switzerland, and the Low Countries (2) **:** GERMAN 2 **b :** of, relating to, or in the Dutch language **c :** of, relating to, or in Afrikaans **3** [influenced in meaning by PaG *deitsch* German, fr. OHG *thiutisc, diutisc*] **:** of or relating to the Pennsylvania Dutch or their language **4** *of a meal* **:** served buffet style

²**dutch** \ˈ"\ *n* [ME *Duche,* fr. *Duche,* adj.] **1** -ES *cap* **a** *archaic* (1) **:** any of the Germanic languages of Germany, Austria, Switzerland, and the Low Countries — compare HIGH GERMAN, LOW GERMAN (2) **:** GERMAN 2 **b :** the Germanic language of the majority of the inhabitants of the Netherlands and the northern half of Belgium — see FLEMISH **c :** AFRIKAANS **2** *pl in constr, cap* **a** *archaic* **:** the Germanic peoples of Germany, Austria, Switzerland, and the Low Countries **b** *archaic* **:** GERMAN 1 **c :** the people of the Netherlands, principally of Frankish, Frisian, and Saxon origin **3** -ES *cap* [PaG *deitsch* German, fr. OHG *thiutisc, diutisc*] **:** PENNSYLVANIA DUTCH **4** -ES *usu cap, slang* **:** DANDER ⟨the fighting tone he used indicated that the President's *Dutch* is up —*Newsweek*⟩ **5** -ES *usu cap* **:** DISFAVOR, WRONG, TROUBLE — used with *in* ⟨the story is accurate, but its publication put me in *Dutch* with the composer in question —Nicolas Slonimsky⟩ ⟨every time he got in *Dutch* —J.T.Farrell⟩ **6** *usu cap* **:** a breed of small rabbits developed in the Netherlands with white blaze, collar, chest, and feet

³**dutch** \ˈ"\ *vt* -ED/-ING/-ES *sometimes cap* [¹*Dutch*] **1 :** to clean and harden (a quill) for use as a pen esp. by plunging in hot sand **2 :** to miscalculate in placing (a series of bets) so as to have a mathematical expectancy of losing rather than winning ⟨the man had ~*ed* his book, as clumsy operators sometimes did in their haste to take bets —*Newsweek*⟩

⁴**dutch** \ˈ"\ *adv, sometimes cap* [¹*Dutch*] **:** with each person treating himself or paying his own way ⟨they went ~ on the check —Truman Capote⟩ ⟨a candidate may drink ~ or even accept drinks from constituents —*Time*⟩

⁵**dutch** \ˈ"\ *n* -ES [prob. by shortening & alter. fr. *duchess*] *slang Brit* **:** WIFE — now used as a term of affection

dutch auction *n, usu cap D* **:** the public offer of property at a high price and then at gradually lowering prices until someone buys it

dutch backgammon *n, usu cap D* **:** a variation of backgammon in which a player's men must all be entered before any can be moved and a blot cannot be hit by a player until at least one of his men has reached home table

dutch bargain *n, usu cap D* **:** a bargain made and sealed while drinking — called also *wet bargain*

dutch barn *n, usu cap D* **:** a roofed farm shelter closed in only on the weather side and often used for storing and curing hay or tobacco

dutch bath *n, usu cap D* **:** a mordant composed of hydrochloric acid and potassium chlorate used in etching

dutch beech *n, usu cap D* **:** WHITE POPLAR 1a

dutch belted *n, usu cap D&B* **:** a breed of medium-sized dairy cattle originating in Holland, the cattle being black with a broad band of white around the body

dutch blue *n, often cap D* **1 :** a variable color averaging a moderate blue that is redder and darker than average copen, redder, lighter, and stronger than azurite blue, and redder and deeper than Dresden blue **2 :** a grayish blue that is redder and paler than electric or copenhagen and lighter than Gobelin

dutch bob *also* **dutch cut** *n, usu cap D* **:** a bob with straight bangs across the front and the rest of the hair cut evenly about earlobe length

dutch bond *n, usu cap D* **:** ENGLISH CROSS BOND

dutch brass *n, usu cap D* **:** LOW BRASS

dutch bulb *n, usu cap D* **:** a bulb or bulbous plant imported from Holland (as the hyacinth, tulip, and daffodil) — compare CAPE BULB

dutch cap *n, usu cap D* **:** a woman's cap with a triangular piece rolled back at each side

dutch cheese *n, usu cap D, North* **:** COTTAGE CHEESE

dutch clinker *also* **dutch brick** *n, usu cap D* **:** a long, narrow, and very hard yellowish brick made in Holland

dutch clover *n, usu cap D* **:** WHITE CLOVER a

dutch colonial *adj, usu cap D* [so called fr. the style prevailing in New York during the Dutch colonial period] *of a style of architecture* **:** characterized by the gambrel roof with widely overhanging eaves

dutch courage *n, usu cap D* **:** courage due to intoxicants or other artificial stimulation ⟨had to nerve himself with *Dutch courage* to face a skilled gunfighter —W.S.Campbell⟩ ⟨singing and crooning old Irish airs to give myself *Dutch courage* —S.J. Roche⟩

dutch curse *n, usu cap D* **:** DAISY 1b

dutch door *n, usu cap D* **:** a door divided horizontally so that the lower part can be shut while the upper remains open — compare DOUBLE DOOR

dutch elm *n, usu cap D* **:** a hybrid European shade tree (*Ulmus hollandica major*) planted for ornament

dutch elm disease *n, usu cap D* **:** a vascular disease of elms caused by a fungus (*Ceratostomella ulmi*) which is transmitted by bark beetles (genera *Scolytus* and *Hylurgopinus*) and which produces destructive toxic substances that are largely responsible for wilting and yellowing of the foliage, defoliation, and death first of local areas then of the entire plant

Dutch door

dutch engine *n, usu cap D* **:** HOLLANDER 3b

dutches *pl of* DUTCH, *pres 3d sing of* DUTCH

dutch flax *n, usu cap D* **:** GOLD OF PLEASURE

dutch foot *n, usu cap D* **:** a foot found on cabriole legs suggesting a hoof in its outward turn and in its thick dislike formation — called also *duck foot;* compare CLUB FOOT, DRAKE FOOT, SNAKE FOOT

dutch frill *n, usu cap D & often cap F* **:** a domestic canary of a variety distinguished by large size, upright carriage, and crimped and ruffled feathers

dutch-ga·bled \ˈ=ˈ=\ *adj, usu cap D* **:** having gables like those of Dutch houses

dutch grass *n, usu cap D* **1 :** COUCH GRASS **2 :** PARA GRASS 1

dutch guianese *also* **dutch guianan** *adj or n, usu cap D&G* [*Dutch Guiana* (older name for Surinam) + E *-ese* or *-an*] **:** SURINAMESE

dutch hoe *n, usu cap D* **:** SCUFFLE HOE

dutchier *comparative of* DUTCHY

dutchies *pl of* DUTCHY

dutchiest *superlative of* DUTCHY

dutch·i·fy \ˈdəchəˌfī\ *vt* -ED/-ING/-ES *often cap* **:** to make Dutch in quality or traits

dutching *pres part of* DUTCH

dutch iris *n, usu cap D* **:** any of certain beardless bulbous irises derived primarily from the species irises (*Iris tingitana* and *I. filifolia*)

dutch lap *n, usu cap D* **:** the lapping of roof shingles not only at their butts but also at their sides

dutch light *n, usu cap D* **:** a removable glazed sash used in the erection of greenhouses

dutch lottery *n, usu cap D* **:** a lottery in which tickets are drawn in certain classes or series for each of which certain prizes increasing in number and value with each class are fixed — called also *class lottery*

dutch lunch *n, usu cap D* **:** an individual serving of assorted sliced cold meats and cheeses — compare COLD CUTS

dutch·ly *adv, often cap* **:** in the manner of the Dutch ⟨streets, concrete and *Dutchly* clean —Bill Redgrave⟩

dutch·man \ˈ=mən\ *n, pl* **dutchmen** [ME *Ducheman,* fr. *Duche* Dutch + *man*] **1** *cap* **a** *archaic* **:** a member of any of the Germanic peoples of Germany, Austria, Switzerland, and the Low Countries **b :** a native or inhabitant of the Netherlands **:** HOLLANDER **c :** a person of Dutch descent born in southern Africa — compare AFRIKANER **d** *slang* **:** GERMAN 1 **2 a :** a contrivance to hide or counteract defective work (as an odd piece inserted to fill an opening) **b :** a short prop for supporting a log esp. to prevent pinching during sawing or to keep logs from falling from a load **c :** a strip of cloth used in the theater to conceal the crack between two scenery flats **d :** a piece of pipe or duct used to replace temporarily a piece of equipment (as a heating unit in a ventilation duct)

dutchman's-breeches \ˈ==ˈ=\ *n pl but sing or pl in constr, usu cap D* [so called fr. the shape of the blossoms] **:** a delicate spring-flowering herb (*Dicentra cucullaria*) of the eastern U.S. having finely divided leaves and cream-white double-spurred flowers

dutchman's log *n, usu cap D* **:** a method of estimating the speed of a boat in which an object that will float (as a piece of wood) is thrown over the bow and calculations are made based on the time that elapses before the stern passes

dutchman's-pipe \ˈ==ˈ=\ *n, pl* **dutchman's-pipes** *usu cap D* **:** a vine (*Aristolochia durior*) with large leaves and early summer flowers having the tube of the calyx curved like the bowl of a pipe

dutch metal *or* **dutch leaf** *or* **dutch gold** *n, usu cap D* **:** low brass esp. in the form of foil **:** imitation gold leaf

Dutchman's-breeches

dutch myrtle *n, usu cap D* **:** SWEET GALE

dutch orange *n, often cap D* **:** a moderate to strong orange yellow that is slightly darker than Indian yellow — called also *Florida gold, orpiment red, realgar orange, yellow carmine*

dutch oven *n, usu cap D* **1 :** a metal utensil for baking fitted with shelves and having one open side that is placed close to the fire **2 :** a brick oven in which cooking is done by the preheated walls **3 a :** a cast-iron usu. three-legged kettle with a tight cover on which coals may be heaped that is used for baking in an open fire **b :** a heavy pot with a tight-fitting domed cover used for braising, steaming, or baking on top of a stove **4 :** a furnace or other heating equipment in which the temperature is stabilized by indirect application of heat

Dutch oven 3b

dutch pink *n, often cap D* **1 :** a yellow lake prepared usu. from Persian berries or from quercitron and used chiefly as an artist's pigment **2 :** a light yellow that is greener and slightly darker than jasmine and greener and stronger than average maize or popcorn — called also *English pink, Italian pink, madder yellow, stil-de-grain yellow, yellow madder*

dutch–process \'ˌ=ˌ=\ *adj, usu cap D* **:** treated with an alkaline substance — used of cocoa and chocolate

dutch process *n, usu cap D* **:** a method of manufacturing white lead in which metallic lead gratings or plates are placed in the upper part of pots containing dilute acid and the pots stacked in fermenting tanbark or manure and left for about three months

dutch quill *also* **dutch pen** *n* **:** a pen made of a quill that has been dutched

dutch rabbit *n, usu cap D* **1 :** a genetic variety of the domestic rabbit characterized by more or less extensive white spotting typically forming a white belt on a dark ground **2 :** DUTCH 6

dutch reformed *adj, usu cap D&R* **:** of or referring to the Reformed Church in America that traces its beginnings to the Dutch communities of New York state as early as 1614 and that took its present name in 1867

dutch roll *n, usu cap D* **1 :** CROSS ROLL **2 :** a combination directional-lateral oscillation of an airplane

dutch rose *n, usu cap D* **:** a cut (as of a diamond or other gem) having 24 triangular facets — see ROSE illustration

dutch rush *n, often cap D* **:** a scouring rush (*Equisitum hyemale*)

dutch scarlet *n, often cap D* **:** CASTILIAN RED

dutch settle *n, usu cap D* **:** a wooden bench whose back may be tipped forward to form a table

dutch straight *n, usu cap D* **:** SKIP STRAIGHT

dutch treat *n, sometimes cap D* **:** a meal, entertainment, or trip for which each person present pays his own way ⟨a *dutch treat* was better than no date at all⟩

dutch 200 *n, pl* **dutch 200s :** a bowling score of exactly 200 made by rolling alternate strikes and spares

dutch uncle *n, usu cap D* **:** one who admonishes or reprimands with great severity and directness **:** a severe mentor ⟨I got mad and talked like a *Dutch uncle* —Joseph Hergesheimer⟩

dutch vermilion *n, often cap D* **:** a vivid reddish orange that is redder and lighter than international orange and redder and deeper than chrome orange — called also *toreador*

dutchware blue \'ˌ=ˌ=-\ *n, often cap D* **:** DELFT 2

dutch wife *n, usu cap D* **:** a long round bolster or an open frame of rattan or cane used in beds in tropical countries as a rest for the limbs and an aid in keeping cool

dutch woodbine *n, usu cap D* **:** a purplish variety (*Lonicera periclymenum belgica*) of the common European honeysuckle

[1]**dutchy** \'dəchē, -chi\ *adj* -ER/-EST *usu cap* [²*Dutch* + *-y*] **:** characteristically Dutch

[2]**dutchy** \"\ *n* -ES *usu cap* **1 :** DUTCHMAN **2 :** GERMAN

du·te·ous \'d(y)üdēəs, -ütēəs *chiefly Brit* -ü·tyəs\ *adj* [irreg. fr. *duty* + *-ous*] **1 :** marked by a sense of duty **:** DUTIFUL ⟨his chaste and ~ wife —Andrew Lang⟩ **2** *obs* **:** OBSEQUIOUS ⟨many a ~ and knee-crooking knave that . . . wears out his time . . . for naught but provender —Shak.⟩ — **du·te·ous·ly** *adv* — **du·te·ous·ness** *n* -ES

du·ti·able \-ēəbəl, -yəb-\ *adj* **:** subject to a duty ⟨~ imports⟩

du·tied \'d(y)üd·ēd\ *adj, archaic* **:** subjected to a duty (as when imported)

du·ti·ful \'d(y)üd·ǀəfəl, -ütǀ, ǀēf-\ *adj* **1 :** filled with or motivated by a sense of duty to one's natural or legal superiors **:** having due respect for one's own moral obligations **:** willingly obedient ⟨a ~ son⟩ ⟨a ~ servant⟩ ⟨she's a wonderfully ~ girl. Her father's wish would be sacred to her —G.B.Shaw⟩ **2 :** proceeding from or expressive of a sense of duty **:** DEFERENTIAL ⟨the tender and ~ manner in which she had supported her parents —W.M.Thackeray⟩ ⟨~ attendance at church⟩ — **du·ti·ful·ness** *n* -ES

du·ti·ful·ly \-f(ə)lē, -li\ *adv* **:** in a dutiful manner **:** from a sense of duty ⟨a promise of secrecy was . . . ~ given —Jane Austen⟩ ⟨a group of sailor boys . . . all ~ saluted —H.A. Chippendale⟩

du·tu·bu·ri \ˌdüd·əˈbürē\ *n* -S [MexSp] **:** a women's ceremonial circle dance of the Tarahumara Indians of Chihuahua, Mexico

[1]**du·ty** \'d(y)üd·ē, -ütē, -i\ *n* -ES [ME *duete, dewte,* fr. AF *dueté, duité,* fr. OF *deu* due + *-té* -ty — more at DUE] **1 a :** conduct due parents and superiors **:** respectful or obedient behavior **:** RESPECT ⟨every prince that has parents owes them as much filial ~ and obedience —John Locke⟩ **b :** conduct or activities showing respect **:** expression of respect ⟨addressed the king with humble ~⟩ **2 a :** obligatory tasks, conduct, service, or functions enjoined by order or usage according to rank, occupation, or profession ⟨*duties* that he knew he would have to do —Joseph Conrad⟩ **b :** service, ministration, or performance enjoined on a clergyman **c :** active military or naval service **:** assigned participation in activity **:** service under orders **d :** responsibility for maintaining continued operation or status **:** supervision of a post, ship, or installation in the interest of normal operation — used with *the* ⟨the commander had the ~ on Monday⟩ **3 a :** behavior required by moral obligation, demanded by custom, or enjoined by feelings of rightness or fitness — compare CATEGORICAL IMPERATIVE **b :** the force of moral obligation **:** feeling for or sense of such obligation ⟨the call of ~⟩ **c :** the conduct or acts of a person motivated by pure goodwill **:** conduct that produces the greatest good — used in axiological philosophy **4 a :** a payment or service imposed by law or custom; *esp* **:** a charge payable to a government **b :** a sum paid as a tax on import, export, manufacture, or consumption of goods ⟨no tax or ~ shall be laid on articles exported from any state —*U.S. Constitution*⟩ **5 a :** work done by a particular machine under certain conditions (as of time or energy) ⟨the ~ of a stamp may be stated as the number of tons of ore crushed to a given degree of fineness in a given time⟩ **b :** a measure of the overall efficiency (as of a machine, engine, pump, power plant, but esp. of a water pump) expressed in terms of the amount of work delivered for a certain quantity of input energy **6** *also* **duty of water :** the quantity of irrigation water required to satisfy the requirements of the area of a particular crop expressed in acre-inches or acre-feet per acre or as acres per second per foot of water **7 a :** service required (as of a machine) under specified conditions of load and rest ⟨intermittent ~⟩ ⟨continuous ~⟩ **b :** USE, SERVICE, FUNCTION ⟨if one chain, one rope, or one bolt was amply strong enough for a particular ~ —O.S.Nock⟩; *esp* **:** service as a replacement or substitute ⟨a big book doing ~ as a doorstop⟩ ⟨making the word do ~ for the thing —Edward Sapir⟩ **syn** see FUNCTION, OBLIGATION, TASK — **in line of duty :** within the scope of one's duties **:** in accordance with assigned duties ⟨feeling that he had acted *in line of duty*⟩ — **off duty :** not assigned to any specific task or duty **:** free from assignment or responsibility ⟨men *off duty* loafing around the barracks⟩ — **on duty :** assigned to a task or duty **:** engaged in or responsible for some specific performance

[2]**duty** \"\ *adj* **1 :** done as a duty ⟨paying ~ calls on his elderly relatives⟩ **2 :** being on duty **:** having the responsibility for certain assigned tasks or functions ⟨the was ~ officer the night of the raid⟩ ⟨a ~ doctor to take care of emergencies⟩

duty mark *n* **:** a punch mark in the form of the sovereign's head which had to be placed on all British wares made of silver or gold from 1784 to 1890 to show that duty had been paid

duty plate *n* **:** the plate that prints the frame, denomination, and sometimes also (as on certain British colonial stamps) the name of the country on a bicolor postage stamp

duty roster *n* **:** a roster of a military unit showing what duties (as guard and kitchen police) each man has performed

du·um·vir \d(y)üˈəmvər, -ˌvi(ə)r\ *n, pl* **duumvirs** \-rz\ *also* **duumvi·ri** \-ˌvəˌrī, -ˌrē\ [L, fr. *duum* of two (gen. of *duo* two) + *vir* man — more at TWO, VIRILE] **1 :** one of two Roman officers or magistrates constituting a board, commission, or court appointed for a specific function **2 :** one of two men jointly holding power or associated in some official position

du·um·vi·rate \-vərət, -ˌrāt\ *n* -S [L *duumviratus,* fr. *duumvir* + *-atus* -ate] **1 :** the office or government of the Roman duumvirs **2 :** two people associated in high office or position **:** a coalition of two people

du·vet \(ˈ)d(y)üˌvā\ *n* -S [F, lit., down, fr. MF, alter. of (assumed) *dumet* (whence later MF *dumet* & Bret *dumed*), dim. of *dum* down, fr. OF, alter. (prob. influenced by *plume* feather) of *dun,* fr. ON *dūnn* — more at DOWN (feathers)] **:** a downy growth characteristic of some fungus cultures

du·ve·tyn \'d(y)üvətən, 'dəvt-\ *also* **du·ve·tyne** \", 'd(y)ü-və,tēn\ *n* -S [F *duvetine,* fr. *duvet* down + *-ine*] **:** a smooth lustrous velvety fabric that has a napped surface which obscures the twill weave and that is made usu. in solid colors from wool, silk, rayon, cotton, or various combinations

du·wa·mish \də'wämish, 'dwä-\ *n, pl* **duwamish** *or* **duwamishes** *usu cap* [fr. the *Duwamish* river, Wash.] **1 :** a Salishan people of the valley of the Duwamish river and its tributaries in the state of Washington **2 :** a member of the Duwamish people

dux \'dəks, 'düks\ *n, pl* **du·ces** \'d(y)üˌsēz, 'düˌkās\ *also* **duxes** \'dəksəz, 'dük-\ [L, lit., leader — more at DUKE] **1 :** a military commander stationed in a province of the later Roman Empire **2** *Brit* **:** the pupil at the academic head of his class or of his school **3 :** the theme of a fugue or canon — compare COMES

d'ux·elles *or* **dux·elles** \(ˈ)dük¦sel, (ˈ)dək-, (ˈ)d(y)ük-, *F* dɯ̈sel\ *n, pl* **d'uxelles** \-lz, *F* -l\ *or* **duxelles** *often cap U in the apostrophized form* [after the Marquis *d'Uxelles,* 17th cent. Fr. nobleman, patron of the Sieur de la Varenne, famous 17th cent. Fr. chef] **:** a garnish or sauce whose principal ingredients are minced mushrooms and tomato puree

duyker *var of* DUIKER

DV *abbr* **1** [L *Deo volente*] God willing **2** distinguished visitor **3** *often not cap* double vibration

dvan·dva \'dvän(ˌ)dvä, də'v-, -vəndvə\ *n, pl* **dvandvas** *or* **dvandva** [Skt *dvandva,* lit., a pair, couple, redupl. of *dva* two — more at TWO] **:** a class of compound words having two immediate constituents that are equal in rank and related to each other as if joined by *and* **:** a compound word belonging to this class (as *bittersweet, secretary-treasurer, sociopolitical*) — see ²COPULATIVE 2

dva·pa·ra yu·ga \ˌdväpərəˈyügə\ *n, usu cap D&Y* [Skt *dvāparayuga,* fr. *dvāpara* third best throw at dice (that of the two) (fr. *dva* two + *para* further) + *yuga* yoke, age of the world — more at TWO, PEREION, YOKE] **:** the third age of a Hindu world cycle

dvi- *comb form* [Skt *dvi-* two — more at TWI-] **:** standing or assumed to stand in the second place beyond (a specified element) in the same family of the periodic table — in names of chemical elements esp. when not yet discovered ⟨*dvi-manganese* (now called *rhenium*)⟩; compare EKA-

dvr *abbr* driver

DW *abbr* **1** deadweight **2** delayed weather **3** distilled water **4** dock warrant **5** dust wrapper

dwai·ble \'dwābəl\ *also* **dwai·bly** \-bli\ *adj* [origin unknown] *chiefly Scot* **:** feeble and shaky **:** UNSTABLE ⟨I would just be a hindrance with my ~ legs —John Buchan⟩

dwale \'dwā(ə)l\ *n* -S [ME, stupefying drink, belladonna, perh. of Scand origin; akin to OSw *dvala* trance, lethargy, delay, Dan *dvale* trance, lethargy, ON *dvöl* short stay, delay — more at DWELL] **:** BELLADONNA 1

dwall \'dwal\ *Scot var of* DWELL

[1]**dwalm** *or* **dwam** \'dwäm\ *n* -S [akin to OE *dwolma* chaos, OHG *twalm* bewilderment, stupefaction, ON *dylminn* careless, indifferent, Goth *dwalmon* to be foolish, insane — more at DWELL] **1** *chiefly Scot* **:** a fainting spell or sudden attack of illness **2** *chiefly Scot* **:** DAYDREAM, REVERIE

[2]**dwalm** *or* **dwam** \"\ *vi* -ED/-ING/-S *chiefly Scot* **:** to fall in a faint **:** become dazed

[1]**dwarf** \'dwȯ(ə)r|f, -ȯ(ə)|\ *n, pl* **dwarfs** \|fs\ *or* **dwarves** \|vz\ [ME *dwerg, dwerf,* fr. OE *dweorg, dweorh;* akin to OFris *dwerch* dwarf, OHG *twerg,* ON *dvergr,* and perh. to Skt *dhvaras* demon, *dhvarati* he bends, injures — more at FRAUD] **1 a :** an abnormally small person; *esp* **:** one of markedly atypical proportions **b :** a person of small or negligible powers or endowments ⟨a literary ~ . . . writing in something that resembles, however inadequately, your style —Osbert Sitwell⟩ **2 :** an animal or plant much below the normal size of its species or kind: as **a :** a small fruit tree reaching a height at maturity of as little as four or five feet and bearing early but normal fruit **b :** a plant of abnormally small size developed by root pruning, starving, pruning of leaders, or other measures that restrict growth **3 :** a legendary manlike being of small stature usu. misshapen and ugly and skilled as an artificer **4** *also* **dwarf star :** a star (as the sun) of ordinary or low luminosity and relatively small mass and size

[2]**dwarf** \"\ *vb* -ED/-ING/-S *vt* **1 a :** to make dwarf in size **:** stunt in growth ⟨malnutrition had ~*ed* these children⟩ ⟨an arid climate ~*ing* oaks into mere shrubs⟩; *specif* **:** to make (a plant) dwarf by grafting a scion of standard size to a dwarf stock **b :** to cause the intellectual or moral development of (a person) to be hindered or stunted ⟨incessant repetition of the same handwork ~*s* the man —R.W.Emerson⟩ **2 :** to cause to appear smaller or inferior in any way in relation to some other individual or thing ⟨~*ed* the chair in which he sat⟩ ⟨~ the achievements of his predecessors⟩ **~** *vi* **:** to become dwarf

[3]**dwarf** \"\ *adj* -ER/-EST **1** *of a plant or animal* **:** extremely small as contrasted with related species or varieties **2 :** resembling a dwarf **:** characterized by smallness or insignificance of size, proportion, scope, strength, or power **:** DIMINUTIVE ⟨the farmer on a ~ holding . . . must supplement his income by working off his own land —J.M.Mogey⟩ ⟨what is man but a species . . . dominant over other species on a ~ planet —W.R.Inge⟩

[4]**dwarf** \"\ *also* **dwarf disease** *n* -S **:** any of various diseases of plants characterized by shortened internodes and generally reduced size of the plants ⟨rice ~ is a virus disease known chiefly from Japan⟩

dwarf agave *n* **:** a lechuguilla (*Agave lecheguilla*)

dwarf alder *n* **1 :** a small American buckthorn (*Rhamnus alnifolia*) with leaves resembling those of the alder **2 :** a shrub (*Fothergilla gardeni*) of the southeastern U.S. with white flowers

dwarf apple *n* **1 :** a small apple tree produced by grafting a scion of a standard variety onto a dwarfing rootstock **2 :** any of several horticultural apple varieties marked by trees of low stature

dwarf ash *n* **1 :** GOUTWEED **2 :** SINGLE-LEAF ASH

dwarf banana *n* **:** a low-growing banana (*Musa nana* or *M. cavendishii*) cultivated esp. in the West Indies and distinguished by its compact growth habit and its six-angled curved fragrant fruit — called also *Canary banana, Cavendish banana, Chinese banana*

dwarf bean *n* **:** any of various beans that form a comparatively small plant; *esp* **:** BUSH BEAN

dwarf bilberry *or* **dwarf blueberry** *n* **:** a low-growing tufted blueberry (*Vaccinium caespitosum*) of northern and alpine No. America with deep pink to coral red flowers followed by light blue primrose edible berries

dwarf birch *n* **:** any of several low shrubs of the genus *Betula* (esp. *B. pumila, B. glandulosa,* and *B. nana*)

dwarf box *n* **1 :** any of several Australian eucalypts (as *Eucalyptus bicolor*) **2 :** SAND MYRTLE **3 :** a dwarf variety (*Buxus sempervirens suffruticosa*) of the box with small leaves

dwarf buckeye *n* **:** BOTTLEBRUSH BUCKEYE

dwarf buffalo *n* **1 :** ANOA **2 :** CONGO BUFFALO

dwarf bunt *n* **:** a bunt disease of wheat that causes dwarfing

dwarf buttercup *n* **:** any of several small or low-growing buttercups; *esp* **:** a weak-stemmed buttercup (*Ranunculus pygmaeus*) that is native to Europe but widely distributed in moist rocky northern and alpine parts of America and that usu. has several stems each bearing a single flower

dwarf canadian primrose *n, usu cap C* **:** MISTASSINI

dwarf cassia *n* **:** SENSITIVE PEA

dwarf cherry *n* **:** any of several small usu. shrubby cherries: as **a :** the wild sour cherry **b :** any of certain sand cherries (esp. *Prunus cuneata*)

dwarf chestnut *n* **:** a low-growing shrubby chestnut; *esp* **:** CHINQUAPIN 1a

dwarf chestnut oak *n* **:** a low shrubby chestnut oak (*Quercus prinoides*)

dwarf chinquapin oak *n* **:** CHINQUAPIN OAK b

dwarf cornel *n* **:** either of two red-berried perennial herbs of the genus *Cornus:* **a :** a creeping plant (*C. canadensis*) having whorled leaves and white floral bracts **b** *or* **dwarf honeysuckle :** a closely related plant (*C. suecica*) with opposite leaves and purple bracts

dwarf crab *n* **:** a tiny pear-shaped hairy crab (*Pelia tumida*) found among seaweeds along the west coast of Central America and Mexico

dwarf cudweed *n* **:** a white-tomentose alpine or circumboreal perennial herb (*Gnaphalium supinum*) with mostly basal leaves and yellowish flowers

dwarf cypress *n* **:** an alpine and circumboreal club moss (*Lycopodium alpinum*)

dwarf dandelion *n* **:** KRIGIA 2

dwarf eggplant *n* **:** a small straggling herb (*Solanum melongena depressum*) with thin scarcely lobed leaves, small flowers, and obovoid to pyriform dark purple fruit

dwarf elder *n* **1 :** DANEWORT **2 :** GOUTWEED **3 :** BRISTLY SARSAPARILLA

dwarf elm *n* **:** SIBERIAN ELM

dwarf false musk *n* **:** a low tufted perennial figwort (*Mazus pumilio*) with small bluish white flowers

dwarf fan palm *n* **:** any of several usu. low-growing fan palms; *esp* **:** a hemp palm (*Chamaerops humilis*)

dwarf forest *n* **:** a low usu. deciduous forest — compare CHAPARRAL, KRUMMHOLZ

dwarf french pink *n, usu cap F* **:** DEPTFORD PINK

dwarf ginseng *n* **:** a small herbaceous perennial (*Panax trifolius*) having stalkless leaves and a globular root — called also *groundnut*

dwarf goldenrod *n* **:** a dyer's-weed (*Solidago nemoralis*)

dwarf gourami *n* **:** a small Indian anabantid fish (*Colias lalia*) the male of which is light blue and barred with orange-red stripes and the female less brilliant

dwarf gray willow *n* **:** SAGE WILLOW

dwarf horse chestnut *n* **:** BOTTLEBRUSH BUCKEYE

dwarf houseleek *n* **:** a prostrate European herb (*Sedum reflexum*) with yellow flowers that is sparingly adventive in the eastern U.S.

dwarf huckleberry *n* **:** BUSH HUCKLEBERRY

dwarfing *pres part of* DWARF

dwarfing stock *n* **:** a stock used in budding or grafting that produces a dwarf tree

dwarf iris *n* **:** any of several low-growing American irises (as *Iris verna* and *I. cristata*); *also* **:** any of several exotic irises common in cultivation (as *I. pumila*)

dwarf·ish \'dwȯrfish, -ȯ(ə)f-, -fēsh\ *adj* **:** of or like a dwarf ⟨a bewhiskered, button-faced ~ man —R.S.Harper⟩ **:** very small ⟨sounded in the distance like an elf upon his ~ drum —G.K.Chesterton⟩ — **dwarf·ish·ly** *adv* — **dwarf·ish·ness** *n* -ES

dwarf·ism \-ˌfizəm\ *n* -S **:** the condition of stunted growth **:** NANISM ⟨~ results from a recessive gene —Merrill Gregory⟩

dwarf japanese quince *n, usu cap J* **:** a low Japanese shrub (*Chaenomeles japonica*) cultivated chiefly for its early blooming orange-scarlet flowers

dwarf juniper *n* **:** any of several low-growing or prostrate shrubs of the genus *Juniperus:* as **a :** SAVIN 1 **b :** a horticultural variety (*J. communis depressa*) of the common juniper

dwarf larkspur *n* **:** a No. American larkspur (*Delphinium tricorne*) with blue or white flowers

dwarf laurel *n* **1 :** SHEEP LAUREL **2 :** MEZERON 1

dwarf lemur *n* **:** any of several very small Malagasy lemurs constituting the genus *Microcebus*

dwarf·ling \-ȯrfliŋ, -ȯ(ə)f-\ *n* -S **:** a little dwarf

dwarf lupine *n* **:** a low-growing plant of the genus *Lupinus; esp* **:** an alpine (*L. minimus*) of the Rocky mountains

dwarf male *n* **1 :** a small plant of algae of the family Oedogoniaceae that consists of a few cells, develops from an androspore near the oogonium, is usu. attached to the cell below it, and produces only spermatozoids — called also *nannander* **2 :** COMPLEMENTAL MALE

dwarf mallow *n* **:** a prostrate European weedy plant (*Malva rotundifolia*) having long-stalked roundish leaves, blue flowers, and small flat fruits — called also *blue mallow;* compare CHEESE 4

dwarf maple *n* **:** a low shrubby maple (*Acer glabrum*) of the Rocky mountain region

dwarf milkweed *n* **:** WHORLED MILKWEED

dwarf mistletoe *n* **:** AMERICAN MISTLETOE 1

dwarf mountain fir *or* **dwarf mountain pine** *n* **:** MUGHO PINE

dwarf mulberry *n* **1 :** CLOUDBERRY 1 **2 :** a low-growing mulberry that is a variety of the white mulberry (*Morus alba*) used for silkworm culture

dwarf·ness *n* -ES **:** the quality or state of being a dwarf **:** DWARFISM

dwarf nettle *n* **:** SMALL NETTLE

dwarf nipplewort *n* **:** LAMB SUCCORY

dwarf oak *n* **1 :** any of various trees of the genus *Teucrium* **2 :** a shrubby tree of the genus *Quercus; esp* **:** CHINQUAPIN OAK b

dwarf palmetto *n* **1 :** BLUE PALMETTO **2 :** a low-growing palm (*Sakal minor*) of the southeastern U.S. with subterranean rootstock and a short underground trunk from which flat-bladed leaves project in a crown

dwarf partition *n* **:** a partition that does not extend up to the ceiling

dwarf pea *n* **:** CHICK-PEA 2

dwarf phlox *n* **:** MOSS PINK

dwarf pine *n* **1 :** MUGHO PINE **2** *in California* **:** BISHOP PINE

dwarf pocket rat *n* **:** any of several small No. American pouched rats (genus *Microdipodops*)

dwarf rafter *n* **:** JACK RAFTER

dwarf raspberry *n* **:** any of several low prostrate or trailing plants of the genus *Rubus; esp* **:** a No. American plant (*R. pubescens*) with reddish purple fruit

dwarfs *pl of* DWARF, *pres 3d sing of* DWARF

dwarf salamander *n* **:** a small tailed amphibian (*Manculus quadridigitatus*) of the southern U.S.

dwarf salmon *n* **:** a landlocked salmon of western No. America

dwarf senna *n* **:** SENSITIVE PEA

dwarf signal *n* **:** a low home signal for railroad trains — called also *backup signal*

dwarf solomon's seal *n, usu cap 1st S* **:** FALSE LILY OF THE VALLEY

dwarf spurge *n* **:** a European erect or depressed annual spurge (*Euphorbia exigua*) adventive in the northeastern U.S.

dwarf star *n* **:** DWARF 4

dwarf sumac *n* **:** a common nonpoisonous shrub (*Rhus copallina*) of eastern No. America having green paniculate flowers, red fruit, and compound leaves — called also *black sumac*

dwarf tapeworm *n* **:** the common hymenolepidid tapeworm (*Hymenolepis nana*) of man — compare HYMENOLEPIS

dwarf tiger lily *n* **:** BLACKBERRY LILY

dwarf upland willow *n* **:** SAGE WILLOW

dwarf wall *n* **:** a low toe wall built to retain the slope of an excavation or embankment

dwarf water plantain *n* **:** a low aquatic or marsh plant (*Helianthium parvulum*) of the family Alismataceae common in No. America and having long-stalked lanceolate leaves and white flowers

dwarf weasel *n* **:** LEAST WEASEL

dwarf whin *n* **:** a low spiny almost leafless furze (*Ulex nanus*) of western Europe with yellow flowers

dwarf willow *n* **:** any of several low-growing willows: as **a :** a widely distributed alpine or boreal shrubby willow (*Salix*

herbacea) with partially underground creeping stems and bright green lustrous reticulate-veined leaves **b :** SAGE WILLOW
dwarf yew *n* **:** GROUND HEMLOCK
dwarves *pl of* DWARF
DWC *abbr* deadweight capacity
dwee·ble \'dwēbəl\ *var of* DWAIBLE
[1]**dwell** \'dwel\ *vb* **dwelt** \-lt\ *also* **dwelled** \-lt, -ld\ **dwelt** *also* **dwelled; dwelling; dwells** [ME *dwellen*, fr. OE *dwellan* to lead astray, go astray; akin to OHG *twellen* to tarry, hesitate, ON *dvelja* to delay, *dvöl* delay, Goth *dwalmōn* to be mad, OE *dol* foolish — more at DULL] *vi* **1 a :** LIVE, RESIDE ⟨~ for years in the same town⟩ **b :** to be or continue in some state or condition ⟨*dwelt* in bondage to his mother —Edmund Fuller⟩ **c :** to exist or be present ⟨wisdom must ~ in a mind so honest⟩ **d :** CONSIST, LIE ⟨the poem's main interest ~*s* in its unusual imagery⟩ **2 a :** to linger over something (as with the mind or eyes) — used with *on* or *upon* ⟨sights on which the eyes may ~ with pleasure⟩ ⟨her mind *dwelt* on his good qualities —Ellen Glasgow⟩ **b :** to speak or write with emphasis or at length — used with *on* or *upon* ⟨~*ing* eloquently on the power of Milton's prose style⟩ **~** *vt, obs* **:** to inhabit or occupy as a place of residence **syn** see RESIDE
[2]**dwell** \"\ *n* -s **1 :** a short interruption or intermission in the motion of a part of a machine that gives time for its own proper operation or for the operation of another part **2 :** the time during which material is subjected to a particular operation (as in a manufacturing process) ⟨the ~ during heat sealing of plastic⟩; *specif* **:** the time during which material to be printed is in contact with the printing surface
dwell·er \-lə(r)\ *n* -s [ME, fr. *dwellen* to dwell + *-er*] **:** one that dwells **:** INHABITANT, RESIDENT ⟨a vast number of services available for city and town ~*s* — J.B.Conant⟩
dwell·ing \'dweliŋ, -lēŋ\ *n* -s [ME, fr. gerund of *dwellen* to dwell — more at DWELL] **:** a building or construction used for residence **:** ABODE, HABITATION
dwelling house *n* **:** a house or sometimes part of a house that is occupied as a residence in distinction from a store, office, or other building and that may legally include associated or connected buildings within the same curtilage
dwg *abbr* **1** drawing **2** dwelling
dwight-lloyd \'dwī¦lȯid\ *adj, usu cap D&L* [after A.S.*Dwight* †1946 and R.L.*Lloyd* *b*1870 Am. mining engineers] **:** relating to a process for roasting and sintering fine ores whereby the ore is ignited in a thin layer on a traveling grate which passes over a suction box
[1]**dwin·dle** \'dwindᵊl, ÷-nᵊl\ *vb* **dwindled; dwindled; dwindling** \-(ᵊ)liŋ\ **dwindles** [prob. freq. of *dwine*] *vi* **:** to become steadily less **:** diminish in size, amount, or quality **:** SHRINK ⟨the boat gradually *dwindled* to a speck⟩ ⟨population is *dwindling*⟩ ⟨the novel ~*s* away to a most unsatisfactory ending⟩ **~** *vt* **:** to make steadily less **:** reduce in any way ⟨~*s* all other developments to insignificance⟩ **syn** see DECREASE
[2]**dwindle** \"\ *n* -s **:** DECREASE, DECLINE
dwine \'dwīn\ *vi* -ED/-ING/-S [ME *dwinen*, fr. OE *dwīnan;* akin to MD *dwīnen* to disappear, languish, faint, ON *dvīna* to dwindle or pine away, OIr *dīth* end, death, Arm *di* corpse, ON *deyja* to die — more at DIE] *now chiefly dial* **:** to waste or pine away **:** LANGUISH
dwt *abbr* [*denarius* + *weight*] pennyweight
DWT *abbr, often not cap* deadweight ton
DX \(')dē¦eks\ *abbr or n* -ES distance — used of long-distance radio transmission
dy- *or* **dyo-** *comb form* [LL *dy-* & G *dyo-*, fr. Gk *dy-*, *dyo-*, fr. *dyo* — more at TWO] **:** two ⟨*dy*archy⟩ ⟨*dy*aster⟩ ⟨*dyo*theism⟩
dy *abbr* **1** delivery **2** [L *denarius* + E *penny*] penny **3** deputy
Dy *symbol* dysprosium
dyable *var of* DYEABLE
[1]**dy·ad** *also* **di·ad** \'dī,ad, -īəd\ *n* -s [LL *dyad-*, *dyas* two (n.), fr. Gk, fr. *dyo* two — more at TWO] **1 :** two units treated as one **:** COUPLE, PAIR; *specif* **:** a pair of individuals (as husband and wife, teacher and pupil) maintaining a sociologically significant relationship **2 :** a bivalent element, atom, or radical **3 :** a meiotic chromosome after separation of the two homologous members of a tetrad **4** *math* **:** an operator indicated by writing the symbols of two vectors without a dot or cross between (as AB)
[2]**dy·ad** *var of* DIAD
[1]**dy·ad·ic** *also* **di·ad·ic** \(')dī¦adik\ *adj* [*dyad*, *diad* + *-ic*] **:** of, having reference to, or concerning a dyad **:** being of two parts or elements **:** involving two in its formation ⟨a ~ relation between the spectator and the experience —Daniel Bell⟩ ⟨~ arithmetic⟩ ⟨cultural importance, intimate nature, and ~ character of the family —J.G.March⟩ ⟨a ~ relation between a sign and an object —R.S.Wells⟩
[2]**dyadic** \"\ *n* -s **:** a sum of dyads
dyak *usu cap, var of* DAYAK
dy·a·kis·dodecahedral \¦dīəkəs, dī¦akəs+\ *adj* **:** having the shape or the symmetry of a diploid
dy·a·kis·dodecahedron \"+\ *n* -s [ISV *dyakis* (fr. Gk *dyakis* twice, fr. *dyo* two) + *dodecahedron*] **:** DIPLOID
dy·ar·chic \(')dī¦ärkik\ *also* **dy·ar·chi·cal** \-rkəkəl\ *or* **dy·ar·chal** \-rkəl\ *adj* **:** of or having reference to a dyarchy
dy·ar·chy *also* **di·ar·chy** \'dī,ärkē\ *n* -ES [*dy-* or *di-* + *-archy*] **:** a government in which power is vested in two rulers or authorities; *specif* **:** a dual form of government established first in the provinces of India and now used in some British colonies in which the British government shares power and responsibility with native ministers responsible to a locally elected legislature
dy·as·sic \(')dī¦asik\ *adj* [NL *Dyas* Permian system (fr. LL, two, n.) + E *-ic* — more at DYAD] **:** PERMIAN
dyaster *n* -s [*dy-* + *-aster* (star)] **:** DIASTER
dyb·buk *or* **dib·buk** \'dibək\ *n, pl* **dybbu·kim** *or* **dibbu·kim** \¦dibu̇¦kēm, di'bu̇kim\ *also* **dybbuks** *or* **dibbuks** \'dibəks\ [Heb *dibbūq*, fr. *dābhaq* to cling, cleave] **:** an evil spirit or the wandering soul of a dead person believed in Jewish folklore to enter the body of a man and control his actions until exorcised by a religious rite
[1]**dye** \'dī\ *n* -s [ME *dehe*, fr. OE *dēah*, *dēag;* akin to OE *dīegol* secret, hidden, OS *dōgalnussi* secret, hiding place, OHG *tugōn* to become variegated, *tougan* dark, hidden, secret, L *fumus* smoke — more at FUME] **1 :** color produced by dyeing **2 :** a natural or esp. a synthetic coloring matter whether soluble or insoluble that is used to color materials (as textiles, paper, leather, or plastics) usu. from a solution or fine dispersion and sometimes with the aid of a mordant — called also *dyestuff;* compare PIGMENT, STAIN, TINT; see DYE table — **of deepest dye** *or* **of the deepest dye :** of the worst kind ⟨a scoundrel *of the deepest dye*⟩ **:** of the most pronounced kind ⟨an intellectual *of the deepest dye*⟩

DYES

The dyes listed include most of the synthetic dyes and pigments manufactured in the U.S., a very few domestic natural dyes that continue to be important, and six representative foreign-made fiber-reactive dyes. The American-made dyes have been taken from the *Technical Manual of the American Association of Textile Chemists and Colorists* (AATCC), in which all American dye manufacturers voluntarily list their domestic products. Only synthetic dyes and pigments have been selected whose compositions have been disclosed in the *Colour Index* (CI), 2d ed., compiled and published jointly by the Society of Dyers and Colourists of Great Britain and the American Association of Textile Chemists and Colorists.

The dyes in the table are arranged in the first column in accordance with the names assigned to them in part I of the *Colour Index*, 2d ed. These names are derived from the use classes described after the table, and within each use class the dyes are arranged coloristically in the following order: yellow, orange, red, violet, blue, green, brown, and black. Within each use class and color, dyes are differentiated from one another by serial arabic numbers, which are a part of the name. For example, Methylene Blue 2B becomes Basic Blue 9 in the new system of nomenclature, and that dye can be unequivocally designated by that name instead of by one of the commercial names, many of which contain a trademark.

In the second (double) column the small number to the left indicates the type of chemical structure to which the dye on that line belongs, the number referring to one of the 31 structure types given at the end of this paragraph. Each number to the right, which always has 5 digits, indicates the structural formula—if known—that is shown for the dye in part II, volume III, of the *Colour Index*. Structure Types:

1	nitroso	17	indamine
2	nitro	18	indophenol
3	monoazo	19	azine
4	disazo	20	oxazine
5	trisazo	21	thiazine
6	polyazo	22	sulfur
7	azoic diazo component	23	lactone
8	azoic coupling component	24	amino ketone
9	stilbene	25	hydroxy ketone
10	diphenylmethane	26	anthraquinone
11	triarylmethane	27	indigoid
12	xanthene	28	thioindigoid
13	acridine	29	phthalocyanine
14	quinoline	30	natural organic
15	methine or polymethine	31	oxidation base
16	thiazole		

In the third column is given at least one commercial or common name for each dye under which the dye may be defined in the body of the dictionary. This name has been selected because it may be the one given to it by the first manufacturer (and may thus often be reflected in the names given by other manufacturers) or because it may be considered as most used in old literature. However, United States trademarks are usually replaced by other appropriate names. Final letters often indicate shade (as R for reddish and G for greenish or yellowish, the latter from the German *gelb*). Numbers with the letters or doubled letters indicate the extent of redness, greenness, and so on; thus "Blue 5R" indicates a very reddish blue.

Each number given in the last column is either the old *Colour Index* number (CI No.) of the first edition or the Prototype number (Pr No.) assigned to the dye in question by the AATCC.

The uses of the various dyes are given in general under the descriptions of each use class after the table.

DYE TABLE I

Part I Colour Index Generic Name	Chemical Structure Type	Part II Colour Index No.	Commercial Name	Old Colour Index No. or Prototype No.
ACID				
Yellow 1	2	10,316	Naphthol Yellow S Ext D&C Yellow No. 7	CI 10
Yellow 2	14	47,010	Quinoline Yellow KT	CI 802
Yellow 3	14	47,005	Quinoline Yellow D&C Yellow No. 10	CI 801
Yellow 7	24	56,205	Brilliant Sulpho Flavine FF	Pr 224
Yellow 9	3	13,015	Fast Yellow	CI 16
Yellow 11	3	18,820	Fast Light Yellow Ext D&C Yellow No. 3	CI 636
Yellow 17	3	18,965	Xylene Light Yellow	CI 639
Yellow 23	3	19,140	Tartrazine D&C Yellow No. 5 FD&C Yellow No. 5	CI 640
Yellow 29	3	18,900	Acid Yellow 3 GL	Pr 474
Yellow 34	3	18,890	Fast Light Yellow	CI 636
Yellow 36	3	13,065	Metanil Yellow Ext D&C Yellow No. 1	CI 138
Yellow 38	4	25,135	Milling Yellow O	Pr 139
Yellow 40	3	18,950	Acid Yellow 2G	CI 642
ACID—*Continued*				
Yellow 42	4	22,910	Acid Yellow R	Pr 187
Yellow 44	4	23,900	Milling Yellow H5G	Pr 138
Yellow 54	3	19,010	Acid Fast Yellow ELN	Pr 330
Yellow 63	3	13,095	Azo Yellow	CI 146
Yellow 73	12	45,350	Fluorescein, Uranine Ext D&C Yellow Nos. 10 and 11	CI 766
Yellow 99	3	13,900	Acid Yellow GR	Pr 316
Orange 1	3	13,091	Azo Flavine RR	CI 145
Orange 3	2	10,385	Amido Yellow E	CI 11
Orange 7	3	15,510	Orange II D&C Orange No. 4	CI 151
Orange 8	3	15,575	Orange R	CI 161
Orange 10	3	16,230	Orange G D&C Orange No. 3	CI 27
Orange 11	12	45,370	Eosine H8G	
Orange 12	3	15,970	Croceine Orange G	CI 26
Orange 20	3	14,600	Orange I Ext D&C Orange No. 3	CI 150
Orange 24	4	20,170	Resorcin Brown D&C Brown No. 1	CI 234
Orange 45	4	22,195	Acid Orange R	Pr 152
Orange 49	4	23,260	Acid Orange GS	Pr 151
Orange 50	3	13,150	Milling Orange G	Pr 137
Orange 51	4	26,550	Acid Brown 5R	Pr 562
Orange 52	3	13,025	Methyl Orange	CI 142
Orange 56	4	22,895	Acid Orange G	Pr 186
Orange 74	3	18,745	Acid Fast Orange GN	Pr 315
Orange 76	3	18,870	Acid Orange R	Pr 146
Red 1	3	18,050	Amido Naphthol Red G Ext D&C Red No. 11	CI 31
Red 4	3	14,710	Azo Eosine G	CI 114
Red 12	3	14,835	Diamond Blue 3B	CI 180
Red 14	3	14,720	Azo Rubine Ext D&C Red No. 10	CI 179
Red 17	3	16,180	Fast Red B	CI 88
Red 18	3	16,255	Cochineal Red A	CI 185
Red 25	3	16,050	Croceine Scarlet 3BX	CI 183
Red 26	3	16,150	Ponceau R D&C Red No. 5	CI 79
Red 27	3	16,185	Amaranth FD&C Red No. 2	CI 184
Red 29	3	16,570	Chromotrope 2R	CI 29
Red 32	3	17,065	Fast Light Rubine BL	Pr 188
Red 33	3	17,200	Fast Acid Fuchsine B Ext D&C Red No. 23	CI 30
Red 34	3	17,030	Guinea Fast Red 8BL	Pr 102
Red 35	3	18,065	Acid Red 3B	Pr 193
Red 37	3	17,045	Guinea Fast Red BL	Pr 101
Red 51	12	45,430	Erythrosine Bluish FD&C Red No. 3	CI 773
Red 52	12	45,100	Sulpho Rhodamine B	CI 748
Red 66	4	26,905	Ponceau 3RB	CI 280
Red 73	4	27,290	Brilliant Croceine M Ext D&C Red No. 13	CI 252
Red 80	26	68,215	Alizarine Rubinol R	CI 1091
Red 85	4	22,245	Acid Red G	CI 430
Red 87	12	45,380	Eosine G or Y D&C Red Nos. 22 and 23	CI 768
Red 88	3	15,620	Fast Red A Ext D&C Red No. 8	CI 176
Red 89	4	23,910	Milling Scarlet 4R	CI 487
Red 92	12	45,410	Phloxine B D&C Red No. 28	CI 778
Red 94	12	45,440	Rose Bengal B	CI 779
Red 95	12	45,425	Erythrosine Yellowish D&C Orange No. 11	CI 772
Red 97	4	22,890	Acid Anthracene Red G	CI 443
Red 99	4	23,285	Acid Red	CI 430
Red 106	3	18,110	Brilliant Acid Red	CI 32
Red 115	4	27,200	Cloth Red B	CI 262
ACID—*Continued*				
Red 133	3	17,995	Acid Chrome Red B	Pr 360 and 649
Red 134	4	24,810	Acid Bordeaux B	CI 430
Red 137	3	17,755	Paper Red A	Pr 148
Red 151	4	26,900	Cloth Scarlet G	CI 275
Red 179	3	19,351	Acid Bordeaux R	Pr 145
Red 182	—	—	Acid Red B	Pr 591
Red 183	3	18,800	Acid Red GRE	Pr 391
Red 186	3	18,810	Acid Fast Pink BN	Pr 326
Violet 1	3	17,025	Victoria Fast Violet RR	Pr 197
Violet 3	3	16,580	Victoria Violet 4BS	CI 53
Violet 6	3	16,600	Chromotrope 6B	CI 56
Violet 7	3	18,055	Amido Naphthol Red 6B Ext D&C Red No. 1	CI 57
Violet 9	12	45,190	Fast Acid Violet R	CI 758
Violet 12	3	18,075	Guinea Carmine B	Pr 100
Violet 13	3	16,640	Chromotrope 10B	CI 90
Violet 14	3	17,080	Acid Fast Red 6BL	Pr 453
Violet 17	11	42,650	Formyl Violet S4B	CI 698
Violet 19	11	42,685	Acid Fuchsine Acid Magenta	CI 692
Violet 34	26	61,710	Anthraquinone Violet	CI 1080
Violet 43	26	60,730	Alizarine Acid Violet R Ext D&C Violet No. 2	CI 1073
Violet 49	11	42,640	Acid Violet 6B FD&C Violet No. 1	CI 697
Violet 56	3	16,055	Acid Fast Violet 3RN	Pr 328
Violet 58	3	16,260	Acid Fast Violet 5RN	Pr 329
Blue 1	11	42,045	Azure Blue VX	CI 672
Blue 5	11	42,052	Patent Blue A	CI 714
Blue 7	11	42,080	Azure Blue Z	CI 673
Blue 9	11	42,090	Azure Blue AEG FD&C Blue No. 1	CI 671
Blue 13	11	42,571	Fast Acid Violet 10B	CI 696
Blue 15	11	42,645	Brilliant Milling Blue B	Pr 37
Blue 20	19	50,405	Induline	CI 861
Blue 22	11	42,755	Soluble Blue	CI 707
Blue 23	26	61,125	Alizarine Light Blue 4GL	Pr 485
Blue 25	26	62,055	Alizarine Supra Blue A	Pr 12
Blue 27	26	61,530	Alizarine Starry Blue B	CI 1075
Blue 40	26	62,125	Alizarine Direct Blue A2G	Pr 10
Blue 41	26	62,130	Alizarine Direct Blue AR	Pr 11
Blue 43	26	63,000	Alizarine Saphirol SE	CI 1053
Blue 45	26	63,010	Alizarine Saphirol B Ext D&C Blue No. 4	CI 1054
Blue 47	26	62,085	Cyananthrol R	CI 1076
Blue 59	19	50,315	Wool Fast Blue BL	CI 833
Blue 74	27	73,015	Indigotine IA Indigo Carmine FD&C Blue No. 2	CI 1180
Blue 75	11	42,576	Acid Cyanine A	CI 699
Blue 78	26	62,105	Alizarine Sky Blue B	CI 1088
Blue 81	26	64,515	Anthraquinone Blue SR	CI 1089
Blue 83	11	42,660	Brilliant Indocyanine 6B	Pr 222
Blue 89	3	13,405	Acid Blue B	CI 209
Blue 90	11	42,655	Brilliant Indocyanine G	Pr 223
Blue 92	3	13,390	Acid Blue R	CI 208
Blue 93	11	42,780	Methyl Cotton Blue	CI 706
Blue 102	19	50,320	Wool Fast Blue GL	CI 833
Blue 104	11	42,735	Brilliant Wool Blue FFR	Pr 40
Blue 109	11	42,740	Brilliant Wool Blue FFB	Pr 39
Blue 110	11	42,750	Alkali Blue	CI 704
Blue 113	4	26,360	Acid Cyanine 5R	CI 289

Part I Colour Index Generic Name	Chemical Structure Type	Part II Colour Index No.	Commercial Name	Old Colour Index No. or Prototype No.
ACID—*Continued*				
Blue 118	4	26,410	Acid Cyanine G	CI 288
Blue 120	4	26,400	Acid Cyanine GR	CI 289
Blue 158	3	14,880	Acid Fast Blue GGN	Pr 144
Blue 158A	3	15,050	Acid Blue 2G	Pr 144
Blue 161	3	15,076	Acid Fast Blue BN	Pr 318
Green 1	1	10,020	Naphthol Green B Ext D&C Green No. 1	CI 5
Green 3	11	42,085	Guinea Green B Acid Green B FD&C Green No. 1	CI 666
Green 5	11	42,095	Light Green SF Yellowish FD&C Green No. 2	CI 670
Green 7	11	42,055	Acid Green A	Pr 688
Green 9	11	42,100	Brilliant Milling Green B D&C Green No. 7	CI 667
Green 11	11	42,038	Fast Green Extra Bluish	CI 691
Green 12	3	13,425	Acid Fast Green BLN	Pr 321
Green 16	11	44,025	Naphthalene Green V	CI 735
Green 20	4	20,495	Amido Black Green B	CI 247
Green 22	11	42,170	Alkali Fast Green 10G	Pr 131
Green 25	26	61,570	Alizarine Cyanine Green G D&C Green No. 5	CI 1078
Green 35	3	13,361	Acid Dark Green B	Pr 560
Green 50	11	44,090	Wool Green S	CI 737
Brown 13	2	10,410	Acid Brown 3GL	Pr 579
Brown 14	4	20,195	Resorcin Dark Brown	CI 235
Black 1	4	20,470	Naphthol Blue Black Naphthylamine Black 10B D&C Black No. 1	CI 246
Black 2	19	50,420	Nigrosine	CI 865
Black 7	4	26,300	Naphthylamine Black D	CI 308
Black 24	4	26,370	Acid Cyanine Black B	CI 307
Black 26B	4	26,690	Nerol 2B	CI 304
Black 31	3	17,580	Acid Black BR	Pr 189
Black 35	4	26,320	Acid Black R	CI 271
Black 41	4	20,480	Naphthol Blue Black S	Pr 141
Black 47	24	56,055	Acid Gray G	Pr 705
Black 48	26	65,005	Alizarine Fast Gray BBLW	Pr 206
Black 52	3	15,711	Acid Black WA	Pr 143
AZOIC				
Yellow 1		37,610+37,090	Azoic Yellow G	Pr 171
Yellow 2		37,610+37,120	Azoic Yellow GG	Pr 353
Yellow 3		37,610+37,558	Azoic Golden Yellow R	Pr 345
Orange 2		37,520+37,005	Azoic Orange G	Pr 348
Orange 3		37,558+37,010	Azoic Orange R	Pr 349
Red 1		37,558+37,090	Azoic Scarlet RS	Pr 170
Red 2		37,530+37,120	Azoic Red R	Pr 169
Red 6		37,520+37,090	Azoic Red GS	Pr 168
Red 12		37,550+37,150	Azoic Red ITR	Pr 402
Red 16		37,520+37,100	Azoic Bordeaux R	Pr 165
Violet 1		37,505+37,165	Azoic Violet B	Pr 351
Violet 3		37,540+37,160	Azoic Corinth IB	Pr 511
Blue 6		37,505+37,175	Azoic Blue B	Pr 163
Blue 7		37,505+37,155	Azoic Blue R	Pr 342
Green 1		37,585+37,175	Azoic Green B	Pr 347
Brown 2		37,545+37,010	Azoic Brown IR	— —
Brown 10		37,550+37,605	Azoic Black Brown IT	Pr 340
Black 1		37,235+37,175	Azoic Black MG	Pr 339
Coupler 2	8	37,505	Naphthol AS	Pr 302
Coupler 3	8	37,575	Naphthol AS-BR	Pr 304
Coupler 4	8	37,560	Naphthol AS-BO	Pr 303
Coupler 5	8	37,610	Naphthol AS-G	Pr 309
Coupler 7	8	39,565	Naphthol AS-SW	Pr 313
Coupler 8	8	37,525	Naphthol AS-TR	Pr 314
Coupler 9	8	37,625	Naphthol AS-L4G	Pr 647
Coupler 10	8	37,510	Naphthol AS-E	Pr 308
Coupler 11	8	37,535	Naphthol AS-RL	Pr 312
Coupler 12	8	37,550	Naphthol AS-ITR	Pr 310
Coupler 13	8	37,595	Naphthol AS-SG	Pr 388
Coupler 14	8	37,558	Naphthol AS-PH	Pr 557
Coupler 15	8	37,600	Naphthol AS-LB	Pr 387
Coupler 16	8	37,605	Naphthol AS-DB or AS-BT	Pr 307
Coupler 17	8	37,515	Naphthol AS-BS	Pr 305
Coupler 18	8	37,520	Naphthol AS-D	Pr 306
Coupler 19	8	37,545	Naphthol AS-BG	Pr 385
Coupler 20	8	37,530	Naphthol AS-OL	Pr 311
Coupler 21	8	37,526	Naphthol AS-KB	Pr 604
Coupler 22	8	37,511	Naphthol AS-MCA	Pr 693
Coupler 23	8	37,555	Naphthol AS-LC	Pr 460
Coupler 24	8	37,540	Naphthol AS-LT	Pr 506
Coupler 25	8	37,590	Naphthol AS-SR	Pr 558
Coupler 27	8	37,516	Naphthol AS-AN	Pr 692
Coupler 29	8	37,527	Naphthol AS-MX	Pr 556
Coupler 30	8	37,559	Naphthol AS-RP	Pr 694
Coupler 31	8	37,521	Naphthol AS-RT	Pr 695
Coupler 33	8	37,620	Naphthol AS-L3G	Pr 555
Coupler 34	8	37,531	Naphthol NEL	Pr 559
Coupler 35	8	37,615	Naphthol AS-LG	Pr 505
Coupler 36	8	37,585	Naphthol AS-GR	Pr 386
Diazo 1	7	37,135	Fast Bordeaux GP Base or Salt	Pr 260
Diazo 2	7	37,005	Fast Orange GC Base or Salt	Pr 264
Diazo 3	7	37,010	Fast Scarlet 2G Base or Salt	Pr 94
Diazo 4	7	37,210	Fast Garnet GBC Base or Salt	CI 17
AZOIC—*Continued*				
Diazo 5	7	37,125	Fast Red B Base or Salt	CI 117
Diazo 6	7	37,025	Fast Orange GR Base or Salt	Pr 265
Diazo 7	7	37,030	Fast Orange R Base or Salt	CI 38
Diazo 8	7	37,110	Fast Red GL Base or Salt	CI 69
Diazo 9	7	37,040	Fast Red 3GL Base or Salt	Pr 269
Diazo 10	7	37,120	Fast Red RC Base or Salt	Pr 271
Diazo 11	7	37,085	Fast Red TR Base or Salt	Pr 273
Diazo 12	7	37,105	Fast Scarlet G Base or Salt	CI 68
Diazo 13	7	37,130	Fast Scarlet R Base or Salt	CI 118
Diazo 20	7	37,175	Fast Blue BB Base or Salt	Pr 258
Diazo 22	7	37,240	Diazo Blue Salt RT	Pr 358
Diazo 23	7	37,205	Fast Black LB Base	Pr 257
Diazo 24	7	37,155	Fast Blue RR Base or Salt	Pr 498
Diazo 27	7	37,215	Fast Garnet GC Base or Salt	Pr 501
Diazo 28	7	37,151	Fast Red PDC Base or Salt	Pr 501
Diazo 32	7	37,090	Fast Red KB Base or Salt	Pr 270
Diazo 33	7	37,075	Fast Red FR Base or Salt	Pr 671
Diazo 34	7	37,100	Fast Red RL Base or Salt	Pr 272
Diazo 35	7	37,255	Diazo Blue Salt B	Pr 357
Diazo 36	7	37,275	Fast Red AL Salt	Pr 267
Diazo 37	7	37,035	Fast Red 2G Base or Salt	CI 44
Diazo 38	7	37,190	Fast Black K Salt	Pr 256
Diazo 39	7	37,220	Fast Corinth V Salt	Pr 261
Diazo 40	7	37,170	Fast Bordeaux BD Salt	Pr 259
Diazo 41	7	37,165	Fast Violet B Base or Salt	Pr 274
Diazo 42	7	37,150	Fast Red ITR Base or Salt	Pr 378
Diazo 44	7	37,000	Fast Yellow GC Base or Salt	Pr 275
Diazo 46	7	37,080	Fast Scarlet TR Base	Pr 442
Diazo 48	7	37,235	Fast Blue B Base or Salt	CI 499
BASIC				
Yellow 1	16	49,005	Thioflavine T	CI 815
Yellow 2	10	41,000	Auramine	CI 655
Yellow 9	13	46,040	Euchrysine GG	CI 797
Yellow 11	15	48,055	Methine Basic Yellow 3G	— —
Orange 1	3	11,320	Chrysoidine R	CI 21
Orange 2	3	11,270	Chrysoidine G	CI 20
Orange 10	13	46,035	Brilliant Phosphine G	CI 789
Orange 14	13	46,005	Acridine Orange NO	CI 788
Orange 15	13	46,045	Phosphine	CI 793
Orange 21	15	48,035	Methine Basic Orange G	— —
Red 1	12	45,160	Rhodamine 6G	CI 752
Red 2	19	50,240	Safranine	CI 841
Red 9	11	42,500	Para Fuchsine Para Magenta Para Rosaniline	CI 676
Violet 1	11	42,535	Methyl Violet B	CI 680
Violet 2	11	42,520	New Fuchsine	CI 678
Violet 3	11	42,555	Crystal Violet Gentian Violet	CI 681
Violet 4	11	42,600	Ethyl Violet	CI 682
Violet 5	19	50,205	Methylene Violet 3R	CI 842
Violet 10	12	45,170	Rhodamine B Ext D&C Red No. 21	CI 749
Violet 13	11	42,536	Benzyl Violet	CI 683
Violet 14	11	42,510	Fuchsine Magenta Rosaniline	CI 677
Blue 1	11	42,025	Basic Blue 6G	CI 658
Blue 5	11	42,140	Brilliant Basic Blue 5B	CI 663
Blue 6	20	51,175	Meldola's Blue New Blue R	CI 909
Blue 7	11	42,595	Victoria Pure Blue B	Pr 198
Blue 9	21	52,015	Methylene Blue B Ext D&C Blue No. 1	CI 922
Blue 11	11	44,040	Victoria Blue R	CI 728
Blue 12	20	51,180	Basic Blue A	CI 913
Blue 26	11	44,045	Victoria Blue B	CI 729
Green 1	11	42,040	Brilliant Green	CI 662
Green 4	11	42,000	Malachite Green	CI 673
Green 5	21	52,020	Methylene Green B	CI 924
Brown 1	4	21,000	Bismarck Brown G	CI 331
Brown 2	4	21,030	Phoenix Brown Leather Brown 5RT	Pr 552
Brown 4	4	21,010	Bismarck Brown R	CI 332
DEVELOPER				
1	—	—	Developer Z	Pr 597
5	8	37,500	Beta Naphthol	Pr 586
8	—	—	Beta Oxy Naphthoic Acid 3-Hydroxy-2-naphthoic Acid Developer BON	Pr 587
14	31	76,035	Developer MTD	Pr 602
DIRECT				
Yellow 1	4	22,250	Chrysamine G	CI 410
Yellow 4	4	24,890	Brilliant Yellow	CI 364
Yellow 5	14	47,035	Direct Quinoline Yellow	Pr 533
Yellow 6	9	40,001	Mikado Yellow G	CI 622
Yellow 7	16	49,010	Thioflavine S	CI 816
DIRECT—*Continued*				
Yellow 8	3	13,920	Direct Yellow 5G	Pr 249 and 492
Yellow 9	3	19,540	Naphthamine Pure Yellow G	CI 813
Yellow 11	9	40,000	Curcumin S	CI 620
Yellow 12	4	24,895	Chrysophenine G	CI 365
Yellow 19	9	40,030	Diphenyl Chrysoine G	CI 631
Yellow 20	4	22,410	Cresotine Yellow G	CI 411
Yellow 26	4	25,300	Cotton Yellow G Benzo Fast Yellow 5GL	CI 346
Yellow 27	3	13,950	Direct Supra Yellow 5GL	Pr 99
Yellow 28	3	19,555	Direct Yellow	CI 814
Yellow 29	3	19,556	Direct Supra Yellow RT	CI 814
Yellow 41	4	29,005	Direct Fast Yellow RL	Pr 54
Yellow 50	4	29,025	Direct Supra Yellow R	Pr 582
Yellow 59	16	49,000	Primuline	CI 812
Yellow 62	6	36,900	Diazo Fast Yellow GG	Pr 251
Orange 1	4	22,375/430	Direct Fast Orange G	CI 653
Orange 6	4	23,375	Toluylene Orange G	CI 478
Orange 8	4	22,130	Benzo Orange R	CI 415
Orange 10	4	23,370	Alkali Orange RT	CI 446
Orange 15	9	40,002/3	Mikado Orange	CI 621
Orange 18	4	20,216	Diamine Orange B	CI 409
Orange 26	4	29,150	Benzo Fast Orange S	CI 326
Orange 29	4	29,155	Benzo Fast Orange WS	CI 326
Orange 37	9	40,265	Diamine Fast Orange ER	Pr 73
Orange 39	9	40,215	Direct Supra Orange GGL	Pr 276
Orange 41	9	40,235	Direct Supra Orange RRL	Pr 576
Orange 73	4	25,200	Direct Orange R	Pr 173
Orange 74	4	28,255	Direct Orange RR	Pr 435
Orange 75	3	17,840	Diazo Brilliant Orange GR	Pr 376
Red 1	4	22,310	Diamine Fast Red F	CI 419
Red 2	4	23,500	Benzopurpurine 4B	CI 448
Red 4	4	29,165	Benzo Fast Scarlet GS	CI 326
Red 7	4	24,100	Benzopurpurine 10B	CI 495
Red 10	4	22,145	Congo Corinth G	CI 375
Red 13	4	22,155	Diamine Bordeaux B	Pr 67
Red 16	4	27,680	Benzo Bordeaux 6B	Pr 19
Red 17	4	22,150	Congo Rubine	CI 376
Red 20	3	15,075	Diamine Pink BD	CI 128
Red 23	4	29,160	Benzo Fast Scarlet 4BS	CI 327
Red 24	4	29,185	Benzo Fast Scarlet S	CI 326
Red 26	4	29,190	Benzo Fast Scarlet 8BS	CI 326
Red 28	4	22,120	Congo Red	CI 370
Red 31	4	29,100	Benzo Rose Red B	Pr 31
Red 32	4	28,395	Direct Fast Rubine B	Pr 539
Red 37	4	22,240	Diamine Scarlet B	CI 382
Red 39	4	23,630	Diamine Scarlet 3B	CI 382
Red 43	4	22,205	Benzo Fast Red 9BL Diamine Brilliant Bordeaux R	CI 400
Red 44	4	22,500	Bordeaux COV	CI 385
Red 45	3	14,780	Thiazine Red R	CI 225
Red 46	4	23,050	Acetopurpurine 8B	CI 436
Red 47	3	14,985	Erica GGN	CI 126
Red 51	3	14,990	Erica B	CI 130
Red 53	4	22,405	Oxamine Brilliant Red B	Pr 393
Red 75	4	25,380	Benzo Fast Pink 2BL	CI 353
Red 76	9	40,270	Direct Supra Scarlet GG	Pr 577
Red 79	4	29,065	Direct Fast Red 6BLL	Pr 428
Red 80	6	35,780	Direct Fast Red 5BRL	Pr 246
Red 81	4	28,160	Benzo Fast Red 8BL	CI 278
Red 83	4	29,225	Direct Fast Violet 2RLL	Pr 491
Red 84	6	35,760	Direct Supra Brown 3RL	Pr 575
Red 120	4	25,275	Diazo Rubine B	Pr 89
Red 121	4	28,250	Diazo Fast Bordeaux FBL	Pr 438
Red 122	4	29,210	Diazo Brilliant Scarlet BBL	Pr 79
Red 123	3	17,820	Diazo Brilliant Scarlet ROA	Pr 80
Red 148	4	25,005	Direct Bordeaux B	Pr 404
Red 149	4	29,110	Diazo Bordeaux 7B	Pr 77
Red 152	4	28,360	Diazo Fast Red 8BL	Pr 84
Red 153	4	28,210	Diazo Fast Red 7BL	Pr 85
Red 155	4	25,210	Diazo Brilliant Scarlet 5BLN	Pr 377
Red 189	4	28,400	Direct Rubine G	Pr 681
Violet 1	4	22,570	Diamine Violet N	CI 394
Violet 9	4	27,885	Brilliant Benzo Violet B	Pr 35
Violet 12	4	22,550	Oxamine Violet	CI 393
Violet 14	4	29,105	Benzo Direct Red 3B	Pr 32
Violet 22	4	22,480	Direct Violet B	CI 387
Violet 47	4	25,410	Direct Supra Red Violet RL	Pr 277
Violet 51	4	27,905	Brilliant Benzo Fast Violet BL	Pr 367
Blue 1	4	24,410	Chicago Blue 6B Diamine Sky Blue FF	CI 518
Blue 2	4	22,590	Diamine Black BH	CI 401
Blue 3	4	23,705	Oxamine Blue 3R	CI 471
Blue 4	4	24,380	Chicago Blue B	CI 516
Blue 6	4	22,610	Benzo Blue BB	CI 406

Part I Colour Index Generic Name	Chemical Structure Type	Chemical Structure Part II Colour Index No.	Commercial Name	Old Colour Index No. or Prototype No.
DIRECT—*Continued*				
Blue 8	4	24,140	Benzo Azurine C	CI 502
Blue 14	4	23,850	Diamine Blue 3B	CI 477
Blue 15	4	24,400	Diamine Pure Blue	CI 520
Blue 21	4	23,710	Diamine Blue BX	CI 472
Blue 22	4	24,280	Chicago Blue RW Benzo Blue RW	CI 512
Blue 25	4	23,790	Direct Blue B	CI 466
Blue 26	5	31,930	Benzo Chrome Black Blue B	Pr 20
Blue 27	4	23,750	Direct Blue R	CI 464
Blue 30	5	31,955	Congo Fast Blue B	CI 576
Blue 41	11	42,700	Brilliant Sky Blue 5G Cotton Pure Blue B	CI 710
Blue 55	4	27,940	Brilliant Congo Blue BFL	Pr 417
Blue 63	5	31,910	Congo Fast Blue R	CI 567
Blue 64	4	22,595	Benzo Cyanine R	CI 405
Blue 71	5	34,140	Benzo Supra Blue FFL	Pr 71
Blue 81	5	34,215	Direct Supra Blue BL	Pr 594
Blue 86	29	74,180	Durazol Blue 8G	Pr 278
Blue 98	4	23,155	Direct Supra Blue FBGL	Pr 443
Blue 120	5	34,085	Diazo Indigo Blue BR	Pr 74
Blue 120A	5	34,090	Diazo Indigo Blue M	Pr 74
Blue 126	5	34,010	Diaminogen Blue NA	Pr 529
Blue 127	5	34,080	Diazo Indigo Blue 4GL	—
Blue 130	4	27,110	Diazo Brilliant Blue BBL	Pr 436
Blue 133	5	34,005	Diazo Indigo Blue 4RL	Pr 87
Blue 136	4	24,065	Diazo Sky Blue B	Pr 90
Blue 138	4	26,650	Diazo Sky Blue 3GL	Pr 91
Blue 175	6	35,465	Direct Blue BB	Pr 675
Green 1	5	30,280	Diamine Dark Green N	CI 583
Green 6	5	30,295	Diamine Green B	CI 593
Green 8	5	30,315	Diamine Green G	CI 594
Green 11	4	27,540	Brilliant Benzo Green B	Pr 368
Green 12	5	30,290	Direct Green B	CI 589
Green 26	5	34,045	Direct Fast Green BLL	Pr 425
Green 28	3	14,155	Direct Fast Green 5GLL	Pr 616
Green 38	4	28,280	Diazo Brilliant Green 3G	Pr 78
Green 39	5	30,220	Diazo Olive G	CI 595
Green 51	5	34,260	Diazo Fast Green GF	Pr 530
Brown 1	5	30,045	Benzo Chrome Brown G Benzamine Brown 3GO	CI 596
Brown 2	4	22,311	Diamine Brown M	CI 420
Brown 6	5	30,140	Congo Brown G	CI 598
Brown 21	5	30,155	Congo Brown R	CI 601
Brown 27	5	31,725	Benzo Chrome Brown G	Pr 364
Brown 29	9	40,505	Diphenyl Catechine G	CI 628
Brown 30	3	17,630	Direct Brown B	Pr 208
Brown 33	6	35,520	Diamine Catechine B	Pr 68
Brown 57	5	31,705	Cotton Dark Brown T Direct Brown B	CI 560
Brown 58	4	22,340	Diphenyl Brown BBN	CI 422
Brown 59	4	22,345	Diamine Brown B	CI 423
Brown 74	6	36,300	Diamine Catechine 3G	Pr 70
Brown 95	5	30,145	Direct Supra Brown BRS	Pr 47
Brown 101	5	31,740	Benzo Chrome Brown G	Pr 365
Brown 106	6	36,200	Direct Supra Brown G	Pr 28
Brown 112	4	29,166	Direct Fast Brown 8RLL	Pr 423
Brown 132	5	31,505	Diazo Brown 3RB	Pr 83
Brown 138	5	31,500	Diazo Brown 3R	Pr 250
Brown 151	5	31,685	Para Brown V	Pr 397
Black 3	4	27,710	Neutral Gray G	CI 267
Black 4	5	30,245	Direct Deep Black RW	CI 582
Black 9	5	31,560	Columbia Black FF	CI 539
Black 17	4	27,700	Zambesi Black D	Pr 201
Black 19	6	35,255	Naphthamine Fast Black RF	CI 619
Black 22	6	35,435	Cotonerol A	Pr 372
Black 29	4	22,580	Diamine Black RO	CI 395
Black 38	5	30,235	Direct Deep Black EW Columbia Black EAW	CI 581
Black 41	5	30,260	Chrome Leather Fast Black S	Pr 371
Black 51	4	27,720	Benzo Fast Black L	Pr 24
Black 56	5	34,170	Diphenyl Fast Gray B	CI 403
Black 71	4	25,040	Direct Supra Gray VGL	Pr 379
Black 74	5	34,180	Benzo Fast Gray BL	Pr 416
Black 75	6	35,870	Direct Supra Gray R	Pr 96
Black 78	5	30,015	Zambesi Black V	Pr 202
Black 80	5	31,600	Oxydiaminogen OB	Pr 147
Black 83	5	31,850	Diazo Blue Black RS	CI 552
DISPERSE				
Yellow 1	2	10,345	Disperse Fast Yellow RR	Pr 243
Yellow 3	3	11,855	Disperse Fast Yellow G	Pr 242
Yellow 5	3	12,790	Disperse Yellow 5G	Pr 245
Yellow 11	24	56,200	Disperse Brilliant Yellow FF	Pr 369
Yellow 23	—	—	Disperse Fast Yellow 4RL	Pr 583
DISPERSE—*Continued*				
Yellow 31	15	48,000	Disperse Fast Yellow 7G	Pr 420
Yellow 33	—	—	Disperse Fast Yellow GLF	Pr 537
Orange 1	3	11,080	SRA Orange I	Pr 637
Orange 3	3	11,005	Disperse Orange GR	Pr 43
Orange 5	3	11,100	Disperse Fast Brown 3R	Pr 230
Orange 11	26	60,700	SRA Orange II	Pr 638
Orange 13	4	26,080	Disperse Golden Orange I	Pr 635
Orange 15	2	10,350	SRA Fast Golden Orange III	Pr 636
Red 1	3	11,110	Disperse Scarlet B	Pr 244
Red 4	26	60,755	Disperse Fast Pink RF	Pr 370
Red 5	3	11,215	Disperse Fast Rubine 3B	Pr 239
Red 9	26	60,505	SRA Red VI–X	Pr 639
Red 11	26	62,015	Disperse Fast Pink FF3B	Pr 235
Red 13	3	11,115	Disperse Fast Rubine B	Pr 238
Red 15	26	60,710	SRA Fast Red VII	Pr 234
Red 17	3	11,210	SRA Red VIII	Pr 236
Red 31	3	11,250	Disperse Scarlet G	Pr 63
Red 32	3	11,190	Disperse Fast Brown 5R	Pr 231
Violet 1	26	61,100	Disperse Fast Red Violet RN	Pr 237
Violet 4	26	61,105	Disperse Fast Violet 6B	Pr 241
Violet 6	26	61,140	SRA Fast Red FSI	Pr 640
Violet 8	26	62,030	Disperse Fast Violet B	Pr 240
Violet 13	3	11,195	Disperse Violet R	Pr 641
Blue 1	26	64,500	Disperse Sapphire Blue G	Pr 62
Blue 3	26	61,505	Disperse Fast Blue FFR	Pr 228
Blue 7	26	62,500	Disperse Fast Blue Green B	Pr 229
Blue 9	26	61,115	Disperse Fast Blue FR	Pr 227
Blue 19	26	61,110	Disperse Direct Blue RS	Pr 642
Black 1	3	11,365	Disperse Diazo Black STN	Pr 630
Black 2	3	11,255	Disperse Diazo Black B	Pr 58
Black 6	7	37,235	Disperse Diazo Navy B (Fast Blue B Base)	CI 499
Black 7	3	11,035	Disperse Diazo Black NS	Pr 41
FIBER-REACTIVE				
Red	—	—	Cibacron Brilliant Red 3B	—
Red	—	—	Procion Brilliant Red H3B	—
Red	—	—	Remazol Red 3B	—
Blue	—	—	Cibacron Blue 3G	—
Blue	—	—	Procion Brilliant Blue R	—
Blue	—	—	Remazol Brilliant Blue R	—
FLUORESCENT				
Brightener 1	9	40,630	Brightener BVA	Pr 698
Brightener 5	6	36,900	Diazo Fast Yellow GG	Pr 251
Bright-ener 30	9	40,600	Brightener R	Pr 690
Bright-ener 34	9	40,605	Direct White 2GT	—
Bright-ener 41	16	49,015	Brightener RS	Pr 710
Bright-ener 74	12	45,550	Fluorol 5G (Solvent Green No. 4)	Pr 542
FOOD				
Yellow 3	3	15,985	FD&C Yellow No. 6	Pr 674
Red 1	3	14,700	FD&C Red No. 4	Pr 673
Red 6	3	16,155		CI 80
Green 3	11	42,053	FD&C Green No. 3	Pr 672
INGRAIN				
Blue 1	29	74,240	Alcian Blue 8GX	—
Blue 2	29	74,160	Phthalogen Brilliant Blue IF3G	—
MORDANT				
Yellow 1	3	14,025	Alizarine Yellow 2G	CI 36
Yellow 3	3	14,095	Chrome Yellow D	CI 195
Yellow 5	3	14,130	Chrome Flavine A	CI 219
Yellow 8	3	18,821	Acid Alizarine Flavine R	Pr 1
Yellow 10	3	14,010	Chrome Yellow G	Pr 56
Yellow 14	3	14,055	Azo Alizarine Yellow GP	CI 52
Yellow 16	4	25,100	Anthracene Yellow C	CI 343
Yellow 20	3	14,110	Crumpsall Yellow	CI 197
Yellow 26	4	22,880	Chromocitronine R	CI 441
Yellow 30	3	18,710	Chrome Yellow ME	Pr 317
Yellow 36	3	14,135	Diamond Flavine G	CI 110
Yellow 38	3	14,080	Alizarine Yellow 5G	CI 122
Orange 1	3	14,030	Alizarine Yellow R	CI 40
Orange 4	3	18,940	Chrome Fast Orange 3RL	Pr 247
Orange 6	4	26,520	Acid Alizarine Orange GR Milling Orange	CI 274
Red 3	26	58,005	Alizarine Red S	CI 1034
Red 5	3	14,290	Acid Alizarine Garnet R	CI 168
Red 7	3	18,760	Chrome Red B	CI 652
Red 8	4	23,095	Anthracene Red	CI 431
Red 9	3	16,105	Acid Alizarine Red B	CI 216
MORDANT—*Continued*				
Red 11	26	58,000	Alizarine VI D&C Orange No. 15	CI 1027
Red 19	3	18,735	Metachrome Red G Metachrome Red 5G	Pr 135
Red 21	3	17,995	Acid Chrome Red B	Pr 360
Violet 1	11	43,565	Naphthochrome Violet R	Pr 461
Violet 5	3	15,670	Acid Alizarine Violet N	CI 169
Violet 11	11	43,550	Mordant Brilliant Violet B	Pr 484
Blue 1	11	43,830	Chrome Azurol B	CI 720
Blue 3	11	43,820	Chrome Cyanine R	CI 722
Blue 7	3	17,940	Chrome Cyanine BLL	Pr 603
Blue 8	26	58,805	Anthracene Blue WGG	CI 1060
Blue 9	3	14,855	Acid Chrome Blue RR	Pr 7
Blue 10	20	51,030	Gallocyanine	CI 883
Blue 13	3	16,680	Fast Mordant Blue B	Pr 93
Blue 32	26	58,605	Anthracene Blue WR	CI 1062
Blue 51	21	52,055	Brilliant Alizarine Blue G	CI 931
Blue 54	3	16,685	Acid Chrome Blue 3G	Pr 408
Blue 56	20	51,120	Delphine Blue B	CI 878
Green 9	3	19,515	Acid Chrome Green G	Pr 527
Green 12	4	27,520	Diamond Green B	CI 302
Green 17	3	17,225	Chrome Fast Green G	CI 99
Green 26	3	18,180	Metachrome Olive BL	Pr 254
Brown 1	4	20,110	Anthracene Chromate Brown EB	Pr 14
Brown 4	3	11,335	Metachrome Brown B	CI 101
Brown 13	3	13,225	Acid Alizarine Brown B	CI 167
Brown 15	3	14,870	Acid Anthracene Brown KE	Pr 203
Brown 18	4	20,150	Anthracene Acid Brown G	CI 238
Brown 19	3	14,250	Chrome Brown DKL	Pr 253
Brown 21	3	19,600	Acid Anthracene Brown TBL	Pr 584
Brown 22	3	14,235	Acid Anthracene Brown WSG	Pr 205
Brown 33	3	13,250	Acid Anthracene Brown RH	CI 98
Brown 35	3	14,765	Acid Anthracene Brown V	Pr 3
Brown 40	3	17,590	Acid Anthracene Brown PG	Pr 4
Brown 42	26	58,200	Anthracene Brown Anthragallol	CI 1035
Brown 61	3	16,070	Chrome Fast Brown V	Pr 634
Black 1	3	15,710	Chrome Black A	CI 204
Black 3	3	14,640	Chrome Blue Black B	CI 201
Black 5	4	26,695	Diamond Black F	CI 299
Black 9	3	16,500	Diamond Black PV	CI 170
Black 10	4	21,720	Acid Alizarine Black SE	CI 336
Black 11	3	14,645	Chrome Black T	CI 203
Black 13	26	63,615	Alizarine Blue Black B	CI 1085
Black 17	3	15,705	Chrome Blue Black R	CI 202
Black 38	3	18,160	Metachrome Black Blue G	Pr 299
NATURAL				
Yellow 8	30	75,660	Osage Orange	—
Yellow 10	30	75,720	Quercitron, Flavine	CI 1233
Yellow 11	30	75,240	Fustic, Old Fustic	CI 1232
Red 4	30	75,470	Carmine, Cochineal	CI 1239
Red 24	30	75,280	Extract of Brazil-wood	CI 1243
Brown 1	30	75,620	Young Fustic	CI 1231
Brown 3	30	75,250	Cutch, Gambier, Catechu	CI 1249
Black 1	30	75,290	Hematine, Logwood	CI 1246
Black 4	30	75,291	Steam Black Logwood Printing Black	CI 1253
OXIDATION				
Base 1	19	50,440	Aniline Oil, Aniline Salt, Aniline Black	CI 870
Base 2	31	76,085	Diphenyl Black Base	CI 871
PIGMENT				
Yellow 1	3	11,680	Pigment Yellow G Ext D&C Yellow No. 5	Pr 103
Yellow 3	3	11,710	Pigment Yellow 10G	Pr 105
Yellow 10	3	12,710	Pigment Yellow R	—
Yellow 12	4	21,090	Benzidine Yellow	Pr 518
Yellow 13	4	21,100	Vulcan Fast Yellow GR	Pr 479
Yellow 14	4	21,095	Vulcan Fast Yellow G	Pr 478
Yellow 16	4	20,040	Permanent Fast Yellow NCG	—
Orange 1	3	11,725	Pigment Yellow 3R Ext D&C Orange No. 1	Pr 280
Orange 2	3	12,060	Ortho Nitraniline Orange	Pr 697
Orange 5	3	12,075	Permanent Red GG Ext D&C Orange No. 6	Pr 657
Orange 13	4	21,110	Vulcan Fast Orange G	Pr 475
Orange 14	4	21,165	Vulcan Fast Orange GG	—
Orange 16	4	21,160	Diane Orange Pulp Y-25	Pr 663
Red 1	3	12,070	Paranitraniline Red	CI 44
Red 2	3	12,310	Permanent Red FRR	—
Red 3	3	12,120	Toluidine Red Toner D&C Red No. 35	CI 69
Red 4	3	12,085	Permanent Red R D&C Red No. 36	Pr 541
Red 5	3	12,490	Permanent Carmine FB	Pr 398

Part I Colour Index Generic Name	Chemical Structure Type	Part II Colour Index No.	Commercial Name	Old Colour Index No. or Prototype No.
PIGMENT—*Continued*				
Red 7	3	12,420	Permanent Red F4RH	—
Red 10	3	12,440	Permanent Red FRL	—
Red 12	3	12,385	Permanent Bordeaux FRR	—
Red 15	3	12,465	Romanesta Red MT-2544	Pr 701
Red 18	3	12,350	D&C Red No. 38	Pr 661
Red 22	3	12,315	Pigment Orange R	CI 68
Red 23	3	12,355	Textile Red WD-263	Pr 708
Red 32	3	12,320	Vulcan Fast Rubine BF	—
Red 38	4	21,120	Vulcan Fast Red B	Pr 476
Red 40	3	12,170	Pigment Bordeaux N	CI 82
Red 41	4	21,200	Vulcan Fast Red BBE	Pr 664
Red 48	3	15,865	Permanent Red 2B	Pr 563
Red 49	3	15,630	Lithol Red R Toner Ext D&C Red Nos. 17, 18, 19, and 20	CI 189
Red 50	3	15,500	Lake Red D	CI 214
Red 51	3	15,580	Pigment Red RMT	Pr 112
Red 52	3	15,860	Lithol Red 2G	CI 166
Red 53	3	15,585	Lake Red C Ext D&C Red Nos. 15 and 16	CI 165
Red 54	3	14,830	Double Ponceau R	CI 84
Red 55	3	15,820	Cabarine Red MB	Pr 651
Red 57	3	15,850	Lithol Rubine B D&C Red Nos. 6 and 7	CI 163
Red 60	3	16,105	Pigment Scarlet 3B Acid Alizarine Red B	CI 216
Red 63	3	15,880	Lake Bordeaux B D&C Red No. 34	CI 190
Red 64	3	15,800	Brilliant Lake Red R D&C Red No. 31	CI 35
Red 81	12	45,160	Rhodamine 6G Toner	CI 752
Red 83	26	58,000	Madder Lake Alizarine Lake D&C Orange No. 15	CI 1027
Red 84	26	58,210	Pigment Fast Rubine RL	Pr 407
Red 87	28	73,310	Indo Red MV-6632	Pr 686
Red 100	3	13,058	D&C Red No. 39 Alba Red	Pr 662
Violet 1	12	45,170	Rhodamine B Lake	CI 749
Violet 3	11	42,535	Methyl Violet B Lake Gentian Violet Lake	CI 680
Violet 5	26	58,055	Pigment Fast Rubine 4BL	Pr 406
Violet 12	26	58,050	Quinizarin	CI 1028
Blue 1	11	42,595	Victoria Pure Blue BO Lake	Pr 198
Blue 2	11	44,045	Victoria Blue B Lake	CI 729
Blues 5 and 14	11	42,600	Ethyl Violet Lake	CI 682
Blue 9	11	42,025	Basic Blue 6G Lake	CI 658
Blue 15	29	74,160	Phthalocyanine Blue B	Pr 481
Blue 16	29	74,100	Phthalocyanine Blue G	Pr 482
Blue 21	26	69,835	Pigment Blue BCS	CI 1114
Blue 24	11	42,090	Peacock Blue Lake D&C Blue No. 4	CI 671
Blue 25	4	21,180	Diane Blue Pulp B-34 Pigment Blue WNL	Pr 699
Green 1	11	42,040	Brilliant Green Lake	CI 662
Green 4	11	42,000	Malachite Green Lake	CI 657
Green 7	29	74,260	Phthalocyanine Green G	Pr 483
Green 8	1	10,006	Pigment Green B	Pr 149
Green 10	3	12,775	Pigment Fast Yellow GD Virescent Gold	Pr 691
Brown 2	3	12,071	Paratone Brown ZUS	Pr 709
Brown 3	4	21,010	Bismarck Brown Lake	CI 332
Brown 5	3	15,800	Ginger Brown T-5902	CI 35
Black 1	19	50,440	Pigment Black B (Aniline Black)	CI 870
SOLVENT				
Yellow 1	3	11,000	Aminoazobenzene Oil Yellow B Spirit Yellow G	CI 15
Yellow 2	3	11,020	Butter Yellow O Oil Yellow	CI 19
Yellow 3	3	11,160	Aminoazotoluene Spirit Yellow R	CI 17
Yellow 5	3	11,380	Oil Yellow AB Ext D&C Yellow No. 9	CI 22
Yellow 6	3	11,390	Oil Yellow OB Ext D&C Yellow No. 10	CI 61
Yellow 14	3	12,055	Sudan I Sudan Orange R	CI 24
Yellow 19	3	13,900A	Solvent Fast Yellow GR Zapon Fast Yellow GR	Pr 216
Yellow 29	4	21,230	Sudan Yellow GRN	Pr 472
Yellow 30	4	21,240	Sudan Yellow GR Conc	Pr 703
Yellow 33	14	47,000	Quinoline Yellow Spirit-Soluble D&C Yellow No. 11	CI 800
Yellow 34	10	41,000B	Auramine Base	CI 655
Orange 2	3	12,000	Ext D&C Orange No. 4	—
Orange 3	3	11,270B	Chrysoidine G Base	CI 20
Orange 5	3	18,745A	Solvent Fast Orange G Zapon Fast Orange G	Pr 211
Orange 7	3	12,140	Sudan II Ext D&C Red No. 14	CI 73
Orange 18	12	45,371	D&C Orange No. 16	Pr 656
Red 1	3	12,150	Sudan R Pigment Purple A	CI 113
Red 8	3	12,715	Zapon Fast Red BE Solvent Fast Red BE	Pr 488
Red 22	4	21,250	Sudan Red GG	Pr 471

Part I Colour Index Generic Name	Chemical Structure Type	Part II Colour Index No.	Commercial Name	Old Colour Index No. or Prototype No.
SOLVENT—*Continued*				
Red 23	4	26,100	Sudan III D&C Red No. 17	CI 248
Red 24	4	26,105	Sudan IV	CI 258
Red 26	4	26,120	Oil Red OB	Pr 696
Red 27	4	26,125	Oil Red O D&C Red No. 18	Pr 658
Red 35	3+12	16,260+45,170	Zapon Fast Red 3B	Pr 213
Red 41	11	42,510B	Fuchsine Base Magenta Base Rosaniline Base	CI 677
Red 42	12	45,366	D&C Red No. 24	Pr 659
Red 43	12	45,380A	D&C Red No. 21	CI 768
Red 48	12	45,410A	Phloxine B D&C Red No. 27	CI 778
Red 49	12	45,170B	Rhodamine B Base Ext D&C Red No. 22	CI 749
Red 52	26	68,210	Alizarine Rubinol G Base Solvent Oil Red R	CI 1091
Red 72	12	45,370A	Dibromofluorescein Ext D&C Orange No. 5	—
Red 73	12	45,425A	Erythrosine G D&C Orange No. 10	CI 772
Violet 8	11	42,535B	Methyl Violet Base	CI 680
Violet 9	11	42,555B	Crystal Violet Base	CI 681
Violet 10	12	45,190A	Solvent Violet R Base Ext D&C Red No. 3	CI 758
Violet 13	26	60,725	Alizarine Violet IR Spirit-Soluble D&C Violet No. 2	CI 1073
Blue 3	11	42,775	Spirit Blue B	CI 689
Blue 4	11	44,045B	Victoria Blue B Base	CI 729
Blue 5	11	42,595B	Victoria Pure Blue B Base	Pr 198
Blue 6	11	44,040B	Victoria Blue R Base	CI 728
Blue 7	19	50,400	Induline Spirit-Soluble	CI 860
Blue 11	26	61,525	Alizarine Sky Blue B Base	CI 1075
Blue 12	26	62,100	Alizarine Pure Blue B Base	CI 1088
Green 1	11	42,000	Victoria Green Base Malachite Green Base	CI 657
Green 3	26	61,565	Alizarine Cyanine Green G Base D&C Green No. 6	CI 1078
Green 4	12	45,550	Fluorol 5G	Pr 542
Brown 12	4	21,010B	Bismarck Brown Base	CI 332
Black 3	4	26,150	Sudan Black BT	Pr 610
Black 5	19	50,415	Nigrosine Spirit-Soluble	CI 864
Black 7	19	50,415B	Nigrosine Base B	CI 864
SULFUR				
Yellow 1	22	53,040	Thiochem Sulfur Yellow R	CI 950
Yellow 2	22	53,120	Sulfur Yellow G	CI 951
Yellow 3	22	53,125	Kryogen Yellow G	CI 952
Yellow 4	22	53,160	Sulfur Yellow GG	CI 955
Red 1	22	53,721	Sulfur Bordeaux G	CI 1012
Red 5	22	53,830	Sulfur Red Brown CL3R	Pr 702
Red 6	22	53,720	Sulfur Red Brown 3B	CI 1012
Blues 1, 5, and 11	22	53,235	Sulfur Direct Blue RL	CI 956
Blue 7	22	53,440	Sulfur Indone R	CI 959
Blue 9	12	53,430	Sulfur Pure Blue Sulfur Brilliant Blue CLB	CI 957
Blue 10	22	53,470	Sulfur New Blue FBL	Pr 285
Blue 13	22	53,450	Sulfur Indigo	CI 961
Blue 15	22	53,540	Sulfur Green Blue CV	Pr 65 and 129
Green 1	22	53,166	Sulfur Dark Green B	Pr 707
Green 2	22	53,571	Sulfur Green BB	CI 1006
Green 3	22	53,570	Sulfur Green GG	CI 1006
Green 8	22	53,175	Sulfur Olive B	Pr 706
Green 11	22	53,165	Italian Green Sulfur Olive G	CI 1002
Brown 1	22	53,000	Cachou de Laval	CI 933
Brown 2	22	53,060	Sulfur Brown B	CI 937
Brown 10	22	53,055	Sulfur Orange C	CI 949
Brown 12	22	53,721	Sulfur Bordeaux G	CI 1012
Brown 14	22	53,246	Sulfur Black Brown A	Pr 545
Brown 26	22	53,090	Sulfur Yellow D	CI 948
Black 1	22	53,185	Sulfur Black T	CI 978
Black 2	22	53,195	Cross Dye Black RX	CI 978 and 983
Black 6	22	53,295	Sulfur Black CLG	Pr 126
Black 10	22	53,190	Sulfur Black 3G	CI 978
Black 11	22	53,290	Sulfur Black CLS	Pr 126
VAT				
Yellow 1	26	70,600	Vat Yellow G	CI 1118
Yellow 2	26	67,300/1	Anthraflavone GC	Pr 9
Yellow 3	26	61,725	Vat Yellow GK	CI 1132
Yellow 4	26	59,100/1	Vat Golden Yellow GK	Pr 291
Yellow 5	24	56,006	Vat Ester Yellow HCG	CI 1176
Yellow 9	26	66,510	Vat Yellow GF	Pr 451
Yellow 12	26	65,405	Vat Yellow 3GF	Pr 549
Yellow 13	26	65,425	Vat Yellow 4G	—
Yellow 21	26	69,705	Vat Yellow R	CI 1170
Yellow 28	26	69,000	Vat Yellow FFRK	Pr 450
Orange 1	26	59,105/6	Vat Golden Yellow RK	Pr 292
Orange 2	26	59,705/6	Vat Orange RRT	CI 1098
Orange 3	26	59,300	Vat Brilliant Orange RK	Pr 116
Orange 4	26	59,710	Vat Orange 4R	Pr 381
Orange 5	28	73,335/6	Thioindigo Orange RF	CI 1217
Orange 7	26	71,105	Vat Brilliant Orange GR	—

Part I Colour Index Generic Name	Chemical Structure Type	Part II Colour Index No.	Commercial Name	Old Colour Index No. or Prototype No.
VAT—*Continued*				
Orange 9	26	59,700	Vat Golden Orange G	CI 1096
Orange 11	26	70,805	Vat Yellow 3R	Pr 452
Orange 15	26	69,025	Vat Golden Orange 3G	Pr 290
Orange 16	26	69,540	Vat Orange F3R	Pr 446
Orange 21	26	69,700	Vat Orange R	CI 1169
Red 1	28	73,360/1	Thioindigo Pink R D&C Red No. 30	Pr 109
Red 10	26	67,000/1	Vat Red FBB	Pr 296
Red 13	26	70,320	Rubine R	Pr 124
Red 14	26	71,110	Vat Scarlet GG	—
Red 15	26	71,100	Vat Bordeaux RR	—
Red 29	26	71,140	Vat Scarlet R	Pr 449
Red 32	26	71,135	Vat Scarlet B	Pr 409
Red 35	26	68,000	Vat Red RK	CI 1162
Red 41	28	73,300	Thioindigo Red B Vat Red 5B	CI 1207
Red 45	28	73,860	Thioindigo Scarlet G	CI 1228
Violet 1	26	60,010/1	Vat Brilliant Violet RR	CI 1104
Violet 2	28	73,385/6	Thioindigo Red Violet RH	CI 1212
Violet 3	28	73,395/6	Thioindigo Red Violet RRN	Pr 503
Violet 9	26	60,005	Vat Brilliant Violet 3B	Pr 288
Violet 13	26	68,700	Vat Violet BN or FFBN	CI 1163
Violet 14	26	67,895	Vat Red Violet RRK	CI 1161
Violet 17	26	63,365	Vat Brilliant Violet RK	CI 1135
Blue 1	27	73,000	Indigo D&C Blue No. 6	CI 1177
Blue 1	27	73,001	Indigo White (leuco)	CI 1178
Blue 1	27	73,002	Solubilized Indigo O	CI 1178
Blue 4	26	69,800	Indanthrone Vat Blue RS	CI 1106
Blue 5	27	73,065	Brilliant Indigo 4B	CI 1184
Blue 5	27	73,066	Solubilized Indigo O4B	CI 1184
Blue 6	26	69,825/6	Vat Blue BCS D&C Blue No. 9	—
Blue 7	26	70,305/6	Vat Blue 3G	CI 1173
Blue 9	27	73,071	Solubilized Indigo O6B (ester)	CI 1185
Blue 12	26	69,840	Vat Blue 3G	CI 1109
Blue 14	26	69,810	Vat Blue GCD	—
Blue 16	26	71,200	Vat Dark Blue G	Pr 522
Blue 18	26	59,815	Alizanthrene Navy Blue R	CI 1100
Blue 20	26	59,800	Vat Dark Blue BO Violanthrone	CI 1099
Blue 29	29	74,140	Vat Brilliant Blue 4G	Pr 623
Blue 35	27	73,060	Indigo Blue B Indigo Blue R	CI 1182/3
Blue	30	75,800	Tyrian Purple (natural isomer of Vat Blue 35)	CI 1182/3
Blue 41	27	73,040	Brilliant Indigo BASF/B	Pr 528 CI 1190
Blue 43	22	53,630	Carbazole Blue R	CI 969
Green 1	26	59,825/6	Vat Jade Green	CI 1101
Green 2	26	59,830/1	Vat Brilliant Green GG	Pr 632
Green 3	26	69,500/1	Vat Olive Green B	Pr 293
Green 7	26	58,825	Vat Olive G	CI 1167
Green 8	26	71,050	Vat Khaki GG	Pr 122
Green 9	26	59,850	Anthra Green B Vat Black B	CI 1102
Brown 1	26	70,800/1	Vat Brown BR	Pr 118
Brown 3	26	69,015/6	Vat Brown R	CI 1151
Brown 5	28	73,410/1	Thioindigo Brown RRD	Pr 121
Brown 25	26	69,020	Vat Red Brown 5RF	Pr 448
Brown 31	26	70,695	Vat Red Brown R	Pr 447
Black 1	28	73,671	Solubilized Thioindigo Gray IBL (ester)	Pr 295
Black 9	26	65,230	Vat Direct Black RB	Pr 289
Black 25	26	69,525	Vat Olive T	Pr 547
Black 27	26	69,005	Vat Olive R	CI 1150

The dyes on the market may be classified as follows with respect to the properties that determine their use:

Acid dyes (as Naphthol Blue Black) dye wool and silk directly in an acid bath; the degree of acidity necessary for effective dyeing and the resultant fastness (as to light and washing) vary widely with the type of dye. *Milling acid dyes* are simple acid dyes fast to fulling on wool. The acid dyes that give the best washfastness on wool and silk and in many cases are also very fast to light are the premetallized acid dyes. Acid dyes are also dyed on acrylic, nylon and other polyamide, and regenerated protein fibers. They are employed for economical shades of poor wetfastness on bast fibers (as jute) and other lignocellulosic fibers (as coir). Acid dyes may likewise be printed on fibers on which they can be dyed. Other important uses include the dyeing of leather, paper, and anodized aluminum and the coloring of wood stains, varnishes, inks, plastics, foods, drugs, and cosmetics. A few serve as biological stains and as chemical indicators. Some acid dyes are made into pigments.

Azoic compositions contain both an azoic coupling component and an azoic diazo component in a stabilized condition of such a nature that the two do not couple to form an insoluble azoic dye in situ until printed onto the fabric and steamed in an atmosphere of organic acid. The fastness properties are the same as those of the azoic dyeings produced from azoic coupling components and azoic diazo components.

Azoic coupling components (as Naphthol AS) are water-insoluble but dissolve in dilute alkali and couple with diazotized azoic diazo components after being padded or exhausted on cotton to form azoic dyes in situ in and on the fiber. These ingrain azoic dyeings are known for very good wetfastness and for economy in deep shades, especially among red, scarlet, and orange hues, in which vat dyes appear to less advantage than in other colors. Although azoic dyeings have very good fastness to washing, they vary widely in fastness to chlorine and light, and the color, esp. when badly applied, tends somewhat to crock. Azoic dyeings are employed mostly on cotton, rayon, linen, and other cellulosic textiles, but are employed also to some extent on silk, acetate, nylon and other polyamide fibers, polyester fibers, and even on wool, fur, and leather.

Azoic diazo components (fast color bases or salts) are aromatic amines that require diazotization with nitrite and acid for use or that are stabilized diazo salts of those amines. A diazo component in the diazotized state couples with an azoic coupling component to produce an azoic dye in situ on the fiber.

Basic dyes (as Methylene Blue B) dye wool and silk directly and cotton if the cotton is first mordanted with tannin and tartar emetic. Basic dyes display very high tinctorial value and brightness of color rather than good fastness. They now find very little use on cotton but are still used on jute, coir, raffia, and other lignocellulosic fibers, which they dye directly without mordanting. Basic dyes are used to some extent on silk, esp. for colored discharges printed on a colored ground or colored patterns printed on white. They are printed also on acetate, nylon, and polyester textiles. Basic dyes are applied to a slight extent on wool yarns but virtually not at all on wool piece goods. Newer basic dyes (as the polymethine types) and a few of the better older ones are used on acrylic fibers, on which they have adequate lightfastness and wetfastness. Although of minor importance for textiles, basic dyes have a greater variety of other uses than any other dye type. They are applied directly on leather, furs, sheepskin, and paper. The free bases or oleates of basic dyes are used as solvent dyes. Basic dyes are employed for coloring hectograph papers, spirit inks, varnishes, aqueous and spirit wood stains, carbon paper, and typewriter ribbons; as biological stains, chemical indicators, and food colors; and for medicinal and photographic purposes. Many basic dyes are manufactured into pigments.

Developers (as Developer Z, which is methyl-phenyl-pyrazolone, or Developer BON, which is 3-hydroxy-2-naphthoic acid) couple with a diazotized direct dye on cotton or other cellulosic fiber or with a diazotized disperse dye on acetate for improvement of wetfastness and other fastness properties and for deepening of the color.

Direct cotton dyes (as Direct Deep Black EW) dye cotton directly in the presence of a suitable quantity of common salt. They vary widely in lightfastness but most are poor in washfastness. Aftertreatment with developers, formaldehyde, copper or chromium salts, or diazotized *para*-nitroaniline improves the lightfastness, washfastness, or both of some direct dyes on cotton. Besides dyeing cotton, direct dyes are employed for dyeing and printing rayon, linen, and other cellulosic fibers, jute and other lignocellulosic fibers, silk, wool, and nylon, and for dyeing paper and leather. Some direct dyes are converted into pigments, and some are useful as chemical indicators and biological stains.

Disperse dyes (as Disperse Fast Blue FFR) are only slightly soluble in water but are readily dispersed in water with the aid of sulfated oil. Disperse dyes partition themselves in a solubility equilibrium between water and certain fibers (as acetate and nylon) in the dyeing process. Some disperse dyes on acetate are subject to acid fading in air containing traces of nitrogen oxides (as in combustion gases). Disperse dyes are used on nylon knit goods (as hosiery and sweaters) rather than acid dyes in spite of poorer fastness to washing because they do not show up knitting streaks as acid dyes do. Disperse dyes are used also to dye polyester fibers in the presence of a carrier, acrylic fibers, cellulose triacetate fiber, and vinylidene chloride polymer. Disperse dyes are also printed on acetate and nylon. Some disperse dyes are employed for dyeing pastels on wool, sheepskins, and furs, some for the surface dyeing of thermoplastic resins, and a few for coloring oils, fats, and waxes when in a pure state.

Fiber-reactive dyes have the ability to combine with cellulose by covalent bonds to form esters or ethers. Derivatives of cyanuric chloride and of vinyl sulfone have been utilized for this purpose. As fiber-reactive dyes are applied by hydrolysis in alkaline solution, a considerable proportion of the activated dye reacts with water before it can react and combine with cellulose, and thus is wasted. Fiber-reactive dyes are employed mostly on cotton, rayon, and other cellulosic fibers but are also suggested for use on wool and even silk.

Fluorescent brighteners are colorless water- or solvent-soluble aromatic compounds with affinity for fibers of various kinds. They have the property of transforming ultraviolet radiation into radiation of 400 to 500 millimicrons visible as violet, blue, and blue-green colors and are capable of increasing both the blueness and the brightness of a substrate with a resulting marked whitening effect. Brighteners are used on white papers and on wool and silk as well as cellulosic textiles; they are especially useful for improving white discharges and the brightness of tints. Brighteners are incorporated into detergents of all kinds for washing textiles to enhance the apparent cleansing action of the detergent and to obviate the need for bluing.

Food colors in the *Colour Index*, 2d ed., are those dyes and pigments that find important use in foods throughout the world where food colors are under regulation. Because all but a very few of these are also classified in the *Colour Index* under other names (as Acid Blue 74 and Solvent Yellow 5) only those are listed under *Food* in the first Column of table I that are not given under another use type. See table II.

Ingrain dyes taken as a separate subgroup are those that form water-insoluble dyes in situ upon being suitably printed or dyed on cellulosic textiles and properly fixed, respectively, in subsequent steaming or by treatment in solution. Those that belong to the azoic class are entered under *Azoic* in the table.

Mordant dyes (as Alizarine) dye wool, silk, and cotton that have been mordanted with compounds of polyvalent metals (as chromium or tin). This kind of mordant dye is no longer of importance in America for dyeing or printing textiles and is fast losing importance throughout the world. Most mordant dyes now in use are mordant acid dyes (as Chrome Black T) which dye wool and silk in an acid bath after, during, or before treatment of the fiber with a mordanting salt like sodium dichromate or chromium fluoride to give dyeings with better wetfastness and also lightfastness than most dyeings of acid dyes on wool or silk. Chrome dyeings in general are faster to fulling on wool than either metallized or simple acid dyes. Mordant acid dyes are used also for dyeing nylon, leather, and anodized aluminum and for Vigoureux printing as well as for the ordinary printing of wool, silk, and cellulosic fabrics. Some mordant dyes are used to some extent for coloring paper and furs, for the manufacture of pigments, and as indicators, biological stains, cosmetics, and food dyes.

Natural dyes are organic substances of plant or animal origin that are used mainly for dyeing and printing textiles and for dyeing leather. Many natural dyes could be classified also among the other use types described here or among the chemical structures listed in the second column of the table.

Oxidation bases (as Aniline Black) are in most cases aromatic amines but in some cases amino phenols or aromatic diols. When suitably oxidized after being applied mainly on furs and to some extent on textiles they yield various shades of black, gray, and brown of good wetfastness and lightfastness.

Organic pigments are water-insoluble azo, vat, and other dye types that are usu. insoluble in some organic solvents or are lakes prepared from acid, basic, direct, mordant, or mordant acid dyes or from other dye types by precipitation with a suitable precipitant. Some water-soluble dyes that are more important for the preparation of lakes than for dyeing textiles are listed under Pigments though they are often sold to the lake manufacturer in water-soluble form. Toners are full-strength organic pigments that have not been extended with a solid diluent. Pigments have a great many uses, all of which depend upon the incorporation of the pigment into a medium in which it is usu. rather insoluble. They are employed in coating compositions of many kinds, including oil paints, emulsion paints, lacquers of many types, enamels, leather finishes, poster colors, and water colors. Pigments are esp. important in the manufacture of letterpress and intaglio inks and many inks for special purposes (as for wallpaper and metal foil). In the printing of textiles the pigment is bonded to the fabric with synthetic resins. Viscose-rayon, acetate, and other man-made fibers can be colored in the mass with pigments before being spun through a spinneret. Paper is colored in the beater with pigments and is also coated with compositions containing pigments. Detergents, soap, candles, wax compositions, modeling clay, chalk, wax crayons, and colored pencils are all often colored with pigments. Builders' items colored with pigments include cement for concrete, roofing granules, linoleum, and tiles of asphalt, rubber, or vinyl. Rubber, other elastomers, plastics, molding powders, and casting resins are also colored with pigments, and foods, drugs, and cosmetics are permitted to be colored with selected pigments.

Solvent dyes are generally insoluble in water but dissolve in varying degree in different organic media in liquid, molten, or solid form, including alcohols, esters, ketones, aliphatic or aromatic hydrocarbons, chlorinated hydrocarbons, oils, fats, and waxes. Solvent dyes do not normally contain a sulfonic or carboxylic group unless the dye has been combined with an organic base that imparts solubility in organic solvents. Basic dyes become somewhat solvent-soluble when prepared as the free base, but generally the free base is melted in about two parts of oleic acid before commercial use as a solvent-soluble dye. The uses of a particular solvent dye depend not only upon fastness to light and adequate solubility in a required solvent but often also on other properties (as stability to heat, acid, or alkali, or freedom from bleeding in water). Solvent dyes are used in spirit and oil wood stains and varnishes, in transparent lacquers of various kinds, in shellac, in inks, on copying paper and typewriter ribbons, in printing inks, in ball-point inks, in candles and sealing waxes, and in polishes for shoes and other purposes. Gasoline, soap, cosmetics, foods, drugs, fuel oil, and signaling smokes are other materials colored with solvent dyes. Molding powders and various resinous and plastic materials are also colored with solvent dyes.

Sulfur dyes are usu. dissolved and then dyed on cotton and also on rayon and other cellulosic fibers in a hot dilute solution containing sodium sulfide and sodium carbonate. Salt is required for exhaustion. Sulfur dyes are occasionally dyed on silk and less often on wool, and sometimes on leather and paper. Sulfur dyeings are limited in brightness, the oranges, reds, and violets being quite dull, while the yellows are less fast than the other colors. The blacks, browns, blues, and greens display fair to good and very good fastness to light, esp. when aftertreated with copper sulfate and acetic acid. Sulfur dyeings have reasonably good fastness to washing, which is also often improved considerably by aftertreatment with dichromate and acetic acid. *Solubilized sulfur dyes* are ordinary sulfur dyes that have been prepared in strong prereduced leuco form either as a liquid or as a powder or that have been premixed with a suitable alkaline reducing mixture that dissolves them when they are placed in hot water. They are not listed separately in table I from the sulfur dyes from which they are derived and which they yield in dyeing.

Vat dyes are water-insoluble aromatic organic compounds containing at least two symmetrically located carbonyl groups in the molecule. They dissolve in water when vatted with an alkaline solution of the reducing agent sodium hydrosulfite; many require salt for good exhaustion on cotton from such an aqueous solution. In the printing of textiles reduction and dyeing in the areas of the printed pattern take place in the steam atmosphere of a neutral vat ager by the reducing action of sodium formaldehydesulfoxylate and potash printed on the cloth with the dye in a printing paste also containing gums. Upon subsequent oxidation and soaping the vat dye is regenerated in the fiber. Many vat dyeings, but not those from indigo, display excellent fastness to light, washing, and dilute hypochlorite and peroxide and thus are among the fastest dyes for cotton, rayon, linen, and other cellulosic fibers. Some vat dyes are applied by special methods on silk, wool, nylon, and acrylic textiles. Some are now finding increasing use as lightfast pigments, and a few as food, drug, and cosmetic colors. *Solubilized vat dyes* are the sodium salts of the sulfuric monoesters of the leuco compounds of vat dyes, are more expensive than ordinary vat dyes, and hence are used mainly for dyeing pastels on cotton, rayon, and linen when the best possible levelness and penetration in addition to fastness are demanded. Bright blue or green solubilized vat dyes are often printed on cotton alongside azoic dyes, which are deficient in brightness in the blue-green range. Solubilized vat dyes are occasionally applied on silk, wool, acetate, acrylic, polyester, and polyamide fibers when the very best fastness properties are required. An advantage of these dyes for fibers that are sensitive to alkali is that they are applied in neutral or slightly acid solution. Dyeings on all fibers must finally be oxidized and hydrolyzed, for example with sodium nitrite and dilute sulfuric acid. Only a few are listed in table I because all of the solubilized vat dyes have *Colour Index* names and structural numbers closely related to those of the dyes from which they are derived and yield those vat dyes on the fiber upon development in dyeing. Thus Solubilized Vat Blue 6 with the structural formula 69,826 is the leuco ester of Vat Blue 6 with the structural formula 69,825.

COLORS PERMITTED FOR
FOODS, DRUGS, AND COSMETICS

In the U.S. only selected acid, mordant acid, direct, basic, and solvent dyes and selected pigments are permitted by the Food and Drug Administration for use in foods, drugs, and cosmetics that enter into interstate commerce. Further, each batch of permitted color must be analyzed and certified as free from certain deleterious impurities. There are three separate categories of these permitted colors: (1) Food, Drug, and Cosmetic Colors (FD&C); (2) Drug and Cosmetic Colors (D&C); and (3) External Drug and Cosmetic Colors (Ext D&C). The colors of group 3 may be used in drugs and cosmetics for external parts of the body, but not on mucous membranes. For example, colors of group 3 may not be used in lipstick.

In the first column are listed the permitted dyes and pigments by the names that have been assigned to them by the Food and Drug Administration, and in the second column the *Colour Index* generic names of the corresponding dyes from which batches of permitted colors are purified.

DYE TABLE II

Permitted Color	Colour Index Generic Name
FD&C	
Yellow No. 5	Acid Yellow 23
Yellow No. 6	Food Yellow 3
Red No. 2	Acid Red 27
Red No. 3	Acid Red 51
Red No. 4	Food Red 1
Violet No. 1	Acid Violet 49
Blue No. 1	Acid Blue 9
Blue No. 2	Acid Blue 74
Green No. 1	Acid Green 3
Green No. 2	Acid Green 5
Green No. 3	Food Green 3
D&C	
Yellow No. 5	Acid Yellow 23
Yellow No. 10	Acid Yellow 3
Yellow No. 11	Solvent Yellow 33
Orange No. 3	Acid Orange 10
Orange No. 4	Acid Orange 7
Orange No. 10	Solvent Red 73
Orange No. 11	Acid Red 95
Orange No. 15	Mordant Red 11 Pigment Red 83
Orange No. 16	Solvent Orange 18
Red No. 5	Acid Red 26
Red Nos. 6 and 7	Pigment Red 57
Red No. 17	Solvent Red 23
Red No. 18	Solvent Red 27
Red No. 21	Solvent Red 43
Red Nos. 22 and 23	Acid Red 87
Red No. 24	Solvent Red 42
Red No. 27	Solvent Red 48
Red No. 28	Acid Red 92
Red No. 30	Vat Red 1
Red No. 31	Pigment Red 64
Red No. 34	Pigment Red 63
Red No. 35	Pigment Red 3
Red No. 36	Pigment Red 4
Red No. 38	Pigment Red 18
Red No. 39	Pigment Red 100
Violet No. 2	Solvent Violet 13
Blue No. 4	Pigment Blue 24
Blue No. 6	Vat Blue 1
Blue No. 9	Vat Blue 6
Green No. 5	Acid Green 25
Green No. 6	Solvent Green 3
Green No. 7	Acid Green 9
Brown No. 1	Acid Orange 24
Black No. 1	Acid Black 1
EXT D&C	
Yellow No. 1	Acid Yellow 36
Yellow No. 3	Acid Yellow 11
Yellow No. 5	Pigment Yellow 1
Yellow No. 7	Acid Yellow 1
Yellow No. 9	Solvent Yellow 5
Yellow No. 10	Solvent Yellow 6
Yellow Nos. 11 and 12	Acid Yellow 73
Orange No. 1	Pigment Orange 1
Orange No. 3	Acid Orange 20
Orange No. 4	Solvent Orange 2
Orange No. 5	Solvent Red 72
Orange No. 6	Pigment Orange 5
Red No. 1	Acid Violet 7
Red No. 3	Solvent Violet 10
Red No. 8	Acid Red 88
Red No. 10	Acid Red 14
Red No. 11	Acid Red 1
Red No. 13	Acid Red 73
Red No. 14	Solvent Orange 7
Red Nos. 15 and 16	Pigment Red 53
Red Nos. 17, 18, 19, and 20	Pigment Red 49
Red No. 21	Basic Violet 10
Red No. 22	Solvent Red 49
Red No. 23	Acid Red 33
Violet No. 2	Acid Violet 43
Blue No. 1	Basic Blue 9
Blue No. 4	Acid Blue 45
Green No. 1	Acid Green 1

[2]**dye** \"\ *vb* **dyed; dyed; dyeing; dyes** [ME *dyen*, fr. OE *dēagian, dēgian*, fr. *dēag, dēah*] *vt* **1 :** to color throughout **:** impart a new and often permanent color to esp. by impregnating with a dye — compare DYEING 1; STAIN, TINT **2 a :** to impart (a color) by dyeing ⟨~ a blue over a yellow⟩ **b :** to cause (a dye) to be applied **3 :** to color or tinge in any way ⟨a warm flush *dyed* her cheeks —Ellen Glasgow⟩ **:** STAIN ⟨*dyed* his hands in the blood of innocents⟩ **~** *vi* **:** to take up or impart color in dyeing ⟨wool ~*s* readily with acid dyes⟩ ⟨level ~*ing* properties of acid dyes⟩

dye·able *also* **dy·able** \ˈdīəbəl\ *adj* **:** capable of being dyed

dye base *n* **:** an organic base that is itself a dye or that with acids forms salts which are dyes — called also *color base;* compare LEUCO BASE

dyebath \ˈ=ˌ=\ *n* **:** a solution containing a dye used in dyeing

dyebeck \ˈ=ˌ=\ *n* [[1]*dye* + *beck* (vat)] **:** a large shallow dye vat equipped with a winch and used for dyeing pieces of fabric in rope form

dye–bleach process *n* **:** any of several processes of color photography in which dyes are destroyed in the presence of a metallic image by the application of chemical agents — distinguished from *bleach-out process*

dye·crete process \ˈdīˌkrēt-\ *n* [[2]*dye* + con*crete*] **:** a process for coloring cement and concrete with organic dyes which are insoluble in water and fast to light, moisture, and atmospheric effects

dyed–in–the–wool \ˌ===ˈ=\ *adj* **1 :** dyed before spinning **2 :** DEVOTED ⟨a *dyed-in-the-wool* fisherman⟩ **:** firm and uncompromising in principle ⟨a *dyed-in-the-wool* conservative⟩

dyehouse \ˈ=ˌ=\ *n* **:** a building, department, or plant in which dyeing and related processes or operations are carried out

dyeing *n* -s **1 :** the process or art of applying (as to textile fibers or leather) a coloring matter usu. in a solution or fine dispersion in a liquid (as water) so that the coloring matter is taken up from the dyebath and the color imparted is not readily removed by washing **2 :** a product of dyeing **:** a substance colored with a dye or a color produced by dyeing ⟨this red ~ is fast⟩

dye intermediate *n* **:** an organic compound (as aniline or a naphthol) that is prepared for use in synthesizing dyes

dyeleaves \ˈ=ˌ=\ *n pl* **1 :** SWEETLEAF **2 :** INKBERRY 1

dyer \ˈdī(ə)r, -īə\ *n* -s [ME, fr. *dighere, dyere*, fr. *dyen* to dye + *-ere* -er] **:** one that dyes (as fabrics, leather, hats, fur, or wooden articles)

dyer·ma *also* **djer·ma** \dēˈermə, ˈdyer-\ *n, pl* **dyerma** *or* **dyermas** *usu cap* **1 a :** a Negroid people of the middle Niger valley **b :** a member of such people **2 :** the Songhai language of the Dyerma people

dyer's alkanet *n* **:** ALKANET 1

dyer's barberry *n* **:** an Indian barberry (*Berberis aristata*) yielding a yellow dye

dyer's–broom \ˌ==ˈ=\ *n, pl* **dyer's–brooms :** WOODWAXEN

dyer's broom *n* **:** a light to moderate greenish yellow that is less strong than acacia and redder and less strong than liqueur green — called also *broom, dyewood, genestrole, genet*

dyer's buckthorn *n* **:** any of several shrubs of the genus *Rhamnus* (esp. *R. infectoria*) yielding a yellow dye

dyer's cleavers *n* **:** MADDER

dyer's furze *or* **dyer's genista** *or* **dyer's greenweed** *or* **dyer's greenwood** *n* **:** WOODWAXEN

dyer's grape *n* **:** POKEWEED

dyer's mulberry *n* **:** FUSTIC

dyer's oak *n* **1 :** an Asiatic tree (*Quercus infectoria*) the galls of which yield a dye **2 :** a black oak (*Quercus velutina*)

dyer's rocket *also* **dyer's mignonette** *n* **:** a European mignonette (*Reseda luteola*) cultivated for its yellow dye and naturalized in No. America

dyer's saffron *n* **:** SAFFLOWER 1

dyer's–weed \ˈ==ˌ=\ *n, pl* **dyer's–weeds 1 :** any of several dye-yielding plants (as the dyer's rocket, the woodwaxen, the dyer's woad) **2 :** any of certain plants of the genus *Solidago* (esp. *S. nemoralis* and *S. rugosa*) whose yellow flowers are occas. used in dyeing

dyer's whin *n* **:** WOODWAXEN

dyer's woad *n* **:** a woad (*Isatis tinctoria*) that yields an indigo

dyer's woodruff *n* **:** a perennial woodruff (*Asperula tinctoria*) having a creeping rootstock that is sometimes used as a substitute for madder

dyes *pl of* DYE, *pres 3d sing of* DYE
dye shell *n* **:** DOG WHELK b
dyestuff \'ˌ=\ *n* [prob. trans. of G *farbstoff*] **:** DYE 2
dye toning *n* **:** the process of altering the color of a developed image by converting it into a mordant and then bathing in a suitable dye solution
dye transfer *n* **1 :** a color printing process in which dyed images (cyan, magenta, and yellow) on three matrices are transferred successively in register onto a paper surface **2 :** a print made by the dye transfer process
dyeweed \'ˌ=\ *n* **1 :** WOODWAXEN **2 :** a small American weedy herb (*Eclipta alba*) of the family Compositae with yellowish white flowers
dyewood \'ˌ=\ *n, often attrib* **1 :** a wood (as logwood or fustic) from which coloring matter is extracted for dyeing ⟨~ extract⟩ **2 :** DYER'S BROOM
dying *adj* [ME, fr. pres. part. of *dien* to die — more at DIE] **1 a :** passing from life **:** being about to die ⟨a ~ man⟩ **:** gradually ceasing to be **:** EXPIRING ⟨the ~ day⟩ ⟨a ~ fire⟩ **b :** having reached an advanced or ultimate stage of decay or disuse ⟨a ~ civilization⟩ ⟨a ~ tradition⟩ **2 :** of or relating to death or dying ⟨recorded his ~ words⟩ ⟨promised to fulfill his ~ wishes⟩ ⟨the ~ crisis of a decadent culture⟩
dying declaration *n* **:** a declaration made by a person in the immediate prospect of death and having no hope of recovery **:** an antemortem statement
dykage *var of* DIKAGE
dyke *var of* DIKE
-dym·ia \'dimēə\ *n comb form* -S [NL, fr. *-dymus* + *-ia*] **:** condition of being a pair of twin terata joined at (a specified body part) ⟨cephalo*dymia*⟩
-dy·mus \dəməs\ *n comb form* -ES [NL, irreg. fr. Gk *didymos* twin, fr. *dyo* two — more at TWO] **:** pair of twin terata joined at (a specified body part) ⟨sterno*dymus*⟩
dyn *abbr* **1** dynamics **2** dynamo
dy·na·graph \'dīnə,graf, -răf\ *n* -S [Gk *dyna*mis power + E *-graph*] **:** an apparatus in a railroad car for recording the condition of a line of track, the resistance of a train, its speed, and other features of its performance
dynam- *or* **dynamo-** *comb form* [prob. fr. F, fr. Gk, fr. *dynamis*] **:** power ⟨*dynam*ism⟩ ⟨*dynamo*graph⟩
-dy·nam·ia \,dī'namēə, ,də'-, -nām-\ *n comb form* -S [NL, fr. Gk, fr. *dynamis* + *-ia* -y] **:** strength **:** condition of having (such) strength ⟨a*dynamia*⟩ ⟨myo*dynamia*⟩
¹dy·nam·ic \(')dī¦namik, -mēk *sometimes* də'n-\ *also* **dy·nam·i·cal** \-məkəl, -mēk-\ *adj* [F *dynamique*, NL *dynamicus*, & G *dynamisch*, fr. Gk *dynamikos* powerful, fr. *dynamis* power (fr. *dynasthai* to be able) + *-ikos* -ic, -ical] **1** *in Kantianism* **:** relating to the grounds or reasons for the existence of a sense presentation ⟨the ~ categories of relation⟩ **2 a :** of or relating to power **:** relating to physical force or energy ⟨the ~ theory of heat⟩ **b :** of or relating to dynamics **:** of or relating to forces producing motion **:** ACTIVE — compare POTENTIAL, STATIC **3 :** FUNCTIONAL 1b (1) ⟨a ~ disease⟩ **4 a :** characterized by continuous movement, advance, or expansion ⟨a ~ economy⟩ ⟨a ~ population⟩ **:** characterized by continuous change ⟨an unstable ~ age⟩ or tending to produce change ⟨the ~ force of technology⟩ **:** having or relating to a nonphysical force or energy ⟨every social behavior pattern ... contains a ~ component —S.F.Nadel⟩ **:** FORCEFUL, ENERGETIC ⟨a ~ personality⟩ **b :** having reference to change or behavior ⟨the ~ relationship between man and institutions —Abram Kardiner⟩; *specif* **:** relating to a system or culture marked by continuous alteration and a resulting lack of equilibrium of its elements ⟨a ~ system like a human individual or social group —H.V.Dicks⟩ **c :** characterized by a concern with or interest in cultural change or process and the patterns of cultural change ⟨wrote social history of the static sort, as opposed to the ~ interpretative variety —J.B.Hedges⟩ **5 a :** producing an effect of energetic movement or progression ⟨a ~ line⟩ ⟨~ brushwork⟩ **b :** characterized by an aesthetic equilibrium of parts which considered separately are unstable **6 :** taking time into account as an explicit factor in economic processes so that variables at different points in time are functionally related **7 :** characterized by variations of accent dependent on variation in force of expiration or stress — compare EXPIRATORY, STRESS ACCENT **8 :** relating to volume of musical sound or to relative loudness and softness ⟨the ~ range of the piano⟩ — **dy·nam·i·cal·ly** \-mək(ə)lē, -mēk-, -li\ *adv*
²dynamic \"\ *n* -S [prob. fr. F *dynamique*, fr. *dynamique*, adj.] **1 a :** DYNAMICS 2 a ⟨convert its ~ of grievance and discontent into revolutionary class struggle —A.L.Locke⟩ **b :** a particular dynamic force ⟨the generative force, the historical ~ of their country —Archibald MacLeish⟩ **2 :** DYNAMICS 3
dynamical parallax *n* **:** the parallax of a binary star determined by the use of the relation between mass and absolute magnitude
dynamic augment *n* **:** the force produced by centrifugal action of the incompletely balanced weight of reciprocating parts of a steam locomotive
dynamic brake *n* **:** a brake operating by dynamic braking
dynamic braking *n* **:** a system of braking (as in electric trains or machinery) in which the driving motor is converted into a generator and is driven by the kinetic energy of the vehicle thus exerting a retarding force
dynamic factor *n* **:** the ratio between the load carried by any part of an aircraft when accelerating or otherwise subjected to abnormal conditions and the load carried in normal flight
dynamic geology *n* **:** a branch of geology that deals with the causes and processes of geological change
dynamic head *n* **:** VELOCITY HEAD
dynamic isomerism *n* **:** TAUTOMERISM
dynamic load *n* **:** a live load (as a motor vehicle in motion) on a structure (as a bridge)
dynamic metamorphism *n, geol* **:** metamorphism characterized by shear movements as well as elevated temperature — compare CONTACT METAMORPHISM
dynamic meteorology *n* **:** a branch of meteorology that deals with motions of the atmosphere and the forces that cause them
dynamic microphone *n* **:** a microphone in which the sound waves cause a movable wire or coil to vibrate in a magnetic field and thus induce a current
dynamic model *or* **dynamic scale model** *n* **:** a copy (as of an airplane) usu. smaller than the original and having linear dimensions, weight, and moments of inertia reproduced to scale in proportion to those of the original
dynamic monarchianism *n, usu cap D&M* **:** the doctrine that Christ was a mere man who was made son of God by adoption — called also *dynamistic monarchianism*
dynamic oceanography *n* **:** the science that deals with ocean waves, currents, and tides
dynamic pressure *n* **1 :** the pressure on a surface at which a flowing fluid is brought to rest in excess of the pressure on it when the fluid is not flowing **2 :** the quantity of air measured by most airspeed instruments and equal to the product ½ ρV^2 where ρ is the density of the air and V is the relative speed of the air
dynamic psychology *n* **:** a psychological approach or system affirming that human acts are understandable and predictable only through an analysis of the previous experiences and motivational states of the organism rather than through a simple description of the objective stimuli temporally preceding human acts — compare PSYCHOANALYSIS
dynamic range *n* **:** the ratio of the loudest to the weakest sound intensity which can be transmitted or reproduced by a recording or broadcasting system
dynamic refraction *n* **:** the reciprocal of the near-point distance of the eye — compare STATIC REFRACTION
dynamic reproducer *n* **:** a phonograph pickup whose electrical output is produced when the stylus moves a coil in a magnetic field
dy·nam·ics \dī'namiks, -mēks *sometimes* də'-\ *n pl but often sing in constr* [F *dynamique*, fr. *dynamique*, adj., dynamic — more at DYNAMIC] **1 :** a branch of mechanics that deals with forces and their relation primarily to the motion but sometimes also to the equilibrium of bodies of matter — compare KINEMATICS, KINETICS, STATICS **2 a :** the driving physical, moral, or intellectual forces of any kind or the laws that relate to them ⟨the principal ~ of climatic change is the sun —Gerard Piel⟩ ⟨the ~ of an acquisitive society⟩ **b :** PSYCHODYNAMICS **3 a :** the pattern of any process of sociocultural growth and change ⟨the study of population ~⟩ **:** the pattern of response or adaptation to environment by an individual or group ⟨insights into cultural ~ can be obtained ... why certain common elements of Spanish culture were accepted by one group, rejected by a second, and profoundly modified by a third —G.M.Foster⟩ **b :** the pattern of change or growth of any object or phenomenon ⟨the ~ of these storms⟩ **c :** economic analysis that stresses the sequence of phenomena, the rate at which phenomena occur, and the functional relationships of variables at different points in time **4 :** variation and contrast in force or intensity (as in music, in the use of color, or in the execution of a dance)
dynamic speaker *n* **:** ELECTRODYNAMIC SPEAKER
dynamic viscosity *n* **:** COEFFICIENT OF VISCOSITY
dy·na·mis \'dīnəməs\ *n, pl* **dyna·mes** \-,mēz\ [Gk — more at DYNAMIC] **:** the state of that which is not yet fully realized **:** POWER, POTENTIALITY — contrasted with *energeia*
dy·na·mism \'dīnə,mizəm\ *n* -S [prob. fr. F *dynamisme*, fr. *dynam-* + *-isme* -ism] **1 a :** a theory or doctrine that explains the universe in terms of forces and their interplay (as immanent forces that are irreducible to matter and its motion) — used esp. of ancient hylozoistic doctrines and Leibnizianism; contrasted with *mechanism;* compare ENERGETICS **b :** a theory that considers becoming, change, motion, or energy as fundamental to the constitution of the universe **2 a :** a dynamic or expansionist quality ⟨a ~ threatening the balance of power in Europe⟩ **:** a quality of insistent restless drive or movement esp. in a particular direction ⟨found in the 12th century an escape from the ~ of the 20th⟩ **:** FORCE, ENERGY ⟨a passionate person filled with an incredible ~⟩ **b :** a quality in artistic representation that conveys (as to the observer or auditor) an impression of dynamic movement ⟨the ~ of the Gothic architectural style⟩ ⟨his readings of Beethoven have never been surpassed in fluency and ~⟩ **c :** DYNAMICS 3
dy·na·mist \-məst\ *n* -S [prob. fr. F *dynamiste*, fr. *dynam-* + *-iste* -ist] **:** an adherent of dynamism — **dy·na·mis·tic** \¦dīnə¦mistik, -tēk\ *adj*
dynamistic monarchianism *n, usu cap D&M* **:** DYNAMIC MONARCHIANISM
dy·na·mi·tard \¦dīnəmə¦tärd\ *n* -S [¹*dynamite* + *-ard*] **:** one that uses dynamite for anarchistic or other political acts of violence
¹dy·na·mite \'dīnə,mīt, *usu* -īd·+V\ *n* -S [ISV *dynam-* + *-ite;* orig. formed as Sw *dynamit*] **1 :** a solid blasting explosive used esp. in mining, quarrying, and engineering that contains nitroglycerin incorporated with a base which increases the safety of handling: as **a :** an explosive in which the base (as kieselguhr) is inert **b :** an explosive in which the base is active and consists essentially of a carbonaceous combustible material (as wood pulp) and an oxidizing material (as sodium nitrate) — called also *straight dynamite* **c :** a strong explosive similar to a straight dynamite but containing ammonium nitrate in place of part of the nitroglycerin and often part of the oxidizing material — called also *ammonia dynamite* **d :** GELATIN DYNAMITE **2 :** a blasting explosive used similarly to dynamite but containing an essential constituent (as nitrostarch) other than nitroglycerin **3 :** one that is characterized by notable vitality, power, or effectiveness ⟨box-office ~ —Steve McNeil⟩ ⟨not only is he tough and ruthless; he is also ~ with the ladies —*Saturday Rev.*⟩; *also* **:** something that has great potential (as for causing strife or trouble) ⟨devaluation is ~ and politicians don't like its sound —M.A.Heilperin⟩ ⟨this letter is ~ —Erle Stanley Gardner⟩
²dynamite \"\ *vt* -ED/-ING/-S **1 :** to charge with dynamite **2 :** to blow up or shatter with dynamite **3 :** to cause the utter failure or destruction of ⟨it is easy to ~ an industrial system —M.R.Cohen⟩ ⟨the board has *dynamited* its own findings in two particulars —B.H.Kizer⟩
dy·na·mit·er \-īd·ə(r), -ītə-\ *n* -S **1 :** one that blasts with dynamite **2 :** DYNAMITARD
dy·na·mit·ic \¦dīnə¦mid·ik\ *also* **dy·na·mit·i·cal** \-mid·əkəl\ *adj* **:** of, like, or relating to dynamite
dy·na·mi·za·tion \,dīnəmə'zāshən, -,mī'z-\ *n* -S **:** the act or an instance of dynamizing
dy·na·mize \'dīnə,mīz\ *vt* -ED/-ING/-S [*dynam-* + *-ize*] **1 :** to make (a drug) effective (as by comminution or dilution) **2 :** to make dynamic **:** endow with force
dy·na·mo \'dīnə,mō\ *n* -S [short for *dynamo machine* & *dynamoelectric machine;* trans. of G *dynamomaschine* & *dynamoelektrische maschine*] **1 :** GENERATOR 3; *esp* **:** a direct-current generator **2 :** an individual possessing great or unusual force or energy ⟨this stubby ~ of thirty-four organizes unions, writes poetry —George Weller⟩

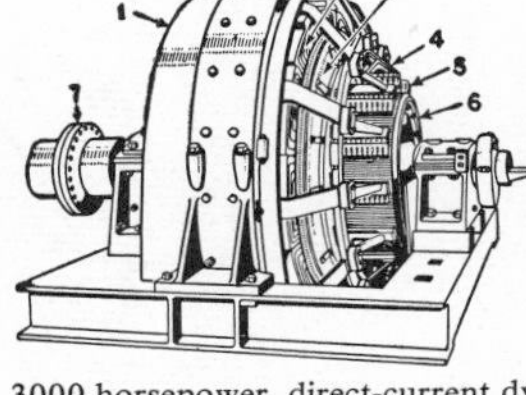

3000 horsepower, direct-current dynamo: *1* frame, *2* field, *3* armature, *4* brush rigging, *5* brushes, *6* commutator, *7* coupling

dynamo- — see DYNAM-
dy·na·mo·electric \¦=ˌ=+\ *adj* [ISV *dynam-* + *electric;* orig. formed as G *dynamoelektrisch*] **:** relating to the conversion by induction of mechanical energy into electrical energy or vice versa
dy·na·mo·genesis \,=ˌ=+\ *n, pl* **dynamogeneses** [NL, fr. *dynam-* + *-genesis*] **:** an increase of mental and motor activity resulting from stimulation of any sense organ
dy·na·mo·gen·ic \¦dīnəmō¦jenik\ *also* **dy·na·mog·e·nous** \-¦mäjənəs\ *adj* [*dynam-* + *-genic, -genous*] **:** relating to or instrumental in dynamogenesis
dy·na·mog·e·ny \,dīnə'mäjənē\ *n* -ES [ISV *dynam-* + *-geny*] **:** DYNAMOGENESIS
dy·na·mo·metamorphic \¦dīnə(,)mō+\ *adj* [*dynam-* + *metamorphic*] **:** of or belonging to dynamometamorphism
dy·na·mo·metamorphism \¦dīnə(,)mō+\ *n* [*dynam-* + *metamorphism*] *geol* **:** metamorphism in which mechanical energy (as exerted in pressure and movement) is the principal agent — contrasted with *hydrometamorphism*, and *pyrometamorphism*
dy·na·mom·e·ter \,dīnə'mäməd·ə(r)\ *n* -S [F *dynamomètre*, fr. *dynam-* + *-mètre* -meter] **1 :** an instrument for measuring mechanical forces or torques usu. by the elastic deformation produced (as a machine for testing the strength of materials or of a man's grip) **2 :** an apparatus for measuring mechanical power (as of an engine, an electric motor, or a draft animal) **:** ERGOMETER — see TRANSMISSION DYNAMOMETER **3 :** ELECTRODYNAMOMETER
dynamometer car *n* **:** a laboratory car with equipment for measuring and recording drawbar pull, horsepower, brake-pipe pressure, and other information on locomotive performance and train operation
dy·na·mo·met·ric \¦dīnəmō¦me·trik\ *or* **dy·na·mo·met·ri·cal** \-rəkəl\ *adj* **:** of, belonging to, or measured by dynamometry
dy·na·mom·e·try \-ämə·trē\ *n* -ES [ISV *dynam-* + *-metry*] **:** an art or process of measuring forces doing work; *specif* **:** measurement of the strength of muscular contraction
dy·na·mo·static \¦dīnəmō+\ *adj* [*dynam-* + *static*] *adj* **:** of or relating to a machine for producing static electricity by the use of a direct or alternating current
dy·na·motor \'dīnə+,-\ *n* [*dynamo* + *motor*] **:** a motor generator combining the motor and generator in a single machine with one field magnet and with two armatures or with one armature with two windings one of which receives current as a motor and the other of which generates current as a dynamo
-dy·na·mous \¦dīnəməs\ *adj comb form* [prob. fr. NL *-dynamus*, fr. Gk *-dynamos* having (such) power, fr. *dynamis* power — more at DYNAMIC] *bot* **:** having developing power of a (specified) type ⟨andro*dynamous*⟩
dy·nast \'dī,nast, ¦nəst, ¦naa(ə)st *sometimes* 'di¦\ *n* -S [L *dynastes*, fr. Gk *dynastēs*, fr. *dynasthai* to be able] **1 :** a ruler over a state; *esp* **:** a hereditary ruler **:** one of a line of kings or princes **2 :** a person that founds or belongs to a family powerful in a particular field ⟨a ~ in the field of international finance⟩
dy·nas·tes \dī'na(,)stēz, də'-\ *n, cap* [NL, fr. L, dynast] **:** a genus (the type of the family Dynastidae) of large chiefly tropical lamellicorn beetles having large mandibles and commonly greatly elongated pointed processes on the head and prothorax of the males — see RHINOCEROS BEETLE
dy·nas·tic \(')dī¦nastik, də'n-, -naas-, -tēk\ *also* **dy·nas·ti·cal** \-təkəl, -tēk-\ *adj* [Gk *dynastikos*, fr. *dynastēs* + *-ikos* -ic, -ical] **:** of or belonging to a dynasty ⟨ended two centuries of ~ rule⟩ ⟨debated Europe's tangled ~ relations⟩ — **dy·nas·ti·cal·ly** \-tək(ə)lē, -tēk-, -li\ *adv*
dy·nas·ti·cism \dī'nastə,sizəm, də'-, -naas-\ *n* -S **:** the theory, practice, or an instance of dynastic government ⟨nationalism ... lost the implication of liberalism which it had had so long as it figured as the opponent of ~ —G.H.Sabine⟩
dy·nas·ty \'dī¦nəstē, -ti *also* ¦,nas- *or* ¦,naas- *sometimes* 'di¦\ *n* -ES [Gk *dynasteia*, fr. *dynastēs* + *-eia* -y] **1 :** a succession of rulers of the same line of descent **2 a :** a group or class of individuals having power or authority in some sphere of activity and able to choose their successors ⟨a literary ~, dictating to the country in matters of taste⟩ ⟨a tightly knit ~ of industrialists and bankers⟩ **b :** a family that establishes and maintains predominance in a particular field of endeavor for generations ⟨a famed theatrical ~⟩
dy·na·tron \'dīnə,trän\ *n* -S [Gk *dynamis* power + E *-tron* — more at DYNAMIC] **:** a four-electrode vacuum tube in which the secondary emission of electrons from the plate results in a decrease in the plate current as the plate voltage increases
dyne \'dīn\ *n* -S [F, fr. Gk *dynamis* power — more at DYNAMIC] **:** the unit of force in the cgs system equal to the force that would give a free mass of one gram an acceleration of one centimeter per second per second
Dy·nel \(')dī¦nel\ *trademark* **1** — used for a fiber made in staple form from vinyl chloride and acrylonitrile and characterized by great resistance to burning **2 :** a yarn or fabric made of Dynel fiber
dy·node \'dī,nōd\ *n* -S [Gk *dynamis* power + E *-ode*] **:** one of the electrodes in an electron multiplier each of which in turn increases by its secondary emission the total flux of electrons
dyo- — see DY-
dy·oph·y·site \dī'äfə,sīt\ *n* -S *usu cap* [LGk *Dyophysitai*, *Diphysitai*, pl., fr. *dyo-* dy- or *di-* + *-physitai* (fr. *physis* nature) — more at PHYSIC] **:** one who maintains the Chalcedonian doctrine that full deity and full humanity exist in the person of Jesus Christ as two natures without confusion or change — compare MONOPHYSITE — **dy·oph·y·sit·ic** \(¦)dī¦äfə¦sid·ik\ *adj, usu cap*
dy·o·the·ism \'dīə(,)thē,izəm, ,==ˌ=,==\ *n* -S [*dy-* + *-theism*] **:** a doctrine or system recognizing two gods
dy·oth·e·lite \dī'äthə,līt\ *or* **dy·oth·e·lete** \-lēt\ *n* -S *usu cap* [*dy-* + *-thelite, -thelete* (as in *Monothelite, Monothelete*)] **:** an adherent of Dyothelitism
dy·oth·e·lit·ism \-līd-,izəm\ *or* **dy·oth·e·let·ism** \-lēd-\ *n* -S *usu cap* **:** the theological doctrine that in Christ there were two wills, the human and the divine — opposed to *Monothelitism*
dyp·none \'dip,nōn\ *n* [*di-* + *hypnone*] **:** a liquid ketone $C_6H_5COCH{:}C(CH_3)C_6H_5$ formed by the condensation of two molecules of acetophenone and used as a plasticizer
dys- *prefix* [alter. (influenced by L & Gk *dys-*) of ME *dis-*, fr. MF & L; MF *dis-*, fr. L *dys-*, fr. Gk; akin to OE *tō-*, *te-* apart, to pieces, OHG *zi-*, *zir-* apart, to pieces, ON *tor-* difficult, Goth *tuz-* (in *tuzwerjan* to doubt), Skt *dus-* difficult, bad] **1 a :** abnormal **:** diseased ⟨*dys*hidrosis⟩ ⟨*dys*plasia⟩ **b :** difficult ⟨*dys*menorrhea⟩ ⟨*dys*uria⟩ **:** with difficulty ⟨*dys*oxidizable⟩ **:** poorly ⟨*dys*crystalline⟩ — sometimes opposed to *eu-* **c :** faulty **:** impaired ⟨*dys*function⟩ ⟨*dys*pepsia⟩ **d :** bad **:** unfavorable ⟨*dys*pathy⟩ ⟨*dys*phemism⟩ — sometimes opposed to *eu-* **2 :** absence or reverse of ⟨*dys*teleology⟩
dys·acou·sia \,disə'küzh(ē)ə\ *also* **dys·acou·sis** \-üsəs\ *n, pl* **dysacousias** \-üzh(ē)əz\ *also* **dysacou·ses** \-ü,sēz\ [NL, fr. *dys-* + *-acousia* or Gk *akousis* act of hearing — more at -ACOUSIA] **:** a condition in which ordinary sounds produce discomfort or pain
dys·adaptation \dəs, (¦)dis+\ *n* [*dys-* + *adaptation*] **:** an impaired ability of the iris and retina to adapt properly to variations in light intensities that is often indicative of vitamin-A deficiency
dys·ar·thria \də'särthrēə\ *n* -S [NL, fr. *dys-* + *arthr-* + *-ia*] **:** difficulty in articulating words due to disease of the central nervous system — compare DYSPHASIA — **dys·ar·thric** \də'särthrik, (')di¦s-\ *adj*
dys·arthrosis \¦dis+\ *n, pl* **dysarthroses** [NL, fr. *dys-* + *arthr-* + *-osis*] **1 :** a condition of reduced joint motion due to deformity, dislocation, or disease **2 :** DYSARTHRIA
dys·che·zia *also* **dys·che·sia** \də'skē¦zēə, -kel, ¦zh(ē)ə\ *n* -S [NL, fr. *dys-* + Gk *chezein* to defecate + NL *-ia* — more at GATE] **:** constipation associated with a defective reflex for defecation and accompanied by accumulation of feces in the rectum — **dys·che·zic** \də'skēzik, (')di¦s-, -kez-\ *adj*
dys·chon·dro·pla·sia \də,skändrō'plāzh(ē)ə, (¦)di,-\ *n* -S [NL, *dys-* + *chondr-* + *-plasia*] **:** CHONDRODYSPLASIA
dys·chromatopsia \dəs, (¦)dis+\ *n* [NL, fr. *dys-* + *chromatopsia*] **:** incomplete color blindness — **dys·chromatoptic** \"+\ *adj*
dys·cra·sia \də'skrāzh(ē)ə\ *n* -S [NL, fr. ML, mixture of the humors in bad proportions, fr. Gk *dyskrasia*, fr. *dys-* + *-krasia* (fr. *krasis* mixing, combination, temperature, temperament) — more at CRASIS] **:** an abnormal condition of the body **:** an imbalance of physiologic or constitutional elements esp. of the blood — opposed to *eucrasia*
dys·cra·site \'diskrə,sīt\ *n* -S [alter. of F *discrase* (fr. *dis-* dys- + *crase*, fr. Gk *krasis* mixing, combination) + E *-ite*] **:** a native compound Ag_3Sb of antimony and silver usu. massive and silver-white
dys·crystalline \dəs, (')dis+\ *adj* [*dys-* + *crystalline*] **:** poorly crystallized — used of rocks
dys·der·cus \dəs'dərkəs\ *n, cap* [NL, prob. fr. Gk *dysderkēs* ugly, hard to see, fr. *dys-* + *-derkēs* (fr. *derkesthai* to see, flash)] **:** a genus of long-legged slender-bodied usu. brightly colored bugs (family Pyrrhocoridae) that feed chiefly in the developing seed of cotton causing discoloration of the lint — see COTTON STAINER
dys·en·ter·ic \¦disᵊn¦terik\ *adj* [L *dysentericus*, fr. Gk *dysenterikos*, fr. *dysenteria* + *-ikos* -ic] **:** of or relating to dysentery **:** having dysentery ⟨a ~ patient⟩ ⟨~ symptoms⟩
dys·en·ter·i·form \-erə,fȯrm\ *adj* [*dysentery* + *-form*] **:** resembling that of dysentery ⟨~ stool⟩ ⟨~ symptoms⟩
dys·en·tery \'disᵊn,terē, -,teri *also* -,t(ə)r-\ *n* -ES [ME *dissenterie*, fr. L *dysenteria*, fr. Gk, fr. *dys-* + *enteron* intestine + *-ia* -y — more at INTER-] **1 :** an often epidemic or endemic disease characterized by severe diarrhea with passage of mucus and blood and often with intestinal ulceration and generalized toxemia, marked by abdominal pain and tenesmus, and usu. caused by infection with pathogenic bacteria or protozoans that are spread chiefly through contaminated food or water — see AMEBIC DYSENTERY; compare SHIGELLOSIS **2 :** DIARRHEA; *esp* **:** severe diarrhea of domestic animals **3 :** any of various infectious or nutritive disorders of insects (as honeybees or silkworms) characterized by the passage of excessive amounts of usu. atypical frass
dys·er·gia \də'sərj(ē)ə\ *also* **dys·er·gy** \'di,sərjē, də's-\ *n, pl* **dysergias** *also* **dysergies** [NL *dysergia*, fr. Gk, difficulty in working, inability to exert oneself, fr. *dys-* + *-ergia* -ergy] **:** lack of muscular coordination due to defect in innervation
dys·esthesia \¦dis+\ *n* -S [NL, fr. *dys-* + *esthesia*] **:** impairment of sensitivity esp. to touch — **dys·esthetic** \"+\ *adj*
dys·function *also* **dis·function** \dəs, (')dis+\ *n* [*dys-* or ¹*dis-* + *function*] **1 :** impaired or abnormal functioning (as of an organ of the body) **2 :** a nonadaptive trait or condition; *esp* **:** one failing to serve a useful or adjustive purpose in society — **dys·functional** \dəs, (')dis+\ *adj*
dys·genesis \dəs, (')dis+\ *n, pl* **dysgeneses** [NL, fr. *dys-* + *genesis*] **:** infertility esp. between hybrids that remain fertile with either parent but not with one another
dys·gen·ic *also* **dis·gen·ic** \dəs'jenik, (')dis¦j-\ *adj* [*dys-* or ¹*dis-* + *-genic*] **:** detrimental to the hereditary qualities of a stock (as of man) or tending to counteract racial improvement through an influence bearing on reproduction **:** biologically

defective or deficient — contrasted with *eugenic* — **dys·gen·i·cal·ly** \-nə̇k(ə)lē\ *adv*

dys·gen·ics \də̇s'jeniks\ *n pl but sing in constr* : the study of racial degeneration

dys·ger·mi·no·ma \dəs,jərmə'nōmə, (,)dis-\ *n, pl* **dysgerminomas** *or* **dysgerminomata** [NL, fr. *dys-* + L *germin-, germen* sprout, bud, germ + NL *-oma* — more at GERM] : a malignant tumor of the ovary arising from undifferentiated germinal epithelium

dys·gonic \dəs'gänik, (')dis¦g-\ *adj* [*dys-* + *gon-* + *-ic*] : growing with difficulty on artificial media — used chiefly of certain strains of tubercle bacilli; opposed to *eugonic*

dys·hi·dro·sis \¦dis,hī¦drōsə̇s, -s·hə̇¦\ *or* **dys·idro·sis** \-s,ī¦-, -sə̇¦-\ *n, pl* **dyshidro·ses** *or* **dysidro·ses** \-ō,sēz\ [NL, fr. *dys-* + *hidrosis*] : an abnormality of sweat production

dys·keratosis \dəs, (¦)dis+\ *n, pl* **dyskeratoses** [NL, fr. *dys-* + *kerat-* + *-osis*] : faulty development of the epidermis with abnormal keratinization — **dys·ker·a·tot·ic** \-,kerə¦täd·ik\ *adj*

dys·ki·ne·sia \,diskə̇'nēzh(ē)ə, -,kī'-\ *n* -s [NL, fr. Gk *dyskinēsia* difficulty in moving, fr. *dys-* + *-kinēsia* (fr. *kinēsis* motion + *-ia*) — more at KINESIS] : impaired or abnormal motion of voluntary or involuntary muscle — **dys·ki·net·ic** \¦=(,)=¦ned·ik\ *adj*

dys·la·lia \də̇'slālēə, -lal-\ *n* -s [NL, fr. *dys-* + *-lalia*] : defect in articulative power caused by malformation of or imperfect distribution of nerves to the organs of articulation

¹**dys·lec·tic** \də'slektik, (')di¦s-\ *adj* [fr. NL *dyslexia*, after such pairs as LL *apoplexia* apoplexy: E *apoplectic*] : suffering from dyslexia

²**dyslectic** \"\ *n* -s : a dyslectic person

dys·lex·ia \də̇'sleksēə\ *n* -s [NL, fr. *dys-* + *-lexia*] : a disturbance of the ability to read — **dys·lex·ic** \də'sleksik, (')di¦s-\ *adj*

dys·lex·i·ac \də̇'sleksē,ak\ *n* -s [NL *dyslexia* + E *-c* (as in *maniac*)] : one affected with dyslexia

dys·lo·gia \də̇'slōj(ē)ə\ *n* -s [NL, fr. *dys-* + *-logia*] : difficulty in expressing ideas through speech caused by impairment of the power of reasoning (as in certain psychoses and feeblemindedness)

dys·lo·gis·tic *also* **dis·lo·gis·tic** \¦dislə¦jistik\ *adj* [*dys-* or ¹*dis-* + *-logistic* (as in *eulogistic*)] : UNCOMPLIMENTARY, DISPARAGING ⟨~ terms like *nitwit* and *scalawag*⟩ — opposed to *eulogistic* — **dys·lo·gis·ti·cal·ly** \-tə̇k(ə)lē\ *adv*

dys·lu·ite \'di(,)slü,īt, də̇'s-\ *n* -s [irreg. fr. *dys-* + Gk *lyein* to loosen, dissolve + E *-ite* — more at LOSE] : a brown variety of gahnite

dys·men·or·rhea *also* **dys·men·or·rhoea** \(¦)di,smenə¦rēə, də,==ˈ==\ *n* -s [NL, fr. *dys-* + *meno-* + *-rrhea, -rrhoea*] : painful menstruation — **dys·men·or·rhe·al** \(¦)di¦smenə¦rēəl, də¦s-\ *or* **dys·men·or·rhe·ic** \-ēik\ *adj*

dys·met·ria \də̇'sme·trēə\ *n* -s [NL, fr. *dys-* + Gk *metron* measure + NL *-ia* — more at MEASURE] : impaired ability to estimate distance in muscular action

dys·o·dile \'disə,dīl\ *n* -s [F, fr. Gk *dysōdēs* ill-smelling (fr. *dys-* + *-ōdēs*, fr. *ozein* to smell) + F *-ile* — more at ODOR] : a hydrocarbon mineral occurring in thin flexible folia and emitting a highly fetid odor when burning

dys·o·don·ta \,disə'däntə\ [NL, fr. *dys-* + *-odonta*] *syn of* ANISOMYARIA

dys·ontogenetic \dəs, (¦)dis+\ *adj* [*dys-* + *ontogenetic*] : involving abnormal growth and differentiation of cells or tissues (as in the formation of certain cysts or tumors)

dys·ostosis \¦dis+\ *n, pl* **dysostoses** [NL, fr. *dys-* + *-ostosis*] : defective formation of bone

dys·pareunia \¦dis+\ *n* [NL, fr. *dys-* + *pareunia*] : difficult or painful coitus

dys·pa·thy \'dispəthē\ *n* -ES [prob. fr. obs. F *dispathie*, fr. *dis-* dys- + *-pathie* -pathy] : lack of sympathy : ANTIPATHY

dys·pep·sia \də̇'spepshə, -epsēə\ *n* -s [L, fr. Gk, fr. *dyspeptos* hard to digest (fr. *dys-* + *peptos* cooked, fr. *peptein, pessein* to cook) + *-ia* — more at COOK] : a condition of disturbed digestion characterized by nausea, heartburn, pain, gas, and a sense of fullness due to local causes or to disease elsewhere in the body : INDIGESTION — opposed to *eupepsia*

dys·pep·sy \-epsē\ *n* -ES [F or L; F *dyspepsie*, fr. L *dyspepsia*] *now chiefly dial* : DYSPEPSIA

¹**dys·pep·tic** \də'speptik, (')di¦s-\ *also* **dys·pep·ti·cal** \-tə̇kəl, -tēk-\ *adj* [Gk *dyspeptos* + E *-ic, -ical*] **1** : relating to dyspepsia : having dyspepsia ⟨a ~ symptom⟩ — opposed to *eupeptic* **2 a** : gloomy or negative ⟨took a ~ view of the whole affair⟩ **b** : ILL-TEMPERED, MOROSE

²**dyspeptic** \"\ *n* -s : a person having dyspepsia

dys·pha·gia \də̇'sfāj(ē)ə\ *n* -s [NL, fr. *dys-* + *-phagia*] : difficulty in swallowing — **dys·phag·ic** \də'sfajik, (')di¦s-\ *adj*

dys·pha·sia \də̇'sfāzh(ē)ə\ *n* -s [NL, fr. *dys-* + *-phasia*] : loss of or deficiency in the power to use or understand language caused by injury to or disease of the brain — **dys·pha·sic** \-āzik\ *n or adj*

dys·phe·mia \də̇'sfēmēə\ *n* -s [NL, fr. *dys-* + *-phemia*] : STAMMERING

dys·phe·mism \'disfə,mizəm\ *n* -s [*dys-* + *-phemism* (as in *euphemism*)] : substitution of a disagreeable, offensive, or disparaging word or expression for an agreeable or inoffensive one (as of *axle grease* for *butter*, *old man* for *father*, or *heap* for *car*); *also* : a word or expression so substituted — contrasted with *euphemism*

dys·pho·nia \də̇'sfōnēə\ *n* -s [NL, fr. *dys-* + *-phonia*] : impairment of the voice manifested by hoarseness or other defects of phonation due to organic, functional, or psychic causes — **dys·phon·ic** \də̇'sfänik, (')di¦s-\ *adj*

dys·pho·ria \də̇'sfōrēə\ *n* -s [NL, fr. Gk, malaise, vexation, fr. *dysphoros* hard to bear (fr. *dys-* + *-phoros*, fr. *pherein* to bear) + *-ia* — more at BEAR] : a generalized state of feeling unwell or unhappy — opposed to *euphoria* — **dys·phor·ic** \də'sfȯrik, (')di¦s-\ *adj*

dys·pho·tic \də'sfōd·ik, (')di¦s-\ *adj* [*dys-* + Gk *phōt-, phōs* light + E *-ic* — more at FANCY] : having feeble illumination : occurring where the light is very limited (as at marine depths)

dys·phra·sia \də̇s'frāzh(ē)ə\ *n* -s [NL, fr. *dys-* + *-phrasia*] : defective speech due to impairment of intellect

dys·pla·sia \də̇'splāzh(ē)ə\ *n* -s [NL, fr. *dys-* + *-plasia*] : abnormal growth or development (as of organs, tissues, or cells); *broadly* : anatomic structure that presents some abnormality as a result of such growth — **dys·plas·tic** \də'splastik, (')di¦s-\ *adj*

dysp·nea *also* **dysp·noea** \'dis(p)nēə *also* də̇s(p)'nēə\ *n* -s [L *dyspnoea*, fr. Gk *dyspnoia*, fr. *dyspnoos, dyspnous* short of breath (fr. *dys-* + *-pnoos, -pnous*, fr. *pnoē* breathing, fr. *pnein* to breathe) + *-ia* — more at SNEEZE] : difficult or labored respiration — distinguished from *eupnea* — **dysp·ne·ic** *or* **dysp·noe·ic** \(')dis(p)¦nēik, dəs(p)'n-\ *adj*

dys·pro·si·um \də̇'sprōzēəm\ *n* -s [NL, fr. Gk *dysprositos* hard to get at (fr. *dys-* + *prositos* approachable) + NL *-ium*] : a trivalent metallic element of the rare-earth group that forms compounds which are among the most highly magnetic known, and of which the oxide is white and the salts yellowish — symbol *Dy;* see ELEMENT table

dys·rhyth·mia \də̇s'rith̲mēə *sometimes* -th-\ *n* -s [NL, fr. *dys-* + L *rhythmus* rhythm + NL *-ia* — more at RHYTHM] : abnormal rhythm; *specif* : disordered rhythm in the brain waves as disclosed by an electroencephalogram — **dys·rhyth·mic** \(')dis¦rith̲mik, dəs'r- *sometimes* -th-\ *adj*

dys·se·ba·cia \,dis(s)ə̇'bāsh(ē)ə\ *n* -s [NL, fr. *dys-* + ISV *sebaceous (gland)* + NL *-ia*] : a disorder of the sebaceous glands marked by reddening and accumulation of greasy flaky scales on affected areas and often indicative of vitamin deficiency

dys·so·dia \də̇'sōdēə\ *n, cap* [NL, modif. of Gk *dysōdia* foul smell, fr. *dysōdēs* ill-smelling + *-ia* — more at DYSODILE] : a small genus of prairie herbs (family Compositae) found in the central part of No. America with fetid finely dissected leaves and small yellow heads of tubular and ray flowers

dys·synergia \¦di(s)+\ *also* **dys·synergy** \(¦)di(s), də+\ *n, pl* **dyssynergias** *also* **dyssynergies** [NL *dyssynergia*, fr. *dys-* + *syn-* + *-ergia*] : DYSKINESIA — **dys·synergic** \¦di(s)+\ *adj*

dys·teleological \dəs, (¦)dis+\ *adj* : of or relating to dysteleology : PURPOSELESS

dys·teleology \"+\ *n* [G *dysteleologie*, fr. *dys-* + *teleologie* teleology] **1** : absence of purpose in nature esp. as manifested in rudimentary or nonfunctional structures; *also* : the doctrine of purposelessness in nature — compare TELEOLOGY **2 a** : frustration or evasion of a normal functional end **b** : a vestigial organ

dys·thy·mia \də̇'sthīmēə\ *n* -s [NL, fr. Gk, despondency, fr. *dysthymos* despondent (fr. *dys-* + *-thymos*, fr. *thymos* spirit, mind, courage) + *-ia* -y — more at FUME] : morbid anxiety and depression accompanied by obsession — **dys·thy·mic** \-mik\ *adj*

dys·to·cia \də̇'stōsh(ē)ə\ *or* **dys·to·kia** \-ōkēə\ *n* -s [NL, fr. Gk *dystokia*, fr. *dys-* + *tokos* childbirth, parturition + *-ia;* akin to Gk *teknon* child — more at THANE] : slow or difficult labor or delivery — opposed to *eutocia* — **dys·to·cial** \də̇'stōsh(ē)əl\ *adj*

dys·to·nia \də̇'stōnēə\ *n* -s [NL, fr. *dys-* + *-tonia*] : a state of disordered tonicity of tissues (as of muscle) — **dys·ton·ic** \də'stänik, (')di¦s-\ *adj*

dys·trophic \dəs, (')dis+\ *adj* **1** : relating to or caused by faulty or imperfect nutrition **2** *of a lake* : brownish in color with much dissolved humic matter, a small bottom fauna, and a notably high oxygen consumption — compare EUTROPHIC, OLIGOTROPHIC

dys·tro·phy \'distrəfē, -fi\ *also* **dys·tro·phia** \də̇'strōfēə\ *n, pl* **dystrophies** *also* **dystrophias** [NL *dystrophia*, fr. *dys-* + *-trophia* -trophy] : imperfect or faulty nutrition; *specif* : any of several neuromuscular disorders — see MUSCULAR DYSTROPHY

dys·uria \də̇'shu̇rēə, də̇s'yu̇-\ *n* -s [NL, fr. Gk *dysouria, dysouriē*, fr. *dys-* + *-ouria, -ouriē* -uria] : difficult or painful discharge of urine — **dys·uric** \də̇'shu̇rik, dəs'yu̇-, (')dis¦yu̇-\ *adj*

dy·syn·tri·bite \də̇'sin·trə,bīt\ *n* -s [*dys-* + Gk *syntribein* to rub together, shatter, crush (fr. *syn-* + *tribein* to rub) + E *-ite* — more at THROW] : a variety of pinite

-dy·tes \‿də,tēz\ *also* **-dy·ta** \‿dəd·ə, ‿dətə\ *n comb form* [NL, fr. Gk *dytēs*, fr. *dyein* to enter, dive in, sink — more at ADYTUM] : diver — in generic names chiefly of birds ⟨Aptenodytes⟩

dy·tis·cid \dī'tisə̇d, də̇'-\ *n* -s [NL *Dytiscidae*] : one of the Dytiscidae : DIVING BEETLE

dy·tis·ci·dae \-sə,dē\ *n pl, cap* [NL, fr. *Dytiscus*, type genus + *-idae*] : a family of predacious aquatic beetles of oval flattened form with filamentous antennae comprising the diving beetles, being notably voracious, and feeding on aquatic insects, worms, and even young fish — see WATER DEVIL

dy·tis·cus \-skəs\ *n, cap* [NL, irreg. fr. Gk *dytikos* able to dive, fr. (assumed) Gk *dytos* (verbal of Gk *dyein* to enter, dive in, sink) + Gk *-ikos* -ic — more at ADYTUM] : the type genus of Dytiscidae including many of the larger and better-known American diving beetles

dyu·la \dē'üլə, 'dyü-\ *n, pl* **dyula** *or* **dyulas** *usu cap* **1 a** : a Negro people who live widely scattered among other peoples in the Ivory Coast, Upper Volta, and neighboring parts of West Africa, many of whom are active traders **b** : a member of such people **2** : a Mande language of the Dyula people that is widely used as a trade language in the Ivory Coast and Upper Volta — compare MANDINGO

dy·vour \'dīvər\ *n* -s [ME (Sc dial.) *dyour*] *Scot* : a man in debt : BANKRUPT

dz *abbr* dozen

dzau·dzhi·kau \(d)zau̇'jē,kau̇\ *adj, usu cap* [fr. *Dzaudzhikau*, U.S.S.R.] : of or from the city of Dzaudzhikau, U.S.S.R. : of the kind or style prevalent in Dzaudzhikau

dzeggetai *var of* CHIGETAI

dze·ren \(d)zə'ren, '(d)zerə̇n\ *or* **dze·ron** \(d)zə'rän, '(d)zerən\ *also* **dze·rin** \(d)zə'rin, '(d)zerə̇n\ *n* -s [Russ *dzeren*, fr. Kalmuck *zērn*] : a gregarious fawn-colored black-tailed gazelle (*Procapra gutturosa*) of Central Asia, Tibet, and China

dzer·zhinsk \d(y)ə(r)'zhinzk, (d)zə-, -n(t)sk\ *adj, usu cap* [fr. *Dzerzhinsk*, U.S.S.R.] : of or from the city of Dzerzhinsk, U.S.S.R. : of the kind or style prevalent in Dzerzhinsk

dzo \'(d)zō\ *or* **zho** \'zhō\ *n, pl* **dzos** *also* **dzo** *or* **zhos** *also* **zho** [Tibetan *wdzo*] : a hybrid between the yak and the domestic cow

dzun·gar \'(d)zu̇ŋ,gär, -zəŋ-\ *n* -s *cap* : a native of Dzungaria

1e \ˈē\ *n, pl* **e's** *or* **es** *also* **ees** \ˈēz\ *often cap, often attrib* **1 a :** the fifth letter of the English alphabet **b :** an instance of this letter printed, written, or otherwise represented **c :** a speech counterpart of orthographic *e* (as long *e* in *equal*, short *e* in *let*, or *e* in German *mehl*) **2 a :** the keynote of E major or E minor **b :** the tone E **3 :** a printer's type, a stamp, or some other instrument for reproducing the letter e **4 :** someone or something arbitrarily or conveniently designated *e*, esp. as the fifth in order or class: as **a :** the base of the natural system of logarithms being the *x*th root of the expression $1+x$ as *x* approaches the limit 0 and having the approximate numerical value 2.71828 **b :** the eccentricity of a curve **c :** the enlarging of a variable of a function in the calculus of finite differences by 1 so that fx becomes $f(x+1)$ **d :** the second-class Lloyd's rating for the quality of a merchant ship **5 a :** a grade assigned by a teacher or examiner rating a student's work as falling in the fifth highest class in a scale of 5 or of 6 classes and usu. constituting a conditional pass ⟨received an *E* in Latin⟩ **b :** one graded or rated with an E ⟨one of the *E's* in the class⟩ **6 :** something having the shape of the letter E **7 :** an award usu. in the form of a pennant bearing a symbolic E for excellence or exceptional merit (as in performance, production, or product) given usu. to an industrial organization by an agency of the U. S. government (as one of its armed forces)

2e *abbr, often cap* **1** earl **2** early **3** earth **4** easily **5** east; easterly; eastern **6** Easter **7** eccentricity **8** edge **9** educated **10** efficiency; efficient **11** Egyptian **12** elasticity **13** eldest **14** ell **15** empty **16** end **17** energy **18** engine; engineer; engineering **19** English **20** entrance **21** equatorial **22** erg **23** error **24** escudo **25** estimate; estimated **26** excellence; excellency; excellent **27** export **28** exposure

3e *symbol* **1** *cap* Elohistic or Ephraimitic — used in biblical criticism ⟨the *E* source in the Hexateuch⟩ ⟨an *E* psalm⟩ **2** *cap* Young's modulus of elasticity **3** *cap* electric intensity **4** *cap* illumination **5** the charge of an electron **6** *cap* oxidation-reduction potential **7** *cap* einsteinium

e- *prefix* [ME, not, out, forth, away, fr. OF & L; OF, out, forth, away, fr. L, fr. *ex-* — more at EX-] **1 a :** not ⟨*ecarinate*⟩ ⟨*erostrate*⟩ **b :** missing **:** absent ⟨*Ecardines*⟩ ⟨*edental*⟩ **2 :** out **:** on the outside ⟨*escribe*⟩ **3 :** thoroughly ⟨*evaporize*⟩ **4 :** forth ⟨*eradiate*⟩ **5 :** away ⟨*eluvium*⟩

ea \ˈē(ə)\ *n* -s [ME *æ, ee,* fr. OE *ēa* — more at ISLAND] *dial Eng* **:** RIVER, STREAM

ea *abbr* each

EA *abbr* **1** economic adviser **2** educational age **3** enemy aircraft

eace·worm \ˈēs,=\ *n* [E dial. *eace, easse* earthworm (fr. ME *ees* bait, carrion, fr. OE *ǣs*) + E *worm;* akin to OHG *ās* carrion, L *esca* food, bait, Lith *edesis* food, OE *etan* to eat — more at EAT] *NewEng* **:** EARTHWORM

1each \(ˈ)ēch\ *adj* [ME *ech,* fr. OE *ǣlc;* akin to OHG *iogilīh* each; both fr. a prehistoric WGmc compound whose first and second constituents respectively are represented by OE *ā* always and by OE *gelīc* alike — more at AYE, LIKE] **:** being one of two or more distinct individuals having a similar relation and often constituting an aggregate **:** this as well as that or the next or any other of two or more separate but similar individuals ⟨a boat . . . hung from the ceiling by ropes attached at ~ end —J.G.Frazer⟩ ⟨the little chipmunk . . . with a piñon nut in ~ cheek pouch —*Nature Mag.*⟩ ⟨~ day was like every other one —H.D.Skidmore⟩ ⟨~ year the Cape has a summer inundation of people —R.W.Hatch⟩ ⟨a program flexible enough to be tailored to ~ individual employee —A.J.Nickerson⟩ ⟨giving to ~ syllable an equal stress —Max Beerbohm⟩ ⟨some publishers . . . will have books to show in ~ category —James Britton⟩

2each \"\ *pron* [ME *ech,* fr. OE *ǣlc,* fr. *ǣlc,* adj.] **1 :** each one — usu. used with reference to a preceding substantive or followed by *of* ⟨shot after shot, ~ missing by inches⟩ ⟨~ of them is to pay his own fine⟩ ⟨~ of them are to pay their own fine⟩ **2 :** each person **:** EVERYBODY — used with indefinite or vaguely implicit reference ⟨whatever their faults ~ believes in the gods of his father⟩ **3 :** all considered one by one — used following a series ⟨your songs, your thoughts, your doings, ~ divide this perfect beauty —Amy Lowell⟩

3each \"\ *adv* **:** to or for each **:** APIECE ⟨allow two helpings ~⟩ ⟨the reports cost a dollar ~⟩

each and every *pron, Midland* **:** EVERYBODY

each other *pron* [ME *ech other,* fr. OE *ǣlc ōther,* fr. *ǣlc* each + *ōther* other] **:** each of two or more in reciprocal action or relation **:** ONE ANOTHER — used esp. in the possessive case or as the object of a verb or preposition to indicate that of the two or more persons or things referred to by two or more substantives or by a plural or collective substantive any particular one performs the same action upon or stands in the same relation to one or more of the others as one or more of the others do to him ⟨army officers salute *each other*⟩ ⟨when he and I saw *each other's* faces⟩ ⟨the two are now writing to *each other* daily⟩; sometimes used with only *other* in the possessive case or as the object of a verb or preposition and with *each* in a different construction typically as subject of a verb or in apposition with the subject of a verb ⟨*each* at *other* looked —John Keats⟩ ⟨*each* for *other* they were born —R.W.Emerson⟩

ead *abbr* [L *eadem*] the same

-e·ae \ˌē,ē, ˈē,ē\ *n pl suffix* [NL, fr. L (fem. pl. of *-eus* -eous)] **:** those belonging to (such a group) — in biological taxonomic names of groups (as tribes) larger than the genus ⟨*Diatomeae*⟩ ⟨*Florideae*⟩ ⟨*Uredineae*⟩

1ea·ger \ˈēgə(r)\ *adj, sometimes* -ER/-EST [ME *egre* sharp, sour, eager, fr. OF *aigre,* fr. L *acer* sharp, sour, spirited, zealous; akin to Gk *akros* highest, extreme, Skt *aśri* corner, edge — more at EDGE] **1 :** marked of its kind by reason of notable development of some quality (as sourness, savor, fierceness, violence, chill, or vigor) — obs. except of weather phenomena ⟨an ~ breeze ruffled the lake⟩ ⟨a nipping and an ~ air —Shak.⟩ **2 :** having or characterized by strong and urgent interest, desire, ardor, enthusiasm, or impatience ⟨an ~ lad determined to make his mark⟩ ⟨they were ~ to get on their way before the storm broke⟩ **3** *obs, of metal* **:** BRITTLE **:** lacking in ductility or temper

syn AVID, KEEN, ANXIOUS, AGOG, ATHIRST: EAGER is likely to imply ardor, enthusiasm, and impatient reluctance at delay ⟨the parent, moreover, is likely to be too *eager* and too much interested in his child's progress —Bertrand Russell⟩ ⟨when the boys saw one another taking their seats, they were as *eager* as before they had been slow; and they hustled each other at the bottom of the table —Anthony Trollope⟩ AVID may have suggestions of intense desire or insatiability ⟨the westward-moving settlers, *avid* for land —D.E.Clark⟩ ⟨outward satiety such as follows a too *avid* thirst for pleasure —G.W.Russell⟩ ⟨she watched him eagerly, *avid* for any gleam of surprise or disapproval —Margery Allingham⟩ KEEN suggests sharp and lively interest marked by lasting intensity and ready responsiveness ⟨I was making the acquaintance of my shipmates, and so *keen* on learning my new duties that the days were all too short —C.B.Nordhoff & J.N.Hall⟩ ⟨she was a *keen* horticulturist, and won prizes at all the local flower shows —John Buchan⟩ ANXIOUS may suggest deep desire intermixed with worry and fear of frustration or disappointment ⟨the average immigrant was pathetically *anxious* to become an American —Allan Nevins & H.S.Commager⟩ ⟨the schoolmasters may be pathetically *anxious* to guide boys right, and to guard them from evil —A.C.Benson⟩ ⟨I am particularly *anxious* in this lecture not to assume the role of Christian apologist —W.R. Inge⟩ AGOG suggests excited or impatient expectancy ⟨awaiting him impatiently, *agog* with curiosity —Fred Majdalany⟩ ⟨a greenhorn who arrives in Australia, all *agog* to begin life as a station owner —Leslie Rees⟩ ATHIRST may suggest yearning or longing ⟨on naturalism and materialism a constant war is waged by one or two great souls *athirst* for pure aesthetic rapture —Clive Bell⟩ ⟨older boys and girls eager for the universities, all of them *athirst* for experience —*Saturday Rev.*⟩

2eager *var of* EAGRE

eager beaver *n* **:** one who is overzealous, overdiligent, and impatient not only to perform his part with promptness but to volunteer for more

ea·ger·ly *adv* [ME *egrely,* fr. *egre* + *-ly*] **:** in an eager manner **:** with urgent desire or enthusiasm

ea·ger·ness *n* -ES [ME *egrenesse,* fr. *egre* + *-nesse* -ness] **1 :** the quality or state of being eager **:** ARDOR, ENTHUSIASM **2 :** an act or instance of being eager

1ea·gle \ˈēgəl\ *n* -s [ME *egle,* fr. OF *egle, aigle,* fr. L *aquila*] **1 :** any of various large diurnal birds of prey (family Accipitridae) noted for their strength, size, graceful figure, keenness of vision, and powers of flight — see AQUILA, BALD EAGLE, GOLDEN EAGLE, HARPY EAGLE, IMPERIAL EAGLE, SEA EAGLE **2 :** any of various figures or representations of an eagle esp. when used as an emblem or symbol: as **a :** the standard of the ancient Romans **b :** the seal or standard of any nation having an eagle as emblem (as the U.S. or France under the Bonapartes) **c** *or* **eagle lectern :** a lectern whose brass or wooden book support is shaped like an eagle with outspread wings **d :** one of a pair of silver insignia of rank worn by a colonel in the army, marine corps, or air force and by a captain in the navy or coast guard **e :** a green conventionalized figure of an eagle that is used as the identifying symbol of the fifth suit in 5-suit packs of playing cards manufactured in the U. S. **f** *or* **eaglebird** \ˈ=,=\ **:** a compartment on some roulette wheels marked with an eagle and equivalent to the zero and double zero of other wheels **3 :** a gold coin of the U. S. bearing an eagle on the reverse and worth 10 dollars, first issued 1795, last issued 1933 **4 :** CLOVE BROWN 2 **5 :** a golf score of two strokes less than par on any hole but a par-three hole

eagle 2d

2eagle \"\ *adj* **:** like that of an eagle ⟨hooked ~ nose⟩ ⟨a bright ~ glance⟩; *esp, of the eye* **:** keen-sighted, bright, and piercing

3eagle \"\ *vt* -ED/-ING/-S **:** to shoot (a hole in golf) in two strokes under par ⟨*eagled* the 510-yard par five 13th hole —*United Press International*⟩

eagle boat *n* **:** an antisubmarine warship smaller than a destroyer

eagle dance *n* **:** a widespread American Indian ritual dance esp. for rain among the Pueblos and for cure and peace among the Iroquois that is derived from the calumet dance and is performed by two or four men commonly with artificial wings bound to their arms and with movements which are imitative of eagles

eagle eye *n* **1 :** the ability to see or observe with exceptional keenness **2 :** one that sees or observes with exceptional keenness ⟨her sewing would never pass that *eagle eye* without stern criticism —Flora Thompson⟩

eagle-eyed \ˈ=ˌ=ˈ=\ *adj* **:** keen of vision or insight ⟨the *eagle-eyed* scout watched the distant dust cloud⟩ ⟨an *eagle-eyed* appraisal of the situation⟩

eagle fern *n* **:** a common brake (*Pteridium aquilinum*)

eagle-hawk \ˈ=,=,=\ *n* **1 :** any of numerous tropical American birds of prey (family Accipitridae) intermediate in size between the typical hawks and eagles and often crested **2** *Austral* **:** WEDGE-TAILED EAGLE

eagle-kite \ˈ=,=,=\ *n* **:** BRAHMINY KITE; *also* **:** any of several closely related birds

eagle owl *n* **:** any of numerous large horned owls constituting the genus *Bubo; specif* **:** a very large Old World owl (*B. bubo*) that is widely distributed in Europe and northern Asia

eagle ray *n* **:** any of several large active stingrays of the family Myliobatidae having broad pectoral fins like wings and being represented by several species that are widely distributed esp. in warm seas — see SPOTTED EAGLE RAY

eagle scout *n* **:** a boy scout who has been awarded 21 merit badges — compare STAR SCOUT

eaglestone \ˈ=,=,=\ *n* **:** a concretionary nodule of clay ironstone about the size of a walnut that the ancients believed an eagle takes to her nest to facilitate egg-laying

ea·glet \ˈēglət\ *n* -s [MF *aiglet,* fr. *aigle* eagle + *-et*] **:** a young eagle

eagle vulture *n* **:** a large black-and-white western African bird (*Gypohierax angolensis*) intermediate in some characters between eagles and vultures and feeding on the fruit of oil palms and on carrion (as fish) — called also *vulturine sea eagle*

eaglewood \ˈ=,=,=\ *n* [prob. trans. of F *bois d'aigle,* prob. trans. (influenced by Pg *águia* eagle) of Pg *pao d'águia,* lit., agalloch wood] **:** AGALLOCH

ea·gre *or* **ea·ger** *also* **ae·gir** \ˈēgə(r), ˈāg-\ *n* [alter. of earlier *higre,* fr. (assumed) ME *higre* (whence ML *higra*)] **:** a tidal flood or flow **:** BORE

eal·der·man *or* **eal·dor·man** *archaic var of* ALDERMAN

ea·ling \ˈēliŋ\ *adj, usu cap* [fr. *Ealing,* municipal borough in England] **:** of or from the municipal borough of Ealing, England **:** of the kind or style prevalent in Ealing

ean \ˈēn\ *vb* -ED/-ING/-S [ME *enen,* fr. OE *ēanian* — more at YEAN] *dial Eng* **:** YEAN

-ean — see -AN

E and OE *abbr* errors and omissions excepted

E and P *abbr* extraordinary and plenipotentiary

eanling *n* -s [*ean* + *-ling*] *obs* **:** YEANLING

EAON *abbr* except as otherwise noted

1ear \ˈi(ə)r, ˈiə\ *n* -s [ME *ere,* fr. OE *ēare;* akin to OHG *ōra* ear, ON *eyra,* Goth *auso,* L *auris,* Gk *ous,* Lith *ausis*] **1 a :** the characteristic vertebrate organ of hearing and equilibrium consisting in the typical mammal of a sound-collecting outer ear separated by a membranous drum from a sound-transmitting middle ear which in turn is separated from a sensory inner ear by membranous fenestrae, the whole being variously simplified in lower vertebrates in which the outer ear is frequently absent, the middle often modified or absent, and the inner in some cases reduced to the structures concerned with equilibrium **b :** any of various organs (as an otocyst or a chordotonal organ) capable of detecting vibratory motion esp. of frequencies higher than several vibrations per second that is taking place in the surrounding medium whether this detection takes the form of hearing as commonly understood or not — compare HEARING, LABYRINTHINE SENSE; ORGAN OF CORTI **2 :** the external ear of man and most mammals **3 a :** the sense or act of hearing ⟨a keen ~⟩ **:** perception of sound **b :** refinement or acuity of the sense of hearing ⟨a nice ~ for pitch⟩ **c :** the ability to catch and retain or reproduce music by hearing it ⟨to play by ~⟩; *often* **:** the ability to imagine aurally a tone or group of tones with correct relative pitch ⟨a violinist must have a good ~⟩ **4 :** something resembling in shape or position a mammalian ear: as **a :** a projecting part (as a lug, plate, or handle) or either of a pair of such parts that is suitable for lifting, transporting, adjusting, or fixing in position the object of which it is a part (as the handle of a pitcher or platter or tub the cannon of a bell, or the leather pull for tightening the cord of a drum) **b (1) :** a process on an animal body **:** AURICLE **(2) :** either of a pair of tufts of lengthened feathers on the head of certain birds **(3) :** the tuft of specialized feathers associated with the ear opening in some birds **c :** CROSSETTE 1 **d :** either of the lateral scrolled ends of the cresting of a Chippendale chair or mirror **e :** a projecting tag inadvertently formed during deep-drawing of sheet metal **f :** a device usu. in the form of a grooved bronze casting for supporting a trolley wire **g :** a projection on certain printed letters (as the right-hand projection of the upper part of *g*) **h :** the projecting part of a typesetter's composing rule — called also *neb* **i :** either of two right-angled projections at the uppermost edge of a linotype matrix **j :** one of the boxes or spaces in the upper corners of the front page of a newspaper usu. containing advertising of the paper itself or a weather forecast **5 a :** HEARING, AUDIENCE; *esp* **:** compassionate and favorable attention ⟨give ~ to my plea⟩ ⟨I seek the merciful ~ of our Lord⟩ **b :** AWARENESS, ATTENTION ⟨when her kindness came to the ~ of her enemies, they were bowed with shame⟩ ⟨it has come to my ~ that you have missed several classes⟩ **6 :** the stiff reflexed end of an oriental composite bow — **by the ears** *adv* **:** in or into discord ⟨set the whole neighborhood *by the ears*⟩ — **in one ear and out the other** *or* **in at one ear and out at the other :** through the mind without making an impression ⟨everything you say to him goes *in one ear and out the other*⟩ — **on one's ear 1** *slang* **:** into a state of irritation or rage ⟨his insults really put me *on my ear*⟩ **2 :** head over heels **:** UNCEREMONIOUSLY ⟨if you ever made that mistake you went out *on your ear* — Nicholas Monsarrat⟩ — **to the ears** *adv* **:** to the limit of capacity ⟨drunk *to the ears*⟩ — **up to the ears** *or* **up to one's ears :** heavily or deeply involved **:** implicated or concerned to a greater degree than is safe or proper ⟨*up to his ears* in the conspiracy⟩ ⟨*up to the ears* in debt⟩

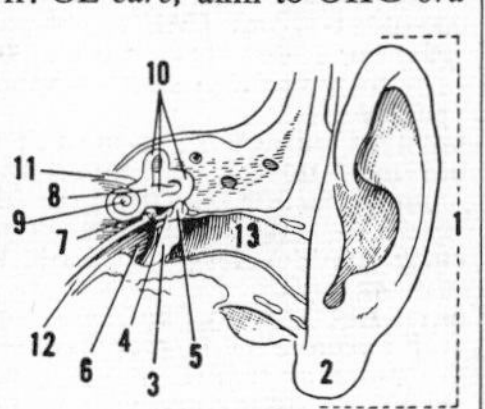

ear: *1* pinna, *2* lobe, *3* tympanic membrane, *4* incus, *5* malleus, *6* tympanum, *7* stapes, *8* vestibule, *9* cochlea, *10* semicircular canals, *11* auditory nerve, *12* eustachian tube, *13* auditory meatus

2ear \"\ *vt* -ED/-ING/-S [ME *eren,* fr. OE *erian;* akin to OHG *erien* to plow, ON *erja,* Goth *arjan,* L *arare,* Gk *aroun,* Lith *arti*] *now dial Eng* **:** to plow or till **:** CULTIVATE

3ear \"\ *n* -s [ME *ere, er,* fr. OE *ēar;* akin to OHG *ahir* ear, ON *ax,* Goth *ahs* ear, L *acus* chaff, Gk *achnē* chaff, OE *ecg* edge — more at EDGE] **:** the fruiting head of a cereal (as Indian corn, wheat, or rye) including both the kernels of grain and protective and supporting structures ⟨plump golden ~s of wheat rustling in the breeze⟩

4ear \"\ *vi* -ED/-ING/-S [ME *eren,* fr. *ere, er,* n.] **:** to form ears in the course of growing ⟨this corn ~s well⟩ — often used with *up* ⟨the rye should soon be ~*ing* up⟩

5ear \(ˈ)ār, (ˈ)er, ər\ *var of* 1ERE

6ear \ˈi(ə)r, ˈiə\ *dial var of* YEAR

earache \ˈ=,=\ *n* **:** an ache or pain in the ear **:** OTALGIA

ear·age \ˈirij\ *n* -s **:** length of ears measured from tip to tip across the top of the head — used of certain dogs and rabbits

ear banger *n* [so called fr. the practice of talking as much as possible to someone who is influential or has rewards at his disposal] *slang* **:** a person who is overanxious to please his superiors or seniors

earbash \ˈ=,=\ *vt* -ED/-ING/-ES *Austral* **:** HARANGUE, LECTURE ⟨a treat to have an authentic account after having been ~*ed* by those other blowhards —*Sydney* (*Australia*) *Bull.*⟩

earbob \ˈ=,=\ *n* -s **:** EARRING

ear-brisk \ˈ=,=\ *adj, of a horse* **:** carrying the ears pricked forward

ear canker *n* [1*ear*] **:** CANKER 7a

earclip \ˈ=,=\ *n* **:** an earring with a clip fastener

earcockle \ˈ=,=,=\ *n* **:** a disease of wheat caused by a nematode (*Anguina tritici*) that invades the developing ear and causes galls to form

ear conch *n* [1*ear*] **:** PINNA 2b

ear covert *n* **:** EAR 4b(3)

ear crystal *n* [1*ear*] **:** OTOLITH, OTOCONIUM

ear defender *n* **:** a device (as an earplug) designed to lessen the transmission of excessive or damaging sound to the auditory receptors of the inner ear

eardrop \ˈ=,=\ *n* **1** *also* **eardropper** \ˈ=,=,=\ **:** EARRING; *esp* **:** one with a pendant **2 eardrops** *pl but sing or pl in constr* **a :** a plant of the genus *Dicentra* (esp. *D. spectabilis*) — called also *bleeding heart* **b :** FUCHSIA 2 **c :** BUCKWHEAT VINE **3 eardrops** *pl* **:** medicine in liquid form to be instilled by drops into the external auditory meatus

eardrop tree *n* **:** CONACASTE

eardrum \ˈ=,=\ *n* [1*ear*] **:** TYMPANUM 1a(1)

ear dust *n* [1*ear*] **:** OTOCONIA

1eared \ˈi(ə)rd, ˈiəd\ *adj* [ME *ered,* fr. *ere* ear + *-ed* — more at 1EAR] **1 :** having ears; *usu* **:** having external ears esp. of a specified character — often used in combination ⟨long-*eared*⟩ ⟨pink-*eared*⟩ ⟨flop-*eared*⟩ **2 :** having projecting processes: as **a :** having tufts of feathers resembling ears in form or position ⟨an ~ owl⟩ **b** *of a heraldic shield* **:** having small triangular projections at the two upper corners

2eared \"\ *adj* [ME *ered,* past part. of *eren* to ear — more at 4EAR] **1** *of cereal plants* **:** having ears usu. of a specified character ⟨~ wheat stalks bending in the breeze⟩ — used chiefly in combination ⟨golden-*eared* grain⟩ ⟨full-*eared* corn⟩ **2 :** being in ear **:** come into ear ⟨an ~ field of corn⟩

eared grebe *n* **:** a rather small grebe (*Colymbus nigricollis* or *Colymbus caspicus* or *Podiceps caspicus*) having yellow ear tufts of fan shape and a black neck and being represented by various subspecies in Europe, Asia, southern Africa, and western No. America — called also *black-necked grebe*

eared pheasant *n* **:** any of several pheasants (genus *Crossoptilon*) having a tuft of bright feathers projecting from each side of the head and being native to eastern and central Asia but now often bred as ornamentals

eared seal *n* **:** any of various seals comprising the family Otariidae, including the sea lions and fur seals, having the hind limbs independent and mobile so that they are able to move with some facility on land, and being distinguished from other seals by small but well-developed external ears

earflap \ˈ=,=\ *n* [1*ear*] **1 :** PINNA 2b **2 :** a warm covering for the ear; *esp* **:** an extension on the lower edge of a cap that may be folded up or down

earflap 2

earflower \ˈ=,=\ *n* [1*ear*] **:** SACRED EARFLOWER

ear fly *n* [1*ear*] **:** DEERFLY

ear·ful \ˈi(ə)r,fu̇l, ˈiə,-\ *n* -s **1 a :** an astonishing and usu. unexpected oral response ⟨the probers got an ~ —Vance Packard⟩ **b :** an outpouring of news or gossip often unwanted **2 :** a sharp reprimand **:** TALKING-TO

ear fungus *n* [1*ear* + *fungus;* fr. the shape of the sporophores] **:** a fungus of the order Auriculariales; *esp* **:** JEW'S-EAR

earhead \ˈ=,=\ *n* **:** the ear of grain — used esp. of millets and sorghums

earhole \ˈ=,=\ *n* [1*ear*] **:** the orifice of the external auditory meatus; *broadly* **:** the meatus itself

ear·ing *or* **ear·ring** \ˈir(,)iŋ, ˈirēŋ\ *n* -s [perh. fr. 1*ear* + *-ing*] **1 :** a line used to fasten the upper corners of a sail to the yard or gaff — called also *head earing* — see SAIL illustration **2 a :** a line for hauling the reef cringle to the yard — called also *reef earing* **3 :** a line fastening the corners of an awning (as on a ship) to the rigging or stanchions

earjewel \ˈ=,=,=\ *n* [1*ear*] **:** JEWELWEED

earl \ˈər(-ə)l, ˈəl, ˈəil\ *n* -s [ME *erl,* fr. OE *eorl* warrior, nobleman; akin to OS *erl* man, ON *jarl* warrior, nobleman ranking next to a king, and perh. to OE *rīsan* to rise — more at RISE] **1** *in Anglo-Saxon England* **a :** a man of noble rank **b :** the governor of one of the great divisions of England established by Canute **2** *obs* **:** a feudal noble or prince **:** COUNT **3 :** a member of the third grade of the peerage in Great Britain ranking below a marquess and above a viscount — compare COUNT; see COUNTESS

ear·land·ite \ˈirlən,dīt, ˈər-\ *n* -s *often cap E* [Arthur *Earland* †1958 Eng. civil servant + E *-ite*] **:** a mineral $Ca_3(C_6H_5O_7)_2 \cdot 4H_2O$ consisting of a hydrous citrate of calcium found in ocean-bottom sediments from the Weddell sea

earlap \ˈi(ə)r,lap\ *n* [ME *erelappe,* fr. OE *ēarlæppa,* fr. *ēar-* (fr. *ēare* ear) + *læppa* lap — more at 1EAR, LAP] **:** EARFLAP

earl·dom \ˈərldəm, ˈəl-, ˈəil-\ *n* -s [ME *erldom,* fr. OE *eorldōm,* fr. *eorl* earl + *-dōm* -dom] **1 :** the domain or territory of an earl or countess **2 :** the rank or dignity of an earl or countess

ear-leaved umbrella tree \ˈ=,=-\ *n* **:** a slender tree (*Magnolia fraseri*) having oblong spatulate leaves that are auriculate at the base

ear·less \ˈi(ə)rləs, ˈiəl-\ *adj* **1 :** lacking ears **2 :** deficient in auditory acuity esp. in respect to music

earless seal *n* **:** a seal of the family Phocidae — compare EARED SEAL

ear·let \-lət\ *n* -s [1*ear* + *-let*] **1 :** a small ear (as of a plant leaf) **2 :** the tragus esp. when exceptionally large (as in the ears of some bats)

earlier on *adv* **:** PREVIOUSLY, BEFORE ⟨I told you yes *earlier on*⟩

earlike \ˈ=,=\ *adj* **:** projecting like or otherwise like an ear

earlily *adv* [*early,* adj. + *-ly*] *obs* **:** EARLY

ear·li·ness \ˈərlēnəs, ˈəl-,ˈəil-, -lin-\ *n* -ES **:** the quality or state of being early; *esp* **:** the ability of a plant to produce the product (as flowers or fruit) for which it is cultivated at an earlier period in the growing season than is usual of related plants ⟨a sweet corn of superior ~ and good flavor⟩

earl marischal *n, pl* **earls marischals** *or* **earl marischals** *or* **earls marischal :** a marshal of Scotland from the 15th century to 1716 — compare EARL MARSHAL; see MARISCHAL

earl marshal *n, pl* **earls marshals** *or* **earl marshals** *or* **earls marshal** [ME *erl marshal*, fr. *erl* earl + *marshal*] **1 :** a marshal of England who since 1194 has always been at least an earl in rank, who in medieval times was a principal military officer of the crown, but who in more recent times has been chiefly an attendant upon the sovereign at the opening and closing of Parliament arranging the order of state processions (as for coronations and royal marriages and funerals) and as head of the College of Arms appointing kings of arms, heralds, and pursuivants **2 :** a former marshal of Scotland or of Ireland when office was held by an earl — compare EARL MARISCHAL

earl marshal's court *n, usu cap E&M, often cap C* **:** the English court of chivalry since the time when it has been held before the earl marshal alone — called also *Marshal's court;* compare COURT OF THE CONSTABLE AND MARSHAL

earlobe \ˈ=,=\ *n* **1 :** the dependent part of the pinna of the ear of man or certain apes **2 :** a fleshy appendage below the ear of a fowl

earlock \ˈ=,=\ *n* **:** a lock or curl of hair hanging in front of the ear ⟨with ~s down to the collarbone —I.M.Lask⟩

earl of coventry *n, usu cap E&C* **:** SNIPSNAPSNORUM

earl palatine *n* **:** COUNT PALATINE 2

earl·ship \ˈərl,ship, ˈə̄l-, ˈəil-\ *n* **:** the rank or dignity of an earl

1ear·ly \ˈərlē, ˈə̄l-, ˈəil-\ *adv* -ER/-EST [ME *erly,* fr. OE *ǣrlīce,* fr. *ǣr* early, soon + *-līce* -ly — more at ERE] **1 a :** near the beginning of a period of time ⟨this great and salutary reaction began ~ in the present century —H.T.Buckle⟩ ⟨awoke ~ in the morning⟩ **b :** near the beginning of a course, process, or series ⟨is too ~ to guess the outcome⟩ ⟨~ in his senatorial career⟩ **c :** in a distant past time ⟨were men of education and business experience and their stamp on the village gave it a degree of culture that ~ eliminated many frontier crudities —*Amer. Guide Series: Minn.*⟩ ⟨~ discovered the use of fire⟩ **2 a :** before the expected or usual time ⟨retired from business quite ~ for a lawyer⟩ ⟨the train arrived ~⟩ **b** *archaic* **:** in the near future **:** SOON ⟨that from these may grow a hundredfold, who, having learnt thy way, ~ may fly the Babylonian woe —John Milton⟩ **c :** at a time sooner than related forms ⟨these apples bear ~ and heavy⟩

2early \"\ *adj* -ER/-EST [ME *erly,* fr. *erly,* adv.] **1 :** of, relating to, or occurring near the beginning of a period of time ⟨in the ~ Renaissance⟩ ⟨the ~ morning⟩ **b :** of, relating to, or occurring near the beginning of a development, movement, or series ⟨work on the thymus gland is still in an exceedingly ~ experimental stage —Morris Fishbein⟩ ⟨the ~ days of the West⟩ **c** (1) **:** distant in past time ⟨the ~ character of the state⟩ (2) **:** PRIMITIVE ⟨~ art forms⟩ ⟨~ tools found in recent excavations⟩ **2 a :** occurring before the expected or usual time ⟨taking an ~ walk before breakfast —W.F.De Morgan⟩ ⟨planned an ~ dinner before the concert⟩ ⟨an ~ death⟩ **b :** occurring in the near future ⟨other commitments making it impossible for him to schedule an ~ production of the play —*Current Biog.*⟩ ⟨hope for an ~ improvement in international relations⟩ **c :** maturing or producing sooner than related forms ⟨~ flowers and vegetables —Geoffrey Boumphrey⟩ ⟨an ~ sweet corn⟩

3early \"\ *n* -ES **:** one that arrives, produces, or is ready early; *esp* **:** a plant that matures its economic part (as flowers or fruit) more rapidly than the average

early ambulation *n* **:** a technique of postoperative care in which a patient gets out of bed and engages in light activity (as sitting, standing, or walking) as soon as possible after an operation

early american *adj, usu cap E&A* **1 :** built or produced during the colonial period in the American colonies — used chiefly of buildings, furniture, and domestic articles **2 :** of the type built, produced, or used in the American colonies

early bird *n* [so called fr. the proverb "the early bird catches the worm"] **1 :** an early riser **2 :** one that arrives beforehand esp. before possible competitors ⟨a bargain sale for *early birds*⟩

early bite *n, Brit* **:** pasturage adapted to or in condition for grazing early in the season

early blight *n* **:** any of several blights of plants in which symptoms appear early in the season: as **a :** a leaf spot esp. of the potato and tomato that is caused by a fungus (*Alternaria solani*) — compare LATE BLIGHT **b :** a leaf spot of celery caused by a fungus (*Cercospora apii*) — see CELERY BLIGHT

early coralroot *n* **:** a small parasitic orchid (*Corallorhiza trifida*) of the eastern U. S. having flowers with a 3-lobed lip

early-day \ˈ==ˌ=\ *adj* **:** of an earlier or former period ⟨the *early-day* settlers of New England⟩

early english style *or* **early english** *n, usu cap both E's* **:** the first of the pointed Gothic architectural styles used in England (as from 1180 to about 1250) — see ARCHITECTURE table

early foot *n* **:** a vigorous start (as in a race or contest) — used esp. of racehorses

early germ *n* **:** a cleaving zygote up to the completion of blastulation

early goldenrod *n* **:** a smooth early flowering No. American goldenrod (*Solidago juncea*) with oval lanceolate toothed leaves and yellow flower heads in branched clusters

early hawkweed *n* **:** RATTLESNAKE WEED 1

ear·ly·ish \ˈərlēish, ˈə̄l-, ˈəil-, -li·ish\ *adj* **:** somewhat early; *often* **:** early enough ⟨don't go; it's ~ yet⟩

early meadow parsnip *or* **early parsnip** *n* **:** GOLDEN MEADOW PARSNIP

early meadow rue *n* **:** a delicate No. American spring-flowering meadow rue (*Thalictrum dioicum*) with greenish to purple apetalous flowers

early on *adv* **1** *Brit* **:** at or during an early stage (as in a process) ⟨the reasons were obvious *early on* in the experiment⟩ **2** *Brit* **:** SOON ⟨he could see very *early on* that it would be impossible⟩

early saxifrage *n* **:** a small sticky white-flowered herb (*Saxifraga virginiensis*) common on rocky ledges in eastern No. America

early scorpion grass *n* **:** a small dry-land forget-me-not (*Myosotis virginica*) of eastern No. America with hairy foliage and white flowers

early wake-robin *n* **:** a low perennial white-flowered trillium (*Trillium nivale*) of the southeastern U. S.

early-warning radar *n* **:** a set or line of radar sets operating in air defense on the perimeter or outward from the defended area to give the earliest possible warning of approaching airplanes

early winter cress *also* **early cress** *n* **:** a biennial European weedy cress (*Barbarea verna*) that is naturalized widely in No. America, has pinnatifid leaves and deep yellow flowers, and is sometimes used for a salad plant or potherb

earlywood \ˈ===,=\ *n* **:** SPRINGWOOD

ear mange *n* **:** canker of the ear esp. in cats and dogs usu. caused by a rather large long-legged strictly parasitic ear mite (*Otodectes cynotes*)

1earmark \ˈ=,=\ *n* [ME *ere mark,* fr. *ere* ear + *mark* — more at 1EAR, MARK] **1 :** a mark of identification (as a cropping or slitting) on the ear esp. of a domestic animal **2 :** a distinguishing or a characteristic mark **:** an indicative sign ⟨all the ~s of poverty⟩ ⟨a book with the ~s of a doctoral dissertation⟩ — **under earmark :** EARMARKED ⟨gold *under earmark* for a foreign account⟩

common earmarks of cattle: *1* crop, *2* oversquare, *3* undersquare, *4* swallow fork, *5* steeple fork, *6* overslope, *7* underslope, *8* split, *9* underbit, overbit

2earmark \"\ *vt* **1 a :** to mark (as livestock) with an earmark **b :** to mark (something) in a distinguishing manner esp. as one's property ⟨dissipation ~s a man⟩ ⟨Satan ~s his own⟩ **2 a :** to designate or set aside (funds) for a specific use or owner ⟨the part of income that is ~ed for financing expansion⟩ ⟨a gift ~ed for a new dormitory⟩ — used esp. of gold held by one central bank for and as the property of another central bank or government **b :** to designate, hold, or recognize as the property of another ⟨the postmastership is traditionally ~ed for a leading politician⟩ ⟨goods ~ed for future delivery⟩

ear-minded \ˈ=;==\ *adj* **:** having one's mental imagery predominantly auditory **:** inclined to remember and think of things in terms of their sounds **:** AUDILE — compare EYE-MINDED

ear mite *n* **:** any of various mites attacking the ears of mammals — compare CANKER 7a

ear mold *n* **1 :** any of various fungi (as *Diplodia zeae*) that resemble molds and attack ears of grain; *esp* **:** fungus of the genus *Fusarium* that causes diseases of Indian corn **2 :** a disease caused by an ear mold

earmuff \ˈ=,=\ *n* **:** one of a pair of ear coverings connected by a strip of cloth, elastic band, or flexible metal strap and worn as protection against cold **2 :** EARFLAP

1earn \ˈərn, ˈə̄n, ˈəin\ *vb* -ED/-ING/-S [ME *ernen,* fr. OE *earnian;* akin to OHG *arnōn* to reap, ON *önn* working season, Goth *asans* harvest, OSlav *jesenĭ* autumn] *vt* **1 a :** to receive as equitable return for work done or services rendered **:** have accredited to one as remuneration **b :** to come to be duly worthy of or entitled to as remuneration for work or services ⟨he has ~ed his promotion, but we cannot give it to him now⟩ **c :** to bring in by way of return — used of income-producing property ⟨money in bonds may ~ less but it is more secure⟩ ⟨this block of stocks should ~ $5000 a year⟩ **2 a :** to come to be duly worthy of or entitled or suited to by way of reward, praise, penalty, or censure ⟨she had once ~ed a scolding from her nurse by filling her stockings with mud —G.B.Shaw⟩ ⟨his wasteful heedless ways ~ed him the name of a spendthrift⟩ **b :** to receive as ostensibly due by way of praise or blame **c :** to obtain (as a degree or a number of credits) at an educational institution by fulfilling the requirements and meeting definite standards **d :** to play in such a way as to score (as a point or run) in a sports contest; *esp* **:** to score (a run in baseball) without benefit of error by the opponent **~** *vi* **:** to obtain income by labor or as a return on capital ⟨so many students must now ~ in order to attend school⟩ ⟨stocks that do not ~ regularly are rarely a good investment⟩ **syn** see DESERVE

earmuff

2earn *vb* -ED/-ING/-S [prob. alter. of *yearn*] *obs* **:** to yearn or grieve

earn *abbr* earnings

earned income *n* [*earned* fr. past part. of 1*earn*] **:** income (as wages, salary, professional fees, or commissions) that results from the personal labor or services of an individual — compare UNEARNED INCOME

earned premium *n* **:** the pro rata share of a total insurance premium for the expired portion of a policy term

earned run average *n* **:** the average number of earned runs per game scored off a pitcher determined by dividing the total of earned runs scored against him by the total number of innings pitched and multiplying by nine

earned surplus *n* **:** the net accumulated balance of earnings of a corporation that remains after deducting losses, distributions to stockholders, and transfers to capital stock accounts and that includes appropriated surplus (as reserve for contingencies) as well as unappropriated surplus — called also *retained income*

earn·er \ˈərnə(r), ˈə̄nə(r, ˈəin-\ *n* -S **:** one that earns esp. money ⟨however trite they may be Westerns are among the motion-picture industry's best ~s⟩ — often used in combination ⟨wage *earners*⟩

1ear·nest \ˈərnəst, ˈə̄n-, ˈəin-\ *n* -S [ME *ernest,* fr. OE *eornost;* akin to OHG *ernust* seriousness, ON *ern* vigorous, Goth *arniba* safely and prob. to OE *rīsan* to rise — more at RISE] **1 :** a serious and intent mental state; *usu* **:** grave and intense attention, interest, or purpose **:** SERIOUSNESS — usu. used with *in* and often contrasted with *jest* ⟨and given in ~ what I begged in jest —Shak.⟩ ⟨are you sure you're in ~ about this⟩ **2** *archaic* **:** serious matter or expression

2earnest \"\ *adj* [ME *ernest,* fr. OE *eornoste,* fr. *eornost,* n.] **1 :** characterized by or proceeding from an intense and serious state of mind **:** not light, flippant, playful, or jesting ⟨~ attention⟩ ⟨an ~ plea⟩ **2 :** of a grave or important nature **:** not trivial ⟨life is real, life is ~ —H.W.Longfellow⟩ **syn** see SERIOUS

3earnest \"\ *adv, obs* **:** EARNESTLY

4earnest \"\ *n* -S [ME *ernest,* prob. by folk etymology (influence of ME *ernest* seriousness) fr. *ernes,* modif. of OF *erres,* pl. of *erre* earnest, fr. L *arra,* short for *arrabon-, arrabo,* fr. Gk *arrhabōn,* fr. Heb *ʽērābōn*] **1 :** something of value given by a buyer to a seller to bind a bargain — compare EARNEST MONEY, GOD'S PENNY **2 :** a token or installment of what is to come **:** PLEDGE ⟨the Resurrection which was an ~ of the coming redemption of the world —G.W.H.Lampe⟩ ⟨his whole expression was an ~ of his good intentions⟩ **syn** see PLEDGE

earnestful *adj* [ME *ernestful,* fr. *ernest,* n. + *-ful*] *obs* **:** EARNEST — **earnestfully** *adv, obs*

ear·nest·ly *adv* [ME *ernestly,* fr. OE *eornostlīce,* fr. *eornoste* earnest + *-līce* -ly — more at 2EARNEST] **:** in an earnest manner **:** with intent and serious mind **:** not lightly, casually, or flippantly

earnest money *n* [4*earnest*] **:** money paid as earnest

ear·nest·ness *n* -ES **:** intent and serious state or quality (as of mind) **:** ardor and firmness (as of purpose) ⟨he worked with great ~⟩ ⟨the unshakable ~ of their outlook⟩

earn·ful \ˈərnfəl\ *adj* [prob. alter. of *yearnful*] *now dial Eng* **:** YEARNING

earn·ing \ˈərniŋ, ˈə̄n-, ˈəin-, -nēŋ\ *n* -S [ME *erning* merit, fr. OE *earnung* merit, recompense, fr. *earnian* to earn + *-ung* -ing — more at 1EARN, -ING] **1 earnings** *pl* **a :** something (as wages or dividends) earned as compensation for labor or the use of capital ⟨his ~s never amounted to more than $2000 a year⟩ ⟨corporation ~s are up⟩ **b :** the balance of revenue for a specific period that remains after deducting related costs and expenses incurred — compare PROFIT **2 :** the act or process of acquiring (as a reward or honor) or of fitting oneself to receive (as a commendation or rebuke) ⟨the ~ of his high position was not easy⟩ ⟨he seemed to set himself doggedly to the ~ of his degree⟩

earning asset *n* [*earning* fr. pres. part. of 1*earn*] **:** an asset (as a loan or security) of a bank on which interest is received — usu. used in pl.

earning power *n* [*earning* fr. gerund of 1*earn*] **:** the relative ability of an individual or an organization to command earnings in return for services or goods ⟨a corporation with good *earning power*⟩ ⟨the general rise in all *earning power* has tended to divorce the worker from the specific job by minimizing the importance of wage differentials —*Management Rev.*⟩

earns *pres 3d sing of* EARN

ea·rock \ˈē,räk, ˈērək\ *n* -S [ScGael *eireag* & IrGael *eireog*] *Scot & Irish* **:** PULLET

earphone \ˈ=,=\ *n* -S **:** any device that converts electrical energy into sound waves and is worn over or inserted into the auditory opening

earpick \ˈ=,=\ *n* [ME *erepik,* fr. *ere* ear + *pik* pick — more at 1EAR, PICK] **:** a device often of precious metal for removing wax or foreign bodies from the ear

earpiece \ˈ=,=\ *n* **1 :** a piece (as of a helmet or cap) intended to cover and protect the ear **2 :** a part of an instrument (as a stethoscope or hearing aid) to which the ear is applied; *esp* **:** EARPHONE **3 :** one of the two sidepieces that support eyeglasses by passing over or behind the ears

ear piercer *n* [1*ear*] **:** one that pierces the ear

ear-piercing \ˈ=;==\ *adj* **:** shrill and irritating to the ear ⟨an *ear-piercing* shriek⟩

earplug \ˈ=,=\ *n* **1 :** an ornament often of spool shape inserted in the lobe of the ear esp. to distend it **2 :** a device of pliable material for insertion into the outer opening of the ear (as for protection against water or to deaden sound)

1earring \ˈi(,)riŋ, ˈirēŋ, ˈir,riŋ\ *n* -S [ME *erering,* fr. OE *ēarhring,* fr. *ēar-* (fr. *ēare* ear) + *hring* ring — more at 1EAR, RING] **:** an ear ornament with or without a pendant attached to a pierced earlobe by a loop of wire or to an unpierced earlobe by a screw or a clip

earrings: *1* for pierced ears, *2* screw type, *3* clip type

2earring *var of* EARING

earringed \-ŋd\ *adj* [1*earring* + *-ed*] **:** wearing earrings

ear rot *n* **:** a condition marked by decay or molding of ears of Indian corn and caused usu. by fungi of the genera *Diplodia, Fusarium,* or *Gibberella*

ears *pl of* EAR, *pres 3d sing of* EAR

earscrew \ˈ=,=\ *n* **:** an earring with a screw fastener

ear shell *n* [so called fr. the shape] **:** ABALONE

earshot *also* **earreach** \ˈ=,=\ *n* **:** the range within which the unaided voice may be heard

ear snail *or* **ear shell** *n* [so called fr. the shape] **:** any gastropod mollusk of the family Ellobiidae

earsplitting \ˈ=,==\ *adj* **:** distressingly or intolerably loud or shrill **:** DEAFENING ⟨the ice let go with an ~ roar⟩ **syn** see LOUD

earspool \ˈ=,=\ *n* **:** a spool-shaped earplug worn buttoned through a hole in the earlobe esp. by the ancient Hopewell and Copena people

ear stone *n* [1*ear*] **:** OTOLITH

eartab \ˈ=,=\ *n* [1*ear*] **:** EARFLAP 2

ear tag *n* [1*ear* + *tag*] **:** a metal identification tag attached to the ear of an animal

ear-tag \ˈ=,=\ *vt* [*ear tag*] **:** to mark (an animal) for future identification with an ear tag

1earth \ˈərth, ˈə̄th, ˈəith\ *n* -S *often attrib* [ME *erthe,* fr. OE *eorthe;* akin to OHG *erda* earth, ON *jörth,* Goth *airtha,* OHG *ero* earth, Gk *eraze* to earth, W *erw* acre] **1 a :** the fragmental material composing part of the surface of the globe **:** SOIL, GROUND ⟨give him a little ~ for charity —Shak.⟩ — usu. distinguished from *bedrock* **b :** soil for cultivating ⟨good ~ in a sheltered valley⟩ ⟨a clayey ~ difficult to drain⟩ **c :** one of the four elements of the alchemists **2 :** the sphere of mortal life comprising the world with its lands and seas as distinguished from spheres of spirit life — compare HEAVEN, HELL **3 a :** areas of land uncovered by water **b :** the solid footing formed of earth ⟨good to feel the ~ under his feet again⟩ **c :** the solid materials that make up the physical globe **4** *archaic* **:** a particular region of the world **:** COUNTRY, LAND ⟨would I had never trod this English ~ —Shak.⟩ **5** *often cap* **:** the planet upon which we live and which being about 93 million miles from the sun is the third in order of distance from the sun and which having a diameter at the equator of 7927 miles is the fifth in size among the planets **6 a :** the people of the planet earth **b :** the mortal body of man — distinguished from *soul, spirit* **c :** the pursuits, interests, and allurements of earthly life **:** worldly as distinguished from spiritual concerns **7 :** the burrow of a burrowing animal **8 a :** a difficultly reducible metallic oxide (as alumina, zirconium oxide, yttrium oxide) formerly classed as an element — see ALKALINE EARTH, RARE EARTH **b :** EARTH COLOR ⟨red ~⟩ **c :** a clay or substance resembling clay used chiefly as an adsorbent ⟨active ~s⟩ — see BLEACHING CLAY, FULLER'S EARTH **9** *chiefly Brit* **:** GROUND 7 — **on earth :** among numberless possibilities **:** EVER — used as an intensive ⟨where *on earth* can he be?⟩ ⟨I can't imagine who *on earth* would do such a thing⟩ ⟨what *on earth* shall we do?⟩

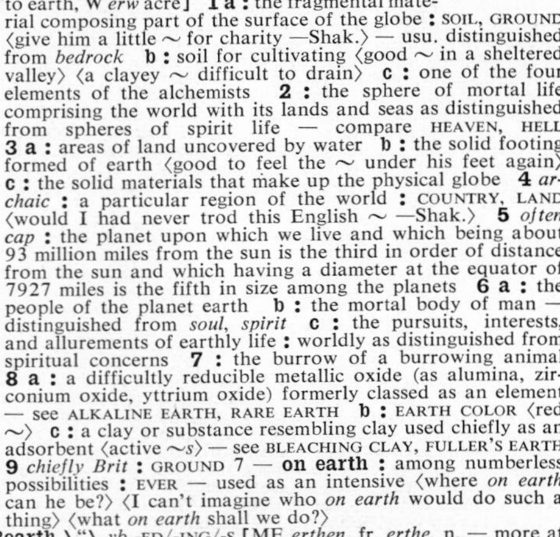

ear snail

2earth \"\ *vb* -ED/-ING/-S [ME *erthen,* fr. *erthe,* n. — more at 1EARTH] *vt* **1** *now dial Brit* **:** BURY, INTER **2 :** to hide (as oneself) or cause to hide (as an animal) in the earth or in a burrow or den **3 :** to draw soil about (plants) **:** cultivate so as to throw soil toward (as a row crop) **:** BANK, RIDGE — often used with *up* ⟨potatoes should be ~ed up before blooming⟩ ⟨soil should be kept out of the heart when ~*ing* celery⟩ **4** *chiefly Brit* **:** GROUND *vt* 6 **~** *vi* **:** to hide in the ground (as in an earth or den) **:** go to ground — used esp. of a hunted animal

3earth \", ˈi(ə)rth, ˈiəth\ *n* -S [ME *erth, erthe,* fr. OE *earth, yrth,* fr. *erian* to plow — more at 2EAR] *now dial Brit* **:** an act of plowing **:** a stirring or tilling of soil in preparation for planting

earth almond *n* **:** CHUFA

earth apple *n* **1 :** POTATO **2 :** JERUSALEM ARTICHOKE

earth-ball \ˈ=,=\ *n* **:** any of certain usu. tuberous subterranean fruiting bodies of fungi (as a truffle or the hard-skinned fruit of members of the family Sclerodermataceae)

earthborn \ˈ=,=\ *adj* **1 :** coming into life by emergence from the ground — used chiefly of certain mythological persons ⟨the ~ sons of the dragon's teeth⟩ **2 :** born on this earth **:** of mortal race **:** HUMAN — compare ANGELIC, IMMORTAL **3 :** associated with earthly life or occasioned by earthly objects ⟨~ cares and sorrows⟩; *broadly* **:** arising from or typical of earth ⟨~ storms⟩

1earthbound \ˈ=,=\ *adj* [1*earth* + *bound* (fastened)] **1 a :** fast in or to the soil ⟨~ roots⟩ **b :** restricted to land or to the surface of earth ⟨armies are no longer ~⟩ **c :** restricted to the planet Earth ⟨man is still an ~ creature⟩ **2 :** lacking in freedom (as of expression) or in imagination ⟨a competent but ~ performance⟩; *sometimes* **:** EARTHY, HOMELY ⟨~ peasant speech⟩ **3 :** bound by earthly interests **:** lacking in spiritual quality ⟨an ~ outlook⟩ ⟨the ~ soul of man⟩

2earthbound \"\ *adj* [1*earth* + *bound* (going)] **:** on the way to or toward earth ⟨an ~ meteor⟩ ⟨~ cosmic rays⟩

earth bread *n* **:** MANNA LICHEN 1; *often* **:** a food prepared from one of these lichens (esp. *Lecanora esculenta*)

earthbred \ˈ=,=\ *adj* **1 :** bred in or on the earth **2 :** lacking in elevated or spiritual quality; *often* **:** EARTHY, LOW, VULGAR

earth closet *n, chiefly Brit* **:** a privy in which earth is used as a covering or as an absorbing or deodorizing agent

earth club *n* [1*earth* + *club* (staff)] **:** SQUAWROOT 1

earth coal *n, obs* **:** COAL 3a — distinguished from *charcoal*

earth color *n* **:** a colored mineral (as an ocher) used as a pigment

earth current *n* **:** an electric current flowing through the ground that is set up by either natural or man-made differences of potential — called also *ground current*

earth eating *n* **:** GEOPHAGY

earth·en \ˈərth|ən, ˈə̄th|, ˈəith|, -t͟h|\ *also* **earth·ern** \|ə(r)n\ *adj* [*earthen* fr. ME *erthen,* fr. *erthe* earth + *-en; earthern* alter. of *earthen* — more at 1EARTH] **1 a :** made of earth ⟨an ~ dam⟩ ⟨~ walls rammed firm⟩ **b :** made of fired clay ⟨glazed ~ tiles⟩ ⟨an ~ jug⟩ **2 :** characteristic of earth esp. in human or mortal quality **:** EARTHLY

earthenware \ˈ==,=\ *n, often attrib* **:** vessels and other utensils or ornaments made of low-fired clay that is slightly porous, opaque, and lacking sonority and commonly covered with a nonporous glaze — compare CHINA, PORCELAIN

earthfall \ˈ=,=\ *n* **:** LANDSLIDE

earthfast \ˈ=,=\ *adj* **:** EARTHBOUND

earth flax *n* **:** AMIANTHUS

earthflow \ˈ=,=\ *n* **:** a landslide consisting of unconsolidated surface material that moves down a slope when saturated with water — compare MUDFLOW

earth foam *n* [trans. of F *écume de terre*] **:** soft or earthy aphrite

earth god *n* **:** a deity concerned with vegetation and fertility and usu. with the underworld

earth goddess *n* **:** a goddess concerned with vegetation and fertility and usu. with the underworld

earth hog *n* [trans. of obs. Afrik *aardvark*] **:** AARDVARK

earth house *n* [ME *erthehous,* fr. OE *eorthhūs,* fr. *eorth-* (fr. *eorthe* earth) + *hūs* house] **:** a dwelling built into or covered with earth: as **a :** PICTS' HOUSE **b :** EARTH LODGE

earth hunger *n* **:** a desire or craving to possess or control land

earth·ian \-thēən, -t͟h-\ *n* -S **:** an inhabitant of the earth

earthier *comparative of* EARTHY

earthiest *superlative of* EARTHY

earth·i·ly \-thəlē, -li *sometimes* -t͟h-\ *adv* **:** in an earthy manner

earth inductor *n* **1 :** an inclinometer (sense 1) whose indications depend on the current generated in a coil revolving in the earth's magnetic field **2** *or* **earth inductor compass** **:** INDUCTION COMPASS

earth·i·ness \-thēnəs, -thin- *sometimes* -t͟h-\ *n* -ES [ME *erthynesse*, fr. *erthy* earthy + *-nesse* -ness] **:** the quality or state of being earthy: as **a :** a realistic or matter-of-fact or human quality (as of a literary or dramatic production) **b :** an anomalous or off flavor (as of wines or certain foods) suggestive of soil

earthing *pres part of* EARTH

earth lichen *n* **:** a lichen growing in soil; *esp* **:** any of various ascolichens (genus *Baeomyces*) with fruiting bodies filled with cottony hairs or nearly solid

earthlight *var of* EARTHSHINE

earthlike \ˈ⸗,⸗\ *adj* **:** resembling earth or something earthly ⟨an ~ atmosphere⟩ ⟨drab ~ coloring⟩

earth·li·ness \-thlēnəs, -lin-\ *n* -ES **:** the quality or state of being earthly ⟨the deep original materialism or ~ of human nature itself —Walter Pater⟩

earth·ling \-thliŋ, -lēŋ\ *n* -s **1 :** an inhabitant of the earth; *esp* **:** a mortal human **2 :** a worldly-minded person **:** WORLDLING

earth–lit \ˈ⸗,⸗\ *adj* **:** illuminated by earthshine

earth lodge *n* **:** a dwelling (as a hogan) constructed of earth or sod, often supported on a wooden frame, and often placed partially below the surface of the ground

earth louse *n* [trans. of L *pediculus terrae*] **:** any of numerous aphids that feed on the roots of plants

earth·ly \-thlē, -li\ *adj* [ME *erthely, erthly*, fr. OE *eorthlīc*, fr. *eorth-* (fr. *eorthe* earth) + *-līc* -ly] **1 a :** characteristic of or belonging to this earth — often distinguished from *heavenly* ⟨no ~ sovereign can do what he pleases —M.R. Cohen⟩ ⟨there could be a new order based on vital harmony and the ~ millenium might approach —E.M.Forster⟩ **b :** relating to man's actual life on this earth **:** REALISTIC, FACTUAL, WORLDLY **:** not ideal, spiritual, or utopian **2** *archaic* **:** EARTHEN **3 :** existing, living, or occurring on or in the ground ⟨airplane travel would have remained a merely minor quantitative improvement over ~ locomotion —Maya Deren⟩ **4 :** conceivable according to actualities and facts **:** POSSIBLE ⟨there is no ~ doubt that men degenerate —J.B.Cabell⟩ ⟨not an ~ chance to win⟩

syn TERRESTRIAL, TERRENE, EARTHY, MUNDANE, WORLDLY, SUBLUNARY: EARTHLY is generally an opposite for *heavenly* or *spiritual* ⟨the high gods, who dwell remote from the fret and fever of this *earthly* life —J.G.Frazer⟩ ⟨we felt that the holy calm that lay like sunshine over the wasted face and form was only an *earthly* token and symbol of the calm that was to reign forever —Bram Stoker⟩ TERRESTRIAL, sometimes a sonorous or scientific close synonym for EARTHLY, is often an opposite for *celestial*. It may be used to designate land in contrast to water or air or to indicate planets nearer the sun in contrast to those more distant ⟨it was probably not the first time that struggles for *terrestrial* power were carried on in terms of celestial ideology; it certainly has not been the last —L.A.White⟩ ⟨strictly *terrestrial*, being from the nature of its claws unable to climb trees —James Stevenson-Hamilton⟩ TERRENE is an uncommon synonym for EARTHLY and for TERRESTRIAL in general nonscientific applications ⟨and so the empyrean element, lying smothered under the *terrene*, and yet inextinguishable there, made sad writings —Thomas Carlyle⟩ ⟨all that was mixed and reconciled in Thee . . . of high with low, celestial with *terrene* —William Wordsworth⟩ EARTHY differs from EARTHLY in centering attention on the soil or ground of the earth rather than on the earth as a planet or as the habitat of mankind; it may imply grossness, crudeness, concern with material things, and lack of anything exalted ⟨he smelled the *earthy* fragrance rising up out of the furrows —Pearl Buck⟩ ⟨these native passion plays are more *earthy* than religious, are enlivened with a good many broadly comic touches —Green Peyton⟩ ⟨with much *earthy* dross in her, she was yet preeminently a creature of "fire and air" —John Buchan⟩ MUNDANE is opposed to *spiritual, lofty, exalted*, or *elevated;* it centers attention on practical affairs and concerns, immediate objectives, base or basic needs and pleasures, and occas. routine or humdrum activity ⟨she did not allow them to talk of *mundane* affairs on these expeditions to and from church —Archibald Marshall⟩ ⟨the real meaning of the play is evidently the triumph of the spiritual over the *mundane* —Grenville Vernon⟩ ⟨such *mundane* activities as washing dishes or driving an automobile —Ralph Linton⟩ WORLDLY may suggest indifference to and obliviousness about matters spiritual and attention to success, pleasure, sophistication, and gain ⟨the obvious thing to say of her was that she was *worldly;* cared too much for rank and society and getting on in the world—which was true in a sense —Virginia Woolf⟩ ⟨our medieval universities were founded not for laymen but for monks and clerics whose business was primarily not with *worldly* affairs but with the eternal hereafter —M.R.Cohen⟩ SUBLUNARY is a rather literary synonym for TERRESTRIAL or, sometimes, for EARTHLY ⟨the quakes and *sublunary* conflicts of this negligible earth —L.P.Smith⟩ ⟨the contrast between the transcendental, immutable, and eternal heavens, the home of the blest, on the one hand, and the *sublunary* sphere of the earth, the scene of birth, change, decay, and death on the other —G.C.Sellery⟩

earthly–minded \ˈ⸗⸗ˈ⸗⸗\ *adj, archaic* **:** WORLDLY-MINDED

earth·man \-th,man, -ˌmən\ *n, pl* **earthmen :** a human native or resident of the planet Earth

earth metal *n* **:** a metal whose oxide is classed as an earth

earth mother *n, often cap E&M* **:** the earth viewed (as in primitive theology) as the divine source of terrestrial life **:** the female principle of fertility

earth movement *n* **:** differential movement of the earth's crust **:** elevation or subsidence of the land **:** DIASTROPHISM, FAULTING, FOLDING

earthmover \ˈ⸗,⸗⸗\ *n* **:** a machine (as a bulldozer or power shovel) for excavating, pushing, or transporting large quantities of earth (as in road building)

earthnut \ˈ⸗,⸗\ *n* [ME *erthenote*, fr. OE *eorthnutu*, fr. *eorth-* (fr. *eorthe* earth) + *nutu, hnutu* nut — more at NUT] **1 :** any of various roots, tubers, or subterranean pods: as **a :** the tuber of a common southern European plant (*Conopodium denudatum*) of the family Umbelliferae having the flavor of roasted chestnuts **b :** CHUFA **c :** PEANUT **d** *also* **earthnut pea :** the root of the heath pea **2 :** any plant producing earthnuts **3 :** TRUFFLE

earthnut oil *n* **:** PEANUT OIL

earth oil *n, archaic* **:** PETROLEUM

earth people *n, usu cap E&P* **:** the living humans and the witches and ghosts who according to Navaho religion inhabit the profane world — called also *Earth Surface People;* contrasted with *Holy People*

earth physics *n pl but sing or pl in constr* **:** GEOPHYSICS

earth pig *n* [trans. of obs. Afrik *aardvark*] **:** AARDVARK

earth pillar *also* **earth pyramid** *n* **:** a column of unconsolidated earth materials that is formed by differential erosion and that typically tapers upward and is often capped by a stone — called also *demoiselle*

earth pitch *n* [trans. of G *erdpech*] **:** MALTHA 2a

earth plate *n* **:** GROUND PLATE 2

earth plum *n* **1 :** any of several leguminous plants (genera *Astragalus* and *Geoprumnon*) of the southwestern U. S. and adjacent Mexico with pods which suggest plums and are edible when unripe **2 :** the pod of an earth plum

earth quadrant *n* **:** a fourth of the earth's circumference

earthquake \ˈ⸗,⸗\ *n, often attrib* [ME *erthequake*, fr. *erthe* earth + *quake*] **:** a shaking or trembling of the earth that accompanies mountain building or other crustal movements including those caused by deposition of heavy loads of sediment on the sea bottom; that usu. has an actual double amplitude of vibration of less than one millimeter, though a range of 76 millimeters is on record and the amplitude is commonly increased in unconsolidated surface material; and that is divisible into the two major classes volcanic and tectonic according to the major precipitating factor — see AFTERSHOCK, FOCUS 7, FORESHOCK

earth·quaked \-kt\ *or* **earth·quak·en** \-kən\ *adj* [*earthquaked* fr. *earthquake* + *-ed; earthquaken* fr. *earthquake* + *-en* (as in *shaken*)] **:** shaken by earthquakes **:** subject to earthquakes

earthquake insurance *n* **:** insurance against loss resulting from damage to buildings and their contents by earthquake, volcanic eruption, or both

earthquake–proof \ˌ⸗⸗ˈ⸗\ *adj* **:** designed to withstand the shattering effect of an earthquake ⟨an *earthquake-proof* building⟩

earthquake sea wave *n* **:** TSUNAMI

earthquake wave *n* **:** a seismic wave

earthquaking \ˈ⸗,⸗⸗\ *adj* [partly fr. ¹*earth* + *quaking*, pres. part. of *quake;* partly fr. *earthquake* + *-ing*] **1 :** causing the earth to shake ⟨an ~ roar⟩ **2 :** EARTHQUAKED

earthquaky \ˈ⸗,⸗⸗\ *adj* [*earthquake* + *-y*] **:** suggesting the effects or the characteristic movement of an earthquake

earths *pl of* EARTH, *pres 3d sing of* EARTH

earth science *n* **1 :** a science (as geology, geography, geophysics, geomorphology, geochemistry, meteorology, or oceanography) that deals with the earth or with one or more of its parts — often used in pl. **2 :** any one of the earth sciences

earthshaker \ˈ⸗,⸗⸗\ *n* **:** something outstanding in merit, importance, or stature

earthshaking \ˈ⸗,⸗⸗\ *adj* **:** of fundamental importance ⟨~ proposals⟩

earthshine *or* **earthlight** \ˈ⸗,⸗\ *n* **:** sunlight reflected by the earth that faintly illuminates the dark part of the moon and is best seen during the moon's crescent phases

earthshock \ˈ⸗,⸗\ *n* **:** an earthquake esp. when sharply localized ⟨the ~ following a heavy explosion⟩

earth–smoke \ˈ⸗,⸗\ *n* [trans. of ML *fumus terrae*] **:** FUMITORY

earth sounds *n pl* **:** audible deep-pitched vibrations accompanying an earthquake that are prob. caused by the transmission of earth vibrations to the air

earth spirit *n* [prob. trans. of G *erdgeist*] **1 :** the earth personified either poetically or as a deity supposed to live in or under the earth **2 :** a humanoid long-lived or immortal entity (as a gnome)

earthstar \ˈ⸗,⸗\ *n* **:** a fungus of the genus *Geastrum* in form suggesting a puffball with a double peridium the outer layer of which splits into the shape of a star and the inner one forms a ball containing the dustlike spores

earth stopper *n* **:** one that stops up fox holes prior to a hunt

earth surface people *n, usu cap E&S&P* **:** EARTH PEOPLE

earth table *n* **:** the course of stones in a building next above the ground — called also *ground table*

earth tide *n* **:** a periodic alteration in the conformation of the earth's crust caused by the same forces that produce ocean tides

earth tilting *n* **:** a change in attitude of any portion of the earth's surface whether temporary or undulatory (as in some earthquakes) or permanent (as in areas of block faulting); *esp* **:** one in which the inclination of the surface is increased

earthtongue \ˈ⸗,⸗\ *n* [trans. of NL *Geoglossum*] **:** any fungus of a genus *Geoglossum* having ascomata that resemble the sporophores of the simpler club fungi and grow on decaying logs or damp soil

earth tremor *n* **:** an earthquake esp. of low or moderate intensity

earth·ward \ˈ⸗wə(r)d\ *or* **earth·wards** \-dz\ *adv* [ME *ertheward*, fr. *erthe* earth + *-ward*] **:** toward the earth

earth wave *n* **1 a :** an elastic vibration of the material of the earth **b :** a visible undulation of alluvial or unconsolidated material at the surface of the earth that has been reported to occur in severe earthquakes **2 :** an immobile undulation on the earth's surface

earth wax *n* [trans. of G *erdwachs*] **:** OZOKERITE

earth wire *n* **:** GROUND WIRE 1

earth wolf *n* [trans. of Afrik *aardwolf*] **:** AARDWOLF

earthwork \ˈ⸗,⸗\ *n* **1 :** a field fortification made chiefly of earth **2 a :** the operations connected with excavations and embankments of earth (as in preparing foundations of buildings or in constructing canals, railroads) **b :** an embankment or other construction made of earth

earthworm \ˈ⸗,⸗\ *n* [ME *ertheworm*, fr. *erthe* earth + *worm*] **1 :** any terrestrial annelid worm of the class Oligochaeta; *esp* **:** any of numerous widely distributed tapering segmented hermaphroditic worms that constitute the family Lumbricidae and that lack true appendages but move through the soil by means of setae, feed on decaying organic matter, and are an important factor in loosening and aerating the upper layers of soil in which they dwell — called also *angleworm* **2** *archaic* **:** a mean sordid person **:** WORM

earthy \ˈərthē, ˈōth-,ˈəith-, -thi *sometimes* -t͟h-\ *adj* -ER/-EST [ME *erthy*, fr. *erthe* earth + *-y*] **1 :** consisting of or resembling earth **:** having a property or properties characteristic of soil: as **a :** suggesting or resembling earth in a manner directly perceptible by the senses ⟨a stale ~ smell⟩ ⟨wine with an ~ flavor⟩ ⟨clad in dull ~ hues⟩ **b** *of a mineral* **:** without luster or dull and roughish to the touch **c :** containing earthlike impurities **2 a** *archaic* **:** of or relating to the earth **:** TERRESTRIAL; *esp* **:** WORLDLY — distinguished from *spiritual, heavenly* **b :** characteristic of or associated with mortal life on the earth **:** not predominantly spiritual, ideal, or ethereal ⟨a vigorous ~ woman⟩ **3 :** characterized by realistic material attitudes ranging from the matter-of-fact and practical to the unrefined, gross, and low ⟨my anger and disgust at his gross ~ egoism —W.H.Hudson †1922⟩ **4 :** having a cold and dry complexion **:** predominating in the elements earth and water — used with reference to phenomena and bodies as understood by the old natural philosophers and of signs of the zodiac; compare HUMOR **5 :** relating to an earth oxide

syn see EARTHLY

earthy cobalt *n* **:** ASBOLITE

ear tick *n* **:** any of several ticks infesting the ears of mammals, including man; *esp* **:** SPINOSE EAR TICK

ear tree *n* [prob. trans. of Nahuatl *cuauhnacaztli*] **:** CONACASTE

ear trumpet *n* **:** a trumpet-shaped instrument used for collecting and intensifying sounds to aid a person with defective hearing

ear tuft *n* **:** EAR 4b(2)

ear wagon *n* **:** a wagon having a bangboard

ear warden *n* [¹*ear*] **:** EARPLUG

earwax \ˈ⸗,⸗\ *n* [ME *erewax*, fr. *ere* ear + *wax* — more at ¹EAR] **:** CERUMEN

¹**ear·wig** \ˈi(ə)r,wig, ˈiə,-\ *n* -s [ME *erwigge*, fr. OE *ēarwicga*, fr. *ēar-* (fr. *eare* ear) + *wicga* insect; prob. fr. a belief that the insect creeps into the human ear — more at ¹EAR, VETCH] **1 a :** any of numerous insects of the order Dermaptera having slender many-jointed antennae, a pair of large forceps at the end of the body the use of which is unknown, the fore wings when wings are present modified into elytra, and nymphs that are very similar to the adults **b :** any of various small centipedes (as those of the genus *Geophilus*) **2 a** *archaic* **:** a whispering busybody **:** TOADY, FLATTERER **b :** EAVESDROPPER

²**earwig** \"\ *vt* **earwigged; earwigged; earwigging; earwigs :** to annoy or attempt to influence by private talk

ear·wig·gy \-wigē\ *adj* [¹*earwig* + *-y*] **:** full of earwigs ⟨an ~ hostelry on the outskirts of the town —W.J.Locke⟩

earwitness \ˈ⸗,⸗⸗\ *n* **:** a person who does or can testify to something heard by himself

earworm \ˈ⸗,⸗\ *n* **:** any of certain larval insects (as the corn earworm) that feed in the developing maize ear

eas *pl of* EA

¹**ease** \ˈēz\ *n* -s [ME *ese*, fr. OF *aise* comfort, opportunity, fr. L *adjacent-, adjacens* neighboring place, fr. *adjacent-, adjacens*, pres. part. of *adjacēre* to lie near — more at ADJACENT] **1 :** the state of being comfortable: as **a :** freedom from pain or discomfort ⟨with all the ~ of wearing an old, comfortable . . . dressing gown —H.V.Gregory⟩ ⟨a special seat mounting for ~ in riding —*Motor Transportation in the West*⟩ **b :** freedom from care or worry **:** TRANQUILLITY, SECURITY ⟨~ of mind⟩ ⟨there is ~ in the family and in the village —Abram Kardiner⟩ **c :** freedom from labor, effort, inconvenience, or burden **:** RELAXATION ⟨shallow waters where she could swim with ~ —Agnes Repplier⟩ ⟨she took her ~ on Sunday⟩ **d :** freedom from embarrassment, constraint, or formality **:** NATURALNESS ⟨he experiences ~ among his friends⟩ ⟨with an ~ of manner sportsmen are apt to have —A.W.Long⟩ **2 :** relief from or mitigation of discomfort, pain, constraint, or obligation ⟨the medicine brought almost instant ~⟩ ⟨there seemed to him to be no ~ from the burdens of life⟩ **3 :** FACILITY, EFFORTLESSNESS ⟨she rides a horse with ~⟩; *esp* **:** stylistic smoothness in literary or artistic expression ⟨the ~ and polish of the best 18th century English prose⟩ **4 a :** EASEMENT 3 **b :** an allowance of fullness that is usu. placed across the back shoulders, over the bust, and about the hips in a garment to permit free motion of the body **5 :** an act of easing (as of a restriction) or state of being eased (as of a market) ⟨credit ~ tends to promote buying⟩; *esp* **:** a lowering trend in prices ⟨the grain market showed considerable ~ last week⟩ — **at ease 1 :** free from pain or discomfort ⟨after the doctor's visit, the patient felt more *at ease*⟩ **2 a** *or* **at one's ease :** free from restraint or formality **:** RELAXED ⟨the quiet and the solitude of the place put the visitor *at his ease*⟩ **b** (1) *of a man in military ranks* **:** standing silently with the right foot in place — often used as a command to assume this position (2) *of a man marching* **:** silent but relaxed from attention and free to break step — often used as a command to proceed in this manner **3** *or* **at one's ease :** as and when one wishes ⟨he was allowed to complete the task *at his ease*⟩ **syn** see REST

²**ease** \"\ *vb* **eased; eased; easing; eases** [ME *esen*, fr. OF *aaisier* & *aisier;* OF *aaisier* fr. *a-* (fr. L *ad-*) + *aisier*, fr. *aise*, n.] *vt* **1 a :** to free from something that pains, disquiets, or burdens **:** relieve esp. from toil or care ⟨*eased* and comforted the sick⟩ — usu. used with *of* ⟨let him ~ you of your troubles⟩ **b** *obs* **:** to provide with food and lodging **:** ENTERTAIN **c :** to take something away from easily **:** ROB ⟨a pickpocket slipped up and *eased* him of his purse⟩ **2 :** to take away **:** LESSEN, ALLEVIATE ⟨took an aspirin to ~ the pain⟩ ⟨we cannot ~ taxes while every special interest demands more money⟩ **3 a :** to lessen the pressure or tension of (as by slackening, lifting, or shifting) ⟨~ the spring gently⟩ **:** adjust by gradual movements so as to relieve strain or avoid injury or damage ⟨*easing* himself into his chair⟩ **:** maneuver gently or carefully ⟨they *eased* the heavy block into position⟩ — often used with a directional word ⟨~ in that line⟩ ⟨~ your clutch in slowly⟩ ⟨he *eased* the bolt in carefully⟩ **b :** to moderate or reduce esp. in amount, intensity, or rate of performance ⟨*easing* the flow from the faucet until he could hear what she said⟩ **:** make more gentle, gradual, or slow ⟨*eased* his climb with a brief rest by the side of the path⟩; *often* **:** to cause to slow down or stop ⟨~ the car down to 20 miles an hour on this curve⟩ **c :** to adjust (fullness in a garment) by pulling, gathering, or pleating so that a longer and a shorter part join smoothly; *broadly* **:** to provide (a garment) with requisite ease **4 :** to make less difficult **:** FACILITATE **5 a :** to bring (a ship) into position to meet a wave bow on (as by putting the helm alee or by regulating the sails) **b :** to let (a helm or rudder) come back a little after having been put hard over ~ *vi* **1 :** to give freedom or relief (as from pain or discomfort) **:** lessen pain or oppressiveness ⟨a hot bath often ~*s* and relaxes⟩ **2 :** to move or pass with freedom from abruptness or awkwardness or with little resistance — sometimes used with a directional word (as *along, over*) **3 :** MODERATE, SLACKEN, DIMINISH; *also* **:** STOP, DESIST — now usu. used with an expletive (as *off, up*)

eased–up \ˈ⸗ˈ⸗\ *adj* **1 :** relieved from strain or tension **:** RELAXED ⟨she looked comfortable and *eased-up*⟩ **2** *of a racehorse* **:** not running all out

ease·ful \ˈēzfəl\ *adj* [ME (Sc) *esful*, fr. ME *es, ese* ease + *-ful* — more at ¹EASE] **1 :** suitable for affording ease or rest **:** RESTFUL ⟨a quiet ~ corner⟩ ⟨~ plenty⟩ **2 :** characterized by or full of ease ⟨a poised ~ manner⟩ ⟨a placid ~ life⟩ — **ease·fully** \-fəlē\ *adv*

ea·sel \ˈēzəl\ *n* -s *often attrib* [D *ezel* ass, donkey, fr. MD *esel;* akin to OE *esol* ass, OS & OHG *esil*, Goth *asilus;* all fr. a prehistoric Gmc word borrowed with modification fr. L *asinus* ass — more at ASS] **:** a frame for supporting something at a desired angle: as **a :** a wooden, metal, or plastic frame to hold a canvas upright or inclined at a proper level for the painter's convenience in working **b :** a display frame for advantageous exhibition (as of a painting, a piece of china, or a poster) **c :** a frame for holding photographic paper flat in enlarging or copying **d :** the sheet of plain glass on which the constituent pieces of a work of stained glass are first assembled

easel a

easelback \ˈ⸗⸗,⸗\ *n* **:** a back by which a flat object (as a framed picture) may be made to stand upright or suitably inclined usu. by means of a tab or prop made fast with the back above and pulled out at an angle below — **easel–backed** \ˌ⸗⸗ˈ⸗\ *adj*

ea·seled \ˈēzəld\ *adj* **:** mounted on an easel

ease·less \ˈēzləs\ *adj, archaic* **:** subject to no relief or rest **:** UNCEASING

easel painting *n* **1** *or* **easel picture :** a painting of a size and on a material suitable for framing — often distinguished from *mural* **2 :** the practice of painting easel paintings

ease·ment \ˈēzmənt\ *n* -s [ME *esement*, fr. MF *aaisement* & *aisement;* MF *aaisement* fr. *aaise-* (fr. *aaisier*) + *-ment;* MF *aisement* fr. *aise-* (fr. *aisier*) + *-ment*] **1 :** an act or means of easing or relieving (as from pain, discomfort, or burdens) ⟨a long needed ~ of taxation⟩ ⟨an ~ of international tension⟩ **2** *obs* **:** food and lodging **:** ENTERTAINMENT **3 :** a curved structural member used to prevent abrupt change of direction (as in a baseboard or handrail) **4 :** an incorporeal usu. nonprofitable interest granted by deed or created by will, deed, or prescription that is held by one person in land owned by another and that entitles its holder to a specific limited use or enjoyment (as the right to cross the land or to have a view continue unobstructed over it) — compare SERVITUDE

easement appurtenant *n* **:** an easement that is intended to and does benefit the possessor of a particular tract of land in the physical use and enjoyment made of that land and that is described as appurtenant to that land

easement curve *n* **:** a curve (as on a highway) whose degree of curvature is varied either uniformly or according to a definite pattern to give a gradual transition between a tangent and a simple curve which it connects or between two simple curves

easement in gross : an easement (as the right to take or sell water from another's land) that exists for the benefit of the holder independently of his possession of any land and that does not benefit any particular land possessed by the holder

ease off *vt* **:** to lessen the tension of **:** SLACKEN ⟨*eased off* the rope⟩ ~ *vi* **:** to become less tense, vigorously active, or engaged **:** decrease in intensity ⟨she lowered the flame and the boiling *eased off*⟩ ⟨as I grow older I find I have to *ease off* now and then⟩ ⟨the weather bureau said the storm . . . would *ease off* today —*Associated Press*⟩

eas·er \ˈēzə(r)\ *n* -s **:** one that eases: as **a :** a bar for slackening threads in a loom **b** *or* **easer rail :** a railroad rail placed close to the running rail to provide a bearing for the overhang of worn wheel treads

eases *pl of* EASE, *pres 3d sing of* EASE

easied *past of* EASY

easier *comparative of* EASY

easies *pres 3d sing of* EASY

easiest *superlative of* EASY

eas·i·ly \ˈēz(ə)lē, -li\ *adv* [ME *esily*, fr. *esy* easy + *-ly*] **1 :** in an easy manner **:** without difficulty, discomfort, or reluctance **:** READILY, SMOOTHLY, GENTLY **2 :** without question **:** by far ⟨~ the most original thinker of his generation⟩ ⟨this is ~ the best course⟩

eas·i·ness \ˈēzēnəs, -zin-\ *n* -ES [ME *esinesse*, fr. *esy* easy + *-nesse* -ness] **1 :** freedom from difficulty or hardship ⟨the ~ of the trip astonished them⟩ ⟨the ~ of the earlier puzzles⟩ **2 a :** freedom from harshness **:** gentle indulgent quality **:** KINDNESS ⟨a certain ~ of temper⟩ **b :** relaxed easy poise (as of manner or style) ⟨entered the room with a quiet ~ of bearing⟩ ⟨a pleasant ~ of style marks his presentation⟩ **c :** casual unconcern or indifference **:** indolent disregard ⟨his losses were largely due to his foolish ~⟩ **d** *archaic* **:** susceptibility to influence **:** CREDULITY **3 :** a state of economic weakness characterized by declining prices and usu. by reduced volume of trade ⟨rubber futures closed slightly steadier after ~ —*Wall Street Jour.*⟩

eas·ing *n* -s [ME *esing*, fr. *esen* to ease + *-ing*] **1 a :** the act or process of an easer **b :** an instance of such act or process **2 :** EASEMENT 3

ea·sings \ˈēzᵊnz, ˈāz-, -zənz\ *n pl* [pl. of obs. & E dial. *easing* eaves of a building, fr. ME *esing*, contr. of *evesing*, fr. *eves* eaves + *-ing* — more at EAVE] *dial Brit* : the eaves of a building

ea·sing sparrow \ˈēz|ᵊnz-, ˈāz|, |zən-\ *n* [E dial. *easing* eaves of a building + E *sparrow*] *dial Brit* : HOUSE SPARROW

eas·sel \ˈēsəl, ˈās-\ *adv* [irreg. fr. *east*] *Scot* : EASTWARD

[1]**east** \ˈēst\ *adv* [ME *est*, fr. OE *ēast*; akin to OHG *ōstar* to the east, ON *austr* to the east, L *aurora* dawn, Gk *ēōs*, Skt *uṣas*] : to, toward, or in the east : EASTWARD

[2]**east** \"\ *adj* [ME *est*, fr. OE *ēast-*, fr. *ēast*, adv.] **1 a** : situated toward or at the east ⟨the ~ gate⟩ **b** [ME *est*, fr. OE *ēastan-*, fr. *ēastan*, adv; akin to OHG *ōstana* from the east, ON *austan*; derivative fr. the root of E [1]*east*] : coming from the east ⟨the ~ wind⟩ **2** : situated in the direction of the altar from the nave of a church : being or situated in that part of a church containing the chancel

[3]**east** \"\ *n* -s [ME *est*, fr. *est*, adv.] **1 a** : the general direction of sunrise : the direction toward the right of one facing north **b** : the part of the sky in which celestial bodies rise; *specif* : the place on the horizon where the sun rises when it is near one of the equinoxes **c** : the cardinal point directly opposite to west — abbr. *E*; see COMPASS CARD **d** : the point of the horizon having an azimuth or bearing of 90° and marking one intersection of the horizon and the celestial equator : the direction of the earth's daily rotation : the direction on the celestial sphere opposite to its apparent rotation : the direction of increasing right ascension or celestial longitude : the direction of revolution around the sun of the earth and the principal planets when seen from the north side of their orbits **2** *usu cap* **a** : regions or countries lying to the east of a specified or implied point of orientation ⟨the worn mountains of the *East*⟩ **b** : something (as people, culture, or institutions) characteristic of the East ⟨the *East* is strongly opposed to these innovations⟩ ⟨the *East* has produced some of our most original thinkers⟩ **3** : the east wind **4** *often cap* : the one of four positions at 90-degree intervals that lies toward the east; *often* : a person (as a bridge player or a Masonic officer) occupying this position in the course of a specific activity

[4]**east** \"\ *vb* -ED/-ING/-S [[1]*east*] : to move or veer toward the east : ORIENT

[5]**east** \"\ *n* -s [by alter.] *dial* : YEAST

eastabout \ˈ==,=\ *adv* (*or adj*) : about in tacking so as to head east; *broadly* : toward the east : EASTWARD

east african cedar *n, usu cap E&A* : a tropical African timber tree (*Juniperus procera*) with fragrant wood

east african hunting dog *n, usu cap E&A* : AFRICAN HUNTING DOG

east african yellowwood *or* **east african pine** *n, usu cap E&A* : a tropical African timber tree (*Podocarpus gracilior*) that is related to the yews and is sometimes cultivated as a greenhouse ornamental

[1]**east anglian** *adj, usu cap E&A* **1** : of or relating to the Anglo-Saxon kingdom of East Anglia, its people, or their language **2** : of or belonging to the modern region of East Anglia, England, corresponding to Norfolk and Suffolk counties

[2]**east anglian** *n, cap E&A* **1** : a native or resident of East Anglia **2** : the speech of East Anglia; *esp* : the Middle English dialect characteristic of this region

eastbound \ˈ=,=\ *adj* : traveling or headed in an easterly direction; *broadly* : headed east or north — used of freight cars in railroad accounting

[1]**east by north** : a compass point that is one point north of due east : N 78° 45′ E — abbr. *E b N, E by N;* see COMPASS CARD

[2]**east by north** *adv* (*or adj*) **1** : toward east by north **2** : from east by north

[1]**east by south** : a compass point that is one point south of due east : S 78° 45′ E — abbr. *E b S, E by S;* see COMPASS CARD

[2]**east by south** *adv* (*or adj*) **1** : toward east by south **2** : from east by south

east coast fever *n* : an acute highly fatal febrile disease of cattle esp. of eastern and southern Africa that is caused by a protozoan (*Theileria parva*) transmitted by ticks (genus *Rhipicephalus*) and is marked by intense fever, labored breathing, gastrointestinal hemorrhage, swelling of the lymph glands, and generalized weakness and emaciation

[1]**eas·ter** \ˈēstə(r)\ *n* -s *usu cap, often attrib* [ME *ester, estre*, fr. OE *ēaster, ēastre;* akin to OHG *ōstarun* (pl.) Easter; both fr. the prehistoric WGmc name of a pagan spring festival, derived fr. the root of E [1]*east*] **1** : an annual church celebration that commemorates Christ's resurrection and is observed with variations of date due to different calendars on the first Sunday after the full moon on or next after March 21 or one week later if the full moon falls on Sunday **2** : the Easter season : EASTERTIDE

EASTER DATES[1]

YEAR	GOLDEN NUMBER	EPACT	DOMINICAL LETTER	PASCHAL FULL MOON[2]	ASH WEDNESDAY	EASTER
1960	4	2	CB	Apr 11	Mar 2	Apr 17
1961	5	13	A	Mar 31	Feb 15	Apr 2
1962	6	24	G	Apr 18	Mar 7	Apr 22
1963	7	5	F	Apr 8	Feb 27	Apr 14
1964	8	16	ED	Mar 28	Feb 12	Mar 29
1965	9	27	C	Apr 16	Mar 3	Apr 18
1966	10	8	B	Apr 5	Feb 23	Apr 10
1967	11	19	A	Mar 25	Feb 8	Mar 26
1968	12	0	GF	Apr 13	Feb 28	Apr 14
1969	13	11	E	Apr 2	Feb 19	Apr 6
1970	14	22	D	Mar 22	Feb 11	Mar 29
1971	15	3	C	Apr 10	Feb 24	Apr 11
1972	16	14	BA	Mar 30	Feb 16	Apr 2
1973	17	25	G	Apr 17	Mar 7	Apr 22
1974	18	6	F	Apr 7	Feb 27	Apr 14
1975	19	17	E	Mar 27	Feb 12	Mar 30
1976	1	29	DC	Apr 14	Mar 3	Apr 18
1977	2	10	B	Apr 3	Feb 23	Apr 10
1978	3	21	A	Mar 23	Feb 8	Mar 26
1979	4	2	G	Apr 11	Feb 28	Apr 15
1980	5	13	FE	Mar 31	Feb 20	Apr 6
1981	6	24	D	Apr 18	Mar 4	Apr 19
1982	7	5	C	Apr 8	Feb 24	Apr 11
1983	8	16	B	Mar 28	Feb 16	Apr 3
1984	9	27	AG	Apr 16	Mar 7	Apr 22
1985	10	8	F	Apr 5	Feb 20	Apr 7

[1]As established by the first Nicene Council, Easter is always the first Sunday after the full moon on or next after the vernal equinox, fixed as March 21 for this calculation. If the full moon falls on Sunday, Easter is observed one week later.

[2]The paschal full moon is determined according to certain calendar rules and may differ from that of the astronomical full moon.

[2]**east·er** \"\ *n* -s [[2]*east* + *-er*] : a storm or gale coming from the east

easter anemone *n, usu cap E* : PASQUEFLOWER

easter bell *n, usu cap E* : GREATER STITCHWORT

easter cactus *n, usu cap E* : a So. American cactus (*Schlumbergera gaertneri*) with oblong joints and coral-red flowers

easter candle *n, usu cap E* : PASCHAL CANDLE

easter daisy *n, usu cap E* : a low-growing ash-gray perennial herb (*Townsendia exscapa*) of western No. America with linear or linear-oblanceolate leaves arranged in a rosette and sessile white flower heads that appear at about Easter season

easter duty *n, usu cap E* : the obligation in the Roman Catholic Church of receiving Communion during Easter time

easter egg *n, usu cap 1st E* : an egg given as a present at or used to celebrate Easter and often dyed with bright colors or otherwise decorated; *broadly* : a symbolic representation of an egg (as in confectionery or the jeweler's art) similarly used

easter even *n, usu cap both Es* [ME *ester even*, fr. *ester* Easter + *even* eve — more at EVEN (eve)] : the 24-hour period preceding Easter

easter flower *n, usu cap E* **1** : PASQUEFLOWER **2** : DAFFODIL 1

easter lily *n, usu cap E* **1** : any of certain predominantly white cultivated lilies that bloom or can be forced into bloom in early spring: as **a** : MADONNA LILY **b** : BERMUDA LILY **2** : any of several native or cultivated spring-flowering plants (as the daffodil, the atamasco lily, or the dogtooth violet)

eas·ter·li·ness \-ēnəs, -in-\ *n* -ES : the situation of being easterly

[1]**east·er·ling** \ˈēstərliŋ -təl-,-tᵊl-\ *n* -s [ME *esterling*, fr. *ester*, *estern* eastern + *-ling*] : a native of a country eastward of another — used esp. of German merchants from Baltic cities who traded in England or competed with the English in foreign ports

[2]**easterling** \"\ *n* -s [alter. (influenced by [1]*easterling*) of *sterling;* fr. a belief that it was coined by German merchants from Baltic cities] **1** *or* **easterling penny** : a medieval English silver coin **2** : the weight of an easterling : PENNYWEIGHT : 1/20 ounce

[1]**east·er·ly** \ˈēstərlē, -li; *-R* -təl- *sometimes* -tᵊl-\ *adj* [obs. E *easter* eastern (fr. ME *ester, estern*) + E *-ly*] **1** : situated toward the east ⟨the ~ shore⟩ **2** : blowing from the east

[2]**easterly** \"\ *adv* **1** : from the east ⟨the wind blew ~⟩ **2** : toward the east ⟨sailed ~ for a week⟩

[3]**easterly** \"\ *n* -ES : a wind from the east

easter mackerel *n, usu cap E* : CHUB MACKEREL

easter monday *n, usu cap E&M* [ME *ester monday* Monday after Easter, fr. *ester* Easter + *monday* Monday] : the Monday after Easter observed as a legal holiday in North Carolina, England, Wales, Northern Ireland, the Republic of Ireland, Canada, Australia, New Zealand, and the Republic of So. Africa

east·er·most \ˈēstə(r),mōst, *esp Brit also* -,məst\ *adj* [obs. E *easter* eastern + E *-most*] *archaic* : EASTERNMOST

[1]**east·ern** \ˈēstə(r)n, *-R also* -tᵊn\ *adj* [ME *estern*, fr. OE *ēasterne;* akin to OHG *ōstrōni* eastern, ON *austrœnn;* derivative fr. the root of E [1]*east*] **1** *often cap* : of, relating to, originating or dwelling in, or characteristic of any region conventionally designated East (as the Orient, the more easterly or northeasterly part of the U.S., or the predominantly Slavic part of Europe) ⟨proposals for settling the ~ question⟩ ⟨~ beef⟩ **2** *usu cap* **a** : of, relating to, or being the totality of Christian churches originating in the church of the Eastern Roman Empire and comprising various Eastern Orthodox, Uniate, Monophysite, and Nestorian churches **b** : Eastern Orthodox **3 a** : lying toward the east ⟨dawn breaking in the ~ sky⟩ ⟨the ~ boundary of the state⟩ **b** : coming from the east ⟨an ~ wind⟩ **4** *often cap* : being or characterizing the native speech of eastern New England and of the r-dropping population of New York City and its suburbs

[2]**eastern** \"\ *n* -s *usu cap* **1** : an inhabitant of the East; *esp* : ORIENTAL **2** : a member of the Eastern Church **3** : eastern American speech

eastern apple box *n, sometimes cap E* : a wooden box with protective pads that is used esp. for apples from eastern orchards of the U.S.

eastern bluestem *n* : BLUESTEM 2b

eastern brook trout *n* : BROOK TROUT

eastern crow *n* : the common crow (*Corvus brachyrhynchos brachyrhynchos*) of northeastern No. America

eastern crown *or* **eastern coronet** *n* : ANTIQUE CROWN

east·ern·er *-R* -tə(r)nər, *-R* -tənə(r *also* -tᵊnə(r\ *n* -s *usu cap* : a native or inhabitant of the East; *esp* : a native or resident of the eastern part of the U.S.

eastern gall rust *n, usu cap E* : a disease of various hard pines (as shortleaf and scrub pine) that is caused by a rust fungus (*Cronartium quercuum*) and characterized by formation of globose galls on the stems

eastern hemisphere *n* : the vertical half of the earth that lies chiefly to the east of the Atlantic ocean and includes Europe, Asia, Africa, and minor landmasses

eastern hemlock *n* : a common forest tree (*Tsuga canadensis*) of the eastern U.S. and Canada that has leaves narrowed toward the apex and with pale stomatal lines beneath, yields a soft, splintery, but moisture-resistant lumber, and is largely used for pulp production

eastern hindi *n, cap E&H* : a group of Indic dialects in northern India including Awadhi

east·ern·ism \-,nizəm\ *n* -s *usu cap* : ORIENTALISM

east·ern·ize \-,nīz\ *vt* -ED/-ING/-S *sometimes cap* **1** : to imbue with qualities native to or sometimes associated with residents of eastern U.S. **2** : ORIENTALIZE

eastern kingbird *n* : a common American kingbird (*Tyrannus tyrannus*) that breeds in much of No. America from coast to coast and winters in tropical America and is distinguished from related birds by a wide white band on the tip of the tail and an orange-red crest which is usu. obscured

eastern larch *n* : a tamarack (*Larix laricina*)

east·ern·ly \-,nlē, -li\ *adv* (*or adj*) **1** : EASTERLY **2** *often cap* : in the Eastern manner : ORIENTALLY

eastern mermaid *n* : a fake stuffed animal usu. consisting of the foreparts of a monkey sewed to the hindpart of a fish

east·ern·most \-n,mōst *esp Brit also* -,məst\ *adj* : farthest to the east : most eastern

eastern orthodox *adj, usu cap E&O* : of, relating to, or being the body of Eastern churches in communion with the ecumenical patriarch of Constantinople that includes the churches of the ancient patriarchates of Constantinople, Alexandria, Antioch, and Jerusalem and a number of autocephalous often national churches (as the Greek and Russian Orthodox churches) and that adheres to the Niceno-Constantinopolitan Creed and to a rite having the same liturgies in different languages, Communion under both kinds, an ecclesiastical year including days for Old Testament saints and based on the Julian calendar, and a married parish clergy

eastern phoebe *n* : a common phoebe (*Sayornis phoebe*) of eastern No. America that is grayish brown above with darker head and grayish white breast

eastern pickerel *n* : CHAIN PICKEREL

eastern red cedar *n* : RED CEDAR 1a

eastern roll *n, usu cap E* : a method of high jumping in which the jumper approaches the bar at right angles, takes off from his outside foot while flinging the leading leg forward and upward, and lands on the outside foot — compare BARREL ROLL, WESTERN ROLL

eastern spruce *n* **1** : WHITE SPRUCE 1a **2** : RED SPRUCE **3** : BLACK SPRUCE 1

eastern sudanic *n, usu cap E&S* : a language group containing the Nilotic and Nubian languages and constituting a subfamily of the Chari-Nile language family

eastern tent caterpillar *n* : the gregarious web-building larva of a reddish brown American moth (*Malacosoma americanum*) hatching in spring, feeding on the young foliage of apple, wild cherry, and related trees, and building community nests of silk in crotches of the trees invaded

eastern time *or* **eastern standard time** *n, often cap E* : the time of the 5th time zone west of Greenwich based on the 75th meridian and used in the eastern parts of Canada and the U.S. — abbr. *ET, EST*

eastern white pine *n* : WHITE PINE 1a

easters *pl of* EASTER

easter sepulcher *n, usu cap E* **1** : a shallow recess in the north side of the chancel in some churches in which formerly the sacred elements were reserved from Maundy Thursday to Easter **2** : a tomb in medieval churches in which the altar crucifix was buried from Good Friday to Easter Sunday

easter sunday *n, usu cap E&S* : the Sunday on which Easter falls

easter term *n, usu cap E* **1** : the term from April 15 to May 8 during which the superior courts of England were formerly open — compare HILARY TERM, TRINITY TERM **2** *also* **easter sitting** : the sitting of the High Court of Justice of England between April 21 and May 29

eas·ter·tide \ˈēstə(r),tīd\ *also* **easter time** *n, usu cap E* [*Eastertide* fr. ME *estertide* Easter season, fr. OE *ēastertīd*, fr. *ēaster* Easter + *tīd* time; *Easter time* fr. ME *ester time* period from Easter to Whitsunday, fr. *ester* Easter + *time* — more at TIDE] : a period extending from Easter to Ascension Day, to Whitsunday, or to Trinity Sunday

easter water *n, usu cap E* : water blessed with special ceremonies on Holy Saturday (as in the Roman Catholic Church) a part of which is set aside for use as a sacramental in the church and at home, the remainder being ceremonially mixed with consecrated oils and used for baptisms in the church

east germanic *n, cap E&G* [prob. trans. of G *ostgermanisch*] : a now extinct division of the Germanic languages containing Gothic and prob. also certain languages of which no connected written records survive, esp. those of the Burgundians and Vandals — see INDO-EUROPEAN LANGUAGES table

east goth *n, cap E&G* : OSTROGOTH

east ham \ˈēst¦ham, ˈē¦stam, -aa(ə)m\ *adj, usu cap E&H* [fr. *East Ham*, county borough in England] : of or from the county borough of East Ham, England : of the kind or style prevalent in East Ham

east india company *n, usu cap E&I&C* [*East India*, collective name applied loosely and vaguely to India, Indochina, and the Malay archipelago] : any of several companies organized chiefly during the 17th and 18th centuries for carrying on trade with the East Indies

east india kino *or* **east indian kino** *n, usu cap E&I* : KINO 1a

east indiaman *n, usu cap E&I* [*East India* + E *man*] : a sailing ship formerly running to the East Indies; *esp* : a large fast sailing ship used on this run

[1]**east indian** *adj, usu cap E&I* [*East India* + E *-an*] **1** : of, relating to, or characteristic of the East Indies **2** : of, relating to, or characteristic of India or Pakistan

[2]**east indian** *n, cap E&I* **1** : a native or inhabitant of the East Indies; *sometimes* : EURASIAN **2** : a native or inhabitant of India or Pakistan; *also* : a person of East Indian ancestry

east indian arrowroot *n, usu cap E&I* : INDIAN ARROWROOT 2b

east indian lotus *n, usu cap E&I* : INDIAN LOTUS

east indian rhubarb *n, usu cap E&I* : CHINESE RHUBARB

east indian rosewood *n, usu cap E&I* : BLACKWOOD b

east indian satinwood *n, usu cap E&I* : SATINWOOD 1

east indian sumbul *n, usu cap E&I* : BOMBAY SUMBUL

east indian walnut *n, usu cap E&I* **1** : LEBBEK **2** : the wood of the lebbek that resembles and is used similarly to walnut

east india resin *also* **east india** *n, usu cap E&I* : any of several pale to black hard semifossil dammar resins

east india root *n, usu cap E&I* : the rhizome of a galingale (*Alpinia officinarum*)

east indies *adj, usu cap E&I* [fr. *East Indies*, the former Netherlands Indies (in some usage, the entire Malay archipelago; in some usage, India, Indochina, and the Malay archipelago)] : of or from the East Indies : of the kind or style prevalent in the East Indies : EAST INDIAN

east·ing \ˈēstiŋ\ *n* -s [[1]*east* + *-ing*] **1** : difference in longitude to the east from the last preceding point of reckoning **2** : easterly progress : a going eastward ⟨weeks of snow . . . and not for anything can you keep an ~ —Joseph Hergesheimer⟩

east·lake \ˈēst,lāk\ *adj, usu cap* [after Sir Charles L. *Eastlake* †1865 Eng. painter and art critic] *of furniture* : being machine-made after a style characterized by sturdy rectangular lines

east·lin \ˈēstlən\ *or* **east·ling** \", -liŋ\ *adj* [[1]*east* + *-ling*] *Scot* : EASTERLY

east·lins \-nz\ *or* **east·lings** \-nz,-ŋz\ *adv* [[1]*east* + *-lings*] *Scot* : to the east

east london boxwood *n, usu cap E&L* [after *East London*, city in the Union of So. Africa] **1** : a box (*Buxus macowani*) that grows in nearly pure stands at East London, Union of South Africa **2** : the wood of East London boxwood

east lo·thi·an \-ˈlōthēən, -thyən\ *adj, usu cap E&L* [fr. *East Lothian*, county in Scotland] : of or from the county of East Lothian, Scotland : of the kind or style prevalent in East Lothian

east midland *n, cap E&M* : the branch of the Midland dialect of Middle English that is the basis of modern standard English

east·most \ˈēs(t),mōst, *esp Brit also* -,məst\ *adj* [ME *estmest*, fr. OE *ēastemest, ēastmest*, fr. *ēast-* east + *-mest* -most — more at [2]EAST] : EASTERNMOST

east·ness \ˈēs(t)nəs\ *n* -ES : the quality or state of being east

[1]**east-northeast** \(¦)=¦=¦=\ *adv* (*or adj*) [ME *est northest*, fr. *est* east + *northest* northeast — more at [1]EAST] **1** : toward east-northeast **2** : from east-northeast

[2]**east-northeast** \"\ *n* : a compass point that is two points north of due east : N 67°30′ E — abbr. *ENE;* see COMPASS CARD

eas·ton·ite \ˈēstə,nīt\ *n* -s *often cap* [*Easton*, city in eastern Pennsylvania, its locality + E *-ite*] : a mineral $K_2Mg_5AlSi_5Al_3O_{20}(OH)_4$ consisting of basic silicate of potassium, aluminum, and magnesium and being an end-member of the biotite system

easts *pl of* EAST, *pres 3d sing of* EAST

eastside \ˈ=¦=\ *adj, often cap* [fr. the *East Side*, the eastern part of Manhattan] : of, relating to, or situated in the eastern part of Manhattan ⟨~ tenements⟩

east-sid·er \ˈēs(t)¦sīdə(r)\ *n, often cap E&S* [*East Side*, the eastern part of Manhattan borough, New York City + E *-er*] : a native or resident of the East Side of New York City

east slavic *n, cap E&S* : a subdivision of the Slavic languages that includes Russian, Ukrainian, and Belorussian — see INDO-EUROPEAN LANGUAGES table

[1]**east-southeast** \(¦)=¦=¦=\ *adv* (*or adj*) [ME *est southest*, fr. *est* east + *southest* southeast — more at [1]EAST] **1** : toward east-southeast **2** : from east-southeast

[2]**east-southeast** \"\ *n* : a compass point that is two points south of due east : S 67° 30′ E — abbr. *ESE;* see COMPASS CARD

[1]**east·ward** \ˈēstwə(r)d\ *adv* (*or adj*) [ME *estward*, fr. OE *ēastweard*, fr. *ēast* east + *-weard* -ward — more at [1]EAST] : toward the east ⟨turned ~ down the slope⟩ ⟨~ movement of the herd⟩

[2]**eastward** \"\ *n* -s : eastward direction or part ⟨sail to the ~⟩

east·ward·ly *adv* (*or adj*) : toward or from the east : EASTERLY

east·wards \-dz\ *adv* [*eastward* + *-s* (fr. ME *-es*, adverbially functioning gen. sing. ending of nouns) — more at -s] : EASTWARD

east-west \ˈ=¦=\ *adv* (*or adj*) : from east to west : from or along a line of geographic latitude ⟨the first *east-west* railroad⟩

east-windy \ˈ=¦=\ *adj* [*east wind* (fr. [2]*east* + *wind*) + *-y*] : BLEAK, UNPLEASANT

[1]**easy** \ˈēzē, -zi\ *adj* -ER/-EST [ME *esy*, fr. OF *aaisié* (past part. of *aaisier* to ease) & *aisié* (past part. of *aisier* to ease) — more at [2]EASE] **1** : causing, exacting, or involving little difficulty, exertion, hardship, or discomfort to execute or cope with : performed, accomplished, achieved, solved, coped with, taken, acted on, or cared for with ready ease ⟨it was ~ to sit on a camel's back without falling off but very difficult to get the best out of her —T.E.Lawrence⟩ ⟨ritual is not ~ compliance with detailed and punctilious rule —W.G.Sumner⟩ ⟨an ~ victim . . . of this good-natured diplomatist —W.M. Thackeray⟩ ⟨feeding this outfit would have been ~ for an old hand —*Amer. Guide Series: Ariz.*⟩ ⟨the St. Lawrence route is . . . ~ of navigation —B.K.Sandwell⟩ **2 a** : not severe, not stern, not harsh : readily assuaged or placated : MILD, LENIENT, COMPLAISANT ⟨you are . . . so ~ that every servant will cheat you —Jane Austen⟩ ⟨we really ought to be ~ on him because everybody makes mistakes —V.G.Heiser⟩ **b** : marked by gentle gradual change or variation making for ease in traversing or following : not steep, not abrupt, not sharp ⟨this is the ~ country of the pass where the stream flows gently —Ernest Hemingway⟩ ⟨terraced steps rise in ~ flights —*Amer. Guide Series: Mich.*⟩ ⟨a pleasant ~ angle —Richard Jefferies⟩ **c** : marked by ease and convenience in going from one place to another usu. by short distances at a time ⟨brought him back by ~ stages —Willa Cather⟩ **d** : not difficult to endure or undergo : not burdensome or onerous : complied with or fulfilled without marked discomfort ⟨an ~ penalty⟩ ⟨an ~ contract⟩ ⟨William Pitt . . . condemned the Peace of Paris as too ~ —Stringfellow Barr⟩ **e** : readily prevailed on : overcome without difficulty: as (1) : yielding quickly to sexual importunities ⟨women of the ~ kind, the lusty kind, the ardent and the impudent —T.H.Raddall⟩ (2) : not difficult to trick, deceive, or take advantage of ⟨fell an ~ prey to her wiles⟩ (3) : especially susceptible (as to disease or predation ⟨in winter upland game birds are ~ victims to predators where cover is poor⟩ ⟨exhausted by overwork he was an ~ victim to infection⟩ **f** (1) : obtained or obtainable with ease : not involving especial effort, inconvenience, or anguish ⟨he won an ~ victory⟩ (2) *of money, credit, or commodities* : available in such large quantities that interest rates or prices are depressed ⟨farmers generally want *easier* money⟩ ⟨the hog market has been irregular and ~ for several days⟩ — compare [2]EASY-MONEY **g** : clear and without complexity or difficulty : very readily understood although often without challenge or reward ⟨~ language — no strain upon either adult or youthful reader —J.D.Hart⟩ **3 a** : marked by ease, by peace, comfort, and placid rest ⟨retired and living

an ~ life⟩ ⟨the ~ warmth of most southern cities —Green Peyton⟩ **b :** not hurried, not ruffled, not strenuous **:** marked by or suited to placid calm or mild, slow, or gentle activity ⟨an ~ walk through the meadow⟩ ⟨the ~ climate of the island⟩ ⟨a stretch of ~ water —C.S.Forester⟩ **4 a :** free from pain, distress, annoyance, discomfort ⟨the patient was *easier* after the sedative⟩ **b :** marked by social ease **:** constituting or facilitating ready natural sociability **:** calm, smooth, and without restraint, formality, embarrassment, or harshness ⟨~ and familiar manners of men who had worked for years together —Sir Winston Churchill⟩ ⟨the ~ carriage of a man born to a dignified place in life —Jack London⟩ **c :** marked by or arising from a complaisant desire for ease or by an attitude of careless casual acquiescence **:** showing a disinclination to energetic individual action or resolute independent thought ⟨his ~ disposition made him fall in unresistingly with the family courses —George Eliot⟩ ⟨the ~, irreligious gay society which jumped the life to come —H.O.Taylor⟩ **d :** free from mental or emotional agitation **:** unruffled and not harassed by discontent, anxiety, doubt, or fear **:** TRANQUIL ⟨an ~ and dignified calm, far removed from the intensity of life —Thomas Hardy⟩ ⟨men who fish for a living must have an ~ courage —Mary H. Vorse⟩ **e :** enjoying or showing comfortable assured tranquillity about money and expenses **:** rich enough for comfort or luxury ⟨he married an heiress and found himself in ~ circumstances —*Times Lit. Supp.*⟩ **f :** marked by ready facility at smooth composition or performance without labored effort **:** EFFORTLESS ⟨he wrote in an ~, rapid, flowing style —H.S.Robinson⟩ **g :** felt, experienced, or attained to readily, naturally, and spontaneously without guided or forced effort **:** not conscious, purposive, or factitious ⟨an ~ familiarity with his subject⟩ ⟨~ emotions⟩ **h :** no less than — used with the indefinite article and terms denoting quantity (as of years of age) ⟨looking an ~ 35 in the harsh light⟩ ⟨an ~ two hours' work⟩ ⟨weighs an ~ 200⟩ **5 a :** conducive to or facilitating ease, comfort, relaxation, or surcease from discomfort, inconvenience, or vexation ⟨~ furniture⟩ ⟨an ~ arrangement of the room⟩ **b** (1) **:** supportable with ease **:** not onerous or burdensome ⟨got very ~ terms from his creditors⟩ (2) *of payments* **:** designed to be made in installments over a period of time and from regular income ⟨furnished his house on an easy-payment plan⟩ **c** *of a garment* **:** fitting comfortably with due allowance for motion of the body **:** not tight or constricting ⟨an ~ shoe⟩ ⟨an ~ fit⟩ **6 a :** evenly divided — used of the aces in a no-trump contract in auction bridge when each partnership holds two **b** *Austral* **:** willing to consider or participate but not enthusiastic

syn FACILE, SIMPLE, LIGHT, EFFORTLESS, SMOOTH: EASY applies to persons and to things making demands answerable without much effort or difficulty ⟨he found his studies too *easy* to require serious attention, and, being very large and strong, he devoted his energies to athletics —E.S.Bates⟩ ⟨the English owe more to their national home than do most nations. Its insular situation made it readily accessible in time of peace and *easy* to defend in time of war —Kemp Malone⟩ FACILE, sometimes a close synonym of EASY, now applies to execution, accomplishment, or performance seemingly without effort or with very little effort; sometimes it is derogatory in implying undue haste or careless execution ⟨full of *facile* theories, with glib explanations of everything —Bertrand Russell⟩ ⟨Chrétien is a *facile* narrator, with little sense of the significance that might be given to the stories —H.O.Taylor⟩ SIMPLE stresses ease in comprehending and freedom from complexity or intricacy ⟨feeding this outfit would have been easy for an old hand, but it was far from *simple* to me —*Amer. Guide Series: Ariz.*⟩ ⟨the English mother or the English nurse has a *simpler* job. She must teach her charge to start as few fights as possible and that there are rules. That is enough —Margaret Mead⟩ LIGHT involves freedom from the onerous or burdensome ⟨college teaching job — preferably where your formal duties are as *light* as you can decently make them —W.G.Carleton⟩ ⟨it was no *light* thing to encounter the rage and despair of fifty thousand fighting men —T.B.Macaulay⟩ EFFORTLESS suggests appearance of ease and often implies perfected artistry or mastery ⟨so that attention became concentration, and concentration became at first *effortless*, then involuntary —Charles Morgan⟩ ⟨that *effortless* grace with which only a true poet can endow his work —Martha O. Smith⟩ SMOOTH suggests absence of obstacles, hindrances, unevennesses, interruptions ⟨the *smooth* advance of the German Army into France in 1940 —S.L.A.Marshall⟩ ⟨by the time he had warmed up his motors, the sky had cleared and it was day. The takeoff was *smooth* as cream —John Dos Passos⟩ **syn** see in addition COMFORTABLE

²easy \ˈ"\ *adv* -ER/-EST [ME *esy*, fr. *esy*, adj.] **1 :** EASILY ⟨~ come, ~ go⟩ ⟨take it ~⟩ ⟨my boots went on ~⟩ **2 :** without undue speed **:** SLOWLY ⟨go ~ here, the road is very rough⟩ ⟨worked ~ until his muscles loosened up⟩ **:** without undue excitement — often used interjectionally to suggest proceeding with caution ⟨~, the road's washed out just ahead⟩ or calming down ⟨~, there's nothing to be afraid of now⟩

³easy \ˈ"\ *vb* -ED/-ING/-ES [¹*easy*] **:** EASE

⁴easy \ˈ"\ *vb* -ED/-ING/-ES [²*easy*] *vi* **:** to stop rowing ⟨the crew *easied* on approaching the dock⟩ — often used as a command, sometimes with *all* ⟨~ all⟩ **~** *vt* **:** to command (an oarsman or crew) to stop rowing

⁵easy \ˈ"\ *usu cap* — a communications code word for the letter *e*

easy chair *n* **:** a roomy usu. upholstered chair designed for comfortable relaxation

easy-does-it \ˌēzēˈdəzət, -zi-, *usu* -əd·+V\ *adj* **:** free from strain and tension **:** comfortable and pleasantly relaxing ⟨an *easy-does-it* approach to a problem⟩

easygoing \ˌ==ˈ=\ *adj* **1** *of a horse* **:** having a comfortable gait **2 :** taking life easily **:** PLACID, CALM ⟨an ~ man, rarely stirred to anger⟩: as **a :** indolent and careless ⟨those ~ slipshod ways would not do today⟩ **b :** not bound by rigid standards of conduct or morals ⟨a country that, for all its reputation of being ~, has often set a moral example to the rest of Europe —*Manchester Guardian Weekly*⟩ **3 :** free from onerous demands or exactions **:** casually pleasant and comfortable ⟨the ~ way of 19th century cultured living⟩ ⟨an ~ unhurried tempo⟩ ⟨the ~ demands of the present public taste —Kenkichi Yoshida⟩ — **easy·go·ing·ness** *n* -ES

easylike \ˈ==,=\ *adv* **:** with ease **:** GENTLY, CAUTIOUSLY ⟨leaned ~ against the fence⟩ ⟨crept forward ~ until we could hear what was said⟩

easy mark *n* [so called fr. the similarity to a target that can easily be hit] **:** one easily imposed upon, duped, or overcome

easy money *n* **:** money obtained without especial hardship or effort; *often* **:** money obtained unfairly or improperly (as by trickery or crime)

easy-money \ˈ==ˈ==\ *adj* [*easy money*] **:** devoted to or concerned with increasing the availability of money and credit ⟨the present *easy-money* policy of the government⟩ — compare ¹EASY 2f(2)

easy-osey *or* **easy-osie** \ˈēziˈōzi\ *adj* [redupl. of ¹*easy*] *Scot* **:** EASYGOING, CASUAL

easy rider *n, slang* **:** a parasitical hanger-on; *esp* **:** PIMP

easy street *n, sometimes cap E&S* **:** a situation marked by financial independence — usu. used with *on* ⟨if I get that contract I'll be on *easy street* for months⟩

easy virtue *n* **:** sexually promiscuous behavior or habits

¹eat \ˈēt, *usu* ˈēd·+V\ *vb* **ate** \ˈāt *chiefly in substand speech* ˈet, *usu* |d·+V; *Brit* ˈet *sometimes* ˈāt\ *or dial* **eat** \ˈelt, ˈēt, *usu* |d·+V\ *also* **et** \ˈet, *usu* ˈed·+V\ **eat·en** \ˈēt³n\ *or dial* **eat** \ˈelt, ˈēlt, *usu* |d·+V\ *also* **et** \ˈet, *usu* ˈed·+V\ **eat·ing** \ˈēd·iŋ, ˈētiŋ\ **eats** \ˈēts\ [ME *eten*, fr. OE *etan*; akin to OHG *ezzan* to eat, ON *eta*, Goth *itan*, L *esse*, *edere*, Gk (Homeric) *edmenai* to eat, Skt *atti* he eats, *admi* I eat] *vt* **1 a :** to take in through the mouth as food ⟨sat *eating* a ripe plum⟩ **:** ingest, chew, and swallow (food) — used of solids and then contrasted with *drink* ⟨he *ate* his sandwich and drank a glass of milk⟩ or broadly of both solids and liquids ⟨he ~s dinner at noon⟩ ⟨~ your soup⟩ **b :** to use as food **:** make a food of **:** obtain nourishment from ⟨the carnivores ~ meat⟩ ⟨~ whatever is put before you⟩ **2 :** destroy, use up, or waste by or as if by eating **:** DEVOUR, CONSUME, RAVAGE ⟨time ~s the strongest walls⟩ ⟨the wooded hills were *eaten* by fire⟩ ⟨locusts *ate* the country bare⟩ ⟨an inheritance *eaten* up by debt⟩ **3 :** to take in in order to obtain some benefit (as nourishment, wisdom, or comfort) ⟨Thy words were found, and I *ate* them —Jer. 15:16 (RSV)⟩ **4 a :** to consume gradually ⟨waves ~*ing* the cliffs⟩ **:** waste or wear away ⟨*eaten* by a high fever⟩ **:** CORRODE ⟨acid ~*ing* the surface of a metal plate⟩ **b** *slang* (1) **:** to consume with vexation ⟨what's ~*ing* her now⟩ (2) **:** to defeat decisively ⟨our team can ~ those chumps⟩ **5 a** *obs* **:** to submit tamely to (as insult or abuse) **:** accept as one's portion — compare EAT CROW, EAT DIRT **b** *slang* **:** to accept unquestioningly **:** believe uncritically — usu. used with *up* ⟨he *ate* up the stories of our journeys⟩ **6 a :** to gnaw, perforate, or bore into ⟨the timber was so *eaten* by termites as to be useless⟩ **b :** to bring (as oneself) to a particular state by eating ⟨he *ate* himself sick⟩ ⟨the peach was *eaten* hollow by Japanese beetles⟩ ⟨he'll ~ us out of house and home⟩ **~** *vi* **1 :** to take food or a meal ⟨where shall we ~ this evening⟩; *broadly* **:** BOARD ⟨I ~ at the little café around the corner⟩ **2 :** to present a specified quality or characteristic when eaten ⟨crackers alone ~ very dry⟩ ⟨the beef *ate* surprisingly tender⟩ **3 a :** to affect something by a gradual destructive action — used with *into* ⟨the acid *ate* into the metal⟩ ⟨an ulcer *ate* into the flesh⟩ **b :** to use up in part esp. over a period of time — used with *into* ⟨smokers ~ greedily into dollar reserves —*English Digest*⟩ ⟨his extravagances *ate* into his inheritance⟩ **4** *slang* **:** to annoy or irritate someone — used with *on* ⟨what's ~*ing* on her⟩

syn SWALLOW, INGEST, DEVOUR, CONSUME: EAT is a general term, often without especial connotation; figuratively, it may indicate a wasting or wearing away, often gradual ⟨the river has been *eating* away its west bank rather than east —*Amer. Guide Series: La.*⟩ ⟨poor Mother, the farm has *eaten* away her life —Ellen Glasgow⟩ SWALLOW may focus attention on passage down the throat without chewing or without much chewing ⟨chewing pemmican and *swallowing* army bread —F.V.W.Mason⟩ Figuratively, it implies a seizing, taking in, engulfing, encompassing, or dominating so that existence or identity of the object concerned is threatened or lost ⟨in opera the music *swallows* the words and the other arts of the theater —Susanne K. Langer⟩ ⟨Detroit burst its bounds, *swallowed* other sizable cities —*Amer. Guide Series: Mich.*⟩ INGEST indicates with comprehensiveness and indefiniteness any process of taking through the mouth and into the stomach ⟨does a man dine well because he *ingests* the requisite number of calories? —Walter Lippmann⟩ ⟨anyone who accidentally *ingests* some of the fluid should not go untreated —H.G. Armstrong⟩ Figuratively, it likewise stresses the fact of reception, absorption, or assimilation without more specific suggestion ⟨*ingested* the statement slowly, thought, and then began to express surprise —Elizabeth Bowen⟩ ⟨the U.S.S.R. wants to annex and *ingest* as many satellite nations as possible —B.A. Javits⟩ DEVOUR indicates an eating up wholly, typically with force, intemperance, greed, or rapacity ⟨it is only when an object in the water is still that a shark can *devour* it —H.A. Chippendale⟩ ⟨crossties are of steel, since the customary wooden ties would be quickly *devoured* by insects —Tom Marvel⟩ Figuratively, it implies greedy or very avid seizing or using ⟨an omnivorous reader, *devouring* history, biography, philosophy, science, and fiction —A.F.Harlow⟩ CONSUME may stress the fact of using up entirely by eating or drinking or otherwise employing or assimilating ⟨taking a piece of asparagus in her hand, she was deeply mortified at seeing her hostess *consume* the vegetable with the aid of a knife and fork —G.B.Shaw⟩ ⟨one famous class of British locomotives *consumed* about 52 pounds of coal per mile on ordinary express duty —O.S.Nock⟩ It may indicate utter consumption accomplished forcefully, fiercely, or wastefully ⟨the first two buildings occupying this site were destroyed by fire, the last being *consumed* in the flames that swept the city in 1794 —*Amer. Guide Series: La.*⟩

— **eat crow :** to accept what one has fought against **:** recede from a position taken — **eat dirt :** to be or become grovelingly submissive — **eat high on the hog :** to live well — **eat one's head off 1 :** to eat excessively or gluttonously **2** *slang* **:** to nag or grumble at one **:** scold or pick at one ⟨she *ate his head off* when he came in late⟩ — **eat one's heart out :** to grieve bitterly and without hope — **eat one's words :** to retract what one has said — **eat out of one's hand :** to accept habitually and supinely the domination of another — **eat someone's salt :** to partake of someone's hospitality — **eat stick :** to suffer a beating (as with a rod or bastinado) — **eat the air** *obs* **:** to have vain hopes

²eat \ˈēt, *usu* ˈēd·+V\ *n* -S [ME *et*, fr. OE *ǣt*; akin to OHG *āz* food, ON *āt*, Russ *eda*; derivative fr. the root of E ¹*eat*] **:** something to eat **:** FOOD — usu. used in pl. ⟨saw the jolly hand come waltzing in for ~s —Sinclair Lewis⟩

¹eat·able \ˈēd·əbəl, ˈētəb-\ *adj* [ME *etable*, fr. *eten* to eat + *-able* — more at ¹EAT] **:** fit to be eaten: **a :** such as can be taken as food without risk or utter revulsion though usu. without pleasure ⟨a piece of bread, stale and slightly moldy but ~⟩ **b :** pleasant to eat ⟨her cherry cobbler is very ~⟩

²eatable \ˈ"\ *n* -S **1 :** something to eat **2 eatables** *pl* **:** FOOD

eat·age \ˈēd·ij\ *n* -S [prob. by folk etymology (influence of ¹*eat* and *-age*) fr. *eddish*] **1 :** eatable growth of grass for horses and cattle esp. after a second mowing **2 :** right of using grassland for pasturage

eat away *vt* **:** to consume by eating **:** ERODE ⟨wind *eating away* the dunes⟩ **~** *vi* **:** to eat heartily or to repletion ⟨they *ate away* with right good will⟩ ⟨*eat away*, children, you're welcome to all you want⟩

eaten *past part of* EAT

eaten-out \ˈ==ˈ=\ *adj, of grazing land* **:** grazed beyond capacity for recovery **:** rendered barren by overgrazing ⟨the miles of *eaten-out* range attest our incapacity to manage natural resources⟩

eat·er \ˈēd·ə(r), ˈētə-\ *n* -S [ME *etere*, fr. OE, fr. *etan* to eat + *-ere* -er — more at ¹EAT] **:** one that eats or is accustomed to eat ⟨a heavy ~⟩ ⟨careless ~s⟩ ⟨the dog is basically a meat ~⟩

eat·ery \ˈēd·ərē, ˈētə-, -ri\ *n* -ES **:** LUNCHROOM, RESTAURANT

eath *or* **eith** \ˈēth\ *adv (or adj)* [ME *eth*, *ethe*, fr. OE *ēath*, *ēathe*; akin to OHG *ōdi* easy, *ōdo* perhaps, ON *auth-* easily, and perh. to L *avēre* to long for — more at AVID] *Scot* **:** EASY

eath·ly *or* **eith·ly** \-li\ *adv* [ME *etheliche*, fr. OE *ēathelīce*, fr. *ēathelīc* (adj.) easy, fr. *ēathe* + *-līc* (adj. suffix) -ly] *Scot* **:** EASILY

¹eating *n* -S [ME *etinge*, fr. OE *eting*, fr. *etan* to eat + *-ing*] **1 :** the act of one that eats ⟨the daintiness of her ~⟩ **2 :** food to eat ⟨there's no better ~ than fried chicken and fresh green peas⟩ ⟨lobster makes hard ~ for a young child⟩

²eating \ˈ"\ *adj* [ME *eting*, fr. *eten* to eat + *-ing*] **1 :** CONSUMING, DEVOURING, GNAWING, CORROSIVE, FRETTING ⟨~ cares⟩ **2** [¹*eating*] **a :** used for eating ⟨an ~ room⟩ ⟨~ utensils⟩ **b :** suitable for eating; *often* **:** being for or of the kind used for human food ⟨~ corn is sweeter than field corn⟩ **c :** fit to be eaten raw — distinguished from *cooking* ⟨these are excellent mild ~ apples but I like something a little tarter for pie⟩

eating house *n* [ME *etinge house*, fr. *etinge* eating + *hous* house — more at ¹EATING] **:** a place where cooked food is served; *often* **:** a cheap or inferior restaurant

eat out *vt* **1 :** to consume the herbage from esp. to excess ⟨the marsh was badly *eaten out* by muskrats⟩ **2** *slang* **:** to reprimand (a person) severely **~** *vi* **:** to eat away from home, esp. at a restaurant ⟨we usually *eat out* on Thursdays⟩

eat-out \ˈ=,=\ *n* -S [*eat out*] **:** an area of marsh denuded of vegetation by the feeding of an excessive population (as of muskrats or waterfowl)

eats *pres 3d sing of* EAT, *pl of* EAT

eat up *vt* [ME *eten up*, fr. *eten* to eat + *up*] **1 :** to eat completely and without delay ⟨*eat up* your dinner before it gets cold⟩ ⟨the locusts *ate up* the bean crop⟩ **2 :** DISTRESS, STRAIN, EXHAUST ⟨a tedious monotonous job *eats* a person *up*⟩ **3 :** to consume entirely ⟨her savings were *eaten up* by illness⟩ ⟨a man so *eaten up* with vanity as to be scarcely human⟩ **4** *slang* **:** to exhibit avid interest in or enjoyment of ⟨the crowd *ate up* the maudlin scene⟩ ⟨the jury will *eat up* the lurid testimony⟩ ⟨even sensible men *ate up* the chance to get in on such a good thing⟩

eau \ˈō\ *n, pl* **eaux** \ˈō(z)\ [F, lit., water, fr. L *aqua* — more at ISLAND] **:** a watery solution (as of perfume); *esp* **:** a liqueur of moderate density and sweetness

eau de co·logne \ˌōdəkəˈlōn\ *n, pl* **eaux de cologne** \ˌō(z)d-\ *sometimes cap E&C* [F, lit., Cologne water, fr. *Cologne*, Germany, where it was manufactured] **:** COLOGNE 1

eau de ja·vel green \ˌōdə,zhaˈvel-, -ˌzhaˈ-\ *n, often cap J* **:** JAVEL GREEN

eau de javelle \ˌ==(,)=ˈ=\ *or* **eau de javel** \ˈ"\ *n, pl* **eaux de javelle** \ˌō(z)d-\ *usu cap J* [F, lit., Javel water, fr. *Javel*, former town now included in Paris, France] **:** JAVELLE WATER

eau de nile \ˌōdəˈnē(ə)l, -nī(-\ *n, pl* **eaux de nile** \ˌō(z)d-\ *often cap N* [F *eau de Nil*, lit., Nile water, fr. *Nil* Nile, river in northeast Africa] **:** NILE

eau-de-vie \ˌōdəˈvē\ *n, pl* **eaux-de-vie** \ˌō(z)d-\ [F, lit., water of life, trans. of ML *aqua vitae*] **:** a spirit distilled from grape wine or other fermented fruit juice **:** BRANDY

eau-de-vie de marc \ˌōdə,vēdəˈmärk\ *n* [F] **:** MARC 2

eave \ˈēv\ *n* -S *often attrib* [back-formation fr. *eaves* (taken as a plural), fr. ME *eves*, fr. OE *efes*; akin to OHG *obasa* portico, ON *ups* eaves, Goth *ubizwa* portico, Goth *uf* under — more at UP] **1** *usu* **eaves** *pl but sing or pl in constr* **a :** the lower border of a roof that overhangs the wall ⟨worn by the dripping from the ~⟩ ⟨the ~s are neatly boxed⟩ **b :** the corresponding overhang of thatch (as on a stack of fodder) **2** *usu* **eaves** *pl but sing or pl in constr* **:** a projecting edge (as of a hill or a hat)

eave 1a

eaved \-vd\ *adj* **:** having eaves esp. of an indicated kind ⟨deep-*eaved*⟩ ⟨steep-*eaved*⟩

eaves board *also* **eave board** *n* [ME *evesbord*, fr. *eves* + *bord* board] **:** an arris fillet nailed across the rafters at the eaves of a building in order to raise the starter course of slates or tiles

¹eaves·drop \ˈēvz,dräp *sometimes* -v,d-\ *vb* [prob. back-formation fr. *eavesdropper*] *vi* **:** to listen secretly to what is said in private — usu. used with *on* ⟨*eavesdropping* on the senate conference⟩ ⟨he hid under the table and *eavesdropped* on his sister and her sweetheart⟩ **~** *vt* **1** *archaic* **:** to learn or overhear by eavesdropping **2 :** to eavesdrop on (as a conversation) ⟨I've just *eavesdropped* two demographers or geopoliticians —Christopher Morley⟩

²eavesdrop \ˈ"\ *also* **eaves·drip** \-,drip\ *n* [*eavesdrop* fr. ME *evesdrop*, fr. *eves* + *drop*; *eavesdrip* fr. *eaves* + *drip*] **1 :** the water that falls in drops from the eaves of a house **2 :** the ground on which the water falls from the eaves **3 :** a servitude formerly required in England before one could build so that water from one's eaves could fall directly on the land of another

eaves·drop·per \-pə(r)\ *n* [ME *evesdropper*, fr. *evesdrop*, n. + *-er*] **:** one that eavesdrops

eaves lath *also* **eave lath** *n* [ME *eveslath*, fr. *eves* + *lath*] **:** EAVES BOARD

eaves molding *also* **eave molding** *n* **:** a molding below the eaves of a building that acts as a cornice or part of a cornice

eaves swallow *also* **eave swallow** *n* **:** a swallow that nests under the eaves of buildings (as the cliff swallow or the common European martin)

eaves tile *also* **eave tile** *n* **:** roofing tile used for the row along the eaves of a building — called also *starter*

eaves trough *also* **eave trough** *n* **:** a gutter along the eaves

EB *abbr* eastbound

éba·no \ˈābə,nō, ˈeb-\ *n* -S [AmerSp, fr. Sp, ebony, fr. L *ebenus* — more at EBON] **:** any of several Mexican and Central American timber trees of the genus *Caesalpinia* (esp. *C. sclerocarpa*)

ébauche \āˈbōsh\ *n* -S [F, fr. *ébaucher* to rough out, outline, roughhew, fr. MF *esbocher*, fr. *es-* (fr. L *ex-*) + *-bocher* (fr. OF *-bauchier*, fr. *bauch*, *bauc* beam) — more at DEBAUCH] **:** an incomplete watch movement consisting of plates, bridges, wheels, and barrels to be finished and fitted with jewels, escapement, mainspring, hands, and dial

ébau·choir \ˌā(,)bōshˈwär\ *n* -S [F, fr. *ébaucher*] **:** a chisel used to roughhew sculpture

¹ebb \ˈeb\ *n* -S [ME *ebbe*, fr. OE *ebba*; akin to OFris *ebba* ebb, MD *ebbe*, OS *ebbia* ebb, ON *efja* river bend in which the current flows backwards, OE *of* from — more at OF] **1 :** the reflux or flowing back of the tide **:** return of the tidal wave toward the sea ⟨the boats will go out on the ~⟩ — opposed to *flood* **2 :** a point or condition of gradual decline from a higher to a lower level (as of activity) or from a better to a worse state — often used in the phrase *at the ebb* ⟨faith in the possibilities of mankind . . . is at the ~ —B.R.Redman⟩ or *at a low ebb* ⟨Federalism in New York was at a low ~ —L.B.Mason⟩

²ebb \ˈ"\ *vb* -ED/-ING/-S [ME *ebben*, fr. OE *ebbian*, fr. *ebba*, n.] *vi* **1 :** to recede from its flood (as of the water of a tide toward the ocean) — opposed to *flow* **2 a :** to fall gradually from a higher to a lower level (as of activity) or from a better to a worse state **:** DECLINE ⟨his energy seemed to ~⟩ **:** draw to a close **:** DIMINISH, LESSEN ⟨capacity to resist ~*ed* away —Oscar Handlin⟩ **b :** RETURN, REVIVE — used with *back* ⟨his courage ~*ed* back again —O.E.Rölvaag⟩ **~** *vt* **:** to dry by the recession of the tide ⟨an ~*ed* beach⟩

³ebb \ˈ"\ *adj* [ME *eb* being at ebb, fr. *eb*, *ebbe*, n.] *dial Brit* **:** SHALLOW

ebb and flow *n* **1 :** the alternate ebb and flood of the tide **2 :** a condition or rhythm of alternate forward and backward movement or of alternate decline and renewed advance ⟨the *ebb and flow* of battle⟩ ⟨the *ebbs and flows* of business⟩

ebb-and-flow structure *n* **:** stratified rock structure characterized by alternating horizontal and cross-bedded layers thought to be produced by tidal ebb and flow

eb·bet \ˈebət\ *n* -S [alter. of earlier *evat*, *evet* newt, fr. ME *evete* — more at EFT] **:** the common green newt (*Triturus viridescens*) of the eastern U.S.

ebb tide *n* **1 :** the tide while ebbing or at ebb — opposed to *flood tide* **2 :** a period or state of decline ⟨civilization at its *ebb tide*⟩

eb·e·na·ce·ae \,ebəˈnāsē,ē\ *n pl, cap* [NL, fr. L *ebenus* ebony + NL *-aceae* — more at EBON] **:** a family of plants (order Ebenales) comprising trees and shrubs (as the ebony and persimmon) with very hard wood, entire leaves, and dioecious or rarely perfect flowers succeeded by fleshy berries — **eb·e·na·ceous** \ˌ==ˈnāshəs\ *adj*

eb·e·na·les \ˌ==ˈnā(,)lēz\ *n pl, cap* [NL, fr. L *ebenus* + NL *-ales*] **:** an order of dicotyledonous shrubs or trees having flowers with united petals and superior ovary and stamens borne on the corolla tube and constituting the families Ebenaceae, Sapotaceae, Styracaceae, and Symplocaceae

eb·e·ne·zer \,ebəˈnēzə(r)\ *n* -S [Heb *ebhen hā-ʿezer* stone of help; fr. the application of this name by Samuel to the stone which he set up in commemoration of God's help to the Israelites in their victory over the Philistines at Mizpah (1 Sam 7:12)] **1** *usu cap* **:** a commemoration of divine assistance ⟨here I raise mine *Ebenezer*; hither by Thy help I'm come —Robert Robinson⟩ **2** *dial* **:** ANGER, TEMPER ⟨he must have had a tempestical time of it for she had got her ~ up —T.C. Haliburton⟩

eber·hard effect \ˈebər,härd-, ˈābər,härt-\ *n, usu cap 1st E* [after Gustav *Eberhard* †1940 Ger. astronomer] **:** an effect observed in developed photographic images in which the density of small equally exposed areas varies with their size — compare ADJACENCY EFFECT

eb·er·thel·la \,ebə(r)ˈthelə\ *n, cap* [NL, fr. Karl J. *Eberth* †1926 Ger. bacteriologist + NL *-ella*] *in many classifications* **:** a genus of motile aerobic gram-negative bacteria (family Enterobacteriaceae) forming acid but no gas on many carbohydrates, including certain pathogens (as *E. typhosa* which causes typhoid fever in man), and being sometimes replaced by *Salmonella* or *Bacterium*

ebi·o·nism \ˈēbēə,nizəm, ˈeb-\ *n* -S *cap* [*ebion-* (fr. *Ebionite*) + *-ism*] **:** the principles and practices of the Ebionites

ebi·o·nite \-,nīt\ *n, usu cap* [ME, fr. ML *ebionita*, fr. Heb *ebyōn* poor + L *-ita* -ite] **:** one of a Judaistic Christian Gnostic sect of the 2d century A.D. that observed the Jewish law in part, rejected St. Paul, accepted only the Gospel of Matthew, and held an adoptionist Christology — **ebi·o·nit·ic** \ˌ===ˈnid·ik\ *adj, usu cap*

ebi·o·nit·ism \ˈ≈≈≈,nīd‚izəm\ *n* -s *cap* : EBIONISM

ebo *or* **eboe** \ˈē(‚)bō\ *n, pl* **ebo** *or* **ebos** *or* **eboe** *or* **eboes** *usu cap* : IBO

¹eb·on \ˈebən\ *n* -s [ME *eban*, fr. L *ebenus*, fr. Gk *ebenos*, fr. Egypt *hbnj*] *archaic* : ¹EBONY

²ebon \"\ *adj* : ²EBONY

eb·on·ite \-‚nīt\ *n* -s [¹*ebon* + *-ite*] : hard rubber esp. when left black — sometimes used only of unfilled compositions

eb·on·ize \-‚nīz\ *vt* -ED/-ING/-S : to make black or stain black in imitation of ebony

¹eb·o·ny \ˈebənē, -ni\ *n* -ES [prob. alter. of ME *hebenyf*, modif. of LL *hebeninus*, *ebeninus* of ebony, fr. Gk *ebeninos*, fr. *ebenos* ebony] **1** : a hard heavy durable wood yielded by various trees of the genus *Diospyros* in tropical Asia and Africa **2** : a tree from which ebony is obtained **3** : any of several trees yielding wood resembling ebony (as green ebony) **4** : a variable color averaging a dark grayish olive that is almost black — called also *teak*

²ebony \"\ *adj* **1** : made of or like ebony ‹an ~ handle› **2** *of color* : of very low lightness : BLACK, DARK ‹a lanky man with an ~ face —R.G.Hubler›

ebony brown *n* : a reddish black

ebony family *n* : EBENACEAE

ebony spleenwort *n* : a common No. American fern (*Asplenium platyneuron*) with polished black stipes

éboule·ment \ābülmäⁿ\ *n* -s [F, fr. MF *esboulement*, fr. *esbouler* to cause to crumble down (fr. OF *esboeler* to disembowel, fr. *es-* — fr. L *ex-* — + *-boeler*, fr. *boel* bowel) + *-ment* — more at BOWEL] : LANDSLIDE

ebracteate \(ˈ)ē+\ *also* **ebrac·te·at·ed** \-ktē‚ād‚əd\ *adj* [*ebracteate* fr. NL *ebracteatus*, fr. *e-* + *bracteatus* bracteate; *ebracteated* fr. NL *ebracteatus* + E *-ed*] : being without bracts

ebracteolate \(ˈ)ē+\ *adj* [NL *ebracteolatus*, fr. *e-* + *bracteolatus* bracteolate] : being without bracteoles

ebri·e·ty \əˈbrīəd‚ē, ēˈ-, -ətē, -i\ *n* -ES [ME *ebriete*, fr. MF or L; MF *ebrieté*, fr. L *ebrietat-*, *ebrietas*, fr. *ebrie-* (fr. *ebrius* drunk) + *-tat-*, *-tas* -ty — more at SOBER] : INEBRIETY

ébril·lade \ˌābrēˈyäd\ *n* -s [obs. F *ébrillade*, *esbrillade*, fr. It *sbrigliata*, fr. *sbrigliare* to jerk the rein, unbridle, fr. *s-* (fr. L *ex-*) + *-brigliare*, fr. *briglia* bridle, prob. of Gmc origin; akin to OE *brigdils* bridle, OHG *brittil* rein — more at BRIDLE] : a checking of a horse by means of jerking one rein when he refuses to turn

ebri·os·i·ty \‚ēbrēˈäsəd‚ē, -ətē, -i\ *n* -ES [L *ebriositat-*, *ebriositas*, fr. *ebriosus* addicted to drink (fr. *ebrius* drunk + *-osus* -ose) + *-itat-*, *-itas* -ity] : habitual intoxication

ebul·lience \əˈbu̇lyən(t)s, ēˈ-,eˈ- *also* -ˈbəl- *or* -lēə-\ *n* -s [fr. *ebullient*, after such pairs as E *confluent: confluence*] : the quality of lively or animated expression of thoughts or feelings : high spirits : ENTHUSIASM, EXUBERANCE ‹exhorted with his characteristic ~ and bluntness —G.H.Bolsover›

ebul·lien·cy \-nsē, -si\ *n* -ES [*ebullient* + *-cy*] : EBULLIENCE

ebul·lient \-nt\ *adj* [L *ebullient-*, *ebulliens*, pres. part. of *ebullire* to come bubbling out, fr. *e-* + *bullire* to bubble, boil, fr. *bulla* bubble — more at POLL (head)] **1** : BOILING, AGITATED ‹indicates the presence of ~ internal energy —E.A.Armstrong› **2** : characterized by ebullience ‹three acts of ~ breezy music —C.M.Smith› — **ebul·lient·ly** *adv*

ebul·li·om·e·ter \ə‚bu̇lēˈämədə(r), ē‚-, e‚- *also* -‚bəl-\ *n* -s [ISV *ebullio-* (fr. L *ebullire*) + *-meter*] : an instrument for the usu. precise determination of either the absolute or the differential boiling points of liquids used esp. for determining the molecular weight of a solute dissolved in a liquid, the purity of liquids, and the alcoholic content of beverages

ebul·li·o·met·ric \≈ˌ≈lēəˈme·trik\ *adj* [*ebulliometry* + *-ic*] : relating to or by means of ebulliometry

ebul·li·om·e·try \≈‚≈lēˈämə·trē\ *n* -ES [ISV *ebullio-* + *-metry*] : the determination of boiling points of liquids or the change of boiling point of a liquid owing to the presence of dissolved material

ebul·lio·scope \≈ˈ≈lēə‚skōp, -lyə-\ *n* [ISV *ebullio-* + *-scope*; orig. formed as F *ébullioscope*] : EBULLIOMETER

ebul·li·o·scop·ic \≈ˌ≈(≈)≈ˈskäpik\ *adj* [ISV *ebullioscope* + *-ic*] : EBULLIOMETRIC

ebul·li·os·co·py \≈‚bu̇lēˈäskəpē, -‚bəl-\ *n* -ES [ISV *ebullio-* + *-scopy*] : EBULLIOMETRY

eb·ul·li·tion \‚ebəˈlishən, ‚ēb-\ *n* -s [LL *ebullition-*, *ebullitio*, fr. L *ebullitus* (past part. of *ebullire*) + *-ion-*, *-io* -ion] **1** : the act, process, or state of boiling or bubbling up **2** : a sudden and violent outburst or display ‹an ~ of chivalry, indignation, and racial solidarity —Douglas Stewart›

eb·ur·nat·ed \ˈebər‚nād‚əd, ˈē(‚)bər-; əˈbər-, ēˈ-,eˈ-\ *adj* [fr. *eburnation*, after such pairs as E *creation: created*] : hard and dense like ivory ‹~ bone› ‹~ cartilage›

eb·ur·na·tion \‚ebərˈnāshən, ‚ē(‚)bər-\ *n* -s [fr. (assumed) NL *eburnation-*, *eburnatio*, fr. L *eburnus*, *eburneus* of ivory (fr. *ebur* ivory) + *-ation-*, *-atio* -ation — more at IVORY] : a diseased condition in which bone or cartilage is eburnated

ebur·ne·an \əˈbərnēən, ēˈ-,eˈ-\ *or* **ebur·ne·ous** \-ēəs\ *adj* [*eburnean* fr. L *eburneus* + E *-an*; *eburneous* fr. L *eburneus*] : resembling ivory in color

¹ec- *prefix* [ME, fr. OF, fr. L, fr. Gk *ek*, fr. *ex* — more at EX-] : out of : outside of : outside ‹*ec*cyesis›

²ec- *or* **eco-** *also* **oec-** *or* **oeco-** *or* **oiko-** *comb form* [earlier also *yco-*, fr. MF & LL; MF *yco-*, fr. LL *oeco-*, *oiko-*, fr. Gk *oik-*, *oiko-*, fr. *oikos* house, habitation — more at VICINITY] **1 a** : household ‹*eco*nomy› **b** : economic and ‹*eco*-cultural› **2** : habitat or environment esp. as a factor significantly influencing the mode of life or the course of development ‹*eco*species› ‹*eco*system› ‹*ec*ad›

ec *abbr* economics

EC *abbr* **1** east central **2** error corrected **3** established church **4** [L *exempli causa*] for example

ecad \ˈē‚kad, ˈe‚-\ *n* -s [²*ec-* + *-ad*, n. suffix] **1** : an organism or kind of organism (as a species) modified by environment **2** : a nonheritable somatic modification induced by environment : an acquired character

ecalcarate \(ˈ)ē+\ *adj* [*e-* + L *calcar* spur + E *-ate* — more at CAUDATE] *biol* : being without a spur

ecan·da \əˈkandə\ *n* -s [prob. fr. Umbundu *ekanda*] : a tropical African vine (*Raphionacme utilis*) of the family Asclepiadaceae that yields rubber

ecardinal \(ˈ)ē+\ *adj* [*e-* + L *cardin-*, *cardo* hinge + E *-al* — more at CARDINAL] : being without a hinge — used of inarticulate brachiopods or their shells

ecardines \(ˈ)ē+\ [NL, fr. *e-* + *-cardines* creatures having (such) a hinge, fr. L *cardines*, pl. of *cardin-*, *cardo* hinge] *syn of* INARTICULATA

ecarinate \(ˈ)ē+\ *adj* [*e-* + *carinate*] *biol* : being without a carina or keel

¹écar·té \ˌāˌkärˈtā, āˈkär‚tā\ *n* -s [F, fr. past part. of *écarter* to discard, fr. *é-* (fr. L *ex-*) + *-carter* (fr. *carte* card) — more at CARD] : a two-handed card game which is played with a 32-card pack and in which each player is dealt 5 cards and has the right to replace any or all of them before play can begin, the object being to win at least 3 tricks in a given hand

²écarté \"\ *adj* [F, past part. of *écarter* to separate, spread apart, fr. OF *escarter*, fr. (assumed) VL *exquartare* to divide into four parts, fr. L *ex-* + (assumed) VL *-quartare*, fr. L *quartus* fourth — more at QUART] *ballet, of the legs* : held wide apart with an oblique side extension of one foot and the same arm

ecaudata \ˌē+\ [NL, fr. neut. pl. of *ecaudatus*] *syn of* SALIENTIA

ecaudate \(ˈ)ē+\ *adj* [NL *ecaudatus*, fr. *e-* + ML *caudatus* having a tail — more at CAUDATE] : having no tail

ec·bol·ic \ekˈbälik\ *n* -s [ISV *ecbol-* (fr. Gk *ekbolē* expulsion, fr. *ekballein* to throw out, fr. *ek* out of, out — fr. *ex* — + *ballein* to throw) + *-ic* — more at EX-, DEVIL] : a drug (as ergot) that tends to increase uterine contractions and that is used esp. to facilitate delivery

ec·ce \ˈ≈(‚)≈ — *see* ECCE HOMO\ *interj* [L, see, behold, fr. *ec-* (prob. akin to Gk *ekeinos* that one, Russ *eto* this, Skt *adaḥ* that, L *iterum* again) + *-ce* (akin to L *cis* on this side) — more at ITERATE, HE] — used to call attention often to one persecuted unjustly

ec·ce ho·mo \ˌe(‚)chāˈhō(‚)mō (*usu in the Catholic Church*), ˌe(‚)kā-, ˌek(‚)sē-\ *n* [L, behold the man; fr. the Vulgate version of the words spoken by Pilate in presenting Christ wearing the crown of thorns to the Jews (Jn 19:5)] : a picture in which the central figure is Christ crowned with thorns

¹ec·cen·tric \ikˈsen·trik, (ˈ)ekˈs-, -rēk\ *n* -s [ME *excentryke*, fr. MF & ML; MF *excentrique*, fr. ML *excentricus*, *eccentricus*, fr. *eccentricus*, adj.] **1** *in the Ptolemaic system of astronomy* : the circular orbit of the sun around the earth, the latter not being at the center of the circle; *also* : the orbit or deferent of the epicycles of the moon or a planet **2** : a mechanical device consisting of a disk through which a shaft is keyed eccentrically and a circular strap which works freely round the rim of the disk for communicating its motion to one end of a rod the other end of which is compelled to move in a straight line so as to produce reciprocating motion **3 a** : a person that deviates from conventional or accepted conduct esp. in odd or whimsical ways ‹an ~ who cluttered his estate with statues of himself› **b** : a person or thing that varies from some established type, pattern, or rule in any way ‹Milton seems to me . . . the greatest of all ~s —T.S.Eliot›

²eccentric \"\ *or* **ex·cen·tric** \"\ *adj* [ML *eccentricus*, fr. Gk *ekkentros* not having the earth as center, eccentric (fr. *ek* out of, out — fr. *ex* — + *-kentros*, fr. *kentron* center of a circle) + L *-icus* -ic — more at CENTER] **1** : not having the same center — used of circles, cylinders, spheres, and certain other figures; opposed to *concentric* **2** : deviating from some established type, pattern, or rule ‹his goods were so ~ that only he could ever sell them —Wolf Mankowitz› : deviating from conventional or accepted usage or conduct esp. in odd or whimsical ways ‹famed for his ~ spelling› ‹~ behavior made him the butt of many jokes› **3 a** : deviating or departing from the center or from the line of a circle ‹an ~ orbit› : relating to deviation from the center or from circular motion **b** : located elsewhere than at the geometrical center : having its axis or support so located ‹~ wheel› **4** : being away or remote from a center ‹their ~ location makes it . . . costly to get oil from there —Ellsworth Huntington & Samuel Van Valkenburg› : OFF-CENTER ‹~ loading occurs when force on a member such as a column is not applied at the center of the column —*Army Tech. Manual 5-230*› **5** : of or relating to an eccentric : driven by an eccentric ‹an ~ strap› ‹an ~ rod›

syn see STRANGE

ec·cen·tri·cal \-rəkəl\ *archaic var of* ECCENTRIC

ec·cen·tri·cal·ly \-rək(ə)lē, -rēk-, -li\ *adv* : in an eccentric way

ec·cen·tric·i·ty \‚ek‚senˈtrisəd‚ē, -ətē, -i *sometimes* ‚eksən- *or* ik‚sen- *or* ek‚sen-\ *n* -ES [ML *eccentricitat-*, *eccentricitas*, fr. *eccentricus* + L *-itat-*, *-itas* -ity] : the condition, degree, or an instance of being eccentric: as **a** *in machinery* : the distance of the center of figure of a body from an axis about which it turns : THROW — compare ¹ECCENTRIC 2 **b** : deviation from an established pattern, rule, or norm ‹speaking French with an ~ that could not be ignored —F.M.Ford› : odd or whimsical behavior ‹mild and retiring to the point of ~ —C.B. Forcey› **c** : the ratio of the distances from any point of a conic section to a focus and the corresponding directrix, being less than one in the ellipse, greater than one in the hyperbola, equal to one in the parabola, and equal to zero in the circle

eccentric-shaft press *n* : a punch press in which pressure is applied to the slide by means of an eccentric shaft

ec·chy·mosed \ˈekə‚mōzd, -ōst\ *adj* [*ecchymosis* + *-ed*] : affected with ecchymosis

ec·chy·mo·sis \‚ekəˈmōsəs\ *n, pl* **ecchymo·ses** \-ō‚sēz\ [NL, fr. Gk *ekchymōsis*, fr. *ekchymousthai* to extravasate blood (fr. *ek* out of, out — fr. *ex* — + *-chymousthai*, fr. *chymos* juice) + *-osis* — more at EX-, CHYME] : the escape of blood into the tissues from ruptured blood vessels marked by a livid black-and-blue or purple spot or area; *also* : the discoloration so caused — compare PETECHIA — **ec·chy·mot·ic** \ˌ≈≈ˈmäd·ik\ *adj*

eccl *abbr* **1** ecclesiastical **2** ecclesiology

ec·cle \ˈekəl\ *n* -s [alter. of *hickwall*] *dial Eng* : GREEN WOODPECKER

ec·cles cake \ˈekəlz-\ *n, usu cap E* [*Eccles*, municipal borough in Lancashire, England] *Brit* : a rich cake with fruit filling (as currants)

ecclesi- *or* **ecclesio-** *comb form* [ME *ecclesi-*, fr. LL, fr. *ecclesia* church, fr. L, assembly of citizens of a Greek state, fr. Gk *ekklēsia* church, assembly of citizens of a Greek state, fr. *ekkalein* to call forth, summon, fr. *ek* out of, out (fr. *ex*) + *kalein* to call — more at EX-, LOW (moo)] : church ‹*ecclesi*arch› ‹*ecclesio*graphy›

ec·cle·sia \əˈklēzēə, eˈ-, -lēzh(ē)ə\ *n, pl* **ecclesi·ae** \-lēz(h)ē‚ē, -lāzē‚ī\ [in sense 1, fr. L, fr. Gk *ekklēsia*; in other senses, fr. LL, church, fr. L] **1** : a political assembly of citizens of ancient Greek states; *esp* : the periodic meeting of the Athenian citizens for conducting public business and for considering affairs proposed by the council **2** : CHURCH 4d, 4e **3** : one of the local organizations of the Christadelphians

ec·cle·si·arch \-lēzēˌärk\ *n* -s [*ecclesi-* + *-arch*] **1** : a high church official or ruling prelate **2** [MGk *ekklēsiarchēs*, fr. Gk *ekklēsia* church + *-archēs* -arch] : a sacristan in the Eastern Church

ec·cle·si·ast \-zē‚ast, -ēəst, -ē‚aa(ə)st\ *n* -s [ME *ecclesiaste*, fr. LL *ecclesiastes*, fr. Gk *ekklēsiastēs*, lit., member of a Greek ecclesia, fr. *ekklēsia* church, ecclesia + *-astēs* -ast] **1** : ECCLESIASTIC **2** : a member of the Athenian ecclesia

ec·cle·si·as·tic \ə‚klēzēˈastik, e‚-, -ˈaas-, -tēk\ *n* -s [LL *ecclesiasticus*, fr. *ecclesiasticus*, adj.] : a person in holy orders or consecrated to the service of the church : CLERGYMAN, PRIEST

ec·cle·si·as·ti·cal \≈ˌ≈≈ˈ≈tәkәl, -tēk- *or* **ec·cle·si·as·tic** \-tik‚-tēk\ *adj* [*ecclesiastical* fr. ME, fr. LL *ecclesiasticus* ecclesiastical + ME *-al*; *ecclesiastic* fr. MF *ecclesiastique*, fr. LL *ecclesiasticus*, fr. Gk *ekklēsiastikos*, lit., of an ecclesia, fr. *ekklēsiastēs* + *-ikos* -ic] **1 a** : of or relating to a church esp. as a formal and established institution ‹whether tried in an ~ or a civil court› ‹~ history› **b** : belonging to, suggestive of, or suitable for use in a church building or service of worship ‹roofing material ideal for ~ work› ‹~ music› : CHURCHLY ‹spoke with an ~ solemnity› **2** : of or relating to the formal and established institutions or government of any religion ‹the festivals of the ~ year in ancient Athens› ‹the Jewish board that gives ~ endorsement to chaplaincy candidates› — **ec·cle·si·as·ti·cal·ly** \-tək(ə)lē, -tēk-, -li\ *adv*

ecclesiastical calendar *n* : a lunisolar calendar used in Roman Catholic and many Protestant countries for determining the times of Easter and other movable feasts

ecclesiastical corporation *n* : a corporation concerned only with religious matters and consisting wholly of ecclesiastics (as the dean and chapter of a cathedral church) — contrasted with *lay corporation*

ecclesiastical court *n* : a court having jurisdiction in ecclesiastical affairs : a tribunal in an ecclesiastical body — called also *Court Christian*

ecclesiastical law *n* : the law established by a church or religious denomination and administered in its courts : CANON LAW : the law whether of ecclesiastical or civil law origin applied to a church

ecclesiastical mode *n* : an ascending diatonic musical scale of eight notes or tones comprising an octave and consisting of a pentachord and a tetrachord of which the highest tone of one is the lowest tone of the other — called also *Gregorian mode, medieval mode*; see DORIAN MODE, HYPODORIAN MODE, HYPOMIXOLYDIAN MODE, HYPOPHRYGIAN MODE, LYDIAN MODE, MIXOLYDIAN MODE, PHRYGIAN MODE; MODE illustration

ec·cle·si·as·ti·cism \ə‚klēzēˈastə‚sizəm, e‚-, -ˈaas-\ *n* -s : excessive attachment to ecclesiastical forms, methods, and practices ‹the struggle between religion and ~›

ec·cle·si·ast·ry *pronunc at* ECCLESIAST + rē\ *n* -ES : ecclesiastical matters

ec·cle·si·ol·a·try \ə‚klēzēˈälə·trē, -e‚-\ *n* -ES [*ecclesi-* + *-latry*] : excessive devotion to the church

ec·cle·si·o·log·i·cal \≈ˌ≈zēəˈläjəkəl\ *also* **ec·cle·si·o·log·ic** \-jik\ *adj* [*ecclesiology* + *-ical*, *-ic*] : of or relating to ecclesiology — **ec·cle·si·o·log·i·cal·ly** \-jək(ə)lē\ *adv*

ec·cle·si·ol·o·gist \≈ˌ≈≈ˈäləjəst\ *n* -s [*ecclesiology* + *-ist*] : a specialist in ecclesiology

ec·cle·si·ol·o·gy \-jē\ *n* -ES [*ecclesi-* + *-logy*] **1** : the science or study of ecclesiastical art and antiquities esp. with reference to the adornment and equipment of churches **2** : the study of the doctrine of the church **3** : church policy ‹a venture in practical ~ in southern India›

ec·co·pro·ti·co·phor·ic \‚ekō‚prōd·əkōˈfōrik, -präd-·\ *adj* [obs. E *eccoprotic*, n., laxative (fr. assumed NL *eccoproticum*, fr. neut. of assumed NL *eccoproticus*, adj., laxative, fr. Gk *ekkoprōtikos*, fr. assumed Gk *ekkoprōtos* — verbal of *ekkoproun* to empty of excrement, fr. *ek* out of, out, fr. *ex* + *-koproun*, fr. *kopros* excrement, dung — + Gk *-ikos* -ic) + E *-o-* + *-phoric* — more at EX-, COPR-] : exhibiting the properties of a laxative

ec·cri·na·les \‚ekrəˈnā(‚)lēz\ *n pl, cap* [NL, fr. *Eccrina*, genus of fungi + *-ales*] : an order of fungi (class Phycomycetes) containing lower fungi that occur as parasites in the alimentary canals of arthropods, that have slender coenocytic hyphae with funnel-shaped attachment disks, and that reproduce by endospores

ec·crine \ˈekrən; -‚krin, -īn,-ēn\ *adj* [ISV ¹*ec-* + *-crine* (fr. Gk *krinein* to separate) — more at CERTAIN] : producing a fluid secretion without removing cytoplasm from the secreting cells : produced by an eccrine gland — compare APOCRINE, MEROCRINE

eccrine gland *n* : any of the rather small sweat glands that produce an eccrine secretion, are restricted to the human skin, and are lined with cuboidal epithelium surrounded by contractile myoepithelial cells — compare APOCRINE GLAND

ec·cri·nid \ˈekrənəd, -‚nid\ *n* -s [NL *Eccrina* + E *-id*] : a fungus of the order Eccrinales

ec·cri·nol·o·gy \‚ekrəˈnäləjē\ *n* -ES [F *eccrinologie*, fr. *eccrino-* (fr. Gk *ekkrinein* to secrete, fr. *ek* out of, out + *krinein* to separate) + *-logie* -logy] : a branch of physiology that deals with secretion and secretory organs

ec·cy·cle·ma \‚eksəˈklēmə\ *n* -s [Gk *ekkyklēma*, fr. *ekkyklein* to wheel out, fr. *ek* out of, out + *kyklein* to wheel, revolve, fr. *kyklos* wheel — more at WHEEL] : a machine used to display an interior scene (as dead bodies after a murder) in the classic theater

ec·de·mite *or* **ek·de·mite** \ekˈdē‚mīt, ˈekdə‚m-\ *n* -s [Sw *ekdemit*, fr. Gk *ekdēmos* being away from home (fr. *ek* + *dēmos* deme, populace) + Sw *-it* -ite — more at DEM-] : a yellow or green lead arsenate and chloride of uncertain composition occurring in crystals, masses, and crusts

ec·dys·i·al \(ˈ)ekˈdizēəl, -izh(ē)əl\ *adj* [*ecdysis* + *-al*] : of, relating to, or functioning in ecdysis ‹an ~ gland›

ec·dys·i·ast \ekˈdizē‚ast, -ēəst\ *n* -s [*ecdysis* + *-ast*] : STRIPTEASER

ec·dy·sis \ˈekdəsəs\ *n, pl* **ecdy·ses** \-ə‚sēz\ [NL, fr. Gk *ekdysis* act of getting out, escape, fr. *ekdyein* to take off, strip off (fr. *ek* out of, out + *dyein* to dive in, put on, don) + *-sis* — more at ADYTUM] : the act of molting or shedding an outer cuticular layer (as in insects and crustaceans) — opposed to *endysis*

ece \ˈēs\ *n* -s [Gk *oikos* house, habitation — more at VICINITY] : HABITAT

ECE *abbr* extended coverage endorsement

ece·sic \əˈsēsik, ēˈ-\ *adj* [*ecesis* + *-ic*] : of, relating to, or engaging in ecesis

ece·sis \-ēsəs\ *n* -ES [Gk *oikēsis* act of inhabiting, fr. *oikein* to inhabit (fr. *oikos*) + *-sis*] : ESTABLISHMENT 5

ECG *abbr* electrocardiogram

ec·go·nine \ˈekgə‚nēn, -nən\ *n* -s [ISV *ecgon-* (fr. Gk *ekgonos* born of, sprung from, fr. *ek* out of, out + *gonos* child) + *-ine*; akin to Gk *gignesthai* to be born — more at KIN] : a crystalline alkaloid $C_9H_{15}NO_3$ obtained by hydrolysis of cocaine; tropine-carboxylic acid

ech *abbr* echelon

échap·pé \ˌā‚shaˈpā, āˈsha‚pā\ *adj* [F, fr. past part. of *échapper* to escape, fr. (assumed) VL *excappare* — more at ESCAPE] *ballet, of the legs* : opened from closed position

échappée \"\ *n* -s [F, fr. fem. of *échappé*, past part. of *échapper* to escape] : ESCAPE NOTE

ech·ard \ˈe‚kärd\ *n* -s [Gk *echein* to hold, withhold + *ardein* to water — more at SCHEME, ARDELLA] : the soil water that is unavailable to plant organisms — compare CHRESARD, HOLARD

eche *vt* -ED/-ING/-S [ME *echen* — more at EKE (to increase)] *obs* : INCREASE, ENLARGE

eche·lette \ˌeshəˈlet, ˌāsh-\ *n* -s [F *échelette* small rack, fr. MF *eschelette* small ladder, fr. *eschele*, *eschiele* ladder + *-ette*] : a reflection grating made by ruling parallel V-shaped grooves in a polished metal plate so that light is reflected from the corresponding faces of successive grooves

echel·i·dae \əˈkelə‚dē, ēˈ-\ *n pl, cap* [NL, prob. fr. *Echelus*, type genus (prob. modif. of Gk *enchelys* eel) + *-idae* — more at ANGUIS] : a family of small tropical eels comprising the worm eels

¹echelle \āˈshel\ *n* -s [F *échelle* ladder] : a lacing of ribbons on the stomacher of a 17th century costume

²echelle \"\ *n* -s [F *échelle* ladder, fr. OF *eschiele*, fr. LL *scala* — more at SCALE] : a diffraction grating made by ruling narrow flat steps on a plane metallic mirror and having a grating space and resolving power intermediate between an echelette and an echelon

¹ech·e·lon \ˈeshə‚län\ *n* -s *often attrib* [F *échelon*, lit., rung of a ladder, fr. OF *eschelon*, fr. *eschele*, *eschiele* ladder] **1 a** : an arrangement of a body of troops with its units each somewhat to the left or right of the one in the rear like a series of steps; *also* : any similar formation of units or individuals ‹a long ~ of wild geese —H.L.Davis› — often used with *in* ‹long staggering line of north canoes turned in ~ —Walter O'Meara› **b** : a flight formation in which each airplane flies at a certain elevation above or below and at a certain distance behind and to the right or left of the airplane ahead **c** : one of a number of military units in echelon formation; *also* : any military or nonmilitary unit or group of individuals acting or appearing to act in a disciplined, organized, or united manner ‹the first ~s in an amphibious assault —*Aero Digest*› **2 a** : a group of individuals having a particular responsibility or occupying a particular level or grade (as of command, authority, or leadership) in an organization, profession, or field of activity ‹the financial, supply, and training ~s of the European Army —*Newsweek*› ‹the lower ~s of the bureaucracy› ‹the higher ~s of the Social Register —Alva Johnston› **b** : one of a series of levels or grades (as of leadership or responsibility) in an organization or field of activity ‹permits employees on every ~ to participate in the development of policy› **3** : a diffraction grating giving spectra of very high order and dispersion and used mainly in the study of fine structure that consists of a series of plane-parallel glass plates of exactly equal thickness each wider than its neighbor by the same small amount and thus forms a miniature stairway, light normally entering at the widest plate and emerging at the successive risers of the stairway **4** : an arrangement of geologic features (as mountains, folds, fractures) in a pattern resembling that of a military echelon

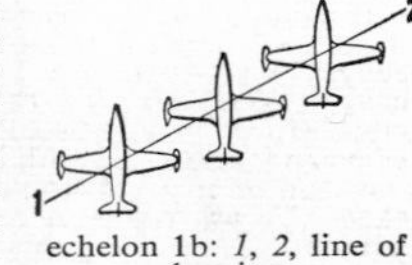

echelon 1b: *1, 2,* line of bearing

²echelon \"\ *vb* -ED/-ING/-S [F *échelonner*, fr. *échelon*] *vt* : to place (as troops or fortifications) in echelon ~ *vi* : to take position in echelon

ech·e·lon·ment \-nmənt, ˌ≈≈ˈ≈≈\ *n* -s [F *échelonnement*, fr. *échelonner* + *-ment*] : the timing or positioning of troops or supplies to provide uninterrupted flow to the front

ech·e·ne·id \‚ekəˈnēəd\ *n* -s [NL *Echeneid-*, *Echeneis*] : a fish of the genus *Echeneis*; *broadly* : REMORA

ech·e·ne·is \-ēəs\ *n, cap* [NL, fr. L, remora, fr. Gk *echenēis*, fr. *echenēis* that detains ships, fr. *eche-* (fr. *echein* to hold) + *-nēis* (fr. *naus* ship); fr. a supposed ability to slow down ships — more at SCHEME, NAVE] : a genus (the type of the family Echeneididae or Echeneidae) of marine fishes comprising the typical remoras

ech·e·ve·ria \‚echəvəˈrēə, -rīə\ *n* [NL, after *Echeveria*, 19th cent. Mex. botanical illustrator] **1** *cap* : a large genus of tropical American succulent plants (family Crassulaceae) having flowers with erect petals that spread only at the tips and axillary flower clusters **2** -s : any plant of *Echeveria* or of the closely related genus *Cotyledon*

¹echid·na \əˈkidnə, ēˈ-,eˈ-\ *n* [NL, fr. L, viper, fr. Gk — more at ANGUIS] **1** -s **a** : an oviparous burrowing nocturnal mammal (*Tachyglossus aculeatus*) of the order Monotremata native to Australia, Tasmania, and New Guinea that is somewhat larger than a hedgehog and has the hair of the skin mingled with spines on the upper part of the body, the snout long and tapering, the mouth wholly toothless with a long extensile tongue adapted for feeding on ants, the salivary glands enlarged, and the claws long and heavy **b :** a member of a related New Guinea genus (*Zaglossus*) having three claws on each foot **2** *cap* **:** a genus of moray eels that are usu. rather small with strikingly marbled and reticulated patterns on the body surface

[2]**echidna** \"\ [NL, fr. L, viper] *syn of* TACHYGLOSSUS

[3]**echidna** \"\ [NL, fr. L, viper] *syn of* BITIS

[1]**echid·ni·dae** \-nə,dē\ [NL, fr. *Echidna* genus of moray eels + *-idae*] *syn of* MURAENIDAE

[2]**echidnidae** \"\ [NL, fr. [2]*Echidna* + *-idae*] *syn of* TACHYGLOSSIDAE

echid·noph·a·ga \,ē,kid'näfəgə, ,e,-\ *n, cap* [NL, prob. fr. *echidno-* (fr. Gk, fr. *echidna*) + *-phaga* (fem. of *-phagus* -phagous, fr. Gk *-phagos*)] **:** a genus comprising fowl fleas (as the sticktight flea) of which the female remains attached to the host

echim·y·ine \ə'kimē,īn, ē'-,e'-, -mēən\ *adj* [NL *Echimys* + E *-ine*] **:** of or relating to *Echimys*

echi·mys \-'kīməs, 'ekə,mis\ *n, cap* [NL, irreg. fr. Gk *echinos* hedgehog + *mys* mouse — more at ANGUIS, MOUSE] **:** a genus (the type of the family Echimyidae) of hystricomorph rodents of So. and Central America comprising various spiny rats or urares

echin- *or* **echino-** *comb form* [L *echin-* prickle, fr. *echinus* sea urchin, fr. Gk *echinos* hedgehog, sea urchin] **1 :** prickle **:** prickly ⟨*Echino*cactus⟩ **2 a :** sea urchin ⟨*echin*al⟩ ⟨*echino*chrome⟩ **b :** echinoderm ⟨*echino*logy⟩

ech·i·na·cea \,ekə'nāshēə\ *n* [NL, fr. *echin-* + *-acea* (fem. of *-aceus* -aceous)] **1** *cap* **:** a small genus of coarse herbs (family Compositae) having thick rough leaves and long-stalked flower heads with showy purplish, crimson, or yellow rays **2 :** the dried rhizome and roots of either of two herbs (*Echinacea pallida* and *E. angustifolia*) formerly used in the treatment of ulcers and boils

echi·nal \ə'kīnᵊl, ē'-,e-; 'ekənᵊl\ *adj* [*echin-* + *-al*] **:** relating to a sea urchin

echi·nate \-nət, -,nāt\ *also* **echi·nat·ed** \-,nād·əd\ *adj* [*echinate* fr. L *echinatus*, fr. *echin-* + *-atus* -ate; *echinated* fr. L *echinatus* + E *-ed*] **:** densely covered with stiff bristles or spines **:** prickly like a hedgehog — compare ECHINULATE, MURICATE

eching *pres part of* ECHE

echini *pl of* ECHINUS

echi·nid \ə'kīnəd, ē'-,e'-\ *n* -S [NL *Echinidae*] **:** SEA URCHIN

echin·i·dae \-'kinə,dē\ *n pl, cap* [NL, fr. *Echinus*, type genus + *-idae*] **:** a family (order Centrechinoida) including a large number of widely distributed sea urchins a few of which are used as food — see ECHINUS

ech·i·nid·ea \,ekə'nidēə\ [NL, fr. *Echinus* + *-idea*] *syn of* ECHINOIDEA

ech·i·nite \'ekə,nīt; ə'kī,-, ē'-,e'-\ *n* -S [NL *echinita*, fr. L *echinus* sea urchin + *-ita* -ite] **:** a fossil sea urchin

echi·no- *in pronunciations below*, ≈≈≈ = ə¦kīnō *or* ē¦- *or* e¦ *or* -nə *or* ¦ekə(,)nō\ — see ECHIN-

echi·no·cactus \≈≈≈ *at* ECHINO- + \ *n* [NL, fr. *echin-* + *Cactus*] **1** *cap* **:** a large genus of globular or cylindrical strongly ribbed and usu. very spiny cacti that occur from the southwestern U.S. to Brazil **2 :** any plant of the genus *Echinocactus*

echi·no·car·is \" + 'ka(a)rəs\ *n, cap* [NL, fr. *echin-* + *-caris*] **:** a genus of extinct crustaceans (order Nebaliacea) the tail spines of which are common in various Devonian rocks

echi·no·ce·re·us \" + 'sirēəs\ *n* [NL, fr. *echin-* + *Cereus*] **1** *cap* **:** a genus of low ribbed cacti **2** *pl* **echinoce·rei** \-ē,ī\ **:** any plant of the genus *Echinocereus* having single or few usu. short joints and spiny ovaries and flower tubes

ech·i·noch·loa \,ekə'näkləwə\ *n, cap* [NL, fr. *echin-* + Gk *chloa, chloē* young verdure, fr. *chloos* light green color; fr. the prickly awns — more at GLOW] **:** a genus of succulent grasses found in warm regions — see BARNYARD GRASS, JAPANESE MILLET

echi·no·chrome \≈≈≈ *at* ECHINO- + ,krōm\ *n* -S [*echin-* + *-chrome*] **:** any of several red to brown respiratory pigments found in certain sea urchins

echi·no·coc·cic \"+¦käk(s)ik\ *adj* [ISV *echinococc-* (fr. NL *Echinococcus*) + *-ic*] **:** of, relating to, or involving *Echinococcus* or hydatids

echi·no·coc·co·sis \"+(,)kä'kōsəs\ *n, pl* **echinococco·ses** \-ō,sēz\ [NL, fr. *Echinococcus* + *-osis*] **:** infestation with or disease caused by a small tapeworm (*Echinococcus granulosus*); *esp* **:** HYDATID DISEASE

echi·no·coc·cus \"+'käkəs\ *n* [NL, fr. *echin-* + *-coccus*] **1** *cap* **:** a genus of tapeworms (family Taeniidae) that alternate a minute adult usu. having no more than three proglottids and living as a harmless commensal in the intestine of dogs and other carnivores with a hydatid larva invading tissues esp. of the liver of cattle, sheep, swine, and man, and acting as a serious often fatal pathogen **2** *pl* **echinococ·ci :** any worm of the genus *Echinococcus; sometimes* **:** HYDATID

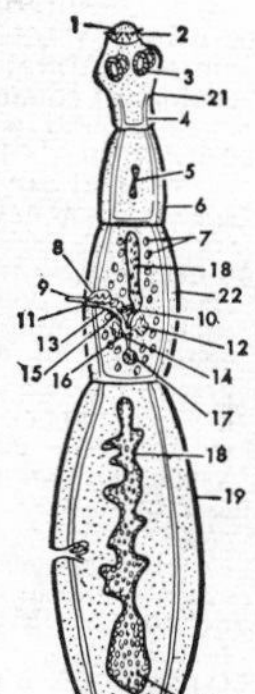

echinococcus: *1* rostellum, *2* hooklets, *3* sucker, *4* neck, *5* germinal mass, *6* immature proglottid, *7* testes, *8* cirrus pouch, *9* cirrus, *10* vas deferens, *11* genital pore, *12* ovary, *13* vagina, *14* vitelline duct, *15* seminal receptacle, *16* ootype, *17* vitelline gland, *18* uterus, *19* gravid proglottid, *20* eggs

echi·no·cys·tis \"+'sistəs\ *n* [NL, fr. *echin-* + *-cystis;* fr. the spiny globular fruit] **1** *cap* **:** a genus of prostrate or climbing American herbaceous plants (family Cucurbitaceae) with greenish white flowers followed by densely spiny oblong to ovate fruits **2** -ES **:** any plant of the genus *Echinocystis*

echi·no·cys·toi·da \"+sə'stȯidə\ *n pl, cap* [NL, irreg. fr. *Echinocystites*, fossil genus of Echinodermata (fr. *echin-* + *-cystis* + *-ites* -ite) + *-oida*] **:** an order of Silurian fossil echinoids having small irregular spheroidal or flattened tests

echi·no·der \"+,de(ə)r\ *n* -S [NL *Echinodera*] **:** KINORHYNCH

ech·i·nod·era \,ekə'nädərə\ [NL, fr. *Echinoderes*] *syn of* KINORHYNCHA

ech·i·nod·er·es \-,rēz\ *n, cap* [NL, fr. *echin-* + *-deres* (fr. Gk *derē, deirē* neck) — more at DER-] **:** a genus (the type of the family Echinoderidae) of minute segmented spinous marine worms that is the first-known and best-known representative of the class Kinorhyncha

ech·i·nod·er·id \-,rəd, -,rid\ *n* -S [NL *Echinoderidae* (family including the genus *Echinoderes*), fr. *Echinoderes*, type genus + *idae*] **:** KINORHYNCH

echi·no·derm \≈≈≈ *at* ECHINO- + ,dərm\ *n* -S [NL *Echinodermata*] **:** one of the Echinodermata

echi·no·der·ma \"+'dərmə\ [NL, fr. *echin-* + *-derma* (fr. Gk *derma* skin) — more at DERM-] *syn of* ECHINODERMATA

echi·no·der·ma·ta \-məd·ə\ *n pl, cap* [NL, fr. *echin-* + *-dermata*] **:** a phylum of radially symmetrical coelomate marine animals consisting of the starfishes, sea urchins, and their related forms all having a calcareous exoskeleton, a blood-vascular system, a nervous system, and a water-vascular system that through small tubular appendages of the body connecting with these vessels provides tentacles and organs of locomotion — compare TUBE FOOT — **echi·no·der·ma·tous** \-¦dərməd·əs\ *adj*

ech·i·nod·o·rus \,ekə'nädərəs\ *n, cap* [NL, fr. *echin-* + Gk *doros* leather bag, fr. *derein* to skin; fr. the form of the ovary — more at TEAR] **:** a genus of chiefly American aquatic or marsh herbs (family Alismataceae) having long-stalked often spotted leaves, delicate white flowers in racemes or panicles, and spiny clusters of beaked fruits

echi·noid \ə'kī,nȯid, ē'-,e'-, 'ekə,-\ *n* -S [NL *Echinoidea*] **:** SEA URCHIN

ech·i·noi·dea \,ekə'nȯidēə\ *n pl, cap* [NL, fr. *echin-* + *-oidea*] **:** a class of motile bottom-dwelling echinoderms comprising the sea urchins and related forms having a disk-shaped shell formed of regular and usu. united plates studded with tubercles bearing spines and with pedicellariae and pores through which the tube feet emerge and most having a characteristic complicated system of pentamerous jaws in the mouth — compare ARISTOTLE'S LANTERN, CENTRECHINOIDA, CIDAROIDA, EXOCYCLOIDA

ech·i·nol·o·gy \,ekə'näləjē\ *n* -ES [*echin-* + *-logy*] **:** a branch of zoology that deals with echinoderms

echi·no·mys \≈≈≈ *at* ECHINO- + ,mis\ [NL, alter. (influenced by Gk *echinos* hedgehog) of *Echimys*] *syn of* ECHIMYS

ech·i·nop·a·nax \,ekə'näpə,naks\ *n, cap* [NL, fr. *echin-* + *Panax*] **:** a small genus of prickly shrubs of the family Araliaceae

echi·no·pa·ryph·i·um \≈≈≈ *at* ECHINO- + pə'rifēəm\ *n, cap* [NL, fr. *echin-* + *-paryphium* (fr. Gk *paryphē* border woven along a robe, fr. *para-* + *hyphē* web); akin to Gk *hyphainein* to weave — more at WEAVE] **:** a genus of digenetic trematodes (family Echinostomatidae) infesting the small intestine of waterfowl and domestic poultry and sometimes carnivorous mammals or man

echi·no·pluteus \"+\ *n* [NL, fr. *echin-* + *pluteus*] **:** the pluteus larva of an echinoid

ech·i·nops \'ekə,näps; ə'kī,näps, ē'-,e'-\ *n, cap* [NL, fr. *echin-* + *-ops*] **:** a large genus of Mediterranean herbs (family Compositae) comprising the globe thistles that have one-flowered heads aggregated in dense globular clusters

ech·i·nop·sine \,ekə'näp,sēn, -,sən\ *n* -S [ISV *echinops-* (fr. NL *Echinops*) + *-ine*] **:** a crystalline alkaloid $C_{10}H_9NO$ derived from quinoline occurring in the seeds of globe thistles and having a physiological effect like that of strychnine and brucine

echi·no·rhin·i·dae \≈≈≈ *at* ECHINO- + 'rinə,dē *or* 'rīn-\ [NL, fr. *Echinorhinus* + *-idae*] *syn of* SQUALIDAE; see ECHINORHINUS

echi·no·rhi·nus \-'rīnəs\ *n, cap* [NL, fr. *echin-* + Gk *rhinos* skin; akin to OE *wrītan* to write — more at WRITE] **:** a genus of sharks (family Squalidae) comprising the bramble sharks and sometimes being made type of a separate family Echinorhinidae

echi·no·rhyn·chus \-'riŋkəs\ *n, cap* [NL, fr. *echin-* + *-rhynchus*] **:** a genus (the type of the family Echinorhynchidae) of small cylindrical acanthocephalan worms that are parasitic in various vertebrates

echi·no-so·rex \-'sōr,eks\ *n, cap E* [NL, fr. *echin-* + *Sorex*] **:** a genus of ratlike southern Asiatic insectivores including only the moonrat

echi·no·sto·mat·i·dae \,stō'mad·ə,dē\ *n pl, cap* [NL, fr. *Echinostomat-, Echinostoma*, type genus (fr. *echin-* + *-stoma*) + *-idae*] **:** a family of digenetic trematode worms (type genus *Echinostoma*) that are rare in man but common and widely distributed as parasites of birds and lower vertebrates and are distinguished by having the anterior end modified and armed with spines

echi·no·stome \≈≈≈ *at* ECHINO- + ,stōm\ *n* -S [NL *Echinostoma*] **:** one of the Echinostomatidae — **ech·i·nos·to·moid** \¦ekə¦nästə,mȯid\ *adj*

echi·no·sto·mi·a·sis \"+stə'mīəsəs; *or* ,ekə,nästə'-\ *n, pl* **echinostomia·ses** \-ə,sēz\ [NL, fr. *Echinostoma* + *-iasis*] **:** infestation with or disease caused by worms of the family Echinostomatidae

echi·no·zoa \≈≈≈ *at* ECHINO- + 'zōə\ *n pl, cap* [NL, fr. *echin-* + *-zoa*] *in some classifications* **:** a major division of Echinodermata consisting of the Echinoidea and Holothurioidea

echin·u·late \ə'kinyələt, ē'-,e'-, -'kīn-, -,lāt\ *also* **echin·u·lated** \-,lād·əd\ *adj* [*echinulate* prob. fr. (assumed) NL *echinulatus*, fr. (assumed) NL *echinulus* small prickle (fr. L *echin-* prickle + *-ulus* -ule) + L *-atus* -ate; *echinulated* fr. (assumed) NL *echinulatus* + E *-ed* — more at ECHIN-] **:** set with small spines or prickles — compare ECHINATE — **echin·u·la·tion** \≈,≈≈'lāshən\ *n* -S

echi·nus \ə'kīnəs, ē'-,e'-\ *n* [ME, fr. L, fr. Gk *echinos* hedgehog, sea urchin — more at ANGUIS] **1 a** *pl* **echi·ni** \-,nī\ **:** SEA URCHIN **b** *cap* [NL, fr. L] **:** the type genus of Echinidae that comprises numerous sea urchins including the common edible European urchin (*E. esculenta*) **2** [L, echinus of a capital, sea urchin; prob. fr. its shape] **a :** the rounded molding forming the bell of the capital in the Greek Doric order and having in profile a peculiar elastic curve; *also* **:** a similar member in other orders, the Ionic having the egg-and-dart ornament **b :** a quarter-round molding **c :** EGG AND DART

ech·is \'ekəs, 'ēk-\ *n, cap* [NL, fr Gk, viper; akin to Gk *echidna* viper — more at ANGUIS] **:** a genus of vipers found in India, Arabia, and No. Africa

echi·tes \-'kīd·ēz\ *n, cap* [NL, irreg. fr. Gk *echis* viper; fr. the coiling stem of some species] **:** a large genus of woody vines (family Apocynaceae) chiefly of tropical America having a 5-lobed disk in the flowers and a glandular or fine-scaled calyx

ech·i·um \'ekēəm\ *n* [NL, fr. Gk *echion* echium, fr. *echis* viper] **1** *cap* **:** a genus of bristly herbs and some shrubs (family Boraginaceae) having an irregular corolla and unequal exserted stamens **2** -S **:** any plant of the genus *Echium*

ech·i·u·ri·da \,ekē'yu̇rədə\ [NL, fr. *Echiurus* + *-ida*] *syn of* ECHIUROIDEA

[1]**ech·i·u·roid** \-u̇,rȯid\ *n* -S [NL *Echiuroidea*] **:** one of the Echiuroidea

[2]**echiuroid** \¦≈≈¦≈,≈\ *adj* **:** of or relating to the Echiuroidea

ech·i·u·roi·dea \,ekēyə'rȯidēə\ *n pl, cap* [NL, fr. *Echiurus* + *-oidea*] **:** a group of marine worms of obscure position though commonly classed as a division of Gephyrea and distinguished by a sensitive but nonretractile proboscis overlying the mouth which in some forms (as some worms of the genus *Bonellia*) may attain great size

ech·i·u·rus \,ekē'yu̇rəs\ *n, cap* [NL, fr. Gk *echis* viper + NL *-urus*] **:** a common genus (the type of the family Echiuridae) of echiuroid worms — compare ECHIUROIDEA

[1]**echo** \'e(,)kō\ *n* -ES [ME *ecco*, fr. MF & L; MF *echo*, fr.L, fr. Gk *ēchō;* akin to L *vagire* to cry (said of a child), Gk *ēchē, ēchos* sound, and perh. Skt *vagnu* sound, cry] **1 :** the repetition of a sound caused by reflection of sound waves **:** the sound due to such reflection **2 a :** a repetition or imitation (as of the style or ideas) of another **:** REFLECTION ⟨you catch the ~ everywhere of this strong sense of purpose —Joseph Alsop⟩ ⟨containing strong ~*es* from the work of older and greater poets⟩ **:** REPERCUSSION, RESULT ⟨the economic collapse had dangerous political ~*es*⟩ **:** SURVIVAL, TRACE, VESTIGE ⟨~*es* of an older culture linger in the area⟩ **:** RESPONSE ⟨his appeal would find a sympathetic ~ in most minds —Roger Fry⟩ **b :** one who closely imitates or repeats another's words, ideas, or acts ⟨the minister may . . . become a pious ~ of their opinions —W.L.Sperry⟩ **3 :** the repetition of a sound, syllable, word, or phrase for rhetorical or poetic purposes; *esp* **:** repetition in imitation of an echo popular in 16th and 17th century poetry at the end of a line or stanza — see ECHO VERSE **4 a :** a soft repetition of a musical phrase **b :** ECHO ORGAN **c :** ECHO STOP **d :** a mute used to soften and modify the tone of brass wind instruments **5 a :** a signal in whist play in response to a signal given by one's partner; *specif* **:** the trump signal by a player whose partner has previously given the trump signal **b :** the play or discard in bridge of an unnecessarily high card followed by a lower one — compare HIGH-LOW **6 a :** the repetition of a received radio signal a perceptible time after the signal is first received due to the travel of the radio waves over a path (as the indirect path when the waves are reflected from an ionized layer of the atmosphere) other than the most direct path between transmitter and receiver **b** (1) **:** the reflection of transmitted radar signals by an object (2) **:** the visual indication of this reflection as seen on a radarscope **:** BLIP, PIP — **to the echo** *adv* **:** to the point of causing an echo **:** LOUDLY ⟨cheered him *to the echo* —Henry Irving⟩

[2]**echo** \", *in pres part* " *or* 'ekəw\ *vb* -ED/-ING/-ES *vi* **1 a :** to resound with echoes ⟨woods ~*ing* with the chopping of axes⟩ **:** produce echoes or become repeated by echoes ⟨the sound of battle ~*ed* over all the hills —Farley Mowat⟩ **b :** to repeat like an echo ⟨"a fine life", he said . . . "a fine life", he ~*ed*, drowsily —Laura Krey⟩ **2 :** REPEAT ⟨a theme which ~*es* throughout the novel —Ruth Suckow⟩ **:** become reflected or find renewed expression ⟨the effects of this revolutionary change still ~ throughout human anatomy and physiology —Weston La Barre⟩ **3 :** to make an echo in a game of cards (as bridge) ~ *vt* **1 :** REPEAT, IMITATE ⟨~*ing* the words and ideas of his famous father⟩ ⟨cushions in faint colors that ~ the carpet —Rumer Godden⟩ **2 :** to send back or repeat (a sound) by the reflection of sound waves

[3]**echo** \'e(,)kō\ *usu cap* — a communications code word for the letter *e*

echo box *n* **:** CAVITY RESONATOR

echo chamber *n* **:** a room with sound-reflecting walls used for producing hollow or echoing sound effects

echo·gram \'ekō,gram\ *n* -S [[1]*echo* + *-gram*] **:** the record made by an echograph

echo·graph \-raf,-räf\ *n* -S [[1]*echo* + *-graph*] **:** a sonic depth finder that automatically records depths

echo·ic \ə'kōik, e'-\ *adj* [[1]*echo* + *-ic*] **:** of, relating to, or being an echo; *specif* **:** formed in imitation of some natural sound **:** IMITATIVE, ONOMATOPOEIC

echo·ing·ly *adv* **:** in the manner of something echoing

echo·ism \'ekō,izəm, -kə,wi-\ *n* -S [[1]*echo* + *-ism*] **1 :** the formation of echoic words **:** ONOMATOPOEIA **2 :** the phonetic assimilation of a following to a preceding sound (as a vowel)

echo·ki·ne·sia \,e(,)kōkə'nēzh(ē)ə, -,kī'-\ *or* **echo·ki·ne·sis** \-nēsəs\ *n, pl* **echokinesias** *or* **echokineses** [NL, fr. L *echo* + NL *-kinesia* or *kinesis*] **:** ECHOPRAXIA

echo·la·lia \,ekō'lālēə, -lal-\ *n* -S [NL, fr. L *echo* + NL *-lalia*] **:** the often pathological repetition of what is said by other people as if echoing them — **echo·lal·ic** \¦≈≈¦lalik, -lāl-\ *adj*

echo·less \'ekōləs\ *adj* **:** having or producing no echo ⟨the hollow and ~ darkness —K.L.Patton⟩

echolocation \¦≈(,)≈≈¦≈≈\ *n* [[1]*echo* + *location*] **1 :** a process that is used by an animal (as a bat) to orient itself and avoid obstacles esp. in darkness and that involves emission of high-frequency sounds which are reflected back from environing surfaces and thus indicate the relative distance and direction of such surfaces **2 :** a technical process (as in sounding or seismography) for locating a distant object by measuring the time a wave takes to travel to and from the object

echo·me·ter \'ekō,mēd·ə(r)\ *n* -S [[1]*echo* + *-meter*] **:** an apparatus for measuring depths of objects in water or underground by timing the echoes of sound reflected from them

echo·mim·ia \,ekō'mimēə\ *n* -S [NL, fr. L *echo* + *mimus* mime + NL *-ia* — more at MIME] **:** ECHOPRAXIA

echo organ *n* **:** a division of a pipe organ situated at a distance from the rest of the instrument and containing soft stops suitable for echo effects

echoppe \ā'shäp, -shȯp\ *n* -S [F *échoppe*, by folk etymology (influence of F *échoppe* booth, fr. OF *escope*, fr. MD *schoppe*) fr. obs. F *eschople*, alter. of MF *eschalpre* scraping or graving tool, fr. L *scalprum* chisel, knife — more at SCALPEL, SHOP] **:** an engraver's needle beveled to an oval facet at the end and used to reopen previously incised lines

echo·prac·tic \¦ekō¦praktik\ *adj* [fr. *echopraxia*, after such pairs as E *ataxia: atactic*] **:** of or relating to echopraxia **:** suffering from echopraxia

echo·prax·ia \,ekō'praksēə\ *n* -S [NL, fr. L *echo* + NL *-praxia*] **:** pathological repetition of the actions of other people as if echoing them

echo ranging *n* **:** determination of the distance and direction of an object (as under water) by means of an echo (as of sound) returned by the object — compare ECHO SOUNDING, SONAR

echo sounder *n* **:** SONIC DEPTH FINDER

echo sounding *n* **:** sounding a body of water by means of a sonic depth finder or of a radar device

echo stop *n* **1 :** a stop on a harpsichord for producing the soft effect of distant sound **2 :** an organ stop having its pipes enclosed for echoic effects

echo verse *n* **:** poetry that uses the device of an echo

[1]**echt** \'äkt, 'ekt\ *adj* [ME *eghte, eighte* — more at EIGHT] *Scot* **:** EIGHT

[2]**echt** \'ekt\ *adj* [G, fr. LG, fr. MLG *echt, echte* lawful; akin to OFris *aft* lawful, OHG *ēhaft;* all fr. a prehistoric WGmc compound whose first constituent is represented by OE *ǣ, ǣw* law, OFris *ēwa, ā, ē*, OS *ēo*, OHG *ēwa* and whose second constituent is represented by OE *hæft*, adj., captive, OHG *haft* captive, bound, Goth *hafts* united; first constituent prob. akin to Goth *aiws* time, eternity, second constituent akin to OHG *heffen, hevan* to raise — more at AYE, HEAVE] **:** GENUINE, AUTHENTIC ⟨as performances these are ~ masterpieces —*Metronome*⟩

eciliate \(')ē+\ *adj* [*e-* + *ciliate*] **:** having no cilia

ec·i·ton \'esə,tän\ *n, cap* [NL] **:** a genus of blind polymorphic ants containing the American army ants

ecize \'ē,sīz\ *vi* -ED/-ING/-S [[2]*ec-* + *-ize*] *of a migrant organism* **:** to become established in and adjusted to a new habitat **:** COLONIZE

eck·er·mann·ite \'ekə(r)mə,nīt\ *n* -S [Sw *eckermannit*, fr. Claes W. H. von *Eckermann* b1886 Swed. professor + Sw *-it* -ite] **:** a mineral $Na_3(Mg,Li)_4(Al,Fe)Si_8O_{22}(OH,F)_2$ consisting of an amphibole containing magnesium, lithium, iron, and some fluorine

eck·ert projection \'ekə(r)t-\ *n, usu cap E* [after Max *Eckert* †1938 Ger. cartographer] **:** any of several projections developed by Max Eckert in which the poles are parallel straight lines half the length of the equator

eck fistula \'ek-\ *n, usu cap E* [after N.V.*Eck*, 19th cent. Russ. physiologist] **:** an artificial anastomosis between the portal vein and inferior vena cava by which blood from the intestinal region is diverted from the liver to flow directly to the heart

ecl *abbr* **1** eclectic **2** eclogue

éclair \(')ā¦kla(a)|(ə)r, -le|, |ə, ə'k-\ *n* -S [F, lit., lightning, fr. OF *esclair* lightning, light, fr. *esclairier* to light, shine, flash, fr. (assumed) VL *exclariare*, alter. of L *exclarare* to light up, illuminate, fr. *ex-* + *clarare* to make clear, make bright, fr. *clarus* clear, bright — more at CLEAR] **:** a usu. chocolate-frosted oblong cream puff with whipped cream or custard filling

éclair·cisse·ment \āklersēsmäⁿ\ *n, pl* **éclaircissements** \-äⁿ(z)\ [F, fr. MF *esclaircissement*, alter. (influenced by MF *cler, clair* clear, bright) of OF *esclarcissement*, fr. *esclarciss-* (stem of *esclarcir* to light up, illuminate, fr. — assumed — VL *exclaricire*, alter. of — assumed — VL *exclaricare*, fr. L *ex-* + *claricare* to glow, gleam, fr. *clarus*) + *-ment*] **:** the clearing up of something obscure **:** ENLIGHTENMENT

ec·lamp·sia \e'klampsēə, ə'-\ *n* -S [NL, modif. (influenced by NL *-ia*) of Gk *eklampsis* brightness, shining forth, fr. *eklampein* to shine forth (fr. *ek* out of, out, forth — fr. *ex* — + *lampein* to shine) + *-sis* — more at EX-, LAMP] **:** a convulsive state **:** an attack of convulsions: as **a :** toxemia of pregnancy esp. when severe and marked by convulsions and coma — compare PREECLAMPSIA **b :** a condition comparable to milk fever of cows occurring in domestic animals (as dogs and cats) — **ec·lamp·tic** \(')e¦klam(p)tik, ə'k-\ *adj*

éclat \(')ā¦klä, -lȧ\ *n* -S [F, splinter, fragment, explosion, ostentation, fr. OF *esclat* splinter, fr. *esclater* to splinter, burst, prob. fr. (assumed) VL *exclapitare*, fr. L *ex-* + (assumed) VL *clapitare*, prob. of imit. origin] **1 :** dazzling effect **:** BRILLIANCE ⟨the stern imagery and rhetorical ~ of the first stanza —Robert Lowell⟩ **:** display of pomp or pageantry ⟨arrived with much ~, entering the capital in a coach of state drawn by eight milk-white horses —C.G.Bowers⟩ **:** DASH, ENERGY ⟨the croupiers . . . spin the wheel with ~ —Joseph Wechsberg⟩ **2 a :** public display or ostentation **:** PUBLICITY ⟨this letter was sprung . . . with great ~ . . . in public hearing —*New Republic*⟩ **b** *archaic* **:** NOTORIETY, SCANDAL ⟨with the object of saving an ~ —Lord Byron⟩ **3 :** brilliant or conspicuous success ⟨dominated the House of Commons with ~ —C.H.Driver⟩ **:** FAME, RENOWN ⟨handed down to posterity with all the ~ of a proverb —Jane Austen⟩ **:** APPLAUSE ⟨gave me more ~ than my efforts merited —S.H.Adams⟩ **syn** see FAME

[1]**ec·lec·tic** \(')e¦klektik, ə'kl-,ē'kl-\ *adj* [Gk *eklektikos*, fr. *eklektos* picked out, select (verbal of *eklegein* to pick out, select, fr. *ek* out of, out + *legein* to pick up, gather) + *-ikos* -ic — more at LEGEND] **1 :** selecting what appears to be best or true in various and diverse doctrines or methods **:** rejecting a single, unitary, and exclusive interpretation, doctrine, or method **:** of or relating to eclecticism **:** SELECTIVE ⟨an ~ painter, mirroring the restlessness of his times, on a constant search for varied experience —H.D.Walker⟩ ⟨her taste was ~ in music as in persons —Osbert Sitwell⟩ **2 :** composed of

elements drawn from various sources ⟨a party with an ~ program —*Time*⟩ ⟨an ~ liturgy . . . incorporating such usages of . . . other churches as he might consider most profitable —F.M.Stenton⟩ — **ec·lec·ti·cal·ly** \-tək(ə)lē, -tēk-, -li\ *adv*

2eclectic \"\ *n* -s [Gk *eklektikos*, fr. *eklektikos*, adj.] **:** one who uses an eclectic method or approach in any field of thought or activity ⟨~s who derive most of their theory from Freud but add a little of Jung or Adler —*Time*⟩

ec·lec·ti·cism \ˌ=ˈ=tə,sizəm\ *n* -s [1*eclectic* + *-ism*] **1 :** the theory or practice of an eclectic method **:** the selection of doctrines or elements from various and diverse sources according to their presumed utility or validity usu. for the purpose of combining them into a satisfying or acceptable style, system of ideas, or set of practices; *also* **:** the eclectic style, system of ideas, or method formed in this manner **2 :** a system of medicine once popular in the U.S. that depended primarily on plant remedies

eclectic resinoid *n* **:** RESINOID 2a

ec·lec·tus parrot \(ˈ)eˌkl|ektəs-, əˈkl|, ēˈkl|\ *n* [NL *Eclectus*, fr. Gk *eklektos* picked out, select] **:** any of certain parrots of the southwest Pacific constituting a genus (*Larius*, formerly *Eclectus*) and being distinguished by having males predominantly green and females predominantly red

ec·leg·ma \eˈklegmə\ *n* -s [NL, alter. of L *ecligma* electuary, fr. Gk *ekleigma*, fr. *ekleichein* to lick up — more at ELECTUARY] *archaic* **:** a syrup on licorice root sucked for the relief of cough

1eclipse \əˈklips, ēˈk- *sometimes* ˈē,k-\ *n* -s [ME, fr. OF, fr. L

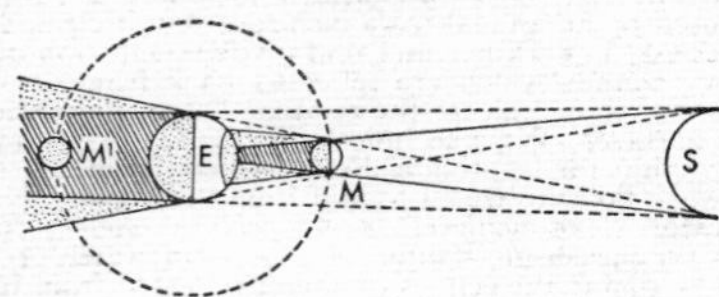

diagram of eclipse: sun, *S;* earth, *E;* moon in a solar eclipse, *M;* moon in a lunar eclipse, *M*¹

eclipsis, fr. Gk *ekleipsis*, lit., abandonment, cessation, fr. *ekleipein* to leave out, abandon, cease, fr. *ek* out of, out (fr. *ex*) + *leipein* to leave — more at EX-, LOAN] **1 a :** the obscuration of one celestial body by another ⟨an ~ of the sun by the moon⟩ **:** the passing into the shadow of a celestial body ⟨an ~ of the moon in the earth's shadow⟩ **:** the cutting off of some or all of the light from one celestial body by another (as in an eclipsing variable) — compare ANNULARITY, APPULSE, CONTACT, OCCULTATION, SHADOW TRANSIT, TOTALITY, TRANSIT **b :** the period or phase of darkness of an occulting light **2 :** the act or process or an instance of falling into obscurity, disuse, or disgrace **:** a temporary or permanent disappearance **:** DECLINE, DOWNFALL ⟨mourned the ~ of the hereditary upper class⟩ ⟨the ~ of the familiar essay will be slow —Clifton Fadiman⟩ **:** a period or condition of obscurity or disgrace ⟨returned to Versailles after a temporary ~ at court —Evelyn G. Cruickshanks⟩ or of decline or decay ⟨in the seventeenth century science came out of a long ~ —R.W.Livingstone⟩ **3 :** the assuming of dull eclipse plumage after the mating season (as by the normally brilliantly colored males of certain ducks); *also* **:** the state of a bird in such plumage

2eclipse \"\ *vb* -ED/-ING/-S [ME *eclipsen*, fr. *eclipse*, n.] *vt* **1 :** to cause the obscuration of **:** darken by or as if by an eclipse ⟨the moon ~s the sun⟩ ⟨when the sun is artificially *eclipsed* in a special telescope —Hugh Odishaw⟩ **2 a :** to reduce esp. in importance or repute **:** cast down (as into obscurity or disgrace) ⟨this . . . monocled military order was only *eclipsed* but never eliminated by the Versailles Treaty —G.W.Speyer⟩ **:** EXTINGUISH ⟨whose sudden death . . . *eclipsed* the gaiety of so many of his faithful readers —*Times Lit. Supp.*⟩ **b :** to make insignificant by comparison **:** throw into the shade ⟨whose history ~s that of the English colonies as a stirring and fascinating romance —A.L.Burt⟩ **:** SURPASS, EXCEL ⟨a new quarterly aluminum-production record . . . *eclipsing* the previous record —*Wall Street Jour.*⟩ **3 :** to cause eclipsis of (a sound) **~** *vi* **:** to suffer an eclipse **syn** see OBSCURE

eclipse plumage *n* **:** comparatively dull plumage usu. of seasonal occurrence in birds that exhibit a distinct nuptial plumage; *specif* **:** dull plumage developed in the adult male following a postnuptial molt — compare NUPTIAL PLUMAGE

eclips·er \-sə(r)\ *n* -s **:** one that eclipses; *specif* **:** the occulting screen for a lighthouse light

eclipse series *n* **:** SAROS SERIES

eclipse year *n* **:** the interval of 346.62 sidereal days between two successive conjunctions of the sun with the same node of the moon's orbit

eclipsing variable *also* **eclipsing double star** *or* **eclipsing binary** *n* [*eclipsing* fr. pres. part. of *2eclipse*] **:** a binary star in which the orbit plane lies near the line of sight so that one or both of the stars may eclipse the other as they revolve and produce rhythmic fluctuations in the total light of the system

eclip·sis \əˈklipsəs, ēˈ-,eˈ-\ *n, pl* **eclip·ses** \-p,sēz\ *or* **eclipsises** [Gk *ekleipsis* omission, eclipse, abandonment — more at 1ECLIPSE] **:** an omission or suppression of words or sounds

1eclip·tic \əˈkliptik, (ˈ)ēˌk-, -tēk\ *adj* [ME *ecliptik*, fr. LL *eclipticus*, fr. L, of an eclipse, fr. Gk *ekleiptikos*, fr. *ekleipsis* eclipse] **1 :** of or relating to the ecliptic **2** [L *eclipticus*] **:** of or relating to an eclipse

2ecliptic \"\ *n* -s [ME *ecliptik*, fr. ML *ecliptica*, fr. LL, fem. of *eclipticus*, adj.; fr. the fact that eclipses occur on this circle] **1 :** the great circle of the celestial sphere that is the apparent path of the sun among the stars or of the earth as seen from the sun **:** the plane of the earth's orbit extended to meet the celestial sphere — see OBLIQUITY **2 :** a great circle drawn on a terrestrial globe making an angle of about 23° 27′ with the equator and used for illustrating and solving astronomical problems

eclip·ti·cal \-təkəl\ *adj* [1*ecliptic* + *-al*] **:** ECLIPTIC

ecliptic coordinate *n* **:** one of the coordinates in the ecliptic system of coordinates

ecliptic pole *n* **:** either of the poles in the ecliptic system of coordinates

ecliptic system of coordinates : a system of celestial coordinates based on the ecliptic — compare CELESTIAL LATITUDE, CELESTIAL LONGITUDE

ec·lo·gite \ˈeklə,jīt\ *n* -s [F *éclogite*, fr. Gk *eklogē* selection + F *-ite*] **:** a metamorphic rock consisting of soda-rich pyroxene and magnesia-rich garnet as essential minerals

ec·logue \ˈe,klȯg *also* -läg\ *n* -s [partly alter. (influenced by L *ecloga*) of earlier *eglog*, fr. MF *eglogue*, fr. L *ecloga* eclogue, short poem, choice extract or group of extracts from a literary work, fr. Gk *eklogē* selection, choice extract or group of extracts from a literary work, fr. *eklegein* to pick out, select; partly fr. ME *eclog*, fr. L *ecloga* — more at ECLECTIC] **:** a poem in which shepherds are introduced conversing **:** BUCOLIC, IDYL

eclose \ēˈklōz\ *vi* -ED/-ING/-S [back-formation fr. *eclosion*] *of an insect* **:** to emerge from the eggshell or pupal case

eclo·sion \-ōzhən\ *n* -s [F *éclosion*, fr. *éclore* to hatch, fr. (assumed) VL *excludere* to hatch out (transitive), alter. (influenced by L *claudere* to close) of L *excludere* to hatch out (transitive), exclude — more at EXCLUDE, CLOSE] **1** *of a full-grown insect* **:** the act of emerging from the pupal case **2** *of an insect larva* **:** the act of hatching from the egg

eco- — see 2EC-

ECO *abbr* electron-coupled oscillator

eco·bi·ot·ic \ˌekō, ˌēkō+\ *adj* [2*ec-* + *-biotic*] **:** tending to produce or associated with adjustment to a particular mode of life ⟨~ adaptation⟩

eco·climate \ˈekō, ˈēkō+,-\ *n* [2*ec-* + *climate*] **:** climate as an ecological factor; *specif* **:** the actual climatic condition of a habitat ⟨the ~ of a coniferous forest⟩ — **eco·climatic** \ˌ==+\ *adj*

eco·clinal \ˌekōˌklīnᵊl, ˌēk-\ *adj* [*ecocline* + *-al*] **:** of, relating to, or inducing an ecocline ⟨~ variation⟩

eco·cline \ˈ==,klīn\ *n* [2*ec-* + *cline*] **:** a series of intergrading forms produced within a group in a zone of intergradation between two distinctive ecological niches — compare GENOCLINE

ecod \ēˈkäd, iˈ-\ *interj* [by alter.] *archaic* **:** EGAD

ec·o·deme \ˈekō,dēm, ˈēk-\ *n* [2*ec-* + *deme*] **:** a population occupying a particular ecological niche

ecog·ra·phy \ēˈkägrəfē, əˈ-\ *n* -ES [2*ec-* + *-graphy*] **:** the descriptive phase of ecology

ecoid *or* **oe·coid** \ˈē,kȯid\ *n* -s [ISV *ec-* (fr. Gk *oikos* house) + *-oid* — more at VICINITY] **:** the colorless stroma of a red blood cell

ec·o·log·i·cal \ˌekəˈläjəkəl, ˌēk-, -jēk-\ *also* **ec·o·log·ic** \-jik\ *adj* [*ecology* + *-ical*, *-ic*] **1 :** of or relating to the science of ecology **2 :** of or having to do with the environments of living things or with the pattern of relations between living things and their environments ⟨these then are the ~, the environmental diseases —*Science*⟩ **3 :** relating to or characterized by the interdependence of organisms ⟨departure from sound ~ principles in labeling hawks as good or bad . . . without any recognition of their essential role in all wildlife communities —I.R.Barnes⟩ — **ec·o·log·i·cal·ly** \-jək(ə)lē, -jēk-, -li\ *adv*

ecological subspecies *n* **:** PHYSIOLOGIC RACE

ecol·o·gist \ēˈkäləjəst, əˈ-\ *n* -s [*ecology* + *-ist*] **:** a specialist in ecology

ecol·o·gy *also* **oe·col·o·gy** *or* **ae·col·o·gy** \-jē, -ji\ *n* -ES [G *ökologie*, fr. *ök-* 2*ec-* + *-logie* -logy] **1 :** a branch of science concerned with the interrelationship of organisms and their environments esp. as manifested by natural cycles and rhythms, community development and structure, interaction between different kinds of organisms, geographic distributions, and population alterations — see AUTECOLOGY, GENECOLOGY, SYNECOLOGY; compare BIOGEOGRAPHY, PHYTOSOCIOLOGY **2 :** the totality or pattern of relations between organisms and their environment ⟨the ~ of a mountain pine⟩ ⟨assist the peasants . . . in improving their ~ and technology —R.A. Hall *b*.1911⟩ **3 :** HUMAN ECOLOGY

econ *abbr* economic; economics; economy

econ·o·met·ric \ēˌkänəˈme·trik, əˌk-\ *adj* [*economy* + *-metric* (as in *barometric*)] **:** of or relating to econometrics

econ·o·me·tri·cian \ˌ=ˌ==məˈtrishən\ *n* -s **:** a specialist in econometrics

econ·o·me·trics \-ˈme·triks\ *n pl but sing in constr* [fr. *econometric*, after such pairs as E *economic: economics*] **:** the application of mathematical form and statistical techniques to the testing and quantifying of economic theories and the solution of economic problems — **econ·o·met·rist** \-trəst; ˌekəˈnämə·tr-, ˌēk-\ *n* -s

ec·o·nom·ic \ˌekəˈnämik, ˌēk-, -mēk\ *also* **ec·o·nom·i·cal** \-məkəl, -mēk-\ *adj* [*economic* fr. LL *oeconomicus* of or relating to a divine dispensation, fr. LGk *oikonomikos*, fr. Gk, skilled in the management of a household, frugal, fr. *oikonomos* steward + *-ikos* -ic; *economical* fr. LL *oeconomicus* + E *-al* — more at ECONOMY] **1** *usu economical*, *archaic* **:** of or relating to a household or its management **:** of or relating to a divine dispensation or system of government **2** *usu economical* **:** given to thrift ⟨a sturdy, handsome, high-colored woman . . . *economical* and sensible —Carl Van Doren⟩ **:** productive of saving ⟨sea power is the . . . most *economical* form of military power —*Time*⟩ **:** sparing in quantity (as of words) ⟨a style as *economical* and exact as a theorem in geometry —Richard Harrity⟩ **3 a :** of or relating to the science of economics ⟨rejected the ~ doctrines of Ricardo⟩ **:** of, relating to, or concerned with the production, distribution, and consumption of commodities ⟨a program to prevent inflation and ~ collapse⟩ ⟨a council of ~ advisers⟩ **:** MATERIAL ⟨moved exclusively by ~ motives⟩ **b :** having practical or industrial significance, uses, or application ⟨the ~ plants of a region⟩ **:** affecting or liable to affect material resources or welfare ⟨two ~ pests were intercepted by . . . inspectors during recent weeks —*Farm Chemicals*⟩ **c :** operated or produced on a profitable basis **:** producing an excess of returns over expenditures ⟨reactor types which might be developed to produce ~ power —*U.S. Code*⟩ **:** capable of or liable to profitable exploitation ⟨~ beds of phosphate are found only under marine conditions —A.M.Bateman⟩ **:** PROFITABLE ⟨barely ~, since she paid a nurse almost as much as she made herself —Elizabeth Janeway⟩ **syn** see SPARING

ec·o·nom·i·cal·ly \-mək(ə)lē, -mēk-, -li\ *adv* **:** in an economic or economical way or manner

economic botany *n* **:** a division of botany that deals with the utilization of plants

economic council *n* **:** a body that is composed of representatives of all economic groups including both management and labor and that acts as an advisory governmental body or has direct governing power

economic cycle *n* **:** BUSINESS CYCLE

economic determinism *n* **:** ECONOMIC INTERPRETATION OF HISTORY

economic geography *n* **:** a branch of geography that deals with the relations of physical and economic conditions to the production and distribution of commodities

economic geology *n* **:** a branch of geology that deals with geological materials of economic utility — see MINING GEOLOGY, PETROLEUM GEOLOGY

economic good *n* **:** a commodity or service that is useful to man but that must be paid for — usu. used in pl.

economic interpretation of history : the theory that in the last analysis economic factors including esp. the level of technology attained by a particular society and the economic relations into which men enter on the basis of that technology exert a decisive influence on the course of political, social, and intellectual evolution — compare HISTORICAL MATERIALISM

economic life *n* **:** the period during which an economic good retains its utility

economic man *n* **:** an imaginary individual created in classical economics and conceived of as behaving rationally, regularly, and predictably in his economic activities with motives that are egoistic, acquisitive, and short-term in outlook

economic poison *n* **:** a substance or mixture of substances (as an insecticide, fungicide, rodenticide, or herbicide) for control of plants or animals that have economic significance as pests (as in agriculture, industry, or households) **:** PESTICIDE

economic rent *n* **:** the return for the use of a factor in excess of the minimum required to bring forth its service — compare CONSUMER SURPLUS, RENT

ec·o·nom·ics \ˌekəˈnämiks, ˌēk-, -mēks\ *n pl but usu sing in constr* [modif. (influenced by E *-s*, pl. ending) of NL *oeconomica*, fr. Gk *oikonomika*, fr. neut. pl. of *oikonomikos* skilled in the management of a household — more at ECONOMIC] **1** *obs* **:** a science or art of managing a house or household **2 a :** a social science that studies the production, distribution, and consumption of commodities **b :** economic aspect or significance ⟨the ~ of the tideland issue was relatively simple —T.H.White *b* 1915⟩ **:** considerations of cost and return ⟨standards by which the ~ of electric vs. manual typewriters could be evaluated —H.B.Averill⟩

economic science *n* **:** ECONOMICS

economic strike *n* **:** a strike by employees over wages, hours, or working conditions as opposed to one called in protest against unfair practices by an employer

econ·o·mism \ēˈkänə,mizəm, əˈ-\ *n* -s [F *économisme*, fr. *économie* economy (alter. — influenced by such forms as ML *economus* steward — of MF *yconomie*) + *-isme* -ism] **:** a theory or viewpoint that attaches decisive or principal importance to economic goals or interests

econ·o·mist \-məst\ *n* -s [*economy* + *-ist*] **1** *archaic* **a :** one who manages household affairs **:** HOUSEKEEPER **b :** one who practices or advocates economy ⟨~s even to parsimony —Edmund Burke⟩ **2** [F *économiste*, fr. *économie* economy + *-iste* -ist] *archaic* **:** PHYSIOCRAT **3 :** a specialist in or student of economics

econ·o·mite \-,mīt\ *n* -s *cap* [*Economy* (now Ambridge), Pennsylvania + E *-ite*] **:** one of a group of Harmonites who in 1803 settled in Pennsylvania, who in 1825 formed the settlement of Economy, Pennsylvania, and whose religious community came to an end in 1903 following the introduction of celibacy in 1807

econ·o·mize \-,mīz\ *vb* -ED/-ING/-S *see -ize in Explan Notes* [*economy* + *-ize*] *vi* **:** to practice economy: **a :** to use more sparingly ⟨it was necessary to ~ in the running of diesel engines —G. de Q.Robin **b :** to effect a saving — usu. used with *on* ⟨the larger animal . . . can ~ on brain, eyes, and certain other organs —J.B.S.Haldane⟩ **~** *vt* **1 :** to use more economically **:** SAVE ⟨regenerators which ~ fuel —E.B.Shand⟩ **2 :** to give economic value to **:** utilize to the best advantage ⟨they learned how to ~ the soil —Richard Koebner⟩

econ·o·miz·er \-zə(r)\ *n* -s **:** an apparatus for utilizing heat otherwise wasted; *specif* **:** a system of water tubes in the breeching of a boiler to heat the feedwater — compare REGENERATOR

econ·o·my \ēˈkänəmē, əˈ-, -mi\ *n* -ES *often attrib* [alter. (influenced by such forms as ML *economus* steward, fr. LL *oeconomus*, fr. Gk *oikonomos*) of earlier *yconomie*, fr. MF, fr. ML *oeconomia*, fr. Gk *oikonomia*, fr. *oikonomos* steward (fr. *oikos* house + *-nomos* manager, fr. *nemein* to distribute, manage) + *-ia* -y — more at VICINITY, NIMBLE] **1 a** *obs* **:** an art of managing a household **b** *archaic* **:** the management of the affairs of a group, community, or establishment with a view to insuring its maintenance or productiveness **c :** God's plan or system for the government of the world ⟨the Incarnation would be no accident in the divine ~ —P.E.More⟩; *also* **:** a special divine dispensation suited to the needs of a nation or period **d :** the management of a person's household or private affairs **2 a :** thrifty or economical use or administration of material resources **:** frugality in expenditures sometimes verging on parsimony ⟨the great cathedrals after 1200 show ~, and sometimes worse —Henry Adams⟩; *also* **:** an instance or a means of economizing **:** SAVING ⟨a small ~ if achieved at the expense of quality⟩ **b** (1) **:** cautious, selective, or partial exposition of facts or principles esp. to avoid causing displeasure — used chiefly in the phrase *economy of truth* ⟨either suffering from a lapse of memory or practicing an official ~ of truth —*Times Lit. Supp.*⟩ (2) **:** the efficient and sparing use of nonmaterial resources ⟨~ of effort⟩ ⟨~ of motion⟩ **:** the reduction to a minimum of the steps or processes required to achieve some end or reach some conclusion (as in logical reasoning); *also* **:** the saving achieved thereby (3) **:** conciseness in verbal or artistic expression **:** elimination of all unnecessary details so as to produce the maximum artistic effect ⟨every device of ~ known to musical expression —Virgil Thomson⟩ ⟨the incidents are treated with dramatic ~ —Hector Chevigny⟩ **3 a :** the system of arrangement or mode of operation or functioning of anything **:** ORGANIZATION ⟨the individual's psychic ~⟩ ⟨the place of the university in the educational ~ of the state⟩ **b** (1) **:** the natural ordering or system of operation of the processes of anabolism and catabolism in living bodies ⟨the ~ of the cell⟩ (2) **:** the body of an animal or plant as an organized whole ⟨disorganizing wide segments of the body ~ —Leonard Engel⟩ **4 a :** the structure of economic life in a country or area **:** an economic system ⟨the ~ was rising to new peaks of production and employment —F.B.Wilde⟩; *also* **:** a segment of an economic system ⟨sweeping changes in our farm ~⟩ **b :** a particular type of economic system or stage of economic development ⟨a money ~⟩ ⟨a pastoral ~⟩ **syn** see SYSTEM

economy coil *n* **:** a high-inductance coil shunted around series lamps to prevent an open circuit in case a lamp burns out

ec·o·phene \ˈekō,fēn, ˈēk-\ *n* -s [2*ec-* + *-phene* (fr. *phenotype*)] **:** ECAD

eco·phenotype \ˌekō, ˌēkō+\ *n* [2*ec-* + *phenotype*] **:** a phenotype modified by specific adaptive response to environmental factors **:** ECAD

écor·ché \ˌā,kȯrˈshā, āˈkȯr,shā\ *n* -s [F, fr. past part. of *écorcher* to skin, fr. OF *escorchier* to skin, peel, fr. LL *excorticare* to peel, fr. L *ex-* + LL *-corticare* (fr. L *cortic-*, *cortex* bark) — more at CUIRASS] **:** an anatomical figure or manikin showing the muscles and bones that are visible with the skin removed

ecorticate \(ˈ)ē+\ *adj* [*e-* + *corticate*] **:** being without a cortex; *specif* **:** being without an external tough investment ⟨~ lichens⟩

eco·species \ˈekō, ˈēkō+ ,-\ *n* [2*ec-* + *species*] **:** a subdivision of a cenospecies that is capable of free gene interchange between its members without impairment of fertility but is less capable of fertile crosses with members of other subdivisions of the cenospecies and that is typically more or less equivalent to the taxonomic species

eco·specific \ˌ==+\ *adj* **:** of, relating to, or like an ecospecies

ecos·saise \ˌā kōˈsāz, -ˌkō|, -ˌkə|-\ *n* -s [F *écossaise*, fr. fem. of *écossais* Scottish, fr. *Écosse* Scotland] **1 :** an old-fashioned dance in slow three-quarter time **2 :** a lively dance tune in duple rhythm

ecostate \(ˈ)ē+\ *adj* [*e-* + *costate*] *of a leaf* **:** having no midvein

eco·system \ˈekō, ˈēkō+ ,-\ *n* [2*ec-* + *system*] **:** an ecological community considered together with the nonliving factors of its environment as a unit

ec·o·ton·al \ˌekəˈtōnᵊl, ˌēk-\ *adj* [*ecotone* + *-al*] **:** of, relating to, or constituting an ecotone

ec·o·tone \ˈ==,tōn\ *n* [2*ec-* + *-tone* (fr. Gk *tonos* tension) — more at TONE] **:** a transition area between two adjacent ecological communities (as forest and grassland) usu. exhibiting competition between organisms common to both

ec·o·top·ic \ˌ==ˈtäpik\ *adj* [2*ec-* + *-topic* (fr. Gk *topos* place) — more at TOPIC] **:** tending to or involving adjustment to specific local habitat conditions ⟨~ divergence among common songbirds⟩

ec·o·type \ˈ==,tīp\ *n* [2*ec-* + *type*] **:** a subdivision of an ecospecies that comprises individuals which are interfertile with each other and with members of other ecotypes of the same ecospecies but which maintain their individuality as a distinct group through environmental selection and isolation and that is when morphologically distinct comparable with a taxonomic subspecies — **ec·o·typ·ic** \ˌ==ˈtipik\ *adj* — **ec·o·typ·i·cal·ly** \-pək(ə)lē\ *adv*

ec·pho·ne·sis \ˌekfəˈnēsəs\ *n, pl* **ecphone·ses** \-ē,sēz\ [Gk *ekphōnēsis*, fr. *ekphōnein* to cry out (fr. *ek* out of, out — fr. *ex* — + *phōnein* to speak, sound, fr. *phōnē* sound, voice) + *-sis* — more at EX-, BAN] **:** EXCLAMATION

ec·phore *or* **ek·phore** \ˈek,fō(ə)r\ *vt* -ED/-ING/-S [prob. back-formation fr. *ecphoria*, *ecphorize*] **:** ECPHORIZE

ec·pho·ria \ekˈfōrēə\ *n, pl* **ecphorias** \-ēəz\ *or* **ecpho·riae** \-ē,ē\ [G *ekphorie*, fr. *ek-* 1*ec-* + *-phorie* (fr. Gk *-phoria* action of bearing) — more at -PHORIA] **:** the rousing of an engram or system of engrams from a latent to an active state (as by repetition of the original stimulus or by mnemic excitation)

ec·pho·rize \ˈekfə,rīz\ *vt* -ED/-ING/-S [*ecphoria* + *-ize*] **:** to revive or rouse (an engram or system of engrams) from latency

ecra·se *or* **écra·sé** \ˌā(,)kräˈzā, -ˌkrə|-\ *adj* [F *écrasé*, past part. of *écraser* to crush, fr. MF *escraser*, fr. *e-* (fr. L *ex-*) + *-craser* (prob. fr. E 1*craze*)] **:** CRUSHED, FLATTENED — used esp. of fabrics or leather

écre·visse \ākrəvēs\ *n* -s [F, fr. OF *escrevice*, *crevice* — more at CRAYFISH] **:** CRAYFISH

ecri·bel·la·tae \ˌēkrəbəˈlā,tē\ *n pl, cap* [NL, fr. *e-* + *cribellum* + L *-atae* (fem. pl. of *-atus* -ate)] *in some classifications* **:** a group of arachnomorph spiders comprising those which lack a cribellum

1ecribellate \(ˈ)ē+\ *adj* [NL *cribellum* + E *-ate*] **:** lacking a cribellum **:** of or relating to the Ecribellatae

2ecribellate \"\ *n* -s **:** an ecribellate spider

ec·ru \ˈe(,)krü, ˈā(,)-, =ˈ=\ *n* -s [F *écru* unbleached, fr. OF *escru*, fr. *es-* completely — fr. L *ex-* — + *cru* raw, fr. L *crudus* — more at RAW] **1 :** a grayish yellow that is greener and paler than chamois or old ivory **2** *of a textile* **:** a light grayish yellowish brown that is yellower and lighter than gravel

ecru silk *n* **:** a partially degummed silk with little luster and some harshness

ec·sta·si·ate \ekˈstāz(h)ē,āt\ *vb* -ED/-ING/-S [F *extasier* to cause to go into an ecstasy (fr. MF, fr. *extasie* ecstasy) + E *-ate*] **:** ECSTASIZE

ec·sta·size \ˈekstə,sīz\ *vb* -ED/-ING/-S [*ecstasy* + *-ize*] *vt* **:** to cause to go into an ecstasy ⟨*ecstasizing* her audience⟩ **~** *vi* **:** to go into an ecstasy

1ec·sta·sy *also* **ec·sta·cy** \ˈekstəsē, -si\ *n* -ES [ME *extasie*, fr. MF, fr. LL *extasis*, *ecstasis*, fr. Gk *ekstasis*, fr. *existanai* to put out of place, derange, fr. *ex* out of, out + *histanai* to cause to stand — more at EX-, STAND] **1 :** a state of being beyond reason and self-control through intense emotional excitement, pain, or other sensation **:** obsession by powerful feeling ⟨in an ~ of pain —Ludwig Bemelmans⟩ ⟨whose eyes kept sweeping in an ~ of fear from side to side —Irwin Shaw⟩

2 : a state of exaltation or rapturous delight manifested either demonstratively ⟨sending their shrill, diamond-hard cries of ~ streaming across the streets —Kay Cicellis⟩ or in a profound calm or abstraction of mind ⟨a state of quiet ~ which illuminated his whole being —E.S.Bates⟩ **3 :** a trance state in which intense absorption in divine or cosmic matters is accompanied by loss of sense perception and voluntary control ⟨at the sight of a crucifix . . . she would at once fall into an ~ —Norman Douglas⟩

syn ECSTASY, RAPTURE, and TRANSPORT agree in designating a feeling or state of intense, often extreme, mental and emotional exaltation. ECSTASY in one sense signifies an exalted state resembling a trance in which contemplation of what inspires the exaltation makes one oblivious of all else, and in another sense signifies an overmastering exalting joy or similar intense emotion ⟨this picture of Fra Angelico in a state of religious *ecstasy* —*Time*⟩ ⟨these were thrilling words, and wound up Catherine's feelings to the highest points of *ecstasy* —Jane Austen⟩ ⟨such a success threw us into a perfect *ecstasy* of hilarity —Ben Riker⟩ ⟨their faces were fixed in a calm *ecstasy* of malevolence —Elinor Wylie⟩ ⟨a drunken *ecstasy*, compounded of superstition, greed, bloodlust, seized upon the hundreds of servitors of the goddess —Maurice Samuel⟩ RAPTURE implies intense bliss or beatitude, sometimes connoting an accompanying ecstasy ⟨he was familiar with the passionate *rapture* of lovers on the stage, in books, and in pictures —William Black⟩ ⟨he put little of this personal *rapture* of holiness into his published works —P.E.More⟩ ⟨continual ups and downs of *rapture* and depression —Edith Wharton⟩ TRANSPORT applies to any violent or powerful emotion that lifts one out of oneself and usu. provokes vehement expression ⟨thronged about him and embraced and kissed him, with such joy and *transport*, as he said, that he always looked upon that moment as the happiest of his life —Van Wyck Brooks⟩ ⟨a periodical that is weekly moved to *transports* of delight about contemporary America —Bruce Bliven b.1889⟩ ⟨the first *transports* of love⟩

²ecstasy \"\ *vt* -ED/-ING/-ES **:** to fill with ecstasy or rapture **:** ENRAPTURE ⟨the most *ecstasied* order of holy . . . spirits —Jeremy Taylor⟩

¹ec·stat·ic \(ˈ)ek¦stad·|ik, ək'sᵊ-, -at|, |ēk\ *adj* [ML *ecstaticus*, fr. Gk *ekstatikos*, fr. *existanai*] **1 :** of or relating to ecstasy ⟨the ~ element in medieval religion⟩ **2 :** caused by, expressing, or causing ecstasy ⟨the first taste of the water in his mouth was ~ —Norman Mailer⟩ ⟨looked at her with an ~ stare⟩ **:** in a state of ecstasy ⟨~ at his new possession —Nevil Shute⟩

²ecstatic \"\ *n* -s **:** a person who is subject to states resembling trances

ecstatical *adj* [ML *ecstaticus* + E *-al*] *obs* **:** ECSTATIC

ec·stat·i·cal·ly \|ək(ə)lē, |ēk-, -li\ *adv* **:** in an ecstatic manner

ect- *or* **ecto-** *comb form* [NL, fr. Gk *ekto-* outside, fr. *ektos*, fr. *ex* out of, out — more at EX-] **1 :** outside **:** external ⟨*ecto*stosis⟩ ⟨*ecto*plasm⟩ — compare END-, EXO- **2 :** out of place ⟨*ecto*cardia⟩

ECT *abbr* electroconvulsive therapy

ec·tad \ˈek,tad\ *adv* [*ect-* + *-ad*, adv. suffix] *anat* **:** OUTWARD

ec·ta·de·ni·um \,ektəˈdēnēəm\ *n, pl* **ectade·nia** \-nēə\ [NL, fr. *ect-* + Gk *aden-*, *adēn* gland + NL *-ium* — more at ADEN-] **:** one of the ectodermal accessory reproductive glands of male insects — compare MESADENIUM

ec·tal \ˈektᵊl\ *adj* [*ect-* + *-al*] *anat* **:** EXTERIOR, OUTER — opposed to *ental* — **ectal·ly** \-ᵊlē\ *adv*

ec·ta·sia \ekˈtāzh(ē)ə\ *n* -s [NL, modif. (influenced by NL *-ia*) of Gk *ektasis*] **:** the expansion of a hollow or tubular organ

ec·ta·sis \ˈektəsəs\ *n, pl* **ecta·ses** \-ə,sēz\ [LL, fr. Gk *ektasis* extension, stretching, lengthening of a short syllable, fr. *ekteinein* to stretch out, fr. *ek* out of, out (fr. *ex*) + *teinein* to stretch — more at EX-, THIN] **1 :** the lengthening of a short syllable **2** [NL, fr. Gk] **:** DILATATION, ECTASIA

ec·tat·ic \(ˈ)ek¦tad·ik\ *adj* [fr. (assumed) NL *ectaticus*, fr. Gk *ektatos* capable of extension (verbal of *ekteinein*) + L *-icus* -ic] **:** of, relating to, or involving ectasia

ectene *var of* EKTENE

ect·epicondylar \(ˈ)ek¦t+-\ *adj* [*ect-* + *epicondyle* + *-ar*] **:** relating to the external condyle of the distal end of the humerus

¹ect·ethmoid \(ˈ)ek¦t+-\ *n* [*ect-* + *ethmoid*, n.] **:** either of two lateral parts of the ethmoid bone lying on either side of the mesethmoid and forming part of the anterior wall of the orbit

²ectethmoid \"\ *also* **ect·ethmoidal** \(ˈ)ek¦t+-\ *also* **ec·to·ethmoid** \¦ektō+\ *adj* **:** lateral or external to the ethmoid

ec·thlip·sis \ekˈthlipsəs\ *n, pl* **ecthlip·ses** \-p,sēz\ [LL, fr. Gk *ekthlipsis* loss of a sound or letter in a word, squeezing out, fr. *ekthlibein* to squeeze out (fr. *ek* out of, out — fr. *ex* — + *thlibein* to squeeze, alter. — influenced by Gk *thlan* to crush, bruise — of Gk — Aeol & Ion — *phlibein* to squeeze) + *-sis*; Gk *thlan* akin to Czech *dlasmati* to press and perh. to Skt *dṛṣad*, *dhṛṣad* millstone — more at EX-, PROFLIGATE] *Latin prosody* **:** the elision of a final *m* with a preceding short vowel before a word beginning with *h* or a vowel

ec·thy·ma \ekˈthīmə\ *n* -s [NL *ecthymat-*, *ecthyma*, fr. Gk *ekthymat-*, *ekthyma* pimple, fr. *ekthyein* to break out, fr. *ek* + *thyein* to rage, seethe; akin to L *fumus* smoke — more at FUME] **1 :** a cutaneous eruption marked by large flat pustules that have a hardened base surrounded by inflammation, heal with pigmented scar formation, and occur esp. on the lower legs **2 :** sore mouth of sheep — **ec·thym·a·tous** \(ˈ)ekˈthiməd·əs, -thīm-\ *adj*

ec·to·blast \ˈektə,blast\ *n* [ISV *ect-* + *-blast*] **:** EPIBLAST — **ec·to·blas·tic** \¦==¦blastik\ *adj*

ec·to·can·thi·on \,ektōˈkan(t)thēən\ *n* -s [*ect-* + *-canthion* (irreg. fr. LL *canthus* corner of the eye) — more at CANTHUS] **:** the point at which the outer ends of the upper and lower eyelids meet — compare ENDOCANTHION

ec·to·car·dia \-ˈkärdēə\ *n* -s [NL, fr. *ect-* + *-cardia*] **:** abnormal position of the heart

ec·to·car·pa·ce·ae \-,kärˈpāsē,ē\ *n pl, cap* [NL, fr. *Ectocarpus*, type genus + *-aceae*] **:** a cosmopolitan family of chiefly epiphytic marine brown algae (order Ectocarpales) that includes algae with a thallus of erect branching filaments arising from a creeping filament or layer or sometimes being compacted into a pseudoparenchymatous thallus — see ECTOCARPUS — **ec·to·car·pa·ceous** \¦==,=¦pāshəs\ *adj*

ec·to·car·pa·les \,==,=ˈpā(,)lēz\ *n pl, cap* [NL, fr. *Ectocarpus* + *-ales*] **:** a large order of rather simple heterotrichous brown algae that lack true oogamy — see ECTOCARPACEAE

ec·to·car·pic \¦ektō¦kärpik\ *adj* [NL *Ectocarpus* + E *-ic*] **:** of or relating to algae of the genus *Ectocarpus*

ec·to·car·pous \-pəs\ *adj* [*ect-* + *-carpous* having such fruit — more at -CARPOUS] **:** having reproductive organs developed from the ectoderm — used of hydromedusae

ec·to·car·pus \,==ˈ=pəs\ *n, cap* [NL, fr. *ect-* + *-carpus*] **:** the type genus of Ectocarpaceae containing numerous more or less branched filamentous brown algae that are esp. abundant in cold seas and are sometimes considered the most primitive of living brown algae

ec·to·chon·dral \¦==¦kändrəl\ *adj* [*ect-* + *chondr-* + *-al*] **:** on the surface of cartilage ⟨an ~ lesion⟩ ⟨~ bone formation⟩

ec·to·commensal \¦ek(,)tō+\ *n* [*ect-* + *commensal*] **:** an organism that lives as a commensal on the surface of the body of another organism

ec·to·condyle \¦ektō+\ *n* [*ect-* + *condyle*] **:** the lateral condyle of a bone — **ec·to·condyloid** \"+\ *adj*

ec·to·co·nus \,ektəˈkōnəs\ *n, cap* [NL, fr. *ect-* + L *conus* cone — more at CONE] **:** a genus of primitive ungulate mammals (order Condylarthra) of the Paleocene of No. America thought to have been forest-dwelling browsers

ec·to·cornea \¦ektō+\ *n* [NL, fr. *ect-* + ML *cornea*] **:** the external layer of the cornea

ec·to·cranial \"+\ *adj* [*ect-* + *cranial*] **:** of or relating to the exterior of the skull

ec·to·cyst \ˈektə,sist\ *n* [ISV *ect-* + *cyst*] **:** the external layer of the walls of a zooecium

ec·to·derm \-tə,dərm\ *n* -s [ISV *ect-* + *-derm*] **1 :** the outer cellular membrane of a medusa or other diploblastic animal **2 :** the outermost of the three primary germ layers of an embryo **:** the source of neural tissue and sense organs, of the outer layer of the skin, and of minor adult structures **:** EPIBLAST; *also* **:** any tissue wherever located derived from this germ layer — compare EPIDERMIS — **ec·to·der·mal** \¦==¦dərməl\ *or* **ec·to·der·mic** \-mik\ *adj*

ec·to·der·moi·dal \¦==(,)dərˌmȯidᵊl\ *adj* [*ectoderm* + *-oidal*] **:** resembling ectoderm

ec·to·dynamomorphic *or* **ek·to·dynamomorphic** \¦ektō+\ *adj* [*ect-* + *dynam-* + *-morphic*] *of a developing soil* **:** characterized by changes brought about by external (as climatic) forces or agencies — opposed to *endodynamomorphic*

ec·to·entad \"+\ *adv* [*ect-* + *entad*] *anat* **:** from without inward

ectoethmoid *var of* ECTETHMOID

ec·to·gen·e·sis \,ektō+\ *n* [NL, fr. *ect-* + L *genesis*] **:** development outside the body; *esp* **:** development of a mammalian embryo in an artificial environment — **ec·to·genetic** \¦==+\ *adj*

ec·to·gen·ic \¦==¦jenik\ *adj* [prob. fr. G *ektogen* ectogenic (fr. *ekt-* ect- — fr. NL — + *-gen* -genic, -genous, fr. Gk *-genēs* born) + E *-ic* — more at -GEN] **1** *of disease* **:** EXOGENOUS **2** *of an organism* **:** ECTOGENOUS

ec·tog·e·nous \(ˈ)ek¦täjənəs\ *adj* [prob. fr. G *ektogen* + E *-ous*] **:** capable of development apart from the host — used chiefly of pathogenic bacteria

ec·tog·na·thous \(ˈ)ek¦tägnəthəs\ *adj* [*ect-* + *-gnathous*] **:** having the mouthparts exserted; *sometimes* **:** THYSANURAN — compare ENTOGNATHOUS

ec·to·lecithal \¦ektō+\ *adj* [ISV *ect-* + *lecith-* + *-al*] **:** CENTROLECITHAL

ec·to·loph \ˈektə,läf\ *n* -s [*ect-* + *-loph*] *zool* **:** one of the principal crests of a lophodont molar extending from the paracone to the metacone — compare METALOPH, PROTOLOPH

-ec·tome \ˈek,tōm\ *n comb form* -s [NL *-ectomus*, fr. *-ectomia*, after NL *-tomia* -tomy: *-tomus* -tome] **:** instrument used in surgical removal of (a specified organ or part) ⟨neur*ectome*⟩ ⟨tonsill*ectome*⟩

ec·to·meninx \¦ektō+\ *n, pl* **ectomeninges** [NL, fr. *ect-* + Gk *mēninx* membrane — more at MEMBER] **:** the layer of mesoderm from which the dura mater and much of the membrane bone of the skull develop in the higher vertebrate embryo

ec·to·mere \ˈektə,mi(ə)r\ *n* -s [*ect-* + *-mere*] **:** a blastomere destined to form ectoderm — **ec·to·mer·ic** \¦==¦merik\ *adj*

ec·to·mesenchyme \¦ektō+\ *n* [*ect-* + *mesenchyme*] **:** mesenchyme derived from ectoderm

ec·to·mesoblast \"+\ *n* [*ect-* + *mesoblast*] **:** an undifferentiated layer of cells destined to produce both epiblast and mesoblast

ec·to·mesoderm \"+\ *n* [*ect-* + *mesoderm*] **1 :** ECTOMESENCHYME **2 :** ECTOMESOBLAST — **ec·to·mesodermal** \"+\ *adj*

ec·to·mo·lare \¦ektōmōˌla(ə)rē\ *n* -s [*ect-* + *-molare* (irreg. fr. L *molaris* molar) — more at MOLAR] *anthrop* **:** the most lateral point on the exterior surface of the alveolar border

ec·to·morph \ˈektə,mȯrf\ *n* -s [*ectoderm* + *-morph*] **:** an ectomorphic individual

ec·to·mor·phic \¦==¦mȯrfik\ *adj* [*ectoderm* + *-morphic*] **:** characterized by predominance of the structures developed from the ectodermal layer of the embryo, the skin, nerves, sense organs, and brain **:** of a light or asthenic type of body build — compare ENDOMORPHIC, MESOMORPHIC — **ec·to·mor·phy** \ˈ==,=fē\ *n* -ES

-ec·to·my \ˈektəmē, -mi\ *n comb form* -ES [NL *-ectomia*, fr. *ec-* + *-tomia* -tomy] **:** cutting out **:** surgical removal ⟨gas*trectomy*⟩

ec·to·nephridium \¦ek(,)tō+\ *n* [NL, fr. *ect-* + *nephridium*] **:** a nephridium of ectodermal origin (as that of certain mollusks)

ec·to·parasite \¦ektō+\ *n* [ISV *ect-* + *parasite*] **:** a parasite that lives on the exterior of its host — opposed to *endoparasite* — **ec·to·parasitic** \"+\ *adj*

ec·toph·a·gous \(ˈ)ek¦täfəgəs\ *adj* [*ect-* + *-phagous*] **:** feeding from without: **a** *of a parasitoid insect larva* **:** developing external to and feeding on the surface of the host — compare ENDOPHAGOUS **b :** consuming vegetation or plant debris by ingestion (as by browsing) rather than by disintegrating it from within

ec·to·phlo·ic \¦ektə¦flōik\ *adj* [*ect-* + *phloem* + *-ic*] *bot* **:** having phloem only external to the xylem — used of the siphonostele of certain vascular plants; compare AMPHIPHLOIC

ec·to·phyte \ˈ==,fīt\ *n* -s [ISV *ect-* + *-phyte*] **:** an ectoparasitic plant — **ec·to·phyt·ic** \¦==¦fid·ik\ *adj*

ec·to·pia \ekˈtōpēə\ *n* -s [NL, fr. Gk *ektopos* away from a place (fr. *ek* out of, out — fr. *ex* — + *topos* place) + NL *-ia* — more at EX-, TOPIC] **:** an abnormal congenital or acquired position of an organ or part ⟨~ of the heart⟩

ec·top·ic \(ˈ)ek¦täpik, -tōp-\ *adj* [ISV *ectopia* + *-ic*] **:** exhibiting ectopia ⟨an ~ kidney⟩ **:** occurring in an unusual position ⟨~ lesions⟩ or in an unusual manner or form ⟨~ heartbeat⟩ — compare ENTOPIC

ectopic pregnancy *n* **:** gestation elsewhere than in the uterus (as in a fallopian tube or in the peritoneal cavity)

ec·to·placenta \¦ektō+\ *n* [NL, fr. *ect-* + *placenta*] **:** TROPHOBLAST — **ec·to·placental** \"+\ *adj*

ec·to·plasm \ˈektə,plazəm\ *n* -s [ISV *ect-* + *-plasm*] **1 :** the outer relatively rigid granule-free layer of the cytoplasm usu. held to be a thixotropic gel — compare ENDOPLASM **2 :** the emanation from a spiritualistic medium that is believed to effect telekinesis and similar phenomena — **ec·to·plasmatic** \¦==+\ *or* **ec·to·plasmic** \"+\ *adj*

ec·to·plast \ˈ==,plast\ *n* -s [*ect-* + *-plast*] **1 :** PLASMA MEMBRANE I **2 :** the ectoplasmic content of a cell

ec·to·proct \ˈ==,präkt\ *n* -s [NL *Ectoprocta*] **:** a bryozoan of the group Ectoprocta

ec·to·proc·ta \,==ˈpräktə\ *n pl, cap* [NL, fr. *ect-* + ¹*-procta*] *in some classifications* **:** an order or subclass coextensive with Bryozoa — used by those who use Bryozoa as a division of Molluscoidea — **ec·to·proc·tous** \¦==¦təs\ *adj*

ec·to·pterygota \¦ektō+\ [NL, fr. *ect-* + Gk *pterygōta*, neut. pl. of *pterygōtos* winged — more at PTERYGOTA] *syn of* HEMIMETABOLA

ec·to·rhinal \"+\ *adj* [*ect-* + *rhinal*] **:** of, related to, or located on the outside of the nose ⟨the ~ fissure⟩

ec·to·sarc \ˈektə,särk\ *n* -s [*ect-* + *-sarc*] **:** the semisolid external layer of protoplasm in some unicellular organisms (as the amoeba) **:** ECTOPLASM — **ec·to·sar·cous** \¦==¦särkəs\ *adj*

ec·to·som·al \¦==¦sōməl\ *adj* **:** of or relating to the ectosome

ec·to·some \ˈ==,sōm\ *n* -s [*ect-* + *-some*] **:** the cortical part of a sponge

ec·to·sphenotic \¦ek(,)tō+\ *adj* [*ect-* + *sphenotic*] **:** of or relating to the external part of the sphenotic bone

ec·to·sphere \ˈektə,sfi(ə)r\ *n* [*ect-* + *sphere*] **:** the cortical zone of the attraction sphere

ect·osteal \(ˈ)ek¦t+-\ *adj* [*ect-* + *osteal*] **1 :** of, produced by, or relating to ectostosis **2 :** of or relating to the surface of a bone — **ect·osteally** *adv*

ect·os·to·sis \,ek,t+\ *n, pl* **ectostoses** [NL, fr. *ect-* + *-ostosis*] **:** bone formation beginning immediately beneath the perichondrium and surrounding or replacing the underlying cartilage — compare ENDOSTOSIS

ec·to·symbiont *or* **ec·to·symbiote** \¦ek(,)tō+\ *n* [*ect-* + *symbiont* or *symbiote*] **:** a symbiont dwelling on the surface of or physically separate from its host — **ec·to·symbiosis** \"+\ *n* — **ec·to·symbiotic** \"+\ *adj*

ec·to·therm \ˈektə,thərm\ *n* -s [*ect-* + *-therm*] **:** a cold-blooded animal **:** POIKILOTHERM

ec·to·ther·mic \¦==¦thərmik\ *adj* **:** deriving heat from without the body **:** COLD-BLOODED

ec·to·thrix \ˈ==,thriks\ *adj* [NL, fr. *ect-* + Gk *thrix* hair — more at TRICHINA] **:** occurring on the surface of hair ⟨~ fungi⟩ — compare ENDOTHRIX

ec·to·trophic *also* **ec·to·tropic** \¦ektō+\ *adj* [*ect-* + *-trophic* or *-tropic*] *of a mycorrhiza* **:** growing as a close web on the surface of the associated root — opposed to *endotrophic*

ec·to·zoa \,ektəˈzōə\ *n pl, often cap* [NL, fr. *ect-* + *-zoa*] **:** external animal parasites — often used as if a taxon — **ec·to·zo·an** \¦==¦zōən\ *adj or n*

ec·to·zo·ic \¦==¦zōik\ *adj* [NL *ectozoa* + E *-ic*] **:** living on the surface of an animal **:** ECTOZOAN

ec·to·zo·on \,==ˈzō,än\ *sing of* ECTOZOA

ectro- *comb form* [NL, fr. Gk *ektrōsis* miscarriage, fr. *ektitrōskein* to miscarry, fr. *ek* out of, out (fr. *ex*) + *titrōskein* to wound, damage; akin to Gk *tribein* to rub — more at EX-, THROW] **:** congenitally absent — in teratological terms chiefly indicating absence of a particular limb or part ⟨*ectro*dactylism⟩

ec·tro·dactylism *also* **ec·tro·dactylia** *or* **ec·tro·dactyly** \¦ektrō+\ *n, pl* **ectrodactylisms** *also* **ectrodactylias** *or* **ectrodactylies** [*ectrodactylism* fr. *ectro-* + *-dactylism*; *ectrodactylia & ectrodactyly* fr. NL *ectrodactylia*, fr. *ectro-* + *-dactylia*] **:** congenital complete or partial absence of one or more digits — **ec·tro·dac·ty·lous** \¦==¦daktələs\ *adj*

ec·tro·me·lia \,ektrōˈmēlēə\ *n* -s [NL, fr. *ectro-* + *-melia*] **1 :** congenital absence or imperfection of one or more limbs **2 :** MOUSEPOX

ec·tro·mel·ic \¦==¦melik, -mēl-\ *adj* [*ectromelia* + *-ic*] **:** marked by or having ectromelia

ec·tro·pi·on \ekˈtrōpē,än, -ēən\ *n* -s [NL, fr. Gk *ektropion*, fr. *ek* out of, out (fr. *ex*) + *-tropion* (fr. *trepein* to turn) — more at TROPE] **:** an abnormal turning out of a part (as an eyelid)

ec·tro·pi·um \-ēəm\ *n* -s [NL, fr. Gk *ektropion*] **:** ECTROPION

ec·typ·al \ˈek,tīpəl, -,təp-\ *adj* **:** having the characteristics of an ectype

ec·type \ˈek,tīp\ *n* [*ec-* coming from something else, derivative (fr. Gk *ek* out of, out, fr. *ex*) + *-type* (as in *archetype*) — more at EX-] **1 :** a copy from an original **:** an imitation or reproduction (as an impression of a seal) **2 a :** something in the world of external reality as distinguished from its eternal and ideal archetype or prototype **b** *Lockeanism* **:** an idea or impression more or less corresponding to some external reality

ecu \(ˈ)āˈkyü, ākˈü\ *n* -s [MF *ecu*, *escu* ecu, shield, fr. OF *escu* shield, fr. L *scutum* — more at ESQUIRE] **1 :** any of an old French coin having a shield as part of the design: **a :** a gold coin worth three livres issued from the 14th century until the introduction of the louis d'or in 1640 **b :** a silver crown-sized coin first issued in 1642 as equivalent to three livres but later varied arbitrarily esp. under Louis XIV between five, six, and eight livres **2 :** a silver piece worth five francs after introduction of the franc in 1795; *also* **:** the 20-franc silver piece issued 1929–38 **3 :** a unit of value equivalent to one ecu coin ⟨the captain's pay was one thousand ~*s*⟩ ⟨a ½-*ecu* coin⟩

ec·ua·dor \ˈekwə,dȯ(ə)r, -ō(ə)\ *adj, usu cap* [fr. *Ecuador*, republic in So. America] **:** of or from the Republic of Ecuador **:** of the kind or style prevalent in Ecuador **:** ECUADORIAN

¹ec·ua·dor·i·an \¦ekwə¦dōrēən, -dȯr-\ *also* **ec·ua·dor·an** \-¦dōrən\ *or* **ec·ua·dor·e·an** \-¦dōrēən, -dȯr-\ *adj, usu cap* **1 :** of, relating to, or characteristic of Ecuador **2 :** of, relating to, or characteristic of the people of Ecuador

²ecuadorian \"\ *also* **ecuadoran** \"\ *or* **ecuadorean** \"\ *n* -s *cap* **:** a native or inhabitant of Ecuador

ecuelle \āˈkwel\ *n* -s [F *écuelle*, fr. (assumed) VL *scūtella* drinking bowl, alter. of L *scūtella* — more at SCUTTLE] **:** a 2-handled bowl used for soup

ec·u·mene \ˈekyə,mēn, eˈkyüməˌ(,)nē\ *n* -s [Gk *oikoumenē*, fr. fem. of *oikoumenos* inhabited, pres. part. middle of *oikein* to inhabit, fr. *oikos* house, habitation — more at VICINITY] **1 a :** the permanently inhabited portion of the earth as distinguished from the uninhabited or temporarily inhabited area ⟨but that the southern limit of the ~ should be pushed southward, to about latitude 68° S, in Graham Land —*Geog. Rev.*⟩ **b :** the nuclear area or center of maximum activity of a state having the densest population and the closest network of transportation routes ⟨Russia's ~ is on the same grand scale as that of the U.S. —Derwent Whittlesey⟩ **2** *anthrop* **:** a nuclear area of high culture to which neighboring regions stand in a relation of cultural backwardness or dependence **:** CIVILIZATION

ec·u·men·ic *also* **oec·u·men·ic** \¦ekyə¦menik, -nek *sometimes* ¦ēk-\ *adj* [LL *oecumenicus*, fr. LGk *oikoumenikos*, fr. Gk *oikoumenē* + *-ikos* -ic] **:** ECUMENICAL

ec·u·men·i·cal *also* **oec·u·men·i·cal** \-nəkəl, -nēk-\ *adj* [LL *oecumenicus* ecumenical + E *-al*] **1 :** worldwide, general, or universal in extent or influence ⟨dreamed of re-creating an ~ church⟩ or in application ⟨the shrewdest political and ~ comment of our time —Christopher Morley⟩ **2 a :** of, relating to, representing, or governing the whole of a body of churches ⟨an ~ council⟩ **b :** of or relating to the ecumenical movement ⟨~ leaders⟩ ⟨~ discussions⟩ **c :** promoting or tending toward worldwide Christian unity ⟨~ thinking⟩ ⟨~ activity⟩ **d :** of, relating to, or being a chiefly 20th century movement toward worldwide interconfessional Christian unity originating in Protestantism and now focused in a world council of churches that is supported by many Protestant, Eastern Orthodox, and other church bodies and that promotes through functional organizations cooperation on such common tasks as missions and work among students and through conferences mutual understanding on fundamental issues in belief, worship, and polity and a united witness on world problems **syn** see UNIVERSAL

ec·u·men·i·cal·ism \,==ˈ==kə,lizəm\ *n* -s **:** the principles and practices of ecumenical Christianity; *esp* **:** those underlying the ecumenical movement

ec·u·men·i·cal·ly \¦==¦=nək(ə)lē, -nēk-, -li\ *adv* **:** in an ecumenical manner **:** in a manner that demonstrates ecumenical principles

ecumenical patriarch *n* **:** the patriarch of Constantinople who is the acknowledged highest ecclesiastical official in the Eastern Orthodox Church by virtue of a primacy of honor

ecumenical patriarchate *n* **:** the office of the ecumenical patriarch

ec·u·men·i·cism \,==ˈ=nə,sizəm\ *n* -s **:** ECUMENICALISM

ec·u·men·i·cist \-nəsəst\ *n* -s **:** one who favors ecumenicity esp. as expressed through the ecumenical movement

ec·u·me·nic·i·ty \,ekyəməˈnisəd·ē, ,ēk-, -(,)meˈ-\ *n* -ES [*ecumenic* + *-ity*] **:** the quality or state of being ecumenical; *esp* **:** the condition of being ecumenically united in a worldwide interconfessional and interdenominational Christian fellowship **:** ecumenical Christianity

ec·u·men·ics \,==ˈmeniks, -nēks\ *n pl but sing in constr* [fr. *ecumenic*, after such pairs as *economic: economics*] **:** the study of the nature, mission, problems, and strategy of the Christian church from the perspective of its ecumenical character as a worldwide Christian fellowship, often including within its scope an emphasis on the contributions of Christian mission work to the rise of the ecumenical movement

ec·u·me·nism \ˈekyəmə,nizəm, eˈkyüm- *sometimes* ˈēkyəm-\ *n* -s [ISV *ecumenic* + *-ism*] **:** ecumenical principles and practices particularly as exemplified in the ecumenical movement

ec·u·me·nist \-,nəst\ *n* -s [ISV *ecumenic* + *-ist*] **:** an advocate of ecumenism

ecus *pl of* ECU

ec·ze·ma \÷igˈzēmə, ˈeksəmə, ˈegzəmə, egˈzēmə\ *n* -s [NL *eczemat-*, *eczema*, fr. Gk *ekzemat-*, *ekzema*, fr. *ek* out of, out (fr. *ex*) + *zemat-*, *zema* fermentation, boiling, fr. *zein* to boil — more at EX-, YEAST] **:** an acute or chronic noncontagious inflammatory condition of the skin that is characterized by redness, itching, and oozing vesicular lesions which become scaly, crusted, or lichenified and that is often associated with exposure to chemical or other irritants

eczematization \ig,zeməd·əˈzāshən, eg-, -zem-\ *n* -s [ISV *eczemat-* (fr. NL *eczemat-*, *eczema*) + *-ize* + *-ation*] **:** an eczematous skin lesion complicating a noneczematous dermatitis

ec·ze·ma·to·gen·ic \ig¦zeməd·ō¦jenik, eg-, -zem-\ *or* **ec·ze·ma·tog·e·nous** \-mə¦täjənəs\ *adj* [NL *eczemat-*, *eczema* + E *-o-* + *-genic* or *-genous*] **:** giving rise to eczema

ec·ze·ma·toid \-ˈ=mə,tȯid\ *adj* [ISV *eczemat-* + *-oid*] **:** resembling eczema

ec·ze·ma·tous \igˈzeməd·əs, (ˈ)egˈz-, -zem-, -mətəs\ *adj* [ISV *eczemat-* + *-ous*] **:** relating to eczema ⟨~ dermatitis⟩ **:** having the characteristics of eczema ⟨~ eruption⟩ **:** affected with eczema ⟨an ~ skin⟩

¹-ed \d *after infinitive forms ending in a vowel or in* b, g, j, ŋ, th, v, z, zh, *or* r (r *in such position is usually regarded as a vowel*); t *after infinitive forms ending in* ch, f, k, p, s, sh, *or* th; əd *sometimes* (,)ed *after infinitive forms ending in* d *or* t; *after a few infinitives ending in* l, m, *or* n, *the pronunciation* d *is alternative to* t *and the spelling* -ed *to* -t (dwell, kneel, spell, dream, burn, lean, learn); *some forms that are* -d *or* -t *when used as verbs are alternatively, sometimes only,* -əd *or* -(,)ed *when used* *as adjectives (blessed, cursed, forked, striped, learned); adjectivally used forms in which -ed (often written -èd) follows infinitive terminals other than* d *and* t *are sometimes* -əd *or* -(ˌ)ed *in poetry for the sake of the meter; -ed forms that are regularly* -d *or* -t *are often alternatively* -əd *or* -(ˌ)ed *when -ly or -ness is added, the tendency to the latter pronunciations being in general in proportion to the difficulty of the consonantal cluster of which* l *or* n *is the final member*\ *vb suffix or adj suffix* [ME, fr. OE *-ed, -od, -ad,* fr. *-e-, -o-, -a-* (thematic vowels of various classes of weak verbs) + *-d,* past part. ending of weak verbs; akin to OHG *-t,* past part. ending of weak verbs, ON *-thr,* Goth *-ths,* L *-tus,* past part. ending, Gk *-tos,* suffix forming verbal adjectives, Skt *-ta,* past part. ending] **1** — used to form the past participle of regular weak verbs ⟨end*ed*⟩ ⟨follow*ed*⟩ ⟨dress*ed*⟩; regularly accompanied by coalescence with final *e* of the base word ⟨fad*ed*⟩, change of final postconsonantal *y* of the base word to *i* ⟨tri*ed*⟩, or doubling of the final consonant of the base word immediately after a short stressed vowel ⟨patt*ed*⟩ **2** — used to form adjectives of identical or nearly identical meaning from Latin-derived adjectives ending in *-ate* ⟨crenulat*ed*⟩ ⟨pinnat*ed*⟩ **3 a :** having **:** provided or furnished with **:** characterized by — in adjectives formed from nouns ⟨balconi*ed*⟩ ⟨cultur*ed*⟩ ⟨money*ed*⟩ ⟨wing*ed*⟩ or from combinations having a noun as final constituent ⟨two-legg*ed*⟩ ⟨deep-chest*ed*⟩ ⟨three-stori*ed*⟩ **b :** having the characteristics of — in adjectives formed from nouns ⟨bigot*ed*⟩ ⟨dogg*ed*⟩

²-ed \"\ *vb suffix* [ME *-ede, -de,* fr. OE *-ede, -ode, -ade,* past ending (1st pers. sing. indic.) of weak verbs, fr. *-e-, -o-, -a-* (thematic vowels of various classes of weak verbs) + *-de,* past ending (1st pers. sing. indic.) of weak verbs; akin to OHG *-ta,* past ending (1st pers. sing. indic.) of weak verbs, ON *-tha,* Goth *-da,* and prob. to OE *-d,* past part. ending of weak verbs] — used to form the past tense of regular weak verbs; regularly accompanied by coalescence with final *e* of the base word ⟨judg*ed*⟩, change of final postconsonantal *y* of the base word to *i* ⟨deni*ed*⟩, or doubling of the final consonant of the base word immediately after a short stressed vowel ⟨dropp*ed*⟩

ed *abbr* **1** edited; edition; editor **2** educated; education

ED *abbr* **1** election district **2** ex dividend **3** extra duty

eda·cious \əˈdāshəs, ēˈ-\ *adj* [L *edac-, edax* (fr. *edere* to eat) + E *-ious* — more at EAT] **:** relating to eating **:** VORACIOUS, DEVOURING ⟨time may have its ~ way even with those who deal in . . . absolute truths —Clifton Fadiman⟩

edac·i·ty \-ˈdasədē\ *n* -ES [L *edacitas,* fr. *edac-, edax* + *-itas* -ity] **:** the quality or state of being edacious **:** APPETITE, VORACITY ⟨the ~ of vultures⟩

edam \ˈēdəm, ˈēˌdam, ˈēˌdaa(ə)m\ *or* **edam cheese** *n* -S *usu cap E* [fr. *Edam,* Netherlands] **:** a Dutch pressed cheese of yellow color and mild flavor made in balls weighing up to 10 pounds and usu. colored dark red outside

edaph·ic \əˈdafik, ēˈ-\ *adj* [ISV *edaph-* (fr. Gk *edaphos* bottom, ground, soil) + *-ic;* prob. akin to Gk *hezesthai* to sit — more at SIT] **1 :** of or relating to the soil ⟨~ relations⟩ ⟨~ factors in forest development⟩ **2 a** *of ecological formations* **:** resulting from or influenced by factors inherent in the soil (as salinity, alkalinity, or drainage) — opposed to *climatic;* see EDAPHIC CLIMAX **b :** AUTOCHTHONOUS 1 — **edaph·i·cal·ly** \-fək(ə)lē\ *adv*

edaphic climax *n* **:** an ecological climax resulting from soil factors and commonly persisting through cycles of climatic and physiographic change — compare PHYSIOGRAPHIC CLIMAX

ed·a·phol·o·gy \ˌedəˈfäləjē\ *n* -ES [Gk *edaphos* + E *-logy*] **:** PEDOLOGY

ed·a·phon \ˈedəˌfän\ *n* -S [ISV *edaph-* (fr. Gk *edaphos*) + *-on* (as in *plankton*); orig. formed in G] **:** the animal and plant life present in soils — compare PLANKTON

ed·a·pho·sau·ria \ˌedəfōˈsȯrēə\ *n pl, cap* [NL, fr. Gk *edaphos* bottom, ground, soil + NL *-sauria*] **:** a suborder of Pelycosauria that includes Edaphosauridae and certain related families of extinct reptiles — compare EDAPHOSAURUS

¹ed·a·pho·sau·rid \ˌ≈≈≈ˈsȯrəd\ *adj* [NL *Edaphosauridae* family of reptiles, fr. *Edaphosaurus,* type genus + *-idae*] **:** of or relating to Edaphosauria or to reptiles of this group

²edaphosaurid \"\ *n* -S **:** a reptile or fossil of the suborder Edaphosauria

ed·a·pho·sau·rus \ˌ≈≈≈ˈsȯrəs\ *n, cap* [NL, fr. Gk *edaphos* + NL *-saurus*] **:** a genus (the type of the family Edaphosauridae) of heavy-bodied prob. herbivorous late Paleozoic reptiles having a bony dorsal sail or crest resembling that characteristic of the genus *Dimetrodon*

edd *abbr* editions; editors

ed·dic \ˈedik\ *also* **ed·da·ic** \(ˈ)eˈdāik\ *adj, usu cap* [ON *Edda* (prob. fr. *edda* great-grandmother) + E *-ic;* prob. akin to MHG *eide* mother, ON *eitha,* Goth *aithei*] **1 :** of or relating to the Old Norse *Edda* which is a 13th century collection of mythological, heroic, and gnomic poems many of which were composed at a much earlier date **2 :** having the characteristics of the alliterative strophic poetry of the *Edda* that is relatively simple in syntax and imagery — compare SKALDIC

ed·dish \ˈedish\ *n* -ES [ME *eddysche,* prob. fr. OE *edise* enclosed pasture; perh. akin to OE *ed-* again — more at EDDY] **1** *now dial Brit* **:** second-growth hay **:** AFTERMATH **2** *dial Eng* **:** STUBBLE ⟨a field of wheat ~⟩

ed·do \ˈe(ˌ)dō\ *n* -ES [of African origin; akin to Twi *o¹de³* yam, Fanti *o¹do³*] **1 :** TARO **2 :** the edible root or stem of any of several aroids; *esp* **:** the root of taro

¹ed·dy \ˈedē, -di\ *n* -ES [alter. of ME (Sc dial.) *ydy,* prob. fr. ON *itha;* akin to OE & OS *ed-* again, OHG & ON *ith-* again, Goth *ith* but, L *et* and, Gk *eti* yet, still, Skt *ati* beyond, very; basic meaning: beyond] **1 :** a current of air or water running contrary to the main current; *esp* **:** one moving circularly **:** WHIRLPOOL **2 a :** a movement or school (as of thought or policy) that is static and unprogressive or that runs counter to the main trend ⟨this was merely an ~ in the stream of American foreign policy —P.C.Jessup⟩ ⟨shows a minute acquaintance with the minor *eddies* of the periodical literature —P.B.Rice⟩ **b :** a stagnant provincial region **:** a region that is remote from the main center of life and activity — often used with *back* ⟨when civilization moved northward and westward, Rome became a back ~ in European affairs —C.L.White & G.T.Renner⟩ **c :** an agitated or spasmodic movement (as of controversy or conflict); *esp* **:** one that is haphazard, aimless, or unproductive ⟨*eddies* and flurries of tribal strife ruled out the possibility of a topographical survey —J.V.Harrison⟩ **3 :** a material substance or group of individuals moving in a swirling or circular manner within a relatively limited area ⟨a constant wind whined through the tunnels, whipping *eddies* of coal dust into our eyes —Franc Shor⟩ ⟨little *eddies* of people were dancing with each other in the streets —L.C.Stevens⟩

²eddy \"\ *vb* -ED/-ING/-ES *vt* **:** to cause to move in an eddy ~ *vi* **:** to move in an eddy or in the manner of an eddy ⟨at the base of which the river swirls and *eddies* in a manner dangerous to small craft —Tom Marvel⟩ ⟨a crowd of blue-gowned men ~*ing* as starlings do about a tree —Patrick O'Donovan⟩ **syn** see TURN

eddy chamber *n* **:** a chamber where a fluid is caused to whirl in eddies

eddy current *n* **:** an electric current induced by an alternating magnetic field in a massive conductor (as the core of an armature or a transformer) — called also *Foucault current*

eddy–current brake *n* **:** a speed-control dynamometer in which the resistance to rotation is produced by eddy currents generated by the relative rotation of copper disks and magnets **:** an electromagnetic brake — compare MAGNETIC DAMPING

eddy–current loss *n* **:** loss of energy (as in electrical machinery or transformers) due to eddy currents in cores or conductors — compare CORE LOSS

ed·dy·root \ˈedēˌ, -diˌ≈\ *n* [by folk etymology fr. *eddo* + *root*] **:** TARO

ede- *or* **edeo-** *comb form* [NL *aedoe-, aedoeo-,* fr. Gk *aidoi-* & LGk *aidoio-,* fr. Gk *aidoia* genitals, fr. neut. pl. of *aidoios* worthy of reverence or compassion, fr. *aidōs* reverence, shame; prob. akin to OE *ār* honor, reverence, OHG *ēra* honor, reverence, ON *eir* clemency, Goth *aistan* to respect, Skt *īḍe* I praise] **:** genitals ⟨*ede*itis⟩ ⟨*edeo*scopy⟩

edel·e·a·nu process \əˌdelēˈä(ˌ)nü-\ *n, usu cap E* [after L. *Edeleanu* †1941 Romanian chemist] **:** a process for refining petroleum fractions (as kerosine or heavier oils) by extraction with liquid sulfur dioxide

edel·weiss \ˈādᵊlˌwīs, -ˌvīs\ *n* -ES [G, fr. *edel* noble (fr. OHG *edili*) + *weiss* white (fr. OHG *hwīz, wīz*); akin to OE *æthelu* nobility — more at ATHELING, WHITE] **1 :** a small perennial herb (*Leontopodium alpinum*) having a dense woolly white pubescence and growing high in the Alps **2 :** a New Zealand herb (*Leucogenes leontopodium*) related to and closely resembling the European edelweiss **3 :** any of various plants of the genus *Gnaphalium*

ede·ma *also* **oe·de·ma** \əˈdēmə, ēˈ-\ *n, pl* **edemas** \-məs\ *also* **edem·a·ta** \-ˈdeməd·ə, -ˈdēm-, -ətə\ *or* **oedemas** *or* **oedemata** [NL, fr. Gk *oidēma* swelling, tumor, fr. *oidein, oidan* to swell; akin to Gk *oidos* swelling, tumor — more at ATTER] **1 :** an abnormal accumulation of serous fluid in connective tissue causing puffy swelling or in a serous cavity (as the peritoneal or pleural) causing distention and compression of the contents that is usu. associated with defective circulation either primary or secondary to other conditions (as nephritis) **2 a :** extended swelling of plant organs or parts of organs from an overdevelopment of cells induced by an excess of water combined with unfavorable light and temperature relations **b :** any of various specific diseases of plants (as the tomato) characterized by such swellings — compare INTUMESCENCE

edem·a·tous \-ˈdeməd·əs, -ˈdēm-, -ətəs\ *adj* [NL *edemat-, edema* + E *-ous*] **:** relating to, affected by, or having edema

eden \ˈēdᵊn\ *n* -S *usu cap* [fr. *Eden,* the garden where Adam and Eve resided before the Fall (Gen 2:8), fr. LL, fr. Heb *ʽĒdhen*] **:** PARADISE 2

eden·ic \(ˈ)ēˈdenik\ *adj, usu cap* **:** of or relating to an Eden **:** PARADISIACAL

eden·ite \ˈēdᵊnˌīt\ *n* -S [G *edenit,* fr. *Edenville,* N.Y. + G *-it* -ite] **:** a light-colored variety of aluminous amphibole

eden·tal \(ˈ)ēˈdentᵊl\ *or* **eden·ta·lous** \-ᵊləs\ *adj* [*edental* fr. *e-* + *dent-* + *-al; edentalous* fr. *edental* + *-ous*] **:** EDENTATE

eden·ta·ta \ˌēˌdenˈtädə, -ˈtādə\ *n pl, cap* [NL, fr. L, neut. pl. of *edentatus,* past part. of *edentare* to make toothless, fr. *e* out of (fr. *ex*) + *dent-, dens* tooth — more at EX-, TOOTH] **:** an order of Eutheria comprising mammals with teeth if present few and small, a small unconvoluted cerebrum, and the skin hairy or covered with bony plates and including the sloths, armadillos, and New World anteaters and formerly also the pangolins, the aardvark, and sometimes other forms

¹eden·tate \(ˈ)ēˈdenˌtāt\ *adj* [in sense 1, fr. L *edentatus;* in sense 2, fr. NL *Edentata*] **1 :** lacking teeth ⟨an ~ animal⟩ ⟨an ~ leaf⟩ **2 :** belonging to the Edentata

²edentate \"\ *n* -S **:** one of the Edentata

eden·tu·late \(ˈ)ēˈdenchələt, -ˌlāt\ *adj* [L *edentulus* + E *-ate*] **:** lacking teeth **:** EDENTATE — used esp. of animals

eden·tu·lous \-ləs\ *adj* [L *edentulus,* fr. *e-* out of + *dent-, dens* tooth + *-ulus* -ulous] **:** lacking teeth; *esp* **:** having lost teeth previously present

edeo- — see EDE-

edes·san \əˈdesᵊn, ēˈ-\ *also* **edes·sene** \-ˌsēn\ *adj, usu cap* [*Edessa,* Mesopotamia + E *-an* or *-ene*] **:** of or relating to Edessa (modern Urfa), a city of ancient Mesopotamia

edes·tin \əˈdestən, ē-\ *n* -S [ISV *edest-* (fr. Gk *edestos* eatable, fr. *edein* to eat) + *-in* — more at EAT] **1 :** a crystalline globulin found in many edible seeds (as in oats or rye) — not used technically **2 :** a crystalline globulin obtained esp. from hempseed that contains all of the essential amino acids

ed·gar \ˈedgə(r)\ *n* -S *usu cap* [after *Edgar* Allan Poe †1849 Am. poet and story writer known as the father of the detective story] **:** any of several small busts of Edgar Allan Poe awarded annually by a professional organization of writers to authors in various branches of mystery writing

¹edge \ˈej\ *n* -S *often attrib* [ME *egge,* fr. OE *ecg;* akin to OS *eggia* edge of a blade, edge, OHG *ecka,* ON & OFris *egg,* L *acies* sharp edge, point, *acer* sharp, Gk *akmē* point, edge, LGk *akē* point, Skt *aśri* corner, angle, edge] **1 a :** the cutting side of the blade of an instrument ⟨the ~ of an ax⟩ **b** *archaic* **:** an edged weapon or tool **c :** the sharpness or degree of sharpness of a blade ⟨the sickle has no ~⟩ **d** (1) *obs* **:** ardor or inclination esp. for battle (2) **:** FORCE, EFFECTIVENESS ⟨local resistance blunted the ~ of radical legislation at Washington⟩ **:** vigor or energy esp. of mind and body ⟨he looked and acted flabby; the ~ of him was gone —Carleton Beals⟩ **:** incisive or penetrating quality (as of thought or expression) ⟨the cutting ~ of Machiavelli's irony —E.R.Bentley⟩ **:** a quality of hardness, harshness, or bite ⟨his voice had an ~ like ice —John Buchan⟩ ⟨your goodness must have an ~ in it — else it is none —R.W. Emerson⟩ (3) **:** keenness or intensity esp. of desire or enjoyment ⟨when they'd taken the ~ off their own hunger —Kenneth Roberts⟩ **:** RELISH, ZEST, SAVOR ⟨flying bombs . . . gave a brilliant ~ of chance to homely days and nights —Audrey Barker⟩ **:** SPUR, STIMULUS ⟨to give more ~ to the contest, he felt for his rival the bitter hate that . . . was typically Venetian —T.B.Costain⟩ **2 a :** the extreme verge or brink (as of a cliff or precipice) **b :** the crest of a ridge of hills **:** the escarpment of a plateau **3 a :** the line or point where a material object or area begins or ends **:** BORDER ⟨the town stands on the ~ of a plain⟩ ⟨a smoldering hulk, burned to the water's ~ —H.A.Chippendale⟩; *also* **:** the portion of the surface of an object or area that is adjacent to its border ⟨walked on the ~ of the deck⟩ **b :** a point near the beginning or the end (as of an era, condition, subject, or action) **:** a dividing line or line of transition from one state or condition to another **:** MARGIN — often used in the phrase *on the edge* ⟨science stood on the ~ of a major theoretical advance⟩ ⟨her body hovered delicately on the last ~ of childhood —Scott Fitzgerald⟩ ⟨many of the ranches . . . are on the ~ of bankruptcy —H.W. Baldwin⟩ ⟨was on the ~ of screaming⟩ **4** *obs* **:** EDGING, BORDER **5 :** a terminating border ⟨the ~ of a tablecloth⟩ **:** a line that is the intersection of two plane faces of a solid object ⟨the ~*s* of a pyramid⟩ **:** the relatively thin surface or side of any object bounded by plane surfaces ⟨the ~ of a book⟩ **6 a :** the inside or outside verge of the blade of a skate **b :** a skating stroke including appropriate body lean made on one edge of the blade of a skate ⟨a forward inside ~⟩; *also* **:** the resultant pattern cut in the ice **7 :** the privilege in poker of betting last after the other players have revealed their intentions — called also *age* **8 :** a favorable margin **:** ADVANTAGE ⟨had the ~ on top speed —A.S.Kramer⟩ ⟨the open spaces that gave the suburb . . . an ~ over the city — Lewis Mumford⟩ ⟨a decisive ~ in military strength⟩ **9** *slang* **:** a condition of being intoxicated **:** degree of intoxication ⟨got a good ~ on —Ernest Hemingway⟩ **syn** see BORDER — **on edge :** NERVOUS, ANXIOUS, UNEASY ⟨as a conductor . . . he kept the singers uncomfortably *on edge* —*Time*⟩

²edge \"\ *vb* -ED/-ING/-S [ME *eggen,* fr. *egge, n.*] *vt* **1 :** to give an edge to ⟨asked him to ~ the ax⟩ ⟨hurt resentment *edged* his wife's voice —G.G.Carter⟩ **2** *obs* **:** to set (one's teeth) on edge **3 a** (1) **:** to finish (an edge) with a binding, band, strip, or trimming ⟨~ a blouse with lace⟩ ⟨~ a plywood counter⟩ (2) **:** to decorate an edge of (as a book) (3) **:** to level an edge of (a rafter); *also* **:** to square an edge of **b :** to serve as a border to **:** FRINGE ⟨warehouses and terminals ~ the 25-mile waterfront —L.A.Borah⟩ **:** be on an edge of ⟨grew up in a community still *edging* the wilderness —H.M.Kallen⟩ ⟨now *edging* sixty, he retains all his vigor⟩ **4** *archaic* **:** to urge or egg on **5 :** to move gradually or by pressing forward edgewise ⟨*edged* his master out of hearing —George Meredith⟩ ⟨~ him off the road⟩ **:** force (as from a position) by the application of pressure ⟨*edging* his foes out of every position of influence⟩ **:** DISPLACE ⟨machine-made muslins and calicoes have been *edging* out native-made muslins —John Murra⟩ **6 a :** to strike (a bowled ball) in cricket with the edge of the bat **b :** to incline (a ski) sideways so that one edge cuts into the surface of the snow ~ *vi* **:** to move in one direction by degrees ⟨*edged* over the open plains toward the western extremities of the country —Oscar Handlin⟩ ⟨~ away from his responsibilities⟩ **:** move edgeways ⟨began to ~ along the front of the bureau —Berton Roueché⟩

edgebone *var of* AITCHBONE

edged \ˈejd *sometimes* ˈejəd\ *adj* **1 :** having a specified kind of edge, boundary, or border ⟨black-*edged*⟩ ⟨rough-*edged*⟩ ⟨scalloped-*edged*⟩ or number of edges ⟨two-*edged*⟩ **2 :** SHARP, CUTTING ⟨an ~ knife⟩ **:** TRENCHANT ⟨an ~ remark⟩ ⟨~ satire⟩

edge effect *n* **1 :** the result of the presence of two adjoining plant communities (as in an ecotone) on the numbers and kinds of animals present in the immediate vicinity **2 :** a special physical condition (as of electric surface density or turbulence) existing at the edge of an area (as a charged metal plate) or region

edge–grain \ˈ≈,≈\ *or* **edge–grained** \ˈ≈;≈\ *adj* **:** QUARTERSAWED

edge in *vt* **:** to work in **:** INTERPOLATE ⟨with difficulty *edging in* a word of his own⟩

edge iron *n* **:** a gardener's tool for cutting turf along a border (as of a walk or flower bed)

edge joint *n* **:** a joint formed by uniting two edges or two surfaces (as by welding) esp. making a corner

edge·less \ˈejləs\ *adj* **:** lacking an edge **:** DULL, BLURRED

edge lighting *n* **:** the ability of a transparent substance (as plastic) to transmit light (as from the edge of a sheet or the end of a rod) so that it remains invisible until it emerges at the far edge or end regardless of bends or turns in the substance

edge mill *n* **1 :** an ore-grinding machine of the Chile-mill type **2 :** a narrow plain milling cutter

edge on *adv* **:** EDGEWAYS **:** on an edge ⟨receive a blow *edge on*⟩

edge out *vt* **:** to defeat or surpass by a small margin ⟨coming from behind to *edge out* the opposing team by one point⟩ ⟨*edged* his opponent *out* by 367 votes in a total vote of 40,000⟩

edge protector *n* **:** a right-angle piece of metal or hard fiber placed over the edge (as of a shipping case, crate, box, or bale) to prevent cutting by metal strapping or wire

edg·er \ˈejə(r)\ *n* -S **1 a :** a worker who stitches or finishes the edge of a garment **b :** an operator of a burnishing machine for finishing the skived edge of a shoe upper to make it appear rolled or for setting the edge of the forepart of a sole **c :** a person who bevels or grinds the edge of optical glass **d :** STRANDER 2 **e :** an operator of a lumber-edging machine **2 a :** a machine for edging lumber; *esp* **:** one with feed rolls, press rolls, and several circular saws **b :** a wood-sanding machine adapted to work around an edge (as of a floor) **c :** a tool used to trim an edge (as of a lawn) along a sidewalk or curb **3 :** BREAKDOWN 5

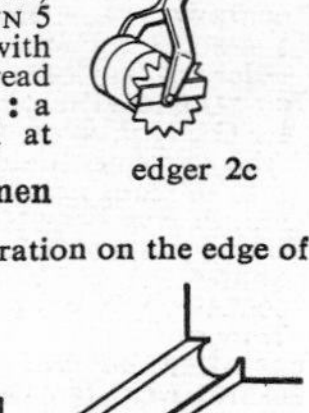

edger 2c

edge rail *n* **1 :** a railroad rail set on edge with which a flanged wheel with a conoidal tread is used — contrasted with *tram rail* **2 :** a guardrail laid alongside the main rail at a switch

edg·er·man \ˈ≈≈mən\ *n, pl* **edgermen :** EDGER 1

edge roll *n* **1 a :** a tool for rolling in decoration on the edge of a book cover **b :** a decoration made with an edge roll **2 :** a molding of semicircular section replacing the arris at the edge of a member

edge roll 2

edge runner *n* **1 :** a stone or metal wheel in an edge mill **2 :** a machine consisting of one or more heavy steel rolls or grindstones set on a horizontal shaft rotating round a pan or trough that is used for crushing stone, fibrous material for papermaking, or other material

edges *pl of* EDGE, *pres 3d sing of* EDGE

edgeshot \ˈ≈,≈\ *adj* [¹*edge* + *shot,* past part. of *shoot* (to plane)] **:** having an edge planed

edgestitch \ˈ≈;≈\ *vt* **:** to seam or stitch for decoration along a fold line of (a piece of cloth)

edgestone \ˈ≈,≈\ *n* **1 :** CURBSTONE **2 :** a stone roller in an edge mill

edge strip *n* **:** a strap for a butt joint in riveted plate work esp. when used for a fore-and-aft joint in a ship's hull

edge tone *n* **:** a tone produced by an air stream deflected by a sharp edge (as in a flute)

edge tool *n* **1 :** a tool with a sharp cutting edge (as a chisel, plane, knife, or gouge) **2 :** a tool for forming or dressing an edge **:** an edging tool

edge trim *n* **:** a contour (as bevel or round) given in finishing the edge of a sole

edgewater \ˈ≈,≈≈\ *n* **:** water underlying petroleum in an oil-bearing sand — compare EDGE WELL

edgeways *or* **edgewise** \ˈ≈,≈\ *adv* **:** with the edge toward or foremost **:** on, by, or with the edge ⟨saw a plank ~⟩; *also* **:** as if by an edge **:** BARELY — chiefly used in the phrase *get a word in edgeways* ⟨had to raise his voice to get a word in ~ —George Bellairs⟩

edge well *n* **:** a well on the edge of an oil or gas pool

edg·i·ly \ˈejəlē, -li\ *adv* **:** in an edgy manner

edg·i·ness \ˈejēnəs, -jin-\ *n* -ES **1 :** sharpness or angularity of outline ⟨the ~ of a fresh-cut gem —R.C.B.Brown⟩ **2 :** the condition of being on edge **:** NERVOUSNESS

edging *n* -S [¹*edge* + *-ing*] **1 :** something that forms an edge or border: as **a :** a narrow piece of lace, fringe, or braid usu. with one straight edge used to finish or decorate an edge or joining on clothing, upholstery, or curtains **b :** a border of plants, wood, metal or bricks used to define an edge (as of a bed or lawn) or the material used for such a border **c :** small solid wood squares set into the edge of a veneered top to protect the veneer **d :** a narrow rounded or right-angled strip (as of metal) on the edge of a flat surface (as a table top or ski) for decoration or protection **2 :** a piece of waste wood produced in edging

edging box *n* **:** a dwarf box (*Buxus sempervirens* var. *suffruticosa*) that is used esp. for edging (as around a bed in a garden)

edging grinder *n* **:** a cutting machine for grinding up refuse wood

edg·ing·ly *adv* **:** little by little **:** GRADUALLY

edgy \ˈejē, -ji\ *adj* -ER/-EST **1 :** SHARP, EDGED ⟨often displayed a perceptive, ~ wit —*New Yorker*⟩ ⟨the vocal quality on this occasion was raw and ~ —Irving Kolodin⟩ **:** hard or angular in line or outline **2 :** being on edge **:** TENSE, NERVOUS, IRRITABLE ⟨looked well, though a little tired and ~ —H.L.Davis⟩ ⟨the ~ days before World War I —*Saturday Rev.*⟩ ⟨tempers became ~ —Gordon Webber⟩

edh *or* **eth** \ˈeth\ *n* -S [Icel *eth*] **:** a letter ð formed with a stroke across the simple *d* used in Old English and in Icelandic writing to represent an interdental fricative and in the International Phonetic alphabet to represent the voiced interdental fricative (as in *then*) — compare THORN 3

ed·i·bil·i·ty \ˌedəˈbilədē, -ətē, -i\ *n* -ES **:** the quality or state of being edible

¹ed·i·ble \ˈedəbəl\ *adj* [LL *edibilis,* fr. L *edere* to eat + *-ibilis* -ible — more at EAT] **:** suitable by nature for use as food esp. for human beings **:** NONPOISONOUS, EATABLE — **ed·i·ble·ness** *n* -ES

²edible \"\ *n* -S **:** something that is edible ⟨state police rushed food to stricken families . . . only cold ~*s* were transported —*N.Y.Times*⟩

edible bird's nest *n* **:** the nest of various small swifts (genus *Collocalia*) of southern Asia and neighboring islands that is made chiefly of the dried glutinous secretion of the salivary glands of the birds and is used in making soup

edible canna *n* **:** an Asiatic herb (*Canna edulis*) cultivated for its starchy rootstocks — see TOUS-LES-MOIS

edible dormouse *n* **:** any of various common European dormice (genus *Glis*) esp. of the Mediterranean region

edible frog *n* **:** a European frog (*Rana esculenta*)

edible galingale *n* **:** CHUFA

edible–podded pea \ˈ≈≈≈,≈≈-\ *or* **edible pod pea** \ˈ≈≈≈,≈-\ *n* **:** a pea of a variety (*Pisum sativum macrocarpon*) with edible pods

edible snail *n* **:** a snail used as food (as *Helix pomatia* and *H. aspersa* of Europe)

edict \ˈē(ˌ)dikt, ˈēdēkt, *archaic* ≈ˈ≈\ *n* -S [L *edictum,* fr. neut. of *edictus,* past part. of *edicere* to declare, decree, fr. *e-* + *dicere* to say — more at DICTION] **1 a :** a public notice issued by official ecclesiastical or state authority **:** a public command or ordinance by the sovereign power **:** the proclamation of a law or rule of conduct made by competent authority — compare DECREE, RESCRIPT **b :** an order or command esp. when suggesting such an official public notice ⟨so the wife won't notice it and issue bitter ~*s* about slovenliness —*Fortnight*⟩ **2 :** the order of the court in Scots and Roman Dutch law commanding that notice of a pending civil or criminal suit be given to an absent or nonresident defendant by citation and specifying in what manner it should be given — compare EDICTAL CITATION

edic·tal \(ˈ)ēˌdiktᵊl, əˈd-\ *adj* [LL *edictalis*, fr. L *edictum* + *-alis* -al] **:** relating to or consisting of an edict **:** announced by an edict

edictal citation *n* **:** a citation or summons in Scots and Roman Dutch law proclaimed, published, or deposited in a public place and summoning nonresident or absent defendants to court in civil or criminal cases

edic·tal·ly \-ᵊlē\ *adv* **:** by means of an edict

ed·i·cule \ˈedəˌkyül\ *var of* AEDICULA

ed·i·fi·ca·tion \ˌedəfəˈkāshən\ *n* -s [ME *edificacioun*, fr. LL & L; LL *aedification-, aedificatio* spiritual improvement, fr. L, construction, fr. *aedificatus* (past part. of *aedificare* to construct) + *-ion-, -io* -ion — more at EDIFY] **1 a :** a building up of the mind, character, or faith **:** intellectual, moral, or spiritual improvement ⟨images of ~ are offered to our eyes —E.R. Bentley⟩ **b :** ENLIGHTENMENT ⟨examples of good quality in our public museums for the ~ of the man off the street —S.L. Faison⟩ **2** *archaic* **:** construction esp. of a building ⟨the assured ~ of his church —Joseph Hall⟩

edif·i·ca·to·ry \əˈdifəkəˌtōrē, ēˈdif-, edəf-; ˈedəfəˌkādˌərē\ *adj* [LL *aedificatorius*, fr. *aedificatus* (past part. of *aedificare* to edify) + L *-orius* -ory — more at EDIFY] **:** intended or suitable for edification ⟨a minister given to the writing of ~ epistles to his congregation⟩; *also* **:** EDIFYING ⟨the ~ force of an oration⟩

ed·i·fice \ˈedəfəs\ *n* -s [ME, fr. MF, fr. L *aedificium*, fr. *aedificare* to construct — more at EDIFY] **1 :** BUILDING; *esp* **:** a large or massive structure (as a church or government building) **2 :** something built up in a manner analogous to the erection of an architectural structure ⟨on this argument he based his ~ of faith —A.N.Whitehead⟩ ⟨does not feel that the whole ~ of science has collapsed and crumbled —G.B. Shaw⟩

ed·i·fi·cial \ˌedəˈfishəl\ *adj* [LL *aedificialis*, fr. L *aedificium* + *-alis* -al] **1 :** relating to an edifice **:** STRUCTURAL **2 :** IMPOSING

ed·i·fi·er \ˈedəˌfī(ə)r, -īə\ *n* -s [ME, fr. *edifien* + *-er*] **:** one that edifies

ed·i·fy \ˈedəˌfī\ *vb* -ED/-ING/-S [ME *edifien, edefien*, fr. MF *edifier, edefier*, fr. LL & L; LL *aedificare* to instruct or improve spiritually, fr. L, to erect a house, construct, fr. *aedes* temple, house, building (prob. orig. "hearth") + *-ficare* -fy; akin to OE *ād* funeral pyre, fire, OHG *eit* funeral pyre, fire, G dial. *aitel*, a kind of bright fish, Sw *id* ide (fish), L *aestas* summer, Gk *aithein* to ignite, burn, Skt *inddhe* he ignites] *vt* **1** *archaic* **a :** BUILD ⟨a holy chapel *edified* —Edmund Spenser⟩ ⟨*edified* fourteen hundred mosques —Edward Gibbon⟩ **b :** ORGANIZE, ESTABLISH **2 :** to instruct and improve esp. in moral and religious knowledge **:** ENLIGHTEN, ELEVATE, UPLIFT ⟨the object of these paintings . . . was to instruct and ~ all who came into the church, even if they could not read —O. Elfrida Saunders⟩ ⟨believe myself to be *edified* by the old liturgy —D.W.Brogan⟩ ~ *vi* **1** *obs* **:** GROW, PROSPER **2 a** *obs* **:** to profit spiritually **:** IMPROVE **b** *archaic* **:** to gain knowledge **:** LEARN

ed·i·fy·ing·ly \ˈ==ˌ===, ˌ=ˈ===\ *adv* **:** so as to edify **:** in an edifying manner

ed·i·fy·ing·ness \ˈ==ˌ===, ˌ=ˈ===\ *n* -ES **:** the quality or state of being edifying

edile *var of* AEDILE

ed·in·burgh \ˈedᵊnˌbər·ə, -ˌbə·r|, |ō *also* -ˌbərg *or* -ˌbəg *or* -ˌbəig\ *adj, usu cap* [fr. *Edinburgh*, Scotland] **:** of or from Edinburgh, the capital of Scotland **:** of the kind or style prevalent in Edinburgh

ed·ing·ton·ite \ˈediŋtəˌnīt\ *n* -s [after *Edington*, 19th cent. Scot who found it] **:** a grayish white zeolitic mineral $BaAl_2Si_3O_{10}.4H_2O$ consisting of hydrous aluminum barium silicate (hardness 4–4.5, sp. gr. 2.69)

ed·i·son battery \ˈedəsən-\ *or* **edison storage battery** *n* [fr. *Edison*, a trademark] **:** a storage battery employing a solution of caustic potash as the electrolyte, nickel hydroxide and iron as the active agents of the plates, and nickel-plated steel as the framework and container

edison cell *n* [fr. *Edison*, a trademark] **:** a cell of an Edison battery

edison effect *n, usu cap E* [after Thomas A. *Edison* †1931 Am. inventor] **:** the thermionic current observed when an additional electrode is introduced into an incandescent-lamp bulb and connected externally with the positive terminal through a galvanometer

ed·it \ˈedət, *usu* -əd·+V\ *vt* -ED/-ING/-S [back-formation fr. *editor*] **1 a :** to prepare an edition of **:** select, emend, revise, and compile (as literary material) to make suitable for publication or for public presentation ⟨~*ed* the complete poetic works⟩ ⟨the newsroom staff ~*s* the bulletins for radio broadcasts⟩ ⟨this old opera was recently revived and ~*ed*⟩ ⟨~*s* his thoughts before speaking⟩ **b :** to assemble (a photographic film sequence or tape recording) by cutting, rearranging, and combining its component parts ⟨the ~*ed* film is a selected assembly of many "bits and pieces" of all kinds . . . the result is a smooth-flowing continuity —W.H.Offenhauser⟩ ⟨~*ed* the tape recording to fit a 15-minute program⟩ **c :** to alter, adapt, or refine esp. to bring about conformity to a standard or to suit a particular purpose ⟨~*s* the finished creations with an architect's eye for line and proportion —*Fashion Digest*⟩ ⟨famous last words are usually ~*ed* after the fact —John Hersey⟩ ⟨took the liberty of ~*ing* the information that was presented to the committee at the hearing⟩ **2 :** to superintend or direct the publication of ⟨~*ed* the daily paper⟩ ⟨~*ed* scientific journals⟩ **3 :** OMIT, DELETE, ELIMINATE — usu. used with *out* ⟨~*ing* clichés out of other people's writing —Max Ascoli⟩ ⟨has mistakenly ~*ed* out of his book a wealth of characterization and anecdote that his original research must have provided —R.N.Denney⟩ ⟨~ out undesirable film⟩

edi·tion \əˈdishən, ēˈ-\ *n* -s [MF & ML; MF *edition*, fr. ML *edition-, editio*, fr. L, act of bringing forth, fr. *editus* (past part. of *edere* to bring forth, produce, proclaim, publish, fr. *e-* + *-dere* to put or *-dere*, fr. *dare* to give) + *-ion-, -io* -ion — more at DO, DATE] **1** *obs* **a :** the action of publishing **b :** the action or result of bringing into existence: (1) **:** EXTRACTION, ORIGIN (2) **:** CREATION ⟨can we treat the absolute ~ of the world as a legitimate hypothesis? —William James⟩ **2 :** the form in which a literary work (as an edited text) or group of works (as the works of several poets) is published: as **a :** the whole number of bound copies printed from a single setting of type or from plates made therefrom **b :** PRINTING **c :** a printed production the same as an earlier one in title but with substantial changes in or additions to the text **d :** a set of copies differing in some way from others of the same published text ⟨a thumb-indexed ~⟩ ⟨an india-paper ~⟩ **e :** an arbitrarily limited number of copies or complete sheets of an impression **3 a :** one of the forms in which something is issued or otherwise presented to the public ⟨most of the standard ~*s* of the older music contain few staccato marks —Warwick Braithwaite⟩ ⟨the Spanish Civil War ~ of the Goya etchings —H.L.Matthews⟩ ⟨this year's ~ of the annual charity ball⟩ **b :** the whole number of articles of one style put out at one time ⟨a limited ~ of custom-made radiophonographs⟩; *specif* **:** the number of stamps or of items of a particular piece of postal stationery in one issue **c :** something that resembles another in its main characteristics **:** REPRODUCTION, COPY, VERSION ⟨the Southern Uplands form a softer and kindlier ~ of the Highlands —L.D.Stamp⟩ ⟨her younger sister, a weaker ~ of Octavie —Dorothy C. Fisher⟩ **4 :** all the copies printed in a single pressrun of a newspaper — see CITY EDITION, FINAL EDITION, FIRST EDITION, MAIL EDITION

edition bindery *n* **:** a plant specializing in machine binding of complete editions or large quantities of books as distinguished from a plant doing job binding or hand binding

edition binding *n* **:** the binding of books in uniform style usu. by mass-production methods and in relatively large quantities esp. as contrasted with hand binding or library binding; *also* **:** a book so bound — called also *publisher's binding, trade binding*

edi·tio prin·ceps \əˈdidˌēˌōˈprinˌkeps; əˈdishēˌōˈprinˌseps, ēˈ-\ *n, pl* **edi·ti·o·nes prin·ci·pes** \əˌdidˌēˈōˌnāsˈpriŋkəˌpās; əˌdishēˈō(ˌ)nēzˈprin(t)səˌpēz, ēˌd-\ [NL, lit., first edition] **:** the first printed edition esp. of a work that circulated in manuscript before printing became common ⟨the *editio princeps* of the Greek New Testament —*Times Lit. Supp.*⟩

ed·i·tor \ˈedəd·ə(r), -ətə(r)\ *n* -s [LL, publisher, fr. L *editus* (past part. of *edere* to bring forth, produce, proclaim, publish) + *-or* — more at EDITION] **1 a :** one who revises, corrects, or arranges the contents and style of the literary, artistic, or musical work of others for publication or presentation ⟨the ~ of some early English ballads⟩ ⟨an ~ of Aristotle⟩ ⟨the ~ of a film⟩ **b :** one who alters or revises another's work to make it conform to some standard or serve a particular purpose ⟨some ~ had bowdlerized th letter before publishing it⟩ **c :** one who directs or supervises the expressive policies or the preparation of a publication (as a newspaper, periodical, reference work) **d :** one who has contextual supervision of a section, special department, or feature of a publication ⟨the sports ~ of the evening paper⟩ ⟨the fiction ~ of a magazine⟩ **e :** one who handles the written product as distinct from other matters (as sales) in many publishing concerns ⟨the ~*s* and the sales and business personnel of the magazine stayed on friendly terms⟩ **2 :** a device usu. consisting of a splicer and viewer and used in editing film

[1]**ed·i·to·ri·al** \ˌedəˈtōrēəl, -ȯr-\ *adj* [*editor* + *-ial*] **1 a :** being an editor or consisting of editors ⟨an ~ staff⟩ **b :** of or relating to an editor or his functions ⟨an ~ job⟩ ⟨the ~ desk⟩ ⟨the punctuation is ~ —R.H.Robbins⟩ **2 a :** of, befitting, or resembling an editorial **:** expressive of an opinion ⟨an ~ broadcast⟩ ⟨an ~ statement⟩ **b :** of, relating to, or constituting the literary contents of a publication ⟨the ~ content of a woman's magazine sandwiched in among the ads⟩

[2]**editorial** \"\ *n* -s **:** a newspaper or periodical article that is usu. given a special or significant place and that intentionally expresses the views of those in control of the publication on a matter of current interest; *also* **:** an expression of opinion that resembles such an article

ed·i·to·ri·al·ist \ˌ==ˈ==ələst\ *n* **:** a writer of editorials

ed·i·to·ri·al·i·za·tion \ˌ==ˌ==əlᵊˈzāshən, -ˌlīˈz-\ *n* -s **:** the action of editorializing

ed·i·to·ri·al·ize \ˌ=ˈ==əˌlīz\ *vi* -ED/-ING/-S **1 :** to express an opinion in the form of an editorial ⟨all the local papers *editorialized* on the subject⟩ **2 :** to introduce opinion into the reporting of facts (as by overt comment or by slanting the report) ⟨the interpretative function of a newspaper or a radio news program need entail no *editorializing*⟩ **3 :** to express an opinion (as on a controversial issue) ⟨the advertisement did not so much sell goods as ~ on local issues⟩

ed·i·to·ri·al·iz·er \-zə(r)\ *n* -s **:** one that editorializes

ed·i·to·ri·al·ly \ˌ=ˈ== əlē, -li\ *adv* **1 :** in editorials or in an editorial manner ⟨the evening paper commented ~ on his appointment⟩ **2 :** in the capacity of editor ⟨he was ~ connected with the publication for many years⟩

editor in chief \ˈ===ˈ=\ *n, pl* **editors in chief :** an editor who is the head of the entire editorial staff of a publication

ed·i·tor·ship \ˈ===ˌship\ *n* **1 a :** the position and functions of an editor ⟨he had the ~ of the magazine⟩ **b :** the tenure of such a position ⟨the publication thrived during his ~⟩ **2 :** editorial revision or alteration ⟨it was hard to tell the extent of the Russian ~ of the reports⟩

ed·i·tress \ˈedə·trəs\ *n* -ES [*editor* + *-ess*] **:** a female editor

edits *pres 3d sing of* EDIT

EDL *abbr* edition deluxe

ed·mon·ton \ˈedməntən, -ntᵊn\ *adj, usu cap* **1** [fr. *Edmonton*, England] **:** of or from the municipal borough of Edmonton, England **:** of the kind or style prevalent in Edmonton, England **2** [fr. *Edmonton*, Alberta, Canada] **:** of or from Edmonton, the capital of Alberta **:** of the kind or style prevalent in Edmonton, Alberta

edn *abbr* **1** edition **2** education

ednl *abbr* educational

edo \ˈe(ˌ)dō\ *n, pl* **edo** *or* **edos** *usu cap* **1 a :** a Negro people of the province of Benin in southern Nigeria **b :** a member of such people **2 :** a Kwa language of the Edo people

edom·ite \ˈēdəˌmīt\ *n* -s *usu cap* [*Edom* (Esau), eponymous ancestor of the Edomites (Gen 36) + *-ite*] **:** a member of an ancient people who were descended from Esau and who lived southeast of the Dead sea — **edom·it·ic** \ˌēdəˈmid·ik\ *adj*

ed·reo·benthos \ˌedrēō+\ *n* [*edreo-* (fr. Gk *hedraios* sedentary, fr. *hedra* seat, sitting) + *benthos*; akin to Gk *hezesthai* to sit — more at SIT] **:** obligatorily sedentary organisms of the benthos (as mussels and rock oysters)

ed·ri·as·ter·oi·dea \ˌedrēˌastəˈroidēə\ *syn of* EDRIOASTEROIDEA

[1]**ed·rio·as·ter·oid** \ˌedrēōˈastəˌrȯid\ *adj* [NL *Edrioasteroidea*] **:** of or relating to the Edrioasteroidea

[2]**edrioasteroid** \"\ *n* -s **:** an echinoderm of the class Edrioasteroidea

ed·rio·as·ter·oi·dea \ˌ===ˌ==ˈrȯidēə\ *n pl, cap* [NL, fr. *edrio-* (fr. Gk *hedraios* sedentary, stationary) + *Asteroidea*] **:** a class of extinct echinoderms (subphylum Pelmatozoa) with a plated but flexible body resembling a sac

ed·ri·oph·thal·ma \ˌedrēˌäfˈthalmə\ *n pl, cap* [NL, fr. *edri-* (fr. Gk *hedraios*) + *-ophthalma*] *in some classifications* **:** a superorder of Malacostraca that includes forms with sessile eyes and is coextensive with the orders Isopoda and Amphipoda — compare ARTHROSTRACA — **ed·ri·oph·thal·ma·tous** \ˌ==ˌ=ˈ=məd·əs\ *or* **ed·ri·oph·thal·mous** \-məs\ *adj*

ed·ri·oph·thal·ma·ta \ˌedrēˌäfˈthalməd·ə\ [NL, irreg. fr. *edri-* + Gk *ophthalmos* eye] *syn of* EDRIOPHTHALMA

[1]**ed·ri·oph·thal·mi·an** \ˌ==ˌ=ˈ=mēən\ *n* -s [NL *Edriophthalma* + E *-ian*] **:** a crustacean of the superorder Edriophthalma

[2]**edriophthalmian** \ˌ|==ˌ|===\ *adj* **:** of or relating to the Edriophthalma

EDTA *abbr* ethylenediaminetetraacetic acid

educ *abbr* **1** educated **2** education

ed·u·ca·bil·ia \ˌejəkəˈbilyə, -lēə\ *n pl, cap* [NL, fr. L *educare* to bring up, rear, educate + *-abilia* (neut. pl. of *-abilis* -able) — more at EDUCATE] *in former classifications* **:** a superorder of placental mammals having the large cerebrum overlapping the cerebellum and optic lobes and including the higher mammals (as the Primates, Carnivora, Ungulata) — **ed·u·ca·bil·ian** \ˌ==ˈbilyən, -lēən\ *adj*

ed·u·ca·bil·i·ty \ˌejəkəˈbiləd·ē, -ətē, -i\ *also* **ed·u·cat·abil·i·ty** \-ˌkād·əˈb-, -ˌkātə-\ *n* -ES **:** the quality or state of being educable

ed·u·ca·ble \ˈejəkəbəl\ *also* **ed·u·cat·able** \-ˌkād·əbəl, -ˌkātə-, ˌ==ˈ===\ *adj* [*educate* + *-able*] **:** capable of being educated ⟨molders of young, still ~ Americans —Austin Warren⟩

ed·u·cand \ˌejəˈkand\ *n* -s [L *educandus*, gerundive of *educare*] **:** one that is to be educated **:** STUDENT

ed·u·cate \ˈejəˌkāt, *usu* -ād·+V\ *vb* -ED/-ING/-S [ME *educaten*, fr. L *educatus*, past part. of *educare* to rear, bring up, educate, fr. *e-* + *-ducare* (fr. *ducere* to lead) — more at TOW] *vt* **1** *obs* **:** to bring up (as a child or animal) **:** REAR **2 a :** to develop (as a person) by fostering to varying degrees the growth or expansion of knowledge, wisdom, desirable qualities of mind or character, physical health, or general competence esp. by a course of formal study or instruction **:** provide or assist in providing with knowledge or wisdom, moral balance, or good physical condition esp. by means of a formal education ⟨many more things than a formal schooling serve to ~ a man⟩ ⟨~ their children by tutors⟩ ⟨*educated* rather by wide experience than by books⟩ ⟨the poverty of the institutions which ~ her mind and her body —Virginia Woolf⟩ **:** provide with formal schooling ⟨*educated* at a prep school and then at college⟩ **b :** to train by formal instruction and supervised practice esp. in a trade, skill, or profession ⟨~*s* physically handicapped children for useful work —*Amer. Guide Series: Mich.*⟩ ⟨~ a dog to sit up and beg⟩ ⟨felt that he needed to ~ himself more before he could understand the larger machines the factory operated⟩ **c :** to provide with information **:** INFORM ⟨can . . . ~ himself as to the most desirable attributes of the good field-trial dog —W.F.Brown b. 1903⟩ **d :** to bring about an improvement in or refinement of ⟨one of the most important arenas for the exercise of intelligence, in purging and *educating* our values —P.W.Bridgman⟩ ⟨psychoanalysis has *educated* our sensibilities —Abram Kardiner⟩ **3 a :** ACCUSTOM ⟨the absence of an accustomed stimulant to which she had *educated* his nerves —Francis Hackett⟩ **b** (1) **:** to condition or persuade to feel, believe, or react in a particular way by providing with often selective information or knowledge ⟨spent some time trying to ~ the club membership to place more responsibility and trust in the club officers⟩ ⟨~ stockholders and keep them eager to support the companies they own —*Time*⟩ ⟨~ people to call the police without hesitation —V.A.Leonard⟩ ⟨furniture manufacturers . . . put on a national drive to ~ people to desire homes that are more attractive and livable —N.C. Brown⟩ (2) **:** to make willing to accept (as by providing with knowledge, information, or experience) — used with *in* or *to* ⟨*educating* the leaders in the wisdom of a change —L.S.B. Leakey⟩ ⟨people of the world are more *educated* to international organization —André Schenker⟩ ⟨~ the Filipinos to the necessity of giving blood —Irene Kuhn⟩ **4 :** to make (as a person) competent in the handling of or in dealing with by preparation, discipline, or expansion of knowledge or competence — used with *to* and a secondary object ⟨a greater moral perceptiveness and a will *educated* to a new social responsibility —Lucius Garvin⟩ **5 a :** to remove (as from a person's makeup) by education — used with *out of* ⟨the fundamental preference for one's own race and breed neither is wholly educated into one nor can be wholly *educated* out of one —Katharine F. Gerould⟩ ⟨~ bad manners out of a child⟩ **b :** to raise (as to a higher social or cultural level) by education ⟨*educating* underprivileged children up to a better level of opportunity⟩ ~ *vi* **:** to educate a person, a thing, or a group ⟨the belief that a teacher should confine himself to *educating* and avoid proselytizing⟩ **syn** see TEACH

educated *adj* **1 :** possessing an education; *esp* **:** having information or knowledge beyond the average **2 a :** marked by perfection of performance that is the result of training and practice **:** SKILLED ⟨Doc worked over him with his ~ fingers —Budd Schulberg⟩ **b :** befitting one that is educated esp. by much formal schooling ⟨colorless voices of ~ conversation —Thomas Munro⟩ **c :** based on some knowledge of fact ⟨the precise results to be attained by modern aerial warfare could only be an ~ guess —G.C.Marshall⟩ **d :** consisting of people of education ⟨in ~ circles⟩

ed·u·cat·ee \ˌejəˌkādˈē, -āˈtē, -ˌkəˈtē\ *n* -s [*educate* + *-ee*] **:** a recipient of education

ed·u·ca·tion \ˌejəˈkāshən\ *n* -s [L *education-, educatio*, fr. *educatus* (past part. of *educare*) + *-ion-, -io* -ion] **1 :** the act or process of educating or of being educated: as **a** *obs* **:** the act or process of rearing or bringing up (as a child or animal) or developing physically from childhood or of being reared, brought up, or developed in this way **b :** the act or process of providing with knowledge, skill, competence, or usu. desirable qualities of behavior or character or of being so provided esp. by a formal course of study, instruction, or training ⟨the child received his ~ at home from a governess until he was nearly 10⟩ ⟨a prominent man whose ~ ended in grade school⟩ ⟨devoting himself to the ~ of adults who never got any formal schooling⟩ ⟨an ~ in dealing with his fellowmen⟩ ⟨an ~ in the handling of farm machinery⟩ **c :** a conditioning, strengthening, or disciplining esp. of the mind or faculties ⟨the ~ of the will⟩ ⟨the ~ of an audience to appreciate modern music⟩ ⟨the ~ of the muscles to respond faster⟩ **2 a :** a process or course of learning, instruction, or training that educates or is intended to educate ⟨a man too busy to give any time to an ~ other than hard experience⟩; *esp* **:** a formal course of instruction or training offered by an institution (as a college) primarily designed to provide an education ⟨~ in the high school⟩ ⟨a college ~⟩ — often used with a modifier specifying the type or field of instruction or training ⟨physical ~⟩ ⟨health ~⟩ ⟨driver ~⟩ — see ADULT EDUCATION, HIGHER EDUCATION; GENERAL EDUCATION, LIBERAL EDUCATION **b :** a system of formal education as a whole (as in a particular area) ⟨investigating ~ in several states⟩ **3 :** the product of an education **:** the totality of the knowledge, skill, competence, or qualities of character gained by education ⟨these groups acquired a great deal of their ~ by discussion, talking over and analyzing all aspects of life —H.R.Douglass⟩ ⟨formerly most of the child's ~ was obtained in the home —H.C.McKown⟩ ⟨he obtained his ~ in the local schools and college⟩ **4 :** the field of study that concerns itself primarily with the principles and methods of teaching or of learning esp. in formal education ⟨a professor of ~ in a small college⟩

ed·u·ca·tion·al \ˌejəˈkāshənᵊl, -shnəl\ *adj* **1 :** of, relating to, or concerned with education or the field of education ⟨~ concept⟩ ⟨~ TV⟩ ⟨~ adviser⟩ ⟨~ theorists⟩ **2 :** serving to further education ⟨the documentary subject is really an ~ film for pupils of all ages —Andrew Buchanan⟩

educational age *n* **:** ACHIEVEMENT AGE

ed·u·ca·tion·al·ly \-ᵊlē, -əlē, -li\ *adv* **:** with reference to education ⟨backward and ~ subnormal children —*Brit. Book News*⟩

educational psychology *n* **:** a field of study that deals with the application of objective psychological methods and esp. of standardized tests to such problems as the selection of students for advanced or specialized training, the assessment of a student's progress, and the development of more effective methods of instruction

educational quotient *n* **:** ACHIEVEMENT QUOTIENT 1

educational sociology *n* **:** the sociology of education **:** study of educational objectives and organization in the light of an analysis of the group life as a whole

educational test *n* **:** a test that measures achievement in subjects of study

ed·u·ca·tion·ist \ˌejəˈkāsh(ə)nəst\ *also* **ed·u·ca·tion·al·ist** \-shənᵊləst, -shnəl-\ *n* -s **1** *chiefly Brit* **:** EDUCATOR ⟨~*s* are agreed that the medium of instruction in schools must be the local language —*Times Lit. Supp.*⟩ ⟨if progress is to be not only rapid but of a high standard many more *educationalists* are needed —Harold Ingrams⟩ **2 :** an educational theorist ⟨pragmatism was foisted on the American people by the ~*s* —F.M.Hechinger⟩ — usu. used disparagingly

ed·u·cat·ive \ˈejəˌkād·iv, -āt|, |ēv *also* |əv\ *adj* **1 :** having to do with education **:** EDUCATIONAL ⟨the problem is also an ~ one —John Dewey⟩ **2 :** tending to educate **:** INSTRUCTIVE ⟨much that is ~ occurs outside the school —Paul Woodring⟩ ⟨the able editor . . . makes his paper a real ~ force in community and nation —F.L.Mott⟩

ed·u·ca·tor \-ˌkād·ə(r), -ātə- *sometimes* ˌ==ˈkāˌtō(ə)r *or* -ō(ə)\ *n* -s [L, fr. *educatus* + *-or*] **1 :** one skilled in teaching **:** TEACHER **2 a :** a student of the theory and practice of education **:** EDUCATIONIST 2 **b :** an administrator in education

ed·u·ca·to·ry \ˈejəkəˌtōrē, -ȯr-, -ri, *chiefly Brit* ˌ==ˈkātəri *or* -ā·tri\ *adj* **:** EDUCATIVE

educe \ēˈd(y)üs, iˈ-\ *vt* -ED/-ING/-S [L *educere* to lead forth, draw out, fr. *e-* + *ducere* to lead — more at TOW] **1 :** to bring into manifestation (as a form, quality, or law conceived to be present in a latent, potential, or undeveloped state) **:** ELICIT, EVOLVE ⟨they want to ~ and cultivate what is best and noblest in themselves —Matthew Arnold⟩ ⟨*educing* power from confusion —H.O.Taylor⟩; *sometimes* **:** EVOKE ⟨from the reader, he can only ~ pity, not respect or interest —V.A.Young⟩ **2 :** to arrive at (as from reasoning) ⟨seem to be able to ~ from common sense a more or less clear reply to the questions raised —Henry Sidgwick⟩ ⟨~ the conclusion —O.W.Holmes †1935⟩

syn EDUCE, EVOKE, ELICIT, EXTRACT, and EXTORT agree in meaning to draw out what is hidden, latent, or reserved. EDUCE usu. implies the bringing out of something potential or latent, often by inference but usu. by means of development ⟨polls rarely *educe* future attitudes —E.L.Bernays⟩ ⟨constantly straining on to *educe* further salutary meaning from the text —H.O.Taylor⟩ ⟨aimed to *educe* the innate capabilities of the student —Reyner Banham⟩ EVOKE now implies some strong agency that can produce a particular effect, usu. immediately, or that serves as a stimulus in arousing (as an emotion, a passion, or an interest) ⟨choose the right words to *evoke* the right mood⟩ ⟨there was melody in it, such as a woodpecker knows how to *evoke* from a smooth dry branch —John Burroughs⟩ ⟨words *evoking* concrete imagery —Alice Bensen⟩ ⟨there is much in this volume to *evoke* a smile —*N.Y.Herald Tribune Bk. Rev.*⟩ ⟨*evoke* the hope that you were going to see more —O.W.Holmes †1935⟩ ELICIT, often interchangeable with EVOKE, usu., however implies care, trouble, or skill in drawing something forth or out, often against resistance ⟨which *elicited* alternate jeers and applause from the shilling audience below —G.B.Shaw⟩ ⟨no subject *elicits* a more animated response than some question about a woman's work —A.R.Williams⟩ ⟨to make a study of blank verse alone would be to *elicit* some curious conclusions —T.S.Eliot⟩ ⟨the inductive method of *eliciting* general laws —A.N.Whitehead⟩ ⟨*elicit* information by cross-examination⟩ EXTRACT, in this context, implies an action, force, or effort resembling the physical use of pressure or suction ⟨we journeyed on, fed by food *extracted* from the peasants —Bertrand Russell⟩ ⟨eke out her personal adornment by gifts which she managed to *extract* from her admirers —Mary Austin⟩ ⟨in spite of incessant questioning, all he had been able to *extract* from this young girl was the story that the admiral had offered to lend her his house —Edith Sitwell⟩ EXTORT implies a wringing or wresting, esp. from someone reluctant or resisting ⟨*extort* money by blackmail⟩ ⟨his perfect command of all his faculties *extorted* praise from those who neither loved nor esteemed him —T.B. Macaulay⟩ ⟨whose income is ample enough to *extort* obsequiousness from the vulgar of all ranks —Arnold Bennett⟩

educ·ible \-səbəl\ *adj* : capable of being educed

educt \ˈē,dəkt\ *n* -s [L *eductus*, past part. of *educere* to lead forth, draw out — more at EDUCE] : something that is educed: **a** *chem* : a substance separated from material in which it already existed — distinguished from *product* **b** : INFERENCE

educ·tion \ēˈdəkshən, iˈ-\ *n* -s [LL *eduction-, eductio* act of leading forth, drawing out, fr. L *eductus* + *-ion-, -io* -ion] **1** : the action or process of educing, eliciting, or directly inferring **2** : the result of the process of educing : INFERENCE **3** : the action or process of conducting a fluid away from a container (as oil from a tank car)

educ·tive \-ktiv\ *adj* [L *eductus* + E *-ive*] : relating to eduction

educ·tor \-ktə(r)\ *n* -s [LL, one that leads forth, fr. L *eductus* + *-or*] : one that educes: as **a** : EJECTOR 2 **b** : a device similar to an ejector for mixing two fluids (as air and water)

edul·co·rate \əˈdəlkə,rāt, ēˈ-\ *vt* -ED/-ING/-S [NL *edulcoratus*, past part. of *edulcorare*, blend of LL *edulcare* to sweeten (fr. L *e-* + LL *dulcare* to sweeten, fr. L *dulcis* sweet) and *dulcorare* to sweeten, fr. LL *dulcor* sweetness, fr. L *dulcis* — more at DULCET] **1** *obs* : to make (food) sweet **2** *archaic* : to free from acids, salts, or other soluble substances by washing **3** : to free from harshness (as of attitude) : make pleasant ⟨cozened and flattered and *edulcorated* the Turks —Vincent Sheean⟩ — **edul·co·ra·tion** \=,==ˈrāshən\ *n* -s

[1]**ed·war·de·an** *or* **ed·war·di·an** \(ˈ)eˈdwärdēən, -wȯd-, -wȯ(r)d-\ *adj, usu cap* [Jonathan *Edwards* †1758 Am. Congregational clergyman and theologian + E *-ean* or *-ian*] : of or relating to the Calvinistic theological doctrines of Jonathan Edwards : derived from such doctrines : accepting such doctrines

[2]**edwardean** *or* **edwardian** \"\ *n* -s *usu cap* : an adherent of the theology of Jonathan Edwards

[1]**edwardian** \"\ *adj, usu cap* [*Edward* VII †1910 king of England + E *-ian*] : of, relating to, or having the characteristics of the era of Edward VII of England (1901–10): as **a** : characterized by opulence and a complacent sense of material security **b** : marked by a socially analytical and critical frame of mind **c** *of clothing* : marked by the hourglass silhouette for women and the long narrow fitted suits for men that were popular during this period

[2]**edwardian** \"\ *n* -s *usu cap* : one belonging to or as if to the Edwardian era

ed·ward·ine \ˈedwə(r)dīn, -dēn\ *adj, usu cap* [*Edward* VII + E *-ine*] : EDWARDIAN

ed·ward·sia \eˈdwärdzēə, -wȯd-,-wȯ(r)d-\ *n, cap* [NL, fr. Henri Milne-*Edwards* †1885 Fr. zoologist + NL *-ia*] : a genus (the type of the family Edwardsiidae) of sea anemones having eight mesenteries and living in tubes in the sand

ed·ward·si·an \(ˈ)=ˈ=zēən\ *adj, usu cap* [Jonathan *Edwards* + E *-ian*] : EDWARDEAN

ee \ˈē\ *n, pl* **een** \ˈēn\ [ME (northern dial.), fr. OE *ēage* — more at EYE] *Scot* : EYE

[1]**-ee** \(ˈ)ē\ *n suffix* -s [ME *-e*, fr. MF *-é*, fr. OF, fr. *-é*, past part. ending of some verbs, fr. L *-atus*, past part. ending of 1st conj. verbs — more at -ATE (adj. suffix)] **1** : animate and usu. human undergoer, recipient, or beneficiary of (a specified action) ⟨appoint*ee*⟩ ⟨draft*ee*⟩ ⟨grant*ee*⟩ ⟨train*ee*⟩ ⟨trust*ee*⟩ **2** : person furnished with (a specified thing) ⟨patent*ee*⟩ **3** : person that performs (a specified action) ⟨escap*ee*⟩ ⟨stand*ee*⟩

[2]**-ee** \"\ *n suffix* -s [prob. alter. of *-ie*] **1** : one associated with ⟨barg*ee*⟩ ⟨goal*ee*⟩ ⟨town*ee*⟩ **2** : a particular esp. small kind of ⟨boot*ee*⟩ ⟨coat*ee*⟩ **3** : one resembling or suggestive of ⟨goat*ee*⟩

EE \(ˈ)=ˈ=\ *abbr or n* -s electrical engineer

EE *abbr* **1** envoy extraordinary **2** errors excepted

ee·bree \ˈē,brē\ *n* -s [*ee* + *bree*] **1** *chiefly Scot* : EYEBROW **2** *chiefly Scot* : EYELASH — usu. used in pl.

EEG *abbr* electroencephalogram

[1]**eel** \ˈēl, *esp before pause or consonant* ˈēəl\ *n, pl* **eels** *also* **eel** [ME *ele*, fr. OE *ǣl*; akin to OS & OHG *āl* eel, ON *āll*] **1 a** : any of numerous voracious elongate snakelike teleost fishes that constitute the order Apodes and that have a smooth slimy skin often without scales, are destitute of pelvic and sometimes of pectoral fins, and have the median fins confluent around the tail — see ANGUILLA, CONGER EEL, LEPTOCEPHALUS, MORAY **b** : any of numerous elongate fishes more or less resembling the true eels (as those of the order Symbranchii) —see ELECTRIC EEL, SAND EEL, SNAKE EEL **2** : any of various nematodes or eelworms ⟨the vinegar ~⟩ **3** : a person or thing that is slippery or elusive

[2]**eel** \"\ *vi* -ED/-ING/-S **1** : to fish for eels **2** : WORM 2

eel-back flounder *n* : a small flounder (*Liopsetta putnami*) of the coasts of northern New England and the Maritime Provinces

eelboat \ˈ=,=\ *n* : SCHUYT

eel cat *n* : a broad-headed catfish (*Ictalurus anguilla*) of the lower Mississippi and Ohio valleys — compare CHANNEL CAT

eel·ery \ˈēlərē\ *n* -ES [[1]*eel* + *-ery*] : a place for catching eels

eelfare \ˈ=,=\ *n* [[1]*eel* + *fare* (journey)] : the migration of young eels up a stream

eelgrass \ˈ=,=\ *n* **1** : a submerged marine plant (*Zostera marina*) with very long narrow leaves that is found in abundance along the No. Atlantic coast — called also *grass wrack* **2** : TAPE GRASS

eelgrass family *n* : ZOSTERACEAE

eel·like \ˈē(ə)l,līk\ *adj* : like an eel in sinuosity, swimming ability, or evasiveness

eelpot \ˈ=,=\ *n* : a trap like a box with funnel-shaped openings for catching eels

eelpout \ˈ=,=\ *n* [[1]*eel* + *pout* (fish)] **1** : any of various marine fishes resembling blennies and constituting the family Zoarcidae: as **a** : a viviparous blenny (*Zoarces viviparus*) of Northern Europe **b** : MUTTONFISH 2 **2** : BURBOT

eelspear \ˈ=,=\ *n* : a barbed spear for spearing eels

eelworm \ˈ=,=\ *n* : a nematode worm; *esp* : any small free-living or plant-parasitic roundworm, some of which are serious pathogens of cultivated plants — see BULB EELWORM

eely \ˈēlē, -li\ *adj* -ER/-EST : resembling an eel (as in being wriggly or slippery)

[1]**een** \(ˈ)ēn\ *Scot var of* ONE

[2]**een** \ˈēn\ *pl of* EE

[1]**e'en** \(ˈ)ēn\ *adv* [by contr.] : EVEN

[2]**e'en** *or* **een** \ˈēn\ *n* -s [contr. of [1]*even*] *chiefly Scot* : EVENING

[1]**-een** \ˈēn\ *n suffix* -s [prob. partly fr. the *-een* of *ratteen* and partly alter. of the *-ine* of *armozine, bombazine*] : inferior fabric resembling (a specified fabric) : imitation ⟨sat*een*⟩ ⟨velvet*een*⟩

[2]**-een** \"\ *n suffix* -s [IrGael *-īn*] *chiefly Irish* : small one : dear one : petty or contemptible one — in diminutive nouns ⟨bird*een*⟩ ⟨buck*een*⟩ ⟨squir*een*⟩

een·a·most \ˈēnə,mōst\ *adv* [*e'en* + *amost*, alter. of *almost*] : even almost : NEARLY

eence \ˈēn(t)s\ *Scot var of* ONCE

eend \ˈēnd\ *dial var of* END

-eer \ˈi(ə)r, ˈiə\ *n suffix* -s [MF *-ier*, fr. L *-arius* — more at -ARY (n. suffix)] **1** : one that deals in, is concerned with professionally, manages, conducts, or produces ⟨auction*eer*⟩ ⟨pamphlet*eer*⟩ — often in words with derogatory meaning or connotation ⟨sonnet*eer*⟩ **2** : contemptible one ⟨profit*eer*⟩

e'er \(ˈ)e(ə)r, (ˈ)a(ə)r, |ə\ *adv* [by contr.] : EVER

ee·rie *also* **ee·ry** \ˈirē, ˈēr-, -ri\ *adj* -ER/-EST [ME (northern dial.) *eri*, fr. OE *earg* cowardly, lazy, slow, wretched — more at ARGH] **1** *dial Brit* : affected with fear esp. of the supernatural : FRIGHTENED ⟨when I sleep I dream, when I wake I'm ~ —Robert Burns⟩ **2** : unusual, unexpected, or unnatural to such a degree as to inspire fear : WEIRD, FRIGHTENING ⟨it is an ~ experience to drive for miles through ghostly ranks of . . . cypress woods —*Amer. Guide Series: Fla.*⟩ ⟨an uncomfortable and ~ stillness had settled over the piazza —Alan Moorehead⟩; *also* : STRANGE, MYSTERIOUS, UNCANNY ⟨blue and yellow flames that at night cast an ~ glow over the landscape —*Amer. Guide Series: Pa.*⟩ ⟨the *eeriest* mystery in modern court records—a persistent riddle —*Life*⟩ ⟨the clarinet sings, in its ~, plaintive tone —Sara R. Watson⟩ **3** *Scot* : GLOOMY, DISMAL **syn** see WEIRD

ee·ri·ly \-rəlē, -li\ *adv* : in an eerie manner : MYSTERIOUSLY, WEIRDLY ⟨the sea moaned ~ as if in anticipation of what was to come —G.G.Carter⟩

ee·ri·ness \-rēnəs, -rin-\ *n* -ES **1** : inexplicable fear ⟨private distresses, a streak of ~, dark moods —*Times Lit. Supp.*⟩ **2** : the quality or state of being eerie

ees *pl of* E *or of* EE

-ees *pl of* -EE

[1]**ef** *also* **eff** \ˈef\ *n* -s : the letter *f*

[2]**ef** \(ˈ)ef, əf\ *dial var of* IF

ef- — see EX-

EF *abbr* **1** English finish **2** expeditionary force **3** extra fine; extremely fine

ef·a·tese \ˌefəˈtēz, eˈfä,t-, -ēs\ *n, pl* **efatese** *usu cap* [*Efate*, one of the New Hebrides islands in the So. Pacific + E *-ese*] **1 a** : a Melanesian people of Efate in the New Hebrides islands **b** : a member of such people **2** : the language of the Efatese people

efe \ˈefā, ˈfā, ˈe,-\ *n* -s *cap* : the central Sudanic language of the Mbuti pygmies of the Belgian Congo

eff *abbr* **1** effect; effective **2** efficiency; efficient

ef·fa·ble \ˈefəbəl\ *adj* [L *effabilis*, fr. *effari* to speak out, fr. *ex-* + *fari* to speak, say — more at BAN] : capable of being uttered or expressed

[1]**ef·face** \əˈfās, eˈ-, ēˈ-\ *vt* -ED/-ING/-S [MF *effacer*, fr. *ef-* (fr. L, fr. *ex-*) + *face* — more at FACE] **1 a** : to eliminate clear evidence of (something written, painted, or otherwise marked upon a surface) by abrasive or leveling action ⟨the "murals" have long since been *effaced* by rock slides and the weathering of the cliff's wall —*Amer. Guide Series: Pa.*⟩ **b** : to cause to disappear : eliminate completely : wipe out : DESTROY, ERADICATE ⟨his year . . . of peace had *effaced* all the ill effects of his previous suffering —Samuel Butler †1902⟩ ⟨fire suppression . . . and a comprehensive program of reforestation have *effaced* the worst of the scars —*Amer. Guide Series: Mich.*⟩ **2** : to remove from cognizance, consideration, or memory ⟨he had left a mark on the affairs of the church which would not easily be *effaced* —R.W.Southern⟩; *also* : to make insignificant : OVERSHADOW ⟨the bloodthirsty aspect of the tyrant is becoming *effaced* —Norman Douglas⟩ **3** : to withdraw (oneself) entirely from attention : make (oneself) inconspicuous and modestly or shyly unnoticeable ⟨the wife of a man who had done anything disgraceful in business had only one idea: to ~ herself, to disappear with him —Edith Wharton⟩ **syn** see ERASE

[2]**ef·fa·cé** \ˌefəˈsā\ *adj* [F, fr. past part. of *effacer* to stand apart, stand sideways, fr. *ef-* (fr. L, fr. *ex-*) + *face*] *ballet* : facing the audience obliquely, sometimes with opposite arm and leg raised

ef·face·able \əˈfāsəbəl, eˈ-,ēˈ-\ *adj* : capable of being effaced

ef·face·ment \-smənt\ *n* -s : the act or process of effacing : the state of being effaced; *esp* : reduction to insignificance

ef·fac·er \-sə(r)\ *n* -s : one that effaces

[1]**ef·fect** \əˈfekt, eˈ-,ēˈ-\ *n* -s [ME, fr. MF & L; MF, fr. L *effectus*, fr. *effectus*, past part. of *efficere* to bring about, accomplish, effect, fr. *ex-* + *-ficere* (fr. *facere* to make, do) — more at DO] **1** : something that is produced by an agent or cause : something that follows immediately from an antecedent : a resultant condition : RESULT, OUTCOME ⟨low mortality, the ~ of excellent social services available in every village —William Petersen⟩ ⟨as tolerance develops, the addict needs more and more of the drug to give him the same ~ he originally obtained from a small dose —D.W.Maurer & V.H.Vogel⟩ ⟨his feet in the most appalling state from the ~s of porcupine quills —James Stevenson-Hamilton⟩ **2 a** : PURPOSE, INTENTION, END ⟨as a boy he had gone to work early to the ~ that he might help out his parents⟩ **b** : the result of purpose or intention : ADVANTAGE ⟨employed his knowledge to little ~ in the development of his organization⟩ **3** : an outward sign : MANIFESTATION, APPEARANCE ⟨the sky ~s by day and night are grander —Wilfrid Eggleston⟩ **4** *obs* : ACCOMPLISHMENT, FULFILLMENT **5** *obs* : something acquired as the expected result of an action **6** : REALITY, FACT — now used only in the phrase *in effect* ⟨the guilder became in ~ convertible with other currencies in free Continental Europe —Alan Valentine⟩ **7** : power to bring about a result : operative force : INFLUENCE ⟨the ~ of wind in changing tide levels —*Geog. Rev.*⟩ ⟨the ~ of great demand upon supply⟩ ⟨all of the children in the schoolroom felt the ~ of her happiness —Sherwood Anderson⟩ **8 effects** *pl* : movable property : GOODS ⟨her household ~s were sold at auction but her clothing, jewelry, and other personal ~s were given away⟩ **9 a** : a distinctive impression upon the human senses ⟨a concentration on detail at a cost to total ~ —Irving Kolodin⟩ ⟨achieves amazing ~s with his woodcuts —José Gómez-Siere⟩ ⟨decorated in yellow, which increased the ~ of lightness —Sheila Kaye-Smith⟩; *also* : the creation of a desired impression ⟨her sobs were purely for ~⟩ **b** : something designed to produce such an impression ⟨never have we been so bombarded with trick ~s—3-D, cinemascope, panoramic screens —John Baker⟩ ⟨the technique of sound ~s was extremely limited and used only . . . for such things as doorbells —Richard Hubbell⟩ **10** : the quality or state of being operative ⟨the subcommittee's recommendations were quickly given ~ —W.R.Langdon⟩ ⟨the court will not give ~ to a judgment based on unfair proceedings⟩; *specif* : OPERATION ⟨a commission was set up to carry the new proposals into ~⟩ ⟨the agreement will have to be approved by a majority before it can go into ~⟩ ⟨the same excises and corporate tax rates that are now in ~ —William Fellner⟩ — compare *take effect* at TAKE **11** : basic meaning : TENOR, ESSENCE **12** : a specific scientific phenomenon named usu. for its discoverer ⟨Faraday ~⟩ **13** : one in a series of evaporators

syn RESULT, CONSEQUENCE, UPSHOT, AFTEREFFECT, AFTERMATH, SEQUEL, ISSUE, OUTCOME, EVENT: these ten nouns are similar in signifying something, usu. a condition, situation, or occurrence, ascribable to a cause or combination of causes. EFFECT is the correlative of the word *cause* and in general use implies something necessarily and directly following upon or occurring by reason of the cause, generally applying to intangibles such as bodily or social conditions or states of mind or feeling ⟨the *effect* of the medicine was an intermittent dizziness⟩ ⟨the *effect* of the speech was immediate governmental reform⟩ ⟨tanning is the *effect* of exposure to sunlight⟩ ⟨the *effects* of the hurricane were visible in roofless houses and uprooted trees⟩ RESULT, close to EFFECT in meaning, implies a direct relationship with an antecedent action or condition though possibly less direct than EFFECT, usu. suggesting an effect in the character of a termination of the operation of a cause, and applying more commonly than EFFECT to tangible objects ⟨the *result* of the investigation was a scandalous exposure of corruption⟩ ⟨his limp was the *result* of an automobile accident⟩ ⟨the *result* of the marriage was a family of seven children⟩ ⟨the subsiding flood or surface waters cause mineral deposits and the *result* is a mound —Alice Duncan-Kemp⟩ CONSEQUENCE may suggest a direct but looser or more remote connection with a cause than either EFFECT or RESULT, usu. implying an adverse or calamitous effect and often suggesting a chain of intermediate causes or a complexity of effect ⟨one of the *consequences* of his ill-advised conduct was a loss of prestige⟩ ⟨his poor health is a *consequence* of early privation⟩ ⟨both good and bad *consequences* can follow upon the acquisition of much leisure⟩ UPSHOT often implies a climax or conclusion in a series of consequent occurrences, or the most conclusive point of a single complex gradual consequence ⟨we spent the time swimming at Glenelg and dancing at the Palais Royal in the city. The *upshot* was that, before we left . . . we were engaged —Rex Ingamells⟩ ⟨they won the battle, and the *upshot* was a short-lived bourgeois republic —Roy Lewis & Angus Maude⟩ ⟨the *upshot* of the whole matter was that there was no wedding —Padraic Colum⟩ AFTEREFFECT and AFTERMATH both usu. designate secondary rather than direct or immediate effects. AFTEREFFECT besides designating a secondary effect sometimes suggests a side effect but more generally implies an effect ascribable to a previous effect that has become a cause ⟨the *aftereffects* of an atomic-bomb explosion —*Current Biog.*⟩ ⟨although the pioneer effort had reached a dead end, its *aftereffects* were all too apparent —Dayton Kohler⟩ ⟨to the left of the highway the blackened appearance is the *aftereffect* of a fire that has recently swept across the flat —G.R. Stewart⟩ ⟨the *aftereffects* of the war were a general disorder and confusion⟩ AFTERMATH, often suggesting a more complex effect or generalized condition than AFTEREFFECT, usu. carries the notion of belated consequences that appear after the effects, esp. disastrous effects, seem to have passed ⟨the serious dislocations in the world as an *aftermath* of war —*U.S.Code*⟩ ⟨the *aftermath* of the epidemic in Memphis was worse than the dismal days of Reconstruction —*Amer. Guide Series: Tenn.*⟩ ⟨asbestos dust has the same effect as silica, the resulting disease being known as "asbestosis", with pulmonary tuberculosis as the *aftermath* —V.M.Ehlers & E.W.Steel⟩ SEQUEL is usu. used to signify a result that follows after an interval ⟨spinal curvature . . . may be a symptom or a *sequel* to many different diseases —Morris Fishbein⟩ ⟨she lay rigid experiencing the *sequel* to the pain, an ideal terror —Jean Stafford⟩ ISSUE, the way something, for example an argument, comes out, carries strongly the notion of result as a solution or resolution ⟨a contest of wits between the criminal and the police—usually aided in fiction by a quicker-witted private detective—a contest in which the *issue* is still the greatest and gravest of all, life or death —A.C.Ward⟩ ⟨the war was by then obviously proceeding toward a successful *issue* —F.M.Ford⟩ OUTCOME, interchangeable with RESULT or with ISSUE, possibly carries the notion of less finality than does ISSUE ⟨the *outcome* of the presidential election⟩ ⟨the enduring organisms are now the *outcome* of evolution —A.N.Whitehead⟩ ⟨one *outcome* of this report was the formation of the Southern Conference for Human Welfare —*Current Biog.*⟩ ⟨his book is the *outcome* of two years' travels in India, China, and Siam —*Geog. Jour.*⟩ EVENT, rare and somewhat archaic in the sense pertinent here, of *outcome* or *result*, usu. carries the notion of an unpredictable or unforeseeable outcome ⟨the happiness of Rome appeared to hang on the *event* of a race —Edward Gibbon⟩ ⟨he employed himself at Edinburgh till the *event* of the conflict between the court and the Whigs was no longer doubtful —T.B.Macaulay⟩ ⟨the calm assumption that I should live long enough to carry out my extensive plan at leisure . . . has in the *event* been justified —Havelock Ellis⟩ — **in effect** *adv* : in substance : VIRTUALLY ⟨these tribal bodies included the entire soldiery of the tribe; *in effect*, the nation in arms —W.J.Shepard⟩ ⟨though stated in polite terms his reply was, *in effect*, a flat refusal⟩ — **to the effect** : with the meaning ⟨speculations *to the effect* that Shakespeare did the grand tour —D.W.Brogan⟩ ⟨his comments about the incident were less coherent but *to the* same *effect*⟩

[2]**effect** \"\ *vt* -ED/-ING/-S **1** : to cause to come into being : PRODUCE ⟨specific genes ~ specific bodily characters⟩ **2 a** : to bring about esp. through successful use of factors contributory to the result : ACCOMPLISH, EXECUTE ⟨passage could be ~*ed* only by way of certain transverse valleys and high passes —W.G.East⟩ ⟨the Romans who, with superb political skill, ~*ed* the unification of Italy —Benjamin Farrington⟩ ⟨minor repairs to the road were ~*ed* during the summer⟩ — compare [3]AFFECT 1 **b** : to put into effect ⟨consistently taken the position that the function of the president is to ~ the public will —R.H.Rovere⟩ **syn** see PERFORM

effecter *var of* EFFECTOR

ef·fect·ful \-tfəl\ *adj* : creating effects : EFFECTUAL

ef·fect·ible \-təbəl\ *adj, archaic* : capable of being effected

[1]**ef·fec·tive** \əˈfektiv, eˈ-, ēˈ-, -tēv *also* -təv\ *adj* [ME, fr. MF or LL; MF *effectif*, fr. LL *effectivus*, fr. L *effectus* (past part. of *efficere* to bring about, accomplish, effect) + *-ivus* -ive — more at EFFECT] **1 a** : capable of bringing about an effect : productive of results ⟨an air-cooled motor was more ~ than a witch's broomstick for rapid long-distance transportation —Lewis Mumford⟩ ⟨a new organization which would be strong where the league had been weak, . . . ~ where the league had been fumbling —G.L.Kirk⟩ ⟨his arm was too badly injured to deliver an ~ blow —L.C.Douglas⟩ **b** : capable of having its normal effect : able to function normally ⟨at 26,000 feet none are able to retain ~ consciousness . . . without oxygen —C.H.Best & N.B.Taylor⟩ **2** : marked by the quality of being influential or exerting positive influence: **a** : exerting authority : carrying weight ⟨the countries represented had virtually all the ~ power in the world —M.W.Straight⟩ ⟨his ~ career began inauspiciously⟩ **b** : able to accomplish a purpose : EFFICIENT ⟨persons who will do nothing unless they get something out of it for themselves are often highly ~ persons of action —G.B.Shaw⟩ **c** : IMPRESSIVE, COGENT, TELLING ⟨an ~ if not eloquent preacher —E.W.Knight⟩ ⟨equally ~ in portraiture, landscape, and still life —*Current Biog.*⟩ **d** : PLEASING, SATISFYING ⟨a most ~ substitute for the conventional Christmas tree —*Amer. Guide Series: La.*⟩ **3 a** : capable of being used to a purpose ⟨his handwriting was still so bad he couldn't take ~ notes —Sloan Wilson⟩ ⟨the ~ value of our annual income for scholarship endowment has been diminished —J.B.Conant⟩ **b** : equipped and ready for service — used esp. of military forces ⟨the fort was held by about 100 ~ soldiers⟩ **4** : ACTUAL ⟨committed the blunder of confusing the increased load of equipment and the increased expenditure with the quantity of ~ work done —Lewis Mumford⟩ ⟨the number of ~ wage earners, excluding workers absent for the whole of one week, fluctuated —*Collier's Yr. Bk.*⟩ ⟨a gain in housing units in response to ~ demand⟩ **5** *of a verb form or aspect* : expressing the final point of an action or state or a result attained **6** : taking effect : VALID, OPERATIVE ⟨the following resignations were accepted ~ during the academic year under review —J.B.Conant⟩ ⟨the order was ~ as of June 7⟩ **7** *of the publication of a taxon* : accompanied by sale, exchange, or other distribution of printed matter containing a new taxon or new combination — see VALID 5b **8** *of a natural population* : INTERBREEDING

syn EFFECTUAL, EFFICIENT, EFFICACIOUS: EFFECTIVE may indicate the power to produce an effect or the actual production of an effect ⟨we are calling on men and women and property and money to join in making our defense *effective* —F.D. Roosevelt⟩ ⟨Bob had rebuked him after all, and his rebuke, though less hurtful than Sir James's, had been even more *effective* —Archibald Marshall⟩ EFFECTUAL may apply to what has accomplished an intended result and may approach the connotations of *decisive* ⟨the powers of sovereignty and the eminent domain were ceded with the land. This was essential, in order to make it *effectual*, and to accomplish its objects —R.B.Taney⟩ ⟨an appeal to the emotions is little likely to be *effectual* before luncheon —W.S.Maugham⟩ EFFICIENT may designate that which is actually operative; it may apply to smooth operation with a maximum of work or output accomplished with a minimum of effort ⟨it should be obvious that it is the conditions producing the end effects which must be regarded as the *efficient* causes of them —M.F.A.Montagu⟩ ⟨a strong tendency to break up cumbersome estates into small, *efficient* farms —Allan Nevins and H.S.Commager⟩ ⟨since the steam engine requires constant care on the part of the stoker and engineer, steam power was more *efficient* in large units than in small ones: instead of a score of small units, working when required, one large engine was kept in constant motion —Lewis Mumford⟩ EFFICACIOUS may suggest possession of potent, powerful, or proper qualities productive of effective power ⟨in their opinion, the flesh and blood of an enemy killed in battle is the most *efficacious* of all charms and makes a first-rate drug —J.G.Frazer⟩ ⟨the pained expression that he had long since found to be much more *efficacious* than anger —Edith Wharton⟩

[2]**effective** \"\ *n* -s : one that is effective: as **a** : a soldier equipped, fit, and ready for active service ⟨the troop figure includes quartermasters, MPs, and signal, transportation, and medical corpsmen to a total of perhaps half its ~s —T.H. White b. 1915⟩ **b** : an effective aspect of a verb or an effective verb form

effective aperture *n* **:** the diameter of the entrance pupil of an optical system; *specif* **:** the apparent diameter of the diaphragm opening in a camera lens as seen through the front of the lens

effective current *n* **:** the value of an alternating or otherwise variable current that would result in the same heat production in a circuit as that of a direct current in the same length of time **:** the square root of the means of the squares of the instantaneous values of an alternating current

effective horsepower *n* **:** the net horsepower required to move a vehicle or boat that is the part of the total propelling engine horsepower that remains after deducting losses due to engine friction and propeller and other inefficiencies

ef·fec·tive·ly \-tə̇vlē, -li\ *adv* [ME, fr. *effective* + *-ly*] **:** in an effective manner **:** with great effect ⟨he knows how to communicate his ideas ~⟩; *also* **:** COMPLETELY ⟨rain . . . blotting out the landscape as ~ as a fog would do —C.S.Forester⟩

ef·fec·tive·ness \-tivnə̇s, -tēv- *also* -təv-\ *n* -ES **1 :** the quality or state of being effective ⟨declining public interest caused laws to lose ~ —J.W.McConnell⟩ **2 :** power to be effective **:** EFFICACY

effective pitch *n* **:** the distance an airplane advances along its flight path for one revolution of the propeller **:** PITCH

effective range *n* **:** the range of an airplane under the specific requirements of a special mission

effective rate *n, of interest* **:** the excess over unity of the accumulation factor for a year, furnishing the rate at simple interest which would yield in one year the same amount as the actual or nominal rate at compound interest

effective resistance *n* **:** ALTERNATING-CURRENT RESISTANCE

effective value *n* **:** the value of an alternating current or voltage equal to the square root of the arithmetic mean of the squares of the instantaneous values taken throughout one complete cycle

ef·fec·tiv·i·ty \ˌeˌfek'tivəd·ē, ə̇-, ē-\ *n* -ES **:** EFFECTIVENESS

ef·fect·less \ə̇'fektlə̇s, e'-,ē'-\ *adj, archaic* **:** lacking effect **:** FECKLESS

ef·fec·tor \ə̇'fektə(r), e'-,ē'-\ *n* -S **1** *also* **ef·fect·er** \"\ **:** one that effects ⟨sheer force of personality as an ~ of discipline —Nathaniel Burt⟩ **2 :** a bodily organ that becomes active in response to stimulation — distinguished from *receptor*

effects *pl of* EFFECT, *pres 3d sing of* EFFECT

ef·fec·tu·al \-'fekch(əw)əl, -ksh-\ *adj* [ME *effectuel, effectual,* fr. MF & ML; MF *effectuel,* fr. ML *effectualis,* fr. L *effectus* effect + *-alis* -al — more at EFFECT] **1 :** characterized by adequate power to produce an intended effect **:** productive of a result or effect **:** EFFECTIVE ⟨a man to whom painting was but another and less ~ way of writing dramas, novels, or history —Aldous Huxley⟩ ⟨no Oriental veil could be more ~ than her beautiful Catholic quiet —H.G.Wells⟩ **2** *obs* **:** impressively earnest or pertinent ⟨the ~ fervent prayer of a righteous man availeth much —Jas 5:16 (AV)⟩ **3 :** ACTUAL ⟨the ~ truth of the matter⟩ ⟨sufficient to supply the ~ demand and no more —Adam Smith⟩ **syn** see EFFECTIVE

effectual calling *n* **:** the action of the Holy Spirit in producing conviction of sin and bestowing the gift of faith in Christ according to Calvinist theology

ef·fec·tu·al·i·ty \-ˌfekchə'waləd·ē, -ksh-, -ətē, -i\ *n* -ES **:** EFFECTUALNESS

ef·fec·tu·al·ly \-'fekch(əw)əlē, -ksh-, -li\ *adv* [ME *effectuelly, effectually,* fr. *effectuel, effectual* + *-ly*] **:** in an effectual manner **:** with great or decisive effect; *also* **:** COMPLETELY

ef·fec·tu·al·ness \-lnə̇s\ *n* -ES **:** the quality or state of being effectual

ef·fec·tu·ate \=ˈ==ˌwāt, *usu* -ād·+V\ *vt* -ED/-ING/-S [ML *effectuatus,* past part. of *effectuare,* fr. L *effectus* effect] **:** EFFECT 2 ⟨strove successfully to ~ a settlement not by force but by reason —F.D.Roosevelt⟩ ⟨the question was still open as to the extent to which the courts would ~ the change —B.N. Cardozo⟩

ef·fec·tu·a·tion \ə̇ˌfekchə'wāshən, (ˌ)eˌf-, ēˌf-, -ksh-\ *n* -S **:** the action of putting into effect **:** ACCOMPLISHMENT ⟨the court did not enjoin the ~ of the plan absolutely —*Corporation Jour.*⟩

ef·feir \ə̇'fēr\ *Scot var of* AFFAIR

ef·fem·i·na·cy \ə̇'femənəsē, e'-,ē'-, -si\ *n* -ES [*effeminate* + *-cy*] **:** the quality or state of being effeminate **:** a womanlike delicacy, weakness, or softness in a man, in a thing produced by a man (as a painting), or in something generally classified as male

¹ef·fem·i·nate \-nə̇t, *usu* -əd·+V\ *adj* [ME *effeminat,* fr. L *effeminatus,* past part. of *effeminare* to make effeminate, fr. *ex-* + *femina* woman — more at FEMININE] **1 :** marked by qualities more characteristic of and suited to women than to men **:** lacking manly strength and purpose **:** exhibiting or proceeding from delicacy, weakness, emotionalism **:** marked by luxuriousness or voluptuousness ⟨such men practiced extravagances and affectations, and are generally described as ~ —W.G.Sumner⟩ ⟨had found in his nature strange depths of love for the little mite . . . and thought the exhibition of it ~ —Ruth Park⟩ ⟨blessed with all good things, these godchildren soon became ~ and suffered all manner of misfortunes —*Amer. Guide Series: La.*⟩ **2** *obs* **:** TENDER, SOFT, DELICATE **3** *of wool* **:** overdelicate or oversoft **syn** see FEMALE

²ef·fem·i·nate \-ˌnāt, *usu* -ād·+V\ *vt* -ED/-ING/-S [L *effeminatus*] **:** to make effeminate **:** WEAKEN ⟨it will not corrupt or ~ children's minds —John Locke⟩

³ef·fem·i·nate \-ˌnə̇t, *usu* -əd·+V\ *n* -S [¹*effeminate*] **:** an effeminate person

ef·fem·i·nate·ly \-nə̇tlē, -li\ *adv* **:** in an effeminate manner

ef·fem·i·nate·ness *n* -ES **:** the quality or state of being effeminate

ef·fem·i·na·tion \ə̇ˌfemə'nāshən, (ˌ)eˌf-, ēˌf-\ *n* -S [LL *effemination-, effeminatio,* fr. L *effeminatus* + *-ion-, -io* -ion] **:** the act or process of making or becoming effeminate; *specif* **:** the taking on by a man of the mental characteristics of a woman

ef·fem·i·nize \=ˈ==ˌnīz\ *vt* -ED/-ING/-S [¹*effeminate* + *-ize*] **:** to make effeminate ⟨he has become *effeminized,* without having the virtues of being frankly feminine —Sinclair Lewis⟩

ef·fen·di \ə̇'fendē, e'-, -di\ *n* -S [Turk *efendi,* fr. NGk *aphentēs,* alter. of Gk *authentēs* murderer, master, doer — more at AUTHENTIC] **1 :** MASTER, SIR — used in Turkey until 1935 as a title of respect esp. for a state official but often as a courtesy title for an educated man or a man of the upper classes **2 a :** one of a class of feudal landowners in an eastern Mediterranean country; *esp* **:** an Arab landowner **b :** a member of the upper classes or an educated man in such a country **3 :** a white-collar worker in an eastern Mediterranean or esp. an Arab country

ef·fer·ence \'ef(ə)rən(t)s\ *n* -S **:** efferent activity

¹ef·fer·ent \-nt\ *adj* [F *efférent,* fr. L *efferent-, efferens,* pres. part. of *efferre* to carry outward, fr. *ex-* + *ferre* to carry — more at BEAR] **:** bearing or conducting outward from a part or an organ; *specif* **:** conveying nervous impulses from a nerve center to an effector **:** CENTRIFUGAL, MOTOR — opposed to *afferent* — **ef·fer·ent·ly** *adv*

²efferent \"\ *n* -S **:** an efferent part (as a blood vessel or nerve fiber)

ef·fer·vesce \ˌefə(r)¦ves\ *vi* -ED/-ING/-S [L *effervescere,* fr. *ex-* + *fervescere* to begin to boil, incho. of *fervēre* to boil — more at BURN] **1 :** to bubble and hiss (as of fermenting liquors or carbonated water); *also* **:** to issue in bubbles (as of the escaping gas from carbonated water) **2 :** to exhibit (as in speech or action) almost unrestrainable enthusiasm or happy emotion **:** bubble over ⟨I was full and *effervescing* with joy of creation —Mary Austin⟩ ⟨the honeymooners hectically *effervesced* into small talk — Owen Wister⟩

ef·fer·ves·cence \ˌ==¦ves°n(t)s\ *n* -S [L *effervescere* + E *-ence*] **1 :** the action or process of effervescing **:** the commotion of a liquid produced by effervescing **2 :** inner excitement or turmoil usu. finding expression in lively action **:** the quality or state of being effervescent ⟨London today, even with all the grimness, has a sort of early New Deal intellectual ~ —J.R. Chamberlain⟩ ⟨continued in a state of ~ —Edith Wharton⟩

ef·fer·ves·cent \¦==¦ves°nt\ *adj* [L *effervescent-, effervescens,* pres. part. of *effervescere*] **1 :** marked by or expressing a state of effervescence **:** impossible or difficult to restrain or suppress **:** BUBBLING, EXUBERANT ⟨his fertile ~ mind never ceased thinking of new and more effective ways to organize workers and win strikes —C.A.Madison⟩ **2 :** having the property of effervescing ⟨~ wine⟩ ⟨~ salts⟩ **syn** see ELASTIC

ef·fer·ves·cent·ly *or* **ef·fer·vesc·ing·ly** *adv* **:** in an effervescent manner

ef·fer·vesc·ible \¦==¦vesəbəl\ *adj* **:** able or ready to effervesce

ef·fete \ə̇'fēt, e'-\ *adj* [L *effetus* fr. *ex-* + *fetus* pregnant, breeding, fruitful — more at FEMININE] **1 :** exhausted of fertility **:** no longer able to produce young or fruit **:** UNFRUITFUL ⟨eroded ~ earth⟩ **2 :** marked by lack or deprivation of some inherent characteristic **:** ENERVATED: **a** *of a substance* **:** having lost its unique quality (as flavor) **b :** exhausted of physical energy **:** worn out **:** SPENT ⟨~, weary, burned-out revolutionists —H.F.Mooney⟩ **c :** having lost character, courage, strength, stamina, or vitality ⟨~ literary critics and dogmatic professors —J.T.Farrell⟩ **:** DEGENERATE ⟨a soft, ~, and decadent race —R.P.Parsons⟩ **d :** totally devoid of an original positive drive or purposiveness ⟨vaguely educated for minor diplomatic or other governmental posts in an ~ struggle to maintain position —Janet Flanner⟩ **e :** soft or decadent as a result of overrefinement of living conditions or laxity of mental or moral discipline ⟨the ~ householder who wants things done for him —*New Yorker*⟩ ⟨the ~ gentility that lay like a blight on the critical writing of the nineties —C.I.Glicksberg⟩ **f :** OUT-OF-DATE, OUTMODED ⟨an old but by no means ~ statute —Edward Jenks⟩ — **effetely** *adj* — **effeteness** *n* -ES

ef·fi·ca·cious \ˌefə¦kāshəs\ *adj* [L *efficac-, efficax* (fr. *efficere* to bring about, accomplish, effect) + E *-ious* — more at EFFECT] **:** characterized by qualities giving power to bring about an intended result ⟨written propaganda is less ~ than the habits and prejudices, the class loyalties . . . of the readers —Aldous Huxley⟩ ⟨an ~ law⟩ **syn** see EFFECTIVE

ef·fi·ca·cious·ly *adv* **:** in an efficacious manner **:** EFFECTIVELY

ef·fi·ca·cious·ness *n* -ES **:** the quality of being efficacious **:** EFFECTIVENESS

ef·fi·cac·i·ty \ˌefə'kasəd·ē, -ətē, -i\ *n* -ES [ME *efficacite,* fr. L *efficacitas,* fr. *efficac- efficax* + *-itas* -ity] **:** EFFICACY, EFFECTIVENESS

ef·fi·ca·cy \'efə̇kəsē, -fēk-, -si\ *n* -ES [L *efficacia,* fr. *efficac-, efficax* + *-ia* -y] **:** the power to produce an effect **:** EFFECTIVENESS ⟨the ~ of prayer⟩ ⟨~ of medicine⟩ ⟨the ~ of the Security Council in safeguarding world security —Vera M. Dean⟩

efficience *n* -S [L *efficientia*] *obs* **:** efficient action; *also* **:** EFFICACY

ef·fi·cien·cy \ə̇'fishənsē, e'-,ē'-, -si\ *n* -ES [L *efficientia,* fr. *efficient-, efficiens* (pres. part. of *efficere* to bring about, accomplish, effect) + *-ia* -y — more at EFFECT] **1 :** the power, characteristic quality, or manner of operation of an efficient cause ⟨it is absurd to credit inert mass with ~ —James Ward⟩ **2 a :** EFFECTIVENESS; *esp* **:** capacity to produce desired results with a minimum expenditure of energy, time, money, or materials ⟨increasing recognition of the unfairness of such scales of pay is corroding the ~ of the economic system —J.A. Hobson⟩ ⟨the despairing conclusion that their evil ~ knows no limits —S.L.A.Marshall⟩ **b :** suitability for a task or purpose ⟨the ~ of the drawing board is in no way impaired —*Gadgets Annual*⟩ **3 :** efficient operation as measured by a comparison of actual results with those that could be achieved with the same expenditure of energy ⟨structural changes may take place to enable the respiratory organs to remain in a state of ~ —W.H.Dowdeswell⟩ ⟨the invention of instruments for assessing degrees of ~ in communication —Barbara Wootton⟩: as **a :** the ratio of the useful energy delivered by a dynamic system (as a machine, engine, or motor) to the energy supplied to it over the same period or cycle of operation **b :** performance of a task with little or no waste effort **c :** economic productivity **:** YIELD — used esp. of the average number of times a unit of money serves to effect an exchange in a specified period **d :** the relative effective operation of a biological system as measured by the ratio of energy released in product (as milk, muscular effort, or wool) to the energy consumed (as in food) — called also *feed efficiency* **4** *or* **efficiency apartment :** a small usu. furnished apartment having minimal kitchen and bath facilities

efficiency engineer *also* **efficiency expert** *n* **:** one who analyzes methods, procedures, and jobs in order to devise means for securing maximum efficiency of equipment and personnel

¹ef·fi·cient \-nt\ *adj* [ME, fr. MF or L; MF *efficient,* fr. L *efficient-, efficiens*] **1 :** serving as or characteristic of an efficient cause **:** causally productive **:** OPERANT ⟨the ~ action of heat⟩ **2 :** marked by ability to choose and use the most effective and least wasteful means of doing a task or accomplishing a purpose **:** COMPETENT ⟨her education made it likely that she would be a typist more ~ than the average —W.S. Maugham⟩ ⟨the ~ housewife takes the best possible care of her utensils⟩ **3 :** marked by qualities, characteristics, or equipment that facilitate the serving of a purpose or the performance of a task in the best possible manner **:** eminently satisfactory in use **:** effective to an end ⟨the most ~ kind of phrase for the purpose of communicating these subtle, complex impressions —H.J.Muller⟩ ⟨the new barn is more ~ —S.H.Holbrook⟩ **syn** see EFFECTIVE

²efficient *n* -S *obs* **:** EFFICIENT CAUSE ⟨the great ~ of the world —Joseph Hall⟩

efficient cause *n* **:** the immediate agent in the production of an effect ⟨I have a free morning, and this is the *efficient cause* of the chance for talk with you —H.J.Laski⟩

ef·fi·cient·ly *adv* **:** in an efficient manner **:** with success, competence, or adequate effect ⟨a church where he considered the mass ~ performed —T.S.Eliot⟩ ⟨failed to meet the requirements of his position ~⟩

ef·fig·ial \ə̇'fij(ē)əl, e'-\ *adj* [*effigy* + *-al*] **:** of or resembling an effigy

ef·fig·i·ate \-jēˌāt\ *vt* -ED/-ING/-S [LL *effigiatus,* past part. of *effigiare,* fr. L *effigies*] **:** to form or represent in or as if in an effigy — **ef·fig·i·a·tion** \=ˌ==ē'āshən\ *n* -S

ef·fi·gi·es \ə̇'fijēˌēz, e'-, -jēz\ *n, pl* **effigies** [L] **:** EFFIGY

ef·fig·u·rate \(')e, ə̇ +\ *adj* [*ex-* + *figurate*] *bot* **:** having a definite form **:** not effuse ⟨~ lichens⟩ — **ef·fig·u·ra·tion** \(¦)e, ə̇ +\ *n* -S

¹ef·fi·gy \'efə̇jē, -ji\ *n* -ES [MF *effigie,* fr. L *effigies,* fr. *effingere* to form, fashion, portray, fr. *ex-* + *fingere* to form, shape — more at DOUGH] **:** a full or partial representation esp. of a person: as **a :** a sculptured likeness ⟨the old man himself sits in bronze ~ on a cornerstone —Lawrence Constable⟩ **b :** a portrait on a coin ⟨in those distant days when the only representation of the sovereign was a rough-drawn ~ on coin or seal —R.T.B.Fulford⟩ **c :** a crude figure often in the form of a stuffed dummy that is tortured or disposed of (as by burning or hanging) to represent treatment felt to be due to a person who is the object of hatred — see ⁴GUY 1

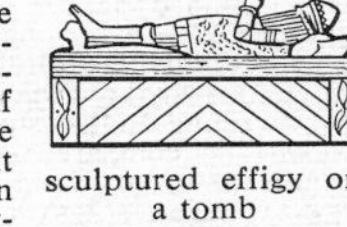

sculptured effigy on a tomb

²effigy \"\ *vt* -ED/-ING/-ES **:** to represent by an effigy

effigy mound *n* **:** a prehistoric American Indian burial mound shaped like an animal (as a bird or serpent)

ef·fleu·rage \ˌeflə'räzh, -(ˌ)flü¦-\ *n* -S [F, fr. *effleurer* to stroke lightly (fr. *ef-* — fr. L, fr. *ex-* — + *fleur* flower, surface, fr. OF *flour, flur, flor*) + *-age* — more at FLOWER] **:** a light stroking movement used in massage

ef·flo·resce \ˌeflə¦res\ *vi* -ED/-ING/-S [L *efflorescere,* fr. *ex-* + *florescere* to begin to blossom — more at FLORESCENCE] **1 a** *obs* **:** BLOSSOM **b :** to burst forth or become manifest as if flowering **2** *chem* **a :** to change on the surface or throughout to a whitish mealy or crystalline powder from the loss of water of crystallization on exposure to the air ⟨Glauber's salt ~*s*⟩ **b :** to become covered with a powdery crust or hard coating ⟨bricks may ~ owing to the deposition of soluble salts⟩

ef·flo·res·cence \ˌ==¦res°n(t)s\ *n* -S [F, fr. MF, fr. L *efflorescere* + MF *-ence*] **1 :** the period or state of flowering **:** ANTHESIS **2 a :** the action or process of developing and unfolding as if coming into flower **:** BLOSSOMING ⟨his concern for the organic roots of architecture and its eventual ~ in beauty —Lewis Mumford⟩ ⟨periods of higher prosperity and intellectual and artistic ~ —Julian Huxley⟩ **b :** an instance or example of developmental growth ⟨that amazing ~ of genius —DeLancey Ferguson⟩ ⟨perhaps the most astonishing ~ of intellectual adventure in the history of mankind —Lancelot Hogben⟩ **c :** the result or culminating feature of a developmental process **:** OUTGROWTH, FLOWER ⟨the change in art is merely the ~ of certain long prepared and anticipated effects —Roger Fry⟩ ⟨shows how the rich ~ of civilization in the West was achieved —*Times Lit. Supp.*⟩ **3** *chem* **a :** the process of efflorescing **b :** the powder or crust thus formed **4 :** a redness of the skin **:** eruption (as in a rash)

ef·flo·res·cent \¦==¦res°nt\ *adj* [F or L: F, fr. L *efflorescent-, efflorescens,* pres. part. of *efflorescere*] **:** forming or resembling an efflorescence **:** EFFLORESCING

ef·flu·ence \'eˌflüən(t)s, 'efləwən-\ *n* -S [L *effluere* to flow out + E *-ence*] **1 :** the action or process of flowing out **:** EMANATION, EFFLUX ⟨the ~ of power rather than the conscious application of it —John Burroughs⟩ **2 :** something that flows out (as from a person or substance) — usu. used of something having an effect ⟨some ~ from its ageless hills and waters laid a spell upon me which has never been broken —John Buchan⟩

¹ef·flu·ent \-nt\ *adj* [L *effluent-, effluens,* pres. part. of *effluere* to flow out, fr. *ex-* + *fluere* to flow — more at FLUENT] **:** flowing out **:** EMANATING, OUTGOING ⟨the Pigeon river, whose blackened waters are flecked with white foam, ~ from the mill —*Amer. Guide Series: N.C.*⟩ ⟨~ vein⟩ ⟨~ stream⟩

²effluent \"\ *n* -S **:** something that flows out: as **a :** an outflowing branch of a main stream or lake — compare AFFLUENT **b :** liquid discharged as waste (as water used in an industrial process or sewage)

ef·fluve \'eˌflüv; e'f-,ə̇'f-\ *n* -S [F, fr. L *effluvium*] **:** a feeble electric discharge due to convection in a fluid dielectric under high voltage

ef·flu·vi·um \e'flüvēəm, ə̇'-\ *also* **ef·flu·via** \-vēə\ *n, pl* **ef·flu·via** \-vēə\ *or* **effluviums** *also* **effluvias** [L, act of flowing out, outlet, fr. *effluere* to flow out — more at EFFLUENT] **1 :** something esp. subtle and invisible that flows out or issues forth **:** EMANATION: as **a :** EFFLUX 1b(1) **b :** a hypothetical imponderable formerly believed to be manifest as an efflux from electrified bodies and magnets and to be responsible for their powers of attraction and repulsion **c :** an exhalation or smell esp. when unpleasant ⟨emerging from the barbershop, his jowls gray with powder, moving in an ~ of pomade —William Faulkner⟩ ⟨the mingled *effluvia* of rotting leaves and manure heaps . . . drifted toward her —Ellen Glasgow⟩; *also* **:** gaseous waste **:** EXHAUST ⟨carbon monoxide is generously present in the *effluvia* of all internal-combustion engines, most industrial plants, and many mines, mills, or workshops —Berton Roueché⟩ **2 :** a by-product usu. in the form of waste ⟨the big rum distillery just below the town sweetens the air with a luscious smell of molasses when the *effluvia* are being run off into the river —Francis Ratcliffe⟩ ⟨most of the most admired literature . . . has been to all appearance the ~ of a sick society —Elmer Davis⟩

ef·flux \'eˌfləks\ *n* -ES [L *effluxus,* past part. of *effluere*] **1 a :** something that emanates in or as if in a stream **:** EFFUSION ⟨many wished to touch the relics and so absorb their healing ~*es* —E.H.Short⟩ ⟨used secretly to think ourselves the Wordsworth and Coleridge of an endless ~ of lyrical ballads —Christopher Morley⟩ **b** (1) **:** an emanation supposed by Empedocles and the Sophists to be continually given off by external objects and to be the cause of our perception of them (2) **:** EMANATION 1b **2 a :** the action or process of flowing or seeming to flow out ⟨large underground ~ of salt water from the lake —*Geog. Jour.*⟩ ⟨the influx and ~ of gold —R.F.Harrod⟩ ⟨the annual ~ of men and women for work —V.G.J.Sheddick⟩ **b :** a lapse or passing of time ⟨the influx and ~ of life, which we call the seasons —A.C.Benson⟩ ⟨for a brief second, for an inexpressibly curtailed ~ of time —Anthony Powell⟩; *also* **:** END, EXPIRATION

ef·flux·ion \e'fləkshən, ə̇'-\ *n* -S [LL *effluxion-, effluxio* act of flowing out, fr. L *effluxus* + *-ion-, -io* -ion] **:** EFFLUX — used esp. of time ⟨mere ~ of time has given him a long range of observation⟩ ⟨his term of office expired by ~ of time previously fixed⟩

ef·fo·di·en·tia \(ˌ)eˌfōdē'ench(ē)ə, ə̇ˌ-\ *n pl, cap* [NL, fr. L neut. pl. of *effodient-, effodiens,* pres. part. of *effodere* to dig out, fr. *ex-* + *fodere* to dig — more at BED] *in former classifications* **:** the Edentata as most broadly conceived excepting only the sloths; *sometimes* **:** an order or other group comprising the pangolins and the aardvark

efforce *vt* [MF *efforcer,* fr. OF *esforcier,* fr. *es-* (fr. L *ex-*) + *forcier* to force — more at FORCE] *obs* **:** FORCE

ef·form \(')e¦fō(ə)rm\ *vt* [LL *efformare,* fr. L *ex-* + *formare* to form — more at FORM] *archaic* **:** FORM, SHAPE — **efformation** *n, obs*

ef·fort \'efə(r)t *also* -ˌfȯr| *or* -ˌfō(ə)| *sometimes* -ˌfōr| *or* -ˌfōə|; *usu* |d·+V\ *n* -S [MF, fr. OF *esfort, esforz,* fr. OF *esforcier* to force (as in *s'esforcier* to exert oneself) — more at EFFORCE] **1 a :** conscious exertion of physical or mental power ⟨the constant ~ of the dreamer to attain his ideal —Henry Adams⟩ ⟨the church was built through community ~⟩ ⟨the speech of the Southerner appears to ignore ~ in its slow, carelessly articulated syllables —*Amer. Guide Series: N.C.*⟩ **b :** expenditure of energy toward a particular end **:** forceful attempt ⟨his clumsy ~*s* at certain rural tasks —A.C.Cole⟩ ⟨made one last ~ to obtain Negro suffrage in the South —Carol L. Thompson⟩ ⟨the company's ~*s* to improve working conditions —Daily Worker⟩ **c :** hard work ⟨an A for ~⟩ ⟨the work is highly skillful . . . one feels, what was absent from the previous work, a distinct sense of ~ —F.J.Mather⟩ **2 :** the product or result of expenditure of energy — used esp. of a literary or artistic creation ⟨their magnificent churches being justly ranked among the most wonderful ~*s* of the human hand —H.T. Buckle⟩ ⟨one of his television ~*s* —J.P.Shanley⟩ **3 a :** active or effective force ⟨muscular ~⟩ **b :** the force applied to a simple machine (as a lever) as distinguished from the force exerted by it against the load **4 :** the total energy expended and work done to achieve a particular purpose or result **:** UNDERTAKING ⟨the war ~⟩ ⟨an unsuccessful rescue ~⟩

syn EFFORT, EXERTION, PAINS, and TROUBLE can signify in common the active expenditure of physical or mental power in producing or attempting to produce a desired result. EFFORT implies conscious attempt or a toiling or straining to achieve ⟨to divorce the worker's income from any dependence on the *efforts* he makes —*Time*⟩ ⟨modern science, with infinite *effort,* has discovered and announced that man is a bewildering complex of energies —Henry Adams⟩ ⟨made an *effort* to increase his income⟩ EXERTION stresses the active, often vigorous, exercise of a power or faculty ⟨his work was done with remarkable grace, but with *exertions* which it was painful to witness —Margaret Deland⟩ ⟨prodigious *exertions* were made to bring in the cargoes and to protect the ships —Sir Winston Churchill⟩ ⟨by a violent *exertion* of his powers of self-command he reassumed his tranquillity —Elinor Wylie⟩ PAINS implies toilsome or solicitous effort ⟨taken unusual *pains* to inform himself beforehand concerning the subject matter of the conference —Vera M. Dean⟩ ⟨exercising great *pains* to improve one's speech⟩ TROUBLE implies exertion that inconveniences ⟨a lazy man's expedient for ridding himself of the *trouble* of thinking and deciding —B.N.Cardozo⟩ ⟨no need to go to all the *trouble* of pushing through a constitutional amendment —Zechariah Chafee⟩ ⟨for the *trouble* of looking, . . . you will acquire the warm and palpitating facts of life —R.L.Stevenson⟩

ef·fort·ful \'efə(r)tfəl\ *adj* **:** marked by the presence of or necessity for an expenditure of effort **:** LABORED ⟨a dry subject that makes for ~ reading⟩ ⟨he answered with an ~ smile⟩ ⟨~ reporting of fact⟩ — **ef·fort·ful·ly** \-fəlē, -li\ *adv*

ef·fort·less \-tlə̇s\ *adj* **1 :** requiring no effort ⟨a style the layman and the immature reader can absorb with ~ pleasure —*Saturday Rev.*⟩ **2 :** having the effect by virtue of ease, mastery, artistry, or smoothness of performance of being or having been accomplished without effort ⟨even the swallows, the restless swallows, glided in an ~ way through the busy air —Richard Jefferies⟩ ⟨she walked with ~ grace⟩ ⟨this writer of ~, often casual, verses —Arna W. Bontemps⟩ **syn** see EASY

ef·fort·less·ly *adv* **:** in an effortless manner

ef·fort·less·ness *n* -ES **:** the quality of being effortless **:** absence of strain or apparent difficulty

effort syndrome *n* **:** CARDIAC NEUROSIS

ef·frac·tion \e'frakshən, ə̇'-\ *n* -S [F, modif. (influenced by F *-ion*) of LL *effractura,* fr. L *effractus* (past part. of *effringere* to break open, fr. *ex-* + *-fringere,* fr. *frangere* to break) + *-ura*

-ure — more at BREAK] **:** the action of making forcible entry ⟨criminal ~ of a house⟩ ⟨~ into a store⟩
ef·fron·tery \ə'frəntərē, e'-,ē'-, -ri\ *n* -ES [F *effronterie*, fr. MF, fr. *effronté* shameless (fr. LL *effront-, effrons* — fr. L *ex-* + *front-, frons* forehead — + MF *-é*, fr. L *-atus* -ate) + *-erie* -ery — more at FRONT] **:** flagrant boldness that is offensive or insolent in its crass discourtesy or utter presumption **:** GALL ⟨the ~ to propound three such heresies —*Times Lit. Supp.*⟩
syn see TEMERITY
effs *pl of* EFF
ef·fulge \e'fŭlj, ə'-,ē'-, -'fəlj\ *vi* -ED/-ING/-S [L *effulgēre*, fr. *ex-* + *fulgēre* to shine, flash — more at FULGENT] **:** to shine forth **:** RADIATE
ef·ful·gence \-jən(t)s\ *n* -S [LL *effulgentia*, fr. L *effulgent-, effulgens* + *-ia* -y] **:** strong radiant light **:** glorious splendor **:** BRILLIANCE ⟨that crimson flow, that ~ at the solemn twilight hour —Willa Cather⟩
ef·ful·gent \-nt\ *adj* [L *effulgent-, effulgens*, pres. part. of *effulgēre*] **:** marked by or as if by brightly shining light **:** impressive in resplendence **:** extremely radiant **:** BRILLIANT ⟨her ~ beauty —Arnold Bennett⟩ ⟨the same little ~ flash of intuition —J.D.Salinger⟩ **syn** see BRIGHT
ef·fund \e'fənd\ *vt* -ED/-ING/-S [ME *effunden*, fr. L *effundere*] *archaic* **:** EFFUSE
[1]**ef·fuse** \e'fyüz, ə'-,ē'-\ *vb* -ED/-ING/-S [L *effusus*, past part. of *effundere*, fr. *ex-* + *fundere* to pour — more at FOUND] *vt* **1 :** to pour out (a liquid) **2 :** to give off **:** SHED, RADIATE ⟨the drawing room . . . *effused* an atmosphere of unhappiness and discontent —I.V.Morris⟩ ~ *vi* **:** to flow out **:** EMANATE
[2]**ef·fuse** \(ˈ)e¦fyüs, ə'f-,ē'f-\ *adj* [L *effusus*, past part.] **1 :** poured out freely **:** overflowing without restraint **:** PROFUSE ⟨so should our joy be very ~ —Isaac Barrow⟩ **2** *bot* **:** DIFFUSE; *specif* **:** spread out flat without definite form ⟨~ lichens⟩ — compare EFFIGURATE **3 :** having the lips separated by a gap — used of certain shells
[3]**effuse** *n* -S [¹*effuse*] *obs* **:** EFFUSION
ef·fu·si·om·e·ter \ə,fyüzē'ämәd·ə(r)\ *n* [*effusion* + *-meter*] **:** an apparatus for determining the effusion velocities of gases and hence their densities
ef·fu·sion \ə'fyüzhən, e'-,ē'-\ *n* -S [ME *effusioun*, fr. MF or L; MF *effusion*, fr. L *effusion-, effusio*, fr. *effusus* + *-ion-, -io* -ion] **1 :** the action or process of effusing or of being poured out ⟨desirous to stop the ~ of British blood —C.G.Bowers⟩: as **a :** escape of a fluid into a tissue or part (as the pleural cavity) by rupture of a vessel or by exudation through the walls **:** EXTRAVASATION **b :** the flow of a gas through an aperture whose diameter is small as compared with the distance between the molecules of the gas ⟨~ through a plug of unglazed porcelain⟩ **2 :** unrestrained expression of feelings ⟨greeted her with great ~ —Olive H. Prouty⟩ ⟨in the first ~ of self-admiration —J.A.Froude⟩ **3 a :** something that is poured out with little or no restraint — used esp. of evidences of self-expression ⟨she bore with the ~*s* of his endless conceit —Jane Austen⟩ ⟨literary and critical ~*s* —Rex Ingamells⟩ **b :** the liquid that escapes in extravasation
ef·fu·sive \-üsiv, -üz|, |ēv *also* |əv\ *adj* **1** *archaic* **:** pouring freely ⟨washed with the ~ wave —Alexander Pope⟩ **2 :** expressing or marked by unrestrained emotion **:** unduly demonstrative **:** GUSHING ⟨at the sight of the stranger he sprang to his feet and darted forward, his hands outstretched, smiling with all his teeth, ~ —Aldous Huxley⟩ ⟨insincere and ~ demonstrations of sentimental friendship —Dean Acheson⟩ **3 :** characterized or formed by a nonexplosive outpouring of lava ⟨~ volcano⟩ ⟨~ eruption⟩ ⟨~ rock⟩ — **ef·fu·sive·ly** \|əvlē, -lī\ *adv* — **ef·fu·sive·ness** \|ivnəs |ēv- *also* |əv-\ *n* -ES
ef·ik \'efik\ *n, pl* **efik** *or* **efiks** *usu cap* **1 a :** a Negro people of southeastern Nigeria **b :** a member of such people **2 :** a dialect of Ibibio that is used as the literary language throughout the Ibibio area and in some neighboring areas and by the Efik people as their language
e flat \'ᵊ⸗ᵊ\ *n, usu cap E* **1 :** the keynote of E-flat major or E-flat minor **2 :** the tone a half step below E
e-flat major \'⸗,⸗'⸗⸗\ *n, usu cap E* **:** the major musical key having a signature of three flats
e-flat minor *n, usu cap E* **:** the minor musical key having a signature of six flats
efoveolate \(ˈ)ē+\ *adj* [*e-* + *foveolate*] **:** not foveolate
ef·reet *var of* AFREET
efs *pl of* EF
[1]**eft** \'eft\ *n* -S [ME *evete, ewte*, fr. OE *efete*] **1** *obs* **:** LIZARD **2 :** NEWT; *esp* **:** the terrestrial phase of a predominantly aquatic newt
[2]**eft** \"\ *adv* [ME, fr. OE *eft, æft*; akin to OE *æfter* after — more at AFTER] **1** *archaic* **:** AGAIN **2** *archaic* **:** AFTER, AFTERWARD
ef·ter \'eftər\ *chiefly Scot var of* AFTER
eft·soons \(ˈ)eft¦sünz\ *also* **eft·soon** \-ün\ *adv* [ME *eftsones* (fr. *eft* + *sone* immediately, soon + *-s*, adverbial suffix) & *eftsone*, fr. *eft* + *sone* — more at SOON, -S] **1** *archaic* **:** a second time **:** AGAIN **2** *archaic* **:** soon afterward **:** QUICKLY **3** *archaic* **:** from time to time **:** OFTEN
ef·wa·ta·ka·la grass \,efwə'täkəlә-\ *n* [Kongo *efwatakala*] *Africa* **:** MOLASSES GRASS
e g *abbr* [L *exempli gratia*] for example
EG *abbr* edge grain
egad \ē'gad, i'-, -gaa(ə)d\ *interj* [prob. euphemism for *oh God*] — used as a mild oath
egal \'egəl\ *adj* [ME, fr. MF, fr. L *aequalis* — more at EQUAL] *archaic* **:** EQUAL
[1]**egal·i·tar·i·an** \(¦)ē¦galə¦terēən, ə̇'g-, -taar-,-tār-\ *adj* [F *égalitaire* (fr. *égalité* equality — fr. L *aequalitat-, aequalitas* — + *-aire* -ary) + E *-ian* — more at EQUALITY] **:** marked by or believing in egalitarianism **:** DEMOCRATIC ⟨an ~ age can have no place for the snobbish and feudal notion that one occupation can be of greater worth than another —Christopher Hollis⟩
[2]**egalitarian** \"\ *n* -S **:** one who believes in egalitarianism
egal·i·tar·i·an·ism \(,)ē,⸗⸗'⸗⸗ə,nizəm, ə̇,-\ *n* -S **1 :** a belief in human equality: **a :** a belief that all men are equal in intrinsic worth and are entitled to equal access to the rights and privileges of their society; *specif* **:** a social philosophy advocating the leveling of social, political, and economic inequalities ⟨the theory of English ~ has . . . postulated a process of leveling up, not down; of increasing, not diminishing, the middle classes —Roy Lewis & Angus Maude⟩ **b :** the belief that men are born equal in aptitudes and capacities ⟨Plato's view of human nature was such as to be clearly opposed to ~. . . . Men are naturally unequal —H.E.Barnes & H.P.Becker⟩ **2 :** the suppression of all distinctions between individuals and groups as inherently unjust **:** an extreme social and political leveling ⟨the Tiv people of Nigeria . . . are nurtured in a "fierce and rather brutal ~", and dislike anything that singles anybody out for special attention —Barbara Wooton⟩ **3 :** social, political, or economic equality ⟨the ~ of the early Christian communities, where distinctions of class were disregarded and even a slave could hold an important position —H.E.Barnes & H.P.Becker⟩
éga·li·té \ägälētä\ *also* **egal·i·ty** \ē'galəd·ē, ə̇'-\ *n* -S [F *égalité* equality] **:** social or political equality; *esp* **:** an extreme social and political leveling
egally *adv* [ME, fr. *egal* equal + *-ly* — more at EGAL] *obs* **:** EQUALLY
eg·ba \'egbə\ *n, pl* **egba** *or* **egbas** *usu cap* **1 :** a Yoruba-speaking people of southwestern Nigeria primarily concentrated in the vicinity of Abeokuta **2 :** a member of the Egba people
eger·an \'ägərən, -,ran\ *n* -S [G, fr. *Eger* (Cheb), Czechoslovakia, its locality + *-an*] **:** a brown idocrase
ege·ria \ə̇'jirēə, ē'-\ *n* -S *usu cap* [after *Egeria*, mythical adviser of Numa Pompilius, legendary 2d king of Rome, fr. L] **:** a woman adviser or companion ⟨listening to the promptings of his *Egeria* —*Encyc. Britannica*⟩ ⟨the most highly esteemed as an *Egeria* by his old friends —Janet Flanner⟩
egest \(ˈ)ē¦jest, ə̇'j-\ *vt* -ED/-ING/-S [L *egestus*, past part. of *egerere* to carry outside, discharge, fr. *e-* + *gerere* to carry, bear — more at CAST] **:** to cast out (indigestible matter) from the digestive tract; *broadly* **:** to rid the body of (waste matter) by any normal route (as the skin, lungs, or kidneys)
eges·ta \ə̇'jestə\ *n pl* [NL, fr. L, neut. pl. of *egestus*] **:** something egested from the body **:** DEJECTA, EXCRETA — opposed to *ingesta*
eges·tion \ə̇'jes(h)chən\ *n* -S [ME *egestioun*, fr. MF or L; MF *egestion*, fr. L *egestion-, egestio*, fr. *egestus* + *-ion-, -io* -ion] **:** the act or process of egesting
[1]**egg** \'eg, 'āg\ *vt* -ED/-ING/-S [ME *eggen*, fr. OE *eggian*, fr. ON *eggja*, fr. *egg* edge of a blade, edge — more at EDGE] **:** to provoke or goad to action **:** INCITE, TEMPT, ENCOURAGE — usu. used with *on* ⟨his vanity ~*ed* him on —O.S.J.Gogarty⟩ ⟨~ their governments on to spend hundreds of millions —G.B. Shaw⟩ **syn** see URGE
[2]**egg** \"\ *n* -S *often attrib* [ME *egge*, fr. ON *egg*; akin to OE *ǣg* egg, OHG *ei*, Crimean Goth *ada*, L *ovum*, W *wy*, Gk *ōion*, OPer *xāya* and perh. to L *avis* bird — more at AVIARY] **1 a** (1) **:** the hard-shelled reproductive body produced by a bird, esp. by domestic poultry ⟨a dozen new-laid ~*s*⟩ (2) **:** the content of such an egg used as food ⟨I like an ~ for breakfast⟩ **b :** an animal reproductive body (as of reptiles, birds, and most insects) consisting of an ovum together with its nutritive and protective envelopes and being capable of development that results in the production and release of a new individual capable of independent existence — used esp. of such bodies when enclosed in a firm membrane or shell and able to withstand exposure to air **c :** OVUM 1 **d :** the pupa of certain insects — not used technically **2 :** something resembling an egg: as **a :** an incipient idea ⟨that a handful of men . . . carry in their brains the ovarian ~*s* of the future —Van Wyck Brooks⟩ **b** *slang* **:** a military explosive; *esp* **:** an aerial bomb ⟨the fighter-bombers . . . dropped their ~*s* —G.S. Patton⟩ **3** *slang* **:** FELLOW, GUY ⟨a good ~⟩ ⟨a bad ~⟩ **4 :** ACID EGG

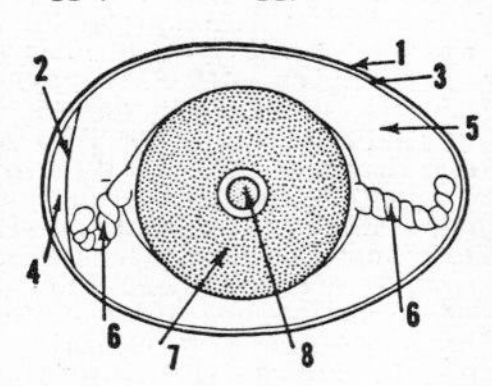

diagram of hen's egg: *1* shell, *2* inner shell membrane and *3* outer shell membrane enclosing air space *4*, *5* albumen or white, *6* chalazas, *7* yolk, *8* blastodisc

[3]**egg** \"\ *vb* -ED/-ING/-S *vt* **1 :** to cover with egg ⟨slices of meat, ~*ed*, crumbed, and fried⟩ **2 :** to pelt with eggs ~ *vi* **:** to gather the eggs of wild birds
egg albumin *n* **1 :** the albumin of eggs; *esp* **:** OVALBUMIN 1 **2 :** dried whites of eggs (as of hen's eggs) obtained usu. as yellowish lumps or powder and containing ovalbumin and other proteins
egg and dart *also* **egg and tongue** *or* **egg and anchor** *n* **:** a carved ornamental design in relief consisting of an ovoid figure and a roughly triangular figure usu. approximating a somewhat elongated javelin or arrowhead repeated alternately (as along a molding or cornice)

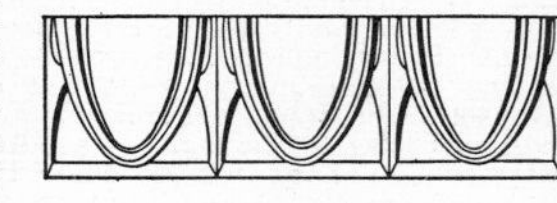
egg and dart

egg apparatus *n* **:** a group of three cells at the micropylar end of the embryo sac in seed plants consisting of the egg and two sterile cells
egg apple *n* **:** EGGPLANT
egg·ar *also* **egg·er** \'egə(r), 'āg-\ *n* -S [*eggar* alter. of *egger*; *egger* fr. ²*egg* + *-er*; fr. the shape of the cocoon] **:** any of various moths of the family Lasiocampidae (as many members of the genera *Eriogaster* and *Lasiocampa*) that have nonfunctional mouthparts as adults and plumose antennae in the males and produce larvae that feed on the foliage of trees
egg axis *n* **:** an embryonic axis passing through the animal and vegetal poles of an egg
eggbeater \'⸗,⸗⸗\ *n* **1 :** a rotary beater operated by hand for beating eggs or cream and other liquids **2 :** HELICOPTER
egg bed *n* **:** an area where many grasshoppers have deposited egg pods
eggberry \'⸗- — see BERRY\ *n* [alter. of *hagberry*] **:** EUROPEAN BIRD CHERRY
egg bird *n* **:** any of various sea birds whose eggs are used for food; *esp* **:** SOOTY TERN
egg bonnet *n* **:** WATER SHIELD 1
[1]**egg-bound** \'⸗,⸗\ *adj* [²*egg* + *bound*] **:** unable to expel eggs in the normal manner — used of a fowl or a fish
[2]**egg-bound** \"\ *n* -S **:** the condition of being egg-bound
eggbox \'⸗,⸗\ *adj, Brit* **:** EGGCRATE ⟨~ screening⟩
egg bread *n, Midland* **:** SPOON BREAD
egg burster *n* **:** a ridge, group of teeth, or other prominence on the body of an insect embryo by which it ruptures the egg membranes in hatching
egg case *n* **1 a** *or* **egg capsule :** a protective case enclosing eggs (as of certain insects and mollusks) **:** OOTHECA — see SEA NECKLACE **b** *or* **egg sac :** a pouch of spun silk in which many spiders carry their eggs **c :** a highly specialized outer envelope that encloses an egg and that is either soft and gelatinous (as in certain amphibians) or strong and horny with special adaptations for the escape of the young (as in skates) — see SEA PURSE **2 :** a container (as of cardboard) for marketing eggs
egg cell *n* **:** the female germ cell — contrasted with *sperm cell*
egg cement *or* **egg glue** *n* **:** a secretion by which eggs (as those of many crustaceans) are fastened together or to some object
egg coal *n* **:** anthracite coal of a large size — see ANTHRACITE table
egg cowry *n* **:** a large smooth spindle-shaped cowry (*Amphiperas ovum*) of the Indian and southwest Pacific oceans that is pure white without and deep brown within the shell and is prized by natives of the area for ornament and as a fertility symbol — called also *shuttle shell*
eggcrate \'⸗,⸗\ *adj* **:** having rectangular cells that direct and diffuse light ⟨an ~ ceiling shuts out direct view of fluorescent lamps⟩
eggcup \'⸗,⸗\ *n* **:** a cup made to hold an egg that is to be eaten from the shell
egg dance *n* **:** an old English dance performed by a blindfolded dancer among eggs
eggeater \'⸗,⸗⸗\ *also* **egg-eating snake** \'⸗,⸗⸗-\ *n* **:** a snake living entirely on eggs: as **a :** a small aglyphous snake (*Dasypeltis scaber*) of Africa **b :** a related Indian snake (*Elachistodon westermanni*) — compare DASYPELTIDAE

eggcup

[1]**egger** *var of* EGGAR
[2]**egg·er** \'egə(r), 'āg-\ *n* -S [³*egg* + *-er*] **:** one that collects the eggs of wild birds esp. for gain
egg flat *n* **:** a partition used between layers in egg crates to prevent breakage
eggfruit \'⸗,⸗\ *n* **1 :** any of several edible fruits of plants of the genus *Ponteria*; *esp* **:** CANISTEL **2 :** EGGPLANT
egghead \'⸗,⸗\ *n* **1 :** one with intellectual interests or pretensions **:** INTELLECTUAL ⟨can be considered an ~ himself (he boned up for covering the Korean war by reading Thucydides) —*Newsweek*⟩ **:** HIGHBROW ⟨radio programming so sophisticated that it appeals only to ~*s*⟩ **2 :** a highly educated person ⟨the know-nothing at the expense of the ~ —William Barrett⟩ **:** THEORIST ⟨a kind of McCarthy ~ not because he is liberal . . . but because he is the theoretician —Harvey Breit⟩ ⟨was a creation of the longhairs, the do-gooders, the ~*s* —Malcolm Cowley⟩
egghot \'⸗,⸗\ *n* -S **:** a hot drink consisting of beer and eggs sweetened and seasoned with nutmeg
egging *pres part of* EGG
egg·ler \'eglə(r)\ *n* -S [¹*egg* + *-ler* (as in *higgler, peddler*)] *dial Brit* **:** an egg dealer
egg·less \'egləs, 'āg-\ *adj* **:** lacking or deprived of eggs
egg membrane *n* **:** a membrane enveloping an egg; *esp* **:** VITELLINE MEMBRANE
eggnog \'⸗,⸗\ *n* -S [²*egg* + *nog*] **:** a drink consisting of eggs beaten up with sugar, milk or cream, and often rum, brandy, or other liquor or sometimes a wine usu. served cold and flavored with grated nutmeg
egg nucleus *n* **:** FEMALE PRONUCLEUS
egg parasite *n* **:** any of numerous small hymenopterons that develop within the eggs of other insects
egg picking *n* **:** a game in which two contestants strike boiled Easter eggs together until one egg is cracked
eggplant \'⸗,⸗\ *n* **1 a :** a hairy upright somewhat woody perennial herb (*Solanum melongena*) that is prob. native to southeastern Asia but is widely cultivated in many horticultural varieties usu. as an annual for its edible purple, white, or occas. yellow or striped fruits which are commonly used as a vegetable — called also *aubergine, brinjal, garden egg* **b :** the usu. smooth ovoid fruit of the eggplant **2 :** a variable color averaging a blackish purple that is bluer and stronger than Burgundy (sense 2b) — called also *aubergine*

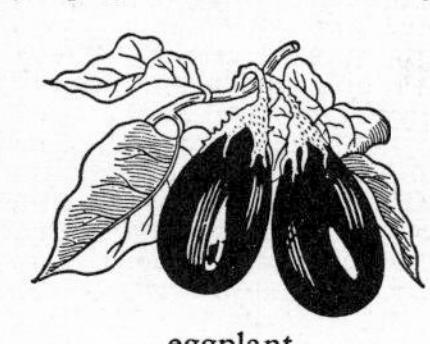
eggplant

egg powder *n* **:** a powder made from dried eggs
egg raft *n* **:** a floating mass of eggs produced by certain fishes and mosquitoes
egg receptor *n* **:** a hypothetical substance in the egg cell that in conjunction with fertilizin and the sperm receptor is held to play a part in the fertilization of the egg
egg roll *n* **:** an egg-dough casing filled with minced vegetables fried in deep fat
egg rolling *n* **1 :** an old European folk custom of rolling eggs down a hill as part of a spring festival **2 :** a frolic for children usu. held during the Easter season
eggs *pres 3d sing of* EGG, *pl of* EGG
egg sac *n* **1 :** EGG CASE 1b **2 :** one of a pair of egg masses that project into the water from the first abdominal segment of certain crustaceans (as most copepods)
eggs-and-bacon \¦⸗⸗'⸗⸗\ *n* -S **:** TOAD FLAX 1
egg sauce *n* **:** any of various sauces containing eggs: as **a :** a sauce made of fish or meat stock and beaten eggs **b :** a drawn butter sauce with beaten egg yolks or minced hard-boiled eggs
eggs ben·e·dict \-'benə,dikt\ *n pl but sing or pl in constr, usu cap B* [prob. fr. the name *Benedict*] **:** poached eggs placed on broiled ham laid on toasted halves of English muffin and topped with hollandaise sauce
[1]**eggshell** \'⸗,⸗\ *n* [ME, fr. *egge* + *shell*] **1 a :** the hard exterior covering of an egg **b :** something resembling an eggshell esp. in fragility ⟨the old carrier was hardly in the ~ class —*Newsweek*⟩ **2** *usu* **egg shell :** any of various smooth somewhat oval gastropod shells of *Ovula* and related genera **3 :** a paper with a relatively rough finish finer than antique and rougher than vellum **4 a :** any of the colors exhibited by the shells of birds' eggs; *esp* **:** those of the hen's egg **b** *of textiles* **:** a variable color averaging a pale yellow that is redder, slightly lighter, and very slightly stronger than ivory and redder and darker than cream
[2]**eggshell** \"\ *adj* **1 :** like an eggshell: **a :** thin and fragile ⟨~ china⟩ ⟨~ porcelain⟩ **b :** having semimat luster ⟨~ paint⟩ ⟨~ enamel⟩ **:** SEMIGLOSS ⟨~ finish⟩ ⟨~ black⟩ **2 :** GENTLE ⟨the helicopter . . . came down to an ~ landing —*Time*⟩
eggshell blue *or* **eggshell green** *n* **:** ROBIN'S-EGG BLUE 2
eggshell nail *n* **:** a thin fingernail turning up at the outer edge seen in some diseases and nutritional disorders
egg timer *n* **:** a small sandglass running about three minutes for timing the boiling of eggs — compare HOURGLASS
egg tooth *n* **:** a hard sharp prominence on the tip of the beak or nose of embryo birds and oviparous reptiles with which they break through the eggshell; *also* **:** an analogous chitinous prominence on the head of an insect
egg tray *n* **:** a usu. square paperboard tray shaped to hold and protect eggs in a shipping case or crate
egg tube *n* **1 :** OVIDUCT **2 :** OVARIOLE
egg urchin *n* **:** a globular thin-shelled sea urchin
egg white *n* **:** the white of an egg (as of a hen or duck) used beaten or unbeaten in cookery ⟨beat an *egg white* until stiff⟩ ⟨separate the *egg whites* from the yolks⟩
egg-white injury *also* **egg-white disease** *n* **:** a vitamin-deficiency disease induced by feeding upon an excess of raw egg white — see AVIDIN, BIOTIN
egis *var of* AEGIS
eg·lan·tine \'eglən,tīn, -tēn\ *n* -S [ME *eglentyn*, fr. MF *aiglent* (fr. — assumed — VL *aculentum*, fr. L *acus* needle, fr. *acer* sharp) + ME *-yn* -ine — more at EDGE] **1 :** SWEETBRIER **2 :** AUSTRIAN BRIER **3 :** DOG ROSE
eg·la·tere \'eglə,ti(ə)r\ *n* -S [ME *eglenter*, fr. MF *eglentier*, *aiglentier*, fr. *aiglent* + *-ier* -er] *archaic* **:** EGLANTINE
eg·le·ston·ite \'egəlztə,nīt, -lst-\ *n* -S [Thomas *Egleston* †1900 Am. mineralogist + E *-ite*] **:** a mineral Hg_4Cl_2O consisting of mercury oxychloride occurring in brownish yellow isometric crystals
eglo·mise *or* **églo·mi·sé** \¦āglō(,)mē¦zā, ¦eg-\ *adj* [F *églomisé*, past part. of *églomiser* to decorate a glass panel by painting on its back, fr. *é-* (fr. L *e-*) + *Glomy*, 18th cent. Fr. decorator + F *-iser* -ize] **:** made of decorative glass on the back of which and showing through is a painted or gilded picture ⟨a mahogany banjo clock with ~ panel⟩
eg·mont buttercup \'eg,mänt-\ *n, usu cap E* [fr. Mt. *Egmont*, New Zealand] **:** a New Zealand crowfoot (*Ranunculus nivicola*) with yellow flowers
ego \'ē(,)gō *sometimes* 'e(- *or* 'ā(-\ *n* -S [NL, fr. L, I — more at I] **1 :** the self esp. as inside one as contrasted with something outside (as another self or the world): as **a** *metaphysical philos* (1) *in Descartes* **:** the soul or an underlying mental or spiritual substance (2) *in Kant* **:** a transcendentally postulated unity either of apperception or of the morally free person — called also *pure ego* (3) *in Fichte* **:** pure self-determining activity positing itself — called also *pure ego* **b** *empirical philos* (1) *in Hume* **:** a complex of ideas or a system of successive mental states (2) *in Kant* **:** the conscious subject of experience (3) **:** the consciousness of an individual's being in distinction from other selves **c :** SELF 3 **2 a :** SELF-ESTEEM ⟨few things are more soothing to a battered ~ than an afternoon's shopping —Ralph Linton⟩ **:** EGOTISM ⟨nice boy . . . not a speck of ~ in him —Clifford Odets⟩ **b :** WILL ⟨Stalin chose Malenkov as the most faithful projection of his own political ~ —*Reporter*⟩ **3** [trans. of G *ich*] *psychoanalysis* **:** the largely conscious part of the personality that is derived from the id through contacts with reality and that mediates the demands of the id, of the superego, and of external everyday reality in the interest of preserving the organism **4** *ethnol* **:** an individual person taken as a point of reference in a particular framework (as a kinship system)
[1]**ego·cen·tric** \¦ēgō¦sen·trik, -gə,-, -trēk *sometimes* ¦eg-\ *adj* [NL *ego* + E *-centric*] **1 :** concerned with the individual person rather than society **:** INDIVIDUALISTIC ⟨this literature reveals two main attitudes, the one, ~ . . . , stresses the horror, waste, and futility of war; the other, ethnocentric, is aware of the comradeship between soldier and soldier —*Canadian Forum*⟩ **2 :** taking the ego as the necessary starting point in philosophy **:** viewed from one's own mind as a center ⟨the new realist revolutionizes philosophic thought by abandoning the ~ position —May Sinclair⟩ **3 a :** limited in outlook or concern to one's own activities or needs or to those of one's group **:** wrapped up in oneself ⟨~ . . . speech shows no concern for the audience —G.A.Miller⟩ ⟨the ~ policy of France . . . bears the germs of a new war —*Nation*⟩ **b :** tending to self-assertion or self-satisfaction **:** SELFISH ⟨~ personalities, lacking in conscience and feeling for others —E.J.Coventry⟩
[2]**egocentric** \"\ *n* -S **:** an egocentric person ⟨~*s* grappling glibly with the world's most ponderous problems —*Saturday Rev.*⟩
ego·cen·tric·i·ty \,⸗⸗(,)sen'trisəd·ē, -,sən-, -ətē, -i\ *n* -ES **:** the quality or state of being egocentric ⟨he sees himself as the hub of the wheel and all of the rest of the people in the world revolve about him and everything leads to him . . . this is the classic formula of ~ —Rudolf Hirschberg⟩
egocentric predicament *n* **:** the epistemological predicament of apparently being unable to get outside one's own mind because all that the knower can know will be what is present to his own mind
ego·cen·trism \,⸗⸗'sen,trizəm\ *n* -S **1 :** EGOCENTRICITY **2 :** the effort to get personal recognition esp. by socially unacceptable behavior **:** psychic overcompensation

egoc·er·us \ē'gäsərəs, ə'-\ [NL, fr. Gk *aigo-, aix* goat + NL *-cerus* — more at AEGIS] *syn of* HIPPOTRAGUS

ego-defense \ˌ≈(ˌ)≈≈ˌ≈, ˌ≈(ˌ)≈'≈ˌ≈\ *n* **:** a psychological mechanism designed consciously or unconsciously to protect one's self-image or self-esteem

ego-expansion \ˌ≈(ˌ)≈≈ˌ≈\ *n* **:** broadening, fulfillment, or realization of the self

ego·hood \'ēgō,hu̇d *sometimes* 'eg- *or* 'äg-\ *n* [NL *ego* + E *-hood*] **:** SELFHOOD

ego ideal *n* **:** the group of positive standards, ideals, goals, and ambitions assimilated from the superego that a person consciously entertains **:** an idealized picture of what one would like to be; *broadly* **:** CONSCIENCE

ego-identity \ˌ≈(ˌ)≈(ˌ)≈ˌ≈≈\ *n* **:** perception of continuity and coherence in one's self-picture and in one's social relations

ego-involve \ˌ≈(ˌ)≈≈ˌ≈\ *vt* **:** to involve (a person) by investing a situation or object with a component that arouses feelings of pride or its opposite **:** MOTIVATE

ego-involvement \ˌ≈(ˌ)≈≈ˌ≈≈\ *n* **:** an involvement of one's self-esteem in the performance of a task or in an object

ego·ism \'ē|gə,wizəm, -(ˌ)gō,iz- *sometimes* 'e|\ *n* -S [F *égoïsme*, fr. NL *egoismus*, fr. L *ego* I + *-ismus* -ism — more at I] **1 a** (1) **:** the philosophic doctrine of some Cartesians and Fichteans that all the elements of knowledge are in the ego and the relations that it implies or provides for (2) **:** SOLIPSISM **b :** the philosophic doctrine (as that held by Fichte) that identifies ultimate reality with an absolute ego **2 a :** the ethical doctrine that individual self-interest is the actual motive of all conscious action — called also *psychological egoism* **b :** the ethical doctrine that individual self-interest is the valid end of all action — called also *ethical egoism;* compare ALTRUISM **3** [by alter.] **:** EGOTISM **4 :** excessive libidinization of the ego — compare NARCISSISM **syn** see CONCEIT

ego·ist \|gəwəst, |(ˌ)gō≈\ *n* -S [F *égoïste*, fr. L *ego* I + F *-iste* -ist] **1 :** a believer in egoism ⟨the psychological ~'s view that every voluntary action is determinately motivated by the agent's desire to benefit himself —C.A.Baylis⟩ **2 :** a person who is egocentric or egotistic ⟨to a selfish or proud man, triumph is pleasant and defeat painful, but to an ~, both are equally interesting, for what matters is not the content of the experience but the fact that it is his —W.H.Auden⟩

ego·is·tic \ˌ≈gə¦wistik, -gō¦is-, -tēk\ *also* **ego·is·ti·cal** \-təkəl, -tēk-\ *adj* **1 :** EGOCENTRIC, EGOTISTIC **2 :** of or relating to the ego or egoism ⟨the interior ~ relations of a single subject —James Martineau⟩ ⟨an ~ interpretation of social behavior, a denial of the existence of altruistic conduct —F.W. Znaniecki⟩ — **ego·is·ti·cal·ly** \-tək(ə)lē, -tēk-, -li\ *adv*

egoistic hedonism *n* **:** the ethical theory that the valid aim of right conduct is one's own happiness — contrasted with *universalistic hedonism*

ego·ity \ē'gōəd·ē, e'-,ə'-\ *n* -ES [NL *ego* + E *-ity*] **1 :** SELFHOOD **2 :** EGO 1a(3)

ego-libido \ˌ≈(ˌ)≈≈ˌ≈(ˌ)≈\ *n* **:** the part of the libido attached to the self — compare OBJECT LIBIDO

ego·ma·nia \ˌēgō'mānēə, -gə-, -nyə *sometimes* ˌeg-\ *n* [NL, fr. *ego* + *-mania*] **:** extreme egocentricity **:** abnormally developed egotism ⟨religious individualism degenerating into egoism and producing even ~ —W.B.Selbie⟩

ego·ma·ni·ac \-nē,ak\ *n* [*ego* + *maniac*] **:** one characterized by egomania ⟨~*s* of incredible selfishness and utter callousness —*Atlantic*⟩ — **ego·ma·ni·a·cal** \ˌ≈≈mə'nīəkəl\ *adj*

ego-oriented \ˌ≈(ˌ)≈ˌ≈≈ˌ≈\ *adj* **:** arousing ego-involvement

egoph·o·ny *also* **ae·goph·o·ny** \ē'gäfənē\ *n* -ES [ISV *ego-* (fr. Gk *aig-, aix* goat) + *-phony* — more at AEGIS] **:** a modification of the voice resembling bleating heard on auscultation of the chest in certain diseases (as in pleurisy with effusion)

ego psychology *n* **:** the study of the ego esp. with regard to mechanisms of defense, transference, reality-testing, and attainment of the ego ideal

egos *pl of* EGO

ego-satisfaction \ˌ≈(ˌ)≈ˌ≈≈ˌ≈\ *n* **:** SELF-SATISFACTION

ego-syntonic \ˌē(ˌ)gō *sometimes* ¦e(- *or* ¦ä(-+\ *adj* **:** compatible with or acceptable to the ego ⟨the *ego-syntonic* profanity of a Rabelais —George Devereux⟩

ego·tism \'ēgə|,tizəm, -gō| *sometimes* 'eg-\ *n* -S [L *ego* I + E *-tism* (as in *idiotism*) — more at I] **1 a :** the practice of speaking or writing of oneself esp. in excess **:** BOASTFULNESS; *specif* **:** the frequent use of the words *I, my,* and *me* ⟨banish the ~ out of your conversation —Earl of Chesterfield⟩ **b :** a sense of self-importance **:** SELF-CENTEREDNESS, SELFISHNESS **2 :** a sense of superiority often accompanied by contempt toward others **:** PRIDE ⟨this ~, this arrogance, this complete indifference to what the rest of the world thinks of him —James Stern⟩ **3** [by alter.] **:** EGOISM 1a **syn** see CONCEIT

ego·tist \|ˌtəst, |d·ə-\ *n* -S **:** one characterized by egotism **:** one marked by boastfulness or arrogance or egocentricity ⟨an atrocious ~ in his disregard of others —G.B.Shaw⟩ — **ego·tis·tic** \ˌ≈gə¦tistik, -gō¦-\ *or* **ego·tis·ti·cal** \-stəkəl, -tēk-\ *adj* — **ego·tis·ti·cal·ly** \-stək(ə)lē, -stēk-, -li\ *adv*

ego·tize \'≈gə,tīz, -gō-\ *vi* -ED/-ING/-S **:** to refer unduly to oneself

egre·gious \ə'grējəs, ē'- *sometimes* -jēəs\ *adj* [L *egregius*, fr. *e* out of (fr. *ex*) + *greg-, grex* flock, herd — more at EX-, GREGARIOUS] **1** *archaic* **:** remarkable for good quality **:** DISTINGUISHED, STRIKING **2 :** conspicuous for bad quality or taste **:** NOTORIOUS ⟨the ~ epicure who condescended to take only one bite out of the sunny side of a peach —J.G.Lockhart⟩ ⟨a bilious combination of brummagem melodrama and synthetic seascapes . . . the picture is ~ —John McCarten⟩ **3 a :** EXTRAORDINARY, EXTREME ⟨a published story which seemed too ~ to be believed —*Economist*⟩ **b :** FLAGRANT ⟨~ errors⟩ ⟨some Germans, conditioned by experience to ~ behavior on the part of their rulers —E.J.Kahn⟩ **4 :** ASOCIAL ⟨it is rather a gregarious instinct to keep together by minding each other's business . . . we must be preserved from becoming ~ —Robert Frost⟩ — **egre·gious·ly** *adv* — **egre·gious·ness** *n* -ES

[1]**egress** \'ē,gres\ *n* -ES [L *egressus*, fr. *egressus*, past part. of *egredi* to go out, come out, fr. *e-* + *-gredi* (fr. *gradi* to step, go) — more at GRADE] **1 :** the act or right of going or coming out (as from a place of confinement) ⟨provided that reasonable means of ingress and ~ be allowed to the livestock —*Farmer's Weekly (So. Africa)*⟩; *specif* **:** the emergence of a celestial object from eclipse, occultation, or transit **2 :** a place or means of going out **:** EXIT, OUTLET ⟨a small room whose only ~ . . . was . . . a mammoth rat hole —A.Gene M. Cleaveland⟩

[2]**egress** \(')ē¦gres\ *vi* -ED/-ING/-ES [L *egressus*, past part.] **:** to go out **:** ISSUE

egres·sion \ē'greshən\ *n* -S [ME *egressioun*, fr. L *egression-, egressio* act of going out, fr. *egressus* (past part.) + *-ion-, -io* -ion] **1 :** an act of emergence or emigration **2** *obs* **:** OUTBURST

egres·sive \-esiv\ *adj* [L *egressus*, past part. + E *-ive*] **:** of or relating to egress **:** OUTGOING

egret \'ēgrə|t, ē'gre|, 'egrə| *also* 'ē,gre| *or* ə'gre|, *usu* |d·+V\ *n* -S [ME, fr. MF *aigrette*, fr. OProv *aigreta*, of Gmc origin; akin to OHG *heigaro* heron — more at HERON] **1 :** any of various herons that bear long plumes on the lower back during the breeding season and commonly have pure white plumage — see AMERICAN EGRET, CATTLE EGRET, SNOWY EGRET **2 :** an egret plume or a plume resembling it **:** AIGRETTE

egret monkey *n* [F *aigrette;* fr. the tuft on top of its head] **:** an East Indian macaque (*Macaca cynomolga*)

egual·men·te \āgwäl'mān·tā\ *adv* [It, equally, even, adv. of *eguale* equal, even, fr. L *aequalis* equal — more at EQUAL] **:** EVENLY — used as a direction in music

eguei·ite \e'gwā,īt\ *n* -S [F *egueïite*, fr. *Egueï* region, Chad territory, French Equatorial Africa + F *-ite*] **:** a mineral that consists of a hydrous basic ferric iron phosphate with a little calcium and aluminum and that occurs in nodules in clay

egypt \'ējəpt\ *adj, usu cap* [fr. *Egypt*, country in northeastern Africa] **:** of or from Egypt **:** of the kind or style prevalent in Egypt **:** EGYPTIAN

egyp·ti·ac \ə'jiptē,ak, (')ē¦j-\ *adj, usu cap* [L *Aegyptiacus*, fr. Gk *Aigyptiakos*, fr. *Aigyptos* Egypt] **:** of or relating to ancient Egypt ⟨*Egyptiac* society . . . became extinct in the 5th century of the Christian era —A.J.Toynbee⟩

[1]**egyp·tian** \-pshən\ *adj, usu cap* [ME *Egipcian*, fr. OF *egipcien*, adj. & n., fr. *Egipte* Egypt (fr. L *Aegyptus*, fr. Gk *Aigyptos*) + OF *-ien* -ian] **1 :** of or relating to Egypt, the Egyptians, or the Egyptian language ⟨*Egyptian* architecture⟩ ⟨*Egyptian* conquest⟩ **2** [fr. the reference in Exod 10:22 to a plague of darkness visited upon Egypt] **:** EXTREME, INTENSE — usu. used in the phrase *Egyptian darkness*

[2]**egyptian** \"\ *n* -S *cap* [ME *Egipcien, Egipcian*, fr. MF *egipcien*] **1 :** a native or inhabitant of Egypt **2 :** the Afro-Asiatic language of the ancient Egyptians from earliest times to about the 3d century A.D. — compare COPTIC, DEMOTIC EGYPTIAN, MIDDLE EGYPTIAN, NEW EGYPTIAN, OLD EGYPTIAN; see AFRO-ASIATIC LANGUAGES table **3 :** the ancient Egyptian system of writing in any of its forms — see DEMOTIC, HIERATIC, HIEROGLYPHIC **4** *obs* **:** GYPSY **5** [so called fr. the fact that Cairo is a principal city] **:** a native or inhabitant of southern Illinois — used as a nickname **6** *often not cap* **:** a heavy typeface having little contrast between thick and thin strokes and thick squared serifs

egyptian alfalfa weevil *n, usu cap E* **:** an Old World weevil (*Hypera brunneipennis*) related to the alfalfa weevil and established in western No. America where it feeds on alfalfa and various clovers

egyptian architecture *n, usu cap E* **:** the architecture of ancient Egypt from approximately 5000 B.C. to early Christian times — see ARCHITECTURE table

egyptian bean *n, usu cap E* **1 a :** INDIAN LOTUS **b :** the seed of the Indian lotus resembling a bean **2 :** HYACINTH BEAN

egyptian black *n, usu cap E* **:** BASALT 2

egyptian blue *n, usu cap E* **:** a blue silicate of copper and calcium used as a pigment by the ancient Egyptians and Romans

egyptian clover *n, usu cap E* **:** BERSEEM

egyptian corn *n, usu cap E* **:** SORGHUM; *esp* **:** DURRA

egyptian cotton *n, usu cap E* **:** a fine long-staple often somewhat brownish cotton grown chiefly in Egypt and believed to be a derivative of sea island cotton from which it is distinguished by shorter fiber length or of Peruvian cotton or possibly a hybrid between these or between one of these and unknown African cottons — see PIMA

egyptian cross *n, usu cap E* **:** TAU CROSS 1

egyptian ginger *n, usu cap E* **:** the root of the taro

egyptian goose *n, usu cap E* **:** a brightly colored bird (*Alopochen aegypticus*) of Africa and Palestine that is related to the sheldrakes but popularly regarded as a true goose and is often bred as an ornamental waterfowl

egyptian grass *n, usu cap E* **1 :** a creeping grass (*Dactyloctenium aegypticum*) with spikes like fingers — called also *crab grass, crowfoot grass* **2 :** JOHNSON GRASS

egyptian green *n, often cap E* **:** a moderate green that is yellower, lighter, and stronger than sea green (sense 1a) and bluer, lighter, and stronger than myrtle green (sense 3a) or average laurel green (sense 1)

egyptian gum *n, usu cap E* **:** GUM ARABIC

egyptian hallel *n, usu cap E&H* **:** HALLEL

egyptian henbane *n, usu cap E* **:** the leaves of an herb (*Hyoscyamus muticus*) used as a source of hyoscyamine

egyptian henna *n, usu cap E* **:** HENNA 1

egyptian indigo *n, usu cap E* **1 :** an indigo yielded by a shrub (*Tephrosia apolinea*) of southern Europe **2 :** the shrub that yields Egyptian indigo

egyp·tian·ism \-shə,nizəm\ *n* -S *usu cap* **:** a quality or group of qualities characteristic of Egypt, its people, or its language

egyp·tian·i·za·tion \≈ˌ≈shənə'zāshən, -ˌnī'z-\ *n* -S *usu cap* **:** the act or process of Egyptianizing or the state of being Egyptianized ⟨decreed the *Egyptianization* of British and French banks —*Newsweek*⟩

egyp·tian·ize \≈'≈≈ˌnīz\ *vt* -ED/-ING/-S *usu cap* [*Egyptian* + *-ize*] **:** to make Egyptian (as in quality, traits, or ownership)

egyptian jackal *n, usu cap E* **:** a large wild dog (*Canis anthus lupaster* or *C. lupaster*) of northern Africa that resembles a wolf in size and proportions

egyptian lotus *n, usu cap E* **1 :** either of two water lilies held sacred by the Egyptians: **a :** a white lily (*Nymphaea lotus*) **b :** a blue lily (*N. caerulea*) **2 :** INDIAN LOTUS

egyptian lupine *n, usu cap E* **:** an erect hairy annual legume (*Lupinus termis*) orig. of the eastern Mediterranean but introduced into certain dry regions of the U.S. that has white flowers tinged with blue on the standard and bluish green on the keel apex

egyptian millet *n, usu cap E* **:** JOHNSON GRASS

egyptian onion *n, usu cap E* **:** TREE ONION

egyptian ophthalmia *n, usu cap E* **:** TRACHOMA

egyptian privet *n, usu cap E* **:** HENNA 1

egyptian red *n, often cap E* **:** a dark red to strong reddish brown

egyptian soaproot *n, usu cap E* **:** a European herb (*Gypsophila struthium*) having a 5-angled inflated calyx

egyptian thorn *n, usu cap E* **:** BABUL 1a — used esp. of the tree as it occurs in the Sudan where it is a source of high-grade gum arabic; compare AMRAD GUM

egyptian vulture *n, usu cap E* **:** a small vulture (*Neophron percnopterus*) with largely white plumage that is widely distributed over much of Africa, southern Europe, and southern Asia — called also *Pharaoh's chicken*

egyptian wheat *n, usu cap E* **1 :** any of certain bearded branching wheats cultivated since ancient times **2 :** PEARL MILLET **3 :** a grain sorghum resembling kafir corn

egyp·tic·i·ty \(ˌ)ē,jip'tisəd·ē, ˌējəp-, ə,jip-\ *n* -ES *usu cap* [*Egypt* + E *-icity* (as in *eccentricity*)] **:** EGYPTIANISM

egypt·ize \'ējəp,tīz, ē'jip-\ *vi* -ED/-ING/-S *often cap* [*Egypt* + E *-ize*] **:** to become Egyptian (as in quality or traits)

egypto- *comb form, cap* [prob. fr. F *égypto-*, fr. Gk *aigypto-*, fr. *Aigyptos* Egypt] **1 :** Egypt ⟨*Egyptology*⟩ **2 :** Egyptian and ⟨*Egypto*-Arabic⟩ ⟨*Egypto*-Greek⟩

egyp·to·log·i·cal \(ˌ)ē¦jiptə¦läjəkəl, ə¦jip-, ¦ējəp-, -ˌläj-, -ējək-\ *adj, usu cap* **:** of or relating to Egyptology ⟨~ studies⟩

egyp·tol·o·gist \(ˌ)ē,jip'täləjəst, ə,jip-, ˌējəp-\ *n* -S *usu cap* **:** a specialist in Egyptology

egyp·tol·o·gy \-ləjē, -ji\ *n* -ES *usu cap* [*Egypto* + *-logy*] **:** the study of Egyptian antiquities

eh \'(h)ā(ⁿ), '(h)ai(ⁿ), '(h)e(e)(ⁿ)(ᵊ), '(h)a(a)(ⁿ)(ᵊ), '(h)ä(ä)(ⁿ)(ᵊ), *all with interrogatory intonation*\ *interj* [ME *ey*] — used to invite confirmation or to express inquiry or slight surprise

Eh \(')ē¦āch\ *symbol* standard oxidation-reduction potential

ehat·i·saht \ā'hädə,sät\ *n, pl* **ehatisaht** *or* **ehatisahts** *usu cap* **1 :** an Indian people of Vancouver Island **2 :** a member of the Ehatisaht people

EHF *abbr, often not cap* extremely high frequency

EHP *abbr* **1** effective horsepower **2** electric horsepower

eh·re·tia \e'rēsh(ē)ə\ *n* [NL, fr. George D. *Ehret* †1770 Ger. botanical illustrator + NL *-ia*] **1** *cap* **:** a large genus (family Boraginaceae) of tropical or subtropical shrubs and trees having cymose usu. white flowers succeeded by fleshy drupes **2** -S **:** any plant of the genus *Ehretia*

eh·rings·dorf man \'eriŋz,dȯrf-, 'ār-\ *n, usu cap E* [fr. *Ehringsdorf*, village near Weimar, Germany] **:** an early Neanderthal man known from skeletal remains found associated with Acheulean and pre-Mousterian artifacts near Weimar

ehr·lich's 606 \'erlik(s)¦sik(ˌ)sō'siks, 'ār-, -li̲k(-\ *n, usu cap E* [after Paul *Ehrlich* †1915 Ger. bacteriologist] **:** ARSPHENAMINE

EHT *abbr* extra high tension

ehu·a·wa \ˌā(ˌ)hü'äwə\ *n* -S [Hawaiian] **:** a sedge (*Cyperus laevigatus*) cultivated as a fiber plant in Hawaii

-ei *pl of* -EUS

EI *abbr* **1** endorsement irregular **2** extra-illustrated

eich·hor·nia \ī'kȯrnēə, īk'hȯ-\ *n, cap* [NL, fr. Johann A. F. *Eichhorn* †1856 Prussian official + NL *-ia*] **:** a genus of chiefly tropical floating aquatic herbs (family Pontederiaceae) having rounded or broad clustered leaves with inflated petioles — see WATER HYACINTH

eicosa- *or* **eicos-** *comb form* [ISV, fr. Gk *eikosa-, eikos-* twenty, fr. *eikosi* — more at VICENARY] **:** containing 20 atoms (as of carbon) ⟨*eicosane*⟩

ei·co·sane \'īkə,sān\ *n* -S [ISV *eicosa-* + *-ane*] **:** any of the isomeric hydrocarbons $C_{20}H_{42}$ of the methane series; *esp* **:** normal eicosane $CH_3(CH_2)_{18}CH_3$ obtained as a colorless solid from paraffin wax

ei·co·sa·no·ic acid \ˌīkəsə¦nōik-\ *n* [ISV *eicosane* + *-o-* + *-ic*] **:** ARACHIDIC ACID

eid- *or* **eido-** *comb form* [Gk, form, fr. *eidos* — more at IDOL] **:** image **:** figure ⟨*eido*ptometry⟩

eide *pl of* EIDOS

ei·dent \'īdᵊnt\ *adj* [ME (northern dial.) *ithen, ithand*, fr. ON *ithinn, īthen*, fr. *ith, īth* work, activity; akin to OE *īdig* busy] *chiefly Scot* **:** diligent and conscientious **:** HARD-WORKING ⟨~ in Scotland's cause⟩ — **ei·dent·ly** *adv*

ei·der \'īdə(r)\ *n* -S [D, G, or Sw, fr. Icel *æthur*, fr. ON *æthr;* akin to Sw dial. *åd, åda* eider duck] **1** *or* **eider duck :** any of several large northern sea ducks constituting *Somateria* and related genera and being distinguished by the profuse fine soft down that forms an insulating layer protecting the body from cold, that is used by the female for lining the nest, and that is eagerly sought by man resulting in near extinction of the birds in some areas **2 :** EIDERDOWN 1

eiderdown \'≈≈,≈\ *n* [prob. fr. G *eiderdaune*, fr. Icel *æthardūnn*, fr. *æthar* (gen. of *æthur*) + *dūnn* down, fr. ON — more at DOWN] **1 :** the down of the eider valued for its lightness, softness, resiliency, and warmth **2 :** a quilt or comforter; *esp* **:** one filled with eiderdown **3 :** a soft lightweight clothing fabric knitted or woven of wool, cotton, or man-made fibers and napped on one or both sides

[1]**ei·det·ic** \(')ī¦ded·ik\ *adj* [Gk *eidētikos*, fr. *eidos* + *-ētikos* -etic] **1 a :** of, relating to, or having the characteristics of eide, essences, forms, or images **b :** INTUITIONIST ⟨phenomenology . . . attempts the construction of a priori sciences on the basis of concrete intuition — pure grammar, pure logic, pure law, the ~ science of the world intuitively apprehended —Maurice Natanson⟩ **2 :** of or relating to voluntarily producible visual images having almost photographic accuracy **:** VIVID, LIFELIKE ⟨perhaps the artists have a greater ~ power than most adults —Franz Boas⟩ — **ei·det·i·cal·ly** \ed·ək(ə)lē\ *adv*

[2]**eidetic** \"\ *n* -S **:** one that experiences eidetic images

eidolo- — see IDOLO-

ei·do·lon \ī'dōlən\ *n, pl* **eidolons** \-lənz\ *or* **eido·la** \-lə\ [Gk *eidōlon* phantom, image, idol — more at IDOL] **1 :** an unsubstantial image ⟨free from her troubles among the ~s of sleep —J.C.Powys⟩ **:** PHANTOM **2 a :** an ideal figure ⟨he had created in the Boss an ~ a half century before this machine-age man became triumphant in history —H.S.Canby⟩ or idealized person ⟨Lincoln . . . the ~ of democracy —G.W. Johnson⟩ **:** EXEMPLAR **b :** IDEAL ⟨psychiatry's ~ of the personality completely . . . at home in the world —Bernard DeVoto⟩ **3 :** a small winged figure human or combining human with animal elements found in Greek vase painting

ei·dos \'ī,däs, 'ā,-\ *n, pl* **ei·de** \'ī,dē, 'ā,dā\ [Gk, lit., shape, form — more at IDOL] **1 :** something that is seen or intuited: **a** *in Platonism* **:** IDEA **b** *in Aristotelianism* (1) **:** FORM, ESSENCE (2) **:** SPECIES **c :** an appearance, conception, or form of intuition **2 :** the cognitive part of cultural structure made up of the criteria of credibility, the logic used in thinking and acting, and the basic ideas by which the members of a culture organize and interpret experience **:** logical structure ⟨the ~ is visible wherever group behavior is characterized by intellectual efforts of a similar kind —S.F.Nadel⟩ — contrasted with *ethos*

ei·fe·li·an \(')ī¦fēlēən\ *adj, usu cap* [*Eifel*, region in western Germany + E *-ian*] **:** of, relating to, or constituting a subdivision of the European Devonian — see GEOLOGIC TIME table

ei·gen-frequency \'īgən+,-\ *n* [part trans. of G *eigenfrequenz*, fr. *eigen-* peculiar to, characteristic (fr. *eigen* own, fr. OHG *eigan*) + *frequenz* frequency — more at OWN] **:** one of the frequencies with which a given oscillatory system is capable of vibrating

ei·gen-function \"+,-\ *n* [part trans. of G *eigenfunktion*, fr. *eigen-* + *funktion* function] **:** the solution of a differential equation (as the Schrödinger wave equation) satisfying specified conditions

ei·gen·state \"+,-\ *n* [part trans. of G *eigenstand*, fr. *eigen-* + *stand* state, condition] **:** a state of a quantized dynamic system (as an atom, molecule, or crystal) in which one of the variables defining the state (as energy or angular momentum) has a determinate fixed value

ei·gen·tone \"+,-\ *n* [part. trans. of G *eigenton*, fr. *eigen-* + *ton* tone] **:** a tone or one of several tones produced by and characteristic of a vibrating body or system

ei·gen·value \"+,-\ *n* [part trans. of G *eigenwert*, fr. *eigen-* + *wert* value] **:** any of the permissible values of a parameter in an eigenfunction (as the discrete values of the energy in the solution of the Schrödinger wave equation)

[1]**eight** \'āt, *usu* 'ād·+V\ *adj* [ME *eighte*, fr. OE *eahta;* akin to OHG *ahto* eight, ON *ātta*, Goth *ahtau*, L *octo*, Gk *oktō*, Skt *aṣṭā*] **:** being one more than seven in number ⟨~ years⟩ — see NUMBER table

[2]**eight** \"\ *pron, pl in constr* [ME *eighte*, fr. OE *eahte*, fr. *eahta*, adj.] **:** eight countable persons or things not specified but under consideration and being enumerated ⟨~ are here⟩

[3]**eight** \"\ *n* -S [ME *eighte*, fr. *eighte*, adj. & pron.] **1 :** twice four **:** four times two **:** the cube of two **2 a :** eight units or objects ⟨a total of ~⟩ **b :** a group or set of eight ⟨arranged by ~*s*⟩ **3 a :** the numerable quantity symbolized by the arabic numeral 8 **b :** the figure 8 **4 :** eight o'clock — compare BELL table, TIME illustration **5 :** the eighth in a set or series: as **a :** a playing card marked to show that it is eighth in a suit **b :** an article of clothing of the eighth size ⟨wears an ~⟩ **6 :** FIGURE EIGHT e **7 :** something having as an essential feature eight units or members: as **a :** an octosyllabic usu. iambic line of verse — usu. used in pl. ⟨a poem in ~*s*⟩ **b eights** *pl* **:** OCTAVO ⟨a book printed in ~*s*⟩ **c** (1) **:** an 8-oared racing boat (2) **:** the crew of such a boat **d :** an 8-cylinder engine or automobile **8 eights** *pl but sing in constr* **:** a game in which each successive player must play a card either of the same suit or of the same rank as that played by the preceding player or may play an eight and call for any suit and in which the object is to get rid of all one's cards first — called also *crazy eights*

eight ball *n* **1 :** a black pool ball numbered 8 **2 :** a game of pool played with a cue ball and 15 object balls in which a player or side must pocket either the balls numbered from one to seven or nine to 15 and in which the winner is the player or side that first pockets its numerical group and then legally pockets the eight ball **3 :** a round black nondirectional microphone **4** *slang* **:** NEGRO — usu. used disparagingly **5** *slang* **:** a soldier often in trouble **:** MISFIT, SAD SACK ⟨for . . . a chronic *eight ball* in perpetual flight from life, going AWOL is an easy decision —Taliaferro Boatwright⟩ — **behind the eight ball :** in a highly disadvantageous position or baffling situation ⟨finds himself *behind the eight ball*, unable to buy the things his family needs —Philip Murray †1952⟩

[1]**eigh·teen** \(')ā(t)¦tēn *sometimes* (')ād·¦ēn *adj* [ME *eightetene, eightene*, fr. OE *eahtatīene, eahtatȳne, eahtatēne* (akin to OHG *ahtozehan* eighteen, ON *ātjān, ātjān*), fr. *eahta* eight + *-tīene, -tȳne, -tēne* (fr. *tīen, tȳn, tēn* ten) — more at EIGHT, TEN] **:** being one more than 17 in number ⟨~ years⟩ — see NUMBER table; used prepositively to designate certain years of the 19th century ⟨the *eighteen*-eighties⟩ ⟨the early *eighteen*-hundreds⟩

[2]**eighteen** \"\ *pron, pl in constr* [ME *eightetene, eightene*, fr. OE *eahtatīene, eahtatȳne, eahtatēne, eahtatȳne*, fr. *eahtatēne*, adj.] **:** 18 countable persons or things not specified but under consideration and being enumerated ⟨~ are here⟩

[3]**eighteen** \"\ *n* -S **1 :** 10 and eight **:** twice nine **:** nine times two **:** three times six **2 a :** 18 units or objects ⟨a total of ~⟩ **b :** a group or set of 18 **3 :** the numerable quantity symbolized by the arabic numerals 18 **4 :** the 18th in a set or series; *esp* **:** an article of clothing of the 18th size ⟨wears an ~⟩ **5 :** EIGHTEENMO — usu. used in pl. ⟨a book printed in ~*s*⟩ **6 :** something having as an essential feature 18 units or members

eigh·teen·mo \≈'≈,mō\ *n* -S [*eighteen* + *-mo* (as in *duodecimo*)] **:** the size of a piece of paper cut 18 from a sheet; *also* **:** paper or a page of this size — abbr. *18mo;* symbol *18°;* see BOOK tables

eighteen-one balkline *n* **:** a carom billiards game in which balklines are 18 inches from the cushions and a player may score only one point when balls are in balk — usu. written *18.1 balkline;* compare EIGHTEEN-TWO BALKLINE

[1]**eigh·teenth** \(')ā(t)¦tēn(t)th *sometimes* (')ād·¦ē-\ *adj* [ME *eightetenthe, eightenthe*, adj. & n., alter. (influenced by *eightetene, eightene*) of *eightetethe, eightethe*, fr. OE *eahtatēotha, eahtēotha* (akin to ON *āttjāndi, ātjāndi* eighteenth), fr. *eahtatiene, eahtatȳne, eahtatēne* eighteen + *-otha, -tha* -th] **1 :** being number 18 in a countable series ⟨the ~ day⟩ — see NUMBER table **2 :** being one of 18 equal parts into which something is divisible ⟨an ~ share of the money⟩

[2]**eighteenth** \"\ *n, pl* **eighteenths** \-n(t)s,-n(t)ths\ [ME *eightetenthe, eightenthe*] **1 :** number 18 in a countable series

⟨the ~ of the month⟩ **2 :** the quotient of a unit divided by 18 **:** one of 18 equal parts of something ⟨one ~ of the total⟩
eighteen-two balkline *n* **:** a carom billiards game in which the balklines are 18 inches from the cushions and a player may score two points when the balls are in balk — usu. written *18.2 balkline;* compare EIGHTEEN-ONE BALKLINE
eight·er from de·ca·tur \ˈād·ə(r)f(r)əmdəˈkād·ə(r), -mdēˈk-\ *usu cap D* [rhyming slang: *Decatur* prob. fr. *Decatur*, Ill.] *slang* **:** the throw of eight in craps
eightfoil \ˈ=,=\ *n* **:** DOUBLE QUATREFOIL
¹eight·fold \ˈāt¦fōld\ *adj* [ME *eightefold*, fr. OE *eahtafeald*, fr. *eahta* eight + *-feald* -fold] **1 :** having eight parts or aspects **2 :** being eight times as large, as great, or as many as some understood size, degree, or amount ⟨an ~ increase⟩
²eightfold \"\ *adv* **:** to eight times as much or as many **:** by eight times ⟨increased ~⟩
eightfold path *n, usu cap E & P* **:** the Buddhist teaching of the means of attaining Nirvana through rightness of belief, resolve, speech, action, livelihood, effort, thought, and meditation — see FOUR NOBLE TRUTHS
eight-foot octave *n* **:** GREAT OCTAVE
eight-foot pitch *n* **:** the pitch of an 8-foot stop on a pipe organ
eight-foot stop *n* **:** a pipe-organ stop sounding the pitches indicated by the notes, the lowest pipe of such a stop being approximately eight feet in length — compare FOUR-FOOT STOP, SIXTEEN-FOOT STOP
eight-four \ˈ=¦=\ *adj* **:** of or relating to a plan of school organization with eight elementary and four secondary grades — compare SIX-THREE-THREE
eight-gauge \ˈ=¦=\ *adj, of a shotgun* **:** having a bore 0.835 inch in diameter
¹eighth \ˈātth, ÷ˈāth\ *adj* [ME *eightethe, eighthe*, adj. & n., fr. OE *eahtotha* (akin to OHG *ahtodo* eighth, ON *āttandi*, Goth *ahtudin*, dat. sing. masc.) fr. *eahta* eight + *-otha, -tha* -th — more at EIGHT] **1 :** being number eight in a countable series ⟨the ~ day⟩ — see NUMBER table **2 :** being one of eight equal parts into which something is divisible ⟨an ~ share of the money⟩
²eighth \"\ *n, pl* **eighths** \ˈāts, ˈātths, ÷ˈāths\ [ME *eightethe, eighthe*] **1 :** number eight in a countable series ⟨the ~ of the month⟩ **2 :** the quotient of a unit divided by eight **:** one of eight equal parts of something ⟨one ~ of the total⟩ **3 a :** OCTAVE **b :** EIGHTH NOTE
³eighth \"\ *adv* **1 :** in the eighth place **2 :** with seven exceptions ⟨the nation's ~ largest city⟩
eighth cranial nerve *or* **eighth nerve** *n* **:** AUDITORY NERVE
eighth·ly \ˈātthlē, -li, ÷ˈāth-\ *adv* **:** in the eighth place ⟨the search is . . . , ~, a search for ideals —R.G.F.Robinson⟩
eighth note *n* **:** a musical note with the time value of one eighth of a whole note — called also *quaver*
eight-hour law *n* **:** a law fixing the working day for specified employments at eight hours frequently coupled with a provision for time and one-half compensation for hours worked after eight hours

eighth notes

eighth pole *n* **:** the furlong pole on a racetrack that is ⅛ of a mile from the finish
eighth rest *n* **:** a musical rest corresponding in value to an eighth note
¹eight·i·eth \ˈād·ēəth, ˈāt¦, ¦iəth\ *adj* [ME *eightetithe, eightithe*, adj. & n., fr. OE *hundeahtatigotha*, fr. *hundeahtatig* eighty + *-otha -tha* -th — more at EIGHTY] **1 :** being number 80 in a countable series ⟨the ~ day⟩ — see NUMBER table **2 :** being one of 80 equal parts into which something is divisible ⟨an ~ share of the money⟩
²eightieth \"\ *n* -s [ME *eightetithe, eightithe*] **1 :** number 80 in a countable series **2 :** the quotient of a unit divided by 80 **:** one of 80 equal parts of something ⟨one ~ of the total⟩
eight·ling \ˈātliŋ\ *n* -s **:** a compound or twin crystal made up of eight individuals
eight·pen·ny nail \ˈāt,penē-, -ni-\ *n* [so called fr. the former price per hundred nails] **:** a nail typically 2½ inches long
eight-pointed cross \ˈ=,==-\ *n* **:** MALTESE CROSS 1b
eights *pl of* EIGHT
eight·some \ˈātsəm\ *n* -s *often attrib* [¹*eight* + *-some*] **:** a Scottish reel for eight dancers
eight-spotted forester \ˈ=,==-\ *n* **:** a familiar day-flying moth (*Alypia octomaculata*) of the eastern U.S. that is black with eight conspicuous pale spots on the wings and has humped and transversely striped larvae which often defoliate ornamental vines and grapevines
eight-square \ˈ=¦=\ *adj* **:** OCTAGONAL ⟨an *eight-square* rifle barrel⟩
¹eighty \ˈād·ē, ˈāt¦, ¦i\ *adj* [ME *eightety, eighty*, fr. OE *eahtatig*, short for *hundeahtatig*, fr. *hundeahtatig*, n., group of 80, fr. *hund* hundred + *eahta* eight + *-tig* group of ten; akin to OHG *-zug* group of ten, ON *tigr*, Goth *-tigjus;* all derivatives fr. the root of OE *tien, tȳn, tēn* ten — more at HUNDRED, EIGHT, TEN] **:** being one more than 79 in number ⟨~ years⟩ — see NUMBER table
²eighty \"\ *pron, pl in constr* [ME *eightety, eighty*, fr. *eightety eighty* adj.] **:** 80 countable persons or things not specified but under consideration and being enumerated ⟨~ are here⟩ ⟨~ were found⟩
³eighty \"\ *n* -ES **1 :** eight tens **:** twice 40 **:** five times 16 **:** four twenties **:** FOURSCORE **2 a :** 80 units or objects ⟨a total of ~⟩ **b :** a group or set of 80 **3 :** the numerable quantity symbolized by the arabic numerals 80 **4 :** the 80th in a set or series **5 :** something having as an essential feature 80 units or members **6 :** an 80-acre tract of land **7 eighties** *pl* **a :** the numbers 80 to 89 inclusive ⟨a golf score in the *eighties*⟩ ⟨all his grades in that subject are in the *eighties*⟩ **b :** the members of a series or set of successive numbers that end in 80 to 89 inclusive ⟨the *eighties* of the preceding century⟩ ⟨lives in the *eighties* in the next block⟩ **c :** the portion of a continuum lying between 80 and 90 on a scale of measurement or segmentation ⟨temperatures in the high *eighties* tomorrow⟩ ⟨a man still vigorous in his *eighties*⟩
¹eighty-eight \¦==¦=\ *adj* **:** being one more than 87 in number ⟨*eighty-eight* years⟩ — see NUMBER table
²eighty-eight \"\ *pron, pl in constr* **:** 88 countable persons or things not specified but under consideration and being enumerated ⟨*eighty-eight* are here⟩ ⟨*eighty-eight* were found⟩
³eighty-eight \"\ *n* **1 :** eight and 80 **:** four times 22 **:** eight times 11 **2 a :** 88 units or objects ⟨a total of *eighty-eight*⟩ **b :** a group or set of 88 **3 :** the numerable quantity symbolized by the arabic numerals 88 **4 :** the 88th in a set or series **5** [so called fr. the standard number of keys] *slang* **:** PIANO **6 :** an 88 millimeter gun
eighty-eighter \,ād·ēˈād·ə(r)\ *n, slang* **:** PIANIST
¹eighty-eighth \¦==¦=\ *adj* **1 :** being number 88 in a countable series ⟨the *eighty-eighth* day⟩ — see NUMBER table **2 :** being one of 88 equal parts into which something is divisible ⟨an *eighty-eight* share of the money⟩
²eighty-eighth \"\ *n* **1 :** number 88 in a countable series **2 :** the quotient of a unit divided by 88 **:** one of 88 equal parts of something ⟨one *eighty-eighth* of the total⟩
¹eighty-fifth \¦==¦=\ *adj* **1 :** being number 85 in a countable series ⟨the *eighty-fifth* day⟩ — see NUMBER table **2 :** being one of 85 equal parts into which something is divisible ⟨an *eighty-fifth* share of the money⟩
²eighty-fifth \"\ *n* **1 :** number 85 in a countable series **2 :** the quotient of a unit divided by 85 **:** one of 85 equal parts of something ⟨one *eighty-fifth* of the total⟩
¹eighty-first \¦==¦=\ *adj* **1 :** being number 81 in a countable series ⟨the *eighty-first* day⟩ — see NUMBER table **2 :** being one of 81 equal parts into which something is divisible ⟨an *eighty-first* share of the money⟩
²eighty-first \"\ *n* **1 :** number 81 in a countable series **2 :** the quotient of a unit divided by 81 **:** one of 81 equal parts of something ⟨one *eighty-first* of the total⟩
¹eighty-five \¦==¦=\ *adj* **:** being one more than 84 in number ⟨*eighty-five* years⟩ — see NUMBER table
²eighty-five \"\ *pron, pl in constr* **:** 85 countable persons or things not specified but under consideration and being enumerated ⟨*eighty-five* are here⟩ ⟨*eighty-five* were found⟩
³eighty-five \"\ *n* **1 :** five and 80 **:** five times 17 **2 a :** 85 units or objects ⟨a total of *eighty-five*⟩ **b :** a group or set of 85 **3 :** the numerable quantity symbolized by the arabic numerals 85 **4 :** the 85th in a set or series
¹eighty-four \¦==¦=\ *adj* **:** being one more than 83 in number ⟨*eighty-four* years⟩ — see NUMBER table
²eighty-four \"\ *pron, pl in constr* **:** 84 countable persons or things not specified but under consideration and being enumerated ⟨*eighty-four* are here⟩ ⟨*eighty-four* were found⟩
³eighty-four \"\ *n* **1 :** four and 80 **:** three times 28 **:** four times 21 **:** six times 14 **:** seven times 12 **:** seven dozen **2 a :** 84 units or objects ⟨a total of *eighty-four*⟩ **b :** a group or set of 84 **3 :** the numerable quantity symbolized by the arabic numerals 84 **4 :** the 84th in a set or series
¹eighty-fourth \¦==¦=\ *adj* **1 :** being number 84 in a countable series ⟨the *eighty-fourth* day⟩ — see NUMBER table **2 :** being one of 84 equal parts into which something is divisible ⟨an *eighty-fourth* share of the money⟩
²eighty-fourth \"\ *n* **1 :** number 84 in a countable series **2 :** the quotient of a unit divided by 84 **:** one of 84 equal parts of something ⟨one *eighty-fourth* of the total⟩
¹eighty-nine \¦==¦=\ *adj* **:** being one more than 88 in number ⟨*eighty-nine* years⟩ — see NUMBER table
²eighty-nine \"\ *pron, pl in constr* **:** 89 countable persons or things not specified but under consideration and being enumerated ⟨*eighty-nine* are here⟩ ⟨*eighty-nine* were found⟩
³eighty-nine \"\ *n* **1 :** nine and 80 **2 a :** 89 units or objects ⟨a total of *eighty-nine*⟩ **b :** a group or set of 89 **3 :** the numerable quantity symbolized by the arabic numerals 89 **4 :** the 89th in a set or series
eighty-niner \,ād·ēˈnīnə(r)\ *n* -s **:** one that entered Oklahoma when it was opened to settlement in 1889
¹eighty-ninth \¦==¦=\ *adj* **1 :** being number 89 in a countable series ⟨the *eighty-ninth* day⟩ — see NUMBER table **2 :** being one of 89 equal parts into which something is divisible ⟨an *eighty-ninth* share of the money⟩
²eighty-ninth \"\ *n* **1 :** number 89 in a countable series **2 :** the quotient of a unit divided by 89 **:** one of 89 equal parts of something ⟨one *eighty-ninth* of the total⟩
¹eighty-one \¦==¦=\ *adj* **:** being one more than eighty in number ⟨*eighty-one* years⟩ — see NUMBER table
²eighty-one \"\ *pron, pl in constr* **:** 81 countable persons or things not specified but under consideration and being enumerated ⟨*eighty-one* are here⟩ ⟨*eighty-one* were found⟩
³eighty-one \"\ *n* **1 :** one and 80 **:** three times 27 **:** nine nines **:** the square of nine **2 a :** 81 units or objects ⟨a total of *eighty-one*⟩ **b :** a group or set of 81 **3 :** the numerable quantity symbolized by the arabic numerals 81 **4 :** the 81st in a set or series
¹eighty-second \¦==¦==\ *adj* **1 :** being number 82 in a countable series ⟨the *eighty-second* day⟩ — see NUMBER table **2 :** being one of 82 equal parts into which something is divisible ⟨an *eighty-second* share of the money⟩
²eighty-second \"\ *n* **1 :** number 82 in a countable series **2 :** the quotient of a unit divided by 82 **:** one of 82 equal parts of something ⟨one *eighty-second* of the total⟩
¹eighty-seven \¦==¦==\ *adj* **:** being one more than 86 in number ⟨*eighty-seven* years⟩ — see NUMBER table
²eighty-seven \"\ *pron, pl in constr* **:** 87 countable persons or things not specified but under consideration and being enumerated ⟨*eighty-seven* are here⟩ ⟨*eighty-seven* were found⟩
³eighty-seven \"\ *n* **1 :** seven and 80 **:** three times 29 **2 a :** 87 units or objects ⟨a total of *eighty-seven*⟩ **b :** a group or set of 87 **3 :** the numerable quantity symbolized by the arabic numerals 87 **4 :** the 87th in a set or series
¹eighty-seventh \¦==¦==\ *adj* **1 :** being number 87 in a countable series ⟨the *eighty-seventh* day⟩ — see NUMBER table **2 :** being one of 87 equal parts into which something is divisible ⟨an *eighty-seventh* share of the money⟩
²eighty-seventh \"\ *n* **1 :** number 87 in a countable series **2 :** the quotient of a unit divided by 87 **:** one of 87 equal parts of something ⟨one *eighty-seventh* of the total⟩
¹eighty-six \¦==¦=\ *adj* **:** being one more than 85 in number ⟨*eighty-six* years⟩ — see NUMBER table
²eighty-six \"\ *pron, pl in constr* **:** 86 countable persons or things not specified but under consideration and being enumerated ⟨*eighty-six* are here⟩ ⟨*eighty-six* were found⟩
³eighty-six \"\ *n* **1 :** six and 80 **:** 43 times two **2 a :** 86 units or objects ⟨a total of *eighty-six*⟩ **b :** a group or set of 86 **3 :** the numerable quantity symbolized by the arabic numerals 86 **4 :** the 86th in a set or series
¹eighty-sixth \¦==¦=\ *adj* **1 :** being number 86 in a countable series ⟨the *eighty-sixth* day⟩ — see NUMBER table **2 :** being one of 86 equal parts into which something is divisible ⟨an *eighty-sixth* share of the money⟩
²eighty-sixth \"\ *n* **1 :** number 86 in a countable series **2 :** the quotient of a unit divided by 86 **:** one of 86 equal parts of something ⟨one *eighty-sixth* of the total⟩
¹eighty-third \¦==¦=\ *adj* **1 :** being number 83 in a countable series ⟨the *eighty-third* day⟩ — see NUMBER table **2 :** being one of 83 equal parts into which something is divisible ⟨an *eighty-third* share of the money⟩
²eighty-third \"\ *n* **1 :** number 83 in a countable series **2 :** the quotient of a unit divided by 83 **:** one of 83 equal parts of something ⟨one *eighty-third* of the total⟩
¹eighty-three \¦==¦=\ *adj* **:** being one more than 82 in number ⟨*eighty-three* years⟩ — see NUMBER table
²eighty-three \"\ *pron, pl in constr* **:** 83 countable persons or things not specified but under consideration and being enumerated ⟨*eighty-three* are here⟩ ⟨*eighty-three* were found⟩
³eighty-three \"\ *n* **1 :** three and 80 **2 a :** 83 units or objects ⟨a total of *eighty-three*⟩ **b :** a group or set of 83 **3 :** the numerable quantity symbolized by the arabic numerals 83 **4 :** the 83d in a set or series
¹eighty-two \¦==¦=\ *adj* **:** being one more than 81 in number ⟨*eighty-two* years⟩ — see NUMBER table
²eighty-two \¦==¦=\ *pron, pl in constr* **:** 82 countable persons or things not specified but under consideration and being enumerated ⟨*eighty-two* are here⟩ ⟨*eighty-two* were found⟩
³eighty-two \"\ *n* **1 :** two and eighty **:** 41 times two **2 a :** 82 units or objects ⟨a total of *eighty-two*⟩ **b :** a group or set of 82 **3 :** the numerable quantity symbolized by the arabic numerals 82 **4 :** the 82d in a set or series
eigne \ˈān\ *adj* [modif. of MF *ainé, aisné, ainsné*, fr. OF, fr. *ainz* before (fr. L *ante*) + *né* born — more at ANTE-, NEE] **:** ELDEST, FIRSTBORN
eijk·man test \ˈīk¦mən-, ˈāk¦\ *n, usu cap E* [after Christiaan *Eijkman* †1930 Dutch physiologist] **:** a test for the identification of coliform bacteria from warm-blooded animals on the basis of their ability to produce gas or glucose media at 46° C
eik \ˈēk, ˈāk, ˈəik\ *var of* EKE
eikon *var of* ICON
eikon- *or* **eikono-** — see ICON-
ei·ko·nom·e·ter \,īkəˈnäməd·ə(r)\ *n* [*icon-* + *-meter*] **1 :** ICONOMETER **2 :** a device to detect aniseikonia or to test stereoscopic vision
¹eild \ˈē(ə)ld\ *var of* ELD
²eild \ˈē(ə)l(d)\ *adj* [ME *yeld*, fr. OE *gelde* barren, sterile — more at GELD] **1** *Scot, of an animal* **:** BARREN **2** *Scot, of a cow* **:** DRY
eil·ding \ˈēldən, -diŋ\ *var of* ELDING
ei·me·ria \īˈmirēə\ *n, cap* [NL, fr. Theodor *Eimer* †1898 Ger. zoologist + NL *-ia*] **:** a genus of coccidia that invade the intestinal wall or other visceral epithelia of many vertebrates and some invertebrates and include serious pathogens — see EIMERIIDAE — **ei·me·ri·al** \(ˈ)ī¦mirēəl\ *adj* — **ei·me·ri·an** \-ēən\ *adj or n*
ei·me·ri·idae \,īməˈrīə,dē\ *n pl, cap* [NL, fr. *Eimeria*, type genus + *-idae*] **:** a family of coccidia that includes several genera (as *Eimeria* and *Isospora*) of medical or veterinary importance and with minor families constitutes a suborder of the order Coccidia
-ein *or* **-eine** *n suffix* -s [ISV, alter. of *-in, -ine*] **:** a compound distinguished from a compound with a name ending in *-in* or *-ine* — usu. *-eine* in names of bases and *-ein* in names of nonbases ⟨nicoteine⟩ ⟨phthalein⟩
eind·ho·ven \ˈīnt,hōvən, ˈānt-\ *adj, usu cap* [fr. *Eindhoven*, Netherlands] **:** of or from the city of Eindhoven, Netherlands **:** of the kind or style prevalent in Eindhoven
ein·kan·ter \ˈīn,käntə(r)\ *n* -s [G, lit., something having one edge, fr. *ein* one (fr. OHG) + *kante* edge + *-er* — more at ONE, DREIKANTER] **:** a stone with a single sharp edge worn by wind-driven sand — compare DREIKANTER, VENTIFACT
ein·korn \ˈīn,kȯrn\ *n* -s [G, fr. OHG, fr. *ein* one + *korn* grain — more at CORN] **:** a one-grained wheat (*Triticum monococcum*) that has a short flat spike like barley, is regarded by some as the most primitive wheat, and is grown esp. in poor soils in central Europe
ein·stein \ˈīnz,tīn, ˈīn,st- *sometimes* ˈīn,sht-\ *n* -s [after *Albert Einstein* †1955 Am. physicist and mathematician] **1** *often cap* **:** the radiant energy of a given frequency required to effect the complete photochemical transformation of one mole of a photosensitive substance being equal to about 0.004 erg second times the frequency in question **2** *usu cap* **:** a mathematical genius ⟨the statistics . . . would give pause to an *Einstein —Official Guide to the Army Air Forces*⟩
einstein-bose statistics *n, usu cap E&B* **:** BOSE-EINSTEIN STATISTICS
einstein-de haas effect \-dəˈhäs-\ *n, usu cap E&H* [after Albert *Einstein* and Arthur E. *de Haas* †1941 Austrian physicist] **:** a rotational impulse imparted to a body upon sudden magnetization — compare BARNETT EFFECT
einstein equation *n, usu cap E* [after Albert *Einstein*] **:** any of several equations in physics: as **a :** MASS-ENERGY EQUATION **b :** EINSTEIN'S PHOTOELECTRIC EQUATION **c :** a formula expressing the diffusion coefficient of suspended colloidal particles as the product of the Boltzmann's constant, the Kelvin temperature, and the particle mobility
ein·stein·ian \ˈ=,=ēən, =ˈ===\ *adj, usu cap* [Albert *Einstein* + E *-ian*] **:** of or relating to Albert Einstein or his theories
ein·stein·ium \ˈ=,=ēəm, =ˈ===\ *n* -s [NL, fr. Albert *Einstein* + NL *-ium*] **:** a radioactive element artificially produced (as by bombardment of plutonium with neutrons) — symbol *Es* or *E;* see ELEMENT table
einstein law of photochemical equivalence *usu cap 1st E* [after Albert *Einstein*] **:** a law in quantum theory: each molecule activated in any photochemical process absorbs one photon of radiant energy — compare EINSTEIN 1
einstein shift *or* **einstein effect** *n, usu cap 1st E* [after Albert *Einstein*] **:** a slight displacement of the lines in the spectra of very dense stars from their normal wavelength positions toward the red — compare RED SHIFT
einstein's photoelectric equation *n, cap 1st E* [after Albert *Einstein*] **:** an equation in physics giving the kinetic energy of a photoelectron emitted from a metal as a result of the absorption of a radiation quantum: $E_k = h\nu - \omega$ where E_k is the kinetic energy of the photoelectron, h is the Planck constant, ν is the frequency associated with the radiation quantum, and ω the work function of the metal
einstein temperature *n, usu cap E* [after Albert *Einstein*] **:** DEBYE TEMPERATURE
einstein theory *n, usu cap E* [after Albert *Einstein*] **:** the theory of relativity
ei·rann \ˈa(a)rən, ˈer-,ˈär-\ *adj, usu cap* [IrGael *Éireannach*, fr. *Éire*] **:** IRISH
ei·re \ˈa(a)rə, ˈer-,ˈär-,ˈīr-, -rē,-ri\ *adj, usu cap* [fr. *Eire* Republic of Ireland, fr. IrGael *Éire*] **:** IRELAND 2
eirenic *var of* IRENIC
ei·ren·i·con *also* **iren·i·con** \īˈrenə,kän, -ək̇ən, *chiefly Brit* -rēn-\ *n* -s [LGk *eirēnikon*, fr. neut. of Gk *eirēnikos* of peace — more at IRENIC] **:** a statement that attempts to harmonize conflicting doctrines (as in a church) **:** RECONCILIATION ⟨can a new ~ be enforced on rival sects by making them share a common ping-pong table —J.E.MacColl⟩
eis·e·ge·sis \,īsəˈjēsə̇s\ *n, pl* **eisege·ses** \-ē,sēz\ [NL, fr. Gk *eisēgēsis* act of proposing, advising, introducing, fr. *eisēgeisthai* to bring in, introduce, propose, advise (fr. *eis* into + *hēgeisthai* to lead) + *-sis;* akin to Gk *en* in — more at IN, SEEK] **:** the interpretation of a text (as of the Bible) by reading into it one's own ideas — compare EXEGESIS — **eis·e·get·i·cal** \¦==¦jed·ək̇əl\ *adj*
ei·sen·how·er jacket \ˈīzᵊn,hau̇(ə)r, ¦ə *sometimes* -zᵊn,au̇\ *n, usu cap E* [after Dwight D. *Eisenhower* *b*1890 Am. general and 34th U.S. president] **:** a short jacket fitting snugly at the waist and cuffs; *specif* **:** one used as a part of a military uniform
ei·se·nia \āˈsēnēə, īˈ-, -nyə\ *n, cap* [NL, fr. Gustav A. *Eisen* †1940 Am. zoologist and archaeologist + NL *-ia*] **:** a widely distributed genus of small earthworms (family Lumbricidae) including the common pink dung worm (*E. foetida*)
ei·stedd·fod \īˈsteth(,)vȯd, (i)ˈs-\ *n* -s [W, lit., session, fr. *eistedd* to sit, sitting (derivative fr. the root of W *sedd* seat) + *bod* to be, being; akin to L *sedēre* to sit and to OIr *brith* to be, being, OE *bēon* to be — more at SIT, BE] **:** a Welsh competitive festival of the arts esp. in singing ⟨adjudicating at a local ~ in Wales where there were three male voice choirs competing in the final —Warwick Braithwaite⟩ — compare FEIS 2, MOD — **ei·stedd·fod·ic** \,ī,steth¦vȯdik\ *adj*
eith \ˈēth\ *var of* EATH
¹ei·ther \ˈēthə(r), *sometimes* ˈīth-; *Eng & Wales* ˈīth-; *Ireland & Scot* ˈāth-\ *adj* [ME *either, aither*, adj. & pron., fr. OE *ǣghwæther, ǣgther* both, each (akin to OHG *iogihwedar* each of two), fr. *ā* always + *ge-*, collective prefix + *hwæther* which of two, whether — more at AYE, CO-, WHETHER] **1 :** the one and the other of the two **:** EACH ⟨flowers blooming on ~ side of the walk⟩ **2 :** the one or the other of the two ⟨use ~ foot, no matter which⟩ ⟨you may take ~ fork of the road⟩
²either \"\ *pron* [ME *either, aither*] **1** *archaic* **a :** each of two or more ⟨at ~ of the three corners is an exquisite . . . bust —W.D.Howells⟩ **b :** each other ⟨as two yoke devils sworn to ~'s purpose —Shak.⟩ **2 :** one of two or more: as **a :** the one or the other ⟨take ~ of the two routes⟩ **b :** any one (of more than two) ⟨three famous talkers . . . ~ of whom would illustrate what I say —O.W.Holmes †1935⟩ — usu. sing. in constr. except when a plural (usu. after *of*) intervenes between *either* and the verb form in which circumstance the verb is often plural in form ⟨of the two forms of address ~ is appropriate to the situation⟩ ⟨~ of them is satisfactory⟩ ⟨~ of them are satisfactory⟩
³either \"\ *conj* [ME *either, aither*, fr. OE *ǣghwæther* (*ge*), *ǣgther* (*ge*) both, fr. *ǣghwæther, ǣgther*, pron.] **1** — used as a function word before two or more coordinate words, phrases, or clauses joined usu. by *or* to indicate that what immediately follows is the first of two or more alternatives that are equally applicable ⟨that voice, which could be used ~ as a glaive or as an organ stop —Victoria Sackville-West⟩ ⟨the man did not kill himself ~ physically or spiritually —E.C.Wagenknecht⟩ ⟨unready, ~ politically, economically, or militarily —H.E. Gaston⟩ or mutually exclusive ⟨the statement as originally worded must be ~ true or false⟩ ⟨the population will ~ die, migrate, or plunge into economic chaos —Herbert Hoover⟩ **2** *obs* **:** OR
⁴either \"\ *adv* [ME *either, aither*, fr. *either, aither*, adj., pron., & conj.] **1 :** at all **:** LIKEWISE, MOREOVER — used for emphasis after a negative ⟨they are the best available and are not expensive ~⟩ esp. one contradicting a previous affirmation ⟨it's raining. It isn't ~⟩ or agreeing with a previous negative statement ⟨I didn't see it. Nor I ~⟩ or supplementing one ⟨you'll not go far in life and you won't be happy ~ —W.J.Reilly⟩ — compare TOO **2 :** for that matter — used for emphasis after an alternative following a question or conditional clause esp. where negation is implied ⟨who answers for the Irish parliament? or army ~? —Robert Browning⟩ ⟨if his father had come or his mother ~ all would have gone well⟩
¹either-or \¦=thə(r) ō(ə)r, -ȯ(ə)\ *adj* **:** of or marked by either-or **:** BLACK-AND-WHITE ⟨has written an *either-or* book in which the good are totally good and the wicked are totally bad⟩
²either-or \"\ *n* -s **:** an unavoidable choice or exclusive division between only two alternatives **:** DICHOTOMY ⟨the problem of specialized versus general courses is not one of *either-or* —*Science*⟩ ⟨no *either-or* between nature and . . . culture —C.K. Kluckhohn⟩
¹ejac·u·late \əˈjakyə,lāt, ēˈ-, *usu* -ād·+V\ *vb* -ED/-ING/-S [L *ejaculatus*, past part. of *ejaculari* to throw out, hurl, fr. *e-* + *jaculari* to throw, fr. *jaculum* dart, javelin, fr. *jacere* to throw — more at JET] *vt* **1 a** *obs* **:** to throw out (as a dart) suddenly and swiftly **:** EJECT **b :** to eject (a fluid) from a living body; *specif* **:** to eject (semen) in orgasm **2 :** to blurt out (as in anger or surprise) ⟨angry and *ejaculating* unfinished sentences —Jean Stafford⟩ **~** *vi* **1 a :** to dart out suddenly and swiftly

b : to eject a fluid (as semen) 2 : to utter an ejaculation : cry out ⟨the seagull flapped away . . . *ejaculating* from time to time as seagulls do —Ethel Wilson⟩ **syn** see EXCLAIM

²**ejac·u·late** \-lət, -,lāt, *usu* |d.+V\ *n* -s 1 : the semen released by one ejaculation 2 : EJACULATION 1

ejac·u·la·tion \ˌ=ˌ=ˈlāshən\ *n* -s [L *ejaculatus* + E *-ion*] 1 a : the act or process of ejaculating; *specif* : the sudden or spontaneous discharging of a fluid (as semen in orgasm) from a duct b : an instance of such an act or process 2 : something ejaculated: as a : a short sudden emotional utterance b : a short urgent prayer ⟨he received a birthday spiritual bouquet from the children advising him that they had offered . . . 10,705 *ejaculations*, 340 sacrifices, and 270 acts of charity in his behalf —E.J.Kahn⟩

ejac·u·la·tio prae·cox \ˌ=ˌ=ˈlāshē,ōˈprē,käks\ *n* [NL] : premature ejaculation in coitus

ejac·u·la·tive \ˌ=ˈ=ˌ=,lād·iv, -ləl, |t|, |ēv *also* |əv\ *adj* : EJACULATORY

ejac·u·la·tor \-,lād·ə(r), -ātə-\ *n* -s : one that ejaculates

ejac·u·la·to·ry \-,lə,tōrē, -ôr-, -ri\ *adj* 1 : casting or throwing out; *specif* : associated with or concerned in physiological ejaculation ⟨~ vessels⟩ 2 : marked by or given to ejaculation ⟨an ~ prayer⟩ ⟨a breathless ~ hotelkeeper who is forcing a traveling salesman to hear her story —*Times Lit. Supp.*⟩

ejaculatory duct *n* : a duct through which semen is ejaculated; *specif* : either of the paired ducts in man that are formed by the junction of the duct from the seminal vesicle with the vas deferens, pass through the prostate, and open into the upper part of the urethra

ejac·u·lum \-,ləm\ *n*, *pl* **ejacu·la** \-lə\ [NL, fr. L *ejaculari* to throw out — more at EJACULATE] : EJACULATE 1

¹**eject** \əˈjekt, ē'-\ *vt* -ED/-ING/-S [ME *ejecten*, fr. L *ejectus*, past part. of *eicere*, fr. *e-* + *-icere* (fr. *jacere* to throw) — more at JET] 1 a : to drive (as a person) out esp. by physical force : EXPEL ⟨he was being ~*ed* for taunting the pianist —Brooks Atkinson⟩ b : to deprive of membership or of a position or office : OUST ⟨the membership ~*ed* the chairman by acclamation⟩ c : to evict from property : DISPOSSESS ⟨~*ed* for nonpayment of rent⟩ 2 a : to throw or force out from within ⟨a mechanism that ~*s* the empty cases from the gun⟩ b : to throw off ⟨an electron ~*ed* from an atom of copper⟩ c *obs* : EMIT ⟨every look . . . mine eyes ~*s* —Ben Jonson⟩

syn EJECT, EXPEL, OUST, EVICT, and DISMISS can mean, in common, to force or thrust (a thing or person) out. EJECT carries the strongest implication of throwing out from within ⟨cones of material *ejected* from the volcanoes —W.E.Swinton⟩ ⟨the solar system had been formed out of matter *ejected* from the sun —S.F.Mason⟩ ⟨no solid bank of smoke *ejected* itself from the breastworks —Kenneth Roberts⟩ ⟨a roaring fire *ejecting* sparks —T.S.Eliot⟩ ⟨cowboys forcibly *eject* the farmers from their places in line —*Amer. Guide Series: Texas*⟩ EXPEL, stressing a thrusting out or driving away, implies more generally a voluntary compulsion than EJECT, indicating more generally an intent to get permanently rid of ⟨*expel* the air from the lungs⟩ ⟨the fish and the bird, which *expel* the egg from the body —H.M.Parshley⟩ ⟨he was arrested . . . then *expelled* from the city with the warning never to come back —*Current Biog.*⟩ ⟨*expelled* from his seat in the Senate for plotting with the British —R.B.Morris⟩ OUST implies removal or dispossession by the power of a law or the exercise of force or compulsion ⟨to *oust* squatters from his property —*Amer. Guide Series: Pa.*⟩ ⟨the first explorers were the Genoese, who had been *ousted* from the Levant trade by the Venetians —S.F.Mason⟩ ⟨Ferdinand . . . *ousted* the local king from Navarre —Francis Hackett⟩ EVICT now means to turn out (of house and home, one's place of business, or the like) by legal or equally effective means, commonly for nonpayment of rent ⟨after two months the landlord had the tenants *evicted* for rowdyism and destruction of property besides nonpayment⟩ ⟨Roger Williams, rebel against the Puritans and *evicted* by them from the sacred confines of Massachusetts —R.W.Hatch⟩ ⟨thousands of crofters were *evicted* to make way for large sheep farms —*London Calling*⟩ DISMISS stresses a getting rid of (something) by refusing it further consideration, ejecting it from the thoughts, or taking steps to ensure its no longer annoying one ⟨nonviolence as a political weapon . . . should not be *dismissed* lightly —*African Abstracts*⟩ ⟨a very downright sort of Yankee, given to *dismissing* people who disagreed with him —Charlton Laird⟩ ⟨*dismiss* an enemy by having him deported⟩

²**eject** \ˈē,jekt\ *n* -s : PROJECTION 8

ejec·ta \əˈjektə, ē'-\ *n pl but sing or pl in constr* [NL, fr. L, neut. pl. of *ejectus*] : material thrown out (as from a volcano)

ejec·ta·men·ta \ə,jektəˈmentə, (,)ē,j-\ *n pl* [NL, fr. L, pl. of *ejectamentum* something thrown out, fr. *ejectare* to throw out (freq. of *eicere*) + *-mentum* -ment] : EJECTA

ejec·tion \əˈjekshən, ē'-\ *n* -s [ME *ejeccioun*, fr. L *ejection-*, *ejectio*, fr. *ejectus* + *-ion-*, *-io* -ion] 1 : the act or process of ejecting : EXPULSION ⟨automatic ~ of empty cartridge cases from revolvers —C.S.Comeaux⟩ 2 *Scots law* : EJECTMENT 2 3 : EJECTA

ejection capsule *n* : a pressurized cockpit designed to be ejected from airplanes in an emergency and equipped with an automatic parachute, survival gear, rations, and radio transmitter

ejection port *n* : an opening in the receiver of a firearm through which the expended cases are thrown from the piece after firing

ejection seat *or* **ejector seat** *n* : an emergency escape seat designed to propel its occupant out and away from an airplane by means of an explosive charge

¹**ejec·tive** \-ktiv, -tēv *also* -təv\ *adj* [¹*eject* + *-ive*] 1 : causing ejection ⟨the ~ force is supplied by an explosive charge under the seat⟩ 2 *of a voiceless consonant* : uttered with simultaneous glottal stop ⟨an ~ explosive is heard when the mouth closure and glottis are released almost simultaneously⟩ — **ejec·tive·ly** \-təvlē, -li\ *adv*

²**ejective** \"\ *n* -s : an ejective consonant

eject·ment \-k(t)mənt\ *n* -s 1 : DISPOSSESSION ⟨the ~ of tenants from their homes⟩ 2 a : a mixed action admissible for the recovery of possession of property and for damages and costs for the wrongful withholding of it b : the writ by which this action is commenced

ejec·tor \-ktə(r)\ *n* -s 1 : one that ejects: as a : the mechanism of a firearm that ejects the empty cartridge b : a device that ejects finished work (as a cast slug) from the mold of a typecasting mechanism or the die of a die-casting mechanism or hydraulic press ⟨the casting is removed by pressure from ~ pins fastened to the ~ plate behind the movable die —David Basch⟩ 2 : a jet pump for withdrawing a gas, fluid, or powdery substance (as air, water, or sand) from a space

ejects *pres 3d sing of* EJECT, *pl of* EJECT

eji·dal \eˈkēthäl, ehē-\ *adj* [MexSp, fr. *ejido* + *-al*] : of or relating to an ejido or the ejido system : COMMUNAL ⟨~ lands⟩ ⟨~ procedure⟩ ⟨~ agriculture⟩

eji·da·ta·rio \-,thäˈtäryō\ *n*, *pl* **ejidatarios** \-yōs\ [MexSp, fr. *ejido*] : a member of an ejido

eji·do \eˈkēthō, eˈhē-\ *n*, *pl* **ejidos** \-ōs\ [MexSp, fr. Sp, common land in a village used for pasturage or threshing, fr. L *exitus* departure, way out — more at EXIT] 1 : a tract of land held in common by the inhabitants of a Mexican village and farmed cooperatively or individually : COMMON 2 a : a Mexican village having an ejido 3 : a system of communal land tenure in Mexico — compare HACIENDA

ejoo \ˈē(,)jü\ *n* -s [Java *ijo*] : GOMUTI 2

ejus·dem ge·ne·ris \ēˈyüs(,)demˈgenərəs, ē,jəs(,)demˈje-\ *adj* [L] : of the same kind or class ⟨the articles here imported are not *ejusdem generis* with the class of articles specifically named in said paragraph 217 —*U.S. Daily*⟩ — usu. used in law to limit the application of a broad term to a specific class of things

eka- \ˈekə, ˈēkə\ *comb form* [Skt *eka* one — more at ONE] : standing or assumed to stand next in order beyond (a specified element) in the same family of the periodic table — in names of chemical elements esp. when not yet discovered ⟨*eka*cesium (now called francium)⟩; compare DVI-

eka·iodine \"+\ *n* [*eka-* + *iodine*] : ASTATINE

eka·ri \äˈkärē\ *n*, *pl* **ekari** *or* **ekaris** *usu cap* 1 : a Papuan people of western New Guinea 2 : a member of the Ekari people

ekdemite *var of* ECDEMITE

¹**eke** \ˈēk\ *adv* [ME, fr. OE *ēac*; akin to OHG *ouh* also, ON & Goth *auk*, L *aut* or, Gk *au* again, Skt *u* and, but] *archaic* : in addition : ALSO, MOREOVER ⟨the most entertaining, ~ the most learned —H.J.Laski⟩

²**eke** *or* **eik** \ˈēk, ˈāk, ˈəik\ *n* -s [ME *eke*, fr. OE *ēaca*; akin to OE *ēacian* to increase] *now chiefly Scot* : an addition or extension: as a : a piece added to increase the size or length of a garment b : an additional drink ⟨an ~ before I go⟩

³**eke** \ˈēk, *Scot* " *or* ˈāk *or* ˈəik\ *vb* -ED/-ING/-S [ME *eken*, *echen*, fr. OE *ēacian* (v.i.) to increase and *ēacan* (v.i.) to increase and *īecan*, *ēcan* (v.t.) to increase, augment, carry out; akin to OHG *ouhhōn* to add, ON *auka* to increase, Goth *aukan*, L *augēre*, Gk *auxein* to increase, Skt *oja* strength] *vt* 1 *or* **eik** *chiefly Scot* a : ADD, INCREASE ⟨*eked* a few words fit for the occasion⟩ ⟨the memory *eked* her sadness⟩ b : to repair by adding material : PATCH, LENGTHEN ⟨let out and ~ the petticoat⟩ 2 a : to supplement or fill (what is felt to be deficient) esp. by a laborious, inferior, or scanty addition — used with *out* ⟨to ~ out his meager pay . . . he turned to writing —*English Digest*⟩ ⟨~ out the information given in the native chronicles and so to reconstruct . . . the society of the first centuries —G.B.Sansom⟩ b : to make (a supply) last by economy ⟨~ out the stores by strict rationing⟩ or partial use of a substitute ⟨this wool could be obtained only in small and uncertain quantities and was often *eked* out as a facing to a core of cedar bark —C.D.Forde⟩ : STRETCH — used with *out* 3 a : to obtain, maintain, or achieve with effort usu. in small quantity : SQUEEZE ⟨he asked about the living conditions . . . and I tried to ~ out the little knowledge I had collected —Christopher Isherwood⟩; *specif* : to make (a living) meagerly and laboriously — used with *out* ⟨from . . . unproductive cutover land many farmers have *eked* out a precarious living —*Amer. Guide Series: Minn.*⟩ b : to live from day to day esp. with boredom or with difficulty — used with *out* ⟨on this, with £1 a month from his father, the boy *eked* out his year —*Sydney (Australia) Bull.*⟩ ~ *vi*, *chiefly Scot* : ADD ⟨it *eked* to his woe⟩ : AUGMENT

eke·name \ˈēk,nām\ *n* [ME — more at NICKNAME] *archaic* : NICKNAME

EKG *abbr*, *often not cap* electrocardiogram

ekhi·mi \eˈkēmē\ *n* -s [native name in Africa] : the grayish brown coarse-grained wood of a tropical African tree (*Piptadenia africana*) used for structural work and inexpensive furniture

ek·ka \ˈe(,)kä, ˈekə\ *n* -s [Hindi *ekā*, *ekkā*, lit., unit, fr. Skt *ekatā*, fr. *eka* one — more at ONE] : a light 2-wheeled one-horse one-passenger carriage used in India

ek·ki \ˈekē\ *n* -s [native name in Africa] 1 : a tropical African timber tree (*Lophira alata* or *L. procera*) of the family Ochnaceae yielding a heavy hard durable reddish brown wood that is used esp. for wharves, railway ties, and flooring 2 : the wood of the ekki

ekoi \ˈē,kȯi\ *n*, *pl* **ekoi** *or* **ekois** *usu cap* 1 a : a Negro people of southeastern Nigeria noted for their carved masks b : a member of such people 2 : the language of the Ekoi people belonging to the Central branch of the Niger-Congo language family

ekphore *var of* ECPHORE

ek·te·ne *or* **ec·te·ne** \,ektəˈnē\ *n* -s [MGk *ektenē*, fr. Gk *ektenēs* assiduous, prolonged, fr. *ekteinein* to stretch out, fr. *ek*, *ex* out + *teinein* to stretch — more at EX-, THIN] : SYNAPTE

ektodynamomorphic *var of* ECTODYNAMOMORPHIC

¹**el** \ˈel\ *n* -s : the letter *l*

²**el** \"\ *n* -s *often cap*, *often attrib* [by shortening] : ELEVATED RAILROAD ⟨the Third Avenue ~⟩

-el \ˈel, ˌəl\ *n suffix* -s [ME, fr. OF *-el*, *-ele*, fr. L *-ellus*, *-ella*, *-ellum*] : small one ⟨cormel⟩

el *abbr* 1 eldest 2 elected 3 electric; electricity 4 element 5 elevated; elevation

¹**elab·o·rate** \əˈlab(ə)rət, ē'-, *usu* -rəd.+V\ *adj* [L *elaboratus*] 1 *archaic* : produced by labor 2 a : planned or carried out with great care and exactness : worked out in detail : COMPLEX ⟨the ~ register of the inhabitants prevented tax evasion —John Buchan⟩ ⟨he began an ~ calculation on his fingers —Dorothy Sayers⟩ b : marked by complexity, fullness of detail, or ornateness : INTRICATE, COMPLICATED ⟨~ wood decorations, mansard roofs, and long porches —Fred Zimmer⟩ c : PAINSTAKING, DILIGENT ⟨an ~ collector of etchings⟩ — **elab·o·rate·ly** *adv* — **elab·o·rate·ness** *n* -ES

²**elab·o·rate** \-bə,rāt, *usu* -ād.+V\ *vb* -ED/-ING/-S [L *elaboratus*, past part. of *elaborare* to work out, labor diligently, acquire by labor, fr. *e-* + *laborare* to labor — more at LABOR] *vt* 1 : to produce by labor : fashion with care 2 *of a living organism* : to alter the chemical makeup of (as a foodstuff) to one more suited to bodily needs (as of assimilation or excretion); *esp* : to build up (complex organic compounds) from simple ingredients ⟨some neoplasms ~ abnormal proteins⟩ ⟨green plants ~ organic compounds from inorganic by means of photosynthesis⟩ 3 a : to work out in detail : DEVELOP ⟨requested all nations to meet to ~ a code of international law⟩ b : to expand, develop, or perfect esp. by analysis or reasoning ⟨the idea of mechanical energy was . . . inherent in Newton's work and was *elaborated* by those who followed him —W.V.Houston⟩ ~ *vi* 1 : to become elaborate ⟨this particular area seems a point where such influences have flowered and *elaborated* —Ruth Underhill⟩ 2 : to expand something in detail : discuss something at length ⟨he never *elaborated* on that remark —Irving Kristol⟩ ⟨declined to ~ in spite of strong hints that he tell all⟩ : dwell on a subject ⟨and then *elaborated* in response to questions —*N.Y.Times*⟩ **syn** see UNFOLD

elab·o·rat·er *or* **elab·o·rator** \-ād·ə(r), -ātə-\ *n* -s : one that elaborates

elab·o·ra·tion \ˌ=ˌ=ˈrāshən\ *n* -s [L *elaboration-*, *elaboratio*, fr. *elaboratus* + *-ion-*, *-io* -ion] 1 a : the act or process of elaborating ⟨scholars were mainly concerned in translation and ~ of texts —H.J.J.Winter⟩ b : the quality or state of being elaborated ⟨reached an extravagant degree of ~ in the 'seventies and 'eighties —James Laver⟩ 2 : something produced by elaborating ⟨can be used to solicit suggestions, to obtain ~*s*, to elicit reasons —S.L.Payne⟩ 3 : psychic interpretation or amplification of the content of dreams and other unconscious processes

elab·o·ra·tive \ˈ=ˌbə,rād·iv, -b(ə)rə|, |t|, |ēv *also* |əv\ *adj* : capable of elaborating : tending to elaborate — **elab·o·ra·tive·ly** \|əvlē, |ēv-, -li\ *adv*

elab·o·ra·to·ry \-b(ə)rə,tōrē, -ôr-, -ri\ *n* -ES [L *elaboratus* + E *-ory*] *archaic* : LABORATORY

el·a·chis·ta·ce·ae \,eləkəˈstāsē,ē\ *n pl*, *cap* [NL, fr. *Elachista*, type genus (fr. Gk *elachistē*, fem. superl. of *elachys* small) + *-aceae* — more at LIGHT (in weight)] : a family of brown algae (order Ectocarpales) found on other marine algae esp. of the family Fucaceae — **el·a·chis·ta·ceous** \ˌ=ˌ=ˌ=ˈstāshəs\ *adj*

el·a·chis·to·don·ti·dae \,elə,kistəˈdäntə,dē\ *n pl*, *cap* [NL, fr. *Elachistodont-*, *Elachistodon*, type genus (fr. Gk *elachistos* superl. of *elachys* — + NL *-odont-*, *-odon*) + *-idae*] : a small family of Indian egg-eating snakes comprising a single genus that is sometimes placed with the egg-eating snakes of southern Africa in the family Dasypeltidae

el·ae·ag·na·ce·ae \,elē,agˈnāsē,ē\ *n pl*, *cap* [NL, fr. *Elaeagnus*, type genus + *-aceae*] : a family of trees or shrubs (order Myrtales) having silvery, scurfy, or stellate-pubescent foliage, small perfect or dioecious flowers, and baccate fruit — **el·ae·ag·na·ceous** \ˌelē,agˈnāshəs\ *adj*

el·ae·ag·nus \,elēˈagnəs\ *n*, *cap* [NL, fr. Gk *elaiagnos*, a kind of willow, fr. *elaia* olive, olive tree + *agnos* chaste tree — more at OLIVE, AGNUS CASTUS] : a genus (the type of the family Elaeagnaceae) of chiefly Asiatic shrubs or trees having alternate leaves and perfect flowers with four stamens — see GOUMI, RUSSIAN OLIVE, SILVERBERRY

elae·is \əˈlēəs\ *n*, *cap* [NL, prob. modif. of Gk *elaïs* olive tree, fr. *elaia* olive] : a genus of pinnate-leaved palms having very dense clusters of crowded flowers and bright red fruits — see AFRICAN OIL PALM

elae·nia \əˈlēnēə\ *n* [NL, modif. of Gk *elainea*, fem. of *elaineos* of the olive, of olivewood, fr. *elaia* olive; fr. the color of the plumage] 1 *cap* : a genus of small crested insectivorous birds (family Tyrannidae) of tropical America and the West Indies 2 -s : any bird of the genus *Elaenia*

elae·o·blast \əˈlēə,blast\ *n* [*elaio-* + *-blast*] : an outgrowth at the posterior end of the embryo of certain tunicates believed to contain nutritive material — **elae·o·blas·tic** \ˌ=ˌ=ˈblastik\ *adj*

elae·o·car·pa·ce·ae \ə,lēō(,)kärˈpāsē,ē\ *n pl*, *cap* [NL, fr. *Elaeocarpus*, type genus + *-aceae*] : a widely distributed family of trees and shrubs (order Malvales) closely related to Tiliaceae — **elae·o·car·pa·ceous** \ˌ=ˌ=(,)=ˈpāshəs\ *adj*

elae·o·car·pus \ˌ=ˌ=ˈkärpəs\ *n*, *cap* [NL, fr. *elaio-* + *-carpus*] : a genus (the type of the family Elaeocarpaceae) of Indian and Australian trees and shrubs having simple leaves and small racemose flowers and including some species valuable as timber trees — see BRISBANE QUANDONG

el·ae·od·o·chon \,eləˈädə,kän\ *n* -s [NL, fr. Gk *elaiodochon*, neut. of *elaiodochos* holding oil, fr. *elaio-* + *dochos* containing, able to hold — more at CHOLEDOCH] : the oil gland of a bird situated near the base of the tail

elaeolite *var of* ELEOLITE

el·ae·om·e·ter \,eləˈämәd·ə(r)\ *n* [prob. fr. F *élaiomètre*, fr. *élaio-* elaio- + *-mètre* -meter] : OLEOMETER

el·ae·oph·o·ra \,eləˈäf(ə)rə\ *n*, *cap* [NL, fr. *elaio-* + *-phora*] : a genus of filarioid nematode worms which infest the arteries of sheep and other ruminants and whose larvae move into the subcutaneous tissues and cause lesions esp. about the head and feet

elaeoptene *var of* ELEOPTENE

elaeostearic acid *var of* ELEOSTEARIC ACID

el·a·id·ic acid \,eləˌidik-\ *n* [*elaio-* + *-ide* + *-ic*] : a white crystalline unsaturated acid $C_{17}H_{33}COOH$ obtained from oleic acid by isomerization; the trans isomer of oleic acid

el·a·i·din \əˈlāədᵊn, -dən\ *n* -s [ISV *elaidic* + *-in*] : a glycerol ester of elaidic acid

el·a·i·din·i·za·tion \ə,lāə,dinəˈzāshən\ *n* -s : the process of elaidinizing

el·a·i·din·ize \əˈlāədᵊn,īz, -də,nīz\ *vt* -ED/-ING/-S : to isomerize (as an unsaturated fatty acid or ester) from the cis form to the trans form (as from oleic acid to elaidic acid)

elaidin reaction *n* : elaidinization used as a test for unsaturated glycerides (as olein) in fatty oils

elaio- *or* **elaeo-** *or* **eleo-** *comb form* [G *eläo-* & NL *elaeo-*, fr. Gk *elaio-* olive oil, oil, fr. *elaion*, fr. *elaia* olive — more at OLIVE] : oil ⟨*elaio*plast⟩ ⟨*elaeo*blast⟩ ⟨*eleo*cyte⟩

elai·o·plast \əˈlīə,plast, -lāə-\ *n* -s [ISV *elaio-* + *-plast*; orig. formed as G *eläoplast*] : a leucoplast that secretes oil

elam·ite \ˈēlə,mīt\ *n* -s *usu cap* [*Elam*, ancient kingdom east of Babylonia + E *-ite*] 1 : one of an ancient people living northeast of Babylonia whose civilization goes back to the fifth millennium B.C. 2 *also* **elam·it·ic** \,ēləˈmid·ik\ : a language of unknown affinities used in Elam and known from texts ranging in date approximately from the 25th to the 4th centuries B.C. and mostly in cuneiform characters — called also *Anzanite*, *Susian*

élan \āˈlänⁿ, (ˈ)āˌlän, -ˈlan\ *n* -s [F, fr. MF *eslan* dash, rush, fr. (*s'*)*eslancer* to rush] : vigor, spirit, or enthusiasm typically revealed by assurance of manner, brilliance of performance, or liveliness of imagination : ARDOR, ZEST ⟨a man of the world of considerable dash and ~ —Frank Sullivan⟩ ⟨performed with great ~ in a sophisticated style —*Dance Observer*⟩ ⟨the ~ that went into the writing of the great novels of the twenties —Perry Miller⟩ **syn** see VIGOR

elance \ēˈl+\ *vt* -ED/-ING/-S [F *élancer*, fr. MF (*s'*) *eslancer* to rush, fr. *es-* (fr. L *ex-*) + *lancer* to hurl, launch — more at EX-, LANCE] *archaic* : THROW ⟨~ a spear⟩ : LAUNCH

eland \ˈēlənd, -,land, -laa(ə)nd\ *n*, *pl* **eland** *or* **elands** [Afrik, elk, eland, fr. D, elk, fr. obs. G *elen*, *elend*, fr. Lith *elnis*; akin to OHG *elaho* elk — more at ELK] : either of two large African antelopes of the genus *Taurotragus* bovine in form and having short spirally twisted horns in both sexes: a : the common dark fawn-colored eland (*T. oryx*) of southern and eastern Africa the male of which sometimes attains six feet in height and weighs 1500 pounds b : the larger dark-striped giant eland (*T. derbianus*) restricted to western equatorial Africa

el·a·nus \ˈelənəs\ *n*, *cap* [NL, fr. LGk *elanos* kite] : a genus of small kites of both the Old and New Worlds that have the tail unforked and the plumage black, white, and gray

élan vi·tal \āˌlänⁿvēˈtäl\ *n* [F] : the vital force or impulse of life ⟨became a firm believer in electricity's curative powers because he regarded it as a kind of *élan vital* —J.H.Plumb⟩; *specif* : the creative principle and fundamental reality held by Bergson to be immanent in all organisms and responsible for evolution — compare CREATIVE EVOLUTION

el·a·phe \ˈeləfē\ *n*, *cap* [NL, prob. fr. Gk *elaphē* deerskin, fr. *elaphos* deer — more at ELK] : a large genus of colubrid snakes comprising the rat snakes that are widely distributed in the northern hemisphere where they are valuable as destroyers of rodents — see COIN SNAKE, FOX SNAKE, LEOPARD SNAKE

el·a·phine \ˈelə,fīn, -,fən\ *adj* [fr. Gk *elaphos* deer + E *-ine*] : of, relating to, or resembling the red deer

elaph·o·dus \əˈlafədəs\ *n*, *cap* [NL, fr. Gk *elaphos* deer + NL *-odus*; fr. the large upper canines of the male] : a genus of mammals (family Cervidae) comprising the tufted deer of China which is related to the muntjacs but lacks frontal glands and has antlers greatly reduced

el·a·pho·glos·sum \,eləfōˈgläsəm\ *n*, *cap* [NL, fr. Gk *elaphos* deer + NL *-glossum* (fr. Gk *glōssa* tongue) — more at ELK, GLOSS] : a large genus of tropical ferns (family Polypodiaceae) having shaggy stipes and firm or thick oblong to paddle-shaped fronds entire or forked, the fertile fronds being covered beneath with a felty layer of sporangia lacking indusia — see ELEPHANT-EAR FERN

el·a·pho·my·ces \ˌ=ˌ=ˈmī,sēz\ *n*, *cap* [NL, fr. Gk *elaphos* deer + NL *-myces*] : a genus (the type of the family Elaphomycetaceae) of subterranean ascomycetous fungi resembling the truffles but having sessile ascocarps which are about the size of walnuts and are often rooted up by animals for food

el·a·phure \ˈelə,fyü(ə)r\ *n* -s [NL *Elaphurus*, genus of deer, fr. Gk *elaphos* deer + NL *-urus*] : PÈRE DAVID'S DEER — **el·a·phu·rine** \,eləˈfyü,rīn, -,rən\ *adj*

¹**el·a·pid** \ˈeləpəd\ *adj* [NL *Elapidae*] : of or relating to the Elapidae

²**elapid** \"\ *n* -s : one of the Elapidae

elap·i·dae \əˈlapə,dē\ *n pl*, *cap* [NL, fr. *Elap-*, *Elaps*, type genus + *-idae*] : a family of front-fanged venomous snakes found in the warmer parts of both hemispheres and including the cobras and mambas, the coral snakes of the New World, and the majority of Australian snakes (as the death adder, black snake, and tiger snake) — see ELAPINAE

el·a·pi·nae \,eləˈpī(,)nē\ *n pl*, *cap* [NL, fr. *Elap-*, *Elaps*, type genus + *-inae*] : the Elapidae when considered as a subfamily of Colubridae — **el·a·pine** \ˈelə,pīn, -,pən\ *adj*

¹**el·a·poid** \ˈelə,pȯid\ *adj* [NL *Elap-*, *Elaps* + E *-oid*] : of, relating to, or resembling the Elapidae

²**elapoid** \"\ *n* -s : one of the Elapidae

elaps \ˈē,laps\ *n*, *cap* [NL *Elap-*, *Elaps*, fr. MGk *elaps*, a fish, alter. of Gk *ellops*, *elops* — more at ELOPS] : a genus (the type of the family Elapidae) of venomous snakes formerly including many of the groove-fanged snakes (as those now placed in *Micrurus*) but now usu. restricted to a few garter snakes of southern Africa

¹**elapse** \əˈlaps, ē'-\ *vb* -ED/-ING/-S [L *elapsus*, past part. of *elabi* to slip away, escape, fr. *e-* + *labi* to fall, slide — more at SLEEP] *vi* : to slip by : glide away : PASS — usu. used of time ⟨after 1330, a whole generation ~*s* before there is another recorded demand for annual parliaments —J.G.Edwards⟩ ~ *vt*, *obs* : to permit (time) to pass : OUTLAST, OVERSTAY

²**elapse** \"\ *n* -s 1 *archaic* : a flowing out : EMANATION 2 *of time* : PASSAGE, EXPIRATION ⟨after the ~ of five years the screen is now permitted to dramatize the greatest news event of the modern age —Louise Mace⟩

elapsed time *n* : the actual time taken by a boat to sail over a course in yacht racing — see CORRECTED TIME

elasm- *or* **elasmo-** *comb form* [F *élasm-* & NL *elasmo-*, fr. Gk *elasmos*; akin to Gk *elaunein* to drive — more at ELASTIC] : metal plate ⟨*Elasmo*branchii⟩

¹**elas·mo·branch** \əˈlazmə,braŋk\ *also* **elas·mo·bran·chi·an** \ˌ=ˌ=ˈbraŋkēən\ *or* **elas·mo·bran·chi·ate** \-kēət, -kē,āt\ *adj* [*elasmobranch* fr. NL *Elasmobranchii*; *elasmobranchian*, *elasmobranchiate* fr. NL *Elasmobranchii* + E *-an*, *-ate*] : of or relating to the Chondrichthyes

²**elasmobranch** \"\ *also* **elasmobranchian** \"\ *or* **elasmobranch** \"\ *n* -s : one of the Chondrichthyes

¹**elas·mo·bran·chii** \ˌ=ˌ=ˈbraŋkē,ī\ [NL, fr. *elasm-* + *-bran-*

chii (fr. L *branchia* gill) — more at BRANCHIA] *syn of* CHONDRICHTHYES

2elasmobranchii \"\ [NL, fr. *elasm-* + *-branchii*] *syn of* EUSELACHII

elas·mo·saur \=ˈ==,sȯ(ə)r\ *n* -s [NL *Elasmosaurus*] **:** a reptile of the genus *Elasmosaurus*

elas·mo·sau·rus \=,==ˈsȯrəs\ *n, cap* [NL, fr. *elasm-* + *-saurus*] **:** a genus of gigantic long-necked marine reptiles (order Sauropterygia) from the Cretaceous of Kansas related to *Plesiosaurus*

elas·mo·there \=ˈ==,thi(ə)r\ *n* -s [NL *Elasmotherium*] **:** a rhinoceros of the genus *Elasmotherium*

elas·mo·the·ri·um \=,==ˈ===\ *n, cap* [NL, fr. *elasm-* + *-therium;* fr. the enamel plates of the molars] **:** a genus of rhinoceroses of the Pleistocene of Russia

elast- *or* **elasto-** *comb form* [NL *elast-*, fr. LGk *elastos* ductile] **1 :** elasticity ⟨*elast*in⟩ **2 :** elastic and ⟨*elasto*viscous⟩

elas·tase \əˈla,stās, ēˈ-, -āz\ *n* -s [*elast*in + *-ase*] **:** an enzyme that decomposes elastin and collagen and has been obtained in crystalline form from the pancreas

1elas·tic \əˈlastik, ēˈ-, -laas-, -tēk *sometimes chiefly Brit* -lȧs-\ *adj* [NL *elasticus* expansive, impulsive, fr. LGk *elastos* ductile, beaten (fr. Gk *elaunein* to drive, beat out) + L *-icus* -ic; akin to Gk *elan* to drive, OIr *luid* went, and perh. to Arm *elanim* I become] **1 a** *of a solid* **:** capable of recovering size and shape after deformation **b** *of a liquid* **:** capable of resisting compression **c** *of a gas* **:** capable of indefinite expansion **2 :** capable of recovering quickly from low spirits, disappointment, or misfortune ⟨a very cheerful and ~ gentleman —T.L. Peacock⟩ **:** marked by buoyancy **:** RESILIENT ⟨one called the young Indians "boys", perhaps because there was something youthful and ~ in their bodies —Willa Cather⟩ **3 :** capable of being easily stretched or expanded and of snapping back or resuming former shape **:** FLEXIBLE ⟨a brave old Panama hat . . . so ~ that upon rolling it up it sprang into perfect shape again —Herman Melville⟩ **4 a :** capable of ready change or easy expansion ⟨left as ~ as possible the constitution of the new institutions —P.J.Noel-Baker⟩ **:** not rigid or constricted ⟨the word *democratic* is doubtless one of the most ~ in the language —D.D.McKean⟩ **b :** receptive to new ideas and willing to modify previous judgments **:** ADAPTABLE ⟨the French mind is ~ and French public opinion tolerant to a degree which shames the prejudice of other peoples —W.C. Brownell⟩ **5 :** enlarging or decreasing readily in demand in response to changes in price ⟨the market is a fixed one in certain ways and quite ~ in other ways —Charles Yerkow⟩

syn EXPANSIVE, RESILIENT, BUOYANT, VOLATILE, EFFERVESCENT: ELASTIC may indicate an ability to recover quickly from discouragement or dejection and enjoy optimism or elation again ⟨the buoyant and *elastic* temper of the French trouveur —J.R. Green⟩ ⟨an *elastic* faculty of throwing off such recollections as would be too painful for endurance —Nathaniel Hawthorne⟩ ⟨to him whose *elastic* and vigorous thought keeps pace with the sun, the day is a perpetual morning —H.D. Thoreau⟩ EXPANSIVE may imply high spirits, optimism, benevolence, geniality, and communicativeness ⟨an *expansive* mood is one of the most familiar and sometimes costly first responses to a Florida winter sun. The person noted for taciturnity in his home community often becomes loquacious —*Amer. Guide Series: Fla.*⟩ RESILIENT may stress speed of return to accustomed good or high spirits after stress, tribulation, or depression ⟨already the shock and horror of it was fading from her *resilient* mind —Ruth Park⟩ ⟨good fighters, outspoken and tenacious of opinion, unsparing in attack, refusing to be browbeaten, *resilient* and tough as seasoned hickory —V.L. Parrington⟩ BUOYANT may indicate a temperamental lightness of spirit incapable of lasting dejection or depression ⟨in the dark days of the Revolution there was a *buoyant* American spirit —*Encyc. Americana*⟩ ⟨no such immaterial burden could depress that *buoyant*-hearted young gentleman for many hours together —George Eliot⟩ VOLATILE suggests lightness, levity, gaiety, or flightiness overcoming the sedate, serious, sober, or downcast ⟨how different from the *volatile* Polynesian in this, as in all other respects, is our grave and decorous North American Indian —Herman Melville⟩ ⟨was suspected of levity, irreverence, disregard, and affectation. He was too *volatile;* he talked too much —*John o' London's Weekly*⟩ EFFERVESCENT suggests a bubbling liveliness and boisterousness over which restraint or suppression is unlikely or impossible ⟨an *effervescent* sort of chap with an enthusiasm that takes off like a rocket —Richard Joseph⟩ **syn** see in addition FLEXIBLE

2elastic \"\ *n* -s **1 a :** ELASTIC WEB **b :** a fabric that is woven usu. of yarns containing rubber and that is used esp. for girdles and elastic hose **c :** something made from such fabric; *esp* **:** GARTER 1 — usu. used in pl. **2 :** easily stretched rubber usu. prepared in cords, strings, or bands: as **a :** RUBBER BAND **b :** a band of elastic placed around a tooth at the gum line in effecting its nonsurgical extraction

elas·ti·ca \-təkə\ *n* -s [NL, fr. fem. of *elasticus*] **1 :** either of two layers of elastic tissue present in the walls of most arteries: **a :** an inner layer between the intima and media **b :** an outer layer between the media and adventitia **2 :** ELASTIC CURVE

elastic afterwork *or* **elastic afterworking** *n* **:** the plastic yielding or creep of certain crystals of a metal on recovery after the release of a stress that has previously caused plastic deformation

elastical *obs var of* 1ELASTIC

elas·ti·cal·ly \-tək(ə)lē, -tēk-, -li\ *adv* **:** in an elastic manner **:** utilizing an elastic quality ⟨could be bent ~ —E.F.Riebling & W.W.Webb⟩

elastic bitumen *n* **:** ELATERITE

elastic cartilage *n* **:** a yellowish flexible cartilage having the matrix infiltrated in all directions by a network of elastic fibers and occurring chiefly in the external ear, eustachian tube, and certain cartilages of the larynx and epiglottis

elastic collision *n* **:** a collision in which the total kinetic energy of the colliding pair remains unchanged and the total momentum is conserved although usu. reapportioned between them

elastic constant *n* **:** one of the constants that express the elastic behavior of a given material — compare BULK MODULUS, ELASTIC LIMIT, POISSON'S RATIO, SHEAR MODULUS, YIELD POINT, YOUNG'S MODULUS

elastic currency *n* **:** a currency that automatically increases and decreases in volume with the demands of business

elastic curve *n* **:** the curve assumed by the longitudinal axis of an originally straight elastic strip or bar bent within its elastic limits by any system of forces

elastic deformation *n* **:** deformation that disappears upon removal of the external forces causing the alteration and the stress associated with it

elastic fiber *n* **:** a thick very elastic smooth yellowish connective tissue fiber that contains elastin and that branches and anastomoses with other similar fibers — see ELASTIC CARTILAGE, ELASTIC TISSUE

elastic glue *n* **:** FLEXIBLE GLUE

elastic hysteresis *n* **:** HYSTERESIS 1b

elas·tic·i·ty \ə,laˈstisəd·ē, (,)ē,l-, -laaˈ-, -ətē, -i *sometimes chiefly Brit* -,ləˈ- *or* ,e(,)l- *or* -,lȧˈ-\ *n* -ES **1 :** the quality or state of being elastic: as **a :** the capability of a strained body to recover its size and shape after deformation in any way **:** SPRINGINESS **b :** RESILIENCE ⟨with the ~ of youth she quickly recovered⟩ **c :** ADAPTABILITY ⟨they do not always perceive that the ~ of democracy is its strength —*New Yorker*⟩ **2 :** the property in paint or varnish that enables the film to follow without breaking changes in the surface to which it is applied **3 :** the responsiveness of a dependent variable to changes in a causal factor ⟨the price ~ of exports and imports may not be adequate to bring about equilibrium —A.H.Hansen⟩ ⟨~ of demand⟩

e·las·ti·cized \=ˈ=stə,sīzd\ *adj* **1 :** woven or knitted with elastic or rubber thread ⟨~ fabrics⟩ **2 :** stitched with elastic thread or made with inserts of elastic ⟨an ~ belt⟩ ⟨~ shoes⟩

elastic limit *n* **1 :** the greatest stress that an elastic solid can sustain without undergoing permanent deformation **2 :** the greatest stress for which the strain of an elastic body is proportional to the stress

elastic membrane *n* **:** a membrane consisting of or containing elastic tissue

elastic modulus *n* **:** MODULUS OF ELASTICITY

elastic scattering *n* **:** a scattering of material particles or photons as the result of elastic collision

elastic stocking *n* **:** STOCKING 2a

elastic tissue *n* **:** tissue consisting chiefly of elastic fibers that is found esp. in certain ligaments and tendons

elastic wave *n* **:** a wave in which the propagated disturbance is an elastic deformation of the medium

elastic web *or* **elastic webbing** *n* **:** a narrow fabric woven of various textile fibers and typically rubber threads and used esp. for garters and suspenders

elas·tin \=ˈ=stən\ *n* -s [ISV *elast-* + *-in;* orig. formed in G] **:** a protein that is similar to collagen and forms the chief constituent of elastic fibers

elas·tique \,ā,laˈstēk\ *n* -s [F *élastique* elastic (adj. and n.), fr. NL *elasticus* expansive, impulsive — more at ELASTIC] **:** a firm fabric resembling cavalry twill that is usu. made of wool or worsted and is used for uniforms and sportswear

elasto- — see ELAST-

elas·to·mer \əˈlastəmə(r), ēˈ-\ *n* -s [*elast-* + *-mer*] **:** an elastic rubberlike substance (as a synthetic rubber or a plastic having some of the physical properties of natural rubber) ⟨polyvinyl ~*s*⟩ — **elas·to·mer·ic** \=¦==¦merik\ *adj*

elas·tom·e·ter \ə,laˈstämәd·ə(r), (,)ē,l-\ *n* [*elast-* + *-meter*] **:** an instrument for measuring elasticity (as of body tissues or rubber) — **elas·tom·e·try** \-mə·trē\ *n* -ES

Elas·to·plast \əˈlastə,plast, ēˈl-\ *trademark* — used for an elastic adhesive bandage used as a dressing or support (as a cast or a corset)

1elas·to·plas·tic \əˈlastə,plastik, ēˈl-\ *n* [*elast-* + *plastic* (n.)] **:** a substance having both elastic and plastic properties **:** a rubberlike plastic

2elastoplastic \"\ *adj* [*elast-* + *plastic* (adj.)] **:** relating to the state of stress between the elastic limit of a material and its breaking strength in which the material exhibits both elastic and plastic properties — **elas·to·plas·tic·i·ty** \=,==,plaˈstisəd·ē\ *n* -ES

elas·to·sis \ə,laˈstōsəs, (,)ē,l-\ *n, pl* **elasto·ses** \-ō,sēz\ [NL, fr. *elast-* + *-osis*] **:** a condition marked by loss of elasticity of the skin in elderly people due to degeneration of the connective tissue

elas·tra·tion \-ˈstrāshən\ *n* -s [blend of 2*elastic* and *castration*] **:** bloodless castration (as of a lamb) by fitting a strong rubber band about the scrotum

1elate \əˈlāt, ēˈ-, *usu* -ād·+V\ *adj* [ME *elat*, fr. L *elatus*] **1** *archaic* **:** of high position **:** LOFTY, PROUD **2 :** in high spirits ⟨who can be alone ~ while the world lies forlorn —Matthew Arnold⟩ **:** EXALTED ⟨the poet's eyes . . . careworn, not ~ —Hugh McCrae⟩

2elate \"\ *vt* -ED/-ING/-S [L *elatus* (suppletive past part. of *efferre* to carry out), fr. *e-* + *latus*, suppletive past part. of *ferre* to bear — more at EFFERENT, BEAR, TOLERATE] **1** *archaic* **:** to raise up **:** LIFT ⟨~ his shady forehead —George Chapman⟩ **2 a :** to raise the spirits of **:** EXCITE, INSPIRE ⟨it was a fine sunny day, the sort of day that ~*s* the heart of young and old —W.S. Maugham⟩ **b :** to flush with triumph or success **:** puff up (as with pride) ⟨*elated* over his great bargain —M.M.Musselman⟩

elated *adj* **:** elevated in spirit **:** excited esp. with pride **:** EXULTANT ⟨I felt at once tranquil and ~ —John Galsworthy⟩ — **elat·ed·ly** *adv* — **elat·ed·ness** *n* -ES

elate·ment \-ātmənt\ *n* -s **:** ELATION

el·a·ter \ˈeləd·ə(r)\ *n* [NL, fr. Gk *elatēr* driver, fr. *elaunein* to drive, beat out — more at ELASTIC] **1** -s *obs* **:** ELASTICITY **2** [NL, fr. Gk *elatēr*] **a** *cap* **:** the type genus of Elateridae **b** -s **:** any beetle of the family Elateridae **:** CLICK BEETLE **3** -s **:** a filamentous plant structure functioning in the distribution of some product (as spores): as **a :** one of the elongated filaments among the spores in the capsule of a liverwort **b :** a filament of the capillitium of a slime mold **c :** one of the filamentous appendages of the spores in the scouring rushes

1elat·er·id \əˈlad·ərəd\ *adj* [NL *Elateridae*] **:** of or relating to the Elateridae

2elaterid \"\ *n* -s **:** a beetle of the family Elateridae **:** CLICK BEETLE

el·a·ter·i·dae \,eləˈterə,dē\ *n pl, cap* [NL, fr. *Elater*, type genus + *-idae*] **:** a large family of elongated tapering beetles that commonly have the ability when overturned to flip into the air by a sudden movement of the prothorax and so produce a distinct clicking — compare CLICK BEETLE, WIREWORM

elat·er·in \əˈlad·ərən\ *n* -s [ISV *elater*ium + *-in*] **:** a bitter white crystalline poisonous cathartic substance obtained esp. from elaterium and colocynth

elat·er·ite \-,rīt\ *n* -s [G *elaterit*, fr. Gk *elatēr* driver + G *-it* -ite] **:** a mineral consisting of a dark brown elastic resin occurring in soft flexible masses — called also *elastic bitumen, mineral caoutchouc*

el·a·te·ri·um \,eləˈtirēəm\ *n* -s [L, fr. Gk *elatērion* (also, squirting cucumber), fr. neut. of *elatērios* driving, driving away, purgative, fr. *elatēr* driver] **:** a purgative substance precipitated as a fine powder from the juice of the squirting cucumber on spontaneous evaporation and used in the form of yellowish cakes

elat·i·na·ce·ae \ə,latᵊnˈāsē,ē, ,elətəˈnā-\ *n pl, cap* [NL, fr. *Elatine*, type genus + *-aceae*] **:** a widely distributed family of aquatic or marsh plants (order Parietales) having opposite leaves and small axillary flowers — **elat·i·na·ceous** \ə¦latᵊn¦āshəs, ¦elətə¦nā-\ *adj*

elat·i·ne \əˈlatᵊn,ē\ *n, cap* [NL, fr. L, a kind of plant, fr. Gk *elatinē*, fr. fem. of *elatinos* of the silver fir, fr. *elatē* silver fir; perh. akin to Arm *elevin* cedar, Russ *yalovets* juniper] **:** a genus (the type of the family Elatinaceae) of aquatic or amphibious creeping herbs having dimerous to tetramerous flowers

elating *pres part of* ELATE

ela·tion \əˈlāshən, ēˈ-\ *n* -s [ME *elacioun*, fr. MF *elation*, fr. L *elation-*, *elatio*, fr. *elatus* (suppletive past part. of *efferre* to carry out) + *-ion-*, *-io* -ion — more at EFFERENT, ELATE] **1 :** the quality or state of being elated: **a :** SELF-EXALTATION, VAINGLORY ⟨when Lincoln was reelected in 1864 he felt no ~, only humility —Ruth P. Randall⟩ **b :** high spirits **:** BUOYANCY, JOY ⟨and within us, tramping over the valley meadows, was the incredible ~ of those who set out before the sun has risen —John Galsworthy⟩ **2 :** pathological euphoria sometimes accompanied by intense pleasure

1ela·tive \ˈēləd·iv, ˈel-\ *adj* [L *elatus* + E *-ive*] *of a grammatical case* **:** denoting motion away from

2elative \"\ *n* -s [L *elatus* + E *-ive*] **1** *linguistics* **:** the absolute superlative **2** [1*elative*] **a :** the elative case of a language **b :** a form in the elative case

e layer *n, cap E* **:** the lowest well-defined layer of the ionosphere regularly occurring during the daytime at about 60 miles above the earth's surface and capable of reflecting radio waves of medium frequency — compare E REGION

1el·bow \ˈel,bō\ *n* -s [ME *elbowe*, fr. OE *elboga*, *elnboga;* akin to OHG *elinbogo* elbow, ON *olbogi*, *ölnbogi*, MD *ellenboge;* all fr. a prehistoric Gmc compound whose constituents are akin to OE *eln* ell and *boga* bow — more at ELL, BOW] **1 a :** the joint between the human forearm and upper arm that supports the outer curve of the arm when bent **b :** a joint in the anterior limb of a vertebrate animal corresponding to the human elbow — see DOG illustration **c :** the portion of the sleeve of a garment that encloses this joint; *esp* **:** the portion that covers the outer bend when the arm is flexed ⟨wearing a tattered coat with holes in the ~*s*⟩ **2 :** something felt to resemble an elbow: as **a :** a sharp bend in a river or coast ⟨north to south through the ~ of the Minnesota river —Meridel Le Sueur⟩ **b** (1) **:** a bend or projection (as in a wall or building) ⟨her starboard quarter . . . hit with a solid thump against the ~ of the brick-faced canal side —C.S. Forester⟩ (2) **:** CROSSETTE 1 **c** *archery* **:** the part of the limb of a reflexed bow that bends sharply away from the string **d :** an angular pipe fitting **:** ELL **3 :** an arm of a chair ⟨he sat leaning backward obliquely in an easy chair with his leg thrown over the ~ of it —*Punch*⟩ — **at one's elbow** *or* **at the elbow :** at one's side **:** close at hand **:** NEARBY, ALONGSIDE ⟨with him *at her elbow*, she became a fine draftsman and a compositional designer of enviable talent —J.T.Soby⟩ — **bend an elbow** *also* **crook an elbow** *or* **lift an elbow :** to drink intoxicating liquor **:** have a drink ⟨don't *bend elbows* with strangers in bars —*Wall Street Jour.*⟩ — **out at elbows 1 :** shabbily dressed **:** RAGGED, SHABBY ⟨the wretched little *out at elbows* youngster with ink smudges on his face —Mary S. Watts⟩ **2 :** in financial straits **:** short of funds ⟨if he is a trifle *out at elbows*, so is the empire itself —G.W.Johnson⟩

pipe elbows

2elbow \"\ *vb* -ED/-ING/-S *vt* **1 :** to shove aside by jabbing with or as if with the elbow **:** press upon **:** PUSH, JOSTLE, NUDGE ⟨they ~*ed*, punched, and insulted each other —Wirt Williams⟩ ⟨little bazaars and shops ~*ed* one another for standing room —L.C.Douglas⟩ **2 a :** to make (one's way) by elbowing people ⟨the boy ~*ed* his way through the crowd⟩ **b :** to force (one's way) forwardly and impudently ⟨a habit of ~*ing* her way into the best social circles⟩ ~ *vi* **1 :** to elbow one's way **:** push or jostle along ⟨~*ing* through the crowd —Robert Westerby⟩ **2 :** to make an angle **:** TURN ⟨the passage ~*ed* and we were in an enormous cellar —Merle Considine⟩

elbow bending *n* **:** the drinking of beer or liquor

elbowboard \ˈ=(,)=,=\ *n* **:** the inside ledge formed by the projecting board covering the bottom of a window frame

elbow chair *n* **:** ARMCHAIR ⟨he was seated before a large fire in an *elbow chair* —*Encore*⟩

el·bowed \ˈel,bōd\ *adj* [1*elbow* + *-ed*] **:** GENICULATE ⟨~ antennae of certain weevils⟩

elbow grease *n* **:** energy vigorously exerted in the performance esp. of manual labor **:** strenuous application of oneself **:** SWEAT ⟨this was the first such expedition not powered solely by the *elbow grease* of oarsmen —*New Yorker*⟩

elbow in hawse : a foul hawse resulting from a 360 degree turn made by a ship riding at two anchors — compare ROUND TURN

elbow of capture : an abrupt turn in the course of a river attributable to stream piracy

elbowroom \ˈ=(,)=,=\ *n* **1 a :** ample room for moving the elbows freely ⟨stepped back to give them ~ —John Fountain⟩ **b :** adequate space for comfortable existence or development **:** sufficient room for work or operation ⟨this plane needs ~ to fly⟩ **2 :** freedom of movement or opportunity **:** LIBERTY ⟨more ~ for interpreting the party line⟩ **syn** see ROOM

elbow stand *n* **:** an acrobatic position in which the body is balanced on the forearms and the legs are held in the air

elbow stone *n* **:** a prehistoric curved stone artifact found in Puerto Rico and the Dominican Republic

el·buck \ˈel(,)bək\ *Scot var of* ELBOW

eld \ˈeld\ *n* -s [ME *elde*, fr. OE *yldo*, *eldo*, *ældo;* akin to OHG *altī*, *eltī* old age, eld, ON *elli;* derivative fr. the root of E *old*] **1 a** *dial Brit* **:** period of life **:** AGE **b** *archaic* **:** OLD AGE **2** *archaic* **:** old times **:** ANTIQUITY ⟨a spirit of immemorial ~ pervades this tavern —Norman Douglas⟩ **3** *archaic* **:** an old person

eld *abbr* eldest

el de·bab \elˈde,bab\ *n* [Ar *al-dhubāb* the flies (the source of the disease)] **:** a trypanosomiasis of northern African camels resembling surra but caused by a distinct parasite (*Trypanosoma soudanense*)

1el·der \ˈeldə(r)\ *n* -s [ME *eldre*, *eller*, *ellern*, fr. OE *ellærn*, *ellen;* prob. akin to OE *alor* alder — more at ALDER] **:** a shrub or tree of the genus *Sambucus; esp, Brit* **:** BOURTREE

2el·der \ˈeldə(r)\ *adj* [ME, fr. OE *yldra*, *ieldra*, *eldra*, compar. of *ald*, *eald* old — more at OLD] **1 :** of earlier birth ⟨much the ~ of the two —Norman Demuth⟩ **:** of greater age ⟨the ~ service flag was a . . . cobwebby bunting —MacKinlay Kantor⟩ **:** OLDER ⟨great, rich, established ~ nations —Joseph Alsop⟩ **2 :** of or relating to earlier times **:** FORMER ⟨his poems are of the ~ New England tradition —H.V.Gregory⟩ **3** *obs* **:** of or relating to a more advanced time of life **:** LATER ⟨I tender you my service raw and young; which ~ days shall ripen —Shak.⟩ **4 :** of greater experience **:** SENIOR ⟨an ~ educator⟩

3elder \"\ *n* -s [ME *eldre*, fr. OE *yldra*, *ieldra*, *eldra*, fr. *yldra*, *ieldra*, *eldra*, adj.] **1 :** one who lived at an earlier period — usu. used in pl. ⟨rules and standards passed down from the ~*s* —Paul Woodring⟩ **2 a :** one who is older **:** SENIOR — usu. used in pl. ⟨young people ski and their ~*s* golf —S.H.Holbrook⟩ **b** *archaic* **:** an aged person ⟨the wither'd ~ hath his Poll claw'd like a Parrot —Shak.⟩ **3** [ME, trans. of LL *senior*] **:** a member of a governing body or ruling class made up of those whose age or experience confers a special dignity on them **:** SUPERIOR — usu. used in pl. ⟨hereditary village ~*s* governing by common consent . . . held political authority beyond the courts —J.M. Van der Kroef⟩ **4** [trans. of LL *presbyter* & Gk *presbyteros*] **:** any of certain church officers or leaders: as **a :** PRESBYTER 1 ⟨at first the Christian churches followed the precedent of the synagogues in their organization and the ~*s* were the official leaders —E.H.Sugden⟩ **b :** a permanent officer elected by a Presbyterian congregation and ordained to serve on the session and assist the pastor at communion **c :** a fully ordained Methodist minister ⟨made a deacon in 1790 and ordained ~ in 1793 —H.E.Starr⟩ **d :** one ordained to the Melchizedek priesthood in the Mormon Church

4elder \"\ *n* -s [Flem; prob. akin to OE *ūder* udder — more at UDDER] *dial* **:** UDDER

elderberry \ˈ==- — *see* BERRY\ *n* [ME *eldreberye*, fr. *eldre* elder (bush) + *berye* berry] **1 a :** the edible berrylike drupe of an elder, (as the European bourtree or the No. American elder blow) that is eaten raw or processed into preserves or wines **b :** an elder bush or tree **2 :** DERBY BLUE

elder blow *n* [1*elder* + *blow* (blossom)] **:** an elder plant; *esp* **:** the No. American elder (*Sambucus canadensis*)

elder fungus *n* **:** JEW'S-EAR

el·der·li·ness \ˈeldə(r)lēnəs, -lin-\ *n* -ES **:** the quality or state of being elderly

el·der·ly \-lē,-li\ *adj* [2*elder* + *-ly*] **1 :** somewhat old: **a :** rather advanced in years **:** past middle age ⟨we must face the problems of an aging population, i.e., where a much larger proportion of the citizens is ~ —Alan Gregg⟩ **b :** OLD-FASHIONED, OUT-OF-DATE, OUTMODED ⟨an ~ office building on lower Fifth Avenue —Dwight Macdonald⟩ **2 :** of, relating to, or characteristic of one past the prime of life ⟨the Frate carried his doctrine rather too far for ~ ears —George Eliot⟩

el·dern \ˈeldərn\ *adj* [ME (Scot dial.), fr. 2*elder* + 1*-en*] *chiefly Scot* **:** ELDERLY

elder statesman *n* **:** an eminent senior member of a group or organization ⟨a much honored *elder statesman* of the geographic profession —*Economic Geog.*⟩; *esp* **:** a retired statesman who unofficially advises national leaders ⟨may hand over the premiership to his younger second-in-command after a year or two in office and stay on in the role of *elder statesman* —*New Yorker*⟩

el·dest \ˈeldəst\ *adj* [ME, fr. OE *yldest*, *ieldest*, *eldest*, superl. of *eald*, *ald* old — more at OLD] **:** of the greatest age or seniority: **a** *archaic* **:** most ancient **:** EARLIEST ⟨let us pay heed to our ~ scientific brothers and shrewdest symbolists, the mathematicians —Weston La Barre⟩ **b :** FIRSTBORN, OLDEST ⟨when their ~ child was arriving at school age —F.L.Allen⟩

eldest born *n* **:** FIRSTBORN

eldest hand *n* **:** the card player who first receives cards in the deal; *specif* **:** the player to the left of the dealer

el·ding \ˈeldən, -diŋ\ *n* -s [ME, fr. ON *elding*, fr. *eldr* fire + *-ing* (n. suffix) — more at ANNEAL] *chiefly Scot* **:** FUEL, FIREWOOD

el·do·ra·do \,eldəˈrä¦(,)dō, -rā¦, -ra¦, -rȧ¦, ¦də\ *n* -s *often cap* [after *El Dorado*, fabulously wealthy city or country that 16th cent. explorers thought existed in So. America, fr. Sp, lit., the gilded one] **:** a place of fabulous wealth, abundance, or opportunity ⟨in the ~ of the New World they quickly amassed wealth and power⟩ ⟨the town is a composer's ~ —Aaron Copland⟩ ⟨orchards which in blossoming time offer an ~ of color —Samuel Van Valkenburg & Ellsworth Huntington⟩

el·dress \ˈeldrəs\ *n* -ES [3*elder* + *-ess*] **:** a female church elder

el·dritch *also* **el·drich** *or* **el·ritch** \ˈel(d)rich\ *adj* [perh. fr. (assumed) OE *ælfrīce* fairyland, fr. OE *ælf* elf + *rīce* kingdom, power; akin to OE *rīce* powerful, rich — more at ELF, RICH] **:** WEIRD, EERIE, UNCANNY ⟨the ~ screech of hunting horns swelled louder —F.V.W.Mason⟩ ⟨its ~ comedy captivated audiences around the world —Lincoln Barnett⟩

elds *pl of* ELD

1el·e·at·ic \¦elē¦ad·ik\ *adj, usu cap* [L *Eleaticus* (also, of Elea), fr. Gk *Eleatikos*, fr. *Eleatēs* of Elea (fr. *Elea* — Velia — ancient town in southern Italy) + *-ikos* -ic] **:** of or relating to a school of Greek philosophers founded by Parmenides and developed by Zeno who principally asserted the unity of being and the unreality of motion or change — compare PARMENIDEAN

²eleatic \"\ *n* -s *usu cap* **:** an Eleatic philosopher
el·e·at·i·cism \-d·ə,sizəm\ *n* -s *usu cap* **:** Eleatic doctrine
elec *abbr* **1** electric; electrical; electricity; electrified **2** electuary
el·e·cam·pane \,eləkam'pān, -kəm-, -lē(,)-; -'kam,pān\ *n* -s [ME *elena campana*, fr. ML *enula campana*, lit., field inula, fr. *enula* inula (alter. of L *inula* elecampane) + *campana*, fem. of *campanus* of the field, fr. L *campus* field + *-anus* -an — more at INULA, CAMP] **:** a large coarse European herb (*Inula helenium*) having yellow ray flowers and being naturalized in the U.S.
¹elect \ə'lekt, ē'l- *sometimes* 'ē,l-\ *adj* [ME, fr. LL & L; LL *electus* chosen of God, fr. L, choice, excellent, selected, fr. past part. of *eligere*] **1 :** chosen esp. by preference or for excellence **:** carefully selected **:** EXCLUSIVE, CHOICE ⟨considered themselves a very ~ group⟩ **2 a :** chosen for office or position but not yet installed — usu. used after the noun ⟨president-*elect*⟩ ⟨delegate-*elect*⟩ **b :** chosen for marriage at some future time to a specified person ⟨bride-*elect*⟩ **3 :** chosen as an object of divine mercy or favor **:** set apart for eternal life — used in theology ⟨to ~ souls a Redeemer comes down who reveals the secret knowledge —W.F.Howard⟩
²elect \ə'l-,ē'l-\ *n, pl* **elect** [ME, fr. LL & L *electus*, adj. & n.] **:** one chosen or set apart: **a :** one chosen by God as the object of mercy or favor ⟨the emperor was the ~ of God —R.M. French⟩ ⟨they were of the ~, those chosen by God —J.C. Brauer⟩ **b :** a select or exclusive group of people ⟨her status changed from that of "outsider" to one of the ~ when her classmates discovered that she could sing F above high C —*Current Biog.*⟩
³elect \"\ *vb* -ED/-ING/-S [ME *electen*, fr. L *electus*, past part. of *eligere* to pick out, choose, select, fr. *e-* + *-ligere* (fr. *legere* to gather, pick out, choose) — more at LEGEND] *vt* **1 :** to make a selection of **:** CHOOSE ⟨having ~*ed* deliberately . . . that stern land and weather —William Faulkner⟩ ⟨concentrators in geological sciences ~ either geology or geography —*Official Register of Harvard Univ.*⟩ **2 :** to choose (a person) for an office, position, or membership ⟨~ a chairman⟩ ⟨~ a leader⟩ ⟨~ a member of a board⟩; *esp* **:** to select (a person) for political office by vote ⟨~ the president of the U.S.⟩ **3 :** to choose (a course of action) esp. by preference **:** decide upon ⟨~*ed* suicide as a preferable fate —*Sydney (Australia) Bull.*⟩ ⟨received the opening kickoff and ~*ed* to punt —Harry Molter⟩ **4 :** to designate or choose as an object of divine mercy or favor ⟨Wyclif argued that the true Church is made up only of those ~*ed* by God —K.S.Latourette⟩ ~ *vi* **:** to make a selection **:** CHOOSE ⟨what is worse still is the power of the big company to ruin the individual as capriciously as it ~*s* —Robert Lekachman⟩ **syn** see DESIGNATE
elect *abbr* **1** electric; electrical; electrician; electricity **2** electuary
elec·tion \ə'lekshən, ē'-\ *n* -s [ME *eleccioun*, fr. MF *election*, fr. LL & L; LL *election-, electio* election to divine favor, fr. L, choice, selection, fr. *electus* (past part. of *eligere* to pick out, choose) + *-ion-, -io* -ion] **1 a :** the act or process of electing **:** CHOICE ⟨the faculty of ~, or the power of free choice —Frank Thilly⟩ ⟨our income-tax system is replete with ~*s* —*Jour. of Accountancy*⟩ **b :** the act or process of choosing a person for office, position, or membership by voting ⟨they had an ~ last week⟩ **c :** an instance of the electorate's exercising its function ⟨the ~ of 1936 was rather uneventful⟩ **d :** divine choice; *specif* **:** predestination of individuals as objects of divine mercy and salvation **e :** the choice of an astrologically favorable time **f :** the selection of a site for or method of surgery **2 :** the fact or status of being elected ⟨an open convention . . . to ratify his ~ to party chief —*Time*⟩ **syn** see CHOICE
election cake *n* **:** a fruitcake usu. made of bread dough, raisins, figs, sugar, egg, and butter and baked in a bread pan
election day *n* **:** a day legally established for the election of public officials; *specif, often cap E&D* **:** the first Tuesday after the first Monday in November in an even year designated for national elections in the U.S. and observed as a legal holiday in most states
election district *n* **1 a :** a district that is created for the administration of elections ⟨all party organization rests ultimately upon the "unit cell" of the precinct or *election district* —W.S.Sayre⟩ **b :** PRECINCT 1c **2 :** a political division of a county in certain states (as Alabama, Florida, Wyoming) in the U.S. — compare JUDICIAL TOWNSHIP
¹elec·tion·eer \ə,lekshə'ni(ə)r, ē'-\ *vi* -ED/-ING/-S [*election* + *-eer* (as in *auctioneer*, v.)] **:** to take an active part in an election campaign: as **a :** to campaign for one's own election ⟨the senator ~*ed* vigorously in his opponent's home county⟩ **b :** to try to sway public opinion esp. by the use of propaganda ⟨skillful, amateur ~*ing* all over the country —*New Republic*⟩ ⟨whip up public feeling for ~*ing* purposes or to launch smear attacks —A.E.Norman⟩
²electioneer \"\ *n* -s **:** one who electioneers
election pink *n* **:** PINXTER FLOWER
election posies *n pl* **:** INDIAN PAINTBRUSH
¹elec·tive \ə'lektiv, -tēv *also* -təv\ *adj* [MF & ML; MF *electif*, fr. ML *electivus*, fr. L *electus* (past part. of *eligere* to pick out, choose) + *-ivus* -ive — more at ELECT] **1 a** (1) **:** chosen by popular election ⟨an ~ legislature⟩ (2) **:** assigned or filled by popular election ⟨first ~ position was as county probate judge —*Current Biog.*⟩ **b :** of or relating to election ⟨all other ~ functions can only be exercised by the General Assembly —Herbert Weinschel⟩ ⟨the ~ franchise⟩ **c :** based on the right or principle of election ⟨governments may be described . . . as either hereditary or ~ —F.L.Windolph⟩ **2 :** that may be elected **:** permitting a choice (as between alternatives) ⟨a law is ~ if the employer is allowed to accept or reject the act —G.W.Miller⟩ **:** OPTIONAL ⟨for the other half day ~ courses are followed in heterogeneous groups — music, art . . . and physical education —Elise Martens⟩ **3 a :** tending to operate on one substance rather than another ⟨~ fermentation⟩ ⟨~ absorption⟩ ⟨~ attraction⟩ **b :** tending toward one object rather than another **:** sympathetically inclined toward ⟨we Southerners lack . . . an ~ affinity with that book —Norman Douglas⟩ — **elec·tive·ly** \-tivlē, -li\ *adv* — **elec·tive·ness** \-tivnəs, -tēv- *also* -təv-\ *n* -ES
²elec·tive \"\ *n* -s **:** an elective course or subject (as in a college curriculum) ⟨in the late seventies, when I was an undergraduate, ~*s* were still unknown in the smaller New England colleges —John Dewey⟩ ⟨his ~*s* included English 136 and Philosophy 101⟩
elec·tor \-tə(r) *also* -,tó(ə)r *or* -,tó(ə)\ *n* -s [ME *electour*, fr. MF *electeur*, fr. L *elector* one that chooses, fr. *electus* (past part. of *eligere* to pick out, choose) + *-or*] **:** one who is entitled to vote esp. in a political election ⟨the numerous unthinking ~*s* who cast ballots in response to superficial and emotional appeals —Alexander Brady⟩: as **a** [MF or ML; MF *electeur*, fr. ML *elector*, fr. L, one that chooses] **:** one of the German princes entitled to take part in choosing the sovereign head of the Holy Roman Empire ⟨the ~ of Hanover⟩ **b :** a member of the electoral college that elects the president and vice-president of the U.S. ⟨in 1860 he was presidential ~ on the Douglas ticket —H.E.Nettles⟩
elec·tor·al \ə'lekt(ə)rəl, ē|; ÷|,lek|tór-, ÷·|tōr-\ *adj* **1 :** belonging to or holding rank as a German elector ⟨the vendors did not enter ~ Saxony —R.H.Bainton⟩ **2 a :** of or relating to an elector ⟨an ~ district⟩ ⟨the ~ vote⟩ **b :** of or relating to election ⟨the ~ system was modified through the Twelfth Amendment —W.S.Sayre⟩
electoral college *n, sometimes cap E&C* **:** a body of electors ⟨the Prussian House of Representatives was chosen by *electoral colleges* —F.A.Magruder⟩; *esp* **:** the group of presidential electors representing the states in the U.S. ⟨the *Electoral College* is composed of as many representatives as there are senators and representatives in Congress —*Voter's Guide*⟩
elec·tor·al·ly \-rəlē, -li\ *adv* **:** in a manner relating to or involving electors or elections
elec·tor·ate \ə'lekt(ə)rə|t, ēl- *sometimes* -tə,rā|; *usu* |d·+V\ *n* -s [F *électorat*, fr. ML *elector* + F *-at* -ate] **1 :** the territory, jurisdiction, or dignity of a German elector **2 :** a body of people entitled to vote ⟨the president appealed directly to the electorate⟩
elec·to·ri·al \ə,lek|tōrēəl, ē|-, |ē,=|=-, -tór-\ *adj* **:** ELECTORAL
electr- *or* **electro-** *comb form* [NL *electr-*, fr. L *electrum* amber] **1 a :** electricity ⟨*electro*meter⟩ **b :** electric ⟨*electr*ize⟩ ⟨*electro*magnet⟩ **:** electric and ⟨*electro*medical⟩ **:** electrically ⟨*electro*positive⟩ **2 :** electrolytic ⟨*electro*analysis⟩ **3 :** electromagnetic ⟨*electro*chronograph⟩ **4 :** electron ⟨*electro*philic⟩
elec·tra complex \ə'lektrə-, ē|\ *n, usu cap E* [after *Electra*, Greek mythological personage who urged her brother Orestes to slay their mother Clytemnestra in revenge for her murder of their father Agamemnon, fr. L, fr. Gk *Ēlektra*] **:** the female counterpart of the Oedipus complex
elec·tress \-rəs\ *n* -ES [fr. earlier *electoress*, fr. *elector* + *-ess*] **:** the wife or widow of a German elector
elec·tret \-rət\ *n* -s [*electricity* + *magnet*] **1 :** a dielectric body in which a permanent state of electric polarization has been set up **2 :** the material of which an electret is composed
¹elec·tric \ə'lektrik, ē'-, -rēk\ *or* **elec·tri·cal** \-rəkəl, -rēk-\ *adj* [NL *electricus* produced from amber by friction, electric, fr. ML, of amber, fr. L *electrum* amber, alloy of gold and silver (fr. Gk *ēlektron*) + *-icus* -ic, -ical; akin to Gk *ēlektōr* beaming sun, Skt *ulkā* fiery phenomenon in the sky, meteor] **1 a :** of, relating to, or produced by electricity ⟨~ supply⟩ ⟨~ output⟩ ⟨*electrical* industry⟩ ⟨*electrical* shock⟩ **b :** of, relating to, or produced by a method of reproducing sound in which the cutting stylus is electrically vibrated — compare ACOUSTIC 3 a(2) **2 a :** operated by an electric motor ⟨an ~ refrigerator⟩ **b :** heated by an electric current ⟨an ~ stove⟩ **c :** charged by an electric potential **3 :** exciting with or as if with electric shock **:** ELECTRIFYING, STIMULATING ⟨when the people are Irishmen and the town is Dublin, the possibilities are fairly ~ —Harry Levin⟩ ⟨a part in which she gave an ~ performance —Brooks Atkinson⟩ ⟨the effect upon the jurors was *electrical* —Erle Stanley Gardner⟩ — **elec·tri·cal·ly** \-rək(ə)lē, -rēk-, -li\ *adv* — **elec·tri·cal·ness** \-kəlnəs\ *n* -ES
²electric \"\ *n* -s **1** *archaic* **:** a nonconductor of electricity (as amber, glass, resin) used to excite or accumulate electricity **2** [*electric (lamp)* or *electric (light)*] **:** an electric light — usu. used in pl. ⟨the church was lit with little ~*s* —Richard Llewellyn⟩ **3 :** an electrically operated vehicle: **a** [*electric (motorcar)*] **:** an electric automobile ⟨nice old ladies driving down . . . Broad Street in their elegant Baker ~*s* —James Thurber⟩ **b** [*electric (railway)*] **:** an electric train or streetcar ⟨~*s* and diesels do not have side rods —John Page⟩ **4** *dial* **:** ELECTRICITY **5** *or* **electric blue** *or* **electric green :** a grayish blue that is greener and deeper than copenhagen, Saxe blue, or old china, redder and deeper than Gobelin, and greener and duller than Quimper
electrical degree *n* **1 :** one 360th of a cycle of an alternating current **2 :** one 360th of the angle subtended at the axis of an alternating current by two consecutive field poles of like polarity
electrical drainage *n* **:** diversion of electric currents from underground pipes to prevent damage by electrolysis
electrical engineer *n* **:** one trained in electrical engineering
electrical engineering *n* **:** a branch of engineering that deals with the practical application of electricity esp. as related to communications, the distribution of power, and the design and operation of machinery and equipment
electrical interlock *n* **:** an interlock operating by the combined action of mechanical and electrical means
electrical precipitation *n* **:** ELECTROSTATIC PRECIPITATION
electrical sheet *n* **:** flat-rolled silicon steel used in electric motors, generators, and transformers
electrical storm *var of* ELECTRIC STORM
electrical transcription *n* **1 :** a phonograph record esp. designed for use in radiobroadcasting **2 :** a radio program broadcast from an electrical transcription
electric board *n* **:** a hard fiberboard used (as in electric switches) for insulation
electric brain *n* **1 :** an electric computing machine; *esp* **:** a punched-card machine that performs complex operations (as sorting and filing) with prepared matter fed into it **2 :** ELECTRONIC BRAIN
electric calamine *n* [so called fr. its strong pyroelectric properties] **:** HEMIMORPHITE
electric catfish *n* **:** a catfish (*Malapterurus electricus*) of northern and tropical Africa attaining a length of about 30 inches and having an electric organ of epidermal origin capable of giving a strong shock — called also *raad*
electric cell *n* **:** CELL 6
electric chair *n* **1 :** a chair used in carrying out the death penalty by electrocution **2 :** the penalty of death by electrocution
electric charge *n* **:** a definite quantity of electricity, either negative or positive, usu. regarded as a more or less localized population of electrons separated or considered separately from their corresponding protons or vice versa **:** the quantity of electricity held by a body and construed as an excess or deficiency of electrons
electric clock *n* **:** any of various clocks operated by electricity: **a :** a clock having a spring or weighted arm that is wound at regular intervals by an electric motor **b :** a clock whose pendulum is kept in vibration by electromagnetic impulse **c :** one of a system of electrically operated clocks consisting of a master clock and a number of sympathetic clocks **d :** a clock connected with an electromagnetic recording apparatus **e :** a clock having neither pendulum nor balance, consisting simply of a small alternating-current motor that drives the clock hands through a reducing train of gearing, and telling time by current controlled at the generator to a definite rate of alternations per second
electric current *n* **:** a movement of positive or negative electric particles (as electrons) accompanied by such observable effects as the production of heat, of a magnetic field, or of chemical transformations — compare ALTERNATING CURRENT, DIRECT CURRENT, DISPLACEMENT CURRENT
electric displacement *n* **:** DISPLACEMENT 3 a
electric double layer *n* **:** a region existing at the boundary of two phases and assumed to consist of two oppositely charged layers (as a layer of negative ions adsorbed on colloidal particles that attracts a layer of positive ions in the surrounding electrolytic solution) — called also *Helmholtz double layer*
electric ear *n* **1 :** a microphone with accessories adapted to the measurement of sound intensity **2 :** an apparatus resembling an electric ear used for the automatic control of machinery
electric eel *n* **:** an eel-shaped cyprinoid fish (*Electrophorus electricus*) of the rivers of the Orinoco and Amazon basins often attaining a length of six feet and said to disable large animals by its shocks produced by electric organs that consist of modified muscle tissue situated along the ventral part of the body
electric eraser *n* **:** a hand-sized machine with an erasing head driven by an electric motor used esp. in drafting and library work
electric eye *n* **1 :** a photoelectric cell with accessories adapted to the automatic performance of a process (as color selection or lighting control) **2 :** a miniature cathode-ray tube that indicates determination of a condition (as the proper tuning of a radio receiver) — called also *electron-ray tube*
electric fence *n* **:** a wire fence electrically charged to give animals touching it a slight warning shock
electric field *n* **:** a region established by the proximity of electric charges or the variation of surrounding magnetic intensity resulting in the application of mechanical force to an electric charge introduced into the region, the direction of the field at any point being that of the force on a small positive charge placed at that point — compare ELECTRIC INTENSITY
electric fire *n, Brit* **:** a small electric space heater for rooms
electric fish *n* **:** any of several fishes (as the electric eel, electric catfish, electric ray) able to communicate an electric shock by means of special organs
electric fluid *n* **:** a hypothetical imponderable fluid to the presence of which electrical phenomena were formerly attributed — compare EFFLUVIUM 1b
electric furnace *n* **:** a furnace that is heated usu. to very high temperatures by an electric current and used esp. in industry for fusing alloys and refractory materials — see ARC FURNACE, INDUCTION FURNACE
electric green *n* **:** ELECTRIC 5
electric guitar *n* **:** a guitar whose tone is magnified electrically by a microphone or pickup device that is built into the instrument or attached externally, by an audio-frequency amplifier, and by a loudspeaker, the volume and resonance being controlled by the player
electric hammer *n* **:** an electrically driven hammer used esp. in riveting or caulking
electric hygrometer *n* **:** a hygrometer that utilizes changes in electrical resistance (as of a film of salt) to indicate changes in atmospheric humidity
elec·tri·cian \ə,lek'trishən, ē,l- *sometimes* ,ē,l-, *chiefly Brit* ,e,lek- *or* ,elik-\ *n* -s [*electr-* + *-ician* (as in *technician*)] **1 :** a specialist in the field of electricity **2 :** one who installs, maintains, operates, or repairs electrical equipment; *specif* **:** a warrant officer in the U.S. Navy whose specialty is supervision of the installation, maintenance, operation, and repair of electrical equipment
electric intensity *n* **:** the strength of an electric field at any point as measured by the force exerted upon a unit positive charge placed at that point
electric iron *n* **:** an electrically heated smoothing or pressing iron
elec·tric·i·ty \ə,lek'trisəd·|ē, ē,l-, -s(ə)t|ē, |i *sometimes* ,ē,l-, *chiefly Brit* ,e,lek- *or* ,elik-\ *n* -ES [NL *electricus* electric + E *-ity* — more at ELECTRIC] **1 :** a fundamental entity of nature consisting of negative and positive kinds composed respectively of electrons and protons or possibly of electrons and positrons, usu. measured in electrostatic units (as the statcoulomb) or electromagnetic units (as the coulomb), observable in the attractions and repulsions of bodies electrified by friction and in certain natural phenomena (as lightning or the aurora borealis), and usu. utilized in the form of electric currents — see NEGATIVE ELECTRICITY, POSITIVE ELECTRICITY, STATIC ELECTRICITY **2 :** a science that deals with the phenomena and laws of electricity **3 :** a contagious feeling of keen excitement or inspiration **:** ENTHUSIASM ⟨you can feel the ~ in the crowd and the band —Bill Simon⟩ **4 :** ELECTRIC CURRENT ⟨heating by ~⟩
electric knife *n* **:** an electrode in the form of a needle that simultaneously cuts and sears tissue
electric lamp *n* **:** a lamp in which electricity is the source of light — compare ARC LAMP, FLUORESCENT LAMP, INCANDESCENT LAMP, NEON LAMP, NERNST LAMP
electric light *n* **:** light produced by an electric lamp; *also* **:** ELECTRIC LAMP
electric light bug *n* [so called fr. the fact that adult bugs are often attracted by bright lights] **:** GIANT WATER BUG
electric lobes *n pl but sing or pl in constr, zool* **:** the part of the medulla of an electric ray that controls the electric organs
electric lock *n* **:** a device to prevent or restrict the movements of a lever, switch, or drawbridge unless the locking member is withdrawn by an electrical device
electric locking *n* **:** the locking by electricity of a railroad mechanism (as a signal or switch) to prevent a change which might endanger an approaching or passing train
electric locomotive *n* **:** an electrically operated locomotive that obtains electric power from an overhead wire, a third rail, or storage battery or that generates its own electric power — compare DIESEL-ELECTRIC LOCOMOTIVE, TURBINE-ELECTRIC LOCOMOTIVE
electric log *n* **1 :** a device for determining the nature of geological strata (as in well digging) by electrical means usu. through resistivity measurements **2 :** the record of tests made by an electric log — compare ¹LOG 3b(3)
electric moment *n* **:** the product of the distance between the centers of the charges composing an electric dipole and the magnitude of either charge
electric organ *n* **1 :** a pipe organ with an electric action **2 :** a specialized tract of tissue in which electricity is generated and which consists of closely packed prisms typically of modified muscle tissue separated by sheaths of connective tissue and abundantly supplied with nerves, each prism in turn being composed of many layers of disklike electroplaxes separated from one another by a layer of gelatinous material into which the nerve fibers enter and from which they are distributed to one surface of an adjacent electroplax
electric oscillation *n* **:** OSCILLATION 3
electric pen *n* **:** a hand pen for making stencils that consists essentially of a puncturing needle and a small magnetoelectric device for making it reciprocate
electric plate *n* **:** ELECTROPLAX
electric potential *n* **:** a quantity that in an electric field is roughly analogous to elevation or level in a gravity field and that is measured at any point by the potential energy of a unit positive charge placed at that point and reckoned with reference to some arbitrary zero of potential (as that at an infinite distance from all electric charges or for practical purposes that of the earth or any well-grounded conductor)
electric railroad *or* **electric railway** *n* **:** a railroad on which the trains are drawn by electric locomotives
electric ray *n* **:** any of numerous bottom-dwelling rays (family Torpedinidae) that are widely distributed in warm seas and have the anterior part of the body round and disklike, a short tail terminating in a rayed fin, and a pair of electric organs composed of modified pectoral muscles and occupying the lateral part of each side between the head and the pectoral fin: as **a :** a ray (*Tetranarce occidentalis*) of the eastern coast of No. America that attains a length of about five feet and is capable of giving a severe shock **b :** a somewhat smaller fish (*T. californica*) of the Pacific coast
electric refrigeration *n* **:** refrigeration by means of a compression machine driven by an electric motor
electrics *pl of* ELECTRIC
electric seal *n* **:** hare or rabbit fur clipped and dyed to simulate sealskin
electric shock *n* **:** ³SHOCK 5
electric shocker *n* **:** a device for stunning freshwater fishes by passing a current of electricity through the water of a stream or pond (as for collecting fishes for transport from one body of water to another or for studying fish population)
electric shock therapy *or* **electric shock treatment** *also* **electric shock** *or* **electric therapy** *n* **:** ELECTROSHOCK THERAPY
electric shovel *n* **:** a power shovel using electric power
electric steel *n* **:** steel refined in an electric furnace — called also *electrosteel*
electric storm *or* **electrical storm** *n* **:** a sudden and violent storm usu. accompanied by rain and characterized by electrical phenomena (as thunder and lightning) that often interfere with communications and electric light systems **:** THUNDERSTORM
electric strength *n* **:** DIELECTRIC STRENGTH
electric switch *n* **:** SWITCH 5
electric tape *n* **:** FRICTION TAPE
electric torch *n, Brit* **:** FLASHLIGHT d
electric varnish *n* **:** a varnish having good insulating properties
electric wave *n* **1 :** ELECTROMAGNETIC WAVE **2 :** a high-frequency alternating-current cycle considered as a wave propagated with definite velocity in a conductor
elec·tri·fi·ca·tion \ə,lektrəfə'kāshən, ē,-\ *n* -s **:** the act or process of electrifying or the state of being electrified: as **a :** the act or process of charging, equipping, or supplying with or operating by electricity or the state of being so charged, equipped, supplied, or operated ⟨the ~ of cloud droplets⟩ ⟨the ~ of rural areas⟩ ⟨the ~ of the railroads⟩ **b :** the act or process of markedly exciting or thrilling or the state of being markedly excited or thrilled ⟨the strange pure ecstasy was not a transient ~ —George Meredith⟩ ⟨his charm wrought a positive ~ of the audience⟩
elec·tri·fi·er \-'=ə,fī(ə)r, -īə\ *n* -s **:** one that electrifies
elec·tri·fy \-,fī\ *vt* -ED/-ING/-S [*electric* + *-fy*] **1 :** to charge with electricity ⟨~ a glass rod⟩ **2 :** to excite suddenly and markedly as if by an electric shock **:** startle, jar, or thrill into total attention or concern ⟨a hunger strike that *electrified* all Egypt —*Holiday*⟩ ⟨the boys cooked up a hair-raising piece of news . . . to ~ the girls —Dixon Wecter⟩ esp. pleasurably ⟨the blue-eyed girl whose silvery tones and immense vitality had *electrified* audiences —Alan Tomkins⟩ **3 :** to equip, operate, or supply with electricity ⟨in Minnesota, where the number of *electrified* farms has risen . . . to 90 percent —A.E. Stevenson b. 1900⟩ ⟨there is waterpower enough to ~ the continent —Waldo Frank⟩
elec·tro \ə'lek(,)trō, e'-\ *n* -s [short for ¹*electrotype*] **1 :** ELEC-

TROTYPE **2 :** a reproduction of a coin made by the electrotype process ⟨an ~ of a 1793 cent⟩
elec·tro- *in pronunciations below,* ≈¦≈≈ = ə¦lek(ˌ)trō *or* ē¦- *or* -trə\ — see ELECTR-
elec·tro·acous·tic *also* **elec·tro·acous·ti·cal** \≈¦≈≈+\ *adj* [*electr- + acoustic, acoustical*] **:** of or relating to electroacoustics
elec·tro·acous·tics \"+\ *n pl but sing in constr* **:** a science that deals with the transformation of acoustic energy into electric energy or vice versa
elec·tro·anal·y·sis \"+\ *n* [NL, fr. *electr- + analysis*] **:** chemical analysis by electrolytic methods involving the use of significant amounts of electrical energy (as for electrodeposition) in distinction from electrical methods (as potentiometry or conductometric methods) that use negligible amounts — **elec·tro·an·a·lyt·ic** \"+\ *or* **elec·tro·an·a·lyt·i·cal** \"+\ *adj*
electrobiological \"+\ *adj* **:** of or relating to electrobiology
electrobiologist \"+\ *n* **:** a specialist in electrobiology
electrobiology \"+\ *n* [*electr- + biology*] **:** a branch of biology that deals with the electrical phenomena of living organisms
electrocapillarity \"+\ *n* [ISV *electr- + capillarity;* orig. formed as F *électrocapillarité*] **:** a change in the surface tension between two immiscible liquids when an electric current passes through the interface from one to the other (as in capillary tubes) — **electrocapillary** \"+\ *adj*
electrocardiogram \"+\ *n* [*electr- + cardiogram*] **:** the tracing made by an electrocardiograph used to determine abnormality in the heart muscle
electrocardiograph \"+\ *n* [*electr- + cardiograph*] **:** an instrument for recording the changes of electrical potential occurring during the heartbeat (as by photographing vibrations of a string galvanometer connected with the right and left hands or with one hand and one foot) used esp. in diagnosing irregularities of heart action — **electrocardiographic** \"+\ *adj* — **electrocardiographically** \"+\ *adv* — **electrocardiography** \"+\ *n*

electrocardiogram: *P*, first upward deflection due to contraction of auricles; *Q, R, S, T*, deflections due to action of ventricles

electrocautery \"+\ *n* [*electr- + cautery*] **1 :** a cautery operated by an electric current **2** *also* **electrocauterization** \"+\ *n* **:** the cauterization of tissue by means of an electrocautery **:** ELECTROCOAGULATION
electrochemical \"+\ *adj* [*electr- + chemical*] **:** of or relating to electrochemistry ⟨~ corrosion⟩ — **electrochemically** \"+\ *adv*
electrochemical equivalent *n* **:** the weight of a substance (as an element) deposited or evolved during electrolysis by the passage of a specified quantity of electricity and usu. expressed in grams per coulomb, the value for silver as the usual standard being 0.001118 gram
electrochemical series *n* **:** ELECTROMOTIVE SERIES
electrochemical telegraph *n* **:** CHEMICAL TELEGRAPH
electrochemist \"+\ *n* [*electr- + chemist*] **:** a specialist in electrochemistry
electrochemistry \"+\ *n* [*electr- + chemistry*] **:** a science that deals with the relation of electricity to chemical changes and with the interconversion of chemical and electrical energy (as in electric cells or in electrolysis) and that has many applications in industry (as in the production of aluminum, alkalies, and chlorine or in electroplating)
electrochromatography \"+\ *n* [*electr- + chromatography*] **:** chromatography involving differential electrical migration produced by application of an electric potential
electroclean \"+\ *vt* [*electr- + clean*] **:** to clean (a metal surface) by immersion in the form of an electrode in the alkaline bath of an electrolytic cell
electrocoagulate \"+\ *vt* [back-formation fr. *electrocoagulation*] **:** to cause the electrocoagulation of
electrocoagulation \"+\ *n* [*electr- + coagulation*] **:** the coagulation of tissue by surgical diathermy; *also* **:** the operation of coagulating tissue in this way **:** ELECTROCAUTERY
electrocoma \"+\ *n* [*electr- + coma* (unconsciousness)] **:** the coma induced in electroshock therapy
electroconductive \"+\ *adj* [*electr- + conductive*] **:** capable of conducting electricity
electroconization \"+\ *n* [*electr- + conization*] **:** CONIZATION
electrocontractility \"+\ *n* [*electr- + contractility*] **:** contractility (as of a muscle) in response to electric stimulation
electroconvulsive \"+\ *adj* [*electr- + convulsive*] **:** of, relating to, or involving convulsive response to electroshock
electroconvulsive therapy *or* **electroconvulsive shock** *n* **:** ELECTROSHOCK THERAPY
electrocorticogram \"+\ *n* -s [*electr- + cortico- + -gram*] **:** an electroencephalogram made with electrodes in direct contact with the brain
electrocortin \"+\ *n* [*electr- + cortin*] **:** ALDOSTERONE
elec·troc·u·lo·gram \əˌlek'träkyələˌgram, ēˌl-\ *n* -s [*electr- + ocul- + gram*] **:** a record of eye movement **:** a recording of the moving eye
elec·tro·cute \ə'lektrəˌkyüt, ē'-, *usu* -üd.+V\ *vt* -ED/-ING/-S [*electr- + -cute* (as in *execute*)] **1 :** to put to death as a legal punishment by causing a fatally large electric current to pass through the body ⟨~ a criminal⟩ ⟨a person may be *electrocuted* for treasonable activities in some states⟩ **2 :** to kill by electric shock ⟨the lineman was *electrocuted* when he happened to touch a power wire⟩
elec·tro·cu·tion \≈ˌ≈≈'kyüshən\ *n* -s **:** the act of killing or putting to death by electric current — **elec·tro·cu·tion·al** \≈¦≈≈¦kyüshənᵊl, -shnəl\ *adj*
electrocutor trap *n* **:** an insect trap that kills the insects attracted to it by electric energy
elec·trode \-ˌtrōd\ *n* -s [*electr- + -ode*] **:** a conductor (as a metallic substance or carbon) used to establish electrical contact with a nonmetallic portion of a circuit (as in an electrolytic cell, a storage battery, an electron tube, or an arc lamp) — see ANODE, CATHODE
electrodecantation \≈¦≈≈ *at* ELECTRO-+\ *n* [*electr- + decantation*] **:** an electrophoretic process utilizing two vertical membranes for concentrating and separating colloidal dispersions by stratification, the layers so formed being separable by decantation into the dispersed particles and the liquid dispersion medium
elec·trode·less discharge \ə¦'lekˌtrōdləs-, ē\ *n* **:** a discharge produced in the neighborhood of a high-frequency alternating current under certain conditions through a gas contained in a closed tube without electrodes
¹electrodeposit \≈¦≈≈ *at* ELECTRO-+\ *n* [*electr- + deposit* (n.)] **:** a deposit (as metal or rubber) formed on or at an electrode by electrolysis (as in electroplating or electroforming)
²electrodeposit \"\ *vt* **:** to deposit (as nickel, copper, or rubber) by electrical action, esp. electrolysis
electrodeposition \≈¦≈≈ *at* ELECTRO-+\ *n* [*electr- + deposition*] **:** the process of electrodepositing
electrode potential *n* **:** the difference in electric potential between an electrode and the electrolyte with which it is in contact
electrodesiccation \≈¦≈≈ *at* ELECTRO-+\ *n* [*electr- + desiccation*] **:** the drying up of tissue by use of a high-frequency electric current applied with a needle electrode
electrodialysis \"+\ *n* [NL, fr. *electr- + dialysis*] **:** dialysis accelerated by an electromotive force applied to electrodes adjacent to the membranes and useful esp. in removing electrolytes from naturally occurring colloids (as proteins) — compare ELECTROOSMOSIS
electrodialyze \"+\ *vt* [*electr- + dialyze*] **:** to subject to electrodialysis
electrodisintegration \"+\ *n* [*electr- + disintegration*] **:** the disintegration of atomic nuclei due to bombardment with electrically charged particles — compare PHOTODISINTEGRATION
elec·tro·dot·ic \"+¦dädˌik\ *adj* [*electr-* + Gk *dotikos* inclined to give, giving freely, fr. *dotos* (verbal of *didonai* to give) + *-ikos* -ic — more at DATE] **:** NUCLEOPHILIC
electrodynamic \"+\ *adj* [F *électrodynamique,* fr. *électro-* electr- + *dynamique* dynamic — more at DYNAMIC] **:** of or relating to electrodynamics ⟨signal voltage . . . obtained from ~ velocity-sampling transducers —B.S.Melton⟩
electrodynamics \"+\ *n pl but usu sing in constr* [F *électrodynamique,* fr. *électrodynamique,* adj.] **:** a branch of physics that deals with the effects arising from the interactions of electric currents with magnets, with other currents, or with themselves
electrodynamic speaker *n* **:** a loudspeaker in which the voice coil is attached to and vibrates with the diaphragm — called also *dynamic speaker*
electrodynamometer \"+\ *n* [ISV *electr- + dynamometer;* prob. orig. formed as G *elektrodynamometer*] **:** an ammeter or galvanometer in which the torque due to the reaction between two coils in series with each other is balanced by a spiral spring
electroencephalogram \"+\ *n* [ISV *electr- + encephalogram;* orig. formed as G *elektrenkephalogramm*] **:** the tracing of brain waves made by an electroencephalograph
electroencephalograph \"+\ *n* [ISV *electr- + encephalograph*] **:** an apparatus for detecting and recording brain waves — **electroencephalographic** \"+\ *adj* — **electroencephalographically** \"+\ *adv* — **electroencephalography** \"+\ *n*
electroendosmosis \"+\ *also* **electroendosmose** \"+\ *n, pl* **electroendosmoses** [NL *electroendosmosis,* fr. *electr- + endosmosis*] **:** ELECTROOSMOSIS — **electroendosmotic** \"+\ *adj*
electroextraction \"+\ *n* [*electr- + extraction*] **:** extraction (as of metals from ores) by electrochemical processes
electrofiltration \"+\ *n* [*electr- + filtration*] **:** ELECTROSTATIC PRECIPITATION
electroform \≈'≈≈+ˌ-\ *vt* [*electr- + form*] **:** to form (shaped articles) by electrodeposition on a mold (as in making electrotypes) — compare ELECTROPLATE
electrogalvanize \≈¦≈≈+\ *vt* [*electr- + galvanize*] **:** to electroplate with zinc
elec·tro·gram \≈'≈≈+ˌgram\ *n* [*electr- + -gram*] **:** a tracing of the electric potentials of a tissue (as the brain) made by means of electrodes placed directly in the tissue instead of on the surface of the body
elec·tro·graph \-ˌgraf, -ˌgrȧf\ *n* [*electr- + -graph*] **1 :** a phototelegraphic apparatus for the electrical transmission of pictures **2 :** a device used for the etching or transfer of pictures or designs by electrolytic means
elec·tro·graph·ic \≈¦≈≈+¦grafik\ *adj* **1 :** relating to an electrograph **2** [*electr- + -graphic*] **:** relating to a method for the analysis of minerals and metals whereby a minute amount of the sample is transferred by electrical means to a suitable surface (as treated paper) where ions are then identified
electrographite \≈¦≈≈ *at* ELECTRO- +\ *n* [ISV *electr- + graphite*] **:** artificial graphite produced by heating carbon (as petroleum coke) in an electric furnace — called also *graphitized carbon*
elec·trog·ra·phy \əˌlek'trägrəfē, ēˌl- *sometimes* ˌēˌl- *or* (ˌ)eˌl-\ *n* -ES [*electr- + -graphy*] **:** the art or process of using an electrograph
electrohysterograph \≈¦≈≈ *at* ELECTRO- +\ *n* [*electr- + hyster- + -graph*] **:** an instrument for recording changes in electric impulses in the contracting uterine muscle during labor and used esp. in the detection of deviations from the normal progress of labor — **electrohysterography** \"+\ *n*
electrojet \≈'≈≈+ˌ-\ *n* [*electr- + jet*] **:** an overhead concentration of electric current that is restricted laterally so that in its effects it resembles a line current, that is found in the regions of strong auroral displays and along the magnetic equator, and that is sensitive to changes in the sun's emission of gases and radiation
electrokinetic \≈¦≈≈+\ *adj* [*electr- + kinetic*] **:** relating to the motion of particles or liquids that results from or produces a difference of electric potential (as in electrophoresis, electroosmosis, or the production of a streaming potential) — **electrokinetically** \"+\ *adv*
electrokinetic potential *n* **:** ZETA POTENTIAL
electrokinetics \"+\ *n pl but sing in constr* [*electr- + kinetics*] **:** a branch of physics that deals with the motion of electricity esp. as governed by the laws of steady currents in circuits and networks or with the motion of electrified particles in electric and magnetic fields
electrokinetograph \"+\ *n* [*electr- + kinet- + -graph*] **:** an instrument for measuring velocities of ocean currents by means of electrical effects of their movement in the earth's magnetic field
electrokymogram \"+\ *n* [*electr-* + Gk *kymo-* cym- + E *-gram*] **:** the tracing made by an electrokymograph
electrokymograph \"+\ *n* [*electr-* + Gk *kymo-* cym- + E *-graph*] **:** an instrument for recording graphically the motion of the heart as seen in silhouette on a fluoroscopic screen — **electrokymographic** \"+\ *adj* — **electrokymographically** \"+\ *adv* — **electrokymography** \"+\ *n*
electro–lethaler \"+¦lēthələ(r)\ *n* -s [*electr- + lethal + -er*] *Brit* **:** an electrically operated device for shocking a slaughter animal into insensibility before killing it
elec·tro·lier \ə¦lektrə¦li(ə)r, ē¦-\ *n* -s [*electr- + -lier* (as in *chandelier*)] **:** a support for electric lamps; *esp* **:** one like a chandelier
Electrolimit Gage \≈¦≈≈ *at* ELECTRO-+ . . .\ *trademark* — used for a gauge in which contact with the work is indicated by an electric signal
elec·trol·o·gist \əˌlek'träləjəst, (ˌ)ēˌ-\ *n* -s [blend of NL *electrolysis* (sense 2) and E *-logist*] **:** one that removes hair, warts, moles, and birthmarks by means of an electric current applied to the body with a needle-shaped electrode
electroluminescence \≈¦≈≈ *at* ELECTRO-+\ *n* [*electr- + luminescence*] **:** luminescence resulting from a high-frequency discharge through a gas or from application of an alternating current to a layer of phosphor — **electroluminescent** \"+\ *adj*
elec·trol·y·sis \əˌlek'träləsəs, ēˌl- *sometimes* ˌēˌl-, *chiefly Brit* ˌeˌlek- *or* ˌelik-\ *n* [NL, fr. *electr- + -lysis*] **1 :** the process of producing chemical changes by passage of an electric current through an electrolyte (as in a cell), the ions present carrying the current by migrating to the electrodes where they may form new substances (as in the deposition of metals or the liberation of gases) — compare ELECTRODEPOSITION, ELECTROFORM, ELECTROPLATE; see FARADAY'S LAW a **2 :** the destruction of hair roots with an electric current
elec·tro·lyte \ə'lektrəˌlīt, ē'-, *usu* -īd.+V\ *n* -s [*electr-* + Gk *lytos* that may be untied, soluble, verbal of *lyein* to loosen, dissolve — more at LOSE] **1 :** a nonmetallic electric conductor (as a solution, liquid, or fused solid) in which current is carried by the movement of ions instead of electrons with the liberation of matter at electrodes **:** a liquid ionic conductor — see ELECTROLYSIS 1 **2 :** a substance (as an acid, base, or salt) that when dissolved in a suitable solvent (as water) or when fused becomes an ionic conductor
electrolyte acid *n* **:** BATTERY ACID
¹elec·tro·lyt·ic \≈¦≈¦lid·ik, ¦≈(ˌ)≈≈-, -lit|, |ēk\ *adj* [*electr-* + Gk *lytikos* able to loose — more at LYTIC] **:** of or relating to electrolysis or an electrolyte ⟨an ~ solution⟩ **:** produced or brought about by electrolysis ⟨~ copper⟩ ⟨~ oxidation and reduction⟩ — **elec·tro·lyt·i·cal·ly** \ək(ə)lē, |ēk-, -li\ *adv*
²electrolytic \"\ *n* -s **1 :** ELECTROLYTE **2 :** a device utilizing an electrolyte; *specif* **:** ELECTROLYTIC CONDENSER
electrolytic cell *n* **:** a cell for use in electrolysis
electrolytic condenser *n* **:** a capacitor in which one plate is formed of a metal (as aluminum) and the other plate by an electrolyte, the separating dielectric consisting of a film of gas deposited on the metal when the metal is used as an anode in a suitable electrolyte
electrolytic interrupter *n* **:** an electrical interrupter consisting of a cell containing two electrodes in an electrolytic solution in which bubbles formed at frequent intervals by application of current to one of the electrodes continually interrupt the passage of current
electrolytic polishing *n* **:** ELECTROPOLISHING
electrolytic rectifier *n* **:** a rectifier having electrodes that are immersed in an electrolyte and permitting the passage of a current in only one direction
electrolytic refining *n* **:** ELECTROREFINING
elec·tro·lyze \ə'lektrəˌlīz, ē'-\ *vt* -ED/-ING/-S [*electr- + -lyze*] **:** to subject to electrolysis
electromagnet \≈¦≈≈ *at* ELECTRO-+\ *n* [*electr- + magnet*] **:** a core of magnetic material (as soft iron) that is surrounded wholly or in part by a coil of wire, that is magnetized when an electric current is passed through the wire, and that retains its power of attraction only while the current is flowing
electromagnetic \"+\ *adj* [*electr- + magnetic*] **:** of, relating to, or produced by electromagnetism — **electromagnetically** \"+\ *adv*
electromagnetic field *n* **:** a field of force that is made up of associated electric and magnetic components, that results from the motion of an electric charge, and that possesses a definite amount of electromagnetic energy
electromagnetic induction *n* **:** the induction of an electromotive force in a circuit by varying the magnetic flux linked with the circuit

electromagnet: *1, 1* current-carrying coils, *2* armature, *3* load

electromagnetic mass *n* **:** the mass that is equivalent to the kinetic energy of a moving charge
electromagnetic radiation *n* **:** a succession of electromagnetic waves
electromagnetics \"+\ *n pl but sing in constr* **:** ELECTROMAGNETISM 2
electromagnetic spectrum *n* **:** the entire range of wavelengths or frequencies of electromagnetic radiation from the shortest gamma rays to the longest radio waves, visible light comprising only a small part of the range
electromagnetic theory of light : a theory in physics: light consists of electromagnetic oscillations perpendicular to the direction of travel of the wave motion
electromagnetic unit *n* **:** any of a system of electrical units based primarily upon the magnetic properties of electric currents, the fundamental cgs unit being the abampere
electromagnetic wave *n* **:** one of the waves that are propagated by simultaneous periodic variations of electric and magnetic field intensity, the two kinds of oscillation being perpendicular to each other, and that include radio waves, infrared, visible light, ultraviolet, X rays, and gamma rays in ascending order of frequency
electromagnetism \"+\ *n* [*electr- + magnetism*] **1 :** magnetism developed by a current of electricity **2 :** a branch of physical science that deals with the physical relations between electricity and magnetism (as the development of magnetism by an electric current or the effect of magnets upon currents)
electromechanical \"+\ *adj* [*electr- + mechanical*] **1 :** of, relating to, or being a mechanical process, device, or assembly of parts actuated or controlled electrically **2 :** of or relating to electromechanics
electromechanics \"+\ *n pl but sing in constr* [ISV *electr- + mechanics*] **:** a branch of electrodynamics that deals with the mechanical forces involved in electric circuits
elec·tro·mer \ə'lektrəmə(r), ē'-\ *n* -s [*electr- + -mer*] **:** one of two or more substances that differ only in the distribution of electrons — compare RESONANCE — **elec·tro·mer·ic** \≈¦≈≈-¦merik\ *adj*
electrometallurgical \≈¦≈≈ *at* ELECTRO-+\ *adj* **:** of or relating to electrometallurgy
electrometallurgist \"+\ *n* **:** a specialist in electrometallurgy
electrometallurgy \"+\ *n* [*electr- + metallurgy*] **:** a branch of metallurgy that deals with the application of electric current either for electrolytic deposition or as a source of heat (as in smelting or refining)
elec·trom·e·ter \əˌlek'trämədˌə(r), (ˌ)ēˌ-\ *n* [*electr- + -meter*] **:** any of various instruments for detecting or measuring electric-potential differences or ionizing radiations by means of the forces of attraction or repulsion between charged bodies — compare CAPILLARY ELECTROMETER, ELECTROSCOPE
electrometer tube *n* **1 :** an amplifier tube of extremely high sensitivity used in a vacuum-tube measuring instrument (as a voltmeter) **2 :** a vacuum tube having high impedance in the grid circuit so as to minimize the undesirable control-grid current
electrometric \≈¦≈≈ *at* ELECTRO-+\ *adj* [*electr- + -metric*] **:** of or relating to electrical measurements esp. of differences of potential **:** measured by an electrometer — **electrometrically** \"+\ *adv*
electromigratetics \≈¦≈≈ *at* ELECTRO-+\ *n pl but usu sing in constr* [*electr- + migratetics*] **:** ELECTRONOGRAPHY
electromigration \"+\ *n* [*electr- + migration*] **:** migration (as of ions or colloidal particles) in an electric field; *specif* **:** an electrolytic process of separating isotopes or ionic species on the basis of their different ionic mobilities
electromotive \"+\ *adj* [*electr- + motive* (adj.)] **:** of, relating to, or tending to produce an electric current
electromotive force *n* **:** something that moves or tends to move electricity **:** the amount of energy derived from an electrical source per unit quantity of electricity passing through the source (as a cell or generator)
electromotive series *or* **electromotive force series** *n* **:** an arrangement of metallic elements or ions usu. in a column or table according to their electrode potentials determined under specified conditions, the order showing the tendency of one metal to reduce the ions of any other metal below it in the series; *also* **:** a similar arrangement including nonmetallic elements or ions as well as metallic elements — called also *electrochemical series*
electromyogram \"+\ *n* [*electr- + myogram*] **:** a tracing made by an electromyograph
electromyograph \"+\ *n* [*electr- + myograph*] **:** an instrument for the simultaneous recording of a visual and sound record of electric waves associated with activity of skeletal muscle that is used in the diagnosis of neuromuscular disorders — **electromyographic** \"+\ *adj* — **electromyographically** \"+\ *adv* — **electromyography** \"+\ *n*
elec·tron \ə'lekˌträn *sometimes* -ˌtrən\ *n* -s [*electr- + -on*] **:** one of the constituent elementary particles of an atom being a charge of negative electricity equal to about 1.602×10^{-19} coulomb, having a mass when at rest of about 9.109×10^{-28} gram or $\frac{1}{1837}$ that of a proton, being the least massive known charged particle, and having a magnetic moment of about 1 Bohr magneton associated with its one half quantum unit of spin
electron affinity *n* **1 :** the degree to which an atom or molecule attracts additional electrons **2 :** the minimum energy required to remove an electron from a negative ion to produce a neutral atom or molecule **3 :** the negative of the energy required to introduce an additional initially free electron into a crystal
elec·tro·nar·co·sis \≈¦≈≈ *at* ELECTRO-+\ *n* [NL, fr. *electr- + narcosis*] **:** unconsciousness induced by passing a weak electric current through the brain and used in treating certain mental disorders
electron ballistics *n* **:** a branch of electronics that deals with the motions of free electrons or other electric particles in electric or magnetic fields
electron cloud *n* **1 :** the system of electrons surrounding the nucleus of an atom **2 :** an electronic space charge in a vacuum tube
electron diffraction *n* **:** an effect due to the wavelike nature of electrons and observed when a narrow beam of them upon passing through a very thin layer of a material (as a metal crystal) is deflected in particular directions and if allowed to fall on a fluorescent screen produces a pattern of light and dark areas, the pattern formed by these areas being characteristic of the material traversed
electronegative \≈¦≈≈ *at* ELECTRO-+\ *adj* [*electr- + negative*] **1 a :** charged with negative electricity **:** having a tendency to pass to the anode in electrolysis **b :** capable of acting as the positive electrode of a voltaic cell **:** CATHODIC — used esp. in electrical engineering **2 a :** having a tendency to attract electrons esp. in the formation of an electrovalent bond **:** ELECTROPHILIC ⟨fluorine is the most ~ of the elements⟩ **b :** capable of acting as the negative electrode of a voltaic cell **:** ANODIC
electronegativity \"+\ *n* **:** the quality, state, or degree of being electronegative; *specif* **:** the power of an atom or radical in a compound to attract electrons esp. in the formation of an electrovalent bond

electron emission *n* **1 :** the issuing of electrons from a substance (as in photoelectric, thermionic, or radioactive processes) **2 :** the rate of electron emission
electroneutral \⸗¦⸗⸗ *at* ELECTRO- + \ *adj* [*electr-* + *neutral*] **:** NEUTRAL 3e — **electroneutrality** \"+\ *n*
electron gas *n* **:** a population of free electrons either in a vacuum or in a metallic conductor whose distribution and motions are subject to laws somewhat analogous to those of gas molecules
electron gun *n* **:** the electron-emitting cathode and its surrounding assembly in a cathode-ray tube for directing, controlling, and focusing the stream of electrons to a spot of desired size
elec·tron·ic \ə̇¦lek¦tränik, ē,l- *sometimes* e¦l- *or* ¦ē,l- *or* ¦e,l-\ *adj* [*electron* + *-ic*] **1 :** of or belonging to an electron ⟨an ~ rectifier⟩ **2 :** of or relating to electronics; *esp* **:** utilizing devices constructed or working by the methods or principles of electronics ⟨an ~ circuit⟩ ⟨an ~ organ⟩ ⟨an ~ clock⟩ ⟨~ control⟩ — **elec·tron·i·cal·ly** \-nək(ə)lē, -nēk-, -li\ *adv*
electronic brain *n* **:** a large computing machine that depends primarily on electronic devices for its operation
electronic carillon *n* **:** CARILLON 1c
electronic heating *n* **:** DIELECTRIC HEATING
elec·tron·ics \ə̇,lek'träniks, ē,l- *sometimes* ,ē,l- *or* (,)e,l-\ *n pl but sing in constr* **:** a branch of physics that deals with the emission, behavior, and effects of electrons in vacuums and gases and with the utilization of electronic devices
electronic tube *n* **:** ELECTRON TUBE
electron lens *n* **:** a device for converging or diverging a beam of electrons by means of either an electric or a magnetic field
electron micrograph *n* **:** a micrograph made with an electron microscope — **electron micrography** *n*
electron microscope *n* **:** an electron-optical instrument in which a beam of electrons focused by means of an electron lens is used to produce an enlarged image of a minute object on a fluorescent screen or photographic plate in a manner analogous to that in which light is used to form the image in a compound microscope — **electron microscopy** *n*
electron multiplier *also* **electron multiplier tube** *n* **:** an electronic device (as an electron tube or a component of an electron tube) that amplifies a corpuscular or photon emission by means of the secondary electron emission produced by it
elec·tron·o·graph·ic \ə̇,lek¦trānə¦grafik, (,)ē,l-\ *adj* **:** done by or designed for electronography ⟨an ~ press⟩ ⟨~ printing⟩
elec·tro·nog·ra·phy \ə̇,lektrə'nägrəfē, ē,l-\ *n* -ES [*electron* + *-o-* + *-graphy*] **:** a printing process in which the ink is transferred by electrostatic action across a gap between printing plate and impression cylinder — called also *onset*
elec·tron–optical \ə̇¦lek,trän, -,tran+\ *adj* **:** of or relating to electron optics
electron optics *n* **:** a branch of electronics that deals with those properties of beams of electrons that are analogous to the properties of rays of light
electron pair *n* **:** a group of two electrons belonging to one atom or shared by two atoms as a chemical bond
electron–ray tube *n* **:** ELECTRIC EYE 2
electron telescope *n* **:** an electron-optical instrument that penetrates obstacles to vision (as fog, smoke, darkness, or distance) by means of infrared rays, the image being focused on a photosensitive cathode that in turn produces the final enlarged electron image on a fluorescent screen
electron tube *n* **:** an electronic device in which conduction by electrons takes place through a vacuum or a gaseous medium within a sealed glass or metal container and which has various common uses (as amplification of electrical energy and the conversion of alternating current to direct current and vice versa) that are based on the controlled flow of electrons
electron volt *n* **:** a unit of energy equal to the energy gained by an electron in passing from a point of low potential to a point one volt higher in potential: 1.60×10^{-12} erg
electrooptic \⸗¦⸗⸗ *at* ELECTRO-+\ *or* **electrooptical** \"+\ *adj* [*electr-* + *optic, optical*] **:** of or relating to electrooptics — **electrooptically** \"+\ *adv*
electrooptics \"+\ *n pl but sing in constr* [ISV *electr-* + *optics*] **:** a branch of optics that deals with the effects of an electric field upon light traversing it
electroosmosis \"+\ *also* **electroosmose** \"+\ *or* **elec·tros·mo·sis** \ə̇¦lektr, ē¦l+\ *n, pl* **electroosmoses** [NL *electroosmosis, electrosmosis,* fr. *electr-* + *osmosis*] **:** the movement of a conducting liquid (as water in clay) through a porous diaphragm under the action of an electromotive force applied to electrodes on opposite sides of the diaphragm — called also *electroendosmosis* — **electroosmotic** \⸗¦⸗⸗ *at* ELECTRO-+\ *adj* — **electroosmotically** \"+\ *adv*
electrooxidation \⸗¦⸗⸗ *at* ELECTRO-+\ *n* [*electr-* + *oxidation*] **:** oxidation at the anode in an electrolytic cell
elec·tro·phil·ic \"+¦filik\ *adj* [*electr-* + *-philic*] **:** having an affinity for electrons **:** electron-seeking **:** CATIONOID — contrasted with *nucleophilic* ⟨~ reagents⟩ ⟨~ attack on a double bond⟩ — **elec·tro·phil·i·cal·ly** \-lək(ə)lē\ *adv*
elec·tro·phone \⸗'⸗⸗,fōn\ *n* [*electr-* + *-phone*] **:** an instrument (as a theremin) that produces musical tones by means of oscillating electric circuits — **elec·tro·phon·ic** \⸗¦⸗⸗¦fänik\ *adj* — **elec·tro·phon·i·cal·ly** \-nək(ə)lē\ *adv*
elec·tro·pho·re·sis \⸗,⸗⸗fə'rēsə̇s\ *n* [NL, fr. *electr-* + *-phoresis*] **:** the movement of suspended particles through a fluid under the action of an electromotive force applied to electrodes in contact with the suspension, important applications being in the separation of colloids (as proteins, clay, humus) and the deposition on one of the electrodes of coatings (as of oxides on cathodes for electron tubes and of rubber and synthetic polymers) — called also *cataphoresis* — **elec·tro·pho·ret·ic** \⸗¦⸗⸗fə¦red·ik\ *adj* — **elec·tro·pho·ret·i·cal·ly** \-d·ək(ə)lē\ *adv*
¹**elec·troph·o·rus** \ə̇,lek'träf(ə)rəs, ē,l- *sometimes* ,ē,l- *or* (,)e,l-\ *n, pl* **electropho·ri** \-fə,rī, -,rē\ [NL, fr. *electr-* + *-phorus* (fr. Gk *-phoros* -phore)] **:** an instrument for the production of electric charges by induction consisting of a disk (as of resin, shellac, or ebonite) that is negatively electrified by friction and a metal plate that becomes charged by induction when placed upon the disk, the repelled negative charge being conducted away by momentary contact (as of the operator's finger) after which the plate with its remaining positive charge is removed by its insulating handle
²**electrophorus** \"\ *n, cap* [NL, fr. *electr-* + *-phorus*] **:** a genus of cyprinoid fishes comprising the electric eel and being included in the family Gymnotidae or sometimes made the type of a separate family
electrophotographic \⸗¦⸗⸗ *at* ELECTRO-+\ *adj* **:** of, relating to, or used in electrophotography
electrophotography \"+\ *n* [*electr-* + *photography*] **:** photography in which images are produced by electrical means (as in xerography)
electrophrenic \"+\ *adj* [*electr-* + *phrenic*] **:** relating to or induced by electrical stimulation of the phrenic nerve ⟨~ respiration⟩
electrophrenic respiration *n* **:** artificial respiration by means of an electrophrenic respirator used esp. in poliomyelitis and other conditions in which the nervous control of breathing is impaired
electrophrenic respirator *n* **:** a device for the regular recurrent electrical stimulation of the phrenic nerve or nerves to induce respiratory movements artificially and induce breathing
electrophysiologic \⸗¦⸗⸗ *at* ELECTRO- +\ *or* **electrophysiological** \"+\ *adj* [ISV *electrophysiology* + *-ic, -ical*] **1 :** of or relating to electrophysiology ⟨~ methods⟩ **2** [*electr-* + *physiologic, physiological*] **:** of, relating to, or involving the electrical aspects of physiological processes ⟨~ phenomena⟩ — **electrophysiologically** \"+\ *adv*
electrophysiologist \"+\ *n* **:** a specialist in electrophysiology
electrophysiology \"+\ *n* [ISV *electr-* + *physiology*] **1 :** a branch of physiology that is concerned with the electric phenomena associated with living bodies and involved in their functional activity **2 :** electric phenomena (as of a body part or organ) ⟨the ~ of synaptic transmission⟩
elec·tro·pism \ə̇'lektrə,pizəm, ē'l-\ *n* [blend of *electr-* and *-tropism*] **:** ELECTROTROPISM
¹**elec·tro·plate** \-,plāt\ *n* [*electr-* + *plate,* n.] **:** something electroplated; *specif* **:** ¹ELECTROTYPE 1
²**electroplate** \"\ *vt* **1 :** to plate with an adherent continuous coating by electrodeposition; *esp* **:** to plate (a metal or metal-coated or graphite-coated nonmetal serving as cathode during the electrolysis) with a metal ⟨~ a wax recording disc⟩ — compare ELECTROFORM **2 :** ELECTROTYPE
elec·tro·plat·er \-ād·ə(r)\ *n* **:** one that electroplates **:** PLATER
elec·tro·plax \-,plaks\ *n* -ES [NL, fr. *electr-* + Gk *plax* anything flat and broad — more at PLANK] **:** one of the flattened plates of modified muscle constituting the typical structural element of the electric organ of some fishes
elec·tro·plexy \-,pleksē\ *n* -ES [*electr-* + *-plexy* (as in *apoplexy*)] *Brit* **:** ELECTROSHOCK THERAPY
elec·tro·pneu·mat·ic \⸗¦⸗⸗ *at* ELECTRO- +\ *adj* [*electr-* + *pneumatic*] **:** of or relating to a combination of electrical and pneumatic effects **:** operated by electric and pneumatic power ⟨an ~ signal⟩ — **electropneumatically** \"+\ *adv*
electropolish \"+\ *vt* [*electr-* + *polish*] **:** to produce a smooth bright surface on (metal) by immersion as an anode in an electrolytic bath
electropositive \"+\ *adj* [*electr-* + *positive*] **1 a :** charged with positive electricity **:** having a tendency to pass to the cathode in electrolysis **b :** capable of acting as the negative electrode of a voltaic cell **:** ANODIC — used esp. in electrical engineering **2 a :** having a tendency to release electrons esp. in an oxidation-reduction reaction **:** NUCLEOPHILIC ⟨sodium is a highly ~ element⟩ **b :** capable of acting as the positive electrode of a voltaic cell **:** CATHODIC
electroprecipitation \"+\ *n* [*electr-* + *precipitation*] **:** ELECTROSTATIC PRECIPITATION
elec·tro·pult \ə̇'lektrə,pəlt, -pu̇lt\ *n* -S [*electr-* + *-pult* (as in *catapult*)] **:** an electrical catapult for accelerating airplanes to takeoff speed on a short runway that consists of a car and a track which react with each other as the stator and rotor of an induction motor to give the car great acceleration when enormous electrical power is supplied for a short time
electropyrexia \⸗¦⸗⸗ *at* ELECTRO- +\ *n* [NL, fr. *electr-* + *pyrexia*] **:** artificial fever induced by electrical means for therapeutic purposes
electroreduction \"+\ *n* [*electr-* + *reduction*] **:** reduction at the cathode in an electrolytic cell
electrorefining \"+\ *n* [*electr-* + *refining*] **:** refining of a metal (as copper) by electrolysis, the crude metal used as the anode going into solution and the pure metal being deposited upon the cathode — called also *electrolytic refining*
electroresection \"+\ *n* [*electr-* + *resection*] **:** resection by electric means **:** ELECTROSURGERY
elec·tro·ret·i·no·gram \"+¦ret·ᵊnə,gram\ *n* [*electr-* + *retina* + *-o-* + *-gram*] **:** a graphic record of the electric activity of the retina used esp. in the diagnosis of conditions of the retina
electros *pl of* ELECTRO
elec·tro·scope \⸗'⸗⸗+,skōp\ *n* [prob. fr. F *électroscope,* fr. *électro-* electr- + *-scope*] **:** any of various instruments for detecting the presence of an electric charge on a body, for determining whether the charge is positive or negative, or for indicating and measuring intensity of radiation by means of the motion imparted to charged bodies (as strips of gold leaf) suspended from a metal conductor within an insulated chamber — compare ELECTROMETER
electroshock \⸗'⸗⸗+\ *n* [*electr-* + *shock*] **1 :** ³SHOCK 5 **2 :** ELECTROSHOCK THERAPY
electroshock therapy *n* **:** the treatment of mental disorder by the induction of coma through use of an electric current
electrosmosis *var of* ELECTROOSMOSIS
electrostatic \⸗¦⸗⸗ *at* ELECTRO- +\ *adj* [ISV *electr-* + *static*] **1 :** of or relating to static electricity or electrostatics **2 :** of, relating to, or characterized by a special type of spray painting utilizing electrically charged paint particles to insure complete coating of an object — **electrostatically** \"+\ *adv*
electrostatic bond *n* **:** a chemical bond (as an electrovalent bond or a hydrogen bond) characterized by electrostatic attraction between ions or molecules
electrostatic field *n* **:** ELECTRIC FIELD
electrostatic generator *n* **:** an apparatus for the production of heavy electrical discharges at very high voltage commonly consisting of an insulated hollow conductor (as a sphere) that accumulates in its interior the charge continuously conveyed from a source of direct current (as a high-voltage rectifier-transformer) by an endless belt of flexible nonconducting material (as silk, rayon, or paper) revolving on insulated motor-driven drums, the voltage thus generated being used esp. for accelerating charged particles in nuclear bombardment
electrostatic induction *n* **:** induction of an electric charge in a conductor due to the proximity of another charged body
electrostatic lens *n* **:** an electron lens that utilizes an electric field
electrostatic precipitation *n* **:** removal of suspended particles (as dust and acid mists) from a gas (as air or blast-furnace gas) by charging the particles and precipitating them by applying a strong electric field (as by passing the gas between collecting and discharge electrodes in a precipitator) — compare COTTRELL PROCESS
electrostatics \⸗¦⸗⸗ *at* ELECTRO- +\ *n pl but sing in constr* **:** a branch of physics that deals with phenomena due to attractions or repulsions of electric charges but not dependent upon their motion
electrostatic unit *n* **:** any of a system of electrical units based primarily upon forces of interaction between electric charges with the fundamental cgs unit being the statcoulomb — abbr. *esu*
electrostatic voltmeter *n* **:** an electrometer of the electrostatic type graduated to read directly in volts or kilovolts
electrosteel \⸗'⸗⸗+,⸗\ *n* [*electr-* + *steel*] **:** ELECTRIC STEEL
electrostimulation \⸗¦⸗⸗+\ *n* [*electr-* + *stimulation*] **:** electroshock administered in nonconvulsive doses
electrostriction \"+\ *n* [*electr-* + *-striction* (as in *constriction*)] **:** deformation of a dielectric body as the result of an applied electric field — compare MAGNETOSTRICTION — **elec·tro·stric·tive** \"+¦striktiv\ *adj*
electrosurgery \"+\ *n* [*electr-* + *surgery*] **:** diathermy for surgical purposes
electrosurgical \"+\ *adj* [*electr-* + *surgical*] **:** of, relating to, or performed by means of electrosurgery
electrosynthesis \"+\ *n* [NL, fr. *electr-* + *synthesis*] **:** synthesis accomplished with the aid of electricity; *esp* **:** synthesis of an organic compound by electrolysis — **electrosynthetic** \"+\ *adj* — **electrosynthetically** \"+\ *adv*
electrotactic \"+\ *adj* [*electr-* + *-tactic*] **:** of or relating to electrotaxis
electrotaxis \"+\ *n* [NL, fr. *electr-* + *-taxis*] **:** movement in which an electric current constitutes the directive factor **:** GALVANOTAXIS
electrotechnic \"+\ *or* **electrotechnical** \"+\ *adj* [*electr-* + *technic, technical*] **:** of or relating to electrotechnology
electrotechnician \"+\ *n* [*electr-* + *technician*] **:** a specialist in electrotechnology
electrotechnics \"+\ *n pl but sing in constr* [*electr-* + *technics*] **:** ELECTROTECHNOLOGY
electrotechnology \"+\ *n* [*electr-* + *technology*] **:** a science that deals with the practical application of electricity
electrotherapist \"+\ *n* **:** one that practices electrotherapy
electrotherapy \"+\ *n* [*electr-* + *therapy*] **:** treatment of disease by means of electricity (as by diathermy or by means of electrically generated heat) — compare ELECTROSHOCK THERAPY
electrothermal \"+\ *or* **electrothermic** \"+\ *adj* [*electr-* + *thermal* or *thermic*] **:** relating to both electricity and heat **:** combining electricity and heat ⟨~ bath⟩; *specif* **:** relating to the generation of heat by electricity — compare THERMOELECTRIC
electrotin \"+¦tin\ *vt* [*electr-* + *tin*] **:** to electroplate with tin
elec·tro·tome \⸗'⸗⸗+,tōm\ *n* [*electr-* + *-tome*] **:** an electric cutting instrument used in electrosurgery
electrotone \"+,⸗\ *n* [*electr-* + *tone*] **:** ELECTROPHONE
electrotonic \⸗¦⸗⸗+\ *adj* [NL *electrotonus* + E *-ic*] **1 :** of, induced by, relating to, or constituting electrotonus ⟨the ~ condition of a nerve⟩ ⟨~ induction of depolarization⟩ **2 :** ELECTROPHONIC — **electrotonically** \"+\ *adv*
electrotonicity \"+\ *n* **:** ELECTROTONUS
elec·trot·o·nus \ə̇,lek'trät·ᵊnəs, ē,l- *sometimes* ,ē,l- *or* (,)e,l-\ *n* [NL, fr. *electr-* + *tonus*] **:** the altered sensitivity of a nerve when a constant current of electricity passes through any part of it — see ANELECTROTONUS, CATELECTROTONUS
electrotropic \⸗¦⸗⸗ *at* ELECTRO- +\ *adj* [*electr-* + *-tropic*] **:** of or relating to electrotropism
elec·trot·ro·pism \ə̇,lek'trä·trə,pizəm, ē,l- *sometimes* ,ē,l- *or* (,)e,l-\ *n* [*electr-* + *-tropism*] **:** bodily orientation in relation to an electric current **:** GALVANATROPISM
¹**elec·tro·type** \ə̇'lektrə,tīp, ē'-\ *n* [*electr-* + *type*] **1 :** a duplicate printing surface made by pressure molding in wax, lead, or other plastic material the surface to be reproduced, dusting the mold with graphite when necessary to make it electroconductive, and electrodepositing on it a thin shell (as of copper) which is then backed up with lead and sometimes given an extra facing of a harder metal (as nickel or chromium) — compare NICKELTYPE **2 :** a print made from an electrotype
²**electrotype** \"\ *vt* **:** to make an electrotype from (a printing surface) ~ *vi* **:** to be reproducible by electrotyping
elec·tro·typ·er \-pə(r)\ *n* **:** one that makes electrotypes
electro–ultrafiltration \⸗¦⸗⸗ *at* ELECTRO- +\ *n* [*electr-* + *ultrafiltration*] **:** ultrafiltration brought about by electroosmosis
electrovalence \"+\ *or* **electrovalency** \"+\ *n* [*electr-* + *valence, valency*] **:** valence characterized by the transfer of one or more electrons from one atom to another with the formation of ions (as in sodium chloride and other simple salts); *also* **:** the number of positive or negative charges acquired by an atom by the loss or gain of electrons — called also *ionic valence;* distinguished from *covalence* — **electrovalent** \"+\ *adj* — **electrovalently** \"+\ *adv*
electrovalent bond *n* **:** a chemical bond formed between ions of opposite charge — called also *ionic bond;* distinguished from *covalent bond*
electroviscosity \"+\ *n* [*electr-* + *viscosity*] **:** the effect of the presence of ions upon the viscosity of a solution or suspension — **electroviscous** \"+\ *adj*
electroviscous effect *n* **:** the increase in viscosity due to an electric charge on solid particles in a solution
electrowinning \"+\ *n* [*electr-* + *winning*] **:** the recovery esp. of metals from solutions by electrolysis
elec·trum \ə̇'lektrəm, ē'-\ *n* -S [ME, fr. L — more at ELECTRIC] **1** *archaic* **:** AMBER 2 **2 :** a natural pale yellow alloy of gold and silver
elects *pres 3d sing of* ELECT
elec·tu·ary \ə̇'lekchə,werē, ē'-, -ri\ *n* -ES [ME *electuarie,* fr. L *electuarium, electarium,* prob. by folk etymology (influence of *electus,* past part. of *eligere* to elect and *-arium* -ary) fr. Gk *ekleikton,* fr. *ekleichein* to lick up, fr. *ek,* ex out + *leichein* to lick — more at ELECT, EX-, LICK] **:** CONFECTION 1b; *esp* **:** a medicated paste prepared with honey or other sweet, used in veterinary practice, and administered by smearing on the teeth, gums, or tongue
el·ee·mos·y·nar \,elə'mäsᵊnə(r) *also* ,elē(ə)'m- *sometimes* -äzᵊn-\ *n* -S [ML *eleemosynarius,* fr. LL *eleemosyna* alms + L *-arius* -ary, -ar (n. suffix) — more at ALMS] **:** one that distributes charity or doles out relief **:** ALMONER
el·ee·mos·y·nary \-ᵊn,erē, -ri\ *adj* [ML *eleemosynarius,* fr. LL *eleemosyna* + L *-arius* -ary (adj. suffix)] **1 :** of or relating to charity **:** CHARITABLE, PHILANTHROPIC ⟨a rich man given to many ~ activities⟩ ⟨~ relief⟩ **2 a :** nonprofit and receiving all or a great part of sustaining funds from donations or gifts ⟨about 90 percent of the hospitals are of a governmental, charitable, or ~ and nonprofit character —*U.S. Code*⟩ ⟨churches, lodges, and other ~ institutions —*Sat. Eve. Post*⟩ **b :** provided by an institution of this nature ⟨an ~ education⟩
eleemosynary corporation *n* **:** a corporation organized for charitable purposes — contrasted with *civil corporation*
el·e·gance \'eləgən(t)s, -lēg-\ *n* -S [MF *elegance,* fr. L *elegantia,* fr. L *elegant-, elegans* + *-ia* -y] **1 a :** refined grace or dignified propriety that expresses good breeding or good taste **:** URBANITY ⟨never looked more radiant, moved with greater ~, ease, or grace, or acted with truer style —John Mason Brown⟩ ⟨waltzes performed with great delicacy and ~ to the music of eight guitars —C.L.Jones⟩ **b :** tasteful richness of design or ornamentation **:** refined luxury ⟨householders who demand ~ in the chambers they sleep in, no matter what the price tags say —*New Yorker*⟩ **c :** dignified gracefulness or restrained beauty of style **:** POLISH ⟨a cultivated man should express himself by tongue or pen with some accuracy and ~ —C.W.Eliot⟩ **d :** scientific precision, neatness, and simplicity ⟨the ~ of a mathematical equation —Lewis Mumford⟩ **2 :** something that is elegant **:** REFINEMENT ⟨I flatter myself that we've always preserved the ~*s,* the finer graces —Elmer Davis⟩ **3** *pharmacy* **:** the quality or state of being elegant or of having elegant characteristics
el·e·gan·cy \-nsē, -si\ *n* -ES [ME *elegancie,* fr. L *elegantia*] **:** ELEGANCE — usu. used in pl. ⟨Lord Chesterfield . . . that arbiter of *elegancies* —P.E.More⟩ ⟨*elegancies* such as silk, porcelain, fans, and screens —Victor Purcell⟩
¹**el·e·gant** \-nt\ *adj* [MF or L; MF *elegant,* fr. L *elegant-, elegans;* akin to L *eligere* to choose, select — more at ELECT] **1 a :** characterized by refined grace or dignified propriety esp. in appearance or manner **:** tastefully correct and refined ⟨she is not conventionally beautiful . . . but she is charming to look at and ~ to her fingertips —John Martin⟩ **b :** characterized by tasteful richness esp. of design or ornamentation **:** luxurious or sumptuous in a refined way ⟨carrying his briefcase, an ~ piece of luggage of excellent leather and the best bronze hardware —Lionel Trilling⟩ ⟨in the glade, still standing in it, many of them after two hundred years, are thirty-nine ~ white houses —*New Yorker*⟩ **c :** characterized by dignified gracefulness and restrained beauty esp. in style or performance **:** POLISHED ⟨an ~ novel, one with the richness, restraint, and subtle obliquity which belong properly to elegance —*Saturday Rev.*⟩ **d :** characterized by scientific precision, neatness, and simplicity ⟨mathematicians say of a problem, a demonstration, or a solution in their science, when it exhibits perfect lucidity and form, that it is ~ —Isabel Paterson⟩ **2** *pharmacy* **:** pleasant in taste, attractive in appearance, and free from objectionable odor ⟨an ~ nontoxic emulsion⟩ **3 :** of a high grade or quality **:** EXCELLENT, FINE, SPLENDID ⟨he agreed with her that it must be an ~ place and he didn't wonder she wanted to go there —J.C.Lincoln⟩ **syn** see CHOICE
²**ele·gant** *or* **élé·gant** \ālāgäⁿ\ *n, pl* **elegants** *or* **élégants** \-äⁿ(z)\ [F *élégant,* fr. *élégant,* adj., fr. MF *elegant*] **:** a fashionable man **:** DANDY
ele·gante *or* **élé·gante** \ālāgäⁿt\ *n, pl* **elegantes** *or* **élégantes** \-t(s)\ [F *élégante,* fr. fem. of *élégant,* adj.] **:** a fashionable woman
el·e·gant·ly \'eləgəntlē, -lēg-, -li\ *adv* **:** in an elegant manner
¹**el·e·gi·ac** \,elə'jīək, -lē'- *also* -ī,ak; *also* ə̇'lējē,ak *or* ē'lē-\ *also* **el·e·gi·a·cal** \,elə'jīəkəl, -lē'-\ *adj* [LL *elegiacus,* fr. Gk *elegeiakos,* fr. *elegeion* elegiac couplet, elegy] **1 a :** consisting of two dactylic hexameter lines the second of which is often felt to be pentameter and is made up of two hemistichs each containing two dactyls and a long syllable **:** consisting of two dactylic hexameter lines the second of which has the short elements omitted in the third and sixth feet — usu. used of classical Greek couplets **b :** comprising or metrically similar to the second line of such a couplet **c** (1) **:** written in or consisting of such couplets (2) **:** noted for having written poetry in such couplets **d :** of or relating to the period in Greece around the seventh century B.C. when poetry written in such couplets flourished **2 :** of, relating to, befitting, or comprising elegy or an elegy ⟨an ~ poem on the death of a friend⟩; *esp* **:** expressing sorrow or lamentation often for something now past **:** PLAINTIVE, NOSTALGIC, MELANCHOLY ⟨an ~ regret for departed youth⟩ ⟨an ~ lament for a long-lost tradition⟩ ⟨~ poignance, excruciating nostalgia —Peggy Bennett⟩ **3 :** being the meter characteristic of a kinah — compare KINAH METER
²**elegiac** \"\ *n* -S **:** an elegiac couplet, verse, or poem
elegiac pentameter *n* **:** an elegiac hexameter verse
elegiac stanza *n* **:** a quatrain in iambic pentameter with alternate lines rhyming
el·e·gi·am·bus \,elə,jī'ambəs, ə̇,lējē'am-\ *n, pl* **elegiam·bi** \-,bī\ [LL, fr. LGk *elegiambos,* fr. Gk *elegeion* + *iambos* iamb — more at IAMB] **:** a verse in classical Greek or Latin poetry composed of half an elegiac pentameter and four iambic feet
el·e·gi·ast \,elə'jīəst, -lē'-, -ī,ast; ə̇'lējē,ast, ē'lē-, -jēəst\ *n* -S [by alter.] **:** ELEGIST
el·e·gist \'eləjə̇st\ *n* -S [*elegy* + *-ist*] **:** a composer of an elegy

ele·git \ə'lējət, ā'lāgət\ *n* -s [L, he has chosen, perf. indic. 3d sing. of *eligere* to choose — more at ELECT] **:** a judicial writ of execution no longer legal in England by which a defendant's goods and if necessary his lands are delivered for debt to the plaintiff until either the debt is paid by the rents and profits or the defendant's interest has expired

el·e·gize \'elə,jīz\ *vb* -ED/-ING/-S [*elegy* + *-ize*] *vi* **:** to lament or celebrate in elegy ~ *vt* **:** to write an elegy upon

el·e·gy \'eləjē, -ji\ *n* -ES [L *elegia*, fr. Gk *elegeia*, *elegeion*, fr. *elegos* song of mourning or lamentation accompanied by the flute, prob. of non-IE origin] **1 a :** a song or poem expressing sorrow or lamentation esp. for one who is dead **b :** something resembling or suggesting such a song or poem ⟨the splendid and sorrowful speech . . . that deserves a place among the world's great *elegies* —Geoffrey Bruun⟩ **2 :** a poem in elegiac couplets **3 a :** a pensive or reflective poem typically highly subjective and usu. sorrowful, nostalgic, or melancholy **b :** a musical composition in pensive or mournful mood

elem *abbr* **1** element **2** elementary

el·e·me figs *or* **el·e·mi figs** \'eləmē-\ *n pl* [Turk *eleme* selected, sifted] **:** Smyrna figs of superior quality packed flat

[1]**el·e·ment** \'eləmənt\ *n* -s [ME, fr. OF & L; OF, fr. L *elementum*] **1 a :** one of the simple substances air, water, fire, and earth of which according to early natural philosophers the physical universe was composed **b :** one of these substances in its natural form or occurrence ⟨the ~ of the fire is quite put out —John Donne⟩ ⟨drank of the pure and limpid ~⟩ **c** (1) **:** one of the celestial spheres of ancient astronomy **:** one of the celestial bodies (2) **:** HEAVENS, SKY **d elements** *pl* **:** weather conditions viewed as activities of the elements; *esp* **:** violent or severe weather ⟨attacked by the full fury of the ~*s*⟩ **e** (1) **:** one of the four elements viewed as a natural habitat ⟨water is the ~ of fishes⟩ (2) **:** the state or sphere natural or suited to any person or thing ⟨in that cloistered academic atmosphere he was in his ~⟩ ⟨mystery was his mental ~ —T.L.Peacock⟩ **2 :** one of the constituent parts, principles, materials, or traits of anything **:** one of the relatively simple forms or units that enter variously into a complex substance or thing ⟨bricks are ~*s* of a wall⟩ ⟨cells are ~*s* of living bodies⟩ **:** one of the simplest parts or principles of which anything consists or into which it may be analyzed: as **a elements** *pl* **:** the bread and wine used in the Eucharist **b elements** *pl* **:** the simplest principles of any art, science, or subject of study **:** RUDIMENTS ⟨mastered the ~*s* of this abstruse and subtle doctrine⟩ ⟨taught him the ~*s* of geometry⟩ **c :** one of a number of distinct or disparate units, parts, traits, or characteristics of which something tangible or intangible is composed ⟨the constitution was oddly compounded of democratic and feudal ~*s*⟩ ⟨there was an ~ of gravity in his appearance⟩; *specif* **:** one of a number of distinct or different groups or classes of which a human community is composed ⟨the criminal ~ in this city⟩ ⟨he obtained the solid support of the laboring ~⟩ **d** (1) **:** a part of a geometric magnitude (as of an area) (2) **:** a generator of a geometric figure (as of a cone) (3) **:** one of a set of numbers (as in a progression) or of symbols (as in a matrix) **e** (1) **:** one of the necessary data or values upon which a system of calculations depends or general conclusions are based ⟨the ~*s* of a planet's orbit⟩ (2) **:** one of the factors or conditions playing a part in or determining the outcome of some process or activity ⟨fine teamwork and hard hitting were key ~*s* in the team's pennant victory⟩ **f :** any of more than 100 fundamental metallic and nonmetallic substances that consist of atoms of only one kind and that either singly or in combination constitute all matter, most of these substances lighter in weight than and including uranium being found in nature and the rest being produced artificially by causing changes in the atomic nucleus (as by bombardment) **:** a substance that is composed exclusively of atoms having the same atomic number and that cannot be separated into simpler substances by ordinary chemical means — compare [3]COMPOUND 2a, ELEMENTARY PARTICLE; see ISOTOPE, PERIODIC TABLE, RADIOELEMENT **g :** a distinct part of a composite device (as the cathode, grid, and plate of a triode, the individual lenses of an objective, or the two metals of a thermocouple) ⟨circuit ~*s* of a doorbell installation⟩ ⟨heating ~ of an electric iron⟩ **h :** one of the basic constituent units of a tissue (as a cell or fiber) **i :** any of the modified cells often lacking the protoplast and with end walls lacking wholly or in part that make up the vessels of xylem or the sieve tubes of phloem; *also* **:** a young protoxylem cell before it has differentiated into a trachea or tracheid **j :** one of the subdivisions of a military unit (as a squad, company, or battalion) **k :** a part of a biota (as a fossil biota) that is usu. associated with a different region or environmental situation ⟨an extrazonal ~ from Moravia —*Biol. Abstracts*⟩ **l :** one of the physical properties or states of the atmosphere (as temperature, humidity, pressure, clouds, wind, or precipitation) **m** (1) **:** a simple component of perception **:** a sensation or sense datum (2) **:** a member of a class in logic

syn COMPONENT, CONSTITUENT, INGREDIENT, INTEGRANT, FACTOR: ELEMENT applies to anything, tangible or intangible, making up a part of a complex or compound whole ⟨the *elements* of a house are the walls, roof, and floors —*Military Engineer*⟩ ⟨the *elements* in an electrical circuit are electrical resistance, inductance, and electrical capacitance —H.F.Olson⟩ ⟨another *element* common to all novels is characterization —R.D.Jacobs⟩ ⟨another useful *element* in the theories of Paracelsus was the doctrine that diseases were highly specific in their action —S.F.Mason⟩ It sometimes indicates irreducible simplicity ⟨resolving the problem into its various *elements*⟩ COMPONENT and CONSTITUENT are often interchangeable in applying to any parts comprising a compounded or complex thing or intangible system, although the first may occas. call attention to the fact of existing as a separate entity, the second to the fact of comprising as a part ⟨he employed numerous workmen to make the lock *components* by hand —S.F.Mason⟩ ⟨in addition to the music-minded who will shop and combine *components* with view entirely to end results, there are those who prefer the convenience of an assembled unit —Irving Kolodin⟩ ⟨the *components* of knowledge can never be harmonized until all the relevant facts are in —Bernard De Voto⟩ ⟨to discover the structure of a chemical molecule it was necessary to know the combining numbers of its *constituent* atoms —S.F.Mason⟩ ⟨the *constituent* elements in the great monopolies found other ways to maintain a community of interest —Allan Nevins & H.S.Commager⟩ ⟨rhythm is a property of words, character a product that needs analysis before a satisfactory account of its effect can be given in terms of its *constituents*, and a product, moreover, that invites extraliterary scrutiny —C.H.Rickword⟩ INGREDIENT is more likely to stress notions of tangible substances that one combines together to form something else than the preceding words are ⟨the *ingredients* of a cake⟩ ⟨the *ingredients* of concrete⟩ ⟨electric power is one of the basic *ingredients* of the nation's industrial and economic welfare —K.W.Hamilton⟩ ⟨using the word "philosophic" to cover the unscientific *ingredients* of philosophy —T.S.Eliot⟩ INTEGRANT may apply to a binding essential component. FACTOR, often not a synonym for other words in this group, may apply to an element or component that exerts effectuating force toward composition, operation, or direction ⟨the mechanical engineer became a dominant *factor* in a civilization based on the utilization of the energy in coal —Waldemar Kaempffert⟩ ⟨only recently has the original Darwinian bias toward an overemphasis of the *factor* of natural selection yielded to the proper evaluation of other factors —Edward Sapir⟩

[2]**element** *vt* -ED/-ING/-S [back-formation fr. *elemented*, fr. ME, fr. [1]*element* + *-ed*] *obs* **:** to compose of elements

[1]**el·e·men·tal** \ˌeləˈmentᵊl\ *adj* [ME *elementall*, fr. ML *elementalis*, fr. L *elementum* + *-alis* -al] **1 a :** of, relating to, or caused by a great force of nature ⟨~ forces important to those engaged in a struggle with the soil —Frank Thilly⟩ ⟨the rains come with ~ force, scourging the earth wrathfully each day —Gertrude Diamant⟩ ⟨and over all the ancient ~ smell of the sea —Al Hine⟩ ⟨a race against hail, cold rains, or some other ~ catastrophe —J.K.Howard⟩ **b** *obs* **:** MATERIAL, PHYSICAL **c :** representing or personifying a force of nature ⟨the worship of ~ spirits⟩ **:** of or relating to a natural force or object conceived as a supernatural power or being ⟨~ religion⟩ **d :** comparable to a force or object of nature (as in power or breadth) **:** characterized by stark simplicity, naturalness, or unrestrained or undisciplined vigor or force **:** not complex or refined **:** CRUDE, PRIMITIVE, FUNDAMENTAL, BASIC, EARTHY ⟨his roughhewn ~ poetry —*Key Reporter*⟩ ⟨this genius who was too wild and ~ ever to conform to any aesthetic convention —H.M.Ledig-Rowohlt⟩ ⟨it was the ~ simplicity of his mind that baffled me —Jack London⟩ ⟨the real Highland world . . . is . . . something raw, stark, and ~ —Richard Joseph⟩ ⟨a creature of flesh and ~ feelings —Nicola Chiaromonte⟩ ⟨had a shrewd knowledge of all those predicaments in which ~ human nature comes to the surface —John Erskine⟩ ⟨the smell was ~, farmyards and manure and sweat —Laura H. Mackenzie⟩ **2 a** (1) **:** of, relating to, or being an element (2) **:** consisting of a single chemical element **:** UNCOMBINED ⟨~ sulfur⟩ (3) **:** of, relating to, or being the ultimate or basic constituent of anything ⟨the ~ stuff . . . out of which the many forms of life have been molded —Jack London⟩ **b :** ELEMENTARY, INTRODUCTORY, RUDIMENTARY ⟨in the new nations they lacked ~ political and civic rights —Oscar Handlin⟩ ⟨this ~ recital of what your Government is doing —F.D. Roosevelt⟩ **c :** forming an integral part **:** INHERENT ⟨such self-assurance is so ~ that it is not even tinged with conceit —Albert Dasnoy⟩ ⟨possessed an ~ sense of rhythm⟩ — **el·e·men·tal·ly** \-ᵊlē, -ᵊli\ *adv*

[2]**elemental** \"\ *n* -s **1 :** SPIRIT, SPECTER, WRAITH ⟨a frightening ~ which appears as a pillar of whirling darkness —G.G.Carter⟩ **2 :** an elementary concern **:** a first principle **:** RUDIMENT — usu. used in pl. ⟨sorrow, deprivation, and dread—those constant ~*s* among the very poor —Sylvia Berkman⟩ ⟨not too much I can teach him . . . but I guess I still remember the ~*s* —Agnes S. Turnbull⟩

el·e·men·tal·ism \ˌ==ˈ=ᵊlˌizəm\ *n* -s **:** a tendency to postulate a separation into independent entities or elements of things (as mind and body, space and time) that can be only verbally so separated — **el·e·men·tal·is·tic** \ˈ==ˈ=ᵊlˈistik\ *adj* — **el·e·men·tal·is·ti·cal·ly** \-tək(ə)lē, -tēk-, -li\ *adv*

el·e·men·tar·i·ly \ˈelə(ˌ)menˈterəlē, -ˌmən-, -li\ *adv* **:** in an elementary manner

el·e·men·ta·ri·ness \ˌelə'mentərēnəs, -n·trē-, -rin-\ *n* -ES **:** the quality or state of being elementary

el·e·men·ta·ry \ˈeləˈmentərē, -n·trē, -ri\ *adj* [ME *elementare*, fr. MF or L; MF *elementaire*, fr. L *elementarius*, fr. *elementum* element + *-arius* -ary — more at ELEMENT] **1 a** *obs* **:** MATERIAL,

CHEMICAL ELEMENTS

ELEMENT	SYMBOL	ATOMIC NUMBER	ATOMIC WEIGHT[1]	SPECIFIC GRAVITY[2]	MELTING POINT[3]	BOILING POINT[3]	DISCOVERY DATE[4]
actinium	Ac	89	[227]	—	1050	—	1899
aluminum	Al	13	26.9815	2.702	660	2057	1754
americium	Am	95	[243]	11.7	<1100	—	1944
antimony	Sb	51	121.75	6.684	630.5	1380	ancient
argon	Ar or A	18	39.948	1.784g/l	−189.2	−185.7	1894
arsenic	As	33	74.9216	5.727	814 (36 atm.)	615 (subl.)	1649
astatine	At	85	[210]	—	—	—	1940
barium	Ba	56	137.34	3.5	850	1140	1774
berkelium	Bk	97	[247]	—	—	—	1949
beryllium	Be	4	9.0122	1.85	1278	2970	1798
bismuth	Bi	83	208.980	9.80	271.3	1560	1737
boron	B	5	10.811	3.33	2300	2550	1702
bromine	Br	35	79.909	2.928	−7.2	58.78	1826
cadmium	Cd	48	112.40	8.642	320.9	767	1817
calcium	Ca	20	40.08	1.55	845	1240	1808
californium	Cf	98	[251]	—	—	—	1949
carbon	C	6	12.01115	2.25(gr.)	3700 (subl.)	4200	ancient
cerium	Ce	58	140.12	6.90	640	1400	1803
cesium	Cs	55	132.905	1.873	28.5	670	1860
chlorine	Cl	17	35.453	3.214g/l	−103	−34.6	1810
chromium	Cr	24	51.996	7.20	1890	2200	1797
cobalt	Co	27	58.9332	8.9	1495	2900	1737
columbium	Cb	(see niobium)					
copper	Cu	29	63.54	8.92	1083	2336	ancient
curium	Cm	96	[248]	7 (?)	—	—	1944
dysprosium	Dy	66	162.50	8.56	—	—	1886
einsteinium	Es or E	99	[254]	—	—	—	1952
erbium	Er	68	167.26	9.16	1250	—	1843
europium	Eu	63	151.96	5.24	1150	—	1901
fermium	Fm	100	[253]	—	—	—	1952
fluorine	F	9	18.9984	1.70g/l	−223	−188	1768
francium	Fr	87	[223]	—	—	—	1939
gadolinium	Gd	64	157.25	7.95	—	—	1886
gallium	Ga	31	69.72	5.904(s)	29.78	1983	1875
germanium	Ge	32	72.59	5.35	958.5	2700	1886
gold	Au	79	196.967	19.3	1063	2600	ancient
hafnium	Hf	72	178.49	13.3	2207	<3200	1923
helium	He	2	4.0026	0.1785g/l	−272.2 (26 atm.)	−268.9	1895
holmium	Ho	67	164.930	8.76	—	—	1879
hydrogen	H	1	1.00797	0.0899g/l	−259.14	−252.8	1671
indium	In	49	114.82	7.30	156.4	2000	1863
iodine	I	53	126.9044	4.93	113.7	184.35	1811
iridium	Ir	77	192.2	22.42	2454	>4800	1804
iron	Fe	26	55.847	7.86	1535	3000	ancient
krypton	Kr	36	83.80	3.708g/l	−156.6	−152.9	1898
lanthanum	La	57	138.91	6.15	826	1800	1839
lawrencium	Lr	103	[257]	—	—	—	1961
lead	Pb	82	207.19	11.344	327.4	1620	ancient
lithium	Li	3	6.939	0.534	186	1336	1817
lutetium	Lu	71	174.97	9.74	—	—	1907
magnesium	Mg	12	24.312	1.74	651	1107	1755
manganese	Mn	25	54.9380	7.20	1260	1900	1774
mendelevium	Md or Mv	101	[256]	—	—	—	1955
mercury	Hg	80	200.59	13.55	−38.87	356.58	ancient
molybdenum	Mo	42	95.94	10.2	2620	5560	1777
neodymium	Nd	60	144.24	6.9	840	—	1885
neon	Ne	10	20.183	0.9002g/l	−248.7	−245.9	1898
neptunium	Np	93	[237]	19.5	640	—	1940
nickel	Ni	28	58.71	8.90	1455	2900	1751
niobium	Nb	41	92.906	8.55	1950	2900	1801
nitrogen	N	7	14.0067	1.2506g/l	−209.9	−195.8	1772
nobelium	No	102	[253]	—	—	—	1957
osmium	Os	76	190.2	22.48	2700	>5300	1804
oxygen	O	8	15.9994	1.429g/l	−218.4	−182.96	1774
palladium	Pd	46	106.4	11.40	1549	2540	1803
phosphorus	P	15	30.9738	1.82 (yell.)	44.1 (yell.)	280	1669
platinum	Pt	78	195.09	21.45	1773	4300	1748
plutonium	Pu	94	[244]	19.82	639.5	3508	1940
polonium	Po	84	[210]	—	—	—	1898
potassium	K	19	39.102	0.86	62.3	760	1702
praseodymium	Pr	59	140.907	6.5	940	—	1885
promethium	Pm	61	[145]	—	—	—	1947
protactinium	Pa	91	[231]	15.37	—	—	1917
radium	Ra	88	[226]	5	960	1140	1898
radon	Rn	86	[222]	9.73g/l	−110	−61.8	1900
rhenium	Re	75	186.2	20.53	3160	—	1925
rhodium	Rh	45	102.905	12.4	1985	>2500	1803
rubidium	Rb	37	85.47	1.532	38.5	700	1861
ruthenium	Ru	44	101.07	12.6	>1950	—	1844
samarium	Sm	62	150.35	6.93	1350	—	1879
scandium	Sc	21	44.956	2.5	1200	2400	1879
selenium	Se	34	78.96	4.82	220	688	1818
silicon	Si	14	28.086	2.42	1420	2600	1824
silver	Ag	47	107.870	10.5	960.8	1950	ancient
sodium	Na	11	22.9898	0.97	97.5	880	1702
strontium	Sr	38	87.62	2.6	757	1150	1790
sulfur	S	16	32.064	2.07(rh)	112.8	444.6	ancient
tantalum	Ta	73	180.948	16.6	3027	4100	1802
technetium	Tc	43	[99]	11.49	—	—	1937
tellurium	Te	52	127.60	6.25	452	1390	1783
terbium	Tb	65	158.924	8.33	—	—	1843
thallium	Tl	81	204.37	11.85	302	1457	1861
thorium	Th	90	232.038	11.2	1750	>3000	1828
thulium	Tm	69	168.934	9.35	—	—	1879
tin	Sn	50	118.69	7.28	231.9	2270	ancient
titanium	Ti	22	47.90	4.5	1800	>3000	1791
tungsten	W	74	183.85	19.3	3370	5900	1783
uranium	U	92	238.03	18.7	1133	3818	1789
vanadium	V	23	50.942	5.96	1710	3000	1831
wolfram	W	(see tungsten)				—	
xenon	Xe	54	131.30	5.851g/l	−112	−107	1898
ytterbium	Yb	70	173.04	7.01	1800	—	1907
yttrium	Y	39	88.905	5.51	1490	2500	1794
zinc	Zn	30	65.37	7.14	419.5	907	1742
zirconium	Zr	40	91.22	6.4	1900	>2900	1789

[1]International chemical atomic weights (C=12) are given which for most elements are those of a naturally occurring mixture of isotopes. Numbers in square brackets are mass numbers of the isotopes of longest known life.
[2]For gases density in grams per liter is given instead of specific gravity.
[3]Temperatures are given in centigrade degrees.
[4]"Ancient" indicates that the element has been known since ancient times and that there is no record of date of discovery.
A dash means that data are not known.
Abbreviations (designations of allotropic forms under SPECIFIC GRAVITY apply to all physical constants):

atm.	=atmospheres	s	=solid
g/l	=grams per liter	subl.	=sublimes
gr.	=graphite	yell.	=yellow
rh	=rhombic		

PHYSICAL **b :** ELEMENTAL 1 ⟨these stark ~ powers . . . this wind, this earth, this sea, this forest —J.C.Powys⟩ **2 :** of, relating to, or treating of the elements, rudiments, or first principles of any subject or thing **:** INTRODUCTORY, RUDIMENTARY, SIMPLE, FUNDAMENTAL, PRIMITIVE ⟨an ~ text in geology⟩ ⟨an ~ precaution of historical research —M.R.Cohen⟩ ⟨the play has a very ~ plot⟩ ⟨the serf had the ~ security of the land itself —Lewis Mumford⟩ ⟨look at those hippopotami —how ~ is their . . . appearance —Llewelyn Powys⟩ **:** BEGINNING ⟨a concise aid to ~ students of Irish literature —G.B. Saul⟩; *specif* **:** of or relating to an elementary school ⟨Alaska's public schools had 765 teachers serving 100 ~ departments —*Americana Annual*⟩ ⟨a skilled craftsman has always . . . been able to earn more than an ~ schoolmaster —Roy Lewis & Angus Maude⟩ **3 a :** ELEMENTAL 2a(2) ⟨an ~ substance⟩ **b :** NUCLEAR ⟨agriculture, fishing, hunting, gathering . . . are carried on by the ~ family —J.B.Watson⟩ **4** *of a hand* **:** coarse and clumsy with the palm large and heavy and with short fingers and short nails usu. held by palmists to indicate low or animal characteristics and very little mental capacity or self-control ⟨the ~ hand rarely rises above the most menial occupations —Alice D. Jennings⟩

elementary algebra *n* **:** the part of algebra dealing with the simple properties (as the fundamental operations, factoring, simple equations)

elementary analysis *n* **:** the detection or determination of the elements composing a substance

elementary body *n* **:** one of the distinguishable units making up an inclusion body and believed to be or to contain the actual infective particles of certain viruses

elementary charge *n* **:** an apparently fundamental constant that is the smallest known quantity of electricity, is either positive or negative (as the positron or the electron), and has a value of about 4.802×10^{-10} statcoulomb or 1.602×10^{-19} absolute coulomb

elementary geometry *n* **:** the part of Euclidean geometry dealing with the simpler properties of straight lines, circles, planes, polyhedrons, the sphere, the cylinder, and the right circular cone

elementary particle *n* **:** any of the submicroscopic constituents of matter and energy (as the electron, pion, proton, or photon) whose existence has not been attributed to the combination of other more fundamental entities

elementary school *n* **:** a school in which elementary subjects (as reading, writing, spelling, and arithmetic) are taught to children from about six to about twelve years of age which in the U.S. covers the first six or eight grades — compare SECONDARY SCHOOL

elementary species *n* **:** SUBSPECIES

elements *pl of* ELEMENT, *pres 3d sing of* ELEMENT

elements of an orbit : a set of numerical quantities that define the orbit of a member of the solar system or of a binary star and permit computation of the body's position at any given time

el·e·mi \ˈeləmē\ *n* -s [alter. of earlier *elimi*, fr. NL, prob. fr. Ar *al-lāmi* the elemī] **:** any of certain fragrant oleoresins obtained from tropical trees of the family Burseraceae and used chiefly in varnishes, lacquers, and printing inks and formerly in medicinal plasters: as **a :** a soft yellowish plastic resin from several African, Asiatic, and Philippine trees of the genus *Canarium*; *esp* **:** MANILA ELEMI — compare BREA 1a(2) **b :** a resin obtained from certain trees of the genus *Protium* and used as incense

elem·i·cin \əˈleməsən\ *n* -s [ISV *elemic* (fr. *elemi* + *-ic*) + *-in*; orig. formed as G *elemizin*] **:** a liquid ether $C_{12}H_{16}O_3$ found in some essential oils (as oil of Manila elemi)

elemi figs *var of* ELEME FIGS

el·e·mol \ˈelə,mōl, -ōl\ *n* -s [*elemi* + *-ol*] **:** a crystalline alcohol $C_{15}H_{25}OH$ obtained from oil of Manila elemi and citronella oil

elench *n* -s [L *elenchus*] **1** *obs* **:** ELENCHUS **2** *obs* **:** SOPHISM

elen·chus \əˈleŋkəs, ēˈ-\ *n, pl* **elen·chi** \-,kī, -,kē\ [L, fr. Gk *elenchos* cross-examination, refutation, fr. *elenchein* to shame, cross-examine, refute; perh. akin to MIr *lang* shame, Latvian *langāt* to scold, Hitt *link-* to swear] **:** REFUTATION; *esp* **:** one cast in syllogistic form — compare IGNORATIO ELENCHI

elenc·tic *or* **elench·tic** \-ŋtik\ *also* **elenc·ti·cal** *or* **elench·ti·cal** \-tə̇kəl\ *adj* [Gk *elenktikos*, fr. *elenktos* (verbal of *elenchein*) + *-ikos* -ic, -ical] **:** serving to refute — used of indirect modes of proof; opposed to *deictic*

el·enge \ˈelənj\ *adj* [ME, fr. OE *ǣlenge*, fr. *ǣ-* (var. of *ā-*, *ar-*, perfective & intensive prefix) + *-lenge* (fr. *lang* long) — more at ABEAR, LONG] *archaic* **:** TEDIOUS, REMOTE, MISERABLE, DREARY

eleo- — see ELAIO-

el·e·och·a·ris \,elēˈäkərə̇s\ *n, cap* [NL, fr. Gk *hele-*, *helos* marsh + *charis* grace, beauty — more at HELODES, CHARISMA] **:** a genus of sedges (family Cyperaceae) with dense spikes of flowers and leaves reduced to basal sheaths

ele·o·cyte \əˈlēə,sīt\ *n* -s [*elaio-* + *-cyte*] **:** a coelomocyte containing numerous fat globules

ele·o·lite *or* **elae·o·lite** \-,līt\ *n* -s [G *eläolith*, fr. *eläo-* elaio- + *-lith* -lite] **:** NEPHELINE

el·e·op·tene *or* **el·ae·op·tene** \,elēˈäp,tēn\ *n* -s [ISV *elaio-* + Gk *ptēnos* winged; akin to Gk *petesthai* to fly — more at FEATHER] **:** the liquid portion of any natural essential oil that partly solidifies in the cold — distinguished from *stearoptene*

el·eo·stearic acid *or* **el·aeo·stearic acid** \,elē(,)ō, əˈlē(,)ō+ . . .\ *n* [ISV *elaio-* + *stearic*] **:** a crystalline unsaturated fatty acid $C_4H_9(CH{:}CH)_3(CH_2)_7COOH$ that exists in two stereoisomeric forms, (1) the alpha acid occurring as the glyceryl ester esp. in tung oil and (2) the beta acid obtained from the alpha acid by irradiation; 9, 11, 13-octa-deca-trien-oic acid

¹el·e·o·trid \,elēˈō·trə̇d\ *adj* [NL *Eleotridae*] **:** of or relating to the Eleotridae

²eleotrid \"\ *n* -s **:** a member of the Eleotridae

el·e·o·tri·dae \,elēˈōtrə,dē\ *n pl, cap* [NL, fr. *Eleotris*, type genus (fr. Gk *eleōtris*, a fish of the Nile river) + *-idae*] **:** a large widely distributed family of chiefly small fishes comprising the sleepers that are closely related to and sometimes included among the gobies from which they are distinguished by pelvic fins that are separate and do not form a cup or disk

el·e·paio \,eləˈpī(,)ō\ *n* -s [Hawaiian *ʻelepaio*] **:** a flycatcher (*Chasiempis sandwichensis*) found on several of the Hawaiian islands

el·e·phant \ˈeləfənt\ *n* -s [ME *olifaunt*, *elephant*, fr. OF & L; OF *olifant* elephant, ivory, fr. L *elephantus*, fr. Gk *elephant-*, *elephas*, perh. of Hamitic origin; akin to Egypt *ʾb(w)* elephant, ivory] **1 a :** any of certain thickset mostly very large nearly hairless four-footed mammals of the family Elephantidae esp. of the genera *Elephas* and *Loxodonta* having the snout prolonged into a muscular trunk, two incisors in the upper jaw developed esp. in the male into long curved tusks which furnish ivory, the head large with much diploic tissue and a well-developed brain, and the feet short and rounded with five toes **b :** an animal of the order Proboscidea — see MAMMOTH, MASTODON **2 :** one that is an uncommonly large specimen of its kind ⟨he was an ~ of a man⟩ **3 :** a size of paper ranging from 20x27 to 23x30 inches **4 :** a grooving and rabbeting machine

Indian elephant

el·e·phan·ta \,eləˈfantə\ *n* -s [Pg *elefante*, lit., elephant, fr. L *elephantus*; fr. the fact that the elephant is a symbol of the Hindu 13th lunar mansion, when such storms occur] **:** a violent East Indian storm at either at the close or at the setting in of the monsoon

elephant apple *n* **1 :** WOOD APPLE 1 **2 :** BEL

elephant beetle *n* **1 :** any of several very large chiefly tropical lamellicorn beetles that bear a forked upwardly curved horn on the front of the head **2** *also* **elephant bug :** WEEVIL

elephant bird *n* **:** AEPYORNIS 2

elephant creeper *n* **:** an East Indian vine (*Argyreia speciosa*) of the family Convolvulaceae that has large cordate leaves with silvery lower surface and funnel-shaped rose-colored flowers and is widely cultivated as an ornamental in tropical areas

elephant-ear fern *n* **:** a tropical American fern (*Elaphoglossum crinitum*) with large simple fronds

elephant-ear sponge *n* **:** a fine soft durable fan-shaped or cup-shaped commercial sponge (*Spongia officinalis lamella*) occurring in the Mediterranean sea

elephant fish *n* **:** a chimaeroid fish (*Callorhynchus callorhynchus*) with an elongated mobile projection of the snout; *broadly* **:** any of various other chimaeras

elephant folio *n* **:** a publication (as a book or atlas) of the largest size

elephant grass *n* **1 :** an Old World cattail (*Typha elephantina*) ranging from southern Europe to the East Indies and having leaves that are used in making baskets and pollen that is used in India for making bread **2 :** NAPIER GRASS

elephant green *n* **:** HUNTER GREEN

elephant gun *n* **:** a rifle of large caliber (as .400 or above) designed primarily for hunting the largest of African or Indian game animals

el·e·phan·ti·as·ic \,eləˌfantēˈasik; -fən·ˈtī,sik, -,fan·ˌ-\ *adj* [NL *elephantiasis* + E *-ic*] **:** affected with or characteristic of elephantiasis

el·e·phan·ti·a·sis \,eləfən·ˈtīəsə̇s, -,fan-\ *n, pl* **elephantia·ses** \-ī̇ə,sēz\ [NL, fr. L, a kind of leprosy in which the skin takes on the appearance of an elephant's hide, fr. Gk, fr. *elephant-*, *elephas* elephant + *-iasis* — more at ELEPHANT] **1 :** enlargement and thickening of tissues; *specif* **:** the enormous enlargement of a limb or the scrotum resulting from obstruction of lymphatics by filarial worms — compare FILARIASIS **2 :** an undesirable enormous growth, enlargement, or overdevelopment ⟨dislikes ~ in labor and in government as much as in industry —Robert Lekachman⟩ ⟨his obsession for self-expression . . . resulted in verbal ~ —*Saturday Rev.*⟩

el·e·phan·tic \,eləˈfantik\ *adj* **:** ELEPHANTINE

el·e·phan·ti·dae \,eləˈfantə,dē\ *n pl, cap* [NL, fr. *Elephant-*, *Elephas*, type genus + *-idae*] **:** a family of bulky mammals (order Proboscidea) comprising the recent elephants and related extinct forms (as the mammoths) that differ from these chiefly in respect to their dentition and in former classifications including also the mastodons

el·e·phan·tine \,eləˈfan,tēn, -faan- *also* -ˈfa(a)n·,tīn *or* ˈeləfən·,tēn *or* ˈeləfən·,tīn\ *adj* [L *elephantinus* of an elephant, of ivory, fr. Gk *elephantinos* of ivory, fr. *elephant-*, *elephas* elephant, ivory + *-inos* -ine — more at ELEPHANT] **1 :** of or relating to an elephant **2 a :** of enormous size or weight **:** uncommonly large **:** IMMENSE, MASSIVE ⟨all his limbs . . . were ~ —George Meredith⟩ **b :** lacking in grace or ease **:** PONDEROUS, CLUMSY, HEAVY-FOOTED ⟨wrote some ~ light verse⟩ ⟨they chat with . . . raucous malevolence and ~ facetiousness —Warren Beck⟩ **syn** see HUGE

elephantine tortoise *n* **:** ELEPHANT TORTOISE 1

elephant iron *n* **:** iron in large semicylindrical sheets of corrugated steel used in roofing (as of dugouts or other military installations)

el·e·phan·toid \,eləˈfan,tȯid, ˈeləfən-\ *adj* **1 :** of or resembling an elephant **2** [NL *elephantiasis* + E *-oid*] **:** resembling or relating to elephantiasis

el·e·phan·to·pus \,eləˈfantəpəs\ *n* [NL, fr. *elephanto-* (fr. L *elephantus* elephant) + *-pus* — more at ELEPHANT] **1** *cap* **:** a genus of alternate-leaved perennial American herbs (family Compositae) with agglomerate bracted heads of blue or purple flowers **2** -ES **:** any plant of the genus *Elephantopus*

elephant seal *n* **1 :** a very large seal (*Mirounga leonina*) formerly abundant along many coasts of the southern hemisphere but hunted nearly to extermination for its oil and having a male that attains a length of 20 feet and has a long inflatable proboscis **2 :** a very similar smaller seal (*Mirounga angustirostris*) formerly abundant along the California and Lower California coast but now restricted to a single herd protected by the Mexican government on the island of Guadalupe

elephant's ear *also* **elephant ear** *n* **:** any of several plants having large one-sided leaves: as **a :** BEGONIA **b :** a plant of the genus *Colocasia*; *esp* **:** TARO

elephant's-foot \ˈ==ˌ=\ *n, pl* **elephant's-foots 1 a :** a plant of the genus *Elephantopus* **b :** a southern African vine (*Dioscorea elephantipes*) having a massive rootstock covered with a deeply fissured bark — called also *tortoise plant*; see HOTTENTOT BREAD **2 :** a ram with a foot for holding the work to the block in a flanging machine

elephant's grass *n* **:** ELEPHANT GRASS

elephant shark *n* **1 :** BASKING SHARK **2 :** ELEPHANT FISH

elephant's-head *or* **elephant head** \ˈ==ˌ=\ *n, pl* **elephant's heads** [so called fr. the shape of the corolla] **:** a lousewort (*Pedicularis groenlandica*) of arctic and western alpine No. America with spikes of crimson flowers

elephant shrew *n* **:** any of several leaping African shrews comprising a family (Macroscelididae) remotely related to both the true shrews and the hedgehogs and having the nose long and flexible like a proboscis

elephant's-tooth \ˈ==ˌ=\ *n, pl* **elephant's-tooths :** TOOTH SHELL

elephant's-trunk plant \ˈ==ˌ=-\ *n* **:** UNICORN PLANT

elephant's-tusk \ˈ==ˌ=\ *or* **elephant's-tusk shell** *n, pl* **elephant's-tusks** *or* **elephant's-tusk shells :** TOOTH SHELL

elephant thorn *n* **:** an East Indian tree (*Acacia tomentosa*) with large spreading brown spines

elephant tortoise *n* **1 :** a giant tortoise (*Testudo gigantea*) of the Aldabra islands **2 :** a tortoise (*Testudo elephantopus*) of the Galápagos islands that is now extinct

elephant tree *n* **:** a spicy-odored small tree or shrub (*Bursera microphylla*) of the southwestern U.S. having a light-gray outer bark, slender zigzag twigs, and white flowers in mostly 3-flowered clusters

elephant trunk *n* **:** a flexible chute used to direct coal onto a pile with limited blowing of dust or to direct concrete with minimum spatter

elephant wood *n* **:** a shrub or small tree (*Pachycormus discolor*) of the family Anacardiaceae found only in Lower California and having a large swollen trunk, a low crown, and clusters of small red flowers

el·e·phas \ˈeləfəs, -,fas\ *n, cap* [NL, fr. Gk, elephant — more at ELEPHANT] **:** the type genus of the family Elephantidae comprising the Asiatic elephant and extinct related forms and formerly being nearly coextensive with Elephantidae

elepidote \(ˈ)ē+\ *adj* [*e-* + *lepidote*] *bot* **:** lacking small scurfy scales

el·et·tar·ia \,eləˈta(a)rēə\ *n, cap* [NL, prob. fr. a native name like Jav *ela-ela* cardamom, prob. redupl. of Skt *elā*] **:** a genus of East Indian herbs (family Zingiberaceae) having lanceolate sheathing leaves and small purple-striped flowers in a long spike — see CARDAMOM

el·eu·si·ne \,elyüˈsī(,)nē\ *n* [NL, fr. Gk *Eleusinē*, a name for Demeter, goddess of grain] **1** *cap* **:** a genus of grasses with digitate or rarely scattered spikes consisting of many-flowered spikelets — see RAGGEE, YARD GRASS **2** -s **:** any plant of the genus *Eleusine*

¹el·eu·sin·i·an \,elyüˈsinēən\ *adj, usu cap* [L *Eleusinius* (fr. Gk *Eleusinios*, fr. *Eleusis*, city of ancient Greece) + E *-an*] **:** of or relating to the ancient city of Eleusis in Attica

²eleusinian \"\ *n* -s *cap* **:** a citizen or inhabitant of the city of Eleusis in ancient Greece

el·e·ut *also* **el·e·uth** \ˈelē,üt\ *n* -s *usu cap* **:** KALMUCK

eleuther- *or* **eleuthero-** *comb form* [Gk, free, fr. *eleutheros* — more at LIBERAL] **1 :** freedom ⟨*eleutheromania*⟩ **2 :** free ⟨*Eleutherozoa*⟩

eleu·thera bark \əˈlüthərə-\ *n* [fr. *Eleuthera* Island, Bahamas] **:** CASCARILLA 1

el·eu·the·ria \,elyəˈthirēə\ *n, cap* [NL, fr. Gk, freedom, fr. *eleutheros* + *-ia* -y] **:** a genus of atypical hermaphroditic hydrozoan jellyfishes

eleu·thero·dac·ty·lus \ə,lüthə(,)rōˈdaktələs\ *n, cap* [NL, fr. *eleuther-* + Gk *daktylos* finger, toe] **:** a large genus of small chiefly tropical New World frogs (family Bufonidae or Leptodactylidae) that commonly complete metamorphosis within the egg

eleu·ther·o·zoa \-thərəˈzōə\ *n pl, cap* [NL, fr. *eleuther-* + *-zoa*] **:** a subphylum or other division of Echinodermata including the Asteroidea, Ophiuroidea, Echinoidea, and Holothurioidea — **eleu·ther·o·zo·an** \ˌ=ˌ===ˈzōən\ *adj or n* — **eleu·ther·o·zo·ic** \-ōik\ *adj*

¹el·e·vate \ˈelə,vāt, -,vət\ *adj* [ME *elevat*, fr. L *elevatus*, past part.] *archaic* **:** ELEVATED

²el·e·vate \ˈelə,vāt, *usu* -ād·+V\ *vb* -ED/-ING/-S [ME *elevaten*, fr. L *elevatus*, past part. of *elevare* to raise up, lighten, fr. *e-* + *levare* to raise, lighten — more at LEVER] *vt* **1 a :** to lift up in space **:** RAISE ⟨materials are *elevated* to the top floor by a hoist⟩ **b :** to lift up (the Host) at Mass **c :** to cause (a structure) to be built **:** ERECT, REAR ⟨*elevated* a palace⟩ **d :** to cause to rise ⟨the gas, being lighter than air, ~s the balloon⟩ **e :** to turn, aim, or direct upward ⟨*elevated* his eyebrows, and looked at him in amazement —Oscar Wilde⟩ **f :** to increase markedly the degree or level of ⟨~ the temperature⟩ **2 a** (1) **:** to raise (a person) in rank, station, or dignity ⟨the appeal of the frontier democracy which had *elevated* Andrew Jackson to the presidency —A.C.Cole⟩ (2) **:** to advance (as an idea or activity) to a higher level of importance or significance ⟨~ an automatic movement of history to the position of supreme arbiter —John Dewey⟩ **b :** to improve or tend to improve (as in morality, taste, culture, or quality) **:** ENNOBLE, EXALT, REFINE ⟨~ backward peoples⟩ ⟨~ the art of reedworking into something more . . . wonderful than it really is —Ben Riker⟩ ⟨claims the artist should not only entertain but ~ his audience⟩ **3** *obs* **:** to mitigate or lessen by depreciation or extenuation **4 :** to cause (the voice) to rise **5 :** to raise the spirits of **:** EXHILARATE, ELATE ⟨the morning air of heaven refreshed and *elevated* me —W.H.Hudson †1922⟩ **:** inspire fervor or excitement in ⟨the subject *elevated* him to more than usual solemnity of manner —Jane Austen⟩ **~** *vi* **:** to raise the moral or intellectual faculties ⟨contended that art and music not only entertain but ~⟩ **syn** see LIFT

¹elevated *adj* **1 a :** raised esp. above the ground or other surface **:** situated at a high level ⟨the house stood on an ~ site⟩ ⟨after the skin becomes ~ and lumpy, pus forms —Morris Fishbein⟩ **b :** increased esp. abnormally (as in degree or amount) ⟨the pulse rate is ~ slightly —D.W.Maurer & V.H. Vogel⟩ ⟨an ~ temperature⟩ **2 a :** morally or intellectually on a high plane **:** aloof from what is mean or ignoble **:** marked by nobility of thought or feeling **:** NOBLE, REFINED, EDIFYING ⟨his ~ mind abominated the luxuries of an effete civilization —Elinor Wylie⟩ ⟨~ ideas⟩ **b :** FORMAL, DIGNIFIED, EXALTED, LOFTY ⟨we must not smile at the ~ diction of this letter —H.S.Canby⟩ ⟨by prose I mean . . . plain, workaday prose, not artistic or ~ prose —J.L.Lowes⟩ **3 a :** exalted in mood or feeling **:** EXHILARATED, EXCITED ⟨she was in one of those moods of ~ feeling, when the soul is upheld by a strange tranquillity —Nathaniel Hawthorne⟩ **b :** TIPSY, INTOXICATED ⟨he drinks much champagne and becomes ~ —Joyce Cary⟩ — **el·e·vat·ed·ly** *adv* — **el·e·vat·ed·ness** *n* -ES

²elevated \"\ *n* -s **:** ELEVATED RAILROAD

elevated pole *n* **:** the one of the two celestial poles that is above the observer's horizon

elevated railroad *or* **elevated railway** *n* **:** a railroad usu. for local transit in urban or interurban areas all or part of which is raised (as on trestlework) above the ground level

elevating *adj* **:** tending to improve morally or intellectually **:** EDIFYING ⟨the discovery that to borrow books and ideas from Europe was . . . ~ in itself —G.W.Pierson⟩ ⟨exercised an ~ influence on society —Wilmot Harrison⟩ ⟨the theory . . . is that a taste for music is an ~ passion —H.L.Mencken⟩ — **el·e·vat·ing·ly** *adv*

elevating arc *n* **:** a vertical graduated arc on a gun or its carriage used in elevating or depressing the gun

el·e·va·tio \,āləˈväd·ē,ō, -ätsē,ō\ *n, pl* **elevati·o·nes** \,==,==-ˈō,nās\ [ML, fr. L, elevation] **:** the rising of a melody beyond the ambitus of the mode in medieval music

el·e·va·tion \,eləˈvāshən\ *n* -s [ME *elevacioun*, fr. L *elevation-*, *elevatio*, fr. *elevatus* + *-ion-*, *-io* -ion] **1 :** the height to which something is elevated: as **a :** the angular distance of a celestial object above the horizon ⟨computing the ~ of the pole⟩ **b** (1) **:** the vertical pointing of an artillery piece; *also* **:** ANGLE OF ELEVATION (2) **:** the height of an arrow's head in relation to the nock in the act of aiming **c :** the height above sea level **:** ALTITUDE **d** (1) **:** a ballet dancer's or skater's leap and illusory suspension in the air (2) **:** the ability of a dancer or skater to attain height in the air (3) **:** the height in the air attained by a dancer or skater; *usu* **:** the distance between the pointed toes and the ground **2 a :** the act or an instance of elevating **:** the act of raising something from a lower to a higher level ⟨the ~ of second-rate . . . scientists to posts of authority —Martin Gardner⟩ ⟨an ~ of the eyebrows⟩ **b** *often cap* **:** a portion of an Eastern or Western Christian liturgy in which the priest solemnly raises one or both of the eucharistic elements for the people to view with homage or adoration **c :** something that is elevated: as (1) **:** an elevated place or station **:** HILL ⟨an ~ of the ground⟩ (2) **:** a swelling esp. on the skin **3 :** the condition or quality of being elevated: as **a :** the condition of being raised in rank, dignity, or importance ⟨overjoyed at his ~ to that honorable post⟩ **b :** the state or an instance of being piously exalted or uplifted ⟨he can never hear the Ave-Mary bell without an ~ —Douglas Bush⟩; *also* **:** a lifting of spirits **:** a state of marked cheerfulness or gaiety **:** EBULLIENCE ⟨he was subject to periods of ~ and wretched depression⟩ **c** (1) **:** dignity or sublimity of style, mood, or thought **:** loftiness of tone ⟨epics, like Greek tragedies, must be rendered with ~ —Dudley Fitts⟩ ⟨the English translation is not good; its failure to convey the very slight ~ of tone is a fundamental failure —Allen Tate⟩ ⟨he is always impressive, and . . . the foreign policy speech reaches an admirable ~ —*Nation's Business*⟩ (2) **:** nobility of character or spirit ⟨he had too much ~ of mind to save himself by informing against others —T.B.Macaulay⟩ **d :** a usu. abnormal increase (as in degree or amount) ⟨an ~ of the pulse rate⟩ ⟨an ~ of temperature⟩ **4 :** a grace used in old English music **:** SLIDE **5 :** a geometrical projection (as of a building) on a plane perpendicular to the horizon **:** orthographic projection on a vertical plane

elevation head *n* **:** head (sense 14b) that corresponds to the potential energy of elevation of a flowing liquid

elevation meter *n* **:** an instrument that combines both odometer and inclinometer features and that when drawn along a hilly road automatically computes and records the net change in elevation as the vehicle proceeds

ele·va·to \,eləˈvä,tō\ *adj (or adv)* [It, fr. L *elevatus*] **:** elevated in tone **:** SUBLIME — used as a direction in music

el·e·va·tor \ˈelə,vād·ə(r), -ātə-\ *n* -s **1 :** one that raises or lifts up anything: as **a :** an endless belt or chain conveyor with cleats, scoops, or buckets for raising material **b :** a cage or platform and its hoisting machinery (as in a building or mine) for conveying persons or goods to or from different levels — see HYDRAULIC ELEVATOR **c :** a building for elevating, storing, discharging, and sometimes processing grain **d :** a compressed-air lift or pump for raising acids **e :** a tool or device for raising or lowering pipe or rods out of or into a well **2 :** a movable auxiliary airfoil usu. attached to the tail plane the function of which is to impress a pitching moment on an airplane thus producing rotation about its lateral axis, positive or downward deflection of the elevator causing the airplane to dive, and negative or upward deflection causing it to climb **3 :** a dental instrument for removing the roots of teeth **4 :** a surgical instrument for raising a depressed part (as of a bone) or for separating contiguous parts **5** *printing* **:** either of two mechanisms in keyboard slugcasting machines for raising set matrices, one used for casting and the other for distribution

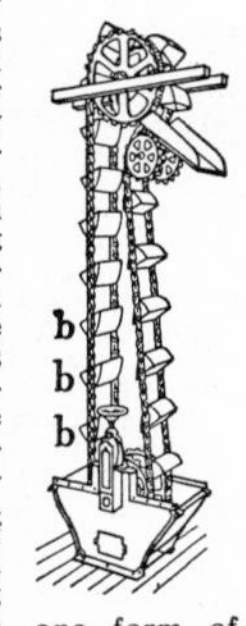

one form of elevator 1a: *b*, *b*, *b*, buckets

elevator dredge *n* **:** a dredge operating by means of a bucket conveyor

el·e·va·tor·ing \-ād·əriŋ, -ā·tr-\ *n* -s **:** passenger elevators

elevator liability insurance *or* **elevator insurance** *n* **:** insurance against loss due to legal liability for bodily injury or property damage resulting from ownership, maintenance, or use of elevators, escalators, lifts, or hoists

elevator shoe *n* [fr. *Elevators*, a trademark] **:** a shoe having a specially constructed raised insole intended to make the wearer look taller

el·e·va·to·ry \'eləvə,tōrē, *chiefly Brit* -,vātəri *or* -,vā·tri\ *adj* **:** tending to elevate ⟨~ forces⟩

[1]**elev·en** \ə'levən, ē'-, -lev^əm,-leb^əm, *rapid* 'le-\ *adj* [ME *enleven, elleven,* fr. OE *endleofan;* akin to OHG *einlif* eleven, OS *ēlleban,* ON *ellifu,* Goth *ainlibim* (dat.); all fr. a prehistoric Gmc compound whose first constituent is represented by OE *ān* one, and whose second constituent is prob. akin to Lith *-lika* (as in *vėnúlika* eleven), OHG *līhan* to lend — more at ONE, LOAN] **:** being one more than 10 in number ⟨~ years⟩ — see NUMBER table

[2]**eleven** \"\ *pron, pl in constr* [ME *enleven, elleven,* fr. OE *endleofane,* fr. *endleofan,* adj.] **:** 11 countable persons or things not specified but under consideration and being enumerated ⟨~ are here⟩ ⟨~ were found⟩

[3]**eleven** \"\ *n* -s [ME *enleven, elleven,* fr. *enleven, elleven,* adj. & pron.] **1 :** 10 and one **2 a :** 11 units or objects ⟨a total of ~⟩ **b :** a group or set of 11 **3 :** the numerable quantity symbolized by the arabic numerals 11 **4 :** a playing team of 11 members; *esp* **:** a football team **5 :** 11 o'clock — compare BELL table, TIME illustration

eleven rule *n* **:** RULE OF ELEVEN

elev·ens·es \-ənziz,-^əmziz\ *n pl* [irreg. pl. of [3]*eleven* (o'clock)] *Brit* **:** a light lunch or sometimes only coffee or tea taken around the middle of the morning

[1]**elev·enth** \-ən(t)th,-^əmth\ *adj* [ME *enlefte, ellefte, enleventhe, elleventhe,* adj. & n., fr. OE *endleofta, endlyfta* (akin to OHG *einlifto* eleventh, ON *ellifti*), fr. *endleofan* eleven + *-tha* -th] **1 :** being number 11 in a countable series — see NUMBER table **2 :** being one of 11 equal parts into which something is divisible ⟨an ~ share of the money⟩

[2]**eleventh** \"\ *n, pl* **elevenths** \-ən(t)s,-^əm(p)s,-ən(t)ths, -^əmths\ [ME *enlefte, ellefte, enleventhe, elleventhe*] **1 :** number 11 in a countable series ⟨the ~ of the month⟩ **2 :** the quotient of a unit divided by 11 **:** one of 11 equal parts of anything ⟨one ~ of the total⟩ **3 a :** the musical interval made up of an octave and a fourth **b :** a tone at this interval

eleventh cranial nerve *or* **eleventh nerve** *n* **:** ACCESSORY NERVE

eleventh hour *n* [so called fr. the parable of the vineyard (Mt 20:1–16) where laborers hired at the "eleventh hour" are paid the same wage as those hired early in the day] **:** the latest possible time ⟨perceived the danger of it at the *eleventh hour* —Louis Eisenmann⟩

el·e·von \'elə,vän\ *n* -s [*elevator* + *-on* (as in *aileron*)] **:** an airplane control surface that combines the functions of elevator and aileron — called also *ailavator*

elf \'elf, 'eu̇lf\ *n, pl* **elves** \|vz\ *also* **elfs** [ME, fr. OE *ælf;* akin to MLG *alf* incubus, MHG *alp* incubus, ON *alfr* elf, and prob. to OE *ælbitu, ielfetu* swan, OHG *alba* insect larva, *albiz, elbiz* swan, ON *elptr, ölpt* swan, L *albus* white, Gk *alphos,* a white skin disease, W *elfydd* earth, world, Russ *lebed'* swan; basic meaning: white] **1 :** a mythical diminutive being in human form endowed with magical powers and given to beneficial or mischievous interference in human affairs **:** FAIRY, SPRITE, PIXIE **2 a :** a small being or creature **:** DWARF; *esp* **:** a small usu. playful or prankish child ⟨the school yard teemed with running, shouting, laughing *elves*⟩ ⟨a little child, a limber ~ —S.T.Coleridge⟩ **b :** a mischievous, sly, or malicious person **3** *also* **elft** \|ft\ *Africa* **:** BLUEFISH 1

elf arrow *also* **elf bolt** *or* **elf dart** *n* **:** a flint arrowhead or similarly shaped stone supposed in some parts of Great Britain to be arrows shot by elves esp. at cattle and to possess magical powers

elf child *n* **:** CHANGELING

elf cup *n* **:** the apothecium of a fungus of the family Pezizaceae

elf dock *n* **:** ELECAMPANE

[1]**elf·in** \'elfən\ *adj* [irreg. fr. *elf*] **1 a :** of, relating to, or produced by an elf ⟨~ bells⟩ ⟨all the little creatures joined in the ~ dance⟩ **b :** of or relating to a small child or to childhood ⟨the ~ and adventurous time when tall weeds closed over us like woods —G.K.Chesterton⟩ **2 a :** small, slight, and delicately made or proportioned **:** DWARFISH ⟨a little ~ man whose reddish hair was beginning to thin and gray —W.A. White⟩ ⟨apparently was obsessed by things ~ and small —Green Peyton⟩ **b :** quick, agile, and delicate (as in movement or thought) ⟨unfailingly shows poetic insight and ~ liveliness of fancy —*Amer. Guide Series: Ind.*⟩ ⟨his touch was light, crisp, and somehow deliciously comic; he could start the keys into ~ life —J.B.Priestley⟩ **c :** good-naturedly or slyly mischievous **:** PLAYFUL, PUCKISH ⟨with ~ delight he perpetuated a successful practical joke —J.A.Morris b. 1904⟩ **d :** having an otherworldly, unearthly, or magical quality **:** FEY ⟨a strange ~ creature⟩ ⟨a tale of ~ charm⟩

[2]**elfin** \"\ *n* -s **1 :** ELF; *also* **:** CHILD, URCHIN **2 :** any of several delicate grayish brown or orange-brown hairstreak butterflies (genus *Incisalia*) flying in early spring

elfinwood \'⸗⸗,⸗\ *n* **:** KRUMMHOLZ

elfin woodland *n* **:** stunted forest growing at higher elevation in warm moist regions and characterized by gnarled stumpy trees heavily burdened with epiphytes and abundant growth of mosses — compare KRUMMHOLZ

elf·ish \'elfish, -fēsh\ *adj* [alter. of *elvish*] **1 :** of or relating to an elf **:** resembling an elf **:** ELFIN ⟨~ figures⟩ **2 :** MISCHIEVOUS, IMPISH, ELVISH ⟨~ pranks⟩ — **elf·ish·ly** *adv*

elf·land \'el,fland\ *n* **:** FAIRYLAND ⟨where earth and ~ meet —Walter de la Mare⟩

elflock \'⸗,⸗\ *n* **:** hair matted as if by elves — usu. used in pl.

el fo *abbr* elephant folio

elf owl *n* **:** a very small insectivorous owl (*Micropallas whitneyi*) living in or about the giant cacti of desert areas of the southwestern U.S. and northern Mexico

[1]**elf–shot** \'⸗,⸗\ *n* [*elf* + *shot,* n.] **:** ELF ARROW

[2]**elf–shot** \"\ *adj* [*elf* + *shot,* past part. of *shoot*] *Scot* **:** afflicted with a disease supposed to result from a wound by an elf arrow

elfwort \'⸗,⸗\ *n* **:** ELECAMPANE

el·gin·shire \'elgən,shi(ə)r, -,shər\ *or* **el·gin** \'elgən\ *adj, usu cap* [*Elginshire, Elgin* (Moray), county in northeast Scotland] **:** MORAY

eliad *obs var of* OEILLADE

elian \'ēlēən, -lyən; *sometimes* 'el-, *which appears to have been the pronunc used by Lamb*\ *adj, usu cap* [*Elia,* pseudonym of Charles Lamb †1834 English essayist and critic + E *-an*] **:** of, relating to, or like the essayist Lamb or his writing ⟨that *Elian* technique —W.H.Gardner⟩

eli·as·ite \'ēlēə,sīt, -līə\ *n* -s [G *eliasit,* fr. the *Elias* mine in Czechoslovakia + G *-it* -ite] **:** GUMMITE

[1]**elicit** *adj* [L *elicitus,* past part.] *obs, of an act* **:** proceeding from the will — contrasted with *imperate*

[2]**elic·it** \ē'lisət, ə'-, *usu* -əd·+V\ *vt* -ED/-ING/-S [L *elicitus,* past part. of *elicere,* fr. *e-* + *-licere* (fr. *lacere* to allure) — more at DELIGHT] **1 a :** to draw or bring out (something latent or potential) ⟨~ a flame by the friction of the word —J.G.Frazer⟩ ⟨*~ed* harmonious sounds from his instrument⟩ ⟨the larger gatherings may have *~ed* more aspects of his thought and revealed more sides of his personality —Lucien Price⟩ **b :** to derive (as a truth or principle) by logical process **:** bring to view (as by reason or argument) ⟨the controversy *~ed* one important truth⟩ **2 :** to call forth or draw out (a response or reaction) **:** EVOKE, PROVOKE, CAUSE ⟨his question *~ed* only a blank stare⟩ ⟨best quality cauliflowers and carrots *~ed* keen bidding —*Farmer's Weekly (So. Africa)*⟩ ⟨his antics *~ed* applause and laughter⟩ ⟨his ability to ~ support from subordinates⟩ **syn** see EDUCE

elic·it·able \-əd·əbəl, -ətə-\ *adj* **:** capable of being elicited

elic·i·tate \-sə,tāt\ *vt* -ED/-ING/-S [L *elicitus* + E *-ate*] **:** ELICIT

elic·i·ta·tion \(,)ē,lisə'tāshən, ə,l-\ *n* -s **:** a drawing forth **:** EVOCATION, EXTRACTION ⟨the ~ of the true story took time⟩

elic·i·tor \ə'⸗səd·ə(r), -sətə(r), -sə,tō(ə)r, -ō(ə)\ *n* -s **:** one that elicits ⟨a skillful ~ of confidential information⟩

elide \ə'līd, ē'-\ *vt* -ED/-ING/-S [L *elidere,* fr. *e-* + *-lidere* (fr. *laedere* to hurt, damage) — more at LESION] **1** *archaic* **:** DESTROY ⟨~ the force of his argument⟩ **:** ANNUL **2 a :** to suppress or alter (as a vowel or syllable) by elision **b :** to strike out (as a written figure, word, or passage) ⟨I write very slowly and ~ a good deal —A.N.Whitehead⟩ ⟨these figures should be *elided* wherever possible, the minimum being used to give the sense —P.G.Burbidge⟩ ⟨sternly *elided* the reference to the fact that he had laughed —John Gunther⟩ **c :** to leave out of consideration **:** pass over **:** IGNORE, OMIT, SUPPRESS ⟨he *~s,* as much as possible, the incest motif —Francis Fergusson⟩ ⟨it may seek to ~, instead of recognizing, the high and solemn function of parliament —Ernest Barker⟩ **d :** CURTAIL, ABRIDGE, SHORTEN, REDUCE, DIMINISH ⟨the two worlds often have the power of mutually *eliding* . . . their effectiveness —Pier-Maria Pasinetti⟩ ⟨the circulating exhibitions are not *elided* versions of the Museum of Modern Art's own shows —Roger Angell⟩

elid·ible \-dəbəl\ *adj* **:** capable of being elided ⟨~ vowels⟩

el·i·gi·bil·i·ty \,eləjə'biləd·ē, -lēj-, -lətē, -i\ *n* -ES **1** *archaic* **:** the quality of being advantageous or preferable **:** ADVANTAGE ⟨this was his plan . . . and he thought it an excellent one, full of ~ —Jane Austen⟩ **2 :** the quality or state of being eligible **:** FITNESS, SUITABILITY, QUALIFICATION ⟨determine the ~ of various nations for loans —*Current Biog.*⟩ ⟨~ of prisoners for repatriation⟩ ⟨~ of a candidate for office⟩

[1]**el·i·gi·ble** \'⸗⸗⸗,bəl\ *adj* [ME, fr. MF & LL; MF, fr. LL *eligibilis,* fr. L *eligere* to choose + *-ibilis* -ible — more at ELECT] **1 :** fitted or qualified to be chosen or used **:** entitled to something ⟨only native-born citizens are ~ to the office of president⟩ ⟨~ for benefits⟩ ⟨the book is not ~ for copyright in this country⟩ ⟨not ~ to play in the championship game⟩ ⟨anyone with an ~ craft . . . is invited to enter —Geneva J. Yockey⟩ **2 :** worthy to be chosen or selected **:** ADVANTAGEOUS, PREFERABLE, DESIRABLE ⟨recorded his wonder that so ~ a spot was not finally chosen —A.T.Quiller-Couch⟩ ⟨commenting upon the ~ circumstances of the paupers —G.E.Fussell⟩ ⟨had chosen this bright Sunday morning as ~ for churchgoing —George Eliot⟩; *specif* **:** suitable or desirable for marriage ⟨flirted with . . . all the bachelor squires who seemed ~ —W. M.Thackeray⟩ ⟨disappointed mothers of other more ~ damsels —Florence Bullock⟩ **3** *archaic* **:** subject to choice or adoption **:** capable of being adopted **:** POSSIBLE ⟨the villainy and shallowness of rulers . . . are just as ~ to these states as to any foreign despotism —Walt Whitman⟩

[2]**eligible** \"\ *n* -s **:** one that is eligible ⟨I hope all the rest of the *~s* register too —A.E.Stevenson b. 1900⟩

el·i·gi·ble·ness *n* -ES **:** ELIGIBILITY

eligible paper *n* **:** notes and bills designated as proper for rediscount by the Federal Reserve banks

el·i·gi·bly \-blē, -li\ *adv* **:** in an eligible manner

eli·jah's chair \ə'līјəz-, ē|\ *n, usu cap E* [after *Elijah,* 9th cent. B.C. Hebrew prophet] **:** an empty chair that is traditionally reserved among Jews for the prophet Elijah during the circumcision ceremony

elijah's cup *n, usu cap E* **:** a cup of wine set on the table at the celebration of the seder on Passover and reserved for the precursor of the Messiah, the prophet Elijah, who according to Jewish tradition may come anytime as a guest

elim·i·na·bil·i·ty \ə,limənə'biləd·ē, ē,-, -lətē, -i\ *n* -ES **:** the quality or state of being eliminable

elim·i·na·ble \ə'⸗⸗nəbəl\ *adj* [*eliminate* + *-able*] **:** capable of being eliminated

[1]**elim·i·nant** \-nənt\ *adj* [L *eliminant-, eliminans,* pres. part. of *eliminare*] *med* **:** promoting elimination

[2]**eliminant** \"\ *n* -s **:** a function of the coefficients of *n* equations connecting *n* symbols, whose vanishing is the necessary and sufficient condition that the equations are consistent — called also *resultant*

elim·i·nate \-,nāt, *usu* -ād·+V\ *vt* -ED/-ING/-S [L *eliminatus,* past part. of *eliminare,* fr. *e-* + *limin-, limen* threshold — more at LIMB] **1** *archaic* **:** to put out of doors **:** thrust out **2 a :** to cast out **:** REMOVE, EXPEL, EXCLUDE, DROP, OUST ⟨the resultant cabinet change *eliminated* twelve ministers —*Current Biog.*⟩ ⟨~ gangster elements from the organization⟩ ⟨the two teams losing two games in succession will be *eliminated* —*N.Y. Times*⟩ ⟨a number of candidates were *eliminated* for poor flying technique⟩ **b :** to cause the disappearance of esp. as a factor or element in a process or situation **:** get rid of **:** ERADICATE ⟨to ~ surprise, the theory goes, is to ~ nuclear war —W.R.Frye⟩ ⟨seek to ~ the odium attaching to the word *materialism* —William James⟩ ⟨succeeded in *eliminating* the city's debt⟩ ⟨~ a distracting noise⟩; *sometimes* **:** to get rid of by killing or destroying ⟨*eliminated* his opponents with ruthless cruelty⟩ **3 :** to set aside as unimportant, invalid, or irrelevant **:** leave out of consideration **:** IGNORE **4** *archaic* **:** to isolate (as a principle) from surrounding or confusing details **:** DEDUCE **5 :** to cause to disappear by combining two or more equations ⟨~ an unknown quantity⟩ **6 :** to expel from the living body **:** EXCRETE, EGEST ⟨*eliminating* toxins from the intestine⟩ ⟨the kidneys ~ urea⟩ **syn** see EXCLUDE

elim·i·na·tion \⸗,⸗⸗'nāshən\ *n* -s *often attrib* **:** the act, process, or an instance of eliminating or discharging: as **a** (1) **:** the act of discharging or excreting waste products or foreign substances from the body (2) **eliminations** *pl* **:** bodily discharges **:** urine, feces, and vomitus **b :** the act of making a quantity disappear from an equation; *esp* **:** the operation of deducing from several equations containing several unknowns a less number of equations containing a less number of unknowns **c :** the removal of logical terms or their symbols by combining or transforming logical equations **d :** the act or process of excluding from a match, tournament, or other contest the losers of any round or heat ⟨~ race⟩ **e :** the removal from a molecule of a simpler molecule in the form of atoms and groups that can combine ⟨the ~ of water from ethyl alcohol in the form of hydrogen and hydroxyl produces ethylene⟩ — compare ADDITION 6 **f** *or* **elimination play :** a process in bridge by which the declarer removes from his hand and dummy all cards of each suit that an opponent might safely lead so as to gain a trick when next an opponent leads — called also *strip, strip play;* compare END PLAY 2, THROW-IN

elim·i·na·tive \⸗'⸗⸗,nād·|iv, -,nə|, |t|, |ēv *also* |əv\ *adj* **:** serving or tending to eliminate; *specif* **:** relating to, operating in the process of, or carrying on bodily elimination ⟨citrous foods aid the ~ organs in their work⟩

elim·i·na·tor \-,nād·ə(r), -ātə-\ *n* -s **:** one that eliminates — **elim·i·na·to·ry** \-,nə,tōrē, -ōr-, -ri, *chiefly Brit* -,nātəri *or* -,nā·tri\ *adj*

el·in·var \'elən,vär\ *n* -s [F *élinvar,* fr. *élasticité invariable* invariable elasticity] **:** an alloy that contains about 50 percent iron, 36 percent nickel, and 12 percent chromium, that has low thermal expansivity and a modulus of elasticity virtually unaffected by changes in temperature, and that is used for springs for watches and other precise instruments

eli·quate \ē'lī,kwāt, ə'-; 'elə,k-\ *vt* -ED/-ING/-S [L *eliquatus,* past part. of *eliquare* to strain, clarify, cause to flow freely, fr. *e-* + *liquare* to strain, liquefy, melt — more at LIQUATE] **1** *obs* **:** to cause to flow freely **:** LIQUEFY **2 a :** LIQUATE, SMELT **b :** to cause to run off by melting

eli·qua·tion \(,)ə,lī'kwāshən, ə,lī'-, ,elə'-, -āzhən\ *n* -s [LL *eliquation-, eliquatio* act of liquefying, fr. L *eliquatus* + *-ion-, -io* -ion] **1** *obs* **:** LIQUEFACTION **2 :** LIQUATION

eli·sion \ə'lizhən, ē'-\ *n* -s [LL *elision-, elisio,* fr. L *elisus* (past part. of *elidere* to elide) + *-ion-, -io* -ion — more at ELIDE] **1 :** the use of a speech form that lacks a final or initial sound that a variant speech form has (as the use of *l'* and not *le* in French *l'été* or the use of *'s* instead of *is* in English *there's*); *specif* **:** the deliberate syllable-reducing suppression or consonantalization of a final proclitic vowel in poetry for the sake of the meter (as in \th(y)ə'presiv'chānz\ for *the* (or *th'*) *oppressive chains* or in \t(w)ə'mēlyə'zīz\ for *to* (or *t'*) *Amelia's eyes*) **2 :** the act or an instance of dropping out or omitting something **:** OMISSION, CUT ⟨~ of false scenery, explanatory essays, useless subplots —V.S.Pritchett⟩ ⟨makes a few *~s* in the ballet . . . but preserves all the solos —Arthur Knight⟩

[1]**elite** \ā'lēt *also* ə'- *sometimes* e'- *or* ē'-; *usu* -lēd·+V\ *n* -s [F *élite,* fr. OF *eslite* choice, fr. fem. of *eslit,* past part. of *eslire* to choose, fr. (assumed) VL *exligere,* alter. (influenced by L *ex-*) of L *eligere* — more at ELECT] **1 :** the choice part or segment **:** FLOWER, CREAM, ARISTOCRACY ⟨an intellectual ~⟩ ⟨the ~ of coffees⟩: as **a :** a segment or group regarded as socially superior ⟨a store catering only to the ~⟩ **b :** highly trained soldiers ⟨threw the ~ of his army at the enemy's weakened flank⟩ **c :** a minority group or stratum that exerts influence, authority, or decisive power ⟨a power ~⟩ ⟨party managers and the leaders of the control groups within the parties are the *~s* —B.J.Loewenberg⟩ **2 :** a size of typewriter type providing 12 characters to the linear inch and 6 lines to the vertical inch

[2]**elite** \"\ *adj* **1 :** of, relating to, or constituting an elite ⟨seeking to attain ~ status⟩ ⟨it cannot . . . be argued that the ~ principle means necessarily a dictatorship —F.G.Wilson⟩ ⟨he has . . . denied holding the ~ theory —G.A.Wagner⟩ ⟨~ troops⟩ **2 :** CHOICE, SUPERIOR, SELECT ⟨it places easily in the ~ class of historical fiction —Edmund Fuller⟩ ⟨an ~ brand of coffee⟩ ⟨all the officers are dressed in most ~ uniforms —Johnny Johnson & P.E.Green⟩

elite seed *n* **:** foundation stock of pure selected seed of a certain crop variety

elit·ism \-lēd,izəm, -lē,tiz-\ *n* -s **1 :** belief in and advocacy of leadership or rule by an elite ⟨in other recent writers . . . one can find a similar ~ and a similar concern with . . . strong leadership —David Riesman⟩; *also* **:** leadership or rule by an elite ⟨will . . . be charged . . . with being undemocratic, or, worse, of advocating ~ —Cormac Philip⟩ **2 :** consciousness of being an elite or one of the elite ⟨they escape the ~ which is characteristic of the administrative class in the national government —C.J.Friedrich⟩ ⟨the new liberalism enjoyed its taste of ~, of being in the know —Louis Filler⟩

[1]**elit·ist** \-lēd·əst, -lētə-\ *n* -s [*elite* + *-ist*] **1 :** one who is an adherent of elitism ⟨the few may rule for the logical reason that they do rule, as some *~s* maintain —C.E.Merriam⟩ **2 :** one who is or regards himself as a member of an elite ⟨he was an ~, who esteemed himself better than Americans from most classes of the population —Louis Filler⟩

[2]**elitist** \"\ *adj* **:** of or relating to elitism **:** characterized by or favorable to elitism ⟨there is a good deal of ~ thinking among those neoliberals —C.J.Friedrich⟩ ⟨these new ~ and totalitarian regimes —F.G.Wilson⟩

elix·ate \ə'lik,sāt\ *vt* -ED/-ING/-S [L *elixatus,* past part. of *elixare,* fr. *elixus* thoroughly boiled, fr. *e-* + *-lixus* (fr. *lixa* water, lye) — more at LIQUID] *archaic* **:** BOIL, SEETHE

elix·a·tion \ə,lik'sāshən\ *n* -s [L *elixatus* + E *-ion*] *archaic* **:** the action of boiling or seething

elix·ir \ə'liksə(r), ē'-\ *n* -s [ME *elixir, elixer,* fr. ML *elixir,* fr. Ar *al-iksīr* the elixir, fr. *al* the + *iksīr* elixir, prob. fr. Gk *xērion* desiccative powder, fr. *xēros* dry — more at SERENE] **1 a :** a substance held esp. in the middle ages to be capable of transmuting metals into gold; *also* **:** a substance or concoction held to be capable of prolonging life indefinitely — used esp. in the phrase *elixir of life* **b :** CURE-ALL, PANACEA ⟨do we have to be persuaded that it is a panacea, an ~, before we take any of it? —Glenway Wescott⟩ **c** *archaic* **:** a strong extract or tincture **d** (1) **:** the quintessence of a thing **:** its driving force or principle ⟨injected one way or another with the élan or ~ of the poet's dominant attitudes —Allen Tate & J.P.Bishop⟩ (2) **:** something (as an experience or idea) that acts potently upon one, invigorating or filling with exuberant energy or cheer ⟨the distant sound of music . . . the bright flash of colored skirts . . . was like a strong ~ —Victor Canning⟩ ⟨an ~ was at work on American colonials . . . they saw life full of opportunities and believed they were alive under a new sky —Adrienne Koch⟩ **2 :** any of a class of sweetened aromatic preparations that contain variable percentages of alcohol and are used either for their medicinal ingredients or in prescriptions for their flavoring quality

elixirate *vt* -ED/-ING/-S [*elixir* + *-ate*] *obs* **:** DISTILL, PURIFY

eliz·a·beth \ə'liz(ə)bəth, ē'-, *rapid* 'li-\ *adj, usu cap* [fr. *Elizabeth,* N. J.] **:** of or from the city of Elizabeth, N. J. ⟨*Elizabeth* refineries⟩ **:** of the kind or style prevalent in Elizabeth

[1]**eliz·a·be·than** \ə¦lizə¦bēthən, ē¦-; *sometimes* -beth-\ *adj, usu cap* [*Elizabeth* I †1603 queen of England + E *-an*] **1 a :** of or relating to Queen Elizabeth I or her reign ⟨the *Elizabethan* age⟩ ⟨*Elizabethan* policy⟩ **b :** of or relating to the Elizabethan age or its culture (as its literature) ⟨studies of *Elizabethan* idiom —C.W.Shumaker⟩ ⟨*Elizabethan* sea power⟩ ⟨an *Elizabethan* lyric⟩ ⟨the *Elizabethan* climate of opinion⟩ **c :** of or relating to a style in women's clothing characterized esp. by long pointed waists and standing collars **2** [*Elizabeth* II *b*1926 queen of England + E *-an*] **:** of or relating to Queen Elizabeth II or her reign

[2]**elizabethan** \"\ *n* -s *usu cap* **:** an Englishman of the age of Elizabeth I; *specif* **:** an Elizabethan poet or dramatist ⟨the intimate lyrics of the *Elizabethans* —F.G.Steiner⟩

elizabethan collar *n, usu cap E* **:** a broad circle of stiff cardboard or other material placed about the neck of a cat or dog to prevent it from licking or biting an injured part

elizabethan style *n, usu cap E* **1 :** an early Renaissance architectural style combining Tudor and Italian features, common in English country houses of Elizabeth's reign, and characterized by large windows, long galleries, tall decorated chimneys, and a profusion of ornamental strapwork **2 :** the Renaissance style of furniture esp. as developed in the Elizabethan era, characterized by massive structure and elaborate carving

[1]**elk** \'elk, 'eu̇k\ *n, pl* **elk** *or* **elks** [ME, prob. fr. OE *eolh;* akin to OHG *elaho* elk, ON *elgr,* Gk *elaphos* deer, OIr *elit* roedeer, Arm *eln* deer, Skt *ṛśya* male of a species of antelope] **1** *pl usu* **elk a :** the largest existing deer (*Alces alces*) of Europe and Asia resembling the moose of No. America but not so large and found in parts of Scandinavia, Germany, Russia, and Siberia **b :** WAPITI **c :** any of various large Asiatic deer (as the sambar) **2 :** soft tanned rugged cattlehide leather used for work shoes, sport shoes — called also *smoked elk* **3** *pl* **elks,** *usu cap* **:** a member of one of the major benevolent and fraternal orders **4 :** LAMA 2

[2]**elk** \"\ *n* -s [origin unknown] *dial Eng* **:** a wild goose or swan

elk bark *n* **:** LARGE-LEAVED MAGNOLIA

el·ke·saite \'elkə,sīt; ,elkə'sā,īt, -'sī,īt\ *n* -s *usu cap* [*Elkesai,* semilegendary author of a 2d or 3d cent. work of religious inspiration + E *-ite*] **:** a member of an Ebionite sect in whose system magic and astrology played a conspicuous role

elkhorn fern \'⸗,⸗-\ *n* **:** STAGHORN FERN; *esp* **:** the Australian staghorn fern (*Platycerium alcicorne*)

elkhound \'⸗,⸗\ *n* **:** NORWEGIAN ELKHOUND

elk kelp *n* **:** a large marine brown alga of the genus *Pelagophycus* (order Laminariales) sometimes reaching a length of 100 feet or more and characterized by blades that are split, the whole structure being somewhat like a tree in shape

elk nut *n* **:** BUFFALO NUT

elk·slip \'elk,slip, 'eu̇k-\ *n* **:** a marsh marigold (*Caltha rotundifolia*) of the northwestern U. S.

elk tree *n* **:** SOURWOOD

elkwood \'⸗,⸗\ *n* **1 :** SOURWOOD **2 a :** the soft wood of the umbrella tree (*Magnolia tripetala*) **b :** UMBRELLA TREE

[1]**ell** \'el\ *n* -s [ME *eln, ellen, elle,* fr. OE *eln;* akin to OHG *elina* ell, ON *eln, öln* forearm, ell, Goth *aleina,* L *ulna* elbow, arm, ell, Gk *ōlenē* elbow, Skt *āṇi* linchpin, part of the leg immediately above the knee] **1 :** an English unit of length chiefly for cloth equal to 45 inches but no longer used **2 :** any of various units of length similar in use to the English ell (as the old Dutch or Flemish unit of about 27 inches, the Scotch unit of about 37 inches, or the modern unit of the Netherlands equal to 1 meter) **3 :** CUBIT

[2]**ell** \"\ *n* -s **1 :** [1]EL **2 :** an extension at right angles to the length of a main building **3 :** an elbow in a pipe or conduit

-el·la \'elə\ *n suffix, pl* **-ellae** *or* **-ellas** [L — more at -EL] **1 :** little one resembling — often in generic names ⟨*Capsella*⟩ **2 :** little one ⟨*squamella*⟩ **3 :** little one belonging to ⟨*Moluccella*⟩

el·la·chick \'elə,chik\ *n* [Nisqualli] **:** a freshwater tortoise (*Clemmys marmorata*) of California used as food

el·lag·ic acid \ə¦lajik-, e¦\ *n* [F *ellagique,* fr. *ellag* (anagram of *galle* gallnut, gall) + *-ique* -ic — more at GALL (excrescence)] **:** a crystalline phenolic dilactone $C_{14}H_6O_8$ obtained from bezoar stones, oak galls, and many tannins and made by oxidation of gallic acid

el·lagi·tannin \ə¦lajə, e¦·+\ *n* [ISV *ellagic* + *tannin*] **:** a tannin occurring in various tanning extracts (as those from myrobalans and divi-divi) and yielding ellagic acid on hydrolysis

el·leck \'elik\ *n* -s [origin unknown] **:** RED GURNARD 1

el·ler \'elə(r)\ *dial var of* [2]ELDER

el·le·stad·ite \'elə,sta,dīt, ⸗⸗'⸗⸗\ *n* -s [Reuben B. *Ellestad* *b*1900 Am. chemist + E *-ite*] **:** a variety of apatite $Ca_5(F,Cl,OH)[(P,Si,S,C)O_4]_3$ containing silicon, carbon, and sulfur replacing some of the phosphorus

el·liot's pheasant \'elēəts-, -lyəts-\ *n, usu cap E* [prob. after Daniel G. *Elliot* †1915 Am. zoologist] **:** a large brilliantly colored barred pheasant (*Syrmaticus ellioti*) native to southeastern China where it is highly regarded as a game bird and extensively bred elsewhere as an ornamental

el·lipse \ə'lips, e'-,ē'-\ *n* -s [alter. of *ellipsis*] **1 :** an elongated circle **:** a regular oval; *specif* **:** a closed plane curve generated by a point so moving that its distance from a fixed point divided by its distance from a fixed line is a positive constant less than 1 **2 :** ELLIPSIS

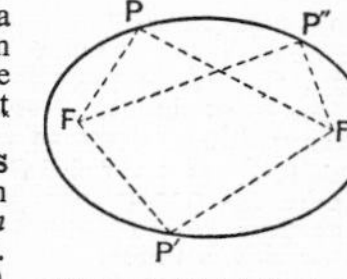

ellipse 1: *F, F′* foci; *P, P′, P″* any point on the curve; $FP + PF' = FP'' + P''F' = FP' + P'F'$

el·lip·sis \-psəs\ *n, pl* **ellip·ses** \-p,sēz\ [Gk *elleipsis*, lit., condition of falling short, defect, fr. *elleipein* to leave in, leave out, fall short (fr. *el-* — fr. *en* in — + *leipein* to leave) + *-sis* — more at IN, LOAN] **1 :** ELLIPSE **2** [L, fr. Gk *elleipsis*] **a** (1) **:** omission of one or more words that are obviously understood but must be supplied to make a construction grammatically complete (as in "all had turned out as expected" for "all had turned out as had been expected") ⟨fine examples of Shakespearean compression and ~ —F.R.Leavis⟩ ⟨a writer . . . whose very syntax is warm with the ~ of spoken speech —Robert Phelps⟩ ⟨uses ~ for poetic and comic effects —*Times Lit. Supp.*⟩ (2) **:** an instance of such omission **:** a grammatical construction marked by ellipsis ⟨the poem's striking *ellipses* offer no impediment to the reader's ear⟩ ⟨a crisp spare style abounding in *ellipses*⟩ (3) **:** the practice or use of ellipsis ⟨a writer much given to ~⟩ **b :** omission of an element (as from a train of thought or a speech) either fortuitously or for artistic effect **:** a leap or sudden passage without logical connectives, from one topic to another ⟨a complicated recital . . . full of grunts and *ellipses* —Hamilton Basso⟩ ⟨~ of both syntax and sense —Robert Browning⟩ **3 :** marks or a mark (as . . . or * * * or ——) showing omission of letters, words, or other material — compare SUSPENSION PERIODS

el·lip·so·graph \-psə,graf, -âf\ *n* [*ellipse* + *-o-* + *-graph*] **:** an instrument used for drawing ellipses

el·lip·soid \-p,sȯid\ *n* -s [F *ellipsoïde*, fr. *ellipse* + *-oïde* -oid] **:** a surface all plane sections of which are ellipses or circles; *also* **:** the corresponding solid

ellipsoid

el·lip·soi·dal \ə¦lip¦sȯidᵊl, e¦-, ē¦-; ¦e(,)lip¦s-\ *adj* **1 :** resembling an ellipsoid **2 :** having a shape like a round pillow — used esp. of lava

ellipsoidal spotlight *n* **:** a spotlight used in theatrical lighting that contains an ellipsoidal reflector and that is particularly designed for long throws and is more efficient than conventional spotlights, reflecting rays that others waste

ellipsoid of revolution *math* **:** a figure generated by the revolution of an ellipse about one of its axes **:** SPHEROID

el·lip·som·e·ter \ə,lip'sämәd·ə(r), e,-, ē,-, ,e(,)-\ *n* [*ellipse* + *-o-* + *-meter*] **:** a polarimeter designed esp. for determining the ellipticity of polarized light

el·lip·tic \ə'liptik, (')e¦l-, ē'l-, -tēk\ *or* **el·lip·ti·cal** \-tәkəl, -tēk-\ *adj* [Gk *elleiptikos* defective, elliptic (grammatical sense), fr. (assumed) *elleiptos* (verbal of *elleipein* to leave out, fall short) + *-ikos* -ic, -ical — more at ELLIPSIS] **1 :** of, relating to, or shaped like an ellipse ⟨an ~ mirror⟩ ⟨an ~ orbit⟩ — see LEAF illustration **2 a** (1) **:** of, relating to, or marked by grammatical ellipsis ⟨the clause of comparison is often *elliptical* —G.O. Curme⟩ (2) **:** of or relating to a statement that is grammatically complete but lacks an element needed to assert a definite proposition (⟨"the car moves now" is *elliptical* for "the car moves now relatively to the earth" —Arthur Pap⟩ (3) **:** of or relating to a mark showing omission (as of words) ⟨many authors use brief phrases, separated by three *elliptical* dots —L.E.Bowling⟩ **b** (1) **:** of, relating to, or marked by a manner of speech or writing characterized by extreme economy of expression or omission of superfluous elements **:** SUMMARY, BRIEF, CONCISE, CONDENSED ⟨the author in her *elliptical* four-page introduction —B.S.Myers⟩ ⟨concise, even *elliptical* to the verge of obscurity —H.O.Taylor⟩ ⟨listened to them talk, in tight, exclusive groups, with their own peculiar, *elliptical* language —Irwin Shaw⟩ (2) **:** of, relating to, or marked by a literary style that cultivates a studied obscurity for artistic effect **:** ENIGMATIC, CRYPTIC, OBLIQUE, OBSCURE ⟨the dialogue between them is stately, ~, and full of dark hints of the metaphysical —Wolcott Gibbs⟩

elliptical galaxy *n* **:** a galaxy of a generally elliptical shape, from round to lenticular, differing chiefly from other types in having no apparent internal structure or spiral arms — called also *spheroidal galaxy*

el·lip·ti·cal·ly \-tәk(ə)lē, -tēk-, -li\ *adv* **1 :** in an elliptic manner **:** in the shape or manner of an ellipse ⟨moves ~ about its orbit⟩ **2 a :** with omission of an element (as one needed to complete a train of thought or speech) **:** without transition or logical connectives **:** CRYPTICALLY, ENIGMATICALLY ⟨one might go ~ . . . from talk of toothache to talk of ships storm-tossed at sea —K.D.Burke⟩ **b :** with great economy of expression **:** CONCISELY ⟨this whole earlier empire-building clan . . . is described so eloquently and so ~ —M.D.Geismar⟩ **c :** in a passing or tangential way ⟨even in the pieces upon which he impinges most ~ —Richard Watts⟩

el·lip·ti·cal·ness \-kəlnəs\ *n* -ES **:** the quality or state of being elliptical

elliptical projection *n* **:** a map of the earth's surface upon the interior of an ellipse

elliptical stern *n* **:** an overhanging ship's stern in which the part above the knuckle line (as the bulwark) is of conical form with a rake aft

elliptic arch *n* **:** an arch whose intrados is or approximates an ellipse

elliptic compass *n* **:** ELLIPSOGRAPH

elliptic gear *n* **:** a change gear consisting of a pair of equal gear wheels which are elliptical in shape and each of which rotates around one of its foci

elliptic arch

elliptic geometry *n* **:** geometry that adopts all of Euclid's axioms except the parallel axiom which is replaced by the axiom that through a point in a plane there pass no lines that do not intersect a given line in the plane

elliptic integral *n* **:** the integral as to *x* of a function rational in *x* and the square root of a polynomial of third or fourth degree in *x*

el·lip·tic·i·ty \ə,lip'tisəd·ē, e,-, ē,-, ,e(,)-\ *n* -ES **1 :** deviation of an ellipse or a spheroid from the form of a circle or a sphere **2 :** the difference between the equatorial and polar semidiameters, divided by the equatorial or occas. by the polar — used esp. in ref. to the figure of the earth ⟨the ~ of the earth is approximately $\frac{1}{300}$⟩

elliptic–lanceolate *adj, bot* **:** intermediate between elliptic and lanceolate

elliptic spring *or* **elliptical spring** *n* **:** a spring composed of laminated steel plates and having an elliptical shape

elliptic springs: *1* half elliptic, *2* elliptic

el·lip·to·cyte \ə'liptə,sīt, e'-, ē'-\ *n* -s [ISV *elliptic* + *-o-* + *-cyte*] **:** an elliptical red blood cell **:** OVALOCYTE

el·lip·to·cy·to·sis \ə,≈≈,sī'tōsəs\ *n, pl* **elliptocy·to·ses** \-ō,sēz\ [NL, fr. ISV *elliptocyte* + NL *-osis*] **:** OVALOCYTOSIS

el·lo·bi·idae \,elə'bīə,dē\ *n pl, cap* [NL, fr. *Ellobium*, type genus + *-idae*] **:** a family of pulmonate snails that have a conoidal shell with a strongly toothed ear-shaped aperture and that are widely distributed in salt marshes chiefly along tropical and subtropical shores

el·lo·bi·um \ə'lōbēəm, e'-\ *n, cap* [NL, fr. Gk *ellobion* that which is in the lobe of the ear, earring, fr. *el-* (fr. *en* in) + *lobos* lobe + *-ion* (dim. suffix) — more at IN, LOBE] **:** the type genus of Ellobiidae

el·lops \'e,läps\ *n, pl* **ellops** *or* **ellopses** [Gk *ellops, elops*, a fish — more at ELOPS] **:** ELOPS

ells *pl of* ELL

ellul *usu cap, var of* ELUL

ell·wand \'elwən(d)\ *n* [ME *elenwand, elle wande, el wande*, fr. *eln, ellen, elle* ell + *wand* — more at ELL] *Scot* **:** a measuring rod one ell long

elm \'elm, 'eùm, *dial or substand* 'eləm\ *n* -s *often attrib* [ME, fr. OE; akin to OHG *elme, elm* elm, ON *almr*, L *ulmus*, MIr *lem* elm, and perh. to L *alnus* alder — more at ALDER] **1 a :** a tree of the genus *Ulmus* — see ROCK ELM, SIBERIAN ELM, SLIPPERY ELM — see TREE illustration **b :** the hard tough wood of this tree used extensively for implements, furniture, and barrel hoops **2 :** any of various chiefly Australian and West Indian trees or shrubs having foliage resembling that of members of the genus *Ulmus*

el man·su·ra \¦el,man¦sůrə\ *adj, usu cap E&M* [fr. *El Mansura*, Egypt] **:** of or from the city of El Mansura, Egypt **:** of the kind or style prevalent in El Mansura

elm bark *n* **:** SLIPPERY ELM 1c

elm bark beetle *n* **:** either of two beetles that are vectors of the fungus which causes Dutch elm disease: **a :** a native beetle (*Hylurgopinus rufipes*) of eastern No. America **b :** a smaller European beetle (*Scolytus multistriatus*) that has become established in the same part of the New World

elm blight *n* **:** DUTCH ELM DISEASE

elm borer *n* **:** any of several beetles having larvae that bore into the elm; *esp* **:** a rather large hairy longicorn beetle (*Saperda tridentata*) of the eastern U.S.

elm calligrapha *n* **:** a coppery green and yellow calligrapha (*Calligrapha scalaris*) that often feeds on the foliage of elm

elm·en \'elmən\ *adj* [ME *elmyn*, fr. *elm* + *-yn* -en] *dial Eng* **:** relating to or made of wood from an elm tree

el·men·dorf test \'elmən,dȯrf-\ *n, usu cap E* [after Armin *Elmendorf* b1890 Am. mechanical engineer, its inventor] **:** a standard test for the tearing strength of paper

el·men·tei·tan \¦elmən-¦tāt°n\ *adj, usu cap* [*Elmenteita* Lake, Kenya + E *-an*] **:** of or relating to an early Neolithic or Mesolithic culture of eastern Africa characterized by obsidian microliths

elm family *n* **:** ULMACEAE

elm green *n* **:** a moderate olive green that is slightly lighter than forest green (sense 2), yellower, lighter, and stronger than cypress, and greener and stronger than Lincoln green

el·min·i·us \el'minēəs\ *n, cap* [NL] **:** a genus of acorn barnacles native to the southern hemisphere but including one form (*E. modestus*) that has recently become established on the English coast where it is a pest of oyster beds

el·mi·ra system \el'mīrə-\ *n, usu cap E* [fr. *Elmira*, N.Y., where the system was adopted in a reformatory in 1876] **:** a system of penology based on the indeterminate sentence with possible commutation

elm leaf beetle *n* **:** a small orange-yellow black-striped Old World chrysomelid beetle (*Pyrrhalta luteola*) that is long established in eastern No. America and is both as adult and larva a leaf-eating pest on elm

elm phloem necrosis *n* **:** PHLOEM NECROSIS c

elm sawfly *n* **:** a large American sawfly (*Cimbex americana*) that has knobbed antennae, orange-tinged tarsi, black head and thorax with somewhat lighter, spotted abdomen, and smoke brown wings, and produces yellowish or greenish white larvae with a dorsal black stripe which are vigorous defoliators chiefly of elm and willow

elm scale *or* **elm scurfy scale** *n* **:** any of several scales that feed on elm trees; *esp* **:** a widely distributed scale (*Chionaspis americana*) of eastern No. America that feeds on elm and hackberry and has the female covered by a dull white scale often darkened anteriorly by secretion

elm tea *n* **:** an infusion prepared from slippery-elm bark that is used as a demulcent

elm water *n* **1 :** a decoction of slippery-elm bark **2 :** a watery exudation from the galls of the English elm

elmy \'elmē, 'eùmē\ *adj, sometimes* -ER/-EST **:** characterized by or abounding in elms

elocular \(')ē+\ *adj* [*e-* + *locular*] **:** having but one cavity **:** not divided by a septum **:** lacking loculi

el·o·cute \'elə,kyüt\ *vb* -ED/-ING/-S [back-formation fr. *elocution*] **:** DECLAIM ⟨the senator ranted and *elocuted* but made little impression on the crowd⟩ ⟨a frail drama superbly acted, and excellently *elocuted* —*N.Y. Times*⟩

el·o·cu·tion \,elə'kyüshən\ *n* -s [ME *elocucioun*, fr. L *elocution-, elocutio*, fr. *elocutus* (past part. of *eloqui* to speak out, orate) + *-ion-, -io* -ion — more at ELOQUENT] **1** *archaic* **a :** literary style or expression **b :** impressive writing or style **:** ELOQUENCE ⟨to express these thoughts with ~ —John Dryden⟩ **2 a :** oratorical, dramatic, or expressive oral delivery ⟨an expert user of ~⟩ **b :** style or manner of speaking ⟨clear concise ~⟩; *sometimes* **:** an affected or overembellished style or manner of speaking **3 :** the art of oratorical or expressive public speaking

el·o·cu·tion·ary \-shə,nerē, -ri\ *adj* **:** of, relating to, or exhibiting elocution ⟨~ recitals⟩ ⟨an ~ Oxonian delivery —E.R.Bentley⟩

el·o·cu·tion·ist \-sh(ə)nəst\ *n* -s **:** a person adept in elocution: as **a :** a teacher of elocution **b :** a professional reciter or reader

elo·dea \ə'lōdēə, ,elə'dēə\ *n* [NL, irreg. fr. Gk *helōdēs* marshy — more at HELODES] **1** *cap* **:** a small genus of submerged aquatic herbs (family Hydrocharitaceae) that are native to No. and So. America and that have leafy stems and small dioecious or polygamous flowers arising from a 2-cleft spathe — see WATERWEED **2** -s **:** any plant of the genus *Elodea*

eloge \ā'lōzh, ālōözh\ *n, pl* **elog·es** \-ōzhəz,-ōözh\ [MF, fr. ML *elogium* (influenced in meaning by ML *eulogium* eulogy), fr. L, maxim, saying, inscription on a tombstone, prob. by folk etymology (influence of L *e-* and Gk *logos* word) fr. Gk *elegeion* elegy — more at EULOGY, LOGIC, ELEGY] **1** *archaic* **:** ENCOMIUM, EULOGY **2 :** a panegyrical funeral oration

el·o·gy \'eləjē, -ləjē\ *also* **elo·gium** \ə'lōj(ē)əm, ē'-,e'-\ *n, pl* **elogies** *also* **elogiums** [in sense 1, fr. L *elogium*; in sense 2 & 3, fr. ML *elogium*] **1** *obs* **:** an inscription esp. on a tombstone **2** *archaic* **:** a characterization or biographical sketch esp. in praise **3** *obs* **:** a funeral oration

elo·him \,elō'hēm, -lō'- 'him; e'lō,him, ə'-\ *n* [Heb *ĕlōhīm*, pl. of *ĕlōah* god] **1** *cap* **:** God esp. as conceived of in the Old Testament or in those Old Testament passages where he is designated in the Hebrew text by the word *ĕlōhīm* **2 elohim** *pl, usu cap* **:** local or minor divinities of the ancient Canaanites and Hebrews

el·o·him·ic \¦elō¦himik\ *adj, cap* **:** ELOHISTIC 2

elo·hism \'elō,hizəm, -lō,-; e'lō,-, ə'-\ *n* -s *cap* **:** the religion and worship of Elohim — compare YAHWISM

¹elo·hist \-,(h)əst\ *n* -s *usu cap* [*elohim* + *-ist*] **1 :** an author of an Elohistic document **2** *archaic* **:** a priestly writer

²elohist \"\ *adj, usu cap* **:** ELOHISTIC

el·o·his·tic \¦elō¦histik\ *adj, usu cap* **1 :** of, relating to, or characteristic of one of the supposed ancient biblical sources (*Elohistic* document) **2 :** characterized by usage in Hebrew of the word *ĕlōhīm* rather than *yahweh* as a designation fo God ⟨Psalms 42–83, the *Elohistic* Psalter⟩ **3 :** of, or characteristic of, or characterized by worship of God as Elohim rather than as Yahweh

eloign \ə'lȯin, ē'-\ *vt* -ED/-ING/-S [ME *eloynen, esloignen*, fr. MF *esloignier*, fr. OF *esloignier*, fr. *es-* (fr. L *ex-*) + *loing* far, fr. L *longe* long, far, adv. fr. *longus* long — more at LONG] **1** *archaic* **:** to take (oneself) far away **2** *archaic* **a :** to convey to a distance or beyond the legal jurisdiction of **b :** CONCEAL ⟨~ goods liable to distress⟩

Elon \'ē,län, ≈'≈\ *trademark* — used for a white soluble powder used as a photographic developer

¹elon·gate \ē'lȯn,gāt, ə'- *also* -läŋ- *sometimes* 'ē,≈,≈; *usu* -ād·+V\ *vb* -ED/-ING/-S [LL *elongatus*, past part. of *elongare*, fr. L *e-* + *longus* long] *vt* **:** to increase the length of **:** stretch out **:** LENGTHEN ⟨he *elongated* his face as he heard their story⟩ ⟨the British *elongating* their defense program —*Economist*⟩ ~ *vi* **:** to grow in length **:** LENGTHEN — used esp. of plants and their parts ⟨rapidly *elongating* internodes⟩ **syn** see EXTEND

²elongate \"\ *adj* [LL *elongatus*, past part.] **:** stretched out **:** LENGTHENED; *esp* **:** having a form notably long in comparison to its width ⟨an ~ tail that tapers to a point —R.E.Coker⟩

³elongate \"\ *vi* -ED/-ING/-S [LL *elongatus*, past part. of *elongare*, fr. L *e-* + *longe* far — more at ELOIGN] **1** *archaic* **:** to go away **:** DEPART, RECEDE **2** *archaic*, *of a celestial body* **:** to appear to recede from its primary or from a particular point in the sky — compare ELONGATION

elongated *adj* **:** ELONGATE

elongate nut shell *n* **:** BEAKED COCKLE

¹elon·ga·tion \(,)ē,lȯŋ'gāshən, ə,- *also* -läŋ-\ *n* -s [ME *elongacioun*, fr. ML *elongation-, elongatio*, fr. LL *elongatus* (past part. of *elongare* to withdraw) + L *-ion-, -io* -ion] **1 a :** the angular distance of a celestial body from another around which it revolves or from a particular point in the sky ⟨the ~ of a planet from the sun⟩ ⟨the ~ of an eclipsing variable⟩ — see GREATEST ELONGATION **b :** the daily extreme east or west position of a star with reference to the north celestial pole ⟨the ~s of the North Star⟩ **2** *obs* **:** removal to a distance **:** REMOTENESS

²elongation \"\ *n* -s [¹*elongate* + *-ion*] **1 a :** a lengthening or state of being lengthened **:** PROTRACTION, EXTENSION ⟨the ~ of a muscle under tension⟩ ⟨~ of the apex of a plant⟩ **b :** the total deformation in the direction of load or per unit of length caused by a tensile force; *sometimes* **:** the maximum permanent stretch per unit of original length induced in a body by a force that causes it to break **2 :** something that is elongated **:** PROLONGATION, CONTINUATION ⟨the arm may be considered a specialized ~ of the earlier fin⟩

elongato- *comb form* [*elongate* + *-o-*] **:** elongated and ⟨*elongato*-ovate⟩

elope \ə'lōp, ē'-\ *vi* -ED/-ING/-S [AF *aloper*, perh. fr. *a-* (fr. OF *es-*, fr. L *ex-*) + MD *lōpen* to run; akin to OE *hlēapan* to leap, jump, run — more at LEAP] **1 a** *of a married woman* **:** to run away from one's husband with a lover **b** *of an unmarried woman* **:** to run away from one's home with the unannounced intention of getting married ⟨she *eloped* with her second cousin and they were married in the next state⟩ **c** *of two persons of opposite sex* **:** to go away secretly with the intention of marrying or establishing a more or less permanent relation of cohabitation ⟨her mother wanted a big wedding but the young people decided to ~⟩ **2 :** to run or slip away (as from a mental institution or training school) **:** ESCAPE, FLEE ⟨he *eloped* from his creditors⟩ — **elope·ment** \-pmənt\ *n* -s

elop·er \-pə(r)\ *n* -s **:** one that elopes

elops \'e,läps, 'ē,-\ *n* [L, fr. Gk *ellops, elops*, a fish; perh. akin to Gk *lepis* scale — more at LEPID-] **1** *pl* **elops** *or* **elopses** *obs* **:** a marine animal sometimes identified as the sturgeon; *also* **:** SEA SERPENT **2** *cap* [NL, fr. L] **:** a genus (the type of the family Elopidae) of fishes of the order Isospondyli that are related to the tarpons and contain the ten-pounder (*E. saurus*)

el·o·quence \'eləkwən(t)s *sometimes* -lēk- *or* -lik-\ *n* -s [ME, fr. MF, fr. L *eloquentia*, fr. *eloquent-, eloquens* + *-ia* -y] **1 a :** discourse marked by force and persuasiveness suggesting strong feeling or deep sincerity; *esp* **:** discourse marked by apt and fluent diction and imaginative fervor ⟨the poetry of western nations is ~ in meter —George Santayana⟩ **b :** the art or power of using such discourse ⟨Plato's ~ and moral fervor —G.R.Morrow⟩ **2 :** forceful or persuasive usu. oral expressiveness ⟨he has fecundity, ~, wit —Matthew Arnold⟩ ⟨the ~ of the photographs —*Times Lit. Supp.*⟩ **3** *archaic* **:** RHETORIC

el·o·quent \-nt\ *adj* [ME, fr. MF, fr. L *eloquent-, eloquens*, fr. pres. part. of *eloqui* to speak out, fr. *e-* + *loqui* to speak] **1 :** adept at skilled easy pleasing communication of a thought, idea, or feeling usu. in a fluent, moving, vivid, or forceful manner ⟨but he was no Emerson, of the grave ~ voice, the noble presence —H.S.Canby⟩ **2 :** clearly and forcefully indicative of some feeling, condition, or character ⟨that paternal pressure on his hand was ~ to him how warmly he was beloved —George Meredith⟩ ⟨a tremulous little man in greenish black broadcloth, ~ of continued depression in some village retail trade —A.T.Quiller-Couch⟩ **syn** see EXPRESSIVE, VOCAL

el·o·quent·ly *adv* [ME, fr. *eloquent* + *-ly*] **:** with eloquence **:** in an eloquent manner

el·o·quent·ness *n* -ES **:** the quality or state of being eloquent

el·o·the·ri·um \,elə'thirēəm\ [NL, irreg. fr. Gk *helos* marsh + NL *-therium* — more at HELODES] *syn of* ENTELODON

elo·ti·llo \,elō'tē(,)(y)ō\ *n* -s [MexSp, dim. of *elote* ear of green corn, fr. Nahuatl *elotl*] **:** SQUAWROOT 1

el paso \el'pa(,)sō\ *adj, usu cap E&P* [fr. *El Paso*, Texas] **:** of or from the city of El Paso, Texas **:** of the kind or style prevalent in El Paso

el paso·an \el'pasəwən\ *n* -s *cap E&P* [*El Paso*, Texas + E *-an*] **:** a native or resident of El Paso, Texas

el·paso·lite \el'pasō,līt\ *n* -s [*El Paso* co., Colo. + E *-lite*] **:** a mineral K_2NaAlF_6 consisting of sodium potassium aluminum fluoride

el·pi·dite \'elpə,dīt\ *n* -s [Sw *elpidit*, fr. Gk *elpid-, elpis* hope + Sw *-it* -ite; fr. the expectation of finding other minerals in the same locality — more at VOLUPTUOUS] **:** a mineral $Na_2ZrSi_6O_{15}.3H_2O$ consisting of a hydrated sodium zirconium silicate

elritch *var of* ELDRITCH

els *pl of* EL

-els *pl of* -EL

el sal·va·dor \el'salvə,dō(ə)r, (,)≈,≈≈'≈\ *adj, usu cap E&S* [fr. *El Salvador*, republic of Central America] **:** of or from the Republic of El Salvador **:** of the kind or style prevalent in El Salvador **:** SALVADORAN

¹else \'els, -lts\ *adv* [ME *elles*, fr. OE; akin to OHG *elles* otherwise, ON *elligai* otherwise, Goth *aljis* other, L *alius* other, *alter* other of two, Gk *allos* other, Arm *ail* other, OE *eall* all — more at ALL] **1 a :** in a different manner ⟨how ~ could he act under the circumstances⟩ **:** in a different place ⟨here and nowhere ~⟩ **:** at a different time ⟨Friday isn't convenient for me so when ~ can we meet⟩ **b :** in an additional manner ⟨how ~ can buildings be heated⟩ **:** in an additional place ⟨where ~ is gold found⟩ **:** at an additional time ⟨Friday is convenient for one of the two weekly lessons but when ~ can we get together⟩ **2 a :** if the facts were different **:** if not **:** OTHERWISE — often preceded by *or* ⟨do what I tell you, or ~ you will be sorry⟩ and used absolutely without a following clause to express a threat of unspecified but presumably dire consequences ⟨do what I tell you or ~⟩ **b :** whether it is not so ⟨house, land, money are things obtainable . . . by clever headwork: ask my father ~ —Robert Browning⟩ **c :** apart from that **:** with the exception of that ⟨a tower of refuge built for the ~ forlorn —William Wordsworth⟩

²else \"\ *adj* [ME *elles*, fr. *elles*, adv.] **:** OTHER: **a :** being different in identity ⟨nothing ~ but the best will do⟩ ⟨such decisions are to be made by the commanding officer and no one ~⟩ **b :** being in addition ⟨what ~ did he say⟩ ⟨did you meet anyone ~⟩ — now usu. used with a preceding pronoun; followed by the possessive ending *'s* when the combination of the pronoun and *else* is in the possessive case dependent on an immediately following noun ⟨somebody ~'s house⟩ ⟨I don't know who ~'s hat it could be⟩ and usu. also when not dependent on an immediately following noun ⟨it couldn't be anybody ~'s⟩ ⟨I don't know who ~'s it could be⟩ ⟨I don't know whose ~ it could be⟩

elseways \'≈,≈\ *adv* [¹*else* + *-ways*] *dial* **:** OTHERWISE

elsewhence \'≈,≈ ≈'≈\ *adv* [¹*else* + *whence*] **:** from another quarter

else·where \'el(t)s,(h)we|(ə)r, -wa(ə)|, |ə, ≈'≈\ *also* **else·wheres** \|(ə)rz, |ez\ *adv* [ME *elleswher*, fr. OE *elles hwǣr*, fr. *elles* else + *hwǣr* where — more at ELSE, WHERE] **:** in or to some or any other place ⟨it is found in town and ~⟩ ⟨we went ~ for dinner⟩ ⟨~ he mentions his dependence on his mother⟩

elsewhither \'≈,≈, ≈'≈≈\ *adv* [ME *elleswhider*, fr. OE *elles hwider*, fr. *elles* else + *hwider* whither — more at WHITHER] **:** to some or any other place in a different direction or toward a different objective ⟨his soul aimed ~⟩

elsewise \'≈,≈, ≈'≈\ *adv* [¹*else* + *-wise*] **:** OTHERWISE

el·sholt·zia \el'shōltsēə\ *n, cap* [NL, fr. Johann S. *Elsholtz* †1688 Ger. physician and botanist + NL *-ia*] **:** a genus of chiefly Asiatic aromatic herbs (family Labiatae) with blue or purple flowers in one-sided spikes

el·sin *or* **el·shin** *or* **el·son** \'els(h)ən\ *n* -s [ME *elsen*, prob.

fr. MD *elsene, else;* akin to OHG *alunsa, alansa* awl, G dial. (Swiss) *alesne,* (assumed) Goth *alisna* (whence OSp *alesna*), ON *alr* — more at AWL] *dial Brit* **:** a shoemaker's awl

el·sin·oë \el'sinə,wē\ *n, cap* [NL] **:** a genus of ascomycetous fungi that have a flat stroma with a gelatinous interior and a crustose rind and that cause various anthracnose and scab diseases of higher plants

el·u·ate \'elyəwət, -,wāt\ *n* -s [L *eluere* to wash out (fr. *e-* + *-luere,* fr. *lavere* to wash) + E *-ate* — more at LYE] **:** the washings obtained by eluting (as a solution containing a formerly adsorbed substance)

elu·ci·date \ə'lüsə,dāt, ē'- *also* ə'lyü- *or* ēl'yü-; *usu* -ād.+V\ *vb* -ED/-ING/-S [LL *elucidatus,* past part. of *elucidare,* fr. L *e-* + *lucidus* clear, bright — more at LUCID] *vt* **:** to make clear; *esp* **:** to make intelligible by clear explanation or careful analysis ⟨*elucidated* the pattern of ancient roadways⟩ ⟨served to ~ the policy of the government⟩ ⟨critical notes that ~ the text⟩ ~ *vi* **:** to provide a clarifying explanation ⟨well, ~, my boy; you know all the answers⟩

elu·ci·da·tion \=,==dāshən\ *n* -s **:** the act, process, or means of elucidating **:** EXPLANATION; *sometimes* **:** identification or determination esp. of the nature of something ⟨~ of the chemical structure of an antibiotic⟩

elu·ci·da·tive \=ˈ==,dād·iv, -,dəl, |t|, |ēv *also* |əv\ *or* **elu·ci·da·to·ry** \-,də,tōrē, -ōr-, -ri, *chiefly Brit* -,dātəri *or* -,dā·tri\ *adj* **:** tending or serving to elucidate **:** EXPLANATORY ⟨~ comments on a difficult passage⟩

elu·ci·da·tor \-,dād·ə(r), -ātə-\ *n* -s **:** one that elucidates

eluctation *n* -s [LL *eluctation-, eluctatio,* fr. L *eluctatus* (past part. of *eluctari* to struggle out, fr. *e-* + *luctari, luctare* to struggle, wrestle) + *-ion-, -io* -ion — more at LOCK (ringlet of hair)] *obs* **:** a bursting or struggling forth

elucubrate \ē, ə+\ *vt* -ED/-ING/-S [L *elucubratus,* past part. of *elucubrare* to compose by lamplight, fr. *e-* + *lucubrare* to work by lamplight — more at LUCUBRATE] **:** to work out or express by studious effort — **elucubration** \(,)ē, ə+\ *n* -s

elude \ē'lüd, ə'- *also* ēl'yüd *or* əl'y-\ *vt* -ED/-ING/-S [L *eludere,* fr. *e-* + *ludere* to play — more at LUDICROUS] **1** *obs* **:** TRICK, DELUDE; *also* **:** BAFFLE, FRUSTRATE **2 :** to avoid slyly or adroitly (as by artifice, stratagem, or dexterity) **:** EVADE ⟨~ a blow⟩ ⟨he ~s law by piteous looks aloft —Robert Browning⟩ ⟨*eluding* their responsibilities⟩ **3 :** to escape the notice or perception of ⟨the reality of human nature is bound to ~ us if we look only at a momentary cross section of it —Walter Lippmann⟩; *esp* **:** to baffle or evade by reason of recondite or inconspicuous character ⟨a sense that ~s definition⟩ **syn** see ESCAPE

elud·er \-də(r)\ *n* -s **:** one that eludes

el·u·ent *or* **el·u·ant** \'elyəwənt\ *n* -s [L *eluent-, eluens,* pres. part. of *eluere* to wash out — more at ELUATE] **:** the solvent used in eluting

elul *or* **el·ul** \'eləl\ *n* -s *usu cap* [Heb *ĕlūl*] **:** the 12th month of the civil year or the 6th month of the ecclesiastical year in the Jewish calendar — see MONTH table

elu·sion \ē'lüzhən, ə'- *also* ēl'yü- *or* əl'y-\ *n* -s [ML & LL; ML *elusion-, elusio* evasion, fr. LL, deception, fr. L *elusus* (past part. of *eludere* to elude) + *-ion-, -io* -ion — more at ELUDE] **1** *obs* **a :** the act of deluding **b :** deceptive quality **c :** ILLUSION **2 :** an instance or act of eluding: as **a :** adroit escape (as by artifice) **b :** an evasion esp. of a problem or an order

elu·sive \=ˈ=s|iv, |ēv *also* |əv\ *adj* [*elusion* + *-ive*] **:** tending to elude **:** EVASIVE: as **a :** tending to avoid or evade grasp or pursuit ⟨shy ~ denizens of the deep woods⟩; *often* **:** incapable of being prolonged ⟨~ pleasures of a sunny afternoon in childhood⟩ **b :** not easily comprehended or defined **:** BAFFLING ⟨that ~ thing, the soul⟩ ⟨an ~ person⟩ **c :** hard to pin down, isolate, or identify ⟨use of egg cultures to isolate certain hitherto ~ viruses⟩ ⟨a haunting ~ odor⟩ ⟨the ~ atomic particles called mesons —John Pfeiffer⟩ — **elu·sive·ly** \|əvlē, -li\ *adv*

elu·sive·ness \|ivnəs, |ēv- *also* |əv-\ *n* -ES **:** the quality or state of being elusive ⟨the author's ~ may at times be construed . . . as evasiveness —J.W.Chase⟩ ⟨brings vividly before us the ~ of the eternal objects of sense —A.N.Whitehead⟩ ⟨resented charges of rough tactics in his base running, maintaining that he developed ~ by his fall-away or fadeaway slide —*Current Biog.*⟩

elu·so·ry \-üs(ə)rē, -üz(-, -ri\ *adj* [ML *elusorius,* fr. L *elusus* + *-orius* -ory] **:** EVASIVE, ELUSIVE

elute \ē'lüt, ə'- *also* ēl'yüt *or* əl'y-\ *vt* -ED/-ING/-S [L *elutus,* past part. of *eluere* to wash out — more at ELUATE] **:** to wash out **:** EXTRACT; *specif* **:** to remove (adsorbed material) from an adsorbent by means of a solvent (as in chromatography)

elu·tion \-üshən\ *n* -s [LL *elution-, elutio* act of washing out, fr. L *elutus* + *-ion-, -io* -ion] **:** the process or action of eluting

elu·tri·ate \-ü·trē,āt\ *vt* -ED/-ING/-S [L *elutriatus,* past part. of *elutriare* to wash out, decant, prob. fr. (assumed) *elutor* one that washes out, fr. *elutus* + *-or*] **:** to subject to elutriation

elu·tri·a·tion \=,==trē'āshən\ *n* -s [L *elutriatus* + E *-ion*] **1 :** the removal of substances from a mixture by washing and decanting ⟨the ~ of liquid sludge⟩ **2 :** the separation of finer lighter particles from coarser heavier particles in a mixture by means of a usu. slow upward stream of fluid so that the lighter particles are carried upward **3 :** the washing away of the lighter or finer particles (as of humus or clay) in a soil esp. by the splashing of raindrops

elu·tri·a·tor \=ˈ==,ād·ə(r)\ *n* -s **:** an apparatus for separating particles (as of clay) according to size by elutriation

elu·vial \(')ē¦lüvēəl, -vyəl *also* (')el¦yü-\ *adj* [NL *eluvium* + E *-al*] **1 :** of, relating to, or composed of eluvium **2 :** of or relating to eluviation or to eluviated materials or areas (as soils or soil horizons)

elu·vi·ate \=ˈ=vē,āt\ *vi* -ED/-ING/-S [NL *eluvium* + E *-ate*] **:** to undergo eluviation

elu·vi·a·tion \(,)=,=vē'āshən\ *n* -s **:** the transportation of dissolved or suspended soil material within the soil by the downward or lateral movement of water when rainfall exceeds evaporation — compare ILLUVIATION

elu·vi·um \=ˈ=vēəm\ *n* -s [NL, fr. L *eluere* to wash out, after such pairs as L *alluere* to wash against: LL *alluvium* — more at ELUATE, ALLUVION] **1 :** rock debris produced by the weathering and disintegration of rock in situ — compare ALLUVIUM **2 :** fine soil or sand deposited by wind (as in dunes)

el·vel·la·ce·ae \,elvə'lāsē,ē\ *syn of* HELVELLACEAE

el·ver \'elvə(r)\ *n* -s [alter. of *eelfare*] **:** a small cylindrical young eel that is more advanced in development than a leptocephalus and that is found chiefly along shores or about estuaries — called also *glass eel*

elves *pl of* ELF

el·vish \'elvish, -vēsh\ *adj* [ME *elvissh,* fr. *elf* + *-issh* -ish] **1 :** of or relating to elves **:** being or like elves ⟨~ tricks disturbed the cattle⟩ ⟨ugly shrunken ~ men⟩ **2 :** characteristic of or like that of elves ⟨~ laughter⟩: as **a :** MISCHIEVOUS **b :** SPITEFUL **c :** IRRITATING — **el·vish·ly** *adv*

el·y·mi \'elə,mī\ *n pl, usu cap* [L, fr. Gk *Elymoi*] **:** an ancient people of northwest Sicily

el·y·mus \-,məs\ *n, cap* [NL, fr. Gk *elymos* millet] **:** a genus of tall tufted perennial grasses comprising the lyme grasses, having closely flowered terminal flower spikes, and being sometimes used as fodder and to bind loose sandy soil — see WILD RYE

ely·sia \ə'lizh(ē)ə, ē'-,e'-, -lēzh-\ *n, cap* [NL, prob. fr. L *Elysium*] **:** the type genus of Elysiidae comprising sea slugs that lack both cerata and gills

ely·sian \-zh(ē)ən\ *adj, often cap* [L *Elysius* (fr. Gk *Ēlysios*) + E *-an*] **1 :** relating to Elysium **2 :** sweetly blissful **:** BEATIFIC ⟨~ peace⟩

elysian fields *n pl, often cap E* **:** ELYSIUM

el·y·si·idae \,elə'sīə,dē\ *n pl, cap* [NL, fr. *Elysia,* type genus + *-idae*] **:** a family of slender creeping sea slugs with distinct head, tapering tail, auriculate tentacles, and lateral body folds functioning as fins when the animal swims

ely·si·um \ə'liz(h)ēəm, ē'-,e'-, -lēz(h)-, -zhəm\ *n, pl* **elysiums** \-z(h)ēəmz,-zhəmz\ *or* **ely·sia** \-z(h)ēə,-zhə\ *often cap* [L, fr. Gk *Ēlysion,* fr. neut. of *Ēlysios* Elysian] **1 :** the dwelling place of happy souls after death as conceived by the ancient Greeks and Romans either as a concrete physical region or a state of existence **2 :** abode or state of ideal delight and happiness **:** PARADISE ⟨lovers sitting cheek by jowl for an hour of idle ~ —John Galsworthy⟩

elytr- *or* **elytri-** *or* **elytro-** *comb form* [prob. fr. NL, fr. *elytron*] **1 :** elytron ⟨*elytroid*⟩ ⟨*elytriferous*⟩ **2 :** vagina ⟨*elytropolykus*⟩

elytra *pl of* ELYTRON

el·y·tral \'elə·trəl\ *adj* [NL *elytron* + E *-al*] **:** of or relating to an elytron

el·y·trif·er·ous \¦elə¦trif(ə)rəs\ *adj* [*elytr-* + *-ferous*] **:** bearing elytra — used esp. of segments of certain polychaetes

elyt·ri·form \ə'li·trə,fȯrm, e'li·t-,'elə·t-\ *adj* [*elytr-* + *-form*] **:** resembling or shaped like an elytron **:** SHIELD-SHAPED

el·y·trig·er·ous \¦elə¦trij(ə)rəs\ *adj* [*elytr-* + *-gerous*] **:** ELYTRIFEROUS

el·y·troid \'elə,trȯid\ *adj* [*elytr-* + *-oid*] **:** resembling an elytron

el·y·tron \'elə,trän\ *or* **elytrum** \'elə·trəm\ *n, pl* **ely·tra** \-,trə\ [NL, fr. Gk *elytron* sheath, wing cover] **1 :** one of the thickened sclerotized anterior wings in beetles and some other insects that serve only to protect the posterior pair — called also *wing cover* **2 :** one of the shielding dorsal scales of various polychaete worms

elyt·ro·phore \ə'li·trə,fō(ə)r, e'li·t-,'elə·t-\ *n* -s [*elytr-* + *-phore*] **:** a modified cuticular prominence to which an elytron of a polychaete worm is attached

el·y·troph·o·rous \¦elə¦träf(ə)rəs\ *adj* [*elytr-* + *-phorous*] **:** having elytra

el·y·trous \'elə·trəs\ *adj* [*elytr-* + *-ous*] **:** resembling or suggestive of an elytron

[1]el·ze·vir \'elzə,vi(ə)r, -lsə-\ *adj, usu cap* [after the *Elzevir* (Elzevier) family, Dutch printers and publishers that flourished in the 16th & 17th centuries] **:** of, relating to, or being books or editions esp. of the Greek New Testament and the classics printed and published by the Elzevir family at Amsterdam or Leiden from about 1583 to 1680

[2]elzevir \"\ *n* -s *usu cap* **:** an Elzevir publication

[1]em \'em\ *n* -s **1 :** the letter *m* **2 :** the set dimension of an em quad used as a unit of measure **3 :** PICA

[2]em \"\ *adj* **1 :** having the form of capital M ⟨an ~ fold⟩ **2 :** of the size of an em ⟨an ~ dash⟩ ⟨a 24 ~ line of type⟩

em- — see EN-

em *abbr* **1** emanation **2** eminence

EM *abbr* **1** earl marshal **2** electromagnetic **3** end matched **4** enlisted man **5** [L *episcopus et martyr*] bishop and martyr

Em *symbol* emanation

'em \,əm; *after* p, b, f, *or* v, ᵊm *or* əm; *an immediately preceding* v *may become* b *by assimilation; thus "save 'em" may be* 'sāvᵊm *or* 'sābᵊm *or* 'sāvəm\ *pron* [ME *hem,* fr. OE *heom, him,* dat. pl. of *hē* he — more at HE] **:** THEM

emacerate \ē, ə+\ *vb* [L *emaceratus,* fr. *e-* + *maceratus,* past part. of *macerare* to soften, macerate — more at MACERATE] *archaic* **:** EMACIATE

[1]ema·ci·ate \ə'māshē,āt, ē'-, *usu* -ād.+V\ *vb* -ED/-ING/-S [L *emaciatus,* past part. of *emaciare,* fr. *e-* + *macies* leanness, thinness, fr. *macer* lean, thin — more at MEAGER] *vt* **1 :** to cause to lose flesh so as to become very lean ⟨his sickness *emaciated* him⟩ **2 :** to make poor and weak or unattractive **:** ATTENUATE ⟨all extraneous light *emaciated* and shattered by the flare of gas and electricity —William Beebe⟩ ⟨consistency . . . is the hobgoblin of foolish nations. It ~s a people's life —M.Y.Buch⟩ ~ *vi* **:** to waste away in body **:** become very lean

[2]ema·ci·ate \-ē,ət, -ēə̇t, *usu* |d.+V\ *adj* [L *emaciatus*] **:** EMACIATED

ema·ci·at·ed \-ē,ād.əd, -ātə̇d\ *adj* **1 :** made lean by impairment (as from hunger) ⟨~ bony hands⟩; *also* **:** MEAGER, NARROW ⟨an ~ outlook on life⟩ ⟨the succession of ~ parsonages —Ellery Sedgwick⟩ **2 :** ENFEEBLED, ATTENUATED ⟨failed to pass even this ~ version of the original bill⟩ ⟨the ~ state of the controversy⟩

ema·ci·a·tion \-,māshē'āshən *also* -āsē- *by* sh-*dissimilation*\ *n* -s **1 :** the process of making or becoming emaciated **2 :** the state of being emaciated; *esp* **:** a wasted condition of the body

em·a·gram \'emə,gram\ *n* -s [[1]*em* + *-agram* (as in *diagram*)] **:** a thermodynamic chart on which temperature is shown on a linear scale as abscissa and pressure on a logarithmic scale as ordinate

email \ā'mī, āmȧȧy\ *n, pl* **emails** \-īz,-ȧȧy\ [F *émail,* fr. OF *esmail, esmal* — more at ENAMEL] **1 :** ENAMEL **2 :** a moderate bluish green to greenish blue that is lighter than gendarme, deeper than cyan blue, and duller than parrot blue — called also *bleu Louise*

ema·ja·gua \,emə'hägwə\ *n* -s [AmerSp, alter. of *demajagua, damajagua* — more at MAJAGUA] **1 :** MAJAGUA **2 :** MOUNTAIN MAHOE **3 :** a small tree (*Daphnopsis philippiana*) of the family Thymelaeaceae that is endemic in Puerto Rico

e major *n, usu cap E* **:** the major musical key having a signature of four sharps

em·a·nant \'emənənt\ *adj* [L *emanant-, emanans,* pres. part. of *emanare*] **:** issuing or flowing forth **:** emerging from or as if from a source ⟨water ~ from the earth⟩ — used esp. of mental acts ⟨an ~ volition⟩

em·a·nate \-,nāt, *usu* -ād.+V\ *vb* -ED/-ING/-S [L *emanatus,* past part. of *emanare,* fr. *e-* + *manare* to flow] *vi* **:** to come out from a source ⟨fragrance ~s from flowers⟩ ⟨much of the criticism against him *emanated* from defeated candidates⟩ ⟨transitory powers *emanating* from an editor's desk —Horace Gregory⟩ ~ *vt* **:** to give out **:** spread abroad as or as if an emanation **:** EMIT ⟨the serenity she *emanated* touched him so warmly —Jean Stafford⟩ ⟨some radioactive substances can ~ dangerous radiations for many years⟩ **syn** see SPRING

em·a·na·tion \,emə'nāshən\ *n* -s [LL *emanation-, emanatio,* fr. L *emanatus* + *-ion-, -io* -ion] **1 a :** the action of emanating **:** a flowing forth ⟨experiencing our consciousness as an ~ of the creative impulse that rules the world —Albert Schweitzer⟩ ⟨the ~ of light from a candle⟩ **b :** the origination of the world conceived in Neoplatonism not as a creation out of nothing but as a series of hierarchically descending radiations from the Godhead to nous and other intermediate stages and ultimately to matter **c :** the procession (as of Jesus Christ or the Holy Spirit) directly from the Godhead — distinguished from *creation* as used of mortal beings **2 :** something that emanates or is produced by emanation **:** EFFLUX: as **a :** a quality or property issuing from a source ⟨the dark ~s of the unconscious —Herbert Read⟩ ⟨the soul may be considered an ~ of divinity lodged in man⟩ **b :** something impalpable (as light, odor, or effluvium) that arises from a material source ⟨the air was tainted with musky ~s from the alligator pens⟩; *esp* **:** a heavy gaseous element produced by radioactive disintegration ⟨radium ~⟩ — symbol *Em;* compare ACTINON, RADON, THORON **c :** CONSEQUENCE, OUTCOME; *esp* **:** any of the specific products of a particular social milieu or cultural level **:** a cultural aspect ⟨the stylized art of the Egyptians was as definite an ~ of their culture as was the heroic naturalism of the Greeks⟩ — **em·a·na·tion·al** \¦emə¦nāshənᵊl, -shnəl\ *adj*

em·a·na·tion·ism \,=ˈ=ˈ=shə,nizəm\ *or* **em·a·na·tism** \'emənə,tiz-\ *n* -s **:** a theory of the origination of the world by emanation

em·a·na·tion·ist \,emə'nāsh(ə)nə̇st\ *n* -s **1** *or* **em·a·na·tist** \'emənətə̇st\ **:** an adherent of the philosophical theory of emanationism **2 :** a sociologist that seeks to derive all human action and belief from the existing cultural orientation

em·a·na·tive \'emə,nād·iv, -,nəl, |t|, |ēv *also* |əv\ *adj* [*emanation* + *-ive*] **1 :** tending to emanate or cause to emanate **2 :** resulting from or relating to emanation — **em·a·na·tive·ly** \|əvlē, -li\ *adv*

em·a·na·tor \-,nād·ə(r), -ātə-\ *n* -s **:** one that emanates

em·a·na·tory \'emənə,tōrē, -ōr-, -ri, *chiefly Brit* -,nātəri *or* -,nā·tri\ *adj* [*emanation* + *-ory*] **1 :** being an emanation ⟨~ matter⟩ **2 :** of or relating to emanation ⟨an ~ theory of the origin of matter⟩

[1]eman·ci·pate \ə'man(t)sə,pāt, ē'-, -maan-, *usu* -ād.+V\ *vt* -ED/-ING/-S [L *emancipatus,* past part. of *emancipare,* fr. *e-* + *mancipare* to deliver as property, transfer, sell — more at MANCIPATE] **1 :** to release (a child) from the paternal power, making the person released sui juris — used chiefly in ancient Roman and civil law **2 :** to set free from the power of another **:** LIBERATE; *specif* **:** to free from bondage ⟨*emancipated* the slaves⟩ **3 :** to free from any controlling influence **4** *obs* **:** to deliver into bondage **:** ENSLAVE **syn** see FREE

[2]eman·ci·pate \-,pāt, -,pət\ *adj* [L *emancipatus*] **:** EMANCIPATED

eman·ci·pat·ed \-,pād·əd, -ātə̇d\ *adj* **:** at liberty **:** FREE, UNTRAMMELED; *often* **:** not bound or formulated by or adherent to currently accepted mores, techniques, or beliefs ⟨those ~ spirits who demand the right to live their lives in their own way⟩

eman·ci·pa·tio \(,)ā,män(t)sə'päd·ē,ō\ *n* -s [L] **:** EMANCIPATION 2

eman·ci·pa·tion \ə,man(t)sə'pāshən, (,)ē,-, -maan-\ *n* -s [L *emancipation-, emancipatio,* fr. *emancipatus* + *-ion-, -io* -ion] **1 :** the act or process of setting or making free **:** LIBERATION ⟨the ~ of slaves⟩; *broadly* **:** deliverance from any onerous and controlling power or influence ⟨~ of the mind from superstition⟩ **2 :** the act or procedure of legally freeing from the paternal power **3 :** gradual segregation of an orig. homogeneous embryo into fields with different specific potentialities for development

eman·ci·pa·tion·ist \-sh(ə)nə̇st\ *n* -s **:** an advocate of emancipation

eman·ci·pa·tor \=ˈ==,pād·ə(r), -ātə-\ *n* -s [LL, fr. L *emancipatus* + *-or*] **:** one that emancipates or advocates emancipation

eman·ci·pa·to·ry \-,pə,tōrē, -ōr-, -ri, *chiefly Brit* -,pātəri *or* -,pā·tri\ *adj* **:** designed or tending to produce emancipation ⟨~ efforts⟩ ⟨~ laws⟩

eman·ci·pist \-'man(t)səpə̇st\ *n* -s [*emancipate* + *-ist*] **:** a prisoner in one of the former Australian convict settlements whose time had expired

emandibulate \¦ē+\ *adj* [*e-* + *mandibulate*] **:** being without functional or well-developed mandibles

emane \ē'mān\ *vb* -ED/-ING/-S [F *émaner,* fr. L *emanare* — more at EMANATE] *archaic* **:** EMANATE

em·a·nom·e·ter \,emə'nämed·ə(r)\ *n* [*emanation* + *-o-* + *-meter*] **:** any of various devices designed to measure quantities or intensity of emanation — **em·a·no·met·ric** \¦emənō¦me·trik\ *adj* — **em·a·nom·e·try** \,emə'nämə·trē\ *n* -ES

emarginate \(')ē+\ *or* **emarginated** \"+\ *adj* [*emarginate* fr. L *emarginatus,* past part. of *emarginare* to deprive of a margin, fr. *e-* + *margin-, margo* edge, margin; *emarginated* fr. L *emarginatus* + E *-ed* — more at MARGIN] **:** having the margin notched: **a :** having a shallow marginal notch (as at the apex of a leaf or in the caudal fin of a fish) — compare OBCORDATE, RETUSE **b** *of a crystal* **:** having truncated edges — **emar·ginate·ly** *adv*

emargination \(,)ē+\ *n* -s **:** a notching at the margin (as of a crustacean's carapace)

emar·gin·ula \,ē,mär'jinyələ\ *n, cap* [NL, fr. ISV *emarginate* + NL *-ula*] **:** a genus of small keyhole limpets

[1]emas·cu·late \ə'maskyə,lāt, ē'-, *sometimes chiefly Brit* -mȧs-; *usu* -ād.+V\ *vt* -ED/-ING/-S [L *emasculatus,* past part. of *emasculare,* fr. *e-* + *masculus* male — more at MALE] **1 :** to deprive of virile or procreative power **:** CASTRATE, GELD **2 :** to deprive of masculine vigor or spirit **:** weaken or attenuate by removal or alteration of potent qualities: as **a :** to divest (language) of vigor and freedom (as by excision, euphemism, or weakening of sense) **b :** to deprive (a law) of force or effectiveness (as by amendment or interpretation) **3 :** to remove the androecium of (a flower) in the process of artificial cross-pollination **syn** see UNNERVE

[2]emas·cu·late \-lə|t, -,lā|t, *usu* |d.+V\ *adj* [L *emasculatus*] **:** EMASCULATED

emas·cu·lat·ed \-,lād·əd, -ātə̇d\ *adj* **:** deprived of or lacking virility, vigor, or characteristic flavor **:** IMPOTENT, INEFFECTIVE, ATTENUATED

emas·cu·la·tion \(,)=,==ˈlāshən\ *n* -s [L *emasculatus* + E *-ion*] **:** the act or process of emasculating **:** the state of being emasculated

emas·cu·la·tome \=ˈ== lə,tōm\ *n* -s [blend of [1]*emasculate* and *-tome*] **:** a pair of double-hinged pincers for castrating domestic animals bloodlessly by crushing the spermatic cord through the unbroken skin — compare EMASCULATOR

emas·cu·la·tor \-,lād·ə(r), -ātə-\ *n* -s **:** one that emasculates; *specif* **:** an instrument often with a broad surface and a cutting edge used in castrating livestock — compare EMASCULATOME

emb *abbr* **1** embankment **2** embargo **3** embark; embarkation **4** embassy **5** embossed **6** embroidered **7** embryo; embryology

em·ba·dom·o·nas \,embə'dämənəs\ *n, cap* [NL, fr. *embado-* (fr. Gk *embad-, embas* slipper, coarse shoe, fr. *embainein* to step in, go on, fr. *em-* [2]*en-* + *bainein* to go) + *-monas;* fr. the shape — more at IN, COME] **:** a genus of small flagellates with two unequal flagella commensal in the intestines of various vertebrates including man

em·bale \əm, em+\ *vt* [[1]*en-* + *bale* (n.)] *archaic* **:** BALE, WRAP

em·ball \"+\ *vt* [[1]*en-* + *ball* (n.)] *archaic* **:** ENCIRCLE

em·bal·lo·nu·ri·dae \(,)em,balə'n(y)urə,dē\ *n pl, cap* [NL, fr. *Emballonura,* type genus (fr. Gk *emballōn* — pres. part. of *emballein* to throw in — + NL *-ura*) + *-idae;* fr. the loose appearance of the tail — more at EMBLEM] **:** a family of insectivorous bats having the face obliquely truncated, no nose leaf, and the tail partly free

em·balm \əm'bä|m, em-, -bȧ| *also* |lm; *archaic* -bam\ *vt* -ED/-ING/-S [ME *enbaumen, enbaumen, embalmen,* fr. MF *embaumer, embalmer,* fr. OF *embasmer, embausmer,* fr. *en-* [1]*en-* + *basme* balm — more at BALM] **1 :** to treat (a dead body) so as to protect from decay or to sterilize: **a :** to prepare for burial by soaking in brine or bitumen often together with packing the body cavities with spices and aromatic substances (as in the preparation of the mummies of ancient Egyptians) **b :** to prepare for burial by injecting into the arterial system and body cavities a preservative and disinfectant fluid (as a solution of formaldehyde) **2 :** to fill with odors ⟨[drying] codfish which had ~*ed* the air for blocks around —Mary H. Vorse⟩; *usu* **:** to make sweet or pleasing with odors **:** PERFUME ⟨spring ~s the woods and fields⟩ **3 a :** to protect from decay or oblivion ⟨his memory is ~*ed* in the hearts of his people⟩ **b :** to preserve (as food) by chemical or other agencies — often used disparagingly ⟨reduced to eating weeviled biscuit and ~*ed* beef⟩ **4 :** to fix in a static condition **:** leave with no opportunity to grow or develop ⟨make them think of it as something living on the stage, not as something ~*ed* in a book —Dorothy De Huneeus⟩ ⟨big fortunes ~*ed* in bank deposits or in tax-exempt bonds —H.E.Stassen⟩

em·balm·er \-mə(r)\ *n* -s **:** one that embalms; *esp* **:** a person whose work is to embalm the dead

em·balm·ment \-mmənt\ *n* -s **1 :** the act or process of embalming **2 :** a preparation used in embalming

em·bank \əm, em+\ *vt* [[1]*en-* + *bank* (n.)] **:** to enclose (as a marsh) or confine (as a stream) by means of embankments

em·bank·ment \"mənt\ *n* -s **1 :** the action or process of embanking **2 :** a structure (as of earth or gravel) raised usu. to prevent water from overflowing a level tract of country, to retain water in a reservoir or a stream in its bed, or to carry a roadway or railroad

em·bar \əm, em+\ *vt* [ME *enbarren,* fr. MF *embarrer,* fr. *em-* [1]*en-* + *barre* bar] **:** to stop, check, or hinder by or as if by enclosing with bars: as **a** *obs* **:** to interrupt or impede (as commerce) by an embargo **b** *archaic* **:** ENCLOSE, IMPRISON **c** *obs* **:** to put a stop to by legal means **:** BAR ⟨~ a claim⟩

em·bar·ca·de·ro \(,)em,bärkə'de(,)rō\ *n* -s [Sp, fr. *embarcado* (past part. of *embarcar* to embark, fr. *em-* — fr. L *im-* [2]*in-* — + *barca* bark, fr. LL) + *-ero* -er — more at BARK (ship)] *West* **:** a landing place **:** WHARF, QUAY; *esp* **:** a landing place on an inland waterway (as a navigable stream)

[1]em·bar·go \əm'bär(,)gō, em-, -'bä(\ *n* -ES [Sp, fr. *embargar* to embargo, fr. (assumed) VL *imbarricare,* fr. L *im-* [2]*in-* + (assumed) VL *-barricare* (fr. *barra* bar)] **1 :** an edict or order of the government prohibiting the departure or entry of ships of commerce at ports within its dominions — compare BLOCKADE; see CIVIL EMBARGO, HOSTILE EMBARGO **2 :** a prohibition imposed by law upon commerce either in general or in one or more of its branches **3 :** STOPPAGE, IMPEDIMENT; *esp* **:** PROHIBITION ⟨an ~ against employment of union labor was notoriously one of the chief obstructions to collective bargaining —Felix Frankfurter⟩ **4 :** an order that is issued by a common carrier or public regulatory agency and that prohibits the acceptance of all or of specified kinds of freight for transportation on its lines or between specified points or areas because of traffic congestion, labor difficulties, or other reasons

[2]embargo \", *in pres part* " *or* -gəw\ *vt* -ED/-ING/-ES **1 :** to lay or put an embargo on (as ships or commerce); *often* **:** to prevent the movement of (as diseased plants or animals) in commerce **2 :** to retain or seize for state purposes or under state authority ⟨~*ing* all batches of vaccine until the source of contamination could be identified⟩ **:** REQUISITION

em·bark \əm'bärk, em-, -bȧk\ *vb* -ED/-ING/-S [MF *embarquer*, fr. OProv *embarcar*, fr. *em-* (fr. L *im-* ²in-) + *barca* bark — more at BARK (ship)] *vt* **1 :** to cause to go on board a boat or airplane **2 :** to engage, enlist, or invest (as persons or money) in an enterprise ⟨he ~*ed* his fortune in trade⟩ ~ *vi* **1 :** to go on board a boat or airplane for transportation ⟨the troops ~*ed* at midnight⟩ **2 :** to make a start **:** COMMENCE — usu. used with *on* or *upon* ⟨after the war the company ~*ed* on a program of expansion⟩ ⟨she had no hesitation about ~*ing* on a new career⟩ ⟨ready to ~ upon any new adventure⟩

em·bar·ka·tion *also* **em·bar·ca·tion** \,em,bär'kāshən, -,bȧ'k-, -,bə(r)'k-\ *n* -S **1 a :** the action or process of embarking ⟨the ~ of troops⟩ **b :** something (as a body of troops) that is embarked **2** *archaic* **:** SHIP, BOAT

em·bark·ment \əm'bärkmənt, em-, -bȧk-\ *n* -S [MF *embarquement*, fr. *embarquer* + *-ment*] **:** EMBARKATION 1a

em·bar·ras *n* [F, obstacle, trouble, embarrassment, fr. *embarrasser* to hinder, embarrass] **1** *like* EMBARRASS\ -ES *archaic* **:** EMBARRASSMENT **2** \ˌäⁿbə'rä\ *pl* **embarras** [LaF, fr. F] **:** snags or packed masses of tree trunks or driftwood (as in a Louisiana bayou)

em·bar·rass \əm'barəs, em- *also* -ber-\ *vt* -ED/-ING/-ES [F *embarrasser*, fr. Sp *embarazar*, fr. Pg *embaraçar*, prob. fr. *em-* (fr. L *im-* ²in-) + *baraça* noose, rope] **1 :** to hamper or impede the movement or freedom of movement of (as a person) ⟨a man who refused to let physical handicaps ~ him⟩; *often* **:** HAMPER, IMPEDE ⟨~*ed* our freedom of movement⟩ ⟨our progress was ~*ed* by mountains of baggage⟩ ⟨they counted on the spring rains to ~ the advance of the enemy⟩ **2 a :** to place in doubt, perplexity, or difficulties ⟨the Government was again ~*ed* from within party ranks by a political speech —*Current Biog.*⟩ ⟨too often preciosity and aimless verbiage ~ the thought and confuse the emotion —Mathurin Dondo⟩ **b :** to involve (as a person or his affairs) in difficulties concerning money matters ⟨we believe the company will be seriously ~*ed* if it does not get this loan⟩ ⟨heavy gambling losses ~*ed* him for years⟩ ⟨the estate was ~*ed* by the prospect of heavy death duties⟩ **c :** to cause to experience a state of self-conscious distress **:** ABASH ⟨their frank discussion of his looks ~*ed* the boy⟩ ⟨it ~*es* many people to walk into a room full of strangers⟩ **d :** to impair the activity of (a bodily function) ⟨his digestion was ~*ed* by overeating and irregular hours⟩ or the function of (a bodily part) ⟨the congestion of pneumonia ~*es* the lungs⟩ **3 :** to make intricate **:** COMPLICATE ⟨a course of legislation had prevailed . . . which weakened the confidence of man in man, and ~*ed* all transactions between individuals —John Marshall⟩ ⟨the courts . . . were not established to . . . enable a few to harass and ~ sovereign action by the government —F.D.Roosevelt⟩

syn DISCOMFIT, ABASH, DISCONCERT, RATTLE, FAZE: EMBARRASS is likely to implicate an agency or influence checking and hampering free choice or action, often with accompanying chagrin, confusion, and loss of face ⟨in immense flood of litigation, which seriously *embarrassed* the courts —T.F.T. Plucknett⟩ ⟨the problems of food, shelter, and sanitation for the impoverished veterans *embarrassed* Washington, and there was latent danger of disorder —J.M.Hanson⟩ ⟨the southern housewife is not unduly *embarrassed* by an unexpected guest —*Amer. Guide Series: N.C.*⟩ DISCOMFIT implies hampering or frustrating and also chagrining, causing loss of self-possession, and confusing ⟨Bradley's polemical irony and his obvious zest in using it, his habit of *discomfiting* an opponent with a sudden profession of ignorance, of inability to understand, or of incapacity for abstruse thought —T.S.Eliot⟩ ⟨she may heckle the dealer, add a running commentary to the demonstrations, or just assume a *discomfiting* smugness —*Fortune*⟩ ABASH suggests the calling up of feelings of shyness, unworthiness, diffidence, shame, and loss of self-pride through some vexation or check ⟨she would feel *abashed* before any woman who had not been rejected like herself —Rebecca West⟩ ⟨as *abashed* as a child interrupted in his game of make-believe —Rudyard Kipling⟩ DISCONCERT implies a bringing about of confused uncertainty and hesitation in proceeding or of loss of composure and assurance ⟨I was *disconcerted* to find that they were locked. I stood there irresolute and uneasy like a baffled thief —Joseph Conrad⟩ ⟨watched the beautiful young man with her solemn unwinking stare that *disconcerted* self-conscious people —Rose Macaulay⟩ RATTLE suggests an utter loss of poise, composure, and accustomed control of a situation, along with disorganization of wonted mental powers ⟨that means that Freddy is *rattled* out of his senses —John Buchan⟩ ⟨*rattled* by hypothetical eyes spying upon her —Jean Stafford⟩ ⟨when other advisers became *rattled*, Mr. Adams was calm —Tris Coffin⟩ FAZE applies to loss of assurance, face, and confidence brought about by a check, retort, sudden difficulty ⟨it hit Marciano flush on the right side of the jaw, but it didn't seem to *faze* him a bit —A.J.Liebling⟩ ⟨he had ice water in his veins. Nothing *fazed* him, not insult or anger or violence or getting his face beat into a hamburger —R.P. Warren⟩

em·bar·rassed·ly \-stlē,-sədlē, -li\ *adv* **:** in an embarrassed manner **:** with embarrassment ⟨he spoke ~⟩

embarrassingly *adv* **:** to an embarrassing degree **:** so as to cause embarrassment ⟨her ~ plain speech⟩

em·bar·rass·ment \-smənt\ *n* -S [F *embarrassement*, fr. *embarrasser* + *-ment*] **1 a :** the state of being embarrassed **:** PERPLEXITY **:** confusion or discomposure of mind ⟨his ~ when he dropped the cake in his lap was pitiful to see⟩ ⟨the ~ of dull minds faced by the complexities of modern life⟩; *often* **:** difficulty or perplexity arising from the want of money to pay debts ⟨financial ~ was chronic in our family⟩ **b :** difficulty in functioning as a result of disease ⟨cardiac ~⟩ ⟨respiratory ~⟩ **2 a :** something that embarrasses **:** IMPEDIMENT, ENCUMBRANCE ⟨a shrill harsh voice is a serious ~ in business and social life⟩ **b :** an excessive quantity from which a selection must be made ⟨an ~ of choice things to see —*N.Y. Times*⟩ — used esp. in the phrase *embarrassment of riches* ⟨an age that builds whole libraries to house the papers of presidents, an ~ of riches —Leon Edel⟩ ⟨the unprejudiced observer would have some difficulty saying just which details might best be dropped, so many wryly devastating moments crop up at every turn — a real ~ of riches —*Saturday Rev.*⟩

em·barren \əm, em+\ *vt* [¹en- + *barren* (adj.)] *archaic* **:** to make barren

em·base \"+\ *vt* [¹en- + *base* (adj.)] *archaic* **:** to lower esp. in rank, dignity, or quality **:** DEBASE

embassade *var of* AMBASSADE

embassador *var of* AMBASSADOR

em·bas·sage \'embəsij\ *n* -S [ME *ambassage*, prob. alter. of *ambassade* — more at AMBASSADE] **1** *archaic* **:** a sending of an ambassador **:** EMBASSY; *also* **:** status as ambassador **2** *archaic* **:** message, errand, business, or charge of an ambassador

em·bas·sy \'embəsē, -si\ *n* -ES *often attrib* [MF *ambassee*, modif. of OIt *ambasciata*, fr. OProv *ambaisada*, fr. (assumed) *ambaisa* mission, of Gmc origin; akin to OE *ambiht* office, service, OHG *ambaht*, ON *embætti*, Goth *andbahti*; all fr. a prehistoric Gmc word of Celt origin; akin to Gaulish *ambactos* vassal, W *amaeth* farmer; both fr. a prehistoric Celt compound whose constituents are akin respectively to W *am-* around, Gk *amphi*, and to OIr *ad-aig* to drive — more at BY, AGENT] **1 a :** the function or position of an ambassador ⟨held the ~ in that country for over nine years⟩ **b :** a journey or stay away from one's homeland or accustomed place undertaken in the character of an ambassador or other envoy ⟨an expeditionary force, or official visit abroad, such as *embassies* or other necessary missions —K.R.Popper⟩ **2 :** the message, charge, or business of an ambassador or other envoy **3 :** an ambassador or other envoy usu. together with his suite **4 :** the official residence and offices of an ambassador

em·bathe \əm, em+\ *vt* [¹en- + *bathe*] **:** to wash freely **:** BATHE, IMMERSE, DRENCH

em·batholithic \(ˌ)em+\ *adj* [²en- + *batholithic*] **:** relating or belonging to or constituting ore deposits formed among closely spaced outcrops of the projecting parts of a batholith where the invaded rocks predominate

¹em·battle \əm, em+\ *vb* [ME *embatailen*, fr. MF *embatailler*, fr. *em-* ¹en- + *batailler* to battle — more at BATTLE] *vt* **1 :** to arrange (as an army) in order of battle **:** array for battle — used chiefly as a participial adjective ⟨*embattled* forces awaiting the dawn⟩ **2 :** to make (as oneself) ready for conflict **:** be prepared to fight ⟨only a hard core of *embattled* trucking firms still refused to give the union the 25-cent-an-hour . . . increase —*Springfield (Mass.) Union*⟩ **3 :** FORTIFY ⟨~ a building⟩ ⟨~ a city⟩ ~ *vi, obs* **:** to prepare for battle

²embattle \"\ *vt* [ME *embatailen*, fr. ¹en- + *batailen* to fortify with battlements — more at BATTLE] **:** to furnish with battlements ⟨received royal permission to ~ [his residence] —Sam Boal⟩

embattled *adj* [ME *embatailed*, fr. past part. of *embatailen* to furnish with battlements] **1 :** having battlements **:** CASTELLATED **2 :** having the edge broken with indentations like the crenels of battlements — used esp of a heraldic device (as a fess or bend)

em·battlement \əm, em+\ *n* [ME *embatailment*, fr. *embatailen* to furnish with battlements + *-ment*] **:** BATTLEMENT

¹em·bay \əm'bā, em-\ *vt* -ED/-ING/-S [¹en- + *bay* (body of water)] **1 a :** to shut in or shelter esp. in a bay ⟨an ~*ed* fleet⟩ **b :** ENCIRCLE, SURROUND **2 :** to form into a bay ⟨an ~*ed* shore⟩

²embay *vt* [prob. fr. ¹en- + *-bay* (alter. of *bathe*)] *obs* **:** BATHE, SUFFUSE

embayed mountain *n* **:** a mountain depressed so that sea water enters the valleys

em·bay·ment \əm'bāmənt, em-\ *n* -S **1 a :** formation of a bay (as by depression of the land about a river mouth so that the sea overflows it) — compare ESTUARY 1 **b :** a bay or a conformation resembling a bay **2 :** an irregular corrosion of a crystal by the magma in which it occurs as a foreign inclusion or as a previously crystallized mineral

emb·den *or* **em·den** \'emdən\ *n* [fr. *Emden*, Germany] **1** *usu cap* **:** a breed of large white domestic geese with an orange-colored bill and deep orange shanks and toes **2** -S *often cap* **:** a goose of the Embden breed

em·bed *or* **im·bed** \əm'bed, em-\ *vb* [¹en- *or* ²in- + *bed* (n.)] *vt* **1 a :** to enclose closely in or as if in a matrix ⟨pebbles *embedded* in silt⟩ ⟨~ brick firmly in mortar⟩ **b :** to place in so as to form an integral part of a whole ⟨~*s* Latin constructions in a passage of Italian —*Publ's Mod. Lang. Assoc. of Amer.*⟩ ⟨the tales of his prowess that have become *embedded* in folklore⟩ **c :** to prepare (as material for microscopic examination) for sectioning (as with a microtome) by infiltrating with and enclosing in a supporting substance (as paraffin or celloidin) **2 :** to surround closely **:** ENCLOSE ⟨a sweet edible pulp ~*s* the seed of plums and related fruits⟩ ~ *vi* **:** to become embedded ⟨dirt ~*s* under their fingernails⟩ ⟨the great bulk of the tree slowly *embedded* into the soft soil⟩

em·bed·ment \-dmənt\ *n* -S **:** the act, process, or product of embedding

em·be·lia \em'bēlyə, -ēlēə\ *n* [NL, prob. fr. native name in Ceylon] **1** *cap* **:** a large genus of Old World tropical woody vines (family Myrsinaceae) with alternate leaves and racemose flowers **2** -S **:** the dried powdered fruit of an Indian vine (*Embelia ribes*) used locally as a tapeworm remedy

¹em·be·lif \ˌembə'lif\ *adj* [ME, fr. MF *en belif*] *heraldry* **:** OBLIQUE

²embelif \"\ *adv* [ME, fr. MF *en belif*] *heraldry* **:** OBLIQUELY

em·be·lin \'embələn\ *also* **em·bel·ic acid** \(ˌ)em'belik-\ *n* -S [NL *Embelia* (genus name of *Embelia ribes*) + E *-in* or *-ic*] **:** an orange phenolic quinone $C_{17}H_{26}O_4$ obtained esp. from embelia and used formerly as an anthelmintic

em·bel·lish \əm'belish, em-, -lēsh, *esp in pres part* -ləsh\ *vt* -ED/-ING/-ES [ME *embelisshen*, fr. MF *embeliss-*, stem of *embelir*, fr. *em-* ¹en- + *bel* beautiful — more at BEAUTY] **1** *obs* **:** to make beautiful **2 :** to make beautiful or elegant with ornaments or ornamentation **:** DECORATE, ADORN ⟨~*ed* a book with pictures⟩ ⟨the faults with which nature has generously ~*ed* us all —Henry Adams⟩ **3 :** to enhance, amplify, or garnish (an account) by elaboration with inessential but decorative or fanciful details ⟨speech . . . ~*ed* with felicitous classical quotations —H.W.H.Knott⟩ ⟨~*ed* his story, distorting and inventing detail to suit himself —Rex Ingamells⟩ **syn** see ADORN

em·bel·lish·er \-shə(r)\ *n* -S **:** one that embellishes

em·bel·lish·ment \-shmənt\ *n* -S **1 :** the act or process of embellishing **:** ORNAMENTATION ⟨money provided for the ~ of the new cathedral⟩ **2 :** something serving to embellish ⟨~ of a literary work⟩ ⟨similes and metaphors as poetical ~*s* —J.L. Lowes⟩ ⟨the graces and ~*s* of the exterior man —Isaac Taylor⟩ ⟨a style stripped of all hyperbole and ~ —Henry Aiken⟩ **3 :** ORNAMENT 5

em·ber \'embə(r)\ *n* -S [ME *eymere*, *eymbre*, modif. of ON *eimyrja*; akin to OE *æmerge* ashes, OHG *eimuria* ember; all fr. a prehistoric NGmc-WGmc compound whose first and second constituents respectively are akin to E *oam*, ON *eimr* steam, vapor and to OE *ysle* spark, ash, ON *ysja* fire, L *urere* to burn, Gk *heuein* to singe, Skt *oṣati* he burns] **1 a :** a lighted coal **:** a glowing fragment of coal, coke, wood, or other solid fuel from a fire; *esp* **:** such a coal smoldering in ashes **b :** the smoldering remains of a fire — usu. used in pl. **2 embers** *pl* **:** slowly cooling emotions, memories, ideas, or responses from past experience that are still capable of being enlivened ⟨~*s* of an old love⟩ ⟨generals . . . who kept alive the ~*s* of resistance —Telford Taylor⟩ **3 :** a moderate red that is yellower and duller than cerise, claret (sense 3a), average strawberry (sense 2a), or Turkey red and yellower and less strong than Harvard crimson (sense 1)

em·ber day \"-\ *n* [ME *ymber day*, *embyr day*, fr. OE *ymbrendæg*, fr. *ymbryne*, *ymbrene* circuit, course, anniversary, fr. *ymb*, *ymbe* around + *ryne* course, running, period of time + *dæg* day; akin to OHG *umbi* around, ON *um*, *umb*, Gk *amphi*, and to OE *rinnan* to run — more at BY, RUN, DAY] **:** a Wednesday, Friday, or Saturday in any of the four weeks commencing on the first Sunday in Lent or on Whitsuntide or including or immediately following September 14 or December 13 set apart for fasting and prayer and observed esp. by the Anglican and Roman Catholic Churches

em·ber·goose \"+\ *n, pl* **embergeese** [*ember* (by folk etymology fr. Norw *ymbre*, *imbre*, *hymber* embergoose, fr. ON *himbrin*) + *goose*] **:** COMMON LOON

em·be·ri·za \ˌembə'rēzə, -rīzə\ *n, cap* [NL, fr. G dial. (Alemannic) *emberitze*, *emmeritz* yellowhammer, fr. MHG *ameriz*, fr. OHG *amarzo*, *amirzo*, dim. of *amaro* — more at YELLOWHAMMER] **:** a genus of passerine birds that includes numerous typical buntings and is made the type of a separate family or included with the finches and related birds in Fringillidae — **em·ber·i·zine** \-ˌzīn, -ˌzən\ *adj*

embetter *vt* [¹en- + *better* (adj.)] *obs* **:** BETTER

em·bez·zle \əm'bezəl, em-\ *vt* **embezzled; embezzled; embezzling** \-z(ə)liŋ\ **embezzles** [ME *embesilen*, fr. AF *embeseiller* to destroy, embezzle, fr. MF *em-* ¹en- + *beseiller* to destroy] **1** *obs* **a :** to make away with **b :** to cause (as a document) to be destroyed, mutilated or falsified **2** *obs* **:** LESSEN; *sometimes* **:** WEAKEN, SQUANDER, DISSIPATE **3 :** to appropriate fraudulently to one's own use (as property entrusted to one's care) ⟨*embezzled* a trust fund⟩ ⟨succeeded in *embezzling* several thousand dollars⟩

em·bez·zle·ment \-zəlmənt\ *n* -S **:** the act of embezzling; *specif* **:** fraudulent appropriation of property by a person to whom it has been entrusted (as of an employer's money by his clerk or of public funds by the officer in charge) — compare LARCENY

em·bez·zler \-z(ə)lə(r)\ *n* -S **:** one that embezzles

em·bi·ar·ia \ˌembē'a(a)rēə\ [NL, fr. *Embia* genus of insects (fr. Gk *embie*, fem. of *embios* having life, fr. *em-* ²en- + *bios* mode of life) + *-aria* — more at QUICK] *syn of* EMBIODEA

em·bi·id \'embēəd\ *n* -S [NL *Embiidae*] **:** one of the Embiodea **:** WEB SPINNER

em·bi·idae \em'bīəˌdē\ *n pl, cap* [NL, fr. *Embia*, type genus + *-idae*] **:** a major family of Embiodea

em·bi·idi·na \ˌembēə'dīnə\ [NL, fr. *Embiidae* + *-ina*] *syn of* EMBIODEA

em·bind \əm, em+\ *vt* [¹en- + *bind*] **:** BIND

em·bi·o·dea \ˌembē'ōdēə\ *n pl, cap* [NL, fr. *Embia* + *-odea*] **:** a small order of slender elongated chiefly tropical insects with large head and 10-segmented abdomen having males that are usu. winged and both nymphs and adults that live in silken webs which they spin with glands in the fore tarsi — see WEB SPINNER

em·bi·op·tera \ˌembē'äpt(ə)rə\ [NL, fr. *embio-* (fr. *Embia*) + *-ptera*] *syn of* EMBIODEA

em·bi·ot·o·cid \-ē'ädəsəd; -ēə'täsəd, -tōs-\ *n* -S [NL *Embiotocidae*] **:** a fish of the family Embiotocidae

em·bi·o·toc·i·dae \ˌembēə'täsəˌdē, -tōs-\ *n pl, cap* [NL, fr. *Embiotoca*, type genus (fr. Gk *embios* having life + *-toca*, fr. *tokos* offspring, fr. *tiktein* to bear, beget) + *-idae* — more at EMBIARIA, THANE] **:** a family of viviparous percoid fishes comprising the surf fishes

em·bi·ra \em'bērə\ *n* -S [Pg, fr. Tupi] **:** any of several Brazilian bast fibers that are derived from trees of the genera *Daphnopsis* (family Thymelaeaceae) and *Xylopia* and are used for making nets

em·bit·ter \əm'bid·|ə(r), em-, -it|\ *also* **im·bit·ter** \əm-\ *vt* -ED/-ING/-S [¹en- *or* ²in- + *bitter* (adj.)] **1 :** to make bitter or more bitter ⟨hops serve to ~ beer⟩ **2 :** to excite bitter feelings or animosities in **syn** see EXACERBATE

em·bit·ter·er \|ərə(r)\ *n* -S **:** one that embitters

em·bit·ter·ment \|ə(r)mənt\ *n* -S **:** the act of embittering or state of being embittered ⟨the ~ that followed his father's needless death persisted for years⟩

¹em·blaze \əm'blāz, em-\ *vt* -ED/-ING/-S [¹en- + *blaze* (to blazon)] **1** *archaic* **:** to set forth in or adorn with heraldic devices **:** EMBLAZON **2 :** to adorn sumptuously **:** EMBELLISH ⟨with gems and golden luster rich *emblazed* —John Milton⟩ **3** *obs* **:** to place among the honored or noteworthy

²emblaze \"\ *vt* [¹en- + *blaze* (fire)] **1 :** to illuminate esp. by a blaze **:** cause to blaze with light **2 :** to set in a blaze **:** KINDLE

em·blaz·er \-zə(r)\ *n* -S **:** one that emblazes

em·bla·zon \əm'blāzᵊn, em-\ *vt* **emblazoned; emblazoned; emblazoning** \-z(ᵊ)niŋ\ **emblazons** [¹en- + *blazon*] **1 :** to inscribe or adorn with heraldic bearings or devices **2 a :** to deck in bright colors **:** set off conspicuously (as by rich or brilliant decorations) **:** display sumptuously ⟨many banners, ~*ed* with the emblem of the cross —G.W.Benson⟩ **b :** to depict or delineate with brightness and approbation **:** CELEBRATE, EXTOL ⟨his subjects ~*ed* the good king's fame to all the world⟩ — **em·bla·zon·er** \-(ᵊ)nə(r)\ *n* -S

em·bla·zon·ment \-ᵊnmənt\ *n* -S **:** heraldic emblazonry — usu. used in pl.

em·bla·zon·ry \-ᵊnrē, -ri\ *n* -ES **1 :** the act or art of emblazoning **2 :** emblazoned figures **:** brilliant decoration ⟨the glowing ~ of the coronation setting⟩

¹em·blem \'embləm *also* -blim *or* -ˌblem\ *n* -S [ME, fr. L *emblema* inlaid work, tesselated work, fr. Gk *emblēma*, lit., insertion, fr. *emballein* to throw in, put in, insert, fr. *em-* ²en- + *ballein* to throw — more at DEVIL] **1 :** a picture with a motto or set of verses intended as a moral lesson or a subject of meditation that was common in the 17th century **2** *obs* **:** inlaid or mosaic work **3 a :** a visible sign of an idea **:** an object or the figure of an object symbolizing and suggesting another object or an idea by natural aptness or by association ⟨a balance is an ~ of justice⟩ ⟨a scepter, an ~ of sovereignty⟩ **b :** a typical representative **:** SYMBOL ⟨evening cooling is an ~ of autumn chill⟩ ⟨trying to find out enough about eagles to keep our national ~ from dying out —Caroline Bird⟩ **4 a :** a symbolic object used as a heraldic device or badge **b :** a device, symbol, design, or figure adopted and used as an identifying mark (as a publisher's colophon) **syn** see SYMBOL

²emblem \"\ *vt* -ED/-ING/-S **:** to represent by or as if by an emblem **:** IMAGE ⟨~*ed* with the state seal⟩

em·ble·ma \em'blēmə, -lāmə,-lemə\ *n, pl* **emblema·ta** \-mədə\ [L] **1 :** a featured picture or ornament in mosaic work used frequently by the ancients for decorating pavement or wall **2 :** separate ornament done in relief and often in precious metal that was attached as decoration (as to a ship or piece of furniture) esp. by the ancient Romans — usu. used in pl.

em·blem·at·ic \ˌemblə'mad·|ik, -at|, |ēk\ *also* **em·blem·at·i·cal** \|əkəl, |ēk-\ *adj* [Gk *emblēmatikos*, fr. *emblēmat-*, *emblēma* + *-ikos* -ic, -ical] **:** relating to, containing, or constituting an emblem **:** SYMBOLIC, REPRESENTATIVE ⟨a crown is ~ of royalty⟩ ⟨the free discussion that is ~ of the democratic process⟩ — **em·blem·at·i·cal·ly** \|ək(ə)lē, |ēk-, -li\ *adv* — **em·blem·at·i·cal·ness** \|əkəlnəs, |ēk-\ *n* -ES

em·blem·a·tist \em'blemədəst\ *also* **em·blem·ist** \'embləməst\ *n* -S [*emblemat-* fr. L *emblemat-*, *emblema* + E *-ist*; *emblemist* fr. ¹*emblem* + *-ist*] **:** a writer, designer, or inventor of emblems

em·blem·a·tize \em'blemə,tīz\ *or* **em·blem·ize** \'emblə,mīz\ *vt* -ED/-ING/-S [*emblematize* fr. L *emblemat-*, *emblema* + E *-ize*; *emblemize* fr. ¹*emblem* + *-ize*] **1 :** to represent by or as if by an emblem **:** SYMBOLIZE **2 :** to be or to serve as an emblem of

emblem book *n* **:** a book consisting of emblems

em·ble·ment \'embləmənt, -bəlm-\ *n* -S [ME *emblayment*, *emblayment*, fr. MF *emblaement*, fr. *emblaer* to sow a field with grain (fr. *em-* ¹en- + *-blaer*, fr. *blee* grain) + *-ment*] **:** the growing crop or vegetable growth resulting from annual manurage and cultivation as distinguished from the produce from old roots (as pasturage) or from trees (as timber or fruit) **:** the profits from such a crop

em·blic \'emblik\ *n* -S [NL *emblica*, fr. Ar *amlaj*, fr. Per *āmlah*] **1 :** an East Indian tree (*Phyllanthus emblica*) used with other myrobalans for tanning **2 :** the fruit of emblic — called also *Indian gooseberry*

em·blossom \əm, em+\ *vt* [¹en- + *blossom* (n.)] **:** to cover or adorn with blossoms ⟨trees ~*ed* by the warmth of spring⟩

em·bod·i·er \əm'bädēə(r), em- -diə-\ *n* -S **:** one that embodies

em·bod·i·ment \-dēmənt, -dəm-\ *n* -S **1 :** the act of embodying or state of being embodied ⟨worked for years toward the ~ of a set of rules that would solve all philosophical problems mathematically⟩ **2 :** a thing in which something (as a soul, idea, principle, or type) is embodied **:** INCARNATION ⟨the ~ of courage⟩ ⟨the ~ of all our hopes⟩ **3 :** organization in an aggregate **:** INCORPORATION ⟨log tables and their immediate ~ in slide rules —Bryan Morgan⟩

em·body \-dē,-di\ *vb* [¹en- + *body* (n.)] *vt* **1 :** to give a body to (a spirit) **:** invest with a body **:** INCARNATE **2 a :** to cause to become material or sensual **:** deprive of spirituality **b :** to make concrete by expression in perceptible form (as in words, acts, institutions, or works of art) ⟨attempted to ~ basic democratic principles in the treaty⟩ ⟨a dictatorship *embodied* in a triumvirate⟩ **3 :** to cause to become a body or part of a body **:** INCORPORATE, ORGANIZE ⟨*embodied* a revenue provision in the new law⟩ ⟨they must ~ their ideas in substantial institutions if they are to survive⟩ **4 :** to represent in human or animal form ⟨*embodied* virtue⟩ **:** PERSONIFY ⟨~*ing* love as Cupid⟩ ~ *vi* **1** *obs* **:** to become embodied or materialized — used esp. of the soul **2 :** to unite in a body or mass **:** COALESCE ⟨fat globules *embodied* into butter⟩

em·bog \əm, em+\ *vt* [¹en- + *bog* (n.)] **:** to sink into or as if into a bog **:** bog down **:** MIRE ⟨the meeting became *embogged* in arguments over precedent⟩

em·boî·té \äⁿbwȧ'tā\ *adj* [F, fr. past part. of *emboîter* to put in a box, encase, fit together, fr. *em-* ¹en- + *boîte* box, fr. OF *boiste* — more at BOIST] *of a ballet step* **:** joined with the feet interlocked

em·boîte·ment \äⁿbwȧtmäⁿ\ *n* -S [F, fr. *emboîter* + *-ment*] **:** ENCASEMENT 1b

embol- *or* **emboli-** *or* **embolo-** *comb form* [NL *embol-*, fr. ML (in *embolismus* intercalation) — more at EMBOLISM] **1 :** embolus ⟨*embolectomy*⟩ ⟨*emboli*form⟩ **2 :** wedge ⟨*Embolomeri*⟩

em·bold·en \əm'bōldən, em-\ *vt* -ED/-ING/-S [¹en- + *bold* + *-en*] **:** to impart boldness or courage to **:** instill with boldness, bravery, or resolution enough to overcome timidity or misgiving ⟨~*ed* by the weakness of the royal governor, an irresponsible mob . . . set upon a squad of ten soldiers —R.W.G. Vail⟩ **syn** see ENCOURAGE

embole *var of* EMBOLY

em·bo·lec·to·my \ˌembə'lektəmē\ *n* -ES [*embol-* + *-ectomy*] **:** surgical removal of an embolus

em·bo·le·mia *also* **em·bo·lae·mia** \-'lēmēə\ *n* -S [NL, fr. *embol-* + *-emia*, *-aemia*] **:** an abnormal state characterized by the presence of emboli in the blood

emboli *pl of* EMBOLUS

em·bol·ic \(ˌ)em'bälik\ *adj* [*embol-* + *-ic*] **1 :** of or relating to an embolus or embolism **2 :** of, relating to, or produced by emboly

em·bo·lism \'embə,lizəm\ *n* -s [ME *embolisme*, fr. ML *embolismus*, fr. *embolismus* intercalary, fr. LL, modif. of Gk *embolimos*, fr. *embolos* stopper, fr. *emballein* to throw in, put in, insert — more at EMBLEM] **1 :** INTERCALATION 1 **2 :** a liturgical expansion of the last two petitions of the Lord's Prayer that is found in many Eastern and Western liturgies with the exception of the Byzantine and Ethiopic **3** [NL *embolismus*, fr. ML] **a :** the sudden obstruction of a blood vessel by an embolus **b :** EMBOLUS — not used technically

em·bo·lis·mic \,;==;lizmik\ *also* **em·bo·lis·mi·cal** \-məkəl\ *adj* **:** relating to, formed by, or including a temporal embolism ⟨any doubt as to when the ~ terms are to be applied must be solved by the calendar Easter new moon —Peter Archer⟩ ⟨an ~ year⟩; *often* **:** inserted as an intercalation ⟨an ~ lunation completing the 13-month Anglo-Saxon year⟩

em·bo·lite \'embə,līt\ *n* -s [G *embolit*, fr. Gk *embolion* + G *-it* -ite] **:** a mineral Ag(Cl, Br) consisting of native silver chloride and bromide and resembling cerargyrite

em·bo·li·um \em'bōlēəm\ *n, pl* **embo·lia** \-ēə\ [NL, fr. Gk *embolion* insertion, embossed ornament, dim. of *embolos*] **:** a narrow piece on the costal margin of the corium of the wings of certain true bugs

em·bo·li·za·tion \,embələ'zāshən, -,lī'z-\ *n* -s **:** the condition of being embolized ⟨pulmonary ~⟩ or of embolizing ⟨~ of a thrombus⟩

em·bo·lize \'embə,līz\ *vb* -ED/-ING/-S [*embol-* + *-ize*] *vt, of an embolus* **:** to lodge in and obstruct (as a blood vessel or organ) ~ *vi* **:** to break up into emboli or become an embolus ⟨marrow fragments *embolized* and were swept to the lung from the site of the fracture⟩

em·bo·lo \'embə,lō\ *n* -s [native name in Africa] **:** the edible bluish fleshy fruit of the Cape ebony

em·bo·lo·la·lia \,embəlō'lālēə, |'lal-\ *also* **em·bo·la·lia** \,embə|\ *n* -s [*embololalia*, NL, fr. *embol-* + *-lalia*; *embolalia*, NL, blend of *embol-* and *-lalia*] **:** the interpolation of meaningless sounds or words into speech

em·bo·lo·mere \'embəlō,mi(ə)r\ *n* -s [NL *Embolomeri*] **:** an animal or fossil of the order Embolomeri

em·bo·lom·eri \,embə'läməˌrī\ *n pl, cap* [NL, fr. *embol-* + *-meri* (fr. Gk *meros* part) — more at MERIT] **:** an order of primitive labyrinthodonts including most of the larger Carboniferous amphibians and having vertebrae in which both intercentra and pleurocentra are complete disks

em·bo·lom·er·ism \-,rizəm\ *n* -s [*embolomerous* + *-ism*] **:** the condition of being embolomerous

em·bo·lom·er·ous \;==;läməras\ *adj* [ISV *embol-* + *-merous*] **1 :** having both centrum and intercentrum present and pierced for passage of the persistent notochord **:** DIPLOSPONDYLIC — used of the vertebrae of various primitive fishes and amphibians **2 :** having embolomerous vertebrae

em·bo·lo·phra·sia \,embəlō'frāzh(ē)ə\ *n* -s [NL, fr. *embol-* + *-phrasia*] **:** EMBOLOLALIA

em·bo·lus \'embələs\ *n, pl* **embo·li** \-,lī, -,lē\ [NL, fr. L, piston of a pump, fr. Gk *embolos* stopper] **1** *archaic* **:** something inserted (as a wedge or the piston of a syringe) **2 a :** a foreign or abnormal material particle circulating in the blood (as a bubble of air or a blood clot) — see EMBOLISM; compare THROMBUS **3 :** a complex chitinous structure that forms the apex of the digital joint of the palpus of a male spider, that contains the terminal portion of the receptacle in which sperm is stored prior to insemination, and that assists in transferring sperm to the female

em·bo·ly *also* **em·bo·le** \'embəlē\ *n, pl* **embolies** *also* **emboles** [Gk *embolē* act of putting into, insertion, fr. *emballein* to throw in, put in, insert — more at EMBLEM] **:** a process of gastrula formation by simple invagination or infolding of the blastula wall that is typical of embryos with holoblastic and approximately equal cleavage

em·bon·point \äⁿbōⁿpwaⁿ\ *n* [F, fr. MF, fr. *en bon point* in good condition] **:** plumpness of person **:** STOUTNESS ⟨firmly corseted ~⟩ ⟨an elderly gentleman of dignified ~⟩ ⟨an actress better known for her ~ than her artistic skill⟩

emborder *vt* [¹*en-* + *border* (n.)] *obs* **:** to enclose with a border **:** EDGE

em·bosk \əm, em+\ *vt* -ED/-ING/-S [¹*en-* + *bosk*] **:** to shroud or conceal esp. with plants or greenery ⟨the summerhouse all ~*ed* with vines⟩

em·bosom *also* **im·bosom** \əm, em+\ *vt* [¹*en-* or ²*in-* + *bosom* (n.)] **1** *archaic* **:** to take into or place in the bosom; *broadly* **:** CHERISH, FOSTER **2 :** to shelter closely **:** ENCLOSE, SURROUND ⟨his house ~*ed* in the grove —Alexander Pope⟩

¹**em·boss** \əm'bäs, em-, -bȯs\ *vt* [ME *embosen* to become exhausted from being hunted, perh. fr. ¹*en-* + MF *bos, bois* forest, of Gmc origin; akin to OHG *busc* bush — more at BUSH] **1** *obs* **:** to drive (as a hunted animal) to bay or to exhaustion **2** *obs* **:** to cause (as an animal) to foam at the mouth with exhaustion or sometimes with rage or other emotion **3** *archaic* **:** to cover or spatter with foam

²**emboss** \"\ *vt* [ME *embosen*, fr. MF *embocer*, fr. *em-* ¹en- + *boce* boss — more at BOSS (protuberance)] **1** *obs* **:** to cause to swell or protrude **:** INFLATE **2 a :** to raise in relief from a surface (as an ornament, a head on a coin, or a device on a letterhead) either by carving or handiwork or now more commonly by mechanical means (as by embossing dies) — opposed to *deboss* **b :** to raise the surface of into bosses or protuberances esp. by pressure against a steel die roller cut or engraved with a pattern **c :** to mark (a postage stamp) with a grill **3 :** to adorn (as leather or metal) with raised work **4 a :** to produce (as braille characters or a notary's seal) in relief usu. by stamping on paper or other impressionable surface **b :** to record (sounds) on a disc record by pushing material to either side without actually removing the material from the disc

³**emboss** *vt* [origin unknown] *obs* **:** ENCLOSE, ENSHEATHE

embossed *adj* [fr. past part. of ²*emboss*] **:** prepared, ornamented, or finished by embossing; *esp, of cloth* **:** having a permanent raised design usu. produced by pressure ⟨an ~ satin blouse⟩ ⟨washable, ~, taffetized cotton sundress —*advt*⟩

embossed book *n* **:** a book with embossed text (as one in braille)

embossed stamp *n* **:** an imprinted stamp with raised lettering and design

em·boss·er \-sə(r)\ *n* -s [²*emboss* + *-er*] **:** one that embosses: as **a :** a punch used in repoussé work for striking metal on the reverse side to raise the relief **b :** an operator of a machine for forming raised designs (as on leather, book covers, textiles, or stationery) **c :** a writer of braille; *esp* **:** one whose work is embossing braille by stereotyping

embossing *n* -s [ME *embosing*, fr. gerund of *embosen* to emboss] **1 :** a product of embossing **:** an embossed figure or design; *sometimes* **:** ¹GRILLE 3 **2 :** the act of or process used by one that embosses; *esp* **:** a calendering process for finishing textiles with a raised, moiré, or other ornamental pattern produced by passing the cloth under heat and pressure between a pair of correspondingly engraved rollers

embossing press *n* **:** a punch press used for embossing (as of book covers)

embossing stylus *n* **:** a stylus that is used in disc recording and that has a rounded tip which pushes the disc material to either side in forming the groove

em·boss·ment \-smənt\ *n* -s [²*emboss* + *-ment*] **1 :** the process of embossing **2 :** BOSS, PROTUBERANCE **3 :** embossed work; *specif* **:** embossed ornamentation

em·both·ri·um \em'bäthrēəm\ *n, cap* [NL, fr. ²*en-* + Gk *bothrion* small pit, dim. of *bothros* pit] **:** a genus of shrubs or small trees (family Proteaceae) with long willowy branches, leathery entire leaves, and showy reddish flowers in terminal racemes

em·bouche·ment \äm'büshmənt\ *n* -s [F, fr. *emboucher* + *-ment*] **:** EMBOUCHURE 1

em·bou·chure \;äm¦bü;shů(ə)r, -bə;-\ *n* -s [F, fr. (s')*emboucher* to flow into, fr. *em-* ¹en- + *bouche* mouth, mouth of a river, fr. L *bucca* cheek — more at POCK] **1 :** the mouth of a river; *also* **:** expansion of a river valley into a plain **2 a :** the position and use of the lips in producing a musical tone on a wind instrument — called also *lip, lipping* **b :** the mouthpiece of a musical instrument **3 :** BOUCHE 2

em·bound *also* **im·bound** \əm, em+\ *vt* [¹*en-* or ²*in-* + *bound* (n.)] **:** BIND

em·bow \əm'bō, em-\ *vt* [ME *embowen*, fr. ¹*en-* + *bowe* bow — more at BOW (arch)] *archaic* **:** to form into an arch or vault

em·bowed \-ōd\ *adj* [ME, fr. past part. of *embowen*] **:** bent like a bow: as **a :** ARCHED, VAULTED ⟨an ~ ceiling⟩ **b** *heraldry, of the arm or leg* **:** represented with the elbow or knee bent to the dexter **c :** curved outward to form a projecting recess ⟨an ~ window bay⟩

em·bowel \əm, em+\ *vt* [¹*en-* + *bowel* (v.)] **1 :** DISEMBOWEL **2** [¹*en-* + *bowel* (n.)] *obs* **:** to hide in the inward parts **:** ENCLOSE, ENCOMPASS ⟨deep ~*ed* in the earth —Edmund Spenser⟩

em·bower *also* **im·bower** \"+\ *vt* [¹*en-* or ²*in-* + *bower* (n.)] **:** to shelter or enclose in or as if in a bower ⟨a house ~*ed* with shrubs⟩

em·box \"+\ *vt* [¹*en-* + *box* (n.)] **:** to enclose in or as if in a box

embr *abbr* **1** embroidered **2** embryo; embryology

¹**em·brace** \əm'brās, em-\ *vb* -ED/-ING/-S [ME *embracen*, fr. MF *embracer*, fr. OF *embracier*, fr. *em-* ¹en- + *brace* two arms — more at BRACE] *vt* **1 a :** to clasp in the arms usu. as a gesture of affection **:** HUG **b :** to copulate with **c** *archaic* **:** to greet or salute by clasping in the arms **2 :** ENCIRCLE, ENCLOSE, ENCOMPASS ⟨a quiet valley *embraced* by dark forests⟩ ⟨the strong walls that ~ the city⟩ **3** *archaic* **:** to take in hand or under consideration **:** UNDERTAKE **4 :** to receive or take up esp. readily or gladly: as **a :** to come to believe in and seek to further, defend, support, or join willingly ⟨a cause which is *embraced* and cherished by so vast a portion of American society —Kenneth Roberts⟩ ⟨finally he *embraced* his father's religion and politics and settled down to be a country gentleman⟩ **b :** to welcome or accept eagerly **:** attach oneself to **:** avail oneself of readily ⟨this life secured for the mind of him who *embraced* it the inestimable advantages of solitude and silence —Joseph Conrad⟩ ⟨an instructor should ~ every opportunity to prepare himself —C.H.Grandgent⟩ ⟨ready to ~ the hard life of a pioneer⟩ **5 :** to attempt to or act so as to influence (as a jury or court) corruptly **6 :** to take in **:** ENFOLD, INCLUDE, COVER **:** treat as part, item, or phase of a larger whole; *sometimes* **:** to be equal or equivalent to **:** total to ⟨called *Summae*, as their scope *embraced* the entire contents of the faith —H.O.Taylor⟩ ⟨my financial assets which *embraced* a few hundred dollars . . . as my immediate assets —Herbert Hoover⟩ ~ *vi* **:** to participate in an embrace ⟨*embracing* tearfully before they parted⟩ **syn** see ADOPT, INCLUDE

²**embrace** \"\ *n* -s **1 a :** a close encircling with the arms and pressure to the bosom esp. as a mark of affection or passion ⟨rushed to the comforting ~ of his mother's arms⟩ ⟨a quick ~ full of love and despair⟩ **b :** COPULATION; *broadly* **:** any close physical relation designed to ensure fertilization of eggs ⟨the amplectic ~ of amphibians⟩ **c :** a clasping with the forelimbs when in conflict — used esp. of an animal ⟨the grim ~ of the grizzly bear⟩ **2 :** ENCIRCLEMENT, ENCLOSURE, GRIP ⟨helpless in the ~ of terror⟩ ⟨a valley lying in the ~ of wooded hills⟩ **3 :** acceptance esp. with favor or approbation ⟨his ready ~ of Communist doctrine⟩

³**embrace** *vt* -ED/-ING/-S [¹*en-* + *brace* (n.)] *obs* **:** to fasten (as armor) with or as if with a brace or buckle

em·brace·able \əm'brāsəbəl, em-\ *adj* **:** suitable for embracing or capable of being embraced; *sometimes* **:** such as may be comprehended and accepted — **em·brace·ably** \-blē\ *adv*

em·brace·ment \-smənt\ *n* -s **:** EMBRACE; *esp* **:** ready or cheerful acceptance (as of an idea, point of view, or method)

em·brace·or \-sə(r)\ *n* -s [AF, fr. MF *embracer* to embrace + *-eor* -or] **:** one guilty of embracery

em·brac·er \"\ *n* -s [ME, fr. *embracen* + *-er*] **:** one that embraces; *esp* **:** EMBRACEOR

em·brac·ery \-s(ə)rē\ *n* -ES [ME *embracerie*, fr. *embracen* + *-erie* -ery] **:** the act of one who attempts to or acts so as to influence a court, jury, or other office or officer corruptly (as by promises, entreaties, money, entertainments, or threats)

embracing *adj* **:** ENCIRCLING, ENCLOSING: as **a** *of a leaf* **:** having the base clasped about the supporting stem of the plant **b :** COMPREHENSIVE, INCLUSIVE ⟨an all-*embracing* glance⟩ — **em·brac·ing·ly** *adv* — **em·brac·ing·ness** *n* -ES

em·brac·ive \-siv\ *adj* **1 :** disposed to embrace **2 :** INCLUSIVE, COMPREHENSIVE

em·brail \əm, em+\ *vt* [¹*en-* + *brail* (n.)] **:** BRAIL 1

em·branch·ment \əm'branchmənt, em-, -raan-,-rain-,-rån-\ *n* -s [F *embranchement*, fr. (s')*embrancher* to branch out (fr. *em-* ¹en- + *branche* branch) + *-ment* — more at BRANCH] **1 :** a branching off or out (as of a valley or a mountain range) **2 :** BRANCH, RAMIFICATION

em·bran·gle *also* **im·bran·gle** \əm'braŋ(g)əl, em-\ *vt* [¹*en-* or ²*in-* + *brangle*] **:** CONFUSE, ENTANGLE ⟨all *embrangled* with this election squabble⟩ ⟨the outside snares and commitments which so *embrangled* him in his first two years —*Isis*⟩ — **em·bran·gle·ment** \-lmənt\ *n* -s

em·bra·sure \əm'brāzhə(r), em-\ *n* -s [F, fr. obs. *embraser* to widen an opening + *-ure*] **1 :** a recess of a door or window; *esp* **:** one sloped or beveled to give an effect of largeness from one side **2 :** an opening with sides flaring outward in a wall or parapet of a fortification usu. for allowing the firing of cannon **3 :** the sloped valley between adjacent teeth (as in the human mouth)

embrasure 1

em·bra·sured \-(r)d\ *adj* **:** having or furnished with embrasures ⟨an ~ fort⟩

em·brave \əm, em+\ *also* **en·brave** \ən, en+\ *vt* [¹*en-* + *brave* (adj.)] **1** *archaic* **:** to make fine or impressive **:** BRIGHTEN **2** *archaic* **:** to inspire with courage **:** make brave or daring

embreathe *vt* [ME *embrethen*, fr. ¹*en-* + *brethen* to breathe — more at BREATHE] **:** INHALE

embrew *obs var of* IMBRUE

embright *vt* -ED/-ING/-S [¹*en-* + *bright* (adj.)] *obs* **:** to make bright **:** ILLUMINATE

em·brighten \əm, em+\ *vt* [¹*en-* + *brighten*] **:** to make brighter **:** BRIGHTEN

embrion *obs var of* EMBRYO

em·bri·thop·o·da \,embrə'thäpədə\ *n pl, cap* [NL, fr. *embritho-* (fr. Gk *embrithēs* weighty) + NL *-poda*] **:** a small order of extinct African ungulate mammals possibly related to the Hyracoidea

em·brittle \əm, em+\ *vb* -ED/-ING/-S [¹*en-* + *brittle* (adj.)] *vt* **:** to make (as metal or plastic) brittle ~ *vi* **:** to become brittle — **em·brit·tle·ment** \"mənt\ *n* -s

em·bro·cate \'embrə,kāt, -rō,-\ *vt* -ED/-ING/-S [LL *embrocatus*, past part. of *embrocare*, fr. Gk *embrochē* embrocation, lotion, fr. *embrechein* to bathe with a lotion, fr. *em-* ²en- + *brechein* to wet] **:** to moisten and rub (a part of the body) with a lotion

em·bro·ca·tion \,==-'kāshən\ *n* -s [LL *embrocatus* + E *-ion*] **:** LINIMENT

embroche *n* -s [Gk *embrochē*] *obs* **:** EMBROCATION

embroglio *var of* IMBROGLIO

em·broi·der \əm'brȯidə(r), em-\ *vb* **embroidered; embroidered; embroidering** \-d(ə)riŋ\ **embroiders** [ME *embroden, embroderen*, fr. MF *embroder*, fr. *em-* ¹en- + *broder* to embroider — more at BROIDER] *vt* **1 a :** to ornament with needlework ⟨~*ed* a sampler⟩ **b :** to form with needlework ⟨~*ing* tiny flowers on a scarf⟩ **2 a :** EMBELLISH, ORNAMENT; *esp* **:** to present (as an account) with florid language or fictitious details **b :** EXAGGERATE ⟨~*ed* the story of his adventures in the jungle —Rudyard Kipling⟩ ~ *vi* **1 :** to make embroidery **2 :** to provide embellishments or ornamentation (as fictitious details) **:** ELABORATE — used with *on* or *upon* ⟨he would take a theme and ~ upon it with . . . drollery —W.S.Maugham⟩ ⟨he develops his subject . . . ~*ing* on rather than deepening its significance —C.D.Lewis⟩

em·broi·der·er \-dərə(r)\ *n* -s [ME *embrawderer*, fr. *embrawderen, embrouderen* to embroider + *-er*] **:** one that embroiders

em·broi·der·ess \-d(ə)rəs\ *n* -ES **:** a woman who embroiders

em·broi·dery \-d(ə)rē, -ri\ *n* -ES *often attrib* [ME *embrouderie*, fr. *embrouderen, embroderen* + *-erie* -ery] **1 a :** the art or process of forming decorative designs in plain or fancy stitches by hand or machine (as on cloth, leather, or paper) **b :** any such design or decoration ⟨enlivened by ~ on the collar and cuffs⟩ ⟨a neckline accented by ~⟩ **c :** an object decorated with embroidery ⟨made a modest living by sale of her *embroideries*⟩ **2 :** elaboration of decorative often fictitious detail **:** EMBELLISHMENT ⟨the succinct statement of economic facts and principles, without ~ —W.B.Shaw⟩ ⟨little time and breath to waste on long speeches, ~, and trivialities —Robert Moses⟩ ⟨a classic case of ~ on fact —*Reporter*⟩ **3 :** diversified ornamentation esp. by contrasts ⟨fields in spring's ~ are dressed —Joseph Addison⟩ **4 :** something pleasing or desirable but superficial and nonessential ⟨most of the content of all cultures consists of *embroideries* which, although they possess use and function, cannot be regarded as direct responses to the basic needs of the society —Ralph Linton⟩ ⟨those who consider the humanities mere educational ~⟩

embroidery hoop *n* **:** either of two hoops fitting snugly one over the other for holding fabric taut while embroidering

embroidery hoops

¹**em·broil** \əm'brȯil, *esp before pause or consonant* -ȯiəl\ *vt* [F *embrouiller*, fr. MF, fr. *em-* ¹en- + *brouiller* to mix, confuse — more at BROIL (mix)] **1 a :** to cause (as a person or affairs) to fall into disorder or confusion ⟨political complications which ~*ed* the whole policy of the great oceanic expeditions —C.P.Fitzgerald⟩ **:** CONFUSE, DISORDER, DISTRACT ⟨her emotions were forever ~*ing* her intellect —V.L.Parrington⟩ ⟨the city was ~*ed* in gigantic traffic bottlenecks —*New Yorker*⟩ **b :** to throw into physical uproar or disorder ⟨the wind ~*ing* the sea⟩ **2 :** to involve esp. in conflict or with a problem, adversaries, or the law ⟨~*ed* in ideological arguments⟩ ⟨found himself ~*ed* with the group investigating the union's finances⟩ ⟨an opinionated and litigious lady who . . . was forever ~*ed* with landlords, travel agencies, and shops —Louis Auchincloss⟩ ⟨often ~*ed* in federal criminal proceedings⟩ ⟨his drinking often ~*s* him with the law⟩

²**embroil** \"\ *n* -s *archaic* **:** EMBROILMENT

em·broil·er \-ȯilə(r)\ *n* **:** one that embroils; *esp* **:** TROUBLEMAKER

em·broil·ment \-ȯi(ə)lmənt\ *n* -s [F *embrouillement*, fr. *embrouiller* + *-ment*] **1 :** the act of embroiling or state of being embroiled; *often* **:** UPROAR, COMMOTION, QUARREL ⟨an ~ that led to a crowded police court the next morning⟩ **2 :** ENTANGLEMENT, PERPLEXITY, INVOLVEMENT ⟨trying to avoid ~ in continental quarrels⟩

em·brown \əm'braůn, em-\ *vt* [¹*en-* + *brown* (adj.)] **1 :** DARKEN ⟨shade ~*ing* a glen⟩ **2 :** to cause to turn brown ⟨drought ~*ed* the leaves⟩

embrue *var of* IMBRUE

embrute *var of* IMBRUTE

embry- *or* **embryo-** *comb form* [LL, fr. Gk, fr. *embryon*] **:** embryo ⟨*embry*ectomy⟩ ⟨*embryo*logy⟩

em·bryo \'embrē,ō\ *n* -s *often attrib* [ML *embryon-, embryo*, modif. of Gk *embryon*, fr. (assumed) Gk *embryein* to swell inside, fr. Gk *em-* ²en- + *bryein* to swell — more at SAUERKRAUT] **1 a** *archaic* **:** a human or other animal offspring at any stage of development prior to birth or hatching as a young individual fundamentally similar to the adult **b :** an animal organism in the early stages of growth and differentiation that are characterized by cleavage, the laying down of fundamental tissues, and the formation of primitive organs and organ systems and that in higher forms (as mammals) merge insensibly into fetal stages but in lower forms are terminated by commencement of larval life, often with a form markedly different from that of the adult — compare FETUS, ZYGOTE **c :** the developing human individual from the time of implantation to the end of the eighth week after conception — compare FETUS, OVUM **2 :** the young sporophyte of a seed plant, resulting from union of the egg and one of the two sperm nuclei, sometimes consisting of only a few cells (as in orchids) but usu. comprising a rudimentary plant with plumule, radicle, and cotyledons, and typically embedded in endosperm that provides nutriment for the developing plant upon germination — called also *germ* **3 :** something as yet undeveloped and lacking final form and differentiation **:** a conception precedent to realization; *often* **:** the state characteristic of such a thing **:** a state of incipience — used esp. in the phrase *in embryo*

em·bryo·car·dia \,embrēō'kärdēə\ *n* [NL, fr. *embry-* + *-cardia*] **:** a symptom of heart disease in which the heart sounds resemble those of the fetal heart

em·bryo·gen·e·sis \-ō'jenəsəs\ *n* [NL, fr. *embry-* + L *genesis*] **:** EMBRYOGENY

em·bryo·gen·ic \;==;jenik\ *also* **em·bry·o·ge·net·ic** \;==-(,)=jə;ned·ik\ *adj* **:** of, relating to, or involved in embryogeny

em·bry·og·e·ny \,embrē'äjənē\ *n* -ES [*embry-* + *-geny*] **:** the formation and development of the embryo whether direct or indirect — compare HETEROBLASTIC, HOMOBLASTIC

em·bry·oid \'embrē,ȯid\ *adj* [ISV *embry-* + *-oid*] **:** resembling an embryo

em·bry·o·log·ic \;embrēə;läjik, -jēk\ *or* **em·bry·o·log·i·cal** \-jəkəl, -jēk-\ *adj* **:** of, relating to, used in, or involving the methods of embryology ⟨~ development⟩ ⟨~ apparatus⟩ ⟨an ~ approach to a problem⟩ — **em·bry·o·log·i·cal·ly** \-jək(ə)lē, -jēk-, -li\ *adv*

em·bry·ol·o·gist \,embrē'äləjəst\ *n* -s **:** a specialist in embryology

em·bry·ol·o·gy \-jē, -ji\ *n* -ES [F *embryologie*, fr. *embry-* + *-logie* -logy] **1 :** a branch of biology that relates to embryogeny in animals and plants **:** the study of the development of the individual from the egg to birth or hatching ⟨a student of ~⟩ — compare ONTOGENY **2 :** the features and phenomena exhibited in the formation and development of an embryo ⟨certain peculiarities of the ~ of the brook trout⟩ **3 :** a treatise on embryology

em·bry·o·ma \,embrē'ōmə\ *n, pl* **embryomas** \-məz\ *or* **embryoma·ta** \-məd·ə\ [NL, fr. *embry-* + *-oma*] **:** a tumor derived from embryonic structures **:** TERATOMA

em·bry·on \'embrē,än\ *n* -s [ML *embryon-, embryo* — more at EMBRYO] **:** EMBRYO — not used technically

embryon- *or* **embryoni-** *comb form* [ML *embryon-, embryo*] **:** embryo ⟨*embryon*ic⟩ ⟨*embryoni*form⟩

em·bry·o·nal \'embrēən°l\ *adj* **:** EMBRYONIC 1 — **em·bry·o·nal·ly** \-°lē\ *adv*

em·bry·o·nary \-,nerē\ *adj* [*embryon-* + *-ary*] **:** EMBRYONIC

em·bry·o·nate \-,nāt\ *vi* -ED/-ING/-S [*embryon-* + *-ate*] *of an egg or zygote* **:** to produce or differentiate into an embryo

em·bry·o·nat·ed \-ād·əd\ *also* **em·bry·o·nate** \-āt\ *adj* [*embryon* + *-ated, -ate*] **:** having an embryo; *esp* **:** far-enough developed to have a perceptible living embryo ⟨growing viruses on ~ hen's eggs⟩

em·bry·o·na·tion \,embrēə'nāshən\ *n* -s **:** the formation of an embryo within an egg

em·bry·on·ic \;embrē;änik, -nēk\ *adj* [*embryon-* + *-ic*] **1 :** of or relating to an embryo **2 :** incipient and rudimentary — **em·bry·on·i·cal·ly** \-nək(ə)lē, -nēk-, -li\ *adv*

embryonic disk *n* **1 a :** BLASTODISC **b :** BLASTODERM **2** *or* **embryonic shield :** the part of the inner cell mass of a blastocyst from which the embryo of a placental mammal develops

embryonic knob *n* **:** INNER CELL MASS

embryonic layer *n* **:** GERM LAYER

embryonic membrane *n* **:** a structure that derives from the fertilized ovum but does not form a part of the embryo, including true membranes (as the amnion and chorion) and other structures (as the placenta and umbilical cord) not usu. considered membranes

embryonic vesicle *n* **:** EGG 1b

em·bry·o·ny \'embrēənē, em'brīə-\ *n* -ES [*embryon-* + *-y*] **:** the condition of having or the production of an embryo — compare MONEMBRYONY, POLYEMBRYONY

em·bry·op·a·thy \,embrē'äpəthē\ *n* -ES [*embry-* + *-pathy*] **:** a congenital but usu. not hereditary malformation

em·bry·o·phore \'embrēə,fō(ə)r\ *n* -s [*embry-* + *-phore*] **:** the outer cellular covering of the hexacanth embryo of a tapeworm; *broadly* **:** the covering and included embryo

em·bry·oph·y·ta \,embrē'äfəd·ə\ *n pl, cap* [NL, fr. *embry-* + *-phyta*] *in some classifications* **:** a primary division or subkingdom of Plantae that comprises all plants producing an embryo and developing vascular tissues and includes all plants except the Myxophyta and Thallophyta — **em·bry·o·phyte** \'embrēə,fīt\ *n* -s

embryos *pl of* EMBRYO
embryo sac *n* **:** the female gametophyte of a seed plant consisting of a thin-walled sac within the nucellus that typically develops from a single functional megaspore and contains several meiotically reduced nuclei which lack separating cell walls and which include the egg nucleus and others that give rise to endosperm on fertilization
em·bry·ot·ic \ˌembrēˈädˌik\ *adj* [*embryo* + *-tic* (as in *patriotic*)] **:** EMBRYONIC 2
em·bry·o·tome \ˈembrēəˌtōm\ *n* -S [*embry-* + *-tome*] **:** an instrument used in embryotomy
em·bry·ot·o·my \ˌembrēˈädəmē\ *n* -ES [F *embryotomie*, fr. *embry-* + *-tomie* -tomy] **1 :** mutilation of a fetus for removal from the uterus when natural delivery is impossible **2 :** dissection of embryos for examination
em·bry·o·troph \ˈembrēəˌträf, -rōf\ *or* **em·bry·o·trophe** \-rōf\ *n* -S [F *embryotrophe*, fr. *embry-* + *-trophe* (fr. Gk *trophos* one that feeds or rears, fr. *trephein* to nourish) — more at ATROPHY] **:** the pabulum of uterine tissue fluids and cellular debris that nourishes the embryo of a placental mammal prior to the establishment of the placental circulation — **em·bry·ot·ro·phy** \ˌembrēˈä·trəfē\ *n* -ES
em·bry·ous \ˈembrēəs\ *adj* [*embry-* + *-ous*] **:** EMBRYONIC
embue *var of* IMBUE
embuia *var of* IMBUIA
em·bus \əm, em+\ *vi* [¹*en-* + *bus* (n.)] **:** to get aboard a bus
em·bus·qué \ˌäm(ˌ)büˈskā, äⁿbüskā\ *n* -S [F, fr. past part. of (*s'*)*embusquer* to lie in ambush, shirk, fr. OF *embuschier* to place in ambush — more at AMBUSH] **:** a person seeking to avoid military service (as by working in a government office) **:** SHIRKER, SLACKER
¹**em·cee** \(ˈ)emˈsē\ *n* -S [¹*em* + *cee* (letter); fr. the initials *M.C.*] **:** MASTER OF CEREMONIES; *esp* **:** a person who conducts a program (as on television) introducing numbers, introducing and interviewing speakers, and usu. providing the continuity
²**emcee** \"\ *vb* **emceed; emceed; emceeing; emcees** *vt* **:** to act as master of ceremonies of ⟨~*ing* a nightly show⟩ ~ *vi* **:** to act as master of ceremonies ⟨a leading comedian will ~⟩
em dash *n* [¹*em*] **:** a dash that is one em wide
emden *usu cap, var of* EMBDEN
eme \ˈēm\ *n* -S [ME, fr. OE *ēam* — more at UNCLE] **1** *chiefly Scot* **:** UNCLE **2** *chiefly Scot* **:** FRIEND
-eme \ˌēm\ *n suffix* -S [F *-ème* thing, unit (in *phonème* speech sound), fr. Gk *-ēmat-*, *-ēma* (in *phōnēmat-*, *phōnēma* utterance), fr. *-ē-* (stem vowel of *phōnein* to sound) + *-mat-*, *-ma* (noun suffix) — more at -MENT] **:** significantly distinctive unit of structure of a (specified) kind in a language or dialect ⟨morph*eme*⟩ ⟨ton*eme*⟩ — compare ALLO-
emeer *var of* EMIR
emend \ēˈmend, əˈ-\ *vt* -ED/-ING/-S [ME *emenden*, fr. L *emendare* — more at AMEND] **1** *archaic* **:** to free from faults or defects **:** BETTER, IMPROVE **2 a :** to correct (as a literary work) usu. by textual alterations ⟨will ~ a chapter here or a verse there —*London Calling*⟩ **b :** to alter (as a literary work) to serve a purpose different from the original ⟨the Roman Paul borrowed Plato's image and ~*ed* it to suit his needs —Henry Silverstein⟩ **syn** see CORRECT
emend·able \-dəbəl\ *adj* **:** capable of being emended **:** RECTIFIABLE; *esp, of offenses against early English law* **:** such as may be forgiven in return for a payment of money
emen·dan·dum \(ˌ)ēˌmenˈdandəm, ˌēmən-, ˌeˌmen-, ˌemən-, əˌmen-\ *n, pl* **emendan·da** \-də\ [L, neut. of *emendandus*, gerundive of *emendare*] **:** CORRIGENDUM
emen·date \ˈēmənˌdāt, ˈēmən-, ˈeˌmen-, ˈemən-, ēˈmen-, əˈmen-, *usu* -ād+V\ *vt* -ED/-ING/-S [L *emendatus*, past part. of *emendare*] **:** EMEND 2a
emen·da·tion \(ˌ)ēˌmenˈdāshən, ˌēmən-, ˌeˌmen-, ˌemən-, əˌmen-\ *n* -S [ME *emendacioun*, fr. L *emendation-*, *emendatio*, fr. *emendatus* + *-ion-*, *-io* -ion] **1 :** the act of emending **:** CORRECTION **2 a :** corrections or alterations made in the emending (as of a text) ⟨a manuscript full of ~*s*⟩ **b :** the word or the matter substituted for incorrect or unsuitable matter in an emended work ⟨I have retained all such ~*s* —Bernard De Voto⟩ **3** *obs* **:** COMPENSATION **4 a :** an alteration of the spelling of a taxonomic name ⟨*Agchylostoma* is an invalid ~ of *Ancylostoma*⟩ **b :** a redefinition of a taxon that alters the composition of that taxon ⟨many taxonomists reject any ~ of Compositae that puts the thistles in a separate family⟩
emen·da·tor *pronunc at* EMENDATE + ə(r)\ *n* -S [L, fr. *emendatus* + *-or*] **:** one that emends
emen·da·to·ry \ēˈmendəˌtōrē, əˈ-, -ōr-, -ri\ *adj* [LL *emendatorius*, fr. *emendatus* + *-orius* -ory] **:** of or relating to emendation **:** CORRECTIVE
emer *abbr* **1** emergency **2** emeritus
¹**em·er·ald** \ˈem(ə)rəld\ *n* -S [ME *emeraude*, *emerallde*, fr. MF *esmeragde*, *esmeraude*, *esmeralde*, fr. (assumed) VL *smaragda*, *smaralda*, fr. L *smaragdus*, fr. Gk *smaragdos*, *maragdos*, prob. of Sem origin; akin to Heb *bāreqet* emerald] **1 a :** a variety of beryl distinguished by a rich green color caused by the presence of chromium and highly prized as a gemstone **b :** any of various green gemstones (as synthetic corundum or demantoid) — used chiefly in combination **2** *or* **emerald green a :** a brilliant green that is the color of emerald green pigment — called also *Mitis green, Vienna green* **b** *of textiles* **:** a strong yellowish green approximating the color of the emerald — called also *emeraude* **c :** a variable color averaging a strong bluish green **3** *Brit* **:** MINIONETTE **4 :** any of various tropical American hummingbirds more or less marked with emerald green
²**emerald** \"\ *adj* **1 :** brightly or richly green ⟨the ~ fields of spring⟩; *sometimes* **:** of the color emerald ⟨an ~ scarf⟩ **2** *of a mineral* **:** gemmy and richly green in color ⟨~ spodumene⟩ **3** *of a jewelry setting* **:** square or rectangular — compare EMERALD CUT
emerald copper *n* **:** DIOPTASE
emerald cuckoo *n* **1 :** a small brilliant green African cuckoo (*Chrysococcyx smaragdineus*) with yellow breast **2 :** a small bright green cuckoo (*Chrysococcyx maculatus*) found from the Himalayas to southern China
emerald cut *n* **:** a step cut in which the contour of the gem is square or rectangular — see CUT illustration
emerald feather *n* **:** a commonly cultivated ornamental asparagus (*Asparagus sprengeri*) with long slender wiry or drooping stems bearing flat slender pointed cladophylls, tiny stellate pink blossoms in axillary inflorescences, and bright red berries
emerald green *n* **1 a :** a clear bright green resembling that of the emerald **b :** EMERALD 2 **2 a :** Paris green for use as a pigment **b :** GUIGNET'S GREEN **c :** BRILLIANT GREEN
¹**em·er·al·dine** \-lˌdēn, -dīn\ *adj* [¹*emerald* + *-ine*] **:** EMERALD 1
²**em·er·al·dine** \-dēn\ *n* -S **:** a blue basic compound yielding bottle-green salts with acids that is formed as an intermediate in the production of aniline black
emerald tint *n* **:** a very pale green that is yellower and lighter than tourmaline, bluer, lighter, and stronger than celadon tint, and yellower, lighter, and slightly stronger than microcline green
emerald whip snake *n* **:** WHIP SNAKE a
em·er·ant \ˈem(ə)rənt\ *dial var of* EMERALD
em·er·aude \ˈeməˌrōd\ *or* **emeraude green** *n* -S [F *émeraude* emerald, fr. OF *esmeragde*, *esmeraude*, *esmeralde* — more at EMERALD] **1 :** EMERALD 2b **2 :** VIRIDIAN 2
emerge \ēˈmərj, əˈ-, -mōj, -məij\ *vi* -ED/-ING/-S [L *emergere*, fr. *e-* + *mergere* to dip, plunge — more at MERGE] **1 :** to rise from or as if from an enveloping fluid **:** come out into view ⟨when land first *emerged* from the sea⟩ ⟨the sun ~*s* from eclipse⟩ ⟨rays *emerging* from a prism⟩ ⟨a road *emerging* from the park⟩ **2 :** to become revealed **:** become manifest **:** become known ⟨a new problem then *emerged*⟩ ⟨it ~*s* that her past behavior was far from irreproachable⟩ ⟨after long study there *emerged* an overall picture of conditions that was extremely disheartening⟩ **3 :** to come forth or rise from an inferior, obscure, or unfortunate position or condition into one of superiority, prominence, or success ⟨as the common people *emerged* from illiteracy⟩ ⟨someone must ~ as a leader⟩ ⟨*emerged* the unchallenged head of the state⟩ ⟨the youngest runner *emerged* the victor⟩ **4 a :** to arise by emergent evolution **b :** to come into being through evolution ⟨certain new viruses appear to have *emerged* in recent years⟩ ⟨there is no certainty as to the ancestors from which vertebrates *emerged*⟩
emer·gence \-jən(t)s\ *n* -S [*emerge* + *-ence*] **1 :** the act or an instance of emerging **:** a coming forth or rising into view ⟨slow ~ from barbarism⟩ ⟨the cold weather delayed the ~ of the apple blossoms⟩: as **a :** the appearance of an emergent or the process of emerging — compare EMERGENT EVOLUTION **b :** the recovering of consciousness (as after anesthesia) **c** *often cap* **:** the issuing forth from an underworld abode of the original ancestors of the human race — used in various No. American Indian mythologies **2** [ML *emergentia*] *archaic* **a :** EMERGENCY **b :** urgent need **3 :** any of various outgrowths (as the prickle of a rose) from superficial layers of plant tissue usu. from both the epidermis and immediately underlying layers — compare ENATION, TRICHOME
emer·gen·cy \-nsē, -si\ *n* -ES *often attrib* [ML *emergentia*, fr. L *emergent-*, *emergens*, (pres. part. of *emergere*) + *-ia* -y] **1 :** an unforeseen combination of circumstances or the resulting state that calls for immediate action ⟨they were far from help when the ~ overtook them⟩: as **a :** a pressing need **:** EXIGENCY ⟨a state of ~ existed during which any help was acceptable⟩ **b :** a sudden bodily alteration such as is likely to require immediate medical attention (as a ruptured appendix or surgical shock) **c :** a usu. distressing event or condition that can often be anticipated or prepared for but seldom exactly foreseen ⟨wait until the ~ is over, prices will go down then⟩ ⟨an ~ water supply⟩ ⟨~ docking facilities⟩ ⟨~ crews working to clear the roads⟩ **2** [*emerge* + *-ency*] *archaic* **:** the act or an instance of emerging **:** EMERGENCE 1 **3 :** the theory of emergent evolution **syn** see JUNCTURE
emergency barrage *n* **:** a standing barrage for which an artillery battery has prepared data and to which it can shift on call
emergency brake *n* **:** a hand brake (as on an automobile) that can be set so that it continues to hold in the driver's absence and is commonly used as a parking brake — compare SERVICE BRAKE
emergency landing field *n* **:** a surface either of water or land that is adapted but not equipped for the landing and taking off of aircraft
emergency money *n* **:** NECESSITY MONEY
emergency power *n* **:** power granted to or used or taken by a public authority to meet the exigencies of a particular emergency (as of war or disaster) whether within or outside a constitutional frame of reference
¹**emer·gent** \-nt\ *adj* [ME, fr. L *emergent-*, *emergens*, pres. part. of *emergere* to emerge — more at EMERGE] **1 :** emerging out of a fluid or something that covers or conceals **:** issuing forth **:** rising into notice ⟨like the lovely goddess ~ from the waves⟩ ⟨~ coastal islands⟩ ⟨the ~ vegetation along the shore⟩ **2 :** suddenly appearing **:** arising unexpectedly; *often* **:** calling for prompt action **:** URGENT ⟨~ danger⟩ ⟨an ~ state in a hemophiliac⟩ **3 :** arising as a natural or logical consequence or outcome ⟨political issues ~ from war⟩ **4 :** appearing as or involving the appearance of something novel in a process of evolution — compare EMERGENT EVOLUTION — **emer·gent·ly** *adv*
²**emergent** \"\ *n* -S **1** *obs* **:** EMERGENCY **2 :** an emergent quality, character, or individual **3 :** a plant (as a tall tree with its crown above the level of the forest) that emerges from its substrate; *esp* **:** any of various plants (as a bulrush) rooted in shallow water and having most of the vegetative growth above water
emergent evolution *n* **:** evolution conceived as characterized by the appearance at different levels of wholly new and unpredictable characters or qualities (as life and consciousness) through a rearrangement of preexistent entities — compare CREATIVE EVOLUTION
emer·gent·ist \-ntəst\ *n* -S **:** an adherent of the theory of emergent evolution
emer·gent·ness *n* -ES **:** the quality or state of being emergent
emerges *pres 3d sing of* EMERGE
emerging *pres part of* EMERGE
emeried *past of* EMERY
emeries *pl of* EMERY, *pres 3d sing of* EMERY
emeril *obs var of* EMERY
emer·il·lon \āˈmerəˌlän, -əˌyäⁿ\ *n, pl* **emerillon** *or* **emerillons** *usu cap* **1 a :** a Tupian people living along the north Brazilian coast from the mouth of the Amazon into French Guiana **b :** a member of such people **2 :** the language of the Emerillon people
¹**emer·i·ta** \əˈmerəd·ə, ēˈ-, -rətə\ *n, cap* [NL, fr. L, fem. of *emeritus*] **:** a genus of anomuran decapod crustaceans (suborder Reptantia) widely distributed along sandy shores of both coasts of No. America and the western coast of So. America — see BAIT BUG
²**emerita** \"\ *adj* [L, fem. of *emeritus*] **:** EMERITUS — used only of the female and esp. in titles ⟨Professor *Emerita* Mary Smith⟩
emer·it·ed \-d·əd, -təd\ *adj* [L *emeritus* + E *-ed*] *archaic* **:** retired from a service or occupation
¹**emer·i·tus** \əˈmerəd·əs, ēˈ-, -rətəs\ *adj* [L, past part. of *emerēre* to obtain by service, to complete one's term, fr. *e-* + *merēre* to earn, serve one's time — more at MERIT] **1 :** holding after retirement (as from professional or academic office) an honorary title corresponding to that held last during active service ⟨he is ~ professor of English at a women's college⟩ ⟨a red-faced ~ cook⟩ **2 :** retired from an office or position esp. after gaining public or professional recognition ⟨an ~ dramatic critic —*N. Y. Times Book Rev.*⟩ — often used postpositively ⟨professor ~⟩ and sometimes converted to *emeriti* after a plural substantive ⟨professors *emeriti*⟩
²**emeritus** \"\ *n, pl* **emeri·ti** \-rəˌtī, -ˌtē\ **:** one retired from professional life but permitted to hold the rank of his last office as an honorary title ⟨joining the ranks of the *emeriti* —W.W.Sweet⟩
em·er·ize \ˈeməˌrīz\ *vt* -ED/-ING/-S [¹*emery* + *-ize*] **:** to nap (fabric) with emery rollers for a surface resembling suede
em·er·od \ˈeməˌräd\ *n* -S [ME *emeroidea*, *emerodes*, pl., fr. MF *emorroides*, fr. L *haemorrhoidae* — more at HEMORRHOID] *archaic* **:** HEMORRHOID
emer·sal \(ˈ)ēˈmərsəl, əˈm-\ *adj* [L *emersus* (past part. of *emergere* to emerge) + E *-al* — more at EMERGE] **:** rising toward or floating at the surface of water — used esp. of aquatic plants or animals or their products ⟨the ~ eggs of many marine fishes⟩; contrasted with *demersal*
emersed \ēˈmərst\ *adj* [L *emersus* + E *-ed*] **:** standing out of or rising above a surface (as of a fluid) ⟨an aquatic plant with flower stalk ~⟩
emer·sion \ēˈmər|zhən, -mə̄|, -məi| *also* |sh-\ *n* -S [L *emersus* + E *-ion*] **1** *archaic* **:** an act of emerging **:** EMERGENCE **2 :** the reappearance of a celestial body after eclipse or occultation or a conjunction with the sun
em·er·so·nian \ˌemə(r)ˈsōnēən, -ōnyən\ *adj, usu cap* [Ralph W. *Emerson* †1882 Am. writer + E *-ian*] **:** like or relating to Ralph Waldo Emerson, his writings, or his theories — see TRANSCENDENTALISM 1b — **em·er·so·nian·ism** \-ēəˌnizəm, -yəˌ-\ *n* -S *usu cap*
¹**em·ery** \ˈem(ə)rē, -ri\ *n* -ES *often attrib* [ME, fr. MF *emeri*, fr. OIt *smiriglio*, fr. ML *smiriglum*, fr. Gk *smyrid-*, *smyris* powdered emery — more at SMEAR] **1 :** a common dark granular corundum that contains varying amounts of magnetite or hematite and that on account of its great hardness is used in the form of powder, grains, or larger masses for grinding and polishing **2 a :** a natural abrasive used in modern gem grinding that is composed of an impure mixture of corundum and magnetite **b :** a hard abrasive powder — not used technically **3** *or* **emery bag :** a small cloth bag filled with powdered emery and used for polishing and sharpening needles **4** *or* **emery board :** a nail file made of cardboard covered with powdered emery
²**emery** \"\ *vt* -ED/-ING/-ES **1 :** to cover with emery (as in the preparation of abrasive papers) **2 :** to roughen or smooth by rubbing with emery
emery ball *n* **:** a baseball illegally roughened by powdered emery or by a piece of emery cloth or emery paper
emery cake *n* **:** powdered emery or a synthetic substitute caked in a binding material
emery stone *n* **1 :** a mixture of powdered emery and a suitable binder that can be molded into grinding wheels and other devices **2 :** WHETSTONE
emery wheel *n* **:** a wheel made of consolidated emery powder or having a surface of emery and used esp. for abrading, grinding, or polishing
emes *pl of* EME
-emes *pl of* -EME
em·e·sa \ˈeməsə\ [NL, fr. *Emesa* (now Homs), ancient city in Syria, fr. L, fr. Gk] *syn of* PLOIARIA
eme·sal \ˌeməˈsäl\ *n, usu cap* [Sumerian] **:** a form or dialect of Sumerian in which many religious texts were written
em·e·sis \ˈeməsəs\ *n, pl* **eme·ses** \-əˌsēz\ [NL, fr. Gk, fr. *emein* + *-sis*] **:** VOMITING
¹**emet·ic** \əˈmed·ik, ēˈ-, -et|, |ēk\ *n* -S [L *emetica*, fr. Gk *emetikē*, fr. fem. of *emetikos*] **:** an agent that induces vomiting
²**emetic** \"\ *also* **emet·i·cal** \|əkəl, |ēk-\ *adj* [LL *emeticus*, fr. Gk *emetikos*, fr. *emetos* vomiting (fr. *emein* to vomit) + *-ikos* -ic, -ical — more at VOMIT] **:** inducing to vomit — **emet·i·cal·ly** \|ək(ə)lē, |ēk-, -li\ *adv*
emetic holly *n* **:** a yaupon (*Ilex vomitoria*)
emetic mushroom *n* **:** a mushroom (*Russula emetica*) with a deep-red or rarely white pileus that grows usu. in the woods and is violently emetic and poisonous
emetic root *n* **:** FLOWERING SPURGE
emetic weed *n* **:** INDIAN TOBACCO
em·e·tine \ˈeməˌtēn, -ətᵊn\ *n* -S [F *émétine*, fr. *émétique* emetic (fr. L *emetica*) + *-ine*] **:** an amorphous alkaloid $C_{29}H_{40}N_2O_4$ extracted from ipecac root and used as an emetic, expectorant, and amebicide
emeu *archaic var of* EMU
émeute \āmœ̄t\ *n* -S [F, fr. OF *esmuete* act of starting up, motion, fr. fem. of *esmuet*, past part. of *esmovoir* to start out, incite — more at EMOTION] **:** an outbreak of disorder or violence; *esp* **:** a popular uprising
EMF *abbr, often not cap* **:** electromotive force
em·gal·la \emˈgalə\ *n* -S [native name in Africa] **:** the southern African wart hog
-e·mia *or* **-ae·mia** \ˈēmēə, *esp Brit* ˈēmyə\ *also* **-hemia** *or* **-haemia** *n comb form* -S [NL *-emia*, *-aemia*, fr. Gk *-aimia*, fr. *haima* blood + *-ia* -y — more at HEM-] **1 :** condition of having (such) blood ⟨leuk*emia*⟩ ⟨septic*emia*⟩ **2 :** condition of having (a specified thing) in the blood ⟨chol*emia*⟩ ⟨ur*emia*⟩
¹**em·i·grant** \ˈeməgrənt, -mēg- *sometimes* -ˌgrant *or* -ˌgraa(ə)nt\ *n* -S [L *emigrant-*, *emigrans*, pres. part. of *emigrare* to depart, emigrate, fr. *e-* + *migrare* to depart, migrate — more at MIGRATE] **1 :** a person who leaves a country or region to establish permanent residence elsewhere; *esp* **:** a pioneer moving esp. during the 19th century from the settled lands of the eastern U.S. to unsettled lands to the west — compare IMMIGRANT **2 :** a plant or animal that is a migrant
²**emigrant** \"\ *adj* [L *emigrant-*, *emigrans*] **1 :** departing from a country or region to settle permanently elsewhere **2 :** of, relating to, concerned with, or for the use of emigrants ⟨~ cars⟩ ⟨~ agents⟩
em·i·grate \ˈeməˌgrāt, *usu* -ād+V\ *vb* -ED/-ING/-S [L *emigratus*, past part. of *emigrare*] *vi* **:** to leave a place of abode (as a country) for life or residence elsewhere **:** be or behave as an emigrant — usu. used with *from* or *to* ⟨*emigrated* to Texas⟩ ⟨*emigrated* from England⟩ ~ *vt* **:** to cause, force, or help to emigrate
em·i·gra·tion \ˌeməˈgrāshən\ *n* -S [LL *emigration-*, *emigratio*, fr. L *emigratus* + *-ion-*, *-io* -ion] **1 :** an act or instance of emigrating **:** departure from a place of abode, natural home, or country for life or residence elsewhere ⟨several separate Oregon ~*s*⟩ ⟨considered the advantage of ~⟩ **2 :** a body of emigrants ⟨the ~ set out in early spring⟩ **3 :** DIAPEDESIS 1
em·i·gra·tion·al \ˌ|;|grāshənᵊl, -shnəl\ *adj* **:** concerned with emigration ⟨~ agencies⟩
em·i·gra·to·ry \ˈeməgrəˌtōrē, -mēg-, -ōr-, -ri\ *adj* **:** relating to or engaged in emigration; *usu* **:** MIGRATORY
émi·gré *or* **emi·gré** *also* **emi·gre** \ˌeməˈgrā, ˌām-, ˌmēˈ-\ *or* **emi·gree** \", ˌeməˈgrē\ *n* -S *often attrib* [F *émigré* (masc.) & *émigrée* (fem.), fr. past part. of *émigrer* to emigrate, fr. L *emigrare*] **:** EMIGRANT; *esp* **:** a person forced to emigrate (as from France or Russia during their revolutions or from Germany under the Nazis) by political or other circumstances beyond his control
emi·lia \əˈmēlyə, ēˈ-, -lēə *also* -mil-\ *n, cap* [NL, prob. fr. the name *Emilia*] **:** a genus of tropical Asiatic and African herbs (family Compositae) resembling *Senecio* but having a simple involucre and fruits with fine acute angles and being widely naturalized in So. America — see TASSEL FLOWER
emim \ˈēˌmim\ *n pl, usu cap* [Heb *ēmīm*, lit., terrible ones] **:** Rephaim orig. inhabiting Moab ⟨like the Anakim they are known as Rephaim, but the Moabites call them *Emim* —Deut 2:11 (RSV)⟩
em·i·nence \ˈemənən(t)s\ *n* -S [ME, fr. MF, fr. L *eminentia*, fr. *eminent-*, *eminens* + *-ia* -y] **1 :** a condition or station of prominence or superiority by reason of rank or office or of personal attainments ⟨her sons have attained the pinnacle of literary ~⟩ ⟨sent her climbing to ~ as an embezzler —R.T. Moriarty⟩ ⟨New York owes its ~ primarily to its natural advantages —Robert Moses⟩ ⟨the ~ of the presidency⟩ **2** *obs* **a :** superiority or superior quality; *esp* **:** UPPER HAND **b :** consideration due an eminent person **:** HOMAGE **3 :** something eminent, outstanding, or lofty: as **a :** a protuberance or projection esp. on a bone **b :** a person of high rank or attainments ⟨the theatrical ~*s* of New York⟩ ⟨a gathering of literary ~*s*⟩ — used as a title or in a mode of address usu. for a cardinal and then usu. cap **c :** a natural elevation **:** a piece of high ground ⟨built his home on an ~ overlooking the city⟩ ⟨reached the ~ of the cliff⟩ **4 :** a dark purple that is bluer, stronger, and slightly lighter than average prune, redder and deeper than mulberry (sense 2a), redder and stronger than mulberry purple, and stronger than plum (sense 6b)
émi·nence grise \āmēnäⁿsəgrēz\ *n, pl* **éminences grises** \"\ [F, lit., gray eminence, nickname of Père Joseph (François Le Clerc du Tremblay) †1638 French monk and diplomat who was confidant of Cardinal Richelieu †1642 Fr. statesman and cardinal who was styled *Éminence Rouge* red eminence; fr. the colors of their respective habits] **:** a confidential agent; *esp* **:** one exercising unsuspected or unofficial power
em·i·nen·cy \ˈemənənsē, -si\ *n* -ES [L *eminentia*] **1 :** *obs* **:** EMINENCE **2 a :** a point in which one excels **:** FORTE ⟨his *eminencies* were kindness and understanding⟩ **b :** outstanding quality **:** PROMINENCE ⟨men of scientific ~⟩
em·i·nent \-nənt\ *adj* [ME, fr. MF or L; MF, fr. L *eminent-*, *eminens*, pres. part. of *eminēre* to stand out, be prominent, fr. *e-* + *-minēre* (akin to L *mont-*, *mons* mountain) — more at MOUNT] **1 :** standing out so as to be readily perceived or noted **:** CONSPICUOUS, EVIDENT, NOTEWORTHY ⟨his ~ services to the party⟩ ⟨a man of ~ fairness⟩ ⟨churches of ~ beauty⟩ **2 :** PROJECTING, PROTRUDING ⟨a house standing ~ near the top of a hill⟩; *sometimes* **:** LOFTY, TOWERING **3 :** exhibiting eminence esp. in standing above others in some quality or position (as birth, office, professional attainment, talent, or virtue) **:** high in public estimation **:** PROMINENT, OUTSTANDING ⟨the ~ conductor of the civic orchestra⟩ ⟨a man ~ in scholarship⟩ ⟨several of our most ~ military authorities⟩ **4** *obs* **:** IMPORTANT, VALUABLE **5** *of a geologic cleavage* **:** capable of complete or perfect division (as into layers)
eminent domain *n* **1 :** superior dominion exerted by a sovereign state over all property within its boundaries that authorizes it to appropriate all or any part thereof to a necessary public use, reasonable compensation being made **2 :** a right wider than angary sometimes considered to exist in international law for one nation to appropriate the territory or property of another as a necessary measure of self-protection
em·i·nen·ter \ˌeməˈnentə(r), ˌāməˈnen,te(ə)r\ *adv* [LL, adv. fr. *eminent-*, *eminens*] **:** EMINENTLY 3
em·i·nen·tia \ˌeməˈnench(ē)ə\ *n* -S [NL, fr. L] **:** EMINENCE 3a
emi·nen·tis·si·mo \ˌeməˌnenˈtisəˌmō, ˌām-, -tēs-\ *n* -S [It, fr. superl. (used as a title for cardinals) of *eminente* eminent, fr. L *eminent-*, *eminens*] **:** a person of superlative eminence
em·i·nent·ly \ˈemənəntlē, -li\ *adv* [ME, fr. *eminent* + *-ly*] **1** *obs* **:** in a high or conspicuous position **:** so as to be readily observed **2 :** to a high degree **:** NOTABLY, EXTREMELY, VERY ⟨an ~ competent workman⟩ ⟨~ practical studies⟩ ⟨did an ~ satisfactory job⟩ ⟨an ~ pleasing state of affairs⟩; *sometimes* **:** WHOLLY, COMPLETELY ⟨a man ~ sane and competent⟩ **3** *philos* **:** in a manner reflecting an overplus of reality or of power

emi·nen·to \ˌeməˈnen·ˌtō\ *n* -s [modif. of It *eminente*] **:** an eminent person

e minor *n, usu cap E* **:** the minor musical key having a signature of one sharp

emir *or* **amir** *also* **ameer** *or* **emeer** \əˈmi(ə)r, (ˈ)āˈm-\ *n* -s [Ar *amīr* commander] **:** a nobleman, independent chieftain, or native ruler esp. in Arabia and Africa — often used as a title ⟨the *Emir* of Kano attended the coronation of Elizabeth II⟩

emir·ate *or* **amir·ate** *also* **ameer·ate** *or* **emeer·ate** \əˈmirət, āˈm-, -ˌrāt\ *n* -s **:** the state or jurisdiction of an emir

em·is·sar·i·um \ˌeməˈsa(a)rēəm\ *n, pl* **emissar·ia** \-ēə\ [L, fr. *emissus* (past part. of *emittere* to send out) + *-arium* — more at EMIT] **:** a subterranean channel used by the ancient Romans for the drainage of a lake lacking a natural outlet

[1]**em·is·sary** \ˈeməˌserē, -ri\ *n* -ES [L *emissarius*, fr. *emissus* + *-arius* -ary] **1 a :** an agent or representative usu. empowered to act more or less independently (as in collecting or conveying information or in negotiating) ⟨sent a special ~ to discuss possible peace terms⟩ ⟨acted as the president's personal ~ to the union leaders⟩ **b :** a spy or other undercover agent ⟨was reported to be nothing but a Communist ~⟩ **c :** MESSENGER ⟨sent an ~ backstage to order quiet⟩ **2 a** *archaic* **:** an outlet esp. of a lake or river **b** *obs* **:** an emissary duct or vessel

[2]**emissary** \"\ *adj* **1** *obs* **:** relating to or acting as an emissary **2 :** leading outward — used esp. of certain veins that pass through apertures in the skull and connect the venous sinuses of the dura mater with veins external to the skull

emis·sile \ēˈmisəl, əˈ-\ *adj* [L *emissus* + E *-ile*] *archaic* **:** capable of being protruded — used esp. of the oral structures of certain worms

emis·sion \ēˈmishən, əˈ-\ *n* -s [L *emission-, emissio*, fr. *emissus* + *-ion-, -io* -ion] **1** *obs* **:** an act of sending forth (as on a mission) **2 a :** an act or instance of emitting (as heat or light) **:** EMANATION ⟨the ~ of the sun's rays⟩ ⟨slow ~ of warmth from a banked fire⟩ **b :** a putting into circulation (as of a coinage) ⟨the ~ of bank notes unbacked by specie⟩ **c** *archaic* **:** publication esp. of a writing **d :** a flow of electrons out of the heated filament or cathode of an electron tube **3 a :** something that is sent forth by or as if by emitting **:** a discharge esp. of electrons **b** (1) **:** a discharge of fluid from the living body (2) **:** EJACULATE 1 — called also *emissio seminis* **c :** EFFLUVIUM, EMANATION ⟨any ~ from the person of the medium such as ectoplasm or odor⟩ ⟨an evil-smelling sticky ~ from the cut surface⟩

emission spectrum *n* **:** an electromagnetic spectrum that derives its characteristics from the material of which the emitting source is made and from the way in which the material is excited — compare ABSORPTION SPECTRUM

emis·sive \-isiv\ *adj* [L *emissus* + E *-ive*] **1 :** sending out **:** EMITTING **2 :** sent out **:** EMITTED

emissive power *n* **:** the energy of thermal radiation emitted in all directions per unit time from each unit area of a surface at any given temperature

emis·siv·i·ty \ˌeməˈsivəd·ē, ˌēm-, -(ˌ)miˈs-\ *n* -ES **:** the relative emissive power of a radiating surface expressed as a fraction of the emissive power of a black-body radiator at the same temperature

emit \ēˈmit, əˈ-, *usu* -id·+V\ *vb* **emitted; emitted; emitting; emits** [L *emittere*, fr. *e-* + *mittere* to send — more at SMITE] *vt* **1 :** to send out **:** DISCHARGE, RELEASE: as **a :** to throw or give off or out (as effluvia, light, heat, gases, or charged particles) ⟨a fire *emitting* heat and smoke⟩ ⟨gamma rays may continue to be *emitted* for years⟩ **b :** EJECT, EXUDE, LOOSE ⟨some puffballs ~ myriads of spores⟩ ⟨aphids ~ a sweet fluid attractive to ants⟩ ⟨a cloudy sky *emitting* occasional drops of rain⟩ **c :** TRANSMIT 2b **2 a :** to cause to be issued (as an order or decree); *esp* **:** to put (as money or bills) into circulation **b** *obs* **:** PUBLISH **3 a :** to give utterance to (as words, ideas, or emotions) **:** EXPRESS ⟨they *emitted* constant complaints over the lack of conveniences⟩ ⟨*emitting* a stream of angry words⟩ ⟨in this book she ~*s* her inmost thoughts concisely and lucidly⟩ **b :** to give voice to (sound) ⟨the cricket *emitting* his shrill chirp⟩ ⟨sound cannot be *emitted* in a complete vacuum⟩ ~ *vi* **:** to come forth **:** ISSUE ⟨a sharp odor *emitting* from a broken gas line⟩

syn EMIT, EXUDE, OOZE, VENT, EXHALE, and REEK agree in meaning to discharge something such as moisture, vapor, or fumes. EMIT is the most inclusive in carrying the base meaning ⟨a small hose *emitting* a dribble of water⟩ ⟨a chimney *emitting* smoke⟩ ⟨to *emit* a groan⟩ ⟨to *emit* a stench⟩ ⟨a boat *emitting* a stream of passengers⟩ EXUDE usu. implies an emitting (as of a liquid) through pores, interstices, cracks, and so on, or an action resembling this ⟨to *exude* a cold perspiration⟩ ⟨the resin is made plastic and *exuded* through a nozzle —J.C.Tarr⟩ ⟨to *exude* confidence —*Newsweek*⟩ ⟨sickened at the evil that a crocodile seems to *exude* —F. Tennyson Jesse⟩ OOZE implies a slow passing (as of a liquid or of gas) through pores or interstices, or a slowness of movement suggesting this ⟨the steam *oozing* out of the leaky joints —C.S.Forester⟩ ⟨the dirt *oozes* out between the flags of the floor —Donat O'Donnell⟩ ⟨a trickle of blood *oozing* down his face —F.V.W.Mason⟩ VENT implies discharge through a relatively small outlet; it stresses the idea of release of what presses for release from within ⟨an exhaust pipe *venting* a blue smoke⟩ ⟨a factory outlet *vents* warm water into the Miami river —G.X.Sand⟩ ⟨the Norman woman would not dare *vent* her hatred on him —T.B. Costain⟩ ⟨*vented* an impatient snort —Cameron Hawley⟩ EXHALE implies a breathing out, often of something delicate or subtle ⟨the pans . . . *exhaled* a sulphurous stench —T.B. Macaulay⟩ ⟨their wet macintoshes . . . *exhaled* a smell of rubber —Rebecca West⟩ ⟨she *exhaled* a style and distinction of her own —Osbert Sitwell⟩ REEK stresses the emission of smoke, fumes, or strong odors, esp. offensive ones ⟨a pipe along a barge was gasping and *reeking* —Frederick Way⟩ ⟨the players, *reeking* of dirt and sweat —J.J.Godwin⟩ ⟨the waiter, a man, was *reeking* with rose water or musk —Ralph Knight⟩

emit·tance \-itᵊn(t)s\ *n* -s **:** EMISSIVITY

emittent *adj* [L *emittent-, emittens*, pres. part. of *emittere*] *obs* **:** EMISSIVE

emit·ter \-id·ə(r), -itə-\ *n* -s **:** one that emits; *often* **:** a substance or electrode that emits particles ⟨radium is an alpha ~⟩ ⟨thermionic ~*s*⟩

em·ma \ˈemə\ *usu cap* [fr. Brit. signalmen's pron. of *M* (as in A.M.)] — a communications code word for the letter *m* — see ACK EMMA, PIP EMMA

em·marble \en, ən+\ *or* **en·marble** *also* **im·marble** \ə+\ *vt* [[1]*en-* or [2]*in-* + *marble* (n.)] **1 :** to change into or embody in marble **2 :** to make like marble

em·marvel \e, ə+\ *vt* [[1]*en-* + *marvel*] *archaic* **:** to cause to marvel

em·me·leia \ˌeməˈlīə\ *n* -s [Gk, lit., harmony, fr. *emmelēs* harmonious, suitable + *-ia* -y] **:** a solemn and stately dance used in ancient Greek tragedy

em·men·a·gog·ic \əˈmenəˈgäjik, (ˌ)e,ˌ=ˈ=, -mēn-, -ägik\ *adj* **:** acting as an emmenagogue **:** promoting menstruation

[1]**em·men·a·gogue** \=ˈ==ˌgäg\ *adj* [Gk *emmēna* menses (fr. neut. pl. of *emmēnos* monthly, fr. *em-* [2]*en-* + *mēn* month) + E *-agogue* (fr. LL *-agogus* promoting the expulsion of) — more at MOON, -AGOGUE] **:** EMMENAGOGIC

[2]**emmenagogue** \"\ *n* -s **:** an agent that promotes the menstrual discharge

em·men·ta·ler *or* **em·men·tha·ler** \ˈemənˌtälə(r)\ *or* **em·men·tal** *or* **em·men·thal** \-äl\ *or* **emmentaler cheese** *or* **emmenthaler cheese** *n* -s *usu cap E* [G *Emmentaler* (formerly spelled *Emmenthaler*) *käse*, lit., Emmental cheese, fr. Emmental, region in Switzerland] **:** SWISS CHEESE

em·mer \ˈemə(r)\ *n* -s [G, fr. OHG *amari* — more at YELLOWHAMMER] **:** a hard red wheat (*Triticum dicoccum*) having spikelets with two kernels that remain in the glumes after threshing and being grown in several varieties in Russia and Germany and to a limited extent in the U.S. as a stock feed; *broadly* **:** any tetraploid wheat — compare SPELT

em·met \ˈemət\ *n* -s *now chiefly dial* [ME *emete* — more at ANT] **:** ANT

em·me·trope \ˈeməˌtrōp\ *n* -s [ISV *emmetr-* (fr. Gk *emmetros* in measure, proportioned, suitable) + *-ope*] **:** a person having emmetropic eyes

em·me·tro·pia \ˌeməˈtrōpēə\ *n* -s [NL, fr. Gk *emmetros* + NL *-opia*] **:** the normal refractive condition of the eye in which with accommodation relaxed parallel rays of light are all brought accurately to a focus upon the retina — distinguished from *astigmatism* and *myopia*

em·me·trop·ic \ˌ==ˈträpik, -rōp-\ *adj, of the eye* **:** having normal refraction **:** exhibiting emmetropia

em·mons·ite \ˈemənˌzīt\ *n* -s [Samuel F. *Emmons* †1911 Am. geologist + E *-ite*] **:** a mineral $Fe_2Te_3O_9.2H_2O$ consisting of a hydrous oxide of iron and tellurium

em·my \ˈemē, -mi\ *n, pl* **emmys** *or* **emmies** *usu cap* [fr. alter. of *Immy*, nickname for *Image Orthicon*] **:** a statuette awarded annually by a professional society for outstanding cultural, educational, or technological achievement in television

an Emmy

em·o·din \ˈemədən, -dᵊn\ *n* -s [ISV *emodi-* (fr. NL *emodi*, specific epithet of *Rheum emodi*) + *-in*] **:** an orange crystalline phenolic compound $C_{14}H_4O_2(OH)_3CH_3$ derived from anthraquinone and obtained esp. from plants (as rhubarb, cascara buckthorn, and senna) yielding cathartic substances — called also *frangula emodin*

emol·li·ate \əˈmälēˌāt, ēˈ-\ *vt* -ED/-ING/-S [L *emollire* to soften + E *-ate*] **:** to make weak, ineffective, or effeminate

emol·lience \-lyən(t)s, -lēə-\ *n* -s **:** the quality or state of being emollient

[1]**emol·lient** \-nt\ *adj* [L *emollient-, emolliens*, pres. part. of *emollire* to soften, fr. *e-* + *mollire* to soften, fr. *mollis* soft — more at MELT] **:** making soft or supple; *also* **:** soothing esp. to the skin or mucous membrane ⟨an ~ cream for the hands⟩ ⟨an ~ preparation to apply to the membranes of the nose⟩ **:** MOLLIFYING ⟨soothe us in our agonies with ~ words —H.L.Mencken⟩ ⟨had an ~ effect on the man's exasperation⟩

[2]**emollient** \"\ *n* -s **:** an emollient agent ⟨an ~ added to a rubber compound to give pliability⟩ ⟨an ~ for the hands⟩

emollition *n* -s [L *emollitus* (past part. of *emollire*) + E *-ion*] *obs* **:** the act, process, or effect of softening

emo·loa \ˌāmōˈlōə, ˌem-\ *n* -s [Hawaiian] **:** a rough tufted tall Hawaiian grass (*Eragrostis variabilis*)

emol·u·ment \əˈmälyəmənt, ēˈ-\ *n* -s [ME, fr. L *emolumentum* profit, gain, lit., sum paid to have grain ground up, fr. *emolere* to grind up (fr. *e-* + *molere* to grind) + *-mentum* -ment — more at MEAL] **1 :** profit or perquisites from office, employment, or labor **:** FEES, SALARY ⟨~ in the form of a wage and tips⟩ ⟨a goose . . . raised to the dignity and ~*s* of a household pet, and carried about in a basket —Agnes Repplier⟩; *also* **:** COMPENSATION ⟨was telling this sympathetic American all about how the coup d'etat had been pulled off, and what territorial ~*s* had been promised his native land —Upton Sinclair⟩ **2** *archaic* **:** ADVANTAGE, BENEFIT ⟨the idol of the people . . . how surprisingly he exerted himself for the ~, convenience, and pleasure of his fellow-citizens —Tobias Smollett⟩ **syn** see WAGE

em·o·ny \ˈemənē\ *n* -ES [by shortening & alter. (resulting from incorrect word division of *anemone*, taken as *an emone*)] *dial Eng* **:** ANEMONE

em·o·ry oak \ˈem(ə)rē-\ *n, usu cap E* [after W.H.*Emory* †1887 Am. soldier and engineer] **:** a low shrubby black oak (*Quercus emoryi*) of the southwestern U.S. with evergreen leaves and very heavy wood

emote \əˈmōt, ēˈ-, *usu* -ōd·+V\ *vi* -ED/-ING/-S [back-formation fr. *emotion*] **:** to give expression to emotion ⟨June is the month when more Americans ~ than at any other time of year —E.A.Weeks⟩ ⟨knowledge about how man ~*s* and about what structures in the brain and what physiological devices therein produce emotions —*Jour. Amer. Med. Assoc.*⟩ esp. in or as if in a play or movie ⟨the producers, realizing that picture audiences unconsciously yearn for a little more expression than is common on the lacquered faces of the contemporary screen stars, make Miss Swanson ~ with a physical abandon —H.E.Clurman⟩ often falsely or in a manner befitting a ham actor ⟨but more often she assaults her readers with rhetoric . . . ~*s*, postures, harangues —*Time*⟩

emot·er \-d·ə(r), -tə-\ *n* -s **:** one that emotes

emo·tion \əˈmōshən, ēˈ-\ *n* -s [MF, fr. *emouvoir* to start out, incite, stir up (after MF *mouvoir* to move: *motion*), fr. OF *esmovoir*, fr. L *exmovēre*, *emovēre* to move out, move away, fr. *ex-* [1]*ex-*, *e-* + *movēre* to move — more at MOVE] **1 a** *obs* **:** a physical or social agitation, disturbance, or tumultuous movement **b :** turmoil or agitation in feeling or sensibility ⟨the nerveless dreamer, who spends his life in a weltering sea of sensibility and ~ —William James⟩ ⟨love between men and women . . . is such a hot, stupid, middling thing, all ~ and no thought —Rose Macaulay⟩ **c :** a physiological departure from homeostasis that is subjectively experienced in strong feeling (as of love, hate, desire, or fear) and manifests itself in neuromuscular, respiratory, cardiovascular, hormonal, and other bodily changes preparatory to overt acts which may or may not be performed — often used in pl. ⟨how can I describe my ~*s* at this catastrophe —Mary W. Shelley⟩ **d :** an instance of such a turmoil or agitation in feeling or sensibility **:** state of strong feeling (as of fear, anger, disgust, grief, joy, or surprise) ⟨he felt a sudden rage but quickly controlled the ~⟩ ⟨overcome with the ~ of grief when he heard of his friend's death⟩ ⟨the girl hardly knew what love was since she had never before experienced so tender an ~⟩ **2 a :** the affective aspect of consciousness **:** FEELING ⟨we are not men of reason, we are creatures of ~ —C.C.Furnas⟩ **b :** a reaction of or effect upon this aspect of consciousness ⟨the essential ~ of the play is the feeling of a son toward a guilty mother —T.S.Eliot⟩ ⟨the ~ of beauty, like all our emotions, is certainly the inherited product of unimaginably countless experiences in an immeasurable past —P.E.More⟩ ⟨reason rather than ~ forms the main basis for his marriage —Nellie Maher⟩ ⟨the mind must have its share in deciding these important matters, not merely the ~*s* and desires —Rose Macaulay⟩ **3 :** the quality (as of a song or painting) that arouses an emotion, esp. a pleasant one ⟨the melody of the song voices the ~, the appeal —Anatole Chujoy⟩ **4 :** an expression of feeling, esp. strong feeling ⟨the king moves anonymously among his men . . . listening to their ~*s* about the war —Delmore Schwartz⟩ **syn** see FEELING

emo·tion·able \-sh(ə)nəbəl\ *adj* **:** capable of being moved by feeling

emo·tion·al \-shənᵊl,-shnəl\ *adj* **1 :** of or relating to emotion, esp. to more than usual emotion: as **a :** dominated chiefly by emotion ⟨a highly ~ condition of mind⟩ **b :** expressing more than usual emotion ⟨~ language used in the heat of argument⟩ ⟨an ~ expression of friendship⟩ **c :** prone to arousal of the emotions ⟨he is intensely ~, is sometimes moved to tears by the pathos of his own words —*Time*⟩ **d :** motivated chiefly by the emotions as opposed to the intellect ⟨an ~ act⟩ ⟨an ~ drive⟩ **:** largely lacking a rational justification ⟨an ~ judgment⟩ **e :** appealing to or arousing the emotions ⟨~ art⟩ **f :** involving emotion ⟨verbal rather than ~ acceptance of social precepts —M.S.Gurvitz⟩ **g :** having particular impact or bearing upon the emotions ⟨the ~ shock of war⟩ ⟨~ security⟩ **2 :** markedly aroused or agitated in feeling or sensibilities ⟨he has been known to get ~ over a . . . piece of costume jewelry —*Time*⟩ — **emo·tion·al·ly** \-ᵊlē,-əlē, -li\ *adv*

emotional insanity *n* **:** PSYCHOPATHIC PERSONALITY

emo·tion·al·ism \-shənᵊlˌizəm, -shnəˌlizəm\ *n* -s **1 a :** undue indulgence in or display of emotions ⟨it is . . . not a curtsy to sentimentality, not a maudlin ~ —C.S.Kilby⟩ **b :** a disposition to indulge in or display emotion unduly ⟨the ~ of adolescent girls⟩ **2 a :** a tendency to regard things emotionally or to respond emotionally as opposed to rationally ⟨a critic whose judgments are marked by ~⟩ **b :** a tendency to overvalue the emotions esp. as expressed in the arts ⟨the romantic ~ characteristic of much early 19th century writing⟩

emo·tion·al·ist \-shənᵊləst, -shnəl-\ *n* -s **1 :** one that tends to rely upon emotion as opposed to reason; *esp* **:** one who bases a theory or policy (as in artistic matters) upon an emotional conviction or justifies it by setting up a certain emotional condition as its end **2 :** one given to emotionalism ⟨an austere and rational way of life hardly palatable to an ~⟩ — **emo·tion·al·is·tic** \=ˌmōshənᵊlˈistik, -shnəˌli-, -tēk\ *adj*

emo·tion·al·i·ty \=ˌmōshəˈnaləd·ē, -ətē, -i\ *n* -ES **:** the quality or state of being esp. unduly emotional ⟨the ~ inspired by barefoot soldiers —N.W.Stephenson & H.W.H.Knott⟩

emo·tion·al·ize \=ˈmōshənᵊlˌīz, -shnəˌlīz\ *vt* -ED/-ING/-S **:** to make emotional: as **a :** to express in a way that arouses emotion ⟨concerned to get his idea across, not to ~ it —Edith Hamilton⟩ **b :** to place in inseparable association with feeling ⟨the birth of his son affected him little until some years later when it suddenly in memory became a highly *emotionalized* experience⟩ **c :** to cause to react emotionally ⟨the various devices of humor furnish convenient ways of *emotionalizing* an audience —A.T.Weaver⟩ **:** cause to be moved or dominated by emotion ⟨trying to handle an extremely *emotionalized* woman⟩ **d :** to motivate by feeling ⟨this firm and highly *emotionalized* touch —F.J.Mather⟩ ~ *vi* **:** to express oneself in a way inspired by or expressive of emotion rather than reason **:** pour forth one's feeling esp. in a disordered way ⟨vagueness or confusion or loose *emotionalizing* —R.H.Pearce⟩

emo·tion·less \=ˈmōshənləs\ *adj* **:** unmoved by feeling ⟨he kept his ~ objectivity and his faith in the cause he served —Vincent Sheean⟩ **:** giving no evidence of emotion ⟨grimly lord of himself, he stood ~ before the world —George Meredith⟩ **:** expressing no emotion ⟨the colonel's words were short and ~ —*Infantry Jour.*⟩ — **emo·tion·less·ness** *n* -ES

emo·tive \əˈmōd·|iv, ēˈ-, -ōt|, |ēv *also* |əv\ *adj* [*emotion* + *-ive*] **1 :** marked by special bearing upon, reference to, or involvement with the emotions ⟨the ~ side of her nature⟩ ⟨an ~ concept of art⟩ ⟨~ associations⟩ **2 a :** evocative of or appealing to the emotions ⟨an ~ utterance⟩ ⟨the ~ use of language⟩; *esp* **:** HORTATORY **b :** expressive of feeling ⟨the rudimentary language of the lower animals seems to be purely ~ —Aldous Huxley⟩ — **emo·tive·ly** \|əvlē, -li\ *adv*

emotive theory *n* **:** a theory according to which value judgments or normative ethical statements are exhortatory rather than cognitive

emo·tiv·ism \|əˌvizəm, |ēˌv-\ *n* -s **:** an emotive theory of ethics or the advocacy of such a theory — **emo·tiv·ist** \-vəst\ *n* -s

emo·tiv·i·ty \ˌē(ˌ)mōˈtivəd·ē, əˌmō, ēˌmō-, -ətē, -i\ *n* -ES **:** the quality or state of being emotive ⟨a musical rendition marked by great ~⟩

emp *abbr* **1** emperor; empire; empress **2** employment

empale *var of* IMPALE

em·pa·na·da \ˌempəˈnädə, -äthə\ *n* -s [AmerSp, fr. Sp, fem. of *empanado*, past part. of *empanar* to put a crust of dough around, fr. *em-* (fr. L, [1]*en-*) + *pan* bread, fr. L *panis* — more at FOOD] **:** a turnover filled with meat

empanel *var of* IMPANEL

em·panoply \əm, em+\ *vt* [[1]*en-* + *panoply* (n.)] **:** to enclose in a full suit of armor

emparadise *var of* IMPARADISE

emparl *var of* IMPARL

em·pa·thet·ic \ˌempəˈthed·|ik, -et|, |ēk\ *adj* [fr. *empathy*, after such pairs as *sympathy: sympathetic*] **:** EMPATHIC — **em·pa·thet·i·cal·ly** \|ək(ə)lē, |ēk-, -li\ *adv*

em·path·ic \(ˈ)emˈpathik, əmˈp-, -thēk\ *adj* **:** involving, characterized by, or based on empathy ⟨an ~ understanding of others⟩ — **em·path·i·cal·ly** \-thək(ə)lē, -thēk-, -li\ *adv*

em·pa·thize \ˈempəˌthīz\ *vb* -ED/-ING/-S *vt* **:** to regard with empathy ~ *vi* **:** to experience empathy

em·pa·thy \ˈempəthē, -thi\ *n* -ES [[2]*en-* + *-pathy*; trans. of G *einfühlung*] **1 :** the imaginative projection of a subjective state whether affective, conative, or cognitive into an object so that the object appears to be infused with it **:** the reading of one's own state of mind or conation into an object (as an artistic object) ⟨without ~ an artistic emotion is purely intellectual and associative —W.H.Wright⟩ **2 :** the capacity for participating in or a vicarious experiencing of another's feelings, volitions, or ideas and sometimes another's movements to the point of executing bodily movements resembling his ⟨the goal of all reading is ~ with the content and the spirit of the material read —Stella Center⟩ ⟨an example of ~ is a feeding situation in which a fright experienced by the mother results in eating disturbances on the part of the child —G.S.Blum⟩ **syn** see SYMPATHY

empearl *var of* IMPEARL

[1]**em·ped·o·cle·an** \əmˌpedəˈklēən, em-ˌ, ˌem,==ˈ==\ *adj, usu cap* [*Empedocles*, 5th cent. B.C. Greek philosopher and statesman + E *-an*] **:** of, relating to, or befitting the philosopher Empedocles or his philosophy according to which change takes place through the uniting and dividing forces of love and hate upon the elements earth, air, fire, and water

[2]**empedoclean** \"\ *n* -s *usu cap* **:** one whose philosophy is Empedoclean

em·pei·ne \emˈpā(ˌ)nā\ *n* -s [MexSp, fr. Sp, impetigo, fr. ML *impedigin-, impedigo*, alter. of L *impetigin-, impetigo* — more at IMPETIGO] **:** PINTID

em·pen·nage \ˌämpəˈnäzh, ˌem-\ *n* -s [F, feathers of an arrow, empennage, fr. *empenner* to put feathers on an arrow (fr. *em-* [1]*en-* + *penne* feather, fr. L *pinna*) + *-age* — more at PEN] **:** the tail assembly of an aircraft

empeople *vt* [[1]*en-* + *people* (n.)] *obs* **:** POPULATE, PEOPLE

em·per·or \ˈemp(ə)rə(r), -ri\ *n* -s [ME *emperour*, fr. OF *empereor*, fr. L *imperator*, fr. *imperatus* (past part. of *imperare* to command, fr. *im-* [2]*in-* + *parare* to prepare, order) + *-or* — more at PARE] **1 :** the sovereign or supreme monarch of an empire ⟨George VI was the last British king to be called *Emperor* of India⟩ **2** *obs* **:** COMMANDER, IMPERATOR **3 :** the largest size of handmade paper, commonly 48×72 inches **4 :** EMPEROR BUTTERFLY **5 :** EMPEROR MOTH

emperor boa *n* **:** a Central American boa (*Constrictor constrictor imperator*)

emperor butterfly *n* **:** any of several large richly colored butterflies of the family Nymphalidae (as the purple emperor)

emperor fish *n* **:** a large brilliantly colored edible butterfly fish (*Holacanthus imperator*) of the Japanese seas

emperor goose *n* **:** a medium-sized goose (*Philacte canagica*) of the coast of Alaska and adjacent islands having ashen gray plumage barred with black and white, a white head and nape, black foreneck, and yellow-orange feet

emperor moth *n* **:** a moth of the family Saturniidae; *esp* **:** a large European moth (*Saturnia pavonia*)

emperor penguin *n* **:** the largest known penguin (*Aptenodytes forsteri*) occurring only south of the antarctic circle and noted for its habit of brooding the egg or young between the feet and a fold of abdominal skin resembling a pouch

em·pery \ˈemp(ə)rē, -ri\ *n* -ES [ME *emperie*, fr. OF, fr. *emperer* to command, fr. L *imperare*] **1 a** *obs* **:** the position or the dominion of an emperor **b** *archaic* **:** the territory of an emperor or of an absolute ruler **2 :** SOVEREIGNTY, EMPIRE; *also* **:** CONTROL, DOMINION

em·pest \əm, em+\ *vt* -ED/-ING/-S [[1]*en-* + *pest* (n.)] **:** to infect with or as if with a contagion ⟨sleeping in an ~*ed* atmosphere —Aldous Huxley⟩

em·pe·tra·ce·ae \ˌempəˈtrāsēˌē\ *n pl, cap* [NL, fr. *Empetrum*, type genus + *-aceae*] **:** a small family of heathlike shrubs (order Sapindales), having small diclinous flowers and drupes that resemble berries — compare CROWBERRY 1a — **em·pe·tra·ceous** \ˌ==ˈ=shəs\ *adj*

em·pe·trum \ˈempəˌtrəm\ *n, cap* [NL, fr. Gk *empetron*, neut. of *empetros* growing on rock, fr. *em-* [2]*en-* + *-petros* (fr. *petra* rock)] **:** a genus (the type of the family Empetraceae) of low shrubs having flowers scattered and solitary or few in the axils — see CROWBERRY

em·pha·sis \ˈem(p)fəsəs\ *n, pl* **empha·ses** \-fəˌsēz\ [L, fr. Gk, exposition, significance, implied meaning, fr. *emphainein* to exhibit, display, indicate (fr. *em-* [2]*en-* + *phainein* to show) + *-sis* — more at FANCY] **1 a :** a forcefulness of expression that gives special impressiveness, calls to special attention, or gives special significance ⟨writing with commendable ~ on the need for reform⟩ **b :** a particular prominence given in reading or speaking to one or more words or syllables (as by voice stress or pitch) to attract attention to or focus attention on their special emotional or logical importance (as when words or the things they represent are contrasted) ⟨the speaker's ~ was on the word *conciliation*⟩ **c :** stress or relative importance given to a certain part or feature of a literary work (as by its prominent position in the whole or its fullness of presentation) ⟨the biography gave considerable ~ to his early life⟩ **2** *obs* **:** an implied meaning in a word **3 a :** special consideration of or stress or insistence upon something ⟨his father's ~ had always been on discipline⟩ ⟨the ~ of the campaign was to be on the elimination of graft⟩ ⟨he disliked the school's ~ on classics —*Current Biog.*⟩ ⟨the first congress at which special ~ is laid on tropical forestry —Hilary Phillips⟩ **b :** something given such emphasis ⟨good citizenship, another chief ~ in the Camp Fire program —*Collier's Yr. Bk.*⟩ **4 :** PROMINENCE, DISTINCTNESS, VIVIDNESS ⟨the altering of the colors in the painting caused the main figure to lose all ~⟩

em·pha·size \-fəˌsīz\ *vt* -ED/-ING/-S *see -ize in Explan Notes* [*emphasis* + *-ize*] **:** to give emphasis to or place emphasis upon **:** STRESS ⟨which is to be *emphasized* — morale or efficiency —W.H.Whyte⟩ ⟨I ~ that many of the figures quoted in the succeeding paragraphs . . . are little more than estimates —W.B. Fisher⟩ ⟨*emphasizing* the importance and desirability of fairness in the conduct of congressional investigations —J.D. Morris⟩ ⟨he had swung one knee above the other, *emphasizing* the trimness of his fur-topped boots —T.B.Costain⟩

em·phat·ic \əm'fad·|ik, em'-, -at|, |ēk\ *adj* [Gk *emphatikos* forcible, expressive, var. of *emphantikos*, fr. (assumed) *emphantos* (verbal of Gk *emphainein*) + *-ikos* -ic] **1 a :** marked by emphasis **:** uttered with emphasis **:** made prominent by stress ⟨an ~ word⟩ ⟨an ~ argument⟩ **b :** commanding attention by prominence, forcefulness, or insistence ⟨even more ~ is the chapter . . . which comes out frankly for rescuing the Adirondack country from destruction at the hands of eager tourists —C.L.Carmer⟩ ⟨unfolding a still more vast and ~ display in blue and yellow —Dorothy L. Sayers⟩ ⟨this document, which may be termed New Jersey's first constitution, contained a particularly ~ guarantee of religious liberty —*Amer. Guide Series: N.J.*⟩ **c :** INSISTENT ⟨the point is one worth being rather ~ about —A.A.Hill⟩ **2 a :** tending to express oneself in emphatic speech or to take habitually brusque or decisive action ⟨a little ~ man —Charles Dickens⟩ ⟨I wish I were unflinching and ~, and had big, bushy eyebrows and a Message for the Age —L.P.Smith⟩ **b :** markedly forceful ⟨used an ~ blue pencil freely —W.L.McAtee⟩ **3 a :** attracting special attention **:** strikingly conspicuous ⟨some ~ feather or brooch —John Galsworthy⟩ ⟨government of the U.S. had been so commonly on dead center, with not even a party able to enact its wish, that its contrast to government by parliament and cabinet was ~ —F.L.Paxson⟩ **b :** clearly delineated **:** definite in outline or features ⟨the line of tall fir trees at the lake's edge casting their ~ shadows on the ice —Jean Stafford⟩ **4** *of a linguistic form* **:** expressive of special emphasis ⟨the ~ article in Samoan⟩; *esp* **:** constituting or belonging to a set of tense forms in English that consist of the auxiliary *do* followed by an infinitive without *to* and are used to facilitate rhetorical inversion (as *did see* in "only then did he see the danger"), to take the place of a simple verb form normally in negative or interrogative sentences (as *did believe* in "he did not believe it" or *do think* in "what do you think?"), or to emphasize (as *does work* in "but I tell you he does work hard") **5** *of some Semitic consonants* **:** differing from the other member of a pair through being velarized and alveolar rather than dental or being pharyngeal rather than velar — **em·phat·i·cal·ly** \|ək(ə)lē, |ēk-, -li\ *adv* — **em·phat·i·cal·ness** \|əkəlnəs, |ēk-\ *n* -ES

em·phat·i·cal \|əkəl, |ēk-\ *archaic var of* EMPHATIC

emphatic pronoun *n* **:** INTENSIVE PRONOUN

emphatic state *n* **:** the state or form of a noun in Syriac and Aramaic that makes it determinate or definite — compare ABSOLUTE STATE, CONSTRUCT STATE

em·phy·se·ma \ˌem(p)fə'sēmə, -'zē-\ *n* -S [NL, fr. Gk *emphysēma* inflation or swelling of a part of the body, fr. *emphysan* to inflate, fr. *em-* [2]en- + *physan* to blow — more at FOG] **:** a condition characterized by air-filled expansions like blisters in interstitial or subcutaneous tissues; *specif* **:** a local or generalized condition of the lung marked by distention, progressive loss of elasticity, and eventual rupture of the alveoli and accompanied by labored breathing, a husky cough, and frequently by impairment of heart action

em·phy·sem·a·tous \¦==¦s|emədəs, ¦==¦z|, |ēm-\ *adj* [NL *emphysemat-*, *emphysema* + E *-ous*] *adj* **1 :** relating to, being, or resembling emphysema **:** SWELLED, BLOATED **2** *bot* **:** inflated like a bladder **:** BLADDERY

emphysematous anthrax *or* **emphysematous gangrene** *n* **:** BLACKLEG 1

em·phy·teu·sis \ˌem(p)fə'tyüsəs, -fə·'tyü-\ *n, pl* **emphyteu·ses** \-üˌsēz\ [LL, fr. LGk, fr. Gk *emphyteuein* to implant (fr. *em-* [2]en- + *phyteuein* to plant, fr. *phyton* plant) + *-sis* — more at PHYT-] **:** a Roman and civil law contract by which a grant is made of a right either perpetual or for a long period to the possession and enjoyment of orig. agricultural land subject to the keeping of the land in cultivation or from depreciation, the payment of a fixed annual rent, and some other conditions; *also* **:** the heritable and alienable right so granted or the tenure by which it is held

em·phy·teu·ta \-üd·ə\ *n, pl* **emphyteu·tae** \-d·ˌē\ [LL, fr. LGk *emphyteutēs*, fr. Gk *emphyteuein*] **:** one holding land by emphyteusis

em·phy·teu·tic \¦==¦tüd·ik, ¦==·¦tyü-\ *adj* [LL *emphyteuticus*, fr. *emphyteuta* + L *-icus* -ic] **:** being or in tenure by an emphyteusis

em·pid \'empəd\ *n* -S [NL *Empidae*] **:** one of the Empididae

em·pi·dae \'empəˌdē\ [NL, fr. *Empis* + *-idae*] *syn of* EMPIDIDAE

em·pid·i·dae \em'pidəˌdē\ *n pl, cap* [NL, fr. *Empid-*, *Empis*, type genus (fr. Gk *empid-*, *empis* mosquito, gnat) + *-idae*] **:** a large family of small predaceous brachycerous flies that fly in swarms with a dancing movement in the mating season, the males of many species courting the females with prey captured in silken balloons or webs produced from silk glands on their forelegs

em·pi·do·nax \ˌempə'dōˌnaks, em'pidᵊnˌaks\ *n, cap* [NL, irreg. fr. Gk *empid-*, *empis* + *anax* lord, master] **:** a genus of small olivaceous American flycatchers comprising several familiar birds (as the least flycatcher and the Acadian flycatcher

em·piece·ment \əm'pēsmənt, em-\ *n* -S [[1]*en-* + *piece* + *-ment*] **:** a piece of material inserted in a garment usu. as trimming or ornamentation

em·pierce \əm, em-+\ *vt* [[1]*en-* + *pierce*] *archaic* **:** PIERCE, PENETRATE

[1]**em·pire** \'emˌpī(ə)r, -īə; *sense 4 &* [2]EMPIRE *are more often* (')äm¦pi(ə)r *or* (')ȯm- *or* -iə\ *n* -S [ME, fr. OF *empire*, *empirie*, fr. L *imperium*, fr. *imperare* to command — more at EMPEROR] **1 a :** an extended territory usu. comprising a group of nations, states, or peoples under the control or domination of a single sovereign power: as (1) **:** a state comprising a dominating conquering people and the conquered people dominated ⟨the Babylonian ~⟩ ⟨the Aztec ~⟩ (2) **:** a state comprising a confederacy in which one strong member dominates its confederates or its confederates, conquests, and colonies ⟨the Athenian ~⟩ ⟨the Roman ~⟩ (3) **:** a state that has a great extent of territory and a great variety of peoples under one rule and often has a ruler with the title of emperor ⟨the former Japanese ~⟩ **b :** the territory or peoples under such control or domination ⟨the former large colonial ~ of Spain⟩ ⟨the colonial ~ proper numbers some 60,000,000 in Asia, America, and Africa —*New Republic*⟩ **c :** REALM, PROVINCE, TERRITORY ⟨fish in their watery ~⟩ ⟨the ~ of gnats and midges⟩ ⟨primarily an inland ~, Texas nevertheless has the third longest coastline of the States —*Amer. Guide Series: Texas*⟩ ⟨a whole ~ of enjoyment is yours to command —*N.Y.Times*⟩ **2 a :** supreme or absolute power esp. of an emperor **:** imperial dominion, sway, or sovereignty ⟨the problems of a colonial administration in retreat from ~ —*N.Y.Times Book Rev.*⟩ ⟨the first Ptolemies were consolidating their ~ over Egypt —Benjamin Farrington⟩ **b :** DOMINATION, CONTROL ⟨reckless revolt against the ~ of business and convention —E.K.Brown⟩ ⟨even as a child her ~ over her two sisters and her half-brothers . . . was complete —*Times Lit. Supp.*⟩ ⟨the ~ of strong emotion —C.W.Cunnington⟩ **3 a :** an extended territory or an extensive enterprise or group of related enterprises dominated or significantly controlled by a single person, family, or group of interested persons ⟨a cattle ~ of several thousand acres⟩ ⟨a fabulous ~, with no strings attached, was given to the railroads, to encourage the construction of transportation facilities —J.E. Lawrence⟩ ⟨state officials . . . nor competitors had been able to halt the growth of his branch-banking ~ —*Newsweek*⟩ ⟨the breakup of the former . . . utilities ~ —*Wall Street Jour.*⟩ ⟨a motion-picture ~ that at one time included a leading film-producing company, hundreds of theaters, and a newsreel organization —*Americana Annual*⟩ ⟨one of the world's greatest industrialists, a man who created a billion-dollar ~ —Paul Marcus⟩ **b :** control over such territory or enterprises ⟨this ~ of crime . . . enforces its rule by systematic murder and terrorism —Malcolm Johnson⟩ **4** *often cap* [[2]*empire*] **:** CADMIUM GREEN — distinguished from *Empire green* and *Empire blue*

[2]**empire** *see* [1]EMPIRE\ *adj, usu cap* [F *Empire*, fr. (*le premier*) *Empire*, the First Empire of France (1804–1814)] **:** of, relating to, or befitting the style popular in France in the early 19th century: as **a** *of clothing* **:** having the characteristics of the French Directoire style but usu. with richer fabrics, greater formality, and elaborate accessories **b** *of furniture* **:** characterized by classic and oriental motives, long curving lines, some carving, and ornamentation in brass and ivory — see DIRECTOIRE b

empire blue *n, often cap E* [[2]*empire*] **:** a moderate blue that is greener and duller than average copen or Dresden blue, redder and deeper than azurite blue, and redder and darker than pompadour

empire builder *n* **:** one whose aim or achievement is the formation of an empire: as **a :** one whose aim and activities are chiefly designed to and usu. do notably increase the territory of or controlled by a country or notably enhance a country's authority and dominion **b :** one whose aim and achievement is the extension of his control (as financial or political) over a large territory or an extensive enterprise or set of related enterprises

empire building *n* **:** the activities of an empire builder ⟨our forefathers were often too busy with *empire building* to worry about their souls⟩

empire cloth *n* **:** a cloth treated with oxidized oil for use as an electrical insulator

empire day *n, usu cap E&D* [fr. (*British*) *Empire*] **1 :** May 24 observed in most of the countries of the British Commonwealth as the anniversary of Queen Victoria's birthday — called also *Victoria Day* **2 :** the last school day before Victoria Day in Canada when special patriotic observances are held in the schools

empire green *n, often cap E* [[2]*empire*] **:** a dark grayish green to dark yellowish green that is yellower than Danube green

empire red *n, often cap E* [[2]*empire*] **:** vermilion or a color resembling it

empire wine *n, usu cap E* [fr. (*British*) *Empire*] **:** a wine produced within the British Empire and shipped to England for sale

empire yellow *n, often cap E* [[2]*empire*] **:** a light to brilliant yellow that is lighter than orpiment

em·pir·ic \əm'pirik, em-, -rēk\ *n* -S [L *empiricus*, fr. Gk *empeirikos*, fr. *empeirikos* experienced, fr. *empeiros* (fr. *em-* [2]en- + *-peiros*, fr. *peiran* to try, attempt, experiment) + *-ikos* -ic — more at FEAR] **1 a :** a member of an ancient sect of physicians who based their practice on experience alone disregarding all theoretical and philosophic considerations **b** *archaic* **:** one that in any walk of life disregards or deviates from the rules of science or accepted practice **:** QUACK, CHARLATAN **2 :** one who follows an empirical method **:** one who relies upon practical experience

em·pir·i·cal \əm'pirəkəl, (')em¦p-, -rēk-\ *or* **em·pir·ic** \-rik,-rēk\ *adj* **1** *archaic* **a :** following or used in the practice of the empirics **b :** relying on experience or observation alone without proper regard for considerations of system, science, and theory **c :** being or befitting a quack or charlatan **2 a :** originating in or relying or based on factual information, observation, or direct sense experience usu. as opposed to theoretical knowledge ⟨~ law⟩ ⟨an ~ equation⟩ ⟨an ~ basis for an ethical theory⟩; *also* **:** relying on or proceeding on the information to be derived from experience and observation for lack of other knowledge **:** proceeding strictly experimentally or by the trial and error method ⟨an ~ treatment of a disease about which little is known⟩ ⟨much medical lore had had an ~ origin . . . centuries of trial-and-error gropings after remedies —R.H.Shryock⟩ ⟨agriculture from its primitive beginnings has been an individualistic, unorganized, ~ business —*Yrbk. of Agriculture*⟩ **b :** EXPERIENTIAL; *broadly* **:** OBSERVATIONAL, FACTUAL ⟨~ data⟩ ⟨the psychoanalysts have had no trouble in finding ~ confirmation for their theories —H.M.Parshley⟩ ⟨an immense mass of evidence, gathered by ~ investigation —*Newsweek*⟩ **3 :** capable of being confirmed, verified, or disproved by observation or experiment ⟨~ statements or laws⟩ — **em·pir·i·cal·ly** \-rək(ə)lē, -rēk, -li\ *adv* — **em·pir·i·cal·ness** \-rəkəlnəs, -rēk-\ *n* -ES

empirical formula *n* **:** a chemical formula based on analysis but not on molecular weight and showing merely the simplest ratio of elements in a compound rather than the total number of atoms in the molecule ⟨CH_2O is the *empirical formula* of formaldehyde, acetic acid, methyl formate, and glucose⟩ — compare MOLECULAR FORMULA

empirical truth *n* **:** exact conformity as learned by observation or experiment between judgments or propositions and externally existent things in their actual status and relations — called also *actual truth*, *contingent truth*

em·pir·i·cism \əm'pirəˌsizəm, em-\ *n* -S **1 a :** a former school of medical practice founded on experience without the aid of science or theory **b :** QUACKERY, CHARLATANRY **2 a :** the practice of emphasizing experience esp. of the senses or the practice or method of relying upon observation, experimentation, or induction rather than upon intuition, speculation, deduction, dialectic, or other rationalistic means in the pursuit of knowledge **b :** a tenet arrived at empirically **3 a :** the theory associated esp. with the British philosophers John Locke, George Berkeley, and David Hume that all knowledge originates in experience **b :** logical empiricism, radical empiricism, or scientific empiricism — compare PHENOMENALISM, POSITIVISM, PRAGMATISM, SENSATIONALISM

em·pir·i·cist \-ˌsəst\ *n* -S **:** one that advocates or practices empiricism **:** EMPIRIC ⟨remained a stubborn ~, one whose theories were always open to revision in the light of fresh experience —*Times Lit. Supp.*⟩

em·pir·ics \-'piriks\ *n pl but sing in constr* **:** empirical practices or beliefs; *broadly* **:** the science of empirics

empirio- *also* **empirico-** *comb form* [*empirio-* fr. G, fr. Gk *empeiria* experience (fr. *empeiros* experienced + *-ia* -y) + G *-o-*; *empirico-* fr. *empiric*, adj. + *-o-*] **1 :** experience **:** experiment ⟨*empirio*genic⟩ **2 :** empirical and ⟨*empirico*inductive⟩

em·pir·io·critical \əm¦pirē(ˌ)ō, em-+\ *adj* [*empirio-* + *critical*] **:** of, relating to, or advocating empiriocriticism

em·pir·io·criticism \"+\ *n* [part trans. of G *empiriokritizismus*, fr. *empirio-* + *kritizismus* criticism] **:** a scientifically oriented phenomenalistic form of empiricism that endeavors to reduce knowledge to a description of pure experience and eliminate all aspects of apriorism, metaphysics, and dualism

em·pir·io·logical \"+\ *adj* [F *empiriologique*, fr. *empirio-* + *logique* logical, fr. L *logicus* — more at LOGICAL] **:** emphasizing or based on procedures that are both logical and empirical (as those employing mathematics and experiments) ⟨~ in contrast to ontological methods⟩

em·pi·rism \'empəˌrizəm\ *n* -S [*empiric* + *-ism*] **:** EMPIRICISM 2, 3 — **em·pi·ris·tic** \¦==¦ristik\ *adj*

em·place \əm'plās, em-\ *vt* [back-formation fr. *emplacement*] **:** to put into position ⟨where thick glacial deposits were *emplaced* by ice moving —W.R.Hansen⟩ ⟨the deeply *emplaced*, presbytic eyes, peering out from under the dark brows —A.J.Liebling⟩ ⟨two artificial harbors to be *emplaced* off the beaches —G.C.Marshall⟩ ⟨a smooth sea enabled us to get more troops ashore and to ~ some artillery —*Time*⟩ ⟨an area where the annoying guns were evidently thought to be *emplaced* —E.J.Kahn⟩

em·place·ment \-smənt\ *n* [F, fr. obs. F *emplacer* to put in place (fr. MF, fr. *em-* [1]en- + *place*) + F *-ment* — more at PLACE] **1 :** the situation or location of something (as of a building) ⟨a pile of embers marking the ~ of the fort and the little village —*Amer. Guide Series: Mich.*⟩ ⟨the clue to the genesis of the continents must lie in the origin and ~ of granite —C.M.Nevin⟩ ⟨took his flock of llamas to a sheltered ~ . . . for the night —*Springfield (Mass.) Union*⟩ **2 :** a prepared position for weapons (as a gun or group of guns) or military equipment from which they can operate effectively ⟨a concealed gun ~⟩ **3** [*emplace* + *-ment*] **:** a putting into position **:** PLACEMENT ⟨~ of the panels on the steel frames of the buildings involves little more than lifting the panels into position and inserting bolts —*Civil Engineering*⟩ ⟨the ore ~ has been chiefly by cavity filling —A.M.Bateman⟩

emplane *var of* ENPLANE

emplant *var of* IMPLANT

[1]**em·plas·tic** \(')em¦plastik, əm'p-\ *adj* [Gk *emplastikos*, fr. *emplastos* (verbal of *emplassein* to plaster up, make stick, fr. *em-* [2]en- + *plassein* to mold, form, plaster — more at PLASTER] **:** ADHESIVE

[2]**emplastic** \"\ *n* **:** an emplastic substance

emplead *archaic var of* IMPLEAD

em·plec·tite \əm'plekˌtīt, em-\ *n* -S [G *emplektit*, fr. Gk *emplektos* inwoven + G *-it* -ite] **:** a grayish or white metallic-looking mineral consisting of a compound of copper, bismuth, and sulfur $CuBiS_2$ occurring in thin prisms

em·ple·o·ma·nia \ˌempleō'mānēə, emˌplēə'-\ *n* [Sp *empleomanía*, fr. *empleo* employment, use, public office (fr. *emplear* to employ, use, fr. OSp, fr. OF *empleoir*, *emploiier*) + *-manía* (fr. NL *-mania*)] **:** a mania for holding public office

[1]**em·ploy** \əm'plȯi, em-\ *vt* -ED/-ING/-S [ME *emploien*, fr. MF *emploier* fr. OF *empleoir*, *emploiier*, fr. L *implicare* to infold, involve, implicate, engage, fr. *in-* [2]in- + *plicare* to fold — more at PLY] **1 a :** to make use of ⟨~ a pen for sketching⟩ ⟨~ metal girders in building construction⟩ ⟨~ questionable methods in business⟩ ⟨craftsmen were finding in the new land raw materials on which they could ~ all their artistry —*Amer. Guide Series: Pa.*⟩ ⟨atomic energy could be ~*ed* for military purposes —*Current Biog.*⟩ ⟨office buildings are beginning to ~ whole banks of elevators which . . . run without operators or starters —John Lear⟩ **b :** to use or occupy (as time) advantageously ⟨~ your leisure in reading⟩ ⟨possible fields where the capacities and interests of the student might best be ~*ed* —Bates Boyle⟩ **c :** to use or engage the services of ⟨~ a lawyer to straighten out a legal tangle⟩; *also* **:** to provide with a job that pays wages or a salary or with a means of earning a living ⟨he is ~*ed* by a local plumbing concern⟩ **d :** to devote to or direct toward a particular activity or person ⟨~ all his talent to the creation of frivolities⟩ ⟨all his caddishness was ~*ed* against her —J.F.Gore⟩ **e :** OCCUPY, BUSY ⟨~ oneself in charitable activities⟩ ⟨~ the child at cutting out paper dolls⟩ **2** *obs* **a :** COMPRISE, INCLUDE, ENCLOSE **b :** SIGNIFY, IMPLY **3** *obs* **:** to dispatch (a person) with a commission **syn** see USE

[2]**employ** \" *sometimes* 'emˌp-\ *n* -S **1** *archaic* **a :** something on which one is employed or with which he is occupied; *also* **:** USE, PURPOSE ⟨that war chest . . . which had been accumulated by the late king for the proposed Spanish war, and which had now no ~ —Hilaire Belloc⟩ **b :** BUSINESS, OCCUPATION, TRADE, PROFESSION **2 :** the state of being employed esp. for wages or a salary by someone or something (as an employer or a business firm) ⟨in the ~ of a trucking company⟩ ⟨professors of science, though not actually in the government's ~ —Waldemar Kaempffert⟩ **3** *archaic* **:** an official public position

em·ploy·abil·i·ty \əmˌplȯiə'biləd·ē, (ˌ)em-, -ətē, -i\ *n* -ES **:** the quality or state of being employable

em·ploy·able \əm'plȯiəbəl, em-\ *adj* **:** capable of being employed; *specif* **:** physically and mentally capable of earning a wage at a regular job and available for hiring

em·ploy·ee *or* **em·ploye** \əmˌplȯ(i)'ē, (ˌ)emˌ='=, əm'plȯi(ˌ)ē, -'plȯˌē, -'plȯi, em'=(ˌ)=, *sometimes* (ˌ)äm- *or* -ȯi'ā *or* -ȯi(ˌ)ā\ *n* -S [F *employé*, fr. past part. of *employer* to employ, fr. OF *empleoir*, *emploiier*] **1 :** one employed by another usu. in a position below the executive level and usu. for wages **2** *in labor relations* **:** any worker who is under wages or salary to an employer and who is not excluded by agreement from consideration as such a worker

em·ploy·er \əm'plȯi(y)ə(r), em'-, -ȯyə-\ *n* -S **:** one that employs something or somebody: as **a** (1) **:** the owner of an enterprise (as a business or manufacturing firm) that employs personnel for wages or salaries (2) **:** such an enterprise itself **b :** an agent acting for such an enterprise in employing persons

employers' association *n* **:** an organization of owners of business or manufacturing enterprises employing personnel or of their agents for the purpose of concerted action (as in labor negotiations)

employer's liability insurance *n* **:** insurance against loss an employer may suffer from his common-law liability for injury to an employee excluding liability imposed by a workmen's compensation act

em·ploy·ment \-ȯimənt\ *n* -S [ME *employement*, fr. *emploien* to employ + *-ment* — more at EMPLOY] **1 :** USE, PURPOSE **2 a :** activity in which one engages and employs his time and energies ⟨her baby will give her ~ enough now —Rachel Henning⟩ ⟨those in public office usually had to attend to their private ~*s* —C.L.Jones⟩: as (1) **:** work (as customary trade, craft, service, or vocation) in which one's labor or services are paid for by an employer ⟨~ as a mechanic⟩ ⟨in the ~ of the contractor⟩ (2) **:** temporary or occasional work or service for pay ⟨went from town to town, working when I could get ~ —Oliver Goldsmith⟩ (3) **:** occasional activity engaged in as an avocation, pastime, habit, or expedient **b :** an instance of such activity ⟨no sooner did he get an ~, however lowly, than his employer turned out to be a Communist —F.M.Ford⟩ ⟨in blitz war, the tactical ~*s* of the airplane are many and varied —S.L.A.Marshall⟩ **3 a :** the act of employing someone or something or the state of being employed ⟨the ~ of a pen in sketching⟩ ⟨the ~ of all means to an end⟩ ⟨the ~ of new workers⟩ ⟨walk to a distant table, and, leaning there in pretended ~, try to subdue the feelings —Jane Austen⟩ ⟨the routine ~ of blood transfusion —*Current Biog.*⟩ ⟨the next four essays examine the way in which the ~ of myth, belief, or even manners give meaning and form to the novel —W.V. O'Connor⟩ **b :** the degree or extent to which the persons needing employment or available for employment are provided with it or lack it because of the prevailing economic conditions ⟨~ in the particular area is likely to increase or decrease with the economic condition of the country as a whole⟩ ⟨efforts to increase ~ by stimulating local industry⟩ **syn** see WORK

employment agency *n* **:** an agency whose business is to find jobs for those seeking them or people to fill jobs that are open

employment agent *n* **:** one that runs an employment agency or as a business finds jobs for those seeking them or people to fill jobs that are open

employment bureau *n* **1 :** EMPLOYMENT AGENCY **2 :** an office (as in a school) that places applicants in jobs or gets and makes available information on job opportunities

employment certificate *n* **:** an authorization issued by school authorities for a child of school age to work at a job paying wages or salary

employment exchange *n* **:** any of the offices established in England for the collection of labor statistics, for the placing of employees, and for handling part of the system of unemployment insurance

emplume *var of* IMPLUME

em·po·as·ca \ˌempō'askə\ *n, cap* [NL] **:** a cosmopolitan genus of leafhoppers (family Cicadellidae) having the ocelli vestigial or wanting and including numerous serious pests of cultivated plants (as the potato leafhopper)

em·pocket \əm, em+\ *vt* [[1]*en-* + *pocket* (n.)] **:** to put into one's pocket

em·po·di·um \əm'pōdēəm, em-\ *n, pl* **empo·dia** \-ēə\ [NL, fr. [2]*en-* + *-podium*] **:** a small median appendage between the claws of the tarsi of many insects and arachnids

em·poison \əm, em+\ *vt* [ME *empoysonen*, fr. MF *empoisoner*, fr. OF, fr. *em-* [1]en- + *poison* — more at POISON] **1** *archaic* **:** POISON **2 :** EMBITTER ⟨a look of ~*ed* acceptance —Saul Bellow⟩ — **em·poi·son·ment** \"mənt\ *n* -S

em·poisoner *n* [ME *empoysoner*, fr. *empoysonen* + *-er*] *obs* **:** POISONER

em·polder *or* **im·polder** \əm, em +\ *vt* -ED/-ING/-S [D *inpolderen*, fr. *in-* [1]in- (akin to OE *in-*) + *polder* — more at IN-,

POLDER] : to make (land that is underwater or periodically flooded) cultivable by the erection of banks or levees to prevent or control inundation and by adequate drainage

em·po·ri·um \əm'pōrēəm, em-, -ór-\ *n, pl* **emporiums** \-ēəmz\ *also* **empo·ria** \-ēə\ [L, fr. Gk *emporion*, fr. *emporos* traveler, trader, fr. *em-* ²en- + *-poros* (fr. *poros* path, road, journey — more at FARE] **1 a :** a place of trade : MARKETPLACE, MART; *esp* : a commercial center ⟨the ~ of the innumerable kinds of merchandise which are exchanged between China, Central Asia, and Europe —W.H.G.Kingston⟩ ⟨it has been primarily an industrial city rather than a commercial ~ —Lewis Mumford⟩ **b :** an esp. sizable place of business or center of activity that serves customers ⟨earning his living at the local furniture ~ —William McFee⟩ ⟨he has built and equipped two eating ~*s* with a combined capacity of more than 200 food consumers at a sitting —Fred Hawthorne⟩ ⟨a hardware ~⟩ **c :** a store, shop, or similar enterprise making claim to fanciness or special commercial significance ⟨drinking and gambling ~ —*Amer. Guide Series: Oregon*⟩ ⟨found his once sedate carriage shop transformed into a sort of Hollywood hot-rod ~ —Hugh Humphrey⟩ ⟨the dresses in the windows of the dry-goods ~ —Hamilton Basso⟩ ⟨one of the shiny movie ~*s* —P.E.Deutschman⟩ ⟨a Chinese chop-suey ~ —Bennett Cerf⟩ **2 :** a store carrying a great diversity of merchandise ⟨the general ~ which catered to a variety of human needs —Della Lutes⟩ ⟨an air-conditioned news, candy, and soda-fountain ~ —J.P.Marquand⟩

empory *obs var of* EMPORIUM

em·power \əm, em +\ *vt* [¹*en-* + *power* (n.)] **1 :** to give official authority to : delegate legal power to : COMMISSION, AUTHORIZE ⟨~*ed* the Supreme Court and the district courts of the U.S. to issue writs of habeas corpus in circumstances involving the exercise of jurisdiction by Federal authorities —C.B.Swisher⟩ ⟨these courts of appeal are also ~*ed* to review and enforce orders of federal administrative bodies —W.S. Sayre⟩ ⟨the department was ~*ed* by the legislature to begin courses in medicine —*Amer. Guide Series: Minn.*⟩ **2 :** to give faculties or abilities to : ENABLE ⟨the emotion which ~*s* artists to create significant form —Clive Bell⟩ ⟨~*ed* by long training, the young priest blotted himself out of his own consciousness and meditated upon the anguish of his Lord —Willa Cather⟩ — **em·pow·er·ment** \"mənt\ *n* -s

em·pre·sa·rio \ˌemprə'särēˌō, -sa(a)r-, -ser-, -sär-\ *n* -s [Sp, contractor, manager, prob. fr. It *impresario* — more at IMPRESARIO] : one who before Texas became part of the U.S. entered into a contract with the Spanish or Mexican government to settle a certain number of families in Texas in exchange for sizable grants of land

¹**em·press** \'emprəs\ *n* -ES [ME *emperesse*, fr. OF, fem. of *empereor* emperor — more at EMPEROR] **1 :** the wife or widow of an emperor **2 :** a woman who holds an imperial title in her own right ⟨in 1876 Parliament conferred the title *Empress* of India on Queen Victoria⟩

²**empress** *obs var of* ²IMPRESS

em·presse·ment \äⁿpresmäⁿ\ *n, pl* **empressements** \-mäⁿ(z)\ [F, fr. (*s'*)*empresser* to hurry, be eager (fr. *em-* ¹en- + *presser* to hurry) + *-ment* — more at PRESS] : emotional interest or involvement : FERVOR ⟨lively, too lively, fond of showing off, exhibiting abundance of ~ in everything —W.G.Hammond⟩ ⟨if I hear anything very sinister and dramatic related with great ~ —Ngaio Marsh⟩ : WARMTH, CORDIALITY ⟨came forward to welcome her with considerable ~ —Agatha Christie⟩ ⟨his manner lacked ~ —Elizabeth Bowen⟩

em·press·ite \'emprəˌsīt\ *n* -s [*Empress* Josephine mine, Kerber creek dist., Colorado + E *-ite*] : a mineral AgTe consisting of telluride of silver

empress tree *n* [¹*empress*; after Anna Pavlovna, after whom the genus *Paulownia* was named — more at PAULOWNIA] : a paulownia (*Paulownia tomentosa*)

em·prise \em'prīz\ *n* -s [ME, fr. MF, fr. OF, fem. of *empris*, past part. of *emprendre* to undertake, fr. (assumed) VL *imprehendere*, fr. L *im-* ²in- + *prehendere* to seize — more at GET] **1 :** UNDERTAKING, ENTERPRISE ⟨when a nation of men starts making literature it invariably starts on the difficult ~ of verse, and goes on to prose as by an afterthought —A.T. Quiller-Couch⟩; *esp* : adventurous, daring, or chivalric enterprise ⟨the deep-breathed glory of high ~ —S.E.White⟩ **2 :** an instance of esp. adventurous or daring emprise ⟨in a high ~ that to the rest of us is at once a challenge and a solace —R.M.Neal⟩

em·pros·thot·o·nos \ˌem,präs'thätᵊnəs\ *n* -ES [NL, fr. Gk drawn forward and stiffened, fr. *emprostho-* (fr. *emprosthen* before, in front) + *-tonos* (fr. *tenein* to stretch)] : a tetanic spasm which bends the body ventralward

empt \'em(p)t\ *vb* -ED/-ING/-S [ME *empten*, *emptien*, fr. OE *ǣmtian*, *ǣmettigian* to empty, be at leisure, fr. *ǣmtig*, *ǣmettig* empty, unoccupied — more at EMPTY] *now dial* : EMPTY

emptied *past of* EMPTY

¹**emptier** *comparative of* EMPTY

²**emp·ti·er** \'em(p)tēə(r)\ *n* -s : one that empties

empties *pres 3d sing of* EMPTY, *pl of* EMPTY

emptiest *superlative of* EMPTY

emp·ti·ly \'em(p)tə̇lē, -tᵊl, |i\ *adv* : in an empty manner ⟨gazing ~ at television —Perry Miller⟩ ⟨the play after that ~ thins down —Stark Young⟩

emp·ti·ness \-tēnə̇s, -tin-\ *n* -ES [ME *emptinesse*, fr. *empty* + *-nesse* -ness] **1 a :** the quality or state of being empty **b :** the quality or state of lacking or being devoid of contents (as typical or customary) ⟨the ~ of the coal bin⟩ ⟨the ~ of the garage⟩ **c :** the quality or state of being uninhabited, unfrequented, or containing no human beings ⟨the ~, the blankness of great solitudes —Laurence Binyon⟩ ⟨the peculiar ~ of the green meadows and the tiny hidden lanes —Margery Allingham⟩ **2 a :** BARRENNESS ⟨a life . . . ghastly in its ~ and sterility —Aldous Huxley⟩; *esp* : lack of imagination or creative ability ⟨paintings marked by simplicity but not ~⟩ **b :** lack of something necessary to spiritual growth or sustenance ⟨the vulgarity, the cheapness, the showy pretentiousness, the dreadful ~ of life for the middle classes during the uneasy peace —W.L. Shirer⟩ ⟨the spiritual ~ of army life will have deeply affected the thinking habits of many men —B.B.Seligman⟩ **c :** INANITY, FOOLISHNESS, SENSELESSNESS ⟨he realized the ~ of mere opposition to the U.S. on such questions —A.F.Buchan⟩ **d :** lack of significant purposefulness : an engaging in purposeless or inane activity ⟨life without a customary companion was ~, ennui, restiveness and fidget —Francis Hackett⟩ **3 :** HUNGER ⟨the family had sat down, ill-humored from ~, to dinner at four o'clock —Ellen Glasgow⟩ **4 a :** LACK ⟨they were glad to overlook its frequent ~ of content —Van Wyck Brooks⟩ **b :** lack of warmth, love, or affection ⟨with her children she feels affectionate and at the same time has an impression of ~, which she gloomily interprets as complete indifference —H.M.Parshley⟩ **c :** marked unhappiness deriving from the loss of something loved ⟨the ~ of utter loss —F.R.Leavis⟩ **d :** sense of loss esp. of something desirable ⟨only an ~, a feeling that something was over —Stuart Cloete⟩ **5 :** uninhabited or unknown territory ⟨stood on the shores of this nameless lake at last . . . saying that we should turn back from the ~ which stretched ahead —Farley Mowat⟩ ⟨appears as a sort of outpost, standing almost on the edge of ~ —Green Peyton⟩ **6 :** something lacking significant content : FRIVOLITY 2 ⟨a play that was nothing more than a competent piece of ~⟩ **7** *Buddhism* : NIRVANA

emp·tins \'em(p)tə̇nz\ *or* **emp·tings** \", -tiŋz\ *n pl* [alter. of *emptyings*, pl. of *emptying*, fr. gerund of ²*empty*] *dial* : a liquid leavening usu. made at home from potatoes or hops and kept from one baking to the next

emp·tion \'em(p)shən\ *n* -s [L *emption-*, *emptio*, fr. *emptus* (past part. of *emere* to buy) + *-ion-*, *-io* -ion — more at REDEEM] **1 :** the act of buying : PURCHASE ⟨relieved both of the ~ of stuffs and of the payment of tailors and property-makers —E.K.Chambers⟩ **2 :** RIGHT OF EMPTION — **emp·tion·al** \-shənᵊl\ *adj*

emp·tio-ven·di·tio \'em(p)tē,ō,wen'did·ē,ō\ *or* **emptio et venditio** \-tē,ō(,)et(,)w-\ *n* [L *emptio et venditio* buying and selling] : the consensual contract between two parties for the purchase of something by one party and its sale by the other at an agreed price

emp·tor \'em(p)tər, -ˌtó(ə)r\ *n* -s [L, fr. *emptus* + *-or*] : PURCHASER, BUYER

¹**emp·ty** \'em(p)tē, -ti\ *adj* -ER/-EST [ME, fr. OE *ǣmtig*, *ǣmettig* empty, unoccupied, fr. *ǣmetta* leisure, rest (fr. *ǣ-* not, without + *-metta*, fr. *mōtan* to have to) + *-ig* -y — more at MUST] **1 a :** containing nothing : devoid of contents : not filled ⟨an ~ box⟩; *esp* : lacking typical, expected, or former contents ⟨a cold ~ stove⟩ ⟨an ~ pantry⟩ ⟨an ~ purse⟩ ⟨an ~ chair⟩ ⟨shows the ~ cross and the distant rising sun —T.A. Stafford⟩ **b :** VACANT, UNOCCUPIED ⟨an ~ house⟩ ⟨an ~ lot⟩ ⟨~ factory space⟩ **c :** devoid of people ⟨an ~ theater⟩ ⟨along the road that had been so quiet and ~ the night before, but was now crowded with people —Archibald Marshall⟩ : UNINHABITED ⟨colonize ~ lands where the Red Indian nomad would be the only person aggrieved —G.M.Trevelyan⟩ ⟨most of the northeast coast is ~ except for the villages —P.E.James⟩ : UNFREQUENTED ⟨seemed less disagreeable when one could walk in quiet, ~ places after dark —W.B.Yeats⟩ ⟨the muddy waters are ~, except for an occasional small ship such as the one taking me away —H.W.Carter⟩ **d** *of a female domestic animal* : not bearing a fetus : not pregnant ⟨an ~ heifer⟩ **e** *logic, of a class* : having no members : NULL **2 :** having nothing to carry or to transport : not loaded or burdened ⟨an ~ truck⟩ ⟨an ~ mail pouch⟩ : lacking cargo ⟨an ~ freighter⟩ ⟨an ~ camel train⟩ **3 a :** destitute of reality or substance ⟨an ~ dream⟩ ⟨~ lip service⟩ **b :** destitute of value : HOLLOW, VAIN ⟨an ~ pleasure⟩ ⟨confirmation of appointments by the senate is anything but an ~ form —*Amer. Guide Series: N.J.*⟩ ⟨~ bragging and all the playacting that springs from insincerity —H.M.Parshley⟩ ⟨an ~ display of erudition —Benjamin Farrington⟩ ⟨unless our party is reunited . . . the nomination for presidency will be purely an ~ honor —F.D.Roosevelt⟩ ⟨the idle or ~ use of God's name —*Interpreter's Bible*⟩ **c :** destitute of effect or force ⟨~ threats⟩ **d :** devoid of sense : MEANINGLESS, FOOLISH ⟨a speech made up of ~ and platitudinous ideas⟩ ⟨if all that cannot be understood or satisfactorily explained is to be dismissed as impossible or unreal, life will be an ~ thing indeed —W.F.Hambly⟩ **e :** devoid of knowledge, intelligence, or sense ⟨where a member of the aristocracy may be as husky of body and as ~ of mind as the most menial of the working caste —W.C.Allee⟩ **f :** devoid of expression or of any sign of intelligence ⟨an ~ face⟩ **4 :** HUNGRY ⟨after missing lunch the children were very ~ by suppertime⟩ **5 a :** lacking meaningful occupation or activity ⟨she wakened in the morning with a slight feeling of anticipation, a faint stirring of hope, instead of the horror and dread of another ~ day —Dorothy Witton⟩ ⟨summer in the city was an ~ season —Nancy Cardozo⟩ : not occupied with any purposeful activity : IDLE ⟨to fill the ~ hours, her daughter asked her to embroider a worsted picture —*Current Biog.*⟩ ⟨she enjoys turning her ~ leisure into a bountiful offering —H.M.Parshley⟩ **b :** having no purpose : USELESS ⟨a certain amount of ~ mileage is unnecessarily run —*Brit. Transport Rev.*⟩ **c :** yielding no return ⟨it was tedious work and involved following a lot of ~ leads —*Best True Fact Detective*⟩ **6 a :** marked by the absence of human life or activity or anything providing comfort or human warmth ⟨the ~ silence of the night⟩ ⟨a cold and ~ wasteland⟩ ⟨blank and ~ fields —Pearl Buck⟩ **b :** lacking human affection, warmth, or love ⟨it had been an acrid ~ home with everyone growing alien to one another —Norman Mailer⟩ **7 :** DESTITUTE, DEVOID ⟨~ of all purpose or meaning⟩ ⟨the streets are ~ of automobiles —Jean Stafford⟩ ⟨did the roads look peculiarly ~ of traffic —Meridel Le Sueur⟩ ⟨the air was never ~ of their sweet, sad calling —Mary Webb⟩ ⟨~ of meaning⟩ **8 a :** marked by a strong sense of loss or unhappy purposelessness ⟨the weeks after his wife's death were ~ and desolate⟩ : experiencing a marked and unsatisfied emotional need ⟨one evening you are lonely and ~ because the moon is shining and there is a strange beauty over the land —Charlton Laird⟩ **b :** incapable of experiencing further emotion : emotionally dulled or exhausted ⟨his outburst had left him completely ~, like a shaken sack —Liam O'Flaherty⟩

syn VACANT, BLANK, VOID, VACUOUS: EMPTY is a general term describing something lacking content; its usual antonyms are *full* or *filled* ⟨an *empty* basket⟩ ⟨an *empty* room from which the furniture had been moved⟩ ⟨the dark and *empty* auditorium of a theater in the morning when only one or two cleaners are moving about —Alan Moorehead⟩ Figuratively, EMPTY indicates lack of content or significance ⟨when words came they did not break the silence. The wall remained. The words that came were *empty*, meaningless words —Sherwood Anderson⟩ ⟨the unthinking mind is not necessarily dull, rude, or impervious; it is probably simply *empty* —C.W.Eliot⟩ VACANT describes what is without an occupant, incumbent, tenant, inmate, or person or thing appropriately settled or fixed within ⟨a *vacant* room ready for a new tenant⟩ ⟨the nook among the brambles where his van had been standing was as *vacant* as ever the next morning —Thomas Hardy⟩ ⟨a *vacant* throne⟩ ⟨a *vacant* professorship⟩ Figuratively VACANT may indicate lack of an agency or attribute considered as a usual occupant ⟨her partner, the poor snail, was a *vacant* creature, scarcely more than half-witted — and the hard work, of course, was put off on her —Willa Cather⟩ ⟨his *vacant* eye, his lack of interest in what went on about him, and his strange gestures and mutterings were symptoms of a failing mind —C.B. Nordhoff & J.N.Hall⟩ BLANK describes what is free from writing or marking ⟨a *blank* book⟩ ⟨a *blank* page⟩ In more figurative uses it may indicate lack of signs of expression, comprehension, or meaning ⟨she had not a word to say, and in *blank* astonishment she beheld the carriage drive off —William Black⟩ ⟨their utterances are more or less seriously taken because the public, equally ignorant, is just as *blank* and undiscriminating —C.H.Grandgent⟩ VOID intensifies the notions of EMPTY ⟨*void* barren desert⟩ ⟨a large smooth shining face, *void* of a sign of mustache or whiskers —Henry James †1916⟩ ⟨*void* of human interest or poetic quality, as yet unstirred by a breath of life —H.O.Taylor⟩ VACUOUS may suggest the emptiness of a vacuum; in figurative applications to persons and their notions, it is a synonym of *inane* ⟨the substances are dried in a bell jar or desiccator over concentrated sulfuric acid. The drying takes place more rapidly if the containing vessel is rendered *vacuous* —J.F.Thorpe & Martha A. Whiteley⟩ ⟨to see whether he could detect any surprise or suspicion. There was nothing to be read in the *vacuous* face, blank as a school notice-board out of term —Graham Greene⟩

syn see in addition VAIN

²**empty** \"\ *vb* -ED/-ING/-ES *vt* **1 a :** to make empty, devoid of contents, or vacant : deprive of contents, furnishings, or inhabitants ⟨~ a box⟩ ⟨~ a truck⟩ ⟨~ a house⟩ ⟨~ a city⟩ **b :** DEPRIVE, DIVEST ⟨~ a phrase of all meaning⟩ ⟨*emptied* himself of all power to control⟩ ⟨the Christ who *emptied* Himself of His glory and accepted humiliation and suffering —R.M. French⟩ ⟨his eyes *emptied* themselves of light and intelligence —R.H.Newman⟩ ⟨a style *emptied* of human content —Anthony Blunt⟩ ⟨the curriculum can be *emptied* of all the studies and the disciplines which relate to faith and to morals —Walter Lippmann⟩ **c :** to discharge (itself) of contents ⟨the stream *empties* itself into the river⟩ ⟨the water pipe *emptied* itself into the rain barrel with a gurgling sound⟩ **d :** to fire (a repeating firearm) until empty ⟨he leaped to his feet and *emptied* his gun through the broken window —S.H.Holbrook⟩ **2 :** to remove from what holds, encloses, or contains (as by carrying, pouring, or leading out) ⟨~ the grain from a sack⟩ ⟨~ the money from a purse⟩ ⟨~ the furniture from a house⟩ ⟨~ the cattle from a stable⟩ **3 :** to place, deposit, carry, dump, or pour by emptying from what holds, encloses, or contains ⟨~ grain into a bin⟩ ⟨~ his armful of packages onto the table⟩ ⟨~ the sacks from the truck onto the porch⟩ ⟨no waste, garbage, or refuse may be *emptied* on highways —*Amer. Guide Series: N. H.*⟩ ~ *vi* **1 :** to become empty ⟨the theater *emptied* rapidly after the show ended⟩ **2 :** to empty or discharge its contents ⟨the river *empties* into the ocean⟩ **3 :** to defecate or urinate : EVACUATE

³**empty** \"\ *n* -ES : something that is empty; *esp* : an empty container (as a box, bottle, cask) or vehicle (as a cab or car) ⟨an engine pulling five full boxcars, one coal car, and several *empties*⟩ ⟨always drunk two quarts of wine a day on the job, tossing his *empties* into the basement —Clifford Aucoin⟩

empty-cell process *or* **empty-cell treatment** *n* : a method of treating wood so that the chemical preservative coats the cell walls, the cell cavities remaining nearly or quite empty — compare FULL-CELL PROCESS

empty glume *n* : GLUME

empty-handed \¦==¦==\ *adj* : being without gain or acquisition : having acquired or gained nothing ⟨went out to win a fortune but came home *empty-handed*⟩ ⟨lack of mining equipment and geological data forced him to sail home *empty-handed* —*Amer. Guide Series: Mich.*⟩

empty-headed \¦==¦==\ *adj* : uninformed and scatterbrained ⟨an *empty-headed* wriggle-hipped blonde —*Time*⟩

emptyhearted \¦==¦==\ *adj* : having an empty heart ⟨hardly consistent with the levity of that society, alike ~ and empty=headed —James Martineau⟩

empty out *vt* : EMPTY ⟨*empty out* the water barrel to clear it of sediment⟩ ⟨*empty* a boat *out* by beaching it and turning it over⟩

empty weight *n* : the weight of the structure, power plant, and fixed equipment of an airplane in flying condition

empty word *n* : FUNCTION WORD

em·purple \əm, em+\ *vb* [¹*en-* + *purple* (adj.)] *vt* **1 a :** REDDEN ⟨blood from a deep cut *empurpling* the leg⟩ **b :** to make flushed (as with effort or embarrassment) ⟨broke off, his red face *empurpled*, mouthing speechlessly —J.E.Macdonnell⟩ **2 :** to make purple (as with cold or anger) ⟨a dying sun *empurpling* the distant hills⟩ ⟨a face *empurpled* by exposure⟩ ~ *vi* : to become red or flushed ⟨face *empurpled*, and the sweat poured down as she toiled away with the cranky thing —C.S. Forester⟩

empurpled *adj* : marked by purple passages ⟨a lush and ~ prose⟩ ⟨a writer of ~ literature⟩

em·pu·sa \em'pyüsə, -üzə\ [NL, fr. Gk *empousa* hobgoblin, specter] *syn of* ENTOMOPHTHORA

em·py·e·ma \ˌem,pī'ēmə, -pē'ē-\ *n, pl* **empyema·ta** \-'ēmədə, -'em-\ *or* **empyemas** [LL, fr. Gk *empyēma*, fr. *empyein* to suppurate] : the presence of pus in a bodily cavity (as the pleural cavity) : purulent pleurisy — **em·py·e·mic** \¦=,=¦ēmik -¦em-\ *adj*

em·py·re·al \ˌem,pī'rēəl, -,pə¦-; (ˈ)em¦pirēəl, -¦pīr-\ *adj* [LL *empyreus*, *empyrius* (fr. LGk *empyrios*, fr. Gk *empyros* fiery, fr. *em-* ²en- + *-pyros*, fr. *pyr* fire) + E *-al* — more at FIRE] **1 :** of or relating to the empyrean : CELESTIAL **2 :** SUBLIME ⟨well-meaning ineptitude, that rises to ~ absurdity —M.S. Dworkin⟩

¹**em·py·re·an** \-ēən\ *adj* [LL *empyreus*, *empyrius* + E *-an*] : EMPYREAL ⟨the earthly perfection of the individual to a height no less ~ than Luther's ideal of religious salvation —Helen Sullivan⟩ ⟨~ aplomb —Hamilton Basso⟩

²**empyrean** \"\ *n* -s **1 a :** the highest heaven or heavenly sphere in ancient and medieval cosmology usu. described as a sphere of fire or light — compare ELEMENT 1; ETHER, HEAVEN **b :** the true and ultimate heavenly paradise — used chiefly by certain Christian writers (as John Milton) **2 :** FIRMAMENT : HEAVENS ⟨an inhabitant of Mars guiding his spaceship through the ~ —Lucius Garvin⟩ ⟨the blue and cloudless ~ —F.L. Allen⟩ **3 :** a transcendentally sublime or lofty otherworldly place esp. from which lofty ideas may be thought to derive ⟨forever to inhabit an ~ of blithe intellectual play, of charming fancies and biting good sense —Edmund Wilson⟩ ⟨he alone stands still while the whole ~ of Greek life circles about him —J.J.Chapman⟩ ⟨the social theorist high in the ~ of pure ideas uncontaminated by mundane facts —R.K.Merton⟩

empyreum *n* -s [ML, fr. neut. of LL *empyreus*] *obs* : EMPYREAN 2

em·py·reu·ma \ˌempə'rümə, -pē'-, -,pī'-\ *n, pl* **empyreuma·ta** \-mədə\ [Gk, live coal covered with ashes, fr. *empyreuein* to light a fire, fr. *em-* ²en- + *pyreuein* to light, fr. *pyr*] : the peculiar odor of the products of organic substances burned in closed vessels

em·py·reu·mat·ic \¦=(,)=,rü¦mad·ik\ *also* **em·py·reu·mat·i·cal** \-d·ə̇kəl\ *adj* [Gk *empyreumat-*, *empyreuma* + E *-ic*, *-ical*] : being or having an odor of burnt organic matter as a result of decomposition at high temperatures ⟨creosote and other ~ oils⟩

em quad *n* [¹*em*] : a quad whose point dimension and set dimension are the same or very nearly the same : a quad with a square or almost square body

ems *pl of* EM

emu \'ē(,)myü *sometimes* -mü\ *n* -s [modif. of Pg *ema*] **1 :** a large Australian ratite bird (*Dromiceius novae-hollandiae*) now almost wholly restricted to northern and western Australia and being the largest existing bird next to the closely related ostrich, inhabiting open forests and plains, and having rudimentary wings and plumage of slender drooping feathers with greatly developed aftershafts and a head and neck feathered and without wattles **2 :** any of various tall flightless birds (as the rhea and cassowary)

EMU *abbr*, *usu not cap* electromagnetic unit

emu apple *n* : an Australian tree (*Owenia acidula*); *also* : its subacid fruit that is about as large as a small nectarine

emu bush *n* **1 :** an Australian tree of the genus *Pholidia* of the family Myoporaceae (esp. *P. longifolia*) **2 :** an Australian tree (*Heterodendron oleaefolium*) of the family Sapindaceae

emul *abbr* emulsion

¹**em·u·late** \'emyəˌlāt, *usu* -ād·+V\ *vb* -ED/-ING/-S [L *aemulatus*, past part. of *aemulari*, fr. *aemulus* rivaling, envious, akin to Gk *aitia* cause — more at ETIOLOGY] *vt* **1 a :** to strive to equal or excel : imitate with the intention of equaling or outdoing ⟨a simplicity *emulated* without success by numerous modern poets —T.S.Eliot⟩ **b :** IMITATE ⟨book-covering materials which one way or another ~ leather —*Book Production*⟩ ⟨some of the early Protestant congregations *emulated* this custom, but soon gave up the practice —*Amer. Guide Series: La.*⟩ **2** *obs* : to be jealous of : ENVY **3 :** to equal or approach equality with : RIVAL ⟨her companions she loved and admired, but could not ~, for they were wise about things she knew not of —Rose Macaulay⟩ ⟨modern watercolor in the West, when it tries, as it often does, to ~ the force and solidity of oil painting, only succeeds in sacrificing its own special felicities —Laurence Binyon⟩ ⟨he became president . . . at the age of 32, *emulating* his father's election to the post when he was 34 —H.T.Brundidge⟩ ~ *vi*, *obs* : STRIVE, ENDEAVOR

²**emulate** *adj* [L *aemulatus*, past part.] *obs* : EMULOUS

em·u·la·tion \ˌemyə'lāshən\ *n* -s [L *aemulation-*, *aemulatio*, fr. *aemulatus* + *-ion-*, *-io* -ion] **1 a :** a striving by imitation to equal others in accomplishment or quality ⟨earlier there was rivalry and even antagonism between the two nations of British culture but there was little ~ —Edward Shils⟩ ⟨creating manufacturing industries in ~ of the U. S. —George Wythe⟩; *also* : IMITATION ⟨slavish ~ of the elite —M.D.Geismar⟩ ⟨native military traditions tolerated no blind ~ of a foreign prototype —Hajo Holborn⟩ **b :** a striving to excel others in accomplishment or quality : RIVALRY ⟨the spirit of ~ enters into the majority of games, and usually the contest element masks other features of the games —*Notes & Queries on Anthropology*⟩ **c** *archaic* : the ambition to equal or excel in accomplishment or quality **d** *obs* : contentious rivalry **2** *archaic* : JEALOUSY, ENVY

em·u·la·tive \'emyəˌlād·|iv, -ˌlə|, |t|, |ēv *also* |əv\ *adj* : characterized by emulation ⟨a son's ~ drive to achieve the same success as his father⟩ : tending to emulation ⟨a man's character marked by strong ~ qualities⟩ : deriving from emulation or the impulse or drive to emulation ⟨the exploitation of materialistic drives and ~ anxieties —D.M.Potter⟩ — **em·u·la·tive·ly** \|ə̇vlē, -li\ *adv*

em·u·la·tor \-ˌlād·ə(r), -ātə-\ *n* -s [L *aemulator*, fr. *aemulatus* + *-or*] : one that emulates : IMITATOR, RIVAL

em·u·la·to·ry \'emyələˌtōrē, -ór-, -ri, *chiefly Brit* -ˌlātəri *or* -ˌlā·tri\ *adj* : EMULATIVE

emulge \ə̇'məlj, ē'-\ *vt* -ED/-ING/-S [L *emulgēre* to milk out] *archaic* : to draw off the fluid from (a bodily organ)

emul·gent \-jənt\ *adj* [L *emulgent-*, *emulgens*, pres. part. of *emulgēre* to milk out, fr. *e-* + *mulgēre* to milk — more at MILK] : that provides a drain for or strains out the product of something (as the kidneys)

em·u·lous \'emyələs\ *adj* [L *aemulus* rivaling, envious — more at EMULATE] **1 a :** ambitious or eager to emulate : striving for an accomplishment or quality equal or superior to that of another : marked by a desire to imitate or rival ⟨~ suitors⟩ **b :** inspired by or deriving from a desire to emulate ⟨~ fervor⟩ **2** *obs* : JEALOUS, ENVIOUS **3** *archaic* : ZEALOUS — **em·u·lous·ly** *adv* — **em·u·lous·ness** *n* -ES

emul·si·fi·abil·i·ty \ə̇,məlsə,fīə'bilad·ē\ *or* **emul·si·bil·i·ty** \-sə'bil-\ *n* -ES : capacity for being emulsified

emul·si·fi·able \ə'məlsə,fīəbəl, ē'-, ⸗,⸗⸗'⸗⸗⸗\ *or* **emul·si·ble** \⸗'⸗səbəl\ *adj* **:** capable of being emulsified ⟨~ oils⟩
emul·si·fi·ca·tion \-səfə'kāshən\ *n* -s **:** the process of emulsifying
emul·si·fi·er \-'məlsə,fī(ə)r, -īə\ *n* -s **1 :** an emulsifying agent **:** a surface-active agent (as a soap) for promoting the formation and stabilization of an emulsion **2 :** a machine (as a mixer) for emulsifying — compare HOMOGENIZER
emul·si·fy \-,fī\ *vt* -ED/-ING/-ES [*emulsion* + *-ify*] **:** to convert (as an oil) into an emulsion — compare HOMOGENIZE
emul·sin \-'məlsən\ *n* -s [G, fr. L *emulsus* + G *-in*] **:** any of various enzyme preparations that are obtained usu. from plants (as almonds and mold fungi) as white amorphous powders and that contain glycosidases active on beta-glycosides (as amygdalin or cellobiose)
emul·sion \ə'məlshən, ē'-\ *n* -s [NL *emulsion-, emulsio,* fr. L *emulsus* (past part. of *emulgēre* to milk out) + *-ion-, -io* -ion — more at EMULGENT] **1 a :** a milky fluid made by rubbing almonds or other seeds with water and used as a demulcent **b :** any of various milky liquids **2 a** (1) **:** an intimate mixture of two incompletely miscible liquids (as oil and water) in which one of the liquids in the form of fine droplets is dispersed in the other usu. with the aid of an emulsifier **:** a disperse system in which both phases are liquids ⟨milk is an oil-in-water ~⟩ (2) **:** an intimate mixture consisting of a semisolid or solid (as a resinous or bituminous material) dispersed in a liquid ⟨an ~ of asphalt in water⟩ — compare FOAM 1, SUSPENSION 2b (3) **b :** an emulsion of a liquid or solid substance in an aqueous liquid with an emulsifier (as a gum or gelatin) used esp. to improve the palatability of a medicine ⟨~ of cod-liver oil⟩ **3 :** a suspension of a finely divided sensitive silver salt (as silver bromide) or a mixture of silver halides in a viscous medium (as a gelatin solution) used for coating photographic plates, films, and paper; *also* **:** the resultant coating when dried
emulsion paint *n* **:** a paint having water usu. as the volatile phase with various nonvolatile substances (as a linseed-oil varnish) in emulsion as the binder — compare LATEX PAINT
emul·sive \-lsiv\ *adj* [*emulsion* + *-ive*] **:** constituting or yielding an emulsion ⟨~ insecticidal spray oils⟩
emul·soid \-,sȯid\ *n* -s [ISV *emulsion* + *-oid*] **1 :** a colloidal system consisting of a liquid dispersed in a liquid — not used scientifically; compare SUSPENSOID **2 :** a lyophilic sol (as a gelatin solution) — used esp. in biology — **emul·soi·dal** \ə'məl,sȯidᵊl, ē'-; ,ē,məl'⸗-\ *adj*
emul·sor \ə'məlsə(r), ē'-\ *n* -s [*emulsion* + *-or*] **:** EMULSIFIER 2 ⟨centrifugal ~s⟩
emunc·to·ry \ə'məŋ(k)t(ə)rē, ē'-\ *n* -ES [NL *emunctorium,* fr. L *emunctus* (past part. of *emungere* to blow or wipe the nose, fr. *e-* + *-mungere,* akin to *mucus*) + *-orium* -ory — more at MUCUS] *archaic* **:** an organ or part of the body (as the kidneys or skin) that serves to carry off body wastes
emundation *n* -s [LL *emundation-, emundatio,* fr. L *emundatus* (past part. of *emundare* to clean out, fr. *e* + *mundare* to clean, fr. *mundus* clean) + *-ion-, -io* -ion — more at MOTHER (membrane)] *obs* **:** ceremonial cleansing
emus *abbr* [L *eminentissimus*] most eminent
emu wren *n* **:** any of several small Australian warblers (genus *Stipiturus*) that resemble wrens but have the tail feathers long and loosely barbed like emu feathers
emyd·ea \ə'midēə, ē'\ *n pl, cap* [NL, fr. *Emyd-, Emys*] *in former classifications* **:** a group of turtles nearly coextensive with the family Emydidae
em·y·did \'emə,did; ə'midəd, ē'-\ *adj* [NL *Emydidae*] **:** of or relating to the Emydidae
emyd·i·dae \ə'midə,dē, ē'-\ *n pl, cap* [NL, fr. *Emyd-, Emys,* type genus + *-idae*] **:** a family of chelonians comprising most of the freshwater aquatic tortoises and terrapins and closely related to Testudinidae in which it has often been included as a subfamily
em·y·do·sau·ria \,emədō'sȯrēə\ [NL, fr. Gk *emyd-, emys* + NL *-o-* + *-sauria*] *syn of* LORICATA
¹em·y·do·sau·ri·an \¦⸗⸗⸗'sȯrēən\ *adj* [NL *Emydosauria* + E *-an*] **:** of or relating to the Loricata **:** CROCODILIAN
²emydosaurian \"\ *n* -s **:** LORICATE
emys \'ēməs, 'em-\ *n, cap* [NL, fr. Gk *emys* freshwater tortoise] **:** a small genus of turtles (family Emydidae) including the common European pond tortoise (*E. orbicularis*) and a No. American tortoise (*E. blandingii*)
¹en \'en\ *n* -s **1 :** the letter *n* **2 :** the set dimension of an en quad used esp. in Great Britain as a unit of measure of a typesetter's production
²en \ən, ᵊn, ˌēn\ *dial Eng var of* HIM
³en \'en, 'ān, 'əi(ə)n\ *Scot var of* END
⁴en \(ˈ)äⁿ(n), (ˌ)än, (ˌ)en, (ˌ)in\ *prep* [F, lit., in, fr. L *in*] **:** in the form or manner of — see EN BLOC, EN BROSSE, EN CABOCHON
¹en- *also* **em-** *prefix* [ME, fr. OF, fr. L *in-, im-,* fr. *in* — more at IN] **1 :** put into ⟨*en*cradle⟩ **:** put on to ⟨*en*throne⟩ **:** cover or surround with ⟨*en*verdure⟩ **:** go into or on to ⟨*em*bus⟩ — in verbs formed from nouns **2 :** cause to be ⟨*en*glad⟩ ⟨*en*slave⟩ — sometimes in verbs that also have the suffix *-en* ⟨*em*bolden⟩; in verbs formed from adjectives or nouns **3 :** provide with ⟨*en*collar⟩ ⟨*em*power⟩ — in verbs formed from nouns **4 :** so as to cover or surround ⟨*en*wrap⟩ **:** thoroughly ⟨*en*tangle⟩ — often in verbs differing little or not at all in meaning from the corresponding verb without prefix ⟨*en*tame⟩; in verbs formed from verbs; in all senses usu. *em-* before *b, m,* or *p* and *en-* in other circumstances
²en- *also* **em-** *prefix* [ME, fr. L, fr. Gk, fr. *en* in — more at IN] **:** in **:** within **:** inside ⟨*en*dermic⟩ ⟨*en*gram⟩ ⟨*en*zootic⟩ — usu. *em-* before *b, m,* or *p* (*em*batholithic) and *en-* in other circumstances
³en- — see OEN-
⁴en- *comb form* [ISV, fr. *-ene*] **:** chemically unsaturated; *esp* **:** having one double bond ⟨*en*amine⟩
¹-en \ən, ᵊn *sometimes* ᵊm *after* p, b, f, *or* v *sometimes* ᵊŋ *after* k *or* g\ *also* **-n** \n\ *adj suffix* [ME, fr. OE; akin to OHG *-īn* made of, ON *-inn,* Goth *-eins* made of, of or belonging to, L *-inus* (with long *ī*) of or belonging to, Gk *-inos* made of, of or belonging to, Skt *-īna* of or belonging to] **:** made of **:** consisting of ⟨earth*en*⟩ ⟨wool*en*⟩ — now relatively infrequent because of the widespread attributive use of nouns or of adjectives formed from nouns without the addition of a suffix (as in *gold* cup, *wheat* cake) and to be found chiefly in adjectives which are obsolete ⟨tinn*en*⟩ or archaic ⟨oak*en*⟩ or in which a sense other than the literal one has become prominent ⟨gold*en*⟩ ⟨wood*en*⟩; usu. *-n* after *-er* ⟨silver*n*⟩
²-en \"\ *vb suffix* -ED/-ING/-S [ME *-nen,* fr. OE *-nian* (as in *fæstnian* to fasten); akin to OS *-nōn,* final segment of certain transitive infinitives (as in *fastnōn* to fasten), OHG *-inōn* (as in *festinōn* to fasten), ON *-na* (as in *fastna* to pledge, betroth)] **1 a :** cause to be ⟨sharp*en*⟩ — sometimes in verbs that also have the prefix *en-* ⟨*em*bold*en*⟩; in transitive verbs formed from adjectives **b :** cause to have ⟨length*en*⟩ — in transitive verbs formed from nouns **2 a :** come to be ⟨steep*en*⟩ — in intransitive verbs formed from adjectives **b :** come to have ⟨length*en*⟩ — in intransitive verbs formed from nouns
en *abbr* enemy
en *symbol* ethylenediamine — in chemical formulas ⟨[Co(en)₃]-Br₃⟩
EN *abbr* exception noted
en·able \ə'nābəl, e'-\ *vt* **enabled; enabled; enabling** \-b(ə)liŋ\ **enables** [ME *enablen,* fr. ¹*en-* + *able,* adj.] **1 a :** to render able ⟨~ a person to earn a living⟩ **:** give power, strength, or competency ⟨his particular theology *enabling* him to overcome some of the difficulties —S.F.Mason⟩ **b :** to make possible, practical, or easy ⟨*enabled* passage of the anti-poll-tax law —H.F. & Katharine Pringle⟩ **2 a** *archaic* **:** to give authority or sanction to **:** ENDOW **b :** to give legal capacity to **3 :** to give the opportunity to **:** ALLOW ⟨examinations so designed that high-school graduates are *enabled* to pass⟩
en·abler \-b(ə)lə(r)\ *n* -s **:** one that enables
enabling *adj* [fr. pres. part. of *enable*] **:** giving or providing legal power or sanction esp. beyond usual bounds in order to meet the demands of an unusual or anomalous situation ⟨an ~ act⟩ ⟨an ~ resolution⟩
¹en·act \ə'nakt, e'-\ *vb* [ME *enacten,* fr. ¹*en-* + *acte* act, formal record — more at ACT] *vt* **1** *obs* **:** to enter into the public records **:** CHRONICLE **2 :** to establish by legal and authoritative act **:** make into a law; *esp* **:** to perform the last act of legislation upon (a bill) that gives the validity of law **3 :** to act out **:** REPRESENT, PLAY ⟨a lot of history has been ~*ed* within my view —Douglas Carruthers⟩ ⟨this scene being ~*ed* in the courtroom —Beatrice Griffith⟩ ~ *vi* **:** to act on or as if on the stage **:** PERFORM
²enact *n* [ME *enacte,* fr. *enacten,* v.] *obs* **:** ENACTMENT
enacting clause *n* [*enacting* fr. pres. part. of ¹*enact*] **:** the clause of an act that formally expresses the legislative sanction and that usu. appears after the title or preamble of the act
en·ac·tion \ə'nakshən, e'-\ *n* [¹*enact* + *-ion*] **:** ENACTMENT
en·act·ment \-k(t)mənt\ *n* -s **1 :** the act or action of enacting **:** PASSING ⟨the ~ of a bill by the legislature to aid private industry⟩ **2 :** something that has been enacted (as a law, bill, or statute)
en·ac·tor \-ktə(r)\ *n* **:** one that enacts ⟨the new laws . . . fulfilled the fondest hopes of their ~*s* —Oscar Handlin⟩
enacture *n* -s *obs* **:** ENACTMENT, RESOLUTION
en·a·lid \'enᵊləd\ *n* -s [ISV *enal-* (fr. Gk *enalios* of the sea, fr. *en-* ²*en-* + *halios* of the sea, fr. *hal-, hals* sea) + *-id;* akin to Gk *hals* salt — more at SALT] **:** a submerged marine plant (as eelgrass)
en·al·i·or·nis \ə,nalē'ȯrnəs\ *n, cap* [NL, fr. *enali-* (fr. Gk *enalios* of the sea) + *-ornis*] **:** a genus comprising Cretaceous swimming birds from the Greensand formations of England and related to *Hesperornis*
en·al·i·o·saur \ə'nalēə,sȯ(ə)r\ *n* -s [NL *Enaliosauria*] **:** a marine reptile of the division Enaliosauria
en·al·i·o·sau·ria \⸗,⸗⸗⸗'sȯrēə\ *n pl, cap* [NL, fr. *enalio-* (fr. Gk *enalios* of the sea) + *-sauria*] *in some classifications* **:** a division of extinct marine reptiles comprising the Ichthyosauria and the Plesiosauria and other forms — **en·al·i·o·sau·ri·an** \⸗¦⸗⸗⸗¦sȯrēən\ *adj or n*
en·a·lite \'enᵊl,īt\ *n* -s [*Ena,* town in central Honshu, Japan + E *-lite*] **:** a uraniferous thorite
enam \ə'näm\ *n* -s [Hindi *in'ām* enam, gift, favor, fr. Per, fr. Ar] *Hindu law* **:** a grant of land to be held rent free or on favorable rent; *specif* **:** such a grant in perpetuity — compare JAGIR
enam·dar \-,där\ *n* -s [Hindi *in'āmdār,* fr. Per, fr. *in'ām* + *-dār* holder — more at BHUMIDAR] **:** the holder of an enam
¹enam·el \ə'naməl, e'-\ *vt* **enameled** *or* **enamelled; enameled** *or* **enamelled; enameling** *or* **enamelling** \-m(ə)liŋ\ **enamels** [ME *enamelen,* fr. MF *enameler, enamailler,* fr. *en-* ¹*en-* + *esmaillier, amaillier* to enamel, fr. OF *esmaillier,* fr. *esmail, esmal* enamel, of Gmc origin; akin to OHG *smelzan* to melt — more at SMELT] **1 :** to cover or inlay with enamel **2 :** to beautify or adorn with or as if with a colorful bright surface ⟨sun . . . ~*ed* the whole scene —*London Calling*⟩ **3 :** to form or produce a glossy surface upon (as paper, leather, or cloth) **4 :** to apply enamel to (the face or nails)
²enamel \"\ *n* -s [ME, fr. *enamelen,* v.] **1 :** a usu. opaque or semiopaque vitreous composition applied by fusion to the surface of metal, glass, or pottery for ornament or protection or as a basis for decoration — see CHAMPLEVÉ, CLOISONNÉ; compare GLAZE **2 :** a surface, exterior, or outer covering that resembles or suggests enamel **3 :** a paint that flows out to a smooth hard coat when applied, that contains a specially prepared vehicle instead of raw oil, and that usu. dries with a glossy appearance **4 :** something that is enameled **:** enameled ware **5 :** a cosmetic intended to give the appearance of a smooth and beautiful complexion or to produce a glossy appearance **6 :** the intensely hard calcareous substance that forms a thin layer capping or partly covering the teeth of most mammals (as man) and many other vertebrates, being the hardest substance of the animal body and consisting of minute prisms that are secreted by ameloblasts, are arranged at right angles to the surface, and are bound together by a cement substance — see TOOTH illustration **7 a :** the coating of carbonized glue or shellac that forms the acid-resisting portion of a metal photoengraving plate **b :** the facing material of coated paper
enamel cell *n* **:** AMELOBLAST
enameled brick *n* [*enameled* fr. past part. of ¹*enamel*] **:** a brick having a smooth impervious easily cleaned surface secured by coating with a special wash before burning and used in bathrooms, hotel kitchens, and swimming pools
enameled leather *n* **:** leather having a hard varnished surface; *specif* **:** PATENT LEATHER
enam·el·er *or* **enam·el·ler** \-m(ə)lə(r)\ *n* -s **:** one that applies enamel: as **a :** one that fuses enamel into jewelry settings **b :** one that coats cast-iron sanitary units with enamel
enameling *or* **enamelling** *n* -s [ME *enamelinge,* fr. *enamelen* to enamel + *-inge* -ing] **1 :** ENAMEL; *specif* **:** enamel ornamentation **2 a :** the application of enamel **b :** the process or technique of applying enamel
enam·el·ist *or* **enam·el·list** \-məlǝst\ *n* -s **:** ENAMELER
enamel kiln *n* **:** a muffle kiln used by enamelers in which colors and gold applied over the glaze are fired **:** a decorating kiln
enamel organ *n* **:** an ectodermal ingrowth from the dental ridge that forms a cap with two walls separated by a reticulum of stellate cells, encloses the anterior part of the developing dental papilla and the cells of the inner enamel layer adjacent to the papilla, and differentiates into columnar ameloblasts which lay down the enamel rods of the tooth
enamel painting *n* **:** painting with enamel colors that are fixed with heat usu. upon a surface of fired enamel
enamel rod *n* **:** one of the elongated prismatic bodies making up the enamel of a tooth
enamelware \⸗'⸗⸗,⸗\ *n* **:** ware (as iron cooking utensils) coated with enamel for protection (as from rust or the action of acids)
en·am·or \ə'namə(r), e'-\ *vt* **enamored; enamored; enamoring** \-m(ə)riŋ\ **enamors** *see -or in Explan Notes* [ME *enamouren,* fr. OF *enamourer,* fr. *en-* ¹*en-* + *amour, amor* love — more at AMOUR] **:** to inflame with love **:** CHARM, CAPTIVATE — usu. used in the passive with *of* ⟨tourists were ~*ed* of the town⟩ and sometimes with *with* ⟨a beautiful Indian girl with whom he was ~*ed* —Walter Havighurst⟩
en·am·ored·ness \-mə(r)dnəs\ *n* -ES **:** the state of being enamored
enan·thal·de·hyde *or* **oe·nan·thal·de·hyde** \,ē,nan'thaldə,hīd\ *n* [ISV *enanth-, oenanth-* (as in *enanthic acid*) + *aldehyde*] **:** a pungent oily compound $CH_3(CH_2)_5CHO$ obtained by pyrolysis of castor oil and used esp. in making artificial cognac — called also *heptaldehyde, heptanal*
enan·thate *or* **oe·nan·thate** \ə'nan,thāt, ē'-\ *n* -s [ISV *enanth-, oenanth-* + *-ate*] **:** a salt or ester of enanthic acid
en·an·them \ə'nan(t)thəm, e'-\ *or* **en·an·the·ma** \,e,nan'thēmə\ *n, pl* **enanthems** \-thəmz\ *or* **enanthe·ma·ta** \-'thēmədə, -'them-\ [NL *enanthema,* fr. ²*en-* + *-anthema*] **:** an eruption upon a mucous surface — **en·an·them·a·tous** \¦⸗¦⸗'themədəs, -¦thēm-\ *adj*
enan·thic acid *or* **oe·nan·thic acid** \ə¦'nan(t)thik-, ē¦-\ *n* [ISV *enanth-, oenanth-* (fr. L *oenanthe* wild grape, fr. Gk *oinanthē* grape blossom, fr. *oinē* grapevine + *anthē* blossom) + *-ic;* akin to Gk *oinos* wine and to Gk *anthos* flower — more at WINE, ANTHOLOGY] **:** an oily fatty acid $CH_3(CH_2)_5COOH$ usu. made by oxidizing enanthaldehyde and used chiefly in making esters for flavoring materials — called also *heptanoic acid*
enantio- *comb form* [NL, fr. Gk, fr. *enantios,* fr. *enanti* in the presence of, fr. *en* in + *anti* against — more at IN, ANTE-] **1 :** opposite ⟨*enantio*tropy⟩ **2 :** antagonistic ⟨*enantio*biosis⟩
en·an·ti·o·bi·o·sis \ə,nantēō,bī'ōsəs, e,-\ *also* **en·an·to·bi·o·sis** \-tō,b-\ *n, pl* **enantiobioses** *also* **enantobioses** [NL, fr. *enantio-* + *-biosis*] **:** antagonistic symbiosis
en·an·ti·o·blas·tic \ə¦nantēō¦blastik, e¦-\ *also* **en·an·ti·o·blas·tous** \-stəs\ *adj* [*enantio-* + *-blastic* or *-blastous* (fr. *-blast* + *-ous*)] **:** originating at the end of a seed opposite the hilum — used of an embryo
en·an·ti·o·mer \ə'nantēəmər, e'-, -,me(ə)r\ *n* -s [*enantio-* + *-mer*] **:** ENANTIOMORPH 2
en·an·ti·o·mer·ic \-¦nantēō¦merik\ *adj* [*enantio-* + *-meric*] **:** ENANTIOMORPHOUS
en·an·ti·o·morph \⸗'⸗⸗⸗,mȯrf\ *n* -s [ISV *enantio-* + *-morph;* orig. formed as G] **1 :** either of two enantiomorphous crystals **2 :** either of two crystalline forms or compounds exhibiting enantiomorphism — called also *optical antipode;* distinguished from *diastereoisomer;* compare RACEMIC
en·an·ti·o·mor·phism \⸗,⸗⸗⸗'mȯr,fizəm\ *n* -s [*enantio-* + *-morphism*] **:** the phenomenon of mirror-image relationship exhibited by right-handed and left-handed crystals (as of quartz) or by the molecular structures of two stereoisomeric compounds (as *dextro*-tartaric acid and *levo*-tartaric acid) — distinguished from *diastereoisomerism;* compare ASYMMETRIC CARBON ATOM, OPTICAL ISOMERISM
en·an·ti·o·mor·phous \⸗¦⸗⸗⸗¦mȯrfəs\ *or* **en·an·ti·o·mor·phic** \-fik\ *adj* [*enantio-* + *-morphous* or *-morphic*] **:** of, relating to, or exhibiting enantiomorphism
en·an·ti·o·trop·ic \⸗¦⸗⸗⸗¦träpik\ *adj* [*enantio-* + *-tropic*] **:** of, relating to, or exhibiting enantiotropy
en·an·ti·ot·ro·py \⸗,⸗⸗'ä·trəpē\ *n* -ES [ISV *enantio-* + *-tropy*] **:** the relation of two different forms of the same substance (as two allotropic forms of tin) that have a definite transition point and can therefore change reversibly each into the other — compare MONOTROPY
en·arched \ə'närcht, e'-\ *adj* [fr. past part. of obs. *enarch* to provide with an arch or arches, fr. ME *enarchen,* fr. ¹*en-* + *arche,* n., arch] *heraldry* **:** bent into a curve or arch ⟨an ~ fess⟩
en·ar·gite \ə'när,jīt, 'enər-\ *n* -s [G *enargit,* fr. Gk *enargēs* visible (fr. *en* in + *argēs* bright) + G *-it* -ite; fr. its cleavage; akin to Gk *argos* white — more at ARGENT] **:** a grayish black or iron-black copper arsenic sulfide (Cu_3AsS_4) of metallic luster occurring in small orthorhombic crystals or massive and often containing antimony
en·arm \ə'närm, e'-\ *vt* [ME *enarmen,* prob. fr. ¹*en-* + *armen* to arm] *archaic* **:** to equip with arms or armor
en·arme \"\ *n* -s [obs. F, fr. OF, fr. *enarmer* to provide (a shield) with straps through which an arm may be passed, fr. (assumed) VL *inarmare,* fr. L *in* + (assumed) VL *-armare* (fr. L *armus* shoulder) — more at IN, ARM] **:** the strap or the set of straps by which a shield was held on the arm — usu. used in pl.
enar·ra·tion \,ē,na'rāshən, ,e,n-\ *n* -s [L *enarration-, enarratio* detailed exposition, fr. *enarratus* (past part. of *enarrare* to explain in detail, fr. *e-* + *narrare* to narrate) + *-ion-, -io* -ion — more at NARRATE] *archaic* **:** a detailed exposition or description
en ar·rière \äⁿnäryeer\ *adv (or adj)* [F, behind, backward, in arrears] **1** *heraldry* **:** from the back ⟨an eagle proper *en arrière*⟩ **2** *ballet* **:** toward the back **:** BACKWARD — used of a movement or of the execution of a step ⟨a glissade *en arrière*⟩
en·ar·thro·di·al \¦e,när¦thrōdēəl\ *adj* [NL *enarthrodia* enarthrosis (fr. ²*en-* + *arthrodia*) + E *-al*] **:** of, relating to, or having the form of an enarthrosis
en·ar·thro·sis \⸗,⸗'thrōsəs\ *n, pl* **enarthro·ses** \-ō,sēz\ [NL, fr. Gk *enarthrōsis,* fr. *en-* ²*en-* + *arthrōsis* arthrosis] **:** an articulation in which the rounded head of one bone fits into a cuplike cavity of the other and admits movement in any direction **:** a ball-and-socket joint (as the hip joint)
enas·cent \ē, ə+\ *adj* [L *enascent-, enascens,* pres. part. of *enasci* to spring up, sprout, fr. *e-* + *nasci* to be born — more at NATION] *archaic* **:** NASCENT
¹enate \'ē,nāt\ *adj* [L *enatus,* past part. of *enasci*] **1 :** growing out **2 :** ENATIC
²enate \"\ *n* -s [L *enatus,* past part. of *enasci*] **:** one related on the mother's side — compare AGNATE
enat·ic \(ˈ)ē¦nad·ik\ *adj* [L *enatus* (past part. of *enasci*) + E *-ic*] **:** descended from the same mother **:** related on the mother's side ⟨~ clans⟩
ena·tion \ē'nāshən\ *n* -s [L *enatus* (past part. of *enasci*) + E *-ion*] **1 :** an outgrowth from the surface of an organ ⟨a plant virus forming ~*s* on leaves⟩ **2 :** kinship on the mother's side
enation mosaic *n* **:** mosaic (as of tobacco, potato, and tomato) in which raised pin-shaped corrugated outgrowths appear chiefly on the lower surface of the leaves
en avant \äⁿnäväⁿ\ *adv (or adj)* [F, in front, forward] *ballet* **:** in front **:** FORWARD — used of a movement or of the execution of a step
en axe \äⁿnäks\ *adj* [F, on the axis] **:** placed symmetrically in or upon the axis — used with *with* ⟨pillars *en axe* with the central aisle⟩
en banc \äⁿbäⁿ\ *adv (or adj)* [F, on the bench] **:** in full court **:** with full judiciary authority ⟨in the recent . . . case all seven circuit judges sat *en banc* —Archibald Cox⟩
en bas \äⁿbä\ *adv (or adj)* [F, below, down] *ballet* **:** in a low position — used of the arms
en bloc *pronunc at* ⁴EN + 'bläk\ *adv (or adj)* [F] **1 :** as a whole **:** in a lump or mass ⟨forced the islanders . . . to move *en bloc* —D.B.Forrester⟩ ⟨one escape for harassed editors is to buy a group of strips *en bloc* from some syndicate —Coulton Waugh⟩ **2 :** in one piece **:** as a unit ⟨an engine with cylinders cast *en bloc*⟩
enbrave *var of* EMBRAVE
en bro·chette \¦äⁿbrō¦shet\ *adv (or adj)* [F] **:** on a skewer ⟨broiled kidney *en brochette*⟩
en brosse \äⁿbrȯs\ *adv (or adj)* [F, lit., in the manner of a brush] **:** in a manner resembling the short erect bristles of a brush — used of a man's hair style ⟨his black hair . . . stood up *en brosse* —Hugh Walpole⟩ ⟨his very thick graying hair *en brosse* added an extra inch to his stature —Kathryn Grondahl⟩
enc *abbr* **1** enclosed; enclosure **2** encyclopedia
en cab·o·chon \en'kabə,shän\ *adv* [F, in the manner of a cabochon] **:** in convex form but not faceted ⟨a ruby cut *en cabochon*⟩
en·cae·nia \en'sēnyə, in'-, -nēə\ *n pl but sing or pl in constr, sometimes cap* [NL, fr. L, dedication festival, fr. Gk *enkainia,* fr. *en* in + *-kainia* (fr. *kainos* new) — more at IN, RECENT] **:** an annual university ceremony (as at Oxford University) of commemoration with recital of poems and essays and conferring of degrees
en·cage \ən, en+\ *vt* [¹*en-* + *cage,* n.] **:** CAGE 1
en·camp \ən, en+\ *vb* [¹*en-* + *camp,* n.] *vt* **:** to form into or place in a camp ⟨~ soldiers⟩ ~ *vi* **:** to form or occupy a camp **:** prepare and settle in temporary habitations (as tents or huts)
en·camp·ment \"mənt\ *n* -s **1 a :** the action of encamping **b :** the state of being encamped **2 a :** the place where a body of troops or campers is encamped **:** CAMP ⟨was not enthusiastic over the choice of Valley Forge as a winter ~ —F.V.W. Mason⟩ ⟨a well-fortified ~⟩ ⟨the ~ of migratory workers outside the city⟩ **b :** the individuals that make up an encampment ⟨the whole ~ was in an uproar⟩ **3 :** COMMANDERY 3 **4 :** a convention of a national association of ex-servicemen
en·cap·su·late \ən'kapsə,lāt, en- *also* -syə-\ *also* **en·capsule** \ən, en+\ *vb* -ED/-ING/-S [*encapsulate* fr. ¹*en-* + *capsule,* n. + *-ate,* vb. suffix; *encapsule* fr. ¹*en-* + *capsule,* n.] *vt* **:** to surround, encase, or protect in or as if in a capsule **:** CAPSULE ⟨the tissues of the body surround the [trichina] organisms and ~ them —Morris Fishbein⟩ ⟨in his youth he was *encapsulated* in affection —H.L.Mencken⟩ ~ *vi* **:** to become encapsulated ⟨a bacillus that ~*s* in the human body⟩ ⟨some very small poikilotherms desiccate and ~ for protection —Samuel Brody⟩ — **en·capsulation** \ən, (,)en+\ *n*
encapsulated *adj* [fr. past part. of *encapsulate*] *biol* **:** surrounded by a gelatinous or membranous envelope ⟨~ water bacteria⟩
encaptive *vt* [¹*en-* + *captive,* n. or adj.] *obs* **:** to make captive
encarnadine *var of* INCARNADINE
en·carnalize \ən, en+\ *vt* [¹*en-* + *carnalize*] **:** to make carnal ⟨grossness *encarnalizing* a conversation⟩
en·car·pus \en'kärpəs\ *n, pl* **encar·pi** \-,pī, -,pē\ [alter. (influenced by Gk *enkarpos*) of earlier *encarpa* festoons as an architectural ornament, fr. L, fr. Gk *enkarpa,* neut. pl. of *enkarpos* containing fruit, fr. *en-* ²*en-* + *-karpos* -carpous] **:** an ornament on a frieze or capital consisting of festoons (as of fruit or flowers)
en car·ré \äⁿkärā\ *adv* [F, lit., in the form of a square] **:** on the intersection of four numbers in roulette so as to include all four — used of a bet
en·case *also* **in·case** \ən'kās, en-\ *vt* [¹*en-* or ²*in-* + *case,* n.] **1 :** to enclose in, place in, or provide with a case ⟨each product *encased* in leatherette⟩ **2 :** to cover or surround with or as if with something solid, impermeable, or confining ⟨the neurotic loneliness of a woman *encased* in her ambition —*Saturday Rev.*⟩
encased knot *n* [*encased* fr. past part. of *encase*] **:** a dead or

loose knot or portion of a branch partially or entirely embedded in the bole of a tree

encased postage stamp *n* **:** a postage stamp mounted in a metal case with a transparent face (as of mica) for use as a piece of money

en·case·ment *also* **in·case·ment** \-mənt\ *n* **1 a :** the act or process of encasing or the state of being encased **b :** the supposed enclosure in a living germ of the germs of all future generations that might develop from it — compare PREFORMATION **2 :** CASE, COVERING

en·cash \ən, en+\ *vt* [¹*en-* + *cash*, n.] *Brit* **:** CASH — **en·cash·able** \"əbəl\ *adj, Brit* — **en·cash·ment** \-mənt\ *n* -S *Brit*

en casserole *pronunc at* ⁴EN+\ *adv (or adj)* [F] **:** in a casserole — used of foods so cooked and served ⟨chicken *en casserole*⟩ ⟨ham cooked *en casserole*⟩

en·cas·tage \äⁿkästäzh\ *n* -S [F, action of placing pieces of pottery in saggers, fr. *encaster* to place (pieces of pottery) in saggers (irreg. fr. *en-* ¹en- + *casette* sagger, fr. *case* compartment, square of a chessboard — fr. Sp *casa* square of a chessboard, house, fr. L, hut, cabin — + *-ette*) + *-age* — more at CASA] **:** the placing of pottery in a kiln for firing

en·cas·tre \äⁿkästrā\ *adj* [F *encastré*, past part. of *encastrer* to embed, fit into a recess, fr. It *incastrare*, fr. LL, fr. L *in* + *castrare* to trim, cut off, castrate — more at CASTRATE] **:** built in at the supports ⟨standing on an ~ beam⟩

¹en·caus·tic \ən'kȯstik, (')en¦k-, -tēk\ *adj* [L *encausticus*, fr. Gk *enkaustikos*, fr. *enkaustos* painted in encaustic (fr. *enkaiein* to burn in, paint in encaustic, fr. *en-* ²en- + *kaiein* to burn) + *-ikos* -ic — more at CAUSTIC] **:** of or relating to encaustic ⟨the ~ method⟩ ⟨an ~ picture⟩ — **en·caus·ti·cal·ly** \-tək(ə)lē, -tēk-, -li\ *adv*

²encaustic \"\ *n* **1 :** a paint mixed with melted beeswax and after application fixed by heat **2 :** the method involving the use of encaustic; *also* **:** a picture produced by this method

encaustic tile *n* **1 :** a tile decorated with colored clays inlaid and fired **2 :** colored tile laid in a wall or floor to form a pattern — usu. used in pl.

en·cave \ən'kāv, en-\ *vt* [¹*en-* + *cave*, n.] **:** to hide in or as if in a cave

-ence \ən(t)s, ᵊn(t)s, *in some words* " *or* -,en(t)s; "-*erence*" *is often* ərn(t)s\ *n suffix* -S [ME, fr. OF, fr. L *-entia*, fr. *-ent-*, *-ens* -ent + *-ia* -y] **1 :** action or process ⟨abstin*ence*⟩ ⟨emerg*ence*⟩ ⟨conflu*ence*⟩ **:** instance of an action or process ⟨refer*ence*⟩ ⟨reminisc*ence*⟩ **2 :** quality or state ⟨condescend*ence*⟩ **:** one having a (specified) quality or being in a (specified) state ⟨standing on an emin*ence*⟩ ⟨depend*ence*⟩

¹en·ceinte \(')äⁿ¦saⁿt, (')än¦-, -sent,-sänt, F äⁿsaⁿt\ *adj* [MF, fr. (assumed) VL *incienta*, alter. of L *incient-*, *inciens* being with young, fr. *in* + *-cient-*, *-ciens* (akin to Gk *kyein* to be pregnant) — more at CAVE] **:** being with child **:** PREGNANT

²enceinte \"\ *n* -S [F, enclosed area, fr. OF, enclosing wall or fence, fr. fem. of *enceint*, past part. of *enceindre* to enclose, fr. L *incingere* to gird, surround, fr. *in* + *cingere* to gird — more at CINCTURE] **1 :** a line of fortification enclosing a castle or town **2 :** the area or town enclosed by an enceinte

en·ce·lia \ən'sēlēə\ *n* [NL] **1** *cap* **:** a genus of shrubs (family Compositae) of the southwestern U.S. and northern Mexico having linear leaves, radiate flower heads, and flat achenes — see BRITTLEBUSH **2** -S **:** any plant of the genus *Encelia* — see INCIENSO

encephal- *or* **encephalo-** *comb form* [F *encéphal-*, fr. Gk *enkephal-*, fr. *enkephalos* brain] **1 :** brain ⟨*encephal*itis⟩ ⟨*encephalo*cele⟩ **2 :** of or belonging to the brain and ⟨*encephalo*spinal⟩

encephala *pl of* ENCEPHALON

en·ceph·a·lar·tos \ən,sefə'lärd·əs\ *n* [NL, fr. Gk *enkephalos* heart of the date palm, brain + *artos* bread — more at ARTO-] **1** *cap* **:** a genus of arborescent African cycads (family Cycadaceae) having stout cylindrical trunks and a terminal crown of mostly long spiny pinnate leaves — see KAFFIR BREAD **2** -ES **:** any plant of the genus *Encephalartos*

-encephali *pl of* -ENCEPHALUS

-en·ce·pha·lia \,ensə'fālyə, -lēə\ *n comb form* -S [NL, fr. *-encephalus* + *-ia* -y] **:** condition of having (such) a brain ⟨scler*encephalia*⟩

en·ce·phal·ic \,ensə¦falik, -lēk\ *adj* [F *encéphalique*, fr. *encéphal-* encephal- + *-ique* -ic] **:** of or relating to the brain; *also* **:** lying within the cranial cavity

-encephalies *pl of* -ENCEPHALY

en·ceph·a·lit·ic \ən¦sefə¦lid·ik, (,)en, -it|, |ēk\ *adj* [ISV *encephalit-* (fr. NL *encephalitis*) + *-ic*] **:** relating to, affected with, or characteristic of encephalitis

en·ceph·a·li·tis \⸗,⸗⸗'līd·əs, -ītəs\ *n, pl* **encephalit·i·des** \-'lid·ə,dēz, -itə-\ [NL, fr. *encephal-* + *-itis*] **:** inflammation of the brain esp. when due to infectious agents or their toxins; *specif* **:** any of several diseases of man in which a virus of any of several related strains normally parasites of lower vertebrates and commonly transmitted by biting arthropods invades the brain causing inflammatory and degenerative lesions commonly accompanied by apathy, muscular weakness, and lethargy passing into more or less profound somnolence — see SLEEPING SICKNESS

encephalitis le·thar·gi·ca \-lə'thärjəkə, -le'-\ *n* [NL, lethargic encephalitis] **:** epidemic virus encephalitis in which somnolence is marked

en·ceph·a·li·to·gen·ic \⸗¦⸗⸗¦līd·ə¦jenik\ *also* **en·ceph·a·li·tog·e·nous** \⸗,⸗⸗,lī¦täjənəs\ *adj* [*encephalito-* (fr. NL *encephalitis*) + *-genic* or *-genous*] **:** tending to cause encephalitis ⟨an ~ strain of virus⟩

en·ceph·a·li·to·zo·on \⸗,⸗⸗,līd·ə'zō,än, -ōən\ *n* [NL, fr. *encephalito-* (fr. *encephalitis*) + *-zoon*] **1** *cap, in some classifications* **:** a genus of microorganisms of uncertain systematic position that are known from intracellular bodies in neural and visceral structures of various mammals (as the rabbit) in which they are associated with an encephalitis and sometimes a nephritis **2** *pl* **encephalito·zo·a** \-ōə\ **:** an organism or intracellular body assigned to the genus *Encephalitozoon*

en·ceph·a·lo·cele *also* **en·ceph·a·lo·coele** \⸗'sefəlō,sēl\ *n* -S [*encephalocele* ISV *encephal-* + *-cele; encephalocoele* alter. (influenced by *-coele*) of *encephalocele*] **:** hernia of the brain either congenital or due to trauma

encephalocoele \"\ *n* -S [*encephal-* + *-coele*] **:** the ventricles of the brain

en·ceph·a·lo·gram \,gram\ *n* -S [ISV *encephal-* + *-gram*] **:** an X-ray picture of the brain made by encephalography

en·ceph·a·lo·graph \-,graf, -äf\ *n* -S [*encephal-* + *-graph*] **1 :** ENCEPHALOGRAM **2 :** ELECTROENCEPHALOGRAPH

en·ceph·a·lo·graph·ic \⸗¦⸗⸗¦grafik\ *adj* [*encephalography* + *-ic*] **:** of, relating to, or by means of encephalography — **en·ceph·a·lo·graph·i·cal·ly** \-fək(ə)lē\ *adv*

en·ceph·a·log·ra·phy \⸗⸗⸗'lägrəfē\ *n* -ES [ISV *encephal-* + *-graphy*] **:** roentgenography of the brain after the cerebrospinal fluid has been replaced by air or other gas

en·ceph·a·loid \⸗'⸗⸗,lȯid\ *adj* [ISV *encephal-* + *-oid*; prob. orig. formed as F *encéphaloïde*] **:** resembling the material of the brain

en·ceph·a·lo·malacia \⸗¦⸗⸗(,)lō+\ *n* [NL, fr. *encephal-* + *malacia*] **:** softening of the brain due to degenerative changes in nervous tissue (as in crazy chick disease) — **en·ceph·a·lo·ma·lac·ic** \"+mə¦lasik\ *adj*

en·ceph·a·lo·meningitis \"+\ *n* [NL, fr. *encephal-* + *meningitis*] **:** MENINGOENCEPHALITIS

en·ceph·a·lo·mere \⸗'⸗⸗,mi(ə)r\ *n* -S [*encephal-* + *-mere*] **:** a segment of the embryonic brain — **en·ceph·a·lo·mer·ic** \⸗¦⸗⸗¦merik\ *adj*

en·ceph·a·lo·myelitic \⸗¦⸗⸗+\ *adj* [*encephalomyelitis* + *-ic*] **:** of, relating to, or of the nature of encephalomyelitis

en·ceph·a·lo·myelitis \"+\ *n* [NL, fr. *encephal-* + *myelitis*] **:** concurrent inflammation of the brain and spinal cord; *specif* **:** any of several serious enzootic arthropod-transmitted virus diseases of horses characterized by fever, sluggishness, incoordination, and damage to the central nervous system and represented in the U.S. by a severe eastern and a milder western form caused by distinct viruses either of which may produce encephalitis in man — called also *infectious equine encephalomyelitis, sleeping sickness*

en·ceph·a·lon \ən'sefə,län, en-, -lən\ *n, pl* **encepha·la** \-lə\ [NL, modif. of Gk *enkephalos* brain, fr. *en* in + *kephalē* head — more at IN, CEPHALIC] **:** the vertebrate brain

en·ceph·a·lop·a·thy \⸗,⸗⸗'läpəthē\ *n* -ES [NL *encephalopathia*, fr. *encephal-* + *-pathia* -pathy] **:** a disease of the brain; *esp* **:** one involving alterations of brain structure

en·ceph·a·lo·phone \⸗'⸗⸗⸗+,fōn\ *n* -S [*encephal-* + *-phone*] **:** an apparatus that emits a continuous hum whose pitch is changed by interference of brain waves transmitted through oscillators from electrodes attached to the scalp and that is used to diagnose abnormal brain functioning

en·ceph·a·lo·sis \-'lōsəs\ *n, pl* **encephalo·ses** \-ō,sēz\ [NL, fr. *encephal-* + *-osis*] **:** ENCEPHALOPATHY

-en·ceph·a·lous \(,)en¦sefələs, ən-, ᵊn-\ *adj comb form* [Gk *-enkephalos*, fr. *enkephalos* brain] **:** having (such) a brain ⟨micr*encephalous*⟩

-en·ceph·a·lus \⸗'⸗⸗⸗\ *n comb form, pl* **-encepha·li** \-,lī\ [NL, fr. Gk *-enkephalos* -encephalous] **1 :** fetus having (such) a brain ⟨pseud*encephalus*⟩ **2 :** condition of having (such) a brain ⟨micr*encephalus*⟩

-en·ceph·a·ly \⸗'⸗⸗lē, -li\ *n comb form* -ES [NL *-encephalia*] **:** condition of having (such) a brain ⟨an*encephaly*⟩

-ences *pl of* -ENCE

en·chafe \ən'chāf, en-\ *vt* [ME *enchaufen*, fr. ¹*en-* + *chaufen* to chafe] *archaic* **:** CHAFE, HEAT, EXCITE

en·chain \ən'chān, en-\ *vt* [ME *encheynen*, fr. MF *enchaëner*, *enchainer*, fr. OF, fr. *en-* ¹en- + *chaeine* chain] **1 :** to bind with or put in chains **:** restrain with or as if with chains **:** FETTER ⟨men ~*ed* by reason of their greed⟩ **2 :** to attract and hold (as the attention or emotions) ⟨a speaker hoping to ~ the attention of the audience⟩ **3** *obs* **:** to link together **:** CONNECT

en·chaîne·ment \äⁿshānmäⁿ, -shen-\ *n* -S [F, enchainement, fr. MF *enchainement* series, action of binding with chains, fr. MF *enchainement* chain, fr. *enchainer* + *-ment*] **:** a short series of steps in ballet comprising a phrase which can be repeated or varied

en·chain·ment \ən'chānmənt, en-\ *n* -S [*enchain* + *-ment*] **1 :** the act or action of linking together **2 :** the quality or state of being linked together

en·chant \ən'chant, en-, -aa(ə)-,-ai-,-à-\ *vb* [ME *enchanten*, fr. MF *enchanter*, fr. L *incantare*, fr. *in* in, against + *cantare* to sing — more at IN, CHANT] *vt* **1 :** to influence by or as if by charms and incantation **:** BEWITCH ⟨a princess ~*ed* by a cruel sorcerer⟩ ⟨the scene ~*ed* her to the point of tears —Elinor Wylie⟩ **2 :** to thrill or enrapture **:** DELIGHT ⟨new talent to ~ viewers this coming television season —Goodman Ace⟩ **3 :** to endow with charm **:** infuse, permeate, or transfix with allure, fascination, or attraction ⟨the rare smile that ~*ed* her whole face —Edith Wharton⟩ ~ *vi* **1 :** to employ or practice magic or sorcery **2 :** to be charming **:** create delight **syn** see ATTRACT

en·chant·er \-t·ə(r)\ *n* -S [ME, alter. (influenced by ME *-er*) of *enchantour*, fr. OF *enchanteor*, fr. LL *incantator*, fr. L *incantatus* (past part. of *incantare*) + *-or*] **1 :** one that practices sorcery **:** WITCH, MAGICIAN **2 :** one that fascinates or delights

enchanter's nightshade *n* **:** any plant of the genus *Circaea* (esp. *C. lutetiana*) of the family Onagraceae characterized by inconspicuous white flowers and bristly fruit

en·chant·ing *adj* [fr. pres. part. of *enchant*] **:** CHARMING, FASCINATING ⟨~ dinner dresses —*New Yorker*⟩ — **en·chant·ing·ly** *adv* — **en·chant·ing·ness** *n* -ES

en·chant·ment \-tmənt\ *n* -S [ME *enchantement*, fr. OF, fr. L *incantamentum* incantation, fr. *incantare* + *-mentum* -ment] **1 a :** the act or action of enchanting **:** BEWITCHMENT **b :** the quality or state of being enchanted **:** FASCINATION ⟨having missed almost everything that lent ~ to a normal childhood —L.C.Douglas⟩ **2 :** something that fascinates, bewitches, or charms ⟨the dangers and ~*s* of mountainous country⟩

en·chant·ress \-ntrəs\ *n* -ES [ME *enchaunteresse*, fr. MF *enchanteresse*, fr. OF, fr. *enchanteor* enchanter + *-esse* -ess] **1 :** a woman who practices magic **:** SORCERESS **2 :** a fascinating or bewitching woman

en·charge \ən, en+\ *vt* [ME *enchargen*, fr. MF *enchargier*, fr. (assumed) VL *incarricare*, fr. L *in* + LL *carricare* to charge, load — more at IN, CHARGE] **1** *archaic* **:** to give into the charge of a person ⟨*encharging* him the custody and defense thereof —Robert Barret⟩ **2 :** to give a responsibility, duty, or task to **:** ENTRUST — usu. used with *with* ⟨found himself *encharged* with the bringing up of a young nobleman —R.H. Quick⟩

en·chase \ən'chās, en-\ *vt* [ME *enchasen* to emboss, fr. MF *enchasser* to enshrine (as a holy relic), set (as a jewel), fr. OF, fr. *en-* ¹en- + *chasse* reliquary, fr. L *capsa* box, case — more at CASE] **1 :** ENCASE, ENCLOSE ⟨~ a gem⟩ **:** SET ⟨a diamond *enchased* in a gold ring⟩ **2 :** ORNAMENT, DECORATE: as **a :** to cut or carve (as figures or designs) in relief **:** ENGRAVE **b :** INLAY ⟨a table *enchased* with ivory⟩ **3** *obs* **:** to enclose solemnly **:** ENSHRINE

en·chas·er \-sə(r)\ *n* **:** one that enchases

encheason *n* -S [ME *enchesoun*, fr. OF *enchaison*, alter. (influenced by OF *en-* ¹en-) of *achaison*, modif. (influenced by OF *a-*, fr. L *ad-*) of L *occasion-*, *occasio* — more at OCCASION] *obs* **:** OCCASION, CAUSE, REASON

en·cheer \ən, en+\ *vt* [¹*en-* + *cheer*] *archaic* **:** CHEER

en·chel·y·ceph·a·li \(,)en¦kelə'sefə,lī\ *n pl, cap* [NL, fr. Gk *enchelys* eel + NL *-cephali* (pl. of *-cephalus*) — more at ANGUIS] *in some classifications* **:** a suborder of Apodes including the common eels

en·chi·la·da \,enchə'lädə, -ladə\ *n* -S [AmerSp, fr. fem. of *enchilado*, past part. of *enchilar* to season with chili, fr. Sp *en-* ¹en- (fr. L *in-*) + *chile* chili] **:** a tortilla topped or rolled up with a highly seasoned meat or other filling and served with tomato sauce seasoned with chili

en·chi·rid·i·on *also* **en·chei·rid·i·on** \,en|,kī'ridēən, ,eŋ|, |,kə'-, -ē,än\ *n* -S [LL *enchiridion*, fr. Gk *encheiridion*, fr. *en* in + *cheir* hand + *-idion* -idium — more at IN, CHIR-] **:** HANDBOOK, MANUAL ⟨a bulky ~ for pious women —Israel Zangwill⟩

¹en·cho·don·tid \¦eŋkə¦däntəd\ *or* **en·cho·don·toid** \-n-,tȯid\ *adj* [*enchodontid* fr. NL *Enchodontidae*, fr. *Enchodont-*, *Enchodus*, type genus + *-idae*; *enchodontoid* fr. NL *Enchodont-*, *Enchodus* + E *-oid*] **:** of or relating to the genus *Enchodus* or the Enchodontidae

²enchodontid *or* **enchodontoid** \"\ *n* -S **:** an enchodontid fish

en·cho·dus \'eŋkədəs\ *n, cap* [NL, fr. Gk *enchos* spear + NL *-odus*] **:** a genus (the type of the family Enchodontidae) of large-mouthed Cretaceous stomiatoid fishes with spear⸗shaped teeth

en·chondral \(')en (')eŋ+\ *adj* [ISV ²*en-* + *chondral*] **:** ENDOCHONDRAL

en·chon·dro·ma \,en,kän'drōmə, ,eŋ,k-\ *n, pl* **enchondromas** *or* **enchondroma·ta** \-məd·ə\ [NL, fr. ²*en-* + *chondr-* + *-oma*] **:** a tumor consisting of cartilaginous tissue; *esp* **:** one arising where cartilage does not normally exist — **en·chon·drom·a·tous** \¦⸗,⸗'drämədəs, -rōm-\ *adj*

en·chon·dro·sis \¦⸗,⸗'drōsəs\ *n, pl* **enchondro·ses** \-ō,sēz\ [NL, fr. ²*en-* + *chondr-* + *-osis*] **:** a cartilaginous outgrowth; *also* **:** CHONDROMA

en·cho·ri·al \(')en¦kōrēəl, (')eŋ¦k-\ *adj* [Gk *enchōrios* of the country, native, domestic (fr. *en-* ²en- + *-chōrios*, fr. *chōra* place, land, country) + E *-al*; akin to Gk *chēros* left, bereaved — more at HEIR] **:** DEMOTIC 2 a

en·chy·le·ma \,en,kī'lēmə, ,eŋ,k-\ *n* -S [ISV ²*en-* + *chyle* + *-ma* (as in *-oma*); in sense 1 prob. orig. formed as G *enchylem*; in sense 2 prob. orig. formed as F *enchylème*] **1 :** HYALOPLASM **2 :** KARYOLYMPH — **en·chy·lem·a·tous** \¦⸗¦⸗¦lemədəs, -lēm-\ *adj*

-en·chy·ma \'eŋkəmə, 'enk-\ *n comb form, pl* **-enchymata** *or* **-enchymas** [NL, fr. *-enchyma* (in *parenchyma*)] **:** cellular tissue of a (specified) type ⟨coll*enchyma*⟩ ⟨cyst*enchyma*⟩

en·chym·a·tous \en'kimədəs, eŋ'k-\ *adj* [NL *enchymat-*, *enchyma* infusion (fr. Gk, fr. *enchein* to pour in, infuse, fr. *en* in + *chein* to pour) + E *-ous* — more at IN, FOUND] *of gland cells* **:** distended with secretion

-en·chyme \ən,kīm, 'eŋ,k-, 'en,k-\ *n comb form* -S [NL *-enchyma*] **:** -ENCHYMA ⟨coll*enchyme*⟩

en·chy·trae \'eŋkə,trē, 'enk-\ *n pl* [irreg. fr. NL *Enchytraeus*] **:** worms belonging to the genus *Enchytraeus* and used as food for aquarium fishes

¹en·chy·trae·id \⸗¦⸗'trēəd\ *adj* [NL *Enchytraeidae*] **:** of or relating to the genus *Enchytraeus* or to the Enchytraeidae

²enchytraeid \"\ *n* -S **:** a worm of the genus *Enchytraeus*

en·chy·trae·idae \⸗,⸗'trēə,dē\ *n pl, cap* [NL, fr. *Enchytraeus*, type genus + *-idae*] **:** a family of oligochaete worms including the genus *Enchytraeus*

en·chy·trae·us \-ēəs\ *n, cap* [NL, fr. ²*en-* + Gk *chytraios* of earthenware, fr. *chytra* earthen pot, fr. *chein* to pour] **:** a genus of small white worms (family Enchytraeidae) comprising both terrestrial and aquatic forms, often found in sewage filters, and widely propagated as food for aquarium fishes

-encies *pl of* -ENCY

en·ci·na \ən'sēnə, en-\ *n* -S [AmerSp, fr. Sp, holm oak, modif. of LL *ilicina*, fem. of *ilicinus* of holm oak, fr. L *ilic-*, *ilex* holm oak + *-inus* -ine — more at ILEX] **1 :** COAST LIVE OAK **2 :** LIVE OAK a

en·ci·nal \¦en(t)sə¦nal, -näl\ *n* -S [AmerSp, fr. Sp, grove of holm oak, fr. *encina*] **:** an oak grove or an area marked primarily by the growth of oaks

en·cincture \ən, en+\ *vt* [¹*en-* + *cincture*, n.] **:** to encircle with or as if with a girdle **:** GIRD ⟨a lake *encinctured* with a belt of forest⟩

en·ci·ni·llo \,en(t)sə'nē(,)(y)ō\ *n* -S [AmerSp, dim. of Sp *encina* holm oak] **:** an endemic Puerto Rican shrub (*Drypetes ilicifolia*) of the family Euphorbiaceae with leathery leaves, inconspicuous flowers, and drupaceous fruit

en·cipher \ən, en+\ *vt* [¹*en-* + *cipher*, n.] **:** to convert (a message) into cipher

en·cipherer \"+\ *n* -S **:** one that enciphers

enciphering alphabet *n* [*enciphering* fr. gerund of *encipher*] **:** a substitution alphabet with its plain component in normal alphabetic order — see ALPHABET 1j, CONJUGATE ALPHABET

en·ci·pher·ment \"mənt\ *n* -S **1 :** the act or process of enciphering **2 :** the result of enciphering **:** CIPHERTEXT

en·circle \ən, en+\ *vt* [¹*en-* + *circle*, n.] **1 :** to form a circle about ⟨insert each comma in your shorthand notes and ~ it —L.A.Leslie⟩ **:** enclose within a circle **:** SURROUND ⟨a ring *encircled* her finger⟩ ⟨a camp *encircled* by enemies⟩ **2 :** to make a circuit about **:** go around ⟨as a hungry wolf might have *encircled* . . . the firelit camp of a hunter —Sherwood Anderson⟩ **syn** see SURROUND

en·cir·cle·ment \"mənt\ *n* -S **:** the act or process of encircling, surrounding, or encompassing ⟨the ~ of the globe by an airplane⟩ ⟨the ~ of a wound by scar tissue⟩; *specif* **:** the policy of one or more countries of gradually enveloping or isolating another country ⟨ridden by the nightmare of ~ —*Yale Rev.*⟩

encl *abbr* enclosed; enclosure

en clair \äⁿkle(ə)r\ *adv (or adj)* [F, lit., in clear] **:** in plain language ⟨the message was in cipher, not *en clair* —E.O. Hauser⟩ — used esp. of diplomatic messages sent by telegraph

en·clasp *also* **in·clasp** \ən, en+\ *vt* [¹*en-* or ²*in-* + *clasp*] **:** to seize and hold **:** CLASP ⟨he ~*ed* her waist in his arm⟩

¹en·clave \'e|n,klāv, 'ä| *also* |ŋ,k- *sometimes* "ä . . . läv *or* "ä . . . lāv\ *n* -S [F, fr. MF, fr. *enclaver*, v.] **1 :** a tract or territory enclosed within foreign territory; *also* **:** a district or region (as in a city) inhabited by a particular race or sect apart for a special purpose — compare EXCLAVE **2 a :** something enclosed in an organ or tissue but not a continuous part thereof **b :** a small often relict community of one kind of plant in an opening of a larger plant community

²enclave \"\ *vt* -ED/-ING/-S [F *enclaver*, fr. OF, fr. (assumed) VL *inclavare* to enclose, lock up, fr. L *in* + (assumed) VL *-clavare* (fr. *clavis* key); akin to L *claudere* to close — more at CLOSE] **:** to enclose within or encircle or surround by alien or foreign territory

en·cli·sis \'eŋkləsəs, 'enk-\ *n, pl* **encli·ses** \-ə,sēz\ [LL, fr. Gk *enklisis*, fr. *enklinein*] **:** pronunciation as an enclitic

¹en·clit·ic \(')en¦klid·|ik, in'k-, -lit|, |ēk *also* (')eŋ¦- *or* iŋ'-\ *adj* [LL *encliticus*, fr. Gk *enklitikos*, fr. *enklinein* to cause to incline, pronounce as an enclitic, fr. *en* in + *klinein* to lean — more at IN, LEAN] **1 :** leaning or dependent with reference to accent: **a** *of a word or particle in Greek or Latin grammar* **:** being without independent accent and being attached in pronunciation to a preceding word in which it may cause certain accentual changes (as Greek *te* in *anthrōpoi te*, Latin *-ne* in *videsne*) **b** *of a word or particle in the grammar of languages other than Greek and Latin* **:** treated in pronunciation as forming a part of the preceding word (as English *thee* in *prithee* and *not* in *cannot*) — compare PROCLITIC **2 :** INCLINED — used of the relation of the planes of the fetal head to those of the maternal pelvis — compare SYNCLITIC

²enclitic \"\ *n* -S **:** an enclitic word or particle

enclog *vt* [¹*en-* + *clog*, v.] *obs* **:** CLOG

encloister *vt* [¹*en-* + *cloister*, n.] *obs* **:** to immure esp. in a cloister **:** CONFINE

en·close *or* **in·close** \ən'klōz, en-\ *vt* [ME *enclosen*, *inclosen*, prob. fr. *enclos*, *inclos*, adj., enclosed, fr. MF *enclos*, past part. of *enclore* to enclose, fr. (assumed) VL *includere*, alter. (influenced by L *claudere* to close) of L *includere* to enclose, include — more at INCLUDE, CLOSE] **1 a :** to close in ⟨~ a porch with glass⟩ **:** SURROUND ⟨~ a yard with a fence⟩; *specif* **:** to fence off or in (common land) in order to appropriate to individual use **b :** ENVELOP, ENFOLD ⟨mountains *enclosed* the town⟩ ⟨*enclosed* in a circle of candlelight —Stuart Cloete⟩ **c :** to hem in **:** CONFINE ⟨a convict *enclosed* within walls for life⟩ **:** subject (a religious or a building or an area) to the rules of enclosure ⟨an *enclosed* order of nuns⟩ ⟨~ the chapel⟩ **d :** to complete the shell of (a building under construction) so as to make weatherproof and secure from intrusion **2 :** to place (as a document, note, or bill) in a parcel or envelope ⟨a check *enclosed* with a letter⟩ **3 :** to seize or grasp securely **:** HOLD ⟨his fingers *enclosed* the money⟩

syn ENVELOP, FENCE, PEN, COOP, CORRAL, CAGE, WALL: ENCLOSE is a general word without rich or specific connotation or definite limitation ⟨their prey *enclosed* within a ring —William Wordsworth⟩ ⟨the study of the history of ideas and their *enclosing* words —C.A.Beard⟩ ENVELOP implies complete enclosure on all sides, esp. one opaque or translucent but yielding and penetrable ⟨the sweet, often incense-laden atmosphere . . . *enveloped* her like a warm and healing garment —Rose Macaulay⟩ ⟨the great chilly unused drawing room whose spacious ceremoniousness seemed to embrace and *envelop* her —J.C.Powys⟩ The remaining words in this set are closely connected with cognate nouns and may show regional variations. In general, FENCE is to close off as if with a fence; it suggests an area barred to entrance or exit and somewhat protected. It is wide and often figurative in use ⟨a Kirghiz tent, with all its muffled walls . . . would not suffice to *fence* out that insistent sunlight —Sacheverell Sitwell⟩ ⟨*fencing* off a corner of the sea with dikes —*N.Y.Times*⟩ PEN is to enclose in a pen esp. to prevent straying. It expresses irksome restriction, but ideas of confinement are stronger in the following words ⟨pigs and geese are *penned* up for the night⟩ ⟨practically the whole of the population is *penned* in on a narrow coastal strip —W.A. Lewis⟩ COOP reinforces notions of prevention of straying, stresses structure rather than area, and more strongly implies narrow and cramped limitation inhibiting activity ⟨poultry *cooped* up⟩ ⟨they feel themselves in a state of thralldom, they imagine that their souls are *cooped* and cabined in —Edmund Burke⟩ ⟨sent their whole army over here onto this island and *cooped* it up so it couldn't get away —Kenneth Roberts⟩ CORRAL suggests prevention of straying or escape by enclosing in larger, less cramping, but stronger and more secure quarters ⟨to *corral* rodeo broncos⟩ It usu. connotes difficulty in driving or controlling whatever is corralled and is often figurative ⟨the vitamins are being *corralled* one by one and the proteins are being brought under control —C.C.Furnas⟩ ⟨to *corral* as many liberal and mutually hostile groups of voters as he can —*New Republic*⟩ CAGE connotes prevention of escape by confinement in a strong small structure; it suggests more inexorable confinement ⟨*caged* eagles⟩ ⟨as sullen as a beast new⸗*caged* —Alfred Tennyson⟩ ⟨the feeling of *caged* muscular tightness has provoked a fairly widespread desire to emigrate from Britain —J.R.Chamberlain⟩ WALL suggests strong impenetrable construction barring entrance or exit and guaranteeing confinement or security ⟨when towns were so small that they were *walled* in as gardens are now —G.B.Shaw⟩ ⟨an artificial universe . . . *walled* off from the world of nature —Aldous Huxley⟩

enclosed arc lamp *n* [*enclosed* fr. past part. of *enclose*] **:** an arc lamp having electrodes protected from the atmosphere by a close-fitting globe that much reduces their rate of consumption

enclosed rhyme *or* **enclosing rhyme** *n* [*enclosing* fr. pres. part. of *enclose*] **:** the rhyming pattern *a b b a* found in certain quatrains

en·clos·er \-zə(r)\ *n* **:** one that encloses

en·clo·sure *or* **in·clo·sure** \ən'klōzhə(r), en-\ *n* -s [ME *enclosure*, fr. MF, fr. OF, fr. *enclos* + *-ure*] **1 :** the act or action of enclosing: as **a :** the separation of land from common ground by a fence or barrier **b :** separation (as for fire protection) of one part of a building from others **2 :** the quality or state of being encompassed or shut up ⟨books musty and damp from long ~⟩ **3 :** something that encloses (as a barrier) **4 a :** something enclosed in a package or letter ⟨each envelope contained miscellaneous ~s⟩ **b :** an enclosed or fenced-in area ⟨a ranch and its outlying ~s⟩ **c :** the part of a monastery or convent strictly reserved for the religious of the community to the exclusion of outsiders or of certain outsiders (as those of the opposite sex) **5 :** the regulation that establishes and is designed to preserve the enclosure of a monastery or convent ⟨an order with a very strict ~⟩

enclosure wall *n* **:** CURTAIN WALL 2

en·clothe \ən, en+\ *vt* [¹*en-* + *clothe*] **:** to cover with or as if with clothing

en·code \ən'kōd, en-\ *vt* [¹*en-* + *code*, n.] **:** to transfer (as a body of information) from one system of communication into another ⟨~ chemical data on punched cards⟩; *esp* **:** to convert (a message) into code

en·code·ment \-mənt\ *n* -s **:** the process or result of encoding

en·cod·er \-də(r)\ *n* **:** one that encodes; *esp* **:** CIPHER MACHINE

en·coffin \ən, en+\ *vt* [¹*en-* + *coffin*, n.] **:** to shut up in or as if in a coffin

en·coi·gnure \ən'känyər, än'k-, -kōin-, *F* äⁿkônyüer\ *n* -s [F, fr. MF, corner formed by the junction of two walls, fr. *encoigner* to put into a corner (fr. OF *encoignier*, fr. *en-* ¹en- + *coing* corner) + *-ure* — more at COIN] **:** a small piece of furniture (as a cabinet) made to fit into a corner

en·col·pion *or* **en·kol·pion** \eŋ'kōlp,yōn\ *n, pl* **encol·pia** *or* **enkol·pia** \-,yä\ [MGk *enkolpion*, fr. Gk, neut. of *enkolpios* in or on the bosom, fr. *en* in + *-kolpios* (fr. *kolpos* bosom) — more at IN, GULF] **:** a medallion bearing a sacred picture that is worn on the breast of a bishop of the Eastern Orthodox Church

en·co·lure \¦äŋkə¦lü(ə)r\ *n* -s [F, neck of an animal, fr. MF, fr. *en* in (fr. L *in*) + *col* neck + *-ure* — more at COL] **:** the mane of a horse

en·co·men·de·ro \(,)en,kōmən'de(,)rō, -käm-\ *n* -s [Sp, fr. *encomienda*] **:** the holder of an encomienda

en·co·mi·ast \ən'kōmē,ast, en-, -ē,aa(ə)st, -ēəst\ *n* -s [Gk *enkōmiastēs*, fr. *enkōmiazein* to praise, fr. *enkōmion* laudatory ode, eulogy] **:** one that praises **:** PANEGYRIST ⟨he was not a true mystic . . . but rather an ~ of piety —A.J.Arberry⟩

¹**en·co·mi·as·tic** \ən¦==¦astik, (,)en,=ˈ==, -tēk\ *also* **en·co·mi·as·ti·cal** \-təkəl, -tēk-\ *adj* [*encomiastic* fr. Gk *enkōmiastikos*, fr. *enkōmiastēs* + *-ikos* -ic; *encomiastical* fr. Gk *enkōmiastikos* + E *-al*] **:** of, belonging to, or bestowing praise **:** EULOGISTIC ⟨~ remarks⟩ — **en·co·mi·as·ti·cal·ly** \-tək(ə)lē, -tēk-, -li\ *adv*

²**encomiastic** \"\ *n* -s *archaic* **:** PANEGYRIC

en·co·mic \(')en¦kōmik\ *adj* [²*en-* + *coma* + *-ic*] *of human hair* **:** KINKY, CRINKLED

en·co·mi·en·da \(,)en,kōmē'endə, -,käm-; ,enkəm'yen-\ *n* -s [Sp, fr. *encomendar* to entrust, fr. *en-* ¹en- (fr. L *in-*) + obs. Sp *comendar* to entrust, fr. L *commendare* — more at COMMEND] **:** an estate of land and the inhabiting Indians formerly granted to Spanish colonists or adventurers in America for purposes of tribute and evangelization — compare REPARTIMIENTO

en·co·mi·o·log·ic \ən¦kōmēə¦läjik\ *adj* [LL *encomiologicus*, fr. Gk *enkōmiologikos*, lit., of a laudatory ode, fr. *enkōmion* + *-logikos* -logic] **:** of or having to do with a compound verse in Greek and Latin prosody that is made up of a dactylic penthemimer followed by an iambic penthemimer

encomion *n, pl* **encomia** *or* **encomions** [Gk *enkōmion*] *obs* **:** ENCOMIUM

en·co·mi·um \ən'kōmēəm, en-\ *n, pl* **encomiums** \-ēəmz\ *or* **enco·mia** \-ēə\ [L, fr. Gk *enkōmion* laudatory ode, fr. *en* in + *-kōmion* (fr. *kōmos* revel, celebration) — more at IN, COMEDY] **:** an often formal expression of warm or high praise **:** EULOGY, PANEGYRIC ⟨an unstinted ~ of a national hero⟩

en·compass \ən, en+\ *vt* [¹*en-* + *compass*, n.] **1 a :** to form a circle about **:** ENCIRCLE ⟨with the rising of ~*ing* mountain ranges the Mojave became a cooped-in desert —*Amer. Guide Series: Calif.*⟩ **b** *obs* **:** to make a circuit around **:** go completely around **2 a :** ENVELOP, ENWRAP ⟨a thick fog ~*ed* the building⟩ ⟨have ~*ed* him with every protection —Charles Dickens⟩ **b :** to hem or box in **:** CONFINE ⟨~*ed* by hostile natives⟩ **c :** to bring within **:** INCLUDE, COMPREHEND ⟨in the telling are ~*ed* . . . the philosophy, the traditions, and the ritual beauty of that ancient land —*Saturday Rev.*⟩ **3** *obs* **:** to get the better of **:** OUTWIT **4 :** to bring to completion, fruition, or perfection **:** ACCOMPLISH ⟨a difficult dramatic part few actors can ~⟩ **syn** see SURROUND

en·com·pass·ment \"mənt\ *n* -s **1 :** the act or action of encompassing ⟨the president's adroit ~ of each difficulty⟩ **2 :** the quality or state of being encompassed ⟨had a feeling of complete ~ by unfriendly forces⟩

en·cop·re·sis \,en(,)kä'prēsəs, ,kə'-\ *n, pl* **encopre·ses** \-ē,sēz\ [NL, fr. *en-* (as in *enuresis*) + *copr-* + *-esis*] **:** involuntary defecation of psychic origin

en co·quille \¦äⁿkō¦kē\ *adv (or adj)* [F] **:** in the shell — used esp. of oysters baked in their shells

en·cor·bel·ment *or* **en·cor·bell·ment** \ən'kō(r)bəlmənt, en-\ *n* -s [F *encorbellement*, fr. MF *encorbelement*, fr. *en* in (fr. L *in*) + *corbel* + *-ment* — more at CORBEL] **:** projection of each course of masonry over the one below it

¹**en·core** \'än,kō(ə)r, -ō(ə)r, -ōə, -ō(ə) *sometimes* 'äŋ,k-\ *n* -s *often attrib* [F, still, yet, in addition, prob. fr. (assumed) VL *hinc ad horam*, fr. L *hinc* from here (fr. *hic* this) + *ad* to + *horam* (accus. of *hora* hour) — more at AT, HOUR] **1 a :** a request usu. indicative of approbation made by an audience (as by clapping or calls of *encore*) for the further appearance of a performer or the repetition of a particular performance — often used interjectionally **2 :** the further appearance of a performer or an additional performance requested by an audience

²**encore** \"\ *vt* -ED/-ING/-S **:** to request (as by clapping or calls of *encore*) a repetition or the further appearance of ⟨~ a song⟩ ⟨~ a singer⟩

¹**en·coun·ter** \ən'kau̇ntə(r), en'-\ *vb* **encountered; encountered; encountering** \-nt(ə)riŋ *also* -n·triŋ\ **encounters** [ME *encountren*, fr. OF *encontrer*, fr. ML *incontrare*, fr. LL *incontra* toward, against, fr. L *in* + *contra* against — more at COUNTER (adv.)] *vt* **1 a :** to meet in the role of an adversary or enemy **:** CONFRONT **b :** to engage in conflict with ⟨enemy raiding parties were ~*ed* and driven back⟩ **2 :** to come upon face to face **:** MEET ⟨~ an old acquaintance on the street⟩ **3 :** to come upon accidentally or unexpectedly ⟨~ difficulties⟩ ~ *vi* **1** *obs* **:** to meet in a hostile manner **2 :** to come together by chance **syn** see MEET

²**encounter** \" *sometimes* 'en,k-\ *n* -s [ME *encountre*, fr. OF *encontre*, fr. *encontrer*, v.] **1 a :** a meeting between hostile factions or persons **b :** a sudden often violent clash **:** BATTLE ⟨a bloody ~⟩ **2 a :** a chance meeting **:** an unexpected often direct coming upon **b :** a direct often momentary meeting **:** momentary or temporary contact **3 :** the coming of one molecule within the sphere of action of another with consequent change of direction or velocity of motion — see COLLISION 2d

encounterer *n* -s *obs* **:** OPPONENT, ADVERSARY

en·cour·age \ən'kər·ij, en-, -kə·r\|, \|ēj, *chiefly in pres part* \|əj\ *vt* -ED/-ING/-S [ME *encoragen*, fr. MF *encoragier*, fr. OF, fr. *en-* ¹en- + *corage* courage — more at COURAGE] **1 :** to give courage to **:** inspire with courage, spirit, or hope **:** HEARTEN ⟨an example that *encouraged* struggling peoples to fight for liberty⟩ **2 :** to spur on **:** STIMULATE, INCITE ⟨the conversation was . . . skillfully *encouraged* by host and hostess —Lucien Price⟩ **3 :** to give help or patronage to **:** FOSTER ⟨government grants designed to ~ conservation⟩ **4 :** to call forth **:** PRODUCE, CREATE ⟨sharp competition among newsmen . . . tends to ~ sensationalism —F.L.Mott⟩

syn INSPIRIT, CHEER, HEARTEN, EMBOLDEN, NERVE, STEEL: ENCOURAGE suggests generally instilling with courage, confidence, and purpose or fostering enough of these characteristics by advice, inducement, or similar influence to perform or endure as indicated ⟨so much is she overshadowed by her husband, who, indeed, did little himself to *encourage* her personality beyond the home —H.S.Canby⟩ ⟨the treatment should begin by *encouraging* him to utter freely even his most shocking thoughts —Bertrand Russell⟩ INSPIRIT, a rather literary word, indicates imparting of a spirit, esp. one of courageous or optimistic resolution ⟨the marches [of Sousa] were most *inspiriting* . . . and so patriotic —Osbert Sitwell⟩ ⟨an astonishing and *inspiriting* record of what human ingenuity can accomplish —Basil Davenport⟩ CHEER indicates lifting up in spirit, either from a degree of sadness or discouragement or to a degree of courage, optimism, and hope needed to continue or persevere ⟨doctored the sick, *cheered* the downhearted . . . and by sheer force of character made himself their indispensable leader —G.H.Genzmer⟩ HEARTEN suggests imparting new or renewed courage, ardor, energy, and optimism ⟨gifts . . . which both strengthen our resources and *hearten* our endeavors —J.B.Conant⟩ ⟨*heartened* by the arrival of three great soldiers —Kenneth Roberts⟩ EMBOLDEN is likely to suggest overcoming timidity, reticence, or reservation and imparting sufficient boldness for whatever is under consideration ⟨on seeing a carriage drive up to the Abbey, she was *emboldened* to descend and meet him under the protection of visitors —Jane Austen⟩ ⟨the government, *emboldened* by this first victory, now aimed a blow at an enemy of a very different class —T.B. Macaulay⟩ NERVE and STEEL are likely to indicate an imparting or collecting of qualities of moral strength, resolution, and courage for some special occasion, accomplishment, task, or duty; they may differ in that STEEL may be stronger in indicating an inflexible resolution or utter insensibility to what would enervate or mollify ⟨this commercial opportunity *nerved* the Ottawas to an unaccustomed doing —Bernard De Voto⟩ ⟨*nerving* myself with the thought that if I got crushed by the fall I should probably escape a lingering and far more painful death, I dropped into the cloud of foliage —W.H.Hudson †1922⟩ ⟨the aspirant must school and *steel* himself to sniffs and sneers —H.L.Mencken⟩ ⟨it taught them to *steel* their wills, to discipline their habits, to work intensively —A.R.Williams⟩ **syn** see in addition FAVOR

en·cour·age·ment \-mənt\ *n* -s **1 :** the act or action of encouraging ⟨the government's ~ of new industries⟩ **2 :** the quality or state of being encouraged **3 :** something that encourages **:** INCENTIVE ⟨gifts of money and other ~s⟩

en·cour·ag·er \-jə(r)\ *n* -s **:** one that encourages

encouraging *adj* [fr. pres. part. of *encourage*] **:** giving hope or promise **:** INSPIRITING, FAVORING — **en·cour·ag·ing·ly** *adv*

en·cra·tism \'eŋkrə,tizəm, 'enk-\ *n* -s *usu cap* [*encratite* + *-ism*] **:** the doctrines or tenets of the Encratites

en·cra·tite \-,tīt\ *n* -s *usu cap* [LL *encratita*, fr. LGk *enkratitēs*, fr. Gk *enkratēs* self-disciplined (fr. *en* in + *-kratēs*, fr. *kratos* strength) + *-itēs* -ite — more at IN, HARD] **:** a member of certain 2d century ascetic sects that condemned sexual intercourse, clericalism, and the use of animal food and strong drink — compare APOSTOLICI

en creux \äⁿ 'krə̄, -rər(·), *F* -rœ\ *adj* [F, lit., in the hollow] **:** being in intaglio **:** sunk below the surface ⟨an engraving *en creux*⟩

en·cri·nal \(')en¦krīnᵊl, (')eŋ¦-\ *adj* [NL *Encrinus* + E *-al*] **:** of, relating to, or made up of encrinites

en·crin·ic \(')en¦krinik, (')eŋ¦-\ *or* **en·cri·nit·al** \¦eŋkrə¦nīdᵊl, ¦enk-\ *adj* [*encrinic* fr. NL *Encrinus* + E *-ic*; *encrinital* fr. *encrinite* + *-al*] **:** ENCRINAL

en·cri·nite \'eŋkrə,nīt, 'enk-\ *n* -s [NL *encrinites*, fr. *Encrinus* + *-ites* -ite] **:** CRINOID; *esp* **:** a fossil crinoid (as one belonging to or like one belonging to the genus *Encrinus*) — **en·cri·nit·ic** \¦==¦nidik\ *or* **en·cri·nit·i·cal** \-d·əkəl\ *adj*

en·cri·noid \'eŋkrə,nȯid, 'enk-; en'krī,n-, eŋ'k-\ *adj* [NL *Encrinus* + E *-oid*] **:** ENCRINAL

en·cri·nus \en'krīnəs, eŋ'-\ *n* [NL, fr. ²*en-* + *-crinus* (fr. Gk *krinon* lily)] **1** *cap* **:** a genus (the type of the family Encrinidae) of extinct stalked crinoids whose remains are abundant in some Triassic formations (as in beds of limestone formed chiefly of fragments of their stalks) **2** *pl* **encri·ni** \-,nī\ **:** a crinoid of the genus *Encrinus*

¹**en·croach** \ən'krōch, en-\ *vi* -ED/-ING/-ES [ME *encrochen* to get, seize, fr. MF *encrochier* to seize, hang up, set aloft, fr. OF, fr. *en-* ¹en- + *croc* hook, of Scand origin; akin to ON *krōkr* hook — more at CROOK] **1 :** to enter by gradual steps or by stealth into the possessions or rights of another **:** TRESPASS, INTRUDE — usu. used with *on* or *upon* ⟨~ on the territory of a neighboring country⟩ **2 :** to advance beyond desirable or normal limits **:** take undue liberties — usu. used with *on* or *upon* ⟨a governor ~*ing* upon the liberties of his people⟩ **syn** see TRESPASS

²**encroach** \"\ *n* -ES **:** ENCROACHMENT ⟨the ~ of fungi into crevices⟩

en·croach·ment \-mənt\ *n* -s [ME *encrochement*, fr. AF, fr. MF *encrochier* + *-ment*] **1 :** the act or action of encroaching ⟨the gradual ~ of the white people upon the Indian territories⟩ **2 :** an instance of encroaching (as the building of a structure in a public park or a fence that projects over a neighbor's land)

en·crust *also* **in·crust** \ən'krəst, en-\ *vb* [*encrust* prob. alter. (influenced by ¹*en-*) of *incrust*, fr. L *incrustare*, fr. *in* + *crustare* to encrust, fr. *crusta* crust — more at CRUST] *vt* **1 :** to form a crust on the surface of **:** crust over ⟨the rust of ages ~*ed* the hull⟩ ⟨ice ~*ed* the edges of the pool⟩ **2 a :** COVER, OVERLAY ⟨~ a wall with marble⟩ ⟨~ glass with gold leaf⟩ **b :** to inlay esp. jewels into the surface of **3 :** to conceal or obscure as if with a layer or crust ⟨words that are so heavily ~*ed* with images and feelings that we forget that after all they are only words —J.C.Powys⟩ ~ *vi* **:** to form a crust ⟨salt had ~*ed* on the bottom of the kettle⟩

¹**en·crust·ant** *also* **in·crust·ant** \-stənt\ *adj* **:** forming a crust ⟨hidden by layers of ~ dirt⟩

²**encrustant** *also* **incrustant** \"\ *n* -s **:** something that forms a crust

encrustation *var of* INCRUSTATION

en·crypt \ən'kript, en-\ *vt* -ED/-ING/-S [¹*en-* + *-crypt* (fr. *cryptogram*, *cryptograph*)] **:** to encipher or encode

en·cul·tu·rate \ən'kəlchə,rāt, en-\ *vt* -ED/-ING/-S [prob. back-formation fr. *enculturation*] **:** to modify or condition by enculturation ⟨*enculturated* to the established norms of behavior —M.J.Herskovits⟩

en·cul·tu·ra·tion \ən,kəlchə'rāshən, (,)en-\ *n* -s [¹*en-* + *-culturation* (as in *acculturation*)] **:** the process by which an individual learns the traditional content of a culture and assimilates its practices and values — compare SOCIALIZATION — **en·cul·tu·ra·tive** \=ˈ==,rā\|d·iv, -,rə\|\ *adj*

en·cum·ber \ən'kəmbə(r), en-\ *vt* **encumbered; encumbered; encumbering** \-b(ə)riŋ\ **encumbers** [ME *encombren*, fr. MF *encombrer* to obstruct, burden, fr. OF, fr. *en-* ¹en- + (assumed) *combre* abatis (whence MF *combre* barrier constructed in the bed of a river to hold back fish or protect the banks), perh. of Celt origin; akin to the source of ML *combrus* abatis and to MIr *commar* confluence; both these fr. a prehistoric Celt compound whose first constituent is represented by OIr *com-* together and whose second constituent is akin to L *ferre* to carry — more at CO-, BEAR] **1 a :** to weigh down ⟨a man ~*ed* with parcels⟩ **:** BURDEN ⟨shock troops ~*ed* with mortars, grenades, and flamethrowers⟩ **b :** to load to excess **:** OVERBURDEN ⟨a summer resort . . . ~*ed* with great clapboard-and-stucco hotels —A.J.Liebling⟩ **2 :** to impede or hamper the natural or requisite function or activity of ⟨elaborate ritual ~*ing* international diplomacy⟩ **:** HINDER ⟨a project ~*ed* by lack of funds⟩ **3 :** to load with debts or other legal claims ⟨~ an estate with mortgages⟩ **syn** see BURDEN

en·cum·ber·ing·ly *adv* [*encumbering* (pres. part. of *encumber*) + *-ly*] **:** in a manner to encumber

en·cum·brance \-brən(t)s *also* -bər-\ *n* -s [ME *encombraunce*, fr. OF *encombrance*, fr. *encombrer* + *-ance*] **1** *obs* **:** the quality or state of being encumbered **:** PERPLEXITY, TROUBLE **2 :** something that encumbers **:** a burden that impedes action or renders it difficult **:** IMPEDIMENT **3** *or* **in·cum·brance** \"\ **a :** a burden or charge upon property **:** a claim or lien upon an estate that may diminish its value; *specif* **:** any interest or right in land existing to the diminution of the value of the fee but not preventing the passing of the fee by conveyance **b :** a dependent person (as a child)

en·cum·branc·er \-nsə(r)\ *n* -s **:** one that holds an encumbrance

-en·cy \ənsē, ᵊn-, -si\ *n suffix* -ES [ME *-encie*, fr. L *-entia* — more at -ENCE] **1 :** quality or state ⟨effici*ency*⟩ ⟨expedi*ency*⟩ **2 :** one having a (specified) quality or being in a (specified) state ⟨a depend*ency* with limited self-government⟩ ⟨His Excell*ency*⟩ **3 :** instance of a (specified) quality or state ⟨repeated inadvert*encies*⟩

ency *or* **encyc** *abbr* encyclopedia

¹**en·cyc·li·cal** \ən'sikləkəl, en-, -lēk-\ *also* **en·cyc·lic** \-klik, -lēk\ *adj* [*encyclical* fr. LL *encyclicus* + E *-al*; *encyclic* fr. LL *encyclicus*, modif. (influenced by L *-icus* -ic) of Gk *enkyklios* circular, general, fr. *en* in + *kyklos* circle, wheel — more at IN, WHEEL] **:** sent to many persons or places **:** intended for many or for a whole order **:** GENERAL ⟨an ~ letter⟩

²**encyclical** \"\ *also* **encyclic** \"\ *n* -s **:** an encyclical letter (as sent by a bishop or high church official) that treats a matter of grave or timely importance and is intended for extensive circulation; *specif* **:** such a letter issued by a pope

en·cy·clo·pe·dia *also* **en·cy·clo·pae·dia** \ən,sīklə'pēdēə, (,)en-, *in rapid speech sometimes* -dē *in some contexts, as in "Encyclopaedia Britannica"*\ *n* -s [ML *encyclopaedia* course of general education, fr. a supposed Gk *enkyklopaideia* (in MSS of the Roman rhetorician Quintilian), fr. Gk *enkyklios paideia* general education, fr. *enkyklios* general + *paideia* education, rearing of a child, fr. *paid-, pais* child — more at FOAL] **:** a work that treats comprehensively all the various branches of knowledge and that is usu. composed of individual articles arranged alphabetically; *also* **:** such a work treating only a particular branch of knowledge ⟨an ~ of agriculture⟩ ⟨an ~ of religion⟩

en·cy·clo·pe·di·ast *also* **en·cy·clo·pae·di·ast** \-ēdē,ast, -,əst\ *n* -s [*encyclopedia, encyclopaedia* + *-ast*] **:** ENCYCLOPEDIST

en·cy·clo·pe·dic *also* **en·cy·clo·pae·dic** \ən¦==¦pēdik, (¦)en-, -dēk\ *also* **en·cy·clo·pe·di·cal** *also* **en·cy·clo·pae·di·cal** \-dəkəl, -dēk-\ *adj* [*encyclopedia, encyclopaedia* + *-ic, -ical*] **:** of, relating to, resembling, or suggestive of an encyclopedia or its methods of treating or covering a subject: as **a :** embracing or informed in a wide range of subjects ⟨an ~ mind⟩ **b :** comprehensive in treatment or knowledge of a subject ⟨an ~ article on the Egyptian religion⟩ — **en·cy·clo·pe·di·cal·ly** *also* **en·cy·clo·pae·di·cal·ly** \-dək(ə)lē, -dēk-, -li\ *adv*

en·cy·clo·pe·dism *also* **en·cy·clo·pae·dism** \=,==ˈpē,dizəm\ *n* -s [*encyclopedia, encyclopaedia* + *-ism*] **1 :** possession of a wide range of knowledge **2** *often cap* **:** the writings, views, and influence on thought of the encyclopedists

en·cy·clo·pe·dist *also* **en·cy·clo·pae·dist** \-ēdəst\ *n* -s [*encyclopedia, encyclopaedia* + *-ist*] **1 :** one who compiles or assists in the compilation of an encyclopedia **2** [F *encyclopédiste*, fr. *encyclopédie* encyclopedia (fr. ML *encyclopaedia*) + *-iste* -ist] **a** *often cap* **:** one of the writers of the French *Encyclopédie ou Dictionnaire raisonné des Sciences, des Arts, et des Métiers* (1751-80) who were identified with the Enlightenment and advocated deism and scientific rationalism **b :** one who adheres to or displays affinities with 18th century rationalism

¹**en·cyr·tid** \ən'sərd·əd, (')en¦s-\ *adj* [NL *Encyrtidae*] **:** of or relating to the Encyrtidae

²**encyrtid** \"\ *n* -s **:** a fly of the family Encyrtidae

en·cyr·ti·dae \ən'sərd·ə,dē, en-\ *n pl, cap* [NL, fr. *Encyrtus*, type genus (fr. Gk *enkyrtos* curved, crooked, fr. *en* in + *kyrtos* convex, bulging) + *-idae*; akin to L *curvus* curved — more at IN, CROWN] **:** a large cosmopolitan family of small chalcid flies parasitic in the eggs or later stages of many insects

en·cyst \ən'sist, en-\ *vb* -ED/-ING/-S [¹*en-* + *cyst*, n.] *vt* **:** to enclose in or as if in a cyst or capsule ⟨an ~*ed* tumor⟩ ~ *vi* **:** to form or become enclosed in a cyst or capsule ⟨protozoans ~*ing* in order to resist desiccation⟩

en·cys·ta·tion \,en,si'stāshən, ən-\ *n* -s **:** ENCYSTMENT

en·cyst·ment \ən'sis(t)mənt, en-\ *n* -s **:** the process of forming a cyst or becoming enclosed in a capsule

¹**end** \'end\ *n* -s [ME *ende*, fr. OE; akin to OHG *enti* end, ON *endir*, Goth *andeis* end, L *ante* before, Gk *anti* against, Skt *anta* end, Hitt *hanz* front] **1 a (1) :** the portion of an area or territory that lies at or by the termination and that often serves as a delimitation or boundary; *specif* **:** a section of a city not within the center portion ⟨the East *End* of London⟩ **(2) :** the extreme, ultimate, or most remote section or area ⟨a criminal hunted to the very ~s of the earth⟩ **b (1) :** a point that marks the extent of something **:** LIMIT ⟨no ~ of good things⟩ ⟨gifts without ~ showered upon the newcomers⟩ **(2) :** the point where something possessed of or exhibiting temporal progression ceases to exist ⟨the ~ of the fiscal year⟩ ⟨the ~ of a bullet's flight⟩ **c (1) :** a narrow, sharp, or pointed part of something longitudinal or slender ⟨the ~ of a pencil⟩ ⟨the ~s of a pole⟩ ⟨the dangerous ~ of a knife⟩ **(2) :** the extreme or last part lengthwise ⟨the ~ of a board⟩ ⟨~ of a garden⟩ ⟨~ of a rope⟩ ⟨the rear ~ of an automobile⟩ **d (1) :** the terminal unit of something spatial that is marked off by or exhibits a progression of units ⟨the ~ of a series⟩ **(2) :** the portion of a distillate (as from petroleum) at either extremity of its distillation range ⟨the light or low ~s are the most volatile portions⟩ **(3) :** END MAN **(4) :** a player stationed at the extremity of a line or team (as in football) **e (1) :** the heading of a barrel or the lid of a metal can or drum **(2) :** either half of a domino face **(3) :** either extremity of a cricket pitch ⟨batsmen changing ~s after a run⟩ **2 a :** cessation of a course of action, pursuit, or activity ⟨the ~ of a war⟩ ⟨working and never seeing the ~ in sight⟩ **b (1) :** termination of being **:** DEATH ⟨an opponent of taxation until his very ~⟩ **(2) :** the dissolution of structural or functional existence **:** DESTRUCTION, DEMOLITION ⟨a freighter that met its ~ in a hurricane⟩ **c (1) :** the ultimate state **:** final condition ⟨the ~ being utter oblivion⟩ **(2) :** the result of an activity **:** ISSUE ⟨the ~ of the matter being general agreement⟩ **d :** the complex of events, parts, or sections that forms an extremity, termination, or finish ⟨the frontal attacks that marked the ~ of the war⟩ **3 :** something incomplete, fragmentary, or undersize: as **a :** a leftover or scrap **:** REMNANT ⟨the ~s of meat⟩ — see ODDS AND ENDS **b :** a short or half piece of cloth — see MILL END **c :** a deal or batten of timber less than eight feet long **4 a :** an outcome worked toward esp. with forethought, deliberate planning, and organized effort **:** PURPOSE ⟨the ~ being complete mastery of the subject⟩ ⟨a politician working to the ~ that all debts be paid off⟩ **b (1) :** the goal, ultimate intention, or purpose for the attainment of which an agent does something or ought to be acting **(2) :** the object by virtue of which or the objective for the sake of which an event or a series of events happens or is said to take place **:** a final cause **5 a :** a particular duty **:** share in an undertaking — used with *keep* and *up* ⟨he was able to keep his ~ up⟩ **b :** a department or particular phase of an undertaking, business, or organization ⟨the advertising ~ of insurance⟩ **6 a :** a unit or turn in shooting (as in archery) **b :** an inning in a game played from one limit of a course toward the other (as in bowls) **7 a (1) :** a warp thread or yarn **(2) :** a single sliver, roving, or yarn while in the process of manufacture on a textile machine **b :** WAXED END **8 :** the number of arrows (as three in England and six in America) shot by an archer during his turn

syn TERMINATION, ENDING, TERMINUS: END, the most common and most inclusive of the terms, may apply to the finish or the final limit in nearly any application ⟨the *end* of a meal⟩ ⟨the *end* of a book⟩ ⟨the *end* of a road⟩ ⟨the *end* of a life⟩ ⟨the *end* of a play⟩ ⟨the *end* of a journey⟩ ⟨the *end* of a friendship⟩ ⟨the *end* of one's endurance⟩ TERMINATION or ENDING usu. applies to an end in time or, less often, in space, of something that is brought to a close as by having set bounds or by being completed or no longer purposeful, ENDING often also including a portion prior to the exact terminal point ⟨the *termination* of a lease⟩ ⟨the *termination* of a moratorium⟩ ⟨the *ending* of a play⟩ ⟨the *ending* of vacation⟩ ⟨to change the *ending* of a song⟩ ⟨a long *ending* to a symphony⟩ TERMINUS applies to an end, usu. a definite point or place, to which something moves or progresses or beyond which it does not go ⟨the modern city hall is the *terminus* of the tour⟩ ⟨an airline *terminus*⟩ ⟨the northern *terminus* of the natural-gas pipeline⟩ ⟨the eighth grade is for many the *terminus* of religious teaching —C.T.H. Sherlock⟩ **syn** see in addition INTENTION

— **end for end** *adv* **:** with the ends reversed **:** upside down ⟨it will fit if you turn it *end for end*⟩ — **end of one's rope :** the limit of one's endurance, patience, or resources — **in the end** *adv* **:** after all **:** ULTIMATELY — **no end** *adv* **:** AWFULLY, EXCEEDINGLY ⟨the whole crowd was *no end* put out by the poor spirit of the home team⟩ — **on end** *adv* **1 :** with the end down or on the bottom ⟨a box standing *on end*⟩ **2** : without a break or stop : with no letup ⟨rained for days *on end*⟩

²end \"\ *vb* -ED/-ING/-S [ME *enden*, fr. OE *endian*; akin to OHG *entōn* to end, ON *enda*; denominative fr. the root of E ¹*end*] *vt* **1** *obs* : to carry out : perform fully **2 a** : to bring to an end : TERMINATE ⟨the speech ~*ed* the ceremonies⟩ **b** : to bring about the death of : KILL ⟨hit him with the edge of it behind the skull, and he lay still and ~*ed* —B.T.Cleeve⟩ **3** : to make up the end of : constitute the last element of ⟨*k* ~*s* the word *back*⟩ ⟨a brass band ~*ed* the parade⟩ **4** : to place on end : UPEND **5** : to stand as the supreme example of — usu. used in the infinitive ⟨a novel to ~ all novels⟩ **6** : to attach the top and bottom pieces of (a set-up paper box) ⟨containers ~*ed* by hand⟩ ~ *vi* **1 a** : to come to an end : reach a final or ultimate point ⟨the song ~*ed* on a high note⟩ — often used with *up* ⟨the party ~*s* up with dancing⟩ or *in* ⟨his efforts ~*ed* in failure⟩ **b** : to come to a conclusion or ultimate state or situation ⟨the poem stops rather than ~*s*⟩ — often used with *up* ⟨the whole gang ~*ed* up in jail⟩ **2** : DIE ⟨his parents ~*ed* in the . . . gas ovens —Joseph Alsop⟩ — sometimes used with *up* **syn** see CLOSE

³end \"\ *vt* [prob. alter. of ³*in*, v.] *now dial Eng* : to put (grain or hay) into a barn or stack

end *abbr* endorsed; endorsement

end- *or* **endo-** *comb form* [F, fr. Gk, fr. *endon* within, at home, fr. *en* in + *-don* (perh. akin to L *domus* house) — more at IN, TIMBER] **1 a** : within : inside ⟨*Endamoeba*⟩ ⟨*endoscope*⟩ **b** : taking in : requiring ⟨*endergonic*⟩ — opposed to *exo-* **2** *endo-* **a** : forming a bridge between two atoms in a cyclic system or having a bond or bivalent radical regarded as a bridge ⟨*endoethylenic* bridge⟩ ⟨1,4-*endo*methylene-cyclohexane⟩ **b** *sometimes ital* : having one or more substituents directed inward — in names of stereoisomeric compounds containing a 6-membered ring in its boat form ⟨2,5-methylene-*endo*-cyclohexyl-amine⟩; compare EXO- b **3** : endocardium and ⟨*endo*pericarditis⟩

end–all \'ˌˌ\ *n* -s : something that stands as the ultimate goal or conclusion ⟨elucidating . . . may not be the *end-all* of philosophical activity —Morris Weitz⟩

en·damage \ən, en+\ *vt* [ME *endamagen*, prob. fr. ¹*en-* + *damage*, n.] : to cause loss or damage to : HARM, INJURE ⟨testimony sufficient to ~ a reputation⟩ — **en·dam·age·ment** \"mənt\ *n* -s

end·amebiasis *or* **end·amoebiasis** \ˌend+\ *n* [NL *endamoebiasis*, fr. *Endamoeba* + *-iasis*] : infection with or disease caused by amoebas of the genus *Endamoeba* : AMEBIASIS

end·amoeba \ˌend+\ *n* [NL, fr. *end-* + *amoeba*] **1** *cap* : the type genus of the family Endamoebidae comprising amoebas parasitic in the intestines of insects and in some classifications various parasites of vertebrates including the amoeba (*E. histolytica*) that causes amebic dysentery in man — see ENTAMOEBA **2** *also* **end·ame·ba** \"+\ : any amoeba of the genus *Endamoeba* including *Entamoeba* — **end·amoebic** *also* **end·amebic** \"+\ *adj*

end·amoe·bi·dae \ˌendəˈmēbəˌdē\ *n pl, cap* [NL, fr. *Endamoeba*, type genus + *-idae*] : a large family of endoparasitic amoebas (order Amoebina) that invade the digestive tract of vertebrates and invertebrates and are typically passed from host to host in a resistant cyst through the medium of contaminated food or drink — compare ENDAMOEBA, ENTAMOEBA

end–and–end \ˌˌˈˌ\ *adj, of textiles* : woven with warp threads of alternating white and color and filling threads of one color or alternating white and color for a striped or checked effect

en·dan·ger \ənˈdānjə(r), en-\ **endangered**; **endangered**; **endangering** \-j(ə)riŋ\ **endangers** *vt* [ME *endaungeren*, fr. ¹*en-* + *daunger* power, jurisdiction — more at DANGER] **1** *obs* : to subject to another's power; *also* : to make liable to punishment or arrest **2** : to bring into danger or peril of probable harm or loss : imperil or threaten danger to ⟨he condemned the abolitionists as agitators who actually ~*ed* the cause of freedom —A.C.Cole⟩ **syn** see VENTURE

en·dan·ger·ment \-jə(r)mənt\ *n* -s : the act of placing in danger or the state of being placed in danger ⟨an act that constituted an ~ of the state⟩ ⟨had never been in a position of ~ before⟩

end·aortic \ˌend+\ *adj* [*end-* + *aortic*] : of or relating to the interior of the aorta or to its lining membrane

en·darch \ˈenˌdärk\ *adj* [*end-* + *-arch*] : formed or taking place from the center outward — used of the primary xylem (as of a root) or its development; compare EXARCH, MESARCH — **en·dar·chy** \-kē\ *n* -ES

endark *or* **endarken** *vt* [*endark* fr. ME *endarken*, fr. ¹*en-* + *derk*, *dark* dark; *endarken* fr. ¹*en-* + *darken* — more at DARK (adj.)] *obs* : DARKEN

end around *n* : a football play in which an offensive end comes behind the line of scrimmage to take a hand-off and attempts to carry the ball around the opposite flank

end·arterial \ˌend+\ *adj* [*end-* + *arterial*] : of or relating to the intima of an artery

end·arteritis \ˌend+\ *n* [NL, fr. *end-* + *arteritis*] : inflammation of the intima of one or more arteries

endarteritis ob·lit·er·ans \-əˈblidəˌranz\ *n* [NL, obliterating endarteritis] : endarteritis in which the intimal tissue proliferates and ultimately plugs the lumen of an affected artery

end·ar·te·ri·um \ˌendärˈtirēəm\ *n, pl* **endarte·ria** \-ēə\ [NL, fr. *end-* + L *arterium* artery, alter. of *arteria* — more at ARTERY] : the intima of an artery

endartery \ˈˌ(ˌ)ˌ\ *n* [¹*end* + *artery*; trans. of G *endarterie*] : a terminal artery supplying all or most of the blood to a body part without significant collateral circulation

en dash *n* [¹*en*] : a dash that is one-half the length of an em dash

endball \ˈˌ\ *n* [¹*end* + *ball*] : a game played with a basketball on a divided court with one third of each team standing in its own end zone and the remaining players occupying the opposite playing area and attempting to score by tossing the ball over the opponents to their teammates in the end zone

end batter *n* : the mashing and wear of a rail at a rail joint caused by the repeated passing of railroad-car wheels

endboard \ˈˌ\ *n* : TAILBOARD

endbrain \ˈˌ\ *n* [trans. of NL *telencephalon*] : the anterior subdivision of the forebrain : TELENCEPHALON

end brush *n* : END PLATE

end bud *n* **1** : END BULB 1 **2** : the knob of tissue undifferentiated into germ layers that forms the primitive knot and later forms posterior portions of the body of an embryo

end bulb *n* **1** *also* **end corpuscle** : one of the bulbous bodies in which some of the sensory nerve fibers end in certain parts of the skin and mucous membranes **2** : BOUTON

end cell *n* : one of those cells of a storage battery which may be switched in or out of the circuit to adjust the voltage

end construction *n* : hollow structural blocks or tiles laid with the cells running vertically — compare SIDE CONSTRUCTION

end–cut brick *n* : brick having the end surfaces wire-cut — compare SIDE-CUT BRICK

end–dump \ˈˌ\ *adj* : having a truck body that tips up and discharges its contents from the rear end ⟨an *end-dump* truck⟩

en·dear \ənˈdi(ə)r, en-, -iə\ *vt* -ED/-ING/-S [¹*en-* + *dear*, adj.] **1** *obs* : to make higher in cost, value, or estimation **2** *obs* : to value highly or hold in affection or love **3** : to make dear, beloved, or esteemed ⟨his humor ~*ed* him to the public⟩ ⟨they ~*ed* themselves to the whole town⟩

endearing *adj* [fr. pres. part. of *endear*] : arousing affection, tenderness, or admiration ⟨~ smile⟩ ⟨~ qualities⟩ — **en·dear·ing·ly** *adv* — **en·dear·ing·ness** *n* -ES

en·dear·ment \-di(ə)rmənt, -diəm-\ *n* -s **1** : the act or process of endearing ⟨the passionate embrace, the joy in personal ~ —H.A.Overstreet⟩ **2** : something that endears or manifests affection ⟨a term of ~⟩ ⟨peculiarly lavish of ~*s* —D.H.Lawrence⟩ : CARESS **3** *obs* **a** : ENHANCEMENT **b** : attachment through love or gratitude

¹en·deav·or *also* **en·deav·our** \ənˈdevə(r), en-\ *vb* **endeavored**; **endeavored**; **endeavoring** \-v(ə)riŋ\ **endeavors** [ME *endeveren*, fr. ¹*en-* + *dever* duty — more at DEVOIR] *vt* **1** *obs* : to exert (oneself) strenuously **2** *obs* : to strive to achieve or reach **3** *obs* : to make an attack against ~ *vi* **1** *obs* : to exert oneself : STRIVE **2** : to work with set purpose : make an effort ⟨however much he ~*ed*, the goal stayed unattained⟩ — often used with the infinitive ⟨she walked up and down the room, ~*ing* to compose herself —Jane Austen⟩ **syn** see TRY

²endeavor *also* **endeavour** \"\ *n* -s [ME *endevour*, fr. *endeveren*, v.] : a serious determined effort ⟨an ~ to bring about national economic stabilization —B.F.Fairless⟩

endeavor river pear *n, cap E&R* [fr. *Endeavour river*, Queensland, Australia] : an Australian plant (*Eugenia eucalyptoides*) having fruit used in jam

endecasyllabic *var of* HENDECASYLLABIC

en·de·cha \enˈdächə\ *n* -s [Sp, prob. fr. L *indicta*, neut. pl. of *indictus*, past part. of *indicere* to proclaim, announce, fr. *in* + *dicere* to say — more at DICTION] : a short mournful Spanish song usu. having four lines of six or seven syllables

ended *past of* END

en de·dans \äⁿd(ə)däⁿ\ *adv (or adj)* [F, inside] : INWARD — used of a circular ballet movement of arms or legs leading toward the body or of the position in which the toes are turned in

en de·hors \äⁿdə(h)ȯr\ *adv (or adj)* [F, outside] : OUTWARD — used of a circular ballet movement of arms or legs leading away from the body or of the position in which the toes are turned out

en·dek \ˈenˌdek\ *n* -s *usu cap* [Pol, fr. *en* (name of the letter *n*, here standing for the initial letter of the first word of *Narodowa Demokracja* National Democratic party, lit., National Democracy) + *-dek* (irreg. fr. the *d* and *k* in *Demokracja*)] : a member of the fascist anti-Semitic National Democratic party of Poland

en·del·lion·ite \enˈdelyəˌnīt\ *n* -s [G *endellionit*, fr. *Endellion*, Cornwall, England, its locality + G *-it* -ite] : BOURNONITE

en·dell·ite \ˈendəˌlīt\ *n* -s [prob. fr. a name *Endell* + E *-ite*] : a clay mineral consisting of hydrous silicate of aluminum with varying amounts of water and being more hydrous than halloysite

en·de·mi·al \(ˈ)enˈdēmēəl\ *adj* [Gk *endēmios* native, endemic (fr. *en* in + *dēmos*) + E *-al*] : ENDEMIC

¹en·dem·ic \(ˈ)enˈdemik, -mēk *sometimes* -dēm-\ *also* **en·dem·i·cal** \-məkəl, -mēk-\ *adj* [*endemic* fr. F *endémique*, fr. *endémie*, n., endemic (fr. Gk *endēmia* action of dwelling or staying, fr. *endēmos*, adj., native, endemic — fr. *en* in + *dēmos* deme, populace — + *-ia* -y) + *-ique* -ic; *endemical* fr. F *endémique* + E *-al* — more at DEM-] **1** : belonging or native to a particular people or country : not introduced or naturalized ⟨the many shades of radicalism ~ in Spain —*Harper's*⟩ **2** : restricted to or native to a particular area or region : INDIGENOUS — used of kinds of organisms ⟨the islands have a number of interesting ~ species⟩; compare EXOTIC **3** : peculiar to a locality or region — used of a disease that is constantly present to a greater or less extent in a particular place; distinguished from *epidemic, sporadic* **syn** see NATIVE

²endemic \"\ *n* -s **1** : an endemic disease or an instance of its occurrence **2** : an organism or kind of organism (as a species) that is endemic : INDIGENE

en·dem·i·cal·ly \-mək(ə)lē, -mēk-, -li\ *adv* : in an endemic manner : natively and not by introduction from outside or by naturalization : as a phenomenon restricted or peculiar to a particular locality

en·de·mic·i·ty \ˌendəˈmisədē\ *n* -ES [ISV ¹*endemic* + *-ity*] : ENDEMISM

en·de·mism \ˈendəˌmizəm\ *n* -s [ISV *endem-* (fr. ¹*endemic*) + *-ism*] : the quality or state of being endemic

en·den·i·za·tion \ənˌdenəˈzāshən, (ˌ)enˌd-\ *n* -s [¹*en-* + *denize* + *-ation*] *archaic* : the act or process of naturalizing : DENIZATION

endenize *vt* [¹*en-* + *denize*] *obs* : ENDENIZEN

en·denizen \ən, en+\ *vt* [¹*en-* + *denizen*, n.] : to admit to the privileges of a denizen : NATURALIZE

end·er·gon·ic \ˌen(ˌ)dərˈgänik\ *adj* [*end-* + Gk *ergon* work + E *-ic* — more at WORK] : requiring work or the expenditure of energy — opposed to *exergonic*; used of a chemical reaction occurring in biological processes

en·der·mat·ic \ˌendə(r)ˈmad·ik\ *adj* [²*en-* + *dermat-* + *-ic*] : ENDERMIC

en·der·mic \(ˈ)enˈdərmik\ *adj* [ISV ²*en-* + *derm-* + *-ic*] : acting through the skin or by direct application to the skin ⟨~ ointment⟩ or applied in the skin ⟨~ injection⟩ : INTRADERMAL — **en·der·mi·cal·ly** \-mək(ə)lē, -mēk-, -li\ *adv*

en dés·ha·bil·lé \äⁿdāzäbēyā\ *adv (or adj)* [F] : in a state of undress

en·dew *obs var of* ENDUE

end–fire array *n* : a radio antenna with strong directional properties consisting of a number of antenna elements arranged in a line

end fly *n* : TAIL FLY

end fold *n* : the portion of a wrapper that is folded and adhered to the bottom of the package

end foot *n* : BOUTON

end game *n* **1** : the last stage (as the last three tricks) in playing a bridge hand **2** : the final phase of a board game; *specif* : the stage of a chess game following serious reduction of forces

endgate \ˈˌ\ *n* : TAILBOARD

endgate seeder *n* : a seeding machine attached to the rear of a wagon or truck and used to broadcast seeds

endgate spreader *n* : a 2-wheeled machine attached to the rear of a truck or wagon that distributes ground limestone or fertilizer by means of gears activated by the wheels

end–grain \ˈˌ\ *adv (or adj)* : with the end of the wood grain outward : across the grain

end–grain nailing *n* : nailing in which the nail shanks run parallel to the grain of the wood

end group *n* : a group at the end of a chain of a molecule; *esp* : a functional group at the end of the chain of a linear polymer ⟨the amino and carboxyl *end groups* in a polypeptide⟩

endhand \ˈˌ\ *n* [trans. of G *hinterhand*] : the last skat player in turn to bid — called also *hinterhand*

end hardening *n* : the treating by heat of the upper part of a railhead at the end to minimize end batter

end·ing \ˈendiŋ, -dēŋ\ *n* -s [ME *ending*, *endinge*, fr. OE *endung*, fr. *endian* to end + *-ung* -ing — more at ²END] : something that constitutes an end: as **a** : CONCLUSION **b** : death or destruction **c** (1) : one or more letters or syllables added to a word base (as in inflection) (2) : a sound or class of sounds peculiar to or found in final syllables **syn** see END

¹en·dite \ənˈdīt, en-\ *n, archaic var of* INDITE

²en·dite \ˈenˌdīt\ *n* -s [*end-* + *-ite*] **1** : one of the appendages of the inner side of the limb of an arthropod **2** : the chewing ridge on the inner surface of the pedipalpus or maxilla of many arachnids

end–item \ˈˌˌ\ *n* : a manufactured product that can be put to use without further work being done on it ⟨military *end-items*⟩

en·dive \ˈenˌdīv *sometimes* ˈänˌdēv *or* änˈdēv\ *n* -s [ME, fr. MF, fr. LL *endivia*, alter. of L *intubus*, *intibus*, perh. of Sem origin; akin to Ar *hindab* endive] **1** : an annual or biennial herb (*Cichorium endivia*) probably native to India but widely cultivated as a salad plant and occurring in cultivation in two forms distinguished by one having deeply lobed and laciniate leaves and the other having much-curled but entire leaves — called also *escarole* **2** : the developing crown of chicory when blanched for use as salad — called also *French endive, witloof*

endive blue *n* : ²IRIS 3

end lap *n* **1** *or* **end lap joint** : a joint (as of two boards) made by cutting away half the thickness of each member so that each overlaps the other — called also *half lap* **2** : the overlapping parts of successive aerial photographs of contiguous areas in a line of flight

endleaf \ˈˌ\ *n* : ENDPAPER

end·less \ˈen(d)ləs\ *adj* [ME *endelees*, fr. OE *endelēas*, fr. *ende* end + *-lēas* -less — more at ¹END, -LESS] **1** : having no end : BOUNDLESS, INFINITE ⟨~ duration⟩ ⟨an ~ line⟩ ⟨~ praise⟩ **2** : extremely numerous : very many ⟨~ waves⟩ ⟨~ scraps⟩ **3** : united at the ends so as to form a continuous whole ⟨an ~ chain⟩ — **end·less·ly** *adv*

endless belt *n* : a conveyor in the form of a continuous belt traveling around a set of pulleys

end·less·ness *n* -ES [ME *endelesnesse*, fr. *endeles*, *endelees* endless + *-nesse* -ness] : the quality or state of being endless : PERPETUITY

end·lich·ite \ˈen(d)liˌkīt, ˈentl-\ *n* -s [F. M. *Endlich*, 19th cent. American + E *-ite*] : a mineral $Pb_5Cl[(As,V)O_4]_3$ in composition falling between mimetite and vanadinite and consisting of lead arsenate, vanadate, and chloride

end line *n* : a line marking an end or boundary: as **a** : a line at either end of a football field 10 yards beyond and parallel with the goal line — see FOOTBALL illustration **b** : either of the lines running at right angles to the sidelines and marking the two ends of a basketball court — see BASKETBALL illustration

end loader *n* : a pneumatic or hydraulic platform elevator that lifts loads to the level of the rear of a truck

endlong \ˈˌ\ *adv* [ME *endelong*, by folk etymology (influence of *ende* end) fr. *andlong*, fr. OE *andlang*, adv., along, fr. *andlang*, prep., along — more at ALONG] *archaic* : LENGTHWISE

end man *n* : the last man in a row; *esp* : the man at each end of the line of performers who with the interlocutor creates the comic repartee of a minstrel show

end–match \ˈˌ\ *vt* : to finish (as flooring) at the end with a tongue and groove

end matter *n* : BACK MATTER

end–member \ˈˌˌ\ *n* : a pure chemical compound in some cases hypothetical but regarded as a component entering into solid solution with other pure chemical compounds to form an isomorphous series of minerals ⟨fayalite Fe_2SiO_4 and forsterite Mg_2SiO_4 are *end-members* of the olivine series $(Mg,Fe)_2SiO_4$⟩

end mill *n* : a milling cutter having cutting teeth on the end of a cylindrical shank and usu. spiral blades on the lateral surface — see MILLING CUTTER illustration

end moraine *n* : a moraine deposited by a glacier at its end — compare TERMINAL MORAINE

end·most \ˈen(d)ˌmōst\ *adj* : situated at the very end : FARTHEST

endnote \ˈˌ\ *n* : a note placed at the end of the text (as of an article or chapter) — compare FOOTNOTE

en·do \ˈen(ˌ)dō\ *adj* [*end-*] : being, having, or characterized by valence bonds of a 6-membered ring in its boat form that are directed inward ⟨the ~ form of dicyclopentadiene⟩ — compare END- 2b

endo- — see END-

en·do·adaptation \ˌen(ˌ)dō+\ *n* [*end-* + *adaptation*] : modification of an organism resulting in more effective interaction between its various parts — compare EXOADAPTATION

en·do·basal body \ˌendō+ . . . -\ *n* [*end-* + *basal*] : an intranuclear body serving as a centrosome (as in protozoans)

en·do·basion \ˌendō+\ *n* [*end-* + *basion*] : the most anterior point of the edge of the foramen magnum at the level of its smallest diameter

en·do·batholithic \ˌen(ˌ)dō+\ *adj* [*end-* + *batholithic*] : of or relating to ore deposits formed in and near the roof pendants of a large batholith where the intrusive rock predominates

en·do·biotic \"+\ *adj* [ISV *end-* + *-biotic*] : dwelling within the tissues of a host as parasite or symbiont

en·do·blast \ˈendəˌblast\ *n* -s [ISV *end-* + *-blast*] : HYPOBLAST — **en·do·blas·tic** \ˌˌˈblastik\ *adj*

en·do·bronchial \ˌen(ˌ)dō+\ *adj* [*end-* + *bronchial*] : located within a bronchus ⟨~ tuberculosis⟩ — **en·do·bronchially** \"+\ *adv*

en·do·cannibalism \"+\ *n* [ISV *end-* + *cannibalism*; orig. formed as G *endokannibalismus*] : cannibalism of members of one's own family or tribe — contrasted with *exocannibalism*

en·do·can·thi·on \ˌendōˈkan(t)thēən, -ēˌän\ *n* -s [*end-* + *-canthion* (irreg. fr. LL *canthus* corner of the eye) — more at CANTHUS] : the point at which the inner ends of the upper and lower eyelid meet — compare ECTOCANTHION

en·do·cardiac \ˌen(ˌ)dō+\ *adj* [ISV *end-* + *cardiac*] : ENDOCARDIAL

en·do·car·di·al \ˌendōˈkärdēəl\ *adj* [*end-* + Gk *kardia* heart + E *-al* — more at HEART] : situated within the heart : of, relating to, or involving the endocardium

en·do·carditis \ˌendō+\ *n* [NL, fr. *end-* + *carditis*] : inflammation of the lining of the heart and its valves produced by bacterial infection or other causes

en·do·car·di·um \ˌendōˈkärdēəm\ *n, pl* **endocar·dia** \-ēə\ [NL, fr. *end-* + *-cardium*] : a thin serous membrane lining the cavities of the heart

en·do·carp \ˈendəˌkärp\ *n* -s [F *endocarpe*, fr. *end-* + *-carpe* -carp (fr. NL *-carpium*)] : the inner layer of the pericarp when it consists of two or more layers of different texture or consistency (as in the apple or orange) — compare EPICARP, MESOCARP — **en·do·car·pal** \ˌˌˈkärpəl\ *or* **en·do·car·pic** \-pik\ *adj*

vertical section of a cherry, showing *1* epicarp, *2* mesocarp, *3* endocarp, *4* seed. *1*, *2*, and *3* together form the pericarp

en·do·car·poid \-ˌpȯid\ *adj* [NL *Endocarpon* genus of lichens having the apothecia immersed in the thallus (fr. *end-* + *-carpon*, fr. Gk *-karpon*, neut. of *-karpos* -carpous) + E *-oid*] *of lichens* : having the apothecia immersed in the thallus

en·do·cellular \ˌen(ˌ)dō+\ *adj* [ISV *end-* + *cellular*] : INTRACELLULAR

en·do·centric \ˌendō+\ *adj* [*end-* + *-centric*] : having the same grammatical function as one of its immediate constituents that does not modify the other immediate constituent — used of a compound or construction (as *blackbird* or *my little Mary*); compare EXOCENTRIC

en·doc·er·as \enˈdäsərəs\ *n, cap* [NL, fr. *end-* + *-ceras*] : a genus (the type of the family Endoceratidae) of Ordovician and Silurian nautiloid cephalopods with a straight shell having a very large siphuncle and endocones and reaching a length of 12 feet — **en·do·cer·a·tid** \ˌendōˈserəd·əd\ *adj or n*

en·do·cer·a·tite \ˌˌˈserəˌtīt\ *n* -s [NL *Endocerat-*, *Endoceras* + E *-ite*] : a fossil of the genus *Endoceras* — **en·do·cer·a·tit·ic** \ˌˌˌˈtid·ik\ *adj* — **en·do·cer·a·toid** \ˌˌˈˌtȯid\ *n* -s

en·do·cervical \ˌen(ˌ)dō+\ *adj* [*end-* + *cervical*] : of, relating to, or affecting the endocervix

en·do·cervicitis \"+\ *n* [NL, fr. *end-* + *cervicitis*] : inflammation of the lining of the uterine cervix

en·do·cervix \"+\ *n, pl* **endocervices** [NL, fr. *end-* + *cervix*] : the epithelial and glandular lining of the uterine cervix

en·do·chondral \ˌen(ˌ)dō+\ *adj* [ISV *end-* + *chondr-* + *-al*] : occurring within the substance of cartilage — used chiefly of bone and bone formation; compare PERICHONDRAL

endochondral ossification *n* : ossification taking place from centers arising in cartilage and involving deposition of lime salts in the cartilage matrix followed by secondary absorption and replacement by true bony tissue — compare INTERMEMBRANOUS OSSIFICATION

en·do·chorion \ˌˌ+\ *n* [NL, fr. *end-* + *chorion*] : the inner of the two layers usu. making up the chorion of an insect egg

en·do·chrome \ˈendəˌkrōm\ *n* [ISV *end-* + *-chrome*] : coloring matter within a cell; *specif* : coloring matter other than chlorophyll in plant cells

en·do·coele *or* **en·do·coel** \-ˌsēl\ *n* -s [*end-* + *-coele*] : the space between a pair of mesenteries in certain anthozoans — **en·do·coel·ic** \ˌˌˈsēlik\ *adj*

en·do·commensal \ˌen(ˌ)dō+\ *n* [*end-* + *commensal*] : a commensal dwelling within the body of its host

en·do·condensation \"+\ *n* [*end-* + *condensation*] : condensation occurring within a molecule

en·do·cone \ˈendəˌkōn\ *n* [*end-* + *cone*] : one of the concentric conical structures developed within the calcareous siphuncle of certain cephalopod shells (as of the genus *Endoceras*)

en·do·conidium \ˌen(ˌ)dō+\ *n, pl* **endoconidia** [NL, fr. *end-* + *conidium*] : an endogenous conidium

en·do·corpuscular \"+\ *adj* [*end-* + *corpuscular*] : located within a corpuscle; *specif* : located within a red blood cell ⟨~ parasites of malaria⟩

en·do·cranial \ˌendə+\ *adj* [*endocranium* + *-al*] : of or belonging to the endocranium

endocranial cast *n* : a cast of the cranial cavity showing the approximate shape of the brain

en·do·cranium \"+\ *n, pl* **endocrania** [NL, fr. *end-* + *cranium*] **1** : the processes of the inner surface of the cranium of certain insects : TENTORIUM **2 a** : DURA MATER **b** : the inner surface of the cranium

en·do·cri·nal \ˌendəˈkrīnᵊl, -rēn-, -rin-\ *adj* : ENDOCRINE

¹en·do·crine \ˈendəkrən; -ˌkrin, -ˌrīn, -ˌrēn\ *adj* [ISV *end-* +

-crine (fr. Gk *krinein* to separate) — more at CERTAIN] **1 :** secreting internally; *specif* **:** producing secretions that are distributed in the body by way of the blood stream rather than discharged through ducts — used of glands (as the thyroid, suprarenal, and pituitary) that secrete hormones **2 :** of, relating to, or associated with a hormone **3 :** of or belonging to or relating to an endocrine gland **:** like that of an endocrine gland

²endocrine \" *also* **en·do·crin** \-ˌkrən, -ˌkrin\ *n* -s **1 :** a secretion leaving the gland producing it by way of the circulatory system **:** HORMONE **2 :** ENDOCRINE GLAND

endocrine gland *n* **:** a gland that produces an endocrine secretion — called also *gland of internal secretion*

endocrine system *n* **:** the glands and parts of glands that produce endocrine secretions

en·do·crin·ic \ˌendəˈkrinik, -nēk\ *adj* **:** ENDOCRINE

en·do·crin·o·log·ic \ˌ==ˌkrinᵊlˈäjik, -rīn-, -rēn-\ *also* **en·do·crin·o·log·i·cal** \-jəkəl\ *adj* [*endocrinology* + *-ic*, *-ical*] **:** involving or relating to the endocrine glands or secretions or to endocrinology

en·do·cri·nol·o·gist \ˌ==krəˈnäləjəst, -ˌkrī-, -ˌkrē-\ *n* -s [*endocrinology* + *-ist*] **:** one specializing in endocrinology

en·do·cri·nol·o·gy \-jē\ *n* -ES [ISV *endocrine* + *-o-* + *-logy*] **:** a science or study of the internal secretions and endocrine glands and their physiology and pathology as related to each other and to the organism as a whole

en·do·crin·o·path \ˌ==ˈkrinəˌpath, -rīn-, -rēn-\ *n* -s [ISV *endocrine* + *-o-* + *-path*] **:** one suffering from endocrinopathy

en·do·crin·o·path·ic \ˌ==ˌ==ˈpathik\ *adj* [ISV *endocrine* + *-o-* + *-pathic*] **:** involving endocrinopathy

en·do·cri·nop·a·thy \ˌ== ˌkrəˈnäpəthē, -ˌkrī-, -ˌkrē-\ *n* -ES [ISV *endocrine* + *-o-* + *-pathy*] **:** a disease marked by disorder in action or function of one or more of the endocrine organs

en·doc·ri·nous \(ˈ)enˈdäkrənəs\ *adj* **:** ENDOCRINE

en·do·cuticle \ˈendō+\ *n* [*end-* + *cuticle*] **:** the inner layer of a cuticle; *specif* **:** the colorless flexible highly chitinized inner layer of the exoskeleton of an insect — compare EPICUTICLE — **en·do·cuticular** \"+\ *adj*

en·do·cu·tic·u·la \ˌ==kyüˈtikyələ\ *n*, *pl* **endocuticu·lae** \-ˌlē\ [NL, fr. *end-* + L *cuticula*] **:** ENDOCUTICLE

en·do·cyclic \ˈendō+\ *or* **endocyclical** *adj* [*endocyclic* fr. NL *Endocyclica*; *endocyclical* fr. NL *Endocyclica* + E *-al*] **:** of or relating to the Regularia

en·do·cyc·li·ca \ˌ==ˈsikləkə\ [NL, fr. *end-* + *-cyclica* (fr. Gk *kyklika*, neut. pl. of *kyklikos* circular, cyclic) — more at CYCLIC] *syn of* REGULARIA

en·do·cyst \ˈendəˌsist\ *n* [ISV *end-* + *-cyst*] **1 :** the soft layer of the body wall of a bryozoan lining the ectocyst and consisting of ectoderm with a layer of mesoderm **2 :** the lining membrane of a hydatid cyst from which larvae are budded off

en·do·derm \-ˌdərm\ *n* -s [F *endoderme*, fr. *end-* + Gk *derma* skin, fr. *derein* to skin — more at TEAR] **:** the innermost of the three primary germ layers of an embryo and the source of the epithelium of the digestive tract and its derivatives **:** HYPOBLAST; *also* **:** any tissue wherever located that is derived from this germ layer

en·do·der·mal \ˌ==ˈdərməl\ *or* **en·do·der·mic** \-mik\ *adj* **:** of or derived from endoderm or from endodermis

endoderm disk *n* **:** an unpaired thickening on the posterior ventral surface of the crayfish embryo

en·do·der·mis \ˌ==ˈ==məs\ *n* [NL, fr. *end-* + *-dermis*] **:** the innermost tissue of the cortex in the majority of roots and some stems consisting usu. of a single layer of living cells with no intercellular spaces and with walls in part at least suberized or cutinized and often thickened in bands radially and transversely and supposedly functioning as a controlling element in the movement of water and other substances into and out of the stele — called also *starch sheath*; compare CASPARIAN STRIP

en·do·der·mi·za·tion \ˌ==ˌ==məˈzāshən\ *n* -s [*endoderm* + *-ize* + *-ation*] **:** excessive formation of endoderm due to experimental modification of the course of development

endoderm lamella *n* **:** a thin sheet of endoderm extending from the gastric cavity to the circular canal between adjacent radial canals in a medusa and separated from the ectoderm on either side by mesoglea

en·do·don·tia \ˌ==ˈdänch(ē)ə\ *n* -s [NL, fr. *end-* + *-odontia*] **:** a branch of dentistry concerned with the diagnosis and treatment of diseases of the pulp — **en·do·don·tic** \ˌ==ˈdäntik\ *adj* — **en·do·don·tist** \ˌ==ˈdäntəst\ *n* -s

en·do·don·tics \ˌ==ˈdäntiks\ *n pl but sing in constr* [by alter. (influence of *-ics*)] **:** ENDODONTIA

en·do·dynamomorphic \ˌen(ˌ)dō+\ *adj* [*end-* + *dynam-* + *-morphic*] *of a developing soil* **:** characterized by changes brought about by inherent properties of the parent rock rather than by external forces or agencies — opposed to *ectodynamomorphic*

en·do·ectothrix \ˌendō+\ *adj* [NL, fr. *end-* + *ectothrix*] **:** occurring in and on hair

en·do·enzyme \ˈendō+\ *n* [ISV *end-* + *enzyme*] **:** an enzyme that acts within the cell (as in most higher plants) **:** an intracellular enzyme — distinguished from *exoenzyme*

en·do·epithelial \ˌen(ˌ)dō+\ *adj* [*end-* + *epithelial*] **:** occurring within epithelial cells ⟨~ parasites⟩

en·do·er·gic \ˌendōˈərjik\ *adj* [*end-* + *erg-* + *-ic*] **:** absorbing energy **:** ENDOTHERMIC ⟨~ nuclear reactions⟩ — opposed to *exoergic*

en·do·erythrocytic \ˌen(ˌ)dō+\ *adj* [*end-* + *erythrocytic*] **:** occurring within red blood cells — used chiefly of stages of malaria parasites

en·do-form \ˈendō+ˌ-\ *n* [*end-* + *form*] **:** a rust producing spores in the aecia which have the appearance of aeciospores but which germinate like teliospores by a promycelium — compare EU-FORM

en·do·gam·ic \ˌendōˈgamik\ *adj* [*endogamy* + *-ic*] **:** ENDOGAMOUS

en·dog·a·mous \(ˈ)enˈdägəməs\ *adj* [*end-* + *-gamous*] **:** of, relating to, or characterized by endogamy

en·dog·a·my \ˈ=ˈ==mē\ *n* -ES [*end-* + *-gamy*] **1 :** marriage within a specific group as required by custom or law — contrasted with *exogamy* **2 a :** sexual reproduction between near relatives; *esp* **:** pollination of a flower by pollen from another flower of the same plant — compare AUTOGAMY, EXOGAMY **b :** fertilization by union of two female gametes

en·do·gastric \ˌen(ˌ)dō+\ *adj* [*end-* + *gastric*] **:** of or relating to the inside of the stomach — **en·do·gastrically** \"+\ *adv*

en·do·gen \ˈendəjən, -ˌjen\ *n* -s [F *endogène*, fr. *endogène* endogenous, fr. *end-* + *-gène* (fr. Gk *-genēs* born) — more at -GEN] **:** a plant that develops by endogenous growth (as most monocotyledons)

en·do·genesis \ˌendə+\ *n* [NL, fr. *end-* + L *genesis*] **:** ENDOGENY

en·do·genetic \ˌ==+\ *adj* [*end-* + *genetic*] **1 :** of or having to do with rocks formed by solidification from fusion, precipitation from solution, or sublimation — compare CLASTIC **2 :** ENDOGENOUS

en·do·gen·ic \ˌ==ˈjenik\ *adj* [modif. (influenced by E *-ic*) of G *endogenisch*, fr. *end-* + *-genisch* (fr. Gk *-genēs* born + G *-isch* -ish, fr. OHG *-isc*, *-isk*)] **:** of or having to do with the processes of metamorphism taking place within the earth — compare EXOGENOUS e

en·do·ge·nic·i·ty \ˌ==jəˈnisəd·ē\ *n* -ES [*endogenous* + *-ic* + *-ity*] **:** endogenous quality or origin

en·dog·e·nous \(ˈ)enˈdäjənəs\ *adj* [F *endogène* endogenous + E *-ous*] **1 a :** growing from or on the inside ⟨~ tissues⟩ **:** developing within the cell wall ⟨~ spores⟩ **b :** originating within the body ⟨an ~ disease⟩ **:** arising from internal structural or functional causes ⟨~ malnutrition⟩ ⟨~ mental deficiency⟩ **c :** constituting or relating to metabolism of the nitrogenous constituents of cells and tissues — compare EXOGENOUS **2 :** of, relating to, or resembling an endogen **3 :** originating in the individual's own psychodynamics rather than through other causes — **en·dog·e·nous·ly** *adv*

en·dog·e·ny \enˈdäjənē\ *n* -ES [*end-* + *-geny*] **:** growth from within or from a deep-seated layer

en·dog·nath \ˈendägˌnath, -ˌdäg-\ *n* -s [*end-* + Gk *gnathos* jaw; akin to Gk *genys* jaw — more at CHIN] **:** the inner and principal branch of an oral appendage of a crustacean

en·dog·na·thal \(ˈ)enˈdägnəthəl\ *adj* [*end-* + Gk *gnathos* + E *-al*] **1 :** of or relating to the endognath **2 :** situated within the jaw

en·do·gnathion \ˌendō+\ *n* [NL, fr. *end-* + *gnathion*] **:** the medial segment of the premaxilla situated on each side of the midline of the palate and bearing the medial incisor

en·do·li·max \ˌendəˈlīˌmaks\ *n*, *cap* [NL, fr. *end-* + L *limax* slug, snail — more at LIMAX] **:** a genus of amoebas commensal in vertebrate intestines including a species (*E. nana*) found in man

en·do·lith·ic \ˌendəˈlithik\ *adj* [ISV *end-* + *lithic*] **:** living within rocks or other stony substance (as mollusk shells or coral) ⟨~ algae⟩

en·do·lymph \ˈendə+\ *n* [ISV *end-* + *lymph*] **:** the watery fluid in the membranous labyrinth of the ear

en·do·lym·phat·ic \ˌendəˌlimˈfad·ik\ *adj* [fr. *endolymph*, after E *lymph*: *lymphatic*] **:** of or containing endolymph ⟨~ duct⟩

en·do·meninx \ˌendō+\ *n*, *pl* **endomeninges** [NL, fr. *end-* + Gk *mēninx* membrane — more at MEMBER] **:** the layer of embryonic mesoderm from which the arachnoid coat and pia mater of the brain develop

en·do·mere \ˈendəˌmi(ə)r\ *n* -s [*end-* + *-mere*] **:** a blastomere forming endoderm

en·do·mesoderm \ˌendō+\ *n* [*end-* + *mesoderm*] **:** MESENDODERM — **en·do·mesodermal** \"+\ *adj*

en·do·me·tri·al \ˌendəˈmētrēəl\ *adj* [ISV *endometri-* (prob. fr. NL *endometrium*) + *-al*] **:** of, belonging to, or consisting of endometrium

en·do·me·tri·o·ma \ˌ==ˌmētrēˈōmə\ *n*, *pl* **endometriomas** *or* **endometrioma·ta** \-məd·ə\ [NL, fr. *endometri-* (fr. *endometrium*) + *-oma*] **1 :** a tumor containing endometrial tissue **2 :** ENDOMETRIOSIS — used chiefly of isolated foci of endometrium outside the uterus

en·do·me·tri·o·sis \-ˈōsəs\ *n*, *pl* **endometrioses** [NL, fr. *endometri-* + *-osis*] **:** the presence of functioning endometrial tissue in places where it does not belong esp. where (1) invading the myometrium or (2) forming multiple foci and invading any organ within the pelvic cavity — called also respectively (1) *internal endometriosis*, *adenomyosis*; (2) *external endometriosis*

en·do·me·tri·tis \ˌ==məˈtrīd·əs\ *n* [NL, fr. *endometr-* (prob. fr. *endometrium*) + *-itis*] **:** inflammation of the endometrium

en·do·me·tri·um \ˌ==ˈmētrēəm\ *n*, *pl* **endome·tria** \-rēə\ [NL, fr. *end-* + *-metrium*] **:** the mucous membrane lining the uterus

en·do·mic·tic \ˌendəˈmiktik\ *adj* [fr. *endomixis*, after such pairs as E *apomixis*: *apomictic*] **:** of or relating to endomixis

en·do·mitosis \ˌendə+\ *n* [ISV *end-* + *mitosis*] **1 :** division of chromosomes in a nucleus without subsequent nuclear division resulting in duplication of the chromosome complex **2 :** PROMITOSIS — **en·do·mitotic** \"+\ *adj* — **en·do·mitotically** \"+\ *adv*

en·do·mix·is \ˌendəˈmiksəs\ *n* -ES [NL, fr. *end-* + *-mixis*] **:** a periodic nuclear reorganization in certain ciliated protozoans marked by degeneration of the macronucleus and its replacement by a product of micronuclear origin; *broadly* **:** any of several nuclear reorganization activities (as autogamy or hemixis) in ciliates that are distinct from conjugation

en·do·mo·lare \ˌendōmōˈla(a)rē\ *n* -s [*end-* + *-molare* (irreg. fr. L *molaris* molar) — more at MOLAR] **:** the most lateral point on the lingual aspect of the alveolar process of the jaw

en·do·morph \ˈendəˌmȯrf\ *n* -s [ISV *end-* + *-morph*] **1 :** a crystal of one species enclosed in one of another **2** [*endoderm* + *-morph*] **:** an endomorphic individual

en·do·mor·phic \ˌ==ˈmȯrfik\ *adj* [*end-* + *-morphic*] **1 a :** of or relating to an endomorph **b :** of, relating to, or produced by endomorphism — opposed to *exomorphic* **2** [*endoderm* + *-morphic*] **:** characterized by predominance of the structures (as the internal organs) developed from the endodermal layer of the embryo **:** of a pyknic type of body build — compare ECTOMORPHIC, MESOMORPHIC — **en·do·mor·phy** \ˈ==ˌ=fē\ *n* -ES

en·do·mor·phism \ˌ==ˈ=ˌfizəm\ *n* -s [ISV *end-* + *-morphism*; orig. formed as F *endomorphisme*] **:** a change (as in texture or in chemical composition by assimilation of foreign material) produced in an intrusive rock by reaction with the wall rock

en·do·my·ces \ˌendəˈmīˌsēz\ *n*, *cap* [NL, fr. *end-* + *-myces*] **:** a genus (the type of the family Endomycetaceae) of fungi having very simple structure with spirally wound gametangia which fuse apically

en·do·my·ce·ta·ce·ae \-ˌmīsəˈtāsēˌē\ *n pl*, *cap* [NL, fr. *Endomycet-*, *Endomyces*, type genus + *-aceae*] **:** a family of fungi (order Endomycetales) having the characteristics of the genus *Endomyces* and the asci 4-spored and borne directly on the hyphae

en·do·my·ce·ta·les \-ˈtā(ˌ)lēz\ *n pl*, *cap* [NL, fr. *Endomycet-*, *Endomyces* + *-ales*] **:** an order of ascomycetous fungi (subclass Hemiascomycetes) having a zygote or a single cell developing directly into an ascus

en·do·my·si·um \ˌendəˈmiz(h)ēəm\ *n*, *pl* **endomy·sia** \-ēə\ [NL, fr. *end-* + Gk *mys* muscle, mouse + NL *-ium* — more at MOUSE] **:** the delicate connective tissue surrounding the individual muscular fibers within the smallest bundles — compare EPIMYSIUM

end on *adv* **:** with an end pointing in a given direction or toward the eye of an observer — opposed to *broadside*

end-on \ˈ=ˈ=\ *adj* [*end on*] *of a coal working* **:** parallel in direction to the course of the main cleavage planes

en·do·neu·ri·al \ˌendōˈn(y)u̇rēəl\ *adj* [*endoneurium* + *-al*] **:** of or consisting of endoneurium

en·do·neu·ri·um \ˌ==ˈ=rēəm\ *n*, *pl* **endoneu·ria** \-ēə\ [NL, fr. *end-* + *neur-* + *-ium*] **:** the delicate connective tissue network holding together the individual fibers of a nerve trunk

en·do·parasite \ˌen(ˌ)dō+\ *n* [ISV *end-* + *parasite*] **:** a parasite that lives in the internal organs or tissues of its host — opposed to *ectoparasite* — **en·do·parasitic** \"+\ *adj* — **en·do·parasitism** \"+\ *n*

en·do·peptidase \"+\ *n* [*end-* + *peptidase*] **:** any of a group of enzymes that hydrolyze peptide bonds inside the long chains of protein molecules **:** PROTEINASE — distinguished from *exopeptidase*

en·do·pericardial \"+\ *adj* [*end-* + *pericardi-* + *-al*] **:** of or involving the endocardium and pericardium ⟨~ infection⟩

en·do·peridial \ˌen(ˌ)dō+\ *adj* [*endoperidium* + *-al*] **:** of or relating to the endoperidium

en·do·peridium \"+\ *n*, *pl* **endoperidia** [NL, fr. *end-* + *peridium*] **:** the inner peridium when consisting of two layers (as in the puffballs) — compare EXOPERIDIUM

en·doph·a·gous \(ˈ)enˈdäfəgəs\ *adj* [*end-* + *-phagous*] **:** feeding from within: **a** *of a parasitoid insect larva* **:** developing within and feeding on the internal organs and tissues of the host — compare ECTOPHAGOUS **b :** consuming vegetation or plant debris by burrowing in and disintegrating plant structures (as in the tunneling of leaves by leaf miners)

en·do·pha·sia \ˌendəˈfāzh(ē)ə\ *n* -s [It *endofasia*, fr. *end-* + *-fasia* -phasia] **:** speech that is not audible or visible **:** implicit speech — contrasted with *exophasia*

en·do·phragm \ˈ==ˌfram\ *n* -s [ISV *end-* + *-phragm* (as in *diaphragm*)] **:** SEPTUM; *specif* **:** one formed by the apodemes of the crustacean thorax — **en·do·phrag·mal** \ˌ==ˈfragməl\ *adj*

en·do·phyl·lum \ˌ==ˈfiləm\ *n*, *cap* [NL, fr. *end-* + *-phyllum*] **:** a genus (type of the family Endophyllaceae) of rusts producing teliospores in chains in cuplike spore fruits

en·do·phyte \ˈ==ˌfīt\ *n* -s [ISV *end-* + *-phyte*; prob. orig. formed in F] **:** a plant living within another plant but not necessarily parasitic upon it

en·do·phyt·ic \ˌ==ˈfid·ik\ *adj* [ISV *endophyte* + *-ic*] **1 :** of, relating to, or being an endophyte ⟨an ~ plant⟩ **2 :** situated or occurring within plant tissues ⟨oviposition in Odonata is often ~⟩ ⟨~ development⟩ **3 :** tending to grow inward into tissues in fingerlike projections from a superficial site of origin — used of certain tumors; opposed to *exophytic* — **en·do·phyt·i·cal·ly** \-d·ək(ə)lē\ *adv*

en·doph·y·tous \(ˈ)enˈdäfəd·əs\ *adj* [*endophyte* + *-ous*] **:** living within the tissues of plants ⟨~ insects⟩ ⟨~ fungi⟩

en·do·plasm \ˈendəˌplazəm\ *n* [ISV *end-* + *-plasm*] **:** the inner relatively fluid part of the cytoplasm — compare ECTOPLASM — **en·do·plas·mic** \ˌ==ˈplazmik\ *adj*

en·do·plas·ma \ˌ==ˈplazmə\ *n* [prob. fr. G, fr. *end-* + *-plasma* -plasm] **:** ENDOPLASM

en·do·plast \ˈ==ˌplast\ *n* -s [ISV *end-* + *-plast*] **1 :** ENDOPLASM **2 :** NUCLEUS 2a — **en·do·plas·tic** \ˌ==ˈplastik\ *adj*

en·do·plastron \ˌen(ˌ)dō+\ *n* [*end-* + *plastron*] **:** ENTOPLASTRON

en·do·pleu·ra \ˌendəˈplu̇rə\ *n* [NL, fr. *end-* + *-pleura*] **:** the inner coating or integument of a seed — called also *tegmen* — **en·do·pleu·ral** \ˌ==ˈ=rəl\ *adj*

en·do·pleu·rite \ˌ==ˈ=ˌrīt\ *n* -s [ISV *end-* + *pleurite*] **1 :** the portion of an apodeme of a crustacean developed from the interepimeral membrane **2 :** one of the lateral infoldings on the thorax of an insect which extend into the body cavity — **en·do·pleu·rit·ic** \ˌ==(ˌ)plu̇ˈrid·ik\ *adj*

en·do·pod \ˈendəˌpäd\ *n* -s [*end-* + *-pod*] **:** ENDOPODITE

en·dop·o·dite \enˈdäpəˌdīt\ *n* [ISV *end-* + *-podite*] **:** the mesial or internal branch of a typical limb of a crustacean that is borne upon the protopodite and that in the thoracic limbs of the higher Decapoda forms the entire limb — **en·dop·o·dit·ic** \(ˌ)=ˌ==ˈdid·ik\ *adj*

en·do·polyploid \ˌen(ˌ)dō+\ *adj* [*end-* + *polyploid*] **:** of or relating to endopolyploidy

en·do·pol·y·ploi·di·za·tion \ˌ=(ˌ)=ˌpäləˌplȯidəˈzāshən\ *n* -s [*endopolyploid* + *-ize* + *-ation*] **:** the act or process of becoming endopolyploid

en·do·polyploidy \ˌ=(ˌ)=+\ *n* [*end-* + *polyploidy*] **:** the polyploid state characteristic of cells, tissues, or individuals in which the chromosomes have divided repeatedly without mitosis or subsequent cell division

en·do·proct \ˈendəˌpräkt\ *n or adj* [NL *Endoprocta*] **:** ENTOPROCT

en·do·proc·ta \ˌ==ˈ=tə\ [NL, fr. *end-* + *-procta*] *syn of* ENTOPROCTA

en·do·proc·tous \ˌ==ˈ=təs\ *adj* [NL *Endoprocta* + E *-ous*] **:** ENTOPROCTOUS

en·do·psychic \ˌendō+\ *adj* [*end-* + *psychic*] **:** arising or existing within the mind

en·do·pterygota \ˌen(ˌ)dō+\ [NL, fr. *end-* + Gk *pterygōta*, neut. pl. of *pterygōtos* winged — more at PTERYGOTA] *syn of* HOLOMETABOLA

en·do·pterygote \"+\ *adj* [NL *Endopterygota*] **:** HOLOMETABOLOUS

end·oral \(ˈ)end+ˌ-\ *adj* [ISV *end-* + *oral*] **:** situated within a mouth or stoma ⟨~ groove⟩

end organ *n* **:** a structure forming the peripheral terminus of a path of nerve conduction and consisting of an effector or a receptor with its associated nerve terminations

en·do·rhe·ic *or* **en·do·re·ic** \ˌendəˈrēik\ *adj* [ISV *end-* + *-rheic*, *-reic* (fr. Gk *rhein* to flow + ISV *-ic*)] **:** relating to or characterized by endorheism

en·do·rhe·ism *or* **en·do·re·ism** \ˌ==ˈrēˌizəm\ *n* -s [ISV *end-* + *-rheism*, *-reism* (fr. Gk *rhein* to flow + ISV *-ism*) — more at STREAM] **:** interior drainage **:** the condition of a region in which little or none of the surface drainage reaches the sea

en·dors·able \ənˈdȯ(r)səbəl, en-\ *adj* **:** that can be endorsed

¹en·dorse *or* **in·dorse** \ənˈdȯ(ə)rs, en-, -ō(ə)s\ *vt* -ED/-ING/-S [*endorse* alter. (influenced by *indorse*) of *endoss*, fr. ME *endosen*, fr. MF *endosser*, fr. OF, to put on one's back, fr. ¹*en-* + *dos* back, fr. L *dorsum*; *indorse* fr. ME *indorsen*, fr. ML *indorsare*, fr. L *in* in, on + ML *-dorsare* (fr. L *dorsum* back)] **1 a :** to write on the back of (a commercial document): as (1) **:** to sign one's name as payee on the back of (a check) in order to obtain the cash or credit represented on the face (2) **:** to register payments of interest on (as a note or bill) by writing the amounts on the back with the signature of the one receiving the payment **b :** to inscribe (one's signature) on a check, bill, note, or other commercial document **:** SIGN ⟨he *endorsed* his name on the check⟩ **c :** to inscribe (as an official document) with a title, direction, memorandum, or explanation ⟨mail not delivered at the original address must be *endorsed* to show the next address —*Postal Term Glossary*⟩; *specif* **:** to write an endorsement on (a letter) in military communication **d :** to make over to another (the value represented in a check, bill, or note) by inscribing one's name on the document sometimes with specific directions for transfer **e :** to acknowledge receipt of (all or part of a sum specified in a note or bill) by one's signature on the document with proper notation **2** *obs* **:** to load upon the back **3 :** to express definite approval or acceptance of ⟨*endorsed* happiness, parenthood, and babies —Jack Gould⟩ **:** support or aid explicitly by or as if by signed statement **:** vouch for **:** UNDERWRITE ⟨a lot of people will ~ a good idea, but . . . few will fight for it —Owen Lattimore⟩ ⟨all of these measures had been *endorsed* by the governor —G.C. Wright⟩ **syn** see APPROVE — **endorse in blank :** to write one's name on the back of (a note or bill) without adding restrictions as to endorsee or manner of payment

²endorse \"\ *n* -s [perh. fr. past part. of ¹*endorse*] *heraldry* **:** a cotise paralleling a pale

endorsed *adj* [perh. fr. past part. of ¹*endorse*] **1 :** ADDORSED **2** *of a heraldic pale* **:** enclosed between two endorses

endorsed bond *n* [*endorsed* fr. past part. of ¹*endorse*] **:** a bond the payment of which is guaranteed by endorsement

en·dors·ee \ənˌdȯrˈsē, ˌenˌd-, -dō(ə)ˈ-\ *n* -s **:** one to whom a note or bill is endorsed or assigned by endorsement

en·dorse·ment \ənˈdȯrsmənt, en-, -ō(ə)s-\ *n* -s **1 :** the act or process of writing on the back of a note, bill, or other written instrument **2 a :** something that is written (as a name or an order for or a receipt of payment) on the back of a note, bill, or other document; *esp* **:** a writing usu. on the back but sometimes on the face of a negotiable instrument by which the property therein is assigned and transferred **b :** a provision added to an insurance contract altering its scope or application that takes precedence over printed portions of the policy in conflict therewith **3 a :** SANCTION, SUPPORT, APPROVAL ⟨the president's wholehearted ~ of a policy⟩ ⟨against his father's judgment but with his mother's sympathetic ~, he decided to be a missionary —K.S.Latourette⟩ **b :** RECOMMENDATION **4 :** a reply, comment, or forwarding note added to a letter by an officer or headquarters staff in military communication

en·dors·er \-sə(r)\ *n* -s **:** one that endorses: as **a :** a holder or payee who transfers title to a bill or note by endorsement **b :** one who signs a negotiable instrument (as a check or note) as an accommodation to enable another to obtain money or credit — compare COMAKER

en·dors·ing·ly *adv* [*endorsing* (pres. part. of ¹*endorse*) + *-ly*] **:** so as to endorse

en·do·salpinx \ˌen(ˌ)dō+\ *n*, *pl* **endosalpinges** [NL, fr. *end-* + *salpinx*] **:** the mucous membrane lining the fallopian tube

en·do·sarc \ˈendəˌsärk\ *n* -s [*end-* + *-sarc*] **:** the central usu. semifluid part of the protoplasm of some unicellular organisms (as amoebas) **:** ENDOPLASM — **en·do·sar·cous** \ˌ==ˈsärkəs\ *adj*

en·do·sclerite \ˌen(ˌ)dō+\ *n* [*end-* + *sclerite*] **:** a sclerite that is part of the internal skeleton of an insect or other arthropod

en·do·scope \ˈendəˌskōp\ *n* [ISV *end-* + *-scope*; prob. orig. formed in F] **1 :** an instrument for visualizing the interior of a hollow organ or part (as the rectum or urethra) — compare BRONCHOSCOPE, CYSTOSCOPE, OTOSCOPE **2 :** an optical instrument for examining the interior surface of a hole drilled through a pearl and used to distinguish between cultured and natural pearls

en·do·scop·ic \ˌ==ˈskäpik\ *adj* [*endoscope* + *-ic*] **1 :** of, relating to, or by means of the endoscope or endoscopy **2** [*end-* + *-scopic*] *bot* **:** having the apex of the embryo pointing toward the base of the archegonium — compare EXOSCOPIC

en·dos·co·pist \enˈdäskəpəst\ *n* -s **:** a physician specializing in the use of the endoscope

en·dos·co·py \-pē, -pi\ *n* -ES [ISV *endoscope* + *-y*] **:** examination with the endoscope

en·do·sep·sis \ˌendəˈsepsəs\ *n*, *pl* **endosep·ses** \-pˌsēz\ [NL, fr. *end-* + Gk *sēpsis* putrefaction, decay] **:** an internal rotting of figs caused by a fungus (*Fusarium moniliforme fici*) introduced by the fig wasp during pollination

en·do·siphon \ˌen(ˌ)dō+\ *n* [*end-* + *siphon*] **:** ENDOSIPHUNCLE — **en·do·siphonal** \"+\ *adj* — **en·do·siphonate** \"+\ *adj*

en·do·siphuncle \"+\ *n* [*end-* + *siphuncle*] **:** an inner tube in the calcareous siphuncle of certain fossil cephalopods

en·do·skeletal \"+\ *adj* [*endoskeleton* + *-al*] **:** of or belonging to an endoskeleton

en·do·skeleton \"+\ *n* [*end-* + *skeleton*] **:** an internal skeleton or supporting framework in an animal ⟨as the system of apodemes in an insect or the internal system of articulated bones in a vertebrate⟩ — compare EXOSKELETON

end·osmometer \ˌen,d+\ *n* [ISV *endosmo-* (fr. F *endosmose*) + *-meter*] : an instrument for measuring endosmosis — **endosmometric** \"+\ *adj*

endosmosis \ˌen,d+\ *n, pl* **endosmoses** [alter. (influenced by Gk *-sis*) of earlier *endosmose*, fr. F, fr. *end-* + Gk *ōsmos* action of thrusting or pushing, fr. *ōthein* to push; akin to Skt *vadhati* he strikes, kills] **1 :** passage (as of a surface-active substance) through a membrane from a region of lower to a region of higher concentration — used chiefly in biology; compare EXOSMOSIS 2 **2 :** osmotic diffusion toward the inside of a cell or vessel **3 :** infiltration or permeation of one cultural group by members of another — **endosmotic** \"+\ [fr. *endosmosis*, after such pairs as E *narcosis: narcotic*] *adj* — **endosmotically** \"+\ *adv*

en·do·some \ˈendə,sōm\ *n* -s [*end-* + *-some*] **1 :** the central body of a vesicular nucleus whether a karyosome or a plasmosome (as in various protozoan nuclei) **2 :** the inner part of the body of various higher sponges that contains flagellated chambers and few if any supporting spicules

en·do·sperm \-,spərm\ *n* [F *endosperme*, fr. *end-* + *sperme* sperm] **1 :** a nutritive tissue in seed plants formed around the embryo within the embryo sac by proliferation of the endosperm nucleus to form a mass of thin-walled triploid cells rich in carbohydrates which may be absorbed by the developing embryo or may remain until the seed germinates **2 :** any storage tissue within the seed regardless of its origin (as the female gametophyte tissue in gymnospermous seeds) — **en·do·sper·mic** \ˌ==ˈspərmik\ *adj* — **en·do·sper·mous** \-məs\ *adj*

endosperm nucleus *n* **:** the triploid nucleus formed in the embryo sac of a seed plant by fusion of a sperm nucleus with the two polar nuclei or with a nucleus produced by their prior fusion — compare DOUBLE FERTILIZATION

en·do·sphae·ra·ce·ae \ˌen(,)dōsfəˈrāsē,ē\ *n pl, cap* [NL, fr. *end-* + *sphaer-* + *-aceae*] **:** a family of irregularly shaped unicellular green algae (order Chlorococcales) living as endophytes or parasites within other algae, mosses, or seed plants

en·do·spore \ˈendə+,-\ *n* [ISV *end-* + *spore*] **1 :** an asexual spore developed within the cell esp. in bacteria — compare EXOSPORE **2 :** INTINE **3 :** the thin inner layer surrounding the protoplast of a sporozoan spore — **en·do·spor·ous** \ˌ==ˈspōrəs, (ˈ)enˈdäspərəs\ *adj* — **en·do·spor·ous·ly** *adv*

en·do·spo·ri·um \ˌendəˈspōrēəm\ *n, pl* **endospo·ria** \-ēə\ [NL, fr. *end-* + *-sporium*] **:** INTINE

en·do·sporulation \ˌendə+\ *n* [fr. *endospore*, after E *spore: sporulation*] **:** the production of endospores

en·doss \ənˈdäs, en-, -ˈdȯs\ *vt* [ME *endosen* — more at ¹ENDORSE] *archaic* **:** ENDORSE

end·osteal \(ˈ)enˌd+,-\ *adj* [*endosteum* + *-al*] **1 :** of, relating to, or involving the endosteum **2 :** located within bone or cartilage ⟨~ bone formation⟩ — **end·osteally** \"+\ *adv*

end·osteitis \ˌen,d+,-\ *or* **end·ostitis** \"+\ *n* -ES [NL, fr. *endosteum* + *-itis*] **:** inflammation of the endosteum

en·do·sternite \ˌen(,)dō+\ *n* [ISV *end-* + *sternite*] **:** a part of the endoskeleton of an arthropod: **a :** the part of one apodeme of a crustacean derived from the intersternal membrane **b :** ENTOSTERNITE **c :** one of the ventral segmental parts of the insect endoskeleton

en·os·te·um \enˈdästēəm\ *n, pl* **endos·tea** \-ēə\ [NL, fr. *end-* + Gk *osteon* bone — more at OSSEOUS] **:** the layer of vascular connective tissue lining the medullary cavities of bone

en·dos·to·ma \enˈdästəmə\ *n, pl* **endosto·ma·ta** \ˌen,däˈstōmədə, ˌendəˈs-\ *or* **endostomas** \enˈdästəməz\ [NL, fr. *end-* + *stoma*] **:** a plate which supports the labrum in some crustaceans

en·do·stome \ˈendə,stōm\ *n* -s [ISV *end-* + *-stome*; prob. orig. formed in F] **1 a :** the opening in the inner integument of an ovule having two integuments **b :** the inner part of the peristome of a moss **2** [NL *endostoma*] **:** ENDOSTOMA

end·ostosis \ˌen,d+\ *n, pl* **endostoses** [NL, fr. *end-* + *-ostosis*] **:** ossification beginning in the substance of a cartilage — compare ECTOSTOSIS

end·os·tra·cal \(ˈ)enˈdästrəkəl\ *adj* [*endostracum* + *-al*] **:** consisting of or involving an endostracum ⟨~ layers of the shell⟩ ⟨a marked ~ luster⟩

end·os·tra·cum \ˈ==kəm\ *n, pl* **endostra·ca** \-kə\ [NL, fr. *end-* + Gk *ostrakon* hard shell; akin to Gk *osteon* bone] **:** the inner layer of a shell esp. of a crustacean

en·do·style \ˈendə,stīl\ *n* [ISV *end-* + *style*] **:** a pair of parallel longitudinal folds projecting into the pharyngeal cavity and bounding a furrow lined with glandular ciliated cells in lower chordates (as amphioxus and the tunicates) that is believed to be morphologically equivalent to the thyroid of higher forms — **en·do·sty·lic** \ˌ==ˈstīlik\ *adj*

en·do·symbiont *or* **en·do·symbiote** \ˌen(,)dō+\ *n* [*end-* + *symbiont* or *symbiote*] **:** a symbiont dwelling within the body of its symbiotic partner

en·do·symbiosis \"+\ *n, pl* **endosymbioses** [NL, fr. *end-* + *symbiosis*] **:** symbiosis between endosymbionts

en·do·symbiotic \"+\ *adj* [*end-* + *symbiotic*] **:** of, relating to, or engaged in endosymbiosis

en·do·tergite \ˌen(,)dō+\ *n* [*end-* + *tergite*] **:** a dorsal phragma of the insect skeleton to which muscles are attached

en·do·theca \ˌendə+\ *n, pl* **endothecae** [NL, fr. *end-* + *theca*] **:** the tissue that partly fills the interior of the interseptal chambers of most madreporarian corals — **en·do·thecal** \"+\ *adj* — **en·do·the·cate** \"+\ *adj*

en·do·the·ci·al \ˌ==ˈthēsh(ē)əl, -sēəl\ *adj* [*endothecium* + *-al*] **1 :** of or belonging to an endothecium **2 :** having asci enclosed in an ascocarp

en·do·the·ci·um \ˌ==ˈthēs(h)ēəm\ *n, pl* **endothe·cia** \-ēə\ [NL, fr. *end-* + *-thecium*] **1 :** the middle of three layers that make up the young anther wall in a flowering plant becoming at maturity of the anther the innermost layer because of disintegration of the original inner wall cells **2 :** the central mass of cells within the young sporophyte in mosses and liverworts that develops into sporogenous tissue — compare AMPHITHECIUM

endotheli- *or* **endothelio-** *comb form* [ISV, fr. NL *endothelium*] **:** endothelium ⟨*endothelio*cyte⟩ ⟨*endothelio*ma⟩

en·do·the·li·al \ˌendəˈthēlēəl\ *adj* [ISV *endotheli-* + *-al*] **:** of, relating to, or produced from endothelium

en·do·the·lio·chorial \ˌendə,thēlē(,)ō+\ *adj* [*endotheli-* + *chorial*] *of a placenta* **:** having fetal epithelium enclosing maternal blood vessels (as in carnivores and some insectivores) — compare EPITHELIOCHORIAL, HEMOCHORIAL, SYNDESMOCHORIAL

en·do·the·li·o·cyte \ˌ==ˈlēə,sīt\ *n* -s [*endotheli-* + *-cyte*] **1 :** MONOCYTE **2 :** HISTIOCYTE

en·do·the·li·o·ma \ˌ==,=ˈlēˈōmə\ *n, pl* **endotheliomas** *or* **endothelioma·ta** \-mədə\ [NL, fr. *endotheli-* + *-oma*] **:** a tumor developing from endothelial tissue

en·do·the·li·um \ˌ==ˈlēəm\ *n, pl* **endothe·lia** \-ēə\ [NL, fr. *end-* + *-thelium* (as in *epithelium*)] **1 :** an epithelium of mesoblastic origin composed of a single layer of thin flattened cells that lines internal body cavities (as the serous cavities or the interior of the heart) **2 :** the inner layer of the seed coat of certain plants whose cells upon disorganization of the nucellus elongate radically and form a nutritive layer around the embryo sac — **en·do·the·loid** \ˌ==ˈ=,lȯid\ *adj*

en·do·therm \ˈendə,thərm\ *n* [*end-* + *-therm*] **:** a warm-blooded animal

en·do·thermal \ˌ==+\ *adj* [*end-* + *thermal*] **:** ENDOTHERMIC 1

en·do·thermic \"+\ *adj* [ISV *end-* + *thermic*] **1 :** characterized by or formed with absorption of heat **:** ENDOERGIC ⟨~ chemical reactions⟩ — opposed to *exothermic* **2** [*endotherm* + *-ic*] **:** WARM-BLOODED, HOMOIOTHERMIC — **en·do·ther·mic·al·ly** \"+\ *adv* — **en·do·ther·mism** \"+ˈthər,mizəm\ *n* -s

en·do·ther·my \ˈendə,thərmē\ *n* -ES [ISV *end-* + *-thermy*] **:** DIATHERMY

en·doth·ia \enˈdäthēə, -dōth-\ *n, cap* [NL, fr. Gk *endothen* within, from within (fr. *endon* within) + NL *-ia*; fr. the immersed perithecia — more at END-] **:** a genus of ascomycetous fungi (family Melogrammataceae) having ellipsoid 2-celled ascospores and including the fungus (*E. parasitica*) that causes chestnut blight

endothia canker *n, cap E* **:** CHESTNUT BLIGHT

en·do·thoracic \ˌendə+\ *adj* [fr. *endothorax*, after E *thorax: thoracic*] **:** of or relating to an endothorax

en·do·thorax \"+\ *n* [ISV *end-* + *thorax*] **:** the system of apodemes in the thorax or cephalothorax of an arthropod

¹en·do·thrix \ˈendə,thriks\ [NL, fr. *end-* + *-thrix*] *syn of* TRICHOPHYTON

²endothrix \"\ *n, pl* **endothrixes** \-səs\ *or* **endothri·ces** \ˌ==ˈthrī,sēz\ [NL *Endothrix*] **:** TRICHOPHYTON 2

³endothrix \"\ *adj* [NL, fr. *end-* + Gk *thrix* hair — more at TRICHINA] **:** occurring within a hair — compare ECTOTHRIX

en·do·toxic \ˌen(,)dō+\ *adj* [*endotoxin* + *-ic*] **:** of, relating to, or acting as an endotoxin

en·do·toxin \"+\ *n* [ISV *end-* + *toxin*] **:** a toxin of internal origin; *specif* **:** any of a class of poisonous substances present in bacteria (as of typhoid fever) but separable from the cell body only on its disintegration — compare EXOTOXIN

en·do·toxoid \"+\ *n, often attrib* [*endotoxin* + *-oid*] **:** a toxoid derived from an endotoxin

en·do·tracheal \ˌen(,)dō+\ *adj* [*end-* + *tracheal*] **1 :** placed within or passed inside of the trachea ⟨an ~ tube⟩ **2 :** applied or effected through the trachea ⟨~ anesthesia⟩ ⟨~ aspiration⟩

en·do·tro·phi \ˌen(,)dōˈtrō,fī\ [NL, fr. *end-* + *trophi*] *syn of* ENTOTROPHI

en·do·troph·ic \ˌendəˈträfik, -rōf-\ *also* **en·do·trop·ic** \-ˈräpik\ *adj* [*end-* + *-trophic* or *-tropic*] *of a mycorrhiza* **:** penetrating into the associated root and ramifying between the cells — opposed to *ectotrophic*

en·do·venous \ˌen(,)dō+\ *adj* [ISV *end-* + *venous*] **:** INTRAVENOUS

en·dow \ənˈdau̇, en-\ *vb* -ED/-ING/-S [ME *endowen*, fr. AF *endouer*, fr. MF *en-* ¹en- + *douer* to endow, fr. L *dotare*, fr. *dot-, dos* gift, dower — more at DOWER] *vt* **1** *obs* **:** to furnish with a dower **2 :** to furnish with (as an institution) with an income ⟨a millionaire who ~*ed* several hospitals⟩ **3 a :** to provide or equip gratuitously — usu. used with *with* ⟨nature ~*ed* him with good eyesight⟩ **b :** ENRICH, HEIGHTEN, ENHANCE — usu. used with *with* ⟨Shakespeare took these words . . . and ~*ed* them with new significance —C.S.Kilby⟩ **c :** to consider usu. favorably as the possessor of a quality **:** CREDIT 5a — usu. used with *with* ⟨he ~*ed* each girl he met with the beauty of a goddess⟩ ⟨during the 19th century the ether was ~*ed* with some very remarkable properties —W.V.Houston⟩ **~** *vi, of an insurance policy* **:** to mature or become payable

en·dow·ment \-mənt\ *n* -s [ME *endowement*, fr. AF *endouement*, fr. *endouer* + MF *-ment*] **1 :** the act or process of bestowing a dower, fund, or permanent provision for support **2 :** something that is endowed; *specif* **:** the portion of an institution's income usu. in the form of dividends from invested funds that is derived from donations **3 :** natural capacity, power, or ability ⟨a duty for men of great ~s . . . to sow the seed of the mind freely and lavishly —A.C.Benson⟩ **4 :** a course of instruction in the Mormon Church concerning past and present dispensations and their associated ordinances and given in the temples only **5 :** PURE ENDOWMENT

endowment insurance *n* **:** life insurance that promises to pay a stated amount to a designated beneficiary if the insured dies within a stipulated time or to the insured himself if he survives

en·do·xerosis \ˌen(,)dō+\ *n, pl* **endoxeroses** [NL, fr. *end-* + *xer-* + *-osis*] **:** a physiological disease of citrus causing the juice sacs esp. in the stylar end of the fruit to collapse and leave a hollow region — **en·do·xerotic** \"+\ *adj*

en·do·zoa \ˌendəˈzōə\ *n pl* [NL, fr. *end-* + *-zoa*] **:** ENTOZOA

en·do·zo·ic \ˌ==ˈzōik\ *adj* [ISV *end-* + *-zoic*] **:** living within or involving passage through an animal ⟨~ distribution of weeds⟩

endpaper \ˈ=,==\ *n* **:** a folded sheet of paper in books being plain or printed and having one leaf that forms a pastedown endpaper and one that forms a flyleaf — called also *endleaf, endsheet*

endpiece \ˈ=,=\ *n* **:** a piece at or forming an end

end pin *n* **1 :** the button of a violin **2 :** the usu. adjustable peg on which a cello or contrabass in use rests on the floor

end plate *n* **:** a flat plate or structure at the end of something: as **a :** a complex terminal arborization of a motor nerve fiber — called also *end brush* **b :** one of the main end timbers of a shaft set in a mine **c :** a surface attached approximately perpendicular to and near the end of an airfoil in order to produce an effective increase in the aspect ratio of the airfoil

¹end play *n* **1 :** slight endwise movement (as of a shaft or axle); *also* **:** room for such movement **2 a :** any of various plays in bridge usu. made on the eleventh trick and occurring when a declarer forces an opponent to make a lead favorable to the declarer and after the declarer has first eliminated all cards not essential to the play — compare COUP, ELIMINATION, SQUEEZE, THROW-IN **b :** THROW-IN 2 **c :** END GAME

²end play *vt* **1 :** to execute a throw-in when playing (a bridge hand) **2 :** to force (a bridge opponent) to win a trick and make a subsequent lead unfavorable to him

endpleasure *n* **:** pleasurable excitement that results from the release of tensions at the culmination of an act — compare FOREPLEASURE

end point *n* **:** a point marking the completion of a process or stage of a process **:** a final point **:** RESULTANT: as **a :** a point in a titration at which a definite effect is observed (as the change of color of an indicator in the neutralization of an acid by a base) **b** (1) **:** the highest temperature observed in a distillation esp. in the analysis of various petroleum products (as gasoline) (2) **:** the temperature at which liquid ceases to distill over **c :** the greatest dilution (as of a virus or a vitamin) that will produce a specified effect in a biological system (as the production of a disease or the alleviation of an avitaminosis) and that is usu. determined in bioassay as the 50 percent end point at which the specified effect appears in one half of the test subjects

end post *n* **:** a piece of nonconducting material used to provide electrical insulation between adjoining rail ends

end product *n* **1 :** the final product of a series of changes, processes, or operations ⟨industry whose *end product* — yarns and fabrics — has been Britain's bread and butter for centuries —Sam Pollock⟩ **2 :** the ultimate result of a series of activities, experiences, or tendencies ⟨every culture . . . is the *end product* of a long series of events occurring mostly in other cultures —A.L.Kroeber⟩

end–rack \ˈ=,=\ *vt* **:** to stack (as lumber) on end esp. for drying

end reaction *n* **:** a reaction that occurs only at the end of a process or as the final stage of a series of reactions

end rhyme *n* **:** rhyme of terminal syllables of verses

en·drin \ˈendrən\ *n* -s [prob. fr. ²*en-* + *-drin* (as in *aldrin*)] **:** an insecticide $C_{12}H_8Cl_6O$ that is a stereoisomer of dieldrin and resembles dieldrin in toxicity and other properties

end ring *n* **:** the ring at either end of an induction motor rotor to which the copper or aluminum bars are connected

end rot *n* **:** a disease of the cranberry caused by an imperfect fungus (*Fusicoccum putrefaciens*) and characterized by decay starting at either end of the fruit

end·rumpf \ˈent‚ru̇m(p)f; ˈen,drəm-, -dru̇m-\ *n* -s [G, fr. *ende* end (fr. OHG *enti*) + *rumpf* trunk, torso (fr. MHG *rumph*) — more at END, RUMP] **:** PENEPLAIN

end run *n* **1** *or* **end sweep :** a football play in which the ball carrier attempts to run wide around his own left or right flank **2 :** an evasive trick **:** an artful move

ends *pl of* END, *pres 3d sing of* END

end scraper *n* **:** a prehistoric flint scraper with scraping edge at one or both ends

ends down *n pl* **:** breaks in sliver, roving, or yarn during manufacture

endseal \ˈ=,=\ *n* **:** an adhesively applied label placed over the folded ends of a wrapper to increase durability and make a smooth closure

endsheet \ˈ=,=\ *n* **:** ENDPAPER

end–shrink \ˈ=ˌ=\ *vi* **:** to shrink in length (as of lumber)

end stone *n* **:** a polished flat unpierced jewel in a timepiece that limits a pivot's end play and acts as a bearing

end–stopped *adj* **:** marked by a grammatical pause at the end — used of verse, esp. of blank verse; compare RUN-ON

end table *n* **:** a small table used beside a larger piece of furniture

end thrust *n* **:** THRUST 3b

end–to–end \ˌ=ˈ=ˈ=\ *adj* **1 :** characterized by having the end of one object placed against the end of another ⟨an *end-to-end* position⟩ **2 :** effected by suturing one severed end (as of intestine) to the other **3 :** END-AND-END

en·due *or* **in·due** \ənˈd(y)ü, en-\ *vt* -ED/-ING/-S [ME *endewen, enduen, induen* (in sense 1 influenced in meaning by ME *endowen* to endow), fr. MF *enduire* to bring in, introduce, digest, fr. L *inducere* to bring in, introduce, induce — more at INDUCE] **1 a** (1) **:** PROVIDE, SUPPLY ⟨the coasts . . . are nearly everywhere badly *endued* by Nature —E.D.Laborde⟩ — usu. used with *with* (2) **:** INVEST — usu. used with *with* ⟨the court *endued* him with the full rights of a citizen⟩ **b :** IMBUE, TRANSFUSE — usu. used with *with* ⟨~ an object with life⟩ **2** [ME *induen* to take upon oneself, clothe, fr. L *induere* to put on, don, fr. *ind-* (fr. OL *indu, endo* in) + *-uere* (as in *exuere* to take off) — more at INDIGENOUS, EXUVIAE] **a :** to put on **:** DON **b :** CLOTHE — usu. used with *with* ⟨*endued* with gorgeous robes⟩ **3** *obs* **:** DIGEST — used chiefly of hawks

en·du·ra \ənˈd(y)u̇rə, en-\ *n* -s [ML, fr. OProv, fast, fr. *endurar* to fast, endure, fr. (assumed) VL *indurare* to last, continue] **:** a hunger strike against evil carried out by the Cathari and usu. leading to death

en·dur·able \ənˈd(y)u̇rəbəl, en-\ *adj* **:** capable of being endured **:** BEARABLE, TOLERABLE ⟨~ burdens⟩ ⟨our table manners were reasonably ~ —W.A.White⟩ — **en·dur·a·ble·ness** \-bəlnəs\ *n* -ES — **en·dur·a·bly** \-blē, -li\ *adv*

en·dur·ance \-rən(t)s\ *n* -s *often attrib* **1 :** PERMANENCE, DURATION ⟨a political confederacy of variable ~ —Fredrik Barth⟩ **2 a** (1) **:** the ability to withstand hardship or tribulation ⟨the great physical ~ of mountain troops⟩ (2) **:** the ability of a person or thing to continue to perform esp. under adverse conditions ⟨the five-mile cross-country stretch . . . becomes under these conditions a supreme test of ~ —Frank Weldon⟩ ⟨~ swimming⟩ **b** (1) **:** the power of holding out **:** STAMINA ⟨a hike beyond the ~ of most of us⟩ (2) **:** the capability of acting with moral courage and strength **:** FORTITUDE ⟨the indescribable look of high ~, which used to mark the sailing-ship seamen —John Masefield⟩ **3 :** SUFFERING ⟨the ~ of the inequalities of life by the poor is the marvel of human society —J.A.Froude⟩ **4 :** an instance of enduring (as hardship or tribulation) **:** TRIAL ⟨all these grim sights of tragic birth and tragic death, and the deep solitary ~s among the beasts of the field —J.C.Powys⟩ **5 :** the maximum time of performance, function, or operation esp. at an efficient level; *specif* **:** the maximum length of time an aircraft can remain in the air under given conditions without refueling

endurance limit *n* **:** FATIGUE LIMIT

endurance ratio *n* **:** FATIGUE RATIO

endurance strength *n* **:** FATIGUE STRENGTH

en·dur·ant \-rənt\ *adj* **:** capable of enduring adversity, severity, or hardship ⟨an ~ animal⟩

en·dure \ənˈd(y)u̇(ə)r, en-, -u̇ə\ *vb* -ED/-ING/-S [ME *enduren*, fr. MF *endurer*, fr. (assumed) VL & L; (assumed) VL *indurare* to last, continue, fr. L *indurare* to harden, fr. *in-* + *durare* to harden, fr. *durus* hard — more at DURE] *vi* **1 :** to continue in essentially the same state **:** LAST ⟨laws that have *endured* for centuries⟩ **2 :** to attain to or retain position or stature **:** maintain permanent recognition ⟨the question of why one novel ~s and another does not⟩ **3 a :** to remain firm under adversity **:** bear up (as under tribulation) without yielding ⟨*enduring* despite criticism⟩ **b :** to continue to act or function esp. under adverse conditions ⟨~ to the bitter end⟩ **~** *vt* **1** *obs* **:** to make hard, callous, or tough **:** STRENGTHEN **2 :** to undergo (as a hardship or difficulty) esp. without faltering, giving in, or breaking **:** SUFFER ⟨~ tension⟩ ⟨we must try to ~ all this in the fashion of philosophers —Louis Bromfield⟩ **3 :** to be compatible with **:** ALLOW, PERMIT ⟨a poem that will not ~ a facile interpretation⟩ **4 a :** to allow to stand **:** COUNTENANCE, TOLERATE — often used with a negative ⟨a century ago hospitals were charnel houses, presenting a spectacle no one could ~ today —*Saturday Rev.*⟩ **b :** to face with equanimity or tolerance **:** put up with — often used with a negative ⟨unable to ~ jazz⟩ **syn** see BEAR, CONTINUE

en·dur·er \-u̇rə(r)\ *n* -s **:** one that endures

¹en·dur·ing \-riŋ,-rēŋ\ *prep* [ME *enduringe*, fr. *enduringe* (pres. part. of *enduren*), fr. *enduren* + *-inge* -ing (pres. part. suffix)] *dial* **:** through the course of **:** DURING ⟨keep track of him ~ the holidays —Maristan Chapman⟩

²enduring \"\ *adj* [fr. *enduring* (pres. part. of *endure*), fr. ME *enduringe* (pres. part. of *enduren*)] **1 :** LASTING, PERMANENT ⟨an ~ novel⟩ **2 :** capable of existing without deterioration **:** DURABLE ⟨an ~ substance⟩ **3 :** PATIENT, LONG-SUFFERING ⟨an ~ disposition⟩ **4** *dial* **:** LIVELONG, ENTIRE — often used with *whole* ⟨he stayed the whole ~ day⟩

en·dur·ing·ly *adv* **:** LASTINGLY, PERMANENTLY

en·dur·ing·ness *n* -ES **:** lasting quality **:** PERMANENCE

enduring of *prep, dial* **:** ENDURING

end use *n* **:** the ultimate specific use to which a manufactured product (as paper) is put or restricted

endways \ˈ=,=\ *adv (or adj)* **1 :** with the end forward (as toward the observer) **:** END ON ⟨with houses built ~⟩ **2 :** in or toward the direction of the ends **:** LENGTHWISE ⟨~ pressure⟩ **3 :** at or on the end ⟨poles leaning ~ against a wall⟩ **4** *chiefly Scot* **:** well along **:** AHEAD ⟨couldn't get ~ with the job⟩

endwise \ˈ=,=\ *adv (or adj)* **:** ENDWAYS

en·dy·ma \ˈendəmə\ *n* -s [NL, fr. Gk *endyma* garment, fr. *endyein*] **:** EPENDYMA — **en·dy·mal** \-məl\ *adj*

en·dy·sis \ˈendəsəs\ *n, pl* **endy·ses** \-ə,sēz\ [NL, fr. Gk, act of putting on, fr. *endyein* to put on, don (fr. *en* in, on + *dyein* to dive in, put on, don) + *-sis* — more at IN, ADYTUM] **:** the act or process of developing a new coat of hair or a new set of feathers — opposed to *ecdysis*

end zone *n* **1 :** the area at each end of a football field bounded by the end line, the goal line, and the side lines — see FOOTBALL illustration **2 :** the part of an ice-hockey rink between each zone line and the nearer end of the rink — see ICE HOCKEY illustration

-ene \ˌēn *sometimes* ˈēn\ *n suffix* -s [ISV, fr. Gk *-ēnē* (fem. patronymic suffix)] **:** unsaturated carbon compound ⟨ben*zene*⟩; *esp* **:** carbon compound characterized by the presence of one double bond ⟨prop*ene*⟩ — in names of straight-chain hydrocarbons; distinguished from *-ane, -yne;* compare -YLENE

ENE *abbr* east-northeast

en echelon \ˌän+\ *adv (or adj)* [F *en échelon*] **:** in the arrangement or order of an echelon ⟨*en echelon* faults⟩

-ened *past of* -EN

ene·di·ol \ˈēn,dī,ōl, -ōl, =ˈ=,=\ *n* -s *often attrib* [ISV *ene-* (fr. *-ene*) + *diol*] **:** an organic compound characterized by the grouping >C(OH)—C(OH)< containing 2 hydroxyl groups adjacent to a double bond ⟨a reducing sugar can form an ~⟩

en·e·ma \ˈenəmə\ *n, pl* **enemas** *also* **enem·a·ta** \əˈnemədə, eˈ-,ēˈ-, -mətə\ [LL, fr. Gk, fr. *enienai* to send in, inject, fr. *en* in + *hienai* to send — more at JET] **1 :** the injection of liquid into the intestine by way of the anus for cleansing, examination, or other purpose **2 :** material for injection or injected as an enema — see BARIUM ENEMA

en·e·my \ˈenəmē, -mi\ *n, pl* **enemies** *often attrib* [ME *enemi*, fr. OF *enemi, inimi*, fr. L *inimicus*, fr. *in-* not + *amicus* friend — more at UN-, AMIABLE] **1 :** one that seeks the injury, overthrow, or failure of a person or thing to which he is opposed **:** ADVERSARY, OPPONENT ⟨the two brothers were political *enemies*⟩ **2 :** something injurious, harmful, or deadly ⟨drink was his greatest ~⟩ **3 a :** a military foe ⟨the ~ was driven off⟩ ⟨meet the ~ on equal terms⟩ — sometimes pl. in constr. ⟨the ~ were in large force⟩ **b :** a hostile unit, ship, tank, or aircraft ⟨after a running battle the ~ was sunk by a direct hit at 1000 yards⟩ **c** *pl* **enemy :** a member of a hostile force ⟨30 to 40 ~ engaged a friendly patrol —*N.Y. Times*⟩

syn ENEMY and FOE both signify a thing, person, or group that is hostile to one. ENEMY usu. stresses antagonism manifest in a desire to harm or destroy although it may suggest only an active dislike or habit of preying upon ⟨to amass adequate air power to deter our *enemies* from immediate attack⟩ ⟨let the teacher appear always the ally of the pupil, not his natural *enemy* —Bertrand Russell⟩ ⟨time is at once the *enemy* and the ally of life and of love —F.B.Millett⟩ ⟨the mortal *enemies* of man are . . . the aspects of the physical world that limit or challenge his control —W.C.Allee⟩ ⟨germ-bearing insects and other *enemies* of mankind⟩ FOE generally implies active warfare, usu. figurative ⟨the intransigent *foe* of hypocrisy and false standards —Gene Baro⟩ ⟨laughter is by no means a *foe* of reason —H.A.Overstreet⟩ ⟨the representative from Michigan has a reputation as a *foe* of waste, particularly in the armed services —*Current Biog.*⟩ In application to an opponent in war, ENEMY is the common word and FOE is chiefly poetic or

rhetorical ⟨he had fresh troops and superior numbers and forced the *enemy* back until they abandoned the field —C.H. Lanza⟩ ⟨donning his sword and buckler to fight the *foe*⟩
enemy alien *n* **:** a foreigner resident in a country with which his country is at war
eneolithic *usu cap, var of* AENEOLITHIC
en·epidermic \(ˌ)en+\ *adj* [²*en-* + *epidermic*] **:** applied to the unbroken skin for medicinal purposes
ener·geia \ˌenər'jīə, -r'gī, |āə, |ē(y)ə; e'ner(ˌ)gä,ä\ *n* -s [Gk, activity, operation — more at ENERGY] **:** ENERGY 4a — contrasted with *dynamis*
en·er·get·ic \ˌenə(r)|jed·|ik, -et|, |ēk\ *adj* [Gk *energētikos* active, fr. (assumed) *energētos* (verbal of *energein* to be in action, effect, fr. *energos* active, effective) + *-ikos* -ic] **1 :** exhibiting energy **:** STRENUOUS ⟨an ~ administration of business affairs⟩ **:** marked by energy ⟨an ~ walk⟩ ⟨an ~ campaigner⟩ **2 :** operating with force, vigor, or effect ⟨~ laws⟩ ⟨an ~ oxidizing agent for the creation of high temperatures⟩ **3 :** possessing energy **:** having the capacity for action or exerting force ⟨the volcanoes that raised the islands are still ~ in places⟩ **4 :** of, relating to, based on, or in terms of energy ⟨~ stability⟩ ⟨~ equation⟩ **syn** see VIGOROUS
en·er·get·i·cal \|əkəl, |ēk\ *adj* [Gk *energētikos* + E *-al*] **:** ENERGETIC — **en·er·get·i·cal·ly** \|ək(ə)lē, |ēk-, -li\ *adv*
en·er·get·i·cist \ˌ=='jed·əsəst, -et|\ *n* -s [fr. *energetics*, after such pairs as E *physics: physicist*] **:** a specialist in energetics
en·er·get·ics \|iks, |ēks\ *n pl but sing in constr* **:** a branch of mechanics that deals primarily with energy and its transformations ⟨nuclear ~⟩
en·er·ge·tis·tic \ˌenə(r)ˌjed·ə'tistik, -je'tis-, -tēk\ *adj* [*energetics* + *-ist* + *-ic*] **:** relating to energetics
ener·gic \(')e'nərjik, ə'n-,ē'n-\ *adj* [*energy* + *-ic*] **:** ENERGETIC
en·er·gid \'enə(r)jəd, -(ˌ)jid\ *n* -s [ISV *energ-* (fr. Gk *energos* active) + *-id*; orig. formed as G *energid*] **:** a nucleus and the body of cytoplasm with which it interacts — called also *protoplast*
en·er·gism \'enə(r)ˌjizəm\ *n* -s [G *energismus*, fr. *energie* energy (fr. LL *energia*) + *-ismus* -ism] **1 :** a doctrine that certain phenomena (as mental states) are explicable in terms of energy **2 :** an ethical theory that the supreme good consists in the efficient exercise of normal human faculties rather than in happiness or pleasure **:** SELF-REALIZATIONISM
en·er·gist \-jəst\ *n* -s **:** an adherent of energism
en·er·gize *also* **en·er·gise** \-ˌjīz\ *vb* [*energy* + *-ize*] *vi* **:** to put forth energy **:** ACT ~ *vt* **1 :** to impart energy to **:** make active ⟨~ the will⟩ **2 :** to make energetic or vigorous ⟨~ the administration of an office⟩ **3 :** to make an electric circuit alive electrically by applying voltage to ⟨allow current to flow from the battery to ~ the windings —Joseph Heitner⟩ **syn** see STRENGTHEN, VITALIZE
en·er·giz·er \-zə(r)\ *n* -s **:** one that energizes; *specif* **:** a metal carbonate (as barium carbonate) mixed with charcoal in a carburizing compound to increase carburizing speed
en·er·gu·men \ˌenə(r)'gyümən\ *n* -s [LL *energumenus* one possessed by an evil spirit, fr. LGk *energoumenos*, fr. Gk, worked on, being the object of an action, pres. middle part. of *energein* to be in action, effect, fr. *energos* active, effective] **1 :** a person possessed by or as if by an evil spirit **:** DEMONIAC; *specif* **:** one belonging to a Christian church in the first centuries and placed in a special class ministered to by exorcists and allowed limited participation in common worship **2 :** a fanatical devotee, adherent, or enthusiast ⟨military ~s⟩
en·er·gy \'enə(r)jē, -ji\ *n* -ES [LL *energia*, fr. Gk *energeia* activity, operation, fr. *energos* active, effective, fr. *en* in + *ergon* work — more at IN, WORK] **1** *of language or style* **:** imaginative or affective force **:** VITALITY **2 :** the capacity of acting, operating, or producing an effect **:** inherent power ⟨an individual of great intellectual ~⟩ ⟨he expended his *energies* in useless tasks⟩ **3 :** power efficiently and forcefully exerted **:** vigorous or effectual operation **:** VIGOROUSNESS ⟨the ~ and success of an argument⟩ **4 a :** the realized state of potentialities as opposed to their unrealized state — compare ENTELECHY **b** (1) **:** ACTIVITY; *esp* **:** psychical activity (2) **:** the product of activity **:** EFFECT **5 :** an entity rated as the most fundamental of all physical concepts and usu. regarded as the equivalent of or the capacity for doing work either being associated with material bodies (as a coiled spring or speeding train) or having an existence independent of matter (as light or X rays traversing a vacuum), its physical dimensions being the same as those of work $ML^2 \div T^2$ where M is mass, L length, and T time, usu. being expressed in work units (as foot-pounds or ergs), and in any form being endowed with the properties of mass (as inertia, momentum, gravitation) by relativity which assigns to the energy E an equivalent mass m by the equation $m = E \div c^2$ where c is the speed of light — see CONSERVATION OF ENERGY, KINETIC ENERGY, POTENTIAL ENERGY **6 :** MUZZLE ENERGY **syn** see POWER
energy balance *n* **:** the relation between intake of food and output of work (as in muscular or secretory activity) that is positive when the body stores extra food as fats and negative when the body draws on stored fat to provide energy for work
energy density *n* **:** the amount of energy (as in a beam of radiation) per unit volume
energy level *or* **energy state** *n* **:** one of the stable states of constant energy that may be assumed by a physical system — used esp. of the quantum states of electrons in atoms or molecules, of nuclei, or of other systems of interacting elementary particles
energy spectrum *n* **:** an arrangement of particle energies (as of alpha particles or photoelectrons) in a heterogeneous beam that is analogous to the arrangement of frequencies in an optical spectrum
¹**ener·vate** \ē'nərvət, ə'n-,e'n-\ *adj* [L *enervatus*, past part. of *enervare*] **:** ENERVATED
²**en·er·vate** \'enə(r)ˌvāt, *usu* -ād·+V\ *vt* -ED/-ING/-S [L *enervatus*, past part. of *enervare* to make weak or effeminate, fr. *e* out of, out + *-nervare* (fr. *nervus* sinew, nerve) — more at E-, NERVE] **1** *obs* **:** to cut the nerves or tendons of; *specif* **:** HAMSTRING **2 :** to lessen the nerve, vitality, or strength of **:** ENFEEBLE ⟨heat ~s people⟩ **3 :** to reduce the mental or moral vigor of **:** WEAKEN ⟨a government *enervated* by corruption⟩ **syn** see UNNERVE
en·er·vat·ed \'enə(r)ˌvād·əd, -ātəd\ *adj* [fr. past part. of ²*enervate*] **:** lacking physical, mental, or moral vigor **:** ENERVATE **syn** see LANGUID
en·er·va·tion \ˌenə(r)'vāshən\ *n* -s [LL *enervation-, enervatio*, fr. L *enervatus* + *-ion-, -io* -ion] **1 :** the act or action of enervating **2 :** the quality or state of being enervated
en·er·va·tor \'enə(r)ˌvād·ə(r), -ātə-\ *n* -s **:** one that enervates
enerve *vt* [F *énerver*, fr. L *enervare*] *obs* **:** ²ENERVATE
-enes *pl of* -ENE
eneuch *or* **eneugh** \ə'n(y)ük, -'(y)ük, -'(y)ək\ *Scot var of* ENOUGH
enew *vt* -ED/-ING/-S [ME *enewen*, fr. AF *enewer* to moisten, fr. OF *en-* ¹en- + *ewe, eve, aigue* water (fr. L *aqua*) — more at ISLAND] *obs, of a hawk* **:** to drive or plunge (a fowl) into the water
en face \äⁿfäs\ *adj* [F, opposite] **1 :** facing forward **:** having face or front forward ⟨a portrait *en face*⟩ **2 :** OPPOSITE ⟨a collection of French poems with English translation *en face*⟩
en·face \ən'fās, en-\ *vt* [*en-* (as in *endorse*) + *face*, n.] *Brit* **:** to write or print on the face of (a draft or bill) ⟨~ drafts with memoranda⟩; *also* **:** to write or print (a memorandum or direction) on the face of a draft or bill
en·face·ment \-mənt\ *n* -s *Brit* **:** the act of enfacing; *also* **:** something (as a note or bill) that is enfaced — compare ENDORSEMENT
en·fant ter·ri·ble \äⁿfäⁿterēbl(ᵊ), -b(lə)\ *n, pl* **enfants terribles** \"\ [F, terrible child] **1 :** a child whose inopportune remarks cause embarrassment **2 :** a person who compromises his cause or party by rash actions
en·fa·ti·co \äm'fätē(ˌ)kō\ *adj* [It, fr. LL *emphaticus* forcible, expressive, fr. Gk *emphatikos* — more at EMPHATIC] **:** EMPHATIC, FORCEFUL — used as a direction in music
en·fee·ble \ən'fēbəl, en-\ *vt* **enfeebled; enfeebled; enfeebling** \-b(ə)liŋ\ **enfeebles** [ME *enfeblen*, fr. MF *enfeblir*, fr. OF, fr. *en-* ¹en- + *feble, foible* feeble — more at FEEBLE] **:** to make feeble ⟨a man *enfeebled* by hunger⟩ **:** deprive of strength **:** reduce the strength of ⟨a country *enfeebled* by civil war⟩ **syn** see WEAKEN

en·fee·ble·ment \-bəlmənt\ *n* -s **1 :** the action of enfeebling **2 :** the quality or state of being enfeebled
en·fee·bler \-b(ə)lə(r)\ *n* -s **:** one that enfeebles
en·feoff \ən, en +\ *vt* -ED/-ING/-S [ME *enfeffen, enfeoffen*, fr. AF *enfeffer, enfeoffer*, fr. OF *en-* ¹en- + *fief*, n., fee — more at FEE] **1 :** to invest with a fief or fee **:** invest (a person) with a freehold estate by feoffment ⟨the holdings in which a baron ~*ed* his leading tenants —F.M.Stenton⟩ **2** *obs* **:** to give into vassalage
en·feoff·ment \"mənt\ *n* -s [ME *enfeffement*, fr. AF, fr. *enfeffer* + MF *-ment*] **1 :** the act of enfeoffing **2 :** the instrument or deed by which one is enfeoffed
en fête \äⁿ'fāt\ *adj* [F, in festival] **:** being in festal dress **:** making a holiday showing
en·fetter \ən, en +\ *vt* [¹*en-* + *fetter*, n.] **:** to bind in fetters
¹**en·field** \'enˌfēld\ *adj, usu cap* [fr. *Enfield*, urban district in Middlesex, England] **:** of or from the urban district of Enfield, England **:** of the kind or style prevalent in Enfield
²**enfield** \"\ *or* **enfield rifle** *n* -s *usu cap E* [fr. *Enfield*, Middlesex, Eng., where it was orig. manufactured] **1 :** a muzzle-loading rifled musket of .577 caliber used by the British during the Crimean War and by U.S. troops in the Civil War **2 :** a .303 caliber magazine rifle of bolt type used by the British **3 :** a .30 caliber rifle used by U.S. troops in World War I — see RIFLE illustration
¹**en·fi·lade** \'enfəˌlād, -ˌäd, -ˌäd *also* 'äⁿ...äd *or* 'äⁿ...äd; ˌ=='=\ *n* -s [F, series, row, military enfilade, fr. *enfiler* to thread, string, rake with gunfire in a lengthwise direction (fr. OF, to thread, fr. *en-* ¹en- + *fil*, n., thread) + *-ade* — more at FILE] **1 :** arrangement (as of rooms, doorways, trees) in opposite and parallel rows **2 a :** a condition permitting the delivery of fire at an objective (as a trench or line of troops) from a point on or near the prolongation of its longest axis **b :** a position favorable for enfilade firing
²**enfilade** \"\ *vt* -ED/-ING/-S **1 :** to arrange (as trees or rooms) to form an enfilade **2 :** to rake or be in a position to rake (as a fortification or column of troops) with gunfire in a lengthwise direction
en·file \ən'fī(ə)l, en-\ *vt* [ME *enfilen*, fr. MF *enfiler*] *archaic* **:** to put on a string **:** THREAD
enfiled *adj* [fr. past part. of *enfile*] *heraldry* **:** passed or thrust through — used with *with* or *of* ⟨two branches ~ with a baron's coronet⟩ ⟨~ with a chaplet of roses —Edward Almack⟩
en·fire \ən, en +\ *vt* [ME *enfiren*, fr. *en-* ¹en- + *fir*, n., fire — more at FIRE] *archaic* **:** KINDLE
enflame *var of* INFLAME
en·flesh \ən, en +\ *vt* [¹*en-* + *flesh*, n.] **:** to clothe with or as if with flesh ⟨~ the idea of spirit —H.O.Taylor⟩
en·fleu·rage \ˌäⁿflœ'räzh\ *n* -s [F, fr. *enfleurer* to saturate with the perfume of flowers (fr. *en-* ¹en- + *fleur*, n., flower, fr. L *flor-, flos*) + *-age* — more at BLOW (to bloom)] **:** a process of obtaining fragrant oils for perfumes by exposing successive batches of freshly picked flowers to layers of fat (as a mixture of lard and tallow) coated on stacked glass plates and finally extracting usu. with alcohol the resulting pomade
en·fold \ən'fōld, en-\ *vt* **enfolded; enfolded** *or archaic* **enfolden; enfolding; enfolds** [alter. (influenced by ¹*en-*) of *infold*] **1 a :** to surround with a covering **:** CONTAIN ⟨gilded tombs do worms ~ —Shak.⟩ ⟨~*ed* within the covers of this volume —*N.Y.Herald Tribune Bk. Rev.*⟩ **b :** to cover with or as if with folds **:** ENVELOP ⟨the new atmosphere that seemed to ~ her —Helen R. Martin⟩ ⟨blackness moved up the walls till night ~*ed* the pass —Zane Grey⟩ ⟨she lay *enfolden* in the warm shadow of her loveliness —P.B.Shelley⟩ **2 a :** to clasp with or within the arms **:** EMBRACE ⟨arms ~*ing* bunches of flowering branches —Angélica Mendoza⟩ **b :** to take in and hold ⟨either ~ them as respectable . . . members of a commercial society or drive them on —Russell Lord⟩ **3 :** to make or put a fold in **:** fold over or back ⟨~*ed* margins⟩
en·fold·er \-də(r)\ *n* -s **:** one that enfolds
enfolding *n* **:** a folding in **:** FOLD, CREASE
en·fold·ment \-l(d)mənt\ *n* -s **:** an action of enfolding
en·force \ən'fō(ə)rs, en-, -ō(ə)rs,-ōəs, -ō(ə)s\ *vt* [ME *enforcen*, fr. MF *enforcier* to strengthen, force, fr. OF, fr. *en-* ¹en- + *force*, n., strength & *forcier*, v., to attack — more at FORCE (n.), FORCE (v.)] **1 :** to give force to **:** REINFORCE ⟨his comment is enough to confirm and ~ the significance attributed to a free ballot⟩ **2 a :** to urge with energy ⟨~ arguments⟩ **b** *obs* **:** ENCOURAGE, INSPIRE **3** *obs* **:** to use force upon **:** ASSAIL, ASSAULT **4** *obs* **:** to fling or drive forcibly **5 :** CONSTRAIN, COMPEL ⟨~ obedience from children⟩ **6** *obs* **:** to make or obtain by force ⟨~ a passage⟩ **7 :** to put in force **:** cause to take effect **:** give effect to esp. with vigor ⟨~ laws⟩ ⟨a government unable to ~ its national interests⟩ ⟨*enforced* his rule by cruel methods —C.S.Forester⟩
syn IMPLEMENT: ENFORCE refers to requiring operation, observance, or protection of laws, orders, contracts, and agreements by authority, often that of a whole government or of its executive or legal branches ⟨this law is seldom *enforced*⟩ ⟨in order to make the papal bureaucracy disciplined and fit for such duties he *enforced* the hated rule of celibacy upon his clergy —Herbert Agar⟩ ⟨the mediator's request for troops to back up its resolutions and *enforce* the truce —*Collier's Yr. Bk.*⟩ IMPLEMENT suggests performance of such acts as are necessary to bring into actual effect or operation some agreed-on plan or measure ⟨the estimates of public accountants that the actual cost of *implementing* the bill would be about double the amount the president forecast —*Current Biog.*⟩ ⟨he also urged that military equipment be given to the nations of Western Europe to *implement* the Brussels pact —*Current Biog.*⟩ ⟨to *implement* the prison's group activities by providing films, books, and pamphlets —*Saturday Rev.*⟩
en·force·abil·i·ty \ˌ=ˌ=ə'bilәd·ē, -ətē, -i\ *n* -ES **:** the quality or state of being enforceable
en·force·able \=ˈ=səbəl\ *adj* **:** capable of being enforced
en·forced \-st\ *adj* [fr. past part. of *enforce*] **:** COMPELLED, FORCED ⟨~ obedience⟩ ⟨~ idleness⟩ — **en·forced·ly** \-sədlē, -stlē, -li\ *adv*
en·force·ment \-smənt\ *n* -s [MF *enforcement*, fr. OF, fr. *enforcier* + *-ment*] **:** the act of enforcing: as **a :** compulsion esp. by physical violence **b :** forcible urging or argument ⟨the ~ of a reasonable claim⟩ **c :** the compelling of the fulfillment (as of a law or order)
en·forc·er \=ˈ=sə(r)\ *n* -s **:** one that enforces; *specif* **:** a gunman used to enforce discipline within a gang
en·forc·ive \=ˈ=siv\ *adj, obs* **:** tending to enforce
enforest *vt* [¹*en-* + *forest*, n.] *obs* **:** AFFOREST
enfouldred *adj* [¹*en-* + obs. E *fouldre* thunderbolt, lightning (fr. ME *fouldre, foudre*, fr. MF, fr. L *fulgur*) + E *-ed*; akin to L *flagrare* to burn — more at BLACK] *obs* **:** mixed with or emitting lightning
en·frame \ən'frām, en-\ *vt* [¹*en-* + *frame*, n.] **:** FRAME — **en·frame·ment** \-āmmənt\ *n* -s
enfranch *vt* [prob. by shortening] *obs* **:** ENFRANCHISE
en·fran·chise \ən'franˌchīz, en-, -raan- *sometimes* -īs\ *vt* [ME *enfraunchisen*, fr. MF *enfranchiss-*, stem of *enfranchir*, fr. OF, fr. *en-* ¹en- + *franc* free — more at FRANK] **1 :** to set free (as from slavery, prison, or obligation) **2 a :** to endow with a franchise **:** admit to the privileges of a freeman or citizen **b :** NATURALIZE **3 :** to admit (a town or city) to political privileges **:** give political rights to (a town or city) **4 :** to make (lands) freehold under feudal law **syn** see FREE
en·fran·chise·ment \-mənt, -chəzmənt *sometimes* -chəsm- *or* ən,fra(a)n'chī- *or* (ˌ)en,fra(a)n'chī- *or* ,enfran'chī-\ *n* **:** the act of enfranchising: as **a :** the releasing from slavery or custody **b :** admission to the freedom of a corporation or body politic **c :** the making of lands (as copyhold) freehold under feudal law
en·fran·chis·er \=ˈ=ˌchīzə(r) *sometimes* -īsə-\ *n* -s **:** one that enfranchises
enfume *vt* [F & L; F *enfumer*, fr. L *infumare*, fr. *in* + *fumus* smoke — more at FUME] *obs* **:** to envelop in smoke
¹**eng** \'eŋ\ *n* -s [native name in Burma] **:** a large timber tree (*Dipterocarpus tuberculatus*) of Burma and parts of India that produces a hard strong heavy straight-grained reddish brown timber
²**eng** \"\ *n* -s **:** the symbol ŋ that is widely used in pronunciation alphabets for the velar nasal consonant which is the sound of *ng* in English *thing* and of *n* in English *think*
eng *abbr* **1** engine; engineer; engineering **2** engraved; engraver; engraving

en·gage \ən'gāj, en-\ *vb* -ED/-ING/-S [ME *engagen*, fr. MF *engager, engagier*, fr. OF *engagier*, fr. *en-* ¹en- + *gage* pledge, pawn — more at GAGE] *vt* **1 a** *obs* **:** MORTGAGE, PAWN, PLEDGE **b :** to offer (as one's life or word) as backing to a cause or aim **:** expose to risk for the attainment or support of some end ⟨*engaged* his all in the king's cause⟩ ⟨I would like to drop out of this undertaking but my word is *engaged*⟩ **2 a** *obs* **:** to involve or entangle (as a person) in some affair or enterprise **b** *obs* **:** to entangle or entrap in or as if in a snare or bog **c :** to attract and hold ⟨*engaged* his attention by a series of sprightly comments⟩ **d :** to make (an architectural member) fast; *esp* **:** to partially incorporate (a column) in a wall **e :** to come into contact or interlock with **:** MESH ⟨the teeth of one gear wheel *engaging* those of another to transmit power⟩; *also* **:** to cause (parts) to engage ⟨~ the gears, then slowly let in your clutch⟩ **3 a** *obs* **:** to commit (as a person) as surety (as for the payment of a debt or performance of an obligation) **b :** to bind (as oneself) to do or to forbear doing something by or as if by a formal promise or contract ⟨he *engaged* himself not to call on his father for help⟩; *esp* **:** to bind (as oneself) by a pledge to marry ⟨a girl who *engaged* herself to three different men in as many months⟩ — usu. used passively ⟨they had been *engaged* for over six years⟩ **c :** to pledge or commit (as oneself) to participate in some social or business activity ⟨*engaged* herself to attend the meeting⟩; *often* to bind by a previous commitment ⟨I would like to go with you but I am *engaged* that evening⟩ ⟨a popular hairdresser whose time is *engaged* weeks in advance⟩ **4 a :** to provide occupation for (as a person, his interest, or labor) **:** require the use of ⟨it *engaged* all their strength to budge the stone⟩ ⟨to fix the attention, but not to ~ the mind, is a precise statement of the advertiser's formula —D.M.Potter⟩ ⟨subsistence farming ~s the major efforts of the settlers⟩ ⟨his family had been *engaged* in trade for generations⟩ **b :** to arrange to obtain the services of usu. for a wage or fee ⟨she was *engaged* to play the leading role in the new opera⟩ ⟨you will need to ~ a cook and two extra maids if you take that house⟩; *also* **:** to enter (oneself) into an agreement to serve ⟨he *engaged* himself with the new company for two years⟩ **c :** to arrange or arrange to secure (as accommodations, goods, or aid) ⟨we will ~ a suite at the hotel⟩ ⟨have your agent ~ wheat for fall delivery⟩ ⟨I have *engaged* the help of the local chief in order to recruit enough porters⟩ **d :** to gain over **:** win and attach **:** ATTRACT ⟨his gentle persistence gradually *engaged* all the neighbors⟩ ⟨she ~s everyone with her pretty girlish ways⟩ **5 a** *archaic* **:** to call upon **:** EXHORT, INDUCE, PERSUADE **b :** to hold the attention of **:** ENGROSS, OCCUPY ⟨the puzzle *engaged* him all evening⟩ ⟨we were *engaged* in cleaning the cottage until just before you came⟩ **c :** to induce to participate **:** draw out ⟨I *engaged* him in conversation⟩ **6 a :** to enter into contest with **:** bring to conflict ⟨ordered to seek out and ~ the enemy fleet⟩ **b :** to bring together or interlock (weapons) ⟨*engaged* their foils after a preliminary pass or two⟩ ⟨the battling stags ~ their heavy antlers and strive for mastery⟩ ~ *vi* **1 a :** to promise or pledge oneself ⟨*engaged* to free the Holy Land⟩ **:** enter into or take on an obligation ⟨they *engaged* to sell our grain at the best possible price⟩ ⟨the Indians *engaged* to keep the peace⟩ **b :** to become pledged or answerable **:** GUARANTEE, PROMISE — usu. used with *for* ⟨he'll be there on time but that's all I can ~ for⟩ ⟨he ~s for the honesty of his brother⟩ **2 a :** to begin and carry on an enterprise, esp. a business or profession ⟨he *engaged* in trade for several years⟩ **b :** to employ or involve oneself ⟨he *engaged* in one long round of pleasure as long as his money lasted⟩ **c :** to take part **:** PARTICIPATE ⟨he *engaged* in a long-winded dispute⟩ ⟨*engaging* in a hog-calling contest⟩ **3 a :** to enter into conflict **:** join battle **b :** to bring together or interlock weapons — used esp. of fencers **4** *archaic* **:** to become involved or entangled **5** *of machinery* **:** to be or become in gear (as of two gear wheels working together) **:** interlock and interact **syn** see PROMISE
en·gaged \-jd\ *adj* [fr. past part. of *engage*] **1 :** OCCUPIED, EMPLOYED **2 :** pledged or promised esp. in marriage **:** BETROTHED **3 :** greatly interested **:** EARNEST **4 :** involved esp. in a hostile encounter ⟨the ~ ships continued the fight⟩ **5** *of an architectural member* **a :** partly embedded or bonded (as in a wall) ⟨an ~ column⟩ **b :** FITTED, FRAMED **6 a** *of machinery* **:** being in gear **b** *of gears* **:** MESHED — **en·gaged·ly** \-jədlē, -jdlē, -li\ *adv* — **en·gaged·ness** \-jədnəs, -j(d)n-\ *n* -ES
en·gage·ment \-jmənt\ *n* -s **1 a :** the act of engaging or state of being engaged **:** a pledging or pledged state **:** INVOLVEMENT, ATTACHMENT **b :** BETROTHAL **2 a :** something that engages (as an engrossing occupation, an obligation) ⟨his ~s kept him very busy⟩ **b :** PREPOSSESSION, BIAS **:** favorable attachment ⟨religion, which is the chief ~ of our league —John Milton⟩ **3 a :** a promise to be present at a specified time and place **:** APPOINTMENT ⟨a previous ~⟩ **b :** employment esp. by contract for a stated time ⟨an ~ as leading lady⟩ **4 engagements** *pl* **:** pecuniary liabilities **:** OBLIGATIONS **5 :** the act of crossing fencing blades in any of the eight positions **6 :** the state of being in gear or in such contact that motion may be transmitted ⟨one part of a clutch is brought into ~ with the other part⟩ **7 :** the phase of parturition in which the fetal head passes into the pelvic canal **8 a :** hostile encounter between military forces ⟨forces . . . reported small patrol ~s during the day —*N.Y.Times*⟩ **b :** a duel or other single combat
syn ENGAGEMENT, APPOINTMENT, RENDEZVOUS, TRYST, ASSIGNATION, DATE can apply, in common, to an agreement or commitment to be in a specific place at a specific time for a specified purpose. ENGAGEMENT is the general term interchangeable in basic meaning with any of the rest ⟨his *engagement* with the duke —F.M.Stenton⟩ ⟨an *engagement* with the doctor at 2 p.m.⟩ ⟨an *engagement* to meet secretly after dark⟩ APPOINTMENT applies chiefly to an engagement with someone, as a doctor or executive, who must apportion his time in order to meet all commitments ⟨an *appointment* with the dentist⟩ ⟨an *appointment* to see the governor⟩ ⟨an *appointment* with fate⟩ RENDEZVOUS, now commonly an agreed-upon meeting or meeting place, can still signify a pledge, often implicit, to meet someone or something usu. at a specific place and time which honor makes inescapable ⟨I have a *rendezvous* with Death —Alan Seeger⟩ ⟨this generation of Americans has a *rendezvous* with destiny —F.D.Roosevelt⟩ TRYST, now chiefly poetic, applies generally to a lovers' agreement to meet at a particular place or time ⟨young women kept *trysts* with their beaux here —*Amer. Guide Series: N.C.*⟩ An ASSIGNATION is commonly a tryst but is usu. illicit or clandestine ⟨make *assignations* for them with ladies of the street —G.B.Shaw⟩ DATE is interchangeable with but more current in speech than ENGAGEMENT, often suggesting a more casual agreement esp. between young men and women ⟨remembering suddenly he had a riding *date* with the major's wife at 12:30 —James Jones⟩ ⟨she has a *date* with a boy⟩
engagement ring *n* **:** a ring given in token of betrothal; *esp* **:** a diamond solitaire so given by a man to his fiancée

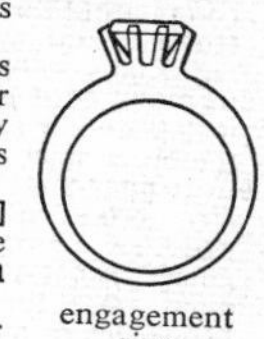
engagement ring

en·gag·er \-jə(r)\ *n* -s **:** one that engages: as **a** *obs* **:** a person who acts as a guarantor **:** SURETY **b :** one that engages in an activity or occupation **c :** a person who engages another's service **:** EMPLOYER
engaging *adj* [fr. pres. part. of *engage*] **:** tending to draw favorable attention or the affections **:** ATTRACTIVE ⟨~ manners⟩ **syn** see SWEET
en·gag·ing·ly *adv* **:** in an engaging manner **:** CHARMINGLY
en·gag·ing·ness *n* -ES **:** the quality of being engaging
en·garland \ən, en+\ *vt* [¹*en-* + *garland*, n.] **:** to deck or encircle with or as if with a garland
engastrimyth *n* -s [MF *engastrimythe*, fr. Gk *engastrimythos*, fr. *en* in + *gastr-* + *mythos* speech — more at IN, MYTH] *obs* **:** VENTRILOQUIST
en·gas·tri·myth·ic \ən|gastrə|mithik, en-\ *adj* **:** relating to or like ventriloquism
en·gaud \ən, en+\ *vt* -ED/-ING/-S [¹*en-* + *gaud*, n.] **:** to make showy; *esp* **:** to lend a false glamor to ⟨lowly occupations ~*ed* by pompous names⟩
en·gel·man·nia \ˌeŋgəl'manēə\ *n, cap* [NL, fr. George *Engelmann* †1884 Am. botanist born in Germany + NL *-ia*] **:** a genus of No. American herbs (family Compositae) resembling sun-

flowers and having pinnatifid leaves and large yellow flower heads

en·gel·mann ivy \ˈeŋgəlmən-\ *n, usu cap E* **:** a Virginia creeper (*Parthenocissus quinquefolia engelmannii*) that is distinguished by small thick leathery leaves

engelmann spruce *also* **engelmann's spruce** *n, usu cap E* **:** a large mountain spruce (*Picea engelmanni*) of the Rocky mountain region and British Columbia that yields a light-colored wood used chiefly as rough lumber and for boxes

engelmann spruce beetle *n, usu cap E* **:** a very destructive reddish brown or blackish bark beetle (*Dendroctonus obesus*) that feeds in the cambium of Engelmann spruce

en·gel's law \ˈeŋ(g)əlz-\ *n, usu cap E* [after Ernst *Engel* †1896 Ger. statistician and economist] **:** a generalization in economics: as family income increases, the percentage spent for food decreases, that spent for clothing, rent, heat, and light remains the same, while that spent for education, health, and recreation increases

en·gen·der \ən'jendə(r), en-\ *vb* **engendered; engendered; engendering** \-d(ə)riŋ\ **engenders** [ME *engendren*, fr. MF *engendrer*, fr. L *ingenerare*, fr. *in* + *generare* to beget — more at GENERATE] *vt* **1 :** to produce by the union of the sexes **:** BEGET, PROCREATE, PROPAGATE **2 :** to cause to exist or to develop **:** bring forth **:** sow the seeds of **:** PRODUCE ⟨angry words ~ strife⟩ ⟨the class struggle tends to ~ fear and hatred⟩ ~ *vi* **1** *archaic* **a** *of disease* **:** ORIGINATE, STEM **b :** COPULATE **c :** to breed, multiply, or develop **2 :** to assume form **:** come gradually into being ⟨a storm was ~*ing* in the mountains⟩

en·gen·der·er \-d(ə)rə(r)\ *n* -s [ME *engendrer*, alter. (influenced by ME *-er, -ere* -er) of *engendrour*, fr. MF *engendreur*, fr. OF *engendreor*, fr. *engendrer* to engender + *-eor* -or] **:** one that engenders **:** PRODUCER, PRECURSOR ⟨flies are often ~*s* of disease⟩

en·gen·drure\ -drər, -ˌdrü(ə)r\ *also* **en·gen·dure** \-dyər, -ˌdyü(ə)r\ *n* -s [*engendrure* fr. ME, fr. MF, fr. OF *engendreure*, fr. *engendrer* to engender + *-ure; engendure* fr. ME, alter. of *engendrure*] **1** *obs* **:** the act of engendering **2** *archaic* **:** DESCENT, PARENTAGE; *also* **:** ORIGIN, SOURCE

engg *abbr* engineering

en·gild \ən, en+\ *vt* [ME *engilden*, fr. [1]*en-* + *gilden* to gild] **1** *archaic* **:** GILD **2** *obs* **:** to make bright with or as if with light

engin *abbr* **1** engineer **2** engineering

[1]**en·gine** \ˈenjən\ *n* -s [ME *engin*, fr. OF, skill, trick, mechanical contrivance, fr. L *ingenium* natural capacity, natural disposition, fr. *in* + *-genium* (akin to L *gignere* to beget) — more at KIN] **1** *obs* **a :** natural capacity **:** ABILITY, SKILL **b :** ingenuity or an instance or product of it; *often* **:** cunning or evil contrivance **:** ARTIFICE, WILE ⟨all the ~*s* of her wit —Edmund Spenser⟩ **2** *archaic* **:** something that is used to effect a purpose **:** AGENT, MEANS, METHOD ⟨all these ~*s* of lust —Shak.⟩ **3 a :** a mechanical contrivance or tool: as (1) **:** an instrument or machine of war (2) *obs* **:** a torture implement; *esp* **:** RACK (3) *obs* **:** a net, trap, or similar device (4) *obs* **:** MACHINE 1e **b :** MACHINERY, APPARATUS **c :** any of various mechanical appliances — often used in combination; see FIRE ENGINE, ROSE ENGINE, RULING ENGINE **4 :** a machine for converting energy (in such forms as heat, chemical energy, nuclear energy, radiation energy, and the potential energy of elevated water) into mechanical force and motion **5 :** a railroad locomotive **6 :** ENGINE COMPANY **syn** see MACHINE

[2]**engine** \"\ *vt* -ED/-ING/-S [ME *enginen* to contrive, deceive, fr. OF *enginier*, fr. *engin*] **1** *obs* **:** CONTRIVE, PLAN **2** [[1]*engine*] **:** to equip with an engine ⟨such planes were not *engined* for high-altitude combat⟩ ⟨a 4-*engined* bomber⟩

engine bell *n* **1 :** a bell on a locomotive used in signaling train and locomotive movements **2 :** a part of the engine-room telegraph of a ship

engine burn fracture *n* **:** a progressive fracture in a rail that originates at spots where the driving wheels of a locomotive have slipped or spun

engine company *n* **:** a fire-department company having charge of one or more fire engines

engine control *n* **:** a device used by the pilot of an airplane in controlling or modulating the power output of an engine

engine driver *n, Brit* **:** ENGINEER 4; *esp* **:** one in charge of a railroad locomotive

[1]**en·gi·neer** \ˌenjəˈni(ə)r, -iə\ *n* -s [alter. (influenced by *-eer*) of earlier *enginer*, fr. ME, alter. (influenced by ME *-er, -ere* -er) of *enginour*, fr. MF *engigneor*, fr. OF *engignier* to contrive + *-eor* -or] **1 a** *obs* **:** a builder of military engines **b** *obs* **:** a designer or builder of military works (as fortifications) **c** (1) *obs* **:** ARTILLERYMAN (2) **:** a member of a military group devoted to engineering work (as in building bridges or roads, removing land mines, or preparing airfields) **2** *obs* **a :** a person who designs, invents, or contrives **b :** a crafty schemer **:** PLOTTER **3 a :** a designer or builder of engines, esp. steam engines or heavy machinery **b :** a person who is trained in or follows as a calling or profession a branch of engineering (as civil, military, electrical, mining, structural, or sanitary engineering) — in some jurisdictions legally restricted in technical use to a person who has completed a prescribed course of study and complied with requirements concerning registration or licensing **c :** a person who carries through an enterprise or brings about a result esp. by skillful or artful contrivance ⟨a political ~ of some note⟩ ⟨the ~ of the compromise that settled the dispute⟩ ⟨a skilled ~ of the economy of the nation —Frank Paddock⟩ **d :** a person who is trained or skilled in the technicalities of some field (as sociology or insurance) not usu. considered to fall within the scope of engineering and who is engaged in using such training or skill in the solution of technical problems **e :** a person with or without technical training who affects technical knowledge to further his endeavors (as in selling) **4 :** a person who runs or supervises engines or other complex technical machinery or apparatus: as **a :** a person in charge of the engines of a ship **b :** the driver of a locomotive **c :** STATIONARY ENGINEER **5 a :** a person engaged in any of various occupations commonly regarded as requiring little skill or special knowledge — often used with a qualifying word ⟨the white-coated ~*s* who sweep the streets of the city⟩

[2]**engineer** \"\ *vb* -ED/-ING/-S *vi* **1 :** to perform the work of an engineer **2 :** CONTRIVE, MANEUVER ~ *vt* **1 a :** to act as an engineer in the laying out, construction, or management of ⟨he ~*ed* some great dams⟩ **b :** to design or produce by the methods of engineering ⟨with the day approaching when fabrics can be ~*ed* for any desired purpose —Henry Lesesne⟩ ⟨~*ing* bigger and faster ships and longer and wider docks⟩ **2 a :** to contrive or plan out usu. with more or less subtle skill or craft ⟨~*ed* a daring jailbreak⟩ ⟨Roosevelt skillfully ~*ed* events —Louis Morton⟩ ⟨a hundred men could carry out such a plan for one who could ~ it⟩ **b :** to guide the course of **:** manage or supervise during production or development ⟨~*ing* a bill through congress⟩ ⟨~*ed* a corner in grain futures⟩ ⟨the prenatal health clinic was ~*ed* by the joint effort of local physicians and philanthropists⟩ **syn** see GUIDE

engineer boot *n* **:** a boot with a supporting strap across the instep and a strap-adjusted gusset on the outer side

engineer boot

en·gi·neer·ing \ˌenjəˈniriŋ, -rēŋ\ *n* -s [fr. gerund of [2]*engineer*] **1 :** the activities or the function of an engineer; *esp* **:** the art of managing engines **2 :** the science by which the properties of matter and the sources of energy in nature are made useful to man in structures, machines, and products — see CHEMICAL ENGINEERING, CIVIL ENGINEERING, ELECTRICAL ENGINEERING, HYDRAULIC ENGINEERING, INDUSTRIAL ENGINEERING, MECHANICAL ENGINEERING, MUNICIPAL ENGINEERING, SANITARY ENGINEERING

engineering geology *n* **:** a branch of geology that deals with the application of geology to engineering

en·gi·neer·ing·ly *adv* **:** from the point of view of the engineering problems involved ⟨an ~ feasible project⟩

engineer's brake valve *n* **:** a valve in the cab of a locomotive for operating the air brake

engineer's chain *n* **:** a chain (sense 1c(1)) 50 or 100 feet long consisting of one-foot links

engineer's hammer *n* **:** any of various hand hammers used by engineers and metalworkers and resembling a machinist's hammer but heavier

engineer's level *n* **:** SURVEYOR'S LEVEL

engineer's scale *also* **engineer's rule** *n* **:** a scale that is commonly of triangular cross section and has different decimal scales on its edges

enginehouse \ˈ==ˌ=\ *n* **:** a building for housing an engine (as a fire engine, a railroad locomotive, or a stationary engine)

engine lathe *n* **:** a screw-cutting lathe equipped with a back-geared cone-driven headstock or with a headstock of the geared-head type

en·gine·less \ˈ==ləs\ *adj* **:** lacking an engine

en·gine·man \ˈenjənˌman, -ˌmaa(ə)n, -ˌmən\ *n, pl* **enginemen 1 :** a man who supervises, operates, tends, or tests an engine (as a locomotive engineer or fireman) **2 :** ENGINE DRIVER

engine mount *n* **:** a framework that is usu. of steel tubing, is used to mount the engine of an airplane, and is attached to the airplane in such a manner as to be readily detachable

engine room *n* **:** a room (as on a steamer) in which an engine is located

engine-room telegraph *n* **:** a signaling device for transmitting orders from an officer on the bridge of a ship to the engineer in charge relating to the direction and speed of the engine

en·gine·ry \ˈenjənrē, -ri\ *n* -ES [[1]*engine* + *-ery, -ry*] **1** *obs* **:** the art of constructing or managing engines, esp. military engines **2 a :** instruments of war **b :** machines, tools, and mechanical devices (as of a plant or an industry or for the carrying out of a process) ⟨the complex ~ of a modern refining plant⟩; *broadly* **:** PLANT 3a ⟨the physical elements of this marvelous ~ for multiplying man's powers and possibilities are three — tracks, trains, locomotive power —R.S.Henry⟩ **c :** things that underlie and form a basis for the functioning of something **:** MACHINERY 4 ⟨Keats was beginning . . . to bring forward the vast ~ of his mind to attack the riddle of life in its deeper aspects, when death cut him short —G.M.Trevelyan⟩ ⟨the subtler and cruder ~ of threat —H.A.Overstreet⟩ ⟨a ponderous ~ of statistics, graphs, and mathematical devices⟩

engines *pl of* ENGINE, *pres 3d sing of* ENGINE

engine sand *n* **:** TRACTION SAND

engine-size \ˈ==ˌ=\ *vt* **:** BEATER-SIZE

engine-turn \ˈ==ˌ=\ *vt* **:** to ornament or finish with engine turning

engine turning *n* [fr. gerund of *engine-turn*] **1 :** a method of ornamentation of a surface (as of a watch) by means of a rose engine or lathe **2 :** ornamentation in the form of a pattern of fine lines produced by engine turning

engining *pres part of* ENGINE

enginous *adj* [ME *enginous*, fr. MF *engigneus*, fr. L *ingeniosus* ingenious, talented — more at INGENIOUS] *obs* **:** contrived with care **:** INGENIOUS, CRAFTY

en·gird \ən, en+\ *vt* [[1]*en-* + *gird*, v.] **:** GIRD, ENCOMPASS

en·girdle \ən, en+\ *vt* [[1]*en-* + *girdle*, n.] **:** GIRDLE

engirt *vt* [[1]*en-* + *girt*, v.] *obs* **:** ENVELOP, ENCIRCLE, ENGIRD

en·glacial \ən, (ˈ)en+\ *adj* [[2]*en-* + *glacial*] **:** embedded in a glacier ⟨~ drift⟩ **:** being within the body of a glacier ⟨an ~ stream⟩ — **en·glacially** \"+\ *adv*

en·glamour \ən, en+\ *vt* -ED/-ING/-S [[1]*en-* + *glamour*] **:** to surround with or as if with illusions **2 :** to render glamorous

en·gland \ˈiŋglənd *also* |ŋl- *sometimes* ˈe|\ *adj, usu cap* [fr. *England*, south part of the island of Great Britain, excluding Wales, fr. ME *Engeland*, fr. OE *Engla land*, lit., land of the Angles, fr. *Engla* (gen. of *Engle*, pl., Angles) + *land* — more at ANGLE] **:** of or from England **:** of the kind or style prevalent in England **:** ENGLISH

en·gland·er \-də(r)\ *n* -s *cap* **:** a native of England

en·gler flask \ˈeŋ(g)lə(r)-\ *n, usu cap E* [after Karl *Engler* †1925 Ger. chemist] **:** a standard distilling flask usu. of 100-milliliter capacity used to determine the volatility characteristics of petroleum products (as gasoline, naphtha, or kerosine)

en·gler·o·phoenix \ˌeŋglərō+\ *n, cap* [NL, fr. Adolf *Engler* †1930 Ger. botanist + NL *-o-* + *Phoenix* genus of palms — more at PHOENIX] **:** a genus of tropical American pinnate-leaved palms with linear pinnae

[1]**en·glish** \ˈiŋglish, -lēsh *also* |ŋl- *sometimes* ˈe|\ *adj, usu cap* [ME, fr. OE *englisc*, fr. *Engle*, pl., Angles + *-isc* -ish] **1 :** of or from England **:** of the kind or style prevalent in England ⟨*English* earth⟩ ⟨fine *English* tailoring⟩ ⟨*English* customs⟩ — often used in English-speaking areas outside the British isles to identify that one of two or more kinds of plant or animal sharing a common vernacular to which the vernacular is applied in England without regard to actual prevalence or origin ⟨*English* catchfly⟩ ⟨*English* cherry wood⟩ **2 :** of, relating to, or characteristic of the English language ⟨beauties of *English* expression⟩ ⟨*English* studies⟩ ⟨a literal *English* translation⟩ ⟨vagaries of the *English* colloquial idiom⟩ **3 :** BRITISH

[2]**english** \"\ *n* -ES *see sense 2* [ME, fr. OE *englisc*, fr. *englisc*, adj.] **1** *cap* **a :** the language of the people of England and the U.S. and most of the British colonies and dominions — see ANGLO-SAXON, MIDDLE ENGLISH, OLD ENGLISH, INDO-EUROPEAN LANGUAGES table **b :** a particular variety of English (as that characteristic of a nation, locality, class of people, or an individual) distinguished by peculiarities (as of pronunciation, vocabulary, idiom, syntax, or style) ⟨speaking a beautiful precise *English*⟩ ⟨the archaic *English* that often lingers in isolated communities⟩ ⟨the comparative informality of American *English*⟩ ⟨the *English* of the gutter⟩ **c :** English language, literature, or composition or a part thereof regarded as a field of study or teaching ⟨most colleges require all freshmen to take a course in *English*⟩ ⟨he found *English* a difficult subject⟩ **2** *pl in constr, cap* **:** the people of England; *esp* **:** native Englishmen irrespective of residence ⟨the chill formality of the *English* is no more than a caricaturist's generalization⟩ ⟨the *English* and their tea are matched by the Swedes and their coffee⟩ **3** *usu cap* **a :** an English translation or rendering **:** the English equivalent (as of a foreign word) ⟨tell me the *English* for *gluteus*⟩; *sometimes* **:** CRIB, PONY **b :** idiomatic or intelligible English; *often* **:** the plain sense of something obscure, involved, technical, or pedantic ⟨give me the *English* of it⟩ — compare GREEK 2c **4** *often cap* **:** an old size of type approximately 2 points larger than pica **5** *usu cap* **:** a spinning or rotary motion round the vertical axis given to a ball by striking it to the right or left of its center (as in pool) or by releasing it in such a way as to produce this rotary motion (as in bowling) — called also *side*

[3]**english** \", *chiefly in pres part* -ləsh\ *vb* -ED/-ING/-ES *often cap* [ME *englishen*, fr. *english*, adj. & n.] *vt* **1 :** to translate into English ⟨regretfully spent his holiday ~*ing* 500 lines of Virgil⟩ **2** *obs* **:** to interpret or set forth plainly ⟨those gracious acts . . . may be *Englished*, more properly, acts of fear and dissimulation —John Milton⟩ **3 :** to adopt into English **:** ANGLICIZE ⟨our language expands chiefly by coining new words and ~*ing* the words already in other languages⟩ ~ *vi* **:** to be translatable into English

[4]**english** *adv, usu cap* [[1]*english*] *obs* **:** ENGLISHLY

english basement *n, usu cap E* **:** a high basement that is usu. mainly above ground, is often adapted to living quarters or domestic offices, but does not contain the principal entrance of the house

english billiards *n pl but usu sing in constr, usu cap E* **:** billiards which is played on a table with six pockets and in which points are scored by cannons and pocketed balls

english bluebell *n, usu cap E* **:** WOOD HYACINTH

english bluegrass *n, usu cap E* **1 :** WIRE GRASS a **2 :** MEADOW FESCUE

english bond *n, usu cap E* **:** a masonry bond in which courses consist alternately of headers and stretchers

English bond

english breakfast tea *also* **english breakfast** *n, usu cap E* **:** CONGOU; *broadly* **:** a black tea or blend of similar character

english bulldog *or* **english bull** *n, usu cap E* **:** BULLDOG

english camomile *or* **english chamomile** *n, usu cap E* **:** a pleasantly strong-scented European downy perennial herb (*Anthemis nobilis*) that is widely cultivated and often escaped

english cavalry saddle *n, usu cap E* **:** ENGLISH SADDLE

english chop *n, usu cap E* **:** a lamb or mutton chop cut across the undivided loin with the bone removed and usu. the kidney rolled in

english corn *n, usu cap E* **:** wheat or other small grain — contrasted with *Indian corn* and now chiefly of historical interest

english cowslip *n, usu cap E* **:** COWSLIP 1a

english cross bond *n, usu cap E* **:** a modification of English bond in which the stretcher courses break joints with each other

english daisy *n, usu cap E* **:** DAISY 1a

english disease *n, usu cap E, archaic* **:** RICKETS

english elm *n, usu cap 1st E* **:** a broad spreading rough-leaved elm (*Ulmus procera*) common throughout western Europe and planted elsewhere — compare WYCH ELM

english equatorial *n, usu cap 1st E* **:** a telescope with its main tube supported in a split or yoke-type polar axle that rests on north and south pedestals permitting continuous observation across the meridian and eliminating the declination counterweight

en·glish·er \-lishə(r), -lēsh-\ *n* -s [[1]*english* + *-er*] **1** *cap* **:** ENGLISHMAN ⟨not in very good humour with the *Englishers* —E.B. Ramsay⟩ **2** *usu cap* [[3]*english* + *-er*] **:** a person who translates into English

english finish *n, usu cap E* **:** a finish on paper that is smooth but not glossy; *specif* **:** a finish intermediate between machine finish and supercalendered

english flute *n, usu cap E* **:** RECORDER 3a

english foot *n, usu cap E* **:** a hosiery foot that has a seam on each side of the sole — compare FRENCH FOOT

english foxhound *n* **1** *usu cap E & F* **:** a breed of foxhounds developed in England and characterized by a large heavily boned form, rather short ears, and lightly fringed tail **2** *usu cap E* **:** any dog of the English Foxhound breed

English foxhound

english garden wall bond *n, usu cap E* **:** a masonry bond employing three courses of stretchers to one of headers

english gooseberry *n, usu cap E* **:** a stocky Eurasian shrub (*Ribes grossularia*) with greenish flowers and pubescent and glandular fruit that is the source of most of the European cultivated gooseberries and a parent of many of those grown in America and is often an escape in eastern No. America

english grain aphid *n, usu cap E* **:** a pale green aphid (*Macrosiphum avenae*) with dark markings that is native to Europe but widespread in No. America and that feeds on grasses and small grains, being esp. destructive when feeding on the developing heads of grain

english grass *n, usu cap E* **:** any of various hay or forage grasses (as timothy or some bluegrasses) orig. introduced (as into the U. S. or Australia) from England

english green *n, often cap E* **1 :** DEEP BRUNSWICK GREEN **2 :** SCHEELE'S GREEN 2 **3 :** EMERALD 2

english guitar *n, usu cap E* **:** a cittern popular in England in the 18th century

english harvest *n, usu cap E, obs* **:** harvest of wheat

english hawthorn *n, usu cap E* **:** either of two Eurasian hawthorns (*Crataegus oxyacantha* and *C. monogyna*) that have deeply cleft leaves and bright red fruits, that are extensively cultivated as ornamentals and under cultivation have developed varied plant forms and flower form and color, and that are established as escapes in much of eastern No. America

english hay *n, usu cap E* **:** hay from English grass; *broadly* **:** cultivated hay as distinguished from native hay

english herring *n, usu cap E, in Maine* **:** the common herring (*Clupea harengus*) of the No. Atlantic

english holly *n, usu cap E* **:** a Eurasian tree or shrub (*Ilex aquifolium*) with thick glossy spiny-margined leaves, bright red persistent berries, and a fine-grained white wood — compare AMERICAN HOLLY

english horn *n, usu cap E* **1 :** a double-reed woodwind musical instrument similar to the oboe but a fifth lower in pitch with a rich and somber tone quality **2 :** an organ stop with a tone similar to that of the English horn

English horn

englishing *n* -s *usu cap* [ME, fr. [3]*english* + *-inge, -ing* -ing] **:** the act of translating or a translation into English ⟨the earliest *Englishing* of the Bible⟩ ⟨*Englishings*, in the most original and least second-hand fashion, of the peculiar verse stories —George Saintsbury⟩

english iris *n, usu cap E* **:** a bulbous iris (*Iris xiphioides*) that is native to the Pyrenees but is now widely cultivated for its large delicate flowers which are typically dark purple marked with yellow but in cultivation sometimes white, blue, or wine red but never yellow — compare DUTCH IRIS, SPANISH IRIS

en·glish·ism \-ˌshizəm\ *n* -s *usu cap* **1 :** a quality, characteristic, or mode of procedure peculiar to the English **2 :** a form of expression peculiar to English as spoken in England **:** ANGLICISM **3 :** attachment to that which is English

en·glish·ite \-ˌshīt\ *n* -s *usu cap* [George L. *English* †1944 Am. mineral dealer and collector + E *-ite*] **:** a mineral perhaps in the relation $K_2Ca_4Al_8(PO_4)_8(OH)_{10}.9H_2O$ consisting of hydrous basic phosphate of potassium, calcium, and aluminum

english ivy *n, usu cap E* **:** IVY 1a

en·glish·ize \-ˌshīz\ *vt* -ED/-ING/-S *often cap* **:** ANGLICIZE

english last *n, usu cap E* **:** a shoe last with a low heel and long tapering toe

english laurel *n, usu cap E* **:** CHERRY LAUREL 1

english loose *n, usu cap E* **:** MEDITERRANEAN RELEASE

en·glish·ly *adv, usu cap* [ME, fr. [1]*english* + *-ly*] **:** in the manner of the English ⟨people whose chief value to the community lay, oddly but *Englishly*, in their sturdy individualism —W.B.Adams⟩

english maidenhair *n, usu cap E* **:** MAIDENHAIR SPLEENWORT

en·glish·man \-shmən\ *n, pl* **englishmen** [ME, fr. OE *englisc-man*, fr. *englisc* English + *man* — more at ENGLISH] **1** *cap* **:** a native or inhabitant of England **2** *usu cap* **:** an English ship **3** *usu cap* **:** a marine percoid food fish (*Chrysoblephus anglicus*) of southern Africa having the snout truncate and suggestive of a forehead

englishman's knot *n, usu cap E* **:** FISHERMAN'S KNOT

english maple *n, usu cap E* **:** HEDGE MAPLE

english muffin *n, usu cap E* **:** bread dough rolled and cut into rounds and baked on a griddle

en·glish·ness *n* -ES *usu cap* **:** the distinctive qualities or characteristics that set apart or are felt to set apart the English people, their works, or institutions ⟨Oxford and Cambridge are the very essence of *Englishness*, on a par with the monarchy, Parliament, the Church of England —*Newsweek*⟩

english oak *n, usu cap E* [ME *english oke*, fr. [1]*english* + *oke*, *ook* oak] **1 a :** a medium-sized to large tree (*Quercus robur*) having glabrous leaves with very short petioles and rounded lobes **b :** the strong durable hard straight-grained wood of this tree that is used in structural work and cabinetwork and tends to darken with prolonged exposure from pale yellowish brown almost to black **2 :** a moderate brown that is paler and slightly yellower than bay, lighter than auburn, and redder, lighter, and slightly stronger than chestnut brown

english ocher *n, often cap E* **:** YELLOW OCHER

english opera *n, usu cap E* **:** BALLAD OPERA

english pea *n, usu cap E, South & Midland* **:** PEA 1a — used esp. to distinguish this vegetable from the black-eyed pea

english pink *n, often cap E* **:** DUTCH PINK 2

english plantain *n, usu cap E* **:** a ribgrass (*Plantago lanceolata*)
english pool *n, usu cap E* **:** a pool game in which each player draws one of the colored balls which he uses as cue ball and must play on the color next in a fixed order, being put out of the game when his ball is pocketed three times — called also *color-ball pool*
english primrose *n, usu cap E* **:** a low-growing perennial European primrose (*Primula vulgaris*) that is widely cultivated for its early bloom which in the wild is usu. single, solitary, and yellow but has developed many divergent forms and colors under cultivation
english rabbit *or* **english spotted** *n, usu cap E* **:** a breed of white domestic rabbits having distinctive dark markings
english red *n* **1** *usu cap E* **:** an iron-oxide pigment **2** *often cap E* **a :** a dark reddish orange to strong brown that is stronger than ferruginous — called also *Forest of Dean red, madder red* **b :** COLCOTHAR 2 **c :** GOYA
english rite *n, usu cap E & often cap R* **:** YORK RITE
english robin *n, usu cap E* **:** ROBIN 1a
en·glish·ry \-shrē, -ri\ *n* -ES *usu cap* [ME *englisherie, englishrie,* fr. ¹*english* + *-erie, -rie* -ry] **1 :** the state or fact of being of English birth **2 :** people of English descent esp. in Ireland **3 :** English ways (as of speech or conduct); *also* **:** bias toward English ways
english ryegrass *n, usu cap E* **:** PERENNIAL RYEGRASS
english saddle *n, usu cap E* **:** a saddle with long side bars, steel cantle and pommel, no horn, and a leather seat supported by webbing stretched between the saddlebow and cantle — called also *English cavalry saddle*

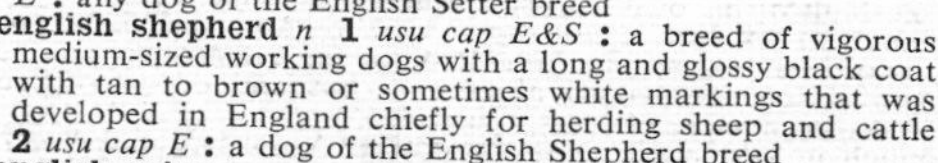
English saddle

english saxon *n, cap E & S, obs* **:** ANGLO-SAXON
english setter *n* **1** *usu cap E&S* **:** a breed of bird dogs characterized by a silky coat that is flat, moderately long, and white or white with color (as black, lemon, or orange) and by feathering on the tail and legs, a long moderately domed skull with marked stop, a height of 21 to 23 inches, and a weight when in condition of 35 to 55 pounds **2** *usu cap E* **:** any dog of the English Setter breed
english shepherd *n* **1** *usu cap E&S* **:** a breed of vigorous medium-sized working dogs with a long and glossy black coat with tan to brown or sometimes white markings that was developed in England chiefly for herding sheep and cattle **2** *usu cap E* **:** a dog of the English Shepherd breed
english snipe *n, usu cap E* **:** WILSON'S SNIPE
english sole *n, usu cap E* **1 :** an important pale brown market flatfish (*Parophrys vetulus*) of the Pacific coast of No. America distinguished by a projecting snout **2 :** PETRALE SOLE
english sonnet *n, usu cap E* **:** a sonnet in which the lines are grouped into three quatrains and a couplet and the rhyme scheme is *abab, cdcd, efef, gg*
english sparrow *n, usu cap E* **:** HOUSE SPARROW
english springer *also* **english springer spaniel** *n, usu cap E* **:** a springer spaniel of a breed supposed to have originated in Spain characterized by deep-bodied muscular build with weight to 45 pounds when in good condition and a moderately long straight or slightly wavy silky coat of typically black and white hair
english system *n, usu cap E* **:** BRADFORD SYSTEM
english thistle *n, usu cap E* **:** WILD TEASEL
english toy spaniel *n* **1** *usu cap E&T&S* **:** a breed of small blocky spaniels of English origin with well-rounded upper skull projecting forward toward the short turned-up nose — see BLENHEIM SPANIEL, KING CHARLES SPANIEL, RUBY SPANIEL **2** *usu cap E* **:** any dog of the English Toy Spaniel breed
english turbot *n, usu cap E* **:** WINDOWPANE 2
english vermilion *n, often cap E* **1 :** GOYA **2 :** VERMILION 1a; *esp* **:** a pigment of a light brilliant shade
english violet *n, usu cap E* **:** SWEET VIOLET
english wallflower *n, usu cap E* **:** a short-lived perennial wallflower (*Cheiranthus cheiri*) with white, yellow, brown, or reddish to purplish single or double flowers
english walnut *n, usu cap E* **1 :** a Eurasian walnut (*Juglans regia*) that is valued for its large edible nut and its hard richly figured wood — called also *Circassian walnut, French walnut, Persian walnut* **2 a :** the fruit of the English walnut **b :** CIRCASSIAN WALNUT 1
english wheat *n, usu cap E* **:** POULARD WHEAT
english white *n, usu cap E* **:** whiting used as a pigment
englishwoman \'==,==\ *n, pl* **englishwomen** *usu cap* [ME, fr. ¹*english* + *woman*] **:** a woman of English birth, nationality, or origin
english yew *n, usu cap E* **:** a large evergreen tree (*Taxus baccata*) that is native to Eurasia and northern Africa but cosmopolitan in cultivation and is the chief source of yew lumber — called also *European yew*
en·globe \ən'glōb, en-\ *vt* [¹*en-* + *globe,* n.] **1 :** to enclose in or as if in a globe **2 :** INGEST ⟨bacteria *englobed* by leukocytes⟩ — **en·globe·ment** \-mənt\ *n* -S
¹**en·glut** \ən'glət, en-\ *vt* [MF *engloutir,* fr. LL *ingluttire,* fr. L *in* + *gluttire* to swallow — more at GLUTTON] **:** to gulp down **:** SWALLOW
²**englut** \"\ *vt* [¹*en-* + *glut,* v.] *archaic* **:** to satiate or surfeit esp. with food or pleasure
eng·lyn \'eŋlən\ *n, pl* **englyns** \-nz\ *also* **englyn·ion** \eŋ'lin,yōn\ [W] **:** a usu. epigrammatic quatrain in Welsh poetry consisting of 30 syllables in lines of 10, 6, 7, and 7 syllables, the last three lines rhyming usu. with the 6th syllable of the first line whose final syllable has no rhyme
en·gobe \(')än¦gōb\ *n* -S [F, fr. *engober* to cover with slip, fr. *en-* ¹en- + *gober* to swallow, gulp down; akin to OF *gobet* mouthful, bite, piece — more at GOBBET] **:** white or colored slip applied to pottery usu. for decoration or to improve the surface texture
en·gore \ən, en+\ *vt* [¹*en-* + *gore,* n.] **:** to make bloody **:** dabble or stain with blood
en·gorge \ən, en+\ *vb* [MF *engorgier* to feed to repletion, devour, fr. OF, to devour, fr. *en-* ¹en- + *gorge* throat — more at GORGE] *vt* **1 :** GORGE, GLUT: as **a :** to feed (as oneself or an animal) to repletion ⟨a working horse should not be *engorged* on the weekend⟩ **b :** to fill with blood to the point of congestion — usu. used in passive ⟨the gastric mucosa was greatly *engorged*⟩ **2 :** to swallow with greediness **:** DEVOUR, ENGULF ~ *vi* **1 :** to feed with eagerness or voracity **2** *of a bloodsucking invertebrate* **:** to feed on blood to the limit of body capacity ⟨larvae which had *engorged* . . . previously on an infected guinea pig, transmitted a fatal infection —*Jour. of Infectious Diseases*⟩
en·gorge·ment \"mənt\ *n* -S [obs. F *engorgement* action of devouring & F *engorgement* congestion, fr. MF *engorgement* action of devouring, fr. *engorgier* + *-ment*] **1 :** the act of engorging or state of being engorged **2 :** overfullness of the vessels of some part of the body ⟨~ of the breast⟩ **:** CONGESTION, HYPEREMIA
engorgement colic *n* **:** colic in horses caused by the ingestion of excessive quantities of food, too rapid eating, or the failure of the stomach to pass the food on into the intestines
en·gou·lée *also* **en·gou·led** \ä"gülä\ *or* **en·gouled** \(')än¦güld\ *adj* [*engoulée* fr. F, fem. of *engoulé,* fr. past part. of *engouler* to swallow up, fr. OF *engoler,* fr. *en-* ¹en- + *gole* throat, mouth, fr. L *gula* throat; *engoulé* fr. F, fr. past part. of *engouler; engouled* modif. (influenced by E *-ed*) of F *engoulé* — more at GLUTTON] *heraldry* **:** having the extremities issuing from the mouths of animals — used of an ordinary
engr *abbr* **1** engineer **2** engraved; engraver; engraving
en·grace \ən, en+\ *vt* [¹*en-* + *grace,* n.] **:** to endue with grace
engraff *vt* [ME *engraffen, ingraffen,* fr. ¹*en-* or ²*in-* + *graffen* to graft, insert (a scion) — more at GRAFF] *obs* **:** ENGRAFT
en·graft *also* **in·graft** \ən, en+\ *vt* [¹*en-* or ²*in-* + *graft,* v.] **1 :** GRAFT 1, 2 **2 :** to implant (a reflective matter) into a host
en·graf·ta·tion \,en,graf'tāshən\ *or* **en·graft·ment** \ən'graf(t)mənt, en-, -raaf-,-raif-,-räf-\ *n* -S **:** the act of engrafting
en·grail \ən'grāl, en-, *chiefly before pause or consonant* -āəl\ *vt* -ED/-ING/-S [ME *engrelen,* fr. MF *engresler,* fr. *en-* ¹en- + *gresle, graisle* slender, fr. L *gracilis* — more at GRACILE] **1 a :** to indent (as a heraldic ordinary) with small curves — see ENGRAILED **b :** to ornament esp. with a pattern indented on the edge **2** *obs* **:** to carve in intaglio **3 a** *obs* **:** ROUGHEN **b :** to cause to appear serrated ⟨a scene ~*ed* by three tall peaks⟩
engrailed *adj* [ME *engreled,* fr. *engrelen* + *-ed*] **1 :** indented at the edge with small concave curves ⟨an ~ heraldic bordure⟩ **2 :** made of raised dots ⟨an ~ circle on a coin⟩ **:** bordered by a circle of raised dots ⟨an ~ coin⟩
en·grain \ən'grān, (')en¦g-\ *vt* [ME *engreinen,* fr. ¹*en-* + *grain, grein* kermes; in senses 2 and 3 influenced in meaning by E *grain* texture — more at GRAIN] **1** *obs* **:** to dye with kermes or cochineal or a fast color **2 :** INGRAIN 2 ⟨his swart forefinger, deeply ~*ed* with gunpowder —Charles Dickens⟩ ⟨Judaism, Catholicism, and Protestantism are too deeply ~*ed* in the habits of men to be superseded by some newfangled religious institution —S.P.Lamprecht⟩ **3 :** to color in imitation of the grain of the wood — compare GRAIN *vt* 3
en·grained \-nd\ *adj* [fr. past part. of *engrain*] **:** deeply incorporated or infused **:** DEEP-DYED — **en·grained·ly** \-n(ə)dlē, -li\ *adv*
en·gram *also* **en·gramme** \'en,gram, 'eŋ,g-\ *n* -S [ISV ²*en-* + *-gram;* orig. formed as G *engramm*] **:** a memory trace; *specif* **:** a protoplasmic change in neural tissue hypothesized to account for the persistence of memory — **en·gram·mic** \(')=¦gramik\ *adj*
en·gran·dize \ən'gra(a)n,dīz, en-; 'engrən-, 'eŋgrən-\ *or* **in·gran·dize** \ən'gra(a)n-\ *vt* -ED/-ING/-S [modif. (influenced by *-ize*) of obs. F *engrandiss-,* stem of *engrandir,* fr. OF, fr. *en-* ¹en- + *grant, grand* great, large — more at GRAND] **:** to make great or grandiose
en·gran·dize·ment \ən'gra(a)ndəzmənt, en-, -,dīz-; 'en-,gra(a)n,dīz-, ,en,gra(a)n'dīz-\ *n* -S **:** an act of engrandizing or the state of being engrandized
en·grau·li·dae \en'grȯlə,dē\ *n pl, cap* [NL, fr. *Engraulis,* type genus (fr. Gk *engraulis* anchovy) + *-idae*] **:** a family of small fishes related to the herrings and comprising the anchovies
en·grave \ən'grāv, en-\ *vb* **engraved** \-vd\ **engraved** \"\ *or archaic* **en·grav·en** \-vən\ **engraving; engraves** [MF *engraver,* fr. *en-* ¹en- + *graver* to engrave, of Gmc origin; akin to OHG *graban* to dig; E *engrave* influenced in inflection (note past part. *engraven*) by *grave,* v. — more at GRAVE (v.)] *vt* **1 a :** to produce (as letters, figures, or devices) by means of incised lines, spaces, or points ⟨~ an inscription on stone⟩ **b :** to impress deeply **:** infix as if with a graver ⟨~ principles in men's minds —John Locke †1704⟩ **2 a :** to cut upon (as wood, stone, or metal) with a graving instrument in order to form an inscription or pictorial representation either of the incised lines, spaces, or points (as in copperplate engraving) or of the surface left in relief (as in wood engraving) **b :** to incise (a metal plate or wooden surface) for the purpose of printing therefrom ⟨*engraved* the plates for a new series of banknotes⟩ **c :** to print from an engraved plate ⟨an *engraved* calling card⟩ — used esp. when raised printing results **d :** PHOTOENGRAVE **3** *obs* **:** to represent (as a scene) in sculpture ~ *vi* **1 :** to make engravings ⟨busily *engraving* on wood⟩ **2 :** to be suitable for engraving ⟨that clear classic profile would ~ well⟩
engraved *adj* [fr. past part. of *engrave*] **:** having the surface marked or ornamented with impressed lines — used esp. of the hard exterior coverings of certain insects
engraved glass *n* **:** glass ornamented with intaglio cutting that is usu. left unpolished — compare CUT GLASS
en·grave·ment \-vmənt\ *n* -S **:** ENGRAVING
engraven *vt* [by alter.] *obs* **:** ENGRAVE
en·grav·er \ən'grāvə(r), en-\ *n* -S **1 :** one that engraves; *esp* **:** one whose work is the production of engraving (as on silverware or on plates for use in printing) by hand or mechanical processes **2 a :** PHOTOENGRAVER **b :** ENGRAVER BEETLE — usu. used in combination ⟨fir ~*s*⟩
engraver beetle *n* **:** any of numerous bark beetles that make furrows often arranged in specific patterns in the wood of trees under the bark; *esp* **:** a beetle of *Scolytus* or a related genus that lives chiefly on young trees — compare DENDROCTONUS
engraver's block *n* **:** a heavy metal turntable with clamps for securing articles to be engraved
engravery *n* -ES [*engrave* + *-ery*] *obs* **:** ENGRAVING
engraving *n* -S [fr. gerund of *engrave*] **1 :** the act or process of one that engraves — compare ANAGLYPTOGRAPH, ANASTATIC, DRYPOINT, MEZZOTINT, XYLOGRAPHY; ETCHING **2 :** something that is engraved: as **a :** an engraved printing surface ⟨prepared the ~*s* for the new banknotes⟩ **b :** engraved work ⟨decorated with delicate ~⟩ **3 :** a print or impression from an engraved printing surface
engreaten *vt* [¹*en-* + *great,* adj. + *-en*] *obs* **:** to make great
en·groove \ən'grüv, en-\ *vt* [¹*en-* + *groove,* n.] **:** to fit or form into a groove
en·gross \ən'grōs, en-\ *vt* -ED/-ING/-ES [in sense 1, fr. ME *engrossen,* fr. AF *engrosser,* prob. fr. ML *ingrossare,* fr. L *in* + ML *grossa* engrossment (of a document), fr. L, fem. of *grossus* thick; in sense 2, fr. ME *engrosen, engrossen,* fr. MF *en gros* in large quantities, at wholesale, fr. OF, fr. *en* in (fr. L *in*) + *gros* whole quantity, fr. *gros* thick, plentiful, fr. L *grossus;* in sense 3, fr. ME *engrosen,* alter. of *ingrossen,* fr. ML *ingrossare,* fr. L *in* + *grossus* thick — more at GROSS] **1 a :** to copy or write in a large hand **:** write a fair copy of in a hand formerly used in formal documents, derived from the court hand, and nearly illegible to all but experts or now usu. in a distinct and legible hand **b** *obs* **:** to inscribe the name of **:** include in a list **:** NAME **c :** to prepare the text of (a bill, resolution, treaty, or other official document) by whatever process (as handwriting or printing) may be officially permitted or prescribed; *specif* **:** to prepare the text of (a bill) for the third reading in a legislature — distinguished from *enroll* **2 a :** to purchase either the whole or large quantities of (commodities) so as to control the market, enhance the price, and make a monopoly profit **b :** to obtain control of (a market) in this way — compare FORESTALL, REGRATE **c** *obs* **:** AMASS, COLLECT **d :** to take or assume to the exclusion of others **:** concentrate in one's possession **:** take the whole of ⟨a few families ~*ed* the power of the state⟩ ⟨the new customer ~*ed* his attention⟩ **3 a** *obs* **:** to make dense, thick, or large **:** increase in bulk or quantity **:** THICKEN **b** *archaic* **:** to render gross in body or mind **syn** see MONOPOLIZE
en·grossed \-st\ *adj* [fr. past part. of *engross*] **1 :** completely occupied or absorbed ⟨~ in her humble task⟩ ⟨an ~ look of rapt delight⟩ **2 :** PREOCCUPIED ⟨answered briefly without raising her ~ eyes from the book⟩ — **en·grossed·ly** \-sədlē, -stl-, -li\ *adv*
engrossed bill *n* **:** a bill printed or written in the final form in which it is presented for the third reading in a house or chamber of a legislative body — compare ENROLLED BILL
en·gross·er \-sə(r)\ *n* -S [ME, fr. *engrossen* + *-er, -ere* -er] **1 :** a monopolist or a person who attempts to establish a monopoly (as of goods or power) **2 :** one that engrosses documents
engrossing *adj* [fr. pres. part. of *engross*] **1 :** monopolizing or tending to monopolize **2 :** taking up the time or attention completely **:** ABSORBING, FASCINATING ⟨hidden under the ~ surface of the story —Harrison Smith⟩ **syn** see INTERESTING
en·gross·ing·ly *adv* **:** so as to engross
en·gross·ing·ness *n* -ES **:** the quality of being engrossing
en·gross·ment \-smənt\ *n* -S **1 a :** the engrossing of a document **b :** an engrossed document **2 a :** the buying up or hoarding of a commodity esp. for speculative purposes **b :** the taking up of common or public lands (as by enclosure or purchase) often for speculative purposes **3 :** the state of being absorbed or occupied ⟨his ~ with the nation's problems⟩
engs *pl of* ENG
en·gulf \ən, en+\ *vt* [¹*en-* + *gulf,* n.] **1 a :** to flow over and enclose **:** OVERWHELM ⟨a man ~*ed* by fear⟩ ⟨the mounting seas threatened to ~ the island⟩ **b :** to take in (food) by or as if by flowing over and enclosing ⟨the amoeba ~*s* particulate matter with its pseudopodia⟩ ⟨snakes ~ their food whole⟩ **2 :** to plunge (as oneself) into something ⟨~*ing* himself in the political mire⟩ ⟨to be ~*ed* in the whirling, curving, backing fleet of cars at the station —Eve Langley⟩ **syn** see OVERPOWER
en·gulf·ment \"mənt\ *n* -S **:** the act of engulfing or state of being engulfed
en·gys·seismology \,enjə, ¦eŋg, ¦ē + \ *n* [Gk *engys* near + E *seismology*] **:** a branch of seismology that deals with the records of earthquake shocks registered in or near the region of disturbance — compare TELESEISMOLOGY
en·gys·to·mat·i·dae \(,)en,jistə'mad·ə,dē, (,)eŋ,gistə'm-; ,enj-¦əstō'm. ,eŋg|, |ēstō'm-\ [NL, fr. *Engystomat-, Engystoma* (prob. influenced in meaning by G *eng* narrow, fr. OHG *engi*), former name of an included genus (fr. Gk *engys* near + NL *-stomat-, -stoma* -stoma) + *-idae* — more at ANGER] *syn of* BREVICIPITIDAE
en·halo \ən, en+\ *vt* [¹*en-* + *halo,* n.] **:** to honor or surround with or as if with a halo ⟨a figure ~*ed* with misty light⟩ ⟨an enlightened clergyman who . . . ~*es* the ticket collectors, bus conductors, waitresses —E.M.Forster⟩
en·hance \ən'han(t)s, en-, -haa(ə)n-,-hain-,-hān-\ *vt* -ED/-ING/-S [ME *enhauncen,* fr. AF *enhauncer,* alter. of OF *enhaucier,* fr. *en-* ¹en- + *haucier* to raise, fr. (assumed) VL *altiare,* fr. L *altus* high — more at OLD] **1** *obs* **a :** RAISE, LIFT **b :** to exalt esp. in rank or spirit; *also* **:** EXTOL **2 :** ADVANCE, AUGMENT, ELEVATE, HEIGHTEN, INCREASE ⟨our pleasure was *enhanced* by our hostess's care⟩ ⟨his gracious courtesy *enhanced* his scholarship⟩ **3 a :** to increase the worth or value of ⟨an estate *enhanced* by careful management⟩ **b :** ORNAMENT, BEAUTIFY ⟨proposed to ~ the paneling with gilt medallions⟩ ⟨a young girl should avoid trying to ~ her looks with heavy makeup⟩ **syn** see INTENSIFY
enhanced *adj* [fr. past part. of *enhance*] *of a heraldic charge* **:** placed higher than is usual — opposed to *abased*
en·hance·ment \-smənt\ *n* -S **:** the act of enhancing or state of being enhanced **:** AUGMENTATION, INTENSIFICATION: as **a :** induced increase in some chemical or physical property ⟨the current ~ by gas filling may be greater by 20 to 30 percent for infrared light —V.K.Zworykin & E.G.Ramberg⟩ ⟨~ of the virulence of a virus by egg passage⟩ **b :** accentuation or exaggeration of tonal or positional characteristics of a sound recording
en·hanc·er \-sə(r)\ *n* -S [ME *enhauncere,* fr. *enhauncen* + *-er, -ere* -er] **:** one that enhances
en·hanc·ive \-siv\ *adj* **:** tending to enhance
en·harden \ən, en+\ *vt* [¹*en-* + *harden,* v.] *archaic* **:** HARDEN ⟨nor hath conversation, age or travel been able to . . . ~ me —Sir Thomas Browne⟩
¹**en·harmonic** \,en+\ *adj* [F *enharmonique,* fr. MF *enarmonique, enharmonique,* modif. (influenced by MF *-ique* -ic) of Gk *enarmonios,* fr. *en* in + *harmonia* joint, concord, musical scale — more at IN, HARMONY] **1 a** *in ancient Greek music* **:** relating to that genus or scale employing quarter tones **b** *of a Greek tetrachord* **:** comprising a major third and two quarter tones — compare CHROMATIC **2 :** relating to a written change of notes that sound the same on all instruments using the tempered scale ⟨the ~ change from A flat to G sharp⟩ **3 :** relating to the difference in pitch that results from the exact tuning of a diatonic scale and its transposition into another key — **en·harmonically** \,en+\ *adv*
²**enharmonic** \"\ *n* **:** an enharmonic note or chord
enharmonic diesis *n* **1** *in ancient Greek music* **:** QUARTER TONE **2 :** the difference between three conjunct major thirds and an octave (ratio 125:128)
enharmonic modulation *n* **:** a modulation in which by enharmonically altering one or more notes the harmonic relation of a chord is changed so as to lead to a new key
en haut \ä"ō\ *adv* [F, above, up] *ballet* **:** in a high position — used of the arms
en·hearten \ən, en+\ *vt* [¹*en-* + *hearten*] **:** to give or restore strength and courage to ⟨their cheerfulness ~*ed* his saddened spirit⟩
en·hedge \ən'hej, en-\ *vt* [¹*en-* + *hedge,* n.] **:** to enclose or surround with or as if with a hedge
enherit *obs var of* INHERIT
en·horror \ən, en+\ *vt* -ED/-ING/-S [¹*en-* + *horror,* n.] **:** HORRIFY
en·hunger \ən, en+\ *vt* [¹*en-* + *hunger,* n.] **:** to make hungry ⟨passions . . . ~*ed* to feed on innocence —James Martineau⟩
en·hy·dra \en'hīdrə\ *n, cap* [NL, irreg. fr. Gk *enydris* otter, fr. *enydros* living in water, fr. *en* in + *hydōr* water — more at IN, WATER] **:** a genus of carnivorous mammals (family Mustelidae) that contains only the sea otter
en·hy·drite \-,drīt\ *n* -S [ISV *enhydr-* (fr. *enhydrous*) + *-ite*] **1 :** ENHYDROS **2 :** a mineral or rock containing water — **en·hy·drit·ic** \,en,hī¦drid·ik\ *adj*
en·hy·dros \-īdrəs\ *n* -ES [NL, fr. L, enhydrus mineral, fr. Gk *enydros*] **:** a hollow nodule of chalcedony containing water
en·hy·drous \(')en¦hīdrəs\ *adj* [LL *enhydrus,* fr. Gk *enydros* containing water, living in water] *of certain crystalline minerals* **:** having water within **:** containing fluid drops
en·hy·po·sta·sia \,en,hīpə'stāzh(ē)ə\ *also* **en·hy·pos·ta·sis** \,en(,)hī'pästəsəs\ *n* -S [NL, fr. Gk *enypostatos* substantial (verbal of *enyphistasthai* to subsist in, fr. *en* in + *hyphistasthai* to subsist, exist, stand under), after Gk *statos* standing, fixed: *-stasia* and Gk *statos: stasis* condition of standing, stoppage — more at IN, HYPOSTASIS, -STATE, -STASIA, STASIS] **:** the dependence of the human nature of Christ upon his divine nature in such fashion that the second is the subsistent hypostasis of the first postulated (as in early Orthodox theology) as a doctrine of hypostatic union excluding an independent and impersonal existence of the human nature and emphasizing its subsistence from the beginning in the person of the Logos — **en·hy·po·stat·ic** \,en,hīpə¦stad·ik\ *adj*
enig·ma *also* **ae·nig·ma** \ə'nigmə, ē'-,e'-\ *sometimes* 'enigmə *or* 'eneg-\ *n, pl* **enigmas** \-məz\ *also* **enigma·ta** \-məd·ə, -mətə\ [L *aenigma,* fr. Gk *ainigma,* fr. *ainissesthai* to speak in riddles, fr. *ainos* tale, fable] **1 :** an intentionally obscure statement (as a riddle or complex metaphor) that depends for full comprehension on the alertness and ingenuity of the hearer or reader; *broadly* **:** an obscure speech or writing ⟨the new . . . novel is a brilliant ~ —Mark Schorer⟩ **2 :** an inexplicable circumstance, event, or occurrence ⟨the ~ of human reason⟩ **:** an unsolved problem ⟨the ~*s* of American prehistory⟩ **:** MYSTERY **3 :** a person not readily understood **:** an inscrutable person; *often* **:** one that exhibits an incomprehensible mixture of opposed qualities **syn** see MYSTERY
enigma canon *or* **enigmatic canon** *or* **enigmatical canon** *n* **:** RIDDLE CANON
enig·mat·ic \¦e(,)nig¦mad·|ik, -,nēg-, -at|, |ēk *also* ¦ē(- *or* ¦i(-\ *also* **enig·mat·i·cal** \|əkəl, |ēk-\ *adj* [*enigmatic* fr. LL *aenigmaticus,* fr. Gk *ainigmatikos,* fr. *ainigmat-, ainigma* enigma + *-ikos* -ic; *enigmatical* fr. LL *aenigmaticus* + E *-al*] **:** relating to or resembling an enigma **:** INEXPLICABLE, PUZZLING ⟨know everything possible about our ~ ally —E.J. Simmons⟩ **syn** see OBSCURE
enig·mat·i·cal·ly \|ək(ə)lē, |ēk-, -li\ *adv* **:** in an enigmatic manner
enig·ma·tite *also* **ae·nig·ma·tite** \ə'nigmə,tīt, ē'-,e'-\ *n* -S [G *ainigmatit, änigmatit,* fr. Gk *ainigmat-, ainigma* + G *-it* -ite] **:** an imperfectly known mineral formerly classed with the amphibole group that occurs in black triclinic crystals and is essentially a silicate of iron, titanium, and sodium (sp. gr. 3.74–3.80)
enig·ma·tize \-,tīz\ *vt* -ED/-ING/-S [*enigmatic* + *-ize*] **:** to make enigmatic ⟨it is the very humanity of man that ~*s* him for the true ascetic⟩
enig·ma·tog·ra·pher \=,==ˈtägrəfə(r)\ *n* -S [*enigmato-* (fr. L *aenigmat-, aenigma* enigma) + *-grapher*] **:** a propounder of enigmas
enig·ma·tog·ra·phy \-fē\ *n* -ES [*enigmato-* + *-graphy*] **:** the art of composing enigmas
enig·ma·tol·o·gy \-täləjē\ *n* -ES [*enigmato-* + *-logy*] **:** the investigation or analysis of enigmas
eni·ma·gá \¦enəmə¦gä\ *n, pl* **enimagá** *or* **enimagás** *usu cap* [Sp, of AmerInd origin] **:** MACÁ
enin *var of* OENIN
-ening *pres part of* -EN
en·isle \ən, en+\ *vt* [¹*en-* + *isle,* n.] **1 :** to place apart (as on an island) **2 :** to make an island of
en·jail \ən, en+\ *vt* [¹*en-* + *jail,* n.] *archaic* **:** to shut up in or as if in prison
en·jambed \ən'jamd, en-\ *adj* [fr. *enjambment,* after such pairs as E *refinement: refined*] **:** marked or characterized by enjambment
en·jamb·ment *or* **en·jambe·ment** \-mmənt\ *n* -S [F *enjambement,* fr. MF, encroachment, fr. *enjamber* to encroach, straddle (fr. *en-* ¹en- + *jambe* leg) + *-ment* — more at JAMB]

: continuation in prosody of the sense in a phrase beyond the end of a verse or couplet : the running over of a sentence from one line into another so that closely related words fall in different lines — compare RUN-ON

enjeopard *vt* -ED/-ING/-S [¹en- + jeopard, v. or jeopardy, n.] *obs* : JEOPARDIZE

en·jewel \ən, en +\ *vt* [¹en- + jewel, n.] : BEJEWEL

en·join \ən'jȯin, en-\ *vt* [ME *enjoinen*, fr. OF *enjoindre*, fr. L *injungere*, fr. *in* + *jungere* to join — more at YOKE] **1** : to direct, prescribe, or impose by order typically authoritatively and compellingly and with urgent admonition ⟨he was bound to avenge his father, the god Apollo had ~*ed* it —G.L. Dickinson⟩ ⟨his leader had sternly ~*ed* him to avoid any weakness —George Meredith⟩ **2** *obs* : to join together **3 a** : FORBID, PROHIBIT ⟨church synods repeatedly ~*ed* the use of the Roman service books —M.H.Shepherd⟩ ⟨a person who found himself attacked — yet ~*ed* by conscience from deliberately taking human life —Lucius Garvin⟩ **b** : to prohibit or restrain by a judicial order or decree : put an injunction on **syn** see COMMAND, FORBID

en·join·der \-ȯində(r)\ *n* -S [*enjoin* + *-der* (as in *rejoinder*)] **1** : an authoritative request : COMMAND **2** : INTERDICTION, PROHIBITION; *often* : INJUNCTION

en·join·ment \-ȯinmənt\ *n* -S *archaic* : PROHIBITION, INJUNCTION

en·joy \ən'jȯi, en-\ *vb* -ED/-ING/-S [ME *enjoien*, fr. MF *enjoir*, fr. OF, fr. *en-* ¹en- + *joir* to derive benefit or pleasure, fr. L *gaudēre* to rejoice — more at JOY] *vi* **1** *obs* : to feel or manifest joy : REJOICE **2** : to have a good time ~ *vt* **1** : to take pleasure or satisfaction in : experience or possess with pleasure ⟨~*ing* a comfortable chat by the fire⟩ ⟨they ~*ed* the beat of the rain on the roof⟩ ⟨foolish men who having wealth do not ~ it⟩ **2 a** : to have in possession for one's use or satisfaction ⟨he ~*ed* a good salary for many years⟩ ⟨the right to ~ liberty and the pursuit of happiness⟩ **b** : to have the benefit of (as a right, a desirable thing or quality, or something profitable) ⟨she ~*s* a life interest in her husband's estate⟩ ⟨they ~*ed* the esteem of their fellows⟩ ⟨~*ed* the income from a nice little family business⟩ **c** : to undergo the experience of (a change for the better) ⟨dried skim milk ~*ed* an enormous rise —Vance Packard⟩ **3 a** : to make happy ⟨~*ed* themselves at the party⟩ **b** *chiefly dial* : ENTERTAIN **4** : to copulate with (a woman) **5** : to be immediately aware of (as an emotion or psychic reaction) not as an object of thought but as a phase or ingredient of one's own conscious state or activity — compare CONTEMPLATE 4 **syn** see HAVE, LIKE

en·joy·able \-ȯiəbəl\ *adj* : capable of being enjoyed : being a source of pleasure or enjoyment ⟨an ~ afternoon at the seaside⟩ ⟨those ~ traits of character that make us humanly weak but strongly human⟩ — **en·joy·able·ness** \-bəlnəs\ *n* -ES — **en·joy·ably** \-blē, -li\ *adv*

en·joy·er \-ȯi(ə)r,-ȯiə\ *n* -S : one that enjoys

en·joy·ing·ly *adv* [*enjoying* (pres. part. of *enjoy*) + *-ly*] : with enjoyment or satisfaction

en·joy·ment \-ȯimənt\ *n* -S **1 a** : the action or state of enjoying something : the deriving of pleasure or satisfaction (as in the possession of anything) **b** : possession and use ⟨the ~ of civic rights⟩ **2** : something that gives pleasure or keen satisfaction ⟨the poorest life has its ~*s* and pleasures⟩ **3** : the mind's immediate consciousness of aspects of itself **syn** see PLEASURE

en·ki·an·thus \,eŋkē'an(t)thəs\ *n, cap* [NL, fr. *enki-* (perh. irreg. fr. Gk *enkyos* pregnant, fr. *en* in + *kyos* fetus) + *-anthus*; akin to L *cavus* hollow — more at IN, CAVE] : a genus of erect Asiatic shrubs (family Ericaceae) that have whorled branches, leaves which are mostly clustered at the twig ends, and nodding flowers in terminal clusters and that are often cultivated as ornamentals

en·kindle \ən, en +\ *vb* [¹en- + *kindle*] *vt* **1** : to set (as fuel) on fire : cause to ignite **2** : to make bright and glowing ⟨his passionate conviction . . . ~*s* his book —H.L.Shapiro⟩ ~ *vi* : to take fire : FLAME

en·kindler \"+\ *n* -S : one that enkindles

enkolpion *var of* ENCOLPION

enl *abbr* **1** enlarged **2** enlisted; enlistment

en·lace \ən'lās, en-\ *vt* [ME *enlacen*, fr. MF *enlacier*, fr. OF, fr. *en-* ¹en- + *lacier* to lace — more at LACE] **1** : ENCIRCLE, ENFOLD **2** : ENTANGLE, ENTWINE, INTERLACE

en·lace·ment \-mənt\ *n* -S : INTERLACEMENT

en l'air \äⁿ 'l + *pronunc at* AIR\ *adv (or adj)* [F, in the air] *ballet* : in the air — opposed to *par terre*

enlard *vt* [¹en- + *lard*, n.] *obs* : LARD

¹en·large \ən, en +\ *vb* -ED/-ING/-S [ME *enlargen*, fr. MF *enlargier*, fr. OF, fr. *en-* ¹en- + *large*, adj. — more at LARGE] *vt* **1 a** : to make larger : increase in quantity or dimensions : extend in limits : MAGNIFY ⟨the body is *enlarged* by nutrition⟩ ⟨*enlarging* his fortune by speculation⟩ ⟨such an experience ~*s* your point of view⟩ **b** : to reproduce in larger form ⟨~ a picture⟩ **2 a** : to increase the capacity of : give free scope or greater scope to : EXPAND ⟨he *enlarged* his plan as he grew in experience⟩ **b** : to dilate esp. with joy, affection ⟨his sorrow *enlarged* her heart⟩ **3** : to set at large : set free (as a captive) **4 a** : to make an extension of (as the time for a legal action) **b** : to extend the time limit of (as a lease, order, rule) **c** : to increase the scope of (an estate) — usu. used of a release that operates to convert a life interest or an estate for years into a fee ~ *vi* **1** : to grow large or larger : become more extended : EXPAND ⟨as the city *enlarged* its slums came down to the river⟩ ⟨the embryo gradually ~*s* and differentiates⟩ **2** : to speak or write at length: as **a** : to present in detail something previously outlined — often used with *on* or *upon* ⟨let me ~ on this basic theme⟩ ⟨these gentlemen can ~ upon the scheme I mentioned⟩ **b** : to be diffuse in speech or writing : DILATE, EXPATIATE ⟨the preacher *enlarged* interminably in a dull dry voice⟩ **syn** see INCREASE

²enlarge \"\ *n* -S *archaic* : ENLARGEMENT

en·large·able \"əbəl\ *adj* : suitable for enlargement

en·larged \-jd\ *adj* [fr. past part. of *enlarge*] : larger or greater than that formerly, usually, or normally present ⟨an ~ joint⟩ ⟨the ~ authority of the committee⟩ — **en·larged·ly** \-j(ə)dlē, -li\ *adv* — **en·larged·ness** \-jədnəs, -j(d)n-\ *n* -ES

en·large·ment \-jmənt\ *n* -S **1** : an act or instance of enlarging or the state of being enlarged: as **a** : increase in bulk or extent : AUGMENTATION, EXPANSION, EXTENSION **b** : expansion or intensification of mental powers : increase or breadth esp. of knowledge or sympathies **c** : a setting at large : release from confinement, servitude, or distress : LIBERATION **d** : diffusive quality or expatiation in discourse; *often* : amplification esp. by copious illustration or detailed description **e** *archaic* : freedom from constraint (as in prayer) **2** : something that enlarges or is enlarged: as **a** *obs* : RIGHT, PRIVILEGE **b** : something added ⟨building an ~ on his new house⟩ **3** : a photographic print larger than the negative that is made by projecting through a lens an image of the negative upon a photographic printing surface

en·larg·er \-jə(r)\ *n* -S : one that enlarges; *specif* : an optical projector used to produce a photographic enlargement

¹enlarging *adj* [fr. pres. part. of *enlarge*] : making larger : EXTENDING, AUGMENTING — **en·larg·ing·ly** *adv*

²enlarging *n* -S [ME, action or process of making larger, fr. *enlargen* + *-inge*, *-ing* -ing] : the process of making photographic enlargements

en·leg·end·ed \ən'lejəndəd, en-\ *adj* [¹en- + *legend*, n. + *-ed*] : LEGENDARY, FABULOUS

en·lève·ment \äⁿlevmäⁿ\ *n, pl* **enlèvements** \-mäⁿ(z)\ [F, action of lifting, fr. MF *enlevement*, fr. *enlever* to lift, raise (fr. OF, to raise, fr. *en* from that place — fr. L *inde*, akin to L *is* he and to L *de* from — + *lever* to raise) + *-ment* — more at ITERATE, DE-, LEVER] : the lift into the air of a ballerina by her supporting male dancer

enlight \ən, en+\ *vt* -ED/-ING/-S [¹en- + *light*, n.] *archaic* : ENLIGHTEN

en·light·en \ən'līt°n, en-\ *vb* **enlightened; enlightened; enlightening** \-t(°n)iŋ\ **enlightens** [¹en- + *light*, n. + *-en*] *vt* **1** *archaic* : to supply with light : ILLUMINATE ⟨His lightnings ~*ed* the world —Ps 97:4 (AV)⟩ **2** *obs* : to cause to shine or give light : make luminous : ENKINDLE **3 a** : to furnish with useful information : INSTRUCT, INFORM ⟨radio should ~ the listener as well as entertain him⟩ **b** : to supply with spiritual insight or light ⟨the divine mercy can ~ the blackest spirit⟩ ~ *vi* : to give information

enlightened \-t°nd\ *adj* [fr. past part. of *enlighten*] : freed from ignorance and misinformation ⟨an ~ people⟩; *often* : based on full comprehension of the problems involved ⟨an ~ judgment⟩ — **en·light·ened·ly** \-t°n(ə)dlē, -li\ *adv* — **en·light·ened·ness** \-t°ndnəs, -t°n(d)nəs\ *n* -ES

enlightened self-interest *n* : behavior based on awareness that what is in the public interest is eventually in the interest of all individuals and groups ⟨polls that are kept honest only by the *enlightened self-interest* of the pollsters⟩

en·light·en·er \-t(°)nə(r)\ *n* -S : one that enlightens

enlightening *adj* [fr. pres. part. of *enlighten*] : tending to dissipate ignorance or increase knowledge and awareness ⟨an ~ glimpse of government in action⟩ — **en·light·en·ing·ly** *adv*

en·light·en·ment \-t°nmənt\ *n* -S **1** : the act or means of enlightening : the state of being enlightened ⟨the gradual attaining of spiritual ~⟩ **2 a** *usu cap* : a philosophic movement of the 18th century characterized by an untrammeled but frequently uncritical use of reason, a lively questioning of authority and traditional doctrines and values, a tendency toward individualism, and an emphasis on the idea of universal human progress and on the empirical method in science — used with *the* **b** : a mental attitude in the spirit of the Enlightenment; *also* : a movement or period resembling the Enlightenment **3** : the ultimate goal of the Taoist and Buddhist religious life: **a** *Taoism* : the state of being in harmony with the laws of the universe **b** *Buddhism* : the realization of ultimate universal truth

en·link \ən'liŋk, en-\ *vt* [¹en- + *link*, v.] : to bring together and make fast as if links of a chain : connect by or as if by links

en·list \ən'list, en-\ *vb* [¹en- + ⁶*list*] *vt* **1** : to engage (a person) for military or naval service usu. for a definite period **2** : to secure the support and aid of : employ or utilize in advancing some interest ⟨~ you in a good cause⟩ ⟨~ photography for educational purposes⟩; *broadly* : ATTRACT ⟨a compilation of Collects to ~ the interest of busy people —*Philosophic Abstracts*⟩ ⟨personal participation ~*s* belief in the objectivity of an experience⟩ ~ *vi* **1** : to enroll oneself for military or naval service esp. voluntarily and for a definite period ⟨he ~*ed* for three more years of service in the navy⟩ **2** : to participate heartily (as in a cause or effort) ⟨~*ed* in the cause of world peace⟩ ⟨~*ing* in the argument raging between science and theology⟩

enlisted *adj* [fr. past part. of *enlist*] : of, relating to, for, or constituting the part of a military or naval force ranked below commissioned officers, warrant officers, and persons (as cadets or midshipmen) who are in the course of qualifying as commissioned officers ⟨many officers holding temporary commissions reverted to ~ status after the war⟩ ⟨~ men and women⟩ ⟨~ quarters⟩

enlisted specialist *n* : an enlisted person in U. S. armed forces classified as an occupational specialist

en·list·ee \ən,li'stē, en-; |en,li|stē\ *n* -S **1** : a person who enlists esp. for military or naval service **2** : a member of the enlisted ranks of a military or naval force

en·list·ment \ən'lis(t)mənt, en-\ *n* -S **1** : the act of enlisting or state of being enlisted **2** : a period of service in a military or naval force for which an individual can volunteer ⟨the 2-year ~ was discontinued⟩

en·live \ən'līv, en-\ *vt* [prob. fr. ¹*en-* + *live*, adj.] : ENLIVEN

en·liv·en \ən'līvən, en-\ *vt* **enlivened; enlivened; enlivening** \-v(ə)niŋ\ **enlivens** [prob. fr. ¹*en-* + *live*, adj. + *-en*] **1** : to give life, action, or motion to : make vigorous or active **2** : to give spirit or vivacity to : make sprightly, gay, or cheerful : ANIMATE ⟨*enlivened* by the music⟩ **syn** see QUICKEN

en·liv·en·er \-v(ə)nə(r)\ *n* -S : one that enlivens

enlivening *adj* [fr. pres. part. of *enliven*] : imparting spirit or vivacity : STIMULATING — **en·liv·en·ing·ly** *adv*

en·lock \ən, en+\ *vt* [¹en- + *lock*, v.] : to lock up : ENCLOSE

en masse \(')än'mas, -maa(ə)s,-mais *also* (')äⁿ '- *or* (')in'- *or* (')en'-\ *adv* [F] **1** : in a body ⟨the frogs began to die *en masse*⟩ ⟨the convicts were transported *en masse* to the new prison⟩ **2** : in general : as a whole ⟨viewing the new clothes *en masse*⟩

enmarble *var of* EMMARBLE

en·matter \ən, en+\ *vt* [¹en- + *matter*, n.] : to endue with or confine in matter ⟨the essences treated by physical science may be considered as ~*ed* and formulable⟩

en·mesh \ən'mesh, en-\ *also* **in·mesh** \ən'm\ *or* **im·mesh** \i'm-\ *vt* [¹en- *or* ²in- + *mesh*, n.] : to catch or entangle in or as if in meshes ⟨he was ~*ed* in a series of boundary disputes with his neighbors⟩ — **en·mesh·ment** \-mənt\ *n* -S

en·mi·ty \'enməd·ē, -ətē, -i, *chiefly in substand speech* 'emn\ *n* -ES [ME *enmite*, *enemite*, fr. MF *enemité*, *enemistié*, fr. OF *enemistié*, *enemistié*, fr. *enemi* enemy, after OF *ami* friend: *amistié* amity (whence MF *amité*, *amitié*) — more at ENEMY, AMI, AMITY] **1 a** : ill will such as actuates a personal enemy ⟨his act only increased the ~ of his rival⟩ **b** : a condition marked by such ill will : hatred or antagonism esp. when mutual ⟨men settled in ~ toward their fellows⟩ **c** : an instance of such ill will or hostility ⟨he had an ~ with man —Lord Dunsany⟩ **2** *obs* : something baneful or prejudicial

syn HOSTILITY, ANTIPATHY, ANTAGONISM, ANIMOSITY, RANCOR, ANIMUS: ENMITY indicates ill will, dislike, or hatred that may be overt or concealed and absence of any friendly spirit ⟨farmers began to arrive, some to remain and conquer the *enmity* of cattlemen —*Amer. Guide Series: Texas*⟩ ⟨France's feud with Germany and her *enmity* with England —A.L. Guérard⟩ HOSTILITY may, but does not always, indicate an enmity manifesting itself in open active attack or aggression ⟨the *hostility* with which bishops and parish priests regarded monks and friars —G.M.Trevelyan⟩ ⟨driven from their old homes because of their loyalty to the British Crown and their consequent *hostility* to the Revolution —B.K.Sandwell⟩ ⟨Richelieu in his own mind determined upon overt *hostilities*, upon national war —Hilaire Belloc⟩ ANTIPATHY may apply to a temperamental dislike, aversion, or desire to avoid and shun ⟨inveterate *antipathies* against particular nations and passionate attachments for others should be excluded —George Washington⟩ ⟨as for cats and Negroes, he was inclined to believe that both species knew instinctively of his pronounced *antipathy* for them —Osbert Sitwell⟩ ANTAGONISM may suggest a natural hatred or ill will marked by quick hostility or bitter rivalry or resistance ⟨an *antagonism* existed between the two brothers⟩ ⟨her fragility aroused the chivalry of men, her modesty precluded the *antagonism* of women —Victoria Sackville-West⟩ ANIMOSITY suggests intense, vindictive ill will capable of culminating in hostility ⟨her hatred of the idea of it was intensified into violent *animosity* —Arnold Bennett⟩ ⟨vicious *animosity* of political opponents kept alive an unfortunate mistake that occurred at the time of the Jackson marriage —*Amer. Guide Series: Tenn.*⟩ RANCOR may indicate bitter malevolence, often accompanied by brooding over an injustice or wrong ⟨his most faithful disciple and his most trusted helper, for a dozen years. There is small wonder at her feeling an unchristian *rancor* against the nation which had caused his death —C.S.Forester⟩ ANIMUS applies to dislike, often prejudiced, and ill will, often malevolent or spiteful ⟨a sense that he had been patronized lay behind the *animus* that made him a "defiant American", when he was minister to England —Van Wyck Brooks⟩

enmove *vt* [¹en- + *move*, v.] *obs* : to move inwardly : cause to feel emotion

enmun *often cap*, *var of* ONMUN

ennea- *comb form* [Gk, fr. *ennea* — more at NINE] : nine ⟨enneagon⟩ ⟨enneapetalous⟩

en·ne·ad \'enē,ad, -ēəd\ *n* -S [Gk *ennead-*, *enneas*, fr. *ennea* nine + *-ad-*, *-as* -ad] : a group of nine; *esp* : any of several groups of nine gods that were considered to be associated in the mythology and religion of ancient Egypt

en·ne·ad·ic \|enē|adik\ *adj* : of or relating to an ennead

en·nea·style \'enēə,stīl\ *adj* [*ennea-* + *-style*] : marked by columniation with nine columns across the front — compare DISTYLE

en·nea·sty·los \|enēə|stīləs\ *n* -ES [*ennea-* + Gk *-stylos* -style] : an enneastyle building

en·nea·syllabic \|enēə+\ *adj* [Gk *enneasyllabos* enneasyllabic (fr. *ennea-* + *syllabē* syllable) + E *-ic* — more at SYLLABLE] : having or composed of lines having nine syllables

-en·nial \|enēəl, |enyəl\ *adj comb form* [ME *-eniale*, fr. MF *-ennial*, fr. L *-ennium* (as in *biennium* period of two years) + MF *-al* — more at BIENNIAL] : recurring at or marking intervals of (so many) years ⟨*biennial*⟩ ⟨*centennial*⟩

en·no·ble \ə'nōbəl, e'-\ *vt* **ennobled; ennobled; ennobling** \-b(ə)liŋ\ **ennobles** [ME *ennobelen*, fr. MF *ennoblir*, fr. OF, fr. *en-* ¹en- + *noble*, adj.] **1** : to make noble : elevate in degree or excellence ⟨what can ~ sots, or slaves, or cowards —Alexander Pope⟩ ⟨our buildings are thus *ennobled* by the devotion to service which they proclaim —Joseph Hudnut⟩ **2** : to raise to the rank of nobility ⟨was *ennobled* by Charles II⟩ **3** *archaic* : to make noted or conspicuous **4 a** : to transmute (a base metal) into a noble metal ⟨the . . . conception of *ennobling* metals by a process of death and resurrection —S.F. Mason⟩ **b** : to make (a metal, as iron) resistant to corrosion

en·no·ble·ment \-bəlmənt\ *n* -S : an act of ennobling or the state of being ennobled

ennobling *adj* [fr. pres. part. of *ennoble*] : tending to ennoble ⟨the ~ influence of cultured surroundings⟩ — **en·no·bling·ly** *adv*

ennoblish *vt* [MF *ennobliss-*, stem of *ennoblir*] *obs* : ENNOBLE, HONOR, DISTINGUISH

¹en·nui \(')än|wē *sometimes* |än(y)ə|wē\ *n* -S [F, fr. OF *enui* annoyance — more at ANNOY] **1** : a feeling of weariness and dissatisfaction : languor or emptiness of spirit : TEDIUM, BOREDOM ⟨the moment we indulge our affections, the earth is metamorphosed; . . . all tragedies, all ~*s* vanish —R.W. Emerson⟩ **2 a** : an instance or period of ennui **b** : something that causes ennui ⟨the effort she made was itself an ~⟩

²ennui \"\ *vt* **en·nuied** *or* **en·nuyed** \-|wēd\ **ennuied** *or* **ennuyed** \"\ **en·nuy·ing** \-|wēiŋ, -|wē-ēŋ\ **en·nuies** \-|wēz\ : to afflict with ennui : BORE — used chiefly in the past participle

¹en·nuyé \|än(,)wē|(y)ā\ *adj* [F, past part. of *ennuyer* to affect with ennui, fr. OF *enuier* to annoy — more at ANNOY] : affected with ennui

²en·nuyé \"\ *n, pl* **ennuyés** *or* **ennuyé** : one affected with ennui

eno- — see OEN-

enoch ar·den \|ēnə|kärd°n, -nē|k-, -kəd-\ *n, usu cap E&A* [after *Enoch Arden*, hero of the poem *Enoch Arden* (1864) by Tennyson] : a person missing and believed dead usu. through no fault of his own who subsequently is found alive

enoch arden law *n, usu cap E&A* : a statute providing for divorce or exempting from liability for remarriage on the ground of unexplained absence of husband or wife for a specified number of years, usu. seven

enoch·ic \(')ē|näkik\ *also* **eno·chi·an** \-nōkēən, -näk-\ *adj, usu cap* [*Enoch*, patriarch mentioned in Gen 5:18–24 + E *-ic* or *-ian*] : of, relating to, or in the manner of any of the various apocryphal or pseudepigraphical books bearing the name of the patriarch Enoch

enol \(')ē|nōl, -ōl\ *n* -S [ISV *ene-* (fr. *-ene*) + *-ol*] : an organic compound containing a hydroxyl group adjacent to a double bond and usu. characterized by the grouping >C:C(OH)– — compare ETHYL ACETOACETATE

eno·lase \'ēnə,lās, -āz\ *n* -S [ISV *enol* + *-ase*] : a crystalline enzyme that may be obtained from muscle and yeast and that plays an important role in the metabolism of carbohydrates by promoting a reversible dehydration of phosphoglyceric acid to phosphopyruvic acid

eno·late \-āt\ *n* -S [*enol* + *-ate*] : a metallic derivative of an enol

eno·lic \(')ē|nōlik, -näl-\ *adj* [ISV *enol* + *-ic*] : of or relating to an enol

eno·liz·able \|ēnə|līzəbəl\ *adj* : capable of being enolized

eno·li·za·tion \,ēnələ'zāshən, -,lī'z-\ *n* -S [ISV *enolize* + *-ation*] : the process of enolizing

eno·lize \'ēnə,līz\ *vb* -ED/-ING/-S [ISV *enol* + *-ize*] *vt* : to convert (as a ketone) into an enol : convert (as a carbonyl group) into an enolic hydroxyl group ~ *vi* : to become enolized

enol–keto tautomerism *n* : KETO-ENOL TAUTOMERISM

enol·o·gist \ē'näləjəst\ *n* -S [*enology* + *-ist*] : a specialist in enology

enol·o·gy *or* **oenology** \ē'näləjē\ *n* -S [*enology* alter. of *oenology*; *oenology* fr. *oen-* + *-logy*] : a science that treats of wine making or wine

en·oph·thal·mos *also* **en·oph·thal·mus** \,e,näf'thalməs, -näp'th-, -,mäs\ *n* -ES [NL, fr. ²*en-* + Gk *ophthalmos* eye or NL *-ophthalmus*] : a sinking of the eyeball into the orbital cavity

en·op·la \e'näplə\ *n pl, cap* [NL, fr. Gk, neut. pl. of *enoplos* armed, fr. *en-* ²en- + *-hoplos* (fr. *hoplon* tool, weapon) — more at HOPLITE] : a class or other division of Nemertea including the orders Hoplonemertea and Bdellonemertea and comprising nemertine worms in which the mouth is anterior to the brain and the proboscis is armed with one or more stylets

en·op·li·da \e'näplədə\ *n pl, cap* [NL, fr. *Enoplus*, genus of nematodes (fr. Gk *enoplos* armed) + *-ida*] : an order of Aphasmidia that comprises nematode worms with the esophagus divisible into two regions and the amphids saccular or poriform and that is usu. divided into the suborders Enoplina, Dorylaimina, and Dioctophymatina — compare CHROMADORIDA — **en·op·loid** \(')e|näplȯid\ *n* -S

en·op·li·na \,e,näp'līnə, -lēnə\ *n pl, cap* [NL, fr. *Enoplus* + *-ina*] : a suborder of Enoplida including free-living nematode worms that usu. lack a buccal stylet but have setae on the head — compare DIOCTOPHYMATINA, DORYLAIMINA

en·op·li·on \e'näplē,än, -ēən\ *n* -S [Gk, neut. of *enoplios* martial, fr. *enoplos* armed] : an acatalectic hemiepes preceded by one or two short syllables or a long — see PROSODIAC

en·op·tro·man·cy \e'näptrə,man(t)sē\ *n* -ES [F *énoptromancie*, fr. Gk *enoptron* mirror (fr. *en-* ²en- + *op-* — as in *optikos* optic — + *-tron*) + F *-mancie* -mancy] : divination by means of a mirror

en·organic \|en+\ *adj* [²*en-* + *organic*] : arising within or inherent in the organism

enorm \ə'nȯ(ə)rm, ē'-\ *adj* [ME *enorme*, fr. MF, fr. L *enormis*] **1** *obs* : ABNORMAL, EXTRAORDINARY **2 a** *obs* : OUTRAGEOUS, MONSTROUS **b** *archaic* : ENORMOUS, VAST **3** *Scots law* : legally excessive : constituting a legal enormity — used of an injury sustained by one by reason of being party to a contract or deed

enormious *adj* [ME, fr. L *enormis* + ME *-ous*] *obs* : ENORMOUS

enor·mi·ty \ə'nȯ(r)məd·ē, -ətē, -i\ *n* -ES [MF *enormité*, fr. L *enormitat-*, *enormitas*, fr. *enormis* + *-itat-*, *-itas* -ity] **1** : the quality or state of exceeding a measure or rule or of being immoderate, monstrous, or outrageous ⟨the ~ of the offense⟩ **2** : a grave offense against order, right, or decency **3** *obs* **a** : ABNORMALITY **b** : something abnormal or eccentric **4 a** : HUGENESS, IMMENSITY **b** : a thing of huge size

¹enor·mous \-məs\ *adj* [L *enormis* (fr. *e* out of, out + *norma* rule) + E *-ous* — more at E-, NORMAL] **1** *archaic* **a** : exceeding the usual rule, norm, or measure : out of due proportion : INORDINATE ⟨wallowing unwieldy, ~ in their gait —John Milton⟩ **b** : breaking set norms of conduct : exceedingly wicked, monstrous, shocking : extreme in some bad quality or way ⟨these easy terms on which absolution is obtained certainly encourage the repetition of the most ~ crimes —Tobias Smollett⟩ **2** : marked by extraordinarily great size, amount, number, degree, scope, intensity, or significance : exceeding or transcending usual bounds or commonly accepted notions ⟨the ~ size of the Pacific ocean —F.D.Roosevelt⟩ ⟨~ panoramic views of mountain ranges —*Amer. Guide Series: Calif.*⟩ ⟨the big industries with their vast over-capitalization and their ~ overhead —Lewis Mumford⟩ **syn** see HUGE

²enormous \"\ *adv* : EXTREMELY, VERY

enor·mous·ly *adv* : to an enormous degree : EXCEEDINGLY, VASTLY

enor·mous·ness *n* -ES : vast or excessive bulk or size — compare ENORMITY

eno·sis \ə'nōsəs, e'-,ē'-\ *n* -ES [NGk *henōsis*, fr. Gk, union, fr. *henoun* to unite (fr. *hen-*, *heis* one) + *-sis* — more at SAME] : UNION; *specif* : a movement designed to secure the political union of Greece and Cyprus — **eno·sist** \-ōsəst\ *n* -S

¹enough \ə'nəf, ē'nəf; *after* t, d(·), s, z, " *or* 'n'əf\ *adj* [ME *ynough*, *inough*, fr. OE *genōg*; akin to OHG *ginuog* enough, ON *gnōgr*, Goth *ganohs*; all fr. a prehistoric Gmc compound whose first constituent is represented by OE *ge-* (perfective, associative, and collective prefix) and whose second constituent is akin to L *nancisci* to get, Gk *enenkein* to carry, Skt *naśati* he attains — more at CO-] **:** marked by or present or occurring in such quantity, quality, or scope as to satisfy fully the demands, wants, or needs of a situation or of a proposed use or end ⟨there is ~ food today for all of us —F.D.Roosevelt⟩ **syn** see SUFFICIENT

²enough \"\ *adv* [ME *ynough, inough,* fr. OE *genōg,* fr. *genōg,* adj.] **1 :** in or to a degree or quantity that satisfies or is sufficient or necessary to satisfaction **:** SUFFICIENTLY ⟨unstable ~ to react with moisture in the air⟩ **2 :** FULLY, QUITE — used to express slight to marked augmentation of the positive degree ⟨he is ready ~ to embrace the offer⟩ **3 :** in a tolerable degree — used to express mere acceptance or acquiescence and usu. implying some degree of derogation ⟨she sang well ~⟩ ⟨this dress is good ~ for that party⟩

³enough \"\ *n* -s [ME *ynough, inough,* fr. OE *genōg,* fr. *genōg,* adj.] **:** a quantity that satisfies desire, is adequate to the want, or is equal to the power **:** SUFFICIENCY ⟨we have ~ for all our needs⟩ ⟨~ is as good as a feast⟩ — often used interjectionally usu. with an implication that what has gone before has exceeded any proper sufficiency ⟨~! how dare you insult our queen⟩

enounce \ē'naůn(t)s, i'-\ *vt* -ED/-ING/-S [F *énoncer,* fr. L *enunciare, enuntiare* to report, declare, express — more at ENUNCIATE] **1 :** to set forth or state as a proposition or argument ⟨the principles of criticism first *enounced* by Aristotle —Malcolm Cowley⟩ **:** state formally or publicly ⟨the angel *enounced* the coming of Christ⟩ **2 :** ENUNCIATE 2

¹enow \ə'naů, ē'naů; *after* t, d(·), s, z, " *or* ᵊn'aů\ *adv (or adj)* [ME *inow, ynow, inowe, ynowe,* partly fr. OE *genōg,* adj & adv. and partly fr. OE *genōge,* pl. of *genōg,* adj.] *archaic* **:** ENOUGH

²enow \ē(n)'nü, i'nü\ *adv* [contr. of *even now*] **1** *dial Brit* **:** just now **2** *Brit* **:** PRESENTLY

en pas·sant \äⁿpä'säⁿ\ *adv* [F] **:** in passing **:** in the course of a procedure **:** INCIDENTALLY ⟨he mentioned *en passant* that his brother was then in Rome⟩ — used in chess of the capture of a pawn as it makes a first move of two squares by an enemy pawn in a position to threaten the first of these squares; abbr. *e. p.*

en pen·sion \äⁿpäⁿsyōⁿ\ *adv (or adj)* [F, lit., on boarding contract] **:** at a fixed rate for board and lodging **:** on the American plan ⟨possible to live quite reasonably *en pension* in many of the smaller hotels⟩ ⟨argued over *en pension* terms⟩

¹en·phy·tot·ic \,en,fī,täd·ik\ *adj* [²*en-* + *phyt-* + *-otic*] *of a plant disease* **:** occurring regularly among the plants of a district but only in moderate severity

²enphytotic \"\ *n* -s **:** an enphytotic disease or an outbreak of such disease

en pla·card \äⁿplȧkȧr\ *adj* [F, lit., on the document] *of a seal* **:** affixed directly to the face of a document rather than pendent from a ribbon or other fastener **:** PLAQUÉ

en·plane \ən'plān, en-\ *or* **em·plane** \əm-,em-\ *vi* [¹*en-* + *plane* (airplane)] **:** to board an airplane for purposes of travel

en plein \äⁿplaⁿ\ *adv* [F, lit., in full] **:** on a single number, side, or chance — used of a bet (as in roulette)

en prince \äⁿpraⁿs\ *adv* [F] **:** in a princely manner; *usu* **:** LAVISHLY, LUXURIOUSLY

en prise \äⁿprēz\ *adj* [F] *of a chess piece* **:** exposed to capture

en quad \'en,=\ *n* [*en*] **:** a quad whose set dimension is one half that of an em quad

enquest *obs var of* INQUEST

enquire *var of* INQUIRE

en·rage \ən'rāj, en-\ *vb* [MF *enrager* to become mad, fr. OF *enragier,* fr. *en-* ¹en- + *rage* — more at RAGE] *vt* **1** *obs* **a :** to make (as the sea) violent **:** cause (as a disease) to become more virulent **:** EXACERBATE **b :** to cause to become fevered or swollen **:** produce heat in (as a lesion) **2 :** to cause to become furious **:** fill with rage **:** MADDEN ⟨the child's teasing *enraged* the animal⟩ *sometimes* **:** to make angry **:** EXASPERATE **:** seriously annoy **~** *vi* **1** *obs* **:** to become distracted or maddened (as by pain or distress) **2 a** *archaic* **:** to become furiously angry **b** *obs* **:** to become intense (as of plague, famine, or tyranny) **:** RAGE

en·raged \-jd\ *adj* [ME, fr. past part. of *enragen*] **:** INFURIATED, MADDENED — **en·raged·ly** \-j(ə)dlē, -li\ *adv*

en·rage·ment \-mənt\ *n* -s [MF, fr. *enrager* + *-ment*] **:** the act of enraging or state of being enraged

en·ra·ma·da \,enrə'mädə\ *n* -s [Sp, fr. fem. of *enramado,* past part. of *enramar* to roof with branches, fr. *en-* (fr. L *in-* ²in-) + *ramo* branch, fr. L *ramus* — more at RAMIFY] *Southwest* **:** a roofed open-sided shelter often used for dances

en·rank \ən, en+\ *vt* [¹*en-* + *rank* (n.)] **:** to place in ranks or in order

en rap·port \äⁿra'pȯ(ə)r, -ō(ə)r,-ȯ(ə),-ōə\ *adj* [F] **:** in harmony **:** in a state of mutual accord and sympathetic understanding ⟨the lecturer was completely *en rapport* with his auditors⟩

en·rapt \ən'rapt, en-\ *adj* [¹*en-* + *rapt*] **:** absorbed in or as if in ecstatic contemplation **:** ENRAPTURED ⟨fools listen to him, silent, ~, sighing when he is done —Alan Paton⟩

en·rap·ture \ən'rapchə(r), en-, -psh-\ *vt* **enraptured; enraptured; enrapturing** \-pchəriŋ,-psh(ə)r-\ **enraptures** [¹*en-* + *rapture*] **:** to fill with delight **:** gratify completely

enraptured *adj* **:** characterized by or full of poetic fancy ⟨the ~ strain of her allegoric prose⟩ — **en·rap·tured·ly** \-ə(r)dlē, -li\ *adv*

en·ravish \ən, en+\ *vt* [¹*en-* + *ravish*] **:** to transport with delight **:** ENRAPTURE

en·regiment \ən, en+\ *vt* [¹*en-* + *regiment* (n.)] **:** to subject to discipline and orderly control **:** REGIMENT

en·register \ən, en+\ *vt* [MF *enregistrer,* fr. OF, fr. *en-* ¹en- + *registre* register — more at REGISTER] **:** to record in a register **:** to put on record — **en·registration** \ən, (,)en+\ *n*

en·rich \ən'rich, en-\ *also* **en·rich·en** \-chən\ *vt* **enriched** *also* **enrichened; enriched** *also* **enrichened; enriching** \-chiŋ\ *also* **enrichening** \-ch(ə)niŋ\; **enriches** *also* **enrichens** [ME *enrichen,* fr. MF *enrichir,* fr. OF, fr. *en-* ¹en- + *riche* rich — more at RICH] **1 a :** to make (as oneself) rich or richer ⟨he ~*ed* himself at the expense of his brothers⟩ ⟨the expanding economy gradually ~*ed* the workers⟩ **b :** to increase the intellectual or spiritual riches of ⟨his life was ~*ed* by his charity⟩ ⟨returning home ~*ed* by this new experience⟩ **c :** to fill with things of value **:** add to the valuable contents of ⟨sun and rain ~ the harvest⟩ ⟨his several expeditions ~*ed* the museum's collections of tropical fauna⟩ **d :** to add to or improve by additions ⟨our language has been ~*ed* from many sources⟩ ⟨physical science is constantly being ~*ed* by new discoveries⟩ **2 a :** to supply with ornament ⟨a collar ~*ed* with embroidery⟩ **:** ADORN, DECK ⟨he plans to ~ the ceiling with frescoes⟩ **b :** to ornament (as an architectural member) with carving ⟨paneling ~*ed* with raised garlands of fruits and leaves⟩ **3 a :** to make richer in some quality (as in nutritive value, savor, or beauty) ⟨~ the gravy with a little flour browned in butter⟩ ⟨the blooming laurel ~*es* the hill⟩ ⟨~*ing* culture media for fastidious microorganisms⟩ **b :** to make (soil) more productive esp. by increasing the supply of plant nutrients ⟨the desert can be ~*ed* and given new life by irrigation⟩; *usu* **:** FERTILIZE ⟨~ the compost with well-rotted manure or bone meal⟩ **c :** to improve (a food) in nutritive value by addition of vitamins and minerals in processing; *esp* **:** to restore part of the thiamine, nicotinic acid, iron, and riboflavin removed in processing (wheat flour or cornmeal) **4 :** to increase the proportion of valuable metal or mineral in (as by concentration or smelting) **5 :** to expand (a course of study) esp. in an elementary or secondary school by increasing the variety of subjects as well as the depth of treatment ⟨bright pupils are given an ~*ed* curriculum and are expected to cover much more than the normal amount of material at their grade level —J.D.Russell & C.H.Judd⟩

en·rich·er \-chə(r)\ *n* -s **:** one that enriches

en·rich·ing·ly *adv* **:** so as to enrich ⟨the silt carried by the river spread ~ over the delta⟩

en·rich·ment \-chmənt\ *n* -s **1 a :** the act of enriching or state of being enriched (as by the addition of ornamentation, wealth, or nutrients) ⟨the ~ of soil by green-manuring⟩ **b :** something (as decorations or possessions) that enriches ⟨old oaken panels carved with linenfold ~*s*⟩ **2 :** the natural process by which sulfide-ore deposits gain additions of valuable metals through the descent of metalliferous solutions from the zone of oxidation and through their chemical reaction with the original sulfides below the level of underground water or below the depth to which atmospheric oxygen can penetrate

enridged *adj* [¹*en-* + *ridged*] *obs* **:** formed into ridges **:** WAVY

en·ring \ən, en+\ *vt* [¹*en-* + *ring*] **1 :** ENCIRCLE **2 :** to put a ring on

en·robe \ən'rōb, en+\ *vt* [¹*en-* + *robe* (n.)] **1 :** to invest or adorn with or as if with a robe; *broadly* **:** ATTIRE **2 :** to cover (confections) with a coating (as of chocolate)

en·rob·er \-bə(r)\ *n* **:** one that enrobes

En·rob·er \"\ *trademark* — used for a machine that coats candies and other foods with a coating esp. of chocolate

en·rock·ment \ən'räkmənt, en-\ *n* -s [¹*en-* + *rock* + *-ment*] **:** a mass of large stones thrown into water to form a base (as for a pier)

en·roll *or* **en·rol** \ən'rōl, en-\ *vb* **enrolled; enrolled; enrolling; enrolls** *or* **enrols** [ME *enrollen,* fr. MF *enroller,* fr. *en-* ¹en- + *rolle* roll, register — more at ROLL] *vt* **1 a :** to insert, register, or enter (as a person or a fact) in a list, catalog, or roll (as of a court) ⟨nearly 10 percent of our population is ~*ed* in the elementary schools⟩ ⟨the surprising speed with which men were ~*ed* for the draft⟩ ⟨are they likely to ~ a newcomer on the jury list⟩ **b :** to enlist (oneself) for or as if for military service ⟨he ~*ed* himself with those who were determined to stamp out ignorance and poverty⟩ **2 :** to write out in formal or legal form; *esp* **:** to prepare in written or printed form a final perfect copy of (a bill passed by a legislature) — distinguished from *engross* **3 :** to roll, coil, or wrap up; *sometimes* **:** ENFOLD **~** *vi* **:** to enroll oneself or cause oneself to be enrolled (as in a military organization, on a list of voters, or for a course of study) ⟨~*ing* in the law school⟩ ⟨hundreds ~*ed* in the military reserve forces⟩

enrolled bill *n* **:** a copy of a bill enacted by a U.S. governing body that embodies all changes introduced before enactment and that is filed away as evidence of what the law is

en·roll·ee \ən,rō'lē, en-\ *n* -s **:** a person who is enrolled (as in a military force or a course of study)

en·roll·ment *or* **en·rol·ment** \-'rōlmənt\ *n* -s [ME *enrollement,* fr. MF *enrollement,* fr. *enroller* + *-ment*] **1 a :** the act or process of enrolling (as at enlistment or registration) ⟨the problems involved in the ~ of millions of men for the draft⟩ **b :** the state of being enrolled ⟨my college ~ was approved yesterday⟩ **c :** the number enrolled ⟨the course will have a maximum ~ of 20⟩ **2 :** a writing or an entry in which something is enrolled **3 :** the enrolling of a boat engaged in the domestic commerce or fisheries of the U. S. or in navigating the waters on the northern, northeastern, and northwestern frontiers otherwise than by sea

en·root \ən, en+\ *vb* [¹*en-* + *root* (n.)] *vt* **:** to fix by or as if by roots **:** ESTABLISH ⟨the Negro, an immigrant like the white man and now as ~*ed —Geographical Rev.*⟩; *often* **:** to implant firmly or deeply (as in the mind or a social milieu) ⟨the concept of the fundamental dichotomy of good and evil is ~*ed* in modern European thought⟩ **~** *vi* **:** to take root and grow **:** become established and develop ⟨spots where the free mind can ~ and grow —J.R.MacGillivray⟩

en·rough \ən, en+\ *vt* [¹*en-* + *rough* (adj.)] *archaic* **:** to make rough **:** ROUGHEN

enround *vt* [ME *enrounden,* fr. ¹*en-* + *round* anything round] *obs* **:** SURROUND

en route \(')än'rüt *also* (')en'rüt *or* ən'rüt *or* (')äⁿ'rüt *or* (')ōⁿ'rüt; *sometimes* (')en'raů *or* ən'raů *or* (')ōⁿ'rüt *or* (')ōⁿ'rüt; *usu* \d+V\ *adv (or adj)* [F] **:** on or along the way ⟨noticed while *en route* to church⟩ ⟨in spite of various *en route* delays we arrived safe but tired⟩

¹ens \'enz, 'en(t)s\ *n, pl* **en·tia** \'enchēə, 'entēə, 'en(t)sēə\ [ML, fr. L, irreg. pres. part. of *esse* to be — more at IS] **1 a** (1) **:** abstract being (2) **:** the being of a thing — compare ESSE **b** (1) **:** an existent being **:** ENTITY (2) **:** something that can be conceived **:** a conceptual being **2 :** something supposed by alchemists to condense within itself all the virtues and qualities of a substance from which it is extracted **:** ESSENCE

²ens *pl of* EN

-ens *pres 3d sing of* -EN

ens *abbr* ensign

en·saffron \ən, en+\ *vt* [¹*en-* + *saffron* (adj.)] **:** to make strongly or richly yellow

en·saint \ən, en+\ *vt* [¹*en-* + *saint* (n.)] **:** to make saintly or make a saint of

en·sa·la·da \,ensə'lädə, -äthə\ *n* -s [Sp, lit., salad, fr. *en-* (fr. L *in-* ²in-) + *sal* salt (fr. L) + *-ada* -ate — more at SALT] **:** a burlesque madrigal consisting of several popular tunes sung as a quodlibet that was cultivated in Spain in the 16th century

en·sample \ən, en+\ *n* [ME *ensaumple,* fr. MF *ensample, essample, exemple* — more at EXAMPLE] **:** a pattern or model for imitation or warning **:** EXAMPLE, INSTANCE

en·sanguine \ən, en+\ *vt* -ED/-ING/-S [¹*en-* + *sanguine* (color)] **1 :** to stain or cover with blood **:** make bloody **2 :** to stain or color blood red ⟨the setting sun *ensanguined* the western sky⟩

en·sate \'en,sāt\ *adj* [L *ensis* sword + E *-ate*] **:** ENSIFORM

en·sche·de \'enz|kə,dā, -ns|, |k-\ *adj, usu cap* [fr. *Enschede,* Netherlands] **:** of or from the city of Enschede, Netherlands **:** of the kind or style prevalent in Enschede

en·sconce \ən'zkän(t)s, en-, -n'sk-\ *vb* -ED/-ING/-S [¹*en-* + *sconce* (n.)] *vt* **1** *obs* **:** to cover or shelter esp. with a fort **2 :** to place or hide (as oneself) securely **:** CONCEAL ⟨he *ensconced* himself behind the sofa to hear what went on⟩ **3 :** to establish or settle firmly, comfortably, or snugly ⟨the statue was finally *ensconced* in its niche⟩ ⟨such foolish customs tend to ~ themselves in the life of a people⟩ ⟨comfortably *ensconced* before the fire⟩ **~** *vi, obs* **:** to take shelter esp. behind a fortification **syn** see CONCEAL

en·scroll *also* **in·scroll** \ən'zkrōl, en-, -n'sk-\ *vt* [¹*en-* or ²*in-* + *scroll* (n.)] **:** to inscribe in or as if in a scroll; *broadly* **:** RECORD

ense \'en(t)s, 'enz\ *adv* [alter. of Sc *an* than, else (alter. of *than*) + *else*] *Scot* **:** OTHERWISE, ELSE

en·seal \ən, en+\ *vt* [ME *enselen,* fr. MF *enseeler,* fr. *en-* ²en- + *seel* seal — more at SEAL] **1** *obs* **a :** to impress (as a document) with or as if with a seal **b :** RATIFY **2** *archaic* **:** to seal up (as a box or house)

¹en·seam \ən'sēm, en-\ *vb* [ME *enseymen,* alter. of MF *essaimer,* fr. *es-* (fr. L *ex-*) + *saim* fat, grease, fr. ML *sagimen,* fr. L *sagina* food, stuffing, fatness] *vt, archaic* **:** to free (as a hawk or horse) of superfluous fat **:** bring into hard condition **~** *vi, obs, of a hawk* **:** to lose excess weight **:** come into condition

²enseam \"\ *vt* [MF *ensaimer,* fr. *en-* ¹en- + *saim* fat] *archaic* **:** to fill or cover with grease — usu. used as past part.

³enseam \"\ *vt* [¹*en-* + *seam* (n.)] **:** to mark (as a person) with or as if with seams ⟨an old tomcat, his ears ~*ed* with scars⟩

en·search \ən, en+\ *vb* [ME *enserchen,* fr. MF *encercher,* fr. OF *encerchier,* fr. *en-* ¹en- + *cerchier* to search — more at SEARCH] *vi, archaic* **:** to make search **~** *vt* **1** *archaic* **:** to examine (as a place or document) attentively **:** SEARCH, SCRUTINIZE **2** *obs* **:** to search for **:** seek out

en·seat \ən, en+\ *vt* [¹*en-* + *seat* (n.)] **:** ENTHRONE

¹en·sem·ble \(')än'sämbəl, (')äⁿ'sämbəl, (')äⁿ'säⁿbl(ə), (')äⁿ'säⁿb(l)ə\ *sometimes* (')äⁿ'säm\ *n, pl* **ensembles** \-bəlz, -bl(ə), -b(lə), -mz\ *often attrib* [F, fr. *ensemble* together, fr. L *insimul,* fr. *in-* ²in- + *simul* together — more at SAME] **1 :** a system of items that constitute an organic unity **:** a congruous whole: as **a :** AGGREGATE 5 **b :** concerted music of two or more parts (as a quartet) **c** (1) **:** a complete costume including a basic garment (as a dress or suit) and the accessories (as gloves, shoes, ornaments, and hat) worn with it for a total harmonious effect (2) **:** two or more articles of clothing designed to complement one another when worn together ⟨a dress-and-jacket ~⟩ ⟨her ~ consisted of a smooth fawn wool suit under a darker coat lined with the suit color⟩ **d :** a group of furnishings (as for a room) designed to harmonize when used together; *sometimes* **:** SUITE 3b **2 :** a group of persons acting together to produce some particular effect or result: as **a :** the musicians engaged in the performance of a musical ensemble **b :** a group of supporting players, singers, or dancers; *esp* **:** CORPS DE BALLET **3 a :** the bringing together of items into an ensemble **:** UNIFICATION ⟨the company develops a sense of ~ and the producer can cast his plays better as he comes to know his actors —Martin Feinstein⟩ **b :** distinctive quality imparted by such bringing together; *esp* **:** the quality of a concerted musical performance as such ⟨the quartet's members were individually excellent but the ~ was somewhat inferior⟩

²ensemble \"\ *vt* -ED/-ING/-S **:** to bring together and coordinate (as clothing or furnishings) into a congruous whole

ensemble acting *n* **:** a system of theatrical presentation in which balanced casting, accurate historical reference, and careful integration of the whole performance replace the star system

en·sepulcher \ən, en+\ *vt* [¹*en-* + *sepulcher* (n.)] **:** BURY, ENTOMB, ENGULF

en·serf \ən, en+\ *vt* -ED/-ING/-S [¹*en-* + *serf*] **:** to force into serfdom **:** deprive of liberty and personal rights — **en·serf·ment** \"mənt\ *n* -s

en·sete \'en(t)sət\ *n* -s [Amharic *ensat*] **:** ABYSSINIAN BANANA

en·sheathe *also* **en·sheath** *or* **in·sheathe** *or* **in·sheath** \ən, en+\ *vt* [¹*en-* or ²*in-* + *sheathe* or *sheath*] **:** to cover with or as if with or enclose in or as if in a sheath ⟨bud scales *ensheathing* the growing point⟩ ⟨the bony core is *ensheathed* by horny tissue⟩

en·shield \ən, en+\ *vt* [¹*en-* + *shield* (v.)] **:** SHIELD

en·shrine \ən, en+\ *vt* [¹*en-* + *shrine* (n.)] **1 a :** to enclose in or as if in a shrine ⟨*enshrined* the cheese in close folds of bright tinfoil⟩ **b :** to preserve or cherish as or as if something sacred ⟨robes of shadowy silver or *enshrining* light —P.B. Shelley⟩ ⟨certain nearly meaningless traditional expressions that are *enshrined* in English usage⟩ **2 :** to serve as a shrine for ⟨my heart ~*s* his memory⟩

en·shrine·ment \"mənt\ *n* -s **:** the act of enshrining or the state of being enshrined

en·shroud \ən, en+\ *vt* [¹*en-* + *shroud* (n.)] **:** to cover with or as if with or enclose by or as if by a shroud ⟨much of the aura of haziness which still tends to ~ animal ecology is due to the imperfection of our present knowledge —W.H.Dowdeswell⟩ ⟨darkness ~*ed* the earth⟩ ⟨his life became ~*ed* in legend⟩

en·si·form \'en(t)sə,fȯrm\ *adj* [F *ensiforme,* fr. L *ensis* sword + F *-forme* -form] *biol* **:** having sharp edges and tapering to a slender point **:** having a shape suggesting a sword ⟨the ~ leaf of the gladiolus⟩ — see LEAF illustration

ensiform cartilage *or* **ensiform process** *also* **ensiform appendix** *n* **:** XIPHOID PROCESS

¹en·sign \'en(t)sən, 'en,sīn *sometimes* 'enzən; *in the United States & Brit navies* 'en(t)sən *sometimes* 'enzən\ *n* -s [ME *ensigne,* fr. MF *enseigne,* fr. L *insignia,* pl. of *insigne,* fr. neut. of *insignis* having a distinctive mark, outstanding, fr. ²*in-* ²in- + *-signis* (fr. *signum* mark, sign) — more at SIGN] **1 :** a flag that has been established by a national authority for display as the symbol of nationality by ships or airplanes and that also may be flown sometimes with a distinctive badge added to its design by a military installation, by an organization (as the customs service, a harbor board, or a marine insurance company) having nautical associations, or by an overseas colony or dominion **2 a :** a badge of office, rank, or power; *sometimes* **:** heraldic bearings — usu. used in pl. **b :** EMBLEM, SYMBOL, SIGN ⟨that ~ of tutorial authority, the hickory stick⟩ **3 a** *archaic* **:** STANDARD-BEARER; *esp* **:** a commissioned officer of the British army before 1871 who acted as a standard-bearer **b :** the most junior naval commissioned officer ranking just below a lieutenant junior grade and above a chief warrant officer **c :** a onetime infantry officer of the lowest commissioned rank **4 :** a dark to blackish blue **syn** see FLAG

ensign 1: Royal Air Force

²en·sign \ən'sīn, en'-\ *vt* [MF *enseigner,* fr. ML *insignare,* fr. L *in-* ²in- + *signum* mark, sign] **1 :** to distinguish by a mark or ornament ⟨a sail ~*ed* with an ornamental device⟩ **2 :** to distinguish (as a heraldic charge) by a significant mark (as a granted badge or a crown or miter); *specif* **:** to surmount (as a shield) with such a mark

ensign armorial *n, pl* **ensigns armorial :** a heraldic bearing or emblem

ensign bearer *n* **1 :** the bearer of a flag **2** *archaic* **:** ENSIGN 3a

en·sign·cy *pronunc at* ¹ENSIGN + (t)sē,(t)si\ *n* -ES **:** the rank or office of an ensign ⟨purchased an ~ in an Indian regiment⟩

ensign fly *or* **ensign wasp** *n* **:** a parasitic wasp (family Evaniidae) having the abdomen carried high on a long pedicel and larvae that live in the ootheca of cockroaches and feed on their eggs

en·sign·ry \-rē,-ri\ *n* -ES **:** ensigns and banners

ensign staff *n* **:** the staff at the stern of a ship from which the national flag is flown

en·sil·abil·i·ty \ən,sīlə'bilədē, (,)en-\ *n* -ES **:** fitness or suitability for ensiling ⟨the ~ of lush young growth rich in protein can be improved by adding carbohydrates⟩

¹en·si·lage \'en(t)s(ə)lij, -lēj\ *n* [F, fr. *ensiler* + *-age*] **1 :** the process of preserving fodder by ensiling **2 :** SILAGE

²ensilage \"\ *vt* **:** ENSILE

ensilage blower *n* **:** a machine that elevates cut green forage into a silo by an air blast

ensilage cutter *n* **:** a machine that chops green fodder for ensilage and usu. incorporates a device for elevating it into the silo

en·sile \ən'sīl, (')en|s-, *chiefly before pause or consonant* -ᵊl\ *vt* -ED/-ING/-S [F *ensiler,* fr. *en-* ¹en- + *silo,* fr. Sp *silo* — more at SILO] **:** to prepare (fodder) usu. by chopping and storing so as to exclude air by compression in a tight silo or pit often with additives (as certain acids, preservatives, or carbohydrates) so as to induce conversion to silage

en·sis \'en(t)səs\ *n, cap* [NL, fr. L, sword] **:** a common genus of razor clams

en·sky \ən'skī, en-, -n'skī\ *vb* **enskied** *or* **enskyed; enskied** *or* **enskyed; enskying; enskies** [¹*en-* + *sky* (n.)] *vt* **1 :** to elevate to or as if to heaven ⟨we view George Eliot *enskied* in fame and time —Sylvia T. Warner⟩ ⟨that wonderful voice is forever ~*ing* him —Amy Lowell⟩ **2 :** to raise into or toward the skies ⟨leaves that ~ themselves —Padraic Colum⟩ **~** *vi* **:** to become enskied

en·slave \ən'slāv, en-\ *vb* [¹*en-* + *slave* (n.)] *vt* **1 :** to reduce to slavery **:** make a slave of ⟨free peasants reduced to serfdom or *enslaved*⟩; *broadly* **:** to hold in an inferior or subject state **:** SUBJUGATE ⟨millions of people held in subjugation, *enslaved* by poverty and illiteracy —W.O.Douglas⟩ ⟨millions of workers . . . pay tribute . . . and their money is being used further to ~ the American people —M.K.Hart⟩ **2 :** to obtain such influence over as to make slavishly subject ⟨drugs that ~ the will⟩ ⟨even the most pleasant indulgences can end by *enslaving* the indulger⟩ **~** *vi* **:** to make a person slavish ⟨declares that sex ~*s* —G.A.Chapman⟩ ⟨routine duties that bind but do not narrow or ~ —R.B.Perry⟩

en·slave·ment \-mənt\ *n* -s **1 :** the act or process of enslaving ⟨the gradual ~ of primitive peoples⟩ **2 :** the state of being enslaved **:** BONDAGE, SERVITUDE

en·slav·er \-və(r)\ *n* **:** one that enslaves

ens·len's vine \'enzlənz-, 'en(t)s|\ *n, usu cap E* [after Aloysius *Enslen,* 19th cent. botanist] **:** SAND VINE

en·snare \ən'sna(a)(ə)r, en-, -sne|, |ə\ *vt* [¹*en-* + *snare* (n.)] **:** to take in or as if in a snare **:** SNARE ⟨birds *ensnared* in a net⟩ ⟨a simplicity which it would be easy to ~ with the romanticism embodied in him —Victor Canning⟩ **syn** see CATCH

en·snare·ment \rmənt, |əm-\ *n* -s **:** ENTRAPMENT

en·snar·er \|rə(r)\ *n* -s **:** one that ensnares

en·snar·ing·ly *adv* **:** so as to ensnare **:** for the purpose of ensnaring

en·snarl \ən, en+\ *vt* [¹*en-* + *snarl* (n.)] **:** to entangle in or into or as if in or into a snarl ⟨trees all ~*ed* with vines and bushes —A.J.Liebling⟩ ⟨ended up by ~*ing* himself in a hopeless love affair⟩

en·sof *or* **en·soph** \ān'sōf, en'sōf\ *n, cap E&S* [Heb *ēn sōph* without end] **:** the absolutely infinite God — used in cabalistic doctrine

en·sor·cell \ən'sȯrsəl, en-\ *or* **ensorcel** *vt* **ensorcelled** *or* **ensorceled; ensorcelled** *or* **ensorceled; ensorcelling** *or* **ensorceling** \-rs(ə)liŋ\ **ensorcells** *or* **ensorcels** [MF *ensorceler*, alter. of OF *ensorcerer*, fr. *en-* ¹en- + *-sorcerer*, fr. *sorcier* sorcerer — more at SORCERER] **:** BEWITCH, ENCHANT ⟨she would not do him any hurt or ~ him —Sir Richard Burton⟩; *broadly* **:** to make rapt with delight or interest **:** FASCINATE ⟨the quiet beauty of the hill country will relax and ~ you⟩ — **en·sor·cell·ment** \-rsəlmənt\ *n* -S

en·sor·cer·ize \ən'sȯrs(ə),rīz, en-\ *vt* -ED/-ING/-S [¹*en-* + *sorcerize*] **:** ENSORCELL

en·soul *also* **in·soul** \ən, en+\ *vt* -ED/-ING/-S [¹*en-* or ²*in-* + *soul* (n.)] **1 :** to receive, put, or cherish in the soul **2 :** to endow or imbue with a soul ⟨the spirit of man is . . . ~*ed* spirit —W.R.Inge⟩

en·sphere *also* **in·sphere** \ənz'fi(ə)r, en-, -n'sf-, -iə\ *vt* -ED/-ING/-S [¹*en-* or ²*in-* + *sphere* (n.)] **1 :** to place or enclose in or as if in a sphere **:** ENVELOP, ENCIRCLE ⟨his ample shoulders in a cloud *ensphered* —George Chapman⟩ ⟨its very concrete symbolism seems sometimes to ~ the intended truths of spirit —H.O.Taylor⟩ **2 :** to form into a sphere

enspirit *var of* INSPIRIT

ens ra·ti·o·nis \ˌenz,rashē'ōnəs; ˌen(t)s,räd·ē'-, -ätsē'-\ *n* [ML, lit., being of the mind] **:** an abstract logical entity usu. having no positive existence outside the mind — compare ENS REALE

ens re·ale \ˌenzrē'ā(,)lē, ˌen(t)srā'ä(,)lā\ *n* [ML, lit., real being] **:** an entity that has either actual or potential existence beyond the confines of the finite mind — compare ENS RATIONIS

en·stamp \ənz'tamp, en-, -n'st-, -taa(ə)mp,-taimp\ *vt* [¹*en-* + *stamp* (n.)] *archaic* **:** to imprint or impress with or as if with a stamp

enstar *var of* INSTAR

enstate *var of* INSTATE

en·sta·tite \'enztə,tīt, 'en(t)stə-\ *n* -S [G *enstatit*, fr. Gk *enstatēs* adversary + G *-it* -ite] **:** an orthorhombic mineral $MgSiO_3$ of the pyroxene group consisting of magnesium silicate usu. occurring massive and varying from grayish white to olive green and brown — compare BRONZITE — **en·sta·tit·ic** \ˌ==ˈtid·ik\ *adj*

en·steel \ənz'tē(ə)l, en-, -n'st-\ *vt* [¹*en-* + *steel* (n.)] **:** to make hard and strong ⟨frost ~*ed* the soil⟩

ensteep *obs var of* INSTEEP

en·stool \ənz'tül, en-, -n'st-\ *vt* [¹*en-* + *stool* (seat of a chief)] **:** to install (a ruler of any of several native African groups) in office — contrasted with *destool* — **enstoolment** *n* -S

enstyle *vt* [¹*en-* + *style* (v.)] *obs* **:** STYLE, NAME

en·su·ant \ən'süənt, en-\ *adj* [*ensue* + *-ant*] **:** following as a consequence ⟨the ~ response to his appeal was very satisfying⟩ — often used postpositively and with *on* ⟨the privations and disorders ~ on war⟩

en·sue \ən'sü, en-\ *vb* -ED/-ING/-S [ME *ensuen*, fr. MF *ensivre, ensuivre, ensuire* (3d sing. *ensuit, ensiut*), fr. OF, fr. *en-* ¹en- + *sivre, suivre* to follow — more at SUE] *vt* **1** *obs* **a :** to correspond to **:** take the place of or be commensurate with **b :** to take after **:** follow the lead of **:** IMITATE **c :** to follow after **:** be subsequent to **:** SUCCEED **d :** to carry through or on (as a train of thought or a profession) **2 :** to pursue or strive to attain ⟨within certain limits he *ensued* and sometimes attained perfection —John Buchan⟩ ~ *vi* **:** to take place afterward: **a :** to follow as a chance, likely, or necessary consequence **:** RESULT ⟨when his mind fails to stay the pace set by its inventions, madness must ~ —C.D.Lewis⟩ **b :** to follow in chronological succession **syn** see FOLLOW

en·su·ing·ly *adv, obs* **:** in an ensuing manner **:** AFTERWARD

en suite \(')äⁿ ˈswēt, *usu* -ēd·+V; *F* äⁿswᵞēt\ *adv (or adj)* [F] **:** in a succession, series, or set: **a :** in an integrated functional unit ⟨rooms arranged *en suite*⟩ ⟨a pleasant sewing room with lavatory *en suite*⟩ **b :** in a coordinated set ⟨a Chippendale wing chair with footstool designed *en suite* —*Antiques*⟩ ⟨heavy tray and sugar bowl *en suite*⟩

ensurance *n* -S [ME *ensuraunce*, fr. AF *ensurance*, prob. alter. of MF *assurance* — more at ASSURANCE] *obs* **:** the act or means of ensuring; *specif* **:** INSURANCE

en·sure \ən'shů(ə)r, en-, -ůə\ *vt* -ED/-ING/-S [ME *ensuren*, fr. AF *enseurer*, prob. alter. of OF *aseurer* to assure — more at ASSURE] **1** *obs* **a :** to make (one) sure (as by pledging, guaranteeing, convincing, or declaring) **:** ASSURE **b :** AFFIANCE, BETROTH; *sometimes* **:** MARRY, ESPOUSE **2 :** INSURE 2 **3 :** to make sure, certain, or safe **:** GUARANTEE ⟨good farming practices go far to ~ good crops⟩ ⟨provisions to ~ the rank and file a voice in union policies⟩ ⟨his industry and ability will ~ his success in life⟩

syn INSURE, ASSURE, SECURE: ENSURE, INSURE, and ASSURE all indicate a making of an outcome or event sure, certain, or inevitable as a consequence or concomitant ⟨certain rules of conduct for the purpose of *ensuring* the safety and victory of the absent warriors —J.G.Frazer⟩ ⟨for the remainder of his life he so constrained the expression of his thoughts as to *ensure* safety —H.O.Taylor⟩ ⟨shipbuilders, who wished to *insure* a profitable career for their vessels —*Amer. Guide Series: Mich.*⟩ ⟨the structural division of the buildings, with no more than four apartments opening on any hallway, *insures* privacy and quiet —*Amer. Guide Series: N.Y. City*⟩ ⟨protected by game laws and reared in state hatcheries, this bird is now *assured* a permanent place among the game birds of the state —*Amer. Guide Series: Tenn.*⟩ ⟨policies and plans for *assuring* the necessary labor force for defense and essential civilian production —*Current Biog.*⟩ ASSURE is the usual form to express the notion of removal of doubt, uncertainty, or worry from a person's mind ⟨I *assured* him that I was far from advising him to do anything so cruel —Joseph Conrad⟩ ⟨*assured* the inhabitants that France intended to grant autonomy —*Current Biog.*⟩ INSURE is now the general word for reference to making certain arrangements for indemnification for loss by contingent events ⟨to *insure* the car against theft and fire damage⟩ SECURE implies purposive action to ensure safety, protection, or certainty against adverse contingencies ⟨lock the door to *secure* us from interruption —Charles Dickens⟩ ⟨one other battalion moved up to *secure* the first battalion's flank —Walter Bernstein⟩

en·sur·er \-ůrə(r)\ *n* -S **:** one that ensures

en sur·tout \ˌäⁿ(,)sər'tü, äⁿ 'sər,tü\ *adv (or adj)* [F, lit., as a centerpiece] **:** in a centered position on another as if laid on top of it — used of one coat of arms in respect to another, esp. of that of a wife in respect to that of her husband

en·swathe \ən, en+\ *vt* [¹*en-* + *swathe*] **:** SWATHE, ENVELOP, ENWRAP ⟨swelling buds still *enswathed* in their furry overcoats⟩ ⟨his head *enswathed* in bloody bandages⟩

en·sweep \ən, en+\ *vt* [¹*en-* + *sweep*] *archaic* **:** to sweep over or across

ent- *or* **ento-** *comb form* [NL & Gk; NL, fr. Gk *entos*; akin to L *intus* within, Gk *en* in — more at IN] **:** inner **:** within ⟨entad⟩ ⟨entoblast⟩

¹-ent \ənt, ³nt; *in some words chiefly with stress on the antepenult or by syncope on the penult* (*as "president"*) *sometimes* ,ent; *in common words "-erent" preceded by stressed vowel and consonant* (*as in "different"*) *often* ərnt\ *n suffix* -S [ME, fr. OF, fr. L *-ent-, -ens*, fr. pres. part. suffix of the 2d & 3d conjugations, fr. *-e-* (vowel of the 2d & 3d conjugations) + *-nt-, -ns*, pres. part. suffix — more at -ANT] **:** one that performs (a specified action) ⟨regent⟩ ⟨resident⟩ ⟨tangent⟩ — compare ¹-ANT

²-ent \"\ *adj suffix* [ME, fr. OF, fr. L *-ent-, -ens*, pres. part. suffix] **:** doing, behaving, existing (in the way specified) **:** -ing ⟨apparent⟩ ⟨reverent⟩ ⟨subsequent⟩ — with verbs or verbal roots; compare ²-ANT

ent *abbr* **1** entered; entrance **2** entertainment **3** entomology

en·tab·la·ture \ən'tabləˌchů(ə)r, en-, -ˌchůə, -ləchə(r), -lə-,tyů-, -lə,tů-\ *n* [obs. F, modif. of It *intavolatura*, fr. *intavolato* (past part. of *intavolare* to put on a board or table, fr. *in-* — fr. L *in-* ²in- — + *tavola* board, table, fr. L *tabula*) + *-ura* -ure — more at TABLE] **1 :** an architecturally treated wall consisting of the architrave, the frieze, and the cornice that in classical architecture rests upon the capitals of the columns and supports the pediment or roof plate according to its position on the front or flank of the building; *also* **:** a similar part in a post-and-lintel construction **2 :** an elevated support for certain parts of a machine (as the upper portion of a forging press)

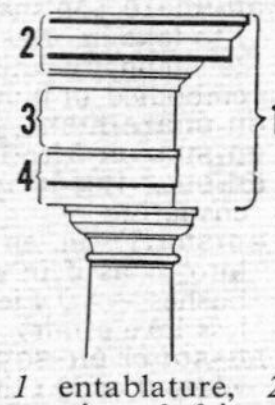

1 entablature, *2* cornice, *3* frieze, *4* architrave

en·tab·la·tured \"+d\ *adj* **:** having an entablature

en·ta·ble·ment \ən'tābəlmənt, en-\ *n* -S [F, fr. OF, fr. *en-* ¹en- + *table* + *-ment* — more at TABLE] **:** a platform supporting a statue and above the dado

en·tad \'en,tad\ *adv* [*ent-* + *-ad*] *anat* **:** INWARD

en·ta·da \en'tädə\ *n, cap* [NL, prob. fr. native name in India] **:** a small genus of tropical woody vines (family Leguminosae) with small flowers in clustered spikes and large woody pealike pods containing large highly polished seeds — see SNUFFBOX BEAN

¹en·tail \ən'tāl, en-, *chiefly before pause or consonant* -āəl\ *vt* -ED/-ING/-S [ME *entailen, entaillen*, fr. ¹*en-* + *taile, taille* limitation — more at TAIL (limitation)] **1 a :** to restrict (property) as to course of descent upon the owner's death by limiting the inheritance to the owner's lineal descendants or to a particular class thereof (as to his male children) **b :** to convert (an estate in certain property) into a fee-tail estate **:** create such an estate in (property) **c :** to settle (land) upon a person in a way designed to preserve for possession in his family as far as legally possible **2 a :** to confer, assign, or transmit as if by entail **:** burden indefinitely with ⟨lament the stupid commonplace and often ribald names ~*ed* upon the rivers and other features of the great West —Washington Irving⟩ **:** FASTEN ⟨blood revenge . . . could be ~*ed* for many generations —A.P. Davies⟩ — often used with *on* or *upon* ⟨~*ed* on them indelible disgrace —Robert Browning⟩ ⟨helped to ~ upon them the ridicule of their neighbors —Tobias Smollett⟩ **b** *obs* (1) **:** to attach inseparably to something **:** TACK (2) **:** to fix (a person) permanently in some status or condition **:** make (a person) the hereditary successor ⟨~ him and his heirs unto the crown —Shak.⟩ ⟨the method ~*ed* upon medieval thought by its scholastic . . . character —H.O.Taylor⟩ **3 a :** to impose, involve, or require as a necessary accompaniment or result ⟨the work ~*s* expense⟩ ⟨political democracy ~*s* a cultural democracy —K.I.L.Lansner⟩ ⟨believed that the wrong faith would ~ hellfire —R.H.Bainton⟩ **b :** to imply with strict logical necessity ⟨a sentence *s* is said to ~ a sentence *t* when the proposition expressed by *t* is deducible from the proposition expressed by *s* —A.J.Ayer⟩

²en·tail \", 'en,t-\ *n* -S [ME *entaile, entaille*, fr. *entailen, entaillen*, v.] **1 a :** an entailing esp. of lands **:** a settling of an estate tail **b :** an estate settled in fee tail or limited in descent to a particular class of issue **c :** the rule by which the descent is fixed **:** the fixed line of devolution **2 a :** irremediable or assured transmission (as of a good or bad quality) ⟨the ~ of ignorance and vice on children born in such surroundings⟩ **b :** something (as a quality) that is transmitted as if by entail **:** LEGACY, INHERITANCE ⟨the doctrine . . . that every child coming into the world is born with an ~ of sin —H.G.Goodykoontz⟩ **c :** logical or necessary consequence or sequence ⟨an evil with a most unfortunate ~ for the future —E.D.Soper⟩

en·tail·er \ən'tālə(r), en-\ *n* -S **:** one that entails

en·tail·ment \-ā(ə)lmənt\ *n* -S **1 :** the act of entailing ⟨~ of property upon a certain heir⟩ **2 :** strict, logical, or analytical implication (as between two statements so that one can be deduced from the other on purely logical grounds)

en·tal \'ent³l\ *adj* [*ent-* + *-al*] *anat* **:** INNER — opposed to *ectal*

en·tame \ən-, en+\ *vt* [¹*en-* + *tame* (adj.)] *archaic* **:** TAME

ent·amebiasis *or* **ent·amoebiasis** \ˌen,t+-\ *n* [NL, fr. *Entamoeba* + *-iasis*] **:** endamebiasis esp. of a vertebrate **:** AMEBIASIS

ent·amoeba \ˌent+\ *n* [NL, fr. *ent-* + *Amoeba*] **1** *cap, in some classifications* **:** a genus of parasitic amoebas (family Endamoebidae) that includes those members of the genus *Endamoeba* which are parasites of vertebrates — used chiefly in medical literature **2** *also* **entameba :** an endamoeba esp. of a vertebrate — **entamoebic** *also* **entamebic** *adj*

en·tangle \ən-, en+\ *vt* [ME *entanglen*, fr. ¹*en-* + *tanglen* to tangle — more at TANGLE] **1 a :** to twist or interweave so as to make separation difficult **:** make tangled and intricate **:** SNARL ⟨~ yarn⟩ **b :** to make complicated or difficult of comprehension **:** CONFUSE ⟨his explanation did not so much clarify as ~ the question⟩ **2 a :** to involve so as to impede physical movement or make extrication difficult **:** ENMESH, ENSNARL ⟨~ a bird in the coils of a net⟩ ⟨*entangled* themselves in a maze of woods and marshes⟩ ⟨*entangled* his feet in the train of her dress⟩ **b :** to involve in a perplexing or troublesome situation from which escape is difficult **:** ENTRAP ⟨*entangling* the country in a vicious circle of wars⟩ ⟨*entangled* himself in a ruinous litigation⟩ ⟨*entangled* his victims in a real-estate scheme that cost them dearly⟩ ⟨had *entangled* the king in a false marriage with her —Edith Sitwell⟩ **c :** to confuse mentally **:** PERPLEX, BEWILDER ⟨*entangled* his listeners in a maze of sophistries⟩ **d** *archaic* **:** ENCUMBER ⟨died . . . leaving an *entangled* estate, due to loans and back rentals —R.J.Porcell⟩

en·tan·gled \-gəld\ *adj* **1 a :** twisted together **:** INTERTWINED, INTERWOVEN, SNARLED ⟨the ropes became ~⟩ ⟨toiled through the ~ growths of scrub oak and mesquite —*Amer. Guide Series: Texas*⟩ **b :** placed in a situation that impedes physical movement or from which extrication is difficult **:** caught fast **:** ENSNARED, ENMESHED ⟨~ in machinery⟩ ⟨one of the hares was ~, and endeavoring to disengage himself —William Cowper⟩ ⟨~ and even lost in the maze of swamps —Frank Debenham⟩ **c :** INTRICATE, COMPLICATED, CONFUSED ⟨moved in a thicker and more ~ machinery of government —Sacheverell Sitwell⟩ ⟨become ~ with still wider social and political problems —J.B.Conant⟩ **2 :** involved in an embarrassing, troublesome, or compromising situation ⟨~ in an affair with another man's wife⟩ ⟨became ~ in a costly litigation⟩ — **en·tan·gled·ly** *adv* — **en·tan·gled·ness** *n* -ES

en·tan·gle·ment \-gəlmənt\ *n* -S **1 a :** the action or an instance of physically entangling **:** the state of being entangled or snarled ⟨walnut legs . . . placed so far under the table that any ~ with the diners' legs is . . . avoided —*New Yorker*⟩ ⟨such waste often causes ~*s* and the breaking of whole batches of threads —J.J.Sussmuth⟩ **b :** something that entangles physically; *specif* **:** an obstacle consisting of specially constructed barbed-wire fences for impeding the advance of foot troops **c :** something that is closely interwoven or tangled ⟨there stand the trees . . . their leafy ~*s* thickly loaded —F.R.Leavis⟩ **2 a :** the condition or an instance of being deeply involved or closely linked usu. in an embarrassing or compromising way ⟨his boy's ~ with . . . the child of a gypsy mother —Edith Sitwell⟩ ⟨a well-known ~ with shady elements seriously injured his chances of reelection⟩ ⟨mistrust of foreign ~*s*⟩ **b** (1) **:** something that involves or preoccupies **:** COMMITMENT, CARE ⟨lamented that the exigencies and ~*s* of business prevented him from giving exclusive attention to chemical research —C.A.Browne⟩ ⟨to Paris she would return whenever she could free herself from the ~*s* of the village —L.C.Powys⟩ (2) **:** something that confuses, complicates, or ensnares **:** ALLURE, COMPLICATION, COMPLEXITY, CONFUSION ⟨contriving many ~*s* to catch the souls of poor sinners⟩ ⟨a plot full of ~*s*⟩ ⟨I cannot look upon the circumstances of this country, without being persuaded that I discern in them an ~ . . . never met with in the history of any other —William Cowper⟩

en·tan·gler \-g(ə)lə(r)\ *n* -S **:** one that entangles

en·tan·gling \-g(ə)liŋ\ *adj* **:** tending to entangle ⟨~ briers⟩; *esp* **:** tending to compromise, involve, or commit in an undesirable way — often used in the phrase *entangling alliance* ⟨~ alliances with foreign powers⟩ ⟨with a boy of eighteen there was always the danger of some ~ alliance —Hamilton Basso⟩

en·ta·sis \'entəsəs\ *n, pl* **enta·ses** \-ə,sēz\ [Gk, lit., distention, stretching, fr. *enteinein* to stretch tight (fr. *en-* ²en- + *teinein* to stretch) + *-sis* — more at THIN] **:** a slight convexity (as in the shaft of a column); *esp* **:** one that begins at the base of a shaft and continues to the top and that is greatest a little below the middle point ⟨the ~ of the columns at the corner of the peristyle —Vincent Sheean⟩

entd *abbr* entered

en·té en point *also* **enté en pointe** \ˌen·ˌtā,en'pȯint\ *adj* [F] **1** *heraldry* **:** constituting or occupying a point — used of a coat marshaled with two or more others that are conjoined by impalement or quartering ⟨the arms of Spain include León and Castile quartered with those of Granada *enté en point*⟩ **2** *heraldry* **:** including a coat enté en point — used of an escutcheon in which three or more coats are marshaled ⟨the arms of Spain are *enté en point* of the arms of Granada⟩

en·te·lech·i·al \ˌentəˌlekēəl\ *adj* **:** being or relating to an entelechy

en·tel·e·chy \en'teləkē, ən-\ *n* -ES [LL *entelechia*, fr. Gk *entelecheia*, prob. fr. *enteles echein* to be complete (fr. *enteles* — neut. of *entelēs* complete, full — + *echein* to have) + *-ia* -y] **1** *in Aristotle* **a :** the full realization of form-giving cause or energeia as contrasted with mere potential existence **b :** the form that actuates this realization **2 a** *in modern philosophy* **:** something that contains or realizes an end or final cause **b :** a supposititious immanent but immaterial agency held by some vitalists to regulate or direct the vital processes of an organism esp. toward the achievement of maturity — compare ÉLAN VITAL

en·tel·lus \en'teləs, ən-\ *n* -ES [NL, prob. fr. L *Entellus*, a Sicilian hero famous as a pugilist] **:** HANUMAN

en·tel·o·don \en'telə,dän\ *n, cap* [NL, fr. Gk *entelēs* complete, full + NL *-odon*] **:** a genus (the type of the family Entelodontidae) of giant pigs widespread in the Oligocene of Europe — compare DINOHYUS

en·tel·o·dont \-änt\ *n* -S [NL *Entelodontidae*, fr. *Entelodont-*, *Entelodon*, type genus + *-idae*] **:** a member of a family (Entelodontidae) of giant pigs that appeared in the Eocene and reached their highest development in the Oligocene of the northern hemisphere — compare DINOHYUS, ENTELODON

en·temple \ən-, en+\ *vt* [¹*en-* + *temple* (n.)] *archaic* **:** ENSHRINE

entender *vt* [¹*en-* + *tender* (adj.)] *obs* **:** to make tender in feeling

en·tente \(')äⁿ'tänt, (')äⁿ ˌtä(ä)ⁿt\ *n, pl* **ententes** \-änts, -ä(ä)ⁿt(s)\ [F, lit., understanding, fr. OF, intent, effort, understanding, fr. fem. of *entent*, past part. of *entendre* to intend, be attentive, perceive, understand — more at INTEND] **1 :** a written or unwritten international understanding or agreement providing for or marked by a common course of action or policy in foreign affairs but usu. less definite or formally binding than an alliance ⟨it changes the ~ into an alliance, and alliances . . . are not in accordance with our traditions —Edward Grey⟩ **2 :** a coalition of parties to an entente ⟨the three powers formed an extremely powerful ~⟩

entente cor·diale \-ˌkȯrd'yäl, -yȧl\ *n* [F] **:** cordial understanding esp. between two governments in regard to foreign affairs

¹en·ter \'entə(r)\ *vb* **entered; entered; entering** \'entəriŋ, 'en·triŋ\ **enters** [ME *entren*, fr. OF *entrer*, fr. L *intrare* to enter, fr. *intra* on the inside, within; akin to *inter* between — more at INTER-] *vi* **1 a :** to go or come into a material place **:** make a physical entrance or penetration ⟨knock on the door before you ~⟩ ⟨no evil thing approach nor ~ in —John Milton⟩ **b** (1) **:** to come into the mind or feelings ⟨a strange idea ~*ed* into his head⟩ ⟨a spirit of tenderness ~*ed* into his heart⟩ (2) **:** to come into something intangible ⟨a tone of menace ~*ed* into her voice⟩ **c :** to pass or come into some particular state ⟨by the Lord's favor he ~*ed* into a state of grace⟩ ⟨~*ed* into a deep coma⟩ **d :** to come into a group **:** gain admission **:** become a member **:** JOIN ⟨asked at what school he would ~⟩ ⟨a debutante ~*ing* into society⟩ **2 a :** to make a beginning **:** take the first steps **:** ENGAGE, START ⟨~*ed* into business⟩ ⟨~*ing* upon a career⟩ ⟨~*ed* upon a wearisome account of his travels⟩ ⟨~*ed* into negotiations with the enemy⟩ **b :** to begin to consider a subject ⟨he had barely ~*ed* into the matter when the bell rang⟩ ⟨once he had ~*ed* upon a question, he would never stop⟩ **c :** to make an entrance (as in a fugue) **:** BEGIN **3 :** to go in upon lands as a formal act of ownership **:** take possession **4 :** to come upon the stage — often used as a stage direction in the subjunctive ⟨~ Hamlet⟩ ⟨~ four clowns⟩ **5 :** to play a part **:** be a factor **:** have a bearing **:** CONTRIBUTE ⟨all for the best: . . . sentiment won't ~ in —Elizabeth Bowen⟩ ⟨many processes ~ into the making of this product⟩ ⟨much anxious thought ~*ed* into the framing of this document⟩ ⟨factors other than habitat ~ in this varied adaptation —M.J.Herskovits⟩ **6 :** to register or enroll in a competition **:** become a candidate in a competition ⟨two days before the race he decided not to ~⟩ ⟨candidates may ~ for more than one scholarship⟩ ~ *vt* **1 a :** to come or go into **:** pass into the interior of **:** pass within the outer cover or shell of **:** PENETRATE, PIERCE ⟨~ a house⟩ ⟨rivers ~ the sea⟩ **b :** to come into (the mind) **:** occur to ⟨it never ~*ed* his head that he might be wrong⟩ ⟨a new doubt ~*ed* his mind⟩ **c :** to come into (something intangible) ⟨the shadow of passion ~*ed* her voice —Louis Bromfield⟩ ⟨an extraordinarily beautiful girl who never ~*ed* his life —V.H.Brombert⟩ **2 a** (1) **:** to inscribe or make a record of **:** REGISTER ⟨~ the names of qualified voters⟩ ⟨~ a notation in a journal⟩ ⟨~ a book in a catalog⟩ (2) **:** SKETCH, DEPICT ⟨even ~*ed* these four mountains on the map he sent back —Frank Debenham⟩ **b :** to cause to go into or be received into something **:** cause to be admitted **:** ENROLL ⟨~ a boy at a school⟩ ⟨~ a horse in a race⟩ **c :** to put in **:** INSERT ⟨~ a wedge into a log⟩ ⟨she ~*ed* the key in the door —E.F.McGuire⟩ **d** *of a male animal* **:** to copulate with **3 a :** to make a beginning in **:** take up **:** START, BEGIN ⟨the troops ~*ed* battle⟩ ⟨~ the legal profession⟩ **b :** to pass within the limits of (a particular period of time) ⟨we are ~*ing* a new era⟩ **4 a :** to employ for the first time in actual hunting, racing, hawking **:** exercise initially **:** TRAIN; *specif* **:** to break in (a horse) **b** *archaic* **:** to introduce to a subject **:** INITIATE **5 a :** to become a member of **:** JOIN ⟨~ the army⟩ ⟨~ the university⟩ **b** (1) **:** to become an active participant in ⟨~ a war⟩ ⟨~ a discussion⟩ (2) **:** to become a candidate in (a contest or competition) ⟨~ a race⟩ ⟨~ a short-story contest⟩ **6 :** to go into (a subject) **:** EXAMINE, CONSIDER ⟨for the moment I will not ~ the question of how this decision is to be formulated precisely —M.G.White⟩ **7 a :** to become a part of **:** merge with ⟨the hemlock that killed Socrates . . . is significant only because it ~*s* the context of human cultural history —L.A. White⟩ **b :** to have an intuitive sympathy with **:** identify oneself with **:** UNDERSTAND ⟨few Americans can ~ the poem completely —William Power⟩ ⟨it is hard to ~ the feelings of another⟩ **8 :** to make report of (a ship or her cargo) at the customhouse **:** submit a statement of (imported goods) with the original invoices to the proper officer of the customs for estimating the duties — see ENTRY 6 **9 a :** to place in regular form before a law court usu. in writing **:** put upon record in proper form and order ⟨~ a writ⟩ ⟨~ a judgment⟩ **b :** to file or inscribe upon the records of the land office the required particulars concerning (a quantity of public land) in order to secure the right of preemption **c :** to deposit for copyright the title or description of (as a book, picture, map) ⟨~*ed* according to act of congress⟩ **10 :** to go into or upon and take actual possession of (as lands) **11 :** to put on record (a statement of one's position) **:** present formally or informally **:** ADVANCE, INTERJECT ⟨~*ing* a solemn protest against this forcible intrusion⟩ ⟨~*ed* a caution against excessive haste⟩; *specif* **:** to submit (an offer of a price) in competition with others — used chiefly in the phrase *enter a bid* ⟨~ a bid at an auction⟩ **12 a :** to bring into play (a man that is on the bar) in backgammon **b :** to cause (one's own hand or dummy) to win a trick in bridge in order to lead to the next trick

syn PENETRATE, PIERCE, PROBE: ENTER is a general term without definite implications ⟨one *enters* the apartment through a hallway⟩ ⟨thieves *entered* the apartment and ransacked it⟩ but sometimes, esp. when the object is a thing, it may suggest a pushing through a resisting medium ⟨the bullet *entered* his chest⟩ PENETRATE is applicable to entrance or passage through motivated by an impelling force or facilitated by strength, acuteness, or resolution ⟨a fiber that the ordinary needle will not *penetrate*⟩ ⟨*penetrating* the defense in this sector⟩ ⟨the third attack of the Mexicans succeeded in gaining a breach in the walls. The Mexicans now *penetrated* into the interior of the fortress —*Amer. Guide Series: Texas*⟩ ⟨serving our potential enemies, spreading dissension and confusion; they have *penetrated* to high and sensitive places —Vannevar Bush⟩ ⟨a mind capable of making great and *penetrating* analyses of the nature of the human spirit —William Barrett⟩ PIERCE is likely to suggest the entering, running through, or cutting through of a sharp pointed instrument ⟨to *pierce* the skin with a lancet⟩ ⟨a sword blade that *pierced* me through and through —Vachel Lindsay⟩ ⟨able, with the glittering lance of his

paradoxes, to *pierce* many a weak point in the modernist armor —F.B.Millett⟩ PROBE may suggest exploratory or investigating penetration with or as if with a pointed instrument ⟨a dentist *probing* a cavity⟩ ⟨with surgical objectivity . . . *probes* every detail of his early life and education —Stuart MacClintock⟩ ⟨a squadron of Federal men . . . have been *probing* into his financial affairs —H.H.Martin⟩
— **enter into** 1 **:** to inquire into (a subject) **:** EXAMINE, CONSIDER ⟨regrettable that the book does not *enter into* the moral aspect of the issue⟩ 2 **:** to make oneself a party to or in ⟨*entered into* a solemn treaty and covenant⟩ 3 **:** to form a constituent part or element of **:** become a part of ⟨tin *enters into* the composition of pewter⟩ ⟨forbidden . . . to make use of words . . . which *enter into* the names of dead kings —J.G. Frazer⟩ ⟨a combination of brightness, stupidity, and mediocrity probably *enters into* the mental pattern of most children —R.J.Williams⟩ ⟨regarded her with an admiration *into* which awe *entered* —Donn Byrne⟩ 4 a **:** to participate or share in ⟨didn't *enter into* the conversation, but lounged . . . haughtily in his chair —Scott Fitzgerald⟩ ⟨cheerfully *entered into* the tasks of the household⟩ b **:** to be in tune or sympathy with **:** identify oneself with **:** UNDERSTAND ⟨*entered into* the festive spirit of the occasion⟩ ⟨to *enter into* the mood of this subtle poem requires both sensitivity and study⟩ ⟨no one can *enter into* an alien culture short of many years' experience —Stuart Chase⟩ ⟨we need to *enter into* the scene imaginatively and sympathetically —J.D.Peter⟩ — **enter into force :** to come to have binding effect or validity ⟨the treaty *enters into force* next month⟩ — **enter the lists :** to accept a challenge **:** engage in contest ⟨*enter the lists* against the forces of corruption⟩

²**enter** \"\ *n* -s **:** the entrance of a character upon the scene in a play

enter- *or* **entero-** *comb form* [L & Gk; L *entero-*, fr. Gk *enter-*, *entero-*, fr. *enteron* — more at INTER-] 1 **:** intestine ⟨*enteritis*⟩ ⟨*entero*crinin⟩ 2 **:** intestinal and ⟨*entero*hepatic⟩

en·ter·able \ˈentərəbəl\ *adj* **:** capable of being entered ⟨the building is ~ on the street side⟩ **:** suitable or eligible for entry ⟨~ in tomorrow's race⟩ ⟨~ on the books as an allowable charge⟩

en·ter·al \ˈentərəl\ *adj* [*enter-* + *-al*] **:** ENTERIC — **en·ter·al·ly** \-rəlē\ *adv*

en·ter·al·gia \ˌentəˈralj(ē)ə\ *n* -s [NL, fr. *enter-* + *-algia*] **:** pain in the intestines **:** COLIC

en·ter·ec·to·my \ˌentəˈrektəmē\ *n* -ES [ISV *enter-* + *-ectomy*] **:** the surgical removal of a portion of the intestine

entered *past of* ENTER

entered apprentice *n* 1 **:** the first degree of Freemasonry 2 **:** one who has taken the degree of entered apprentice — compare BLUE LODGE

en·ter·er \ˈentərə(r)\ *n* -s 1 **:** one that enters or makes entries 2 **:** DRAWER-IN

en·ter·ic \(ˈ)enˈterik, inˈt-\ *adj* [Gk *enterikos*, fr. *enter-* + *-ikos* -ic] 1 **:** of, relating to, or being a medicinal preparation treated so that it will pass through the stomach unaltered to be disintegrated in the intestines ⟨an ~ pill⟩ **:** INTESTINAL 2 **:** of, or relating to the enteron **:** INTESTINAL

enteric fever *n* **:** typhoid fever or a closely related febrile condition

entering *n* -s [ME *entring* act of entering, fr. gerund of *entren* to enter — more at ENTER] **:** DRAWING-IN

entering port *n* **:** a port cut down to the level of the gun deck (as in old battleships) for convenience in landing or in entering the ship

en·ter·it·i·dis \ˌentəˈridədəs, -ritə-\ *n* -ES [NL, fr. specif. epithet of *Salmonella enteritidis*, fr. *enteritis*] **:** enteritis esp. in young animals that is related to food poisoning in man, is accompanied by diarrhea or scouring, and is caused by the Gaertner bacillus or one of its varieties

en·ter·i·tis \ˌentəˈrīdəs, -ītəs\ *n*, *pl* **enterit·i·des** \-ˈridə-ˌdēz, -ˈritə-\ *or* **enteritises** [NL, fr. *enter-* + *-itis*] 1 **:** inflammation of the intestines, esp. of the human ileum **:** ILEITIS 2 **:** any disease of domestic animals marked by enteritis and diarrhea (as panleukopenia of cats or necrotic enteritis of swine)

enterlude *obs var of* INTERLUDE

en·tero·bacteriaceae \ˌentə(ˌ)rō+\ *n pl* [NL, fr. *enter-* + *Bacteriaceae*] 1 *cap* **:** a large family (order Eubacteriales) of gram-negative straight bacterial rods that ferment glucose with the production of acid or acid and gas and that include the common coliform organisms and other saprophytes as well as a number of serious pathogens of man, lower animals, and plants — see EBERTHELLA, ERWINIA, ESCHERICHIA, SALMONELLA 2 **:** members of the family Enterobacteriaceae

en·tero·bi·a·sis \ˌentə(ˌ)rōˈbīəsəs\ *n*, *pl* **enterobia·ses** \-əˌsēz\ [NL, fr. *Enterobius* + *-iasis*] **:** infestation with or disease caused by pinworms of the genus *Enterobius*, common in children and when the infection is heavy marked by toxemic symptoms with wasting, fatigability, irritability, night sweats, feverishness, and often cough and poor appetite **:** human oxyuriasis

en·te·ro·bi·us \ˌentəˈrōbēəs\ *n*, *cap* [NL, fr. *enter-* + *-bius*] **:** a genus of small nematode worms (family Oxyuridae) including the common pinworm of the human intestine

en·ter·o·cele \ˈentərōˌsēl\ *n* -s [L, fr. Gk *enterokēlē*, fr. *enter-* + *kēlē* tumor, hernia — more at -CELE] **:** a hernia containing a portion of the intestines

en·ter·o·coc·cal \ˌentərōˈkäkəl\ *adj* [NL *enterococcus* + E *-al*] **:** of, relating to, or caused by enterococci

¹**en·ter·o·coc·cus** \ˌentərōˈkäkəs\ [NL, fr. *enter-* + *-coccus*] *syn of* STREPTOCOCCUS

²**enterococcus** \"\ *n*, *pl* **enterococ·ci** \-äˌkī, -äkē, -äkˌsī, -äksē\ **:** STREPTOCOCCUS 2; *esp* **:** a streptococcus (as *Streptococcus faecalis*) normally present in the intestine

en·ter·o·coe·la \ˌentərōˈsēlə\ *n pl*, *cap* [NL, fr. *enter-* + *-coela* (fr. Gk *koilos* hollow) — more at CAVE] *in some classifications* **:** a group comprising all the invertebrate animals (as echinoderms and coelenterates) in which the sole bodily cavity is the digestive cavity — compare COELOMATA, PSEUDOCOELOMATA; ENTEROCOELE

en·ter·o·coele *or* **en·ter·o·coel** \ˈentərōˌsēl\ *n* -s [*enter-* + *-coele*, *-coel*] **:** a coelom that originates by outgrowth from the archenteron (as in the echinoderms) — compare SCHIZOCOEL — **en·ter·o·coe·lic** \ˌ=ˌ=ˈsēlik\ *adj* — **en·ter·o·coe·lous** \-ləs\ *adj*

en·tero·colitis \ˌentə(ˌ)rō+\ *n* [NL, fr. *enter-* + *colitis*] **:** enteritis affecting both the small and large intestine

en·ter·o·cri·nin \ˌentərōˈkrīnən *also* -rōˈkrin- *or* -ˈräkrən-\ *n* -s [*enter-* + endo*crine* + *-in*] **:** an intestinal hormone found in several animals that stimulates the digestive glands of the small intestine

en·ter·o·derm \ˈentərōˌdərm\ *n* -s [*enter-* + *-derm*] **:** the endoderm of the alimentary canal

en·ter·o·gas·trone \ˌentərōˈgaˌstrōn\ *n* -s [*enter-* + *gastr-* + hor*mone*] **:** a hormone obtained from the upper intestinal mucosa that has an inhibitory action on gastric motility and secretion

en·ter·og·e·nous \ˌentəˈräjənəs\ *adj* [ISV *enter-* + *-genous*] **:** produced within the intestine

en·ter·o·gram \ˈentərōˌgram\ *n* -s [*enter-* + *-gram*] **:** a graphic representation (as by a tracing) of the motion of the intestine

en·tero·hepatic \ˌentə(ˌ)rō+\ *adj* [*enter-* + *hepatic*] **:** of or involving the intestine and liver

en·tero·hepatitis \"+\ *n* [NL, fr. *enter-* + *hepatitis*] **:** ¹BLACKHEAD 3

en·tero·kinase \"+\ *n* [ISV *enter-* + *kinase*] **:** an enzyme obtained esp. from the upper intestinal mucosa that activates trypsinogen by converting it to trypsin

en·ter·o·lith \ˈentərōˌlith\ *n* -s [ISV *enter-* + *-lith*] **:** a calculus occurring in the intestine

en·ter·o·lo·bi·um \ˌentərōˈlōbēəm\ *n*, *cap* [NL, fr. *enter-* + Gk *lobos* capsule, pod + NL *-ium*] **:** a small genus of tropical American timber trees (family Leguminosae) with finely dissected compound leaves, globose heads of small flowers with exserted stamens, and spirally coiled pods — see CONACASTE

en·ter·o·mor·pha \-ˈmȯrfə\ *n*, *cap* [NL, fr. *enter-* + *-morpha*] **:** a genus of green algae (family Ulvaceae) having a hollow tubular thallus with a wall one cell in thickness and often growing on the bottoms of ships

en·ter·on \ˈentəˌrän, -ˌrən\ *n* -s [NL, fr. Gk, intestine — more at INTER-] **:** ALIMENTARY CANAL, ALIMENTARY SYSTEM — used esp. of the incompletely differentiated structures of the embryo or fetus

en·tero·nephric \ˌentə(ˌ)rō+\ *adj* [*enter-* + *nephric*] *of an excretory system* **:** discharging into the intestine (as in certain annelid worms)

en·ter·op·neust \ˈentəˌräpˌn(y)üst\ *or* **en·ter·op·neus·tan** \ˌ=ˌ=ˈn(y)üstən\ *n* -s [*enteropneust* fr. NL ¹*Enteropneusta*; *enteropneustan* fr. NL *Enteropneusta* + E *-an*] **:** an animal of the order Enteropneusta

¹**en·ter·op·neus·ta** \ˌ=ˌ=ˈn(y)üstə\ *n pl*, *cap* [NL, fr. *enter-* + *-pneusta*] **:** an order or other division of hemichordate worms consisting of *Balanoglossus* and related genera

²**enteropneusta** \"\ [NL, fr. *enter-* + *-pneusta*] *syn of* HEMICHORDATA

en·ter·op·to·sis \ˌentəˌräpˈtōsəs\ *n*, *pl* **enteropto·ses** \-ōˌsēz\ [NL, fr. *enter-* + *ptosis*] **:** an abnormal sagging or downward displacement of the intestines — **en·ter·op·tot·ic** \ˌ=ˌ=ˌ=ˈtäd·ik\ *adj*

en·ter·or·rha·gia \ˌentərəˈrāj(ē)ə\ *n* -s [NL, fr. *enter-* + *-rrhagia*] **:** bleeding from the intestine **:** intestinal hemorrhage

en·ter·os·to·my \ˌentəˈrästəmē\ *n* -ES [ISV *enter-* + *-stomy*] **:** the surgical formation of an opening into the intestine through the abdominal wall

en·tero·toxemia \ˌentə(ˌ)rō+\ *n* [NL, fr. *enter-* + *toxemia*] **:** a disease attributed to absorption of a toxin from the intestine (as pulpy kidney disease of lambs)

en·tero·toxigenic \"+\ *adj* [*enterotoxin* + *-genic*] **:** producing enterotoxin ⟨an ~ strain of bacteria⟩

en·ter·o·toxin \ˌentərō+\ *n* [*enter-* + *toxin*] **:** a toxic substance produced by microorganisms (as certain staphylococci) that is responsible for the gastrointestinal symptoms of some forms of food poisoning

en·ter·o·zoa \ˌentərəˈzōə\ *n pl*, *usu cap* [NL, fr. *enter-* + *-zoa*] **:** ENTOZOA

en·ter·o·zo·an \ˌ=ˌ=ˌ=ˈzōən\ *adj or n* [NL *enterozoa* + E *-an*] **:** ENTOZOAN

¹**en·ter·prise** *also* **en·ter·prize** *R* ˈentə(r)ˌprīz, *-R* -təp-\ *n* -s [ME, fr. MF *entreprise*, fr. fem. of *entrepris*, past part. of *entreprendre* to undertake, fr. *entre-* inter- (fr. L *inter-*) + *prendre* to take, fr. L *prehendere* to seize, grasp — more at GET] 1 a **:** a plan or design for a venture or undertaking ⟨his friends judged his novel ~ to be impractical and urged him to forget it⟩ b **:** VENTURE, UNDERTAKING, PROJECT; *esp* **:** an undertaking that is difficult, complicated, or has a strong element of risk ⟨indicate the . . . important ~s in which he had been engaged, probably battles, expeditions, or treaties of peace —W.A.Mason⟩ ⟨his new ~, a restaurant on Fifth avenue, met with complete failure⟩ ⟨exploring the English character has long been a favorite ~ of literary men —H.S. Commager⟩ ⟨a military ~ of major scope⟩ c **:** a unit of economic organization or activity (as a factory, a farm, a mine); *esp* **:** a business organization **:** FIRM, COMPANY ⟨an old ~ specializing in scientific textbooks —*Current Biog.*⟩ ⟨proposed to encourage the growth of small independent ~s⟩ d **:** any systematic purposeful activity or type of activity ⟨agriculture is the principal economic ~ among these people⟩ ⟨history, more than any other literary ~, puts the writer in the debt of other people —J.K.Galbraith⟩ ⟨the . . . problem of the nature of philosophy and the philosophical ~ itself —J.E.Smith⟩ 2 **:** readiness to attempt or engage in what requires daring or energy **:** a bold energetic questing spirit **:** independence of thought **:** INITIATIVE, ENERGY ⟨the public rarely shows ~ when in search of entertainment —Tyrone Guthrie⟩ ⟨complained of his lack of ~⟩

²**enterprise** \"\ *vb* -ED/-ING/-S *vt* **:** to venture upon **:** UNDERTAKE, LAUNCH ⟨new churches are being *enterprised* in every area in America —*Time*⟩ ~ *vi*, *archaic* **:** to undertake an enterprise

en·ter·prise·less \-ləs\ *adj* **:** lacking enterprise **:** UNAMBITIOUS

en·ter·pris·er \-zə(r)\ *n* -s **:** one who undertakes an enterprise; *specif* **:** ENTREPRENEUR

enterprising *adj* **:** characterized by a bold daring energetic spirit or by independence or originality of thought **:** prompt or ready to undertake or experiment **:** ENERGETIC ⟨distrusted ~ thinkers who . . . can never be satisfied with the status quo —*Britain Today*⟩ ⟨~ peasants who . . . added to their land by purchase or lease —Hans Nabholz⟩ **:** reflecting or attesting to a daring or energetic spirit ⟨there is no question but that he made a number of ~ journeys —*Geog. Jour.*⟩ — **en·ter·pris·ing·ly** *adv*

enters *pres 3d sing of* ENTER, *pl of* ENTER

¹**en·ter·tain** \ˌentə(r)ˈtān\ *vb* -ED/-ING/-S [ME *entertinen*, fr. MF *entretenir*, fr. *entre-* inter- + *tenir* to hold, fr. (assumed) VL *tenire*, alter. of L *tenēre* to hold — more at THIN] *vt* 1 a *archaic* **:** to keep up **:** cause (as a custom) to be maintained ⟨~ a friendly correspondence with his brother⟩ ⟨wished to ~ peace with all his neighbors⟩ b *obs* **:** to treat in a specified manner c *obs* **:** to give reception to (a person) **:** RECEIVE d *obs* **:** to enter upon **:** take upon oneself **:** engage in 2 **:** to show hospitality to **:** to provide for the needs of (a guest) ⟨~ your in-laws over the weekend⟩ ⟨~ a friend at lunch⟩ — often used with *to* in England ⟨~*ed* to dinner by the entire Bench and Bar —E.M.Lustgarten⟩ 3 a *obs* **:** to maintain or support in one's service ⟨you, sir, I ~ for one of my hundred —Shak.⟩ b *archaic* **:** HIRE, ENGAGE c *obs* **:** to meet in battle 4 a **:** to keep, hold, or maintain in the mind with favor **:** keep in the mind **:** HARBOR, CHERISH ⟨~*s* the friendliest sentiments toward him⟩ ⟨~ hopes of a peaceful settlement⟩ ⟨~*s* no grievance against her⟩ b (1) **:** to receive and take into consideration (as an idea or proposal) ⟨if it had not been for that woman you would never have ~*ed* this teaching scheme at all —Thomas Hardy⟩ ⟨the chairman will ~ nominations⟩ ⟨refused to ~ her plea⟩ (2) **:** TREAT, CONSIDER ⟨~ a subject⟩ ⟨I am not here going to ~ so large a theme as the philosophy of Locke —Thomas De Quincey⟩ 5 **:** to cause the time to pass pleasantly for (someone) **:** AMUSE, DIVERT ⟨fortunately he was able to ~ his nurses as well as provoke them —Virginia D. Dawson & Betty D. Wilson⟩ ⟨~*ed* troops overseas with songs and skits⟩ ~ *vi* **:** to provide entertainment esp. for guests ⟨even the smallest child is accustomed to ~ without self-consciousness —Nora Waln⟩ **syn** see AMUSE

²**entertain** \"\ *n* -s *obs* **:** ENTERTAINMENT

en·ter·tain·er \ˌentə(r)ˈtānə(r)\ *n* -s **:** one that entertains ⟨the rest of the stories are mostly well-written slick-magazine ~s —Taliaferro Boatwright⟩; *specif* **:** one who entertains professionally ⟨sent a troupe of ~s to the fighting front⟩

entertaining *adj* **:** providing entertainment **:** DIVERTING ⟨an ~ and instructive volume⟩ ⟨an ~ speaker⟩ ⟨spent an ~ evening⟩ — **en·ter·tain·ing·ly** *adv* — **en·ter·tain·ing·ness** *n* -ES

en·ter·tain·ment \ˌentə(r)ˈtānmənt\ *n* -s 1 **:** the act of entertaining: as a **:** the act of receiving as a guest **:** hospitable reception ⟨delighted in ~ of friends and relatives⟩ b **:** the act of receiving or considering (as an idea or proposal) ⟨his serious ~ of angelology . . . reveals the complications of a too strictly biblical theology —L.W.Norris⟩ c **:** the act of diverting, amusing, or causing someone's time to pass agreeably **:** AMUSEMENT ⟨engaged a concert pianist for the ~ of her guests⟩ ⟨started a brisk argument for the ~ of the company⟩ 2 a *archaic* **:** the manner or means of providing for the needs of someone (as a guest or lodger) **:** PROVISION ⟨ten pounds is the usual pension in these convents; but nothing can be more wretched than their ~ —Tobias Smollett⟩ b *obs* **:** the condition of being in someone's service **:** EMPLOYMENT c *obs* **:** provision for the support of persons in service **:** PAY 3 **:** something that diverts, amuses, or occupies the attention agreeably ⟨this book is first-rate ~⟩ ⟨provide ~ for his guests, whimsical as well as culinary —O.S.J.Gogarty⟩ ⟨a serious novel as opposed to an ~ —*Times Lit. Supp.*⟩ ⟨the stream of life is the most permanently available of free ~s —Fred Majdalany⟩: as a **:** a social gathering or reception ⟨last night another of these pleasant social ~s was given . . . at her home —D.D.Martin⟩ b **:** a public performance designed to divert or amuse ⟨Negro orchestras are in demand at white ~s —*Amer. Guide Series: Fla.*⟩ ⟨still frequently produced at school or Sunday-school ~s —H.R.Reichard⟩

en·thal·py \ˈenˌthalpē, enˈth-, ənˈth-\ *n* -ES [Gk *enthalpein* to warm in (fr. *en-* ²en- + *thalpein* to heat, warm) + E *-y*] **:** a thermodynamic quantity that is the sum of the internal energy of a body and the product of its volume multiplied by the pressure: $H=U+pV$ — called also *heat content*

en·thrall *also* **en·thral** \ənˈthrȯl, en-\ *vt* **enthralled**; **enthralled**; **enthralling**; **enthralls** *also* **enthrals** [ME *enthrallen*, fr. ¹en- + *thral* thrall (n.) — more at THRALL] 1 **:** to hold in slavery **:** reduce to the condition of a slave ⟨the bars survive the captive they ~ —Lord Byron⟩ 2 **:** to hold spellbound **:** CHARM, CAPTIVATE ⟨his ringing laugh and humorous anecdotes ~*ed* his companions —T.S.Lovering⟩

en·thrall·ing *adj* **:** capable of holding spellbound **:** intensely absorbing or interesting **:** ENGROSSING, THRILLING ⟨it was the most ~ race . . . I've seen all season —G.F.T.Ryall⟩ ⟨this . . . painful little tale of failure and futility is ~ —David Cecil⟩ ⟨music is the most ~ . . . phenomenon in the world —Susanne K. Langer⟩ — **en·thrall·ing·ly** *adv*

en·thrall·ment *also* **en·thral·ment** \-lmənt\ *n* -s **:** the act of enthralling **:** the state of being enthralled ⟨mourned the ~ of his country by a foreign foe⟩ ⟨gazed at her with delight and ~⟩

en·throne \ənˈthrōn, en-\ *vt* [¹*en-* + *throne* (n.)] 1 a **:** to seat on a throne **:** exalt to the seat of royalty or high authority ⟨~ a king⟩; *specif* **:** to install a high ecclesiastic in office b **:** to seat in a place associated with some position of authority or influence ⟨*enthroned* at the end of the table as moderator of the evening —Louis Auchincloss⟩ c **:** to seat on a high object or in a high commanding place ⟨old salts . . . *enthroned* on mackerel barrels —Van Wyck Brooks⟩ ⟨prompters are *enthroned* in the loft —*Amer. Guide Series: Conn.*⟩ 2 **:** to assign supreme virtue or value to **:** EXALT ⟨the frontiersman *enthroned* work as a god and worshiped it —W.P.Webb⟩

en·throne·ment \-mənt\ *n* -s **:** an act or instance of enthroning; *esp* **:** the ceremony of installing a high ecclesiastic in office ⟨the service for the ~ of the archbishop of Canterbury⟩

en·thron·iza·tion \ənˌthrōnəˈzāshən, (ˌ)enˌthrō\|, ˌenthrə\|, \|ˌnīˈz-\ *n* -s **:** ENTHRONEMENT

en·thron·ize \ənˈthrōˌnīz, enˈthrō-, ˈenthrə-\ *vt* -ED/-ING/-S [ME *entronizen*, *intronisen*, fr. MF *entroniser*, fr. LL *enthronizare*, fr. Gk *enthronizein*, fr. *en-* ²en- + *thronos* throne + *-izein* -ize — more at THRONE] **:** ENTHRONE

en·thuse \ənˈth(y)üz, en-\ *vb* -ED/-ING/-S [back-formation fr. *enthusiasm*, *enthusiast*, *enthusiastic*] *vt* 1 **:** to make enthusiastic ⟨~ her with the potential pleasing power of the merchandise at her disposal —*Fashion Accessories*⟩ 2 **:** to express (as an opinion) with enthusiasm ⟨"a sweet little town", he *enthused* —Lawrence Constable⟩ ~ *vi* **:** to grow enthusiastic **:** express enthusiastic sentiments ⟨they are always ready to ~ over arms, the romance of heraldry and the family —L.G.Pine⟩

en·thu·si·asm \-üzēˌazəm *sometimes* -zēəzəm\ *n* -s [Gk *enthousiasmos*, fr. *enthousiazein* to be inspired, fr. *entheos*, *enthous* inspired, fr. *en-* ²en- + *-theos*, *-thous* (fr. *theos* god) — more at THE-] 1 *archaic* **:** inspiration by a god or other superhuman power **:** divine possession or frenzy 2 *archaic* **:** a state of impassioned emotion **:** exaltation of feelings **:** TRANSPORT, ECSTASY; *esp* **:** excessive or extravagant display of religious emotion ⟨conservative churchmen frowned on the ~ and mystical tendency of his sermons⟩ 3 a **:** strong excitement of feeling on behalf of a cause or a subject **:** ardent zeal or interest **:** FERVOR ⟨supported the party's candidate with ~⟩ ⟨the play aroused his ~⟩ b **:** something that inspires or is pursued or regarded with ardent zeal or fervor ⟨his ~ is sailing⟩ ⟨the great literary realists were his ~s⟩ **syn** see PASSION

en·thu·si·ast \-zēˌast, -zēəst, -zēˌaa(ə)st\ *n* -s [Gk *enthousiastēs*, fr. *enthousiazein*] 1 **:** a person who is or believes himself to be inspired or possessed by a divine power or spirit ⟨a society of ~s dominated by the conviction that they were spirit-possessed —G.W.H.Lampe⟩ 2 **:** a person who is visionary, extravagant, or excessively zealous in his religious views or emotions **:** FANATIC ⟨took to task mystics and ~s whose faith transcended the bounds of reasonableness —Andrew Brown⟩ 3 a **:** a person who is ardently attached to a cause, object, or pursuit ⟨a former mountain-climbing ~ —*Current Biog.*⟩ ⟨an impassioned ~ for both literature and painting —*Times Lit. Supp.*⟩ b **:** a person of an ardent enthusiastic cast of mind **:** one who tends to give himself completely to whatever engages his interest ⟨we are a nation of ~s —Oden Meeker⟩

syn FANATIC, ZEALOT, BIGOT: ENTHUSIAST in early use may designate one claiming inspiration or showing such signs as rapture, madness, or marked emotionalism; now it is likely to indicate a person showing keen, ardent, or devoted interest ⟨was not in the least an *enthusiast*, which literally means "possessed by God". He was a casuist and a theorist —Francis Hackett⟩ ⟨he had been in his youth an *enthusiast* for liberty, and had hailed the dawn of the French Revolution —T.L. Peacock⟩ ⟨a chess *enthusiast*⟩ ⟨a sailing *enthusiast*⟩ FANATIC is often used hyperbolically for ENTHUSIAST ⟨a baseball *fanatic*⟩ It may suggest a mad or irrational devotion and concentration, with resolute determination and uncompromising fixity ⟨a virtuous *fanatic*, regarding all ways as wrong but his own, and thinking all men who would not walk as he prescribed wicked as well as mistaken —J.A.Froude⟩ ⟨a utopia about which he was utterly dogmatic—which he explained to me with *fanatic* zeal—as dogmatic, as undeviating as the most rabid Communist —Carleton Beals⟩ ZEALOT applies to one showing ardent devotion to and vehement activity for protecting or furthering a cause ⟨the reopening of village churches that had been closed by the action of local *zealots* —A.R.Williams⟩ BIGOT applies to one blindly and obstinately devoted to his own creed or belief with stern, stiff-necked, dogged disdain, contempt, and intolerance of others ⟨not that the modern *bigot* is any more tolerant or less cruel than her ancestors —G.B.Shaw⟩

¹**en·thu·si·as·tic** \ənˌth(y)üzēˈastik, (ˌ)en-, -ēˈaas-, -tēk\ *adj* [Gk *enthousiastikos*, fr. (assumed) Gk *enthousiastos* (verbal of Gk *enthousiazein*) + Gk *-ikos* -ic] 1 **:** relating to enthusiasm (senses 1, 2) ⟨~ ministers and their hearers preferred extempore or inspired preaching —Douglas Bush⟩ 2 **:** filled with, characterized by, or manifesting enthusiasm **:** ZEALOUS, ARDENT ⟨the chair was received with ~ praise⟩ ⟨an ~ supporter of the president⟩ ⟨an ~ golfer and fisherman⟩ 3 **:** having an ardent, receptive, responsive temperament **:** tending to give oneself wholly to whatever engages one's interest or liking ⟨one of the most generous and ~ men I ever met —O.S.J.Gogarty⟩

²**enthusiastic** *n* -s *archaic* **:** ENTHUSIAST, ZEALOT

en·thu·si·as·ti·cal \-stəkəl, -stēk-\ *adj*, *archaic var of* ENTHUSIASTIC

en·thu·si·as·ti·cal·ly \-stək(ə)lē, -stēk-, -li\ *adv* **:** in an enthusiastic manner

en·thy·me·mat·ic \ˌen(t)thə(ˌ)mēˈmad·ik\ *adj* [L *enthymemat-*, *enthymema* + E *-ic*] **:** relating to or constituting an enthymeme ⟨the ~ form of the conventional syllogism —J.T. Clark⟩

en·thy·meme \ˈen(t)thəˌmēm\ *n* -s [L *enthymema*, fr. Gk *enthymēma*, fr. *enthymeisthai* to keep in mind, consider, fr. *en-* ²en- + *thymos* mind] 1 **:** an argument or truncated syllogism in which one of the propositions, usu. a premise, is understood but not stated (as *we are dependent; therefore we should be humble*) 2 *Aristotelianism* **:** a rhetorical syllogism which is probable and persuasive but may not be valid

entia *pl of* ENS

en·tice \ənˈtīs, en-\ *vt* -ED/-ING/-S [ME *enticen*, fr. OF *enticier*, fr. (assumed) VL *intitiare*, fr. L *in-* ²in- + *titio* firebrand] 1 *obs* **:** INCITE, INSTIGATE 2 a **:** to draw on by arousing hope or desire **:** ALLURE, ATTRACT ⟨with her . . . high-mindedness she *enticed* him into a sphere of spirituality that was not his native realm —E.L.Stahl⟩ ⟨a vivid dark face that ~s attention —Claudia Cassidy⟩ b **:** to draw into evil ways **:** lead astray **:** TEMPT ⟨it was . . . your uncle . . . who *enticed* me, saying that you had good horses stored up —Pearl Buck⟩ **syn** see LURE

en·tice·ment \-mənt\ *n* -s [ME, fr. OF, fr. *enticier* + *-ment*] 1 *obs* **:** INCITEMENT 2 **:** the act of enticing 3 **:** something that entices **:** a means or method of enticing

enticing *adj* **:** ALLURING, ATTRACTIVE, BEGUILING ⟨they cannot say no to an ~ advertisement or an excited review —Howard Taubman⟩ ⟨~ opportunities for Christian missionary activity —J.W.Pratt⟩ — **en·tic·ing·ly** *adv* — **en·tic·ing·ness** *n* -ES

en·ti·fi·ca·tion \ˌentəfəˈkāshən\ *n* -s **:** the process of entifying

en·ti·fy \ˈentəˌfī\ *vt* -ED/-ING/-ES [ML *ent-*, *ens* + E *-i-* + *-fy* — more at ENS] **:** REIFY, HYPOSTATIZE

¹en·tire \ən'tī(ə)r, (ˈ)en¦t-, -īə *sometimes* 'in,t-\ *adj* [ME *entere, entier, entire,* fr. MF *entier, entir,* fr. L *integer,* fr. ³in- + -*teger* (fr. *tangere* to touch) — more at TANGENT] **1 :** with no element or part excepted : WHOLE, COMPLETE ⟨made careful notes on the ~ proceeding⟩ ⟨remained alone the ~ day⟩ ⟨the ~ mechanism of the ship was intact⟩ **2 a :** complete in degree : UNDIMINISHED, UNIMPAIRED, TOTAL ⟨the ~ control of the enterprise rests with the mayor⟩ ⟨his ~ ignorance of the subject⟩ ⟨his ~ devotion to his family⟩ ⟨he was an ~ stranger to her⟩ ⟨~ freedom of choice⟩ **b** *obs* **:** sincerely and unreservedly devoted : FAMILIAR, INTIMATE **3 a :** consisting of one piece : CONTINUOUS, UNDIVIDED ⟨the diamond was ~ and free from flaws⟩ ⟨here the river is ~, but later it divides into two branches⟩ **b :** wholly of one kind : without mixture or alloy : PURE, HOMOGENEOUS ⟨the book is short, ~ in mood, and gives the impression of a single afternoon's reverie —*Times Lit. Supp.*⟩ ⟨their primitive speech has come down ~, without admixture of any kind⟩ **c** *archaic* **:** having unimpaired strength or vigor : SOUND, HEALTHY **d** (1) **:** with no part lacking : INTACT ⟨conveniently passed on his estates to his heir ~⟩ ⟨strove to keep the collection ~ and even to augment it⟩ (2) *heraldry* **:** without difference or cadency mark : UNDIFFERENCED (3) *heraldry* **:** extending to the edges of the field : THROUGHOUT **4** *obs* **:** morally unblemished : BLAMELESS ⟨so ~ are all your deeds and you —John Donne⟩ **5** *of a male animal* **:** not castrated **6 :** having the margin continuous or not broken by divisions, teeth, or serrations ⟨an ~ leaf⟩ **syn** see WHOLE

²entire \"\ *adv* **:** in entirety : COMPLETELY ⟨was to shatter our little universe ~ —Deneys Reitz⟩

³entire \"\ *n* -s **1** *archaic* **:** the whole : ENTIRETY **2 :** an uncastrated male domestic animal; *esp* **:** an uncastrated male horse **3** *brewing, Brit* **:** PORTER **4 a :** a whole cover bearing a nonadhesive postage stamp **b :** any cover — **on entire :** on cover

en·tire·ly *adv* [ME *enterely, entierly, entirely,* fr. *entere, entier, entire* + -*ly*] **1** *obs* **:** EARNESTLY, SINCERELY **2 :** WHOLLY, COMPLETELY, FULLY ⟨agreed with me ~⟩ ⟨an ~ noble and disinterested person⟩ ⟨lives ~ in the past⟩ ⟨you are ~ welcome⟩ **3 :** EXCLUSIVELY, SOLELY ⟨it is his fault ~⟩

en·tire·ness \ˌ=ˈ=nəs\ *n* -ES [ME *enternesse, entiernesse,* fr. *entere, entier* entire + -*nesse* -ness] **1 :** the quality or state of being entire : COMPLETENESS ⟨an individual marked by the ~ and passion of his commitment to his cause⟩ **2** *obs* **:** spiritual wholeness or oneness : UNITY, INTIMACY

entire sanctification *n* **:** the religious doctrine of perfect holiness in which there is no sin

en·tire·ty \ən'tīrəd·ē, en-, ¦t¦, ¦i *also* -ī(ə)r¦ *or* -īə¦\ *n* -ES [ME *enterte,* fr. MF *entiereté,* fr. L *integritat-, integritas,* fr. *integr-, integer* + -*itat-, -itas* -ity] **1 :** the state of being entire or complete ⟨his grasp of the singular ~ of medieval civilization —Henry Adams⟩ ⟨his fortunate ~ which made woman as a complement unnecessary to him —Audrey Barker⟩ **2 :** SUM TOTAL, WHOLE ⟨its compelling theme and skillful development are not the ~ of this extraordinary play⟩ — **in its entirety :** as a whole ⟨view the problem *in its entirety*⟩

entirety of contract : the indivisibility of a contract — used esp. of a judicial doctrine that if a holder of a fire-insurance policy has violated the terms of his policy so as to render it void as to any of the property thereunder insured it will be void as to all

entire wheat flour *n* **:** WHOLE WHEAT FLOUR

en·ti·ta·tive \'entə,tād·iv, -təl\ *adj* [NL *entitativus,* fr. ML *entitat-, entitas* entity + L -*ivus* -ive — more at ENTITY] **1 :** considered as mere entity abstracted from all circumstances or relations **2 :** being an entity : having real existence — **en·ti·ta·tive·ly** *adv*

en·title \ən'tīd·ᵊl, en-, -īt·ᵊl\ *vt* **entitled; entitled; entitling** \-īd·ᵊliŋ, -īt(ᵊ)liŋ\ **entitles** [ME *entitlen, entitulen,* fr. MF *entitler, entituler,* fr. LL *intitulare,* fr. L *in-* ²in- + *titulus* title] **1 :** to give a title to : affix a name or designation to ⟨his discussion . . . was contained in a sermon *entitled* Popular Government by Divine Right —S.W.Chapman⟩ **2 :** to give a right or legal title to : qualify (one) for something : furnish with proper grounds for seeking or claiming something ⟨his age ~s him to a pension⟩ ⟨you are *entitled* to your opinion⟩ ⟨the work ~s him to a place among the great novelists⟩ **3** *obs* **a :** to regard or represent as holding title, right, or responsibility **b :** ASSIGN, IMPUTE, ASCRIBE

en·ti·tle·ment \-ᵊlmənt\ *n* -s **1 a :** the act of entitling **b :** NAME, DESIGNATION **2 a :** the condition of being entitled : RIGHT; *specif* **:** the right to benefits under state unemployment-compensation laws or federal old-age and survivors insurance **b :** an allowance of money due to someone ⟨~s of local school districts came to $30 million —E.J.McGrath⟩

en·ti·ty \'entəd·ē, -ətē, -i\ *n* -ES [ML *entitas,* fr. L *ent-, ens* (irreg. pres. part. of *esse* to be) + -*itat-, -itas* -ity — more at IS] **1 a :** BEING, EXISTENCE; *esp* **:** independent, separate, or self-contained existence ⟨seeking to preserve their ~ and individuality⟩ ⟨successfully maintain their tribal ~⟩ ⟨the policy of the government of the U.S. is to seek . . . to preserve Chinese territorial and administrative ~ —G.F.Kennan⟩ **b** (1) **:** the existence of something as contrasted with its attributes or properties (2) **:** the essence, fundamental nature, or real being of something ⟨for some philosophers, actual *entities* are the ultimate facts of reality⟩ **2 :** something that has objective or physical reality and distinctness of being and character : something that has independent or separate existence : something that has a unitary and self-contained character ⟨whether the common cold is an ~ has been debated —*Yr. Bk. of Med.*⟩ ⟨my thoughts were chiefly occupied with the idea of the train, that luxurious complete ~ —Arnold Bennett⟩ ⟨the individual churches are considered independent and autonomous *entities* —*Current Biog.*⟩ ⟨sees Germany as a unified state, an ~ rather than a regional confederation —*N.Y.Times*⟩ **3 :** an abstraction, ideal conception, object of thought, or transcendental object : SUBSISTENT ⟨such *entities* as love, reason, and beauty⟩ ⟨such *entities* as numbers, particularized relations, and chimeras are classified as subsistent but not existent —R.J.Butler⟩

ento- — see ENT-

en·to·blast \'entə,blast\ *n* -s [*ent-* + -*blast*] **1 :** HYPOBLAST **2 :** a blastomere producing endoderm — **en·to·blas·tic** \¦=ˌ=¦blastik\ *adj*

en·to·bronchium \¦en(,)tō+\ *n, pl* **entobronchia** [NL, fr. *ent-* + *bronchium*] **:** one of the ventral branches of the main bronchi in the lungs of a bird

en·to·coele *or* **en·to·coel** \'entə,sēl\ *n* -s [*ent-* + -*coele, -coel*] **:** ENDOCOELE — **en·to·coe·lic** \¦=ˌ=¦sēlik\ *adj*

en·to·commensal \¦en(,)tō+\ *n* [*ent-* + *commensal*] **:** ENDOCOMMENSAL

en·to·condyle \"+\ *n* [*ent-* + *condyle*] **:** the medial condyle of a bone on the side next the body

en·to·cone \'entə,kōn\ *n* [*ent-* + *cone*] **:** the posterointernal cusp of the talon of an upper molar tooth

en·to·co·nid \ˌ=ˌ='kōnəd\ *n* -s [*ent-* + *con-* + -*id*] **:** the posterointernal cusp of the talon of a lower molar tooth

en·to·cornea \¦en(,)tō+\ *n* [NL, fr. *ent-* + *cornea*] **:** DESCEMET'S MEMBRANE

en·to·cyth·ere \,entō'sithə(,)rē\ *n, cap* [NL, fr. *ent-* + *Cythere* genus of crustaceans, fr. *Cythere,* epithet of Aphrodite, fr. L, fr. Gk *Kytherē,* fr. *Kythēra* (Cythera), island in the Aegean] **:** a genus of parasitic ostracods found in the gill cavities of various No. American crayfishes

en·to·derm \'entə,dərm\ *n* [*ent-* + -*derm*] **:** ENDODERM

en·to·der·mal \¦=ˌ=¦dərməl\ *or* **en·to·der·mic** \-mik\ *adj* **:** ENDODERMAL

en·to·gastric \¦en(,)tō+\ *adj* [ISV *ent-* + *gastric*] **:** relating to the interior of the stomach

en·tog·na·thous \(ˈ)en¦tägnəthəs\ *adj* [*ent-* + -*gnathous*] *of an insect* **:** having the mouthparts sunk below the surface of the head — compare ECTOGNATHOUS

en·to·hy·al \¦entō¦hīəl\ *adj* [*ent-* + Gk *hyalos* transparent stone, glass] **:** BASIBRANCHIAL

en·toil \ən, en +\ *vt* [¹*en-* + *toil* (n.)] **:** ENSNARE, ENTRAP ⟨a last desperate attempt to ~ his love —Anne Green⟩ ⟨~*ed* by the . . . least desirable human emotions —Llewelyn Powys⟩

en·to·le·ter \'entə,lēd·ə(r)\ *n* -s [fr. *Entoleter,* a trademark] **:** a machine for disinfestation in flour processing in which insect eggs remaining in sifted flour are destroyed on impact as the flour is thrown against the lugs and case of a rotor revolving at a high rate of speed

en·to·lo·ma \,entə'lōmə\ *n, cap* [NL, fr. *ent-* + Gk *lōma* fringe] **:** a genus of pink-spored agarics lacking both volva and annulus, having the gills notched or separating from the fleshy stem, and including some (as *E. lividum*) that are distinctly poisonous

entom- *or* **entomo-** *comb form* [F, fr. Gk *entomon* — more at ENTOMOLOGY] **:** insect ⟨*entomo*phagous⟩ ⟨*entomo*stracan⟩

en·tomb \ən'tüm, en-\ *vt* [ME *entoumben,* fr. MF *entomber,* fr. *en-* ¹en- + *tombe* tomb — more at TOMB] **1 :** to deposit in a tomb : BURY, INTER, INHUME ⟨sixty men were ~*ed* by the mine explosion⟩ **2 :** to serve as a tomb for ⟨a rocky hillside ~s the fallen hero⟩ ⟨the sea ~s the lost schooner and her crew⟩

en·tomb·ment \-ümmənt\ *n* -s **1 :** the act or process of entombing : BURIAL ⟨~ services will be held on Friday⟩ **2 :** the condition of being entombed ⟨the shell, though . . . of chitin, is usually modified by its long ~ —W.E.Swinton⟩

en·to·mere \'entə,mi(ə)r\ *n* -s [*ent-* + -*mere*] **:** ENDOMERE — **en·to·mer·ic** \¦=ˌ=¦merik, -mir-\ *adj*

en·to·mesoderm \¦en(,)tō+\ *n* [*ent-* + *mesoderm*] **:** MESENDODERM

en·tom·ic \(ˈ)en¦tämik\ *adj* [*entom-* + -*ic*] **:** relating to insects

en·to·mi·on \en'tōmē,än, -ēən\ *n, pl* **ento·mia** \-ēə\ [NL, fr. Gk *entomē* notch (fr. fem. of *entomos,* verbal of *entemnein* to cut in, cut up) + -*ion* (dim. suffix) — more at ENTOMOLOGY] **:** the tip of the thickened angular part of the parietal bone that articulates with the mastoid portion of the temporal bone — see CRANIOMETRY illustration

entomo- — see ENTOM-

en·to·mo·cecidium \¦entə(,)mō+\ *n* [NL, fr. *entom-* + *cecidium*] **:** a gall caused by an insect

en·to·mo·fauna \"+\ *n* [NL, fr. *entom-* + *fauna*] **:** a fauna of insects : the insects of an environment or region

en·to·mog·e·nous \¦entə¦mäjənəs\ *adj* [*entom-* + -*genous*] **:** growing on or in the bodies of insects ⟨~ fungi⟩

en·to·mo·log·i·cal \¦entəmə¦läjəkəl, -jēk-\ *also* **en·to·mo·log·ic** \-jik,-jēk\ *adj* [F *entomologique,* fr. *entomologie* + -*ique* -ic, -ical] **:** of or relating to entomology — **en·to·mo·log·i·cal·ly** \-jək(ə)lē, -jēk-, -li\ *adv*

en·to·mol·o·gist \,entə'mäləjəst\ *n* -s [F *entomologiste,* fr. *entomologie* + -*iste* -ist] **:** one specializing in entomology : a student of insects

en·to·mol·o·gize \-,jīz\ *vi* -ED/-ING/-S **:** to study entomology : collect insects

en·to·mol·o·gy \-jē, -ji\ *n* -ES [F *entomologie,* fr. Gk *entomon* insect (fr. neut. of *entomos* cut up, cut in, fr. *entemnein* to cut in, cut up, fr. *en-* ²en- + *temnein* to cut) + F -*logie* -logy — more at TOME] **1 :** zoology that deals with insects **2 :** a treatise on insects

en·to·moph·a·gous \¦entə¦mäfəgəs\ *adj* [*entom-* + -*phagous*] **:** feeding on insects

en·to·moph·i·lous \-fələs\ *adj* [*entom-* + -*philous*] **:** normally pollinated by insects — compare ANEMOPHILOUS — **en·to·moph·i·ly** \-lē\ *n* -ES

en·to·moph·tho·ra \ˌ=ˌ='mäfthərə\ *n, cap* [NL, fr. *entom-* + -*phthora*] **:** a genus (the type of the family Entomophthoraceae) comprising fungi that are parasitic on insects

en·to·moph·tho·ra·ce·ae \ˌ=ˌ=ˌ=¦rāsē,ē\ *n pl, cap* [NL, fr. *Entomophthora,* type genus + -*aceae*] **:** a family of mostly parasitic lower fungi (order Entomophthorales) that typically develop in the bodies of insects, have a reduced mycelium which tends to break up into hyphal bodies, reproduce asexually by usu. plurinucleate conidia and in a few instances sexually with the formation of zygospores, and commonly also produce thick-walled chlamydospores under unfavorable conditions — see ENTOMOPHTHORA

en·to·moph·tho·ra·ceous \¦=ˌ=¦=¦rāshəs\ *adj* [NL *Entomophthoraceae* + E -*ous*] **:** of or relating to the genus *Entomophthora* or family Entomophthoraceae

en·to·moph·tho·ra·les \-ā(,)lēz\ *n pl, cap* [NL, fr. *Entomophthora* + -*ales*] **:** an order of phycomycetous fungi (subclass Zygomycetes) coextensive with the family Entomophthoraceae

en·to·moph·tho·rous \-thərəs\ *adj* [NL *Entomophthora* + E -*ous*] **:** relating to or caused by a fungus of the order Entomophthorales

en·to·mo·spo·ri·um \,entə(,)mō'spōrēəm\ *n, cap* [NL, fr. *entom-* + -*sporium*] **:** a form genus of imperfect fungi (family Melanconiaceae) having 4-celled spores with slender appendages, thus somewhat resembling insects

en·to·mos·tra·ca \,entə'mästrəkə\ *n pl, cap* [NL, fr. *entom-* + -*ostraca* (fr. Gk *ostrakon* earthen vessel, potsherd, shell)] *in some classifications* **:** a subclass of Crustacea comprising the Branchiopoda, Ostracoda, Copepoda, and Cirripedia, groups regarded by most modern systematists as too diverse for inclusion in a single subclass, the name then being used as a term of convenience without taxonomic implications — **en·to·mos·tra·can** \¦=ˌ=¦=kən\ *adj or n* — **en·to·mos·tra·cous** \-kəs\ *adj*

en·to·parasite \¦en(,)tō+\ *n* [*ent-* + *parasite*] **:** ENDOPARASITE

en·top·ic \(ˈ)en¦täpik\ *adj* [ISV *entop-* (fr. Gk *entopos* in a place, fr. *en-* ²en- + *topos* place) + -*ic*] *anat* **:** occurring in the usual place — compare ECTOPIC

en·to·plasm \'entə,plazəm\ *n* [ISV *ent-* + -*plasm*] **:** ENDOPLASM — **en·to·plas·tic** \¦=ˌ=¦plastik\ *adj*

en·to·plastral \¦entō+\ *adj* [*entoplastron* + -*al*] **:** of or relating to an entoplastron

en·to·plastron \"+\ *n, pl* **entoplastra** [*ent-* + *plastron*] **:** a median bony plate of the anterior part of the plastron of turtles that is considered homologous with the interclavicle of other reptiles

¹en·to·proct \'entə,präkt\ *adj* [NL *Entoprocta*] **:** of or relating to the Entoprocta

²entoproct \"\ *n* -s **:** an animal of the phylum Entoprocta

en·to·proc·ta \,entə'präktə\ *n pl, cap* [NL, fr. *ent-* + -*procta*] **:** a phylum of pseudocoelomate animals resembling the Bryozoa but lacking a true coelom and having the anus adjacent to the mouth — **en·to·proc·tous** \¦=ˌ=¦präktəs\ *adj*

ent·op·tic \(ˈ)ent·+\ *adj* [ISV *ent-* + *optic*] **:** lying or originating within the eyeball — used esp. of visual sensations due to the shadows of retinal blood vessels or of opaque particles in the vitreous humor falling upon the retina

en·to·retina \¦en(,)tō+\ *n* [NL, fr. *ent-* + *retina*] **:** the internal or neural portion of the retina

en·to·sarc \'entə,särk\ *n* -s [*ent-* + -*sarc*] **:** ENDOSARC

en·to·sclerite \¦en(,)tō+\ *n* [*ent-* + *sclerite*] **:** ENDOSCLERITE

en·to·sphe·nal \¦entō¦sfēnᵊl\ *adj* [*ent-* + *sphen-* + -*al*] **:** BASISPHENOID

en·to·sternal \¦en(,)tō+\ *adj* [NL *entosternum* + E -*al*] **:** relating to the entosternum

en·to·sternite \"+\ *n* [NL *entosternum* + E -*ite*] **:** a cartilaginous structure giving attachment to muscles in the cephalothorax of various arachnids and of limuli

en·to·sternum \"+\ *n, pl* **entosterna** [NL, fr. *ent-* + *sternum*] **:** an internal process or system of processes of the sternum of an insect or other arthropod

en·to·thorax \"+\ *n* [NL, fr. *ent-* + *thorax*] **:** ENDOTHORAX

ent·otic \(ˈ)ent·+\ *adj* [*ent-* + -*otic* (of the ear)] **:** of or relating to the interior of the ear

en·to·trophi \¦entə+\ *n pl, cap* [NL, fr. *ent-* + *trophi*] **:** an order of primitively wingless, eyeless, unpigmented insects that are related to the Symphyla and Thysanura, that have the mouthparts largely concealed within the head and the abdomen ending in a pair of filamentous or forceps-shaped cerci, and that live in the soil

en·tou·rage \¦äntə¦räzh, ¦äⁿ-(,)tü¦-, ¦äⁿ-(,)tü¦-, -räzh\ *n* -s [F, fr. MF, fr. *entourer* to surround (fr. *entour* around, fr. *en* in — fr. L *in* — + *tour* turn, circuit) + -*age* — more at IN, TURN] **1 :** one's attendants ⟨each matador's ~ is getting things ready —Claudia Cassidy⟩ ⟨the bridesmaid's ~⟩ or associates ⟨talks over national and international problems . . . with members of his ~ —*New Yorker*⟩ **2 :** the surroundings of a building (as terraces, steps, or planting) ⟨landscape planting played an important part in the ~ of the attractive clubhouse⟩

en tour·nant \¦äⁿ,tür¦näⁿ\ *adv* [F] *ballet* **:** while turning — used of the body or of movement of the leg inward or outward

¹en-tout-cas \¦äⁿ,tü'kä\ *n* -ES [F, lit., in any case] **:** a combination parasol and umbrella

²en-tout-cas \"\ *adj, of a tennis court* **:** having a composition surface that dries quickly (as after a rain)

en·to·zoa \,entə'zōə\ *n pl, often cap* [NL, fr. *ent-* + -*zoa*] **:** internal animal parasites; *esp* **:** the intestinal worms — often used as if a taxon though not a natural group — **en·to·zo·an** \¦=ˌ=¦zōən\ *adj or n*

en·to·zo·ic \-ōik\ *or* **en·to·zo·al** \-ōəl\ *adj* [*entozoic* fr. *ent-* + -*zoic*; *entozoal* fr. *ent-* + *zo-* + -*al*] **:** living within an animal **:** ENTOZOAN

en·to·zo·on \,=ˌ='zō,än\ *sing of* ENTOZOA

en·tr'acte \'än,trakt, 'äⁿ-, -räkt, -råkt, ˌ='=\ *n* -s [F, fr. *entre-* inter- (fr. L *inter-*) + *acte* act] **1 :** the interval between two acts of a play **2 :** a dance, piece of music, or interlude performed between two acts of a play

en·tra·da \ən'trädə, en-\ *n* -s [Sp, lit., entry, entrance, fr. fem. of *entrado* (past part. of *entrar* to enter), fr. L *intratus,* past part. of *intrare* to enter — more at ENTER] **:** an expedition or journey into unexplored territory ⟨before beginning the long ~, the trappers killed three deer —R.G.Cleland⟩; *esp* **:** a Spanish exploring or conquering expedition in America ⟨through the many ~s and colonization attempts, to the final conquest after the great Maya revolt —*Science*⟩ ⟨nothing was left except the deeply engraved routes of their remarkable ~s —Frank Waters⟩

en·trail \'en·trəl, -rāl\ *n* -s [ME *entraille,* fr. MF, fr. ML *intralia,* alter. of L *interanea,* pl. of *interaneum* intestine, fr. neut. of *interaneus* interior, inner, fr. *inter* between + -*aneus* (as in *extraneus* external) — more at INTER-] **1** *archaic* **:** an internal part of an animal body **2 entrails** *pl* **:** BOWELS, GUTS, VISCERA **3 entrails** *pl* **:** the interior or internal parts of something ⟨hairy ~s of the sofa —Berton Roueché⟩ ⟨whole mountains had their ~s torn out —Wyn Roberts⟩

¹en·train \ən'trān, en-\ *vt* [MF *entrainer,* fr. *en-* ¹en- + *trainer* to draw, drag — more at TRAIN] **1 a :** to draw away with or after oneself ⟨the tribes they had ~*ed* with themselves on their long migrations to the West —K.H.Menges⟩ **b :** to bring on as a result : result in ⟨change embodied in . . . inventions . . . ~s change in the ways of applying human effort —G.B.Hurff⟩ ⟨~*ed* only my own ruin, my own bankruptcy —Henry Miller⟩ **2 :** to carry along or over esp. mechanically (as fine drops of liquid in vapors during distillation or evaporation) **3 :** to collect and transport (a substance) by the flow of a fluid moving at high velocity ⟨air is ~*ed* by a stream of water in a jet pump⟩ **4 :** to incorporate (air in the form of bubbles) into concrete (as for making resistant to the action of frost or to the effects of chemicals used for the removal of ice and snow)

²entrain \"\ *vb* [¹*en-* + *train* (n.)] *vt* **:** to put aboard a railroad train ⟨took the mail to the station to be ~*ed*⟩ ~ *vi* **:** to board a railroad train ⟨immediately after the game the team ~*ed* for New York⟩

en·train·er \-ānə(r)\ *n* [¹*entrain* + -*er*] **:** one that entrains; *specif* **:** a liquid added as a third component to liquid mixtures for aiding their separation by fractional distillation (as by the formation of an azeotrope)

en·train·ment \-ānmənt\ *n* -s **:** the act or process of entraining; *specif* **:** the process of carrying along or over (as in distillation or evaporation)

en·trammel \ən-, en-+\ *vt* [¹*en-* + *trammel* (net)] **:** to entangle or hamper : FETTER ⟨allowed himself to become ~*ed* by convention and society —R.S.Hillyer⟩ ⟨the eternal melancholy of the ~*ed* Irish soul —Liam O'Flaherty⟩

¹en·trance \'en·trən(t)s\ *n* -s [ME *entraunce,* fr. MF *entrance,* fr. *entrer* to enter + -*ance* — more at ENTER] **1 a :** the act or an instance of physical entering : INGRESS ⟨looked up at her ~ into the room⟩ ⟨the ~ of the army into the city⟩ ⟨made an ~ through the window⟩ ⟨the ~ of air and sunshine is desirable⟩ **b :** the means or place for physical entering (as a door, gate, or passage) ⟨all ~s to the city are guarded by armed men⟩ ⟨ships threaded their way down this narrow ~ into the bay⟩ **c :** a particular mode or manner of entering ⟨so many . . . were trying to copy that ~ —Barnaby Conrad⟩ ⟨though he had given no thought to an ~, he could not have perfected a better one —Hamilton Basso⟩ **2 a :** the act or fact of entering (as upon an office or course of action) ⟨made his ~ into office one month after the election⟩ ⟨the ~ of new firms into a highly competitive field⟩ ⟨marked the nation's ~ into the role of a great power⟩ ⟨a country's ~ into war⟩ ⟨~ into college was a great event in his life⟩ **b :** a means of entering (as upon a condition or pursuit) ⟨schools of nursing are the principal ~ to the profession⟩ ⟨books were for the child the ~ to a new and kindlier world⟩ **3 :** liberty, power, or permission to enter : ADMISSION ⟨applied for ~ at a number of schools⟩ ⟨he did not have the price . . . but figured he could wangle an ~ —Harold Sinclair⟩ **4 :** the first part or commencement of a period of time ⟨at the ~ of the night silence fell upon the village⟩ ⟨at the ~ of the holiday season an unwonted bustle and activity began⟩ **5** *cap* [trans. of LGk *eisodos*] **:** a solemn procession through the body of the church to the bema in the liturgy of the Eastern Church — see GREAT ENTRANCE, LITTLE ENTRANCE **6 a :** the point at which a voice or instrument part begins in ensemble music esp. after a rest ⟨a difficult ~⟩ **b :** the manner in which such a beginning is made ⟨a ragged ~⟩ **7 :** the bow or entire forepart of a ship below the waterline — compare RUN — see SHIP illustration **8 a :** the first appearance of an actor in a scene **b :** an opening at the side or rear of a stage scene by which to enter or exit

²en·trance \ən'tran(t)s, en-, -raa(ə)n-,-rain-,-rån-\ *vt* -ED/-ING/-S [¹*en-* + *trance* (n.)] **1 :** to put into a trance ⟨the loud, rapid breathing of the *entranced* medium —A.G.N.Flew⟩ **2 :** to overpower or carry away with emotion (as with delight, wonder, or rapture) ⟨the beauty of the land *entranced* them —Joseph Baily⟩ ⟨able to hold an audience *entranced* for 20 minutes at a time —W.S.Maugham⟩

entrance cone *n* **1 :** the protuberance of cytoplasm through which the fertilizing sperm enters an egg **2 :** the portion of a wind tunnel from which the air flows to the test section

en·trance·ment *pronunc at* ²ENTRANCE + mənt\ *n* -s **1 :** the act or process of entrancing **2 :** the condition of being entranced

entrance path *n* **:** the course of the sperm or male pronucleus through the egg cytoplasm toward the female pronucleus

entrance pupil *n* **:** the stop in an optical instrument or the virtual image of the stop that determines the angular diameter of the bundle of rays traversing the instrument from a given point in the object space — compare EXIT PUPIL

entranceway \ˌ=ˌ=,=\ *n* **:** ENTRYWAY

entrancing *adj* [fr. pres. part. of ²*entrance*] **:** giving or capable of giving delight : DELIGHTFUL ⟨antique papers of the most ~ design —*New Yorker*⟩ ⟨~ shades of pink and yellow⟩ ⟨~ descriptions . . . of a happy boyhood and youth —Dorothy C. Fisher⟩ — **en·tranc·ing·ly** *adv*

¹en·trant \'en·trənt\ *n* -s [F, fr. pres. part. of *entrer* to enter — more at ENTER] **:** one that enters ⟨an illegal ~ into the country⟩ ⟨new ~s into a highly competitive field⟩ ⟨deficiencies of the ~s in the basic skills needed for college study —I.L. Kandel⟩; *esp* **:** one that enters a competition ⟨~s include leading athletes from many countries⟩

²entrant \"\ *adj* **:** being an entrant

en·trap \ən'trap, en-\ *vt* [MF *entraper,* fr. *en-* ¹en- + *trape* trap — more at TRAP] **1 a :** to catch in or as if in a trap ⟨the pit had *entrapped* big beetles —William Beebe⟩ ⟨*entrapped* by falling timbers⟩ ⟨*entrapped* by ice floes⟩ **b :** to capture and hold (a substance) ⟨a system for *entrapping* the furnace fumes as a safety measure —*Monsanto Mag.*⟩ ⟨wool's tendency to produce lofty fabrics which ~ air —G.E.Hopkins⟩ **2 :** to lure or maneuver into a difficult, hopeless, or compromising situation : bring into one's power by stratagem : ENSNARE ⟨it was now too late to ~ and annihilate the Chinese armies —Owen & Eleanor Lattimore⟩ ⟨some women get married easily; but others . . . are driven to every possible trick . . . to ~ some man —G.B.Shaw⟩; *specif* **:** to lure into an erroneous, contradictory, or compromising statement ⟨the whole intent of the questioning was to ~ the defendant⟩ ⟨*entrapped* him into making a very damaging admission⟩ **syn** see CATCH

en·trap·ment \-mənt\ *n* -s **1 :** the act or process of entrapping ⟨had the good luck to be witness to the ~ of a species . . . not seen in these parts for some years⟩ ⟨the ~ of air contaminated with unwanted gases —*Ceramic Abstracts*⟩; *specif* **:** the luring by an officer of the law of a person into the commission of a crime in order that he may be prosecuted for the offense ⟨brutality, third degree, duress, and ~ are vigorously condemned —J.E.Hoover⟩ **2 :** the condition of being entrapped ⟨did I have the right to risk the ~ in the ice of our 276 men —Glen Jacobsen⟩ ⟨his ~ into marriage to a Southern girl whom he did not really love —James Hilton⟩

en·trap·ping·ly *adv* [*entrapping* (pres. part. of *entrap*) + *-ly*] **:** so as to entrap

entreasure *vt* [[1]*en-* + *treasure* (n.)] *obs* **:** to store in a treasury

[1]**en·treat** \ən'trēt, en-- *usu* -ēd.+V\ *vb* [ME *entreten*, fr. MF *entraitier* to treat of, fr. *en-* [1]en- + *traitier* to treat — more at TREAT] *vt* **1** *archaic* **:** to treat or conduct oneself toward **:** deal with **:** USE ⟨all those knights . . . she foully doth ~ —Edmund Spenser⟩ **2 :** to ask earnestly **:** petition or supplicate urgently **:** beg for ⟨~ him to hold his revengeful hand —L.M.Montgomery⟩ ⟨~*ed* permission to introduce his friend —Jane Austen⟩ ⟨I must . . . ~ both the patience and attention of the reader —Adam Smith⟩ **3** *obs* **a :** to beseech or supplicate successfully **:** prevail upon by pleading **:** PERSUADE **b :** to make a concern of **:** occupy or be occupied with ~ *vi* **1** *obs* **a :** to negotiate esp. for a treaty **b :** TREAT, DISCOURSE ⟨in those old times of which I do ~ —Edmund Spenser⟩ **2 :** to make an earnest petition or request **:** PLEAD ⟨accustomed to command, not to ~ —Willa Cather⟩ **syn** see BEG

[2]**entreat** *n, obs* **:** ENTREATY

en·treat·ing·ly *adv* [*entreating* (pres. part. of [1]*entreat*) + *-ly*] **:** in an entreating manner

entreatment *n* **1** *obs* **:** TREATMENT **2** *obs* **:** favor entreated ⟨set your ~*s* at a higher rate than a command to parley —Shak.⟩

en·treaty \ən'trēd·ē, en--, -rētē, -i\ *n* [ME *entrety*, fr. *entreten* + *-y*] **1** *obs* **a :** TREATMENT **b :** ENTERTAINMENT **2 :** the act of entreating **:** earnest petition or solicitation **:** PLEA ⟨before she could reply to . . . *entreaties* . . . that she would sing again —Jane Austen⟩

en·tre·chat \ˌäⁿtrəˌshä, ˌäⁿ-t-, -shä\ *n* -s [F, by folk etymology fr. It (*capriola*) *intrecciata*, lit., intertwined caper, fr. fem. of *intrecciato*, past part. of *intrecciare* to interlace, intertwine, fr. *in-* [2]in- (fr. L) + *treccia* tress] **:** a leap during which a ballet dancer repeatedly crosses the legs, sometimes beating them together while crossed

en·tre·cote \ˌäⁿtrəˌkōt\ *n, pl* **entrecotes** \"\ [F *entrecôte*, fr. *entre-* inter- (fr. L *inter*) + *côte* rib, fr. L *costa* — more at UNDER, COAST] **:** a steak cut from between the ribs; *sometimes* **:** SIRLOIN

en·tre·deux \ˌäⁿtrəˌdə, -dǝ̄, -ˌdər(·), *F* äⁿtrədœ\ *n, pl* **entre·deux** \-ə(z),-ǝ̄(z),-ər·,-ərz,-œ\ [F, fr. *entre-* + *deux* two, fr. L *duos*, acc. of *duo* — more at TWO] **:** something placed between two things; *specif* **:** INSERTION 2b

en·trée *or* **en·tree** \'än,trā *also* ='=\ *n* -s [F *entrée*, fr. OF *entree* — more at ENTRY] **1 a :** the act or manner of entering **:** ENTRANCE ⟨makes her ~ into society this spring⟩ ⟨making a graceful ~ into the parlor⟩ **b :** freedom of access **:** permission or right to enter ⟨he had ~ into the best society —Ludwig Bemelmans⟩ ⟨commented on the ~ which his son had with the president —J.P.Kennedy b. 1888⟩ **c :** something that qualifies one for entrance **:** means of gaining access ⟨the mere . . . possession of money is no ~ —Bentz Plagemann⟩ ⟨a thief-girl . . . who served as an ~ to underworld circles in that city —D.W.Maurer⟩ **2 a :** a dish served between the main courses **b :** a made dish served before the roast in England **c :** the principal dish of the meal in the U. S. ⟨this chicken casserole is an excellent ~⟩ **3 a** *obs* **:** a short musical composition in slow march rhythm, usu. in two repeated parts, often accompanying the entry of a procession in an opera or ballet **b :** the opening movement of an opera or ballet following the overture **c :** an introductory musical movement of any kind **4 :** one of the ballet numbers in a divertissement

en·tre·fer \ˌäⁿtrəˌfe(ə)r\ *n* -s [F, fr. *entre-* + *fer* iron, fr. L *ferrum* — more at FARRIER] **:** an air gap between the armature and the field magnets of a dynamo or motor

en·tre·més \ˌentrəˈmās\ *n, pl* **entreme·ses** \-ˈmā,sās\ [Sp, fr. Catal *entremès*, fr. L *intermissus*, past part. of *intermittere* to intermit — more at INTERMIT] **1 :** an interlude sometimes inserted in Spanish mystery plays of the middle ages **2 a :** a short comic piece usu. with music and dancing in the Spanish theater

en·tre·mets *in sing constr* ˌäntrəˌmā *or* ˌäⁿ-t-, *in pl constr* -mā(z)\ *n pl but sing or pl in constr* [F, fr. OF *entremés*, fr. L *intermissus*, past part.] **:** dishes (as vegetables or savories) served in addition to the main course of a meal ⟨precisely the same dinner, down to the ~ that she provided six months ago —*Time*⟩

en·trench *or* **in·trench** \ən'trench, en--\ *vb* [[1]*en-* or [2]*in-* + *trench* (n.)] *vt* **1 a :** to place within or surround with a trench esp. for defensive purposes ⟨the enemy ~*ed* himself strongly along the river⟩ ⟨~ a town⟩ **b :** to place (oneself) in any position that has strong military defensive advantages ⟨the settlers ~*ed* themselves behind a high stout stockade⟩ ⟨an enemy platoon ~*ed* itself in a half-destroyed factory⟩ **c :** to establish so solidly or strongly as to make dislodgment or change extremely difficult **:** CONFIRM ⟨~*ing* a practice⟩ **:** implant firmly **:** STRENGTHEN ⟨the landed interest ~*ed* itself on the steps of the throne —Ernest Barker⟩ ⟨Caucasian contacts gave the Indians more comforts, but also ~*ed* them more firmly as hunters —A.L.Kroeber⟩ ⟨the presence of Louisiana pirates . . . probably ~*ed* the term *bayou* in the Texas gulf area —R.C.West⟩ ⟨this thought is . . . firmly ~*ed* in the minds of many —Louis Tuft⟩ ⟨an ~*ed* habit⟩ **2 :** to cut into **:** FURROW; *specif* **:** to erode downward so as to form a trench ~ *v* **1 :** to dig a trench for defensive purposes **:** place oneself in a trench ⟨the platoon ~*ed* and awaited the enemy attack⟩ **2 :** to encroach upon or take possession of something reserved for other use or belonging to another person **:** TRESPASS — used with *on* or *upon* ⟨it does not appear that he ~*ed* upon his own or his mother's private fortune —John Buchan⟩ **syn** see TRESPASS

entrenched meander *n* **:** INCISED MEANDER; *specif* **:** one with slopes of about the same steepness on each side of the stream — compare INGROWN MEANDER

en·trench·ment *also* **in·trench·ment** \-chmənt\ *n* -s **1 a :** the act of entrenching ⟨used this delay for the ~ of the town⟩ **b :** the condition of being entrenched **2 a :** a defensive work consisting of a trench and a parapet **b :** any defense or protection ⟨municipal government is usually regarded as one of the great ~*s* of democracy —R.M.Dawson⟩ **3** *obs* **:** ENCROACHMENT, INFRINGEMENT **4 a :** the process whereby streams become incised, ingrown, or entrenched **b :** the results of this process

en·tre nous \ˌäⁿtrəˌnü, ˌäⁿ-t-\ *adv* [F] **:** between us **:** in confidence

en·tre·pôt \-rəˌpō\ *n* -s [F, fr. *entreposer* to put in a warehouse (fr. *entre-* + *poser* to put, place, rest), after F *déposer* to deposit: *dépôt* depot — more at POSE] **:** a place serving as an intermediary center for the collection and distribution of goods **:** a transshipment center or point ⟨upon the free flow of goods through this ~ hung the welfare of every farm in the west —Oscar Handlin⟩

en·tre·pre·neur \ˌäntrəp(r)əˈnər, +V -nər-, ˌäⁿ-t-, -nǝ̄(r, -n(y)ü(ə)r, -üə\ *n* -s [F, fr. OF, fr. *entreprendre* to undertake + *-eur* -or — more at ENTERPRISE] **1 :** the organizer of an economic venture; *esp* **:** one who organizes, owns, manages, and assumes the risks of a business ⟨he aimed at . . . increased opportunities for the small ~ —A.M.Schlesinger b. 1917⟩ **2 :** one that organizes, promotes, or manages an enterprise or activity of any kind **:** PRACTITIONER, PROMOTER ⟨a doctor or lawyer, who, as an independent ~, provides service to a client —Bernard Goldstein⟩ ⟨an ~ of the theater⟩ ⟨alert historical ~*s* —J.D.Hicks⟩ ⟨the Yankee ~ . . . who descended on the desolated South to make his fortune —*Holiday*⟩ **3 :** one who serves as an intermediary **:** MIDDLEMAN, GO-BETWEEN ⟨New York is . . . becoming world-city and ~ between Europe and the American hinterland —Donald Davidson⟩ ⟨they are . . . the ~*s*, the links between the businessmen . . . and the fanatics —Eric Ambler⟩

en·tre·pre·neur·i·al \-nər·ēəl, -n(y)ür- *also* -nǝ̄r-\ *adj* **:** of or relating to an entrepreneur ⟨~ history⟩ ⟨~ risks and rewards⟩

en·tre·pre·neur·ship \-nər,ship, -nǝ̄,sh-, -n(y)ü(ə)r,sh-, -üə-,sh-\ *n* -s **:** the condition of being an entrepreneur **:** the role or function of the entrepreneur **:** entrepreneurial ability or activity ⟨recent American experiences have proved how imaginative private ~ can continue to be —L.M.Hacker⟩ ⟨voices a plea for the study of ~ in history —W.C.Scoville⟩ ⟨it is now generally accepted that ~ consists in the meeting of uncertainty —Donald Dewey⟩

en·tre·pre·neuse \-ˌnə(r)z, -ˌnǝ̄z, -ˌnəiz, -ˌn(y)üz\ *n* -s [F, fem. of *entrepreneur*] **:** a woman entrepreneur

en·tre·sol \'entə(r)ˌsäl, 'en,trə,s-, 'än·trə,s-, 'äⁿ·trə,s-, -sōl\ *n* -s [F, fr. *entre-* + *sole* story, floor, alter. of OF *suele*, fr. (assumed) VL *sola*, fr. L *solea* sandal, sole, sill — more at SOLE] **:** MEZZANINE

en·tro·pi·on \en·'trōpē,än, -ēən\ *n* -s [NL, fr. Gk *entropē* act of turning toward, turning in + *-ion* (dim. suffix)] **:** inversion or turning inward against the eyeball of the border of the eyelids

en·tro·py \'en·trəpē, -pi\ *n* -ES [ISV [2]*en-* + *-tropy*] **1** *in thermodynamics* **:** a quantity that is the measure of the amount of energy in a system not available for doing work, numerical changes in the quantity being determinable from the ratio dQ/T where dQ is a small increment of heat added or removed and T is the absolute temperature ⟨the ~ of dry air is proportional to its potential temperature —A.H.Thiessen⟩ **2** *in statistical mechanics* **:** a factor or quantity that is a function of the physical state of a mechanical system and is equal to the logarithm of the probability for the occurrence of the particular molecular arrangement in that state **3** *in communication theory* **:** a measure of the efficiency of a system (as a code or a language) in transmitting information, being equal to the logarithm of the number of different messages that can be sent by selection from the same set of symbols and thus indicating the degree of initial uncertainty that can be resolved by any one message **4 :** the ultimate state reached in the degradation of the matter and energy of the universe **:** state of inert uniformity of component elements **:** absence of form, pattern, hierarchy, or differentiation ⟨cultural diversity and heterogeneity counteracts the tendency to cultural ~ —David Bidney⟩ ⟨~ is the general trend of the universe toward death and disorder —J.R.Newman⟩

en·truck \ən·'trək, en--\ *vb* [[1]*en-* + *truck* (n.)] *vi, of troops* **:** to get into a truck ~ *vt* **:** to put (troops) into trucks

en·trust *or* **in·trust** \ən·'trəst, en--\ *vt* [[1]*en-* or [2]*in-* + *trust* (n.)] **1 :** to confer a trust upon **:** deliver something to (another) in trust ⟨~*ed* him with responsibility for completing the work⟩ ⟨~*ed* him with my money⟩ **2 :** to commit or surrender to another with a certain confidence regarding his care, use, or disposal of ⟨~*ed* money to him⟩ **syn** see COMMIT

en·trust·ment \-s(t)mənt\ *n* -s **1 :** the act of entrusting or the condition of being entrusted **2 :** something with which one is entrusted **:** TRUST ⟨encouraged and imparted Christian spiritual ~*s* —*Time*⟩

en·try \'en·trē, -ri\ *n* -ES [ME *entre*, fr. OF *entree*, fr. fem. of *entré*, past part. of *entrer* to enter — more at ENTER] **1 :** the act of entering **:** ENTRANCE, INGRESS ⟨~ into the conflict disposed of the immediate issue of foreign policy —Oscar Handlin⟩ ⟨helps smooth his ~ into group life —*N.Y. Times*⟩ ⟨the Roman conquest of Britain began by an ~ in the southeast —L.D.Stamp⟩ **2 :** the right or privilege of entering **:** ADMISSION, ENTREE ⟨managed to gain ~ to an exclusive club⟩ ⟨I wandered into Symphony Hall and after some difficulty (for the house was sold out, as usual) obtained ~ —Virgil Thomson⟩ **3 a :** the place or point at which entrance is made ⟨at the ~ to the bridge stand two imposing pillars⟩**:** as (1) **:** VESTIBULE, PASSAGE, HALLWAY ⟨they had played hide-and-seek dodging . . . in and out of the *entries* of apartment houses —Jean Stafford⟩ (2) **:** DOOR, GATE ⟨the procession entered the church by the south ~⟩ (3) **:** the mouth of a river ⟨the French controlled both the St. Lawrence and the Mississippi *entries* to the great interior plain —B.K.Sandwell⟩ **b :** a section of a building (as a college dormitory) that is divided into several sections each with its own entrance ⟨it was the only bathtub in her ~ —George Santayana⟩ **4** *dial Brit* **:** a short lane or alley **5 a :** the act of making or entering a record ⟨~ of a sale⟩ **b :** something that is entered: as (1) **:** a record or notation (as in a journal, diary, or account book) of a particular day's occurrences or of some transaction or proceeding ⟨made no ~ in his logbook for that day⟩ ⟨the *entries* for that year reveal the growing scale of the firm's operations⟩ ⟨one ~ records a vote of censure against the speaker of the house⟩ (2) **:** a descriptive record in a catalog or listing of a book, periodical, or other item in a library's collection (3) **:** HEADWORD; *also* **:** a headword with its appended definitional and informational matter — see VOCABULARY ENTRY (4) **:** one of various similar objects composing a total or series **:** ITEM, OFFERING ⟨the *entries* in this anthology are of uneven worth⟩ ⟨fortunately, this ~ has little in common with the other stories —James Stern⟩ ⟨the latest ~ of the theater season is a very slight comedy⟩ **6 a :** the exhibition or depositing (as by a ship's officer at the customhouse) of the papers required by law to procure license to land or import goods **b :** the giving an account esp. of a ship's cargo to the officer of the customs and obtaining his permission to land or import it — see ENTER *vt* 8 **c :** BILL OF ENTRY **7 a :** a person or thing entered in a contest (as a race) **b :** the aggregate of persons or things so entered ⟨a large ~ is attracted, with the best men and dogs from England —Roy Saunders⟩ **8 :** a main passageway for haulage and ventilation in a mine **9 a :** the actual taking possession of lands or tenements by entering or setting foot on them **b :** a putting upon record in proper form and order **c :** the act in addition to breaking essential to constitute burglary consisting of the introduction of the least part of the person or of any instrument for the purpose of committing a felony **10 a :** ENTRANCE 6 **b :** the entrance of a voice in a fugue esp. after a rest **c :** ENTRÉE 3 **11 :** ENTRANCE 8a **12 a :** the act or means of winning a trick so as to lead to the next trick in bridge **b** *or* **entry card :** the card with which such a trick is or can be won — compare REENTRY

en·try·man \-mən\ *n, pl* **entrymen 1 :** one who enters upon public land with intent to secure an allotment under homestead, mining, or other laws **2 :** a coal miner engaged in driving a haulageway, airway, or passageway

entry table *n* **:** a conveyor that feeds material or objects (as bottles to be capped or labeled) into a processing machine

entryway \'=ˌ=\ *n* **:** a passage for entrance **:** ENTRY

entry word *n* **:** HEADWORD

-ents *pl of* -ENT

ent·wick·lungs·ro·man \ent·ˌvik(ə)luŋ(k)srō'mä än\ *n, pl* **entwicklungsroma·ne** \-nə\ *often cap* [G, fr. *entwicklung* development + *roman* novel] **:** an often autobiographical novel treating of the development of a character from childhood to maturity

en·twine *also* **in·twine** \ən·'twīn, en--\ *vb* [[1]*en-* or [2]*in-* + *twine*] *vt* **1 a :** to twine together ⟨flowers and vines solidly *entwined*⟩ **b :** to twine or twist around **:** ENCIRCLE, WREATHE ⟨*entwined* a pretty garland about her arms⟩ ⟨a pillar *entwined* by ivy⟩ **2 :** to interweave, attach, or involve inextricably in sentiment or thought ⟨she knows how to ~ herself in your affections —Henry Miller⟩ ⟨these elements of action are so many and so closely *entwined* —McGeorge Bundy⟩ ~ *vi* **:** to become twisted or twined **syn** see WIND

en·twine·ment \-mənt\ *n* -s **:** the action of entwining **:** the condition of being entwined

en·twist *also* **in·twist** \ən·'twist, en--\ *vt* [[1]*en-* or [2]*in-* + *twist*] **:** to twist or wreathe round **:** ENTWINE

en·ty·lo·ma \ˌentᵊl'ōmə\ *n, cap* [NL, fr. [2]en- + Gk *tylōma* callus] **:** a genus of parasitic fungi (family Tilletiaceae) that produce abundant conidia on long conidiophores and that comprise the white smuts

en·ty·py \'entəpē\ *n* -ES [[2]*en-* + *-typy*] **:** a method of amnion formation in certain mammals in which the embryonic knob invaginates into the yolk sac and no amniotic folds are formed — compare AMNION

[1]**enucleate** \(')ē+\ *vt* [L *enucleatus*, past part. of *enucleare* to remove a kernel from, to clarify, fr. *e-* + *nucleus* kernel — more at NUCLEUS] **1** *archaic* **:** to bring out the meaning or sense of **:** CLARIFY, EXPLAIN **2 :** to deprive of a nucleus **3** *med* **:** to remove without cutting into ⟨~ a tumor⟩ ⟨~ the eyeball⟩ **:** shell out from a capsule — **enucleation** \(ˌ)ē+\ *n* -s — **enucleator** \(')ē+\ *n* -s

[2]**enucleate** \(')ē+\ *adj* [L *enucleatus*, past part.] *biol* **:** ENUCLEATED

enu·mer·a·ble \ē'n(y)üm(ə)rəbəl, ə̇'-\ *adj* [*enumerate* + *-able*] **:** DENUMERABLE

enu·mer·ate \ə̇'n(y)üməˌrāt, ē'-, *usu* -ād.+V\ *vt* -ED/-ING/-S [L *enumeratus*, past part. of *enumerare*, fr. *e-* + *numerare* to count, fr. *numerus* number — more at NIMBLE] **1 :** to ascertain the number of **:** COUNT ⟨more gulls than I could ~ —E.A.Weeks⟩ ⟨the census . . . *enumerated* 247,450 persons of Hungarian birth —L.M.Sears⟩ ⟨the bank *enumerated* 57 overseas offices in addition to 71 New York branches —*Investor's Reader*⟩; *specif* **:** to make a census of the population of ⟨the population in 1820 when Mississippi was first *enumerated* as a state —*U. S. Census*⟩ **2 :** to relate one after another **:** LIST, SPECIFY ⟨it is not necessary to ~ all the bitter and factious disputes which marked this unhappy quarter century —B.K.Sandwell⟩ ⟨*enumerated* the advantages of his new position⟩ ⟨*enumerated* the necessary qualities of a good general —Eric Linklater⟩ ⟨the *enumerated* and implied powers of Congress⟩ ⟨the circumstances may be roughly *enumerated* as follows —G.G.Coulton⟩ **syn** see COUNT

enu·mer·a·tion \ə̇ˌ==ˈrāshən, (ˌ)ē,-\ *n* -s [MF or L; MF, fr. L *enumeration-, enumeratio*, fr. *enumeratus* + *-ion-, -io* -ion] **1 a :** the act of listing one after the other **:** DETAILING ⟨the rebel leader's effective ~ of popular grievances⟩ **:** the act of mentioning as an item in a total or series ⟨not so entwined with the government as to warrant ~ as a separate element of the constitutional system —F.A.Ogg & Harold Zink⟩ **b :** an itemized list or detailed or seriatim account **:** CATALOG ⟨the modern way to learn English . . . is to absorb a phrase-by-phrase ~ of all that might be conceivably said in ordinary talk —J.M.Barzun⟩ ⟨a careful ~ of the circumstances that led to the tragedy⟩ ⟨the author provides complete ~*s* . . . of the opinions of Cartesian scholars on disputed questions of interpretation —W.F.Doney⟩ **2 a :** the act of counting **:** NUMBERING ⟨as the faculty of speech developed . . . the art of ~ or counting would begin —J.A.N.Friend⟩ **b :** a count of something (as a population) **:** CENSUS ⟨the decennial ~ is only one of the many censuses it conducts —*Current Biog.*⟩ **3** *logic* **:** examination of the instances falling under a universal ⟨total ~ in perfect induction⟩

enu·mer·a·tive \ə̇'n(y)üməˌrā|d·|iv, ē'-, -m(ə)rəl, |t|, |ēv *also* |əv\ *adj* **:** enumerating or concerned with enumeration

enumerative induction *n* **:** inductive verification of a universal proposition by enumeration and examination of all the instances to which it applies — called also *perfect induction*

enu·mer·a·tor \ə̇'n(y)üməˌrād·ə(r), -ātə-\ *n* -s **:** one that enumerates; *esp* **:** a census taker

enun·cia·ble \ē'nən(t)sēəbəl, -nənch(ē)əb- ə̇'-\ *adj* [*enunciate* + *-able*] **:** capable of being enunciated

enun·ci·ate \-nən(t)sēˌāt *sometimes* -nənchē-, *usu* -ād.+V\ *vb* -ED/-ING/-S [L *enunciatus, enuntiatus*, past part. of *enunciare, enuntiare* to report, declare, express, fr. *e-* + *nunciare, nuntiare* to announce, relate, inform, fr. *nuncius, nuntius* messenger, message] *vt* **1 a :** to make a definite or systematic statement of **:** FORMULATE ⟨Descartes was the first to ~ the modern principle of inertia —S.F.Mason⟩ ⟨emphasized . . . and *enunciated* a materialistic theory of the universe —*Encyc. Americana*⟩ **b :** ANNOUNCE, PROCLAIM, DECLARE ⟨he *enunciated* the aims of the paper —*Current Biog.*⟩ ⟨*enunciated* the principles to be followed by his administration⟩ **2 :** UTTER, ARTICULATE, PRONOUNCE ⟨*enunciating* their words with peculiar and offensive clarity —Geoffrey Household⟩ ~ *vi* **:** to utter articulate sounds ⟨should children be taught to ~ correctly —Bertrand Russell⟩

enun·ci·a·tion \(ˌ)ē,==ˈāshən, ə̇,==-\ *n* -s [L *enunciation-, enunciatio, enuntiation-, enuntiatio*, fr. *enunciatus, enuntiatus* + *-ion-, -io* -ion] **1 a :** the act of formulating or stating (as a law or principle) in a definite systematic way ⟨the ~ of the exclusion principle resolved the apparent contradiction within the . . . theory —G.H.Wannier⟩ **b :** the act of producing or declaring publicly ⟨we have a national penchant for ~ of broad, idealistic goals —A.B.Lans⟩ **2 :** manner of uttering, articulating, or pronouncing esp. as regards ease of perceptibility ⟨a region of literacy and slurred ~ —James Thurber⟩ ⟨detected in his ~ some slight influence of the brandy —Glenway Wescott⟩ **3 :** something that is enunciated **:** STATEMENT, ANNOUNCEMENT, EXPRESSION ⟨a tentative ~ to a theme which was to become important —G.J.Becker⟩ ⟨contained an ~ . . . of all the traditional freedoms —J.P.Humphrey⟩

enun·cia·tive \=ˈ==,ā|d·|iv, |t|, |ēv *also* |əv *sometimes* -nənch(ē)ə|\ *adj* [L *enunciativus, enuntiativus*, fr. *enunciatus, enuntiatus* + *-ivus* -ive] **1 :** serving to enunciate **:** DECLARATIVE **2 :** relating to enunciation — **enun·cia·tive·ly** \|əvlē, -li\ *adv*

enun·ci·a·tor \-nən(t)sēˌād·ə(r), -ātə- *sometimes* -nənchē-\ *n* -s [LL *enunciator, enuntiator*, fr. L *enunciatus, enuntiatus* + *-or*] **:** one that enunciates

enure *var of* INURE

en·u·re·sis \ˌenyəˈrēsəs\ *n* -ES [NL, fr. Gk *enourein* to urinate in, to wet the bed (fr. *en-* [2]en- + *ourein* to urinate, fr. *ouron* urine) + NL *-esis* — more at URINE] **:** an involuntary discharge of urine **:** incontinence of urine — called also *bed-wetting* — **en·u·ret·ic** \ˌ==ˈred·|ik, -et|, |ēk\ *adj or n*

env *abbr* **1** envelope **2** envoy

envassal *vt* [[1]*en-* + *vassal* (n.)] *obs* **:** to reduce to vassalage

enveigle *chiefly Brit var of* INVEIGLE

en·veil *also* **in·veil** \ən, en +\ *vt* [[1]*en-* or [2]*in-* + *veil*, n.] **:** to cover with or as if with a veil

en·vel·op *also* **en·vel·ope** \ən'veləp, en-\ *vt* **enveloped; enveloped; enveloping; envelops** *also* **envelopes** [ME *envolupen*, fr. MF *envoluper, enveloper, enveloper*, fr. OF, fr. *en-* [1]en- + *voluper, voleper, veloper* to wrap up] **1 a :** to enclose completely with a garment or other covering **:** wrap up ⟨a shroud ~*ed* her form —Mary W. Shelley⟩ ⟨drew off his coat and ~*ed* him in a white robe —Laura Krey⟩ ⟨other folks ~ the meat in the leaves —E.J.Banfield⟩ **b :** to enclose or surround with a nonsolid material or medium (as air or darkness) **:** obscure or conceal by covering or shrouding ⟨distant hills ~*ed* in a blue haze⟩ ⟨large black clouds ~*ed* the moon⟩ ⟨flames ~*ed* the building⟩ ⟨a snug . . . warmth ~*ed* him —O.E.Rölvaag⟩ **c :** to surround or enfold with something immaterial (as a mood or atmosphere) **:** POSSESS, DOMINATE ⟨the Presbyterian culture that ~*ed* me when I was a boy —St. Clair McKelway⟩ ⟨the drowsy silence that ~*ed* the yacht —Scott Fitzgerald⟩ ⟨she had been ~*ed* in profound peace —Ellen Glasgow⟩ ⟨then she would . . . ~ me in the great, soft, spicy tide of her affection —R.P.Warren⟩ ⟨a feeling of gloom and self-pity ~*ed* him⟩ ⟨he was ~*ed* by that strange sense of detachment —Walter O'Meara⟩ **2** \" *or* 'envə,lōp *or* 'änve,lōp\ **:** to put in an envelope ⟨she scrawled across the bottom of the letter the word NO and ~*ed* it for return mailing —E.P.O'Donnell⟩ **3 :** to attack or move to attack (one or both of an enemy's flanks) ⟨there were indications that they intended to ~ the northern wing of Army Group South —W.R.Desobry⟩ **syn** see ENCLOSE

en·ve·lope \'envəˌlōp, 'än-\ *also* **en·vel·op** \ən'veləp, en'v-, 'en,veləp, 'env(ə)ləp, 'änv(ə)ləp\ *n* -s [F *enveloppe*, fr. MF *envelope*, fr. *enveloper*] **1 :** something that envelops **:** WRAPPER, CONTAINER, ENCLOSURE ⟨one of these graves . . . may contain the earthly ~ of some immortal mind —Kathleen Freeman⟩ ⟨the ~ of air around the earth⟩ **2 :** a flat flexible usu. paper container in many sizes and constructions made by die cutting and gluing with an overlapped back seam and with bottom and closure flaps both adhering to the back portion **3 a :** the wrapper or cover for a phonograph record or electrical transcription **b :** ENVELOPE STAMP **4 :** something (as a woman's handbag) shaped like a letter envelope ⟨wistfully fingered her . . . narrow beadwork ~ —Maeve Brennan⟩ **5 a :** the outer covering of an aerostat **b :** the bag which contains the gas in a balloon or airship **6** *biol* **:** any enclosing covering (as a membrane, shell, integument, or surrounding leaves) **7 a :** a curve that is tangent to each one of a family of curves **b :** a surface that is tangent to each one of a family of surfaces **8 :** the suggestion of atmosphere surrounding the subject of a painting or sculpture (as by modulation of tone or by shallow and simplified cutting of the form) **9 :** the

envelope 2

container or housing of glass, quartz, or metal that encloses the working elements of a vacuum tube **10** : JACKET 3b(2)

envelope stamp *n* : an embossed postage stamp on an envelope

envelope table *n* : a small table having a triangular drop leaf or leaves

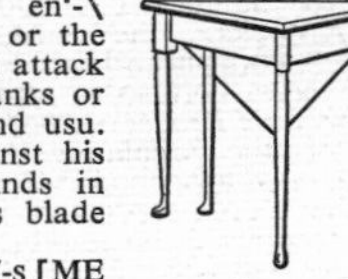
envelope table

en·vel·op·ment \ən'veləpmənt, en'-\ *n* -s **1** : the act of enveloping or the state of being enveloped **2** : an attack directed against one or both flanks or the rear of the enemy's forces and usu. accompanied by an attack against his front **3** : two consecutive binds in fencing carrying the opponent's blade in a complete circle

en·venom \ən, en+\ *vt* -ED/-ING/-S [ME *envenimen*, fr. OF *envenimer*, fr. *en-* ¹en- + *venim* venom — more at VENOM] **1** *obs* : to poison esp. by a venomous bite **2 a** : to taint or impregnate with venom or any substance harmful to life : make poisonous ⟨thoroughly ~*ed* a whole pound of hamburger —Jean Stafford⟩ **b** : to infuse bitterness, malice, or hatred into : EMBITTER ⟨~*ing* the relations between the two countries⟩ ⟨a countenance ~*ed* with jealousy and rage⟩

en ven·tre sa mère \äⁿ,väⁿ·trəsä'me(ə)r\ [AF] *of an infant* : in utero and therefore for beneficial purposes legally born

en·verdure \ən, en+\ *vt* -ED/-ING/-S [¹*en-* + *verdure* (n.)] : to clothe or cover with verdure ⟨a country *enverdured* with palms and bamboos —Rose Macaulay⟩

en·vermeil \"+\ *vt* -ED/-ING/-S [¹*en-* + *vermeil* (adj.)] *archaic* : to color with or as if with vermilion

en·vi·able \'envēəbəl, -viə-\ *adj* [²*envy* + *-able*] : being such as to attract envy or desire to possess or resemble : highly desirable ⟨an ~ reputation for integrity⟩ ⟨found himself in an ~ position⟩ — **en·vi·able·ness** \-nəs\ *n* -ES

en·vi·ably \-blē, -li\ *adv* : in an enviable manner

envied *past of* ENVY

en·vi·er \-ēə(r), -iə-\ *n* -s [ME, fr. *envien* to envy + *-er*] : one that envies

envies *pl of* ENVY, *pres 3d sing of* ENVY

en·vi·ous \'envēəs, -viəs\ *adj* [ME, fr. OF *envieus, envious*, fr. L *invidiosus*, fr. *invidia* envy + *-osis* -ous — more at ENVY] **1** : characterized by, exhibiting, or reflecting envy : feeling or motivated by envy : maliciously covetous or resentful of the possessions or good fortune of another ⟨tried to look disappointed and angry but . . . only succeeded in looking ~ —Hervey Allen⟩ ⟨the sterile and ~ principle of artificial equality —*Time*⟩ ⟨examining the tire with ~ appreciation —M.M.Musselman⟩ **2** *archaic* **a** : EMULOUS **b** : ENVIABLE ⟨theirs was an ~ gift, but lightly held —Thomas Cole⟩

syn JEALOUS: ENVIOUS is likely to suggest a grudging of another's possessions and accomplishments, a spiteful desiring of their loss, or, most frequently, a malicious or cankerous coveting of them ⟨his successes were so repeated that no wonder the *envious* and the vanquished spoke sometimes with bitterness regarding them —W.M.Thackeray⟩ JEALOUS may suggest distrustful, suspicious, angry, or malcontent intolerance of the notion of anyone else's coming to possess what is viewed as belonging to or befitting oneself ⟨France, *jealous* as it was of his greatness and covetous of his Gascon possessions, he could hold at bay —J.R.Green⟩ ⟨I know that religion, science, and art are all *jealous* of each other because each of them claims, in a sense, to cover the whole field, that is, to interpret all experience from its own point of view —W.R.Inge⟩ It may be used without derogation to indicate cherishing and vigilantly guarding or maintaining ⟨proud of their calling, conscious of their duty, and *jealous* of their honor —John Galsworthy⟩

en·vi·ous·ly *adv* [ME, fr. *envious* + *-ly*] : in an envious manner

en·vi·ous·ness *n* -ES [ME *enviousnes*, fr. *envious* + *-nes* -ness] : the quality or state of being envious

en·vi·ron \ən'vīrən, en-, -ī(ə)rn\ *vt* -ED/-ING/-S [ME *envirounen*, fr. MF *environner*, fr. *environ* around, about, fr. *en* in, (fr. L *in*) + *viron* circle, circuit, fr. *virer* to turn, fr. (assumed) VL *virare*, prob. alter. (influenced by L *vibrare* to shake or *vertere* to turn) of L *gyrare* to turn around — more at IN, VIBRATE, WORTH, GYRATE] **1 a** : ENCIRCLE, ENVELOP : form a ring around ⟨the seas ~*ing* the island⟩ ⟨a city ~*ed* by pleasant and extensive plains⟩ **b** : to stand close around : cluster or press near ⟨ladies in waiting ~*ed* the queen⟩ **2** : to surround or enfold with a condition, atmosphere, or other intangible thing : surround permeatingly ⟨the heavy pressure of the cultural influences that ~ us⟩ ⟨made light of the dangers that ~*ed him*⟩ **syn** see SURROUND

en·vi·ron·ment \-īrənmənt, -ī(ə)rnmə-, *rapid* -īrəmə-\ *n* -s **1** : something that environs : SURROUNDINGS ⟨relaxed . . . in a cosy ~ of apple-green furniture and art linoleum —*Punch*⟩ ⟨sat at the mahogany table surrounded by the ~*s* of his wealth —E.S.Gardner⟩ **2** : the surrounding conditions, influences, or forces that influence or modify: as **a** : the whole complex of climatic, edaphic, and biotic factors that act upon an organism or an ecological community and ultimately determine its form and survival — compare HABITAT **b** : the aggregate of social and cultural conditions (as customs, laws, language, religion, and economic and political organization) that influence the life of an individual or community

en·vi·ron·men·tal \ən¦vīrən¦mentᵊl, (,)en-, -ī(ə)rn¦me-, *rapid* -īrə¦me-\ *adj* : of, relating to, or produced by environment — **en·vi·ron·men·tal·ly** \-ᵊlē, -ᵊli\ *adv*

en·vi·ron·men·tal·ism \(,)⸗,⸗(⸗)'mentᵊl,izəm\ *n* -s : a theory that views environment rather than heredity as the important factor in the development of the individual or a group — compare HEREDITARIANISM — **en·vi·ron·men·tal·ist** \-ᵊləst\ *n or adj* — **en·vi·ron·men·tal·is·tic** \-,mentᵊl'istik\ *adj*

environmental resistance *n* : the sum of the environmental factors (as drought, mineral deficiencies, competition) that tend to restrict the biotic potential of an organism or kind of organism and impose a limit on numerical increase

en·vi·rons \ən'vīrənz, en'-, -'vī(ə)rnz *also* 'en,vī- *or* 'envərənz *or* 'envə,ränz\ *n pl* [F, pl. of *environ*, fr. MF, fr. *environ*, adv. & prep., around, about — more at ENVIRON] **1** : the enclosing limits or boundaries : COMPASS ⟨some 2483 concerns . . . were located within the ~ of the various cities —N.R.Heiden⟩ ⟨subsequent administrative developments have further enlarged the ~ of these towns —A.D.Rees⟩ **2 a** : the suburbs or districts round about a city or other populated place ⟨an adequate system of parks . . . for the national capital and its ~ —*Current Biog.*⟩ **b** : any adjoining or surrounding region or space : VICINITY, NEIGHBORHOOD ⟨strange biblical duds being worn by the natives in the ~ of the pyramids —Erskine Johnson⟩ **c** : environing things : SURROUNDINGS ⟨foliage . . . serves to give a relief to the tree, to make it stand out from among its ~ —Richard Semon⟩

en·vis·age \ən'vizij, en-, -zēj, *chiefly in pres part* -zəj\ *vt* -ED/-ING/-S [F *envisager*, fr. *en-* ¹en- + *visage* — more at VISAGE] **1** *archaic* : to meet squarely : CONFRONT, FACE **2 a** : to conceive of : grasp mentally : view or regard in a particular way ⟨*envisaging* man as simply the locus of a polytheism —Aldous Huxley⟩ ⟨of all the points of view from which we may ~ their brilliant activity —G.L.Dickinson⟩ ⟨in the beginning a science is quantitative . . .; only later does it ~ its problems mathematically —Edward Sapir⟩ **b** : to have a mental picture in advance of realization : look forward to : have in view : CONTEMPLATE, FORESEE ⟨the plan *envisaged* lavish use of mechanical equipment of all kinds —M.A.Abrams⟩ ⟨*envisaged* a single, centralized state embracing all the former colonies⟩ ⟨men of the . . . mental stature to ~ and carry out so great a work —Yvonne Adamson⟩ ⟨I ~ that in the event of a German collapse the need . . . to undertake this work will be all the more apparent —F.D.Roosevelt⟩ **syn** see THINK

en·vis·age·ment \-mənt\ *n* -s : the act or an instance of envisaging : CONCEPTION ⟨all the main ~*s* or images of us as a nation . . . had begun at least dimly to emerge —*Amer. Quarterly*⟩

en·vision \ən, en+\ *vt* [¹*en-* + *vision* (n.)] : to have a mental image of esp. in advance of realization : picture to oneself : look forward to : ENVISAGE, FORESEE ⟨~*ed* the perfectibility of man through a long process of . . . evolution —*Amer. Scholar*⟩ ⟨she ~*ed* a career in teaching and research —Leonard Engel⟩ ⟨reading this essay, I automatically ~*ed* some accomplished slick writer —F.O.Baker⟩ ⟨he came to the end his prophetic schoolmaster had ~*ed* —C.B.Driscoll⟩ **syn** see THINK

en·voi \'en,vȯi, 'äṅ-\ *n* -s [F, fr. OF *envei, envoy*] **1** : the usu. explanatory or commendatory concluding remarks to a poem, essay, or book; *specif* : a short fixed final stanza of a poem (as a ballade) pointing the moral and usu. addressing the person to whom the poem is written **2** : parting word ⟨each one's ~ to his successors ended on a note of frustration and defeat —Cleve Hallenbeck⟩ ⟨Dick's muttered ~ . . . fell . . . with the effect of a stunning blow —Mary McCarthy⟩

en·voûte·ment \äⁿvütmäⁿ\ *n, pl* **envoûtements** \-mäⁿ(z)\ [F, fr. MF *envoutement*, fr. *envouter* to cast a spell on, practice envoûtement on (fr. OF, fr. *en-* ¹en- + *vout* face, image, fr. L *vultus* face) + *-ment*] : the magical practice of using an image or likeness of a person to influence his actions or destiny usu. with malevolent intent

¹**en·voy** \'en,vȯi, 'äṅ-\ *n* -s [ME, fr. MF *envei, envoy* message, envoi, fr. *enveier, envoier* to send, fr. (assumed) VL *inviare*, fr. L *in-* ²in- + *via* way — more at VIA] : ENVOI 1

²**envoy** \"\ *n* -s [alter. of earlier *envoyée, envoyé*, fr. F *envoyé*, fr. past part. of *envoyer* to send, fr. OF *enveier, envoier*] **1 a** *also* **envoy extraordinary** : a minister plenipotentiary accredited to a foreign government ranking between an ambassador and a minister resident **b** : any person deputed to represent one sovereign or government in its intercourse with another **2** : MESSENGER, AGENT, REPRESENTATIVE ⟨the mutineers sent an ~ to deal with the captain⟩

¹**en·vy** \'envē, -vi\ *n* -ES [ME *envie*, fr. OF, fr. L *invidia*, fr. *invidus* envious (fr. *invidēre* to look askance at, envy, fr. *in-* ²in- + *vidēre* to see) + *-ia* -y — more at WIT] **1** *obs* **a** : MALICE, SPITE **b** : OPPROBRIUM, UNPOPULARITY **2 a** : painful or resentful awareness of an advantage enjoyed by another, accompanied by a desire to possess the same advantage ⟨his lavish style of living . . . provoked half-contemptuous ~ among his brothers —Willa Cather⟩ ⟨I have a wild ~ of the man in the taxi with her —Hollis Alpert⟩ **b** **envies** *pl* : instances of envious feeling ⟨the attack . . . was due not only to the jealousies and *envies* —Hilaire Belloc⟩ **c** : an object of envious notice or feeling ⟨my brother and I were the ~ of all our friends —Margaret Bean⟩

²**envy** \"\ *vb* -ED/-ING/-ES [ME *envien*, fr. MF *envier*, fr. *envie*] *vt* **1** : to feel envy toward or on account of : be painfully or resentfully aware of the advantage of (another) with a desire to possess the same advantage : be envious of ⟨I often ~ the writer who works in a university —V.S.Pritchett⟩ ⟨she pretended to deplore her compatriots' escapades, which actually she *envied* desperately —Jean Stafford⟩ **2** *obs* : BEGRUDGE ~ *vi, obs* : to feel or show envy

en·vy·ing·ly *adv* [*envying* (pres. part. of ²*envy*) + *-ly*] : so as to feel or show envy

enweave *var of* INWEAVE

enwheel *vt* [¹*en-* + *wheel* (n.)] *obs* : ENCIRCLE

en·wind *also* **in·wind** \ən, en+\ *vt* **enwound; enwound; enwinding; enwinds** [¹*en-* or ²*in-* + *wind* (v.)] : to wind in or about : encircle with windings : ENFOLD ⟨his legs *enwound* with bandages following the accident⟩

en·womb \ən, en+\ *vt* -ED/-ING/-S [¹*en-* + *womb* (n.)] **1** *obs* : to make pregnant : carry in the womb **2** : to bury, hide, or contain in the depths or recesses of something ⟨you may ~ yourself in words —Emery Neff⟩

enwoven *var of* INWOVEN

en·wrap *also* **in·wrap** \ən, en+\ *vt* [ME *enwrappen, inwrappen* (trans. of L *involvere*), fr. ¹*en-* or ²*in-* + *wrappen* to wrap — more at WRAP] **1 a** : to wrap or enfold in a garment or other covering ⟨a shabby overcoat *enwrapped* his body⟩ ⟨designed to ~ luxury items —*Modern Packaging*⟩ ⟨the little packet *enwrapped* in a faded yellow envelope —Stephen Crane⟩ **b** : to enfold in or closely surround with any physical or material substance or condition : ENVELOP ⟨only the coldness of the empty house *enwrapped* her —Edith Sitwell⟩ ⟨a house *enwrapped* in flowers⟩ **2 a** : to wrap in or surround with something immaterial (as a mood or atmosphere) ⟨sat there *enwrapped* in a sullen defiance⟩ ⟨silence *enwrapped* the sleeping town⟩ **b** : to enfold in a trance, slumber, or deep thought : engross or absorb mentally ⟨*enwrapped* in fond dreams of a bright future⟩

en·wreathe \ən, en+\ *vt* [¹*en-* + *wreathe*] : WREATHE, ENVELOP

enwrought *var of* INWROUGHT

en·zed \(')en¦zed\ *adj, usu cap* [¹*en* + *zed*; fr. the initials N.Z.] *Austral* : NEW ZEALAND

en·zed·der \-də(r)\ *n* -s *cap, Austral* : NEW ZEALANDER

¹**en·zo·ot·ic** \¦enzə¦wäd·ik, -zō¦ä-\ *adj* [²*en-* + *zo-* + *-otic*] *of animal diseases* : peculiar to or constantly present in a locality — compare ENDEMIC, EPIZOOTIC — **en·zo·ot·i·cal·ly** \|ək(ə)lē\ *adv*

²**enzootic** \"\ *n* -s : an enzootic disease

enzootic ataxia *n* : swayback of lambs

enzootic marasmus *n* : cobalt deficiency of sheep and cattle in western Australia — compare ¹PINE 3

en·zygotic \¦en+\ *adj* [²*en-* + *zyg-* + *-otic*] *of twins* : IDENTICAL

en·zy·mat·ic \¦enzə¦mad·ik *also* -,zī- *or* **en·zy·mic** \(')en¦zīmik, -zim-\ *adj* [*enzyme* + *-atic* (as in *automatic*) *or -ic*] : of, relating to, or produced by an enzyme ⟨~ activity⟩ ⟨~ digestion⟩ — **en·zy·mat·i·cal·ly** \-mad·ək(ə)lē\ *or* **en·zy·mi·cal·ly** \-mək(ə)lē\ *adv*

en·zyme \'en,zīm\ *n* -s [G *enzym*, fr. MGk *enzymos* leavened, fr. Gk *en-* ²en- + *zymē* leaven; perh. akin to L *jus* broth, soup — more at JUICE] **1** : any of a very large class of complex proteinaceous substances (as amylases or pepsin) that are produced by living cells, that are essential to life by acting like catalysts in promoting at the cell temperature usu. reversible reactions (as hydrolysis and oxidation) without themselves undergoing marked destruction in the process but frequently requiring the presence of activators (as metal ions) or of coenzymes, and that can act also outside of living organisms and therefore are useful in many industrial processes (as fermentation, tanning of leather, and production of cheese) — see -ASE; APOENZYME, FERMENT 1, SUBSTRATE **2** : an active system comprising an enzyme usu. together with a coenzyme : HOLOENZYME

en·zy·mol·o·gist \,enzə'mäləjəst, -,zī-\ *n* -s : a person trained in or engaged in enzymology

en·zy·mol·o·gy \-jē\ *n* -ES [ISV *enzyme* + *-o-* + *-logy*] : a branch of science that deals with enzymes and with their chemical nature, biochemical activity, and biological significance

eo- *comb form* [Gk *ēō-* dawn, fr. *ēōs* — more at EAST] : earliest : oldest ⟨*Eohippus*⟩ ⟨eolithic⟩; *specif* : first of two or three subdivisions of geologic time ⟨*Eocene*⟩ — compare MES-, MI-, NE-, PLEIO-

EO *abbr* **1** errors and omissions **2** executive officer **3** executive order **4** ex officio

eo·acanthocephala \¦ē(,)ō+\ *n pl, cap* [NL, fr. *eo-* + *Acanthocephala*] : an order of Acanthocephala comprising parasites of aquatic vertebrates having the proboscis hooks in quincuncial arrangement and the cement-producing glands syncytial

eo·an \(')ē¦ōən\ *adj* [L *eous* (fr. Gk *ēōios*, fr. *ēōs* dawn) + E *-an*] : of or relating to the dawn or the east

eo·an·thro·pus \,ē(,)ō'an(t)thrəpəs, -,an'thrōpəs\ *n, cap* [NL, fr. *eo-* + *-anthropus*] *in some classifications* : a genus of the family Hominidae comprising only the Piltdown man

eo·carboniferous \¦ē(,)ō+\ *adj or n, usu cap* [*eo-* + *carboniferous*] *geol* : MISSISSIPPIAN

¹**eo·cene** \'ēə,sēn\ *adj, usu cap* [*eo-* + *-cene*] : of or relating to the second principal subdivision of the Tertiary — used commonly of the epoch following the Paleocene and preceding the Oligocene but sometimes of all the Cenozoic era preceding the Miocene — see GEOLOGIC TIME table

²**eocene** \"\ *n* -s *usu cap* **1** : the Eocene epoch **2** : the series deposited during the Eocene epoch

eo·dis·cid \,ēō'disəd\ *n* -s [NL *Eodiscida*] : a member of *Eodiscus* or a related genus

eo·dis·cus \-skəs\ *n, cap* [NL, fr. *eo-* + *-discus*] : a genus of minute Cambrian trilobites that with related forms constitute a distinct order of small-eyed trilobites resembling those of the order Agnostida

EOE *abbr* errors and omissions excepted

eo·hip·pus \,ēō'hipəs\ *n* [NL, fr. *eo-* + *-hippus*] **1** *cap* : a genus of small primitive 4-toed horses from the Lower Eocene of the western U.S. that is now often included in the European genus *Hyracotherium* — see EQUIDAE illustration **2** -ES : an animal or a fossil of the genus *Eohippus*

EOHP *abbr* except as otherwise herein provided

eo·la·tion \,ēə'lāshən\ *n* -s [*Aeolus* god of the winds (fr. L, fr. Gk *Aiolos*) + E *-ation*] : the action of wind on land surfaces

eo·la weed \'ē'ōlə-,\ *n, usu cap E* [prob. fr. the place name *Eola*] : KLAMATH WEED

eo·li·an *also* **ae·o·li·an** \ē'ōlēən, -lyən\ *adj* [*Aeolus* + E *-ian*] : borne, deposited, produced, or eroded by the wind ⟨~ sand⟩ ⟨~ rock sculpture⟩

eo·lian·ite \ē'ōlyə,nīt, -lēə-\ *n* -s : a sedimentary rock of eolian origin

eol·ic \ē'älik\ *adj* [*Aeolus* + E *-ic*] : EOLIAN

eo·li·enne \,ē(,)ōlē'en, (,)ā,ōlē'en, (,)ē,ō-\ *n* -s [F *éolienne*, fr. fem. of *éolien* Aeolean (of Aeolus), fr. *Aeolus* + F *-ien* -ian] : a lustrous lightweight dress fabric woven with a silk warp and coarser filling threads of wool, rayon, or cotton that make a fine cross rib

eolipile *var of* AEOLIPILE

eo·lith \'ēə,lith\ *n* -s [*eo-* + *-lith*] : a very crudely or irregularly chipped flint assumed by some archaeologists to have been used by early man

eo·lith·ic \¦ēə¦lithik, -thēk\ *adj, usu cap* [*eo-* + *-lithic*] : of or relating to the earliest period of the Stone Age and the earliest assumed stage of human culture characterized by the use of eoliths

eolotropic *var of* AEOLOTROPIC

EOM *abbr* end of month

eon *var of* AEON

eonian *var of* AEONIAN

eon·ism \'ēə,nizəm\ *n* -s [Chevalier d'*Éon* (Charles Eon de Beaumont) †1810 Fr. political adventurer who for many years posed as a woman + E *-ism*] : TRANSVESTISM

eo no·mi·ne \,ē(,)ō'nämə(,)nē, ¦ā(,)ō'nōmə,nā\ [L] : by or under that name

eo·paleozoic *or* **eo·palaeozoic** \¦ē(,)ō+\ *adj, usu cap* [*eo-* + *Paleozoic, Palaeozoic*] : being or relating to the early part of the Paleozoic

eo·sin \'ēəsən\ *or* **eo·sine** \", -,sēn\ *n* -s [ISV *eos-* (fr. Gk *ēōs* dawn) + *-in, -ine*; orig. formed as G *eosin*; fr. the color it gives to silk — more at EAST] **1 a** : a red crystalline fluorescent dye $C_{20}H_8Br_4O_5$ made by bromination of fluorescein and used chiefly in cosmetics and as a toner; tetrabromo-fluorescein — called also *bromo acid* **b** *often cap* : the red to brown crystalline sodium or potassium salt of this dye used chiefly in making pink or red organic pigments, in microscopy as a biological stain, and in pharmaceutical preparations — called also *Eosine G, Eosine Y, Eosine Yellowish*; see DYE table I (under *Acid Red 87*) **2** *often cap* : any of several dyes related chemically to eosin ⟨*Eosine B* or *Eosine* Bluish⟩ ⟨*Eosine* H8G⟩ — see DYE table I (under *Acid Orange 11*)

eo·sin·o·cyte \,ēə'sinə,sīt\ *n* -s [ISV *eosin* + *-o-* + *-cyte*] : EOSINOPHIL

eo·sin·o·pe·nia \,ēə,sinə'pēnēə, -pēnyə\ *n* -s [NL, fr. ISV *eosin* + NL *-o-* + *-penia*] : an abnormal decrease in the number of eosinophils in the blood — **eo·sin·o·pe·nic** \¦⸗⸗¦⸗⸗¦pēnik\ *adj*

eo·sin·o·phil \,ēə'sinə,fil\ *or* **eo·sin·o·phile** \-,fīl\ *n* -s [*eosin* + *-o-* + *-phil, -phile*] : a leukocyte or other granulocyte with cytoplasmic inclusions readily stained by eosin — called also *acidophile* — **eo·sin·o·phil·ic** \-¦sinə¦filik\ *adj*

eosinophile \"\ *or* **eosinophil** \"\ *adj* : staining readily with eosin — used chiefly of cells or cell constituents

eo·sin·o·phil·ia \,⸗,⸗⸗'filēə\ *n* -s [NL, fr. ISV *eosinophile* + NL *-ia*] : an abnormal increase in the number of eosinophils in the blood characteristic of allergic states and various parasitic infestations — **eo·sin·o·phil·ic** \¦⸗⸗¦⸗⸗¦filik\ *adj*

eosinophilic granuloma *n* : a disease of adolescents and young adults marked by the formation of granulomas in bone and the presence in them of histiocytes and eosinophile cells with secondary deposition of cholesterol

eo·sper·ma·top·ter·is \,ē(,)ō,spərmə'täptərəs\ *n, cap* [NL, fr. *eo-* + *spermat-* + *-pteris*] : a genus of fossil seed ferns of the Devonian Lavive structure and terminal sporangia similar to those of Psilophyton but lacking the leafiness of the Carboniferous and later ferns

eos·pho·rite \ē'äsfə,rīt\ *n* -s [Gk *heōsphoros* bringer of dawn, morning star (fr. *heōs, ēōs* dawn) + E *-ite*; fr. its pink color — more at EAST] : a hydrous aluminum manganese phosphate $(Mn,Fe)Al(PO_4)(OH)_2.H_2O$ occurring in prismatic crystals or massive that is generally rose-pink in color

eo·su·chia \,ēō'sükēə\ *n pl, cap* [NL, fr. *eo-* + Gk *souchos*, a kind of crocodile + NL *-ia*] : an order of Reptilia comprising primitive extinct 2-arched reptiles (subclass Lepidosauria) from the Upper Permian that are sometimes considered ancestral to modern lizards and snakes — **eo·su·chi·an** \¦⸗⸗¦⸗⸗ən\ *adj or n*

eöt·vös balance \'ət|(,)vəsh-, 'et|, 'ōt,vōsh-, 'ōtvəsh-\ *n, usu cap E* [after Roland *Eötvös* †1871 Hung. physicist] : a sensitive torsion balance used for the measurement of variations in the density of the underlying rocks that records the horizontal gradient of gravity

eötvös unit *n, usu cap E* : a unit for expressing horizontal gradients of gravity (as in geophysical prospecting) equal to 10^{-9} gal per horizontal centimeter

-eous \ēəs, yəs; *or as when the e influences the pronunciation of the preceding consonant as in "cretaceous"*\ *adj suffix* [L *-eus* composed of, of the nature of or resembling (a specified substance); akin to Gk *-eos* composed of, Skt *-aya*] : like : resembling : of the nature of ⟨aqueous⟩ ⟨vitreous⟩

eo·zo·ic \¦ēə¦zōik\ *adj or n, usu cap* [*eo-* + *-zoic*] **1** : PRECAMBRIAN **2** : Proterozoic or Algonkian

eo·zo·on \,ēə'zō,än\ *n, pl* **eozoons** \-nz\ *or* **eo·zoa** \-ōə\ [NL, fr. *eo-* + *-zoon*] : a banded arrangement of various ophicalcites associated with the Grenville series of Canada and formerly regarded as the remains of an animal (*Eozoon canadense*) related to the existing Foraminifera — **eo·zo·on·al** \¦ēə¦zōənᵊl\ *adj*

ep- — see EPI-

ep *abbr* **1** [LL *episcopus*] bishop **2** epistle

EP *abbr or n* -s extended play

EP *abbr* **1** electroplate **2** endpaper **3** endpoint **4** [F *en passant*] in passing **5** estimated position **6** evening prayer **7** excess profits **8** extreme pressure

¹**ep·a·crid** \'epəkrəd\ *adj* [NL *Epacridaceae*] : of or relating to the Epacridaceae

²**epacrid** \"\ *n* -s : a plant of the family Epacridaceae

ep·a·cri·da·ce·ae \,epəkrə'dāsē,ē\ *n pl, cap* [NL, fr. *Epacrid-, Epacris*, type genus + *-aceae*] : a large family of Australasian heathlike shrubs, small trees, and woody vines (order Ericales) having flowers with usu. five stamens adnate to the corolla tube and the ovary surrounded by a hypogynous disk or five free scales — **ep·a·cri·da·ceous** \¦⸗⸗⸗¦dāshəs\ *adj*

ep·a·cris \'epəkrəs\ *n* [NL, fr. Gk *epakros* pointed at the end; fr. the sharply pointed leaves] **1** *cap* : a genus (the type of the family Epacridaceae) of plants having a disk of five scales around the ovary and as fruit a small globular capsule with numerous minute seeds **2** -ES : any plant of the genus *Epacris*

epact \'ē,pakt, 'e,-\ *n* -s [MF *epacte*, fr. LL *epacta*, fr. Gk *epaktē*, fr. fem. of *epaktos*, verbal of *epagein* to bring in, lead on, intercalate, teach by induction, fr. *epi-* + *agein* to lead, drive — more at AGENT] **1 a** : the number of days' difference between a lunar year and a solar year — called also *annual epact* **b** : the number of days' difference between a lunar month and a calendar month — called also *menstrual epact* **2** : the age in number of days of the moon at the beginning of the calendar year used in determining the date of Easter

epac·tal \(')ē¦paktᵊl, (')e¦p-, ə'p-\ *adj* [prob. fr. F *épactal*, fr. Gk *epaktos* + F *-al*] *of a bone* : occurring irregularly in the sutures of the skull — compare WORMIAN BONE

ep·a·go·ge \'epə,gōjē *sometimes* -gäjē *or* ,⸗⸗'⸗⸗\ *n* -s [LL, fr. Gk *epagōgē*, fr. *epagein*] : logical induction from all the particulars comprised under the inferred generalization : induction by simple enumeration — compare BACONIAN INDUCTION — **ep·a·gog·ic** \¦⸗⸗¦gäjik\ *adj*

ep·a·gom·e·nal \¦epə¦gämənᵊl\ *adj* [Gk *epagomenos* (pres.

part. pass. of *epagein*) + E *-al*] **:** INTERCALARY — used esp. of certain days of the Egyptian solar calendar

epalpate \(ˈ)ē+\ *adj* [*e-* + *palpate*] **:** lacking palpi

ep·a·naph·o·ra \ˌepəˈnaf(ə)rə\ *n* [LL, fr. LGk, fr. Gk, reference, act of referring, fr. *epanapherein* to refer to, ascribe, fr. *epi-* + *anapherein* to carry up — more at ANAPHORA] **:** ANAPHORA 1a

ep·a·nor·thi·dae \ˌepəˈnȯ(r)thəˌdē\ [NL, fr. *epi-* + Gk *anorthos* upright, erect + NL *-idae*] *syn of* CAENOLESTIDAE

ep·a·nor·tho·sis \-ˌnȯ(r)ˈthōsə̇s\ *n* -ES [LL, fr. Gk *epanorthōsis* correction, revision, fr. *epanorthoun* to correct, revise (fr. *ep-* + *anorthoun* to restore, correct, fr. *ana-* + *orthoun* to straighten, fr. *orthos* straight, right — more at ORTH-] **:** a substitution of a more emphatic word or phrase for one just preceding (as in "Most brave, nay, most heroic act!")

epapillate \(ˌ)ē+\ *adj* [*e-* + L *papilla* nipple + E *-ate* — more at PAPULE] **:** being without papillae

ep·apophysis \ˌep+\ *n, pl* **epapophyses** [NL, fr. *epi-* + *apophysis*] **:** a median dorsal process of the centrum of a vertebra

epappose \(ˈ)ē+\ *adj* [*e-* + *pappose*] **:** not pappose

ep·arch \ˈeˌpärk\ *n* -S [Gk *eparchos*, fr. *epi-* + *archos* ruler — more at ARCHI-] **:** the chief official of a Greek eparchy **2 :** a bishop in the Eastern Orthodox Church

ep·arch·ate \-kə̇t, -ˌkāt\ *n* -S **:** EPARCHY

ep·ar·chi·al \(ˈ)eˈpärkēəl\ *adj* **:** of or relating to an eparchy

ep·archy \ˈeˌpärkē\ *n* -ES [Gk *eparchia*, fr. *eparchos* + *-ia* -y] **1 :** a subdivision of a nomarchy **2 :** a diocese in the Eastern Orthodox Church

ep·arcuale \(ˌ)ep+\ *n, pl* **eparcualia** [NL, fr. *epi-* + *arcuale*] **:** any of the ossification centers from which the spines of the vertebrae develop — compare ARCUALE

ep·arterial \ˌep+\ *adj* [*epi-* + *arterial*] **:** situated above an artery; *specif* **:** of or relating to the first branch of the right bronchus — compare HYPARTERIAL

épau·lé \ˌāpōˈlā\ *adj* [F, fr. past part. of *épauler* to place the shoulder forward, fr. *épaule* shoulder] *ballet* **:** having one shoulder forward

epaule·ment \āpōlmäⁿ\ *n, pl* **epaulements** \-äⁿ(z)\ [F *épaulement*, fr. *épaule* + *-ment*] **1 :** a barricade of earth like a rough parapet used mainly as cover from flanking fire **2** *usu* **épaulement** \"\ [F, fr. *épauler* + *-ment*] *ballet* **:** a shoulder movement performed by turning the body from the waist upward and bringing one shoulder forward and the other back

ep·au·let *also* **ep·au·lette** \ˌepəˈle|t, ˈepəl|, *usu* |d.+V\ *n* -S [F *épaulette*, dim. of *épaule* shoulder, fr. OF *espaule*, fr. LL *spatula*, *spathula* shoulder blade, spoon for stirring, dim. of L *spatha* wooden spoon, sword, fr. Gk *spathē* blade of a loom, oar, or sword — more at SPADE] **1 :** something that ornaments or protects the shoulder: as **a :** an ornamental fringed usu. gold-colored shoulder pad on a uniform (as the full-dress uniform formerly worn by military officers) **b :** any one of the small articulated shoulder pieces on a suit of plate armor — compare PAULDRON **c :** an ornamental strip sewn across the shoulder of a dress **d :** a shoulder loop (as on a trench coat) **2 :** a 5-sided step cut of a gem

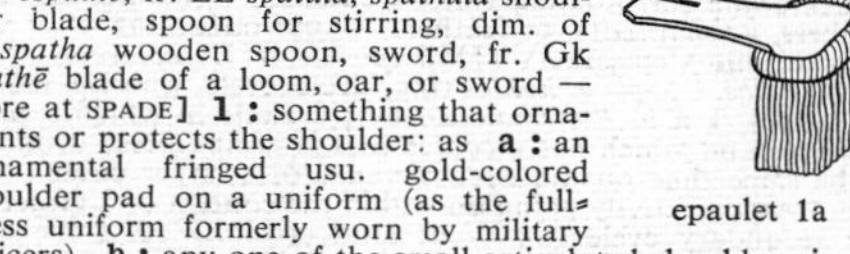
epaulet 1a

epaulet bat *n* **:** any of several African fruit bats having males distinguished by shoulder glands overlaid with tufts of white hair and constituting *Epomophorus* and related genera

epaulet fish *n* **:** a highly esteemed percoid food fish (*Glaucosoma scapulare*) of the southern Queensland coast of Australia

epaulette tree *n* **:** a tree (*Pterostyrax hispida*) of the family Styracaceae having alternate stalked leaves, hanging clusters of white fragrant flowers, and bristly 10-ribbed fruit

épau·lière \ˌāˌpōlˈye(ə)r\ *n* -S [F, fr. OF *espaulliere*, fr. *espaule*] **:** the part of a suit of armor covering the shoulder **:** shoulder plate ⟨they were armed to the teeth . . . with heavy ~s on their shoulders and iron morions on their heads —T.B.Costain⟩

ep·ax·i·al \(ˈ)eˈpaksēəl\ *also* **ep·ax·on·ic** \ˌeˌpakˈsänik\ *adj* [*epaxial* fr. *epi-* + *axial*; *epaxonic* fr. *epi-* + Gk *axon-*, *axōn* axle, axis + E *-ic* — more at AXIS] **:** located above or on the dorsal side of an axis — **ep·ax·i·al·ly** \(ˈ)eˈpaksēəlē\ *adv*

EPC *abbr* editor's presentation copy

EPD *abbr* excess profits duty

épée \ˈeˌpā, ˈāˌpā, ≠ˈ≠\ *n* -S [F, fr. L *spatha* wooden spoon, sword — more at EPAULET] **1 :** a fencing or dueling sword having a bowl-shaped guard and a rigid 35-inch blade with no cutting edge that has a fluted triangular section tapering to a sharp point blunted with a metal stop for fencing and weighing more than a foil or saber **2 :** the art or practice of fencing with the épée that includes the whole body as the target

épée

épée·ist \-āəst\ *n* -S [F *épéiste*, fr. *épée* + *-iste* -ist] **:** one that uses an épée

¹epei·ra \ə̇ˈpīrə\ [NL, fr. *epi-* + *-eira* (fr. Gk *eirein* to fasten in rows, string together) — more at SERIES] *syn of* ARANEA

²epeira \"\ *n* -S **:** a spider of the genus *Aranea* **:** GARDEN SPIDER

epei·ric \ə̇ˈpīrik, (ˈ)eˌp-\ *adj* [Gk *ēpeiros* mainland, continent + E *-ic*] *of a shallow sea* **:** that covers a large part of a continent while remaining connected with the ocean — compare EPICONTINENTAL

¹epei·rid \-rə̇d\ *adj* [NL *Epeiridae*] **:** of or relating to the Argiopidae

²epeirid \"\ *n* -S **:** a spider of the family Argiopidae

epei·ri·dae \ə̇ˈpīrəˌdē\ [NL, fr. *Epeira* + *-idae*] *syn of* ARGIOPIDAE

epei·ro·gen·e·sis \ə̇ˌpīrō+\ *n, pl* **epeirogeneses** [NL, fr. Gk *ēpeiro-* (fr. *ēpeiros* mainland, continent) + L *genesis*] **:** EPEIROGENY — **epei·ro·ge·net·ic** \ə̇ˈpīrō+\ *adj*

epei·ro·gen·ic *also* **epi·ro·gen·ic** \ə̇ˌpīrōˈjenik\ *adj* **:** of or relating to epeirogeny

ep·ei·rog·e·ny *also* **ep·i·rog·e·ny** \ˌeˌpīˈräjənē\ *n* -ES [Gk *ēpeiro-* + E *-geny*] **:** the deformation of the earth's crust by which the broader features of relief (as continents, ocean basins, and greater plateaus) are produced — compare DIASTROPHISM, OROGENY

epeirot *var of* EPIROTE

ep·ei·so·di·on \ˌeˌpīˈsōdēˌän\ *n, pl* **epeiso·dia** \-ēə\ [Gk — more at EPISODE] **:** EPISODE 1a

ep·embryonic \(ˌ)ep+\ *adj* [*epi-* + *embryonic*] **:** of or relating to biological stages immediately following the embryonic

ep·encephalon \ˌep+\ *n, pl* **epencephala** [NL, fr. *epi-* + *encephalon*] **1 :** METENCEPHALON **2 :** RHOMBENCEPHALON

ependym- *or* **ependymo-** *comb form* [NL, fr. *ependyma*] **:** ependyma ⟨*ependymitis*⟩ ⟨*ependymoepithelium*⟩

ep·en·dy·ma \eˈpendəmə\ *n* -S [Gk, upper garment, fr. *epi-* + *endyma* garment, fr. *endyein* to put on, fr. *en-* ²en- + *dyein* to sink, get into (clothes), put on] **:** an epithelial membrane lining the ventricles of the brain and the canal of the spinal cord — **ep·en·dy·mal** \(ˈ)eˈpendəməl\ *adj* — **ep·en·dy·mary** \-dəˌmerē\ *adj*

ep·en·dy·mo·ma \eˌpendəˈmōmə\ *n, pl* **ependymomas** \-məz\ *also* **ependymoma·ta** \-mədə\ [NL, fr. *ependym-* + *-oma*] **:** a glioma arising in or near the ependyma

ep·en·the·sis \ə̇ˈpen(t)thəsə̇s, eˈp-\ *n, pl* **epenthe·ses** \-əˌsēz\ [LL, fr. Gk, fr. *epentithenai* to insert a letter, fr. *epi-* + *entithenai* to put in, fr. *en-* ²en- + *tithenai* to put, place — more at DO] **1 :** the occurrence of an intercalated consonant (as a homorganic stop after a nasal consonant) or vowel in a succession of speech sounds without a counterpart in etymon or in orthography (as \t\ in \ˈfents\ *fence;* \ə\ in \ˈathəˌlēt\ *athlete*) **2 :** an insertion of a letter in a word to make spelling conform to epenthetic pronunciation (as *b* in *nimble*, earlier *nimel*) — compare ANAPTYXIS

ep·en·thet·ic \ˌepənˈthed·|ik, -et|, |ēk\ *adj* [Gk *epenthetikos*, fr. (assumed) Gk *epenthetos* (verbal of *epentithenai* + Gk *-ikos* -ic] **:** inserted by, relating to, or constituting epenthesis — compare INTRUSIVE

epergne \ə̇ˈpərn, ēˈ-,āˈ-, -pə̄n,-pəin\ *n* -S [prob. fr. F *épargne* economy, saving, fr. *épargner* to save, fr. OF *espargnier*, *esparner*, of Gmc origin; akin to OHG *sparōn* to save — more at SPARE] **:** a composite centerpiece of silver or glass used esp. on a dinner table for serving or decoration: as **a :** a stand holding a large central dish or vase, several smaller dishes or vases, and sometimes candles **b :** a 2-tiered center dish or dish and vase

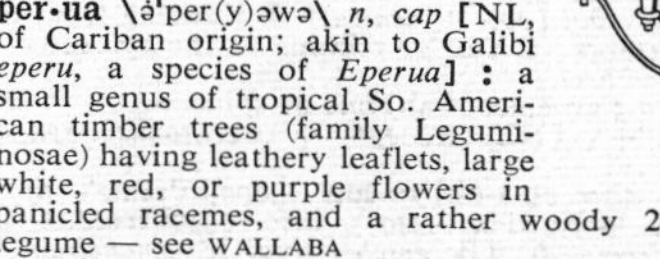
epergne a

eper·ua \ə̇ˈper(y)əwə\ *n, cap* [NL, of Cariban origin; akin to Galibi *eperu*, a species of *Eperua*] **:** a small genus of tropical So. American timber trees (family Leguminosae) having leathery leaflets, large white, red, or purple flowers in panicled racemes, and a rather woody 2-valved 2-seeded legume — see WALLABA

ep·eryth·ro·zo·on \ˌepəˌrithrəˈzōˌän\ *n* [NL, fr. *epi-* + *erythr-* + *-zoon*] **1** *cap* **:** a genus of blood parasites of vertebrates commonly considered to be rickettsiae related to the organism causing Oroya fever in man **2** *pl* **eperythrozoa** \-ōə\ **:** an organism of the genus *Eperythrozoon*

ep·eryth·ro·zo·on·o·sis \-ˌzōəˈnōsə̇s\ *n* [NL, fr. *Eperythrozoon* + *-osis*] **:** infection with or disease caused by parasites of the genus *Eperythrozoon* that is esp. severe in young pigs in which it takes the form of an anemia accompanied by jaundice and often terminates fatally

ep·exegesis \(ˌ)eˌp+ˌ-\ *n, pl* **epexegeses** [Gk *epexēgēsis*, fr. *epi-* + *exēgēsis* — more at EXEGESIS] **:** an explanation following a word or larger part of a text that limits its application or clarifies its meaning (as *the great river, the river Euphrates*) **:** additional information

ep·exegetical *also* **ep·exegetic** \"+\ *adj* [fr. *epexegesis*, after such pairs as E *exegesis: exegetical, exegetic*] **:** constituting epexegesis ⟨the temptation of . . . piling up *epexegetic* clauses —George Saintsbury⟩

eph- — see EPI-

ephah \ˈēfə, ˈefə\ *also* **ephi** \-ˌfī\ *or* **epha** \-ˌfə\ *n* -S [Heb *ēphāh*, fr. Egypt *ipt*] **:** an ancient Hebrew unit of dry measure equal to 1/10 homer or a little over a bushel — compare ³BATH

eph·apse \ˈeˌfaps\ *n* -S [Gk *ephapsis* act of touching, knot, fr. *epi-* + *apsis* loop, wheel — more at APSE] **:** a point of contact between neurons; *esp* **:** the lateral contact between parallel fibers in a nerve or fiber tract — **eph·ap·tic** \(ˈ)eˈfaptik\ *adj*

ep·har·mone \(ˈ)epˈhärˌmōn\ *n* -S [back-formation fr. *epharmony*] **:** an organism that has undergone adaptation to a particular habitat **:** ECAD

ep·harmonic \ˌep+\ *adj* **:** of, relating to, or constituting epharmony

ep·harmony \(ˈ)ep+\ *n* [ISV *epi-* + *harmony;* orig. formed in F] **:** the immediate acquirement by an organism of a morphological or physiological alteration that enables it to exist in an altered environment

eph·ebe \ˈeˌfēb; ə̇ˈfēb, eˈ-\ *n* -S [L *ephebus*, fr. Gk *ephēbos*, fr. *epi-* + *hēbē* early manhood, youth] **:** a young man; *specif* **:** EPHEBUS

eph·e·be·um \ˌefəˈbēəm\ *n* -S [L, fr. Gk *ephēbeion*, fr. neut. of *ephēbeios* youthful, fr. *ephēbos*] **:** a place for gymnastic exercises in ancient Greek palaestrae or Roman thermae; *specif* **:** the exercise court for ephebi

ephe·bic \ə̇ˈfēbik, (ˈ)eˈf-\ *adj* [Gk *ephēbikos*, fr. *ephēbos* + *-ikos* -ic] **1 :** of or relating to the ephebi ⟨~ oath⟩ ⟨~ inscriptions⟩ **2** *biol* **:** being between the neanic and gerontic stages **:** ADULT

ephe·bus \ə̇ˈfēbəs, eˈ-\ *n, pl* **ephe·bi** \-ˌbī\ [L] **:** a youth of ancient Greece; *esp* **:** an Athenian 18 or 19 years old receiving military and gymnastic training in preparation for full citizenship

ephec·tic \ə̇ˈfektik, (ˈ)eˈf-\ *adj* [Gk *ephektikos*, fr. *ephektos*, verbal of *epechein* to hold back, fr. *epi-* + *echein* to hold, have — more at SCHEME] **:** given to suspense of judgment — used of a school of ancient skeptics; compare EPOCHE

ephed·ra \ə̇ˈfedrə, ˈefədrə\ *n* [NL, fr. L, horsetail, fr. Gk, fr. *ephedros* sitting upon, fr. *epi-* + *hedra* seat — more at SIT] **1** *cap* **:** a large genus of jointed nearly leafless desert shrubs (family Gnetaceae) having the leaves reduced to opposite or verticillate scales at the nodes — see MAHUANG **2** -S **:** any plant of the genus *Ephedra*

ephed·rine \ə̇ˈfedrə̇n, eˈf-; ˈefəˌdrēn, ˈefədrən\ *n* -S [ISV *ephedra-* (fr. NL *Ephedra*, genus name of *Ephedra sinica*) + *-ine*] **:** a white crystalline alkaloid $C_6H_5CHOHCH(CH_3)NHCH_3$ extracted esp. from mahuang or made synthetically and used often in the form of a salt (as the sulfate) chiefly in relieving hay fever, asthma, and nasal congestion

ephe·lis \ə̇ˈfēlə̇s\ *n, pl* **ephe·li·des** \-ləˌdēz, -feləˌ-\ [NL, fr. Gk *ephēlis*] **:** FRECKLE

¹ephem·era \ə̇ˈfem(ə)rə\ *n* [NL, fr. Gk *ephēmerē*, fem. of *ephēmeros*] **1 a** *cap* **:** a genus (the type of the family Ephemeridae) of mayflies with shining transparent wings and strong functional legs **b** *pl* **ephemeras** \-rəz\ *or* **ephemer·ae** \-məˌrē\ **:** MAYFLY, EPHEMERID **2** *pl* **ephemeras** *or* **ephemerae** **:** ²EPHEMERAL

²ephemera *pl of* EPHEMERON

¹ephem·er·al \ə̇ˈfem(ə)rəl, ēˈf-, (ˈ)eˈf-, *chiefly Brit* -fēm-\ *adj* [Gk *ephēmeros*, lit., lasting a day, daily (fr. *epi-* + *hēmera* day) + E *-al* — more at HEMERA] **1 a :** lasting or existing briefly **:** TEMPORARY ⟨~ boundaries⟩ ⟨their floors and ceilings . . . thin and ~ in appearance as a card palace —Roderick Cameron⟩ **:** FLEETING ⟨jazz is perishable, ~, elusive —Whitney Balliett⟩; *specif* **:** lasting only one day ⟨~ fever⟩ ⟨~ blossom⟩ **b :** of interest or value for only a short time **:** TOPICAL ⟨were not local and ~ . . . but universal and timeless —J.P.Boyd⟩ **c :** existing in an immaterial form ⟨~ data, the businessman's unrecorded wealth of experiential knowledge of the behavior of consumers⟩ **:** INTANGIBLE **2 :** devoted to what is of temporary interest ⟨a medium so ~ as radio⟩ ⟨prose drama is the most ~ of the arts . . . practically all plays find their resting places on the library shelves after their brief day or few decades in the theater —R.A.Cordell⟩ **syn** see TRANSIENT

²ephemeral \"\ *n* -S **:** something ephemeral; *specif* **:** a plant that grows, flowers, and dies in a few days (as many desert and arctic annuals)

ephemeral fever *n* **:** a three-day fever of cattle

ephem·er·al·i·ty \ə̇ˌfeməˈralədˌē, ēˌf-, (ˌ)eˌf-, -ətē, -i, *chiefly Brit* -fēm-\ *n* -ES **1 :** the quality or state of being ephemeral ⟨a sense of ~, of pale erratic fragility —D.H.Lawrence⟩ **2 :** ²EPHEMERAL — usu. used in pl. ⟨"Barrack-Room Ballads" . . . clever *ephemeralities* —Henry Austin⟩

ephem·er·al·ly \ə̇ˈfem(ə)rəlē, ēˈf, (ˈ)eˈf-, -li, *chiefly Brit* -fēm-\ *adv* **:** in an ephemeral manner ⟨~ popular⟩

ephem·er·al·ness \-əlnə̇s\ *n* -ES **:** the quality or state of being ephemeral

ephemeral stream *n* **:** a stream that flows only briefly during and following a period of rainfall in the immediate locality

ephem·er·an \ə̇ˈfem(ə)rən\ *n* -S [Gk *ephēmeros* + E *-an*] **:** EPHEMERID 1

¹ephem·er·id \-rə̇d\ *adj* [NL *Ephemerida*] **:** of or relating to the Plectoptera

²ephemerid \"\ *n* -S **1 :** one of the Plectoptera **:** MAYFLY **2** [Gk *ephēmeros* + E *-id*] **:** ²EPHEMERAL

eph·e·mer·i·da \ˌefəˈmerədə\ [NL, fr. *Ephemera* + *-ida*] *syn of* PLECTOPTERA

eph·e·mer·i·dae \-əˌdē\ *n pl, cap* [NL, fr. *Ephemera*, type genus + *-idae*] **:** a family of mayflies once made coextensive with the order Plectoptera but now restricted to forms having shining transparent wings as adults and as naiads very large mandibles curved out at the tips, gills extending dorsally over the abdomen, and antennae with long cilia

ephem·er·is \ə̇ˈfem(ə)rə̇s\ *n, pl* **eph·e·mer·i·des** \ˌefəˈmerəˌdēz\ [L, diary, journal, ephemeris, fr. Gk *ephēmeris*, fr. *ephēmeros* daily — more at EPHEMERAL] **1 a :** a publication giving the computed places of the celestial bodies for each day of the year or for other regular intervals and including other data for the astronomer and navigator **:** an astronomical almanac ⟨the annual ~ —Paul Herget⟩ **b :** any tabular statement of the assigned places of a celestial body for regular intervals — compare SEARCH EPHEMERIS **c** *archaic* **:** an almanac or calendar ⟨cures plagues, piles and pox by the *ephemerides* —Ben Jonson⟩ ⟨he wrote an ~ of the Irish saints —Thomas Fuller⟩ **2** *archaic* **:** DIARY, JOURNAL **3 :** ²EPHEMERAL

ephemeris time *n* **:** a uniform measure of time defined by the orbital motions of the planets and determined by correcting mean solar time for the irregularities arising from variations in the rate of rotation of the earth

ephem·er·on \ə̇ˈfeməˌrän\ *n, pl* **ephem·era** \-m(ə)rə\ *also* **ephemerons** \-məˌränz\ [NL, fr. Gk *ephēmeron* May fly, fr. neut. of *ephēmeros* lasting a day, short-lived, daily] **1 :** EPHEMERID **2 :** ²EPHEMERAL

ephem·er·op·tera \ə̇ˌfeməˈräpt(ə)rə\ [NL, fr. Gk *ephēmeros* + NL *-ptera*] *syn of* PLECTOPTERA

ephem·er·op·ter·an \≠ˌ≠≠ˈ≠t(ə)rən\ *adj* [NL *Ephemeroptera* + E *-an*] **:** PLECTOPTERAN

ephem·er·ous \ə̇ˈfem(ə)rəs, ēˈf-, (ˈ)eˈf-, *chiefly Brit* -fēm-\ *adj* [Gk *ephēmeros* — more at EPHEMERAL] **:** EPHEMERAL

¹ephe·sian \ə̇ˈfēzhən, ēˈ-,eˈ- *sometimes* -zhēən\ *adj, usu cap* [L *Ephesius* (fr. Gk *Ephesios*, fr. *Ephesos* Ephesus, ancient city of Asia Minor) + E *-an*] **:** of or belonging to Ephesus

²ephesian \"\ *n* -S **1** *cap* **:** a native or inhabitant of Ephesus **2** *usu cap* **:** a boon companion ⟨it is thine host, thine *Ephesian*, calls —Shak.⟩

eph·e·sine \ˈefəˌsin, -ˌsēn, -ˌsōn\ *adj, usu cap* [*Ephes*us + *-ine*] **:** EPHESIAN

ephes·tia \ə̇ˈfestēə\ *n, cap* [NL, fr. Gk, fem. of *ephestios* situated by the hearth, of the house or family, fr. *epi-* + *estia* hearth] **:** a genus of small dull-colored or mottled moths (family Pyralididae) having larvae that spin silken tunnels in and feed on a variety of stored food products — see ALMOND MOTH, RAISIN MOTH

eph·ete \ˈeˌfēt\ *n, pl* **ephe·tae** \ˈefəˌtē\ *or* **ephe·tai** \-ˌtī\ *usu cap* [Gk *ephetēs*, fr. *ephienai* to command, fr. *epi-* + *hienai* to send] **:** a member of an ancient Athenian court that tried certain murder cases — compare AREOPAGITE

ephi *var of* EPHAH

eph·i·al·tes \ˌefēˈalˌtēz\ *n, pl* **ephialtes** [Gk *ephialtēs*] *archaic* **:** NIGHTMARE 1, 2

ephip·pi·al \ə̇ˈfipēəl, (ˈ)eˈf-\ *adj* [NL *ephippium* + E *-al*] **:** of or relating to an ephippium

ephip·pi·dae \ə̇ˈfipəˌdē, eˈf-\ *n pl, cap* [NL, fr. *Ephippus*, type genus (fr. Gk *ephippos* on horseback, riding, fr. *epi-* + *hippos* horse) + *-idae* — more at EQUINE] **:** a family of chiefly tropical percoid fishes comprising the spadefishes

ephip·pi·um \-pēəm\ *n, pl* **ephip·pia** \-pēə\ [NL, fr. Gk *ephippion* saddlecloth, saddle, fr. neut. of *ephippios* for putting on a horse, fr. *epi-* + *hippios* of a horse, fr. *hippos* horse] **1 :** SELLA TURCICA **2 :** a saddlelike chitinous thickening over the brood pouch of various cladocerans that when shed forms a bivalve capsule containing the winter eggs

eph·od \ˈeˌfäd, ˈēˌfäd, ˈefəd\ *n* -S [Heb *ēphōd*] **1 :** a linen apron worn by ancient Hebrews in religious ceremonies; *specif* **:** an ornate vestment of the Jewish high priest consisting of a garment like an apron suspended from the shoulders and fastened with a band ⟨make the ~ of gold, of blue and purple and scarlet stuff, and of fine twined linen, skillfully worked —Exod 28:6 (RSV)⟩ **2 :** an Old Testament instrument of priestly divination (as an image of deity or a box)

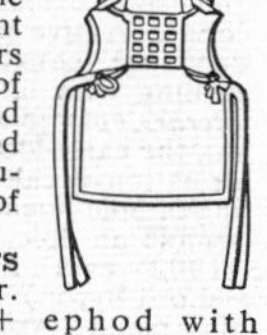
ephod with breastplate attached

eph·or \ˈefər, ˈeˌfȯ(ə)r, ˈēˌfȯ-\ *n, pl* **ephors** \-rz\ *also* **epho·ri** \ˈefəˌrī\ [L *ephorus*, fr. Gk *ephoros*, fr. *ephoran* to oversee, fr. *epi-* + *horan* to see — more at WARY] **1 :** a magistrate in various ancient Dorian states; *esp* **:** one of a body of five magistrates chosen by the Spartans to exercise a controlling power over the king **2 :** a government official in modern Greece **:** OVERSEER

eph·or·al·ty \ˈefəraltē\ *n* -ES [*ephor* + *-alty* (as in *mayoralty*)] **:** EPHORATE

eph·or·ate \ˈefəˌrāt, -ˌrōt\ *n* -S **1 :** the office of ephor **2 :** the body of ephors

¹ephra·im·ite \ˈēfrēəˌmīt\ *n* -S *usu cap* [*Ephraim*, younger son of Joseph (Gen 41:50–52), the eponymous ancestor of the Ephraimites (Josh 16) + E *-ite*] **1 :** a member of the Hebrew tribe of Ephraim — compare MANASSITE **2 :** a native or inhabitant of the ancient northern kingdom of Israel

²ephraimite \"\ *adj, usu cap* **:** EPHRAIMITIC

ephra·im·it·ic \ˌ≠≠≠ˈmid·ik\ *adj, usu cap* **:** of or belonging to the Ephraimites or to the northern kingdom of Israel

ephra·ta \ˈefrəd·ə\ *adj, usu cap* [fr. *Ephrata*, Pa., where the community was established] **:** of or relating to a monastic community of German Seventh-Day Baptists founded in Pennsylvania in the early part of the 18th century

eph·rath·ite \ˈefrəˌthīt\ *n* -S *cap* [*Ephrath* (Bethlehem), Palestine + E *-ite*] **1 :** BETHLEHEMITE **2 :** EPHRAIMITE 1

eph·tha·lite \ˈefthəˌlīt\ *also* **heph·tha·lite** \ˈhe-\ *n* -S *usu cap* **:** a member of the western branch of the Yueh-chi-Tocharians that ruled Russian Turkestan and northwest India in the 5th and 6th centuries A.D. — called also *White Hun*

eph·y·da·tia \ˌefəˈdāsh(ē)ə\ *n, cap* [NL, fr. Gk, fem. of *ephydatios* of the water, in the water, fr. *epi-* + *hydat-*, *hydōr* water — more at WATER] **:** a common genus of freshwater encrusting sponges (family Spongillidae) often bright green from included symbiotic algae

¹ephyd·rid \ə̇ˈfidrə̇d, eˈ-; ˈefədrə̇d, -ˌdrid\ *adj* [NL *Ephydridae*] **:** belonging or relating to the Ephydridae

²ephydrid \"\ *n* -S **:** one of the Ephydridae

ephyd·ri·dae \ə̇ˈfidrəˌdē, eˈ-\ *n pl, cap* [NL, fr. *Ephydra*, type genus (fr. Gk *ephydrē*, fem. of *ephydros* living on the water, fr. *epi-* + *-hydros*, fr. *hydōr* water) + *-idae*] **:** a large family of small dark-colored two-winged flies that usu. lack bristles, live in moist places, and have cylindrical larvae having mouth hooks and living in fresh or salt water or ocean. in plants — see BRINE FLY

eph·y·ra \ˈefərə\ *n, pl* **eph·y·rae** \-ˌrē\ *or* **ephyras** [NL, fr. *Ephyra*, a nymph, fr. L, fr. Gk] **:** a free-swimming larva of a scyphozoan jellyfish formed by transverse fission of a scyphistoma and growing into a medusa — compare STROBILA

ephyr·u·la \ə̇ˈfir(y)ələ\ *n, pl* **ephyru·lae** \-ˌlē\ [NL, fr. *Ephyra*, a nymph + NL *-ula*] **:** EPHYRA

épi \(ˈ)āˈpē\ *n* -S [F, lit., ear of grain, fr. OF *espi*, fr. L *spica*, *spicum* point, head, tuft — more at SPIKE] **:** a covering for the apex of a sharp-pointed roof usu. in a finial

epi- *or* **ep-** *also* **eph-** *prefix* [*epi-* fr. ME, upon, fr. MF & ML; MF, fr. ML, fr. L, fr. Gk, fr. *epi* on, upon, to; *ep-* fr. MF, fr. L, fr. Gk, fr. *epi; eph-* fr. L, fr. Gk, fr. *epi;* akin to OE *eofot* crime, Goth *ifturna* next, following, L *ob* to, before, on account of, Skt *api* besides] **1 :** upon ⟨*epiphyte*⟩ **:** besides ⟨*epenthesis*⟩ **:** near to ⟨*epencephalon*⟩ **:** over ⟨*epicenter*⟩ **:** outer ⟨*epidermis*⟩ **:** anterior ⟨*epicnemial*⟩ **:** prior to ⟨*epacme*⟩ **:** after ⟨*epembryonic*⟩ — *epi-* before consonants other than *h*, and sometimes *ep-* before vowels and *eph-* before *h* (which is not repeated), but sometimes *epi-* even before *h* or a vowel **2 :** chemical compound or group related in some manner to a (specified) chemical compound or group: as **a :** epimer of a (specified) chemical compound ⟨*epicholesterol*⟩ ⟨*epirhamnose*⟩ **b :** chemical compound or group distinguished from a (specified) chemical compound or group by having a bridge connection ⟨*epichlorohydrin*⟩ ⟨9,10-*epidioxyanthracene*⟩ **3 :** altered — in petrographic terms ⟨*epidiorite*⟩ **4 :** resting on as a geological stratum **:** following in time — in names of geological eras, periods, systems, series, or formations ⟨*Eparchean*⟩

ep·i·an·drum \ˌepēˈandrəm\ *n* -S [NL, fr. *epi-* + *-andrum* (fr. neut. of *-andrus* -androus)] **:** the genital orifice of a male arachnid

epi·basal \ˌepə̇, ˌepē+\ *adj* [ISV *epi-* + *basal*] *bot* **:** situated anterior to the basal wall ⟨the ~ lower segment of a developing embryo⟩ — compare HYPOBASAL

epi·basidium \"+\ *n* [NL, fr. *epi-* + *basidium*] **1 :** a superior prolongation of each cell of the basidium of various heterobasidiomycetous fungi (as members of the order Tremellales) that bears the spore **2 :** PROMYCELIUM

epi·batholithic \"+\ *adj* [*epi-* + *batholithic*] *of an ore deposit* **:** located near the periphery of a batholith

epi·benthos \"+\ *n* [*epi-* + *benthos*] **:** the fauna and flora of the sea bottom between low-water mark and the mesobenthos down to a lower limit of about 100 fathoms

ep·i·bi·ont \ˌepəˈbīˌänt, ˌepēˈ-\ *n* -S [*epi-* + *-biont*] **:** an organism that lives on the body surface of another

¹epi·biotic \ˌepə̇, ˌepē+\ *adj* [*epi-* + *biotic*] **:** living on the surface of plants or living animals usu. parasitically — used esp. of fungi; compare EPIPHYTIC, EPIZOIC

²**epibiotic** \"\ *adj or n* : RELICT

ep·i·blast \ˈepə,blast\ *n* -s [*epi-* + *-blast*] **1** : the outer layer of the blastoderm : ECTODERM — compare GERM LAYER **2** : a small outgrowth shaped like a claw that lies in front of the plumule and opposite the scutellum in many grasses and has been considered to be a second cotyledon — **ep·i·blas·tic** \ˌepəˈblastik\ *adj*

ep·i·blem \ˈepə,blem\ *or* **ep·i·ble·ma** \ˌepəˈblēmə\ *n* -s [NL *epiblema*, fr. Gk *epiblēma* covering, fr. *epi-* + *blēma* throw, coverlet, fr. *ballein* to throw — more at DEVIL] : the superficial layer of tissue replacing the true epidermis in most roots and in stems of submerged aquatics

ep·i·bol·ic \ˌepəˈbälik\ *adj* : of, relating to, produced by, or involving epiboly ⟨~ invagination⟩ ⟨~ growth⟩

epib·o·ly *also* **epib·o·le** \əˈpibəlē, eˈ-\ *n, pl* **epibolies** *also* **epiboles** [Gk *epibolē* act of throwing or laying on, something thrown or laid on, fr. *epiballein* to throw on, fr. *epi-* + *ballein* to throw] : the growing of one part about another during embryogenesis, such growth of the dorsal lip area being one of the fundamental movements of gastrulation — compare INVAGINATION, INVOLUTION

¹**epi·branchial** \ˌepə, ˌepē+\ *adj* [*epi-* + *branchial*] : of or belonging to the segment next below the pharyngobranchial in a branchial arch

²**epibranchial** \"\ *n* -s : an epibranchial cartilage or bone

¹**ep·ic** \ˈepik, -pēk\ *also* **ep·i·cal** \ˈepəkəl, -pēk-\ *adj* [L *epicus*, fr. Gk *epikos*, fr. *epos* word, speech, epic poem + *-ikos* -ic, -ical — more at VOICE] **1 a** : of, relating to, or befitting an epic ⟨~ poets⟩ ⟨an ~ hero⟩ : HEROIC ⟨the ~ period in Greek history⟩ **b** : having the characteristics of, resembling, or suggestive of an epic ⟨they are heroic poems . . . but that they are ~ in any save the most general sense . . . is not quite clear —W.P.Ker⟩ **2** : extending beyond the usual or ordinary esp. in size or scope ⟨transforms the conventional length of bread into an ~ loaf —Rosamund Frost⟩ : undertaken on a grand scale ⟨the final paragraph of this ~ biography —W.L. Shirer⟩ : IMPOSING, IMPRESSIVE ⟨improvisation . . . that ranges from out-and-out burlesque to ~ grandeur of scene and action —Saxe Commins⟩ ⟨a faithful record of an ~ expedition —C.A. Lejeune⟩ ⟨a strange . . . human being of rather ~ proportions —Richard Watts⟩

²**epic** \"\ *n* -s **1** : a long narrative poem recounting the deeds of a legendary or historical hero: **a** : a long narrative poem (as Homer's *Iliad*) recounting heroic deeds set against a background of war and the supernatural, having a serious theme developed in a coherent and unified manner, written in a dignified style, and marked by certain formal characteristics (as a beginning in medias res, the invocation to the muse, and the use of extended similes) — called also *classical epic* **b** : a long narrative poem (as Milton's *Paradise Lost*) having the structure, conventions, and tone of the classical epic but dealing with later or different subject matter — called also *literary epic* **c** : a long narrative poem (as *Beowulf*) expressing the early ideals, characteristics, and traditions of a people or nation — called also *folk epic* **d** : the literary genre consisting of epic poems ⟨~ and romance⟩ **2** : something felt to resemble an epic ⟨an ~ in stone and marble —Samuel Butler †1902⟩: as **a** : a long narrative poem ⟨an ~ . . . every spring —Lord Byron⟩ **b** : a prose narrative (as a novel), play, or motion picture ⟨voluminous ~s on the moral conquest of poverty —E.S.Bates⟩ ⟨a Broadway ~ —Wolcott Gibbs⟩ ⟨eager for short features to exhibit along with the full-length Hollywood ~s —*Dun's Rev.*⟩; *esp* : one embodying a nation's ideals or historical traditions or centering around the adventures or achievements of a single person or character ⟨*Moby Dick* is an American ~ —Richard Chase⟩ **3** : a series of events or body of legend or tradition felt to form the proper subject of an epic ⟨revives the memories of the great American ~, the winning of the West —William Clark⟩ **4** *usu cap* : OLD IONIC

ep·i·cal·ly \-pək(ə)lē, -pēk-, -li\ *adv* : in an epic manner

epi·calyx \ˌepə, ˌepē+\ *n* [*epi-* + *calyx*] : an involucre resembling the true calyx but consisting simply of a whorl of bracts below the calyx (as in mallows) or resulting from the union of the sepal appendages (as in roses)

epi·can·thic fold \ˌepəˌkan(t)thik-, ˌepē\ *n* [NL *epicanthus* + E *-ic*] : a prolongation of a fold of the skin of the upper eyelid over the inner angle or both angles of the eye — called also *eye fold, Mongolian fold*

epi·canthus \ˌepə, ˌepē+\ *n* [NL, fr. *epi-* + *canthus*] : EPICANTHIC FOLD

ep·i·car·dia \ˌepəˈkärdēə\ *n* -s [NL, fr. *epi-* + Gk *kardia* heart — more at HEART] : the short part of the esophagus extending from the diaphragm to the stomach

ep·i·car·di·al \ˌ=ˈ=dēəl\ *also* **ep·i·car·di·ac** \-ē,ak\ *adj* [NL *epicardia* & *epicardium* + E *-al* or *-ac* (as in *cardiac*)] : of or relating to an epicardium or an epicardia

ep·i·car·di·um \ˌ=ˈ=dēəm\ *n, pl* **epicar·dia** \-ēə\ [NL, fr. *epi-* + *-cardium* (fr. Gk *kardia* heart)] **1** : the visceral part of the pericardium that closely invests the heart **2** : a tubular posterior prolongation of the bronchial sac of certain compound ascidians that takes part in the process of gemmation

¹**ep·i·car·id** \ˌepəˈkarəd\ *or* **ep·i·car·i·dan** \-rədᵊn\ *adj* [*epicarid* fr. NL *Epicaridea*; *epicaridan* fr. NL *Epicaridea* + E *-an*] : of or relating to the Epicaridea

²**epicarid** \"\ *or* **epicaridan** \"\ *n* -s : a crustacean of the suborder Epicaridea

ep·i·ca·rid·ea \ˌepəkəˈridēə\ *n pl, cap* [NL, fr. *epi-* + *-caridea* (fr. Gk *karid-, karis* shrimp)] : a suborder of Isopoda comprising isopods (as those of the family Bopyridae) of which the enlarged and modified females are parasites on other crustaceans while the minute males usu. live attached to the females

ep·i·car·i·des \ˌepəˈkarə,dēz\ [NL, fr. *epi-* + *-carides* (fr. Gk *karid-, karis* shrimp)] *syn of* EPICARIDEA

ep·i·carp \ˈepə,kärp\ *n* -s [F *épicarpe*, fr. *épi-* epi- + *-carpe* -carp] : the outermost layer of the pericarp of a fruit — see ENDOCARP illustration

ep·i·cau·ta \ˌepəˈkȯd·ə\ *n, cap* [NL, fr. Gk *epikautē*, fem. of *epikautos* burned at the tip, fr. *epikaiein* to burn on the surface, burn at the top, fr. *epi-* + *kaiein* to burn — more at CAUSTIC] : a cosmopolitan genus of blister beetles that feed on various cultivated plants as adults and that as larvae are predacious in egg masses or nests of insects

epic caesura *n* : a feminine caesura following an extra unstressed syllable intruded into accentual iambic meter under cover of the caesural pause which is there longer than usual (as in Shakespeare's "but how of Cawdor? ‖The Thane of Cawdor lives") — contrasted with *lyric caesura*

epic drama *n* : a modern episodic drama that seeks to provoke objective understanding of a social problem through a series of loosely connected scenes that avoid illusion and often interrupt the action to address the audience directly with analysis or argument (as by a narrator) or with documentation (as by a film) — compare LIVING NEWSPAPER

ep·i·cede \ˈepə,sēd\ *or* **ep·i·ce·di·um** \ˌ=ˈsēdēəm\ *n, pl* **epicedes** \ˈ=,sēdz\ *or* **epice·dia** \ˌ=ˈsēdēə\ [L *epicedium*, fr. Gk *epikēdeion*, fr. neut. of *epikēdeios* of a funeral, fr. *epikēdeia* funeral, fr. *epi-* + *kēdeia* funeral, mourning, fr. *kēdos* grief, trouble, sadness + *-eia* -y — more at HATE] : a funeral song or ode : DIRGE, ELEGY ⟨Lycidas . . . formed a part of a collection of ~s on Edward King —George Saintsbury⟩

ep·i·ce·di·al \ˌ=ˈsēdēəl\ *also* **ep·i·ce·di·an** \-ēən\ *adj* : of or relating to an epicede : ELEGIAC

epicele *var of* EPICOELIA

¹**ep·i·cene** \ˈepə,sēn\ *adj* [ME, fr. L *epicoenus*, fr. Gk *epikoinos*, fr. *epi-* + *koinos* common — more at CO-] **1** : having but one form to indicate either male or female sex (as Latin *bos* "a bull, ox, or cow") — used of a noun **2** : having characteristics typical of the other sex : INTERSEXUAL ⟨his brothers suspect the ~ wife because of her masculine arms —R.H.Lowie⟩ : EFFEMINATE **3** : lacking the typical characteristics of either sex : SEXLESS ⟨perpetual children . . . happy ~ Peter Pans —Dwight Macdonald⟩ **4** : lacking vigor ⟨recent ~ treatises . . . withdraw from the major task of evaluating significance —Ephraim Fischoff⟩ : lacking vigorous masculinity ⟨the hearty sportsman . . . really ~ beneath his tweeds —Wolcott Gibbs⟩ : DELICATE ⟨a swift ~ felicity of wit —Evelyn Waugh⟩

²**epicene** \"\ *n* -s : one who is epicene

ep·i·cen·ism \-ē,nizəm\ *n* -s : the quality or state of being epicene

epi·center \ˌepə, ˌepē+\ *n* [NL *epicentrum*, fr. *epi-* + L *centrum* center — more at CENTER] **1** *also* **epi·centrum** \"+\ : the part of the earth's surface directly above the focus of an earthquake **2** : CENTER 2 ⟨the White House, that ~ of world power —Stewart Alsop⟩

¹**epi·central** \"+\ *adj* [*epi-* + *central*] **1** : arising from the centrum of a vertebra **2** : of or relating to the epicenter of an earthquake ⟨~ area⟩

²**epicentral** \"\ *n* : an epicentral bone or spine

epi·ceratodus \"+\ [NL, fr. *epi-* + *Ceratodus*] *syn of* NEOCERATODUS

ep·i·chei·re·ma *also* **ep·i·chi·re·ma** \ˌepə,kīˈrēmə\ *n, pl* **epicheirema·ta** \-ˈrēməd·ə, -rem-\ *also* **epichiremas** [L & Gk; L *epichirema*, fr. Gk *epicheirēma*, fr. *epicheirein* to endeavor, attempt to prove, fr. *epi-* + *cheir* hand — more at CHIR-] : a syllogism in which some statement supporting one or both of the premises is introduced with the premises themselves

ep·i·chil·i·um \ˌepəˈkilēəm\ *also* **ep·i·chil** \ˈepə,kil\ *or* **ep·i·chile** \ˈ=,kīl\ *n, pl* **epichil·ia** \ˌ=ˈkilēə\ [NL *epichilium*, fr. *epi-* + Gk *cheilos* lip + NL *-ium*] : the terminal lobe of the labellum in some orchids

epi·chlorohydrin \ˌepə, ˌepē+\ *n* [*epi-* + *chlorohydrin*] : a volatile liquid toxic epoxide C_3H_5ClO having an odor like chloroform, made usu. by alkaline hydrolysis of dichlorohydrins, and used chiefly in making epoxy resins

epi·chondrosis \"+\ *n* [NL, fr. *epi-* + *chondrosis*] : a cartilaginous growth upon periosteum ⟨an antler arising from an ~⟩ — **epi·chon·drot·ic** \ˌ==ˌkänˈdräd·ik\ *adj*

epi·chordal \ˌepə, ˌepē+\ *adj* [ISV *epi-* + *chordal*; orig. formed in G] : located upon or above the notochord — used esp. of vertebrae or elements of vertebrae on the dorsal side of the notochord

ep·i·cho·ric \ˌepəˈkōrik, -kȯr-, -kär-\ *adj* [Gk *epichōrios* of a certain country, in a certain country, local (fr. *epi-* + *-chōrios*, fr. *chōra* land, country, place) + E *-ic*] : peculiar to a limited area : LOCAL — used of ancient Greek alphabets ⟨every town, certainly every region, had its own ~ script —H.M.Hoenigswald⟩

epi·christian \ˌepə, ˌepē+\ *adj* [*epi-* + *Christian*] : of or relating to the period immediately after the lifetime of Christ

ep·i·cist \ˈepəsəst\ *n* -s [²*epic* + *-ist*] : an epic poet

epi·clastic \ˌepə, ˌepē+\ *adj* [ISV *epi-* + *-clastic*] *of rocks* : formed at the surface of the earth by consolidation of fragments of preexisting rocks

ep·i·cle·sis *or* **ep·i·kle·sis** \ˌepəˈklēsəs\ *n, pl* **epicle·ses** *or* **epikle·ses** \-ē,sēz\ *often cap* [LGk *epiklēsis*, fr. Gk, surname, title, invocation, fr. *epikalein* to summon, invoke, call by a surname (fr. *epi-* + *kalein* to summon) + *-ēsis* -esis] : a liturgical invocation of the Holy Spirit for the purpose of consecrating the eucharistic elements found particularly in Eastern liturgies where it follows the words of institution and is regarded as the point at which the eucharistic bread and wine become the body and blood of Christ

ep·i·cne·mi·al \ˌepə(k)ˈnēmēəl, ˌepē(k)-\ *adj* [*epi-* + Gk *knēmē* tibia + E *-al*] : of or belonging to the anterior part of the tibia

epi·coelia \ˌepə, ˌepē+\ *also* **ep·i·coele** *or* **ep·i·cele** \ˈepə,sēl\ *n, pl* **epicoeliae** *also* **epicoeles** *or* **epiceles** [*epicoelia*, NL, fr. *epi-* + *coelia*; *epicoele, epicele* fr. *epi-* + *-coele, -cele*] : the cavity of the metencephalon : the anterior part of the 4th ventricle of the brain

ep·i·coe·lo·ma \ˌepəsēˈlōmə\ *also* **epi·coelom** \ˌepə, ˌepē+\ *n* -s [NL, fr. *epi-* + *coelom*] : the part of the coelom nearest the notochord

epi·colic \ˌepə, ˌepē+\ *adj* [ISV *epi-* + *colic* (of the colon)] : situated upon or over the colon — used esp. of the region of the abdomen adjacent to the colon

epi·condyle \ˌepə, ˌepē+\ *n* [F *épicondyle*, fr. *épi-* epi- + *condyle*] **1** : the lateral condyle at the distal end of the humerus **2** : the medial condyle — **epi·con·dyl·i·an** \-ˌkänˈdilēən\ *adj* — **epi·con·dyl·ic** \-lik\ *adj*

epi·continental \ˌepə, ˌepē+\ *adj* [*epi-* + *continental*] : found or lying upon a continent or a continental shelf ⟨~ sedimentation⟩ ⟨a partly landlocked ~ sea⟩ ⟨the North sea is ~⟩ — compare EPEIRIC

epi·cor·a·co·humeral \ˌepəˌkȯrə(ˌ)kō, ˌepē+\ *adj* [¹*epicoracoid* + *humeral*] : of or connecting the epicoracoid and humerus

¹**epi·coracoid** *also* **epi·coracoidal** \ˌepə, ˌepē+\ *adj* [*epi-* + *coracoid, coracoidal*] : lying at the sternal end of the coracoid — used of a cartilaginous or bony element lying in the shoulder girdle of some vertebrates (as various reptiles, amphibians, and monotreme mammals)

²**epicoracoid** \"\ *n* [*epi-* + *coracoid*, n.] : an epicoracoid bone or cartilage

ep·i·cor·mic \ˌepəˈkȯrmik\ *adj* [*epi-* + *corm* + *-ic*] : growing from a dormant bud exposed to light and air ⟨new ~ branches on thinned forest trees⟩

ep·i·cot·yl \ˈ=ˌkäd·ᵊl, ˌ=ˈ=\ *n* -s [*epi-* + *cotyledon*] : the portion of the axis of a plant embryo or seedling above the cotyledonary node — compare HYPOCOTYL, PLUMULE

ep·i·cotyledonary \ˌepə+\ *adj* [*epi-* + *cotyledonary*] : situated above the cotyledons; *often* : of or relating to the epicotyl

epi·cranial \ˌepə+\ *adj* [NL *epicranium* + E *-al*] **1** : situated on the cranium **2** : belonging to the epicranium

epi·cranium \" +\ *n, pl* **epicrania** [NL, fr. *epi-* + *cranium*] **1** : the dorsal wall of the head of an insect **2** : the structures covering the vertebrate cranium

ep·i·cra·ni·us \ˌepəˈkrānēəs\ *n, pl* **epicra·nii** \-ē,ī\ [NL, fr. *epi-* + *-cranius* (fr. *cranium*)] : OCCIPITOFRONTALIS

¹**epic·ri·sis** \əˈpikrəsəs\ *n* [NL, fr. Gk *epikrisis* determination, judgment, fr. *epikrinein* to decide, fr. *epi-* + *krinein* to judge, discern — more at CERTAIN] : a critical or analytical summing up esp. of a medical case history

²**epi·crisis** \ˌepəˈkrīsəs, ˌepē-\ *n* [*epi-* + *crisis*] *med* : something that follows a crisis; *specif* : a secondary crisis

ep·i·crit·ic \ˌepəˈkrid·ik\ *adj* [Gk *epikritikos* determinative, fr. *epikritos* (verbal of *epikrinein*) + *-ikos* -ic] **1** *of cutaneous reception* : marked by accurate discrimination between small degrees of sensation (as of heat, cold, and pain) **2** *of cutaneous sensory receptors* : adapted to or subserving epicritic reception **3** *of cutaneous reactivity* : dependent on epicritic reception or receptors — compare PROTOPATHIC

epics *pl of* EPIC

epic simile *n* : an extended simile often running to several lines used typically in epic poetry to intensify the heroic stature of the subject (as by contrast) and to serve as decoration — called also *Homeric simile*

ep·ic·te·tian \ˌepəkˈtēshən, -pēk-\ *adj, usu cap* [Gk *Epiktētos* (fr. *Epiktētos* Epictetus 1st cent. A.D. Greek Stoic philosopher) + E *-an*] : of or relating to Epictetus or to his doctrine that the greatest good lies in independence of external things and in reliance upon the inner life or character

epic theater *n* : EPIC DRAMA

ep·i·cure \ˈepə,kyu̇(ə)r, -pē,k-, -ùə\ *n* -s [after *Epicurus* (fr. L, fr. Gk *Epikouros*) †270 B.C. Greek philosopher] **1** *usu cap, obs* : EPICUREAN; *specif* : one that disbelieves in any concern of deity with man ⟨were I an ~ I could bate swearing —George Herbert⟩ **2** *archaic* : one devoted to sensual pleasure (as eating) : SYBARITE ⟨an ~ is for his wine or women or feasts continually —Thomas Traherne⟩ **3** : one with sensitive and discriminating tastes (as in food, wine, music) : CONNOISSEUR ⟨an ~ in many of the delights of the senses —H.S.Canby⟩

syn GOURMET, GOURMAND, GLUTTON, BON VIVANT, GASTRONOME, GASTRONOMER: EPICURE refers to a choice connoisseur of the pleasurable, luxurious, or sensual, esp. in matters of food and drink ⟨the *epicure* is conscious of much more than the taste of the food. Rather, there enter into the taste, as directly experienced, qualities that depend upon reference to its source and its manner of production in connection with criteria of excellence —John Dewey⟩ GOURMET may be close to EPICURE; it may stress delicate taste and steady attempt to savor to the fullest. GOURMAND implies a hearty appetite for good food and drink, not without discernment but with less than a gourmet's ⟨eating habits . . . of a determined *gourmet*, verging at times on those of a *gourmand* —E.J.Kahn⟩ ⟨quality, not quantity, is the source of the attraction; it appeals to the *gourmet* rather than the *gourmand* —C.W.H.Johnson⟩ GLUTTON indicates a voracious eater having a very heavy and quite indiscriminate appetite ⟨skillfully made delicacies from many countries in Europe and Asia . . . in such vast array this season that they threaten to turn the *gourmet* into a *glutton* —Jane Nickerson⟩ BON VIVANT suggests one who takes habitual lively pleasure in dining and drinking with others ⟨somewhat of a *bon vivant*, and his wine was excellent —Sir Walter Scott⟩ GASTRONOME and GASTRONOMER are synonyms for EPICURE; they may suggest undue ritual about the appreciation of fine food ⟨the thing for U.S. *gourmets* to do, of course, would be to wash the illustrious birds down with a full cup of English mead; piment, said *gastronomes*, would go best with grouse —*Time*⟩

epicureal *or* **epicurial** *obs var of* EPICUREAN

¹**ep·i·cu·re·an** \ˌepəkyəˈrēən, -pēk-, -ˈkyu̇rē-\ *adj* [L *Epicureus* (fr. Gk *Epikoureios*, fr. *Epikouros*) + E *-an*] **1** *usu cap* : of Epicurus or Epicureanism **2 a** : given to the pursuit of pleasure or to the attainment of sensuous gratification : SENSUAL ⟨an ~ family⟩ **b** : stimulating and satisfying to the senses ⟨~ dishes⟩ **c** : of or relating to an epicure : LUXURIOUS ⟨an ~ life⟩ **syn** see SENSUOUS

²**epicurean** \"\ *n* -s **1** *usu cap* : a follower of Epicurus **2** *often cap* : EPICURE 3 ⟨his adventures . . . had wasted his spirit, leaving him morally languid, a graceful and prudent ~ —Francis Hackett⟩ **3** *usu cap* : APIKORES

ep·i·cu·re·an·ism \ˌ==kyəˈrēə,nizəm, -ˈkyu̇rēə-\ *n* -s **1** *usu cap* **a** : the philosophy of Epicurus and his followers who within a framework of modified Democritean atomism subscribed to a hedonistic ethics that considered ataraxy the highest good, held intellectual pleasures superior to others, and advocated the renunciation of momentary in favor of more permanent pleasures **b** : a mode of life in consonance with Epicureanism **2** : EPICURISM 2 **3** : the attitude or practice of an apikores : worldly-mindedness

ep·i·cu·re·ous \ˌ==ˈkyu̇rēəs\ *adj* [L *Epicureus*] *archaic* : EPICUREAN 2

ep·i·cur·ism \ˈepə,kyu̇,rizəm, -pē,k-\ *n* -s [prob. fr. F *épicurisme*, fr. *Epicurus* + *-isme* -ism] **1** *usu cap, archaic* : EPICUREANISM 1 **2** : the habits or tastes of an epicure

epicurize *vi* -ED/-ING/-S *obs* : to profess or practice Epicureanism

epi·cuticle \ˌepə, ˌepē +\ *n* -s [*epi-* + *cuticle*] **1** *also* **epi·cuticula** \" +\ [*epicuticula*, NL, fr. *epi-* + *cuticula* cuticle] : the outermost nonchitinous waxy layer of the insect exoskeleton — compare ENDOCUTICLE **2** : an outer resistant membrane surrounding various cuticular structures (as wool fibers, animal hairs, or feathers) — **epi·cuticular** \" +\ *adj*

ep·i·cy·cle \ˈepə,sīkəl\ *n* [ME *epicicle*, fr. LL *epicyclus*, fr. Gk *epikyklos*, fr. *epi-* + *kyklos* ring, circle, cycle, wheel — more at WHEEL] **1 a** *in Ptolemaic astron* : a circle in which a planet moves and which has a center that is itself carried around at the same time on the circumference of a larger circle **b** : a process or activity going on within the context of a larger one : secondary cycle ⟨an ~ of land erosion⟩ **2** : the circle generating an epicycloid or hypocycloid

ep·i·cy·clic \ˌ==ˈsīklik, -sik-\ *also* **ep·i·cy·cli·cal** \-ləkəl\ *adj* : relating to, resembling, or having the motion of an epicycle

epicyclic train *n* : a train (as of gear wheels or belt pulleys) designed to have one or more parts travel around the circumference of another fixed or revolving part

ep·i·cy·cloid \ˌ==ˈsī,klȯid\ *n* -s [prob. fr. F *épicycloïde*, fr. *épicycle* (fr. LL *epicyclus*) + *-oïde* -oid] : a curve traced by a point on a circle that rolls on the outside of a fixed circle — compare HYPOCYCLOID

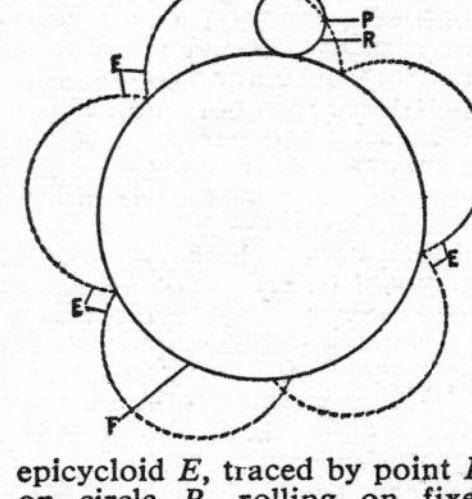

epicycloid *E*, traced by point *P*, on circle *R*, rolling on fixed circle *F*

ep·i·cy·cloi·dal \ˌ==ˌsīˈklȯidᵊl\ *adj* : relating to or having the properties of the epicycloid

ep·i·cyte \ˈepə,sīt\ *n* -s [ISV *epi-* + *-cyte*; orig. formed as F *épicyte*] **1** : the investing membrane of a cell **2** : an epithelial cell

ep·i·deic·tic \ˌepəˈdīktik\ *adj* [Gk *epideiktikos*, fr. (assumed) Gk *epideiktos* (verbal of Gk *epideiknynai* to exhibit, show off, display, fr. *epi-* + *deiknynai* to show) + Gk *-ikos* -ic — more at DICTION] : designed primarily for rhetorical effect : DEMONSTRATIVE ⟨~ style of writing⟩ ⟨the Indian speeches are . . . more of the nature of the forensic and, occasionally, ~ or panegyric, than of deliberative oratory —H.J.C.Grierson⟩ — used esp. of ceremonial orations of praise or blame

ep·i·de·mi·al \ˌepəˈdēmēəl\ *adj* [*epidemy* + *-al*] *archaic* : EPIDEMIC

¹**ep·i·dem·ic** \ˌepəˈdemik, -mēk\ *also* **ep·i·dem·i·cal** \-məkəl, -mēk-\ *adj* [F *épidémique*, fr. MF *epidemique*, fr. *epidemie* epidemic (n.) (fr. LL *epidemia*, fr. Gk *epidēmia* visit, epidemic, fr. *epidēmos* visiting, prevalent, epidemic — fr. *epi-* + *dēmos* deme, populace — + *-ia* -y) + *-ique* -ic, -ical — more at DEM-] **1 a** *of a communicable disease* (1) : affecting or tending to affect many persons within a community, area, or region at one time ⟨many children died that winter of ~ fevers⟩ ⟨typhoid was ~⟩; *broadly* : PANDEMIC — distinguished from *endemic* (2) : epiphytotic or epizootic — not used technically **b** : prevalent esp. to a degree felt to be excessive ⟨padded shoulders became ~ in the late thirties —Lois Long⟩ : COMMON; *specif, of economic insects* : present in such numbers as to constitute a plague ⟨this defoliator became ~ in 1949⟩ **c** : CONTAGIOUS 3 ⟨an ~ personality⟩ ⟨~ laughter⟩ **2** : of, relating to, or constituting an epidemic ⟨the outbreak was of ~ proportions⟩ ⟨the ~ phase of the grasshopper cycle⟩ — **ep·i·dem·i·cal·ly** \-mək(ə)lē, -mēk-, -li\ *adv*

²**epidemic** \"\ *n* -s **1 a** : an outbreak of epidemic disease ⟨the Indonesian malaria ~⟩ ⟨plagues, ~s, heat, and other trials⟩ **b** : an outbreak of something felt to resemble an epidemic disease esp. in its rapid spread ⟨harnessed Niagara did not start a hydroelectric ~ —Roger Burlingame⟩ ⟨the ugly ~ of rioting which flared clear across the nation —E.A.Gray⟩ **2** : a product of epidemic spread, growth, or development; *specif* : a natural population (as of insects) suddenly and greatly enlarged

ep·i·de·mic·i·ty \ˌepə,deˈmisəd·ē, -ˌdəˈm-, -ətē, -i\ *n* -ES : the quality or state of being epidemic; *specif* : the relative ability to spread from one host to others ⟨~ of typhoid bacteria⟩

epidemic parotitis *n* : MUMPS

epidemic pleurodynia *n* : an acute virus infection that is characterized by sudden onset with fever, headache, and acute diaphragmatic pain and that is believed to be caused by the Coxsackie virus

epidemic tremor *n* : AVIAN ENCEPHALOMYELITIS

ep·i·de·mi·o·log·ic \ˌepəˌdēmēəˈläjik, -dem-\ *or* **ep·i·de·mi·o·log·i·cal** \-jəkəl\ *adj* : of, relating to, or involving epidemiology ⟨characteristic ~ features⟩ — **ep·i·de·mi·o·log·i·cal·ly** \-jək(ə)lē\ *adv*

ep·i·de·mi·ol·o·gist \ˌ==ˌ=mēˈäləjəst\ *n* -s : a specialist in epidemiology

ep·i·de·mi·ol·o·gy \-jē\ *n* -ES [ISV *epidemio-* (fr. LL *epidemia*) + *-logy*] **1** : a science that deals with the incidence, distribution, and control of disease in a population (as of animals or plants) **2** : the sum of the factors controlling the presence or absence of a disease or pathogen ⟨the ~ of the common cold⟩ : the ecology of a disease or pathogen

epidemy *n* -ES [ME *epidemie*, fr. MF & LL; MF, fr. LL *epidemia* — more at EPIDEMIC] *archaic* : EPIDEMIC

ep·i·den·drum \ˌepəˈdendrəm\ *n* [NL, fr. *epi-* + Gk *dendron* tree; akin to Gk *drys* tree — more at TREE] **1** *cap* : a very large genus of highly variable chiefly epiphytic American orchids having flowers of which the lip has a spreading and usu. deeply lobed limb and a claw adnate to the column, being chiefly tropical but including a few forms native to the southeastern U.S., and often grown in the greenhouse for their brightly colored flowers **2** *or* **ep·i·den·dron** \-rən\ -s : any orchid of the genus *Epidendrum*

ep·i·derm \ˈepə,dərm\ *n* -s [LL *epidermis*] **:** EPIDERMIS

epiderm- *or* **epidermo-** *comb form* [*epidermis*] **:** epidermis ⟨*epidermolysis*⟩

ep·i·der·mal \ˌepəˈdərməl, -dəm-,-dəim-\ *also* **ep·i·der·mic** \-mik,-mēk\ *or* **ep·i·der·mi·cal** \-məkəl, -mēk-\ *or* **ep·i·der·mous** \-məs\ *adj* **:** of, relating to, or arising from the epidermis ⟨~ cells⟩ ⟨~ system⟩ ⟨~ structures⟩

ep·i·der·mat·ic \ˌepə(ˌ)dərˈmadˌik\ *adj* [Gk *epidermat-, epiderma* epidermis (fr. *epi-* + *dermat-, derma* skin) + E *-ic*] **1** *also* **ep·i·der·ma·tous** \-ˈdərmədˌəs\ [*epidermatous* fr. Gk *epidermat-, epiderma* + E *-ous*] **:** EPIDERMAL **2** *of an ointment* **:** acting only upon the outer surface of the skin — compare DIADERMAL, ENDERMIC

ep·i·der·ma·toid \-ˈdərmə,tȯid\ *adj* [Gk *epidermat-, epiderma* + E *-oid*] **:** EPIDERMOID

ep·i·der·mi·cal·ly \ˌepəˈdərmək(ə)lē\ *adv* [*epiderm* + *-ical* + *-ly*] **1 :** on the epidermis **:** on the skin **2 :** with regard to kind of skin

ep·i·der·mi·dal·i·za·tion \ˌepəˌdərmədᵊlə̇ˈzāshən\ *n* -s [*epidermidal* epidermal (fr. LL *epidermid-, epidermis* + E *-al*) + *-ization*] **:** the transformation of cuboidal cells derived from the stratum germinativum into flattened cells of the outer horny layer of the skin

ep·i·der·mis \ˌepəˈdərmə̇s, -dəm-,-dəim-\ *n* -ES [LL, fr. Gk, fr. *epi-* + *-dermis* (fr. *derma* skin, fr. *derein* to skin) — more at TEAR] **1 a :** the outer epithelial layer of the external integument of the animal body that is derived from the embryonic epiblast; *specif* **:** the outer nonsensitive and nonvascular layer of the skin of a vertebrate that overlies the corium, consists of numerous layers of squamous epithelial cells of which the outer are progressively more compressed and horny, and is often modified into specialized outgrowths (as hair, feathers, nails, and hoofs) **b :** any of various animal integuments; *esp* **:** PERIOSTRACUM **2 :** a layer of primary tissue in higher plants that is commonly one cell thick, often cutinized on its outer surface, and continuous in young plants except over the stomata, that provides protection to underlying parts against mechanical injury and desiccation, and that is largely replaced (as by periderm or exodermis) in older plants except on leaves and herbaceous stems

ep·i·der·mi·za·tion \-ˌdərməˈzāshən\ *n* -s [*epiderm* + *-ization*] **:** EPITHELIZATION

ep·i·der·moid \ˌepəˈdər,mȯid\ *also* **ep·i·der·moi·dal** \ˌ⸗⸗(ˌ)⸗ˈmȯidᵊl\ *adj* [*epiderm-* + *-oid, -oidal*] **:** resembling epidermis or epidermal cells **:** made up of elements like those of epidermis ⟨~ neoplasms⟩

epidermoid cyst *or* **epidermoid** *n* **:** a cystic tumor containing epidermal or similar tissue — see CHOLESTEATOMA; compare DERMOID CYST

ep·i·der·mol·y·sis \ˌepə(ˌ)dərˈmäləsə̇s\ *n, pl* **epidermoly·ses** \-lə,sēz\ [NL, fr. *epiderm-* + *-lysis*] **:** a state of detachment or loosening of the epidermis

ep·i·der·mo·my·co·sis \ˌepəˌdərmōˌmīˈkōsə̇s\ *n* -ES [NL, fr. *epiderm-* + *mycosis*] **:** DERMATOMYCOSIS

ep·i·der·moph·y·tid \ˌepə(ˌ)dərˈmäfəd·əd\ *n* -s [NL *Epidermophyton* + E *-id*] **:** a skin eruption accompanying infection with a dermatophyte

ep·i·der·moph·y·ton \-fə,tän\ *n, cap* [NL, fr. *epiderm-* + Gk *phyton* plant] *in some classifications* **:** a genus comprising dermatophytes that are held to be causative agents of athlete's foot and tinea cruris, now usu. being considered to include a single species (*E. floccosum*, syn. *E. inguinale* and *E. cruris*), and sometimes suppressed as a synonym of *Trichophyton*

ep·i·der·mo·phy·to·sis \ˌepə(ˌ)dərˌmäfəˈtōsə̇s\ *n, pl* **epidermophyto·ses** \-ō,sēz\ [NL, fr. *Epidermophyton* + *-osis*] **:** a disease of the skin or nails caused by a dermatophyte

ep·i·di·a·scope \ˌepəˈdīə,skōp\ *n* [ISV *epi-* + *dia-* + *-scope*] **1 :** a projector for images of both opaque and transparent objects **2 :** EPISCOPE — **ep·i·di·a·scop·ic** \ˌ⸗⸗ˌ⸗⸗ˈskäpik\ *adj*

epididym- *or* **epididymo-** *comb form* [NL, fr. *epididymis*] **:** epididymal and ⟨*epididymodeferential*⟩

ep·i·did·y·mal \ˌepəˈdidəməl\ *adj* [NL *epididymis* + E *-al*] **:** of or relating to the epididymis

ep·i·did·y·mis \ˌepəˈdidəmə̇s\ *n, pl* **epididymi·des** \-ˈdidəmə,dēz; -də̇ˈdimə-, -ˌdīˈdimə-\ [NL, fr. Gk, fr. *epi-* + *-didymis* (fr. *didymos* twin, testicle) — more at DIDYM-] **:** an elongated mass at the back of the testis composed chiefly of the greatly convoluted efferent tubes of that organ — see VASA EFFERENTIA

ep·i·did·y·mite \-ˈdidə,mīt\ *n* -s [G *epididymit*, fr. *epi-* + *-didymit* (as in *eudidymit* eudidymite) — more at EUDIDYMITE] **:** a silicate $NaBeSi_3O_7(OH)$ of sodium and beryllium

ep·i·did·y·mi·tis \-ˌdidəˈmīd·ə̇s\ *n* -ES [NL, fr. *epididym-* + *-itis*] **:** inflammation of the epididymis

epi·diorite \ˌepə, ˌepē +\ *n* -s [ISV *epi-* + *diorite*; orig. formed as G *epidiorit*] **:** a variety of diorite formed by metamorphism from pyroxenic igneous rocks and often being somewhat schistose

ep·i·do·site \ˌepəˈdō,sīt, əˈpidə,s-\ *n* -s [G *epidosit*, fr. Gk *epidosis* free giving, free gift, contribution, advance (fr. *epididonai* to give besides, increase, advance) + G *-it* -ite] **:** a schistose metamorphic rock composed of green epidote with some quartz

ep·i·dote \ˈepə,dōt\ *n* -s [F *épidote*, fr. (assumed) Gk *epidotos*, verbal of Gk *epididonai* to give besides, increase, fr. *epi-* + *didonai* to give — more at DATE] **:** a yellowish green mineral $Ca_2(Al,Fe)_3Si_3O_{12}OH$ consisting of a silicate of calcium, aluminum, and iron and occurring massive or in grains, columns, and monoclinic crystals (hardness 6–7, sp. gr. 3.25–3.50)

ep·i·dot·ite \ˈepə,dōd,ˌīt\ *n* -s **:** a rock composed mostly of epidote

ep·i·dot·i·za·tion \ˌepəˌdōdə̇ˈzāshən\ *n* -s [*epidote* + *-ization*] **:** metamorphism in which epidote is formed from other minerals

ep·i·dot·ized *or* **ep·i·dot·ised** \ˈepədōd,ˌīzd\ *adj* **:** changed by metamorphism into epidote

epi·du·ral \ˌepəˈd(y)u̇rəl, ˌepē-\ *adj* [*epi-* + *dural*] **:** situated upon or administered outside the dura mater ⟨an ~ abscess⟩ ⟨~ block⟩ — **epi·du·ral·ly** \-rəlē\ *adv*

epidural anesthesia *n* **:** CAUDAL ANESTHESIA

ep·i·ei·keia \ˌepēˌīˈkīə\ *or* **ep·i·keia** \ˌepəˈkīə\ *n* -s [Gk *epieikeia* reasonableness, equity, fr. *epieikēs* suitable, reasonable + *-ia* -y] **:** interpretation of a law of the Roman Catholic Church that presumes it not applicable in a case of hardship felt to violate natural law (as when a mother presumes she may miss mass rather than leave her baby alone) **:** EQUITY ⟨the ~ of the church⟩

ep·i·fa·gus \ˌepəˈfāgəs\ *n, cap* [NL, fr. *epi-* + L *fagus* beech — more at BEECH] **:** a genus of slender purplish brown leafless herbs (family Orobanchaceae) having whitish flowers and being parasitic on the roots of beech trees — see BEECHDROPS

epi·focal \ˌepə, ˌepē +\ *adj* [*epi-* + *focal*] **:** EPICENTRAL 2

epi·folliculitis \"+\ *n* -ES [NL, fr. *epi-* + *folliculitis*] **:** inflammation of hair follicles

ep·i·gaea \ˌepəˈjēə\ *n, cap* [NL, fr. Gk *epigaios* upon the earth, fr. *epi-* + *-gaios* (fr. *gaia* earth)] **:** a genus of half-evergreen creeping or trailing woody plants (family Ericaceae) with white or rose-colored flowers in small axillary and terminal clusters — see ARBUTUS 3

ep·i·gam·ic \ˌepəˈgamik\ *adj* [Gk *epigamos* marriageable (fr. *epi-* + *gamos* marriage, wedding) + E *-ic*] **:** tending to attract the opposite sex during the breeding seasons ⟨~ colors of birds⟩

epig·a·mous \əˈpigəməs, (ˈ)eˈp-\ *adj* [Gk *epigamos*] **:** EPITOKOUS

ep·i·gas·ter \ˈepə,gastə(r), ˌ⸗⸗ˈ⸗⸗\ *n* -s [NL, fr. *epi-* + Gk *gastēr* stomach] **:** the posterior part of the embryonic intestine from which the colon develops

ep·i·gas·tric \ˌepəˈgastrik\ *or* **ep·i·gas·tri·cal** \-rə̇kəl\ *or* **ep·i·gas·tri·al** \-rēəl\ *also* **ep·i·gas·tral** \-rəl\ *adj* [NL *epigastrium* + E *-ic, -ical* or *-al*] **1 :** lying upon or over the stomach **2 a :** of or relating to the anterior walls of the abdomen ⟨~ veins⟩ **b :** of or relating to the region of the abdomen lying between the hypochondriac regions and above the umbilical region ⟨~ sensation⟩ — see ABDOMINAL REGION illustration

epigastric artery *n* **:** one of three arteries supplying the anterior walls of the abdomen, (1) one being a direct downward continuation of the internal mammary, (2) another arising from the external iliac near Poupart's ligament and ascending along the inner margin of the internal abdominal ring, and (3) a third arising from the femoral, passing through the saphenous opening in the fascia lata, and then ascending upon the lower part of the abdomen — called also respectively (1) *superior epigastric artery*, (2) *inferior epigastric artery* or *deep epigastric artery*, and (3) *superficial epigastric artery*

epigastric fold *n* **:** a fold of peritoneum on the anterior abdominal wall covering the deep epigastric artery

epigastric plexus *n* **:** SOLAR PLEXUS

ep·i·gas·tri·um \ˌ⸗⸗ˈgastrēəm\ *also* **ep·i·gas·trae·um** \-ˌgaˈstrēəm\ *n, pl* **epigas·tria** \-ˈgastrēə\ [NL, fr. Gk *epigastrion*, fr. *epi-* + *gastrion*, dim. of *gastr-, gastēr* stomach] **1 :** the epigastric region **2 :** the ventral side of the mesothorax and metathorax of an insect

ep·i·ge·al \ˌepəˈjēəl\ *or* **ep·i·ge·ous** \-ēəs\ *also* **ep·i·ge·an** *or* **ep·i·gae·an** \-ēən\ *or* **ep·i·ge·ic** \-ēik, -ēēk\ *adj* [Gk *epigaios* upon the earth + E *-al* or *-ous* or *-an* or *-ic* — more at EPIGAEA] **1 a** *of a plant or a plant part* **:** growing above the surface of the ground ⟨green ~ stalks of asparagus⟩; *esp, of a cotyledon* **:** forced above ground by elongation of the hypocotyl **b** *of plant germination* **:** characterized by the production of epigeal cotyledons **2 :** living near or on the surface of the ground — used esp. of an insect; distinguished from *aerial, hypogeal*

ep·i·gene \ˈepə,jēn\ *adj* [F *épigène*, fr. Gk *epigenēs* growing after, fr. *epigignesthai* to be born after — more at EPIGONE] **1** *of a crystal* **:** not natural to the substance in which it is found **2 :** formed, originating, or taking place on or not far below the surface of the earth — opposed to *hypogene*

ep·i·gen·e·sis \ˌepəˈjenəsə̇s\ *n* [NL, fr. *epi-* + L *genesis*] **1 a :** development involving gradual diversification and differentiation of an initially undifferentiated entity (as a zygote or spore) — compare PREFORMATION **b :** THEORY OF EPIGENESIS **2 :** change in the mineral character of a rock owing to outside influences — compare METAMORPHISM

ep·i·gen·e·sist \-sə̇st\ *n* -s [irreg. fr. NL *epigenesis* + E *-ist*] **:** an adherent of epigenesis

ep·i·ge·net·ic \ˌepəjəˈned·ik\ *adj* [*epi-* + *genetic*] **1 :** of, relating to, or produced by epigenesis ⟨the ~ nature of vertebrate development⟩ **2** *or* **ep·i·gen·ic** \ˌepəˈjenik\ *of deposit or structure* **:** formed after the laying down of the enclosing rock **:** POSTDEPOSITIONAL ⟨~ structures are formed after deposition of the sediment, as certain concretions . . . and large scaled features as folds and faults —W.C.Krumbein & L.L.Sloss⟩ ⟨~ changes — both solution and precipitation —F.J.Pettijohn⟩ — compare SYNGENETIC — **ep·i·ge·net·i·cal·ly** \-jəˈned·ək(ə)lē\ *adv*

epigenetic drainage *n* **:** drainage by streams whose courses have been determined by the conditions of an older land surface now eroded — compare AUTOGENETIC DRAINAGE

epig·e·nist \əˈpijənə̇st\ *n* -s [by alter.] **:** EPIGENESIST

epig·e·nite \-,nīt\ *n* -s [G *epigenit*, fr. Gk *epigenēs* growing after + G *-it* -ite — more at EPIGENE] **:** a sulfide perhaps $(Cu,Fe)_5AsS_6$ of copper, iron, and arsenic

epig·e·nous \əˈpijənəs, (ˈ)eˈp-\ *adj* [ISV *epi-* + *-genous*] **:** growing upon the surface esp. the upper surface of a leaf or other organ of a plant — compare HYPOGENOUS

ep·i·glot·tal \ˌepəˈglädᵊl, -ätᵊl\ *also* **ep·i·glot·tic** \-ik, -ēk\ *adj* [NL *epiglottis* + E *-al* or *-ic*] **:** of, relating to, or produced with the aid of the epiglottis

ep·i·glot·tid·e·an \ˌepə(ˌ)gläˈtidēən\ *adj* [NL *epiglottid-, epiglottis* + E *-ean*] **:** EPIGLOTTAL

ep·i·glot·tis \ˌepəˈgläd·ə̇s, -ätə̇s, ˈ⸗⸗ˌ⸗⸗\ *n* [NL, fr. Gk *epiglōttis*, fr. *epi-* + *glōttis* glottis — more at GLOTTIS] **1 a :** a thin lamella of yellow elastic cartilage that ordinarily projects upward behind the tongue and just in front of the glottis and that with the arytenoid cartilages serves to cover the glottis during the act of swallowing **2 :** the epistome of a bryozoan **3 :** the epipharynx of an insect

ep·i·glot·ti·tis \ˌepəˌgläˈtīd·ə̇s\ *n* -ES [NL, fr. *epiglottis* + *-itis*] **:** inflammation of the epiglottis

epig·o·nal \əˈpigənᵊl, (ˈ)eˈp-\ *adj* **1 :** EPIGONIC **2** *usu cap* **:** of or belonging to a prehistoric culture of coastal Peru and Chile that is part of the Tiahuanaco culture **:** coastal Tiahuanaco

ep·i·go·na·tion \ˌepēgōˈnäˌtyȯn\ *n* -s [NGk, dim. of LGk *epigonatis* kneecap, fr. Gk *epi-* + *gonat-, gony* knee — more at KNEE] *Eastern Orthodox Church* **:** a rhombic vestment usu. of stiff material worn by a bishop or certain other ecclesiastical dignitaries on the right hip as a sign of authority and rank

¹ep·i·gone \ˈepə,gōn\ *also* **ep·i·gon** \-,gän\ *n, pl* **epigones** *or* **epigons** [G *epigone*, fr. L *epigonus*, one of the seven sons of seven leaders in Greek legend who were defeated at Thebes and who themselves marched against Thebes, fr. Gk *epigonos*, lit., one born after, fr. *epigonos* born after, fr. *epigignesthai* to be born after, fr. *epi-* + *gignesthai* to be born — more at KIN] **:** an imitative follower; *esp* **:** an inferior imitator of a distinguished writer, philosopher, musician, or artist ⟨the obsequious literature of the ~s —Vincent Sheean⟩

²epigone \"\ *n* -s [NL *epigonium*] **:** EPIGONIUM

ep·i·gon·ic \ˌepəˈgänik\ *or* **epig·o·nous** \əˈpigənəs, (ˈ)eˈp-\ *adj* **:** of an epigone **:** IMITATIVE ⟨the body of ~ poetry which now bulks largest derives from the Georgians—W.V.O'Connor⟩

ep·i·go·nich·thys \ˌepəgəˈnikthə̇s\ *n, cap* [NL, fr. *epi-* + *gon-* + *-ichthys*] **:** a genus (the type of the family Epigonichthyidae) of lancelets having gonads only on the right side of the body

epig·o·nism \əˈpigəˌnizəm, eˈ-; ˈepə,gō,n-, ˈepə,gä,n-\ *n* -s **:** artistic, literary, or intellectual imitation esp. by a later generation than the artist, writer, or thinker imitated ⟨your verse . . . supports a primitive traditionalism and ~ —W.R. Benét⟩

ep·i·go·ni·um \ˌepəˈgōnēəm\ *n* -s [NL, fr. *epi-* + Gk *gonē* seed + NL *-ium*] **:** CALYPTRA; *esp* **:** the cover enclosing the young sporangium of a liverwort

epig·o·nos \əˈpigənəs, eˈ-, -,näs\ *n, pl* **epigo·noi** \-,nȯi\ [Gk] **:** ¹EPIGONE

epig·o·nus \-nəs\ *n, pl* **epigo·ni** \-,nī, -,nē\ [L — more at EPIGONE] **:** ¹EPIGONE

ep·i·gram \ˈepə,gram, -raa(ə)m\ *n* -s [ME *epigrame*, fr. L *epigramma*, fr. Gk, fr. *epigraphein* to write on, inscribe, fr. *epi-* + *graphein* to write — more at CARVE] **1** *obs* **:** EPIGRAPH 1 **2 a :** a short poem treating concisely, pointedly, and often satirically of a single thought or event and often ending with a witticism or ingenious turn of thought ⟨the Earl of Rochester's ~ on Charles II: "here lies our sovereign lord the king, whose word no man relies on; he never says a foolish thing nor ever does a wise one"⟩ **b :** a terse, sage, or witty often paradoxical saying ⟨speaks in a characteristically paradoxical ~ of the "sacred duty of lawlessness" —G.L.Kline⟩ — compare APHORISM, APOTHEGM **c :** epigrammatic expression ⟨his conversation . . . was a cascade of wit, ~, and poetic images —G.H. Genzmer⟩ **3 :** a small piece of meat (as of lamb, game, poultry) usu. breaded and fried and served with a sauce and vegetables as an entree

ep·i·gram·mat·ic \ˌepəgrəˈmad·ik, -pēg-, -at\, \ēk\ *also* **ep·i·gram·mat·i·cal** \ə̇kəl, \ēk-\ *adj* [LL *epigrammaticus*, fr. L *epigrammat-, epigramma* + *-icus* -ic, -ical] **1 :** having the form of, resembling, or suggestive of an epigram ⟨the ~ expression — "some are too foolish to commit follies"⟩ ⟨the ~ simplification by means of which fables please and . . . instruct —*Times Lit. Supp.*⟩ **:** PITHY ⟨~ style⟩ **2 :** marked by or given to the use of epigrams ⟨fairly short, extremely compact, ~ essays —Antonio Iglesias⟩ ⟨a jaunty, bulbous, ~ Parisian of eighty —*Holiday*⟩ — **ep·i·gram·mat·i·cal·ly** \ə̇k(ə)lē, \ēk-, -li\ *adv*

ep·i·gram·ma·tism \ˌepəˈgramə,tizəm\ *n* -s [*epigrammatic* + *-ism*] **:** epigrammatic quality ⟨the playfulness and ~ of the general style —Jane Austen⟩

ep·i·gram·ma·tist \-məd·ə̇st, -mətə̇-\ *also* **ep·i·gram·mist** \ˈepə,gramə̇st, -graam-\ *n* -s [*epigrammatist* fr. LL *epigrammatista*, fr. L *epigrammat-, epigramma* + *-ista* -ist; *epigrammist* fr. *epigram* + *-ist*] **:** a maker of epigrams

ep·i·gram·ma·tize \ˌepəˈgramə,tīz\ *vb* -ED/-ING/-S [*epigrammatic* + *-ize*] *vt* **1 :** to express epigrammatically ⟨he *epigrammatized* the same thought⟩ **2 :** to make an epigram about (as a person) ~ *vi* **:** to make an epigram ⟨*epigrammatizing* on passing events⟩

ep·i·gram·ma·tiz·er \-zə(r)\ *n* -s **:** EPIGRAMMATIST

ep·i·gramme \ˈepə,gram, -raa(ə)m\ *n* -s [F *épigramme*, lit., epigram, fr. L *epigramma*] **1 :** EPIGRAM 3 **2 :** a dish of small pieces of one kind of meat (as lamb) prepared in two different ways (as some breaded and fried and others broiled)

ep·i·graph \ˈepə,graf, -āf\ *n* [Gk *epigraphē*, fr. fem. of *epigraphos* inscribed, fr. *epigraphein* to write on, inscribe — more at EPIGRAM] **1 :** INSCRIPTION; *esp* **:** an inscription engraved in durable material (as on an ancient temple or monument or a coin) **2 :** a quotation set at the beginning of a literary work (as a novel) or a division of it to suggest its theme **:** MOTTO ⟨a passage from the *Divine Comedy* provided the ~ of the novel —R.P.Warren⟩

epig·ra·pher \əˈpigrəfə(r), eˈ-\ *n* -s **:** EPIGRAPHIST

ep·i·graph·ic \ˌepəˈgrafik, -fēk\ *also* **ep·i·graph·i·cal** \-fə̇kəl, -fēk-\ *adj* **1 :** of, consisting of, or bearing inscriptions ⟨Syria has begun to produce its ~ wealth of cuneiform tablets —J.H.Iliffe⟩ **2 :** of or relating to epigraphy ⟨archaeological, ~, and philological studies⟩ **3 :** of a style characteristically used in inscriptions ⟨a block of basalt engraved with a text . . . in Greek ~ characters —M.R.Dobie⟩ — **ep·i·graph·i·cal·ly** \-fə̇k(ə)lē, -fēk-, -li\ *adv*

epig·ra·phist \əˈpigrəfə̇st, eˈ-\ *n* -s **:** a specialist in epigraphy

epig·ra·phy \-fē, -fi\ *n* -ES [irreg. (influence of *-graphy*) fr. *epigraph* + *-y*] **1 a :** EPIGRAPHS, INSCRIPTIONS **b :** the style of lettering used in inscriptions ⟨on the basis of the ~ and the language this monument has been assigned to the first half of the eighth century —J.H.Fisher⟩ **2 :** a study or science of inscriptions; *esp* **:** the deciphering and interpretation of ancient inscriptions ⟨paleography or the decipherment of documents and ~ . . . have been indispensable keys to the history of the alphabet —Edward Clodd⟩

epig·y·nous \əˈpijənəs, eˈ-\ *adj* [*epi-* + *-gynous*] **1** *of stamens, petals, and sepals* **:** adnate to the surface of the ovary and appearing to grow from the top of it **2** *of a flower* **:** having epigynous floral parts — compare HYPOGYNOUS, PERIGYNOUS

epig·y·num \-nəm\ *also* **ep·i·gyne** \ˈepə,jīn\ *n* -s [NL *epigynum*, fr. *epi-* + *-gynum* (fr. Gk *-gynon*, neut. of *-gynos* -gynous)] **:** the female genital opening of an arachnid; *also* **:** a chitinous plate overlying this opening in a spider

epig·y·ny \əˈpijənē, eˈ-\ *n* -ES [*epi-* + *-gyny*] **:** the condition of being epigynous

epi·hip·pus \ˌepəˈhipəs, ˌepē-\ *n, cap* [NL, fr. *epi-* + *-hippus*] **:** a genus of ancestral horses of the Upper Eocene known only from fragmentary remains and having the middle toe of each foot prominent and the side toes rather slender

ep·i·hy·al \-ˈhīəl\ *n* -s [*epi-* + *hyoid* + *-al*] **:** an element of the hyoid arch lying between the stylohyal and the ceratohyal that in man is the stylohyoid ligament and in many vertebrates forms a distinct bone

epi·ianthinite \ˌepē+\ *n* [*epi-* + *ianthinite*] **:** a mineral occurring as an alteration product of ianthinite

epikeia *var of* EPIEIKEIA

epiklesis *var of* EPICLESIS

epil *abbr* epilogue

epi·labrum \ˌepə, ˌepi+\ *n, pl* **epilabra** [NL, fr. *epi-* + *labrum*] **:** a transverse process at the side of the labrum of certain myriopods

ep·i·lach·na \ˌepəˈlaknə\ *n, cap* [NL, fr. *epi-* + *-lachna* (fr. Gk *lachnē* soft woolly hair)] **:** a genus of ladybirds that feed on plants both as larvae and adults — see MEXICAN BEAN BEETLE

epi·lamellar \ˌepə, ˌepi+\ *adj* [*epi-* + *lamellar*] *anat* **:** outside the basement membrane

ep·i·lat·ing wax \ˈepə,lād·iŋ-\ *n* [fr. pres. part. of *epilate* "to remove hair", back-formation fr. *epilation*] **:** a mixture of resins and waxes designed to remove cosmetically undesirable hair by being applied hot to a surface and pulled away with the embedded hairs after cooling

ep·i·la·tion \ˌepəˈlāshən\ *n* -s [F *épilation*, fr. *épiler* to remove hair (fr. *é-* e- + L *pilus* hair) + *-ation* — more at PILE] **:** the loss or removal of hair from any cause or for any reason — compare DEPILATION

ep·i·la·tor \ˈepə,lād·ə(r)\ *n* -s **:** DEPILATORY; *specif* **:** EPILATING WAX

ep·i·lem·ma \ˌepəˈlemə\ *n* -s [NL, fr. *epi-* + *-lemma*] **:** the sheath covering a terminal nerve fibril — **ep·i·lem·mal** \ˌepəˈleməl\ *adj*

ep·i·lep·sy \ˈepə,lepsē, -si\ *n* -ES [MF *epilepsie*, fr. LL *epilepsia*, fr. Gk *epilēpsia*, fr. *epilēptos* (verbal of *epilambanein* to seize, attack, fr. *epi-* + *lambanein* to take, seize) + *-ia* -y — more at LATCH] **:** a chronic nervous disorder of man and other animals that involves changes in the state of consciousness and of motion and that is due either to an inborn defect which produces convulsions of greater or lesser severity with clouding of consciousness or to an organic lesion of the brain produced by tumor, injury, toxic agents, or glandular disturbances — see GRAND MAL, PETIT MAL; JACKSONIAN EPILEPSY

epilept- *or* **epilepti-** *or* **epilepto-** *comb form* [F *épilept-*, fr. L *epilept-*, fr. Gk *epilēpt-*, fr. *epilēptos*] **:** epilepsy ⟨*epileptoid*⟩ ⟨*epileptogenic*⟩

¹ep·i·lep·tic \ˌepəˈleptik, -tēk\ *adj* [F *épileptique*, fr. LL *epilepticus*, fr. Gk *epilēptikos*, fr. *epilēptos* + *-ikos* -ic] **1 :** relating to, affected with, or having the characteristics of epilepsy **2 :** suggestive of epilepsy ⟨the effect on the public mind was ~ —C.W.Ferguson⟩ **:** CONVULSIVE ⟨his dancing was . . . ~ —*Springfield (Mass.) Republican*⟩ — **ep·i·lep·ti·cal·ly** \-tə̇k(ə)lē, -tēk-, -li\ *adv*

²epileptic \"\ *also* **ep·i·lept** \ˈepə,lept\ *n* -s **:** one affected with epilepsy

ep·i·lep·ti·form \ˌepəˈleptə,fȯrm\ *adj* [*epilept-* + *-form*] **:** resembling that of epilepsy ⟨an ~ convulsion⟩

ep·i·lep·to·gen·ic \ˌepəˌleptəˈjenik\ *adj* [*epilept-* + *-genic*] **:** inducing or tending to induce epilepsy

ep·i·lep·toid \-,tȯid\ *adj* [*epilept-* + *-oid*] **:** EPILEPTIFORM ⟨an ~ symptom⟩ **:** exhibiting symptoms resembling those of epilepsy ⟨an ~ criminal⟩

ep·i·lim·net·ic \ˌepəˌlimˈned·ik\ *also* **ep·i·lim·ni·al** \-mnēəl\ *adj* [NL *epilimnion* + E *-etic* or *-al*] **:** of, relating to, or constituting an epilimnion

ep·i·lim·ni·on \ˌepəˈlimnē,än, -ēən\ *n, pl* **epilim·nia** \-ēə\ [NL, fr. *epi-* + *-limnion*] **:** the layer of water that overlies the thermocline of a lake and is subject to the action of wind — compare HYPOLIMNION

ep·i·lith·ic \ˌepəˈlithik\ *adj* [*epi-* + *-lithic*] **:** growing upon stone or stonelike material ⟨~ mosses⟩ ⟨~ lichens⟩

ep·i·lo·bi·um \ˌepəˈlōbēəm\ *n* [NL, fr. *epi-* + Gk *lobos* lobe, pod + NL *-ium* — more at SLEEP] **1** *cap* **:** a large genus of widely distributed herbs (family Onagraceae) with pink or rarely yellow flowers, slender lanceolate leaves, and seeds with a silky coma **2** -s **:** any plant of the genus *Epilobium* **:** WILLOW HERB 1

ep·i·lo·bous \ˌepəˈlōbəs; əˈpiləbəs, eˈ-\ *adj* [*epi-* + *-lobous* (fr. Gk *lobos* lobe, pod)] *of an annelid prostomium* **:** set off by a groove and overlapping the first true segment

epil·o·gist \əˈpiləjə̇st, eˈ-; ˈepə,lȯgə̇st *also* -,läg-\ *n* -s [*epilogue* + *-ist*] **:** the writer or speaker of an epilogue

¹ep·i·logue *also* **ep·i·log** \ˈepə,lȯg *also* -pē,- *or* -pi- *or* -läg\ *n* -s [ME *epiloge*, fr. MF *epilogue*, fr. L *epilogus*, fr. Gk *epilogos*, fr. *epilegein* to say in addition, fr. *epi-* + *legein* to speak, gather — more at LEGEND] **1 :** the final part that serves typically to round out or complete the design of a nondramatic literary work **:** CONCLUSION ⟨only in prefaces, ~s and topical interjections . . . did they achieve ease and force —Boris Ford⟩ — called also *afterword*; compare FOREWORD, PREFACE **2 a** (1) **:** a speech often in verse addressed to the audience by one or more of the actors at the end of a play ⟨a good play needs no ~ yet . . . good plays prove the better by the help of good ~s —Shak.⟩ — compare PROLOGUE (2) **:** the actor speaking such an epilogue ⟨it is not the fashion to see the lady the ~ but it is no more unhandsome than to see the lord the prologue —Shak.⟩ **b :** the final scene of a play whose main action is set within a framework ⟨the ~ reassembles the characters of the prologue, their experience enriched by the insight that the main body of the play has given them —F.H. O'Hara & Marguerite Bro⟩ **3 :** something felt to resemble an epilogue: as **a :** an incident or series of events that completes, rounds out, or gives point to a previous incident or series of events ⟨the story can be regarded either as an ~ to the history of Roman Britain or as a prologue to the history of Saxon England —F.M.Stenton⟩ **b :** the concluding section of a musical composition **:** CODA

²epilogue \"\ *vt* -ED/-ING/-S : to supply with an epilogue
epiloguize *vi* -ED/-ING/-S *obs* : to speak an epilogue
ep·i·loia \ˌepəˈlȯiə\ *n* -S [NL] : a dominant genetic anomaly in man marked by mental deficiency and multiple tumor formation of the skin and brain and perpetuated by high mutation rate
ep·i·ma·ni·kion \ˌepēmə'nēk,yȯn\ *n, pl* **epimani·kia** \-yə\ [MGk, fr. Gk *epi-* + LGk *manikion* sleeve, dim. of *manika*, fr. L *manica* — more at MANCHE] : a cuff worn as a liturgical vestment over each sleeve of the sticharion by ecclesiastics of the Eastern Orthodox Church
ep·i·me·di·um \ˌepəˈmēdēəm\ *n, cap* [NL, fr. L *epimedion*, an unknown plant, fr. Gk *epimēdion*, fr. *epi-* + *mēdion*, a species of *Campanula*] : a small genus of nearly woody herbs (family Berberidaceae) having pinnately compound leaves and flowers with eight sepals in two whorls and four petals that are mostly transformed into nectaries
ep·i·me·lete \ˌepəˈmeˌlēt\ *n, pl* **epimele·tae** \-ˌməˈlēˌtē\ [Gk *epimelētēs*, lit., curator, fr. *epimelesthai* to be careful, attentive] : an ancient Greek civil or religious official
ep·i·men·i·de·an \ˌepəˌmenəˈdēən\ *adj, usu cap* [*Epimenides*, 7th cent. B.C. Cretan poet and philosopher who according to legend slept for 57 years in a cave + E *-an*] : being or resembling that of the Cretan poet and philosopher Epimenides ⟨the *Epimenidean* paradox that "All Cretans are liars"⟩
ep·i·mer \ˈepəmə(r)\ *also* **epim·er·ide** \əˈpiməˌrīd\ *n* -S [*epimer* fr. *epi-* + *-mer*; *epimeride* fr. *epimer* + *-ide*] : either of two stereoisomers of a compound containing more than one asymmetric carbon atom that differ in the arrangement of groups around only one of the asymmetric carbons; *specif* : either of the stereoisomers of a sugar or sugar derivative that differ in the arrangement around the asymmetric carbon next to the carbonyl or carboxyl group ⟨glucose and mannose are ~*s*⟩
ep·i·me·ral \ˌepəˈmirəl\ *adj* [NL *epimeron* + E *-al*] : of or relating to an epimeron
ep·i·mere \ˈepəˌmi(ə)r\ *n* -S [ISV *epi-* + *-mere*] : the dorsal portion of a mesodermal segment of a chordate embryo that functions as the source of myotome and sclerotome
ep·i·mer·ic \ˌepəˈmerik\ *adj* [*epimer* + *-ic*] : having the relationship of an epimer or epimers ⟨3-α-coprosterol is ~ with 3-β-coprosterol⟩
epim·er·ite \əˈpiməˌrīt, eˈ-\ *n* -S [ISV *epi-* + *mer-* + *-ite*] : an anterior prolongation of the protomerite of many gregarines bearing organelles for attachment to the host — **epim·er·it·ic** \=ˌ==ˈrid·ik\ *adj*
ep·i·mer·i·za·tion \ˌepəmərəˈzāshən\ *n* -S : the process of epimerizing
ep·i·mer·ize \ˈepəməˌrīz\ *vt* -ED/-ING/-S [*epimer* + *-ize*] : to change into an epimer
ep·i·me·ron \ˌepəˈmiˌrän\ *n, pl* **epime·ra** \-irə\ [NL, fr. *epi-* + *-meron* (fr. Gk *meros* thigh) — more at MEMBER] **1** : a lateral part of the wall of a somite of an arthropod that is situated between the tergum and the insertion of the appendages **2** : the posterior sclerite of a pleuron of an insect
ep·i·mor·pha \ˌepəˈmȯrfə\ *n pl, cap* [NL, fr. *epi-* + *-morpha*] : a division of centipedes commonly considered a subclass, comprising forms having 21 or more leg-bearing segments and young born with the adult number of legs — compare ANAMORPHA
ep·i·mor·phic \ˌepəˈmȯrfik\ *adj* [*epi-* + *-morphic*] : having the same form (as the same number of body segments) in successive stages of growth — used of insects and other arthropods undergoing incomplete metamorphosis
ep·i·mor·pho·sis \ˌepəˈmȯrfəsəs *sometimes* -ˌmȯrˈfōs-\ *n* [NL, fr. *epi-* + *-morphosis*] **1** : regeneration of a part or organism involving extensive cell proliferation followed by differentiation — compare MORPHALLAXIS **2** : development without fundamental changes of form (as without adding segments) — compare METAMORPHOSIS
epi·myocardium \ˌepə, ˌepē+\ *n* [NL, fr. *epi-* + *myocardium*] : the undifferentiated splanchnic mesodermal layer of the embryonic heart that subsequently differentiates into myocardium and epicardium
ep·i·my·si·um \ˌepəˈmiz(h)ēəm\ *n, pl* **epimy·sia** \-ēə\ [NL, fr. *epi-* + Gk *mys* mouse, muscle + NL *-ium* — more at MOUSE] : the external connective-tissue sheath of a muscle — compare ENDOMYSIUM, PERIMYSIUM
epi·naos \ˌepə, ˌepē+\ *n, pl* **epinaoi** [*epi-* + *naos*] : a room in the rear of the cella of an ancient Greek temple — compare PRONAOS
epi·nard \āpēnäär\ *n, pl* **epinards** \"\ [F *épinard*, alter. (influenced by *-ard*) of MF *espinache* — more at SPINACH] : SPINACH
ep·i·nas·tic \ˌepəˈnastik\ *adj* [ISV *epinasty* + *-ic*] : of, relating to, or caused by epinasty — **ep·i·nas·ti·cal·ly** \-tək(ə)lē\ *adv*
ep·i·nas·tism \ˌepəˈnaˌstizəm\ *n* -S : EPINASTY
ep·i·nas·ty \ˈepəˌnastē\ *n* -ES [ISV *epi-* + *-nasty*; orig. formed as G *epinastie*] : a nastic movement by which a plant part is bent outward and often downward (as in the unfolding of a flower petal) ⟨the opening of the bud is brought about by . . . ~ —B.S.Meyer & D.B.Anderson⟩
ep·i·ne·phel·i·dae \ˌepənəˈfeləˌdē\ *n pl, cap* [NL, fr. *Epinephelus*, type genus + *-idae*] *in some classifications* : a family of percoid fishes comprising *Epinephelus* and other genera that are usu. placed in Serranidae
ep·i·neph·e·lus \ˌepəˈnefələs\ *n, cap* [NL, fr. Gk *epinephelos* clouded, overcast, fr. *epi-* + *nephelē* cloud — more at NEBULA] : a large genus of fishes of warm seas including a number of typical groupers — see SERRANIDAE
ep·i·neph·rine \ˌepəˈnefrən, -ˌfrēn, -ˌfrən\ *also* **ep·i·neph·rin** \-ˌfrən\ *n* -S [ISV *epi-* + *nephr-* + *-ine*, *-in*] : a colorless crystalline feebly basic compound $(HO)_2C_6H_3CH(OH)CH_2NHCH_3$ existing in three optically different forms; 1-(3,4-dihydroxy-phenyl)-2-methylamino-ethanol; *esp* : the levorotatory form constituting the principal blood-pressure-raising hormone of the medulla of the adrenal glands, prepared from adrenal extracts and also synthetically, and used chiefly as a heart stimulant, as a vasoconstrictor in controlling hemorrhages of the skin and in prolonging the effects of local anesthetics, and as a muscle relaxant in bronchial asthma — called also *adrenaline*, *adrenin*
epi·neritic \ˌepə, ˌepē+\ *adj* [*epi-* + *neritic*] : of, relating to, or constituting the upper portion of the neritic zone usu. to a depth of 120 feet — opposed to *infraneritic*
épi·nette \āpēnet\ *n* -S [CanF, dim. of F *épine* thorn, spine, fr. L *spina* — more at SPINE] **1** *dial* : any of several No. American spruces; *esp* : WHITE SPRUCE 1 **2** *dial* : a tamarack (*Larix laricina*)
¹epi·neural \ˌepə, ˌepē+\ *adj* [*epi-* + *neural*] **1** : arising from the neural arch of a vertebra **2** : overlying nervous tissue; *specif* : above the ventral nerve cord of an arthropod
²epineural \"\ *n* : a spine or process arising from the neural arch of a vertebra
epineural canal *n, zool* : a canal derived from the ambulacral groove and running between the radial nerve and the external epithelium in ophiuroids and echinoids
ep·i·neu·ri·um \ˌepəˈn(y)u̇rēəm\ *n* -S [NL, fr. *epi-* + *neur-* + *-ium*] : the external connective-tissue sheath of a nerve trunk
epin·gle \āˈpaŋ,glā; -paŋ;-\ *n* -S [F *épinglé*, fr. past part. of *épingler* to pin, fr. *épingle* pin, fr. L *spinula* small thorn, dim. of *spina* thorn, spine — more at SPINE] : a silk, rayon, or worsted clothing fabric in plain weave characterized by alternating wide and narrow cross ribs
ep·i·ni·cian \ˌepəˈnishən\ *or* **ep·i·nik·i·an** \-ˈnikēən\ *adj* [Gk *epinikios* + E *-an*] : celebrating victory ⟨an ancient ~ ode⟩
ep·i·ni·ci·on \ˌepəˈnis(h)ēˌän\ *or* **ep·i·nik·i·on** \-ˈnikē-\ *n, pl* **epini·cia** \-ēə\ *or* **epinik·ia** \-ēə\ [Gk *epinikion*, fr. neut. of *epinikios* of victory, fr. *epi-* + *-nikios* (fr. *nikē* victory)] : a song of triumph or a choral ode in honor of a victor in war or games (as in the Olympian or Pythian games)
ep·i·nine \ˈepəˌnēn, -nən\ *n* -S [*epinephrine*] : a colorless crystalline compound $(OH)_2C_6H_3CH_2CH_2NHCH_3$ used as a substitute for epinephrine
epinychium *or* **epionychium** *var of* EPONYCHIUM
epi·organism \ˌepē+\ *n* [*epi-* + *organism*] : a complex of interacting individuals regarded as a functional entity (as in colonial protozoans or a hive of bees)

¹epi·ornithic \ˌepē+\ *adj* [*epi-* + *ornithic*] : affecting many birds of one kind at the same time — compare EPIDEMIC
²epiornithic \"\ *n* -S **1** : an epiornithic disease **2** : an outbreak of epiornithic disease
¹epi·otic \ˌepē+\ *adj* [*epi-* + *-otic* (of the ear)] : belonging to or constituting the upper and outer element of the bony capsule of the internal ear that in man forms a part of the temporal bone
²epiotic \"\ *n* -S : one of the small cartilage bones of the capsule of the inner ear in birds and lower vertebrates that is represented in mammals by a part of the temporal bone
ep·i·pac·tis \ˌepəˈpaktəs\ *n, cap* [NL, fr. Gk *epipaktis* rupturewort] : a genus of orchids with simple stems, plicate clasping leaves, and greenish or purplish irregular flowers in leafy-bracted racemes
epi·paleolithic \ˌepə, ˌepē+\ *adj, usu cap* [ISV *epi-* + *paleolithic*] : MESOLITHIC
epiparasite \"+\ *n* [*epi-* + *parasite*] **1** : ECTOPARASITE **2** : HYPERPARASITE — **epi·parasitic** \"+\ *adj* — **epi·parasitism** \"+\ *n*
epi·pelagic \"+\ *adj* [*epi-* + *pelagic*] : of, relating to, or constituting the part of the oceanic zone into which enough light for photosynthesis penetrates
epi·peripheral \"+\ *adj* [*epi-* + *peripheral*] *of a bodily sensation* : originating upon the external surface of the body
epi·petalous \"+\ *adj* [*epi-* + *-petalous*] : having stamens inserted on the corolla
ep·i·phan·ic \ˌepəˈfanik\ *adj* [²*epiphany* + *-ic*] : of or having the character of an epiphany ⟨~ events⟩
epiph·a·nize \əˈpifəˌnīz, eˈ-,eˈ-\ *vt* -ED/-ING/-S [²*epiphany* + *-ize*] : to represent in a literary epiphany ⟨Joyce once *epiphanized* a whole sermon, audience, theme, and preacher in nine words: 'Pilate! Wy don't you old back that owlin mob?' —Hugh Kenner⟩
¹epiph·a·ny \əˈpifənē, ēˈ-,eˈ-, -ni\ *n* -ES *usu cap* [ME *epiphanie*, fr. MF *epiphanie*, fr. LL *epiphania*, fr. LGk *epiphania*, pl., fr. neut. pl. of *epiphanios* manifest, fr. Gk *epiphainein* to display, make manifest, fr. *epi-* + *phainein* to show — more at FANCY] : a Christian feast celebrated on Jan. 6 orig. and still in the Eastern Church commemorating the baptism of Christ and secondarily the marriage feast at Cana but since the 5th century in the Western Church commemorating the coming of the Magi as the occasion of the first manifestation of Christ to the Gentiles — called also *Twelfth Day*
²epiphany \"\ *n* -ES [Gk *epiphaneia*, lit., appearance, manifestation, fr. *epiphanēs* coming to light, appearing (fr. *epiphainein*) + *-ia* -y] **1 a** : an appearance or revelatory manifestation of God or of a divine being or a god ⟨the ~ of Jesus at the Transfiguration⟩ ⟨the prophetess of the ancient Greeks prophesied on the day of the god's ~⟩ **b** : an incarnation of God or a god in earthly form ⟨the ~ of God in Christ⟩ ⟨Greek goddesses that had rabbit and pig *epiphanies*⟩ **2 a** : a usu. sudden manifestation or perception of the essential nature or meaning of something ⟨its soul, its whatness leaps to us from the vestment of its appearance . . . the object achieves its ~ —James Joyce⟩ : an intuitive grasp of reality through something usu. simple and striking (as a commonplace event or person) ⟨Stephen's brothers and sisters, formerly seen as separate entities . . . became the essence of childhood; in the performance of his labor, Joyce progressed from things to *epiphanies* of things —J.W. Aldridge⟩ **b** : a literary representation of an epiphany : a symbolically revealing work or part of a work ⟨the ~ in *Oedipus*, the final tableau of the blind old man with his incestuous brood . . . conveys the moral truth which underlay the action —Francis Fergusson⟩
¹epi·pharyngeal \ˌepə, ˌepē+\ *adj* [*epi-* + *pharyngeal*] **1** : of or relating to the epipharynx **2** : belonging to the dorsal aspect of the pharynx : upon the pharynx; *specif* : PHARYNGOBRANCHIAL
²epipharyngeal \"\ *n* : PHARYNGOBRANCHIAL
epi·pharynx \"+\ *n* [NL, fr. *epi-* + *pharynx*] : a median lobe beneath the labrum of certain insects
ep·i·phe·gus \ˌepəˈfēgəs\ [NL, fr. *epi-* + Gk *phēgos* oak — more at BEECH] *syn of* EPIFAGUS
epi·phenomenal \ˌepə, ˌepē+\ *adj* [*epi-* + *phenomenal*] : having the character of or relating to an epiphenomenon : DERIVATIVE ⟨social currents of which the war was only an ~ symptom —J.G.Jenkins⟩ — **epi·phenomenally** \"+\ *adv*
epi·phenomenalism \"+\ *n* : the doctrine that consciousness or mental processes accompany and are determined by brain processes but cannot influence them — compare INTERACTIONISM
epi·phenomenalist \"+\ *n* : one who believes in epiphenomenalism ⟨that behaviorist may . . . be also an ~ —*Jour. of Philosophical Studies*⟩ ⟨an ~ view of the mind-body relation⟩
epi·phenomenon \"+\ *n, pl* **epiphenomena** *also* **epiphenomenons** [*epi-* + *phenomenon*] **1** : a secondary phenomenon accompanying another phenomenon and thought of as caused by it ⟨fate determines what will happen to us, while ideas, convictions, and intentions are no more than phosphorescent *epiphenomena* —J.W.Krutch⟩ **2** : an accidental or accessory event or process occurring in the course of a disease but not necessarily related to that disease
ep·i·phloe·dal \ˌepəˈflēdᵊl\ *or* **ep·i·phloe·dic** \-ēdik\ *adj* [irreg. fr. *epi-* + Gk *phloios* bark + E *-al* or *-ic*] : growing upon the surface of bark ⟨an ~ lichen⟩
ep·i·pho·ne·ma \ˌepəfōˈnēmə\ *n, pl* **epiphonemas** \-məz\ *or* **epiphone·mae** \-ˌmē\ [L, fr. Gk *epiphōnēma*, fr. *epiphōnein* to mention, fr. *epi-* + *phōnein* to speak, fr. *phōnē* sound — more at FAME] : an exclamatory sentence or striking esp. summary comment concluding a discourse
epiph·o·ra \əˈpifərə\ *n* -S [NL, fr. *epi-* + *-phora*] : a watering of the eyes due to excessive secretion of tears or to obstruction of the lacrimal passages
ep·i·phragm \ˈepəˌfram\ *n* -S [Gk *epiphragma* covering, lid, fr. *epiphrassein*, *epiphrattein* to block up, stop up, fr. *epi-* + *phrassein*, *phrattein* to enclose, fence in, block — more at FARCE] **1** : a membranous or calcareous septum with which many inoperculate gastropods close the shell aperture in hibernation or aestivation **2 a** : a taut membrane attached to the tips of the peristome teeth and closing the aperture of the capsule in mosses of the family Polytrichaceae — called also *tympanum* **b** : a delicate membrane closing the cuplike sporophore in fungi of the family Nidulariaceae
ep·i·phyll \ˈepəˌfil\ *n* -S [*epi-* + Gk *phyllon* leaf — more at BLADE] : an epiphyte growing on the surface esp. the upper surface of a leaf — see EPIGENOUS
epi·phyllous *also* **epi·phylline** \ˌepə, ˌepē+\ *adj* [*epi-* + *-phyllous* or *phylline*] : EPIGENOUS
ep·i·phyl·lum \ˌepəˈfiləm\ *n* [NL, fr. *epi-* + *-phyllum*] **1** *cap* : a small genus of tropical American cacti having flattened jointed irregularly branching stems and showy tubular flowers — see ORCHID CACTUS **2** -S : any plant of the genus *Epiphyllum*; *esp* : CRAB CACTUS
epiph·y·sary \əˈpifəˌserē\ *adj* [NL *epiphysis* + E *-ary*] : EPIPHYSEAL
epiph·y·se·al \əˈpifəˈsēəl, -ˈzē- *also* ˌepəˈfizē- *also* **ep·i·phys·i·al** \ˌepəˈfizē-\ *adj* [*epiphyseal* alter. of *epiphysial*; *epiphysial* fr. NL *epiphysis* + E *-al*] : of or belonging to an epiphysis : occurring toward an epiphysis ⟨~ end of a bone⟩ : taking place at an epiphysis ⟨~ formation of bone⟩
epiphyseal arch *n* : an arched structure in the embryonic third ventricle marking the site of development of the pineal body
epiphyseal cartilage *n* : the cartilage containing an epiphysis and uniting it with the shaft
epiphyseal line *n* : the line marking the site of the epiphyseal cartilage
epiphyseal separation *n* : EPIPHYSIOLYSIS
epiph·y·si·od·e·sis \əˌpifəsēˈädəsəs, ˌepəˌfizē-\ *n, pl* **epiphysiode·ses** \-dəˌsēz\ [NL, fr. *epiphysio-* (fr. *epiphysis*) + *-desis*] : the surgical reattachment of a separated epiphysis to the shaft of its bone
epiph·y·si·ol·y·sis \-ˈäləsəs\ *n, pl* **epiphysioly·ses** \-əˌsēz\ [NL, fr. *epiphysio-* + *-lysis*] : abnormal separation of the epiphysis from the bone shaft — called also *slipped epiphysis*
epiph·y·sis \əˈpifəsəs\ *n, pl* **epiphy·ses** \-əˌsēz\ [NL, fr. Gk, fr. *epiphyesthai* to grow on (fr. *epi-* + *phyesthai* to grow, pass. of *phyein* to bring forth) + *-sis* — more at BE] **1** : a part or process of a bone that ossifies separately and later becomes ankylosed to the main part of the bone; *esp* : one of the ends of the long bones of the limbs in higher vertebrates — distinguished from *diaphysis* **2** : PINEAL BODY **3** : a movable process of the tibia of certain lepidopterous insects
epiph·y·si·tis \əˌpifəˈsīd·əs\ *n* -ES [NL, fr. *epiphysis* + *-itis*] : inflammation of an epiphysis
ep·i·phyte \ˈepəˌfīt\ *n* -S [*epi-* + *-phyte*] **1** : a plant that grows upon another plant (as a tree) nonparasitically or sometimes upon some other object (as a building or telegraph wire), derives its moisture and nutrients from the air and rain and sometimes from debris accumulating around it, and is found in the temperate zone (as many mosses, liverworts, lichens, and algae) and in the tropics (as many ferns, cacti, orchids, and bromeliads) — called also *air plant* **2** : a plant ectoparasitic on a human or animal body
ep·i·phyt·ic \ˌepəˈfid·ik\ *also* **ep·i·phyt·al** \-fīd·ᵊl\ *adj* **1** : relating to or being an epiphyte **2** : living on the surface of plants ⟨an ~ marine commensal⟩ ⟨an ~ insect⟩ — **ep·i·phyt·i·cal·ly** \-fid·ək(ə)lē\ *adv*
ep·i·phy·tol·o·gy \ˌepəˌfīˈtäləjē\ *n* -ES [*epiphyt*otic + *-ology*] **1** : a science that deals with character, ecology, and causes of outbreak of plant diseases esp. of epiphytotic nature **2** : the sum of the factors controlling the presence or absence of a disease or pathogen of plants ⟨aspects of ~ and control of tomato fruit rot⟩
¹ep·i·phy·tot·ic \ˌepəˌfīˈtäd·ik\ *adj* [*epi-* + *phyt-* + *-otic*] **1** *of an infectious plant disease* : tending to recur sporadically usu. over a wide area and to affect large numbers of susceptible plants whenever present ⟨an ~ blight of potatoes⟩ **2** : of, relating to, or tending to produce an epiphytotic ⟨the disease exhibited an ~ tendency⟩ ⟨~ conditions associated with a single-crop agriculture⟩
²epiphytotic \"\ *n* -S : an outbreak of epiphytotic disease
epi·pi·al \ˌepəˈpīəl, ˌepē-\ *adj* [*epi-* + *pia* (*mater*) + *-al*] : situated upon the pia mater
epi·plankton \ˌepə, ˌepē+\ *n* [*epi-* + *plankton*] : the portion of the plankton occurring from the surface of the sea to a depth of about 100 fathoms — **epi·planktonic** \"+\ *adj*
ep·i·plasm \ˈepəˌplazəm\ *n* [ISV *epi-* + *-plasm*] : the remnants of cytoplasm left in the ascus of ascomycetous fungi after spore formation — **ep·i·plas·mic** \ˌepəˈplazmik\ *adj*
epi·plastron \ˌepə, ˌepē+\ *n, pl* **epiplastra** *or* **epiplastrons** [*epi-* + *plastron*] : one of the first pair of lateral bony plates in the plastron of a turtle sometimes considered homologous with the clavicles of other vertebrates
¹epi·pleural \"+\ *adj* [*epi-* + *pleural*] **1** : arising from or attached to a rib **2** [NL *epipleuron* + E *-al*] : of or in the region of the epipleurals or epipleura
²epipleural \"\ *n* : a spine or bone arising from the rib of a fish and passing toward the lateral line
epi·pleuron \"+\ *n, pl* **epipleura** [NL, fr. *epi-* + *pleuron*] : a part of the outer margin of an elytron of a beetle turned down on the side of the thorax and abdomen
ep·i·plo·ic \ˌepəˈplōik\ *adj* [NL *epiploon* + E *-ic*] : of or associated with the epiploon
epiploic foramen *n* : the only opening between the omental bursa and the general peritoneal sac — called also *foramen of Winslow*
epip·lo·on \əˈpipləˌwän\ *n, pl* **epip·loa** \-ləwə\ [NL, fr. Gk] **1** : OMENTUM; *specif* : GREATER OMENTUM **2** : FAT BODY 2
¹ep·i·po·di·al \ˌepəˈpōdēəl\ *adj* [NL *epipodium* + E *-al*] : of or relating to an epipodium
²epipodial \"\ *adj* [*epipodite* + *-al*] : of or relating to an epipodite
³epipodial \"\ *adj* [NL *epipodiale*] : of or relating to an epipodiale
ep·i·po·di·a·le \ˌepəˌpōdēˈā(ˌ)lē\ *n, pl* **epipodia·lia** \-ālēə, -ālyə\ [NL, fr. *epi-* + Gk *podion* (dim. of *pod-*, *pous* foot) + L *-ale* (neut. of *-alis* -al) — more at FOOT] : any one of the bones of either the forearm or shank
epip·o·dite \əˈpipəˌdīt, eˈ-\ *n* [*epi-* + *-podite*] : a branch of the basal joint of the protopodite of the thoracic limbs of many arthropods often highly modified and commonly absent in higher and terrestrial forms — **epip·o·dit·ic** \=ˌ==ˈdid·ik\ *adj*
ep·i·po·di·um \ˌepəˈpōdēəm\ *n, pl* **epipo·dia** \-ēə\ [NL, fr. *epi-* + *-podium*] : a lateral ridge or fold along either side of the foot in various gastropods (as members of the Rhipidoglossa) sometimes bearing appendages, sensory organs, and pigment spots
epi·precoracoid \ˌepə, ˌepē+\ *adj* [*epi-* + *precoracoid*] : of, relating to, or constituting a cartilaginous element of the pectoral girdle of some turtles situated at the ventral end of the precoracoid
ep·i·proct \ˈepəˌpräkt\ *n* [*epi-* + Gk *prōktos* anus — more at PROCT-] : a plate above the anus of certain insects that is usu. the dorsal part of the 11th segment
ep·i·pter·ic \ˌepə(p)ˈterik, ˌe,pipˈt-, ˌepēˈt-\ *adj* [*epi* + *pter-* + *-ic*] : relating to or being a small Wormian bone sometimes present in the human skull between the parietal and the great wing of the sphenoid
¹epi·pterygoid \ˌepə, ˌepē+\ *adj* [*epi-* + *pterygoid*] : situated above or upon the pterygoid : relating to or being a slender bone in the skull of most lizards and some other reptiles that extends between the pterygoid and the parietal or anterior end of the pro-otic
²epipterygoid \"\ *n* -S : the epipterygoid bone — called also *columella cranii*
epi·pubic \ˌepə, ˌepē+\ *adj* [*epi-* + *pubic*] : borne on the pubis; *specif* : relating to or being the epipubis or other cartilage, bone, or pair of bones attached in front of the pubis (as the marsupial bones of marsupials and monotremes)
epipubis \"+\ *n, pl* **epipubes** [NL, fr. *epi-* + *pubis*] : an unpaired cartilage or bone in front of the pubis in some amphibians and other vertebrates
epirogeny *var of* EPEIROGENY
epi·rote \əˈpīˌrōt, ēˈ-, eˈ-; ˈepəˌrōt, ˈeˌpīˌ-\ *also* **epei·rot** \əˈpīrət, ēˈpī-\ *n* -S [L *Epirotes*, fr. Gk *Ēpeirōtēs*, fr. *Ēpeiros* Epirus + *-ōtēs* -ote] : a native or inhabitant of ancient or modern Epirus in northwestern Greece
epi·rotulian \ˌepə, ˌepē+\ *adj* [*epi-* + *rotula* + *-ian*] : situated upon or superficial to the patella
ep·ir·rhe·ma \ˌepiˈrēmə\ *n* -S [Gk *epirrhēma*, fr. *epi-* + *rhēma* word, saying — more at WORD] : an address usu. about public affairs spoken by the coryphaeus after the parabasis in old Greek comedy — **ep·ir·rhe·mat·ic** \ˌepə(ˌ)rēˈmad·ik, -rə-\ *adj*
épis *pl of* ÉPI
epis *or* **episc** *abbr* episcopal
epi·scia \əˈpish(ē)ə\ *n* [NL, fr. Gk *episkia*, fem. of *episkios* shaded, dark, fr. *epi-* + *-skios* (fr. *skia* shade, shadow) — more at SHINE] **1** *cap* : a genus of tropical American herbs (family Gesneriaceae) having soft hairy foliage and flowers with four stamens and a staminodium **2** -S : any plant of the genus *Episcia*
epi·sclera \ˌepə, ˌepē+\ *n* -S [NL, fr. *epi-* + *sclera*] : the layer of connective tissue between the conjunctiva and the sclerotic coat of the eye
epi·scleral \"+\ *adj* [*epi-* + *scleral*] **1** : situated upon the sclerotic coat of the eye **2** [NL *episclera* + E *-al*] : of or relating to the episclera
epi·scle·ri·tis \ˌ==skləˈrīd·əs\ *n* -ES [NL, fr. *epi-* + *sclera* + *-itis*] : inflammation of the superficial layers of the sclera
epis·co·pa·cy \əˈpiskəpəsē, ēˈ-, -si\ *n* -ES [¹*episcopate* + *-cy*] **1** : government of the church by bishops or by a hierarchy (as of bishops, priests, and deacons) ⟨tough Presbyterian Scots who had overthrown the ~ —George Willison⟩ **2** : the state of being a bishop : episcopal rank **3** : DIOCESE **4** : EPISCOPATE 3
¹epis·co·pal \-pəl\ *adj* [ME, fr. LL *episcopalis*, fr. *episcopus* bishop + L *-alis* -al — more at BISHOP] **1** : of, being, or suited to a bishop ⟨~ jurisdiction⟩ ⟨~ chairman of the education department⟩ ⟨an ~ voice⟩ ⟨an ~ class⟩ : DIOCESAN ⟨~ lands⟩ **2 a** : of, advocating, or governed by an episcopacy ⟨subject to neither presbyterian nor ~ system⟩ ⟨did not save the ~ author from royal displeasure —Douglas Bush⟩ ⟨entertains friendly feelings for the Old Catholic and Lutheran ~ churches —*Sobornost*⟩ : HIERARCHICAL ⟨the church of the first few centuries had an ~ type of government —E.A.Nida⟩ **b** *usu cap* : of or relating to the Protestant Episcopal Church or

the Episcopal Church in Scotland ⟨an ~ rector⟩; *sometimes* **:** ANGLICAN — **episcopally** *adv*

²**episcopal** \"\ *n* -s *usu cap* **:** EPISCOPALIAN — not often in formal use

¹**epis·co·pa·lian** \ə͵piskə'pālyən, ē͵pisk-, -lēən\ *n* -s [¹*episcopal* + *-ian*] **1 :** an adherent of the episcopal form of church government **2** *usu cap* **:** a member of an episcopal church (as the Protestant Episcopal Church)

²**episcopalian** \"\ *adj, usu cap* **:** EPISCOPAL 2b

epis·co·pa·lian·ism \"'pālyə͵nizəm, -lēə͵-\ *n* -s *cap* **:** the doctrine and usages of Episcopalians

epis·co·pal·ism \ə'piskəpə͵lizəm\ *n* -s **:** the theory that in church government supreme authority resides in a body of bishops and not in any one individual — compare GALLICANISM

epis·co·pate \-pə̇|t, -͵pā|, usu |d+V\ *n* -s [LL *episcopatus*, fr. *episcopus* + L *-atus* -ate] **1 a :** the office of a bishop ⟨he held the ~ for 10 years⟩ **b :** the institution of episcopacy ⟨the abortive effort to introduce the ~ in the colonies —M.H. Shepherd⟩ **2 :** DIOCESE ⟨in administrative matters the ~ is an autonomous organization —F.S.Mead⟩ **3 :** the body of bishops (as in a country) ⟨the ~ and the nobility⟩ **4 :** the period of a bishop's office ⟨he spent almost all his ~ in journeys through his province —S.V.Troitsky⟩

ep·i·scope \'epə͵skōp\ *n* -s [ISV *epi-* + *-scope*] **:** a projector for images of opaque objects — **ep·i·scop·ic** \͵epə'skäpik\ *adj*

epis·co·pize \ə'piskə͵pīz, ē'-\ *vb* -ED/-ING/-S [LL *episcopus* bishop + E *-ize* — more at BISHOP] *vt* **1 :** to make a bishop of **2 :** to make episcopalian ~ *vi* **:** to act as bishop

ep·i·sco·tis·ter \͵epə͵skō'tistə(r)\ *n* -s [fr. (assumed) Gk *episkotistos* (verbal of Gk *episkotizein* to shadow, darken, fr. *epi-* + *skotizein* to darken, fr. *skotos* dark + *-izein* -ize) + E *-er* — more at SHADE] **:** a device for reducing the intensity of light in known ratio by means of rapidly rotating opaque and transparent sectors

epi·sematic \͵epə̇, ¦epē+\ *adj* [*epi-* + *sematic*] **:** serving to assist animals of the same species in recognizing each other — used of colors or structures; compare APOSEMATIC

epi·sepalous \"+\ *adj* [ISV *epi-* + *-sepalous*] *of stamens* **:** growing on or adnate to the sepals

episio- *comb form* [NL, fr. Gk *epision, episeion* pubic region] **:** vulva ⟨*episiotomy*⟩ **:** vulva and ⟨*episioperineal*⟩

ep·i·si·ot·o·my \͵epə͵sī'ädəmē\ *n* [ISV *episio-* + *-tomy*] **:** surgical incision of the vulvar orifice for obstetrical purposes during parturition

epi·skeletal \͵epə̇, ¦epē+\ *adj* [*epi-* + *skeletal*] **:** above or outside the endoskeleton

ep·i·sode \'epə͵sōd *sometimes* -pē| *or* -pi| *or* |͵zōd\ *n* -s [Gk *epeisodion*, fr. neut. of *epeisodios* coming in besides, fr. *epi-* + *eisodios* coming in, going in, fr. *eis* in + *-odios* (fr. *hodos* road, way, journey); akin to Gk *en* in — more at IN, CEDE] **1 :** a usu. brief unit of action in a dramatic or literary work: as **a :** the part of an ancient Greek tragedy between two choric songs and equivalent to any developed situation in a modern play **b :** a developed situation that is integral to but separable from a continuous narrative (as a novel or play) **:** INCIDENT ⟨that childhood visit . . . to "dog town" is a perfect little ~ —M.G.Geismar⟩ **:** SCENE **c :** one of a series of loosely connected stories or scenes ⟨his novels . . . tend to resolve themselves into a series of ~*s* resembling beads on a string —Malcolm Cowley⟩ **d :** the part of a radio, television, or motion-picture serial presented at one performance ⟨a TV film series of 30 ~*s*⟩ **2 :** an occurrence or connected series of occurrences and developments which may be viewed as distinctive and apart although part of a larger or more comprehensive series ⟨considers her war work an ~, not equal in quality to her lifework —Christina Baker⟩: as **a :** a distinctive and significant event or series of events in the geological history of a region or feature ⟨fourth glacial ~ of the Quaternary period⟩ ⟨volcanic ~⟩ ⟨two high-water ~*s*⟩ **b :** an occurrence of a usu. recurrent pathological abnormal condition ⟨a febrile ~⟩ ⟨a coronary ~⟩ **3 :** a digressive subdivision in a musical composition that is either derived from the chief thematic material (as in a fugue) or is completely new material (as in a rondo) **syn** see OCCURRENCE

ep·i·sod·ic \¦epə¦sädik, -dek *sometimes* -¦zä-\ *also* **ep·i·sod·i·cal** \-də̇kəl, -dēk-\ *or* **ep·i·sod·al** \-¦sōdᵊl *sometimes* -¦zō-\ *adj* **1 :** made up of separate esp. loosely connected episodes ⟨the book is ~ and the various incidents don't always hang together —Alberta Eiseman⟩ ⟨most of these symphonies are not truly symphonic . . .; their structure is ~ —Winthrop Sargeant⟩ ⟨an ~ life⟩ **2 :** having the form of an episode ⟨mixture of ~ adventure, satire, and learned discourses —Douglas Bush⟩ **:** INCIDENTAL ⟨compresses the five acts of the original into three, eliminates all ~ material —E.H. Zeydel⟩ **3 :** of or limited in duration or significance to a particular episode **:** TEMPORARY, EPHEMERAL ⟨a reform movement that made only an ~ appearance in the life of the city⟩ ⟨the meeting if it is to be historic rather than ~ must usher in an era of peaceful change —J.F.Dulles⟩ ⟨his accounts . . . are more concerned with ~ events such as the succession of rulers and peoples —W.W.Taylor⟩ **4 :** occurring, appearing, or changing at usu. irregular intervals **:** OCCASIONAL, CAPRICIOUS ⟨their ideal of national union was ~ combined resistance to an intruder —T.E.Lawrence⟩ ⟨~ in his affections⟩

ep·i·sod·i·cal·ly \-¦sädə̇k(ə)lē, -dēk-, -li *sometimes* -¦zä-\ *adv* **1 :** in an episodic manner **2 :** in the form of a series of episodes ⟨would present . . . the man in relation to his work — even if only in facets and perhaps somewhat ~ —*Americas*⟩

ep·i·spa·di·as \͵epə'spādēəs\ *n* -ES [NL, fr. *epi-* + *-spadias* (as in *hypospadias*)] **:** a congenital defect in which the urethra opens upon the upper surface of the penis

¹**ep·i·spas·tic** \¦epə¦spastik\ *adj* [Gk *epispastikos* drawing in, fr. *epispastos* drawn in (fr. *epispan* to draw after, draw in, fr. *epi-* + *span* to draw) + *-ikos* -ic — more at SPAN] **:** causing a blister or producing a serous discharge by producing inflammation

²**epispastic** \"\ *n* -s **:** VESICANT 1

ep·i·sperm \'epə͵spərm\ *n* [*epi-* + *-sperm*] **:** TESTA

ep·i·spore \-͵spō(ə)r\ *n* [*epi-* + *-spore*] **1 a :** the covering or outer membrane of a spore (as the membrane surrounding the megaspore in heterosporous ferns) **b :** EXOSPORE 2 **2 :** the outer layer of a sporocyst

ep·i·spo·ri·um \͵epə'spōrēəm\ *n, pl* **epispo·ria** \-ēə\ [NL, fr. *epi-* + *-sporium*] **:** EXOSPORE 2

epi·stapedial \͵epə̇, ¦epē+\ *adj* [*epi-* + *stapedial*] **:** situated on the stapes ⟨the ~ cartilage⟩

epis·ta·sis \ə'pistəsə̇s\ *n, pl* **epista·ses** \-tə͵sēz\ [NL, fr. Gk, act of stopping, stoppage, fr. *ephistanai* to set on, set over, stop, fr. *epi-* + *histanai* to place, set — more at STAND] **1** *med* **a :** suppression of a secretion or discharge **b :** a scum on the surface of urine **2 :** suppression of the effect of a gene by a nonallelic gene ⟨the role of ~ in polygenic inheritance⟩

epis·ta·sy \-təsē\ *n* -ES [NL *epistasis* + E *-y*] **1 :** EPISTASIS 2 **2 :** exhibition of greater phylogenetic modification by one of two related groups

epis·ta·tes \ə'pistə͵tēz\ *n, pl* **epista·tae** \-stə͵tē, -͵tī\ [Gk *epistatēs*, fr. *ephistanai*] **:** an administrative official in ancient Greece and the Hellenic world

ep·i·stat·ic \¦epə¦stad·ik\ *adj* [after NL *epistasis*, after such pairs as E *emphasis: emphatic*] **1** *of a gene* **:** exhibiting epistasis toward another gene ⟨the gray coat-color gene is ~ to all other color genes in horses⟩ ⟨~ genes in fruit flies⟩ **2** *of a hereditary character* **:** induced by epistasis **:** appearing dominant over another character due to mediation by epistatic genes ⟨pea and rose comb are not dominant to single comb but . . . ~ to it —F.B.Hutt⟩ **3 :** serving to suppress a gene or its expression ⟨semidominants whose expression is suppressed by the ~ effect of the genotype —I.L.Dordick⟩

ep·i·stax·is \͵epə'staksə̇s\ *n* -ES [NL, fr. Gk, fr. *epistazein* to drop on, to bleed at the nose again, fr. *epi-* + *stazein* to drop, drip] **:** NOSEBLEED

ep·i·ste·me \͵epə'stē(͵)mē\ *n* -s [Gk *epistēmē* understanding, knowledge, fr. fem. of *epistēmōn* understanding, knowing, fr. *epistanai* to understand, know, fr. *epi-* + *histanai* to set, place — more at STAND] **:** KNOWLEDGE; *specif* **:** intellectually certain knowledge

ep·i·ste·mic \¦epə¦stēmik, -tem-\ *adj* [Gk *epistēmikos* of knowledge, capable of knowledge, fr. *epistēmē* + *-ikos* -ic] **:** of, having the character of, or relating to episteme, knowledge, or knowing as a type of experience **:** purely intellectual or cognitive; *also* **:** SUBJECTIVE ⟨the ~ conditions in our present state of knowledge⟩ ⟨the ~ as contrasted with the phenomenological sense⟩ — **ep·i·ste·mi·cal·ly** \-mə̇k(ə)lē\ *adv*

epis·te·mo·log·i·cal \ə¦pistəmə¦läjə̇kəl, (͵)e¦-, ē¦-\ *adj* **1 :** of, relating to, or based on epistemology ⟨the ~ problem⟩ ⟨~ position⟩ ⟨~ type of definition⟩ **2 :** EPISTEMIC ⟨to transcend the confines of his own civilization . . . is an ~ impossibility —H.J.Morgenthau⟩ — compare ONTOLOGICAL

epis·te·mo·log·i·cal·ly \-jə̇k(ə)lē\ *adv* **:** in regard to epistemology ⟨~ he is a dualist⟩

epis·te·mol·o·gist \"'mäləjə̇st\ *n* -s **:** one devoted to or skilled in epistemology

epis·te·mol·o·gy \-jē\ *n* -ES [*epistemo-* (fr. Gk *epistēmē*) + *-logy*] **:** the study of the method and grounds of knowledge esp. with reference to its limits and validity; *broadly* **:** the theory of knowledge — compare GNOSEOLOGY

epis·te·mo·phil·ia \-͵mō'filēə\ *n* -s [NL, fr. *epistemo-* + *-philia*] **:** love of knowledge; *specif* **:** excessive striving for or preoccupation with knowledge — **epis·te·mo·phil·i·ac** \-lē͵ak\ *n* -s — **epis·te·mo·phil·ic** \"'filik\ *adj*

epi·sternal \͵epə̇, ¦epē+\ *adj* [*epi-* + *sternal*] **1 :** located on or above the sternum **2 :** of or relating to the episternum

epi·ster·na·lia \͵epə͵stər'nālēə, -pē͵-, -lyə\ *n pl* [NL, fr. *epi-* + *stern-* + *-alia*] **:** two small centers of ossification sometimes developing between the clavicles and sternum and fusing with the sternum

epi·ster·nite \-'stər͵nīt\ *n* -s [NL *episternum* + E *-ite*] **:** an anterior cuticular sidepiece of a somite of an insect

epi·sternum \͵epə̇, ¦epē+\ *n, pl* **episterna** [NL, fr. *epi-* + *sternum*] **1 a :** INTERCLAVICLE **b :** any of several other sternal elements of similar origin or position (as the presternum of a mammal or the epiplastron of a turtle) **2 :** a lateral division or piece of a somite of an arthropod; *specif* **:** the anterior sclerite of the pleuron of an insect — compare EPIMERON **3 :** MANUBRIUM 1a

epi·stilbite \͵epə̇, ¦epē+\ *n* [G *epistilbit*, fr. *epi-* + *stilbit* stilbite] **:** a zeolitic mineral $CaAl_2Si_6O_{16}5H_2O$ consisting of aluminosilicate of calcium and occurring in usu. white prismatic crystals or granular forms

¹**epis·tle** \ə'pisəl, ē'-\ *n* -s [ME *epistel, epistle, epistole*, fr. OF, LL & L; OF *epistle*, fr. LL *epistola, epistula* biblical epistle, fr. L, letter, fr. Gk *epistolē* order, message, epistle, fr. *epistellein* to send to, order, fr. *epi-* + *stellein* to make ready, send — more at STALL] **1** *usu cap* **a :** one of the letters of the New Testament ⟨the General *Epistles* follow Paul's *Epistles* —Madeleine S. & J.L.Miller⟩ **b :** a lection usu. from one of the New Testament Epistles and read or sung as part of a Christian liturgical service (as in Roman Catholic and Anglican churches) ⟨the subdeacon sings the *Epistle* for the day at high Mass⟩ **2 a :** LETTER ⟨flinging the journal into the farthest corners and sitting down to indite ~*s* —H.A.Overstreet⟩ ⟨Pope Gelasius . . . in his ~ mentioning the legend —G.C.Sellery⟩ **b :** a composition in prose or poetry written in the form of a letter to a particular person or group ⟨in spite of Bacon's disclaimer, in a dedicatory ~ to Andrewes —Douglas Bush⟩ ⟨a digressive verse ~⟩

²**epistle** \"\ *vt* -ED/-ING/-S *archaic* **:** WRITE

epis·tler \-s(ə)lə(r)\ *n* -s [¹*epistle* + *-er*] **:** EPISTOLER

epistle side *n* **:** the right side of an altar or chancel as one faces it **:** south side ⟨the priest goes to the *epistle side*, pours wine into the chalice —C.W.Currier⟩ ⟨one sees the pulpit o' the *epistle side* —Robert Browning⟩ — used esp. of churches in which the Epistle and the Gospel are read or sung from different sides

epistolar *adj* [LL *epistolaris*, fr. L *epistola* + *-aris* -ar] *obs* **:** EPISTOLARY

¹**epis·to·lary** \ə'pistə͵lerē, ē'-, -ri\ *also* **epis·to·la·to·ry** \-tələ͵tōrē, -ōr-, -ri\ *adj* [*epistolary* fr. F or LL; F *épistolaire*, fr. LL *epistolarius*, fr. L *epistola* + *-arius* -ary; *epistolatory* alter. of *epistolary*] **1 :** of, relating to, or suitable to a letter or epistle ⟨the ordinary Greek ~ salutation is the infinitive of the verb "rejoice" —E.J.Goodspeed⟩ ⟨retain their ~ prowess —*New Republic*⟩ ⟨an ~ style⟩ **2 :** contained in or carried on by letters ⟨qualifying statements (chiefly ~) . . . which amount to a confession of polemical overstatement —G.L.Kline⟩ ⟨an endless sequence of . . . ~ love affairs —*Times Lit. Supp.*⟩ **3 :** written in the form of a series of letters ⟨the ~ novel⟩ ⟨an ~ short story⟩

²**epistolary** \"\ *or* **epis·to·lar·i·um** \"'la(a)rēəm\ *n, pl* **epistolaries** *or* **epistolariums** [ML *epistolarium*, fr. LL *epistola* + L *-arium* -ary] **:** a lectionary containing the liturgical Epistles

epis·to·ler \ə'pistələ(r)\ *n* -s [LL & L *epistola* + E *-er*] **1** *or* **epis·to·list** \-lə̇st\ [*epistolist* fr. L *epistola* + E *-ist*] **:** a writer of epistles **2 :** the reader of the Epistle at Holy Communion esp. in Anglican churches

ep·is·tol·ic \¦epə¦stälik\ *or* **ep·is·tol·i·cal** \-lə̇kəl\ *adj* [L *epistolicus*, fr. Gk *epistolikos*, fr. *epistolē* + *-ikos* -ic] **:** EPISTOLARY

epis·to·lize \ə'pistə͵līz, ē'-\ *vb* -ED/-ING/-S [L *epistola* letter + E *-ize* — more at EPISTLE] *vi* **:** to write a letter ~ *vt* **:** to write a letter to ⟨forgive and ~ me —Edward Gibbon⟩

epis·to·liz·er \-zə(r)\ *n* -s **:** EPISTOLER

epis·to·lo·graph·ic \ə¦pistə(͵)lō¦grafik, ē¦p-\ *adj* [LGk *epistolographikos*, fr. Gk *epistolo-* (fr. *epistolē*) + *-graphikos* -graphic] **:** DEMOTIC 2a

epis·to·log·ra·phy \"'lägrəfē\ *n* -ES [Gk *epistolo-* + E *-graphy*] **:** the art or practice of writing epistles **:** letter writing ⟨the study of Renaissance ~⟩

ep·i·stom·al \¦epə¦stōməl, ə'pistəm-\ *adj* **:** of or relating to an epistome

ep·i·stome \'epə͵stōm\ *also* **epis·to·ma** \ə'pistəmə\ *n, pl* **ep·i·stomes** \-͵stōmz\ *also* **ep·i·sto·ma·ta** \͵epə'stōmədə\ [NL *epistoma*, fr. *epi-* + *-stoma*] **1 a :** the region between the antennae and the mouth of a crustacean **b :** a plate covering this region **2 a :** the region between the labrum and the epicranium of an insect **b :** CLYPEUS **3 :** the region just above the mouth of some two-winged flies **4 :** a labiate organ covering the mouth in various bryozoans **5 :** an anterior median plate on the doublure of some trilobites

epis·tro·phe \ə'pistrə(͵)fē\ *n* [Gk *epistrophē*, lit., turning about, fr. *epi-* + *strophē* turning — more at STROPHE] **:** repetition of the same word or expression at the end of successive phrases, clauses, or sentences for rhetorical effect (as *government of the people, for the people, and by the people*) — compare ANAPHORA

ep·i·stro·phe·al \¦epə¦strōfēəl\ *adj* [NL *epistropheus* + E *-al*] **:** of or relating to an axis (sense 3a(1))

ep·i·stro·phe·us \͵epə'strōfēəs\ *n* -ES [NL, fr. Gk, fr. *epistrephein* to turn about, fr. *epi-* + *strephein* to turn — more at STROPHE] **:** AXIS 3a(1)

ep·i·sty·lar \¦epə¦stīlə(r)\ *adj* **:** of or having the function of an epistyle ⟨~ arcuation⟩

ep·i·style \'epə͵stīl\ *also* **ep·i·sty·li·um** \͵epə'stīlēəm\ *n, pl* **epistyles** \"͵stīlz\ *or* **episty·lia** \"'stīlēə\ [L *epistylium*, fr. Gk *epistylion*, fr. *epi-* + Gk *stylos* pillar + *-ion* (dim. suffix) — more at STOW] **:** ARCHITRAVE 1

ep·i·sty·lis \͵epə'stīlə̇s\ *n, cap* [NL, fr. *epi-* + *-stylis* (fr. Gk *stylos*)] **:** a genus (the type of the family Epistylidae) of fixed colonial peritrichous ciliates ectocommensal on aquatic animals and including both solitary and colonial forms

epi·syllogism \͵epə̇, ¦epē +\ *n* [*epi-* + *syllogism*] **:** a syllogism one or both of whose premises is the conclusion of a preceding syllogism — compare PROSYLLOGISM

epi·synaloephe \"+\ *n* [LGk *episynaloiphē*, fr. Gk *epi-* + *synaloiphē* synaloepha — more at SYNALOEPHA] *Greek & Latin prosody* **1 :** the elision of a vowel at the end of a verse before a vowel beginning the next **2 :** SYNERESIS 1a

ep·i·syn·the·ton \͵epə'sin(t)thə͵tän\ *n* -s [Gk, fr. *epi-* + *syntheton*, neut. of *synthetos* put together, compounded, composed — more at SYNTHETIC] *Greek & Latin prosody* **:** a meter made up of cola of different kinds of feet

epit *abbr* **1** epitaph **2** epitome

¹**ep·i·taph** \'epə͵ta|f, -taa(ə)|, -͵tä|\ *n, pl* **epitaphs** \|fs *sometimes* |vz\ [ME *epitaphe, epitaphie*, fr. MF & ML; MF *epitaphe*, fr. ML *epitaphium*, fr. L, funeral oration, fr. Gk *epitaphion*, fr. neut. of *epitaphios* being at a tomb or funeral, fr. *epi-* + *-taphios* (fr. *taphos* tomb, funeral); akin to Gk *thaptein* to inter, bury, Arm *damban* grave] **1 :** an inscription on or at a tomb or a grave in memory or commendation of the one buried there **2 :** something felt to resemble an epitaph: as **a :** a brief statement (as a phrase or sentence) commemorating or epitomizing a deceased person or something past ⟨a book of ~*s* on the death of the knight⟩ ⟨an extemporal ~ on the death of the deer —Shak.⟩ ⟨all over but the recounts: that was the somewhat sardonic American ~ on the mid-term congressional election —Christopher Serpell⟩ **b :** something that commemorates or serves as a final judgment ⟨the abstract style has not replaced representative art; the show . . . must serve more as an ~ than accolade —Lincoln Kirstein⟩

²**epitaph** \"\ *vt* -ED/-ING/-S **:** to commemorate by an epitaph ⟨the bishop was ~*ed* in a pair of lovely couplets⟩

ep·i·taph·i·al \¦epə¦tafēəl\ *also* **ep·i·taph·ic** \-fik\ *adj* **:** of or having the character of an epitaph

ep·i·taph·less \'epə͵taflə̇s, -taaf-, -täf-\ *adj* **:** lacking an epitaph

epit·a·sis \ə'pid·əsə̇s\ *n, pl* **epita·ses** \-ə͵sēz\ [Gk, lit., stretching, increase in intensity, fr. *epiteinein* to stretch upon, stretch over, fr. *epi-* + *teinein* to stretch — more at THIN] **:** the part of a play developing the main action and leading to the catastrophe — compare CATASTASIS, PROTASIS

ep·i·tax·i·al \¦epə¦taksēəl\ *or* **ep·i·tax·ic** \-sik\ *adj* **:** having orientation controlled by the crystal substrate — used of crystals and of the relation between them and their substrate

ep·i·taxy \'epə͵taksē\ *n* -ES [*epi-* + *-taxy*] **:** the oriented growth of one crystalline substance on a substrate of a different crystalline substance

ep·i·ten·din·e·um \͵epə͵ten'dinēəm\ *n* -s [NL, fr. *epi-* + *-tendineum* (fr. F *tendineux* or E *tendinous*) — more at TENDINOUS] **:** white fibrous tissue covering a tendon

ep·i·tha·lam·ic \¦epəthə¦lamik\ *also* **ep·i·tha·la·mi·al** \-lāmēəl\ *adj* [*epithalamium* + *-ic* or *-al*] **:** of or being an epithalamium **:** NUPTIAL ⟨an ~ ode⟩

ep·i·tha·la·mi·um \͵epəthə'lāmēəm\ *also* **ep·i·tha·la·mi·on** \-mēən, -ē͵än\ *or* **ep·i·thal·a·my** \-'thaləmē\ *n, pl* **epithalamiums** \-thə'lāmēəmz\ *or* **epithala·mia** \-thə'lāmēə\ *also* **epithalamies** \-'thaləmēz\ [L & Gk; L *epithalamium*, fr. Gk *epithalamion*, fr. neut. of *epithalamios* nuptial, fr. *epi-* + *-thalamios* (fr. *thalamos* room, woman's apartment, bridal chamber)] **:** a nuptial song or poem in honor or praise of a bride and bridegroom

epi·thalamus \͵epə̇, ¦epē+\ *n, pl* **epithalami** [NL, fr. *epi-* + *thalamus*] **:** a dorsal segment of the diencephalon containing the habenula and the pineal body

epi·theca \"+\ *n* [NL, fr. *epi-* + *-theca*] **1 :** an external calcareous layer investing the lower portion of the theca of many corals **2 :** the outer or upper half or valve of the diatom frustule — compare HYPOTHECA — **epi·thecal** \"+\ *or* **epi·thecate** \"+\ *adj*

epi·thecium \"+\ *n, pl* **epithecia** [NL, fr. *epi-* + *thecium*] **:** the surface layer of the fruiting body in many fungi and lichens that in fungi is usu. equivalent to the hymenium and in lichens forms a film over the hymenium — compare HYPOTHECIUM

epithel- *comb form* [NL *epithelium*] **:** epithelium ⟨*epithelize*⟩ ⟨*epitheloid*⟩

epitheli- *or* **epithelio-** *comb form* [NL *epithelium*] **:** epithelium ⟨*epithelioma*⟩ **:** epithelial and ⟨*epitheliog*landular⟩

ep·i·the·lial \¦epə¦thēlēəl, -thēlyəl\ *adj* [NL *epithelium* + E *-al*] **:** of or belonging to epithelium

epithelial body *n* **:** PARATHYROID GLAND

epithelial germ *n* **:** one of the clusters of embryonic dermal ectoderm cells that are precursors of hairs, sebaceous glands, and apocrine glands of the skin

epithelial pearl *n* **:** a small firm body that is translucent like a pearl and is formed within an epithelioma

ep·i·the·lio·chorial \͵epə¦thēlē(͵)ō+\ *adj* [*epitheli-* + *chorial*] *of a placenta* **:** having maternal and fetal epithelium in contact (as in horses and whales) — compare ENDOTHELIOCHORIAL, HEMOCHORIAL, SYNDESMOCHORIAL

ep·i·the·li·oid \¦epə¦thēlē͵ȯid\ *adj* [*epitheli-* + *-oid*] **:** resembling epithelium **:** like that of epithelium ⟨~ cells⟩

ep·i·the·li·o·ma \͵epə͵thēlē'ōmə\ *n, pl* **epitheliomas** \-məz\ *or* **epithelioma·ta** \-məd·ə\ [NL, fr. *epitheli-* + *-oma*] **:** a benign or malignant tumor derived from epithelial tissue — **ep·i·the·li·om·a·tous** \͵epə͵thēlē¦ämədəs, -lē¦ōm-\ *adj*

ep·i·the·lio·muscular \͵epə¦thēlē(͵)ō+\ *adj* [*epitheli-* + *muscular*] **:** of or being an epithelial cell of coelenterates that is modified to function in contraction and has an elongated fibrillar base that functions in the same manner as a muscle cell

ep·i·the·lio·trop·ic \͵epə¦thēlēə¦träpik\ *adj* [*epitheli-* + *-tropic*] **:** having an affinity for epithelium — used esp. of viruses

ep·i·the·li·um \͵epə'thēlēəm\ *n, pl* **epithe·lia** \-lēə\ *also* **epitheliums** [NL, fr. *epi-* + Gk *thēlē* nipple + NL *-ium* — more at FEMININE] **1 :** a cellular animal tissue that covers a free surface or lines a tube or cavity, that consists of one or more layers of cells forming a sheet practically unbroken by intercellular substance and either smoothly extended (as in epidermis) or much folded on a basement membrane and compacted (as in glands), and that serves esp. to enclose and protect the other parts of the body, to form the most essential part of the sense organs, to produce secretions and excretions, and to function in assimilation — see ENDOTHELIUM **2 :** any of certain layers of plant tissue one or more cells thick consisting of parenchyma that line an internal cavity or tube (as in a resin canal where they excrete the resin into the cavity)

ep·i·the·li·za·tion \͵epə͵thēlə̇'zāshən\ *or* **ep·i·the·lial·i·za·tion** \-lēələ'z-, -lyəl-, -͵lī'z-\ *n* -s **:** the process of becoming epithelized ⟨rapid and healthy ~ of wounds⟩ ⟨~ of mesenchyme⟩

ep·i·the·lize \͵epə'thē͵līz\ *also* **ep·i·the·lial·ize** \-ēlēə͵līz, -ēlyə͵-\ *vb* -ED/-ING/-S [*epithel-* or *epithelial* + *-ize*] *vt* **:** to cover (as an open wound) with or convert (another tissue) to epithelium ⟨a completely *epithelized* lesion⟩ ~ *vi* **:** to become covered with epithelium ⟨the denuded surface rapidly *epithelized*⟩

ep·i·the·loid \¦epə¦thē͵lȯid\ *adj* [*epithel-* + *-oid*] **:** EPITHELIOID

ep·i·them \'epə͵them\ *n* -s [ME *epithima, epithime*, fr. L *epithema*, fr. Gk, fr. *epitithenai* to put on, add, fr. *epi-* + *tithenai* to set, place, put — more at DO] **1** *also* **ep·i·theme** \-͵thēm\ *archaic* **:** an external local application to the body (as a poultice) **2 :** a group of thin-walled loosely arranged cells beneath the epidermis of the leaves of many angiosperms that constitutes an internal hydathode ⟨the ~*s* through which guttation occurs in the tomato leaf⟩

ep·i·the·ma \͵epə'thēmə, ə'pithəmə\ *n, pl* **epithe·ma·ta** \-thēməd·ə, -them-\ [NL, fr. Gk *epithema* something put on, fr. *epitithenai*] **:** a horny excrescence on the bill of some birds (as the casque of a hornbill)

epi·thermal \͵epə̇, ¦epē +\ *adj* [*epi-* + *thermal*] **1 :** deposited from warm waters at rather shallow depth under conditions in the lower ranges of temperature and pressure — used of mineral veins and ore deposits; compare HYPOTHERMAL, MESOTHERMAL **2 :** having translational speeds and energies greater than those usu. due to thermal agitation but less than those required for nuclear fission ⟨~ neutrons⟩

¹**ep·i·thet** \'epə͵the|t *also* -pē- *or* -pi- *or* -͵thə|; *usu* |d·+V\ *n* -s [L *epitheton*, fr. Gk, fr. neut. of *epithetos* added, fr. *epitithenai*] **1 a** *also* **epith·e·ton** \ə'pithə͵tän, e'-\ **:** a characterizing word or phrase ⟨~*s* applied to gorillas by psychologists . . .: cautious, conservative, not skillful mechanically or manually —A.L.Kroeber⟩ ⟨the ~ of "the most unsordid act in history" —*Economist*⟩: as (1) **:** such a word or phrase joined often by fixed association to the name of a person or thing ⟨identified more familiarly by his ~ as Richard Lionheart than by his number as Richard the First⟩ ⟨such stock ornamental ~*s* in Homer as "wine-dark" that regularly precedes "sea"⟩ (2) **:** such a word or phrase used as a name for a person or thing ⟨uses the ~ "the Eternal" instead of the usual title "the Lord"⟩ **b :** a disparaging or abusive word or phrase ⟨his sneering tone made "professor" an ~⟩ ⟨hurled the ~*s* "slave-labor law" and "un-American" at the proposed bill⟩ **c :** the part of a scientific name identifying the species, variety, or other subunit within a genus ⟨in the scientific name *Rosa chinensis longifolia*, *chinensis* is the specific ~ and

longifolia is the varietal ~⟩ **2** obs **:** EXPRESSION ⟨suffer love! a good ~ . . . for I love thee against my will —Shak.⟩ **3 :** the use of epithets; esp **:** NAME-CALLING ⟨loud denunciation, ~, and abuse —A.E.Stevenson †1965⟩

[2]epithet \"\ vt -ED/-ING/-S **:** to describe with an epithet ⟨"woeful woman", as he ~ed her⟩ ⟨whose appearance she ~ed "untimely"⟩

ep·i·thet·ic \¦==¦thed·ik\ or **ep·i·thet·i·cal** \-d·ə̇kəl\ adj **1 :** using epithets **2 :** of or having the character of an epithet ⟨the poetry . . . was conservatively epithetical, containing only about seven adjectives in ten lines —Josephine Miles⟩

ep·i·thet·ize \'epə,thed·,īz, -,thə̇d·-; ə̇'pithə,tīz, e'-\ vt -ED/-ING/-S **:** EPITHET ⟨dared ~ him with that insolent character —Miles Davies⟩

ep·i·thu·met·ic \¦epəth(y)ü¦med·ik\ adj [irreg. fr. Gk epithymētikos, fr. epithymētos desired (fr. epithymein to long for, desire, covet, fr. epi- + thymos desire, mind, soul) + -ikos -ic — more at FUME] **:** of or relating to appetite or desire **:** SENSUAL ⟨the ~ part of human nature⟩

ep·i·toke \'epə,tōk\ n -S [Gk epitokos fruitful, fr. epi- + -tokos (fr. tiktein to bear)] **:** the posterior sexual part of various polychaete worms that develops from the anterior sexless part — compare ATOKE — **epit·o·kous** or **epit·o·cous** \ə̇'pid·əkəs, (')e¦p-\ adj

epit·o·ma·tor \ə̇'pid·ə,mād·ə(r), ē'-,e'-, -itə-, -ātə-\ n -S [LL epitomatus (past part. of epitomare to epitomize, fr. L epitome) + E -or] **:** EPITOMIST

epit·o·me \ə̇'pid·ə(,)mē, ē'-,e'-, -itə-, -,mi\ n -S [L, fr. Gk epitomē, fr. epitemnein to cut short, abridge, fr. epi- + temnein to cut — more at TOME] **1 a :** a summary of a written work **:** ABRIDGMENT, ABSTRACT ⟨purporting to be a translation from a French original although it is in fact but a meager ~ of it —Mary D. Anderson⟩ **b :** a brief presentation of a broad topic **:** COMPENDIUM ⟨a convenient ~ of much current knowledge and belief —H.S.Bennett⟩ **c :** a brief statement expressing the essence of something ⟨"five years of fighting and ninety-five of winding up barbed wire" . . . was a fair ~ of war's aftermath —Dixon Wecter⟩ **2 :** a typical representation or ideal expression **:** EMBODIMENT ⟨his manner of receiving my aunt and myself was an ~ of his urbane and appreciative attitude toward the universe —Siegfried Sassoon⟩ ⟨the British monarchy itself is the ~ of tradition —Richard Joseph⟩ ⟨my community . . . considers a man in uniform to be the living ~ of heroism —Lucius Garvin⟩ **3 :** brief or miniature form — used esp. in the phrase in epitome ⟨the spectator does in ~ and without halt what the artist did slowly and by process of trial and error —F.J.Mather⟩ **syn** see ABRIDGMENT

ep·i·tom·i·cal \¦epə¦tämə̇kəl\ or **ep·i·tom·ic** \-mik\ adj **:** of, relating to, or having the characteristics of an epitome ⟨our literature is rich in ballads, a form ~ of the epic and dramatic —Elizabeth B. Browning⟩

epit·o·mist \ə̇'pid·əmə̇st, ē'-,e'-, -itə-\ n -S **:** a writer of an epitome

epit·o·mize \-,mīz\ vt -ED/-ING/-S **1 :** to make or give an epitome of **:** SUMMARIZE ⟨his personal and political creed is epitomized by his own comment —A.C.Gordon⟩ ⟨assertions which ~ one of the richest and boldest metaphysical theories ever invented —Gregory Vlastos⟩ **2** obs **:** to reduce in number, size, or degree **3 :** to serve as the typical representation or ideal expression of **:** EMBODY, TYPIFY, SYMBOLIZE ⟨a young, dynamic, aggressive leader who ~s many of the self-reliant American virtues —E.D.Raff⟩ ⟨epitomized in himself the merits and the defects of the statesmanship of his country —Ernest Barker⟩

epit·o·miz·er \-zə(r)\ n -S **:** EPITOMIST

ep·i·to·ni·idae \,epətə'nīə,dē\ n pl, cap [NL, fr. Epitonium, type genus + -idae] **:** a family of marine gastropod mollusks (suborder Taenioglossa) having an elongated conical shell with many whorls and elevated ribs, a horny operculum, and a short siphon and including the wentletraps

ep·i·to·ni·um \,epə'tōnēəm\ n, cap [NL, fr. Gk epitonion turncock, peg] **:** the type genus of Epitoniidae

epi·toxoid \¦epə̇, ¦epē +\ n [epi- + toxoid] **:** a toxoid weaker in affinity for antitoxin than is the corresponding toxin

ep·i·tra·che·lion \,epētrə'kēlyȯn\ n -S [MGk epitrachēlion, fr. neut. of epitrachēlios, fr. Gk epi- + -trachēlios (fr. trachēlos neck)] **:** a long narrow stole worn by bishops and priests of the Eastern Orthodox Church

ep·i·trich·i·um \,epə'trikēəm\ n -S [NL, fr. epi- + trich- + -ium] **:** an outer layer of the epidermis of the fetus of many mammals beneath which the hair develops

ep·i·trite \'epə·,trīt\ n -S [LL epitritos, fr. Gk, fr. epitritos 1⅓, having a ratio of 4:3, having 4 long and 3 short syllables, fr. epi- + tritos third; akin to Gk treis three — more at THREE] **:** a foot in Greek and Latin prosody consisting of three long and one short syllables — **ep·i·trit·ic** \¦epə·¦trid·ik\ adj

ep·i·trix \'epə,triks\ n, cap [NL, fr. epi- + -trix (fr. Gk thrix hair) — more at TRICH-] **:** a widely distributed genus of flea beetles including pests of various cultivated plants and some that are vectors of virus diseases — see POTATO FLEA BEETLE, TUBER FLEA BEETLE

epi·trochlea \¦epə̇, ¦epē +\ n [NL, fr. epi- + trochlea] anat **:** the medial epicondyle at the distal end of the humerus — **epi·trochlear** \"+\ adj

epi·trochoid \"+\ n [epi- + trochoid] **:** a plane curve traced by a point on the radius or extended radius of a circle rolling on the outside of a fixed circle — compare EPICYCLOID, HYPOTROCHOID — **epi·trochoidal** \"+\ adj

ep·i·troph·ic \¦epə¦träfik, -rōf-\ adj **:** characterized by epitrophy

epit·ro·phy \ə̇'pi·trəfē\ n -ES [ISV epi- + -trophy] **:** increased increments of growth upon the upper side of horizontal or ascending branches or roots — opposed to hypotrophy

epi·tuberculosis \¦epə̇, ¦epē+\ n [NL, fr. epi- + tuberculosis] **:** an abnormal state of the tissues near a tuberculous lesion that is caused by the spread of products therefrom, occurs usu. in children, and is not associated with severe symptoms — **epi·tuberculous** \"+\ adj

epi·tympanic \"+\ adj [epi- + tympanic] **1 :** situated above the tympanic membrane **2 :** HYOMANDIBULAR

epi·tympanum \"+\ n [NL, fr. epi- + tympanum] **:** the upper portion of the middle ear — compare HYPOTYMPANUM

ep·i·typh·li·tis \,epətə̇'flīd·ə̇s\ n -ES [NL, fr. epityphlon vermiform appendix (fr. epi- + Gk typhlon cecum) + -itis] **:** APPENDICITIS

epiural var of EPURAL

ep·i·vag \'epə,vaj\ n -S [by shortening] Africa **:** EPIVAGINITIS

epi·vaginitis \,epə+\ n [NL, fr. epi- (as in epididymitis) + vaginitis] **:** a widespread venereal disease of southern African cattle that is marked by inflammation and discharges from the genital organs and by sterility and that takes the form of an epididymitis in the male

epi·valve \'epə̇, 'epē + ,-\ n [epi- + valve] **1 :** the apical half of the shell of certain dinoflagellates **2 :** the epitheca of a diatom

ep·i·xy·lous \¦epə¦zīləs\ adj [epi- + xyl- + -ous] **:** growing on wood ⟨~ fungi⟩

ep·i·zeux·is \,epə'züksə̇s\ n -ES [LL, fr. Gk, lit., act of fastening together, fr. epizeugnynai to fasten together (fr. epi- + zeugnynai to join, yoke) + -sis] Greek and Latin prosody **:** the joining of two successive ionics a minore so that the syllables that come together exchange quantities (as when ∪∪––|∪∪–– becomes ∪∪–∪|–∪––)

ep·i·zoa \,epə'zōə\ n pl [NL, fr. epi- + -zoa] **1 :** ECTOZOA **2** cap **:** a group consisting of the fish lice — **ep·i·zo·al** \¦epə¦zōəl\ adj — **ep·i·zo·an** \-ōən\ adj or n

epi·zoanthus \¦epə̇, ¦epē+\ n, cap [NL, fr. epi- + Zoanthus] **:** a genus of zoanthidean anemones — see CARCINOECIUM

ep·i·zo·ic \¦epə¦zōik\ adj [epi- + -zoic] **:** dwelling upon the body of an animal ⟨an ~ plant parasite⟩ ⟨an ~ commensal⟩ — compare EPIPHYTIC 2 — **ep·i·zo·ism** \,epə'zō,izəm, '==,=-\ n -S — **ep·i·zo·ite** \-ō,īt\ n -S

ep·i·zo·on \,epə'zō,än\ n, pl **epi·zoa** \-ōə\ [NL, fr. epi- + -zoon] **:** an animal epizoite

[1]ep·i·zo·ot·ic \¦epəzə¦wäd·ik, -zō¦ä-, in sense 3 -¦züd·-\ n -S [epi- + zo- + -otic (fr. -otic, adj. suffix)] **1 :** an outbreak of epizootic disease **2 :** an epizootic disease; specif **:** EQUINE INFLUENZA **3** dial **:** AILMENT, MISERY — often used in pl. ⟨he's not here today — must have the ~s⟩

[2]epizootic \"\ adj, of a disease **:** affecting many animals of one kind at the same time — compare EPIDEMIC — **ep·i·zo·ot·i·cal·ly** \-d·ə̇k(ə)lē\ adv

epizootic abortion n **:** CONTAGIOUS ABORTION

epizootic lymphangitis n **:** a chronic contagious inflammation chiefly of the superficial lymphatics and lymph nodes of horses, mules, and donkeys that is characterized by enlargement and thickening of the vessels and softening and purulent ulceration of the nodes and is caused by a yeast (Cryptococcus farciminosus)

ep·i·zo·oti·o·log·i·cal \¦epə(,)zō¦ōd·ēə¦läjə̇kəl\ also **ep·i·zo·oti·o·log·ic** \-jik\ or **ep·i·zo·oto·log·ic** \-¦zōəd·ə¦läjik\ or **ep·i·zo·olog·i·cal** \¦epə,zōə¦läjə̇kəl\ adj **:** of or relating to epizootiology — **ep·i·zo·oti·o·log·i·cal·ly** or **ep·i·zo·olog·i·cal·ly** \-jə̇k(ə)lē\ adv

ep·i·zo·oti·ol·o·gy \,epə(,)zō,ōd·ē'äləjē\ or **ep·i·zo·otol·o·gy** \-,zōə'täləjē\ or **ep·i·zo·ol·o·gy** \-,zō'äləjē\ n -ES [epizootio-, epizooto- or epizoo- (fr. [1]epizootic) + -logy] **1 :** a science that deals with epizootics and the factors involved in the occurrence and spread of the diseases of animals — compare EPIDEMIOLOGY **2 :** the sum of the factors controlling the presence or absence of a disease or pathogen of animals ⟨the ~, symptoms, and prognosis of fowl cholera⟩

ep·i·zo·oty \,epə'zōəd·ē\ n -ES [prob. fr. F épizootie, fr. E [1]epizootic + F -ie -y] **:** EPIZOOTIC

EPNS abbr electroplated nickel silver

ep·och \'epək also 'e,päk sometimes 'ē,päk or 'epik or 'epēk\ n -S [ML or NL epocha, fr. Gk epochē stoppage, cessation, suspension of judgment, position in space or fixed point in time, fr. epechein to hold back, pause, fr. epi- + echein to hold, have — more at SCHEME] **1 a** obs (1) **:** the fixed point from which years are numbered in a system of chronology (as in the Greek olympiads) usu. determined by an important event (as the birth of Christ) ⟨a different ~ to account by, . . . the hegira they have from Muhammad —Thomas Herbert⟩ (2) **:** ERA 1 **b** astron **:** an instant of time or a date selected as a point of reference for which are given values of the data under consideration ⟨the heliocentric position at a certain zero ~, say 1950.000 —Popular Astronomy⟩ **2 a :** an event or a time marked by an event that begins a new period or development **:** a new beginning ⟨we two . . . made an ~ in the criticism of the theater . . . by making it a pretext for a propaganda of our own views of life —G.B.Shaw⟩ **:** TURNING POINT **b :** a memorable event or date ⟨the child's first sight of the circus parade was an ~ in his life⟩ **c :** TIME 8a ⟨the ~ of the completion of a thousand years from the birth of Christ —C.E.Norton⟩ **3 :** an extended period of time usu. characterized by a distinctive development or by a memorable series of events ⟨the feudal ~⟩ ⟨the Napoleonic ~⟩ ⟨Dante's work . . . initiated a new ~ in literature —R.A.Hall b. 1911⟩ ⟨his college years were a happy ~ in his life⟩: as **a :** a division of geologic time **:** EPISODE; specif **:** a division of geologic time less than a period and greater than an age ⟨the Niagara ~ of the Silurian period⟩ — see GEOLOGIC TIME table **b :** a period of time during which a particular type of culture is dominant in an area ⟨Magdalenian ~⟩ **4 a :** the value of the phase angle of a periodic process (as an alternating current or small oscillations of a pendulum) at the selected zero of time **b :** TIDAL EPOCH **syn** see PERIOD

ep·o·cha \'epəkə\ archaic var of EPOCH

ep·och·al \'epəkəl also 'e,päk- sometimes (')ē¦päk- or 'epik- or 'epēk- or ə̇¦päk- or e'päk-\ adj **1 :** of or relating to an epoch **2 a :** bringing about or marking the beginning of a new development or era ⟨the ~ venture of Christopher Columbus —I.M.Price⟩ **b :** uniquely or highly significant (as in a historical development) **:** MOMENTOUS ⟨his fights to advance . . . democracy during his three ~ years in the assembly —C.G. Bowers⟩ **:** UNPARALLELED ⟨the American delegates . . . have fallen for it out of their almost ~ dumbness —J.T.Flynn⟩ — **ep·och·al·ly** \-kəlē, -li\ adv

ep·o·che \'epə,kē\ n -S [Gk epochē — more at EPOCH] **:** suspension of judgment: **a** in ancient skepticism **:** the act of refraining from any conclusion for or against anything as the decisive step for the attainment of ataraxy **b :** the methodological attitude of phenomenology in which one refrains from judging whether anything exists or can exist as the first step in the phenomenological recognition, comprehension, and description of sense appearances **:** transcendental reduction

epoch–making \'=(,)=,==\ adj **:** EPOCHAL 2

ep·ode \'e,pōd\ n -S [L epodos, fr. Gk epōidos, fr. epōidos, sung or said after, fr. epaidein to sing to, lit., to sing after, fr. epi- + aidein to sing — more at ODE] **1 :** a verse form composed of two lines differing in construction and often in meter, the second shorter than the first ⟨the ~s of Horace's Fifth Book of Odes⟩ **2 :** the third part of triadically constructed Greek odes following the strophe and the antistrophe

epol·li·cate \(')ē¦pälə̇kə̇t, -lə,kāt\ adj [e- + L pollic-, pollex thumb + E -ate — more at POLLEX] **1 :** lacking a thumb **2 :** lacking a hind toe — used of certain birds

ep·o·moph·o·rus \,epə'mäfərəs\ n, cap [NL, fr. epi- + om- + -phorus] **:** a genus of African fruit bats including several typical epaulet bats

eponge \āpōⁿzh\ n -S [F éponge, lit., sponge, fr. L spongia sponge — more at SPONGE] **:** a soft fabric of wool, silk, rayon, or cotton loosely woven in a plain weave with one or two sets of nubby ply yarns for a rough uneven appearance

ep·o·nych·i·um also **ep·i·nych·i·um** \,epə'nikēəm\ or **ep·i·o·nych·i·um** \,epēō'n-\ n -S [NL, fr. epi- + -onychium] **1 :** the thickened layer of epidermal tissue over the developing fetal fingernail or toenail that disappears before birth except over the base of the nail where it persists as the perionychium **2 :** the quick of a nail

ep·o·nym \'epə,nim\ n -S [Gk epōnymos, fr. epōnymos eponymous] **1 :** one for whom or which something is named or supposedly named **:** name giver: as **a :** the usu. mythical ancestor or totem animal or object that a social group (as a tribe) holds to be the origin of its name ⟨it is now the opinion of biblical scholars that . . . the grandchildren of Noah are tribal ~s —A.R.Wagner⟩ **b :** an Assyrian official whose name was used in chronology of the period 893–666 B.C. to designate his year of office — called also limmu **2** [influenced in meaning by E -onym] **:** a name derived from the name of an eponym ⟨taking the name of the totem animal as an ~ —M.J. Herskovits⟩ ⟨the ~ "Weil's disease" assumes that Weil was the first to describe the disease accurately⟩

epon·y·mate \e'pänəmə̇t, -,māt\ n -S **:** the year of office of an Assyrian eponym

epon·y·mous \ə̇'pänəməs, (')e¦p-\ also **ep·o·nym·ic** \¦epə¦nimik\ adj [eponymous fr. Gk epōnymos, fr. epi- + -ōnymos (fr. onyma, onoma name); eponymic fr. eponym + -ic — more at NAME] **:** bearing the name of, being, or relating to an eponym (sense 1) ⟨~ clan⟩ ⟨~ disease⟩ ⟨~ ancestor⟩ ⟨eponymic patron saint⟩ ⟨she played the ~ role in the play⟩ ⟨eponymic myths which account for the parentage of a tribe by turning its name into the name of an imaginary ancestor —E.B.Tylor⟩ — compare [3]NAME, [3]TITLE

epon·y·my \='=nəmē\ n -ES [Gk epōnymia, fr. epōnymos + -ia -y] **1** or **epon·y·mism** \-nə,mizəm\ [eponymism fr. eponym + -ism] **:** the explanation of a proper name (as of a tribe or town) by supposing it to be derived from a fictitious eponym **2 :** EPONYMATE

ep·oophoron \¦ep+\ n [NL, fr. epi- + oophoron] **:** a rudimentary organ homologous with the male epididymis lying in the broad ligament of the uterus and consisting of a number of small tubules that are the remains of the tubules of the wolffian body of the embryo and that open into a larger tube, a remnant of the upper part of the wolffian duct

ep·o·pea \,epə'pēə\ or **ep·o·pe·ia** \-'pē(y)ə\ n -S [Gk epopoiia] **:** EPOPEE

ep·o·pee \'epə,pē\ n -S [F épopée, fr. Gk epopoiia, fr. epopoios writer of epics (fr. epos + -poios, fr. poiein to make) + -ia -y — more at POET] **:** EPIC; esp. **:** an epic poem

ep·opt \'e,päpt\ n -S [Gk epoptēs, lit., overseer, watcher, fr. epopteuein to watch, supervise, be admitted to the highest grade of the Eleusinian mysteries, fr. epi- + opteuein to see] **1** pl also **epop·tae** \e'päp,tē\ or **epop·tai** \e'päp,tī\ **:** an initiate in the highest grade of the Eleusinian mysteries **2 :** one instructed in a secret system

epop·tic \(')e¦päptik\ adj [Gk epoptikos, fr. epoptēs + -ikos -ic] **1 :** of or designed for an epopt **:** SECRET **2 :** of or being the interference figures exhibited by idiophanous crystals

ep·or·nit·ic \¦e,pȯr¦nid·ik\ adj or n [by alter.] **:** EPIORNITHIC — **epor·nit·i·cal·ly** \-d·ə̇k(ə)lē\ adv

ep·os \'e,päs\ n -ES [Gk, word, speech, epic poem — more at VOICE] **1 :** a body of poetry expressing the tradition of a people; specif **:** a number of poems that treat parts of an epic theme but are not formally united ⟨the age of ~ is followed by that of epopee —George Grote⟩ **2 :** EPIC 1 ⟨a wide variety of genre from the simple . . . to the more complex (ceremonial songs and the heroic ~) —T.G.Wiener⟩

ep·oxidation \(¦)e,p+,-\ n [epi- + oxidation] **:** the process of epoxidizing

ep·oxide \(')e¦p+,-\ n [epi- + oxide] **:** an epoxy compound **:** a cyclic ether

ep·oxidize \"+,-\ vt [epi- + oxidize] **:** to convert (as an unsaturated compound) into an epoxide ⟨epoxidized oils⟩

ep·oxy \(')e¦päksē\ adj [epoxy-] **:** containing oxygen attached to two different atoms already united in some other way; specif **:** containing a 3-membered ring consisting of one oxygen and two carbon atoms (as in ethylene oxide)

epoxy- comb form [epi- + oxy-] **:** epoxy

epoxy resin also **epoxy** n -ES **:** any of various usu. thermosetting resins that are made by polymerization of an epoxide (as ethylene oxide or epichlorohydrin) esp. with a diphenol, that are characterized by good adhesiveness, flexibility, and resistance to chemicals, and that are used chiefly in coatings and adhesives

epp abbr epistles

eprou·vette \¦ā,prü¦vet\ n -S [F éprouvette, fr. éprouver to test, try (fr. OF esprover, fr. — assumed — VL exprobare, fr. L ex- + probare to try, approve, prove) + -ette — more at PROVE] **:** an apparatus (as a mortar) formerly used for testing the strength of gunpowder

epruinose \(')ē+\ adj [e- + pruinose] biol **:** not pruinose

EPs pl of EP

ep·si·lon \'epsə,län also -,lən, chiefly Brit ep'sīlən\ n -S [Gk e psilon, lit., simple e] **1 :** the fifth letter of the Greek alphabet — symbol Ε or ϵ; see ALPHABET table **2** in mathematical analysis **:** an arbitrarily small positive quantity

ep·som·ite \'epsə,mīt\ n -S [F, fr. Epsom, England, its locality + F -ite] **:** a mineral $MgSO_4.7H_2O$ consisting of native Epsom salts usu. occurring massive or in crusts (hardness 2.0–2.5, sp. gr. 1.75)

ep·som salts \'epsəm-\ n pl but usu sing in constr, or **epsom salt** usu cap E [fr. Epsom, England] **:** a bitter colorless or white crystalline salt consisting of magnesium sulfate heptahydrate $MgSO_4.7H_2O$, having cathartic qualities, and used esp. in medicine and in the leather and textile industries (as in dyeing and finishing)

EPT abbr excess-profits tax

ep·tes·i·cus \ep'tesə̇kəs\ n, cap [NL] **:** a nearly cosmopolitan genus of vespertilionid bats that includes the big brown bat and other common forms

ep·thi·a·nu·ra \,epthēə'n(y)u̇rə\ n [NL, perh. irreg. fr. Gk ephthien oura the tail has wasted away] **1** cap **:** a genus of very small short-tailed Australian birds (family Sylviidae) **2** -S **:** any bird of the genus Epthianura **:** CHAT 3b

ep·u·la·tion \,epyə'lāshən\ n -S [L epulation-, epulatio, fr. epulatus (past part. of epulari to feast, fr. epulum feast) + -ion-, -io -ion; akin to L opus work — more at OPERATE] **:** FEASTING, BANQUETING

epu·lis \ə̇'pyülə̇s\ n, pl **epuli·des** \-lə,dēz\ [NL, fr. Gk epoulis, fr. epi- + -oulis (fr. oulon gum)] **:** a tumor or tumorous growth of the gum — **ep·u·loid** \'epyə,lȯid\ or **ep·u·loi·dal** \¦epyə¦lȯidᵊl\ adj

ep·u·lo \'epyə,lō, 'āpə,-\ n, pl **epulo·nes** \-pyə'lō,nēz, -pə'lō,nās\ [L, fr. epulum] **:** a member of a college of ancient Roman priests who had charge of the sacrificial banquets

epupillate \(')ē+\ adj [e- + L pupilla pupil + E -ate — more at PUPIL] zool, of a color spot **:** having no dark central dot

[1]ep·ural \(')e¦pyu̇rəl\ or **epi·ural** \¦epē¦y-\ adj [epi- + Gk oura tail + E -al] **:** situated on the dorsal side of the tail

[2]epural \"\ or **epiural** \"\ n -S **:** an epural bone or cartilage on a fish

ep·u·rate \'epyə,rāt\ vt -ED/-ING/-S [F épurer to purify (fr. OF epurer, fr. e- + pur pure) + E -ate — more at PURE] **:** PURIFY

ep·u·ra·tion \,epyə'rāshən\ n -S [F épuration, fr. épurer + -ation] **:** PURIFICATION; specif **:** the criminal prosecution of French and Italian officials held after World War II to have been fascists or collaborators

epure \(')ā¦pyu̇(ə)r\ n -S [F épure, fr. épurer] archit **:** a full-scale pattern of work to be done usu. traced on a wall or floor **:** CARTOON 1

epus abbr [L episcopus] bishop

epyl·li·on \e'pilēən, -ē,än\ n, pl **epyl·lia** \-ēə\ or **epyllions** [Gk, dim. of epos word, speech, epic poem — more at VOICE] **:** a relatively short narrative poem resembling an epic in theme, tone, or style ⟨Arnold's emulation of certain Homeric qualities in his ~ Sohrab and Rustum⟩

eq abbr **1** equal **2** equation **3** equator; equatorial **4** equerry **5** equipment **6** equitable; equity **7** equivalent

EQ abbr educational quotient

eqpt abbr equipment

eq·ua·bil·i·ty \,ekwə'biləd·ē, -lətē, -i also ,ēk-\ n -ES [L aequabilitas, fr. aequabilis + -itas -ity] **1 :** the quality or condition of being equable ⟨~ of temperature⟩ **:** EQUANIMITY ⟨they lacked our gusto as surely as we lacked their ~ —John Mason Brown⟩ **2** archaic **:** comparability as equals or on equal terms

eq·ua·ble \'ekwəbəl also 'ēk-\ adj [L aequabilis, fr. aequare to make level, make equal (fr. aequus level, equal) + -abilis -able] **1 a :** marked by lack of variation or change **:** UNIFORM **b :** showing regular or consistent movement, occurrence, operation, or character ⟨an ~ stride⟩ **2 :** marked by lack of noticeable, unpleasant, or extreme variation, inequality, or fluctuation ⟨for rest and recreation a warm, ~ climate is doubtless most delightful —Ellsworth Huntington⟩ ⟨my affections tend to be deep and ~ and calm —Havelock Ellis⟩ **syn** see STEADY

eq·ua·ble·ness n -ES **:** the quality or condition of being equable

eq·ua·bly \-blē, -li\ adv **:** in an equable manner ⟨studied much, slept little, . . . and was ~ cheerful —Charles Dickens⟩

[1]equal \'ēkwəl\ adj [ME, fr. L aequalis, fr. aequus level, equal + -alis -al] **1 a** (1) **:** of the same measure, quantity, amount, or number as another or others **:** LIKE ⟨~ quantities of bread for each man⟩ ⟨each placed an ~ distance from the door⟩ ⟨~ pay for ~ work⟩ (2) **:** identical in mathematical value or logical denotation **:** EQUIVALENT — often used with to ⟨set each factor ~ to zero⟩ ⟨class a is ~ to class b if a is included in b and b is included in a —M.R.Cohen & E. Nagel⟩ ⟨the temperature there must have been ~ to the freezing point of the sea —Valter Schytt⟩ **b :** like, as great as, or the same as another or others in degree, worth, quality, nature, ability, or status ⟨held men to be ~ in the sight of God⟩ ⟨work ~ to his best⟩ ⟨premature babies . . . eventually . . . become ~ to children born after a normal time —Morris Fishbein⟩ ⟨of ~ interest with the first book⟩; specif **:** receiving or entitled to the same treatment or privileges any other individual has or is entitled to ⟨all men are created ~ —U. S. Declaration of Independence⟩ **c :** like, as great, or the same for each member of a group or class ⟨failing to provide ~ opportunities⟩ **:** uniform in quantity or quality, measure or degree ⟨an ~ pressure throughout the system⟩ ⟨the song of the birds . . . is not ~ as to melody and force —Richard Semon⟩ **2 :** regarding or affecting all objects in the same way **:** IMPARTIAL ⟨in ~ care to nourish lord in hall or beast in stall —Sidney Lanier⟩ ⟨authors of the past and present should be judged with ~ eyes —F.O.Matthiessen⟩ **:** FAIR, JUST ⟨~ laws⟩ **3 :** free from extremes **:** EQUABLE: as **a :** tranquil of mind or mood **:** showing tranquillity ⟨with ~ mind . . . they fell upon their swords —Philip Murray †1952⟩ **b :** not showing variation in appearance, structure, or proportion ⟨architecture, always hard, logical, and ~ —Osbert Sitwell⟩ **:** LEVEL ⟨the ~ plains of . . . Sicily —Elizabeth B. Browning⟩ **4 a :** capable of meeting the requirements of a situation or a task ⟨neither their financial resources nor their military organization were ~ to the task —A.C.Flick⟩ **:** capable of meeting a demand upon one's ability or resources ⟨he was ~ to extended walks by this time —T.B. Costain⟩ **b :** SUITABLE, COMMENSURATE ⟨work not ~ to his abilities⟩ **5** archaic **:** not a matter of concern (as between alternatives) ⟨it was ~ to him whether he fell by his enemies in the field or by his creditors in the city —Oliver Goldsmith⟩ **syn** see SAME

²equal \"\ *n* -s **1 :** one that is equal in status (as social position), achievement, or a particular quality **:** MATCH ⟨humankind as the law views it is a society of ~s —B.N.Cardozo⟩ ⟨hardly a man his ~ in the field —Elizabeth M. Roberts⟩ ⟨he has no ~ in common sense and honesty⟩ **2** *obs* **:** CONTEMPORARY ⟨profited in the Jews' religion above many my ~s in mine own nation —Gal 1:14 (AV)⟩ **3 :** an equal quantity or number ⟨if ~s are taken from ~s, the remainders are equal⟩ **4 :** one of two or more playing cards held by one player that are consecutive or equivalent in rank

³equal \"\ *vb* **equaled** *or* **equalled; equaled** *or* **equalled; equaling** *or* **equalling; equals** *vt* **1 a** *archaic* **:** to compare or regard as equal esp. in quality ⟨~*ing* the pleasures of war to social festivity —Sharon Turner⟩ **b** *archaic* **:** to make equal esp. in ability or condition **:** EQUALIZE ⟨the fair democracy of flowers that ~s cot and palace —J.G.Whittier⟩ **c** *obs* **:** to make equal in height (as with the ground) **:** LEVEL ⟨cities have been ~*ed* with the ground —Robert Hill⟩ **2 :** to be equal to (as in quantity or quality) ⟨the migrant population ~*ed* the native population⟩ ⟨for sheer relaxation and comfort I don't know anything to ~ it —Keith Munro⟩; *specif* **:** to be identical in value to ⟨two times two ~s four⟩ ⟨if the curve *xy* ~s the arc *AB*⟩ — symbol = **3 a :** to make or produce something equal to ⟨~ that if you can⟩ **b** *obs* **:** to make equal return to ⟨the ardent passion . . . which if he failed to ~ —Henry Fielding⟩ ~ *vi, obs* **:** to be equal ⟨we are so a body strong enough, even as we are, to ~ with the king —Shak.⟩ **syn** see MATCH

⁴equal \"\ *adv, obs* **:** EQUALLY ⟨he is ~ ravenous as he is subtle —Shak.⟩

equal–area \¦==¦===\ *adj, of a map projection* **:** maintaining constant ratio of size between quadrilaterals formed by the meridians and parallels and the quadrilaterals of the globe thereby preserving true areal extent of forms represented

equaling file *n* **:** a blunt almost parallel but slightly bulging double-cut file of rectangular section used esp. in fine toolmaking

equal·i·tar·i·an \(,)ē¦kwälə¦terēən, ə¦k-, ¦ē,k- *also* -wȯl- *or* -ta(a)r- *or* -tär-\ *adj or n* [*equality* + *-arian*] **:** EGALITARIAN

equal·i·tar·i·an·ism \(,)ē,==¦===ə,nizəm, ə,-\ *n* -s **:** EGALITARIANISM

equal·i·ty \ē'kwälədē, ə'-, -ətē, -i\ *n* -ES [ME *equalite*, fr. MF *equalité*, fr. L *aequalitat-, aequalitas*, fr. *aequalis* equal + *-itat-, -itas* -ity — more at EQUAL] **:** the quality or state of being equal: as **a :** sameness or equivalence in number, quantity, or measure ⟨~ of size⟩ **b :** likeness or sameness in quality, power, status, or degree ⟨legal ~ of states was accepted in spite of physical inequality —Herbert Weinschel⟩ ⟨master and servant associating in ~⟩ **c :** evenness or uniformity esp. of a surface or of a process or motion **d :** equability of temper **e** *logic* **:** IDENTITY — compare EQUIVALENCE

equality sign *var of* EQUAL-SIGN

equal·i·za·tion \,ēkwələ'zāshən, -,lī'z-\ *n* -s **:** the act of equalizing or the state of being equalized ⟨~ of conditions of employment in agriculture and industry⟩ ⟨~ of brake pressure on all wheels⟩; *specif* **:** the adjustment of the tax valuation of property so as to make the tax burden in different districts proportionate to the value of the taxable property in the district

equalization fund *n* **1 :** a fund for equalizing payments or income to various classes of persons; *specif* **:** a fund raised by tariff duties on certain products and used for equalizing the income of producers of those products in proportion to their respective ratios of production **2** *or* **equalization account :** STABILIZATION FUND

equalization period *n* **:** a period when a previously unmanaged forest will yield regular and continuous crops

equal·ize \'ēkwə,līz\ *vb* -ED/-ING/-S *see -ize in Explan Notes* [¹*equal* + *-ize*] *vt* **1** *archaic* **:** EQUAL 1a, 1b, 2 **2 :** to make equal **:** cause to be like in amount or degree **:** make of equal status ⟨extended Roman citizenship to all provincials . . . *equalizing* the conquered peoples with their conquerors —Clyde Pharr⟩ ⟨~ educational opportunities⟩ **3 a :** to reduce or bring up to a normal level **:** compensate for ⟨she has an instinct to ~ an inequality which "nature" may have left —Reinhold Niebuhr⟩ **b :** to make uniform; *specif* **:** to distribute evenly or uniformly ⟨a bar to ~ the pressure on a set of springs⟩ ⟨~ the burden of taxation⟩ **c :** to adjust or correct the frequency characteristics of (an electronic signal) by restoring to their original level high frequencies that have been attenuated in recording or transmission or by other means ~ *vi* **:** to make something equal; *specif, chiefly Brit* **:** to tie the score in a sports match ⟨the score was still 2–1, but then Hofman *equalized* —Jimmy Hogan⟩

equal·iz·er \-zə(r)\ *n* -s **1 :** one that equalizes esp. by equal distribution (as of force): as **a** *or* **equalizing bar** (1) **:** a bar to which the whippletrees of a vehicle are attached to equalize the pull of the draft animals (2) **:** a beam connecting two axle springs of a railway locomotive or car to distribute the weight equally on both axles **b** (1) **:** a device for equalizing the pull of electromagnets (2) **:** a conductor of low resistance joining points of equal potential in the armature winding of a dynamoelectric machine **c :** a device for equalizing an electronic signal **d** *or* **equalizer brake :** a device for distributing braking force between independent brakes of a motor vehicle **e** (1) **:** a machine for sawing wooden stock to uniform lengths (2) **:** an operator of an equalizer **2** *railroading* **:** a straight-arm crank used in interlocking **3** *slang* **:** PISTOL **4 :** a tying score in a sports contest ⟨he scored the ~ with two out in the sixth⟩

equalizer set *n* **:** BALANCER SET 1

equalizing basin *n* **:** a small irrigation reservoir that receives water from a pump and is used to maintain uniform water flow during brief pumping interruptions and to permit temporary water withdrawal in excess of the pump capacity

equalled *past of* EQUAL

equalling *pres part of* EQUAL

equal·ly \'ēkwəlē, -li\ *adv* [ME, fr. *equal* + *-ly*] **1 :** in an equal manner or way: **a :** in equal amounts or shares ⟨divided ~ between girls and boys⟩ **b :** with equal treatment for each **:** JUSTLY, IMPARTIALLY ⟨so to use them as . . . their merits and our safety may ~ determine —Shak.⟩ **c :** UNIFORMLY, EVENLY ⟨distribute the heat ~ through the room⟩ **d :** in the same way **:** LIKEWISE, SIMILARLY ⟨endeavor to encourage learning and ~ to protect students from distracting influences⟩ **2 :** to an equal degree ⟨two ~ undesirable alternatives —Vera M. Dean⟩ **:** ALIKE ⟨respected ~ by young and old⟩ ⟨affecting city governments ~ with states⟩ ⟨~ opposed to Communism as to Fascism —*Ecclesiastical Rev.*⟩

equal·ness \-əlnəs\ *n* -ES *archaic* **:** EQUALITY

equals *pres 3d sing of* EQUAL, *pl of* EQUAL

equal–sign \'==,=\ *also* **equals sign** *or* **equality sign** *n* **:** a sign = indicating mathematical or logical equivalence

equal temperament *n* **:** the division of the octave into twelve equal half steps

equa·nim·i·ty \,ēkwə'nimədē, ,ek-, -ətē, -i\ *n* -ES [L *aequanimitas*, fr. *aequus* equal + *animus* mind, soul (in the phrase *aequo animo ferre* to bear with equal mind) + *-itas* -ity — more at ANIMATE] **1** *obs* **:** fairness or justness of judgment **:** EQUITY **2 :** evenness of mental disposition **:** emotional balance esp. under stress ⟨the inner life where the rational soul may cultivate ~ in defiance of all outward circumstances —Reinhold Niebuhr⟩ **3 :** right disposition **:** BALANCE ⟨rest restored the strained muscles to physical ~ —Richard Jefferies⟩ ⟨perfection . . . was nothing but perfect ~ and harmony —John Galsworthy⟩

syn COMPOSURE, PHLEGM, SANGFROID: EQUANIMITY suggests a habitual or constitutional emotional balance or poise that is disturbed only by the most trying of circumstances ⟨Stoicism teaches men . . . to accept with proud *equanimity* the misfortunes of life —W.R.Inge⟩ ⟨even direct insult did not disturb his *equanimity*⟩ COMPOSURE usu. suggests the achievement or the maintenance of self-possession or the appearance of self-possession by design or by effort of will, esp. under trying circumstances ⟨we have to call upon our whole people — men, women, and children alike — to stand up with *composure* and fortitude to the fire of the enemy —Sir Winston Churchill⟩ ⟨in the *composure* of his manner, he was unaltered —Charles Dickens⟩ PHLEGM signifies an imperturbability usu. ascribable to a certain sluggishness or slowness of mental or emotional response ⟨to react to terrible news with *phlegm*⟩ ⟨Clare was always restless; she had none of Jane's *phlegm* and stolidity —Rose Macaulay⟩ SANGFROID usu. suggests a constitutional coldness or a preternatural self-possession, esp. under strain ⟨in his feeling that most men were fools, in his *sangfroid* and his scorn of what "folks would say" —Van Wyck Brooks⟩ ⟨Rachmaninoff, who in spite of his apparent *sangfroid* had a very sensitive nervous system —Charles O'Connell⟩

equan·i·mous \(')e¦kwanəməs, (')ē¦k-, ə'k-\ *adj* [LL *aequanimus*, back-formation fr. *aequanimitas*] **:** possessing or displaying equanimity ⟨a good-humored, ~ individual —*Current Biog.*⟩ — **equan·i·mous·ly** *adv*

equant \'ēkwənt, -,kwant\ *adj* [L *aequant-, aequans*, pres. part. of *aequare*] **:** of, being, or relating to a crystal having equal or nearly equal diameters in all directions ⟨~ grain⟩ ⟨~ habit⟩

equat·abil·i·ty \(,)ē,kwād·ə'biləd·ē, ə,k-\ *n* -ES **:** the quality or state of being equatable

equat·able \(')ē¦kwād·əbəl, ə'k-\ *adj* **:** capable of being equated ⟨different but ~ terminologies —Ethel Albert⟩

equate \(')ē¦kwāt, ə'k-, *usu* -ād·+V\ *vb* -ED/-ING/-S [ME *equaten*, fr. L *aequatus*, past part. of *aequare* — more at EQUABLE] *vt* **1 a :** to make equal **:** EQUALIZE ⟨Turkey has had difficulties *equating* exports and imports —Welles Hangen⟩ **:** make equal in specific respects ⟨two groups *equated* as to age and sex⟩; *specif* **:** to establish equality with respect to (one or more attributes between colors evoked by different stimuli) ⟨when matching colors in quantitative experiments, hue, brilliance, and saturation must each be *equated*⟩ **b :** to make such an allowance or correction in as will reduce to a common standard or obtain a correct result; *specif* **:** to make allowance for grading or curving (a railroad track or sections of it) by adding a specified distance for each degree of curvature or foot of ascent esp. in obtaining a basis for division of charges between different sections of a through route **c :** to make comparable **:** show the relationship between ⟨~ the production of poetry to the forms of society —J.G. Fletcher⟩ **2 a :** to treat, represent, or regard as equal, equivalent, or comparable ⟨a superior . . . had unbent so far as to ~ her with herself —José Durand⟩ ⟨tend to ~ . . . "good" with "European" —Rosalind Murray⟩; *specif* **:** to put in the form of an equation ⟨not to be . . . *equated* by the mathematician —John Ruskin⟩ **b :** to regard as necessarily or properly associated ⟨they ~ goodness with unhappiness, as some ladies . . . ~ culture with seriousness —O.S.J.Gogarty⟩ ~ *vi* **:** to correspond as equal (as in meaning) ⟨little men from space ~ neatly with our own projected dreams —L.C.Eiseley⟩

equated date *n* **:** AVERAGE DUE DATE

equa·tion \ē'kwāzhən, ə'- *also* -āsh-\ *n* -s [ME *equacioun*, fr. L *aequation-, aequatio*, fr. *aequatus* + *-ion-, -io* -ion] **1 a :** the act or process of equating **:** EQUALIZATION ⟨the ~ of service pay and civilian wages⟩ ⟨~ of colors⟩ **:** IDENTIFICATION ⟨the king's ~ of himself with his country⟩ **b** (1) **:** a quantity added or subtracted in equating a computation ⟨~ of the equinoxes⟩ (2) **:** an element affecting a process **:** FACTOR ⟨solely on the merits of their performances on that occasion, and no other ~s should enter into his decisions —W.F.Brown b. 1903⟩ (3) **:** a complex of variable factors ⟨sociologists . . . taking into account motives, values, norms, ends — the whole social ~ that fundamentalists in science have considered merely a source of error —H.J.Muller⟩ — compare HUMAN EQUATION, PERSONAL EQUATION **c :** a state of being equated **:** BALANCE ⟨diplomats who work out the delicate ~s of power⟩; *specif* **:** a state of association or identification of two or more things ⟨the dreamer . . . can put into symbolic ~ any two diverse things —Weston La Barre⟩ **2 a :** usu. formal statement of equivalence: **a :** a statement of equality between two mathematical expressions (as numbers, functions, magnitudes, operations), the sign = usu. being placed between them **b :** an expression representing a chemical reaction quantitatively by means of chemical symbols, the formulas of the reacting substances being placed on the left and those of the products on the right of the sign → or = or of the sign ⇆ or ⇌ if the reaction is reversible all of which signs should be read "give," not "are equal to" **c** (1) *logic* **:** a formal expression of the sameness of reference of two expressions (2) *symbolic logic* **:** the expression of a proposition or of the relation between propositions in a form analogous to an algebraic equation **d :** the mathematical expression of the proportions in which color stimuli must be mixed for equation of colors

equa·tion·al \-zhənᵊl, -zhnəl *also* -sh-\ *adj* **1 :** of, using, or involving equations **2 a :** dividing into two equal parts — used esp. of the mitotic cell division following reduction in meiosis **b :** occurring in or resulting from an equational division ⟨~ splits appear early in each chromosome⟩ ⟨each ~ half⟩ **3 :** having a subject and predicate not linked by a verb ⟨~ sentence⟩ — **equa·tion·al·ly** \-ᵊlē, -əl|, |i\ *adv*

equation clock *n* **:** a timepiece made to exhibit the differences between mean solar time and apparent time

equation of continuity : a partial differential equation whose derivation involves the assumption that matter is neither created nor destroyed

equation of exchange : a formulation in economics: the quantity of money in circulation times its average rate of turnover is equal to the average price level times the quantity of goods exchanged

equation of light : LIGHT-TIME

equation of motion : an equation that enters into the calculation of the position of a point or of a body as a function of time

equation of state : an equation that expresses the relation between the pressure, temperature, and volume of a gas or liquid — compare GAS LAW c

equation of the center : the difference between the place of a planet as supposed to move uniformly in a circle and its place as moving in an ellipse

equation of time : the difference between mean solar time and apparent time usu. expressed as a correction which is to be added to apparent time to give local mean solar time and which never exceeds +16 minutes

¹equat·ive \(')ē¦kwād·iv, ə'k-\ *adj* [*equate* + *-ive*] **1 :** belonging to or constituting a degree of comparison (as in Welsh) that denotes an equal level of the quality, quantity, or relation expressed by the adjective or adverb compared ⟨the ~ degree⟩ ⟨an ~ form⟩ **2** *of a grammatical case* **:** denoting likeness or identity

²equative \"\ *n* -s **1 :** the equative degree of comparison in a language **:** a form in the equative degree **2 :** the equative case in a language **:** a form in the equative case

equa·tor \ē'kwād·ə(r), ə'k- *also* 'ē,k-\ *n* -s [ME, fr. ML *aequator*, fr. L *aequatus* (past part. of *aequare* to make equal) + *-or* — more at EQUABLE] **1 :** the great circle of the celestial sphere whose plane is perpendicular to the axis of the earth **:** CELESTIAL EQUATOR **2 :** the great circle midway between the poles of rotation of a planet, star, or other celestial body; *specif* **:** a great circle of the earth that is everywhere equally distant from the two poles and divides the earth's surface into the northern and southern hemispheres and that is the line from which latitudes are reckoned, its own latitude being everywhere 0 degrees — see ZONE illustration **3 :** a circle or circular band dividing the surface of a body into two usu. equal and symmetrical parts ⟨the rainfall ~⟩; *esp* **:** a circle about a body at the place of its greatest width ⟨~ of a balloon⟩ ⟨~ of an egg⟩ ⟨~ of the eyeball⟩ **4 :** the circle on a surface of revolution that bisects its meridians; *specif* **:** GREAT CIRCLE

equator coordinate *n* **:** a member of the equator system of coordinates

¹equa·to·ri·al \¦ēkwə¦tōrēəl, ¦ek-, -tȯr-\ *adj* [*equator* + *-ial*] **1 a :** of, at, or relating to the equator or an equator ⟨~ regions⟩ ⟨~ diameter⟩ **b :** of, in, originating in, or suggesting the region around the geographic equator ⟨~ forests⟩ ⟨~ origin⟩ ⟨~ air masses⟩ ⟨~ heat⟩ **2 :** being or having a support that includes two axles at right angles to each other, one being parallel to the earth's axis of rotation so that motion of the instrument supported in right ascension and declination is possible — used of a telescope or other astronomical instrument **3 :** extending in a direction essentially in the plane of a cyclohexane or similar cyclic structure; *also* **:** characterized by bonds extending in this manner ⟨~ bonds⟩ ⟨~ hydrogen atoms⟩ — distinguished from *axial*

²equatorial \"\ *n* -s **:** a telescope with an equatorial mounting

equatorial current *n* **1 :** an ocean current flowing westward just north or just south of the equator — called respectively *north equatorial current* and *south equatorial current* **2 :** a tidal current occurring when the moon is over the equator

equatorial guin·ea \-'ginē, -ni\ *adj, usu cap E&G* [fr. *Equatorial Guinea*, country in western Africa] **:** of or relating to Equatorial Guinea **:** of the kind or style prevalent in Equatorial Guinea

equatorial horizontal parallax *n* **:** the geocentric parallax of a celestial body seen on the horizon by an observer at the earth's equator

equa·to·ri·al·ly \-rēəlē, -li\ *adv* **:** in an equatorial manner ⟨a telescope ~ mounted⟩

equatorial plane *n* **:** a plane perpendicular to a mitotic spindle and equidistant from the centrosomes

equatorial plate *n* **:** the chromosomes of a cell when arranged in the equatorial plane of the spindle during mitosis

equatorial tide *n* **:** a tide occurring when the moon is over the equator

equator of heat : THERMAL EQUATOR

equator system of coordinates : the system of celestial coordinates based on the celestial equator, its coordinates being declination and right ascension

¹equa·tor·ward *also* **equa·tor·wards** *pronunc at* EQUATOR + wə(r)d(z)\ *adv* [*equator* + *-ward, -wards*] **:** toward the equator ⟨air flowing ~⟩

²equatorward \"\ *adj* **:** lying nearer to or moving toward the equator ⟨~ winds⟩

eq·uer·ry \'ekwərē, -ri; ə'kwer-, ē'-,e'-\ *n* -ES [alter. (influenced by L *equus* horse) of earlier *esquiry, escurie*, fr. *esquiry, escurie* stable, fr. MF *escuirie, escurie* collection of squires, office of a squire, stable, fr. *escuier* squire + *-ie* -y — more at ESQUIRE] **1 :** an officer of princes or nobles charged with the care of their horses **2 a :** a man usu. of social or military rank in regular attendance upon a member of royalty; *specif* **:** one of the officers of the British royal household in the department of the master of the horse in regular attendance on the sovereign or another member of the royal family (as for carrying messages, receiving formal social correspondence, or announcing guests) — compare LADY-IN-WAITING

eques \'e,kwes, 'ē,kwēz\ *n, pl* **equi·tes** \'ekwə,tās, -,tēz\ [L, lit., horseman, fr. *equus* horse — more at EQUINE] **:** a member of a Roman order between the senatorial order and the ordinary citizen serving orig. as cavalry, having entrance requirements based on wealth, and having during some periods exclusive rights to certain judicial, financial, and military positions — called also *knight*

¹eques·tri·an \ə'kwestrēən, ē'-,e'-\ *adj* [L *equestr-, equester* of a horseman, of an eques (fr. *eques*) + E *-ian*] **1 a :** of, relating to, or featuring horseback riding **b** *archaic* **:** riding on horseback **:** MOUNTED **c :** representing a person on horseback ⟨an ~ statue⟩ ⟨~ portrait⟩ ⟨~ seal as the reverse of his heraldic seal⟩ **2 :** of, relating to, or composed of knights **:** KNIGHTLY ⟨a 14th century book of Spanish ~ arms⟩

²equestrian \"\ *n* -s **:** one who rides on horseback **:** HORSEMAN, RIDER; *specif* **:** an equestrian acrobat

equestrian director *n* **:** an official of a circus or carnival who is the stage manager and master of ceremonies of the performance and has general responsibility for the performers — compare RINGMASTER

eques·tri·an·ism \-rēə,nizəm\ *n* -s **:** the art or practice of riding a horse **:** HORSEMANSHIP

eques·tri·enne \ə¦kwestrē¦en, ē¦k-, e¦k-, ,e,==¦=\ *n* -s [²*equestrian* + *-enne* (as in *tragedienne*)] **:** a female equestrian

equi- *also* **aequi-** *comb form* [ME *equi-*, fr. MF & L; MF *equi-*, fr. L *aequi-*, fr. *aequus* level, equal] **:** equal ⟨*equi*distribution⟩ **:** equally ⟨*equi*sided⟩

equi·angular \¦ēkwə, -wē *sometimes* ¦ekwə *or* ¦ekwē *or* ¦ē,kwī +\ *adj* [*equi-* + *angular*] **:** having all or corresponding angles equal ⟨an ~ triangle⟩ ⟨~ polygons⟩ — **equi·angu·larity** \,=(,)=+\ *n* -ES

equiangular spiral *n* **:** a plane curve that cuts all its radii vectores at the same angle — called also *logarithmic spiral*

equi·axed \"+,akst\ *adj* [F *équiaxe* (fr. *équi-* equi- + *axe* axis, fr. L *axis*) + E *-ed* — more at AXIS] **:** having approximately equal dimensions in all directions — used esp. of a crystal grain in a metal

equi·caloric \"+\ *adj* [*equi-* + *caloric*] **:** capable of yielding equal amounts of energy in the bodily economy ⟨~ high and low protein diets⟩

equi·cohesive temperature \"+. . .-\ *n* [*equi-* + *cohesive*] **:** the temperature below which fracture of a metal does not occur at crystal boundaries and above which it does occur at such boundaries

equi·crural \"+\ *adj* [LL *aequicrurius* (fr. L *aequi-* equi- + LL *-crurius*, fr. L *crur-, crus* leg) + E *-al* — more at CRUS] *archaic* **:** ISOSCELES

eq·uid \'ekwəd, 'ēk-\ *n* -s [NL *Equidae*] **:** one of the Equidae

eq·ui·dae \'ekwə,dē\ *n pl, cap* [NL, fr. *Equus*, type genus + *-idae*] **:** a family of perissodactyl ungulate mammals consisting of the horses, asses, and zebras and various extinct related animals, all recent members being distinguished from the other existing perissodactyls by their comparatively slender and agile build, hypsodont grinding teeth with the grooves between the ridges filled with cement, reduced ulna and fibula fused with the radius and tibia respectively to form in turn a rigid slender forearm and shank, and esp. by the reduction of each foot to a single enlarged functional middle digit upon the tip of which they walk, the other digits being entirely wanting except for rudimentary splint bones of the metapodials of the second and fourth — see EQUUS

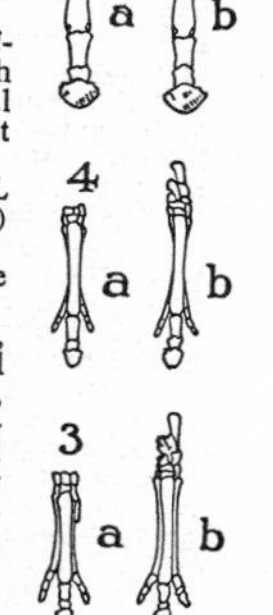

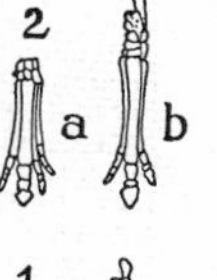

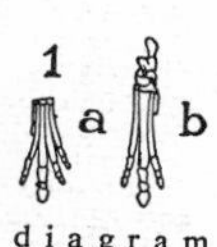

1 a b

diagram showing evolution of the Equidae: *a* lower fore leg and foot, *b* lower hind leg and foot: *1 Hyracotherium*, Lower Eocene; *2 Eohippus*, Lower Eocene; *3 Mesohippus*, Oligocene; *4 Protohippus*, Miocene; *5 Equus*, Pleistocene to recent

equi·distant *as at* EQUIANGULAR +\ *adj* [MF or LL; MF, fr. LL *aequidistant-, aequidistans*, fr. L *aequi-* + *distant-, distans*, pres. part. of *distare* to stand apart, be distant — more at DISTANT] **1 :** being at an equal distance **:** equally distant — often used with *from* ⟨points on a circle are ~ from its center⟩ ⟨houses ~ from the street⟩ **2 :** representing map distances true to scale in all directions from a given point or along or at right angles to a given meridian or parallel (as the equator) ⟨2-point ~ diagram⟩ ⟨the limited ~ quality of a cylindrical projection⟩ — see AZIMUTHAL EQUIDISTANT PROJECTION — **equidistantly** *adv*

equi·final *as at* EQUIANGULAR +\ *adj* [*equi-* + *final*] **:** having the same effect or outcome from initially different events

equi·finality \,=(,)=+\ *n* [*equi-* + *finality*] **:** the property of allowing or having the same effect or result from different events

equi·form \'ēkwə,fȯrm, 'ek-\ *or* **equi·for·mal** \¦==¦fȯrməl\ *adj* [*equiform* fr. LL *aequiformis*, fr. L *aequi-* equi- + *-formis* -form; *equiformal* fr. LL *aequiformis* + E *-al*] **:** like in shape or function **:** UNIFORM ⟨~ crystals⟩ ⟨~ phonemes⟩ ⟨those plants that radiate from the same center have progressive *equiformal* areas of different size —S.A.Cain⟩ — **equi·for·mi·ty** \,==¦fȯrməd·ē\ *n* -ES

equi·glacial line *as at* EQUIANGULAR + . . .-\ *n* [*equi-* + *glacial*] **:** a line on a map or chart to show coincidence of ice conditions (as in lakes, rivers, or harbors) at a given time — see ISOPAG, ISOPECTIC, ISOTAC

equi·granular *as at* EQUIANGULAR +\ *adj* [*equi-* + *granu-*

lar] **:** having or characterized by crystals of nearly the same size ⟨a rock of ~ texture⟩

equi·lat·er \ˌēkwəˌlad·ə(r), ¦ek-\ *adj* [LL *aequilaterus*, fr. L *aequi-* equi- + LL *-laterus* (fr. L *later-, latus* side) — more at LATERAL] **:** EQUILATERAL 1

¹equi·lateral *as at* EQUIANGULAR +\ *adj* [LL *aequilateralis*, fr. L *aequi-* equi- + *lateralis* lateral — more at LATERAL] **1 a :** having all the sides equal ⟨an ~ triangle⟩ ⟨an ~ polygon⟩ **b** *of a polyhedron* **:** having all the faces equal **2 :** bilaterally symmetrical; *specif, of a bivalve shell* **:** divisible into two equal and symmetrical parts by a transverse line drawn through the apex of the umbo

equilateral triangle

²equilateral \"\ *n* -s **1 :** a side exactly corresponding or equal to others **2 :** a figure of equal sides

equilateral arch *n* **:** a two-centered pointed arch in which the chords of the curves are equal to the span — see TWO-CENTERED ARCH illustration

equilateral cross *n* **:** GREEK CROSS

equilateral hyperbola *n* **:** a hyperbola with its asymptotes at right angles

equi·laterally \"+\ *adv* **:** in an equilateral manner

eq·ui·len·in \ˌekwəˈlenən, əˈkwilənən\ *n* -s [blend of *equilin* and ³*en-*] **:** a crystalline weakly estrogenic hormone that is a phenolic steroid ketone $C_{18}H_{18}O_2$ and is obtained from the urine of pregnant mares

equil·i·brant \əˈkwiləbrənt, ēˈk- *sometimes* ˌēkwəˈlibrənt *or* ˌekwə- *or* -wəˈlib-\ *n* -s [*equilibrate* + *-ant*] **:** a force or system of forces capable of balancing a given force or system of forces

equil·i·brate \-ˌbrāt, *usu* -ād·+V\ *also* **equi·lib·ri·ate** \ˌēkwəˈlibrēˌā- *also* ˌek-\ *vb* -ED/-ING/-S [*equilibrate* fr. LL *aequilibratus*, past part. of *aequilibrare*, fr. L *aequilibris* in equilibrium; *equilibriate* fr. *equilibrium* + *-ate* — more at EQUILIBRIUM] *vt* **:** to bring into or keep in equilibrium **:** BALANCE ⟨the resulting relationship . . . tends to ~ the status of men and women in Hopi society —Laura Thompson⟩ ⟨the gas is measured to ~ the liquid⟩ **~** *vi* **:** to bring about, come to, or be in equilibrium ⟨the forces that ~⟩ ⟨the distribution of the . . . sample will not ~ owing to absorption and excretion —*Science*⟩ ⟨while its weight ~*s* with the other weight⟩

equil·i·bra·tion \əˌkwiləˈbrāshən, ēˌk- *sometimes* ˌēkwələˈb- *or* ˌekwə- *or* -wəˌlīˈb-\ *n* -s [LL *aequilibration-, aequilibratio*, fr. *aequilibratus* + L *-ion-, -io* -ion] **1 :** a bringing into, keeping in, or coming to equilibrium **:** the action of equilibrating ⟨the ~ . . . of solutions of nonvolatile solutes in the same solvent —F.W.Leavitt & Saul Kaye⟩ ⟨an artful ~ . . . of particular interest for the sake of the wider community —Reinhold Niebuhr⟩ **2 :** the state of being equilibrated **:** EQUILIBRIUM ⟨the pilot maintains his ~ in space by controlling the attitude of his machine —H.G.Armstrong⟩

equil·i·bra·tor *pronunc at* EQUILIBRATE + ə(r)\ *n* -s **:** any of various devices for maintaining equilibrium (as in an airplane or on a piece of artillery)

equil·i·bra·to·ry \əˈkwiləbrəˌtōrē, ēˈk-; ˌēkwəˈlib-, ˌekwə-, -wəˈlīb-\ *adj* **:** serving to cause or maintain equilibrium ⟨~ reactions in the form of wing positions that differ from the . . . normal —*Biol. Abstracts*⟩

equilibre *n* -s [F *équilibre*, fr. L *aequilibrium* — more at EQUILIBRIUM] *archaic* **:** EQUILIBRIUM

equi·lib·rio \ˌēkwəˈlibrēˌō *also* ˌek-\ *n* [L *aequilibrio* (as in *in aequilibrio*), ablative of *aequilibrium*] *archaic* **:** EQUILIBRIUM ⟨in uncertain ~ between soberness and its reverse —Herman Melville⟩ — used esp. in the phrase *in equilibrio*

equi·lib·ri·ous \ˌ=ˌ=ˈlibrēəs\ *adj* [L *aequilibrium* + E *-ous*] *archaic* **:** characterized by equilibrium **:** BALANCED

equi·lib·rist \ˌ=ˌ=ˈlibrəst; əˈkwiləb-, ēˈk-\ *n* -s [F *équilibriste*, fr. *équilibre* + *-iste* -ist] **:** one who practices balancing **:** BALANCER; *esp* **:** one who balances himself in unnatural positions and hazardous movements (as in ropedancing)

equi·lib·ri·stat \ˌēkwəˈlibrəˌstat *also* ˌek-\ *n* -s [*equilibrium* + *-stat*] **:** an apparatus consisting essentially of a U-tube with capillary ends designed to test the equilibrium of a railroad car when rounding a curve and measure any deviation therefrom

equil·i·bris·tic \əˌkwiləˈbristik, eˌk-; ¦ēkwəˌliˈb-, ¦ek-\ *adj* **:** of or being an equilibrist ⟨a gravity-defying ~ wonder was the hit performer of the show⟩

equi·lib·ri·um \ˌēkwəˈlibrēəm *also* ˌek-\ *n, pl* **equilibriums** \-ēəmz\ *or* **equi·lib·ria** \-ēə\ [L *aequilibrium*, fr. *aequilibris* in equilibrium, fr. *aequi-* equi- + *-libris* (fr. *libra* pound, weight, balance)] **1 :** a state of balance between or among opposing forces or processes resulting in the absence of acceleration or the absence of net change: as **a :** a state of static balance of a body or system acted upon by forces whose resultant is zero **b :** a state of dynamic balance attained in a reversible chemical reaction when the velocities in both directions are equal **c :** a state of dynamic balance (as of a liquid at the boiling point) in which two or more simultaneous opposing processes (as vaporization and condensation) proceed at the same rate and thereby cancel each other's effects **d :** uniformity of temperature throughout a body or system **e :** a state of a system in which no spontaneous change can take place, the temperature and pressure being the same throughout **2 a :** a state of adjustment between or among opposing or divergent elements ⟨the introduction of a new and mighty force had disturbed the old ~ and had turned one limited monarchy after another into an absolute monarchy —T.B.Macaulay⟩ **b :** a state of intellectual or emotional balance: (1) **:** a state of equanimity **:** POISE ⟨he was speechless with anger and did not recover his ~ for a week —Sherwood Anderson⟩ (2) **:** a state of doubt, indecision, or indifference resulting from the balancing of motives or reasons ⟨freedom of thought has brought us to an ~, a center of indifference, far removed from the whirl of continental anticlericalism —G.G.Coulton⟩ (3) **:** a state of dynamic stability of mind or temper **:** TENSION ⟨a certain internal ~ of impulsions . . . that mutually excite and reinforce one another —John Dewey⟩ **c** (1) **:** a condition in which opposing economic forces are so balanced that there is no tendency to change in one way or another (2) **:** a normative position toward which economic forces impel or about which fluctuations occur **d :** a state of society characterized by a balance of antagonistic or noncomplementary elements (as attitudes, sentiments, and associations) and the stable operation of a common system of social norms **e :** the normal oriented state of the animal body in respect to the substrate that represents automatic adjustment to changing spatial and gravitational relationships through the labyrinthine sense or through the equivalent static senses in lower forms **3 :** BALANCE 6 a(1) ⟨those constant miracles of precision and of exact ~ that a first-class modern orchestra is capable of —Virgil Thomson⟩ **syn** see BALANCE

equilibrium moisture content *n* **:** the condition of balance with the moisture content of the air, being in wood equivalent to about 15 percent of moisture at which level wood neither takes on nor loses moisture when exposed to air

equilibrium price *n* **:** the price at which supply and demand are equal

equilibrium sense *n* **:** LABYRINTHINE SENSE

equil·i·brize \əˈkwiləˌbrīz, ēˈ-\ *vt* -ED/-ING/-S [*equilibrium* + *-ize*] **:** EQUILIBRATE

eq·ui·lin \ˈekwələn\ *n* -s [L *equi-* horse (fr. *equus*) + connective *-l-* + E *-in* — more at EQUINE] **:** a crystalline estrogenic hormone that is a phenolic steroid ketone $C_{18}H_{20}O_2$ and is obtained from the urine of pregnant mares; dihydro-equilenin

equi·molal *as at* EQUIANGULAR +\ *adj* [*equi-* + *molal*] **1 :** having equal molal concentration **2 :** EQUIMOLAR 1

equi·molar \"+\ *adj* [*equi-* + *molar*] **1 :** of or relating to an equal number of moles ⟨an ~ mixture of chlorine and sulfur dioxide⟩ **2 :** having equal molar concentration

equi·molecular \"+\ *adj* [*equi-* + *molecular*] **1 :** containing an equal number of molecules **2 :** EQUIMOLAR 1

equi·nal \(ˈ)ē¦kwīnᵊl, (ˈ)e¦-\ *adj* [L *equinus* + E *-al*] *archaic* **:** EQUINE

¹equine \ˈēˌkwīn, ˈe,-\ *adj* [L *equinus*, fr. *equus* horse + *-inus* -ine; akin to OE *eoh* horse, OS *ehu*skalk horse servant, ON *jōr* horse, Goth *aihwa*tundi thornbush (lit., horse-tooth), Gk *hippos* horse, OIr *ech*, Skt *aśva*] **1 :** resembling a horse **2** [NL *Equus* + E *-ine*] **a :** of or relating to the Equidae **b :** of or being one of the Equidae — **equine·ly** *adv*

²equine \"\ *n* -s **:** one of the Equidae; *specif* **:** HORSE

equine antelope *n* **:** ROAN ANTELOPE

equine encephalomyelitis *n* **:** either of two virus-induced encephalomyelitides chiefly attacking equines and man in various parts of No. America — called also *eastern equine encephalomyelitis, western equine encephalomyelitis* according to the region of usual occurrence

equine influenza *n* **:** shipping fever of horses

equine plague *n* **:** AFRICAN HORSE SICKNESS

equine syphilis *n* **:** DOURINE

equine variola *n* **:** HORSEPOX

equin·ia \əˈkwinēə, ēˈ-,e'-\ *n* -s [NL, fr. L *equinus* equine + NL *-ia* — more at EQUINE] **:** FARCY 1

equin·i·ty \-nəd·ē\ *n* -ES **:** equine nature or character

¹equi·noc·tial \ˌēkwə¦näkshəl *also* ˌek-\ *adj* [ME *equinoccial, equinoxial*, fr. MF & L; MF *equinocial, equinoctial*, fr. L *aequinoctialis*, fr. *aequinoctium* equinox + *-alis* -al — more at EQUINOX] **1 :** relating to an equinox or to a state or the time of equal day and night **2 :** relating to the regions or climate of the equinoctial line or equator **:** being in or near that line ⟨~ heat⟩ **3 :** relating to the time when the sun passes an equinoctial point ⟨an ~ storm⟩ **4** *of a sign of the zodiac* **:** beginning at one of the equinoxes

²equinoctial \"\ *n* -s [ME *equinoccial, equinoxial*, fr. MF & ML; MF *equinocial, equinoctial*, fr. ML *aequinoctialis*, fr. L *aequinoctialis*, adj.] **1 a :** EQUATOR 1 **b** *obs* **:** EQUINOX **c** *archaic* **:** the terrestrial equator **2 :** an equinoctial gale or storm

equinoctial circle *or* **equinoctial line** *n* **:** CELESTIAL EQUATOR

equinoctial colure *n* **:** the circle of 0 and 12 hours right ascension passing through the equinoctial points of the celestial sphere

equinoctial point *n* **:** EQUINOX 2

equinoctial tide *n* **:** a tide that occurs near the time of an equinox

equinoctial year *n* **:** TROPICAL YEAR

equi·nox \ˈēkwəˌnäks *also* ˈek-\ *n* -ES [ME, fr. MF or ML; MF *equinoxe*, fr. ML *equinoxium*, alter. of L *aequinoctium*, fr. *aequi-* equi- + *-noctium* (fr. *noct-, nox* night) — more at NIGHT] **1 :** either of the two times each year when the sun crosses the equator and day and night are everywhere of equal length, being about March 21 and September 23 — called also respectively *vernal equinox, autumnal equinox* **2 :** either of the two points on the celestial sphere where the celestial equator intersects the ecliptic — compare PRECESSION OF THE EQUINOXES

equip \əˈkwip, ēˈ-\ *vt* **equipped**; **equipped** *also* **equipt**; **equipping**; **equips** [MF *equiper*, fr. OF *esquiper, eschiper* to embark, launch a ship, equip a ship, of Gmc origin; akin to OE *scipian* to embark, equip a ship, fr. *scip* ship — more at SHIP] **:** to provide with what is necessary, useful, or appropriate: as **a** (1) **:** to supply with material resources (as implements or facilities) **:** fit out ⟨a ship *equipped* with every mechanical aid to navigation⟩ ⟨a park *equipped* with a playground, ball fields, riding trails, and a historical museum⟩ ⟨he . . . was *equipped* with letters that opened every European door —Van Wyck Brooks⟩ (2) **:** to provide with clothing or ornament ⟨*equipt* in the . . . national dress of the Scottish people —Sir Walter Scott⟩ ⟨the long fitted jacket . . . is *equipped* with a notched cape collar —*New Yorker*⟩ (3) **:** to provide with intellectual or emotional resources (as concepts or traits) ⟨thus *equipped* with a philosophy Emerson was prepared to begin work as a critic —V.L.Parrington⟩ **:** ENDOW ⟨she was *equipped* with an acute business sense —*Current Biog.*⟩ **b :** to make ready or competent for service or action or against a need **:** PREPARE ⟨most junior colleges are well *equipped* to engage . . . in such programs —L.L.Medsker⟩ **:** QUALIFY, FIT ⟨so young and so badly *equipped* to console someone so beset that she could not utter a word —Jean Stafford⟩; *specif* **:** to prepare by training or experience with the necessary skills or knowledge ⟨went back to school to ~ himself for a career as a telegrapher⟩ ⟨his own ordeal *equipped* him to understand and appreciate his friend's suffering⟩ **syn** see FURNISH

¹eq·ui·page \ˈekwəpij, *chiefly in pl* -wəpəj; *also* ÷əˈkwipij *or* ēˈkwip- *sometimes* ˈekwəˌpäzh *or* ˈekwəˌpäj\ *n* -s [MF, fr. *equiper* + *-age*] **1** *obs* **:** EQUIPMENT 1 ⟨hastens the ~ of the galleys —*London Gazette*⟩ ⟨to put himself in ~ for that . . . voyage —James Howell⟩ **2 a** (1) **:** material or articles used in equipping an organized group ⟨the expense of providing arms, ordnance stores, quartermaster stores, and camp ~ —*US Code*⟩ (2) *archaic* **:** a collection of equipment **:** OUTFIT ⟨the queen had ordered a little ~ of all things necessary for me —Jonathan Swift⟩ **:** SET, SERVICE ⟨a complete tea and coffee ~ —*Chelsea Catalog of 1756*⟩ (3) *archaic* **:** ETUI ⟨little ~ of silver gilt containing scissors, thimble, nail trimmer —C.G.D.Roberts⟩ **b** *archaic* **:** a set of clothing and accessories **:** UNIFORM ⟨the ~ of a well-armed trooper of the period —Sir Walter Scott⟩ **:** TRAPPINGS ⟨first strip off all her ~ of pride —Alexander Pope⟩ **3** *archaic* **:** RETINUE ⟨an ~ indeed . . . a hundred servants in ordinary attendance —Thomas Fuller⟩ ⟨Death the crowned phantom with all the ~ of his terrors —Thomas De Quincey⟩ **4** *archaic* **:** ceremonious display **:** STYLE, POMP ⟨kings have their entrance in due ~ —Thomas Heywood⟩ **5** [F *équipage*, fr. MF *equipage*] **a :** an elegant horse-drawn carriage with its retinue of servants **b :** such a carriage without its retinue

²equipage \"\ *vt* -ED/-ING/-S *archaic* **:** to furnish with an equipage ⟨a goodly train of squires and ladies *equipaged* well —Edmund Spenser⟩

equi·partition *as at* EQUIANGULAR +\ *n* [*equi-* + *partition*] **1 :** EQUIPARTITION OF ENERGY **2 :** distribution of a solute equally between two immiscible solvents

equipartition of energy : an ideal condition postulated as existing among the molecules, atoms, and ions of a gas or vapor wherein the total heat energy is equally apportioned among the various degrees of freedom possessed by those particles, the realization of this ideal at lower temperatures often being impaired by quantum restrictions

eq·ui·pluve \ˈekwəˌplüv, ˈēk-\ *n* -s [*equi-* + *-pluve* (fr. L *pluvia* rain) — more at PLUVIAL] **:** a line on a rainfall map connecting places where the same fraction of their several annual rainfalls occurs during any specified portion of the year (as a given month)

equip·ment \əˈkwipmənt, ēˈ-\ *n* -s **1 a :** the equipping of a person or thing ⟨the development and ~ of a library extension program⟩ **b :** the state of being equipped ⟨the institution did not spring in full maturity and ~ —J.H.Burton⟩ **2 a :** the physical resources serving to equip a person or thing ⟨funds for buildings and ~⟩ ⟨the vocal ~ of a singer⟩ ⟨a new jail became part of the municipal ~ —*Amer. Guide Series: Va.*⟩: as (1) **:** the implements (as machinery or tools) used in an operation or activity **:** APPARATUS ⟨where a tractor is standard ~⟩ ⟨sports ~⟩ (2) **:** all the fixed assets other than land and buildings of a business enterprise ⟨the plant, ~, and supplies of the factory⟩ (3) **:** the rolling stock of a railway **b :** a collection of such equipment ⟨having its own uniform, flag, and . . . a standardized ~ —S.B.Fay⟩ **c :** a piece of such equipment ⟨manufactured . . . an air-conditioning ~ for beds —*Current Biog.*⟩ ⟨in what a desperate condition the Virginia troops were as regarded clothing and ~*s* —H.E.Scudder⟩ **3 a :** mental or emotional traits or resources ⟨prejudice, intolerance, and bigotry . . . soon become a part of a child's ~ —*Episcopal Churchnews*⟩ **:** PREPARATION ⟨some knowledge of the facts of biology should be an essential part of the ~ of every educated man —*Nineteenth Century & After*⟩ **b :** an aspect of one's mental or emotional makeup **:** ENDOWMENT ⟨a ready repartee is also a valuable ~ for anyone seeking high office —V.L. Albjerg⟩

syn EQUIPMENT, APPARATUS, MACHINERY, PARAPHERNALIA, OUTFIT, TACKLE, GEAR, MATÉRIEL can signify, in common, all the things used in a given work or useful in effecting a given end. EQUIPMENT usu. covers everything, except personnel, needed for efficient operation or service, often applying also to human qualities and skills useful in this way ⟨the marines took with them full combat *equipment*, including tanks, artillery, jeeps, trucks, and flamethrowers —*Time*⟩ ⟨other *equipment* in the park includes tables, benches, and playground apparatus —*Amer. Guide Series: Minn.*⟩ ⟨the only essential *equipment* for softball is a bat and a ball —J.H.Shaw⟩ ⟨innate *equipment* of the child (sensory, neural and glandular) —*Psychological Abstracts*⟩ ⟨the heroine, typically named Virginia, has no *equipment* for life but loveliness and innocence —Carl Van Doren⟩ APPARATUS, a very general term, usu. in this connection covers instruments, tools, machines, and appliances used in a craft or profession, or the equipment used in a sport or recreation, or, more generally, any contrivance or device or set of them commonly used in any activity ⟨a collection of safecracking *apparatus*⟩ ⟨drill, X-ray machine, and other dental *apparatus*⟩ ⟨punitive *apparatus* — bilboes, stocks, pillories, and ducking stools —*Amer. Guide Series: Mass.*⟩ ⟨she had insisted on leaving in his room the materials and *apparatus* for a light meal —Arnold Bennett⟩ MACHINERY covers all devices, means, or agencies which permit a thing to function or accomplish an end ⟨the *machinery* of criminal identification⟩ ⟨the treaty must be given the kind of *machinery* which will permit it to operate efficiently —*New Republic*⟩ ⟨the *machinery* of advertising and propaganda —Jerome Stone⟩ ⟨the *machinery* of recruitment — written examinations, interviews, internal promotions or transfers —*Times Lit. Supp.*⟩ PARAPHERNALIA, sometimes contemptuous in implication, usu. suggests a collection of miscellaneous articles or belongings constituting the usual, often necessary, appurtenances of a particular activity or person engaged in it ⟨a golden chalice, vestments and cruets, all the *paraphernalia* for celebrating Mass —Willa Cather⟩ ⟨family allowances, maternity grants, and all the *paraphernalia* of social security —Roy Lewis & Angus Maude⟩ ⟨little piles of wheels, strips of unworked iron and steel, blocks of wood, the *paraphernalia* of the inventor's trade —Sherwood Anderson⟩ ⟨the chivalric romances . . . are of course replete with adventure of every kind: warlike knight-errantry, magic forests and fountains, enchanted castles, magicians, and all the other *paraphernalia* —R.A.Hall b. 1911⟩ OUTFIT is more colloquially interchangeable with EQUIPMENT but generally is confined to the personal effects necessary for a given occupation, recreation, function, or type of life ⟨a fireman's *outfit*⟩ ⟨a camper's *outfit* consisting of high boots, poncho, sleeping bag, and cooking utensils⟩ ⟨a college girl's *outfit*⟩ ⟨a bride's *outfit*⟩ ⟨a soldier's *outfit*⟩ TACKLE is colloquially interchangeable with APPARATUS ⟨toothbrush and shaving *tackle* in the bedroom —Graham Greene⟩ or EQUIPMENT ⟨fishing *tackle*⟩ GEAR may be interchangeable with EQUIPMENT, often transportable equipment or luggage ⟨housekeeping *gear* —Dorothy C. Fisher⟩ ⟨we had a collapsible stage that broke down into boxes and battens and about a ton of *gear* which travelled with us in a large ancient but very game delivery van —Barry Carman⟩ ⟨we gathered together our *gear* and prepared to make our way back to the railroad station —Thomas Barbour⟩ or with OUTFIT, often in specific reference to wearing apparel ⟨when cowboy *gear* became so popular —D.C.Morrill⟩, or may signify one's belongings collectively ⟨the student immediately stowed all his *gear* in his new room⟩ MATÉRIEL, confined usu. to military or industrial use, is a comprehensive term to designate everything but the personnel ⟨a heavy drain on both the manpower and *matériel* resources —*N.Y. Times*⟩ ⟨the latest developments in artillery *matériel* —*Combat Forces Jour.*⟩

equipment bond *n* **:** a railroad bond secured by rolling stock

equipment ground *n* **:** an electrical grounding connection that is required for equipment that may become energized if the winding insulation fails

equipment note *n* **:** a note issued by a railroad to purchase equipment (as locomotives)

equipment obligation *n* **:** a bond, certificate, or share serving as a direct lien on a specific lot of railroad rolling stock

equipment trust *n* **:** a trust established for the ownership and lease of equipment

equipment trust certificate *n* **:** an interest in an equipment trust on which payments are made out of rentals received from lease of the equipment

¹eq·ui·poise \ˈekwəˌpȯiz, ˈēk-\ *n* [*equi-* + *poise*] **1 :** a state of equilibrium or balance ⟨weights in ~⟩ ⟨an ~ of social classes⟩ ⟨the adventure . . . upset the ~ of his sensitive nature —James Joyce⟩ **2 :** COUNTERBALANCE ⟨the aristocracy served as an ~ to the clergy⟩ **syn** see BALANCE

²equipoise \"\ *vt* **1 :** to serve as an equipoise to ⟨an opposition that nearly *equipoised* the party in power⟩ **2 :** to put or hold in equipoise ⟨an effort to ~ the opposing interests of the two groups⟩

equipoised *adj* **:** lacking lateral dominance **:** neither right-handed nor left-handed ⟨~ children⟩

equi·pol·lence \ˌēkwəˈpälən(t)s, ˌek-\ *also* **equi·pol·len·cy** \-nsē\ *n, pl* **equipollences** *also* **equipollencies** [*equipollence* fr. ME, fr. MF, fr. ML *aequipollentia*, fr. L *aequipollent-, aequipollens* + *-ia* -y; *equipollency* fr. *equipollence* + *-y*] **:** the quality of being equipollent ⟨the ~ of the two propositions⟩

¹equi·pol·lent \ˌ=ˌ=ˈ=lənt\ *adj* [ME, fr. MF, fr. L *aequipollent-, aequipollens*, fr. *aequi-* equi- + *pollent-, pollens*, pres. part. of *pollēre* to be strong, be able — more at POLLEX] **1 :** equal in force, power, or validity ⟨our poets put into a foot two ~ syllables —T.S.Omond⟩ ⟨a sea power ~ with France⟩ **2 :** the same in effect or signification ⟨implying that money could be dispensed with if something ~ were provided⟩; *specif* **:** EQUIVALENT 2 b — **equi·pol·lent·ly** *adv*

²equipollent \"\ *n* -s **:** something that is equipollent (as in signification) ⟨a term having no exact ~ in any European language⟩

equi·pon·der·ant \-¦pändərənt\ *adj* [ML *aequiponderant-, aequiponderans*, pres. part. of *aequiponderare*] **:** of equal weight, force, or power **:** evenly balanced ⟨three ~ branches of government⟩

¹equi·pon·der·ate \ˌ=ˌ=ˈ=ˌ=ˌrāt\ *vb* -ED/-ING/-S [ML *aequiponderatus*, past part. of *aequiponderare*, fr. L *aequi-* equi- + *ponderare* to weigh — more at PONDER] *vi* **:** to be equal in weight or force ⟨the point at which the forces ~⟩ **~** *vt* **:** to equal or make equal in weight **:** COUNTERBALANCE, BALANCE ⟨until it ~*s* the weight of the same quantity of water⟩ ⟨~ pleasure and duty⟩

²equi·pon·der·ate \¦=ˌ=¦=ˌ=rət\ *adj* [ML *aequiponderatus*] *archaic* **:** EQUIPONDERANT

equi·pon·der·a·tion \ˌ=ˌ=ˌ=ˈrāshən\ *n* -s **:** a state of being equiponderated **:** BALANCE

equiponderous *adj* [*equi-* + L *ponder-, pondus* weight + E *-ous* — more at PONDER] *obs* **:** having equal weight

equi·potent *as at* EQUIANGULAR +\ *adj* [*equi-* + *potent*] **1 :** having equal effects or capacities ⟨~ genes⟩ ⟨~ doses in different solvents⟩ **2** *of egg protoplasm* **:** potentially capable of developing into any tissue **:** UNDIFFERENTIATED

equi·potential \"+\ *adj* [*equi-* + *potential*] **1 :** having the same potential ⟨~ points⟩ of uniform potential throughout ⟨an ~ surface⟩ **2 :** EQUIPOTENT 2 — **equi·potentiality** \"+\ *n*

equipped *past of* EQUIP

equip·per \əˈkwipə(r), ēˈ-\ *n* -s **:** one that equips a person or thing

equipping *pres part of* EQUIP

equi·probabilism *as at* EQUIANGULAR +\ *n* [fr. *equiprobable*, after E *probable: probabilism*] **:** a theory that in moral questions where certainty is impossible and the arguments for both courses are equiprobable either course may be followed — compare PROBABILIORISM, PROBABILISM

equi·probability \"+\ *n* **:** the state of being equiprobable ⟨determining the ~ of a set of alternatives⟩

equi·probable \"+\ *adj* [*equi-* + *probable*] **:** having the same degree of logical or mathematical probability **:** equally probable ⟨two alternatives are ~ if there is no sufficient reason why one rather than the other should be realized —Arthur Pap⟩ — **equi·probably** \"+\ *adv*

equips *pres 3d sing of* EQUIP

equipt *past part of* EQUIP

equipt *abbr* equipment

eq·ui·se·ta·ce·ae \ˌekwəsəˈtāsēˌē\ *n pl, cap* [NL, fr. *Equisetum*, type genus + *-aceae*] **:** the sole surviving family of the order Equisetales appearing first in the Carboniferous and represented in the recent flora by the single genus *Equisetum* — **eq·ui·se·ta·ceous** \¦=ˌ=ˌ=ˈtāshəs\ *adj*

eq·ui·se·ta·les \ˌ=ˌ=ˈ=ˈtā(ˌ)lēz\ *n pl, cap* [NL, fr. *Equisetum* + *-ales*] **:** an order of lower tracheophytes (subdivision Sphenopsida) that have the sporangiophores inserted directly on the axis and have existed since the Devonian — see CALAMARIACEAE, EQUISETACEAE; compare ARCHAEOCALAMITES

eq·ui·se·tic \ˌekwəˈsēd·ik, -sed·-\ *adj* [NL *Equisetum* + E *-ic*] : of or relating to the genus *Equisetum*

eq·ui·se·tin·e·ae \ˌekwəsəˈtinēˌē\ *n pl, cap* [NL, fr. *Equisetum* + *-ineae*] : a class of lower tracheophytes coextensive with the subdivision Sphenopsida

eq·ui·se·ti·tes \ˌekwəsəˈtīd·(ˌ)ēz\ *n, cap* [NL, fr. *Equisetum* + L *-ites* -ite] : a form genus of fossil pteridophytes closely related and possibly belonging to *Equisetum*

eq·ui·se·tum \ˌekwəˈsēd·əm\ *n* [NL, fr. L *equisaetum* horsetail (plant), fr. *equi-* (fr. *equus* horse) + *-saetum* (fr. *saeta, seta* bristle) — more at EQUINE, SINEW] **1** *cap* : the type genus of Equisetaceae comprising perennial plants that spread by creeping rhizomes, are homosporous and asexual, and have leaves reduced to more or less conspicuous nodal sheaths on the hollow jointed grooved shoots that may all bear asexual spores provided with elaters in sporangia arranged on conical spikes or in some cases may be differentiated into sterile and fertile shoots **2** *pl* **equisetums** \-d·əmz\ *or* **equise·ta** \-d·ə\ : any plant of the genus *Equisetum*

equi·signal *as at* EQUIANGULAR +\ *adj* [*equi-* + *signal*] : of or relating to a radio system used in navigation in which two distinguishable signals of different amplitude emitted by a radio range station merge and become indistinguishable when the receiver is in the on-course region

equi·sonance \"+\ *n* [*equi-* + *sonance*] *music* : consonance of the unison or its octaves — **equi·sonant** \"+\ *adj*

eq·ui·ta·ble \ˈekwəd·əbəl, -wətə- *sometimes* (ˈ)eˌkwid·ə- *or* -ˌkwitə-\ *adj* [F *équitable*, fr. MF *equitable*, fr. *equité* equity + *-able* — more at EQUITY] **1** : characterized by equity : fair to all concerned ⟨an ~ pay scale⟩ ⟨an ~ price⟩ : without prejudice, favor, or rigor entailing undue hardship ⟨it depended wholly on their individual characters whether their terms of office were ~ or oppressive —John Buchan⟩ **2** : that can be sustained or made effective in a court of equity or upon principles of equity jurisprudence : existing or valid in equity as distinguished from law ⟨~ suits⟩ ⟨~ jurisdiction⟩ **3** : characterized by evenness (as in temper or climate) : EQUABLE **syn** see FAIR

equitable assets *n pl* : assets that are charged with or have become a fund for the payment of debts only by operation of equity; *specif* : assets charged with the payment of debts by a debtor that would be exempted by law (as real estate of a decedent)

equitable assignment *n* : an assignment that is not recognizable at law but will be enforced in equity subject to equities

equitable attachment *n* : an attachment of debts, choses in action, or other property that cannot be attached at law or secured under statute, by injunction, or by other equitable process : an attachment effected in a suit in equity or by a court of equity

equitable conversion *n* : CONVERSION 3d

equitable dower *or* **equitable jointure** *n* : a provision made and accepted by a woman (not being an infant) before her marriage in lieu of dower that will generally be enforced in equity as a bar to dower

equitable election *n* : the choice that must be made by a party whether he will accept a benefit under an instrument with any burdens imposed by it (as the giving away of property of his own) or remain free of the burden or loss and go without the benefits

equitable estate *n* : the estate of one who has a beneficial right in property the legal ownership of which is vested in a trustee or a person treated by equity as a trustee (as in the case of a use, trust, or power) that has under modern statutes some of the characters of a legal estate

equitable fraud *n* : FRAUD 1a(2)

equitable garnishment *n* : a proceeding under statutory provisions by a judgment creditor to compel discovery of property of, due to, or held in trust for the judgment debtor and to secure payment from it

equitable interest *n* : an interest in or with respect to property of the sort recognized by a court of equity (as an interest arising because of fraud)

equitable levy *n* : the putting of a lien on a judgment debtor's assets by means of process under a creditor's bill

equitable lien *n* : a security interest in real or personal property that does not require possession of the property and that can be reached in an equitable proceeding to prevent unjust enrichment

equitable mortgage *n* : a conveyance of or right in property such that it will be treated as a mortgage in equity though not constituting a common-law mortgage (as a deposit of title deeds with a creditor in England or a conveyance nominally absolute but intended merely as a security)

eq·ui·ta·ble·ness *n* -ES : the quality or state of being equitable

equitable right *n* : a right enforceable in a court having equity jurisdiction or equity powers : a right cognizable in a court of equity

equitable title *n* : the title or right by which an equitable estate is held

eq·ui·ta·bly \-əblē, -li\ *adv* : according to the principle or the system of equity : in an equitable manner ⟨the cost of the . . . improvements shall be shared ~ between the participants in proportion to the benefit which each will receive —*U.S. Code*⟩ ⟨property ~ owned⟩

eq·ui·tant \ˈekwəd·ənt, -wətənt *also* -wətᵊnt\ *adj* [L *equitant-*, *equitans*, pres. part. of *equitare* to ride on horseback, fr. *equit-*, *eques* horseman — more at EQUES] *of leaves* : overlapping each other transversely at the base (as in an iris)

eq·ui·ta·tion \ˌekwəˈtāshən\ *n* -S [MF, fr. L *equitation-*, *equitatio*, fr. *equitatus* (past part. of *equitare*) + *-ion-*, *-io* -ion] : the act or art of riding on horseback : school horsemanship

equites *pl of* EQUES

eq·ui·time point \ˈek|wəˌtīm- *also* ˈēk-\ *n* [*equi-* + *time*] : the point in the course of a long airplane flight at which the alternatives of returning to base or proceeding to destination involve equal risks and beyond which the pilot must not turn back — see HOWGOZIT CURVE

eq·ui·ty \ˈekwəd·ē, -wətē, -i\ *n* -ES *often attrib* [ME *equite*, fr. MF *equité*, fr. L *aequitat-*, *aequitas*, lit., equality, fr. *aequus* equal + *-itat-*, *-itas* -ity] **1 a** : a free and reasonable conformity to accepted standards of natural right, law, and justice without prejudice, favoritism, or fraud and without rigor entailing undue hardship : justice according to natural law or right : FAIRNESS ⟨prompted by considerations of ~ to honor claims not legally valid⟩; *specif* : IMPARTIALITY ⟨tax adjustment for the sake of ~⟩ ⟨presenting both sides of the issue with ~⟩ **b** : something that conforms to the principle of equity (as an equitable act) : an instance of equity ⟨the inequities produced by the system being outweighed by the *equities*⟩ **2 a** : a system of law (as in England and the U.S.) originating in the English chancery and comprising a settled and formal body of legal and procedural rules and doctrines that supplement, aid, or override common and statute law and are designed to protect rights and enforce duties fixed by substantive law **b** : trial or remedial justice under or by the rules and doctrines of equity administered in a separate court (as in some states) or in a court of law (as in the federal court system) ⟨a suit or proceeding at law or in ~⟩ **c** : a body of legal doctrines and rules (as the Roman praetorian law) developed to enlarge, supplement, or override a system of law that has become too narrow and rigid in its scope; *specif* : a set of rules or treaties accepted or acknowledged in international relations as imposing certain obligations in the mutual conduct of affairs between politically organized peoples **3 a** : a right, claim, or interest existing or valid in equity ⟨the wife's ~ to a settlement of a portion of the property⟩ **b** : the money value of a property or of an interest in a property in excess of claims or liens (as mortgaged indebtedness) against it **c** : a risk interest or ownership right in property; *specif* : EQUITY SECURITY ⟨~ investment⟩ ⟨~ finance⟩

equity capital *n* : VENTURE CAPITAL

equity of redemption **1** : the right of a mortgagor to redeem his property after the term of the mortgage has expired but before an absolute foreclosure has been authorized **2** : the interest or estate remaining to the mortgagor in property mortgaged by him or the value of such interest

equity security *also* **equity** *n* -ES : a stock issue; *esp* : the common stock of a corporation

equiv·a·lence \əˈkwivələn(t)s, ēˈ-\ *also* **equiv·a·len·cy** \-nsē, -si\ *n, pl* **equivalences** *also* **equivalencies** [MF & ML; MF *equivalence*, fr. ML *aequivalentia*, fr. LL *aequivalent-*, *aequivalens* + L *-ia* -y] **1 a** : the state or property of being equivalent : EXCHANGEABILITY, CORRESPONDENCE ⟨the ~ of paper money and coins⟩ ⟨the ~ between the hero's career and that of the author⟩ : EQUATABILITY ⟨the ~ of mass and energy⟩ : geologic contemporaneity ⟨time *equivalency* of the Sly Gap to a portion of the Devonian of Iowa is suggested by new paleological evidence —*Jour. of Geol.*⟩ **b** : an equivalent or an instance of equivalence ⟨a series of logical *equivalences*⟩ **2** *logic* **a** : sameness in truth value; *specif* : the logical relationship holding between two statements if they are either both true or both false — called also *material equivalence;* compare BICONDITIONAL **b** : mutual deducibility or reciprocal entailment; *specif* : the relationship holding between two statements if to affirm one and to deny the other would result in a contradiction — called also *logical equivalence, strict equivalence* **3** : equality in metrical value of a regular foot and one in which there are substitutions (as of a long syllable for two short syllables in quantitative verse or of two or more light unaccented syllables for the normal unaccented syllable in accentual or syllabic verse)

equivalence principle *n* : PRINCIPLE OF EQUIVALENCE

equivalence zone *n* : the part of the range of possible proportions of interacting antibody and antigen in which neither or but small traces of both remain uncombined in the medium

[1]equiv·a·lent \-nt\ *adj* [ME, fr. MF or LL; MF, fr. LL *aequivalent-*, *aequivalens*, pres. part. of *aequivalēre* to have equal power, be equivalent, fr. L *aequi-* equi- + *valēre* to be strong, be worth — more at WIELD] **1** : equal in force or amount ⟨the misery of such a position is ~ to its happiness⟩ ⟨a new TV film series that has the ~ footage of 13 feature pictures⟩; *specif, of a quantity* : equal in area or volume but not admitting of superposition ⟨a square ~ to a triangle⟩ **2 a** : like in signification or import ⟨~ but differently worded statements of the two writers⟩ : SYNONYMOUS ⟨substituted a term ~ with it but more familiar⟩ **b** *logic* : having equivalence : implying each other **3 a** : equal in value : COMPENSATIVE, CONVERTIBLE ⟨a person who consumes goods or accepts services without producing ~ goods or performing ~ services in return inflicts . . . injury —G.B.Shaw⟩ ⟨a sum ~ to $250 in our currency⟩ ⟨a vitamin pill ~ to four oranges⟩ ⟨the decimal 0.75 is ~ to the fraction ¾⟩ **b** : corresponding or virtually identical esp. in effect or function ⟨a bureau of the French army ~ to the intelligence division of the American general staff⟩ : TANTAMOUNT ⟨where winning the primary is ~ to election⟩; *specif, math* : that can be set in one-to-one correspondence with another or each other ⟨an ~ aggregate⟩ ⟨a pair of ~ quadratic forms⟩ **4** *obs* : equal in might or authority ⟨ancestors who stood ~ with mighty kings —Shak.⟩ **5** *chem* : having the same combining capacity ⟨~ quantities of two elements⟩ **6** : contemporaneous in deposition; *sometimes* : containing the same fauna or flora — used of strata **7** *of a map projection* : EQUAL-AREA **syn** see SAME

[2]equivalent \"\ *n* -S **1** : one that is equivalent (as in value, meaning, or effect) ⟨a price that was the ~ of 10-years rent⟩ ⟨two years of high-school Latin or the ~⟩ ⟨a word with no ~ in English⟩ ⟨the prose ~ of a poem⟩ ⟨the secret Australian ballot . . . and its mechanical ~, the voting machine —H.R. Penniman⟩ : COUNTERPART ⟨the Chinese ~*s* of Boston, New York, and Philadelphia⟩ ⟨the governor of Jerusalem (the modern ~ of Pontius Pilate) —H.J.Laski⟩ **2** *or* **equivalent weight a** : the relative weight of an element that has the same combining capacity as a given weight of another element, the standard now usu. being eight for oxygen but formerly one for hydrogen : the atomic weight divided by the valence — called also *combining weight* **b** : the relative weight of a radical or compound that combines with a given weight of an element, radical, or compound ⟨one ~ of a base reacts with one of an acid to form a normal salt⟩; *esp* : the weight of a compound that reacts with one equivalent of an element **3** : a psychopathological symptom replacing the usual one in a given disorder ⟨a twilight state may be an epileptic ~⟩

equivalent circuit *n* : an electric circuit made up of the basic elements resistance, inductance, and capacitance in a simple arrangement such that its performance would duplicate that of a more complicated circuit or network

equivalent evaporation *n* : the rate in pounds per hour at which water would be vaporized in a given steam boiler if supplied and evaporated at the normal boiling point and normal atmospheric pressure

equivalent focal length *or* **equivalent focus** *n* : the focal length of a single thin lens that would best duplicate the images formed by a given thick lens, compound lens, or lens system

equiv·a·lent·ly *adv* : to an equivalent degree : in an equivalent manner : EQUALLY ⟨another room ~ bare⟩

equivalent weight *n* **1** : [2]EQUIVALENT 2 **2** : ATOMIC WEIGHT — used when atomic weights were more or less conjectural

equi·valve \ˈēkwə, ˈek-+ˌ-\ *adj* [ISV *equi-* + *valve*] *of a bivalve mollusk* : having valves equal in size and form — opposed to *inequivalve;* compare EQUILATERAL

equiv·o·ca·cy \əˈkwivəkəsē, ēˈ-\ *n* -ES [*equivocal* + *-cy*] : EQUIVOCALITY 1

[1]equiv·o·cal \əˈkwivəkəl, ēˈ-\ *adj* [LL *aequivocus* (fr. *aequi-* equi- + *-vocus*, fr. *voc-*, *vox* voice) + E *-al* — more at VOICE] **1 a** : having two or more significations : capable of more than one interpretation : of doubtful meaning : AMBIGUOUS ⟨an ~ word⟩ ⟨an ~ statement⟩ — compare UNIVOCAL **b** : uncertain as an indication or sign : INCONCLUSIVE ⟨the evidence from bacteriologic analysis was ~⟩ **2** *obs* : called by the same name but differing in nature or function : NOMINAL ⟨they being subject to the oversight of the ephori were but ~ kings —James Ussher⟩ **3 a** : of uncertain nature or classification : of a nature that does not admit of definite classification : INDETERMINATE ⟨the ~ objects painted by surrealists⟩ **b** (1) : of uncertain disposition toward a person or thing : UNDECIDED, INSCRUTABLE ⟨the ~ behavior of the officials increased the uneasiness of the riot victims⟩ ⟨something ~ about him contrasting with the other's straightforward manner⟩ (2) : characterized by a mixture of opposite feelings : AMBIVALENT ⟨an ~ attitude toward the proposal⟩ **c** : open to question regarding advantage, validity, genuineness, or moral rectitude : QUESTIONABLE, DUBIOUS ⟨popularity is an ~ crown —A.L.Guérard⟩ ⟨his conscience reproached him with the ~ character of the union into which he had forced his son —Anna Jameson⟩ **syn** see OBSCURE

[2]equivocal \"\ *n* -S : something equivocal; *esp* : an equivocal word or term ⟨regards the term *being* as an analogical ~⟩

equivocal generation *n* : ABIOGENESIS

equiv·o·cal·i·ty \=ˌ==ˈkaləd·ē, -ətē, -i\ *n* -ES **1** : an equivocal character ⟨the ~ of a law that does not specify the agency having primary authority⟩ **2** : EQUIVOQUE ⟨unlikely that any reader would see an ~ in the statement⟩

equiv·o·cal·ly \=ˈ=vək(ə)lē, -li\ *adv* : in an equivocal manner : AMBIGUOUSLY ⟨an ~ worded reply⟩

equiv·o·cal·ness \-kəlnəs\ *n* -ES : the quality or state of being equivocal : AMBIGUITY

equiv·o·cate \-vəˌkāt, *usu* -ād·+V\ *vi* -ED/-ING/-S [ME *equivocaten*, fr. ML *aequivocatus*, past part. of *aequivocare*, fr. LL *aequivocus*] **1** : to use equivocal language esp. with intent to deceive ⟨avoided both persecution and outright lying by *equivocating* with their questioners⟩ **2** : to avoid committing oneself in what one says : speak evasively ⟨he would anger them with frankness before he would ~⟩ : be willfully misleading esp. by the use of double meanings **syn** see LIE

equiv·o·ca·tion \=ˌ==ˈkāshən\ *n* -S [ME *equivocacioun*, fr. ML *aequivocation-*, *aequivocatio*, fr. *aequivocatus* + L *-ion-*, *-io* -ion] **1** : an equivocal state or character : AMBIGUITY; *esp* : duplicity of meaning in a word ⟨~ in the word "fallible"⟩ **2** : an act or instance of equivocating : UNCERTAINTY, EVASIVENESS, PREVARICATION ⟨bold and forthright thinking and action are . . . needed; ~, compromise, pussyfooting . . . are no longer to be tolerated —I.M.Ives⟩ : confusion of terms or ideas similar in meaning ⟨the evils arising from the ~ between faith and intellectual . . . insight —S.T.Coleridge⟩ ⟨a lie may be told by silence, by ~, . . . by a glance of the eye —John Ruskin⟩ **3** : a fallacy in logical reasoning arising from an ambiguous use of a word or phrase — contrasted with *amphibology*

equiv·o·ca·tor \=ˈ==ˌkād·ə(r), -ātə-\ *n* -S : one that equivocates ⟨an ~ who could be quoted on either side of almost any question —John Mason Brown⟩

eq·ui·voc·i·ty \ˌekwəˈväsəd·ē, ˌēk-\ *n* -ES [LL *aequivocus* + E *-ity*] : the character of being equivocal in signification or predication

eq·ui·voque *also* **eq·ui·voke** \ˈ==ˌvōk\ *n* -S [F *équivoque*, fr. *équivoque* equivocal, fr. LL *aequivocus*] **1** : an equivocal word or phrase; *specif* : PUN ⟨ready with quip and ~⟩ **2 a** : duplexity or confusion of meaning : double meaning : the fallacy of equivocation ⟨the ~ in applying indiscriminately to the word *church* the predicates of both the actual and the ideal church⟩ **b** : EQUIVOCATION 2 ⟨an ~ in which the magician offers a choice of right or left without saying whose⟩; *specif* : WORDPLAY

eq·uoid \ˈeˌkwȯid, ˈēˌ-\ *or* **equoi·de·an** \eˈkwȯidēən, əˈk-, ēˈk-\ *adj* [*equoid* fr. NL *Equoidea; equoidean* fr. NL *Equoidea* + E *-an*] **1** : of or relating to the Hippoidea **2** : EQUINE

equoi·dea \eˈkwȯidēə, əˈk-,ēˈk-\ [NL, fr. *Equus* + *-oidea*] *syn of* HIPPOIDEA

eq·uus \ˈekwəs, ˈēk-\ *n, cap* [NL, fr. L, horse — more at EQUINE] : a genus that comprises the horses, asses, zebras, and related recent and extinct animals and that is the type and only surviving genus of the family Equidae — see EQUIDAE illustration

er \ˈə(ə), ˈə̄(ə̄), ˈă(ă), ˈȧ(ȧ); *the* ˈər, *usu prolonged, used by many R speakers when they encounter "er" as they read aloud is not an accurate reproduction of the sound that the spelling, introduced by – R speakers, is intended to convey*\ *interj* — used to express hesitation ⟨said shyly, "I — ~ — don't know"⟩

[1]-er \ə(r), *after some vowels* (ə)r *in R speech, after* ŋ gə(r) (*but after* ŋ [2]-ER *is* ə(r))\ *adj suffix or adv suffix* [ME *-er*, *-ere*, *-re*, fr. OE *-ra* (in adjectives), *-or* (in adverbs); akin to comparative suffixes OHG *-iro*, *-ōro* (in adjectives), *-ōr* (in adverbs), ON *-ri*, *-ari* (in adjectives), *-r*, *-ar* (in adverbs), Goth *-iza*, *-oza* (in adjectives), *-is*, *-os* (in adverbs), L *-ior* (in adjectives), Gk *-iōn* (in adjectives), Skt *-īyas* (in adjectives)] — used to form the comparative degree of adjectives and adverbs of one syllable ⟨hott*er*⟩ ⟨dri*er*⟩ ⟨lat*er*⟩ ⟨soon*er*⟩ ⟨cold*er*⟩ and of certain adjectives and adverbs of two syllables ⟨abl*er*⟩ ⟨complet*er*⟩ ⟨gentli*er*⟩ ⟨happi*er*⟩ ⟨yellow*er*⟩ and sometimes of longer ones; regularly accompanied by coalescence with final *e* of the base word, change of final postconsonantal *y* of the base word to *i*, or doubling of the final consonant of the base word immediately after a short stressed vowel; compare [2]MORE

[2]-er \ə(r) — *compare* [1]-ER\ *also* **-ier** \ēə(r), yə(r)\ *or* **-yer** \yə(r)\ *n suffix* -S [ME *-er*, *-ere*, fr. OE *-ere;* akin to D & G *-er*, OHG *-āri*, ON *-ari*, Goth *-areis;* all fr. a prehistoric Gmc suffix borrowed fr. L *-arius* [1]-ary; in sense 1, partly fr. ME *-er*, *-ier*, *-ere*, *-iere*, fr. AF *-er*, *-ere* & OF *-ier*, *-iere*, fr. L *-arius*, *-aria*, *-arium* [1]-ary; in sense 2, partly fr. ME *-er*, *-ere*, fr. MF *-ere*, fr. L *-ator* (suffix denoting an agent) — more at -ARY, -OR] **1 a** : person occupationally connected with ⟨hatt*er*⟩ ⟨jail*er*⟩ ⟨furri*er*⟩ ⟨hosi*er*⟩ ⟨law*yer*⟩ **b** : person or thing belonging to, related to, or associated with ⟨head*er*⟩ ⟨old-tim*er*⟩ ⟨high school*er*⟩ **c** : native of : resident of : one coming from ⟨cottag*er*⟩ ⟨London*er*⟩ ⟨Maryland*er*⟩ ⟨New York*er*⟩ **d** : one that has ⟨three-deck*er*⟩ ⟨the baby is a ten-pound*er*⟩ **e** : one that produces or yields ⟨pork*er*⟩ ⟨veal*er*⟩ ⟨wool*er*⟩ **2 a** : one that does or performs (a specified action) ⟨mak*er*⟩ ⟨play*er*⟩ ⟨report*er*⟩ ⟨transform*er*⟩ ⟨range find*er*⟩ — sometimes added to both elements of a compound ⟨build*er*-upp*er*⟩ ⟨try*er*-out*er*⟩ **b** : one that is a suitable object of (a specified action) ⟨broil*er*⟩ ⟨fry*er*⟩ **3** : one that is ⟨foreign*er*⟩ ⟨gon*er*⟩ ⟨western*er*⟩ ⟨down-and-out*er*⟩ — *-yer* in a small number of words after *w*, *-ier* in a small number of words after other letters, otherwise *-er; -er* and *-ier* regularly accompanied by doubling of the final consonant of the base word immediately after a short stressed vowel, *-ier* regularly accompanied by omission of final *e* of the base word, *-er* regularly accompanied by coalescence with final *e* of the base word and sometimes accompanied by change of final postconsonantal *y* of the base word to *i* ⟨fli*er*⟩ ⟨fly*er*⟩

ER *abbr* **1** earned run **2** educational ratio **3** en route

Er *symbol* erbium

era \ˈirə, ˈerə, ˈērə\ *n* -S [LL *aera*, fr. L, counters, pl. of *aer-*, *aes* copper, brass, money — more at ORE] **1** : a system of chronological notation computed from a given date as basis ⟨the Roman ~ is computed from the date when Rome was supposedly founded⟩ ⟨from the beginnings of history to the 5th century of our ~⟩ **2 a** : a fixed point in time from which a series of years is reckoned : the basic date of a chronological era ⟨a hundred years before the Christian ~⟩ **b** : a memorable or important date or event; *esp* : one that begins a new period in the history of a person or thing ⟨June 1585 marked an ~ in the foreign policy of Elizabeth —J.A.Symonds⟩ **3** : a period in the history of a person or thing ⟨the seven years . . . form one of the greatest ~*s* in the annals of British statesmanship —Ernest Barker⟩: as **a** : a period set off or typified by some prominent figure or characteristic feature ⟨a style popular in the Victorian ~⟩ ⟨dates back to the ~ of the horse and buggy⟩ ⟨calls the twenties an ~ of extravagance⟩ **b** : a period of existence or prevalence of something (as a process, quality, or group) ⟨another ~ of rapid expansion in industry⟩ ⟨an ~ of prosperity⟩ ⟨the relatively brief cowboy ~⟩ : DAY **c** : a stage in the development of a person or thing (as a nation, institution, or art) ⟨during the first ~ of the nation's existence⟩ ⟨a new ~ in the development of the textbook⟩; *specif* : one of the five major divisions of geologic time — see GEOLOGIC TIME table **syn** see PERIOD

ERA *abbr* earned run average

eradiate \(ˈ)ē+\ *vt* -ED/-ING/-S [*e-* + *radiate*] : RADIATE 1 — **eradiation** \(ˌ)ē+\ *n* -S

erad·i·ca·ble \əˈradəkəbəl, ēˈr,- -dēk-\ *adj* [*eradicate* + *-able*] : that can be eradicated ⟨whether the habit is ~ or ineradicable⟩ — **erad·i·ca·bly** \-blē, -li\ *adv*

[1]erad·i·cant \-kənt\ *adj* [*eradicate* + *-ant*] : acting or tending to act as a pesticidal eradicant ⟨an ~ spray⟩

[2]eradicant \"\ *n* -S : an agent of eradication; *esp* : a pesticidal spray used to destroy a parasitic organism at its source before it reaches the suscept ⟨an ~ applied to scab-infested apple leaves on the ground⟩ — compare PROTECTANT

erad·i·cate \-dəˌkāt, *usu* -ād·+V\ *vt* -ED/-ING/-S [L *eradicatus*, past part. of *eradicare*, fr. *e-* + *radic-*, *radix* root — more at ROOT] **1** : to pull up (as a weed) by the roots : UPROOT ⟨perennial creeping rootstocks that are difficult to ~⟩ **2** : to do away with (something not wanted) : root out : destroy completely ⟨aerial sprays that ~ weeds, diseases, and insect pests from the wheat fields⟩ ⟨a campaign that virtually *eradicated* illiteracy in the country⟩ **syn** see EXTERMINATE

eradicated *adj, heraldry* : depicted with roots exposed as though pulled up ⟨an oak tree ~ vert⟩

erad·i·ca·tion \=ˌ==ˈkāshən\ *n* -S [LL *eradication-*, *eradicatio*, fr. L *eradicatus* + *-ion-*, *-io* -ion] : the act or process of eradicating ⟨the ~ of weeds⟩ ⟨the ~ of opposition groups⟩ ⟨the ~ of white pine blister rust depends on destruction of the intermediate host⟩

erad·i·ca·tive \=ˈ==ˌkā|d·|iv, -ˌkə|, |t|, |ēv *also* |əv\ *adj* : tending or serving to eradicate ⟨~ and preventive measures against trachoma⟩

erad·i·ca·tor \-ˌkād·ə(r), -ātə-\ *n* -S [ML, fr. L *eradicatus* + *-or*] : one that eradicates; *specif* : a chemical preparation used for removing marks or stains (as of ink or rust)

er·a·gros·tis \ˌerəˈgrästəs\ *n, cap* [NL, fr. Gk *eros* love + *agrōstis*, a kind of grass] : a genus of grasses resembling the bluegrasses but having flattened spikelets and deciduous lemmas

eran·the·mum \əˈran(t)thəməm\ *n* [NL, fr. Gk *ēranthemon*, a plant resembling camomile, fr. *ēr*, *ear* spring + *anthemon* flower, fr. *anthos* — more at ANTHOLOGY, VERNAL] **1** *cap* : a small genus of tropical Asiatic shrubs or perennial herbs (family Acanthaceae) having flowers with a 5-parted limb and two stamens **2** -S : any plant of the genus *Eranthemum*

eran·this \-thəs\ *n, cap* [NL, fr. Gk *ēr*, *ear* + NL *-anthis* (fr. Gk *anthos*)] : a genus of Eurasian herbs (family Ranunculaceae) with tuberous rootstocks, palmately dissected mostly basal leaves, and solitary yellow flowers — see WINTER ACONITE

eras *pl of* ERA

eras·abil·i·ty \ə,rāsə'bilәd·ē, ē,r-, *chiefly Brit* -āzə-\ *n* -ES **:** the property or degree of being erasable ⟨~ is important in good typing paper⟩ ⟨compared the ~ of different tapes⟩

eras·able \ə'==bəl\ *adj* **:** capable of being erased esp. without traces or damage that would impair reuse ⟨~ tracing paper⟩ ⟨a signal too loud to be ~ in a single pass through the erase head⟩

erase \ə'rās, ē'-, *chiefly Brit* -āz\ *vb* -ED/-ING/-S [L *erasus*, past part. of *eradere*, fr. *e-* + *radere* to scratch, scrape — more at RAT] *vt* **1 a** (1) **:** to rub or scrape out (as letters or figures written, engraved, or painted) ⟨*erased* the chalk marks⟩ ⟨a typing error neatly *erased*⟩ (2) **:** to remove (a magnetic pattern) from the surface of a recording tape or wire so as to make the surface available for a new magnetic pattern **:** DEMAGNETIZE ⟨the recording can be *erased* and the tape used again⟩ **b :** to remove marks, symbols, or other communicating devices from ⟨the school children *erased* the blackboard⟩ ⟨~ a tape for a new recording⟩ **2 a :** to remove from existence or memory as if by erasing **:** wipe out **:** OBLITERATE ⟨a plan to ~ the boundary between the countries⟩ ⟨time had *erased* the bitter memories⟩; *specif* **:** to get rid of (a person) by murder ⟨the efforts of a group of murderers to ~ a blinded man —Anthony Boucher⟩ **b :** to nullify the effect or force of **:** remove from the necessity of consideration **:** make quite insignificant or inconsequential **:** ANNUL ⟨the . . . statement had *erased* in one day months of patient work —W.J. Jordan⟩ **c :** OFFSET, NEUTRALIZE, BALANCE ⟨profit taking *erased* most of these gains —*Wall Street Jour.*⟩ **~** *vi* **1 :** to yield to being erased ⟨marks that ~ easily⟩ ⟨tape that ~*s* when recorded over⟩ **2 :** to remove marks or signals from something ⟨an assistant who ~*s* while the lecturer is away from the blackboard⟩ ⟨a tape recorder that ~*s* at a higher speed⟩

syn EXPUNGE, BLOT (*out*), EFFACE, OBLITERATE, DELETE, CANCEL: ERASE stresses the fact of removal of symbols or impressions without important damage to the surface involved and may imply a resulting blank usable for a new symbol or impression ⟨*erase* a misspelled word⟩ ⟨a child *erasing* numbers from a slate⟩ ⟨so violently have they hated the soul of the modern man that they have wished to *erase* from the record of history every thought and deed since the Renaissance —J.W.Krutch⟩ EXPUNGE, esp. in relation to tangible and simple action, has been influenced by *sponge* and stresses a complete washing out or off of whatever is affected or indicates its complete removal from consideration ⟨*expunge* a false report⟩ ⟨irrelevant testimony *expunged* from a court proceeding⟩ ⟨a woman's history, you know: certain chapters *expunged* —George Meredith⟩ BLOT (*out*) suggests the complete covering or obscuring of an impression by smearing or blurring over ⟨lines of the manuscript *blotted out* by spilled ink⟩ ⟨the same process by which Communist literature first blackened, and then *blotted out* altogether, Trotsky's exploits in the civil war —*Times Lit. Supp.*⟩ EFFACE suggests complete removal of an impression, sometimes through slow attrition and wear ⟨inscriptions on a pyramid *effaced* by time⟩ ⟨a cliché, a worn counter of a word, with its original meaning all *effaced*, and even its secondary meaning now only just visible —Havelock Ellis⟩ OBLITERATE is perhaps the most forceful of this group in connoting utter, complete, and inexorable removal or elimination of all traces of impressions ⟨a flash of lightning *obliterated* the first letter of 'Caesar' on a statue of Augustus —John Buchan⟩ ⟨the Navajo was careful to *obliterate* every trace of their temporary occupation —Willa Cather⟩ With no suggestion of either the destruction or the preservation of the marks or symbols involved, DELETE now stresses simple exclusion ⟨*delete* a word unnecessarily repeated⟩ ⟨whenever you feel an impulse to perpetrate a piece of exceptionally fine writing, obey it — wholeheartedly — and *delete* it before sending your manuscript to press —A.T.Quiller-Couch⟩ CANCEL, formerly indicating to cross out, now stresses invalidation, nullification, or reduction to insignificance ⟨the laboratory door does not lock behind him and bar his return any more than it swung shut to imprison Darwin and forever *cancel* his status as a naturalist —*Amer. Naturalist*⟩ Many of these words show semantic developments to ideas of destroying, killing, annihilating ⟨the killers may in time succeed in *erasing* me —V.A. Kravchenko⟩ ⟨the few survivors of the brilliant generation of young Englishmen *expunged* by the first World War —Jack Winocour⟩ ⟨they [enemy soldiers] were just *blotted out* —Nevil Shute⟩ and to ideas of balancing, offsetting, equaling, nullifying with equal opposing force ⟨the . . . mixture of races *canceling* each other's beliefs —T.S.Eliot⟩ ⟨a hideous phrase which no amount of palliation can ever quite *obliterate* —P.E.More⟩ These semantic extensions may retain nuances of meaning implied in older uses.

erased *adj, heraldry* **:** depicted with jagged extremities as if torn off — used esp. of the head or leg of an animal ⟨a lion's head ~ proper⟩; compare COUPED

erase head *or* **erasing head** *n* **:** a device mounted on a magnetic recorder that obliterates previous recordings on the magnetic medium by demagnetization just before a new recording is made

erase·ment \-smənt, *chiefly Brit* -zm-\ *n* -s **:** ERASURE

eras·er \-sə(r), *chiefly Brit* -zə-\ *n* -s **:** one that erases: as **a :** an instrument with a handle and sharp blade used to scrape out writing quickly — called also *steel eraser* **b :** a piece of a rubber composition usu. containing vulcanized oil and pumice for erasing pencil, ink, or other marks ⟨a wood-encased ~ of pencil shape⟩ ⟨a ferrule secures the ~ to the pencil⟩ ⟨a typewriter ~ with brush⟩ **c :** a block of absorbent material (as felt strips or sponge rubber) usu. fastened to a hard back and used for removing chalk marks from a slate or blackboard **d :** a wooden instrument with a flat smooth point used to obliterate braille dots by pressure **e :** a chemical solution for removing ink marks **:** ERADICATOR

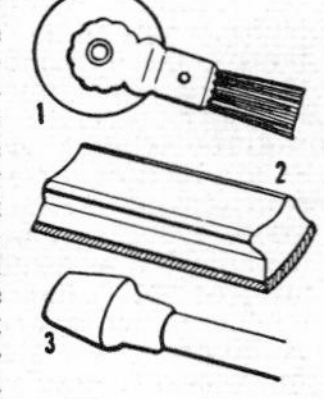

erasers: *1* typewriter, *2* blackboard, *3* pencil

eraser shield *or* **erasing shield** *or* **erasure shield** *n* **:** a thin plate (as of metal or celluloid) with holes usu. of several sizes used to confine an erasure to a limited area

erases *pres 3d sing of* ERASE

erasing *pres part of* ERASE

era·sion \-āzhən, -āsh-\ *n* -s **1 :** ERASURE 1 ⟨the signatures have been erased . . . not without leaving signs of ~ —Agatha Christie⟩ **2 :** surgical removal of diseased tissue by scraping or curetting

¹eras·mi·an \ə'razmēən, -ē'r-\ *adj, usu cap* [Desiderius *Erasmus* (Geert Geerts) †1536 Dutch scholar + E *-ian*] **:** of, relating to, or in the manner of Desiderius Erasmus ⟨the *Erasmian* movement⟩ ⟨*Erasmian* humor⟩ — **eras·mi·an·ism** \-,nizəm\ *n* -s

²erasmian \"\ *n* -s *usu cap* **:** a follower of Erasmus

¹eras·tian \ə'rastēən, ē'r-, -schən\ *adj, usu cap* [Thomas *Erastus* (Lieber or Liebler) †1583 German-Swiss physician and Zwinglian theologian + E *-ian*] **1 :** of or relating to the physician and theologian Erastus or his doctrines **2 :** of, characterized by, or advocating Erastianism ⟨an ~ doctrine of the relation of church and state⟩ ⟨~ arguments⟩

²erastian \"\ *n* -s *usu cap* **:** a supporter of Erastian doctrines; *esp* **:** an upholder of state supremacy in ecclesiastical affairs ⟨the 17th century English *Erastians*⟩

eras·tian·ism \-,nizəm\ *n* -s *usu cap* **:** the doctrine that the state is supreme over the church in ecclesiastical affairs — compare BYZANTINISM, CAESAROPAPISM

era·sure \ə'rāshə(r), ē'- *sometimes* -āzh-\ *n* -s [*erase* + *-ure*] **1 :** an act or instance of erasing **:** a rubbing or scratching out **:** OBLITERATION ⟨prevents accidental ~ of the tape⟩ ⟨errors and ~*s* in the typescript⟩ ⟨the bomb spelled ~ of the world —D.D.Eisenhower⟩ **2 :** the place where something has been erased ⟨a feathering of the ink at the ~⟩

er·bi·um \'ərbēəm\ *n* -s [NL, fr. *Ytterby*, Sweden, where gadolinite is found + NL *-ium*] **:** a trivalent metallic element of the rare-earth group that occurs with yttrium (as in gadolinite and fergusonite) and forms a pink oxide and reddish salts — symbol *Er;* see ELEMENT table

er·cles vein \'ər,klēz-\ *n, usu cap E* [*Ercles*, alter. of *Hercules*, ancient Greco-Roman hero, fr. L, fr. Gk *Hēraklēs*] **:** a rousing somewhat bombastic manner of public speaking or writing ⟨could not write in the *Ercles vein* if he would, and he had chosen to give his inaugural address an agreeably quiet tone —*Nation*⟩

erd \'erd\ *dial var of* EARTH

erd shrew *n* **:** the common European shrew (*Sorex vulgaris*)

erdvark *var of* AARDVARK

¹ere \'ar, 'er\ *adv* [ME *er, ar*, fr. OE *ǣr*, adv. (historically compar. but used as positive and compar.), prep. & conj.; akin to OHG *ēr* earlier, ON *ār* early, Goth *air* early, *airis* earlier, Gk *ēri* early, Av *ayarə* day; basic meaning: day, morning] **1** *chiefly Scot* **:** EARLY **2** *chiefly Scot* **:** SOON

²ere \(')e(ə)r, (')a(ə)|, |ə\ *prep* [ME *er, ar*, fr. OE *ǣr*] **:** ²BEFORE 1a ⟨virtues . . . contrived ~ the beginning of the world —Norman Douglas⟩

³ere \"\ *conj* [ME *er, ar*, fr. OE *ǣr*] **:** ³BEFORE ⟨supersedes it ~ the twentieth century ends —C.H.Moehlman⟩ ⟨I will be thrown into Etna . . . ~ I will leave her —Shak.⟩

⁴ere *var of* ²EAR

⁵ere \'a(ə)|(ə)r, 'e|, |ə\ *dial var of* THERE

ereb *or* **erev** \'erəv, 'e,rev\ *n* -s [Heb *'erebh*] **:** EVE: **a :** the part of the day or the day immediately preceding the Jewish Sabbath or a Jewish holiday **b :** an indefinite period preceding the Sabbath or a Jewish holiday ⟨as busy as a housewife on ~ Yom Kippur⟩

er·ech·ti·tes \,erək'tīd·(,)ēz, ,e,rek-\ *n* [NL, fr. Gk *erechthitis* groundsel, fr. *erechthein* to rend, break] **1** *cap* **:** a genus of coarse herbs (family Compositae) commonly with whitish discoid flower heads and a silky pappus that facilitates their wide distribution as weeds **2** *pl* **erechtites :** any plant of the genus *Erechtites*

¹erect \ə'rekt, ē'-\ *adj* [ME, fr. L *erectus*, past part. of *erigere* to erect, fr. *e-* + *-rigere* (fr. *regere* to lead straight, guide, direct) — more at RIGHT] **1 a :** vertical in position **:** UPRIGHT ⟨he is in an ~ position and flying parallel to the earth's surface —H.G.Armstrong⟩ **:** STANDING ⟨buried their dead ~⟩ ⟨a column still ~ amid the ruins⟩ ⟨his armorial crest bore a sword ~ proper⟩; *specif* **:** not spreading or decumbent ⟨an ~ stem⟩ — contrasted with *prone* **b :** standing up or out from the body ⟨hair ~ from fright⟩; *specif* **:** being in a state of erection **c** *of an image* **:** normal rather than inverted in position **:** right side up ⟨in this device the image is observed ~⟩ **d :** characterized by firm or rigid straightness in bodily posture **:** not leaning or bent **:** not slouching or stooped ⟨the ~ bearing of one . . . accustomed to official uniform —A. Conan Doyle⟩ **2** *archaic* **:** directed upward **:** UPLIFTED ⟨with face ~ against the sun —George Chapman⟩ **3** *obs* **:** characterized by alertness **:** WATCHFUL ⟨bid her well be . . . ~ lest by some fair-appearing good surprised she dictate false —John Milton⟩ **4 :** characterized by aspiration or rectitude **:** NOBLE, UPRIGHT ⟨an ~ mind⟩ ⟨an ~ life⟩ — **erect·ly** *adv*

²erect \"\ *vb* -ED/-ING/-S [ME *erecten*, fr. L *erectus*, past part.] *vt* **1 a** (1) **:** to put up (as a building or machine) by the fitting together of materials or parts **:** cause to stand ready for use **:** BUILD ⟨the settlers ~*ed* walls of field stones⟩ ⟨when the state ~*s* a new bridge⟩ ⟨a building ~*ed* in 1920⟩; *specif* **:** to hoist and bolt in place fabricated parts of (a ship's structure) before riveting or welding (2) **:** to fix in an upright position (as a statue, signpost, or plaque) **:** put up ⟨~ a flagpole⟩ ⟨~*ed* a marker over the grave⟩ (3) **:** to cause to stand up or out **:** RAISE ⟨~*ed* himself to full height⟩ ⟨the porcupine ~*s* its quills⟩ ⟨~ the hood of the camera⟩ ⟨an armorial crest bearing a ship at anchor, her oars ~*ed*⟩ **b** *archaic* **:** to direct upward **:** lift up ⟨to stand with their mouths open and ~*ed* —Jonathan Swift⟩ **c :** to change (an image) from an inverted to a normal position ⟨a microscope attachment that ~*s* the image seen⟩ **2 :** to elevate in status **:** raise to a higher office or dignity **:** EXALT, MAGNIFY ⟨~*ed* the worship of nationality into a religion usurping the ancient religion —Hilaire Belloc⟩ ⟨~ methods into dogmas⟩ ⟨has been ~*ed* into a great poet of the 13th century —George Saintsbury⟩; *specif* **:** to hold up as an ideal ⟨the doctrine which ~*s* pleasure as the end of human action —G.D.H. Cole⟩ **3 a :** to bring into existence as if by raising or building ⟨~ social barriers along religious lines⟩ **:** ESTABLISH **:** set up ⟨~ the attempt to ~ political authority upon the basis of self-interest —John Dewey⟩ **:** build up **:** DEVELOP ⟨~ a complex philosophical system⟩ ⟨~ a civilization⟩ **b :** to give legal existence to (as a unit of civil or church government) by a formal act of authority **:** CONSTITUTE, CREATE ⟨Indiana and Illinois were ~*ed* into territories during Jefferson's first term —H.L.Mencken⟩ ⟨the Holy See alone ~*s* dioceses, cathedral churches, abbeys of monks or nuns, archconfraternities —*Catholic Dict.*⟩ **c :** to set up (a taxonomic category) ⟨has ~*ed* a new genus on a recently discovered species⟩ **4** *obs* **:** to stir up (as the mind or spirits) **:** ALERT, ENCOURAGE, EMBOLDEN ⟨better counsels might ~ our minds and teach us to cast off this yoke —John Milton⟩ **5 a :** to draw or construct (a perpendicular or figure) upon a given base **b :** to calculate (a horoscope) by astrology **~** *vi* **:** to rise to an erect position **:** stand up or out ⟨will make thy hair like . . . bristles to ~ —Robert Burns⟩ **syn** see BUILD

erec·tile \-t°l, -,tīl, -(,)til\ *adj* [F *érectile*, fr. L *erectus* + F *-ile*] **:** capable of being raised to an erect position or state ⟨~ feathers⟩; *esp* **:** CAVERNOUS 3

erec·til·i·ty \ə,rek'tilәd·ē, (,)ē,r-\ *n* -ES **1 :** the state of being erectile **2 :** capacity for erection

erec·tion \ə'rekshən, ē'r-\ *n* -s [ME *erecciound*, fr. L *erection-, erectio*, fr. *erectus* + *-ion-, -io* -ion] **1 :** the act or process of erecting **:** CONSTRUCTION ⟨the ~ of a new building⟩ **:** ESTABLISHMENT ⟨the ~ of tariffs⟩ ⟨the ~ of an international economic union⟩ **2 a :** the state of a previously flaccid bodily part containing cavernous tissue when that tissue becomes dilated with blood marked by firm turgid form and erect position **b :** an occurrence of such a state in the penis or clitoris **3 :** something erected; *esp* **:** EDIFICE ⟨an imposing ~ of red brick rising above the other houses⟩

erection tower *n* **:** a temporary framework like a tower built to support hoisting equipment for the erection of a building or other structure

erect·ness \-k(t)nəs\ *n* -ES **:** the quality or state of being erect

erec·tor \-ktə(r)\ *n* -s [LL, fr. L *erectus* + *-or*] **:** one that erects or supervises erection: as **a :** a muscle that raises or keeps a part erect — see ERECTOR PILI **b** (1) **:** a workman who works on a structure (as a steel building or bridge) by assembling fabricated parts; *specif* **:** SHIPFITTER (2) **:** a workman who assembles machines, tests the equipment in operation, and makes adjustments (3) **:** a workman who assembles electrical equipment **c :** a machine for erecting (as a derrick)

erector pi·li \-'pī,lī -'pi,lē\ *n* -s [NL, lit., hair-raiser] **:** one of the small fan-shaped smooth muscles associated with the base of each hair that contract when the body surface is chilled and erect the hairs, compress an oil gland above each muscle, and produce the appearance of gooseflesh

erects *pres 3d sing of* ERECT

e region *n, usu cap E* **:** the part of the ionosphere occurring between 40 and 90 miles above the surface of the earth and containing the daytime E layer and the sporadic E layer

erelong \(')=¦=\ *adv* **:** before long **:** SOON ⟨a man . . . following the stag ~ slew him —Edmund Spenser⟩

erem- *or* **eremo-** *comb form* [NL, fr. Gk *erēm-, erēmo-*, fr. *erēmos* lonely, solitary and *erēmia* desert, fr. *erēmos* + *-ia* -y — more at RETINA] **:** solitary ⟨*Eremurus*⟩ **:** desert ⟨*eremology*⟩ — chiefly in terms in biology

er·e·ma·cau·sis \,erəmə'kȯsəs\ *n* -ES [NL, fr. Gk *ērema* gently, softly, slowly + *kausis* burning, fr. *kaiein* to burn — more at RIM, CAUSTIC] **:** gradual oxidation of organic matter from exposure to air and moisture

eremeyevite *var of* JEREMEJEVITE

ere·mi·an \ə'rēmēən\ *adj, usu cap* [Gk *erēmia* solitude, desert + E *-an*] **:** of, relating to, or constituting a division of the Palaearctic region including northern Africa, northern Arabia, and Asiatic desert regions

ere·mic \-ēmik, -em-\ *adj* [*erem-* + *-ic*] **:** of or relating to deserts or sandy regions

er·e·mite \'erə,mīt, *usu* -īd·+V\ *n* -s [ME *eremite, ermite, heremite, hermite* — more at HERMIT] **:** HERMIT; *esp* **:** a Christian living for religious reasons in solitary retirement

er·e·mit·ic \¦==¦mid·|ik, -it|, |ēk\ *or* **er·e·mit·i·cal** \|əkəl, |ēk-\ *adj* **1 :** of, relating to, or befitting a hermit ⟨the ~ legend⟩ ⟨~ austerities⟩ **2 :** characterized by ascetic solitude in mode of life **:** SOLITARY ⟨~ or corporate monastic life⟩ ⟨the ~ element in the life of the religious colony⟩ — contrasted with *cenobitic*

er·e·mit·ish \'==,mīd·ish\ *adj* **:** resembling an eremite **:** suitable to an eremite

er·e·mit·ism \-īd,izəm\ *n* -s **:** the practice of living in solitary retirement ⟨a long tradition of monasticism and ~⟩ ⟨the poet's voluntary ~⟩

er·e·mol·o·gy \,erə'mäləjē\ *n* -ES [*erem-* + *-logy*] **:** a science concerned with the desert and its phenomena

er·e·moph·i·la \-äfələ\ *n* [NL, fr. *erem-* + *-phila* (fem. of *-philus*)] **1** *cap* **:** a genus of shrubs or trees (family Myoporaceae) having large solitary or paired often spotted flowers one species of which (*E. latrobei*) is important in Australia as a stock-poisoning plant **2** -s **:** any plant of the genus *Eremophila*

er·e·mo·phyte \'erəmō,fīt, ə'rēmə,f-\ *n* -s [*erem-* + *-phyte*] **:** DESERT PLANT

er·e·mop·ter·is \,erə'mäptərəs\ *n, cap* [NL, fr. *erem-* + *-pteris*] **:** a form genus of fossil ferns or pteridosperms represented by leaves of Carboniferous age

er·e·mu·rus \-'myůrəs\ *n* [NL, fr. *erem-* + *-urus*] **1** *cap* **:** a small genus of Asiatic herbs (family Liliaceae) with leaves in a basal rosette and flowers in racemes at the tops of long naked stalks **2** *pl* **eremu·ri** \-,rī\ **:** any plant of the genus *Eremurus* — called also *desert candle, foxtail lily*

erep·sin \ə'repsən\ *n* -s [ISV *er-* (prob. fr. L *eripere* to take away) + *pepsin;* orig. formed in G] **:** a proteolytic enzyme obtained esp. from the intestinal juice and now known to be a mixture of peptidases

ereth·ic \ə'rethik, e'r-\ *adj* [*erethism* + *-ic*] **:** of, relating to, or tending to produce erethism **:** RESTLESS ⟨the most ~ of all its fantasies, wealth —Rebecca West⟩

er·e·thism \'erə,thizəm\ *n* -s [F *éréthisme*, fr. Gk *erethismos* irritation, fr. *erethein, erethizein* to provoke, excite, irritate; akin to Gk *ornynai* to urge on, incite, call forth — more at RISE] **:** abnormal irritability or responsiveness to stimulation whether generalized or restricted to a particular body part ⟨cardiac ~⟩ ⟨expressed his view . . . with such an effluence of ~ —*Psychiatry*⟩ — **er·e·this·mic** \¦==¦thizmik\ *adj*

er·e·thi·zon \,erə'thīz°n, -,zän\ *n, cap* [NL, fr. Gk *erethizōn*, pres. part. of *erethizein*] **:** the type genus of Erethizontidae comprising the No. American porcupine

er·e·thi·zon·ti·dae \,erəthə'zäntə,dē\ *n pl, cap* [NL, fr. *Erethizont-, Erethizon*, type genus + *-idae*] **:** a family of chiefly arboreal hystricomorph rodents comprising the typical New World porcupines with the tail more or less prehensile and the soles of the feet specialized for climbing

er·et·moch·e·lys \,e,ret'mäkələs\ *n, cap* [NL, fr. Gk *eretmon* oar + *chelys* turtle — more at ROW (propel a boat)] **:** a genus of aquatic turtles including only the hawksbill

erev *var of* EREB

erevan *usu cap, var of* YEREVAN

erewhile *also* **erewhiles** \(')=¦=\ *adv* [ME *erwhile*, fr. *er* ere (prep.) + *while*] *archaic* **:** some time ago **:** a little while before **:** HERETOFORE ⟨I am as fair now as I was ~ —Shak.⟩

er·e·whon·i·an \,erə¦(h)wänēən, -wōn-\ *adj, usu cap* [*Erewhon* (anagram of *nowhere*), fictitious land described in the utopian novel *Erewhon* (1872) by Samuel Butler †1902 British writer + E *-ian*] **:** of or suggestive of the utopia described in the book *Erewhon* whose people dealt with disease as a crime and destroyed machinery lest machines destroy them ⟨an *Erewhonian* fear of automation⟩

erf \'e(ə)rf\ *n, pl* **er·ven** \'ervən\ [Afrik, fr. MD *erf, erve* plot of ground, inheritance; akin to OHG *erbi* inheritance — more at ORPHAN] *Africa* **:** a plot of land usu. about half an acre in size; *specif* **:** BUILDING LOT

er·furt \'erfərt, -,fůrt\ *adj, usu cap* [fr. *Erfurt*, Germany] **:** of or from the city of Erfurt, Germany **:** of the kind or style prevalent in Erfurt

¹erg \'ərg, 'əg, 'əig *sometimes* 'e(ə)rg\ *n* -s [Gk *ergon* work — more at WORK] **:** an absolute cgs unit of work representing the work done by a force of one dyne acting through a displacement of one centimeter in the direction of the force — compare JOULE

²erg \'e(ə)rg\ *n, pl* **ergs** \'e(ə)rgz\ [F, of Hamitic origin, akin to Amharic *'arăgă* rise, ascend] **:** a desert region of shifting sand ⟨the dunes of the Saharan ~*s*⟩

erg- *or* **ergo-** *comb form* [Gk, fr. *ergon*] **:** work ⟨*ergo*phobia⟩ ⟨*erg*odic⟩

er·ga·sia \,ər'gāzh(ē)ə\ *n* -s [NL, fr. Gk work, business, fr. *ergazesthai* to work, labor, fr. *ergon* work] **:** organismic activity **:** BEHAVIOR ⟨held mental illness to involve an ~ of the total organism rather than a physiological function of the brain alone⟩

er·gas·tic \¦ər¦gastik\ *adj* [Gk *ergastikos* able to work, industrious, fr. (assumed) *ergastos* (verbal of *ergazein*) + *-ikos* -ic] **:** constituting the nonliving by-products of protoplasmic activity ⟨~ materials⟩ — used chiefly of intracellular deposits (as of starch or fat) or of extracellular secretions; compare METAPLASM

er·gas·to·plasm \,ər'gastə,plazəm\ *n* [ISV *ergasto-* (fr. — assumed — Gk *ergastos*) + *-plasm;* orig. formed as F *ergastoplasme*] **:** basophilic cytoplasmic material — **er·gas·to·plas·mic** \¦=¦=¦=¦plazmik\ *adj*

er·gas·tu·lum \,ər'gaschələm, -stəl-\ *n, pl* **ergastu·la** \-lə\ [L, prob. modif. of Gk *ergastērion* workshop, fr. *ergazesthai* to work] **:** a dungeon on a large Roman farm in which slave laborers were confined

ergat- *or* **ergato-** *comb form* [ISV, fr. Gk *ergat-*, fr. *ergatēs*, fr. *ergazesthai* to work — more at ERGASIA] **:** worker ⟨*ergat*oid⟩ ⟨*ergato*morphic⟩

er·ga·tan·dro·morph \,ərgə'tandrə,mȯrf\ *n* -s [*ergat-* + *andr-* + *-morph*] **:** ERGATANER — **er·ga·tan·dro·mor·phic** \¦==¦==¦mȯrfik\ *adj*

er·ga·tan·drous \¦==¦tandrəs\ *adj* [*ergat-* + *-androus*] **:** having wingless males — used of ants — **er·ga·tan·dry** \'==,=drē\ *n* -ES

er·ga·ta·ner \,ərgə¦tānər, -¦tä¦ne(ə)r\ *n* -s [NL, fr. *ergat-* + Gk *anēr* man (male person) — more at ANDR-] **:** a male ant that resembles a worker

er·gate \'ər,gāt\ *n* -s [Gk *ergatēs* worker] **:** an ant of one of the worker castes

¹er·ga·tive \'ərgəd·iv\ *adj* [ISV *ergat-* + *-ive*] *of a grammatical case* **:** denoting agency or instrumentality

²ergative \"\ *n* -s **1 :** the ergative case of a language **2 :** a form in the ergative case

er·gat·o·gyne \,ər'gad·ə,jīn, 'ərgəd·ō,j-\ *n* -s [ISV *ergat-* + *-gyne*] **1 :** a wingless queen ant resembling a worker **2 :** a worker or soldier ant that develops female characteristics esp. as a result of the attack of parasitic worms — **er·gat·o·gy·nic** \,=¦=¦=¦jīnik, ¦==¦=-, -jin-\ *adj* — **er·ga·tog·y·nous** \¦ərgə¦täjənəs\ *adj* — **er·ga·tog·y·ny** \,ərgə'täjənē\ *n* -ES

¹er·ga·toid \'ərgə,tȯid\ *adj* [ISV *ergat-* + *-oid*] **:** having wingless fertile sexual individuals of either sex ⟨~ ants⟩

²ergatoid \"\ *n* -s **:** a wingless sexually perfect ant; *specif* **:** ERGATOGYNE 1

er·gat·o·morph \,ər'gad·ə,mȯrf, 'ərgəd·ō,m-\ *n* -s [*ergat-* + *-morph*] **:** an ergatomorphic ant — **er·gat·o·mor·phism** \,=¦=¦=¦mȯr,fizəm, ,==¦=-\ *n* -s

er·gat·o·mor·phic \,=¦=¦=¦mȯrfik, ¦==¦=-\ *adj* [*ergat-* + *-morphic*] **:** resembling a worker — used of male and female ants

ergh \'erk\ *Scot var of* ARGH

-ergies *pl of* -ERGY

¹er·go \'e(ə)r|(,)gō, 'ər|, 'eə|, 'ə|, 'əi|\ *adv* [L, fr. (assumed) OL *e rogo* from the direction (of)] **:** THEREFORE, HENCE ⟨they fight no battles; ~ in a certain . . . sense they are noncombatant —T.O.Heggen⟩ — often used to emphasize the illogical nature of an inference ⟨if they were not familiar with German theology . . . there just wasn't any; ~, the "Dutch" were just dumb —R.H.Shryock⟩

²ergo \"\ *n* -s **:** an inferred conclusion

¹ergo- — see ERG-
²ergo- *comb form* [F, fr. *ergot*] **:** ergot ⟨*ergo*sterol⟩
er·go·calciferol \ˌər(ˌ)gō+\ *n* -s [²*ergo-* + *calciferol*] **:** VITAMIN D₂ — used in the system of nomenclature adopted by the International Union of Pure and Applied Chemistry
er·go·cor·nine \ˌərgōˈkȯrˌnēn, -ˌnən\ *n* -s [G *ergokornin*, prob. fr. *ergo-* ²ergo- + *korn* grain, rye or L *cornu* horn + G *-in*] **:** a crystalline tripeptide alkaloid $C_{31}H_{39}N_5O_5$ separated from ergotoxine — see DIHYDROERGOCORNINE
er·go·cris·tine \-ˈkriˌstēn, -stən\ *n* -s [G *ergokristin*, fr. *ergo-* ²ergo- + *kristall* crystal + *-in*] **:** a crystalline tripeptide alkaloid $C_{35}H_{39}N_5O_5$ separated from ergotoxine
er·god·ic \ˌərˈgädik\ *adj* [*erg-* + Gk *hodos* way, journey + E *-ic* — more at CEDE] **1 :** of or relating to a process in which every sequence or sizable sample is the same statistically and therefore equally representative of the whole **2 :** involving or relating to the probability that any state will recur — **er·go·dic·i·ty** \ˌərgəˈdisəd·ē\ *n* -ES
er·go·gen·ic \ˌərgəˈjenik\ *adj* [*erg-* + *-genic*] **:** increasing capacity for bodily or mental labor esp. by eliminating fatigue symptoms ⟨an ~ drug⟩
er·go·gram \ˈ==ˌgram\ *n* [ISV *erg-* + *-gram;* orig. formed as It *ergogramma*] **:** a record of muscular work obtained by use of the ergograph
er·go·graph \-raf, -rȧf\ *n* [ISV *erg-* + *-graph;* orig. formed as It *ergografo*] **:** an apparatus or instrument with a recording device used to measure the work capacity of a muscle or group of muscles (as when exercised to exhaustion in the study of fatigue) ⟨a weight ~ attached to a finger repeatedly clasped to the palm⟩ ⟨a spring ~ for measuring handgrip⟩ — compare DYNAMOMETER — **er·go·graph·ic** \ˌ==ˈgrafik\ *adj*
er·go·ma·nia \ˌ==ˈmānēə\ *n* [NL, fr. *erg-* + *-mania*] **:** excessive devotion to work esp. as a symptom of mental disorder — **er·go·ma·ni·ac** \-ēˌak\ *n*
er·gom·e·ter \ˌərˈgäməd·ə(r)\ *n* [*erg-* + *-meter*] **:** an apparatus or instrument with a recording device used to measure the work performed by a group of muscles under control conditions as to time, rate, or resistance (as in comparing the energy yield of different diets) ⟨performed on a bicycle ~ in the minimum time work equivalent to a one-mile ride⟩ — compare DYNAMOMETER
er·go·met·rine \ˌərgəˈme\|·ˌtrēn, -mē\|, \|·trən\ *n* [²*ergo-* + *metr-* + *-ine*] **:** ERGONOVINE
er·gone \ˈərˌgōn\ *n* -s [*erg-* + *-one* (as in *hormone*)] **:** a substance that when present in minute quantities promotes a physiological activity
er·go·nom·ic \ˌərgəˈnämik\ *adj* [*erg-* + eco*nomic*] **:** BIOTECHNOLOGICAL
er·go·nom·ics \ˌ==ˈ=miks\ *n pl but sing or pl in constr* [*erg-* + eco*nomics*] **:** BIOTECHNOLOGY
er·go·no·vine \ˌərgəˈnōˌvēn, -ˌvən\ *n* -s [²*ergo-* + *nov-* + *-ine*] **:** a crystalline alkaloid $C_{19}H_{23}N_3O_2$ from ergot that has the pharmacological action of ergot and is used chiefly in the form of its maleate — called also *ergometrine*
er·go·phobe \ˈərgəˌfōb\ *n* [*erg-* + *-phobe*] **:** one suffering from ergophobia
er·go·pho·bia \ˌ==ˈfōbēə\ *n* [NL, fr. *erg-* + *-phobia*] **:** fear of or aversion to work
er·gos·ter·ol \(ˌ)ərˈgästəˌrōl, -ˌrōl\ *n* [ISV ²*ergo-* + *sterol*] **:** a crystalline steroid alcohol $C_{28}H_{43}OH$ that occurs esp. in yeast, molds, and ergot and that is converted by ultraviolet irradiation into isomeric products leading to vitamin D_2
er·got \ˈərgə\|t, ˈōg-, ˈəig-, -ˌgä\|, *usu* \|d·+V\ *n* -s [F, lit., cock's spur (which the sclerotium resembles), fr. OF *argos*, *argoz*, pl., spurs of a horse's hoofs] **1 a :** the black or dark purple sclerotium of fungi of the genus *Claviceps* that occurs as a club-shaped body which replaces the seed of various grasses (as rye) **b :** any fungus of the genus *Claviceps* **2 :** a disease of rye and other cereals caused by fungi of the genus *Claviceps* and characterized by the presence of ergots in the seed heads **3 a :** the dried sclerotial bodies of an ergot fungus grown on rye and containing several alkaloids (as ergonovine, ergotamine) **b :** any of the ergotic alkaloids with pharmacologic effect on peripheral arterioles and esp. on the uterus that are used in therapeutic doses mainly to induce contraction of the uterine muscle after delivery of the fetus and placenta and that may in overlarge doses or from natural sources (as infected rye) produce contraction of peripheral arterioles sometimes leading to gangrene — compare ²ERGOTISM **4 :** a soft horny stub about the size of a chestnut occurring as a normal growth in the tufts of hair on the back of the fetlock in the horse
er·got·a·mine \(ˌ)ərˈgäd·əˌmēn, -ˌmən\ *n* [ISV *ergot* + *amine*] **:** a crystalline tripeptide alkaloid $C_{33}H_{35}N_5O_5$ from ergot that has the pharmacological action of ergot and is used chiefly in the form of its tartrate in treating migraine
er·go·therapy \ˈərgō+\ *n* [*erg-* + *therapy*] **:** the treatment of disease by physical work and recreation
er·go·thi·o·ne·ine \ˌər(ˌ)gōˌthīˈōnēˌēn, -īˈän-, -nēən\ *n* [ISV *ergo-* + *thion-* + *-eine;* orig. formed as F *ergothionéine*] **:** a crystalline betaine $HSC_3H_2N_2CH_2CH[N(CH_3)_3]^+COO^-$ derived from a mercapto-histidine and found esp. in ergot and blood
er·got·ic \ˌərˈgäd·ik, ərˈg-\ *adj* **:** of, relating to, or produced by ergot
er·got·i·nine \(ˌ)ərˈgätᵊnˌēn, -tᵊnən\ *n* -s [ISV *ergotine*, an extract of ergot (ISV *ergot* + *-ine*) + *-ine*] **:** a crystalline tripeptide alkaloid $C_{35}H_{39}N_5O_5$ from ergot that is relatively inactive pharmacologically
ergotised *chiefly Brit var of* ERGOTIZED
¹er·go·tism \ˈergəˌtizəm, ˈər-\ *n* -s [F *ergotisme*, fr. *ergoter* to quibble, cavil (fr. OF *argoter*, fr. L *ergo* therefore) + *-isme* -ism — more at ERGO] **:** logical or sophistical reasoning
²er·got·ism \ˈərgəd·ˌizəm, -ˌgäd·-\ *n* -s [*ergot* + *-ism*] **:** a toxic condition produced by eating grain, grain products (as rye bread), or grasses infected with ergot fungus or by chronic excessive use of the drug ergot and characterized by cramps of the muscles or dry gangrene — see SAINT ANTHONY'S FIRE
er·go·tize \ˈergəˌtīz, ˈər-\ *vi* -ED/-ING/-S [F *ergoter* + E *-ize*] **:** to argue logically or sophistically
er·got·ized \ˈərgəd·ˌīzd, -ˌgäd·-\ *adj* [*ergot* + *-ize* + *-ed*] **1 :** affected by ergotism ⟨~ cattle⟩ **2 :** containing ergot
er·go·toxine \ˌərgə+\ *n* -s [²*ergo-* + *toxine*] **1 :** a crystalline pharmacologically active alkaloid $C_{35}H_{39}N_5O_5$ from ergot that is stereoisomeric with ergotinine **2 :** a mixture of isomorphous pharmacologically active alkaloids from ergot — called also *ergotoxine group;* see ERGOCORNINE, ERGOCRISTINE
ergot poisoning *n* **:** ²ERGOTISM
ergs *pl of* ERG
-er·gy \ə(r)jē, ˌərj-, ˌōj-, ˌəij-, -ji\ *n comb form* -ES [LL *-ergia*, fr. Gk *-ergeia*, *-ergia*, fr. *ergon* work + *-eia*, *-ia* -y — more at WORK] **:** work ⟨syn*ergy*⟩ **:** effect ⟨all*ergy*⟩
eri·an \ˈirēən, ˈēr-, -riən\ *adj, usu cap* [*Erian*, subdivision of the American Devonian, fr. Lake *Erie*, one of the Great Lakes of No. America + E *-an*] **:** of, relating to, or constituting a subdivision of the American Devonian — see GEOLOGIC TIME table
er·i·an·thus \ˌerēˈan(t)thəs\ *n* [NL, fr. Gk *eri* wool (short for *erion*, *eirion*, dim. of *eiros* fleece) + NL *-anthus*] **1** *cap* **:** a genus of reedlike grasses having spikes crowded in a panicle clothed with long silky hairs **2** -ES **:** any plant of the genus *Erianthus* — called also *plume grass*
er·ic \ˈerik, ˈār-\ *also* **eric fine** *n* -s [IrGael *ēiric*, fr. OIr *ēric*] **:** a payment imposed for homicide in medieval Irish law upon the slayer and his kin consisting of a fixed price for the life of the slain and the honor price of the slayer **:** BLOOD FINE — compare CRO, GALANAS, WERGILD
er·i·ca \ˈerəkə; əˈrīkə, əˈrēkə\ *n* [NL, fr. L *erice* heather, fr. Gk *ereikē* — more at BRIER] **1** *cap* **:** a large genus (the type of the family Ericaceae) of low much-branched evergreen shrubs comprising the true heaths and having whorled scalelike or needlelike leaves and sepals shorter than the petals **2** -s **:** any plant of the genus *Erica*
er·i·ca·ce·ae \ˌerəˈkāsēˌē\ *n pl, cap* [NL, fr. *Erica*, type genus + *-aceae*] **:** a family of plants (order Ericales) comprising the heaths and various related plants, being predominantly shrubs, and having usu. distinct stamens borne on a disk and an ovary with four or more locules — **er·i·ca·ceous** \ˌ==ˈ=shəs\ *adj*
er·i·cad \ˈerəˌkad; əˈrīkəd, əˈrēkəd\ *n* -s [NL *Erica* + E *-ad*] **:** a plant of the family Ericaceae
erica dye *n, usu cap E* **:** either of two direct dyes — see DYE table I (under *Direct Red 47* and *51*)
er·i·ca·les \ˌerəˈkā(ˌ)lēz\ *n pl, cap* [NL, fr. *Erica* + *-ales*] **:** an order comprising chiefly gamopetalous dicotyledonous plants characterized by regular flowers with stamens in two whorls free from the corolla and with a compound ovary and containing the families Ericaceae, Clethraceae, Pyrolaceae, Diapensiaceae, Lennoaceae, and Epacridaceae
er·i·ce·tal \ˌerəˈsēd·ᵊl\ *adj* [NL *ericet*um heath, moorland (fr. L *erice* heather + NL *-etum*) + E *-al*] **:** composed of or containing heaths ⟨an ~ flora⟩
er·i·ce·tic·o·lous \ˌerəsəˈtikələs\ *adj* [NL *ericet*um + E *-i-* + *-colous*] **:** inhabiting a heath or similar habitat
erich·thoi·di·na \əˌrikˌthȯiˈdīnə, -dēnə\ *n* -s [NL, fr. ISV *erichthoid* (fr. NL *Erichthus* + ISV *-oid*) + NL *-ina* (fem. of *-inus* -ine)] **:** a larva of a stomatopod crustacean intermediate between pseudozoea and erichthus
erich·thus \əˈrikthəs\ *n* -ES [NL, fr. Gk *ēri* early + NL *-ichthus* (fr. Gk *ichthys* fish) — more at ERE, ICHTHUS] **:** a late larva of a stomatopod crustacean
eri·cius \əˈrish(ē)əs\ *n* -ES [L — more at URCHIN] **:** HEDGEHOG 1 ⟨bittern and ~ shall possess it —Isa 34:11 (NCE)⟩
er·i·coid \ˈerəˌkȯid\ *adj* [NL *Erica* + E *-oid*] **:** resembling heath; *esp* **:** narrow and recurved — used of leaves ⟨the ~ leaf of the juniper⟩
er·i·co·phyte \ˈerəkōˌfīt, əˈrīkəˌf-\ *n* [*erico-* (fr. L *erice* heather) + *-phyte*] **:** a plant that grows on a heath or moor
¹erie \ˈirē, ˈēr-, -ri\ *n, pl* **erie** *or* **eries** *usu cap* **1 a :** an Iroquoian people of northern Ohio, northwestern Pennsylvania, and western New York **b :** a member of such people **2 :** the language of the Erie people
²erie \"\ *adj, usu cap* [fr. *Erie*, Pa.] **:** of or from the city of Erie, Pa. ⟨an *Erie* resident⟩ **:** of the kind or style prevalent in Erie
-eries *pl of* -ERY
erig·er·on \əˈrijərən, -jəˌrän\ *n* [NL, fr. L, groundsel, fr. Gk *ērigerōn*, fr. *ēri-* early + *gerōn* old man; fr. the hoary down of some species — more at ERE, CHURL] **1** *cap* **:** a widely distributed genus of herbs (family Compositae) having flower heads resembling asters but with fewer and narrower involucral bracts — see DAISY FLEABANE **2** -s **a :** any plant of the genus *Erigeron* **b :** the leaves and tops of plants of the genus *Erigeron* occas. and esp. formerly used as a diuretic and as a hemostatic in uterine hemorrhage **c :** ERIGERON OIL
erig·er·on oil \əˈrijə\|ˌrän-, \|ˌrən-\ *n* **:** a volatile oil distilled from the horseweed (*Erigeron canadense*) and sometimes used medicinally
er·i·glos·sa \ˌerəˈgläsə, -lȯsə\ *n pl, cap* [NL, fr. Gk *eri-* very much, high + NL *-glossa*] *in some classifications* **:** a suborder including all the Lacertilia except the chameleons — **er·i·glos·sate** \ˌ==ˈ=sət, -ˌsāt\ *adj*
erig·na·thus \əˈrignəthəs\ *n, cap* [NL, fr. Gk *eri-* + NL *-gnathus*] **:** a genus of mammals comprising the bearded seal
er·ik·ite \ˈerəˌkīt\ *n* -s [G or Dan *erikit*, fr. *Erik* (Eric) the Red, 10th cent. Norwegian-Icelandic explorer who organized the first white settlements of Greenland, the mineral's locality + G or Dan *-it* -ite] **:** a mineral consisting of a silicate and phosphate of the cerium metals that is of uncertain composition and occurs in brown orthorhombic crystals
er·i·na·ceous \ˌerəˈnāshəs\ *adj* [L *erinaceus*, n., hedgehog, fr. *er* hedgehog + *-inaceus* (as in *gallinaceus* cock, fr. *gallinaceus* of a cock) — more at URCHIN, GALLINACEOUS] **:** like or relating to the hedgehog
er·i·na·ceus \ˌ==ˈ=sēəs, -sh(ē)əs\ *n, cap* [NL, fr. L, hedgehog] **:** a genus (the type of the family Erinaceidae) of Old World spiny-coated mammals consisting of the true hedgehogs
erin·e·um \əˈrinēəm\ *n, pl* **erin·ea** \-ēə\ *or* **erineums** [NL, fr. Gk *erineon*, *eirineon*, neut. of *erineos*, *eirineos* woolen, fr. *erion*, *eirion* wool, dim. of *eiros* fleece] **:** an abnormal felty growth of hairs from the leaf epidermis of plants caused by various mites
erineum mite *n* **:** any of various mites chiefly of the family Eriophyidae that feed on plants and induce the formation of erinea
er·in·ite \ˈerəˌnīt\ *n* -s [*Erin* Ireland + E *-ite*] **:** a mineral $Cu_5(OH)_4(AsO_4)_2$ consisting of emerald-green basic copper arsenate
er·i·nose \ˈerəˌnōs\ *n* -s [NL *erine*um + E *-ose*] **1 :** a disease of plants (as grape, walnut, mountain maple) characterized by the presence of erinea **2 :** ERINEUM
erio- *comb form* [Gk *erio-*, *eirio-*, fr. *erion*, *eirion*] **:** wool ⟨*Erio*gonum⟩ ⟨*erio*meter⟩
er·i·o·bot·rya \ˌerēōˈbä·trēə\ *n, cap* [NL, fr. *erio-* + *-botrya* (fr. Gk *botrys* bunch of grapes)] **:** a small genus of Asiatic evergreen trees (family Rosaceae) having paniculate white flowers and a fruit with large seeds and a thin endocarp — see LOQUAT 1
er·i·o·cau·la·ce·ae \-ōˌkȯˈlāsēˌē\ *n pl, cap* [NL, fr. *Eriocaulon*, type genus + *-aceae*] **:** a family of chiefly tropical monocotyledonous aquatic or bog herbs (order Xyridales) having clustered or tufted linear leaves and minute flowers in dense heads — **er·i·o·cau·la·ceous** \ˌ===ˈ=ˈ=shəs\ *adj*
er·i·o·cau·lon \ˌ===ˈkȯˌlän\ *n, cap* [NL, fr. *erio-* + *-caulon* (fr. Gk *kaulos* stalk, stem) — more at HOLE] **:** a genus (the type of the family Eriocaulaceae) of widely distributed acaulescent herbs having flowers with glandular petals and 4 to 6 stamens
er·i·o·chalcite \ˈ===+\ *n* [*erio-* + *chalcite*] **:** a mineral $CuCl_2.2H_2O$ consisting of hydrous copper chloride
er·i·o·coc·ci·dae \ˌ===ˈkäk(s)əˌdē\ [NL, fr. *Eriococcus* (fr. *erio-* + *Coccus*) + *-idae*] *syn of* PSEUDOCOCCIDAE
er·i·o·dic·ty·ol \ˌ===ˈdiktēˌōl, -ˌōl\ *n* -s [*eriodictyon* + *-ol*] **:** a colorless crystalline compound $C_{15}H_{12}O_6$ derived from flavanone and found esp. in the leaves of some resinous shrubs of the genus *Eriodictyon* — see CITRIN, HESPERITIN
er·i·o·dic·ty·on \-ēˌän\ *n* [NL, fr. *erio-* + Gk *diktyon* net, fr. *dikein* to throw; fr. the woolly netlike leaves] **1** *cap* **:** a small genus of resinous shrubs (family Hydrophyllaceae) of southwestern No. America having finely reticulated leaves often woolly beneath and white or bluish flowers in scorpioid cymes — see YERBA SANTA **2** -s **:** any plant of the genus *Eriodictyon*
er·i·og·o·num \ˌerēˈägənəm\ *n* [NL, fr. *erio-* + *-gonum* (fr. Gk *gony* knee); fr. the woolly stems of some species — more at KNEE] **1** *cap* **:** a genus of No. American herbs (family Polygonaceae) with small clustered flowers subtended by an involucre **2** -s **:** any plant of the genus *Eriogonum*
er·i·om·e·ter \ˌerēˈäməd·ə(r)\ *n* [*erio-* + *-meter*] **:** an instrument for measuring the diameters of minute particles or fibers from the size of the colored diffraction rings or fringes produced by them in monochromatic light
er·i·o·nite \ˈerēəˌnīt\ *n* -s [Gk *erion* wool + E *-ite* — more at ERINEUM] **:** a mineral $NaKCaAl_4Si_{12}O_{32}.12H_2O$ consisting of zeolitic aluminosilicate of sodium, potassium, and calcium occurring in aggregates of orthorhombic fibrous white crystals resembling wool (sp. gr. 2)
er·i·oph·o·rum \ˌerēˈäfərəm\ *n* [NL, fr. *erio-* + *-phorum* (neut. of *-phorus*)] **1** *cap* **:** a genus of bog sedges (family Cyperaceae) characterized by cottony masses of spikelets, the perianth consisting of soft bristles **2** -s **:** any plant of the genus *Eriophorum* — called also *cotton grass*
er·i·oph·y·es \-fēˌēz\ *n, cap* [NL, fr. *erio-* + *-phyes* (fr. Gk *phyē* growth, stature)] **:** the type genus of Eriophyidae formerly containing a great number of gall and blister mites most of which are now placed in other genera
¹er·i·oph·y·id \-fēəd\ *adj* [NL *Eriophyidae*] **:** of or relating to the genus *Eriophyes* or the family Eriophyidae
²eriophyid \"\ *n* -s **:** an eriophyid mite
er·i·o·phy·i·dae \ˌerēōˈfīəˌdē\ *n pl, cap* [NL, fr. *Eriophyes*, type genus + *-idae*] **:** a large family of minute wormlike plant-feeding mites with two pairs of legs placed far anterior, lacking a respiratory system, some forming galls, others feeding on leaves and often causing blisters
er·i·o·phyl·lous \ˌerēōˈfiləs\ *adj* [ISV *erio-* + *-phyllous*] **:** having leaves with a cottony pubescence
er·i·o·so·mat·i·dae \ˌerē(ˌ)ōsəˈmad·əˌdē\ *n pl, cap* [NL, fr. *Eriosomat-*, *Eriosoma*, type genus (fr. *erio-* + *-somat-*, *-soma*) + *-idae*] **:** a family of plant lice having the cornicles reduced or absent and the wing venation simplified and including forms that cause leaf rolling and distortion of host growth and often produce quantities of woolly wax (as the woolly apple aphid)
eris·ma·tu·ra \əˌrizməˈtu̇rə, -mə·ˈtyu̇rə\ *n* -s [NL *Erismatura* former genus of birds containing the ruddy duck, fr. Gk *ereismat-*, *ereisma* prop, support (fr. *ereisis* propping, supporting, fr. *ereidein* to prop, support) + NL *-ura*] **:** RUDDY DUCK
eris·ta·lis \əˈristələs\ *n, cap* [NL] **:** a genus of large syrphid flies having larvae of the rat-tailed type and including the drone fly (*E. tenax*) — compare RAT-TAILED LARVA
¹eris·tic \əˈristik, (ˈ)eˈr-, -tēk\ *also* **eris·ti·cal** \-təkəl, -tēk-\ *adj* [Gk *eristikos* fond of wrangling, fr. *eristos* (verbal of *erizein* to wrangle, vie with, fr. *eris* quarrel, strife) + *-ikos* -ic, -ical] **:** characterized by disputatious often subtle and specious reasoning (as in argument) ⟨not . . . in any ~ temper, but in order to increase mutual understanding, desiring to get as well as to give —Walter Moberly⟩ — compare APODICTIC, CONTROVERSIAL, DIALECTICAL — **eris·ti·cal·ly** \-tək(ə)lē, -tēk-, -li\ *adv*
²eristic \"\ *n* -s **1 :** a person devoted to logical disputation **:** CONTROVERSIALIST; *specif* **:** a Megarian philosopher **2 :** the art or practice of disputation and polemics (as in Aristotelian logic) esp. as based on specious grounds ⟨a kind of ~, training the student to use the processes of thought and their expression . . . to attain an end, commonly argumentative —H.O.Taylor⟩
erith·a·cus \əˈrithəkəs\ *n, cap* [NL, fr. Gk *erithakos*, a bird, probably the robin] **:** a genus of Old World thrushes including the European robin and various related Asiatic birds
er·i·trea \ˌerə·ˈtrēə, -trāə\ *adj, usu cap* [fr. *Eritrea*, country in northeastern Africa] **:** of or from Eritrea **:** of the kind or style prevalent in Eritrea
er·i·tre·an \ˌ==ˈ=ən\ *adj, usu cap* [*Eritrea* + E *-an*] **:** of or relating to Eritrea
erivan *usu cap, var of* YEREVAN
eri·zo \əˈrē(ˌ)zō, -)sō\ *n* -s [Sp, lit., hedgehog, fr. L *ericius* — more at URCHIN] **1 :** any of several porcupine fishes **2** [AmerSp, fr. Sp] **a :** the strong bast fiber of a So. American timber tree (*Apeiba tibourbou*) of the family Tiliaceae **b :** the tree that yields erizo
erk \ˈərk, ˈōk\ *n* -s [alter. of *airc*, short for *aircraftsman*] *Brit* **:** a member of the lowest rank in the Royal Air Force (as on the ground crew) **:** AIRCRAFTSMAN
er·len·mey·er flask \ˈərl\|ənˌmī(ə)r-, ˈerl\|\ *n, usu cap E* [after Emil *Erlenmeyer* †1909 Ger. chemist] **:** a flat-bottomed conical flask whose shape allows the contents to be shaken laterally without danger of spilling

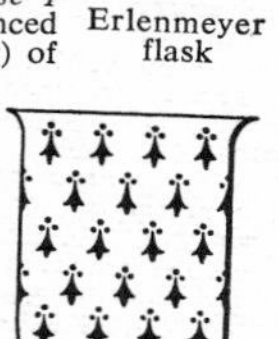
Erlenmeyer flask

erm *abbr* ermine
er·me·lin \ˈərmələn\ *n* -s [prob. modif. (influenced by *ermine*) of G *hermelin*, fr. MHG *hermelīn*, fr. OHG *harmilī* weasel, dim. of *harmo* — more at ERMINE] *archaic* **:** ERMINE
er·mi·line \-ˌlēn, -ˌlən\ *n* -s [alter. of *ermelin*] **:** white rabbit fur processed to simulate ermine
¹er·mine \ˈərmən, ˈōm-, ˈəim-\ *n* -s *see sense 1* [ME, fr. OF *ermine*, *hermine*, modif. (influenced by *ermin*, *hermin* Armenian, fr. L *Armenius*) of a Gmc word akin to OE *hearma* weasel, OS & OHG *harmo* weasel; akin to Rhaeto-Romanic *carmún* weasel, Lith *šarmuõ*, *šermuõ* weasel, and perh. to OHG *hornunc* February, ON *hjarn* frozen snow, Lith *šir̃vas* gray; basic meaning: gray, white] **1** *or pl* **ermine :** any of several weasels that assume white winter pelage usu. with more or less black on the tail: **a :** a large European weasel (*Mustela erminea*) — called also *stoat* **b :** LEAST WEASEL **c :** any of the more northerly dwelling forms of the long-tailed weasel; *esp* **:** NEW YORK WEASEL **2 a :** the fine white fur of the ermine in winter pelage prized for ornament (as on the official robes of judges and peers) **b :** a trimming or garment made of ermine **3 :** a rank (as of a king or lord) or office (as of a judge) of which the ceremonial or official robe is ornamented with ermine emblematic of authority and dignity or of purity and honor **4 a :** a heraldic fur consisting of black spots of one of various conventional shapes representing ermine tails set on a white field **b :** any of the heraldic furs having ermine spots — see ERMINES, ERMINITES, ERMINOIS, PEAN

ermine 4a

²ermine \"\ *adj* [ME, fr. MF *ermin*, *ermine*, *hermin*, *hermine*, fr. *ermine*, *hermine*, n.] **1 a :** of or relating to the ermine or its fur **b :** of the heraldic fur ermine — abbr. *erm.* **2 :** pure white
er·mined \-nd\ *adj* [ME, fr. *ermine* + *-ed*] **1 :** trimmed or lined with ermine ⟨a robe with ~ sleeves⟩ **2 a :** clothed in an ermined robe (as a judge or peer) **b :** made a judge or peer ⟨a newly ~ Labourite⟩ **3 :** having heraldic ermine spots of the tincture specified ⟨a roundel sable ~ argent⟩
ermine moth *n* **1 :** any of several small white moths (genus *Yponomeuta*) with black spots suggesting ermine **2 :** any of various rather large moths of the family Arctiidae with markings suggesting ermine
¹er·mines \-nz\ *also* **er·mi·nees** \ˈ=mənēz\ *n* [irreg. fr. ¹*ermine*] **:** a heraldic fur consisting of white ermine spots on a black field
²ermines \"\ *adj* **:** of the heraldic fur ermines
ermine spot *n* **:** a heraldic representation of an ermine tail
er·min·ette \ˌ=məˈnet\ *n* -s [¹*ermine* + *-ette*] **:** rabbit fur processed to simulate ermine
er·min·ites \ˈ=məˌnīts\ *n* [MF *erminite*, *herminite*, fr. *ermine*, *hermine*] **:** a heraldic fur consisting of black ermine spots with a red hair on each side on a white field
¹er·mi·nois \ˌ=məˈnȯiz\ *n* [MF *erminois*, *herminois*, fr. *ermine*, *hermine*] **:** a heraldic fur consisting of black ermine spots on a golden field
²erminois \"\ *adj* **:** of the heraldic fur erminois
erne *or* **ern** \ˈərn, ˈe(ə)rn\ *n* -s [ME *ern* eagle, fr. OE *earn;* akin to OHG *aro*, *arn* eagle, ON *ari*, *örn*, Goth *ara*, OIr *irar* eagle, Gk *ornis* bird, Lith *erẽlis* eagle, Arm *oror* seagull] **:** EAGLE; *esp* **:** WHITE-TAILED SEA EAGLE
erode \əˈrōd, ēˈ-\ *vb* -ED/-ING/-S [L *erodere* to erode, fr. *e-* + *rodere* to gnaw — more at RAT] *vt* **1 :** to diminish or destroy by degrees **:** eat into or away: **a :** to eat into or away by slow destruction of substance (as by acid, infection, or cancer) **:** CORRODE ⟨acids that ~ the teeth⟩ ⟨cancer had *eroded* the bone⟩ **b** (1) **:** to wear down or away by separation of small particles ⟨friction ~*s* the moving parts of machinery⟩ **:** rub or scrape away; *specif* **:** to remove with an abrasive ⟨a dental tool that quickly ~*s* the decayed tooth area⟩ (2) **:** to wear away (as land) by the action of water, wind, or glacial ice ⟨drainage quickly ~*s* the fine soil of the plowed hillside⟩ ⟨a mountain range that has been *eroded* into low hills⟩ **c :** to cause to deteriorate or disappear as if by eating or wearing away **:** destroy by degrees ⟨his commitment to a world of conferences . . . and agitation has *eroded* his family life —Anthony West⟩ **:** WEAR ⟨the institution is *eroded* away . . . person by person —R.T.LaPiere⟩ **:** IMPAIR ⟨~ the purchasing power of wages⟩ **:** UNDERMINE ⟨repeated compromises that ~ the basic principle of freedom of worship⟩ **2 :** to produce or form by eroding ⟨glaciers ~ U-shaped valleys⟩ ~ *vi* **1 :** to undergo erosion (as by weathering) ⟨where the land has *eroded* away⟩ **2 :** to deteriorate or disappear as if by eating or wearing away ⟨when the rights of any . . . are chipped away the freedom of all ~*s* —Earl Warren⟩ ⟨his regional accent has nearly *eroded*⟩
eroded *adj* **1 :** marked by or subject to erosion **2 :** EROSE
erod·ibil·i·ty *also* **erod·abil·i·ty** \=ˌrōdəˈbiləd·ē\ *n* -ES **:** the quality or degree of being erodible; *esp* **:** rate of soil erosion ⟨the ~ of soils varies with their composition⟩
erod·ible *also* **erod·able** \=ˈrōdəbəl\ *adj* **:** capable of or subject to being eroded (as by action of water and wind) ⟨~ soils⟩ ⟨~ parts of the channel⟩
ero·di·um \-dēəm\ *n* [NL, fr. Gk *erōdios* heron; fr. the long-beaked fruit — more at ARDEA] **1** *cap* **:** a large genus of herbs (family Geraniaceae) having pinnate or pinnatifid leaves, small flowers, and long bearded twisted tails on the carpels — see ALFILARIA **2** -s **:** any plant of the genus *Erodium* — called also *heron's-bill*, *storks-bill*
erog·e·ne·i·ty \əˌräjəˈnēəd·ē, ēˌr-, (ˌ)eˌr-; ˌerəjə-\ *n* -ES [*erogenous* + *-eity* (as in *homogeneity*)] **:** the quality of being erogenous ⟨the ~ of the lips⟩

ero·genesis \ˌerə+\ *n* [NL, fr. Gk *erōs* sexual love + NL *-genesis*] : EROTOGENESIS

erog·e·nous \əˈräjənəs, ēˈr-, (ˈ)eˈr-\ *also* **er·o·gen·ic** \ˌerəˈjenik\ *adj* [Gk *erōs* + E *-genous, -genic*] **1** : producing sexual excitement or libidinal gratification when stimulated : sexually sensitive ⟨~ zones of the human skin⟩ **2** : of or arousing sexual feelings : sexually stimulating ⟨~ pleasure⟩ ⟨an ~ quality⟩

erog·e·ny \əˈräjənē, ēˈr-, eˈr-\ *n* -ES [Gk *erōs* + E *-geny*] : EROTOGENESIS

eros \ˈeˌräs, ˈiˌ-, ˈēˌ-, ˈāˌ-; ˈirəs\ *n* -ES *see sense 1* [Gk *erōs* sexual love; akin to Gk *erasthai* to love, desire ardently] **1** *pl also* **ero·tes** \əˈrōˌtēz, ēˈr-,eˈr-\ *usu cap* [fr. *Eros*, Greek god of love, fr. Gk *Erōs*, fr. *erōs* sexual love] : CHERUB 3, CUPID **2 a** *usu cap* : the aggregate of pleasure-directed life instincts whose energy is derived from libido — contrasted with *Thanatos* **b** *often cap* : aspiring self-fulfilling love often having a sensuous quality : DESIRE, YEARNING ⟨animated by the true scientific ~ . . . for the task of scientific investigation —C.S.Peirce⟩ ⟨~ . . . calculates its relations to others from the standpoint of its own need of others —Reinhold Niebuhr⟩ — compare AGAPE

erose \əˈrōs, ēˈ-\ *adj* [L *erosus*, past part.] : IRREGULAR, UNEVEN; *specif, bot* : having the margin irregularly notched as if gnawed — **erose·ly** *adv*

ero·si·bil·i·ty \əˌrōzəˈbiləd·ē, ēˌr-\ *n* -ES : ERODIBILITY

ero·si·ble \əˈ≡zəbəl\ *adj* [*erosion* + *-ible*] : ERODIBLE

ero·sion \əˈrōzhən, ēˈ-\ *n* -S [MF, fr. L *erosion-, erosio*, fr. *erosus* (past part. of *erodere* to erode) + *-ion-, -io* -ion — more at ERODE] **1 a** (1) : the superficial destruction of a surface area of tissue (as mucous membrane) by inflammation, ulceration, or trauma ⟨~ of the uterine cervix⟩ ⟨gizzard ~ in chicks⟩ (2) : progressive loss of the hard substance of a tooth **b** : CORROSION 1a **2 a** : the general process whereby materials of the earth's crust are worn away and removed by natural agencies including weathering, solution, corrasion, and transportation; *specif* : land destruction and simultaneous removal of particles (as of soil) by running water, waves and currents, moving ice, or wind ⟨stream ~⟩ ⟨glacial ~⟩ — compare DENUDATION **b** : surface destruction of a metal or refractory material effected by the abrasive or the corrosive and abrasive action of a moving liquid or gas and often accelerated by solid particles in suspension ⟨range errors due to gun ~⟩ ⟨severe ~ of the furnace lining caused by the scouring motion of molten slag⟩ **c** : even disintegration of a paint surface caused by chalking and washing away **3** : an instance or product of erosion ⟨a circular ~ on the skin half an inch in diameter⟩ ⟨a canyon with red tower-shaped ~s⟩ **4** : progressive impairment or destruction as if by eating or wearing away (as of resources, strength, or effectiveness) : DEPLETION, DETERIORATION ⟨~ of real earnings by inflation⟩ ⟨the great ideals of liberty and equality are preserved against . . . the ~ of small encroachments —B.N. Cardozo⟩

ero·sion·al \-zhənᵊl,-zhnəl\ *adj* : of, relating to, or produced by erosion ⟨the ~ and depositional work of the ocean⟩ ⟨~ materials on the valley floor⟩

erosion cycle *n* : the succession of stages through which a newly uplifted land mass must pass before it is worn down to a peneplain or a surface near sea level including juvenile stages in which the original surface is sharply cut by canyons, mature stages in which the original surface may disappear and the topography be characterized by high steep hills and fairly open valleys, and old-age stages in which the land is so worn down that the streams meander sluggishly across a lowland

ero·sion·ist \-zhənəst\ *n* -S : a supporter of the now obsolete theory that the contour of the land is mainly the result of erosion

erosion pavement *n* : a surficial concentration of pebbles and rock fragments tending to protect the underlying soil from further erosion

erosion remnant *n* : a feature of the landscape standing above the general level to which erosion has reduced its surroundings ⟨as the shoreline is cut landward stacks, caves, islands, and other typical *erosion remnants* may be left standing —P.G. Worcester⟩

erosion surface *n* : a surface generally of low relief shaped by erosion — compare PENEPLAIN, UNCONFORMITY

ero·sive \əˈrōsiv, ēˈ-, -ōz|, |ēv *also* |əv\ *adj* [L *erosus* + E *-ive*] **1** : tending to erode : effecting erosion ⟨nervous fussing and fretting . . . exercise upon the character an ~ effect —Osbert Sitwell⟩ : ERODIBLE ⟨dangerously ~ soil⟩ **2** : soil-exposing ⟨alternate ~ with soil-protecting crops⟩

ero·sive·ness \-vnəs\ *or* **ero·siv·i·ty** \əˌrōˈsivəd·ē, (ˌ)ēˌr-\ *n* -ES **1** : the quality or degree of effecting erosion : the power of eroding ⟨the greater ~ of water on steep slopes⟩ **2** : ERODIBILITY

erosive stomatitis *n* : VESICULAR STOMATITIS

erotes *pl of* EROS

¹erot·ic \əˈräd·|ik, ēˈ-,eˈ-, -ät|, |ēk\ *also* **erot·i·cal** \|əkəl, |ēk-\ *adj* [F & Gk; F *érotique*, fr. Gk *erōtikos*, fr. *erōt-, erōs* sexual love + *-ikos* -ic, -ical — more at EROS] **1** : of, devoted to, or tending to arouse sexual love or desire: as **a** : treating of or depicting sexual love (as by sensuous or voluptuous description) : AMATORY ⟨a poem ~ rather than lyric that delights in feminine beauty and amorous feelings⟩ ⟨~ folk dances depicting courtship with mock teasing and coaxing⟩ **b** : tending to excite sexual pleasure or desire ⟨~ dreams⟩ ⟨the ~ power of perfume⟩ **c** : directed toward sexual gratification ⟨his ~ adventures with prostitutes⟩ ⟨a personality with strong ~ drives⟩ **d** : strongly affected by sexual desire ⟨an ~ person⟩ **2** : of or relating to eros ⟨the dominance of the ~ over the death instinct⟩ — **erot·i·cal·ly** \|ək(ə)lē, |ēk-, -li\ *adv*

²erotic \"\ *n* -S **1** : a theory or doctrine of love ⟨developed a mystical ~⟩ **2** : an erotic person ⟨sex-filled paperbacks suggesting the prevalence of ~s⟩

erot·i·ca \|əkə\ *n pl* [NL, fr. Gk *erōtika*, pl. of *erōtikos*] : literary or artistic items having an erotic theme; *esp* : books treating of sexual love in a sensuous or voluptuous manner — compare PORNOGRAPHY

erot·i·cism \|əˌsizəm\ *also* **er·o·tism** \ˈerəˌtizəm\ *n* -S **1** : the arousal of or the attempt to arouse sexual feeling by means of suggestion, symbolism, or allusion in an art form **2** : a state of sexual arousal or anticipation (as from stimulation of erogenous zones) **3 a** : sexual impulse or desire ⟨the robust *erotisms* that stir deeply in the very autonomic nervous system of the normal individual —Weston La Barre⟩ **b** : abnormally insistent sexual passion

erot·i·cize \əˈräd·əˌsīz, ēˈr-,eˈr-, -ätə-\ *vt* -ED/-ING/-S : to render erotic ⟨a film version that ~s the original story⟩

er·o·ti·za·tion \ˌerəd·əˈzāshən, -rəˌtīˈz-\ *n* -S **1** : the act or process of erotizing **2** : the state of being erotized

er·o·tize \ˈerəˌtīz\ *vt* -ED/-ING/-S : to invest with erotic significance or sexual feeling ⟨a highly ambivalent and *erotized* attachment to a mother —Adelaide Johnson & Dora Fishback⟩

eroto- *comb form* [NL, fr. Gk *erōto-, erōt-, erōs* sexual love — more at EROS] : sexual desire ⟨*erotomania*⟩

ero·to·genesis \əˌrōd·ə, ēˌr-,eˌr-, -rädə+\ *n* [NL, fr. *eroto-* + *-genesis*] : arousal of sexual feeling

ero·to·gen·ic \≡ˌ≡≡+ˈjenik\ *adj* [*eroto-* + *-genic*] : EROGENOUS

ero·to·ge·nic·i·ty \≡ˌ≡≡jəˈnisəd·ē\ *n* -ES : EROGENEITY

ero·to·ma·nia \≡ˌ≡≡+ˈmānēə\ *n* [NL, fr. *eroto-* + *-mania*] : excessive sexual desire esp. as a symptom of mental disorder — **ero·to·ma·ni·ac** \-ēˌak\ *n*

ero·to·path \≡ˈ≡≡+ˌpath\ *n* -S [*eroto-* + *-path*] : one affected with erotopathy

er·o·top·a·thy \ˌerəˈtäpəthē\ *n* -ES [*eroto-* + *-pathy*] : an abnormality of sexual desire

erot·y·lid \əˈrōd·ᵊləd, -räd-\ *n* -S [NL *Erotylidae*] : a beetle of the family Erotylidae

er·o·tyl·i·dae \ˌerəˈtiləˌdē\ *n pl, cap* [NL, fr. *Erotylus*, type genus (fr. Gk *erōtylos* darling, sweetheart, fr. *erōt-, erōs* sexual love) + *-idae* — more at EROS] : a family of elongate oval hairy beetles having larvae that live in fungi or bore in higher plants

er·pe·to·ich·thys \ˌərpəˌtōˈikthəs\ *n, cap* [NL, irreg. fr. *herpet-* + Gk *ichthys* fish — more at ICHTHUS] : a genus of fishes (order Cladistia) that contains only the African reedfish and is often isolated from the related genus *Polypterus* in a monotypic family

err *R* ˈe(ə)r, ˈər (+V ˈər·) *sometimes* ˈa(ə)r; *-R* ˈeə (+*suffixal vowel* ˈer, +*vowel in a following word* ˈer *or* ˈeə), ˈə̄ (+*suffixal vowel* ˈər· *also* ˈə̄r, +*vowel in a following word* ˈər· *or* ˈə̄ *also* ˈə̄r)\ *vi* -ED/-ING/-S [ME *erren*, fr. OF *errer*, fr. L *errare*; akin to OE *ierre, yrre* wandering, angry, *iersian* to be angry, OHG *irri* gone astray, angry, *irrōn* to go astray, OS *irri* angry, Goth *airzeis* led astray, deceived, ON *rās* race — more at RACE] **1** *archaic* **a** : to turn aside from the proper path : STRAY ⟨all we as sheep ~*ed* —John Wyclif⟩ **b** : to go about aimlessly : WANDER, ROAM **2** : to deviate from a standard (as of wisdom, morality, accuracy) : be or do wrong: as **a** : to make a mistake ⟨~*ed* on the side of caution in judging the supplies inadequate⟩ **b** : to violate an accepted standard of conduct : SIN, OFFEND ⟨if you ~ and do not observe all these commandments which the Lord has spoken —Num 15:22 (RSV)⟩ **c** : to be inaccurate ⟨a gauge that must not ~ by more than 0.01 mm.⟩

err·abil·i·ty \ˌerəˈbiləd·ē, ˌərə- *sometimes* ˌarə- *or* ˌə̄rə-\ *n* -ES : liability to error

err·able \ˈ≡≡bəl\ *adj* : liable to error : FALLIBLE

er·ran·cy \ˈerənsē, -si *sometimes* ˈər·ə- *or* ˈarə- *or* ˈə̄rə-\ *n* -ES : a state, practice, or instance of erring ⟨denies the ~ of scripture⟩ ⟨the boy's ~ consisted of pranks⟩ ⟨his first ~ from the straight and narrow path —S.H.Adams⟩

er·rand \ˈerənd\ *n* -S [ME *erend* message, business, fr. OE *ǣrend*; akin to OE *ār* messenger, OS *ēr* messenger, OHG *ārunti* message, ON *eyrendi, erendi, ōrendi* message, *ārr* messenger, Goth *airus*] **1** *archaic* : an oral message entrusted to a person ⟨tell your king from me this ~ —Richard Stanyhurst⟩ **2** : a trip made in order to deliver a message or purchase or attend to something ⟨gone to the shopping center on an ~⟩ ⟨run an ~ for his employer⟩ **3 a** *archaic* : MISSION, EMBASSY **b** : the object or purpose of a short trip ⟨do several ~s of my own in town⟩ **c** : a service, favor, or piece of business undertaken for another ⟨running ~s for his mother⟩

¹er·rant \ˈerənt *sometimes* ˈər·ə- *or* ˈarə- *or* ˈə̄rə-\ *adj* [ME *erraunt*, fr. MF *errant*, pres. part. of *errer* to travel, wander (fr. ML *iterare*, fr. L *iter* way, journey) & *errer* to err — more at EYRE, ERR] **1 a** : traveling or given to traveling (as on a mission of chivalry) ⟨an ~ knight⟩ ⟨~ those exiles . . . who with their burden traverse hill and dale —William Wordsworth⟩; *specif* : itinerant in an official capacity ⟨~ officials who traveled a quarterly circuit⟩ **b** : quixotically adventurous ⟨her temerity in such an ~ undertaking —Thomas Hardy⟩ **2** *obs* : ARRANT 2a ⟨he is so ~ a whig that he strains even beyond his author in his passion for liberty —Henry Cromwell⟩ **3 a** : straying outside the proper path or bounds ⟨in this labyrinth of tunnels the farmer found his ~ pigs —*Amer. Guide Series: Minn.*⟩ **b** : moving about aimlessly or irregularly : WANDERING ⟨an ~ breeze⟩; *specif* : having an irregular course — used formerly in astronomy to distinguish a planet from a star ⟨seven . . . ~ stars in the lower orbs of heaven —Sir Thomas Browne⟩ **c** : deviating from a standard (as of behavior) : ERRING ⟨a parent scolding an ~ child⟩ **d** : liable or inclined to error : FALLIBLE ⟨his instincts being basically sound but like those of all natural men somewhat ~ —Gilbert Millstein⟩ **4** : of or relating to the Errantia — **er·rant·ly** *adv*

²errant \"\ *n* -S : one that is errant ⟨separates the one-time ~ from the long-term philanderer —*Time*⟩; *specif* : KNIGHT-ERRANT

er·ran·tia \eˈranch(ē)ə, -ntēə\ *n pl, cap* [NL, fr. L, neut. pl. of *errant-, errans*, pres. part. of *errare* to wander, err — more at ERR] *in some classifications* : a division of Polychaeta comprising free-swimming worms (as those of the genera *Aphrodite, Nereis*, and *Polynoe*) usu. with well-developed parapodia and sense organs and without special respiratory structures

er·rant·ry \ˈerəntrē, -ri *sometimes* ˈər·ə- *or* ˈarə- *or* ˈə̄rə-\ *n* -ES : WANDERING; *esp* : a roving in quest of knightly adventure ⟨set out on their tour with a sense of ~⟩

er·ra·ta \eˈräd|ə, əˈr-, -rā|, |tə *also* -ra| *or* -rā\ *n* -S [fr. pl. of *erratum*] **1** : ERRATUM **2** : a list of corrigenda or a page bearing such a list

¹er·rat·ic \əˈrad·|ik, (ˈ)eˈr-, ēˈr-, -at|, |ēk\ *also* **er·rat·i·cal** \|əkəl, |ēk-\ *adj* [*erratic* fr. ME *erratik*, fr. MF or L; MF *erratique*, fr. L *erraticus*, fr. *erratus* (past part. of *errare* to wander, err) + *-icus* -ic; *erratical* fr. *erratic* + *-al* — more at ERR] **1 a** : having no fixed course : WANDERING ⟨an ~ comet⟩ **b** *archaic* : having no fixed residence : NOMADIC ⟨those savages although ~ must remain long enough in one position to cultivate this grain —Z.M.Pike⟩ **2** : transported by a glacier from an original resting place ⟨~ boulder⟩ ⟨~ block⟩ **3 a** : characterized by lack of consistency, regularity, or uniformity : UNPREDICTABLE, CAPRICIOUS ⟨~ as an unroped steer —*New Republic*⟩ : FLUCTUATING ⟨the hog market was ~ but pork remained steady⟩ : UNEVEN ⟨the pitcher showed ~ control, throwing too many wild pitches⟩; *specif* : marked by irregular changes of direction ⟨the ~ course of the river⟩ ⟨streets that run at ~ angles⟩ **b** : deviating from what is ordinary or standard (as in nature, behavior, or opinion) : ODD, ECCENTRIC ⟨the key to the code was the ~ punctuation⟩ ⟨he must have been . . . scandalously ~ from the Puritan point of view —*Amer. Guide Series: Mass.*⟩ **syn** see STRANGE

²erratic \"\ *n* -S : one that is erratic ⟨we have ~s, unscholarly foolish persons —Joseph Cook⟩; *specif* : an erratic boulder or block of rock

er·rat·i·cal·ly \|ək(ə)lē, |ēk-, -li\ *adv* : in an erratic manner ⟨a tiny spark was glowing ~ upon the river —J.H.Wheelwright⟩

er·rat·i·cism \≡ˈ≡d·əˌsizəm, ≡ˈ≡tə,-\ *n* -S : a state or instance of being erratic; *esp* : a wayward act or tendency ⟨what ~s mere self-respect can lead to —Edwin Kennebeck⟩

er·ra·tum \eˈräd·əm, əˈr-, -rā|, |təm *also* -ra| *or* -rā|\ *n, pl* **erra·ta** \|d·ə, |tə\ [L, fr. neut. of *erratus*, past part.] **1** *archaic* : an error (as a misstatement or misprint) in something published or written **2** : CORRIGENDUM ⟨the ~ directing its deletion was placed on the verso —J.H.Sledd & G.J.Kolb⟩ ⟨incorporating *errata* in text during reprinting —*Library Science Abstracts*⟩

erred *past of* ERR

¹er·rhine \ˈeˌrīn\ *n* -S [Gk *errhinon*, fr. *er-* (fr. *en-* ²en-) + *-rhinon* (fr. *rhin-, rhis* nose) — more at RHIN-] : STERNUTATOR

²errhine \"\ *adj* [Gk *errhinos*, fr. *er-* + *-rhinos* (fr. *rhin-, rhis*)] : STERNUTATORY

erring *adj* [ME, fr. pres. part. of *erren* to err — more at ERR] : that errs (as in behavior) ⟨extend to ~ youth the same legal protection as adult delinquents have⟩; *specif* : ADULTEROUS ⟨an ~ wife⟩ — **err·ing·ly** *adv*

er·ro·neous \əˈrōnēəs, eˈr- *also* -nyəs\ *adj* [ME, fr. L *erroneus*, fr. *errare* to err — more at ERR] **1** *archaic* : moving about irregularly or aimlessly : WANDERING ⟨on the . . . field I fall ~, there to wander —John Milton⟩ **2** : deviating from what is true, correct, right, or wise: **a** : being or containing an error : FALLACIOUS, MISTAKEN, INACCURATE ⟨an ~ doctrine⟩ ⟨received an ~ impression⟩ ⟨a stamp collection of ~ issues⟩ **b** : characterized by error : ERRING ⟨our own sad species . . . lapsed and ~ humanity —L.P.Smith⟩ — **er·ro·neous·ly** *adv* — **er·ro·neous·ness** *n* -ES

er·ror \ˈerə(r) *sometimes* ˈeˌrō(ə)r *or* -ō(ə)\ *n* -S [ME *errour*, fr. OF *error, errour*, fr. L *error*, fr. *errare* to err] **1 a** : an act or condition of often ignorant or imprudent deviation from a code of behavior : violation of ritual holiness, moral rectitude, or social convention : SIN ⟨entice with licentious passions of the flesh men who have barely escaped from those who live in error —2 Pet 2:18 (RSV)⟩ : OFFENSE, FAULT ⟨the official's ~s of nepotism and acceptance of large gifts from lobbyists⟩ **b** : an act involving an unintentional deviation from truth or accuracy : a mistake in perception, reasoning, recollection, or expression ⟨made an ~ in adding up the bill⟩ ⟨gunnery ~s⟩ **c** : an act that through ignorance, deficiency, or accident departs from or fails to achieve what should be done ⟨got lost when he made the ~ of turning left at the fork⟩ ⟨an ~ of judgment⟩ ⟨the ~ of writing last year's date early in January⟩: as (1) : a misplay (as a fumble or a wild throw) by a baseball player when normal play would have resulted in an out or prevented an advance by a base runner — not used of a passed ball or wild pitch ⟨an ~ is charged against a fielder at the discretion of the official scorer⟩ (2) : a failure in bowling to make a spare when the previous ball left no split (3) : a failure in a racket game to return the ball to the opponent's court after touching it with the racket (as in tennis by hitting it into the net or outside the court) **d** (1) : a mistake in the proceedings of a court of record in matters of law or of fact (2) : WRIT OF ERROR (3) : proceedings for a writ of error **2 a** : the quality or state of erring; *esp* : the act of believing or of setting forth what is not true ⟨the firm is in ~ as to the facts of the case⟩ ⟨the map is in ~ regarding the junction⟩ **b** *Christian Science* : illusion about the nature of reality that is the cause of human suffering : the contradiction of truth ⟨~ is a supposition that pleasure and pain, that intelligence, substance, life are existent in matter —Mary B. Eddy⟩ **c** : an instance of false belief : a mistaken idea or system of ideas ⟨an opposite ~ . . . is the belief that children are naturally virtuous —Bertrand Russell⟩ **d** : the body of false beliefs : FALSEHOOD ⟨hope to reduce ~ by promoting education⟩ **3** : something (as a misstatement or misprint) produced by mistake ⟨a typographical ~⟩; *specif* : a postage stamp released for use that shows flaw in its manufacture (as in differing in color or paper from others of its issue and denomination) **4** *archaic* : an irregular course : WANDERING ⟨brooks rolling with mazy ~ —John Milton⟩ **5 a** *math* : the difference between an observed or calculated value of a quantity and the true value; *specif, statistics* : variation in the measurements, calculations, or observations of a quantity due to mistakes or to usu. uncontrollable factors — see PROBABLE ERROR, STANDARD ERROR **b** *in artillery fire* : the divergence of a point of impact from the center of impact in a dispersion of shots : the distance of a shot from the target **c** : the amount of deviation from a standard or specification ⟨weights used to determine the ~ of a scale⟩ ⟨the allowable ~ in milling a machine part is called its tolerance⟩ **6** : a deficiency or imperfection in structure or function : DEFECT ⟨an ~ in vision may cause headaches⟩

syn MISTAKE, BLUNDER, SLIP, LAPSE, FAUX PAS, BULL, HOWLER, BONER: ERROR indicates a deviation from correct, sanctioned, approved belief, procedure, practice, or course ⟨the *errors* in their beliefs⟩ ⟨an *error* in reasoning⟩ ⟨it is a common *error* to speak of the doctrine of science when what is meant is naturism —W.R.Inge⟩ ⟨an *error* in addition⟩ ⟨sent by *error* to the wrong department⟩ MISTAKE suggests a misunderstanding, wrong decision, or inadvertent wrong action; it may apply to the unimportant or momentary but does not always do so ⟨a *mistake* in reading the road map⟩ ⟨a *mistake* in admitting these students⟩ ⟨a *mistake* in copying the list⟩ BLUNDER may imply ignorance, stupidity, or culpable lack of foresight and care ⟨fortunate to be acquitted by a court-martial after he had made a tragic *blunder* and lost many of his own men —Peter Forster⟩ ⟨we usually call our *blunders mistakes* and our friends style our *mistakes blunders* —H.B. Wheatley⟩ SLIP may apply to a trivial readily forgivable mistake, inadvertence, or accident ⟨a *slip* of the pen⟩ ⟨a list such as a busy and not very well educated library clerk might make, with many *slips* and grammatical mistakes —R.W. Southern⟩ LAPSE may suggest forgetfulness, inattention, or weakness ⟨you gave natives bits to copy under all possible threats against *lapses* of accuracy, only to discover at the end that they had embroidered the work pleasantly to their own fancy —Mary Austin⟩ FAUX PAS now usu. indicates a social blunder as a violation of etiquette or an instance of tactlessness ⟨John and I, horrified, hustled him out before he could commit any further *faux pas* —S.H.Adams⟩ BULL usu. applies to a blunder marked by stupidity although it is often applied to a remark purposely contrived to contain an amusing incongruity ⟨the well-known *bull* stating that "one man is just as good as another — and sometimes more so"⟩ ⟨"the next train to Dublin has just gone", the stationmaster said and laughed at his own *bull*⟩ HOWLER usu. applies to a ludicrous blunder made through ignorance or dim-wittedness ⟨a schoolboy *howler* that turns the title "Intimations of Immortality" into "Imitations of Immorality"⟩ ⟨refused to go on a quiz show for fear he'd make *howlers*⟩ BONER suggests a blunder made through thoughtlessness as well as dim-wittedness ⟨made the *boner* of inviting his boss to dinner on the night his wife's bridge group was due to meet at his house⟩ ⟨pulled a real *boner* when he said the American Civil War was in the 18th century⟩

er·ror·ist \ˈerərəst\ *n* -S : one who holds to and propagates error

er·ror·less \ˈerə(r)ləs\ *adj* : done, played, or performed without an error ⟨an ~ baseball game⟩

error-measuring device *n, in automation and feedback controls* : the means by which departure is detected and measured for correction in the system

error of closure 1 : the ratio of the distance by which a survey fails to close to the perimeter of the tract surveyed **2** : the sum of the angles of a traverse as measured minus the true sum required by geometry — called also *closing error*

error of estimate : an error made by using the equation of a regression line to estimate the values of the dependent variable from those of the independent variable

errs *pres 3d sing of* ERR

ers \ˈərs, ˈe(ə)rs\ *n* -ES [MF, fr. OProv, fr. LL *ervor-, ervus*, alter. of L *ervum*, prob. of non-IE origin like OS *erwit* pea, OHG *araweiz, arwiz*, ON *ertr* pea, Gk *orobos* chick-pea] : a vetch (*Vicia ervilia*) grown in Mediterranean and Asiatic countries as a forage plant and stock food — called also *kersenneh*

-ers *pl of* -ER

er·sar \erˈsär\ *n, pl* **er·sa·ri** \erˈsärē\ *usu cap* : one of a Turkoman people in Bukhara

¹er·satz \ˈerˌz|äts *sometimes* -ˌs| *or* |ats *or* ≡ˈ≡\ *adj* [G *ersatz-*, fr. *ersatz*, n.] **1** : SUBSTITUTE, SYNTHETIC ⟨~ flour . . . developed from sawdust and vegetable waste —Jackson Martindell⟩ ⟨construction will be largely with ~ materials, iron, steel, and copper being needed for armaments —*Newsweek*⟩ ⟨turn . . . any form of art into an ~ religion —W.K.Wimsatt⟩ : SIMULATED ⟨the model . . . nestles on ~ waves —*Newcastle (Australia) Morning Herald*⟩ : COUNTERFEIT ⟨since few dared talk about the real issue, there had to be an ~ issue —*New Republic*⟩ **2** : of, relating to, or marked by the use of substitute products ⟨Germany's wartime ~ economy⟩

²ersatz \"\ *n* -ES [G, substitute, compensation, fr. MHG (Swiss dial.) *ersaz* commensurate punishment, fr. *ersetzen* to replace, fr. OHG *irsezzen*, fr. *ir-* (perfective prefix) + *sezzen* to set — more at ABEAR, SET] **1** : an artificial replacement for a natural product ⟨rayon is an outstanding example of the ~ become . . . a synthetic textile fiber in its own right —*Economist*⟩ : a substitute differing in kind from and often inferior in quality to what it replaces **2** : something similar in only a superficial or partial way to what it is represented to be : something not genuine ⟨a piece of poetic ~ offering sentimentalism for genuine feeling⟩ **3** : the discovery and use of substitute products : SUBSTITUTION ⟨international trade . . . of little importance in a nation skilled in the art of ~ —K.E.Poole⟩

ersatz reserve *n* : a reserve of the German army (as in World War II) drawn upon when necessary to fill out regular units and made up of men not qualified for the regular army or the landwehr

¹erse \ˈərs\ *adj, usu cap* [ME (Sc dial.) *Erisch, Ersch*, var. of *Irish* — more at IRISH] **1 a** : of, relating to, or characteristic of the Gaelic-speaking people of Scotland **b** : of, relating to, or characteristic of the language of such people **2** : Irish Gaelic

²erse \"\ *n* -S *usu cap* [ME (Sc dial.) *Erisch, Ersch*, fr. *Erisch, Ersch*, adj.] **1** : Scottish Gaelic **2** : Irish Gaelic

erst \ˈərst\ *adv* [ME *erest* earliest, soonest, first, formerly, fr. OE *ǣrest*, superlative of *ǣr* early, soon — more at ERE] *archaic* : FORMERLY

¹erstwhile \(ˈ)≡ˈ≡\ *adv* [*erst* + *while*] : in the past : FORMERLY: **a** : in a time past : of old : ONCE ⟨found an apartment house where ~ stood his childhood home⟩ : a short while since : of late : but now ⟨the school-bound child who it seems ~ wailed in your arms⟩ **b** : till then or now : PREVIOUSLY, HERETOFORE ⟨the new cheerfulness of the ~ unhappy man⟩

²erstwhile \ˈ≡ˌ≡\ *adj* **1** : having been or existed at some past time : of the past : ONETIME, SOMETIME, FORMER ⟨the new manager was an ~ machinist who had risen to the top⟩

⟨deserted their ~ friends and allies⟩ **2 :** being, existing, or effective till then or now : PREVIOUS ⟨invading the ~ domain of the specialists⟩

er·te·bol·le \ˌertəˈbälə, -ˈbələ,-ˈbələ\ *adj, usu cap* [fr. *Ærtebølle*, town in Jutland, Denmark, where such mounds were found] **:** of or belonging to an Early Neolithic or Late Mesolithic culture in the Baltic region characterized by large kitchen middens, chipped stone tools, and crude pottery

erub *or* **eruv** \āˈrüv, ˈāˌrəv\ *n, pl* **eru·bin** *or* **eru·vin** \ärüˈvēn, āˈrüvin\ [Heb *ʿērūbh*] **:** a means (as a symbolic alteration of a boundary) provided in Jewish law for extending the strict limits anciently placed upon movements of persons and goods on the Sabbath and so accommodating the laws to the needs of daily life

er·u·bes·cent \ˌer(y)əˈbesᵊnt\ *adj* [L *erubescent-, erubescens*, pres. part. of *erubescere* to grow red, fr. *e-* + *rubescere* to grow red — more at RUBESCENT] **:** REDDENING

er·u·bes·cite \ˌ=ˈbeˌsīt\ *n* -s [L *erubescere* + E *-ite*] **:** BORNITE

eruc \əˈrük\ *n* -s [Tag *iruc*] **:** a cordage fiber derived from a Philippine palm (*Corypha elata*)

eru·ca \əˈrükə\ *n* [L, caterpillar, garden rocket, perh. fr. *er* hedgehog — more at URCHIN] **1** -s **:** CATERPILLAR **2** *cap* [NL, fr. L] **:** a small genus of Old World herbs (family Cruciferae) distinguished by a short 4-angled silique — see GARDEN ROCKET

eruci- *comb form* [ISV, fr. L *eruca*] **:** caterpillar ⟨*eruci*form⟩ ⟨*eruci*vorous⟩

eru·cic acid \əˈrüsik-\ *n* [*erucic* ISV *eruc-* (fr. NL *Eruca*) + *-ic*] **:** a crystalline fatty acid $C_8H_{17}CH{=}CH(CH_2)_{11}COOH$ found in the form of glycerides esp. in oils from the seeds of cruciferous plants (as mustard and rape); *cis*-13-docos·en·oic acid

eru·ci·form \-səˌfȯrm\ *adj* [ISV *eruci-* + *-form*] *of an insect larva* **:** having a soft cylindrical body with a distinct head and usu. having short thoracic legs **:** like a caterpillar in form

eruct \əˈrəkt, ēˈ-\ *vb* -ED/-ING/-S [L *eructare*, fr. *e-* + *ructare* to belch, fr. (assumed) *ructus*, past part. of (assumed) *rugere* to belch (as in LL *erugere*); akin to L *rugire* to roar — more at BRUIT] *vi* **:** BELCH ~ *vt* **1 :** to bring up (gas) from the stomach by belching **2 :** to eject violently ⟨a volcano that ~*s* noxious fumes⟩

eruc·tate \-kˌtāt, *usu* -ād.+V\ *vb* -ED/-ING/-S [L *eructatus*, past part. of *eructare*] **:** ERUCT

eruc·ta·tion \əˌrəkˈtāshən, (ˌ)ēˌr-\ *n* -s [L *eructation-, eructatio*, fr. *eructatus* + *-ion-, -io* -ion] **1 :** the act of belching gas from the stomach **:** BELCH **2 :** a violent belching out or emitting (as of gaseous or other matter from the crater of a volcano) **3 :** something that is emitted by belching

eruc·ta·tive \əˈrəktəd.iv, ēˈr-\ *adj* **:** relating to or given to eructation

eruc·tion \-kshən\ *n* -s **:** ERUCTATION

¹er·u·dite \ˈeryəˌdīt *also* ˈerəˌ-; *usu* -īd.+V\ *adj* [ME *erudit*, fr. L *eruditus* learned, skilled, experienced, fr. past part. of *erudire* to polish, instruct, fr. *e-* + *rudis* rude, unpolished, unskilled, ignorant — more at RUDE] **1 :** possessing or displaying erudition **:** LEARNED ⟨an ~ lawyer⟩ ⟨an unusually winning prologue ... ~ but not academic —Louis Untermeyer⟩; *specif* **:** concerned with unduly specialized information **:** PEDANTIC, BOOKISH ⟨contains a vast amount of information without being ~ —*Liturgical Arts*⟩ ⟨knows about ... sea fighting in a fashion too informed to be ~ —R.J. Purcell⟩ **2 :** characterized by a love of knowledge for its own sake **:** devoted to the pursuit of learning ⟨minutiae that interest only the most ~ scholars⟩

²erudite \"\ *n* -s **:** an erudite person ⟨she was a well-known figure among the ~*s* of the area⟩

er·u·dite·ly *adv* **:** in an erudite manner **:** with erudition

er·u·di·tion \ˌ==ˈdishən\ *n* -s [ME *erudicioun*, fr. L *erudition-, eruditio*, fr. *eruditus* + *-ion-, -io* -ion] **1 a :** extensive often profound or recondite knowledge (as of history, literature, or philosophy) acquired chiefly from books **:** command of a large fund of specialized information **:** LEARNING ⟨for this task he requires the aid of taste, not a mass of facts; an active imagination, not the accumulated weight of ~ —C.I.Glicksberg⟩ **b :** the exhibition of thorough sometimes recondite scholarship **:** an erudite quality of writing or speaking **:** LEARNEDNESS ⟨botanical information of great ~ —Bernard DeVoto⟩ ⟨although this book is the product of long ... study it is not clogged with heavy ~ —Gastón Figueira⟩ **2 :** the practice of scholarly study **:** the pursuit of learning ⟨~ and reflection are complementary in sound scholarship⟩ **syn** see KNOWLEDGE

eruginous *var of* AERUGINOUS

erum·pent \əˈrəmpənt, ēˈ-\ *adj* [L *erumpent-, erumpens*, pres. part. of *erumpere*] **1 :** tending to grow out vigorously from a substrate so as to burst through or rise above its surface ⟨certain ~ fungi that parasitize leaves⟩ **2** *of the fruiting bodies of some fungi and algae* **:** grown or burst through a surface (as of a host's tissue) so as to form a projecting mass ⟨the ~ fruiting bodies of some rusts⟩ ⟨~ acervuli forming black dots on the leaves⟩

erupt \əˈrəpt, ēˈ-\ *vb* -ED/-ING/-S [L *eruptus* past part. of *erumpere* to burst forth, break out, fr. *e-* + *rumpere* to break — more at RUPTURE] *vi* **1 a :** to force out or release suddenly and often violently something pent up (as lava or steam) ⟨a volcano may ~ explosively or quietly⟩ ⟨the man ~*ed* with anger⟩ **b** (1) **:** to burst from or as if from limits or restraint **:** emerge with a sudden often violent rush (as from a volcano or geyser) **:** BURST ⟨towering flames ~ from the oil tank⟩ ⟨steam ~*s* from the geyser⟩ **:** IRRUPT ⟨a new leader ~*s* upon the national scene⟩ ⟨shouting men ~*ed* into the square⟩ (2) *of a tooth* **:** to emerge through the gum **c :** to become active or violent **:** break forth **:** EXPLODE ⟨the village ~*s* into celebration⟩ ⟨the chorus ~*s* into song⟩ ⟨hostility ~*ed* into bloody clashes⟩ ⟨war ~*ed* between the two nations⟩ **2 a :** to break out with or as if with a skin eruption ⟨~*ed* with measles⟩ ⟨the literature of the day ~*ed* with essays on the general depravity of the jazz age —*Esquire's Jazz Bk.*⟩ **b :** to appear in numbers suddenly ⟨pimples ~ all over the skin⟩ **:** BURGEON ⟨the multiplicity of the schemes that seem to ~ all over the place —E.E.Schattschneider⟩ ~ *vt* **:** to force out or release (as something pent up) usu. suddenly and violently **:** cause to erupt **:** throw out **:** EXPEL, EJECT ⟨the volcano ~*ed* lava bombs⟩ ⟨the general ~*ed* orders —Frederic Sondern⟩ ⟨living populations will continue to ~ new biotypes —*American Naturalist*⟩ — **erupt·ible** \-təbəl\ *adj*

erupted *adj* **:** marked by an eruption of the skin or mucous membrane ⟨a badly ~ face⟩

erup·tion \əˈrəpshən, ēˈ-\ *n* -s [ME *erupcioun*, fr. L *eruption-, eruptio*, fr. *eruptus* + *-ion-, -io* -ion] **1 :** an act, process, or instance of erupting ⟨the volcano was in ~⟩ ⟨the ~ of the tooth from the gum⟩ **:** OUTBURST ⟨his loud angry ~*s*⟩ **:** OUTBREAK ⟨the ~ of hostilities⟩ ⟨the ~ of an epidemic⟩ **:** RASH ⟨an ~ of shopping centers has broken out on the countryside —Weare Holbrook⟩; *specif* **:** the breaking out of an exanthem or enanthem on the skin or mucous membrane (as in measles) **2 :** something produced by an act or process of erupting: as **a :** material erupted by a volcano **b :** the condition of the skin or mucous membrane caused by erupting **c :** one of the lesions (as a pustule) constituting this condition **3 :** IRRUPTION **d** — **erup·tion·al** \-shənᵊl, -shnəl\ *adj*

¹erup·tive \-ptiv, -tēv *also* -təv\ *adj* [*eruption* + *-ive*] **1 a :** erupting or tending to erupt **:** bursting forth **:** breaking out ⟨describes a geyser as an intermittently ~ hot spring⟩ ⟨the ~ imagery of the poem⟩ **:** having the character of an eruption ⟨a brawl was the first ~ result of the rising hostility⟩ **b :** characterized by eruption ⟨the ~ stage of smallpox⟩ ⟨~ letters full of outbursts of anger or joking⟩ **2 :** producing eruption ⟨an ~ fever⟩ **3 :** produced by eruption — usu. used of intrusive rocks (as granite, diorite, gabbro) or extrusive rocks (as rhyolite, andesite, basalt) — **erup·tive·ly** \-tə̇vlē, -li\ *adv* — **erup·tive·ness** \-tivnə̇s, -tēv- *also* -təv-\ *n* -ES

²eruptive \"\ *n* -s **:** an igneous rock

eruptive evolution *n* **:** the sudden appearance of varied new stocks from a common ancestral strain

erup·tiv·i·ty \əˌrəpˈtivəd.ē, (ˌ)ēˌr-\ *n* -ES **:** the state of being eruptive ⟨return of the geyser from a dormant phase to ~⟩

eruv *var of* ERUB

erven *pl of* ERF

er·vil \ˈərvəl\ *n* -s [L *ervilia*; akin to L *ervum* bitter vetch — more at ERS] **:** ERS

er·win·ia \ˌərˈwinēə\ *n, cap* [NL, fr. *Erwin* F. Smith †1927 Am. bacteriologist + NL *-ia*] **:** a genus of motile bacteria (family Enterobacteriaceae) that comprises numerous pathogens of plants including forms that cause dry necrosis, galls, wilts, and soft rots

-ery \(ə)rē, (ə)ri\ *n suffix* -ES [ME *-erie*, fr. OF, fr. *-ier* -er + *-ie* -y] **1 :** qualities collectively **:** character **:** -NESS ⟨tomfool*ery*⟩ ⟨snobb*ery*⟩ **2 :** art, practice, trade ⟨mountebank*ery*⟩ — compare -RY **3 :** place of doing, keeping, growing, breeding, selling (the thing specified) ⟨pigg*ery*⟩ ⟨rook*ery*⟩ ⟨fish*ery*⟩ ⟨bind*ery*⟩ ⟨bak*ery*⟩ **4 :** collection **:** aggregate ⟨fin*ery*⟩ ⟨green*ery*⟩ — compare -RY **5 :** state **:** condition ⟨slav*ery*⟩ ⟨monk*ery*⟩ — compare -RY

eryn·gi·um \əˈrinjēəm\ *n* [NL, fr. L *eryngion* eryngo, fr. Gk *ēryngion*, dim. of *ēryngos*] **1** *cap* **:** a genus of coarse bristly herbs (family Umbelliferae) having elongate spinulose-margined leaves and flowers in dense bracted heads — see BUTTON SNAKEROOT, SEA HOLLY **2** -s **:** ERYNGO 2

eryn·go \əˈriŋ(ˌ)gō\ *n* -s [modif. of L *eryngion*] **1 :** candied sea-holly root **2** [NL *Eryngium*] **:** a plant of the genus *Eryngium*; *esp* **:** SEA HOLLY 1

ery·on \ˈerēˌän\ *n, cap* [NL, fr. Gk *eryōn*, pres. part. of *eryein* to draw out, drag; fr. the large carapace] **:** a genus of fossil decapod crustaceans (suborder Reptantia) related to the spiny lobsters and found from the Lias to the Cretaceous esp. in lithographic limestones

ery·op·id \ˌerēˈäpəd\ *n* -s [NL *Eryop-, Eryops* + E *-id*] **:** an amphibian of *Eryops* or a related genus

ery·ops \ˈerēˌäps\ *n, cap* [NL, fr. Gk *eryein* + NL *-ops*] **:** a genus of large Lower Permian labyrinthodont amphibians (order Rhachitomi) known from Texas and New Mexico

erys·i·mum \əˈrisəməm\ *n, cap* [NL, fr. Gk *erysimon*, a kind of mustard, fr. *erysthai* to defend, protect, save; fr. its use as a medicinal herb] **:** a small genus of Old World herbs (family Cruciferae) including several weeds and having alternate leaves, small yellow flowers, and slender terete pods — see WALLFLOWER, WORMSEED MUSTARD

er·y·sip·e·las \ˌerəˈsip(ə)ləs, ˌir-\ *n* -ES [ME *herisipila, erisipila*, fr. L *erysipelas*, fr. Gk, fr. *erysi-* red (akin to *erythros*) + *-pelas* skin (akin to L *pellis*) — more at RED, FELL (hide)] **1 :** an acute febrile disease that is associated with intense often vesicular and edematous local inflammation of the skin and subcutaneous tissues and that is caused by a hemolytic streptococcus — called also *St. Anthony's fire* **2 :** SWINE ERYSIPELAS — used esp. when the disease affects other hosts than swine

er·y·si·pel·a·tous \ˌ==sə̇ˈpeləd.əs\ *adj* [L *erysipelat-, erysipelas* + E *-ous*] **1 :** of or relating to erysipelas **2 :** ERYSIPELOID

¹er·y·sip·e·loid \ˌ==ˈsipəˌlȯid\ *n* -s [ISV *erysipelas* + *-oid*] **:** a localized nonfebrile dermatitis resembling erysipelas, caused by the parasite of swine erysipelas, and occurring esp. about the hands of persons exposed to this organism (as by handling contaminated flesh) — see ERYSIPELOTHRIX

²erysipeloid \ˈ==ˈ==ˌ=\ *adj* **:** resembling erysipelas

er·y·sip·e·lo·thrix \ˌ==ˈsipəlōˌthriks\ *n* [NL, fr. *erysipelas* + *-o-* + *-thrix*] **1** *cap* **:** a genus of microaerophilic, gram-positive, rod-shaped bacteria (family Corynebacteriaceae) forming no spores, tending to produce long filaments, and being usu. considered to include a single form (*E. rhusiopathia*) widespread in nature where nitrogenous matter is disintegrating and the causative agent of swine erysipelas, an arthritis of lambs, and erysipeloid of man **2** -ES **:** a bacterium of the genus *Erysipelothrix*

er·y·si·pha·ce·ae \ˌerəsəˈfāsēˌē\ *n pl, cap* [NL, fr. *Erysiphe*, type genus + *-aceae*] **:** a family of fungi (order Erysiphales) comprising the powdery mildews, being parasitic mostly on leaves, and having delicate hyaline superficial mycelium and perithecia with one to several asci and distinctive appendages — **er·y·si·pha·ceous** \ˈ===ˈfāshəs\ *adj*

er·y·si·pha·les \ˌ===ˈfā(ˌ)lēz\ *n pl, cap* [NL, fr. *Erysiphe* + *-ales*] **:** an order of saprophytic and parasitic ascomycetous fungi (subclass Euascomycetes) that live on plants, have both vegetative and reproductive structures superficial on the host, and include the powdery mildews, many sooty molds, and a few other epiphytic fungi — see ERYSIPHACEAE

er·y·si·phe \ˌerəˈsī(ˌ)fē\ *n, cap* [NL, fr. Gk *erysi-* red + *siphōn* tube — more at ERYSIPELAS, SIPHON] **:** a genus of powdery mildews (family Erysiphaceae) having perithecia with several asci and with usu. unbranched appendages resembling hyphae

er·y·thea \-ˈthēə\ *n* [NL, fr. Gk *Erytheia*, one of the Hesperides] **1** *cap* **:** a genus of Californian and Mexican slender fan palms with smooth trunks and large orbicular leaves whose lobes bear white filaments **2** -s **:** any palm of the genus *Erythea*

er·y·the·ma \-ˈthēmə\ *n* -s [NL, fr. Gk *erythēma*, fr. *erythainein* to redden, fr. *erythros* red — more at RED] **:** abnormal redness of the skin due to capillary congestion (as in inflammation)

er·y·the·mal \ˈ==ˈ=məl\ *adj* [NL *erythema* + E *-al*] **:** relating to or producing erythema ⟨~ radiation⟩

erythema mul·ti·for·me \-ˌməltəˈfȯr(ˌ)mē\ *n* [NL, lit., multiform erythema] **:** a skin disease characterized by papular or vesicular lesions and reddening or discoloration of the skin often in concentric zones about the lesions

erythema no·do·sum \-nōˈdōsəm\ *n* [NL, lit., knotty erythema] **:** a skin condition characterized by small tender reddened nodules under the skin (as over the shin bones) often accompanied by fever and transitory arthritic pains and commonly considered a manifestation of hypersensitivity

erythema so·la·re \-sōˈla(a)(ˌ)rē\ *n* [NL, lit., solar erythema] **:** erythema due to excessive exposure of the skin to ultraviolet rays — compare SUNBURN

er·y·the·ma·to·gen·ic \ˌerəˈthēməd.əˈjenik, -them-\ *adj* [NL *erythemat-, erythema* + E *-o-* + *-genic*] **:** producing erythema

er·y·them·a·tous \ˌerəˈthemad.əs, -thēm-\ *also* **er·y·the·mic** \ˌerəˈthēmik\ *or* **er·y·the·mat·ic** \ˌerəthəˈmad.ik\ *adj* [NL *erythemat-, erythema* + E *-ous* or *-ic*] **:** relating to or marked by erythema

erythr- *or* **erythro-** *comb form* [Gk *erythr-, erythro-*, fr. *erythros* — more at RED] **1 :** red ⟨*erythr*ism⟩ ⟨*erythro*phyll⟩ **2 :** related to erythrose ⟨*erythr*onic acid⟩ **3** *erythro-, usu ital* **:** having the same stereochemical arrangement of atoms or groups about two asymmetric carbon atoms as that in erythrose ⟨DL-*erythro*-3-amino-2-butanol⟩ **4 :** erythrocyte ⟨*erythremia*⟩ ⟨*erythro*poiesis⟩

¹er·y·thrae·an \ˌerəˈthrēən\ *adj, usu cap* [*Erythrae*, ancient city of Asia Minor (fr. Gk *Erythrai*) + E *-an*] **:** of or relating to Erythrae, an ancient Ionian city of Asia Minor that claimed to have been the residence of the sibyl Herophile

²erythraean *or* **erythrean** \"\ *adj* [L *Erythraeus* (fr. Gk *Erythraios*, lit., red, fr. *erythros*) + E *-an*] **:** of or relating to the sea that in ancient geography comprised the Arabian sea, the Red sea, and the Persian gulf

er·y·thrae·idae \ˌerəˈthrēəˌdē\ *n pl, cap* [NL, fr. *Erythraea*, type genus (fr. Gk *erythraia*, fem. of *erythraios*) + *-idae*] **:** a family of Acarina including active hairy usu. reddish mites of predatory habits having the larvae parasitic on insects or on other arachnids

er·y·thras·ma \-ˈthrazmə\ *n* -s [NL, fr. *erythr-* + Gk *-asma* (n. ending)] **:** a chronic contagious dermatitis caused by an actinomycete (*Nocardia minutissima*) and affecting esp. warm moist areas (as the axilla and groin)

eryth·re·de·ma \ə̇ˌrithrəˈdēmə\ *n* [NL, fr. *erythr-* + *edema*] **:** ACRODYNIA

er·y·thre·mia *also* **er·y·thrae·mia** \ˌerəˈthrēmēə\ *n* -s [NL, fr. *erythr-* + *-emia, -aemia*] **:** POLYCYTHEMIA 2

er·y·thri·na \-ˈthrīnə -rēnə\ *n* [NL, fr. *erythr-* + *-ina*] **1** *cap* **:** a genus of tropical shrubs or trees (family Leguminosae) often cultivated and having trifoliolate leaves and chiefly reddish flowers in terminal racemes — see CORAL TREE, KAFFIR BOOM **2** -s **:** any plant of the genus *Erythrina*

er·y·thrine \ˈerəˌthrēn, ə̇ˈriˌth-, -ˌthrən\ *n* -s [F, fr. *erythr-* + *-ine*] **:** ERYTHRITE 1

er·y·thrin·i·dae \ˌerəˈthrinəˌdē\ *n pl, cap* [NL, fr. *Erythrinus*, type genus (fr. Gk *erythrinos*, a kind of fish, fr. *erythr-* + *-inos* -ine) + *-idae*] **:** a family of carnivorous So. American river fishes that resemble the pikes but are related to and often included in the family Characidae

er·y·thrism \ˈerəˌthrizəm, ə̇ˈriˌth-\ *n* -s [ISV *erythr-* + *-ism*] **:** a condition characterized by the exceptional prevalence of red pigmentation (as in skin, hair, or plumage) — **er·y·thris·mal** \ˌerəˈthrizməl\ *adj*

er·y·thris·tic \ˌerəˈthristik\ *adj* **:** of, relating to, or characterized by erythrism

er·y·thrite \ˈerəˌthrīt, ə̇ˈriˌth-\ *n* -s [*erythr-* + *-ite*] **1 :** ERYTHRITOL **2 :** a mineral $Co_3(AsO_4)_2.8H_2O$ consisting of a hydrous cobalt arsenate, occurring in monoclinic crystals isomorphous with annabergite and also in globular and reniform masses and in earthy form, and being usu. rose red

eryth·ri·tol \ə̇ˈrithrəˌtȯl, -ōl\ *n* -s [ISV *erythr-* + *-itol*] **:** a sweet crystalline tetrahydroxy alcohol $HOCH_2(CHOH)_2CH_2OH$ obtained as the optically inactive meso form from lichens, algae, and yeasts or made by reduction of erythrose and used chiefly in the form of its tetranitrate as a vasodilator

erythro- — see ERYTHR-

eryth·ro·blast \ə̇ˈrithrəˌblast\ *n* -s [ISV *erythr-* + *-blast*] **1 :** a polychromatic nucleated cell occurring in red marrow as the first specifically identifiable stage in red blood-cell formation and intermediate in characteristics between hemocytoblast and normoblast **2 :** any of various cells ancestral to red blood cells

eryth·ro·blas·te·mia \=ˌ==ˌblaˈstēmēə\ *n* -s [NL, fr. ISV *erythroblast* + NL *-emia*] **:** the presence of an abnormal number of erythroblasts in the blood

eryth·ro·blas·tic \ə̇ˈ==ˈblastik\ *adj* **:** of, relating to, or characterized by the presence of erythroblasts

eryth·ro·blas·to·sis \=ˌ==ˌblaˈstōsə̇s\ *n, pl* **erythroblastoses** \-ōˌsēz\ [NL, fr. ISV *erythroblast* + NL *-osis*] **:** the abnormal presence of erythroblasts in the circulating blood; *specif* **:** a hemolytic disease of the fetus and newborn that is characterized by destruction of circulating erythrocytes, increase in circulating erythroblasts, and jaundice and that is usu. associated with Rh-factor incompatibility

erythroblastosis fe·ta·lis \-fēˈtaləs\ *n* [NL] **:** erythroblastosis of the fetus

erythroblastosis ne·o·na·to·rum \-ˌnēənəˈtōrəm\ *n* [NL] **:** erythroblastosis of the newborn infant

eryth·ro·blas·tot·ic \ə̇ˌrithrəˌblaˈstäd.ik\ *adj* [fr. NL *erythroblastosis*, after such pairs as NL *hypnosis*: E *hypnotic*] **:** of, relating to, or affected by erythroblastosis ⟨an ~ infant⟩

eryth·ro·ce·bus \ə̇ˈrithrə+\ *n, cap* [NL, fr. *erythr-* + *Cebus*] **:** a genus of reddish African monkeys including the patas

eryth·ro·cru·orin \"+\ *n* [*erythr-* + *cruorin* (old name for hemoglobin)] **:** any of various red respiratory pigments that occur in blood, cells, or body fluids of several invertebrate animals and that are or are related to hemoglobins

eryth·ro·cyte \ə̇ˈrithrəˌsīt\ *n* -s [ISV *erythr-* + *-cyte*] **1 :** a vertebrate blood cell containing hemoglobin and subserving the internal transport of oxygen, in mammals being an enucleated biconcave disk present in numbers up to several millions in each cubic millimeter of blood that are the remains of nucleated cells produced chiefly in red bone marrow — compare LEUKOCYTE **2 :** a cell containing a respiratory pigment (as in some marine worms) — **eryth·ro·cyt·ic** \ə̇ˈ==ˈsid.ik\ *adj*

erythrocyte-maturing factor *n* **:** VITAMIN B_{12}

eryth·ro·cy·the·mia \ə̇ˌrithrəˌsīˈthēmēə\ *n* -s [NL, irreg. fr. ISV *erythrocyte* + NL *-emia*] **:** POLYCYTHEMIA 2

eryth·ro·cy·to·gen·e·sis \=ˌ==ˌsīd.əˈjenəsə̇s\ *n* [NL, fr. ISV *erythrocyte* + NL *-o-* + *-genesis*] **:** ERYTHROPOIESIS

eryth·ro·cy·tom·e·ter \=ˌ==ˌsīˈtämәd.ə(r)\ *n* [*erythrocyte* + *-o-* + *-meter*] **1 :** HEMACYTOMETER **2 :** a device for measuring the diameter of red blood cells

eryth·ro·cy·to·poi·e·sis \=ˌ==ˌsīd.əˌpȯiˈēsə̇s\ *n, pl* **erythrocytopoieses** \-ēˌsēz\ [NL, fr. ISV *erythrocyte* + NL *-o-* + *-poiesis*] **:** ERYTHROPOIESIS

eryth·ro·cy·to·sis \=ˌ==ˌsīd.ˈōsə̇s\ *n, pl* **erythrocytoses** \-ōˌsēz\ [NL, fr. ISV *erythrocyte* + NL *-osis*] **:** POLYCYTHEMIA 1

eryth·ro·der·ma \-ˈdərmə\ *n, pl* **erythrodermas** \-məz\ *or* **erythroderma·ta** \-məd.ə\ [NL, fr. *erythr-* + *-derma*] **:** ERYTHEMA

eryth·ro·der·mia \-mēə\ *n* -s [NL, fr. *erythr-* + *-dermia*] **:** ERYTHEMA

eryth·ro·dextrin *also* **eryth·ro·dextrine** \ə̇ˈrithrō+\ *n* [ISV *erythr-* + *dextrin, dextrine*] **:** a dextrin that gives a red color with iodine

eryth·ro·gen·e·sis \ə̇ˌrithrəˈjenəsə̇s\ *n* [NL, fr. *erythr-* + *-genesis*] **:** ERYTHROPOIESIS

eryth·ro·gen·ic \=ˈ==ˈjenik\ *adj* [*erythr-* + *-genic*] **1 :** producing a color sensation of redness **2 :** ERYTHROPOIETIC **3 :** inducing reddening of the skin ⟨~ toxins⟩

eryth·ro·gone \=ˈ==ˌgōn\ *also* **eryth·ro·go·ni·um** \=ˌ== ˈgōnēəm\ *n* -s [NL *erythrogonium*, fr. *erythr-* + *gonium*] **:** PROMEGALOBLAST

er·y·throid \ˈerəˌthrȯid, ə̇ˈriˌth-\ *adj* [*erythr-* + *-oid*] **:** relating to erythrocytes or their precursors — compare MYELOID

er·y·thro·i·dine \ˌerəˈthrōəˌdēn, -ōəd-ᵊn\ *n* -s [*erythr-* + *-idine*] **:** a crystalline alkaloid $C_{16}H_{19}NO_3$ obtained from plants of the genus *Erythrina* as a mixture of stereoisomers; *esp* **:** beta-erythroidine possessing curariform activity and also acting as a depressant of the central nervous system

er·y·throl \ˈerəˌthrōl, ə̇ˈriˌth-, -ōl\ *n* -s [ISV *erythr-* + *-ol*] **1 :** a liquid unsaturated dihydroxy alcohol $CH_2{=}CHCHOHCH_2OH$ formed by decomposition of erythritol **2 :** ERYTHRITOL — used esp. in pharmacy ⟨~ tetranitrate⟩

eryth·ro·leucosis *or* **eryth·ro·leukosis** \ə̇ˈrithrō+\ *n* [NL, fr. *erythr-* + *leucosis, leukosis*] **:** LEUKOSIS 2

eryth·ro·melalgia \"+\ *n* [NL, fr. *erythr-* + *melalgia*] **:** a state of excessive dilation of the superficial blood vessels of the feet or more rarely the hands accompanied by hyperemia, increased skin temperature, and burning pain

eryth·ro·my·cin \ə̇ˌrithrəˈmīsᵊn\ *n* -s [*erythr-* + *-mycin*] **:** a crystalline weakly basic antibiotic that is produced by an actinomycete (*Streptomyces erythreus*), is similar to penicillin in antibacterial activity, and is also effective in the treatment of amebiasis

er·y·thron \ˈerəˌthrän, ə̇ˈriˌth-\ *n* -s [NL, fr. Gk, neut. of *erythros* red — more at RED] **:** a body organ consisting of the red blood cells and their precursors in the bone marrow — compare LEUKON

eryth·ro·neu·ra \ə̇ˌrithrəˈn(y)u̇rə\ *n, cap* [NL, fr. *erythr-* + *-neura*] **:** a widely distributed genus of leafhoppers containing some that have been implicated in the transmission of virus diseases of cultivated plants — see GRAPE LEAFHOPPER

er·y·thro·ni·um \ˌerəˈthrōnēəm\ *n* [NL, fr. Gk *erythronion*, a kind of plant, fr. *erythros* red — more at RED] **1** *cap* **:** a small genus of chiefly No. American herbs (family Liliaceae) having a corm from which arise a pair of usu. mottled basal leaves and one or more scapose flowers **2** -s **:** any plant of the genus *Erythronium*

eryth·ro·phage \ə̇ˈrithrəˌfāj\ *n* -s [ISV *erythr-* + *-phage*] **:** a phagocyte that ingests red blood cells of the same body

eryth·ro·pha·gia \ˌ==ˈfāj(ē)ə\ *n* -s [NL, fr. *erythr-* + *-phagia*] **:** ERYTHROPHAGOCYTOSIS

eryth·ro·phagocytosis \ə̇ˈrithrə+\ *n* [NL, fr. *erythr-* + *phagocytosis*] **:** consumption of red blood cells by histiocytes and sometimes other phagocytes of the same body

er·y·throph·i·lous \ˌerəˈthräfələs\ *also* **eryth·ro·phile** \ə̇ˈrithrəˌfīl\ *adj* [ISV *erythr-* + *-philous, -phile*] *of a tissue or cell* **:** having especial affinity for red coloring matter

eryth·ro·phle·ine \ə̇ˌrithrəˈflēən, -lēˌēn\ *n* -s [ISV *erythr-* + Gk *phloios* bark + ISV *-ine*] **:** a white crystalline very poisonous alkaloid $C_{24}H_{39}NO_5$ extracted from sassy bark and other plants of the genus *Erythrophloeum*

eryth·ro·pho·bia \-ˈfōbēə\ *n* -s [NL, fr. *erythr-* + *-phobia*] **1 :** morbid avoidance of the color red **2 :** fear of blushing

eryth·ro·phore \=ˈ==ˌfō(ə)r\ *n* -s [*erythr-* + *-phore*] **:** a chromatophore containing a red usu. carotenoid pigment that occurs esp. in some fishes and crustaceans

er·y·thro·pia \ˌerəˈthrōpēə\ *or* **er·y·throp·sia** \-ˈthräpsēə\ *n* -s [NL, fr. *erythr-* + *-opia, -opsia*] **:** a visual disturbance in which all objects appear reddish

eryth·ro·pla·sia \ə̇ˌrithrəˈplāzh(ē)ə\ *n* -s [NL, fr. *erythr-* + *-plasia*] **:** a reddened patch with a velvety surface on the oral or genital mucosa that is considered to be a precancerous lesion

eryth·ro·plastid \ə'rithrə+\ *n* [*erythr-* + *-plastid*] **:** a mammalian red blood cell characterized by absence of the nucleus

eryth·ro·poi·e·sis \ə,rithrə,pȯi'ēsə̇s\ *n* -ES [NL, fr. *erythr-* + *-poiesis*] **:** the production of red blood cells (as from the bone marrow)

eryth·ro·poi·et·ic \ə¦==,=¦ed·ik\ *adj* [*erythr-* + *-poietic*] **:** producing red blood cells

er·y·throp·ter·in \,erə'thräptərə̇n\ *n* -s [*erythr-* + *pterin*] **:** an orange-red pigment $C_9H_9N_5O_5$ found esp. in pierid butterflies

eryth·ro·scope \ə'rithrə,skōp\ *n* [ISV *erythr-* + *-scope;* orig. formed as G *erythroskop*] **:** a device consisting of overlapping yellow and blue glasses through which some shades of green appear red

er·y·throse \'erə,thrōs, ə'ri,th- *also* -ōz\ *n* -s [F *érythrose,* fr. *érythr-* erythr- + *-ose*] **:** a syrupy aldose sugar $HOCH_2(CHOH)_2CHO$ that is the epimer of threose and is obtained by degradation of arabinose

eryth·ro·siderite \ə'rithrə+\ *n* [ISV *erythr-* + *siderite;* orig. formed as It *eritrosiderо*] **:** a mineral $K_2FeCl_5.H_2O$ consisting of hydrous potassium iron chloride and occurring in lavas

eryth·ro·sin *also* **eryth·ro·sine** \ə'rithrəsə̇n, -,sēn\ *n* -s [ISV *erythr-* + *eosin, eosine*] **:** any of several xanthene dyes that are made by iodination of fluorescein and that dye wool, cotton, and silk in reddish shades: as **a :** a brick-red powder $C_{20}H_6I_4Na_2O_5$ that is used esp. in making organic pigments, in coloring foods, as a biological stain, and as a green photographic sensitizer; the sodium salt of tetraiodo-fluorescein — called also *erythrosine bluish;* see DYE table I (under *Acid Red 51*) **b :** a yellowish brown powder $C_{20}H_8I_2Na_2O_5$ used esp. in coloring solutions of drugs and as a biological stain; the sodium salt of diiodo-fluorescein — called also *erythrosine yellowish;* see DYE table I (under *Acid Red 95, Solvent Red 73*)

er·y·thro·sis \,erə'thrōsə̇s\ *n, pl* **erythro·ses** \-ō,sēz\ [NL, fr. *erythr-* + *-osis*] **1 :** a red or purplish color of the skin (as of the face) resulting from vascular congestion (as in polycythemia) **:** PLETHORA **2 :** a hyperplastic condition of tissues that form red blood cells

er·y·throx·y·la·ce·ae \,erə,thräksə'lāsē,ē\ *n pl, cap* [NL, fr. *Erythroxylon,* type genus + *-aceae*] **:** a family of plants (order Geraniales) having monadelphous stamens, a bifid ligulate appendage or callosity on the inner face of each petal, and drupaceous fruit

er·y·throx·y·lon \,=='==,län, -lən\ *n, cap* [NL, fr. *erythr-* + *-xylon*] **:** a large genus of chiefly So. American shrubs and small trees (family Erythroxylaceae) with small white or greenish pentamerous flowers — see COCA

er·y·throx·y·lum \-ləm\ [NL, fr. *erythr-* + *-xylum*] *syn of* ERYTHROXYLON

eryth·ro·zincite \ə'rithrə+\ *n* [ISV *erythr-* + *zincite;* orig. formed as F *érythrozincite*] **:** a manganiferous variety of wurtzite

eryth·ru·lose \ə'rithrə,lōs *also* -ōz\ *n* -s [ISV *erythr-* + *-ule* + *-ose*] **:** a syrupy ketose sugar $HOCH_2CHOHCOCH_2OH$ obtained by bacterial oxidation of erythritol

er·yx \'eriks, 'ir-\ *n, cap* [NL, fr. *Eryx,* a mountain in Sicily, fr. L, fr. Gk] **:** a genus comprising the typical sand snakes — see SAND BOA

er·zah·ler \ert'sālər\ *n* -s [prob. fr. G *erzähler,* lit., narrator, fr. *erzählen* to narrate + *-er*] **:** a gemshorn organ pipe

es *var of* ESS

¹-es *after letters or letter groups whose pronunc is* s, z, sh, *or* ch: ə̇z, *sometimes* ÷,ēz *in some words in which an unstressed syllable precedes, as* "processes"; *after letters whose pronunc is* ē, i, *or* v: z\ *n pl suffix* [ME *-es, -s* — more at ¹-s] **1** — used to form the plural of most nouns that end in *s* ⟨glasses⟩, *z* ⟨fuzzes⟩, *sh* ⟨bushes⟩, *ch* ⟨peaches⟩, or postconsonantal *y* (which changes to *i*) ⟨ladies⟩ and of some nouns ending in *f* (which changes to *v*) ⟨loaves⟩ — compare ¹-s 1 **2 :** ¹-s 2 ⟨Christmases we usually go to grandmother's⟩

²-es *after letters or letter groups whose pronunc is* s, z, sh, *or* ch: ə̇z; *after i:* z\ *vb suffix* [ME (Northern & North Midland) — more at ³-s] **1** — used to form the third person singular present indicative of most verbs that end in *s* ⟨blesses⟩, *z* ⟨fizzes⟩, *sh* ⟨hushes⟩, *ch* ⟨catches⟩, or postconsonantal *y* (which changes to *i*) ⟨defies⟩ — compare ³-s 1 **2** *substand* **:** ³-s 2 ⟨then I rushes over to him⟩

ES *abbr* **1** eldest son **2** electrostatic **3** engine-sized **4** executive secretary **5** extra series

Es *symbol* einsteinium

e's *or* **es** *pl of* E

-es' \(ə̇)z\ *n pl suffix* [ME *-es,* fr. *-e,* older gen. pl. ending (fr. OE *-a*) + *-s,* gen. sing. ending — more at -'s] — used to form the plural possessive of most nouns that end in *s, z, sh, ch,* or postconsonantal *y* and of some nouns ending in *f*

esau \'ē,sȯ\ *n* -s *cap* [after *Esau,* son of Isaac and Rebekah and twin brother of Jacob, to whom he sold his birthright (Gen 25, 27)] **:** one that sacrifices a permanent interest for a more immediate but temporary interest; *also* **:** one that may easily be taken advantage of

esc *abbr* **1** escape **2** escudo **3** escutcheon

es·ca \'eskə\ *n* -s [NL, fr. NGk *ischa*] **:** BLACK MEASLES 2

es·ca·drille \'eskə,dril, -drē(y) *also* ,=='=\ *n* -s [F, flotilla, escadrille, modif. (influenced by F *escadre* squadron) of Sp *escuadrilla,* dim. of *escuadra* squadron, squad — more at SQUAD] **:** a unit of a European esp. French air command usu. six airplanes

¹es·ca·lade \'eskə,lād, -läd, ,=='=\ *n* -s [F, fr. It *scalata,* fr. fem. of *scalato,* past part. of *scalare* to scale, fr. *scala* ladder, fr. LL — more at SCALE (ladder)] **:** the act of scaling

²escalade \"\ *vt* -ED/-ING/-s **:** to climb up or over ⟨forcing them to ~ horrible precipices at midnight on horseback —Norman Douglas⟩ ⟨the storms of rain passed . . . *escalading* the farther bluff —Christina Stead⟩ — **es·ca·lad·er** \-də(r)\ *n* -s

es·ca·la·do \,eskə'lä(,)dō, -lā(-\ *n* -s [modif. of Sp *escalada,* fr. fem. of *escalado,* past part. of *escalar* to scale, fr. *escala* ladder, fr. LL *scala* — more at SCALE (ladder)] *archaic* **:** ESCALADE

es·ca·late \'eskə,lāt\ *vb* -ED/-ING/-s [back-formation fr. *escalator*] **:** to ascend or carry up on or as if on a moving staircase or conveyor belt

es·ca·la·tion \,eskə'lāshən\ *n* -s [*escalator* + *-ion*] **:** an increase (as in the price of an article or in a ship's tonnage) that counteracts an unjust discrepancy (as between the price of a product and the cost of material or between the tonnage of one nation's ships and that of another when both are regulated by the same treaty); *specif* **:** the adjustment of prices proportionally and usu. periodically and automatically to an alteration (as a rise) in the cost of materials or a similar adjustment of wages to an alteration in the cost of living

¹es·ca·la·tor \'eskə,lād·ə(r), -ātə-, *chiefly in substand speech* -kyə-\ *n* -s [fr. *Escalator,* a trademark] **1 :** MOVING STAIRCASE **2 :** a course, means, or agency that carries upward or downward esp. through a series of stages and usu. effortlessly ⟨promised them a place on a never-stopping ~ of economic progress —D.W.Brogan⟩ ⟨rode the ~ right behind him—first to the governorship of his native Veracruz, then to the Ministry of Interior —*Time*⟩ ⟨man had at last found an ~ to heaven . . . had put his foot on the first tread, and time would take care of the rest —*Social Welfare Forum*⟩ **3 :** an escalator clause or provision ⟨many American workers won wage advances, cost-of-living wage ~*s,* various fringe benefits, and strengthening of union security through collective bargaining —*Americana Annual*⟩ ⟨enough to tilt the index into a high bracket and give a million auto-industry workers a cent-an-hour pay increase under the terms of their ~ —J.A.Loftus⟩

²escalator \"\ *adj* **1 :** providing for escalation — used esp. of labor contracts or provisions contained in them ⟨steelworkers whose ~ contracts adjust wages to the government's consumer price index —*Newsweek*⟩ ⟨the introduction of an ~ arrangement tying the base pay of servicemen to living costs and adjustable at one to two-year intervals —*N.Y.Times*⟩ **2 :** providing for periodic and automatic proportionate adjustment similar to escalation ⟨nations seeking loans have asked for ~ clauses which would enlarge the amount of the loan as prices go up —*Newsweek*⟩ ⟨an ~ plan for state colleges under which one grade will be desegregated each year —Eric Sevareid⟩

es·cal·lo·nia \,eskə'lōnēə\ *n* [NL, fr. *Escallon,* 18th cent. Span. traveler in So. Amer. + NL *-ia*] **1** *cap* **:** a genus that is included among the Saxifragaceae or sometimes made type of the separate family Escalloniaceae and that comprises So. American shrubs and trees with simple glossy leaves having gland-tipped teeth, flowers mostly in terminal racemes, and capsular fruits **2** -s **:** any plant of the genus *Escallonia*

es·cal·lo·ni·a·ce·ae \,eskə,lōnē'āsē,ē\ *n pl, cap* [NL, fr. *Escallonia,* type genus + *-aceae*] *in some classifications* **:** a family of shrubs and mostly small trees (order Rosales) that are widely distributed esp. in the southern hemisphere — see ESCALLONIA — **es·cal·lo·ni·a·ceous** \¦==,==¦āshəs\ *adj*

¹es·cal·lop \ə'skäləp, e'-, -kal-\ *var of* SCALLOP

²escallop \"\ *or* **escallop shell** *n* -s [ME, fr. MF *escalope* shell — more at SCALLOP] **:** a decoration in the form of a scallop shell; *specif* **:** a scallop-shell device in heraldry usu. borne as a charge with the fluted edge downward and the convex side toward the viewer

escallop

es·cal·lo·pi·ne \ə,skälə'pēnē, (,)e,s-\ *n* -s [by alter.] **:** SCALLOPINI

es·ca·lope *also* **es·col·lope** \¦eskə¦lōp\ *n* -s [F *escalope,* fr. MF, shell] **:** SCALLOPINI

es·cam·bio \ə'skambē,ō, e'-\ *n* -s [ML, abl. of *escambium, excambium* exchange, fr. *excambiare* to exchange — more at EXCHANGE] **:** a license formerly required in English law for drawing a bill of exchange on a person overseas

es·cam·bron \¦e,skäm¦brōn\ *n* -s [AmerSp *escambrón,* fr. obs. Sp, hawthorn, buckthorn, perh. modif. of L *crabron-, crabro* hornet — more at HORNET] **:** any of several tropical American thorny shrubs or trees: as **a :** COCKSPUR 2b **b** *Puerto Rico* **:** a shrubby vine (*Drepanocarpus lunatus*) of the family Leguminosae with hooked prickles and showy purple flowers **c :** CAT'S-CLAW

es·ca·mo·tage \eskämȯtäazh\ *n* -s [F, fr. *escamoter* to juggle, conjure, make vanish (fr. MF) + *-age*] **:** JUGGLING, SLEIGHT OF HAND, TRICKERY

es·cap·able \ə'skāpəbəl, e'-\ *adj* **:** capable of being escaped **:** AVOIDABLE

es·ca·pade \'eskə,pād, ,=='=\ *n* -s [F, fr. MF, fr. OIt *scappata,* fr. fem. of *scappato,* past part. of *scappare* to escape, fr. (assumed) VL *excappare*] **1** *archaic* **:** escape from, evasion of, or flight from control or confinement **2 :** an adventure or experience involving action that runs counter to set rules of conservative behavior or approved or orthodox conduct **:** a piece of mischief **:** a daring act or unusual experience ⟨childish ~*s* on Halloween⟩ ⟨the ~*s* of the hero in the wilds of Tibet⟩ ⟨he . . . crossed to Greece, where he was initiated into the Eleusinian mysteries, an odd ~ for one of his character —John Buchan⟩

¹es·cape \ə'skāp, e'-\ *vb* -ED/-ING/-s [ME *escapen, ascapen,* fr. ONF *escaper, ascaper,* fr. (assumed) VL *excappare,* fr. L *ex-* + LL *cappa* head covering, cloak — more at CAP] *vi* **1 a :** to get away (as by flight or conscious effort) **:** break away, get free, or get clear ⟨the prisoner *escaped* from prison⟩ ⟨~ from boredom by traveling extensively⟩ ⟨eager to ~ from the army and go back to his home town —Dixon Wecter⟩ ⟨the peculiar merit of this book is that it ~*s* from the conventional attitudes towards the conquest of Mexico —*Times Lit. Supp.*⟩ **b :** to issue from confinement or an enclosure esp. by way of a break (as in a waterpipe) ⟨gas *escaping* from a main⟩ ⟨clamp lips firmly so that no air can ~ —Raymond Zauber⟩ ⟨as the fluid runs through the tile lines, it gradually ~*s* through the open joints —J.R.Dalzell⟩ ⟨her hat was jammed onto the back of her head, her hair *escaping* beneath the crumpled brim —William Faulkner⟩ ⟨the eggs develop in this pouch and the young ~ when they hatch —G.E. & Nettie MacGinitie⟩ **c** *of a plant* **:** to run wild from a condition of cultivation or from a cultivated area **2 :** to avoid or elude an evil that threatens **:** evade imminent pain or misfortune ⟨the infection was so widespread that few *escaped*⟩ ⟨the hunters were so thick any game that *escaped* was lucky⟩ ⟨the crew *escaped,* as usual, but the boat was shattered to pieces —Norman Douglas⟩ ⟨he *escaped* momentarily from the heavy humors which had occupied his mind —T.B.Costain⟩; *specif, of an amateur wrestler* **:** to maneuver from a defensive to a neutral position ~ *vt* **1** *obs* **:** to break away from **:** get free from **2 a :** to get or be out of the way of (something one wishes to avoid) **:** miss or succeed in averting (pain or misfortune) **:** AVOID, ELUDE, EVADE ⟨~ poverty and unhappiness⟩ ⟨the Greeks *escaped* the evils of priestly government —W.R. Inge⟩ ⟨firstborn babies characteristically ~ the disease —E.W. Page⟩ ⟨set sail hastily to ~ possible punishment for his share in the enterprise —*Amer. Guide Series: Maine*⟩ ⟨our family seems to have *escaped* television addiction —John McNulty⟩ ⟨the name of the man ~*s* me entirely⟩ **b :** to be unnoticed by or not obvious, apparent, or recallable to ⟨the more valuable articles *escaped* the eyes of the thieves⟩ ⟨the profounder subtleties of harmony and rhythm more often than not ~ me —Clive Bell⟩ ⟨a veracity that often ~*s* the authors of historical fiction —*Amer. Guide Series: Oregon*⟩ ⟨the myth is a transcendent idea that ~*s* the mental grasp entirely —H.M.Parshley⟩ **3 a :** to issue from ⟨a smile may ~ us in reading Honorius —H.O.Taylor⟩ **b :** to be uttered by (a person) involuntarily ⟨a muffled moan *escaped* the boy —F.V.W.Mason⟩

syn AVOID, EVADE, ELUDE, ESCHEW, SHUN: ESCAPE refers to a getting away from something viewed as dangerous, threatening, or otherwise to be feared or disliked, or, esp. in reference to inanimate or intangible things, to a preventing of being noted, held, confined, or arrested ⟨*escape* from pursuers⟩ ⟨a deer *escaping* from hunters⟩ ⟨*escape* from a prison⟩ ⟨a trap from which no rat can *escape*⟩ ⟨her *escaping* pneumonia by a miracle —Scott Fitzgerald⟩ ⟨that the workings of a parliamentary democracy are intricate and that their true nature sometimes *escapes* even those most practiced in them —*London Calling*⟩ AVOID may be a near synonym of ESCAPE but stresses forethought and caution; it may indicate a keeping well clear of rather than a getting away when exposed to danger ⟨Wang Lung *avoided* them lest some recognize him —Pearl Buck⟩ ⟨by pooling our difficulties, we may at least *avoid* the failures which come from conceiving the problems of government to be simpler than they are —Felix Frankfurter⟩ ⟨life is full of perils, but the wise man ignores those that are inevitable, and acts prudently but without emotion as regards those that can be *avoided* —Bertrand Russell⟩ EVADE suggests cleverness, adroitness, artifice, or occas. subterfuge in avoiding, escaping, or dodging ⟨the king was so far away that his rules might be in large degree *evaded* if not defied —C.L.Jones⟩ ⟨the experience of life shows that people are constantly doing things which must lead to disaster, and yet by some chance manage to *evade* the result of their folly —W.S.Maugham⟩ ELUDE applies to escaping or evading by baffling, shifty, sly, strategic, or abstruse procedure or character ⟨so some biologists, peering into their microscopes, observe remarkable events which somehow *elude* their colleagues —Martin Gardner⟩ ⟨the ruse to which Captain Lyon had resorted to *elude* the writ by transporting his prisoner to Illinois —Winston Churchill⟩ ESCHEW may indicate an avoiding or abstaining from as unwise or distasteful ⟨he says what he has to say in excellent prose, *eschewing* all highflown and arty dithyrambs —*N.Y. Herald Tribune Bk. Rev.*⟩ ⟨*eschewing* melodramatic shortcuts, in spite of the clamor from Rome, he broke the enemy by the only methods possible — starvation, attrition, and a slow, deadly scientific envelopment —John Buchan⟩ ⟨his fundamental respect for human personality makes him instinctively *eschew* the method of authority —M.R.Cohen⟩ SHUN indicates active or pronounced avoidance, usu. with abhorrence, aversion, or contemning as wrong or unwise ⟨a desolate wilderness of maquis, marsh, and coastal swamp, infested with malaria, and *shunned* by people —George Kish⟩ ⟨to *shun* for his health the pleasures of the table —A.T. Quiller-Couch⟩

syn FLY, FLEE, DECAMP, ABSCOND: ESCAPE is the most general in meaning to get out of confinement or to elude or avoid restraint, capture, or, in the verb's broadest application, anything considered dangerous or unpleasant ⟨*escaped* from jail⟩ ⟨*escaped* pursuit⟩ ⟨the first action of the war, in which the British ship . . . *escaped* by superior speed after a sharp fight —Edward Breck⟩ ⟨*escape* from his grief and loneliness —Allen Johnson⟩ ⟨*escape* embarrassment⟩ FLY, used in the sense of *escape* only in the present tense, adds to it the idea of haste, as of one in fear ⟨*fly,* father, *fly!* for all your friends are fled —Shak.⟩ ⟨so absolutely flooded by the Hawkesbury and its tributaries, that the farmers are forced to *fly* for their lives —Anthony Trollope⟩ FLEE implies haste and abruptness of escape, often suggesting not only fear but a certain consequent disorder in the departure ⟨make a boy believe that real work is a thing to *flee* from —C.E.Montague⟩ ⟨founded by men who were *fleeing* from something very like this tyranny —Hugh Gaitskell⟩ ⟨the Irish who *fled* in the famine years —Liam Brophy⟩ ⟨everyone *fled* in summer to escape the swarms of mosquitoes —*Amer. Guide Series: N.C.*⟩ DECAMP does not usu. suggest escape as much as mere, although total, removal from one place to another or complete purposeful departure, applying usu. only with a somewhat humorous connotation to the escape of one in confinement or one avoiding confinement or restraint ⟨other tradesmen came to town, took orders, received advances of goods or money, and then *decamped* —C.L.Jones⟩ ⟨the expectation of his *decamping* as fast as he could from such disgraceful companions —Jane Austen⟩ ⟨might play them false and *decamp* with the entire £100,000 —F.W.Crofts⟩ ABSCOND puts emphasis upon the idea of secrecy, esp. criminal secrecy, in an escape, withdrawal, or departure ⟨a promoter with a salted silver mine sold claims to hundreds, at from $50 to $1000 a claim, and *absconded* with the proceeds —*Amer. Guide Series: Texas*⟩ ⟨he *absconded* from college with his clothes and took refuge in a lonely farmhouse —Van Wyck Brooks⟩ ⟨*abscond* with the family silver⟩

²escape \"\ *n* -s [ME *escap, escape,* fr. *escapen,* v.] **1 :** the act of escaping or the fact of having escaped: as **a :** evasion of or deliverance from what confines, limits, or holds ⟨an ~ from a mental hospital⟩ ⟨~ from the earth's gravitational pull⟩ ⟨how to make ~ from his tight grasp⟩; *specif* **:** an unlawful departure of a prisoner from the limits of his custody esp. when without prison breach — see NEGLIGENT ESCAPE, VOLUNTARY ESCAPE; compare CONSTRUCTIVE ESCAPE **b :** evasion of or deliverance from what injures, threatens, torments, bores, or is otherwise undesirable ⟨find no method of ~ from pain and suffering⟩ ⟨a gradual ~ . . . from the hideous experiences and whirling ideas of his youth —*Times Lit. Supp.*⟩ ⟨the ~ from this legal confusion —H.O.Taylor⟩ ⟨these islands have symbolized ~ from a world that is too much with us —V.G.Heiser⟩ ⟨comedy is an ~ not from truth but from despair —Christopher Fry⟩ **c :** leakage or outflow esp. of steam or a liquid ⟨trying to stop an ~ of gas from a broken conduit⟩ **d :** distraction or relief from the routine or a burdensome aspect of everyday existence, usu. from its irksome responsibilities or its harsher realities ⟨a miserable life that provided no means of ~ but alcohol⟩ ⟨can't think of anything more genuinely pleasurable these days than the pure ~ offered you by a trip in a luxury liner —Richard Joseph⟩; *esp* **:** such mental distraction or relief achieved by flight into idealizing fantasy or fiction that glorifies the self **2 a** *archaic* **:** BLUNDER, MISTAKE **b** *obs* **:** TRANSGRESSION **3** *obs* **:** OUTBURST **4 a :** a means of escape ⟨his ~ was first constant reading and then, when that did not satisfy, day-dreaming⟩ ⟨his moments of intense contemplative vision are not moments of autointoxication or ~ —Douglas Bush⟩ ⟨when he lost all his money there was no ~ left and he finally went to work⟩ **b :** an outlet or gate through which water may be released from a canal or hydraulic structure **c** [by shortening] **:** FIRE ESCAPE; *specif* **:** a wheeled extension ladder used to evacuate a burning building **d :** a maneuver in amateur wrestling that permits a contestant to gain a neutral position from a position of disadvantage **5 :** a commonly cultivated plant that has run wild or has sprung up from self-sown seeds of a cultivated individual **6 :** the action of getting out of a gravitational field ⟨~ by rocket⟩

³escape \"\ *adj* [²*escape*] **1 :** of or relating to escape or to an escape ⟨asked to explain his ~ methods after he got out of the concentration camp⟩ ⟨his work, for all its fantasy and surreality, was never an ~ world: the threat of war, the dark emanations of the unconscious, the grotesque and the erotic, suffering and death, all find a place in his microcosm —Herbert Read⟩ **2 :** providing a means or opportunity of evading a regulation, claim, agreement, or commitment ⟨an ~ clause⟩ ⟨the contract set the price of steel at a low figure but contained an ~ provision for raising the price $2 a ton if the market went up generally⟩; *specif* **:** providing an opportunity to a new employee in a union shop or to union members following the negotiation of a new union contract for quitting the union without penalty ⟨a union contract with a 30-day ~ period⟩ ⟨forced the union to include an ~ clause in the contract that was finally settled upon⟩

⁴escape \"\ *n* -s [F, fr. MF *escappe,* fr. L *scapus* shaft of a column, stalk — more at SHAFT] **:** APOPHYGE

escape artist *n* **:** one (as a showman) markedly and ingeniously adept at releasing himself from confinement esp. as a stunt ⟨earned a living as a magician and *escape artist*⟩; *specif* **:** a criminal noted for his ability to escape from jail ⟨the life story of the bank robber and *escape artist* —*New Yorker*⟩

escape cover *also* **escape covert** *n* **:** vegetation that by reason of strategic location or natural formation assists the escape of animals from their predators ⟨multiflora rose forms excellent *escape cover* and produces some food for game animals⟩

escaped *past of* ESCAPE

es·cap·ee \¦e,skā¦pē; ə,skā'pē, e,s-; *also* ə'skā(,)pē *or* e's- *or* -¸pi; *sometimes* ¦eskə¦pē\ *n* -s [¹*escape* + *-ee*] **:** one that has escaped; *esp* **:** an escaped prisoner

escape hatch *n* **1 :** a hatch providing an emergency exit from an enclosed space (as the cabin of an airplane) **2 :** a means of evading something that is or may prove burdensome (as a responsibility or regulation) **:** a way out of a dilemma or difficulty ⟨an agreement to negotiate with an *escape hatch* allowing for settlement by a third party in the event of a deadlock⟩ ⟨headaches were an *escape hatch* in a world of insurmountable difficulties⟩

es·cape·less \ə'skāplə̇s, e'-\ *adj* **:** incapable of being escaped

escape mechanism *n* **:** a mode of behavior or thinking adopted to evade unpleasant facts or responsibilities **:** MECHANISM OF DEFENSE

es·cape·ment \ə'skāpmənt, e'-\ *n* -s **1 a :** the act of escaping **b** *archaic* **:** a way of escape **:** VENT **2 :** something that escapes; *specif* **:** the number of fish that are permitted to survive and spawn (as by adjustment of fishing seasons or provision of fishways) **3** [alter. (influenced by F *échappement*) of earlier *scapement*] **:** the device in a timepiece which controls the motion of the train of wheelwork and through which the energy of the weight, mainspring, or other power source is delivered to the pendulum or balance by means of impulses that keep the latter in regular vibration and thus permit a tooth to escape from a pallet at regular intervals **4 :** the mechanism in the action of a piano that causes the hammer to rebound after striking **5 :** a ratchet device that permits motion in one direction only in successive equal steps with pauses between (as the spacing mechanism of a typewriter carriage) **6 :** the mechanism that releases the matrices from the magazine of a keyboard-operated slug-casting machine

escapement 3

escape note *or* **escape tone** *n* **:** a nonharmonic note or tone approached by a step from a chord tone and left by a skip in the opposite direction — called also *échappée;* compare CHANGING NOTE

escape opening *n* **:** a secondary means of egress (as from a room) for use only in case of fire

es·cap·er \-pə(r)\ *n* -s **:** one that escapes esp. from enemy custody

escape reaction *n* **:** a physiological or psychological response tending to remove the individual from contact with a noxious stimulus

escapes *pres 3d sing of* ESCAPE, *pl of* ESCAPE

escape valve *n* **:** SAFETY VALVE

escape velocity *n* **:** VELOCITY OF ESCAPE

escapeway \ˈ=ˈ=,=\ *n* [²*escape* + *way*] **:** a channel of escape **:** OUTLET; *also* **:** FIRE ESCAPE
escape wheel *n* **:** a wheel that is last in the train of a timepiece and whose teeth are esp. shaped to impart impulses to a pallet or lever
escaping *pres part of* ESCAPE
es·cap·ing·ly *adv* **:** EVASIVELY
es·ca·pism \əˈskā,pizəm, eˈ-\ *n* -s **1 :** diversion of the mind to purely imaginative activity or entertainment to escape from reality or routine; *esp* **:** habitual diversion of this kind ⟨stigmatized a taste for her books as ~ of the worst variety, headlong flight into vapid unreality —*Times Lit. Supp.*⟩ ⟨the monotony of big-city life and the boredom of an over-regulated existence create a desire for ~, which is the essence of romanticism —Robert Pick⟩ **2 :** an evasion of unpleasant fact or of reality esp. by compensation ⟨it's the old ~ through mockery . . . a hurt pride looking for scapegoats —Ramon Lavalle⟩
¹es·cap·ist \-ˌpəst\ *n* -s [¹*escape* + *-ist*] **:** one that escapes; *specif* **:** one guilty of or given to escapism ⟨the . . . idyllic ecstasy of a romantic primitivist or ~ —Douglas Bush⟩ ⟨he has been called an ~, a perennial tenant of the ivory tower, a man who writes about life while taking great pains to remain aloof from it —W.M.Kunstler⟩ ⟨a daydreamer, an ~, a lover of peace —William Saroyan⟩
²escapist \"\ *adj* **:** befitting an escapist or escapism ⟨~ visions⟩ ⟨~ literature⟩
es·cap·ol·o·gist \əˌskāˈpäləjəst, e,-\ *n* -s [*escape* + *-o-* + *-logist*] **:** one who attempts to avoid reality or serious matters by frivolous self-indulgence and merrymaking — not used technically
es·car·bun·cle \əˈs, eˈs+,-\ *n* [ME, fr. MF *escarbuncle, escarboncle*, modif. (prob. influenced by *esmeraude* emerald) of L *carbunculus* dark red precious stone, small coal — more at CARBUNCLE] **:** a heraldic charge consisting of a center ornament with eight decorated rays to represent the precious stone carbuncle — called also *carbuncle*
es·car·got \eskärgō\ *n, pl* **escargots** \"\ [F, fr. MF *escargot, escargol*, fr. OProv *escaragol*] **:** a snail cooked and served as food
es·car·go·tiere \ˌeˌskärgəˈtye(ə)r\ *n* -s [F *escargotière*, lit., snailery, fr. *escargot* snail] **:** an artificial mound or kitchen midden made up primarily of snail shells but containing artifacts (as found in Algeria)
escarmouche *n* -s [MF — more at SKIRMISH] *obs* **:** SKIRMISH
es·ca·role \ˈeskə,rōl\ *n* -s [F, fr. MF *scariole*, fr. OIt *scariola*, fr. ML, fr. LL *escariola*, fr. L *escarius* of food, for eating (fr. *esca* food — fr. *edere* to eat — + *-arius* -ary) + *-ola* -ole — more at EAT] **:** ENDIVE 1
¹es·carp \əˈskärp, (ˈ)eˈs-\ *n* [F *escarpe*, fr. MF, fr. OIt *scarpa* — more at SCARP] **:** SCARP
²escarp \"\ *vt* [F *escarper*, fr. MF, fr. *escarpe*] **:** SCARP
es·carp·ment \əˈskärpmənt, eˈ-\ *n* -s [F *escarpement*, fr. *escarper* to escarp + *-ment*] **1 :** a steep slope in front of a fortification **2 :** a long cliff or steep slope separating two comparatively level or more gently sloping surfaces and resulting from erosion or faulting
escas *pl of* ESCA
-es·cence \ˈesᵊn(t)s\ *n suffix* -s [MF, fr. L *-escentia*, fr. *-escent-, -escens* + *-ia*] **:** state or process of becoming ⟨obso*lescence*⟩ ⟨convales*cence*⟩
-es·cent \ˈesᵊnt\ *adj suffix* [MF, fr. L *-escent-, -escens* (pres. part. suffix of inchoative verbs ending in *-escere*), fr. *-esc-*, element forming inchoative verbs + *-ent-, -ens*, pres. part. suffix of the 3d conjugation — more at -ENT] **1 :** beginning, beginning to be, becoming, slightly ⟨obsol*escent*⟩ ⟨arbo*rescent*⟩ ⟨alkal*escent*⟩ **2 :** reflecting or emitting light (in a specified way) ⟨opal*escent*⟩ ⟨fluor*escent*⟩
esch·a·lot \ˈeshə,lät\ *n* -s [F *échalote*, fr. MF *eschalotte* — more at SHALLOT] **:** SHALLOT
¹es·char \ˈeˌskär, ˈeskər\ *n* -s [alter. (influenced by F *eschare* & LL *eschara* eschar) of ME *escare* — more at SCAR] **1 :** a dry crust **:** SCAB; *esp* **:** one formed after a burn **2 :** a lesion covered by an eschar
²eschar *var of* ESKER
es·cha·ra \ˈeskərə\ *n* [NL, fr. LL, scab, scar — more at SCAR] **1** *cap* **:** a genus of bryozoans (order Cheilostomata) that produce delicate colonies resembling various fragile corals **2** -s **:** any bryozoan of the genus *Eschara*; *also* **:** an erect 2-layered bryozoan colony — **es·cha·rine** \-,rīn, -,rən\ *adj* — **es·cha·roid** \-,rȯid\ *adj*
¹es·cha·rot·ic \ˌeskəˈrädˌik\ *adj* [F or LL; F *escharotique*, fr. MF, fr. LL *escharoticus*, fr. Gk *escharōtikos*, fr. (assumed) *escharōtos* (verbal of *escharoun* to form an eschar, fr. *eschara* eschar) + *-ikos* -ic — more at SCAR] **:** producing an eschar
²escharotic \"\ *n* -s **:** an agent (as a drug) that produces an eschar
es·chat·o·col \eˈskad·ə,kȯl *also* -,käl *or* -,kōl *or* -d·ōkəl *or* -d·ēkəl\ *n* -s [Gk *eschatos* last, farthest + E *-col* (as in *protocol*)] **:** the concluding part of a protocol
es·chat·o·log·i·cal \eˌskad·əlˈäjəkəl, ˌeskəd-·\ *adj* **:** of, relating to, dealing with, or as regards the ultimate destiny of mankind and the world ⟨~ hope⟩ ⟨~ literature⟩ ⟨~ implications⟩ ⟨~ ideas⟩ — compare ESCHATOLOGY — **es·chat·o·log·i·cal·ly** \-k(ə)lē\ *adv*
es·cha·tol·o·gist \ˌeskəˈtäləjəst\ *n* -s **:** one centrally concerned with eschatology or an eschatological belief, teaching, or interpretation (as of scripture)
es·cha·tol·o·gy \-jē\ *n* -ES [Gk *eschatos* last, farthest + E *-logy*; akin to Gk *ex, ek* out of, from — more at EX-] **1 a :** a study or science dealing with the ultimate destiny or purpose of mankind and the world ⟨a theological student with a dominant interest in ~⟩; *also* **:** central concern for such an ultimate destiny or purpose ⟨it was a big step in the movement away from ~ when Luther formulated his doctrine of baptism without reference to the last things —J.R.Coates⟩ **b :** a doctrine or theory or conclusion concerning the ultimate destiny or purpose of mankind and the world ⟨the horrible ~ which hypnotized even the greatest among medieval philosophers and theologians —G.G.Coulton⟩ ⟨it presupposes an ~ or set of assumptions concerning the end events of history —O.J.Baab⟩; *esp* **:** Christian doctrine or theory or a particular Christian doctrine or theory of this kind ⟨one or other of the Protestant *eschatologies* —*Notes & Queries*⟩ **2 :** ultimate destiny or purpose esp. according to Christian doctrine ⟨man's increasing indifference to ~, his crass mistaking of means for ends —G.M.Hopkins⟩ ⟨in the apocalyptic writings the ~ of the individual comes to the front, although at first associated with an eternal kingdom on earth —L.E.Fuller⟩ **3 :** a science that deals with or a doctrine or theory about things of final importance to mankind ⟨the Marxian economic ~ —B.B.Seligman⟩
¹es·cheat \əs(h)ˈchēt, es(-\ *n* -s [ME *eschete*, fr. AF, fr. OF *eschete, escheoite*, fr. *escheoit*, past part. of *escheoir* to fall, happen, fr. (assumed) VL *excadere* to happen, fall to the lot of, fr. L *ex-* + *cadere* to fall — more at CHANCE] **1 a :** the falling back or reversion of lands in English feudal law to the lord of the fee upon the failure of heirs capable of inheriting under the original grant **b :** the lapsing or reverting of land to the crown in England or to the state in the U.S. as original and ultimate proprietor by reason of failure of persons legally entitled to such land — see INQUEST OF OFFICE **c :** the right of taking property that is subject to such reversion **2 :** escheated property **3 a** *Scotland* **:** CONFISCATION, FORFEITURE — see LIFERENT ESCHEAT **b** *obs* **:** an appropriating unfairly or by force **:** PLUNDERING
²escheat \"\ *vb* -ED/-ING/-S [ME *escheten*, fr. *eschete*, n.] *vt* **1 :** to cause to revert, lapse, pass, or come or go into the possession of another by escheat **2** *Scots law* **:** FORFEIT ~ *vi* **:** to revert, fall, lapse, or pass by escheat
es·cheat·able \-chēd·əbəl\ *adj* **:** subject to escheat or capable of being claimed or taken by escheat ⟨since the unpaid dividends are deposited with a New York bank, it may be inferred that they are also ~ by New York —David Fellman⟩
es·cheat·or \-ēd·ər, -ēd·,ō(ə)r\ *n* -s [ME *eschetour*, fr. AF, fr. OF *escheoit* (past part. of *escheoir* to fall, happen) + *-our* -or] **:** a legal officer formerly appointed to look after escheats
esch·e·rich·ia \ˌeshəˈrikēə\ *n, cap* [NL, fr. Theodor *Escherich* †1911 Ger. physician + NL *-ia*] **:** a genus of aerobic gram-negative rod-shaped bacteria (family Enterobacteriaceae) that form acid and gas on many carbohydrates (as dextrose and lactose) but no acetoin and that include forms (as members of the type species *E. coli*) normally present in the human or various other vertebrate intestines which are occas. pathogenic and indicative of fecal contamination when found in water and other forms which typically occur in soil and water
es·chew \əs(h)ˈchü, es(-\ *vb* -ED/-ING/-S [ME *eschewen, eschuen*, fr. MF *eschiuver, eschiver* to shun, avoid, fr. OF, of Gmc origin; akin to OHG *sciuhen* to frighten off, make timid — more at SHY] *vt* **1 :** to abstain from (as something wrong, inappropriate, distasteful, or harmful) **:** SHUN ⟨trained to ~ private passions and pursuits —E.A.Mowrer⟩ ⟨some of the millionaires ~*ed* palatial magnificence —F.L.Allen⟩ ⟨despite the engagement to ~ violence, disorders and bloodshed took place —*Collier's Yr. Bk.*⟩ ⟨the normal vegetarian only ~*s* fish, flesh, and fowl —N.C.Wright⟩ **2** *obs* **:** to keep free of **:** ESCAPE ~ *vi, obs* **:** ESCAPE **syn** see ESCAPE, FORGO
es·chew·al \-üəl\ *n* -s **:** SHUNNING, AVOIDANCE ⟨the deliberate ~ of virtuous action —Peter Ure⟩ ⟨an ascetic ~ of female luxury —J.G.Cozzens⟩
esch·scholt·zia \eˈshōltsēə\ *n* [NL, fr. J.F.*Eschscholtz* †1831 Ger. naturalist + NL *-ia*] **1** *cap* **:** a genus of showy herbs (family Papaveraceae) of western No. America having leaves ternately dissected several times into linear or oblong segments and sepals coherent into a characteristic pointed hood which is pushed off as the flower buds expand — see CALIFORNIA POPPY **2** -s **:** any plant of the genus *Eschscholtzia*
es·chy·nite *or* **aes·chy·nite** \ˈeskə,nīt\ *n* -s [G *äschynit*, fr. *äschyn-* (fr. Gk *aischynē* shame) + G *-it* -ite] **:** a mineral $(Ce,Ca,Fe,Th)(Ti,Cb)_2O_6$ consisting of a rare oxide of titanium, columbium, cerium, and other metals isomorphous with priorite and found in nearly black prismatic crystals
es·clandre \esklädr(ᵊ), -d(rə)\ *n, pl* **esclandres** \"\ [F, fr. MF, scandal — more at SLANDER] **:** an incident that arouses unpleasant talk or gives rise to scandal **:** a public unpleasant altercation **:** SCENE
es·cla·vage \ˌesklәˈväzh\ *n* -s [F, lit., slavery, fr. MF, slavery, fr. OF *esclave* slave + *-age* — more at SLAVE] **:** a necklace having several rows of chains, beads, or jewels
es·co·bi·lla \ˌeskəˈbē(y)ə\ *n* -s [Sp, lit., little broom, dim. of *escoba* broom] **:** a European plant (*Centaurea salmantica*) naturalized as a weed in California
es·co·bi·ta \ˌeskəˈbēd·ə\ *n* -s [AmerSp, lit., little broom, dim. of *escoba* broom, fr. L *scopa, scopae*] **:** any of several Californian plants of the genus *Orthocarpus* (as *O. purpurascens*)
escocheon *n* -s [ME *escochon* — more at ESCUTCHEON] **1 :** ESCUTCHEON **2 :** INESCUTCHEON
es·co·lar \ˌeskōˈlär\ *n, pl* **escolar** *or* **escolars** [Sp, lit., scholar; from rings like spectacles around the eyes] **:** a fish of the family Gempylidae; *esp* **:** a large rough-scaled fish (*Ruvettus pretiosus*) that resembles a mackerel, is highly prized for food, and lives at a depth of from 100 to 400 fathoms in the Mediterranean, middle Atlantic, and throughout the southern seas and from whose flesh a purgative oil can be extracted — called also *oilfish*
escollope *var of* ESCALOPE
es·con·son \əˈskän(t)sən\ *n* -s [F *écoinçon, écoinson*, fr. MF *escoinson* — more at SCONCHEON] **:** a jamb shaft in the inside arris of a window jamb
es·co·pe·ta \ˌeskəˈpād·ə, -ped·ə\ *n* -s [Sp, fr. OIt *schioppetto*, lit., small explosion, dim. of *schioppo*, lit., explosion] **:** a short firelock musket
es·co·pette \ˌeskəˈpet\ *n* -s [F, fr. MF *eschopette*, fr. OIt *schioppetto*] **:** ESCOPETA
¹es·cort \ˈeˌskȯr\t, -ō(ə)\, *usu* \d·+V\ *n* -s [F *escorte*, fr. MF *escorte, scorte*, fr. OIt *scorta*, lit., act of escorting, fr. *scorgere* to perceive, escort, guide, fr. (assumed) VL *excorrigere* to guide, observe, fr. L *ex-* + *corrigere* to correct, make straight — more at CORRECT] **1 a :** a body of armed men to guard a person or goods on a journey or to accompany as a mark of respect or honor **b :** a protective screen of warships or fighter planes or a single ship or plane attending upon one or more vulnerable craft for fending off enemy attack; *esp* **:** a group of antisubmarine warships accompanying a convoy of merchant ships as protection **c :** protection by an escort ⟨under heavy ~ the big ship made the dangerous trip through the Atlantic and Caribbean to the Panama canal —H.L.Merillat⟩ **2 a :** a body of persons or an individual accompanying another or others as protection or as a mark of honor or courtesy ⟨felt it wise to send an ~ with the group through the more disreputable parts of the city⟩ ⟨included in the Corps of Queen's Messengers is a limited number of ~*s* whose duty it is to accompany and assist the queen's messengers on certain types of journey —*Brit. Information Services*⟩ ⟨I shall give you as many men for an ~ as you think necessary, or you may go entirely alone —Carleton Beals⟩ **b :** the boy or man who goes on a date with a girl or woman ⟨there were many more men in the community than women, and every girl had a choice of ~*s* —David Fairchild⟩ ⟨the older woman left her ~ sitting at the bar⟩ **c :** a man who makes a business of serving as a companion or date for women (as at a restaurant or in attendance at dances or the theater) **3 :** the fact of escorting **:** accompaniment as an escort ⟨he left us, declining our offered ~ —Sheridan Le Fanu⟩ ⟨flying close ~ for the transports —R.L.Scott⟩ **4 :** GUIDE ⟨provide the man with an ~ through the intricate ways of the city⟩; *esp* **:** one who guides visitors to their destination in an industrial establishment
²es·cort \əˈsk-, (ˈ)eˈsk-\ *vt* -ED/-ING/-S **1 :** to accompany as an escort ⟨using it as a base, fighters can ~ all kinds of bombers to and from Japan —*Newsweek*⟩ ⟨each spring they lovingly crate dozens of their finest blooms and ~ them by overnight express to the Royal Horticultural Society's Rhododendron Show in London —D.S.Boyer⟩ ⟨the sacred relic is ~*ed* by the saffron-robed priests around the town —Rex Moorfoot⟩ ⟨the great liner and ~*ing* tugs —*This Week Mag.*⟩ **2 a :** CONDUCT ⟨rescued the men and ~*ed* them to a place of safety⟩ ⟨~*ing* that charming young woman across the terrace —Robert Grant †1940⟩ ⟨~*ed* them to their box with a sort of pompous humility —Oscar Wilde⟩ **:** GUIDE ⟨the tours combine the freedom of traveling by private automobile with the advantages of an ~*ed* tour in such tedious matters as baggage and reservations —*Ford Times*⟩ **b :** to take or lead forcibly ⟨was ~*ed* to headquarters, and almost immediately identified as one of the escaped convicts —*Springfield (Mass.) Union*⟩
escort carrier *n* **:** a small aircraft carrier (as a converted cargo ship) whose primary mission is usu. antisubmarine warfare — called also *baby carrier*
escort fighter *n* **:** an offensive fighter airplane of maximum fuel capacity for escort to heavy bombers on raids
escort wagon *n* **:** a wagon formerly used in the U.S. Army for general hauling
escot *vt, past part* **escoted** [MF *escoter* to share the expense, pay a bill, fr. OF *escot* share of expense, bill, contribution — more at SCOT] *obs* **:** to provide support for (a child) **:** MAINTAIN
escribe \ēˈskrīb, eˈ-\ *vt* [*e-* + L *scribere* to write — more at SCRIBE] **:** to draw (a circle) touching one side of a triangle externally and the other two sides internally
escript *n* [ME, fr. MF — more at SCRIPT] *obs* **:** a written document (as a decree)
es·cri·toire \ˈeskrə,twär, -wå(r, ˌ=ˈ=ˈ=\ *n* -s [F (also, inkstand, writing room), fr. MF *escriptoire* writing room, inkstand, writing case, fr. ML *scriptorium* — more at SCRIPTORIUM] **:** a piece of furniture resembling a bureau or combination bureau and bookcase and providing a writing surface (as by a drawer with a hinged front that drops down) or desk area (as behind a hinged front that drops down to form a writing surface) **:** SECRETARY; *also* **:** the writing drawer or desk area of such a piece of furniture
escrod *var of* SCROD
es·crol *also* **es·croll** \əˈskrōl\ *n* -s [modif. (influenced by E *scroll*) of MF *escroele, escrouelle* small piece, bit, dim. of *escroe, escroue* bit, scroll] **:** a heraldic scroll
¹es·crow \ˈeˌskrō, əˈs-,eˈs-\ *n* -s [MF *escroe, escroue* bit, scroll, strip of parchment — more at SCROLL] **1 :** a deed or bond, money, or a piece of property delivered into the keeping of a third party by one party to a contract or sometimes taken from one party to a contract and put in trust to be returned only upon the performance or fulfillment of some condition of the contract or to insure such performance or fulfillment by some other disposition **2 :** a fund or deposit serving as or designed to serve as an escrow ⟨expenses in connection with an ~ established to ensure the payment of the property tax on the house⟩ ⟨the proposed ~ of funds to ensure completion is acceptable —*Veterans Administration Tech. Bull.*⟩ — **in escrow** *adv (or adj)* **:** in trust as an escrow ⟨cash funds will be placed *in escrow* with the trustee to pay interest on and principal of the notes —*U.S. Investor*⟩ ⟨have over $1000 *in escrow* to pay taxes⟩
²es·crow \əˈs-, (ˈ)eˈs-\ *vt* -ED/-ING/-S **:** to place in escrow ⟨~ a certain amount of money for the payment of taxes⟩ ⟨a certification of loan disbursement showing the loan proceeds which have been ~*ed* —*Veterans Administration Tech. Bull.*⟩
es·crow·ee \ˌeˌskrōˈē; eˌskrōˈē, əˌs-; ˌeskrəˈwē\ *n* -s **:** the one holding an escrow in trust **:** the depository of an escrow
es·cu·age \ˈeˌskyüij, ˈeskyəwij\ *n* -s [MF *escuage*, fr. OF, fr. *escu* shield (fr. L *scutum*) + *-age* — more at ESQUIRE] **1 :** the military service required of a knight incident to his fee **2 :** SCUTAGE
¹es·cu·do \əˈsk(y)ü(,)dō, eˈ-, -kü(,)thō\ *n* -s [Sp, lit., shield, fr. L *scutum* shield — more at ESQUIRE] **1 a :** an old gold coin of Spain and Spanish America worth two pieces of eight or Spanish dollars **b :** a Spanish silver coin of crown or dollar size **2 :** a unit of value equivalent to one escudo coin ⟨a ½-*escudo* coin, 8-*escudo* coin⟩
²es·cu·do \əˈsk(y)ü(,)dō, eˈ-, ishˈkü(,)thü\ *n* -s [Pg, lit., shield, fr. L *scutum*] **1 :** an old Portuguese gold coin similar to the Spanish escudo **2 a :** since 1911 the basic monetary unit of Portugal and Portuguese territories — see MONEY table **b :** a coin representing one escudo unit
esculent \"\ *adj or n* [L *esculentus*, fr. *esca* food (fr. *edere* to eat) + *-ulentus* -ulent — more at EAT] **:** EDIBLE
es·cu·le·tin *or* **aes·cu·le·tin** \ˌeskyəˈlētᵊn\ *n* -s [ISV, blend of *esculin, aesculin* and *-et-*] **:** a crystalline lactone $C_9H_6O_4$ obtained by hydrolysis of esculin; 6,7-dihydroxycoumarin
es·cu·lin *or* **aes·cu·lin** \ˈeskyələn\ *n* -s [It *esculina*, fr. NL *Aesculus* (genus name of *Aesculus hippocastanum*, species that produces it) + It *-ina* -in] **:** a crystalline glucoside $C_{15}H_{16}O_9$ from the inner bark of the horse chestnut and roots of the yellow jessamine (*Gelsemium sempervirens*) that absorbs ultraviolet rays
es·cutch·eon *or* **es·cuch·eon** \əˈskəchən, eˈ-\ *n* -s [ME *escochon*, fr. MF *escuchon, escuçon*, fr. (assumed) VL *scution-, scutio*, fr. L *scutum* shield + *-ion-, -io* -ion — more at ESQUIRE] **1 a :** a defined area on which armorial bearings are depicted, marshaled, or displayed usu. consisting of a shield or something made to resemble a shield — see DEXTER 2, SINISTER; compare BASE, CHIEF, FESS, LOZENGE, NAVEL, NOMBRIL, POINT **b :** the portion of such an area not covered by an armorial bearing **c :** COAT OF ARMS ⟨his haughty, domineering mother, whose family had some claim to an ~ —Theodore Bonnet⟩ **d :** a decorative device or emblem resembling a coat of arms **e :** ²HATCHMENT **2** *or* **escutcheon plate :** a protective or ornamental shield, flange, or border (as around a keyhole or radio dial) **3 :** SHIELD BUDDING **4 :** the part of a vessel's stern on which her name is displayed **5 :** any of certain animal structures shaped somewhat like a shield: **a** (1) **:** an area just above the rear part of the udder of many quadrupeds extending upward and outward to the flanks and being distinguished by the hair which turns upward rather than downward (2) **:** the distinctive hair of such an escutcheon **b :** the mesoscutellum of a beetle or hemipterous insect **c :** the depression behind the beak of certain bivalves

escutcheons 2

es·cutch·eoned \-nd\ *adj* **:** having or decorated with escutcheons
escutcheon of pretense : an inescutcheon on the center of the shield of the husband of an heiress or coheiress
escutcheon pin *n* **:** a small round-headed ornamental usu. brass nail for attaching escutcheon plates
escutellate \(ˈ)ē+\ *adj* [*e-* + NL *scutellum* + E *-ate*] *of insects* **:** having no visible scutellum
esdragol *var of* ESTRAGOLE
¹-ese \ˈēz, ˈēs\ *adj suffix* [Pg *-ês* & It *-ese*, adj. & n. suffix, fr. (assumed) VL *-esis*, fr. L *-ensis*] **:** of, relating to, or originating in (a certain place or country) ⟨Japan*ese*⟩ ⟨Vienn*ese*⟩
²-ese \"\ *n suffix, pl* **-ese** [Pg *-ês* & It *-ese*] **1 :** native or resident (of a specified place or country) ⟨Chin*ese*⟩ **2 a :** the language (of a particular place, country, or nationality) ⟨Siam*ese*⟩ ⟨Canton*ese*⟩ **b :** speech, literary style, or diction peculiar to (a specified place, person, or group) — usu. in words applied in dislike or contempt ⟨Carlyl*ese*⟩ ⟨journal*ese*⟩ ⟨Pentagon*ese*⟩ ⟨federal*ese*⟩
ESE *abbr* east-southeast
es·em·plas·tic \ˌeˌsemˈplastik, ˌesəm-\ *adj* [Gk *es, eis* into (fr. *en* in) + E *em-* (fr. Gk *hen-, heis* one) + E *plastic* — more at IN, HENO-] **:** shaping or having the power to shape disparate things into a unified whole — used of the imagination
eseptate \(ˈ)ē+\ *adj* [*e-* + *septate*] **:** having no septa
es·er·ine \ˈesə,rēn, -,rən\ *n* -s [ISV *eser-* (fr. a native name in Africa) + *-in*; orig. formed as F *ésérine*] **:** PHYSOSTIGMINE — used esp. in biology
es·er·in·ize \ˈesərə,nīz\ *vt* -ED/-ING/-S **:** to treat with physostigmine esp. to enhance the physiologic effect of acetylcholine ⟨proceeded to ~ both eyes of a rabbit —Otto Loewi⟩
es·er·o·line \ˈesərə,lēn\ *n* -s [ISV, blend of *eserine* and *-ol*] **:** a phenolic nitrogenous base $HOC_6H_3C_7H_{14}N_2$ obtained by hydrolysis of physostigmine
e sharp *n, usu cap E* **:** the tone a half step above E and sounding enharmonically the same as F in the tempered scale
eshi-kongo \ˌeshēˈkäŋ(,)gō\ *n pl, usu cap E&K* **:** a division of a Bantu people of Angola descended from the dominant race of the ancient kingdom of Kongo
esh·in \ˈeshən\ *n* -s [perh. irreg. fr. ¹*ashen*] *dial Eng* **:** PAIL, TUB
e silentio *var of* EX SILENTIO
esill \ˈā|səl, ˈē|, |zəl\ *n* -s [ME *eisil, aisil*, fr. OF, vinegar, fr. (assumed) VL *acetulum*, dim. of L *acetum* vinegar, sour wine — more at ACETIC] **1** *archaic* **:** VINEGAR **2** *archaic* **:** a wine made from vinegar
esiphonal \(ˈ)ē+\ *adj* [*e-* + *siphon* + *-al*] *of a bivalve mollusk* **:** having no siphon
esiphonate \"+\ *adj* [*e-* + *siphonate*] **:** ESIPHONAL
-e·sis \ˈēsəs, ˌəsəs\ *n suffix, pl* **-eses** \ˈē(,)sēz, ˌə,sēz\ [ME, fr. OE, fr. L, fr. Gk *-esis, -ēsis*, fr. *-e-, -ē-*, derivational element attached to certain verbs + *-sis*, fem. suffix of action] **:** action **:** process ⟨enur*esis*⟩
es·ker *also* **es·kar** *or* **es·char** \ˈeskə(r)\ *n* -s [Ir *eiscir* ridge] **:** a long narrow often sinuous ridge or mound of sand, gravel, and boulders deposited between ice walls by a stream flowing on, within, or beneath a stagnant glacier — compare KAME
es·ki·mo \ˈeskə,mō\ *n* [Dan *Eskimo* & F *Esquimau*, fr. the name applied by the Algonquians to the tribes north of them; akin to Abnaki *esquimantsic* eaters of raw flesh, Cree *askimowew* he eats it raw] **1** *pl* **eskimo** *or* **eskimos** *usu cap* **a :** a group of peoples of northern Canada, Greenland, Alaska, and eastern Siberia **b :** a member of such people **2** *usu cap* **:** the Eskimo-Aleut language of the Eskimo people **3** -s *often cap* **:** RUSTIC BROWN — **es·ki·mo·an** \ˌeskəˈmōən\ *adj, usu cap*
eskimo-aleut *n, cap E&A* **:** a language stock consisting of Aleut, Inupik, and Yupik
eskimo curlew *n, usu cap E* **:** a New World curlew (*Numenius borealis*) that breeds in northern No. America and winters in So. America and is now prob. extinct
eskimo dog *n, usu cap E* **1 :** a broad-chested powerful dog of a breed native to Greenland and Labrador, where it was developed as a sled dog and hunting dog, and characterized by a heavy double coat, the outer coat long and shaggy and the inner of soft dense wool, by short erect ears, full tail curled across the back, and large hairy paws and averaging 50 to 85 pounds in weight and 20 to 25 inches in height **2 :** any sled dog of American origin
es·ki·moid \ˈeskə,mȯid\ *adj, usu cap* [*Eskimo* + *-oid*] **:** resembling the Eskimo ⟨their longer, narrower . . . faces were more *Eskimoid* than their successors —H.B.Collins⟩

es·ki·mol·o·gist \ˌeskəˈmäləjəst\ *n* -s *usu cap* **:** a specialist in Eskimology

es·ki·mol·o·gy \-jē\ *n* -ES *usu cap* [*Eskimo* + *-logy*] **:** the study of Eskimo culture or language

Eskimo Pie *trademark* — used for a bar of ice cream enclosed in a chocolate shell and often formed on a stick

eskimo potato *n, usu cap E* **:** SPRING BEAUTY 1; *esp* **:** a plant (*Claytonia tuberosa*) of Alaska and high elevations of more southerly western No. America that has a starchy edible tuberous root and bears rosy flowers in clusters in spring

eskimo purchase *n, usu cap E* **:** a crude tackle of looped rawhide rope devised by Eskimos to haul walrus or seal from the water using holes through the ice and the animal's hide in lieu of pulley sheaves

es·ki·se·hir \ˌeskēˌsheˈhi(ə)r\ *adj, usu cap* [fr. *Eskişehir*, Turkey] **:** of or from the city of Eskisehir, Turkey **:** of the kind or style prevalent in Eskisehir

es·march bandage \ˈeˌsmˌärk, ˈezˌm\ *n, usu cap E* [after J. F. A. von *Esmarch* †1908 Ger. surgeon] **:** a tight rubber bandage for driving the blood out of a limb

es·me·ral·da \ˌezməˈraldə\ *n, pl* **esmeralda** *or* **esmeraldas** *usu cap* [AmerSp, fr. Sp, emerald, fr. (assumed) VL *smaragda*; fr. the emeralds found in its territory — more at EMERALD] **:** a now extinct language family of the coast of Ecuador — **es·me·ral·dan** \ˌezməˈraldən\ *adj, usu cap*

es·ne \ˈeznē, -ˌne\ *n* -s [OE; akin to OHG *asni* day laborer, Goth *asneis* day laborer, harvester, *asans* harvest — more at EARN] **:** a laborer or man of the lower classes among the Anglo-Saxons

esnecy *n* -ES [ML *esnescia, aisnecia*, fr. OF *ainsnesse*, fr. *ainsné* eldest, firstborn + *-esse* -ess — more at EIGNE] *Eng law, obs* **:** a prerogative of the eldest coparcener to choose first after an inheritance is divided

eso- *prefix* [Gk *eso-*, fr. *esō* within — more at ESOTERIC] **:** inner ⟨*eso*tropia⟩ ⟨*eso*neural⟩

esoc·i·dae \əˈsäsəˌdē, ēˈ-\ *n pl, cap* [NL, fr. *Esoc-*, *Esox*, type genus + *-idae*] **:** a family of elongated voracious freshwater fishes (order Haplomi) coextensive with the genus *Esox* and comprising the pikes, pickerels, and muskellunges

esoc·i·form \-äsəˌfȯrm\ *adj* [NL *Esoc-*, *Esox*, genus name + E *-iform*] **:** resembling the Esocidae

es·od·ic \(ˈ)eˈsädik, (ˈ)ēˈ-\ *adj* [Gk *esodos, eisodos* entrance (fr. *es, eis* into — fr. *en* in — + *hodos* way) + E *-ic* — more at IN, -ODE] *of nerves* **:** AFFERENT

eso·narthex \ˌesō+\ *n* [*eso-* + *narthex*] **:** the inner narthex of a church — compare EXONARTHEX

esophag- *or* **esophago-** *also* **oesophag-** *or* **oesophago-** *comb form* [Gk *oisophagos* gullet — more at ESOPHAGUS] **:** esophagus ⟨*esophag*ectomy⟩ ⟨*esophago*pathy⟩ **:** esophageal and ⟨*esophago*gastroscopy⟩

esoph·a·ge·al \əˌsäfəˈjēəl, ēˌs-, ˈēˌs- *sometimes* ˈēsəˈfaj(ē)əl\ *also* **esoph·a·gal** \əˈsäfəgəl, (ˈ)ēˈs-\ *or* **oe·soph·a·ge·al** *like* ESOPHAGEAL\ *adj* [NL *esophagus, oesophagus* (fr. Gk *oisophagos*) + E *-eal* (as in *tracheal*), *-al*] **:** of or by means of the esophagus

esophageal artery *n* **:** any of several arteries that arise from the front of the aorta, anastomose along the esophagus, and terminate by anastomosis with adjacent arteries

esophageal gland *n* **:** one of the racemose glands in the walls of the esophagus that in man are small and serve principally to lubricate the food but in some birds secrete a milky fluid on which the young are fed

esophageal ring *n* **:** a circle of nerve tissue surrounding the gullet in many invertebrates (as annelids and arthropods) — called also *circumesophageal ring*

esophageal speech *n* **:** a method of speaking which is used by individuals whose larynx has been removed and in which phonation is achieved by expelling swallowed air from the esophagus

esophageal teeth *n* **:** the series of enamel-tipped hypapophyses of the posterior cervical vertebrae of certain snakes (as *Dasypeltis scaber*) that penetrating the esophagus act as teeth to break the shells of eggs

esoph·a·ge·an *also* **oe·soph·a·ge·an** \əˌsäfəˈjēən, eˌs-, ˈēˌs- *sometimes* ˈēsəˈfaj(ē)ən\ *adj* [NL *esophagus, oesophagus* + E *-ean*] **:** ESOPHAGEAL

esoph·a·gi·tis *also* **oe·soph·a·gi·tis** \əˌsäfəˈjīd·əs, (ˌ)ēˌs-, -fəˈgī-\ *n* -ES [NL, fr. *esophag-, oesophag-* + *-itis*] **:** inflammation of the esophagus

esoph·a·go·gastrostomy \əˌsäfə(ˌ)gō, ēˌs-+\ *n* [ISV *esophag-* + *gastrostomy*] **:** the surgical formation of an artificial communication between the esophagus and the stomach

esoph·a·go·scope *also* **oe·soph·a·go·scope** \ə'==gəˌskōp\ *n* [*esophag-, oesophag-* + *-scope*] **:** an instrument for inspecting the interior of the esophagus — **esoph·a·go·scop·ic** \ə¦===ˈskäpik\ *adj* — **esoph·a·gos·co·pist** \ə,=='gäskəpəst\ *n* -ES

esoph·a·gus *also* **oe·soph·a·gus** \əˈsäfəgəs, ēˈs-\ *n, pl* **esopha·gi** *also* **oesopha·gi** \-ˌgī, -ˌjī, -ˌgē\ [ME *ysophagus*, fr. Gk *oisophagos*, fr. *oiso-* (fr. *oisein*, suppletive future infinitive of *pherein* to carry) + *-phagos*, fr. *phagein* to eat — more at BEAR, BAKSHEESH] **1 :** the tube that leads from the pharynx to the stomach being composed of an outer muscular coat containing both longitudinal and circular fibers, an areolar coat, and an inner mucous coat lined with a stratified pavement epithelium on the surface of which the esophageal glands open, and being in man about nine inches long; passing down the neck between the trachea and the spinal column and behind the left bronchus where it pierces the diaphragm slightly to the left of the middle line and joins the cardiac end of the stomach — see DIGESTION illustration **2 :** PHARYNX 2

es·o·pho·ria \ˌesəˈfōrēə *sometimes* ˌēs-\ *n* -s [NL, fr. *eso-* + *-phoria*] **:** squint in which the eyes tend to turn inward toward the nose **:** LATENT STRABISMUS

¹es·o·ter·ic \ˌesəˈterik, -sō-, -rēk *sometimes* ˈēs-\ *adj* [LL *esotericus*, fr. Gk *esōterikos*, fr. *esōterō* (compar. of *esō* within, fr. *es, eis* into, fr. *en* in) + *-ikos* -ic — more at IN] **1 a :** designed for or understood by the specially initiated alone ⟨types of music . . . that demand special training to be perceived and enjoyed, and its devotees form a cult, so that their art is the most ~ of all arts —John Dewey⟩ ⟨a body of ~ legal doctrine —B.N.Cardozo⟩ ⟨her vocabulary wasn't slimed up with offensive bits of ~ finishing-school slang —R.P.Warren⟩ — opposed to *exoteric* **b :** difficult to understand **:** ABSTRUSE ⟨there are two kinds of classics, the popular and the ~, those that yield their meaning at the first encounter and those that we have to discover by effort and insight —Van Wyck Brooks⟩ ⟨passage involving ~ swordplay —R.L.Taylor⟩ **2 :** holding esoteric doctrines or engaging in esoteric rites ⟨the ~ sects, which guard a mystery known only to the initiated —W.L. Sperry⟩ **:** dealing in or concerned with esoteric matters ⟨an ~ study⟩ ⟨many drivers going through Oak Ridge on their way somewhere else stop to stare at the ~ factories, that, for better or worse, are shaping their futures —Daniel Lang⟩ ⟨the scholarly director of an ~ local research center called the Institute of Jazz Studies —E.J.Kahn⟩ ⟨the museum was an ~, occult place in which a mystic language was spoken —Aline B. Saarinen⟩ **3 a :** confined or limited to a small circle ⟨arctic exploration was an ~ pursuit —E.P.Hanson⟩ ⟨lingers in the twilight of an ~ reputation —H.L.Mencken⟩ **b :** PRIVATE, CONFIDENTIAL ⟨some ~ reason known only to God and himself —Francis Gérard⟩ **4 :** of special, rare, or unusual interest ⟨many are rather ~ items such as aluminum duck presses, mechanical duck pluckers, woolen bands to keep the belly and kidney areas warm when hunting in winter —Bill Wolf⟩ ⟨they would smoke me out and ask me questions, as though I possessed some ~ knowledge of a kind not revealed by the guides —Lawrence Dame⟩ ⟨if the Requiem seems a bit ~ and out of the way for a modern conductor, let us take a symphony —P.H.Lang⟩ ⟨~ colors like taupe or celadon —*New Yorker*⟩ — **es·o·ter·i·cal·ly** \-rək(ə)lē, -rēk-, -li\ *adv*

²esoteric \"\ *n* -s **1** [LGk *esōterikos*, fr. Gk, adj.] **:** an initiate in esoteric doctrines or rites **2 esoterics** *pl* **:** esoteric doctrines or treatises

es·o·ter·i·ca \ˌ==ˈ=rəkə, -ˈrēkə\ *n pl* [NL, fr. Gk *esōterika*, neut. pl. of *esōterikos* esoteric (adj.)] **1 :** esoteric items ⟨such space ~ as the impacts of primary cosmic rays and micrometeorites —*Time*⟩ ⟨persons not familiar with the ~ of maneuvering commands may find the pages of such talk both bewildering and monotonous —Walter Karig⟩ ⟨an American unfamiliar with billabongs, bonzer, and other Australian ~ may find it rough going in spots —Lawrence Griswold⟩ **2 :** PORNOGRAPHY

es·o·ter·i·cism \-rəˌsizəm\ *n* -s **:** esoteric doctrines or practices; *also* **:** the quality or state of being esoteric — **es·o·ter·i·cist** \-səst\ *n* -s

es·o·ter·ism \ˈ==ˌteˌrizəm, ˌ=='=ˌ==\ *n* -s [*esoteric* + *-ism*] **:** ESOTERICISM — **es·o·ter·ist** \ˈ==ˌterəst\ *n* -s

es·o·tery \ˈ==ˌterē\ *n* -ES [*esoteric* + *-y*] **:** ESOTERICISM

es·o·tro·pia \ˌesəˈtrōpēə *sometimes* ˌēs-\ *n* -s [NL, fr. *eso-* + *-tropia*] **:** CROSS-EYE 1 — **es·o·trop·ic** \¦==ˈträpik\ *adj*

esox \ˈēˌsäks, ˈeˌ-\ *n, cap* [NL, fr. L, pike (fish), fr. Gk *isox*, a fish, of Celt origin; akin to OIr *eo, eu* salmon, MW *ehawc*] **:** the type and sole genus of Esocidae

esp \ˈesp\ *dial var of* ASP

esp *abbr* **1** especially **2** [It *espressivo*] with expression

ESP *abbr* extrasensory perception

es·pace·ment \əˈspāsmənt, eˈ-\ *n* -s [F, fr. *espacer* to space (fr. MF, fr. *espace* space) + *-ment* — more at SPACE] *Africa* **:** the distance between a series of things that have been or are to be spaced (as in planting) ⟨when should sunflower seeds be planted and what ~ is usual —*Farmer's Weekly* (*So. Africa*)⟩

es·pa·da \äˈspäthä\ *n* -s [Sp, lit., sword, fr. L *spatha* sword — more at EPAULET] **:** SWORDFISH

es·pa·don \ˌespäˈdōⁿ\ *n* -s [F (also, two-handed sword), fr. MF, sword, fr. OIt *spadone*, aug. of *spada, spata*, fr. L *spatha*] **:** SWORDFISH

es·pa·drille \ˈespəˌdril, ˌ=='=\ *n* -s [F, alter. of *espardille*, fr. Prov *espardilho*, dim. of *espart* esparto, fr. L *spartum* — more at ESPARTO] **:** a flat sandal usu. having a fabric upper and a flexible often rope sole

espadrille

es·pa·gnole \ˌespənˈyōl, -ˌpan-\ *also* **espagnole sauce** *n* -s [F *sauce espagnol, sauce à l'espagnole*] **:** BROWN SAUCE

es·pa·gno·lette \(ˌ)eˌspanyəˈlet, əˌs-\ *n* -s [F, fr. Prov *espagnouleto*, dim. of OProv *espanhol* Spanish, Spaniard, fr. (assumed) VL *Hispaniolus*, fr. L *Hispania* Spain + *-olus* -ole] **1 :** a fastening for a French door or casement window consisting of a long rod with hooks at the top and bottom of the sash both of which are turned by a single handle to hook around fixed pins in the window frame **2 :** a small metal dome with a nipple used as an ornament (as on the top of a cabinet post) in French 18th century furniture making

¹es·pal·ier \əˈspalyər, eˈs-, -spälˌ-, -spal-; -al(ə)ˌyā, -äl-, -lēˌā; ˈespəˈli(ə)r\ *n* -s [F, fr. MF, trellis, fr. OIt *spalliera*, fr. *spalla* shoulder, fr. LL *spatula* shoulder blade — more at EPAULET] **1 :** a fruit tree or other plant trained to grow flat against a building, wall, railing, trellis, or other support **2 :** a railing or trellis on which fruit trees or shrubs are trained to grow flat

²espalier \"\ *vt* -ED/-ING/-s **:** to train to grow flat on or as if on an espalier **:** furnish with an espalier

es·pan·toon \ˌeˌspanˈtün\ *n* -s [alter. of *espontoon*] *in Baltimore* **:** a policeman's club

es·par·cet \ˌeˈspärˈsā\ *also* **es·par·sette** \-rˈset\ *n* -s [F *esparcet, esparcette*, fr. Prov *esparcet*, dim. of OProv *espars* pod, fr. *espars* (past part. of *esparser* to scatter), fr. L *sparsus*, past part. of *spargere* to scatter — more at SPARSE] **:** SAINFOIN 1

es·par·to \eˈspärd·(ˌ)ō, əˈ-\ *or* **esparto grass** *n* -s [Sp *esparto*, fr. L *spartum*, fr. Gk *sparton* — more at SPIRE (spiral)] **1 :** either of two Spanish and Algerian grasses (*Stipa tenacissima* and *Lygeum spartum*) of which cordage, shoes, baskets, and paper are made **2 :** the fiber of esparto grass

esparto paper *n* **:** paper made wholly or in large part from esparto fiber

esparto wax *n* **:** a hard brownish wax obtained from esparto grass and used chiefly in polishes

espath·ate \(ˈ)ēˈspāˌthāt, -paˌth-, -pāˌth-\ *adj* [*e-* + *spathe* + *-ate*] **:** lacking a spathe

es·pa·vé \ˌespəˈvā\ *also* **es·pa·vel** \-vel\ *n* -s [AmerSp] **:** a tropical American timber tree (*Anacardium excelsum*) with reddish rather soft wood used for making dugout canoes

es·pe·cial \əˈspeshəl, eˈ-\ *adj* [ME, fr. MF, fr. L *specialis*, fr. *species* + *-alis* -al — more at SPY] **:** SPECIAL: **a :** not general **:** directed toward a specific end **:** designed or intended for a part, purpose, or occasion ⟨gave ~ greetings to his family⟩ ⟨an ~ ceremony for the holiday⟩ ⟨took ~ pains to make himself clear to the young readers⟩ **b :** of special note **:** EXCEPTIONAL, UNUSUAL, NOTABLE ⟨gave ~ attention to the reactions⟩ **c :** PARTICULAR, PECULIAR ⟨he had an ~ aversion to reform —*New Republic*⟩ ⟨several excellent regional orchestras, each with its own ~ character —T.O.Beachcroft⟩ ⟨personal experience with hospital buildings, where I was able to discover that ~ physical and psychological reactions by patients provided good pointers for ordinary housing —*Current Biog.*⟩ ⟨the special temptation of our ~ way of life —*Amer. Guide Series: Vt.*⟩ **d :** CLOSE, DEAR, INTIMATE ⟨he was supposed to be her ~ friend —Bruce Marshall⟩ ⟨his own and most ~ tree shading his borders —C.G.Glover⟩ **e :** capable of being specified **:** SPECIFIC ⟨he drove with no ~ destination in mind⟩ ⟨chose ~ targets for attack⟩ ⟨is there any ~ piece of furniture that you might care to have —Agatha Christie⟩ **syn** see SPECIAL — **in especial** *adv* **:** in particular ⟨the work of the mind and *in especial* of consciousness —J.H.Muirhead⟩ ⟨it would implicate everybody, the councilors *in especial* being unable to evade —Francis Hackett⟩ ⟨*in especial* we shall be able to see whether the individual is training towards cooperation or against it —Alfred Adler⟩

es·pe·cial·ly \-sh(ə)lē, -li\ *adv* [ME, fr. *especial* + *-ly*] **:** in a special way **:** PARTICULARLY, NOTABLY, EXCEPTIONALLY ⟨an ~ cautious approach to the danger⟩ ⟨an ~ devastating assault by the waters in 1874 —*Amer. Guide Series: Ark.*⟩ ⟨the community declined, ~ after Peter Miller's death —*Amer. Guide Series: Pa.*⟩ ⟨vast amounts of ~ treated water are required —E.R.Riegel⟩

es·pe·cial·ness \-shəlnəs\ *n* -ES **:** the quality or state of being especial **:** SPECIALNESS

esperance *n* -s [ME *esperaunce*, fr. MF *esperance*, fr. (assumed) VL *sperantia*, fr. L *sperant-, sperans* (pres. part. of *sperare* to hope) + *-ia* -y — more at DESPAIR] *obs* **:** HOPE, EXPECTATION

¹es·pe·ran·tist \ˌespəˈrantəst, -ränˌ-, -raan-, -rän-\ *n* -s *usu cap* **:** a specialist in Esperanto; *also* **:** one enthusiastic about the spread of Esperanto as an international language

²esperantist \¦==¦==\ *adj, usu cap* **:** of or relating to Esperanto or Esperantists ⟨the *Esperantist* stock of words —Frederick Bodmer⟩

es·pe·ran·to \ˌ=='=(ˌ)tō\ *n* -s [after Dr. *Esperanto*, pseudonym of Dr. L. L. Zamenhof †1917 Pol. philologist and inventor of the language] **1** *cap* **:** an artificial international language based as far as possible upon words common to the chief European languages **2** *often cap* **:** a usu. artificial language or a set of symbols common to or designed to be common to a widely diverse and esp. international group ⟨acetylsalicylic acid is the universal comforter known in the *Esperanto* of the laboratory as $CH_3CO_2C_6H_4CO_2H$ and almost everywhere else as aspirin —Berton Roueché⟩ ⟨Russian is a second *Esperanto* taught in all schools of the constituent republics —L.A.Triebel⟩ ⟨the language of vision is a ready-made ~, a lingua franca of supreme universality —Martin James⟩ ⟨reached to all corners of the earth as though broadcast in some kind of *Esperanto* of the senses which was understood by all nations and in all tongues —Sacheverell Sitwell⟩

es·pi·al \əˈspīəl, eˈ-\ *n* -s [ME *espiaille*, fr. MF, fr. *espier* to spy + *-aille* -al — more at SPY] **1 :** the act of spying or watching **:** OBSERVATION ⟨Gabriel withdrew from his point of ~ —Thomas Hardy⟩ **2** *obs* **:** one that espies **:** SPY, SCOUT **:** a scouting party **3 :** an act of espying or being espied **:** NOTICE, DISCOVERY, DETECTION

espied *past of* ESPY

es·piè·gle \ˌespyegl(ᵊ), -g(l)ə\ *adj* [F, after *Ulespiegle* (Till Ulenspiegel or Eulenspiegel), Ger. traditional figure and hero of an early 16th cent. chapbook] **:** ROGUISH, FROLICSOME

es·pi·er \əˈspī(ə)r, -īə\ *n* -s [ME *aspiere, espiere*, fr. MF, *aspien*, *espien* to espy + *-ere* -er — more at ESPY] **:** one that espies

espies *pres 3d sing of* ESPY, *pl of* ESPY

es·pi·nil·lo \ˌespəˈnē(ˌ)(y)ō\ *n* -s [AmerSp, dim. of Sp *espino* hawthorn] **:** ESPINO 2

es·pi·no \əˈspē(ˌ)nō\ *n* -s [AmerSp, fr. Sp, hawthorn, fr. L *spinus* blackthorn, fr. *spina* thorn — more at SPINE] **1 :** any of numerous tropical So. American thorny or spiny shrubs or trees esp. of the genus *Zanthoxylum* **2 :** a shrubby acacia (*Acacia cavenia*) used as a hedge plant in southern So. America the pod of which is rich in tannin

es·pi·o·nage \ˈespēəˌnäzh, -ˌnij, -ˌnäzh, ˌ===ˈnäzh, ˌ==='näzh *also* ˈ===ˌnäj *or* ˈ===ˌnäzh *or* ˌ==='näj *or* əˈspēənij *or* eˈspē- *sometimes* əˈspēəˌnä¦zh *or* eˈspē- *or* -nä¦ *or* ¦j *or* -ˈspīənij *chiefly substand* ¦espə(¦)n-\ *n* -s [F *espionnage*, fr. MF, fr. *espionner* to spy (fr. *espion* spy, fr. OIt *spione*, aug. of *spia*, of Gmc origin) + *-age*; akin to OHG *spehōn* to spy — more at SPY] **:** the practice of spying **:** the systematic secret observation of words and conduct; *esp* **:** such spying by special agents upon people of a foreign country or upon their activities or enterprises (as war production or scientific advancement in military fields) and the accumulation of information about such people, activities, and enterprises for political or military uses

es·pla·nade \ˈespləˌnäd, -ˌnād, -ˌnad, ˌ=='=\ *n* -s [F, fr. MF, fr. OIt *spianata*, fr. fem. of *spianato*, past part. of *spianare* to level, fr. L *explanare* — more at EXPLAIN] **1 :** a level open stretch of paved or grassy ground; *esp* **:** one designed for walking or driving and often providing a vista (as over water) **2 a :** a clear space between a citadel and the nearest houses of a town **b :** GLACIS **3** *in Conn* **:** a grassed and landscaped median strip on a highway

es·plees \əˈsplēz\ *n pl* [MF *espleiz*, pl. of *espleit* revenue, profit, fr. OF — more at EXPLOIT] **:** the profits or products that land yields (as hay, pasturage, grain, or rents)

espontoon *var of* SPONTOON

es·pous·al \əˈspau̇zəl, eˈ- *also* -au̇səl\ *n* -s [ME *espousaille*, fr. MF *espousailles*, pl., fr. L *sponsalia*, fr. neut. pl. of *sponsalis* of a betrothal or espousal, fr. *sponsus* betrothed, n. (fr. *sponsus*, past part. of *spondēre* to promise solemnly, betroth) + *-alis* -al — more at SPOUSE] **:** the act of espousing: **a :** BETROTHAL ⟨the ~ of the man's son to a neighbor's daughter⟩ **b :** the marriage ceremony **:** NUPTIALS — often used in pl. **c :** MARRIAGE; *also* **:** a union resembling a marriage ⟨the ~ of the soul to Christ⟩ **d :** a taking up or adopting as a cause or belief ⟨his wholehearted ~ of Indian independence —Herrymon Maurer⟩ ⟨values whose ~ has constituted until now the heart of the distinction between human achievement and merely bestial life —Eliseo Vivas⟩

¹es·pouse \əˈspau̇z, eˈ- *also* -au̇s\ *vt* -ED/-ING/-s [ME *espousen*, fr. MF *espouser*, fr. LL *sponsare* to betroth, espouse, fr. L *sponsus*] **1 a :** to take as spouse **:** WED; *usu* **:** to take as wife **b :** to give in marriage **2** *obs* **:** to promise in marriage **:** BETROTH **3 a :** to come to believe in **:** attach oneself to and seek to maintain, support, further, and defend ⟨the causes we ~ elsewhere must be as true to our ideals and character as those we sponsor here —W.O.Douglas⟩ **b :** to adopt usu. as a matter of policy or practicality ⟨will have to work out some better scheme in repertory than it now ~*s* —*Saturday Rev.*⟩ ⟨Hamlet, the passionate lover of sincerity, has *espoused* insincerity as his weapon and armor —Karl Polanyi⟩ **syn** *see* ADOPT

²espouse *n* -s [ME, fr. MF *espous, espos* (masc.), *espouse, espose* (fem.) — more at SPOUSE] *obs* **:** SPOUSE

es·pous·er \əˈspau̇zə(r), eˈ- *also* -au̇sə-\ *n* -s **:** one that espouses; *esp* **:** SUPPORTER, PARTISAN ⟨an ~ of all good causes⟩

es·pres·si·vo \ˌeˌspreˈsē(ˌ)vō, ˌesprəˈ-\ *adj (or adv)* [It, fr. *espresso* declared, evident, pressed out (fr. *espresso* — past part. of *esprimere* to express, declare, press out — fr. L *expressus*, past part. of *exprimere* to express) + It *-ivo* (fr. L *-ivus* -ive) — more at EXPRESS (adj.)] **:** EXPRESSIVE, EXPRESSIVELY — used as a direction in music

es·pres·so \eˈspre(ˌ)sō\ *n* -s [It (*caffè*) *espresso*, lit., pressed out coffee] **1 :** coffee that is brewed by forcing steam through powdered coffee beans **2 :** a device for brewing espresso coffee **3 :** a neighborhood shop where friends gather to drink espresso

es·pring·al \əˈspriŋəl\ *n* -s [MF *espringale* — more at SPRINGALD (military engine)] **:** SPRINGALD

es·prit \əˈsprē, eˈ-\ *n* -s [F, fr. L *spiritus* spirit, breath — more at SPIRIT] **1** *archaic* **:** quick comprehension **:** INTELLIGENCE **2 :** cleverness and vivacity (as of spirit and mind) **:** sprightly wit **:** an inherent and native lively and colorful quality ⟨among so somber and serious a group his small wit passed for full-fledged ~⟩ ⟨had ~ and for us they filled that difficult patch of childhood with color and life —Rumer Godden⟩ **3** [by shortening] **:** ESPRIT DE CORPS ⟨the ~ of the entire regiment dropped considerably at the news of their transfer⟩ ⟨means that the know-how as well as the ~ of the thousands of uncompensated volunteer workers . . . would be lost —*U.S. Code*⟩ **syn** see VIGOR

es·prit de corps \əˌsprēdəˈkō(ə)r, eˌs-, ˌe(ˌ)s-, -kȯ(ə)r, -kōə, -kȯ(ə)\ *n* [F, lit., corps spirit] **:** the usu. selfless and often enthusiastic and jealous devotion of the members of a group or association of persons to the group or to its purposes ⟨the cultivation in the student body of *esprit de corps*, obedience to orders, acceptance of responsibility —*Bull. of Univ. of Ky.*⟩ ⟨an institution must have an *esprit de corps* which induces its members to put the welfare of the institution above their own —P.F.Drucker⟩ ⟨an *esprit de corps* that often unites senators of differing political views, and sometimes of intense personal rivalry, against the world outside the Senate —R.H. Rovere⟩ ⟨though the development of a strong *esprit de corps* is most desirable, within a small and exclusive group it becomes dangerous . . . assumes the form of a closed club, the members of which can, in each other's eyes, do no wrong —*Political Science Quarterly*⟩

es·pun·dia \eˈspündēə, -pu̇n-\ *n* -s [AmerSp, fr. Sp, fr. L *spongia* sponge — more at SPONGE] **:** leishmaniasis of the mouth, pharynx, and nose prevalent in Central and So. America

¹es·py \əˈspī, eˈ-\ *vb* -ED/-ING/-ES [ME *espien, aspien, spien* — more at SPY] *vt* **1 :** SEE, PERCEIVE, DISCOVER ⟨there among the several horses that whistled at her approach she *espied* the white mustang —Zane Grey⟩; *esp* **:** to see and recognize (something distant, obscure, or covert) ⟨in that moment the duke, turning, *espied* us —Rafael Sabatini⟩ **2** *archaic* **:** to inspect closely **:** WATCH ⟨I would fain have *espied* them, but they stopped up the keyhole —W.S.Gilbert⟩; *also* **:** to spy out ~ *vi, obs* **:** to keep a watch **:** observe or look about closely **syn** see SEE

²espy *n* -ES [ME *espie, aspie, spie* — more at SPY] *obs* **:** SPY

esq *or* **esqr** *or* **esqre** *abbr, often cap* esquire

esquamate \(ˈ)ē+\ *adj* [*e-* + *squamate*] **:** being without scales

esquamulose \(ˈ)ē+\ *adj* [*e-* + *squamulose*] **:** not squamulose

¹-esque \ˈesk\ *adj suffix* [F, fr. It *-esco*, of Gmc origin; akin to OHG *-isc* — more at -ISH] **:** in the manner or style of **:** like **:** -ISH ⟨Roman*esque*⟩ ⟨Kipling*esque*⟩ ⟨Lincoln*esque*⟩ ⟨statu*esque*⟩ ⟨Hardy*esque*⟩

²-esque \"\ *n suffix* -s **:** something in the style of ⟨arab*esque*⟩

es·qui·mau \ˌeskəˌmō\ *n, pl* **esquimau** \-ō\ *or* **esqui·maux** \-ō(z)\ *usu cap* [F — more at ESKIMO] **:** ESKIMO

¹es·quire \ˈeˌskwī(ə)r, əˈs-, eˈs-, -īə\ *n* -s [ME *esquire, esquier, squier*, fr. MF *escuier, esquier* shield bearer, squire, fr. LL *scutarius*, fr. L *scutum* shield + *-arius* -ary; akin to OHG *sceida* sheath — more at SHEATH] **1 :** a member of the English gentry ranking immediately below a knight **2 a** *archaic* **:** SQUIRE 1 **b :** a candidate for knighthood serving as shield bearer to and attendant upon a knight **c :** an attendant upon a king or nobleman in one of several usu. specified offices ⟨~ of the stable⟩ ⟨~ for the body⟩ **3** — used as a title of courtesy that is usu. placed in its abbreviated form after the surname in written address and that is infrequent and of no precise significance in the U.S. except as sometimes applied to certain public officials (as justices of the peace) but that is applied in British usage to anyone (except a member of the nobility or clergy) considered to have the social position of a gentleman; abbr. *Esq.* **4** *archaic* **:** a landed proprietor

²esquire \"\ *vt* [¹*esquire*] **1** *archaic* **:** to attend as an esquire **2 :** to accompany or escort in public

³esquire \"\ *n* -s [MF *esquire, esquierre, esquerre* square, carpenter's square — more at SQUARE] **1** *also* **esquire based :** BASE ESQUIRE **2 :** GYRON; *also* **:** a charge resembling a gyron

esquire's helmet *n, heraldry* **:** a helmet represented in profile without grilles, with the visor closed, and unless another tincture is specified with argent to represent steel

es·quisse \(')e¦skēs\ *n* -s [F, fr. MF *esquiche*, fr. OIt *schizzo* — more at SKETCH] **:** a first usu. rough sketch (as of a picture or model of a statue)

esrog *var of* ETHROG

ess \'es\ *n* -ES **1** *also* **es** \"\ **:** the letter *s* **2 :** something resembling the letter *s* in shape ⟨the great ~*es* the tide left in the estuary —J.M.Brinnin⟩

-ess \ə̇s *sometimes* ¦es\ *n suffix* -ES [ME -*esse*, fr. OF, fr. LL -*issa*, fr. Gk] **:** female ⟨god*dess*⟩ ⟨giant*ess*⟩ — esp. in agent nouns ⟨act*ress*⟩ ⟨poet*ess*⟩

ess *abbr* essence

essart *var of* ASSART

[1]**es·say** \(')e¦sā, ə̇'sā\ *vt* -ED/-ING/-S [MF *essaier, assaier*, fr. OF, fr. *essai, assai* (n.)] **1 a** *archaic* **:** to put to a test **:** try out **b** *obs* **:** to find out by making a test **c :** [2]ASSAY 4a **2 a :** to attempt or endeavor esp. by tentative methods or by appraising, probing, or seeking expedients — used with the infinitive ⟨Dick, being carefully installed in the saddle, ~*ed* to descend —Arnold Bennett⟩ ⟨the heavy butler ~*ed* to speak, but the tremendous blow and the baronet's gesture choked him —George Meredith⟩ **b :** to make an effort to do, accomplish, perform, deal with, or venture upon (something difficult or presenting obstacles) ⟨stayed there all day and in the evening again ~*ed* escape —F.Tennyson Jesse⟩ ⟨the medieval men who ~*ed* the paths of natural science —H.O.Taylor⟩ ⟨the ballerina ~*ed* a dramatic role on televison —*Current Biog.*⟩ ⟨the second part ~*s* to give in sixty-four pages an account of our modern knowledge of the universe —*Times Lit. Supp.*⟩ **syn** see TRY

[2]**es·say** \in sense 2 'e,sā *sometimes* -,sā *or* -,sē *or* -,si *in other senses* (')e¦sā *or* ə̇'sā\ *n* -s [MF *essai, assai*, fr. LL *exagium* act of weighing, weight, balance, fr. L *ex-* + *-agium*, fr. *agere* to do, drive; influenced by L *exigere* to weigh, test, drive out — more at AGENT, EXACT (adj.)] **1 a :** an effort made to do or perform **:** ATTEMPT, ENDEAVOR ⟨make an ~ to assist a friend⟩ ⟨making an ~ to be gallant, "Present company excepted", he said with a smile and a little bow —Aldous Huxley⟩ ⟨nowhere in the book do we find any systematic ~ to characterize this creative partnership —Lee Strasberg⟩ ⟨politics in England is one long ~ in the gentle art of compromise —W.A.Robson⟩; *esp* **:** an initial and tentative effort ⟨the fledgling bird made a small ~ at flying⟩ **b :** the result or product of the effort to do or perform something (as something difficult or presenting unusual obstacles) ⟨Haydn's final ~ in the symphonic form —*Sydney (Australia) Bull.*⟩ ⟨his first ~*s* in the skyscraper and the industrial building, which paved the way for the successful buildings of the middle nineteen-thirties —Lewis Mumford⟩ ⟨turn . . . the monstrously dull Brahms sonata into the heroic ~ it was undoubtedly meant to be —*N.Y. Herald Tribune*⟩; *esp* **:** a usu. tentative and short intellectual or artistic excursion (as into a new field of endeavor) ⟨a schizoid novel . . . an admirable ~ into the picaresque —*New Yorker*⟩ ⟨concertino for pianoforte and orchestra, a charming ~ in the modernized classical vein —Walter Legge⟩ ⟨Brook's first ~ into politics was in the 1932 state elections campaign —*Current Biog.*⟩ **2 a :** an analytic, interpretative, or critical literary composition usu. much shorter and less systematic and formal than a dissertation or thesis and usu. dealing with its subject from a limited often personal point of view ⟨the thesis must not be a mere ~; it must present evidence of a thorough acquaintance with some limited special field, obtained by recourse to original sources —*Bull. of N.Y. Univ.*⟩ ⟨persuasion is more starkly and simply the purpose of the ~ than of fiction or poetry, since the ~ deals always with an idea —Katharine F. Gerould⟩ ⟨in style and structure the three volumes . . . completed are a thousand-page ~ rather than a systematic treatise —Geoffrey Bruun⟩ **b :** something resembling or suggesting such a composition esp. in its presentation of an extended analytic, interpretative, or critical view of something (as by a series of photographs or a documentary film) ⟨a book he did on Europe's postwar children remains one of the most arresting ~*s* of modern photography —*Newsweek*⟩ ⟨the Shelter drawings made during the war are frankly graphic ~*s* done with no thought of sculpture —R.J.Goldwater⟩ ⟨two young dancers whose evident physical talents have not yet received the polish that this ~ in elegant athletics requires —Winthrop Sargeant⟩ **3 :** TRIAL, TEST ⟨make an ~ of the various methods of removing paint⟩ **4 a** *obs* **:** a trial specimen **:** SAMPLE, EXAMPLE **b :** a proof of an unaccepted design for a stamp or piece of paper money

es·say·er *n* -s **1** \(')e¦sāə(r), ə̇'s-\ **:** one that essays **2** *obs* **:** ESSAYIST

es·say·ette \¦e,sā¦et\ *n* -s [[2]*essay* + *-ette*] **:** a short essay

essay examination *or* **essay test** *n* **:** an examination made up of essay questions or a single comprehensive essay question — compare OBJECTIVE TEST

es·say·ist \'e,sāə̇st *sometimes* -,sāə̇- *or* -,sēə̇- *or* -,siə̇- *or* e'sāə̇-\ *n* -s **1 :** one that essays to do something **2 :** a writer of essays

es·say·is·tic \¦e=(,)=¦istik\ *adj* **:** of or relating to an essay or an essayist **:** like an essay in quality or character: as **a :** EXPLANATORY ⟨brief ~ statements of overtly moral intent cannot adequately suggest the interplay of emotional struggles —Carl Benson⟩ ⟨the solid ~ style of a historian —Helmut Schoeck⟩ **b :** more informal, discursive, or personal in its exposition of an idea than a dissertation or treatise ⟨the approach is neither philosophical nor purely historical, but ~ —Alfred Neumeyer⟩ **c :** like a piece of formal exposition ⟨all this is kept from seeming too ~ by the high spirits of the author, the piquant element of caricature with which he flavors his personages, and a complicating twist given to the main character —F.C.Flint⟩

essay question *n* **:** an examination question that requires an answer to be framed in a sentence, paragraph, or short composition and usu. calls for individual analysis, assembling of facts, and interpretation by the student — see ESSAY EXAMINATION

es·se \'esē\ *n* -s [ML, fr. L, to be, exist — more at IS] **1** *in scholastic philosophy* **:** actual being **:** EXISTENCE **2 :** essential nature **:** ESSENCE

es·se est per·ci·pi \'e,sē,est'perkə,pē\ [NL, lit., to be is to be perceived] *Berkeleianism* **:** a tenet that existence consists in the condition of being perceived

es·se·len \'esələn\ *n, pl* **esselen** *or* **esselens** *usu cap* **1 a :** an Indian people of the California coast near Monterey **b :** a member of such people **2 :** an Esselenian language of the Esselen people **3 :** ESSELENIAN

es·se·le·nian \,esə'lēnyən, -ēnēən\ *n, pl* **esselenian** *or* **esselenians** *usu cap* **:** a language family of the Hokan stock comprising only the Esselen language

es·sen \'esᵊn\ *adj, usu cap* [fr. *Essen*, Germany] **:** of or from the city of Essen, Germany **:** of the kind or style prevalent in Essen

es·sence \'esᵊn(t)s\ *n* -s [ME *essencia, essence*, fr. MF & L; MF *essence*, fr. L *essentia*, fr. *esse* to be + *-ent-, -ens* -ent + *-ia* -y — more at IS] **1 :** a basic underlying or constituting entity, substance, or form: as **a** *archaic* **:** ELEMENT 1a **b** (1) **:** the permanent as contrasted with the accidental and variable and hence phenomenal phases or foundation of being **:** metaphysical substance esp. when a substratum that is distinguished from and that supports attributes (2) **:** something that constitutes the individual, real, or ultimate nature or kind often as opposed to the existence of a being or thing ⟨a picture of a tree should represent the ~ of the tree — its ultimate or basic reality, that which makes it what it is, the thing-in-itself or in its intrinsic nature —Hunter Mead⟩ ⟨succeeds in conveying completely the cruel ~ of loneliness —Arthur Knight⟩ ⟨came to the conclusion that the ~ of heat was motion —S.F.Mason⟩ ⟨everything that one has seen or heard or thought or felt leaves a deposit that never filters entirely through the ~ of mind —Ellen Glasgow⟩ ⟨not life in its humdrum, day-by-day existence, but life in its ~, exciting, meaningful, important —L.D.Rubin⟩; *also* **:** the property, attribute, or element or totality of properties, attributes, or elements indispensable or necessary to the nature of a thing ⟨what is individual, what is the peculiar ~ of the man —T.S.Eliot⟩ ⟨the biographical story of his main character, not in the bulk of his million-fold detail but in its ~ —Irving Stone⟩ ⟨the ~ of liberalism—freedom of thought and inquiry, freedom of discussion and criticism —M.R.Cohen⟩ ⟨many of our people, . . . have forgotten the ~ of Americanism —George Sokolsky⟩ — see NOMINAL ESSENCE, REAL ESSENCE (3) **:** an immanent form or metaphysical archetype **:** an Aristotelian formal cause **:** a Platonic idea **c** (1) **:** the properties or attributes that every member of a species or class of things must necessarily have in order to belong to that species or class (2) **:** the totality of those properties or attributes that are indispensable to whatever can be named by a certain term or classified as of a certain class **2** *obs* **:** distinguishing nature or character **3 :** condition or fact of being or existing **:** existence considered as a property of a thing **4 :** something by which another is basically motivated or is maintained or by which it subsists ⟨the enthusiasm of its personnel is the ~ and life of any enterprise⟩ ⟨criticism that will keep in mind that the ~ of a performance is the music as it was written —*Saturday Rev.*⟩ ⟨the camera work, which is the ~ of the coverage . . . was a brilliant job —Gilbert Seldes⟩ ⟨a country where controversy is the ~ of politics —Clifton Daniel⟩ ⟨the trend toward a herd state of which the ~ is the denial of supreme value to the human individual —E.A. Mowrer⟩ ⟨the health of our people is the very ~ of our vitality, our strength, and our progress as a nation —D.D. Eisenhower⟩ **5 :** ENTITY; *esp* **:** an abstract entity ⟨the same true characterization which makes each person in the story an ~ with whom spectators will identify themselves —*Current Biog.*⟩ ⟨own little reviews tranquilly engaged in their endless and placid pursuit of poetry as a timeless ~ —William Barrett⟩ **6 a** (1) **:** the volatile matter constituting perfume (2) **:** PERFUME, ODOR, SCENT ⟨the rice and shrimp in Venice, which breathed with the unmistakable ~ of garlic —Horace Sutton⟩ **b** (1) **:** a volatile spirit (as petroleum spirit or gasoline) (2) **:** a substance resembling a volatile spirit ⟨impregnate it with the volatile ~ of their souls —J.G.Frazer⟩ **c :** AURA, CACHET ⟨a special ~ of authority —S.N.Behrman⟩ ⟨captured in words something of the pattern of life, its color or ~ —Ernest Beaglehole⟩ ⟨the drenched condition of the two women seemed to draw into that little room a desolate melancholy ~ composed of fallen leaves, muddy cart ruts, and clammy mist —J.C.Powys⟩ **7 a :** the most significant element, attribute, quality, property, or aspect of a thing ⟨it is the very ~ of Machiavelli that in politics there is neither good nor evil, of a moral kind —Irving Kristol⟩ ⟨the ~ of Scotland—highlands and lowlands, blue lochs and swift brown streams, grouse moors, tidy farmlands and wild sea cliffs —Alice Campbell⟩; *specif* **:** a central focal issue, argument, or point (as in a law case) upon which all other issues, arguments, or points depend or to which they are subordinate ⟨what he could do superbly was to state a case or extract an ~ in a few clear and compelling words —R.H.Rovere⟩ ⟨appellate argument is the most exacting and concentrated work . . . for it involves the presentation of the ~ of a long trial in an hour or less —A.T.Vanderbilt⟩ ⟨the discernment and understanding with which he penetrates to the heart and ~ of the problem —Margaret E. Hall⟩ **b :** a most significant element, attribute, quality, or property of a thing ⟨speak of his paintings in terms of what they consider his Gallic ~*s*—his sensuousness, his economy in putting his pictures into focus, his infinitely civilized feeling for color and the refinement of line —Janet Flanner⟩ **c :** the essential and most characteristic features of a thing ⟨he believes that deceit and mistrust are the ~ of human relationships —Bergen Evans⟩ ⟨attempts to capture the ~ of our twenty-four-dollar island through extreme close-ups of thirty or more representative New York people —James Kelly⟩ ⟨managed to combine the ~ of jazz, mountain music, and New England church music into one —*Saturday Rev.*⟩ **d :** CENTER, CORE, PITH ⟨such attention to appearances and details rather than to true substance went to the very ~ of the struggle —*Time*⟩ ⟨this takes us to the ~ of national strategy —H.H. Arnold & I.C.Eaker⟩ ⟨here is the ethical ~ of the treaty — the common resolve to preserve, strengthen, and make understood the very basis of tolerance, restraint, and freedom —Dean Acheson⟩ **8 a** (1) **:** a substance considered to possess in high degree the predominant qualities or virtues of a plant, drug, or other natural product from which it is extracted (as by distillation or infusion) (2) **:** an extract (as from fruit) used as flavoring in cooking (3) **:** the concentrated juices of foods obtained in the process of cooking **b** (1) **:** ESSENTIAL OIL (2) **:** an alcoholic solution esp. of an essential oil **:** SPIRIT 21 ⟨~ of peppermint⟩ (3) **:** an artificial preparation (as an alcoholic solution of one or more esters) used esp. in flavoring ⟨pineapple ~⟩ (4) **:** ELIXIR 2 ⟨pepsin ~⟩ **9 :** something that resembles or suggests an extract in possessing the quality, virtue, or value of an original larger substance or thing in concentrated form ⟨it is an ~, a distillation, the very best of all our past reduced, not to a list of physical sights, but to a single emotion —Jerome Weidman⟩ ⟨this spot is the heart and ~ of the Green mountains —Carl Brandt⟩ ⟨the heroine who, in the hands of less eminent novelists, appeared to be the ~ of sentimentality —C.W.Cunnington⟩ — **in essence** *adv* **:** ESSENTIALLY, BASICALLY, FUNDAMENTALLY ⟨from that day onward he became *in essence* a painter —E.O.Malley⟩ ⟨art issues . . . were *in essence* political though presented with masks of aesthetics —*Americana Annual*⟩ ⟨the conflicts between labor and capital often give rise to what are *in essence* lynchings —F.W.Coker⟩ — **of the essence** *adj* **:** of unavoidable importance **:** ESSENTIAL, INDISPENSABLE ⟨in politics, personality is very often *of the essence* —R.H.Rovere⟩ ⟨in a revolution, timing is *of the essence:* temporary expedients are apt to congeal into permanent situations —Gladys Delmas⟩ ⟨it is not enough to say that we are trying to equip young women for life in a self-governing country, though that is clearly *of the essence* —*Smith College President's Report*⟩

es·sence \-n(t)s\ *adj, archaic* **:** SCENTED, PERFUMED

es·sence d'ori·ent \'esᵊn(t)s'dōrēənt, -dȯr-, -ē,ent; esäⁿs-dȯryäⁿ\ *n* [F, lit., essence of the Orient] **:** pearl essence esp. from bleak fish

essence peddler *n* **1 :** a peddler of cure-alls and medicinal preparations **2** *slang* **:** SKUNK

es·sene \'e,sēn, e's-, 'e,s-, e,s-\ *n* -s *usu cap* [Gk *Essēnos*] **:** a member of an ascetic, esoteric, and monastic brotherhood among the Jews of Palestine from the second century B.C. to the second century A.D. who practiced a community of goods and rigorous discipline and for the most part shunned the company of women — **es·se·ni·an** \ə̇'sēnēən, (')e¦s-\ *adj, usu cap* — **es·sen·ic** \ə̇'senik, (')e¦s-, -sēn-\ *adj, usu cap* — **es·sen·ism** \ə̇'sē,nizəm, e's-, 'e,s-\ *n* -s *usu cap*

es·sen·hout \'esᵊn,haùt, -hōt\ *n* -s [Afrik, fr. MD *esschenhout* ash wood, fr. *essche* ash + *hout* wood; akin to OHG *ask* ash and to *holz* wood — more at ASH, WOOD] **:** CAPE ASH

es·sen·tia \ə̇'sench(ē)ə, e'-,ē'-\ *n* -s [L, trans. of Gk *ousia* — more at ESSENCE, OUSIA] **:** ESSENCE 1

[1]**es·sen·tial** \ə̇'senchəl, e'-,ē'-\ *adj* [ME *essencial*, fr. LL *essentialis*, fr. L *essentia* essence + *-alis* -al] **1 :** of or relating to an essence: as **a :** having or realizing in itself the essence of its kind **:** having or consisting of the basic, most fundamental nature, property, quality, or attribute peculiar to or necessary or indispensable to its kind ⟨the problem is to grasp the ~ man —Carl Bridenbaugh⟩ ⟨the sunshine where it fell was a blinding ~ light without color, so that the grass looked like snowdrifts —John Buchan⟩ **b :** forming or constituting the essence of something **:** making up or being the constituent or intrinsic character or very nature of a thing ⟨his eyes were wide, as one who looks at his ~ self through the mask we wear —George Meredith⟩ ⟨wished his work to have no ornament other than its own ~ beauty, without exterior decoration —Aldous Huxley⟩ ⟨our ~ admixture of matter and spirit, emotions and intelligence —*Word Study*⟩ **c :** belonging to or being part of the essence of something **:** belonging to the constituent fundamental character of a thing **:** not accidental to something ⟨stamens are ~ organs of a flower⟩ ⟨has not shown that the merits of puritan thought are ~ and the defects accidental —M.G.White⟩ ⟨the most ~ characteristic of mind is memory —Bertrand Russell⟩ ⟨the great charm of his personality, his ~ sympathy and kindliness —M.R.Cohen⟩ ⟨did much to direct attention to the ~ immorality of lotteries —J.S.Kendall⟩ — compare ACCESSORY 1 **d :** constituting an indispensable structure, core, or condition of a thing **:** BASIC, FUNDAMENTAL ⟨a little excessive to have to sit through so much frankly nonessential repertory in order to hear two short works from the band's ~ repertory —Virgil Thomson⟩ ⟨there was an ~ soundness in his line of reasoning⟩ **2 a :** NECESSARY, INDISPENSABLE ⟨transporting the heavy ore by rail was difficult and expensive; a water route was ~ —Allan Nevins & H.S. Commager⟩ ⟨international scientific meetings are ~ to scientific progress for the reason that no one nation has a monopoly of either ideas or brains —*Saturday Rev.*⟩ ⟨agreed to request uniform standards for deferment of ~ physicians —*Current Biog.*⟩ ⟨Lutherans from the sixteenth century have regarded choir singing as ~ to their ritual —*Amer. Guide Series: Minn.*⟩ **b :** UNAVOIDABLE ⟨a good many ~ tasks are left until the last minute —Stewart Cockburn⟩ ⟨physicians and lawyers may count their purchases of books as ~ expenses of their profession in computing income tax —*Report: (Canadian) Royal Commission on Nat'l Development*⟩ **c :** important in the highest degree **:** demanding maximum attention **:** unavoidably significant ⟨a great reserve of manpower ~ to the defense of the homeland⟩ **d :** minimal but fundamental to the achievement of an end ⟨make yourself a small pocket map showing the ~ landmarks around camp so that you can find your way back —*Boy Scout Handbook*⟩ **3 :** containing the essence of that portion of a plant or substance which is marked by its characteristic odor or virtue **:** being or relating to an essence (sense 8) ⟨an ~ odor⟩ — see ESSENTIAL OIL **4** *of a musical tone* **:** necessary to or determining the tonality of a piece of music ⟨did not alter the ~ tones but added several grace notes and other purely ornamental and passing tones⟩ **5** *med* **:** having no obvious or known cause **:** IDIOPATHIC, INHERENT ⟨~ disease⟩

syn FUNDAMENTAL, VITAL, and CARDINAL all imply maximum importance, indispensability, and necessary priority in considerations, plans, or discussions. Often the words are interchangeable. When they do differ in implication, these differences are suggested by the etymologies. ESSENTIAL may suggest that the matter in question involves the very essence, or being or real nature, of whatever is concerned ⟨but in the epic, lyric, the dramatic . . . ideality in contrast with actuality plays an intrinsic and *essential* part —John Dewey⟩ ⟨undoubtedly correct in concluding that the *essential* emotion of the play [*Hamlet*] is the feeling of a son toward a guilty mother —T.S. Eliot⟩ FUNDAMENTAL may suggest something of the nature of a foundation, something on which a system or structure rests ⟨such *fundamental* methods as induction and deduction, analysis, synthesis, and comparison are common to all types of systematic knowledge —René Wellek & Austin Warren⟩ ⟨recognition of the importance of *fundamental* skills, since in a democracy citizens must be able to compute, read, write, listen, and speak effectively —*N.Y.Times*⟩ VITAL may suggest that which is necessary to continued life or existence of whatever is in question ⟨nitrate, necessary in fertilizers, but *vital* to the manufacturers of explosives in case of war —A.C.Morrison⟩ ⟨barriers within our own country which stand in the way of bringing to Americans resources *vital* to their own safety and interest —C.E.Odegaard⟩ CARDINAL may refer to the decisive or conclusive since it may suggest that on which an outcome hinges or pivots ⟨to one *cardinal* principle Edwards was faithful—the conception of the majesty and sufficiency of God, and this polar idea provides the clue to both his philosophical and theological systems —V.L.Parrington⟩ ⟨the *cardinal* virtue in the Shavian scale . . . is responsibility; every creed he has attacked Shaw has attacked on the grounds of irresponsibility —E.R.Bentley⟩ **syn** see in addition NEEDFUL

[2]**essential** \"\ *n* -s **:** something essential: as **a :** something basic or fundamental esp. belonging to or forming part of the minimal indispensable body, character, or structure of a thing ⟨the ~*s* of the good life⟩ ⟨the ~*s* of astronomy⟩ ⟨gave only the ~*s* of the story⟩ **b :** something necessary, indispensable, or unavoidable ⟨work was an ~ to survival⟩ ⟨a man considered an ~ in his office⟩ ⟨a job that was both a great chore and an ~ to the success of the enterprise⟩ ⟨all that sort of duplicity is an ~ in any handling of men by methods other than direct authority —Hilaire Belloc⟩

essential amino acid *n* **:** any of various alpha amino acids that are required for normal health and growth, are either not manufactured in the body or manufactured in insufficient quantities, are usu. supplied by dietary protein, and in man include isoleucine, leucine, lysine, methionine, phenylalanine, threonine, tryptophan, and valine

essential clause *n* **:** RESTRICTIVE CLAUSE

essential hypertension *n* **:** abnormally high blood pressure, both systolic and diastolic, occurring in the absence of any evident cause and resulting typically in marked hypertrophic and degenerative changes in small arteries, hypertrophy of the heart, and often more or less severe kidney damage — see MALIGNANT HYPERTENSION

es·sen·tial·ism \-chə,lizəm\ *n* -s **1 :** a philosophic theory significantly concerned with and esp. based on a conception of essence or essential things: as **a :** a theory subscribing to the idea that metaphysical essences really subsist and are intuitively accessible — compare REALISM **b :** a theory that assigns priority to essence over existence — contrasted with *existentialism* **2 :** an educational theory holding that certain basic ideas and skills or disciplines essential to our culture are formulable and should be taught to all alike by certain time-tested methods — contrasted with *progressivism*

[1]**es·sen·tial·ist** \-ch(ə)lə̇st\ *n* -s **:** a follower of or believer in essentialism (as in religion, philosophy, or education)

[2]**essentialist** \"\ *adj* **:** of, relating to, subscribing to, or being essentialism **:** of or relating to an essentialist; *also* **:** realist in philosophic theory or point of view — **es·sen·tial·is·tic** \ə̇¦senchə¦listik, (¦)e¦s-,ē¦s-\ *adj*

es·sen·ti·al·i·ty \ə̇,senchē'alə̇d·ē, (,)e,s-,ē,s-, -lətē, -i\ *n* -ES **1 :** the quality or state of being essential ⟨the ~ of certain amino acids in the diet for maximum growth of the tissues —*Jour. Amer. Med. Assoc.*⟩ ⟨the ~ of giving special consideration to the needs of older people —*N.Y. State Legislative Committee on Problems of the Aging*⟩ ⟨are not by tradition fearful or quarrelsome over the ~ of freedom and justice —P.G.Hoffman⟩ **2 a :** the essential nature or character **:** ESSENCE **b :** an essential quality, property, or aspect

es·sen·tial·ize \ə̇'senchə,līz, e'-,ē'-\ *vt* -ED/-ING/-S **:** to express or formulate in essence or in essential form **:** state or present the essence of **:** distill the essence from **:** reduce to essentials

es·sen·tial·ly \ə̇'sench(ə)lē, e'-,ē'-, -li\ *adv* [ME *essencially*, fr. *essencial* essential + *-ly*] **:** in an essential manner **:** by its very nature **:** FUNDAMENTALLY ⟨taught her to play golf in the same grave, methodical but ~ encouraging way —Louis Auchincloss⟩ ⟨the species being ~ an inhabitant of southern waters —W.H.Dowdeswell⟩ ⟨government in New Jersey is ~ the same in general pattern as in each of the other 47 States —*Amer. Guide Series: N.J.*⟩ ⟨painting, ~ a two-dimensional art —Herbert Read⟩

es·sen·tial·ness \-chəlnə̇s\ *n* -ES **:** the quality or state of being essential

essential oil *n* **:** any of a large class of volatile odoriferous oils of vegetable origin that impart to plants odor and often other characteristic properties, that are obtained from various parts of the plants (as flowers, leaves, or bark) by steam distillation, expression, or extraction, that are usu. mixtures of compounds (as terpenoids, aldehydes, or esters), and that are used often in the form of essences in perfumes, flavoring materials, and pharmaceutical preparations — called also *ethereal oil, volatile oil;* distinguished from *fatty oil* and *fixed oil;* see OLEORESIN

essential predication *n* **:** predication in which the predicate is wholly contained in the essence of the subject

essential proposition *n* **:** an analytic proposition

essentiate *vb* [ML *essentiatus*, past part. of *essentiare* to make real or essential, fr. L *essentia* essence — more at ESSENCE] *vt, obs* **:** to form or constitute the essence or being of ~ *vi, obs* **:** to become essence

esses *pl of* ESS *or of* ESSE

-esses *pl of* -ESS

[1]**es·sex** \'esiks, -sēks *sometimes* -,seks\ *adj, usu cap* [fr. *Essex* co., Eng.] **:** of or from the county of Essex, England **:** of the kind or style prevalent in Essex

[2]**essex** \"\ *n* [fr. *Essex* co., Eng. where it was orig. bred] **1** *usu cap* **:** a British breed of small hardy swine that are black with white markings **2** -ES *often cap* **:** any animal of the Essex breed

es·sex·ite \-,sik,sīt, -sēk-\ *n* -s [*Essex* co., Mass. + E *-ite*] **:** granular intrusive igneous rock of various kinds composed chiefly of hornblende, augite, and labradorite with variable amounts of accessory iron ore, biotite, orthoclase, nepheline, or olivine

¹es·sive \ˈesiv\ *adj* [Finn *essiivi*, fr. L *esse* to be + Finn *-ivi* (fr. L *-ivus* -ive) — more at IS] *of a grammatical case* **:** denoting a state of being — used esp. in Finnish and Hungarian grammar

²essive \"\ *n* -s **:** the essive case of a language **:** a form in the essive case

es·soign *or* **es·soine** \əˈsȯin\ *archaic var of* ESSOIN

¹es·soin \"\ *n* -s [ME *essoine*, fr. MF *essoine, essoigne*, fr. ML *essonia, essonium, exonium*, fr. L *ex-* + LL *sonium* care, worry] **1** *Eng law* **a :** an excuse for not appearing in court at the appointed time **b :** an allegation of an excuse of this kind to the court **2** *obs* **:** EXCUSE, EXEMPTION, DELAY

²essoin \"\ *vt* -ED/-ING/-S [ME *essoinen*, fr. MF *essonier, essoignier*, fr. ML *essoniare*, fr. L *ex-* + LL *soniari* to worry, fr. *sonium* care, worry] **:** to offer or allege an essoin **:** excuse or make excuse in behalf of for nonappearance in court

essoin day *n* **:** a day formerly set aside by English law for receiving essoins

es·soin·ee \əˌsȯiˈnē, eˌs-, ˌeˌs-\ *n* -s [AF *essonié, essoignié*, past part. of *essonier, essoignier*, v.] **:** one whose essoin is allowed

es·soin·er \əˈsȯinə(r)\ *n* -s [AF *essonier, essoneour*, fr. *essonier*, v. + *-er, -our* -or] **:** one that essoins another

es·so·nite \ˈesᵊnˌīt\ *also* **hes·so·nite** \ˈhe-\ *n* -s [F, fr. Gk *hēssōn* inferior, less + F *-ite*; fr. its being less hard than true hyacinth] **:** a variety of garnet — called also *cinnamon stone*

est \ˈest\ *n* -s [by alter. (resulting from incorrect division of *a nest*)] *Scot* **:** NEST

¹-est \əst\ *adj suffix or adv suffix* [ME, fr. OE *-st, -est, -ost*; akin to superlative suffixes OHG *-isto, -ōsto* (in adjectives), *-ist, -ōst* (in adverbs), ON *-str, -astr* (in adjectives), *-st, -ast* (in adverbs), Goth *-ists, -osts* (in adjectives), *-ist* (in adverbs), Gk *-istos* (in adjectives), Skt *-iṣṭha* (in adjectives); prob. fr. the suffix represented by E ¹*-er* + the suffix represented by E ¹*-ed*] — used to form the superlative degree of adjectives and adverbs of one syllable ⟨fatt*est*⟩ ⟨lat*est*⟩ ⟨new*est*⟩, of certain adjectives and adverbs of two syllables ⟨lucki*est*⟩ ⟨oft*enest*⟩ ⟨remot*est*⟩ ⟨simpl*est*⟩, and less often of longer ones ⟨beggarli*est*⟩; often attached to words (as participles in adjectival use) that rarely if ever show a corresponding comparative formation in *-er* ⟨cuss*edest*⟩ ⟨fighting*est*⟩ ⟨lying*est*⟩; regularly accompanied by coalescence with final *e* of the base word, change of final postconsonantal *y* of the base word to *i*, or doubling of the final consonant of the base word immediately after a short stressed vowel; compare ²MOST

²-est \əst\ *or* **-st** \st, *after a voiced consonant* zt *or* st\ *suffix* [ME, fr. OE *-est, -ast, -st*, 2d sing. pres. endings of various classes of verbs (fr. earlier *-es, -as, -s* + *-t*, assimilated form of the 2d pers. pron. *thū* thou) & *-est* (fr. earlier *-es* + *-t*), 2d sing. past ending of weak verbs; akin to OHG *-ist, -ōst, -ēst* (fr. earlier *-is, -ōs, -ēs* + *-t*, fr. *thū, thu* thou), 2d sing. pres. endings, *-ōst* (fr. earlier *-ōs* + *-t*), 2d sing. past ending of weak verbs, Goth *-is, -os, -ais*, 2d sing. pres. endings, *-ēs*, 2d sing. past ending of weak verbs, ON *-r, -ar, -ir*, 2d sing. pres. endings, *-ir*, 2d sing. past ending of weak verbs, L & Gk *-s* (preceded by various thematic vowels), 2d sing. pres. ending, Skt *-si*] — used to form the archaic second person singular indicative of English verbs (with *thou*) ⟨get*test*⟩ ⟨di*dst*⟩ ⟨carri*est*⟩ ⟨fail*edst*⟩ ⟨can*st*⟩

est *abbr* **1** established; establishment **2** estate **3** estimate; estimated **4** estuary

EST *abbr* **1** eastern standard time **2** electroshock therapy

es·tab·lish \əˈstablish, eˈs-, -lēsh, *chiefly in pres part* -ləsh\ *vb* -ED/-ING/-ES [ME *establissen*, fr. MF *establiss-*, stem of *establir*, fr. L *stabilire*, fr. *stabilis* firm, stable — more at STABLE] *vt* **1 a :** to make firm or stable **:** fix to prevent or check unsteadiness, wavering, turmoil, or agitation ⟨~ the gun firmly on its base⟩ **b :** to place, install, or set up in a permanent or relatively enduring position esp. as regards living quarters, business, social life, or possession ⟨the family *~ed* itself in a large house⟩ ⟨*~ed* himself in the community as a grain dealer⟩ ⟨stayed with the team long enough to see it *~ed* as a member of a major league⟩ ⟨the first day of 1930 saw me *~ed* in London with a good job on an evening paper —Harold Nicolson⟩ **c :** to found or base securely (as a theory) ⟨*~ed* the moral unity of all people upon the idea of God⟩ ⟨examine critically the foundations of his creed and ~ his theology upon philosophy —V.L.Parrington⟩ **d :** to assist, support, or nurture so that stability and continuance are assured ⟨stayed as principal of the new school until it was well *~ed*⟩ **e :** to fix or implant (itself) in gaining a firm hold ⟨think of the possibilities if this scourge becomes widely *~ed* among our eastern oaks —W.H. Camp⟩ ⟨a vice continued until it *~ed* itself beyond escape⟩ **2 a :** to settle or fix after consideration or by enactment or agreement ⟨a congressional bill *~ing* duties on a wide range of imports⟩ ⟨an act *~ing* quota limits on immigration⟩ **b :** APPOINT, ORDAIN, ENTITLE ⟨*~ed* several European correspondents for the newspaper⟩ ⟨*~ed* a new vice-president for the firm⟩ **3** *obs* **:** to settle (as an estate) upon someone **:** secure (as rights) to a group **4 a :** to bring into existence, create, make, start, originate, found, or build usu. as permanent or with permanence in view ⟨~ a factory on the banks of the river⟩ ⟨*~ed* a cranberry bog —*Amer. Guide Series: Oregon*⟩ ⟨the five studies in this volume have the common purpose of *~ing* a background for an understanding of 18th century English literature —*Univ. of Minn. Press Catalog*⟩ ⟨~ a school for the deaf⟩ ⟨the Italians voted to ~ a republic —*Current Biog.*⟩ ⟨Noah Webster, with his dictionary . . . had *~ed* American usage in the matter of words —Van Wyck Brooks⟩ **b :** to bring about **:** EFFECT ⟨*~ing* friendly relations with the Indians —*Amer. Guide Series: Maine*⟩ **c** (1) **:** PROVIDE **:** set up ⟨it *~ed* a fund of $700,000 to open regional offices —*Current Biog.*⟩ (2) **:** to provide for **:** ENDOW ⟨~ a chair of Oriental studies at the university⟩ **5** *obs* **:** to bring (as anger) to a state of calm **:** QUIET **6 a** *archaic* **:** CONFIRM, VALIDATE **b :** to prove or make acceptable beyond a reasonable doubt ⟨the point the speaker was trying to ~ was the imminence of economic collapse⟩ ⟨the impossibility of spontaneous generation was finally *~ed* as a valuable working principle —J.B.Conant⟩ ⟨~ the fact that he was not there when the murder occurred⟩ **c :** to provide strong evidence for **:** bring unavoidably to the attention ⟨something was said that *~ed* him as being in the contracting business —Hamilton Basso⟩ **d :** to calculate or determine exactly and with certainty the terms, limits, or identity of ⟨the evidence *~ed* the motive for the crime⟩ ⟨~ the weight of the planet⟩ **e :** to provide the mind or comprehension with appropriate information about ⟨the opening shot of the movie *~es* the scene⟩ **7 :** to make a national or state institution of (a church) **8 a :** to provide with a secure reputation esp. as valuable, useful, or certain ⟨screen productions based on *~ed* novels⟩ ⟨*~ed* as the world's tobacco capital —*Amer. Guide Series: N.C.*⟩ **b :** to place in a position of being accepted, respected, or feared ⟨the British authority had been pretty securely *~ed* —B.K.Sandwell⟩ ⟨clearly *~ed* my standing as a man of good character —B.F.Fairless⟩ ⟨upset the *~ed* order in southeast Asia⟩ **c :** to make a norm, a custom, a convention, or a habit ⟨the *~ed* way of addressing a clergyman⟩ ⟨*~ed* art styles⟩ ⟨it was his *~ed* practice to eat an early supper⟩ ⟨an *~ed* conditioned reflex⟩ **9 a :** to set (as a record) as an achievement **b :** to arrive at (as a result) **10 :** to define and record (as a species) by effective publication in systematic biology **11 :** to make such plays in a card game as will permit (a specified card or all remaining cards of a specified suit) to win tricks **~** *vi* **:** to become naturalized **:** enter and persist without care or cultivation — used chiefly of plants ⟨various xerophytes readily ~ on and stabilize coastal dunes⟩ **syn** see FOUND, SET

es·tab·lish·able \-shəbəl\ *adj* **:** capable of being proved or made acceptable to logic or reason ⟨there are certain laws and generalizations ~ by these means —F.L.Will⟩

established *adj* **1 :** introduced from another region and persisting without aid or cultivation **:** NATURALIZED **2 :** surviving and multiplying on a host or substrate

established church *n* **:** a church that is recognized by law as the official church of a nation, that is supported by civil authority, and that receives in most instances financial support from the government through some system of taxation — called also *state church* ⟨the Church of England is the *established church* in England⟩

es·tab·lish·er \-shə(r)\ *n* -s **:** one that establishes

establishing shot *n* **:** a long shot in movie or television photography to establish a scene or locale before photographing specific action or detail

es·tab·lish·ment \-shmənt\ *n* -s **1 :** something that has been established: **a :** a settled arrangement; *esp* **:** a code of laws **:** RULE, DECREE, LAW **b :** ESTABLISHED CHURCH **c :** a permanent civil or military force or organization **d :** a more or less fixed and usu. sizable place of business or residence together with all the things that are an essential part of it (as grounds, furniture, fixtures, retinue, employees) **e :** a public or private institution (as a school or hospital) **2 :** the act of establishing something or the state of being established: as **a** (1) **:** the act of bringing into existence, creating, founding, originating, or setting up so that a certain continuance is assured ⟨the ~ of a custom⟩ ⟨the ~ of a factory⟩ ⟨the ~ of a new set of laws⟩ (2) **:** the act of setting or achieving (as a record) **b** *obs* **:** a settled or stable condition **:** calm security **c :** the making of a church into an established church **d :** a permanent settled position (as in life or business) **3** *archaic* **:** a regular means of support **:** an assured income **4** *also* **establishment of the port :** VULGAR ESTABLISHMENT **5 :** the naturalization of a plant or sometimes an animal in a new habitat or range typically involving successful growth, survival, and reproduction — called also *ecesis*

¹es·tab·lish·men·tar·i·an \ə,ˌ=ˌmən·ˈterēən, -ˌmen-, -ta(a)r-\ *n* -s **:** one who favors the establishment of a state church **:** an adherent of the system by which a government officially recognizes and supports an established church

²establishmentarian \"\ *adj* **:** relating to or favoring religious establishment

es·tab·lish·men·tar·i·an·ism \-ēə,nizəm\ *n* -s **:** the system of giving official state recognition and support to a particular church **:** the setting up of an established church

es·ta·fette \ˌestəˈfet\ *n* -s [F, fr. It *staffetta*, lit., small stirrup, dim. of *staffa* stirrup, of Gmc origin; akin to OHG *stapfo* step, footstep — more at STEP] **:** a mounted courier

es·ta·fia·ta \ˌestəfēˈädə, -fˈyä-\ *n* -s [MexSp *estafiate*, modif. of Nahuatl *iztauhyatl*] **:** WORMWOOD SAGE

es·tall \əˈstȯl\ *vt* -ED/-ING/-S [MF *estaler* to stop, place — more at INSTALLMENT] *archaic* **:** to arrange to pay (as a debt) in installments

es·ta·min \ˈestəmən\ *or* **es·ta·mene** \ˈestə,mēn, ˌ=ˌ=ˈ=\ *n* -s [fr. obs. F *estamine* (now *étamine*), fr. MF, fr. ML *staminia*, fr. L *staminea*, fem. of *stamineus* made of threads, fr. *stamin-*, *stamen* warp, thread, cloth — more at STAMEN] **:** a worsted twilled fabric with a rough face

es·ta·mi·net \estàmēnā\ *n, pl* **estaminets** \-ā(z)\ [F, perh. fr. F dial. (Walloon) *staminet* manger, cow shed, assembly room, fr. *stamon* stake, post, of Gmc origin; akin to OHG *stam* trunk, stem — more at STEM] **:** a small café **:** BISTRO

es·tam·page \ˌe,stämˈpäzh\ *n* -s [F, fr. *estamper* to stamp, pound (influenced in form by It *stampare* to stamp; F, fr. OF, of Gmc origin; akin to OHG *stampfōn* to crush, pound, stamp) + *-age* — more at STAMP] **:** an impression of an inscription made on inked paper

es·tam·pie \ˌe,stämˈpē\ *or* **es·tam·pi·da** \-ēdə\ *n* -s [*estampie* fr. F, fr. OF, modif. of OProv *estampida* noise, chatter, dispute, fr. *estampida*, fem. of *estampit*, past part. of *estampir* to resound, repeat, stamp, of Gmc origin; akin to OE *stempan* to stamp — more at STAMP] **1 :** a slow stamping round dance of Provençal origin that was popular in Europe from the 12th to 15th centuries **2 :** music for the estampie typically having repeated sections and refrain somewhat in the manner of the rondeau

es·tan·cia \eˈstän(t)s(ˌ)yä\ *n* -s [AmerSp, fr. Sp, stay, room, dwelling, fr. (assumed) VL *stantia* — more at STANCHION] **:** a So. American cattle ranch or stock farm

es·tan·cie·ro \ˌe,stän(t)sēˈe(ˌ)rō\ *n* -s [AmerSp, fr. *estancia* + Sp *-ero* (fr. L *-arius* -er)] **:** the owner or manager of an estancia

¹es·tate \əˈstāt, eˈ-, *usu* -ād·+V\ *n* -s [ME *estat*, fr. MF — more at STATE] **1 :** STATE, CONDITION: **a :** the form of existence or state of being of something; *specif* **:** condition or position in respect to a standard of value or to good repute ⟨he wanted to bring painting back to its original ~ —Henry Miller⟩ ⟨discussing what seem to me to be the primary causes behind the low ~ of the public schools —M.B.Smith⟩ ⟨the Civil War . . . brought our ocean marine insurance to a very low ~ —C.K.Knight⟩ **b :** circumstances or situation in life **:** mental, physical, or material condition ⟨a service which would visualize for womanhood its highest domestic ~ —Edward Bok⟩ ⟨a tonic bitterness in such poems as examine man's ~ —Babette Deutsch⟩ ⟨going to be such a field supervisor and later on a district manager, and he must not arrive at his new ~ uninformed —Bernard De Voto⟩ **c** *obs* **:** normal or good condition **2 a** (1) *obs* **:** high social standing or rank (2) **:** social standing or rank ⟨a political platform appealing to people of every ~⟩ **b** *obs* (1) **:** a position or seat of dignity, grandeur, or pomp (2) **:** a canopy, chair, or dais providing this position **c** *obs* **:** a person of high social rank **3 a :** a social or political class or rank **:** a markedly distinguishable class of people in a community or nation esp. when distinguishable by social or political duties or privileges; *specif* **:** one of two or more great classes or orders of a state regarded as part of the body politic who are vested with distinct political powers and whose concurrence is necessary for legislation ⟨generally the three *~s* of Medieval Europe consisted of the nobility, the clergy, and the merchants of the cities⟩ — called also *estate of the realm* **b estates** *pl* **:** an assembly of the governing classes or of their representatives in a nation or state **:** PARLIAMENT ⟨the levying of taxes was subject to the consent of the *~s*⟩ **4 a :** the property or a piece or aggregation of property in lands or tenements and sometimes personalty **:** FORTUNE, POSSESSIONS ⟨a man of small ~⟩ **b** (1) **:** the aggregate of property or liabilities of all kinds that a person leaves for disposal at his death ⟨if you don't make a will, the law makes provision for disposing of your ~ for you —*Have You Made a Will?*⟩ (2) **:** such an aggregate considered as a legal entity ⟨the recoverable portion of the debt does not go to the decedent's ~ but to his heirs⟩ **c :** an interest often varying widely in degree, quality, nature, and extent in land or other property ⟨an ~ for life⟩ ⟨an ~ for years⟩ ⟨system of accumulation of funds for the creation of an ~ for old-age security —C.M.Winslow⟩ **5** *obs* **:** form of government **:** governing constitution **6** *obs* **:** body politic **:** COMMONWEALTH, KINGDOM, STATE **7 a :** a usu. large landed property ⟨the proprietor of a large ~ with ponds, woods, and a sizable house to retire to⟩ **b :** a large farm **:** PLANTATION ⟨orange groves and avocado *~s* lie round about —Aubrey Drury⟩ ⟨European tea *~s* in Africa⟩ **c** *Brit* **:** PROJECT, DEVELOPMENT ⟨trim housing *~s* are being built for the workers —Robert Dunnett⟩

²estate \"\ *vt* -ED/-ING/-S **1** *obs* **:** to bestow as an estate — used with *on* or *upon* **2 a :** to endow with — used with *in* ⟨*estated* half his property in his nephew⟩ **b** *obs* **:** to endow or provide with property

estate agent *n, Brit* **:** a real estate broker or manager

estate at sufferance : the interest in a property held by one who remains in possession of or on the property after his tenancy has terminated — compare TENANCY AT SUFFERANCE

estate at will : an interest in a property subject to termination at the will of another person — compare TENANCY AT WILL

estate bottled *adj, of a wine* **:** bottled on and by the vineyard and labeled with the name of the vineyard or its owner ⟨an *estate bottled* claret⟩

estate car *or* **estate wagon** *n, Brit* **:** STATION WAGON

estate duty *n, chiefly Brit* **:** ESTATE TAX

estate in expectancy : an estate either vested or contingent in which one has a present right or interest but of which the possession is postponed or limited to take effect at some future time or upon some future event

estate in possession : a vested estate

estate of inheritance : an estate that descends to an heir and thus endures throughout two or more lives

estates *pl of* ESTATE, *pres 3d sing of* ESTATE

estates general *n* [trans. of F *états généraux*] **:** STATES GENERAL

estate tail *n* **:** an estate of inheritance held in fee tail

estate tax *n* **:** an excise tax levied often at graduated rates upon the privilege of an owner of property often including life insurance proceeds, property held jointly with right of survivorship, and gifts made in contemplation of death or to take effect in enjoyment after death of transmitting his property to others after his death, measured by the value of his total estate after payment of debts and any deductions permitted by law, and payable from the net estate before its distribution

estating *pres part of* ESTATE

estbd *abbr* established

estd *abbr* **1** established **2** estimated

este *abbr* estate

¹es·teem \əˈstēm, eˈ-\ *n* -s [ME *steem, extyme*, fr. MF *estime*, fr. *estimer* (v.)] **1 a** *archaic* **:** WORTH, VALUE; *also* **:** estimate of value **:** VALUATION **b** *obs* **:** RANK, STANDING **c** *archaic* **:** REPUTATION — used with *of* **d** *archaic* **:** OPINION, JUDGMENT **2 a :** approval and respect often blended with great liking or fondness because of worthy qualities ⟨an aide rising in his superior's ~⟩ **b :** such approval, respect, or liking held generally **:** FAME, RENOWN ⟨the ~ and prestige which nature attaches to excellence —H.W.Dodds⟩ **syn** see REGARD

²esteem \"\ *vb* -ED/-ING/-S [ME *estemen, estimen*, fr. MF *estimer*, fr. L *aestimare, aestumare*, prob. a denominative fr. a prehistoric compound whose first constituent is *aes* copper, bronze, money and whose second constituent is akin to Gk *temnein* to cut — more at ORE, TOME] *vt* **1** *obs* **a :** to form a numerical or quantitative estimate of **b :** to set a value on **:** estimate the worth of **:** APPRAISE **2 :** to regard as being or hold to be (of a particular character or status) **:** DEEM ⟨the enterprise foolish⟩ ⟨preserve my friend from what I *~ed* a most unhappy connection —Jane Austen⟩ ⟨he should have *~ed* it cowardly to hint that he was not happy —Compton Mackenzie⟩ ⟨officials and diplomats . . . likewise *~ed* this their mighty hour —Harry Hansen⟩ **3 :** to set a high value on **:** hold in high regard **:** RESPECT, PRIZE ⟨~ riches⟩ ⟨two of the most *~ed* writers of the twenties —Edward Shils⟩ ⟨*~ed* for its antiquity, like a superannuated piece of furniture —C.H.Grandgent⟩ ⟨society knows what it *~s* and what it despises —W.C.Brownell⟩ **4 a :** to hold in regard to a specified degree ⟨intestines, liver, and other organs are greatly *~ed* and often eaten —Farley Mowat⟩ ⟨should ~ it highly if I might be permitted to place myself during the journey, under that worthy gentleman's protection —Charles Dickens⟩ **b :** to form or hold an opinion or judgment of **c :** to be of the opinion **:** THINK, BELIEVE — used with a clause as object ⟨she *~ed* that she knew what life was, and that it was grim —Arnold Bennett⟩ **~** *vi* **1** *obs* **:** to form or have a favorable regard **2** *obs* **:** to form or have a (particular) opinion **:** REGARD, THINK

es·teem·able \-məbəl\ *adj, archaic* **:** ESTIMABLE

es·ter \ˈestə(r)\ *n* -s [G, fr. *essigäther* acetic ether, fr. *essig* vinegar (fr. OHG *ezzih*, fr. L *acetum*) + *äther* ether, fr. L *aether* — more at ACETIC, ETHER] **:** any of a class of compounds (as ethyl acetate, triphenyl phosphate) that on hydrolysis yield an organic or inorganic acid and an alcohol or phenol and hence may be classified either by their acid constituent (as benzoic esters or nitric esters) or by their alcohol or phenol constituent (as methyl esters or tolyl esters) and that are usu. fragrant liquids if sufficiently volatile, esters of carboxylic acids characterized by the group —COOR being found in essential oils and synthesized esp. for use in artificial fruit essences — see GLYCERIDE, POLYESTER, WAX 2a; compare ACYLAL

es·ter·ase \ˈestə,rās, -āz\ *n* -s [ISV *ester* + *-ase*] **:** any of a class of enzymes that accelerate the hydrolysis or synthesis of esters (as fats or esters of the lower fatty acids) — compare LIPASE, PHOSPHATASE

ester gum *n* **:** a resinous ester or mixture of esters made by combining a resin of acid nature or resin acids with a polyhydric alcohol; *esp* **:** a hard usu. pale substance made by heating rosin with glycerol and used in varnishes, lacquers, and printing inks

es·ter·i·fi·able \eˈsterə,fīəbəl, ˌ=ˌ=ˈ=ˌ=ˌ=\ *adj* **:** capable of being esterified

es·ter·i·fi·ca·tion \e,sterəfəˈkāshən\ *n* -s **:** the process of esterifying or the state of being esterified

es·ter·i·fy \eˈsterə,fī\ *vb* -ED/-ING/-ES [*ester* + *-ify*] **:** to convert into an ester (as by the reaction of a carbolic acid with an alcohol)

es·ter·ize \ˈestə,rīz\ *vb* -ED/-ING/-S **:** ESTERIFY

es·te·ro \eˈste(ˌ)rō\ *n* -s [Sp, fr. L *aestuarium* — more at ESTUARY] **:** an estuary or inlet esp. when marshy; *specif* **:** a tidal channel used as a drainage canal in populated districts

-es·tes \ˈe(ˌ)stēz\ *n comb form* [NL, modif. of Gk *edestēs*, fr. (Homeric) *edmenai* to eat — more at EAT] **:** -eater — in generic names of birds ⟨Sperm*estes*⟩

esth \ˈes(t)th, ˈest\ *n* -s *cap* **:** ESTONIAN

es·tha·cyte *or* **aes·tha·cyte** \ˈesthə,sīt\ *n* -s [*estha-, aestha-* (fr. Gk *aisthanesthai* to perceive) + *-cyte* — more at AUDIBLE] **:** a simple sensory cell (as of a sponge)

es·the·ria \esˈthirēə, eˈsti-\ *n, cap* [NL, prob. fr. the name *Esther* + NL *-ia*] **:** a genus (sometimes made the type of the family Estheriidae) of small branchiopod crustaceans in which the carapace is developed into a bivalve shell not unlike that of some mollusks and enclosing the whole body — **es·the·ri·an** \(ˈ)=ˌ=ˈrēən\ *adj or n*

es·the·sia *also* **aes·the·sia** \esˈthēzh(ē)ə\ *n* -s [NL, back-formation fr. *anesthesia, anaesthesia*] **:** capacity for sensation and feeling **:** the state of feeling or of being sensible **:** SENSIBILITY — opposed to *anesthesia*

esthesio- *or* **aesthesio-** *comb form* [NL, fr. Gk *aisthēsis* sensation, perception, feeling, fr. *aisthanesthai* to perceive, feel — more at AUDIBLE] **:** sensation ⟨*esthesio*neurosis⟩ ⟨*aesthesio*logy⟩

es·the·si·o·blast \esˈthēzēə,blast, -thēsē-\ *n* -s [*esthesio-* + *-blast*] **:** GANGLIOBLAST

es·the·si·om·e·ter \es,thēzēˈämәd·ə(r), -thēsē-\ *n* [*esthesio-* + *-meter*] **:** an instrument for measuring sensory discrimination; *esp* **:** one for determining the distance by which two points pressed against the skin must be separated in order that they may be felt as separate

es·the·si·om·e·try \-mə·trē\ *n* -ES [*esthesio-* + *-metry*] **:** the measurement of sensory (as tactile) discrimination

es·the·sio·physiology \esˌthēzē(ˌ)ō, -thēsē-+\ *n* [*esthesio-* + *physiology*] **:** the physiology of sensation and sense organs

es·the·sis *or* **aes·the·sis** \esˈthēsəs\ *n* -ES [NL, fr. Gk *aisthēsis*] **:** SENSATION; *esp* **:** rudimentary sensation

esthetic *var of* AESTHETIC

es·thi·o·mene \esˈthīə,mēn\ *n* -s [NL *esthiomenus*, fr. Gk *esthiomenos* decayed, infected, fr. pres. part. middle and passive of *esthiein* to eat; akin to Gk (Homeric) *edmenai* to eat — more at EAT] **:** the chronic ulcerated state of the vulva and clitoris characteristic of lymphogranuloma in the female

esthonian *usu cap, var of* ESTONIAN

es·ti·ma·ble \ˈestəməbəl\ *adj* [ME, fr. MF, fr. L *aestimabilis*, fr. *aestimare* to value, estimate + *-abilis* -able — more at ESTEEM] **1** *archaic* **:** of worth **:** VALUABLE **2 :** worthy of esteem or respect **:** deserving good opinion ⟨disappointing her father and jilting an ~ young man —Mary Austin⟩ ⟨a cultivated and eminently ~ dramatic critic —G.J.Nathan⟩ ⟨he is in many ways an admirable and even ~ figure —Irving Howe⟩ ⟨sober ~ paintings —*Time*⟩ — **es·ti·ma·ble·ness** *n* -ES

¹es·ti·mate \ˈestə,māt *sometimes* -,məl; *usu* |d+V\ *vb* -ED/-ING/-S [L *aestimatus*, past part. of *aestimare* to value, estimate] *vt* **1** *archaic* **a :** to consider or judge to be of a particular character or nature **b :** to consider or judge to be of value ⟨a man to ~ and welcome nobleness —George Meredith⟩ **2 :** to make an estimate of: as **a :** to judge the value, worth, or significance of; *esp* **:** to arrive at (a value judgment that is often valid but incomplete, approximate, or tentative) ⟨the egregious error of supposing that the dramatic merit of a dramatic work could be *estimated* without reference to its poetic merit —T.S. Eliot⟩ **b :** to fix sometimes accurately the size, extent, magnitude, or nature of ⟨a method of *estimating* deuterium⟩ ⟨small and manageable numbers of birds must be counted precisely; huge flocks can only be *estimated* —*Time*⟩ ⟨a prehistoric skeleton that is *estimated* by some anthropologists to be at least 20,000 years old —*Amer. Guide Series: Minn.*⟩ ⟨*estimating* the social importance of this movement —C.D.Lewis⟩ **c** (1) **:** to arrive at an often accurate but usu. only approximate statement of the cost of (a job to be done) (2) **:** to arrive at a sometimes only tentative price for which one is willing to undertake (a job to be done) **3 :** JUDGE, CONCLUDE ⟨he checked the chimneys off one by one and *estimated* that the fire was in the kitchen —Hugh MacLennan⟩ ~ *vi* **:** to make an estimate

syn VALUE, EVALUATE, RATE, ASSAY, ASSESS, APPRAISE: ESTIMATE is often used with judgments, either considered or casual, which are not entirely definitive ⟨we have first to *estimate* their effects upon complicated social conditions (largely a matter of guesswork) —John Dewey⟩ ⟨let us dispassionately consider the Codex Sinaiticus and try to *estimate* its position —Aldous Huxley⟩ VALUE may suggest definite but quick and temporary judgments ⟨one may pronounce a play fine or 'rotten'. If one term such direct characterization *valuing*, then criticism is *not valuing* —John Dewey⟩ It may on the other hand suggest more careful judgment ⟨you cannot *value* him alone; you must set him, for contrast and comparison, among the dead. I mean this as a principle of aesthetic . . . criticism —T.S.Eliot⟩ VALUE is used more often than the accompanying words in quick or rash hyperboles ⟨who *values* his own honor not a straw —Robert Browning⟩ EVALUATE has less connotational effect than others in this group. It is often used in situations in which criteria or principles of judgment are specified as new or important ⟨the current debate should be *evaluated*, not in terms of the excess profits tax we had during the last war, but in terms rather of an improved excess profits tax —L.G.Walinsky⟩ ⟨conventional ethical codes are assumed to be invalid or at least impractical for *evaluating* life as it is —C.C.Walcutt⟩ RATE indicates placing in a certain class, status, or bracket, perhaps without much serious reflection ⟨it is a curious thing this friend of yours you *rate* so monstrous high has not come nigh you in your sore affliction —Edna S. V. Millay⟩ ⟨as copper is *rated* very much above its real value, so silver is *rated* somewhat below it —Adam Smith⟩ ASSAY stresses careful analysis before judgment, as with the completeness of scientific methods ⟨alienation in the modern world is a major theme. In his later novels Greene has *assayed* it with acute analysis and philosophical breadth —J.M.Brinnin⟩ ASSESS likewise stresses careful analysis, as though according to better economic principles ⟨long before he arrived in the capital he had cast up his accounts with himself and made his decision. Soberly he *assessed* the elements of his power —John Buchan⟩ More than others in this group, APPRAISE may suggest expert and definitive judgment on difficult or subtle matters ⟨the cool, judicial regard, the scholarly eye of this trained historian resting on and *appraising* the turmoil and hysteria that marked the downfall of Adolf Hitler —Rosemary Benét⟩ ⟨this difficulty of *appraising* literature absolutely —A.T.Quiller-Couch⟩ **syn** see in addition CALCULATE

[2]**es·ti·mate** \ˈestəmə̇t *sometimes* -ˌmā|; *usu* |d.+V\ *n* -s [L *aestimatus*, fr. *aestimatus*, past part. of *aestimare* to value] **1 a :** the act of appraising or valuing **:** VALUATION, CALCULATION ⟨the influence of their work upon the health and well-being of millions of Canadians is beyond ~ —F.C.James⟩ **b** *obs* **:** appraised value **c** *obs* **:** ESTEEM, REPUTE **2 :** an evaluation or judgment (as to the nature, character, or quality of a thing) ⟨an ~ of a man⟩ ⟨by general ~ at the period, the flour ground at the Brandywine Mills possessed an uncommon softness and whiteness —*Amer. Guide Series: Del.*⟩ ⟨in any ~ of human life there are two factors, both of which are extremely difficult to weigh —David Fairchild⟩ ⟨whether it is a benefit at all is a matter of forecast and ~ —O.W.Holmes †1935⟩ ⟨a generous ~ of one of the most intriguing and stimulating characters in modern fiction —Harrison Smith⟩ **:** ESTIMATION ⟨found that he had dropped somewhat in the ~ of the firm⟩ ⟨powerfully influenced an innocent public's ~ of an unfortunate woman—Ruth P. Randall⟩ ⟨in the last eight lines of the first stanza Keats makes one ~ of how this song could have thus affected him —C.S.Kilby⟩ **3 a :** a judgment made from usu. mathematical calculation esp. from incomplete data **:** a rough or approximate calculation (as of the number, amount, or size of anything) ⟨famous for a map of the inhabited earth and for reasonable ~*s* of the heights of mountains —Benjamin Farrington⟩ ⟨production figures for planes, tanks, and shipping actually exceeded the ~*s* projected by the program —*Current Biog.*⟩ ⟨some sort of ~ of the possible future developments —A.G.N.Flew⟩ ⟨impossible to give a precise ~ of the duration of these various Pleistocene ages —W.H. Dowdeswell⟩ **b :** a statement of the often approximate amount for which certain work will be done by one who undertakes it

estimated cost *n* **:** cost in cost accounting estimated in advance of production or construction

estimated weight *n* **:** the weight specified in tariffs and agreed upon by shippers and carriers to be that of certain commodities shipped in specified packages in order to avoid the weighing of each package

es·ti·mat·ing·ly *adv* **:** in an estimating or appraising manner

es·ti·ma·tion \ˌestəˈmāshən\ *n* -s [ME *estimacioun*, fr. MF *estimation* act of estimating, valuation, fr. L *aestimation-, aestimatio*, fr. *aestimatus* (past part. of *aestimare* to value, estimate) + *-ion-, -io* -ion — more at ESTEEM] **1 :** JUDGMENT, OPINION, POINT OF VIEW ⟨but apart from his own ~ of certain modern composers it is a conductor's duty to give all well-written works a trial —Warwick Braithwaite⟩ **2 a :** the act of estimating **:** the act of making an estimate (as of significance, size, or extent) ⟨the thermometer for the measurement of temperature and the barometer for the ~ of atmospheric pressure —S.F.Mason⟩ **b :** the value, number, amount, size, or price arrived at in an estimate **:** EVALUATION, ESTIMATE ⟨felt his ~ of the man was unfair⟩ ⟨staggering ~*s* of the future Canadian population —Aileen D. Ross⟩ **3 a** *archaic* **:** REPUTATION **b :** good reputation **:** ESTEEM, HONOR ⟨after the victory, the victor gained notably in general ~⟩ **c** *archaic* **:** IMPORTANCE, SIGNIFICANCE

es·ti·ma·tive \ˈestəˌmād·iv, -ˌməd-\ *adj* [ME, fr. MF or ML; MF *estimatif*, fr. ML *estimativus*, fr. L *aestimatus* + *-ivus* -ive] **1 :** adapted for and capable of estimating and judging ⟨the ~ power⟩ **2 :** ESTIMATED ⟨send along only an ~ figure rather than an exact calculation of the cost⟩

es·ti·ma·tor \-ˌmād·ə(r), -ātə-\ *n* -s [ML, fr. L *aestimator*, fr. *aestimatus* + *-or*] **:** one that estimates: **a :** one who estimates the amount of material or labor needed to do a given job or the cost of a job or of an item of manufacture **b :** CRUISER 4a

estival *var of* AESTIVAL

estivate *var of* AESTIVATE

es·ti·vo-autumnal *also* **aes·ti·vo-autumnal** \ˌestə(ˌ)vō, eˌstī(-+\ *adj* [*estivo-* or *aestivo-* (fr. L *aestivus* of summer) + *autumnal* — more at AESTIVAL] **:** relating to or occurring in the summer and autumn — used chiefly of a form of malaria

es·toc \(ˈ)eˌstäk\ *n* -s [F (also, tree trunk), fr. OF, tree trunk, sword point, of Gmc origin; akin to OHG *stoc* stump, tree trunk — more at STOCK] **:** a thrusting sword chiefly of the Renaissance

es·to·ca·da \ˌestəˈkädə\ *n* -s [Sp, fr. OSp *estoque* estoc (fr. MF *estoc*) + *-ada* -ade] **:** the thrust of the matador's sword used in the final stage of a bullfight and aimed to pass through the neck and kill by striking the aorta

es·to·fa·do \ˌestəˈfä(ˌ)dō\ *n* -s [Sp, fr. past part. of *estofar* to quilt, make estofado work, fr. *estofa* quilted material, fr. OSp, fr. MF *estoffe* stuff, material — more at STUFF] **:** the technique of finishing sculpture of wood and gesso with gilding, punched patterns, and paint

es·toile \(ˈ)eˌstȯil, -twäl\ *n* -s [MF, star, fr. L *stella* — more at STAR] **:** a star conventionally represented in heraldry usu. with six wavy points

estoile

es·to·lide \ˈestəˌlīd, -lə̇d\ *n* -s [*ester* + *-ol* + *-ide*] **:** any of a class of long-chain esters formed usu. by hydroxy acids by reaction of two molecules either of the same or of different acids

es·to·nia \(ˈ)eˌstōnyə, -nēə\ *adj, usu cap* [fr. *Estonia*, country in northern Europe] **:** of or from Estonia **:** of the kind or style prevalent in Estonia **:** ESTONIAN

[1]**es·to·nian** \(ˈ)eˌstōnyən, -ōnēən\ *also* **es·tho·nian** \(ˈ)esˈthō-, (ˈ)eˌstō-\ *adj, usu cap* [*Estonia, Esthonia* + E *-an*] **:** of or relating to Estonia, the Estonians, or their language

[2]**estonian** \"\ *also* **esthonian** \"\ *n* -s *cap* **1 :** a member of a Finno-Ugric-speaking people living chiefly in the former republic of Estonia on the Baltic sea **2 :** the Finno-Ugric language of the Estonian people — see URALIC LANGUAGES table

es·top \ə̇ˈstäp, eˈ-\ *vt* [ME *estoppen*, fr. MF *estoper, estouper*, fr. (assumed) VL *stuppare*, fr. L *stuppa* tow — more at STUPE] **1** *archaic* **:** to fill up **:** plug up **:** stop up **2 :** PRECLUDE, BAR, PROHIBIT ⟨sought to . . . ~ fighting on Sundays —K.S. Latourette⟩ ⟨if a person is pitch-deaf, he is *estopped* from the skillful use of inflectional change in his voice —A.T.Weaver⟩; *esp* **:** to impede or bar by estoppel

es·top·pel \-pəl\ *n* -s [prob. fr. MF *estoupail* bung, stopper, fr. *estouper*, v.] **:** a legal preclusion or bar by which one is prevented from alleging something he has previously denied in actuality or by implication in his action or from denying something he has similarly alleged

es·to·que \eˈstō,kā\ *n* -s [Sp, fr. MF *estoc* — more at ESTOC] **:** a matador's sword with a flat blade curved at the tip

es·to·vers \ə̇ˈstōvə(r)z, eˈ-\ *n pl* [ME, fr. AF, fr. OF *estoveir, estovoir* to be necessary, fr. L *est opus* there is need, it is necessary] **:** necessary supplies; *esp* **:** wood that a tenant is allowed to take from the landlord's premises for the necessary fuel or implements used by himself and his resident servants or for necessary repairs

es·trade \eˈsträd\ *n* -s [F, fr. Sp *estrado*, fr. L *stratum* bed, covering — more at STRATUM] **:** PLATFORM, DAIS

es·tra·di·ol *also* **oes·tra·di·ol** \ˌestrəˈdīˌȯl, -īˌōl\ *n* -s [ISV *estra-, oestra-* (fr. *estrin, oestrin*) + *-diol*] **:** a white crystalline highly estrogenic hormone that is a phenolic steroid alcohol $C_{18}H_{24}O_2$ found esp. in the follicular fluid of the ovary and in the urine of pregnant mares but is usu. made synthetically (as from estrone by reduction or indirectly from cholesterol) and that is often used in the form of esters esp. in treating menopausal symptoms

es·tra·gole \ˈestrəˌgōl\ *also* **es·dra·gol** \ˈezdrəˌgōl, -gōl\ *n* -s [*estragole* ISV *estragon* + *-ole; esdragol* fr. G, fr. *esdragon, estragon* (fr. F *estragon*) + *-ol* -ole] **:** a liquid ether $C_3H_5C_6H_4OCH_3$ that has an odor like aniseed, occurs in tarragon oil, turpentine, and other essential oils, and is used in perfumes and flavoring materials; *para*-allyl-anisole — called also *methyl chavicol*

es·tra·gon \ˈestrəˌgän\ *n* -s [F, fr. MF, alter. of earlier *targon*, fr. Ar *ṭarkhun* — more at TARRAGON] **:** TARRAGON

estragon oil *n* **:** TARRAGON OIL

estral *var of* ESTROUS

es·trange \ə̇ˈstrānj, eˈ-\ *vt* -ED/-ING/-S [MF *estranger*, fr. OF *estrangier*, fr. ML *extraneare*, fr. L *extraneus* foreign, strange — more at STRANGE] **1 :** to remove or keep at a distance esp. from customary environment or associations ⟨his constant need to travel served to ~ him from most family activities⟩ **2 :** to divert in affection or personal attachment **:** destroy one's confidence in **:** arouse enmity or indifference in where there had been originally love, affection, or friendliness ⟨the difference in religion brought on clashes between the two and ultimately *estranged* them⟩ ⟨the father's need to dominate quickly *estranged* all but one of the children⟩ ⟨poverty and misery had *estranged* him from his background —E.H.Erikson⟩ **3 :** to make alien or a stranger in condition, character, or appearance — now used with *from* ⟨writers who somehow felt *estranged* from their native life when the thread had once been broken —Van Wyck Brooks⟩ ⟨if a young man is not as anxious to work as he might be, let us remember that laws like that have helped ~ him from habits of industry —Elijah Adlow⟩

syn ALIENATE, DISAFFECT, WEAN: ESTRANGE may suggest development of hostility, separation, or divorcement ⟨the *estranging* film of defensive reticence which separates nearly all of us from our friends —C.E.Montague⟩ ALIENATE may not suggest separation but does indicate a changing of affection, sympathy, and interest to coldness, aloofness, or antipathy ⟨the governor and judges, who had *alienated* the people by arrogating to themselves the judicial, legislative, and executive powers of government —*Amer. Guide Series: Mich.*⟩ ⟨the colossal impudence of his comment on his former and now *alienated* associate —E.V.Lucas⟩ DISAFFECT indicates causing loss of warm and ready loyalty and inducing unrest and discontent ⟨the disloyalists tried to *disaffect* the militia, preaching treason —C.G.Bowers⟩ WEAN indicates separating commendably from someone or something that another is weakly dependent on or immaturely preoccupied with ⟨*wean* your minds from hankering after false Germanic standards —A.T.Quiller-Couch⟩ ⟨definitely *weaned* from close emotional dependency on his parents —John Dollard⟩

estranged *adj* **:** marked by or giving evidence of estrangement ⟨suggested a marriage counselor who might help out the ~ couple⟩ ⟨gave him an ~ look⟩

es·tranged·ness \-jə̇dnə̇s, -j(d)n-\ *n* -ES **:** the quality or state of being estranged

es·tran·ge·la \eˈstraŋgələ\ *or* **es·tran·ge·lo** *or* **es·tran·ghe·lo** \-ˌlō\ *n* -s *usu cap* [Syr *estrangelāyē* rounded (letters), fr. Gk *strongylos* rounded; akin to Gk *strangos* twisted — more at STRAIN (draw tight)] **:** the earlier form of the Syriac alphabet — compare SERTA

es·trange·ment \ə̇ˈstrānjmənt, eˈ-\ *n* -s **:** the act of estranging or the condition of being estranged **:** alienation esp. in friendship ⟨the small difference of opinion snowballed into mutual resentment and resulted in final and total ~⟩ ⟨the hero, a middle-aged intellectual and student, has passed through successive ~*s* from bourgeois life —*Time*⟩ ⟨resulted in the almost complete ~ of arts and letters from the sciences —*Scientific American Reader*⟩

estranger *n* -s [ME, fr. MF *estrangier*, fr. OF *estrange* foreign, strange + *-ier* -er — more at STRANGE] *obs* **:** one from another family, district, or country **:** ALIEN, FOREIGNER, STRANGER

es·tra·pe·nia \ˌestrəˈpēnēə, -nyə\ *n* -s [NL, fr. *estra-* (fr. ISV *cholinesterase*) + *-penia*] **:** deficiency of cholinesterase — **es·tra·pe·nic** \ˌestrəˈpēnik\ *adj*

[1]**es·tray** \ə̇ˈstrā, eˈ-\ *vi* [MF *estraier* to roam about without a master — more at STRAY] *archaic* **:** STRAY

[2]**estray** \"\ *n* -s [AF, fr. OF *estraié* wandering, masterless, fr. *estraier*, v.] **1 :** a valuable domestic animal found wandering away from its home or enclosure **:** STRAY **2 :** something that has wandered or gone out of its usual or normal place — compare FREE ASTRAY

[3]**estray** \"\ *adj* [[2]*estray*] **:** being or having gone astray

[1]**es·treat** \ə̇ˈstrēt, eˈ-\ *n* -s [ME *estrete*, fr. AF, fr. OF *estraite*, fem. of *estrait*, past part. of *estraire* to extract, fr. L *extrahere* — more at EXTRACT] **:** a true copy, duplicate, or extract of an original writing or record (as of an amercement)

[2]**estreat** \"\ *vt* -ED/-ING/-S **1 :** to extract from the records of a court so as to enforce or prosecute **2 :** to exact or take by means of a levy or fine

es·trepe \ə̇ˈstrēp, eˈ-\ *vt* -ED/-ING/-S [MF *estreper*, fr. L *exstirpare* to root out — more at EXTIRPATE] **:** to wreak needless destruction or waste upon — compare ESTREPEMENT

es·trepe·ment \-mənt\ *n* -s [AF *estrepement*, fr. OF *estreper*, v. + *-ment*] **:** waste or needless destruction of lands; *esp* **:** such waste in lands, woods, or houses wrought by a tenant for life to the damage of the reversioner

estriate \(ˈ)ē+\ *adj* [NL *estriatus*, fr. L *e-* + *striatus* striated — more at STRIATED] **:** not striated

estrich *or* **estridge** *obs var of* OSTRICH

es·trin *also* **oes·trin** \ˈestrən\ *n* -s [NL *estrus, oestrus* + E *-in*] **:** an estrogenic hormone; *esp* **:** ESTRONE

es·trin·iza·tion \ˌestrənə̇ˈzāshən, -ˌnīˈz-\ *n* -s [*estrin* + *-ization*] **1 :** the uterine and vaginal mucosal alteration characteristic of estrus **2 :** treatment with estrogenic substances

es·tri·ol *also* **oes·tri·ol** \ˈeˌstrīˌȯl, eˈs-, -īˌōl\ *n* -s [blend of *estrin, oestrin* and *-triol*] **:** a white crystalline estrogenic hormone that is a phenolic steroid glycol $C_{18}H_{24}O_3$ and is usu. obtained from the urine of pregnant women — called also *theelol*

es·tro·gen *also* **oes·tro·gen** \ˈestrəjən, -ˌjen\ *n* -s [ISV *estro-, oestro-* (fr. NL *estrus, oestrus*) + *-gen*] **:** a sex hormone (as estradiol, estriol, estrone) produced esp. in the ovaries and usu. characterized by its ability to promote estrus and stimulate the development of secondary sex characteristics in the female; *also* **:** a substance occurring naturally in plants or made synthetically (as benzestrol or diethylstilbestrol) that has similar biological activity — compare ANDROGEN

es·tro·gen·ic *also* **oes·tro·gen·ic** \ˌestrəˈjenik\ *adj* [ISV *estro-, oestro-* + *-genic*] **1 :** promoting estrus **2** [*estrogen, oestrogen* + *-ic*] **:** of, relating to, or caused by an estrogen — **es·tro·gen·i·cal·ly** \-nə̇k(ə)lē\ *adv*

Es·tron \ˈeˌsträn\ *trademark* **1** — used for a fiber made from partly hydrolized cellulose acetate **2 :** a yarn or fabric made of Estron fiber

es·trone *also* **oes·trone** \ˈeˌstrōn\ *n* -s [ISV *estrin, oestrin* + *-one*] **:** a white crystalline estrogenic hormone that is a phenolic steroid ketone $C_{18}H_{22}O_2$ usu. obtained from the urine of pregnant females (as mares or women) and that is used similarly to estradiol — called also *theelin*

es·trous *or* **oes·trous** \ˈestrəs, *chiefly Brit* ˈēs-\ *also* **es·tral** *or* **oes·tral** \-rəl\ *or* **es·tru·al** *or* **oes·tru·al** \-rəwəl\ *adj* [NL *estrus, oestrus* + E *-ous* or *-al*] **1 :** of, relating to, or characteristic of estrus ⟨the ~ state⟩ ⟨~ keratinization of the vaginal mucosa⟩ **2 :** exhibiting estrus **:** being in heat ⟨the ~ bitch⟩

estrous cycle *n* **:** the correlated phenomena of the endocrine and generative systems of a female mammal from the beginning of one period of estrus to the beginning of the next

es·tru·ate *or* **oes·tru·ate** \ˈestrəˌwāt\ *vi* -ED/-ING/-S [back-formation fr. *estruation, oestruation*] **:** to undergo estrus

es·tru·a·tion *or* **oes·tru·a·tion** \ˌestrəˈwāshən\ *n* -s [NL *estrum, oestrum* + E *-ation*] **1 :** the condition of being in estrus **2 :** ESTRUS

es·trus *or* **oes·trus** \ˈestrəs, *chiefly Brit* ˈēs-\ *also* **es·trum** *or* **oes·trum** \-rəm\ *n, pl* **estruses** *or* **oestruses** *also* **estrums** *or* **oestrums** *often attrib* [NL, fr. L *oestrus* gadfly, frenzy, fr. Gk *oistros* — more at IRE] **1 a :** a regularly recurrent state of sexual excitability during which the female of most mammals will accept the male and is capable of conceiving **:** HEAT **b :** a single occurrence of this state ⟨the next ~ was delayed⟩ **2 :** ESTROUS CYCLE

ests *pl of* EST

es·tu·a·rine \ˈes(h)chəwəˌrīn\ *also* **es·tu·ar·i·al** \ˌ==ˈwa(a)rēəl\ *adj* [*estuary* + *-ine, -ial*] **:** of, relating to, or formed in an estuary ⟨~ clays⟩ ⟨~ currents⟩ ⟨~ fisheries⟩ **:** suited to operate in estuaries ⟨*estuarial* craft⟩

estuarine crocodile *n* **:** SALTWATER CROCODILE

es·tu·ary \ˈes(h)chəˌwerē, -ri\ *n* -ES *often attrib* [L *aestuarium*, fr. *aestus* heaving of the sea, tide, boiling, heat + *-arium;* akin to L *aestas* summer — more at AESTIVAL] **1 a :** a water passage (as the mouth of a river) where the tide meets the current of a stream **:** TIDAL RIVER **b :** an arm of the sea at the lower end of a river **2 :** a drowned river mouth caused by the sinking of the land near the coast

estuate *vi* -ED/-ING/-S [L *aestuatus*, past part. of *aestuare* to be in commotion, boil, fr. *aestus*] *obs* **:** HEAVE, SURGE, BOIL — **estuation** *n* -s

es·tu·fa \eˈstüfə\ *n* -s [Sp, lit., stove, warm room, fr. *estufar* to heat an apartment, fr. (assumed) VL *extufare* to heat by steam — more at STOVE] **:** an assembly room or council chamber of a Pueblo Indian dwelling in which a sacred fire is kept burning

ESU *abbr, usu not cap* electrostatic unit

esu·ri·ence \ə̇ˈsu̇rēən(t)s, ēˈs-\ *also* **esu·ri·en·cy** \-nsē\ *n, pl* **esuriences** *also* **esuriencies :** the quality or state of being esurient

esu·ri·ent \-nt\ *adj* [L *esurient-, esuriens*, pres. part. of *esurire* to be hungry, desiderative of *edere* to eat — more at EAT] **:** VORACIOUS, GREEDY ⟨fell into the ~ embrace of a predatory enemy⟩ ⟨regarded the fellow with ~ eyes, the eyes of an avid curiosity —Carl Van Vechten⟩ — **esu·ri·ent·ly** *adv*

esurine *adj* [NL *esurinus*, fr. LL *esuries* hunger (fr. L *esurire* to be hungry) + L *-inus* -ine] **1** *obs* **:** consisting of a mineral acid **:** CORROSIVE **2** *obs* **:** VORACIOUS

et *dial past of* EAT

-et \ˌet, ə̇t, *usu* ˌəd· *or* ə̇d+V\ *n suffix* -s [ME, fr. OF *-et* (masc.) & *-ete* (fem.), fr. LL *-itus* & *-ita*] **1 :** small one **:** lesser one **:** -LET ⟨baronet⟩⟨cellaret⟩⟨singlet⟩ **2 :** group ⟨octet⟩

-et- *comb form* [ISV, fr. *ethyl*] **:** ethyl radical C_2H_5 ⟨phenetidine⟩

ET *abbr* **1** eastern time **2** Easter term **3** electric telegraph **4** electrical transcription

Et *symbol* ethyl

[1]**eta** \ˈā|d·ə, |tə *also* ˈē|\ *n* -s [LL, fr. Gk *ēta*, fr. a Phoenician word akin to Heb *ḥēth*] **:** the seventh letter of the Greek alphabet — symbol Η or η; see ALPHABET table

[2]**eta** \ˈāˌtä\ *n, pl* **eta** *also* **etas** *often cap* [Jap] **1 :** an outcast class formerly segregated in Japan ⟨in pre-Meiji Japan the ~, or pariah class, ranked below the . . . warrior, farmer, artisan, and merchant —J.F.Embree⟩ **2 :** a member of the eta class

-eta *pl of* -ETUM

ETA *abbr or n* -s **:** estimated time of arrival

etac \āˈtäts\ *n* -s [origin unknown] **:** BLAUBOK

éta·gère *or* **eta·gere** \ˌāˌtäˈzhe(ə)r\ *n* -s [F *étagère*, fr. MF *estagiere*, fr. *estage* floor of a building, sojourn, situation + *-iere* -er — more at STAGE] **:** a cabinet consisting of a tier of open shelves **:** WHATNOT

étain blue \ˈāˌtaⁿ-\ *n* [F *étain* tin, pewter, fr. MF *estain*, fr. LL *stagnum, stannum* — more at STANNIC] **:** a very pale green to very pale blue

et al \(ˈ)ed·ˈ|al, (ˈ)eˈt|, -|ȯl, -|äl\ *abbr* **1** [L *et alibi*] and elsewhere **2** [L *et alii* (masc. pl.), *et aliae* (fem. pl.), or *et alia* (neut. pl.)] and others

eta·lon \ˈād·ᵊlˌän, ˈed·-\ *n* -s [F *étalon* standard of weights and measures, fr. MF *estalon, estelon*, prob. of Gmc origin; akin to Fris *stal* shape, form] **:** an interferometer in which two parallel partially silvered glass plates at a fixed distance apart produce by multiple reflection interference spectra of high dispersion and resolution adapted to the fine-structure analysis of spectrum lines

eta·mine \ˈād·əˌmēn, ˈed·-\ *n* -s [F *étamine* — more at ESTAMIN] **:** a light cotton or worsted fabric with an open mesh

etanim *usu cap, var of* ETHANIM

eta·oin shrd·lu \ˈed·|ē,ȯinˈshərd,lü, ˈēd·|, ˈäd·|, |ə,ȯi-, -n-(ˌ)shərdˈlü\ *n* -s **:** a combination of letters set by running a finger down the first and then the second left-hand vertical banks of six keys of a Linotype machine to produce a temporary marking slug not intended to appear in the final printing

eta palm *var of* ITA PALM

etap·ter·is \ə̇ˈtaptərə̇s, āˈ-ˌ,ēˈ-\ *n, cap* [NL, fr. Gk *ēta* eta + NL *-pteris*] **:** a form genus of Paleozoic ferns represented only by fossil leaves which are pinnate and with primary pinnal alternate on the rachis

etat·ism \āˈtäd·ˌizəm\ *or* **éta·tisme** \ātäˈtēsm(ᵊ), -s(mə)\ *also* **état·ism** \āˈtad·ˌizəm\ *n, pl* **etatisms** \-izəmz\ *or* **étatismes** \-sm(ᵊ), -s(mə)\ *or* **étatisms** \-izəmz\ [F *étatisme*, fr. *état* state (fr. MF *estat*) + *-isme* -ism — more at STATE] **:** STATE SOCIALISM

etat·ist *or* **état·ist** \āˈtäd·ə̇st\ *adj* [F *étatiste*, fr. *étatiste*, n., one that favors etatism, fr. *état* state + *-iste* -ist] **:** belonging to or favoring state socialism

etc \ənˈsō,f|ȯrth |ȯrth, |ōth, |ə(ə)th *sometimes* =|=ˈ=; etˈsed·ərə, -setərə,-se·trə *also* ə̇tˈs-\ *abbr* [L *et cetera*] et cetera — sometimes used esp. formerly to shorten a letter-closing formula ⟨I am, Yours, ~⟩

et cet·era *also* **et cae·tera** \etˈsed·ərə, -setərə,-se·trə *also* ə̇tˈs-\ [L] **:** and others esp. of the same kind **:** and so on **:** and so forth ⟨lovely scarves, handbags, *et cetera* —*Mademoiselle*⟩ ⟨children are always catching things from one another, bad manners, germs, *et cetera* —Evelyn Barkins⟩ ⟨amid the new movements, foreign influences, themes, *et cetera* —Stark Young⟩ ⟨other institutional components of a society, such as school, church, *et cetera* —L.S.Cottrell⟩ ⟨climb mountains, cross rivers, swim oceans, *et cetera* —Everett Carter⟩ — abbr. *etc.;* used to imply that other items are to be understood; used also as a reminder that semantic abstractions lack allness

et·cet·era \"\ *n* -s [*et cetera*] **1 :** a number of various unspecified persons or things ⟨a long ~ of illustrious names —Susan E. Ferrier⟩ **2 etceteras** *pl* **:** additional items **:** ODDS AND ENDS, SUNDRIES ⟨she began to pack back her compact, comb and other ~*s* into her handbag —Elizabeth Bowen⟩ ⟨it's roomy enough to hold small parcels, plus your important ~*s* —*Christian Science Monitor*⟩

[1]**etch** \ˈech\ *vb* -ED/-ING/-ES [D *etsen*, fr. G *ätzen* to feed, bite, cause to bite, etch, fr. OHG *azzen* to feed; akin to MD *etten* to put out to graze, ON *etja* to cause to fight, goad on, Goth *fraatjan* to distribute as food; causative fr. the root of E *eat* — more at EAT] *vt* **1 a :** to produce (as a design) usu. on a metal or glass surface by covering it with an acid-resistant ground through which a design is scratched with a

pointed instrument and submitting the surface to an acid bath or other mordant ⟨panels of glass ~*ed* to simulate clouds —*Amer. Guide Series: Minn.*⟩ **b :** to treat (as a copper or zinc plate) in a similar manner to produce a relief printing image by photoengraving — compare HALFTONE **c :** to treat (a lithographic printing surface) with dilute nitric or other acid in order to fix the design and make the exposed parts more repellent to grease **2 :** to corrode the surface of (as a metal) usu. with acid for the purpose of microscopic examination of structural details **3 a :** to draw the main features of (as a face) **:** OUTLINE ⟨a little leaned by the years, and the features a little more sharply ~*ed* —C.I.Lewis⟩ ⟨nor has the relationship between crime and politics been more clearly ~*ed* than in Chicago —Seth Agnew⟩ **b :** to set forth in a clear-cut manner **:** DELINEATE ⟨the most sharply ~*ed* character in the book —*Times Lit. Supp.*⟩ **4 :** to produce (a feature of the landscape) by erosion **:** ERODE, CHISEL ⟨barrier of towering peaks and deeply ~*ed* canyons —R.A.Billington⟩ ⟨streams ~*ed* out new valleys —*Amer. Guide Series: N.J.*⟩ **5 :** to impress usu. on the mind or in the memory **:** IMPRINT ⟨the place, the people, are ~*ed* in our minds to stay —*N.Y. Herald Tribune Bk. Rev.*⟩ ⟨lasting impressions on the American mind, ~*ed* deeply into a national consciousness —J.D.Hart⟩ **~** *vi* **1 :** to practice the art of etching **:** make etchings ⟨has been ~*ing* busily the past month⟩ **2 :** to be susceptible of etching with acid ⟨magnesium is said to ~ faster than copper or zinc⟩

²etch \"\ *n* -ES **1 :** the action or effect of an etching acid on metal or glass **:** BITE **2 :** a chemical agent used in etching; *specif* **:** a solution of acid and gum arabic used in lithography to desensitize the parts of the stone or metal surface that are not intended to print **3 :** TOBACCO ETCH

etch·ant \ˈechənt\ *n* -s [¹*etch* + *-ant*] **:** a reagent (as a dilute solution of an acid) used in etching

etched–out \ˈ≈ˌ≈\ *adj* **:** BURNT-OUT 2

etch·e·min \ˈechəmən\ *n, pl* **etchemin** *or* **etchemins** *usu cap* [F, of AmerInd origin] **:** MALECITE

etch·er \ˈechə(r)\ *n* -s **:** one that etches: as **a :** an artist who hand-etches on metal or glass **b** (1) **:** one that hand-etches copper or steel plates for use in printing (2) **:** a worker who immerses such plates in the acid-etching solution **c :** one that dips a copper roller for use in printing textiles into an acid bath to etch the design previously scratched on its surface **d :** one that etches designs, trademarks, figures, or numbers on cutlery or firearms by hand or machine **e :** a worker who cleans metal airplane parts with an acid to prepare them for welding

etch figure *or* **etching figure** *n* **:** a marking consisting usu. of a minute pit produced by a solvent on the crystal face of a mineral and revealing its molecular structure — usu. used in pl.

etching *n* -s **1 :** the act or process of etching (as a design); *specif* **:** the art of producing pictures or designs by printing from a metal plate prepared by covering with a ground on which the picture is scratched with a needlelike instrument and then etched — compare AQUATINT, CRAYON MANNER, PHOTOENGRAVING, RELIEF, SOFT GROUND **2 :** the result or product of etching: as **a :** an etched plate **b :** a design produced by etching **c :** an impression on paper or a similar substance taken in ink from an etched plate **3 :** a written sketch or impression ⟨a series of ~*s* he wrote —A.W.Long⟩ **4 :** a cracked state of the enamel of a tooth

etching ball *n* **:** a ball of the ground used in etching

etching needle *n* **:** a steel point or stylus used in etching to draw through the ground and expose the metal plate to the acid

etching press *n* **:** COPPERPLATE PRESS

¹et·eo·cretan \ˌēd·ē(ˌ)ō, ˌed-+\ *adj, usu cap* [Gk *Eteokrēt-, Eteokrēs* pre-Greek inhabitant of Crete (fr. *eteos* true + *Krēt-, Krēs* Cretan) + E *-an* — more at SOOTH] **:** of or relating to the pre-Greek inhabitants of Crete — compare MINOAN

²eteocretan \"\ *n* -s *cap* **1 :** a pre-Greek inhabitant of Crete **2 :** a pre-Greek language of Crete preserved in a small amount of inscriptional material partly in hieroglyphic characters

¹eter·nal \əˈtərnᵊl, ēˈ-, -tə̄n-,-təin-\ *adj* [ME, fr. MF *eternal, eternel*, fr. LL *aeternalis*, fr. L *aeternus* (alter. of *aeviternus*, prob. fr. *aevitas* age, lifetime of something, fr. the stem of *aevum* age, eternity + *-itas* -ity) + *-alis* -al — more at AYE] **1 a :** having infinite duration: (1) **:** infinite in past and future duration **:** having no beginning or end ⟨the ~ God is your dwelling place —Deut 33:27 (RSV)⟩ (2) **:** infinite in past duration **:** having no beginning (3) **:** infinite in future duration **:** having no end ⟨the soldiers were convinced that whatever happened, the end of the war would mark the opening of an era of ~ peace —R. de R. de Sales⟩ **b :** having infinite duration and characterized by abiding fellowship with God ⟨good teacher, what must I do to inherit ~ life? —Mk 10:17 (RSV)⟩ **c :** of or relating to eternity ⟨this ~ blazon must not be to ears of flesh and blood —Shak.⟩ **2 a :** continued without intermission **:** CEASELESS, UNCHANGING ⟨and fires ~ in thy temple shine —John Dryden⟩ **b :** seemingly endless often to the point of weariness or disgust **:** constantly recurring **:** INTERMINABLE ⟨there was also the ~ waiting in hotels for appointments with officials —Herbert Hoover⟩ **3** *archaic* **:** INFERNAL, DAMNED — used as an intensive ⟨some ~ villain . . . devised this slander —Shak.⟩ **4 :** valid or existing at all times **:** IMMUTABLE, UNCHANGEABLE ⟨right and wrong were ~ verities . . . which could not be changed and must not be tampered with —O.E.Rölvaag⟩ **5 :** outside or beyond temporal relationships **:** discrete from all times **:** TIMELESS ⟨a color is ~ —A.N.Whitehead⟩

²eternal \"\ *n* -s **1** *cap* **:** ²GOD — used with preceding *the* ⟨the great issue remains man's relationship to the *Eternal* —Ruth Suckow⟩ **2** *obs* **:** ETERNITY **3 :** something that is eternal ⟨the superiority of the spiritual and ~ over the carnal and temporal —H.O.Taylor⟩ — often used in pl. ⟨men so truly spiritual in the ~*s* of their creed —Thomas De Quincey⟩

³eternal *adv, obs* **:** FOREVER

eternal generation *n* **:** the theological doctrine that the Son was begotten of the Father from all eternity and is therefore coeternal with the Father

eter·nal·ism \-ᵊlˌizəm\ *n* -s **:** the doctrine of the eternalists

eter·nal·ist \-ᵊləst\ *n* -s **:** a believer in the eternity of the world, in a transcendent world, or in a transcendental domain — **eter·nal·is·tic** \ə¦≈≈¦istik, ē¦≈-, ˌē¦≈-\ *adj*

eter·nal·i·ty \(ˌ)ēˌtərˈnaləd·ē, əˌt-, -tə̄ˈn-,-təiˈn-, -lətē, -i\ *n* -ES [ME *eternalite*, fr. MF *eternalité*, fr. ML *eternalitas*, fr. LL *aeternalis* eternal + L *-itas* -ity] **:** the quality or state of being eternal ⟨but to realize again the ~, the deathlessness and changelessness of youth —William Faulkner⟩

eter·nal·ize \əˈtərnᵊlˌīz, ēˈ-, -tə̄n-,-təin-\ *vt* -ED/-ING/-S **:** ETERNIZE

eter·nal·ly \-ᵊlē, -ᵊli\ *adv* [ME, fr. *eternal* + *-ly*] **1 :** throughout eternity **:** FOREVER ⟨whosoever liveth and believeth in Him shall not die ~ —*Bk. of Com. Prayer*⟩ **2 :** with continual recurrence **:** CONSTANTLY ⟨he was ~ in need of money —Rudyard Kipling⟩ **3 :** IMMUTABLY, UNALTERABLY ⟨there is such a thing as the ~ right and the unchangeably good —J.P.Hopps⟩

eter·nal·ness \-ᵊlnəs\ *n* -ES **:** ETERNALITY

eternal object *n* **1** *in Whiteheadian philosophy* **:** an enduring potential for becoming **2 :** a subsistent form or idea

eternal recurrence *n* **:** the infinitely cyclical repetition of all things and situations with respect to a finite universe — used in Nietzschean philosophy

eterne \əˈtərn, ēˈt-\ *adj* [ME, fr. MF, fr. L *aeternus* — more at ETERNAL] *archaic* **:** ETERNAL

eter·ni·ty \əˈtərnəd·ē, ēˈt-, -tə̄n-, -tein-, -i\ *n* -ES [ME *eternite*, fr. MF *eternité*, fr. L *aeternitas*, fr. *aeternus* eternal + *-itas* -ity] **1 :** the quality or state of being eternal **:** eternal existence ⟨God enjoys himself only by contemplation of his goodness, ~, infiniteness and power —Izaak Walton⟩ **2 :** a totality of infinite time: **a :** a totality of infinite past and future time **b :** a totality of infinite past time **c :** a totality of infinite future time **3 eternities** *pl* **:** AGES ⟨to unfold through the ages, yea, through the *eternities* —E.H.Sears⟩ **4 :** the condition that begins at death **:** IMMORTALITY ⟨all that lives must die, passing through nature to ~ —Shak.⟩ **5 a :** something that transcends time or involves or includes timeless reality **b :** absolute timelessness **6 :** an indefinite, immeasurable, or seemingly endless period of time ⟨it seemed an ~, not a few hours ago, when her mother had sat there reading —Ellen Glasgow⟩ **7 eternities** *pl* **:** the eternal truths or realities ⟨if a man cannot get some glimpse into the *eternities* —Thomas Carlyle⟩

eternity ring *n* **:** a narrow ring to be worn by a woman and usu. set with a continuous line of gems

eter·nize \əˈtərˌnīz, ēˈ-, -tə̄ˌn-, -təiˌn-; ˈēd·ə(r)ˌnīz, ˈētə-\ *vt* -ED/-ING/-S [MF *eterniser*, fr. *eterne* + *-iser* -ize] **1 a :** to make eternal in duration or character ⟨the mortal soul shall be . . . *eternized* —P.J.Bailey⟩ **b :** to prolong indefinitely **:** PERPETUATE ⟨perpetual quarrels which they take care to ~ —Mary W. Montagu⟩ **2 :** to make forever famous **:** IMMORTALIZE ⟨my verse your virtues rare shall ~ —Edmund Spenser⟩

¹ete·sian \əˈtēzhən, ēˈt-\ *adj, often cap* [L *etesius* (fr. Gk *etēsios*, fr. *etos* year) + E *-an* — more at WETHER] **:** recurring annually — used of northerly winds that blow during the summer over the eastern Mediterranean

²etesian \"\ *n* -s *often cap* **:** an etesian wind — usu. used in pl.

eth *var of* EDH

eth- *or* **etho-** *comb form* [ISV, fr. *ethyl*] **:** ethyl ⟨*eth*aldehyde⟩ ⟨*etho*chloride⟩

¹-eth \əth\ *or* **-th** \th\ *vb suffix* [ME, fr. OE *-eth, -ath, -th*, 3d sing. pres. indic. endings of various classes of verbs; akin to OHG *-it, -ōt, -ēt*, 3d sing. pres. indic. endings, early ON (runic) *-ith, -ith, -ōth, -ēth*, Goth *-ith, -eith, -oth, -aith*, L *-t* (preceded by various thematic vowels), Gk *-ti-*, 3d sing. pres. indic. ending of unthematic verbs, Skt *-ti* (preceded by various thematic vowels or by a consonant), 3d sing. pres. indic. ending] — used to form the archaic third person singular present indicative of verbs ⟨*goeth*⟩ ⟨*doth*⟩ ⟨*thinketh*⟩ ⟨*hath*⟩ ⟨*saith*⟩ ⟨*maketh*⟩ ⟨*leadeth*⟩

²-eth — see -TH

eth *abbr* **1** ether **2** ethical; ethics

eth·a·nal \ˈethəˌnal\ *n* -s [ISV *ethane* + *-al*] **:** ACETALDEHYDE

eth·ane \ˈeˌthān\ *n* -s [ISV *eth-* + *-ane*] **:** a colorless odorless water-insoluble gaseous paraffin hydrocarbon CH_3CH_3 occurring in natural gas, produced as a by-product in the cracking of petroleum, and used chiefly as a fuel or as a source of ethylene by dehydrogenation

eth·a·nim \ˈethəˌnim\ *also* **et·a·nim** \ˈed·ə-\ *n* -s *usu cap* [Heb *Ēthānīm*] **:** the 7th month of the ancient Hebrew calendar corresponding to Tishri

eth·a·nol \ˈethəˌnōl, -nȯl\ *n* -s [ISV *ethane* + *-ol*] **:** ALCOHOL 3 — used in the system of nomenclature adopted by the International Union of Pure and Applied Chemistry

eth·a·nol·amine \ˌethəˈnōləˌmēn, -nȯl-\ *n* [ISV *ethanol* + *amine*] **1 :** a colorless liquid basic amino alcohol $HOCH_2CH_2NH_2$ made usu. from ammonia and ethylene oxide and used chiefly as a solvent, in scrubbing acidic gases from gas streams, in making detergents, and in synthesis (as of pharmaceuticals); 2-amino-ethanol; 2-hydroxyethyl-amine — called also *monoethanolamine* **2 :** an amino alcohol containing hydroxyethyl attached to amino nitrogen — see DIETHANOLAMINE, TRIETHANOLAMINE

eth·a·no·lic \ˌethə¦nōlik, -nȯl-\ *adj* [*ethanol* + *-ic*] **:** of, relating to, containing, or derived from ethyl alcohol **:** ALCOHOLIC 1

eth·a·nol·y·sis \ˌethəˈnäləsəs, -nōl-\ *n, pl* **ethanoly·ses** \-ləˌsēz\ [NL, blend of ISV *ethanol* + NL *-lysis*] **:** alcoholysis with ethyl alcohol

eth·el \ˈethəl\ *n* -s [ME, fr. OE *ēthel, ōthel* — more at ATHELING] **:** ancestral land

etheling *often cap, var of* ATHELING

eth·ene \ˈeˌthēn\ *n* -s [ISV *eth-* + *-ene*] **:** ETHYLENE — used in the system of nomenclature adopted by the International Union of Pure and Applied Chemistry

eth·e·noid \ˈethəˌnȯid\ *adj* [*ethene* + *-oid*] **:** resembling ethylene in chemical properties **:** like ethylene or its double bond in unsaturation **:** characterized by or produced by virtue of a double bond **:** ETHYLENIC ⟨~ fatty acids⟩ ⟨~ resins⟩

etheo·genesis \ˌē¦thēō, ˌe¦+\ *n* [NL *etheo-* (fr. Gk *ēitheos* unmarried youth) + NL *-genesis* — more at WIDOW] **:** male parthenogenesis **:** development of an unfertilized male gamete into an organism

¹ethe·os·to·moid \ˌēthēˈästəˌmȯid, ¦eth-\ *adj* [NL *Etheostoma*, genus of fishes (fr. *etheo-* — fr. Gk *ēthein* to sift, strain — + *-stoma*) + E *-oid* — more at ETHMOID] **:** of or relating to the darters

²etheostomoid \"\ *n* -s **:** DARTER 2

ether *also* **ae·ther** \ˈēthə(r)\ *n* -s [ME *ether*, fr. L *aether*, fr. Gk *aithēr*, fr. *aithein* to kindle, blaze — more at EDIFY] **1 a :** the clear sky **:** HEAVEN, AIR ⟨all the unmeasured ~ flames with light —Alexander Pope⟩ **b :** the element formerly held to form the material of the heavenly spheres and bodies from the moon to the fixed stars **c :** the upper regions of space or the rarefied element formerly held to fill these regions **:** EMPYREAN **2 a :** a medium of unusual qualities (as extreme tenuity, absolute continuity, and high rigidity and elasticity) postulated in the undulatory theory of light as permeating all space and as transmitting transverse waves **b :** the medium of transmission of radio waves ⟨jamming of BBC output became a regular feature of the war in the ~ —J.B.Clark⟩ **3 a :** a light volatile flammable water-insoluble fat-soluble liquid $(C_2H_5)_2O$ that has a characteristic aromatic odor, is obtained by the distillation of alcohol with sulfuric acid, and is used chiefly as a solvent and anesthetic — called also *diethyl ether, ethyl ether, ethyl oxide* **b :** any of a class of relatively inert organic compounds typified by ethyl ether and characterized by an oxygen atom attached to two carbon atoms that are usu. contained in hydrocarbon radicals — see EPOXIDE **c :** ESTER; *esp* **:** ETHYL ESTER — now little used **4 :** something that resembles the medium of ether **:** ATMOSPHERE ⟨the narrator's autoanalysis . . . is the ~ in which the great work exists —Bernard DeVoto⟩

ether alcohol *n* **:** a compound that is both an ether and an alcohol

ether·ate \ˈēthəˌrāt, -rət\ *n* -s [*ether* + *-ate*] **:** a compound with an ether (as ethyl ether) ⟨boron trifluoride ~ $BF_3.(C_2H_5)_2O$⟩

ether drift *n* **:** a relative motion held to exist between a body and the medium of ether

ethe·re·al *also* **ethe·ri·al** *or* **ae·the·re·al** *or* **ae·the·ri·al** \əˈthirēəl, ēˈ-,eˈ-, -thēr-\ *adj* [L *aetherius, aethereus* (fr. Gk *aitherios*, fr. *aithēr* ether) + E *-al*] **1 a :** of or relating to the regions beyond the earth ⟨liberty, far from being an ~ thing, is always . . . related to specific and present situations —Max Ascoli⟩ **b :** CELESTIAL, HEAVENLY ⟨go, heavenly guest, ~ messenger —John Milton⟩ **2 a :** resembling or having the characteristics of the element of ether **:** AIRY, IMMATERIAL ⟨have been obliged to work with physical rather than ~ forms —L.A.White⟩ **b :** characterized by unusual delicacy and refinement **:** DAINTY, EXQUISITE ⟨this smallest, most ~, and daintiest of birds —William Beebe⟩ ⟨a chocolate cake of quite ~ lightness —*New Yorker*⟩ **3 :** of, relating to, or having the characteristics of the medium of ether ⟨~ waves⟩ **4 :** relating to, containing, or resembling the liquid ether or an ether ⟨~ oxygen⟩ ⟨an ~ solution⟩ — **ethe·re·al·ly** \-ēəlē, -li\ *adv* — **ethe·re·al·ness** \-ēəlnəs\ *n* -ES

ethereal blue *n* **:** SKY BLUE

ethe·re·al·i·ty \əˌthirēˈaləd·ē, (ˌ)ēˌth-, eˌth-, -thēr-, -lətē, -i\ *n* -ES **:** the quality or state of being ethereal

ethe·re·al·i·za·tion *or* **ethe·ri·al·i·za·tion** \≈ˌ≈rēələˈzāshən, -ˌlīˈz-\ *n* -s **:** the act or process of etherealizing

ethe·re·al·ize *or* **ethe·ri·al·ize** \≈ˈ≈rēəˌlīz\ *vt* -ED/-ING/-S **:** to make ethereal: **a :** to refine, exalt, or spiritualize ⟨our tastes have been *etherealized*, our perceptions exalted —W.S. Gilbert⟩ **b :** to give an ethereal appearance to ⟨the moonlight cast a kind of dreamy beauty and quite *etherealized* the low brick wall —Olive Schreiner⟩

ethereal oil *n* **1 :** ESSENTIAL OIL **2 :** a mixture of heavy oil of wine with an equal volume of ether

ethereal salt *n* **:** ESTER

ethereal sulfate *n* **:** any of various esters of sulfuric acid that are formed as products of metabolism and excreted in the urine

ethereal tincture *n* **:** a tincture prepared by using a menstruum composed of one volume of ether and two volumes of alcohol

ethe·re·ous \≈ˈ≈rēəs\ *adj* [L *aethereus* ethereal] *archaic* **:** ETHEREAL

ether extract *n* **:** the part of a complex organic material that is soluble in ether and consists chiefly of fats and fatty acids — used esp. in analyses of animal feeds

ethe·ria \əˈthirēə, ēˈ-,eˈ-, -thēr-\ *n, cap* [NL, fr. L *aetheria*, fem. of *aetherius* ethereal — more at ETHEREAL] **:** a genus (the type of the family Etheriidae) of freshwater lamellibranch mollusks of Africa and Madagascar that attach themselves by one valve to rocks in deep water

ether·ic *also* **ae·ther·ic** \əˈtherik, ēˈ-,eˈ-; ˈēthərik\ *adj* [*ether, aether* + *-ic*] **:** ETHEREAL ⟨poetry is to some degree the ~ body of the poet —Edith Sitwell⟩

ether·i·fi·ca·tion \əˌtherəfəˈkāshən, ēˌ-; ˌēthər-\ *n* -s [*ether* + *-i-* + *-fication*] **:** the process of etherifying

ether·i·fy \əˈtherəˌfī, ēˈ-; ˈēthər-\ *vt* -ED/-ING/-ES [*ether* + *-ify*] **:** to convert (an alcohol or phenol) into an ether

ether·in *also* **ae·ther·in** \ˈēthərən\ *n* -s [ISV *ether, aether* + *-in*] **1** *archaic* **:** ethylene believed to be a basic radical and a constituent of alcohol, ether, and various other compounds **2** *archaic* **:** a white crystalline hydrocarbon found in heavy oil of wine

ether·iza·tion \ˌēthərəˈzāshən, -ˌrīˈz-\ *n* -s **1 :** the administration of ether to produce anesthesia **2 :** the exposure of a dormant plant to the fumes of an ether under controlled conditions in order to stimulate growth

ether·ize \ˈēthəˌrīz\ *vt* -ED/-ING/-S **1 :** to treat or anesthetize with ether ⟨couldn't bear to ~ cats and eviscerate frogs —*New Yorker*⟩ **2 :** to make numb as if by anesthetizing **:** TORPIFY ⟨stillness *etherized* the whole train —Truman Capote⟩

ether·iz·er \-zə(r)\ *n* -s **:** one that etherizes

ether·o·phone *also* **aether·o·phone** \ˈēthərəˌfōn; əˈther-, ēˈ-\ *n* -s [*ether, aether* + *-o-* + *-phone*] **:** THEREMIN

eth·ic \ˈethik, -thēk\ *n* -s [ME *etik, ethik*, fr. MF *ethique*, fr. LL *ethica* & L *ethice*, fr. Gk *ēthikē*, fr. *ēthikos*, adj., fem. of *ēthikos* moral, ethic] **1 ethics** *pl but usu sing in constr* **:** the discipline dealing with what is good and bad or right and wrong or with moral duty and obligation ⟨the sphere of ~*s* for the Greeks was not distinguished from the sphere of aesthetics —Havelock Ellis⟩ **2 a :** a group of moral principles or set of values ⟨the Christian ~⟩ ⟨even the code of the gangster . . . has its own ~ —R.P.Warren⟩ ⟨Puritan ~*s*⟩ ⟨Lincoln had been pondering the ~*s* of slavery —A.C.Cole⟩ **b :** a particular theory or system of moral values ⟨a materialistic ~⟩ ⟨naturalistic ~*s*⟩ **c ethics** *pl but sing or pl in constr* **:** the principles of conduct governing an individual or a profession **:** standards of behavior ⟨social ~*s*⟩ ⟨professional ~*s*⟩ ⟨a certain ~*s* makes it impossible for me to review the production . . . which I directed —*New Republic*⟩ **3 :** character or the ideals of character manifested by a race or people ⟨while the rituals . . . are complex and stylized, the meaning behind them and their significance shows how far advanced was Indian religious culture and ~ —Seth Agnew⟩ — compare ETHOS

¹eth·i·cal \ˈethəkəl, -thēk-\ *or* **eth·ic** \-thik,-thēk\ *adj* [ME *etik*, fr. L *ethicus*, fr. Gk *ēthikos*, fr. *ēthos* custom, usage, character, dwelling + *-ikos* -ic, -ical; akin to L *sodalis* comrade, Gk *ethos* custom, habit, Skt *svadhā* self-position, own condition or place, custom, L *sui* of oneself — more at SUICIDE] **1 a :** of or relating to the field of ethics or morality **:** relating to or involving questions of right and wrong ⟨~ principles⟩ ⟨~ theories⟩ **b :** dealing with or concerned with ethics ⟨~ tracts⟩ ⟨modern ~ analysts⟩ ⟨~ literature⟩ **2 :** involving or expressing moral approval or disapproval ⟨~ judgments⟩ **3 a :** being in accord with approved standards of behavior or a socially or professionally accepted code **:** MORAL ⟨~ conduct⟩ ⟨~ practices⟩ **b :** conforming to professionally endorsed principles and practices ⟨an ~ lawyer⟩ ⟨~ medical practice⟩ **4** *of a drug* **:** restricted to sale only on a doctor's prescription ⟨digitalis is an ~ drug but aspirin is not⟩ ⟨the ~ drug business⟩ — compare OVER-THE-COUNTER, PROPRIETARY

syn see MORAL

²ethical \"\ *n* -s **:** an ethical drug

ethical dative *n* **:** a colloquial use of the dative of a pronoun for a person to whom it imputes a vague concern with the matter in question (as German *mir*, literally "for me", in *bleibe mir nur gesund* "I just hope you stay well")

ethical genitive *n* **:** the use of the possessive *your* to impute only a vague concern (as in *she is not at all one of your bluestockings*)

eth·i·cal·i·ty \ˌethəˈkaləd·ē, -lətē, -i\ *n* -ES **:** ethical quality, character, or aspect **:** ethical principle

eth·i·cal·ly \ˈethək(ə)lē, -thēk-, -li\ *adv* **:** in an ethical manner **:** according to ethical principles **:** from an ethical point of view ⟨little can be said ~ . . . for foolish things written —*Saturday Rev.*⟩

eth·i·cal·ness \-kəlnəs\ *n* -ES **:** the quality or state of being ethical

ethical truth *n* **:** NORMATIVE TRUTH

ethi·cian \eˈthishən\ *or* **eth·i·cist** \ˈethəsəst\ *n* -s [*ethics* + *-ian* or *-ist*] **:** a specialist in ethics

eth·i·cize \ˈethəˌsīz\ *vt* -ED/-ING/-S **:** to make ethical or endow with ethical qualities ⟨~ nature⟩

ethico- *comb form* [NL, fr. L *ethicus* moral, ethical — more at ETHICAL] **:** ethical and ⟨*ethico*religious⟩ **:** ethics ⟨*ethico*-centered⟩

eth·ide \ˈeˌthīd, -ˌthəd\ *n* -s [*eth-* + *-ide*] **:** a binary compound of ethyl ⟨sodium ~ C_2H_5Na⟩

ethine *var of* ETHYNE

ethinyl *var of* ETHYNYL

ethinyl estradiol *or* **ethynylestradiol** *n* **:** a white crystalline potent orally effective estrogen $C_{20}H_{24}O_2$ prepared from estrone

eth·iodide \(ˈ)e¦th+ˌ-\ *n* [*eth-* + *iodide*] **:** a compound with ethyl iodide

ethi·on·ic acid \¦e¦thē¦änik-, ¦ē|, |ˌthī|\ *n* [*ethionic* ISV *e-* (fr. *ether*) + *-thion-* (fr. Gk *theion* brimstone) + *-ic* — more at THI-] **:** an unstable diacid $HO_3SCH_2CH_2OSO_3H$ known only in solution and obtainable by adding water to ethionic anhydride

ethionic anhydride *n* **:** a crystalline cyclic compound $C_2H_4O_6S_2$ formed by the action of sulfur trioxide on ethylene or alcohol — called also *carbyl sulfate*

ethi·o·nine \eˈthīəˌnēn, -nən\ *n* -s [*eth-* + *-ionine* (as in *methionine*)] **:** a crystalline amino acid $C_2H_5SCH_2CH_2CH(NH_2)COOH$ that is the ethyl homologue of methionine and is biologically antagonistic to methionine

¹ethi·op \ˈēthēˌäp\ *or* **ethi·ope** \-ēˌōp\ *also* **ae·thi·op** \ˈēth-\ *n* -s *cap* [ME *Ethiope*, fr. L *Aethiops*, fr. Gk *Aithiops*] **:** ETHIOPIAN ⟨*Ethiops* were selling picture postcards —Osbert Sitwell⟩

²ethiop \"\ *adj, usu cap, archaic* **:** black in complexion

ethi·o·pia \ˌēthēˈōpēə\ *adj, usu cap* [fr. *Ethiopia*, country of northeast Africa] **:** of or from Ethiopia **:** of the kind or style prevalent in Ethiopia **:** ETHIOPIAN

¹ethi·o·pi·an \ˌēthēˈōpēən\ *n* -s *cap* [ME *Ethiopien*, fr. *Ethiopia* + ME *-en* -an] **1** *also* **aethiopian :** a member of any of the mythical or actual peoples that the ancient Greeks designated by the name *Aithiopes* usu. described as being dark-skinned and living far to the south; *esp* **:** a native or inhabitant of a country south of Egypt and extending east to the Red sea **2 :** NEGRO **3 :** a native or inhabitant of the modern nation of Ethiopia

²ethiopian \ˈ≈≈≈≈\ *adj, usu cap* **1** *also* **aethiopian a :** of, relating to, or characteristic of the ancient Ethiopians **b :** of, relating to, or characteristic of any of the regions or countries anciently or formerly known as Aethiopia or Ethiopia **2 a :** of, relating to, characteristic of, or being a Negro **b** (1) **:** representing or purporting to represent the Negro esp. of the cultural type found on plantations in the southern U.S. in the 19th cent. — used esp. of entertainers (usu. white men wearing blackface) in Negro minstrel shows and of the entertainment that they offered ⟨*Ethiopian* serenaders⟩ (2) **:** characteristic of, suitable for, or done in the style of the entertainment offered in Negro minstrelsy ⟨*Ethiopian* dialogue⟩ ⟨*Ethiopian* song⟩ **3 :** of, relating to, or being the biogeographic region that includes Africa south of the Sahara, southern Arabia, and sometimes Madagascar and the adjacent islands **4 a :** of, relating to, or characteristic of the modern nation of Ethiopia **b :** of, relating to, or characteristic of the people of the modern nation of Ethiopia **5 :** of or relating to the ancient Monophysite church of Ethiopia that was founded in the 4th century A.D., is governed by an abuna appointed by the Coptic patriarch, and follows Coptic doctrine, discipline, and worship but uses Ethiopic as its liturgical language

[1]**ethi·opic** \ˌēthēˈäpik, -ˈōp-\ *adj, usu cap* [L *Aethiopicus*, fr. Gk *Aithiopikos*, fr. *Aithiopia* Ethiopia + Gk *-ikos* -ic] **1 :** ETHIOPIAN 1, 4 **2 a :** of, relating to, characteristic of, or constituting the language Ethiopic **b :** of, relating to, characteristic of, or constituting a group of related Semitic languages spoken in Ethiopia including the classical Ethiopic, Tigre, Tigrinya, Amharic, Argobba, Harari, and Gurage

[2]**ethiopic** \"\ *n, cap* **1 :** a Semitic language formerly spoken in Ethiopia and still in use as the liturgical language of the Christian church in Ethiopia — called also *Geez* **2 :** the Ethiopic group of the Semitic branch of the Afro-Asiatic family of languages

ethiopic alphabet *n, usu cap E* **:** an alphabet of South Semitic origin in which the vocalization is indicated by modification of the basic character (as by the addition of small appendages or by shortening or lengthening of one of the main strokes) and in use since the 4th century A.D. in writing Ethiopic and since about 1600 in adapted form also for Amharic, Tigre, and Tigrinya

ethiops *n* [NL, fr. L *Aethiops* Ethiopian] *obs* **:** any of various chemical preparations (as metallic salts) of a black or very dark color

ethiops mineral *n* **:** impure black mercuric sulfide prepared by rubbing together mercury and sulfur

ethis·ter·one \əˈthistə,rōn\ *n* -s [*ethi*nyl + *testosterone*] **:** a synthetic crystalline orally effective female sex hormone $C_{21}H_{28}O_2$ administered in cases of deficiency of progesterone; 17-ethynyl-testosterone — called also *anhydrohydroxyprogesterone*

ethmo- *comb form* [Gk *ēthmo-* strainer (influenced in meaning by E *ethmoid*), fr. *ēthmos*] **:** ethmoidal and ⟨*ethmo*frontal⟩ **:** ethmoid and ⟨*ethmo*sphenoid⟩

[1]**eth·moid** \ˈeth,mȯid\ *or* **eth·moi·dal** \(ˈ)ethˈmȯidᵊl\ *adj* [*ethmoid* fr. F *ethmoïde*, fr. MF, fr. Gk *ēthmoeidēs* like a strainer, perforated, ethmoid, fr. *ēthmos* strainer, colander (fr. *ēthein* to sift, strain) + *-oeidēs* -oid; *ethmoidal* fr. F *ethmoïde* + E *-al*; akin to ON *sāld* sieve, MIr *síthlad* act of sifting, W *hidl* strainer, OSlav *sito*, and perh. to L *serere* to sow — more at SOW] **:** of, relating to, or adjoining one or more bones forming part of the walls and septum of the nasal cavity; *also* **:** of or relating to the whole region of the nasal capsule

[2]**ethmoid** \"\ *n* -s **:** ETHMOID BONE

ethmoid bone *n* **:** a delicate essentially cubical cartilage bone of the skull that is made up of thin plates enclosing irregular vacuities, forms much of the walls of the nasal cavity and part of that of the orbits, and is subject to considerable variation in different vertebrate groups

eth·moid·itis \,eth,mȯiˈdīdəs\ *n* -ES [NL, fr. E *ethmoid* + NL *-itis*] **:** inflammation of the ethmoid or its sinuses

eth·mo·lith \ˈethmə,lith\ *n* -s [ISV *ethmo-* + *-lith*] **:** a body of igneous rock intruded into stratified rocks and narrowing downward like a funnel

[1]**eth·mo·turbinal** \ˌeth(,)mō+\ *n* [*ethmo-* + *turbinal*] **:** an ethmoturbinal bone

[2]**eth·mo·turbinal** *also* **eth·mo·turbinate** \"+\ *adj* [*ethmo-* + *turbinal, turbinate*] **:** of, relating to, or consisting of the lateral masses of the ethmoid bone that bear or consist largely of the turbinated bones in mammals

eth·narch \ˈeth,närk\ *n* -s [Gk *ethnarchēs* ruler of a tribe or nation, fr. *ethnos* nation + *-archēs*, fr. *archos* ruler — more at ARCHI-] **:** the governor of a province or people (as of the Byzantine Empire) ⟨the ~ of Cyprus⟩

eth·nar·chy \-kē\ *n* -ES [Gk *ethnarchia* office of ethnarch, fr. *ethnarchēs* ethnarch + *-ia* -y] **:** the dominion of an ethnarch or his office or rank

[1]**ethnic** *n* -s [ME, fr. LL *ethnicus*, fr. Gk *ethnikos*, adj.] *obs* **:** HEATHEN, PAGAN ⟨impure ~s —John Milton⟩

[2]**eth·nic** \ˈethnik, -nēk\ *adj* [ME, fr. LL *ethnicus*, fr. Gk *ethnikos* foreign, gentile, national, fr. *ethnos* nation + *-ikos* -ic — more at ETHNOS] **1 :** of or relating to the Gentiles or to nations not converted to Christianity **:** HEATHEN, PAGAN ⟨ancient ~ revels of a faith long since forsaken —H.W. Longfellow⟩ **2 a :** relating to community of physical and mental traits possessed by the members of a group as a product of their common heredity and cultural tradition ⟨influenced by ~ and cultural ties —J.F.Kennedy⟩ ⟨the boundaries along the West African coast were not plotted with regard to the ancient ~ frontiers —A.H.Young-O'Brien⟩ **b :** having or originating from racial, linguistic, and cultural ties with a specific group ⟨Negroes, Irish, Italians, Germans, Poles, and other ~ groups —F.J.Brown & J.S.Roucek⟩ ⟨displaced persons, 653 of them ~ Germans —*N.Y. Herald Tribune*⟩ **3 :** originating in an exotic primitive culture ⟨~ music⟩

[3]**ethnic** \"\ *n* -s [Gk *ethnikon*, neut. of *ethnikos* national] **:** ETHNICON

eth·ni·cal \-nəkəl, -nēk-\ *adj* [*ethnic* + *-al*] **:** ETHNIC 2, ETHNOLOGIC

eth·ni·cal·ly \-k(ə)lē, -li\ *adv* **:** from an ethnic or ethnologic point of view **:** RACIALLY

eth·ni·cism \ˈethnə,sizəm\ *n* -s *archaic* **:** PAGANISM, HEATHENISM

eth·nic·i·ty \ethˈnisəd·ē\ *n* -ES **:** ethnic quality or affiliation ⟨the influence of ~ upon the character of community status arrangements —G.P.Stone & W.H.Form⟩ ⟨~, occupation, and language spoken are the crucial factors in . . . intermarriage —*Soc. Abstracts*⟩

eth·ni·con *also* **eth·ni·kon** \ˈethnə,kän\ *n, pl* **ethni·ca** *also* **ethni·ka** \-kə\ [Gk *ethnikon*, neut. of *ethnikos* national — more at ETHNIC] **:** the name of a tribe, ethnic group, race, or people (as *Hopi, Ethiopian, Phoenician*) ⟨the ~ *Veneti* is not limited to Italy —Joshua Whatmough⟩

ethno- *comb form* [F, fr. LGk, fr. Gk *ethnos* nation — more at ETHNOS] **1 :** race, people, cultural group ⟨*ethno*graphy⟩ ⟨*ethno*genic⟩ **2 :** characteristic of or believed by a people, race, or group ⟨*ethno*meteorology⟩ **:** used by or related to a people or race ⟨*ethno*biology⟩ ⟨*ethno*flora⟩

eth·no·biological \ˌeth(,)nō+\ *adj* **:** of or relating to ethnobiology

eth·no·biology \"+\ *n* [*ethno-* + *biology*] **:** the branch of biology that deals with the relation between usu. primitive human societies and the plants and animals of their environment

eth·no·botanic *or* **eth·no·botanical** \"+\ *adj* **:** of or relating to ethnobotany

eth·no·botanist \"+\ *n* **:** a specialist in ethnobotany

eth·no·botany \"+\ *n* [*ethno-* + *botany*] **:** the plant lore of a race or people; *also* **:** the systematic study of such lore

eth·no·centric \ˌethnō, -nə+\ *adj* [*ethno-* + *-centric*] **1 :** centering upon race as a chief interest or end ⟨the religion of the future must more and more deal with the salvation of society; it must be ~ —Gamaliel Bradford⟩ **2 a :** inclined to regard one's own race or social group as the center of culture ⟨any profession . . . is somewhat ~ regarding outsiders —L.W. Doob⟩ **b :** exhibiting an incapacity for viewing foreign cultures dispassionately ⟨the ~ view that the rest of the world must become worthy of us by . . . imitating our way of life —G.E.Taylor⟩ ⟨a Greek ~ legend about Persian morals —W.H.Goodenough⟩ — **ethnocentrically** \"+\ *adv* — **ethnocentricity** \"+\ *n* -ES

eth·no·cen·trism \ˌethnōˈsen,trizəm, -thnə-\ *n* -s [*ethno-* + *centr-* + *-ism*] **1 :** a habitual disposition to judge foreign peoples or groups by the standards and practices of one's own culture or ethnic group ⟨this is the more usual form that ~ takes . . . — a gentle insistence on the good qualities of one's own group —M.J.Herskovits⟩ **2 :** a tendency toward viewing alien cultures with disfavor and a resulting sense of inherent superiority ⟨the ~ of national groups . . . causes them to regard their culture as superior to that of all other nations —Mabel Elliott & Francis Merrill⟩ ⟨with perhaps pardonable ~, the Americans have acted on the assumption that the best preparation for freedom is Americanization —Raymond Kennedy⟩ ⟨intolerant ~ and super nationalism can only result in the narrowest sort of isolationism —*Amer. Scholar*⟩

eth·no·flora \ˈethnə+\ *n* [NL, fr. *ethno-* + *flora*] **:** the part of the flora of a region used by its human aborigines

eth·no·gen·ic \ˌethnəˈjenik\ *adj* **:** of or relating to ethnogeny

eth·nog·e·nist \ethˈnäjənəst\ *n* -s **:** an ethnologist who specializes in the study of the origin and evolution of races

eth·nog·e·ny \-jənē\ *n* -ES [F *ethnogénie*, fr. *ethno-* + *-génie* -geny] **:** a branch of ethnology that deals primarily with the evolution of races

eth·no·geographer \ˌeth(,)nō+\ *n* **:** an ethnologist who specializes in ethnogeography

eth·no·geographic \"+\ *adj* **:** of or relating to ethnogeography

eth·no·geography \"+\ *n* [*ethno-* + *geography*] **:** the study of the geographical distribution of races or peoples and their relation to the environments in which they live — compare ANTHROPOGEOGRAPHY

eth·nog·ra·pher \ethˈnägrəfə(r)\ *also* **eth·nog·ra·phist** \-fəst\ *n* -s **:** a specialist in ethnography

eth·no·graph·ic \ˌethnəˈgrafik, -fēk\ *or* **eth·no·graph·i·cal** \-fəkəl, -fēk-\ *adj* **:** of or relating to ethnography — **eth·no·graph·i·cal·ly** \-fək(ə)lē, -fēk-, -li\ *adv*

eth·nog·ra·phy \ethˈnägrəfē, -fi\ *n* -ES [F *ethnographie*, fr. *ethno-* + *-graphie* -graphy] **:** a branch of anthropology that deals historically with the origin and filiation of races and cultures **:** ETHNOLOGY; *specif* **:** a branch of ethnology dealing with description of cultures rather than comparison and analysis **:** descriptive anthropology — compare ANTHROPOGRAPHY

eth·no·historian \ˌeth(,)nō+\ *n* [*ethno-* + *historian*] **:** a specialist in ethnohistory

eth·no·historical *also* **eth·no·historic** \"+\ *adj* [*ethno-* + *historical, historic*] **:** of or relating to ethnohistory

eth·no·history \ˌethnō+\ *n* [*ethno-* + *history*] **:** a study of the development of cultures; *specif* **:** the interpretation of the significance of archaeological findings by means of documentary material

eth·no·linguistic \ˌeth(,)nō+\ *adj* [*ethno-* + *linguistic*] **:** of or relating to ethnolinguistics

eth·no·linguistics \"+\ *n pl but sing in constr* [*ethno-* + *linguistics*] **:** a study of the relations between linguistic and nonlinguistic cultural behavior

eth·no·log·ic \ˌethnəˈläjik\ *or* **eth·no·log·i·cal** \-jəkəl, -jēk-\ *adj* **:** of or relating to ethnology — **eth·no·log·i·cal·ly** \-jək(ə)lē, -jēk-, -li\ *adv*

eth·nol·o·gist \ethˈnäləjəst\ *also* **eth·nol·o·ger** \-jə(r)\ *n* -s **:** a specialist in ethnology

eth·nol·o·gy \-jē, -ji\ *n* -ES [*ethno-* + *-logy*] **1 :** a science that deals with the division of mankind into races, with their origin, distribution, and relations, and with the peculiarities that characterize them — see ETHNOGENY, ETHNOGRAPHY **2 :** cultural or social anthropology including the comparative and analytical study of cultures and excluding the subject matter of archaeology and physical anthropology **3 :** the materials of ethnology ⟨the ~ of the American Indian⟩

eth·no·psychological \ˌeth(,)nō+\ *adj* [*ethno-* + *psychological*] **:** of or relating to ethnopsychology — **ethnopsychologically** \"+\ *adv*

eth·no·psychology \"+\ *n* [*ethno-* + *psychology*; trans. of G *völkerpsychologie*] **:** the psychology of races and peoples **:** folk psychology

eth·nos \ˈeth,näs\ *n* -ES [Gk, nation, people, caste, tribe; prob. akin to Gk *ēthos* custom — more at ETHICAL] **:** an ethnic group — compare DEMOS

eth·no·zoological \ˌeth(,)nō+\ *adj* **:** of or relating to ethnozoology

eth·no·zoology \"+\ *n* [*ethno-* + *zoology*] **:** the animal lore of a race or people; *also* **:** the systematic study of such lore

etho- — see ETH-

etho·hexa·di·ol \ˌe(,)thō,heksəˈdī,ȯl, -ī,ōl\ *n* [*etho-* + *hexane* + *-diol*] **:** an odorless oily glycol $C_8H_{16}(OH)_2$ applied to the skin as an insect repellent; 2-ethyl-hexane-1,3-diol

etho·log·i·cal \ˌethəˈläjəkəl, ˌēth-\ *adj* **:** of or relating to ethology — **etho·log·i·cal·ly** \-jək(ə)lē\ *adv*

ethol·o·gy \ēˈthäləjē, ē-\ *n* -ES [L *ethologia* art of depicting character, fr. Gk *ēthologia*, fr. *ēthos* + *-logia* -logy] **1 :** a systematic study of the formation of human character **2 :** a scientific study of animal behavior

ethos \ˈē,thäs *sometimes* ˈe, *or* -thōs\ *n* -ES [NL, fr. Gk *ēthos* character, delineation of character, custom, accustomed place — more at ETHICAL] **1 :** character, sentiment, or moral nature: **a :** the guiding beliefs, standards, or ideals that characterize or pervade a group, a community, a people, or an ideology **:** the spirit that motivates the ideas, customs, or practices of a people, an epoch, or a region ⟨the general ~ of the people they have to govern . . . determines the behavior of politicians —T.S.Eliot⟩ ⟨every age or epoch is inspired by what may be called its inevitable idea — the ~ of the century —*Life*⟩ ⟨our democratic ~⟩ ⟨the quasi-moral American ~ of production at any cost —William Troy⟩ ⟨the commercial ~ . . . of the 19th century —C.W.Hendel⟩ **b :** the complex of fundamental values that underlies, permeates, or actuates major patterns of thought and behavior in any particular culture, society, or institution ⟨the value system, the ~ of a group —Kurt Lewin⟩; *also* **:** such a complex permeating a literary or scientific work or an intellectual discipline ⟨the ~ of science⟩ **2 a** *in Aristotelian philosophy* (1) **:** the character or personality of a man esp. with respect to a balance between the passions and caution (2) **:** an element (as moral purpose) in dramatic character which determines what a man does in contrast to what he thinks — compare DIANOIA **b :** the disposition, fundamental outlook, moral attitude, or system of values of an individual ⟨that fateful summer of 1940 when Churchill alone, endowed with prophetic ~ and a keen sense of the realities of war and peace, turned the tide —*Atlantic*⟩ ⟨there was a distinctly athletic ~ about her, as if . . . she might have majored in physical education —J.D.Salinger⟩

eth·oxide \eˈth+,-\ *n* -s [*ethoxyl* + *-ide*] **:** a binary compound of ethoxyl; *esp* **:** a base formed from ethyl alcohol by replacement of the hydroxyl hydrogen with a metal ⟨aluminum ~ $Al(OC_2H_5)_3$⟩

eth·oxy \(ˈ)eˈthäksē\ *adj* [*ethoxy-*] **:** relating to or containing ethoxyl

ethoxy- *comb form* [ISV, fr. *ethoxyl*] **:** containing ethoxyl — in names of chemical compounds ⟨*ethoxy*caffeine⟩

ethoxy·carbonyl \(ˌ)eˈthäksē+\ *n* [*ethoxy-* + *carbonyl*] **:** CARBETHOXYL

eth·oxyl \(ˈ)eˈthäksəl\ *n* -s [*eth-* + oxygen + *-yl*] **:** a univalent radical C_2H_5O- composed of ethyl united with oxygen

eth·ox·y·line resin \eˈthäksə,lēn-, -lən-\ *n* [*ethoxyl* + *-ine*] **:** EPOXY RESIN

eth·rog *or* **et·rog** \eˈthrōg, etˈrōg, ˈ=,= *or* **es·rog** \ˈes,rōg\ *n, pl* **eth·ro·gim** *or* **et·ro·gim** \,ethrōˈgim, ,et·r-\ *or* **es·ro·gim** \esˈrōgim\ *or* **ethrogs** *or* **etrogs** *or* **esrogs** [Heb *ethrōgh*] **:** the fruit of the citron (*Citrus medica*) anciently used with the palm branch in the celebration of Sukkoth and still used by Jews as a symbol of that occasion — compare LULAB

eth·yl \ˈethəl, *chiefly by Brit chemists* ˈē,thīl\ *n* -s [ISV *ether* + *-yl*] **:** a univalent hydrocarbon radical C_2H_5 or CH_3CH_2 derived from ethane by removal of one hydrogen atom — compare TETRAETHYL LEAD

ethyl acetate *n* **:** a colorless fragrant volatile flammable liquid ester $CH_3COOC_2H_5$ made from ethyl alcohol and acetic acid and used chiefly as a solvent and in organic synthesis

ethyl acetoacetate *n* **:** a colorless liquid ester with pleasant odor important for its tautomerism [keto form $CH_3COCH_2COOC_2H_5$, enol form $CH_3C(OH)=CHCOOC_2H_5$] and for the numerous condensations it can undergo — called also *acetoacetic ester*

eth·yl·acetylene \ˌethəl+\ *n* [ISV *ethyl* + *acetylene*] **:** BUTYNE a

ethyl alcohol *n* **:** ordinary alcohol **:** ALCOHOL 3

eth·yl·amine \ˌethələˈmēn\ *n* [ISV *ethyl* + *amine*] **1 :** a colorless flammable volatile liquid base $C_2H_5NH_2$ that has an ammoniacal odor, is usu. made from ammonia and ether or alcohol, and is used chiefly in organic synthesis — called also *monoethylamine* **2 :** an amine containing ethyl attached to amino nitrogen — see DIETHYLAMINE, TRIETHYLAMINE

ethyl aminobenzoate *n* **:** BENZOCAINE

[1]**eth·yl·ate** \ˈethə,lāt, -ˌlət\ *n* -s [*ethyl* + *-ate*] **:** ETHOXIDE

[2]**eth·yl·ate** \-,lāt\ *vt* -ED/-ING/-S [*ethyl* + *-ate*, v. suffix] **:** to introduce the ethyl group into (a compound) — **eth·yl·a·tion** \,ethəˈlāshən\ *n* -s

eth·yl·ben·zene \ˌ=,=ˈ=,=, ˌ=,=ˈ=\ *n* [ISV *ethyl* + *benzene*] **:** a liquid hydrocarbon $C_6H_5C_2H_5$ that is made usu. from benzene and ethylene and is used chiefly in the manufacture of styrene

ethyl bromide *n* **:** a volatile liquid compound C_2H_5Br of aromatic odor; bromo-ethane

ethyl butyrate *n* **:** a colorless liquid ester $C_3H_7COOC_2H_5$ with a pineapple odor found in fruits and also synthesized and used in artificial rum, pineapple oil, and perfumes

ethyl carbamate *n* **:** URETHANE

ethyl cellulose *n* **:** any of various white granular tough thermoplastic substances made by ethylating alkali cellulose and used chiefly in making plastics and lacquers

ethyl chaulmoograte *n* **:** a pale-yellow liquid containing a mixture of the ethyl esters of the acids of chaulmoogra oil and formerly used in the treatment of leprosy

ethyl chloride *n* **:** a colorless pungent flammable gaseous or volatile liquid compound C_2H_5Cl that is usu. made from chlorine and ethane or from hydrogen chloride and ethylene or ethyl alcohol and that is used chiefly in synthesis (as of tetraethyl lead and ethyl cellulose) and as a local surface anesthetic — called also *chloroethane*

ethyl cyanide *n* **:** PROPIONITRILE

eth·yl·ene \ˈethə,lēn\ *n* -s [ISV *ethyl* + *-ene*] **1 :** a colorless flammable gaseous olefin hydrocarbon $CH_2=CH_2$ found in coal gas, now usu. obtained by pyrolysis of petroleum hydrocarbons, and used chiefly in organic synthesis (as of ethyl alcohol, polyethylene, and styrene), in promoting growth of plants and ripening of fruits, and as an anesthetic **2 :** a bivalent hydrocarbon radical $-CH_2CH_2-$ derived from ethane by removal of one hydrogen atom attached to each carbon atom or from ethylene by breaking of the double bond

ethylene chlorohydrin *n* **:** a colorless toxic liquid alcohol $ClCH_2CH_2OH$ made usu. by reaction of ethylene with chlorine and water esp. in the presence of alkali and used chiefly in organic synthesis (as of ethylene oxide and ethylene glycol) and as a solvent

ethylene cyanohydrin *n* **:** a straw-colored toxic liquid alcohol $CNCH_2CH_2OH$ made usu. from ethylene oxide and hydrogen cyanide and used chiefly in making acrylonitrile and esters of acrylic acid

eth·yl·ene·diamine \ˌethə,lēn+\ *n* [ISV *ethylene* + *diamine*] **:** a colorless volatile liquid base $NH_2CH_2CH_2NH_2$ that has an ammoniacal odor, is made from ethylene dichloride and ammonia, and is used chiefly as a solvent and in organic synthesis — symbol *en*

ethylenediaminetetraacetate \+ˌte·trə+\ *n* [*ethylenediamine* + *tetra-* + *acetate*] **:** a salt of ethylenediaminetetraacetic acid

ethylenediaminetetraacetic acid \+ˌte·trə+. . .-\ *n* [*ethylenediamine* + *tetra-* + *acetic*] **:** a colorless crystalline acid $(HOOCCH_2)_2NCH_2CH_2N(CH_2COOH)_2$ used esp. in the form of its salts (as the tetrasodium salt or the calcium disodium salt) as a chelating and sequestering agent in industry, in chemical analysis, and in pharmacy and medicine (as in the treatment of lead poisoning) — abbr. *EDTA*

ethylene dibromide *or* **ethylene bromide** *n* **:** a colorless heavy toxic liquid compound $BrCH_2CH_2Br$ made by direct union of ethylene and bromine and used chiefly with tetraethyl lead in antiknock compositions and as a solvent; 1, 2-dibromo-ethane

ethylene dichloride *or* **ethylene chloride** *n* **:** a colorless heavy toxic liquid compound $ClCH_2CH_2Cl$ that has an odor like chloroform, is made usu. by direct union of ethylene and chlorine, and is used chiefly as a solvent (as for fats and oils) and insecticidal fumigant; 1,2-dichloro-ethane

ethylene glycol *n* **:** a thick sweet colorless liquid dihydroxy alcohol $HOCH_2CH_2OH$ made usu. by the hydration of ethylene oxide and used chiefly as an antifreeze, as a coolant (as in airplane engines), in hydraulic fluids, and in the manufacture of dynamites, plasticizers, and resins; 1,2-ethane-diol — called also *glycol*

ethylene linkage *or* **ethylenic linkage** *n* **:** a carbon-to-carbon double bond

ethylene oxide *n* **:** a colorless flammable toxic gaseous or liquid compound C_2H_4O made by reaction of ethylene chlorohydrin and alkali or by catalytic oxidation of ethylene and used chiefly in organic synthesis (as of ethylene glycol and ethanolamines) and in sterilization and fumigation — compare STRUCTURAL FORMULA

H_2C—CH_2 \/ O
ethylene oxide

ethylene series *n* **:** the homologous series of unsaturated hydrocarbons C_nH_{2n} of which ethylene is the lowest member — compare OLEFIN

eth·yl·e·nic \ˌethəˈlēnik\ *adj* [ISV *ethylene* + *-ic*] **:** relating to or derived from ethylene **:** resembling ethylene esp. in having a double bond **:** ETHENOID — **eth·yl·e·ni·cal·ly** \-nək(ə)lē\ *adv*

ethylenic isomerism *n* **:** CIS-TRANS ISOMERISM a

eth·yl·en·imine *or* **eth·yl·ene·imine** \,ethəˈlēnə,mēn\ *n* [ISV *ethylene* + *imine*] **:** a colorless toxic base C_2H_4NH made by dehydration of ethanolamine and used esp. in making finishing agents for textiles

ethyl ester *n* **:** an ester that yields ethyl alcohol on hydrolysis ⟨*ethyl esters* of fatty acids⟩

ethyl ether *n* **1 :** ETHER 3a **2 :** an ether in which one of the radicals united to oxygen is ethyl ⟨an *ethyl ether* of a phenol⟩

eth·yl·hex·o·ate \ˌethəlˈheksə,wāt\ *n* -s [*ethylhexoic* + *-ate*] **:** a salt or ester of ethylhexoic acid — called also OCTOATE

eth·yl·hex·o·ic acid \ˌethəlˌhekˈsōik-\ *n* [*ethyl* + *hexoic*] **:** a colorless liquid acid $CH_3(CH_2)_3CH(C_2H_5)COOH$ made synthetically and used in the form of its salts (as the cobalt or lead salt) chiefly as varnish driers; 2-ethyl-hexanoic acid

ethyl·ic \(ˈ)eˈthilik\ *adj* [ISV *ethyl* + *-ic*] **:** relating to, derived from, or containing ethyl ⟨an ~ ester⟩

eth·yl·i·dene \eˈthilə,dēn, ˈethəl-\ *n* -s [ISV *ethyl* + *-idene*] **:** a bivalent hydrocarbon radical $CH_3CH<$ isomeric with ethylene ⟨~ chloride CH_3CHCl_2⟩

ethyl iodide *n* **:** a colorless liquid compound C_2H_5I made by the interaction of ethyl alcohol, red phosphorus, and iodine and used chiefly in organic synthesis; iodo-ethane

ethyl lactate *n* **:** a colorless water-soluble liquid ester $CH_3CH(OH)COOC_2H_5$ of low volatility used chiefly as a solvent (as for cellulose derivatives in lacquers)

ethyl mercaptan *n* **:** a colorless flammable volatile liquid compound C_2H_5SH of disagreeable odor used as a warning agent in fuel-gas systems; ethane-thiol

ethylmorphine \ˌ=ˌ=ˈ=,=, ˌ=ˌ=ˈ=ˌ=\ *n* [ISV *ethyl* + *morphine*] **:** a synthetic toxic alkaloid $C_{19}H_{23}NO_3$ that is an ethyl ether of morphine and is used esp. in the form of its white crystalline hydrochloride similarly to morphine and codeine

ethyl nitrite *n* **:** a pale-yellow flammable volatile liquid ester C_2H_5ONO of ethereal odor

ethyl nitrite spirit *n* **:** a solution of ethyl nitrite in alcohol formerly used as a diuretic and diaphoretic — called also *spirit of nitrous ether, sweet spirit of nitre*

ethyl oxide *n* **:** ETHER 3a — used esp. of ether not intended for use in anesthesia

ethyl phthalate *n* **:** an ethyl ester of phthalic acid; *esp* **:** DIETHYL PHTHALATE

ethyls *pl of* ETHYL

ethyl silicate *n* **:** a colorless flammable liquid ester $(C_2H_5)_4SiO_4$ that hydrolyzes to silica and ethyl alcohol and is used esp. in paints and coatings (as for weatherproofing stone and cement) and as a bonding agent (as for molds for casting metals) — called also *tetraethoxysilane, tetraethyl orthosilicate*

ethyl sulfate *n* **:** an ethyl ester of sulfuric acid; *esp* the fragrant oily diethyl ester $(C_2H_5)_2SO_4$ made usu. by reaction of ethyl alcohol and oleum and used as an ethylating agent

ethyl vanillin *n* **:** a white crystalline aldehyde $C_2H_5O(OH)C_6H_3CHO$ that is the ethyl analogue of vanillin, has a more intense odor and flavor than vanillin, and is used as a flavoring agent — called also *bourbonal*

ethyl violet *n, usu cap E&V* **:** a basic dye — see DYE table I (under *Basic Violet 4; Pigment Blues 5 & 14*)

eth·yne *also* **eth·ine** \ˈe,thīn, eˈth-\ *n* -s [ISV *eth-* + *-yne*, *-ine*] **:** ACETYLENE

ethy·nyl *or* **ethi·nyl** \eˈthīnᵊl\ *n* -s [*ethyne, ethine* + *-yl*] **:** a univalent unsaturated radical $HC≡C-$ derived from acetylene by removal of one hydrogen atom

ethy·nyl·a·tion \(,)e,thīnᵊlˈāshən\ *n* -s **:** the introduction of the ethynyl radical into a compound usu. by reaction with acetylene ⟨~ of aldehydes yields acetylenic alcohols⟩

ethynylestradiol *var of* ETHINYL ESTRADIOL

-et·ic \ˈed·|ik, ˈet|, |ēk\ *adj suffix* [L & Gk; L *-eticus*, fr. Gk

-etikos, fr. -et-, formative element of certain nouns + -ikos -ic] : -IC ⟨algetic⟩ ⟨epilimnetic⟩ —usu. used to form adjectives corresponding to nouns ending in -esis (as genetic : genesis)

etio- or **aetio-** or **aitio-** comb form [ML aetio-, fr. Gk aitio-, fr. aitia — more at ETIOLOGY] **1** : cause ⟨etiologic⟩ ⟨etiogenic⟩ **2** : formed by chemical degradation of a (specified) compound ⟨etiophyllin⟩

¹eti·o·late \ˈēd·ēə,lāt\ vt -ED/-ING/-S [F étioler + E -ate (v. suffix)] **1** : to bleach and alter or weaken the natural development of (a green plant) by excluding sunlight **2** : to make pale and sickly ⟨remembering how drink hardens the skin and how drugs ~ it —Jean Stafford⟩ **3** : to rob of natural vigor : prevent or inhibit the full physical, emotional, or mental growth of (as by sheltering or pampering) ⟨the shade of Poets' walk, a green tunnel that has etiolated so many . . . poets —Cyril Connolly⟩

²etiolate \"\ adj [F étioler + E -ate (adj. suffix)] : COLORLESS, PALE, ETIOLATED

etiolated adj **1** : grown in absence of sunlight : BLANCHED ⟨~ celery⟩ **2** : lacking in vigor or natural exuberance : lacking in strength of feeling or appetites : EFFETE ⟨~ poetry⟩

eti·o·la·tion \,ēd·ēəˈlāshən\ n -S **1** : the act, process, or result of growing a plant in darkness : the yellowing or whitening of a green plant through lack of sunlight **2** : the loss or lessening of natural vigor : overrefinement of thought or emotional sensibilities : DECADENCE

eti·o·log·ic or **ae·ti·o·log·ic** \ˌē|d·ēəˈläjik, |tē- also ˌe|\ or **eti·o·log·i·cal** or **ae·ti·o·log·i·cal** \-jəkəl, -jēk-\ adj [Gk aitiologikos inquiring into causes, fr. aitiologia + -ikos -ic, -ical] : relating to etiology : assigning or seeking to assign a cause ⟨~ myth⟩ — **eti·o·log·i·cal·ly** or **ae·ti·o·log·i·cal·ly** \-jək(ə)lē, -jēk-, -li\ adv

eti·ol·o·gy or **ae·ti·ol·o·gy** \,==ˈäləjē, -ji\ also **ai·ti·ol·o·gy** \,ī|, ,ā|\ n -ES [ML aetiologia allegation of a cause or reason, fr. Gk aitiologia, fr. aitia cause + -logia -logy; akin to L aemulus rivaling, envious, rival, OIr āes age, Gk ainumai I take, seize, aisa destiny, share, Av aēta- punishment] **1 a** : a science or doctrine of causation or of the demonstration of causes **b** : a branch of science dealing with the causes of particular phenomena **2** : all the factors that contribute to the occurrence of a disease or abnormal condition : CAUSE, ORIGIN ⟨~ of malaria⟩ ⟨~ of crown rot⟩ ⟨~ of an old custom⟩

etio·porphyrin or **ae·tio·porphyrin** \ˌē|d·ē(,)ō also ˌē|+\ n [etio-, aetio- + porphyrin] : any of four isomeric porphyrins $C_{20}H_6N_4(CH_3)_4(C_2H_5)_4$; esp : a violet crystalline pigment occurring in nature (as in petroleum and coal) and formed by degradation of chlorophyll and of heme

et·i·quette \ˈed·ə̇kə̇t, ˈet|, |ēk-, -,ket, usu -kəd· or -ked· +V\ n -S [F étiquette — more at TICKET] **1** : the forms required by good breeding or prescribed by authority to be observed in social or official life : observance of the proprieties of rank and occasion : conventional decorum ⟨the strict ~ of court functions⟩ **2** : an item of behavior prescribed by rule or custom **3** : the rules of conduct, action, or practice binding on members of a profession (as medicine or law) esp. in their relations with one another

et·na \ˈetnə\ n -S [fr. Mt. Etna, Sicily; fr. its cone shape] : a device formerly used for heating liquids and consisting of a cup fixed in a saucer in which alcohol is burned

et·ne·an \(ˈ)etˈnēən\ adj, usu cap [L Aetnaeus, fr. Gk Aitnaios (fr. Aitnē Etna, volcano in Sicily) + E -an] : of or relating to Mt. Etna in Sicily

étoile \āˈtwäl\ n -S [F, fr. MF estoile star — more at ESTOILE] **1** : a star or a pattern in the shape of a star **2** : a principal dancer in a ballet company

eton \ˈētᵊn\ adj, usu cap [fr. Eton College, public school in Eton, Bucks, England] : resembling the clothes or appearance of boys at Eton College ⟨a short Eton crop for women⟩

eton blue n, often cap E [so called fr. its being the school color] : a light bluish green that is bluer and duller than average aqua green (sense 1) or average turquoise green and bluer and deeper than robin's-egg blue (sense 2) — called also Cambridge blue

eton cap n, usu cap E : a boy's cap with a short visor

eton collar n, usu cap E : a wide turnover collar for wear with an Eton jacket

eton game or **eton fives** n, usu cap E : the game of fives played on a court with front and side walls — compare RUGBY GAME

¹eto·ni·an \ēˈtōnēən\ n -S cap [Eton College + E -ian] : a student or former student of Eton College

²etonian \(ˈ)=ˈ===\ adj, usu cap : of or relating to Eton College

eton jacket n, usu cap E [so called fr. its being worn by boys at Eton College] **1** : a black jacket having long sleeves, wide lapels, and an open front and reaching just below the waistline in length **2** also **eton** -S : a woman's jacket that is usu. waist-length, often short-sleeved, and without lapels

eton wall game n, cap E [so called from being originated there] : an early form of English school football played by two teams on a strip of ground bounded on one side by a high wall

Eton jacket 1

étouf·fé \,ā,tüˈfā\ adj [F, fr. past part. of étouffer to stifle, smother, mute, fr. MF estouffer to smother, suffocate] : STIFLED, SMOTHERED — used esp. of a damping or muting of the tone on a stringed instrument (as the harp)

etrog var of ETHROG

etru·me·us \ə̇ˈtrümēəs\ n, cap [NL] : a genus of rather small chiefly tropical marine fishes (family Dussumieriidae) that includes round herrings of economic importance esp. in parts of the Pacific — see JAPANESE HERRING

¹etru·ri·an \ə̇ˈtrurēən, ēˈt-\ n -S cap [L Etruria, ancient country of central Italy + E -an] : ETRUSCAN

²etrurian \"\ adj, usu cap : ETRUSCAN

etru·ria ware \-rēə-\ n, cap E [fr. Etruria, factory in Staffordshire, England, where it was made] : pottery made in Staffordshire, England

¹etrus·can \ə̇ˈtrəskən, ēˈ-\ adj, usu cap [L Etruscus of Etruria, Etruscan + E -an] : of, relating to, or characteristic of Etruria or its inhabitants, art, language, or civilization

²etruscan \"\ n -S **1** cap : a native or inhabitant of ancient Etruria : TYRRHENIAN **2** cap : the language of the Etruscans which is of unknown affiliation and whose surviving records have been imperfectly interpreted **3** often cap : TUSCAN BROWN

etruscan alphabet n, usu cap E : an alphabet derived from the Greek alphabet, used for writing Etruscan, and having 26 letters in its earliest known form of the 7th or 8th century B.C. and subsequently 23 and then 20

etruscan red n, often cap E : a grayish reddish orange that is slightly darker than hyacinth red, yellower and darker than Persian melon, and duller than light persimmon

etruscan ware n, usu cap E : a black ware ornamented with encaustic colors chiefly in red and white and invented by Josiah Wedgwood and patented by him in 1770

etrusco- comb form, cap [L Etruscus] : Etruscan and ⟨Etrusco-Roman⟩

etrus·col·o·gist \(,)ē,trəˈskäləjə̇st, ə̇,-\ n -S usu cap : a specialist in Etruscan language and antiquities

etrus·col·o·gy \-jē\ n -ES usu cap [Etrusco- + -logy] : a study of Etruscan and Etruscan antiquities

-ets pl of -ET

ETS abbr expiration of term of service

et se·quens \etˈse,kwān(t)s, -sē,kwenz, -ˈsēkwənz\ [L] : and the following one — abbr. et seq.

et se·quen·tes \,etseˈkwen-,tās, -səˈkwen(·)tēz\ or **et sequen·tia** \-seˈkwentē,ä, -səˈkwench(ē)ə\ [L et sequentes (masc. & fem. pl.), et sequentia (neut. pl.)] : and those that follow — abbr. et seq., et seqq., et sqq.

-ette \ˈet sometimes ət; usu ˈed· or ˌəd· +V\ n suffix -S [ME, fr. MF, fem. dim. suffix, fr. OF -ete — more at -ET] **1** : little one (of the thing or class specified) : -LET ⟨wagonette⟩ ⟨kitchenette⟩ ⟨dinette⟩ **2** : group of (so many) ⟨octette⟩ **3** : female ⟨majorette⟩ ⟨farmerette⟩ ⟨suffragette⟩ **4** : imitation : substitute ⟨leatherette⟩ — used chiefly in commercial names

et·ter·cap \ˈed·ər,kap\ n -S [ME attercop, attercoppe, fr. OE ātorcoppe, fr. ātor poison, venom + -coppe spider, fr. copp top, summit — more at ATTER, COP] **1** Scot : SPIDER **2** Scot : an ill-tempered or spiteful person

et·tings·hau·sen effect \ˈed·iŋz,haüzᵊn-\ n, usu cap E [fr. the name Ettingshausen] : a transverse temperature gradient produced when a metal in which an electric current is flowing is placed in a magnetic field whose direction is perpendicular to that of the current

¹et·tle \ˈed·ᵊl\ vb [ME ettlen, atlen, fr. ON ætla; akin to OE eahtian to consider, estimate, watch over, eaht consideration, estimation, OHG ahtōn to consider, believe, estimate, ahta consideration, attention, esteem, Goth ahjan to believe, think, aha understanding, mind, Gk oknos hesitation, fear, and perh. to OE ēage eye — more at EYE] vt **1** chiefly Scot : INTEND, PLAN, DESIGN **2** chiefly Scot : ATTEMPT, VENTURE **3** chiefly Scot : GUESS, SUPPOSE ~ vi, chiefly Scot : AIM, ASPIRE, PLAN

²ettle \"\ n -S Scot : INTENT, PURPOSE

³ettle \"\ n -S [by alter. (resulting from incorrect division of a nettle)] dial Eng : NETTLE

et·tring·ite \ˈe·triŋ,īt\ n -S [G ettringit, fr. Ettringen, Rhine Province, Germany, its locality + G -it -ite] : a mineral $Ca_6Al_2(SO_4)_3(OH)_{12}.26H_2O$ consisting of hydrous basic sulfate of calcium and aluminum

et·ua tree \ˈed·əwə-, ˈet·wə-\ n [of African origin; akin to Twi etwa, a prickly plant] : a tropical African tree (Kigelia pinnata) of the family Bignoniaceae with sausage-shaped pods borne on the old wood

étude \ˈā,tüd, ˈā-,tyüd, =ˈ=\ n -S [F, lit., study, fr. MF estude, estudie — more at STUDY] : a piece of music for the practice of some special point of technical execution : STUDY, EXERCISE; also : a composition built upon a technical motive but played for its artistic value ⟨concert ~⟩

etui also **etwee** \āˈtwē, etˈwē, ˈ=,=\ n -S [F étui — more at TWEEZE] : an ornamental case for an article or small articles (as toilet articles, glasses, scissors, needles) in daily use

-e·tum \ˈēd·əm, ˈētəm\ n suffix, pl **-e·ta** \|ə\ or **-etums** [L -etum] **1** : garden or group of a (specified) kind of plant ⟨rosetum⟩ ⟨pinetum⟩ **2** : consocies (of a specified plant genus or family) ⟨characetum⟩

et ux·or \ed·ˈək,sȯ(ə)r\ [L] : and wife — abbr. et ux.

etyma pl of ETYMON

et·y·mol·o·ger \,ed·əˈmäləj(ə)r, ,etə-\ n -S [prob. fr. obs. etymologe, v., to derive etymologically (fr. Gk etymologein, fr. etymon + -logein to discourse, fr. logos speech) + ¹-er — more at ¹LEGEND] archaic : ETYMOLOGIST

et·y·mo·log·i·cal \ˌ==məˈläjəkəl, -jēk-\ also **et·y·mo·log·ic** \-jik, -jēk\ adj [etymological fr. L etymologicus (fr. Gk etymologikos, fr. etymologia + -ikos -ic) + E -al; etymologic fr. L etymologicus] : belonging to, based on, or in accord with etymology — **et·y·mo·log·i·cal·ly** \-jək(ə)lē, -jēk-, -li\ adv

et·y·mo·log·i·con \ˌ===ˈjə,kän, -jē-, -kən\ n -S [Gk etymologikon, fr. neut. of etymologikos] : an etymological dictionary or manual

et·y·mol·o·gist \,ed·əˈmäləjə̇st, ,etə-\ n -S [fr. etymologize, after such pairs as E catechize: catechist] : one that etymologizes : a specialist in etymology

et·y·mol·o·giz·able \-ˌjīzəbəl\ adj : capable of being etymologized

et·y·mol·o·gize \-z\ vb -ED/-ING/-S [ML etymologizare, fr. L etymologia etymology + LL -izare -ize] vt : to discover, formulate, or state an etymology for ~ vi **1** : to study etymology : formulate etymologies **2** : to define etymologically

et·y·mol·o·gy \,ed·əˈmäləjē, ,etə-, -ji\ n -ES [alter. (influenced by L etymologia) of ME ethimologie, prob. fr. ML ethimologia, alter. of L etymologia, fr. Gk, fr. etymon + -logia -logy] **1 a** : the history often including the prehistory of a linguistic form (as a word or morpheme) as shown by tracing its phonetic, graphic, and semantic development since its earliest recorded occurrence in the language where it is found, by tracing the course of its transmission from one language to another, by analyzing it into the component parts from which it was put together, by identifying its cognates in other languages, or by tracing it and its cognates back to a common ancestral form in a recorded or assumed ancestral language **b** : a branch of linguistics concerned with etymologies **2** : ACCIDENCE **3** : the etymological meaning of a word

et·y·mon \ˈ==,män\ n, pl **ety·ma** \-,mä, -,mə\ also **etymons** [L, origin of a word, fr. Gk, literal meaning of a word according to its origin, fr. neut. of etymos true; akin to Gk eteos true — more at SOOTH] **1 a** : the original form of a word either in the same language or in an ancestral language **b** : the word in a foreign language that is the source of a particular loanword ⟨the ~ of English cantata is Italian cantata⟩ **2** : the literal meaning of a word according to its origin **3** : a word or morpheme from which words are formed by composition or derivation

eu- comb form [ME, fr. L, fr. Gk, fr. neut. of eys good; akin to Hitt asus good and perh. to Skt asti he is — more at IS] **1 a** : well : easily ⟨euplastic⟩ — opposed to dys- **b** : good ⟨eudaemon⟩ — opposed to dys- **2 a** : most typical : true ⟨Euascomycetes⟩ ⟨euchromosome⟩ ⟨euglobulin⟩ **b** : truly ⟨eucoelomate⟩ **c** : having a complete life cycle ⟨eu-form⟩ **3** : improved derivative of a (specified) substance ⟨eucodeine⟩

EU abbr entropy unit

Eu symbol europium

eu·arc·tos \yüˈ(w)ärktəs, -,täs\ n, cap [NL, fr. eu- + Gk arktos bear — more at ARCTIC] in some classifications : a genus of bears comprising the American and sometimes the Asiatic black bears — compare SELENARCTOS, URSUS

eu·as·ca·les \,yü,aˈskā(,)lēz\ n pl, cap [NL, fr. eu- + asc- + -ales] in some classifications : an order equivalent to the class Euascomycetes

eu·ascomycetes \(ˌ)yü,(w)+-\ n pl, cap [NL, fr. eu- + Ascomycetes] : a subclass of the Ascomycetes having the asci borne in or on an ascocarp and usu. from ascogenous hyphae — compare HEMIASCOMYCETES, PROTOASCOMYCETES

eu·as·co·my·cet·i·dae \(,)yü,(w)askō,mīˈsed·ə,dē\ [NL, fr. eu- + Ascomycetes + -idae] syn of EUASCOMYCETES

eu·ascomycetous \(ˌ)=+\ adj [NL Euascomycetes + E -ous] : of or relating to the Euascomycetes

eu·aster \(ˈ)yüˈ(w)+-\ n [NL, fr. eu- + aster] : a sponge spicule in the shape of a modified aster in which the rays meet at a common center — compare STREPTASTER

eu·bacteria \ˌyü+\ [NL, fr. eu- + bacteria] syn of EUBACTERIALES

eu·bac·te·ri·a·les \,yü(,)bak,tirēˈā(,)lēz\ n pl, cap [NL, fr. eu- + bacteri- + -ales] : an order of Schizomycetes comprising relatively simple nonfilamentous unbranched bacteria showing no visible sulfur or iron particles and including spherical and rod-shaped forms

eu·bacterium \ˌyü+\ n [NL, fr. eu- + bacterium] : one of the Eubacteriales : a typical bacterium

eu·ba·sid·i·ae \,yübəˈsidē,ē\ n pl, cap [NL, fr. eu- + -basidiae (fr. basidium)] in some classifications : a subclass of fungi (class Basidiomycetes) including the orders Polyporales and Agaricales and characterized by one-celled basidia which produce spores on terminal sterigmata — compare HETEROBASIDIAE, TELIOSPOREAE

eu·ba·sid·ii \-dē,ī\ n pl, cap [NL, fr. eu- + -basidii (fr. basidium)] in some classifications : a subclass of fungi including all those basidiomycetes in which the basidium arises directly from vegetative cells of the diploid mycelium (as the puffballs, jelly fungi, pore fungi, and related forms) — compare HEMIBASIDII, HETEROBASIDIOMYCETES

¹eu·boe·an \(ˈ)yüˈbēən\ adj, usu cap [Euboea, island of Greece northeast of Attica and Boeotia + E -an] : EUBOIC

²euboean \"\ n -S cap [Euboea + E -an] : a native or inhabitant of Euboea

eu·bo·ic \(ˈ)yüˈbōik\ adj, usu cap [L euboicus, fr. Gk euboikos, fr. Euboia Euboea + Gk -ikos -ic] : of or relating to the island of Euboea or the sea which separates it from the Greek coast — compare CHALCIDIAN

eu·branchipus \(ˈ)yü+\ n, cap [NL, fr. eu- + Branchipus] : a genus of freshwater branchiopod crustaceans comprising fairy shrimps formerly classed in the genus Branchipus

eu·bryales \ˌyü+\ n pl, cap [NL, fr. eu- + Bryales] : an order of Musci comprising mosses that have perennial erect gametophores, stems with many rows of leaves, and drooping capsules with a double peristome of well-developed teeth

eu·caine \yüˈkān, ˈ=,=\ n -S [ISV eu- + -caine; orig. formed as G eucain (now eukain)] : a local anesthetic $C_{15}N_{21}NO_2$ derived from piperidine and usu. administered as the white crystalline hydrochloride — called also beta-eucaine

eu·cai·rite also **eu·kai·rite** \yüˈkī,rīt, -kā-\ n -S [Sw eukairit, fr. Gk eukairos seasonable, opportune (fr. eu- + kairos time, season) + Sw -it -ite; fr. its being found soon after the discovery of selenium] : a mineral CuAgSe composed of a grayish metallic-looking copper silver selenide (sp. gr. 7.50)

eu·ca·lypt \ˈyükə,lipt\ n -S [NL Eucalyptus] : a tree of the genus Eucalyptus — **eu·ca·lyp·tic** \ˌ==ˈliptik\ adj

eu·ca·lyp·tog·ra·phy \,yükə,lipˈtägrəfē\ n -ES : a treatise upon or study of the genus Eucalyptus

eu·ca·lyp·tole \,yükəˈlip,tōl\ or **eu·ca·lyp·tol** \-,tōl, -,tōl\ n -S [ISV eucalypt- (fr. NL Eucalyptus) + -ole, -ol] : CINEOLE

¹eu·ca·lyp·tus \,yükəˈliptəs\ n [NL, fr. eu- + Gk kalyptos covered, fr. kalyptein to cover, conceal; fr. the hemispherical or conical covering of the buds — more at HELL] **1** cap : a genus of evergreen timber trees or rarely shrubs (family Myrtaceae) mostly native to western Australia, having rigid entire leaves, umbellate flowers, and rather woody fruits, and yielding gums, resins, oils, and tars as well as useful woods — compare BLOODWOOD, BLUE GUM, CIDER GUM, EUCALYPTUS GUM, PEPPERMINT TREE, STRINGYBARK **2** pl **eucalyp·ti** \-,tī\ or **eucalyptuses** : any tree or shrub of the genus Eucalyptus : EUCALYPT **3** or **eucalyptus green** -ES : a grayish yellow to yellow green

²eucalyptus \ˌ==ˈ==\ adj : of or relating to the eucalyptus : made of eucalyptus wood

eucalyptus gum or **eucalyptus kino** n : a reddish brown dried gummy exudation from a red gum tree (Eucalyptus rostrata) of Australia and several other eucalypts used as a base for lozenges and troches — called also Botany Bay kino, red gum

eucalyptus oil n : any of various essential oils obtained from the leaves of various eucalypts (as Eucalyptus globulus) and used in pharmaceutical preparations (as antiseptics, cough drops), in perfumes, and in the flotation process for concentrating ores

eu·carida \(ˌ)yü+\ n pl, cap [NL, fr. eu- + -carida (fr. L carid-, caris, a kind of sea crab) — more at -CARIS] : an extensive group of crustaceans having the thoracic segments covered by and fused with a carapace and the eyes on movable stalks and constituting the orders Euphausiacea and Decapoda of the subclass Malacostraca

eu·car·pic \(ˈ)yüˈkärpik\ adj [eu- + -carpic] **1** : having only part of the thallus transformed into a fruiting body or sporangium ⟨~ algae⟩ ⟨~ fungi⟩ **2** : gaining nourishment by means of haustoria or rhizoids — compare HOLOCARPIC

eu·cary·ote or **eu·kary·ote** \yüˈka(a)rē,ōt\ adj [eu- + -caryote, -karyote (irreg. fr. kary-)] biol : having a visibly evident nucleus — **eu·cary·ot·ic** or **eu·kary·ot·ic** \(ˌ)yü-ka(a)rēˈäd·ik\ adj

euc·atropine \(ˈ)yüˈk+,-\ n [eucaine + atropine] : a synthetic alkaloid related in structure to eucaine and atropine, obtained in the form of its white crystalline hydrochloride $C_{17}H_{25}NO_3.HCl$, and used as a mydriatic

eu·ceph·a·lous \(ˈ)yüˈsefələs\ also **eu·ce·phal·ic** \ˌyüsəˈfalik\ adj [ISV eu- + -cephalous or -cephalic] : having a well-developed head — used of the larvae of certain flies; compare HEMICEPHALOUS

eu·cestoda \ˌyü+\ n pl, cap [NL, fr. eu- + Cestoda] in some classifications : a subclass of Platyhelminthes comprising the tapeworms and including all the cestodes except the cestodarians

eu·cha·ris \ˈyük(ə)rə̇s\ n [NL, fr. LL, gracious, charming, fr. Gk, fr. eu- + charis grace; akin to Gk chairein to rejoice — more at YEARN] **1** cap : a small genus of So. American scapose herbs (family Amaryllidaceae) having white umbellate flowers — see AMAZON LILY **2** or **eucharis lily** -ES : any plant of the genus Eucharis

eu·cha·rist \ˈyük(ə)rə̇st\ n -S usu cap [ME eukarist, fr. MF eucariste, fr. LL eucharistia, fr. Gk, Eucharist, giving of thanks, gratitude, fr. eucharistos grateful (fr. eu- + — assumed — charistos, verbal of Gk charizesthai to show favor, fr. charis favor, grace) + -ia -y] **1 a** : the sacrament of the Lord's Supper; specif : a central rite in many Christian churches in which bread and wine are consecrated by the officiating clergyman, shared with the people, and consumed as memorials of Christ's death or as symbols for the realization of a spiritual union between Christ and communicant or as the body and blood of Christ — called also Communion, Holy Communion **b** : the consecrated elements of bread and wine **2 a** : an act of giving thanks **b** : an act of worship in which thanksgiving is central **3** Christian Science : spiritual communion with God

eu·cha·ris·tial \ˌyükəˈris(h)chəl\ n -S [ML eucharistiale, fr. neut. of eucharistialis of the Eucharist, fr. LL eucharistia + L -alis -al] : a vessel for consecrated bread : PYX

eu·cha·ris·tic \ˌyükəˈristik, -tēk\ adj [eucharist + -ic] **1** often cap : of, relating to, or resembling the Eucharist **2** : manifesting or expressing praise and thanksgiving ⟨the poem's ~ intent⟩ — **eu·cha·ris·ti·cal·ly** \-tək(ə)lē, -tēk-, -li\ adv : in a eucharistic manner

eu·cha·ris·ti·cal \-təkəl, -tēk-\ archaic var of EUCHARISTIC

eu·cha·rist·ize \ˈyükərə,stīz, ˌ==ˈri,stīz\ vt -ED/-ING/-S [eucharist + -ize] archaic : to consecrate as elements of the Lord's Supper

eu·cheu·ma \yüˈk(y)ümə\ n, cap [NL, fr. eu- + Gk cheuma stream, fr. chein to pour — more at FOUND] : a genus of red algae (family Solieriaceae) having terete or flattened thalli often with abundant spiny branchlets

eu·chite \ˈyü,kīt\ n -S usu cap [LGk euchitēs, fr. Gk euchē prayer, vow (fr. euchesthai to pray, vow) + -itēs -ite — more at VOW] **1** : one of an ecstatic mendicant vagrant Christian sect of the 4th to the 8th centuries in Mesopotamia, Syria, and Asia Minor that believed man's congenital devil could be expelled only by unremitting prayer **2** : one of an 11th century Thracian sect similar to the Euchite and probably descended from it through 8th and 10th century migrations

eu·chlae·na \yüˈklēnə\ n, cap [NL, fr. eu- + Gk chlaina cloak; fr. the bracts around the ear] : a small genus of Mexican grasses that are closely related to and readily hybridize with Indian corn and have the pistillate spike reduced to a row of hard joints resembling seeds — see TEOSINTE

eu·chlo·rin \yüˈklōrə̇n, ˈyüklər-\ n -S [It euclorina, fr. Gk euchlōros greenish (fr. eu- + chlōros greenish yellow) + It -ina -ine; fr. the color — more at YELLOW] : a mineral $(K,Na)_8Cu_9(SO_4)_{10}(OH)_6$ composed of a basic sulfate of copper, sodium, and potassium found in lava at Vesuvius

eu·cho·lo·gion \,efkōˈlōyōn\ n, pl **eucholo·gia** \-yə\ [MGk, fr. eucho- (fr. Gk euchē prayer) + -logion (fr. Gk legein to collect) — more at LEGEND] : a principal service book of liturgies, prayers, and occasional rites used in the Eastern Orthodox Church

eu·chol·o·gy \yüˈkäləjē\ n -ES [MGk euchologion] : EUCHOLOGION

eu·chor·da \yüˈkȯrdə\ n pl, cap [NL, fr. eu- + -chorda (fr. chorda)] in some classifications : a subphylum or other division of Chordata comprising the lancelets and true vertebrates

eu·chordata \ˌyü+\ [NL, fr. eu- + Chordata] syn of EUCHORDA

¹eu·chre also **eu·cher** \ˈyükə(r)\ n -S [origin unknown] **1** : a card game in which each player is dealt five cards and the player or side that makes the trump must take three tricks to win a hand — see BOWER **2** : the action of euchring an opponent

²euchre also **eucher** \"\ vt **euchred** also **euchered**; **euchred** also **euchered**; **euchring** also **euchering** \ˈyük(ə)riŋ\ **euchres** also **euchers** **1** : to prevent (the maker of trump in the game of euchre) from winning three tricks **2** : CHEAT, DECEIVE, TRICK, OUTWIT ⟨euchred me out of a fortune —Richard Stanton⟩

eu·chred \ˈyükə(r)d\ adj [origin unknown] dial : made slightly tart by an acid or spice ⟨~ figs⟩

eu·chro·ite \ˈyükrō,īt\ n -S [G euchroit, fr. Gk euchroos well-colored (fr. eu- + -chroos -chroous) + G -it -ite] : a mineral $Cu_2(AsO_4)(OH).3H_2O$ consisting of a basic copper arsenate in emerald-green orthorhombic crystals (hardness 3.5–4, sp. gr. 3.39)

eu·chromatic \ˌyü+\ adj [euchromatin + -ic] : of or relating to euchromatin

eu·chromatin \(ˈ)yü+\ n [G, fr. eu- + chromatin] : the portion of chromatin that is genetically active and is held to be largely made up of genes and that stains less intensely than heterochromatin

eu·chro·ma·ti·za·tion \yü,krōməd·ə'zāshən\ *n* -s [*euchromat-* (fr. *euchromatin*) + *-ization*] : the transformation of a portion of chromatin into euchromatin — compare HETEROCHROMATIZATION

eu·chromocenter \(ˈ)yü+\ *n* [ISV *eu-* + *chromocenter;* prob. orig. formed as F *euchromocentre*] : PROCHROMOSOME, CHROMOCENTER

eu·chromocentric \(ˌ)yü+\ *adj* : of, relating to, or characterized by the presence of euchromocenters — used esp. of plant-cell nuclei that appear homogeneous during metabolic phases

eu·chromosome \(ˈ)yü+\ *n* [*eu-* + *chromosome*] : AUTOSOME

euchrysine GG *n, usu cap E* [*euchrysine* ISV *eu-* + *chrys-* + *-ine*] : a basic dye — see DYE table I (under *Basic Yellow 9*)

eu·ciliata \(ˌ)yü+\ *n pl, cap* [NL, fr. *eu-* + *Ciliata*] : the subclass of Ciliata comprising protozoans having a trophic macronucleus and a reproductive micronucleus and reproducing sexually by conjugation and including the four orders Holotricha, Spirotricha, Chonotricha, and Peritricha — compare PROTOCILIATA — **eu·ciliate** \(ˈ)yü+\ *adj or n*

eu·cirripedia \(ˌ)yü+\ *n pl, cap* [NL, fr. *eu-* + *Cirripedia*] *in some classifications* : a group of barnacles consisting of the more typical forms as distinguished from the Rhizocephala

eu·clase \'yü,klās, -āz\ *n* -s [F, fr. *eu-* + Gk *klasis* breaking, fr. *klan* to break — more at HALT] : a rare brittle silicate of beryllium and aluminum $BeAlSiO_4(OH)$ occurring in pale-yellow, green, or blue prismatic crystals and sometimes used as a gem

eu·clea \yü'klēə\ *n, cap* [NL, fr. Gk *eukleia* glory, fr. *euklees* famous (fr. *eu-* + *-klees*, fr. *kleos* report, fame) + *-ia* -y; akin to Gk *klytos* famous— more at LOUD] : a genus of African trees and shrubs (family Ebenaceae) having evergreen leaves, dioecious racemose flowers, and hard wood — see CAPE EBONY

[1]**eu·cle·id** \'yüklēəd\ *adj* [NL *Eucleidae*] : of or relating to the Eucleidae

[2]**eucleid** \"\ *n* -s : a moth of the family Eucleidae

eu·cle·i·dae \yü'klēə,dē\ *n pl, cap* [NL, fr. *Euclea*, type genus (fr. Gk *eukleia* glory) + *-idae*] : a family of hairy robust yellow to brown moths often strikingly marked with color and including some with severely urticating hairs — see CUP MOTH

eu·clid \'yüklәd\ *n* -s *often cap* [after *Euclid fl ab* 300 B.C. Greek geometer] : EUCLIDEAN GEOMETRY

eu·clid·e·an *also* **eu·clid·i·an** \(ˈ)yü¦klidēən\ *adj, often cap* : adopting Euclid's assumptions with respect to space : relating to geometry as developed in Euclid's *Elements*

euclidean construction *n, often cap E* : a geometric construction by the use of ruler and compasses

euclidean geometry *n, often cap E* **1** : the geometry based on Euclid's axioms **2** : the geometry of a Euclidean space

euclidean space *n, often cap E* : the space to which Euclid's axioms and definitions (as of straight and parallel lines, angles of plane triangles) apply

eu·clid's algorithm \'yüklədz-\ *n, often cap E* : a rule for finding the greatest common divisor of two positive integers

eu·coelomate \(ˈ)yü+\ *adj* [*eu-* + *coelomate*, adj.] : having a body cavity that is a coelom— distinguished from *acoelomate* and *pseudocoelomate*

eu·co·lite *also* **eu·ko·lite** *or* **eu·ko·lyte** \'yükə,līt\ *n* -s [G *eukolit*, fr. Gk *eukolos* easily satisfied + G *-it* -ite; fr. a conception that its difference in composition from woehlerite is a disadvantage that it has to endure] : a mineral similar to eudialyte but optically negative

eu·com·mia \yü'kämēə\ *n, cap* [NL, fr. *eu-* + *-commia* (fr. Gk *kommi* gum) — more at GUM] : a monotypic genus (coextensive with the family Eucommiaceae of the order Rosales) containing a hardy Chinese tree that yields rubber and has alternate leaves and solitary unisexual flowers in the leaf axils

eu·cone \'yü,kōn\ *also* **eu·con·ic** \(ˈ)yü¦känik\ *adj* [*eucone* ISV *eu-* + *cone; euconic* fr. *eucone* + *-ic*] : having fully developed crystalline cones in the ommatidia — used of the eyes of insects and crustaceans; compare ACONE, EXOCONE, PSEUDOCONE

eu·copepoda \ˌyü+\ *n pl, cap* [NL, fr. *eu-* + *Copepoda*] : an order of copepods consisting of the typical free-swimming forms and the lernaeans as distinguished from the Branchiura

eu·cos·mi·dae \yü'käzmə,dē\ [NL, fr. *Eucosma*, included genus (irreg. fr. Gk *eukosmos* well adorned, fr. *eu-* + *kosmos* order, ornament) + *-idae*] *syn of* OLETHREUTIDAE

eu·cot·y·lid \yü'käd·əˌləd\ *n* -s [NL *Eucotylidae*] : a worm of the family Eucotylidae

eu·co·tyl·i·dae \,yükə'tilə,dē\ *n pl, cap* [NL, fr. *Eucotyle*, type genus (fr. *eu-* + Gk *kotylē* cup, anything hollow) + *-idae* — more at KETTLE] : a family of digenetic trematode worms including numerous parasites of the kidneys and ureters of gallinaceous birds

eu·cra·sia \yü'krāzh(ē)ə\ *n* -s [NL, fr. ML, mixture of the humors in good proportions, fr. Gk *eukrasia*, fr. *eu-* + *-krasia* (fr. *krasis* mixing, combination) — more at CRASIS] : a normal state of health : physical well-being — opposed to *dyscrasia*

eu·cra·site \'yükrə,sīt, -,zīt\ *n* -s [Sw *eukrasit*, fr. Gk *eukrasia* mixture of the humors in good proportions, good temperature + Sw *-it* -ite] : a variety of thorite

eu·crite \'yü,krīt\ *n* -s [G *eukrit*, fr. Gk *eukritos* easily discerned, fr. *eu-* + *kritos* separated, chosen, fr. *krinein* to separate — more at CERTAIN] **1** : a meteorite composed essentially of anorthite and augite **2** : a very basic gabbro whose feldspar contains at least as much lime as does bytownite

eu·crustacea \ˌyü+\ *n pl, cap* [NL, fr. *eu-* + *Crustacea*] *in some classifications* : a primary division of Crustacea comprising all recent and extinct forms which do not have the body divided into median and lateral lobes — used when trilobites are considered crustaceans

eu·cryph·ia \yü'krifēə\ *n, cap* [NL, fr. *eu-* + Gk *kryphia*, fem. of *kryphios* concealed, fr. *kryptein* to conceal, hide — more at CRYPT] : a genus (coextensive with the family Eucryphiaceae of the order Parietales) of tall evergreen trees native to Australia and Chile that have dark shining opposite leaves, large flowers, and a woody or leathery capsular fruit — **eu·cryph·i·a·ceous** \(ˌ)yü¦krifē'āshəs\ *adj*

eu·cryp·tite \yü'krip,tīt\ *n* -s [G *eukryptit*, fr. Gk *eukryptos* easily hidden (fr. *eu-* + *kryptos* hidden) + E *-ite* — more at CRYPT] : a mineral $LiAlSiO_4$ consisting of a colorless or white lithium aluminum silicate occurring in hexagonal crystals (sp. gr. 2.67)

euctical *adj* [Gk *euktikos* constituting a prayer or vow (fr. *euktos* wished for, vowed — fr. *euchesthai* to pray, vow — + *-ikos* -ic) + E *-al* — more at VOW] *obs* : SUPPLICATORY

eu·cyclic \(ˈ)yü+\ *adj* [ISV *eu-* + *cyclic*] *of a flower* : cyclic with alternate isomerous whorls

eu·daemon *also* **eu·demon** \(ˈ)yü+\ *n* [*eu-* + *demon*] : a good spirit : DEMON, ANGEL — opposed to *cacodemon*

eu·dae·mo·nia \,yüdē'mōnēə\ *also* **eu·dai·mo·nia** \-,dī'-, -(ˌ)dā'-\ *n* -s [Gk *eudaimonia*, fr. *eudaimon-*, *eudaimōn* having a good attendant or indwelling spirit, lucky, happy (fr. *eu-* + *daimon-*, *daimōn* spirit) + *-ia* -y— more at DEMON] **1** : WELL-BEING, HAPPINESS **2** *Aristotelianism* : a life of activity governed by reason

eu·dae·mon·ic \ˌyüdē¦mänik, -nēk\ *also* **eu·dae·mon·i·cal** \-nəkəl, -nēk-\ *adj* [*eudaemonic* fr. Gk *eudaimonikos*, fr. *eudaimon-*, *eudaimōn* + *-ikos* -ic; *eudaemonical* fr. Gk *eudaimonikos* + E *-al*] : producing happiness : based on the idea of happiness as the proper end of conduct

eu·dae·mon·ics \ˌ=ˈ=mäniks, -nēks\ *n pl but sing or pl in constr* [Gk *eudaimon-*, *eudaimōn* + E *-ics*] **1** : the practice of eudaemonism : an art or means of attaining happiness **2** : the science of happiness — contrasted with *aretaics*

eu·dae·mon·ism \yü'dēmə,nizəm\ *also* **eu·dai·mo·nism** \-dīm-, -däm-\ *or* **eu·de·mon·ism** \-dēm-\ *n* -s [prob. fr. G *eudämonismus*, fr. Gk *eudaimon-*, *eudaimōn* + G *-ismus* -ism] : an ethical theory that defines moral obligation by reference to happiness or personal well-being esp. through a life governed by reason as distinguished from pursuit of pleasure— compare HEDONISM

eu·dae·mon·ist \-ˌnəst\ *n* -s [prob. fr. G *eudämonist*, fr. Gk *eudaimon-*, *eudaimōn* + G *-ist*] : an adherent of eudaemonism

eu·dae·mon·is·tic \(ˌ)yü¦dēmə¦nistik, -tēk\ *adj* : of or relating to eudaemonism : based on a conception of eudaemonia — **eu·dae·mon·is·ti·cal·ly** \-tək(ə)lē, -tēk-, -li\ *adv*

eu·dae·mo·ny \yü'dēmənē, -ni\ *n* -ES [Gk *eudaimonia*] : EUDAEMONIA

eu·da·lene \'yüdᵊl,ēn\ *n* -s [*eudesmol* + *naphthalene*] : a liquid hydrocarbon $C_{14}H_{16}$ formed from various sesquiterpenoids by dehydrogenation; 7-isopropyl-1-methyl-naphthalene

eu·de·mis moth \'yüdəməs-\ *n* [NL *Eudemis*, former genus name, fr. *eu-* + *-demis* (fr. Gk *demas* body, fr. *demein* to build) — more at TIMBER] : a small European tortricid moth (*Polychrosis botrana*) that is destructive to the grape

eu·den·dri·um \yü'dendrēəm\ *n, cap* [NL, fr. *eu-* + *-dendrium* (fr. Gk *dendrion*, dim. of *dendron* tree) — more at DENDR-] : a genus of hydrozoans (order Anthomedusae) forming a branching colony of pink hydranths with a chitinous perisarc

eu·der·ma \yü'dərmə\ *n, cap* [NL, fr. *eu-* + *-derma*] : a genus of bats containing the jackass bat

eu·des·mol \yü'dez,mōl, -mȯl\ *n* -s [*eudesm-* (fr. NL *Eudesmia* — syn. of *Eucalyptus* —, fr. *eu-* + *desm-* + *-ia*) + *-ol*] : a crystalline sesquiterpenoid alcohol $C_{15}H_{25}OH$ found in eucalyptus oils and used in perfumery as a fixative

eu·de·ve \eü'dā,vā\ *n, pl* **eudeve** *or* **eudeves** *usu cap* [Sp, of AmerInd origin] **1 a** : a division of the Opata people of Mexico **b** : a member of this division **2** : the language of the Eudeve people

eu·di·a·lyte \yü'dīə,līt\ *n* -s [G *eudialyt*, fr. Gk *eudialytos* easy to dissolve, fr. *eu-* + *dialytos* capable of being dissolved, fr. *dialyein* to dissolve — more at DIALYSIS] : a mineral $Na_4(Ca,Fe)_2ZrSi_6O_{17}(OH,Cl)_2$ consisting of a brownish red silicate chiefly of sodium, iron, zirconium, and calcium that occurs in crystals or masses and is optically positive (H.5–5.5, sp. gr. 2.9–3.0)

eu·did·y·mite \yü'didə,mīt\ *n* -s [Norw *eudidymit*, fr. *eu-* + Gk *didymos* twin + Norw *-it* -ite; fr. its occurrence in twin crystals — more at DIDYM-] : a mineral $NaBeSi_3O_7(OH)$ consisting of a white glassy sodium beryllium silicate

eu·di·om·e·ter \,yüdē'äməd·ə(r)\ *n* [It *eudiometro*, fr. Gk *eudia* fair weather, fr. *eu-* + *-dia* weather — akin to L *dies* day) + *-metro* -meter; fr. a former belief that the proportion of oxygen in the air is considerably higher in fair weather than in bad weather — more at DEITY] : an instrument (as a graduated glass tube) for the volumetric measurement and analysis of gases that involves the explosion of one of the components of a mixture by the passage of an electric spark — compare BURETTE 1 — **eu·di·o·met·ric** \ˌyüdēə¦me·trik\ *adj*

eu·dist \'yüdəst\ *n* -s *cap* [F *eudiste*, fr. Jean *Eudes* †1680 Fr. priest and founder + F *-iste* -ist] : a member of the Roman Catholic Congregation of Jesus and Mary established in 1643 for diocesan priests and lay brothers and now devoted chiefly to teaching and missionary work

eu·doc·i·mus \yü'däsəməs\ *n, cap* [NL, fr. Gk *eudokimos* glorious, famous, fr. *eu-* + *dokimos* esteemed, fr. *dokein* to seem good — more at DECENT] : a genus of ibises containing the New World white and scarlet ibises

eu·do·ri·na \,yüdə'rīnə, -rēnə\ *n, cap* [NL, fr. Gk *eudōros* generous (fr. *eu-* + *-dōros*, fr. *dōron* gift) + NL *-ina*; akin to Gk *didonai* to give — more at DATE] : a genus related to *Volvox* and comprising flagellates that produce markedly anisogamous gametes and form spherical or ellipsoidal colonies

eu·dox·ian \yü'däksēən, -kshən\ *n* -s *usu cap* [*Eudoxius* †A.D.370, bishop of Constantinople and a leader of the Anomoeans + E *-an*] : a follower of Bishop Eudoxius

eu·dro·mi·as \yü'drōmēəs\ *n, cap* [NL, fr. Gk, rapid swimmer, fr. *eudromos* swift, running well, fr. *eu-* + *dromos* course, racecourse; akin to Gk *dramein* to run — more at DROMEDARY] : a genus of plovers that includes the common dotterel of Europe

eu·echinoidea \(ˌ)yü+\ *n pl, cap* [NL, fr. *eu-* + *Echinoidea*] *in some classifications* : a division of Echinoidea including all living sea urchins and comprising the orders Cidaroida, Centrechinoida, and Exocycloida— compare PALAEECHINOIDEA

eu–form \'yü,fȯrm\ *n* : a rust having a complete life cycle of pycnial, aecial, uredinial, and telial stages — compare OPSIS-FORM

eu·ge \'eü,gā, 'yü,jē\ *n* -s [L, well done!, fr. Gk, fr. *eu* well — more at EU-] : an act or expression of approval : BRAVO

eu·gene poplar \'yü,jēn-, ˌ=ˈ=-\ *n, usu cap E* [prob. fr. the name *Eugene*] : a hybrid poplar (*Populus canadensis eugenei*) of pyramidal habit originated near Metz in 1832 and used for ornament esp. as a street tree

eu·genesis \ˌyü+\ *n* [NL, fr. *eu-* + L *genesis*] : fertility between hybrids

eu·ge·nia \yü'jēnyə, -nēə\ *n* [NL, fr. *Eugene*, prince of Savoy †1736 Austrian general + NL *-ia*] **1** *cap* : a large genus of tropical trees and shrubs (family Myrtaceae) having aromatic leaves, tetramerous flowers, baccate fruit, and wood that is often hard and valuable — see SURINAM CHERRY **2** -s : any tree of the genus *Eugenia*

eugenia red *n, often cap E* : a moderate red that is yellower and paler than cerise, claret (sense 3a), or average strawberry (sense 2a) and bluer and paler than Turkey red

eu·gen·ic \(ˈ)yü¦jenik, -nēk\ *also* **eu·gen·i·cal** \-nəkəl, -nēk-\ *adj* [Gk *eugenēs* wellborn (fr. *eu-* + *-genēs* born) + E *-ic*, *-ical* — more at -GEN] : relating to or fitted for the production of good offspring : relating to or aiming at the improvement of race or breed — contrasted with *dysgenic* — **eu·gen·i·cal·ly** \-nək(ə)lē, -nēk-, -li\ *adv*

eu·gen·i·cist \yü'jenəsəst\ *n* -s : a student or advocate of eugenics

eu·gen·ics \yü'jeniks, -nēks\ *n pl but usu sing in constr* **1** : a science that deals with the improvement of hereditary qualities in a series of generations of a race or breed esp. by social control of human mating and reproduction — compare EUTHENICS, GENETICS **2** : the process or means of race improvement (as by restricting mating to superior types suited to each other)

eu·gen·ism \yü'je,nizəm, yü'jē,-, 'yüjə,-\ *n* -s [Gk *eugenēs* + E *-ism*] : the combination of influences best suited to improve the hereditary qualities of a race or breed, esp. the human race

eu·gen·ist \-ˌnəst\ *n* -s [Gk *eugenēs* + E *-ist*] : EUGENICIST

eu·ge·nol \'yüjə,nōl, -nȯl\ *n* -s [ISV *eugen-* (fr. *Eugenia caryophyllata*, species of clove that is a source of clove oil) + *-ol*; orig. formed as F *eugénol*] : a colorless aromatic liquid phenol $CH_2CH{:}CH_2C_6H_3(OCH_3)OH$ found esp. in clove oil and cinnamon-leaf oil and used chiefly in flavors and perfumes, in dentistry as an anodyne and disinfectant, and in the synthesis of vanillin; 4-allyl-guaiacol

eu·geosynclinal \(ˌ)yü+\ *adj* : of the nature of or relating to a eugeosyncline

eu·geosyncline \"+\ *n* [*eu-* + *geosyncline*] : a narrow rapidly subsiding geosyncline usu. with volcanic materials mingled with clastic sediments — compare MIOGEOSYNCLINE

eu·glan·di·na \,yü,glan'dīnə, -dēnə\ *n, cap* [NL, fr. *eu-* + *Glandina* genus of snails, fr. L *gland-*, *glans* acorn + NL *-ina* — more at GLAND] : a genus of land snails (family Oleacinidae) found esp. in the southern U.S. and in Mexico that are largely carnivorous in habits

eu·gle·na \yü'glēnə\ *n, cap* [NL, fr. *eu-* + Gk *glēnē* eyeball, socket of a joint; prob. akin to Gk *glainoi* ornaments — more at CLEAN] : a genus (order Euglenoidina) of green flagellates that are often classed as algae, are cosmopolitan in stagnant fresh water, usu. have a distinct pellicle more or less sculptured and striated, and are capable of writhing plastic movement as well as flagellar motility — see EUGLENACEAE

eu·gle·na·ce·ae \yü¦glə'nāsē,ē\ *n pl, cap* [NL, fr. *Euglena*, type genus + *-aceae*] : a family of algae (class Euglenophyceae) that includes *Euglena* and numerous related genera when these are considered to be algae

eu·gle·na·les \ˌ=ə(ˌ)lēz\ *n pl, cap* [NL, fr. *Euglena* + *-ales*] : an order of algae (class Euglenophyceae) comprising forms in which the motile flagellate is the dominant phase in the life cycle — compare COLACIALES

eu·gle·ni·da \yü'glēnədə, -len-\ *or* **eu·gle·noi·di·da** \ˌyüglə'nȯidədə\ [*Euglenida* fr. NL, fr. *Euglena* + *-ida; Euglenoidida* fr. NL, fr. *Euglena* + L *-oides* -oid + NL *-ida*] *syn of* EUGLENOIDINA

eu·gle·nin·e·ae \,yüglə'ninē,ē\ [NL, fr. *Euglena* + *-ineae*] *syn of* EUGLENOPHYCEAE

[1]**eu·gle·noid** \yü'glē,nȯid, 'yüglə,n-\ *adj* [NL *Euglenoidina*] : of or relating to the order Euglenoidina

[2]**euglenoid** \"\ *n* -s [NL *Euglenoidina*] : a flagellate of the order Euglenoidina

eu·gle·noi·di·na \,yüglə,nȯi'dīnə, -dēnə\ *n pl, cap* [NL, fr. *Euglena* + L *-oides* -oid + NL *-ina*] : an order of Phytomastigina comprising extremely varied flagellates that are typically solitary green or colorless stigma-bearing organisms with one or two flagella emerging anteriorly from a well-defined gullet — see EUGLENA

euglenoid movement *n* : writhing usu. nonprogressive protoplasmic movement characteristic of plastic-bodied euglenoids but known to occur in other groups (as certain sporozoans) — called also *metabolic movement*

eu·gle·no·phy·ce·ae \yü,glēnə'fīsē,ē, -'fis-\ *n pl, cap* [NL, fr. *Euglena* + *-o-* + *-phyceae*] : a class (coextensive with a division Euglenophyta) of mostly green and free-swimming algae comprising the family Euglenaceae and related forms

eu·gle·noph·y·ta \,yüglə'näfəd·ə\ *n pl, cap* [NL, fr. *Euglena* + *-o-* + *-phyta*] : a division or other category of algae that is coextensive with the zoological order Euglenoidina

eu·globulin \(ˈ)yü+\ *n* [ISV *eu-* + *globulin*] : a simple protein insoluble in half-saturated ammonium sulfate or sodium sulfate and insoluble in pure water — distinguished from *pseudoglobulin*

eu·gly·pha \'yüglәfə, yü'glifə\ *n, cap* [NL, fr. *eu-* + Gk *glyphē* carving, fr. *glyphein* to carve or hollow out — more at CLEAVE] : a genus (the type of a cosmopolitan family Euglyphidae) of freshwater amoeboid protozoans with a plated test, one or two nuclei, and dichotomously branched filopodia — **eu·gly·phid** \-fəd\ *adj or n*

eu·gon·ic \(ˈ)yü¦gänik\ *adj* [*eu-* + *gon-* + *-ic*] : growing readily on artificial media — used esp. of tubercle bacteria; opposed to *dysgonic*

eu·greg·a·rine \yü'gregə,rīn, -ˌrēn\ *n* -s [NL *Eugregarinina*] : one of the Eugregarinina

eu·gregarinida \(ˌ)yü+\ [NL, fr. *eu-* + *Gregarinida*] *syn of* EUGREGARININA

eu·gregarinina \"+\ *n pl, cap* [NL, fr. *eu-* + *Gregarinina*] : a suborder of Gregarinida comprising sporozoans that do not exhibit asexual schizogonous reproduction — compare SCHIZOGREGARINARIA

eu·harmonic \(ˌ)yü+\ *adj* [*eu-* + *harmonic*] : not tempered : ENHARMONIC 3

eu·he·dral \(ˈ)yü¦hēdrəl\ *adj* [*eu-* + *-hedral*] : IDIOMORPHIC

eu·he·mer·ism \yü'hēmə,rizəm, -hem-\ *n* -s [*Euhemerus*, 4th cent. B.C. Greek mythographer + E *-ism*] **1** *often cap* : a theory held by Euhemerus that the gods of mythology were but deified mortals **2** *sometimes cap* : interpretation of myths as traditional accounts of historical persons and events

eu·he·mer·ist \-ˌrəst\ *n* -s *often attrib* : an advocate of euhemerism — **eu·he·mer·is·tic** \(ˌ)=ˌ=¦ristik\ *adj* — **eu·he·mer·is·ti·cal·ly** \-tək(ə)lē\ *adv*

eu·he·mer·ize \=ˈ==,rīz\ *vt* -ED/-ING/-s : to interpret (mythology) on the theory of euhemerism

eukairite *var of* EUCAIRITE

eukaryote *var of* EUCARYOTE

eu·kinetics \ˌyü+\ *n pl but usu sing in constr* [prob. fr. Gk *eukinētos* easily moved, agile (fr. *eu-* + *kinētos* moving, movable, fr. *kinein* to move, set in motion) + E *-ics* — more at HIGHT] : a science of well-controlled body movement (as of dancers)

eukolite *or* **eukolyte** *var of* EUCOLITE

eu·la·chon *also* **eu·la·chan** \'yülə,kän\ *or* **oo·la·chan** \'ü-\ *n, pl* **eulachon** *or* **eulachons** *also* **eulachan** *or* **eulachans** *or* **oolachan** *or* **oolachans** [Chinook Jargon *ulâkân*] : CANDLEFISH 1

eu·la·lia \yü'lālēə, -lyə\ *n* -s [NL, prob. fr. the name *Eulalia*] : any of several ornamental grasses belonging to the genus *Miscanthus* (esp. *M. sinensis*)

eu·lamellibranch \ˌyü+\ *n* [NL *Eulamellibranchia*] : a eulamellibranchiate mollusk

eu·lamellibranchia \"+\ *n pl, cap* [NL, fr. *eu-* + *Lamellibranchia*] : an order of Lamellibranchia comprising bivalve mollusks that have filamentous gills forming two continuous flattened layers on each side of the body, the foot usu. large, and a byssus reduced or absent and that include the oysters, freshwater mussels, clams, cockles, shipworms, and numerous related mollusks — **eu·lamellibranchiate** \"+\ *adj or n*

eu·lamellibranchiata \"+\ [NL, fr. *eu-* + *Lamellibranchiata*] *syn of* EULAMELLIBRANCHIA

eu·la·mia \yü'lāmēə\ [NL, fr. *eu-* + *Lamia*, former name of a genus of fishes, fr. L *lamia* — more at LAMIA] *syn of* CARCHARHINUS

eu·ler diagram \'ȯilə(r)-\ *or* **eu·ler's diagram** \-)z-\ *n, usu cap E* [after Leonhard *Euler* †1783 Swiss mathematician and physicist] : a graphic method employing circles to represent relations between and operations on classes and the terms of propositions by inclusion, exclusion, and intersection — compare VENN DIAGRAM

euler's equation *n, usu cap E* **1** : an equation in alternating-current theory: $e^{ix} = \cos x + i \sin x$ **2** : any of several differential equations of dynamics

euler's formula *n, usu cap E* : a general engineering formula relating to the strength of a long strut and obtained by mathematical analysis assuming the strut to be initially very slightly bent and neglecting the $\left(\frac{dy}{dx}\right)^2$ term in the curvature equation: $P = c\frac{\pi^2 EI}{l^2}$, where P = axial load, E = Young's modulus, I = moment of inertia of transverse section of strut, l = length of strut, c = a constant depending upon the manner of fixing the ends

eu·littoral \(ˈ)yü+\ *n* [*eu-* + *littoral*] : a landward subdivision of the littoral zone of a body of water; *usu* : the benthic zone that falls between the limits of fluctuation level of a body of water

eu·lo·gia \yü'lōj(ē)ə\ *n, pl* **eulogi·ae** \-jē,ē\ [MGk, fr. Gk, praise, blessing, gift, fr. *eu-* + *-logia* -logy] : ANTIDORON

eu·log·ic \yü'läjik, -lōj-\ *or* **eu·log·i·cal** \-jəkəl\ *adj* [*eulogy* + *-ic* or *-ical*] : EULOGISTIC

eu·lo·gi·ous \yü'lōjēəs\ *adj* [*eulogy* + *-ous*] *archaic* : EULOGISTIC

eu·lo·gism \'yülə,jizəm\ *n* -s [*eulogy* + *-ism*] : an expression of eulogy

eu·lo·gist \-jəst\ *n* -s [*eulogy* + *-ist*] : one that eulogizes

eu·lo·gis·tic \ˌyülə¦jistik, -tēk\ *adj* : of, relating to, or characterized by eulogy : bestowing praise : PANEGYRICAL, LAUDATORY — opposed to *dyslogistic* — **eu·lo·gis·ti·cal·ly** \-tək(ə)lē, -tēk-, -li\ *adv*

eu·lo·gi·um \yü'lōjēəm\ *n, pl* **eulo·gia** \-ēə\ *or* **eulogiums** [ML] : EULOGY

eu·lo·gi·za·tion \,yüləjə'zāshən, -ˌjī'z-\ *n* -s : the act of eulogizing : PRAISE

eu·lo·gize *also* **eu·lo·gise** \'yülə,jīz\ *vt* -ED/-ING/-s [*eulogy* + *-ize*, *-ise*] : to speak or write in strong commendation of : extol in speech or writing : PRAISE ⟨one of those rare days in June *eulogized* by poets —Evelyn Barkins⟩

eu·lo·giz·er \-zə(r)\ *n* -s : one that eulogizes : EULOGIST

eu·lo·gy \'yüləjē, -ji\ *n* -ES [ME *euloge*, fr. ML *eulogium*, alter. (influenced by L *elogium* maxim, saying, inscription on a tombstone) of *eulogia*, fr. Gk, praise, blessing — more at EULOGIA, ELOGE] **1** : a composition (as a set oration) in commendation of someone or something (as of the character and services of a deceased person) : ENCOMIUM **2** : an expression characteristic of eulogies : PRAISE, LAUDATION ⟨mingle ~ with admonition⟩ ⟨the inflated tone of ~ in which their insect authors are lauded —Frances Trollope⟩

[1]**eu·loph·id** \yü'läfəd, 'yüləf-\ *adj* [NL *Eulophidae*] : of or relating to the Eulophidae

[2]**eulophid** \"\ *n* -s : a chalcid fly of the family Eulophidae

eu·loph·i·dae \yü'läfə,dē\ *n pl, cap* [NL, fr. *Eulophus*, type genus (fr. Gk *eulophos* well plumed, fr. *eu-* + *lophos* nape of the neck, crest) + *-idae*] : a large cosmopolitan family of narrow-winged chalcid flies usu. with 4-jointed tarsi that are parasitic as larvae in or on the larvae of various other insects

eu·ly·tite \'yülə,tīt\ *also* **eu·ly·tine** \-,tēn, -ˌtᵊn\ *n* -s [*eulytite* fr. *eulytine* + *-ite; eulytine* fr. G *eulytin*, fr. Gk *eulytos* easily dissolved (fr. *eu-* + *lytos* soluble, fr. *lyein* to dissolve, release) + G -*in* -ine — more at LOSE] **:** a mineral $Bi_4Si_3O_{12}$ consisting of a bismuth silicate occurring usu. in minute dark-brown or grayish tetrahedral crystals (sp. gr. 6.11)

eu·malacostraca \(ˌ)yü+\ *n pl, cap* [NL, fr. *eu-* + *Malacostraca*] **:** a group of malacostracan crustaceans comprising all Malacostraca except the Leptostraca — **eu·malacostracan** \"+\ *adj or n*

eu·me·ces \yü'mē(ˌ)sēz\ *n, cap* [NL, fr. Gk *eumēkēs* tall, long, fr. *eu-* + -*mēkēs* (fr. *mēkos* length); akin to Gk *makros* long — more at MEAGER] **:** a large genus of cosmopolitan diurnal carnivorous lizards (family Scincidae) with opaque scaly eyelids and pterygoid teeth

eu·melanin \(ˈ)yü+\ *n* [ISV *eu-* + *melanin*] **:** a dark melanin pigment — compare PHAEOMELANIN

eu·me·nes \'yüməˌnēz\ *n, cap* [NL, fr. Gk *eumenēs* well disposed, fr. *eu-* + -*menēs* (fr. *menos* spirit, intent) — more at MIND] **:** a widely distributed genus (family Vespidae) comprising chiefly black or black and yellow solitary wasps that build jug-shaped cells of mud singly or in rows and stock them with caterpillars as food for the larval wasps — see POTTER WASP — **eu·me·nid** \'yüməˌnid, yü'menəd\ *adj or n*

eu·men·i·dae \yü'menəˌdē\ *n pl, cap* [NL, fr. *Eumenes*, type genus + -*idae*] *in some classifications* **:** a family of wasps containing those solitary mason wasps and potter wasps that are now usu. included in Vespidae — compare EUMENES

eu·metazoa \(ˌ)yü+\ *n pl, cap* [NL, fr. *eu-* + *Metazoa*] *in some classifications* **:** a major division of the animal kingdom comprising all multicellular forms except the sponges — compare PARAZOA — **eu·metazoan** \"+\ *adj or n*

eu·me·to·pi·as \ˌyümə'tōpēəs\ *n, cap* [NL, fr. *eu-* + Gk *metōpias* having a broad forehead, fr. *metōpon* forehead — more at METOPION] **:** a genus of sea lions including the Australian sea lion and the Steller's sea lion

eu·mitosis \ˌyü+\ *n* [ISV *eu-* + *mitosis*] **:** typical mitosis (as of unicellular organisms)

eu·mitotic \"+\ *adj* [ISV *eu-* + *mitotic*] **1 :** ANASCHISTIC **2 :** of or relating to eumitosis

eu·mol·pique \œmólpēk\ *n* -S [F, fr. Gk *eumolpein* to sing well (fr. *eu-* + -*molpein*, akin to Gk *melpein* to sing) + F -*ique* -ic] **:** a poetic measure consisting of two unrhymed Alexandrines with alternate masculine and feminine endings

eu·mor·phic \(ˈ)yü¦mȯrfik\ *adj* [*eu-* + -*morphic*] **:** MESOMORPHIC 2, ATHLETIC 3 — distinguished from *brachymorphic* and *dolichomorphic*

eu·my·ce·tae \ˌyüˌmī'sēd·(ˌ)ē\ *also* **eu·my·ce·te·ae** \-d·ēˌē\ [NL, fr. *eu-* + -*mycetae*, -*myceteae* (irreg. fr. -*myces*)] *syn of* EUMYCETES

eu·my·cete \yü'mīˌsēt, ¦=ˌ=¦=\ *n* -S [NL *Eumycetes*] **:** a fungus of the subdivision Eumycetes

eu·my·ce·tes \ˌyüˌmī'sēd·ēz\ *n pl, cap* [NL, fr. *eu-* + -*mycetes*] **:** a subdivision of thallophytes comprising all the true fungi as distinguished from myxomycetes and schizomycetes — compare THALLOPHYTA — **eu·my·ce·tic** \¦=ˌ=¦sēd·ik\ *adj*

eu·nec·tes \yü'nek(ˌ)tēz\ *n, cap* [NL, fr. *eu-* + Gk *nēktēs* swimmer, fr. *nēchein* to swim; akin to L *nare* to swim — more at NOURISH] **:** a genus of snakes (family Boidae) comprising the anaconda

eu·ni·ce \yü'nī(ˌ)sē\ *n, cap* [NL, fr. the name *Eunice*] **:** a genus (the type of the family Eunicidae) of marine polychaete worms with complex chitinous jaws including the palolo worm and related forms — **eu·ni·ce·an** \yü'nīsēən, -nis-\ *adj or n* — **eu·ni·cid** \-səd\ *adj or n*

eu·no·mi·an \yü'nōmēən\ *n* -S *usu cap* [LGk *eunomianos*, fr. *Eunomios* Eunomius †*ab*A.D.393 Roman Catholic ecclesiastic who became bishop of Cyzicus in 360] **:** ANOMOEAN

eu·no·mi·an·ism \-ēəˌnizəm\ *n* -S *usu cap* **:** the doctrines of Eunomians **:** extreme Arianism

eu·no·my \'yünəmē\ *n* -ES [Gk *eunomia*, fr. *eunomos* having good laws (fr. *eu-* + *nomos* law) + -*ia* -y — more at NIMBLE] **:** civil order under good laws

eu·no·to·sau·rus \yüˌnōd·ə'sȯrəs\ *n, cap* [NL, prob. fr. Gk *eunōtos* stout-backed (fr. *eu-* + *nōtos*, *nōton* back) + NL -*saurus* — more at NATES] **:** a genus of small generalized reptiles from the Middle Permian of southern Africa that have the vertebrae reduced in number and the ribs broad and somewhat leaf-shaped, are often considered ancestral to the turtles, and are commonly placed in a separate suborder of Chelonia

eu·nuch \'yünək, -nik, -nēk\ *n* -S [ME *eunuk*, fr. L *eunuchus*, fr. Gk *eunouchos*, fr. *eunē* bed + -*ochos* (fr. *echein* to have, have charge of) — more at SCHEME] **1 :** a castrated man in charge of a harem or employed as a chamberlain in a palace; *often* **:** any chamberlain **2 :** a man or boy whose testes or external genitals have been removed or who is deprived of testicular function by other cause (as inflammation or injury) **3 :** CASTRATO **4 :** one who is impotent, ineffective, or lacking in manhood in any respect ⟨intellectual ~⟩ ⟨political ~⟩

eunuch flute *n* **:** KAZOO

eu·nuch·ism \-ˌkizəm\ *n* -S [LL *eunuchismus*, fr. Gk *eunouchismos*, fr. *eunouchos* + -*ismos* -ism] **:** the condition of being a eunuch

eu·nuch·ize \-ˌkīz\ *vt* -ED/-ING/-S [LL *eunuchizare*, fr. Gk *eunouchizein*, fr. *eunouchos* eunuch + -*izein* -ize] **:** EMASCULATE

¹eu·nuch·oid \-ˌkȯid\ *also* **eu·nuch·oi·dal** \¦=ˌ=¦kȯidᵊl\ *adj* [*eunuchoid* fr. Gk *eunouchoeidēs*, fr. *eunouchos* + -*oeides* -oid; *eunuchoidal* fr. *eunuchoid* + -*al*] **:** of, relating to, or characterized by eunuchoidism ⟨~ voice⟩ **:** resembling a eunuch

²eunuchoid \"\ *n* -S **:** a sexually deficient individual; *esp* **:** one lacking in sexual differentiation and tending toward the intersex state

eu·nuch·oid·ism \'==ˌkȯiˌdizəm\ *n* -S [ISV *eunuchoid* + -*ism*] **:** a state suggestive of that of a eunuch in being marked by deficiency of sexual development, by persistence of prepuberal characteristics, and often by the presence of characteristics typical of the opposite sex

eu·nuch·ry \'==ˌkrē, -ri\ *n* -ES **:** the state of being a eunuch

eu·o·nym \'yüəˌnim\ *n* -S [*eu-* + -*onym*] **:** a name well suited to the person, place, or thing named

eu·on·y·min \yü'änəmən\ *n* -S [ISV *euonym-* (fr. NL *Euonymus*, genus name of *Euonymus atropurpureus*) + -*in* — more at EUONYMUS] **:** a mixture of impure active principles derived from a wahoo (*Euonymus atropurpureus*); *also* **:** the dry powdered extract of this plant

eu·on·y·mous \(ˈ)=¦==məs\ *adj* [Gk *euōnymos* having an auspicious name] **:** suitably named

eu·on·y·mus \=ˈ==məs\ *n* [NL, fr. L *euonymus* spindle tree, fr. Gk *euōnymos*, fr. *euōnymos* having an auspicious name, fr. *eu-* + -*ōnymos* (fr. *onyma*, *onoma* name) — more at NAME] **1** *cap* **:** a genus of evergreen shrubs, small trees, or vines (family Celastraceae) of north temperate regions having usu. 4-angled branches, opposite leaves, flowers solitary or in axillary cymes, fruit a lobed capsule, and seed enclosed in a scarlet or orange aril — see SPINDLE TREE, STRAWBERRY BUSH, WAHOO **2** -ES **:** any plant of the genus *Euonymus* **3** -ES **:** the dried bark of the root of a shrub (*Euonymus atropurpureus*) used as a cathartic

euonymus scale *n* **:** a rectangular grayish brown to black scale (*Unaspis euonymi*) that infests euonymus and is common in greenhouses

eu·or·ni·thes \yü'ȯrnəˌthēz, ˌyüˌȯr'nī(ˌ)thēz\ [NL, fr. *eu-* + -*ornithes*] *syn of* NEOGNATHAE

eu·pa·to·ri·a·ceous \ˌyüpə¦tōrē¦āshəs\ *adj* [NL *Eupatorium* + E -*aceous*] **:** of or belonging to *Eupatorium* or related genera

eu·pa·to·rin \ˌyüpə'tōrən\ *n* -S [It *eupatorina*, fr. NL *Eupatorium* + It -*ina* -in] **1 :** a bitter glucoside $C_{35}H_{58}NO_{10}$ occurring in boneset **2 :** an eclectic resinoid prepared from boneset and formerly used as a tonic and expectorant

eu·pa·to·ri·um \ˌyüpə'tōrēəm\ *n* [NL, fr. Gk *eupatorion* hemp agrimony, fr. Mithridates VI *Eupator* †63B.C. king of Pontus] **1** *cap* **:** an immense genus of chiefly tropical herbs (family Compositae) having heads of white or purplish flowers arranged in cymose clusters, a capillary pappus, and 5-angled achenes — see BONESET, HEMP AGRIMONY, JOE-PYE WEED, MISTFLOWER **2** -S **:** any plant of the genus *Eupatorium*

eupatorium purple *n* **:** a moderate reddish purple that is redder, lighter, and stronger than bishop's violet and bluer, lighter, and stronger than heliotrope (sense 4b)

eu·pa·to·ry \'yüpəˌtōrē\ *n* -ES [ME *eupatorie* wild sage, fr. LL *eupatorion* horehound, fr. Gk, hemp agrimony] **:** a plant of the genus *Eupatorium*

eu·pat·rid \yü'pa·trəd, 'yüpə·t-\ *n, pl* **eupatri·dae** \yü'pa·trəˌdē\ *often cap* [Gk *eupatridēs*, fr. *eu-* + *patr-*, *patēr* father + -*idēs*, patronymic suffix — more at FATHER] **:** one of the hereditary aristocrats of ancient Athens who in early times exclusively made and administered the law

eu·pav·er·ine \yü'pavəˌrēn, -rən\ *n* -S [*eu-* + *papaverine*] **:** a synthetic alkaloid $C_{19}H_{15}NO_4$ related to papaverine and used as a relaxant to nonstriated muscle

eu·pep·sia \yü'pepshə, -epsēə\ *also* **eu·pep·sy** \'yüˌpepsē, =ˈ==\ *n, pl* **eupepsias** *also* **eupepsies** [NL *eupepsia*, fr. *eu-* + -*pepsia*] **:** good digestion — opposed to *dyspepsia*

eu·pep·tic \(ˈ)yü¦peptik, -tēk\ *adj* [prob. fr. *eupepsia*, after such pairs as E *dyspepsia: dyspeptic*] **1 :** of, relating to, produced by, or having good digestion — opposed to *dyspeptic* **2 :** CHEERFUL, OPTIMISTIC

eu·phau·si·a·cea \(ˌ)yüˌfȯzē'āshēə\ *n pl, cap* [NL, fr. *Euphausia*, included genus (perh. fr. *eu-* + Gk *pha-* — fr. *phainein* to show — + *ousia* substance) + -*acea* — more at FANCY, OUSIA] **:** an order of small commonly luminescent malacostracan crustaceans (division Eucarida) related to the Decapoda, resembling shrimps, and in some areas forming an important element of marine plankton — **eu·phau·si·id** \(ˈ)yü¦fȯzēəd\ *adj or n* — **eu·phau·si·id** \-zēəd\ *adj or n*

eu·phe·mi·ous \(ˈ)yü¦fēmēəs\ *adj* [Gk *euphēmos* auspicious, sounding good + E -*ious*] **:** EUPHEMISTIC — **eu·phe·mi·ous·ly** *adv*

eu·phe·mism \'yüfəˌmizəm, -fᵊmˌi-\ *n* -S [Gk *euphēmismos*, fr. *euphēmos* auspicious, sounding good (fr. *eu-* + -*phēmos*, fr. *phēmē* speech) + -*ismos* -ism — more at -PHEMIA] **1 :** the substitution of an agreeable or inoffensive word or expression for one that is harsh, indelicate, or otherwise unpleasant or taboo **:** allusion to an offensive thing by an inoffensive expression — contrasted with *dysphemism* **2 :** a polite, tactful, or less explicit term used to avoid the direct naming of an unpleasant, painful, or frightening reality (as *pass away* for *die; underprivileged for poor*)

eu·phe·mis·tic \¦yüfə¦mistik, -fᵊm¦i-, -tēk\ *also* **eu·phe·mis·ti·cal** \-təkəl, -tēk-\ *adj* [fr. *euphemism*, after such pairs as E *optimism: optimistic, optimistical*] **:** relating to or of the nature of euphemism **:** containing a euphemism — **eu·phe·mis·ti·cal·ly** \-tək(ə)lē, -tēk-, -li\ *adv*

eu·phe·mize \'yüfəˌmīz, -fᵊmˌīz\ *vb* -ED/-ING/-S [fr. *euphemism*, after such pairs as E *criticism: criticize*] *vt* **:** to express by a euphemism ⟨the uneasy effort in America to ~ death —W.J.Fisher⟩ ~ *vi* **:** to make use of euphemistic expressions

eu·phe·miz·er \-zə(r)\ *n* -S **:** one that euphemizes

eu·phone \'yüˌfōn\ *n* -S [Gk *euphōnos* sweet-voiced, musical] **:** an 8-foot or 16-foot free-reed organ stop giving a soft expressive tone

¹euphonia *n* -S [LL] *obs* **:** EUPHONY

²eu·pho·nia \yü'fōnēə, -nyə\ [NL, fr. LL, euphony] *syn of* TANAGRA

³euphonia \"\ *n* -S [NL *Euphonia*] **:** a tanager of the genus *Tanagra*

eu·phon·ic \yü'fänik, -nēk\ *adj* [*euphony* + -*ic*] **1 :** of or relating to euphony **:** in accordance with the principles of euphony **2** *of an intervocalic consonant* **:** serving to avoid a hiatus (as \t\ *t* in French \âtē(l)\ *a-t-il*) — **eu·phon·i·cal·ly** \-nək(ə)lē, -nēk-, -li\ *adv*

eu·phon·i·cal \-nəkəl, -nēk-\ *archaic var of* EUPHONIC

eu·pho·nious \yü'fōnēəs, -nyəs\ *adj* [*euphony* + -*ous*] **:** pleasing in sound **:** having euphony — **eu·pho·nious·ly** *adv* — **eu·pho·nious·ness** *n* -ES

eu·pho·ni·um \-nēəm\ *n* -S [Gk *euphōnos* sweet-voiced, musical + E -*ium* (as in *harmonium*)] **1 :** a tenor tuba similar in shape, pitch, and range to the baritone but with a larger bore, a mellower tone quality, and often a double bell **2 :** EUPHONE

euphonium

eu·pho·nize \'yüfəˌnīz\ *vt* -ED/-ING/-S [*euphony* + -*ize*] **:** to make euphonious

eu·pho·nous \'yüfənəs\ *adj* [Gk *euphōnos*] **:** EUPHONIOUS

eu·phony \'yüfənē, -ni\ *n* -ES [F *euphonie*, fr. LL *euphonia*, fr. Gk *euphōnia*, fr. *euphōnos* sweet-voiced, musical (fr. *eu-* + -*phōnos*, fr. *phōnē* voice) + -*ia* -y — more at BAN] **1 :** pleasing or sweet sound **:** the acoustic effect produced by words so formed and combined as to please the ear; *esp* **:** a harmonious succession of words having a pleasing sound or striking the ear as being appropriate to the meaning — opposed to *cacophony* **2 :** tendency to greater ease of pronunciation resulting in regularly observed combinative changes that seem to be caused by increased speed of utterance and economy of effort

eu·phor·bia \yü'fō(r)bēə\ *n* [NL, alter. (influenced by NL -*ia*) of L *euphorbea* euphorbia, fr. *Euphorbus* 1st cent A.D. physician to Juba, king of Mauretania] **1** *cap* **:** a large genus of plants (family Euphorbiaceae) of greatly diverse appearance some being fleshy and like cactus, others leafy and herbaceous or shrubby, but all having milky juice and flowers without a calyx and included in an involucre which surrounds a group of several staminate flowers and a central pistillate flower with 3-lobed pistils **2** -S **:** any plant of the genus *Euphorbia* **:** SPURGE

eu·phor·bi·a·ce·ae \=ˌ==ˈāsēˌē\ *n pl, cap* [NL, fr. *Euphorbia*, type genus + -*aceae*] **:** a widely distributed family of herbs, shrubs, or trees (order Geraniales) with usu. milky often poisonous juice, unisexual flowers, and a superior usu. trilocular ovary and including several medicinal plants (as those yielding castor oil and croton oil), several trees yielding caoutchouc, and the cassava — see HEVEA, MANIHOT — **eu·phor·bi·a·ceous** \=¦==¦āshəs\ *adj*

eu·phor·bi·um \=ˈ=bēəm\ *n* -S [ME *euforbium*, fr. ML, fr. Gk *euphorbion* euphorbium, euphorbia, fr. *Euphorbus*] **:** a yellow or brownish very acrid gum resin derived from a Moroccan spurge (*Euphorbia resinifera*) and other African spurges and formerly employed medicinally as an emetic and cathartic but now used chiefly in veterinary medicine as a vesicant

eu·pho·ria \yü'fōrēə, -fȯr-\ *n* -S [NL, fr. Gk, fr. *eu-* + -*phoria*] **:** a feeling of well-being or elation; *esp* **:** one that is groundless, disproportionate to its cause, or inappropriate to one's life situation

¹eu·pho·ri·ant \-ēənt\ *n* -S [*euphoria* + ¹-*ant*] **:** a drug that tends to induce euphoria

²euphoriant \"\ *adj* [*euphoria* + ²-*ant*] **:** tending to induce euphoria ⟨a ~ drug⟩

eu·phor·ic \yü'fȯrik, -fär-, -fōr-\ *adj* [*euphoria* + -*ic*] **:** characterized by or based on euphoria ⟨a ~ mood⟩

eu·pho·ry \'yüfərē\ *n* -ES [NL *euphoria*] **:** EUPHORIA

eu·pho·tic \(ˈ)yü¦fōd·ik\ *adj* [ISV *eu-* + *photic*] **:** of, relating to, or constituting the upper layers of a body of water into which sufficient light penetrates to permit growth of green plants

eu·phra·sia \yü'frāzh(ē)ə\ *n, cap* [NL, fr. ML *eufrasia* euphrasy] **:** a large genus of hemiparasitic herbs (family Scrophulariaceae) widely distributed outside the tropics and having flowers with the upper lip of the corolla 2-cleft and its margin recurved

eu·phra·sy \'yüfrəsē\ *n* -ES [ME *eufrasie*, fr. ML *eufrasia*, fr. Gk *euphrasia* good cheer, fr. *euphrainein* to gladden, fr. *eu-* + -*phrainein* (fr. *phrēn* mind) — more at FRENZY] **:** an eyebright (*Euphrasia officinalis*)

eu·phra·te·an \yü'frād·ēən\ *adj, cap* [*Euphrates*, river in southwest Asia + E -*an*] **:** of or belonging to the Euphrates river or its valley

eu·phroe \'yüˌfrō\ *n* -S [D *juffrouw*, *juffer* miss, madam, lady, euphroe, fr. MD *joncfrouwe*, *juffrouwe* miss, madam, young lady; akin to OFris *jungfrouwe* young lady, girl, OHG *jungfrouwa*; all fr. a prehistoric WGmc compound whose first constituent is represented by OE *geong* young and whose second constituent is represented by OHG *frouwa* mistress, lady — more at YOUNG, FRAU] **1 :** a block or slat of wood perforated for the passage of the parts of a crowfoot **2 :** TENT SLIDE

eu·phu·ism \'yüfyəˌwizəm\ *n* -S [*Euphues*, character in the prose romances *Euphues, the Anatomy of Wit* (1579) and *Euphues and his England* (1580) by John Lyly †1606 Eng. author + E -*ism*] **1 :** an affected style of conversation and writing fashionable in the time of Elizabeth I and characterized by antithesis, alliteration, similes, and a pervading effort after elegance; *also* **:** an example of such style **2 :** artificial and excessive elegance of language **:** high-flown diction — **eu·phu·ist** \-wəst\ *n* -S — **eu·phu·is·tic** \¦==¦wistik\ *or* **eu·phu·is·ti·cal** \-təkəl\ *adj* — **eu·phu·is·ti·cal·ly** \-k(ə)lē\ *adv*

eu·phu·ize \'==ˌwīz\ *vi* -ED/-ING/-S [*Euphues* + E -*ize*] **:** to use euphuistic language

eu·phyllopoda \¦yü+\ [NL, fr. *eu-* + *Phyllopoda*] *syn of* BRANCHIOPODA

eu·plastic \(ˈ)yü+\ *adj* [*eu-* + *plastic*] **:** adapted to the formation of tissue **:** BLASTEMATIC

eu·plec·tel·la \ˌyüˌplek'telə\ *n, cap* [NL, fr. Gk *euplektos* well plaited (fr. *eu-* + *plektos* plaited, fr. *plekein* to plait) + NL -*ella* — more at PLY] **:** a genus of hyalosponges comprising the Venus's-flower-basket, having a skeleton of interwoven siliceous spicules, and growing in the form of a cornucopia

eu·plex·op·te·ra \ˌyüˌplek'säptərə\ [NL, fr. *eu-* + *plexo-* (fr. L *plexus*, past part. of *plectere* to plait, weave) + -*ptera* — more at PLY] *syn of* DERMAPTERA

¹eu·ploid \'yüˌplȯid\ *adj* [ISV *eu-* + -*ploid*] **:** having a chromosome number that is an exact multiple of the monoploid number

²euploid \"\ *n* -S **:** a euploid individual, strain, or cell; *esp* **:** one having three or more identical genomes

eu·ploidy \-dē\ *n* -ES **:** euploid quality or state

eu·plo·tes \yü'plōd·(ˌ)ēz\ *n, cap* [NL, fr. *eu-* + -*plotes* (prob. irreg. fr. Gk *plōt-*, *plōs* swimmer, fr. *plein* to sail, swim) — more at FLOW] **:** a genus (the type of the family Euplotidae) of large rigid ovoid hypotrichous ciliates extremely common in fresh and salt water — **eu·plo·tid** \-ōd·əd\ *adj or n*

eup·nea *also* **eup·noea** \'yüpnēə, =ˈ=\ *n* -S [NL, fr. Gk *eupnoia*, fr. *eupnoos*, *eupnous* breathing freely (fr. *eu-* + -*pnoos*, -*pnous*, fr. *pnoē* breathing, fr. *pnein* to breathe) + -*ia* — more at SNEEZE] **:** normal respiration — distinguished from *dyspnea* — **eup·ne·ic** \(ˈ)yüp¦nēik\ *adj*

eu·po·li·de·an \¦yüˌpälə¦dēən, ¦yüpəl-; ¦yüpəˌlidē-\ *n* -S *usu cap* [Gk *eupolideion* Eupolidean (fr. neut. of *eupolideios* in the style of Eupolis, fr. *Eupolid-*, *Eupolis* Eupolis, 5th cent. B.C. Greek writer of comedies) + E -*an*] **:** the characteristic meter used by Eupolis composed of two polyschematist choriambic dimeters the second of which is catalectic (as oooo–◡◡– oooo–◡–)

eu·po·ma·tia \ˌyüpə'māsh(ē)ə\ *n, cap* [NL, fr. *eu-* + Gk *pōmat-*, *pōma* lid + NL -*ia* — more at POMACENTRIDAE] **:** a small Australasian genus (the type of the family Eupomatiaceae of the order Ranales) comprising trees and shrubs with large staminodia that resemble petals between the anther-bearing stamens and the stigma so that pollination can only be effected by insects

eu·potamic \¦yü+\ *adj* [*eu-* + *potamic*] *of aquatic organisms* **:** thriving in both flowing and still fresh waters — compare AUTOPOTAMIC, TYCHOPOTAMIC

eu·prac·tic \(ˈ)yü¦praktik\ *adj* [fr. *eupraxia*, after E *apraxia: apractic*] **:** relating to or having normally coordinated muscular performance

eu·prax·ia \yü'praksēə, -kshə\ *n* -S [NL, fr. *eu-* + -*praxia*] **:** normally coordinated muscular performance — contrasted with *apraxia*

eup·tel·ea \yüp'telēə, -tēl-\ *n, cap* [NL, fr. *eu-* + Gk *ptelea* elm — more at PTELEA] **:** a small genus of Asiatic shrubs and trees (family Trochodendraceae) with apetalous showy red flowers

eup·te·ro·ti·dae \ˌyüptə'rōd·əˌdē, -räd-·\ *n pl, cap* [NL, fr. *Eupterote*, type genus (fr. *eu-* + Gk *pterōtē*, fem. of *pterōtos* feathered, fr. *pteron* feather) + -*idae* — more at FEATHER] **:** a family of large moths having strongly pectinate antennae and lacking proboscis and tympanum

eu·pyr·chro·ite \ˌyüpə(r)'krōˌīt\ *n* -S [*eu-* + Gk *pyr* fire + *chroia*, *chroa* color + E -*ite*; akin to Gk *chrōs* skin, color — more at CHROMATIC] **:** a mineral composed of a concretionary variety of apatite

eu·pyrene \(ˈ)yü+\ *adj* [ISV *eu-* + -*pyrene* (fr. Gk *pyrēn* stone of a fruit); prob. orig. formed as G *eupyren*] — more at FURZE] **:** having a normal nucleus ⟨a ~ sperm⟩ — compare APYRENE, OLIGOPYRENE

eu·pyr·i·on \yü'pirēən\ *n* -S [*eu-* + Gk *pyreion* fire stick, fr. *pyr* fire — more at FIRE] **:** an early-19th-century match having a tip coated with sugar and potassium chlorate to be ignited by being dipped in sulfuric acid

eur- *or* **euro-** *comb form, cap* [*Europe*] **:** European and ⟨*Eurafrican*⟩

¹eur·african \(ˈ)yůr+\ *adj, usu cap* [ISV *Eur-* + *African*] **1 :** of or belonging to the continents of Europe and Africa combined **2 :** of or relating to the biogeographic region that includes most of Europe and northern Africa south to the Sahara **3 :** of European and African descent

²eurafrican \"\ *n, cap* **1 :** an assumed prehistoric subrace or type from which originated Mediterraneans of Europe and certain No. African peoples (as in Algeria, Egypt, and Ethiopia); *also* **:** a person of such a subrace or type **2 :** a person of European and African descent

eur·american \¦yůr+\ *or* **euro-american** \¦yů(ˌ)rō+\ *adj, cap E & usu cap A after hyphen* [*Eur-* + *American*] **:** common to Europe and America ⟨*Euramerican* flora⟩ **:** OCCIDENTAL ⟨*Euro-American* culture⟩

euraquilo *usu cap, var of* EUROAQUILO

¹eur·asian \yər, (ˈ)yůr+\ *adj, usu cap* [*Eur-* + *Asian*] **:** relating to Europe and Asia as a whole **:** common to adjacent parts of Europe and Asia or to the whole **:** of a mixed European and Asiatic origin ⟨*Eurasian* race⟩ ⟨*Eurasian* fauna⟩

²eurasian \"\ *n, cap* **:** a person of mixed European and Asian descent — often taken to be offensive esp. in India; compare ANGLO-INDIAN

eur·asiatic \(¦)yůr, yər+\ *adj, usu cap* [fr. *Eurasia*, Europe and Asia as one continent, after *Asia:* E *Asiatic*] **1 :** of or relating to Europe and Asia taken as a unit **:** EURASIAN **2 :** PALAEARCTIC

eu·re·ka \yů'rēkə\ *interj* [Gk *heurēka* I have found, 1st pers. sing. perf. indic. act. of *heuriskein* to find; fr. the exclamation attributed to Archimedes †212B.C., Greek mathematician and inventor, on discovering a method for determining the purity of gold — more at HEURISTIC] — used to express triumph concerning a discovery

eureka red *n* **:** PUCE

eu·rhodine \yə'rōˌdēn, -ˌdᵊn\ *n* -S [ISV *eu-* + *rhod-* (fr. Gk *rhodon* rose) + *ine*; orig. formed as G *eurhodin* — more at ROSE] **:** any of a class of amino-substituted phenazine dyes (as neutral red)

eu·rho·dol \-ˌdȯl, -ˌdōl\ *n* -S [ISV *eurhod-* (fr. *eurhodine*) + -*ol*] **:** any of a class of dyes differing from the eurhodines only in containing hydroxyl in place of an amino group or groups

eurhythmic *var of* EURYTHMIC

eu·rip·i·de·an \yəˌripə¦dēən\ *adj, usu cap* [L *euripideus* Euripidean (fr. Gk *euripideios*, fr. *Euripidēs* Euripides, 5th cent. B.C. Greek playwright) + E -*an*] **:** of, relating to, or characteristic of Euripides or his tragedies

eu·ri·pus \yə'rīpəs\ *n, pl* **euri·pi** \-ˌpī\ [L, fr. Gk *euripos*] **1 :** a narrow tract of water where the tide or a current flows and reflows with violence **:** STRAIT, CHANNEL **2 :** a condition of rapid or dangerous fluctuation

eu·ro \'yů(ˌ)rō\ *n, pl* **euro** *or* **euros** [native name in Australia] **:** a large reddish gray kangaroo (*Macrobus robustus*) — called also *wallaroo*

euro- — see EUR-

euro-american *cap E & usu cap A after hyphen, var of* EURAMERICAN

eu·ro·aq·ui·lo \ˌyůrō'akwəˌlō\ *also* **eur·aq·ui·lo** \yə'rak-\ *n* -S *usu cap* [LL *euroaquilo*, fr. *euro-* (fr. L *eurus* east wind, fr. Gk *euros*) + L *aquilo* north wind] **:** GREGALE

eu·ro·bin \yə'rōbən\ *n* [ISV *euro-* + -*robin* (as in *chrysarobin*); orig. formed in G] **:** the triacetate of chrysarobin formerly used as a substitute therefor in ointments

eu·roc·ly·don \yə'räkləˌdän\ *n* -S *usu cap* [Gk *euroklydōn*, MS var. (in Acts 27:14) of *eurakylōn*, fr. *eur-* (fr. *euros* east wind) + (assumed) Gk *akylōn* north wind, fr. L *aquilon-*, *aquilo*] **:** GREGALE

eu·rope \'yůrəp, 'yůr-\ *adj, usu cap* [fr. *Europe*, continent extending west from Asia] **:** of or from the continent of Europe **:** of the kind or style prevalent in Europe **:** EUROPEAN

1eu·ro·pe·an \ˌyu̇rə¦pēən, ¦yu̇r-\ *adj, usu cap* [L *europaeus* European (fr. Gk *eurōpaios*, fr. *Eurōpē* Europe) + E *-an*] **1 :** of, relating to, or belonging to Europe or its inhabitants **2** *of a plant or animal* **:** native to Europe **:** originating in Europe — used esp. (1) to distinguish Old World forms from New World forms known by the same name ⟨*European* robin⟩ and (2) to distinguish an introduced form from a native New World form ⟨*European* corn borer⟩

2european \"\ *n* -s *cap* **1 a :** a native or inhabitant of Europe **b :** a person of European descent **2 a :** a member of a race inhabiting Europe **b** *in southern and eastern Africa and Asia* **:** a white person **:** CAUCASIAN

european alder *n, usu cap E* **1 :** a tree (*Alnus vulgaris*) with woody fruiting aments and leaves hairy beneath **2 :** GRAY ALDER

european apple sawfly *n, usu cap E* **:** an Old World sawfly (*Hoplocampa testudinea*) now established on both coasts of No. America and becoming a serious pest esp. of early apples

european ash *n, usu cap E* **:** a tall Eurasian tree (*Fraxinus excelsior*) having leaves that are dark green and glabrous above and paler and often pubescent on the veins beneath with 7 to 11 oval leaflets

european aspen *n, usu cap E* **:** a small open-headed tree (*Populus tremula*) of Europe, northern Africa, and Siberia having leaves with rounded irregular notches

european barberry *n, usu cap E* **:** COMMON BARBERRY

european beachgrass *n, usu cap E* **:** a beach grass (*Ammophila arenaria*)

european beech *n, usu cap E* **:** a European tree (*Fagus sylvatica*) with smooth gray bark and minutely toothed often purple leaves widely planted in No. America as an ornamental

european bindweed *n, usu cap E* **:** FIELD BINDWEED

european bird cherry *n, usu cap E* **1 :** a small to medium-sized cherry (*Prunus padus*) closely resembling the chokecherry (*Prunus virginiana*) but having larger flowers and a strongly ridged stone **2 :** the small black fruit of the European bird cherry

european bittersweet *n, usu cap E* **:** BITTERSWEET 2a

european blastomycosis *n, usu cap E* **:** CRYPTOCOCCOSIS

european brooklime *n, usu cap E* **:** WALL INK

european canker *n, usu cap E* **1 :** a disease of the apple, pear, and other fruit and shade trees caused by a fungus (*Nectria galligena*) producing cankers on the trunks and branches characterized by concentric rings of callus **2 :** a disease of poplars caused by a fungus (*Dothichiza populea*)

european chafer *n, usu cap E* **:** an Old World May beetle (*Amphimallon majalis*) now established in parts of eastern No. America where the larvae are a destructive pest feeding on the roots of turf grasses

european chestnut *n, usu cap E* **:** SPANISH CHESTNUT

european chicken flea *n, usu cap E* **:** a flea (*Ceratophyllus gallinae*) native to northern Europe that has become a serious pest of domestic fowls in parts of northern and western No. America

european columbine *n, usu cap E* **:** a common garden columbine (*Aquilegia vulgaris*) with spurred blue flowers

european cranberry *n, usu cap E* **:** a small red-fruited trailing cranberry (*Vaccinium oxycoccus*) found in arctic and cool regions of the northern hemisphere with leaves ovate, acute, and conspicuously whitened beneath, flowers terminal, and fruit ¼ to ⅓ inch in diameter — called also *small cranberry;* compare AMERICAN CRANBERRY

european earwig *n, usu cap 1st E* **:** a large earwig (*Forficula auricularia*) native to Europe but now a pest in various parts of the world

european elder *n, usu cap 1st E* **:** an elder tree or bush native to Europe; *esp* **:** BOURTREE

european elm *n, usu cap 1st E* **:** ENGLISH ELM

european elm scale *n, usu cap 1st E* **:** a reddish brown unarmored scale (*Gossyparia spuria*) introduced into No. America from Europe, feeding esp. on the underside of the limbs of various elms, secreting great quantities of honeydew, and sometimes killing the trees

european fly honeysuckle *n, usu cap E* **:** a cultivated Eurasian shrub (*Lonicera xylosteum*) with twin yellowish white flowers and scarlet fruit

european foulbrood *n, usu cap E* **:** a foulbrood that is caused by a bacillus (*Bacillus alvei*) and that differs from American foulbrood chiefly in the absence of ropiness of affected larvae

european fruit scale *n, usu cap E* **:** an armored scale (*Aspidiotus ostreaeformis*) common on ornamental and deciduous fruit trees in Europe and No. America

european gooseberry *n, usu cap E* **:** ENGLISH GOOSEBERRY

european grape *n, usu cap E* **:** VINIFERA

european honeysuckle *n, usu cap E* **1 :** EUROPEAN FLY HONEYSUCKLE **2 :** a woodbine (*Lonicera periclymenum*)

european house borer *n, usu cap E* **:** a wood-boring beetle (*Hylotrupes bajulus*) native to northern Europe but widely distributed by commerce that feeds as larva and adult in dry timbers and is esp. destructive in soft woods

eu·ro·pe·an·ism \ˌ==ˈ=əˌnizəm\ *n* -s *usu cap* **1 :** traditions, customs, ideals, or traits distinctive of Europeans **2 :** the ideal or advocacy of the political and economic unification of Europe ⟨believes that Germany and France are pursuing, under the guise of *Europeanism* or internationalism, a purely national policy —Hans Kohn⟩

eu·ro·pe·an·iza·tion \-ənəˈzāshən, -əˌnīˈz-\ *n* -s *usu cap* **:** the act, process, or result of Europeanizing

eu·ro·pe·an·ize \-ˈpēəˌnīz\ *vt* -ED/-ING/-S *often cap* **1 :** to modify to accord with a continental European pattern in characteristics, customs, or ideas **2 :** to denationalize and subject (a territory) to the supervision of an agency of a European community of nations

european larch *n, usu cap E* **:** a larch (*Larix decidua*) having pubescent cone scales — compare TAMARACK 1a

eu·ro·pe·an·ly \¦==¦===\ *adv, usu cap* **:** in a European manner

european mountain ash *n, usu cap E* **:** ROWAN TREE 1

european oyster *n, usu cap E* **:** the common edible oyster (*Ostrea edulis*) of northern and western Europe

european partridge *n, usu cap E* **:** HUNGARIAN PARTRIDGE

european pasqueflower *n, usu cap E* **:** a highly variable European perennial herb (*Anemone pulsatilla*) typically having violet or white campanulate flowers in spring

european pine shoot moth *n, usu cap E* **:** an olethreutid moth (*Rhyacionia buoliana*) native to Europe but introduced in eastern No. America and having a larva that feeds on the tips of pines (as the red pine)

european plan *n, usu cap E* **:** a hotel rate whereby guests are charged a fixed sum for lodging and service only and meals are not included — contrasted with *American plan*

european plum *n, usu cap E* **:** any of several cultivated plums derived chiefly from a plum (*Prunus domestica*) of southwestern Asia — compare AMERICAN PLUM

european pond tortoise *or* **european pond turtle** *n, usu cap E* **:** a small European freshwater turtle (*Emys orbicularis*)

european raspberry *n, usu cap E* **:** an upright diffuse red-fruited shrub (*Rubus idaeus*) of Europe extensively cultivated and sometimes an escape in America

european red elder *n, usu cap 1st E* **:** a glabrous European ornamental shrub (*Sambucus racemosa*) with paniculate cymes of yellow or white flowers followed by red fruits

european red mite *n, usu cap E* **:** a very small bright or brownish red oval mite (*Panonychus ulmi*) that is now nearly cosmopolitan in distribution and is a destructive orchard pest that sucks juices and chlorophyll from the leaves of fruit and other trees

european spruce *n, usu cap E* **:** NORWAY SPRUCE

european spruce sawfly *n, usu cap E* **:** a sawfly (*Diprion hercyniae*) native to Europe but introduced into Canada and the northern U.S. the larva of which seriously defoliates spruce

european tortoise *n, usu cap E* **:** a small land tortoise (*Testudo graeca*) of southern Europe with olive carapacial shields bordered in black

european vervain *n, usu cap E* **:** a perennial European herb (*Verbena officinalis*) with small spicate bluish purple flowers — called also *herb-of-the-cross*

european walnut *n, usu cap E* **:** ENGLISH WALNUT

european wheat stem sawfly *n, usu cap E* **:** a sawfly (*Cephus pygmaeus*) native to Europe but now widespread in grain-growing areas that has larvae which bore in the stalks of growing wheat and other small grains

european white birch *n, usu cap E* **:** a birch (*Betula pendula*) with slender pendulous branches and white peeling bark that is often confused with a white birch (*B. alba*)

european wildcat *n, usu cap E* **:** a brown or grayish black-striped wildcat (*Felis sylvestris*) native to most of Europe but now extinct over most of its range and regarded as one of the ancestors of the domestic cat

european winter moth *n, usu cap E* **:** a European geometrid moth (*Operophtera brumata*) introduced in parts of Nova Scotia and having a looper larva very destructive as a defoliator of fruit and other deciduous trees

eu·ro·peo- \ˌyu̇rə¦pē(ˌ)ō, ¦yu̇r-\ *comb form, cap* [L *europaeus* European — more at EUROPEAN] **:** European and ⟨*Europeo-Asiatic*⟩

eu·ro·pic \yəˈrōpik\ *adj* [NL *europium* + E *-ic*] **:** relating to compounds of europium in which it is trivalent

eu·ro·pi·um \yəˈrōpēəm\ *n* -s [NL, fr. *Europe* + NL *-ium*] **:** a bivalent and trivalent metallic element of the rare-earth group found in very small amounts in monazite sand — symbol *Eu;* see ELEMENT table

eu·ro·poid \ˈyu̇rəˌpȯid, ˈyu̇r-; yəˈrōˌp-\ *or* **eu·ro·pid** \ˈyu̇rəˌpid, ˈyu̇r-, -ˌpəd; yəˈrōpəd\ *n* -s *usu cap* [ISV *europ-* (fr. *Europe*) + *-oid* or *-id*] **:** CAUCASOID

eu·ro·pous \yəˈrōpəs\ *adj* [NL *europium* + E *-ous*] **:** relating to compounds of europium in which it is bivalent

euros *pl of* EURO

eu·ro·ti·a·les \yəˌrōd·ēˈā(ˌ)lēz, -ōshē-\ *n pl, cap* [NL, fr. *Eurotium,* included genus (fr. Gk *eurōt-, eurōs* mold + NL *-ium*) + *-ales*] **:** an order (subclass Euascomycetes) of fungi (as the blue molds) having a closed ascocarp with the asci scattered rather than collected into a hymenial layer

eury- *comb form* [NL, fr. Gk, fr. *eurys;* akin to Skt *uru* broad, wide] **:** broad ⟨*eurygnathic*⟩ **:** wide ⟨*eurybenthic*⟩ ⟨*euryhaline*⟩ — opposed to *sten-*

eu·rya \ˈyu̇rēə\ *n, cap* [NL, irreg. fr. Gk *eurys*] **:** a genus of Asiatic evergreen trees and shrubs (family Theaceae) having foliage resembling that of holly, small white flowers, and globose black fruit and being cultivated in mild regions as ornamentals

eu·ry·a·lae \yəˈrīə(ˌ)lē\ [irreg. fr. NL *Euryale*] *syn of* EURYALIDA

eu·ry·a·le \-(ˌ)lē\ *n, cap* [NL, fr. Gk *Euryalē,* one of the Gorgons] **:** a widely distributed genus of basket stars

eu·ry·al·i·da \ˌyu̇rēˈaləda\ *n pl, cap* [NL, fr. *Euryale* + *-ida*] **:** an order or other division of Ophiuroidea comprising the basket stars and related forms with the arms dichotomously branched and capable of acting as tentacles — **eu·ry·al·i·dan** \¦==¦=əd°n\ *adj or n*

eu·ry·apteryx \¦yu̇rē+\ *n, cap* [NL, fr. *eury-* + *Apteryx*] **:** a genus of moas closely related to *Anomalopteryx*

eu·ry·bath·ic \¦yu̇rə¦bathik, -rē¦-\ *adj* [*eury-* + Gk *bathos* depth + E *-ic* — more at BATHOS] **:** living on the bottom of a body of water at varying depths — opposed to *stenobathic*

eu·ry·ben·thic \-¦ben(t)thik\ *adj* [*eury-* + Gk *benthos* depth + E *-ic* — more at BENTHOS] **:** EURYBATHIC

eu·ry·cea \yəˈrish(ē)ə, -isēə\ *n, cap* [NL] **:** a common genus of No. American neotenic salamanders (family Plethodontidae)

eu·ry·ce·phal·ic \¦yu̇rə|sə¦falik, -rē|\ *also* **eu·ry·ceph·a·lous** \-|ˈsefələs\ *adj* [NL *eurycephalus* eurycephalic person (fr. *eury-* + *-cephalus*) + E *-ic* or *-ous*] **:** having a cephalic index of 80 to 84 **:** BRACHYCEPHALIC

eu·ryc·ne·mic \¦yu̇rə(k)¦nēmik, -rē(-\ *adj* [*eury-* + *-cnemic* (as in *platycnemic*)] *of a shinbone* **:** dorsoventrally flattened with a platycnemic index of 70 or more

eu·ry·ene \ˈyu̇rəˌēn, -rēˌēn\ *adj* [G *euryen,* fr. *eury-* + *-en* (fr. Gk *-ēnēs* in *prosēnēs* gentle and *apēnēs* cruel, taken as having the etymological meanings "with face turned toward one" and "with averted face" respectively); perh. akin to Skt *ānana* mouth, face] **:** having a short or broad forehead or both with an upper facial index of 45 to 50 — **eu·ry·eny** \-nē\ *n* -ES

eu·ry·gae·an \¦yu̇rə¦jēən\ *adj, usu cap* [NL *Eurygaea* Palaearctic region (fr. *eury-* + *-gaea*) + E *-an*] **:** PALAEARCTIC

eu·ryg·a·mous \yəˈrigəməs\ *also* **eu·ry·gam·ic** \¦yu̇rə¦gamik\ *adj* [*eury-* + *-gamous* or *-gamic*] *of insects* **:** mating on the wing **:** engaging in a nuptial flight — opposed to *stenogamous*

eu·rygnath·ic \¦yu̇rə(g)¦nathik, -rē(-\ *adj* [F *eurygnathe* eurygnathic (fr. *eury-* + *-gnathe -gnathous*) + E *-ic* or *-ous*] **:** having a wide jaw — **eu·ryg·na·thism** \yəˈrignəˌthizəm\ *n* -s

eu·ry·g·na·thous \yəˈrignəthəs\ *adj* [F *eurygnathe* eurygnathic (fr. *eury-* + *-gnathe -gnathous*) + E *-ic* or *-ous*] **:** having a wide jaw — **eu·ryg·na·thism** \yəˈrignəˌthizəm\ *n* -s

eu·ry·ha·line \¦yu̇rə¦hāˌlīn, -hāˌ-, -lən\ *also* **eu·ry·ha·lin** \-ˌlən\ *adj* [ISV *eury-* + *-haline, -halin* (fr. Gk *halinos* of salt, fr. *hals* salt) — more at SALT] **:** able to live in waters of a wide range of salinity — opposed to *stenohaline*

eu·ry·lai·mi \ˌyu̇rəˈlīˌmī, -lāˌ-\ *n pl, cap* [NL, fr. *Eurylaimus,* included genus, fr. *eury-* + Gk *laimos* throat; perh. akin to OE *lathian* to invite — more at LURE] **:** a suborder (coextensive with the family Eurylaimidae) of Passeriformes consisting of the broadbills

eu·ry·mer·ic \¦yu̇rə¦merik, -rē¦-\ *adj* [*eury-* + *-meric* (as in *platymeric*)] **:** having a broad femur with a platymeric index of 85 to 100

eu·ry·on \ˈyu̇rēˌän\ *n* -s [NL, irreg. fr. Gk *eurys* broad] **:** either of the lateral points marking the ends of the greatest transverse diameter of the skull

eu·ry·pel·ma \ˌyu̇rəˈpelmə\ *n, cap* [NL, fr. *eury-* + Gk *pelma* sole of the foot; akin to L *pellis* skin, hide — more at FELL] **:** a genus of large hairy burrowing spiders (family Theraphosidae) of the western U.S. popularly held to be venomous that includes the typical New World tarantulas

eu·ry·phage \ˈyu̇rəˌfāj\ *n* -s [ISV *eury-* + *-phage*] **:** a euryphagous animal

eu·ryph·a·gous \yəˈrifəgəs\ *adj* [ISV *eury-* + *-phagous*] **:** eating various kinds of foods **:** POLYPHAGOUS — opposed to *stenophagous*

eu·ry·plas·tic \¦yu̇rə¦plastik, -rē¦-\ *adj* [*eury-* + *plastic*] **:** exhibiting great capacity for modification and adaptability to a wide range of environmental conditions **:** capable of great evolutionary differentiation — opposed to *stenoplastic;* compare PSEUDOPLASTIC — **eu·ry·plas·ty** \ˈ==ˌplastē\ *n* -ES

eu·ry·prognathous \¦yu̇rə, -rē+\ *adj* [*eury-* + *prognathous*] **:** having broad prognathous jaws

eu·ry·prosopic \¦yu̇rə, -rē+\ *adj* [G *euryprosop* euryprosopic (fr. *eury-* + Gk *prosōpon* face) + E *-ic* — more at PROSOP-] **:** having a short or broad face or both with a facial index of 80 to 85 — **eu·ry·pros·o·py** \ˌ==+ˈpräsəpē, -ˌprəˈsōpē\ *n* -ES

1eu·ryp·te·rid \yəˈriptərəd\ *adj* [NL *Eurypterida*] **:** of or relating to the Eurypterida

2eurypterid \"\ *n* -s **:** one of the Eurypterida

eu·rypter·i·da \ˌyu̇rə(p)ˈterədə, -u̇rə(-\ *n pl, cap* [NL, fr. *Eurypterus,* included genus (fr. *eury-* + *-pterus*) + *-ida*] **:** an order of aquatic Paleozoic arthropods commonly forming with the related king crabs the class Merostomata, having a cephalothorax with six pairs of limbs of which the last pair were usu. shaped like paddles and a tapering abdomen of 13 segments, and including the largest known arthropods, some exceeding 6 feet in length

1eu·ryp·te·roid \yəˈriptəˌrȯid\ *adj* [NL *Eurypteroidea*] **:** resembling or relating to the Eurypterida

2eurypteroid \"\ *n* -s **:** one of the Eurypterida

eu·ryp·te·roi·dea \yəˌriptəˈrȯidēə\ [NL, fr. *Eurypterus* + *-oidea*] *syn of* EURYPTERIDA

eu·ry·py·ga \ˌyu̇rəˈpīgə\ *n, cap* [NL, fr. *eury-* + *-pyga*] **:** a genus (coextensive with the family Eurypygidae) that includes solely the sun-grebes — compare GRUIFORMES

eu·ry·py·lous \¦yu̇rə¦pīləs\ *or* **eu·ry·pyl·lous** \-¦pil-\ *adj* [*eurypylous* fr. *eury-* + *pyl-* + *-ous; eurypyllous* alter. of *eurypylous*] **:** having a wide opening; *specif, of a sponge* **:** having a direct connection between the flagellated chambers and their apopyles and prosopyles

eu·ry·some \ˈyu̇rəˌsōm\ *also* **eu·ry·so·mat·ic** \¦yu̇rəsō¦mad·ik\ *or* **eu·ry·so·mic** \-¦sōmik\ *adj* [*eurysome* ISV *eury-* + *-some; eurysomatic* prob. alter. (influenced by *somatic*) of *eurysome; eurysomic* prob. fr. *eurysome* + *-ic*] *anthrop* **:** having a broad thickset body build — opposed to *leptosome*

eu·ry·stom·a·tous \¦yu̇rə¦stäməd·əs, -rē¦-, -tōm-\ *adj* [prob. fr. NL *eurystomatus,* fr. *eury-* + *-stomatus* -stomatous] *zool* **:** having a broad mouth **:** having the mouth dilatable

eu·ry·therm \ˈyu̇rəˌthərm\ *n* -s [prob. fr. G *eurytherm* eurythermal, fr. *eury-* + *-therm* (fr. Gk *thermē* heat) — more at THERM] **:** an organism that tolerates a wide range of temperature

eu·ry·ther·mal \¦yu̇rə¦thərməl, -rē¦-\ *or* **eu·ry·ther·mic** \-mik\ *or* **eu·ry·ther·mous** \-məs\ *adj* [prob. fr. G *eurytherm* + E *-al* or *-ic* or *-ous*] **:** able to live in a wide range of temperatures — opposed to *stenothermal*

eu·ryth·mic *or* **eu·rhyth·mic** \(ˈ)yü¦rithmik *sometimes* -th-\ *also* **eu·ryth·mi·cal** *or* **eu·rhyth·mi·cal** \-məkəl\ *adj* [*eurythmy* + *-ic* or *-ical*] **1 :** HARMONIOUS ⟨~ proportions in architecture⟩ **2 :** of or relating to eurythmy or eurythmics

eu·ryth·mics *also* **eu·rhyth·mics** \=ˈ=miks\ *n pl but usu sing in constr* **1 :** the art of harmonious and expressive bodily movement; *specif* **:** this art as applied in music education through expressive timed movements in response to improvised musical effects chiefly according to a system devised by Émile Jaques-Dalcroze **2 :** eurythmy applied to dancing; *specif* **:** a kind of dancing based on musical patterns and used in the study of musical rhythm and phrasing

eu·ryth·my *also* **eu·rhyth·my** \=ˈ=mē, ˈ=ˌ=mē\ *n* -ES [L *eurythmia,* fr. Gk, fr. *eurythmos* rhythmical, well proportioned (fr. *eu-* + *rhythmos* rhythm, proportion) + *-ia* -y — more at RHYTHM] **1 :** harmonious proportion or movement **2** [G *eurhythmie,* fr. L *eurythmia*] **:** a system of harmonious body movement to the rhythm of spoken words devised for dance training by Rudolph Steiner

eu·ry·tom·i·dae \ˌyu̇rəˈtäməˌdē\ *n pl, cap* [NL, fr. *Eurytoma,* type genus (fr. *eury-* + *-toma*) + *-idae*] **:** a family of black or black and yellowish chalcid flies which have the abdomen rounded and compressed and some of which are parasitic on other insects while others are plant feeders and important pests esp. of grains — see JOINTWORM

eu·ry·top·ic \¦yu̇rə¦täpik\ *adj* [prob. fr. G *eurytop* eurytopic (fr. *eury-* + *-top,* fr. Gk *topos* place) + E *-ic* — more at TOPIC] **:** having a wide range of tolerance to variation of one or more environmental factors — compare STENOTOPIC — **eu·ry·to·pic·i·ty** \ˌ==ˌtōˈpisəd·ē\ *n* -ES

eu·ry·tre·ma \ˌyu̇rəˈtrēmə\ *n, cap* [NL, fr. *eury-* + *-trema*] **:** a genus of digenetic trematode worms (family Dicrocoeliidae) infesting the pancreatic and bile ducts of various ruminants, rodents, and primates chiefly in tropical areas

eu·ryzy·gous \¦yu̇rə¦zīgəs, yəˈrizəgəs\ *adj* [*eury-* + *-zygous*] **:** having wide zygomatic arches

-e·us \ēəs\ *n comb form, pl* **-ei** \ēˌī\ *also* **-euses** [NL, fr. L, adj. suffix, composed of, of the nature of, or resembling (a specified substance) — more at -EOUS] **:** muscle that constitutes, has the form of, or joins a (specified) part, thing, or structures ⟨*gluteus*⟩ ⟨*rhomboideus*⟩ ⟨*iliococcygeus*⟩

eu·schis·tus \yüˈskistəs\ *n, cap* [NL, fr. Gk *euschistos* easy to split, fr. *eu-* + *schistos* split, divided, fr. *schizein* to split — more at SHED] **:** a genus of pentatomid bugs some of which cause catfacing of peaches

1eu·se·bi·an \yüˈsēbēən\ *n* -s *usu cap* [*Eusebius* of Nicomedia †*ab* A.D.342 Arian leader and bishop + E *-an,* n. suffix] **:** a follower of Eusebius, bishop of Nicomedia **:** ARIAN

2eusebian \"\ *adj, usu cap* **1** [*Eusebius* of Caesarea †*ab* A.D.340 theologian and church historian + E *-an,* adj. suffix] **:** of or belonging to Eusebius, bishop of Caesarea and church historian **2** [*Eusebius* of Nicomedia + E *-an,* adj. suffix] **:** of or belonging to Eusebius, bishop of Nicomedia, who was a friend and protector of Arius

eusebian canons *n pl, usu cap E* [²*eusebian* (Eusebius of Caesarea)] **:** a set of tables presenting a harmony of the Gospels in outline form by use of section numbers

1eu·selachii \ˌyü+\ *n pl, cap* [NL, fr. *eu-* + *Selachii*] **:** a subclass or other division of Chondrichthyes comprising the recent sharks and rays and certain extinct related forms

2euselachii \"\ [NL, fr. *eu-* + *Selachii*] *syn of* PLEUROTREMATA

eus·ka·ra *or* **eus·ke·ra** \ˈeu̇skəˌrä\ *n* -s *cap* [Basque] **:** the Basque language

eus·kar·i·an \yüˈska(a)rēən\ *n* -s *usu cap* [Basque *euskara* Basque (the language) + E *-ian,* n. suffix] **1 :** the Basque language **2 :** the language family of which Basque is the only member

eu·smi·lus \yüˈsmīləs\ *n, cap* [NL, fr. *eu-* + *-smilus* (fr. Gk *smilē* carving knife) — more at SMITH] **:** a genus of early saber-toothed tigers with extremely large canines known from the Oligocene of Europe and No. America

eu·spongia \(ˈ)yü+\ *n* [NL, fr. *eu-* + *Spongia*] *syn of* SPONGIA

eu·spo·ran·gi·a·tae \ˌyüspəˌranjēˈād·ē, -ˈäd-\ *n pl, cap* [NL, fr. fem. pl. of (assumed) NL *eusporangiatus*] *in some classifications* **:** a group comprising all the ferns in which sporangium formation is eusporangiate — compare LEPTOSPORANGIATAE

eu·spo·ran·gi·ate \¦yüspə¦ranjēət, -ēˌāt\ *adj* [fr. (assumed) NL *eusporangiatus,* fr. NL *eu-* + *sporangium* + L *-atus* -ate] **:** having sporangia which rise from a group of epidermal cells ⟨~ ferns of the families Ophioglossaceae and Marattiaceae⟩ — opposed to *leptosporangiate*

eu·sta·chian \yüˈstāshən *also* -āshēən *or* -ākēən\ *adj, often cap* [Bartolommeo *Eustachio* †1574 Ital. anatomist + E *-an*] **:** of or relating to Eustachio or to the eustachian tube **:** located in or adjoining the eustachian tube

eustachian tonsil *n, often cap E* **:** a mass of lymphoid tissue at the pharyngeal opening of the eustachian tube

eustachian tube *n, often cap E* **:** a bony and cartilaginous tube connecting the cavity of the middle ear with the nasopharynx and serving to equalize air pressure on both sides of the tympanic membrane — see EAR illustration

eustachian valve *n, often cap E* **:** a crescent-shaped fold of the lining membrane of the heart at the entrance of the vena cava inferior that directs the blood through the foramen ovale to the left auricle in the fetus but is rudimentary and functionless in the adult

eu·sta·cy \ˈyüstəsē\ *n* -ES [ISV *eu-* + *-stacy* (irreg. fr. Gk *stasis* condition of standing still) — more at STASIS] **:** worldwide change of sea level as contrasted with local diastrophic uplift or subsidence of the land

eu·sta·sism \ˈyüstəˌsizəm\ *or* **eu·sta·tism** \-təˌtiz-\ *n* -s [*eustasism* prob. irreg. fr. *eustacy* + *-ism; eustatism* ISV *eustat-* (fr. *eustatic*) + *-ism*] **:** EUSTACY

1eu·sta·thi·an \yüˈstāthēən\ *n* -s *cap* **1** [*Eustathius* of Sebaste †*ab* A.D.380 Semi-Arian bishop of Sebaste in Armenia + E *-an,* n. suffix] **:** a follower of the Semi-Arian bishop Eustathius who established a monastic institute which was condemned by the Synod of Gangra in A.D.340 **2** [*Eustathius* of Antioch †*ab* A.D.360 bishop of Antioch in Syria + E *-an,* n. suffix] **:** one of an orthodox party whose protest against the deposition by an Arian synod of Eustathius, bishop of Antioch, led to a schism that lasted till A.D.413

2eustathian \"\ *adj, cap* [*Eustathius* + E *-an,* adj. suffix] **:** of or relating to Eustathius or to a Eustathian

eu·stat·ic \(ˈ)yü¦stad·ik\ *adj* [ISV *eu-* + *static*] **:** relating to or characterized by eustacy — **eu·stat·i·cal·ly** *adv*

eu·stele \(ˈ)yü+\ *n* [*eu-* + *stele*] **:** a stele (as in most higher vascular plants) in which the vascular cylinder is broken up by leaf gaps and interfascicular areas

eu·sternum \"\ *n, pl* **eusterna** [NL, fr. *eu-* + *sternum*] **:** the anterior plate of a sternum of an insect **:** BASISTERNUM; *also* **:** any of certain other sclerites of the ventral part of the insect thorax

eus·the·nop·te·ron \ˌyüsthəˈnäptəˌrän\ *n, cap* [NL, fr. *eustheno-* (fr. Gk *eusthenēs* strong, fr. *eu-* + *-sthenēs,* fr. *sthenos* strength) + Gk *pteron* wing; fr. the strongly developed fins — more at ASTHEN-, FEATHER] **:** a genus of Upper Devonian lobe-finned fishes (order Rhipidistia)

eu·stom·a·tous \(ˈ)yü¦stäməd·əs, -tōm-\ *adj* [prob. fr. (assumed) NL *eustomatus,* fr. NL *eu-* + *-stomatus* -stomatous] **:** having a distinct and well-developed mouth — used esp. of ciliates and larval nematodes

eu·style \ˈyüˌstīl\ *n* [L *eustylos* having columns at the best distances, fr. Gk, fr. *eu-* + *stylos* pillar — more at STOW] **:** an intercolumniation of 2¼ diameters

eu·su·chia \yüˈsükēə\ *n pl, cap* [NL, fr. *eu-* + Gk *souchos* crocodile + NL *-ia*] **:** a suborder or other division of Loricata including the typical members of that group (as the existing gavials, alligators, and crocodiles and post-Cretaceous fossil forms) having the internal nasal opening situated far back and surrounded by the pterygoid bone — **eu·su·chi·an** \-ēən\ *adj*

eu·syn·chite \yü'sin,kīt, -in,k-, 'yüsᵊn,k-\ *n* -s [G *eusynchit*, fr. *eu-* + Gk *syncheint*o commingle, confuse (fr. *syn-* + *chein* to pour) + G *-it* -ite — more at FOUND] : DESCLOIZITE

eu·tae·nia \yü'tēnēə\ [NL, fr. *eu-* + Gk *tainia* band, fillet — more at TAENIA] *syn of* THAMNOPHIS

eu·tamias \(ˈ)yü+\ *n, cap* [NL, fr. *eu-* + *Tamias*] : a genus of rodents comprising the chipmunks of western No. America

eu·tax·ic \(ˈ)yü¦taksik\ *adj* [*eutaxy* + *-ic*] : of or relating to stratified ore deposits — opposed to *ataxic*

eu·taxy \ˈyü,taksē\ *n* -ES [Gk *eutaxia*, fr. *eutaktos* orderly (fr. *eu-* + *taktos* ordered, fr. *tattein, tassein* to put in order) + *-ia* -y — more at TACTICS] : good order or management ⟨whose keeping of Christmas . . . was an annual example of that competent ~ in which her life was ordered —Rose Macaulay⟩

¹**eu·tec·tic** \(ˈ)yü¦tektik\ *adj* [ISV *eutect-* (fr. Gk *eutēktos* easily melted, fr. *eu-* + *tēktos* melted, fr. *tēkein* to melt) + *-ic* — more at THAW] : relating to a eutectic or its composition ⟨~ mixture⟩ or the temperature at which it melts or freezes ⟨~ point⟩

²**eutectic** \"\ *n* -s **1** : an alloy or solution having its components in such proportions that the melting point is the lowest possible with those components **2** : the characteristic microstructure resulting from solidification of metal of eutectic composition — compare EUTECTOID

¹**eu·tec·toid** \yü'tek,tȯid\ *n* -s [ISV *eutect-* (fr. *eutectic*) + *-oid*, n. suffix] : a eutectoid alloy (as pearlite) formed when a solid solution transforms during cooling into new solid phases, the change taking place entirely in the solid state

²**eutectoid** \(ˈ)ˌ=¦=,=\ *adj* : like a eutectic — used esp. of steel in the form of pearlite

eu·tele·genesis \(,)yü,telə+\ *n* [NL, fr. *eu-* + *tel-* + L *genesis*] : ARTIFICIAL INSEMINATION

eu·tely \ˈyüd·ᵊlē; ˈyü,telē, =ˈ==\ *n* -ES [prob. fr. G *eutelie*, fr. Gk *euteleia* thrift, economy, fr. *eutelēs* cheap, frugal, fr. *eu-* + *-telēs* (fr. *telos* end, toll, expenditure) — more at WHEEL] : the condition of having a body made up of a constant number of cells (as in certain rotifers and some lower worms)

eu·ter·pe \yü'tər(,)pē\ *n, cap* [NL, fr. L *Euterpe*, one of the Muses (in late Roman times characterized as the Muse of the flute), fr. Gk *Euterpē*, one of the Muses] : a genus of graceful tropical American pinnate-leaved palms having a small globose fruit about the size of a pea — see ASSAI

eu·ter·pe·an \(ˈ)yü¦tərpēən\ *adj, usu cap* [L *Euterpe* + E *-an*] : relating to the muse Euterpe or to music

eu·tex·ia \yü'teksēə, -ksha\ *n* -s [Gk *eutēxia*, fr. *eutēktos* easily melted + *-ia* -y] **1** : the quality of melting at a minimum temperature **2** : the principle or process of forming from given components the eutectic alloy

eu·tha·mia \yü'thāmēə\ *n, cap* [NL, fr. *eu-* + *tham-* (prob. fr. Gk *thamees* crowded) + *-ia*; akin to Gk *tithenai* to place — more at DO] *in some classifications* : a genus of composite herbs including those members of the genus *Solidago* in which the flower heads are flat topped

eu·tha·na·sia \,yüthə'nāzh(ē)ə\ *n* -s [Gk, easy death, fr. *eu-* + *-thanasia* (fr. *thanatos* death) — more at THANAT-] **1** : an easy death or means of inducing one **2** : the act or practice of painlessly putting to death persons suffering from incurable conditions or diseases — **eu·tha·na·sic** \ˌyüthə¦nāzik\ *adj*

eu·then·ics \yü'theniks\ *n pl but sing or pl in constr* [Gk *euthenein* to thrive (fr. *eu-* + *-thenein* to swell) + E *-ics*; akin to Lith *gana* enough, Skt *ghana* compact, dense] : a science that deals with developing human well-being and efficient functioning through the improvement of environmental conditions — compare EUGENICS

eu·then·ist \yü'thenəst, 'yüthən-\ *n* -s [*euthenics* + *-ist*] : a student or advocate of euthenics

eu·theria \(ˈ)yü+\ *n pl, cap* [NL, fr. *eu-* + *Theria*] : a major division of Mammalia originally coextensive with the subclass Theria but in modern usage an infraclass or other division of Theria comprising the placental mammals as opposed to the Metatheria — **eu·the·ri·an** \(ˈ)yü¦thirēən\ *adj or n*

eu·thermic \(ˈ)yü+\ *adj* [*eu-* + *thermic*] : inducing or promoting warmth

eu·tho·scop·ic \ˌyüthə¦skäpik\ *adj* [*eutho-* (irreg. fr. Gk *euthys* straight) + *-scopic*] *of a photoreceptor* : capable of perceiving the presence, direction, and relative intensity of light but unable to form a visual image

eu·thy·neu·ra \ˌyüthə'n(y)u̇rə\ *n pl, cap* [NL, fr. *euthy-* (fr. Gk, fr. *euthys* straight) + *-neura*] : a large subclass of Gastropoda comprising the Opisthobranchia and Pulmonata — **eu·thy·neu·ral** \ˌ==¦=rəl\ *or* **eu·thy·neu·ran** \-rən\ *or* **eu·thy·neu·rous** \-rəs\ *adj*

eu·thyn·nus \yü'thinəs\ *n, cap* [NL, fr. *eu-* + Gk *thynnos* tunny — more at TUNNY] : a genus of comparatively small tunas with teeth on the palatine bones that includes the little tuna cosmopolitan in tropical seas

eu·thyroid \(ˈ)yü+\ *adj* [*eu-* + *thyroid*] : characterized by normal thyroid function : having a thyroid that functions normally — **eu·thyroidism** \ˌyü+\ *n*

eu·to·cia \yü'tōsh(ē)ə\ *n* -s [NL, fr. Gk *eutokia*, fr. *eutokos* giving birth easily (fr. *eu-* + *tokos* childbirth, parturition) + *-ia*; akin to Gk *teknon* child — more at THANE] : normal parturition — opposed to *dystocia*

eutomous *adj* [*eu-* + *-tomous*] *obs, of a mineral* : cleaving readily or distinctly

eu·to·pia \yü'tōpēə, eu̇'t-\ *n* -s *usu cap* [NL, fr. *eu-* + *-topia* (fr. Gk *topos* place + *-ia*) — more at TOPIC] : a country of ideal felicity and perfection; *sometimes* : UTOPIA — **eu·to·pi·an** \(ˈ)ˌ=¦=pēən\ *adj, usu cap*

eu·tracheata \(¦)yü+\ *n pl, cap* [NL, fr. *eu-* + *Tracheata*] : a group of Arthropoda comprising all arthropods (as insects, chilopods, diplopods, and a few related forms) that have a tracheal respiratory system and a single pair of antennae — **eu·tracheate** \(ˈ)yü+\ *adj or n*

eu·trombicula \ˌyü+\ *n, cap* [NL, fr. *eu-* + *Trombicula*] : a genus of rather large mites (family Trombidiidae) that have the body clearly demarked into cephalothorax and abdomen, are free-living as adults, and have larvae which are typical chiggers

eu·troph·ic \(ˈ)yü¦träfik, -rōf-\ *adj* [prob. fr. *eutrophy* + *-ic*] **1** : relating to or being in a well-nourished condition **2** [prob. fr. G *eutroph* eutrophic (fr. Gk *eutrophos* well nourished, nourishing) + E *-ic*] *of a lake* : rich in dissolved nutrients but frequently shallow and with seasonal oxygen deficiency in the hypolimnion — compare DYSTROPHIC, OLIGOTROPHIC

eu·troph·i·ca·tion \(,)yü,träfə'kāshən, -rōf-\ *n* -s [*eutrophic* + *-ation*] : the process of becoming more eutrophic either as a natural phase in the maturation of a body of water or artificially (as by fertilization)

eu·tro·phy \ˈyü·trəfē\ *n* -ES [Gk *eutrophia*, fr. *eutrophos* well nourished, nourishing (fr. *eu-* + *trophos* feeder, fr. *trephein* to nourish) + *-ia* -y — more at ATROPHY] **1** : healthy nutrition : healthy action of the nutritive functions **2** [prob. fr. G *eutrophie*, fr. Gk *eutrophia*] *of a lake* : the quality or state of being eutrophic

eu·tych·i·an \(ˈ)yü¦tikēən\ *n* -s *usu cap* [*Eutyches* †A.D.454? heresiarch, presbyter, and archimandrite of the Eastern Church in Constantinople + E *-ian*] : a follower of Eutyches in the belief that the divine and the human in the person of Christ so blend as to constitute but one nature so that Christ is of two natures but not in two : MONOPHYSITE — compare NESTORIAN — **eu·tych·i·an·ism** \-,nizəm\ *n* -s *usu cap*

eux·e·nite \'yüksə,nīt\ *n* -s [G *euxenit*, fr. Gk *euxenos* hospitable (fr. *eu-* + *xenos* guest, stranger) + G *-it* -ite; fr. the rare elements it contains] : a brownish black mineral (Y, Ca, Ce, U, Th) (Cb, Ta, Ti)$_2$O$_6$ that consists of oxide of calcium, cerium, columbium, tantalum, titanium, and uranium, that has a metallic luster, and that is isomorphous with polycrase (hardness 6.5, sp. gr. 4.7–5.0)

eux·ine \'yüksən, -,sīn\ *adj, usu cap* [L *euxinus*, fr. Gk *euxeinos* (esp. in *Pontos Euxeinos* Black sea), fr. *euxenos, euxeinos* hospitable] : of, relating to, or having to do with the Black sea

eux·in·ic \(ˈ)yük¦sinik\ *adj* [*euxine* + *-ic*] : relating to a rock facies that includes black shales and graphitic sediments of various kinds

eu·xoa \yük'sōə\ *n, cap* [NL] : a genus of brownish noctuid moths having larvae that are voracious cutworms — see RED-BACKED CUTWORM

ev *abbr* evangelical

EV *abbr, often not cap* electron volt

Evac·tor \ə'vaktə(r), ē'-\ *trademark* — used for a jet pump

¹**evac·u·ant** \ə'vakyəwənt, ē'-\ *n* -s [L *evacuant-, evacuans*, pres. part. of *evacuare*] : an evacuant agent

²**evacuant** \"\ *adj* [L *evacuant-, evacuans*, pres. part. of *evacuare*] : EMPTYING, EMETIC, DIURETIC, PURGATIVE, CATHARTIC

evac·u·ate \ə'vakyə,wāt, ē'-, *usu* -ād.+V\ *vb* -ED/-ING/-S [L *evacuatus*, past part. of *evacuare*, fr. *e-* + *vacuus* empty — more at WANE] *vt* **1 a** : to make empty : empty out ⟨~ an abscess⟩ **b** : DEPRIVE ⟨a naturalistic logic which *evacuated* Christianity of all religious values —*Times Lit. Supp.*⟩ **2** *archaic* : to make void : NULLIFY, VACATE **3** : to discharge through the excretory passages : VOID **4** : to remove something (as a gas or water) from esp. by pumping : EXHAUST ⟨a highly *evacuated* glass tube⟩ **5 a** : to remove (troops equipment, civilians) esp. from a military position or zone : remove (sick and wounded) from a combat area **b** : to withdraw from military occupation of (a fort or region) **c** : to remove (a person or thing) from some place in an organized way esp. as a protective measure ⟨*evacuated* the people of the towns threatened by the forest fire⟩ ⟨~ American citizens from the war-torn land⟩ ⟨during the war their school had been *evacuated* to the country —Margaret Kennedy⟩ ⟨the irreplaceable treasures had been *evacuated* to safety —*Amer. Library Assoc. Bull.*⟩ ⟨the pigs had been *evacuated* and were not brought back —*Time*⟩ **d** : to remove the inhabitants of (a place or area) esp. as a protective measure ⟨~ a city under attack⟩ **e** : to give up the occupancy of (premises) ~ *vi* **1** : to withdraw in an organized way from a place or territory esp. as a protective measure or as a military operation ⟨the decision to ~ was made as flood waters reached a new height⟩ ⟨enemy troops were to ~ in 10 days⟩ **2** : DEFECATE, URINATE

evac·u·a·tion \ə,==ˈwāshən\ *n* -s [ME *evacuacioun*, fr. MF & LL; MF *evacuation*, fr. LL *evacuation-, evacuatio*, fr. L *evacuatus* + *-ion-, -io* -ion] **1** : the act of emptying, clearing of the contents, or discharging ⟨easy and resounding ~ of words —Philip Wylie⟩ ⟨it is very wrong . . . to hold back a natural ~ of joy —Robertson Davies⟩: as **a** : the withdrawal of troops from a town or fortress, of a population from a city or territory, or of sick and wounded from a combat area ⟨demanded the immediate ~ of foreign troops⟩ ⟨~ of the threatened city had begun⟩ **b** : any organized withdrawal or removal (as of persons or things) from a place or area esp. as a protective measure ⟨as flood waters rose ~ of families and farm animals was begun⟩ ⟨advised ~ of the precious art collection to a neutral country⟩ **c** : discharge of any matter by the natural passages of the body or by an artificial opening : DEFECATION **2** : something that is evacuated or discharged by natural or artificial means

evacuation hospital *n* : a mobile or partly mobile hospital where casualties are received usu. from collecting stations and where major medical and surgical treatment can be given before evacuation to rear installations

evac·u·a·tive \ˌ===,wād·iv\ *adj* : of or relating to evacuation

evac·u·ee \ˌ=¦=ˈwē\ *also* **evac·ué** *or* **evac·u·ée** \-wā\ *n* -s [F *évacué* (masc.) & *évacuée* (fem.), fr. past part. of *évacuer* to evacuate, fr. L *evacuare* — more at EVACUATE] : a person who is removed from his home or community in time of war or pressing danger as a protective measure ⟨the villagers fed and housed the ~s from the blitzed city⟩

evad·able \ə'vādəbəl, ē'-\ *adj* : capable of being evaded ⟨these obligations are not easily ~⟩

evade \ə'vād, ē'-\ *vb* -ED/-ING/-S [MF & L; MF *evader*, fr. L *evadere*, fr. *e-* + *vadere* to go, walk — more at WADE] *vi* **1** : to slip away : give someone the slip ⟨submariners have always despised the need to ~ in order to escape —S.D.Cutter⟩ **2** : to take refuge in evasion : use craft or stratagem in avoidance : avoid facing up to something ⟨wisdom consists . . . in learning when to ~, when to stave off, and when to oppose head on —Irving Howe⟩ ⟨the adult who regresses to the infantile . . . ~s —H.A.Overstreet⟩ ~ *vt* **1 a** (1) : to get away from (a pursuer or enemy) by dexterity or stratagem : avoid capture by : shun or avoid contact or confrontation with : ELUDE, ESCAPE, AVOID ⟨*evaded* the police and crossed the border into safety⟩ ⟨he . . . tried to ~ her kisses —Winifred Bambrick⟩ ⟨guiltily *evaded* her accusing look⟩ (2) : to avoid facing up to (a fact or condition) ⟨though she knew . . . her father would never be up again, she united with her mother in *evading* the fact —Ellen Glasgow⟩ ⟨prefers to ~ home truths . . . by saying what he does not really mean —*Va. Quarterly Rev.*⟩ **b** (1) : to manage to avoid the performance of (an obligation) : escape from doing or experiencing (something disagreeable) : CIRCUMVENT, DODGE ⟨I have a horror of the men who *evaded* service during the war —Rose Macaulay⟩ ⟨the French had been limited to a hundred thousand troops . . . but they had managed . . . to ~ this limit —Upton Sinclair⟩ ⟨several very safe and easy methods of *evading* the law —Adam Smith⟩; *specif* : to fail to pay or to minimize (taxes) in violation of law ⟨served a term . . . for *evading* his income tax —H.H.Martin⟩ (2) : to get around (an intellectual obstacle) ⟨the traditional way of *evading* the difficulty . . . is to have recourse to . . . "vitalism" —A.N.Whitehead⟩ **c** : to avoid answering directly (as a question or a questioner) : turn aside : PARRY ⟨tried to ~ his query but he was not to be put off⟩ ⟨tried to ~ this nonsensical demand —Alfred Burmeister⟩ **2** : BAFFLE, ELUDE : be baffling or elusive to ⟨the simple, personal meaning *evaded* them —C.D. Lewis⟩ **syn** see ESCAPE

evad·er \-də(r)\ *n* -s : one that evades ⟨prosecuting tax ~s⟩

eva·ga·tion \,ēvə'gāshən, ,ē(,)vā'-, ,evə'-\ *n* -s [ME *evagacioun*, fr. MF or ML; MF *evagation*, fr. ML *evagation-, evagatio*, fr. L, wandering, fr. *evagatus* (past part. of *evagari* to wander, fr. *e-* + *vagari* to stroll, wander) + *-ion-, -io* ion — more at VAGARY] **1** *obs* : a wandering of the mind **2** [L *evagation-, evagatio*] *archaic* : the act or an instance of wandering

evag·i·na·ble \ə'vajənəbəl, ē'-\ *adj* : capable of being evaginated

¹**evag·i·nate** \-,nāt\ *vb* -ED/-ING/-S [L *evaginatus*, past part. of *evaginare* to unsheathe, fr. *e-* + *vagina* sheath — more at VAGINA] *vt* : to turn (as a body part) inside out : cause (a part) to protrude by eversion of an inner surface ~ *vi, of a part or structure* : to protrude by eversion of an inner surface : turn inside out

²**evag·i·nate** \-,nət, -,nāt\ *adj* [L *evaginatus*, past part.] : EVAGINATED

evag·i·na·tion \ə,vajə'nāshən, (,)ē,v-\ *n* -s [LL *evagination-, evaginatio* act of unsheathing, fr. L *evaginatus* + *-ion-, -io* -ion] **1** : the act or an instance of evaginating **2** : a product of evagination : OUTGROWTH

eval·u·ate \ə'valyə,wāt, ē'v-, *usu* -ād.+V\ *vb* -ED/-ING/-S [back-formation fr. *evaluation*] *vt* **1 a** : to set down or express the mathematical value of : express numerically **b** : to estimate or ascertain the monetary worth of : VALUE ⟨the inspector *evaluated* the horses at thirty-five dollars a head —F.B.Gipson⟩ **2** : to examine and judge concerning the worth, quality, significance, amount, degree, or condition of : APPRAISE, RATE ⟨using trained observers to visit and ~ teachers in their classrooms —*Educational Research Bull.*⟩ ⟨X-ray and radium therapy must be further explored before their efficacy can be *evaluated* —W.S.Middleton⟩ ⟨*evaluated* a new novel⟩ ⟨~ a student's ability⟩ ⟨at the first visit, an attempt should be made to ~ the patient as a whole —*Therapeutic Notes*⟩ ⟨~ a new political trend⟩ ~ *vi* : to make an evaluation ⟨it is not enough to count, we must ~ —Havelock Ellis⟩ ⟨we . . . come . . . as critics, to scrutinize and ~ —R.W. Stallman⟩ **syn** see ESTIMATE

eval·u·a·tion \ə,valyə'wāshən, (,)ē,v-\ *n* -s [F *évaluation*, fr. MF *evaluation*, fr. *evaluer* to evaluate (fr. *e-* + *value*) + *-ation* — more at VALUE] : the act or result of evaluating : JUDGMENT APPRAISAL, RATING, INTERPRETATION ⟨a man can be labeled a security risk for presenting his ~ of a political situation —*Civil Liberties*⟩ ⟨if we examine the great writers, we find that their moral ~s are often either below, or above, the level of their material —William Barrett⟩ ⟨every woman should have a thorough examination, including ~ of the pelvic organs —*Therapeutic Notes*⟩

eval·u·a·tive \ə'==,wā|d·|iv, -,wəl, |t|, |ēv *also* |əv\ *adj* : serving or tending to evaluate ⟨the literary judge uses ~ terms freely —C.W.Shumaker⟩

eval·u·a·tor \-,wād·ə(r), -ātə-\ *n* -s : one that evaluates ⟨an intelligence officer is supposed to be a professional ~ —Perry Miller⟩

ev·a·nesce \ˌevə¦nes, *chiefly Brit* ¦ēv-\ *vi* -ED/-ING/-S [L *evanescere* — more at VANISH] : to dissipate and disappear like vapor : disappear gradually ⟨I touch a scarf and it falls into air and light and seems to ~ —William Goyen⟩ **syn** see VANISH

ev·a·nes·cence \ˌ==ˈnesᵊn(t)s\ *n* -s **1** : the process or fact of evanescing : a vanishing away ⟨the possible ~ of her passion for him —Thomas Hardy⟩ **2** : evanescent quality ⟨the fleeting ~ of all things that are —J.L.Lowes⟩

ev·a·nes·cent \ˌ==¦nesᵊnt\ *adj* [L *evanescent-, evanescens*, pres. part. of *evanescere*] **1** : tending to vanish or pass away like vapor : of short life or duration : VANISHING, FLEETING, IMPERMANENT ⟨slight and ~ as an April storm —Elinor Wylie⟩ ⟨~ isotopes⟩ ⟨an ~ eruption⟩ ⟨~ flowers⟩ **2** *archaic* : becoming imperceptible by diminution : INFINITESIMAL **3** : characterized by extreme delicacy or fineness of form, structure, or texture : light and airy : FRAGILE, DIAPHANOUS, UNSUBSTANTIAL ⟨with the . . . ~ brushwork and psychological clarity since lost in English painting —*New Republic*⟩ ⟨many beautiful creatures, . . . so ~ that they are only discoverable by the faint shadows which they cast on the bottom —William Beebe⟩ **syn** see TRANSIENT

ev·a·nes·cent·ly *adv* : in an evanescent manner

¹**evan·gel** \ə'vanjəl, ē'-, -vaan-\ *n* -s [ME *evangile, evangell*, fr. MF *evangile*, fr. LL *evangelium*, fr. Gk. *euangelion* good news, glad tidings, gospel, fr. *euangelos* bringing good news, fr. *eu-* + *-angelos*, fr. *angelos* messenger — more at ANGEL] **1 a** : the Christian gospel **b** *usu cap* : one of the four Gospels of the New Testament **2** : good news : announcement of good news **3** : a doctrine regarded as having special grace, sanction, or efficacy ⟨a contemporary situation invested atomism . . . with the attributes of an ~ —Benjamin Farrington⟩

²**evangel** \"\ *n* -s [LL *evangelus*, fr. Gk *euangelos*, adj.] : one who proclaims a gospel message : EVANGELIST ⟨never joined in the public confessions of his fellow ~s —*Time*⟩

evan·ge·lary \-,lerē\ *n* -ES [modif. of ML *evangeliarium*, fr. LL *evangelium* + L *-arium* -ary] : EVANGELISTARY

¹**evan·gel·ic** \¦ē,van¦jelik, ¦evən-, ¦ē,vaan-, ¸ē,va(a)n-, ə-,va(a)n-\ *adj* [ME, fr. LL *evangelicus*] : EVANGELICAL

²**evangelic** \"\ *n* -s *archaic* : EVANGELICAL

¹**evan·gel·i·cal** \-lәkəl, -lēk-\ *adj* [LL *evangelicus* (fr. Gk *euangelikos*, fr. *euangelion* + *-ikos* -ic) + E *-al*] **1** : of, relating to, contained in, or in agreement with the Christian gospel esp. as it is presented in the four Gospels of the New Testament **2** *sometimes cap* : PROTESTANT ⟨mobs attacked ~ property⟩ **3** : of, relating to, or being a religious group emphasizing salvation by faith in the atoning death of Jesus Christ through personal conversion, the authority of Scripture, and the importance of preaching as contrasted with ritual **4 a** *usu cap* : of or relating to the Evangelical Church in Germany **b** *sometimes cap* : of or relating to Fundamentalism or Fundamentalists ⟨an ultraconservative ~ message⟩ **c** *usu cap* : of or relating to Low Church adherents in the Church of England and the Protestant Episcopal Church as distinguished from High Church Anglo-Catholics; *also* : of or relating to Wesleyans or Methodists who stand in the tradition of the 18th century evangelical revival in England **5** : characteristic or suggestive of an evangelist : characterized by or reflecting a missionary, reforming, or redeeming impulse or purpose : EVANGELISTIC, ZEALOUS, ARDENT, MILITANT, CRUSADING ⟨did not feel the passion for writing or preaching that more ~ authors have felt —F.A.Swinnerton⟩ ⟨the rise and fall of ~ fervor within the Socialist movement —*Times Lit. Supp.*⟩ ⟨propaganda . . . reinforced the mood of ~ patriotism —J.D. Hart⟩ ⟨the Marxist impulse in American literary criticism was chiefly hortatory and ~ —C.I.Glicksberg⟩ — **evan·gel·i·cal·ness** *n* -ES

²**evangelical** \"\ *n* -s *usu cap* : one holding evangelical principles or belonging to an evangelical party or church

evan·gel·i·cal·ism \ˌ=ˌ=¦=¦=kə,lizəm, ˌ==¦=-, =ˌ=¦=-\ *n* -s *usu cap* : evangelical principles or beliefs; *also* : adherence to the party or churches holding them

evan·gel·i·cal·i·ty \ˌē,va(a)n,jelə'kaləd·ē, ˌevən-\ *n* -ES : the state of being evangelical

evan·gel·i·cal·ly \¦ē,va(a)n¦jelək(ə)lē, ¦evən-, ¸ē,va(a)n-, ə-,va(a)n-, -lēk-, -li\ *adv* : in an evangelical manner : in the manner of an evangelist ⟨~ pleaded for individual regeneration —*Time*⟩

evan·gel·i·cism \ˌ=ˌ=¦=lə,sizəm, ˌ==¦=-, =ˌ=¦=-\ *n* -s *sometimes cap* : EVANGELICALISM

evan·ge·lion \ˌe,vän¦gyelyȯn\ *n* -s [LGk *euangelion*, fr. Gk, good news, gospel — more at EVANGEL] **1** *Eastern Church* : EVANGELISTARY **2** *Eastern Church* : a pericope of a gospel as read in the liturgy

evan·ge·lism \ə'vanjə,lizəm, ē'-\ *n* -s [LGk *euangelismos*, fr. Gk *euangelizesthai, euangelizein* to evangelize] **1** : the proclamation of the gospel; *esp* : the presentation of the gospel to individuals and groups by such methods as preaching, teaching, and personal or family visitation programs **2** : missionary, militant, or crusading zeal for or earnest advocacy of any cause ⟨stumped the state, denouncing the Fugitive Slave law and . . . electrifying his audiences with his Free-Soil ~ —W.E.Smith⟩

evan·ge·list \-ləst\ *n* -s [ME, fr. OF & LL; OF *evangeliste*, fr. LL *evangelista*, fr. Gk *euangelistēs*, fr. *euangelizesthai, euangelizein*] **1** *usu cap* : a writer of any of the four Gospels **2 a** : a member of the primitive church who brought the first news of the gospel message, paving the way for the more systematic work of settled church officers : a traveling missionary or wandering teacher **b** : one who converts (as a nation) to Christianity : EVANGELIZER, APOSTLE **c** : an occasional preacher having no fixed charge : a traveling missionary: as (1) : a minister of the Disciples of Christ who organizes church societies and sets churches and their officers in order (2) : a minister or layman among various Protestant denominations who goes about from place to place preaching at special services to awaken religious interest : REVIVALIST **3** : PATRIARCH 4 **4** : a person characterized by evangelical zeal for and earnest advocacy of any cause ⟨a fervent ~ for the mutual interests of labor and management —*Time*⟩

evan·ge·lis·ta·ry \ˌ==ˈlistərē, -ri\ *n* -ES [ML *evangelistarium*, fr. LL *evangelista* + L *-arium* -ary] : a book consisting of the four Gospels that is used as a lectionary

evan·ge·lis·tic \=¦=¦listik, -tēk\ *adj* **1** : of or relating to evangelism : designed or used for the purpose of evangelization ⟨the ~ concerns of the early church⟩ ⟨an ~ tent⟩ **2** : EVANGELICAL ⟨an ~ interpretation of the Bible⟩ **3** : of, relating to, or led by an evangelist ⟨an ~ service⟩ ⟨~ writings⟩ **4 a** : having a missionary or revivalist character or purpose ⟨the ~ movement on the American frontier⟩ **b** : marked by evangelism — **evan·ge·lis·ti·cal·ly** \-tək(ə)lē, -tēk-, -li\ *adv*

evan·ge·lis·tics \ˌ=ˌ==stiks, -tēks\ *n pl but sing in constr* : the science of the propagation of Christianity

evan·ge·li·za·tion \-lə'zāshən, -,lī'z-\ *n* -s [LL *evangelization-, evangelizatio*, fr. *evangelizatus* (past part. of *evangelizare*) + L *-ion-, -io* -ion] : the act or process of evangelizing : the state of being evangelized

evan·ge·lize \ˌ==,līz\ *vb* -ED/-ING/-S [ME *evangelisen*, fr. LL *evangelizare*, fr. Gk *euangelizesthai, euangelizein*, fr. *euangelion* + *-izesthai, -izein* -ize] *vt* : to instruct in the gospel : to preach the gospel to : convert to Christianity ⟨~ the world⟩ ~ *vi* : to preach the gospel; *esp* : to preach in the manner of an evangelist

evan·ge·liz·er \-zə(r)\ *n* -s [ME *evangeliser*, fr. *evangelisen* + *-er*] : one that evangelizes

evangely *n* [ME *evangelie*, fr. LL *evangelium* — more at EVANGEL] *obs* : ¹EVANGEL

evan·id \ə'vanəd, ē'-\ *adj* [L *evanidus*; akin to L *evanescere* to vanish — more at VANISH] *archaic* : EVANESCENT, FAINT, ILLUSORY

ev·a·ni·idae \ˌevə'nīə,dē\ *n pl, cap* [NL, fr. *Evania*, type genus (fr. Gk *euanios* taking trouble easily, fr. *eu-* + *ania* trouble) + *-idae*] : a family of hymenopterous insects comprising the ensign flies

evan·ish \ə̇, ē+\ *vi* [ME *evanisshen*, fr. MF *esvaniss-*, stem of *esvanir* — more at VANISH] **1 :** VANISH, DISAPPEAR **2 :** to cease to be

evanishment \"+\ *n* **:** the act or process of vanishing **:** DISAPPEARANCE

ev·a·ni·tion \,evəˈnishən\ *n* -s [fr. *evanish*, after such pairs as E *abolish: abolition*] **:** EVANISHMENT

ev·ans blue \ˈevənz-\ *n, usu cap E* [after Herbert M. *Evans* *b*1882 Am. anatomist] **:** a disazo dye $C_{34}H_{24}N_6Na_4O_{14}S_4$ that is obtained as a green, bluish green, or brown powder and that on injection into the blood stream combines with serum albumin and serves as a means of determining blood volume colorimetrically

ev·ans·ite \ˈevən,zīt\ *n* -s [Brooke *Evans* †1862 Eng. nickel refiner + E *-ite*] **:** a massive basic aluminum phosphate $Al_3(PO_4)(OH)_6.6H_2O$

ev·ans'-root \ˈevənz,=\ *n* [by folk etymology fr. *avens*] **:** WATER AVENS

ev·ans·ville \ˈevənz,vil, -,vəl\ *adj, usu cap* [fr. *Evansville*, Ind.] **:** of or from the city of Evansville, Ind. **:** of the kind or style prevalent in Evansville

evap·o·ra·ble \ə̇ˈvap(ə)rəbəl, ēˈ-\ *adj* **:** capable of being evaporated

evap·o·rate \ə̇ˈvapə,rāt, ēˈ-, *usu* -ād.+V\ *vb* -ED/-ING/-S [ME *evaporaten*, fr. L *evaporatus*, past part. of *evaporare*, fr. *e-* + *vapor* steam, vapor — more at VAPOR] *vi* **1 a :** to pass off in vapor **:** escape and be dissipated either as a visible cloud or in particles that are too minute to be visible **b** (1) **:** to pass away or disappear without leaving a trace **:** pass off harmlessly ⟨the principal secret . . . *evaporated* with the advent of the Russian bomb —*Atlantic*⟩ ⟨a book so beguiling that the faintest impulse to criticize ~*s* —Dan Wickenden⟩ ⟨suddenly the anger left him and his pugnaciousness *evaporated* —Erle Stanley Gardner⟩ (2) **:** to shrink or diminish sharply or quickly ⟨the industry's stocks of scrap *evaporated*, leaving only a few days' supply in some areas —*New Internat'l Yr. Bk.*⟩ (3) **:** to grow weak **:** lose in substance, force, or value **:** DECLINE ⟨a thing of infinite beauty in the hands of a master . . . ~*s* into meaningless overrefinement in his imitators —R.A.Hall b.1911⟩ (4) **:** to take sudden leave **:** depart without leaving a trace **:** VANISH ⟨after his first wife *evaporated*, he married the girl —Hugh McGovern⟩ ⟨a foreigner, for the purpose of *evaporating*, paid in advance for the hire of a boat —Norman Douglas⟩ **2** *obs* **:** to issue forth as vapor **:** become exhaled **3 :** to give forth vapor **:** undergo evaporation — compare SUBLIME **~** *vt* **1 a :** to convert from a liquid state into vapor **:** dissipate or draw off in vapor or fumes **b :** to deposit in the form of a film (as a metal or metal salt) by sublimation of the material from a nearby solid source **c :** EXPEL ⟨~ neutrons from a nucleus⟩ ⟨~ electrons from a thermionic filament⟩ **2 :** to cause to disappear **:** do away with **:** DISSOLVE, WEAKEN, DISSIPATE ⟨the contradiction between ends and means . . . is what Marxism and like ideologies pretend to ~ —David Riesman⟩ **3 :** to expel moisture from (as by heat) leaving the solid portions **:** subject to evaporation ⟨~ apples⟩ **4** *obs* **:** to send out as if vapor **:** give vent to **:** give off (as smoke or an odor) **:** EMIT **syn** see VANISH

evaporated milk *n* **:** milk concentrated by evaporation under high pressures and temperature without the addition of sugar to one half or less of its bulk and usu. containing a specified amount of milk fat and milk solids — compare CONCENTRATED MILK, CONDENSED MILK, DRIED MILK

evaporating dish *n* **:** a shallow usu. lipped vessel often of porcelain used esp. for concentrating solutions on a small scale by evaporation of the solvent

evaporating dish

evap·o·ra·tion \ə̇,=ˈrāshən\ *n* -s [ME *evaporacioun*, fr. MF or L; MF *evaporation*, fr. L *evaporation-, evaporatio*, fr. *evaporatus* + *-ion-, -io* -ion] **1 a :** the change by which any substance is converted from a liquid state into and carried off in vapor; *specif* **:** the conversion of a liquid into vapor in order to remove it wholly or partly from a liquid of higher boiling point or from solids dissolved in or mixed with it — compare DISTILLATION 1, SUBLIMATION **b :** the process by which molecules of a heated metal or metallic compound are released to be subsequently deposited as a film on neighboring cooler surfaces **:** SUBLIMATION **c :** the expulsion of particles (as of neutrons from a nucleus or electrons from a thermionic filament) **2 :** the process of evaporating or concentrating by conversion of a part into vapor ⟨~ of syrup⟩ **3** *archaic* **:** the product or result of evaporating **:** vapor formed or a reaction effected by evaporating **4 a :** the process of passing away or off without leaving a trace **:** DISAPPEARANCE, DISSIPATION ⟨~ of the fortune took less time . . . and in the early thirties he was on his uppers —R.H.Rovere⟩ ⟨the gradual ~ of humanitarian and democratic spirit —Carl Landauer⟩ **b :** the process of passing into a weaker, less substantial, or inferior state or form **:** WEAKENING, DECLINE ⟨a danger of ~ into a vague . . . mysticism —P.E.More⟩

evaporation tank *n* **:** an experimental tank used to determine the amount of evaporation from the surface of water under measured or observed climatic and cultural conditions

evap·o·ra·tive \ə̇ˈvapə,rād·iv, ēˈ-, -p(ə)rəl, |t|, |ev *also* |əv\ *adj* [ME, fr. LL *evaporativus*, fr. L *evaporatus* + *-ivus* -ive] **:** relating to, producing, or produced by evaporation ⟨~ coating⟩ — **evap·o·ra·tive·ly** \|əvlē, -li\ *adv*

evap·o·ra·tiv·i·ty \ə̇,vap(ə)rəˈtivəd·ē, ē,v-, -vətē, -i\ *n* -ES **:** tendency to evaporate **:** rate of evaporation

evap·o·ra·tor \ə̇ˈvapə,rād·ə(r), ēˈ-, -ātə-\ *n* -s **:** one that evaporates: as **a :** a workman in charge of an evaporation process **b :** a usu. closed apparatus for driving off superfluous liquid (as in a concentration plant for sugar and syrup) or for evaporating liquid for subsequent condensation to purify it (as from salts held in solution) **c :** the part of a refrigeration system in which cooling is produced by evaporation of the liquid refrigerant **d :** a kiln for evaporating

evap·o·rim·e·ter \ə̇,vapəˈrimǝd·ə(r), ē,-\ *also* **evap·o·rom·e·ter** \-ˈräm-\ *n* [*evaporate* + *-i-* or *-o-* + *-meter*] **:** ATMOMETER

evap·o·rite \ə̇ˈvapə,rīt, ēˈ-\ *n* -s [*evaporation* + *-ite*] **:** a sedimentary rock (as gypsum or salt) that originates by evaporation of sea water in enclosed basins

evap·o·rize \ə̇ˈvapə,rīz, ēˈ-, -vap-\ *vt* [*e-* + *vaporize*] **:** VAPORIZE

evapo·transpiration \ə̇ˈva(,)pō, ēˈ-+\ *n* [*evaporation* + *transpiration*] **:** loss of water from the soil both by evaporation from the surface and by transpiration from the plants growing thereon; *also* **:** the volume of water lost in this way

eva·sé \ˈā,vaˈzā\ *adj* [F *évasé*, fr. past part. of *évaser* to widen the mouth of, flare out, fr. MF *evaser*, fr. *e-* + *vase* — more at VASE] **:** enlarging gradually — used esp. of chimneys or outlet ducts

eva·sion \ə̇ˈvāzhən, ēˈ-\ *n* -s [ME *evasioun*, fr. MF or LL; MF *evasion*, fr. LL *evasion-, evasio*, fr. L *evasus*, (past part. of *evadere* to evade) + *-ion-, -io* -ion — more at EVADE] **1 a :** physical escape or flight ⟨every abolitionist took part in a conspiracy of ~ —S.E.Morison & H.S.Commager⟩ ⟨rented a house . . . for midweek ~*s* of Paris —Janet Flanner⟩ **b :** mental escape ⟨on this basis the springs of action are cleansed without ~ into a false spirituality —A.N.Wilder⟩ **c :** means of escape ⟨war and travel have been the accredited ~ by which a member . . . may relax the pursuit of decorum without derogation of dignity —F.J.Mather⟩ **2 a :** the act or an instance of evading, dodging, or equivocating **:** failure to answer or state one's position directly or candidly ⟨it was not a case of ~, quibbling, or concealment . . . it was sheer, blank, bottomless ignorance —S.H.Adams⟩ ⟨you always come back to my point, in spite of your wrigglings and ~*s* and sophistries —G.B.Shaw⟩ **b :** the act of evading, dodging, or circumventing a law, responsibility, or obligation; *specif* **:** the act of failing to pay taxes or of minimizing taxes in violation of law ⟨opportunities for tax ~ . . . favor self-employment —R.B.Goode⟩

eva·sion·al \-zhənᵊl,-zhnəl\ *adj* **:** constituting an evasion **:** EVASIVE ⟨faces away from his obstacles and seeks his triumph through various ~ procedures —H.A.Overstreet⟩

eva·sive \-ās|iv, |ēv *also* -āz| *or* |əv\ *adj* [*evasion* + *-ive*] **1 a :** tending to evade **:** not direct, candid, or forthright **:** EQUIVOCAL ⟨his answers were brief, constrained, and ~ —T.L.Peacock⟩ ⟨if one persists in merely asking for the truth, they suspect hidden motives and become ~ —Norman Douglas⟩ **b :** avoiding confrontation **:** SHIFTY ⟨the monotonous voice, ~ eyes, and grim, tired face —Peggy Durdin⟩ **2 a :** not easily caught **:** ELUSIVE ⟨dug vigorously for the ~ prey, half fish, half eel —Anne D.Sedgwick⟩ ⟨inspiration is not forever ~ —Warren Beck⟩ **b :** directed toward avoidance of or escape from enemy fire ⟨mentioned . . . for skillful ~ tactics when . . . under attack by German night fighters —*McGill News*⟩ — used esp. in the phrase *evasive action* ⟨all pilots are taught to take ~ action should their ammunition be exhausted —Keith Ayling⟩ **c :** escaping perception or definition **:** VAGUE, NEBULOUS, ELUSIVE ⟨this menace from the north was intangible and ~ —John Buchan⟩ ⟨since she had been brought so close to reality she had had less patience with ~ idealism —Ellen Glasgow⟩

eva·sive·ly \|əvlē, -li\ *adv* **:** in an evasive manner **:** with the use of evasion ⟨answered his questions grudgingly and ~⟩

eva·sive·ness \|ivnə̇s, |ēv- *also* |əv-\ *n* -ES **:** the quality or condition of being evasive ⟨the most crushing blow of all has been the ~ of peace —T.H.Fielding⟩

¹eve \ˈēv\ *n* -s [ME, var. of *even*] **1 :** EVENING ⟨from morn to noon he fell, from noon to dewy ~ —John Milton⟩ **2 :** the evening or the day before a holiday, a saint's day, or any important day **3 :** the period immediately preceding some particular event ⟨believed that America was on the ~ of a tremendous theoretical and cultural development—J.T.Farrell⟩

²eve \"\ *n* -s *usu cap* [ME, after *Eve*, the first woman in the Bible] **:** a woman having qualities typically associated with womankind **:** WOMAN ⟨an effortlessly feminine creature whose personal career never interferes with her role as a charming, eternal *Eve* —*Newsweek*⟩

³evé *usu cap, var of* EWE

evec·tion \ə̇ˈvekshən, ēˈ-\ *n* -s [L *evection-, evectio* act of going up, fr. *evectus* (past part. of *evehere* to carry out, raise up, fr. *e-* + *vehere* to carry) + *-ion-, -io* -ion — more at WAY] **1 :** perturbation of the moon's motion in its orbit due to the attraction of the sun **2** *in certain filamentous algae* **:** displacement of the base of a new branch with respect to its parent cell so as to result in apparent dichotomy — **evec·tion·al** \-shənᵊl,-shnəl\ *adj*

eve green *n, often cap E* [²*eve*] **:** a strong to brilliant yellowish green

evejar \ˈ=,=\ *n* [¹*eve* + *jar*] **:** NIGHTJAR

eve method \ˈēv-\ *n, usu cap E* [after Frank C. *Eve*, 20th cent. Brit. physician] **:** artificial respiration by seesawing the victim head up and head down on a stretcher, the alternating pressure and release of pressure of the abdominal organs against the diaphragm promoting expiration and inspiration

¹even \ˈēvən\ *n* -s [ME *even, eve*, fr. OE *ǣfen*; akin to OFris *ēvend* evening, OS *āband*, OHG *āband*, ON *aptann* evening, and perh. to Gk *epi* on — more at EPI-] **1** *archaic* **:** EVENING **2** *archaic* **:** ¹EVE 2

²even \"\ *adj, sometimes* -ER/-EST [ME, fr. OE *efen*; akin to OFris *even* even, equal, OS *eban*, OHG *eban*, ON *jafn*, Goth *ibns*] **1 a** (1) **:** having a horizontal surface **:** not sloping **:** FLAT, LEVEL ⟨toiling up the mountain they at last came to ~ ground⟩ (2) **:** being without gross deviation from a geometrical plane ⟨pneumatic hammers . . . work across the . . . block, producing a rough but ~ surface —*Amer. Guide Series: Vt.*⟩ **b :** being without break, indentation, roughness, or other irregularity **:** SMOOTH, CONTINUOUS ⟨the coastline was always ~ and unbroken —Valter Schytt⟩ **c :** being in the same plane or line **:** LEVEL, PARALLEL — used chiefly with *with* ⟨the man came ~ with the corner —Robert Murphy⟩ ⟨houses ~ with each other⟩ ⟨that great wind had laid the tree ~ with the ground⟩ **2 a** (1) **:** being without variation or fluctuation **:** REGULAR, SMOOTH, EQUAL, STEADY, UNIFORM ⟨~ distances apart⟩ ⟨the ~ motion of the airplane⟩ ⟨the ~ beat of raindrops on the roof⟩ ⟨his straight nose and clear ~ features went well with his blondness —Louis Auchincloss⟩ (2) **:** uniform or consistent in character or quality ⟨the darkling sky was of an ~ slate color⟩ ⟨the texture of his writing is ~ and finished —*Times Lit. Supp.*⟩ (3) **:** LEVEL 5 **b :** not easily disturbed **:** SERENE, UNRUFFLED, CALM, PLACID ⟨the child . . . was naturally of an ~ temper —Samuel Butler †1902⟩ ⟨the ~ tenor of his life⟩ ⟨speaks in a thoughtful, ~ voice —Stuart Keate⟩ **3 a** *obs* **:** STRAIGHTFORWARD, PLAIN, DIRECT **b :** equal in quality, opportunity, or station ⟨they started out ~, since neither had had any playing experience⟩ **c :** giving no advantage to either side ⟨an ~ exchange⟩ ⟨the ~ balance of its interests —F.L.Paxson⟩ **:** FAIR, IMPARTIAL, JUST **d** (1) **:** leaving nothing due on either side **:** SQUARE, QUITS ⟨we shall not be ~ till you repay my visit⟩ (2) **:** fully revenged — often used in the phrase *get even with* ⟨get ~ with his tormentor⟩ **e :** being in equilibrium **:** BALANCED ⟨the scales hang ~⟩; *specif* **:** being neither loser nor gainer **:** showing neither profit nor loss ⟨the firm has to do an enormous business in order to stay ~ —Harold Koontz & Cyril O'Donnell⟩ **4 :** equal in size, number, or quantity ⟨~ shares⟩ **5 a :** being any member of a sequence of positive integers beginning with two and counting by twos **:** being always exactly divisible by 2 — opposed to *odd* **b :** having an even number as one of a series ⟨an ~ page in a book⟩ ⟨an *even*-pinnate leaf⟩ **c :** containing an even number of individuals ⟨analyzing a committee chairman's tie-breaking function . . . we see that . . . in an ~ committee he is never pivotal —L.S.Shapley & Martin Shubik⟩ **6 :** having neither more nor less than the named or understood amount, extent, or number **:** EXACT ⟨an ~ mile⟩ ⟨an ~ dollar⟩ **7 :** as likely as not **:** nicely balanced **:** FIFTY-FIFTY ⟨it is at least an ~ chance that he will prosper⟩ ⟨he stands an ~ chance of winning⟩ ⟨the chances of success or failure are ~⟩ **syn** see LEVEL, STEADY — **at even hand** *or* **at even hands** *obs* **:** on equal terms — **of even date :** of the same date — used esp. of letters and documents ⟨*of even date* with the treaty was the protocol —J.S.Reeves⟩ — **on even keel** *or* **on an even keel 1** *of a ship* **a :** having approximately the same draft forward and aft; *sometimes* **:** having the load water line of the ship parallel to the surface of the water (as in a ship whose natural draft is much greater aft than forward) **b :** without list **2** *of an aircraft* **:** in proper fore-and-aft trim **3** *usu on an even keel* **:** in a sound or stable condition **:** STABLE, STEADY, UNSHAKEN ⟨struggling to keep the firm *on an even keel* during the dismal depression years⟩ ⟨a man of character, he stayed *on an even keel* while the others panicked⟩

³even \ˈēvən *or except in sense 1b* ˈēᵛm *or* ˈēᵇm\ *adv* [ME *evene, even*, fr. OE *efne*, fr. *efen*, adj.] **1 a** *obs* **:** without disagreement **:** in accord **b** *knitting* **:** without change by increasing or decreasing — used chiefly in the phrase *work even* ⟨work ~ until armhole measures same as back armhole —*Nat'l Needlecraft Bureau*⟩ **2 a :** as well **:** PRECISELY, JUST, EXACTLY ⟨~ as you and I, children need warmth and affection⟩ ⟨some can appreciate character ~ as other men —Nora Waln⟩ **b :** to a degree that extends **:** FULLY, QUITE ⟨~ to the shedding of some natural tears —William Wordsworth⟩ ⟨to be faithful ~ unto death⟩ **c :** at the very time **:** ALREADY ⟨~ as the fish's head fell from the crocodile's munching mouth there was a swoop of white wings —Francis Birtles⟩ ⟨perhaps ~ now the time has arrived —Walt Whitman⟩ **d** *archaic* **:** to be sure **3 a :** TRULY, INDEED, NAY — used as an intensive serving to emphasize the identity or character of something ⟨we, ~ we, henceforth flaunt out masterful —Walt Whitman⟩ ⟨a huge, ~ monstrous animal⟩ **b** — used as an intensive serving to indicate an extreme, hypothetical, or unlikely case or instance of something ⟨corruption is so diffused that no one ~ protests —Gilbert Seldes⟩ ⟨refused ~ to look at her⟩ ⟨~ if help comes, it will be too late⟩ ⟨ravaged it ~ to the precious library and family Bible —*Amer. Guide Series: N.C.*⟩ **c** — used as an intensive serving to stress the comparative degree ⟨did ~ better under the new coach⟩ ⟨emeralds are ~ scarcer than rubies⟩ **4 :** in an even manner

⁴even \ˈēvən\ *vb* **evened; evened; evening** \ˈēv(ə)niŋ\ **evens** [ME *evenen*, fr. OE *efnan*, fr. *efen*, adj.] *vt* **1 a :** to make (a surface) smooth or even ⟨~ out the soil with a spade⟩ **b :** to make regular or uniform **:** free of fluctuations **:** STABILIZE — often used with *out* ⟨giant reservoirs . . . ~ out the flow of the river by controlling floods in winter and releasing water in dry periods —G.R.Clapp⟩ ⟨~ out the activities of the construction industry . . . providing a reasonable level of construction throughout the year —Beardsley Ruml⟩ **2** *archaic* **a :** to regard as being on the same level **:** treat as equal **:** COMPARE **b :** to come up to **:** MATCH, RIVAL **c :** to bring down to a certain level **3** *dial Brit* **:** ASCRIBE, IMPUTE ⟨would you ~ such a thing to him⟩ **4 :** to make even in advantage **:** make (accounts or some other reckoning) balanced **:** make quits ⟨things are ~*ed* up in this world —*Irish Digest*⟩ ⟨his mind . . . is suggestible to suspicious jealousy, and he cannot cease until he is ~*ed* with the Moor wife for wife —*College English*⟩ **~** *vi* **:** to be or become even ⟨odds have probably ~*ed* somewhat between us and the Russians in the air-atomic field —R.W.Frase⟩

even-aged \ˈ==ˈājd\ *adj, of a forest* **:** consisting of trees of a single age

even break *n* **:** an equal chance esp. for success **:** fair chance ⟨a nation that doesn't spy today is not giving its people an *even break* —E.B.White⟩

even court *n*, **:** the right half court in a singles racket game — compare ODD COURT

evendown \ˈ==ˈ=\ *adj* **1** *dial* **:** straight up and down **:** PERPENDICULAR **2** *dial* **:** OUT-AND-OUT, DOWNRIGHT, SHEER ⟨an ~ lie⟩ **3** *dial* **:** STRAIGHTFORWARD, CANDID ⟨an ~ man with an open heart⟩

even·er \ˈēv(ə)nə(r)\ *n* -s **:** one that makes even: as **a :** a pivoting bar of wood which is often reinforced with metal and at each end of which a pivoting singletree is attached **b :** any of various devices on textile machines that regulate the flow or size of material

evenfall \ˈ==,=\ *n* [¹*even* + *fall*] **:** the beginning of evening ⟨all through the quiet ~ —P.G.Wodehouse⟩

even function *n* **:** a function not changed by reversing the sign of its argument: $f(x)=f(-x)$

evenglow \ˈ==,=\ *n* [¹*even* + *glow*] **:** a reddish gray that is yellower and deeper than mist and lighter, stronger, and slightly bluer than opal gray

evenhanded \ˈ==ˈ==\ *adj* **:** FAIR, IMPARTIAL, UNBIASED ⟨~ justice⟩ ⟨~ rulings⟩ — **even·hand·ed·ly** *adv* — **even·hand·ed·ness** *n* -ES

eve·ning \ˈēvniŋ, -nēŋ *sometimes* ÷ -vən-\ *n* -s *often attrib* [ME, fr. OE *ǣfnung*, fr. *ǣfnian* to grow towards evening (fr. *ǣfen* evening) + *-ung* -ing — more at EVEN] **1 a :** the latter part and close of the day and early part of darkness or night **b** *chiefly South & Midland* **:** the time extending roughly from noon to twilight **:** AFTERNOON ⟨it was about 3 o'clock in the ~⟩ **c :** the part of the day from noon to midnight — used in the Bible **d :** the period from sunset or from the evening meal to bedtime **2 :** the latter portion **:** the period of decline ⟨in the ~ of life⟩ ⟨the ~ of his country's glory⟩ **3 a :** the period of an evening's entertainment ⟨an ~ at the theater⟩ ⟨an ~ of bridge⟩ **b :** an evening party **:** SOIREE ⟨their ~ became widely known for the distinction and wit of the people assembled —C.A.Dinsmore⟩

evening campion *or* **evening lychnis** *n* **:** WHITE CAMPION a

evening dress *n* **:** conventional dress for formal or semiformal evening social occasions: as **a :** a woman's gown with skirt usu. of floor or ankle length **b** (1) **:** men's clothing consisting of a tailcoat and matching trousers usu. in black or midnight blue, a white stiff-bosomed shirt, and white bow tie (2) **:** men's clothing consisting of a tuxedo jacket usu. in black, midnight blue, or white, a black bow tie, a stiff-bosomed or soft pleated shirt, and usu. a cummerbund — compare MORNING DRESS

evening dress b(1)

evening emerald *n* **:** PERIDOT

evening grosbeak *n* **:** a grosbeak (*Hesperiphona vespertina*) which is related to the European hawfinch, which is found in western No. America but occas. strays to eastern Canada and New England, and the male of which is chiefly olivaceous and yellow with some black and white

evening prayer *n, often cap E&P* **:** EVENSONG

evening primrose *n* **:** any of several plants of the family Onagraceae and esp. of the genus *Oenothera*; *usu* **:** a coarse biennial herb (*O. biennis*) with yellow flowers that open in the evening

evening-primrose family *n* **:** ONAGRACEAE

evening rose *n* **:** any of several nocturnal flowering plants of the family Onagraceae

eve·nings \-ŋz\ *adv* **:** in the evening repeatedly **:** on any evening ⟨he had seen and listened to them playing their guitars ~ around the quad —James Jones⟩ ⟨teen-agers and adults use the building ~ for recreation —W.A.Kinney⟩

evening school *n* **:** NIGHT SCHOOL

evening-snow \ˈ==ˈ=\ *n* **:** a small California annual herb (*Linanthus dichotomus*) with white flowers

evening star *n* **1 a :** a bright planet (as Venus) seen in the western sky after sunset **b :** any planet that rises before midnight **c :** any of the five planets that may be seen with the naked eye at sunset **2 :** a small bulbous plant (*Cooperia drummondii*) of Texas with grasslike leaves and star-shaped white flowers

evening stock *n* **:** a low-growing annual stock (*Mathiola bicornis*) with small purplish flowers

evening student *n* **:** a student at evening school

evening trumpet flower *n* **:** YELLOW JESSAMINE 2

evenk \ə̇ˈveŋk\ *n, pl* **evenk** \"\ *or* **evenks** \-ks\ *or* **even·ki** \-kē\ *usu cap* [Russ] **:** TUNGUS

even·ly \ˈēvənlē, -li\ *adv* [ME *evenliche, evenly*, fr. OE *efenlīce*, fr. *efen* even + *-līce* -ly — more at EVEN] **1 a :** in an even manner or degree **:** in equal parts ⟨a career ~ divided between stage and screen⟩ **b :** IMPARTIALLY, FAIRLY, JUSTLY ⟨she never talked about politics, but was ~ courteous to everyone —H.E.Scudder⟩ **c :** on an equal basis ⟨hoped to found a Latin-American economic bloc strong enough to bargain ~ with U.S. commercial power —*Time*⟩ **2 :** without variation or fluctuation **:** in the same manner or proportion throughout **:** SMOOTHLY, UNIFORMLY ⟨spread plaster ~⟩ ⟨run ~⟩ ⟨there is no climactic choice in the story; it moves ~ on a chain of circumstances —C.C.Walcutt⟩ **3 :** without raising the voice **:** in a flat expressionless voice **:** QUIETLY, UNEMOTIONALLY ⟨"this is a lie", she said ~ —Guy Fowler⟩ ⟨"I'll raise the bloody roof", he said ~ —Nevil Shute⟩

even money *n* **:** equal stakes in betting **:** the same amount on each side in a wager ⟨he bet him *even money*⟩ ⟨an *even money* proposition⟩ ⟨an *even money* bet⟩

even·ness \ˈēvən(n)ə̇s\ *n* -ES [ME *evennesse*, fr. OE *efennes*, fr. *efen* even + *-nes* -ness] **:** the quality or condition of being even: as **a** *archaic* **:** FAIRNESS, IMPARTIALITY **b :** balanced condition ⟨ensure the ~ of the scales of justice⟩ **c :** freedom from variation or fluctuation **:** UNIFORMITY, CONSISTENCY, REGULARITY ⟨her tone regained . . . its ~ of texture from the bottom register to the top —*Current Biog.*⟩ ⟨pronounced each syllable with great ~⟩ **d :** PLACIDITY, EQUANIMITY ⟨kindness and ~ of temper were two of his salient characteristics⟩ **e :** absence of expression esp. in speech **:** FLATNESS ⟨although deeply moved, he spoke with a strange ~⟩

even on *adv, Scot* **:** all the time **:** CONTINUOUSLY

eve·noo \,ēv(ə)ˈnü, ,āv-\ *adv, Scot* [³*even* + Sc *noo* now] **:** just now **:** in this moment

even pitch *n* **:** the pitch of a screw to be cut having the number of threads per inch a multiple or a submultiple of the number of threads per inch of the lead screw of the lathe used to cut it

¹evens *pres 3d sing of* EVEN, *pl of* EVEN

²evens \ˈēvənz\ *n pl but usu sing in constr* [²*even* + *-s*] **1** *Brit* **:** EVEN TIME ⟨a schoolboy who was repeatedly breaking ~ for 100 yards —*Sydney (Australia) Sunday Telegraph*⟩ **2** *Brit* **:** EVEN MONEY ⟨his prospects became dimmer to round thirty-two when ~ was freely offered about him —*Irish Digest*⟩

evensong \ˈ==,=\ *n, often cap* [ME, fr. OE *ǣfensang*, fr. *ǣfen* evening + *sang* song — more at EVEN, SONG] **1 :** the sixth in a system of seven canonical hours **:** VESPERS **2 :** an evening worship service in the Anglican communion related in origin to vespers and compline — called also *evening prayer*

even-span greenhouse *n* : a greenhouse in which the pitch of the roof is the same on both sides

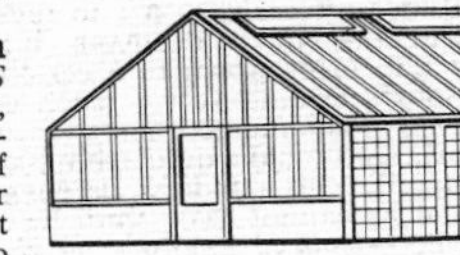
even-span greenhouse

even ste·phen *or* **even ste·ven** \ˌ==ˈstēvən\ *adj, often cap S* [fr. the name *Stephen, Steven,* used as rhyming slang] : having the same score : capable of going one way or the other : TIED, EVEN, FIFTY-FIFTY ⟨at the end of the seventh the two teams were *even Stephen,* no hits, no runs, no errors⟩ ⟨dividing up on an *even Stephen* basis—J.D.Ratcliff⟩ ⟨a few more undecided, and the race will be *even Stephen*—R.L.Neuberger⟩

event \əˈvent, ēˈ- *chiefly South sometimes* ˈē,v-\ *n* -S [MF or L; MF, fr. L *eventus,* fr. *eventus,* past part. of *evenire* to happen, fr. *e-* + *venire* to come — more at COME] **1 a** (1) : something that happens : OCCURRENCE ⟨this day's ~ has laid on me the duty of opening out my heart —William Wordsworth⟩ ⟨such an ~ would shock the conscience of the world⟩ (2) : course of events : ACTIVITY, EXPERIENCE ⟨ending my brief account of long ~ —D.C.Peattie⟩ ⟨from his dark berth he could see without moving this whole immense and immediate theater of human ~ —Thomas Wolfe⟩ — often used in pl. ⟨~*s* proved the folly of such calculations⟩ **b** : a noteworthy occurrence or happening : something worthy of remark : an unusual or significant development ⟨her new book was the intellectual ~ of the year⟩ ⟨the great ~ of his childhood was a voyage to America⟩ ⟨the flat monotonous plains stretch away . . . a single tree becomes an ~ —Alan Moorehead⟩ **2 a** *obs* : the end to which a person or thing comes : FATE **b** (1) *archaic* : the outcome or consequence of anything : ISSUE, CONCLUSION, RESULT ⟨then very doubtful was the war's ~ —Edmund Spenser⟩ ⟨curiosity as to the ~ of an evening which had raised such splendid expectations —Jane Austen⟩ (2) : the issue or outcome of a legal action or proceeding as finally determined **c** : an outcome, condition, or contingency that is assumed or postulated : CASE, EVENTUALITY — used chiefly in the phrase *in the event* ⟨in the ~ of the king's death, the prince succeeds⟩ ⟨in the ~ he has not been told, I will tell him⟩ ⟨in the ~ you are right, I have been tricked and cheated⟩ **3 a** : any one of the contests in a program of sports ⟨track and field ~*s*⟩ **b** : a competitive contest of a specified kind or class ⟨a bow shot in the same manner as in a regulation target ~⟩ **c** : FIXTURE 3a(1) **4** : an occurrence, phenomenon, or complex of processes occupying a restricted portion of four-dimensional space-time : a happening represented by a point designated by *x, y,* and *z* as coordinates of place and *t* as time in the space-time continuum, it being a fundamental assumption of the theory of relativity that all physical measurements reduce to observations of relations between happenings **syn** see EFFECT, OCCURRENCE — **at all events** *adv* : no matter what else may be : in any case ⟨*at all events,* we shall be free of his company⟩ — **in any event** *adv* : at all events : in any case : at any rate : at least : ANYHOW ⟨*in any event,* you will find him in comfortable circumstances⟩ — **in the event** *adv* : as it turns out : in the sequel : in the result ⟨vaguely he expects "something" to happen, but *in the event* hardly anything ever does —*Times Lit. Supp.*⟩ ⟨*in the event* nearly twice as many French prisoners were sent back as English —Olive Anderson⟩

event·ful \-fəl\ *adj* **1** : full of or rich in events ⟨an ~ period of history⟩ **2** : MOMENTOUS : deeply important ⟨an ~ affair that brought two countries to the verge of war⟩ — **event·ful·ly** \-fəlē, -li\ *adv* — **event·ful·ness** \-fəlnəs\ *n* -ES

eventide \ˈ==ˌ=\ *n* [ME, fr. OE *ǣfentīd,* fr. *ǣfen* evening + *tīd* time — more at EVEN, TIDE] : the time of evening : EVENING

eventide home *n, Brit* : a Salvation Army home for old people

eventilate *vt* [L *eventilatus,* past part. of *eventilare* to fan, winnow, fr. *e-* + *ventilare* to fan, winnow — more at VENTILATE] *obs* : VENTILATE — **eventilation** *n* -S *obs*

even time *n* : the running time of exactly 10 seconds for the 100-yard dash

event·less \əˈventləs, ēˈ-\ *adj* : being without event : being without incident ⟨~ weeks passed by⟩

ev·en·tog·na·thi \ˌē,venˈtägnə,thī\ *n pl, cap* [NL, irreg. fr. *eu-* + *ent-* + *-gnathi*] *in some classifications* : an order or other group of soft-finned freshwater fishes comprising the carps, suckers, and loaches — **ev·en·tog·na·thous** \ˌ==ˈ==nəthəs\ *adj*

even·tra·tion \ˌē,venˈtrāshən\ *n* -S [F *éventration,* fr. *é-* e- + *ventre* belly (fr. L *ventr-, venter*) + *-ation* — more at VENTER] : protrusion of abdominal organs through the abdominal wall — compare EVISCERATION

even·tu·al \əˈvench(ə)wəl, ēˈ-, -chəl\ *adj* [L *eventus* event + E *-al* — more at EVENT] **1 a** *obs* : relating to, consisting in, or being an event **b** *obs* : happening to exist : CHANCE, FORTUITOUS **c** *archaic* : dependent or contingent upon certain conditions : CONDITIONAL **2** : taking place, arising, or becoming something at an unspecified later time : ultimately resulting : ULTIMATE, FINAL ⟨hoped for the ~ replacement of the old buildings by others⟩ ⟨predicted the ~ decay and extinction of the monarchical system⟩ ⟨the ~ successor to the presidency⟩ **syn** see LAST

even·tu·al·i·ty \=ˌ=chəˈwalədē, -lətē, -i\ *n* -ES **1** : something that may possibly happen : CONTINGENCY, POSSIBILITY ⟨preparation for the ~ of war⟩ ⟨positions which, in certain *eventualities,* might early become the scene of military operations —*Current History*⟩ **2** : ultimate result or consequence ⟨some *eventualities* we can predict, but not the circumstances of their realization —L.J.Halle⟩

even·tu·al·ly \-ch(ə)lē, -li, -ch(ə)wəl-\ *adv* : at an unspecified later time : in the end : at last : FINALLY, ULTIMATELY ⟨that plan . . . was ~ abandoned as impracticable —Havelock Ellis⟩ ⟨~ achieved success⟩

even·tu·ate \-chə,wāt, *usu* -ād· +V\ *vi* -ED/-ING/-S [L *eventus* + E *-ate*] : to come out finally or in conclusion : come to pass : turn out : RESULT ⟨as things *eventuated* orthodoxy and revolution were not left to fight it out —F.L.Allen⟩ ⟨his illness *eventuated* in death⟩ — **even·tu·a·tion** \=ˌ==ˈwāshən\ *n* -S

¹even-up \ˈ==ˌ=\ *adj* [³*even* + *up*] : EVEN 7

²even-up \"\ *adv* : without odds or a handicap being granted by either side in a bet or competition

eveque \āˈvek\ *n* -S [F *évêque* bishop, fr. LL *episcopus* — more at BISHOP] : MADDER VIOLET

¹ev·er \ˈevə(r)\ *adv* [ME, fr. OE *ǣfre;* prob. akin to OE *ā* always — more at AYE] **1 a** : at all times : ALWAYS, CONSTANTLY, CONTINUOUSLY ⟨he is ~ making the same mistake⟩ ⟨interference in their affairs became ~ less as they became more capable of managing them —B.K.Sandwell⟩ **b** : through all time : through an indefinite time ⟨he will ~ be regarded with gratitude by his countrymen⟩ ⟨I have not seen him ~ since⟩ **c** : in each and every case : INVARIABLY ⟨war and suffering have ~ gone hand in hand⟩ **2** : at any time : on any occasion : at any period or point of time ⟨he is seldom if ~ a visitor⟩ : in any way : by any chance ⟨how could I ~ have lost it⟩ ⟨how can I ~ thank you⟩ : at all ⟨what can I ~ do to repay you⟩ **3 a** : KNOWN — used as an intensive with a superlative ⟨it was New York City and State's worst wreck ~ —*Springfield (Mass.) Union*⟩ **b** (1) — used as an intensive esp. with *so* ⟨the primary data are ~ so often not even cataloged —L.D. Reddick⟩ ⟨does an *ever*-so-cute little dance —*Time*⟩ ⟨thank you ~ so much⟩ ⟨it did him ~ so much good⟩ (2) : EXTREMELY, IMMENSELY — used as an intensive preceding and modifying an adjective after an inverted verb-subject construction ⟨boy . . . was I ~ green —Richard Bissell⟩ ⟨is he ~ proud of it⟩

²ever \"\ *adj* [by shortening] *dial* : EVERY ⟨that's what I say ~ time —Helen Eustis⟩

ever and again *or* **ever and anon** *adv* : from time to time : now and then

everbearer \ˈ==ˌ==, ˈ==ˌ==\ *n* : a plant that is everbearing

everbearing \ˌ==ˈ==\ *adj* : bearing more or less continuously ⟨an ~ strawberry⟩ — compare EVERBLOOMING

everbearing grape *n* : a slender low-growing grape (*Vitis munsoniana*) of the West Indies and the extreme southeastern U.S. that is closely related to the muscadine and ripens its fruit over a long period

everbloomer \ˌ==ˈ==, ˈ==ˌ==\ *n* : an everblooming plant

everblooming \ˌ==ˈ==\ *adj* : blooming more or less continuously throughout the growing season — opposed to *seasonal*

everblooming cherry *n* : ALL SAINTS' CHERRY

everduring \ˌ==ˈ==\ *adj, archaic* : EVERLASTING

ev·er·est \ˈev(ə)rəst, -vərst, -və,rest\ *n* -S *usu cap* [fr. Mount *Everest* in the Himalayas between Nepal and Tibet, the highest mountain in the world] : the highest point : CLIMAX, APEX ⟨has reached an *Everest* of vulgarity that may well stand as a mark —*Time*⟩ ⟨the everlasting *Everest* of all classic puns —*Holiday*⟩

ev·er·ett *also* **ev·er·ette** \ˌevəˈret\ *n* -S [origin unknown] : a man's lounging slipper having a low back and a front reaching to the instep

everett

ev·er·glades kite \ˈevə(r),glādz-\ *or* **everglade kite** \-d-\ *n, often cap E* [fr. the *Everglades,* a large tract of marshland in southern Florida] : a small bluish gray kite (*Rostrhamus sociabilis plumbeus*) ranging from So. America to Florida

¹evergreen \ˈ==ˌ=\ *adj* [¹*ever* + *green*] **1** : remaining verdant ⟨an ~ coniferous tree⟩ ⟨~ tropical plants⟩ — compare DECIDUOUS **2** : ever retaining its freshness, interest, or popularity : ever enduring : PERENNIAL, UNCEASING, PERPETUAL ⟨the plot is the ~ one —Henry Hellssen⟩ ⟨keep us in ~ remembrance of the days of old —Daniel O'Connell⟩ ⟨the . . . author of ~ romances —*Brit. Book News*⟩

²evergreen \"\ *n* **1** : an evergreen plant (as the pine, holly, ivy, laurel, rhododendron, and most tropical plants); *also* : CONIFER **2 evergreens** *pl* : twigs and branches of evergreen plants used for decoration **3 a** : ORPINE **b** : either of two club mosses (*Lycopodium clavatum* and *L. complanatum*) **c** : PIPSISSEWA **d** : CHERRY LAUREL 2 **4** : a dark green that is bluer and less strong than forest green (sense 1) and bluer than average bottle green **5** : something that ever retains its freshness, interest, or popularity ⟨a trio of jazz ~*s* —Wilder Hobson⟩

evergreen beech *n* : a tree of the genus *Nothofagus*

evergreen bittersweet *n* : an Asiatic woody vine (*Euonymus radicans vegetus*) with pinkish fruits

evergreen blueberry *n* : a shrub (*Vaccinium myrsinites*) of the southeastern U.S. with shining evergreen leaves and bluish black fruit

evergreen cherry *n* **1** : CHERRY LAUREL 2 **2** : ISLAY

evergreen grass *n* : TALL OAT GRASS

evergreen magnolia *n* **1** : a magnolia (*Magnolia grandiflora*) of the southern U.S. having evergreen foliage and large white flowers **2** : the wood of the evergreen magnolia

evergreen millet *n* : JOHNSON GRASS

evergreen oak *n* : any of various oaks with foliage that persists for two years so that the plant is more or less continuously green: as **a** : HOLM OAK **b** : COAST LIVE OAK — see LIVE OAK

evergreen thorn *n* **1** : FIRE THORN **2** : an evergreen hawthorn (*Crataegus oxyacantha*) of southeastern Europe

evergreen winterberry *n* : INKBERRY 1

evergreen wood fern *n* **1** : a No. American fern (*Dryopteris marginalis*) with evergreen fronds **2** : CHRISTMAS FERN

¹everlasting \ˌ==ˈ==\ *adj* [ME, fr. ¹*ever* + *lasting,* pres. part. of *lasten* to last — more at LAST] **1** : lasting or enduring through all time : ETERNAL ⟨what a peace is mine, leaning on the ~ arms —E.A.Hoffman⟩ ⟨belief in unchanging and ~ laws governing the physical universe⟩ **2 a** (1) : continuing indefinitely or during a long period : PERPETUAL ⟨reached the zone of ~ snow⟩ ⟨the one thing that seemed to her immutable and ~ was the poverty of the soil —Ellen Glasgow⟩ (2) *of a plant* : retaining its form or color for a long time when dried ⟨~ flowers⟩ **b** : wearisome or tedious from repetition : CONTINUAL ⟨she had grown tired of his ~ whimpering —O.E. Rölvaag⟩ **3** : wearing indefinitely : DURABLE ⟨~ cotton homespun⟩

²everlasting \"\ *n* [ME (*the*) *Everlastinge,* fr. *everlasting,* adj.] **1** *cap* : GOD — used with *the* ⟨the *Everlasting*⟩ **2** : eternal duration : ETERNITY — used chiefly in the phrase *from everlasting* ⟨from ~ thou! —S.T.Coleridge⟩ **3** *or* **everlasting flower a** : any of several plants chiefly of the family Compositae that have flowers which can be dried without loss of form or color: as (1) : LADIES' TOBACCO (2) : STRAWFLOWER 1 (3) : CUDWEED a (4) : a plant of the genus *Anaphalis* (5) : STATICE (6) *usu everlasting flower* : a plant of the Australian genus *Waitzia* **b** : the flower or bloom of any everlasting **4** : a strong durable woolen material of twill or satin weave similar to lasting

ev·er·last·ing·ly *adv* [ME, fr. *everlasting* + *-ly*] **1** : in an everlasting manner ⟨his name will be ~ remembered⟩ ⟨a bird whose plumage remains ~ green —*Publ's Mod. Lang. Assoc. of Amer.*⟩ ⟨this shoe wears ~⟩ ⟨he was ~ whining⟩ **2** : most certainly or completely : IMMEASURABLY ⟨splendidly and ~ right in his determination not to be pressured into war —*New Republic*⟩

ev·er·last·ing·ness *n* [ME *everlastingnesse,* fr. *everlasting* + *-nesse* -ness] : the quality or condition of being everlasting : ETERNITY, IMMORTALITY ⟨a belief in the ~ of our spiritual nature —W.R.Inge⟩

everlasting pea *n* : any of several perennial plants of the genus *Lathyrus* (esp. *L. latifolius*) having usu. purple flowers

everlasting thorn *n* : a fire thorn (*Pyracantha coccinea*)

ev·er·ly \ˈevə(r)lē\ *adv* [ME, fr. ¹*ever* + *-ly*] *dial* : CONTINUALLY

evermore \ˌ==ˈ=\ *adv* [ME *evermo, evermore,* fr. OE *ǣfre mā,* fr. *ǣfre* ever + *mā* more — more at EVER, MORE] **1** : during eternity : at all times : ALWAYS, FOREVER ⟨brightly beams our Father's mercy from his lighthouse ~ —P.P.Bliss⟩ **2** : at any future time : in the future : ever again ⟨means to lead a blameless life ~ —W.S.Gilbert⟩ ⟨I may not ~ acknowledge thee —Shak.⟩ **3** *dial* : CERTAINLY, DEFINITELY ⟨he can ~ ride a horse —R.P.Warren⟩

ever·nia \əˈvərnēə, ēˈ-\ *n, cap* [NL, irreg. fr. Gk *euernēs* sprouting well (fr. *eu-* + *ernos* sprout) + NL *-ia*] : a genus of lichens (family Usneaceae) having a fruticose or pendulous thallus with a cottony medulla

ever-normal granary *n* : stocks of farm products established under a governmental policy of buying and storing surpluses in order to stabilize prices and as a safeguard against crop failures

ever·si·ble \ēˈvərsəbəl, əˈ-, -rzə-\ *adj* [*eversion* + *-ible*] : capable of being everted

ever·sion \-rzhən, -rsh-\ *n* -S [ME *eversioun,* fr. MF, fr. L *eversion-, eversio,* fr. *eversus* (past part. of *evertere*) + *-ion-, -io* -ion] **1** *obs* : the act of everting : DESTRUCTION **2** : the act of turning inside out : the state of being turned inside out ⟨~ of the eyelid⟩ ⟨~ of the bladder⟩ **3** : the condition of being turned outward ⟨~ of the foot⟩

eversporting \ˌ==ˈ==\ *adj, biol* : producing sports repeatedly

evert \ēˈvərt, əˈ-\ *vt* -ED/-ING/-S [L *evertere* to turn out, overturn, overthrow, destroy, fr. *e-* + *vertere* to turn — more at WORTH] **1** : OVERTHROW, UPSET ⟨dash it all! It ~*s* my pet theory —W.H.Wright⟩ **2** : to turn outward (as the foot) or inside out

evertebrate \(ˈ)ē+\ *adj or n* [*e-* + *vertebrate*] : INVERTEBRATE

ever·tor \ēˈvərd·ə(r), əˈ-\ *n* -S [NL, irreg. fr. L *evertere* + *-or*] : a muscle that rotates a part outward

everwhich \ˌ==ˈ=\ *pron* [by alter.] *dial* : WHICHEVER

everwho \ˌ==ˈ=\ *pron* [by alter.] *dial* : WHOEVER

¹ev·ery \ˈevrē, |i *sometimes* ˈevər|\ *adj* [ME *everich, every,* fr. OE *ǣfre ǣlc,* fr. *ǣfre* ever + *ǣlc* each — more at EVER, EACH] **1 a** : being each individual or part of a class or group whether definite or indefinite in number without exception ⟨listened carefully to his ~ word⟩ ⟨~ citizen of the town was there⟩ ⟨has ~ quality needed for success⟩ **b** : being each in a series or succession of similar things ⟨out of ~ five men only two were fit⟩ **c** : being each in a succession of intervals ⟨~ few days⟩ ⟨~ little while⟩ **2** : being all taken severally **3** *archaic* : EVEN — used with *the* and a superlative ⟨~ the least iota⟩ **4** : being each and all within the range of contemplated possibilities ⟨given ~ chance⟩ ⟨~ prospect of success⟩ **5** : COMPLETE, ENTIRE ⟨have ~ confidence in him⟩ — **every now and then** *or* **every now and again** *or* **every so often** : at intervals : OCCASIONALLY, REPEATEDLY ⟨*every now and then* the public gives a great heave of boredom —Cyril Connolly⟩ ⟨dogs sailed out *every so often,* yelping and howling —Marion Hargrove⟩

²every *like* ¹EVERY\ *pron* [ME *everich, every,* fr. *everich, every,* adj.] *archaic* : EVERYONE ⟨occasions given to ~ of us —Richard Hooker⟩

every bit *adv* : in every way : QUITE ⟨the end was *every bit* as good as the beginning —Rumer Godden⟩

ev·ery·body \ˈevrē,bädē, ˈevri,bädi, ˈevrə,b- *sometimes* -(,)bəd-, *chiefly in substand or rapid speech* ˈevə(r)(,)b-\ *pron* [ME, fr. ¹*every* + *body*] **1** : every person : EVERYONE ⟨~ must do what his conscience dictates⟩ ⟨a theory arguing that ~ is motivated by self-interest⟩ **2 a** : every person forming part of a particular group ⟨there is a seat for ~ in the room⟩ — usu. referred to by the third person singular ⟨~ is bringing his own lunch⟩ but sometimes by a plural personal pronoun ⟨~ had made up their minds⟩ **b** : every person considered worthwhile (as in a particular group or in society) ⟨~ will be there⟩

¹everyday \ˈ==ˌ= *sometimes* ˌ==ˈ=\ *adj* [*every day*] **1 a** : used or occurring routinely or typically ⟨the community . . . was once entirely Gaelic speaking and still retains the lilt of it in ~ speech —*Current Biog.*⟩ ⟨the class provides training for meeting and solving ~ problems⟩ ⟨the needs of the ~ movie audience —H.G.Weinberg⟩ **b** *of clothes* : suitable or designed for wear on ordinary days as contrasted with those worn on holidays or special occasions **2** : lacking in unusual or distinctive quality or incident : PLAIN, UNVARNISHED, HOMELY, ORDINARY, COMMONPLACE, DRAB ⟨his characters speak a plain ~ speech, free of literary bombast or rhetoric⟩ ⟨wrote of ~ people who grew out of the soil, not about exceptional individuals —Willa Cather⟩ ⟨feels deeply for such ~ characters as scrubwomen —Wolcott Gibbs⟩ ⟨their life is ordinary and their story is ~ —Katharine Scherman⟩

²everyday \ˌ==ˈ=\ *n* : the typical, routine, or ordinary day : ordinary existence or routine ⟨I wore this dress — I wear it for ~ —Eudora Welty⟩ ⟨the trite and feeble language of ~ —C.S.Kilby⟩

ev·ery·day·ness \ˌ==ˈdānəs\ *n* -ES : everyday quality : COMMONPLACENESS, TYPICALITY ⟨paints the objects themselves in all their vulgar ~ —Roger Fry⟩

everyhow \ˌ==ˈ=\ *adv* [¹*every* + *how*] : in every way

¹ev·ery·man \ˈ==,man, -maa(ə)n\ *pron* [ME *every man*] : EVERYBODY

²everyman \"\ *n, pl* **everymen** *often cap* [after *Everyman,* allegorical character in *The Summoning of Everyman,* 15th cent. English morality play] : the typical or ordinary man ⟨an *Everyman,* salt of the earth, graduate of the school of hard knocks —E.B.Garside⟩

ev·ery·one \ˈ==,wən *sometimes* -ˌwən\ *pron* : EVERYBODY

everyplace \ˈ==ˌ=\ *adv* : in every place : EVERYWHERE

everything \ˈ==ˌ=\ *pron* [ME *every thing*] **1 a** : all that exists or is conceived as existing : ALL ⟨a theory that ~ can be apprehended by the human mind⟩ **b** : every thing forming part of an aggregate ⟨~ in this room belongs to me⟩ **c** : all that relates to the subject under consideration ⟨the substitute housekeeper . . . turned out to be ~ that was wrong —Helen Daringer⟩ ⟨tell the fine gentlemen at court that I know ~, and have marvelous disclosures to make —Max Peacock⟩ **2 a** : something that is most important or excellent : the sum total of all desirable or needed qualities : all that counts ⟨he said that in the theater he thought that the author was ~ —Arnold Bennett⟩ ⟨the Bible was ~ to him —L.C.Powys⟩ ⟨to the Puritan the inward relation of the soul to God is ~ —G.L. Dickinson⟩ ⟨this means ~ to me⟩ ⟨that third baseman has ~⟩ **b** : all of one's capacity or ability : the sum total of one's efforts — often used with following *have* ⟨allowed himself to be persuaded to give a solo item and put ~ he had into a piece —*Irish Digest*⟩ ⟨giving his keynote address ~ he had⟩ **3** : all sorts of other things — used with *and* to indicate the existence of related but unspecified facts or conditions ⟨there's a ticklish situation in the world, with international politics all mixed up and ~ —Sinclair Lewis⟩ ⟨people . . . are not going to shell out any more than about 35 cents for a book, especially if they are hungry and ~ —Mac Hyman⟩ — **like everything** *adv* : with maximum energy, effort, or effect ⟨he ran *like everything*⟩ ⟨it shook him up *like everything*⟩

every-way \ˌ==ˈ=\ *adv* : in every way or respect ⟨his brother is *every-way* superior in talent⟩

everywhen \ˌ==ˈ=\ *adv* : at any or all times ⟨the universal operation of Spirit manifested everywhere and ~ —J.H. Muirhead⟩

¹everywhere \ˈ==ˌ=\ *adv* [ME, fr. *every* + *where*] **1** : in every place : in all places ⟨poverty anywhere is a danger to prosperity and peace ~ —*Current History*⟩ **2** : in every part : THOROUGHLY, ALTOGETHER ⟨his own prose is ~ a vivid demonstration of disdain for brevity —S.E.Fitzgerald⟩ **3** : WHEREVER ⟨~ you go, people are much the same⟩

²everywhere \"\ *n* **1** : every place : all places ⟨~ seemed silent, but for the rattle of trains —D.H.Lawrence⟩ ⟨people came from ~ for the auction⟩ **2** : boundless space ⟨where did you come from, baby dear? out of the ~ into the here —George Macdonald †1905⟩

ev·ery·wheres \-z\ *adv* [*everywhere* + *-s*] *chiefly dial* : EVERYWHERE

every which way *adv* [prob. by folk etymology fr. ME *everich wey,* fr. *everich* every + *wey* way — more at EVERY, WAY] **1** : in every direction ⟨blasting his tanks *every which way* with direct fire —Walter Karig⟩ **2** : in a disorderly manner : IRREGULARLY ⟨big jagged boulders piled up *every which way* —*Jewelers' Circular-Keystone*⟩

¹eves *pl of* EVE

²evés *pl of* EVÉ

eve's constant \ˈēvz-\ *n, usu cap E* [after Arthur S. *Eve* †1948 Brit. physicist] : a measure of the intensity of radioactivity of a given substance consisting of the number of ions produced per second per cubic centimeter of ordinary air at a distance of one centimeter from one gram of the substance when in radioactive equilibrium

eve's needle *or* **eve's-darning-needle** \ˈēvz-\ *n, usu cap E* [after *Eve,* the first woman in the Bible] : ADAM'S NEEDLE 1

eveweed \ˈ=ˌ=\ *n* [¹*eve* + *weed;* fr. its high fragrance in the evening] : DAME'S VIOLET

evg *abbr* evening

evian water \(ˈ)āv,yäⁿ-\ *n, usu cap E* [after *Évian*-les-Bains, town in southeastern France where it is found] : a non-effervescent alkaline mineral water

evict \əˈvikt, ēˈ-\ *vt* -ED/-ING/-S [ME *evicten,* fr. LL *evictus,* past part. of *evincere,* fr. L, to vanquish, win a point in an argument, demonstrate — more at EVINCE] **1 a** : to recover (property) of or from a person by legal process or by virtue of a superior title **b** : to put out (a person) from property by legal process or by virtue of a paramount right or claim of such right : EJECT, OUST **2** : to force out : EXPEL ⟨a heavy counterattack ~*ed* the enemy from the town⟩ **3** [L *evictus*] *obs* **a** : to conquer in disputation : CONFUTE, CONVINCE **b** : to establish by proof : PROVE **syn** see EJECT

evict·ee \=ˌvikˈtē\ *n* -S [*evict* + *-ee*] : one that is evicted ⟨the ~*s* rolled up in a truck with all their furniture —*Time*⟩

evic·tion \=ˈvikshən\ *n* -S [ME, fr. LL *eviction-, evictio,* fr. *evictus* + L *-ion-, -io* -ion] **1** : the act or process of evicting or the state of being evicted **2 a** : the recovery of lands or tenements from another's possession by due course of law — compare EJECTMENT, OUSTER **b** : dispossession in virtue of a paramount title **c** : dispossession of a tenant by his landlord **3** *obs* : conclusive evidence : PROOF

evic·tor \-ktə(r)\ *n* -S [ML, fr. LL *evictus* + L *-or*] : one that evicts

¹ev·i·dence \ˈevədən(t)s *also* -dᵊn- *or* -ˌden-\ *n* -S [ME, fr. MF, fr. LL *evidentia,* fr. L *evident-, evidens* evident + *-ia* -y — more at EVIDENT] **1 a** : an outward sign : INDICATION, TOKEN ⟨~*s* of prosperity⟩ ⟨let's have an ~ of good faith⟩ **b** : something that furnishes or tends to furnish proof : means of making proof : medium of proof : PROOF, TESTIMONY ⟨on every ~ we now have —*N.Y.Times*⟩ ⟨on the ~ of many people who have seen such paintings, . . . their imagery has a very haunting quality —Herbert Read⟩; *specif* : something legally submitted to a competent tribunal as a means of ascertaining the truth of any alleged matter of fact under investigation before it — see CIRCUMSTANTIAL EVIDENCE **2** : one who bears witness; *esp* : one who voluntarily confesses a crime and testifies for the prosecution against his accomplices usu. in the expectation of lenient treatment — see KING'S EVIDENCE, STATE'S EVIDENCE **3** *archaic* : the state of being evident : CLEARNESS — **in evidence 1** : to be seen : PROMINENT, CONSPICUOUS ⟨two members of the committee were not *in evidence*⟩ ⟨he was much *in evidence* during the bitterest fighting of the war —W.H.Wright⟩ ⟨trim lawns and gardens are everywhere *in evidence* —*Amer. Guide Series: N.C.*⟩ **2** : as evidence ⟨papers submitted *in evidence*⟩

²**evidence** \"\ *vb* -ED/-ING/-S *vt* : to offer or constitute evidence of : PROVE, DISPLAY, EVINCE ⟨initiative is *evidenced* by willingness to accept responsibility —A.W.McCann⟩ ⟨certificates *evidencing* stock ownership —*U.S. Code*⟩ ⟨the friendliness she had formerly *evidenced* to the U.S. —V.G.Heiser⟩ ~ *vi*, *archaic* : to give evidence **syn** see SHOW

ev·i·den·cy \-nsē\ *n* -ES [LL *evidentia*] *archaic* : EVIDENCE

¹**ev·i·dent** \-nt\ *adj* [ME, fr. MF, fr. L *evident-*, *evidens*, fr. *e-* + *vident-*, *videns*, pres. part. of *vidēre* to see — more at WIT] **1 a** : capable of being perceived esp. by sight : distinctly visible : being in evidence : DISCERNIBLE ⟨nature in England, slow and ~ in its process, mild in its changes —Francis Hackett⟩ ⟨quaint ways are still ~ in these moneymaking times —F.H.Eliot⟩ ⟨there is no ~ impairment of the organs⟩ ⟨an ~ erasure in the manuscript⟩ ⟨a considerable amount of placer mining is still ~ —*Amer. Guide Series: Oregon*⟩ **b** : clear to the understanding : OBVIOUS, MANIFEST, APPARENT ⟨his leadership qualities soon became ~⟩ ⟨rose with the ~ intention of leaving the room⟩ — often used with impersonal *it* ⟨it is ~ that we do not understand each other⟩ **2** *obs* : CONVINCING, CONCLUSIVE

syn APPARENT, PATENT, MANIFEST, PLAIN, CLEAR, DISTINCT, OBVIOUS, PALPABLE, along with EVIDENT, are often interchangeable without much variation in meaning, implication, or suggestion; any of these words could be substituted for EVIDENT in the sentence "at this point my opponent's disregard for truth becomes *evident*". Since EVIDENT rather naturally suggests *evidence*, it may imply the existence of signs and indications that must lead to an identification or inference ⟨it is abundantly *evident* that American citizens everywhere are demanding and supporting speedy and complete action —F.D. Roosevelt⟩ APPARENT may occas. suggest a longer period of observation or reasoning ⟨as experience accumulated it gradually became *apparent* that the oils of any of the trees ... were equally efficacious —V.G.Heiser⟩ ⟨a few years ago this inconsistency became *apparent* to some —C.H.Grandgent⟩ PATENT may stress ease of sight and lack of any obscuring or concealing factor ⟨to compress and define a character or story and make it *patent* at a glance, within the narrow scope attainable by sculpture —Nathaniel Hawthorne⟩ ⟨in Roosevelt's case the imposture is less *patent;* he died before it was fully unmasked —H.L.Mencken⟩ MANIFEST may add to PATENT suggestions or very open showing or exhibiting and may suggest a shade of purposefulness while PATENT stresses only the fact of openness ⟨the *manifest* will of the king to free himself from parliamentary control estranged the Lower House —J.R.Green⟩ ⟨his May devotions were so largely attended, esp. by the young people of the parish, in whom a notable increase of piety was *manifest* —Willa Cather⟩ PLAIN may connote an ease in perception through absence of confusing adventitious matter ⟨in the unlikely event of any European at all being familiar with the "full inside story" ... it would be his *plain* duty to make his facts known to the police —*Times Lit. Supp.*⟩ CLEAR may suggest easy and assured perception with sharp definiteness and evident certainty ⟨a principle of science based on proof as sharp and *clear* as anything which is known —K.K.Darrow⟩ ⟨until our flow of supplies gives us *clear* superiority we must keep on striking our enemies —F.D.Roosevelt⟩ DISTINCT stresses sharpness of outline, delineation, or definition, and hence unmistakable impression ⟨those shapes *distinct* that yet survive insculptured on the walls of palaces —William Wordsworth⟩ OBVIOUS, often contrasted with *subtle*, stresses ease of perception or interpretation or, more strongly, inevitability of notice ⟨axioms so familiar to us that they seem *obvious* truths —Havelock Ellis⟩ ⟨new mechanical and electrical devices ... automobiles, electric refrigerators, and radios, to mention the most *obvious* examples —J.B.Conant⟩ PALPABLE, in other uses a synonym for *tangible*, may suggest the ease and inevitability of perception associated with solid masses ⟨the least provident of barbaric despots may raise a massive pile of buildings because it is the most *palpable* proof of his present wealth and power —Alfred Marshall⟩ With these words general similarity of meaning is more noteworthy than occasional differences in connotation.

²**evident** \"\ *n* -S [ME (Sc dial.), fr. *evident*, adj.] *archaic* : a thing that serves as evidence

ev·i·den·tial \ˌevəˈdenchəl\ *adj* [ML *evidentialis*, fr. LL *evidentia* evidence + *-alis* -al — more at EVIDENCE] : being, relating to, or affording evidence ⟨conducted an exhaustive examination of the scene for ~ signs of a forced entrance —W.H.Wright⟩ — **ev·i·den·tial·ly** \-ch(ə)lē, -li\ *adv*

ev·i·den·tia·ry \-ch(ə)rē, -ri\ *adj* [LL *evidentia* + E *-ary*] **1** : EVIDENTIAL **2** : determined by, concerning, or deriving its validity from the law of evidence ⟨~ fact⟩ ⟨~ technique⟩ ⟨~ value⟩

ev·i·dent·ly \ˈevədəntlē, ˈevəˌden-, ˌevəˈden-, ˈevədᵊn-, -li\ *adv* [ME, fr. *evident* + *-ly*] : in an evident manner : PERCEPTIBLY, CLEARLY, OBVIOUSLY, PLAINLY ⟨~ the most strenuous exertions must be made by all —Sir Winston Churchill⟩

ev·i·dent·ness \ˈevədəntnəs, -ˌden-\ *n* -ES : evident quality : CLEARNESS ⟨youth's fire surpasses in ~ the settled glow of the forties —Reginald Farrer⟩

¹**evil** \ˈēvəl *sometimes* -(ˌ)vil\ *adj*, *sometimes* **eviler** *or* **eviller**; **evilest** *or* **evillest** [ME *ivel, evel, evil*, fr. OE *yfel;* akin to OFris *evel* evil, OS *ubil*, OHG *ubil*, Goth *ubils* evil, and perh. to OE *ūp* up; fr. the concept that evil is beyond the limits of accepted conduct — more at UP] **1 a** : not good morally : marked by bad moral qualities : violating the rules of morality : WICKED, SINFUL ⟨fell into ~ courses⟩ ⟨never was a more ~ attitude toward life transmitted to the young —Stephen Duggan⟩ ⟨an ~ piece of work⟩ **b** : arising from actual or imputed bad character or conduct ⟨this tribe has acquired an ~ name among its neighbors⟩ ⟨a man of ~ fame⟩ **2 a** *archaic* : unsound or inferior in quality : WORTHLESS, POOR ⟨it is hard to believe this ~ tree could produce so beneficent a wine —Andrew Young⟩ **b** : causing discomfort or repulsion : UNCOMFORTABLE, OFFENSIVE, PAINFUL, FOUL ⟨a liquid with an ~ smell⟩ ⟨awoke with a start from a most realistic and ~ dream⟩ ⟨the strange fruit had an ~ taste⟩ ⟨it was an ~ trip through fever-ridden jungles —S.H.Adams⟩ ⟨forward progress halted because of ice and ~ weather —*All Hands*⟩ **c** : ANGRY, DISAGREEABLE, UNPLEASANT, WRATHFUL, MALIGNANT ⟨found him ailing and in an ~ temper⟩ ⟨cast an ~ glance at his opponent⟩ ⟨he was ever an ~ companion the morning after a drinking bout⟩ **3 a** : causing or tending to cause harm : BANEFUL, HARMFUL, PERNICIOUS ⟨the reaction of the slave system upon the southern people ... was wholly ~ —V.L.Parrington⟩ ⟨people ... remember sins committed secretly and wonder whether they have caused the ~ sequence —John Steinbeck⟩ ⟨other spots ... without the ~ concomitants of lagoon and fever-breeding vapors —Helen T. Lowe⟩ **b** : portending harm or misfortune ⟨messengers ... coming in from all sides with ~ rumors of an immediate attack —T.E.Lawrence⟩ ⟨they spit on the ground to avert the ~ omen —J.G.Frazer⟩ **c** : WRETCHED, MISERABLE, UNFORTUNATE ⟨~ weather caused a postponement⟩ ⟨~ luck was presaged by the flight of a bird past the window —*Amer. Guide Series: Ind.*⟩ ⟨the fish of ~ hap which ... had been caught and frozen fast in the transparent ice —Llewelyn Powys⟩ ⟨found himself in a most ~ plight⟩ **d** : marked or signalized by misfortune or calamity : UNLUCKY, INAUSPICIOUS ⟨the school fell upon ~ days⟩ ⟨made his friendship in an ~ hour⟩ ⟨my days have been few and ~ —Ann E. Bleecker⟩ **syn** see BAD

²**evil** \"\ *adv* [ME *ivel, evel, evil*, fr. OE *yfele, yfle*, fr. *yfel*, adj.] *archaic* : in an evil manner : BADLY

³**evil** \"\ *n* -S [ME *ivel, evel, evil*, fr. *ivel, evel, evil*, adj.] **1 a** : the fact of suffering and wickedness : the totality of undesirable, harmful, wicked acts, experiences, and things ⟨attempts to explain the origin of ~ in the world⟩ ⟨regarding ~ ... as a necessary means of realizing the good —Frank Thilly⟩ **b** : a cosmic force producing evil actions or states **c** (1) : WICKEDNESS, SIN ⟨don't make the mistake of thinking that you are dealing with a woman, ... you happen to be dealing with ~ in its most absolute form —Hamilton Basso⟩ (2) : the wicked or undesirable element or portion of anything ⟨the ~ in that man outweighs the good⟩ **d** (1) : evil actions or deeds — used chiefly with *do* ⟨lived a blameless life, doing no ~ to others, showing charity to all⟩ (2) : slanderous or malicious speech ⟨hearing and speaking no ~⟩ (3) : an evil person : one that embodies or personifies wickedness ⟨it seemed impossible that the ancient ~ was alive after all these years —Archie Binns⟩ **2 a** : something that is injurious to moral or physical happiness or welfare : MISFORTUNE, CALAMITY, DISASTER ⟨if it is an ~ to lose our liberty in a war, it is much worse to sacrifice it ourselves on the altar of fear —M.R.Cohen⟩; *esp* : something (as a condition or practice) that has harmful effects ⟨the narcotics ~⟩ ⟨the drink ~⟩ ⟨erosion of the soil on the slopes ... is one of the great ~*s* in this region —Samuel Van Valkenburg & Ellsworth Huntington⟩ ⟨struggling with the alternate ~*s* of bad seasons and bad markets —G.E.Fussell⟩ **b** : a harmful consequence : ill effect ⟨it is only necessary to remember that the deserts of No. Africa once grew wheat to realize what ~*s* can follow the maltreatment ... of the land —Henry Beresford-Peirse⟩ **3** : MALADY, DISEASE; *esp* : SCROFULA

syn ILL: EVIL is the antithesis of *good*, esp. in moral or moralistic considerations; it may indicate a quality, trait, condition, practice, cause, or desire ⟨obvious *evils:* the beggars, the terrible poverty, the prevalence of disease, the anarchy and corruption in politics —Bertrand Russell⟩ ⟨war is perhaps the greatest of all human *evils* and follies —W.R.Inge⟩ ILL now applies mainly to anything distressing, painful, fretting, or injurious that one suffers ⟨a pathetic lack of medical services, poor housing, poor schooling, and a hundred other *ills* flowing from the same source of poverty —A.E.Stevenson b. 1900⟩ ⟨the diversification of crops long advocated by agricultural economists as a cure for the *ills* of the cotton belt —*Amer. Guide Series: Ark.*⟩

⁴**evil** \"\ *n* -S [prob. fr. OE *geafol, gafol* fork — more at GAFFLE] *dial Eng* : PITCHFORK

evildoer \ˈ==(ˌ)=ˈ==\ *n* [ME *evyl doer*] : one who does evil

evildoing \ˈ==(ˌ)=ˈ==\ *n* : the act or action of doing evil ⟨the recurrent cycle of ~ —O.J.Baab⟩

evil eye *n* : the glance of a person that is believed to be capable of inflicting injury ⟨many people are reputed to ... cause harm by staring at someone with an *evil eye* —Pamela Gulliver & P.H.Gulliver⟩ ⟨contamination by *evil eye* is usually unwitting on the part of ... the causal agent —O.G.Simmons⟩; *also* : a person believed to have such power ⟨what's that *evil eye* up to —Nelson Algren⟩

evilhearted \ˈ==ˈ==\ *adj* : having an evil heart

evil·ly \ˈēvəl(l)ē, -)i *sometimes* -(ˌ)vil-\ *adv* : in an evil manner : WICKEDLY, BADLY ⟨grinning ~ down upon him —Farley Mowat⟩ ⟨the world was an evil place, ... and it had treated him ~ —Max Peacock⟩

evil-minded \ˈ==ˈ==\ *adj* : having an evil disposition or evil intentions : disposed to mischief or sin : MALICIOUS; *also* : tending to interpret words or sayings in a dirty sense — **evil-mind·ed·ly** *adv* — **evil-mind·ed·ness** *n* -ES

evil·ness *n* -ES [ME *ivelnes, evelnes, evilnes*, fr. OE *yfelnes*, fr. *yfel* evil + *-nes* -ness — more at EVIL] : the quality of being evil : BADNESS

evince \əˈvin(t)s, ēˈ-\ *vt* -ED/-ING/-S [L *evincere* to vanquish, win a point in an argument, demonstrate, fr. *e-* + *vincere* to conquer — more at VICTOR] **1** *obs* : CONQUER, SUBDUE **2** *obs* : CONVINCE, CONFUTE **3 a** : to constitute evidence of : PROVE, CONFIRM ⟨the congestion, poverty, and lack of ambition *evinced* by these poor houses on the part of the working people —Samuel Van Valkenburg & Ellsworth Huntington⟩ **b** : to display clearly : EXHIBIT, MANIFEST, REVEAL, EXPRESS ⟨his musical talent *evinced* itself at an early age⟩ ⟨*evinced* the greatest disregard for the feelings of others⟩ **4** : to call forth : OCCASION, PROVOKE ⟨he could ~ no response from his stolid taciturn companion⟩ **syn** see SHOW

evinc·ible \-səbəl\ *adj* : capable of being proved or evinced : DEMONSTRABLE

evin·cive \-siv\ *adj* : tending to prove : DEMONSTRATIVE

Ev·i·pal \ˈevəˌpal, -pȯl\ *trademark* — used for hexobarbital

ev·i·rate \ˈevəˌrāt, ēˈvī-\ *vt* -ED/-ING/-S *archaic* [L *eviratus*, past part. of *evirare*, fr. *e-* + *vir* man — more at VIRILE] : CASTRATE, EMASCULATE

evis·cer·ate \əˈvisəˌrāt, ēˈ-, *usu* -ād.+V\ *vb* -ED/-ING/-S [L *evisceratus*, past part. of *eviscerare*, fr. *e-* + *viscera* — more at VISCERA] *vt* **1 a** : to take out the entrails of : DISEMBOWEL, GUT ⟨~ a turkey⟩ **b** : to deprive of essential or vital content or force : weaken decisively : DEVITALIZE ⟨recklessly ~*s* the ground forces in favor of ... long-range bombers —Walter Millis⟩ ⟨the book is *eviscerated* and left a mere story for boys —Montgomery Belgion⟩ **2** : to remove an organ from (a patient) or the contents of (an organ) ~ *vi* **1** *of a part* : to protrude through a surgical incision **2** *of a patient* : to suffer protrusion of a part through an incision

evis·cer·a·tion \=ˌ==ˈrāshən\ *n* -S [ML *evisceration-*, *evisceratio*, fr. L *evisceratus* + *-ion-*, *-io* -ion] **1** : the act or process of eviscerating **2 a** : protrusion of viscera through the body wall esp. through a surgical incision **b** : removal of an organ or of the contents of an organ

evis·cer·a·tor \=ˈ==ˌrād.ə(r), -ātə-\ *n* -S : one that eviscerates; *specif* : a worker who eviscerates animal carcasses (as poultry or fish)

ev·i·ta·ble \ˈevəd.əbəl, ˈev(ə)təb-\ *adj* [L *evitabilis*, fr. *evitare* to avoid + *-abilis* -able] : AVOIDABLE ⟨even nonhistorical events are ~ —Sidney Hook⟩

evite \əˈvīt, ēˈ-, -vēt\ *vt* -ED/-ING/-S [MF or L; MF *eviter*, fr. L *evitare*, fr. *e-* + *vitare* to shun] *archaic* : SHUN, AVOID ⟨I have *evited* striking you ... under muckle provocation —Sir Walter Scott⟩

eviternal *adj* [L *aeviternus* eternal + E *-al* — more at ETERNAL] *obs* : ETERNAL, EVERLASTING

ev·i·ter·ni·ty \ˌevəˈtərnəd.ē\ *n* -ES : EVERLASTINGNESS

evittate \(ˈ)ē+\ *adj* [*e-* + *vittate*] : destitute of oil tubes — used of the fruit of certain plants; compare VITTA

evng *abbr* evening

ev·o·ca·ble \ˈevəkəbəl, əˈvōk-, ēˈvōk-\ *adj* [F *évocable*, fr. *évoquer* to evoke + *-able* — more at EVOKE] : capable of being evoked

evo·cate \ˈē(ˌ)vōˌkāt, ˈevə-, ˈevō-\ *vt* -ED/-ING/-S [L *evocatus*, past part. of *evocare* — more at EVOKE] *archaic* : EVOKE

evo·ca·tion \ˌē(ˌ)vōˈkāshən, ˌevəˈ-, ˌevōˈ-\ *n* -S [L *evocation-*, *evocatio*, fr. *evocatus* + *-ion-*, *-io* -ion] **1** : the act or fact of evoking or calling forth, out, or up : SUMMONING, CITATION ⟨the most conspicuous result of these four laws was the ~ of protests from many states —W.C.Ford⟩ ⟨both amazed and amused by this ~ of the old Hebrew principle —C.G.Bowers⟩: as **a** : the summoning of a spirit by incantation; *also* : the ritual used in such incantation : SPELL ⟨emotion is an ~ and in ways beyond the senses alters events—creating good and evil luck —W.B.Yeats⟩ **b** : the calling upon a deity for assistance : INVOCATION ⟨there are no prayers, only continuous ~*s* —Negley Farson⟩ **c** *obs* : the summoning of a case from an inferior court by a superior court (as on appeal) **2** : the act or an instance of artistic imaginative re-creation or portrayal (as of a mood, time, place, or personality) esp. in such a manner as to produce a compelling impression of reality or authenticity ⟨a garrulous, gossipy, and engaging ~ of a vanished age —W.H.Hale⟩ ⟨an ~ of the locomotive in musical terms —*Newsweek*⟩ ⟨not so in his most deeply felt portraits, as in that heroic and pathetic ~ of himself in old age —F.J.Mather⟩ ⟨terse and vivid, precise and realistic in its ~ of disagreeable detail —*Amer. Guide Series: Ind.*⟩ ⟨excellent powers of description and ~ —Alexander Klein⟩ **3** *embryol* : INDUCTION 4f; *specif* : initiation of development of a primary embryonic axis — contrasted with *individuation*

evoc·a·tive \əˈväkəd.iv, ēˈ-, -kətiv\ *adj* [LL *evocativus*, fr. L *evocatus* + *-ivus* -ive] **1** : serving or tending to evoke or call forth something ⟨a preface ~ ... of interest —*Times Lit. Supp.*⟩ ⟨the function of alcoholic overindulgence on some individuals ... is not ... ~ of socially or personally disapproved behavior —R.M.Lindner⟩ **2 a** : tending to evoke an emotional response : charged with emotion as well as meaning ⟨the ideas of Thomas Jefferson will always be ~ ... read or heard they inspire and arouse any audience —W.S.Lynch⟩ ⟨spheres of discourse ... rich in ~ or emotive overtones —F.W.Leakey⟩ **b** (1) : tending by artistic imaginative means to re-create (as a mood, time, place, or personality) esp. in such a manner as to produce a compelling impression of reality ⟨superbly ~ account, rooted in fact but crowned with imagination —E.M.Lustgarten⟩ ⟨one of his book's most ~ passages ... describes the effect of this lotus land on the American soldiers —*Time*⟩ ⟨a war novel ... powerful and terse, with ~, minute details of war —Richard Plant⟩ (2) : tending to inspire or evoke vivid memories, recollections, or associations ⟨the old photographs are charmingly ~ —Lee Rogow⟩ ⟨described and illustrated the apples of England: their ~ names, subtle flavors, and the season of highest quality for each —Herbert & Mary Miles⟩

evoc·a·tive·ly *adv* : in an evocative manner

evoc·a·tive·ness *n* -ES : evocative quality ⟨the enormous ~ of the picture and its curious feeling of timelessness —R.M. Coates⟩

evo·ca·tor \ˈē(ˌ)vōˌkād.ə(r), ˈevə-, ˈevō-\ *n* -S [L, fr. *evocatus* + *-or*] : one that evokes; *esp* : the specific chemical constituent responsible for the physiological effects of an inductor or organizer

evoc·a·to·ry \əˈväkəˌtōrē\ *adj* [LL *evocatorius*, fr. L *evocatus* + *-orius* -ory] : EVOCATIVE

evo·dia \əˈvōdēə, ēˈ-\ *n*, *cap* [NL, irreg. fr. Gk *euōdia* fragrance, fr. *euōdēs* fragrant (fr. *eu-* + *-ōdēs*, fr. *ozein* to smell) + *-ia* -y — more at ODOR] : a genus of Asiatic and Australasian shrubs and trees (family Rutaceae) having opposite aromatic leaves, unisexual flowers, and dry fruits

evoke \əˈvōk, ēˈ-\ *vt* -ED/-ING/-S [F *évoquer*, fr. L *evocare*, fr. *e-* + *vocare* to call — more at VOCATION] **1 a** : to call forth or up (a spirit or other supernatural being) : SUMMON ⟨the people avoid mentioning the names of the gods, because ... to name them is to ~ them —J.G.Frazer⟩ ⟨controls his demons largely through ritual which can both ~ and propitiate them —Francis Huxley⟩ **b** : to cite esp. with approval or for support : INVOKE ⟨a list of qualities which men in more religious days *evoked* with familiar approval, but some of which have grown pale —C.W.deKiewiet⟩ ⟨the name of Socrates is not one that would ordinarily be *evoked* by a defender of artists —*Times Lit. Supp.*⟩ **2 a** : to call forth (a response) : ELICIT ⟨his action *evoked* official displeasure⟩ ⟨that remark *evoked* nothing, not even curiosity —Clarissa F. Cushman⟩ **b** : to call into being : cause to arise ⟨these exigencies *evoked* a university in Bologna, Paris, and Oxford —H.O.Taylor⟩ ⟨advertising created modern American radio ..., *evoked* the modern slick periodical —D.M.Potter⟩ **c** : to call up (memories, recollections, associations) ⟨the place ~*s* memories of happier years⟩ ⟨all of them *evoking* historical and literary associations of worldwide fame —Sam Pollock⟩ **3** : to re-create, depict, or suggest by artistic imaginative means esp. in such a manner as to produce a compelling impression of reality : bring to life ⟨the opening chapters of the book, although they contain very few descriptive passages, ~ the place marvelously —Basil Taylor⟩ ⟨the sights, the sounds, the smells of Spain are *evoked* with a vividness that has a physical impact —Harriet de Onís⟩ ⟨to ~ Lincoln the man in marble and bronze was not an easy task for any sculptor —R.P. Basler⟩ **syn** see EDUCE

¹**evo·lute** \ˈevəˌlüt *also* ˈēv- *or* -vəlˌyüt\ *n* -S [L *evolutus*, past part. of *evolvere* to unroll, unfold — more at EVOLVE] **1** *math* : the locus of the center of curvature or the envelope of the normals of another curve — compare INVOLUTE **2** : a curving wavelike scroll used decoratively on friezes and moldings

²**evolute** \"\ *adj* [L *evolutus*, past part.] *bot* : turned back : UNFOLDED

³**evolute** \"\ *vb* -ED/-ING/-S [back-formation fr. *evolution*] : EVOLVE, DEVELOP ⟨if we ever ~ into a really satisfactory political and economic life, we won't like it —*Scribner's*⟩

evo·lu·tion \ˌevəˈlüshən *also* ˌēv- *or* -vəlˈyü-\ *n* -S [L *evolution-*, *evolutio* act of unrolling, fr. *evolutus* + *-ion-*, *-io* -ion] **1 a** : a series of related changes in a certain direction : process of change : organic development : UNFOLDING, MOVEMENT, TRANSFORMATION ⟨the ~ of his hair has been from brown to gray, to bald —*Current Biog.*⟩ ⟨the ~ of a complicated plot⟩ ⟨it should be remembered that even in the biological world, ~ is not always in the direction of progress —A.B.Novikoff⟩ ⟨the ~ of the seasons⟩ ⟨there has been much discussion as to ... the possible ~ of benign adenomas into invasive carcinoma —*Jour. Amer. Med. Assoc.*⟩ **b** (1) : a process of continuous change from a lower, simpler, or worse condition to a higher, more complex, or better state : progressive development : GROWTH, PROGRESS ⟨the ~ of the capitalist forms of business organization, from primitive units to the modern corporation —W.C.Scoville⟩ ⟨the ~ from childhood to manhood⟩ ⟨the ~ of physics from Galileo to Einstein⟩ ⟨the ~ of the rifle⟩ (2) : a process of gradual and relatively peaceful social, political, and economic advance or amelioration — often contrasted with *revolution* ⟨a British pattern of change by ~ ... which contrasts with less attractive changes by revolution in other countries —*Current History*⟩ **c** : the end product of an evolutionary process : something that is evolved ⟨economically it is an ~ of the ancient system of barter —*Encyc. Americana*⟩ ⟨the style of the King James version ... is ... an ~ ..., the resultant of a long selective process —J.L.Lowes⟩ **2** : one of a set of prescribed movements or motions (as those of a skater, dancer, a body of troops, a fleet, or other formation) : any movement designed to effect a new arrangement by passing from one position to another : MANEUVER ⟨~*s* of the eight pink bridesmaids and the eight black ushers —Edith Wharton⟩ **3** : the process of working out or developing (as an idea, design, or theme) ⟨the greatest task facing agricultural scientists in this region is the ~ of an adaptable farming system —*Farmer's Weekly* (*So. Africa*)⟩ **4** *math* : the extraction of roots — opposed to *involution* **5 a** (1) *archaic* : the development of an organism by gradual unfolding of parts (as in the growth of a plant from a seed) (2) : the presumed process of development in which a germ containing the adult parts in miniature was stimulated to differentiate by the action of fertilization — opposed to *epigenesis;* compare ENCASEMENT **b** : the development of a race, species, or other group : PHYLOGENY : the process by which through a series of changes or steps any living organism or group of organisms has acquired the morphological and physiological characters which distinguish it : the theory that the various types of animals and plants have their origin in other preexisting types, the distinguishable differences being due to modifications in successive generations — compare DARWINISM, HEREDITY, MUTATION, NATURAL SELECTION, VARIATION, WEISMANNISM **6 a** : the progressive development of civilization and social institutions in a fixed sequence of stages — called also *unilinear evolution;* see EVOLUTIONISM **b** : a process of cultural change determined esp. by technological factors and marked by a movement from simplicity to complexity and the gradual increase of man's control over his environment **7 a** : the process of the whole universe conceived as a progression of interrelated phenomena **b** : the theory of such progression — compare EMERGENT EVOLUTION, SPENCERIANISM

evo·lu·tion·al \ˌ==ˈlüshənᵊl, -shnəl *also* -vəlˈyü-\ *adj* : EVOLUTIONARY — **evo·lu·tion·al·ly** \-ᵊlē, -əl, |i\ *adv*

evo·lu·tion·ar·i·ly \ˌ==ˌshəˈnerəlē, -li\ *adv* : in an evolutionary way : from the evolutionary point of view ⟨moved ~ some way apart —*Biol. Symposia*⟩

¹**evo·lu·tion·ary** \ˌ==ˈ==shəˌnerē, -ri\ *adj* [*evolution* + *-ary*] : of, relating to, or produced by evolution

²**evolutionary** \"\ *n* -ES : EVOLUTIONIST

evo·lu·tion·ism \ˌ==ˈ==shəˌnizəm\ *n* -S **1** : a theory of evolution (as in philosophy, biology, or sociology) — see DARWINISM **2** : adherence to or belief in evolution esp. of living beings

¹**evo·lu·tion·ist** \ˌevəˈlüsh(ə)nəst, -vəlˈyü-\ *n* -S [*evolution* + *-ist*] : a student of or adherent to a theory of evolution

²**evo·lu·tion·ist** \ˌ==ˈ==(=)=\ *or* **evo·lu·tion·is·tic** \ˌ=ˌ=ˌlüshəˈnistik, -tēk *also* -vəlˌyü-\ *adj* : of or relating to evolution or evolutionists — **evo·lu·tion·is·ti·cal·ly** \-tək(ə)lē, -tēk-, -li\ *adv*

evo·lu·tive \ˌevəˈlüd.iv, -vəlˈyü-\ *adj* [*evolution* + *-ive*] : of, relating to, or promoting evolution or development ⟨~ conditions⟩

evolv·able *pronunc at* EVOLVE +əbəl\ *adj* **:** capable of being evolved

evolve \ə'välv, ē'-, -'vȯlv *also* -'vä(ů)v *or* -'vȯv\ *vb* -ED/-ING/-S [L *evolvere* to unroll, unfold, fr. *e-* + *volvere* to roll — more at VOLUBLE] *vt* **1** *archaic* **a :** UNFOLD, UNROLL **b :** to disclose by degrees to view **:** DISENTANGLE **2 :** to give off **:** EMIT ⟨natural cheese, during the course of its aging, ~s carbon dioxide —*Modern Packaging*⟩ **3 a :** DERIVE, EDUCE ⟨from these premises he *evolved* a startling new set of philosophic axioms⟩ ⟨out of their writings . . . Hitler and his disciples *evolved* the racial myth —Raoul de R. de Sales⟩ **b :** to work out or develop esp. by experience, experimentation, or intensive care or effort ⟨*evolved* . . . a fresh and personal approach to residential design —*Amer. Guide Series: N.Y.*⟩ ⟨I lay awake for an hour or so *evolving* a plan —Irving Stone⟩ ⟨~ a solution for the problem⟩ ⟨independently *evolved* a lamp based upon this principle —S.F.Mason⟩ ⟨*evolved* a new and improved variety of this plant⟩ **c :** to develop or produce by natural evolutionary processes ⟨the Protozoa . . . *evolved* the types that were transitional to higher animals —R.W. Miner⟩ **~** *vi* **:** to develop by or as if by evolution **:** undergo evolutionary change ⟨hygiene . . . has *evolved* into preventive medicine —Victor Robinson⟩ ⟨show . . . that life has *evolved* according to a Creator's plan—J.P.Marquand⟩ **syn** see UNFOLD

evolve·ment \-mənt\ *n* -s **:** the act or process of evolving **:** the state of being evolved

[1]**evon·y·mus** \ə'vänəməs, e'-,ē'-\ [NL, fr. L *euonymos* spindle tree — more at EUONYMUS] *syn of* EUONYMUS

[2]**evonymus** \"\ *n* -ES **:** EUONYMUS 2

evot·o·mys \ə'väd·əməs, e'-,ē-, -vōd-·\ [NL, irreg. fr. *eu-* + *ot-* + *-mys*] *syn of* CLETHRIONOMYS

evul·gate \ə'vəl,gāt, ē'-\ *vt* -ED/-ING/-S [L *evulgatus*, past part. of *evulgare*, fr. *e-* + *vulgare* to spread abroad, publish, divulge, fr. *vulgus* multitude — more at VULGAR] *archaic* **:** PUBLISH, DIVULGE — **evul·ga·tion** \,ē,vəl'gāshən\ *n* -s

evulse \ə'vəls, ē'- *also* -lts\ *vt* -ED/-ING/-S [L *evulsus*, past part. of *evellere*, fr. *e-* + *vellere* to pluck — more at VULNERABLE] **:** to extract forcibly **:** pluck out or root out ⟨~ a tooth⟩

evul·sion \-lshən\ *n* -s [L *evulsion-*, *evulsio*, fr. *evulsus* + *-ion-*, *-io* -ion] **:** the act of plucking out **:** a rooting or casting out

ev·zone \'ev,zōn\ *n* -s [NGk *euzōnos*, fr. Gk *euzōnos* active, lit., well girt, fr. *eu-* + *zōnē* girdle — more at ZONE] **:** a member of a select infantry corps in the Greek army

EW *abbr* enlisted woman

[1]**ewe** \'yü, *esp among farm dwellers* 'yō\ *n* -s [ME, fr. OE *ēowu*; akin to OHG *ou*, *ouwi* ewe, ON *ær* ewe, Goth *awethi* flock of sheep, L *ovis* sheep, Gk *ois*, Skt *avi*] **:** the female of the sheep esp. when mature; *also* **:** the female of various related animals (as goats or the smaller antelopes)

[2]**ewe** *also* **evé** \'ā,wā, 'ā,vā\ *n, pl* **ewe** *or* **ewes** *also* **evé** *or* **evés** *usu cap* **1 a :** a Negro people of Ghana and Togo and border regions of Dahomey **b :** a member of such people **2 :** a Kwa language of the Ewe people

ewe hogg *or* **ewe hogget** *also* **ewe hog** *n, chiefly Brit* **:** a young female sheep usu. between weaning and first shearing

ewe lamb *n* **:** a young usu. unweaned female sheep

ewelease \'₌,₌\ *n, dial Eng* **:** a sheep pasture

ewe-neck \'₌,₌\ *n* **:** a thin sheeplike neck having an insufficient, faulty, or concave arch and occurring as a defect in certain dogs and horses — **ewe-necked** \'₌,₌\ *adj*

[1]**ew·er** \'yüə(r), -ü(ə)r,-üə\ *n* -s [ME, fr. AF, fr. OF *evier*, fr. (assumed) VL *aquarium*, fr. neut. of L *aquarius* of water, fr. *aqua* water + *-arius* -ary — more at ISLAND] **:** a usu. vase-shaped pitcher or jug with a handle and often a spout for ease of pouring

ewer

[2]**ewer** \"\ *n* -s [prob. of Scand origin; akin to OSw *iūwer*, *iūger* udder, ON *jūgr* — more at UDDER] *dial Eng* **:** UDDER

ew·ery \-ərē\ *n* -ES [ME *ewerie*, fr. AF, fr. *ewer* + *-ie* -y] **:** a room for ewers, table linen, and towels (as in a royal palace)

ew·est \'yüəst\ *adj* [ME (Sc dial.), alter. (resulting from incorrect division) of *anewest*, fr. OE *on nēawiste* in the neighborhood] *Scot* **:** NEAREST, NEXT

ew·ing's sarcoma *also* **ewing's tumor** \'yüiŋz-, -üēŋz-\ *n, usu cap E* [after James Ewing †1943 Am. pathologist] **:** a tumor of bone that invades the shaft of a long bone, tends to recur, but rarely metastasizes

[1]**ex** \'eks\ *n* -ES [*ex-*] **:** one that formerly held a specified position or place; *esp* **:** a former spouse ⟨took my ~ and the children to dinner⟩

[2]**ex** \(ˌ)eks\ *prep* [L] **1 :** out of **:** FROM ⟨sturdy plants ~ 3-inch pots⟩: as **a :** from a specified place or source — used chiefly in commerce ⟨the goods will be supplied ~ stock or ~ factory at the option of the buyer⟩ **b** — a function word used by breeders to identify the dam of an animal ⟨a promising calf by Eric XVI ~ Heatherbell⟩ **2 :** free from **:** WITHOUT: as **a :** without an indicated value or right (as a dividend declared, interest accrued, or a preferential right to purchase shares) — used esp. of securities ⟨was willing to buy the shares ~ rights⟩ **b :** free of charges precedent to removal from the specified place, purchaser to provide means of subsequent transportation ⟨~ dock⟩ ⟨~ warehouse⟩ — used also attributively with a hyphen between *ex* and the noun

[3]**ex** \'eks\ *n* -ES **:** the letter *x*

[4]**ex** \"\ *n* -ES [alter. of E dial. *ax*, fr. OE *eax* axis, axle — more at AXIS] *dial* **:** AXLE

[5]**ex** \"\ *n* -ES [by shortening] **1 :** EXPENSE **2 :** EXAMINATION

[1]**ex-** *variants not shown in the pronunciations of "ex-" words below are* ə *or* ē *for the "e" when the prefix is unstressed and esp when a stressed syllable immediately precedes without pause, and* ks *for the "x" in words in which only* gz *is shown, as "exact"*\ *or* **ef-** *prefix* [ME, fr. OF & L; OF, fr. L (also, perfective and intensive prefix), fr. *ex* out of, from; akin to Gk *ex* out of, from, OIr *ess-*, OSlav *iz*, *izŭ*, *is*] **1 :** out of **:** away from **:** outside of ⟨*ex*circle⟩ ⟨*ex*clave⟩ **2 :** without **:** lacking ⟨*ex*alate⟩ ⟨*ex*albuminous⟩ **3** \(ˌ)eks\ [ME *ex-*, fr. LL, fr. L] **:** out of (the office or condition named by the main word) **:** former **:** sometime — usu. joined to second element by a hyphen ⟨*ex*-president⟩ ⟨*ex*-convict⟩; often with phrases ⟨*ex*-child actor⟩ ⟨*ex*-man-about-town⟩; usu. *ef-* in senses 1 & 2 before *f* ⟨*ef*form⟩ ⟨*ef*fuse⟩; always *ex-* in sense 3

[2]**ex-** — see EXO-

ex *abbr* **1** examined **2** example **3** exception **4** exchange **5** excluding **6** excursion **7** executed; executive **8** exempt **9** exercise **10** exhibit **11** export **12** express **13** extra **14** extract **15** extremely

ex·ac·er·bate \ig'z|asə(r),bāt, eg'z|, ek's|, |aas-, *usu* -ād·+V\ *vb* -ED/-ING/-S [L *exacerbatus*, past part. of *exacerbare*, fr. *ex-* [1]ex- + *acerbus* harsh, bitter, unpleasant, fr. *acer* sharp — more at EDGE] *vt* **1 :** to make more violent or bitter **:** intensify the bad qualities of ⟨foolish words *exacerbating* a quarrel⟩ ⟨all the frictions that *exacerbated* the long-drawn-out negotiations —Howard Taubman⟩ **2 :** to cause (a disease or its symptoms) to become more severe ⟨her condition was *exacerbated* by lack of care⟩ **~** *vi* **:** to cause exacerbation ⟨what charms and consoles in the private house may distract and ~ in the public office —Virginia Woolf⟩ — used chiefly as a participial adjective ⟨*exacerbating* factors in modern life⟩

syn EXACERBATE, EMBITTER, *and* SOUR can mean in common to cause to become, or become increasingly, severe or bitter. EXACERBATE stresses intensification in harshness or grievousness or an increase in virulence or violence, as of pain, disease, or hatred ⟨the injuries to his pride, *exacerbated* by her desertion of him —Edith Sitwell⟩ ⟨their prejudices have not been unduly *exacerbated* —Cabell Phillips⟩ ⟨the reduction of diseases may merely *exacerbate* the world's poverty and hunger by increasing the number of people —Eric Larrabee⟩ ⟨they may *exacerbate* rather than cure that unnatural craving for excess and novel thrills —J.D.Adams⟩ EMBITTER implies the making of an experience (esp. a normally pleasant experience) unpleasant or of an unpleasant experience increasingly hard to endure or of a person bitter or resentful ⟨the remoter outcome of the case was that competition was *embittered* rather than allayed —*Times Lit. Supp.*⟩ ⟨his last years were *embittered* by disputes among his sons —*Encyc. Americana*⟩ ⟨violence . . . *embittered* the fight between capitalism and socialism —Stringfellow Barr⟩ ⟨the irresponsibility of privilege that *embitters* even men of goodwill —*Time*⟩ SOUR implies a making or a becoming acidulous, hostile, resentful, peevish, or cynical ⟨his heart was *soured* in his weary old hide, and his hopes had curdled in his breast —Amy Lowell⟩ ⟨they were almost truculent, as if they had been *soured* by heavy and unwelcome duties —John Buchan⟩ ⟨the anxiousness of some might *sour* to enmity under the acerbity of his attack —H.O.Taylor⟩ ⟨the condition of the city government *soured* most of the thinking citizens⟩

ex·ac·er·bat·ing·ly *adv* **:** in an exacerbating manner **:** so as to cause exacerbation

ex·ac·er·ba·tion \ig,₌₌'bāshən, (,)eg-, (,)ek-\ *n* -s [ME *exacerbacioun*, fr. LL *exacerbation-*, *exacerbatio*, fr. L *exacerbatus* + *-ion-*, *-io* -ion] **:** the act of exacerbating or state of being exacerbated

[1]**ex·act** \ig'zakt, eg-\ *vb* -ED/-ING/-S [ME *exacten*, fr. L *exactus*, past part. of *exigere* to drive out, demand, exact (payment), weigh, measure, fr. *ex-* [1]ex- + *-igere* (fr. *agere* to drive, lead, act, do) — more at AGENT] *vt* **1 :** to demand and force or compel (payment, surrender, concession, performance, compliance) **:** WRING, EXTORT, WREST ⟨from them has been ~*ed* the ultimate sacrifice —D.D.Eisenhower⟩ ⟨qualms which ~*ed* rites of expiation —John Dewey⟩ **2 :** to require despite difficulty or reluctance **:** call for as necessary, appropriate, or desirable ⟨a task so delicate ~s the scholar and philosopher —B.N.Cardozo⟩ **3** *archaic* **:** to draw (as a meaning) out **:** EXTRACT **~** *vi, obs* **:** to practice exaction **syn** see DEMAND

[2]**exact** \"\ *adj, often* -ER/-EST [L *exactus*, fr. past part. of *exigere*] **1 :** exhibiting or characterized by strict, particular, and complete accordance with fact, truth, or an established standard or original **:** devoid of any addition, subtraction, or other variation from fact or a standard ⟨the ~ time⟩ ⟨not only is ~ description difficult —Aldous Huxley⟩ ⟨an ~ account of the quarrel⟩ ⟨extremely ~ in conduct⟩ **2 :** characterized or marked by thorough consideration or minute measurement of small factual details usu. leading to incontestably true conclusions **:** not incomplete or approximate ⟨a power of intuition greater than that of an ~ investigator —Havelock Ellis ⟨the ~ measurements of physical science⟩ **syn** see CORRECT

ex·act·able \-təbəl\ *adj* **:** that may be exacted ⟨there is a limit to the interest lawfully ~⟩

exact differential *n* **:** a differential expression of the form $X_1dx_1 + \ldots + X_ndx_n$, where the X's are the partial derivatives of a function $f(x_1 \ldots x_n)$, with respect to $x_1 \ldots x_n$ respectively

exacting *adj* **1 a :** tryingly or unremittingly severe in making demands or requiring the fulfillment of obligations ⟨an ~ employer⟩ **b :** requiring careful attention and precise accuracy ⟨an ~ task⟩ **2 :** unable to thrive except under special conditions (as of nutrition, temperature, or moisture) **:** FASTIDIOUS ⟨an ~ microbe⟩ ⟨certain highly specialized xerophytes are extremely ~ in their requirements⟩ **syn** see ONEROUS

ex·act·ing·ly *adv* **:** in an exacting manner

ex·act·ing·ness *n* -ES **:** the quality or state of being exacting

ex·ac·tion \-kshən\ *n* -s [ME *exaccioun*, fr. L *exaction-*, *exactio*, fr. *exactus* + *-ion-*, *-io* -ion] **1 a :** the act or process of exacting **:** compulsion to furnish **:** a levying esp. by force ⟨the ~ of tribute⟩ ⟨~ of various dues and fees⟩ **b :** the levying or demanding of some benefit (as a fee or gratuity) that is not lawfully or properly due **:** EXTORTION ⟨the ~s of dishonest officials who demand fees to perform their sworn duty⟩ **2 :** something exacted; *usu* **:** a fee, reward, or contribution demanded or levied with severity or injustice

ex·ac·ti·tude \-ktə,tüd, -ə,tyüd\ *n* -s [F, fr. *exact* (fr. L *exactus*) + *-i-* + *-tude*] **:** the quality or an instance of being exact ⟨the ~s of careful expression⟩ ⟨a man of great ~⟩

ex·act·ly \ig'zak(t)lē, eg-, -li\ *adv* **1 a :** in an exact manner **:** precisely according to a rule, standard, or fact **:** ACCURATELY **b :** ENTIRELY, ALTOGETHER ⟨do ~ as you wish this afternoon⟩ ⟨our pleas got us ~ nothing⟩ **2 :** quite so **:** as you say or state — used to express agreement or concurrence

ex·act·ness \-k(t)nəs\ *n* -ES **:** EXACTITUDE, PRECISION ⟨a neat ~ of caricaturing⟩

ex·ac·tor *also* **ex·act·er** \-ktə(r)\ *n* -s [ME *exactour*, fr. L *exactor*, fr. *exactus* + *-or*] **:** one that exacts esp. by authority

exact science *n* **:** a science whose laws are capable of accurate quantitative expression (as physics, chemistry, astronomy)

ex·a·cum \'eksəkəm\ *n* [NL, fr. L, a kind of centaury, fr. Gaulish] **1** *cap* **:** a genus of tropical Asiatic and African plants (family Gentianaceae) including one species (*E. affine*) of herbaceous biennials with bluish to dark lavender flowers that are often cultivated in the greenhouse **2** -s **:** any plant of the genus *Exacum*

ex ae·quo et bo·no \ek,sīkwōet'bō(,)nō, -ōot-\ [L] **:** according to what is equitable and good **:** on the merits of the case — used esp. in international law when a case by agreement of the principals is to be decided on grounds of equity and reason rather than specific points of law

ex·ag·ger·ate \ig'zajə,rāt, eg-, *usu* -ād·+V\ *vb* -ED/-ING/-S [L *exaggeratus*, past part. of *exaggerare*, fr. *ex-* [1]ex- + *aggerare* to pile up, fr. *agger* heap, mound, breastwork, fr. *aggerere* to carry toward, fr. *ad-* + *gerere* to carry — more at JEST] *vt* **1** *obs* **:** to heap up **:** ACCUMULATE **2 :** to enlarge beyond bounds or the truth **:** delineate extravagantly **:** overstate the truth concerning ⟨a friend ~s a man's virtues —Joseph Addison⟩ ⟨*exaggerated* their difficulties in order to enhance their accomplishments⟩ **3 :** to enlarge or increase esp. beyond the normal ⟨the brightly flowered dress ~s her corpulence⟩ ⟨the *exaggerated* crests of certain fowls⟩ **~** *vi* **:** to misrepresent on the side of largeness (as of size, extent, or value) **:** overstate the truth

ex·ag·ger·at·ed·ly *adv* **:** in an exaggerated manner **:** with exaggeration

ex·ag·ger·at·ing·ly *adv* **:** so as to exaggerate ⟨an ~ described incident⟩

ex·ag·ger·a·tion \₌,₌₌'rāshən\ *n* -s [L *exaggeration-*, *exaggeratio*, fr. *exaggeratus* + *-ion-*, *-io* -ion] **1 :** the act of exaggerating **:** a going beyond the bounds of truth, reason, or justice **:** OVERSTATEMENT ⟨their ~ of their wealth caused much later confusion⟩ **2 :** the state or an instance of being exaggerated ⟨this ridiculous ~ was instantly seen through⟩ ⟨the ~ of his height by built-up heels⟩

ex·ag·ger·a·tive \₌'₌₌,rād·|iv, -,rəl, |t|, |ēv *also* |əv\ *adj* **1 :** tending to exaggerate **2 :** given to or involving exaggeration — **ex·ag·ger·a·tive·ly** \|əvlē, -li\ *adv*

ex·ag·ger·a·tor \-,rād·ə(r), -ātə-\ *n* -s **:** one that exaggerates

exagitate *vt* -ED/-ING/-S [L *exagitatus*, past part. of *exagitare*, fr. *ex-* [1]ex- + *agitare* to drive, agitate — more at AGITATE] **1** *obs* **:** to stir up **:** AGITATE **2** *obs* **:** DISCUSS, DEBATE **3** *obs* **:** HARASS, CENSURE —**ex·ag·i·ta·tion** *n* -s *obs*

exalate \(')eks+\ *adj* [[1]*ex-* + *alate*] *bot* **:** lacking winglike appendages

exalbuminous \'ek,s+\ *adj* [[1]*ex-* + *albuminous*] **:** EXENDOSPERMOUS

ex-all \(')₌'₌\ *adv* [[2]*ex* + *all* (pron.)] **:** without any accrued supplementary values, rights, or privileges — used chiefly in respect to transactions in securities ⟨sold his shares *ex-all*⟩

ex·alt \ig'zȯlt, eg-\ *vb* -ED/-ING/-S [ME *exalten*, fr. MF & L; MF *exalter*, fr. L *exaltare*, fr. *ex-* [1]ex- + *altus* high — more at OLD] *vt* **1 :** to raise high **:** put in an eminent position **:** ELEVATE ⟨I will ~ my throne above the stars of God —Isa 14:13(AV)⟩ ⟨sold at ~*ed* prices⟩ **2 :** to raise esp. in rank, dignity, wealth, power, or character ⟨the king ~*ed* his victorious admiral to a place on the privy council⟩ **:** DIGNIFY ⟨a nation ~*ed* by fair dealings⟩ **3 :** to elevate by praise or in estimation ⟨my father ~*ed* dramatic poetry above all other kinds —W.B.Yeats⟩ **:** MAGNIFY, EXTOL, GLORIFY ⟨~ ye the Lord —Ps 99:5(AV)⟩ **4** *obs* **:** to lift up (as with joy, pride, or success) **:** inspire with delight or satisfaction **:** ELATE **5 a :** to enhance the activity of **:** stimulate to greater or higher activity **:** HEIGHTEN, INTENSIFY ⟨~*ing* the imagination to new flights of fancy⟩ **b :** REFINE, CONCENTRATE — used esp. in alchemy **c** *archaic* **:** to make more complete or perfect **d :** to cause (virulence) to increase ⟨virulence ~*ed* by addition of mucin to a bacterial culture⟩; *also* **:** to increase the virulence of ⟨~ a virus by repeated rapid passage through susceptible hosts⟩ **~** *vi* **:** to induce exaltation **:** ELEVATE ⟨the power of brilliant conversation to excite and ~⟩ ⟨the ~*ing* beauty of the forest⟩

syn MAGNIFY, AGGRANDIZE: EXALT may indicate a raising up in prestige or significance, often with concomitant deprecation of something else ⟨crisis government, of course, inevitably *exalts* any agency best situated for supplying vigorous and effective direction of affairs —F.A.Ogg & Harold Zink⟩ MAGNIFY means to increase markedly in actual or apparent size or significance ⟨kind, quiet, nearsighted eyes, which his round spectacles *magnified* into lambent moons —Margaret Deland⟩ ⟨public opinion which thus *magnifies* patriotism into a religion —W.C.Brownell⟩ ⟨to minimize the power of the judiciary and the executive, and *magnify* the power of the legislature —V.L.Parrington⟩ AGGRANDIZE indicates making great in power, authority, sway, or eminence ⟨if we *aggrandize* ourselves at the expense of the Mahrattas —Duke of Wellington †1852⟩

ex·al·ta·tion \,eg,zȯl'tāshən, ,ek,sȯ-\ *n* -s [ME *exaltacioun*, fr. MF or L; MF *exaltation*, fr. LL *exaltation-*, *exaltatio*, fr. L *exaltatus* (past part. of *exaltare*) + *-ion-*, *-io* -ion] **1 :** the part of the zodiac in which in astrology a planet is thought to exert its strongest influence — opposed to *descension* **2 :** an act of exalting or the state of being exalted **:** ELEVATION **3 :** refinement, concentration, or intensification esp. by distilling — used chiefly in old chemistry or alchemy **4** *of larks* **:** FLOCK **5 a :** marked or excessive intensification of a mental state or of the activity of a bodily part or function **b :** an abnormal sense of personal well-being, power, or importance **:** a delusive euphoria **c :** a state of extreme spiritual elevation usu. marked by a more or less transitory sense of unity with the Deity or with all things natural or divine

exaltation of the cross *usu cap E and C* **:** a feast observed in the Roman Catholic and Eastern Orthodox churches on September 14 in commemoration of what is held to be the historical recovery of the true cross from the Persians and its return to Jerusalem in the 7th century — called also *Holy Cross Day*

exalted *adj* **:** exhibiting or characterized by exaltation ⟨~ raptures⟩: as **a :** raised to or having high rank ⟨an ~ personage⟩ **b :** exceedingly or excessively high or favorable ⟨an ~ opinion of his own worth⟩ — often used in negative expressions ⟨took no ~ view of the situation⟩ **c :** marked by nobility of thought or elegance of utterance ⟨an ~ literary style⟩ ⟨we allowed it to be a highly ~ way of telling how so-and-so climbed a hill for a better view —A.T.Quiller-Couch⟩ ⟨the ~ outpourings of a great mind⟩ **d :** CONCENTRATED, STRONG — now used chiefly of seasonings ⟨an ~ essence⟩ ⟨the insipid flesh . . . has need of an ~ seasoning —*Punch*⟩ **e :** partially intoxicated **:** TIPSY — **ex·alt·ed·ly** *adv* — **ex·alt·ed·ness** *n* -ES

ex·alt·er \ig'zȯltə(r), eg-\ *n* -s [ME, fr. *exalten* + *-er*] **:** one that exalts

Ex·al·to·lide \ig'zȯltə,līd, eg-\ *trademark* — used for a crystalline macrocyclic lactone used in perfumes

Ex·al·tone \-,tōn\ *trademark* — used for a crystalline macrocyclic synthetic ketone used in perfumes

ex·am \ig'zam, eg-, -zaa(ə)m\ *n* -s [by shortening] **:** EXAMINATION

ex·a·men \ig'zāmən, eg-\ *n* -s [L, tongue of a balance, consideration, examination, fr. *exigere* to drive out, weigh, measure — more at EXACT] **1 :** examination, inquiry, or investigation esp. when conducted to study or weigh the worth or state of something ⟨a regular ~ of conscience⟩ ⟨show a periodic structure under electron microscope ~ —*Biol. Abstracts*⟩ **2 :** a critical study (as of a writer or a phenomenon) ⟨a sound, often brilliant ~ of the most powerful English poet of this century —Robert Halsband⟩

ex·am·in·able \ig'zam(ə)nəbəl, eg-\ *adj* [LL *examinabilis*, fr. L *examinare* + *-abilis* -able] **:** suitable or fit for examination ⟨an ~ subject⟩

ex·am·i·nant \-mənənt\ *n* -s [L *examinant-*, *examinans*, pres. part. of *examinare*] **1 :** EXAMINER **2** *or* **ex·am·i·nate** \-,nāt, -,nət\ **:** one that is examined or is subject to examination (as a witness or deponent)

ex·am·i·na·tion \ig,zamə'nāshən, eg-\ *n* -s [ME *examinacioun*, fr. MF *examination*, fr. LL *examination-*, *examinatio*, fr. L *examinatus* (past part. of *examinare*) + *-ion-*, *-io* -ion] **1 :** the act or process of examining or state of being examined **:** SEARCH, INVESTIGATION, SCRUTINY ⟨a careful ~ of the terrain showed no signs of human habitation⟩ **2 :** an exercise or a series of exercises designed to examine progress or test qualification: **a :** a test given to a candidate for a certificate or a position and concerned typically with problems to be solved, skills to be demonstrated, or tasks to be performed ⟨a civil service ~⟩ ⟨a driver's ~⟩ **b :** an oral or written test given by a teacher to a class or an individual student to determine the amount and quality of learning over a period of time ⟨the final ~ will decide your grade for the course⟩ ⟨college entrance ~s may be taken in April or June⟩ **3 :** a formal interrogation (as of a witness in a legal action); *also* **:** the deposition or statements made in such an examination

ex·am·i·na·tion·al \₌|₌₌'nāshən°l, -shnəl\ *adj* **:** of or relating to examination ⟨~ methods⟩

examination in chief : DIRECT EXAMINATION

ex·am·i·na·tor \₌'₌₌,nād·ə(r)\ *n* -s [LL, fr. L *examinatus* + *-or*] *chiefly Scot* **:** a person in charge of an examination (sense 2)

ex·am·i·na·to·ri·al \ig|zamənə|tōrēəl, eg-\ *also* **ex·am·i·na·to·ry** \₌'₌₌ə,tōrē\ *adj* [*examinatorial* fr. LL *examinatorius* (fr. L *examinatus* + *-orius* -ory) + E *al*; *examinatory* fr. LL *examinatorius*] **:** of or relating to an examiner or examination

[1]**ex·am·ine** \ig'zamən, eg-\ *vb* **examined; examined; examining** \-ni(ə)niŋ\ **examines** [ME *examinen*, fr. MF *examiner*, fr. L *examinare*, fr. *examin-*, *examen* tongue of a balance, consideration, examination — more at EXAMEN] *vt* **1 :** to test by an appropriate method **:** INVESTIGATE: as **a :** to look over **:** inspect visually or by use of other senses (as for the determination of accuracy, propriety, or quality) ⟨*examining* title deeds⟩ ⟨carefully *examined* his steward's accounts⟩ ⟨*examining* the cloth and its embroidery⟩ **b :** to inspect or test for evidence of disease or abnormality ⟨the doctor *examined* the young men and found them in perfect health⟩ **c :** to inquire into the state of esp. by introspective processes ⟨first ~ your own conscience⟩ ⟨he *examined* his inmost thoughts⟩ **d :** to search (as baggage) esp. for contraband or dutiable items **2 :** to seek to ascertain **:** attempt to determine ⟨attempt to ~ whether and to what extent the enormous growth in the economic welfare of this nation has been . . . aided by our knowledge of economics —Fritz Machlup⟩ ⟨sat brooding and *examining* how he was at fault⟩ **3 :** to interrogate closely (as in a judicial proceeding) **:** try or test by question ⟨*examining* witnesses in court⟩ ⟨*examined* the students in French⟩ ⟨~ a bankrupt regarding the state of his property⟩ **~** *vi* **:** to make or give an examination ⟨the doctor will ~ at the infirmary⟩ — usu. used with *into* ⟨let us ~ into the basic mechanism involved⟩ ⟨spent some time *examining* into the rumor that an underground passage led from the castle to the marsh⟩ **syn** see ASK, SCRUTINIZE

[2]**examine** \"\ *n* -s *archaic* **:** EXAMINATION, SCRUTINY

examined copy *n* **:** a copy (as of a legal document) that has been compared with the original

ex·am·in·ee \ig,zamə'nē, eg-\ *n* -s **:** a person who is examined

ex·am·in·er \₌'zam(ə)nə(r)\ *n* -s **:** one that examines: as **a :** a court officer empowered to administer the oath and take testimony **b :** a person charged with the conducting of examinations into the attainments or qualifications (as of students or applicants) **c :** a person whose work is to inspect usu. a specified thing or situation ⟨the government ~ checked the scene of the crash⟩ ⟨hosiery ~s⟩ ⟨a qualified cable ~⟩ ⟨bank ~⟩

ex·am·in·ing·ly *adv* **:** in an examining manner **:** with careful scrutiny **:** SEARCHINGLY

examplar *archaic var of* [1]EXEMPLAR

[1]**ex·am·ple** \ig'zampəl, eg-, -zaam-,-zaim-,-zȧm-\ *n* -s [ME *exaumple*, fr. MF *example*, *exemple*, alter. (influenced by L *exemplum*) of *essample*, *essemple*, fr. L *exemplum*, fr. *eximere* to take out, remove, fr. *ex-* [1]ex- + *-imere* to take (fr. *emere*

to buy, obtain) — more at REDEEM] **1 :** a particular single item, fact, incident, or aspect that may be taken fairly as typical or representative of all of a group or type ⟨a most outstanding ~ of a war fought with a purpose was our own American Revolution —Wendell Willkie⟩ **2 a :** a pattern or representative action or series of actions tending or intended to induce one to imitate or emulate ⟨we make the mistake of thinking that all can be done by precept, when . . . ~ is no less potent a force —A.C.Benson⟩ **b :** a pattern of action that by its ill result should discourage emulation ⟨learn from me, if not by my precepts, at least by my ~, how dangerous is the acquirement of knowledge —Mary W. Shelley⟩ — often used with a qualifying adjective (as *bad*) **3 :** a parallel or closely similar case, incident, or item esp. when serving as a precedent or model ⟨such temperate order in so fierce a cause doth want ~ —Shak.⟩ **4 a :** an incident or situation in which one individual's punishment or plight may serve to admonish others **b :** an individual so punished ⟨to make an ~ of a malingering soldier⟩ **5 :** an instance (as a problem to be solved) serving to illustrate a rule or precept or to act as an exercise in the application of the rules of any study or branch of science ⟨in mathematics problems assigned are ~*s* designed to test and apply rules previously learned⟩ ⟨we have 10 ~*s* in our homework⟩ **syn** see INSTANCE, MODEL

²example \"\ *vt* **exampled; exampled; exampling** \-p(ə)liŋ\ **examples** [ME *exemplen, exaumplen,* fr. MF *exempler,* fr. LL *exemplare,* fr. L *exemplum*] **1 a :** to serve or use as an example of, for, or to — used in the passive ⟨his novel writing, best *exampled* in the somewhat cruel satire —Fanny Butcher⟩ ⟨their spirit may be *exampled* by the way they help one another⟩ **b** *archaic* **:** to be or set an example to **:** teach through example **2** *obs* **:** to constitute a precedent for **:** PARALLEL, MATCH ⟨I may ~ my digression by some mighty precedent —Shak.⟩

exams *pl of* EXAM

¹ex·animate \(ˈ)eg¦z, (ˈ)ek¦s+‚-\ *adj* [L *exanimatus,* past part. of *exanimare* to deprive of life or courage, terrify, fr. *ex-* ¹ex- + *anima* breath, soul — more at ANIMATE] **1 :** lacking in animation **:** SPIRITLESS **2 :** LIFELESS, DEAD; *also* **:** appearing lifeless

²exanimate *vt* -ED/-ING/-S [L *exanimatus,* past part.] *obs* **:** to deprive of life or of animation — **exanimation** *n* -s *obs*

ex ante \(ˈ)¦=¦==\ *adj* [²*ex* + *ante* (adv.)] **:** based on assumption and prediction and being essentially subjective and estimative ⟨an *ex ante* plan for the budget⟩ ⟨consistency of market behavior, and therefore reasonable conformity of *ex ante* expectations with ex post reality, is basically determined by the social stability of the community —Werner Hochwald⟩ — opposed to *ex post*

ex·an·them \igˈzan(t)thəm, egˈza-, ekˈsa-\ *also* **ex·an·the·ma** \‚eg‚zanˈthēmə\ *n, pl* **exanthems** \-əmz\ *also* **exan·them·a·ta** \-ˈthemədə, -ˈthēm-\ *or* **exanthemas** [NL *exanthema,* fr. LL, skin rash, fr. Gk *exanthēma,* fr. *exanthein* to bloom, to break out (as with a rash), fr. *ex-* (fr. *ex* out of) + *anthein* to bloom, fr. *anthos* flower — more at EX-, ANTHOLOGY] **1 :** an eruptive disease or its symptomatic eruption — used esp. of eruptions attended with fever (as in measles, smallpox, and scarlatina); distinguished from *enanthem* **2** *usu exanthema* **:** a copper-deficiency disease of plants that is esp. prevalent in citrus and olive and is characterized by gummosis often accompanied by dieback and by glossy brownish blotches on leaves and fruit — **ex·an·the·mat·ic** \(ˈ)eg¦zan(t)thə¦mad·ik, (ˈ)ek¦s-\ *or* **ex·an·them·a·tous** \¦==¦themədəs\ *adj*

ex·ant·la·tion \‚eg‚zantˈlāshən, ‚ek‚sa-\ *n* -s [L *exantlatus, exanclatus* (past part. of *exantlare, exanclare* to draw out, fr. Gk *exantlein,* fr. *ex-* + *antlein* to bail out, draw out, fr. *antlos* bilge) + E *-ion*] *archaic* **:** the act of drawing out

ex·a·rate \ˈeksə‚rāt\ *adj* [L *exaratus,* past part. of L *exarare* to plow up, write on a tablet, fr. *ex-* ¹ex- + *arare* to plow — more at EAR] **1 :** grooved or furrowed **2** *of a pupa* **:** having the appendages not cemented to the body — compare OBTECT

ex·a·ra·tion \‚eksəˈrāshən\ *n* -s [LL *exaration-, exaratio,* fr. L *exaratus* + *-ion-, -io* -ion] **:** an act of writing or a product of writing (as a composition or inscription)

¹ex·arch \ˈek‚särk\ *n* -s [LL *exarchus,* fr. LGk *exarchos,* fr. Gk, leader, chief, fr. *exarchein* to begin, take the lead in, rule, fr. *ex-* (fr. *ex* out) + *archein* to begin, rule — more at EX-] **1 :** a viceroy of a province under the Byzantine emperors — used as a title or mode of address **2** *Eastern Church* **a :** the head of a chief see or province during the early periods of church history **b :** a bishop inferior to a patriarch and superior to a metropolitan **c :** a deputy of a patriarch usu. holding the rank of bishop **d :** the head of an independent church — **ex·arch·al** \(ˈ)ek¦särkəl\ *adj*

²exarch \"\ *adj* [¹*ex-* + Gk *archē* beginning] **:** formed or taking place from the periphery toward the center — used of the primary xylem (as of a root) or its development; compare ENDARCH, MESARCH

ex·arch·ate \ˈek‚sär‚kāt, -rkət\ *n* -s [ML *exarchatus,* fr. LL *exarchus* + L *-atus* -ate] **:** the office or the province of an exarch

ex·arch·ist \ˈek‚särkəst\ *n* -s *usu cap* **:** a member of a politico-religious party in Macedonia (1872-1915)

¹ex·as·per·ate \igˈzaspə‚rāt, eg-, -zaas-,-zäs-, *usu* -ād·+V\ *vb* -ED/-ING/-S [L *exasperatus,* past part. of *exasperare,* fr. *ex-* ¹ex- + *asperare* to roughen, irritate, fr. *asper* rough] *vt* **1 :** to excite or inflame the anger of **:** ENRAGE ⟨~ them against the king of France —Joseph Addison⟩; *often* **:** to cause irritation or annoyance to ⟨the general reader will . . . be *exasperated* at a certain cavalier curtness of narrative —C.H.Driver⟩ ⟨she's a good child but her slowness often ~*s* me⟩ **2** *obs* **:** to make grievous or more grievous or malignant **3** *obs* **:** to make harsh or harsher ~ *vi, obs* **:** to become irritated **syn** see IRRITATE

²ex·as·per·ate \-rət, -‚rāt\ *adj* [L *exasperatus,* past part.] **1 :** EXASPERATED **2** *biol* **:** roughened with irregular prickles or elevations ⟨an ~ carapace⟩ ⟨~ seed coats⟩

exasperated *adj* **:** irritated or annoyed esp. to the point of injudicious action — **ex·as·per·at·ed·ly** *adv*

exasperating *adj* **:** causing or tending to cause exasperation — **ex·as·per·at·ing·ly** *adv*

ex·as·per·a·tion \=¦==ˈrāshən\ *n* -s [LL *exasperation-, exasperatio,* fr. L *exasperatus* + *-ion-, -io* -ion] **1 :** the state of being exasperated **:** marked irritation or annoyance ⟨threw the book down in ~⟩ ⟨it should be real anger, and not merely the ~ that comes of fretted nerves or facile emotion —F.A. Swinnerton⟩; *sometimes* **:** violent or bitter anger **:** RAGE **2 :** an act or source of exasperating **:** a cause of irritation ⟨the petty ~*s* of daily life⟩

ex·auc·to·rate \egˈzȯktə‚rāt, ekˈsȯ-\ *vt* -ED/-ING/-S [L *exauctoratus,* past part. of *exauctorare,* fr. *ex-* ¹ex- + (*se*) *auctorare* to hire oneself out, fr. *auctor* author, bail, security — more at AUTHOR] *archaic* **:** to deprive of authority **:** DISMISS — **ex·auc·to·ra·tion** \(‚)=¦===ˈrāshən\ *n* -s *archaic*

ex·au·gu·ral \(ˈ)ek¦sȯgyərəl, ÷ -gər-\ *adj* [¹*ex-* + *-augural* (as in *inaugural*)] **:** occurring at the close of a term of office — opposed to *inaugural* ⟨an ~ message⟩

exc *abbr* **1** excellency; excellent **2** except; excepted; exception **3** exchange **4** exciter **5** [L *excudit*] (he) engraved (it) **6** excuse

ex·calcarate \(ˈ)eks+\ *adj* [¹*ex-* + *calcarate*] **:** ECALCARATE

ex·camb \ekˈskam(b)\ *vb* -ED/-ING/-S [ME (Sc dial.) *excamben,* fr. ML *excambiare,* prob. modif. of OF *eschangier* to exchange — more at EXCHANGE] *Scots law* **:** EXCHANGE

ex·cam·bi·on \-mbēən\ *n* -s [ME (Sc dial.), fr. ML *excambium,* prob. modif. of OF *eschange* — more at EXCHANGE] *Scots law* **:** exchange of land

ex·can·des·cence \‚ekskənˈdesən(t)s, -‚kan-\ *also* **ex·can·des·cen·cy** \-ˈdesənsē\ *n, pl* **excandescences** *also* **excandescencies** [L *excandescentia,* fr. *excandescent-, excandescens* (pres. part. of *excandescere* to grow hot, glow, burn, fr. *ex-* ¹ex- + *candescere* to glow, grow red hot, incho. of *candēre* to shine) + *-ia* -y — more at CANDID] *archaic* **:** a feverish condition brought on by anger or passion

ex·can·ta·tion \‚ek‚skanˈtāshən\ *n* -s [L *excantatus* (past part. of *excantare* to bring out by charms, fr. *ex-* ¹ex- + *cantare* to sing) + E *-ion* — more at CHANT] *archaic* **:** an act of freeing by enchantment

ex·car·di·na·tion \(‚)ek‚skärdənˈāshən\ *n* -s [¹*ex-* + *-cardination* (as in *incardination*)] **:** the transference of a cleric from one diocese to another

excarnate *vt* -ED/-ING/-S [LL *excarnatus,* past part. of *excarnare,* fr. L *ex-* ¹ex- + *carn-, caro* flesh — more at CARNAL] *obs* **:** to deprive or strip of flesh

ex·car·na·tion \‚ek‚skärˈnāshən\ *n* -s **1 :** removal of flesh (as by putrefaction) **2 :** separation of soul from body (as at death)

ex cathedra \(¦)eks+\ *adv* (*or adj*) [L, from the chair] **:** by virtue of or in the exercise of one's office **:** with authority ⟨speaking *ex cathedra*⟩ ⟨an *ex cathedra* pronouncement⟩

ex·ca·vate \ˈekskə‚vāt, *usu* -ād·+V\ *vb* -ED/-ING/-S [L *excavatus,* past part. of *excavare,* fr. *ex-* ¹ex- + *cavare* to make hollow, fr. *cavus* hollow — more at CAVE] *vt* **1 :** to hollow out **:** form a cavity or hole in ⟨*excavating* the side of a hill⟩ ⟨an *excavated* wisdom tooth⟩ **2 :** to form by hollowing **:** shape by removing material so as to leave a space ⟨will ~ the cellar as soon as the frost goes⟩ ⟨*excavated* a tunnel under the river⟩ **3 :** to dig out and remove (as earth or mineral matter) ⟨over a million tons of rich ore were *excavated* from that one pocket⟩ **4 :** to expose to view by or as if by digging away a covering ⟨*excavated* the remains of 10 separate cultures⟩ ⟨*excavated* several forgotten accounts of the brawl⟩ ~ *vi* **:** to make excavations or become hollowed out ⟨the mollusk uses its pointed foot to ~ in the mud⟩ ⟨an area of infarction in soft tissue often tends to ~⟩ **syn** see DIG

ex·ca·va·tion \‚==ˈvāshən\ *n* -s [L *excavation-, excavatio,* fr. *excavatus* + *-ion-, -io* -ion] **1 a :** the act or process of excavating **b :** the removal of superposed material (as earth, stone, or buildings) from the remains or structures of an age or civilization earlier than the present **2 :** a cavity formed by cutting, digging, or scooping **3 a :** an uncovered cutting in the earth — distinguished from *tunnel* **b :** the material dug out in making a channel or cavity

ex·ca·va·tor \ˈ==‚vād·ə(r), -ātə-\ *n* -s **:** one that excavates: as **a :** a worker who digs out material or digs cavities (as in quarrying or for building construction) **b :** any of various machines (as a steam shovel) for excavating earth **c :** an instrument used to open bodily cavities (as in the teeth) or remove material from them

ex·ca·va·to·ry \ˈekskəvə‚tōrē, ekˈskavə-; ¦ekskə¦vād·ərē\ *adj* **:** concerned with excavation or its results ⟨~ archaeology⟩

excecate *vt* -ED/-ING/-S [L *excaecatus,* past part. of *excaecare,* fr. *ex-* ¹ex- + *caecare* to blind, fr. *caecus* blind — more at CECUM] *obs* **:** to blind physically or mentally — **excecation** *n* -s *archaic*

ex·ceed \ikˈsēd, ek-\ *vb* -ED/-ING/-S [ME *exceden,* fr. MF *exceder,* fr. L *excedere,* fr. *ex-* ¹ex- + *cedere* to go, proceed — more at CEDE] *vt* **1 :** to extend outside of or enlarge beyond — used chiefly in strictly physical relations ⟨if this rain keeps up, the river will ~ its banks by morning⟩ **2 a :** to be greater than or superior to **:** SURPASS ⟨his brother ~*s* him in height⟩ ⟨their accomplishment ~*ed* our expectation⟩ ⟨the cost must not ~ one year's income⟩ **b :** to be too much for **:** be beyond the comprehension of ⟨the mercy of God ~*s* our finite minds⟩ **3 :** to go beyond a limit set by (as an authority or privilege) **:** do more than is justified by or allowable under (as a commission or order) ⟨he ~*ed* his authority when he paid his brother's gambling debts with money from the trust⟩ ⟨the captain ~*ed* his orders when he quartered men in private houses⟩ ~ *vi* **1** *obs* **a :** to go too far **:** pass the proper or usual bounds (as of conduct) **b :** to eat or drink to excess **2 :** to stand out among or be more or greater than others **:** PREDOMINATE

syn SURPASS, TRANSCEND, EXCEL, OUTDO, OUTSTRIP: EXCEED indicates a going over or topping what is under consideration in a companion or what is set as a standard or limit ⟨far *exceeding* the production figures from last year⟩ ⟨an Inferno which *exceeds* anything that Dante imagined —Henry Miller⟩ ⟨the number of representatives shall not *exceed* one for every thirty thousand —*U.S. Constitution*⟩ ⟨he seemed to think I'd *exceeded* my authority in disposing of the rebels as I saw fit —Kenneth Roberts⟩ SURPASS is a close synonym of EXCEED; it is likely to be used in reference to superiority in quality, merit, virtue, or skill, although it may be used to describe what is more evil or reprehensible ⟨he wanted himself to *surpass* Caesar in deeds and his legions to *surpass* the achievements of the legions of Caesar —J.T.Farrell⟩ ⟨in the moral essence of tragedy it is safe to say that in this play Middleton is *surpassed* by one Elizabethan alone, and that is Shakespeare —T.S.Eliot⟩ ⟨in the imputation of things evil and in putting the worst construction on things innocent, a certain type of good people may be trusted to *surpass* all others —Rudyard Kipling⟩ ⟨his tyrannies *surpassed* those of his predecessor⟩ TRANSCEND may suggest a rising notably or remarkably above an accustomed standard or level ⟨sorrow *transcending* all sorrows, darker than death, immitigable, eternal —W.H.Hudson †1922⟩ ⟨in Virgil we find that divine afflatus which *transcends* the most balanced wisdom and the deftest technical skill —John Buchan⟩ ⟨certain problems are raised, if an ideal, embodied into law, *transcends* the "realities" too far —Reinhold Niebuhr⟩ In intransitive uses EXCEL implies reaching a preeminence in accomplishment or achievement; in transitive ones it is a close synonym of SURPASS ⟨*excelling* in terse narrative⟩ ⟨*excelling* in athletics⟩ ⟨during their seminary years he had easily *surpassed* his friend in scholarship, but he always realized that Joseph *excelled* him in the fervor of his faith —Willa Cather⟩ ⟨if some *excelled* him in learning and scholarly productivity, not many *surpassed* him in personal attractiveness —H.E.Starr⟩ OUTDO, a more colloquial word, may apply to topping, bettering, or exceeding what has been done before ⟨the military engines he devised for the defense of Syracuse seem never to have been *outdone* in the ancient world —Benjamin Farrington⟩ ⟨a competition in deceit in which, I admit, he *outdid* them —Owen Wister⟩ OUTSTRIP suggests surpassing in a race or competition or similar endeavor ⟨swimming was his chief delight, and so it came about that one day when he was far from land, having *outstripped* all his fellows in a race, he was hardly surprised to see a dolphin plunging alongside of him —Norman Douglas⟩ ⟨bituminous coal had far *outstripped* anthracite in the industrial markets —S.A.Hale⟩ ⟨instead of allowing his reader the easy victory, he takes pride in *outstripping* him completely —Edmund Wilson⟩

ex·ceed·able \-dəbəl\ *adj* **:** suitable for or capable of being exceeded ⟨a safely ~ speed limit⟩

ex·ceed·er \-də(r)\ *n* -s **:** one that exceeds

exceeding *adj* [fr. pres. part. of *exceed*] **:** exceptional in amount, quality, or degree **:** greater than is customary or desirable or predictable ⟨the ~ disorder of the room⟩ ⟨the ~ pallor of her skin⟩

ex·ceed·ing·ly *also* **exceeding** *adv* **:** to a marked degree or extent **:** EXTREMELY, NOTABLY, VERY ⟨ground to an ~ fine powder⟩ ⟨an *exceeding* high hill —Isak Dinesen⟩

ex·cel \ikˈsel, ek-\ *vb* **excelled; excelled; excelling; excels** [ME *excellen,* fr. L *excellere,* fr. *ex-* ¹ex- + *-cellere* to rise, project (akin to L *collis* hill) — more at HILL] *vt* **1 :** to surpass or outshine (as in some quality possessed or activity engaged in) ⟨a charming child who instinctively ~*s* other children in all the social graces⟩ ⟨he *excelled* his brother at sports but not in school⟩ ⟨his journeys *excelled* most . . . of theirs in miles, speed, and comfort —Vilhjalmur Stefansson⟩ **2** *obs* **:** to go beyond ~ *vi* **:** to surpass others esp. in good qualities, laudable actions, or acquirements **:** be distinguishable by superiority — usu. used with *in* ⟨he ~*s* in mathematics⟩ ⟨some painters ~ in precise delineation of detail⟩ ⟨a new melon that ~*s* in flavor⟩ **syn** see EXCEED

ex·cel·lence \ˈeks(ə)lən(t)s\ *n* -s [ME, fr. MF, fr. L *excellentia,* fr. *excellent-, excellens* + *-ia* -y] **1 :** the quality of being excellent **:** the state of possessing good qualities in an eminent degree **2 :** an excellent or valuable quality **:** VIRTUE **3 :** EXCELLENCY 2

syn MERIT, VIRTUE, PERFECTION: EXCELLENCE indicates a high degree or the highest degree of good qualities, of qualities that make for especial worth or merit; it may be limited explicitly by some such word as *particular* or *distinctive* or by its context ⟨spoke of the rude health of their children as if it were a result of moral *excellence;* in a peculiar tone which seemed to imply some contempt for people whose children were liable to be unwell at times —Joseph Conrad⟩ ⟨*excellences* achieved with the sure touch of craftsmanship —*Saturday Rev.*⟩ MERIT, often contrasted with *demerit* in critical estimates, may refer broadly to any good, commendable, worthy, or valuable quality or feature ⟨the result might have been a permanent aristocracy, possessing the *merits* and defects of the Spartans —Bertrand Russell⟩ ⟨the *merits* and defects of Cowper's version —Matthew Arnold⟩ ⟨the subject of my choice has the *merit* of universal appeal —R.W.Chapman⟩ VIRTUE may apply to a peculiar or distinctive power, strength, or efficacy, to a characteristic indicating moral goodness, or to some conspicuous character merit ⟨flexibility and adaptation are the cardinal *virtues* of successful aging —George Lawton⟩ ⟨the fine balance with which Johnson weighed and sustained his judgments of human flaws and virtues —H.V.Gregory⟩ ⟨define as *virtues* those mental and physical habits which tend to produce a good community, and as vices those that tend to produce a bad one —Bertrand Russell⟩ PERFECTION suggests attainment to faultlessness, to the highest excellence ⟨the effort to make such windows was never repeated. Their jeweled *perfection* did not suit the scale of the vast churches of the thirteenth century —Henry Adams⟩ ⟨defective as they are in every branch of knowledge, and in every other species of refinement, it seems wonderful that they should arrive at such *perfection* in the dance —William Cowper⟩

ex·cel·len·cy \-nsē, -si\ *n* -ES [ME *excellencie,* fr. L *excellentia*] **1 :** EXCELLENCE; *usu* **:** outstanding or valuable quality — used chiefly in pl. ⟨noting one another's *excellencies* and defects⟩ **2 :** a person of notable position, dignity, or worth — used in a title or in a mode of address to certain high dignitaries (as a Roman Catholic bishop, a governor of a state, an ambassador, a viceroy) and then usu. cap. ⟨His *Excellency* the Bishop⟩

¹ex·cel·lent \-nt\ *adj, sometimes* -ER/-EST [ME, fr. MF, fr. L *excellent-, excellens,* fr. pres. part. of *excellere* to excel — more at EXCEL] **1** *archaic* **:** excelling or exceeding in kind or degree **2 :** of high station, rank, or office — used as a title or in a mode of address and often cap. ⟨the most ~ chief of the lodge will preside at the meeting⟩ **3 :** meritoriously near the standard or model ; very good of its kind **:** FIRST-CLASS ⟨this vase is an ~ imitation of the antique⟩; *broadly* **:** of great worth **:** eminently good ⟨an ~ man⟩ ⟨~ breeding⟩ ⟨crossbred wool was in ~ demand⟩ ⟨many ~ Americans are fighting this hysteria —Hugh Gaitskell⟩

²excellent \"\ *adv* [ME, fr. ¹*excellent*] *archaic* **:** EXCELLENTLY, EXCEEDINGLY

ex·cel·lent·ly *adv* [ME, fr. ¹*excellent* + *-ly*] **1 :** in an excellent manner **:** to marked advantage **:** very well **:** EFFECTIVELY, FINELY ⟨~ reasoned arguments⟩ ⟨getting along ~⟩ **2 :** to or in a marked or unusual degree **:** EXCEEDINGLY, NOTABLY, VERY ⟨lunched ~ well⟩

ex·cel·lent·ness *n* -ES **:** EXCELLENCE

excelse *adj* [L *excelsus,* fr. past part. of *excellere* to raise, rise, excel — more at EXCEL] *obs* **:** EMINENT, LOFTY

ex·cel·sin \ikˈselsən, ek-\ *n* -s [NL *excelsa* (specific epithet of *Bertholettia excelsa,* fr. fem. of *excelsus* high) + E *-in*] **:** a crystalline globulin obtained from the meat of the Brazil nut

ex·cel·si·or \ikˈselsēə(r), ek- *also* -lts- *sometimes* -lshə- *or* ÷ -l(t)sə- *or* -l(t)sē‚ȯ(ə)r *or* -l(t)sē‚ō(ə)\ *n* -s [L, higher, comparative of *excelsus*] **:** fine curled shavings of wood forming a resilient mass and used esp. for packing fragile items

ex·center \ˈek(s)+‚-\ *n* [¹*ex-* + *center*] **:** the center of an escribed circle

¹ex·centric \ik, (ˈ)ek(s)+\ *var of* ECCENTRIC

²excentric \"\ *or* **ex·central** \ik-, (ˈ)ek(s)+\ *adj* [¹*ex-* + *centric* or *central*] **:** not centrally located **:** ONE-SIDED — used esp. of the relation of stipe to pileus in certain fungi

excentrical *archaic var of* ECCENTRIC

¹ex·cept \ikˈsept, ek-\ *vb* -ED/-ING/-S [ME *excepten,* fr. MF *excepter,* fr. L *exceptare,* fr. *exceptus,* past part. of *excipere,* to take out, make an exception of, take, receive, fr. *ex-* ¹ex- + *-cipere* (fr. *capere* to take) — more at HEAVE] *vt* **1 :** to take or leave out (something) from a number or a whole **:** exclude or omit (as from consideration) ⟨it is desirable to ~ all first-calf heifers in determining butterfat production averages⟩ **2** *obs* **:** to offer as objection; *also* **:** to protest against ~ *vi* **1 :** to take exception **:** OBJECT — usu. used with *to,* sometimes with *against* ⟨~ to a witness⟩ ⟨except thou wilt ~ against my love —Shak.⟩ **2 :** to enter an exception in law

²except \=¦=, *rapid* (‚)sep(t)\ *also* **excepting** *prep* [*except* fr. ME, fr. L *exceptus,* past part.; *excepting* fr. ME, fr. pres. part. of *excepten*] **1 :** with the exclusion or exception of ⟨the stores will remain open daily ~ Sundays⟩ ⟨*excepting* Christmas we did not have one really pleasant holiday⟩ **:** SAVE ⟨he could do little ~ write⟩ **2 :** otherwise, elsewhere, or for other reason than **:** other than **:** BUT ⟨you cannot hope to keep them ~ in sealed containers⟩ ⟨you could never have lost your way ~ by your own carelessness⟩ ⟨I take no orders ~ from the king —G.B.Shaw⟩

³except \"\ *also* **excepting** *conj* [*except* fr. ME, fr. L *exceptus,* past part.; *excepting* fr. *excepting,* prep.] **1 :** on any other condition than that **:** UNLESS ⟨I will not let thee go, ~ thou bless me —Gen 32:26 (AV)⟩ ⟨horses had been man's only means of land travel, ~ he walked —Hugh McCausland⟩ ⟨I wouldn't go near the old gossip ~ I had to⟩ ⟨never does he sit down at table ~ it is crowded with guests —Upton Sinclair⟩ **2 :** ONLY — used with or without *that* ⟨I would buy a new suit ~ I have no money⟩ ⟨a furious energy drove me to all kinds of bodily and mental exercise, without any particular direction ~ that I felt sure I was going to be a great poet —John Reed⟩

⁴except *vt* -ED/-ING/-S [ME *excepten,* fr. L *exceptus,* past part.] *obs* **:** ACCEPT

ex·cept·able \ikˈseptəbəl, (ˈ)ek¦s-\ *adj* [¹*except* + *-able*] **:** fit for excepting or suitable for being excepted

except for *prep* **:** ²EXCEPT 1 ⟨*except for* your presence I would be bored⟩

ex·cep·tio \ikˈsepshē‚ō, ek-, -ptē‚ō; ekˈseptē‚ō\ *n, pl* **ex·cep·ti·o·nes** \ik‚sepshēˈō‚nēz, (‚)ek‚-, -septēˈō‚nēz, -skeptēˈō‚nās\ [L] **:** an exception in pleading at law

ex·cep·tion \ikˈsepshən, ek-\ *n* -s [ME *excepcioun,* fr. MF & L; MF *exception,* fr. L *exception-, exceptio,* fr. *exceptus* (past part. of *excipere* to take out, make an exception) + *-ion-, -io* -ion — more at EXCEPT] **1 :** the act of excepting or excluding **:** exclusion or restriction (as of a class, statement, or rule) by taking out something that would otherwise be included **2 :** one that is excepted or taken out from others ⟨almost every general rule has its ~*s*⟩ ⟨eight of the pups were beauties; the only ~ was a potbellied little male⟩ **3 a :** something offered or offerable as objection or as a ground of objection or taken as objectionable ⟨witnesses whose authority is beyond ~ —T.B.Macaulay⟩ — now usu. used with *take* ⟨taking ~ to the majority vote —Bennett Cerf⟩ ⟨to whose musical ideas one would seldom take ~ —A.T.Davison⟩ **b** *archaic* **:** OFFENSE ⟨she takes ~*s* at your person —Shak.⟩ **4 a :** an oral or written objection (as to a ruling of a judge or something in his charge to a jury) taken in the course of an action or proceeding at law **b :** a clause by which a grantor (as of a deed) excepts something out of what he before granted **5 a :** a special plea in defense in Roman law setting up allegations which if they are true will bar the claim even when the facts on which the claim is based are true, the plea being set up in a formula directing that it be tried first; *also* **:** any plea in defense whether peremptory in complete bar or dilatory in delay of the plaintiff's claim **b :** SPECIAL PLEA IN BAR **c** *Scots law* **:** DEFENSE 1b **d :** an objection alleging insufficiency of some pleading or proceeding in equity

ex·cep·tion·able \-sh(ə)nəbəl\ *adj* **1 :** such as may cause objection **:** OBJECTIONABLE ⟨a thoroughly unpleasant highly ~ piece of writing⟩ **2 :** EXCEPTIONAL — **ex·cep·tion·ably** \-blē, -li\ *adv*

ex·cep·tion·al \-shənᵊl, -shnəl\ *adj* **1 :** forming an exception; *usu* **:** being out of the ordinary **:** UNCOMMON, RARE ⟨they made an ~ group⟩ ⟨there have been an ~ number of rainy days this year⟩ **2 :** better than the average **:** SUPERIOR ⟨his ~ skill⟩ ⟨this is an ~ opportunity⟩ **3** *of a child* **:** requiring special educational or psychological aid in social adjustment whether because of superior ability or because of physical or mental defect — **ex·cep·tion·al·i·ty** \=,=shə'naləd·ē\ *n* -ES — **ex·cep·tion·al·ly** \=ˈ=shənᵊlē, -shnəlē, \i\ *adv* — **ex·cep·tion·al·ness** \-ᵊlnəs, -əl-\ *n* -ES

ex·cep·tion·al·ism \=ˈsepshənᵊl,izəm, -shnə,li-\ *n* -S : a theory or doctrine (as of social or political action) based on the assumption that exceptional circumstances will result in distortion of a generally predictable course in certain instances

ex·cep·tion·al·ist \-ᵊləst, -ələ-\ *n* -S : one that accepts or advocates exceptionalism

ex·cep·tion·less \-shənləs\ *adj* : admitting of no exception

exception principle *n* : a method or plan of supervision (as of a business) under which only significant deviations from normally expected results or conditions are brought to the attention of a supervisor for consideration and decision

ex·cep·tious \-shəs\ *adj* [*exception* + *-ous*] *archaic* : disposed to take exception — **ex·cep·tious·ness** *n* -ES *archaic*

ex·cep·tive \-ptiv, -tēv *also* -təv\ *adj* [ML *exceptivus*, fr. L *exceptus* + *-ivus* -ive] **1** : relating to, containing, or constituting exception : as **a** *of a word* : serving to introduce a verbal exception ⟨an ~ preposition⟩ **b** *of a proposition in logic* : having the subject limited by exception **2** *archaic* : EXCEPTIOUS — **ex·cep·tive·ly** \-təvlē, -li\ *adv*

excepts *pres 3d sing of* EXCEPT

excern *vt* [L *excernere* to sift out, separate, discharge (as feces) — more at EXCRETE] *obs* : EXCRETE, DISCHARGE

[1]**ex·cerpt** \(ˈ)ek¦sərpt, ik'sə|, |əpt, |əipt *sometimes* (ˈ)eg¦z| *or* ig'z|\ *vb* -ED/-ING/-S [L *excerptus*, past part. of *excerpere*, fr. *ex-* [1]ex- + *-cerpere* (fr. *carpere* to gather, pluck, divide) — more at HARVEST] *vt* **1** : to select (passages or details) as typical of a larger store : select for quoting : EXTRACT ⟨a compendium of quotable sayings ~*ed* from the writings of a variety of modern writers —*Book-of-the-Month Club News*⟩ **2** *obs* : to take out : REMOVE **3** : to shorten by selecting parts of ⟨a new biography that is to be ~*ed* for serial publication in three installments⟩ ~ *vi* : to make excerpts

[2]**ex·cerpt** \ˈek,s| *sometimes* ˈeg,z|\ *n* -S [L *excerptum*, fr. neut. of *excerptus*, past part.] : a selection or fragment (as from a writing or a work of music) ⟨played ~*s* from the opera⟩ : a chosen portion or sample ⟨cabled daily ~*s* of life in the Orient⟩

ex·cerp·ta \ek's|, ik's| *sometimes* eg'z| *or* ig'z|\ *n pl* [L, pl. of *excerptum*] : brief bits of writing; *often* : clippings or résumés

ex·cerpt·er *also* **ex·cerp·tor** *pronunc at* [1]EXCERPT+ə(r)\ *n* -S : a maker of excerpts

ex·cerpt·ible *pronunc at* [1]EXCERPT+əbəl\ *adj* : fit or suitable for use as a source of excerpts

ex·cerp·tion \ek's|ərpshən, ik's|, |əp-, |əip- *sometimes* eg'z- *or* ig'z-\ *n* -S [L *excerption-, excerptio*, fr. *excerptus* + *-ion-, -io* -ion] **1** *archaic* : EXTRACT **2** : an act or process of excerpting esp. in the selection of material for an abridgment

[1]**ex·cess** \ik'ses, ˈek,ses, ek'ses\ *n* -ES [ME, fr. MF or LL; MF *excès*, fr. LL *excessus*, fr. L, departure, fr. *excessus*, past part. of *excedere* to go forth, exceed — more at EXCEED] **1 a** : a state of surpassing or going beyond limits : the fact of being in a measure beyond sufficiency, necessity, or duty : SUPERFLUITY, SUPERABUNDANCE ⟨~ of grief⟩ ⟨an ~ of provisions⟩ **b** : something that exceeds what is usual, proper, proportionate, or specified ⟨she was serious almost to ~ —Aldous Huxley⟩ **c** : the amount or degree by which one thing or number exceeds another ⟨there was an ~ of 10 bushels over what was needed to fill the bin⟩ ⟨the ~ of 12 plus 2 over 12 minus 2 is 4⟩ **2** : undue or immoderate indulgence : intemperance esp. in eating and drinking ⟨~ at table is seldom healthful⟩ — often used in pl. ⟨their ~*es* led to their expulsion from the congregation⟩

syn SUPERFLUITY, SURPLUS, SURPLUSAGE, OVERPLUS: EXCESS may be used of any exceeding or going beyond measure, limits, or accustomed bounds ⟨an *excess* of carbon dioxide in the air⟩ ⟨an *excess* of supply over demand⟩ It is often used in connection with culpable lack of moderation, temperance, and restraint ⟨I have a considerable affection for the Empire style, of which I bought a houseful when it could be bought for half nothing. But the *excesses* of the style are terrible —Arnold Bennett⟩ ⟨Washington began with the prestige of a unanimous election and ended, as his farewell address plainly reveals, with a deep abhorrence of the *excesses* of intense party spirit —A.N.Holcombe⟩ SUPERFLUITY may refer to a vain, wasteful, or embarrassing excess, over actual needs ⟨as I have a certain amount of money to spare and am possessed by the strange desire to collect unnecessary objects, I succumb easily to anyone who asks me to buy *superfluities* and luxuries —Aldous Huxley⟩ ⟨not the lack of expressive power, but the *superfluity*. He was profusely and indiscriminately loquacious —Virginia Woolf⟩ SURPLUS applies to whatever is left after all needed has been used or expended; it is often used in reference to money or to valuable commodities ⟨the company books showing a *surplus*⟩ ⟨the Patent Office has become one of the relatively few government establishments that not only pay their way, but normally yield a *surplus* —F.A.Ogg & P.O. Ray⟩ ⟨nearly every farmer had an apple press with which he prepared adequate quantities of cider and vinegar for family consumption, and frequently there were *surpluses* to market —W.M.Kollmorgen⟩ SURPLUSAGE may refer to an unjustified or useless excess ⟨the Senate conferees took the position that the usage of the word "prior" was unnecessary and was mere *surplusage* —*U.S.Code*⟩ OVERPLUS may designate an unnecessary addition or adventitious augmentation ⟨we entered the Rectory drive, the car poked at by the wild *overplus* of vegetation which was certainly not that of a normal garden —Wyndham Lewis⟩

— **in excess of** *prep* : to an amount or degree beyond : OVER ⟨gifts *in excess of* $1,000,000 —T.M.Gordon⟩ ⟨is regarded as *in excess of* that which the law should permit —W.L.Sperry⟩ ⟨made demands on the climbers *in excess of* what was required —E.F.Norton⟩ — **to excess** *adv* : IMMODERATELY ⟨started drinking *to excess* and eventually became an alcoholic —Polly Adler⟩

[2]**ex·cess** \ˈek,ses, ik's-, ek's-\ *adj* [ME, fr. *excess*, n.] **1** : more than or above the usual or specified amount : that constitutes an excess ⟨~ property on hand after a contract ends⟩ ⟨the body tends to rid itself of its ~ nitrogen —H.G.Armstrong⟩ ⟨~ sleep may be a sign of a disturbance —Morris Fishbein⟩ **2** : exceeding in weight or size an allowance transportable without charge ⟨~ baggage⟩

excess condemnation *n* : condemnation under eminent domain of an area of land greater than needed for the immediate purposes for which the land is being condemned

excess insurance *n* **1** : insurance in which the underwriter's liability does not arise until the loss exceeds a stated amount and then only on the excess above that amount **2** : insurance over and above that necessary to meet the requirements of a coinsurance clause

ex·ces·sive \ik'sesiv, (ˈ)ek¦s-, -sēv *also* -esəv\ *adj* [ME, fr. MF *excessif*, fr. ML *excessivus*, fr. L *excessus* (past part.) + *-ivus* -ive] : characterized by or present in excess: as **a** : exceeding the usual, proper, or normal ⟨~ rainfall⟩ ⟨an ~ penchant for intellectual and verbal hairsplitting —J.W. Beach⟩ ⟨gross and ~ language⟩ **b** : very large, great, or numerous : greater than usual ⟨the early rains induced an ~ vegetative growth⟩ **c** : given to excess : INTEMPERATE

syn IMMODERATE, INORDINATE, EXTRAVAGANT, EXORBITANT, EXTREME: EXCESSIVE describes whatever notably exceeds the reasonable, usual, proper, necessary, just, or endurable ⟨outraged farmers had clamored against the railroad monopoly, charging that it gouged them with *excessive* freight charges —Allan Nevins & H.S.Commager⟩ ⟨*excessive* bail shall not be required, nor *excessive* fines imposed, nor cruel and unusual punishments inflicted —*U.S. Constitution*⟩ IMMODERATE may suggest blameworthy lack of restraint and moderation ⟨I can testify that the Mass gave him extreme, I may even say *immoderate*, satisfaction. It was almost orgiastic —T.S.Eliot⟩ ⟨Mr. Hilary saw, at one view, all the circumstances of the adventure, and burst into an *immoderate* fit of laughter —T.L.Peacock⟩ INORDINATE connotes an excess transcending reason or judgment ⟨his pride was *inordinate*. Rather than humble himself, rather than bend, he flings himself to the dogs —Henry Miller⟩ ⟨his insensate wrath seemed to pass all ordinary bounds . . . Even Heath was startled by Rex's *inordinate* malignity —W.H.Wright⟩ EXTRAVAGANT connotes a similar excess; the word may imply a wild, prodigal, or foolish wandering from fit restraints and accustomed bounds ⟨she tore her hair and beat her breast, and abandoned herself to all the violences of *extravagant* emotion —Bram Stoker⟩ ⟨the absence of a customary norm of consumption was most conspicuous in the *extravagant* life of the courts. To externalize the desire for power, wealth, and privilege, the princes of the Renascence lavished upon private luxury and display enormous amounts of money —Lewis Mumford⟩ ⟨altogether too *extravagant* and impossible to be regarded in any other light than as a monstrous joke —Charles Dickens⟩ EXORBITANT likewise suggests a notable excessive departure from the customary; frequently applied to prices asked, demands, or exactions ⟨a continuation of the law for the renegotiation of war contracts — which will prevent *exorbitant* profits and assure fair prices to the government —F.D.Roosevelt⟩ ⟨blinded by so *exorbitant* a lust of gold, the youngster straightway tasked his wits, casting about to kill the lady —Robert Browning⟩ EXTREME may suggest an attaining to, approaching to, and tending toward the greatest excess possible, although it frequently means only to a notably high degree ⟨the fascination of crime is perpetual, especially in its *extreme* form as murder —A.C.Ward⟩ ⟨there are wings *extreme* to the point of anarchy —J.L.Lowes⟩

ex·ces·sive·ly \-səvlē, -li\ *adv* [ME, fr. *excessive* + *-ly*] : to an exceptional or even improper degree : to excess : EXTREMELY ⟨~ fond of fine dress and luxury⟩

ex·ces·sive·ness \-sivnəs, -sēv- *also* -səv-\ *n* -ES : the quality or state of being excessive ⟨the townspeople chafed under the ~ of the tax imposed on them⟩

excessive verdict *n* : a verdict considered by the court as awarding shockingly and unreasonably high damages to the plaintiff even assuming that all the evidence most favorable to the plaintiff is true

excess-loss reinsurance *n* : reinsurance by a company agreeing to bear any loss in excess of a stipulated amount often with some maximum limitation — compare EXCESS INSURANCE, EXCESS REINSURANCE

excess-profits tax *n* : a tax imposed esp. during war on business profits that are in excess of the average profits over a specified base period, of a specified rate of return on invested capital, or of a specified rate of return on certain military contracts

excess reinsurance *n* : reinsurance by a company assuming liability on the risk only for that amount of insurance which is over and above a stated sum with the principle of contribution applying in payment of losses

exch *abbr* **1** exchange **2** exchequer

[1]**ex·change** \iks'chānj, eks'ch *also* ˈeks,ch-\ *n, often attrib* [ME *eschaunge, exchaunge*, fr. MF *eschange*, fr. *eschangier*] **1** : the act of giving or taking one thing in return for another as if equivalent: as **a** : the restoration to their fellows of persons captured during military action usu. by each contesting side in equivalent numbers **b** : the process of reciprocal transfer of ownership (as between persons) : TRADE, BARTER; *broadly* : a complex of transactions that results in the actual interchange of goods and services (as among primitive peoples) even though any one transfer may be widely separated in space and time from another and may take place under the guise of presenting gifts or in consequence of traditional ceremonies — compare KULA **c** : a mutual grant under the law of equal interests one being in consideration of the other **d** : reciprocal transfer (as of military or naval commissions) between individuals usu. with some added gratuity to the individual accepting the less desirable **2 a** : the act of substituting one thing in the place of another ⟨the gradual ~ of her grief for quiet peace⟩ ⟨the startling transformation wrought by the ~ of his rags for royal raiment⟩ **b** : reciprocal giving and receiving (as of courtesies, blows, or words) **c** : a mutual capture of men in chess or checkers **d** : reciprocal interchange of sisters or daughters whereby two men in certain primitive societies obtain wives for themselves or for their brothers or sons ⟨the custom of marriage by ~⟩ **e** : a chemical reaction or process in which one atom, ion, or group changes places with another ⟨isotopic ~⟩ — see ION EXCHANGE; compare DOUBLE DECOMPOSITION, SUBSTITUTION 1d **3** : something offered, given, or received in an exchange (as goods, blows, or words): as **a** : a usu. brief and often heated, acrid, or witty dialogue **b** : a publication (as a periodical) given (as by a publisher or author) in return for another publication; *also* : an item or article reprinted from a newspaper **4 a** : funds (as drafts, checks, or bills of exchange) payable currently at a distant point either in (1) a foreign currency or (2) in domestic currency — called also respectively (1) *foreign exchange*, (2) *domestic exchange* **b** : the amount paid for the collection (as of a draft, bill of exchange, or check drawn in one place upon another) **c** (1) : interchange or conversion of the money of two countries or of current and uncurrent money with allowance for difference in value (2) : RATE OF EXCHANGE (3) : the amount of the difference in value between two currencies or between values at two places — compare ARBITRAGE **d exchanges** *pl* : the items (as drafts, checks) that are presented in a clearinghouse for settlement by mutual interchange of credits and debits and payment of balances **5** : a place where things or services are exchanged: as **a** *obs* : a money changer's place of business **b** : a place devoted to the transaction (as between merchants, bankers, and brokers) of business usu. at the professional level — often used in combination ⟨the grain ~⟩ ⟨a southern stock ~⟩ **c** : an organized market or center for trading in certain commodities at wholesale or on contracts calling for future delivery ⟨a produce ~⟩ **d** : a store or shop where merchandise usu. of a particular type is bought, resold, or repaired ⟨a typewriter ~⟩ **e** : a cooperative store or society ⟨a farmers' ~⟩ **f** *archaic* : BARROOM, SALOON **g** : TELEPHONE EXCHANGE **h** : POST EXCHANGE — **in exchange** *adv* : as a substitute ⟨what will you give me *in exchange*⟩; *sometimes* : as payment ⟨he received $10 *in exchange* for a couple of hours of work⟩

[2]**exchange** \"\ *vb* [ME *eschaungen*, fr. MF *eschangier*, fr. (assumed) VL *excambiare*, fr. L *ex-* [1]ex- + *cambiare* to exchange — more at CHANGE] *vt* **1 a** : to part with, give, or transfer in consideration of something received as an equivalent ⟨the boy *exchanged* his mother's cow for a handful of beans⟩ **b** : to supply (something else) in place of goods returned ⟨do you think the store will ~ something more up-to-date for the high shoes my aunt bought?⟩; *also* : to have (goods returned to the seller) replaced by other merchandise ⟨I'm sure you can ~ the blouse but probably not return it for a refund⟩ **2** : to part with for a substitute ⟨*exchanging* future security for immediate enjoyment⟩ : to lay aside, quit, or resign (something presently possessed) in return for some alternate ⟨*exchanged* his youth and health for the burdens of wealth⟩ ⟨who would not ~ loneliness for happy companionship?⟩ **3** : to give and receive reciprocally (as things of the same kind) : BARTER, SWAP ⟨let's ~ hats⟩ ⟨I would ~ horses if you had a better horse⟩ ⟨if she could ~ natures with her brother⟩ ⟨*exchanging* heated words and finally blows⟩ **4** *obs* : ALTER, CHANGE ~ *vi* **1** : to pass or be received in exchange — used with *for* ⟨when the pound ~*s* for less than $3⟩ **2** : to engage in an exchange esp. of a commission or appointment ⟨anxious to ~ out of that provincial regiment⟩

ex·change·able \-jəbəl\ *adj* **1** : capable of being exchanged : fit or proper to be exchanged **2** : available for making exchanges : RATABLE — **ex·change·ably** \-blē, -li\ *adv*

exchange charge *n* : a small deduction from the face value of a check or draft on a distant point made by the bank that cashes such a document

exchange control *n* : governmental regulation of the conversion of currencies, the purchase of foreign coin or gold, and the transfer of funds between countries

exchange depreciation *n* : reduction of the foreign exchange value of a currency below its true relative value (as for the purpose of stimulating exports)

ex·chang·ee \ˌeks,chān¦jē, iks¦ch-, eks¦ch-\ *n* -S [[2]*exchange* + *-ee*] : a participant or former participant in an exchange program (as of students or teachers)

exchange note *n* : CHANGE NOTE

exchange office *also* **exchange post office** *n* : a post office assigned to and having special facilities for the interchange of mail with foreign countries

ex·chang·er *pronunc at* [1]EXCHANGE +ə(r)\ *n* [ME *eschaungeour*, fr. AF *eschaungeor*, fr. OF *eschangier* to exchange + *-eor* -or] **1** : one that exchanges **2** : MONEY CHANGER, BANKER; *esp* : one formerly appointed in England to exchange plate and bullion for coin under royal authority **3** : an agent or apparatus for carrying out exchange reactions or processes: as **a** : ION EXCHANGER **b** : HEAT EXCHANGER

exchange rate *n* : the ratio at which the principal unit of two currencies may be traded whether arbitrarily established by government action or based on the relative capacity of each currency to buy (as gold) on a free market ⟨an *exchange rate* of nearly 800 to 1⟩ — compare PEG

exchanges *pl of* EXCHANGE, *pres 3d sing of* EXCHANGE

exchange student *n* : a student usu. from a foreign country received free into an institution in exchange for one sent to that country on the same terms

exchange teacher *n* : a teacher teaching at an institution other than his own in exchange with a teacher from that institution

exchange ticket *n* : a slip exchanged between stockbrokers to check accuracy of a transaction — called also *comparison slip*

exchange transfusion *n* : simultaneous withdrawal of the recipient's blood and transfusion with the donor's blood esp. in the treatment of erythroblastosis

exchanging *pres part of* EXCHANGE

excheat *obs var of* ESCHEAT

[1]**ex·che·quer** \ˈeks,chekə(r) *also* iks'ch- *or* eks'ch-\ *n* -S [ME *escheker, exchequer*, fr. AF *escheker, eschekier*, fr. OF *eschequier* chessboard, counting table — more at CHECKER] **1** *usu cap* : a department or office of state in medieval England charged with the collection and management of the royal revenue and the judicial determination of all revenue causes **2** *usu cap* : a former superior court having jurisdiction in England and Wales primarily over revenue matters but also over causes in equity and a concurrent jurisdiction with the courts of common law and now forming a division of the Court of King's Bench **3** *often cap* **a** : the department or office of state in Great Britain and Northern Ireland charged with the receipt and care of the national revenue and headed by a chancellor **b** : the national banking account or purse of this realm **4** : TREASURY; *esp* : a national or royal treasury **5** : pecuniary possessions or resources : PURSE, FINANCES ⟨the ~ is low just now⟩

[2]**exchequer** \"\ *vt* -ED/-ING/-S : to proceed against in the Court of Exchequer

exchequer bill *n* : a former British short-time bill of credit or promissory note issued by governmental authority and bearing interest — compare TREASURY BILL

exchequer bond *n* : a British government interest-bearing bond constituting part of the unfunded debt

exchequer of the jews *usu cap E&J* : a department of the English royal exchequer charged in the 13th century with the supervision of all business with the Jews

ex·cide \ek'sīd, ik-\ *vt* -ED/-ING/-S [L *excidere* — more at EXCISE] : to cut out : EXCISE

[1]**ex·cip·i·ent** \ik'sipēənt, (ˈ)ek¦s-\ *adj* [L *excipient-, excipiens*, pres. part. of *excipere* to take out, make an exception of, take, receive — more at EXCEPT] : taking exception

[2]**excipient** \"\ *n* -S [L *excipient-, excipiens*, pres. part.] : an inert substance (as gum arabic, syrup, lanolin, or starch) that forms a vehicle (as for a drug or antigen); *esp* : one that in the presence of sufficient liquid imparts to a medicated mixture the adhesive quality needed for the preparation of pills or tablets

ex·ci·ple \ˈeksəpəl\ *also* **ex·ci·pule** \-,pyül\ *n* -S [NL *excipulum*, fr. L, a kind of vessel, fr. *excipere*] : a saucer-shaped rim around the hymenium of various lichens formed (1) from the hypothecium or (2) from the upper layer of the thallus — called also respectively (1) *proper exciple*, (2) *thalloid exciple*

ex·cip·u·la·ce·ae \(,)ek,sipyə'lāsē,ē\ *n pl, cap* [NL, fr. *Excipula*, type genus (fr. L *excipulum* receptacle, fr. *excipere* to catch, take out, receive) + *-aceae* — more at EXCEPT] : a family of imperfect fungi (order Sphaeropsidales) characterized by cup-shaped pycnidia

ex·cip·u·li·form \ek'sipyələ,fȯrm\ *adj* [NL *excipulum* + E *-iform*] : resembling or having the shape of an exciple

ex·cip·u·lum \-ləm\ *n, pl* **excipula** [NL] : EXCIPLE

ex·circle \ˈek(s)+,-\ *n* [[1]*ex-* + *circle*] : an escribed circle

ex·cis·able *pronunc at* [1]EXCISE +əbəl\ *adj* [[2]*excise* + *-able*] : subject to excise

[1]**ex·cise** \ˈek,sīz *also* -īs *sometimes* ek's- *or* ik's-\ *n* -S *often attrib* [obs. D *accijs, excijs* (now *accijns*), fr. MD *excijs*, prob. modif. of OF *assise* session, settlement, assessment, tax — more at ASSIZE] **1** *or* **excise tax a** *obs* : DUTY, TOLL, TAX **b** : an internal tax, duty, or impost levied upon the manufacture, sale, or consumption of a commodity within a country and usu. forming an indirect tax that falls on the ultimate consumer **c** : any of various duties or fees levied on producers of excisable commodities **d** : any of various taxes upon privileges (as of engaging in a particular trade or sport, transferring property, or engaging in business in a corporate capacity) that are often assessed in the form of a license or other fee **2** : a former department or bureau of the British public service charged with collection of the excise taxes and now merged in the Bureau of Customs and Excise

[2]**excise** \"\ *vt* -ED/-ING/-S **1** : to lay or impose an excise upon **2** *now dial Brit* : to impose upon : OVERCHARGE

[3]**ex·cise** \(ˈ)ek¦sīz, ik's-\ *vt* -ED/-ING/-S [L *excisus*, past part. of *excidere*, fr. *ex-* [1]ex- + *-cidere* (fr. *caedere* to cut) — more at CONCISE] **1** : to cut out ⟨~ a tumor⟩ : remove by or as if by cutting out : RESECT, EXTIRPATE — compare AMPUTATE **2** : to make an excision in : hollow out — used chiefly as a participial adjective ⟨antenna bases *excised*⟩

ex·cise·man *pronunc at* [1]EXCISE +mən\ *n, pl* **excisemen** [[1]*excise* + *man*] : an officer who inspects and rates articles liable to excise under British law and often collects or enforces payment of excise due

ex·ci·sion \ek'sizhən, ik-\ *n* -S [MF, fr. L *excision-, excisio*, fr. *excisus* + *-ion-, -io* -ion] : the act or procedure of excising: as **a** : EXTIRPATION, DESTRUCTION, ERASURE **b** : excommunication from a church **c** : surgical removal (as of a diseased part) : RESECTION

ex·ci·sion·al \-zhənᵊl, -zhnəl\ *adj* : pertaining to or involving excision ⟨~ surgery⟩

ex·cit·abil·i·ty \ik,sīd·ə'biləd·ē, ek-, -ītə-, -lətē, -i\ *n* -ES : the quality of being excitable

ex·cit·able \ik'sīd·əbəl, ek-, -ītə-\ *adj* [LL *excitabilis*, fr. L *excitare* to call forth, arouse, excite + *-abilis* -able] **1** : capable of being readily roused into action or a state of excitement or irritability **2** *of living tissue or an organism* : capable of being activated by and reacting to stimuli : exhibiting irritability — **ex·cit·able·ness** *n* -ES

[1]**ex·cit·ant** \ik'sītᵊnt, ek'-; ˈeksəd·ənt, -sətənt *also* -sət'nt\ *adj* [L *excitant-, excitans*, pres. part. of *excitare*] : tending to excite : EXCITING ⟨an ~ drug⟩

[2]**excitant** \"\ *n* -S : something that excites; *usu* : an agent that arouses or augments physiologic (as nervous) activity

ex·ci·ta·tion \ˌek,sī'tāshən, ˌeksə'-\ *n* -S [ME *excitacioun*, fr. MF *excitation*, fr. LL *excitation-, excitatio*, fr. L *excitatus* (past part. of *excitare*) + *-ion-, -io* -ion] **1** : the act of exciting or state of being excited : EXCITEMENT ⟨astir with delicious ~ —Agnes Repplier⟩ **2** : electric energizing: as **a** : production of a magnetic field (as in a dynamo, motor, or loudspeaker); *also* : the magnetizing force producing a particular magnetic field **b** : the application of signal voltage to a control electrode of an electron tube; *also* : the voltage so applied **3** : the arousing of activity (as by neural or electrical stimulation) in an individual, organ, or tissue; *broadly* : the disturbed or altered condition resulting from such arousal **4** : the process of exciting an electron, atomic nucleus, atom, molecule, or other particle

ex·cit·ative \ik'sīd·əd·iv, (ˈ)ek¦s-\ *adj* [MF *excitatif*, fr. *exciter* + *-atif* -ative] : having power to excite : tending or serving to induce excitation

ex·cit·a·to·ry \ik'sīd·ə,tōrē, ek-\ *adj* [*excitation* + *-ory*] **1** : EXCITATIVE **2** : exhibiting or marked by excitement or excitation

ex·cite \ik'sīt, ek-, *usu* -īd·+V\ *vt* -ED/-ING/-S [ME *exciten*, fr. MF *exciter*, fr. L *excitare* to call forth, arouse, excite, fr.

ex- ¹ex- + *citare* to put in movement, summon, rouse — more at CITE] **1 a :** to call to activity in any way **:** stir up (as a person or a hive of bees) to combined or general activity **b :** to rouse to feeling **:** kindle to passionate emotion **2 :** to energize (as an electromagnet) **:** produce a magnetic field in ⟨~ a dynamo⟩ **3 :** to arouse or increase the activity of (a living organism or any of its parts) **:** STIMULATE **4 :** to raise (an atomic nucleus, an atom, a molecule, an electron, or other particle) to a higher energy level (as by heating, irradiation, or bombardment) ⟨radiation ~*s* and ionizes the atoms of material through which it passes —R.S.Rochlin⟩ **syn** see PROVOKE

ex·cit·ed·ly *adv* **:** in an excited manner **:** with excitement

ex·cit·ed·ness *n* -ES **:** the quality or state of being excited ⟨experienced a certain ~ at the prospect of a trip⟩

excited state *n* **:** any of the states of a physical system (as of atoms, molecules, atomic nuclei) that is higher in energy than the ground state

ex·cite·ment \-ītmənt\ *n* -S **1 :** the act of exciting or state of being excited **:** AGITATION, STIR **2 a :** something that excites or rouses ⟨the ~*s* of the journey⟩ **b** *archaic* **:** something (as a motive or incitement) that induces action **3 a :** aroused, augmented, or abnormal activity of an organism or functioning of an organ or part **b :** extreme motor hyperactivity (as in catatonic schizophrenia or manic-depressive psychosis)

ex·cit·er \-īd·ə(r), -ītə-\ *n* -S [ME, fr. *exciten* + *-er*] **1 :** one that excites **2 a :** a dynamo or battery that supplies the electric current used to produce the magnetic field in another dynamo or motor **b :** an electrical oscillator that generates the carrier frequency (as for a radar or frequency-modulation transmitter)

exciter lamp *n* **:** a lamp whose light passes through the sound track of a motion-picture film and enters a photoelectric cell causing the current fluctuations that actuate the loudspeaker

exciting *adj, sometimes* -ER/-EST **1 :** being a source of or marked by excitement **:** absorbingly interesting ⟨an ~ adventure⟩ ⟨an ~ period in the history of our nation⟩ **2 :** inducing a state of excitement or excited interest **:** INTRIGUING, STIMULATING ⟨an ~ person to know⟩ ⟨the ~ mystery of Christmas packages⟩ **3 :** having an immediate effect **:** PRECIPITATING — used of various agents or causes (as of disease); contrasted with *remote* ⟨they had long been on bad terms but the ~ cause of the quarrel was her comments on his drinking⟩ ⟨the ~ agent of brucellosis is a specific bacterium⟩ — **ex·cit·ing·ly** *adv*

exciting current *n* **1 :** a current that excites or energizes an electrical apparatus (as the field magnets of a dynamo) **2 :** the current taken by the primary of a transformer on no load

excito- *comb form* [excitor & L *excitare* to excite] **1 :** excitor and ⟨*excito*motory⟩ ⟨*excito*secretory⟩ **2 :** exciting **:** stimulating **:** causing activity (of a specified kind) ⟨*excito*catabolism⟩

ex·ci·ton \ˈeksə,tän\ *n* -S [ISV *excitation* + *-on*] **:** a concentration of energy assumed to exist in crystalline semiconductors under the influence of radiation, to be resident in the electric field between a displaced electron and the hole left by it, to be a mobile unit behaving like a neutral particle with mass and momentum, and to have wave-mechanical characteristics

ex·ci·tor \ikˈsīd·ə(r), ek-, -ītə-\ *n* -S **1** *archaic* **:** EXCITER **2 :** an afferent nerve arousing increased action of the part that it supplies

ex·ci·tron \ˈeksə,trän\ *n* -S [*excitation* + *-tron*] **:** a single-anode mercury-arc rectifier having its output controlled by a grid and an arc that is started by means of a mercury spray

excl *abbr* **1** exclamation **2** excluded; excluding; exclusive

¹ex·claim \ikˈsklām, ek-\ *vb* -ED/-ING/-S [MF *exclamer*, fr. L *exclamare*, fr. *ex-* ¹ex- + *clamare* to cry out, call — more at CLAIM] *vi* **1 :** to cry out or speak in strong or sudden emotion **:** give a cry or utter a word indicative of surprise, pain, anger, delight, or other emotion ⟨~*ed* with wonder as the view unfolded⟩ ⟨~*ing* over the compactness of the trailer⟩ ⟨~*ed* in delight⟩ **2 :** to speak loudly or vehemently (as in blame, mockery, or protest) — used with *against, at, on,* or *upon* ⟨~ against oppression⟩ ⟨~*ed* furiously upon the wickedness of the plot⟩ ~ *vt* **:** to utter sharply, passionately, or vehemently **:** PROCLAIM ⟨powers of air whose tongues ~ dominion —R.P.Warren⟩

syn EXCLAIM, CRY (*out*), EJACULATE, BLURT (*out*), SNORT can mean, in common, to express oneself in sudden, usu. vehement and unpremeditated, utterance. EXCLAIM usu. implies the force of strong emotion, as anger, joy, or surprise, or the sudden force of protest, criticism, praise, or reproach ⟨"Oh, the troubles of the young!" her mother *exclaimed* —Irving Bacheller⟩ ⟨"Well done!" the instructor *exclaimed*⟩ CRY and CRY (*out*) stress loud, exclamatory tones ⟨"I forbid you!" *cried* my master —W.J.Locke⟩ ⟨as we drove past, a man *cried out* that the road ahead was washed out⟩ EJACULATE usu. stresses sudden, forceful, and abrupt utterance as from astonishment, sudden delight, or great disgust ⟨striding up and down in front of her and *ejaculating* horrible oaths —W.J. Locke⟩ ⟨shook his head, and *ejaculated*, "Whew! Whew! Whew!" as though he were overcome with disgust —V.G. Heiser⟩ ⟨"Fifty thousand! My goodness gracious me!" *ejaculated* Mrs. Berry in flattering accents —George Meredith⟩ BLURT (*out*) is similar to EJACULATE but puts more stress upon the impulsiveness of the remark, suggesting an irresistible, often naïve, compulsion to speak ⟨security officers reported overhearing him *blurt out* secret information —*Time*⟩ ⟨stung by his reproaches, I *blurted out* that he had no right to talk to me, even in fun, in such a way —W.H.Hudson †1922⟩ ⟨wished to *blurt out* his indignation —Joseph Conrad⟩ SNORT implies explosive utterance resembling a snort, motivated by contempt, scorn, or indignation ⟨"Running away, and leaving Johnnie to take the blame!" he *snorted* in disgust at himself —Rex Ingamells⟩ ⟨"Talk of his successful son", *snorted* my father, whom I had fairly roused. "He is not fit to black his father's boots" —Samuel Butler †1902⟩ ⟨*snorted* with disdain at such vulgarity —C.S.Forester⟩

²exclaim \"\ *n* -S *archaic* **:** OUTCRY, CLAMOR

ex·claim·er \-mə(r)\ *n* -S **:** one that exclaims

ex·cla·ma·tion \,ekskləˈmāshən\ *n* -S [ME *exclamacioun*, fr. L *exclamation-, exclamatio*, fr. *exclamatus* (past part. of *exclamare*) + *-ion-, -io* -ion] **1 :** the act of exclaiming **:** a sharp or sudden utterance expressive of strong feeling ⟨he uttered an ~ of pain⟩ ⟨amid ~*s* of delight the cake was brought in⟩ **2 :** vehement expression (as of protest, reproach, or complaint) ⟨~*s* of social prejudice —Bernard Smith⟩ **3 :** a word, phrase, clause, or sentence used as an outcry or interjection **4 :** EXCLAMATION POINT — **ex·cla·ma·tion·al** \¦==¦māshənᵊl, -shnəl\ *adj*

exclamation point *or* **exclamation mark** *n* **:** the mark ! used in writing and printing after an interjection, after a sentence or phrase of assertion, wish, or command, and after a direct or indirect question to indicate forceful utterance or strong feeling — called also *mark of exclamation, note of exclamation*

ex·clam·a·tive \ikˈsklamәd·iv, ek-\ *adj* [*exclamation* + *-ive*] *archaic* **:** EXCLAMATORY

ex·clam·a·to·ri·ly \ik¦sklamə¦tōrəlē, (,)ek-, -tȯr-, -li\ *adv* **:** in an exclamatory manner

ex·clam·a·to·ry \=ˈ==mə,tōrē, -tȯr-, -ri\ *adj* [*exclamation* + *-ory*] **1 :** containing, expressing, using, or relating to exclamation ⟨an ~ phrase⟩ ⟨~ speakers⟩ **2 :** showing emotion on the part of speaker or writer by its elliptical form (as in *Oh, for a camera! You an author!*) or by an intensifying expression (as an interrogative pronoun or adverb or other part of speech in an emphatic position like an interjection) ⟨an ~ noun⟩ **3 :** like or having the effect of an exclamation esp. in lending emphasis or focusing attention ⟨set off by a bright ~ scarf⟩

ex·clave \ˈek,sklāv\ *n* -S [¹*ex-* + *-clave* (as in *enclave*)] **:** a portion of a country that is separated from the main part and surrounded by politically alien territory and that is an enclave in respect to the surrounding country ⟨after World War I East Prussia became an ~ of Germany⟩

ex·clo·sure \ekˈsklōzhə(r), ik-\ *n* -S *often attrib* [¹*ex-* + *-closure* (as in *enclosure*)] **:** an area from which intruders (as browsing animals) are excluded by fencing or other means ⟨the ~ plot is used to keep an area in a natural condition, free from grazing by deer or domestic livestock —*Wildlife Management Handbook for Forest Officers*⟩ — compare ENCLOSURE

ex·clud·abil·i·ty \ik,sklüdəˈbiləd·ē, (,)ek-, -ətē, -i\ *n* -ES **:** the condition of being excludable **:** suitability for exclusion ⟨the ~ of certain income for purposes of tax computation⟩

ex·clud·able *or* **ex·clud·ible** \ikˈsklüdəbəl, (ˈ)ek¦s-\ *adj* **:** subject to exclusion ⟨~ classes of aliens include those with certain specified mental or physical defects⟩ ⟨~ income⟩

ex·clude \ikˈsklüd, ek-\ *vt* -ED/-ING/-S [ME *excluden*, fr. L *excludere*, fr. *ex-* ¹ex- + *-cludere* (fr. *claudere* to close) — more at CLOSE] **1 a :** to shut out **:** restrain or hinder the entrance of ⟨immigrants must be screened to ~ the small fraction of undesirables⟩ ⟨if you draw the blind it will ~ the glare⟩ ⟨that high ridge tends to ~ the breezes⟩ **b :** to bar from participation, enjoyment, consideration, or inclusion ⟨there was no need to ~ your brother from our talks⟩ ⟨that request must be *excluded* from further consideration⟩ **c :** to prevent or refuse to tolerate the occurrence, use, or existence of ⟨such words are *excluded* from polite conversation⟩ ⟨true faith ~*s* all doubt⟩ ⟨would ~ any oppressive measures no matter how expedient⟩ **2 a :** to put out **:** expel esp. from a place or position previously occupied ⟨the executed queen's child was specifically *excluded* from the succession⟩ **b :** to eject esp. in giving birth or hatching ⟨as soon as the larva was *excluded* from the egg⟩

syn DEBAR, BLACKBALL, ELIMINATE, RULE (*out*), SHUT (*out*), DISBAR, SUSPEND: EXCLUDE is a general term for shutting out or preventing entrance or admission ⟨*exclude* light from the rooms⟩ ⟨*exclude* hospital visitors⟩ ⟨minority groups who are *excluded* from some activities simply because their ancestors belonged to the less privileged classes in a time when social status was a matter of birth rather than ability —J.R. Everett⟩ ⟨*exclude* these subjects from consideration⟩ DEBAR may suggest the effect of a bar, sometimes literal but usu. figurative, in keeping from belonging or enjoying ⟨the Blue mountains . . . presented a cruel, awful barrier to the earlier settlers, and for a long time *debarred* them from the land beyond —Anthony Trollope⟩ ⟨that movement was condemned as heretical and its adherents were expelled from the Church and *debarred* from the communion —K.S.Latourette⟩ ⟨dangerous and foolish talk — of a sort that should *debar* its author from further serious consideration by intelligent Americans —*New Republic*⟩ BLACKBALL suggests exclusion from membership by adverse vote of those belonging ⟨he was very nearly *blackballed* at a West End club of which his birth and social position fully entitled him to become a member —Oscar Wilde⟩ ELIMINATE indicates a discharging, casting out, or getting rid of something figuring as a constituent member or part or an included element ⟨if children are *eliminated* from the statistics and only persons above the age of fifteen are taken into consideration —Morris Fishbein⟩ ⟨it is always wise to *eliminate* the personal equation from our judgments of literature —J.R.Lowell⟩ RULE (*out*) indicates formal or authoritative exclusion or elimination ⟨a play *ruled out* by the referee⟩ ⟨candidacies *ruled out* by the election laws⟩ ⟨the dean *ruled out* any special celebration⟩ SHUT (*out*) may indicate an effective, forceful, or definitive exclusion ⟨always *shut out* from public office⟩ ⟨the purpose of cartels is to *shut out* newcomers to an industry unless the newcomers are willing to join in and be subjected to cartel arrangements —*Wall Street Jour.*⟩ DISBAR refers to the formal processes whereby a lawyer is prevented from further practice or to similar exclusions ⟨the first proceeding in American history seeking to *disbar* an attorney for having invoked an historic constitutional privilege —*New Republic*⟩ ⟨*disbarred* from further teaching⟩ SUSPEND applies to a temporary elimination or exclusion pending investigation of fitness, occurrence of new developments, or full consideration of the matter ⟨*suspended* from the university for bad conduct⟩

ex·clud·er \-də(r)\ *n* -S **:** one that excludes: as **a :** a person who tries to keep another out of office **b :** a screen with divisions large enough to permit passage of workers but not a queen bee that is placed between chambers or supers of a beehive esp. to control the distribution of brood **c** *Brit* **:** a heavy rubber overshoe **:** GALOSH

ex·clu·si·ble \ikˈsklüzəbəl, ek-\ *adj* [L *exclusus* + E *-ible*] **:** subject to or deserving of exclusion ⟨emergencies, miscellanea, entertainment, such items are not ~ from the well-planned budget⟩

ex·clu·sion \ikˈsklüzhən, ek-\ *n* -S [L *exclusion-, exclusio*, fr. *exclusus* (past part. of *excludere* to exclude) + *-ion-, -io* -ion] **1 :** the act or an instance of excluding **:** the state of being excluded **:** DEBARRING, REJECTION; *specif* **:** refusal of entry into a country by immigration authorities **2 :** an exclusive disjunction

ex·clu·sion·ary \-zhə,nerē, -ri\ *adj* **:** tending to or so as to exclude ⟨~ policy⟩ ⟨~ separation of powers⟩ **:** EXCLUSIVE

exclusion clause *n* **:** a clause in an insurance policy barring certain losses or risks from coverage

¹ex·clu·sion·ist \-zh(ə)nəst\ *also* **ex·clu·sion·er** \-nə(r)\ *n* -S [*exclusion* + *-ist* or *-er*] **:** one who would exclude another from some right or privilege

²exclusionist \"\ *adj* **1 :** of, relating to, or involving exclusion (as from a right or privilege) ⟨~ policies⟩ **2** *of a tariff* **:** designed to reduce competition of foreign goods

exclusion principle *n* **:** PAULI EXCLUSION PRINCIPLE

¹ex·clu·sive \ikˈsklüs|iv, (ˈ)ek¦s-, -üz|, |ēv *also* |əv\ *adj* [MF *exclusif*, fr. ML *exclusivus*, fr. L *exclusus* + *-ivus* -ive] **1 a :** excluding or having power to exclude (as by preventing entrance or debarring from possession, participation, or use) ⟨~ regulations⟩ **b :** limiting or limited to possession, control, or use (as by a single individual or organization or by a special group or class) ⟨~ privileges of the citizens of a country⟩ ⟨the Puritan's God was a somewhat ~ possession —Agnes Repplier⟩ **2 :** excluding or inclined to exclude others (as outsiders) from participation (as in an association or privilege) or from cordial relations ⟨an ~ nation⟩; *sometimes* **:** snobbishly aloof ⟨an ~ clique⟩ ⟨an ~ attitude⟩ ⟨~ standards⟩ **3 a :** admitting of or soliciting only a socially restricted patronage (as of the upper classes) ⟨~ hotels or haberdashers⟩ **b :** STYLISH, FASHIONABLE ⟨~ styles⟩ **c :** EXPENSIVE; *often* **:** restricted in distribution, use, or appeal because of expense ⟨~ suburban neighborhoods⟩ **4 a :** SINGLE, SOLE ⟨an ~ agent⟩ ⟨~ jurisdiction⟩ **b :** UNDIVIDED, WHOLE ⟨giving the question his ~ attention⟩ **c** *of a news item* **:** being an exclusive **5** *in grammar* **:** referring to the speaker and another or some others but excluding the hearer

²exclusive \"\ *n* -S **1 a :** a person who fastidiously limits his acquaintance to a few **b :** an organism restricted in distribution to a single ecological community **2 :** something exclusive: as **a :** a newspaper story at first released to or printed by only one newspaper **b :** an exclusive right (as to sell a particular product in a certain area)

exclusive listing *n* **:** a formal agreement giving a broker the sole right to sell or to rent a property during a specified period of time

ex·clu·sive·ly \|əvlē, -li\ *adv* **:** in an exclusive manner

ex·clu·sive·ness \|ivnəs, |ēv- *also* |əv-\ *n* -ES **:** the quality or state of being exclusive

exclusive of *prep* **:** not taking into account **:** excluding from consideration ⟨there were four of us *exclusive of* the guide⟩ ⟨*exclusive of* artillery⟩

exclusive proposition *n* **:** a proposition in logic whose predicate is asserted to apply to its subject and no other ⟨"none but the brave deserves the fair" is a simple *exclusive proposition*⟩

ex·clu·siv·ism \ikˈsklüs|ə,vizəm, ek-, -üz|, |ē,-\ *n* -S **:** the practice of excluding or of being exclusive

ex·clu·siv·ist \-,vəst\ *n* -S *often attrib* **:** a practitioner of exclusivism — **ex·clu·siv·is·tic** \=¦==¦vistik, -tēk\ *adj*

ex·clu·siv·i·ty \,ek,sklüˈsivəd·ē, -ˈzi-, -vətē, -i\ *n* -ES **1 :** EXCLUSIVENESS **2 :** exclusive rights or services

ex·clu·so·ry \ikˈsklüs(ə)rē, -üz(-, -ri\ *adj* [LL *exclusorius*, fr. L *exclusus* + *-orius* -ory] **:** able to exclude **:** excluding or tending to exclude

excoct *vt* -ED/-ING/-S [L *excoctus*, past part. of *excoquere*, fr. *ex-* ¹ex- + *coquere* to cook, boil, melt — more at COOK] *obs* **:** to obtain, refine, or drive off by heat — **excoction** *n* -S *obs*

ex·coe·car·ia \,ekséˈka(a)rēə\ *n, cap* [NL, irreg. fr. L *excaecare* to blind + NL *-aria* — more at EXCECATE] **:** a genus of timber trees or shrubs (family Euphorbiaceae) of Asia, Africa, and Australia that have a poisonous acrid milky juice and in some species a bark used for dyeing

ex·cog·i·tate \(ˈ)ek¦skäjə,tāt, *usu* -ād·+V\ *vb* [L *excogitatus*, past part. of *excogitare*, fr. *ex-* ¹ex- + *cogitare* to cogitate — more at COGITATE] *vt* **1 :** to examine mentally with thoroughness and care so as to attain thorough grasp and comprehension of ⟨a much-*excogitated* topic⟩ ⟨to consider what ought to be written . . . he must first think and ~ his matter —Samuel Johnson⟩ **2 :** to evolve, invent, or contrive in the mind **:** think out or up ⟨*excogitating* arguments against hard work⟩ ⟨there may have been a time when the scientific inquirer sat still in his chair to ~ science —John Dewey⟩ ⟨socialism was not an ideal . . . *excogitated* by wise men —*Times Lit. Supp*⟩ ~ *vi* **:** COGITATE **syn** see CONSIDER

ex·cog·i·ta·tion \(,)=,==ˈtāshən\ *n* [L *excogitation-, excogitatio*, fr. *excogitatus* (past part. of *excogitare*) + *-ion-, -io* -ion] **1 :** the act of excogitating **2 :** a product of mental analysis and invention **:** something thought out or up **:** CONTRIVANCE

ex·cog·i·ta·tive \=ˈ==,tād·iv\ *adj* **:** of, relating to, or involving excogitation

ex co·mi·ta·te \,ek,skäməˈtād·ē\ [L] **:** from courtesy

ex·com·mu·ni·ca·ble \¦ekskə¦myünəkəbəl, -nēk-\ *adj* [¹*excommunicate* + *-able*] **:** liable to or deserving excommunication

¹ex·com·mu·ni·cate \,ekskəˈmyünə,kāt, *usu* -ād·+V\ *vt* [ME *excommunicaten*, fr. LL *excommunicatus*, past part. of *excommunicare*, fr. L *ex-* ¹ex- + LL *communicare* to communicate — more at COMMUNICATE] **:** to put out of communion or fellowship; *esp* **:** to cut off or shut out by an ecclesiastical sentence from communion with the church

²excommunicate \¦==¦==nəkət, -nēk-; -nə,kāt\ *adj* [LL *excommunicatus*, past part.] **:** interdicted from the rites of the church **:** EXCOMMUNICATED

³excommunicate \"\ *also* **ex·com·mu·ni·cant** \,==ˈ==kənt\ *n* -S [³*excommunicate* fr. ²*excommunicate*; *excommunicant* alter. (influenced by *communicant*) of ³*excommunicate*] **:** an excommunicated person

ex·com·mu·ni·ca·tion \,==,==nəˈkāshən\ *n* [ME *excommunicacioun*, fr. LL *excommunication-, excommunicatio*, fr. *excommunicatus* + L *-ion-, -io* -ion] **:** the act of excommunicating **:** exclusion from fellowship; *esp* **:** an ecclesiastical censure whereby the person against whom it is pronounced is for the time cast out of the communion of the church — see MAJOR EXCOMMUNICATION, MINOR EXCOMMUNICATION

ex·com·mu·ni·ca·tive \,ekskəˈmyünə,kād|iv, -nəkə|, -nēkə|, |t|, |ēv *also* |əv\ *adj* **:** tending toward, decreeing, or favoring excommunication

ex·com·mu·ni·ca·tor \-nə,kād·ə(r), -ātə-\ *n* [LL, fr. *excommunicatus* + L *-or*] **:** one that excommunicates

ex·com·mu·ni·ca·to·ry \-nəkə,tōrē, -nēk-, -tȯr-, -ri\ *adj* [ML *excommunicatorius*, fr. LL *excommunicatus* + L *-orius* -ory] **:** relating to, causing, or declaring excommunication

excommunion *n* [¹*ex-* + *communion*] *obs* **:** EXCOMMUNICATION

ex·conjugant \(ˈ)eks+\ *n* [¹*ex-* + *conjugant*] **:** a protozoan just after the separation following conjugation

ex con·trac·tu \,ekskənˈtrak(,)t(y)ü\ [L] **:** upon or from a contract — used of legal actions or obligations

¹ex·co·ri·ate \ekˈskōrē,āt, ik-, -kȯr-, *usu* -ād·+V\ *vt* -ED/-ING/-S [ME *excoriaten*, fr. LL *excoriatus*, past part. of *excoriare*, fr. L *ex-* ¹ex- + *corium* skin, hide — more at CUIRASS] **1 :** to strip or wear off the skin of **:** FLAY, ABRADE, GALL; *also* **:** to break and remove the cuticle of **2 :** to censure scathingly

²ex·co·ri·ate \-ēət, -ē,āt\ *adj* [LL *excoriatus*, past part.] *archaic* **:** GALLED, ABRADED — used esp. of skin or other covering

ex·co·ri·a·tion \(,)ek,==ˈāshən, ik-\ *n* -S [ME *excoriacioun*, fr. MF & ML; MF *excoriation*, fr. ML *excoriation-, excoriatio*, fr. LL *excoriatus* + L *-ion-, -io* -ion] **1 :** the act of excoriating or state of being excoriated either physically or verbally ⟨marked chafing and ~ of the skin⟩ ⟨his violent ~ of his adversaries⟩ **2 :** an instance or product of excoriation: **a :** a raw irritated lesion (as of the skin or a mucosal surface) **b :** a scathingly censorious utterance

ex·cor·ti·cate \(ˈ)ek¦skȯ(r)də,kāt\ *vt* -ED/-ING/-S [LL *excorticatus*, past part. of *excorticare*, fr. L *ex-* ¹ex- + *cortic-, cortex* bark — more at CORTEX] **:** DECORTICATE

excpt *abbr* exception

¹ex·cre·ment \ˈekskrəmənt\ *n* -S [L *excrementum*, fr. *excre-* (stem of *excernere* to sift out, separate, discharge — as feces—) + *-mentum* -ment — more at EXCRETE] **1 a :** waste matter discharged from the body; *usu* **:** waste discharged from the alimentary canal **:** fecal matter **:** DUNG — compare EXCRETION **b excrements** *pl* **:** DROPPINGS, STOOLS **:** fecal pellets **2** *obs* **:** DREGS, LEES, REFUSE

²excrement *n* -S [LL *excrementum*, fr. L *excre-* (stem of *excrescere* to grow out) + *-mentum* -ment] **1** *obs* **:** an excrescence or appendage esp. of hair or feathers **:** OUTGROWTH **2** *obs* **:** GROWTH, INCREASE

ex·cre·men·ti·tious \,ekskrə,menˈtishəs, -,mən-\ *also* **ex·cre·men·tal** \¦==¦mentᵊl\ *adj* [¹*excrement* + *-itious* or *-al*] **:** of or relating to excrement **:** concerned with or caused by dung ⟨~ odors⟩ — **ex·cre·men·ti·tious·ly** \-shəslē\ *also* **ex·cre·men·tal·ly** \-tᵊlē\ *adv*

ex·cre·men·tous \¦==¦mentəs\ *adj* [¹*excrement* + *-ous*] **:** like or constituting excrement

ex·cres·cence \ekˈskresᵊn(t)s, ik-\ *n* -S [ME, fr. MF *excressance*, fr. L *excrescentia*, pl., fr. neut. pl. of *excrescent-, excrescens*, pres. part. of *excrescere* to grow out, fr. *ex-* ¹ex- + *crescere* to grow, increase — more at CRESCENT] **1 a :** a growing out esp. to an abnormal extent **:** abnormal or excessive increase **b** *archaic* **:** EXCESS, SUPERFLUITY **2 :** an outgrowth or enlargement: as **a :** a natural and normal appendage or development ⟨hair is an ~ from the scalp⟩ ⟨several small glandular ~*s*⟩ **b :** an abnormal outgrowth ⟨warty ~*s*⟩ **3 :** EXCRESCENCY 3

ex·cres·cen·cy \-nsē, -si\ *n* -ES [L *excrescentia*] **1 :** EXCRESCENCE 2 ⟨it would be a well-proportioned house if you stripped off the Victorian *excrescencies*⟩ **2 :** the state of being excrescent; *esp* **:** abnormal protrusion or growth **3 :** occurrence of an excrescent sound or letter

ex·cres·cent \(ˈ)ek¦skresᵊnt, ikˈs-\ *adj* [L *excrescent-, excrescens*, pres. part. of *excrescere*] **1** *archaic* **:** constituting an excess **:** SUPERNUMERARY **2 :** growing out or forming an outgrowth; *usu* **:** forming an abnormal, excessive, or useless outgrowth **:** SUPERFLUOUS ⟨pruning ~ witches'-broom from blueberry bushes⟩ **3** *phonet* **a :** EPENTHETIC, INTRUSIVE **b :** epenthetic but substandard ⟨the ~ second \t\ sound in \ˈwəntst\ for *once*⟩ **c :** epenthetic as a result of folk etymology ⟨the ~ second \r\ sound in *bridegroom*⟩ — **ex·cres·cent·ly** *adv*

ex·cres·cen·tial \¦ekskrə¦senchəl, ¦ek(,)skre¦-\ *adj* [L *excrescentia* + E *-al*] **:** relating to or being an excrescence

excression *n* -S [modif. of LL *excretion-, excretio* — more at EXCRETION (excrescence)] *obs* **:** EXCRESCENCE

ex·cre·ta \ekˈskrēd·ə, ik-, -ētə\ *n pl* [NL, fr. L, neut. pl. of *excretus*, past part. of *excernere*] **:** waste matter eliminated or separated from an organism; *usu* **:** EXCRETIONS — **ex·cre·tal** \(ˈ)ek¦skrēd·ᵊl, ikˈs-, -ētᵊl\ *adj*

ex·crete \(ˈ)ek¦skrēt, ikˈs-, *usu* -ēd·+V\ *vt* -ED/-ING/-S [L *excretus*, past part. of *excernere* to sift out, separate, discharge (as feces), fr. *ex-* ¹ex- + *cernere* to sift — more at CERTAIN] **1 :** to separate and eliminate or discharge (waste, superfluous, or harmful material) from the blood or tissues in animals or from the active protoplasm in plants and animals **2 :** to give off (as something expendable or in some way inferior) ⟨the shell-like covering which our souls have *excreted* to house themselves —Virginia Woolf⟩ ⟨a foundation ~*s* an extraordinary quantity of typed and mimeographed words —*New Yorker*⟩

ex·cret·er \-ēd·ə(r), -ētə-\ *n* -S **:** one that excretes; *esp* **:** one that gives forth from his body an atypical product (as a pathogenic microorganism)

¹ex·cre·tion \ekˈskrēshən, ik-\ *n* -S [*excrete* + *-ion*] **1 :** the process of eliminating useless, superfluous, or harmful matter (as the waste products of metabolism) from the body of an organism or from its protoplasm, usu. through the action of special cells or tissues — compare SECRETION **2 a :** something eliminated by the process of excretion comprising chiefly the urine and sweat in man and other mammals and comparable materials in other animals, characteristically including products of protein degradation (as urea or uric acid), usu. differing from ordinary bodily secretions by lacking any further utility to the organism that produces it, and being distinguished from waste materials (as feces) that have merely passed into or through the alimentary canal without being incorporated into the body proper **b :** a waste product (as urine, feces, vomitus) eliminated from the confines of an animal body **:** EXCREMENT — not used technically **c :** any of various materials stored in or secreted by plants (as certain intracellular crystals, nectar, or the water and carbon dioxide produced in respiration) that are believed to have a basically excretory function

[2]**excretion** *n* -S [LL *excretion-, excretio,* fr. L *excretus* (past part. of *excrescere* to grow out) + *-ion-, -io* -ion — more at EXCRESCENCE] *obs* **:** EXCRESCENCE

ex·cre·to·ry \'ekskrə,tōrē, -tȯr-, -ri, *chiefly Brit* ek'skrētəri *or* ik-\ *adj* [*excrete* + *-ory*] **:** of, relating to, concerned with, or serving for excretion

[1]**ex·cru·ci·ate** \ik'skrüshē,āt, ek- *sometimes* -üsē-, *usu* -ād·+V\ *vt* -ED/-ING/-S [L *excruciatus,* past part. of *excruciare,* fr. *ex-* [1]ex- + *cruciare* to torment, crucify, fr. *cruc-, crux* cross — more at CROSS] **1 a** *obs* **:** to torture esp. by the rack **b :** to inflict intense pain upon **:** subject to the utmost physical suffering ⟨a man *excruciated* by facial neuralgia⟩ **2 :** to subject to intense mental distress **:** irritate or annoy exceedingly ⟨the very sound of his voice ~*s* me⟩ ⟨what panic and gnashing of teeth would ~ the propagandists —Peter Viereck⟩

[2]**excruciate** *adj* [L *excruciatus,* past part.] **1** *obs* **:** suffering intensely **2** *obs* **:** causing intense suffering

excruciating *adj* **1 :** TORTURING, RACKING, AGONIZING **2 :** so intense as to cause great pain or anguish ⟨the ~ spasms of angina⟩ ⟨an ~ fear⟩; *often* **:** very intense **:** EXTREME ⟨~ pain⟩ ⟨the characters are paired off with an ~ regard for balance —Douglas Watt⟩ ⟨~ delight⟩ — **ex·cru·ci·at·ing·ly** *adv*

ex·cru·ci·a·tion \ik,skrüshē'āshən, (,)ek- *also* -üsē-\ *n* -S [LL *excruciation-, excruciatio,* fr. L *excruciatus* + *-ion-, -io* -ion] **:** the act of excruciating or the state or an instance of being excruciated

ex·cul·pate \'ek(,)skəl,pāt, ek's-, ik's-, *usu* -ād·+V\ *vt* -ED/-ING/-S [ML *exculpatus,* past part. of *exculpare,* fr. L *ex-* [1]ex- + *culpare* to blame — more at CULPABLE] **:** to clear from alleged fault or guilt **:** prove to be guiltless ⟨the court *exculpated* him after a thorough investigation⟩ ⟨specifically ~*s* all countries from any special responsibility for bringing on the catastrophe —*Saturday Rev.*⟩

syn ABSOLVE, EXONERATE, ACQUIT, VINDICATE: EXCULPATE indicates a freeing from blame, fault, or guilt, esp. fault or guilt with blameworthy intent ⟨directly Harding was blameless for what was going on. Indirectly he cannot be wholly *exculpated* —S.H.Adams⟩ ABSOLVE indicates a releasing either from charges or suspicions of guilt or from consequences or responsibilities of guilt, often unconfessed guilt ⟨society was at least good-natured and was inclined to take the view that if a fellow had faced his punishment and taken it he was pretty well *absolved* —F.M.Ford⟩ ⟨since the emperor was willing to make the necessary promises, however, he as a priest was bound to *absolve* the contrite sinner —M.W.Baldwin⟩ EXONERATE may imply complete clearance not only from an immediate charge or accusation but from suspicious or attendant denigration ⟨he was subsequently tried for murder, but was completely *exonerated* by the testimony of his crew and passengers, who testified that the ship was in deadly peril of seizure by mutineers —C.C.Cutler⟩ ACQUIT may apply to a formal decision freeing one from a charge ⟨at his trial the next year he was *acquitted* of dishonesty, although his reputation for intelligence suffered —Louise P. Kellogg⟩ VINDICATE may apply to the eventual demonstration by subsequent developments of freedom from guilt, dishonor, wrong, folly, or weakness ⟨both his knowledge and his honesty were *vindicated* when the river was discovered —G.R.Stewart⟩ ⟨then came the fatal letter, the desolating letter, which *vindicated* Constance's dark apprehensions —Arnold Bennett⟩ ⟨*vindicating* the old adage about great minds —Ring Lardner⟩

ex·cul·pa·tion \,ek(,)skəl'pāshən\ *n* -S [ML *exculpation-, exculpatio,* fr. *exculpatus* + L *-ion-, -io* -ion] **1 :** the act or fact of exculpating from alleged fault or crime ⟨his ~ was complete when his partner confessed to the theft⟩ **2 :** an excuse or explanation by way of vindication ⟨this is not said by way of ~ of Aristotle —C.J.O'Neil⟩ ⟨blaming Americans is a familiar ~ —*Time*⟩

ex·cul·pa·to·ry \ek'skəlpə,tōrē, ik-, -tȯr-, -ri\ *adj* **:** tending to exculpate **:** serving as an exculpation ⟨~ testimony⟩ ⟨an ~ statement⟩

ex·current \(')eks+\ *adj* [L *excurrent-, excurrens,* pres. part. of *excurrere* to run out, make an excursion, project, extend, fr. *ex-* [1]ex- + *currere* to run — more at CURRENT] **:** running or flowing out: as **a** *of a plant or plant part* (1) **:** having the axis prolonged to form an undivided main stem or trunk (as in the spruce and other conifers) — opposed to *deliquescent* (2) **:** projecting beyond the apex — used esp. of the midrib of a mucronate leaf **b :** characterized by a current that flows outward — used esp. of those channels in sponges through which water flows toward the osculum ⟨~ canals⟩

[1]**ex·curse** \ek'skərs, '⸗,⸗\ *n* -S [L *excursus,* fr. *excursus,* past part. of *excurrere*] **:** a sally or digression

[2]**excurse** \"\ *vi* [L *excursus,* past part.] **1 :** DIGRESS, RAMBLE **2 :** to journey or pass through **:** make an excursion

[1]**ex·cur·sion** \ik'skər|zhən, ek-, -kə̄|,-kəi|, *chiefly Brit* |shən\ *n* -S [L *excursion-, excursio,* fr. *excursus* (past part.) + *-ion-, -io* -ion] **1 :** a going out or forth as from a place of confinement: as **a :** a military expedition **:** RAID, SORTIE — obs. except in the phrase *alarums and excursions* **b** *in Elizabethan stage directions* **:** a movement of soldiers across the stage **c :** a journey chiefly for recreation **:** a usu. brief pleasure trip; *often* **:** a trip (as by rail or steamship) at special reduced rates ⟨the railway ran Sunday ~*s* to the city⟩ **d :** a trip made with the positive intention of returning to the starting point **:** ROUND TRIP **:** a trip that is not planned to involve prolonged or definite separation from one's usu. or normal place or way of life ⟨his summer ~*s* to the Colorado Rockies⟩ ⟨made several ~*s* into the Amazon valley⟩ **2 :** the persons participating in or going together on an excursion **3 :** departure from a direct or proper course **:** deviation from a definite path; *usu* **:** a wandering from a subject **:** DIGRESSION ⟨his ~*s* into abstruse theory⟩ **4** *obs* **:** a projection or extension (as of a building) **5** *archaic* **:** a sally or outburst (as of wit or feeling) esp. when overstepping accepted or customary bounds **6 :** a movement outward and back or from a mean position or axis **7 a :** a single vibratory motion (as of a diaphragm or membrane); *sometimes* **:** the distance traversed in such a movement **:** AMPLITUDE **b :** one complete movement of inspiratory expansion and expiratory contraction of the lungs and their membranes

[2]**excursion** \"\ *vi* **excursioned; excursioned; excursioning** \-zh(ə)niŋ, -sh(-\ **excursions :** to go on an excursion

[3]**excursion** \"\ *adj* **:** relating to or used for excursions ⟨an ~ rate⟩ ⟨~ trains⟩ ⟨a packed ~ steamer⟩

ex·cur·sion·al \-zhənᵊl, -zhnəl, -sh-\ *or* **ex·cur·sion·ary** \-zhə,nerē, -sh-, -ri\ *adj* **:** of or relating to an excursion ⟨~ fare⟩

ex·cur·sion·ist \-zh(ə)nəst, -sh-\ *n* -S **:** a person who goes on an excursion; *esp* **:** one of a party on a pleasure trip

excursion ticket *n* **:** a special-rate ticket for making a round-trip journey on an excursion

ex·cur·sive \ik'skər|s|iv, (')ek|s-, -kə̄|, -kəi|, |z|, |ēv *also* |əv\ *also* **ex·cur·so·ry** \|(ə)rē, -ri\ *adj* [L *excursus* (past part.) + E *-ive* or *-ory*] **1 :** constituting a digression ⟨his ~ remarks⟩ **2 :** characterized by or prone to digression ⟨an amusingly ~ style⟩ — **ex·cur·sive·ly** \|əvlē, -li\ *adv*

ex·cur·sus \ik'skərsəs, ek-\ *n, pl* **excursuses** *also* **excursus** [L, digression — more at EXCURSE] **1 :** a dissertation that is appended to a work and that contains a more extended exposition of some point or topic **2 :** an incidental discussion **:** DIGRESSION

ex·curvature \(')eks+\ *also* **ex·curvation** \¦eks+\ *n* [[1]*ex-* + *curvature* or *curvation*] **:** excurved state or an excurved part

ex·curved \'eks+,-\ *or* **ex·cur·vate** \'ek,skər,vāt, (')ek¦skərvət\ *adj* [[1]*ex-* + *curved* or *curvate* (fr. [3]*curve* + *-ate*)] **:** curved outward or away from a central part

ex·cus·able \ik'skyüzəbəl, (')ek¦s-\ *adj* [ME, fr. MF, fr. L *excusabilis,* fr. *excusare* + *-abilis* -able] **:** capable of or fit for being excused, forgiven, justified, or acquitted of blame **:** PARDONABLE ⟨an ~ oversight⟩ — **ex·cus·able·ness** \-nəs\ *n* -ES

excusable homicide *n* **:** homicide done by accident or misadventure or in self-defense and without criminal intent

excusable neglect *n, law* **:** neglect for which there is a reasonable excuse

ex·cus·ably \-blē, -li\ *adv* **:** in an excusable manner

ex·cus·al \ik'skyüzəl, ek-\ *n* -S **:** the act or fact of excusing esp. from the payment of an assessment or tax due

excusation *n* -S [ME *excusacioun,* fr. MF & L; MF *excusation,* fr. L *excusation-, excusatio,* fr. *excusatus* (past part. of *excusare*) + *-ion-, -io* -ion] *obs* **:** EXCUSE

ex·cu·sa·tor \'ekskyü,zād·ə(r), ,⸗⸗'⸗⸗\ *n* -S [LL, fr. L *excusatus* + *-or*] **:** APOLOGIST

ex·cus·ato·ry \ik'skyüzə,tōrē, (')ek¦s-, -tȯr-, -ri\ *adj* [LL *excusatorius,* fr. L *excusatus* + *-orius* -ory] **:** making or containing excuse or apology **:** APOLOGETIC

[1]**ex·cuse** \ik'skyüz, ek-, in "*excuse me*" *often* 'sky-\ *vb* -ED/-ING/-S [ME *excusen,* fr. OF *escuser, excuser,* fr. L *excusare,* fr. *ex-* [1]ex- + *-cusare* (fr. *causa* cause, apology) — more at CAUSE] *vt* **1 a :** to offer excuse for **:** make apology for ⟨he *excused* his delay as due to the weather⟩ **b :** to try to remove blame from **:** seek indulgence for **:** seek to extenuate ⟨*excusing* himself for his delay⟩ **2 a :** to seek or obtain exemption or release for ⟨asked the school principal to ~ the boys from religious services⟩ **b** *obs* **:** to serve as a means of exemption from **:** serve as a substitute for **3 :** to accept an excuse for **:** regard as excusable **:** forgive entirely or admit to be little censurable and to overlook **:** PARDON ⟨we ~ irregular conduct when circumstances justify it⟩ **4 :** to regard with indulgence **:** OVERLOOK ⟨it is easy to ~ one's own faults⟩ — often used as an introductory apology (as when interrupting or expressing disagreement) ⟨~ me, but do you mind if I shut the window?⟩ **5 a :** to grant exemption or release to or from **:** free from an obligation or duty ⟨the judge *excused* the young man's fine because of the unusual circumstances⟩ **b :** to permit to leave a place or stop an activity or task ⟨class is *excused*⟩ ⟨you are *excused* the rest of the translation⟩ **6 a :** to serve as excuse for **:** free from imputation of fault **:** clear from guilt **:** EXCULPATE, JUSTIFY ⟨one's own assurance of propriety cannot ~ jeopardizing another's happiness⟩ ⟨perhaps, knowing what you do, you can ~ him⟩ **b** *obs* **:** to release from a charge ~ *vi* **:** to ask or grant excuse ⟨while some accuse, others ~⟩ **:** serve as an excuse ⟨such loving self-sacrifice goes far toward *excusing*⟩

syn CONDONE, PARDON, FORGIVE: EXCUSE indicates a passing over of some fault, omission, neglect, or failure without further consideration, censure, or punishment, redress, or retaliation in view of extenuating conditions ⟨the plea of 'frontier conditions' could no longer *excuse* the lack of an adequate public-school system —*Amer. Guide Series: Mich.*⟩ ⟨guilty of contributory negligence, in default, at least, of special circumstances *excusing* the omission —B.N.Cardozo⟩ ⟨the injustice with which he had been treated would have *excused* him if he had resorted to violent methods of redress —T.B.Macaulay⟩ CONDONE may indicate accepting without protest, censure, or punishment some reprehensible action or condition because of circumstances ⟨those Anglo-Saxon critics of the brutality of the bullfight who *condone* the hunting of the fox or the killing of deer —W.D.Patterson⟩ ⟨often he got into scrapes, but they were the manly scrapes that are easily *condoned* —D.H.Lawrence⟩ ⟨institutionalized suicide, *condoned,* approved, or even exacted by a code and therefore by the culture —A.L.Kroeber⟩ PARDON may indicate waiving of punishment or censure and reinstatement to grace esp. by a superior and in legal, formal, or social situations ⟨*pardoned* by the state governor⟩ ⟨it became necessary for us both to fly for our lives. In the circumstances we could not look to be *pardoned,* even on the score of youth —W.H.Hudson †1922⟩ ⟨the most good-natured of women *pardoned* the error —W.M. Thackeray⟩ FORGIVE may apply to genuine, sincere change of feeling whereby resentment and desire for retaliation on or punishment of an offender are no longer felt ⟨the Mayor invariably gazed stormfully past him, like one who had endured and lost on his account, and could in no sense *forgive* the wrong —Thomas Hardy⟩ ⟨he *forgave* injuries so readily that he might be said to invite them —T.B.Macaulay⟩

[2]**ex·cuse** \ik'skyüs, ek-\ *n* -S [ME, fr. MF, fr. *excuser*] **1 :** the act of excusing (as by apologizing, exculpating, pardoning, or releasing) **:** ACQUITTAL, RELEASE, ABSOLUTION, JUSTIFICATION ⟨pleading so wisely in ~ of it —Shak.⟩ **2 a :** something offered as grounds for being excused **:** a justifying explanation of a fault or defect ⟨what's your ~ for being late this morning?⟩ ⟨he made his ill health an ~ for everything⟩ **b excuses** *pl* **:** an expression of regret for failure to do or participate in something often conveyed through a third party ⟨make my ~*s* to your cousin, I'm sorry to miss her tea⟩ **c :** a note of explanation (as from a parent or teacher) concerning the absence of an individual (as from class or work) **3 a :** something that serves to excuse **:** anything that justifies or extenuates a fault or defect ⟨I suppose his youth is an ~ for his flighty ways⟩ ⟨forgetfulness is no ~ for bad manners⟩ **b :** a purpose or use that justifies **:** JUSTIFICATION, REASON ⟨such loveliness is enough ~ for being⟩ **4 :** an inferior example or instance of a kind specified ⟨finally turned in a blotted ~ for a composition⟩ ⟨this rattletrap is a poor ~ for a car⟩ **syn** see APOLOGY

ex·cuse·less *adj* **1** *obs* **:** having or offering no excuse **2** \-üzləs, -üsl-\ **:** impossible to excuse **:** INEXCUSABLE

ex·cus·er \-üzə(r)\ *n* -S **:** one that excuses

excuses *pres 3d sing of* EXCUSE, *pl of* EXCUSE

ex·cus·ing \(ik)'skyüzᵊn\ *prep* [fr. pres. part. of [1]*excuse*] *chiefly South & Midland* **:** EXCEPT ⟨ain't done much ~ fret and worry —Marjorie K. Rawlings⟩

ex·cus·ing·ly *adv* **:** in an excusing manner

ex·cu·sive \ik'skyüs|iv, ek-, -üz|\ *adj* **:** tending to excuse — **ex·cu·sive·ly** \|əvlē\ *adv*

ex·cuss \ik'skəs, ek-\ *vt* -ED/-ING/-ES [L *excussus,* past part. of *excutere,* fr. *ex-* [1]ex- + *-cutere* (fr. *quatere* to shake) — more at QUASH] **1** *obs* **:** to shake off or out **:** DISCARD **2** *obs* **:** to investigate as if by shaking out **:** DISCUSS **3 :** to proceed against (a principal debtor) before falling back on a surety

excussion *n* -S [LL *excussion-, excussio,* fr. L *excussus* + *-ion-, -io* -ion] *obs* **:** the act of excussing

ex·cyst \(')ek(s)¦sist\ *vi* -ED/-ING/-S [[1]*ex-* + *cyst* (n.)] **:** to emerge from a cyst (as of a protozoan) — **ex·cys·ta·tion** \,ek(s),si'stāshən\ *n* -S — **ex·cyst·ment** \ek(s)'sis(t)mənt\ *n* -S

exd *abbr* examined

ex de·bi·to jus·ti·ti·ae *adj (or adv)* \eks'debə,tō,yu̇'stid·ē,ī\ [NL] **:** of or by reason of an obligation of justice **:** as a matter of right

ex de·lic·to \,eksdə'lik(,)tō\ *adj (or adv)* [LL] **:** of or by reason of a wrong **:** arising from a wrongful act

ex dividend *adv (or adj)* [[2]*ex*] **:** with the value of a pending dividend excluded from the sale price of a security, the buyer not being entitled to the dividend when paid — opposed to *cum dividend;* abbr. *ex div.*

ex·e·at \'eksē,at\ *n* -S [L, let him or her go out, 3d pers. sing. pres. subj. of *exire* to go out, fr. *ex-* [1]ex- + *ire* to go —more at ISSUE] **1** *Brit* **:** a permit for temporary absence (as from a college or monastery) **2 :** a letter of permission allowing a cleric to transfer from one diocese to another **:** a letter of excardination

ex·ec \ig'zek, eg-\ *n* -S [by shortening] **:** EXECUTIVE OFFICER

exec *abbr* executed; execution; executive; executor

ex·e·cra·ble \'eksəkrəbəl, -sēk-\ *adj* [ME, expressing a curse, deserving to be execrated, fr. L *execrabilis, exsecrabilis,* fr. *execrare, exsecrare* + *-abilis* -able] **1** *obs* **:** expressing a curse **2 :** deserving to be execrated **:** DAMNABLE, DETESTABLE, ABOMINABLE, HORRIFYING ⟨~ crimes⟩ **3 :** very bad **:** WRETCHED ⟨~ verses⟩ ⟨~ taste⟩ — **ex·e·cra·ble·ness** \-lnəs\ *n* -ES — **ex·e·cra·bly** \-blē, -li\ *adv*

ex·e·crate \'eksə,krāt, *usu* -ād·+V\ *vb* -ED/-ING/-S [L *execratus, exsecratus,* past part. of *execrari, exsecrari,* fr. *ex-* [1]ex- + *-secrari* (fr. *sacr-, sacer* sacred) — more at SACRED] *vt* **1** *archaic* **:** to call down curses upon **:** put under a curse **:** pronounce accursed **2 :** to declare to be evil or detestable **:** DENOUNCE, DAMN, REVILE ⟨he was *execrated* as a murderer and adulterer⟩ **3 :** to detest utterly **:** ABHOR ⟨finally came to ~ the Victorian values —*New Yorker*⟩ ~ *vi* **:** CURSE, SWEAR ⟨he longed to ~ aloud —James Joyce⟩

syn CURSE, DAMN, ANATHEMATIZE, OBJURGATE: EXECRATE indicates a violent denouncing with intense loathing and, usu., furious passion ⟨for a little while he was *execrated* in Rome; his statues were overthrown, and his name was blotted from the records —John Buchan⟩ ⟨the murder will be added to the many crimes of Egidio Gambara, that posterity may *execrate* his name —Rafael Sabatini⟩ CURSE and DAMN both signify fervent angry denunciation by oaths; the former may seem somewhat more literary than the latter ⟨in literature, with his usual charming violence, he *cursed* Conrad's style —F.A. Swinnerton⟩ ⟨he told me great tales of their cruelty, and he *cursed* them most bitterly —Hugh Walpole⟩ ⟨he mentally *damned* the cook as the real cause of his distress —F.M. Crofts⟩ ⟨*damn* the torpedoes, full speed ahead —David Farragut⟩ ANATHEMATIZE indicates solemn, although perhaps impassioned, formal denunciation or condemnation, as a churchman's denunciation of evil ⟨in the course of the proceedings of the Council, the earlier deposition of Arius by an Alexandrian synod was confirmed and his teachings were *anathematized* —Frank Thilly⟩ OBJURGATE may apply to the chiding of extremists ⟨*objurgating* the present incumbent of the White House⟩

ex·e·cra·tion \,eksə'krāshən\ *n* -S [L *execration-, exsecration-, execratio, exsecratio,* fr. *execratus, exsecratus* + *-ion-, -io* -ion] **1 :** the act of cursing or denouncing ⟨~, if followed by submission, is devoid of motive power —B.N.Cardozo⟩; *also* **:** the curse so uttered ⟨excommunicated with all the somber maledictions, ~*s,* and anathemas —L.K.Anspacher⟩ ⟨the ~*s* of the mob⟩ **2 :** an object of curses **:** a detested thing

ex·e·cra·tive \'eksə,krād·iv, -,krəd·-\ *adj* **:** EXECRATORY — **ex·e·cra·tive·ly** \-d·əvlē\ *adv*

ex·e·cra·tor \-,krād·ə(r)\ *n* -S [LL *execrator, exsecrator,* fr. L *execratus, exsecratus* + *-or*] **:** one that execrates

ex·e·cra·to·ry \'eksəkrə,tōrē\ *adj* **:** of or relating to execration **:** IMPRECATORY

ex·e·cut·able \'eksə,kyüd·əbəl, -ütə-, ,⸗⸗'⸗⸗⸗\ *adj* **:** capable of execution **:** FEASIBLE

[1]**ex·ec·u·tant** \ig'zekyəd·ənt, eg-, ÷ -kə-, -ətənt *also* -ətᵊnt\ *n* -S [F *exécutant,* fr. pres. part. of *exécuter* to execute] **:** one who executes or performs; *esp* **:** one skilled in the technique of an art **:** PERFORMER

[2]**executant** \"\ *adj* [F *exécutant,* pres. part. of *exécuter* to execute, fr. MF *executer*] **1 :** performing esp. for an audience ⟨~ musicians⟩ **2 :** of, related to, or connected with an executant ⟨~ music⟩

ex·e·cute \'eksə,kyüt, *usu* -üd·+V\ *vt* -ED/-ING/-S [ME *executen,* fr. MF *executer,* back-formation fr. *executeur* executor (fr. L *executor, exsecutor*), *execution,* and *executoire* executory (fr. LL *executorius, exsecutorius* executory, putting into effect)] **1 :** to put into effect **:** carry out fully and completely **:** PERFORM, EFFECT ⟨~ a purpose⟩ ⟨~ the king's will⟩ ⟨~ a dance step⟩ ⟨~ a military maneuver⟩ **2** *obs* **a :** to give practical expression to (as a sentiment, a passion) **b :** to make use of (a weapon) **c :** to carry out (as a ceremony) **:** CONDUCT **3 :** to give effect to **:** do what is provided or required by ⟨~ the provisions of a will⟩ **:** perform the requirements of **:** perform the acts necessary to the effectiveness of ⟨~ a decree⟩ **4 :** to inflict capital punishment on **:** put to death in conformity to a legal sentence ⟨*executed* him as a traitor⟩ **5 :** to make or produce (as a work of art) esp. by carrying out a design ⟨a statue *executed* in bronze⟩ ⟨~ a facade in red sandstone⟩ **6 :** COMPLETE ⟨~ legal instrument⟩ **:** perform what is required to give validity to (as by signing and perhaps sealing and delivering) ⟨~ a deed⟩ **7 :** PLAY ⟨~ a piece of music⟩ **syn** see KILL, PERFORM

executed *adj* [fr. past part. of *execute*] **:** carried out **:** carried out legally according to its terms **:** PERFORMED — see EXECUTORY

ex·e·cu·tion \,eksə'kyüshən\ *n* -S [ME *execucioun,* fr. MF *execution,* fr. L *execution-, exsecution-, executio, exsecutio,* fr. *executus, exsecutus* (past part. of *exequi, exsequi* to execute, fr. *ex-* [1]ex- + *sequi* to follow) + *-ion-, -io* -ion — more at SUE] **1 :** the act or process of executing **:** PERFORMANCE, ACCOMPLISHMENT ⟨there was nothing to prevent the ~ of his purpose⟩ ⟨put a new plan into ~⟩ **2 a** *archaic* **:** a punishment ordered legally **b :** a putting to death as a legal penalty **:** CAPITAL PUNISHMENT **3 a :** the process for carrying into effect the judgment or decree of a court; *esp* **:** the enforcement of such judgment or decree by arrest of the person or seizure of the property of a debtor **b :** a judicial writ by which an officer is empowered to carry a judgment into effect — called also *final process* **c :** the act of signing, sealing, and delivering a legal instrument or giving it the forms required to make it valid ⟨the ~ of a deed⟩ ⟨the ~ of a will⟩ **4 :** the act or mode or result of performance in any of the arts or in anything that requires a special skill or technique ⟨~ of a carving⟩ ⟨~ of a violin solo⟩ ⟨the fineness of ~ of the iron balcony and of the railing —*Amer. Guide Series: N.Y. City*⟩ **5 :** effective or destructive action — used usu. with *do* ⟨as soon as day came, we went out to see what ~ we had done —Daniel Defoe⟩ **6** *archaic* **:** the military act of plundering

ex·e·cu·tion·al \¦⸗⸗¦kyüshənᵊl, -shnəl\ *adj* **:** relating to execution

ex·e·cu·tion·er \,⸗⸗'kyüsh(ə)nə(r)\ *n* -S **1 a :** one that executes or performs **b :** one that executes a judgment; *esp* **:** one that inflicts an authorized punishment **2 :** one that puts to death **:** HANGMAN

[1]**ex·ec·u·tive** \ig'zekyəd·iv, eg-, ÷ -kə-, -ətiv *sometimes* ÷ -ktiv *or* ÷ -ktēv\ *adj* **1 :** designed or fitted for or relating to execution or carrying into effect ⟨~ board⟩ ⟨~ skill⟩ ⟨~ plan⟩ ⟨~ committee⟩ **2 :** qualified for, concerned with, or relating to the execution of the laws or the conduct of public and national affairs ⟨~ duties⟩ ⟨~ authority⟩ **:** belonging to the branch of the government that is charged with such powers as diplomatic representation, supreme command of the armed forces, superintendence of the execution of the laws, and appointment of officials and that usu. has some power over legislation (as through the veto, the initiation of legislation, and dissolution of the legislature) ⟨~ department⟩ — distinguished from *judicial* and *legislative* **3 :** active, effectual, or skillful in managing, directing, or accomplishing ⟨the ~ aspects of the ego —Abram Kardiner⟩ ⟨under the supervision of his very strong-minded, ~ wife —Margaret Mead⟩ **4 :** relating or belonging to an executive ⟨~ rewards⟩ ⟨~ suite of offices⟩ — **ex·ec·u·tive·ly** \-əvlē, -li\ *adv* — **ex·ec·u·tive·ness** \-ivnəs, -ēv- *also* -əv-\ *n* -ES

[2]**executive** \"\ *n* -S **1 :** the executive branch of a government; *also* **:** the person or persons who constitute the executive magistracy of a state **2 :** a directing or controlling body of an organization (as a political party, a labor union) **:** an executive council or committee **3 :** one who holds a position of administrative or managerial responsibility in a business or other organization **:** ADMINISTRATOR, OFFICER ⟨chief sales ~⟩

executive agreement *n* **:** an agreement between the U.S. and a foreign government made by the executive branch of the government alone without approval by the Senate and dealing usu. with routine matters not thought to require the formality of a treaty

executive council *n* **1 :** a council constituted to advise or share in the functions of a political executive: as **a :** a council composed of the principal government officials and sometimes unofficial appointees that is constituted to advise the governor of a British colony ⟨the Governor shall . . . preside at all meetings of the *Executive Council* —*Royal Instructions (Nigeria)*⟩ **b :** a council in several member nations of the British Commonwealth that resembles the Privy Council in power and function ⟨in New Zealand . . . the Cabinet and the *Executive Council* have the same membership —Walter Nash⟩ **2 :** a council that exercises supreme executive power **:** a plural executive ⟨in Switzerland . . . the *Executive Council* is not based upon a party majority in the representative bodies —C.J.Friedrich⟩ ⟨replacing the Uruguayan president with an *executive council*⟩

executive officer *n* **1 :** the principal staff officer in a command below division level **2** : the military officer second in command of a company or similar organization **3** : the second in command of a ship, station, or air squadron in the navy

executive order *n* : REGULATION 2b (2)

executive secretary *n* : a secretary having administrative duties; *specif* : a paid full-time official who is responsible for organizing and administering the activities and business affairs of an organization or association

executive session *n* : a usu. closed session of a legislative or other body acting in the function of an executive council (as of the U.S. Senate when considering appointments or the ratification of treaties)

ex·ec·u·tor \ig'zekyəd·ə(r), eg-, ÷ -kə-, -ətə(r), *in sense 1a* " *or* 'eksə,kyüd·ə(r) *or* -,kyütə-\ *n* -s [ME *executour*, fr. OF *executor*, fr. L *executor, exsecutor*, fr. *executus, exsecutus* (past part. of *exequi, exsequi* to execute) + *-or* — more at EXECUTION] **1 a** : one who executes something (as a purpose, duty, function, work of art) : DOER, PERFORMER, AGENT **b** *obs* : EXECUTIONER **2** : the person appointed by a testator to execute his will or to see its provisions carried into effect after his decease

executor-dative \≈¦≈≈≈¦≈≈\ *n* [*executor* + *dative*, adj.] *civil, Scots, & canon law* : an executor or administrator appointed by a bishop or magistrate or ecclesiastical or civil court — distinguished from *executor-nominate*

executor de son tort \-də,sōⁿ'tȯ(ə)r\ *n* [AF, executor of his own wrong] : a person who without legal authority assumes control of a decedent's property as if he were executor

ex·ec·u·to·ri·al \ig¦zekyə¦tōrēəl, (¦)eg-, ÷kə¦-, -tȯr-\ *adj* [ME (Sc), fr. ML *executorialis*, fr. LL *executorius, exsecutorius* executory, putting into effect + L *-alis* -al] **1** *chiefly Scots law* : of or relating to the execution of a mandate or of legal process **2** : of or relating to an executor

executor-nominate \≈¦≈≈¦≈≈(,)≈\ *n, civil, Scots, & canon law* : an executor or administrator nominated in the will — distinguished from *executor-dative*

ex·ec·u·tor·ship \≈'≈≈≈,ship\ *n* : the office of executor

ex·ec·u·to·ry \ig'zekyə,tōrē, eg-, ÷-kə-, -tȯr-, -ri\ *adj* [ME *executorie* operative, being in effect, putting into effect, fr. LL *executorius, exsecutorius* putting into effect, fr. L *executus, exsecutus* (past part. of *exequi, exsequi* to execute) + *-orius* -ory] **1** : relating to administration or to putting the laws in force : EXECUTIVE **2** : designed or of such a nature as to be executed in time to come or to take effect on a future contingency ⟨an agreement to sell is an ~ contract⟩

executory devise *n* : a devise of land which takes effect by terminating a preceding interest

executory interest *n* : an interest that takes effect through an executory limitation

executory limitation *n* : a dispositive provision that becomes effective by divesting a prior interest

ex·ec·u·trix \ig'zekyə,triks, eg-, ÷-kə-\ *n, pl* **executri·ces** \≈,≈≈'trī,sēz\ *or* **executrixes** [ME, executrix of a will, fr. ML, fr. LL, *executrix, exsecutrix* woman that executes something, fem. of L *executor, exsecutor* executor — more at -TRIX] : a woman exercising the functions of an executor

ex·ec·u·try \-(y)ə·trī\ *n* -ES [prob. irreg. fr. *executor* + *-y*] *Scots law* : the movable estate passing to the executor for distribution

exede *vt* -ED/-ING/-S [L *exedere* to eat up, fr. *ex-* ¹ex- + *edere* to eat — more at EAT] *obs* : CORRODE

ex·e·dent \'eksədənt\ *adj* [L *exedent-, exedens*, pres. part. of *exedere*] : WASTING, ULCERATING

ex·e·dra \'eksədrə, ek'sēd-, eks'hēd-\ *n, pl* **exe·drae** \-,drē\ [L *exedra*, fr. Gk, fr. *ex* out of, out + *hedra* seat, fr. *hezesthai* to sit — more at EX-, SIT] **1** *in ancient Greece and Rome* : a room for conversation usu. open like a portico and furnished with seats **2** : a large out-of-door nearly semicircular seat or bench with a solid back — **ex·e·dral** \-rəl\ *adj*

exeem *vt* -ED/-ING/-S [fr. *exemption*, after E *redemption: redeem*] *obs* : EXEMPT

ex·e·ge·sis \,eksə'jēsəs\ *n, pl* **exege·ses** \-ē,sēz\ [NL, fr. Gk *exēgēsis*, fr. *exēgeisthai* to explain, interpret, fr. *ex* out of, out + *hēgeisthai* to lead — more at SEEK] : EXPOSITION, EXPLANATION; *esp* : critical interpretation of a text or portion of Scripture

ex·e·ge·sist \-ēsəst\ *n* -s [*exegesis* + *-ist*] : EXEGETE

ex·e·gete \'eksə,jēt\ *n* -s [Gk *exēgētēs*, fr. *exēgeisthai*] : one who practices exegesis

ex·e·get·ic \¦eksə¦jed·ik\ *or* **ex·e·get·i·cal** \-d·ə̇kəl\ *adj* [*exegetic* fr. Gk *exēgētikos*, fr. *exēgētēs* + *-ikos* -ic; *exegetical* fr. Gk *exēgētikos* + E *-al*] : relating to exegesis : EXPLANATORY, EXPOSITORY — **ex·e·get·i·cal·ly** \ə̇k(ə)lē\ *adv*

ex·e·get·ics \,eksə'jed·iks\ *n pl but sing or pl in constr* : the science of interpretation esp. of the Scriptures

ex·e·get·ist \,eksə'jed·əst, '≈≈,≈≈\ *n* -s [*exegetic* + *-ist*] : EXEGETE

exempla *pl of* EXEMPLUM

¹ex·em·plar \ig'zemplə(r), eg-, -,plär, -,plȧ(r\ *n* -s [ME *exaumplere, exemplar*, fr. MF & L; ME *exaumplere* fr. MF *exemplaire, examplaire*, fr. LL *exemplarium*, alter. of L *exemplar*; ME *exemplar* fr. L, fr. *exemplum* model, example, copy — more at EXAMPLE] : one that serves as a model or example: as **a** : an ideal model ⟨Plato, the classic ~ of the moral theory —Hunter Mead⟩ **b** : a typical or standard specimen **c** : a copy of a book **d** : a manuscript or copy of a text from which other copies were made **e** : a philosophical archetype; *specif* : UNIVERSAL **syn** see MODEL

²exemplar *adj* [L *exemplaris*] *obs* : EXEMPLARY

ex·em·plar·i·ly \,egzəm¦plerəlē, -,zem-, -li, *chiefly Brit* ig'zemplərəli *or* eg'z-\ *adv* : in an exemplary manner : by way of example

ex·em·pla·ri·ness *pronunc at* ¹EXEMPLARY + nə̇s\ *n* -ES : the quality or state of being exemplary

ex·em·plar·ism \ig'zemplə,rizəm, eg-\ *n* -s [¹*exemplar* + *-ism*] : a theological doctrine that the divine ideas are the ontological basis of finite realities and of their knowability

ex·em·plar·i·ty \,eg,zem'plarəd·ē, -,zəm-\ *n* -ES [trans. of It *esemplarità*] : exemplary quality : EXEMPLARINESS

¹ex·em·pla·ry \ig'zemplərē, eg-, -ri *sometimes* 'egzəm,pler- *or* 'eg,zem,pler-\ *n* -ES [ME *exemplarie, exaumplarie*, fr. LL *exemplarium*] : EXEMPLAR

²exemplary \"\ *adj* [L *exemplaris*, fr. *exemplum* + *-aris* -ar] **1 a** : serving as or in the nature of an exemplar, form, or pattern ⟨the realm of ~ ideas⟩ **b** : deserving imitation : COMMENDABLE ⟨the ~ lives of saints⟩ **2** : serving as a warning : MONITORY ⟨~ justice⟩ **3** : serving as an example, instance, or illustration ⟨~ passages⟩ **4** : consisting of or relating to exempla ⟨medieval ~ literature⟩

³exemplary *adv, obs* : EXEMPLARILY

exemplary damages *n pl* : PUNITIVE DAMAGES

ex·em·pli·fi·able \ig'zemplə,fīəbəl, eg-, ≈,≈≈'≈≈≈\ *adj* : capable of being exemplified

ex·em·pli·fi·ca·tion \≈,≈pləfə'kāshən\ *n* -s [ME *exemplificacion*, fr. AF & ML; AF *exemplification*, fr. ML *exemplification-, exemplificatio*, fr. *exemplificatus* (past part. of *exemplificare* to copy, show by example) + L *-ion-, -io* -ion] **1** *law* : an exemplified copy **2 a** : the act or process of exemplifying : a showing or illustrating by example ⟨the formation of a general idea . . . and the observation of its ~ in a variety of occasions —A.N.Whitehead⟩ **b** : a case in point : INSTANCE, EXAMPLE **3** : the presentation or working of degrees (as by the various Masonic bodies) : a setting forth of the work of a lodge or fraternal order for purposes of instruction or conferral of a degree and under the supervision of a qualified officer

ex·em·pli·fi·ca·tive \≈'≈≈≈,kād·iv\ *adj* [ML *exemplificatus* + E *-ive*] : EXEMPLIFYING

ex·em·pli·fi·ca·to·ry \-,kə,tōrē, *chiefly Brit* ≈¦≈≈¦kātəri\ *adj* [ML *exemplificatus* + E *-ory*] : EXEMPLIFYING : designed to exemplify

ex·em·pli·fy \ig'zemplə,fī, eg-\ *vt* -ED/-ING/-ES [ME *exemplifien*, fr. MF *exemplifier*, fr. ML *exemplificare* to copy, show by example, fr. *exempli-* (fr. L *exemplum* model, example, copy) + L *-ficare* -fy — more at EXAMPLE] **1** *obs* : to set an example to **2** : to show or illustrate by example : furnish with examples ⟨the chief value . . . lies not so much in any novelty of thesis as in the instances and insights which ~ and enrich his elaboration —Lucius Garvin⟩ **3** *obs* **a** : to put forward or point to as an example **b** : to make example of by public punishment **4 a** : COPY, TRANSCRIBE **b** : to make an attested copy or transcript of (a document) under seal **5 a** : to be an instance of or serve as an example of : EMBODY ⟨an organism can manifest and ~ mechanical principles in itself —Weston La Barre⟩ **b** : to be typical of : ILLUSTRATE ⟨his works ~ the taste of the period⟩ **6** : to go through the ceremonies and rituals of (as a degree of a fraternal order)

ex·em·pli gra·tia \ig¦zem,plē'gräd·ē,ä, eg-\ *adv* [L] : for the sake of example : for example or instance — abbr. *e.g.*

ex·em·plum \-'zempləm\ *n, pl* **exem·pla** \-lə\ [LL, fr. L, model, example, copy] **1** : an anecdote or short narrative used (as in a medieval sermon) to point a moral or sustain an argument **2** [L] : EXAMPLE, MODEL

¹ex·empt \ig'zem(p)t, eg-\ *adj* [ME, fr. L *exemptus*, past part. of *eximere* to remove, free, fr. *ex-* ¹ex- + *-imere* (fr. *emere* to buy, acquire) — more at REDEEM] **1** *obs* : set apart : cut off : EXCLUDED **2** : not subject to an authority or jurisdiction (as of a bishop) ⟨~ monastery⟩ **3** : free or released from some liability to which others are subject : excepted from the operation of some law or obligation : not subject to : not liable to — used with *from* ⟨goods ~ from execution⟩ ⟨~ from jury service⟩ ⟨tax-*exempt*⟩

²exempt \"\ *vt* -ED/-ING/-S [ME *exempten*, fr. L *exemptus*, past part. of *eximere*] **1** *obs* : to set apart : REMOVE, EXCLUDE **2** : to release or deliver from some liability or requirement to which others are subject : except or excuse from the operation of a law or obligation ⟨~ a man from military service⟩ ⟨~ a student from a generally required course⟩

³exempt \"\ *n* -s [L & F; F *exempt* subordinate in the cavalry commanding in the absence of the higher company officers, fr. *exempt*, adj., fr. L *exemptus*, past part. of *eximere*] **1** : one exempted or freed from duty : one not subject **2 a** : a subordinate in the French cavalry who is in command when the higher company officers are absent and is exempt from common duty; *also* : a similar French police officer **b** : EXON **c** : an honorably discharged fire fighter who enjoys certain exemptions (as from jury duty)

exempt carrier *n* : a transport agency specializing in services (as taxi service) or commodities (as farm products or bulk cargo) exempt from regulation by the Interstate Commerce Act

ex·emp·tion \-m(p)shən\ *n* -s [ME *exempcioun*, fr. MF or ML; MF *exemption*, fr. ML *exemption-, exemptio*, fr. L, removal, fr. *exemptus* (past part. of *eximere*) + *-ion-, -io* -ion] **1** : the act of exempting or state of being exempt : freedom from any charge or obligation to which others are subject : IMMUNITY ⟨~ from an entrance examination⟩ ⟨~ from customs duty⟩ **2** : a cause for exempting (as a portion of taxable income) ⟨claim ~ for a dependent⟩ **3** *Roman Catholicism* : release from the jurisdiction of the ordinary and subjection only to that of the Holy See

ex·emp·tive \-m(p)tiv\ *adj* [²*exempt* + *-ive*] : relating to, securing, or providing exemption

exempt job *n* : a job that is removed from seniority provisions in that while the holder may be laid off he may not be replaced by someone of senior service

ex·endospermous *also* **ex·endospermic** \(¦)eks+\ *adj* [¹*ex-* + *endosperm* + *-ous* or *-ic*] : lacking endosperm — used of seeds ⟨~ beans⟩

¹ex·en·ter·ate \ek'sentə,rāt\ *vt* -ED/-ING/-S [L *exenteratus*, past part. of *exenterare*, modif. of Gk *exenterizein*, fr. *ex* out of, out + *enteron* intestine + *-izein* -ize — more at EX-, INTER-] **1** : DISEMBOWEL, EVISCERATE **2** : to remove the contents of (as the orbit, pelvis, or a sinus) — **ex·en·ter·a·tion** \(,)ek,sentə'rāshən\ *n* -s

²ex·en·ter·ate \(')≈¦≈≈rə̇t\ *adj* [L *exenteratus*, past part. of *exenterare*] : EVISCERATED

ex·e·qua·tur \,eksə'kwād·ə(r), -wäd-\ *n* -s [L *exequatur*, *exsequatur* let him perform, 3d pers. sing. pres. subj. of *exequi*, *exsequi* to perform, execute — more at EXECUTION] **1** : a written official recognition and authorization of a consular officer issued by the government to which he is accredited **2** : permission granted by a sovereign for the exercise of a bishop's functions under papal authority or for the publication of papal bulls

ex·e·qui·al \(')ek¦sēkwēəl\ *adj* [L *exequialis, exsequialis*, fr. *exequiae, exsequiae* + *-alis* -al] : of or relating to funerals : FUNEREAL

ex·e·quy \'eksəkwē\ *n, pl* **exequies** [ME *exequies, exequise*, sing. & pl., fr. MF & L; MF *exequies*, pl., fr. L *exequiae, exsequiae*, pl., fr. *exequi, exsequi* to follow, perform, execute] : a funeral rite or ceremony; *sometimes* : a funeral procession — now chiefly used in pl.

exerce *vb* -ED/-ING/-S [ME *exercen*, fr. L *exercēre*] *obs* : EXERCISE

ex·er·cent \ig'zərsᵊnt, eg-\ *adj* [L *exercent-, exercens*, pres. part. of *exercēre*] *archaic* : EXERCISING, PRACTICING

ex·er·cis·able \'eksə(r),sīzəbəl, ,≈≈'≈≈≈\ *adj* : capable of being exercised ⟨~ right⟩

¹ex·er·cise \'eksə(r),sīz\ *n* -s [ME, fr. MF *exercice*, fr. L *exercitium*, fr. *exercitus*, past part. of *exercēre* to drive on, keep busy, fr. *ex-* ¹ex- + *-ercēre* (fr. *arcēre* to hold off, enclose) — more at ARK] **1 a** : the act of bringing into play or realizing in action : EXERTION, USE ⟨avoid accidents by the ~ of foresight⟩ ⟨the violent . . . ~ of royal authority —T.B. Macaulay⟩ **b** : the discharge of an official function or professional occupation ⟨~ of his judicial duties⟩ **2 a** : regular or repeated appropriate use of a faculty, power, or bodily organ ⟨willpower is strengthened by ~⟩ ⟨muscles atrophy from lack of ~⟩ **b** : bodily exertion for the sake of developing and maintaining physical fitness ⟨he plays golf chiefly for the ~⟩ **3** : something that is performed or practiced in order to develop or improve a specific power or skill: as **a** : a set task (as a piece of writing) designed to improve a pupil's ability or to test his comprehension of a subject ⟨do the ~ at the end of each chapter⟩ ⟨spelling ~⟩ **b** : an artificially devised bodily action or set of actions prescribed for regular or repeated practice as a means of gaining strength, dexterity, suppleness, or all-around competence in some field of performance ⟨finger ~⟩ ⟨bowing ~⟩ ⟨vocal ~*s*⟩ ⟨breathing ~*s*⟩ **4 a** : a composition or work of art performed chiefly in order to practice or display a specific technical point or aspect : STUDY ⟨~ in double-stops⟩ ⟨~ in light and shadow effects⟩ **b** : an artistic or intellectual performance whose value is greater in the doing than in the final result or greater for the performer than for the beholder ⟨a mere literary ~⟩ ⟨to balance forms, calculate proportions, and harmonize colors can be an intellectual ~ rather than an act of creative imagination —Herbert Read⟩ **c** : any performance having a strongly marked or identifiable secondary or ulterior aspect ⟨a biography that . . . is a truly formidable ~ in unrelieved contempt —*New Yorker*⟩ **d** : habitual act : PRACTICE ⟨the casting of metal forms in molds was an ~ older than recorded history⟩ **5** : an act of religious practice esp. in worship (as of preaching, expounding, or praying) ⟨~*s* of devotion⟩ **6** : a public exhibition or ceremony: as **a** : a maneuver, operation, or drill carried out for training and discipline ⟨a field ~⟩ **b** : an academic disputation, oral examination, or discourse required of a candidate for a degree and often carried on in public **c exercises** *pl* : a program including speeches, announcements of awards and honors, and various traditional practices of secular or religious character ⟨commencement ~*s*⟩ **d** : an activity forming part of a regular academic routine ⟨salute the national flag as part of a daily school ~ —Felix Frankfurter⟩

²exercise \"\ *vb* -ED/-ING/-S [ME *exercisen*, fr. *exercise*, n.] *vt* **1 a** : to bring into play : make effective in action ⟨privileges if not *exercised* are often lost⟩ ⟨he failed to ~ good judgment in buying the car⟩ : bring to bear : EXERT ⟨will can only be *exercised* in the presence of something which retards or resists it —W.R.Inge⟩ ⟨~ her influence among all the nations of the world —Norman Angell⟩ **b** *obs* : to carry on (an occupation) or carry out the functions of (an office) **2 a** : to use repeatedly in order to strengthen or develop (a muscle or a bodily faculty) ⟨*exercising* his fingers daily to restore them⟩ **b** : to train (as troops) by drills and maneuvers ⟨Tom was being *exercised* like a raw recruit —George Meredith⟩ **c** : to give exercise to : put through exercises **3 a** : to engage the attention and effort of ⟨a problem which is much *exercising* the minds of the city fathers —Sam Pollock⟩ **b** : to cause anxiety, alarm, or indignation in : VEX, HARASS ⟨was ever a human generation so *exercised* about its education as ours? —C.G.Osgood⟩ ~ *vi* **1** *obs* : to perform one's office **2** : to exert oneself : take exercise : DRILL, TRAIN **3** : to take part in religious exercises **syn** see PRACTICE

ex·er·cis·er \-zə(r)\ *n* -s : one that exercises: as **a** : an apparatus for use in physical exercise **b** : a groom who exercises horses

ex·er·ci·tant \ig'zərsəd·ənt, eg-\ *n* -s [F, prob. fr. LL *exercitant-, exercitans*, pres. part. of *exercitare* to meditate, fr. L, to exercise diligently, fr. *exercitus*, past part. of *exercēre* to drive on, keep busy — more at ¹EXERCISE] : one engaged in spiritual exercises

ex·er·ci·ta·tion \ig,zərsə'tāshən, (,)eg-\ *n* -s [ME *exercitacioun*, fr. L *exercitation-, exercitatio*, fr. *exercitatus* (past part. of *exercitare* to exercise diligently) + *-ion-, -io* -ion] *archaic* : EXERCISE

ex·er·ci·tor \≈'≈səd·ə(r)\ *or* **exercitor ma·ris** \-'ma(a)rə̇s\ *n* -s [*exercitor* fr. L, exerciser, fr. *exercitus* (past part. of *exercēre* to drive on, keep busy) + *-or*; *exercitor maris* fr. NL, lit., exerciser of the sea] *civil & Scots law* : the one (as owner, charterer, or mortgagee in possession) to whom the profits of a ship belong at a particular time

ex·er·ci·to·ri·al \ig¦zərsə¦tōrēəl, (¦)eg¦-\ *adj* : of or relating to an exercitor

ex·er·e·sis \ek'serəsəs, eg'ze-\ *n, pl* **exere·ses** \-ə,sēz\ [NL, fr. Gk *exairesis* removal, taking out, fr. *exairein* to remove, take out (fr. *ex* out of, out + *hairein* to take) + *-sis* — more at EX-, HERESY] : surgical removal of a part or organ (as a nerve)

ex·er·gon·ic \¦ek(,)sər¦gänik\ *adj* [*exo-* + Gk *ergon* work + E *-ic* — more at WORK] : producing work or energy — opposed to *endergonic*; used esp. of a chemical reaction occurring in a biological process

ex·er·gu·al \(')ek¦sərgəl, (')eg¦zər-\ *adj* : relating to the exergue of a coin or medal

ex·er·gue \'ek,sərg, 'eg,zərg, ≈'≈\ *n* -s [F *exergue*, fr. NL *exergum*, fr. Gk *ex* out of, out + *ergon* work] : a space on a coin, token, or medal usu. on the reverse below the central part of the design, sometimes marked off from it by a line, and often containing the date

ex·ert \ig'zər|t, eg-, -zə̄|, -zəi|, *usu* |d.+V\ *vt* -ED/-ING/-S [L *exertus, exsertus*, past part. of *exerere, exserere* to thrust out, fr. *ex-* ¹ex- + *serere* to join together — more at SERIES] **1** *obs* : to thrust forth : EMIT **2 a** : to put forth or put out (as strength, power, or effort) : bring (as a force) into play : set in operation : make effective ⟨he had to ~ all his strength to move the stone⟩ **b** : to put (oneself) into action or to tiring effort ⟨if people are to ~ themselves they must be convinced —A.J.P.Taylor⟩ **3** *obs* : SHOW, REVEAL **4** : to bring (as a force, an influence) to bear esp. with sustained effort or lasting effect ⟨never would have entered the political arena at all if his father had not ~*ed* relentless pressure —Bennett Cerf⟩ ⟨forms which ~*ed* a profound influence on late buildings —*Amer. Guide Series: N.Y. City*⟩ ⟨his long poetic career . . . continues to ~ a special fascination —Delmore Schwartz⟩ **5** : EXERCISE, WIELD ⟨a chance to ~ leadership in a constructive way —*Education Digest*⟩ ⟨disguised aristocracies, where courtiers or even courtesans frequently ~ the real power —M.R.Cohen⟩

ex·er·tion \|shən\ *n* -s : the act of exerting : active exercise of any power or faculty ⟨a diversion requiring little mental ~⟩ : EFFORT; *esp* : a laborious or perceptible effort ⟨panting from the ~ of climbing the stairs⟩ **syn** see EFFORT

ex·ert·ive \|d·iv\ *adj* : having power or a tendency to exert

exes *pl of* EX

ex·e·unt \'eksē(,)ənt, -se,ünt\ [L, they go out, 3d pers. pl. pres. indic. of *exire* to go out — more at EXEAT] : go out : go off the stage — used as a stage direction to specify that all or certain named characters leave the stage; compare MANENT

exeunt om·nes \-(,)ənt'äm,nēz, -,ünt'ōm,näs\ [NL, they all go out] : all go out : all go off the stage — a stage direction to specify that all the characters leave the stage

ex fa·cie \ek'sfākē,ä\ *adv (or adj)* [NL, lit., from the face] : in the light of what is apparent — used in ref. to a legal instrument ⟨the deed appears *ex facie* to be in order⟩

ex·filtration \¦eks+\ *n* [¹*ex-* + *filtration*] : a filtering out : a gradual escape (as through a membrane or a wall) : LEAK

¹ex·flagellant \(¦)eks+\ *adj* [*exflagellate* + *-ant*, adj. suffix] : relating to or marked by exflagellation

²exflagellant \"\ *n* [*exflagellate* + *-ant*, n. suffix] : one that exflagellates

ex·flagellate \(')eks+\ *vi* [back-formation fr. *exflagellation*] **1** *biol* : to cast off cilia or flagella **2** *of sporozoans* : to form microgametes by extrusion of nuclear material into peripheral processes of gametocyte cytoplasm that resemble flagella

ex·flagellation \(¦)eks+\ *n* [¹*ex-* + *flagellum* + *-ation*] : the action or process of exflagellating

ex·fo·li·ate \ek'sfōlē,āt\ *vb* [LL *exfoliatus*, past part. of *exfoliare* to strip of leaves, fr. L *ex-* ¹ex- + *-foliare* (fr. *folium* leaf) — more at BLADE] *vt* **1** : to cast or throw off from the surface in scales, laminae, or splinters **2** : to remove or take off the surface of in scales or laminae **3** : to open, spread, or extend by or as if by opening out leaves ⟨in twenty-three chapters he ~*s* his program of moral transformation —O.L. Reiser⟩ ~ *vi* **1** : to split into or give off scales, laminae, or body cells esp. from the surface **2** : to come off in a thin piece : scale or flake off **3** : to grow or develop by or as if by producing or unfolding leaves ⟨criticism has *exfoliated* until the work of art is sometimes smothered beneath it —Malcolm Cowley⟩

ex·fo·li·a·tion \(,)≈,≈≈'āshən\ *n* [prob. fr. (assumed) ML *exfoliation-, exfoliatio*, fr. LL *exfoliatus* (past part. of *exfoliare* to strip of leaves) + L *-ion-, -io* -ion] : the action or process of unfolding or exfoliating: as **a** : the peeling of the horny layer of the skin (as in some skin diseases) **b** : the shedding of surface components (as cells from internal body surfaces when diseased) **c** : the shedding of a superficial layer of bone (as a sequestrum) or of a tooth or part of a tooth **d** : the phase of weathering that involves the breaking loose of thin concentric shells, slabs, spalls, or flakes from rock surfaces

exfoliation dome *n* : a large dome-shaped rock mass (as of granite) produced by exfoliation

ex·fo·li·a·tive \(')ek¦sfōlē,ād·iv, -lēəd-\ *adj* [F *exfoliatif*, fr. MF, fr. LL *exfoliatus* (past part. of *exfoliare* to strip of leaves) + MF *-if* -ive] : causing or characterized by exfoliation

exfoliative cytology *n* : the study of cells shed from body surfaces esp. for determining the presence or absence of a cancerous condition

ex gr *abbr* [L *exempli gratia*] for example

ex gra·tia \eks'gräd·ē,ä, -grāsh(ē)ə\ *adj (or adv)* [NL, by favor] : as a favor : not compelled by legal right ⟨*ex gratia* pension payments⟩

¹ex·hal·ant *or* **ex·hal·ent** \(')eks¦hālənt\ *adj* [L *exhalant-, exhalans*, pres. part. of *exhalare*] : having the function of exhaling or evaporating : EMISSIVE ⟨the ~ siphon of a clam⟩

²exhalant *or* **exhalent** \"\ *n* -s : an exhaling duct

exhalate *vt* -ED/-ING/-S [L *exhalatus*, past part. of *exhalare*] *obs* : EXHALE

ex·ha·la·tion \,eks(h)ə'lāshən\ *n* -s [ME *exalacioun*, fr. MF & L; MF *exalation*, fr. L *exhalation-, exhalatio*, fr. *exhalatus* (past part. of *exhalare* to exhale) + *-ion-, -io* -ion] **1** : an exhaling or sending forth (as in steam or vapor) : EVAPORATION, EXPIRATION ⟨noisy ~*s* of a locomotive⟩; *specif* : the action of forcing air out of the lungs by means of a complex of essentially reflex actions that involve changes in the diaphragm and in muscles of the abdomen and thorax which cause contraction of the chest cavity and lungs resulting in production of relative positive pressure within the lung so that air flows out until the pressure is restored to equality with that of the atmosphere **2** : something that is exhaled or given off or that rises in the form of gas, fumes, or steam : EFFLUVIUM, EMANATION ⟨a foul ~ from the marsh⟩

¹ex·hale \eks'hāl, *chiefly before pause or consonant* -āəl\ *vb* -ED/-ING/-S [ME *exalen*, fr. L *exhalare*, fr. *ex-* ¹ex- + *halare* to breathe; akin to L *anima* breath — more at ANIMATE] *vt* **1** : to breathe out : let or force out of the lungs ⟨*exhaled* carbon dioxide) ⟨*exhaled* a sigh⟩ **2 :** to give off or give forth (gas or odor) **:** EMIT ⟨the turned earth *exhaled* in the warm sun a delicate fragrance —Mary Austin⟩ **3** *archaic* **:** to draw out (moisture) **:** EVAPORATE **4 :** to discharge through a membranous surface — used in old medical terminology **~** *vi* **1 :** to rise or be given off as vapor ⟨a bad smell *exhaling* from the kitchen —Glenway Wescott⟩ **:** EMANATE; *also* **:** to vanish by or as if by evaporation ⟨dried his hands . . . instead of suffering the moisture to ~ —Sir Walter Scott⟩ **2 :** to breathe out **:** let or force the breath out — opposed to *inhale* **3 :** to percolate through a membrane **:** OOZE — used in old medical terminology **syn** see EMIT

²exhale *vt* [¹*ex-* + *hale* (to draw)] *obs* **:** to draw or force out ⟨and what those sorrows could not thence ~, thy beauty hath, and made then blind with weeping —Shak.⟩

ex·hale·ment \eks'hā(ə)lmənt\ *n* -S [¹*exhale* + *-ment*] *archaic* **:** EXHALATION

¹ex·haust \ig'zȯst, eg-\ *vb* -ED/-ING/-S [L *exhaustus*, past part. of *exhaurire*, fr. *ex-* ¹ex- + *haurire* to draw; akin to MHG *œsen* to empty, ON *ausa* to besprinkle, Gk *exauein* to take out] *vt* **1** *obs* **:** to draw forth (as tears) **2** *obs* **:** to draw in **:** drink up **3 a :** to draw off or let out wholly **:** drain off completely ⟨~ the water of a well⟩ ⟨~ the air from a bell jar⟩ **b :** to empty by drawing off or draining ⟨~ a wine cask⟩ ⟨~ a bank account⟩; *specif* **:** to create a vacuum in (as the receiver of an air pump) **:** EVACUATE 4 **4 a :** to use up the whole supply or store of **:** expend or consume entirely ⟨~ a coal vein⟩ ⟨till her lover had *~ed* his eloquence —T.L.Peacock⟩ **b :** to deprive wholly of strength, patience, or resources **:** tire out **:** wear out **:** WEARY ⟨*~ed* from a day's shopping⟩ ⟨*~ed* himself working in the heat⟩ **c :** to destroy the fertility of ⟨steady cropping *~ed* the soil⟩ **5 a :** to develop (a subject) completely **:** discuss thoroughly **b :** to make use of or try out or otherwise account for the whole number of ⟨*~ed* the possibilities⟩ **c :** to take complete advantage of (legal remedies) ⟨all administrative remedies must be *~ed* before application to the courts can be made⟩ **6 :** to deprive completely of removable ingredients **:** deprive of strength or virtue ⟨~ a photographic developer⟩**:** as **a :** to extract completely with a solvent ⟨~ a drug successively with water, alcohol, and ether⟩ **b :** to free as far as possible from sugar or other ingredient by crystallization ⟨~ molasses⟩ **c :** to transfer dye from (a dyebath) *also* **:** to transfer (a dye) completely from a dyebath onto a fabric **~** *vi* **1 :** DISCHARGE, EMPTY ⟨the engine *~s* through a muffler⟩ **2 :** to flow or pass out ⟨the steam *~s* into the condenser⟩ **3 :** to pass from a dyebath onto a fabric ⟨substantive dyes ~ reasonably well onto cellulose⟩ **syn** see DEPLETE, TIRE

²exhaust \"\ *n* -S **1 a :** the escape or removal of working substance (as gas or vapor) from an engine cylinder after it has done its work on the piston **b :** the gas or vapor thus escaping **c :** the conduit including muffler and stack through which the gases escape **d :** an arrangement (as of fans) for withdrawing undesirable fumes, dusts, or odors from an enclosure (as a factory room or a kitchen) **2 :** the production of a partial vacuum (as by an air pump) **:** EXHAUSTION

exhaust collector ring *n* **:** the exhaust manifold of a radial engine

exhaust cone *n* **:** the tapered exhaust pipe of a jet engine

exhaust draft *n* **:** a draft produced by suction on the outlet side (as of a ventilation system) rather than by pressure on the intake side

ex·haust·er \-tə(r)\ *n* -S **1 :** a fan, pump, or other device for exhausting gases **2 :** one who operates a retort for the final cooking of canned foods **3 :** an operator of an exhaust machine for removing air, gas, and impurities from radio tubes

exhaust-gas analyzer *n* **:** a device for indicating the fuel-air ratio of the fuel mixture of an engine (as of an airplane) that consists of an element sensitive to carbon dioxide placed in the exhaust manifold — called also *fuel-mixture indicator, smoke feeler*

exhaust head *n* **:** a conical casing containing baffle plates that is attached to the end of an exhaust pipe for separating out the entrained oil and water and reducing the noise

ex·haust·ibil·i·ty \ig,zȯstə'bilәd·ē, (,)eg-, -lətē, -i\ *n* -ES **:** the quality or state of being exhaustible

ex·haust·ible \=ˈ=təbəl\ *adj* **:** capable of being exhausted

exhausting *adj* [fr. pres. part. of ¹*exhaust*] **:** producing exhaustion ⟨~ labors⟩ — **ex·haust·ing·ly** *adv*

ex·haus·tion \ig'zȯschən, eg-\ *n* -S [LL *exhaustion-, exhaustio*, fr. L *exhaustus* (past part. of *exhaurire* to exhaust) + *-ion-, -io* -ion — more at EXHAUST] **1 :** the act or process of exhausting or the state of being exhausted ⟨he felt ready to drop from ~⟩ **2 :** neurosis following overstrain or overexertion ⟨combat ~⟩

ex·haus·tive \-stiv, -tēv *also* -təv\ *adj* **:** serving or tending to exhaust **:** testing all possibilities or considering all the elements **:** THOROUGH ⟨an ~ investigation⟩ ⟨~ list⟩ **:** COMPLETE ⟨~ methylation⟩ — **ex·haus·tive·ly** \-tәvlē, -li\ *adv* — **ex·haus·tive·ness** \-tivnəs, -tēv- *also* -təv-\ *n* -ES

ex·haust·less \-tləs\ *adj* **:** not to be exhausted **:** INEXHAUSTIBLE ⟨~ wealth⟩ — **ex·haust·less·ly** *adv* — **ex·haust·less·ness** *n* -ES

exhaust manifold *n* **:** the manifold that receives the exhaust gases from each of several engine cylinders

exhaust nozzle *n* **:** the terminal portion of the tail pipe of a jet engine

exhausts *pres 3d sing of* EXHAUST, *pl of* EXHAUST

exhaust stroke *n* **:** the movement of an engine piston (as of a 4-stroke-cycle engine) that forces the used gas or vapor out through the exhaust ports

exhaust-suction stroke *n* **:** a piston stroke (as of a 2-cycle engine) that simultaneously expels used gases and draws in fresh fuel mixture

exhbn *abbr* exhibition

exhedra *var of* EXEDRA

ex·her·e·da·tion \(,)eks,herə'dāshən\ *n* -S [ME *exheredacioun*, fr. L *exheredation-, exheredatio*, fr. *exheredatus* (past part. of *exheredare*) + *-ion-, -io* -ion] **:** DISINHERITANCE

ex·her·i·date *also* **ex·her·e·date** \=ˈ==,dāt\ *vt* -ED/-ING/-S [L *exheredatus*, past part. of *exheredare*, fr. *exhered-, exheres* disinherited person, fr. *ex-* ¹ex- + *hered-, heres* heir — more at HEIR] **:** DISINHERIT

¹ex·hib·it \ig'zibət, eg-, *usu* -bəd·+V\ *vb* -ED/-ING/-S [ME *exhibiten*, fr. L *exhibitus*, past part. of *exhibēre* to present, show, fr. *ex-* ¹ex- + *-hibēre* (fr. *habēre* to have, hold) — more at HABIT] *vt* **1 :** to present to view **:** SHOW, DISPLAY: as **a :** to show (as a feeling) or display (as a quality) outwardly esp. by visible signs or actions ⟨*~ed* no fear⟩ ⟨*~ed* a mastery of the keyboard⟩ **b :** to have as a readily discernible quality or feature ⟨buildings *~ing* the stark functionalism of a toy village —J.P.Marquand⟩ ⟨in all cultures we know, men ~ an aesthetic sense —H.J.Muller⟩ **c :** to represent or make clear by a drawing, plan, or other visual method esp. so as to show detail or spatial relations **:** PICTURE ⟨orbit is to be diagrammatically *~ed* by a series of dots —A.N.Whitehead⟩ **d :** to show publicly **:** put on display in order to attract notice to what is interesting or instructive or for purposes of competition or demonstration ⟨~ goods in a store⟩ ⟨~ a painting⟩ **:** show off ⟨proudly *~ed* a fine buck he had shot⟩ **2 :** to submit (as a document) to a court or officer in course of proceedings; *also* **:** to present or offer officially or in legal form **:** BRING ⟨~ a charge⟩ **:** file of record **3 a** *obs* **:** to offer (as a sacrifice) or present (as a grant) **b :** to administer as a remedy **c** *obs* **:** ADMINISTER ⟨~ an oath⟩ **4 :** to make clear to the understanding **:** EXPLAIN ⟨article . . . in which he *~s* this distrust as narrow-minded in its origin —B.N.Cardozo⟩ **~** *vi* **:** to display something for public inspection **:** put on an exhibition ⟨he first *~ed* in the salon at the age of 14 —*Amer. Guide Series: Conn.*⟩ **syn** see SHOW

²exhibit \"\ *n* -S **1 :** an act or instance of exhibiting **:** DISPLAY, EXHIBITION ⟨a new ~ in the library⟩ ⟨a school ~⟩ **2 :** something exhibited; *specif* **:** an article or a collection of articles displayed in an exhibition **3 :** a document or material object produced and identified in court or before an examiner for use as evidence; *also* **:** a paper or document referred to by way of explanation or evidence (as in a pleading or petition) ⟨introduced the weapons into evidence as *~s* A and B⟩ **4 exhibits** *pl, Brit* **:** the documents that a clergyman may be required to produce at the first visitation after his admission; *also* **:** the fees then payable

ex·hib·it·able \-bəd·əbəl, -bətə-\ *adj* **:** capable of being exhibited **:** suitable for exhibition

ex·hib·i·tant \-əd·ənt, -ətənt *also* -ət³nt\ *n* -S **:** EXHIBITOR

ex·hi·bi·tion \,eksə'bishən *sometimes* ,egzə-\ *n* -S [ME *exhibicioun*, fr. MF *exhibition, exhibition*, fr. L *exhibition-, exhibitio* presentation, fr. *exhibitus* (past part. of *exhibēre* to present, show) + *-ion-, -io* -ion — more at EXHIBIT] **1 :** an act or instance of showing, evincing, or showing off ⟨an ~ of bad manners⟩ ⟨a notable ~ of courage⟩ ⟨out of training as he was, he was afraid of making an ~ of himself⟩ **2 a** *obs* **:** allowance esp. for food and drink **:** SUSTENANCE, MAINTENANCE **b** *obs* **:** SALARY, PENSION **c** *obs* **:** PRESENT **d :** a grant formerly given by a private benefactor and now drawn from the funds of the institution to help maintain a student at a school, college, or university in the British Commonwealth **3 :** a public show or showing: as **a :** a display esp. of works of art or objects of manufacture — often used with *on* ⟨the coin collection will be on ~ next week⟩; *specif* **:** a display or show where the display itself is the chief object and from which the exhibitor derives or expects to derive a profit ⟨an industrial ~⟩ **b** (1) **:** a public examination of school or college students (2) **:** a public display of the attainments of the pupils of a school **:** EXERCISE **c :** a public display of athletic or other skill often in the form of a contest or game but usu. without importance with respect to winning or losing ⟨a fencing ~⟩ ⟨an ~ baseball game⟩ ⟨an ~ billiards match⟩ **4 :** the act of administering a remedy

ex·hi·bi·tion·er \-sh(ə)nə(r)\ *n* -S **1** *Brit* **:** one who holds an exhibition (sense 2d) **2 :** EXHIBITOR

exhibition game fowl *n* **:** a game fowl of the Modern Game class bred for show and selected esp. for perfection of form, carriage, and feathering — compare PIT GAME FOWL

ex·hi·bi·tion·ism \-shə,nizəm\ *n* -S [ISV *exhibition* + *-ism*] **1 a :** a perversion marked by a tendency to indecent exposure of the person so as to excite or gratify oneself sexually by such exposure **b :** such exposure or an act of such exposure **2 :** the act or practice of behaving so as to attract attention to oneself **:** extravagant or willfully conspicuous behavior

¹ex·hi·bi·tion·ist \-sh(ə)nəst\ *n* -S [ISV *exhibition* + *-ist*] **:** one who engages in or is addicted to exhibitionism

²exhibitionist \;==ˈ=(=)=\ *or* **ex·hi·bi·tion·is·tic** \;== ;bishə;nistik\ *adj* **:** of, relating to, or given to exhibitionism

ex·hib·i·tive \ig'zibəd·|iv, eg-, -ət|\ *adj* [NL *exhibitivus*, fr. L *exhibitus* (past part. of *exhibēre*) + *-ivus* -ive] **:** having the function of exhibiting — **ex·hib·i·tiv·ely** \|əvlē, -li\ *adv*

ex·hib·i·tor *also* **ex·hib·it·er** \|ə(r)\ *n* -S **1 :** one that exhibits (as in an exhibition) **2 :** one who shows motion pictures to the public

ex·hib·i·to·ry \-bə,tōrē, -tȯr-, -ri\ *adj* **:** relating to or intended for exhibition

exhibits *pres 3d sing of* EXHIBIT, *pl of* EXHIBIT

ex·hil·a·rant \ig'zilərənt, eg-\ *adj* [L *exhilarant-, exhilarans*, pres. part. of *exhilarare*] **:** EXHILARATING

ex·hil·a·rate \-ə,rāt, *usu* -ād·+V\ *vt* -ED/-ING/-S [L *exhilaratus*, past part. of *exhilarare*, fr. *ex-* ¹ex- + *hilarare* to cheer, gladden, fr. *hilarus* cheerful — more at HILARITY] **1 :** to make cheerful **:** ENLIVEN, CHEER, GLADDEN ⟨the sun and wind . . . on his back . . . *exhilarated* him —Grace Campbell⟩ **2 :** REFRESH, INVIGORATE, STIMULATE ⟨watching the flood, awed yet somehow *exhilarated* by the terrible, incalculable power of rushing water —Louis Bromfield⟩ **syn** see PLEASE

exhilarating *adj* [fr. pres. part. of *exhilarate*] **:** that exhilarates **:** CHEERING, GLADDENING, INVIGORATING, INTOXICATING ⟨the ~ effect of mountain air⟩ ⟨found something ~ and oddly exciting in all this unusual bright costume —H.G.Wells⟩ — **ex·hil·a·rat·ing·ly** *adv*

ex·hil·a·ra·tion \=,==ˈrāshən\ *n* -S [LL *exhilaration-, exhilaratio*, fr. L *exhilaratus* (past part. of *exhilarare*) + *-ion-, -io* -ion] **1 :** the action of exhilarating **2 :** the feeling or the state of being exhilarated

ex·hil·a·ra·tive \=ˈ==,rād·|iv, -,rəl, |t|, |ēv *also* |əv\ *adj* **:** tending to exhilarate ⟨nature was ~ and restorative —R.L. Cook⟩

ex·hil·a·ra·tor \-ād·ə(r), -ātə-\ *n* -S **:** one that exhilarates

¹ex·hort \ig'z|ȯ(ə)r|t, eg'z|, 'ȯ(ə)| *also* ik's| *or* iks'h| *or* ek's| *or* eks'h|, *usu* |d·+V\ *vb* -ED/-ING/-S [ME *exhorten*, fr. MF *exhorter*, fr. L *exhortari*, fr. *ex-* ¹ex- + *hortari* to incite, urge — more at YEARN] *vt* **:** to incite by argument or advice **:** urge strongly **:** ADVISE, WARN ⟨we have been *~ed* to drive all negative fears out of our minds —W.J.Reilly⟩ **~** *vi* **:** to give warnings or advice **:** make urgent appeal **:** PREACH ⟨ministers and converted Christians rushed about the camp praying and *~ing* —J.C.Brauer⟩ **syn** see URGE

²exhort *n* -S *obs* **:** EXHORTATION

ex·hor·ta·tion \,ek,sȯ(r)'tāshən, ,eg,zȯ(r)-, ,eksə(r)-, ,eks|-,hȯ(r)-\ *n* -S [ME *exhortacioun*, fr. MF & L; MF *exhortation*, fr. L *exhortation-, exhortatio*, fr. *exhortatus* (past part. of *exhortari*) + *-ion-, -io* -ion] **1 :** an act or instance of exhorting **:** SERMON ⟨*~s* to young men to continue their education⟩ **2 :** language intended to incite and encourage **:** ADVICE, COUNSEL; *specif* **:** a liturgical formulary of this nature

ex·hort·ative *pronunc at* ¹EXHORT + əd·|iv *or* ət|\ *adj* [ME, fr. L *exhortativus*, fr. *exhortatus* (past part. of *exhortari*) + *-ivus* -ive] **:** serving to exhort **:** HORTATIVE — **ex·hort·ative·ly** \|əvlē, -li\ *adv*

ex·hort·ato·ry \|ə,tōrē, -tȯr-, -ri\ *adj* [ME, fr. LL *exhortatorius*, fr. L *exhortatus* + *-orius* -ory] **:** HORTATORY

ex·hort·er \|ə(r)\ *n* -S **:** one that exhorts **:** PREACHER; *specif* **:** a layman authorized to exhort under ministerial direction

ex·hort·ing·ly *adv* [*exhorting* (pres. part. of ¹*exhort*) + *-ly*] **:** in the manner of one exhorting ⟨a speech marked by ~ passionate appeals for action⟩

ex·hu·mate \eks'(h)yü,māt, eg'zü-, egz'yü-\ *vt* -ED/-ING/-S [ML *exhumatus*, past part. of *exhumare*] **:** EXHUME

ex·hu·ma·tion \,eks(,)(h)yü'māshən, ,eg(,)zü-, ,egz(,)yü-\ *n* -S [F, fr. *exhumer* + *-ation*] **:** the act or process of exhuming, disinterring, or digging up

ex·hume \ig'züm, igz'yüm, iks'(h)yüm, eg-,ek-\ *vt* -ED/-ING/-S [F or L; F *exhumer*, fr. ML *exhumare*, fr. L *ex-* ¹ex- + *humus* earth — more at HUMBLE] **1 :** to dig out of the ground **:** to take out of a place of burial **:** DISINTER ⟨the body was *exhumed* and burned⟩ **2 :** to bring back from neglect or obscurity **:** REVIVE ⟨~ a minor poet⟩ ⟨~ an old play⟩ **3 :** to uncover or expose by erosion ⟨*exhumed* landscapes⟩ **syn** see DIG

ex·hum·er \-mə(r)\ *n* -S **:** one that exhumes

ex hy·po·the·si \,eks,hī'pıthə,sī\ *adv* [NL, from the hypothesis] **:** by hypothesis **:** HYPOTHETICALLY, THEORETICALLY, SUPPOSEDLY

ex·i·gence \'eksəjən(t)s *also* 'egzə-\ *n* -S [MF *exigence*, fr. ML *exigentia*] **:** EXIGENCY

ex·i·gen·cy \-nsē, -si; ig'zij-,eg'zij-\ *n* -ES [ML *exigentia*, fr. LL, demand, fr. L *exigent-, exigens* + *-ia* -y] **1 :** the quality or state of being exigent **:** PRESSURE, URGENCY ⟨the president is the sole judge of the ~ demanding the use of federal troops —Herman Beukema⟩ **2 :** such need or necessity as belongs to the occasion **:** DEMANDS, REQUIREMENTS — usu. used in pl. ⟨the *exigencies* of French politeness are not necessarily at variance with truthfulness —Norman Douglas⟩ ⟨regret that the *exigencies* of party politics should deprive our government of so much talent —Frank Altschul⟩ **syn** see JUNCTURE

¹ex·i·gent \'eksəjənt *also* 'egzə-\ *n* -S [ME *exigent, exigend*, fr. AF *exigende*, fr. ML *exigenda*, fr. L, fem. sing. or neut. pl. of *exigendus*, gerundive of *exigere* to drive out, demand] *English law* **:** a writ formerly issued summoning a person on pain of outlawry

²exigent *n* -S [ME, prob. fr. L *exigent-, exigens*] *obs* **:** time of crisis or need **:** EXIGENCY, EXTREMITY

³ex·i·gent \'eksəjənt *also* 'egzə- *also* **ex·i·geant** \ägzēzhäⁿ\ *adj* [*exigent* fr. L *exigent-, exigens*, pres. part. of *exigere* to drive out, demand; *exigeant* fr. F, pres. part. of *exiger* to demand, fr. L *exigere* — more at EXACT] **1 :** exacting or requiring immediate aid or action **:** PRESSING, CRITICAL ⟨regarded literary questions as ~ and momentous —H.L. Mencken⟩ **2 :** requiring or calling for much **:** hard to satisfy **:** DEMANDING, EXACTING ⟨they have so much to guard in the way of social status that they have become very ~ in their ideas of what they are willing to do⟩ **syn** see PRESSING

ex·i·gent·ly *adv* **:** in an exigent manner

ex·i·gi·ble \'eksəjəbəl, 'egzə-\ *adj* [F, fr. *exiger* to demand + *-ible*] **:** liable to be exacted **:** REQUIRABLE, DEMANDABLE

ex·i·gi fa·ci·as \,eksə,gē'fākē,äs\ *n* [ML, you should cause to be demanded] **:** ¹EXIGENT

ex·i·gu·i·ty \,eksə'gyüəd·ē, ,egzə-\ *n* -ES [L *exiguitat-, exiguitas*, fr. *exiguus* + *-itat-, -itas* -ity] **:** exiguous state or character **:** SCANTINESS, SMALLNESS ⟨an ~ of cloth that would only allow of miniature capes —George Eliot⟩

ex·ig·u·ous \(ˈ)eg'zigyəwəs, (ˈ)ek'si-\ *adj* [L *exiguus*, fr. *exigere* to drive out, demand, weigh, measure] **:** scanty in amount **:** MEAGER, NARROW ⟨~ budget⟩ **syn** see MEAGER

ex·ig·u·ous·ly *adv* **:** in an exiguous manner **:** MEAGERLY

ex·ig·u·ous·ness *n* -ES **:** EXIGUITY

ex·i·larch \'egzə,lärk, 'eksə,-, -,zī,-, -,sī,-\ *n* -S [¹*exile* + *-arch*; trans. of Aram *rēsh gālūtā*] **:** one of a line of Jewish civil and judicial rulers of the exiles in Babylon from about the third to the tenth centuries A.D. to whom Jews in all countries paid tribute

ex·i·larch·ate \'=(,)=,lärkət, -,kāt, ,=(,)=ˈ=(,)=\ *n* -S **1 :** the office or term of office of an exilarch **2 :** the territory or people ruled by an exilarch

¹ex·ile \'eg,zīl, 'ek,sīl, *chiefly archaic* =ˈ= *or* ig'z- *or* ik's-\ *n* -S [ME *exil*, fr. MF *exil, essil*, fr. L *exilium*, fr. *ex-* ¹ex- + *-ilium* (prob. akin to Gk *alasthai* to wander) — more at AMBLE] **1 a :** forced removal from one's native country **:** expulsion from home **:** BANISHMENT **b :** voluntary absence from one's country **2 a :** a person expelled from his country by authority **b :** one who separates himself from his home **3** *obs* **:** DEVASTATION, RUIN, WASTE

²exile \"\ *vt* -ED/-ING/-S [ME *exilen*, fr. MF *exilier, essilier*, fr. LL *exiliare* to exile, fr. L *exilium*] **1 :** to banish or expel from own country or home **:** drive away ⟨calling home our *exiled* friends abroad —Shak.⟩ **2** *obs* **:** DEVASTATE, RUIN **syn** see BANISH

³exile \=ˈ=, =ˈ=\ *adj* [ME, fr. L *exilis*, prob. fr. *exigere* to drive out, demand, weigh, measure] *archaic* **:** SLENDER, THIN; *also* **:** SCANTY, POOR

ex·il·er \'eg,zīlə(r), 'ek,sī-\ *n* -S [ME *exilere*, fr. *exilen* + *-er, -ere* -er] **:** one that exiles

ex·il·i·an \eg'zilēən *also* ek'si-\ *adj* **:** EXILIC

ex·il·ic \-lik\ *adj* **:** relating or belonging to exile (as that of the Jews in Babylon) ⟨~ books of the Old Testament⟩

exility *n* -ES [ME *exilite*, fr. L *exilitat-, exilitas*, fr. *exilis* + *-itat-, -itas* -ity] **1** *obs* **:** SMALLNESS, MEAGERNESS, SLENDERNESS, FINENESS, THINNESS **2** *obs* **:** TENUITY, SUBTLETY

eximious *adj* [L *eximius*, fr. *eximere* to take out, remove, free — more at EXEMPT] *obs* **:** SELECT, CHOICE, EXCELLENT — **eximiously** *adv, obs*

ex·in·a·ni·tion \(,)eg,zinə'nishən\ *n* -S [L *exinanition-, exinanitio*, fr. *exinanitus* (past part. of *exinanire* to empty, exhaust, fr. *ex-* ¹ex- + *inanire* to empty, fr. *inanis* empty) + *-ion-, -io* -ion] **1** *obs* **:** an emptying or enfeebling **:** EXHAUSTION **2 :** HUMILIATION, ABASEMENT

ex·ine \'ek,s|ēn, |īn\ *also* **ex·tine** \'ek,st|\ *n* -S [*exine* prob. fr. G, fr. L *ex* out of, out; *extine* prob. modif. of. G *exine* — more at EX-] **:** the outer of the two layers forming the wall of certain spores (as pollen grains) — called also *exosporium*; compare INTINE, PERINIUM

ex·i·nite \'eksə,nīt\ *n* -S [*exine* + *-ite*] **:** organic material that occurs in coal and that is composed essentially of spores, spore debris, and cuticular matter

ex·ist \ig'zist, eg-\ *vi* -ED/-ING/-S [L *existere, exsistere* to step forth, emerge, come into being, exist, fr. *ex-* ¹ex- + *sistere* to cause to stand; akin to L *stare* to stand — more at STAND] **1 :** to have actual or real being whether material or spiritual **:** have being in space and time ⟨by whom we ~ and cease to be —Shak.⟩ **2 :** to have being in any specified condition or place or with respect to any understood limitation ⟨salt *~s* in solution in the sea⟩ ⟨queer notions ~ in his mind⟩ **3 :** to continue to be **:** maintain being ⟨some industrial activity does ~ in the urban fringe —N.R.Heiden **4 :** to have life or the functions of vitality **:** LIVE ⟨men cannot ~ without oxygen⟩ **5** [trans. of Dan *eksistere* & G *existieren*] *in existentialism* **:** to have contingent but free and responsible being; *also* **:** to live as one that has such being

ex·is·tence \-tən(t)s\ *n* -S [ME, fr. MF, fr. LL *existentia, exsistentia* state or fact of having being, fr. L *existent-, exsistent-, existens, exsistens* + *-ia* -y] **1** *obs* **:** reality or actuality as opposed to appearance **2 a :** the state or fact of having being esp. as considered independently of human consciousness and as contrasted with nonexistence ⟨the ~ of other worlds⟩ **b :** the manner of being that is common to every mode of being **:** the state common to physical objects, living beings, objects of thought, and anything else ⟨both of noumena and of phenomena we may affirm simple ~ —J.S. Mill⟩ **3 a :** being with reference to some limiting condition or under a particular aspect (as a mode of being, determined being, or a manner of existing) ⟨the ~ of a fictive world⟩ **b :** being as given in experience or in the act of experiencing: (1) *in scholasticism* **:** being in its actuality as contrasted with its essence (2) [trans. of Dan *eksistens* & G *existenz*] *in existentialism* **:** the condition of man in his factuality characterized by a passionate self-consciousness and sense of responsibility in the face of contingency and freedom **4 :** sentient or living being **:** LIFE ⟨God, Nature, Self, are the fundamental facts of ~ —Henry Sidgwick⟩ **5 :** continued or repeated manifestation **:** actual or present occurrence ⟨~ of a state of war⟩ **6 :** something that exists: as **a :** the totality of being **b :** a particular being, individual, or entity **:** EXISTENT ⟨concepts . . . are tyrants rather than servants when treated as real *~s* —B.N.Cardozo⟩

existency *n* -ES [LL *existentia, exsistentia*] *obs* **:** EXISTENCE

¹ex·is·tent \-nt\ *adj* [L *existent-, exsistent-, existens, exsistens*, pres. part. of *existere, exsistere*] **1 :** having existence, being, or actuality **:** EXISTING ⟨chimeras are classified as subsistent but not ~ —R.J.Butler⟩ **2 :** existing now or at the present time **:** CONTEMPORARY, EXTANT ⟨keep abreast with things military as ~ in other nations of the world —H.H.Arnold & I.C.Eaker⟩

²existent \"\ *n* -S **1 :** a particular existing thing, event, person, or entity **2 :** something that exists ⟨to debate whether the ~ is merely appearance⟩ **3** *in existentialism* **:** one who has existence ⟨become aware of oneself as an ~⟩

ex·is·ten·tial \,eg(,)zi'stenchəl, -gzə;-, ;ek(,)si;-, -ksə;-\ *adj* [LL *existentialis, exsistentialis*, fr. *existentia, exsistentia* + L *-alis* -al] **1 :** of, relating to, or dealing with existence ⟨the ~ 'is' which in our logic connects the two parts of a proposition —E.R.Hughes⟩ **2** *logic* **a :** assertive either explicitly or by implication of existence or actuality as opposed to mere possibility, conceivability, or ideality or to mere explication of a meaning ⟨definitions are not ~ propositions⟩ **b :** making an assertion about the extension as opposed to the intension of the subject term **3 a :** grounded in existence **:** having being in time and space ⟨formal logicians . . . are not concerned with ~ matters which are precisely what artists are concerned with —John Dewey⟩ **b :** based on the experience of existence **:** empirical as contrasted with theoretical or abstract ⟨the problem of aesthetic objectivity or, more precisely, the ~ status of aesthetic values —Hunter Mead⟩ **4** [trans. of Dan *eksistentiel* & G *existential*] **:** concerned with or involving human existence or its nature **:** EXISTENTIALIST — **ex·is·ten·tial·ly** \-əlē, -li\ *adv*

ex·is·ten·tial·ism \,=(,)=ˈ=chə,lizəm\ *n* -S **:** an introspective humanism or theory of man that holds that human existence is not exhaustively describable or understandable in either scientific or idealistic terms and relies upon a phenomenological approach that emphasizes the analysis of critical borderline situations in man's life and esp. of such intensely subjective phenomena as anxiety, suffering, and feelings of guilt in order to show the need for making decisive choices through a utilization of man's freedom in an uncertain, contingent, and apparently purposeless world: **a :** a theory stating that man's individual existence precedes his essence and stressing his responsibility for fashioning his self **b :** CHRISTIAN EXISTENTIALISM

¹ex·is·ten·tial·ist \-ləst\ *n* -S **1 :** a proponent or adherent of philosophical existentialism **2 :** a writer who develops or emphasizes in literary form the principles of existentialism

²existentialist \=ˈ=(,)=ˈ===\ *adj* **1 :** dealing with, subscribing to, or based on existential philosophy ⟨~ thought⟩ ⟨~ terminology⟩ ⟨~ writers⟩ **2 :** of, relating to, or involving existentialism or existentialists **:** EXISTENTIAL ⟨an ~ question⟩

⟨the ~ character of his ideas⟩ ⟨an ~ group⟩ — **ex·is·ten·tial·is·tic** \ˌ=(ˌ)=ˈ=chəˈlistik\ *adj* — **ex·is·ten·tial·is·ti·cal·ly** \-tək(ə)lē\ *adv*
ex·is·ten·tial·ize \ˌ=(ˌ)=ˈ=chəˌlīz\ *vt* -ED/-ING/-S : to cause to become existential or transform into existential terms
existential operator *or* **existential quantifier** *n, logic* : a quantifier that asserts at least one value of a variable in a formula
existential philosophy *n* : EXISTENTIALISM
existential psychology *n* : a psychology that emphasizes sensory experience as its object of study — compare CONTENT PSYCHOLOGY, STRUCTURALISM
ex·is·tenz \eksiˈsten(t)s\ *n* -ES [G, fr. LL *existentia, existentia* state or fact of having being — more at EXISTENCE] : EXISTENCE 3b(2)
ex·ist·er \igˈzistə(r), eg-\ *n* -S : one that exists
existimation *n* -S [L *existimation-, existimatio,* fr. *existimatus* (past part. of *existimare* to estimate, esteem, fr. *ex-* ¹ex- + *-istimare,* fr. *aestimare* to value, estimate, esteem) + *-ion-, -io* -ion — more at ESTEEM] *obs* : ESTEEM, OPINION, ESTIMATION
existing *pres part of* EXIST
exists *pres 3d sing of* EXIST
¹**ex·it** \ˈegzət, ˈeksət, *usu* -əd·+V\ [L, he or she goes out, 3d pers. sing. pres. indic. of *exire* to go out — more at EXEAT] : goes out : goes off the stage — used as a stage direction usu. preceding the name of the player ⟨~ Hamlet⟩ ⟨pick up tray and ~ left⟩ — compare MANET
²**exit** \"\ *n* -S [partly fr. ¹*exit,* partly fr. L *exitus* departure, way out, end, fr. *exitus,* past part. of *exire* to go out] **1** : the departure of a player from the stage — compare ENTRANCE **2 a** : the act of going out or going away : act of leaving the scene of action : DEPARTURE **b** : DEATH **3 a** : a way out : a passage out of an enclosed place or space : OUTLET **b** : a door or passage for escape in case of fire **c** (1) : a place of egress from a limited-access highway (2) : a roadway or ramp affording egress from such a highway **4** *card games* : the act or means of losing a trick so as to escape the obligation of leading : a card that when led cannot win the trick
³**exit** \"\ *vi* -ED/-ING/-S **1** : to go out : DEPART **2** : DIE **3** *card games* : to lead a losing card in order to avoid the obligation of leading again
exit cone *n* : the portion of a wind tunnel into which the air flows from the test section
ex·ite \ˈekˌsīt\ *n* -S [*exo-* + *-ite*] : a movable appendage or lobe on the exterior side of the limb of a generalized arthropod (as a branchiopod)
exitial *adj* [L *exitialis,* fr. *exitium* destruction, departure (fr. *exitus,* past part. of *exire*) + *-alis* -al] *obs* : DESTRUCTIVE, FATAL
exit interview *n* : an interview held by a personnel officer with an employee who is leaving the company
exitious *adj* [L *exitiosus,* fr. *exitium* + *-osus* -ose] *obs* : DESTRUCTIVE, FATAL
exit pupil *n* : the image of the entrance pupil of an optical system viewed from the image space (as at the eyepiece)
ex·i·tus \ˈeksəd·əs\ *n, pl* **exitus** [L, departure, way out, end] **1** *obs* : EXIT, EXODUS **2** : ISSUE, OUTCOME, END **3** [ML, fr. L] : an export duty **4** : DEATH; *esp* : fatal termination of a disease **5** [NL, fr. L] : an excretory outlet
ex le·ge \ekˈslāˌgā, -gē\ *adv* [LL, from law] : as a matter of law : by operation of law
¹**exlex** *n* -ES [ML, fr. L, bound by no law, lawless] *obs* : OUTLAW
²**ex·lex** \ˈekˌsleks\ *adj* [G *exlex,* fr. L *exlex* bound by no law, lawless, fr. *ex-* ¹ex- + *lex* law — more at LEGAL] : without legal authority ⟨~ government⟩
ex li·bris \ekˈslēbrəs, -lē(ˌ)brēs *sometimes* -li(ˌ)brēs *or* -librəs *or* -lībrəs\ *n, pl* **ex libris** [NL, from the books; fr. the use of the Latin phrase before the owner's name on bookplates] : BOOKPLATE
ex–li·brism \-ˌbrizəm\ *n* -S [*ex libris* + *-ism*] : the collecting of bookplates
ex–li·brist \-ˌbrəst\ *n* -S [*ex libris* + *-ist*] : a collector of bookplates
ex ma·le·fi·cio \ˌekˌsmäləˈfikēˌō\ *adj* [LL, from wrongdoing] : guilty of malfeasance ⟨a trustee *ex maleficio*⟩
¹**ex·meridian** \ˌeks+\ *adj* [¹*ex-* + *meridian*] : EXTRAMERIDIONAL
²**exmeridian** \"\ *n* : EXTRAMERIDIAN
ex·moor \ˈekˌsmu̇(ə)r, -mō(-\ *n, usu cap* [*Exmoor,* district in Somersetshire, England] **1** *or* **exmoor horn** : a breed of horned sheep of Devonshire, England, that are valuable for mutton **2** *or* **exmoor pony** : a breed of hardy heavy-maned ponies native to the Exmoor district
exmr *abbr* examiner
ex new \(ˈ)=ˈ=\ *adv* (*or adj*) [²*ex*] *Brit* : without the right to claim participation in an issue of new stock — used of a quoted price of a stock
ex ni·hi·lo \ekˈsnēhəˌlō, -ēə,-, -ēhē,- *sometimes* -nihi,- *or* -nī(h)ə,-\ *adv* (*or adj*) [L] : from or out of nothing ⟨creation *ex nihilo*⟩
exo \ˈek(ˌ)sō\ *adj* [*exo-*] *chem* : being, having, or characterized by valence bonds of a 6-membered ring in its boat-shaped conformation that are directed outward ⟨the ~ side of a ring⟩ — compare EXO- 2
exo- *or* **ex-** *comb form* [Gk *exō* out of, out, outside of, outside, fr. *ex* out of — more at ¹EX-] **1 a** : outside ⟨*exogamy*⟩ : outer ⟨*exocarp*⟩ ⟨*exoskeleton*⟩ — opposed to *end-*; compare ECT- **b** : producing ⟨*exergonic*⟩ — opposed to *end-* **2** *exo-, usu ital* : having a 6-membered ring in its boat-shaped conformation with one or more substituents directed outward ⟨2,5-methylene-*exo*-cyclohexyl-amine⟩ — compare END- 2
exo·adaptation \ˌek(ˌ)sō+\ *n* [*exo-* + *adaptation*] *biol* : modification of an organism resulting in more effective interaction with its external environment — compare ENDOADAPTATION
exo·as·ca·ce·ae \ˌek(ˌ)sōaˈskāsēˌē\ [NL, fr. *Exoascus,* type genus + *-aceae*] *syn of* TAPHRINACEAE
exo·as·ca·les \-ā(ˌ)lēz\ [NL, fr. *Exoascus* + *-ales*] *syn of* TAPHRINALES
exo·as·cus \-ōˈaskəs\ *n, cap* [NL, fr. *exo-* + *ascus*] *in some esp former classifications* : a genus of fungi (family Taphrinaceae) distinguished from *Taphrina* by the formation of not more than eight ascospores in each ascus but now usu. included in *Taphrina*
exo·ba·sid·i·a·ce·ae \ˌek(ˌ)sōbəˌsidēˈāsēˌē\ *n pl, cap* [NL, fr. *Exobasidium,* type genus + *-aceae*] : a family comprising fungi parasitic on higher plants and producing their hymenium as a thin coating on the surface of the host plant and without differentiation of a fruiting body — see EXOBASIDIUM, EXOBASIDIALES
exo·ba·sid·i·a·les \-ā(ˌ)lēz\ *n pl, cap* [NL, fr. *Exobasidium* + *-ales*] : an order of Homobasidiomycetes coextensive with the family Exobasidiaceae
exo·basidium \ˌek(ˌ)sō+\ *n, cap* [NL, fr. *exo-* + *basidium*] : the type and chief genus of the family Exobasidiaceae comprising fungi parasitic esp. on various heath plants on which they cause swollen thickenings resembling galls — see FALSE BLOSSOM
exo·cannibalism \"+\ *n* [ISV *exo-* + *cannibalism;* orig. formed as G *exokannibalismus*] : cannibalism of persons from outside one's family or tribe— contrasted with *endocannibalism*
exo·carp \ˈeksōˌkärp\ *n* -S [ISV *exo-* + *-carp*] : EPICARP
¹**ex·occipital** \ˌeks+\ *adj* [ISV *exo-* + *occipital*] : of or relating to a bone or region on each side of the foramen magnum of the skull
²**exoccipital** \"\ *n* : either of a pair of bones lying one on each side of the foramen magnum and free in lower vertebrates but forming in man a part of the occipital bone
exo·centric \ˌeksō+\ *adj* [*exo-* + *-centric*] : not having the same grammatical function as a nonmodifying immediate constituent — used of a compound (as *barefoot*) or construction (as *in the yard* in the sentence "they played in the yard"); compare ENDOCENTRIC
exo·chor·da \ˌeksōˈkȯrdə\ *n, cap* [NL, fr. *exo-* + L *chorda* cord; fr. the free placentary cords supposed to be external to the carpels — more at CORD] : a genus of Asiatic shrubs (family Rosaceae) having spikes of white flowers succeeded by fruits each of which consists of five bony carpels in the form of a star — see PEARLBUSH
exo·chorion \ˌek(ˌ)sō+\ *n, pl* **exochoria** [NL, fr. *exo-* + *chorion*] : the outer of the two layers that form the hardened covering of an insect egg
exo·cli·nal \ˌeksōˈklīnᵊl\ *adj* : relating to or resembling an exocline
exo·cline \ˈ==ˌklīn\ *n* -S [*exo-* + *-cline*] *geol* : an inverted fan fold
exo·coele *or* **exo·coel** \-ˌsēl\ *n* -S [*exo-* + *-coele*] : the space between adjacent pairs of mesenteries in the anthozoan polyp — compare ENDOCOELE — **exo·coe·lic** \ˌ==ˈsēlik\ *adj*
exo·coelom \ˌeksō+\ *n* [ISV *exo-* + *coelom*] : the extra-embryonic part of the body cavity of the embryo of an amniotic vertebrate — **exo·coelomic** \"+\ *adj*
¹**exo·coe·tid** \ˌeksōˈsēd·əd\ *adj* [NL *Exocoetidae*] : of or relating to the Exocoetidae
²**exocoetid** \"\ *n* -S : a flying fish of the family Exocoetidae
exo·coe·ti·dae \ˌ==ˈsēd·əˌdē\ *n pl, cap* [NL, fr. *Exocoetus,* type genus (fr. L, fish that sleeps on the shore, fr. Gk *exōkoitos,* fr. *exō* outside + *koitos* resting place, bed, fr. *keist* to lie) + *-idae* — more at EXO-, CEMETERY] : a family (order Synentognathi) of marine fishes that are closely related to the half-beaks and include all the true flying fishes
exo·cone \ˈeksəˌkōn\ *adj* [*exo-* + *cone*] : having the crystalline cone replaced by an ingrowth of transparent cuticular material from the cornea — used chiefly of insect eyes
exo·cor·tis \ˌeksəˈkȯrd·əs\ *n* -ES [ISV *exo-* + *-cortis* (irreg. fr. *cortex*)] : a disease of oranges that is esp. important in trees grafted on trifoliate stock, is characterized by peeling of the outer bark in narrow dry strips and by dwarfing of the tree, and is caused prob. by either a virus or a genetic factor
ex·o·crine \ˈeksəkrən; -ˌkrīn,-īn,-ēn\ *adj* [ISV *exo-* + *-crine* (fr. Gk *krinein* to separate) — more at CERTAIN] : secreting externally — used of glands that discharge their secretion through a duct; opposed to *endocrine*
exocrine gland *n* : a gland that produces an exocrine secretion — called also *gland of external secretion*
exoculation *n* -S [ML *exoculation-, exoculatio,* fr. L *exoculatus* (past part. of *exoculare* to put out the eyes, fr. *ex-* ¹ex- + *-oculare,* fr. *oculus* eye) + *-ion-, -io* -ion — more at EYE] *obs* : the act of putting out the eyes (as in execution of a judicial sentence)
exo·cuticle \ˌek(ˌ)sō+\ *n* [*exo-* + *cuticle*] : the intermediate layer of a typical cuticle being sometimes considered in insects the outer part of the endocuticle
ex·o·cy·cla \ˌeksōˈsīklə\ *or* **ex·o·cyc·li·ca** \-ˈsikləkə\ [NL, fr. *exo-* + *-cycla* (fr. Gk *kyklos* ring, circle, wheel) *or -cyclica* (fr. Gk *kyklika,* neut. pl. of *kyklikos* circular, cyclic, fr. *kyklos* + *-ikos* -ic) — more at WHEEL] *syn of* EXOCYCLOIDA
ex·o·cy·clic \ˌeksōˈsīklik, -ˈsik-\ *adj* [NL *Exocyclica*] : belonging to or characteristic of the Exocycloida
ex·o·cy·cloi·da \ˌek(ˌ)sōˌsīˈklȯidə\ *n pl, cap* [NL, fr. *exo-* + *cycl-* + *-oida*] : an order of sea urchins comprising forms with the periproct posterior or oral in position and including the heart urchins and sand dollars
ex·ode \ˈekˌsōd, ˈegˌzōd\ *n* -S [F or L; F *exode,* fr. L *exodium,* fr. Gk *exodion* part of a drama following the last song of the chorus, fr. neut. of *exodios* of a departure or exit, fr. *exodos* departure, going out] **1** : a comic afterpiece in the ancient Roman theater : FARCE, TRAVESTY **2** : EXODUS 2
ex·o·derm \ˈeksōˌdərm\ *n* -S [ISV *exo-* + *-derm*] **1** : EXODERMIS **2 a** : ECTODERM **b** : an external integument — **ex·o·der·mal** \ˌeksōˈdərməl\ *adj*
ex·o·der·mis \ˌeksōˈdərməs\ *n* -ES [NL, fr. *exo-* + *-dermis*] **1** : a layer of the outer living cortical cells that by becoming cutinized or suberized takes over the functions of the epidermis in roots such as those of the monocotyledons and some dicotyledons which lack secondary thickening **2** : the single layer of cells just below the corky epidermis of various orchid roots
ex·od·ic \(ˈ)ekˈsädik, (ˈ)egˈzä-\ *adj* [Gk *exodos* departure, going out + E *-ic*] : EFFERENT
ex·o·dist \ˈeksədəst, ˈegzə-\ *n* -S [*exodus* + *-ist*] : EMIGRANT
ex·o·di·um \ekˈsōdēəm, egˈzō-\ *n, pl* **exo·dia** \-ēə\ [L] : EXODE 1
ex·o·don·tia \ˌeksəˈdänch(ē)ə\ *n* -S [NL, fr. ¹*ex-* + *-odontia*] : a branch of dentistry that deals with the extraction of teeth
ex·o·don·tist \-ntəst, ˈ==ˌ==\ *n* -S [NL *exodontia* + E *-ist*] : a specialist in exodontia
ex·o·dus \ˈeksədəs *also* ˈegzə-\ *n* -ES [*Exodus,* Old Testament book that tells of the departure of the Israelites from Egypt, fr. ME, fr. LL, fr. Gk *Exodos,* fr. *exodos* departure, going out, fr. *ex* out of, out + *hodos* way, journey — more at EX-, CEDE] **1** : a mass departure : EMIGRATION ⟨the ~ of the cotton mills from New England to the South —J.A.Morris b. 1918⟩ **2** *also* **ex·o·dos** \-ˌdäs\ [Gk *exodos,* lit., departure] : the part of a Greek drama following the last song of the chorus
ex·o·dy \-ədē\ *n* -ES [Gk *exodia* expedition, journey out, fr. *exodos* + *-ia* -y] : EXODUS
exo·enzyme \ˌeksə̇ˈw+-\ *n* [ISV *exo-* + *enzyme*] : an enzyme that acts outside the cell (as in yeasts) : an extracellular enzyme — distinguished from *endoenzyme*
exo·ergic \ˌeksəˈwərjik\ *adj* [*exo-* + *erg-* + *-ic*] : releasing energy : EXOTHERMIC ⟨~ nuclear disintegration⟩ — opposed to *endoergic*
exo·erythrocytic \ˌeksəw, ˌekˌsō+\ *adj* [*exo-* + *erythrocytic*] : occurring outside of the red blood cells — used of stages of malaria parasites
ex of·fi·cio \ˌeksəˈfishēˌō, -i(ˌ)shō\ *also* **ex offici·is** \-ishēˌēs\ *adv* (*or adj*) [LL] : by virtue or because of an office or offices ⟨all heads of departments . . . are called upon to serve *ex officiis* as members of . . . boards —F.A.Ogg & P.O.Ray⟩ ⟨acting as *ex officio* chairman of the board⟩
ex·o·gam·ic \ˌeksōˈgamik\ *adj* [*exogamy* + *-ic*] : EXOGAMOUS
ex·og·a·mous \(ˈ)ekˈsägəməs\ *adj* [*exo-* + *-gamous*] : of, relating to, or characterized by exogamy
ex·og·a·my \ekˈsägəmē\ *n* -ES [*exo-* + *-gamy*] **1** : marriage outside of a specific group esp. as required by custom or law : OUTBREEDING — contrasted with *endogamy* **2** : sexual reproduction between organisms not closely related
exo·gastrula \ˌeksō+\ *n* [NL, fr. *exo-* + *gastrula*] : an abnormal gastrula that has the presumptive endoderm increased in quantity and incapable of invagination and is therefore unable to develop further — **exo·gastrulation** \"+\ *n*
ex·o·gen \ˈeksəjən, -ˌjen\ *n* -S [F *exogène,* fr. *exogène* exogenous, fr. *exo-* + *-gène* (fr. Gk *-genēs* born) — more at -GEN] : a plant that develops by exogenous growth — compare ENDOGEN
ex·o·gene \ˈeksəˌjēn\ *or* **exo·ge·net·ic** \ˌeksōjəˈned·ik\ *or* **ex·o·gen·ic** \ˌeksōˈjenik\ *adj* [*exogene* prob. fr. F *exogène; exogenetic* fr. *exo-* + *genetic; exogenic* prob. fr. F *exogène* + E *-ic*] : EXOGENOUS
ex·og·e·nism \ekˈsäjəˌnizəm\ *n* -S [*exogenous* + *-ism*] : the state of being exogenous
ex·og·e·nous \(ˈ)ekˈsäjənəs\ *adj* [F *exogène* exogenous + E *-ous*] : produced from without : originating from or due to external causes: as **a** : growing from or on the outside ⟨~ spores⟩ : growing by addition to the exterior ⟨~ stems⟩ **b** *of disease* : having a cause external to the body : not primarily due to structural or functional failure of the body ⟨~ heart disease associated with rheumatic fever⟩ — compare ENDOGENOUS **c** : arising from other than hereditary factors ⟨~ mental deficiency⟩ **d** : of, relating to, or produced by the metabolism of nitrogenous substances obtained from food : DIETARY ⟨~ uric acid⟩ — compare ENDOGENOUS **e** *of rocks* : composed of materials derived from processes of erosion or produced by metamorphism through contact with adjacent igneous intrusion **f** : originating from outside an economic system (as from political, accidental, and technological forces) — compare ENDOGENOUS — **ex·og·e·nous·ly** *adv*
exo·geosyncline \ˌek(ˌ)sō+\ *n* [*exo-* + *geosyncline*] : a transverse basin extending from an orthogeosyncline into a craton
ex·og·nath \ˈeksəgˌnath\ *n* -S [*exo-* + Gk *gnathos* jaw; akin to Gk *genys* jaw — more at CHIN] : EXOGNATHITE
exo·gnathion \ˌeksō+\ *n* [NL, fr. *exo-* + *gnathion*] : the maxilla ~~not including~~ the premaxilla
exo·gnath·ite \ˌeksōˈnaˌthīt, ekˈsägnəˌth-\ *n* [*exo-* + *gnathite*] : the external branch of an oral appendage of a crustacean
ex·o·go·ni·um \ˌeksəˈgōnēəm\ *n, cap* [NL, fr. *exo-* + *-gonium* (fr. Gk *gōnia* corner, angle) — more at DIAGONAL] : a genus of tropical American nearly woody vines (family Convolvulaceae) having showy tubular flowers with exserted stamens and a capitate stigma — see JALAP
ex·o·graph \ˈeksəˌgraf, -räf\ *n* [*exo-* (irreg. fr. *X ray*) + *-graph*] : a radiograph made with X rays
ex·og·y·nous \(ˈ)ekˈsäjənəs\ *adj* [prob. fr. (assumed) NL *exogynus,* fr. *exo-* + *-gynus* -gynous] *bot* : having the style longer than the corolla and exserted beyond it
ex·o·gy·ra \ˌeksəˈjīrə\ *n, cap* [NL, fr. *exo-* + *-gyra* (fr. Gk *gyros* ring, circle, fr. *gyros* round) — more at COWER] : a genus of Upper Jurassic and Cretaceous bivalve mollusks that have thick shells and spirally twisted beak and are related to the true oysters
exolete *adj* [L *exoletus,* past part. of *exolescere* to go out of use, become out of date, fr. *ex-* ¹ex- + *-olescere* (as in *adolescere* to grow up) — more at ADULT] **1** *obs* : DISUSED, OBSOLETE **2** *obs* : STALE, INSIPID, FADED
exolution *n* -S [L *exsolution-, exsolutio,* fr. *exsolutus* (past part. of *exsolvere* to release, fr. *ex-* ¹ex- + *solvere* to loosen, release) + *-ion-, -io* -ion — more at SOLVE] *obs* : a setting free : RELEASE, RELAXATION
ex·o·mol·o·ge·sis \ˌeksəˌmäləˈjēsəs\ *n, pl* **exomologe·ses** \-ēˌsēz\ [LL, fr. LGk *exomologēsis,* fr. Gk, confession, fr. *exomologeisthai* to confess (fr. *ex* out of, out + *homologeisthai,* pres. middle infin. of *homologein* to agree, grant, confess, fr. *homologos* assenting, agreeing) + *-sis* — more at EX-, HOMOLOGOUS] : a penitential rite with public confession of sins that was practiced in the early Christian church
ex·o·mor·phic \ˌeksəˈmȯrfik\ *adj* [*exo-* + *-morphic*] : relating to or produced by exomorphism — opposed to *endomorphic*
ex·o·mor·phism \ˌ==ˈmȯrˌfizəm\ *n* -S [ISV *exo-* + *-morphism;* orig. formed as F *exomorphisme*] : a change (as hardening or the formation of new minerals) produced in a rock mass by igneous intrusion from without : metamorphism by external contact
ex·on \ˈekˌsän\ *n* -S [modif. of F *exempt* subordinate in the cavalry commanding in the absence of the higher company officers — more at EXEMPT] : one of four officers of the yeomen of the British royal guard ranking below ensign who in turn act as resident commanders in the absence of superior officers — called also *exempt*
exo·narthex \ˌeksō+\ *n* [*exo-* + *narthex*] : the outer narthex of a church having two narthexes; *sometimes* : the whole atrium — compare ESONARTHEX
exo·nephric \"+\ *adj* [*exo-* + *nephric*] : having the excretory organs discharge through the body wall (as in some annelid worms)
ex·on·er \igˈzänər, eg-\ *vt* -ED/-ING/-S [L *exonerare*] *Scots law* : EXONERATE
¹**ex·on·er·ate** \igˈzänəˌrāt, eg-\ *vt* -ED/-ING/-S [ME *exoneraten,* fr. L *exoneratus,* past part. of *exonerare* to relieve, free, unload, fr. *ex-* ¹ex- + *onerare* to load, fr. *oner-, onus* load — more at ONEROUS] **1** : to relieve esp. of a charge, obligation, or hardship ⟨no reason for *exonerating* him from the ordinary duties of a citizen —O.W.Holmes †1935⟩ : clear from accusation or blame : EXCULPATE ⟨defendant was *exonerated* from any criminal offense⟩ **2** *obs* : UNLOAD, DISBURDEN, DISCHARGE **syn** see EXCULPATE
²**exonerate** *adj* [L *exoneratus,* past part. of *exonerare*] *obs* : EXONERATED
ex·on·er·a·tion \igˌzänəˈrāshən, eg-\ *n* -S [LL *exoneration-, exoneratio,* fr. L *exoneratus* + *-ion-, -io* -ion] **1** : the act of disburdening, discharging, or freeing morally or legally (as from a charge, imputation, duty, obligation, or responsibility); *also* : the state of being so freed **2 a** : a remedy in equity available to the surety who has discharged the obligation of his defaulting principal or of a prior surety **b** : the right of a surety to require a person or estate subject to a liability prior to his to discharge that liability thus relieving the surety
ex·on·er·e·tur \-ˈrād·ə(r), -ˈrēd-\ *n* -S [L, let him or her be relieved, 3d pers. sing. pres. subj. pass. of *exonerare*] : an entry on a bail piece discharging a surety
exo·peptidase \ˌeksō+\ *n* [*exo-* + *peptidase*] : one of a group of enzymes that hydrolyze peptide bonds formed by the terminal amino acids of peptide chains : PEPTIDASE — distinguished from *endopeptidase;* compare AMINOPEPTIDASE, CARBOXYPEPTIDASE, DIPEPTIDASE
ex ope·re oper·an·tis \ekˈsōpərēˌōpəˈräntəs\ [ML, lit., from the work of the worker] : in virtue of the agent — used of a sacrament considered in relation to the conditions required for its valid administration or for its worthy reception; compare EX OPERE OPERATO
ex opere oper·a·to \-ˈräd·(ˌ)ō\ [ML, lit., from the work done] : in virtue of the action — used of a sacrament considered independently of the merits of the minister or the recipient; compare EX OPERE OPERANTIS
exo·peridium \ˌek(ˌ)sō+\ *n* [NL, fr. *exo-* + *peridium*] : the outer peridium when the peridium has two layers (as in the puffballs) — compare ENDOPERIDIUM
ex·o·pha·sia \ˌeksōˈfāzh(ē)ə\ *n* -S [NL, fr. *exo-* + *-phasia*] : speech that is actually formed with the speech organs : uttered speech : vocalized speech — contrasted with *endophasia* — **ex·o·pha·sic** \ˌeksōˈfāzik\ *adj*
ex·o·pho·ria \ˌeksəˈfōrēə\ *n* -S [NL, fr. *exo-* + *-phoria*] : latent strabismus in which the visual axes tend outward toward the temple — **ex·o·phor·ic** \ˌeksōˈfȯrik\ *adj*
ex·oph·thal·mia \ˌekˌsäfˈthalmēə, ÷-säpˈth-\ *n* -S [NL, fr. Gk *exophthalmos* + NL *-ia*] : EXOPHTHALMOS
ex·oph·thal·mic \ˌ=ˌ=ˈ=mik\ *adj* [ISV *exophthalm-* (fr. NL *exophthalmos*) + *-ic*] : relating to or characterized by exophthalmos
exophthalmic goiter *n* : hyperthyroidism with protrusion of the eyeballs
ex·oph·thal·mos \ˌ=ˌ=ˈ=məs, -ˌmäs\ *also* **exophthal·mus** \-ˌməs\ *n* -ES [NL, fr. Gk *exophthalmos* having prominent eyes, fr. *ex* out of, out + *ophthalmos* eye — more at EX-, OPHTHALMIA] : abnormal protrusion of the eyeball
ex·o·phyt·ic \ˌeksōˈfid·ik\ *adj* [*exo-* + *-phytic* (as in *endophytic*)] **1** : growing on or deposited on the outside of plant tissues **2** : tending to grow outward beyond the surface epithelium from which it originates — used of tumors; opposed to *endophytic*
ex·o·plasm \ˈeksōˌplazəm\ *n* [ISV *exo-* + *-plasm*] : ECTOPLASM 1
ex·op·o·dite \ekˈsäpəˌdīt\ *also* **ex·o·pod** \ˈeksəˌpäd\ *n* [ISV *exo-* + *-podite*] : the external branch on the protopodite of a typical limb of a crustacean — **ex·op·o·dit·ic** \(ˌ)ekˌsäpəˈdid·ik, ˌeksəˌpäˈdi-\ *adj*
ex·op·ter·y·go·ta \ˌekˌsäpˌterəˈgōd·ə, ˌek(ˌ)sōˌter-\ [NL, fr. *exo-* + Gk *pterygōta,* neut. pl. of *pterygōtos* winged — more at PTERYGOTA] *syn of* HEMIMETABOLA
ex·op·ter·y·gote \ˌ=(ˌ)=ˈ==ˌgōt\ *adj* [NL *Exopterygota*] : HEMIMETABOLOUS
exor *abbr* executor
exorable *adj* [L *exorabilis* — more at INEXORABLE] *obs* : capable of being moved by entreaty
ex·or·bi·tance \igˈzȯ(r)bəd·ən(t)s, eg-, -bətən(t)s, *also* -bətᵊn(t)s\ *n* -S [ME *exorbitaunce,* prob. fr. MF *exorbitance,* fr. *exorbitant,* after such pairs as MF *abundant: abundance*] **1** : an exorbitant action or procedure; *esp* : excessive or gross deviation from rule, right, or propriety **2** *archaic* : the fact or action of being exorbitant : irregularity esp. with respect to law or morals **3** : tendency or disposition to be exorbitant : EXTRAVAGANCE ⟨she had earned the right to folly and ~ —V.S.Pritchett⟩
ex·or·bi·tan·cy \-ənsē, -ᵊn-, -si\ *n* -ES [fr. *exorbitance,* after such pairs as E *elegance: elegancy*] *archaic* : EXORBITANCE
ex·or·bi·tant \-nt\ *adj* [ME, fr. MF, fr. LL *exorbitant-, exorbitans,* pres. part. of *exorbitare* to deviate, fr. L *ex-* ¹ex- + LL *-orbitare* (fr. L *orbita* track, rut) — more at ORB] **1** *archaic* : wandering or deviating from the normal or ordinary course : ABNORMAL, IRREGULAR **2** : not within the orbit or scope of the law **3 a** : exceeding in intensity, quality, force, power, scope, or size the customary, due, or appropriate limits ⟨required an ~ quantity of fuel⟩ : EXCESSIVE **b** *of a price, charge, or rate* : grossly exceeding normal, customary, fair, and just limits ⟨~ rent⟩ ⟨~ profits⟩ **syn** see EXCESSIVE
ex·or·bi·tant·ly *adv* : in an exorbitant manner : EXCESSIVELY
exorbitate *vi* -ED/-ING/-S [LL *exorbitatus,* past part. of *exorbitare*] *obs* : to go out of the track : to deviate from the usual orbit
ex·or·ci·sa·tion *or* **ex·or·ci·za·tion** \ˌekˌsȯ(r)səˈzāshən,

,eksə(r)sə'z-, ,eksə(r),sī'z- *also* ,eg,zō- *or* ,egzə-\ *n* -s [ME *exorcisacioun,* fr. MF *exorcization,* fr. LL *exorcization-, exorcizatio,* fr. *exorcizatus* (past part. of *exorcizare*) + L *-ion-, -io* -ion] : EXORCISM

ex·or·cise *also* **ex·or·cize** \'ek,sȯ(r),sīz *also* 'eksə(- *or* 'eg,zȯ- *or* 'egzə-\ *vt* -ED/-ING/-S [ME *exorcisen,* fr. MF *exorciser,* fr. LL *exorcizare,* fr. Gk *exorkizein,* fr. *ex* out of, out + *horkizein* to cause to swear, bind by oath, adjure, fr. *horkos* oath; akin to Gk *herkos* fence, L *sarcire* to patch, mend — more at EX-] **1 a** : to drive out or drive away (an evil spirit) by adjuration esp. by use of a holy name or magic rites **b** : to get rid of (something that is troublesome or menacing or oppressive) ⟨trying to ~ her feeling of alarm —Rebecca West⟩ **2** : to relieve (a person or place) from the presence or influence of an evil spirit : PURIFY **3** *obs* : to address or summon by adjuration : conjure up

ex·or·cis·er *or* **ex·or·ciz·er** \-zə(r)\ *n* -s : EXORCIST

ex·or·cism \-,sizəm\ *n* -s [ME *exorcisme,* fr. MF or LL; MF *exorcisme,* fr. LL *exorcismus,* fr. Gk *exorkismos* administration of an oath, fr. *exorkizein* to administer an oath, conjure, exorcise] **1** : the act or practice of exorcising **2** *obs* : the conjuration of evil spirits **3** : a spell or formula used in exorcising

ex·or·cis·mal \¦=(,)=¦sizməl\ *or* **ex·or·ci·so·ry** \¦=(,)=¦sīzərē\ *adj* [*exorcismal* fr. *exorcism* + *-al; exorcisory* fr. *exorcise* + *-ory*] : of or relating to exorcism

ex·or·cist \'=(,)=,sist, -,səst\ *n* -s [ME *exorciste,* fr. LL *exorcista,* fr. Gk *exorkistēs,* fr. *exorkizein*] **1** : one who exorcises or conjures evil spirits **2 a** : a member of a minor order in the early Christian church **b** : the second highest office of the minor orders in the Roman Catholic Church ranking immediately below that of acolyte

ex·or·cis·tate \¦=(,)=¦si,stāt\ *n* -s : the office or order of exorcist

ex·or·cis·ti·cal \¦=(,)=¦sistəkəl\ *also* **ex·or·cis·tic** \-istik\ *adj* : of or relating to exorcism

ex·or·di·al \(')eg¦zȯ(r)dēəl, (')ek¦sȯ-\ *adj* [*exordium* + *-al*] : relating to an exordium : INTRODUCTORY

ex·or·di·um \=ˈ=dēəm\ *n, pl* **exordiums** \-ēəmz\ *or* **exor·dia** \-ēə\ [L, fr. *exordiri* to begin, begin a web, lay a warp, fr. *ex-* ¹ex- + *ordiri* to begin, begin a web — more at ORDER] : BEGINNING, INTRODUCTION; *esp* : the introductory part of a discourse or composition

ex·organic \¦eks+\ *adj* [¹*ex-* + *organic*] : having lost organic character

exo·rha·son \ek'sȯräsən\ *n* [NGk, fr. Gk *exo-* + MGk *rhason*] : RHASON 2

ex·or·na·tion \,ek,sȯ(r)'nāshən\ *n* -s [L *exornation-, exornatio,* fr. *exornatus* (past part. of *exornare* to embellish, equip, fr. *ex-* ¹ex- + *ornare* to embellish, furnish) + *-ion-, -io* -ion — more at ORNATE] : EMBELLISHMENT, ORNAMENTATION

exo·scop·ic \¦eksō¦skäpik\ *adj* [*exo-* + *-scopic*] *bot* : having the apex of the embryo pointed toward the neck of the archegonium — compare ENDOSCOPIC 2

exo·skeletal \¦ek(,)sō+\ *adj* [*exoskeleton* + *-al*] : of or relating to an exoskeleton

exo·skeleton \"+\ *n* [*exo-* + *skeleton*] **1** : an external skeleton or supportive covering of an animal (as the system of sclerites covering the body of an insect or of bony plates covering an armadillo) — compare ENDOSKELETON **2** : bony or horny parts (as nails, hoofs, or scales) of a vertebrate that are produced from epidermal tissues

ex·osmosis \¦eks+\ *n* [alter. (influenced by Gk *-sis*) of earlier *exosmose,* fr. F, fr. *ex-* ¹ex- + Gk *ōsmos* action of thrusting or pushing — more at ENDOSMOSIS] **1** : osmotic diffusion toward the outside of a cell or vessel **2** : passage of material through a membrane from a region of higher to a region of lower concentration — used chiefly in biology; compare ENDOSMOSIS 1

ex·osmotic \"+\ *adj* [ISV *exosm-* (fr. *exosmosis*) + *-otic*] : of or relating to exosmosis

exo·sphere \'eksō+,-\ *n* [ISV *exo-* + *sphere*] : the outer fringe region of the atmosphere variously estimated to begin at an altitude of 200 to 600 miles

ex·o·spor·al \¦eksə¦spȯrəl, (')ek¦säspər-\ *or* **ex·o·spor·ous** \-rəs\ *adj* : of or relating to an exospore

exo·spore \'eksə+,-\ *n* [ISV *exo-* + *spore*] **1** : EPISPORE 1a **2** : one of the asexual spores formed by abstriction from a parent cell (as in phycomycetous fungi) — compare ENDOSPORE

ex·o·spo·re·ae \,eksə'spȯrē,ē\ *n pl* [NL, fr. *exo-* + *spor-* + *-eae*] : a subclass of fungi (class Myxomycetes) distinguished by having the spores borne externally and germinating to produce a protoplasmic body which then develops a group of eight swarm spores — compare MYXOGASTRES

ex·o·spo·ri·um \-rēəm\ *n, pl* **exospo·ria** \-ēə\ [NL, fr. *exo-* + *-sporium*] : EXINE

exossate *vt* -ED/-ING/-S [L *exossatus,* past part. of *exossare* to deprive of bones, fr. *ex-* ¹ex- + *-ossare* (fr. *oss-, os* bone) — more at OSSEOUS] **1** *obs* : to deprive of bones **2** *obs* : to cause (fruits) to grow without stones

ex·o·ste·ma \,eksə'stēmə\ *n, cap* [NL, fr. *exo-* + LGk *stēma* stamen, fr. Gk, shaft, fr. *histanai* to cause to stand; fr. the exserted stamens — more at STAND] : a genus of tropical American trees or shrubs (family Rubiaceae) with small salverform white flowers and capsular fruits — see PRINCEWOOD

ex·o·stome \'eksə,stōm\ *n* -s [ISV *exo-* + *-stome;* prob. orig. formed in F] **1** *bot* : the opening of the outer integument of an ovule that has two integuments **2** : the outer part of the peristome of a moss

ex·os·tosis \,ek,sä'stōsəs\ *n, pl* **exosto·ses** \-ō,sēz\ [NL, fr. Gk *exostōsis,* fr. *ex* out of, out + *osteon* bone + *-ōsis* -osis — more at EX-, OSSEOUS] **1** : a spur or bony outgrowth from a bone or the root of a tooth **2** : the formation of knots upon the surface of wood in trees

ex·os·tot·ic \¦=,=¦täd·ik\ *adj* [*exostosis* + *-otic*] : of or relating to exostosis

ex·ostracize \eks+\ *vt* [Gk *exostrakizein,* fr. *ex* out of, out + *ostrakizein* to ostracize] : OSTRACIZE

¹**ex·o·ter·ic** \¦eksə¦terik, -rēk\ *adj* [L & Gk; L *exotericus,* fr. Gk *exōterikos,* lit., external, fr. *exōterō* more outside (compar. of *exō* outside) + *-ikos* -ic — more at EXO-] **1 a** : suitable to be imparted to the public : readily comprehensible ⟨the ~ doctrine⟩ — compare ESOTERIC **b** : belonging to the outer or less initiate circle ⟨~ rites⟩ **c** : publicly known : POPULAR **2** : relating to the outside : EXTERNAL, EXTERIOR — **ex·o·ter·i·cal·ly** \-rək(ə)lē, -rēk-, -li\ *adv*

²**exoteric** \"\ *n* -s **1** : LAYMAN, OUTSIDER **2 exoterics** *pl* : doctrines or discourses for the uninstructed or the general public

ex·o·ter·i·ca \,eksə'terəkə\ *n pl* [NL, fr. L, neut. pl. of *exotericus*] : exoteric doctrines or works

ex·o·ter·i·cism \-rə,sizəm\ *n* -s : exoteric doctrines or practices esp. in religion; *also* : the holding of such doctrines or engaging in such practices

exo·thermal \¦eksō+\ *adj* [*exo-* + *thermal*] : EXOTHERMIC — **exo·thermally** \"+\ *adv*

exo·thermic \"+\ *adj* [ISV *exo-* + *thermic*] : characterized by or formed with evolution of heat : EXOERGIC ⟨~ chemical reactions⟩ — opposed to *endothermic* — **exo·ther·mic·i·ty** \,ek(,)sō(,)thər'misəd·ē\ *n* -ES

¹**ex·ot·ic** \ig'zäd·|ik, eg'z-, -ät|, |ēk *sometimes* ik'sä- *or* ek'sä-\ *adj* [L *exoticus,* fr. Gk *exōtikos,* fr. *exō* outside] **1** : from another country : not native to the place where found : FOREIGN ⟨~ flower⟩ ⟨~ fish⟩ ⟨~ dishes⟩ **2** *archaic* : OUTLANDISH, ALIEN **3 a** : strikingly out of the ordinary : rarely met with : STRANGE **b** : excitingly strange : having the appeal of the unknown : MYSTERIOUS, ROMANTIC, PICTURESQUE, GLAMOROUS **c** : strikingly unusual in color or design : RICH, SHOWY, ELABORATE — **ex·ot·i·cal·ly** \|ək(ə)lē, |ēk-, -li\ *adv* — **ex·ot·ic·ness** \|iknəs, |ēk-\ *n* -ES

²**exotic** \"\ *n, pl* **exotics** \-ks\ : one (as a plant or a word) that is exotic

¹**ex·ot·i·ca** \|əkə, |ēkə\ *n* -s [L, fem. of *exoticus*] : an acidanthera (*Acidanthera bicolor*) with creamy-white flowers that are blotched chocolate-brown within

²**exotica** \"\ *n pl* [L, neut. pl. of *exoticus*] : things excitingly different or unusual; *esp* : literary or artistic items having an exotic theme or nature

exotical *adj* [L *exoticus* + E *-al*] *obs* : EXOTIC

ex·ot·i·cism \|ə,sizəm\ *n* -s **1** : the quality or state of being exotic **2** : interest in or adoption of the exotic **3** : a foreign trait of behavior

ex·ot·i·cist \|əsəst\ *n* -s : one who specializes (as in writing) in the exotic : one who exploits the appeal of the exotic

exotic stream *n* : a stream (as the Nile) that has its source in well-watered lands and crosses a desert on its way to the sea

ex·o·tism \'eksə,tizəm, 'egzə-\ *n* -s [*exotic* + *-ism*] : EXOTICISM

exo·toxic \¦eksə+\ *adj* [*exotoxin* + *-ic*] : of, relating to, or acting as an exotoxin

exo·toxin \"+\ *n* [ISV *exo-* + *toxin*] : a soluble poisonous substance that passes into the medium during growth of certain bacilli or other microorganisms ⟨tetanus ~⟩ — compare ENDOTOXIN

ex·o·tro·pia \,eksə'trōpēə\ *n* -s [NL, fr. *exo-* + *-tropia*] : WALLEYE 2b

ex·ot·ro·pism \ek'sä·trə,pizəm\ *n* [ISV *exo-* + *-tropism*] : curvature away from the main axis

exp *abbr* **1** expansion **2** ex parte **3** expense **4** experience **5** experiment; experimental **6** expiration **7** explosive **8** exponential **9** export **10** exposure **11** express

ex·pand \ik'spand, ek-, -paa(ə)nd\ *vb* -ED/-ING/-S [ME *expaunden,* fr. L *expandere,* fr. *ex-* ¹ex- + *pandere* to spread, unfold — more at FATHOM] *vt* **1** : to spread out : open wide : UNFOLD ⟨~*ed* his thick underlip and stared . . . with distended eyes —Liam O'Flaherty⟩ **2** : to increase the extent, size, number, volume, or scope of : ENLARGE ⟨~*ed* this regiment into a brigade —B.I.Wiley⟩ ⟨we need to ~ our factual information concerning the behavior of the economy —L.V.Chandler⟩ ⟨business is ~*ing* its interest in the liberal arts —C.C.Brown⟩ **3 a** : to express fully : develop in detail : AMPLIFY ⟨these views he announced and ~*ed* in three monographs —J.S.Bassett⟩ **b** : to write out in full ⟨contractions have been ~*ed* and spellings modernized —J.L.Clifford⟩ **c** *math* : to state in enlarged form : develop in a series ~ *vi* **1** : to spread itself out : open out ⟨each stalk ~*ing* at the top into a . . . flower head —C.S.Forester⟩ **2** : to increase in extent, size, number, volume, or scope : become larger : GROW ⟨measure how rapidly the water warmed up and ~*ed* while it was warming —K.K.Darrow⟩ ⟨this trend toward conformity will ~ and accelerate —P.H.Odegard⟩ ⟨his mind never ~*ed;* his emotions never deepened —Kenneth Clark⟩ **3** : to speak or write fully or in detail : EXPATIATE — usu. used with *on* or *upon* ⟨I propose . . . to ~ on three of these common problems —W.R.Bascom⟩ **4** : to experience a feeling of well-being : become expansive ⟨the subtle flattery . . . made the eminent Victorian ~ and glow —Osbert Sitwell⟩

syn AMPLIFY, SWELL, DISTEND, INFLATE, DILATE: EXPAND, often interchangeable with others in this list, may indicate any enlarging by opening out, spreading, unfolding, extending, or increasing ⟨the captain established a tavern here, *expanding* it after 10 years into an elaborate stone structure —*Amer. Guide Series: Pa.*⟩ ⟨gradually psalm singing *expanded* into oratorios and concerts of sacred music —*Amer. Guide Series: N.J.*⟩ ⟨she hungered for a full environment in which to *expand* her new powers —Havelock Ellis⟩ AMPLIFY often applies to extending by magnifying the volume or scope or adding details ⟨a pipe organ and an *amplifying* system over which programs can be sent to the entire town —*Amer. Guide Series: Mich.*⟩ ⟨it is on the main argument that the book is to be judged, and I must *amplify* a summary of it —Julian Huxley⟩ SWELL sometimes applies to an abnormal expanding, puffing up or out, or increasing in intensity or volume ⟨now the trickle continued throughout the war, and *swelled* to a flood soon after the war ended —William Clark⟩ ⟨Servia's ambitions had been *swollen* enormously by her successes —A. D.H.Smith⟩ ⟨when at anchor here I ride, my bosom *swells* with pride —W.S.Gilbert⟩ ⟨a great determination *swelled* in him —A.J.Cronin⟩ DISTEND applies to an extending out or a swelling out, often brought about by internal pressures, or to an appearance of swelling or protruding ⟨sails *distended* by the wind⟩ ⟨a stomach *distended* by gas⟩ ⟨her eyes were black with terror, and so *distended* that the white showed all the way round them —Edith Sitwell⟩ ⟨when a piece of oratory intended for a public occasion impresses us as *distended,* which is to say, filled up with repetition, periphrasis, long grammatical forms, and other impediments to directness —R.M. Weaver⟩ INFLATE usu. implies distention or puffing up by or as if by an air or gas or something else relatively insubstantial ⟨*inflate* a balloon⟩ ⟨*inflated* currency⟩ ⟨poems *inflated* with fine language⟩ ⟨the psychological problems of *inflated* national ego, heroic delusions of grandeur, and theories of historical inevitability —R.A.Newhall⟩ DILATE is likely to refer to a swelling or widening of something known or viewed as circular or spherical ⟨arteries *dilated* by the drug⟩ ⟨the pupils of his eyes were *dilated*⟩ ⟨some stirring experience, the drastic stimulus given by some masterpiece in an art or by some personal emotion, may swiftly *dilate* your field of consciousness —C.E.Montague⟩

ex·pand·abil·i·ty \ik,spandə'biləd·ē, ek-, -paan-, -lətē, -i\ *n* -ES : EXPANSIBILITY

ex·pand·able *also* **ex·pand·ible** \=ˈ=dəbəl\ *adj* : capable of being expanded

expanded *adj* [fr. past part. of *expand*] **1 a** : spread out : OUTSTRETCHED, UNFOLDED ⟨then with ~ wings he steers his flight aloft —John Milton⟩ **b** *heraldry* : OPEN, DISPLAYED **c** *of a letter or typeface* : having a somewhat wider face than that of a typeface not so characterized — compare CONDENSED, EXTENDED **2 a** : increased in volume or scope : ENLARGED ⟨~ public-relations programs⟩ **b** : PERIPHRASTIC used of the progressive-tense forms in *-ing* (as *am writing, was writing, is being written*) — **ex·pand·ed·ness** *n* -ES

expanded metal *n* : sheet metal cut and stretched into a lattice

expanded plastic *n* : a lightweight cellular material usu. made by introducing gas into a plastic or resin and used esp. in insulation and lamination — called also *foamed plastic, plastic foam*

expanded metal

ex·pand·er \=ˈ=də(r)\ *n* -s **1** : one that expands: as **a** : an operator of a machine that expands metal tubes **b** : a tool designed to expand a boiler tube at its end so as to fit it snugly into the flue sheet **2** : any of several colloidal substances of high molecular weight (as special preparations of gelatin or dextran) used as a blood or plasma substitute in transfusion for increasing the volume of the circulating blood esp. in the treatment of shock — called also *extender*

expanding *adj* [fr. pres. part. of *expand*] : that expands or may be expanded; *esp* : GROWING ⟨an ~ economy⟩

expanding brake *n* : a brake in which a flexible band or a set of circular segments is sprung outward against the inside rim of a hub or wheel

expanding bullet *n* : a soft-nosed bullet — compare DUMDUM

expanding pulley *n* : a pulley whose diameter can be varied

expanding universe *n* : a relativistic concept of the material universe according to which all celestial bodies are becoming steadily farther apart with the result that those more remote recede from the earth at greater speeds

expands *pres 3d sing of* EXPAND

¹**expanse** *vt* -ED/-ING/-S [L *expansus,* past part. of *expandere* to spread out, expand — more at EXPAND] *obs* : EXPAND

²**ex·panse** \ik'span(t)s, ek-, -paa(ə)n-\ *n* -s [NL *expansum* firmament, fr. L, neut. of *expansus,* past part. of *expandere*] : something that is spread out typically over a wide area: as **a** : FIRMAMENT ⟨moon and stars . . . silvering in the blue ~ —Christopher Smart⟩ **b** : an extensive and usu. unbroken stretch of land or sea ⟨great ~ of country spread around and below —D.H.Lawrence⟩ ⟨majestic ~ of calm water —Tom Marvel⟩

ex·pan·si·bil·i·ty \ik,span(t)sə'biləd·ē, (,)ek-, -paan-, -lətē, -i\ *n* -ES : the quality or state of being expandable

ex·pan·si·ble \=ˈ==,bəl\ *adj* [L *expansus* + E *-ible*] : EXPANDABLE

ex·pan·sile \-n(t)səl, -n,sīl\ *adj* [L *expansus* + E *-ile*] **1** : capable of expansion ⟨gases are more ~ than liquids⟩ **2** : of, relating to, or characteristic of expansion ⟨~ movements⟩

ex·pan·sion \ik'spanchən, ek-, -paan-\ *n* -s [LL *expansion-, expansio,* fr. L *expansus* + *-ion-, -io* -ion] **1** : the act or process of expanding: as **a** (1) : the act or process of spreading out ⟨the easy ~ of the wing of a bird —Nehemiah Grew⟩ (2) : the mushrooming of a bullet upon striking the target **b** (1) : the act or process of increasing in extent, size, number, volume, or scope : ENLARGEMENT, GROWTH ⟨localized pain along nerve trunks may be due to the ~ of the dissolved nitrogen without actual bubble formation —H.G.Armstrong⟩ ⟨the bewildering ~ of science during the last century —C.H. Grandgent⟩ ⟨this desire for territorial ~ is deeply rooted in human history —C.J.Friedrich⟩ (2) *in an electronic sound amplifier* : the widening of the range of an audio-frequency signal by making the gain vary directly with the amplitude of the input signal so that weak sounds become weaker and loud sounds louder **c** (1) : the act of expressing fully or of developing in detail : AMPLIFICATION ⟨these lectures with some slight ~ . . . are here printed as delivered —A.N.Whitehead⟩ (2) *math* : the developed result of an indicated or possible operation : the expression of a function in the form of a series ⟨the ~ of $(a+b)^2$ is $a^2+2ab+b^2$⟩ (3) *logic* : the operation or result of making the terms in a formula more explicit or of introducing new terms without changing the logical significance of the expression **2** : the quality or state of being expanded ⟨the gilded clouds in fair ~ lie —Alexander Pope⟩ **3** : EXPANSE ⟨the sky's serene ~ —Thomas Hood †1845⟩ **4** *obs* : pure space ⟨lost in ~, void and infinite —Richard Blackmore⟩ **5 a** : the increase in volume of working fluid (as steam) in an engine cylinder after cutoff or in an internal-combustion engine after explosion by which it continues to propel the piston while expending part of its internal energy and losing in pressure and temperature **b** : the period during which such expansion occurs **c** : amount of increase of length, area, or volume **6 a** : an expanded part ⟨the great ~ of the St. Lawrence called the Lake of St. Peter —Francis Parkman⟩ **b** : something that results from an act of expanding ⟨this book was an ~ of a notable series of articles —A.C.Ames⟩ **7** : EXPANSIVENESS ⟨gradually tones of careless freedom, moments of reckless ~ come in, though never . . . any trace of sentimentality or of adoration —Havelock Ellis⟩

ex·pan·sion·al \-chən°l, -chnəl\ *adj* : of or relating to expansion

ex·pan·sion·ary \-chə,nerē\ *adj* : tending toward expansion ⟨an ~ factor⟩ ⟨an ~ economy⟩

expansion attic *n* : an unfinished attic area usu. with dormers in an otherwise finished house that is suitable for conversion into habitable space

expansion bit *n* : EXPANSIVE BIT

expansion bolt *n* : a bolt operating in or by an expanding attachment fitted in wood, iron, or masonry

expansion chamber *n* : CLOUD CHAMBER

expansion coupling *n* : EXPANSION JOINT 1

ex·pan·sion·ism \-chə,nizəm\ *n* -s : the policy, practice, or advocacy of expansion, esp. territorial expansion ⟨furnish specific guarantees to countries which lay in the path of Soviet ~ —P.E.Mosely⟩

¹**ex·pan·sion·ist** \-ch(ə)nəst\ *n* -s : one who favors expansionism: as **a** : an advocate of an enlarged paper currency **b** : an advocate of territorial expansion

²**expansionist** \"\ *adj* : practicing, advocating, or tending toward expansion; *specif* : pressing for a policy of extending a nation's political and economic dominance ⟨we must make it perfectly clear that we are not ourselves ~ —H.L.Stimson⟩

ex·pan·sion·is·tic \=,=chə¦nistik\ *adj* : EXPANSIONIST

expansion joint *n* **1** : a coupling (as of steam pipes) designed to permit an endwise movement that compensates for expansion or contraction resulting from temperature changes **2** : a joint or gap (as in concrete work) designed to permit expansion or contraction resulting from temperature changes

expansion shield *n* : a device for anchoring attachments to masonry or concrete surfaces consisting of a metal insert that is driven into a drilled hole and expanded tightly against the sides of the hole

expansion trunk *n* : a trunk that extends above a cargo tank in an oil tanker and that permits the change in volume resulting from temperature changes to be accommodated by a change in the level in the trunk

expansion valve *n* : a valve through which liquid or gas under pressure is allowed to expand to a lower pressure and greater volume

ex·pan·sive \ik'span(t)siv, ek-, -paan-, -sēv *also* -səv\ *adj* [L *expansus* (past part. of *expandere* to expand) + E *-ive* — more at EXPAND] **1** : having a capacity or a tendency to expand ⟨~ materials⟩ **2** : causing or tending to cause expansion ⟨the ~ force of fire⟩ **3 a** : characterized by high spirits or benevolent inclinations : freely communicative : GENIAL ⟨like all secretive persons she could be suddenly ~ at times —Arnold Bennett⟩ ⟨some kindly or helpful act, some ~ expression of fellowship —S.H.Adams⟩ **b** : marked by or indicative of exaggerated euphoria and delusions of self-importance **4** : applying, working by, or capable of expansion ⟨an ~ engine⟩ ⟨an ~ gear⟩ **5** : having considerable extent : BROAD, EXTENSIVE ⟨came abreast of the ~ glittering lake —William Bartram⟩ ⟨a course of lectures on the religions of the world . . . or on something equally ~ —Agnes Repplier⟩ **6** : characterized by largeness or magnificence of scale : AMPLE, SPACIOUS ⟨those glorious days of ~ living were soon curtailed —Frank Monaghan⟩ ⟨they were liberal with good timber in those ~ days —George Farwell⟩ **7** : EXPANSIONIST

syn see ELASTIC

expansive bit *n* : a bit with a cutting blade that can be adjusted

expansive bit

to various sizes — called also *expansion bit*

expansive classification *n* : a library classification using both numbers and letters in its notation and having seven complete schedules each one after the first being more minutely subdivided than the previous one — called also *Cutter classification*

ex·pan·sive·ly \-sȯvlē, -li\ *adv* : in an expansive manner

ex·pan·sive·ness \-sivnəs, -sēv- *also* -səv-\ *n* -ES : the quality or state of being expansive

ex·pan·siv·i·ty \,ek,span'sivəd·ē, ik-, -paan-, -vətē, -i\ *n* -ES **1** : EXPANSIVENESS; *esp* : the capacity to expand **2** : COEFFICIENT OF EXPANSION

ex·pan·sum \ik'span(t)səm\ *n* -s [NL — more at EXPANSE] *archaic* : EXPANSE a

ex·pan·sure \ik'spanchə(r)\ *n* -s [L *expansus* + E *-ure*] **1** *obs* : the process of expanding **2** : EXPANSE ⟨the lowland's dark ~ —T.C.Irwin⟩

ex par·te \(')eks¦pärd·ē\ *adj (or adv)* [ML, on behalf] **1** : on or from one side only — used of such legal matters as injunctions, commissions, hearings, and testimony and ordinarily implying a hearing or examination in the presence of or on papers filed by one party and in the absence of and often without notice to the other party **2** : from a one-sided or partisan point of view ⟨the bully proceeds at once by superior power to enforce his own *ex parte* notion of what is right —*Christian Century*⟩ ⟨was discussed *ex parte* by wehement propagandists on both sides —F.L.Allen⟩

ex·pa·ti·ate \ek'spāshē,āt, ik-, *usu* -ād·+V\ *vb* -ED/-ING/-S [L *expatiatus, exspatiatus,* past part. of *expatiari, exspatiari* to wander from the course, digress, fr. *ex-* ¹ex- + *spatiari* to take a walk, fr. *spatium* space, walk, course — more at SPEED] *vi* **1** : to move about freely or at will : WANDER ⟨fetters to be snapped asunder in order that the human spirit might ~ at liberty —Irving Babbitt⟩ **2** : to speak or write at length or in considerable detail : ELABORATE, ENLARGE — usu. used with *on* or *upon* ⟨his knowledge of the country enabled him to ~ with fluency on the strategical situation —C.S.Forester⟩ ⟨the promoter of the raffle . . . was *expatiating* upon the value of the fabric —Thomas Hardy⟩ ~ *vt* **1** *obs* : EXPAND, SPREAD ⟨princes ~ their dominions —Thomas Adams⟩ **2** *obs* : to allow (oneself) to expatiate ⟨an oration wherein he *expatiated* himself in his praises for the nobility —William Cave⟩ **syn** see DISCOURSE

ex·pa·ti·a·tion \(,)ek,spās(h)ē'āshən, ik-\ *n* -s [*expatiate* + *-ion*] : the act or an instance of expatiating ⟨it is a very risky thing to ask a professional officer . . . to give a weekly ~ on the war —Sir Winston Churchill⟩

¹ex·pa·tri·ate \ek'spā·trē,āt, *usu* -,ād+V, *chiefly Brit* -pa-\ *vb* -ED/-ING/-S [ML *expatriatus,* past part. of *expatriare* to leave one's native country, fr. L *ex-* ¹ex- + LL *-patriare* (fr. L *patria* native country, fr. fem. of *patrius* of a father, paternal, fr. *patr-, pater* father) — more at FATHER] *vt* **1 :** to drive into exile **:** BANISH ⟨this minister after having been *expatriated* outlived his great enemy —Isaac D'Israeli⟩ **2 a :** to withdraw (oneself) from residence in one's native country ⟨*expatriated* himself for years at the Cape of Good Hope —R.W.Emerson⟩ **b :** to withdraw (oneself) from allegiance to one's native country ⟨although the father had . . . *expatriated* himself, the son was appointed a cadet "at large" at West Point —T.M.Spaulding⟩ ~ *vi* **:** to leave one's native country ⟨the population again died out or *expatriated* —George Grote⟩; *specif* **:** to renounce allegiance to one's native country **syn** see BANISH

²ex·pa·tri·ate \(')ᵊ=ᵊ=,ᵊ|t, -ə|t, *usu* |d.+V\ *adj* [ML *expatriatus,* past part. of *expatriare*] **:** living or occurring in a foreign country **:** EXPATRIATED ⟨an indoctrination school for the training of . . . ~ U.S. employees —*Lamp*⟩ ⟨the equivalent in our day of his early ~ experiences in the Twenties —J.W. Aldridge⟩

³expatriate \"\ *n* -S **:** one who lives in a foreign country ⟨there are both disadvantages and attractions to the life of a foreign correspondent: he is an ~ —F.L.Mott⟩; *specif* **:** one who has renounced his native country ⟨becomes a downright ~ and a more or less active agent of anti-American feeling —H.L.Mencken⟩

ex·pa·tri·a·tion \(,)ᵊ,ᵊ=ᵊ'āshən\ *n* -S [F, fr. *expatrier* to expatriate (fr. ML *expatriare* to leave one's native country) + *-ation*] **:** the act or action of expatriating: as **a :** residence in a foreign country ⟨had recently come back from Paris after long years of ~ . . . for an operation —Louis Auchincloss⟩ **b :** renunciation of allegiance to one's native country ⟨the passage of his bill acknowledging the right of ~ —C. G.Bowers⟩

expdn *abbr* expedition

¹ex·pect \ik'spekt, ek-\ *vb* -ED/-ING/-S [L *expectare, exspectare* to await, look forward to, fr. *ex-* ¹ex- + *spectare* to look at, fr. *spectus,* past part. of *specere* to look — more at SPY] *vi* **1** *obs* **:** WAIT ⟨a dog ~*s* till his master has done picking of the bone —Henry More⟩ **2 :** to look forward **:** look with anticipation ⟨we love to ~, and when expectation is disappointed or gratified we want to be again ~*ing* —Samuel Johnson⟩ **3 :** to anticipate the birth of a child **:** be pregnant — used in progressive tenses ⟨his wife is ~*ing*⟩ ~ *vt* **1** *archaic* **a :** to wait for **:** AWAIT ⟨with what anxiety I ~ your news of her health —P.B.Shelley⟩ **b :** to wait in order to see and know ⟨~*ing* what should be the event thereof —Richard Knolles⟩ **c :** to be in store for ⟨if any other fate ~*s* me —Conyers Middleton⟩ **2 :** SUPPOSE, THINK, BELIEVE ⟨I ~ that those Indians are on their way to war —Meriwether Lewis⟩ **3 a :** to look for; *specif* **:** to anticipate the coming or receipt of ⟨she had not ~*ed* the others and there was a great scurrying about to make coffee . . . for them —Louis Bromfield⟩ **b :** to look forward to; *specif* **:** to anticipate the occurrence of ⟨she had spent the night ~*ing* death in the morning, but then was told . . . that she was not to die till noon —Edith Sitwell⟩ **4 a :** to consider probable or certain ⟨he can never ~ . . . that reason will ever hold in leash the emotions —Havelock Ellis⟩ ⟨scurvy was to be ~*ed* in ships that had been long at sea —C.S. Forester⟩ **b :** to consider reasonable, just, proper, due, or necessary ⟨he ~*ed* and demanded hard work of his students —M.H.Thomas⟩ ⟨rich men . . . sometimes ~ a deference which they refuse to claim —J.W.Krutch⟩ **c :** to consider (a person) obligated or in duty bound ⟨England ~*s* every man to do his duty —Horatio Nelson⟩ ⟨a scholar . . . is ~*ed* to know the latest work on his own speciality —T.H. Savory⟩ **5** *obs* **:** DEMAND, REQUIRE ⟨one assertion in it . . . ~*ed* greater evidence —Joseph Boyse⟩

syn EXPECT, HOPE, HOPE (*for*), LOOK (*to*), LOOK (*for*), and AWAIT can mean, in common, to anticipate in the mind a thing or an event more or less likely or certain to occur. EXPECT usu. implies a high degree of certainty to the point of making preparations or anticipating particular things, actions, or feelings ⟨an old three-story brick, nothing like what he had *expected* —Lenard Kaufman⟩ ⟨Bainbridge's men could *expect* to be starved and cold and verminous, as indeed they were —C.S.Forester⟩ ⟨we can *expect* to import only a fraction of the feeding stuffs formerly obtained from abroad —Laurence Easterbrook⟩ ⟨a person of authority, who is awaited, *expected,* and now comes —Virginia Woolf⟩ HOPE and HOPE (*for*) imply little certainty but suggest confidence and sometimes assurance that what one desires or longs for will happen ⟨makes the reading of it as rewarding as anything short of real, bona fide firsthand experience can ever *hope* to be —H.C.Adamson⟩ ⟨I could not remain a moment in the place, although he considerately *hoped* I would stay —Effie Gray⟩ ⟨what I *hope for* and work for today is for a world more favorable to artists than is the present one —E.M.Forster⟩ ⟨a boy who showed intellectual promise was encouraged to *hope for* a college education —H.E.Scudder⟩ LOOK (*to*) implies a freedom from doubt that expectations will be fulfilled ⟨*look to* help from the family in times of uncertainty⟩ ⟨*look to* profit from an enterprise⟩ LOOK (*for*) implies less assurance and suggests an attitude of expectancy and watchfulness ⟨*look for* trouble when the enemy begins to move his forces⟩ ⟨*look for* snags that will almost inevitably occur in putting any theory into practice⟩ AWAIT suggests a being in readiness for something expected or watched for; unlike the preceding words it may have as its subject the thing awaited and as its object the person awaiting ⟨nothing for me to do but *await* their return —A.J.Broadwater⟩ ⟨the punishment which *awaits* unrepented sin —R.A.Hall b. 1911⟩ ⟨the fate that *awaits* a sovereign who would display talents and expert authority —A.M.Young⟩

²expect *n* -S *obs* **:** EXPECTATION

ex·pect·able \-təbəl\ *adj* [L *expectabilis, exspectabilis,* fr. *expectare, exspectare* + *-abilis* -able] **:** to be expected ⟨differences of opinion . . . are quite ~ in the present stage of knowledge —J.H.Steward⟩

ex·pect·ably \-blē, -li\ *adv* **:** as might be expected ⟨the passing years, ~, have made his sense of crisis ever more urgent —Lionel Trilling⟩

ex·pect·an·cy \-tənsē, -si\ *or* **ex·pect·ance** \-n(t)s\ *n, pl* **expectancies** *or* **expectances** [ML *expectantia, exspectantia,* fr. L *expectant-, exspectant-, expectans, exspectans* + *-ia* -y] **1** *archaic* **a :** the act of waiting **b :** the state of waiting **2 a :** the act or action of anticipating ⟨the thirst did feel abatement of its edge e'en from *expectance* —H.F.Cary⟩ **b :** the state of anticipating ⟨suspicion . . . gave way to a more submissive ~ —George Eliot⟩ **3 :** the state of being expected ⟨a large fortune in ~⟩ **4 a** (1) **:** something that is expected **:** the object of expectation or hope ⟨each of us had come . . . with his own purposes and *expectancies* —Esther Warner⟩ (2) **:** the expected amount (as of the number of years of life) based on statistical probability — compare LIFE EXPECTANCY **b** *archaic* **:** something that gives rise to expectations ⟨the ~ and rose of the fair state —Shak.⟩

¹ex·pect·ant \ik'spektənt, (')ek¦s-\ *adj* [ME *expectaunt,* fr. L *expectant-, exspectant-, expectans, exspectans,* pres. part. of *expectare, exspectare* to await, look forward to] **1 a :** characterized by expectation **:** EXPECTING, WAITING ⟨the ~ crowds all curious to catch a glimpse of some familiar face —*London Calling*⟩ ⟨spoke as one ~ of unquestioning obedience —S.H. Adams⟩ **b :** expecting the birth of a child ⟨an ~ father⟩; *specif* **:** PREGNANT ⟨~ mothers⟩ **2 :** having expectations **:** PROSPECTIVE ⟨scruples . . . raised in the mind of the ~ heir —Jonathan Swift⟩ **3 :** existing in expectation **:** in prospect **:** EXPECTED ⟨the fee ~ on his wife's life estate —Thomas Jarman⟩ **4** *of the treatment of disease* **:** involving alleviation of immediate distress without basic interference with the development of the pathologic process **:** CONSERVATIVE

²expectant \"\ *n* -S **:** one who is expectant; *specif* **:** a candidate for a position

ex·pect·ant·ly *adv* **:** in an expectant manner **:** with expectation

ex·pec·ta·tion \,ek,spek'tāshən *also* ik-\ *n* -S [L *expectation-, exspectation-, expectatio, exspectatio,* fr. *expectatus, exspectatus* (past part. of *expectare, exspectare*) + *-ion-, -io* -ion] **1** *archaic* **a :** the act of waiting ⟨a daily ~ at the gate is the readiest way to gain admittance into the house —Robert South⟩ **b :** the state of waiting ⟨sat the livelong day with patient ~ —Shak.⟩ **2 a :** the act or action of looking forward **:** ANTICIPATION ⟨had given rise to a general ~ of their marriage —Jane Austen⟩ **b :** the state of looking forward **:** the mental attitude of one who anticipates ⟨no fear of worse . . . would torment me with cruel ~ —John Milton⟩ **3 :** something that is expected **:** the object of expectancy ⟨the hope and ~ of thy time is ruined —Shak.⟩ **4 a :** the basis for expecting something ⟨my soul, wait thou only upon God; for my ~ is from him —Ps 62:5 (AV)⟩ **b :** prospects of inheritance — usu. used in pl. ⟨a rich old uncle . . . from whom I have the greatest ~*s* —R.B.Sheridan⟩ **5 :** the state of being expected — used esp. in the phrase *in expectation* ⟨benefits in ~⟩ **6 a :** EXPECTANCY 4a(2) **b :** the value of a chance measured by the product of the amount to be received if an event takes place and the probability of the event — called also *mathematical expectation* **7 :** ASSUMPTION, SUPPOSITION, SURMISE ⟨the ~ that you are always from home prevents my writing to you —Thomas Jefferson⟩

expectation of life : LIFE EXPECTANCY

expectation sunday *n, cap E & S* **:** the Sunday before Whitsunday

expectation week *n, cap E&W* [so called fr. its being the period commemorating the apostles' expectation of and prayer for the promised coming of the Holy Spirit] **:** the 10 days between Ascension Day and Whitsunday

¹ex·pect·ative \ik'spektəd·iv, (')ek¦s-, -tətiv\ *adj* [ME (Sc), conferring the right of succession to a benefice, fr. ML *expectativus, exspectativus,* fr. L *expectatus, exspectatus* + *-ivus* -ive] **:** relating to, characterized by, or constituting an object of expectation

²expectative \"\ *n* -S [ML *expectativa, exspectativa* grant of a benefice not yet vacant, fr. fem. of *expectativus, exspectativus*] **:** something that is expected ⟨though blessedness seem to be but an ~, a reversion reserved to the next life —John Donne⟩; *specif* **:** EXPECTATIVE GRACE

expectative grace *n* [alter. of ME (Sc) *grace expectative,* part trans. of ML *gratia expectativa,* fr. L *gratia* grace + ML *expectativa* (fem. of *expectativus*)] **:** a grant of a benefice not yet vacant

expected *past of* EXPECT

expected value *n* **:** the mean value of a random variable

ex·pect·er \ik'spektə(r), (')ek¦s-\ *n* -S **:** one that expects

expecting *pres part of* EXPECT

expectingly *adv* [*expecting* (pres. part. of ¹*expect*) + *-ly*] **:** in an expectant manner

¹ex·pec·to·rant \ik'spektərənt, ek's-\ *adj* [prob. fr. (assumed) NL *expectorant-, expectorans,* pres. part. of (assumed) NL *expectorare*] **:** tending to facilitate expectoration or to promote discharge of mucus from the respiratory tract

²expectorant \"\ *n* -S [prob. fr. (assumed) NL *expectorant-, expectorans,* fr. pres. part. of (assumed) NL *expectorare*] **:** an expectorant agent

ex·pec·to·rate \-,rāt, *usu* -ād+V\ *vb* -ED/-ING/-S [prob. fr. (assumed) NL *expectoratus,* past part. of (assumed) NL *expectorare,* fr. L, to cast out of the mind, fr. *ex-* ¹ex- + *-pectorare* (fr. *pector-, pectus* breast, soul, mind) — more at PECTORAL] *vt* **1** *obs* **:** to bring about the ejection of (phlegm) **2 a** *obs* **:** to cast out of the mind **b** *archaic* **:** to relieve the mind of **3 a :** to eject (as phlegm) from the throat or lungs by coughing or hawking and spitting **b :** SPIT ~ *vi* **1 :** to discharge matter from the throat or lungs by coughing or hawking and spitting **2 :** SPIT

ex·pec·to·ra·tion \ik,spektə'rāshən, (,)ek,s-\ *n* -S [prob. fr. (assumed) NL *expectoration-, expectoratio,* fr. (assumed) NL *expectoratus* + L *-ion-, -io* -ion] **1 :** the act or an instance of expectorating **2 :** expectorated matter

ex·pec·to·ra·tor \ik'spektə,rād·ə(r), ek's-, -ātə-\ *n* -S **:** one that expectorates

expects *pres 3d sing of* EXPECT, *pl of* EXPECT

ex·pede \ek'spēd\ *vt* -ED/-ING/-S [L *expedire* to set free, make ready] *Scots law* **:** to obtain, issue, or take out officially ⟨the letter formerly *expeded* under the dictation of your right honorable mother —Sir Walter Scott⟩

ex·pe·di·ate \ik'spēdē,āt, ek-\ *vt* -ED/-ING/-S [by alter. (influence of *-ate*)] **:** EXPEDITE ⟨fires had been lighted in the grate beneath the climbing boy in order to ~ his efforts —*Ireland's Mag.*⟩

ex·pe·di·en·cy \ik'spēdēənsē, ek-, -si\ *or* **ex·pe·di·ence** \-n(t)s\ *n, pl* **expediencies** *or* **expediences** [*expediency* fr. LL *expedientia* advantage, fr. L *expedient-, expediens* + *-ia* -y; *expedience* fr. ME, advantage, fr. LL *expedientia*] **1** *obs* **:** HASTE, DISPATCH ⟨three thousand men of war are making hither with all due *expedience* —Shak.⟩ **2** *obs* **:** ENTERPRISE, EXPEDITION ⟨let me hear . . . what yesternight our council did decree in forwarding this dear *expedience* —Shak.⟩ **3 :** the quality or state of being suited to the end in view **:** FITNESS, SUITABILITY ⟨the whip of shame and pain could drive her . . . into an appreciation of the ~ of morality —Margaret Deland⟩ **4 :** cultivation of or adherence to means and methods that are opportune or temporarily advantageous as distinguished from those that are right or just; *specif* **:** SELF-INTEREST ⟨the struggle between ethics and politics, between right and ~, had begun —C.W.De Kiewiet⟩ **5 :** a means of achieving a particular end **:** EXPEDIENT ⟨had found a number of simple *expediencies* by which to dissolve what was once the most solemn contract of all —Hamilton Basso⟩

¹ex·pe·di·ent \-nt\ *adj* [ME, fr. MF or L; MF *expedient,* fr. L *expedient-, expediens,* pres. part. of *expedire* to be advantageous, set free, make ready, fr. *ex-* ¹ex- + *-pedire* (fr. *ped-, pes* foot) — more at FOOT] **1 :** characterized by suitability, practicality, and efficiency in achieving a particular end **:** fit, proper, or advantageous under the circumstances ⟨the harvest had been bad, and it was found ~, for their better provision, to disperse the troops over a broader area —J.A.Froude⟩ ⟨it is not necessary, and probably not even ~, to pilfer the secret files of the foreign office —H.J.Morgenthau⟩ **2** *obs* **:** EXPEDITIOUS ⟨I will with all ~ duty see you —Shak.⟩ **3 :** characterized by concern with the opportune or temporarily advantageous as distinguished from the just or right; *specif* **:** governed by self-interest ⟨morality, for the state, means doing what is ~ —H.S.Agar⟩

syn POLITIC, ADVISABLE: EXPEDIENT applies to what is advantageous and opportune under the immediate circumstances in question, often without much regard to ethics ⟨so long as the Stuarts were ruling at St. James's, speculative theocrats found it *expedient* to gloss their principles with nice distinctions between temporal and spiritual overlords —V.L.Parrington⟩ ⟨purely for *expedient* reasons he let the Iroquois alone —Hervey Allen⟩ POLITIC may apply to what is judicious and wise according to the practicalities of the situation ⟨before he faced the head of the Osborne house with the news which it was his duty to tell, Dobbin bethought him that it would be *politic* to make friends of the rest of the family, and, if possible, have the ladies on his side —W.M.Thackeray⟩ ⟨the alacrity with which the German intellectual world submitted to Hitler is proof that, if it knew nothing of politics, it at least knew how to be *politic* —Martin Greenberg⟩ ADVISABLE describes what is practical, prudent, and advantageous and lacks the occas. derogatory implications of EXPEDIENT and POLITIC ⟨in the circumstances, Superintendent, it seems to me *advisable* to adjourn the inquest until you have completed your investigations —Dorothy Sayers⟩ ⟨I do not say that either psychology or medicine or penology has yet arrived at such a stage as to make a revolution in our system of punishment *advisable* —B.N. Cardozo⟩

²expedient \"\ *n* -S [F *expédient,* fr. MF *expedient,* fr. *expedient,* adj.] **1 :** something that is expedient **:** a means to an end ⟨rules of thumb generally . . . are a lazy man's ~ for ridding himself of the trouble of thinking and deciding —B.N. Cardozo⟩ **2 :** a means devised or used in an exigency **:** MAKESHIFT ⟨through so much traveling I had had to learn all sorts of ~*s* and prepare for all sorts of emergencies —V.G.Heiser⟩ **syn** see RESOURCE

ex·pe·di·en·tial \ik¦spēdē¦enchəl, (;)ek¦-\ *adj* [fr. *expediency,* after such pairs as E *potency: potential*] **:** of, characterized by, or governed by expediency ⟨doubtful if government by congressional committees can be justified on either democratic or ~ grounds —E.E.Schattschneider⟩

ex·pe·di·ent·ist \ᵊ'ᵊᵊᵊ,ᵊntəst\ *n* -S **:** one who uses or advocates expedients

ex·pe·di·ent·ly *adv* [ME, fr. *expedient* + *-ly*] **:** in an expedient manner

ex·ped·i·tate \ek'spedə,tāt, ik-\ *vt* -ED/-ING/-S [ML *expeditatus,* past part. of *expeditare,* fr. L *ex-* ¹ex- + ML *-peditare* (fr. L *ped-, pes* foot)] **:** to cut off three claws or the ball of each forefoot of (a dog) so as to prevent the chasing of deer ⟨the mastiffs which were *expeditated* . . . were allowed to be kept in the forest without a special license —Nicholas Biddle⟩

ex·ped·i·ta·tion \(,)ek,spedə'tāshən, ik-\ *n* -S [ML *expeditation-, expeditatio,* fr. *expeditatus* + L *-ion-, -io* -ion] **:** the act of expeditating a dog

¹ex·pe·dite \'ekspə,dīt, *usu* -īd· +V\ *adj* [ME *expedit* accomplished, fr. L *expeditus,* past part. of *expedire*] **1** *obs* **:** QUICK, SPEEDY, PROMPT **2** *obs* **:** free from obstacles, impediments, or difficulties **:** UNHAMPERED, UNIMPEDED **3 a** *obs* **:** ready for action **:** ALERT **b** *archaic* **:** ready for use **:** HANDY **4** *archaic* **:** lightly equipped **:** UNENCUMBERED

²expedite \"\ *vt* -ED/-ING/-S [L *expeditus,* past part. of *expedire* to set free, make ready — more at EXPEDIENT] **1 :** to carry through with dispatch **:** execute promptly ⟨such is my wish: dare thou to ~ it —Bayard Taylor⟩ **2** *obs* **a :** to remove the difficulties from **:** FACILITATE ⟨a broad way now is paved to ~ your glorious march —John Milton⟩ **b :** to set free **:** EXTRICATE ⟨this active gentleman had much ado to ~ himself and save his life —Thomas Fuller⟩ **3 :** to accelerate the process or progress of **:** speed up **:** HASTEN ⟨an administration measure intended to ~ the shipbuilding program —T.W. Arnold⟩ **4 :** to send out **:** ISSUE, DISPATCH ⟨*expedited* a letter under cover to the duke —Fanny Burney⟩

expedite freight *or* **expedited freight** *n* **:** a special railroad freight service giving preference in transportation to specified commodities (as fruit, vegetables, livestock)

ex·pe·dit·er *or* **ex·pe·di·tor** \-īd·ə(r), -ītə-\ *n* -S **:** one that expedites: **a :** one employed to ensure adequate supplies of raw materials and equipment for filling production contracts **b :** one employed to coordinate the flow of materials, tools, parts, and processed goods within a plant in order to facilitate continuous production **c :** one employed to attend to the shipping of products on schedule

ex·pe·di·tion \,ekspə'dishən\ *n* -S [ME *expedicioun,* fr. MF & L; MF *expedition,* fr. L *expedition-, expeditio,* fr. *expeditus* (past part. of *expedire* to set free, make ready) + *-ion-, -io* -ion] **1 a :** a journey, voyage, or excursion undertaken for a specific purpose ⟨had charge of the ~ to observe the transit of Venus in China —W.C.Rufus⟩ ⟨military ~*s*⟩ ⟨an archaeological ~⟩ ⟨a whaling ~⟩ **b :** the group of persons making such an expedition ⟨the gun belongs to the ~ —C.B.Hitchcock⟩ **2 :** efficient promptness **:** SPEED, HASTE ⟨put her things on with remarkable ~ —Arnold Bennett⟩ **3** *obs* **:** the quality or state of being expedited ⟨let us deliver our puissance into the hand of God, putting it straight in ~ —Shak.⟩ **syn** see HASTE

¹ex·pe·di·tion·ary \-shə,nerē, -ri\ *adj* **:** of, relating to, or constituting an expedition; *specif* **:** sent on military service abroad ⟨a British ~ force bound for China was diverted to Calcutta —A.N.Whitehead⟩

²expeditionary \"\ *n* -ES **:** one who goes on an expedition ⟨the *expeditionaries* founded a town . . . and set up the first European colony on the American mainland —*Time*⟩

ex·pe·di·tion·er \-sh(ə)nə(r)\ *n* -S **:** EXPEDITIONARY ⟨the ~*s* left Reykjavik on June 22 —Thomas Foster⟩

ex·pe·di·tion·ist \-sh(ə)nəst\ *n* -S **:** EXPEDITIONARY ⟨a lookout from which Indians as well as returning ~*s* could be watched —*Amer. Guide Series: Minn.*⟩

ex·pe·di·tious \¦ekspə¦dishəs\ *adj* [fr. *expedition,* after such pairs as E *sedition: seditious*] **:** characterized by expedition: **a :** acting or performed with promptness and efficiency **:** SPEEDY ⟨where wages are high . . . we shall always find the workmen more active, diligent, and ~ —Adam Smith⟩ ⟨~ service⟩ **b :** conducive to prompt efficient performance **:** QUICK ⟨stamped out the rebellion by the most ~ means —Virginia W. Valentine⟩ ⟨an ~ system⟩ **syn** see FAST

ex·pe·di·tious·ly *adv* **:** in an expeditious manner **:** with expedition ⟨they traveled as ~ as possible —Jane Austen⟩

ex·pe·di·tious·ness *n* -ES **:** the quality or state of being expeditious ⟨the boss was pleased with the ~ with which the enterprise was completed⟩

ex·ped·i·tive \ek'spedəd·iv\ *adj* **:** EXPEDITIOUS

ex·pel \ik'spel, ek-\ *vt* **expelled; expelled; expelling; expels** [ME *expellen,* fr. L *expellere,* fr. *ex-* ¹ex- + *pellere* to drive — more at FELT] **1 :** to force out from or as if from a receptacle **:** drive out **:** cast out **:** EJECT, DISLODGE ⟨the gigantic explosion . . . *expelled* some four and a half cubic miles of pumice —Howel Williams⟩ ⟨filled her lungs with a long inhalation and *expelled* the smoke —B.A.Williams⟩ ⟨superstitions become lodged in our mental constitutions and sometimes are modified or *expelled* only with the greatest difficulty —F.A.Geldard⟩ **2 :** to drive away from a place or country **:** compel to leave ⟨citizens organized vigilante committees and *expelled* or subdued the undesirables —*Amer. Guide Series: Tenn.*⟩; *specif* **:** DEPORT ⟨an alien within a deportable class had to be *expelled* —*Harvard Law Rev.*⟩ **3 :** to cut off from membership in or the privileges of an institution or society ⟨the boy attended school but was *expelled* for fighting with his teacher —A.F.Harlow⟩ **4** *obs* **:** to dismiss from attention or consideration **:** REFUSE ⟨would you not poor fellowship ~, myself would offer you to accompany —Edmund Spenser⟩ **5** *obs* **:** to keep out **:** EXCLUDE ⟨O, that that earth . . . should patch a wall to ~ the winter's flaw —Shak.⟩ **6** *obs* **:** DISCHARGE, SHOOT ⟨was not slow to ~ the shaft from her contracted bow —John Dryden⟩ **syn** see EJECT

ex·pel·la·ble \-ləbəl\ *adj* **:** capable of being expelled **:** liable to expulsion

¹ex·pel·lant *or* **ex·pel·lent** \-lənt\ *n* -S [*expellant* fr. *expel* + *-ant,* n. suffix; *expellent* fr. L *expellent-, expellens,* pres. part. of *expellere*] **:** an expellant medicine

²expellant *or* **expellent** \"\ *adj* [*expellant* fr. *expel* + *-ant,* adj. suffix; *expellent* fr. L *expellent-, expellens,* pres. part. of *expellere*] **:** tending or serving to expel **:** EXPULSIVE

ex·pel·lee \¦ek,spe¦lē, -,spə¦-; ik¦spe¦lē, ek¦-\ *n* -S **:** a person expelled esp. from his native or adopted country; *specif* **:** one transferred from the country of residence for resettlement in the country with which he is ethnically associated

ex·pel·ler \ik'spelə(r), ek-\ *n* -S **:** one that expels: as **a :** a screw press for expressing vegetable oil from soybeans or other seeds **b :** an operator of a machine for pressing liquid and tallow from tankage

expeller man *n, pl* **expeller men 1 :** EXPELLER b **2 :** an operator of a machine for expressing oil from soybeans

ex·pend \ik'spend, ek-\ *vb* -ED/-ING/-S [ME *expenden,* fr. L *expendere* to weigh out, expend, fr. *ex-* ¹ex- + *pendere* to weigh, pay — more at SPAN] *vt* **1 :** to pay out or distribute **:** SPEND ⟨the social services upon which public revenue is ~*ed* —J.A.Hobson⟩ **2 :** to consume by use **:** use up ⟨little guys — the ones who are ~*ed* — never get to see the broad picture of the war —W.L.White⟩ ⟨still mourns the apparent eclipse of books on which he ~*ed* great energies —Harry Hansen⟩ ~ *vi* **:** to spend money ⟨he rode a horse, lived high, ~*ed* largely —George Meredith⟩ **syn** see SPEND

ex·pend·abil·i·ty \ik,spendə'biləd·ē, (,)ek-, -lətē, -i\ *n* -ES **:** the quality or state of being expendable

¹ex·pend·able \ik'spendəbəl, (')ek¦s-\ *adj* **:** that may be expended: as **a :** normally used up or consumed in service ⟨such ~ supplies as pencils, ink, and paper⟩ **b :** more economically replaced than rescued, salvaged, or protected; *specif* **:** sacrificed according to plan in order to accomplish a military mission ⟨in a war anything can be ~ — money or gasoline or equipment or most usually men —W.L.White⟩

²expendable \"\ *n* -S **:** one that is expendable — usu. used in pl. ⟨when an army is retreating, a small force is left behind to cover the retreat and be sacrificed to the enemy: they are ~*s* —Drew Pearson⟩

ex·pend·er \ᵊ'ᵊdə(r)\ *n* -S **:** one that expends

ex·pen·di·tor \ᵊ'ᵊdəd·ər, -də,tȯ(ə)r\ *n* -S [ML, fr. L *expendere* to expend, prob. after L *vendere* to sell: *venditor* seller] **:** PAYMASTER; *specif* **:** an officer formerly appointed in England to expend the money collected by tax for the repair of sewers

ex·pend·i·ture \ik'spendəchə(r), ek-, -dēchə(r); -də,chu̇(ə)r, -u̇ə, -də,tu̇-, -də-,tyu̇-\ *n* -s [*expendit-* (as in *expenditor*) + *-ure*] **1 :** the act or process of expending ⟨with the ~ of five or six thousand dollars for refurbishing, lighting, advertising, she could have held her own —Mary J. Rolfs⟩ ⟨individual stars which maintain their luminosity by the ~ of nuclear energy —George Gamow⟩ **2 :** something that is expended **:** DISBURSEMENT, EXPENSE ⟨only after ten years of practice did his income equal his ~*s* —R.H.Shryock⟩ **3** *in accrual-basis accounting* **:** an outlay or the creation of a liability for an asset or expense item

¹ex·pense \ik'spen(t)s, ek- *sometimes* 'ek,s-\ *n* -s [ME, fr. AF or LL; AF *expense*, fr. LL *expensa*, fr. L, fem. of *expensus*, past part. of *expendere*] **1 a** (1) *archaic* **:** the act or practice of expending money **:** SPENDING ⟨this exuberance of money displayed itself in wantonness of ~ —Samuel Johnson⟩ (2) *obs* **:** EXTRAVAGANCE ⟨all of them . . . dread a woman of ~ —James Fordyce⟩ **b** (1) *archaic* **:** the act or process of using up **:** CONSUMPTION ⟨the sun is not wasted by ~ of light —Benjamin Franklin⟩ (2) *obs* **:** LOSS ⟨and moan the ~ of many a vanished sight —Shak.⟩ **2 a :** something that is expended in order to secure a benefit or bring about a result ⟨those who have no experience of teaching are incapable of imagining the ~ of spirit entailed by any really living instruction —Bertrand Russell⟩ **b :** the financial burden involved typically in a course of action or manner of living **:** COST ⟨at his own ~ he built a fort and persuaded others to join him there —*Amer. Guide Series: Maine*⟩ ⟨was obliged to spend most of each year earning his tuition and living ~*s* —R.F.Seybolt⟩ **c** (1) **:** the charges that are incurred by an employee in connection with the performance of his duties and that typically include transportation, meals, and lodging while traveling — usu. used in pl. (2) **:** money given to an employee as reimbursement for such charges — usu. used in pl. **d :** an item of outlay incurred in the operation of a business enterprise allocable to and chargeable against revenue for a specific period **3 :** a cause or occasion of expenditure ⟨a country estate is a great ~⟩ **4 :** loss, injury, or detriment as the necessary price of something gained or as the inevitable result or penalty of an action **:** SACRIFICE — usu. used in the phrase *at the expense of* ⟨the spread of the city civilization at the ~ of the villages —Benjamin Farrington⟩ ⟨develop a boy's physique at the ~ of his intelligence —Bertrand Russell⟩

²expense \"\ *vt* -ED/-ING/-S **1 :** to charge with expenses **2 :** to charge to an expense account **:** write off as an expense expenditure

expense account *n* **:** an account of expenses reimbursable to an employee

expense constant *n* **:** a flat amount included in workmen's compensation insurance rates for small risks in order to cover the costs of issuing and servicing the policy

expenseful *adj* **1** *obs* **:** EXPENSIVE **2** *obs* **:** EXTRAVAGANT

ex·pense·less \ə'·ləs\ *adj, archaic* **:** INEXPENSIVE

ex·pen·sive \ik'spen(t)siv, ek-, -sēv *also* -səv\ *adj* **1** *archaic* **:** given to lavish expenditure **:** EXTRAVAGANT ⟨young men of this age are . . . so ~ both of their health and fortune —Richard Steele⟩ **2 :** attended with or involving losses, sacrifices, or continued drains on one's resources **:** COSTLY, DEAR ⟨they . . . tightened credit, raising discount rates and otherwise making it more ~ to borrow —L.H.Haney⟩ ⟨an aggressive foreign policy meant ~ alliances —J.H.Plumb⟩ **3 :** characterized by high price or cost that sometimes exceeds a thing's intrinsic worth or a prospective buyer's financial resources ⟨wind and water power were free; but coal was ~ —Lewis Mumford⟩ ⟨three ~ but flourishing weeklies devoted to absolutely nothing but the life of the rich and titled —Aldous Huxley⟩ **syn** see COSTLY

ex·pen·sive·ly \-səvlē, -li\ *adv* **:** in an expensive manner

ex·pen·sive·ness \-sivnəs, -sēv- *also* -səv-\ *n* -ES **:** the quality or state of being expensive

exper *abbr* **1** experience; experienced **2** experiment; experimental

ex·per·ge·fac·tion \ek¦spərjə¦fakshən\ *n* [LL *expergefaction-, expergefactio*, fr. L *expergefactus* (past part. of *expergefacere* to awaken, fr. *expergisci* to become awake — fr. *ex-* ¹ex- + *-pergisci*, fr. *pergere* to proceed, go on, fr. *per* through + *regere* to lead straight, guide, rule — + *facere* to make, do) + *-ion-, -io* -ion — more at FARE, RIGHT, DO] *archaic* **:** AWAKENING

¹ex·pe·ri·ence \ik'spirēən(t)s, ek-, -pēr-\ *n* -s [ME, fr. MF, fr. L *experientia*, fr. *experient-, experiens* (pres. part. of *experiri* to try, fr. *ex-* ¹ex- + *-periri* — akin to *periculum* attempt, peril) + *-ia* -y — more at FEAR] **1** *obs* **a :** a trial or test ⟨make ~ of my loyalty by some service —James Shirley⟩ **b :** a tentative trial **:** EXPERIMENT ⟨a story of I know not what ~*s* they have made —Walter Blithe⟩ **c :** a conclusive proof **:** DEMONSTRATION ⟨the ~ that Pyrrhus hath given of the Roman power —Walter Raleigh †1618⟩ **2 :** direct observation of or participation in events **:** an encountering, undergoing, or living through things in general as they take place in the course of time ⟨what we call education and culture is . . . the substitution of reading for ~, of literature for life, of the obsolete fictitious for the contemporary real —G.B.Shaw⟩ ⟨she knew by prevision what most women learn only by ~ —Thomas Hardy⟩ **3 a :** the state, extent, duration, or result of being engaged in a particular activity (as a profession) or in affairs generally ⟨ten years' ~ had made my eye learned in the valuing of motion —Thomas De Quincey⟩ ⟨gaining . . . business ~ and developing a character recognized for its industry and ambition —C.W.Mitman⟩ **b** *obs* **:** something approved by or made on the basis of such experience ⟨saw the schools . . . full of pretty curiosities and ~*s*, mechanical, mathematical, and hydraulic —Richard Lassels⟩ **4 :** knowledge, skill, or practice derived from direct observation of or participation in events **:** practical wisdom resulting from what one has encountered, undergone, or lived through ⟨tell him that he ought to get ~, see the world, join a political party, and . . . make sure that he participates in the habitual activities of his society —Delmore Schwartz⟩ **5 a :** the sum total of the conscious events that make up an individual life ⟨all that we know and feel and do, all our facts and theories, all our emotions and ideals and ends may be included in . . . ~ —James Ward⟩ **b :** the sum total of events that make up the past of a community or nation or that have occurred within the knowledge of mankind generally ⟨the organized groups whose life has been the ~ of the peoples of the West —*Official Register of Harvard Univ.*⟩ **6 :** something personally encountered, undergone, or lived through: as **a :** an event observed or participated in ⟨a series of the author's reprinted papers which augment the stories of his personal ~*s* —John Cushing⟩ **b** (1) **:** a state of mind that forms a significant and often crucial part of one's inner religious life and that is sometimes accompanied by intense emotion ⟨in the writings of the earlier Friends, in the diaries and journals that record their intimate and inward ~*s* —Kate W. Tibbals⟩ (2) **:** an account of such an experience — see EXPERIENCE MEETING **c :** illicit sexual relations ⟨a mere nineteen, a kid, when he had his ~ with her —James Jones⟩ **7 :** something by which one is stimulated or moved ⟨the only one of our new playwrights who has given me . . . an ~ in the theater —Louis Kronenberger⟩ ⟨New Mexico was the greatest ~ from the outside world that I have ever had —D.H.Lawrence⟩ **8** *philos* **a :** the act or process of perceiving or apprehending ⟨~ is a matter of the interaction of organism with its environment, and environment that is human as well as physical, that includes the materials of tradition and institutions as well as local surroundings —John Dewey⟩ **b :** the content or the particular result of such experience **c :** the discriminative reaction or the nonconscious response of an organism to events or happenings within its environment **9 :** insurance loss record ⟨the favorable mortality ~ of the past several years —P.M.Fraser⟩

²experience \"\ *vt* -ED/-ING/-S **1 a** *archaic* **:** to put to the test **:** TRY ⟨persuade their governess to ~ their zeal —Thomas Pennant⟩ **b** *obs* **:** to ascertain, prove, or reveal by observation or participation ⟨this trial has . . . *experienced* to me my sad weakness —Rachel Russell⟩ **2** *obs* **:** to teach by experience **:** EXERCISE, TRAIN ⟨~ thy soul in the comforts of Christ's dying —Richard Whitlock⟩ **3 a :** to have experience of **:** meet with **:** FEEL, SUFFER, UNDERGO ⟨the first need for the reader of poetry is to ~ its impact —Mary M. Colum⟩ ⟨the reason death was feared was because no man could twice ~ it —Stuart Cloete⟩ ⟨the cane planters often ~ a lack of workers —P.E.James⟩ **b :** to learn by experience **:** find out **:** DISCOVER ⟨I have *experienced* that a landscape and the sky unfold the deepest beauty —Nathaniel Hawthorne⟩ **4 :** to respond or react discriminatively to (a set of events within the environment) — used of an organism

syn UNDERGO, SUSTAIN, SUFFER: EXPERIENCE indicates an actual living through something and coming to know it first-hand rather than through hearsay or report ⟨a weak and transient feeling to what I now *experienced* —W.H.Hudson⟩ ⟨real people, not labor units, figures in reports, but persons? It is persons who *experience* life —J.B.Priestley⟩ UNDERGO may apply esp. to that which one bears or endures or is subjected to ⟨*undergoing* a major operation⟩ ⟨the air was charged with tension. She saw that he was *undergoing* a difficult struggle —Irving Stone⟩ ⟨part of the ceremony of purification which he must *undergo* before partaking of the new fruits of the season —J.G.Frazer⟩ SUSTAIN in this sense suggests undergoing affliction or infliction without necessarily bearing up with resolution ⟨the two dropped supine into chairs at opposite corners of the ring as if they had *sustained* excessive fatigue —G.B.Shaw⟩ ⟨a few years later he *sustained* something like a heatstroke, which weakened his resistance to climatic conditions —A.D.H.Smith⟩ ⟨the company *sustained* large-scale losses in the venture⟩ SUFFER, often interchangeable in this sense with SUSTAIN, may more strongly implicate wrong or injury ⟨here is a ruthless anatomy of that loneliness which conditions life in the Arctic and is a continuing mystery because the men who *suffer* it gladly have thick enough skins to find an easy shelter —*Times Lit. Supp.*⟩ ⟨women in government are democratic and will not *suffer* the servility of subordination —H.J.Laski⟩ ⟨with frightful atrocities *suffered* mostly by the McCoys —A.F.Harlow⟩

—experience religion : to undergo religious conversion

ex·pe·ri·ence·able \-səbəl\ *adj* **:** capable of being experienced

experienced *adj* [fr. past part. of ²*experience*] **1** *archaic* **:** approved by test **:** TRIED ⟨counteract by ~ remedies every new tendency —Samuel Johnson⟩ **2 :** having experience **:** made skillful or wise through observation of or participation in a particular activity or in affairs generally **:** PRACTICED ⟨advocated so widely by thoughtful and ~ people in all classes —G.B.Shaw⟩ **3 :** encountered or undergone in the course of experience ⟨a cautious and guiltless reformation of ~ grievances —Archibald Alison⟩

ex·pe·ri·ence·less \-sləs\ *adj* **:** being without experience

experience meeting *n* **:** a meeting at which persons relate their religious experiences

ex·pe·ri·enc·er \-sə(r)\ *n* -s **:** one that experiences ⟨signs or symbols calling for one response or another on the part of the ~ —E.M.Bartlett⟩

experience rating *n* **:** merit rating (as in a state unemployment compensation system) that consists of the manual rate modified by the loss experience of the particular risk

experiences *pl of* EXPERIENCE, *pres 3d sing of* EXPERIENCE

experiencing *pres part of* EXPERIENCE

¹ex·pe·ri·ent \-nt\ *adj* [ME, fr. L *experient-, experiens*, pres. part. of *experiri* to try — more at ¹EXPERIENCE] **:** having experience

²experient \"\ *n* -s **:** a person undergoing an experience or having experience

ex·pe·ri·en·tial \ik¦==¦enchəl, (¦)ek¦-\ *adj* [ML *experientialis* experimental, fr. L *experientia* experience, test + *-alis* -al] **:** derived from, based on, or relating to experience **:** EMPIRICAL ⟨the rich ~ content of the teachings of the older philosophers —Benjamin Farrington⟩ — **ex·pe·ri·en·tial·ly** \-chəlē, -li\ *adv*

ex·pe·ri·en·tial·ism \ik,==¦chə,lizəm, (,)ek-\ *n* -s **:** a philosophical theory that experience is the source of all knowledge not purely deductive, formal, or tautological — compare EMPIRICISM

¹ex·pe·ri·en·tial·ist \-chələst\ *n* -s **:** one who believes in experientialism

²experientialist \"\ *or* **ex·pe·ri·en·tial·is·tic** \ik,==¦==¦listik, (,)ek-\ *adj* **:** of or relating to experientialism

experiential time *n* **:** SUBJECTIVE TIME

¹ex·per·i·ment \ik'sperəmənt, ek- *also* ÷-pir-\ *n* -s [ME, fr. MF *experiment*, fr. L *experimentum*, fr. *experiri* to try + *-mentum* -ment] **1 a :** a test or trial ⟨make another ~ of his suspicion —Shak.⟩ **b** (1) **:** a tentative procedure or policy; *esp* **:** one adopted in uncertainty as to whether it will answer the desired purpose or bring about the desired result ⟨is going to put this hope to the test by trying a political ~ of bold proportions —Harold Callender⟩ (2) **:** the tangible result of such a procedure or policy ⟨Benavente's earliest literary ~*s* were four little romantic fantasies published . . . in 1892 —*Current Biog.*⟩ **c :** an act or operation carried out under conditions determined by the experimenter (as in a laboratory) in order to discover some unknown principle or effect or to test, establish, or illustrate some suggested or known truth ⟨the ~*s* of the defendant's experts lead . . . to the opinion that a typhoid bacillus could not survive the journey —O.W.Holmes †1935⟩ **2** *obs* **:** EXPERIENCE ⟨by sad ~ I know how little weight my words with thee can find —John Milton⟩ **3** *obs* **:** EXPEDIENT, REMEDY ⟨you will find it a sure ~ for the quinsy —William Coles⟩ **4 :** the process or practice of trying or testing **:** EXPERIMENTATION ⟨the result of some centuries of ~ tended to raise rather than silence doubt —Henry Adams⟩

²ex·per·i·ment \-,ment, -,mənt —*see* ²-MENT\ *vb* -ED/-ING/-S [ME *experimenten*, fr. *experiment*, n.] *vt* **1** *obs* **:** to have experience of **:** EXPERIENCE, FEEL ⟨thy fatherly mercy . . . so often ~*ed* by me —Henry Hammond⟩ **2** *archaic* **:** to discover by experiment ⟨that may be easily ~*ed* in a small bird —Benjamin Martin⟩ **3** *archaic* **:** to make a trial or test of ⟨several articles were proposed to be ~*ed*, and if found good . . . to be confirmed —John Entick⟩ **~** *vi* **:** to engage in experimentation **:** make experiments ⟨the world has become a laboratory where immature and feverish minds ~ with unknown forces —John Buchan⟩ ⟨studied drawing and painting in an art school . . . and ~*ed* in painting at home —W.H.Downes⟩

¹ex·per·i·men·tal \ik¦sperə¦mentᵊl, ÷-pir-, ek¦-, ,ek,==¦==\ *adj* [ME, fr. ML *experimentalis*, fr. L *experimentum* + *-alis* -al] **1 :** of, relating to, or based on experience **:** EMPIRICAL ⟨misgivings, intensified . . . by ~ knowledge of the difficulties to be overcome, seem to hem me in —Arnold Bennett⟩ **2 a :** founded on, derived from, or discovered by experiment ⟨the heart of the ~ method is the direct control of the thing studied —B.F. Skinner⟩ **b :** given to or skilled in experiment ⟨~ philosophers could only indicate how gravity operated —S.F.Mason⟩ **3 a :** serving the ends of or used as a means of experimentation ⟨~ animals⟩ ⟨the ~ theater⟩ ⟨an ~ school⟩ **b** *of a disease* **:** intentionally produced esp. in laboratory animals for the purpose of study ⟨~ tuberculosis⟩ **4 :** relating to or having the characteristics of experiment **:** TENTATIVE ⟨~ flights will start this autumn — in fact, almost as soon as the two machines can be fitted with floats —*London Calling*⟩ ⟨free verse is not yet out of the ~ stage —J.L.Lowes⟩

²experimental \"\ *n* -s **1** *obs* **:** something learned by experience ⟨as to ~*s* . . . a mere novice —Samuel Richardson⟩ **2 a :** something experimental ⟨don't try ~*s* until you've had plenty of experience with the straight radio play —Josephina Niggli⟩ **b :** a plant or animal used in an experiment — compare CONTROL

experimental design *n* **:** a method of research in the social sciences (as sociology or psychology) in which a controlled experimental factor is subjected to special treatment for purposes of comparison with a factor kept constant

experimental engineer *n* **:** an engineer whose training or specialization is in experimental engineering

experimental engineering *n* **:** research and development work in some branch of engineering

ex·per·i·men·tal·ism \ik,==¦mentᵊl,izəm, (,)ek-\ *n* -s **1 a :** a theory advocating experimental or empirical principles and procedures **b :** pragmatist or instrumentalist theories, principles, and practices; *specif* **:** those of John Dewey and his followers — compare INSTRUMENTALISM, PRAGMATISM **2 :** the practice of relying on experiment

ex·per·i·men·tal·ist \-ᵊst\ *n* -s **1 :** a person conducting scientific experiments **2 :** one who likes to experiment as an innovator, artist, or explorer ⟨a bold ~ with paragraph and punctuation —H.G.Wells⟩

ex·per·i·men·tal·ize \-,īz\ *vi* -ED/-ING/-S **:** to make experiments **:** engage in experimentation

ex·per·i·men·tal·ly *pronunc at* ¹EXPERIMENTAL +ē *or* i\ *adv* **:** in an experimental manner: **a :** by experience **:** as a result of experience ⟨a king . . . ~ acquainted with the ways . . . of flatterers —Robert South⟩ **b :** by experiment **:** as an experiment ⟨the curvature of the runners was determined ~ —E.K. Kane⟩

experimental psychology *n* **:** PSYCHOLOGY 1b

ex·per·i·men·ta·tion \ik,==,mən·tāshən, (,)ek-, -,men-\ *n* -s **1 :** the act, process, or practice of making experiments ⟨a tendency among lay critics to confine ~ to scientists in the laboratory —John Dewey⟩ **2 :** an instance of experimentation **:** EXPERIMENT ⟨an outgrowth and culmination of numerous ~*s* and inventions —William Chomsky⟩

ex·per·i·men·ta·tive \ik,=='mentəd·iv, (,)ek-, -tətiv\ *adj* **:** inclined to experimentation **:** having the characteristics of an experiment

ex·per·i·men·ta·tor \ik'==mən-,tād·ə(r), ek-, -,men-, -ātə-, ik,==(,)=', =, (,)ek,==(,)=''==\ *n* -s [ML, fr. LL *experimentatus* (past part. of *experimentare* to test by experience, fr. L *experimentum* test) + L *-or*] **:** EXPERIMENTER

ex·per·i·men·tee \ik¦=(,)=¦tē, ek-\ *n* -s **:** one subjected to an experiment

ex·per·i·ment·er \='==,mentə(r)\ *or* **ex·per·i·men·tor** \",(,)=,=='men-,tō(ə)r, -ō(ə)\ *n* -s **:** one that experiments or conducts an experiment; *specif* **:** one that conducts an experiment in introspective psychology by arranging and determining the physical conditions of the observer's experience

ex·per·i·men·tize \='==mən-,tīz\ *vi* -ED/-ING/-S **:** EXPERIMENT

experiments *pl of* EXPERIMENT, *pres 3d sing of* EXPERIMENT

experiment station *n* **:** an establishment for scientific research in such fields as agriculture, biology, or meteorology where experiments are carried out, studies of practical application are made, and information is disseminated — called also *field station*

¹ex·pert \'ek,spər|t, -pə̄|, -pəi|, ik's-,ek's-; 'ek spə(r)|; *usu* |d·+V\ *adj* [ME, fr. MF & L; MF *expert*, fr. L *expertus*, past part. of *experiri* to try — more at ¹EXPERIENCE] **1** *obs* **:** proved or approved by test **:** EXPERIENCED ⟨his bark is stoutly timbered and his pilot of very ~ and approved allowance —Shak.⟩ **2 :** having special skill or knowledge derived from training or experience **:** knowing and ready as a result of wide experience or extensive practice **:** CLEVER, SKILLFUL ⟨an ~ bridge player⟩ ⟨an artist ~ in shaping his material into one comprehensive design —S.C.Chew⟩ ⟨had become ~ at learning scientific formulas and principles by heart —Upton Sinclair⟩ **3 a :** involving or displaying special skill or knowledge, extensive practice, or wide experience ⟨the acting was fresh, warm, self-assured . . . , and ~ —John Mason Brown⟩ ⟨the shoemaker whose . . . hands had never been so nimble and ~ —Charles Dickens⟩ **b :** of or relating to an expert ⟨his presence was frequently required in an ~ capacity at the League's general conferences —*Current Biog.*⟩ **syn** see PROFICIENT

²expert *like* ³EXPERT\ *vb* -ED/-ING/-S [in sense *vt* 1, fr. ME *experten*, fr. *expert*, adj.; in other senses, fr. ³*expert*] *vt* **1** *obs* **:** EXPERIENCE **2 :** to serve as an expert for ⟨wanted to know whatever happened to the man who had been sent to ~ their business —*Woman*⟩ **~** *vi* **:** to serve as or set oneself up as an expert ⟨read the newspapers and books of the countries on which they are ~*ing* —*Hispania*⟩

³ex·pert \'ek,spər|t, -pə̄|,-pəi| *also* -,spə(r)|, *usu* |d·+V\ *n* -s [F, fr. *expert*, adj.] **1 :** one who has acquired special skill in or knowledge of a particular subject through professional training or practical experience **:** AUTHORITY, SPECIALIST ⟨being an amateur . . . in philosophy he naturally looks for guidance to the ~*s* and professionals —William James⟩ ⟨this problem . . . was extremely difficult, and an ~ in geodesy was brought from the U.S. —V.G.Heiser⟩; *broadly* **:** one having skill or knowledge not possessed by mankind in general ⟨every man arranged his knapsack and blanket bag . . . with the practiced discretion of an ~ —E.K.Kane⟩ **2 a :** the highest classification given to a member of the military for skill in the use of arms **b :** a soldier having such a classification

syn ADEPT, ARTIST, ARTISTE, VIRTUOSO, WIZARD: each of these six nouns designates a person who shows mastery in a subject, an art, or a profession, or who shows unusual skill in execution, performance, or technique. EXPERT implies experience, knowledge, and achievement, and usu. recognition as an authority in the subject, art, or profession ⟨an *expert* in foreign policy⟩ ⟨an *expert* in mathematics⟩ ⟨an *expert* at skiing⟩ ⟨an *expert* in the art of evasion⟩ ADEPT, usu. connoting understanding of the mysteries of an art or craft or penetration into secrets beyond the reach of exact science, implies, in the most modern use, subtlety or ingenuity ⟨an *adept* in religions of the East⟩ ⟨an *adept* in the Platonic philosophy —Benjamin Farrington⟩ ⟨an *adept* at understatement —John Buchan⟩ ARTIST stresses extraordinary skill in execution usu. involving a high degree of imagination or taste ⟨an *artist* at flower arrangement⟩ ⟨an *artist* in manipulating public opinion —Samuel Lubell⟩ ⟨an *artist* at invective —W.A.Swanberg⟩ ARTISTE, orig. applied to actors, singers, and dancers, is now also often humorously applied to workers in crafts where adeptness and taste are indispensable ⟨a cook, a tragedian, or a music-hall *artiste* —Osbert Sitwell⟩ ⟨a Hollywood musical about life among the radio *artistes* —John McCarten⟩ ⟨a tightrope *artiste* quickly crossing the wire —George Bellairs⟩ VIRTUOSO, usu. applied to musicians, esp. pianists or violinists, stresses the display of great technical skill or brilliance in execution ⟨one of the piano *virtuosos* of international reputation —*Current Biog.*⟩ ⟨a frightfully wonderful *virtuoso* in the old art of love —G.B.Shaw⟩ WIZARD implies a knowledge or skill so great that it seems to border on the magical ⟨a mathematical *wizard*⟩ ⟨a *wizard* with cards —Malcolm Cowley⟩ ⟨a *wizard* in calculating distance —*Current Biog.*⟩

ex·per·tise \,ek,spər'tēz, -per-\ *n* -s [F, fr. MF, expertness, fr. *expert*, adj.] **1 :** expert opinion or commentary ⟨is there an ~ on the question of the relative importance of preserving competition which should induce judges to defer to commissioners? —L.B.Schwartz⟩ **2 :** specialized skill or technical knowledge **:** expertness in a particular field **:** KNOW-HOW ⟨the mental commodity most in demand will be practical wisdom rather than specialized ~ —Walter Moberly⟩ ⟨his bravery, his sure judgment in the most difficult situations, his ~ in the science of war —H.L.Merillat⟩

ex·pert·ism \'ek,spər|d·,izəm, -,spə̄|, -,spəi|, -,spə(r)|, |,tiz-\ *n* -s **:** EXPERTISE 2 ⟨looks like a doctor . . . who in his ~ has discovered . . . how to prolong his years —Janet Flanner⟩

ex·pert·ize \-d·,īz, -,tīz\ *vb* -ED/-ING/-S *vi* **:** to give a professional opinion usu. after careful study or examination ⟨would . . . be pointless for me to ~ on the specific subject —R.F. Cassidy⟩ **~** *vt* **:** to examine and give expert judgment on ⟨a philatelic society which ~*s* the stamps of its members for a moderate fee —R.B.Yardley⟩

ex·pert·ly *pronunc at* ¹EXPERT + lē *or* li\ *adv* **:** in an expert manner **:** ADROITLY

ex·pert·ness *pronunc at* ¹EXPERT +nəs\ *n* -ES **:** the quality or state of being expert **:** SKILL

ex·pi·a·ble \'ekspēəbəl\ *adj* [LL *expiabilis*, fr. L *expiare* to expiate + *-abilis* -able] **:** capable of being expiated **:** ATONABLE

¹ex·pi·ate \'ekspē,āt\ *vb* -ED/-ING/-S [L *expiatus*, past part. of *expiare* to atone for, purify, fr. *ex-* ¹ex- + *piare* to appease, atone for — more at PIOUS] *vt* **1** *obs* **:** to put an end to **:** cause to die out ⟨somewhat to ~ their savage fury —Thomas Adams⟩ **2** *obs* **:** to purify with sacred rites **:** CLEANSE ⟨he lustrated and *expiated* the city —Thomas Stanley⟩ **3 a :** to extinguish the guilt incurred by **:** make propitiation for ⟨trying to ~ by justice and mercy the dark deeds of his bloodstained youth —Charles Kingsley⟩ **b :** to pay the penalty for ⟨the casual offender ~*s* his offense in the company of defectives —B.N.Cardozo⟩ **c :** to make amends for ⟨sought to ~ their failure by adding a few sprigs or posies —Lewis Mumford⟩ **4 :** to ward off by sacred rites **:** AVERT ⟨disaster shall fall upon you, which you will not be able to ~ —Isa 47:11 (RSV)⟩ **~** *vi* **:** to make expiation ⟨we are willing enough to repent, but the Higher Law requires that we ~ —W.L.Sullivan⟩

²expiate *adj* [L *expiatus*, past part. of *expiare*] *obs* **:** fully come ⟨make haste; the hour of death is ~ —Shak.⟩

ex·pi·a·tion \ˌekspēˈāshən\ *n* -s [ME *expiacioun*, fr. L *expiation-*, *expiatio*, fr. *expiatus* + *-ion-*, *-io* -ion] **1 :** the act of making atonement **:** the extinguishing of guilt by suffering or penalty ⟨the tree remains a symbol of agony and ~ —P.B. Sears⟩ **2 :** the means by which atonement is made **:** something done as an act of atonement ⟨the payment of money was ever welcomed as the ready ~ of crime —J.A.Froude⟩ — **ex·pi·a·tion·al** \ˌekspēˈāshənᵊl, -shnəl\ *adj*

ex·pi·a·tive \ˈekspēˌād·iv\ *adj* **:** EXPIATORY

ex·pi·a·tor \-ād·ə(r)\ *n* -s [LL, fr. L *expiatus* + *-or*] *n* -s **:** one that expiates

ex·pi·a·to·ry \ˈekspēəˌtōrē\ *adj* [LL *expiatorius*, fr. L *expiatus* + *-orius* -ory] **:** having power to make expiation **:** serving to expiate **:** ATONING ⟨the sacrifice ~ for our offenses was to be a lamb without blemish —Isaac Barrow⟩

ex·pi·la·tion \ˌekspəˈlāshən, -ˌspīˈ-\ *n* -s [L *expilation-*, *expilatio*, fr. *expilatus* (past part. of *expilare* to plunder, fr. *ex-* ¹ex- + *-pilare*, perh. akin to L *pila* pillar, pier) + *-ion-*, *-io* -ion — more at PILE] *archaic* **:** the act of plundering **:** SPOLIATION ⟨whence . . . proceeds this ravenous ~ of the state —Samuel Daniel⟩

ex·pi·ra·tion \ˌekspəˈrāshən *sometimes* -(ˌ)spīˈ- *or* -ˌspē-, *chiefly Brit* ˌekˌspīˈ-\ *n* -s [ME *expiracioun*, fr. L *expiration-*, *exspiration-*, *expiratio*, *exspiratio*, fr. *expiratus*, *exspiratus* (past part. of *expirare*, *exspirare*) + *-ion-*, *-io* -ion] **1 :** the act, action, or process of expiring: **a** (1) **:** the action or process of releasing air from the lungs through the nose or mouth (2) **:** the escape of carbon dioxide from the body protoplasm (as through the blood and lungs or by diffusion) **b** *obs* **:** the emission of volatile matter **:** EXHALATION ⟨the true cause of cold is an ~ from the globe of the earth —Francis Bacon⟩ **c** *archaic* **:** the last emission of breath **:** DEATH ⟨the attendants did not discern the exact time of his ~ —Samuel Johnson⟩ **2 :** the fact of coming to an end **:** TERMINATION, CLOSE, EXTINCTION ⟨what effect the ~ of the excess-profits tax will have on corporate giving —J.A.Morris b. 1904⟩ **3 :** something that is expired or produced by breathing out ⟨the aspirate "he" which is . . . a gentle ~ —Granville Sharp⟩

ex·pi·ra·tor \ˈ=(ˌ)=ˌrād·ə(r)\ *n* -s [*expire* + *-ator*] **:** one that expires; *specif* **:** an instrument for sending out a stream of air, gas, or vapor

ex·pir·a·to·ry \ikˈspīrəˌtōrē, ek-, -tȯr-, -ri\ *adj* [prob. fr. *expiration*, after such pairs as E *exploration*: *exploratory*] **1 :** of, relating to, or employed in the expiration of air from the lungs ⟨the ~ muscles⟩ **2** *of accent* **:** characterized by variations dependent on variation in force of expiration — compare DYNAMIC, STRESS ACCENT

ex·pire \ikˈspī(ə)r, ek-\ *vb* -ED/-ING/-S [ME *expiren*, fr. MF or L; MF *expirer*, fr. L *expirare*, *exspirare*, fr. *ex-* ¹ex- + *spirare* to breathe — more at SPIRIT] *vi* **1 :** to breathe one's last breath **:** DIE ⟨was carried home by his two old counselors and soon *expired* —D.G.Hoffman⟩ **2 :** to come to an end **:** CEASE: **a :** to reach a close (as of a period of time) **:** TERMINATE ⟨the period of ten years for which the court was established *expired* in 1918 —B.H.Williams⟩ **b :** to become void through the passage of time ⟨now all his powerful patents have *expired* —C.B.Fisher⟩ **c :** to become extinct **:** die out ⟨the title of the daughters *expired* on the birth of the son —William Cruise⟩ **3 :** to emit the breath ⟨the whales . . . *expired* with a rushing sound the instant the blowhole was exposed —P.H.Gosse⟩ **4** *obs* **:** to burst forth **:** fly out with or as if with a blast ⟨furious winds . . . pent in blind caverns, struggling to ~ —George Sandys⟩ ~ *vt* **1** *obs* **:** to breathe out in the act of dying ⟨as soon as their apostle had *expired* his last breath —Jeremy Taylor⟩ **2** *obs* **:** to bring to an end **:** CONCLUDE ⟨would ~ the misery of his unspeakable tormenting uncertainty —Thomas Nash⟩ **3 :** to breathe out from or as if from the lungs **:** release from the nose or mouth in the process of respiration ⟨the basal metabolism test . . . measures the amount of carbon dioxide *expired* by the lungs —J.D. Ratcliff⟩ — distinguished from *inspire* **4** *archaic* **:** to give off **:** EXHALE, EMIT ⟨every shrub ~s perfume —Charles Churchill⟩

ex·pir·ee \ˌekˌspīˈrē; ikˌspīˈrē, ekˌ-\ *n* -s **:** an Australian convict whose time of penal servitude has expired

ex·pir·er \ikˈspīrə(r), ek-\ *n* -s **:** one that expires

ex·pir·ing·ly *adv* [*expiring* (pres. part. of *expire*) + *-ly*] **:** in the manner of one expiring ⟨spoke in an ~ weak voice⟩

ex·pi·ry \ikˈspīrē, ekˈs-, ˈekˌs-; ˈekspərē\ *n* -ES [*expire* + *-y*] **:** EXPIRATION: **a :** exhalation of breath ⟨that deep intake of breath, that brief and passionate ~ were not the components of a sigh —Aldous Huxley⟩ **b :** DEATH ⟨on ~, the rebellious soul shall other bodies enter —P.J.Bailey⟩ **c :** DESTRUCTION, EXTINCTION ⟨ancient history ought . . . not to cease with the ~ of the Roman Empire —William Taylor †1836⟩ **d :** TERMINATION, CLOSE, END ⟨at the ~ of these eight years he dismissed the subject and sold the books —A.N.Whitehead⟩; *esp* **:** the termination of a time or period fixed by law, contract, or agreement ⟨on the ~ of the State Governor's term of office —Noreen Routledge⟩

ex·pis·cate \ˈekspəˌskāt, ekˈspiˌs-\ *vt* -ED/-ING/-S [L *expiscatus*, past part. of *expiscari*, fr. *ex-* ¹ex- + *piscari* to fish, fr. *piscis* fish — more at FISH] *chiefly Scot* **:** to discover by careful examination or investigation **:** search out ⟨has with much ingenuity endeavored to ~ the truth —W.L.Alexander⟩ — **ex·pis·ca·tion** \ˌekspəˈskāshən, -(ˌ)spiˈs-\ *n* -s *chiefly Scot* — **ex·pis·ca·to·ry** \ekˈspiskəˌtōri\ *adj*, *chiefly Scot* **:** tending to expiscate **:** SEARCHING

ex·plain \ikˈsplān, ek-\ *vb* -ED/-ING/-S [ME *explanen*, fr. L *explanare* to level, make plain or clear, fr. *ex-* ¹ex- + *-planare*, fr. *planus* level, flat — more at FLOOR] *vt* **1 a :** to make manifest **:** present in detail **:** EXPOUND, DISCLOSE ⟨promised to ~ the secret of his success⟩ **b :** to make plain or understandable **:** clear of complexities or obscurity **:** INTERPRET, CLARIFY ⟨a commentary that ~s the more difficult passages of the poem⟩ **c :** to give the meaning or significance of **:** provide an understanding of ⟨~*ed* the concept in straightforward language⟩ **d :** to give the reason for or cause of **:** account for ⟨was unable to ~ his strange conduct⟩ **2** *obs* **:** to spread or open out **:** UNFOLD, EXPAND ⟨the horse chestnut is . . . ready to ~ its leaf —John Evelyn⟩ **3 a :** to show the logical development of **:** EXPLICATE ⟨~ an intellectual argument⟩ **b :** to subsume under a scientific theory or exhibit as an instance of a scientific law ⟨~ natural events⟩ **c :** to deduce from stated premises **:** PROVE ⟨~ a mathematical result⟩ **4 :** to state by way of explanation — used in direct or indirect discourse ~ *vi* **1 :** to give an explanation ⟨a poet whose words intimate rather than define, suggest rather than . . . ~ —Irwin Edman⟩ **2** *obs* **:** to speak one's mind ⟨the public . . . begins to ~ upon him —Earl of Chesterfield⟩

syn ACCOUNT (*for*), JUSTIFY, RATIONALIZE: to EXPLAIN is to clarify or make acceptable to the understanding something that it finds mysterious, causeless, or inconsistent ⟨*explain* an inconsistency in a financial report⟩ ⟨there is no comprehensive theory that *explains* these phenomena⟩ ⟨the mountainous character of Greece *explains* its division into a crowd of petty states —Edward Clodd⟩ To ACCOUNT (*for*) suggests a making acceptable by the fitting of the thing to be accounted for into some acceptable scheme (as logical or mathematical consistency, or an order of nature) ⟨their presence could not be *accounted for* by some temporary catastrophe, such as the Mosaic Flood —S.F.Mason⟩ ⟨the presence of buffalo *accounted for* the character of the Indian civilizations frontiersmen encountered when they entered the Great Plains —R.A. Billington⟩ ⟨*account for* the loss of a company's money⟩ To JUSTIFY is to account for or explain, or attempt to account for or explain, to one's or someone's satisfaction, esp. by explaining away guilt or blame ⟨the playhouse was forced to *justify* itself as a serious cultural endeavor —*Amer. Guide Series: Pa.*⟩ ⟨decided after the second day of the hearings that not enough people were watching to *justify* the expense —Gilbert Seldes⟩ ⟨an opinion *justified* by the facts⟩ To RATIONALIZE in an older sense stresses the idea of something acceptable to reason but in modern use signifies frequently to justify by false, esp. self-deceptive, reasoning ⟨cooperation with those from whom we differ is possible only if we *rationalize* our beliefs and thus make them intelligible to those having different backgrounds —M.R.Cohen⟩ ⟨we *rationalize* our cumbersome habit, taking for granted or explaining that this custom is intrinsically and logically best —A.L.Kroeber⟩

— **explain oneself :** to make clear the meaning of one's statements or the reasons for one's conduct

ex·plain·able \-nəbəl\ *adj* **:** capable of being explained

explain away *vt* **1 :** to get rid of by or as if by explanation ⟨was trying to speak some words that . . . would *explain away* all the mistakes and misunderstandings of life —Ellen Glasgow⟩ **2 :** to minimize the significance of by or as if by explanation ⟨evidence which it was hard to *explain away* —A.G.N.Flew⟩

ex·plain·er \-nə(r)\ *n* -s **:** one that explains

ex·pla·nan·dum \ˌeksplәˈnandəm\ *n*, *pl* **explanan·da** \-də\ [NL, fr. L, neut. of *explanandus*, gerundive of *explanare* to explain, make plain or clear] **:** a word or an expression whose meaning is to be explained — used chiefly in philosophy; contrasted with *explanans*

ex·pla·nans \ekˈsplāˌnanz\ *n*, *pl* **ex·pla·nan·tia** \ˌeksplәˈnanchēә\ [NL, fr. L, pres. part. of *explanare*] **:** the meaning of a word or an expression — used chiefly in philosophy; contrasted with *explanandum*

ex·pla·nate \ˈeksplәˌnāt, ekˈsplāˌn-\ *adj* [L *explanatus*, past part. of *explanare* to level] *biol* **:** extending outward in a flat form

ex·pla·na·tion \ˌeksplәˈnāshәn\ *n* -s [ME *explanacioun*, fr. L *explanation-*, *explanatio*, fr. *explanatus* (past part. of *explanare* to level, make plain or clear) + *-ion-*, *-io* -ion] **1 :** the act or process of explaining **:** EXPOSITION, INTERPRETATION, CLARIFICATION ⟨~ consists in successfully comparing new phenomena with older and more familiar ones —J.H. Woodger⟩ **2 :** something that explains or that results from the act or process of explaining; *specif* **:** a statement incorporating an explanation ⟨the ~s offered for mistakes followed a set pattern —V.G.Heiser⟩ **3 :** a mutual discussion designed to correct a misunderstanding or reconcile differences **:** RECONCILIATION ⟨another person I should like an ~ with —Elizabeth Bowen⟩

ex·plan·a·tive \ikˈsplanәd·iv, ek-\ *adj* [LL *explanativus*, fr. L *explanatus* + *-ivus* -ive] **:** EXPLANATORY — **ex·plan·a·tive·ly** \-d·әvlē\ *adv*

ex·pla·na·tor \ˈeksplәˌnād·ә(r)\ *n* -s [L, fr. *explanatus* + *-or*] **:** EXPLAINER

ex·plan·a·to·ri·ly \ikˌsplanәˈtōrәlē, ekˌ-, ˌekˌ==ˈ===, -tȯr-, -li\ *adv* **:** in an explanatory manner **:** by way of explanation

ex·plan·a·to·ry \ikˈsplanәˌtōrē, ek-, -tȯr-, -ri\ *adj* [LL *explanatorius*, fr. L *explanatus* + *-orius* -ory] **:** serving or disposed to explain **:** offering explanation ⟨textual and ~ . . . notes appear at the bottom of the page —I.M.Price⟩ ⟨was surprised to find herself cool, ~, and reasonable —Elizabeth Bowen⟩

¹ex·plant \(ˈ)eks-\ *vt* [*ex-* + *plant*, v.] **:** to remove (living tissue) to a place or medium outside the natural habitat esp. in tissue culture — **ex·plan·ta·tion** \ˌeks+\ *n* -s

²ex·plant \ˈeks+ˌ-\ *n* -s **:** living tissue removed from its place in the body and placed in an artificial medium for tissue culture

ex·ple·ment \ˈeksplәmәnt\ *n* -s [L *explementum* something that fills, fr. *explēre* + *-mentum* -ment] **:** the difference between an angle and 360 degrees — **ex·ple·men·tal** \ˌeksplәˈmentᵊl\ *adj*

ex·ple·men·ta·ry angle \ˌeksplәˌmentәrē-, -n·trē-\ *n* [*explement* + *-ary*] **:** either of two angles whose sum is 360 degrees

explete *vt* -ED/-ING/-S [ME *expleiten*, *expleten*, partly fr. MF *expleiter*, *espleiter*, *exploiter*, *esploiter* to achieve, perform & partly fr. L *expletus*, past part. of *explēre* — more at EXPLOIT] *obs* **:** SATISFY, COMPLETE — **expletion** *n* -s *obs*

¹ex·ple·tive \ˈeksplәd·iv, ǀtiv, *chiefly Brit* ekˈsplē| *or* ikˈs-\ *adj* [LL *expletivus*, fr. L *expletus* (past part. of *explēre* to fill, fr. *ex-* ¹ex- + *plēre* to fill) + *-ivus* -ive; akin to L *plenus* full — more at FULL] **1 a :** serving to fill up or added to fill out ⟨~ phrases . . . to plump his speech —Isaac Barrow⟩ **b** *of a word* **:** used as a grammatical subject or grammatical object **2 :** marked by the use of expletives ⟨resigned his post in a letter of great ~ violence —F.M.Ford⟩

²expletive \"\ *n* -s **1 a :** a syllable, word, or phrase inserted to fill a vacancy (as in a sentence or a metrical line) without adding to the sense ⟨while ~s their feeble aid do join and ten low words oft creep in one dull line —Alexander Pope⟩; *esp* **:** an expletive word (as *it* in "it is easy to say so" or *it* in "make it clear which you prefer") **b :** an exclamatory word or phrase; *esp* **:** one that is obscene or profane ⟨wrote with chalk on the steps and doors the old four-letter Anglo-Saxon ~s —Shelby Foote⟩ **2 :** one that serves as a filler or is added as a filling ⟨a gooseberry tart with other ornamental ~s of the same kind —Richard Graves⟩ ⟨he is a sort of ~ at the table serving to stop gaps —O.W.Holmes †1935⟩

ex·ple·to·ry \ˈeksplәˌtōrē; ekˈsplēd·әrē, ikˈs-\ *adj* [L *expletus* + E *-ory*] **:** EXPLETIVE

ex·plic·a·ble \ekˈsplikәbәl, ikˈs-, ˈek(ˌ)s-, ˈeksplәk-\ *adj* [L *explicabilis*, fr. *explicare* + *-abilis* -able] **:** capable of being explicated **:** EXPLAINABLE

ex·pli·can·dum \ˌeksplәˈkandәm\ *n*, *pl* **explican·da** \-dә\ [NL, fr. L, neut. of *explicandus*, gerundive of *explicare* to explicate] **:** a word or an expression whose meaning is to be explicated — used chiefly in philosophy; contrasted with *explicans*

ex·pli·cans \ˈeksplәˌkanz\ *n*, *pl* **explican·tia** \ˌeksplәˈkanchēә\ [NL, fr. L, pres. part. of *explicare*] **:** the meaning of a word or an expression — used chiefly in philosophy; contrasted with *explicandum*

¹ex·pli·cate \ˈeksplәˌkāt\ *vt* -ED/-ING/-S [L *explicatus*, past part. of *explicare*, lit., to unfold, fr. *ex-* ¹ex- + *plicare* to fold — more at PLY] **1 a :** to give a detailed account of **:** EXPOUND, DISCLOSE ⟨an unfairness . . . which this would not be quite the proper place for *explicating* —Charles Lamb⟩ **b :** to unfold the meaning or sense of **:** INTERPRET, CLARIFY ⟨trying to ~ not vocabulary or techniques but the experience out of which these works were written —Perry Miller⟩ **2** *obs* **:** to lay open **:** UNFOLD, EXPAND ⟨the rose of Jericho will . . . ~ its flowers —Sir Thomas Browne⟩ **3** *obs* **:** DISENTANGLE, EXTRICATE ⟨no way to ~ the Kingdom out of those intricacies —Edward Hyde⟩ **4 :** to develop what is involved or implied in (as a statement or notion) **:** analyze logically ⟨this principle has been *explicated* into three general axioms —Francis Bowen⟩

²explicate *adj* [L *explicatus*, past part. of *explicare*] *obs* **:** EXPLICATED

ex·pli·ca·tion \ˌeksplәˈkāshәn\ *n* -s [L *explication-*, *explicatio*, fr. *explicatus* + *-ion-*, *-io* -ion] **1 :** the act or process of explicating **:** EXPLANATION ⟨he quite naturally brought to the ~ of those principles tastes and principles which were very much of his time —C.S.Singleton⟩ **2 :** something that explicates or that results from the act or process of explicating: as **a :** a detailed description, exposition, or interpretation ⟨a precise ~ of how to drive an automobile —C.A.Fenton⟩ **b :** a statement containing a logical analysis

ex·pli·ca·tion de texte \ˌeksplēkäsyōⁿd(ә)tekst\ *n*, *pl* **explications de texte** \"\ [F, lit., text explanation] **1 :** a method of literary criticism involving a detailed examination of each part of a work and an exposition of the relationship of these parts to each other and to the whole work **2 :** a critical analysis employing explication de texte

¹ex·plic·a·tive \(ˈ)ekˈsplikәd·iv, ikˈs-, ˈeksplәˌkād-\ *adj* **:** serving to explicate **:** EXPLANATORY; *specif* **:** serving to explain logically what is contained in the subject ⟨an ~ proposition⟩ — **ex·plic·a·tive·ly** \-d·әvlē\ *adv*

²explicative \"\ *n* -s **:** an explicative expression

ex·pli·ca·tor \ˈeksplәˌkād·ә(r)\ *n* -s [L, fr. *explicatus* + *-or*] **:** one that explicates **:** EXPOSITOR

ex·pli·ca·to·ry \ekˈsplikәˌtōrē, ikˈs-, ˈeksplәkәˌt-; ˈeksplәˈkād·әrē\ *adj* **:** EXPLICATIVE

ex·pli·ca·tum \ˌeksplәˈkād·әm, -kād-\ *n*, *pl* **explica·ta** \-d·ә\ [NL, fr. L, neut. of *explicatus*, past part. of *explicare*] **:** EXPLICANS

¹ex·pli·cit \ˈeksplәˌkit *sometimes* ekˈsplisәt\ *n* -s [LL, prob. short for L *explicitus* unrolled, past part. of *explicare* to unroll, unfold; fr. the gradual unrolling of a scroll during the course of writing on it and its completely unrolled state when the writing is finished] **:** a statement formerly used at the end of a book or manuscript or section of a book or manuscript (as to indicate authorship or place and date of copying)

²ex·plic·it \ikˈsplisәt, ek-, *usu* -sәd·+V\ *adj* [F or ML; F *explicite*, fr. ML *explicitus*, fr. L, free from obstacles, fr. *explicitus*, past part. of *explicare* to unfold — more at EXPLICATE] **1 :** characterized by full clear expression **:** being without vagueness or ambiguity **:** leaving nothing implied **:** UNEQUIVOCAL ⟨that there might be no mistake as to the meaning of his satire Brackenridge set down . . . an ~ statement of his purpose —V.L.Parrington⟩ — compare IMPLICIT **2 :** clearly and fully developed or formulated **:** DEFINITE ⟨how impossible it is . . . to have a clear and ~ notion of that which is infinite —Robert South⟩ **3** *obs* **:** having no complexities **:** SIMPLE ⟨and that commonly called the plot, whether intricate or ~ —John Milton⟩ **4 :** unreserved and unambiguous in expression **:** speaking fully and clearly **:** OUTSPOKEN ⟨he would not be more ~ about it; the wells of his loquacity were dried up —C.S.Forester⟩ **5 :** externally visible **:** clearly observable ⟨~ movements⟩ ⟨an ~ pattern of culture⟩ **6 :** involving direct payment **:** MONETARY ⟨~ costs⟩ ⟨~ rent⟩

syn DEFINITE, SPECIFIC, EXPRESS, CATEGORICAL: the chief emphasis of the word EXPLICIT is on the notion of plain distinct expression that leaves no need for the reader or hearer to infer; the antonym of this word is *implicit*. It may also connote plainness, frankness, force, or fullness ⟨these things are implicit in Augustine and existed before him: with Gregory they have become *explicit*, elaborated, and insisted on with recurrent emphasis —H.O.Taylor⟩ ⟨he [Hamilton] pointed out that all the powers of the national government could not be set down in *explicit* words, for that would mean intolerable detail —Allan Nevins & H.S.Commager⟩ DEFINITE, which has for its antonym *indefinite*, stresses the clear certainty of wording that leaves nothing unclear or doubtful, certainty sometimes attained by unadorned, flat statement, sometimes by careful limitation or definition ⟨do the quinine derivatives act by attaching themselves to the bacteria or by changing the body fluids? It was a simple, clear, *definite* question —Sinclair Lewis⟩ SPECIFIC indicates on the one hand being specified, particular, or individual or on the other marked by particulars and details sufficiently or amply treated ⟨religion refers to the fundamental issues of human existence, while magic always turns round *specific*, concrete, and detailed problems —B.K.Malinowski⟩ ⟨captions and legends in these pages are often mere generalized comments, devoid of *specific* information — e.g., identification of the illustration as to date, place, photographer —*Saturday Rev.*⟩ EXPRESS stresses the idea that whatever is under consideration has been expressed and not left to tacit understanding; it may suggest stress, cogency, directness, pointedness, or special emphasis in expression ⟨if no *express* acknowledgment of these rights had been made . . . they were practically observed —J.R.Green⟩ ⟨an *express* provision of the act required that the codes should not promote monopolies —F.D.Roosevelt⟩ CATEGORICAL stresses a positive or absolute absence of reserving qualification, demurrer, tentative condition ⟨the question is always *categorical*: is this man guilty or not —W.G.Sumner⟩ ⟨when documentary testimony was not the appropriate answer, Secretary Chapman gave specific *categorical* replies under oath —*Saturday Rev.*⟩

explicit definition *n* **:** a definition giving an exact equivalent for the term defined — contrasted with *contextual definition*

explicit function *n* **:** a mathematical function containing only the independent variable or variables — opposed to *implicit function*

ex·plic·it·ly *adv* **:** in an explicit manner **:** EXPRESSLY

ex·plic·it·ness *n* -ES **:** the quality or state of being explicit **:** CLEARNESS, DIRECTNESS

explicit relation *n* **:** a functional relation in mathematics in which the dependent variable is stated directly in terms of the independent variable

ex·plode \ikˈsplōd, ek-\ *vb* -ED/-ING/-S [L *explodere*, *explaudere*, fr. *ex-* ¹ex- + *plodere*, *plaudere* to clap, applaud] *vt* **1** *archaic* **:** to drive from the stage by noisy disapproval **:** hoot off **2 :** to expose decisively the hollowness or invalidity of **:** bring into disrepute or discredit ⟨*exploding* conventional theories of courtship and marriage —H.L.Myers⟩ ⟨~ a rumor⟩ **3 a :** to cause to explode or burst noisily **:** DETONATE ⟨~ powder⟩ ⟨~ a bomb⟩ **b :** to cause the fibers of (wood chips) to separate into pulp under high steam pressure which is suddenly released **c :** to hit (a golf ball) out of a sand trap with an explosion shot **d :** to separate the covers and panes or leaves of (a stamp booklet) by removing the staples **e :** to utter with explosion (sense 2d) ~ *vi* **1 a** (1) **:** to undergo rapid combustion with sudden release of energy in the form of heat that causes violent expansion of the gases formed and consequent production of great disruptive pressure and a loud noise ⟨dynamite ~s⟩ (2) **:** to undergo an atomic nuclear reaction with similar but more violent results ⟨an atom bomb ~s⟩ (3) **:** to burst violently as a result of pressure from within ⟨a steam boiler may ~⟩ **b :** to hit a golf ball out of a sand trap with an explosion shot **2 :** to give a sudden, strong, and usu. noisy release to an emotion **:** burst forth ⟨*exploded* with wrath⟩ ⟨race tension was *exploding* all around us —H.W.Young⟩ ⟨he is apt to ~ into picturesque profanity —Carl Markwith⟩ **3 :** to resound with a sudden loud noise **4 :** to shatter esp. with a loud report ⟨threw a glass on the stone floor and it *exploded* like a shot —Jean Stafford⟩ **5 :** to suggest an explosion (as in appearance or effect) ⟨clay jars *exploded* with bouquets —Jack Kerouac⟩ ⟨a clever aphorism . . . ~s with a brilliant shower of sparks —V.L.Parrington⟩ ⟨the road inches deep in rough ice and the blizzard *exploding* in the middle of the windshield —Joyce Cary⟩ ⟨when your fist *explodes* against the target —Jack Dempsey⟩ **6 a :** to change state or appearance expansively and suddenly or rapidly ⟨touched by a flicker of flame, the parched woods ~ —W.B.Greeley⟩ **:** break or burst forth ⟨maples have *exploded* into clouds of rosy buds —Walter O'Meara⟩ ⟨~ into a grin⟩ ⟨suburbs are *exploding* outward —*New Republic*⟩ **b :** to come to a sudden violent breaking point or point of release ⟨this situation at last ~s in an overt action —Howard Nemerov⟩ — **explode a bombshell :** to introduce a proposal, theory, statement, or item of information unexpectedly and forcefully so as to compel attention and stimulate action ⟨*exploded a bombshell* that was followed, for the most part, by a stunned silence —Oliver La Farge⟩

exploded *adj* [fr. past part. of EXPLODE] **:** showing the parts (as of an apparatus or machine) separated but in positions that indicate their correct relationship to each other ⟨an ~ view of a carburetor⟩ — compare PHANTOM

ex·plod·ent \-dᵊnt\ *n* -s [*explode* + *-ent*] **:** EXPLOSIVE

ex·plod·er \-dә(r)\ *n* -s **1 :** one that explodes **2 :** a device for firing or detonating an explosive charge: as **a :** BLASTING CAP **b :** BLASTING MACHINE **c :** SQUIB

¹ex·ploit \ˈekˌsplȯit *also* ikˈs- *or* ekˈs-, *usu* -ȯid·+V\ *n* -s [ME *exploit*, *expleit*, *esploit*, *espleit* outcome, success, enterprise, fr. OF, accomplishment, success, revenue, fr. L *explicitum*, neut. of *explicitus*, past part. of *explicare* to unfold, set in order — more at EXPLICATE] **:** DEED, ACT; *esp* **:** a notable or heroic act **:** FEAT ⟨the ~s of Columbus⟩ ⟨a gallant ~⟩

²ex·ploit \ikˈsplȯit, (ˈ)ekˈs-, *usu* -ȯid·+V\ *vt* -ED/-ING/-S [ME *expleiten*, *esploiten*, *espleiten*, fr. MF *exploiter*, *expleiter*, *esploiter*, *espleiter*, fr. OF *exploitier*, *expleitier*, *esploitier*, *espleitier*, fr. *exploit*, *expleit*, *esploit*, *espleit*, n.] **1** *obs* **:** ACHIEVE, PERFORM **2 a** (1) **:** to turn (a natural resource) to economic account **:** WORK, CULTIVATE ⟨~ a mine⟩ ⟨~ the virgin lands of the West⟩ (2) **:** to take advantage of **:** UTILIZE ⟨~*ed* his distinctive talent for book illustration —Herbert Read⟩ ⟨~*ing* the materials . . . and the techniques of our time —*N.Y. Times*⟩ **b :** to make use of meanly or unjustly for one's own advantage or profit **:** take undue advantage of ⟨~s his friends⟩; *specif* **:** to utilize the labor power of (a person) without giving a just or equivalent return ⟨struck by the degree in which the peasant was ~*ed* by the noble —M.H. Dodwell⟩

ex·ploit·able \-ȯid·әbәl, -ȯitә-\ *adj* **:** capable of being exploited

ex·ploi·ta·tion \ˌekˌsplȯiˈtāshәn *sometimes* ˌik-\ *n* -s [F, fr. *exploiter* to exploit (fr. OF *exploitier*, *expleitier*, *esploitier*, *espleitier* to achieve, perform) + *-ation*] **1 :** an act of exploiting ⟨here we get incessant ~ of the author's social and political observations —F.B.Millett⟩ ⟨widespread ~ of antibiotics for nonmedical use —*Americana Annual*⟩: as **a :** utilization or working of a natural resource ⟨the sheep . . . finds its living by ~ of pastures —Allan Fraser⟩ ⟨~ of water power⟩;

sometimes : a wasteful or destructive utilization of a natural resource ⟨the spectacular results of uncontrolled ~ of the soil . . . awakened the American people to their danger —K.D. White⟩ **b** : an unjust or improper use of another person for one's own profit or advantage ⟨~ of the tourist destroys trade —*Americas*⟩; *specif* : utilization of the labor power of another person without giving a just or equivalent return ⟨that magic word "colonies", which means "trusteeship" to an Englishman and ~ in Karachi or Delhi —*Economist*⟩ ⟨capitalist ~⟩ **c** : coaction between organisms in which one is benefited at the expense of the other — used esp. of relationships (as that between an epiphyte and the plant on which it grows) in which the effect is less extreme than in parasitism or predation **2** : PUBLICITY, ADVERTISING ⟨allotted . . . $250,000 for the film's new ~ campaign —*Newsweek*⟩ ⟨the ~ that a dozen American composers are getting today —Deems Taylor⟩ — **ex·ploi·ta·tion·ist** \-sh(ə)nəst\ *adj*

ex·ploit·ative \ik'splȯid·əd·|iv, (')ek¦s-, -ȯitət|\ *adj* [2*exploit* + *-ative*] : relating to exploitation: as **a** : relating to the utilization or working of a natural resource ⟨the ~ activities of this region include lumbering and mining⟩ **b** : relating to the wasteful or destructive utilization of a natural resource ⟨reaping the fruits of an ~ type of agriculture —Bernard Frank & Anthony Netboy⟩ **c** : relating to the utilization of the labor power of a person without giving a just or equivalent return ⟨a stage in the decay of ~ capitalism —*New Republic*⟩ — **ex·ploit·ative·ly** \|əvlē, -li\ *adv*

ex·ploit·ato·ry \ik'splȯid·ə,tōrē, ek-, -tȯr-, -ri\ *adj* [fr. *exploitation*, after such pairs as E *explanation: explanatory*] : EXPLOITATIVE

ex·ploi·tee \¦ek,splȯi¦tē; ik¦s-, ek¦s-\ *n* -s : one that is exploited

ex·ploit·er \ik'splȯid·|ə(r), (')ek¦s-, -ȯit|\ *n* -s : one that exploits

ex·ploit·ive \|iv, |ēv *also* |əv\ *adj* : EXPLOITATIVE

ex·plo·ra·tion \,eksplə'rāshən, -lō'r-,-lȯ'r-\ *n* -s [L *exploration-, exploratio*, fr. *exploratus* + *-ion-, -io* -ion] : an act or an instance of exploring : EXAMINATION, INVESTIGATION, SEARCH ⟨a voyage of ~⟩ ⟨extensive ~s of the psychoneurotic aspects of literature —C.I.Glicksberg⟩ ⟨we encourage ~ and development of additional mineral reserves —*Americana Annual*⟩ ⟨surgical ~ of a visceral organ⟩

ex·plo·ra·tion·al \¦==¦rāshənᵊl, -shnəl\ *adj* : of or relating to exploration

ex·plor·ative \ik'splōrəd·|iv, (')ek¦s-, -lȯr-, -rət|\ *adj* [fr. *exploration*, after such pairs as E *deliberative: deliberation*] : EXPLORATORY — **ex·plor·ative·ly** \|əvlē, -li\ *adv*

ex·plor·ato·ry \ik'splōrə,tōrē, ek-, -lȯr-, -tȯr-, -ri\ *adj* [ME, fr. L *exploratorius*, fr. *exploratus* (past part. of *explorare* to explore, spy out) + *-orius* -ory] : of, relating to, or connected with exploration : serving in or intended for exploration : SEARCHING ⟨an ~ reconnaissance of . . . the least-known inhabited part of the world —R.C.Andrews⟩ ⟨drilling an ~ well in the Gulf of Mexico —*Wall Street Jour.*⟩ ⟨an ~ surgical operation⟩ : designed to orient in or acquaint with the outlines or first elements of a subject : PRELIMINARY ⟨an ~ course in art⟩ ⟨~ talks between diplomats⟩

ex·plore \ik'splō(ə)r, ek-, -ȯ(ə)r,-ōə,-ȯ(ə)\ *vb* -ED/-ING/-S [L *explorare* to explore, spy out, fr. *ex-* 1ex- + *plorare* to cry out, wail, prob. of imit. origin; prob. fr. the outcry of hunters on sighting game] *vt* **1** *obs* : to seek for or after : strive to attain by search **2** : to search through or into : make a first or preliminary study of : INVESTIGATE, EXAMINE ⟨~ archives never before utilized by scholars⟩ ⟨~ the possibilities of reaching an agreement⟩ ⟨~ the economic and social conditions of the period⟩: as **a** : to examine minutely (as by surgery) esp. for diagnostic purposes ⟨operation seemed indicated and the patient was *explored* —J.G.Scannell & L.L.Robbins⟩ **b** : to penetrate into or range over for purposes of geographical discovery ⟨~ a trackless wilderness⟩ ~ *vi* : to make or conduct a systematic search ⟨~ for oil⟩

ex·plor·er \-ōrə(r), -ȯrə-\ *n* -s : one that explores: as **a** : a person who travels or is sent in search of geographical or scientific information ⟨an arctic ~⟩ **b** : a youth of 14 years or over, who participates in an exploring program of the Boy Scouts of America — compare BOY SCOUT, CUB SCOUT **c** : an instrument for exploring cavities esp. in teeth : PROBE 1a

explorer tent *n* : a variously shaped tent having a ridgepole, a maximum amount of floor space, and a minimum of standing room

exploring coil *n* [*exploring* fr. gerund of *explore*] : FLIP COIL

ex·plor·ing·ly *adv* [*exploring* (pres. part. of *explore*) + *-ly*] : in the manner of one that explores

ex·plo·si·bil·i·ty \ik,splōzə'biləd·ē, (,)ek,s-, -lətē, -i\ *n* -ES : the quality of being explosible : capacity for being exploded

ex·plo·si·ble \='=zəbəl\ *adj* [*explos-* (as in *explosive*) + *-ible*] : capable of being exploded

ex·plo·sim·e·ter \,eksplō'zimad·ə(r), -ō'si-\ *n* [*explosi*bility + *-meter*] : an instrument for testing explosibility by measuring the concentration of combustible gases and vapors in air

ex·plo·sion \ik'splōzhən, ek-\ *n* -s [L *explosion-, explosio* action of driving from the stage by noisy disapproval, fr. *explosus* (past part. of *explodere, explaudere* to drive from the stage by noisy disapproval) + *-ion-, -io* -ion — more at EXPLODE] **1** : an act of exposing something as invalid or baseless : REJECTION, COLLAPSE, FIASCO ⟨the ~ of that pseudo philosophy of science —P.E.More⟩ **2 a** : an act of exploding : a violent expansion or bursting that is accompanied by noise and is caused by a sudden release of energy from a very rapid chemical reaction, from a nuclear reaction, or from an escape of gases or vapors under pressure (as in a steam boiler) — compare DEFLAGRATION, DETONATION **b** : the noise made by such bursting **c** (1) : a large-scale, rapid, and spectacular expansion, outbreak, or other upheaval ⟨increasing the world food supply to offset the ~ of population —Bruce Bliven b. 1899⟩ ⟨ideal material for a revolutionary ~⟩ (2) : an outburst of temper manifested by excited language or action ⟨an ~ of national rage shattered the plan forever —*Holiday*⟩ **d** : the release of stoppage-impounded breath that occurs in one kind of articulation of stop consonants (as when a vowel or syllabic consonant immediately follows the stop, as in *mica, sodden*)

explosion gun *n* : an impact tool deriving its thrust from the detonation of a cartridge in its cylinder

explosion shot *n* : a golf shot made by driving the club head into sand just behind the ball

1**ex·plo·sive** \-ōs|iv, |ēv *also* -ōz| *or* |əv\ *adj* [L *explos*us (past part. of *explodere, explaudere*) + E *-ive*] **1 a** : relating to, characterized or operated by, or suited to cause explosion ⟨~ force⟩ ⟨an ~ engine⟩ ⟨the ~ increase of population⟩ ⟨an ~ epidemic of rheumatic fever⟩ **b** : tending to explode ⟨a blustering ~ person⟩ **2** : characterized by explosion — **ex·plo·sive·ly** \|əvlē, -li\ *adv* — **ex·plo·sive·ness** \|ivnəs, |ēv- *also* |əv-\ *n* -ES

2**explosive** \"\ *n* -s **1** : an explosive substance : a substance that on ignition by heat, impact, friction, or detonation undergoes very rapid decomposition (as combustion) with the production of heat and the formation of more stable products (as gases) which exert tremendous pressure as they expand at the high temperature produced; *esp* : a solid chemical compound or mixture of compounds that is used to release energy for performing work (as in blasting or propelling projectiles) — see HIGH EXPLOSIVE, LOW EXPLOSIVE **2** : a consonant characterized by explosion in its articulation when it occurs in certain environments : STOP

explosive evolution *n* : the appearance esp. early in the biological history of a group of a great variety of forms few of which become permanently established as lines within the group

explosive oil *n* : nitroglycerin esp. when mixed with a substance (as a nitrated glycol) that lowers the freezing point for use in dynamite

explosive rivet *n* : a rivet containing an explosive charge that is exploded either by touching the head with a heated iron or placing it in a high frequency electromagnetic field

explosive train *n* : a series of explosive elements of a land mine, bomb, or projectile that serve to set off the detonating charge

expn *abbr* **1** exposition **2** expiration

1**ex·po·nent** \ik'spōnənt, ek's-, 'ek,s-\ *adj* [L *exponent-, exponens*, pres. part. of *exponere* to explain, expound, set forth — more at EXPOUND] : giving exemplification : EXPLAINING ⟨in his characters we find not so much people who are ~ types of a region as personifications of various human qualities —J.W.Wilson⟩

2**exponent** \"\ *n* -s **1** : a symbol written above and to the right of a symbol, expression, or quantity to indicate a mathematical operation to be performed (as in involution where 2 in a^2 indicates how many times the operand is to be taken as a factor: $a \times a$; or in extraction of a root where ⅓ in $a^{1/3}$ indicates a cube root of a: $\sqrt[3]{a}$) **2 a** : an expounder or explainer esp. of a doctrine ⟨an ~ of profound economic truths —*Current Biog.*⟩ : an interpreter esp. of an art ⟨an important ~ of the living Bach as opposed to the dry and pedantic Bach —A.E.Wier⟩ ⟨the most controversial figure in the modern dance and . . . its most successful ~ —Walter Terry⟩ : a representative or practitioner esp. of a profession or other activity ⟨a well-known ~ of the science of anthropology —*Current Biog.*⟩ **b** : one that champions, advocates, or exemplifies ⟨the best known ~ of this use of free association in verse —C.D.Lewis⟩ ⟨a leading ~ of arbitration in labor-management disputes —*Current Biog.*⟩

ex·po·nen·tial \¦ekspə¦nenchəl, -pō¦-\ *adj* [2*exponent* + *-i-* + *-al*] **1** : of or relating to an exponent : involving a variable exponent ⟨an ~ expression⟩ **2** : approximately expressible by an exponential equation ⟨~ distribution⟩ — used esp. in indicating variation in which one variable factor depends upon another variable factor ⟨culture is said to grow in an ~ manner; and the number of inventions is a function of the size of the cultural base —F.H.Hankins⟩ — **ex·po·nen·tial·ly** \-chəlē\ *adv*

exponential curve *n* : a graph of an exponential function

exponential equation *n* : an equation involving exponential functions of a variable

exponential function *also* **exponential** *n* : a mathematical function in which an independent variable appears in one of the exponents

exponential horn *n* : a loudspeaker horn whose sectional area varies exponentially along its length

exponential series *n* : a series derived from the development of exponential expressions; *specif* : the fundamental expansion $e^x = 1 + \frac{x}{1} + \frac{x^2}{1 \cdot 2} + \frac{x^3}{1 \cdot 2 \cdot 3} + \frac{x^4}{1 \cdot 2 \cdot 3 \cdot 4} + \ldots$, absolutely convergent for all finite values of x

1**ex·po·ni·ble** \ik'spōnəbəl, ek's-\ *n* -s [ML *exponibilis*, adj.] : an exponible proposition

2**exponible** \ik's, (')ek¦s-\ *adj* [ML *exponibilis*, fr. L *exponere* + *-ibilis* -ible] **1** : capable of being explained **2** : needing restatement — used of a proposition in logic

1**ex·port** \(')ek¦spō(ə)r|t, ik's-, -ȯ(ə)r|, -ōə|, -ȯ(ə)|, *usu* |d·+V\ *vb* -ED/-ING/-S [L *exportare*, fr. *ex-* 1ex- + *portare* to carry — more at PORT] *vt* **1** : to carry away : REMOVE ⟨only the finer debris is ~*ed* by wind —Arthur Holmes⟩ ⟨the blood . . . ~*s* waste products from the tissues —W.E.Swinton⟩ **2 a** : to carry or send (a commodity) to some other country or place — opposed to *import* **b** : to transmit or cause the spread of (as an idea or institution) to another part of the world ⟨unable to ~ its democratic faith to . . . other nations —A.M. Schlesinger b. 1917⟩ ⟨we cannot even ~ freedom —F.L.Schuman⟩ ~ *vi* : to export something abroad ⟨the U.S. ~*s* to many foreign countries⟩

2**ex·port** \'ek,s-\ *n* -s **1** : something that is exported; *specif* : a commodity conveyed from one country or region to another for purposes of trade **2** : an act of exporting : EXPORTATION ⟨the ~ of wheat or tobacco⟩

3**export** \"\ *adj* [2*export*] : of, relating to, or concerned with exportation or exports ⟨an ~ duty⟩ ⟨the ~ trade⟩ : suitable or designed for exportation ⟨an ~ crop⟩

ex·port·able \(')ek¦spōr|d·əbəl, ik's-, -ȯr|, -ōə|, -ȯ(ə)|, |tə-\ *adj* : capable of being exported

ex·por·ta·tion \,ek,spōr'tāshən, -ȯ(r)'-,-ōə'- *also* -,pə(r)'-\ *n* -s [L *exportation-, exportatio*, fr. *exportatus* (past part. of *exportare*) + *-ion-, -io* -ion] **1** : an act of exporting; *also* : a commodity exported : EXPORT **2** : a direct inference from a statement of the form $pq \supset r$ to one of the form $p \supset (q \supset r)$ — used in formal logic

export bar *n* : a bar or ingot of pure gold used in making gold shipments to settle international exchange balances

export credit *n* : a credit opened by an importer with a bank in the country of an exporter to finance an export transaction — compare IMPORT CREDIT

ex·port·er *pronunc at* 1EXPORT + ə(r)\ *n* -s : one that exports; *specif* : a wholesaler who sells to merchants or industrial consumers in foreign countries

export point *n* : the quotation for a foreign currency on the gold standard at which it pays to export gold in place of buying a bill of exchange — compare GOLD EXPORT POINT, GOLD IMPORT POINT

export tax *or* **export duty** *n* : a tax or duty on articles exported from a country

1**ex·pose** \ik'spōz, ek-\ *vt* -ED/-ING/-S [ME *exposen*, fr. MF *exposer*, modif. (influenced by *poser* to put, place) of L *exponere* to expose, explain, set forth (perfect stem *expos-*), fr. *ex-* 1ex- + *ponere* to put, place — more at POSITION, POSE] **1 a** : to lay open (as to attack, danger, trial, or test) : make accessible to something that may prove detrimental : deprive of shelter, protection, or care ⟨~ him to the weather⟩ ⟨~ troops needlessly⟩ ⟨a coast *exposed* to severe gales⟩ **b** : to submit or subject to an action or influence ⟨~ children to good books⟩ ⟨think . . . they can arrest the fall of rain by *exposing* to it a boulder —J.G.Frazer⟩ ⟨~ a man to new impressions⟩; *specif* : to subject (a sensitive photographic film, plate, or paper) to the action of radiant energy **c** : to abandon (an infant) esp. by leaving in the open : DESERT ⟨the foundation of lying-in hospitals and orphanages . . . kept the children alive, . . . prevented them being *exposed* —J.H. Plumb⟩ **2** : to lay open to view : lay bare : make known : set forth : EXHIBIT, DISPLAY ⟨*exposing* a sun-tanned back⟩ ⟨each had started *exposing* his views —F.M.Ford⟩ ⟨the new display object is to ~ the package —*Printers' Ink*⟩: as **a** : to offer publicly for sale ⟨all of which I shall ~ for sale at public auction —*Detroit Law Jour.*⟩ — sometimes used with *to* ⟨the markets at which the corn, the cattle, the wool . . . of the surrounding country were *exposed* to sale —T.B.Macaulay⟩ **b** : to exhibit (a religious relic or the Host) for public veneration **c** : to reveal the face of (a playing card) — used chiefly in games in which such exposure is contrary to the rules **d** : to conduct (oneself) as an exhibitionist **3 a** : to disclose or reveal the faults, frailties, or unsoundness of : bring to light (as something criminal or shameful) : UNMASK ⟨took a leading part in *exposing* the pretensions of this quack⟩ ⟨has behaved like a cad and ought to be *exposed* —Kingsley Martin⟩ ⟨~ a voting fraud⟩ ⟨~ the abuses of the day —John Mason Brown⟩ **b** *obs* : RIDICULE, SATIRIZE **syn** see SHOW

2**ex·po·sé** *or* **ex·po·se** \¦ek(,)spō¦zā, -,spə¦- *sometimes* ek'spō,zā *or* ik's-\ *n* -s [F *exposé*, fr. past part. of *exposer*] **1** : a formal recital or exposition of facts : STATEMENT ⟨the best ~ of the full Platonic metaphysical synthesis that we know —W.N.Clarke⟩ **2** : an exposure or revelation of something discreditable ⟨novelists were making fictional ~*s* of plutocratic iniquity —W.A.White⟩ ⟨has written a startling ~ of missionary mentality —Lucy Crockett⟩ ⟨a newspaper ~ of crime conditions⟩

ex·posed \ik'spōzd, ek-\ *adj* [fr. past part. of 1*expose*] **1** : open to view ⟨left acres of large flat stones ~ —*Amer. Guide Series: Tenn.*⟩; *specif, of a playing card* : dealt or placed so that its face shows whether legally or illegally **2** : not shielded or protected : so situated as to invite or make likely an attack, injury, or other adverse development ⟨must do something to protect her ~ northeast frontier —Geoffrey Godsell⟩; *specif* : not adequately insulated, guarded, or isolated — used of equipment ⟨an ~ electric wire⟩ **syn** see LIABLE

ex·posed·ness \-z(ə)dnəs\ *n* -ES : the quality or state of being exposed ⟨the very ~ of the position on the stage conduced to mild stage fright⟩

ex·pos·er \-zə(r)\ *n* -s : one that exposes

ex·pos·it \ik'späzət, ek-\ *vt* -ED/-ING/-S [L *expositus*, past part. of *exponere*] : EXPOUND ⟨~*s* a pluralism of interests and corresponding types of criticism —René Wellek & Austin Warren⟩

ex·po·si·tion \,ekspə'zishən, -pō'-\ *n* -s [ME *exposicioun*, fr. MF *exposition*, fr. L *exposition-, expositio*, fr. *expositus* (past part. of *exponere* to explain, expound, set forth) + *-ion-, -io* -ion — more at EXPOUND] **1** : a setting forth of the meaning or purpose (as of a writing or discourse) : an expounding of the sense or intent (as of a law) : an interpretation esp. of a parable : EXEGESIS **2 a** (1) : the art or procedure of expository discourse : the art of presenting a subject matter in detail apart from criticism, argument, or development : ELUCIDATION (2) : a verbal statement or presentation of some subject matter or point of view whether expository, critical, or argumentative ⟨overawed by such a splendid piece of advocacy and ~ —Stewart Cockburn⟩ (3) : presentation or interpretation of any kind ⟨demands a clarity of ~ somewhat foreign to the modern piano —P.H.Lang⟩ **b** : discourse or an example of it designed to convey information or explain what is difficult to understand; *esp* : a statement embodying an analysis of the subject matter and the use of familiar illustrations or analogies **c** : a part of a composition (as of music or drama) in which the theme or subject is presented or opened out: as (1) : the first part of a musical composition in sonata form in which the thematic material of the movement is presented (2) : the opening section of a fugue **3** : an act or an instance of exposing: as **a** : abandonment of an infant **b** : an open display of a religious relic or the Host for public veneration **c** : a public exhibition or show (as of industrial and artistic productions)

ex·po·si·tion·al \¦==¦zishənᵊl, -shnəl\ *adj* : EXPLANATORY

ex·pos·i·tive \ik'späzəd·iv, (')ek¦s-\ *adj* [L *exposit*us (past part. of *exponere* to explain, expound, set forth) + E *-ive* — more at EXPOUND] : DESCRIPTIVE, EXPOSITORY — **ex·pos·i·tive·ly** \-d·əvlē\ *adv*

ex·pos·i·tor \='=zəd·ə(r)\ *n* -s [ME *expositour*, fr. MF *expositeur*, fr. LL *expositor*, fr. L *expositus* + *-or*] : one that expounds or explains : EXPOUNDER, COMMENTATOR — **ex·pos·i·to·ri·al** \ik¦späzə¦tōrēəl, (¦)ek¦-\ *adj* — **ex·pos·i·to·ri·al·ly** \-ēəlē\ *adv*

ex·pos·i·to·ri·ly \ik¦späzə¦tōrəlē, (¦)ek¦-, -tȯr-, -li\ *adv* : in an expository manner ⟨in his book the events were presented ~ rather than with any imaginative or creative alteration⟩

ex·pos·i·to·ry \ik'späzə,tōrē, ek-, -tȯr-, -ri\ *adj* [LL *expositorius*, fr. L *expositus* + *-orius* -ory] : of, relating to, or containing exposition : serving to elucidate or interpret : EXEGETIC ⟨the failure of composition teachers to solve the problem of clean ~ writing —H.L.Creek⟩ ⟨occasional textual and explanatory but not ~ notes —I.M.Price⟩

ex post \(')ek¦spōst\ *adj* [1*ex post (facto)*] : based on knowledge and retrospection and being essentially objective and factual ⟨consistency of market behavior, and therefore reasonable conformity of ex ante expectations with *ex post* reality, is basically determined by the social stability of the community —Werner Hochwald⟩ — opposed to *ex ante*

1**ex post fac·to** \¦ek,spōst¦fak(,)tō\ *adj* [LL, from a thing done afterward] : done, made, or formulated after the fact and on the basis of current premises, conditions, or knowledge : disregarding the previous status or setting of the event or thing concerning which a conclusion is reached or at which action is directed : RETROSPECTIVE, RETROACTIVE ⟨*ex post facto* punishment⟩ ⟨the general gave his *ex post facto* approval —W.H.Upson⟩ ⟨*ex post facto* rationalizations of behavior —Edward Sapir⟩ ⟨the results of scientific inquiry are always subject to *ex post facto* interpretation —H.M.Magid⟩

2**ex post facto** \"\ *adv* : after the fact : in a retrospective or retroactive manner ⟨no lawmaker can alter the fact, *ex post facto* —C.A.Beard⟩

ex post facto law *n* : a criminal or penal statute that imposes a punishment for an act not punishable when committed, or alters to the defendant's disadvantage the punishment prescribed at the time of the act, or takes away from the substantial protection afforded the defendant by the then existing law; *also* : a civil or criminal law enacted with a retrospective effect

ex·pos·tu·late \ik'späschə,lāt, ek-, *usu* -ād·+V\ *vb* -ED/-ING/-S [L *expostulatus*, past part. of *expostulare*, fr. *ex-* 1ex- + *postulare* to ask for, demand — more at POSTULATE] *vt* **1** *obs* : to call for : DEMAND **2** *obs* **a** : DISCUSS, EXAMINE **b** : to complain of ~ *vi* **1** *obs* : to talk earnestly : COMPLAIN **2** : to reason earnestly with a person for purposes of dissuasion or remonstrance : REMONSTRATE ⟨it is useless to ~ with a stubborn man⟩ ⟨send for the maître d'hôtel; you have a right to ~ —Margaret Lane⟩ ⟨reporters at his press conference *expostulated* against playing favorites —*New Republic*⟩ **syn** see OBJECT

ex·pos·tu·lat·ing·ly \ik¦späschə¦lād·iŋlē, ek¦-, ,ek,=='===\ *adv* [*expostulating* (pres. part. of *expostulate*) + *-ly*] : in the manner of one that expostulates ⟨raised a hand ~ to try to stop the flow of abuse⟩

ex·pos·tu·la·tion \ik,späschə'lāshən, (,)ek,-\ *n* -s [L *expostulation-, expostulatio*, fr. *expostulatus* + *-ion-, -io* -ion] **1** : an act or an instance of expostulating with a person : REMONSTRANCE ⟨all his ~*s* proved futile⟩ **2** : a speech or writing of remonstrance or dissuasion ⟨wrote an ~ to the minister of education defending their right to function —*Collier's Yr. Bk.*⟩

ex·pos·tu·la·to·ry \='==,lə,tōrē, -tȯr-, -ri\ *adj* : relating to or containing expostulation

ex·po·sure \ik'spōzhə(r), ek-\ *n* -s [*expose* + *-ure*] **1** : an act of exposing, laying open, or setting forth: as **a** : disclosure to view : DISPLAY ⟨skillful ~ of goods in a store window⟩ ⟨her ~ of a shapely leg⟩ **b** (1) : a disclosure esp. of a weakness or something shameful or criminal : UNMASKING ⟨continued his ~ of electoral frauds⟩ ⟨the battle was finally won with the ~ of the Tory commissioner as a grafter —*Current Biog.*⟩; *also* : the condition of being unmasked or shown up ⟨he feared ~ above all else⟩ (2) : PRESENTATION, EXPOSITION ⟨a dispassionate ~ of fundamental passions of any time and any place —T.S.Eliot⟩ ⟨how terrifying an ~ he was making of the emptiness of life without belief —F.O.Matthiessen⟩ ⟨suites were considered too heavy for ~ in the concert hall —Roland Gelatt⟩ **c** : an act of abandoning (as an infant) esp. in the open ⟨reject all regulation of the birth rate by infanticide, ~, . . . or any other means —H.E.Barnes & Howard Becker⟩ **d** (1) : the act of exposing a sensitized photographic material (2) : a section of a film for an individual picture ⟨a roll containing eight ~*s*⟩ (3) : the total amount of light or other radiant energy received per unit area on the sensitized material — usu. expressed for cameras in terms of the time and the lens *f*-number ⟨an ~ of $\frac{1}{50}$ second at *f*/8⟩ **e** : an act of subjecting to an experience or influence ⟨denounced ~ of children to such corrupting literature⟩ **2 a** : a condition or an instance of being laid bare or exposed to view ⟨particularly striking . . . are the picturesque ~*s* of the somber banded clays —*Earth Science Digest*⟩ **b** : a condition of being exposed to danger or loss : liability or accessibility to something that may affect detrimentally ⟨~ to infection⟩ : RISK, VULNERABILITY ⟨insurable under a policy having less ~ —Charles Ray⟩ ⟨~ to sudden attack by the enemy⟩; *specif* : the condition of being exposed to the elements ⟨she died as a result of ~ suffered after a shipwreck —*Amer. Guide Series: Maine*⟩ ⟨the work is hard . . . and ~ is part of the routine —E.P.Hohman⟩ **c** : a condition or an instance of being subjected to an experience or influence ⟨long ~ to the temperature of boiling water —J.B.Conant⟩ ⟨the permanent effects of his early ~ to Catholicism —William Troy⟩ ⟨wearily cynical from years of ~ to human misery —*N.Y. Times*⟩ **d** : a position with respect to the points of compass or to climatic or weather influences ⟨a kitchen with a western ~⟩ **3** : something (as a bed of mineral material) exposed to view ⟨thousands of ~*s* of many different kinds of rock have been examined —W.E.Swinton⟩ **4** : the product of the flux density of radiation falling upon a surface by the time during which the surface is exposed to the radiation

exposure hazard *n* : the chance that a particular building and its contents may sustain loss or damage from fire in a neighboring property

exposure index *n* : a number that is assigned to a photographic film or plate for use with an exposure meter to aid a photographer in obtaining the correct camera exposure

exposure meter *n* : a device for indicating correct photographic exposure under varying conditions of illumination (as by measuring the light falling on or reflected from the subject by means of a photoelectric photometer)

exposure suit *n* : a suit (as of rubber) designed for a flier forced down at sea and for a person exposed to extreme cold or drenching

ex·pound \ik'spau̇nd, ek-\ *vb* -ED/-ING/-S [ME *expounden, expounen*, fr. MF *expondre, espondre*, fr. L *exponere* to explain, expound, set forth, fr. *ex-* ¹ex- + *ponere* to put, place — more at POSITION] *vt* **1 a :** to set forth : STATE, PRESENT, TEACH ⟨~s his conviction that the economic outlook is brightening⟩ ⟨~ing a philosophy from which she shrank —William McFee⟩ ⟨~ing to the literate but uninformed some of the mysteries of economics —Quincy Howe⟩ ⟨it's the personality of the teacher that counts, far more than the topic he ~s —R.B.Merriman⟩ ⟨~ed with distinguished precision the difference between an extinct and an extirpated bird —Edmund Wilson⟩ **b :** to defend with argument : ADVOCATE ⟨welcomed . . . the suggestions of a union with the Church of England, which some . . . clergymen in the two churches ~ed because of an alleged similarity in spirit and ritual —R.C.Wood⟩ **2 :** to make clear the meaning of : comment on : INTERPRET, EXPLAIN, CONSTRUE, GLOSS ⟨~ed to his monks . . . the religious significance of . . . the Song of Songs —G.C.Sellery⟩ ⟨spent much of his time ~ing the conflict between Christianity and Communism —*Current Biog.*⟩ ⟨used to take me riding before breakfast and ~ my shortcomings —John Buchan⟩ ⟨~ a law⟩ ~ *vi* **1 :** to make a statement : present a view : DISCOURSE, COMMENT — often used with *on* ⟨when executives ~ on the subject their views coincide remarkably —W.H.Whyte⟩ ⟨~ on the many good reasons for getting to know Great Britain —Richard Joseph⟩ ⟨sportsmen will ~ for hours on their observations —G.J.Knudsen⟩ **2 :** to make explanatory comments : EXPLAIN ⟨you speak of the time assigned . . . I . . . would like you to ~ —O.W.Holmes †1935⟩

ex·pound·er \-də(r)\ *n* -S [ME *expoundere, expounere*, fr. *expounden, expounen* + *-er, -ere* -er] : one that expounds

¹ex·press \ik'spres, ek- *sometimes* 'ek,s-\ *adj* [ME, fr. MF *expres, espres*, fr. L *expressus*, past part. of *exprimere* to express, press out, fr. *ex-* ¹ex- + *-primere* (fr. *premere* to press) — more at PRESS] **1 a :** directly and distinctly stated or expressed rather than implied or left to inference : not dubious or ambiguous : DEFINITE, CLEAR, EXPLICIT, UNMISTAKABLE ⟨with the ~ injunction that I was to show them to no one —Anita Pollitzer⟩ ⟨with the ~ provision that they remain away from the coast settlement —Mabel R. Gillis⟩ **b :** exactly represented : EXACT, PRECISE ⟨he was the ~ image of his father⟩ **c** *obs* (1) : OUTSPOKEN (2) : STEADFAST, UNWAVERING **2 a :** specially designed or chosen for its purpose : adapted to its purpose ⟨what a piece of work is man! . . . in form and moving how ~ and admirable! —Shak.⟩ **b :** of a particular or special sort : SPECIFIC ⟨he came for that ~ purpose⟩ **3 a :** dispatched with or traveling at special or high speed; *specif* : traveling between terminal or specified points without stop or with a limited number of stops ⟨an ~ train⟩ ⟨an ~ bus⟩ ⟨an ~ elevator⟩ — compare LOCAL **b :** adapted or suitable for or characterized by travel at special or high speed ⟨an ~ highway⟩; *also* : specially fast ⟨traveling at ~ speed⟩ **c** *Brit* : delivered or to be delivered without delay by special messenger ⟨~ letter⟩ ⟨~ mail⟩; *also* : performing or paying for such service ⟨~ messenger⟩ ⟨~ charges⟩ **4 :** designed for an express rifle — used of a cartridge, load, or bullet and now often of what is a high-velocity loading for a particular cartridge **syn** see EXPLICIT

²express \"\ *adv* [ME *expres*, fr. *expres, express* adj.] **1** *obs* : EXPRESSLY **2** [⁴*express*] : by express ⟨send a package ~⟩

³express \"\ *vb* -ED/-ING/-ES [ME *expressen*, fr. MF & L; MF *expresser, espresser*, fr. OF, fr. *expres, espres*, adj., fr. L *expressus*, past part. of *exprimere* to express] *vt* **1 a :** to make or offer a representation of : show by a copy or likeness : DELINEATE, DEPICT ⟨among the striking patterns in modern printed textiles were seen many geometrical and abstract designs gracefully ~ed —*Americana Annual*⟩ **b** (1) : to represent in words : STATE, UTTER ⟨~ an opinion⟩ ⟨~ his views⟩ (2) : to give expression to (an emotion or feeling) ⟨when I ~ed disgust he and others laughed —David Livingstone⟩ ⟨her countenance ~ed both shame and defiance⟩ **c :** to give or convey a true impression of : display fully or exactly : SHOW, SIGNIFY, EXHIBIT, REFLECT, EMBODY ⟨all these thrusting, driving words became the slogans which ~ed the folk ideals —W.P.Webb⟩ ⟨its proud edifices ~ material riches so overwhelming as to transcend materialism —Gerald Sykes⟩ ⟨no words can ~ the grandeur of that scene⟩ ⟨in Constantinople was ~ed all the life and culture of the Byzantine Empire —W.G.East⟩ **d** *obs* : to give a full and explicit statement of : RECOUNT, DESCRIBE, DESIGNATE, SIGNIFY **e** (1) : to make known the opinions or feelings of (oneself) : declare what is in the mind of (oneself) ⟨~ himself very strongly on that subject⟩ ⟨asked the members of the panel to ~ themselves freely⟩ (2) : to give expression to the artistic or creative impulses or abilities of (oneself) ⟨in one of our modern schools, where the little darlings are supposed to ~ themselves —H.W. Van Loon⟩ **f :** to represent by a sign or symbol : SYMBOLIZE ⟨the sign = ~es equality⟩ **2 a :** to force out by pressure : press or squeeze out (as the juice of a fruit) ⟨estimated that the daily water requirements of one person could be ~ed from six to seven pounds of fish —N.B.Marshall⟩ **b :** to empty by pressure or squeezing : subject to pressure so as to extract something ⟨the seeds . . . are ~ed to yield the neutral liquid fat —C.H.Thienes⟩ **3** [⁴*express*] : to send by express messenger : transport by express service ⟨~ a package⟩ ~ *vi* [⁴*express*] : to travel by express train

syn VENT, UTTER, VOICE, BROACH, AIR, VENTILATE: these can mean, in common, to give some form to in letting out (usu. what one feels or thinks). EXPRESS, the most general and comprehensive, can mean merely to say or put into words, but more generally implies any degree of more comprehensive revelation involving thoughts, feelings, moods, attributes, or qualities and a putting into any form that reveals, as words, gestures, bodily positions or facial aspects, arrangements of line, mass, or color (in painting), variations of tone, tempo, rhythm in the playing of notes, phrases, or harmonic progressions (in music), or the like ⟨*express* one's views⟩ ⟨*express* agreement⟩ ⟨to be an artist means . . . to *express* emotion —C.W.H.Johnson⟩ ⟨*express* surprise and anger⟩ ⟨music *expressing* repose and serenity⟩ ⟨a novel *expressing* character⟩ VENT implies some inner compulsion to express or let out as with a pent-up emotion or powerful passion that demands an outlet or cannot be controlled ⟨*vent* a grievance⟩ ⟨*vent* one's spleen against an enemy⟩ ⟨compensate for a lifetime of frustration by *venting* their aggressive drives against an acceptable villain —Walter Goodman⟩ UTTER stresses the use of the voice though not necessarily speech, generally implying a short, usu. significant, often carefully formulated expression ⟨*utter* a grunt⟩ ⟨the ruler who *uttered* the divine command —B.N.Cardozo⟩ ⟨he *uttered* a spell —J.G.Frazer⟩ ⟨*utter* platitudes⟩ ⟨*utter* a dictum⟩ ⟨his impetuosity and eagerness to *utter* what was in him —H.O.Taylor⟩ VOICE suggests expression or formulation in words though not necessarily in vocal utterance ⟨*voice* an opinion⟩ ⟨*voice* resentment⟩ ⟨poetry *voicing* one's yearnings and frustrations⟩ BROACH stresses mention for the first time, esp. of something long thought over and usu. awaiting an opportune moment for disclosure ⟨the idea of religious radio broadcasts was first *broached* in 1923 —*Current Biog.*⟩ ⟨I *broached*, as a practical measure, in my plan of organization, the system which I had discussed tentatively —A.D.White⟩ ⟨*broach* a touchy subject with care⟩ AIR implies exposure, often a parading of one's views, sometimes a much needed expressing of them as a form of relief or in the hope of gaining attention or, occas., to gain sympathy ⟨*air* one's views⟩ ⟨*air* grievances⟩ VENTILATE implies a thorough scrutiny by bringing to light or exposing all phases or aspects of a matter, usu. suggesting a desire to get at the truth by discovering the real issues or by a careful weighing of pros and cons ⟨persuading their legislative representatives to *ventilate* the question in Parliament —S.O.Eklund⟩ ⟨discussion programs of this kind, whose aim is to *ventilate* economic problems —William Salter⟩

⁴express \"\ *n* -ES [¹*express*] **1 a** *Brit* : a messenger sent on a special errand **b** *Brit* : a dispatch conveyed by a special messenger **c** (1) : an intercity and international system for the prompt and safe transportation of parcels, money, or goods with pickup and delivery service and at rates higher than standard freight charges — compare FREIGHT (2) : a company operating a merchandise freight service (3) : the goods or shipments transported by express **d** *or* **express delivery** *Brit* : delivery of express mail : SPECIAL DELIVERY **2** [³*express*] *obs* : EXPRESSION, MANIFESTATION; *esp* : a verbal manifestation : UTTERANCE, DECLARATION, INJUNCTION **3 :** EXPRESS TRAIN

ex·press·age \-sij\ *n* -S : a carrying of parcels by express; *also* : a charge for such carrying

express assumpsit *n* : an action on contract brought to recover damages on a bilateral contract express or implied in fact — called also *special assumpsit*

express car *n* : a railroad car built for carrying express

expressed *past of* EXPRESS

ex·press·er *or* **ex·pres·sor** \-sə(r)\ *n* -S : one that expresses ⟨the ~ of a minority opinion⟩

expresses *pres 3d sing of* EXPRESS, *pl of* EXPRESS

ex·press·ible *also* **ex·press·able** \-səbəl\ *adj* : capable of being expressed ⟨an ~ emotion⟩ ⟨the presence of natural ~ liquids in the meat —*Meat & Meat Cookery*⟩

expressing *pres part of* EXPRESS

ex·pres·sion \ik'spreshən, ek-\ *n* -S [ME *expressioun*, fr. ML *expression-, expressio*, fr. L, action of pressing out, fr. *expressus* (past part. of *exprimere* to express, press out) + *-ion-, -io* -ion — more at EXPRESS] **1 a :** an act, process, or instance of representing, manifesting, or conveying in words or some other medium : MANIFESTATION, UTTERANCE, ISSUE ⟨the sacred principle of freedom of ~ of ideas⟩ ⟨his anger found ~ in a string of oaths⟩ ⟨his talent found ~ in the plastic arts⟩ **b** (1) : something that manifests, represents, reflects, embodies, or symbolizes something else : SIGN, TOKEN ⟨socialism found its practical ~ in Russia⟩ ⟨an assortment of gifts as ~s of his fans' admiration —*Current Biog.*⟩ ⟨the first clinical ~ of the disease⟩ (2) : a significant word or phrase ⟨he uses some very odd ~s⟩ (3) : a sign or character or a finite sequence of signs or characters (as logical or mathematical symbols) representing a quantity or operation (4) : the detectable effect of a gene; *also* : EXPRESSIVITY **2 a** (1) : a mode, means, or use of significant representation or symbolism ⟨dignified ~ in writing⟩; *esp* : felicitous or vivid indication or depiction of mood or sentiment ⟨read a poem with ~⟩ (2) : a manipulation of formal artistic means or an interpretation of subject matter to reveal forcefully the artist's conception, mood, or attitude (3) : features of musical performance other than mechanical reproduction of the notes commonly including gradations of tempo and dynamics, phrasing and articulation, and nuance whether indicated by expression marks or left to the performer's discretion (4) : use of artistic means or the artistic interpretation of subject matter for the imaginative recreation of objects from nature or life ⟨delightful and illuminating journey through 150 years of graphic ~ —Una E. Johnson⟩ ⟨the aestheticians of romanticism invented the term ~ to describe the artistic purpose to which apparent imitation was subservient —J.W.Krutch⟩ **b** (1) : the quality or fact of being expressive ⟨eyes full of fire and ~⟩ (2) : facial aspect or vocal intonation as indicative of feeling ⟨she tried to read something in his face . . . but was not yet capable of understanding its ~ —Joseph Conrad⟩ **3 :** an act or product of pressing out ⟨~ is a process of forcibly separating liquids from solids —E.F.Cook & E.W.Martin⟩

ex·pres·sion·al \-shənᵊl, -shnəl\ *adj* : of or relating to expression

ex·pres·sion·ism \-shə,nizəm\ *n* -S [G *expressionismus*, fr. F *expression* (fr. ML *expression-, expressio*) + G *-ismus* -ism] **1 :** a theory or practice in art esp. of the late 19th and 20th centuries of seeking to depict not objective reality but the subjective emotions and responses that objects and events arouse in the artist with wide use of distortion, exaggeration, and symbolism — often contrasted with *impressionism* **2 :** a theory or practice in the literature and theater of the 20th century of presenting the subjective or subconscious thoughts and emotions of characters, the struggle of abstract forces, or the inner realities of life by a wide variety of nonnaturalistic techniques that include abstraction, distortion, and symbolism **3 :** a theory or practice in music esp. of the 20th century of avoiding the traditional tonalities and techniques and seeking to express the composer's inner experience — often contrasted with *impressionism*

¹ex·pres·sion·ist \-sh(ə)nəst\ *adj* : of or relating to expressionism ⟨how ~ line and color can give a strong feeling of emotion —A.H.Barr⟩

²expressionist \"\ *n* -S : a practitioner or adherent of expressionism

ex·pres·sion·is·tic \ik¦spreshə'nistik, ek¦-, ,ek,=='==\ *adj* : EXPRESSIONIST ⟨her art has always been highly ~, which is to say that it is basically motivated by psychological forces and not solely by the autonomous demands of plastic form —Rhys Gwyn⟩ — **ex·pres·sion·is·ti·cal·ly** \-tək(ə)lē, -tēk-, -li\ *adv*

ex·pres·sion·less \='=shənləs\ *adj* : lacking expression ⟨eyes . . . as numb and ~ as a brace of gray oysters on the half shell —R.P.Warren⟩ — **ex·pres·sion·less·ly** *adv*

expression mark *n* : a sign or mark used in music to denote a specific expressive quality

ex·pres·sio uni·us est ex·clu·sio al·te·ri·us \ek'spresē,ō-'ünē,ü,se,stek'sklüsē,ō,äl'terē,ùs\ [NL, expression of the one is exclusion of the other] : a principle in law: when one or more things of a class are expressly mentioned others of the same class are excluded

ex·pres·sive \ik'spresiv, ek-, -sēv *also* -səv\ *adj* **1 :** of or relating to expression ⟨the ~ function of language⟩ ⟨architecture . . . has its limitations as an ~ medium —Robin Boyd⟩ **2 :** serving to express, utter, or represent : INDICATIVE ⟨spent much time in Arizona . . . and left many canvases ~ of its vitality and color —*Amer. Guide Series: Ariz.*⟩ ⟨poems and prayers . . . ~ of the deepest religious experiences —*Saturday Rev.*⟩ **3 :** forcefully representing the meaning or feeling meant to be conveyed : full of expression : SIGNIFICANT, EMPHATIC ⟨richly ~ gestures⟩ ⟨an ~ silence⟩ ⟨a homely whistling sound which . . . was terribly ~ —William Zukerman⟩ ⟨still cling to their "'tain't so" and "'twan't nothin'" because their fathers found these so ~ —*Amer. Guide Series: N.C.*⟩

syn ELOQUENT, SIGNIFICANT, MEANINGFUL, PREGNANT, SENTENTIOUS: EXPRESSIVE describes that which clearly shows or communicates an idea, mood, or emotion forcefully or vividly ⟨her forehead had been strikingly *expressive* of an engrossing terror and compassion that saw nothing but the peril of the accused —Charles Dickens⟩ ⟨he used foul and novel terms *expressive* of rage —H.G.Wells⟩ ⟨described by such epithets as vital, characteristic, picturesque, individual — in short, on the element that may be summed up by the epithet *expressive* —Irving Babbitt⟩ ELOQUENT may intensify the notions of EXPRESSIVE, esp. in evoking emotional ideas or arousing deep feeling ⟨no man is *eloquent* save when someone is moved as he listens —John Dewey⟩ ⟨there was a burst of applause, and a deep silence which was even more *eloquent* than the applause —Thomas Hardy⟩ ⟨I could scarcely remove my eyes from her *eloquent* countenance: I seemed to read in it relief and gladness mingled with surprise and something like vexation —W.H.Hudson †1922⟩ SIGNIFICANT is applicable to whatever expresses a meaning, sometimes a covert or hidden meaning, sometimes a clearly ascertainable idea, sometimes an important meaning ⟨those who lay down that every sentence must end on a *significant* word, never on a preposition —Havelock Ellis⟩ ⟨every sentence is doubly *significant*, and the sense of our author is as broad as the world —S.P.Sherman⟩ MEANINGFUL may have the suggestion of SIGNIFICANT; it may be used simply to indicate presence of meaning ⟨some brilliant minds to whom the carefully turned phrase and the *meaningful* metaphor are very important —D.W.Maurer & V. H. Vogel⟩ PREGNANT may describe that which conveys a rich or weighty meaning, often with force or conciseness ⟨who has not had the experience of resolving a difficulty with the help of a sentence *pregnant* with life's meaning, some well-phrased words of wisdom, or a poem that came to mind at a critical moment? —Vivian T. Thayer⟩ ⟨no talent for revealing a character or resuming the significance of an episode in a single *pregnant* phrase —W.S.Maugham⟩ SENTENTIOUS may apply to what is full of significance and expressed tersely ⟨clarity is gained by a brief and almost *sententious* statement at the outset of the problem to be attacked —B.N.Cardozo⟩ ⟨the peculiarly sardonic and *sententious* style in which Don Luis composed his epigrams —Hervey Allen⟩

ex·pres·sive·ly \-sə̇vlē, -li\ *adv* : in an expressive manner ⟨sentiments ~ fashioned into verse⟩

ex·pres·sive·ness \-sivnəs, -sēv- *also* -səv-\ *n* -ES : the quality of being expressive

ex·pres·siv·i·ty \,ek,spre'sivəd·ē, -vətē, -i\ *n* -ES [ISV *expressive* + *-ity*; orig. formed as G *expressivität*] **1 :** the relative capacity of a gene to modify the organism of which it is a part — compare PENETRANCE **2** [*expressive* + *-ity*] : the quality of being expressive ⟨works in which intellectual interest . . . is in perfect balance with ~ —Edward Cushing⟩

ex·press·less \ik'spresləs, (')ek¦s-\ *adj, archaic* : INEXPRESSIBLE

express liner *n* : a fast liner equipped chiefly for carriage of passengers, mails, and high-class cargo

ex·press·ly \ik'spreslē, ek's- *sometimes* 'ek,s-\ *adv* [ME *expresli*, fr. ¹*express* + *-li* -ly] **1 :** in direct or unmistakable terms : in an express manner : EXPLICITLY, DEFINITELY, DIRECTLY ⟨he had ~ rejected at one time or another dialectical materialism —J.G.Colton⟩ **2 :** for the express purpose : PARTICULARLY ⟨the need for a city hospital ~ for the cure of addicts —*Current Biog.*⟩

ex·press·man \ik'spre,sman, ek-, -,smən\ *n, pl* **expressmen** : a person employed in the express business

expressor *var of* EXPRESSER

express rifle *n* [prob. fr. ⁴*express* (train)] : a sporting rifle for use at short ranges employing a large charge of powder and a light bullet

express train *n* **1 :** a train formerly run expressly for the occasion **2 a :** a train of express freight **b :** a passenger train operated at high speed with few stops

express truck *n* : a light motor truck for quick delivery (as of express packages)

express trust *n* [¹*express*] : a trust created directly and explicitly by deed, will, or declaration of trust — compare CONSTRUCTIVE TRUST, RESULTING TRUST

ex·pres·sure \ik'spreshə(r), ek-\ *n* -S [³*express* + *-ure*] *archaic* : EXPRESSION

express wagon *n* **1 :** a wagon used for moving and delivering goods sent by express **2 :** a low 4-wheeled wagon with an open rectangular body like a flat box and a retroflex tongue made for the play or use (as for carrying newspapers) of a child

express wagon 2

expressway \='=,=\ *n* : a high-speed divided highway for through traffic with access partially or fully controlled and grade separations at important intersections with other roads — compare FREEWAY, PARKWAY, TURNPIKE

ex·pro·brate \'eksprō,brāt\ *vt* -ED/-ING/-S [L *exprobratus*, past part. of *exprobrare*, fr. *ex-* ¹ex- + *-probrare* (fr. *probrum* disgraceful act, infamy) — more at OPPROBRIUM] *archaic* : CENSURE, UPBRAID

ex·pro·bra·tion \,==*'brāshən\ *n* -S [ME *exprobracioun*, fr. L *exprobration-, exprobratio*, fr. *exprobratus* + *-ion-, -io* -ion] *archaic* : an instance of reproach : REPROACH

ex·pro·mis·sion \,eksprō'mishən\ *n* -S [NL *expromission-, expromissio*, fr. L *expromissus* (past part. of *expromittere* to promise to pay, fr. *ex-* ¹ex- + *promittere* to promise) + *-ion-, -io* -ion — more at PROMISE] : an act of binding oneself for another's debt and thereby releasing him from obligation — compare INTERCESSION 2

ex·pro·mis·sor \,ekspro'misə(r)\ *n* -S [LL, fr. L *expromissus* + *-or*] : one that performs an act of expromission

ex·pro·pri·ate \ek'sprōprē,āt, ik-, *usu* -ād·+V\ *vt* -ED/-ING/-S [ML *expropriatus*, past part. of *expropriare*, fr. L *ex-* ¹ex- + *propriare* to appropriate, fr. *proprius* own — more at PROPER] **1 :** to deprive of possession or proprietary rights — used esp. of the action of a state; see EXPROPRIATION **2 :** to take (something) out of the possession of another : transfer (the property of another) to one's own possession ⟨the landowners *expropriated* the countryside, but they developed it —Roy Lewis & Angus Maude⟩ ⟨they have also *expropriated* another cherished word from the lexicon of western European peoples —R.G.Cowherd⟩ — used esp. of the action of a state ⟨promulgate laws which tended to ~ Jewish possessions —*Collier's Yr. Bk.*⟩ ⟨the government had *expropriated* nearly 68,000 hectares of privately owned property —*Americana Annual*⟩

ex·pro·pri·a·tion \(,)ek,sprōprē'āshən, ik,-\ *n* -S [ML *expropriation-, expropriatio*, fr. *expropriatus* + L *-ion-, -io* -ion] : an act of expropriating or a state of being expropriated; *specif* : the action of the state in taking or modifying the property rights of an individual in the exercise of its sovereignty (as where property is sold under eminent domain)

ex·pro·pri·a·tor \='==,ād·ə(r), -ātə-\ *n* -S : one that expropriates

ex pro·prio vi·go·re \ek'sprōprē,ōvə̇'gōrē\ [NL] : of its own force

expt *abbr* **1** experiment **2** expert **3** export

exptl *abbr* experimental

exptr *abbr* exporter

expugn *vt* -ED/-ING/-S [ME *expugnen*, fr. L *expugnare*, fr. *ex-* ¹ex- + *pugnare* to fight; akin to L *pugnus* fist — more at PUNGENT] **1** *obs* : to take by storm **2** *obs* : VANQUISH

ex·pugna·ble \ek'spyünəbəl, -'spəgnə-\ *adj* [L *expugnabilis*, fr. *expugnare* + *-abilis* -able] : capable of being conquered or taken by storm

ex·pug·na·to·ry \ek'spəgnə,tōrē\ *adj* [LL *expugnatorius* overpowering, fr. L *expugnatus* + *-orius* -ory] : adapted for attack

ex·pulse \ik'spəl(t)s, ek-\ *vt* -ED/-ING/-S [ME *expulsen*, fr. L *expulsare*, fr. *ex-* ¹ex- + *pulsare* to push — more at PUSH] : EXPEL ⟨the country had just *expulsed* the detested . . . invaders —Galbraith Welch⟩

ex·pul·sion \ik'spəlshən, ek-\ *n* -S [ME *expulsioun*, fr. L *expulsion-, expulsio*, fr. *expulsus* (past part. of *expellere* to expel) + *-ion-, -io* -ion — more at EXPEL] : an act of expelling or a state of being expelled : a driving or forcing out : summary removal (as from membership or association) ⟨on the occasion of my ~ from college —A.J.Liebling⟩ ⟨~ from Germany had cost them their homes —Oscar Handlin⟩

expulsion fuse *n* : an electrical fuse that is blown out of its cartridge by a short circuit

ex·pul·sive \-siv, -sēv *also* -lts- *or* -səv\ *adj* [ME *expulsif*, fr. MF & ML; MF *expulsif*, fr. ML *expulsivus*, fr. L *expulsus* + *-ivus* -ive] : having the power of expelling : serving to expel ⟨the ~ power of an exhausting emotional experience —Hunter Mead⟩

ex·punc·tion \ik'spəŋ(k)shən, ek-\ *n* -S [L *expunctus* (past part. of *expungere*) + E *-ion*] : an act of expunging or a state of being expunged : ERASURE ⟨making some ~ —J.M.Conly⟩

ex·punge \ik'spənj, ek-\ *vt* -ED/-ING/-S [L *expungere* to mark for deletion by dots placed above or below, fr. *ex-* ¹ex- + *pungere* to prick — more at PUNGENT] **1 a :** to strike out, obliterate, or mark for deletion (as a word, line, or sentence) **b :** to obliterate (a material record or trace) by any means ⟨~ the sound of a voice from a tape recording⟩ ⟨~ a man's fingerprints⟩ **c :** DROP, EXCLUDE, DISCARD, OMIT ⟨that condemnation stood for priests to read . . . until the seventeenth century, when it was silently *expunged* —G.G.Coulton⟩ **d :** to cause (something intangible) to be effaced ⟨could not ~ those bitter memories from his mind⟩ ⟨the most primitive ways of thinking may not yet be wholly *expunged* —William James⟩ **2 a :** to cause the physical destruction of : ANNIHILATE ⟨the nuclear explosives that can ~ in a fraction of a second . . . the units of . . . civilization —*Saturday Rev.*⟩ ⟨the race of man *expunging* itself by its own hand —Sara H. Hay⟩ **b :** to treat or cause to be regarded as nonexistent : consign to oblivion : destroy in any manner : ERADICATE ⟨released her with a warning and . . . considered the episode *expunged* —Josephine Johnson⟩ ⟨~ the power of labor in politics —Bruce Bliven b. 1889⟩ ⟨official efforts to ~ the popular hero from history⟩ **syn** see ERASE

ex·pur·gate \'ekspə(r),gāt, *usu* -ād·+V\ *vt* -ED/-ING/-S [L *expurgatus*, past part. of *expurgare* to purge, purify, vindicate, fr. *ex-* ¹ex- + *purgare* to purge, purify — more at PURGE] : to cleanse of something morally harmful, offensive, or erroneous : PURGE; *esp* : to expunge before publication or presentation obscene or otherwise objectionable parts from ⟨~ a book⟩ ⟨~ a play⟩

ex·pur·ga·tion \ˌ==ˈgāshən\ *n* -s [ME *expurgacion*, fr. L *expurgation-*, *expurgatio* vindication, fr. *expurgatus* + *-ion-*, *-io* -ion] : an act of expurgating, purging, or cleansing : purification from something morally harmful, offensive, sinful, or erroneous

ex·pur·ga·tor \ˈ==ˌgād·ə(r), -ātə-\ *n* -s : one that expurgates

ex·pur·ga·to·ri·al \ik¦spərgə¦tōrēəl, ek¦-, ˌek,==ˈ===\ *adj* [NL *expurgatorius* + E *-al*] : relating to expurgation or an expurgator : EXPURGATORY

ex·pur·ga·to·ry \ˈ=ˈgə,tōrē\ *adj* [NL *expurgatorius*, fr. L *expurgatus* + *-orius* -ory] : serving to purify from something morally harmful, offensive, or erroneous : CLEANSING, PURIFYING

¹ex·quis·ite \ek'skwizət, 'ek,skwiz-, 'ekskwəz-, ik'skwiz-, *usu* -zəd.+V\ *adj* [ME *exquisit*, fr. L *exquisitus*, fr. past part. of *exquirere* to search out, seek, fr. *ex-* ¹ex- + *-quirere* (fr. *quaerere* to seek, gain, obtain, ask)] **1 a :** carefully selected or sought out : ingeniously devised : CHOICE, RECHERCHÉ ⟨I have given her the best advice, . . . making the most ~ moral reflections — but to no purpose —Iris Origo⟩ **b** *obs* : FARFETCHED, AFFECTED **2** *archaic* : careful or exact in working or operation : ACCURATE, NICE, EXACT **3 a :** marked by flawless craftsmanship or by beautiful, ingenious, delicate, or elaborate execution ⟨Sung vases and ~ lacquers —James Hilton⟩ ⟨an ~ cameo⟩ ⟨an ~ portrait⟩ **b :** marked by nicest discrimination, keenest appreciation, deepest sensitivity, or most subtle understanding ⟨a far more keen and ~ observer than her brother —J.L.Lowes⟩ ⟨an ~ choice⟩ ⟨an ~ critic⟩ : marked or perceptible by or calling for keenest sensitivity ⟨an ~ sense of hearing⟩ ⟨~ variations in color⟩ **c :** transcending and superlative : marked by acute discrimination and selection, faultless execution, and maximum effectiveness ⟨paints with ~ art the charm of the deep country —John Buchan⟩ ⟨the ~ transparency and delicate finish of her work —P.E.More⟩ **d :** ACCOMPLISHED, FINISHED, PERFECTED ⟨an ~ gentleman⟩ **4 a :** affording or accompanied by keen delight, rapture, or pleasure esp. through beauty, fitness, delicacy, or perfection : DELIGHTFUL, DELECTABLE ⟨the night-blooming cereus . . . an ~ white blossom with a spicy fragrance —*Amer. Guide Series:Ariz.*⟩ ⟨~ brushwork⟩ **b :** perfect and unrelieved : TRANSCENDING, ACUTE, EXTREME, CONSUMMATE ⟨the most ~ pitch of joy and happiness to which life could thrill —Jack London⟩ ⟨an ~ pain shot through his arm⟩ ⟨wondered at the ~ stupidity of the hearers —S.M.Crothers⟩ **c :** marked by uncommon, esoteric, or precious appeal ⟨the ~, the finely drawn, the rich trappings of legend —Sara H. Hay⟩ **syn** see CHOICE

²exquisite \"\ *n* -s : one who is overnice in dress or ornament ⟨young ~s, perfumed and foppish⟩

ex·quis·ite·ly *adv* : in an exquisite manner

ex·quis·ite·ness *n* -ES : the quality of being exquisite

ex·quis·i·tive·ly \ek'skwizəd·ivlē\ *adv, archaic* : EXQUISITELY

exr *abbr* executor

ex·radius \(ˈ)eks+\ *n* [¹*ex-* + *radius*] : a radius of an escribed circle or sphere — opposed to *inradius*

ex re·la·ti·o·ne \ˌeksrā,lād·ē'ōnē\ *prep* [L] : by or on the relation or information of — used in the title of informations and special proceedings to designate the person at whose instance the state or a public officer is acting; abbr. *ex rel.*

ex rights *adv (or adj)* [²*ex*] : without carrying or conferring the right to subscribe to a pending new issue of stock ⟨stock that sells *ex rights*⟩

exrx *abbr* executrix

ex·san·gui·nate \ek(s)'saŋgwə,nāt\ *vt* -ED/-ING/-S [L *exsanguinatus* bloodless, fr. *ex-* ¹ex- + *sanguin-*, *sanguis* blood + *-atus* -ate] : to make bloodless : drain of blood — **ex·san·gui·na·tion** \(ˌ)=ˌ==ˈnāshən\ *n* -s

ex·san·guine \(ˈ)ek(s)¦saŋgwən\ *adj* [irreg. (influence of *sanguine*) fr. L *exsanguis*, fr. *ex-* ¹ex- + *sanguis* blood] : BLOODLESS, ANEMIC — **ex·san·guin·i·ty** \ˌek(s),saŋ'gwinəd·ē, -san'g-\ *n* -ES

ex·san·guin·e·ous \ˌek(s),saŋ¦gwinēəs, -saŋ'g-\ *adj* [¹*ex-* + *sanguineous*] : EXSANGUINE

ex·san·guin·o·transfusion \ek(s)¦saŋgwə,nō+\ *n* [¹*exchange* + *sanguino-* + *transfusion*] : EXCHANGE TRANSFUSION

ex·san·gui·nous \(ˈ)ek(s)¦saŋgwənəs\ *adj* [¹*ex-* + *sanguinous*] : EXSANGUINE

ex·san·gui·ous \(ˈ)ek(s)¦saŋgwēəs\ *adj* [irreg. fr. L *exsanguis*] : EXSANGUINE

ex·scind \ek'sind\ *vt* -ED/-ING/-S [L *exscindere* to cut or tear out, fr. *ex-* ¹ex- + *scindere* to cut, tear — more at SHED (to throw off)] : to cut off or out : EXCISE ⟨these words were ~*ed* from the text⟩

exscribe *vt* [L *exscribere*, fr. *ex-* ¹ex- + *scribere* to write — more at SCRIBE] *obs* : COPY, TRANSCRIBE

ex·sculp·tate \ek'skəlp,tāt\ *adj* [L *exsculptus* (past part. of *exsculpere* to carve out, fr. *ex-* ¹ex- + *sculpere* to carve) + E *-ate* — more at SCULPTOR] : having variable and irregular depressed lines that resemble sculptured work

ex·scutellate \(ˌ)ek(s)+\ *adj* [¹*ex-* + NL *scutellum* + E *-ate*] : ESCUTELLATE

ex·sect \(ˈ)ek¦sekt\ *vt* -ED/-ING/-S [L *exsectus*, past part. of *exsecare*, fr. *ex-* ¹ex- + *secare* to cut — more at SAW] : to cut out : EXCISE ⟨an ~*ed* uterus⟩

ex·sec·tile \(ˈ)ek¦sekt³l, -,tīl, -(ˌ)til\ *adj* : capable of being exsected

ex·sec·tion \(ˈ)ek¦sekshən\ *n* [L *exsection-*, *exsectio*, fr. *exsectus* + *-ion-*, *-io* -ion] : EXCISION

¹ex·sert \(ˈ)ek¦sərt\ *vt* -ED/-ING/-S [L *exsertus*, *exertus*, past part. of *exserere*, *exerere* — more at EXERT] : to thrust forth or out : cause to protrude : cause to project : stick out ⟨a bee ~*ing* its sting⟩

²exsert \"\ *adj* [L *exsertus*, *exertus*, past part.] : EXSERTED

exserted *adj* : projecting beyond an enclosing organ or part ⟨~ stamens⟩

ex·ser·tile \(ˈ)ek¦sərd·³l, -r,tīl, -r(ˌ)til\ *adj* : capable of being exserted ⟨the highly ~ tongue of this snake⟩

ex·ser·tion \(ˈ)ek¦sərshən\ *n* -s : the action of exserting or state of being exserted

ex·sheath \(ˈ)ek(s)¦shēth, -th\ *vb* [¹*ex-* + *sheath* (n.)] *vi* : to escape from the residual membrane remaining from a previous stage of development — used of certain larval nematodes (as filaria) ~ *vt* : to cause (nematode larvae) to exsheath — **ex·sheath·ment** \-mənt\ *n* -s

ex ship *adv (or adj)* [²*ex*] : without shipment costs to the consignee until receipt overside of the shipment at destination, the consignee being required to accept delivery at the ship's side and assume all subsequent liability ⟨the firm agreed to receive the lumber *ex ship*⟩ — compare FREE ON BOARD

ex·sic·ca·tae \ˌeksə'kā,tē, -kā,-, -ä,tī, -ä,-, -ä,tē\ *n pl* [NL, fr. L, fem. & masc. pl. respectively of *exsiccatus*] : a collection or series of dried herbarium specimens

ex·sic·ca·ti \-ä,tī, -ä,-, -ä,tē\ *also* **ex·sic·ca·ti**

ex·sic·cate \'eksə,kāt, ek'si,-\ *vt* -ED/-ING/-S [L *exsiccatus*, past part. of *exsiccare*, fr. *ex-* ¹ex- + *siccare* to dry, fr. *siccus* dry — more at SACK] : to drive moisture from (as by the action of heat) : make dry : DEHYDRATE ⟨*exsiccated* salt⟩ : drain of moisture : dry up ⟨an *exsiccated* swamp⟩ : DESICCATE — now used chiefly in passive — **ex·sic·ca·tion** \ˌeksə'kāshən\ *n* -s

ex·sic·co·sis \ˌeksə'kōsəs\ *n* -ES [NL, fr. L *exsiccare* + NL *-osis*] : insufficient intake of fluids or the state of bodily dehydration produced thereby

ex si·len·tio \ˌek(s)sə'lenchē,ō, -)ˌsī'-\ *also* **e silentio** \ˌēsə-, ˌē,sī-\ *adv (or adj)* [L *ex silentio* from silence] : from the fact of lack of specific evidence (as of written or oral attestation) ⟨an argument that was built up wholly *ex silentio*⟩

ex·solution \ˌek(s)+\ *n* [L *exsolution-*, *exsolutio* release, fr. *exsolutus* (past part. of *exsolvere*) + *-ion-*, *-io* -ion] : the action or process of exsolving

ex·solve \(ˈ)ek(s)+\ *vb* [L *exsolvere* to loosen, untie, release, fr. *ex-* ¹ex- + *solvere* to loosen, release — more at SOLVE] : to separate or precipitate from a solid crystalline phase : UNMIX

ex·stipulate \(ˈ)ek(s)+\ *adj* [¹*ex-* + *stipule* + *-ate*] : having no stipules ⟨~ leaves⟩

ex store *adv (or adj)* [²*ex*] : with shipment costs to be paid by the consignee after the shipment leaves the stock — opposed to *free on board;* compare IN STORE

ex·stro·phy \'ekstrəfē\ *n* -ES [¹*ex-* + *-strophy* (fr. Gk *strephein* to turn + E *-y*) — more at STROPHE] : eversion of a part or organ; *specif* : a congenital malformation of the bladder in which the normally internal mucosa of the organ lies exposed on the abdominal wall because of failure of union between the halves of the pubic symphysis and between the adjacent halves of the abdominal wall

ex·suc·cous \(ˈ)ek(s)¦səkəs\ *adj* [L *exsuccus*, fr. *ex-* ¹ex- + *succus* juice — more at SUCCULENT] : devoid of all juices or sap : having no moisture whatsoever : dried up ⟨a withered ~ piece of fruit⟩

exsudation *obs var of* EXUDATION

ex·suf·fla·tion \ˌeksə'flāshən\ *n* [LL *exsufflation-*, *exsufflatio*, fr. *exsufflatus* (past part. of *exsufflare* to blow away, fr. L *ex-* ¹ex- + *sufflare* to inflate, blow upon) + L *-ion-*, *-io* -ion — more at SUFFLATE] **1 :** the action of breathing forth or blowing; *esp* : this action used as an exorcism in some rites of baptism **2 :** forcible breathing or blowing out (as in clearing the respiratory tract) : forcible expiration

ext *abbr* **1** extended; extension **2** exterior **3** external **4** extinct **5** extinguisher **6** extra **7** extract **8** extreme; extremely

ex·tant \'ekstənt, ek'stant, 'ek,stant, ik'stant, -taa(ə)nt\ *adj* [L *exstant-*, *exstans*, *extant-*, *extans*, pres. part. of *exstare*, *extare* to stand out, project, be in existence, fr. *ex-* ¹ex- + *stare* to stand — more at STAND] **1 a** *archaic* : standing, protruding, or protruding out or above ⟨its naked body half ~ from jecting, or protruding out or above the coarse blanket —George Borrow⟩ **b** *archaic* : standing out in a way that is adapted to physical or mental perception : easily seen or understood : clearly evident ⟨the truth should be visibly ~ —A.W.Kinglake⟩ **2 a :** currently or actually existing : that is in existence ⟨the most charming writer ~ —G.W. Johnson⟩ **b :** still existing : continuing to exist : maintaining existence : not exterminated, destroyed, or lost ⟨in the specimens of graphic art found among ~ barbaric folk —Edward Clodd⟩ ⟨one of the oldest works ~ on that subject⟩

ex·ta·sy *archaic var of* ECSTASY

ext d&c color \'eks(t),dēən,sē-\ *n, usu cap E&D & 1st C* [abbr. of *external drug and cosmetic color*] : any of the synthetic dyes that in certified batches are permitted for use only in drugs and cosmetics to be applied externally — compare D&C COLOR, FD&C COLOR; see DYE table II

ex·tem·po·ral \(ˈ)ek¦stemp(ə)rəl, ik's-\ *adj* [L *extemporalis*, fr. *ex tempore* + *-alis* -al] *archaic* : EXTEMPORANEOUS, EXTEMPORE — **ex·tem·po·ral·ly** \-rəlē\ *adv, obs*

ex·tem·po·ra·ne·i·ty \(ˌ)ek,stempərə'nēəd·ē, ik,-, -ēətē, -i\ *n* -ES : the quality or state of being extemporaneous

ex·tem·po·ra·ne·ous \(ˌ)ek¦stempə¦rānēəs, ik¦-\ *adj* [LL *extemporaneus*, fr. L *ex tempore* + *-aneus* (as in *subterraneus* subterranean)] **1 a :** composed, performed, or uttered on or as if on the spur of the moment ⟨an ~ musical composition⟩ ⟨an ~ piece of verse⟩ : impromptu ⟨~ comment⟩ or apparently impromptu (as by avoiding use of rigid memorization, reading, or notes) ⟨a brilliant ~ speech⟩ : marked by or as if by no previous thought, study, or other preparation : IMPROVISED, UNPREMEDITATED **b :** skilled at, given to, or marked by extemporaneous composing, performance, or utterance ⟨one of the funniest ~ wits of our time —E.J.Kahn⟩ **c :** happening suddenly, often unexpectedly, and usu. without clearly known causes or relationships ⟨a great deal of criminal and delinquent behavior is . . . ~ —W.C.Reckless⟩ **2 :** provided, made, or put to use as a temporary expedient : suggested by or hurriedly adapted to the occasion : MAKESHIFT ⟨preparing an ~ meal⟩ ⟨using an ~ shelter⟩ **3** *of a pharmaceutical preparation* : compounded according to a physician's prescription as needed : prepared when ordered : not ready-made — **ex·tem·po·ra·ne·ous·ly** *adv* — **ex·tem·po·ra·ne·ous·ness** *n* -ES

ex·tem·po·rar·i·ly \ik'stempə,rerəlē, -li, (ˌ)ek,==ˈ==, ek'==-,===\ *adv* : in an extemporary manner

ex·tem·po·rary \ik'stempə,rerē, ek-, -ri, -eri\ *adj* [L *ex tempore* + E *-ary*] : EXTEMPORANEOUS

¹ex·tem·po·re \ik'stempərē, ek-, -ri, -,rē *also* -,rā\ *adv* [L *ex tempore* instantaneously, on the spur of the moment, fr. *ex* out of + *tempore*, abl. of *tempus* time — more at EX-, TEMPORAL] : in an extempore manner : EXTEMPORANEOUSLY

²extempore \"\ *n, pl* **extempores** *also* **extempore** *archaic* : something that is extemporaneous : IMPROVISATION

³extempore \"\ *adj* : EXTEMPORANEOUS ⟨his effusions were genuinely ~ —W.G.Lane⟩

ex·tem·po·ri·za·tion \ik,stempərə'zāshən, (ˌ)ek,-, -ˌrī'z-\ *n* -s **1 :** the act of extemporizing : IMPROVISATION **2 :** something produced or marked by extemporization ⟨ingenious ~s were employed to provide substitutes for customary foods, clothing, and household articles —A.D.Kirwan⟩

ex·tem·po·rize \=ˈ==,rīz\ *vb, see -ize in Explan Notes* [¹*extempore* + *-ize*] *vi* **1 :** to do something extemporaneously : IMPROVISE; *esp* : to speak extemporaneously ⟨he rarely *extemporized* and never on grave occasions —John Buchan⟩ **2 :** to get along in a makeshift manner adapted to the occasion : regularly meet necessity with temporary expedients : live with little or no advance planning ⟨the world, facing the need to organize itself internationally, drifted and *extemporized* —Charles McKinley⟩ ⟨*extemporizing* without a plan has long been regarded by many as a necessary and inherent part of movie making —Hortense Powdermaker⟩ ~ *vt* **1 :** to compose, perform, or utter extemporaneously : IMPROVISE ⟨a cleverly *extemporized* organ accompaniment⟩ ⟨*extemporizing* an after-dinner speech⟩ **2 :** to provide, make, or put to use as a temporary expedient ⟨the ungainly but useful vessels which Caesar had *extemporized* —J.A.Froude⟩ ⟨beyond the *extemporized* bandstand —Graham Greene⟩ : produce, put together, devise, or contrive hurriedly or in a makeshift manner to meet an immediate need or emergency ⟨trying to ~ a competent personnel⟩ ⟨*extemporizing* a plan to overwhelm the opposition⟩

ex·tem·po·riz·er \-zə(r)\ *n* -s : one that extemporizes

ex·tend \ik'stend, ek-\ *vb* -ED/-ING/-S [ME *extenden*, fr. MF or L; MF *estendre*, *extendre*, fr. L *extendere*, fr. *ex-* ¹ex- + *tendere* to stretch — more at THIN] *vt* **1** [ME *extenden*, fr. ML *extendere* (fr. L) or AF *estendre*, fr. OF *estendre*, *extendre*] **a** *Brit* : to assess the value of (as lands or buildings) **b** *Brit* : to take possession of by a writ of extent **c** *obs* : to take by force : SEIZE **2 :** to lay out at full length ⟨with his body ~*ed* on the ground⟩ : put into a horizontal and usu. straight position ⟨~*ing* their arms in front of them⟩ : straighten out (as a limb or other bodily part) : UNBEND ⟨alternately flexing his arm and ~*ing* it⟩ **3 a :** to stretch out esp. forcibly : stretch out to fullest length ⟨with the sails ~*ed* by yards⟩ **b** *obs* : to stretch, fill, or inflate beyond normal limits : STRAIN, DISTEND **c :** to cause (as a horse) to move at full stride ⟨a promising racehorse that had so far never been really ~*ed*⟩ : push to full stride **d :** to apply or exert (oneself) energetically or to full capacity ⟨people who would rather accept federal bounties than ~ themselves —F.L.Allen⟩ ⟨his capacity for handling an immense amount of work without appearing to ~ himself —*Lamp*⟩ **e :** to increase the quantity or bulk of (a product) by the addition of a relatively inexpensive or otherwise readily available substance so as to reduce cost, improve efficiency, or attain other desired effects ⟨~*ing* ground meat with cereal⟩; *sometimes* : ADULTERATE **4 a :** to stretch forth : hold out ⟨his arm ~*ed* both her hands to him —W.F.deMorgan⟩ ⟨a bald eagle with its wings ~*ed*⟩ **b :** to present for acceptance or rejection : make the offer of : PROFFER ⟨~*ing* their greetings⟩ ⟨~*ed* hospitality to them⟩ **c :** to make available (as a fund or privilege) often in response to an explicit or implied request : GRANT ⟨financial aid will be ~*ed* where needed —Paul Wooton⟩ **5 a :** to cause to stretch out or reach (as from one point to another) ⟨~*ing* the railroad to the next city⟩ : cause to span an interval (as of distance, space, or time) ⟨a rope bridge was ~*ed* over the chasm⟩ : push to a farther point ⟨~*ing* the frontiers of knowledge⟩ ⟨city boundaries were ~*ed* to take in the entire county —*Amer. Guide Series: Pa.*⟩ : open out (a compass) **b :** to cause to be longer : LENGTHEN, PROLONG, PROTRACT ⟨~*ing* their visit⟩; *specif* : to prolong the time of payment of (as a debt) beyond the time orig. stipulated **c :** to cause to project in one or more directions : stick out ⟨when disturbed, the creature ~*s* its spines⟩ **d :** to bring to a further degree of development ⟨the Anglo-Saxons ~*ed* the use of the plow —L.D.Stamp⟩ : cause to be more nearly complete or perfect : ADVANCE, FURTHER ⟨~*ing* man's knowledge of the universe⟩ ⟨the rest of the decade consolidated and ~*ed* those gains —Oscar Handlin⟩ **e :** to transfer (figures) from one column to another (as in bookkeeping) : carry forward **f :** to compute the amount of (as in accounting) ⟨the credit balance will be ~*ed* on the accounts⟩ **6 a :** to cause to be of greater area or volume ⟨~*ing* the surface of metal plates by hammering⟩ : increase the size of : ENLARGE : make greater in extent ⟨trying to ~ its staff of trained personnel⟩ **b :** to increase the scope, meaning, or application of ⟨~*ing* the sense of a word⟩ ⟨the name . . . was easily ~*ed* to the new land —P.E.James⟩ ⟨~ the force of the laws⟩ : increase the action or capacity of ⟨beauty, I suppose, opens the heart, ~*s* the consciousness —Algernon Blackwood⟩ : make more comprehensive, inclusive, or intensive : BROADEN, AMPLIFY ⟨~*ing* the range of their duties⟩ **c** *archaic* : to enlarge upon in imagination : EXAGGERATE **d :** to write out (as shorthand notes) in expanded form : write out or set forth in detail ~ *vi* **1 :** to stretch out (as in distance, space, or time) : RANGE ⟨rugged hills and ravines ~ in all directions —*Amer. Guide Series: Minn.*⟩ ⟨occupation of the fortress ~*ed* from the second century B.C. to the first century A.D. —J.E.M.White⟩ : REACH, SPREAD **2 :** to span an interval (as of distance, space, or time) ⟨an ancient bridge ~*s* over the river⟩ **3 :** to jut out : stick out : PROTRUDE, PROJECT ⟨through a cupola . . . ~*s* a thin square chimney —*Amer. Guide Series: Minn.*⟩ ⟨fruit trees that ~*ed* out over the farm fences —Sherwood Anderson⟩ **4** *of a serviceman* : to agree to remain on active duty for another term

syn LENGTHEN, ELONGATE, PROLONG, PROTRACT: EXTEND, like others in this group, applies to a drawing out in length; it may suggest also similar or comparable drawing out in breadth, size, or range ⟨*extend* a road⟩ ⟨an *extended* trip⟩ ⟨*extending* his vacation⟩ ⟨federal grants to the states to *extend* and improve their health and welfare services for mothers and children —*Americana Annual*⟩ LENGTHEN is likely to refer to what constitutes or may be thought of as similar in some way to a line ⟨*lengthen* a road⟩ ⟨a *lengthened* period⟩ ⟨the *lengthening* of the average life span by more than twenty years since the last century —*Collier's Yr. Bk.*⟩ ELONGATE suggests a stretching out resulting in a long narrow frame or shape or to unusual length ⟨*elongated* fibers⟩ ⟨an *elongated* segment⟩ ⟨the old man's gaunt and *elongated* frame⟩ PROLONG is likely to indicate a drawing out or stretching out in duration ⟨a *prolonged* discussion⟩ ⟨withstanding a *prolonged* siege⟩ ⟨a strange, secret life, *prolonged* for half a century in Paris —Van Wyck Brooks⟩ PROTRACT, often close to EXTEND or PROLONG, may suggest needlessness, boredom, vexation, indefiniteness ⟨litigation *protracted* through a decade⟩ ⟨the *protracted* interruption of steel production by labor difficulties —*Americana Annual*⟩ ⟨his temptation will be to *protract* negotiations on the minor points still outstanding —*New Statesman & Nation*⟩

extended *adj* [ME, fr. past part. of *extenden*] **1 a :** drawn out in length ⟨an ~ meandering river⟩ esp. in length of time ⟨their ~ residence in England⟩ ⟨an ~ visit⟩ : LENGTHY ⟨an ~ tale⟩ : PROLONGED, PROTRACTED **b** *of a letter or typeface* : having a face considerably wider than that of a typeface not so characterized — compare CONDENSED, EXPANDED **2 a :** fully stretched out ⟨his ~ limbs raised in an attitude of prayer⟩ : widely spread out ⟨an ~ battle line⟩ **b :** stretched forth : held out ⟨refusing to accept her ~ hand⟩ **c** *of a horse's stride* : FULL ⟨an ~ gallop⟩ — compare COLLECTED 3 **d :** INTENSIVE ⟨the groundwork is laid for more ~ efforts —Dorothy Barclay⟩ ⟨an ~ course in college mathematics⟩ **3 :** having the property of extension : having spatial magnitude ⟨~ substances⟩ **4 :** EXTENSIVE: as **a :** having great area ⟨~ farm lands⟩ : WIDESPREAD, FAR-FLUNG ⟨an ~ empire⟩ **b :** having a wide range : greatly diversified : of great scope ⟨an ~ vocabulary⟩ ⟨a word with ~ meanings⟩ : notable in extent ⟨surgeons who have had ~ experience —Morris Fishbein⟩ **c :** ENLARGED, AMPLIFIED : more complete, comprehensive, or detailed ⟨lectures that were later brought out in ~ book form⟩ — **ex·tend·ed·ly** *adv* — **ex·tend·ed·ness** *n* -ES

extended coverage *n* : coverage extending a fire insurance policy so that additional hazards (as those arising from storms or explosions) are included

extended family *n* : a larger family group which includes near relatives (as patrilineal descendants) and in which collateral lines are kept fairly distinct — distinguished from *clan;* opposed to *nuclear family*

extended harmony *n* : OPEN HARMONY

extended insurance *or* **extended term insurance** *n* : life insurance that after cessation of premium payments is continued in its original amount for the period allowed by the cash value

extended order *n* : an arrangement of troops for skirmishing not in exact formation or at fixed intervals but usu. as widely separated as the tactical situation and the terrain permit — distinguished from *close order*

extended play *n* : a 45-rpm phonograph record that has a playing time of about 6 to 8 minutes obtained by the use of closer groove spacing and utilization of a greater part of the surface area than in the standard 45-rpm record — abbr. *EP*

extended river *or* **extended consequent** *n* : a stream lengthened by the extension of its course downstream across newly emerged land (as on a coastal plain)

ex·tend·er \-də(r)\ *n* -s **1 a :** a substance added to a product esp. in the capacity of a diluent, adulterant, or modifier: as (1) *or* **extender pigment** : a colorless or white mineral pigment (as whiting) used with one or more other pigments usu. to achieve certain physical properties (as improved surface characteristics or working properties in paint or printing ink) — called also *filler, inert* (2) : a substance usu. having some adhesive action (as flour) that is added to an adhesive for reducing the cost or sometimes for improving the viscosity (3) : a substance (as a petroleum oil) used for increasing the bulk or improving the processing characteristics of a rubber compound, a plastic, or a resin **b :** EXPANDER 2 **2** *Brit* : a teacher of university extension classes

ex·tend·ibil·i·ty \ik,stendə'biləd·ē, (ˌ)ek,-, -lətē, -i\ *n* -ES : capability of being extended

ex·tend·ible *or* **ex·tend·able** \ik'stendəbəl, (ˈ)ek¦s-\ *adj* : capable of being extended

extending *pres part of* EXTEND

extends *pres 3d sing of* EXTEND

ex·tense \ik'sten(t)s, (ˈ)ek¦s-\ *adj* [L *extensus*, past part. of *extendere* to extend — more at EXTEND] *archaic* : widely extended

ex·ten·si·bil·i·ty \ik,sten(t)sə'biləd·ē, (ˌ)ek,-, -lətē, -i\ *n* -ES : capability of being extended; *specif* : the extent to which something can be stretched without breaking

ex·ten·si·ble \ik'sten(t)səbəl, (ˈ)ek¦s-\ *adj* [L *extensus* + E *-ible*] : capable of being extended ⟨~ school building⟩; *esp* : capable of being protruded ⟨an ~ tongue⟩ or opened out ⟨an ~ measuring rule⟩

ex·ten·sile \ik'sten(t)səl, (ˈ)ek¦s-, -n,sīl, -n(t)(ˌ)sil\ *adj* [L *extensus* + E *-ile*] : EXTENSIBLE

extensimeter *var of* EXTENSOMETER

ex·ten·sion \ik'stenchən, ek-, *in sense 3c* " *or* estäⁿsyōⁿ\ *n, pl* **extensions** \-ənz, -ōⁿ(z)\ *often attrib* [ME *extensioun*, fr. MF or LL; MF *extension*, fr. LL *extension-*, *extensio*, fr. L *extensus* + *-ion-*, *-io* -ion] **1 a :** the action of extending or state of being extended : a stretching out or stretching forth **b :** a carrying forward : LENGTHENING, FURTHERING, DEVELOPING **b :** the action of spreading out (as in area) or state of being spread out : EXPANSION, ENLARGEMENT, AUGMENTATION, INCREASE **c :** something that is extended **2 a :** the total range over which something extends or can be extended : COMPASS ⟨the ~ of the human mind⟩ **b :** DENOTATION 4 ⟨*plant* is a word with wider ~ than *orchid*⟩ — contrasted with *intension* **3 a :** the stretching of a fractured or luxated limb so as to restore it to its natural position **b :** the straightening out of a flexed limb **c :** a dance movement in which the leg is extended at an angle to the body; *also* : an exercise (as for a ballet dancer) in which this movement is used **4 a :** a property whereby something occupies or apparently occupies a greater or lesser part of space : spatial magnitude **b :** something marked or delimited by the property of extension **5 :** an increase in length of time : increased or continued duration; *specif* : an agreement on or concession of additional time (as for meeting an overdue debt or fulfilling a legal formality) **6 :** the making available of the educational opportunities or other resources of an institution by special programs or methods (as evening classes in a university, off-campus instruction centers, correspondence courses, library branches, or bookmobiles) to persons otherwise unable to take advantage of such opportunities and resources; *also* **:** a service or system by which such opportunities or resources are made available **7 a :** a part that is extended from or attached to a main body or section as an addition, supplement, or enlargement ⟨a house with two ~*s*⟩ or that is capable of being so extended or attached ⟨a table with side ~*s*⟩ **:** a section that forms an additional length ⟨an ~ for an electric-light cord⟩ ⟨the ~ of a railway⟩ **:** PROLONGATION; *also* **:** something having extensions (as a table) **b :** an extra telephone connected to the principal line ⟨they have a downstairs phone and an ~ in each of the bedrooms⟩ **8 :** an indicated figure or amount: as **a :** a figure transferred or carried forward (as in bookkeeping) **b :** an amount computed (as by multiplying a number of units by the cost of each unit) ⟨~*s* on an invoice⟩

extension agent *n* **:** COUNTY AGENT

ex·ten·sion·al \ik'stenchənᵊl, (ˈ)ek¦s-, -chnəl\ *adj* **1 :** of, relating to, or marked by extension; *specif* **:** DENOTATIVE ⟨the ~ meaning of *cow* is the group comprising all existing cows —P.D.Wienpahl⟩ **2 :** of, relating to, or marked by practical values, relationships, and applications **:** PRAGMATIC ⟨an ~ nonsubjective approach to social problems⟩ **:** concerned with objective reality **:** CONCRETE, FACTUAL — **ex·ten·sion·al·ly** \-ᵊlē, -əlē, -li\ *adv*

ex·ten·sion·al·ism \ik'stenchənᵊl,izəm, ek-, -chnə,li-\ *n* -s **:** EXTENSIONALITY

ex·ten·sion·al·i·ty \ik,stenchə'naləd·ē, (,)ek,-\ *n* -ES **:** the quality or state of being extensional

ex·ten·sion·al·iza·tion \ik,stenchənᵊlə'zāshən, (,)ek,-, -chnələ-, -ᵊl,ī'z-, -ə,lī'z-\ *n* -s **:** the act of extensionalizing or condition of being extensionalized

ex·ten·sion·al·ize \ik'stenchənᵊl,īz, ek-, -chnə,līz\ *vt* -ED/-ING/-S **:** to make extensional

extension bolt *n* **:** a bolt set flush and vertically (as at the top or bottom of a door) having a long extended rod by which it may be conveniently slid into place

extension-gap lathe *also* **extension lathe** *n* **:** a gap lathe with an upper extendible bed

ex·ten·sion·ist \ik'stench(ə)nəst, ek-\ *n* -s **:** one that advocates extension

extension jamb *n* **:** a jamb extending beyond the head of a door or window usu. to the ceiling

extension ladder *n* **:** a ladder consisting of usu. two sections arranged so that they fit together or extend on a sliding mechanism almost to the full length of the two sections

ex·ten·sion·less \-chənləs\ *adj, philos* **:** having no extension ⟨~ time⟩

extension rule *n* **:** a sliding attachment to a folding rule for the measuring of inside distances between objects

extension spring *n* **:** a closely coiled spring made to resist a

extension spring

force pulling in the direction of its length

extension table *n* **:** a table that can be extended in length by the insertion of a leaf

ex·ten·si·ty \ik'sten(t)səd·ē, ek-\ *n* -ES [L *extensus* + E *-ity*] **1 :** the quality of having extension ⟨two characteristic facts about an emotional experience . . . are its intensity and its ~ —H.H.Britan⟩ **:** degree of extension **:** RANGE ⟨changes in the severity and ~ of punishment for crimes —P.A.Sorokin⟩ **2** *psychol* **:** an attribute of sensation whereby space or size are perceived

ex·ten·sive \ik'sten(t)siv, (ˈ)ek¦s-, -sēv *also* -səv\ *adj* [LL *extensivus,* fr. L *extensus* (past part. of *extendere* to extend) + *-ivus* -ive — more at EXTEND] **1** *obs* **:** capable of being extended **:** APPLICABLE ⟨inability . . . may be more general and ~ to all acts —Jonathan Edwards⟩ **2 :** of, relating to, or marked by logical extension ⟨an ~ proposition⟩ or spatial extension ⟨the ~ nature of the physical world⟩ **:** EXTENSIONAL **3 a :** widely extended in scope or application **:** broad in range **:** WIDE, COMPREHENSIVE ⟨~ reading in literature⟩ ⟨~ repairs⟩ ⟨~ privileges⟩ **:** very complete **:** THOROUGH, FAR-REACHING ⟨an ~ knowledge of languages⟩ ⟨taking ~ precautions⟩ **b :** widely extended in area ⟨~ farms and prairies⟩ **:** extending over a large surface or space ⟨~ stretches of ocean —S.F.Mason⟩ **:** ranging over a wide area ⟨~ travels in Europe⟩ **c :** marked by considerable length ⟨a book with an ~ introduction⟩ ⟨an ~ trip⟩ or detail ⟨an ~ report on the trial⟩ **d :** large in amount ⟨~ funds will be needed⟩ or extent ⟨an ~ business⟩ ⟨~ railroad development⟩ ⟨~ efforts⟩ **e :** considerable in number **:** NUMEROUS ⟨~ examples of picture writing⟩ **4 :** of, relating to, or involving farming in which large areas of land are utilized with minimum outlay and labor ⟨producing wheat under ~ conditions⟩ ⟨agriculture of the ~ type⟩ — opposed to *intensive* — **ex·ten·sive·ly** \-səvlē, -li\ *adv* — **ex·ten·sive·ness** \-sivnəs, -sēv- *also* -səv-\ *n* -ES

ex·ten·siv·i·ty \(,)ek,sten'sivəd·ē, ik,-\ *n* -ES **:** the quality or state of being extensive

ex·ten·som·e·ter \(,)ek,sten'sämәd·ə(r), ik,-\ *also* **ex·ten·sim·e·ter** \-sim-\ *n* [*extension* + *-o-* or *-i-* + *-meter*] **:** an instrument for measuring minute deformations of test specimens under stress (as of tension, compression, bending, or twisting)

ex·ten·sor \ik'sten(t)sər, ek-, -n,sȯ(ə)r\ *n* -s [NL, fr. L *extensus* + *-or*] **:** a muscle that serves to extend a limb or other bodily part — opposed to *flexor*

extensor thrust *n* **:** a sudden reflex extension of a leg in response to upward pressure applied to the sole

ex·tent \ik'stent, ek-\ *n* -s [ME *extente,* fr. AF & MF; AF *estente, extente* valuation, fr. MF, extension, area, land survey, fr. fem. of *estent, extent,* past part. of *estendre, extendre* to extend — more at EXTEND] **1 a** *archaic* **:** valuation or assessment (as of land) in Great Britain esp. when made for the purpose of taxation ⟨an ~ of the realm made on the king's behalf —R.H.I.Palgrave⟩; *also* **:** an instance or record of such valuation or assessment **b** *archaic* **:** the value assigned by such an extent **:** assessed value **2** *obs* **:** the act of exercising (as justice) or showing (as courtesy) ⟨the ~ of equal justice —Shak.⟩ **3 a :** seizure (as of land) in execution of a writ of extent in Great Britain or the condition of being so seized; *also* **:** the right of making such an extent **b :** WRIT OF EXTENT **c :** a writ giving to a creditor temporary possession of his debtor's property (as lands) **4** *obs* **:** ASSAULT ⟨this uncivil and unjust ~ against thy peace —Shak.⟩ **5 a** (1) **:** the range (as of inclusiveness or application) over which something extends **:** SCOPE, COMPASS, COMPREHENSIVENESS ⟨within the ~ of human knowledge⟩ ⟨the ~ of his authority⟩ ⟨the ~ of the law⟩ (2) **:** the point or degree to which something extends ⟨they spent money to the ~ of $1500⟩ **:** the limit to which something extends ⟨exerting the full ~ of his power⟩ ⟨to a certain ~ she was fond of him⟩ **b :** the amount of space which something occupies or the distance over which it extends **:** the length, width, height, thickness, diameter, circumference, or area of something **:** DIMENSIONS, PROPORTIONS, SIZE, MAGNITUDE, SPREAD ⟨a farm of considerable ~⟩ ⟨the ~ of a bird's wings⟩ ⟨20 square miles in ~⟩ **c** (1) **:** something that is extended esp. in area **:** a usu. level stretch or expanse ⟨sailing over the vast ~ of the sea⟩ **:** an extended tract or region ⟨the sloping ~ of the forest⟩ ⟨in the whole ~ of France⟩ (2) **:** DENOTATION 4

syn see SIZE

¹extenuate *adj* [ME *extenuat,* fr. L *extenuatus,* past part.] *obs* **:** EXTENUATED

²ex·ten·u·ate \ik'stenyə,wāt, ek-, *usu* -ād.+V\ *vt* -ED/-ING/-S [L *extenuatus,* past part. of *extenuare,* fr. *ex-* ¹ex- + *tenuare* to make thin or small, fr. *tenuis* thin, small — more at THIN] **1 a** *archaic* **:** to treat as of small importance **:** make light of ⟨not by *extenuating* or by exaggerating the damage —Isaac Taylor⟩ **:** UNDERRATE, UNDERESTIMATE **b** (1) **:** to lessen or to try to lessen the real or apparent seriousness of (as a crime, offense, or fault) or extent of (guilt) by making partial excuses ⟨they neither concealed nor *extenuated* their crime⟩ or by affording a basis for excuses ⟨the fact of his extreme youth certainly *extenuated* the act⟩ **:** MITIGATE (2) **:** to make partial excuses for **:** try to justify (as by making partial excuses) ⟨he thought it necessary to ~ the length of time he kept the dinner on the table —Charles Lamb⟩ **c** *obs* **:** to lessen the worth of **:** DISPARAGE, BELITTLE ⟨every man seemed wholly bent to ~ the sum which fell to his share —Henry Fielding⟩ **2** *archaic* **a :** to make (as a person) thin or emaciated ⟨peasants were . . . *extenuated* by hunger —W.E.H.Lecky⟩ **b :** to lessen the strength or extent of **:** WEAKEN, DIMINISH ⟨in friendship the individual element is intensified, in fraternity it is *extenuated* —W.C.Brownell⟩ **3 a** *obs* **:** to diminish esp. in size, number, or amount **b** *archaic* **:** to lessen the force or effect of (as a law) **4** *archaic* **:** to make (as a liquid or gas) less concentrated **:** lessen the density of ⟨*extenuating* the air —Samuel Vince⟩ **:** thin out **:** ATTENUATE, RAREFY **syn** see PALLIATE, THIN

extenuating *adj* **:** that extenuates ⟨an ~ circumstance⟩ — **ex·ten·u·at·ing·ly** *adv*

ex·ten·u·a·tion \ik,stenyə'wāshən, (,)ek,-\ *n* -s [MF or L; MF, fr. L *extenuation-, extenuatio,* fr. *extenuatus* + *-ion-, -io* -ion] **1 :** the act of extenuating or state of being extenuated; *esp* **:** partial justification ⟨there is surely much to be said in ~ of it —Stewart Cockburn⟩ **2 :** something that extenuates; *esp* **:** a partial excuse ⟨it was a comfort to him, this ~ —Audrey Barker⟩

ex·ten·u·a·tive \ik'stenyə,wād·iv, ek-, -,wəd-·\ *adj* **:** EXTENUATING

ex·ten·u·a·tor \-,wād·ə(r)\ *n* -s **:** one that extenuates

ex·ten·u·a·to·ry \-,wə,tōrē\ *adj* [LL *extenuatorius,* fr. L *extenuatus* + *-orius* -ory] **:** tending to extenuate

¹ex·te·ri·or \(ˈ)ek¦stirēə(r), -tēr-, ik's-\ *adj* [L, comp. of *exter, exterus* outward, on the outside, foreign, strange, fr. *ex* out of, from — more at EX-] **1 :** EXTERNAL; *esp* **:** situated at and forming the outer surface or limit ⟨the ~ surface of a tennis ball⟩ or a part of the outer surface or limit ⟨the ~ slope of a mountain⟩ — opposed to *interior* **2 a :** of or relating to an exterior ⟨an ~ appearance of happiness⟩ **b :** suitable for use on outside surfaces (as of a house) **:** capable of withstanding normal wear and tear of weather conditions for a considerable period of time ⟨an ~ paint⟩ ⟨an ~ finish for the clapboarding⟩ **syn** see OUTER

²exterior \"\ *n* -s **1 :** something that is exterior: as **a** *archaic* **:** exterior features **:** EXTERNALS — usu. used in pl. **b :** exterior part (as of a building) ⟨the house has an old ~⟩ or surface ⟨the ~ of a tennis ball⟩ or appearance ⟨under a cheerful ~ I have got a spirit that is angry —Mark Twain⟩ **2 a :** a representation of an outdoor scene (as a stage or motion-picture set) ⟨remarkably realistic ~*s*⟩ **b :** a background or acting sequence photographed or played outdoors (as for motion pictures or television) ⟨~*s* for the movie will be filmed in Arizona⟩

exterior angle *n* **1 :** the angle between any side of a polygon and an adjacent side prolonged **2 :** an angle between a line crossing two parallel lines and either of the latter on the outside

a b c d e f g h

ega, egb, fhc, fhd
exterior angles

exterior ballistics *n pl but usu sing in constr* **:** a science that deals with the factors affecting the behavior of a projectile after the projectile leaves the muzzle of the firing weapon (as the initial velocity of the projectile, the force of gravity, and atmospheric conditions) — compare INTERIOR BALLISTICS

exterior caste *n* **:** UNTOUCHABLES

exterior crest *n* **:** the line of intersection of the superior and the exterior slopes of a fortification

ex·te·ri·or·i·ty \(,)ek,==ˈȯrəd·ē, ik,-, -ˈär-, -rətē, -i\ *n* -ES **:** the quality or state of being exterior or exteriorized **:** EXTERNALITY — contrasted with *interiority*

ex·te·ri·or·iza·tion \-rēərə'zāshən, -rēə,rī'z-\ *n* -s **:** the act of exteriorizing or the state of being exteriorized

ex·te·ri·or·ize \='==rēə,rīz\ *vt* -ED/-ING/-S *see -ize in Explan Notes* **1 :** to make exterior **:** EXTERNALIZE **2 :** to bring (an organ) out of the abdomen (as for surgery) ⟨*exteriorizing* the colon⟩

exterior lines *n pl* **:** lines of operations of one or more armed forces converging upon a centrally situated opponent

ex·te·ri·or·ly *adv* **:** on or with regard to the exterior **:** EXTERNALLY ⟨situated ~⟩ ⟨quite unobjectionable ~⟩

exterior planet *n* **:** SUPERIOR PLANET

exterior slope *n* **:** the slope connecting the exterior crest of a fortification with the berm

ex·ter·mi·nate \ik'stərmə,nāt, ek-, -stə̄m-, -stəim-, *usu* -ād.+V\ *vt* -ED/-ING/-S [L *exterminatus,* past part. of *exterminare,* fr. *ex-* ¹ex- + *terminus* boundary, limit, end — more at TERM] **1** *obs* **:** to drive out or away (as from the boundaries of a country) **:** BANISH, EXPEL **2 :** to get rid of (as by killing) ⟨*exterminating* rats⟩ **:** put an end to **:** root out **:** ERADICATE, EXTIRPATE ⟨*exterminating* every error⟩ **:** put out of existence **:** utterly destroy **:** ANNIHILATE ⟨the cataclysm *exterminated* all life⟩

syn EXTERMINATE, EXTIRPATE, ERADICATE, UPROOT, DERACINATE, and WIPE (*out*) can mean to bring about the destruction or abolition of something. EXTERMINATE implies utter extinction usu. by killing off ⟨using every feeble attempt at retaliation as an excuse to *exterminate* whole tribes —R.A.Billington⟩ ⟨following the attempt of the people to *exterminate* feudalism —*Amer. Guide Series: N.J.*⟩ EXTIRPATE usu. applies to the extinction of a race, family, species, or growth, often by the destruction or removal of the means by which a thing is propagated ⟨the gray wolf and the black bear have been *extirpated* —*Amer. Guide Series: Mass.*⟩ ⟨the trailing arbutus . . . has been almost *extirpated* —*Amer. Guide Series: Del.*⟩ ⟨the ancient Athenians had been *extirpated* by repeated wars and massacres —Robert Graves⟩ ⟨another set of measures are intended to get closer to the roots of the evil and to *extirpate* them —Frank Gorrell⟩ ERADICATE implies the driving out or elimination of something that has taken root or has established itself ⟨federal and municipal housing groups are cooperating to *eradicate* slums —*Amer. Guide Series: N.Y. City*⟩ ⟨if you *eradicate* a fault, you leave room for a worse one to take root and flourish —L.P.Smith⟩ UPROOT suggests a forcible removal as by tearing up by the roots, not often suggesting elimination ⟨a tribe *uprooted* by war and famine and forced to settle in new territory⟩ ⟨nor was it going to be easy to *uproot* deep-seated tendencies toward corruption —*Collier's Yr. Bk.*⟩ DERACINATE implies an uprooting or, more commonly, a separation from a rootstock ⟨he is not the *deracinated* and rootless author he has sometimes been thought to be —R.B.West⟩ ⟨although the author is himself a Negro, his book is so *deracinated,* without any of the lively qualities of the imagination peculiar to his people —*Commentary*⟩ WIPE (*out*) is often interchangeable with EXTERMINATE but often applies to a canceling or obliteration as by payment or retaliation or by exhaustion of supplies ⟨discover which species still survive and which have been *wiped out* —*Manchester Guardian Weekly*⟩ ⟨a nerve gas that could *wipe out* the populations of enemy cities —*N.Y. Times*⟩ ⟨*wipe out* corruption⟩ ⟨*wipe out* a debt⟩ ⟨the depression *wiped out* his savings⟩

ex·ter·mi·na·tion \ik,=='nāshən, (,)ek,-\ *n* -s [LL *extermination-, exterminatio,* fr. L *exterminatus* + *-ion-, -io* -ion] **1** [ME *exterminacioun* (influenced in meaning by L *exterminare* to banish), fr. LL *extermination-, exterminatio* annihilation, destruction] *obs* **:** BANISHMENT, EXPULSION **2 :** the act of exterminating or the condition of being exterminated **:** total destruction **:** ERADICATION, ANNIHILATION

ex·ter·mi·na·tive \='==,nād·iv, -,nəd-·\ *adj* **:** EXTERMINATORY

ex·ter·mi·na·tor \-,nād·ə(r), -ātə-\ *n* -s [LL, fr. L *exterminatus* + *-or*] **:** one that exterminates: as **a :** one that rids a place of vermin by fumigating — called also *fumigator* **b :** something (as a chemical preparation) used for exterminating

ex·ter·mi·na·to·ry \-,nə,tōrē, -tȯr-, -ri\ *adj* **:** of, relating to, or marked by extermination ⟨an ~ war⟩ **:** tending to exterminate ⟨harsh ~ political moves⟩

extermine *vt* -ED/-ING/-S [ME *exterminen,* fr. MF or L; MF *exterminer,* fr. L *exterminare* — more at EXTERMINATE] *obs* **:** EXTERMINATE

¹ex·tern \(ˈ)ek¦stərn\ *adj* [MF or L; MF *externe,* fr. L *externus*] *archaic* **:** of, relating to, or situated on or at the outside **:** EXTERNAL, OUTER

²ex·tern *also* **ex·terne** \ˈek,stərn\ *n* -s [F *externe,* fr. *externe,* adj.] **1 :** a person connected with an institution but not living or boarding in it: as **a :** a day student of a school **b :** a nonresident doctor or medical student at a hospital **2 :** a nun of a strictly enclosed order (as the Carmelites) that lives within the convent but outside the enclosure and attends to the convent's outside affairs

ex·ter·na \ek'stərnə\ *n, pl* **exter·nae** \-,nē, -,nī\ *or* **externas** [NL, fr. L, fem. of *externus*] **:** the outer layer of a blood vessel made up chiefly of connective tissue — compare INTIMA, MEDIA

¹ex·ter·nal \(ˈ)ek¦stərnᵊl, ik's-, -tə̄n-,-təin-\ *adj* [ME, fr. L *externus* (fr. *exter, exterus* outward, on the outside) + ME *-al* — more at EXTERIOR] **1 a** (1) **:** of, relating to, or consisting in outward form, appearance, or action ⟨the ~ aspect of religion⟩ (2) **:** capable of being perceived outwardly **:** BODILY, PHYSICAL, VISIBLE ⟨~ signs of a disease⟩ **b** (1) **:** merely outward and lacking in or totally devoid of inner nature, spirit, or motivation **:** having the appearance of something with little or none of the reality **:** SUPERFICIAL ⟨her gaiety was of a conventional ~ kind —J.C.Powys⟩ (2) **:** not intrinsic or essential **:** ACCIDENTAL ⟨~ circumstances⟩ ⟨~ factors affecting their decision⟩ **2 a** (1) **:** of, relating to, or connected with the outside or an outer part ⟨the ~ features of the building are very attractive⟩ (2) **:** situated at, on, or near the outside ⟨an ~ protective covering⟩ ⟨an ~ muscle⟩ **b** (1) **:** acting on or exerted upon the outside ⟨sunbaths and other ~ treatments⟩ ⟨the box collapsed after prolonged ~ pressure⟩ (2) **:** directed toward the outside ⟨~ perception⟩ **:** having an outside object ⟨eyesight and the other ~ senses⟩ **c :** used by applying to the outside ⟨an ~ lotion⟩ **3 a** (1) **:** of, relating to, or connected with something outside, apart, or beyond ⟨~ evidence⟩ ⟨the club's ~ activities⟩ (2) **:** situated outside, apart, or beyond ⟨people almost always want something ~ to themselves —Samuel Butler †1902⟩; *specif* **:** situated away from the mesial plane ⟨the ~ condyle of the humerus⟩ (3) **:** arising or acting from outside **:** having an outside origin ⟨~ force⟩ ⟨~ causes⟩ ⟨~ stimuli⟩ **b :** of or relating to dealings or relationships with foreign countries **:** FOREIGN ⟨~ policies⟩ ⟨~ commerce⟩ ⟨the ~ exchange position of the dollar⟩ ⟨~ affairs⟩ **c :** of, relating to, or consisting of something outside the mind **:** having existence independent of the mind **:** belonging to the spatio-temporal world ⟨sensations aroused by ~ phenomena⟩ ⟨~ reality⟩ ⟨man's efforts to understand the workings of the ~ world —James Jeans⟩

syn see OUTER

²external \"\ *n* -s **1 :** something that is external: as **a** *archaic* **:** an outer part **:** OUTSIDE, EXTERIOR **b :** an external feature or aspect — usu. used in pl. ⟨the ~*s* of religion⟩ **2 :** a house organ designed for circulation among outsiders (as dealers, customers, stockholders)

external account *n* **:** an account of a firm or corporation with any outside party

external acoustic meatus *n* **:** EXTERNAL AUDITORY MEATUS

external angle *n* **:** EXTERIOR ANGLE

external audit *n* **:** INDEPENDENT AUDIT

external auditory meatus *n* **:** the passage leading from the external-ear opening to the eardrum

external ballistics *n pl but usu sing in constr* **:** EXTERIOR BALLISTICS

external brake *n* **:** a brake in which the lining operates on the outside of the brake drum

external capsule *n* **:** CAPSULE 1b(2)

external carotid *n* **:** the branch of the carotid artery that supplies the face, tongue, and external parts of the head

external-combustion engine *n* **:** a heat engine that derives its heat from fuel consumed outside the engine cylinder (as a steam engine or hot-air engine) — compare INTERNAL-COMBUSTION ENGINE

external degree *n* **:** a degree granted by a university to a student who has studied at another institution affiliated with or approved by it — compare INTERNAL DEGREE

external ear *n* **:** the parts of the ear that are external to the eardrum; *also* **:** PINNA 2b

external examination *n* **:** an examination prepared by someone outside the faculty of the school where the examination is given (as by a testing bureau)

external gill *n* **:** a gill that projects from the surface of the body and is not enclosed by the body wall and that is characteristic of certain larval fishes and amphibians

ex·ter·nal·ism \ek'==,izəm, ik-\ *n* -s **1 a :** EXTERNALITY 1a **b :** attention to externals; *esp* **:** excessive preoccupation with externals ⟨the ~ of some religions⟩ **2 :** a doctrine dealing only with immediate experience and with objects of sense perception and discounting the validity of other knowledge **:** PHENOMENALISM

ex·ter·nal·ist \-,əst\ *n* -s **:** one that practices or adheres to externalism

ex·ter·nal·i·ty \,ek,stər'naləd·ē\ *n* -ES **1 a :** the quality or state of being external or externalized; *esp* **:** OBJECTIVITY ⟨the ~ of some writers⟩ **b :** EXTERNALISM 1b **2 :** something that is external (as an external object, event, or feature) ⟨the *externalities* of wealth, of friends, of fame —Irwin Edman⟩

ex·ter·nal·iza·tion \(,)ek,stərnᵊlə'zāshən, ik,-, -ᵊl,ī'z-\ *n* -s **1 a :** the action or process of externalizing **b :** the quality or state of being externalized **2 :** something that has been externalized

ex·ter·nal·ize \='==,īz\ *vt* -ED/-ING/-S *see -ize in Explan Notes* **1 a :** to make external **:** embody in an outward form ⟨spoken language ~*s* thought⟩ **b :** to consider or treat as if consisting only of externals ⟨a tendency to ~ all religions⟩ **2 a :** to transform from a mental image into an apparently real object (as in hallucinations) **:** attribute (a mental image) to external causation ⟨*externalizing* an obsession⟩ **b :** to invent an explanation for (an inner conflict, emotion, or problem whose actual basis is known only subconsciously) by attributing to causes outside the self **:** RATIONALIZE, PROJECT ⟨*externalized* his inability to succeed⟩ **3 :** to direct outward socially **:** EXTROVERT ⟨attempts to ~ the individual and to divert his energies into social and recreational channels —L.R. Wolberg⟩

external loan *n* **:** a loan that a government obtains by selling its securities in a foreign country

external lobe *n* **:** the median lobe of the suture on the venter of an ammonoid

ex·ter·nal·ly \(ˈ)ek¦stərnᵊlē, ik's-, -tə̄n-,-təin-, -ᵊli\ *adv* **:** in an external manner

externally fired boiler *n* **:** a boiler whose furnace is neither wholly nor partly surrounded by water — compare INTERNALLY FIRED BOILER

external oblique *n* **:** a chiefly subcutaneous sheet of diagonally arranged abdominal muscle on each side of the trunk

external phase *n* **:** DISPERSION MEDIUM

external relation *n* **:** a relation that is external to the terms or things it relates; *specif* **:** one that does not affect its relata or is not a part of its relata — contrasted with *internal relation*

external respiration *n* **:** exchange of gases (as oxygen and carbon dioxide) between the external environment and some distributing system (as the lungs of higher vertebrates or the tracheal tubes of insects) of the animal body; *also* **:** the exchange of such gases in higher vertebrates between the blood and the alveolae of the lungs — compare INTERNAL RESPIRATION

externals *pl of* EXTERNAL

external student *n* **:** a student studying outside the university at which he has matriculated and from which he expects to receive a degree — compare INTERNAL STUDENT

external thread *n* **:** a screw thread on the outside of a cone or cylinder (as the thread on a plug gage)

external work *n* **:** work done (as by expanding) against a contrary external force

externas *pl of* EXTERNA

ex·ter·na·tion \,ek,stər'nāshən\ *n* -s [¹*extern* + *-ation*] *archaic* **:** EXTERNALIZATION

externe *var of* EXTERN

ex·ter·ni·ty \ek'stərnəd·ē\ *n* -ES [¹*extern* + *-ity*] *archaic* **:** EXTERNALITY

ex·ter·ni·za·tion \(,)ek,stərnə'zāshən\ *n* -s *archaic* : EXTERNALIZATION
ex·ter·nize \ek'stər,nīz\ *vt* -ED/-ING/-S [¹*extern* + -*ize*] *archaic* : EXTERNALIZE
ex·ter·no·median \ek'stər(,)nō, ,ek,stərnō+\ *adj* [L *externus* external + E -*o*- + *median* — more at EXTERNAL] : exterior to a median line or plane
externs *pl of* EXTERN
ex·ter·o·cep·tive \,ekstərō'septiv\ *adj* [L *exter* outward, on the outside + E -*o*- + -*ceptive* (as in *receptive*) — more at EXTERIOR] : activated by, relating to, or constituting stimuli impinging on the organism from outside (as in touch, smell, or sight) — distinguished from *interoceptive* and *proprioceptive*
ex·ter·o·cep·tor \-ptə(r)\ *n* -s [NL, fr. L *exter* + NL -*o*- + -*ceptor* (as in *receptor*)] : a sense organ excited by stimuli arising outside the body (as those of touch, temperature, smell, vision, or hearing) — compare INTEROCEPTOR, PROPRIOCEPTOR
ex·ter·o·fec·tive \-'fektiv\ *adj* [L *exter* + E -*o*- + -*fective* (as in *effective*)] : of, relating to, dependent on, or constituting the cerebrospinal nervous system — distinguished from *interofective*
ex·terrestrial \¦eks+\ *adj* [¹*ex*- + *terrestrial*] : EXTRATERRESTRIAL
ex·territorial \(¦)eks+\ *adj* [¹*ex*- + *territorial*] : EXTRATERRITORIAL — **ex·territorially** \"+\ *adv*
ex·territoriality \(¦)eks+\ *n* : EXTRATERRITORIALITY
ex·territorialize \¦eks+\ *vt, see -ize in Explan Notes* : EXTRATERRITORIALIZE
ex·till \ek'stil\ *vb* -ED/-ING/-S [L *exstillare, extillare*, fr. *ex*- ¹ex- + *stillare* to drip, trickle — more at DISTILL] *archaic* : EXUDE, DISTILL
ex·ti·ma \'ekstəmə\ *n, pl* **exti·mae** \-,mē, -,mī\ *or* **extimas** [NL, fr. L, fem. of *extimus*, superl. of *exter, exterus* outward, on the outside — more at EXTERIOR] : EXTERNA
extimulate *vt* -ED/-ING/-S [L *exstimulatus, extimulatus*, past part. of *exstimulare, extimulare*, fr. *ex*- ¹ex- + *stimulare* to goad, stimulate — more at STIMULATE] *obs* : to stir up : spur on : INCITE — **extimulation** *n* -s *obs*
¹ex·tinct \ik'stiŋ(k)t, (')ek¦s-\ *adj* [ME, fr. L *exstinctus, extinctus*, past part. of *exstinguere, extinguere* to extinguish — more at EXTINGUISH] **1 a** : no longer burning : put out : EXTINGUISHED, QUENCHED ⟨he threw his ~ cigarette into the rapid brown water —C.S.Forester⟩ ⟨all hope was ~⟩ **b** *of a volcano* : marked by total cessation of eruptions : no longer active **2 a** : no longer living : DECEASED, DEAD ⟨~ relatives and friends⟩ **b** : that has died out altogether ⟨an ~ nation⟩ : lacking living representatives : lacking survivors ⟨an ~ royal family⟩ ⟨~ prehistoric animals⟩ : no longer to be found : no longer in existence : VANISHED ⟨a truly kind person of a type almost ~⟩ **c** : that no longer exists in its original form ⟨members of an ~ Indian people now living on a reservation⟩ **3 a** : gone out of use : SUPERSEDED ⟨like a woman dressed in a fashion long ~ —William Beebe⟩ ⟨an ~ language⟩ ⟨~ laws and customs⟩ : OBSOLETE ⟨~ verb suffixes⟩ **b** *of a title of nobility* : being without a qualified claimant ⟨an ~ dukedom⟩
²extinct \"\ *vt* **extincted**; **extincted** *or* **extinct**; **extincting**; **extincts** [ME *extincten*, fr. L *exstinctus, extinctus*, past part.] *archaic* : EXTINGUISH ⟨give renewed fire to our ~*ed* spirits —Shak.⟩
ex·tinc·teur \,ek,staŋk'tər(·)\ *n* -s [F, fr. L *exstinctor, extinctor* one that extinguishes, fr. *exstinctus, extinctus* + -*or*] : a chemical fire extinguisher
ex·tinc·tion \ik'stiŋ(k)shən, ek-\ *n* -s [ME *extinccioun*, fr. L *exstinction-, exstinctio, extinction-, extinctio*, fr. *exstinctus, extinctus* + -*ion-*, -*io* -ion] **1 a** : the act of making extinct or causing to be extinguished : QUENCHING, SUPPRESSION, EXTERMINATION, DESTRUCTION, ANNIHILATION ⟨the ~ of all life in the region⟩ : CANCELLATION, ABOLITION ⟨~ of a debt⟩ **b** : the condition or fact of being extinct or extinguished ⟨~ of a species⟩ **2 a** : progressive decrease in the intensity of radiation (as of the light of the sun) by absorption and scattering in the medium (as the atmosphere) traversed **b** : the condition of a crystal of appearing dark when viewed in polarized light with crossed nicols **3** : elimination of a conditioned response by not reinforcing the response
extinction angle *n* : the angle through which a crystal is revolved from a definite line (as that of the crystallographic axis) to the plane of maximum extinction
extinction coefficient *n* : the sum of the absorption coefficient and the scattering coefficient for a medium that both absorbs and scatters radiation
extinction meter *n* : an exposure meter that indicates the intensity of light usu. by gradually attenuating the light until a selected design (as a number superimposed on a ground-glass screen) is barely visible or disappears completely
ex·tinc·tive \ik'stiŋ(k)tiv, (')ek¦s-, -tēv *also* -təv\ *adj* [²*extinct* + -*ive*] : capable of making extinct or of extinguishing : tending to make extinct or to extinguish ⟨an ~ factor⟩
extine *var of* EXINE
ex·tin·guish \ik'stiŋgwish, -wēsh, *chiefly in pres part* -wəsh; ÷-ŋw-\ *vb* -ED/-ING/-ES [L *exstinguere, extinguere* (fr. *ex*- ¹ex- + *stinguere* to extinguish) + E -*ish* (as in *abolish*); akin to L *instigare* to urge on, incite — more at STICK] *vt* **1 a** : to cause (as a fire or light) to cease burning : put out : QUENCH ⟨~*ing* the flames⟩ ⟨threw water on the glowing coals to ~ them⟩ ⟨the lamps were all ~*ed*⟩ **b** (1) : to bring (as life or hope) to an end : make an end of : cause to die out : do away with entirely : blot out of existence : wipe out : make extinct : DESTROY, ANNIHILATE ⟨a way of life which one might expect to have been ~*ed* almost two generations ago —E.H.Spicer⟩ ⟨death will not ~ us —W.L.Sullivan⟩ ⟨~*ing* the last glimmer of hope⟩ : suppress (an institution or an official position) ⟨~*ing* monasteries by an act of the king⟩ ⟨whose office of paymaster of works was ~*ed* by these efforts —John Craig⟩ (2) : to reduce to silence or ineffectiveness : choke off : STIFLE, SMOTHER ⟨a very nearly ~*ed* voice —Elizabeth Bowen⟩ ⟨~*ing* his opponents with a single word⟩ : make powerless or inoperative : CRUSH, CHECK ⟨a point at which the popular will is ~*ed* —T.E.Utley⟩ (3) : to cause extinction of (a conditioned response) ⟨the more specific a response the easier it is to ~ it —Ralph Linton⟩ **c** : to cause the brightness of to appear relatively dim or to disappear altogether (as by setting next to a superior brilliancy) : cause to seem lackluster or tawdry : ECLIPSE ⟨a glittering costume that ~*ed* all the others⟩ ⟨her face looked pale and ~*ed*, as if dimmed by the rich red of her dress —Edith Wharton⟩ **2 a** : to cause (as a claim or right) to be void : make legally nonexistent : NULLIFY, ABOLISH ⟨titles to the land had not been ~*ed* —C.G.Bowers⟩ **b** : to get rid of (a debt or other liability) by payment or other compensatory adjustment — compare SUSPEND, TRANSFER ~ *vi, archaic* : to become extinguished : die out **syn** see ABOLISH, CRUSH
ex·tin·guish·able \-shəbəl\ *adj* : capable of or subject to being extinguished
ex·tin·guish·ant \-shənt\ *n* -s : an agent (as water) that extinguishes fire
ex·tin·guish·er \-shə(r)\ *n* -s **1** : one that extinguishes; *specif* : EXTINGUISHANT **2 a** : a hollow conical cap typically of metal that is used for extinguishing the flame of a candle, lamp, or torch **b** : a mechanical device that throws out fire-extinguishing chemicals : FIRE EXTINGUISHER
ex·tin·guish·ment \-shmənt\ *n* -s : the act of extinguishing or the state of being extinguished : EXTINCTION ⟨the ~ of the Indians' rights to lands —D.E.Clark⟩
extirp *vt* -ED/-ING/-S [ME *extirpen*, fr. L *exstirpare, extirpare*] *obs* : EXTIRPATE
ex·tir·pate \'ekstə(r),pāt *also* ek'stər,p- *or* ik's- *or* -'stə,p- *or* -'stəi,p- *or* '≈,≈;≈; *usu* -ād·+V\ *vt* -ED/-ING/-S [L *exstirpatus, extirpatus*, past part. of *exstirpare, extirpare*, fr. *ex*- ¹ex- + *stirp-, stirps* trunk, root — more at TORPID] **1 a** : to pull up or out by or as if by the roots or stem : pluck out : root out : ERADICATE ⟨serpent worship which the Mosaic curse and Christianity alike have not succeeded in *extirpating* —Norman Douglas⟩ **b** : to destroy totally : wipe out : kill off : make extinct : EXTERMINATE ⟨many species have been *extirpated* from large areas —William Vogt⟩ **c** : to cut out by surgery **2** *obs* : to drive away : EXPEL **syn** see EXTERMINATE

ex·tir·pa·tion \,ekstə(r),pāshən *also* -,stə'p- *or* -,stəi'p-\ *n* -s [ME *extirpacioun*, fr. L *exstirpation-, exstirpatio, extirpation-, extirpatio*, fr. *exstirpatus, extirpatus* + -*ion-*, -*io* -ion] : the act of extirpating or state of being extirpated ⟨~ of weeds⟩ ⟨~ of evil⟩
ex·tir·pa·tor *pronunc at* EXTIRPATE +ə(r)\ *n* -s [L *exstirpator, extirpator*, fr. *exstirpatus, extirpatus* + -*or*] : one that extirpates
extl *abbr* external
ex·tol *also* **ex·toll** \ik'stōl, ek- *sometimes* -tāl *or* -tōl\ *vt* **extolled**; **extolled**; **extolling**; **extols** *also* **extolls** [ME *extollen*, fr. L *extollere*, fr. *ex*- ¹ex- + *tollere* to lift up — more at TOLERATE] **1** : to praise highly : GLORIFY, LAUD, EULOGIZE ⟨they ~ the largely nonexistent virtues of bygone eras —Adam Abruzzi⟩ **2** *obs* : to lift up : raise up : ELEVATE
ex·tol·ler \-lə(r)\ *n* -s : one that extols
ex·tol·ling·ly *adv* : in an extolling manner
ex·tol·ment \-lmənt\ *n* -s *archaic* : the act of extolling
ex·torsion \(')eks+\ *n* [¹*ex*- + *torsion*] : outward rotation (as of a body part) about an axis or fixed point — compare INTORSION
ex·tor·sive \ik'stȯrsiv, (')ek¦s-\ *adj* [L *extors-* (stem of *extorquēre*) + E -*ive*] : serving for or obtained by extortion — **ex·tor·sive·ly** \-səvlē\ *adv*
ex·tort \ik'stȯ(ə)r|t, ek-, -ȯ(ə)|, *usu* |d.+V\ *vb* **extorted**; **extorted** *or obs* **extort**; **extorting**; **extorts** [L *extortus*, past part. of *extorquēre* to wrench out, obtain by force, extort, fr. *ex*- ¹ex- + *torquēre* to twist — more at TORTURE] *vt* **1 a** (1) : to obtain from an unwilling or reluctant person by physical force, intimidation, or the abuse of legal or official authority : get by compelling : FORCE, EXACT ⟨till the injurious Romans did ~ this tribute from us we were free —Shak.⟩ (2) : to obtain from an unwilling or reluctant ⟨~ bribes⟩ (2) : to obtain from an unwilling or reluctant person by importunity, argument, or ingenuity ⟨~ a confession⟩ ⟨she did at last ~ from her father an acknowledgment that the horses were engaged —Jane Austen⟩ ⟨~*ed* his resignation⟩ **b** : to elicit from someone in exchange —Seymour Freidin⟩ **b** : to elicit from someone unwilling by the obvious or apparent existence of an intrinsic compelling force ⟨his intelligence ~*ed* the admiration even of his worst enemies⟩ **2** : to derive (as a meaning or conclusion) by strained or perverse reasoning ⟨they ~*ed* a bizarre sense from the few words that had been spoken⟩ ~ *vi, archaic* : to obtain something forcibly from someone unwilling **syn** see EDUCE
ex·tor·tion \|shən\ *n* -s [ME *extorsioun, extorcioun*, fr. MF or ML; MF *extorsion, extortion*, fr. ML *extorsion-, extorsio*, *extortion-, extortio*, fr. LL *extortion-, extortio* torture, fr. L *extortus* (past part. of *extorquēre*) + -*ion-*, -*io* -ion] **1** : the act or practice of extorting esp. money or other property; *specif* : the offense committed by an official who practices extortion **2** : something that is extorted; *esp* : a gross overcharge
ex·tor·tion·ary \-shə,nerē\ *adj, archaic* : EXTORTIONATE, EXORBITANT
ex·tor·tion·ate \-sh(ə)nət, *usu* -əd·+V\ *adj* : characterized by extortion : EXCESSIVE, EXORBITANT ⟨~ prices⟩ ⟨~ fees⟩ — **ex·tor·tion·ate·ly** *adv*
ex·tor·tion·er \-sh(ə)nə(r)\ *n* -s [ME *extorsiouner, extorciouner*, fr. *extorsioun, extorcioun* + -*er*] : one that practices or is given to extortion
ex·tor·tion·ist \-sh(ə)nəst\ *n* -s : EXTORTIONER
extortious *adj, obs* : EXTORTIONATE
ex·tort·ive \ik'stȯrd·iv, (')ek¦s-\ *adj* : of, relating to, or using extortion : EXTORTIONATE
extr *abbr* extruded; extrusion
¹ex·tra \'ekstrə, *chiefly in substand speech* -rē *or* -ri\ *adj* [prob. short for *extraordinary*] **1 a** : beyond or greater than what is due, usual, expected, necessary, or essential : SPECIAL, ADDITIONAL ⟨doing ~ work⟩ ⟨using ~ effort⟩ **b** : subject to or marked by an additional charge ⟨room service is ~⟩ **2** : better than ordinary : SUPERIOR ⟨~ quality⟩; *specif* : marked by superiority of hand workmanship and material ⟨an *extra*-bound leather book⟩
²extra \"\ *n* -s **1** : something extra or additional: as **a** : an added charge or fee ⟨television is available in each of the hotel rooms as an ~⟩ ⟨the basic cost and the ~*s*⟩ **b** : a special edition of a newspaper issued in addition to the regular editions or at a time different from that of the regular editions ⟨the city was flooded with ~*s* that screamed the news⟩ **c** : an additional point : an additional score; *specif* : a run in the game of cricket that is scored but is not made from a hit (as a run made from a bye) **d** : an additional worker; *specif* : one hired for a motion picture or stage production to augment the number of people in a crowd or group scene **2** : something of superior quality or grade ⟨a hi-fi set that is a real ~⟩
³extra \"\ *adv* **1** : to a degree or extent beyond the usual : UNUSUALLY, UNCOMMONLY, EXTREMELY ⟨those who may be ~ gullible about witches and demons —W.W.Howells⟩ : very particularly : ESPECIALLY ⟨he was ~ glad to see them⟩ **2** : in excess of a usual, regular, or specified size or amount ⟨these trousers are ~ long⟩
extra- \¦≈≈\ *prefix* [ME, fr. L, fr. *extra*, adv. & prep., outside, except, beyond, fr. *exter* outward, on the outside — more at EXTERIOR] : outside : beyond — esp. in adjectives formed from adjectives ⟨*extra*cranial⟩ ⟨*extra*legal⟩ ⟨*extra*vascular⟩ ⟨*extra*-urban⟩ ⟨*extra*historic⟩
extra-base hit *n* : a hit in baseball or softball good for more than one base
extra binder *n* : one that produces extra bindings — compare ¹EXTRA 2
ex·tra·branchial \¦≈≈+\ *adj* [*extra-* + *branchial*] : situated outside the branchial arches
ex·tra·bronchial \¦≈≈+\ *adj* [*extra-* + *bronchial*] : situated outside the bronchial tubes
ex·tra·bulbar \¦≈≈+\ *adj* [*extra-* + *bulbar*] : situated or originating outside the medulla oblongata
ex·tra·canonical \¦≈≈+\ *adj* [*extra-* + *canonical*] : being outside the body of officially accepted writings : not included in a list of authorized books; *specif* : being outside a canon of books held to be sacred ⟨an ~ writing⟩
ex·tra·capsular \¦≈≈+\ *adj* [*extra-* + *capsular*] : situated outside a capsule; *esp* : situated outside a capsular ligament
ex·tra·cellular \¦≈≈+\ *adj* [*extra-* + *cellular*] : situated or occurring outside a cell or the cells of the body — **ex·tra·cellularly** \¦≈≈+\ *adv*
ex·tra·chance \¦≈≈+\ *adj* [*extra-* + *chance* (n.)] : greater than could be anticipated on a basis of chance : showing a level of frequency or uniformity beyond what can reasonably be attributed to coincidence ⟨wherever parapsychology can yield ~ results —G.R.Price⟩
ex·tra com·mer·cium \¦≈≈kə'mərsh(ē)əm\ *adj* [L, lit., outside of commerce] *Roman & civil law* : not subject to private ownership or acquisition (as of the air, navigable waters, property owned by the government) — opposed to *in commercio*
extra cover *or* **extra cover point** *n* : a position in the game of cricket between cover point and mid off; *also* : a fieldsman playing this position — see CRICKET illustration
¹ex·tract \ik'strakt, ek's-, *in sense 3a usu & in other senses sometimes* 'ek,s-\ *vt* **extracted**; **extracted** *or obs* **extract**; **extracting**; **extracts** [ME *extracten*, fr. L *extractus*, past part. of *extrahere*, fr. *ex*- ¹ex- + *trahere* to draw, pull — more at DRAW] **1 a** : to draw forth ⟨~*ing* a letter from his pocket⟩; *esp* : to pull out (as something embedded or otherwise firmly fixed) forcibly or with great effort ⟨~*ing* a tooth⟩ ⟨~*ing* the stump of a tree⟩ **b** : to obtain (as money or knowledge of a secret) by much maneuvering and effort from or as if from someone unwilling ⟨before you try to ~ money from anyone —Edith Sitwell⟩ ⟨~*ing* a promise⟩ ⟨~*ing* information⟩ ⟨~*ing* the truth⟩ **c** : to derive (as pleasure) or deduce (as the meaning of a word) from a specified source as if by drawing forth ⟨~*ing* happiness from what many would consider a humdrum existence⟩ ⟨~*ing* a strange meaning from what she had said⟩ **d** : to separate or otherwise obtain (as constituent elements or juices) from a substance by treating with a solvent (as alcohol), distilling, evaporating, subjecting to pressure or centrifugal force, or by some other chemical or mechanical process ⟨~*ing* an essence⟩ ⟨~*ing* the juice of apples⟩ ⟨~*ed* honey⟩ — compare LEACH 1b **e** : to treat with a solvent so as to remove soluble substances ⟨adrenal cortex is ~*ed* with acetone⟩ — compare LEACH 1a

f : to separate (an ore or mineral) from a deposit; *also* : to separate (a metal) from an ore **g** : to separate (flour) from broken grain kernels in the process of grinding grain **h** : to separate (a particular genetic character) in the form of a homozygote from a heterozygous strain ⟨~*ed* albinos⟩ ⟨~*ed* dominants and recessives⟩ **2** : to determine (the root of a number or quantity) by mathematical calculation ⟨~*ing* the square root of 64⟩ **3 a** : to make out an extract (sense 1b) of **b** : to select (excerpts) and copy out or cite ⟨I have ~*ed* out of that pamphlet a few notorious falsehoods —Jonathan Swift⟩ **4** : to subject to any action or process of extracting **syn** see EDUCE
²ex·tract \'ek,strakt\ *n* -s [ME, fr. ML *extractus, extracta, & extractum*, fr. L, masc., fem., & neut. respectively of the past part. of *extrahere*] **1 a** *obs* : SUMMARY, OUTLINE **b** : a certified copy of a document that forms part of or is preserved in a public record **c** : a selection from a writing or discourse : EXCERPT, QUOTATION **2** : something extracted: as **a** : a preparation obtained by evaporation (as of a solution of a drug or the juice of a plant) **b** : the portion of a mixture that is dissolved by a solvent and later separated from part or from all of the solvent (as by distillation) **c** : a solution in alcohol of flavor and odor constituents (as from an aromatic plant) ⟨the use of vanilla ~ and lemon ~ in cooking⟩ **d** : a preparation containing the essence of the substance from which it is derived : ESSENCE, CONCENTRATE ⟨beef ~⟩ **e** : the total soluble constituents of beer with the exception of alcohol and carbon dioxide **3** *obs* : EXTRACTION 2
³extract *or* **extracted** *adj* [fr. past part. of ¹*extract*] *obs* : derived or descended
ex·tract·abil·i·ty \ik,straktə'biləd·ē, (,)ek,-\ *n* -ES : capability of being extracted
¹ex·tract·able *also* **ex·tract·ible** \ik'straktəbəl, (')ek¦s-\ *adj* [¹*extract* + -*able* or -*ible*] : capable of being extracted
²extractable *also* **extractible** \"\ *n* -s : EXTRACTIVE
ex·tract·ant \-≈'tənt\ *n* -s [¹*extract* + -*ant*] : a solvent (as alcohol or sulfuric acid) used in extracting
ex·trac·tion \ik'strakshən, ek-\ *n* -s [ME *extraccioun*, fr. LL *extraction-, extractio*, fr. L *extractus* + -*ion-*, -*io* -ion] **1 a** : the act or process of extracting ⟨~ of a tooth⟩ **b** *obs* : EXTRACT 2 **2** [MF (also, act of extracting), fr. LL *extraction-, extractio*] : ORIGIN, LINEAGE, DESCENT, BIRTH ⟨a workman of German ~⟩ **3 a** (1) : the proportion of ore that can be separated from the total mined mass of an ore occurrence (2) : the proportion of valuable metal or mineral recovered from an ore **b** : the proportion of flour obtained from each 100 pounds of milled grain ⟨an ~ of 74 percent⟩
extraction turbine *n* : a steam turbine provided with taps through which steam may be drawn off at various stages for purposes (as heating) other than driving the turbine
¹ex·trac·tive \ik'straktiv, (')ek¦s-, -tēv *also* -təv\ *adj* [¹*extract* + -*ive*] **1 a** : of, relating to, involving, or making use of extraction : marked by extraction ⟨~ processes⟩ ⟨~ industries⟩ **b** : tending to or resulting in withdrawal of natural resources by extraction with no provision for and often no possibility of replenishment of the resources ⟨mining, quarrying, and other ~ occupations⟩ ⟨~ agriculture⟩ **2 a** : capable of being extracted ⟨the ~ constituents of aromatic plants⟩ **b** (1) : of, relating to, or having the nature of an extract ⟨an ~ substance⟩ (2) : containing extractive matter ⟨a full-bodied and highly ~ beer⟩
²extractive \"\ *n* -s **1 a** : something extracted or capable of being extracted; *specif* : an extractable substance that gives a characteristic flavor to meat **b** : a substance that can be separated from an extract ⟨these ~*s* are recovered by removal of the solvent⟩ **2** : a dark-colored insoluble substance produced in the preparation of extracts by evaporation
extractive distillation *n* : a combined continuous fractional distillation and extraction in which a relatively high-boiling solvent (as furfural) flowing down the distillation column selectively scrubs one or more of the components from a mixture of compounds of similar vapor pressures (as butanes and butylenes)
ex·trac·tor \ik'straktə(r), (')ek¦s-\ *n* -s **1** : one that extracts: as **a** : a forceps or other instrument used in extraction (as of a tooth) **b** : a device for withdrawing a cartridge or spent cartridge case from the chamber of a firearm **c** : a machine that exerts centrifugal force in extraction (as of honey from honeycombs or moisture from wet materials) **d** : a device to pull ferrules from tube plates **e** : an apparatus for extracting substances by means of solvents **f** : a device used for extracting fruit juice (as by squeezing) **2** : a worker who operates an extractor
extract printing *n* : DISCHARGE PRINTING
extracts *pres 3d sing of* EXTRACT, *pl of* EXTRACT
extract wool \'ek,strakt-\ *n* : wool fiber extracted from material containing both wool and cotton or rayon by carbonizing the cotton or rayon
ex·tra·curricular *also* **extracurriculum** \¦ekstrə+\ *adj* [*extra-* + *curricular* or *curriculum*] **1** : outside a regular curriculum : not falling within the scope of a regular curriculum; *specif* : of or relating to officially or semiofficially approved and usu. organized student activities (as athletics, dramatics, or publication of a school newspaper) connected with the students' school and usu. carrying no academic credit **2 a** : outside the regular duties of one's job or profession; *esp* : outside and in pleasant contrast to such duties ⟨reading detective stories as an ~ pastime⟩ **b** : outside and in direct opposition to or violation of the conventionally established limits or rights of one's position ⟨the ~ activities of a philandering husband⟩
ex·tra·cystic \¦≈≈+\ *adj* [*extra-* + *cystic*] : situated or originating outside a cyst or bladder
ex·tra·dit·able \'ekstrə,dīd·əbəl, -ītə-, ,≈≈'≈≈≈\ *adj* **1** : subject or liable to extradition ⟨an ~ criminal⟩ **2** : making liable to extradition ⟨an ~ offense⟩
ex·tra·dite \'ekstrə,dīt, *usu* -īd·+V\ *vt* -ED/-ING/-S [back-formation fr. *extradition*] **1** : to deliver up to extradition : subject to extradition **2** : to obtain the extradition of **syn** see BANISH
ex·tra·di·tion \,ekstrə'dishən\ *n* -s [F, fr. *ex*- ¹ex- + L *tradition-, traditio* act of handing over, surrendering — more at TRADITION] **1** : the surrender or delivery of an alleged criminal usu. under the provisions of a treaty or statute by one country, state, or other power to another having jurisdiction to try the charge **2** : localization of a sensation at a point removed from the center of the sensation
ex·tra·dos \'ekstrə,däs, -,dōs, -,dō; ek'strā|,däs, -rā|, |,dəs\ *n, pl* **extrados** \-,dōz\ *or* **extradoses** \-äsəz,-ōsəz,-əsəz\ [F, fr. L *extra* outside + F *dos* back — more at EXTRA-, DOSSIER] **1** : the exterior curve of an arch; *specif* : the upper curved face of the body of voussoirs which forms the arch **2** : the outer surface of a vault — compare INTRADOS

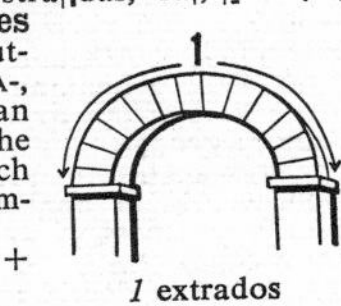

1 extrados

ex·tra·dotal \¦ekstrə+\ *adj* [*extra-* + *dotal*] : PARAPHERNAL
extra dry *adj* [³*extra*] *of a beverage* : having little or no sweetness; *specif* : EXTRA SEC
ex tra·du·ce \ek'strädü,kā\ *adj* [LL *ex traduce*, lit., from a vine layer] *archaic, of the soul* : having direct origin from the souls of the parents
ex·tra·dural \¦ekstrə +\ *adj* [*extra-* + *dural*] : situated or occurring outside the dura mater but within the skull ⟨an ~ hemorrhage⟩
ex·tra·embryonic *also* **ex·tra·embryonal** \¦≈≈+\ *adj* [*extra-* + *embryonic, embryonal*] : situated outside the embryo proper; *esp* : developed from the zygote but not part of the embryo ⟨~ membranes⟩
extraembryonic coelom *n* : the space between the chorion and amnion which in early stages is continuous with the coelom of the embryo proper
ex·tra·enteric \¦ekstrə +\ *adj* [*extra-* + *enteric*] : situated outside the enteron : PERIVISCERAL
ex·tra·familial \¦≈≈+\ *adj* [*extra-* + *familial*] : lying outside the family or its control ⟨~ interests⟩
ex·tra-fare \¦≈≈+\ *adj* [*extra fare*] **1** : requiring or involving an extra fare **2** : providing better than regular accommodation or service

ex·tra·fascicular cambium \ˌekstrə +. . .-\ n [extra- + fascicular] : SECONDARY CAMBIUM

ex·tra·floral \ˌekstrə +\ adj [extra- + floral] of a plant part : not forming part of a flower : located elsewhere than in the flower ⟨~ nectaries⟩

ex·tra·foraneous \ˌ==+\ adj [extra- + ML foraneous external, fr. L foris, fores door — more at DOOR] : OUTDOOR

ex·tra·galactic \ˌ==+\ adj [ISV extra- + galactic] : lying or coming from outside the Milky Way

extragalactic nebula n : GALAXY 1b

ex·tra·genic \ˌ==+\ adj [extra- + genic] : not involving or not entering into the composition of the genes ⟨mutations due to ~ causes⟩

ex·tra·genital \ˌ==+\ adj [ISV extra- + genital] : situated or originating outside the genital region or organs ⟨~ sexual responses⟩

ex·tra·hepatic \ˌ==+\ adj [extra- + hepatic] : situated or originating outside the liver ⟨~ jaundice⟩ — compare INTRAHEPATIC

ex·tra-illustrate \ˌ==+\ vt [[3]extra + illustrate] : to illustrate (as a book) by inserting material (as photographs or engravings) collected from other sources (as books) — compare GRANGERIZE — **ex·tra-illustration** \"+\ n

ex·tra·judicial \ˌ==+\ adj [extra- + judicial] **1 a** : lying outside or beyond court proceedings : forming no valid part of a case before a court ⟨an ~ investigation⟩ **b** (1) : not made before a judge or court in due course of legal proceedings ⟨an ~ confession⟩ ⟨an ~ oath⟩ (2) : not made or delivered officially : INFORMAL, PRIVATE ⟨the judge made it clear that the opinion he voiced was ~⟩ **2** : lying outside, beyond, or contrary to the ordinary course of law or justice : not legally authorized ⟨~ infliction of the death penalty⟩ — **ex·tra·judicially** \"+\ adv

ex·tra·lateral \ˌ==+\ adj [extra- + lateral] : of or relating to the right of a lode locator on the public domain to certain portions of all veins apexing within his claim though these portions lie in adjoining land

ex·tra·lecithal \ˌ==+\ adj [extra- + lecithal] of an egg : having the yolk arranged in a layer superficial to the protoplasm

ex·tra·legal \ˌ==+\ adj [extra- + legal] : being beyond the province of law : not regulated by law ⟨~ law of the mining camps —P.S.Fritz⟩ ⟨voluntary ~ associations of educational institutions which exist for the purpose of improving education —Norman Burns⟩ — **ex·tra·legally** \"+\ adv

ex·tra·limital \ˌ==+\ adj [extra- + [1]limit + -al] : not present in a given area — used esp. of organisms or kinds of organisms (as species)

ex·tra·literary \ˌ==+\ adj [extra- + literary] : lying outside what is literary : lying outside the province of literature ⟨a book whose merits are both literary and ~⟩

ex·tral·i·ty \ekˈstraləd·ē\ n -ES [by alter.] : EXTRATERRITORIALITY

ex·tra·marginal \ˌekstrə+\ adj [extra- + marginal] : lying outside or beyond a margin; specif : lying outside or beyond the margin of awareness ⟨~ perception⟩

ex·tra·marital \ˌ==+\ adj [extra- + marital] : relating to sexual relationship with another than one's spouse : ADULTEROUS ⟨involved in ~ experiences⟩

ex·tra·mastoid \ˌ==+\ adj [extra- + mastoid] : situated on or affecting the outer surface of the mastoid bone ⟨~ infection⟩

ex·tra·matrical \ˌ==+\ adj [extra- + matrical] : lying or growing outside a substratum ⟨~ branches from the body of the host plant⟩ — used chiefly of aerial parts of parasitic fungi

ex·tra·matrimonial \ˌ==+\ adj [extra- + matrimonial] : EXTRAMARITAL

ex·tra·medullary \ˌ==+\ adj [ISV extra- + medullary] : lying outside a medulla; esp : EXTRABULBAR

ex·tra·mental \ˌ==+\ adj [extra- + mental] : existing outside the mind ⟨the ~ world⟩

ex·tra·meridian \ˌ==+\ n [back-formation fr. extrameridional] : an observation of a celestial body when it is near the meridian

ex·tra·meridional \ˌ==+\ adj [extra- + meridional] : of or relating to deviation from the meridian : taken near the meridian

ex·tra·metrical \ˌ==+\ adj [extra- + metrical] : exceeding the usual or prescribed number of syllables in a given meter : not counted in metrical analysis

ex·tra·morainic also **ex·tra·morainal** \ˌ==+\ adj [extra- + morainic, morainal] : situated outside the area occupied by a glacier and its lateral and terminal moraines ⟨~ deposits⟩

ex·tra·mundane \ˌ==+\ adj [LL extramundanus, fr. L extra, adv. & prep., outside, beyond (as in extra mundum beyond the world) + mundanus of the world — more at MUNDANE] : EXTRATERRESTRIAL

[1]ex·tra·mural \ˌ==+\ adj [extra- + mural] **1** : existing outside or beyond the walls, boundaries, or precincts of an organized unit ⟨an ~ basilica⟩ ⟨~ hospital care and treatment⟩ **2 a** : of, relating to, or taking part in extension courses or facilities ⟨~ classes⟩ ⟨the ~ department of a university⟩ **b** : relating to or taking part in informal interschool contests arranged for competition between special groups or classes rather than varsities ⟨~ athletics⟩ — opposed to intramural; distinguished from intercollegiate and interscholastic **3** : EXTRACURRICULAR 2b ⟨a husband's ~ affair —J.W.Krutch⟩ — **ex·tra·murally** \"+\ adv

[2]extramural \"\ n : an extramural contest

ex·tra·ne·i·ty \ˌekstrəˈnēəd·ē, -(ˌ)strāˈ-\ n -ES : the quality or state of being extraneous

ex·tra·ne·ous \(ˈ)ekˈstrānēəs, ikˈs-\ adj [L extraneus — more at STRANGE] **1 a** : existing or originating outside or beyond : external in origin : coming from the outside ⟨~ light in a camera⟩ ⟨protecting the contents of the container from ~ moisture⟩ ⟨no premiums or other ~ inducements⟩ **b** : brought in, introduced, or added from an external source or point of origin ⟨a valley bottom covered with ~ soil⟩ ⟨relying upon an ~ income⟩ **2 a** : not forming an essential or vital part : not belonging to something as a proper or natural part : not intrinsic : ACCIDENTAL, FOREIGN ⟨~ sounds⟩ ⟨they considered art to be ~ to reality⟩ ⟨a ballet that struck me as ~ and somewhat out of keeping with the rest of the play —Wolcott Gibbs⟩ ⟨~ incidents in a novel⟩ ⟨a building with ~ ornamentation⟩ **b** : having little or no relevance : IRRELEVANT : not pertinent ⟨an unexpected and altogether ~ remark⟩ ⟨an ~ digression⟩ **c** : having little or no interdependence or connection : UNRELATED ⟨a series of ~ books⟩ ⟨~ events⟩ **syn** see EXTRINSIC

ex·tra·ne·ous·ly adv : in an extraneous manner

ex·tra·ne·ous·ness n -ES : the quality or state of being extraneous

ex·tra·ne·us he·res \ekˈstrānēəsˈhi(ˌ)rēz\ n, pl **extra·nei here·des** \-nēˌīhəˈrē(ˌ)dēz\ [L, lit., outside heir] : an heir other than a suus heres either of an intestate or under a will in whom the inheritance can be vested only upon his definite acceptance

ex·tra·nuclear \ˌekstrə+\ adj [extra- + nuclear] : situated in or affecting the parts of a cell external to the nucleus : CYTOPLASMIC ⟨~ viruses⟩

ex·tra·ocular muscle \ˌekstrə+. . .-\ n [extra- + ocular] : any of the six small voluntary muscles that pass between the eyeball and the orbit and control the movements of the eyeball in relation to the orbit

ex·traor·di·nar·i·ly \ikˌstrȯ(r)dᵊnˌerəlē, (ˌ)ekˌ-, -li also ˌekstrəˌȯ- sometimes -dəˌne-\ adv : in an extraordinary manner : to an extraordinary degree

ex·traor·di·nar·i·ness \ikˈstȯ(r)dᵊnˌerēnəs, ekˈs-, -rin-, also ˌekstrəˌȯ- sometimes -dəˌne-\ n : the quality, state, or fact of being extraordinary

[1]ex·traor·di·nary \-erē,-eri sometimes -dˌner-\ adj [ME extraordinarie, fr. L extraordinarius, fr. extra, adv. & prep., outside, beyond (as in extra ordinem out of course, in an extraordinary manner) + ordinarius ordinary — more at EXTRA-, ORDINARY] **1 a** : more than ordinary : not of the ordinary order or pattern ⟨ordinary and ~ expenses⟩ : going beyond what is usual, regular, common, or customary : not following the general pattern or norm ⟨held the office for an ~ period of time⟩ ⟨giving ~ powers to the president⟩ **b** (1) : exceptional to a very marked extent : most unusual : far from common ⟨enjoying ~ popularity⟩ ⟨an ~ capacity for work⟩ : very outstanding ⟨an ~ leader⟩ : very remarkable ⟨~ technical progress⟩ : rarely equaled : SINGULAR, PHENOMENAL ⟨a woman of ~ beauty⟩ : strikingly impressive : ARRESTING ⟨an ~ family resemblance⟩ (2) : having little or no precedent and usu. totally unexpected ⟨an ~ combination of circumstances⟩ (3) : very curious, strange, or surprising : AMAZING ⟨how ~ that she should not understand⟩ **2 a** : of, relating to, or having the degree of care, caution, or diligence typical of that exercised by an extremely prudent person ⟨revealing an ~ foresight⟩ **b** : of, relating to, or having the nature of a proceeding or action not normally required by law or not prescribed for the regular administration of the law ⟨an ~ session of a legislature⟩ ⟨an ~ court⟩ ⟨~ jurisdiction⟩ **c** : of, relating to, or having the nature of an occurrence (as an accident or casualty) or risk of a kind other than what ordinary experience or prudence would foresee **3 a** : serving in addition to the regular officials or employees : having a special and usu. occasional rather than regular function : entrusted with a special responsibility : employed for or sent upon an unusual service ⟨an ambassador ~⟩ ⟨appointed as an ~ professor⟩ **b** obs : EXTRA

[2]extraordinary \"\ n, archaic : something extraordinary

[3]extraordinary \"\ adv, archaic : EXTRAORDINARILY ⟨the quite ~ large quantity of furniture —Osbert Lancaster⟩

extraordinary ray n : the part of a ray divided in two by double refraction that does not follow the ordinary laws of refraction because its speed varies with its direction in the doubly refracting medium

extraordinary writ n : PREROGATIVE WRIT

ex·tra·organismal \ˌekstrə+\ adj [extra- + organismal] : situated or originating outside an organism ⟨~ conflicts⟩ ⟨~ infective agents⟩

extra pat·ri·mo·ni·um \-ˌpa·trəˈmonēəm\ adj [L, lit., outside of inheritance] : EXTRA COMMERCIUM

ex·tra·physical \"+\ adj [extra- + physical] : not subject to physical laws or methods

ex·tra·planetary \"+\ adj [extra- + planetary] : situated or originating outside the region of the planetary orbits; also : relating to space outside this region

extra point n **1** : a point scored in football after a touchdown esp. by drop-kicking or place-kicking from scrimmage over the bar between the goalposts **2 extra points** pl : a score of two points gained after a touchdown in football by advancing the ball across the goal line in one play from scrimmage

ex·trap·o·late \ikˈstrapəˌlāt, ek-, usu -ād·+V\ vb -ED/-ING/-S [L extra outside, beyond + E -polate (as in interpolate) — more at EXTRA-] vt **1** : to infer from a trend within an already observed interval (the usu. probable values of a mathematical variable in an unobserved interval) : calculate from the terms of a known series (the terms not included in the series) **2 a** (1) : to project, extend, or expand (known data or experience) into an area not known or experienced so as to arrive at a usu. conjectural knowledge of the unknown area by inferences based on an assumed continuity, correspondence, or other parallelism between it and what is known ⟨events . . . can be traced in the past and extrapolated into the future —D.J.Bogue⟩ ⟨extrapolating the present geological state of the earth to its state billions of years ago⟩ (2) : to extend to a greater length or into a new area ⟨~ a straight line⟩ (3) : to cause to move further, develop, or expand on the basis of often unwarranted assumptions or speculations : draw out or amplify ⟨extrapolating some unpleasant personal experience into a generalized slur on his hosts —L.G.Crocker⟩ ⟨metaphysicians that ~ themselves to the point of absurdity⟩ **b** : to gain knowledge of (an area not known or experienced) by extrapolating : estimate or predict by or as if by extrapolating : CONJECTURE, SURMISE ⟨extrapolating public opinion from the public's known reactions to other issues⟩ ~ vi : to perform the act or process of extrapolating — compare INTERPOLATE

ex·trap·o·la·tion \ikˌstrapəˈlāshən, (ˌ)ekˌ-\ n -S : the act or process of extrapolating : PROJECTION, EXTENSION

extrapolation chamber n : an ionization chamber used as a dosimeter and having adjustments that permit the accurate determination of dosage over a surface by means of extrapolation from measurements on finite layers

ex·trap·o·la·tive \ikˈstrapəˌlād·iv, ek-\ adj : of, relating to, or obtained by extrapolation

ex·trap·o·la·tor \-ād·ə(r)\ n -S : one that extrapolates

ex·trap·o·la·to·ry \-pələˌtōrē\ adj : EXTRAPOLATIVE

ex·tra·psychic or **ex·tra·psychical** \ˌekstra+\ adj [extra- + psychic, psychical] : being or occurring outside the psyche, the mind, or the personality — **extrapsychically** adv

ex·tra·punitive \ˌekstrə+\ adj [extra- + punitive] : tending to direct blame or punishment toward persons other than the self — opposed to intropunitive — **extrapunitiveness** n -ES

ex·tra·pyramidal \ˌ==+\ adj [ISV extra- + pyramidal] : situated outside or independent of the pyramidal tracts ⟨~ brain lesions⟩

ex·tra-regarding \ˌ==+\ adj [[1]extra] : ALTRUISTIC

extra river n : a diamond of the very highest grade

extras pl of EXTRA

ex·tra·scientific \ˌ==+\ adj [extra- + scientific] : lying outside what is scientific : lying outside the province of science ⟨an ~ area of experience⟩

extra sec adj [[3]extra] of champagne : containing from 1.5 to 3 percent sugar by volume : somewhat dry : drier than sec and sweeter than brut

ex·tra·sensorial \ˌ==+\ adj [extra- + sensorial] : EXTRASENSORY — **ex·tra·sensorially** \"+\ adv

ex·tra·sensory \ˌ==+\ adj [extra- + sensory] : residing beyond or outside the ordinary senses : not limited to the senses ⟨mental telepathy and other instances of ~ perception⟩

ex·tra·systole \ˌ==+\ n [NL, fr. L extra outside, beyond + NL systole — more at EXTRA-, SYSTOLE] : a premature beat of one of the chambers of the heart that leads to momentary arrhythmia, the fundamental rhythm being maintained — **ex·tra·systolic** \"+\ adj

ex·tra·tension \ˌ==+\ n [extratensive + -ion] : the state or fact of having extratensive qualities or responses

ex·tra·tensive \ˌ==+\ adj [extra- + tensive] : showing a predominance of color responses on the Rorschach test and characterized by the urge to live in the world outside oneself, by restless motility, and by unstable affective reactions — contrasted with introversive

ex·tra·terrestrial \ˌ==+\ adj [extra- + terrestrial] : originating or existing outside the earth or its atmosphere ⟨the possibility of ~ life⟩

ex·tra·territorial \ˌ==+\ adj [extra- + territorial] : situated outside the territorial limits of a jurisdiction — **ex·tra·territorially** \"+\ adv

ex·tra·territoriality \ˌ==+\ n : a quality, state, or privilege of general or partial exemption from the application of local law or jurisdiction of local tribunals ⟨the ~ of diplomats⟩

ex·tra·territorialize \ˌ==+\ vt, see -ize in Explan Notes : to cause to be extraterritorial

ex·tra·tropical cyclone \ˌ==+. . .-\ n [extra- + tropical] : a cyclone in the middle latitudes being often 1500 miles in diameter and usu. containing a cold front that extends toward the equator for hundreds of miles from the center of low pressure and that divides the warmer humid winds of the forward portion from the cooler dry winds of the rear portion

ex·tra·tubal \ˌ==+\ adj [extra- + tubal] : situated outside a body duct or esp. outside the fallopian tube ⟨~ pregnancy⟩

ex·tra·tympanic \ˌ==+\ adj [extra- + tympanic] : situated outside the middle ear

ex·tra·uterine pregnancy \ˌ==+. . .-\ n [ISV extra- + uterine] : pregnancy in which the fetus develops outside the uterus (as in a fallopian tube)

ex·trav·a·gance \ikˈstravəgən(t)s, ek-, -vēg-\ n -S [F, fr. MF, fr. extravagant] **1** obs : a wandering away from a set course : DEVIATION **2 a** : an instance of excess or prodigality ⟨have never observed any of the ~s of a lover in your conduct —G.B.Shaw⟩; esp : a very great or excessive outlay of money or other resources ⟨living simply and avoiding ~⟩ **b** : something that is extravagant ⟨that coat is an ~ you can't afford⟩ **3** : the quality, condition, or fact of being extravagant : excess or prodigality ⟨living in idle ~⟩ ⟨words that to some might seem wild, even insane in their ~ —W.H.Hudson †1922⟩

ex·trav·a·gan·cy \-nsē, -si\ n -ES [extravagant + -cy] : EXTRAVAGANCE

[1]ex·trav·a·gant \-nt\ adj [ME extravagaunt, fr. MF extravagant, fr. ML extravagant-, extravagans, fr. L extra- + vagant-, vagans, pres. part. of vagari to wander about — more at VAGARY] **1 a** archaic : wandering away : VAGRANT ⟨rare ~ spirits —R.W.Emerson⟩ **b** obs : spreading or projecting beyond usual limits **c** obs : differing greatly : widely divergent **d** obs : STRANGE, CURIOUS **2 a** : exceeding the limits of reason or necessity : exceeding proper bounds : going beyond what is justifiable ⟨an ~ theory⟩ ⟨demanding ~ privileges⟩ ⟨usurping ~ power⟩ ⟨making ~ claims⟩ **b** (1) : almost totally lacking in moderation, balance, and restraint : wildly excessive : going much too far ⟨~ generalizations⟩ : INTEMPERATE ⟨~ praise⟩ ⟨~ enthusiasm⟩ (2) : extremely and often excessively impetuous and vehement and marked by sudden and abrupt changes ⟨the ~ language of a lover⟩ (3) : extremely or excessively elaborate, vivid, and showy and colored by startling and often apparently capricious contrasts ⟨a play filled with ~ dialogue⟩ ⟨gazing at the ~ display of the setting sun⟩ **c** : wildly exaggerated often to the point of absurdity : pushed beyond credibility : utterly fantastic ⟨~ accusations⟩ ⟨~ reports of what they had seen⟩ **3 a** : spending or tending to spend much more than necessary : spending lavishly, recklessly, or wastefully : spending improvidently like a spendthrift : PRODIGAL ⟨~ in everything she bought⟩ ⟨to keep up appearances they became ~⟩ **b** : pouring forth liberally : very bountiful : exceedingly or excessively generous in giving or spending : PROFUSE ⟨he can be counted on to be ~ toward the poor⟩; often : excessively effusive or exuberant ⟨without wishing to be ~ in expressing their admiration⟩ **c** : marked by great abundance often to an extreme or excessive degree : most plentiful ⟨a tropical island with ~ vegetation⟩ **4** : extremely and often unreasonably high in price : costing an excessive amount ⟨interested only in ~ clothes⟩ : EXORBITANT ⟨~ prices⟩ : LAVISH ⟨an ~ new musical⟩ **syn** see EXCESSIVE

[2]extravagant \"\ n -S archaic : one that is extravagant

ex·trav·a·gant·ly adv : in an extravagant manner

ex·trav·a·gan·za \ikˌstravəˈganzə, (ˌ)ekˌ- sometimes -găn- or -gȧn-\ n -S [It estravaganza, stravaganza, lit., extravagance, fr. estravagante, stravagante extravagant, fr. ML extravagant-, extravagans] **1** : a literary fantasy that is freely imaginative in subject, structure, and development and that often includes elements of burlesque or parody **2 a** : a musical composition marked by freedom of form and by elements of burlesque or parody **b** : a lavish or spectacular show or event ⟨a winter sports ~⟩; esp : a lavish musical production (as a stage show or motion picture) typically marked by spectacular and elaborate settings, unusual scenic effects, costly costuming, a large cast of singers and dancers, extensive choral numbers and choreography, and a loosely unifying theme or plot that is usu. light and comic **3 a** : a decorative article of clothing or a clothing accessory designed or used for a striking ornamental effect ⟨such ~s as hats of velvet and dresses sprinkled with sequins⟩ **b** : an object that is strikingly unusual and often bizarre; esp : a usu. large and opulent architectural structure of freely imaginative design and striking ornamental effects **4** : an effusion or burst of activity that captures or holds one's attention like an extravaganza ⟨another ~ of fun —Ernest Beaglehole⟩

ex·trav·a·gate \=ˈ==ˌgāt\ vi -ED/-ING/-S [extravagant + -ate] **1** archaic **a** : to wander off : STRAY **b** : to wander about without control : ROAM **2** archaic : to go beyond the limits of what is reasonable, necessary, or proper — **ex·trav·a·ga·tion** \=ˌ==ˈgāshən\ n -S

ex·tra·vaginal \ˌekstrə+\ adj [extra- + vaginal] : bursting through an enclosing sheath ⟨the ~ shoots of many grasses⟩

[1]ex·trav·a·sate \ikˈstravəˌsāt, ek-\ vb -ED/-ING/-S [L extra outside + vas vessel + E -ate (v. suffix) — more at EXTRA-] vt **1** : to force out (as blood) or cause to escape from a proper vessel or channel (as a blood vessel) **2** : to cause (as molten lava) to pour out or erupt (as from a vent in the earth) ~ vi **1** : to pass by infiltration or effusion from a proper vessel or channel into surrounding tissue (as of blood from a blood vessel) **2** : to pour out or erupt (as of lava from a vent in the earth)

[2]extravasate \"\ adj [L extra + vas + E -ate (adj. suffix)] archaic : EXTRAVASATED

[3]extravasate \"\ n -S : an extravasated fluid (as blood) or a deposit (as of solidified lava) formed from extravasation

ex·trav·a·sa·tion \ikˌstravəˈsāshən, (ˌ)ekˌ-\ n -S [[1]extravasate + -ion] **1** : the action of extravasating : the condition of being extravasated ⟨the ~ of lava from a volcano⟩ : EFFUSION, ERUPTION **2** : an extravasated fluid or a deposit formed from extravasation : EXTRAVASATE

ex·tra·vascular \ˌekstrə+\ adj [extra- + vascular] **1** anat : not contained in vessels **2** anat : destitute of vessels : NONVASCULAR

ex·trav·ased \ikˈstravəst\ adj [F extravaser to extravasate (fr. L extra + vas) + E -ed] archaic : EXTRAVASATED

extraversion var of EXTROVERSION

extravert var of EXTROVERT

ex·tra·visceral \ˌekstrə+\ adj [extra- + visceral] : situated or originating outside the viscera ⟨~ abdominal pain⟩

ex·tra·visible \ˌ==+\ adj [extra- + visible] : lying outside the range of visible wavelengths ⟨the ~ regions of the spectrum⟩

ex·tra·zonal \ˌ==+\ adj [extra- + zonal] : lying outside a zone ⟨in the American sector of the region and in the ~ part⟩

extrema pl of **extremum**

[1]ex·treme \ikˈstrēm, ekˈ-, in "extreme unction" often ÷ˌek(ˌ)strēm\ adj, often -ER/-EST [ME, fr. MF, fr. L extremus, superl. of exter, exterus on the outside, outward — more at EXTERIOR] **1 a** : existing in the highest or the greatest possible degree : very great : very intense ⟨living in ~ poverty⟩ ⟨the ~ cold of the polar regions⟩ **b** : marked by great severity or violence : most severe : most stringent : DRASTIC, DESPERATE ⟨resorting to ~ measures to combat crime⟩ ⟨an ~ action that crushed their spirits⟩ **c** (1) : going to great or exaggerated lengths : UNCOMPROMISING, RADICAL, FANATICAL ⟨he was quite ~ in his views on the matter⟩ (2) : going beyond the limits of reason, necessity, or propriety : IMMODERATE ⟨avidly following the most ~ fashion in clothes⟩ ⟨a religion whose tenets were austere and ~⟩ : exceeding the ordinary, usual, or expected : EXCESSIVE ⟨an ~ descent⟩ **d** : having an implied or specified characteristic to the fullest possible extent ⟨the nature of real need can be studied best in ~ cases⟩ ⟨in politics he sits at the ~ right⟩ **2** archaic : LAST, FINAL ⟨thy ~ hope, the loveliest and the last —P.B.Shelley⟩ **3 a** : situated at the farthest possible point from a center : most remote : FARTHEST, OUTERMOST ⟨the ~ edge of the city⟩ ⟨traveling to the ~ borders of the country⟩ ⟨an ~ outpost⟩ **b** : situated at the very tip of either of two ends (as of a line) ⟨the ~ end of the road⟩ **4 a** : farthest advanced in any direction : most advanced : UTMOST ⟨standing at the ~ edge of the river⟩ **b** : MAXIMUM ⟨a folding table with an ~ length of 6 feet⟩ **syn** see EXCESSIVE

[2]extreme \"\ n -S **1 a** : an extreme state or condition ⟨an ~ of poverty⟩ **b extremes** pl, obs : critical circumstances : STRAITS, HARDSHIPS ⟨resolute in most ~s —Shak.⟩ **2 a** (1) : an extreme variation ⟨~s of behavior weaving into one another as if to spite all moralists —Irving Howe⟩ : something situated at, serving to mark, or terminating one end or the other of a total range or extent ⟨the temperature in the desert ranges astonishingly between ~s of heat and cold⟩ (2) : one of two things related in some way (as by nature, condition, or position) and at the same time removed from, contrasting with, or opposed to each other to a very great extent or as far as possible ⟨the ~s of passion that are called love and hatred⟩ **b** (1) : the first term or the last term of a mathematical proportion (2) : the greatest or the least of several magnitudes **c** logic : a term appearing in an extreme position: as (1) : the subject or predicate of a proposition — contrasted with copula (2) : the major term or minor term of a syllogism — compare MIDDLE TERM **3** archaic : a terminal part of a body : EXTREMITY **4 a** (1) : a very pronounced or excessive degree ⟨there is no need to grieve to such an ~⟩ ⟨a more stable and democratic regime with less ~s of wealth and poverty —William Clark⟩ ⟨he aroused ~s of admiration and hostility —Robert Lawrence⟩ : EXCESS ⟨this world of violent ~s —Huntington Hartford⟩ (2) : the utmost conceivable or tolerable degree : the utter limit ⟨enthusiasm that was carried to an ~⟩ : MAXIMUM ⟨prejudice is found at its ~ in that century⟩ **b** : an extreme measure or expedient : an extreme step ⟨forced to an unpleasant ~⟩ : utmost length ⟨he went to ~s to satisfy their curiosity —P.J.O'Brien⟩; also : an extreme instance or case ⟨an ~ they could not visualize⟩

—**in the extreme** : to the greatest possible extent or degree ⟨would find the task wearisome *in the extreme* —Lionel McColvin⟩
³extreme \"\ *adv, archaic* : EXTREMELY
extreme and mean ratio *n* : GOLDEN SECTION
extreme breadth *n* : BREADTH EXTREME
extreme fiber *n* : one of the longitudinal elements of a structural member (as a beam) that are at the greatest distance from the neutral axis
extreme fiber stress *n* : the stress per unit of area in an extreme fiber of a structural member subjected to bending
ex·treme·ly *adv* : in an extreme manner : to an extreme extent
extremely high frequency *n* : a radio frequency in the highest range of the radio spectrum — see RADIO FREQUENCY table
ex·treme·ness *n* -ES : the quality or state of being extreme ⟨the ~ of the measures to combat crime was almost as bad as the crime itself⟩
extremer *comparative of* EXTREME
extremest *superlative of* EXTREME
extreme unction *n, often cap E&U* : a sacrament (as in the Roman Catholic Church) that consists of praying over and anointing a person who is in danger of death
ex·tre·mism \ik'strē,mizəm, ek-\ *n* -S : the quality or state of being extreme; *specif* : RADICALISM
¹ex·trem·ist \-ēməst *sometimes* -em-\ *n* -S [²*extreme* + -*ist*] : an adherent or advocate of extremism; *esp* : RADICAL
²extremist \"\ *also* **ex·trem·is·tic** \;=(,)=¦mistik\ *adj* : of, relating to, or favoring extremism or extremists
ex·trem·i·ty \ik'stremǝd-ē, ek-, -mǝtē, -i\ *n* -ES [ME *extremite*, fr. MF *extremité*, fr. L *extremitat-, extremitas*, fr. *extremus* extreme + -*itat-, -itas* -ity — more at EXTREME] **1** : something that is extreme: as **a** (1) : an outlying or terminal part, section, or point ⟨one ~ of the mountain range is located to the east⟩ : the farthest or most remote part, section, or point : the most advanced part : the farthest extent : the farthest projection ⟨the region's wooded northern ~⟩ ⟨the inhabitants of the southern ~ of the continent⟩ : the very end ⟨at the ~ of a small path —William Black⟩ ⟨the sting at the ~ of a scorpion's tail⟩ (2) : a limb (as of the body) or other appendage : an arm or leg ⟨circulation of blood in the *extremities*⟩; *usu* : a hand or foot ⟨coldness in the *extremities*⟩ **b** (1) : a condition of extreme urgency or necessity : a highly crucial state of affairs : a time of extreme danger or critical need : extreme adversity ⟨in this ~ she took refuge in grief —G.B.Shaw⟩ ⟨to whom in the depths of his ~ he turned for sympathy —F.W.Crofts⟩ (2) : a moment marked by imminent destruction or dissolution ⟨anchors thrown out by a vessel in its last ~ —A.C.Clarke⟩ (3) *archaic* : the point of death ⟨the king was at ~ —G.P.R. James⟩ **c** (1) : an extremely intense degree (as of emotion or pain) : extreme intensity ⟨in his first ~ of grief —H.G.Wells⟩ ⟨enduring *extremities* of torture —Edith Sitwell⟩ (2) : a culminating point (as of emotion or pain) : HEIGHT, APEX, CLIMAX ⟨some went so far as to kneel on the sharp stones in the very ~ of terror —Elinor Wylie⟩ ⟨an ~ of passion⟩ (3) *archaic* : extreme severity or rigor : ASPERITY **d** *obs* : an instance or act of extravagant behavior : EXTRAVAGANCE **e** : the fullest possible extent : utmost limit : utmost degree ⟨the thought worried her to the ~ of her endurance⟩ ⟨they were definitely provoked to ~ before they did this deed —Rex Ingamells⟩ **f** (1) : a very severe, violent, drastic, or desperate act or measure ⟨reduced to the ~ of telling everything they knew⟩ ⟨forced to *extremities*⟩ (2) : a single remaining source of help or plan of action : sole recourse : final resort ⟨as a last ~ there's only one thing that can be done⟩ **2** : the quality or state of being extreme ⟨avoiding *extremities*⟩ ⟨they vied with one another in the ~ of their opinions —H.G.Wells⟩ ⟨the ~, violence, and anguish which have characterized much of the literature —K.I. Lansner⟩ — **in extremities** : at the end of one's resources : in a most crucial or dangerous condition or position : at the point of death — **to the last extremity** : to the point of death : to the death
ex·tre·mum \ik'strēməm\ *n, pl* **extre·ma** \-ēmə\ [NL, fr. L, end, fr. neut. of *extremus*] : a stationary value of a mathematical function that is either a maximum or a minimum
ex·trica·ble \ek'strikəbəl, ik'strik-, 'ekstrə-, 'ek(,)strik-\ *adj* [L *extricare* + E -*able*] : capable of being extricated
ex·tri·cate \'ekstrə,kāt, *usu* -ād-+V\ *vt* -ED/-ING/-S [L *extricatus*, past part. of *extricare*, fr. *ex-* ¹ex- + *tricae* trifles, impediments, perplexities; perh. akin to L *torquēre* to twist — more at TORTURE] **1 a** *archaic* : to separate the tangled threads of : UNRAVEL, DISENTANGLE **b** : to distinguish (one thing) from a related thing by recognition of common and variant elements : DISCRIMINATE, DIFFERENTIATE ⟨a plant that cannot easily be *extricated* from similar ones⟩ ⟨*extricating* the typical culture of a people from its behavior patterns⟩ **c** *archaic* : to clear up the involved condition of : clear of complication or confusion **2 a** : to draw out from or forth from and set free of a tangled, jumbled, confused, or otherwise involved heap, mass, or situation : separate and set aside ⟨*extricating* the one unbroken dish from the pile of fragments⟩ **b** (1) : to draw out from or as if from a fixed position : remove with effort ⟨he *extricated* the two heavy gas cylinders from the bottom of the boat —C.S.Forester⟩ : pull out : get out ⟨many who were trapped perished before they could be *extricated* —O.S.Nock⟩ : EXTRACT ⟨the horse could not ~ its foot from the mudhole⟩ ⟨the kind of dust that, once it infiltrates one's lungs, seems never to be altogether *extricated* —E.J.Kahn⟩ (2) : to release from or as if from a confining, restraining, difficult, embarrassing, dangerous, or otherwise undesirable condition or situation : get free : DISENGAGE, LIBERATE ⟨*extricating* himself from the straitjacket⟩ ⟨golf players *extricating* themselves from a sand trap⟩ ⟨what he expected of me was to ~ him from a difficult situation —Joseph Conrad⟩ ⟨my success in having *extricated* myself from an awkward predicament —Victor Heiser⟩ ⟨trying to ~ themselves from debt⟩ **3** *archaic* : to set (as a gas) free from a state of combination

syn EXTRICATE, DISENTANGLE, UNTANGLE, DISENCUMBER, and DISEMBARRASS can mean in common to free or release from what binds or holds one back. EXTRICATE implies an entanglement, as in difficulties or perplexities, a restraining from free action so great that only force, ingenuity, or persistence will bring release ⟨on the point of *extricating* itself from the snarls of conflicting claims —*Amer. Guide Series: N. J.*⟩ ⟨give us what aid you can in *extricating* a generous young man from such a pair of schemers as this father and daughter seem to be —W.M. Thackeray⟩ ⟨personality is to be *extricated* from the loyalties which disintegrate it —Donald Meyer⟩ DISENTANGLE is similar to EXTRICATE but often stresses more the things, esp. intricately complex, which entangle other things ⟨*disentangle* one's foot from a fish net⟩ ⟨so picturesque a figure that biography is unable to *disentangle* him from legend —*Amer. Guide Series: N. C.*⟩ ⟨a moralization which must be slowly *disentangled* from the driftings and confusions of everyday life —V.S.Pritchett⟩ ⟨he can *disentangle* facts from impressions —J.G.Cozzens⟩ UNTANGLE is often popularly used in the sense of DISENTANGLE, with the same implications ⟨*untangle* one's foot from a fish net⟩ DISENCUMBER implies a freeing from what weighs down, clogs, or imposes a heavy burden ⟨they *disencumber* themselves of many garments —George Meredith⟩ ⟨he cannot *disencumber* himself of his lifelong methods of composition —H.O.Taylor⟩ ⟨*disencumber* oneself of a weight of debts⟩ DISEMBARRASS implies a release from what impedes, hampers, or hinders ⟨I was glad to *disembarrass* myself of the bag and give it to a duty officer —Basil Black⟩ ⟨decide to *disembarrass* themselves of him by killing or banishing him —Merriam McCulloch⟩ ⟨*disembarrass* ourselves of the curse of ignorance and learn to work together —Alvin Johnson⟩
ex·tri·ca·tion \,=='kāshən\ *n* -S [LL *extrication-, extricatio*, fr. L *extricatus* + -*ion-, -io* -ion] **1** : the action of extricating **2** : the process of being extricated
ex·trin·sic \(')ek¦strinz|ik, ik's-, -n(t)s|, |ēk\ *adj* [F & LL; F *extrinsèque*, fr. LL *extrinsecus*, fr. L, adv., from without, on the outside, fr. (assumed) L *extrim* (fr. L *exter, exterus* outward, on the outside) + L -*secus* (fr. *sequi* to follow) — more at EXTERIOR, SUE] **1 a** : lying outside : not forming part of or belonging properly to : not contained in or occurring in : EXTRANEOUS ⟨~ to native capacities⟩ **b** (1) : arising outside : originating or operating from or on the outside ⟨looking for ~ aid⟩ ⟨disdaining ~ pressure groups⟩; *specif* : originating outside a part and acting upon the part as a whole ⟨the ~ muscles of the tongue⟩ (2) : derived from an external source : not inherent : not essential : ACCESSORY, ADVENTITIOUS ⟨~ evidence⟩ : ACCIDENTAL, CONTINGENT **2** : of or relating to the outside of : OUTER, OUTWARD, EXTERNAL ⟨an ~ feature of the new building⟩

syn EXTRANEOUS, FOREIGN, ALIEN: EXTRINSIC applies to what is definitely not contained in something else, esp. not contained in or derived from its essential nature ⟨that style is something *extrinsic* to the subject, a kind of ornamentation laid on to tickle the taste —A.T.Quiller-Couch⟩ ⟨the special quality of such presuppositions is that they are inherent and not *extrinsic* —Walter Moberly⟩ EXTRANEOUS applies to what is exterior or unrelated but may be interjected with or interpreted as part of an intrinsic essence ⟨simony was no *extraneous* stain to be washed off from the body ecclesiastic, but rather an element of its actual constitution —H.O.Taylor⟩ ⟨it is simply a close rendering of the Latin text, and it contains little, if any, *extraneous* matter of the kind which in other works illustrates the character of Alfred's thought —F.M.Stenton⟩ ⟨no *extraneous* beauty or vigor was ingrafted on the decaying stock —T.B. Macaulay⟩ FOREIGN applies to what is exterior, notably different, or unlikely to be assimilated with or to become part of ⟨the mysticism so *foreign* to the French mind and temper —W.C.Brownell⟩ ⟨executive inaction in such a situation, courting national disaster, is *foreign* to the concept of energy and initiative in the executive as created by the founding fathers —*Current History*⟩ ALIEN may be stronger than FOREIGN in suggesting opposition, incompatibility, repugnance, or irreconcilability ⟨an emotional quality totally *alien* to the austerity of the rest of the sermon⟩ ⟨though such frankness would, in the past, have been wholly *alien* to her nature, she now began to tell him of her experience —Francis King⟩
ex·trin·si·cal \|əkəl, |ēk-\ *adj* [F *extrinsèque* or L *extrinsecus* + E -*al*] *archaic* : EXTRINSIC
ex·trin·si·cal·ly \|ək(ə)lē, |ēk-, -li\ *adv* : in an extrinsic manner : with regard to what is extrinsic : from the outside : EXTERNALLY
extrinsic factor *n* : a dietary substance that was thought to interact with the intrinsic factor of the gastric secretion to produce the antianemic factor and that is now known to be vitamin B_{12}
extrinsic fraud *n* : fraud (as that involved in making a false offer of compromise) that induces one not to present a case or deprives one of the opportunity of being heard; *also* : fraud that is not involved in the actual issues presented to a court or jury and that prevents a full and fair hearing
extro- *prefix* [modif. (influenced by *intro-*) of L *extra* — more at EXTRA-] : outside : outward ⟨*extro*vert⟩ — opposed to *intro-*
ex·trorse \'ek,strȯrs, ek'strȯ(ə)rs\ *adj* [prob. fr. (assumed) NL *extrorsus*, fr. LL *extrorsum*, adv., outward, fr. L *extra* + -*orsus* (as in *introrsus* inward) — more at INTRORSE] : turned away from the axis of growth ⟨an ~ anther⟩ — compare INTRORSE — **ex·trorse·ly** *adv*
ex·tro·spec·tion \'ekstrə¦spekshən, -rō¦-\ *n* -S [*extro-* + -*spection* (as in *introspection*)] : examination or observation of what is outside oneself — opposed to *introspection*
ex·tro·spec·tive \-ktiv\ *adj* [*extro-* + -*spective* (as in *introspective*)] : of, relating to, or marked by extrospection — opposed to *introspective*
ex·tro·ver·sion \,ekstrə'vər|zhən, -trō'-, -vǝ|, -vəi| *also* |shən\ *n* -S [*extro-* + L *versus* (past part. of *vertere* to turn) + E -*ion* — more at WORTH] **1** : EXSTROPHY **2** *also* **ex·tra·ver·sion** \-trə-'\ [G, fr. *extra-* (fr. L) or *extro-* (alter. of *extra-*) + L *versus* + G -*ion*] **a** (1) : the act of directing attention toward and obtaining gratification from what is outside the self (2) : the state of being wholly or predominantly concerned with and interested in what is outside the self **b** : an habitual tendency toward such extroversion — opposed to *introversion*
ex·tro·ver·sive *also* **ex·tra·ver·sive** \¦==¦=|siv *also* |ziv\ *adj* : of, relating to, or tending to extroversion — opposed to *introversive* — **ex·tro·ver·sive·ly** \|sәvlē, |zә-\ *adv*
¹ex·tro·vert *also* **ex·tra·vert** \'==,vər|t, -vǝ|, -vəi|, ,=='=, *usu* |d.+V\ *vb* -ED/-ING/-S [in sense 1, fr. *extro-* or *extra-* + L *vertere*; in other senses fr. ²,³*extrovert*] *vt* **1** *archaic* : to turn or push outward **2** : to cause to be extroversive : make an extrovert of : cause to be extrovert : produce extroversion in — opposed to *introvert* ~ *vi* : to become extroversive : become an extrovert : act in an extroversive manner
²extrovert *also* **extravert** \'==,=\ *adj* [modif. of G *extrovertiert, extravertiert*, fr. *extra-* or *extro-* + -*vertiert* (fr. L *vertere*)] : EXTROVERTED
³extrovert *also* **extravert** \"\ *n* -S **1** : one whose attention and interests are directed wholly or predominantly toward what is outside the self : one characterized by extroversion — opposed to *introvert* **2** [*extro-* or *extra-* + L *vertere*] : an extrusile proboscis (as that of certain marine and parasitic worms)
extroverted *also* **extraverted** \'==,==, ,=='==\ *adj* [modif. of G *extrovertiert, extravertiert*] : having the characteristics of an extrovert : marked by extroversion — opposed to *introverted*
ex·tro·vert·ish \'==,=ish\ *adj* : somewhat extroverted
ex·tro·ver·tive *also* **ex·tra·ver·tive** \¦==¦vərd·iv\ *adj* : EXTROVERSIVE
ex·trude \ik'strüd, ek-\ *vb* -ED/-ING/-S [L *extrudere*, fr. *ex-* ¹ex- + *trudere* to thrust, push — more at THREAT] *vt* **1 a** (1) : to thrust out : cause to protrude : stick out ⟨an insect *extruding* its proboscis⟩ (2) : to cause to emerge by or as if by squeezing out : press out ⟨mollusks *extruding* fecal pellets⟩ : cause to move to or appear at the surface or the outside ⟨a land upheaval that *extruded* molten rock⟩ **b** : to cast out or get rid of forcibly or violently by or as if by pushing or shoving : throw out : EJECT, EXPEL ⟨the offender . . . is *extruded* as unworthy of an honorable calling —R.M.MacIver⟩ **2** : to shape (as metal, plastic, rubber) by forcing through a specially designed opening often after a previous heating of the material or of the opening or of both — compare DRAW *vt* 4e ~ *vi* **1 a** : to jut out as or as if a result of being extruded : PROTRUDE, PROJECT ⟨land masses *extruding* into the sea⟩ **b** : to move to or appear at the surface or the outside : EMERGE ⟨lava *extruding* from early fissures⟩ **2** : to undergo shaping done by the process of extruding ⟨a material that does not ~ well⟩
ex·trud·er \-də(r)\ *n* -S : one that extrudes; *specif* : a machine that shapes materials by the process of extruding
ex·tru·si·ble \-üsəbəl, -üzə-\ *adj* [L *extrusus* + E -*ible*] : EXTRUSILE
ex·tru·sile \ik'strü,sil,|s|īl, ek-, -,|s|əl, -(,)|s|il, |z|\ *adj* [L *extrusus* + E -*ile*] : capable of being extruded
ex·tru·sion \ik'strüzhən, ek-\ *n* -S [ML *extrusion-, extrusio*, fr. L *extrusus* (past part. of *extrudere*) + -*ion-, -io* -ion] **1 a** : the act or process of extruding **b** : the fact of being extruded : subjection to the act or process of extruding **2 a** : an article or product (as of metal, plastic, rubber) made by the process of extruding **b** : something (as lava or mud) forced out (as through a fissure) upon the earth's surface
¹ex·tru·sive \ik'strüsiv, (')ek¦s-, -üziv\ *adj* [*extrusion* + -*ive*] : of, relating to, or produced by geological extrusion ⟨volcanic ~ rocks formed after eruptions and other ~ phenomena⟩ ⟨~ lava reached the earth's surface⟩ — contrasted with *intrusive*
²extrusive \"\ *n* -S : a mass (as an igneous rock) produced by geological extrusion
ex·tu·bate \'ekst(y)ü,bāt, '=,=,=\ *vt* -ED/-ING/-S [¹*ex-* + *tube* + -*ate*] : to take a tube out of (as the larynx) — **ex·tu·ba·tion** \,=,=,='bāshən\ *n* -S
ex·tu·ber·ance \ik'st(y)übərən(t)s, ek-\ *n* -S [L *extuberare* to swell out (fr. *ex-* ¹ex- + *tuber* hump, swelling) + E -*ance* — more at TUBER] *archaic* : PROTUBERANCE
ex·tu·ber·ant \-nt\ *adj* [L *extuberant-, extuberans*, pres. part. of *extuberare*] *archaic* : swelled out
ex·u·ber·ance \ig'züb(ə)rən(t)s, eg-\ *n* -S [F *exubérance*, fr. L *exuberantia*, fr. *exuberant-, exuberans* + -*ia* -y] **1** : the quality or state of being exuberant **2** : an act or expression that is marked by exuberance : an individual instance of exuberance
ex·u·ber·an·cy \-nsē, -si\ *n* -ES [L *exuberantia*] : EXUBERANCE
ex·u·ber·ant \-nt\ *adj* [ME *exuberaunt*, fr. MF *exuberant*, fr. L *exuberant-, exuberans*, pres. part. of *exuberare* to be abundant, fr. *ex-* ¹ex- + *uberare* to be fruitful, fr. *uber* fruitful, fertile, fr. *uber* udder — more at UDDER] **1 a** (1) : joyously unrestrained and enthusiastic : extremely or excessively high-spirited and uninhibited ⟨there were plays which he wrote with an ~ gaiety —Van Wyck Brooks⟩ ⟨her ~ capacity for pleasure —Paul Roche⟩ : full of life : VIVACIOUS ⟨his warm ~ personality —Douglas Cleverdon⟩ (2) : diffuse and undisciplined ⟨~ remarks⟩ : effusively inflated : excessively ornate or otherwise overdone : TURGID, PROFUSE, FLAMBOYANT ⟨a reporter who overwrote his story with ~ images and exaggerated figures —F.L.Mott⟩ ⟨heaping ~ praise on them⟩ **b** : extreme or excessive in degree, size, or extent : surpassing fixed, usual, or expected limits ⟨a person of ~ talent⟩ ⟨the nation enjoyed ~ prosperity⟩ ⟨mountains of ~ bulk⟩ ⟨~ zeal⟩ **c** : LAVISH, EXTRAVAGANT, PRODIGAL ⟨that ~ vista of gilding and crimson velvet —Max Beerbohm⟩ **2 a** (1) : extremely luxuriant : produced in extreme or excessive abundance : PLENTIFUL ⟨~ foliage and vegetation⟩ ⟨~ crops⟩ ⟨an ~ growth of hair⟩ (2) *med* : characterized by excessive proliferation ⟨~ warts⟩ **b** : extremely fertile or creative : richly productive : FECUND, FRUITFUL, PROLIFIC ⟨gifted with an ~ imagination⟩ **syn** see PROFUSE
ex·u·ber·ant·ly *adv* : in an exuberant manner
ex·u·ber·ant·ness *n* -ES : EXUBERANCE
ex·u·ber·ate \-bə,rāt, *usu* -ād-+V\ *vi* -ED/-ING/-S [L *exuberatus*, past part. of *exuberare*] **1** *archaic* : OVERFLOW ⟨one whose . . . breast *exuberated* with human kindness —W.M. Thackeray⟩ **2** : to be exuberant : feel exhilarated ⟨*exuberating* in the knowledge of having contributed to victory⟩ : show exuberance ⟨an actor who knows how to ~ —James Agate⟩
¹ex·u·date \'eksə,dāt, -k(,)sü,- *sometimes* -ksyə- *or* -ks(,)yü-; 'egzə-, -g(,)zü,- *sometimes* -gzyə- *or* -gz(,)yü-\ *vb* -ED/-ING/-S [L *exsudatus, exudatus*, past part. of *exsudare, exudare* — more at EXUDE] *archaic* : EXUDE
²exudate \"\ *n* -S [*exude* + -*ate* (n. suffix)] : exuded matter; *specif* : the material composed of serum, fibrin, and white blood cells in variable amounts that escapes from blood vessels into a superficial lesion or an area of inflammation
ex·u·da·tion \,=(,)='dāshən\ *n* -S [LL *exsudation-, exsudatio, exudation-, exudatio*, fr. L *exsudatus, exudatus* + -*ion-, -io* -ion] **1** : the process of exuding **2** : EXUDATE
exudation pressure *n* : ROOT PRESSURE
ex·ud·a·tive *pronunc at* EXUDE +əd·iv\ *adj* : of, relating to, or marked by exudation
ex·u·da·to·ri·um \ig,züdə'tōrēəm, eg- *sometimes* ik,sü- *or* ek,sü- *or* -gz,yü- *or* -ks,yü-\ *n, pl* **exudato·ria** \-ēə\ [NL, fr. L *exsudatus, exudatus* + NL -*orium*] : one of the papillae present on certain ant and termite larvae that secrete substances attractive to adults of the same species
ex·ude \ig'züd, eg- *sometimes* ik'süd *or* ek'süd *or* -gz'yüd *or* -ks'yüd\ *vb* -ED/-ING/-S [L *exsudare, exudare*, fr. *ex-* ¹ex- + *sudare* to sweat — more at SWEAT] *vi* **1 a** : to ooze out slowly in small drops through openings (as pores) : emerge like drops of sweat ⟨beads of moisture *exuding* from the clammy walls⟩ **b** : to flow slowly out : issue slowly forth ⟨a sticky substance *exuded* from the end of the cut branch⟩ **2** : to undergo diffusion (as of an odor) : EMANATE ⟨an air of respectability *exuded* from them⟩ ~ *vt* **1 a** : to discharge slowly in small drops through openings : cause to ooze out or to emerge like drops of sweat ⟨pine trees *exuding* resin⟩ **b** : to cause to flow slowly out ⟨tar was *exuded* through the cracks⟩ **2** : to cause (as a vapor or odor) to spread out in all directions ⟨the bubbling stew *exuded* a delicious aroma⟩ : DIFFUSE : breathe forth : give off ⟨*exuding* the charm which is held to be Irish —John Mason Brown⟩ ⟨a voice that ~s confidence —Vance Packard⟩ : EXHALE ⟨shawls . . . *exude* the odor of moth balls —John Steinbeck⟩ **syn** see EMIT
¹ex·ulcerate \egz+\ *vt* -ED/-ING/-S [L *exulceratus*, past part. of *exulcerare*, fr. *ex-* ¹ex- + *ulcerare* to ulcerate — more at ULCERATE] *archaic* : EXULCERATE
²exulcerate *adj* [L *exulceratus*, past part.] *obs* : ULCERATED
ex·ult \ig'zəlt, eg-\ *vb* -ED/-ING/-S [MF *exulter*, fr. L *exsultare, exultare*, lit., to leap up, fr. *ex-* ¹ex- + -*sultare* (fr. *saltare* to leap) — more at SALTANT] *vi* **1** *obs* : to leap for joy **2** : to be extremely joyful : be very glad or elated : feel great delight : experience great happiness ⟨~*ing* over their good luck⟩ : feel jubilant : rejoice very much esp. with feelings and often an outward display of triumph or exuberant self-satisfaction : GLORY ⟨~*ing* in their victory⟩ ⟨one who had once ~*ed* in abundant strength —Arnold Bennett⟩ ⟨Indian warriors ~*ing* over their slain enemies⟩ ~ *vt* : to cause to exult : GLADDEN, DELIGHT ⟨it did not exactly ~ him —W.A.White⟩
ex·ult·ance \-t°n(t)s, -tən-\ *or* **ex·ult·an·cy** \-nsē, -si\ *n, pl* **exultances** *or* **exultancies** [LL *exsultantia, exultantia*, fr. L *exsultant-, exsultans, exultant-, exultans* + -*ia* -y] : EXULTATION
ex·ult·ant \-nt\ *adj* [L *exsultant-, exsultans, exultant-, exultans*, pres. part. of *exsultare, exultare*] : filled with extreme joy : manifesting triumphant elation : JUBILANT ⟨he was ~ and could not conceal his delight —Sherwood Anderson⟩ ⟨the ~ laugh of youth —Ellen Glasgow⟩ — **ex·ult·ant·ly** *adv*
ex·ul·ta·tion \,eksəl'tāshən, ,egzəl- *also* -k,s- *or* -g,z-\ *n* -S [ME *exultacioun*, fr. MF *exultation*, fr. L *exsultation-, exsultatio, exultation-, exultatio*, fr. *exsultatus, exultatus* (past part. of *exsultare, exultare*) + -*ion-, -io* -ion] **1 a** : the act of exulting **b** : the state of being exultant **2** : very great or triumphant joy : joyous transport ⟨the ~ of victory and the thrill of power —John Buchan⟩
ex·ul·tet \ig'zül,tet, eg-\ *n* -S *usu cap* [L *exsultet, exultet* let (it) rejoice, 3d pers. sing. pres. subj. of *exsultare, exultare*] : a hymn of praise sung in the Roman Catholic Church at the blessing of the paschal candle on Easter eve
ex·ult·ing·ly *adv* : in an exultant manner
ex·um·brel·la \'ek(,)səm¦brelə\ *n* [NL, fr. *exo-* + *umbrella*] : the top of the umbrella of a jellyfish — **ex·um·brel·lar** \-lə(r)\ *adj*
ex·un·da·tion \,ek(,)sən'dāshən\ *n* -S [L *exundation-, exundatio*, fr. *exundatus* (past part. of *exundare* to overflow, fr. *ex-* ¹ex- + *undare* to surge, overflow, fr. *unda* wave, billow) + -*ion-, -io* -ion — more at WATER] *archaic* : OVERFLOW, FLOODING
exuperance *n* -S [L *exsuperantia, exuperantia*, fr. *exsuperant-, exsuperans, exuperant-, exuperans* (pres. part. of *exsuperare, exuperare* to excel, surpass, fr. *ex-* ¹ex- + *superare* to rise above, surmount exceed, excel, surpass) + -*ia* -y — more at SUPERABLE] *obs* : the amount by which one thing exceeds another; *also* : SUPERABUNDANCE
ex·urb \'ek,sərb, 'eg,zərb\ *n* -S [¹*ex-* (out of) + -*urb* (as in *suburb*)] : a region or district outside a city and usu. beyond its suburbs that is inhabited chiefly by well-to-do families ⟨the ~ is generally further from New York than the suburb on the same railway line —A.C.Spectorsky⟩ ⟨the city, the suburbs, and the ~s —H.S.Commager⟩
ex·ur·ban·ite \ek'sərbə,nīt, eg'zər-, ig'z-\ *n, often attrib* [¹*ex-* + -*urbanite* (as in *suburbanite*)] : one that chooses to live in an exurb after residence in the city, that cherishes and preserves an urban manner of living, and that derives income chiefly from urban businesses (as publishing)
ex·ur·bia \-bēə\ *n* -S [¹*ex-* + -*urbia* (as in *suburbia*)] : the generalized region of exurbs ⟨commuting to New York from ~⟩
ex·ute \ig'züt\ *vt* -ED/-ING/-S [L *exutus*, past part. of *exuere*] *archaic* : STRIP ⟨*exuted* of all his preferments —Robert Southey⟩
ex·u·vi·ae \ig'züvē,ē, eg-\ *n pl* [L, fr. *exuere* to take off, fr. *ex-* ¹ex- + -*uere* to put on; akin to ORuss *izuti* to take off shoes and stockings, Arm *aganim* I put on, Av *aothra-* shoe, and perh. to OIr *fuan* coat] : the natural covering of an animal (as the skin of a snake) after it has been sloughed off — **ex·u·vi·al** \-vēəl\ *adj*
ex·u·vi·ate \-vē,āt\ *vb* -ED/-ING/-S [*exuvial* + -*ate*] : MOLT — **ex·u·vi·a·tion** \ig,==='āshən, (,)eg,-\ *n* -S
¹ex-vo·to \eks'vōd·(,)ō, -vō(,)tō\ *n* -S [L *ex voto* according to a vow] : a votive offering
²ex-voto \(')=¦=(,)=\ *adj* : VOTIVE
exx *abbr* **1** examples **2** executrix
-ey — see -Y, -IE
ey·ak \'ī,ak, 'ē,-\ *n, pl* **eyak** *or* **eyaks** *usu cap* [fr. *Eyak*, lake, village, & river in Alaska] **1 a** : an Indian people of the Copper river delta in Alaska **b** : a member of such people **2 a** : the language of the Eyak people **b** : a language stock of the Na-dene phylum comprising only Eyak
ey·as *or* **ey·ess** \'īəs\ *n* -ES [ME, alter. (resulting fr. incorrect division of *a neias*) of *neias, nyesse*, fr. MF *niais* fresh from the nest, fr. (assumed) VL *nidax* nestling, fr. L *nidus* nest — more at NEST] **1** : an unfledged bird; *specif* : a nestling hawk

2 : a hawk or falcon taken young from the nest for training — compare HAGGARD

¹eye \ˈī\ *n* -s [ME *eie, eye, eighe,* fr. OE *ēage;* akin to OHG *ouga* eye, ON *auga,* Goth *augo,* L *oculus* eye, Gk *osse* (two) eyes, *ōps* eye, face, Skt *akṣi* eye] **1 a** (1) **:** an organ of sight consisting typically of a light-recipient mechanism that by variation of state of pigmentation or refractive index or by muscular or other adjustment regulates the light that reaches a light-sensitive region which projects sensory stimuli due to impinging light to the central nervous system **:** PHOTORECEPTOR **:** the human eyeball protected by movable upper and lower eyelids, movable in its bony orbit by means of four rectus and two oblique muscles, and having externally a tough fibrous sclerotic coat of which the anterior one sixth forms the transparent cornea, a middle highly vascular coat modified anteriorly into the iris, ciliary body, and related structures separated from the cornea by the anterior chamber of the eye and posteriorly into the choroid that underlies the retina, and the retina which is an inner receptive layer, lining the posterior and lateral walls of the large posterior chamber of the eye and on which light passing through the cornea and pupil of the iris is focused by a crystalline lens to form an inverted image of objects in the visual field that is transmitted along sensory paths of the optic nerves to the brain — see ACCOMMODATION 6, VISION 3b; compare FOCUS 2, IMAGE 2a (2) **:** the eye and any closely associated supporting or protective structures (as an eyelid, eyelash, or eyebrow) **:** the whole region within and surrounding the orbit of the eye (3) **:** the iris of the eye; *specif* **:** the distinctively colored anterior surface of the iris ⟨a girl with blue ~*s*⟩ **b** (1) **:** the faculty of seeing with or as if with the eyes ⟨a keen ~ for significant detail —C.A.Lejeune⟩ **:** SIGHT, VISION **:** power of perceiving physically or mentally ⟨a good ~ for what is essential⟩ (2) **:** the ability to see very keenly or with special clarity **:** keen discernment **:** keen discrimination and appreciation ⟨an ~ for beauty⟩ ⟨he has an artist's ~⟩ (3) **:** range of vision **:** VISUAL FIELD **c** (1) **:** LOOK, GLANCE, GAZE, VIEW ⟨peering through the window with an eager ~⟩ ⟨universities have cast a critical ~ on both the methods and the materials —R. de Kieffer⟩ ⟨they were often in the public ~⟩ (2) **:** a very attentive look **:** close watch **:** close observation or supervision **:** SCRUTINY ⟨the workmen were at almost all times immediately under the ~ of their employers —Ben Riker⟩ ⟨I've got to keep an ~ on the road —Ellen Glasgow⟩ **d :** POINT OF VIEW **:** way of looking at something **:** JUDGMENT ⟨in the ~ of the law⟩ ⟨in his ~*s* she was beautiful —Edith Sitwell⟩ **2 :** something having an appearance suggestive of an eye: as **a** (1) **:** the hole through the head of a needle (2) **:** a hole designed to receive a rope, shaft hook, or other object; *specif* **:** a hole in an implement (as an ax or hammer) designed for the insertion of a handle (3) **:** the hole in an upper millstone (4) **:** the central opening in a centrifugal impeller **b :** one of the holes formed in some cheeses (as Swiss cheese) during ripening **c** (1) **:** a usu. circular marking (as on a peacock's tail or on the wings of a butterfly); *also* **:** a small dark spot (as on an egg) (2) **:** a bright spot, band, or circular area (as of light) ⟨the trolley car rumbled toward them, a clanking ~ of light in the distance —Irwin Shaw⟩ (3) **:** an aggregate of minerals exposed in the surface of a rock and having an appearance contrasting with the surface so as to form a more or less conspicuous area **d** (1) **:** a loop (as at the end of a rope) (2) **:** a loop (as of thread) or other catch (as a transverse piece of metal) designed to receive a hook (as for fastening together the opposite edges of a garment) ⟨hooks and ~*s* on a dress⟩ (3) **:** a bound or stitched slit or a loop through which a button is passed **:** BUTTONHOLE (4) **:** a ring through which a rod (as for a curtain) is passed (5) **:** a loop at either end of the bowstring of an archer's bow used for attaching the string to the bow (6) **:** a loop bent in the end of the shank of a fishhook or a hole drilled through the shank for attaching a line or leader **e** (1) **:** an undeveloped bud (as on a potato) (2) **:** the depression at the calyx end of some fruits (as apples or pears) (3) **:** the hilum (as of a bean) **f eyes** *pl* **:** CRAB'S-EYE **g** (1) **:** the opening from which the water of a spring wells out of the earth (2) **:** an opening that leads into a mine shaft (3) **:** an opening at the top of a cupola — compare OCULUS (4) **:** a peephole in the walls of a furnace (5) **:** an aperture through which light enters; *specif* **:** the lens of a camera **h :** an area like a hole or column in the center of a tropical cyclone marked by only light winds or complete calm with no precipitation and sometimes by a sunlit clear sky ⟨the ~ of a hurricane⟩ **i :** the center of a flower esp. when differently colored or marked **:** the disk in composites **j** (1) **:** the indentation on the inside of a bivalve shell (as the oyster) where the adductor muscle is inserted **:** CICATRIX (2) **:** the adductor muscle of a bivalve mollusk esp. when used as food ⟨the ~*s* of scallops⟩ (3) **:** the osculum of a fibrous sponge **k** (1) **:** a triangular piece of beef cut from between the top and bottom of the round (2) **:** the chief muscle of a chop (3) **:** a compact mass of muscular tissue usu. embedded in fat in a rib or loin cut of meat **l :** a very small nugget of gold or platinum **m :** a device (as a photoelectric cell) that functions in a manner analogous to human vision **:** ELECTRIC EYE **3 :** something that is central or is felt to be central (as in location or importance) **:** focal point **:** CENTER **4** *obs* **:** a light touch of color **:** TINGE **5 a :** the direction from which the wind is blowing ⟨sailing into the wind's ~⟩ **b eyes** *pl* **:** the forward part in the bows of a ship near the hawseholes **6** *slang* **:** DETECTIVE ⟨a private ~⟩ **7 :** MELATOPE — **all eyes :** marked by rapt attention to something seen or about to be seen ⟨she was *all eyes* as I unwrapped the package⟩ — **all one's eye** *or* **all the eye** *or* **all in the eye** *chiefly Brit* **:** utter nonsense ⟨their opinions are *all my eye*⟩ — **at eye :** at a glance **:** without effort — **cut an eye 1** *archaic* **:** to cast a look **:** GLANCE **2** *archaic* **:** to make eyes — **do in the eye :** to take complete and unfair advantage of (as by trickery) ⟨born to *do* the other fellow *in the eye* and enjoy life —Alva Johnston⟩ — **give an eye to :** look after **:** give attention to ⟨go into the garden and *give an eye to* your children —Katherine Mansfield⟩ — **give the big eye :** to make eyes — usu. used with *to* — **give the eye to :** to look at ⟨people walk past here just to *give me the eye* —Joseph Mitchell⟩ esp. in admiration or with a more or less open display of sexual interest ⟨sailors *giving the eye to* every girl in the port⟩ — **have an eye to 1 :** to look after **:** give attention to **2 :** to have as an objective ⟨*having an eye to* the furnishing of a new flat —Sam Pollock⟩ — **have eyes only for 1 :** to look at nothing else but **2 :** to desire nothing else but — **have in one's eye :** to have in mind **:** have a mental picture of ⟨I *have* one particular friend *in my eye* at this moment —A.C.Benson⟩ — **have one's eye on 1 :** to look at **2 :** to watch constantly and attentively **:** keep one's eyes on **3 :** to have as an objective — **in a pig's eye** *slang* **:** by no means **:** under no circumstances **:** NEVER — **keep an eye out :** to be on the lookout **:** keep watch attentively and expectantly ⟨*keep an eye out* for modern trends in school design —Cecile Starr⟩ — **keep one's eyes open** *or* **keep one's eyes peeled** *also* **keep one's eyes skinned :** to be on the alert **:** be watchful **:** be careful — **make eyes :** to look with a more or less open display of sexual interest **:** gaze amorously **:** FLIRT, OGLE ⟨a waitress *making eyes* at every customer⟩ — **my eye** — used to express mild disagreement or sometimes surprise ⟨you can do it as well as he can, *my eye!*⟩ — **see eye to eye :** to be in entire agreement **:** agree without exception ⟨we *see eye to eye* in everything we do⟩ — **set one's eyes by :** to have a great affection for **:** esteem highly — **throw eyes at** *or* **throw the eye at** *chiefly Austral* **:** to make eyes at ⟨jealous because her young man began to *throw eyes at* me —Rex Ingamells⟩ — **to the eye :** in appearance **:** on the surface **:** APPARENTLY ⟨prejudices that *to the eye* are rather complex —W.S.White⟩ — **up to one's eyes** *or* **up to the eyes :** extremely busy **:** very much occupied **:** deeply immersed ⟨*up to their eyes* in paper work⟩ — **with an eye to :** with a view to ⟨*with an eye to* the future⟩ **:** with the object of ⟨*with an eye to* robbing him —S.M.Fitzgerald⟩ — **with half an eye :** with only a hurried glance **:** without paying full attention ⟨*with half an eye* he could see what their plan was⟩

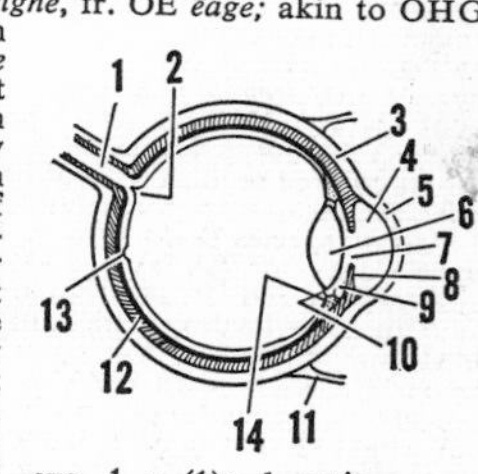

eye, 1 a (1): *1* optic nerve, *2* blind spot, *3* sclera, *4* anterior chamber, *5* cornea, *6* lens, *7* pupil, *8* iris, *9* posterior chamber, *10* suspensory ligament, *11* conjunctiva, *12* choroid, *13* macula and fovea, *14* ciliary muscle

²eye \"\ *vb* **eyed; eyed; eyeing** *or* **eying; eyes** [ME *eyen,* fr. *eie, eye,* n.] *vt* **1 a :** to fix the eyes on **:** turn the eyes toward ⟨after speaking with her he *eyed* the letter she was carrying⟩ **:** look at **:** look upon **:** VIEW **:** gaze upon ⟨the child *eyed* the wonder from a safe distance —Edison Marshall⟩ **:** stare at ⟨the detective *eyed* the bald man searchingly —T. M.Johnson⟩ **b** *archaic* **:** to have a visual perception of **:** get a look at **:** catch sight of **:** SEE **2 a :** to keep a close watch on **:** watch carefully **:** study closely **:** keep an eye on ⟨*eyeing* every change in the stock market⟩ **b :** to have or keep (as an objective or point of reference) in view **:** look to ⟨the cold calculations of statesmen *eyeing* the national advantage —Oscar Handlin⟩ **:** aim at **3 :** to furnish with an eye **:** make an eye in **4 :** to remove the undeveloped buds of (a potato) ~ *vi* **1** *obs* **:** to appear to the eye **:** SEEM, LOOK ⟨this doth not ~ well to you —Shak.⟩ **2 :** to become eyed ⟨in 30 to 45 days the eggs begin to ~ up —*Scientific American*⟩

eye·able \ˈīəbəl\ *adj* **1** *archaic* **:** that may be seen **2** *archaic* **:** visually attractive

eye agate *n* **:** ALEPPO STONE

eye appeal *n* **:** visual attractiveness — **eye–appealing** \ˈ=,=ˈ=\ *adj*

eye backer *or* **eye bender** *n* **:** an operator of a machine for forming the eyes of leaf springs

¹eyeball \ˈ=,=\ *n* [¹*eye* + *ball*] **:** the more or less globular capsule of the eye of vertebrates that is formed by the sclera and cornea together with its contained structures **:** the ball of the eye **:** the eye proper

²eyeball \"\ *vt, slang* **:** to look at intently or fixedly **:** stare at **:** EYE ⟨his triggermen huddled over a table in the corner, ~*ing* me —Milton Mezzrow & Bernard Wolfe⟩

eyebalm \ˈ=,=\ *n* **:** GOLDENSEAL

eye bank *n* **:** a storage place for a reserve supply of human corneas removed from the newly dead for transplanting to the eyes of those blinded because of defects of the cornea

eyebar \ˈ=,=\ *n* **:** a metal bar that is usu. rectangular in cross section and that is enlarged at each end for holes forming eyes; *sometimes* **:** I BAR

eye–beam \ˈ=,=\ *n, archaic* **:** a radiant glance of the eye

eyebeam \ˈ=,=\ *n* [by folk etymology] **:** I BEAM

eyeberry \ˈī–*see* BERRY\ *n* **1 :** PARTRIDGEBERRY 1 **2 :** WINTERGREEN 2a

eyebolt \ˈ=,=\ *n* **:** a bolt with a looped head or an opening in the head

eye bone *n* **:** one of the ossified plates in the sclera of the eye that are esp. well developed in birds and many reptiles

eyebolt

eyebright \ˈ=,=\ *n, pl* **eyebrights** *or* **eyebright 1 :** any of several herbs of the genus *Euphrasia* (esp. *E. officinalis* of Europe) formerly regarded as a remedy for eye ailments **2 a :** SCARLET PIMPERNEL **b :** INDIAN TOBACCO **c :** INDIAN PIPE **d :** GERMANDER SPEEDWELL **e :** a sundew (*Drosera rotundifolia*) **f :** BLUET 1c(1)

¹eyebrow \ˈ=,=\ *n* [ME, fr. *eie, eye* eye + *browe*] **1 a :** the arch or ridge over the eye; *also* **:** the covering of hair growing on this ridge **b :** the narrow surface between the upper border of the orbit and the orbital cavity of fiddler crabs **2 a :** a molding over a window **b :** FILLET 4 **c :** a low dormer over which the roofing is carried in wave line **3 :** a projection above an air port to divert water trickling down the side of a ship — called also *wriggle* **4 :** fibrous waste that accumulates on machines during the spinning of yarn and that often forms defects in the yarn

²eyebrow \"\ *vi* **:** to form eyebrow (sense 4)

eyebrow pencil *n* **:** a cosmetic pencil for the eyebrows

eye–catcher \ˈ=,==\ *n* **:** something that strongly attracts the eye ⟨ads that were real *eye-catchers*⟩

eye–catching \ˈ=,==\ *adj* **:** strongly attracting the eye **:** STRIKING ⟨*eye-catching* posters⟩

eye color *n* **:** pigmentation of the iris in man

eyecup \ˈ=,=\ *n* **1 a :** a small oval cup that has a rim curved to fit the orbit of the eye and that is used for bathing the eyes or for applying liquid remedies to them **b :** an oval part shaped like a cup that extends backward from each of the rims of a pair of goggles and that is designed to fit snugly about the orbit of the eye so as to give the eye added protection from sparks or other hazards **2 :** a round hollowed piece with a peephole in it on the rear sight of a firearm

eyecup 1a

eyed \ˈīd\ *adj* [ME *eied, eyed,* fr. *eie, eye* + *-ed*] **1 a :** having eyes ⟨now they were swimming, making a long ~ line —A.B.Guthrie⟩ or an eye ⟨an ~ fishhook⟩ **b :** having markings suggestive of eyes ⟨~ like a peacock —John Keats⟩ **2** *of a fish egg* **:** developed to the point that the eyes are clearly visible

eye dialect *n* **:** the use of misspellings that are based on standard pronunciations (as *sez* for *says* or *kow* for *cow*) but are usu. intended to suggest a speaker's illiteracy or his use of generally nonstandard pronunciations

eyed·ness \ˈīdnəs\ *n* -ES **:** preference for the use of one or the other eye (as in sighting a gun) — compare HANDEDNESS

eye doctor *n* **:** OPTOMETRIST

eye draft *n* **:** a drawing made from sight

eyedropper \ˈ=,==\ *n* **:** DROPPER 4a

eye·drop·per·ful \ˈ=,==,fu̇l\ *n* -S **:** the amount held by an eyedropper

eyed skate *n* **:** WINTER SKATE

eyed skink *n* **:** a bronzy insectivorous skink (*Chalcides ocellatus*) marked with black spots that is native to Asia Minor but sometimes kept in terraria

eye–ear plane *n* **:** a conventional position in which a human skull is placed for craniometric study marked so that the lower margin of the orbits is on the same horizontal plane as the upper margin of the auditory meatus — called also *Frankfurt horizontal*

eye–filling \ˈ=,==\ *adj* **:** visually attractive **:** EYE-APPEALING

eye fold *n* **:** EPICANTHIC FOLD

eye·ful \ˈī,fu̇l\ *n* -S **1 a :** a full or completely satisfying view **:** a good look **:** all that one could want to see ⟨they wanted to see life in the raw and they got a real ~⟩ **b :** something or someone visually attractive; *esp* **:** a strikingly beautiful woman ⟨a statuesque blond ~ —*New Yorker*⟩ **2 :** a quantity of something thrown into the eye

eyeglass \ˈ=,=\ *n* **1 a** *obs* **:** the lens of the eye **b :** the eyepiece of an optical instrument (as a microscope or a telescope) **c :** a lens for personal wear that is used to aid vision or correct defects of vision; *specif* **:** MONOCLE **d eyeglasses** *pl* **:** GLASSES, SPECTACLES **2 :** EYECUP 1a

eye·glassed \ˈī,glast, -laa(ə)st,-laist,-läst\ *adj* [*eyeglasses* + *-ed*] **:** wearing eyeglasses

eye·glassy \-sē\ *adj* [*eyeglass* (monocle) + *-y*] **:** SNOBBISH

eye gnat *or* **eye fly** *n* **:** a small fly attracted (as by lachrymal secretions) to the eyes of man or other animals — compare CHLOROPIDAE

eyeground \ˈ=,=\ *n* **:** the fundus of the eye; *esp* **:** the retina as viewed through an ophthalmoscope

eyehole \ˈ=,=\ *n* **1 :** one of the orbits of the skull **2 :** a hole (as in a mask) through which one looks **:** PEEPHOLE

eye indexing *n* **:** the indexing of potatoes that is done by preplanting an eye of each potato — called also *tuber indexing*

eyeing *pres part of* EYE

eye·ish \ˈīish, ˈēsh\ *n, pl* **eyeish** *usu cap* [Sp *ayas,* of AmerInd origin] **1 a :** a Caddo people of northeastern Texas **2 :** a member of the Eyeish people

eyelash \ˈ=,=\ *n* **:** the fringe of hair that edges the eyelid; *usu* **:** a single hair of this fringe

eye lens *n* **:** the lens nearest the eye in an eyepiece

eye·less \ˈīləs\ *adj* **1 a** (1) **:** having no natural eyes **:** lacking eyes ⟨~ fishes in caves⟩ (2) **:** being without an eye or eyes ⟨an ~ needle⟩ **b :** no longer having one's natural eyes **:** having had the eyes removed **:** deprived of one's eyes **:** made sightless **:** BLINDED ⟨blind as an ~ beggar —Dorothy Sayers⟩ **2 a :** lacking sight **:** BLIND ⟨the dread of being ~⟩ **b :** not using the eyes **:** failing to use the eyes **:** moving or acting blindly ⟨an ~ leader⟩ — **eye·less·ness** *n* -ES

¹eye·let \ˈīlət, *usu* -əd.+V\ *n* -S [ME *oilet,* fr. MF *oillet,* dim. of *oil* eye, fr. L *oculus* — more at EYE] **1 a :** a small hole usu. round and buttonholed and designed to receive a cord, lace, pin, or button shank or used only for decoration (as in embroidery) **b** (1) **:** a small ring of durable material typically metal that is inserted into an eyelet to reinforce it **:** GROMMET; *also* **:** a small barrel-shaped piece of such material (2) **:** an eyelet (as of a shoe or a mailbag or at the edge of a sail) that is reinforced with such a ring or piece or that is lined with such material **2 :** a small hole (as in a wall) usu. used for observation **:** PEEPHOLE, EYEHOLE, LOOPHOLE **3 :** a small eye; *specif* **:** OCELLUS

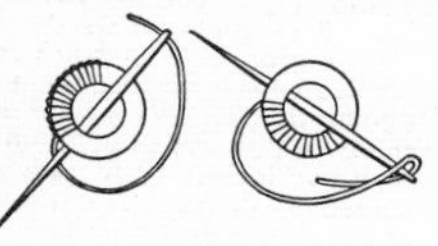
eyelets 1a

²eyelet \"\ *vt* **eyeleted** *also* **eyeletted; eyeleted** *also* **eyeletted; eyeleting** *also* **eyeletting; eyelets :** to make an eyelet in **:** equip with eyelets — **eye·let·er** *also* **eye·let·ter** \-ləd·ə(r), -lətə-\ *n* -S

eye·le·teer \ˌīləˈti(ə)r\ *n* -S **:** a small instrument with a sharp point used in making eyelet holes

eyelid \ˈ=,=\ *n* [ME *eielid, eyelid,* fr. *eie, eye* + *lid*] **:** one of the movable lids of skin with which an animal covers or uncovers the eyeball, most vertebrates above fishes having both an upper lid and a lower lid and many of them having also a nictitating membrane

eyelike \ˈ=,=\ *adj* **:** resembling or suggestive of an eye ⟨~ markings on a butterfly's wings⟩

eyeline \ˈ=,=\ *n* **1 :** the level of the eyes **:** eye level ⟨above his ~ he saw her frown —Richard Llewellyn⟩ **2 :** a linear ridge connecting each eye with the glabella in most early trilobites

eye–minded \ˈ=ˈ==\ *adj* **:** marked by a predominance of visual imagery in one's thought processes or mental productions **:** given to extensive or excessive visualization in one's mental operations — compare EAR-MINDED, MOTOR-MINDED — **eye–mind·ed·ness** *n* -ES

eye muscle *n* **:** either of two long large muscles one of which runs along the right side of the backbone and the other along the left side of the backbone — called also *longissimus dorsi*

ey·en \ˈīən\ *archaic pl of* EYE

eye–opener \ˈ=,=(=)=\ *n* **1 :** a drink intended to wake one up fully or clear one's head esp. when taken early in the day or shortly after awakening **2 a :** something that opens one's eyes with astonishment or that causes one to stare or gape **b :** something (as a sudden or unexpected disclosure, experience, or occurrence) that causes great surprise and that makes inescapably clear or certain what had not been realized ⟨news of the industry's collapse was an *eye-opener*⟩ **:** something very enlightening or revealing ⟨the book was an *eye-opener* to complacent party members⟩ **c :** something or someone of remarkable and often startling visual attractiveness ⟨she was a real *eye-opener*⟩

eye–opening \ˈ=,=(=)=\ *adj* **:** that opens the eyes (as with astonishment) **:** most surprising or enlightening

eyepiece \ˈ=,=\ *n* **1 :** the lens or combination of lenses at the eye end of an optical instrument (as a telescope) through which the image is viewed — see PRISM BINOCULAR illustration **2 a :** a piece of transparent material (as mica) that resists intense heat and that is mounted and fitted in the side of a furnace to permit a view of the interior **b :** a piece of transparent material (as glass) that is mounted and fitted in the facepiece of a gas mask or other respirator to permit vision

eyepiece micrometer *n* **:** a scale in the field of vision of an eyepiece used as a measuring device — called also *ocular micrometer*

eyepit \ˈ=,=\ *n* **:** EYEHOLE

eyepoint \ˈ=,=\ *n* **:** the point at which the eye is placed in using an optical instrument (as a microscope) and which is coincident with the exit pupil of the instrument

eye–popper \ˈ=,==\ *n* **1 :** something that astonishes **:** EYE-OPENER **2 :** something thrilling or exciting ⟨a Western novel that's a surefire *eye-popper*⟩

eye–popping \ˈ=,==\ *adj* **1 :** EYE-OPENING **2 :** thrilling or exciting ⟨the climber has an *eye-popping* view the full length of Zion Canyon —L.F.Clark⟩

ey·er \ˈī(ə)r, ˈīə\ *n* -S **:** one that eyes

eye relief *n* **:** the distance of the eye from the eye lens of an optical instrument that is best suited to the use of the instrument

eye rhyme *n* **:** an imperfect rhyme that appears to have identical vowel sounds from similarity of spelling (as *move* and *love* or *bough* and *though*) or that arises from a former similarity of vowel sound (as *far* and *war*)

eye–ring \ˈ=,=\ *n* **:** the inner margin of the eyelids of a fowl

eyeroot \ˈ=,=\ *n* **:** GOLDENSEAL

eyes *pl of* EYE, *pres 3d sing of* EYE

eye screw *n* **:** a screw (as a wood screw) that has a head in the form of an eye; *often* **:** such a screw with a head that is not closed

eye–servant \ˈ=,==\ *n, archaic* **:** one that attends to duty only when watched

eye–server \ˈ=,==\ *n, archaic* **:** EYE-SERVANT

eye–service \ˈ=,==\ *n, archaic* **:** attendance to duty only when being watched

eyeshade \ˈ=,=\ *n* **:** a visor for shielding the eyes from strong light that is held on the head by a band

eye shadow *n* **:** a cosmetic cream in various colors that is applied to the eyelids to accent the eyes

eyeshine \ˈ=,=\ *n* **:** reflection of light from the inner surface of an eye through the pupil so that the eye has a luminous appearance (as in a cat)

eyeshade

eyeshot \ˈ=,=\ *n* **1 :** the range of the eye **:** the distance that the eye can see **:** SIGHT ⟨there wasn't a living soul walking or standing or sitting anywhere within ~ —Dorothy Sayers⟩ **2** *archaic* **:** a look of the eye **:** GLANCE

eyesight \ˈ=,=\ *n* [ME *eiesight, eyesight,* fr. *eie, eye* + *sight*] **1 a :** the faculty of seeing **:** ability to see **:** SIGHT, VISION ⟨a young man with good ~⟩ **b** *archaic* **:** the act of seeing or looking **:** OBSERVATION **2** *archaic* **:** EYESHOT

eye socket *n* **:** ORBIT 1a

eye·some \ˈīsəm\ *adj* [¹*eye* + *-some*] *archaic* **:** visually attractive

eyesore \ˈ=,=\ *n* [ME *eiesor, eyesor* soreness or disease of the eye, fr. *eie, eye* + *sor* sore] **:** something offensive to the sight ⟨the old church and historic burying ground had fallen into decay and had become an ~ —L.H.Beck⟩

eye splice *n* **:** a splice formed by bending a rope's end back and splicing it into the rope so that a loop is formed

eyespot \ˈ=,=\ *n* **1 a :** a simple visual organ in many invertebrates that consists of pigment or pigmented cells covering a sensory termination **:** OCELLUS **b :** a small pigment body in various unicellular algae that is supposedly sensitive to light **2 a :** a usu. small spot of color (as on the wings of certain butterflies) **b :** a darkish area around the hilum of a seed (as some beans and cowpeas) **3 :** any of several fungous diseases of plants characterized by yellowish oval lesions on the leaves and stems; *esp* **:** a disease of sugarcane and various other grasses caused by a fungus (*Helminthosporium sacchari*)

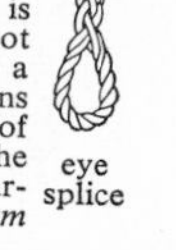
eye splice

eye–spotted \ˈ=,==\ *adj* **:** marked by spots of color **:** having eyespots

eye–spotted bud moth *n* **:** a dark brown tortricid moth (*Spilonota ocellana*) with a light band on each wing and a dark brown black-headed larva that feeds in a web on fruit buds, leaves, and fruit (as apples or plums)

eyess *var of* EYAS

eyestalk \'=,=\ *n* **:** one of the movable peduncles bearing the eyes at the tip in a decapod crustacean

eyestrain \'=,=\ *n* **:** weariness or strained condition of the eye (as from overuse or uncorrected defects of vision)

eyestrings *n pl, obs* **:** organic eye attachments (as muscles of the eye) once popularly viewed as causing blindness by breaking or as breaking at death

eye·tie *also* **ey·tie** \'īd·ē, 'ī,tī\ *adj or n, usu cap* [by shortening & alter.] **:** ITALIAN — usu. used disparagingly

eyetooth \'=¦=\ *n, pl* **eyeteeth** **1 :** a canine tooth of the upper jaw **2** *eyeteeth, pl* **:** something of great value — used in the phrase *give one's eyeteeth* ⟨many a young reporter would give his *eyeteeth* for a foreign assignment —F.L.Mott⟩

[1]**eyewash** \'=,=\ *n* [[1]*eye* + *wash*] **1 a :** a liquid used in bathing the eyes **:** an eye douche **b :** a medicinal solution for the eyes **:** an eye lotion **2 a :** statements, actions, or procedures designed to distract attention from or conceal ulterior motives or actual conditions ⟨the ~ handed out by dictators⟩ **b :** statements, actions, or procedures undertaken merely to make a good impression **:** empty display ⟨disgusted with all the ~ of political campaigns⟩ **c :** pretentious nonsense **:** DRIVEL, CLAPTRAP ⟨preposterous claims that were the purest ~⟩

[2]**eyewash** \"\ *vt* **:** to give a misleading appearance to **:** doctor up **:** PRETTIFY ⟨he'll line up his peg tents and ~ his base camps with the old parade-ground touch —J.W.Bellah⟩

eyewater \'=,==\ *n* **1** *archaic* **a :** TEARS **b :** AQUEOUS HUMOR **2** *archaic* **:** EYEWASH 1

eyewhite \'=,=\ *n* **:** WHITE 2a(2)

eyewink \'=,=\ *n* **1 :** a wink of the eye **2** *obs* **:** LOOK, GLANCE

eyewinker \'=,==\ *n* **1 :** EYELASH; *also* **:** EYELID **2 :** something (as a foreign particle lodged in the eye) that irritates the eye and causes winking

[1]**eyewitness** \'=¦==\ *n, often attrib* [[1]*eye* + *witness*] **1 :** one that sees or has seen an occurrence or an object with his own eyes and so is able to give a firsthand report on it **:** one that gives a report on or testifies to what he has actually seen ⟨an ~ of the crime⟩ **2** *obs* **:** a report by an eyewitness

[2]**eyewitness** \"\ *vt* **:** to see with one's own eyes ⟨correspondents who ~*ed* the recent riots —*Time*⟩

eye worm *n* **:** a parasitic worm found in the eye: as **a :** either of two slender nematode worms (*Oxyspirura mansoni* and *O. petrowi*) living beneath the nictitating membrane of the eyes of chickens or other birds **b :** a member of a genus (*Thelazia*) of spiruroid nematodes living in the tear duct and beneath the eyelid of dog, cat, sheep, man, and other mammals and sometimes causing blindness **c :** an African filarial worm (*Loa loa*) that migrates through the subdermal tissues and eyeball of man — compare CALABAR SWELLING

eyewort \'=,=\ *n* [so called fr. its use as a remedy for eye ailments] **:** EYEBRIGHT 1

eying *pres part of* EYE

eyne \'īn\ *archaic pl of* EYE

eyot \'ā(ə)t\ [ME *ait, eit* — more at AIT] *var of* [1]AIT

ey·ra \'ārə\ *n* -s [AmerSp & Pg, fr. Tupi *eirara, irara*] **:** a solid-colored reddish wildcat usu. regarded as a color phase of the jaguarundi but sometimes considered to constitute a separate species (*Felis eyra* or *Herpailurus eyra*)

eyre \'a(a)|(ə)r, 'e|, |ə\ *n* -s [ME *eire*, fr. AF, fr. OF *erre* trip, journey, round, fr. *errer* to travel — more at ERR] **1 :** the circuit court held by justices in eyre **2 :** the record of an eyre

eyrie *var of* AERIE

ey·rir \'ā,rir\ *n, pl* **au·rar** \'œuæ,rär\ [Icel, fr. ON, ounce (usu. of silver), money (in pl.), prob. fr. L *aureus*, a gold coin — more at AUREUS] **1 :** a unit of monetary value in Iceland worth $\frac{1}{100}$ of a krona — see MONEY table **2 :** a small coin representing one eyrir unit

ey·ry *like* EYRIE — *see* AERIE\ *archaic var of* AERIE

-eys *pl of* -EY

ey·sell \'ā|səl, 'ē|, |zəl\ *var of* ESILL

eytie *var of* EYETIE

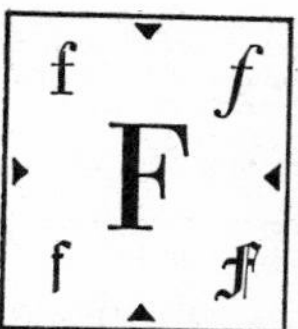

¹f \'ef\ *n, pl* **f's** *or* **fs** \'efs\ *often cap, often attrib* **1 a :** the sixth letter of the English alphabet **b :** an instance of this letter printed, written, or otherwise represented **c :** a speech counterpart of orthographic *f* (as *f* in *fife, wafer*, or Spanish *fuero*) **2 a :** the keynote of F major or F minor **b :** the tone F **3 :** a printer's type, a stamp, or some other instrument for reproducing the letter *f* **4 :** someone or something arbitrarily or conveniently designated *f* esp. as the sixth in order or class **5 a :** a grade assigned by a teacher or examiner rating a student's work as so inferior as to be failing ⟨no student with more than one *F* in a major subject may be advanced to a higher grade without a special examination⟩ **b :** one graded or rated with an F ⟨an *F* student in history⟩ **6 :** something having the shape of the letter F

²f *abbr, often cap* **1** [L *fac*] make **2** Fahrenheit **3** failure **4** fair **5** family **6** farad **7** farthing **8** father **9** fathom **10** fawn **11** feast **12** [L *fecit*] he made **13** fellow **14** female **15** feminine **16** [L *fiat*] let it be done; let it be made **17** fiction **18** field **19** fighter **20** [L *filius*] son **21** filly **22** finance; financial **23** fine **24** finish **25** fire **26** firm **27** fixed **28** flat **29** fleet **30** florin **31** flower **32** fluid **33** fluid ounce **34** fog **35** folio **36** following **37** foot **38** for **39** force **40** forma **41** formed **42** formula **43** forte **44** forward **45** foul **46** fragile **47** fragmentation **48** franc **49** [L *frater*] brother **50** French **51** frequency **52** friar **53** from **54** fuel **55** full **56** function **57** furlong

³f *symbol* **1** *cap* Faraday **2** *cap* luminous flux **3** *cap* filial; filial generation **4** *cap* fluorine **5** focal length **6** *cap* folio **7** the relative aperture of a photographic lens — often written *f/* or *f:*

fa \'fä\ *n, pl* **fas** *or* **fa's** [ME, fr. ML, fr. L *famuli* servants, a word sung to this note in a medieval hymn to St. John the Baptist] **1 :** the fourth tone of the diatonic scale in solmization **2 :** the tone *F* in the fixed-do system

fa' \'fä, 'fȯ\ *chiefly Scot var of* FALL

FA *abbr* **1** field artillery **2** financial adviser **3** football association **4** forage acre **5** free alongside **6** free astray **7** free of all average **8** freight agent

FAA *abbr* free of all average

faags \'fägz, 'fagz\ *var of* FEGS

fab *abbr* fabricated

¹fa·ba \'fābə\ *n, cap* [NL, fr. L, bean — more at BEAN] *in some classifications* **:** a genus of leguminous plants comprising the broad bean and now usu. included in *Vicia*

²faba *var of* FAVA

fa·ba·ce·ae \fə'bāsē,ē\ *n pl, cap* [NL, fr. *Faba*, type genus + *-aceae*] *in some classifications* **:** a large nearly cosmopolitan family that comprises the peas, beans, and related herbaceous or woody plants with pealike flowers and a legume as fruit and that is now usu. included in the family Leguminosae

fa·ba·ceous \-āshəs\ *adj* [LL *fabaceus*, fr. L *faba* bean + *-aceus* -aceous] **1 :** of or relating to the Leguminosae **:** LEGUMINOUS **2 :** relating to, like, or being a bean

fabe \'fāb\ *n* -s [prob. alter. of ME *theve* bramble, gooseberry — more at FEABERRY] *dial Brit* **:** GOOSEBERRY 1a

fa·bel·la \fə'belə\ *n, pl* **fabel·lae** \-e,lē\ [NL, dim. of L *faba*] **:** a small fibrocartilage ossified in many animals and sometimes in man in the tendon of the gastrocnemius muscle, behind one or both of the femoral condyles

¹fa·bi·an \'fābēən\ *adj, usu cap* [L *fabianus*, fr. Quintus *Fabius* Maximus Cunctator †203 B.C. Roman dictator and general + L *-anus* -an] **1 a :** of, relating to, or in the manner of the Roman general Quintus Fabius Maximus who defeated Hannibal in the Second Punic War by avoiding decisive contests and harassing him by marches and countermarches **b :** notably conservative and cautious in making advances or changes **2** [*Fabian (Society)*; fr. the members' belief in slow orderly rather than revolutionary change in government] **:** being or belonging or relating to a society of socialists organized in England in 1884 to spread socialistic principles gradually

²fabian \"\ *n* -s *usu cap* **:** a member of or sympathizer with the Fabian Society of socialists

fa·bi·ana \,fābē'anə, -'ä- *also* -'ā-\ *n, cap* [NL, after Francisco *Fabián* y Fuero †1801 Span. archbishop and naturalist] **:** a genus of heathlike evergreen shrubs (family Solanaceae) of Central and So. America that have numerous small white or lavender tubular flowers and are sometimes cultivated in the cool greenhouse or in the open in frost-free areas

fa·bi·an·ism \'fābēə,nizəm\ *n* -s *usu cap* **:** the doctrines or principles of the Fabian socialists

fa·bi·form \'fābə,fȯrm\ *adj* [L *faba* bean + E *-iform*] **:** shaped like a bean

¹fa·ble \'fābəl\ *n* -s [ME, fr. MF, fr. L *fabula* conversation, narrative, tale, play, fable, fr. *fari* to speak, say — more at FAME] **1 :** a fictitious narrative or statement **:** an invented tale **:** FICTION: as **a :** UNTRUTH, FALSEHOOD ⟨the ~*s* and misrepresentations of this pamphlet⟩ **b :** a story of supernatural or highly marvelous happenings (as in legend, myth, or folklore) **c :** a narration intended to enforce some useful truth or precept; *esp* **:** one in which animals and even inanimate objects speak and act like human beings ⟨the ~ of the fox in the barnyard⟩ — see BEAST FABLE **d :** casual, idle, or foolish report or talk ⟨old wives' ~*s*⟩; *broadly* **:** common talk **2 a :** a subject of fable **:** something (as a mysterious event) productive of fabulous accounts or explanations; *broadly* **:** a theme of popular talk and speculation ⟨he became the chief ~ of the village⟩ **b :** a product of fable **:** something having reality only in fabulous accounts ⟨if personal immortality is not a ~⟩ **3 :** the plot, story, or connected series of events forming the theme of a literary work (as an epic poem or play) **syn** see ALLEGORY, FICTION

²fable \"\ *vb* **fabled; fabled; fabling** \-b(ə)liŋ\ **fables** [ME *fablen*, fr. MF *fabler*, fr. L *fabulari* to talk, fr. *fabula*] *vi* **1 a :** to compose or tell fictitious tales **b** *obs* **:** to talk idly **2** *archaic* **:** to write or speak what is not true **:** utter falsehoods **:** LIE ~ *vt* **:** to devise and recount as if real **:** report as if literally true ⟨it is *fabled* that Norsemen built the tower⟩ ⟨the bird of paradise was *fabled* to have no feet⟩ ⟨how he fell from Heaven they *fabled* —John Milton⟩

fabled *adj* **1 :** told or mentioned in fable **:** MYTHICAL, LEGENDARY **2 :** having no real existence **:** FICTITIOUS ⟨~ sorrows⟩

fa·ble·ist \-b(ə)ləst\ *n* -s **:** a teller or writer of fables **:** FABULIST

fa·bler \-b(ə)lə(r)\ *n* -s [ME, fr. MF *ableur*, fr. *fabler* + *-eur* -or] **:** FABULIST

fab·li·au \'fablē,ō\ *also* **fa·bleau** \fa'blō\ *n, pl* **fabli·aux** *also* **fa·bleaux** \-ō(z)\ [F, fr. OF *fablel, fableau, fabliau*, dim. of *fable*] **:** a short metrical tale of a type composed chiefly by jongleurs for and about the lower classes; *also* **:** the genre of such metrical tales being usu. comic, frankly coarse, and often cynical esp. in their treatment of women

fabling *n* -s [ME, fr. gerund of *fablen* to fable] **:** an act of one who fables **:** ROMANCING, PREVARICATION

fa·braea \fa'brēə\ *n, cap* [NL, prob. after Jean H. *Fabre* †1915 Fr. entomologist] **:** a genus of ascomycetous fungi (family Mollisiaceae) that includes several leaf parasites with multicellular ascospores

¹fab·ric \'fabrik, -rēk\ *n* -s [MF *fabrique*, fr. *fabriquer* to fabricate, fr. L *fabricari*, fr. *fabrica* artisan's workshop, skillfully wrought object, building — more at FORGE] **1 a :** a product of building (as a house or ship) ⟨four high houses . . . of the sort lane-dwellers call ~*s* —Daniel Corkery⟩ **b :** underlying structure **:** FRAMEWORK ⟨the work of restoring the ~ of Westminster Abbey —Conrad Voss Bark⟩ ⟨the very ~ of daily life⟩ ⟨whether the political ~ had the strength to withstand war —S.E.Morrison & H.S.Commager⟩ **2** *obs* **:** CONTRIVANCE, DEVICE; *esp* **:** a military engine **3 :** an act of constructing **:** CONSTRUCTION, ERECTION; *specif* **:** the construction and maintenance of a church building **4 a :** structural plan or style of construction ⟨the whole complex ~ of flowers and floral organs that makes up the head of a composite plant⟩ ⟨soil ~ (arrangement of the constituents of the soil in relation to each other) —L.D.Baver⟩ **b :** TEXTURE, QUALITY — used chiefly of textiles ⟨a linen cloth of fine silky ~⟩ **c :** the form of the planchet of a medal or coin ⟨a coin with thick ~⟩ **5 a** *archaic* **:** something made by man **:** ARTIFACT, PRODUCT ⟨the earliest ~ of the Venetian glassblowers⟩ **b :** CLOTH 1a **c :** cloth of a particular kind ⟨satin is a ~ with a smooth shining surface⟩ or for a particular use ⟨a sheer curtain ~⟩ **d :** a material (as leather or woven wire) that in some respect resembles cloth **6 :** a place devoted to manufacture **:** FACTORY ⟨the chief shapes manufactured in this ~ were bowls —V.G.Childe⟩ **7:** structural material ⟨the more usual ~ was timber or coursed masonry⟩ ⟨using a ~ of silken threads the spider builds her web⟩ **8 :** the appearance or pattern that is produced by the shapes and arrangement of the crystal grains or of these with glass in a rock and that includes those orientation features which are not evident from grain shape alone

²fabric *vt* **fabricked; fabricked; fabricking; fabrics** [F *fabriquer*] *obs* **:** FRAME, BUILD, CONSTRUCT

fab·ri·cant \'fabrəkənt\ *n* -s [F, fr. L *fabricant-, fabricans*, pres. part. of *fabricari*] **:** a maker or producer esp. of a commercial product **:** MANUFACTURER

fab·ri·cate \-ə,kāt, *usu* -d·+V\ *vt* -ED/-ING/-S [ME *fabricaten*, fr. L *fabricatus*, past part. of *fabricari* — more at FABRIC] **1 a :** to form by art and labor **:** MANUFACTURE, PRODUCE ⟨*fabricated* some of the finest English pottery⟩ ⟨an organization devoted to *fabricating* deluxe editions of the classics⟩ **b :** to form into a whole by uniting parts **:** CONSTRUCT, BUILD ⟨*fabricated* a bridge of steel beams⟩ ⟨planning to ~ a house of wholly synthetic materials⟩; *often* **:** to build up into a whole by uniting interchangeable standardized parts ⟨*fabricating* automobiles on the assembly line⟩ **2 a :** to make, shape, or prepare (parts) according to standardized specification so as to be interchangeable ⟨*fabricate* brake assemblies for one of the new cars⟩ **b :** to cause (raw material or stock) to be manufactured **:** SHAPE ⟨*fabricating* sheet steel into plates⟩ ⟨what steel to use or how to ~ it —*Dun's Rev.*⟩ **3 a :** INVENT, FORMULATE ⟨philosophers *fabricating* new theories of the universe⟩ **:** CREATE ⟨his brave attempts to ~ something permanent and holy out of his personal animal feelings —T.S. Eliot⟩ **b** (1) **:** to make up with intent to deceive ⟨*fabricated* an involved explanation of his absence⟩ (2) **:** FORGE **syn** see MAKE

fab·ri·ca·tion \,==ˈkāshən\ *n* -s [ME *fabricacioun*, fr. L *fabrication-, fabricatio*, fr. *fabricatus* + *-ion-, -io* -ion] **1 :** the act or process of fabricating: as **a :** the assembly of materials into a structure ⟨~ of a bridge⟩ **b :** the invention or utterance of something calculated to deceive ⟨the unconscious ~ of an honest man trying to put his best foot forward⟩ **c :** the process of converting one form of metal into another (as ingots into rolled shapes, rolled shapes into structural members, castings into weldments, wire into springs, forgings into gears) **2 :** a product of fabrication: as **a :** FALSEHOOD, DECEIT, FORGERY ⟨all the petty ~*s* with which he hoped to fool his fellows⟩ **b :** a fabricated structure or structural element ⟨the whole ~ of the house⟩ **syn** see FICTION

fabrication-in-transit \=,==ˈ==ˈ==\ *n* **:** an arrangement by which a continuous through rate is charged by a transporting agent (as a railway) for articles that are made up into a new form at some point on the way — compare MILLING-IN-TRANSIT

fab·ri·ca·tive \'fabrə,kād·iv\ *adj* **:** tending or able to fabricate **:** concerned with manufacture

fab·ri·ca·tor \-ād·ə(r), -ātə-\ *n* -s [L, fr. *fabricatus* + *-or*] **:** one that fabricates: as **a :** one that invents a false statement or commits forgery **:** LIAR, FORGER **b :** an implement for fabricating; *specif* **:** a neolithic flint used as a tool for fashioning other implements **c :** a workman who shapes, finishes, or assembles objects **d :** a firm or establishment that converts metal from one form into another — compare FABRICATION 1c

fabricature *n* -s *obs* **:** CONSTRUCTION, STRUCTURE

fabric tire *n* **:** a pneumatic tire having a carcass with a woven fabric — compare CORD TIRE

Fab·ri·koid \'fabrə,kȯid\ *trademark* — used for an imitation leather

fa·bro·ni·a·ce·ae \fə,brōnē'āsē,ē\ *n pl, cap* [NL, fr. *Fabronia*, type genus (after G.V.M. *Fabroni* †1822 Ital. naturalist) + *-aceae*] **:** a family of chiefly tropical mosses (order Hypnobryales) that grow on tree trunks and have erect branches and exserted capsules with the operculum beaked

fab·u·la \'fabyələ\ *n, pl* **fabu·lae** \-yə,lē\ [L — more at FABLE] **:** STORY; *usu* **:** a traditional tale **:** FOLKTALE

fabula pal·li·a·ta \-,palē'äd·ə, -'äd·ə\ *n, pl* **fabulae pallia·tae** \-äd·,ē, -äd·,ē\ [L, lit., drama in himations; fr. the Greek himations worn by the actors] **:** an ancient Roman comedy based on a Greek model and treating a Greek subject — compare FABULA TOGATA

fabula prae·tex·ta \-prē'tekstə-\ *also* **fabula prae·tex·ta·ta** \-(,)prē,tek'städ·ə, -äd·ə\ *n, pl* **fabulae praetex·tae** \-,stē\ [L, lit., drama in praetextae; fr. the praetexta worn by the actors] **:** an ancient Roman drama with a theme from Roman history or legend

fab·u·lar \'fabyələ(r)\ *adj* [L *fabularis*, fr. *fabula* + *-aris* -ar] **:** like or relating to fable

fab·u·la·tion \,==ˈlāshən\ *n* -s [*fabulous* + *-ation*] **:** the act of inventing or retailing false or fantastic tales ⟨unrestrained ~*s* and several otherworldly visions —Susan A. Taubes⟩

fabula to·ga·ta \-tō'gäd·ə, -äd·ə\ *n, pl* **fabulae toga·tae** \-äd·,ē, -äd·,ē\ [L, lit., drama in togas; fr. the togas worn by the actors] **:** ancient Roman comedy based on a Greek model but treating native Roman subjects — compare FABULA PALLIATA

fab·u·la·tor \'fabyə,lād·ə(r)\ *n* -s [L, fr. *fabulatus* + *-or*] *archaic* **:** FABULIST

fab·u·list \-,ləst\ *n* -s [MF *fabuliste*, fr. L *fabula* tale, fable + MF *-iste* -ist — more at FABLE] **1 :** a creator or writer of fables esp. that carry a moral lesson **2** *obs* **:** a professional teller of tales **3 :** an inventor of falsehoods **:** LIAR, PREVARICATOR

fab·u·lize \-,līz\ *vt* -ED/-ING/-S [L *fabula* + E *-ize*] **:** FABLE; *esp* **:** to give a false account of

fab·u·los·i·ty \,==ˈläsəd·ē\ *n* -ES [L *fabulositas*, fr. *fabulosus* fabulous + *-itas* -ity] **1 :** fabulous quality or character **2** *archaic* **:** a fabulous statement or tale **:** FABLE

fab·u·lous \'fabyələs\ *adj* [ME, fr. L *fabulosus*, fr. *fabula* + *-osus* -ous] **1 :** given to telling fables **2 :** celebrated or known from fables only **:** belonging to fables alone **:** not real, actual, or historical ⟨the ~ mill which ground old people young —Charles Dickens⟩ ⟨the ~ German smith, who made feather clothes for flight —Lewis Mumford⟩ **3 a :** characteristic of fables **:** like the contents of fables in being marvelous, incredible, absurd, extreme, exaggerated, or approaching the impossible ⟨a hero who, after many ~ exploits . . . , bolted to the Spanish Main —G.B.Shaw⟩ ⟨[Lincoln] grows vaguer and more ~ as year follows year —H.L.Mencken⟩ **b :** outstanding or remarkable esp. in some acceptable or pleasing quality ⟨a ~ year for the Republicans —*New Republic*⟩ ⟨the ~ view of the mountains from her porch⟩ ⟨~ jewelry⟩ ⟨a career . . . recognized as the most famous and ~ in U.S. diplomacy —Claude Pepper⟩ **syn** see FICTITIOUS

fab·u·lous·ly *adv* **:** in a fabulous manner **:** to a fabulous degree or extent **:** VERY, EXTREMELY, EXCESSIVELY ⟨~ expensive clothes⟩

fab·u·lous·ness *n* -ES **:** the quality or state of being fabulous

fab·ur·den \'fabə(r)d°n\ *n* -s [ME *faburdoun*, fr. MF *faux-bourdon* — more at FAUXBOURDON] **:** FAUXBOURDON

fac *abbr* **1** facsimile **2** factor **3** factory **4** faculty

fa·cade *also* **fa·çade** \fə'säd, -sād *also* fa'-\ *n* -s [F *façade*, fr. It *facciata*, fr. *faccia* face (fr. — assumed — VL *facia*) + *-ata* -ade] **1 a :** the front of a building **b :** a face (as a flank or rear facing on a street or court) of a building that is given emphasis by special architectural treatment **2 :** a false, superficial, or artificial appearance or effect ⟨maintaining a ~ of contentment⟩ ⟨in the winter of 1929 the brilliant ~ of American prosperity fell into ruin almost overnight —*Times Lit. Supp.*⟩ **:** FACE, FRONT; *often* **:** FALSE FRONT 1

facade 1a

²facade *also* **façade** \"\ *vt* -ED/-ING/-S **:** to impose a facade on ⟨*facading* civilization with formalities⟩ ⟨a building *facaded* with white tile⟩

¹face \'fās\ *n* -s *often attrib* [ME, fr. OF, fr. (assumed) VL *facia*, fr. L *facies* form, shape, face, fr. *facere* to make, do — more at DO] **1 a :** the front part of the human head including the chin, mouth, nose, cheeks, eyes, and usu. forehead **:** VISAGE, COUNTENANCE **b :** the corresponding part of the head of a lower animal **c :** the part of the vertebrate skull in front of and below the cranium and including the nasal region, jaws, and associated structures **d :** the part of the insect head lying anterior to the vertex, above the mouth, and between the compound eyes **2** *archaic* **:** PRESENCE, SIGHT, VIEW ⟨thou fleddest from the ~ of Esau —Gen 35:1 (AV)⟩ **3 a :** cast of features as expressing emotion or character **:** expression of countenance ⟨a grave stern ~⟩ ⟨turned an angry ~ on his erring son⟩ **b :** beauty or glory of countenance ⟨in ~ far exceeding her sisters⟩ ⟨the Lord make his ~ shine upon thee —Num 6:25 (AV)⟩ **4 a :** outward appearance or aspect **:** SEMBLANCE ⟨the whole village presented a ~ of placid contentment⟩ **:** visible or apparent state or condition ⟨his report put a new ~ on the matter⟩; *also* **:** a cursory or superficial examination or its result ⟨this testimony is false on the ~ of it⟩ ⟨on the ~ of your report I have no valid objection to raise⟩ **b :** an outward appearance of dignity or prestige or of freedom from abashment, confusion, anger, or distress ⟨though he was obviously distressed he put the best ~ he could on the matter⟩; *broadly* **:** DISGUISE, PRETENSE **c :** ASSURANCE, CONFIDENCE ⟨maintaining a firm ~ in spite of adversity⟩; *often* **:** brash or bold conduct or outlook **:** EFFRONTERY ⟨how anyone could have the ~ to ask such a question⟩ — compare CHEEK, NERVE **d :** DIGNITY, PRESTIGE ⟨a man of considerable ~ in the local community⟩ ⟨trying to save ~⟩; *also* **:** concern for or preservation of one's prestige ⟨~ is sometimes a major consideration in diplomatic negotiations⟩ **5 a :** GRIMACE, MOUE; *esp* **:** an expression of distaste ⟨made a ~ at the taste of the medicine⟩ **b :** MASK ⟨the children bought some funny ~*s* for the party⟩ **c :** facial makeup ⟨she'll be here as soon as she gets her ~ on⟩ **6 a :** the surface of something esp. where only one surface is commonly considered ⟨mist moving over the ~ of the water⟩ ⟨driven from the ~ of the earth⟩ **b** (1) **:** the physical features (as of a country) (2) *obs* **:** a description of a country in its physical features **7 :** a front, upper, or outer surface or a surface presented to view or regarded as principal: as **a :** the front of anything having two or four sides — opposed to *back;* usu. distinguished from *side* **b :** the facade esp. of a building **c :** an exposed surface of rock (as in a wall or a cliff) **d :** one of the broad surfaces of a coin **:** an obverse or reverse ⟨lettering on the edge as well as on the ~ of a coin⟩; *also* **:** the obverse of a currency note **e :** the dial of a watch or clock ⟨a watch with a black enamel ~ and raised gold figures⟩ **f :** any of the plane surfaces that bound a polyhedron (as a crystal) or other geometrical solid **g :** the grille of a hot-air or cold-air register **8 a :** a side or surface dressed, finished, or specially prepared: as **a :** the principal dressed surface (as of a plate, disk, or pulley) **b :** the dressed side of a board finished only on one surface; *sometimes* **:** the side having the better appearance or quality when both are dressed **c :** the right side (as of cloth or leather); *esp* **:** the front side of a fabric in which that side is distinguished from the back by differences of finish, weave, or appearance **d :** the inscribed or printed side of something (as a document or a leaf bearing a map or illustration) that has one blank surface; *broadly* **:** the side of something inscribed or printed on both sides that can be considered the front (as by reason of containing major matter) ⟨the ~ of a stock certificate⟩ **e :** the variously colored scoring surface of a target **f :** the front side of a book or book cover **g :** the side of a playing card that is marked to designate its rank and suit **h :** the top or bottom layer of fruit or vegetables in a container esp. as arranged for purposes of display **i :** the flat surface of a propeller blade that corresponds to the undersurface of a wing **9 :** an acting surface (as of a tool or implement): as **a :** the edge of a cutting implement (as a knife) **b :** the striking surface of the head (as of a hammer or golf club) **c :** the grinding surface of a molar tooth **d** (1) **:** the uppermost part of a relief printing surface (as type or a plate) that receives the ink and transfers it to the paper — see TYPE (2) **:** TYPEFACE — often used in combination ⟨bold*face*⟩ ⟨light*face*⟩ **10 a :** the end or wall of a mine tunnel, drift, or excavation at which work is progressing or was last done **:** BREAST — called also *working face* **b :** the working surface of a pit or quarry **11 a :** the part of the acting surface of a gear tooth that projects beyond the pitch line **b :** the width of a pulley or the length of a gear tooth from end to end **c :** the sole of a carpenter's plane **12** *astrology* **:** one third of a zodiacal sign or 10 degrees of longitude **13 :** FACE CARD — used chiefly in the expression *neither ace nor face* **14 :** FACE VALUE **15 :** a cut made in a pine or other tree from which resin exudes **16 :** FACE-OFF

syn COUNTENANCE, VISAGE, PHYSIOGNOMY, MUG, PUSS: these six nouns can all designate the front part of the head including the mouth, nose, eyes, cheeks, and, usu., the forehead. FACE is the most general, having the common meaning of the group ⟨a person with a pale *face*⟩ ⟨a dog with white markings about the *face*⟩ COUNTENANCE, applied only to the human face, stresses appearance, esp. as revealing or seeming to reveal an inner condition, as thoughts, character, mood, or frame of mind ⟨their hideous *countenances* were all bloody and sweaty —Charles Dickens⟩ ⟨an expressive *countenance*⟩ ⟨something of dignity in his *countenance* —Jane Austen⟩ ⟨a benign *countenance*⟩ ⟨serious illness and suffering stared from his dark *countenance* —A.C.Cole⟩ In an older use it can mean a normal, composed expression and suggest a composed state ⟨far beyond them all in person, *countenance*, air, and walk —Jane Austen⟩ VISAGE, a bookish term very close to COUNTENANCE in meaning, stresses appearance and often suggests attention to the shape and proportion of the face or to the general impression of character or frame of mind it gives, often distinctive or esp. significant ⟨the very *visage* of a man in love —Edna S. V. Millay⟩ ⟨more horrible and cruel than the *visages* of the wildest savages —Charles Dickens⟩ ⟨withered, wrinkled, and loathsome of *visage* —Oscar Wilde⟩ PHYSIOGNOMY is chiefly used when the interest is the contours of face, shape of features, or characteristic expression as indicating race, temperament, or general character; it is applied today, however, more frequently to the distinguishing aspect or features of things other than the face ⟨a man of saturnine *physiognomy*⟩ ⟨a few of many features from two to three thousand years old which have given Chinese civilization a *physiognomy* all its own —A.L.Kroeber⟩ MUG has a humorous intent in suggesting an ugly, though usu. not displeasing, physiognomy ⟨getting your *mug* in the papers is one of the shameful ways of making a living —Norman Mailer⟩ PUSS, Irish in origin, is as symptomatic as any of a wealth of slang words (*map, kisser, pan, mush*) applying to the face or the central area of it, the nose and mouth, and signifying pretty much what the tenor of the remark containing it would suggest, from a mere synonym for FACE to a humorous or grim implication of ugliness or offensiveness ⟨she put on a very sour *puss* when she saw the priest along with me —Frank O'Connor⟩

— **in the face of** *or* **in face of :** in opposition to **:** in defiance of **:** DESPITE ⟨succeed *in the face of* great difficulties⟩ ⟨the aggression was seen *in face of* all evidence as a defensive war⟩ — **to one's face :** in one's presence or so that one is fully aware of what is going on **:** OPENLY, FRANKLY, BOLDLY

²face \"\ *vb* -ED/-ING/-S [ME *facen*, fr. *face*, n.] *vt* **1 :** to confront, controvert, or maintain impudently, brashly, or with excessive assurance **:** BROWBEAT, BULLY — now usu. used with *down* or *out* ⟨the look with which she *faced* down all opposition in the club⟩ ⟨determined to ~ out the situation he answered all questions curtly⟩ **2 a :** to stand or sit opposite to **:** occupy a position with the face toward ⟨the audience *faced* the speaker⟩ ⟨he stood *facing* the window⟩ ⟨a large mirror *faced* the door⟩ **b :** to be face-to-face with ⟨they *faced* one another for the last time⟩; *often* **:** to be on the page opposite to ⟨the color plate *facing* page 857⟩ **c :** to front on or toward ⟨the house *faced* the river⟩ ⟨a sheltered valley that ~*s* the morning sun⟩ **3 :** to meet face-to-face without shrinking, cringing, or withdrawing ⟨I can't bear to ~ your sister after what has happened⟩ ⟨gone with a clear conscience to ~ his Lord⟩: as **a :** to meet or oppose firmly and without evasion ⟨we must ~ the facts⟩ **b :** to meet for the purpose of stopping or opposing ⟨such untrained militia can never hope to ~ veterans successfully⟩ **c :** to master, check, or bring to heel by confronting with firm assurance and steady determination to resist or control — used with *down* ⟨*facing* down the forces of reaction⟩ ⟨we must ~ down every aggressor⟩ ⟨she *faced* down the rebellious students and sent them back to their books⟩ **4 a :** to recognize or contemplate as an often unpleasant or difficult eventuality confronting one ⟨*facing* the risk of the operation and weighing it against the certainty of continued suffering⟩ ⟨*facing* the need to retrench he decided to give up luxuries⟩ **b :** to be likely or possible and often imminent to or for ⟨extermination ~*s* many of the larger mammals as urbanization destroys their habitats⟩ ⟨the king was *faced* with the loss of his throne unless immediate reforms were instituted⟩ **c :** to be an immediate prospect for **:** THREATEN ⟨death ~*s* everyone sooner or later⟩ ⟨our gambling losses left us *faced* with ruin⟩ **5 :** to cover the front or surface of with something (as a protective or ornamental coating) ⟨a building *faced* with marble⟩ ⟨several water-resistant fabrics are *faced* with plastics⟩ **6 :** to bring directly to the attention of **:** CONFRONT — used with *with* ⟨*faced* him with evidence of his treachery⟩ ⟨*faced* by two tragic alternatives⟩ **7 :** to finish an edge of (a textile article) by applying a lining **:** reinforce (as a section of a garment) by applying a piece of cloth on the inside **8 :** to improve the appearance of (cheaper grades of green tea) by use of additives (as coloring matter and soapstone) **9 :** to position (a full-page illustration) at right angles to the text — see ²DOWN 10b, ¹UP 13c **10 :** to turn face up: as **a :** to turn (a playing card) so that the face is exposed usu. deliberately — compare EXPOSE *vt* **b :** to arrange (mail) so that addresses on all pieces in a batch face the same way **11 :** to arrange (fruits or vegetables) in a container so as to display a face ⟨berries are much more salable when neatly *faced*⟩ **12 a :** to make the surface of flat or smooth **:** dress the face of (as a stone or a casting) — often used with *off* **b :** to shape or smooth the flat as distinguished from the cylindrical surface of (an object being made on a lathe) — often used with *up* **13 :** to cause (troops) to face in a particular direction on command ⟨the captain *faced* his company to the left⟩ **14 :** to put (a lacrosse ball) in play by dropping between the crosses of two opposing forwards each of whom stands with his left toward the goal he is attacking; *also* **:** to put (a hockey puck) in play by a similar method **~** *vi* **1** *obs* **:** to present a false appearance **:** play the hypocrite **2 a :** to turn the face ⟨quickly *faced* to her right⟩ **b :** to have or lie so as to have a face or front in a specified direction ⟨the house *faced* south⟩ **3 :** to face the puck or ball in certain sports

syn BRAVE, CHALLENGE, DARE, BEARD, DEFY: FACE means to confront face-to-face or as if face-to-face. It may imply either resolution and fortitude or realistic appraisal of one's situation ⟨I shuddered, but unflinchingly *faced* an awful possibility —Rose Macaulay⟩ ⟨here we are together *facing* a group of mighty foes —Sir Winston Churchill⟩ BRAVE stresses the fact of underlying courage, fortitude, or bravado inciting one to dare or endure ⟨though Archbishop Warham mournfully assured the Queen that "the anger of the King is death", not a few Englishmen were increasingly ready to *brave* his anger —Francis Hackett⟩ ⟨if you find yourself in trouble before them, call on your courage and resolution: *brave* out every difficulty —Kenneth Roberts⟩ CHALLENGE expresses the notion of confronting to invite into competition or contest or to oppose by imputing weakness or fault ⟨Henry IV . . . had in a manner curbed Bouillon's power, but he tolerated it, and he hesitated to *challenge* it —Hilaire Belloc⟩ ⟨the best medical practitioner turned out by the school, who once dared to *challenge* the power of the chief of the witch doctors —V.G.Heiser⟩ DARE may imply venturesomeness, daring, boldness, love of danger, or even vainglory in risking or tempting fate or retribution ⟨those who *dare* an enemy greatly should be prepared for the fullest consequences —S.L.A.Marshall⟩ BEARD suggests a bold confronting, resolute daring, or mocking of someone or something dangerous or powerful ⟨a bold heart yours to *beard* that raging mob —Alfred Tennyson⟩ ⟨for years she led the life of a religious tramp, *bearding* bishops and allowing herself many eccentricities which . . . brought her more than once into serious suspicion of Lollardy —G.G. Coulton⟩ DEFY suggests confronting an opponent with resolution, boldness, and confident assertiveness, sometimes with mocking, arising from the feeling that the strongest efforts thus provoked will fail ⟨fiend, I *defy* thee . . . Foul tyrant both of Gods and Humankind, one only being shalt thou not subdue —P.B.Shelley⟩ ⟨*defy* the enemies of our constitution to show the contrary —Edmund Burke⟩ **syn** see in addition MEET

— **face the music :** to meet resolutely an unpleasant situation, a danger, or the consequences of one's actions ⟨had made a mistake and now had to *face the music*⟩

face·able \ˈfāsəbəl\ *adj* **:** capable of or fit for being faced

face-about \ˌ=ˈ=ˌ=\ *n* -s [fr. *face about!*] **:** ABOUT-FACE

face and fill *n* **:** a method of packing fresh fruit or vegetables in containers with only the surface layer regularly arranged

face angle *n* **:** an angle formed by two edges of a polyhedral angle

face-bedded \ˈ=ˌ=ˌ=\ *adj* **:** bedded in masonry so that the naturally horizontal surface forms the face of the work — used of a quarried stone; compare JOINT-BEDDED

face bone *n* **:** CHEEKBONE

face·bow \ˈfās,bō\ *n* **:** a device used in dentistry to determine the positional relationships of the maxillary arch of a patient

facebread \ˈ=ˌ=\ *n* [trans. of Heb *leḥem happānīm*] **:** SHEWBREAD

face brick *n* **:** brick used in the face of a wall; *usu* **:** brick made esp. for facing purposes by selecting clays to produce desired color or by special surface treatment

face card *n* **:** a playing card bearing a stylized picture of a king, queen, or knave

face-centered \ˈ=ˌ=ˌ=\ *adj* **:** relating to a crystal space lattice in which each cubic unit cell has an atom at the center and at the corners of each face

facecloth \ˈ=ˌ=\ *n* **1 a :** a cloth laid over the face of a corpse **b :** a small cloth used for washing one's face or person **:** WASHCLOTH **2 a :** a cloth with warp threads predominating on the surface **b :** a cloth with a distinctly better appearance on one side often produced by napping or finishing

face cord *n* **:** a cubic measure for wood equivalent to a pile whose length is 8 feet, whose height is 4 feet, and whose width varying with the length of the pieces is usu. from 12 to 36 inches

faced \ˈfāst\ *adj* [¹*face* + *-ed*] **:** provided with a face or a facing ⟨a neatly ~ terrace⟩ ⟨a well-*faced* lapel⟩ — used chiefly in combination with an attributive noun or adjective indicating a particular kind of face or facing ⟨a marble-*faced* brick building⟩ ⟨satin-*faced* lapels⟩ ⟨a dog-*faced* boy⟩ ⟨rosy-*faced* dawn⟩

facedown \ˈ=ˈ=\ *adv* **:** with the face downward ⟨coasting ~⟩

faced wall *n* **:** a wall in which the masonry facing and backing are so bonded as to exert common action under load

face flannel *n*, *Brit* **:** WASHCLOTH

face gear *n* **:** a gear having teeth on its face

face guard *n* **:** a guard for the face; *usu* **:** a complete or partial mask (as one worn by workmen exposed to heat or flying particles of metal or by football players or fencers)

face-harden \ˈ=ˌ==\ *vt* **:** to harden the face or surface of

face joint *n* **:** a joint in the face of a wall usu. more carefully struck or pointed than one less visible

face·less \ˈfāsləs\ *adj* **:** lacking a face: as **a** *obs* **:** COWARDLY **b :** regarded as a member of a category and as such lacking individuality ⟨he might have been any barber in town — ~, pleasant, trusted —Luke Short⟩ ⟨the ~ men who make up statistics⟩ **c :** unidentified or unidentifiable esp. by deliberate intent ⟨the ~ accusers of the police state⟩

face·less·ness *n* -ES **:** faceless state or quality; *esp* **:** lack of individuality

face-lift \ˈ=ˌ=\ *vt* **:** to engage in or perform a face-lifting of ⟨some manufacturers usually just *face-lift* their cars when bringing out new models⟩

face-lifting \ˈ=ˌ==\ *also* **face-lift** \ˈ=ˌ=\ *n* -s **1 :** a plastic operation for removal of facial wrinkles, sagging skin, and certain other defects usu. associated with aging **2 :** an alteration (as of a building) or restyling (as of an automobile design) intended to modernize or to increase comfort or salability

fa·cel·lite \fəˈse,līt\ *n* -s [It, fr. Gk *phakelos* bundle, faggot + It *-lite*] **:** KALIOPHILITE

facemaking \ˈ=ˌ==\ *n* -s **:** GRIMACING

face·man \ˈfāsmən, -ˌman\ *n*, *pl* **facemen :** a worker (as in a quarry or coal mine) who actually works the face as distinguished from one who serves in various supplementary capacities (as in mucking, loading, or hauling)

face mill *n* **:** a cutter for face milling

face milling *n* **:** the process of milling flat surfaces that are at right angles to the axis of rotation of the cutter

face mite *n* **:** FOLLICLE MITE, DEMODEX

face mold *n* **:** the template used to outline forms to be cut out of wood, metal, or other sheet material (as by carpenters or sheet-metal workers); *esp* **:** a pattern for the practical projection of a wreath in stair building

face-nail \ˈ=ˌ=\ *vt* **:** to fasten by means of face nailing ⟨the boards should be *face-nailed* solidly at each bearing point — *Amer. Builder*⟩

face nailing *n* **:** nailing in which the nailheads are exposed to view and which is used in the fastening of facing wood to a base

face-off \ˈ=ˌ=\ *n* -s [fr. *face off*, v.] **:** the act of facing the playing piece (as a puck or ball) in certain games (as hockey)

facepiece \ˈ=ˌ=\ *n* **1 a :** the part of an overcheck that connects the bit with the cavesson and overcheck rein **b :** an ornamental harness brass placed pendant from the cavesson **2 :** the part of a gas mask or other respirator that fits over the face and is provided with eyepieces and a breathing device

face pit *n* **:** FACIAL PIT

faceplate \ˈ=ˌ=\ *n* **1 :** a disk fixed with its face at right angles to the live spindle of a lathe and provided with holes, slots, and other devices for the attachment of the work which thus rotates with the spindle **2 a :** a protective plate for a machine or device (as a door lock) **b :** a protective covering for the human face (as of a diver)

faceplate jaw *n* **:** a dog attachment for a faceplate to convert it into a chuck

face play *or* **face playing** *n* **:** display or simulation of emotion by use of the muscles of the face (as in certain styles of acting)

face presentation *n* **:** presentation of the fetus face first at the mouth of the uterus during parturition

fac·er \ˈfāsə(r)\ *n* -s **1** *obs* **:** one that puts on a false show **:** BRAGGART, SWAGGERER **2** *obs* **:** a tankard esp. when filled **:** BUMPER **3 a :** a blow in the face (as in boxing) **b :** a severe or stunning check or defeat ⟨his refusal to participate was a ~ for me⟩ **4 :** one (as a machine or worker) that faces: as **a :** a cutter for facing or surfacing or a machine-tool attachment for holding such a cutter **b :** a garment worker who sews facings and reinforcements **c :** a worker who polishes the faces of jewel bearings **5 :** something that forms or acts as a face: as **a :** FACE TITLE **b :** a selected specimen for use in facing (as of a pack of fruit or vegetables) **c :** any of certain broad low-growing plants used in border plantings to hide unattractive basal parts of larger background items

faces *pl of* FACE, *pres 3d sing of* FACE

face-saver \ˈ=ˌ==\ *n* **:** something that saves face; *usu* **:** something that constitutes such grounds or justification as to permit compromise or compliance without jeopardizing the dignity or prestige of the compromising or complying parties

face-saving \ˈ=ˌ==\ *n* **:** the act or an instance of preserving one's prestige or dignity ⟨he often effected compromises which, in permitting a certain *face-saving*, did not yield the right —Merle Curti⟩

face spanner *n* **:** a spanner with pins at the ends for fitting into holes in the face of the part to be adjusted

face stone *n* **:** a stone used or usable as part of a facing

face string *n* **:** the outermost string of a stair often of superior material and separate from the roughstrings which in a wooden stair it conceals

¹**fac·et** \ˈfasət, ˈfaas-, *usu* -əd.+V\ *also* **fa·cette** \fəˈset\ *n* -s [F *facette*, dim. of *face* — more at FACE] **1 a :** one of the small plane surfaces produced on a diamond or other precious stone in cutting esp. to enhance its brilliance and beauty — see BRILLIANT illustration **b :** a similar surface on other material (as one cut on a pebble by natural forces) **2 :** any of the sharply defined or definable aspects that make up a subject or object of consideration **:** PHASE ⟨no other ~ of his leadership could be more revealing⟩ **3** *anat* **:** a smooth flat or nearly flat circumscribed surface ⟨the articular ~ of a bone⟩ **4 :** the fillet between the flutes of a column **5 a :** the external corneal surface of an ommatidium of a compound eye **b :** OMMATIDIUM **syn** see PHASE

²**facet** \"\ *vt* **faceted** *or* **facetted** \-səd·əd,-sətəd\ **faceted** *or* **facetted**; **faceting** *or* **facetting**; **facets :** to cut facets upon ⟨the skill with which he ~*ed* the great diamond⟩

facet *abbr* **1** facetiae **2** facetious

fa·cete \fəˈsēt\ *adj* [L *facetus* courteous, elegant, witty, facetious] *archaic* **:** FACETIOUS, WITTY — **fa·cete·ly** *adv*, *archaic*

fac·et·ed *also* **fac·et·ted** \ˈfasəd·əd, ˈfaas-, -sətəd\ *adj* **:** having or made with facets

facet head *n* **:** a device to aid in orienting the facets being cut on a gemstone

fa·ce·ti·ae \fəˈsēshē,ē\ *n pl* [L, pl., of *facetia* jest, witticism, fr. *facetus* + *-ia* -y] **1 :** witty or humorous writings or sayings **2 a :** short humorous frequently obscene tales **b :** EROTICA

face tile *n* **:** tile with one surface designed for use on a face and usu. specially finished or treated (as to enhance appearance, ease of cleaning, or resistance to weathering)

fa·ce·ti·os·i·ty \fə,sēshēˈäsəd·ē, -ətē, -i\ *n* -ES [fr. *facetious*, after such pairs as E *ponderous: ponderosity*] **:** a facetious quality or item ⟨the ponderous ~ of his pronouncements⟩

fa·ce·tious \fəˈsēshəs\ *adj* [MF *facetieux*, fr. *facetie* jest (fr. L *facetia*) + *-eux* -ous] **1 a :** given to jesting that is sometimes crude ⟨a ~ companion⟩ **b** *obs* **:** gay and witty **2 :** characterized by pleasantry or levity **:** exciting laughter **:** JOCOSE ⟨a ~ story⟩ ⟨his impudently ~ reply⟩ **syn** see WITTY

fa·ce·tious·ly *adv* **:** in a facetious manner

fa·ce·tious·ness *n* -ES **:** the quality or state of being facetious

face title *n* **:** a left-hand page facing the title page of a book; *esp* **:** such a page bearing advertising matter (as a list of titles by the same author or publisher)

face-to-face \ˌ=ˌ=ˈ=\ *adv (or adj)* [ME] **1 :** within each other's sight or presence **:** involving close contacts **:** in person ⟨a *face-to-face* meeting of the two leaders⟩ ⟨we met *face-to-face* for the first time⟩ **2 :** under the necessity of having to make a decision or to take action ⟨surgeon *face-to-face* with an emergency case⟩ **3 :** OPPOSITE ⟨printed *face-to-face*⟩

face towel *n* **:** a towel that is smaller than a bath towel, is often of smooth-surfaced material (as linen), and is used esp. for drying the face

face up *vi* **:** to confront or meet something or someone esp. boldly ⟨he *faced up* and considered his situation⟩ — usu. used with *to* ⟨finally *faces up* to the young hoods terrorizing these subway riders —A.H. Weiler⟩

faceup \ˈ=ˈ=\ *adv* **:** with the face upward ⟨floating ~⟩

face validity *n* **:** apparent but untested statistical validity

face value *n* **1 :** the value indicated on the face of an instrument: as **a :** the principal amount of a bond or note **b :** the maturity value of a life-insurance policy **c :** the par value of a municipal bond **2 :** the apparent value ⟨if their results may be taken at *face value*⟩

face wall *n* **:** BREAST WALL

facework \ˈ=ˌ=\ *n* **:** the often ornamental or superior material of the outside or front side (as of a wall) **:** FACING

face worker *n* **:** a miner who works at the face of a mine drift

facia *var of* FASCIA

¹**fa·cial** \ˈfāshəl\ *adj* [ML *facialis*, fr. L *facies* form, shape, face + *-alis* -al] **1 :** of, relating to, situated in, or affecting the face ⟨~ neuralgia⟩ **2 :** of or relating to an outer surface **:** SUPERFICIAL ⟨a ~ layer of grime⟩ **3 :** concerned with or used in improving the appearance or freshness of the human face esp. by the use of massage or cosmetics ⟨~ pack⟩ — **fa·cial·ly** \-shəlē, -li\ *adv*

²**facial** \"\ *n* -s **1 :** a treatment or massage for the face **2 :** a facial part (as a nerve or artery)

facial angle *n* **:** a measure of relative prognathism made by determining the angle at which a line connecting the nasion and prosthion intersects the eye-ear plane

facial artery *n* **:** the external branch of the maxillary artery

facial bone *n* **:** any of the bones of the facial region of the skull that do not take part in forming the braincase and that in man include 14 bones: two nasals, two maxillaries, two lacrimals, two zygomatics, two palatines, two inferior conchae, one vomer, and one mandible

facial canal *n* **:** a passage in the petrous part of the temporal bone that extends from the internal auditory meatus to the stylomastoid foramen and transmits various branches of the facial nerve

facial colliculus *n* **:** a medial eminence situated on the floor of the fourth ventricle of the brain and produced by the nucleus of the abducent nerve and the genu of the facial nerve

facial disk *n* **:** the disk of an owl

facial index *n* **:** the ratio of the breadth of the face to its length multiplied by 100, the breadth used being usu. the bizygomatic and the length either that from ophryon to gnathion or that from nasion to gnathion

facial nerve *n* **:** either of the seventh pair of cranial nerves leaving the cranium on either side by the internal auditory meatus, passing through the facial canal, emerging at the stylomastoid foramen to supply motor fibers to the facial muscles and to the stylohyoid and posterior belly of the digastric, and sending a separate mixed branch to the tongue that carries the gustatory fibers from the anterior two thirds of the tongue and parasympathetic fibers to the sphenopalatine and submaxillary ganglia

facial pit *n* **1 :** a gland-containing depression of the skull surface in front of the orbit in certain ruminants **2 :** one of the paired sensory pits of a pit viper — compare JACOBSON'S ORGAN

facial vein *n* **:** any of several veins draining the face and neighboring parts

facial vision *n* **:** an awareness of obstacles independent of vision that is often considerably developed in blind persons and probably dependent on tactile perception of reflected sound waves

fa·ci·a·tion \ˌfāshēˈāshən\ *n* -s [L *facies* + E *-ation*] **:** a subdivision of an ecological association that is characterized by the codominance of two or more but not all the dominant forms of the association and that constitutes a community of considerable extent, its area usu. being related to a climatic variation within the area of the association — compare LOCIATION

fa·cient \ˈfāshənt\ *n* -s [L *facient-*, *faciens*, pres. part.] **:** one that does something **:** DOER, AGENT

-fa·cient \ˈfāshənt\ *adj comb form* [L *facient-*, *faciens*, pres. part. of *facere* to do, make (as in *calefacere* to warm) — more at DO, CHAFE] **:** making **:** causing ⟨somni*facient*⟩ ⟨sorbe*facient*⟩

facier *comparative of* FACY

fa·ci·es \ˈfāshē,ēz, ˈfāshēz\ *n*, *pl* **facies** [NL, fr. L, form, shape, face — more at FACE] **1 a :** the general appearance or makeup esp. of a natural group (as a fauna) **b :** a particular local aspect or modification of an ecological community **c :** a specialized and commonly localized segment of a cultural community **2 :** an appearance and expression of the face characteristic or indicative of a disease or abnormal condition ⟨peptic ulcer ~⟩ ⟨adenoid ~⟩ **3 a** *geol* **:** a group of stratified beds differing in lithologic character or fossil contents from other beds of the same age **b :** a rock or group of rocks that differ from comparable rocks (as in composition, fabric, or age)

facies-suite \ˈ==ˌ=ˌ=, ˈ==ˌ=\ *n* **:** a collection or group of rocks that exhibits variations in a single rock mass

faciest *superlative of* FACY

fac·ile \ˈfasəl *also* -(ˌ)sil, *chiefly Brit* -ˌsīl\ *adj* [MF, fr. L *facilis*, fr. *facere* to make, do + *-ilis* -ile — more at DO] **1 a :** easily accomplished or attained **:** involving no special difficulty or expenditure of skill or effort **:** EASY ⟨a ~ victory⟩; *sometimes* **:** SPECIOUS, SUPERFICIAL ⟨the work is well-organized but the conclusions and interpretations are often unduly ~⟩ ⟨I am not concerned . . . with offering any ~ solution for so complex a problem —T.S.Eliot⟩ **b :** used or comprehended with ease ⟨the techniques of paper chromatography have provided ~ means of separating complex organic mixtures⟩ ⟨the report proved to be surprisingly ~ reading⟩ **c** *of feelings, emotions, attitudes* **:** readily experienced or manifest and often lacking sincerity, depth, or real basis ⟨sick of words and phrases and ~ emotions and situations and insincerities —Rose Macaulay⟩ ⟨we must possess a peculiarly ~ turn of mind when we can virtuously condemn the cruelties perpetrated in other countries, while . . . we avert our eyes from the cruelties we ourselves continue to condone —Farley Mowat⟩ **2 a** *archaic* **:** easily led or prevailed upon **:** COMPLIANT, DOCILE, YIELDING **b** *Scots law* **:** so easily influenced as to require curatorship or guardianship — used of the mentally weak; compare FACILITY 3b **3 :** mild or pleasing in manner or disposition: **a** *archaic* **:** lenient and gentle **:** not stern, severe, or harsh **b** *obs* **:** kind and affable **c :** exhibiting ease of bearing or manner **:** ASSURED, POISED **4 :** free and unrestrained in performing or expressing **:** READY, RESOURCEFUL, QUICK, FLUENT, EXPERT **:** not hesitant, barren, slow, or awkward ⟨a man ~ in expedients⟩ ⟨the most ~ and prolific of humorists —Alfred Kreymborg⟩ **syn** see EASY

fac·ile·ly \-əl(l)ē, -il(l)|, -īl(l)|, |ī\ *adv* **:** in a facile manner **:** with ease or assurance

fac·ile·ness \-əlnəs, -iln-, -īln-\ *n* -ES **:** the quality or state of being facile ⟨impressed by the ~ of the man's mind⟩

fa·cil·i·tate \fəˈsilə,tāt, *usu* -ād.+V\ *vt* -ED/-ING/-S [F *faciliter* fr. MF, fr. OIt *facilitare*, fr. *facilità* facility, fr. L *facilitat-*, *facilitas*) + E *-ate*) — more at FACILITY] **1 :** to make easier or less difficult **:** free from difficulty or impediment ⟨~ the execution of a task⟩ ⟨*facilitating* free cultural interchange⟩ ⟨measures intended to ~ economic recovery⟩ **2 :** to lessen the labor of (as a person) **:** ASSIST, AID

fa·cil·i·ta·tion \fə,siləˈtāshən\ *n* -s **1 :** the act of facilitating **:** the state of being facilitated ⟨the ~ of trade that results from free intercourse of peoples⟩ ⟨social ~ is essentially an adaptive condition⟩ **2 :** something that facilitates **:** AID, HELP ⟨such notes provide a real ~ to the memory⟩ **3 a :** the lowering of the threshold for reflex conduction by the passage of another preceding or simultaneous stimulation esp. from a reflex of different origin **b :** the lowering of the threshold for reflex conduction along a particular neural pathway that results from repeated use of that pathway **c :** SUMMATION 3

fa·cil·i·ta·tive \ˈ=ˈ==,tād·iv\ *adj* **:** tending to facilitate

fa·cil·i·ta·tor \fəˈsilə,tād·ə(r)\ *n* -s **:** one that facilitates

fa·cil·i·ta·to·ry \fəˈsilətə,tōrē, fə¦silə¦tād·ərē\ *adj* **:** tending to induce or involved in facilitation esp. of reflex action

facilities contract *n* **:** a lease, rental agreement, or other contractual agreement governing the acquisition, use, or disposition of government-owned machinery, tools, building installations, or other property furnished to or acquired by a war contractor for war production purposes other than incorporation in a finished product

fa·cil·i·ty \fəˈsiləd·ē, -ətē, -i\ *n* -ES [ME *facilite*, fr. MF & L; MF *facilité*, fr. L *facilitat-*, *facilitas*, fr. *facilis* easy + *-itat-*, *-itas* -ity — more at FACILE] **1 :** the quality of being easily performed **:** freedom from difficulty **:** EASE **2 :** ease in performance **:** readiness proceeding from skill or use **:** DEXTERITY ⟨practice gives a wonderful ~⟩ **3 a :** easiness to be persuaded **:** READINESS, COMPLIANCE, PLIANCY **b** *Scots law* **:** mental weakness, compliancy, or responsiveness to undue influence sufficient to justify curatorship or guardianship **4** *archaic* **:** easiness in manner **:** AFFABILITY, GRACIOUSNESS **5 a :** something that promotes the ease of any action, operation, transaction, or course of conduct — usu. used in pl. ⟨excellent *facilities* for graduate study⟩ **b :** something (as a hospital, machinery, plumbing) that is built, constructed, installed, or established to perform some particular function or to serve or facilitate some particular end

facility of payment clause : a provision in an industrial life-insurance policy permitting the company to pay the death benefit to a relative of the insured or any other person entitled thereto by reason of his having paid expenses in the insured's behalf

¹fac·ing \'fāsiŋ\ *n* -s [fr. gerund of ²*face*] **1** : the act of one that faces ⟨his brave ~ of the enemy⟩; *also* : an instance of such act **2 a** : a plain or decorative lining applied to an edge of a textile article (as a garment or drapery) and turned either to the inside (as for hems or slashes) or to the outside (as for revers or cuffs) **b facings** *pl* : the collar, cuffs, and trimmings of some military or other uniform coats commonly of a color different from that of the coat and often prescribed for a particular group (as an arm of the service, a regiment, or a hotel staff) **3 a** : a covering in front usu. for ornament or protective purposes : an exterior covering or sheathing ⟨a ~ of stone blocks on an earthen dam⟩ ⟨had to replace the clutch ~ on his car⟩ **b** : a front of porcelain or plastic used in dental crowns and bridgework to face the metal replacement and simulate the natural tooth **4** : material used or suitable for facing ⟨you will need 12 yards of ribbon ~ for the ruffles⟩ **5** : a powdered substance (as graphite) applied to the face of a mold or mixed with the sand that forms the mold to give a smooth surface to the casting **6** : a turning of men in formation to face in a given direction usu. at command

²facing *adj* [fr. pres. part. of ²*face*] **1** : used for or suitable for use in facing ⟨a strong ~ sateen⟩ **2** : arranged or placed opposite one another ⟨the ~ ornaments on the mantel⟩

facing brick *n* : FACE BRICK

facing distance *n* : the minimum distance (as 14 inches) between men necessary to make the facings in military drill

facing-point lock *n* : a mechanical lock for a railroad switch, derail, or movable-point frog comprising a plunger stand and a plunger which engages a lock rod attached to the switch point to lock the operated unit

facing-point switch *n* : a railroad switch so set that a train faces the points as it passes them — distinguished from *trailing-point switch*

facing sand *n* : sand in contact with a foundry pattern

facing slip *n* : a printed or written direction slip or label to be attached to a package of mail

facing tile *n* : FACE TILE

fa·cin·o·rous \fə'sinərəs\ *also* **fac·i·ne·ri·ous** \,fasə'nirēəs\ *adj* [L *facinorosus, facinerosus*, fr. *facinor-, facinus* deed, evil deed, crime (fr. *facere* to do) + *-osus* -ous — more at DO] *archaic* : atrociously wicked : INFAMOUS — **fa·cin·o·rous·ness** *n* -ES *archaic*

facio- *comb form* [ISV, fr. L *facies* form, shape, face — more at FACE] **1** : facial and ⟨*facio*lingual⟩ **2** : facial ⟨*facio*plegia⟩

fa·cio ut des \'fākē,ō,ůt'dās\ *n* [L, I do that you may give] : a commutative contract in which one party performs something in order that another may give something in return

facio ut fa·ci·as \-'fākē,äs\ *n* [L, I do that you may do] : a commutative contract in which one party performs something in order that another may perform something in exchange

fack \'fak\ *dial var of* FACT

fack·el·tanz \'fäkəl,tänts\ *n, pl* **fackeltän·ze** \-,tentsə\ [G, fr. *fackel* torch (fr. OHG *faccala, facchela*, fr. L *facula* small torch) + *tanz* dance, fr. MHG, fr. OF *dance* — more at FACULA, DANCE] **1** : a pavane for a ceremonial torchlight procession formerly celebrating a royal marriage in certain German courts **2** : POLONAISE

fa·con \fä'kōn\ *n* -ES [AmerSp *facón*, aug. of Sp *faca* large knife, prob. fr. Pg, knife] : a large heavy belt knife carried by So. American gauchos

¹fa·con·ne \,fasə'nā\ *adj* [F *façonné*, fr. past part. of *façonner* to work, fashion, fr. *façon* make, fashioning, manner, fr. L *faction-, factio* action of making, company, faction — more at FASHION] *of textiles* : having a pattern that consists of small scattered figures or a fancy weave

²faconne \"\ *n* -s [F *façonné*, fr. *façonné*, adj.] **1** : a faconne fabric (as a jacquard) **2** : the pattern or a figure of the pattern on a faconne fabric

¹fac·sim·i·le \fak'siməlē, -li\ *n* -s *often attrib* [L *fac simile!* make something similar!, fr. *fac* (imp. of *facere* to make, do) + *simile*, neut. of *similis* like, similar — more at DO, SAME] **1** : an exact and detailed copy of something (as of a book, document, painting, or statue) **2** : the process of transmitting and reproducing (as printed matter or still pictures) orig. by facsimile telegraph but now chiefly by a system of radio communication in which the subject matter is scanned by a pinprick of light and differences between light and dark are noted by a photoelectric cell, transmitted by radio broadcast, and intercepted by a radio receiver equipped with a stylus or other device that produces a printed record on paper ⟨a ~ recorder⟩

²facsimile \"\ *vt* -ED/-ING/-S **1** : to be an exact copy of **2** : to make a facsimile of or reproduce by the process of facsimile

facsimile signature *n* : a signature produced by mechanical means but recognized as valid by law for many banking, financial, and business transactions

facsimile telegraph *n* : a telegraphic apparatus that reproduces matter (as messages, drawings, or pictures) in facsimile

fac·sim·i·list \-ləst\ *n* -s : a maker of facsimiles (as in the preparation of lithographs)

fac·sim·i·lize \-ə,līz\ *vt* -ED/-ING/-S : FACSIMILE

fact \'fakt\ *n* -s [L *factum*, fr. neut. of *factus*, past part. of *facere* to do, make — more at DO] **1** : a thing done : DEED: as **a** *obs* : an action in general : ACTION, CONDUCT **b** *obs* : a meritorious or valorous deed **c** : a wrong or unlawful deed : CRIME — used in the phrase *after the fact* ⟨an accessory after the ~⟩ **2** *obs* : DOING, MAKING, PREPARING, PERFORMING, ACT **3 a** : something that has actual existence : EVENT **b** : an occurrence, quality, or relation the reality of which is manifest in experience or may be inferred with certainty; *specif* : an actual happening in time or space ⟨~ in its primary meaning, as an object of direct experience, is distinguished from truth⟩ ⟨stubborn ~s⟩ ⟨given ~s⟩ **c** : a verified statement or proposition; *also* : something that makes a statement or a proposition true or false **4 a** : the quality or character of being actual or of being made up of facts : ACTUALITY ⟨a question of ~ hinges on the actual evidence⟩ **b** : physical actuality or practical experience as distinguished from imagination, speculation, or theory ⟨the realm of ~ is distinct from fancy⟩ **5** : an assertion, statement, or information containing or purporting to contain something having objective reality ⟨you must marshal your ~s to combat his assertions⟩; *broadly* : something presented rightly or wrongly as having objective reality ⟨his ~s are open to question⟩ **6** *usu pl* **a** : any of the circumstances of a case at law as it exists or is alleged to exist in reality : something proved by the evidence to be or alleged to be of actual occurrence **b** : the reality of events or things the actual occurrence or existence of which is to be determined by evidence — **in fact** *adv* : in truth : ACTUALLY, REALLY ⟨painters who are *in fact* anything but unsophisticated —Cyril Ray⟩ ⟨these tests *in fact* marked an important stage in the development of atomic weapons —J.G.Palfrey⟩

facta *pl of* FACTUM

fac·ta·ble \'fak,tābəl\ *n* -s [alter. of earlier *fractable, fract table*, fr. L *fractus* (past part. of *frangere* to break) + E *table* — more at BREAK] : ¹COPING

fact finder *n* : one occupied in determining the realities of a particular case, situation, or relationship; *often* : an impartial examiner appointed by a government agency to investigate and appraise the facts underlying a dispute between labor and management

fact-finding \'=,==\ *n* : the action of a fact finder or a group or committee of fact finders

Fac·tice \'faktəs\ *trademark* — used for a vulcanized oil

fac·ti·cide \'faktə,sīd\ *n* -s [*fact* + *-i-* + *-cide*] : perversion of fact; *also* : a perverter of fact

fac·tic·i·ty \fak'tisəd·ē\ *n* -ES [F or G; F *facticité*, fr. G *faktizität*, fr. *faktum* fact (fr. L *factum*) + *-izität* (fr. L *-icitat-, -icitas* -icity)] : the quality or state of being a fact (as an inescapable and unalterable fact) : FACTUALITY

fact in controversy : a fact other than a fact in issue that is collateral to the issue and controverted between the parties (as evidential facts merely of aid in reaching a verdict) — distinguished from *fact in issue*

fact in issue : a fact that is raised by the pleadings directly and is necessary to be determined by the decision so that it will become res judicata — distinguished from *fact in controversy*; compare ISSUE OF LAW

¹fac·tion \'fakshən\ *n* -s [MF & L; MF *faction*, fr. L *faction-, factio* action of making, company, faction — more at FASHION] **1** : a party, combination, or clique (as within a state, government, or other association) often contentious, self-seeking, or reckless of the common good **2** : party spirit or tumult esp. as manifested in discord, dissension, or intrigue ⟨~, or the irreconcilable conflict of parties —Ernest Barker⟩ **3** *obs* **a** : ACTION, DEED, BEHAVIOR **b** : a set or class of persons **c** : DISPUTE, QUARREL, INTRIGUE **4** : one of the divisions of charioteers contesting in the ancient Roman circus and distinguished by the color of their costumes; *often* : the part of the populace favoring and supporting one of these factions

²faction *also* **factionate** *vb* -ED/-ING/-S *vi, obs* : to act factiously : INTRIGUE ~ *vt, obs* : to gather into factions

-fac·tion \,fakshən\ *n comb form* -s [ME *-faccioun*, fr. MF & L; MF *-faction*, fr. L *-faction-, -factio* (as in *satisfaction-, satisfactio* satisfaction) — more at SATISFACTION] : making : -FICATION ⟨*rarefaction*⟩ — in nouns derived from verbs ending in *-fy*

fac·tion·al \'fakshən°l, -shnəl\ *adj* **1** : of or relating to a faction ⟨a ~ leader⟩ **2 a** : characterized by faction **b** : occurring between factions ⟨~ disputes within the party⟩ — **fac·tion·al·ism** \-°l,izəm, -ə,li-\ *n* -s — **fac·tion·al·ly** \-°lē, -əlē, |li\ *adv*

fac·tion·al·ist \-°ləst, -əl-\ *n* -s : an advocate of or adherent to factionalism

¹fac·tion·ary \'fakshə,nerē, -ri\ *n* -ES [¹*faction* + *-ary* (n. suffix)] : PARTISAN

²factionary \"\ *adj* [¹*faction* + *-ary* (adj. suffix)] : of or relating to a faction : PARTISAN

fac·tion·eer \,fakshə'ni(ə)r\ *n* -s [¹*faction* + *-eer*] : PARTISAN

fac·tion·ist \'faksh(ə)nəst\ *n* -s : a person who promotes factions or engages in faction

fac·tious \'fakshəs\ *adj* [MF or L; MF *factieux*, fr. L *factiosus*, fr. *factio* faction + *-osus* -ous — more at FASHION] **1** : given to faction : addicted to form parties or factions and raise dissensions; *sometimes* : SEDITIOUS **2** : relating to faction : proceeding from or characterized by faction ⟨~ and detailed political or moral analyses —Frances Keene⟩ **syn** see INSUBORDINATE

fac·tious·ly *adv* : in a factious manner

fac·tious·ness *n* -ES : the quality or state of being factious

fac·ti·tial \(')fak'tishəl\ *adj* [by alter.] : FACTITIOUS; *usu* : induced by deliberate human action with or without intention to produce a lesion or disease ⟨~ rectal lesions following irradiation⟩ ⟨a ~ hyperthyroidism resulting from surreptitious ingestion of thyroid products⟩

fac·ti·tious \-shəs\ *adj* [L *facticius, factitius*, fr. *factus* (past part. of *facere* to make, do) + *-icius, -itius* -itious — more at DO] **1** : produced by human art, skill, or effort : not occurring or arising through unaided nature ⟨it seems probable that several of the mounds are ~⟩ — compare FACTITIAL **2 a** : formed by or adapted to an artificial or conventional standard ⟨~ tastes and values⟩ ⟨a ~ report on a situation⟩ **b** : produced artificially or by special effort (as for a particular situation) : not natural or spontaneous ⟨~ popular enthusiasm in the totalitarian state⟩ ⟨a ~ delicacy of speech⟩ **syn** see ARTIFICIAL

fac·ti·tious·ly *adv* : in a factitious manner ⟨prepared to be ~ gay⟩ : with factitious quality : ARTIFICIALLY

fac·ti·tious·ness *n* -ES : the quality of being factitious; *often* : studied quality : ARTIFICIALITY

¹fac·ti·tive \'faktəd·iv, -tət|\ *adj* [NL *factitivus*, irreg. fr. L *factus* (past part. of *facere* to make, do) + *-ivus* -ive — more at DO] **1 a** : being or relating to a transitive verb that in certain constructions requires besides its object an adjective complement (as in "he made the water wine", "they called him Teddy", "boil the eggs hard") **b** : serving as objective predicate ⟨a ~ adjective⟩ ⟨the ~ object in this sentence⟩ **2** : indicating that the subject of a verb causes an action to be performed or a condition to come into being — compare CAUSATIVE — **fac·ti·tive·ly** \|əvlē, -li\ *adv*

²factitive \"\ *n* -s : a factitive verb

¹fac·tive \'faktiv, -tēv, -təv\ *adj* [ML *factivus*, fr. L *factus* + *-ivus* -ive] **1** *obs* : having power to make : CONSTRUCTIVE **2 a** *of a grammatical case* : denoting a process of becoming or transmutation **b** : FACTITIVE

²factive \"\ *n* -s : the factive case of a language; *also* : a form in the factive case

-fac·tive \,faktiv, -tēv, -təv\ *adj comb form* [MF *-factif*, fr. *-faction* + *-if* -ive] : making : causing : -POIETIC ⟨putre*factive*⟩

fac·to \'fak(,)tō\ *adv* [L, abl. of *factum* deed, act — more at FACT] : in or by the fact

fact of life 1 facts of life *pl* : the fundamental physiological processes and reactions involved in sex and reproduction ⟨the mistake of bringing up children in ignorance of the *facts of life*⟩ **2** : something that exists and must be taken into consideration (as in developing a plan of action or comprehending a situation) ⟨that communism has a real appeal to the Asian is a *fact of life* that we cannot afford to disregard⟩

¹fac·tor \'faktə(r) *also* -,tō(ə)r *or* -ō(ə)\ *n* -s [ME *factour*, fr. MF *facteur*, fr. L *factor*, maker, doer, fr. *factus* + *-or*] **1** : a person that acts or transacts business for another : AGENT, DEPUTY: as **a** : a commercial agent who sells or buys goods for others on commission : CONSIGNEE; *esp* : one permitted to buy and sell in his own name and entrusted with the possession and control of goods — compare BROKER **b** *now chiefly Scot* : a steward or bailiff of an estate; *also* : one appointed by law to have charge of forfeited or sequestered property **c** : an employee of the former East India Company of Britain that ranked above a writer and below a merchant **d** : the agent in charge of a trading post of the Hudson's Bay Company who adds to the usual duties of a factor the care of the company's territory and often exercises a quasi police control of the surrounding region **e** : a commercial banker or finance company specializing in financial services to producers and dealers (as the discounting of accounts receivable) **2** *obs* **a** : PARTISAN, ADHERENT **b** : a maker, author, or doer of anything **3 a** : something (as an element, circumstance, or influence) that contributes to the production of a result : CONSTITUENT, INGREDIENT ⟨people and people's doings are the essential ~ —I.J.C.Brown⟩ ⟨such ~s as availability of adequate power, transportation, and a labor source must be considered in appraising an industrial site⟩ ⟨hereditary predisposition, malnutrition, and overexertion are common ~s in the development of many diseases⟩ **b** *or* **factor of production** : a good or service (as land, labor, or capital) used in the process of production **c** : one of the elements determined in job evaluation to be essential to a job (as skill and training required, effort demanded, responsibility and working conditions involved) — called also *job factor* **4 a** : GENE **b** : a presumed equivalent of a gene (as a plasmagene) ⟨some authorities recognize more than one kind of cytoplasmic ~⟩ **5 a** : any of the numbers, quantities, or symbols in mathematics that when multiplied together form a product **b** : the number by which a given time is multiplied in photography to give the complete time for exposure or development **c** : a number that converts by multiplication the weight of one substance into the chemically equivalent weight of another substance — called also *gravimetric factor* **6** : a substance (as a hormone or vitamin) promoting or functioning in a particular physiological process; *esp* : such a substance of which the exact nature or mode of action is unknown ⟨the role of extrinsic ~s in blood formation⟩ **syn** see ELEMENT

²fac·tor \-,tə(r)\ *vb* **factored**; **factored**; **factoring** \-t(ə)riŋ\ **factors** *vi* **1** : to resolve into factors : FACTORIZE **2** : to act as factor for ⟨~*ed* his cousin's estate after he got out of the army⟩ ~ *vi* : to act as a factor esp. in discounting accounts receivable ⟨~*ing* in connection with automobile installment accounts is a big business today⟩

fac·tor·able \-t(ə)rəbəl\ *adj* : capable of representation as the product of numbers of a given field — opposed to *prime*

fac·tor·age \-tərij\ *n* -s [¹*factor* + *-age*] **1 a** : the charges made by a factor for his services : commission or allowance of a factor **b** : the functions or business of a factor **2** : factors esp. of a situation

factor analysis *n* : a statistical method for the identification of each of several statistical variables that fluctuate together and for the determination of their relative contribution to a mingled influence

factoress *n* -ES *obs* : a female factor

¹fac·to·ri·al \fak'tōrēəl, -tȯr-\ *adj* [¹*factor* + *-ial*] **1 a** : of, relating to, or involving the use of factorials ⟨~ mathematics⟩ **b** : involving or based on replication with a variable introduced in each replicate ⟨a ~ experiment⟩ ⟨~ study of mental processes⟩ **2** : of, relating to, or involving a factor ⟨advantages of ~ supervision of an estate⟩ — **fac·to·ri·al·ly** \-ēəlē, -li\ *adv*

²factorial \"\ *n* -s [¹*factor* + *-ial*] : a function of a positive integer *n* denoted by *n!* and defined by the relation *n!* = 1·2·3···*n* with the convention that *o!* is usu. assigned the value one

fac·to·ried \'fakt(ə)rēd, -rid\ *adj* : having or characterized by factories ⟨~ towns along the rivers⟩

factoring *n* -s **1** : the act or process of resolving something (as a mathematical expression) into its constituent factors **2** : the purchase of accounts receivable from a business by a factor who thereby assumes the risk of loss in return for some agreed discount

fac·tor·ist \'faktərəst\ *n* -s [¹*factor* + *-ist*] : an adherent to the theory that mental abilities depend on several factors, some specific and affecting success with one kind of task only, others general and affecting all undertakings

fac·tor·i·za·tion \,faktərə'zāshən, -,rī'z-\ *n* -s : the act or process or an instance of factorizing

fac·tor·ize \'faktə,rīz\ *vt* -ED/-ING/-S **1** : GARNISHEE 1 **2** : ²FACTOR 1

factor of production : FACTOR 3b

factor of safety : the ratio of the ultimate strength of a member or piece of material (as in an airplane) to the actual working stress or the maximum permissible stress when in use

factors *pl of* FACTOR, *pres 3d sing of* FACTOR

fac·tor·ship \'faktə(r),ship\ *n* : the office or status of a factor

fac·to·ry \'fakt(ə)rē, -ri\ *n* -ES *often attrib* [MF *factorie*, fr. *facteur* factor + *-erie* -ery — more at FACTOR] **1** : an establishment (as a trading station) where factors or agents reside and transact business for their employers **2 a** : a building or collection of buildings with facilities (as power-driven machinery) for the manufacture of goods often from raw materials : a place where work is done in the fabricating of goods, wares, or utensils **b** *or* **factory ship** : a ship equipped to process at sea whales or fishes brought to it by other ships **c** : a place that is a seat of some kind of production ⟨the leaf is a ~ for carbohydrate production⟩ ⟨the vice *factories* of the slums⟩ **3** *chiefly Scot* : the office or function of a factor : FACTORSHIP **4** *now dial* : unbleached muslin

factory committee *n* : a group in each Soviet Russian factory elected by the workmen that at first managed the factory but later acted as the local organ of the trade union — compare SHOP COMMITTEE

factory farm *n* : a farm managed and operated like a factory

factory lumber *n* : lumber for or of a grade suitable for further processing (as in making sashes and doors)

factory mutual *n* : a mutual insurance company organized for the purpose of insuring factories and factory properties exclusively

factory system *n* : the system of manufacturing that began in the 18th century with the development of the power loom and the steam engine and is based on concentration of industry into large establishments — contrasted with *domestic system*

fac·to·tum \fak'tōd·əm, -ōtəm\ *n* -s [NL, fr. L *fac totum!* do everything!, fr. *fac* (imp. of *facere* to do, make) + *totum*, neut. of *totus* all — more at DO] **1** : a person having many diverse activities or responsibilities : a general servant **2** : an ornamental oversize capital letter used in printing

fac·trix \'faktriks\ *n* -ES *Scots law* : a female factor

facts *pl of* FACT

fac·tu·al \'fakch(əw)əl, -ksh-; -kshwəl\ *adj* [*fact* + *-ual* (as in *actual*)] **1** : of, relating to, or concerned with facts ⟨~ considerations⟩ ⟨the ~ aspects of the case⟩ **2** : restricted to, involving, or based on fact esp. as opposed to the imaginative or theoretical ⟨a carefully ~ presentation of the evidence⟩ ⟨~ studies⟩ ⟨a ~ account⟩ — **fac·tu·al·ly** \-əlē, -li\ *adv*

fac·tu·al·ism \-ə,lizəm\ *n* -s **1** : adherence or dedication to facts ⟨the ~ of the scientist⟩ **2** : a theory based on or emphasizing the importance of facts

fac·tu·al·ist \-ələst\ *n* -s : an adherent of factualism — **fac·tu·al·is·tic** \;=(=)=;=;=\ *adj*

fac·tu·al·i·ty \,fakchə'waləd·ē, -ətē, -i\ *also* **fac·tu·al·ness** *n* -ES : the quality or state of being fact or factual ⟨the ~ of his report⟩

fac·tum \'faktəm\ *n, pl* **fac·ta** \-tə\ *also* **factums** [NL, fr. L, act, deed — more at FACT] **1** *law* : a man's own act and deed: as **a** : an instrument under seal **b** : the due execution of a will **2** [LL, fr. L] **a** : FACT, EVENT **b** : a statement of facts (as of a case in court) : MEMORIAL

fac·ture \'fakchə(r), -ksh-\ *n* -s [ME, fr. MF, fr. L *factura* act of making, formation — more at FEATURE] **1** : the manner in which something is made or finished : EXECUTION; *often* : the quality or handling of a surface (as in painting) ⟨Dali's neat, tight Vermeerish ~ has its aesthetic as well as Picasso's bold, plangent viscous brushwork —Herbert Read⟩ **2** *archaic* : the act or process of making something **3** : INVOICE

fact verdict *n* : SPECIAL VERDICT

facty \'faktē, -ti\ *adj* -ER/-EST : filled with facts

fac·u·la \'fakyələ\ *n, pl* **facu·lae** \-yə,lē\ [NL, fr. L, small torch, dim. of *fac-, fax* torch] : any of the bright regions of the sun's photosphere seen most easily near the sun's edge and occurring most frequently in proximity to sunspots — **fac·u·lar** \-lə(r)\ *adj* — **fac·u·lous** \-ləs\ *adj*

fac·ul·ta·tive \'fakəl,tād·iv\ *adj* [F *facultatif*, fr. *faculté* faculty + *-atif* -ative] **1 a** : having relation to or concerned with the grant of a privilege ⟨~ legislation or enactments⟩ : involving permission rather than compulsion ⟨the licensing provision is purely ~⟩ **b** *of money* : used for convenience and having no status as legal tender ⟨at one time local subdivisions of France issued ~ coins of small value⟩ **c** : OPTIONAL ⟨~ courses in the sciences⟩ **2 a** : having characteristics that permit alternate responses (as of doing or not doing or of happening or not happening) under different conditions ⟨there is no ~ plurality in the mind; it is a single organ of true judgment —James Martineau⟩ ⟨~ homosexuals⟩ **b** : able to live or thrive under more than one set of conditions ⟨certain ~ parasites that are capable of a free-living saprophytic existence⟩ ⟨many bacteria are ~ anaerobes⟩ **3** : of or relating to the faculties **4** : NONDISTINCTIVE

fac·ul·ta·tive·ly *adv* : in a facultative manner : not obligatorily ⟨~ parasitic fungi⟩

facultative referendum *n* : OPTIONAL REFERENDUM

facultative reinsurance *n* : a separate reinsurance agreement drawn up for a single risk

fac·ul·ty \'fakəltē, -ti\ *n* -ES *often attrib* [ME *faculte*, fr. MF *faculté*, fr. ML & L; ML *facultat-, facultas* branch of learning, academic faculty, fr. L, ability, power, abundance, supply, property, fr. OL *facul* (neut. of L *facilis* easily done, easy) + L *-tat-, -tas* -ty — more at FACILE] **1 a** *obs* : a branch of learning **b** : a branch of teaching or learning in an institution usu. involving the interaction of several academic departments and providing education leading to a particular degree ⟨in medieval universities the *faculties* usually recognized were theology, law, medicine, and arts⟩ **c** *archaic* : something in which one is trained or qualified (as an art, craft, trade, or profession) **2 a** : the holders of graduate degrees and often the student candidates for degrees in theology, law, medicine, or arts **b** : the members of a profession or calling ⟨the medical ~⟩ **c** : the teaching staff and those members of the administrative staff having academic rank in a college, university, or other educational institution or one of its divisions ⟨an excellent mathematics ~⟩ **3** : pecuniary state as evidenced by ability to pay; *often* : MEANS, PROPERTY, RESOURCES ⟨the levying of ~ taxes〉 **4 a :** ability to act or do whether inborn or cultivated 〈man . . . how infinite in ~ —*Shak.*〉 **b :** an inherent capability, power, or function — now used chiefly of the living body or its parts 〈the ~ of hearing〉 〈the digestive ~〉 **c :** one of the powers or agencies into which psychologists formerly divided the mind (as will, reason, instinct) and through the interaction of which they endeavored to explain all mental phenomena **d** *obs* **:** personal characteristics or capacity **:** DISPOSITION **e :** natural aptitude 〈he has a ~ for saying the right thing〉 **f :** executive ability **:** COMPETENCE 〈a natural ~ for managing a household〉 **g :** a special mental endowment 〈Coleridge employed his analytical ~ frequently and brilliantly upon the works of Shakespeare —James Benziger〉 **5 a :** power, authority, or prerogative given or conferred (as by a superior) 〈by its constituting authority the state has the ~ to define treason〉 **b :** a permit from the consistory in the Church of England without which no considerable alterations can be made in a church's fabric, ornaments, or monuments **c :** a right, authority, license, or dispensation granted or delegated by ecclesiastical authority — often pl. in constr. even when sing. in meaning **d** *Scots law* **:** a power or ability created by one to be exercised at any time by another in accordance with the terms of the instrument creating it; *specif* **:** a power to make provision for the support of someone or to apportion or appoint property in which the holder of the power need not necessarily have any ownership **syn** see GIFT

faculty psychology *n* **:** an outmoded school of psychology that attempted to account for human behavior by positing various mental powers or agencies on an a priori basis — compare FACULTY 4c

faculty theory *n* **:** a theory of taxation: every individual should contribute to the support of the public burdens according to his ability

fac·und \ˈfakənd, fəˈkənd\ *adj* [ME *facound*, fr. L *facundus*, fr. *fari* to speak — more at FAME] **:** ELOQUENT

fa·cun·di·ty \fəˈkəndədē, fəˈ-\ *n* -ES [L *facunditas*, fr. *facundus* + *-itas* -ity] **:** ELOQUENCE

facy \ˈfāsi\ *adj* -ER/-EST [¹*face* + *-y*] *now dial Brit* **:** BRASH, IMPUDENT, INSOLENT

fad \ˈfad, ˈfaa(ə)d\ *n* -S [origin unknown] **1 :** a pursuit or interest followed usu. widely but briefly and capriciously with exaggerated zeal and devotion 〈the fancy, fashionable cleverness and egocentric brilliance of each passing modern ~ —Peter Viereck〉 **2 :** the object of a fad **:** RAGE 〈crossword puzzles were the ~ of the year〉 **syn** see FASHION

FAD \ˌefˌāˈdē\ *abbr or n* -S **:** flavin adenine dinucleotide

FAD *abbr* free air delivered

fad·ding *var of* ¹FADING

fad·dish \ˈfadish, ˈfaad-,-ēsh\ *adj* **1 :** inclined to take up fads 〈~ wealthy widows〉 **2 :** constituting or resembling a fad 〈~ collecting of special stamps〉 — **fad·dish·ly** *adv*

fad·dism \-ˌdizəm\ *n* -S **:** inclination to take up fads **:** fondness or enthusiasm for fads 〈aping another's scale out of snobbery or ~ —Hayward Keniston〉

fad·dist \-dəst\ *n* -S **:** one that is inclined to take up fads 〈the literary ~*s* — those people who affect newness of manner —Lodwick Hartley〉; *often* **:** one that enthusiastically accepts and practices quack notions 〈food ~*s* who like to live on strangely restricted diets —Morris Fishbein〉 — **fad·dis·tic** \(ˈ)faˈdistik,(ˈ)faa!-\ *adj*

fad·dle \ˈfadᵊl\ *n* -S [origin unknown] *chiefly dial* **:** NONSENSE, FOOLISHNESS

fad·dy \ˈfadē, ˈfaad-, -di\ *adj* -ER/-EST **:** FADDISH

¹**fade** \ˈfād,ˈfad\ *adj* [ME, fr. OF, fr. (assumed) VL *fatidus*, alter. (influenced by L *sapidus* wise, tasty & *vapidus* flat-tasting) of L *fatuus* foolish, silly, tasteless — more at SAGE, VAPID, BAT (club)] **:** INSIPID, VAPID, TRITE, COMMONPLACE 〈a sauce . . . which . . . struck me as rather more ~ than delicate —*New Yorker*〉

²**fade** \ˈfād\ *vb* -ED/-ING/-S [ME *faden*, fr. MF *fader*, fr. *fade*] *vi* **1 a :** to lose freshness, vigor, vitality, or health **:** LANGUISH, WITHER, DROOP 〈the old flowers in the vase were *fading*〉 **b :** to undergo loss of the appeal or attractiveness of the young or new 〈Mexican wives are expected to do all the domestic work, and ~ early —*Amer. Guide Series: Texas*〉 〈a *fading* child star in Hollywood〉 〈the metaphors contained in countless words *faded* so long, long ago —E.S.McCartney〉 **c :** to decline with or as if with approaching death or invalidism 〈a fell disease from which . . . she was now *fading* —F.M.Ford〉 **d :** to lose force and drive and cease to be a contender 〈the horse *faded* in the stretch〉 **e :** to lose strength **:** suffer loss of significance, consequence, or effectiveness **:** become enervated, unsubstantial, immaterial, or unreal 〈as optimism and security *faded* in the Thirties —Anthony Boucher〉 〈as the dream of building a society of Saints *faded* —Carl Bridenbaugh〉 〈countless small towns had boomed for a few years and then *faded* into ghosts —*Amer. Guide Series: Ark.*〉 **f** *of an automobile brake* **:** to lose braking power gradually (as because of wear or temperature change of parts) — often used with *out* **2 a** (1) **:** to lose freshness of color **:** become dingy 〈there were vivid paintings on the entrance walls . . . they have not entirely *faded* —Green Peyton〉 〈a little mill village with *faded* wooden houses —*Amer. Guide Series: Vt.*〉 (2) **:** to lose brilliance **:** change color by decreasing in saturation or increasing in lightness or both **:** DIM 〈the fabrics *faded* in the strong sunshine〉 〈at about half-past seven, when the light was beginning to ~ —Nevil Shute〉 〈the long Roman twilight *faded* into darkness —Herbert Agar〉 **b** *of a sound* **:** to dwindle or die away gradually 〈heard at night, when daytime sounds have *faded* —Tom Marvel〉 **3 a :** to recede into indistinctness and lack of clarity of outline and detail **:** BLUR 〈now ~*s* the glimmering landscape on the sight —Thomas Gray〉 〈we stood out to sea till the coastline itself began to ~ —Kenneth Roberts〉 **b :** to disappear slowly and die out in effect **:** lapse gradually into desuetude **:** pass gradually from clear consideration or memory 〈memories of transatlantic antecedents *faded* —Oscar Handlin〉 〈this story seems to have *faded* out of the popular mind —Norman Douglas〉 **c :** to undergo gradual disappearance or gradual change or transition **:** become gradually submerged or absorbed **:** BLEND 〈the mountains ~ into lowlands —L.D.Stamp〉 〈that nationalism might gradually ~ into a universal humanism —Bertrand Russell〉 **4 a :** to pass gradually from a certain stage, condition, or situation 〈murmuring to herself and visibly *fading* back into the mist in which she lived —Marcia Davenport〉 **b :** to dwindle away gradually **:** vanish slowly **:** melt away 〈his audience . . . had *faded* away like snow before the sun —Ernest Beaglehole〉 〈the smile *faded* from his face〉 **c :** to draw back **:** go away or backward typically quietly, unobtrusively, or furtively **:** RETREAT, LEAVE 〈the protective plumage that enabled him to ~ effortlessly into the background —Hamilton Basso〉 〈you can ~ away and the sergeant and I will take over —F.W.Crofts〉 **d** *of a football back* **:** to move back from the line of scrimmage 〈the quarterback *faded* back and threw a pass〉 **e** *of a ball* **:** to swerve from a true course **:** CURVE **f** *of a coin* **:** to wear away so that the design becomes indistinct or vanishes **5 :** to switch focus of attention 〈you can immediately ~ to the detective questioning members of the household —Richard Harrison〉 **6 a :** to change gradually in loudness or visibility — used of a motion-picture image or of an electronics signal or image and usu. with *out* to specify change from loud to soft or bright to dark and with *in* to specify change from soft to loud or dark to bright **b :** to begin to operate or to cease to operate — used esp. of a camera or piece of sound equipment and usu. with *out* to specify decreasing operation and with *in* to specify increasing operation ~ *vt* **1 :** to cause to lose freshness or vitality **:** WITHER 〈time has not completely *faded* the humor of these verses —G.H.Genzmer〉 **2 :** to cause to alter and esp. decrease in brightness, loudness, intensity, or distinctness: as **a :** to cause to change color by decreasing in saturation or increasing in lightness or both **b** (1) **:** to cause (as a motion-picture, radio, or television sound or image) to change gradually in loudness or visibility — usu. used with *in* or *out* (2) **:** to cause (as a camera or piece of sound equipment) to begin gradually to operate or to cease to operate — usu. used with *in* or *out* **3 :** to accept a bet offered by (one gambling) **:** COVER 19; *esp* **:** to cover all or a specified part of the center bet of (a crapshooter) **4 :** to curve (a ball) to the player's off side (as in golf or bowling) — opposed to *hook* **syn** see VANISH

³**fade** \"\ *n* -S **1 a :** FADE-IN **b :** FADE-OUT **2 :** a gradual changing of one picture to another in a motion-picture or television sequence **3 :** a fading of an automobile brake

fadeaway \ˈ=ˌ=\ *n* -S [fr. *fade away*, v.] **1 :** an act or instance of fading away **2 a :** a baseball pitch that breaks downward and toward a right-handed batter **b :** a slide in which a base runner throws his body sideways to avoid the tag

fad·ed·ly *adv* **:** in the manner of one that has faded 〈a ~ handsome woman〉

fad·ed·ness *n* -ES **:** the quality or state of being faded

faded rose *n* **:** OCHER RED

fade-in \ˈ=ˌ=\ *n* -S [fr. *fade in*, v.] **:** an act or instance of fading in **:** gradual emergence of a picture from darkness to full visibility or of a sound from silence to full volume

fade·less \ˈfādləs\ *adj* **:** exempt from fading **:** not susceptible to fading 〈the ~ blooms of youth —Thomas Moore〉 — **fade·less·ly** *adv*

Fade-Om·e·ter \fāˈdämədə(r)\ *trademark* — used for an apparatus containing a carbon-arc lamp that emits radiation approximating sunlight for use in accelerated tests of lightfastness under controlled conditions

fade-out \ˈ=ˌ=\ *n* -S [fr. *fade out*, v.] **1 a :** gradual decrease in visibility or distinctness of a motion-picture or television image esp. for signaling transition or conclusion **b :** diminution or disappearance of sound impulse sent by radio either purposive for dramatic effect or natural as caused by ionospheric disturbances **2 a :** the concluding scene of or as if of a motion picture 〈the standard *fade-out* kiss —*Current Biog.*〉 **b :** gradual disappearance from prominence 〈the slow *fade-out* of auction bridge〉 **c :** VANISHING, DISAPPEARING

fad·er \ˈfādə(r)\ *n* -S **1 :** one that fades **2 a :** a device for varying the volume of reproduced sound of a motion picture **b :** an electronic device by which fade-in or fade-out can be controlled

fades *pres 3d sing of* FADE, *pl of* FADE

¹**fadge** \ˈfaj\ *n* -S [ME (Sc dial.) *faige*] **1 a** *chiefly Scot* **:** a round thick loaf of bread **b** *chiefly Irish* **:** potato cake or bread **2 :** BUNDLE **3** *Austral* **:** an irregular package of wool weighing from 60 to 150 pounds

²**fadge** \"\ *vi* -ED/-ING/-S [origin unknown] **1 a** *archaic* **:** to fit surroundings and consequently to thrive or avail **b** *obs* **:** SUIT, AGREE **2 a** *obs* **:** to be compatible **b** *archaic* **:** SUCCEED

¹**fad·ing** \ˈfadiŋ\ *n* -S [origin unknown] *archaic* **:** an Irish dance

²**fad·ing** \ˈfādiŋ\ *n* -S [fr. gerund of ²*fade*] **:** fluctuation in intensity of received radio waves while the adjustments of sending and receiving apparatus remain unchanged

fad·ing·ly *adv* **:** in the manner of one that is fading 〈a ~ attractive beauty of yesterday〉

fa·do \ˈfä(ˌ)thü\ *n* -S [Pg, lit., fate, fr. L *fatum* — more at FATE] **:** a Portuguese folk song typically plaintive or mournful

fads *pl of* FAD

fady \ˈfādē, -i\ *adj* -ER/-EST **:** tending to fade

¹**fae** \ˈfā\ *prep* [alter. of *frae*] *Scot* **:** FROM

²**fae** \"\ *archaic Scot var of* FOE

faecal *var of* FECAL

faem \ˈfām\ *Scot var of* FOAM

fa·e·na \fäˈānə\ *n* -S [Sp, lit., task, fr. obs. Catal (now *feina*), fr. L *facienda* things to be done, fr. neut. pl. of *faciendus*, fut. passive participle of *facere* to do, make — more at DO] **:** the series of final passes by the matador with sword and muleta leading to the kill

fae·nus *or* **fe·nus** *or* **foe·nus** \ˈfēnəs\ *n* [L; prob. akin to L *femina* woman — more at FEMININE] *Roman law* **:** INTEREST 3a

faenus nau·ti·cum \-ˈnȯdəkəm\ *n* [LL, lit., maritime interest] *Roman law* **:** interest paid on maritime loans to be repaid only when a ship and its cargo safely reach port

fa·en·za ware \fäˈenzə-, -ntsə-\ *n, usu cap F* [fr. *Faenza*, commune in northern Italy] **:** pottery of majolica technique made at Faenza, Italy, in the 16th century

fa·er·ie *also* **fa·ery** \ˈfā(ə)rē, ˈfa(a)r-,ˈfer-, -ri\ *n, pl* **faeries** [MF *faerie* fairyland, enchantment — more at FAIRY] **1 :** the imagined realm of fairies **:** an imaginary land of enchantment **2 :** FAIRY

¹**faero·ese** *or* **faro·ese** \ˌfa(a)rəˈwēz, ˌfer-, -ēs\ *adj, usu cap* [*Faeroes*, islands in the north Atlantic comprising a county of Denmark + E *-ese*] **:** of or relating to the Faeroese people or their language

²**faeroese** *or* **faroese** \"\ *n, pl* **faeroese** *or* **faroese** *cap* **1 a :** the Germanic people inhabiting the Faeroes **b :** a member of such people **2 :** the North Germanic language of the Faeroese people

fa·ery *also* **fa·er·ie** \ˈfā(ə)rē, ˈfa(a)r-,ˈfer-, -ri\ *adj* **:** of, relating to, or suggesting faerie 〈pines and crags ~ with September mists —Hervey Allen〉

faex com·pres·sa \ˈfekskəmˈpresə\ *n* [L] **:** COMPRESSED YEAST

FAF *abbr* flyaway factory

faff \ˈfaf\ *vi* -ED/-ING/-S [imit.] *dial Brit* **:** to make a fuss over nothing

¹**fag** \ˈfag, -aa(ə)g,-aig\ *n* -S [ME *fagge* flap, knot in cloth] **1 :** FAG END **2 :** CIGARETTE; *sometimes* **:** a cheap cigarette

²**fag** \"\ *vb* **fagged; fagged; fagging; fags** [obs. E *fag* to droop, perh. fr. ¹*fag*] *vi* **1 :** to become weary **:** TIRE, FLAG **2 :** to work to exhaustion **:** DRUDGE, TOIL 〈*fagging* away at all the extra work〉 **3 a :** to be a fag **:** serve as a fag 〈*fagging* for older boys during his first year〉 **b :** to serve as a fag in the field in British school games (as cricket) ~ *vt* **1 :** to compel to serve as a fag 〈what right have the fifth-form boys to ~ us —Thomas Hughes〉 **2 :** to exhaust by toil, drudgery, or sustained heavy activity — often used with *out* 〈the long march *fagged* them out〉 **3 :** to make (the end of a rope) frayed or untwisted **syn** see TIRE

³**fag** \"\ *n* -S **1** *chiefly Brit* **:** a fatiguing task **:** DRUDGERY 〈it is such a ~; I came back tired to death —Jane Austen〉 **2 a :** an English public-school boy who acts as servant to another boy in a higher form **b :** MENIAL, DRUDGE, SERVITOR

⁴**fag** \"\ *or* **fag·got** \ˈfagət\ *n* -S [origin unknown] *slang* **:** HOMOSEXUAL

fa·ga·ce·ae \fəˈgāsēˌē\ *n pl, cap* [NL, fr. *Fagus*, type genus + *-aceae*] **:** a family of trees and shrubs (order Fagales) having the staminate flowers in cymose heads or drooping aments and pistillate flowers with an urn-shaped to oblong perianth that occur singly or in clusters and are succeeded by one-seeded nuts — see CASTANEA, FAGUS, QUERCUS — **fa·ga·ceous** \-ˈāshəs\ *adj*

fa·ga·les \fəˈgā(ˌ)lēz\ *n pl, cap* [NL, fr. *Fagus* + *-ales*] **:** an order of dicotyledonous trees and shrubs distinguished chiefly by the inferior unilocular ovary containing two or more ovules

fa·ga·ra \fəˈgärə\ [NL, fr. Ar] *syn of* ZANTHOXYLUM

fa·ge·lia \fəˈjēlēə, -lyə\ [NL, fr. Kaspar *Fagel* †1688 Dutch statesman + NL *-ia*] *syn of* CALCEOLARIA

fag end *n* [¹*fag*] **1 a :** the last part or coarser end of a web of cloth **b :** the untwisted end of a rope **c :** an end or other part showing poor quality or spoiled condition **2 :** a worn, poor, or useless ending or remnant unlikely to afford either pleasure or profit

fag·gery \ˈfagərē, -ri\ *n* -ES [³*fag* + *-ery*] **:** the fagging system formerly common in English public schools

fa·gin \ˈfāgən\ *n* -S *often cap* [after *Fagin*, a fence and trainer of children as pickpockets in the novel *Oliver Twist* (1837-39) by Charles Dickens †1870 Eng. novelist] **:** an adult who instructs others in crime; *esp* **:** one who teaches children to steal 〈a kindly ~ who harbors a nest of adolescent thieves as runners for his goods —*Time*〉

fa·gine \ˈfaˌjēn,-jən\ *n* -S [NL *Fagus* + E *-ine*] **:** a volatile narcotic principle present in the husks of beechnuts

fagmaster \ˈ=ˌ==\ *n* [³*fag* + *master*] **:** a schoolboy who has a fag

fag·o·py·rism \ˌfagōˈpīˌrizəm\ *also* **fag·o·py·ris·mus** \-ˌpīˈrizməs\ *n, pl* **fagopyrisms** *also* **fagopyris·muses** [G *fagopyrismus*, fr. NL *Fagopyrum* + G *-ismus* -ism] **:** a photosensitization esp. of swine and sheep that is due to eating large quantities of buckwheat and that appears principally on the nonpigmented parts of the skin as an intense redness and swelling with severe itching and the formation of vesicles and later sores and scabs — compare BIGHEAD 1 b, HYPERICISM

fag·o·py·rum \-ˈpīrəm\ *n, cap* [NL, fr. L *fagus* beech + NL *-o-* + *-pyrum* (fr. Gk *pyros* wheat) — more at BEECH, FURZE] **:** a genus of European and Asiatic annual plants (family Polygonaceae) having the achene much exceeding the perianth but otherwise resembling members of the genus *Polygonum* — see BUCKWHEAT

¹**fag·ot** *or* **fag·got** \ˈfagət,ˈfaig-, *usu* -əd.+V\ *n* -S [ME *fagot*, fr. MF *fagot*, prob. fr. OProv, perh. fr. (assumed) VL *facus*, modif. of Gk *phakelos*] **1 :** a bundle of sticks or twigs esp. as used for fuel, as a fascine, or as a means of burning heretics alive **2 :** BUNDLE, BUNCH **3 :** a bundle of pieces of wrought iron to be worked over into bars or other shapes by rolling or hammering at high temperature **4 :** an unpleasant or objectionable woman **5** *obs* **:** a person paid for use of his name to complete a roster **6** *Brit* **:** FAGOT VOTE **7 a :** BOUQUET GARNI **b :** a portion of the viscera of the hog, chopped, seasoned with herbs, shaped into a ball or stick, and fried or baked

fagot 1

²**fagot** \"\ *or* **faggot** *vb* **fagoted** *or* **faggoted; fagoted** *or* **faggoted; fagoting** *or* **faggoting; fagots** *or* **faggots** *vt* **1 :** to set fagots around (as a heretic) preparatory to execution by burning **2 :** to make a fagot of **:** bind together into a bundle 〈~*ed* sticks〉 〈he ~*ed* all the pamphlets together〉 **3 :** to embroider or work in fagoting **:** seam with fagoting ~ *vi* **:** to make fagots

fagot cinnamon *n* **:** a cinnamon bark from an Asiatic tree (*Cinnamomum burmanni*) — called also *Batavia cassia*

fag·ot·er \ˈfagədə(r)\ *n* -S **:** one that makes fagots or works with fagoting: as **a :** one who sews together or decorates with fagoting by hand or by machine **b :** a sewing machine attachment for making fagoting

fag·ot·ing *or* **fag·got·ing** \-ədiŋ\ *n* -S **1 a :** an embroidery produced by pulling threads in one direction and tying the exposed threads into groups of an hourglass shape **b :** a decorative openwork stitching forming a ladderlike or zigzag line that is used esp. in seams of garments and table linens **2 :** the act or operation of cutting up puddled iron into lengths and piling in a reheating furnace for subsequent heating and rolling or hammering into bars

fagoting 1a

fagot iron *n* **:** iron in bars or masses made from fagots

fa·gott \fəˈgȯt\ *n, pl* **fa·got·te** \-ȯtə\ [G, fr. It *fagotto*] **:** BASSOON — **fa·got·tist** \fəˈgädəst\ *n* -S

fa·got·ti·no \ˌfägəˈtē(ˌ)nō\ *n* -S [It, dim. of *fagotto*] **:** TENOROON

fa·got·to \fəˈgäd.(ˌ)ō\ *It* fäˈgȯt(ˌ)tō\ *n, pl* **fa·got·ti** \-äd.(ˌ)ē, -ȯt(ˌ)tē\ [It, lit., fagot, fr. Prov *fagot* — more at FAGOT] **1 :** BASSOON **2 :** an 8-foot pipe-organ stop of the same general quality as the bassoon

fagot vote *n, Brit* **:** the vote of one made a property holder for party purposes to qualify him as a voter

fags *pl of* FAG, *pres 3d sing of* FAG

fa·gus \ˈfāgəs\ *n, cap* [NL, fr. L, beech — more at BEECH] **:** a genus of trees (family Fagaceae) having the staminate flowers in small pendulous heads and the fruit sharply 3-angled — compare CASTANEA, QUERCUS; see BEECH, COPPER BEECH

fah *abbr, usu cap* Fahrenheit

fa·ham \ˈfäˌhäm\ *n* -S [F, fr. a native name in the Mascarene islands] **1 :** the leaves of an orchid (*Angrecum fragrans*) of Réunion and Mauritius used in France as a substitute for Chinese tea **2 :** the plant that produces faham leaves

fahl·band \ˈfälˌbänt, -band\ *n* [G, fr. *fahl* pale, faded, dun-colored (fr. OHG *falo*) + *band*, fr. OHG *bant*; fr. its pale color at decomposition — more at FALLOW, BAND] **:** a band or stratum in crystalline rock containing metallic sulfides

fahl·erz \ˈfäˌlerts\ *also* **fahl·ore** \-ˌlō(ə)r\ *n, pl* **fahler·ze** \-tsə\ *also* **fahlores** [*fahlerz* fr. G, fr. *fahl* + *erz* ore, fr. OHG *aruz, aruzzi*; akin to OS *arut* ore, ON *örtog*, a small coin; all prob. of non-IE origin; akin to Sumerian *urud* copper; *fahlore* part trans. of G *fahlerz*] **:** TETRAHEDRITE

fah·lun·ite \ˈfäləˌnīt\ *n* -S [Sw *fahlunit*, fr. *Fahlun* (Falun), Sweden + Sw *-it* -ite] **:** an altered form of cordierite

fahr *abbr, usu cap* Fahrenheit

¹**fahr·en·heit** \ˈfarənˌhīt *also* ˈfer-, *usu* -īd.+V\ *adj, usu cap* [after Gabriel D. *Fahrenheit* †1736 Ger. physicist] **:** relating or conforming to a thermometric scale on which under standard atmospheric pressure the boiling point of water is at 212 degrees and the freezing point at 32 degrees above the zero of the scale, the zero point approximating the temperature produced by mixing equal quantities by weight of snow and common salt (10° *Fahrenheit*) — abbr. *F, Fah, Fahr*

²**fahrenheit** \"\ *n* -S *usu cap* **:** a Fahrenheit thermometer or scale

fai·blesse \fāblės\ *n, pl* **fai·blesses** \"\ [F, fr. OF *flebesse, feblesse, foiblesse*, fr. *flebe, feble, foible* weak — more at FEEBLE] **:** WEAKNESS, FOIBLE

fa·ience *or* **fa·ïence** *also* **fa·yence** \fāˈän(t)s, -äⁿs, ˈ=ˌ=\ *n* -S [F, fr. *Faenza*, city in northern Italy] **:** earthenware decorated with opaque colored glazes

faïence d'oi·ron \fäyäⁿsdwärōⁿ\ *n, usu cap O* [F, lit., faïence from Oiron (commune in western France)] **:** SAINT-PORCHAIRE FAÏENCE

faik \ˈfāk\ *vt* -ED/-ING/-S [short for Sc *defaik*, alter. of E *defalk*] *Scot* **:** SPARE, EXCUSE

¹**fail** \ˈfāl, *esp before pause or consonant* -āəl\ *vb* -ED/-ING/-S [ME *faillen, failen*, fr. OF *faillir*, fr. (assumed) VL *fallire*, alter. of L *fallere* to deceive, be concealed from, escape observation, be ignorant of; prob. akin to Gk *phēlos* deceitful, Skt *hrunāti* he gets lost, OSlav *zŭlŭ* bad, evil] *vi* **1 a :** to undergo loss of vigor or activity **:** lose strength, power, vitality, or intensity **:** become enfeebled 〈his health ~*ed* and he retired young〉 〈the breeze ~*ed* and we were becalmed〉 〈the warm sun is ~*ing* . . . the pale flowers are dying —P.B.Shelley〉 〈the never ~*ing* river of student life —J.B.Conant〉 **b :** to diminish in amount or quantity to a point of inadequacy **:** dwindle away **:** run short 〈the supplies of the defenders ~*ed*〉 **c :** to cease to be encountered **:** be or become nonexistent 〈should the rains ~ . . . the numbers of the game depreciate —James Stevenson-Hamilton〉 **d :** to become extinct **:** die away 〈until our family line ~*s*〉 **e :** to be inadequate 〈time ~*s* for recounting all his exploits〉 **f :** to lose strength and control rapidly as a prelude to dying 〈the old man was ~*ing* and they decided to spare him the shock of the news〉 **g :** to grow dim and difficult or impossible to perceive 〈the radio signals ~*ed*〉 〈the landward marks have ~*ed* —Rudyard Kipling〉 **h :** to weaken and come to function very imperfectly 〈his eyesight was ~*ing*〉 〈the senile old woman's mind was ~*ing*〉 **i :** to stop functioning 〈the patient's heart ~*ed*〉 〈one of the plane's engines ~*ed*〉 **j :** to fall away from an expected or hoped-for yield 〈the peach crop ~*ed*〉 **2 a :** to miss attainment **:** fall short of achievement or realization — usu. used with *of* 〈this chronicle . . . may ~ of effect —Clifton Fadiman〉 〈the senator ~*ed* of reelection〉 〈music that ~*s* of beauty〉 **b :** to miss success in some effort **:** become forced to leave incomplete an attempt or enterprise — used with infinitive 〈he ~*ed* to finish the race〉 〈when a rainmaker ~*s* to produce rain —J.G.Frazer〉 **c :** to neglect to do something **:** leave something undone **:** be found wanting in not doing something — used with infinitive 〈the janitor had ~*ed* to call the fire department〉 〈had criminally ~*ed* to latch the street door —Arnold Bennett〉 〈if our civilization has ~*ed* to enable us to look further than our own egoistic ends —Havelock Ellis〉 **d :** to miss success **:** be unavailing **:** MISCARRY — used of things, devices, and arrangements 〈the commission ~*ed* to settle the refugee question〉 〈the jack ~*ed* to raise the truck〉 **e :** to end without success **:** miss successful achievement of a result 〈I ~*ed*, yet still I clung to the hope —Mary W. Shelley〉 〈the neurotic personality wishes to ~〉 **f :** to leave some possible or expected action unperformed or some condition unachieved 〈he usually ~*s* to remember his dreams〉 〈they could hardly ~ to meet〉 〈explosive statements that rarely ~*ed* to startle his hearers —D.D.Eisenhower〉 〈meals that ~ to satisfy〉 〈a . . . section that the continental glacier ~*ed* to cover —*Amer. Guide Series: Minn.*〉 〈a rise in prices that ~*ed* to develop〉 **3 a :** to be deficient or inadequate **:** LACK 〈Aristophanes could ridicule all the literary Homeric

gods but must never ~ in respect to Athena —Gilbert Murray⟩ **b :** to prove inadequate, deficient, or unavailing on trial **:** give way or break down ⟨the attack *~ed*⟩ ⟨the supporting brace *~ed*⟩ **c :** to become unable to meet financial engagements; *esp* **:** to become bankrupt or insolvent ⟨banks were *~ing*, unemployment was soaring —N.M.Clark⟩ **d :** to be deficient or unable to meet a test or standard of attainment ⟨he *~ed* in arithmetic⟩ ⟨a *~ing* term paper⟩ **4** *obs* **:** to err in judgment **:** be in error **~** *vt* **1 :** to disappoint the expectations or trust of **:** be found wanting at the time of need of (a person) **:** miss performing expected or hoped-for service, assistance, or function for ⟨his allies *~ed* him when the battle started⟩ ⟨if a man's English subordinates ~ him in India, he comes to a hard time indeed —Rudyard Kipling⟩ ⟨she reached for a chair and sat down suddenly, as if her legs had *~ed* her —Ellen Glasgow⟩ ⟨for once his ready wit *~ed* him⟩ **2 :** to be deficient in **:** LACK ⟨our youth . . . never *~ed* an invincible courage —Douglas MacArthur⟩ **3** *obs* **:** to leave undone or unperformed ⟨his morning prayer, which he never *~ed*⟩ **4** *archaic* **:** to disappoint or leave unfulfilled (a trust, hope, or expectation) ⟨the book *~s* the reader's hopes⟩ **5 a :** to prove so deficient in knowledge or skill as not to pass (as a test or course) ⟨she *~ed* her driving test⟩ ⟨he *~ed* chemistry⟩ **b :** to rate (as a pupil) as deficient in achievement for not meeting the standard required for passing ⟨the teacher *~ed* only his two worst students⟩

[2]**fail** *n* [ME *faille*, *faile*, fr. OF *faille*, fr. (assumed) VL *fallia*, fr. LL *fallire*] **1 a** *obs* **:** failure to occur **b :** omission of doing or performing something — usu. used in the phrase *without fail* **2** *obs* **:** want of success

failance *n* -s *obs* **:** FAILURE

failed *adj* **:** having failed **:** having been unsuccessful ⟨a ~ candidate⟩ ⟨a ~ novelist⟩

[1]**failing** *n* -s [ME *failling*, *failing*, fr. gerund of *faillen*, *failen* to fail] **:** an often slight or venial disadvantageous foible, personality defect, or character weakness ⟨has all the *~s* of our common lot —Ronald Rubinstein⟩ **syn** see FAULT

[2]**failing** *prep* [fr. pres. part. of [1]*fail*] **:** in absence, default, or lack of **:** in case of nonoccurrence of **:** WITHOUT ⟨~ specific instructions, use your own judgment⟩ ⟨~ brothers and sisters, cousins may inherit⟩

fail·ing·ly *adv* **:** in the manner of one that is failing ⟨a ~ dim beam of light⟩ ⟨a ~ faint cry⟩

faille \\'fīl, *esp before pause or consonant* -īəl\\ *n* -s [F] **:** a semilustrous closely woven fabric with good draping qualities for use in clothing and interior decoration that is made in plain weave of silk, rayon, or cotton and is characterized by slight flat ribs in the weft

fails *pres 3d sing of* FAIL

fail spot *or* **fail place** *n* **:** a place where forest reproduction has failed

fail·ure \\'fālyə(r)\\ *n* -s [alter. (influenced by *-ure*) of earlier *failer*, fr. AF *failer*, fr. OF *faillir* to fail — more at FAIL] **1 a :** omission of performance of an action or task; *esp* **:** neglect of an assigned, expected, or appropriate action ⟨the mechanic's ~ to adjust the brake⟩ ⟨the ~ of students to write complete sentences⟩ ⟨the scout's ~ to rejoin the party⟩ **b :** the fact of a certain action or process not having occurred **:** the fact of nonoccurrence ⟨~ of the water to pass through the pipe⟩ ⟨the ~ of the drug to have a harmful effect⟩ **2 :** want of success **:** lack of satisfactory performance or effect ⟨the ~ of the attack on the fort⟩ ⟨the ~ of the candidate in the election⟩ **3** *obs* **:** FAILING, LAPSE **4 a :** DEFICIENCY, LACK **:** the fact of being cumulatively inadequate or not matching hopes or expectations ⟨the crop *~s* brought on near famine⟩ **b :** ABSENCE, NONEXISTENCE ⟨through ~ of heirs, most of the state societies had disintegrated —A.F.Harlow⟩ **c :** marked weakening **:** the fact of becoming exhausted or enfeebled **:** DETERIORATION ⟨any impairment or ~ of his bodily vigor through sickness or age —J.G.Frazer⟩ **d** *med* **:** inability to perform a vital function ⟨heart ~⟩ **e :** a collapsing, fracturing, or giving way under stress **:** inability of a material or structure to fulfill an intended purpose **5 a :** BANKRUPTCY ⟨the ~ of the company⟩ ⟨the ~ of a friend whose note he had endorsed⟩ **b :** a venture financially unsuccessful ⟨although a contribution to literature, the play was a box-office ~⟩ **6 :** a person or thing that has failed ⟨people who were either *~s* or had had no ambitions —Louis Bromfield⟩ ⟨the war against the confederation was a ~⟩ **7 a :** the fact of failing in a test or course **b :** a failing grade **c :** a student who has failed

syn NEGLECT, DEFAULT, MISCARRIAGE, DERELICTION: FAILURE implies a lack or absence of something expected esp. in performance or achievement ⟨the *failure* of the courts in the past to formulate any principle for drawing a boundary line around the right of free speech —Zechariah Chafee⟩ ⟨the ailing civilization pays the penalty for its *failure* of vitality by becoming disintegrated —A.J.Toynbee⟩ ⟨nutritional *failure* due to inadequate intake of proteins and vitamins —*Jour. Amer. Med. Assoc.*⟩ NEGLECT implies carelessness or inattentiveness resulting in incompleteness or inadequacy of performance or achievement ⟨any *neglect* to take into consideration the relations of the social framework can only lead to a defective understanding —M.F.A.Montagu⟩ ⟨so intent on taking care of the physical mechanics of getting things done, their creative and imaginative faculties suffer from *neglect* —*Phoenix Flame*⟩ ⟨driven to extreme bitterness by public *neglect* of his work —*Amer. Guide Series: N.Y.*⟩ DEFAULT, now chiefly in legal context, implies a failure to perform something required, usu. by total omission of any action at all ⟨some of our decisions . . . are arrived at by *default* — that is, by "letting things go" —W.J.Reilly⟩ ⟨betraying by *default* the privileges of citizenship in a democratic society —Vera M. Dean⟩ ⟨in some *default* of faith too base for words —William Alfred⟩ MISCARRIAGE is often used when one cannot assign or wishes to avoid assigning specific blame for a failure ⟨it seems to me a *miscarriage* of the artist's job if his reputation does his work for him —William Arrowsmith⟩ ⟨we fear . . . some *miscarriage* in the details of our plan —J.W.Krutch⟩ ⟨a *miscarriage* of justice⟩ DERELICTION is extremely strong in signifying or implying a neglect or nonobservance amounting to a reprehensible abandonment of a morally compelling duty, law, or principle ⟨there is a moral *dereliction* in failure by any member of a profession to apply in professional practice the standards which, by consensus of opinion in the profession, are necessary —*Jour. Amer. Med. Assoc.*⟩ ⟨every good reporter knows that his friendship for a news source must never extend so far as disregard of official *dereliction* or incompetence —F.L.Mott⟩ ⟨a manager who fails to throw out hour-old coffee and replace it with fresh coffee is warned not to repeat his *dereliction* —Jack Alexander⟩

failure of issue : a lack of living descendants (as of a designated person) resulting from death or from complete lack of issue — see DEFINITE FAILURE OF ISSUE, INDEFINITE FAILURE OF ISSUE

faim·ly \\'fāmli\\ *Scot var of* FAMILY

[1]**fain** \\'fān\\ *adj* -ER/-EST [ME *fagen*, *fayn*, fr. OE *fægen;* akin to OS *fagin*, *fagan* glad, happy, OHG *faginōn* to rejoice, ON *fegiun* happy, Goth *faginon* to rejoice, OE *fæger* beautiful — more at FAIR] **1** *archaic* **:** PLEASED, HAPPY ⟨if thou wouldst grant his asking and make his heart full ~ —William Morris⟩ **2 a :** GLAD, WILLING **:** INCLINED, DESIROUS ⟨men and birds are ~ of climbing high —Shak.⟩ ⟨something which the scientists approached with reluctance and which they were ~ to leave to the linguists —C.B.Tinker⟩ **b** *archaic* **:** OBLIGED, CONSTRAINED, COMPELLED ⟨such a clamor that we were ~ to comply —Tobias Smollett⟩ **3** *Scot* **:** FOND — **fain·ly** *adv*

[2]**fain** \\"\\ *adv* [ME *fagen*, *fayn*, fr. *fagen*, *fayn*, adj.] **1 :** HAPPILY, JOYFULLY **:** with glad preference ⟨~ would I woo her —Shak.⟩ **2 :** by preference or acquiescence in view of the circumstances ⟨Macbeth, who, though he would ~ repent —H.S.Wilson⟩

[3]**fain** \\"\\ *interj* [by alter.] *chiefly Brit* **:** [3]FEN

fai·naigue \\fə'nāg\\ *vi* -ED/-ING/-S [origin unknown] **1** *dial Brit* **:** RENEGE **2** *dial Brit* **:** to shirk work

fai·ne·an·cy \\'fānēənsē\\ *also* **fai·ne·ance** \\-ēən(t)s\\ *n*, *pl* **faineancies** *also* **faineanc·es :** remiss indolence **:** INACTIVITY ⟨~ and neglect of civic affairs⟩

[1]**fai·ne·ant** \\-nt\\ *n* -s [F *fainéant*, fr. MF *fait-nient*, lit., (he) does nothing, by folk etymology fr. *faignant*, fr. pres. part. of *feindre*, *faindre* to feign, shirk, be inactive (as in *se feindre* to be lazy) — more at FEIGN] **:** an irresponsible or weak idler

[2]**faineant** \\"\\ *adj* **:** showing a faineant's character **:** idle and ineffectual **:** INDOLENT ⟨~ kings under whose rule the country languished⟩ **syn** see LAZY

fainéant deity *n* **:** a deity not acting in human affairs

fai·né·an·tise \\fānāäⁿtēz\\ *n*, *pl* **fainéan·tises** \\"\\ [F, fr. *fainéant*] **:** FAINEANCY

fain·ness \\'fānnəs\\ *n* -ES [ME *faynnesse*, fr. *fayn* fain + *-nesse* -ness] **:** WILLINGNESS, EAGERNESS

fains \\'fānz\\ *or* **fain it** *or* **fains I** *interj* [alter. of [3]*fen*] *chiefly Brit* **:** [3]FEN

[1]**faint** \\'fānt\\ *adj* -ER/-EST [ME *faint*, *feint* (also, deceitful, feigned), fr. OF, fr. past part. of *faindre*, *feindre* to feign, shirk — more at FEIGN] **1 :** lacking courage and spirit **:** COWARDLY, SPIRITLESS — now usu. used in the phrase *faint heart* **2 :** feeble, dizzy, and likely to faint through or as if through hunger, illness, pain, shock, or emotion ⟨he felt suddenly ~ . . . he had eaten nothing —Pearl Buck⟩ ⟨sick and ~ from the pain —Jack London⟩ ⟨~ with her happiness —Ethel Wilson⟩ **3 a :** having an appearance of underlying weakness **:** lacking vigor or strength ⟨fair young man, with a long, pale nose, a ~ chin —Booth Tarkington⟩ **b :** performed, acted, or accomplished in a weak, feeble, or hesitant manner **:** marked by halfhearted forcelessness ⟨believed the assertion at once, but he made a ~ effort to resist conviction —G.B.Shaw⟩ ⟨damning with ~ praise⟩ **4 :** likely to make one faint **:** OPPRESSIVE ⟨the ~ atmosphere of a tropical port⟩ **5 a :** making only a feeble impression on the senses **:** hardly perceptible **:** INDISTINCT, BLURRED, DIM ⟨he tied his shoelaces in hard knots because he couldn't see in the ~ light —Erskine Caldwell⟩ ⟨a ~ hissing sound became audible —H.G.Wells⟩ **b :** not making or accompanied by a clear mental impression **:** OBSCURE ⟨these ~ lights of intuition —G.W.Russell⟩ ⟨a ~ clue to the origin of these mystery people —R.W.Murray⟩ ⟨had not the *~est* idea what was meant⟩

[2]**faint** \\"\\ *n* -s [ME *faint*, *feint*, fr. *faint*, *feint*, adj.] **:** the act or condition of fainting **:** SWOON ⟨the classic signs of the ordinary ~ — marked facial pallor and moist cold skin —*Today's Health*⟩

[3]**faint** \\"\\ *vb* -ED/-ING/-S [ME *fainten*, *feinten*, fr. *faint*, *feint*, adj.] *vi* **1** *archaic* **:** to lose heart **:** become discouraged or afraid **:** give way **:** FLAG **2** *archaic* **:** to grow weak or feeble **:** DECLINE ⟨but his strength dwindled and *~ed*⟩ **3 :** to suffer syncope **:** SWOON **4 a :** to lose brilliance, color, or intensity ⟨the aroma soon *~s*⟩ **b :** to lose distinctness and clarity **~** *vt*, *archaic* **:** to make faint **:** DEPRESS, ENFEEBLE ⟨it *~s* me to think what follows —Shak.⟩

[4]**faint** \\"\\ *adv* [[1]*faint*] **:** FAINTLY

[5]**faint** *var of* FEINT

[1]**faintheart** \\'=,=\\ *adj* [alter. of *fainthearted*] **:** COWARDLY, TIMID, IRRESOLUTE

[2]**faintheart** \\"\\ *n* **:** a timorous or irresolute person **:** COWARD ⟨the *~s* who broke and ran —Bruce Catton⟩

fainthearted \\'=¦==\\ *adj* [ME *feint herted*] **:** lacking courage or resolution **:** FAINTHEART ⟨the ~ wished to surrender —J.A. Froude⟩ — **faint·heart·ed·ly** *adv* — **faint·heart·ed·ness** *n*

fainting *n* -s [ME *fainting*, *feinting*, fr. gerund of *fainten*, *feinten* to faint] **:** the act of one who faints: **a :** a growing faint **:** DEPRESSION **b :** loss of consciousness resulting from arrest of the blood supply to the brain **:** SYNCOPE

fainting fit *or* **fainting spell** *n* **:** FAINTING, SWOON, SYNCOPE

faint·ing·ly *adv* **:** in the manner of one that faints ⟨a ~ weak voice⟩

faint·ly *adv* **1 :** in a faint manner ⟨for a few seconds he ~ struggled with the man —Charles Dickens⟩ ⟨his senses alive so ~ as to be useless —Nigel Dennis⟩ **2 :** to a faint degree **:** SLIGHTLY, INDISTINCTLY ⟨showing ~ at the right of the picture —G.R.Stewart⟩ ⟨~ blue hills —Hugh Walpole⟩ ⟨rumors . . . which weren't even ~ true —Scott Fitzgerald⟩

faint·ness *n* -ES [ME *faintnesse*, *feintnesse*, fr. *faint*, *feint* + *-nesse* -ness] **:** the quality or state of being faint: as **a :** loss of strength **:** partial or near loss of consciousness **b :** lack of courage or spirit ⟨~ of heart⟩ **c :** feebleness of impression or of intensity of color or contrast **:** lack of distinctness ⟨~ of an old photograph⟩ ⟨~ of his recollection of the event⟩

faints *var of* FEINTS

fainty \\'fāntē\\ *adj* [ME *ffaynty*, fr. *faint*, *feint* + *-y*] *chiefly dial* **:** liable to faint **:** FEEBLE

fa·i·pu·le \\fī'pü,lā\\ *n* -s [Samoan, fr. *fai* to do, make + *pule* rule] **:** a Samoan native councillor heading a political district and belonging to a fono

[1]**fair** \\'fa(a)|(ə)r, 'fe|, |ə\\ *adj* -ER/-EST [ME *fager*, *fair*, fr. OE *fæger;* akin to OS & OHG *fagar* beautiful, ON *fagr* beautiful, Goth *fagrs* suitable, and perh. to MHG *vegen* to clean, sweep, ON *fāga* to clean, decorate, Lith *puošti* to decorate] **1 a :** attractive in appearance **:** pleasant to view **:** BEAUTIFUL, HANDSOME, COMELY ⟨the innkeeper had two ~ daughters⟩ ⟨forever wilt thou love and she be ~ —John Keats⟩ ⟨bedecked with garlands and flowers ~⟩ ⟨our ~ city⟩ ⟨settle down in such a ~ fat land and call good acres his own —Charles Kingsley⟩ **b** *archaic* **:** DEAR, KIND — used in formal salutation chiefly in the phrase *fair sir* ⟨your servant, ~ sir —Max Peacock⟩ **c :** FEMININE ⟨the ~ sex⟩ ⟨his ~ companions⟩ **2 :** pleasing to hear **:** inspiring hope or confidence often delusively **:** GRACIOUS, AFFABLE, CIVIL, SPECIOUS ⟨in an evil hour she trusted his ~ promises⟩ ⟨trusted the enemy's ~ words, and were immediately murdered —J.A.Froude⟩ **3 a :** having attraction or admirable qualities **:** pleasant to contemplate **:** AGREEABLE, RICH, CONSIDERABLE, WORTHY ⟨the ~ life of ancient Athens⟩ ⟨a ~ estate⟩ ⟨cheapening a ~ cause with shabby tactics⟩ **b :** somewhat above average **:** moderately numerous or large **:** pretty good **:** being without marked lack or defect **:** SATISFACTORY, PASSABLE, SUFFICIENT, ADEQUATE ⟨a ~ proportion of the people . . . could read and write —G.M. Trevelyan⟩ ⟨a ~ knowledge of English and a smattering of Latin —W.E.Smith⟩ ⟨made some ~ guesses about the shape . . . of the universe —B.J.Bok⟩ ⟨a crop of scrub pine, grown already to a ~ height —Ellen Glasgow⟩ ⟨received a grade of ~ in English⟩ ⟨his work is only ~, certainly not distinguished⟩ **c** *of livestock* (1) **:** of middling quality; *specif* **:** third grade (2) **:** reasonably plentiful in supply **:** not scarce **4 a :** free from spots or dirt **:** not sullied ⟨a sheet of ~ white paper⟩ **b** *of water, archaic* **:** not dirtied, soiled, or contaminated **:** PURE **c :** free from moral stain **:** UNSULLIED, UNBLEMISHED ⟨her ~ name⟩ **d** (1) **:** DISTINCT, LEGIBLE ⟨easily deciphering the old manuscript written in a ~ hand⟩ (2) **:** free from corrections **:** being the final draft ⟨no private bill is permitted to be sent up . . . until a certificate is endorsed on the ~ printed bill —T.E.May⟩ **e :** straight or smoothly curving **:** having no sudden angular deviation **f :** properly aligned **:** fitting together ⟨~ rivet holes⟩ **5 a :** not stormy or foul **:** FINE, CLOUDLESS ⟨a ~ sky⟩ ⟨a ~ day⟩ **b :** free or nearly free from rain, hail, or snow — used in the predictions issued by the U.S. Weather Bureau even if the weather is cloudy and threatening if less than one hundredth of an inch of precipitation occurs **6 :** not dark or brunet **:** LIGHT, CLEAR, BLOND ⟨~ . . . with great wavy masses of golden hair —Bram Stoker⟩ **7 a :** characterized by honesty and justice **:** free from fraud, injustice, prejudice, or favoritism ⟨you will find him a very ~ man⟩ ⟨determined to win by ~ means or foul⟩ **b** (1) **:** conforming to an established commonly accepted code or rules of a game or other competitive activity ⟨observers disagreed as to whether the blow was ~⟩ ⟨believes in ~ play in sports and business⟩ (2) *of a baseball field* **:** lying between the foul lines (3) **:** equitable as basis for exchange **:** REASONABLE ⟨a ~ valuation⟩ ⟨a ~ wage⟩ (4) **:** conforming to its merits or importance **:** DUE ⟨the subject has received its ~ share of attention⟩ (5) **:** having a certain basis in evidence or of reason **:** JUSTIFIED, VALID ⟨a ~ assumption that regularities occur in history⟩ ⟨he has a ~ complaint⟩ (6) **:** being a sufficient, equitable, or adequate basis for judgment or evaluation **:** TYPICAL, REPRESENTATIVE ⟨a ~ sample of his work⟩ ⟨that is not a ~ example⟩ **c :** legitimately open to attack or pursuit ⟨the hypocrite is ~ game to the satirist⟩ **8 a** (1) **:** PROMISING, AUSPICIOUS, LIKELY ⟨his prospects of future wealth were exceedingly ~ —Jane Austen⟩ ⟨in a ~ way to realize a profit —Arnold Bennett⟩ ⟨its cultures and institutions seem ~ to become stabilized —Clark Wissler⟩ (2) *of the wind* **:** favorable to a ship's course ⟨sailed for France with a ~ wind⟩ (3) *of the tide* **:** running in the general direction of a ship's course **b :** neither favorable and promising nor unfavorable and discouraging **:** EVEN ⟨a ~ bet that his team would win⟩ **9** *archaic* **:** free from obstacles **:** UNOBSTRUCTED, OPEN **10** *archaic* **:** plainly visible **:** DISTINCT **11 :** UTTER, REAL, COMPLETE, FULL, STARK, ABSOLUTE ⟨a ~ miracle⟩ ⟨a ~ treat to watch him outsnob the snobs —*New Republic*⟩ ⟨when a ~ month had elapsed I did meet him again —James Stephens⟩

syn FAIR, JUST, EQUITABLE, IMPARTIAL, UNBIASED, DISPASSIONATE, UNCOLORED, and OBJECTIVE can apply, in common, to judgments, judges, or acts resulting from judgments, and signify freedom from improper influence. FAIR, the most general of the terms, implies a disposition in a person or group to achieve a fitting and right balance of claims or considerations that is free from undue favoritism even to oneself, or implies a quality or result in an action befitting such a disposition ⟨a *fair* trial for all offenders⟩ ⟨a *fair* distribution of profits⟩ ⟨a *fair* judge in a criminal trial⟩ ⟨a *fair* estimate of his achievements⟩ JUST stresses, more than FAIR, a disposition to conform with or conformity with the standard of what is right, true, or lawful, despite strong, esp. personal, influences tending to subvert that conformity ⟨a severe but *just* decision of the court⟩ ⟨a *just* estimate of her personal qualities⟩ ⟨a *just* statement of the facts⟩ ⟨he was *just* — but not charitable; he was magnanimous — but not tolerant —H.S.Commager⟩ EQUITABLE implies fair and equal treatment of all concerned, suggesting often a less rigid standard than JUST, as one that provides relief where rigid adherence to law would make for unfairness ⟨the *equitable* distribution of essential commodities —*U.S. Dept. of State Bull.*⟩ ⟨develop an *equitable* and adequate tax structure throughout the country —*Collier's Yr. Bk.*⟩ ⟨techniques that will make for more *equitable* access to higher education and vocational opportunity —W.H.Hale⟩ IMPARTIAL stresses an absence of favor or prejudice in judgment ⟨judges as a rule sincerely and ardently desire to be *impartial* and just —M.R.Cohen⟩ ⟨the law provides for the examination by neutral, *impartial* psychiatric experts of all persons indicted for a capital offense —*Current Biog.*⟩ UNBIASED emphasizes even more strongly than IMPARTIAL the absence of prejudice, favoritism, or prepossession ⟨to furnish the cabinet with *unbiased* and helpful advice on matters of state —R.M. Dawson⟩ ⟨it is difficult to convince the average spectator or juror that the law enforcement officer is an *unbiased* objective witness —Paul Wilson⟩ DISPASSIONATE usu. implies freedom from all unduly influencing feeling or preconception, often implying temperateness or coolness, even coldness, in judgment ⟨the *dispassionate* study of history —John Baillie⟩ ⟨a *dispassionate* and objective description of the region —G.M. Foster⟩ ⟨an economic report studiously *dispassionate* in temper and analytic in mode —Robert Leckachman⟩ UNCOLORED stresses a freedom from influences as prejudices or impulses to dramatize or embellish that detract from truthfulness or accuracy, as of news report ⟨it is often difficult to find a newspaper with *uncolored* accounts of the news⟩ ⟨to strive to give an *uncolored* report of one's experiences⟩ OBJECTIVE implies a looking at something as apart, as disentangled from all personal feeling, prejudice, or opinion ⟨he is not *objective* . . . but the slightest insight into historical processes to discover that objectivity, in the usual sense of that term, is unattainable in a serious political struggle —Philip Rahv⟩ ⟨it has no direct interest in the construction industry and could be expected to approach the problem from a purely *objective* standpoint —*Housing & Home Finance Agency Technical Bull.*⟩ ⟨we shall be like ice when relating passions and adventures . . . we shall be . . . *objective* and impersonal —William Troy⟩ **syn** see in addition BEAUTIFUL

— **fair to middling :** just average **:** pretty good **:** TOLERABLE ⟨the food is *fair to middling*⟩

[2]**fair** \\"\\ *adv* -ER/-EST [ME *faire*, *fair*, fr. OE *fægre*, fr. *fæger*, adj.] **1 a :** in a fair manner **:** in an attractive or agreeable manner **:** PLEASANTLY ⟨the sun shone ~⟩ **b :** GRACIOUSLY, COURTEOUSLY — used chiefly in the phrase *speak (one) fair* ⟨the sheriff felt that he must speak the prisoner ~ —C.W. Chesnutt⟩ **c :** in an equitable manner ⟨play ~⟩ **d :** AUSPICIOUSLY, PROMISINGLY ⟨events promise ~⟩ **e :** CLEARLY, PLAINLY ⟨write ~⟩ **2** *obs* **:** QUIETLY, MODERATELY **3 :** EVENLY, SQUARELY, FULL, PLUMP, STRAIGHT ⟨the torpedo had struck ~ on the starboard side —*Time*⟩ ⟨the gabled houses leaned out over the streets, planted ~ upon sturdy timbers —Lord Dunsany⟩ ⟨you could have thrashed a battleship ~ down midstream —C.E.W.Bean⟩ **4 :** QUITE, COMPLETELY, ABSOLUTELY ⟨he ~ spurned the earth with arrogance —J.H.Wheelright⟩ ⟨~ take one's breath away —David Hardman⟩ ⟨~ blinding you with headlights —Richard Llewellyn⟩

[3]**fair** \\"\\ *vb* -ED/-ING/-S [ME *fairen*, fr. *fair*, adj.] *vt* **1** *obs* **:** to make beautiful **:** BEAUTIFY **2 :** to make smooth without hollows or bumps **:** even out (a curve or line) **:** SHAPE ⟨~ a ship's lines⟩ — often used with *up* or *off* ⟨it'll take a lot of . . . cookery to ~ out the hollows in your outline —Llewellyn Howland⟩ **3 a :** to join one part of a structure with (another part) in such a way that there is a smooth blending of external surfaces — often used with *into* ⟨an engine *faired* into a wing⟩ ⟨a radiator from another make car with the original hood *~ed* into it —B.H.Scott⟩ **b :** to provide (an airplane part) with a fairing **~** *vi*, *of the weather* **:** CLEAR ⟨it *~ed* as the night went on —R.L.Stevenson⟩ — often used with *up* or *off* ⟨stopped on this porch till it *~ed* up —*Reader's Digest*⟩ ⟨it's *~ed* off . . . we'll have a clear day tomorrow —Jessamyn West⟩

[4]**fair** \\"\\ *n* -s [ME, fr. OE *fæger*, fr. *fæger*, adj.] **1** *obs* **:** FAIRNESS, BEAUTY **2** *archaic* **:** a lovely woman **:** SWEETHEART **3** *archaic* **:** something that is fair or fortunate **:** good fortune ⟨~ befall thee —Shak.⟩ — **for fair** *adv* **:** to the greatest extent or degree **:** CERTAINLY, DEFINITELY, FULLY ⟨opened up with everything they had . . . and caught the bomber *for fair* —Alfred Friendly⟩ ⟨the rush was on *for fair* —R.L.Neuberger⟩ — **no fair :** something that is not according to the rules **:** something that is not right or proper ⟨that's *no fair*⟩ — often used interjectionally ⟨you mustn't peek! *no fair!*⟩

[5]**fair** \\"\\ *n* -s [ME *feire*, *faire*, fr. OF *feire*, *foire*, fr. ML *feria* (also, weekday), fr. LL, festal day (also, day of the week), back-formation fr. L *feriae* days of rest, holidays, festivals — more at FEAST] **1 a :** a gathering of buyers and sellers at a particular place at a fixed time for purposes of trade ⟨the village has a ~ once a month —J.M.Mogey⟩ **b :** a competitive exhibition (as of wares, farm products, livestock) with prizes for excellence ⟨an agricultural ~⟩ — see COUNTY FAIR **c :** an exhibition designed to acquaint prospective buyers or the public at large with the range and quality of currently available or planned products ⟨a book ~⟩ ⟨a shoe ~⟩ **2 :** a bazaar or sale of a collection of articles usu. for some charitable purpose ⟨a church ~⟩

fair and square *adj* (*or adv*) **:** marked by honesty and fairness ⟨be so much easier too if he weren't so damn *fair and square* —Sinclair Lewis⟩ **:** in an honest and fair manner ⟨see that everything was done *fair and square* —S.E.Fletcher⟩

fair ball *n* **:** a batted baseball that settles within the foul lines in the infield, that first touches fair territory in the outfield, or that is on or over fair territory when bounding to the outfield past first or third base

fair catch *n* **1 :** a catch of a kicked football by a player who having given a prescribed signal forfeits his right to advance the ball and may not be tackled **2** *rugby* **:** a catch made direct from a kick or knock-on by a player of the opposing side who at the same time marks with his heel the spot where the catch is made — called also *mark*

fair·child·ite \\'fa(a)r,chīl,dīt, 'fer,-\\ *n* -s [John G. *Fairchild* *b*1882 Am. chemist + E *-ite*] **:** a mineral $K_2Ca(CO_3)_2$ consisting of carbonate of potassium and calcium that is found in fused wood ash in partly burned trees

fair comment *or* **fair criticism** *n* **:** the legal privilege everyone has to criticize and comment on matters of public interest provided he states facts truly and without malice and expresses his opinion honestly and provided any criticism he makes imputes no corrupt or dishonorable motive not reasonably warranted by the facts notwithstanding that such criticism may be voiced in a style calculated to attract attention and to entertain and may involve some exaggeration, humor, or irony

fair competition *n* **:** competition reasonable in view of the interests of those competing and the public and not involving practices condemned by law as inimical to the public interest — compare UNFAIR COMPETITION

fair copy *n* **:** a neat and exact copy esp. of a corrected or revised draft of a document; *also* **:** the form of such a copy

fair cow *n, slang Austral* **:** something exceedingly troublesome or unpleasant

fair dinkum *adj* [²*fair*] *slang Austral* **:** unquestionably good or genuine **:** EXCELLENT — often used as a general expression of approval ⟨these cigars are good — *fair dinkum*⟩

fair employment *n* **:** employment of workers on a basis of equality without discrimination or segregation esp. because of race, color, or creed

fairer *comparative of* FAIR

fairest *superlative of* FAIR

fair–faced \ˈ=ˌ=\ *adj* **1 :** having a light complexion **:** beautiful of countenance **2** *Brit, of a brick wall* **:** not plastered

fair·field·ite \ˈfa(a)rˌfēlˌdīt, ˈfer-,-\ *n* -S [*Fairfield* co., Conn. + E *-ite*] **:** a mineral $Ca_2Mn(PO_4)_2.2H_2O$ consisting of a white or pale yellow hydrous calcium manganese phosphate and usu. occurring foliated or fibrous (sp. gr. 3.07–3.15)

fairgoer \ˈ=ˌ=(=)\ *n* **:** one that attends a fair

fairground \ˈ=ˌ=\ *n* **:** an enclosure where outdoor fairs, circuses, or exhibitions are held — sometimes used in pl. with sing. constr. ⟨what a spot for a ~*s* —W.L.Gresham⟩

fair–haired \ˈ=ˌ=\ *adj* **1 :** having fair or light-colored hair **2 :** specially favored **:** DARLING — used chiefly in the phrase *fair-haired boy* ⟨I was something of a *fair-haired* boy with my employer —P.B.Williamson⟩

fair hearing *or* **fair trial** *n* **:** a hearing conducted impartially in accordance with due process of law of which a party has had reasonable notice as to the time, place, and issues or charges, for which he has had a reasonable opportunity to prepare, at which he is permitted to have the assistance of a lawyer, and during which he has a right to present his witnesses and proof, to cross-examine his adversary's witnesses, to argue that a decision be made in accordance with the law and the evidence, and often to have a trial before a jury

fairies *pl of* FAIRY

fairies'–butter \ˈ==ˌ==\ *n* **:** a blue-green alga (*Nostoc commune*) forming gelatinous sheets or pellets

fairies'–table \ˈ==ˌ==\ *n* **1 :** the meadow mushroom or any of several similar fungi **2 a :** a European marsh pennywort (*Hydrocotyle vulgaris*) **b :** the flat peltate leaf of the European marsh pennywort

fair·i·ly \ˈfa(a)rəlē, ˈfer-,ˈfār-, -li\ *adv* **:** in the manner of a fairy **:** lightly and delicately

¹**fair·ing** \ˈfa(a)riŋ, ˈfer-\ *n* -S [⁵*fair* + *-ing*] *Brit* **:** a present, cake or sweet, or souvenir purchased at a fair ⟨a ~ to be bought for those at home —Flora Thompson⟩

²**fairing** *n* -S [fr. gerund of ³*fair*] **:** a member or structure the primary function of which is to produce a smooth outline and to reduce drag or head resistance (as on an airplane)

fair·ish \ˈfa(a)rish, ˈfer-, -rēsh\ *adj* [¹*fair* + *-ish*] **:** tolerably good or large ⟨serves ~ food at controlled prices —Bruce Bliven b. 1889⟩ ⟨a ~ demand for . . . rarer items —Clifton Fadiman⟩ — **fair·ish·ly** *adv*

fair isle *n, often cap F&I* [fr. *Fair Isle,* one of the Shetland islands, where it originated] **:** a style of knitting consisting of simple geometric patterns in two or more colors forming horizontal bands

fair·lead \ˈ=ˌlēd\ *n* **1 a** *also* **fair·lead·er** \-ēdə(r)\ **:** a block, ring, or strip of plank with holes that serves as a guide for the running rigging or any ship's rope and keeps it from chafing **b :** a course of running ship's rope that avoids all chafing **2 :** an insulating tube through which the antenna passes from outside to the inside of an airplane; *also* **:** a guide or support for an airplane control cable that prevents chafing or fouling **3 :** a device that consists of pulleys or rollers arranged to permit reeling in of a cable from any direction and that is used in conjunction with winches and similar apparatus esp. in logging

fair leather *n* **:** leather not artificially colored

fair·ly *adv* [ME, fr. ¹*fair* + *-ly*] **1 a** (1) **:** HANDSOMELY, BEAUTIFULLY ⟨she likes to be overlooking the table with its ~ set dishes and silver —Eve Langley⟩ (2) *of writing* **:** in the manner of a final draft **:** NEATLY, ELEGANTLY ⟨one little essay . . . written out ~ for the press but never published —Richard Garnett †1906⟩ ⟨you excelled in writing ~ —George Lillo⟩ **b** *obs* **:** SOFTLY, QUIETLY, GENTLY **c** *obs* **:** COURTEOUSLY **2 a :** to the full degree or extent **:** CLEARLY, DEFINITELY, ACTUALLY, PLAINLY, DISTINCTLY, FULLY ⟨when the captain is on board and we are ~ off —Rachel Henning⟩ ⟨amongst the boys scurrying to their ten-o'clocks I ~ caught sight of him —*Atlantic*⟩ ⟨when I had him ~ seated in a hackney coach with me —James Boswell⟩ ⟨the chestnut, finding himself ~ in for it, struck out gamely —Henry Lapham⟩ ⟨badly wounded before the battle had ~ begun⟩ **b :** as it were **:** so to speak **:** ABSOLUTELY, POSITIVELY, DOWNRIGHT ⟨the pages ~ quiver with indignation —Alban Baer⟩ ⟨its waters . . . are ~ alive with crocodiles —Tom Marvel⟩ ⟨~ boiling over with pride —Dorothy C. Fisher⟩ ⟨~ lifted the waters of the gulf and hurled them through the city —A.F.Harlow⟩ **c :** SQUARELY, CLEANLY ⟨one of her 8-inch salvos smashed ~ into a large warship —*Time*⟩ **3 a :** in conformity with the evidence, with reason, or with one's merits **:** JUSTIFIABLY, PROPERLY, LEGITIMATELY, RIGHTFULLY ⟨our business is to show that the doctrine is false and this we may ~ claim to have done —A.J.Ayer⟩ ⟨his services have ~ earned him promotion⟩ **b** (1) **:** in a just or lawful manner **:** without fraud, injury, or unfair advantage **:** EQUITABLY ⟨fought and beat him ~⟩ ⟨come by something ~⟩ (2) **:** without bias or distortion **:** IMPARTIALLY, CANDIDLY, ACCURATELY, OBJECTIVELY ⟨the merits of the plea were ~ considered⟩ ⟨~ described as all very decayed and horrible⟩ **4 :** TOLERABLY, MODERATELY, RATHER ⟨a ~ difficult scientific text⟩ ⟨a ~ steady diet of lamb and beef⟩ **:** moderately well ⟨how are you getting along? Only ~⟩ **:** PLEASANTLY ⟨the evening passed away very ~ —Henry Lapham⟩

fairm \ˈfärm, ˈferm\ *Scot var of* FARM

fair maid *n* [by folk etymology fr. *fumado*] **:** a scup (*Stenotomus aculeatus*)

fair–maids–of–france \ˌ=ˈ==ˈ=\ *n pl but sing or pl in constr, cap 2d F* **:** the double garden form of any of several European plants (as garden buttercup, sneezewort, meadow saxifrage, or ragged robin)

fair–minded \ˈ=ˈ=\ *adj* **:** UNPREJUDICED, JUST, JUDICIAL, HONEST ⟨a *fair-minded* man⟩ ⟨his *fair-minded* and dispassionate analysis —*Times Lit. Supp.*⟩ ⟨attempt to be as *fair-minded* as possible —W.L.Sperry⟩

fair–mindedness *n* -ES **:** the quality or state of being fair-minded ⟨his resolute refusal to retaliate, his restraint and *fair-mindedness* won out —S.H.Adams⟩

fair·ness *n* -ES [ME *fairnesse,* fr. OE *fægernes,* fr. *fæger* fair + *-nes* -ness — more at FAIR] **1 :** the quality or state of being fair; *esp* **:** fair or impartial treatment **:** REASONABLENESS ⟨the guarantees of ~ contained in the judicial process —*Harvard Law Rev.*⟩ **2 :** the degree of streamlining (as of an airplane)

fairn·tick·le \ˈfernˌtikəl\ *var of* FERNTICKLE

fair play *n* **:** equitable or impartial treatment **:** JUSTICE ⟨passage of the *fair-play* amendment abolishing the practice of contested delegates voting in their own and other delegate contests —Roscoe Drummond⟩

fairs *pres 3d sing of* FAIR, *pl of* FAIR

fair shake *n* **:** fair chance ⟨give the negative side a *fair shake* —S.L.Payne⟩

fair–spoken \ˈ=ˈ==\ *adj* [ME *faire-spoken*] **:** using fair speech or uttered with fairness **:** BLAND, CIVIL, COURTEOUS, PLAUSIBLE

fairstitcher \ˈ=ˌ==\ *n* **:** an operator of a fair-stitching machine

fair stitching *n* **:** stitching that appears on the extension of a welt shoe to ornament and to bind the outsole to the welt

fair trade *n* **:** trade in conformity with a fair-trade agreement ⟨a *fair-trade* product⟩ ⟨abandonment of price fixing in small home appliances was a staggering blow to *fair trade* —A.R. Zipser⟩

fair–trade \ˈ=ˈ=\ *vt* [*fair trade*] **:** to market (a commodity) in compliance with the provisions of a fair-trade agreement — **fair trader** *n*

fair–trade agreement *n* **:** an agreement between a producer and a vendor (as a manufacturer and a retailer) that commodities bearing a trademark, label, or brand name of that producer be sold at or above a certain price, the agreement often being binding on all vendors in a state after one vendor has signed

fair–traded *adj* **:** protected or covered by a fair-trade agreement ⟨working for a law designed to end price cutting of *fair-traded* books⟩

fair–trade law *n* **:** a law authorizing fair-trade agreements

fair use *n* **:** a legal doctrine that portions of copyrighted materials may be used (as by publishing) without permission of the copyright owner provided the use is fair and reasonable, does not substantially impair the value of the materials, and does not curtail the profits reasonably expected by the owner, such use often being accompanied by fair comment

fair value *n* **:** a reasonable value (as set by courts and regulatory commissions) for property — used esp. in application to public-utility property for rate-making purposes

fairwater \ˈ=ˌ==\ *n* [³*fair* + *water*] **1 :** a device (as a sleeve about a propeller shaft) that is used to fair the lines of an underwater fitting **2 :** a streamlined bridge and conning tower of a submarine

fairway \ˈ=ˌ=\ *n* **1 a :** a navigable part of a river or bay through which boats enter or depart **:** a part of a harbor or channel that is kept open and unobstructed **b :** a stretch of clear or open water adjacent to an airport and used by seaplanes in landing and taking off **2 :** a clear or open path or space ⟨situated . . . in the very ~ of migrating bird hosts —Douglas Carruthers⟩ ⟨the ~ for cars is often choked by stream-lined hummocks of clay —G.W.Murray⟩ **3 :** a part of a golf course exclusive of tees, putting greens, and hazards that is prepared for play by cutting the grass to provide a fair lie for the ball — compare ROUGH

fair–weather \ˈ=ˈ==\ *adj* [*fair weather*] **1 :** suitable for, done during, or made in fair weather ⟨a *fair-weather* sail⟩ **2 :** active, effective, suitable or loyal only during a time of prosperity or when no danger or hardship is involved ⟨a *fair-weather* friend⟩ ⟨our banking system was often spoken of as a *fair-weather* system —E.W.Kemmerer⟩

fair white *n* **:** a light-complexioned or blond white person

¹**fairy** \ˈfa(a)rē, ˈfer-,ˈfār-, -ri\ *n* -ES [ME *faierie, fairie* fairyland, fairy people, enchantment, fr. OF *faerie, faierie,* fr. *fee, feie, fayee* fairy (fr. L *Fata* goddess of fate, fr. *fatum* fate) + *-erie* -ery — more at FATE] **1 :** a mythical being of folklore and romance usu. having diminutive human form and magic powers and dwelling on earth in close relationship with man: **a :** a dwarf creature typically having green clothes and hair, living underground or in stone heaps, and usu. exercising his magic powers to benevolent ends **b :** a diminutive sprite usu. in the shape of a delicate beautiful ageless winged woman dressed in diaphanous white clothing, inhabiting fairyland, but making usu. benevolent intervention in personal human affairs **c :** a tiny mischievous and protective creature in a household usu. associated with the hearth — compare BROWNIE, ELF, GOBLIN, LEPRECHAUN, PUCK **2 :** FAIRY GREEN **3** *slang* **a :** HOMOSEXUAL **b :** a markedly effeminate man suspected of homosexual tendencies

²**fairy** \ˈ\ *adj* **1 :** of or relating to a fairy **:** being a fairy ⟨the sprite made his ~ home in the cleft of an ancient tree⟩ ⟨the nuptials of the ~ queen⟩ **2 :** resembling or suggestive of a fairy in its delicacy or grace ⟨their porcelains . . . showed a subtle ~ fragility —*Time*⟩ ⟨the viaduct comes into view, so slender, so exquisitely graceful, that . . . it seems a mere ~ thing —O.S.Nock⟩

fairy arrow *n* **:** a flint arrowhead — compare THUNDERSTONE

fairy bell *n* **1** *also* **fairy cap** *or* **fairy finger** *or* **fairy glove :** FOXGLOVE 1 **2 :** a woodland herb (*Disporum lanuginosum*) of eastern No. America with terminal greenish flowers and red pulpy berries

fairy bluebird *n* **:** any of several largely brilliant blue Indian or East Indian passerine birds related to the leafbirds and constituting the genus *Irena*

fairy bouquet *n* **:** TOADFLAX 1

fairy butter *n* **1 :** any of various fungi (order Tremellales) having a gelatinous fruiting body (as *Exidia glandulosa* or *E. albida*) **2 :** FAIRIES'-BUTTER

fairy candle *n* **:** a bugbane (*Cimicifuga racemosa*)

fairy circle *n* **1 :** FAIRY RING **2 :** a shrubby form of the common juniper that often grows in ring-shaped masses

fairy club *n* **:** CLUB FUNGUS

fairy creeper *n* **:** CLIMBING FUMITORY

fairy cup *n* **1 :** COWSLIP 1a **2 :** BLOOD CUP **3 :** a miterwort (*Mitella diphylla*) of northeastern No. America usu. with two opposite leaves on the erect flowering stem that terminates in an upright raceme of white flowers

fairy fans *n pl but sing or pl in constr* **:** an annual Californian herb (*Clarkia breweri*) with showy pink fan-shaped petals

fairy flax *n* **:** PURGING FLAX

fairy–fringe \ˈ==ˌ=\ *n* **:** PURPLE-FRINGED ORCHID a

fairy godmother *n* **:** a generous friend or benefactor; *esp* **:** one that appears unexpectedly or at a time of urgent need ⟨our needy unemployed would be cared for when, as, and if some *fairy godmother* should happen on the scene —F.D.Roosevelt⟩

fairy gold *or* **fairy money** *n* **1 :** money held to be given by fairies but turned into rubbish when put to use **2 :** wealth or prosperity that may vanish as swiftly as it is acquired **:** precarious or illusory wealth ⟨was to have been, according to those who profited most from its *fairy gold,* an era that would transcend the business cycle —Stringfellow Barr⟩

fairy green *also* **fairy** *n* -ES **:** a moderate yellowish green that is greener and paler than tarragon, paler than malachite green, and less strong and slightly yellower than verdigris

fairy·ism \-ˌizəm\ *n* -S **:** the state of being or of being like a fairy

fairy lamp *n* **:** a candle-burning night-light usu. of colored glass with separate base and shade

fairy·land \ˈ==ˌland, -aa(ə)nd\ *n* **1 :** the land or habitat of fairies **2 :** a place of delicate beauty or magical charm ⟨a winter ~ of iced boughs and sparkling snow⟩

fairy lantern *n* **:** any of various plants of the genus *Calochortus* (esp. *C. alkus*)

fairylike \ˈ==ˌ=\ *adj* **:** resembling a fairy or what is made or done by fairies ⟨the ~ beauty of the moonlit glade⟩ ⟨a delicate ~ butterfly⟩

fairy lily *n* **1 :** ATAMASCO LILY **2 :** a rain lily (*Cooperia pedunculata*); *also* **:** its white flower resembling a lily

fairy lint *n* **:** PURGING FLAX

fairy martin *n* **:** an Australian swallow (*Hylochelidon ariel*) that builds flask-shaped nests of mud on cliffs

fairy palm *n* **:** a common shallow-water solitary hydroid (*Corynomorpha palma*) of the Pacific coast of No. America

fairy primrose *n* **1 :** a Chinese primrose (*Primula malacoides*) with long-stalked leaves and lilac or rose flowers **2 :** a European alpine primrose (*Primula minima*)

fairy prion *n* **:** a small Australian prion (*Pachyptila turtur*)

fairy ring *n* **1 :** a ring of mushrooms (*Marasmius oreades* or other basidiomycetes) that is produced at the periphery of mycelium which has grown centrifugally from an initial growth point and that increases in diameter from year to year; *also* **:** a ring of luxuriant vegetation associated with these mushrooms that also increases in diameter from year to year **2** *or* **fairy–ring mushroom :** a mushroom (esp. *Marasmius oreades*) that commonly grows in fairy rings

fairy ring spot *n* **:** a disease of carnations found esp. in the greenhouse and caused by a fungus (*Heterosporium echinulatum*) that produces on the leaves bleached spots with concentric dark zones

fairy rose *n* **:** any of various dwarf roses constituting a variety (*Rosa chinensis minima*) of the China rose and having small single or double flowers

fairy shrimp *n* **:** any of several freshwater branchiopod crustaceans (order Anostraca) so called from their delicate colors, transparency, and graceful motions (as the European *Eubranchipus diaphanus* or the No. American *E. vernalis*)

fairy slipper *n* **:** a bog orchid (*Calypso bulbosa*) native to Eurasia and established widely in No. America

fairy stone *n* **1 :** a stone arrowhead **2 :** any of various concretions and fossils of odd or fantastic shape: as **a :** a staurolite crystal **b :** a fossil sea urchin

fairy tale *or* **fairy story** *n* **1 a :** a simple narrative dealing with supernatural beings (as fairies, magicians, ogres, dragons) that is typically of folk origin and written or told for the amusement of children ⟨these ten short *fairy tales* to read aloud to younger children are in an old-fashioned mood —Louise S. Bechtel⟩ **b :** a more sophisticated narrative containing supernatural or obviously improbable events, scenes, and personages and often having a whimsical, satirical, or moralistic character ⟨an unusual adult *fairy tale* well designed to while away an evening —*N.Y. Times Book Rev.*⟩ **2 :** an implausible, incredible, or lying story **:** a story designed to delude or mislead ⟨*fairy tales* about atrocities committed by a barbarous enemy⟩ ⟨in spite of various *fairy tales* that have been spread . . . your power system is still paying taxes to the community —F.D.Roosevelt⟩

fairy–tale \ˈ==ˌ=\ *adj* [*fairy tale*] **:** characteristic of or suitable to a fairy tale **:** marked by exquisite or unreal beauty, grace, or perfection ⟨a thing of beauty, a *fairy-tale* body of water surrounded by little houses with red roofs —J.A.Michener⟩ ⟨its magnificent *fairy-tale* settings —Curtis Harrington⟩ ⟨the sort of *fairy-tale* dresses most women dream about —*Time*⟩ ⟨the *fairy-tale* America manufactured in Hollywood —J.W. Aldridge⟩

fairy tern *n* **:** any of various small terns: **a :** either of two pure white terns constituting a genus (*Gygis*) and living in tropical seas **b :** a small white black-capped tern (*Sterna nereis*) of the Australian region

fairy thimbles *n pl* **:** the blossoms of the foxglove

fairy wand *n* **:** a blazing star (*Chamaelirium luteum*) with a spike of white to greenish or yellow flowers

fairy wren *n* **:** any of numerous small Australian warblers (genus *Malurus*) having the male usu. brilliantly colored and the female drably brown

fais–do–do \ˌfāˌdōˈdō\ *n* -S [LaF, fr. F (baby-talk) *fais dodo!* go to sleep!; prob. fr. the fact that small children who attend the dances are expected to go to sleep during the festivities] **:** a country-dance or dancing party held usu. on a Saturday night in southern Louisiana

fait \ˈfāt\ *n* -S [ME, fr. MF, fr. L *factum* — more at FACT] **:** a legal deed, writing, or fact

fait ac·com·pli \fātakōⁿplē\ *n, pl* **faits accomplis** \-ē(z)\ [F, accomplished fact] **:** a thing accomplished and presumably irreversible **:** an accomplished fact ⟨intended to present the people with a *fait accompli* —Tor Myklebost⟩ ⟨was only asking formal approval of a *fait accompli* —*Current History*⟩

¹**faith** \ˈfāth\ *n, pl* **faiths** \-āths *also* -āt͟hz\ [ME *feith, fey,* fr. OF *feid* (*d* prob. pronounced \t͟h\), *fei, foi,* fr. L *fides;* akin to *fidere* to trust — more at BIDE] **1 a :** the act or state of wholeheartedly and steadfastly believing in the existence, power, and benevolence of a supreme being, of having confidence in his providential care, and of being loyal to his will as revealed or believed in **:** belief and trust in and loyalty to God ⟨people earnestly prayed in the ages of ~ . . . to be delivered from sudden death —J.A.Pike⟩ ⟨lost his ~ at an early age⟩ **b** (1) **:** an act or attitude of intellectual assent to the traditional doctrines of one's religion **:** orthodox religious belief (2) **:** a decision of an individual entrusting his life to God's transforming care in response to an experience of God's mercy **c** *among Roman Catholic theologians* **:** a supernatural virtue by which one believes on the authority of God himself all that God has revealed or proposes through the Church for belief **2 a** (1) **:** firm or unquestioning belief in something for which there is no proof ⟨for the scientist ~ can be no virtue, because it is inconsistent with the resolution to accept the fact as supreme —P.W.Bridgman⟩ ⟨clinging to the ~ that her missing son would one day return⟩ (2) **:** uncritical grounds for belief — used chiefly in the phrase *on faith* ⟨you will have to accept my statements on *faith*⟩ **b :** CONFIDENCE; *esp* **:** firm or unquestioning trust or confidence in the value, power, or efficacy of something ⟨have ~ in prayer⟩ ⟨~ in his medical skill⟩ ⟨the ~ on which science rests, the ~ in the value of truth seeking —H.T.Muller⟩ **3 a :** an assurance, promise, or pledge of fidelity, loyalty, or performance ⟨gave his ~ that he would come on the appointed day⟩ — often used in the phrases *to keep faith* or *to break faith* ⟨to have hitchhiked would have been breaking ~, for all who use the country's youth hostels are honor bound to reach them under their own power —H.V.Morton⟩ **b :** fidelity to one's promises **:** allegiance to a duty or a person **:** sincerity or honesty of intentions **:** LOYALTY — often used with the qualifiers *good* or *bad* to specify a state of mind of one trying to be honest and faithful ⟨observed perfect good ~ and strictly fulfilled their engagements —Marjory S. Douglas⟩ or of one trying to deceive, mislead, or defraud ⟨accused him of bad ~⟩ **4** *obs* **:** AUTHORITY, CREDIT, CREDIBILITY **5 :** something that is believed or adhered to esp. with strong conviction: as **a** (1) **:** a system of religious beliefs **:** RELIGION ⟨an individual of the Jewish ~⟩ (2) **:** the body of believers **:** an organized church or denomination ⟨a movement supported by all the great ~*s*⟩ **b :** the cherished values, ideals, or beliefs of an individual or people **:** WELTANSCHAUUNG, CREED, CREDO ⟨a free world which is strong in its ~ and in its material progress —Dean Acheson⟩ **c :** the fundamental tenets, views, or beliefs of an individual or group on a particular subject or in a particular field ⟨a profession of literary ~⟩ ⟨I state my own ~ at once . . . organic union under the Crown is vital —R.G.Menzies⟩ ⟨she visits the prisoners of her own political ~ —Katharine A. Porter⟩ **6** *often cap* **:** the true religion from the point of view of the speaker — usu. used with *the* ⟨the king, temporal head of the ~⟩ **syn** see BELIEF, RELIGION, TRUST — **in faith :** by my faith **:** VERILY

²**faith** \ˈ\ *vt* -ED/-ING/-S [ME *feithen,* fr. *feith,* n.] *archaic* **:** BELIEVE, TRUST

faith cure *n* **:** a method or practice of treating diseases by prayer and exercise of faith in God **:** a cure held to have been achieved by this method

fai·ther \ˈfāt͟hər, ˈfet͟h-\ *dial var of* FATHER

¹**faith·ful** \ˈfāthfəl\ *adj* [ME *feithful,* fr. *feith* faith + *-ful*] **1** *archaic* **:** full of faith **:** ready to believe esp. in the declarations and promises of God **2 :** true and constant in affection or allegiance **:** LOYAL ⟨a ~ friend⟩ ⟨a ~ dog⟩ **3 :** firm in adherence to promises, oaths, or undertakings **:** firm and thorough in the observance of duty **:** CONSCIENTIOUS ⟨a ~ public official⟩ ⟨~ to his plan of economy —W.M.Thackeray⟩ **4 :** given with strong or solemn assurances **:** BINDING ⟨a ~ promise⟩ **5 :** conforming to the facts or to an original **:** worthy of credence **:** ACCURATE, RELIABLE, EXACT, CREDIBLE ⟨the book presents a ~ picture of life in that century⟩ ⟨the painter . . . concerned . . . with the ~ rendering of the observed facts —*Encounter*⟩ ⟨a very ~ source⟩

syn LOYAL, LEAL, TRUE, CONSTANT, STAUNCH, STEADFAST, RESOLUTE: FAITHFUL implies firm and unhesitating adherence to whatever one is bound to by ties of honor, friendship, allegiance, or love ⟨the story of Lilla, *faithful* thane, who flung himself between his Northumbrian king, Edwin, and the sword of the assassin —H.O.Taylor⟩ ⟨she proved a good and *faithful* helpmate, assisted me much by attending the shop; we throve together, and have ever mutually endeavored to make each other happy —Benjamin Franklin⟩ LOYAL may indicate a continuing, reliable faithfulness and allegiance secure against wavering and temptation ⟨a trained and *loyal* army willing to sacrifice for the good of a common discipline —F.D.Roosevelt⟩ ⟨there was no man more *loyal* to his commander. On the morning of the mutiny there had not been a moment's hesitation in deciding where his duty lay —C.B.Nordhoff & J.N. Hall⟩ LEAL is a Scots or archaic form of *loyal* ⟨thou, Scotland's son, that would'st be *leal* and true —J.S.Blackie⟩ TRUE may add implications of deep inner fidelity and devotion ⟨goodhearted and *true,* full of sturdy, homely sense, willing to take care of a man's money, and make him a straightforward wife —George Moore⟩ ⟨in my judgment the Quakers are the *truest* Christians in the modern world —W.R.Inge⟩ CONSTANT indicates the fact of firm attachment or adherence but implies less than other words in this set about resolution or deep feeling ⟨if he will be *constant* and kind, and not forsake her —W.M.Thackeray⟩ ⟨his last and most *constant* love was for a Roman girl named Morosina —R.A.Hall b. 1911⟩ STAUNCH suggests resolution, fortitude, and conviction in adherence and imperviousness to influences which would weaken it ⟨*staunch* adherence to majority decisions and determination at all costs to preserve the unity of the party in the face of the political enemy are their forte —Woodrow Wyatt⟩ ⟨ever a *staunch*

Federalist, he viewed the policies of Jefferson and his followers with repugnance —E.E.Curtis⟩ STEADFAST indicates unwavering adherence unchanged over a period; like STAUNCH it may imply resolution ⟨hundreds of obscure martyrs now followed in the same path to another world, where surely they deserved to find their recompense if *steadfast* adherence to their faith, and a tranquil trust in God amid tortures and death too horrible to be related, had ever found favor above —J.L. Motley⟩ ⟨if President Lowell had not stood *steadfast* against alumni pressure, we would have today a giant stadium built in the gay twenties on borrowed money —J.B.Conant⟩ RESOLUTE implies steady firm determination to adhere ⟨an earthquake in the midst of the proceedings terrified every prelate but the *resolute* primate —J.R.Green⟩ ⟨your clients, sir, are happy in having so *resolute* a guardian of their confidence —Bram Stoker⟩

²**faithful** \"\ *n, pl* **faithful** *or* **faithfuls** **:** one that is faithful: as **a :** one of the adherents of a system of religious belief ⟨an Eastern Orthodox ~ is expected to attend church regularly⟩ ⟨sectarian schools supported by the fees and contributions of the ~ —C.A. & Mary Beard⟩ **b :** baptized Christians as opposed to catechumens — used with *the* ⟨the division between the liturgy of the catechumens and the liturgy of the ~ is still preserved in the Eastern Orthodox Church⟩ **c :** church members in full communion and good standing — used with *the* **d :** the body of adherents of the Muslim religion — used with *the* ⟨the Muslim congregation of all the ~ is a democratic one —Percival Spear⟩ **e :** a devoted or loyal follower of a cause or member of an organization ⟨only the party ~*s* and ignorant, duped immigrants ... favored his cause —M.D. Hirsch⟩ ⟨Dixieland jazz itself was losing popularity, except with the ~ who gathered in small, smoky cellar clubs to listen to it —Grady Johnson⟩ ⟨party ~*s* will prepare tea and meals for them —Ernie Hill⟩

faith·ful·ly \-fəlē, -li\ *adv* [ME *feithfully,* fr. *feithful* + *-ly*] **:** in a faithful manner: **a :** DUTIFULLY, LOYALLY **b :** ACCURATELY

faith·ful·ness \-fəlnə̇s\ *n* -ES [ME *feithfulnesse,* fr. *feithful* + *-nesse* -ness] **:** the quality or state of being faithful

faith healer *n* **:** one that practices faith healing

faith healing *n* **:** a method or practice of treating diseases by prayer and exercise of faith in God

faith·less \'fāthlə̇s\ *adj* [ME *feithles,* fr. *feith* faith + *-les* -less] **1** *archaic* **:** not believing **:** not giving credence **2 a** *archaic* **:** not believing in God or religion **b :** being without a faith **:** lacking strong convictions ⟨we live in a skeptical and ~ time⟩ **3 :** false to promises or agreements **:** not true to allegiance or duty **:** PERFIDIOUS, TREACHEROUS, DISLOYAL ⟨few of its teachers ... have been ~ to their society —C.W. de Kiewiet⟩ ⟨he abandoned one wife and was ~ to another — J.R.Green⟩ **:** INCONSTANT, FICKLE ⟨she had been too successful, and a ~ public was tired of her —Carl Van Vechten⟩ **4 a :** not to be relied on **:** UNSTABLE, ERRATIC ⟨they are at the mercy of an unseen instructor who can simulate violent weather and ~ machinery —*Time*⟩ **b :** not conforming to a standard or to an original **:** not true or accurate ⟨the disc has a heavy surface and the tone is ~ —Edward Sackville-West & Desmond Shawe-Taylor⟩

syn FALSE, DISLOYAL, TRAITOROUS, TREACHEROUS, PERFIDIOUS: FAITHLESS applies to any lack of adherence or devotion to a vow, pledge, allegiance, or loyalty ⟨the *faithless* conduct of the allies toward this dethroned monarch, who, after giving himself generously up to their mercy, was consigned to an ignoble and cruel banishment —W.M.Thackeray⟩ ⟨a woman who has been deserted by her lover will make a straw effigy of the *faithless* gallant —J.G.Frazer⟩ FALSE may center attention on the fact of failing to be true, reasons ranging from fickle negligence to cold treachery ⟨from the first hour of Edward's rule the threads of his diplomacy ran over Europe in almost inextricable confusion. And to all who dealt with him he was equally *false* and tricky —J.R.Green⟩ ⟨men, when they're *false,* and try to deceive young girls, and are playing their own wicked game with them, do not like to be bothered about such things —Anthony Trollope⟩ DISLOYAL indicates lack of complete faith, loyalty, and adherence to a person, cause, or country ⟨they had already assumed a tone in their correspondence which must have seemed often *disloyal,* and sometimes positively insulting, to the governor —J.L.Motley⟩ ⟨the *disloyal* subject who had fought against his rightful sovereign — T.B.Macaulay⟩ TRAITOROUS applies to committing, countenancing, or contemplating actual treason or similar serious betrayal ⟨*traitorous* generals collaborating with the enemy⟩ ⟨charged with *traitorous* contempt of the emperor —S.T. Coleridge⟩ TREACHEROUS is wider and less specific than TRAITOROUS; it may refer to any serious betrayal or inclination to betray or to anything likely to bring sudden peril or disaster unless one is quite wary ⟨thy kin of the days of old were an evil and *treacherous* folk, and they lied and murdered for gold —William Morris⟩ ⟨lighthouses were placed on *treacherous* parts of the coast —Lewis Mumford⟩ PERFIDIOUS may add to FAITHLESS implications of a base incapacity for fidelity; the word now seems rather declamatory or oratorical ⟨betrayed by his *perfidious* allies⟩ ⟨a *perfidious* violation of a treaty⟩ ⟨*perfidious* Mrs. Albion who had her spouse, Albion I, murdered by a lover acquired for the purpose —Claudia Cassidy⟩

faith·less·ly *adv* **:** in a faithless manner

faith·less·ness *n* -ES **:** the quality or condition of being faithless

faiths *pl of* FAITH, *pres 3d sing of* FAITH

fai·tour \'fād·ə(r)\ *n* -S [ME, fr. AF, fr. OF *faitor* founder, perpetrator, fr. L *factor* maker, doer — more at FACTOR] *archaic* **:** CHEAT, IMPOSTOR

fai·tours grass \'fād·ə(r)z-\ *n* [ME *faytowrys gresse*] **:** LEAFY SPURGE

faits *pl of* FAIT

faize \'fāz\ *Scot var of* ²FEAZE

fa·ja \'fä(,)hä\ *n* -S [Sp, sash, band, prob. fr. Catal *faixa,* fr. L *fascia* band, bandage — more at FASCIA] **:** a wide bright sash worn around the waist by Spaniards and Latin Americans

¹**fake** \'fāk\ *or* **flake** \'flāk\ *vt* -ED/-ING/-S [ME *faken*] **:** to coil (as a ship's rope, line, or hawser or a fire hose) in fakes esp. by winding in layers usu. of zigzag or figure-eight form, to prevent twisting and fouling when running out — often used with *down* ⟨~ down line⟩ or *out* ⟨there's an old twelve-inch hawser *faked* out down there —Chesley Wilson⟩

²**fake** \"\ *or* **flake** \"\ *n* -S **:** one loop of a coil (as of ship's rope) that is coiled free for running

³**fake** \"\ *vb* -ED/-ING/-S [origin unknown] *vt* **1 :** to alter, manipulate, or treat so as to impart a false character to for legitimate or illegitimate reasons **:** cause to appear something other than it is **:** tamper with **:** DOCTOR, COLOR ⟨the well-known biologist who did ~ his results was driven to suicide by the disgrace of exposure —H.J.Muller⟩ ⟨~ the fight until the twelfth round, for the sake of the money —Donn Byrne⟩ ⟨~ the perspective in such a way that the stage appears grander the farther one is from it —*Atlantic*⟩ — often used with *up* ⟨in consequence of the *faked*-up narrative the world of Columbus's discovery would be named America —S.E. Morison⟩ ⟨two small beds *faked* up to look like an enormous bed —Daniel Curley⟩ **2 a :** to counterfeit or make a counterfeit of with fraudulent intent ⟨~ a painting⟩ **b :** to devise an acceptable substitute for ⟨a printer may ~ a foreign accent not carried in stock⟩ **3 a :** to create the illusion of the reality or existence of **:** cause (something inexistent) to appear as real or existing **:** CONCOCT, FABRICATE, SIMULATE, PRETEND ⟨*faked* 38 claims ... for damages incurred in mythical automobile accidents —Henry La Cossitt⟩ ⟨*faked* his own kidnapping in order to avoid extradition to England —M.S.Mayer⟩ ⟨had *faked* an interview with the prime minister that caused a sensation⟩ ⟨*faked* a surprise that was transparently bogus⟩ **b :** to deceive (an opponent) in a sports contest by a simulated movement ⟨busily *faking* two other men out of position —Roy McHugh⟩ **4** *slang* **:** IMPROVISE, AD-LIB ⟨whistle a few bars ... and I'll ~ the rest —Robert Sylvester⟩ ⟨~ a bass accompaniment⟩ ~ *vi* **:** to engage in faking something **:** PRETEND ⟨she's not sick, he's just *faking*⟩

⁴**fake** \"\ *n* -S **1 a :** an article or object simulating one that is genuine; *often* **:** a worthless or spurious imitation passed off as genuine to deceive esp. for gain ⟨experts called the priceless antique a ~⟩ **b :** a report, story, or account spurious in its details, conclusions, or presentation; *esp* **:** one intended to delude for gain or advantage ⟨the adventures of the spy turned out to be a series of ~*s*⟩ **c :** a device, plan, stratagem, or act designed to fool, trick, or defraud **:** FEINT, TRICK, HOAX ⟨the new wonder gasoline was a complete ~⟩: as (1) **:** a simulated movement in a sports contest (as a pretended kick or pass) designed to deceive an opponent (2) *or* **feke** \"\ **:** a device or apparatus used by a magician to achieve the illusion of magic in a trick **d :** a person passing himself off for what he is not **:** PRETENDER, IMPOSTOR, CHARLATAN ⟨medical ~ — Agnes N. Keith⟩ **2 :** a genuine postage stamp fraudulently treated in an attempt to convert it into a more valuable philatelic variety **3 :** a mixture of waxes and dressing for finishing edges and bottoms of shoe soles **syn** see IMPOSTURE

⁵**fake** \"\ *adj* [⁴*fake*] **:** simulating the genuine person, thing, or article **:** being a fake **:** FALSE, SHAM, SPURIOUS, COUNTERFEIT, PRETENDED ⟨skirt is supplied with flap pockets that are completely ~ —*New Yorker*⟩ ⟨a phony physicist and one ~ air force colonel —Greer Williams⟩ ⟨~ patriotism⟩ ⟨~ amnesia victims⟩ ⟨hand-screened prints and crusts of ~ diamonds and pearls —*advt*⟩ **syn** see COUNTERFEIT

fake·ment \-mənt\ *n* -S [³*fake* + *-ment*] **:** something faked **:** a contrivance or device used to deceive

fak·er \'fākə(r)\ *n* -S [³*fake* + *-er*] **:** one that fakes: as **a :** a person who makes fakes ⟨sought by the genealogical scholar and the pedigree ~ alike —A.R.Wagner⟩ **b :** a street or fair vendor who seeks to deceive by ascribing great value or efficacy to cheap or worthless products **:** FRAUD, SWINDLER ⟨the business objective of the old medicine-show ~*s* was to ... defraud the public —C.M.Babcock⟩ **c :** one that passes himself off as something other than he is or pretends to qualities or abilities that he does not possess **:** PRETENDER, IMPOSTOR, PHONY ⟨more honest than the majority of art lovers and concertgoers, most of whom he regards as ... cultural ~*s* —Hunter Mead⟩

fak·ery \-k(ə)rē, -ri\ *n* -ES [³*fake* + *-ery*] **:** the practice or a product of faking ⟨this, according to insurance men, was something unique in ~ —Henry La Cossitt⟩ ⟨were persuaded that the bells were not cast-iron *fakeries* only after sledgehammers failed to crack them —*Time*⟩

fakey \'fākē, -ki\ *adj* [⁴*fake* + *-y*] **:** FAKE

fa·kir \fə'ki(ə)r *or* fä'- *or* fa'- *or* -iə, *in sense 2* 'fākə(r)\ *n* -S [Ar *faqīr* poor] **1** *or* **fa·qir** *or* **fa·quir** \"\ **:** a Muslim mendicant or ascetic; *also* **:** an itinerant wonder-worker of other religions **2** [by folk etymology fr. *faker*] **:** FAKER; *esp* **:** SWINDLER ⟨the ~*s* who accompany a circus came up in full force to ply their games —D.D.Martin⟩ **3 :** PEACHBLOW 1

fa la *also* **fal la** \(')fä(l)¦lä\ *n* -S [fr. *fa-la,* frequent meaningless syllables in the refrains of such songs] **:** a 16th and 17th century part-song that is like a dance in character **:** BALLAD ⟨another kind of ballets commonly called *fa las* —Thomas Morley⟩

fal·a·na·ka \,falə'näkə\ *also* **fal·a·nouc** \¦falə¦nük\ *n* -S [Malagasy] **:** a viverrine mammal (*Eupleres goudotii*) of Madagascar closely related to the Asiatic palm civet

fa·lan·gist \fə'lanjə̇st *also* 'fā,l- *or* fä'l-\ *n* -S *often cap* [Sp *Falangista,* fr. *Falange* (*Española*) Spanish Phalanx, a Spanish fascist organization; Sp *falange,* fr. L *phalang-, phalanx* — more at PHALANX] **:** a member of the Spanish fascist organization Falange

fa·la·sha \fə'läshə\ *n, pl* **falasha** *or* **falashas** *usu cap* [Amharic *fälasha,* fr. *fälasi* sojourner, stranger] **1 :** a people in Ethiopia that are Jewish in religion but similar in biological type to the Galla **2 :** a member of the Falasha people

fal·ba·la \'falbələ\ *n* -S [F, fr. F dial. *ferbelà, farbélla*] **:** a flounce or trimming for a woman's garment (as a petticoat, apron, or scarf)

fal·ca·ta \fal'käd·ə, fōl-, -kād·ə\ [NL, fr. L, *falcatus* falcate] *syn of* AMPHICARPA

fal·cate \'fal,kāt, 'fōl-\ *adj* [L *falcatus,* fr. *falc-, falx* sickle, scythe + *-atus* -ate] **:** hooked or curved like a sickle ⟨a ~ leaf⟩ ⟨a ~ claw⟩ — used also of the moon or an inferior planet when less than half its disk is illuminated

fal·cat·ed \-,kād·ə̇d\ *adj* [L *falcatus* + E *-ed*] **:** FALCATE

falcated teal *also* **falcated duck** *n* **:** a teal (*Anas falcata*) of Asia, the male having an iridescent bronze head with slightly shaggy crest and drooping scapulars

falces *pl of* FALX

fal·chion \'fōlchən, -lsh-\ *n* -S [ME *fauchoun,* fr. OF *fauchon,* fr. *fauchier* to mow, fr. (assumed) VL *falcare,* fr. L *falc-, falx* sickle, scythe] **1** *archaic* **:** a broad-bladed slightly curved sword used in the middle ages **2** *archaic* **:** a sword of any kind

fal·cial \'falshəl, 'fōl-, -lch-\ *adj* [NL *falc-, falx* + E *-ial*] **:** of or belonging to a falx

fal·ci·form \'falsə,fȯrm, 'fōl-\ *adj* [L *falc-, falx* sickle + E *-iform*] **:** having the shape of a scythe or sickle

falciform ligament *n* **:** an anteroposterior fold of peritoneum attached to the under surface of the diaphragm and sheath of the rectus muscle and along a line on the anterior and upper surfaces of the liver extending back from the notch on the anterior margin

fal·cip·a·rum malaria \fal¦'sipərəm-, fōl¦\ *n* [*falciparum,* NL (specific epithet of *Plasmodium falciparum*), fr. L *falci-* (fr. *falc-, falx* sickle) + L *-parum* (neut. of *-parus* -parous)] **:** severe malaria caused by a malaria parasite (*Plasmodium falciparum*) and marked by recurrence of paroxysms usu. in less than 48 hours — called also *malignant malaria, subtertian malaria;* compare VIVAX MALARIA

fal·co \'fal(,)kō, 'fōl-\ *n, cap* [NL, fr. LL, falcon] **:** the type genus of Falconidae comprising the typical falcons

¹**fal·con** \'falkən *also* 'fōlk- *sometimes* 'fōk-\ *n* -S [ME *faucoun, falcon,* fr. OF *faucon, falcon,* fr. LL *falcon-, falco,* prob. of Gmc origin; akin to OHG *falcho* falcon, MLG *valke,* and to the masculine name *Falco* attested among Lombards, Visigoths, and Franks; prob. fr. a prehistoric Gmc compound whose constituents are akin respectively to OHG *falo* pale, faded, dun-colored and OHG *-h, -ch* (suffix designating a bird) — more at FALLOW] **1 a :** any of various hawks trained or adapted for use in the sport of hawking; *esp* **:** PEREGRINE FALCON — used technically only of a female; see TIERCEL; compare IGNOBLE HAWK, NOBLE HAWK **b :** any of various hawks of the family Falconidae distinguished by their long wings, by having a distinct notch and tooth or sometimes two teeth on the edge of the upper mandible where it begins to bend down, and by their usu. plunging down on their prey from above in hunting — compare ACCIPITER **c :** HAWK 1a **2 :** a light piece of ordnance used from the 15th to the 17th centuries

²**falcon** \"\ *vi* **falconed; falconed; falconing** \-k(ə)niŋ\ **falcons :** to hunt with falcons

falcon-beaked \¦==¦=\ *adj* **:** having a curved beak

fal·con·er \-k(ə)nə(r)\ *n* -S [ME *fauconer,* fr. OF *fauconier,* fr. *faucon* + *-ier* -er — more at FALCON] **:** a person who breeds or trains hawks for taking birds or game **:** one who follows the sport of fowling with hawks

fal·co·nes \fal'kō(,)nēz, fōl-\ *n pl, cap* [NL, fr. pl. of *Falcon-, Falco*] **:** a suborder of Falconiformes comprising the hawks, falcons, eagles, Old World vultures, ospreys, caracaras, and secretary birds — compare CATHARTAE

fal·con·et \¦falkə¦net, ¦fōlk-, ¦fōk-\ *n* -S [¹*falcon* + *-et*] **1 :** a smaller type of falcon (sense 2) **2 :** any of several very small Asiatic falcons constituting a genus (*Microhierax*) **3 :** any of several Australian insectivorous passerine birds (genus *Falcunculus*) — called also *shrike tit*

falcon-gentle \¦==¦==\ *n* [ME *faucoun gentil* peregrine falcon, fr. MF *faucon gentil,* lit., noble falcon] **:** the female peregrine falcon — used in the technical language of falconry

fal·con·i·dae \fal'känə,dē, fōl-, -kōn-\ *n pl, cap* [NL, fr. *Falcon-, Falco,* type genus + *-idae*] **:** a family of diurnal birds of prey now usu. restricted to the long-winged swift-flying falcons and the caracaras but formerly including most hawks, eagles, buzzards, Old World vultures, and related forms — compare ACCIPITRIDAE

fal·co·ni·for·mes \(,)fal,kōnə'fȯr(,)mēz, (,)fōl-\ *n pl, cap* [NL, fr. *Falcon-, Falco* + *-iformes*] **:** an order of chiefly diurnal flesh-eating birds having short stout hooped bills and strong feet with four toes, the young being helpless at hatching and fed in the nest, and including the hawks, eagles, vultures, and related birds — see CATHARTAE, FALCONES

fal·co·nine \'falkə,nīn, 'fōlk-,'fōk-\ *adj* [¹*falcon* + *-ine*] **:** belonging to or resembling a falcon

fal·con·ry \-kənrē, -ri\ *n* -ES [F *fauconnerie,* fr. *faucon* falcon + *-erie* -ery — more at FALCON] **1 :** the art of training falcons to pursue and to attack wild fowl or game **2 :** the sport of taking wild fowl or game by the use of falcons — called also *hawking*

fal·cu·la \'falkyələ, 'fōl-\ *n* -S [L, lit., small sickle, dim. of *falc-, falx* sickle] **:** a curved and sharp-pointed claw or process (as of a cat); *specif* **:** the cerebral falx

fal·cu·lar \-lə(r)\ *adj* [L *falcula* + E *-ar*] **1 :** shaped like a sickle **2 :** belonging to or indicating a falcula or falx ⟨~ cilia⟩

fal·cu·late \-,lāt\ *adj* [L *falcula* + E *-ate*] *zool* **:** curved and sharp-pointed

faldage *var of* FOLDAGE

falderal *var of* FOLDEROL

faldistory *n* -ES [ML *faldistorium*] *obs* **:** FALDSTOOL 1

fald·stool \'fōl(d),stül\ *n* [part trans. of ML *faldistolium, faldistorium,* of Gmc origin; akin to OS *faldistōl* folding chair — more at FAUTEUIL] **1 :** a folding stool or chair; *specif* **:** such a chair used by a bishop when not occupying his throne or when officiating outside his own cathedral church **2 :** a similar stool or small desk at which one kneels during devotions; *esp* **:** one used by the king of England at his coronation **3 :** the desk from which the litany is read in churches of the Anglican Communion

faldstool 1

¹**fa·le·ri·an** \fə'lirēən\ *adj, usu cap* [*Falerii,* ancient city of central Italy (now Civita Castellana) + E *-an*] **:** of or relating to ancient Falerii

²**falerian** \"\ *n* -S *cap* **1 :** an inhabitant of Falerii **2 :** FALISCAN

fa·ler·ni·an \fə'lərnēən\ *adj, usu cap* [L *falernus* Falernian + E *-ian*] **:** of or coming from a district of Campania called Falernus ager by the Romans — used esp. of a wine celebrated by Horace

Fa·ler·num \fə'lərnəm\ *trademark* — used for a sweet white flavoring syrup of low alcoholic content often used as a cocktail ingredient

¹**fa·lis·can** \fə'liskən\ *adj, usu cap* [L *Faliscus* + E *-an*] **:** of or relating to the Falisci who inhabited the city of Falerii and its region in ancient Etruria; *also* **:** relating to or constituting their dialect **:** FALERIAN

²**faliscan** \"\ *n* -S *cap* **1 :** one of the Falisci **2 :** the dialect of Latin of the Faliscans that is known from a small body of inscriptions written in an alphabet of Etruscan origin and is sometimes regarded as a language

fa·lis·ci \fə'li,sī, -li,skē\ *n pl, cap* [L] **:** an ancient people of Italic origin who were located in southern Etruria in the 5th century B.C. and whose chief town was Falerii

¹**fall** \'fōl\ *vb* **fell** \'fel\ **fall·en** \'fōlən *also in poetry & sometimes + V in prose* -ln\ *also dial* **fell; falling; falls** [ME *fallen,* fr. OE *feallan;* akin to OFris & ON *falla* to fall, OS & OHG *fallan,* and perh. to Lith *pulti* to fall, OPruss *aupallai* he finds, Arm *p'ul* fall, plunge] *vi* **1 a** (1) **:** to descend by the force of gravity when freed from suspension or support **:** DROP ⟨the rain ~*s*⟩ ⟨ripe fruit ~*ing* off a tree⟩ (2) **:** to pass downward in a certain direction **:** drop in a guided descent ⟨the water ~*s* over the ledge⟩ ⟨the mercury ~*s* in the thermometer⟩ ⟨the lash *fell* on his shoulders⟩ (3) **:** to hang freely **:** extend downward ⟨her hair ~*s* loosely⟩ ⟨his cloak ~*s* from his shoulders⟩ (4) **:** to let oneself down usu. swiftly and suddenly to a sitting, reclining, or kneeling position ⟨she *fell* on the window seat by the coat closet and began to sob —Louis Auchincloss⟩ ⟨I was her slave; I *fell* at her feet —A.W.Long⟩; *sometimes* **:** to leap from a great height ⟨the column was popular with suicides, some of whom *fell* to their death before the top was enclosed in a cage —*Sydney (Australia) Bull.*⟩ **b** (1) **:** to become born — now usu. used of lambs (2) **:** to drop to a lower degree ⟨the temperature *fell*⟩ or level ⟨blood pressure *fell* to 140 systolic⟩ (3) **:** to decrease in volume of sound **:** drop in pitch ⟨his voice *fell*⟩ ⟨the music rose and *fell*⟩ (4) **:** ISSUE — used of speech ⟨the excellent advice that *fell* from his lips⟩ (5) **:** to come or come to pass as if by falling ⟨an ominous stillness *fell* upon the room⟩ ⟨night *fell* upon the village⟩ ⟨a heavy vengeance *fell* upon the rebels⟩ (6) **:** to become lowered — used of a glance or the eyes **2 a :** to drop suddenly and involuntarily ⟨~ down on the ice⟩ ⟨slipped and *fell* heavily to the ground⟩ **b** (1) **:** to enter as if blindly or unawares into a dangerous or undesirable state or situation **:** STUMBLE, STRAY — used with *in* or *into* ⟨*fell* into the enemy ambush⟩ ⟨~*ing* into the moral snares of a great city⟩ ⟨*fell* into grave doctrinal errors⟩ ⟨the novel ~*s* into a cloying sentimentality⟩ (2) *of a structure* **:** to collapse esp. in fragments ⟨many houses *fell* as a result of the earthquake⟩ ⟨the building *fell* of its own weight⟩ (3) **:** to drop to the ground wounded or dead ⟨men were ~*ing* all about him under the enemy fire⟩; *esp* **:** to die in battle ⟨the *fallen* included numerous officers⟩ ⟨*fell* in the first skirmish of the war⟩ (4) **:** to suffer destruction, capture, or total military defeat **:** COLLAPSE ⟨scholars still argue about why the Roman Empire *fell*⟩ ⟨the city *fell* after a siege of many months⟩ (5) **:** to lose office esp. as a result of an adverse parliamentary vote — used of a government or ministry ⟨the coalition government *fell* after only 6 months in office⟩ (6) **:** to suffer ruin, defeat, or failure **:** fail utterly ⟨we will stand or ~ together⟩ — used chiefly of projects or undertakings and in the phrase *fall through* ⟨your paper's ~*ing* through for no money and you want me to give you some? —Josephine Johnson⟩ ⟨I do not remember why the deal *fell* through —A.L.Guérard⟩ (7) **:** LAPSE, EXPIRE **:** PERISH, DISAPPEAR ⟨the conversation *fell* for a few minutes —Arnold Bennett⟩ ⟨his anger suddenly *fell*⟩ — often used with *away* ⟨if you have some other witness ... this difficulty will ~ away —*Farmer's Weekly (So. Africa)*⟩ (8) *card games* **:** to become played — used of a card whose holder must legally though unwillingly play it (9) *cricket, of a wicket* **:** to become lost by the dismissal of a batsman ⟨the first wicket *fell* with 50 runs on the board⟩ **c :** to yield to temptation **:** commit an immoral act ⟨if ~*ing* were all that ever happened to a good man, all his days would he a simple matter of striving and repentance —Owen Wister⟩; *esp* **:** to lose one's chastity **3 a** (1) *of a river* **:** to flow down **:** DEBOUCH, EMPTY — used with *into* ⟨the rivers that ~ into the sea⟩ (2) **:** to move or extend in a generally downward direction ⟨the land ~*s* to a river⟩ — often used with *away* ⟨the ridge ~*s* away quickly where it approaches the sea —Norman Cousins⟩ ⟨the ground ~*ing* away from the highest point —Osbert Lancaster⟩ **b** (1) **:** to cease to be violent **:** SUBSIDE, ABATE ⟨the flames rose and *fell*⟩ ⟨the wind *fell*⟩ **:** EBB ⟨the ~*ing* tide⟩ (2) **:** to decline in quality, character, activity, or quantity ⟨the party's representation in the legislature *fell* from seven seats to six⟩ ⟨after his book on the circulation of the blood came out ... he *fell* mightily in his practice —John Aubrey⟩ ⟨greater increases would merely influence traffic to ~ more sharply —*Collier's Yr. Bk.*⟩ ⟨how low can a man ~⟩ — often used with *off* or *away* ⟨the tourist trade *fell* off markedly in January —R.F.Warner⟩ ⟨the play ~*s* off toward the end⟩ ⟨his work *fell* off badly⟩ ⟨subscriptions *fell* away —C.L.R.James⟩ ⟨the poem does not ~ away from its opening line —Oscar Cargill⟩ (3) **:** to lose physical tone, condition, or weight **:** become wasted — usu. used with *off* or *away* ⟨the cattle have *fallen* off badly in the drouth⟩ ⟨you'd scarcely believe anybody could ~ off so rapidly —Ellen Glasgow⟩ ⟨she's *fallen* away terribly⟩ (4) **:** to assume a look of shame, disappointment, or dejection — used of the face ⟨his face *fell*⟩ (5) **:** to decline in financial value or price **:** suffer a decline in prices ⟨stocks *fell* several points⟩ ⟨the market is ~*ing*⟩ **c :** to make a hostile move or attack physically or verbally — now used with *on* or *upon* ⟨*fell* upon the enemy and routed him⟩ ⟨the opposition speakers *fell* clamorously on the tottering government⟩ **4 a** (1) **:** to come or occur at a certain time **:** ARRIVE ⟨prevent the harvest seasons from coming in time to ~ outside of their proper agricultural seasons —T.H.Gaster⟩ ⟨the beginnings of his career *fell* at the period ... when the vogue of field games ... was beginning —E.P.Tanner⟩ (2) **:** to come by chance

: happen to come ⟨it *fell* into my mind to write you a letter⟩ ⟨hurried me frequently into intrigues with low women that *fell* in my way —Benjamin Franklin⟩ **b** (1) **:** to come or pass by lot, assignment, inheritance, or as a burden or duty **:** DEVOLVE ⟨the estate *fell* to his brother⟩ ⟨the lot *fell* on him⟩ ⟨it *fell* to him to break the news⟩ (2) *dial Brit* **:** to have need or occasion **:** become obliged or due — used with *to* **c** *archaic* **:** to come or be due in the course of events — followed by *to be* and usu. a participle **d** (1) **:** to lie in a certain position ⟨the point ~*s* to the right of a given line⟩ **:** have the proper place or station ⟨the accent ~*s* on the second syllable⟩ (2) **:** to come within the limits, scope, or jurisdiction of something **:** have a definite position in a classificatory system or arrangement — often used with *into, within,* or *under* ⟨this word ~*s* into the class of verbs⟩ ⟨obviously *fell* within the Soviet sphere of influence —Max Ascoli⟩ ⟨~*s* within the jurisdiction of this city⟩ ⟨species ~ under genera⟩ (3) **:** to divide naturally — usu. used with *into* ⟨his creative output ~*s* into three distinct classes⟩ ⟨the area ~*s* into a number of physiographic regions⟩ (4) **:** to break up **:** SEPARATE ⟨they *fell* into two factions —R.A.Billington⟩ ⟨under the enemy thrust, the division *fell* to pieces⟩ **5 a :** to pass usu. somewhat suddenly and passively into a certain state of body or mind or a new condition or relation **:** BECOME ⟨*fell* at musing —Hugh McCrae⟩ ⟨I *fell* silent⟩ ⟨*fell* prey to dangerous diseases⟩ ⟨the brittle dish *fell* apart⟩ ⟨the tax ~*s* due this month⟩ ⟨*fell* heir to the estate⟩ ⟨*fell* in love⟩ — often used with *into* ⟨*fell* into a heavy slumber⟩ ⟨ran a street or two . . . and then *fell* into a walk —Arthur Morrison⟩ ⟨the word *fell* into disuse⟩ **b :** to come by chance into close or friendly dealings with a particular individual or group **:** have a chance encounter ⟨at college he *fell* into a congenial crowd of artistic and literary young men⟩ — often used in the phrases *fall among* or *fall in with* ⟨a bluff and simple country gentleman who had inadvertently *fallen* among politicians —C.H.Driver⟩ ⟨*fell* in with a Russian gentleman and his daughter —Norman Douglas⟩ ⟨he thought he was close to land when he *fell* in with a ship —Walter Hayward⟩ **c :** to set about usu. heartily or actively **:** BEGIN — often used with an infinitive of action ⟨*fell* to work⟩ or a verbal noun after the prefix *a-* ⟨*fell* a-laughing⟩ **6** *archaic* **a :** to revert to a feudal superior — used of a benefice **b :** to become vacant — used of an office **7 :** to have a certain direction or point of incidence **:** STRIKE, IMPINGE ⟨a ray of light *fell* on the table⟩ ⟨music ~*ing* on the ear⟩ ⟨the shot *fell* a great distance from its target⟩ **8 a :** to form an ardent and usu. sudden attachment **:** become passionately or blindly fond or enamored ⟨one look at the girl and he *fell* — but hard⟩ — usu. used with *for* ⟨have you *fallen* for that young female grasshopper . . . at your age —Sinclair Lewis⟩ ⟨he has *fallen* for the ravishing widow —C.J.Rolo⟩ **b :** to become victim of a hoax or deception **:** become gulled or deceived ⟨they just don't ~ any more —Reed Whittemore⟩ — usu. used with *for* ⟨a reform movement that has *fallen* for a panacea —F.L. Allen⟩ **9** *slang* **:** to undergo arrest ⟨he *fell* twice, for theft and burglary —Wallace Beene⟩ **~ *vt* 1** *archaic* **:** to let drop or bring down (as tears or a weapon) **2** *dial Eng* **:** to receive as one's share **:** GET **3 :** FELL *vt* 1

syn FALL, DROP, SINK, SLUMP, and SUBSIDE can mean in common to go or to let go downward freely. FALL, intransitive, suggests a descent by the force of gravity, always implying a loss of support opposing gravity in extension applying to anything extending downward or going figuratively in a downward direction ⟨let a glass *fall* to the ground and shatter⟩ ⟨the supports gone, the structure *fell* in a heap⟩ ⟨the roof had *fallen* in on another speaker —Bennett Cerf⟩ ⟨hair *falling* over a woman's shoulders⟩ ⟨the birthrate *fell* over a 6-month period, then rose⟩ ⟨let *fall* a remark about the weather⟩ DROP usu. stresses a speed, directness, unexpectedness, or casualness in falling or allowing to fall ⟨*dropped* a coin into a pond⟩ ⟨*dropped* seeds into holes⟩ ⟨*dropping* to the ground at the sound of an air-raid warning⟩ ⟨*dropping* a hint of coming trouble⟩ ⟨income figures *dropped* during the slow winter season⟩ SINK implies a gradual descending motion, esp. into something, often to the point of total submersion ⟨the ship *sank* gradually into the placid sea⟩ ⟨the float on the fish line *sank* a moment, then bobbed furiously⟩ ⟨the thermometer *sank* to far below zero —Douglas Carruthers⟩ ⟨*sinking* to her knees from exhaustion⟩ SLUMP now implies a falling or collapsing as of someone suddenly powerless or suddenly totally enervated ⟨*slumping* to the ground, unconscious⟩ ⟨*slumped* in his seat⟩ ⟨prices *slumped* badly in the winter⟩ ⟨when a bird falls asleep, it relaxes and *slumps* down until its body rests against the perch —J.H.Baker⟩ SUBSIDE suggests a gradual descent or return to a normal or usual position, action, or condition after an undue rising, expanding, boiling up; often it can suggest a sinking below a normal or usual level ⟨a wind rising then *subsiding*⟩ ⟨he lost a quarter of an hour waiting for the flood to *subside* —Mary Austin⟩ ⟨the bustle *subsides* and relative calm is resumed —*Amer. Guide Series: N.C.*⟩ ⟨the child's quick temper *subsided* into listlessness —Agnes Repplier⟩ ⟨after the boom prices *subsided* to a level far below normal⟩

—fall a cropper : to come a cropper — **fall by the wayside 1 :** to fall from grace **2 :** to suffer defeat esp. in a contest ⟨many party stalwarts *fell by the wayside* on election day⟩ ⟨some *fell by the wayside* in encounters with unconquered squads —*N.Y. Times*⟩ — **fall down :** to sail or drift down (as a river or harbor) — **fall flat :** to produce no response or result **:** fail of the intended effect ⟨his homespun jokes . . . *fell flat* on those grim-faced men —R.W.Thorp⟩ — **fall foul 1 :** to have a collision **:** become entangled — used chiefly of ships **2 :** to have a quarrel **:** CLASH — often used with *of* ⟨*fell foul* of one another⟩ **3** *archaic* **:** to make an attack — **fall from** *obs* **:** fail in duty to **:** DESERT — **fall from grace 1 :** to forfeit one's state of acceptance with God ⟨some believe that it is not possible for a saved person to *fall from grace* —J.C. Swaim⟩ **2 :** BACKSLIDE — **fall home :** to curve inward — used of the timbers or upper parts of a ship's side that are much within a perpendicular; compare TUMBLE HOME — **fall into line 1 :** to fall in **2 :** to comply or concur with a certain course of action or policy — **fall off the roof :** MENSTRUATE — **fall on** *or* **fall upon :** to meet with (a particular and usu. unfortunate kind of experience) **:** come upon ⟨an aristocratic girl . . . *fallen on* hard times —*Newsweek*⟩ ⟨*fell on* evil days⟩ — **fall on one's face :** to fail completely or resoundingly **:** fail so completely as to appear ridiculous ⟨efforts to increase production have up to now *fallen on their face*⟩ — **fall over oneself** *or* **fall over backward :** to display great or excessive eagerness ⟨*fell over themselves* in their efforts to accommodate the new administration —*Atlantic*⟩ ⟨juries *fell over backward* in favor of progressive art —Aline B. Saarinen⟩ — **fall short 1 :** to become or be deficient ⟨the expedition's supplies began to *fall short*⟩ **2 :** to fail to attain, reach, arrive at, or perform something ⟨the shot *fell short*⟩ ⟨our efforts have *fallen short*⟩

²**fall** \"\ *n* -s [ME, fr. OE *feall;* akin to OFris, OS, & OHG *fal* fall, ON *fall,* deverbatives fr. the root of E ¹*fall*] **1 a** (1) **:** the act of dropping or descending by the force of gravity ⟨the ~ of a stone⟩ ⟨a ~ from a horse⟩ ⟨the leading cause of home deaths continued to be ~*s* —*Americana Annual*⟩ ⟨a ~ on the ice⟩ (2) **:** a guided descent or drop through the air ⟨the ~ of an ax⟩ ⟨the ~ of a man's foot⟩; *specif* **:** a descent to the floor in modern-dance technique that can be effected in a variety of ways and that resolves into a recovery or rise (3) **:** a position in which a wrestler's scapular area is held in contact with the mat for a given period of time; *also* **:** the act of putting an opponent in this position for the prescribed time **b** (1) **:** a falling out, off, or away **:** DROPPING, SHEDDING ⟨the ~ of leaves⟩ ⟨a ~ of snow⟩ (2) **:** the season when leaves fall from trees **:** AUTUMN (3) **:** the approach or onset esp. of night or darkness ⟨he came along the road in the chill ~ of the evening —Padraic Colum⟩ **c** (1) **:** a thing or quantity that falls or has fallen ⟨examined the ~ of earth at the mouth of the tunnel —G.A.Wagner⟩ ⟨a freak 20-inch ~ of rain⟩; *specif* **:** one or more meteorites or their fragments that have fallen together at one place and time (2) **:** birth or production by birth; *also* **:** something which is so produced ⟨a good ~ of lambs⟩ **d :** something that hangs down ⟨pushed back the ~ of hair from her forehead —Berton Roueché⟩: as (1) **:** a costume decoration of lace or thin fabric arranged to hang loosely and gracefully esp. from the back edge of a bonnet (2) **:** a very wide collar of fine fabric and lace worn in the 17th century esp. by Cavaliers (3) **:** the part of a turned-over collar from the crease to the outer edge — compare STAND (4) **:** a wide front flap on trousers (as those worn by sailors) (5) **:** the freely hanging lower edge of the skirt of a coat — often used in pl. ⟨would have done it . . . had I not taken him by the ~*s* of his skirt —Hugh McCrae⟩ (6) **:** one of the three outer and often drooping segments of the flower of an iris — usu. used in pl. (7) **:** long hair overhanging the face of certain terriers (8) **:** a hoisting-tackle rope or chain; *esp* **:** the part of it to which the power is applied (9) **:** BOAT FALL **e :** the manner in which something hangs down ⟨the ~ of a woman's hair⟩ **2 a :** loss of greatness, power, status, influence, or dominion **:** COLLAPSE, DOWNFALL ⟨the ~ of the Roman Empire⟩ ⟨the rise and ~ of business firms —*Economic Jour.*⟩; *specif* **:** loss of office by a government or ministry esp. as a result of an adverse parliamentary vote ⟨the ~ of a government on a vote of confidence⟩ **b :** the surrender or capture of a besieged fortress or town ⟨the ~ of Troy⟩ **c** (1) **:** lapse or departure from innocence or goodness **:** spiritual ruin ⟨~ from virtue⟩ — used with *the* and often cap. in reference to the fall of man reported in Gen 3 (2) **:** loss of a woman's chastity (3) **:** the cause of falling from virtue, grace, or power ⟨his stubbornness was his ~⟩ **3 a :** the descent of land or a hill **:** downward direction **:** SLOPE, DECLIVITY ⟨the well-remembered ~ of the land, dropping away to the old rice fields —Hamilton Basso⟩ **b :** precipitous descent of water **:** CASCADE, CATARACT, WATERFALL ⟨the first ~ is about 60 feet high —*Amer. Guide Series: Tenn.*⟩ — usu. pl. but often sing. in constr. ⟨the ~*s* of Niagara⟩ ⟨the upper ~*s* has a sheer plunge of 20 feet —*Jour. of Geol.*⟩ **c** (1) **:** a musical cadence (2) **:** DOUBLE APPOGGIATURA **d :** a falling-pitch intonation in speech **4 :** diminution or decrease in size, quantity, or degree **:** DECLINE ⟨the persistently steep ~ in immigration —Peter Scott⟩ ⟨it was a compensation for a ~ in excitement and satisfaction in their . . . lives —W.D. Howells⟩ ⟨the main ~ in the average family size . . . had already taken place —Roy Lewis & Angus Maude⟩ ⟨the steady ~ in purchasing power⟩; *specif* **:** diminution or decrease in price or value ⟨recent heavy ~*s* in the stock market⟩ ⟨a ~ of rents⟩ **5 a :** the distance or extent to which something falls or slopes **:** the difference between levels ⟨a cultivated field . . . with a ~ of five feet in a hundred feet —J.B.Robson⟩ ⟨a ~ of five points in the price of a stock⟩ ⟨the Mississippi has a ~ of 620 feet between Minnesota and the Gulf —*Amer. Guide Series: Minn.*⟩ **b :** INCLINATION, PITCH ⟨a flat roof with a barely perceptible ~⟩ ⟨adjust the ~ of the gutter so the water would run along it faster⟩ **6 a :** the act of felling **b :** the quantity of trees cut down **7** *Scot* **:** something that befalls one **:** FORTUNE, LOT ⟨may good fortune be your ~⟩ **8** *slang* **:** ARREST ⟨served time on narcotics and prostitution ~*s* —Jack Lait & Lee Mortimer⟩ — **take a fall out of** *or* **get a fall out of :** to cause the discomfiture of **:** get the best of ⟨some of his sharper-tongued confreres occasionally *took a fall out of* him —S.H.Adams⟩

³**fall** \"\ *adj* **:** of fall or autumn **:** being such as occurs, matures, is done, or is suited for use or wear in the fall ⟨bought a ~ coat⟩ ⟨brisk ~ weather⟩

fall- *or* **fallo-** *comb form* [*Fallopian*] **:** fallopian tube ⟨*fallectomy*⟩ ⟨*fallotomy*⟩

fal la *var of* FA LA

fal·la·cious \fəˈlāshəs\ *adj* [MF *fallacieux,* fr. L *fallaciosus,* fr. *fallacia* + *-osus* -ous] **1 :** embodying or presenting a fallacy ⟨the demand was plausible, but the more I thought upon it the more . . . ~ . . . it seemed —A.D.White⟩ ⟨some ~ conclusions regarding drugs and crime —D.W.Maurer & V.H.Vogel⟩ ⟨read him a second time in order that I might state . . . articulately the points at which I thought he became ~ —O.W.Holmes †1935⟩ **2 :** DECEPTIVE, MISLEADING, DELUSIVE, DISAPPOINTING ⟨the ~ hope that the propriety of going to bed may at any moment dawn upon the paternal mind —W.L.Alden⟩ ⟨a region . . . where . . . the ~ colocynth, the wild melon, scatters its globes of bitter gold —Norman Douglas⟩ — **fal·la·cious·ly** *adv*

fal·la·cious·ness *n* -ES **:** the quality of being fallacious

fal·la·cy \ˈfaləsē, -si\ *n* -ES [L *fallacia,* fr. *fallac-, fallax* deceitful (fr. *fallere* to deceive) + *-ia* -y — more at FAIL] **1 a** *obs* **:** GUILE, TRICKERY **b :** deceptive or false appearance **:** something that misleads the eye or the mind **:** DECEPTION ⟨it appears that . . . the descent is perpendicular but this . . . is a ~ of the eye caused by the distance —Anthony Trollope⟩ **2 a :** a false or erroneous idea ⟨parents console themselves by the American ~ that one can only be young once —Elizabeth Bowen⟩ **b :** erroneous or fallacious character **:** ERRONEOUSNESS ⟨the ~ of such a suit for military use should at once be apparent —H.G.Armstrong⟩ **3 :** a plausible reasoning that fails to satisfy the conditions of valid argument or correct inference — see FORMAL FALLACY, MATERIAL FALLACY, VERBAL FALLACY

fallacy of accident : the fallacy that consists in arguing from some accidental character as if it were essential or necessary (as in *the food you buy you eat; you buy raw meat; therefore you eat raw meat*)

fallacy of composition : the fallacy of arguing from premises in which a term is used distributively to a conclusion in which it is used collectively or of assuming that what is true of each member of a class or part of a whole will be true of all together (as in *if my money bought more goods I should be better off; therefore we should all benefit if prices were lower*)

fallacy of division : a fallacy in which a term taken collectively is used as if taken distributively

fallacy of the antecedent : the logical fallacy of denying the antecedent **:** DENIAL OF THE ANTECEDENT

fallacy of the consequent : the logical fallacy of affirming the consequent **:** AFFIRMATION OF THE CONSEQUENT

fal-lal \(ˈ)fa(l)ˌlal, -ˌläl, fəˈl-\ *n* -s [perh. alter. of *falbala*] **:** an ornament or trimming esp. in dress

fall armyworm *n* **:** the larva of an American noctuid moth (*Spodoptera frugiperda*) that migrates northward as far as New England and is destructive esp. to grasses and small grains

fall away *vi* **1 a :** to withdraw friendship or support ⟨they had only been the companions of his pleasures and would be the surest to *fall away* in affliction —Marcia Davenport⟩ — often used with *from* ⟨the party leaders *fell away* from him, and his popularity seemed on the wane⟩ **b :** to renounce one's faith **:** APOSTATIZE ⟨those who had *fallen away* during the recent persecutions —K.S.Latourette⟩ **2 a :** to diminish in size or height **:** grow gradually smaller ⟨although the limbs are long and powerful . . . the animal *falls away* behind —James Stevenson Hamilton⟩ **b :** to swerve or drift off a line of direction ⟨the boat kept *falling away* to starboard⟩ ⟨*falling away* from the second baseman's tag and hooking the base with his toe as he slid past⟩

fallaway \ˈ⸗⸗ˌ⸗\ *n* -s [*fall away*] **:** a ballroom position in which both partners face in the same direction

fall back *vi* **:** to give way **:** RETREAT, RECEDE ⟨the infantry *fell back* before the determined enemy attack⟩ ⟨rivers . . . were *falling back* from their flood peaks —E.L.Dale⟩ — **fall back on** *or* **fall back upon 1 :** to retreat to (a stronger position) **2 :** to have recourse to (a reserved fund or some available expedient or support) ⟨it's always good to have at least two things you can do because . . . if one folds, you can always *fall back on* the other —Eamonn Andrews⟩

fallback \ˈ⸗ˌ⸗\ *n* [*fall back*] **1 :** a falling back **:** RETREAT ⟨there would be a rapid and orderly ~ to break contact —*N.Y. Times*⟩ **2 :** something on which one can fall back **:** RESERVE ⟨there is a certain ~ against the risk of failure . . . on the part of the Allies —H.V.Hodson⟩

fall block *n* **:** a pulley block used with a fall (sense 1d(8))

fall board *n* **:** the cover of a piano keyboard

fall cankerworm *n* **:** a green or brown white-striped looper that is the larva of a small widespread No. American geometrid moth (*Alsophila pometaria*) with gray-winged males and wingless females and that is a destructive defoliator of fruit trees and deciduous shade trees

fall chronometer *n* **:** an instrument used in experimental psychology having a body which may fall practically without friction and which makes or breaks electrical contacts as it drops so that time intervals can be determined

fall dandelion *n* **:** a European scapose herb (*Leontodon autumnalis*) naturalized in the U.S.

fall down *vi* **1 :** to prostrate oneself in worship **2 :** to fail or disappoint expectation — often used with *on* ⟨he *fell down* on the job⟩

fall duck *n* **:** any of various migratory ducks (as the pintail, the teal, the redhead)

fallen *past part of* FALL

fallen star *n* **:** any of various blue-green algae of the family Nostocaceae growing on moist ground

fallen wool *n* **1 :** wool rubbed off the backs of sheep and collected from the ground or elsewhere **2 :** wool taken from dead sheep

fall·er \ˈfȯlə(r)\ *n* -s [ME, one that falls, fr. *fallen* to fall + *-er* — more at FALL] **1 :** a logger who fells trees — called also *feller* **2 :** a machine part that acts by falling: as **a :** the activating part of some stop motions **b :** a falling or controlling device (as the hammer in a fulling machine, a tensioning device on a mule-spinning machine, or one of a series of pins in a gill box)

fallfish \ˈ⸗ˌ⸗\ *n* **:** any of several common No. American cyprinoid fishes; *esp* **:** a fish (*Semotilus corporalis*) of the streams of northeastern No. America — compare CHUB

fall front \ˈ⸗ˌ⸗\ *n* **:** DROP FRONT

fall grain *n* **:** grain sown in the autumn and harvested the following spring or summer

fall guy *n* **1 :** one who assumes or on whom is placed the blame or responsibility **:** one who takes the rap **:** SCAPEGOAT ⟨public officials use the correctional institution as a *fall guy* for their own apathy, inertia, and ignorance —C.W.Leonard⟩ ⟨becoming the *fall guy* for the ring which operated the houses of prostitution in that district —R.M.Lindner⟩ **2 :** one that is made the victim of a swindle or deception **:** one that is easily gulled or victimized ⟨his friends were laughing at him . . . had he been marked early for a *fall guy* —Irving Stone⟩

fall herring *n* **:** a herring (*Pomolobus mediocris*) of the Atlantic coast from Cape Cod south

fal·li·bi·lism \ˈfaləbəˌlizəm\ *n* -s [ML *fallibilis* + E *-ism*] **:** a theory that it is impossible to attain absolutely certain empirical knowledge because the statements constituting it cannot be ultimately and completely verified — opposed to *infallibilism* — **fal·li·bi·list** \-ˌləst\ *n* -s — **fal·li·bi·lis·tic** \ˌ⸗⸗⸗ˈlistik\ *adj*

fal·li·bil·i·ty \ˌfaləˈbilədˌē, -lətē, -i\ *n* -ES **:** liability or proneness to err ⟨the critics of the romantic period were pioneers, and exhibit the ~ of discoverers —T.S.Eliot⟩ ⟨the ~ of human perceptions —A.S.Eddington⟩

fal·li·ble \ˈfaləbəl\ *adj* [ME, fr. ML *fallibilis,* fr. L *fallere* to deceive + *-ibilis* -ible — more at FAIL] **1 :** liable to err ⟨all men are ~⟩ **2 :** liable to be erroneous or inaccurate ⟨a ~ rule⟩ — **fal·li·ble·ness** \-bəlnəs\ *n* -ES — **fal·li·bly** \-blē, -li\ *adv*

fall in *vi* **1 :** to sink inward ⟨the roof *fell in*⟩ **2 a :** to come to an end **:** TERMINATE, LAPSE — used of a lease or annuity **b :** to come into the owner's possession after a lease **c :** to become operative or available (as of a reversion) **3** *obs* **:** to rush in or come in **4** *archaic* **:** OCCUR, HAPPEN **5 :** to take one's proper place in a military formation and come to the position of attention **~** *vt* **:** to cause (troops) to take proper positions in ranks **:** cause (a military unit) to form ranks — **fall in for :** to come in for **:** INCUR ⟨*fell in for* the major share of the blame⟩ — **fall in with 1 :** to agree or concur with **:** yield to **:** conform to ⟨I had to *fall in with* her wishes as much as possible —Frank Sargeson⟩ ⟨requested me to *fall in with* the custom of the day —Tyrone Power †1841⟩ **2 :** to harmonize with **:** join with ⟨it *falls in* exactly *with* my views⟩

falling *adj* [fr. pres. part of ¹*fall*] **:** passing from a more vigorous to a less vigorous physical condition **:** DECLINING — used esp. of domestic livestock; compare RISING

falling asleep *n, usu cap F&A* [trans. of MGk *koimēsis*] **:** an Eastern Church feast celebrating the corporeal assumption of the Virgin Mary that is observed on August 15 and that corresponds to the Western feast of the Assumption

falling band *n* **:** FALL 1d(2)

falling diphthong *n* **:** a diphthong with less stress on the second element than on the first (as \ȯi\ in \ˈnȯiz\ *noise*) — compare RISING DIPHTHONG

falling disease *n* **:** the typical terminal manifestation of severe copper deficiency in which an animal collapses and dies apparently from heart failure consequent to myocardial damage

falling evil *n* [ME *falling evil*] **:** EPILEPSY

falling fit *n* **:** an epileptic seizure of a domestic animal — compare EPILEPSY

falling hinge *n* **:** a horizontal hinge (as for a trapdoor)

falling leaf *n* **:** an aerobatic flight maneuver in which an airplane is allowed to stall and is then slipped successively to the right and left, the nose being held to point in the same direction throughout

falling mold *n* **:** a pattern for templating the side of a wreath after using the face mold in stairbuilding

falling of the womb : prolapse of the uterus into the vagina

falling-out \ˌ⸗⸗ˈ⸗\ *n, pl* **fallings-out** *or* **falling-outs** [fr. gerund of *fall out*] **:** an instance of falling out **:** QUARREL ⟨Papa had *falling-outs* with a lot of people —Alan Le May⟩

falling rhythm *n, prosody* **:** rhythm with stress occurring regularly on the first syllable of each foot — opposed to *rising rhythm;* compare CADENCE 5

falling sickness *n* **1 :** FALLING FITS **2 :** EPILEPSY

falling star *n* **:** METEOR 2a

falling weather *n, chiefly Midland* **:** weather characterized by heavy rain, snow, or hail **:** bad weather

falling wedge *n* **:** a wedge to drive into the kerf of a tree in order to direct its fall — called also *felling wedge*

fall leaf *n* **:** the drop leaf of a table

fall line *n* **1 :** a line joining the waterfalls on a number of rivers that marks the point where each river descends from the upland to the lowland and the limit of its navigability **2 :** the natural downward course (as for skiing) between two points on a slope

fall meadow rue *n* **:** TALL MEADOW RUE

fall money *n, slang* **:** money set aside or deposited with some other person by a professional criminal or group of criminals for use in an emergency (as for legal fees)

fallo- — see FALL-

fall off *vi* **1 :** to step aside **:** WITHDRAW **2 :** TREND — used of a coastline **3** *of a ship* **:** to deviate or trend to leeward of the point to which her head was directed

falloff \ˈ⸗ˌ⸗\ *n* -s [*fall off*] **:** a decline esp. in quantity ⟨a ~ in exports which helped to pay for Europe's vital imports —*Newsweek*⟩

fall of the hammer : the customary stroke of the hammer or gavel made by an auctioneer to denote that the sale is closed and the highest previous bid is accepted — compare *by inch of candle* at ¹INCH

fal·lo·pi·an \fəˈlōpēən\ *adj, often cap* [Gabriel *Fallopius* (Gabriello *Fallopio*) †1562 Ital. anatomist + E *-an*] **:** relating to or discovered by Fallopius

fallopian aqueduct *or* **fallopian canal** *n, often cap F* **:** FACIAL CANAL

fallopian tube *n, often cap F* **:** the oviduct in mammals **:** either of the pair of tubes that conduct the egg from the ovary to the uterus, have at the upper end a funnel-shaped expansion receiving the egg as it escapes from the ovary, and are continuous with the uterus at the lower end

fall out *vi* **1 :** to turn out **:** RESULT, OCCUR, HAPPEN ⟨as it *fell out,* the building was deserted at the time of the explosion⟩ ⟨all *fell out* very well indeed⟩ ⟨this strangeness of life, this unexpected and even perverse element of things as they *fall out* —G.K.Chesterton⟩ **2 :** to have a quarrel **:** DISAGREE **3 a :** to leave one's place in the ranks **b :** to leave a building to meet a formation ⟨you will *fall out* of the barracks in 10 minutes for retreat⟩

fallout \ˈ⸗ˌ⸗\ *n* -s [*fall out*] **1 :** the descent through the atmosphere of often radioactive particles stirred up by or resulting from a nuclear explosion **2 :** the particles that descend through the atmosphere following a nuclear explosion

fall over *vi, Scot* **:** to go to sleep

¹**fal·low** \ˈfa(ˌ)lō, -lə, *often* -ləw+V\ *adj* [ME *falow,* fr. OE *fealo, fealu;* akin to OHG *falo* pale, faded, dun-colored,

fallow, OS *falu*, ON *fölr* pale, fallow, L *pallēre* to be pale, Gk *polios* gray, Skt *palita* gray, hoary, OSlav *plavŭ* white] **:** of the color fallow ⟨a ~ greyhound⟩; *also* **:** of any pale color or warm hue

[2]**fallow** \"\ *n* -s **:** a light yellowish brown that is lighter and slightly redder and stronger than khaki, less strong and slightly yellower and darker than walnut brown, yellower and paler than cinnamon, and less strong than manila

[3]**fallow** \"\ *n* -s [ME *falwe, falow*, fr. OE *fealg, fealh* — more at FELLY] **1** *obs* **:** plowed land or a piece of it **2 :** land ordinarily used for crop production when allowed to lie idle either in a tilled or untilled condition during the whole or the greater portion of the growing season **3 :** the plowing or tilling of land without sowing it for a season; *also* **:** the state or period of being fallow ⟨summer ~ is a method of destroying weeds⟩

[4]**fallow** \"\ *vt* -ED/-ING/-S [ME *falwen, falowen*, fr. OE *fealgian*, fr. *fealg*, n.] **1** *obs* **:** to plow (land) for sowing **2 :** to plow, harrow, and break up (land) without seeding for the purpose of destroying weeds and conserving soil moisture

[5]**fallow** \"\ *adj* [ME *falwe, falow*, fr. *falwe, falow*, n.] **1 :** left untilled or unsown after plowing **:** UNCULTIVATED ⟨~ ground⟩ **2** *obs* **:** fit for cultivation **:** plowed ready for sowing **3 a :** not pregnant ⟨a ~ sow⟩ **b :** marked by the absence of pregnancy ⟨a long ~ period followed by the birth of two sons in rapid succession⟩ **4 a :** having large potential value or utility but being unused — used esp. in the phrase *to lie fallow* ⟨at this very moment there are probably important inventions lying ~ —*Harper's*⟩ ⟨the skills of the men displaced by . . . up-to-date machinery will not lie ~ for long —Sam Pollack⟩ **b :** characterized by a state of creative or recuperative rest or dormancy **:** gathering strength while lying idle — used esp. in the phrase *to lie fallow* ⟨and now the period of lying ~, of incorporating a new approach, came to an end —Dorothy Lee⟩ ⟨the spirit that actuated the grandfather having lain ~ in the son and being refreshed by repose so as to be ready for fresh exertion in the grandson —Samuel Butler †1902⟩

[6]**fallow** \"\ *Scot var of* FELLOW

fallowchat \ˈ==,=\ *n* [[3]*fallow* + *chat*] **:** WHEATEAR

fallow deer *n* [[1]*fallow*] **:** a European deer (*Dama dama*) much smaller than the red deer that has the antlers palmate near the ends and the coat spotted with white in summer and that is commonly domesticated in England where it is often kept in private parks — see DEER illustration

fal·low·ness *n* -ES [[5]*fallow* + *-ness*] *archaic* **:** the state of being unused or unworked

fall phonometer *n* **:** an instrument used in experimental psychology designed to furnish sounds whose intensities are in known ratios by permitting balls to drop from different heights upon plates of metal or slate

fall-pipe \ˈ=,=\ *n* **:** DOWNSPOUT

fall-plow \ˈ=ˌ=\ *vt* **:** to plow (land) in autumn

fall riv·er \(ˈ)fȯlˈrivə(r)\ *adj, usu cap F&R* [fr. *Fall River*, Mass.] **:** of or from the city of Fall River, Mass. ⟨a *Fall River* resident⟩ **:** of the kind or style prevalent in Fall River

fall rope *n* **:** a rope used for hoisting (as in a derrick)

fall rose *n* **:** CHINA ASTER

falls *pres 3d sing of* FALL, *pl of* FALL

fall snipe *n* **:** RED-BACKED SANDPIPER

fall-sow \ˈ=ˌ=\ *vt* **:** to sow (seed or land) in autumn

falltime \ˈ=,=\ *n* **:** AUTUMN

fall to *vi* **:** to set about doing something esp. actively: as **a :** to begin to fight **b :** to begin to eat ⟨*fell to* as soon as dinner was served⟩

fall together *vi* **:** to become identical **:** become leveled — used of speech sounds or forms

fall-trap \ˈ=,=\ *n* **:** a trap with a door or a weight that falls upon the victim

fall webworm *n* **:** a pale yellow dusky-striped hairy caterpillar that is the larva of either of two common white arctiid moths (*Hyphantria cunea* and *H. textor*) and that lives gregariously in nests of webbing at the ends of branches of many deciduous trees — compare TENT CATERPILLAR

fall wheat *n* **:** WINTER WHEAT

fall wind *n* **:** a katabatic wind

fall witchgrass *n* **:** a tufted No. American perennial grass (*Leptoloma cognatum*) with flat leaves, brittle culms, and very diffuse terminal panicles that break away at maturity and become tumbleweeds

fall zone *n* **:** FALL LINE

fals *var of* FELS

fal·sa·ry \ˈfȯl(t)sərē\ *n* -ES [ME *falsarie*, fr. L *falsarius*, fr. *falsus* + *-arius* -ary] *archaic* **:** FALSIFIER, DECEIVER; *specif* **:** FORGER

[1]**false** \ˈfȯls *also* -lts\ *adj* -ER/-EST [ME fals, *faus*, fr. OF & L; OF *fals, faus*, fr. L *falsus*, past part. of *fallere* to deceive — more at FAIL] **1 a :** not corresponding to truth or reality **:** not true **:** ERRONEOUS, INCORRECT ⟨his assumption that this is the only possible interpretation is demonstrably ~ —M.R.Cohen⟩ **b :** intentionally untrue **:** LYING ⟨~ claims are frequently made of automobile ownership —S.L.Payne⟩ ⟨the ~ testimony of suborned witnesses⟩ **2 a :** speaking falsehood **:** not truthful **:** DISHONEST, DECEITFUL ⟨slanders of her ~ accusers —Shak.⟩ ⟨especially heavy consequences for people . . . attracted to unworthy, ~, and callous persons —H.E.Salisbury⟩ **b** (1) **:** made or tampered with to deceive ⟨~ scales⟩ ⟨~ dice⟩ ⟨~ bottom of a glass⟩ (2) *archaic* **:** tending to distort **:** DEFECTIVE ⟨tears are ~ spectacles —John Donne⟩ (3) **:** inaccurate in pitch **:** out of tune **c :** tending to mislead **:** DECEPTIVE, ILLUSORY ⟨the ~ warmth of the January thaw —Louis Bromfield⟩ **3 :** not faithful or loyal (as to obligations, allegiance, or vows) **:** TREACHEROUS, PERFIDIOUS ⟨a ~ friend⟩ ⟨a ~ lover⟩ **4 a** (1) **:** being other than what is purported or apparent **:** assumed or designed to deceive **:** not genuine or real **:** COUNTERFEIT, ARTIFICIAL, SHAM, FORGED, SPECIOUS ⟨~ tears⟩ ⟨~ modesty⟩ ⟨privateersmen sailing under ~ colors⟩ ⟨~ deeds of ownership⟩ ⟨the ~ glamor of war⟩ ⟨listening to ~ prophets⟩ (2) **:** artificially made or assumed ⟨a set of ~ teeth⟩ ⟨buying ~ hair from impoverished country girls —Lois Long⟩ **b :** BLANK 5b ⟨a ~ door⟩ ⟨a ~ window⟩ **c :** of a kind related to, resembling, or having properties similar to another species that commonly bears the unqualified vernacular — used in plant names ⟨~ oats⟩ ⟨a ~ pea⟩ **d** (1) **:** not essential or permanent — used of parts of a structure that are temporary or supplemental ⟨~ siding⟩ ⟨~ pillar⟩ ⟨~ roof⟩ (2) **:** fastened to or fitting over a main part to strengthen it, to protect it or anything that comes in contact with it, or to disguise its appearance ⟨~ deck⟩ ⟨~ jaw of a chuck or vise⟩ ⟨~ post⟩ **e :** formed through unawareness or misunderstanding of the etymology ⟨pea is a ~ singular formed from the real singular *pease*⟩ **f :** VOIDED 2 **g :** lacking realism, naturalness, or authenticity **:** failing to produce an effect of artistic rightness or inevitability **:** appearing forced, strained, or incongruous **:** ARTIFICIAL, UNCONVINCING ⟨there are only two seriously ~ scenes . . . and they occur toward the end —V.S. Pritchett⟩ ⟨a vocabulary affected and often . . . ludicrously ~ —Gilbert Highet⟩ **5 a :** not based on facts or correct premises **:** not well founded **:** IMPRUDENT, UNWISE, INCORRECT ⟨our time is for the most part spent in hesitation, ~ starts, and painful retracing of our steps —M.R.Cohen⟩ ⟨make a ~ turn in his canoe —*Amer. Guide Series: La.*⟩ ⟨practice ~ economy⟩ ⟨this marriage is ~ —George Meredith⟩ ⟨a sense of ~ security⟩ **b :** appearing inconsistent with one's true character or intentions **:** COMPROMISING, AWKWARD ⟨by accepting the support of such dubious elements he put himself in an extremely ~ position⟩ **6** *dial Eng* **:** SHARP, CLEVER ⟨it's a ~ child that knows its own father⟩ **syn** see FAITHLESS

[2]**false** \"\ *vt* -ED/-ING/-S [ME *falsen, fausen*, fr. OF *falser, fausser*, fr. LL *falsare*, fr. L *falsus*] *obs* **:** FEIGN

[3]**false** \"\ *adv* [ME *false, fals*, fr. *fals, faus*, adj.] **1** *archaic* **:** ERRINGLY, INCORRECTLY, WRONGLY **2 :** FAITHLESSLY, TREACHEROUSLY — usu. used with *play* ⟨his wife played him ~⟩

false acacia *n* **:** LOCUST 3a (2)

false alarm *n* **:** one who raises but fails to meet expectations ⟨rising to attention on waves of their discoverers' ardor, most of them soon . . . sink back to the sea of *false alarms* —*Yale Rev.*⟩

false albacore *n* **:** LITTLE TUNA

false aloe *n* **1 :** any of various plants of the genus *Agave; esp* **:** a bulbous herb (*Agave virginica*) of the southeastern U. S. **2 :** a colicroot (*Aletris farinosa*)

false alumroot *n* **:** a hairy perennial herb (*Tellima grandiflora*) of the western U. S. with racemes of greenish flowers that have fringed petals and that gradually turn pink or reddish as they fade — compare ALUMROOT

false angostura bark *n* **:** the bark of the nux vomica tree

false annual ring *n* **:** FALSE RING

false arborvitae *n* **:** a tree or shrub of the genus *Thujopsis*

false arch *n* **:** a member having the appearance of an arch though not of arch construction; *specif* **:** CORBEL ARCH

false arrest *n* **:** an arrest not justifiable under law

false asphodel *n* **:** a plant of the genus *Tofieldia*

false attic *n* **:** a compartment that is situated like an attic immediately under a roof but does not have windows and does not enclose rooms

false azalea *n* **:** a shrub (*Menziesia ferruginea*) of the Rocky mountains having foliage with a bluish tinge and bell-shaped inconspicuous flowers

false baby's breath *n* **:** any of various plants of the genus *Galium; esp* **:** WILD MADDER 2a

false banana *n* **:** PAPAW 2a

false bark *n* **:** a bark used commercially as a substitute for cinchona

false bearing *n* **:** a bearing (as of a lintel or beam) not directly on a vertical support

false-bedded \ˈ=ˈ==\ *adj* **:** CROSS-BEDDED — **false bedding** *n*

false beechdrops *n* **:** a pinesap (*Monotropa hypopiths*)

false bittersweet *n* **:** BITTERSWEET 2b

false blossom *n* **1 :** a disease of the cranberry caused by a fungus (*Exobasidium oxycocci*) producing erect flower buds which produce malformed flowers that set no fruit or are sometimes replaced by a whorl of leaves or a branch — called also *rosebloom* **2 :** a similar disease of cranberries caused by a virus and transmitted by a leafhopper (*Scleroracus vaccinii*) — called also *Wisconsin false blossom*

false body *n* **:** a higher apparent consistency exhibited on standing than that resulting from stirring or brushing; *also* **:** the property or phenomenon of exhibiting such a change in consistency **:** THIXOTROPY — used esp. of paints and varnishes

false boneset *n* **:** a plant of the genus *Kuhnia; esp* **:** a perennial resinous No. American herb (*K. eupatorioides*) with purplish white flowers

false box *or* **false boxwood** *n* **:** a small tree or shrub (*Gyminda grisebechii*) of the southeastern U.S., Mexico, northern So. America, and parts of the West Indies having small leathery leaves resembling those of the box (*Buxus sempervirens*)

false branching *n* **:** a branched arrangement of the cells of certain filamentous bacteria and algae resulting from a slipping of the end of one cell past that of another following cell division, from continued growth of the free end of a trichome through the sheath in various blue-green algae, or esp. from continued growth of parts of a filament separated by one or more intervening dead cells or by heterocysts — compare TRUE BRANCHING

false branching in an alga

false bromegrass *n* **:** either of the two European fodder grasses (*Brachypodium pinnatum* and *B. sylvaticum*)

false buckthorn *n* **:** a spiny tree (*Bumelia lanuginosa*) of the southern U.S. having oblong to obovate leaves with the undersurface dull and woolly, small greenish white flowers followed by dark globular fruits, and very hard tough wood

false buckwheat *n* **:** an American herbaceous vine (*Polygonum scandens*) with seeds resembling buckwheat

false buffalo grass *n* **:** a low tufted grass (*Munroa squarrosa*) of the western U.S. with stiff leaves and wiry branches

false bugbane *n* **:** a tall herb (*Trautvetteria carolinensis*) of the family Ranunculaceae of the eastern U.S. with large basal leaves and white apetalous flowers

false cadence *n* **:** DECEPTIVE CADENCE

false-card \ˈ=ˈ=\ *n* **:** a card played with the intention of deceiving an opponent as to the content of one's hand

falsecard \"\ *vi* [*false card*] **:** to play a false-card

false cast *n* **:** a cast made when fly-fishing in which neither fly nor line touches the water

false cedar *n* **:** any of several trees resembling cedars of the genus *Thuja* esp. in odor; *specif* **:** SPANISH CEDAR

false ceiling *n* **:** a ceiling that is hung some distance below the ceiling joists

false chamomile *n* **:** a plant of the genus *Boltonia*

false chinaroot *n* **:** AMERICAN CHINAROOT

false chinch bug *n* **:** a small dark bug (*Nysius ericae*) resembling the related chinch bug in appearance and habits though commonly feeding on weeds and not often seriously destructive to cultivated crops

false cirrus *n* **:** a cirrus cloud of appreciable thickness originating from a cumulonimbus cloud — called also *thunderstorm cirrus*

false claims statute *n* **:** a statute penalizing the maker of knowingly false claims against the government or any department or agency thereof

false cockle *n* **:** CARDITA 2

false coltsfoot *n* **:** WILD GINGER 2a

false cypress *n* **:** any of several coniferous shrubs or trees (as members of the genus *Chamaecyparis*) with foliage resembling that of a cypress

falsed *past of* FALSE

false dandelion *n* **:** any of various American herbs (family Compositae) having flower heads resembling those of a dandelion

false dawn *n* **:** a faint light on the eastern horizon sometime before dawn; *often* **:** ZODIACAL LIGHT

false death cap *n* **:** an agaric (*Amanita mappa*) often confused with the death cup (*A. phalloides*) but having the cap usu. lemon yellow or white with no trace of green and a very bulbous stem base with the volva separated from the stem by a distinct groove

false dichotomy *n* **:** a branching in which the main axis appears to divide dichotomously at the apex but is in reality suppressed, the growth being continued by lateral branches (as in the dichasium)

false dragonhead *n* **1 :** a plant of the genus *Physostegia* **2 :** DRAGONHEAD

false face \ˈ=,=\ *n* **:** a caricature of human or animal features that is made of cloth, plaster, or similar material and worn over the face **:** MASK

false-face \"\ *adj* **:** disguised by a false face

false flax *n* **:** a plant of the genus *Camelina* — see GOLD OF PLEASURE, SMALL-SEEDED FALSE FLAX

false floor *n* **:** a floor usu. with open cracks placed about 18 inches above the main floor of a farm fruit or vegetable storage to facilitate free circulation of air

false foot *n* **:** PSEUDOPODIUM

false foxglove *n* **:** any of several gerardias having yellow flowers that resemble those of a foxglove

false front *n* **1 :** a facade extending beyond and esp. above the true dimensions of a building to give it a more imposing appearance **2 :** false hair usu. used for bangs or curls at the front hairline **3 :** appearance or manner intended to deceive

false fruit *n* **:** ACCESSORY FRUIT

false galena *n* **:** SPHALERITE

false garlic *n* **:** a bulbous herb (*Nothoscordum bivalve*) of the southern U. S. and the West Indies

false gid *n* **:** a disease of sheep that resembles gid and is caused by larvae of a botfly (*Oestrus ovis*) in the nasal chambers

false goatsbeard *n* **:** a plant of the genus *Astilbe*

false goldenrod *n* **:** a No. American herb (*Solidago sphacelata*) having sessile or subsessile heads in glomerules along the branches

false gromwell *n* **:** a plant of the genus *Onosmodium*

false guinea grass *n* **:** JOHNSON GRASS

false header *n* **:** SNAP HEADER

falsehearted \ˈ=ˈ==\ *adj* **:** having a disloyal heart ⟨a ~ traitor —Shak.⟩

false heather *n* **1 :** any of several ericaceous plants that resemble true heather; *esp* **:** BEACH HEATHER **2 :** a small heath-like So. American solanaceous shrub (*Fabiana imbricata*) that is sometimes cultivated as an ornamental usu. in the coolhouse

false hedge hyssop *n* **:** a plant of the genus *Ilysanthes*

false heliotrope *n* **:** GARDEN HELIOTROPE 1

false hellebore *n* **1 :** WHITE HELLEBORE **2 :** PHEASANT'S-EYE 1

false hemp *n* **1 :** HEMP NETTLE **2 :** SUNN

false·hood \ˈfȯl(t)s,hu̇d\ *n* [ME *falshede, falshod*, fr. *fals* false + *-hede, -hod* -hood — more at FALSE] **1 a :** absence of truth or accuracy **:** FALSITY ⟨the ~ of this doctrine must be patent to any careful student⟩ **b :** an untrue assertion esp. when intentional **:** LIE ⟨told two flat ~s about what had happened in secret session —Elmer Davis⟩ **c :** the practice of lying **:** MENDACITY ⟨it is a trite . . . observation that courts are the seat of ~ and dissimulation —Earl of Chesterfield⟩ **2** *Scots law* **:** the fraudulent imitation or suppression of truth by words, writing, or conduct to the damage of another

false hoof *n* **:** a hoof terminating a vestigial digit in many ungulates (as deer and pigs)

false hybrid *n* **:** an individual produced by an essentially parthenogenetic process from an egg of one species activated by a sperm of another without the entry of sperm chromosomes to form a synkaryon

false imprisonment *n* **:** the imprisonment of a person contrary to law; *also* **:** any unlawful interference with another's right of free location

false indigo *n* **1 :** a shrub of the genus *Amorpha:* as **a :** a shrub (*A. fruticosa*) of the eastern U.S. **b :** a shrub (*A. californica*) of the Pacific coast **2 :** INDIGO BROOM

false indusium *n* **:** the revolute margin of some fern pinnae (as in the bracken and maidenhair ferns)

false ipecac *n* **1 :** an herb of the genus *Gillenia* that has properties similar to those of ipecac **2 :** BLOODFLOWER 1

false keel *n* **:** a thin keel or strip below the main keel used to serve as a protection and to increase a ship's lateral resistance — see SHIP illustration

false key *n* **:** PICKLOCK

false killer whale *n* **:** a small cosmopolitan toothed whale (*Pseudorca crassidens*) resembling and closely related to the killer whale

false labor *n* **:** pains resembling those of normal labor but without effacement or dilation of the cervix

false larch *n* **:** a tree of the genus *Pseudolarix; esp* **:** GOLDEN LARCH

false leaf *n* **:** CLADOPHYLL

false leg *n* **:** PROLEG

false ligaments *n pl* **:** folds of peritoneum assisting to retain the bladder in position

false lily of the valley *n* **:** a small 2-leaved herb (*Maianthemum canadense*) of the northern U. S. and parts of Canada

false logwood *n* **:** a West Indian timber tree (*Haemocharis haematoxylon*) of the family Theaceae with red wood

false loosestrife *n* **:** an American plant of the genus *Ludwigia*

false lupine *n* **:** an American plant of the genus *Thermopsis* with yellow pealike flowers — called also *golden pea, yellow pea*

false·ly *adv* [ME *falsly*, fr. *fals* false + *-ly*] **:** in a false manner: as **a :** WRONGLY, INCORRECTLY ⟨~ assumed that he was familiar with the subject⟩ **b :** not truthfully **:** DISHONESTLY ⟨recently cleared of a murder charge to which he had ~ confessed as a result of police brutality —Curtis Bok⟩ ⟨swore ~ that he had seen me that morning⟩ **c :** without cause **:** UNJUSTLY ⟨led to the exoneration of a man ~ convicted of forgery —*Current Biog.*⟩ **d :** DECEITFULLY, INSINCERELY ⟨smiled ~ at her unwelcome visitor⟩ **e :** not genuinely **:** SPECIOUSLY ⟨the difficulty in presenting Elizabethan plays is that they are liable to be made too modern or ~ archaic —T.S.Eliot⟩

false mallow *n* **1 :** an American plant of the genus *Malvastrum* **2 :** GLOBE MALLOW **3 a :** INDIAN MALLOW 2 **b :** any of several other plants of the genus *Sida*

false mange *n* **:** severe seborrhea of domestic animals

false manna *n* **:** a product similar to the manna from ash trees but obtained from other plants

false membrane *n* **:** a fibrinous deposit with enmeshed necrotic cells formed esp. in croup and diphtheria

false mermaid *n* **:** a plant of the genus *Floerkea; esp* **:** a slender annual aquatic herb (*F. proserpinacoides*) of eastern No. America with small white flowers

false-mermaid family *n* **:** LIMNANTHACEAE

false mesquite *n* **:** a dwarf somewhat prostrate shrub (*Calliandra eriophylla*) sometimes used for forage in the western U. S.

false mildew *n* **:** DOWNY MILDEW

false mistletoe *n* **:** MISTLETOE 2a

false miterwort *n* **:** an American white-flowered woodland spring-blooming herb (*Tiarella cordifolia*) — called also *coolwort, foamflower*

false music *n* **:** MUSICA FICTA

false·ness *n* -ES [ME *falsnesse*, fr. *fals* false + *-nesse* -ness] **:** the quality or state of being false: as **a :** contrariety to the fact **:** INACCURACY ⟨the ~ of a wicked rumor⟩ **b** (1) **:** UNFAITHFULNESS, TREACHERY, PERFIDY ⟨upbraided him for his ~ to his wife⟩ (2) **:** lack of integrity or uprightness **:** INSINCERITY ⟨there is a certain ~ about the man that I dislike⟩

false nettle *n* **:** any of several plants of the genera *Boehmeria* and *Laportea*

false nostril *n* **:** a blind pouch two or three inches long of unknown function lying between the nasal and premaxillary bones of the horse and related animals

false nutmeg *n* [so called fr. the shape of the fruit] **:** a tree of the genus *Torreya*

false oat grass *n* **1 :** TALL OAT GRASS **2 :** YELLOW OAT GRASS

false paca *n* **:** any of several So. American rodents constituting a genus *Dinomys* closely related to the pacas and chiefly distinguished by their long tails — called also *long-tailed paca*

false-packed \ˈ=ˈ=\ *adj* **:** containing other than the specified grade or amount — used of a bale of cotton

false papers *n pl* **:** documents carried by a ship giving false representations respecting her cargo, destination, or other matters for the purpose of deceiving

false pareira *n* **:** the root of a tropical vine (*Cissampelos pareira*) that is sometimes used like So. American pareira

false parenchyma *n* **:** PSEUDOPARENCHYMA

false pelvis *n* **:** the upper broader portion of the pelvic cavity

false pennyroyal *n* **:** an American annual mint (*Isanthus brachiatus*) with sticky entire leaves and blue flowers

false pimpernel *n* **1 :** CHAFFWEED **2 :** a plant of the genus *Ilysanthes* **3 :** a plant of the genus *Lindernia* (family Scrophulariaceae) with usu. purplish flowers having only two fertile stamens

false position *n* **:** a method of solution of a problem that uses the result obtained by replacing the unknown by trial values

false-positive \ˈ=ˈ=(=)=\ *n* **:** an individual under test whose laboratory data or scores classify him esp. because of imperfection or hypersensitivity of the method in a reference group or diagnostic category he does not belong in

false pregnancy *n* **:** PSEUDOCYESIS, PSEUDOPREGNANCY

false pretenses *n pl* **:** false representations concerning past or present facts or events for the purpose of defrauding another

false proscenium *n* **:** a frame within the fixed proscenium used to make smaller the exposed area of the inner stage

false quantity *n* **:** faulty pronunciation or metrical use of a vowel with respect to its quantity (as in reading Latin verse)

false quarter *n* **:** a cleft in the quarter of a horse's foot

falser *comparative of* FALSE

false ragweed *n* **1 :** a plant of the genus *Franseria* having spiny seeds and resembling a ragweed **2 :** BURWEED MARSH ELDER

false relation *n* **:** the discrepancy in traditional harmony caused by using in different musical voice parts either simultaneously or in successive chords any given tone and one of its chromatic derivatives — called also *cross relation*

false representation *n* **1 :** an untrue representation willfully made to deceive another to his damage **2 :** a representation in fact untrue but recklessly made when the maker has no knowledge as to its truth or falsity **3 :** a promise made with no intention of carrying it out — see DECEIT, FRAUD

false return *n* **1 :** an incorrect report ⟨*false returns* on an income-tax blank⟩ **2 :** an untrue return made to a legal process by the officer to whom it was delivered for execution

false rib *n* **:** any of the ribs with cartilages which unite indirectly or not at all with the sternum

false ring *also* **false annual ring** *n, forestry* **:** a layer of wood

less than a full season's growth and sometimes not all around the trunk — compare ANNUAL RING
false rue anemone *also* **false rue** *n* **:** a slender white-flowered herb (*Isopyrum biternatum*) of the family Ranunculaceae of eastern No. America closely resembling meadow rue
falses *pres 3d sing of* FALSE
false saffron *n* **:** SAFFLOWER
false sandalwood *n* **1 :** a small spiny often shrubby tropical tree (*Ximenia americana*) that has an astringent bark rich in tannins, leathery opposite leaves, whitish flowers, and a yellow to orange edible fruit which resembles a plum and contains a very oily seed and that yields a very dense heavy aromatic wood **2 :** the wood of the false sandalwood sometimes substituted for sandalwood
false sanicle *n* **:** FAIRY CUP 3
false sarsaparilla *n* **:** any of several American plants of the genus *Aralia:* as **a :** WILD SARSAPARILLA 1 **b :** FALSE SOLOMON'S SEAL
false scab *n* **:** severe seborrhea of domestic animals
false scorpion *n* **:** BOOK SCORPION
false sisal *n* **:** a fiber derived from a plant (*Agave decipiens*) closely related to sisal
false smut *n* **1 :** GREEN SMUT **2 :** a disease of palms (as those of the genus *Phoenix*) that is caused by a fungus (*Graphiola phoenicis*) and characterized by small cylindrical protruding pustules surrounded often by yellowish leaf tissue
false solomon's seal *n, usu cap 1st S* **:** a plant of the genus *Smilacina* differing from Solomon's seal in having the flowers in a terminal raceme or panicle
false spider mite *n* **:** any of several phytophagous mites that do not web the plants on which they feed
false spikenard *n* **:** a false Solomon's seal (*Smilacina racemosa*)
false spirea *n* **:** a plant of the genus *Sorbaria*
falsest *superlative of* FALSE
false sting *n* **:** a virus disease of apples causing malformation of the fruit which resembles injury from insect feeding
false stripe *n* **:** a seed-borne virus disease of barley that causes light brown linear mottling of the leaves
false sunflower *n* **:** BURWEED MARSH ELDER
false syringa *n* **:** MOCK ORANGE 1
false tack *n* **:** a coming up into the wind and filling away again on the same tack
false tamarisk *n* **:** GERMAN TAMARISK
false title *n* **:** HALF TITLE 1
false topaz *n* **:** a yellow transparent variety of quartz **:** CITRINE
false truffle *n* **:** the subterranean basidial fruit of various fungi (families Sclerodermataceae and Hymenogastraceae) somewhat like the ascus fruit of the truffle
[1]**fal·set·to** \fȯl'sed·(,)ō, -e(,)tō\ *n* -S [It, fr. *falso* false, (fr. L *falsus*) + *-etto* (dim. suffix) — more at FALSE] **1 :** an artificially high voice; *esp* **:** an artificially produced singing voice that overlaps and extends above the range of the full voice esp. of a tenor and is noticeably less rich, expressive, and powerful than the full voice **2 :** a singer (as a male alto) who uses falsetto — contrasted with *castrato*
[2]**falsetto** \"\ *adj* **:** relating to falsetto
[3]**falsetto** \"\ *adv* **:** in falsetto ⟨to sing ~⟩
false umbel *n* **:** a cyme in which the main axis is of the same length as the secondary axes (as in various pelargoniums)
false unicorn root *also* **false unicorn** *or* **false unicorn plant** *n* **1 :** BLAZING STAR b **2 :** a colicroot (*Aletris farinosa*)
false vampire bat *n* **:** any of various carnivorous bats of the families Megadermatidae and Phyllostomatidae
false violet *n* **:** DEWDROP
false vocal cord *n* **:** either of the upper pair of vocal cords that are not directly concerned with speech production
false wall cress *n* **:** a purple-flowered or violet-flowered perennial herb (*Aubrietia deltoidea*) of southern Europe used as an ornamental
false water lily *n* **:** WATER SOLDIER 1
false wild oats *n* **:** FATUOID
false willow *n* **:** a shrub (*Baccharis glutinosa*) with viscid lanceolate leaves
false wing *n* **:** BASTARD WING
false wintergreen *n* **:** a widely distributed shinleaf (*Pyrola rotundifolia americana*) — called also *wild lily of the valley*
false winter's bark *n, usu cap W* **:** CANELLA BARK
false wireworm *n* **:** a slender hard-coated brownish or yellowish grub that is the larva of any of various tenebrionid beetles (genus *Eleodes*) and that is often destructive to germinating wheat in western No. America
falsework \'=,=\ *n* **1 :** temporary construction work on which a main work is wholly or partly built and supported until it is made strong enough to support itself ⟨~ of a bridge⟩ **2 :** a temporary framework used to support a part or all of a structure during demolition
fal·si cri·men \,fȯl,sē'krēmən, -sī'krīm-, -,men\ *n* [LL, crime of falsifying] **:** the infamous crime of falsifying including in Roman law every crime committed by fraud and deceit, in modern civil law mainly forgery but also perjury and similar offenses, and in English and U. S. law also counterfeiting — called also *crimen falsi*
fal·sie \'fȯl(t)sē, -si\ *n* -S ['*false* + *-ie*] **:** a breast-shaped usu. fabric or rubber cup that is used to pad a brassiere — usu. used in pl.
fal·si·fi·abil·i·ty \,fȯl(t)sə,fīə'bilədē, -bilətē, -i\ *n* -ES **:** the quality or state of being falsifiable
fal·si·fi·able \'==,=əbəl, ,==ˈ===\ *adj* **:** capable of being proved false **:** DEFEASIBLE
fal·si·fi·ca·tion \,fȯl(t)səfə'kāshən\ *n* -S [MF, fr. ML *falsification-, falsificatio*, fr. *falsificatus* (past part. of *falsificare*) + L *-ion-, -io* -ion] **1 :** the act or an instance of falsifying: as **a :** a counterfeiting (as of a work of art) **b :** a usu. willful misstatement or misrepresentation **:** DISTORTION ⟨a far-reaching and fateful ~ of German cultural history —W.A.Kaufmann⟩ ⟨of *Othello* . . . one can say bluntly . . . that it suffers in current appreciation an essential ~ —F.R.Leavis⟩ **2 :** the act or an instance of showing something to be false or erroneous **3 :** a fraudulent alteration of or tampering with (as an account or judgment)
fal·si·fi·er \'==,fī(ə)r, -īə\ *n* -S **:** one that falsifies
fal·si·fy \-,fī\ *vb* -ED/-ING/-ES [ME *falsifien*, fr. MF *falsifier*, fr. ML *falsificare*, fr. L *falsus* false + *-ificare* -ify — more at FALSE] *vt* **1 :** to prove to be false **:** CONFUTE ⟨other records or traces which seemed to ~ the hypothesis based on the records that I found —H.N.Lee⟩; *specif* **:** to prove false so as legally to avoid, defeat, or rectify ⟨~ a judgment⟩ **2 a :** to make false by mutilation or addition **:** tamper with ⟨~ a passport⟩ ⟨~ a will⟩ **b :** COUNTERFEIT, FORGE, ADULTERATE ⟨producing *falsified* champagne for sale to hotels⟩ **3** *obs* **:** to cause (as one's word) to be violated or betrayed **4 :** to prove unsound or untrue by experience **:** DISAPPOINT, FRUSTRATE ⟨its spacious promises of a new era have almost every one of them been *falsified* —W.M.Citrine⟩ **5 :** to represent falsely **:** MISREPRESENT, DISTORT ⟨contended that the history of early Virginia had been *falsified* by the Court party in England —T.J.Wertenbaker⟩ ⟨a low-priced sunglass lens said to be completely effective without ~*ing* the colors seen through it —*Newsweek*⟩ ⟨the novelist has distorted the characters and *falsified* their motives —Bernard De Voto⟩ ~ *vi* **1 :** to violate the truth **:** tell lies ⟨impressed with the fact that he has *falsified* in his answer —H.G.Armstrong⟩ **2 :** to engage in misrepresentation or distortion ⟨his account *falsifies* from beginning to end⟩
falsing *pres part of* FALSE
fal·si·ty \'fȯl(t)səd·ē, -sətē, -i\ *n* -ES [ME *falsete, falste*, fr. OF *falseté, falsité*, fr. LL *falsitat-, falsitas*, fr. L *falsus* + *-itat-, -itas* -ity] **1 a :** the character or quality of not conforming to the truth or facts **:** UNTRUTH ⟨truth (or ~) is a property of declarative statements —Philip Hallie⟩ **b :** DECEITFULNESS, UNTRUSTWORTHINESS, FAITHLESSNESS ⟨the ~ of an ally⟩ **c :** specious, artificial, insincere, or unreal character ⟨the ~ of her smile⟩ ⟨the contrast between the reality of history and the ~ of the most commercialized and popular art of the times —J.T. Farrell⟩ **2 :** something that is false or unreal **:** FALSEHOOD, LIE, SHAM ⟨here we do not escape reality into a pleasant ~ —M.S.Dworkin⟩
fal·staff·ian \(')fȯlz¦tafēən, -l¦st-, -taaf-, -taif-, -täf-\ *adj, usu cap* [Sir John *Falstaff*, character in Shakespeare's *Merry Wives of Windsor* and *Henry IV* + E *-ian*] **1 :** resembling the fat, jovial, humorous, dissolute Shakespearean character Sir John Falstaff ⟨a *Falstaffian* figure, fantastically overfed and fat —C.G.Bowers⟩ **:** like that of Sir John Falstaff ⟨the romanticism of Brahmin culture with all *Falstaffian* vulgarity deleted —V.L.Parrington⟩ **2 :** resembling the ragged regiment raised by Sir John Falstaff
fal·sum \'fȯl(t)səm\ *n* -S [L, fr. neut. of *falsus*, past part. of *fallere* to deceive — more at FAIL] **:** FALSI CRIMEN
falt·boat \'fält,=, 'fȯl-\ *n* [part trans. of G *faltboot* folding boat, fr. *falten* to fold (fr. OHG *faldan*) + *boot* boat — more at FOLD] **:** a small collapsible canoe made of rubberized sailcloth stretched over a knockdown framework — called also *foldboat*
[1]**fal·ter** \'fȯltə(r)\ *vb* **faltered; faltered; faltering** \-ltəriŋ, -l·tr-\ **falters** [ME *falteren*, perh. of Scand origin; akin to Icel *faltrask* to be burdened, be unsure, Faeroese *fjaltra* to tremble] *vi* **1 a :** to walk in an unsteady or wavering manner **:** STUMBLE, STAGGER ⟨the naked stranger ~*s* out of the thicket and drops to his knees —Dudley Fitts⟩ **b :** to be unsteady on one's feet **:** give way **:** TOTTER ⟨being eighty-nine, he had a chair . . . but . . . he stood without complaint or ~*ing* —Joseph Bryan⟩ ⟨he could feel his legs ~⟩ **c :** to move waveringly or unsteadily as if uncertain ⟨her eyes ~*ed* away from his —Erle Stanley Gardner⟩ ⟨forced to bail out of ~*ing* airplanes over the Alps —*Nat'l Geographic*⟩ **2 :** to speak brokenly or weakly **:** HESITATE, STAMMER ⟨his voice ~*ed* just the least bit —Joseph Conrad⟩ **3 a :** to hesitate in purpose or action **:** WAVER, FLINCH ⟨never ~*ed* in his determination to make good⟩ ⟨warned the Western democracies to suffer no division or ~*ing* in their duty —*Current Biog.*⟩ **b :** to lose drive, effectiveness, or momentum in some way **:** WEAKEN, DECLINE, FAIL ⟨his powers of musical invention never ~ or flag⟩ ⟨when a symbolist poem ~*s* for a moment it is irretrievably lost —Burns Singer⟩ ⟨Britain's vaunted prosperity was ~*ing* —*Time*⟩ ~ *vt* **:** to utter with hesitation or in a broken, trembling, or weak manner ⟨~ an excuse⟩
syn see HESITATE
[2]**falter** \"\ *n* -S **:** the act or an instance of faltering ⟨I managed to do what was required of me without ~ —Lonnie Coleman⟩; *esp* **:** QUAVER ⟨a ~ in her voice⟩
fal·ter·er \-tərə(r)\ *n* -S **:** one that falters
fal·ter·ing·ly *adv* **:** in a faltering manner **:** HESITANTLY, UNCERTAINLY ⟨she gave her answer ~⟩
falus *pl of* FELS
falx \'falks, 'fȯl-\ *n, pl* **fal·ces** \-l,sēz\ [NL, fr. L, lit., sickle] **:** a sickle-shaped part or structure; *esp* **:** either of two folds of the dura mater separating the hemispheres of the brain, the larger being between the cerebral hemispheres and containing the sagittal sinuses, the smaller between the lateral lobes of the cerebellum — called also respectively *falx ce·re·bri* \-k(s)'serə,brī\, *falx ce·re·bel·li* \-),serə'be,lī\
fam *abbr* **1** familiar **2** family **3** famous
FAM *abbr* foreign airmail
fa·ma·ti·nite \,famə'tē,nīt, ,fäm-\ *n* -S [G *famatinit*, fr. Sierra de *Famatina*, mountain range in northwest Argentina + G *-it* -ite] **:** a mineral Cu_3SbS_4 consisting of a reddish gray copper antimony sulfide (sp. gr. 4.57)
[1]**fame** \'fām\ *n* -S [ME, fr. OF, fr. L *fama;* akin to Gk *phēmē* utterance, report; derivative fr. the root of L *fari* to speak, Gk *phanai* to say, *phōnē* sound — more at BAN] **1 a :** public estimation of a person or thing **:** REPUTATION ⟨ought to . . . inquire into her former and present ~ —John Chamberlayne⟩ **b :** general recognition for outstanding achievement **:** popular acclaim **:** GLORY, RENOWN ⟨~ is the thirst of youth —Lord Byron⟩ **c :** recognition of an unfavorable kind **:** NOTORIETY ⟨achieved ~ . . . when its school board became the first in the state to require a loyalty oath from the officers of all organizations seeking to use the school facilities —David Clinton⟩ **2** *archaic* **:** common talk **:** RUMOR ⟨and the ~ thereof was heard in Pharaoh's house —Gen 45:16 (AV)⟩
syn NOTORIETY, REPUTATION, REPUTE, CELEBRITY, ÉCLAT, HONOR, RENOWN, GLORY: in this set FAME is a general term used to indicate a state of being quite widely known. It is likely to be favorable in its connotations but, perhaps more than any of the accompanying words, may be qualified widely ⟨he still shines when the light of his successors is fading away; they had celebrity, Spinoza has *fame* —Matthew Arnold⟩ ⟨*fame* is proof that people are gullible —R.W. Emerson⟩ NOTORIETY, sometimes still neutral in its suggestions and indicating the fact of being widely known, is likely to suggest being widely known for evil, shameful, reprehensible, or eccentric behavior ⟨if the occupation of steamboats be a matter of such general *notoriety* that the court may be presumed to know it —John Marshall⟩ ⟨that brilliant, extravagant, careless Reverend Doctor Dodd who acquired some fame and much *notoriety* as an eloquent preacher —Havelock Ellis⟩ REPUTATION usu. suggests the commonly circulated and accepted judgment of one's character; unmodified, it may suggest a quite good reputation, a measure of fame on some particular account ⟨the downfall of his first political *reputation* following the disaster of the Dardanelles expedition —*New Republic*⟩ ⟨he went on writing war poetry and gained a good deal of *reputation* as one of our soldier poets —Rose Macaulay⟩ REPUTE may suggest high esteem ⟨the *repute* which a classical Latin style and the ancient classics had acquired in Renaissance Italy —G.C.Sellery⟩ CELEBRITY in this sense may suggest sudden fame and widespread popularity which may turn out to be ephemeral ⟨there was a time in London when no one could afford to say he had not read the *Poems Descriptive of Rural Life and Scenery*, but that was in the spring of 1820, and the season of *celebrity* was often quite as short then as it is today —H.V.Gregory⟩ ÉCLAT in this sense may suggest a certain suddenness whereby something becomes well known or a certain brilliancy or flashiness in its reputation ⟨this letter was sprung, with great *éclat*, in public hearing —*New Republic*⟩ ⟨consider what luster and *éclat* it will give you . . . to be the best scholar, of a gentleman, in England —Earl of Chesterfield⟩ HONOR in this sense indicates widespread fame and esteem through achievement or position ⟨wherever the bright sun of heaven shall shine, his *honor* and the greatness of his name, shall be, and make new nations —Shak.⟩ ⟨admirals all, for England's sake, *honor* be yours and fame —H.J. Newbolt⟩ RENOWN means much the same as HONOR; it may imply additional acclaim ⟨filled with a nation's praise, filled with *renown* —Alfred Tennyson⟩ GLORY is the strongest and most complimentary word in this group; it suggests lasting, extreme, and deserved fame ⟨there he [Washington] lived in noble simplicity; there he died in *glory* —Edward Everett⟩
[2]**fame** \"\ *vt* -ED/-ING/-S [ME *famen*, fr. *fame*, n.] **1 :** to report, consider, or repute — usu. used in passive ⟨the fancy cannot cheat so well as she is *famed* to do —John Keats⟩ **2 a :** to make famous or renowned — usu. used in passive ⟨an inn . . . that was *famed* for its corn bread —*Amer. Guide Series: Md.*⟩ **b** *obs* **:** to make notorious or infamous ⟨foes enough would ~ thee in their hate —Ben Jonson⟩
[3]**fame** \"\ *Scot var of* FOAM
famed *adj* [fr. past part. of [2]*fame*] **:** FAMOUS ⟨development of the world's most ~ garden spot —*Monsanto Mag.*⟩
fameflower \'=,=\ *n* ['*fame* + *flower;* prob. fr. the transitoriness of its petals] **:** a linear-leaved herb (*Talinum teretifolium*) of the eastern U. S. with scapes of ephemeral pink flowers
fame·less \'fāmləs\ *adj* **:** little known **:** OBSCURE, UNDISTINGUISHED
fames *pl of* FAME, *pres 3d sing of* FAME
fa·meuse \fə'myüz\ *n* -S *usu cap* [F, fem. of *fameux* famous] **:** any of various apples having deep red stripes and crisp white flesh
fa·mil·ia \fə'milēə, -lyə\ *n, pl* **famili·ae** \-lē,ē, -lē,ī\ [L — more at FAMILY] **1** *Roman law* **:** the paterfamilias, his legitimate descendants and their wives, and all persons adopted into his family and their wives — compare POTESTAS **2** *Old English law* **a :** the servants of one master **b :** a quantity of land adequate for the maintenance of one family
fa·mil·ial \fə'milyəl, -lēəl\ *adj* [F, fr. L *familia* family + F *-al*] **1 :** of, relating to, or having the characteristics of a family ⟨children of the same ~ background —E.L.Volpe⟩ **2 :** having a tendency to occur in different members of a family to a degree greater than chance would allow ⟨a ~ disease⟩ — compare CONGENITAL, HEREDITARY
[1]**fa·mil·iar** \fə'milyə(r), *chiefly in substand speech* fər'milyər\ *n* -S [ME *familier* member of one's household, intimate associate, fr. OF, member of one's household, fr. *familier*, adj.] **1 :** an intimate associate **:** COMPANION ⟨with ~*s* he has the unvarnished candor of old people and children —Janet Flanner⟩ **2 :** a member of the household of a high official **:** one who belongs to an official family ⟨a mile away 269 . . . ~*s* or courtiers were buried —V.G.Childe⟩; *specif* **:** a layman employed as a resident servant in a Roman Catholic institution or in the household of a high dignitary of the Roman Catholic church **3 :** a confidential officer of the Inquisition whose task was to apprehend and imprison the accused **4 :** a supernatural spirit often embodied in an animal and at the service of a person ⟨the loathsome toad, the witches' ~ —Harvey Graham⟩ **5 a :** one who is well acquainted with something ⟨~*s* of the measure —C.G.Poore⟩ **b :** one who frequents a place ⟨~*s* of the embassy —Rebecca West⟩
[2]**familiar** \"\ *adj* [ME *familier, familiar*, fr. OF *familier*, fr. L *familiaris*, fr. *familia* + *-aris* -ar — more at FAMILY] **1 :** closely associated **:** INTIMATE: as **a :** on a family footing ⟨his ~ friend —Marjory S. Douglas⟩ **b :** having a supernatural relationship with people ⟨a prayer to the ~ sharks . . . who have exchanged souls with living men —C.E.Fox⟩ **c :** sexually intimate ⟨the girl with whom he has been ~ having to leave school —Evelyn M. Duvall⟩ **2** *obs* **:** affable and courteous **:** SOCIABLE ⟨bland and ~ to the throne he came —Alexander Pope⟩ **3 a :** of or relating to a family ⟨~ domestic happenings —G.F. Whicher⟩ ⟨it is convenient to refer to many of the natural acids by their ~ names —T.P.Hilditch⟩ **b :** designed for family use **:** frequented by families ⟨a ~ resort . . . favored by couples with children —Betty de Sherbinin⟩ **4 :** of an informal nature **:** UNCEREMONIOUS: as **a :** free and easy ⟨a child's ~ access to his eminent . . . circle —W.V.O'Connor⟩ **b :** marked by informality and nonadherence to rigid structure ⟨he learned to write a passable ~ essay —J.W.Krutch⟩ ⟨functional varieties may roughly be grouped together in the two classes ~ and formal writing and speaking —J.S.Kenyon⟩ **c :** overly free and unrestrained **:** PRESUMPTUOUS ⟨he was rather noisily ~ with them —Robertson Davies⟩ **5** *of a wild animal* **:** used to human company **:** not alarmed by proximity to people **:** moderately tame ⟨he is tame and ~ and sings on the tree over your head or on the rock a few paces in advance —John Burroughs⟩ **6 a :** frequently seen or experienced **:** easily recognized ⟨he was a ~ figure at the opera —Edna Yost⟩ ⟨some ~ scent can carry one back to early childhood —Stuart Chase⟩ **b :** of everyday occurrence **:** COMMON, ORDINARY ⟨emotions which he has never experienced will serve his turn as well as those ~ to him —T.S.Eliot⟩ **c :** currently accepted or previously tested **:** WELL-KNOWN ⟨America's most ~ poet —Lewis Leary b. 1906⟩ ⟨the new can be learned successfully only in terms of the ~ —W.M.Mason⟩ **7 :** well acquainted through personal knowledge or study **:** CONVERSANT ⟨~ with what is being taught to our children in schools —Vera M. Dean⟩
syn INTIMATE, CONFIDENTIAL, CLOSE, THICK, CHUMMY: FAMILIAR may suggest natural ease, informality, lack of reserve, constraint, or stiffness, ensuing from long acquaintanceship, as among members of a family ⟨she was constantly referring to dear friends by their Christian names, in a casual and *familiar* way —Havelock Ellis⟩ ⟨the *familiar*, if not rude tone, in which people addressed her —Nathaniel Hawthorne⟩ INTIMATE always indicates closeness of relationship and it usu. suggests a closeness, warmth, personal nearness, or emotionalism which transcends and intensifies the more factual suggestion of FAMILIAR ⟨*intimate* as man is with his habitat —L.A.White⟩ ⟨the *intimate* political relation subsisting between the President of the U. S. and the heads of departments —John Marshall⟩ ⟨*intimate* letters . . . love letters which were never written to be published —Havelock Ellis⟩ ⟨man never derives any *intimate* help, any heart sustenance, from his brother man, but from woman —Nathaniel Hawthorne⟩ CONFIDENTIAL stresses a reposing of confidence, a willingness to confide innermost thoughts and feelings ⟨the growing harmony and *confidential* friendship which daily manifest themselves between their majesties —William Pitt †1778⟩ ⟨a tone as sad and *confidential* as if he were . . . preluding a declaration of love —W.M.Thackeray⟩ CLOSE in this sense suggests strong liking and accustomed agreement and compatibility leading to steady association ⟨I would be with Adam a lot . . . she'd tag along, for she and Adam were very *close* —R.P.Warren⟩ ⟨being *close* to Peggy, [he] was aware that she . . . acted by her own secret intuitions —Morley Callaghan⟩ THICK indicates an accustomed close association or cooperation, often in devious ways or for dishonest purposes ⟨he . . . does a lot of bail bond business . . . and is pretty *thick* with . . . the chief of police —Dashiell Hammett⟩ ⟨he'd told me that you and Pamela Dean were as *thick* as thieves —Dorothy Sayers⟩ CHUMMY takes its color from the word *chum* and describes easy, steady, confidential association with compatibility of interests ⟨an unprecedented thing . . . for a captain to be *chummy* with the cook —Jack London⟩ **syn** see in addition COMMON
fa·mil·iar·ism \-yə,rizəm\ *n* -S *archaic* **:** COLLOQUIALISM
fa·mil·iar·i·ty \fə,mil'yarəd·ē, -lē'(y)ar-,-lə'yar-, -rətē-, -i *also* -(y)er-\ *n* -ES [ME *familiarite*, fr. OF *familiarité*, fr. L *familiaritat-, familiaritas*, fr. *familiaris* + *-itat-, -itas* -ity] **1 a :** a state of close personal relationship **:** INTIMACY ⟨they never exposed their idolatry to the test of domestic ~ —G.B.Shaw⟩ **b** *obs* **:** a circle of intimate friends or relatives ⟨leaving of parents or other ~ —John Milton⟩ **2 a :** absence of ceremony **:** INFORMALITY ⟨began to treat him first with ~ and then with contumely —Robert Graves⟩ **b :** an overly informal act or expression **:** IMPROPRIETY ⟨employs insulting *familiarities* —*New Republic*⟩ **c :** sexual intimacy ⟨she is unwise enough to permit affectionate *familiarities* when she is with boys —Valeria H. Parker⟩ **3 :** close acquaintance with or knowledge of something ⟨~ with the forces in the world which tend to define our policies —W.A.Parker⟩
fa·mil·iar·iza·tion \fə,milyərə'zāshən, -,rī'z-\ *n* -S **:** the act or process or an instance of familiarizing
fa·mil·iar·ize \fə'milyə,rīz\ *vb* -ED/-ING/-S *see -ize in Explan Notes, vt* **1 :** to make known through experience or repetition **:** remove strangeness from ⟨Shakespeare . . . ~*s* the wonderful —Samuel Johnson⟩ **2** *archaic* **:** to accustom to something **:** HABITUATE ⟨intending to ~ my parishioners to it little by little —J.H.Newman⟩ **3 a** *archaic* **:** to make more affable **:** cause to unbend ⟨for the cure of this particular sort of madness it will be necessary to . . . ~ his carriage by the use of a good cudgel —Richard Steele⟩ **b** *archaic* **:** to introduce as a friend ⟨I should be glad . . . to be *familiarized* to the ladies of your family —Samuel Richardson⟩ **4 :** to make well acquainted **:** make conversant ⟨~ students with the use of periodicals —Frances Eldredge⟩ **5** *archaic* **:** to bring into common use **:** POPULARIZE ⟨I have *familiarized* the terms of philosophy —Samuel Johnson⟩ ~ *vi, archaic* **:** to act in an informal way **:** make oneself agreeable ⟨he . . . *familiarized* with his equals —Roger North⟩
fa·mil·iar·ly *adv* [ME *familierly*, fr. *familier*, adj. + *-ly* — more at [2]FAMILIAR] **1 :** in a familiar manner: as **a :** INTIMATELY ⟨he was widely known to many but ~ acquainted with few⟩ **b :** COMMONLY ⟨the frankfurter is ~ called a hot dog⟩ **c :** INFORMALLY ⟨hailed him ~ by his nickname⟩ **d :** PRESUMPTUOUSLY ⟨pinched her cheek ~ when they were introduced⟩ **2 :** without shyness or fear **:** BOLDLY ⟨the phoebe bird . . . comes ~ about the house —John Burroughs⟩
fa·mil·iar·ness *n* -ES **:** the quality or state of being familiar
familiar spirit *n* **1 :** a supernatural often malignant spirit in the service of an individual ⟨medicine men . . . can summon to their aid at any time their *familiar spirits* —G.P.Murdock⟩ — compare DEMON **2 :** the spirit of a dead person invoked by a medium to advise or prophesy ⟨a consultor with *familiar spirits* —Deut 18:11 (AV)⟩ — compare [2]CONTROL 3d
familiar verse *n* **:** LIGHT VERSE
fam·i·lism \'famə,lizəm\ *n* -S [*family* + *-ism*] **1** *sometimes cap* **:** the tenets and practices of the familists ⟨men who follow Anabaptism, ~, antinomianism, and other fanatic dreams —John Milton⟩ **2 :** a social pattern in which the family and familial solidarity, tradition, and social status tend to assume a position of ascendance over individual rights and interests within society ⟨the reduced emphasis on ~ of the middle-class family —M.B.Sussman⟩
fam·i·list \-ləst\ *n* -S *often cap* [*family* + *-ist*] **:** a member of a mystical and somewhat antinomian sect of 16th and 17th century Europe

fam·i·lis·tic \ˌfamə'listik\ *adj* [*familist* + *-ic*] **:** of, relating to, or based on a family or familism; *specif* **:** based on the family as a primary unit ⟨such stories as those of . . . Joseph and his brethren, and the prodigal son had a direct bearing upon life in a ~ society —A.D.Rees⟩

fa·mille jaune \fə,mē'zhōn\ *n* [F, lit., yellow family] **:** Chinese porcelain the decoration of which has a rich yellow background

famille noire \-mēn,wär, -mēnə'wär\ *n* [F, lit., black family] **:** Chinese porcelain the decoration of which has a black background

famille rose \-mē'rōz\ *n* [F, lit., pink family] **:** Chinese porcelain in the decoration of which a rose color predominates

famille verte \-mē've(ə)rt\ *n* [F, lit., green family] **:** Chinese porcelain in the decoration of which green predominates

¹fam·i·ly \'fam(ə)lē, 'faamlē, -li\ *n* -ES [ME *familie*, fr. L *familia* servants of a household, household including not only the servants but also the head of the household and all persons in it related to him by blood or marriage, fr. *famulus* servant; perh. akin to Skt *dhāman* dwelling place, *dadhāti* he puts, places — more at ¹DO] **1 a** *archaic* **:** a group of persons in the service of an individual ⟨he had a great ~, that is to say . . . many slaves who worked in his bronze foundry —Maurice Samuel⟩ **b :** the retinue or staff of a nobleman or high official ⟨invited . . . to join his military ~ as aide-de-camp —H.E. Scudder⟩ **c :** a group of people bound together by philosophical, religious, or other convictions **:** FELLOWSHIP ⟨belongs to the Kantian ~ —W.E.Schlaretzki⟩ **d :** a body of employees or volunteer workers united in a common enterprise ⟨reference is made not just to the administrators, but to every single member of the community hospital ~ —G.W.Gilbert⟩ **2 a :** a group of persons of common ancestry **:** CLAN ⟨let us assail the ~ of York —Shak.⟩; *specif* **:** a group of persons of distinguished lineage ⟨the office has always been held by men of ~ —Oswald Banon⟩ **b :** a people or group of peoples regarded as deriving from a common stock **:** RACE ⟨the worldwide ~ of human beings —K.F.Mather⟩ **3 a :** a group of individuals living under one roof **:** HOUSEHOLD ⟨the ~ includes a poodle —*TV Guide*⟩ **b :** the body of persons who live in one house and under one head including parents, children, servants, and lodgers or boarders; *specif* **:** a group of persons sharing a common dwelling and table considered for census purposes to include at one extreme a single person living alone and at the other the residents of a hotel or the inmates of a prison **4 :** a group of things having common features or properties: as **a** (1) *in the classification of languages of the eastern hemisphere* **:** a number of related languages comprising all those held to be demonstrably descended from a single ancestral language that itself is not demonstrably related to any other language by descent from a common ancestral language ⟨the Afro-Asiatic language ~⟩ (2) *in the classification of languages of the western hemisphere* **:** a number of related languages comprising all those held to be demonstrably descended from a single ancestral language believed to have existed approximately 5 to 25 centuries ago **b :** musical instruments having the same basic method of tone production ⟨the double-reed ~⟩ ⟨the viol ~⟩ **c :** a set of typefaces of the same name and basic design that are cast in various sizes, weights, and widths ⟨the Cheltenham ~⟩ — compare FONT, SERIES **d :** a closely related series of elements or chemical compounds: (1) **:** a subgroup in the periodic table ⟨the chromium ~⟩ (2) **:** RADIOACTIVE SERIES ⟨the radium ~⟩ (3) **:** a homologous series of organic compounds ⟨the paraffin ~⟩ **e :** a group of rocks of the same general mineralogical and chemical composition **f** (1) **:** a group of asteroids whose orbits have similar characteristics which remain little changed over long periods of time prob. because of their common origin (2) **:** a group of comets whose aphelion points are near that of one of the major planets prob. as a result of successive gravitational encounters with the planet **g :** a group of soils that have similar profiles and include one or more series — called also *soil family* **5 a :** the basic biosocial unit in society having as its nucleus two or more adults living together and cooperating in the care and rearing of their own or adopted children ⟨the association of adults . . . is the necessary nucleus of any ~ —Ralph Linton⟩ **b :** one's children ⟨a young mother scouring her numerous ~ with flat pancakes of . . . river clay —Marguerite Steen⟩ **c :** a male and female animal with their young ⟨the typical gorilla band has as many as five associated *families* —Weston La Barre⟩ **6 a :** a group of related plants or animals forming a category ranking above a genus and below an order, usu. comprising several to many genera, but sometimes including a single genus of notably distinctive characters **b** *in livestock breeding* (1) **:** the descendants or line of a particular individual esp. of some outstanding female (2) **:** an identifiable strain within a breed **c :** an ecological community consisting of a single kind of organism and usu. being of limited extent and representing an early stage of a succession **7** *math* **:** an infinite set — used of curves and surfaces

²family \"\ *adj* **1 :** of or relating to a family ⟨a strong ~ resemblance⟩ **2 :** adapted to family use or participation ⟨a ~ room⟩ ⟨~ dances⟩

family allowance *n* **:** a grant to an employee made typically by a government or an employer in addition to regular salary and graded according to occupation and the number of dependent children

family altar *n* **1 :** a place of family devotions **2 :** the custom of family devotions

family bible *n, usu cap B* **:** a large Bible usu. having special pages for recording births, marriages, and deaths

family car doctrine *or* **family purpose doctrine** *n* **:** the legal doctrine whereby the owner of an automobile is liable for the negligence or misconduct of a member of his family who while using the automobile with the owner's permission though not as his agent or servant causes injury to another

family circle *n* **:** a gallery in a theater or opera house usu. located above or behind a gallery containing more expensive seats

family contract *or* **family settlement** *n* **:** a contract between the members of a family settling the distribution or descent of its estates

family court *n* **:** COURT OF DOMESTIC RELATIONS

family doctor *or* **family physician** *n* **:** a general practitioner regularly called by a family in time of illness

family expense *n* **:** an expense incurred for whatever is used or kept for use in the family whether necessaries or luxuries — used in statutes making both husband and wife legally liable for such an expense

family fare *n* **:** a special transportation rate offered by public carriers on certain light-traffic days whereby a wife or children each pay half fare when accompanying a full-fare passenger — called also *family fare plan, family travel plan*

family farm *n* **:** a farm on which the farmer and members of his family do a substantial part of the work

family flour *n* **:** ALL-PURPOSE FLOUR

family income policy *n* **:** a term insurance policy on the life of a breadwinner providing special income benefits beyond the face amount that continue for the remainder of the child-rearing period after the death of the insured

family maintenance policy *n* **:** a term insurance policy on the life of a breadwinner providing special income benefits in addition to the face amount that continue for a specified number of years after the death of the insured

family man *n* **1 :** a man who has a family, esp. a wife and children living with him and dependent upon him **2 :** a responsible man of domestic habits

family meeting *n* **:** a formal meeting of not less than five relatives or next friends of a minor or other person held by official appointment under civil law to consider and give advice in his interest

family name *n* **1 :** SURNAME 2a **2 :** the name of an individual that identifies him with his family **3 :** a male forename that is the surname of another family (as of the mother or grandmother)

family of nations **1 :** the group of nations recognized as having equal status under international law ⟨oceans are regarded as the common property of the *family of nations*⟩ **2 :** a group of nations united by common historical, political, or ideological ties ⟨members of the British *family of nations* —Herbert Dorn⟩

family of orientation : the family of one's parents and relatives

family of procreation : the family created by marriage

family romance *n* **:** a childhood fantasy in which the individual believes that his actual parents are not his own and that he is really of higher birth

family skeleton *n* **:** a secret or hidden source of embarrassment or disgrace to a family — compare SKELETON IN THE CLOSET

family style *adv (or adj)* **:** with the food placed on the table in serving dishes from which those eating may help themselves as often as they like ⟨meals are served *family style*⟩ ⟨a *family style* dinner⟩

family tree *n* **1 :** GENEALOGY ⟨my services were enlisted by a wealthy snob . . . who was anxious to pursue his *family tree* —Wallace Clare⟩; *specif* **:** the relationships of languages of common parent stock **2 :** a schematic description of genealogical relationships ⟨the totem pole was their *family tree* —L.H.Appleton⟩; *specif* **:** a diagram showing the relationships of languages of common parent stock

family-tree theory *n* [trans. of G *stammbaumtheorie*] **:** a theory in linguistics: at various periods branches (as Germanic) sprang from a parent language (as Indo-European) and subsequently forked into subbranches (as West Germanic, North Germanic) that later split up into the various modern languages (as English, German, Swedish) — called also *pedigree theory*; compare WAVE THEORY

family wage *n* **1 :** the total income of a family **2 :** the income needed for the subsistence of a family

family way *n* **:** condition of being pregnant — used with *in* and *the* or *a* ⟨she is in the *family way* again —Mary W. Shelley⟩ ⟨she gets herself in a *family way* and is then, as a matter of course, married off —G.H.Shuster⟩

fam·ine \'famən\ *n* -S [ME, fr. MF, fr. (assumed) VL *famina*, fr. L *fames* hunger — more at DAZE] **1 :** a severe food shortage **:** a period of extreme scarcity of food ⟨six seasons of dearth approaching ~ —Samuel Van Valkenburg & Ellsworth Huntington⟩ **2** *archaic* **:** lack of food **:** extreme hunger **:** STARVATION ⟨horses . . . recovered from past ~ and fatigue —Washington Irving⟩ **3** *archaic* **:** a ravenous appetite ⟨death grinned . . . to hear his ~ should be filled —John Milton⟩ **4 :** a great scarcity or shortage of something ⟨a ~ of television sets —Irwin Edman⟩

famine bread *n* **:** a lichen (*Umbilicaria arctica*) found in arctic regions and sometimes used as food

famine fever *n* **:** RELAPSING FEVER

faming *pres part of* FAME

fam·ish \'famish, -mēsh, *esp in pres part* -məsh\ *vb* -ED/-ING/-ES [ME *famishen*, prob. alter. (influenced by such verbs as *finishen* to finish) of *famen* to famish, starve, modif. of MF *afamer*, fr. (assumed) VL *affamare*, fr. L *ad-* + (assumed) VL *-famare* (fr. L *fames* hunger)] *vt* **1 :** to reduce to extremities for lack of food or other necessities — usu. used in passive ⟨both were dirty, travel-weary, ~*ed* for food and slumber —David Walden⟩ **2** *archaic* **:** to kill by withholding food or water **:** cause to starve ⟨did he marry me to ~ me? —Shak.⟩ ~ *vi* **1** *archaic* **:** to die for lack of food **:** STARVE ⟨they suffer us to ~ and their storehouses crammed with grain —Shak.⟩ **2** *archaic* **:** to suffer for lack of something necessary ⟨you are all resolved rather to die than to ~ —Shak.⟩ ⟨you ~ for promotion —Benjamin Disraeli⟩

fam·ish·ment \-shmənt\ *n* -S [ME *famishement*, fr. *famishe-* (fr. *famishen*) + *-ment*] **1 :** the quality or state of being famished **2 :** the act or process of famishing

fam·meni·an \fə'mēnēən, fa'm-, -men-\ *adj, usu cap* [irreg. fr. *Famenne*, district in Belgium + E *-ian*] **:** of, relating to, or constituting a subdivision of the European Devonian — see GEOLOGIC TIME table

fa·mose \fə'mōs\ *vt* -ED/-ING/-S [ME *famosen*, fr. *famose*, adj., famous, fr. L *famosus*] *archaic* **:** FAMOUS

¹fa·mous \'fāməs\ *adj* [ME, fr. MF *fameux*, fr. L *famosus*, fr. *fama* fame + *-osus* -ose — more at FAME] **1 a :** much talked about **:** WELL-KNOWN ⟨puffer fish . . . are ~ for their ability to inflate themselves when annoyed —S.W.Tinker⟩ **b :** honored for achievement **:** CELEBRATED ⟨he knows innumerable ~ people from the theatrical world⟩ **c :** discreditably renowned **:** NOTORIOUS ⟨~ for her shrewish tongue —Peggy Durdin⟩ **2** *obs* **:** COMMON, USUAL ⟨taking the word . . . in its most ~ signification —John Lewis⟩ **3 :** EXCELLENT, FIRST-RATE ⟨a ~ dinner⟩

²famous \"\ *vt* -ED/-ING/-ES *archaic* **:** to make famous ⟨the painful warrior ~*ed* for fight —Shak.⟩

fa·mous·ly *adv* **1 :** in a celebrated manner **:** NOTABLY ⟨he was a novelist and dramatist but most ~ a poet⟩ **2 :** in a superlative fashion **:** EXCELLENTLY ⟨asked how he was bearing up under the strain of his relentless schedule . . . he replied that he was doing ~ —Robert Shaplen⟩ **3 :** to an unusual degree **:** VERY ⟨the cost of good TV time is ~ high —Walter Goodman⟩

fa·mous·ness *n* -ES **:** the quality or state of being famous

fam·u·lus \'famyələs\ *n, pl* **famu·li** \-,lī\ [G, academic assistant to a university professor, fr. L, servant — more at FAMILY] **:** a private secretary or attendant esp. upon a scholar or magician

¹fan \'fan, 'faa(ə)n\ *n* -S *often attrib* [ME, fr. OE *fann*, fr. L *vannus* — more at WINNOW] **1 a :** a basket or wooden shovel formerly used for tossing grain into the air to let the chaff be blown away **b :** any of various devices for winnowing grain **2 :** an instrument or device for producing an artificial current of air (as by a wafting or revolving motion of a broad surface): as **a :** a device for cooling the person usu. having the form of a segment of a circle and consisting of material (as feathers, paper, or silk) mounted on thin rods or slats moving about a pivot so that the device may be closed compactly when not in use **b :** any revolving vane used for producing a current of air (as in blowing a fire or ventilating a room or for governing rapid rotary motion by the resistance of the air) **c :** a fan wheel revolved to cool the radiator of an automobile engine **d :** a fly that controls the striking mechanism of a clock **e :** one of the small vanes on a smock windmill that receive the impulse of the wind and are so located as to keep the large sails in the direction of the wind **f** *slang* **:** an aircraft propeller **3 :** something felt to resemble an open fan: as **a :** a fan-shaped leaf (as of certain palms) **b :** the wing of a bird **c :** the tail of a bird **d :** any of several fan-shaped architectural members; *esp* **:** FANLIGHT **e :** a gently sloping fan-shaped body of detritus commonly at a place where there is a notable decrease in gradient; *usu* **:** one deposited by a stream **:** ALLUVIAL FAN

fan 2a

²fan \"\ *vb* **fanned; fanned; fanning; fans** [ME *fannen*, fr. OE *fannian*, fr. *fann*, n.] *vt* **1 a :** to separate and drive away the chaff of (grain) by means of a current of air **b :** to eliminate (as chaff) by winnowing **2 :** to move or impel (air) with or as if with a fan **3 :** to blow or breathe upon ⟨the breeze *fanned* her hair⟩ **4 :** to direct a current of air upon with or as if with a fan: as **a :** to cool and refresh by moving the air with a fan ⟨*fanned* her perspiring face⟩ **b :** to drive or scare with or as if with a fan ⟨~ away the smoke with a newspaper⟩ **c :** to force or seek to force to glow or flame up by a draft of air ⟨*fanning* the coals into a brisk blaze⟩ **d :** to stir up to activity as if by fanning **:** STIMULATE ⟨this conduct *fanned* his rage⟩ ⟨they tried to ~ our interest with coy hints⟩ **5** *archaic* **:** to move to and fro like a fan **:** WAVE **6** *slang* **:** BEAT, TAN, WHIP **7 a :** to spread like a fan — often used with *out* ⟨*fanning* out the cards in his hand⟩ **b :** to spread (as the leaves of an unbound book) with one edge of each element extending slightly beyond the next — often used with *out*, sometimes with *over* or *up* **8** *slang* **:** to feel (a person's clothing) in order to locate prospective loot; *broadly* **:** to search or examine (as a person or place) ⟨the guards found a gun when they *fanned* the cell block⟩ ⟨routinely *fanning* him for weapons⟩ **9 :** to strike (a batter) out in baseball or softball **10 :** to fire (a revolver) by squeezing the trigger and striking the hammer to the rear with the free hand thereby rotating the cylinder so that a new cartridge is detonated when it lines up with the firing pin ~ *vi* **1 :** to move like a fan **:** FLAP, FLUTTER ⟨muslin curtains *fanning* in the breeze⟩ ⟨white butterflies were *fanning* on the goldenrod⟩ **2 :** to spread like a fan — often used with *out* ⟨the glacial debris *fanned* out over the slope⟩ ⟨picnickers ~ out along each highway⟩ **3 a :** to drift gently as if in a current of air produced by a fan **b** *dial* **:** to move briskly **:** HUSTLE **4** *of a batter* **:** to strike out in a baseball or softball game

³fan \(')fan, fən\ *Scot var of* WHEN

⁴fan \'fan, 'faa(ə)n\ *var of* FEN

⁵fan *usu cap, var of* FANG

⁶fan \'fan, 'faa(ə)n\ *n* -S *often attrib* [prob. short for *fanatic*] **1 :** an enthusiastic devotee of a sport (as baseball) or diversion (as ballet) usu. as a spectator rather than a participant **2 :** an ardent admirer or champion (as of a person, technique, or pursuit) **:** ENTHUSIAST ⟨the president's thousands of ardent ~*s*⟩ ⟨camera ~*s*⟩ ⟨science-fiction ~*s*⟩ ⟨~ clubs⟩

fa·na \fə'nä\ *n* -S [Ar *fanā'* annihilation, dissolution] *Islam* **:** the annihilation (as in Sufism) of the individual human will before the will of God

fa·na·ga·lo \ˌfänəgə'lō\ *or* **fa·na·ka·lo** \-nəkə-\ *n* -S *cap* **:** a pidgin language based on Xhosa, Zulu, English, and Afrikaans and spoken in the mines in So. Africa

fa·nal \fə'nal, -näl, 'fanᵊl, 'fānᵊl\ *n* -S [It *fanale*, fr. MGk *phanarion*, fr. Gk *phanos* torch, fr. *phanos* bright; akin to Gk *phainein* to show — more at FANCY] *archaic* **:** a beacon on a ship or lighthouse

fan·a·lo·ka \ˌfanᵊl'ōkə\ *n* -S [prob. native name in Madagascar] **:** a civet (*Fossa fossa*) of Madagascar

fa·nam \fə'näm\ *n* -S [prob. modif. of Tamil *paṇam*, prob. fr. Skt *paṇa* bet, reward, wealth] **1 a :** an old gold or silver coin of southern India **b :** a silver coin of Travancore worth ⅛ of a rupee issued up until Indian independence in 1947 **2 :** a unit of value corresponding to a fanam

fanariot *usu cap, var of* PHANARIOT

¹fa·nat·ic \fə'nad·ik, -at|, |ēk\ *or* **fa·nat·i·cal** \|əkəl, |ēk-\ *adj* [*fanatic* fr. L *fanaticus* frantic, inspired by a deity, fr. *fanum* sanctuary, temple — more at FEAST] **1** *obs* **:** possessed by or as if by a demon; *broadly* **:** CRAZED, FRANTIC, MAD **2 :** governed, produced, or characterized by too great zeal ⟨~ enthusiasms⟩ **:** EXTRAVAGANT, UNREASONABLE **:** excessively enthusiastic esp. on religious subjects ⟨certain ~ sects⟩ — **fa·nat·i·cal·ly** \|ək(ə)lē, |ēk-, -li\ *adv* — **fa·nat·i·cal·ness** \|əkəlnəs, |ēk-\ *n* -ES

²fanatic \"\ *n* -S **1** *obs* **a :** LUNATIC **b :** a religious maniac **c :** an English nonconformist — used derogatorily esp. in the 17th century **2 :** a person exhibiting excessive enthusiasm and intense uncritical devotion usu. toward some controversial matter (as in religion, politics, or philosophy) and commonly urging his beliefs zealously and with unreasonable and uncompromising insistence; *broadly* **:** ENTHUSIAST ⟨the duchess became a boating ~⟩ **syn** see ENTHUSIAST

fa·nat·i·cism \|ə,sizəm\ *n* -S **:** fanatic outlook or behavior esp. as exhibited by excessive enthusiasm, unreasoning zeal, or wild and extravagant notions on some subject

fa·nat·i·cize \-,sīz\ *vb* -ED/-ING/-S *vt* **:** to cause to become a fanatic **:** imbue with fanaticism — used chiefly as a participial adjective ⟨a *fanaticized* mob⟩ ~ *vi* **:** to act or feel like a fanatic

fa·na·tism \'fanə,tizəm\ *archaic var of* FANATICISM

¹fanback \'=,=\ *adj, of a chair* **:** having a fan-shaped back; *esp, of a Windsor chair* **:** having the spindles of the back spread fanwise from the seat to the top rail

²fanback \"\ *n* **:** a fanback chair

fanback

fan blower *n* **:** a wheel with vanes on a rotating shaft in a case or chamber used to create a blast of air for a forge or a current for draft and ventilation — called also *fanner*

fan brake *n* **:** a fan or propeller used to provide resistance for its driving mechanism (as an engine or a dynamometer for measuring power)

fan·chon·ette \ˌfanchə'net\ *n* -S [F, fr. *Franchonette*, dim. of *Franchon*, nickname of *Françoise* Frances] *n* -S **:** an open tart covered with meringue or sometimes whipped cream

fan·ci·able \'fan(t)sēəbəl, 'faan-, 'fain-, -siə-\ *adj* **1 :** IMAGINABLE **2 :** ATTRACTIVE

fan·ci·cal \-sökəl\ *adj* [*fancy* + *-ic* + *-al*] *adj, now dial Eng* **:** FANCIFUL

fancied *adj* [fr. past part. of ²*fancy*] **1 :** formed or conceived by the fancy **:** IMAGINED, UNREAL ⟨a ~ wrong⟩ **2 :** FAVORITE, CHOSEN ⟨mounted on a ~ horse⟩ **3** *archaic* **:** artistically devised **:** FANCIFUL, ORNAMENTAL

¹fan·ci·er \'fan(t)sē(ə)r, 'faan-, 'fain-, -siə-\ *n* -S [²*fancy* + *-er*] **1 a :** one that has a special liking for or interest in a particular object, subject, or field **:** ENTHUSIAST ⟨~*s* of liturgical music⟩ **b :** a person who breeds or grows some kind of animal or plant with the intent of approaching some standard of excellence ⟨a pigeon ~⟩ ⟨the multitude of African violet ~*s*⟩ **2 :** one that employs or depends upon imagination (as in artistic designing or reaching decisions) **:** IMAGINER ⟨a ~ of foolish schemes⟩

²fancier *comparative of* FANCY

fancies *pl of* FANCY; *pres 3d sing of* FANCY

fanciest *superlative of* FANCY

fan·ci·fi·ca·tion \ˌfan(t)səfə'kāshən, ˌfaan-, ˌfain-\ *n* -S [fr. *fancify*, after such pairs as E *gratify: gratification*] **:** the art or an instance of making fanciful esp. by ornate elaboration ⟨a stilted ~ of language⟩

fan·ci·ful \'fan(t)səfəl, -aan-, -ain-, -sēf-\ *adj* **1 :** given to fancy, unrestrained imagination, or whim **:** guided by fancy, imagination, or illusion rather than by reason, experience, or fact ⟨I am not a ~ person, but . . . I seemed to hear Moriarty's voice screaming at me —A. Conan Doyle⟩ **2 a :** marked by fancy and unrestrained imagination in conception, thought, or consideration **:** not governed or ascertained by facts, realities, and reason ⟨~ image of primitive man, uncontaminated by science or art, undepraved by thought —C.H. Grandgent⟩ **b :** existing in fancy only **:** having no existence in fact ⟨the falsehood about some ~ secret treaties —F.D. Roosevelt⟩ **3 :** marked by or as if by fancy, whim, or imagination in design, construction, or execution ⟨the thin blue wreaths of smoke that curled up in such ~ whorls —Oscar Wilde⟩ **syn** see IMAGINARY

fan·ci·ful·ly \-f(ə)lē, -li\ *adv* **:** in a fanciful manner

fan·ci·ful·ness \-fəlnəs\ *n* -ES **:** fanciful quality **:** WHIMSICALITY

fan·ci·fy \-sə,fī\ *vb* -ED/-ING/-ES [¹*fancy* + *-fy*] *vt* **:** to make ornate, elaborate, or fancy ⟨a substantial dish and one easily *fancified* for a buffet supper⟩ ~ *vi* **:** to indulge in fancies ⟨resisting an impulse to ~ she turned back to work⟩

fan·ci·less \-sələs, -sil-\ *adj* **:** being without ideas or imagination **:** purely factual and lacking fancy or fanciful quality

fan·ci·ly \-səlē, -li\ *adv* **1 :** with fancy or imagination esp. when studied or affected ⟨a play with a sound plot but much too ~ developed⟩ **2 :** ELABORATELY, ORNATELY ⟨a ~ embroidered smock⟩ ⟨~ carved ornaments⟩

fan·ci·ness \-sēnəs, -sin-\ *n* -ES **:** fancy quality or form; *often* **:** overly elaborate or studied quality (as of literary style)

fan coral *n* **:** any of several gorgonians (as of the genus *Rhipidogorgia*) that form flat colonies resembling fans

fan-crested \'=ˌ==\ *adj, of a bird* **:** having a median erectile crest of feathers resembling a fan

¹fan·cy \'fan(t)sē, -aan-, -ain-, -si\ *n* -ES [ME *fantsy*, contr. of *fantasie* fantasy, fancy, fr. MF, fantasy, fr. LL *phantasia* imagination, fr. L, mental image, fr. Gk, appearance, image, faculty of imagination, fr. *phantazein* to make visible, present to the mind, fr. *phainein* to show; akin to OE *gebōned* polished, MD *boenen* to scour, scrub, Gk *phaos*, *phōs* light, Skt *bhāti* it shines] **1 a :** a liking formed by caprice rather than reason **:** INCLINATION ⟨a ~ for a stroll by the river this evening⟩ ⟨how does this strike your ~?⟩ ⟨had a ~ for rich delicacies⟩ **b :** amorous fondness **:** love or desire ⟨sometimes the queen took a ~ to handsome lads about the court⟩ **2 a :** an opinion or notion formed without much reflection **:** CAPRICE, WHIM ⟨the prediction of his return is based on a mere ~⟩ **b :** an image or representation of something formed in the mind ⟨what sorry *fancies* trouble you so?⟩ **c :** a product of mental conception (as an invention, device, or design) ⟨what a pretty ~ her drawing is⟩ ⟨an excellent trout fly, my father's own ~⟩ **3 :** a short instrumental composition of impromptu character — compare FANTASIA **4** *archaic* **:** fantastic quality or state **5 a** *obs* **:** something that pleases or entertains the taste or caprice **:** CONCEIT **b :** a fabric or an article of clothing manufactured to meet the demand of temporary styles and characterized by novelty in weave, color, design **c :** a diamond of gemstone quality and a color other than white or blue-white **6 a :** imagination esp. of a capricious sort; *often* **:** ILLUSION **:** delusive imagination **b :** the power of conception and representation used in artistic expression (as by a poet or painter) **:** IMAGINATION; *esp* **:** the power of conceiving and giving artistic form to that which is not existent, known, or experienced **c :** the invention of the novel and the unreal by recombining the elements found in reality so that life is represented in alien surroundings or essentially changed in natural physical and mental constitution (as in centaurs or giants) — distinguished from *imagination* **d :** the conceiving power which concerns itself with imagery (as figures of speech and details of a decorative design) **:** CONCEIT **7 :** judgment or taste (as in matters of art or dress) ⟨a person of delicate ~⟩ **8 :** a plant having variegated or parti-colored flowers; *also* **:** a variegated or parti-colored flower **9 a :** persons who pursue or are enthusiastic over some particular art, practice, or amusement: as (1) **:** sporting characters (2) **:** the followers of pugilism (3) **:** fanciers of animals ⟨the bulldog ~⟩ **b :** the object of interest of such a fancy; *esp* **:** PUGILISM **10** *also* **fancy roller :** a carding roller with long teeth used to raise fiber to the top of the main cylinder

syn FANCY, FANTASY, PHANTASY, PHANTASM, VISION, DREAM, DAYDREAM, and NIGHTMARE can signify, in common, a vivid idea or image present in the mind but having no concrete or objective reality. FANCY applies to anything conceived purely in the imagination whether it combines the elements of reality or is pure invention, usu. however, carrying the implication of something consequently more or less trifling ⟨was this only the *fancy* of a visionary, or . . . would it come true in the end? —Ellen Glasgow⟩ ⟨the status of archeological fact and *fancy* in the world today —W.W.Taylor⟩ FANTASY is an imaginative product (often extended and often in literary or artistic form) the greater part or the significant part of which has no correspondence with an objective reality, usu. implying an unrestrained inventiveness ⟨lost himself in a pictured *fantasy* of a London working-class shopping district on a Saturday night —C.S.Forester⟩ ⟨understood Bloom's mind as a river of nonsequiturs and *fantasies* of fear, guilt and desire —*Time*⟩ ⟨intoxicated by *fantasies* of world conquest —Nathaniel Peffer⟩ ⟨to cleanse our minds of all *fantasy* and daydream —*Economic Council Letter*⟩ PHANTASY, generally interchangeable with FANTASY, sometimes applies more to the psychological image-making power in general or its product, often also standing as a clearer antonym of *truth* or *reality* ⟨the distinctions between dream and reality, imagination and fact are blurred, and the speeches and activities of his characters are a further acting out of the schizophrenic's lonely *phantasy*-life, a charade in which the fixed meaning is contactlessness —Isaac Rosenfeld⟩ ⟨on the stage *phantasy*, a strange persuasive illusion, reigns —Leonide Zarine⟩ ⟨probably in his life, certainly in his poetry, there is no sharp boundary between *phantasy* and reality —H.S.Canby⟩ PHANTASM may apply to a phantasy, a mental image, or to a fantasy, esp. a hallucination ⟨held that only the Supreme Being exists and all that we call the natural world is illusion, a *phantasm* of the human mind having no real existence of its own —Radhagovinda Basak⟩ ⟨the figures in the rooming house, in the bars and cabarets slid out of his thoughts like *phantasms* that had no real existence —Donn Byrne⟩ VISION generally applies to what the mind sees so clearly or concretely as to suggest concrete reality, as if revealed by a supernatural power or by vivid intuition, sometimes applying to an image of something one wishes strongly to realize, often suggesting something spiritual in essence and therefore beyond the general grasp of the senses ⟨what *visions* and revelations God may have granted —Willa Cather⟩ ⟨*visions* of suddenly acquired wealth began to float in their minds —Sherwood Anderson⟩ ⟨our *vision* of world law and some sort of worldwide law enforcement agency —*Saturday Rev.*⟩ DREAM applies to the ideas and esp. the images present to the mind in sleep. Figuratively, like DAYDREAM, it suggests vague or idle, commonly happy, imaginings of future events or imaginative projections of the ideal self or life; unlike DAYDREAM, however, DREAM can apply to a serious, though usu. idealized, envisioning of a realizable, often planned, future event or state of affairs ⟨to wake from a bad *dream*⟩ ⟨were it not for the oppressions and monotonies of daily experience, the realm of *dream* and reverie would not be attractive —John Dewey⟩ ⟨a *dream* of a better society in which to live⟩ ⟨the shock that will bring them out of their *daydreams* into today's realities —*Science News Letter*⟩ ⟨a *daydream*, which is wishful thinking and an attempt to escape the experience of oneself —*Life*⟩ ⟨*daydreams* of a better world —*Fortune*⟩ NIGHTMARE applies to any frightful and oppressive dream which occurs in sleep or by extension to any vision or experience which inspires terror or cannot easily be shaken off ⟨to wake in a cold sweat from a *nightmare*⟩ ⟨how many of our daydreams would darken into *nightmares*, were there a danger of their coming true —L.P.Smith⟩ ⟨a marriage might be a *nightmare* to both partners —F.L.Allen⟩ **syn** see in addition IMAGINATION

²fancy \"\ *vb* -ED/-ING/-ES *vt* **1 a :** to be pleased with esp. on account of external appearance or manners **:** LIKE, ENJOY **:** have a taste for ⟨it's natural to ~ people who agree with us⟩ ⟨could ~ a bowl of chowder right now⟩ **b** *obs* **:** to love or desire (a person) **2** *obs* **a :** to suit the fancy of **:** PLEASE **b :** to arrange according to a conception of fancy **:** DESIGN, DEVISE **3 :** to form a conception of **:** IMAGINE — used imperatively to imply surprise ⟨~ that⟩ or to attract attention (as to a point of view) ⟨~ our embarrassment⟩ ⟨just ~ how we felt⟩ **4 :** to believe without any evidence or on the basis of false evidence or misconception **5 :** to believe without being certain **:** be inclined to think ⟨I ~ he will act quickly⟩ **6 :** to transform in fancy **:** visualize or interpret as ⟨I had such a scare; I *fancied* that rock was a crouching wolf⟩ — often used with *to be* ⟨I *fancied* myself to be a child once more⟩ ~ *vi* **1 :** to believe or imagine something without proof or proper grounds **:** build up fancies ⟨idly ~*ing* about all sorts of things as we drowsed in the shade⟩ ⟨let me ~ while I may⟩ **2** *obs* **:** to experience love or desire **syn** see LIKE, THINK

³fancy \"\ *adj* -ER/-EST **1 :** dependent or based on fancy **:** WHIMSICAL, IRREGULAR ⟨a ~ display of bad manners⟩ **2 a :** adapted to please the fancy or senses; *usu* **:** ornamental or elegant rather than utilitarian — often opposed to *plain* ⟨skilled in plain sewing and ~ needlework⟩ ⟨~ shoes with satin bows and 3-inch heels⟩ **b :** of particular excellence **:** of a quality distinctly above the average **:** specially selected — used esp. of foodstuffs and in some schemes of grading designating the highest of a series of grades of quality ⟨~ peaches packed in heavy syrup⟩ ⟨~ fresh fruits and vegetables⟩ **c** *of a gem* **:** of a color other than that usu. considered standard ⟨~ diamonds occur in red, green, blue, and golden to brownish yellow and include the most costly gemstones⟩ **d** *of an animal or plant* **:** bred for special qualities esp. such as lack practical utility ⟨~ goldfish with bulging eyes and immense fins⟩ **3 :** based on conceptions of the fancy rather than reality ⟨~ sketches of nature⟩ **4 a :** dealing in fancy goods ⟨a ~ department stocking notions, bric-a-brac, and other fripperies⟩ or in goods of fancy quality ⟨in the long run it often pays to patronize a ~ butcher who properly grades and trims his meats⟩ ⟨a ~ delicatessen⟩ **b :** above real value or the usual market price ⟨they ask ~ prices at that stand but everything is fresh and good⟩ **:** PREMIUM, TOP; *often* **:** EXCESSIVE, EXTRAVAGANT ⟨during the war ~ rents were paid for mere hovels⟩ **5 :** executed with manner or method requiring technical skill and with superior grace, ease, and harmony ⟨~ diving⟩ ⟨~ techniques in schooling horses⟩ **6** *of a plant or plant part* **:** PARTI-COLORED ⟨~ carnations⟩

fancy bread *n* **:** bread in other form than the conventional yeast-raised loaf; *esp* **:** any of various raised breads enriched (as with eggs, sweetenings, or nuts and fruit) and often baked in some other shape than an elongated loaf (as a braid or twist or an individual portion)

fancy-bred \ˈ=ˌ=\ *adj* **1 :** evoked by fancy **2** *of an animal* **:** having a highly desirable pedigree ⟨*fancy-bred* bulls should produce good progeny⟩

fancy dan \ˈ=ˌ=ˈdan, -daa(ə)n\ *n, often cap D* [³*fancy* + *Dan*, nickname of *Daniel*] **:** a showy fellow more impressive than effective; *esp* **:** a boxer who depends on technical skill and lacks hitting power

fancy dive *n* **:** DIVE 1a (1)

fancy dress *n* **:** a costume (as for a masquerade or party) departing from currently conventional style and usu. representing a fictional or historical character, an animal, the fancy of the wearer, or a particular occupation; *sometimes* **:** formal evening dress

fancy dress ball *also* **fancy ball** *n* **:** a ball at which persons appear in fancy dress

fancy-free \ˈ=ˌ=ˈ=\ *adj* [¹*fancy*] **:** free to imagine or fancy ⟨stage designers, in exercising their *fancy-free* talents —Donald Oenslager⟩ **:** not centering thoughts or attentions on one object; *usu* **:** free from amorous attachment or engagement

fancy geranium *n* **:** MARTHA WASHINGTON GERANIUM

fancy goods *n pl* **1 :** ¹FANCY 5b **2 :** items (as novelties, accessories, or notions) that are primarily ornamental or designed to appeal to taste or fancy rather than essential

fancy house *n* **:** BROTHEL

fancy line *n* **1 :** a line rove through a block at the jaws of a gaff to haul it down **2 :** any of several short lines used chiefly on shipboard for various purposes (as the control of sash windows)

fancy man *n* **1 a** *archaic* **:** a male sweetheart **b :** a woman's paramour **c :** a man who lives on the earnings of a prostitute **:** PIMP **2** *archaic* **:** a man who is a member of a fancy **3 :** DECORATOR d

fancy meat *n* **:** VARIETY MEAT

fancy pants *n pl but sing in constr* **:** an overly elegant, affected, and often somewhat epicene man

fancy roller *n* **:** FANCY 10

fancysick \ˈ=ˌ=ˌ=\ *adj* **:** LOVE-SICK

fancy up *vt* [³*fancy*] **:** to add superficial adornment esp. in order to refurbish ⟨that dress will do if you *fancy* it *up* with a bright scarf⟩

fancy woman *or* **fancy girl** *or* **fancy lady** *n* **:** a woman of questionable morals or reputation; *specif* **:** PROSTITUTE

fancywork \ˈ=ˌ=ˌ=\ *n* **:** decorative needlework (as embroidery and crocheting)

fand \ˈfand\ *chiefly Scot past of* FIND

fan dance *n* **:** a solo dance act performed in or as if in the nude, the dancer using one or more large fans for covering — compare BUBBLE DANCE

fan·dan·gle \fanˈdaŋgəl, ˈ=ˌ==\ *n* -s [perh. alter. of *fandango*] **1 :** an ornate or fantastic ornament ⟨stitched all over . . . with ~*s* in fruit-colored threads —Audrey Barker⟩ **2 :** NONSENSE, TOMFOOLERY

¹fan·dan·go \fanˈdaŋ(ˌ)gō, faan-, -daiŋ-\ *n* -s [Sp, perh. fr. (assumed) Pg *fadango*, fr. Pg *fado* — more at FADO] **1 a :** a lively Spanish or Spanish-American dance usu. performed by a man and a woman with castanets and in triple time **b :** music for such a dance **2** *chiefly Southwest* **:** a ball or other party featuring dancing **3 :** tomfoolery esp. in public affairs or other matters of serious import **:** ridiculous or childishly improper behavior or speech ⟨the continued ~*s* of this committee are subjecting the whole senate to public contempt⟩

²fandango \"\ *vi* -ED/-ING/-ES **:** to dance a fandango or to move or comport oneself as if dancing a fandango ⟨fighter planes ~*ing* in the sky⟩

F and D *abbr* freight and demurrage

fan delta *n* **:** an alluvial fan merging with a delta — called also *delta fan*

F and F *abbr* furniture and fixtures

fan·dom \ˈfandəm, ˈfaan-\ *n* -s **:** all the fans (as of a particular sport) ⟨~ impatiently awaits publication of the new football rules⟩

¹fane \ˈfān\ *n* -s [ME, fr. OE *fana* banner, flag — more at VANE] *archaic* **:** FLAG, PENNANT, BANNER; *also* **:** WEATHERCOCK

²fane \"\ *n* -s [ME, temple, fr. L *fanum* — more at FEAST] **1 :** TEMPLE **2** *archaic* **:** CHURCH

fa·ne·ga \faˈnāgə\ *n* -s [Sp, fr. Ar *fanīqah* large sack] **1 :** any of various units of capacity used in Spain and Spanish-American countries; *esp* **:** one of about 1.6 bushels **2 a :** any of various Spanish units of land area (as of 1.59 acres) **b :** a Mexican land area of 8.81 acres

fan·fa·rade \ˌfanfəˈrād\ *n* -s [*fanfare* + *-ade*] **:** FANFARE

¹fan·fare \ˈfan,fa(a)(ə)r, ˈfaan-, -fe(, |ə\ *n* [F, prob. of imit. origin] **1 :** a sounding of trumpets (as in coming into the lists); *specif* **:** a short and lively air performed on hunting horns during the chase **2 :** a showy outward display or motion **:** FLOURISH ⟨such devout phrases could easily be classed as introductory ~ —Paul Blanshard⟩ ⟨great political ~⟩ **3 :** an orchestral passage in which the brass instruments are prominent

²fanfare \"\ *vt* **:** to make public or call attention to with much clamor ⟨the crash of trees *fanfared* the spread of material civilization —R.G.Lillard⟩

fan·fa·ron \ˈfanfə,rän\ *n* -s [Sp *fanfarrón*, prob. of imit. origin] **1 :** an empty boaster **:** BRAGGART, SWAGGERER **2 :** FANFARE

fan·far·o·nade \ˌfan,farəˈnād, -näd\ *n* -s [F *fanfaronnade*, fr. Sp *fanfarronada*, fr. *fanfarrón* + *-ada* -ade (fr. LL *-ata*)] **1 :** SWAGGERING **:** empty boasting **:** BLUSTER; *often* **:** ostentatious or gaudy display **2 :** FANFARE

fanflower \ˈ=ˌ=\ *n* **:** a tropical shrub (*Scaevola koenigii*) of the family Goodeniaceae having white flowers

fan fold *n* [¹*fan* + *fold*, n.] **:** a fold of geologic strata in which both limbs are overturned forming an anticline if the limbs dip toward each other or a syncline if they dip away from each other

fanfold \ˈ=ˌ=\ *n, often attrib* [¹*fan* + *fold*, n.] **:** a collection of sheets or forms (as for billing) interleafed with carbon paper so as to permit a multiple record (as of a transaction) to be made with a single written or typed impression

fanfoot \ˈ=ˌ=\ *also* **fanfooted gecko** \ˈ=ˌ==-\ *n* -s **:** a gecko with toes expanded into lobes for adhesion; *esp* **:** a harmless Egyptian gecko (*Ptyodactylus hasselquistii*) that is thought by natives to have venomous toes

¹fang \ˈfaŋ\ *vb* -ED/-ING/-S [ME *fangen, fongen*, alter. of *fon* (past *feng*, past part. *fangen, fongen*), fr. OE *fōn* (past *fēng*, past part. *fangen, fongen*) — more at PACT] *vt* **1** *now dial Brit* **:** to lay hold of **:** SEIZE **2** *obs* **a :** to get into one's power or possession **:** SNARE, CAPTURE, OBTAIN, PROCURE **b :** to receive as a guest **c :** to set about **:** COMMENCE, UNDERTAKE, BEGIN **d :** TAKE, CONSUME **3** *now dial Eng* **:** to receive as due **:** EARN ~ *vi, dial Eng* **:** to act as sponsor at baptism — usu. followed by *to*

²fang \ˈfaŋ, ˈfaiŋ\ *n* -s [ME, fr. OE; akin to OHG *fang* seizure, ON *fang* grip; derivative fr. the root of OE *fōn* to seize] **1** *chiefly Scot* **:** BOOTY, PLUNDER **2** *obs* **:** a seizing or capture **:** CATCH; *also* **:** GRIP, GRASP **3 a :** a long sharp tooth by which the prey of an animal is seized and held or torn **:** a long pointed tooth; *esp* **:** one of the long, hollow or grooved, and often erectile, teeth of venomous serpents **b :** one of the chelicerae of a spider at the tip of which a poison gland opens **4 :** the root of a tooth or one of the processes or prongs into which a root divides **5 :** any of various sharp or elongated processes: as **a** *dial Eng* **:** TALON, CLAW **b :** a projecting tooth or prong (as on a lock, the plate of a belt clamp, or the end of a tool) **c :** a branch on a normally unbranched thickened tap root (as of a sugar beet or carrot) **6** *obs* **:** VANG

1 fangs 3a

³fang \"\ *vt* -ED/-ING/-S **1 :** to strike with or as if with fangs ⟨he jumped aside but the snake ~*ed* him⟩ ⟨the wind . . . ~*ed* his ears —Countee Cullen⟩ **2 :** to supply (a pump) with water so as to make it work **:** PRIME **3 :** to fit with or as if with fangs ⟨the gray rocks were ~*ed* with long icicles —Victor Canning⟩

⁴fang \ˈfäŋ, ˈfaŋ\ *or* **fan** \ˈfän\ *n, pl* **fang** *or* **fangs** *or* **fan** *or* **fans** *usu cap* [F *Fan*, perh. modif. of Fang *Mpangwe*] **1 a :** an African people occupying the Ogowe basin, French Equatorial Africa and noted for their carved and painted religious masks **b :** a member of such people — called also *Pahouin, Pangwe* **2 :** a Bantu language of the Fang people

fang bolt *n* **:** a bolt having for a nut a triangular plate with sharp fangs projecting from its corners and used for attaching iron to wood — compare JAG BOLT

fanged \ˈfaŋd, ˈfaiŋd\ *adj* [²*fang* + *-ed*] **:** having fangs or processes resembling fangs ⟨the ice-*fanged* eaves⟩

¹fan·gle \ˈfaŋgəl, ˈfaiŋ-\ *n* -s [prob. fr. *newfangle*, adj.] **1 :** a fashion esp. when foppish or silly — used with *new* and usu. derogatorily **2** *obs* **:** a silly or fantastic contrivance **:** GEWGAW, GAUD

²fangle \"\ *vt* -ED/-ING/-S *now dial* **:** FASHION, DRESS **:** deck out

fan·gle·ment \-mənt\ *n* -s **1 :** CONTRIVANCE, DEVICE **2 :** FRIPPERY, GEWGAW

fang·less \ˈfaŋləs, ˈfaiŋ-\ *adj* **:** having no fangs; *also* **:** having lost the power to do harm

fan·glom·er·ate \(ˈ)fanˈglām(ə)rət\ *n* -s [¹*fan* + *-glomerate* (as in *conglomerate*)] **:** the material of an alluvial fan in which the rock fragments are only slightly waterworn — **fan·glom·er·at·ic** \ˌ=ˌ=məˈrad·ik\ *adj*

fan·go \ˈfaŋ(ˌ)gō, ˈfäŋ-\ *n* -s [It, mud, of Gmc origin; akin to Goth *fani* clay — more at FEN] **:** MUD, MIRE; *esp* **:** a clay mud from hot springs at Battaglio, Italy, that is used in the form of hot external applications in certain medical treatments

fang shih \ˈfäŋˈshē\ *n, pl* **fang shih** [Chin *fang¹ shih⁴*, fr. *fang¹* prescription, formula + *shih⁴* scholar, teacher] **:** a priest-magician flourishing in China 249 B.C.–A.D. 220 whose office was to provide divinational and magical formulas to those seeking immortality and supernatural powers

fangy \ˈfaŋē, ˈfaiŋ-, -ŋi\ *adj* -ER/-EST [²*fang* + *-y*] **:** having fangs; *specif, of certain root crops* **:** producing roots with fangs ⟨sugar beets are often ~ on acid soil⟩

fan·ion \ˈfanyən\ *n* -s [F, fr. *fanon* maniple, pennon — more at FANON] **:** a small flag used orig. by horse brigades and now by soldiers and surveyors to mark positions

fank \ˈfaŋk\ *n* -s [ScGael *fang*, prob. fr. E ²*fang*] *Scot* **:** SHEEPFOLD

fanleaf palm \ˈ=ˌ=-\ *n* **:** FAN PALM; *esp* **:** WASHINGTON PALM

fan letter *n* **:** a letter sent to a public figure (as in sports or the theater) by an admirer

fanlight \ˈ=ˌ=\ *n* **:** a semicircular window made with radiating sash bars like the ribs of a fan and placed over a door or window; *broadly* **:** a window over a door or window

fanlighted \ˈ=ˌ==\ *adj* **:** surmounted by a fanlight

fanlike \ˈ=ˌ=\ *adj* **1 :** resembling a fan or the action of a fan ⟨a ~ motion⟩ **2 :** folded up like a closed fan **:** PLICATE — used esp. of leaves

fanlight

fan magazine *n* **:** a magazine devoted to the exploitation of popular interest in the personalities of the sports or entertainment world (as movie, radio, TV)

fan mail *n* **:** FAN LETTERS

fan·man \ˈ=ˌman, maa(ə)n\ *n, pl* **fanmen :** a worker who operates a ventilation system (as by fans for cooling kilns or for forcing hot air through furnaces)

fan marker *n* **:** a radio beacon located near an airport and on a radio range that transmits a vertical fan-shaped beam with distinctive code signal usu. crossing one leg of the range station as an aid to landing — compare RADIO MARKER

fan mussel *n* [so called fr. the shape of the shell] **:** PEN SHELL

fanned *past of* FAN

fan·ner \ˈfanə(r), ˈfaan-\ *n* -s **:** one that fans: as **a** (1) **:** FAN WHEEL (2) **:** FAN BLOWER (3) **:** FANNING MILL **b :** KESTREL **c** [so called fr. its early use as a winnowing basket] *dial* **:** a broad flat basket esp. for carrying or displaying fresh produce **d :** a stationary engineer who tends the ventilation system of a mine

fan-nerved \ˈ=ˈnərvd\ *adj* **:** having the nerves or veins radially disposed ⟨a *fan-nerved* leaf⟩

fan·nia \ˈfanēə\ *n, cap* [NL, perh. irreg. fr. Gk *phanos* bright, conspicuous + NL *-ia*; akin to Gk *phainein* to show — more at FANCY] **:** a genus of two-winged flies (family Anthomyiidae) resembling but smaller than the common housefly and including the lesser housefly and the latrine fly

fanning *n* -s [ME, winnowing of grain, fr. gerund of *fannen* to fan, winnow] **1 :** the act of one that fans **2 :** an instance or product of fanning: as **a fannings** *pl* **:** coarse tea siftings **b :** a whipping or beating

fanning mill *n* **:** a machine for winnowing

fan·ny \ˈfanē, -aan=\ *n* -ES [fr. *Fanny*, nickname of *Frances*] **1** *slang Brit* **:** ³BILLY **2** *also* **fany** \"\ *usu cap* [*fanny* irreg. (influence of the nickname *Fanny*) fr. *F*irst *A*id *N*ursing *Y*eomanry; *fany* fr. *F*irst *A*id *N*ursing *Y*eomanry] **:** a member of a British women's ambulance unit **3 :** BUTTOCKS

fan·on \ˈfanən, fəˈnōn\ *n* -s [ME *fanoun* maniple, fr. MF *fanon*, of Gmc origin; akin to OHG *fano* cloth — more at VANE] **:** any of several articles used in religious ceremonials: as **a :** MANIPLE **b :** an oblation cloth for carrying vessels and bread for the Eucharist **c :** ¹CORPORAL **d :** a vestment that resembles a short cape and is worn by a Roman pontiff at solemn pontifical mass — called also *orale* **e :** INFULA 2a

fan palm *n* **:** a palm having simple fan-shaped leaves (as the cabbage palmetto of the southern U.S., the hemp palm of Europe, the talipot of Asia, the Chinese fan palm, and the Washington palm of California) — called also *fanleaf palm;* see DWARF FAN PALM

fan roof *n* **:** a vaulted roof with fan tracery

fans *pl of* FAN, *pres 3d sing of* FAN

fan-shaped \ˈ=ˌ=\ *adj* **:** shaped like a fan and often having or made up of radiating parts (as wings, ribs, or individuals) that are felt to resemble the supporting sticks of a fan

fan shell *n* **1 :** a scallop or its shell **2 :** PEN SHELL

fantad *var of* FANTOD

fantail \ˈ=ˌ=\ *n, often attrib* **1 :** a tail or end with the shape of a fan **2 a** *often cap* **:** a domestic pigeon of a variety characterized by a broad rounded tail often having 30 or 40 feathers instead of the usual 12 **b :** any of numerous flycatchers constituting a genus *Rhipidura* of the family Muscicapidae of Asia, Australia, and the southwest Pacific and having a fanlike tail that is often widely spread during flight **c** *often cap* **:** a goldfish of a fancy breed having double anal and tail fins **d :** a wild or low grade range horse **3 :** an architectural part resembling or likened to a fan; *specif* **:** a centering (as of an arch) of radiating struts **4 :** a counter or after overhang of a ship that is shaped like a duck's bill

fantail deer *also* **fantail** *n* **:** a small white-tailed deer (*Odocoileus virginianus couesi*) of the southwestern U.S. and western Mexico

fan-tailed \ˈ=ˌtāld\ *adj* **:** having a tail broadly expanded and suggesting a fan — used esp. of birds and fishes

fan-tailed darter *n* **:** a small darter (*Catonotus flabellaris*) of the central U.S.

fan-tailed pigeon *n* **:** FANTAIL 2a

fan-tailed warbler *n* **:** any of various small Old World warblers (genus *Cisticola*) that build delicate nests woven of cobwebs and down

fantail joint *n* **:** DOVETAIL JOINT

fantail mullet *or* **fan-tailed mullet** *n* **:** a mullet (*Querimana trichodon*) found from Brazil to Key West where it is used as food

fan-tan \ˈfan,tan\ *n* -s [Chin *fan¹-t'an¹*] **1 :** a Chinese gambling game in which a banker counts off a large handful of small objects (as beans) in fours and the players bet on what number from one to four will be left at the end of the count **2 :** a card game in which the object is to play sevens and other cards that form sequences in the same suits as the sevens and to be first to have played all one's cards — called also *sevens*

fan·ta·sia \fan-ˈtāzhə, faan- *also* \|z(h)ēə *sometimes* fän- *or* fan- *or* fən- *or* -ˈtä| *or* -tá| *or* -ta(i)|; ˌfantəˈzēə, faan-, ˌfän-, ˌfàn-, -teˈsēə\ *also* **fan·ta·sie** \ˌfäntəˈzē, ˌfan-, ˌfaan-, ˌfän- *or like* FANTASY\ *n* -s [It *fantasia*, lit., fancy, fr. LL *phantasia* imagination, fr. L, mental image — more at FANCY] **1 a :** an instrumental composition of the 16th and 17th centuries written in contrapuntal style and akin to the motet **b :** a free instrumental composition not in strict form (as the development section of sonata form) **c :** FREE FANTASIA **d :** a composition based generally on one theme ⟨~ on spring⟩ **e :** a potpourri of operatic arias or familiar airs ⟨~ on Christmas carols —Ralph Vaughan Williams⟩ **2 :** a work (as a poem or play) in which the author's fancy roves unrestricted by set form or verisimilitude **3 :** something strange or foreign by reason of grotesque, bizarre, or seemingly unreal qualities ⟨psychologists like to dismiss myths as mere ~ —Robert Graves⟩ ⟨the jungle's boggy ~ —*Time*⟩ **4 :** an Arab performance featuring dancing and often evolutions on horseback, gun firing, and shouting all in a rapid rhythm

fan·ta·sied *or* **phan·ta·sied** \'fantəs|ēd, 'faan-, -təz|, |id\ *adj* [fr. past part. of *fantasy*, v.] **1 :** existing only in the imagination **:** FANCIED — now used esp. in psychiatry **2** *obs* **:** full of fancies or strange whims

fantasies *pl of* FANTASY, *pres 3d sing of* FANTASY

fan·ta·sie·stück \ˌfäntä'zēˌshtuek\ *n, pl* **fantasie·stücke** \-kə\ [G *fantasiestück, phantasiestück*, fr. *phantasie* fantasia (fr. It *fantasia*) + *stück* piece, fr. OHG *stucki* — more at STOCK] **:** FANTASIA 1b **:** CHARACTER PIECE

fan·ta·sist \fan·'täzhəst; 'fantəsəst, -təzə-\ *n* -s [*fantasy*, n. + *-ist*] **:** a composer of fantasias or fantasies

fan·ta·size \'fantəˌsīz\ *vb* -ED/-ING/-S [*fantasy*, n. + *-ize*] *vt* **1 :** FANTASY 1 **2 :** to view as fantastic ⟨nothing will be gained by *fantasizing* our position⟩ ~ *vi* **:** to create or develop imaginative and often fantastic views, ideas, or explanations — often used with *about* ⟨*fantasizing* about her neighbors⟩

fantasm *var of* PHANTASM

[1]fan·tasque \(')fan·¦task\ *n* -s [F, fr. *fantasque*, adj.] **:** FANCY, FANTASY, WHIM

[2]fantasque \"\ *adj* [F, fr. MF, prob. contr. of *fantastique*] **:** FANTASTIC, FANCIFUL

fan·tast *or* **phan·tast** \'fan·ˌtast\ *n* -s [G *phantast, fantast*, prob. fr. (assumed) ML *fantasta*, prob. back-formation fr. ML *fantasticus*] **1 :** VISIONARY, DREAMER **2 a :** a fantastic or eccentric person **b :** FANTASIST

[1]fan·tas·tic \(')fan·¦tastik, -aan-, fən·'t-, -taas-, -stēk\ *also* **fan·tas·ti·cal** \-stəkəl, -stēk-\ *or* **phan·tas·tic** *or* **phan·tas·ti·cal** *adj* [*fantastic* fr. ME *fantastic, fantastik*, fr. MF & ML; MF *fantastique*, fr. ML *fantasticus*, fr. LL *phantasticus* imaginary, fr. Gk *phantastikos* able to produce a mental image, fr. *phantazein* to make visible; *fantastical* fr. ME, fr. *fantastic, fantastik* + *-al* — more at FANCY] **1** *obs* **:** of, belonging to, or constituting fantasy; *esp* **:** PHANTASMAL **2** *usu fantastic* **a :** based on fantasy rather than reason **:** IMAGINARY, IRRATIONAL, UNREAL ⟨this ~ assumption of neutralism is not unknown among some ritualistic liberals —Sidney Hook⟩ *broadly* **:** FOOLISH, UNREALISTIC ⟨a ~ idea of his own importance⟩ **b :** conceived or giving the impression of having been conceived by unrestrained fancy ⟨~ new space and nuclear weapons —Jack Raymond⟩ **:** exhibiting strange, grotesque, inappropriate, or startlingly novel characteristics ⟨~ as the situation was — a landlubber second in command —Jack London⟩; *often* **:** UNSUITABLE, QUAINT, ECCENTRIC ⟨a ~ costume for street wear⟩ **c :** so extreme as to challenge belief esp. by reason of magnitude or extent **:** UNBELIEVABLE ⟨the bomb did ~ damage⟩ ⟨a ~ industrial complex of steel, coal, machine tools, and other heavy industries —M.S.Handler⟩; *broadly* **:** exceedingly or excessively large or great ⟨spent ~ sums on his library⟩ ⟨the housing shortage reached ~ proportions —Gerda Luft⟩ **3 a** *sometimes fantastical* **:** given to or marked by extravagant fantasy, unrestrained imagination, or extreme individuality and deviation from some accepted norm **:** ODD, ECCENTRIC ⟨one need not have a very ~ imagination to see spirits there —Thomas Gray⟩ ⟨a strange ~ mind⟩ ⟨a man *fantastical* in dress⟩ **b :** following no set pattern **:** CAPRICIOUS ⟨~ acts of kindness⟩ ⟨the ~ irregularity of the dunes⟩

syn BIZARRE, GROTESQUE, ANTIC: FANTASTIC suggests unrestrained imagination and unbridled fancy, extravagant conception, or wild or highly imaginative remoteness from reality ⟨explosions, *fantastic*, far off, bright green or violet or golden —C.P.Aiken⟩ ⟨*fantastic* figures, with bulbous heads, the circumference of a bushel, grinned enormously in his face —Nathaniel Hawthorne⟩ ⟨helped their panic as best he could by sending Congo natives over to the Tanganyika side to spread the most *fantastic* rumors he could dream up —Joseph Millard⟩ BIZARRE applies to the sensationally, colorfully queer or strange, often through violent contrasts and incongruities ⟨temple sculpture became *bizarre* — rearing monsters, fiery horses, great pillared halls teeming with sculptures —*Atlantic*⟩ ⟨the restaurants of *bizarre* design — one like a hat, another like a rabbit, a third like an old shoe, another a fish —*Amer. Guide Series: Calif.*⟩ ⟨it was *bizarre* in the extreme. It was as if a judge, wearing the black cap, had suddenly put out his tongue at the condemned —J.C.Powys⟩ GROTESQUE applies to the incongruously distorted, to ridiculous ugliness or incompatibility ⟨there was a *grotesque* look in his face, as if it had been pulled out of shape by some sudden twist —Ellen Glasgow⟩ ⟨the crescendo and diminuendo of the planes, the agitated noise of patrol vessels and the vicious challenge of the guns were all *grotesque* against the still serenity of the moonlight —Eleanor Dark⟩ ⟨*grotesque* serpents eight fathoms long that churned the seas, huge reptiles that beat the air with wings of nightmare breadth —P.E.More⟩ ANTIC, now less common than others in this set, may suggest ludicrous clownish exuberance of action ⟨the Friday-night Mad Arts Balls, Mad Hatters Balls, Pagan Routs, and similar *antic* gatherings —Lillian Ross⟩ ⟨in the course of Kaye's *antic* fun with this plot, he makes an entrance with his head on a platter, gorges himself in fast motion at a feast, keeps a roomful of conspirators hidden from one another, tugs frantically at a sword that refuses to come out of its scabbard —*Time*⟩ **syn** see in addition IMAGINARY

[2]fantastic \"\ *n* -s **1** *archaic* **:** a person with fantastic ideas **2** *obs* **:** a person given to fantastic behavior (as in choice of dress or in manners)

fan·tas·ti·cal·i·ty \(ˌ)=ˌ=stə'kaləd·ē\ *n* -ES **1 :** fantastic quality ⟨consider the ~ of enforcing loyalty by oath —W.T. Hastings⟩ **2 :** a fantastic incident, event, or account ⟨an amusing volume of natural *fantasticalities*⟩

fan·tas·ti·cal·ly \(')fan·¦tastək(ə)lē, -aan-, fən·'t-, -taas-, -stēk-, -li\ *adv* **1 :** in a fantastic manner **:** GROTESQUELY, ODDLY **2 :** to a fantastic degree **:** UNBELIEVABLY, EXTREMELY ⟨~ expensive clothes⟩ **3** *archaic* **:** CAPRICIOUSLY

fan·tas·ti·cal·ness *n* -ES **:** the quality or state of being fantastic **:** ECCENTRICITY, WHIMSICALITY ⟨the charm and ~ of these little sketches⟩ ⟨the sheer ~ of their behavior⟩

fan·tas·ti·cate \='=stəˌkāt\ *vb* -ED/-ING/-S *vi* **:** to indulge in fantastic notions ~ *vt* **:** to render fantastic ⟨time and climate *fantasticated* the cliffs⟩ ⟨*fantasticating* life far beyond the limits of pure drama —W.B.Adams⟩ — **fan·tas·ti·ca·tion** \(ˌ)=ˌ=='kāshən\ *n* -s

fan·tas·ti·cism \='=stəˌsizəm\ *n* -s **:** adherence to or employment of fantasy (as in literature or art)

fantasticly *obs var of* FANTASTICALLY

fan·tas·tic·ness *archaic var of* FANTASTICALNESS

fan·tas·ti·co \fan·'tastəˌkō, fən-\ *n* -ES [It, fantastic (adj.), fr. ML *fantasticus*] **:** a pretentiously fantastic person

[1]fan·ta·sy *or* **phan·ta·sy** \'fantəs|ē, -aan-, -təz|, |i\ *n* -ES [ME *fantasie* — more at FANCY] **1** *obs* **a :** the act or function of forming images or representations whether in direct perception or in memory; *also* **:** an image or impression derived through sensation **b :** HALLUCINATION; *sometimes* **:** PHANTOM, APPARITION **c :** DESIRE, INCLINATION **2 :** imagination or fancy; *esp* **:** the free play of creative imagination as it affects perception and productivity usu. as expressed in an art form or as elicited by projective techniques of formal psychology **3 :** a product of imagination or fantasy: as **a :** an image esp. when illusory **:** PHANTASM **b :** a creation of the imaginative faculty whether merely conceived (as in the mind) or expressed (as in a work of art); *broadly* **:** an ingenious or fantastic design or invention ⟨a ~ of delicate tracery⟩ **c :** an imagined fulfillment of a desire (as in daydreaming) ⟨building *fantasies* and castles in the air⟩ **d :** a chimerical or fantastic notion **e :** FANTASIA 1 **f** *also* **fantasy fiction :** imaginative fiction dependent for effect on strangeness of setting (as other worlds or times) and of characters (as supernatural or unnatural beings); *sometimes* **:** SCIENCE FICTION **4 :** mood or mental prepossession; *often* **:** a whimsical or capricious mood **5** *usu phantasy* **:** the power, process, or result of creating mental images (as of previously perceived persons, objects, or events) modified by need, wish, or desire ⟨the ~ of daydreams⟩ or through the action of drugs or of disease on the central nervous system **syn** see FANCY, IMAGINATION

[2]fantasy *or* **phantasy** \"\ *vb* -ED/-ING/-ES [ME *fantasien*, fr. *fantasie*, n.] *vt* **1 :** to portray in the mind **:** FANCY, IMAGINE **2** *obs* **:** to have a fancy for ~ *vi* **1 :** to indulge in reverie **:** DAYDREAM **2 :** to improvise in playing a musical instrument **:** play fantasias

fan·tee *also* **fan·ti** \'fantē\ *adj* [*Fanti*] *chiefly Brit* **:** wild, unrestrained, or primitive — used chiefly as a predicate adjective and usu. in the phrase *go fantee*

fan·ti *or* **fan·te** *also* **fan·tee** \", 'fän-\ *n, pl* **fanti** *or* **fante** *or* **fantis** *or* **fantes** *cap* **1 a :** an African Negro nation of Ghana **b :** a member of such nation **2 :** a dialect of Akan spoken by the Fanti people **3 :** a literary language based on the Fanti dialect and used by the Fanti and related peoples

fan·tigue *or* **fan·teeg** \fan·'tēg\ *n* -s [perh. blend of *fantastic* and *fatigue*] *dial chiefly Eng* **:** a state of excitement or great tension ⟨his nerves were in a proper ~ —John Galsworthy⟩

fan·toc·ci·ni \ˌfäntə'chēnē, ˌfan-\ *n pl* [It, pl. of *fantoccino*, dim. of *fantoccio* doll, lay figure, aug. of *fante* servant, boy, child, fr. L *infant-, infans* infant — more at INFANT] **1 :** puppets moved by strings or mechanical devices **2 :** puppet shows in which fantoccini are used

fan·tod \'fan·ˌtäd\ *also* **fan·tad** \-tad\ *n* -s [perh. alter. of *fantigue*] **1** *usu* **fantods** *pl* **a :** a state of irritability, fidget, and tension; *sometimes* **:** a state of acute worry and distress **b :** a state of bodily or mental disorder esp. when ill-defined and more or less chronic **2** *sometimes* **fantods** *pl* **a :** an instance or occurrence of the fantods **b :** a violent or irrational outburst **3 :** a fidgety fussy officer of a ship

fantom *var of* PHANTOM

fan tracery *n* **:** decorative tracery on fan vaulting

fan–trained \'=¦=\ *adj, of a tree or vine* **:** trained in growing so that the main branches radiate in one plane like the sticks of a fan

fan tree *n* **1 :** FAN PALM **2 :** a fan-trained tree

fan truss *n* **:** a truss (as of a roof) characterized by the radiating lines of the king post and appended struts or of the queen posts and appended struts

fan vault *n* **:** a vault produced by fan vaulting

fan vaulting *n* **:** an elaborate system of vaulting in which the ribs diverge somewhat like the rays of a fan and that was used esp. in the latest English Gothic architecture

fan vaulting

fanweed \'=ˌ=\ *n* **:** PENNYCRESS

fan wheel *n* **:** the wheel of a fan blower

fan window *n* **:** a window (as a fanlight) with radiating sash bars like the sticks of a fan

fan–wing fly *n* **:** an artificial dry fly with fan-shaped wings

fanwise \'=ˌ=\ *adv* (*or adj*) **:** over a segment of a circle **:** in the manner or position of the sticks of an open fan ⟨highways arranged ~ to the north of the city⟩ ⟨the ~ spread of the turkey gobbler's tail⟩

fanwork \'=ˌ=\ *n* **:** FAN TRACERY

fanwort \'=ˌ=\ *n* **:** a plant of the genus *Cabomba; esp* **:** WATER SHIELD

fany *usu cap, var of* FANNY

fan·zine \(')fan¦zēn\ *n* -s [[6]*fan* + *magazine*] **:** a periodical that is written and edited by science-fiction and fantasy enthusiasts and that is frequently prepared by mimeographing

faon \fän\ *n* -s [F, fawn, fr. OF *faon, feon* young of an animal — more at FAWN] **:** FAWN 3

fap \'fap\ *adj* [origin unknown] *archaic* **:** INTOXICATED

FAP *abbr* first-aid post

fape \'fāp\ *n* -s [prob. by shortening & alter. fr. *feaberry*] *dial Brit* **:** GOOSEBERRY 1a

FAQ *abbr* **1** fair average quality **2** free at quay

fa·qih \fä'kē\ *n, pl* **faqihs** \-ēz\ *or* **fu·qa·ha** \fü'käˌhä\ [Ar *faqīh* (pl. *fuqahā'*)] **:** a Muslim theologian versed in the religious law of Islam

faqir *or* **faquir** *var of* FAKIR

[1]far \'fär, 'fȧ(r\ *adv* **far·ther** \'fär<u>th</u>ər, 'fȧ<u>th</u>ə(r\ *or* **fur·ther** \'fər<u>th</u>ər, 'fə̄<u>th</u>ə(r, 'fəi<u>th</u>ə(r, *in southern US often* 'fə<u>th</u>ə(r *or* 'fə<u>th</u>ər\ **far·thest** \-<u>th</u>əst\ *or* **fur·thest** \-<u>th</u>əst\ [ME *fer*, fr. OE *feorr;* akin to OHG *ferro* far, ON *fjarri*, Goth *fairra* far, OE *faran* to go — more at FARE] **1 a :** to a considerable distance in space **:** to a remote place ⟨wandered ~ from home⟩ ⟨the force of the gale was felt ~ inland⟩ **b :** at a considerable distance in space **:** at a remote place ⟨lived ~ up the mountain⟩ **2 :** at a considerable distance in time ⟨this was not ~ from the year 1115 —H.O.Taylor⟩ **3 a :** to a great extent **:** MUCH — often used with comparatives and superlatives ⟨the book is ~ richer than any of the others I have recommended —M.R.Ridley⟩ **b :** by a broad space **:** WIDELY ⟨the new site is never ~ distant from the old —C.D. Forde⟩ **c :** of a distinctly different quality or attitude — usu. used with *from* ⟨it is ~ from easy to say what makes a nominee . . . emerge as the successful candidate —H.J.Laski⟩ ⟨news reporters are ~ from blind —F.L.Mott⟩ **4 a :** to an advanced point or extent **:** a long way ⟨if the right peace officer is assigned to this contact work he can go ~ —Spencer Parratt⟩ ⟨went ~ toward determining the schedule and character of all his subsequent service —J.C.Archer⟩ ⟨drove the stake ~ into the ground⟩ **b :** to a late hour ⟨works or reads ~ into the night —Gertrude Samuels⟩ — **by far** *adv* **:** far and away — **how far :** to what extent, degree, or distance ⟨didn't know *how far* to trust him⟩ — **so far** *adv* **1 :** to a certain extent, degree, or distance ⟨when the water has risen *so far* the pumps will be brought into action⟩ **2 :** up to the present ⟨he has written only one novel *so far*⟩ — **thus far** *adv* **:** so far ⟨good luck *thus far* in fixing plumbing⟩

[2]far \"\ *adj* **farther** *or* **further**; **farthest** *or* **furthest** [ME *fer*, fr. OE *feorr;* akin to OFris *fīr* far, OS *ferr;* derivative fr. the root of OE *feorr*, adv.] **1 a :** remote in space **:** DISTANT ⟨snow is shining on the ~ volcanoes —Muriel Rukeyser⟩ **b :** distinctly different in quality or relationship — often used with *cry* ⟨a ~ cry from earlier isolationist policies —A.O. Wolfers⟩ **c :** remote in time ⟨go back in the ~ past to a common origin —A.L.Kroeber⟩ **2 a :** of a considerable distance **:** LONG ⟨a ~ journey⟩ **b :** of notable extent **:** COMPREHENSIVE ⟨a man of ~ vision and deep convictions —*Catalog of Hollins Coll.*⟩ **3 :** the more distant of two ⟨on the near side was a tobacconist's and on the ~ a public house —F.W.Crofts⟩

[3]far \"\ *dial Brit var of* WHERE

far *abbr* **1** farad **2** farthing

far·ad \'faˌrad, -ˌrəd\ *n* -s [after Michael *Faraday* †1867 Eng. physicist] **1 :** the practical mks unit of capacitance equal to the capacitance of a capacitor between whose plates there appears a potential of one volt when it is charged by one coulomb of electricity, the unit being taken as the standard in the U.S. **2 :** a unit of capacitance that is equal to .999505 farad and that was formerly taken as the standard in the U.S. — called also *international farad*

far·a·day \'farəˌdā *also* -ˌdē *or* -ˌdi\ *also* **faraday constant** *n* -s *sometimes cap F* [after Michael *Faraday*] **:** the quantity of electricity transferred in electrolysis per equivalent weight of any element or ion, being equal to about 96,500 coulombs per gram equivalent

faraday cage *n, usu cap F* **:** a grounded metallic screen completely surrounding a space to protect it from external electrostatic influence

faraday dark space *n, usu cap F* **:** a dark space of low light intensity between the positive column and the negative glow from the cathode in a vacuum tube

faraday disk *n, usu cap F* **:** a metal disk through which a current of electricity is passed and in which an induced current occurs as the disk rotates on a metal axis between the poles of a magnet

faraday effect *n, usu cap F* **:** the optical rotation produced in a beam of polarized light traversing certain isotropic media along the lines of force of a magnetic field

faraday shield *n, usu cap F* **:** a number of parallel wires arranged in one plane, connected at one end, and usu. grounded to provide electrostatic shielding

faraday's law *n, cap F* **:** either of two laws in physics: **a :** the mass of any substance deposited or dissolved by electrolysis is proportional to the product of the equivalent weight of the substance multiplied by the quantity of electricity passed during the reaction **b :** the electromotive force induced in a circuit by variation of the magnetic flux through the circuit is proportional to the negative of the time rate of change of the magnetic linkage

fa·rad·ic \fə'radik, (')fa¦ra-\ *also* **far·a·da·ic** \¦farə¦dāik\ *adj* [*faradic* fr. F *faradique*, fr. Michael *Faraday* + F *-ique* -ic; *faradaic* fr. Michael *Faraday* + E *-ic*] **:** of or relating to an asymmetric alternating current of electricity produced by an induction coil; *also* **:** produced by or using such a current — distinguished from *galvanic*

far·a·dism \'farəˌdizəm\ *also* **far·a·di·za·tion** \ˌfarədə'zāshən, -ˌdī'z-\ *n* -s [*faradism* fr. F *faradisme*, fr. Michael *Faraday* + F *-isme* -ism; *faradization* fr. F *faradisation*, fr. *faradiser* to faradize + *-ation*] **:** the application of a faradic current of electricity (as for therapeutic purposes)

far·a·dize \'farəˌdīz\ *vt* -ED/-ING/-S [F *faradiser*, fr. Michael *Faraday* + F *-iser* -ize] **:** to treat by faradism — **far·a·diz·er** \-zə(r)\ *n* -s

faradmeter \'=(ˌ)=ˌ==\ *n* **:** an electrical instrument for measuring capacitances and usu. having a scale graduated in farads

farado- *comb form* [*faradic* + *-o-*] **:** resulting from or involving faradic stimulus ⟨*farado*contractility⟩ ⟨*farado*therapy⟩

fa·ran·cia \fə'ranch(ē)ə, -n(t)sēə\ *n, cap* [NL] **:** a genus of snakes (family Colubridae) including only the No. American hoop snake

far and away *adv* **:** by a considerable margin **:** DECIDEDLY ⟨*far and away* the best player on the team⟩

farandine *n* -s [F *ferrandine*, fr. *Ferrand*, 17th cent. Fr. inventor] *obs* **:** a fabric of silk mixed with wool or hair

far·and·man \'farən(d)ˌman\ *n, pl* **farandmen** [ME (Sc), fr. ME (northern dial.) *farand* (pres. part. of ME *faren* to go, travel) + ME *man* — more at FARE] *Scot* **:** WAYFARER; *usu* **:** a traveling peddler or merchant

far and near *or* **far and wide** *adv* **:** on all sides **:** in every direction **:** EVERYWHERE ⟨searched for the child *far and near*⟩ ⟨the story spread *far and wide* —F.D.Ommanney⟩

far·an·dole \'farənˌdōl, ˌ=='=\ *also* **fa·ran·do·la** \fə'randələ\ *n* -s [F *farandole*, fr. Prov *farandoulo*] **1 :** a lively Provençal chain dance in sextuple measure and serpentine path **2 :** the music for a farandole

fa·ra·on \ˌfäˌrä'ōn\ *n, pl* **faraon** \"\ *or* **fara·o·nes** \-ōˌnās\ *usu cap* [AmerSp *faraón*, prob. fr. Sp, pharaoh, fr. LL *Pharaon-, Pharao* — more at PHARAOH] **:** MESCALERO

[1]faraway \¦==¦=\ *adj* [*far away* (adverbial phrase), fr. ME *fer away*, fr. *fer* far (adv.) + *away* (adv.)] **1 a :** distant in space ⟨~ places⟩ **b :** remote in time ⟨the ~ future⟩ **c :** coming or seeming to come from a distance — used esp. of sounds ⟨the ~ tinkle of a cowbell⟩ **2 :** DREAMY, ABSTRACTED — used esp. of a look or the eyes ⟨a ~ expression⟩

[2]faraway \"\ *n* -s **1 :** something remote (as from physical or mental vision) **2 :** the unknown

far·away·ness *n* -ES **:** remoteness esp. from experience or comprehension ⟨~ from life —Dan Levin⟩

far back *adv* (*or adj*) **1 :** at a considerable distance to the rear ⟨from our *far-back* position⟩ ⟨we stood *far back*⟩ **2 :** in or into the remote past ⟨a *far-back* ancestor⟩ ⟨venturing *far back* we can perhaps explore the beginnings of reason⟩

far between *adj* **:** separated by considerable intervals ⟨good workhorses are few and *far between* these days⟩

[1]farce \'färs, 'fȧs\ *vt* -ED/-ING/-S [ME *farsen*, fr. MF *farcir*, fr. L *farcire* to stuff; akin to MIr *barc* attack, Gk *phrassein, phrattein* to enclose, fence in] **1** *obs* **a :** to stuff (as poultry) with forcemeat or other stuffing **b :** to stuff (as oneself) with food **:** GORGE **c :** to make full **:** CRAM, STUFF **2 a** *obs* **:** to fatten or enlarge by or as if by cramming **b :** to enlarge, amplify, or expand (as a literary work) by interpolation or addition often of witty material or quotations; *esp* **:** FARSE

[2]farce \"\ *n* -s [ME *farse*, fr. MF *farce*, fr. (assumed) VL *farsa*, fr. L, fem. of *farsus*, past part. of *farcire*] **1 :** FORCEMEAT; *broadly* **:** any savory stuffing (as for poultry or roasts) **2 a :** a light dramatic composition of satirical or humorous cast in which great latitude is allowed as to probability of happenings and naturalness of characters ⟨an amusing ~ based on confused relationships⟩ **b :** the class or form of drama made up of such compositions ⟨the place of ~ in the modern theater⟩ **3 a :** the element of broad humor that goes to make up theatrical farce **:** comic trait, feature, or characteristic **b :** a passage containing such comic element ⟨the father's speech is sheer ~⟩ **4 :** ridiculous or empty show ⟨the authorities have indulged in a ~ of stubborn resistance —Bosley Crowther⟩; *often* **:** something so much less than it could or should be as to constitute a mockery ⟨a procedure . . . that would have revived the ~ of the veto —A.P.Ryan⟩ ⟨observance and upholding of the law became a ~⟩

farce–comedy \'=ˌ===\ *n* **:** comedy of a marked farcical character

farc·er \'färsər\ *n* -s [[2]*farce* + *-er*] **:** FARCEUR

far·ceur \(')fär¦sər(·)\ *n* -s [F, fr. MF *farseur*, fr. *farser, farcer* to joke, fr. OF, fr. (assumed) OF *farce* theatrical farce (whence MF *farce*), fr. OF *farce* forcemeat — more at FARCE] **1 :** JOKER, WAG **2 :** a person skilled in farce, esp. in the writing or acting of a farce

far·ceuse \(')fär¦sərz, -¦sə̄z, -¦süz, -¦səz\ *n* -s [F, fem. of *farceur*] **:** a woman who is a farceur; *esp* **:** an actress skilled in playing farce

[1]far·ci *or* **far·cie** \(')fär¦sē\ *adj* [F *farci* (masc.), *farcie* (fem.), fr. *farci*, past part. of *farcir*] *of food* **:** stuffed esp. with forcemeat — usu. used postpositively ⟨oysters ~⟩

[2]farci \"\ *n* -ES **:** a stuffed dish (as a roast or fowl)

[1]far·ci·cal \'färsəkəl, 'fȧs-, -sēk-\ *adj* [[2]*farce* + *-ical*] **1 :** constituting or resembling farce in boisterous or nonsensical disregard of the serious or through extravagance or unnaturalness ⟨a wild ~ exuberance of the clownish and swinish side of man —W.L.Sullivan⟩ **2 :** receiving or meriting laughter or amused scorn as utterly without claim to serious consideration or as laughably inept ⟨am I such a ~ bungler . . . that I should erect an obvious dummy and expect that some of the sharpest men in Europe would be deceived? —A. Conan Doyle⟩ **syn** see LAUGHABLE

[2]farcical \"\ *adj* [*farcy* + *-ical*] **:** of, relating to, or affected with farcy

far·ci·cal·i·ty \ˌfärsə'kaləd·ē, ˌfȧs-, -lətē, -i\ *n* -ES **:** farcical quality

far·ci·cal·ly \'=sək(ə)lē, -sēk-, -li\ *adv* **:** in a farcical manner

far·ci·cal·ness \-kəlnəs\ *n* -ES **:** the quality or state of being farcical

far·cied \'färsēd\ *adj* **:** suffering from or affected with farcy ⟨a badly ~ horse⟩

farcin *obs var of* FARCY

far·cist \'färsəst\ *n* -s **:** a maker of farces

far–come \'=¦=\ *adj* **:** come from a distance

far corner *n* **:** a distant and usu. obscure place — used esp. in the phrase *far corners of the world*

farc·tate \'färkˌtāt\ *adj* [L *farctus* (past part. of *farcire* to stuff) + E *-ate*] *of the stipe of certain fungi* **:** having the center solid but softer in consistency than the peripheral layers

far·cy \'färsē\ *n* -ES [ME *farsi, farsin*, fr. MF *farcin*, fr. LL *farcimen*, fr. L, sausage, fr. *farcire* to stuff — more at FARCE] **1 :** GLANDERS; *esp* **:** cutaneous glanders **2 :** a chronic ultimately fatal disease of cattle that is caused by an actinomycete (*Nocardia farcinica* or *Actinomyces farcinicus*), that is marked by indurative lymphadenitis and lymphangitis of the subcutaneous tissues leading to cold abscess formation, and that usu. terminates in pulmonary involvement — called also *bovine farcy, cattle farcy*

farcy bud *also* **farcy button** *n* **:** a swollen subcutaneous lymph gland characteristic of cutaneous glanders

farcy pipe *n* **:** a hard corded sometimes ulcerating subcutaneous lymphatic vessel characteristic of cutaneous glanders

[1]fard \'färd\ *vt* -ED/-ING/-S [ME *farden*, fr. MF *farder*, of Gmc origin; akin to OHG *faro* colored — more at PERCH (fish)] **1 :** to paint (the face) with cosmetics — now used only as a participial adjective ⟨thickly ~*ed* cheeks⟩ **2** *archaic* **:** to gloss over (as a fault)

[2]fard \"\ *n* -s [MF, fr. OF, fr. *farder*, v.] *archaic* **:** paint used on the face

[3]fard \"\ *or* **fardh** \"\ *n* -s [Ar *fard*] **:** a shiny dark brown date grown in eastern Arabia and in California

[1]far·del \'färdᵊl\ *n* -s [ME, fr. MF, fr. OF, fr. *farde* bundle, load, prob. fr. Ar *fardah* bundle, bale of goods] **1 a :** a bundle or parcel (as of raw silk) **b** *archaic* **:** BURDEN **2 a :** a miscellaneous lot or collection **3** *dial* **:** OMASUM

[2]**fardel** *vt* **1** *obs* **:** to make up into a bundle **2** *obs* **:** FURL

[3]**far·del** \'färdᵊl\ *n* -s [ME (Sc), contr. of ME (northern dial.) *ferde del* fourth part, fr. ME (northern dial.) *ferde* fourth (fr. OE *fēartha, fēortha*) + ME *deel, del* part — more at FOURTH, DEAL] **1** *now dial* **:** a fourth part of something **:** QUARTER **2** *now dial* **:** a piece or fragment ⟨a ~ of bread⟩

fardel–bound \'==,=\ *adj* [[1]*fardel* + *bound*] *dial, of cattle* **:** COSTIVE

far·den \'färdᵊn\ *dial Brit var of* FARTHING

farder *obs var of* FARTHER

fardest *obs var of* FARTHEST

far·din·gale \'färdᵊn,gāl, -diŋ,g-\ *archaic var of* FARTHINGALE

far·dle \'färdᵊl\ *archaic or dial var of* FARDEL

far–down \'=,=\ *or* **far–downer** \"+ə(r)\ *n* -s **:** a native of the north of Ireland — often used disparagingly

[1]**fare** \'fa(a)|(ə)r, 'fe|, |ə\ *vi* -ED/-ING/-s [ME *faren*, fr. OE *faran*; akin to OHG *faran* to go, travel, ON *fara*, Goth *faran* to go, travel, L *per* through, *portare* to carry, Gk *peran* to pass through, *poros* ford, passage, path, *poreuein* to convey, Skt *piparti* he brings over] **1 :** to go or travel ⟨~ into the marshes . . . and shoot partridges —Kenneth Roberts⟩ ⟨*faring* on through the fading dusk⟩; *often* **:** to commence on a course or journey — usu. used with *forth* ⟨*fared* forth daily into the streets —C.G.Bowers⟩ ⟨*fared* forth regretfully from his childhood home⟩ **2 :** to get along **:** make out or turn out **:** SUCCEED, PROGRESS ⟨went to see how the lambs were *faring* on the upper pastures⟩ ⟨it is hard to guess how minorities will ~ at the hands of the new government⟩ ⟨a concise characterization usually ~*s* well at the hands of the critics⟩ ⟨the admiral *fared* no better than his predecessors⟩ **3 :** to consume food **:** EAT, DINE ⟨they *fared* very plainly, eating on a few cents a day to stretch their funds⟩ ⟨we all *fared* alike⟩ **4** *dial Eng* **:** APPEAR, SEEM ⟨how does he ~ to feel about it?⟩ ⟨they don't ~ to remember⟩

[2]**fare** \"\ *n* -s [ME, fr. OE *faru* & OE *fær*; OE *faru* akin to OFris *fere* journey, MHG *var* (fem.), ON *fōr*; OE *fær* akin to MHG *var* (neut.) shore, ferry, ON *far* ship, passage, track; derivatives fr. the root of OE *faran*] **1** *obs* **a :** a journey or expedition **:** GOING, PASSAGE **b :** PATH, TRACK, WAY **2 a :** the price charged to transport a person or persons usu. together with a limited amount of baggage or goods **b** *obs* **:** the price charged to transport goods from one place to another **c :** the passenger or passengers hiring a public vehicle ⟨he drove his ~ home⟩ **3** *archaic* **:** state of things **:** FORTUNE ⟨what ~? what news abroad —Shak.⟩ **4 a :** range or stock of food **:** DIET ⟨the ~ in this restaurant⟩ ⟨a rich and delicate ~⟩ **b :** material provided for use, consumption, or enjoyment — used esp. of entertainment media ⟨the current literary ~⟩ ⟨much of our everyday ~ is Bach —Marcia Davenport⟩ ⟨the reviewing of theater ~ —*Theatre Arts*⟩ **5 :** the catch taken by a fishing boat

[3]**fare** \"\ *n* -s [obs. *fare*, v., to farrow, alter. of *farrow*, v.] *dial Eng* **:** a litter of pigs

far eastern *adj, usu cap F&E* **:** of, relating to, or concerned with the countries of the Far East — used of (1) China, Japan, Korea, Manchuria, Mongolia, and eastern Siberia or (2) the Asian countries bordering on the Pacific ocean and including the Philippines and Indonesia or (3) the countries of eastern and southern Asia including those of the Indian subcontinent, Tibet, the Malay peninsula and archipelago, China, Japan, Korea, Manchuria, Mongolia, and eastern Siberia; compare MIDDLE EASTERN, NEAR EASTERN

far·er \'fa(a)rə(r), 'fer-\ *n* -s [ME *-farere* (in *weyfarere* wayfarer), fr. *faren* to go + *-er, -ere* -er] **:** TRAVELER — used esp. in combination ⟨sea*farer*⟩ ⟨way*farer*⟩

fare–thee–well *or* **fare–you–well** *also* **fare–ye–well** \'=(,)=¦=\ *n* -s **1 :** a state of perfection and completion ⟨the cake was done to a *fare-thee-well*⟩ ⟨he took off his uncle's brusque mannerisms to a *fare-thee-well*⟩ **2 :** the utmost degree ⟨worked to a *fare-you-well*⟩ ⟨he drubbed the little pest to a *fare-ye-well*⟩

fareway *dial var of* FAIRWAY

[1]**farewell** \(')=¦=\ *v imper* [ME *farewel, fare wel*, fr. *fare* (imper. of *faren* to go, get along, succeed) + *wel* well — more at FARE] **:** get along well — used interjectionally to or by one departing (as from a place, a group, or a way of life) and often separated by a pronoun ⟨*fare you well*⟩ ⟨~ old year, welcome new⟩

[2]**farewell** \"\ *n* -s [ME *farewel*, fr. *farewel*, v. imper.] **1 :** a wish of happiness or welfare at parting **:** GOOD-BYE, ADIEU ⟨as soon as the visitors had made their ~*s* and left⟩ **2 a :** act of departure **:** LEAVE-TAKING ⟨his ~ to life⟩ ⟨before I take my ~ of the subject —Joseph Addison⟩ **b :** a formal event or ceremonial occasion for honoring a person about to withdraw from the public eye ⟨held a great ~ for the retiring senator⟩; *often* **:** a gala performance honoring a theatrical personality about to retire **3** *dial* **:** AFTERTASTE ⟨the coffee left a good ~ in his mouth⟩

[3]**farewell** \"\ *vb* -ED/-ING/-s [[1]*farewell*] *vt* **:** to bid farewell ⟨~*ing* the parting guests⟩ ~ *vi* **:** to take one's leave **:** say farewell

[4]**farewell** \"\ *adj* [[1]*farewell*] **:** PARTING, VALEDICTORY, FINAL ⟨a ~ concert⟩ ⟨one ~ gift⟩ ⟨made his ~ bow⟩

farewell–summer \,=¦=,=\ *n* **1 :** SOAPWORT **2 :** any of certain late-flowering asters; *esp* **:** HEATH ASTER

farewell–to–spring \(,)=,=¦=\ *n* **:** a summer-flowering annual herb (*Godetia amoena*) cultivated for its showy flowers

far–famed \'=¦=\ *adj* **:** widely and favorably known ⟨this *far-famed* hostelry —John Galsworthy⟩

far·fa·ra \'färfərə\ *n* -s [NL (specific epithet of the coltsfoot *Tussilago farfara*), fr. ML, coltsfoot, alter. of L *farferum, farfarum*] **:** the dried leaves of coltsfoot (sense a) used in folk medicine for coughs and as a tonic

far·fel \'färfəl\ *or* **fer·fel** \'fer-\ *n, pl* **farfel** *or* **ferfel** [Yiddish (pl.), fr. MHG *varveln* (pl.) noodles, noodle soup] **:** noodle dough in the form of small pellets or granules

farfet *adj* [ME *fer-fet*, fr. *fer* far + *fet*, past part. of *fetten* to fetch — more at FAR, FET] *obs* **:** FARFETCHED

[1]**farfetch** *n* [back-formation fr. *farfetched*] *obs* **:** a deep or complicated and obscure stratagem

[2]**farfetch** \'=¦=\ *vb* [back-formation fr. *farfetched*] *vt* **:** to derive (as a word) in a farfetched manner ~ *vi* **:** to make farfetched derivations

farfetched \'=¦=\ *adj* [[1]*far* + *fetched*, past part. of *fetch*] **1 a :** brought from a distance ⟨oranges and other ~ delicacies were rarities in those days⟩ **b** *obs* **:** from a remote time or place **2 :** not easily or naturally deduced or introduced **:** not based on probable or reasonable grounds or relationships **:** FORCED, STRAINED ⟨a ~ theme for a play⟩ ⟨such ~ ideas⟩ ⟨his stand seemed ~ and unreasonable⟩ — **far·fetched·ness** \-ch(t)nəs, -chəd-n-\ *n* -ES

far–flung \'=¦=\ *adj* **1 :** widely spread or distributed **:** having a wide range (as in space, time, or variation) **:** covering a large area ⟨the *far-flung* mountain ranges of the West⟩ ⟨*far-flung* trading operations⟩ ⟨the *far-flung* research fields of this foundation⟩ **2 :** distant from a point of reference ⟨this *far-flung* corner of the continent⟩ **:** REMOTE ⟨a *far-flung* tributary of the Nile⟩

far–forth \'=¦=\ *adv* [ME *ferforth*, fr. *fer* far + *forth*, adv. — more at FAR, FORTH] **:** to a great or definite distance, degree, or extent **:** FAR

fargoing \'=¦==\ *adj* **:** having extended influence **:** FAR-REACHING ⟨the ~ effects of this legislation⟩

[1]**far–gone** \'=¦=\ *adj* **:** remote in some respect (as from a standard or a beginning) ⟨*far-gone* places⟩ **:** nearing an end ⟨sitting in the *far-gone* night over their rum⟩: as **a :** nearing complete exhaustion or death ⟨too *far-gone* to raise his head⟩ **b :** nearly worn out ⟨my shoes were *far-gone* but I patched the soles with cardboard each night⟩

[2]**far–gone** \"\ *adv, dial* **:** by far **:** UNQUESTIONABLY ⟨known to be *far-gone* the best hound —Vereen Bell⟩

fa·ri·na \fə'rēnə *also chiefly Brit* -rīnə\ *n* -s [L, meal, flour, fr. *far* spelt — more at BARLEY] **1 a :** a fine meal of vegetable matter (as cereal grains, nuts, or sea moss) used chiefly for puddings or as a breakfast cereal **b :** the coarsely ground bolted endosperm of wheats other than durum, free from fine flour and from bran **c** *chiefly Brit* **:** starch esp. from the potato **2 :** any of various powdery substances that suggest flour or meal: as **a :** the pollen of a plant — not now used technically **b** *archaic* **:** a pruinous coating on various plants and insects

far·i·na·ceous \¦farə¦nāshəs\ *adj* [L *farinaceus*, fr. *farina* + *-aceus* -aceous] **1 a** *archaic* **:** containing or made of meal or flour **b :** containing or rich in starch **:** STARCHY ⟨~ foods⟩ ⟨a ~ diet lacking in animal protein⟩ **2 :** having a powdery surface that appears to be covered with meal — used esp. of plant and insect parts ⟨elytra ~⟩ **3 :** like meal in texture or quality ⟨a ~ surface⟩; *also* **:** having an odor like that of freshly ground wheat — **far·i·na·ceous·ly** *adv*

farinaceous ipecacuanha *n* **:** the emetic root of the Mexican clover (*Richardia scabra*)

fa·rine \fə'rēn\ *n* -s [modif. of Pg *farinha*] **:** FARINA 1a; *esp* **:** edible meal made from cassava root

faring *n* -s [fr. gerund of [1]*fare*] *dial Eng* **:** [2]FARE 4a

fa·ri·nha \fə'rēnyə\ *n* -s [Pg, cassava meal, meal, flour, fr. L *farina* meal, flour] **:** cassava meal

fa·ri·no·gram \fə'rēnə,gram\ *n* [ISV *farino-* (fr. L *farina*) + *-gram*] **:** a graphic record of the quality of a dough by means of a farinograph

fa·ri·no·graph \-af, -àf\ *n* [ISV *farino-* (fr. L *farina*) + *-graph*] **:** a recording dough mixer designed to measure qualitatively and record automatically the dough-forming properties of different wheats under controlled conditions of temperature — **fa·ri·no·graph·ic** \=¦==¦grafik\ *adj* — **fa·ri·nog·ra·phy** \,farə'nägrəfē\ *n* -ES

far·i·no·sae \,farə'nō(,)sē\ [NL, fr. LL, fem. pl. of *farinosus* mealy] *syn of* XYRIDALES

far·i·nose \'farə,nōs\ *adj* [LL *farinosus* mealy, fr. L *farina* + *-osus* -ose] **1 a :** yielding farina ⟨~ roots⟩ **b :** like farina esp. in texture **2 :** covered with a whitish mealy powder ⟨~ leaves⟩ ⟨the ~ bodies of certain insects⟩ **:** MEALY, FARINACEOUS — **far·i·nose·ly** *adv*

far·ish \'färish\ *adj* [[2]*far* + *-ish*] *dial* **:** somewhat far (as in age or drunkenness) — used with *on* ⟨he's ~ on for so early in the evening⟩

far·kle·ber·ry \'färkəl— *see* BERRY\ *n* [prob. alter. of *whortleberry*] **:** a shrub or small tree (*Vaccinium arboreum*) of the southeastern U.S. having coriaceous often evergreen leaves and a black dry berry with hard stony seeds — called also *sparkleberry*

farl *or* **farle** \'färl\ *n* -s [contr. of [3]*fardel*] **1** *Scot* **a :** a wedge of oatcake **b :** the fourth part of a bannock **2** *Scot* **:** a small scone

far·leu \'fär(,)lü\ *or* **far·ley** \-lē\ *n* -s [origin unknown] **:** money or chattels given by a feudal tenant to his lord in lieu of a heriot

far·ley maidenhair \'färlē-\ *n, usu cap F* [*Farley* Hill, country house in Barbados where it was discovered] **:** a brittle maidenhair of a widely cultivated variety (*Adiantum tenerum farleyense*)

[1]**farm** \'färm, 'fàm\ *vt* -ED/-ING/-s [ME *fermen*, fr. OE *feormian* to cleanse; akin to OHG *āfermī* filth] *dial Eng* **:** CLEANSE, EMPTY

[2]**farm** \"\ *n* -s *often attrib* [ME *ferme* rent, lease, fr. OF, lease, fr. *fermer* to make a contract, fix, fasten, fr. L *firmare* to make firm, fr. *firmus* firm — more at FIRM] **1** *obs* **:** a sum or due fixed in amount and payable at fixed intervals (as by way of rent or tax) **2 a :** a fixed sum payable at set intervals (as yearly) by a person in lieu of taxes or other dues that he has authority to collect **b :** a sum assessed upon a municipality or place as the amount to be paid from taxes to be collected within its limits **c :** a letting out of revenues or taxes for a fixed sum to one authorized to collect and retain them **d :** the farmers of public revenues **3 a :** the condition of being let out at a fixed rent **b** *obs* **:** LEASE **4 :** a district or division of a country leased out for the collection of the revenues of government **5 a :** a piece of land held under lease for cultivation **b :** any tract of land whether consisting of one or more parcels devoted to agricultural purposes generally under the management of a tenant or the owner **:** any parcel or group of parcels of land cultivated as a unit **6 a :** a plot of land devoted to the raising of domestic or other animals ⟨a chicken ~⟩ ⟨a fox ~⟩ **b :** a tract of water reserved for the artificial cultivation of some aquatic life-form ⟨an oyster ~⟩ **c :** TREE FARM **7 :** FARMHOUSE — obs. except in proper names **8 a :** FARMER 5 — used with *the* **b :** the pool in the game of farmer **9 :** a minor-league baseball club associated with a major-league club as a subsidiary to which recruits are assigned until needed or for further training **10 :** a rurally located rest home for alcoholics or other psychiatric patients

[3]**farm** \"\ *vb* -ED/-ING/-s [ME *fermen*, fr. *ferme*, n.] *vt* **1** *obs* **:** RENT **2 :** to collect and take the fees or profits of (an occupation or business) on payment of a fixed sum **3 :** to give up (as an estate, a business, or the revenue) to another on condition of receiving in return a fixed sum **4 :** to contract for the maintenance and care of (a person or thing) at a fixed price ⟨the town ~*s* its paupers⟩ — see FARM OUT **5 a :** to devote (land) to agriculture ⟨they decided to clear and ~ the north forty⟩ **b :** to manage and cultivate (land) as a farm ⟨he ~*ed* a small holding beside the river⟩ ~ *vi* **:** to engage in the business of raising crops or livestock ⟨he ~*ed* for nearly 50 years⟩ **:** manage or conduct a farm **:** work as a farmer

farm belt *n, sometimes cap F&B* **:** an area (as of the north central U.S.) devoted to large-scale commercial farming

farm bloc *n* **:** a combination of members of the U.S. Congress that transcends party lines in order to support the special interests of agriculture

farm·er \-mə(r)\ *n* -s [ME *fermour, fermer*, fr. MF *fermier, fermier* lessee, renter, fr. OF, fr. *ferme* lease + *-ier* -er — more at FARM] **1 :** a person who pays a fixed sum for some privilege or source of income: as **a :** one that obtains the right to collect taxes, customs, excises, or other duties, paying a fixed sum and retaining the moneys collected **b** *obs* **:** a lessee or renter **c :** the lessee of a government monopoly **2 :** a person who cultivates land or crops or raises livestock: as **a :** one that as steward, bailiff, or agent cultivates or supervises the cultivation of the lands of another **b :** one that rents or leases land for cultivation **:** TENANT FARMER **c :** a person whose primary occupation is the raising of crops or livestock — see GENTLEMAN FARMER; compare RANCHER **d :** a person engaged in a particular kind of farming ⟨fruit ~*s*⟩ ⟨a leading dairy ~⟩ **3 :** a person that agrees to perform certain duties for a fixed sum; *specif* **:** one that agrees to keep babies or paupers for a fixed sum per head **4 a :** an ignorant rustic **:** YOKEL, BUMPKIN **b :** a clumsy stupid fellow **:** DOLT **c** *slang* **:** a green hand inexperienced or incompetent in the trade at which he is working **5 :** a variation of twenty-one in which the object is to draw cards totaling sixteen in value; *also* **:** the dealer in this game

farmer cheese *n* **:** a pressed cheese of whole milk or partly skimmed milk made on farms

farm·er·ess \-mərəs\ *n* -ES **1** *archaic* **:** a female farmer **2** *archaic* **:** a farmer's wife

farm·er·ette \¦=mə¦ret\ *n* -s **:** a woman or girl who farms or works on a farm; *esp* **:** one that does farm labor as a civic duty during emergencies

farmer–general \¦==¦=(=)=\ *n, pl* **farmers–general** [trans. of F *fermier général*] **:** one of the men who farmed certain taxes in France from 1697 to 1789

farmer in the dell : a ring game in which one player chosen as the farmer occupies the center of the ring, others being called to join him as wife, child, nurse, cat, rat, and cheese and then sent away in reverse order while the players remaining in the ring circle about the farmer singing appropriate verses

farmer–laborite \,==¦==,=\ *n* -s *usu cap F&L* **:** a member of the Farmer-Labor party which is a minor political party in the U.S.

farm·er·ly \'färmərlē, 'fàməlē, -li\ *adj* **:** befitting or suggesting a farmer ⟨a tall ~ fellow —Lewis Nordyke⟩

farmer's lung *n, chiefly Brit* **:** an acute pulmonary disorder that is characterized by sudden onset, fever, cough, expectoration, and breathlessness and that results from the inhalation of dust from moldy hay or straw

farmers' mutual *n* **:** a mutual insurance company organized for the purpose of insuring farmers and farm property exclusively

far·mer's reducer \'färmərz-, 'fàməz-\ *n, usu cap F* [after E. Howard *Farmer* †1944 Eng. photographic technician who originated it] **:** a 20 to 25 percent solution of hypo to which a few drops of a 10 percent solution of potassium ferricyanide are added and which is used for reducing the image density and fog density of photographic negatives and prints

farmer's satin *n* **:** a lustrous durable fabric in satin weave with a cotton warp and a worsted or cotton filling used esp. for linings and dresses

farm·ery \'färmərē\ *n* -ES [[2]*farm* + *-ery*] *chiefly Brit* **:** the buildings and yards of a farm **:** FARMSTEAD

farmhand \'=,=\ *n* **1 :** a farm laborer; *esp* **:** a hired laborer on a farm **2 :** a baseball player assigned to a farm team

farmhold \'=,=\ *or* **farmholding** \'=,==\ *n* -s [*farmhold* fr. ME *fermehold*, fr. *ferme* rent, lease + *hold* land that is held; *farmholding* fr. [2]*farm* + *holding*, n. — more at FARMS, HOLD] *archaic* **:** a tract of land cultivated as a farm

farmhouse \'=,=\ *n* **1 :** the dwelling on a farm as distinguished from utility buildings (as a barn, corncrib, milk house) ⟨took the milk from the cow shed up to the ~⟩ **2 :** the dwelling and adjacent buildings (as a barn) on a farm

farming *n* -s [fr. gerund of [3]*farm*] **:** the practice of agriculture

farm labor camp *n* **:** any of certain residential facilities provided chiefly by government agencies for migratory or seasonal farm labor

farmland \'=,land\ *n* **:** land used or suitable for farming ⟨the decreasing supply of good ~⟩

farm loan bond *n* **:** a bond issued by a U.S. Federal Land bank and secured by a first mortgage on farmland

farm management *n* **:** the phase of agricultural economics dealing with the management of a farm

farmost \'=,=\ *adj* **:** FARTHEST

farm out *vt* **1 :** to turn over for performance (as a job or part of an operation) or for use (as a property or privilege) usu. on contract or for some agreed payment to one not usu. responsible for such performance or entitled to such use ⟨it is often desirable to *farm out* highly specialized operations⟩ ⟨the candidate was willing to *farm out* a few votes to check the rise of the new party⟩ **2 a :** to put (as children or prisoners) into the hands of a private individual for care in return for a fee ⟨*farmed out* the baby with her grandmother and went to work in town⟩ ⟨state wards are often *farmed out* to private families⟩ **b :** to send (a professional athlete) to a farm team **3 a :** to exhaust (land) by farming, esp. by continued cropping under a monoculture system ⟨much of the foothills has been *farmed out* with tobacco⟩ **b :** to drill (oil wells) on a piece of ground to the extent permitted by law, the terms of a lease, or circumstances

farmout \'=,=\ *n* -s [*farm out*] **:** a sublease granted by an oil company to another for drilling on partially proven ground

farmplace \'=,=\ *n* **:** a farmhouse or farmstead

farms *pres 3d sing of* FARM, *pl of* FARM

farmstead \'=,=\ *also* **farmsteading** \'=,==\ *n* -s **1 :** the buildings and adjacent service areas of a farm; *broadly* **:** a farm with its buildings **2 :** a farmhouse or a rural or suburban residence designed to suggest a farmhouse

farm system *n* **:** the several minor-league baseball clubs subsidiary to a single major-league club; *also* **:** the practice of having such subsidiary clubs

farmwife \'=,=\ *n, pl* **farmwives :** the mistress of a farm; *esp* **:** a farmer's wife

farmyard \'=,=\ *n* **:** space immediately adjoining and often more or less enclosed by the buildings making up a farmstead; *esp* **:** BARNYARD

far·ne·sol \'färnə,sōl, -,zl, |ōl\ *n* -s [ISV *farnes-* (fr. NL *farnesiana* — specific epithet of the huisache *Acacia farnesiana* — after Odoardo *Farnese* *fl* 1600 Ital. cardinal) + *-ol*; orig. formed in G] **:** a liquid alcohol $C_{15}H_{25}OH$ that has a floral odor, occurs in various essential oils (as neroli oil, citronella oil, and oil of amber seed), and is used in perfumes

far·ness *n* -ES [ME *fernesse*, fr. *fer* far + *-nesse* -ness — more at FAR] **1 :** the quality or state of being far off **:** remote site or situation ⟨the ~ of her house from the station⟩ **2** *archaic* **:** distant parts or regions ⟨from the ~ of the stars⟩

faro \'fa(a)|(,)rō, 'fe|\ *n* -s [prob. alter. of *pharaoh*] **:** a banking game in which players place bets on a special layout as to which cards will be winners or losers as they are drawn one at a time from a dealing box, each two cards drawn constituting a turn after which bets are settled

faro bank *n* **1 :** an establishment where faro is played **2 :** FARO

faro banker *n* **:** the proprietor or conductor of a faro bank

faroese *cap, var of* FAEROESE

far·oe step \'fa(a)|(,)rō, 'fe|\ *n, usu cap F* [*Faroe* islands (Faeroes), islands in the north Atlantic comprising a county of Denmark] **:** a dance step similar to the branle used in sung rounds of the Faroe islands

far–off \'=¦=\ *adj* [*far off* (adverbial phrase), fr. ME *fer of*, fr. *fer* far (adv.) + *of* off (adv.) — more at FAR, OFF] **1 :** remote in time or space **:** DISTANT ⟨*far-off* happier times⟩ ⟨rumblings of *far-off* thunder⟩ **2 :** directed toward the distance **:** ABSTRACTED ⟨*far-off* wandering thoughts⟩

fa·rol \fə'rōl, -rȯl\ *n, pl* **farols** \-lz\ *or* **fa·ro·les** \-,lās\ [Sp, lit., lantern, prob. modif. of Catal *faró*, fr. Gk *pharos* lighthouse — more at PHAROS] **:** a pase in bullfighting in which the matador swirls the cape back over his head, drawing the bull closely around

fa·rouche \fə'rüsh\ *adj* [F, shy, unwilling to make friends, wild, fr. OF *farouche, forasche*, fr. LL *forasticus* having come from elsewhere, fr. L *foras* out of doors, out; akin to L *foris, fores* door — more at DOOR] **:** lacking social graces and experience **:** marked by shyness and lack of polish ⟨their manners . . . were ~ beyond reason —Rose Macaulay⟩; *sometimes* **:** wild or disorderly ⟨an extremely ~ bohemian household⟩ — **fa·rouche·ness** *n* -ES

far point *n* **:** the point farthest from the eye at which an object is accurately focused on the retina when the accommodation is completely relaxed, being theoretically equatable with infinity or, for practical purposes in respect to the normal eye, with any distance greater than 6 meters or 20 feet — compare NEAR POINT; see RANGE OF ACCOMMODATION

far·rag·i·nous \fə'rajənəs\ *adj* [L *farragin-, farrago* + E *-ous*] **:** formed of various materials in no fixed order or arrangement ⟨the report is a ~ mass of disordered detail⟩ **:** forming a disordered whole ⟨a ~ body of complex ceremonial⟩

far·ra·go \fə'rä(,)gō, -rā(-, -ra(-\ *n* -ES [L *farragin-, farrago* mixed fodder for cattle, mash, mixture, fr. *far* spelt — more at BARLEY] **1 :** MIXTURE, MEDLEY ⟨a ~ of protein, fiber, and mineral salts —*New Yorker*⟩ **2 a :** a confused, disordered, or irrational assemblage (as of words or ideas) ⟨his ~ of facts would need sifting —O.W.Holmes †1935⟩ ⟨arranged as 'South is London of Brighton' they make a ~ which is neither true nor false, but nonsense —Gilbert Ryle⟩ **b :** a presentation (as of mingled fact and fancy) designed to deceive ⟨a ~ of half-truths intended to put the party line in the best light⟩ ⟨tricked many shrewd men with his wistful ~*es* of the helpless orphan girl⟩

far·rand \'farənd\ *or* **far·rant** \-nt\ *adj* [ME *farand, farende*, pres. part. of *faren* to go, get along, turn out — more at FARE] *chiefly Scot* **:** having a specified appearance or disposition ⟨he was ill, ~, and revengeful⟩ — **far·rand·ly** *or* **far·rant·ly** *adv*

farrash *var of* FERASH

farre *archaic var of* FAR

far–reaching \'=¦==\ *adj* **:** having a wide range or scope **:** having an influence or effect that reaches far in space, time, or relationships ⟨a *far-reaching* reform⟩ ⟨*far-reaching* forests⟩ ⟨*far-reaching* influence⟩ — **far–reach·ing·ly** *adv*

far·ri·er \'farēə(r)\ *n* -s [prob. alter. (influenced by *-er, -ier, -yer*, n. suffix) of obs. *ferrer*, fr. ME *ferrour* blacksmith who shoes horses, veterinarian, fr. MF, blacksmith who shoes horses, fr. OF *ferreor*, fr. *ferrer* to fit with iron, fr. (assumed) VL *ferrare*, fr. L *ferrum* iron, prob. of southwest Asiatic origin; akin to the source of Heb & Phoenician *barzel* iron, Syr *parzlā*, Akkadian *parzillu*] **1** *chiefly Brit* **:** one that attends a sick horse; *broadly* **:** a veterinarian esp. when practicing without full qualification **2** *chiefly Brit* **:** BLACKSMITH 1b **3 :** a noncommissioned officer in a cavalry regiment who has charge of the horses or their shoeing

farrier's hammer *n* **:** a hammer with a curved head having a flat poll at one end and a plain claw at the other

far·ri·er's knife *n* **:** a knife with curved blade and handle that has a square-cut hook on the end of the blade and is used for trimming hooves during shoeing (as of horses)

far·ri·ery \-ēərē\ *n* -ES [*farrier* + *-y*] **:** the art or practice of a farrier

[1]far·row \'fa(,)rō, -,rə *also* 'fe(-, *often* -,rəw+V\ *vb* -ED/-ING/-S [ME *farwen*, fr. (assumed) OE *feargian*, fr. OE *fearh* young pig; akin to OHG *farah* young pig, L *porcus* domestic pig, Lith *paršas* barrow] *vt* **:** to give birth to (a farrow) **~** *vi, of swine* **:** to bring forth young — often used with *down* ⟨planned to have the gilts ~ down about the end of March⟩

[2]farrow \"\ *n* -S **1 :** a litter of pigs **2 :** an act of farrowing

[3]farrow \"\ *adj* [ME (Sc) *ferow, ferrow*, prob. fr. (assumed) MD (Flemish dial.) *verwe-, varwe-* (whence Flem *verwe-, varwe-* in *verwekoe, varwekoe* cow that has ceased bearing); prob. akin to OE *fearr* bull, ox — more at PARE] *of a cow* **:** not in calf **:** not settled

far·ru·ca \fə'rükə\ *n* -S [Sp, fr. fem. of *farruco* Galician or Asturian outside of his native region, fr. *Farruco*, nickname of *Francisco* Francis] **:** a Spanish gypsy dance having sudden changes of mood and tempo

far·sakh \'fär,sak\ *or* **far·sagh** \-ag\ *also* **far·sang** \-aŋ\ *n, pl* **farsakh** [Ar & Per; Ar *farsakh*, fr. Per *farsang*] **:** a Persian unit of distance equal to about 4 miles; *also* **:** a Persian metric unit equal to 10 kilometers or 6.21 miles

[1]farse *obs var of* FARCE

[2]farse \'färs\ *n* -S [ML *farsa*, fr. (assumed) VL *farsa* forcemeat — more at FARCE] **:** an interpolation (as an explanatory phrase) inserted in a liturgical formula; *usu* **:** an addition or paraphrase, often in the vulgar language, formerly permitted in the sung portions of the Mass

[3]farse \"\ *vt* -ED/-ING/-S **:** to amplify (a liturgical formula) by interpolation **:** insert a farse in; *also* **:** to interpolate (a farse)

farseeing \'=¦==\ *adj* **1 :** able to see to a great distance **:** FARSIGHTED **2 :** having foresight

far·si \'fär(,)sē\ *n, pl* **farsi** *or* **farsis** *cap* [Per *fārsī*, fr. *Fārs* Persia] **:** a native or inhabitant of Fars, Iran

far side *n* **:** the farther side — **on the far side of :** BEYOND ⟨just *on the far side of* middle age⟩

far–sight \'=,=\ *n* **:** ability to see far

farsighted \'=¦==\ *adj* **1 a :** seeing or able to see to a great distance **b :** having foresight **:** able to anticipate and plan for the future; *broadly* **:** having good judgment **:** SAGACIOUS ⟨a state under the leadership of ~ men⟩ **2 :** HYPEROPIC — **far·sight·ed·ly** *adv*

far·sight·ed·ness *n* -ES **1 :** the quality or state of being farsighted **2 :** HYPEROPIA

[1]fart \'fär\|t, 'fȧ\|, *usu* \|d·+V\ *vi* -ED/-ING/-S [ME *ferten, farten;* akin to OHG *ferzan* to break wind, ON *freta*, Gk *perdesthai*, Skt *pardate* he breaks wind] **:** to expel intestinal gas from the anus **:** break wind — usu. considered vulgar

[2]fart \"\ *n* -S [ME *fert, fart*, fr. *ferten, farten*; v.] **:** an expulsion of intestinal gas — sometimes used of a person as a generalized term of abuse; usu. considered vulgar

[1]far·ther \'färthər, 'fȧthə(r\ *adv* [ME *ferther*, alter. (influenced by *ferre* — compar. of *fer*, adv., far —, fr. OE *fierr, fyrr*, compar. of *feorr*, adv., far) of *further* — more at FURTHER (adv.), FAR] **1 a :** to a greater distance in space **:** to a more remote place ⟨drive ~ north⟩ ⟨swallows . . . are gathering to fly ~ away —Padraic Colum⟩ **b :** at a greater distance in space **:** at a more remote place ⟨~ down the corridor —Willa Cather⟩ **c :** at a greater distance in time ⟨it may go back still ~ to racial Druid memories —Marjorie K. Rawlings⟩ **d :** more divergent ⟨nothing had been ~ from his thoughts —C.S. Forester⟩ **2 :** to or at a more advanced point **:** beyond a given limit ⟨if he could go a little ~ . . . he might become a very fine poet —C.P.Aiken⟩ **3 :** [1]FURTHER 3 **4 :** to a greater degree or extent ⟨we do not extend the one-man idea any ~ than we have to —G.F.Eliot⟩

[2]farther \"\ *adj* [ME *ferther*, fr. *ferther*, adv.] **1 a :** more distant in space **:** REMOTER ⟨the ~ side of town⟩ ⟨flood the ~ parts of your fields —Oliver La Farge⟩ **b :** more divergent in character or relationship ⟨the ~ the machines get from immediate and practical application —Robert Bendiner⟩ **c :** more remote in time ⟨a memory of a ~ childhood —*Yale Rev.*⟩ **2 :** [2]FURTHER 2 **3 :** the more distant of two ⟨the ~ side —C.E.Craddock⟩ ⟨her glance fixed itself . . . upon the ~ room —Virginia Woolf⟩

[3]farther \"\ *vt* -ED/-ING/-S [ME *fertheren*, fr. *ferther*, adv. & adj.] **:** FURTHER

far·ther·most \'==,mōst *also chiefly Brit* -,məst\ *adj* **:** most remote **:** FARTHEST

[1]far·thest \'färthəst, 'fȧth-\ *adj* [ME *ferthest*, fr. *ferther*, after comparatives and superlatives in ME *-er: -est* — more at -ER, -EST] **1 a :** most distant in space **:** REMOTEST ⟨the rage for these authors had traveled to the ~ frontier —Van Wyck Brooks⟩ ⟨to their ~ caverns sent —Matthew Arnold⟩ **b :** most remote in time **:** LATEST ⟨a few months or a year at ~ —Mary S. Watts⟩ **2 :** most advanced **:** ULTIMATE ⟨girls in beach pajamas already making the ~ use of their smiles —Hortense Calisher⟩

[2]farthest \"\ *adv* [ME *ferthest*, fr. *ferthest*, adj.] **1 a :** to or at the greatest distance in space **:** REMOTEST ⟨see who could jump the ~⟩ ⟨chose the seat ~ from the door⟩ **b :** at the greatest distance in time ⟨~ reach of memory⟩ **c :** of the most divergent quality ⟨~ thing from the ordinary —*New Republic*⟩ **2 :** to the most advanced point ⟨goes ~ toward giving us sculpture —G.L.K.Morris⟩ **3 :** by the greatest degree or extent **:** MOST ⟨the essay ~ removed from this reviewer's comprehension —*Saturday Rev.*⟩

far·thing \'färthiŋ, 'fȧth, -thēŋ\ *n* -S [ME *ferthing*, fr. OE *fēorthung;* akin to OFris *fiardunge, fiardeng* one fourth of a mark, MHG *vierdunc, vierdinc* fourth part, ON *fjōrthungr;* derivative fr. the root of OE *fēortha* fourth — more at FOURTH (adj.)] **1 a :** a British unit of value equal to ¼ of a penny **b :** a coin orig. of silver, later of copper, and after 1860 of bronze representing this unit **2 a :** an ancient English gold coin worth ¼ noble **b :** a somewhat later coin worth ¼ of a ryal **3 :** any very small Roman bronze coin (as a quadrans) **4 a** *obs* **:** a very small quantity **b :** something of small value **:** MITE ⟨I don't care a ~⟩ **5** *obs* **:** any of various measures or quantities of land (as a quarter of an acre or of a virgate)

far·thin·gale \'färthən,gāl, -thiŋ,g-\ *n* -S [modif. of MF *verdugale*, modif. of OSp *verdugado*, fr. *verdugo* young shoot of a tree, fr. *verde* green, fr. L *viridis* — more at VERDANT] **:** a support (as of hoops or a padded roll) worn esp. in the 16th century beneath a skirt to swell out and extend it at the hip line

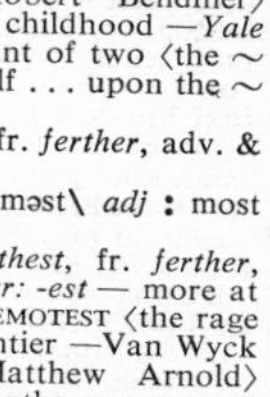

farthingale

farthingale chair *n, often cap F* **:** a broad-seated chair without arms, current in England during the reigns of Elizabeth I and James I

far·thing·deal \'färthiŋ,dēl\ *n* [by folk etymology (influence of *farthing*) fr. earlier *farthendele*, fr. ME *ferthendel*, fr. OE *fēorthandǣl* fourth part, fr. *fēorthan* (accus. of *fēortha* fourth) + *dǣl* part — more at FOURTH, DEAL] *archaic* **:** one fourth acre **:** ROOD

far·thing·land \-,land\ *n, archaic* **:** a farthingdeal or other measure of land

farting *pres part of* FART

far to seek : hard to find **:** RARE ⟨a really conscientious man is *far to seek*⟩ — usu. used negatively ⟨the causes of this oversight were not *far to seek*⟩

far–traveled \'=¦==\ *adj* **:** having traveled far esp. to varied and widely separated places

farts *pres 3d sing of* FART, *pl of* FART

far–western \(')=¦==\ *adj* **:** of, relating to, or situated in the part of the U.S. west of the Mississippi river or esp. west of the Great Plains

fas *or* **fa's** *pl of* FA

FAS *abbr* **1** firsts and seconds **2** free alongside ship

fasc *abbr* fascicle

fas·ces \'fa,sēz\ *n pl but often sing in constr* [L, fr. pl. of *fascis* bundle; akin to L *fascia* band] **1 :** a bundle of rods having among them an ax with the blade projecting, borne before Roman magistrates as a badge of authority in ancient Rome **2 :** the authority symbolized by the fasces

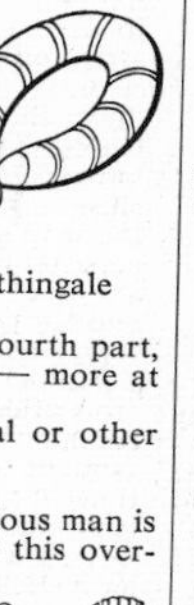

fas·cet \'fasət\ *n* -S [origin unknown] **:** a tool (as a rod or wire basket) used in glass manufacturing to carry bottles to the annealing furnace

fasces

fasci *pl of* FASCIO

fas·cia *or* **fa·cia** \'fash(ē)ə, 'fāsh-, *in sense 1c usu* 'fāsh-\ *n, pl* **fasci·ae** \-shē,ē\ *or* **fascias** *or* **facias** \-sh(ē)əz\ [It *fascia* band, bandage, architectural fascia, fr. L, band, bandage; akin to MIr *basc* necklace] **1 a :** a flat horizontal member of an order or building having the form of a flat band or broad fillet; *esp, in the Ionic order* **:** one of the three bands which make up the architrave — see MOLDING illustration **b** *usu facia* **:** a plate or tablet over the front of a shop (as one bearing the name or business of the owner) **c** *usu facia, also* **facia board** *or* **fascia board** *Brit* **:** the dashboard of an automobile **2** *usu fascia* [L] **:** a band, sash, or fillet (as on a garment) **3** *usu fascia* [NL, fr. L] **:** a broad and well-defined band of color (as on the wing of an insect) **4** *usu fascia* [NL, fr. L] **:** a sheet or layer of more or less condensed connective tissue covering, ensheathing, supporting, or binding together internal parts or structures of the body and being continuous with the other connective-tissue structures (as the ligaments, periosteum, or tendons); *also* **:** tissue of this character — see APONEUROSIS, DEEP FASCIA, SUPERFICIAL FASCIA

fascia board *n* **:** a horizontal board fascia covering the joint between the top of a wall and the projecting eaves

fas·cial \'fash(ē)əl\ *adj* [NL *fascialis*, fr. *fascia* + L *-alis* -al] **:** of or relating to a fascia ⟨~ planes of the neck⟩ **:** taking place through a fascia ⟨a ~ hernia⟩

fascia la·ta \,=(=)='läd·ə, -ād·ə\ *n, pl* **fasciae la·tae** \¦==,=-'läd·,ē, -'lād·,ē\ [NL, wide fascia] **:** the deep fascia that forms a complete sheath for the thigh and presents in front, just below Poupart's ligament, the saphenous opening

fas·ci·ate \'fashē,āt,-ēət\ , *or* **fas·ci·at·ed** \-,ād·əd\ *adj* [*fasciate* prob. fr. (assumed) NL *fasciatus*, fr. NL *fascia* + L *-atus* -ate; *fasciated* prob. fr. (assumed) NL *fasciatus* + E *-ed*] **1 :** banded or striped; *esp* **:** broadly banded with color **2 a :** FASCICLED **b :** exhibiting fasciation

fas·ci·a·tion \,=='āshən\ *n* -S [prob. fr. (assumed) NL *fasciation-, fasciatio*, fr. (assumed) NL *fasciatus* + L *-ion-, -io* -ion] **:** malformation (as in stems of plants) resulting from more or less disorganized tissue growth commonly manifested as enlargement and flattening and sometimes spiral curving as if several stems were fused and often accompanied by an abnormal number and arrangement of floral organs

fas·ci·cle \'fasəkəl\ *n* -S [L *fasciculus* small bundle, dim of *fascis* bundle — more at FASCES] **1 :** a small bundle or collection **:** a compact cluster: as **a :** an inflorescence consisting of a compacted cyme that is less capitate than a glomerule; *broadly* **:** any compact cluster of similar plant parts ⟨a ~ of larch needles⟩ **b :** BUNDLE 1d **c :** FASCICULUS 1 **2 :** one of the divisions of a book published in parts — called also *fascicule*

fas·ci·cled \-kəld\ *adj* **:** arranged in fascicles ⟨~ leaves of the larch⟩

fas·cic·u·lar \fə'sikyələ(r), fa'-\ *adj* [fr. *fascicle*, after such pairs as E *auricle: auricular*] **:** of or belonging to a fascicle **:** made up of fasciculi ⟨~ plant tissues⟩ **:** FASCICLED; *specif* **:** relating to or consisting of bundles of acicular crystals in a rock — **fas·cic·u·lar·ly** *adv*

fascicular cambium *n* **:** cambium within the vascular bundle — compare INTERFASCICULAR CAMBIUM

fascicular tissue *n* **:** VASCULAR TISSUE

fas·cic·u·late \fə'sikyələt,-,lāt,fa'-\ *or* **fas·cic·u·lat·ed** \-,lād·əd\ *adj* [*fasciculate* fr. LL *fasciculatus*, past part. of *fasciculare* to bundle, fr. L *fasciculus* small bundle; *fasciculated* fr. LL *fasciculatus* + E *-ed*] *biol* **:** FASCICLED — **fas·cic·u·late·ly** *adv*

fas·cic·u·la·tion \=,=='lāshən\ *n* -S [prob. fr. (assumed) NL *fasciculation-, fasciculatio*, fr. LL *fasciculatus* + L *-ion-, -io* -ion] **1** *zool* **:** the condition of being fascicled **2** [*fasciculus* + *-ation* (as in *fibrillation*)] **:** muscular twitching involving contiguous groups of muscle fibers — compare FIBRILLATION

fas·ci·cule \'fasə,kyül\ *n* -S [F, fr. L *fasciculus*] **:** FASCICLE 2

fas·cic·u·lus \fə'sikyələs,fa'-\ *n, pl* **fascicu·li** \-,lī\ [NL, fr. L] **1** *anat* **:** a slender bundle of fibers: **a :** a bundle of skeletal muscle cells bound together by fasciae and forming one of the constituent elements of a muscle **b :** a bundle of nerve fibers coursing together but not necessarily having like functional connections (as in certain subdivisions of the funiculi of the spinal cord) **c :** TRACT 2b(2) **2** [L] **:** FASCICLE 2

fas·ci·nate \'fasᵊn,āt,'faas-, *usu* -ād·+V\ *vb* **fascinated; fascinated; fascinating** \-sᵊn,ād·iŋ, -ātiŋ *also* -,snā-\ **fascinates** [L *fascinatus*, past part. of *fascinare*, prob. modif. (influenced by L *fari* to speak) of Gk *baskainein* to bewitch, speak evil of, fr. *baskanos* sorcerer, slanderer, prob. fr. a Thracian or Illyrian word akin to Gk *phaskein* to say, *phanai* to say — more at BAN] *vt* **1** *obs* **:** to cast a spell over **:** BEWITCH, ENCHANT **2 a :** to transfix and hold spellbound by or as if by an irresistible power ⟨believed that the serpent was capable of *fascinating* its prey before striking⟩ ⟨the changing vivid colors of the sunset *fascinated* the eye⟩ ⟨the younger and weaker man was *fascinated* and helpless before the creeping approach of so monstrous a wrath —G.D.Brown⟩ ⟨the bright light of a hooded lantern or a flashlight ~*s* the fleet-footed animal, making him a target for the huntsman's bullet —*Amer. Guide Series: Maine*⟩ **b :** to command the attention or interest of strongly or irresistibly often by the artful, subtle, challenging, strange, or piquant ⟨was *fascinated* by the personality of the tall, dark-haired young actress —J.K.Newnham⟩ ⟨men . . . who were not either *fascinating* women or obeying them —G.K.Chesterton⟩ **~** *vi* **:** to have or exercise the power of charming, alluring, or enthralling **:** be irresistibly attractive or interesting **:** engage and powerfully hold the attention or interest ⟨the very style of the book ~*s*, never mind the content⟩ ⟨since she had proved that she could farm as well as a man there was less need for her to endeavour to ~ as a woman —Ellen Glasgow⟩ **syn** see ATTRACT

fascinated *adj* [fr. past part. of *fascinate*] **:** FASCINATING, ENTHRALLING ⟨the ~ interest of her new novel⟩ ⟨an atmosphere of ~ suspense —W.H.Bucher⟩

fas·ci·nat·ed·ly *adv* [*fascinated* (past part. of *fascinate*) + *-ly*] **:** in the manner of one that is fascinated ⟨watched the man ~ as he juggled seven plates at a time⟩

fascinating *adj* [fr. pres. part. of *fascinate*] **:** holding the interest as if by a spell **:** ENTHRALLING **:** extremely interesting or charming ⟨~ old shops and alleys with the dust of another century upon them —*Amer. Guide Series: Maine*⟩ ⟨a ~ man of varied talents —Green Peyton⟩ ⟨the fickle yet ~ moods of British weather —L.D.Stamp⟩ ⟨India is an astounding and ~ country —Gerald Priestland⟩

fas·ci·nat·ing·ly *adv* **:** in a manner that fascinates

fas·ci·na·tion \,fasᵊn'āshən,,faas-\ *n* -S [L *fascination-, fascinatio*, fr. *fascinatus* + *-ion-, -io* -ion] **1** *obs* **:** the act of placing under a spell or the state of being under a spell; *also* **:** SPELL, ENCHANTMENT **2 a:** the quality of fascinating **:** the quality of holding the interest strongly esp. as if by a spell **:** the ability to enthrall **:** irresistible attraction or charm ⟨attracted by the ~ of discovery and the prospect of spiritual conquest —*Amer. Guide Series: Minn.*⟩ ⟨the Rio Grande . . . offers ~*s* for geologists and bird lovers —Stanley Walker⟩ ⟨it is so dreadful, in fact, that it begins to have its own morbid ~ and it is almost impossible . . . to put it down —B.R.Redman⟩ ⟨they found a certain ~ in combat —Mack Morriss⟩ **b :** a characteristic or peculiarity that gives this quality or ability ⟨tired of her ~*s* . . . he began to blame her for all his misfortunes —Edith Sitwell⟩ **3 :** the state of being fascinated **:** the state of feeling an intense interest in ⟨his lifelong ~ for clowns and their art —*Current Biog.*⟩ ⟨James's ~ by brutality and violence —John Farrelly⟩ ⟨Hunt's ~ with the mechanics and engineering of public opinion —T.H.White b. 1915⟩ **4 :** one form of the game of solitaire

fas·ci·na·tor \'==,ād·ə(r)\ *n* -S **1 :** one that fascinates **2 :** a woman's light head scarf usu. of crochet or lace

[1]fas·cine \fa'sēn,fə'-\ *n* -S [F, fr. L *fascina* bundle of sticks, fr. *fascis* bundle — more at FASCES] **:** a long cylindrical bundle of wooden sticks bound together at intervals by a choker or withy and used for filling ditches, strengthening ramparts, or making parapets, revetments or mats for river banks, dams or jetties

[2]fascine \"\ *vt* -ED/-ING/-S **:** to cover, protect, or strengthen with fascines

fa·scio \'fä(,)shō\ *n, pl* **fa·sci** \-(,)shē\ *sometimes cap* [It, bundle, political group, local branch of the Fascisti, fr. L *fascis* bundle] **:** a local branch of the Fascisti

fas·ci·o·la \fə'sēələ, -sīə-\ *n* [NL, fr. L, small bandage, dim. of *fascia* bandage — more at FASCIA] **1** *pl* **fascio·lae** \-,lē\ *or* **fasciolas :** a narrow fascia or band of color **2** *cap* **:** a genus (the type of the family Fasciolidae) of digenetic trematode worms including common liver flukes of ruminants and various other mammals including man

fas·ci·o·lar \-lə(r)\ *adj* **:** of or relating to a fasciola

fas·ci·o·lar·ia \,fasēə'la(a)rēə\ *n, cap* [NL, fr. L *fasciola* small bandage + NL *-aria*] **:** a genus (the type of the family Fasciolariidae) of large stenoglossate marine snails comprising the typical band shells

fas·ci·ole \'fas(h)ē,ōl\ *n* -S [NL *fasciola*, fr. L, small bandage] **:** a band of minute tubercles bearing modified commonly ciliated spines on the test of certain sea urchins

fas·ci·o·li·a·sis \fə,sēə'līəsəs,fə,sī-\ *also* **fas·ci·o·lo·sis** \-lōsəs\ *n, pl* **fasciolia·ses** \-ə,sēz\ *also* **fasciolo·ses** \-ō-,sēz\ [NL, fr. *Fasciola* + *-iasis*] **:** infestation with or disease caused by liver flukes (genus *Fasciola*) **:** LIVER ROT, DISTOMATOSIS

fas·ci·o·li·ci·dal \fə¦sēələ¦sīdᵊl,fə¦sīə-\ *adj* **:** of or belonging to a fasciolicide ⟨~ effect⟩ ⟨~ efficacy⟩

fas·ci·ol·i·cide \fə'sēələ,sīd,fə'sī-\ *n* -S [NL *Fasciola* + E *-i-* + *-cide*] **:** an agent that destroys liver flukes of the genus *Fasciola*

fas·ci·ol·i·dae \,fasē'äla,dē\ *n pl, cap* [NL, fr. *Fasciola*, type genus + *-idae*] **:** a cosmopolitan family of digenetic trematodes chiefly infesting the livers of mammals and typically having a flattened leaf-shaped body with the ventral sucker near the anterior end — see FASCIOLA, FASCIOLOIDES, FASCIOLOPSIS

fas·ci·o·loid \fə'sēə,lȯid, fə'sī-\ *adj* [NL *Fasciola* + E *-oid*] **:** of, relating to, or resembling worms of the genus *Fasciola* or the family Fasciolidae

fas·ci·o·loi·des \fə,sēə'lȯi(,)dēz,fə,sī-\ *n, cap* [NL, fr. *Fasciola*, genus name + L *-oides* -oid] **:** a genus of trematode worms (family Fasciolidae) including the giant liver flukes of ruminant mammals that are serious pests of livestock and game in parts of western No. America

fas·ci·o·lop·si·a·sis \-,läp'sīəsəs\ *n* -ES [NL, fr. *Fasciolopsis* + *-iasis*] **:** infestation with or disease caused by the large intestinal fluke (*Fasciolopsis buski*) of man

fas·ci·o·lop·sis \-'läpsəs\ *n, cap* [NL, fr. *Fasciola* + *-opsis*] **:** a genus of trematode worms (family Fasciolidae) that includes an important intestinal parasite of man and swine that is prevalent in much of eastern Asia

fas·cism \'fa\|,shizəm, 'faa\|, 'fai\| *also* \|,si- *sometimes* 'fä\| *or* 'fȧ\|\ *n* -S [It *fascismo*, fr. *fascio* bundle, political group + *-ismo* -ism] **1** *often cap* **:** the principles of the Fascisti; *also* **:** the movement or governmental regime embodying their principles **2 a :** any program for setting up a centralized autocratic national regime with severely nationalistic policies, exercising regimentation of industry, commerce, and finance, rigid censorship, and forcible suppression of opposition **b :** any tendency toward or actual exercise of severe autocratic or dictatorial control (as over others within an organization) ⟨the nascent ~ of a detective who is not content merely to do his duty —George Nobbe⟩ ⟨early instances of army ~ and brutality —J.W.Aldridge⟩ ⟨a kind of personal ~, a dictatorship of the ego over the more generous elements of the soul —Edmond Taylor⟩

fa·scis·mo \fä'shez(,)mō\ *n* -S *often cap* [It] **:** FASCISM

[1]fas·cist \'fa\|shəst, 'faa\|, 'fai\| *also* \|səst *sometimes* 'fä\| *or* 'fȧ\|\ *n* -S *often cap* [It *fascista*, fr. *fascio* + *-ista* -ist] **:** one who adheres to, advocates, or practices fascism

[2]fascist \"\ *or* **fas·cis·tic** \(')=¦\|shistik, fə'\| *also* \|si-\ *adj* **1** *usu cap* **:** of or belonging to the Fascisti, their organization, or their program **2** *sometimes cap* **a :** of, belonging to, sponsored by, or embodying fascism **:** according with or favoring fascism **b :** of or belonging or relating to fascists — **fas·cis·ti·cal·ly** \(')=¦\|shistək(ə)lē, fə'\|, \|si-, -tēk-, -li\ *adv*

fa·scis·ta \fä'shēs(,)tä\ *n, pl* **fascis·ti** \-(,)tē\ [It] **1** *usu cap* **:** a member of an Italian political organization that was founded in 1919 and was dedicated to violently nationalistic and totalitarian principles and that under Benito Mussolini gained control of Italy and reorganized its political and social structure to accord with fascism — compare BLACKSHIRT **2 :** a member of an organization similar to that of the Italian Fascisti **:** FASCIST

fa·scis·ti·za·tion \,fa\|s(h)əstə'zāshən, ,faa\|, ,fai\| -,stī'z\| *sometimes* ,fä\| *or* ,fȧ\|\ *n* -S **:** the act or process of fascistizing or the state of being fascistized

fa·scis·tize \'==,stīz\ *vt* -ED/-ING/-S **:** to make over or transform into a fascista **:** convert to the principles of fascism

fasels *n pl* [ME *fasele* (sing.) kidney bean, fr. L *phaselus* — more at FRIJOL] **1** *obs* **:** KIDNEY BEANS **2** *obs* **:** CHICK-PEAS

[1]fash \'fash\ *vb* -ED/-ING/-ES [MF *fascher*, fr. (assumed) VL *fastidiare* to disgust, fr. L *fastidium* loathing, disgust — more at FASTIDIOUS] *vt, chiefly Scot* **:** INCONVENIENCE, TROUBLE, BOTHER ⟨don't ~ yourself about me⟩ **~** *vi, chiefly Scot* **:** to take trouble or pains ⟨no need to ~⟩ — **fash one's beard** *or* **fash one's head** *or* **fash one's thumb** *dial Brit* **:** to trouble oneself

[2]fash \"\ *n* -ES *chiefly Scot* **:** fuss and bother **:** ANNOYANCE ⟨if you don't want to hear it, I am saved the ~ of telling it⟩

[3]fash \"\ *n* -ES [prob. alter. of obs. *fas* tassel, fr. ME, tassel, rootlets of a leek, fr. OE *fæs* fringe; akin to MD *vese* fringe, frayed edge, OHG *faso, fasa* fiber, fringe, Russ *pasmo* part of a skein of yarn] **:** an irregular seam on a boat

fash·er·ie *or* **fash·ery** \fash(ə)ri\ *n, pl* **fasheries** [MF *fascherie*, fr. *fascher* + *-erie* -ery] **1** *dial Brit* **:** ANNOYANCE, BOTHER **2** *dial Brit* **:** unnecessary ornament or ceremony

[1]fash·ion \'fashən, 'faash-, 'faish-\ *n* -S [ME *facioun, fasoun* shape, manner, fr. OF *façon*, fr. L *faction-, factio* action of making, company, faction, fr. *factus* (past part. of *facere* to make) + *-ion-, -io* -ion — more at DO] **1 a :** the form of something or the way it is constructed **:** appearance or mode of structure **:** STYLE, SHAPE ⟨do not like the ~ of your garments —Shak.⟩; *also* **:** a distinctive or peculiar form, shape, or cut (as of attire) ⟨the cut of the coat was a ~ of his own⟩ **b** *archaic* **:** KIND, SORT **2 a :** MANNER, WAY ⟨expressed himself in a striking ~⟩ ⟨turn out munitions in wholesale ~ following the outbreak of war —R.L.Buell⟩ ⟨the phonetics of Chinese are introduced in summary ~ in the first weeks —*Georgetown Univ. Bull.*⟩ **b :** mode of action or operation **:** ⟨threshing grain after the old ~⟩; *also, archaic* **:** DEMEANOR, BEARING, BEHAVIOR **c :** a distinctive or peculiar and often habitual manner, way, gesture, or action ⟨defending demagogy after his ~ —E.R. Bentley⟩ ⟨Carlyle's bad ~ of ignoring the best forces of his own age —Bliss Perry⟩ **d** *archaic* **:** SHOW, PRETENSE **3** *obs* **:** the act or process of making something (as an ornamentation on silver) **:** CRAFTSMANSHIP **4 a :** a prevailing usu. short-lived custom, usage, or style **:** FAD ⟨there are ~*s* in kinds of novels and ~*s* in ways of writing them —Bernard DeVoto⟩ ⟨not even changing ~*s* in warfare have diminished the island's strategic importance —Franc Shor⟩ ⟨Classicism, the Enlightenment, Romanticism, Realism, were not mere literary ~*s* —A.L.Guérard⟩ ⟨in six weeks she was the ~ of the town —Willa Cather⟩ ⟨there was a ~ for it some forty years ago as a depressant in cases of mania —Margery Allingham⟩ **b :** the prevailing or accepted style or group of styles in dress or personal decoration established or adopted during a particular time or season **:** VOGUE ⟨the ~ in hairdressing of the preceding century⟩ ⟨jewelry and clothing ~*s* vary with the season⟩ ⟨a high forehead from which swept back thick bronze hair scrupulously trimmed according to the day's ~ —W.J.Locke⟩ ⟨followed the line and general ~ of female court clothes of the day —Anatole Chujoy⟩; *also* **:** a garment in such a style ⟨we tried on the latest ~*s* today⟩ **c** *often cap* **:** such prevailing customs or styles considered as an abstract force ⟨a woman who lets *Fashion* dictate most of her actions⟩ ⟨as for the peculiar stamp of the scientific thought of an age, we must make due allowance for ~ and the example of leaders —*Times Lit. Supp.*⟩ **d :** social standing or prominence esp. as signalized by dress or conduct that meticulously accords with the most approved prevalent style or mode ⟨the captain, who was speaking a few parting words to some passengers of ~ —Winston Churchill⟩

syn FASHION, STYLE, MODE, VOGUE, FAD, RAGE, CRAZE, DERNIER CRI, CRY can mean, in common, a way of dressing, behaving, dancing, decorating, or an interest (as in a recreation) that is considered esp. up-to-date or noticeably following the contemporary trend in such activities. FASHION, in this context, is the prevailing conventional usage or custom ⟨dressed in the height of *fashion*⟩ ⟨the gloom of modern writing is no more than a *fashion*, which will pass as all fashions pass —Douglas Stewart⟩ ⟨one of a group of elegant, narrative biographies which may be setting a modern *fashion* —*Saturday Rev.*⟩ STYLE, often interchangeable with FASHION, can suggest the elegant or distinguished way of dressing, behaving, and so on, characteristic of those of taste in a given period ⟨dressed in the current *style*⟩ ⟨a house in the *style* of the late 19th century architecture⟩ ⟨the . . . house . . . has space, simplicity, *style* —Lillian Hellman⟩ ⟨a woman of both beauty and *style*⟩ MODE stresses, more than the others, the peak of contemporary fashion especially in dress and behavior, often suggesting a certain transciency ⟨its three bedrooms . . . all done in the modern *mode* —*Monsanto Mag.*⟩ ⟨the romantic landscape of England became a *mode* accepted without question in Sydney —Bernard Smith⟩ ⟨the rule of taste results in the tyranny of the *mode* —W.C.Brownell⟩ VOGUE, when it is not interchangeable with FASHION, often puts stress upon obvious popularity and wide acceptance, esp. of dress or decoration ⟨when fanciful scrollwork trim, cupolas, and brackets were in *vogue* —*Amer. Guide Series: Ariz.*⟩ ⟨the fashionable *vogue* for ultramodern art —*Encyc. Americana*⟩ ⟨a *vogue* at the moment of the red ties and red skirts —Frank Gorrell⟩ FAD designates a fashion that is usu. short lived, and connotes capriciousness in the interest and quick decline of interest shown in it ⟨unconcerned with *fads*, with whims of the moment —Clifton Fadiman⟩ ⟨a *fad* is a small fashion in some secondary matter or detail —N.A.Brisco⟩ ⟨whether the long skirts, high necks, pinched waists, padded hips, and bulky hats are here to stay for a while, or are merely a passing *fad* —*Modern Beauty Shop*⟩ RAGE and CRAZE designate a fad adopted with short lived but intense enthusiasm, often implying a certain senselessness ⟨one of the very latest *rages* — sterling silver charm bracelets that spell out your name —*N.Y. Times Mag.*⟩ ⟨for part of the Grimaldi period, performing dogs were the *rage* —Robert Turley⟩ ⟨the current *craze* for cyclecars —*Current Biog.*⟩ ⟨to satisfy the *craze* for wild-bird feathers on women's hats —J.H.Baker⟩ DERNIER CRI, sometimes with the French article *le*, and the equivalent English CRY (as in the phrase *all the cry*) designate the very latest style, fashion, or fad, esp. in art or clothes ⟨women garbed in the *dernier cri* from Paris —S.J.Perelman⟩ ⟨purporting to be the quintessence of scholarly research, the *dernier cri* in intelligent social theory and practice —*Current History*⟩ ⟨the last *cry* today may be a far cry from that of yesterday⟩ **syn** see in addition METHOD

— **after a fashion** *adv* : in an approximate or rough way ⟨became an artist *after a fashion* but never achieved distinction⟩

²fashion \"\ *vb* **fashioned; fashioned; fashioning** \-sh(ə)niŋ\ **fashions** [ME *faciounen*, fr. *facioun*, n.] *vt* **1 a :** to give shape or form to : FORM, MOLD ⟨~ the clay in the figure of a donkey⟩ ⟨sit once more at the feet of the ancient wisdom and ~ their lives upon the principle that the soul is more than the meat and the body than raiment —V.L.Parrington⟩ ⟨human nature is ~*ed* to a large extent by surrounding cultural configurations —Bernard Rosenberg⟩ ⟨as intelligent creatures, ~*ed* by the hand and in the image of an all-wise God —W.F. Hambly⟩ **b :** ALTER, MODIFY, TRANSFORM ⟨new frontiers were established which ~*ed* the political and social institutions of the old —W.P.Webb⟩ **c :** to mold into a particular character by influencing, instructing, training, or conditioning ⟨the teacher ~*ed* the student into a fine pianist⟩ ⟨the painful metaphysical struggle or religious revolt that ~*ed* Joyce's soul in youth and first manhood —Sean O'Faolain⟩ ⟨choose a dog specifically designed by nature, and ~*ed* by man, to hunt —*Holiday*⟩ **d :** MAKE, CONSTRUCT ⟨~*ed* a canoe from a huge pine —R.S.Monahan⟩ ⟨~ out of paper a representation of the person whom the magician wishes to injure —J.G.Frazer⟩ ⟨well-kept houses of brick ~*ed* from the red clay —*Amer. Guide Series: Pa.*⟩ ⟨each writer had to find or ~ for himself an artistic credo —Max Lerner & Edwin Mims⟩ ⟨his ability to ~ personal triumphs from the most unlikely materials —R.H. Rovere⟩ **2 :** FIT, ADAPT, ACCOMMODATE ⟨she was always ~*ed* to the subtle, disguising whalebone of common sense —V.S. Pritchett⟩ **3 a** *obs* **:** to bring about by devising : CONTRIVE **b :** REPRESENT, PICTURE ⟨the subordinate characters are expertly ~*ed* too —T.C.Chubb⟩ **c** *obs* **:** to make pretense of : COUNTERFEIT **4 :** to make up : CONSTITUTE ⟨from these yards was recruited Noah Brown's heroic band who ~*ed* Commodore Perry's fleet for the Battle of Lake Erie —*Amer. Guide Series: N. Y. City*⟩ **5 :** to increase or decrease stitches in ~ *vi, dial Eng* **:** to have the nerve : DARE **syn** see MAKE

³fashion *n* [by folk etymology fr. obs. *farcin* farcy, fr. ME *farsin* — more at FARCY] *obs* **:** FARCY

fash·ion·a·bil·i·ty \ˌfash(ə)nəˈbilədē, ˌfaash-, ˌfaish-, -lətē, -ī\ *n* -ES **:** FASHIONABLENESS

¹fash·ion·a·ble \ˈfash(ə)nəbəl, ˈfaash-, ˈfaish-\ *adj* [¹*fashion*, ²*fashion* + *-able*] **1 a :** conforming to the custom, fashion, or established mode esp. in dress or behavior : observant of the fashion : dressing or behaving according to the prevailing fashion ⟨a ~ lady⟩ ⟨a ~ society⟩ : in accordance with prevailing form or fashion : STYLISH, MODISH ⟨a ~ dress⟩ ⟨a ~ hairdo⟩ **b :** of or belonging to the world of fashion : frequented or patronized by persons of fashion or by those who conform to fashion ⟨the ~ stores⟩ ⟨a ~ vacation spot⟩ : popular among those who conform to fashion ⟨during the height of St. Martinville's ~ period, steamboats landed passengers regularly at its door —*Amer. Guide Series: La.*⟩ ⟨eventually became a ~ surgeon —*Time*⟩ ⟨there are some ~ books that one must read, because they are ingredients of the talk of the day —T.L.Peacock⟩ ⟨went to Europe because it was the ~ thing to do⟩ ⟨asking the ~ questions of the moment —Max Beloff⟩ **c :** merely echoing or imitating thoughtlessly or irresponsibly a contemporary fashion rather than acting responsibly or with a full awareness of essential issues ⟨the martyr-toned, bogus moralizing now ~ among scientists and their hero worshipers —*Time*⟩ ⟨it is ~ — and easy — to define tolerance in such a way as to evade all responsibility —Paul Blanshard⟩ ⟨an Age of Anxiety in which "escape" itself is becoming increasingly frequent and even ~ —*College English*⟩ ⟨a ~ neurosis —Miriam Allott⟩ **2** *obs* **:** capable of being shaped or molded **3** *obs* **:** of or belonging to mere outward show or form **4** *obs* **:** of good appearance — **fash·ion·a·ble·ness** \-bəlnəs\ *n* -ES — **fash·ion·a·bly** \-blē, -li\ *adv*

²fashionable \"\ *n* -s **:** a fashionable person ⟨trying to keep up with the young ~*s* of Rome —Grace Frick⟩ ⟨the ~*s* were now arriving, including a number of chic Muslims wearing tasseled chechias above their handsomely tailored European clothes —A.J.Liebling⟩

fash·ion·er \-nə(r)\ *n* -s **:** one that fashions, forms, or gives shape to something ⟨the ~*s* of the screens, choir stalls, corbels, and hammer posts of the great cathedrals —L.F.Herreshoff⟩ ⟨for the mind (the "spiritual") is a maker and a ~ of quite formidable proportions —Weston La Barre⟩ ⟨America's most expert ~ of the wholesome love story —*Time*⟩; *esp* **:** one that makes clothing

fashion gray *n* **:** a dark gray that is darker than Oxford gray, Dover gray, or pelican — called also *cruiser, pilgrim, Plymouth*

fash·ion·ist \-sh(ə)nəst\ *n* -s **:** a maker, leader, specialist in, or follower of fashions

fash·ion·less \-shənləs\ *adj, archaic* **:** without a definite shape : SHAPELESS

fashion mark *n* **:** the stitch distortion resulting from an increase or decrease in full-fashioned knitting

fashionmonger \ˈ=,==\ *n* **:** one that studies, imitates, or sets the fashion ⟨~*s* say they must adapt their production and advertising to irrational consumer behavior —P.M.Gregory⟩

fashion piece *n* **:** one of the timbers at the ends of the transom that define the shape of a ship's stern

fashion plate *n* **1 :** an illustration of a clothing style **2 :** a person who dresses in the newest fashion ⟨the wealthy woman who . . . is little more than an animated *fashion plate* —H.A. Overstreet⟩

fashions *pl of* FASHION, *pres 3d sing of* FASHION

fash·ious \ˈfashəs\ *adj* [MF *fascheux*, fr. *fascher* to trouble, bother + *-eux* -ous — more at ¹FASH] *dial Brit* **:** TROUBLESOME, ANNOYING

fasnacht *var of* FASTNACHT

fa·so·la \ˌfäˌsōˈlä\ *n* -s [*fa* + *so* + *la*] **:** a system of solmization used in England and America in the 17th and 18th centuries using of the original six Guidonian syllables only the four fa, sol, la, and mi and often used in conjunction with the shape-note system of musical notation

fas·sa·ite \ˈfasəˌīt\ *n* -s [G *fassait*, fr. Val di *Fassa*, Venezia Tridentina, northeast Italy + G *-it* -ite] **:** a mineral consisting of a pale green to dark green variety of augite

fas·set \ˈfasət, *also* -əd·+V\ *dial var of* FAUCET

¹fast \ˈfast, -aa(ə)-, -ai-, -ȧ-\ *adj* -ER/-EST [ME, *fr.* OE *fæst*; akin to OHG *festi* firm, ON *fastr*, Arm *hast* firm, Skt *pastyā* homestead] **1 a :** firmly fixed : immovable or moved only with the greatest difficulty ⟨the roots of the tree were so ~ in the ground we left them there⟩ ⟨a flagpole set ~ in its concrete socket⟩ ⟨a gun ~ in its carriage⟩ ⟨a ~ and impassable barrier between them⟩ **b :** tightly shut : unable to be opened or very difficult to open ⟨after the damp weather all the drawers became ~⟩ ⟨the trunk lid was ~ so that even after the key was turned it would not budge⟩ : FASTENED, LOCKED ⟨the windows and doors were all ~ so that thieves could not enter⟩ **c :** unable to be separated after being fastened together ⟨the boards were ~ a few hours after being glued together⟩ ⟨made the ropes ~ with a solid square knot⟩ **d :** not easily extricated or freed : STUCK ⟨when his foot went through the rotten floor it became ~ between two of the floor timbers⟩ ⟨a shell ~ in the chamber of a gun⟩ **e :** not able to leave something — usu. used in combination ⟨bed*fast*⟩ **f :** BUSY, ENGAGED **g :** somewhat permanently settled : STABLE **h :** UNCHANGEABLE ⟨hard and ~ rules⟩ **2** *obs* **a** *of a fortification* **:** UNYIELDING, IMPREGNABLE **b** *of a place* **:** secure against attack **3 :** turned from one's purpose only with great difficulty: as **a :** firmly loyal : STAUNCH, STEADFAST — used in the phrase *fast friend* **b** *archaic* **:** UNREMITTING — used in the phrase *fast foe* **4 a** *obs* **:** COMPACT, DENSE, SOLID **b** *archaic* **:** frozen over solid **5 a :** characterized by quick motion: (1) **:** moving or able to move rapidly : FLEET, SWIFT ⟨a ~ car⟩ ⟨a ~ horse⟩ (2) *of a baseball* **:** thrown at the pitcher's highest speed ⟨threw more ~ balls than curves⟩ (3) **:** moving ahead swiftly ⟨a society that was ~ as far as improvement is concerned⟩ (4) **:** taking a comparatively short time ⟨a ~ race⟩ (5) **:** following in rapid succession ⟨took two ~ shots⟩ (6) **:** imparting quickness of motion ⟨a ~ bowler⟩ ⟨a ~ mechanism on the gun trigger⟩ (7) **:** accomplished or capable of being accomplished quickly ⟨~ work⟩ (8) **:** marked by abrupt decision or action esp. as impelled by a quick temper or irascible nature ⟨a bit too ~ with his fists in an argument⟩ (9) *of a dramatic or literary work* **:** holding the interest by reason of the sustained conflict, vivid writing, or the rapid advancement of a story ⟨a taut and ~ play⟩ ⟨a ~ rollicking tale⟩ (10) **:** agile of mind ⟨an excellent witness — eloquent, confident, ~ beyond belief —Michael Straight⟩ (11) **:** having a rapid effect ⟨the medicine was a ~ one⟩ ⟨the acid was chosen because it was ~⟩ **b :** having qualities which are conducive to rapidity of play or action ⟨a ~ track⟩ ⟨a ~ tennis court⟩ ⟨a ~ gun holster⟩ ⟨the roads were ~ between the towns⟩: as (1) *of a wicket* **:** in such condition as to cause a bowled cricket ball to leave the ground swiftly after landing — contrasted with *slow;* compare FIERY (2) **:** allowing the rapid passage of a gas or fluid ⟨a ~ nipple on the baby bottle⟩ **c** (1) *of timepieces or time reports* **:** indicating time in advance of what is correct (2) *of weighing instruments* **:** registering more than the correct weight of the thing weighed (3) **:** according to daylight saving time **d :** contributing to a shortening of exposure time — used of a photographic lens or photographic emulsion **e** *slang* (1) *of money or profits* **:** acquired with unusually little effort and usu. in a rapid transaction ⟨made a ~ fortune in real estate⟩ ⟨made some ~ money on horseracing⟩ and often by shady or dishonest methods ⟨made a ~ dollar in a con scheme⟩ (2) **:** involving unusually little effort in proportion to the money gained thereby ⟨tried to think of a show he could do for a ~ thirteen weeks that would pay for the baby —Pete Martin⟩ (3) **:** unusually quick and ingenious or cunning in finding or recognizing and profiting by easy and often shady ways of making or acquiring money ⟨a particularly ~ man with a buck —*Time*⟩ (4) **:** marked by trickery and unfairness ⟨worked a ~ deal on a friend⟩ **6 a :** securely attached or fixed to someone or something ⟨a rope ~ to the wharf⟩ ⟨when the handcuffs were snapped on, the culprit was ~ to the police officer⟩ **b :** TENACIOUS ⟨a ~ hold on the purse⟩ **c** (1) *of a knot* **:** firmly tied (2) *of an alliance or agreement* **:** not easily broken or betrayed : CERTAIN, SECURE **d** (1) *of a harpoon* **:** stuck securely in a whale (2) *of a whale* **:** secured by a harpoon; *esp* **:** harpooned securely by a certain crew and consequently the rightful possession of that crew regardless of subsequent claims (3) *of a whaleboat* **:** secured to a whale by harpoon **7 a** *archaic* **:** sound asleep **b** *of sleep* **:** not easily disturbed : SOUND ⟨fell into a ~ sleep⟩ **8 a :** not fading or changing color readily : permanently dyed : COLORFAST ⟨~ colors⟩ ⟨~ dyeings⟩ **b :** yielding colors of this kind — used esp. of the diazo components of azoic dyes ⟨~ color bases⟩; see DYE table I (under *Acid, Azoic, Diazo, Disperse, Mordant*) **c :** proof against fading under exposure to a particular agency or action ⟨the dye is made ~ to perspiration —*Know Your Merchandise*⟩ ⟨a color that is ~ to sunlight⟩ — often used in combinations ⟨sun*fast*⟩ ⟨boil*fast*⟩ ⟨wash*fast*⟩ **9 a :** marked by or given to living that is unusually active ⟨his health would not allow so ~ a life and he was forced to slow down⟩ esp. in pursuit of excitement or pleasure ⟨~ living⟩ **b** (1) **:** DISSIPATED, WILD ⟨associating with a pretty ~ bunch⟩ (2) **:** markedly or promiscuously given to a flouting of the proprieties in the matter of personal behavior esp. in sexual relations — usu. used of a woman ⟨he thought how in 1910 a painted woman was said to be ~ —T.H.Raddall⟩ (3) **:** of or characteristic of a person of this kind ⟨a lot of ~ talk and promiscuous behavior⟩ **10 :** resistant to change, esp. to destructive action — used chiefly of organisms and in combination with the name of the agent resisted ⟨acid-*fast* bacteria⟩ ⟨arsenic-*fast* insects⟩ ⟨a streptomycin-*fast* patient⟩

syn RAPID, SWIFT, FLEET, QUICK, SPEEDY, HASTY, EXPEDITIOUS: FAST and RAPID are often interchangeable; FAST often describes moving objects or creatures and may suggest constant speedy course, flight, or procedure; RAPID may refer to actions and their rate of speed and suggest successful course ⟨a *fast* runner⟩ ⟨a *fast* horse⟩ ⟨a *fast* train⟩ ⟨a *fast* worker⟩ ⟨a *rapid* approach⟩ ⟨a *rapid* gait⟩ ⟨*rapid* progress⟩ ⟨*rapid* operations⟩ SWIFT may suggest speed or rapidity accompanied by easy facility, sure flight, brisk activity, or lack of interference and delay ⟨flawless and chaste and *swift* in their machined perfection which even the airplane has never been able to rival —Robert Payne⟩ ⟨so *swift* was Caesar that his greatest exploits were measured by days —J.A.Froude⟩ ⟨the flight of his imagination is very *swift;* the following of it often a breathless business —C.D. Lewis⟩ FLEET, sometimes rather poetic or literary, may suggest nimble or graceful lightness and swiftness ⟨the Indian bands swept over the hills on their *fleet* little ponies and wiped out emigrant wagon trains —*Amer. Guide Series: Ariz.*⟩ ⟨how the *fleet* creature would fly before the wind —Herman Melville⟩ QUICK applies to lively action with alacrity or to prompt occurrence with short duration ⟨am a *quick* man with my hands, and in a minute and a half I had done what I wanted to do —G.K.Chesterton⟩ ⟨a *quick* brain for intrigue —John Buchan⟩ ⟨in passing *quick* rather than deliberate judgment on the literature of the day —M.R.Cohen⟩ SPEEDY may suggest velocity or quickness along with promptness, dispatch, or haste ⟨orders for the fastest plane, the swiftest motorboat, the *speediest* racing car that money and American ingenuity could produce —Gerald Beaumont⟩ ⟨industries where there is a need for exceptionally *speedy* reinforcement —Sir Winston Churchill⟩ ⟨in all criminal prosecutions the accused shall enjoy the right to *speedy* and public trial —*U.S. Constitution*⟩ HASTY suggests precipitate hurried rapidity, sometimes ineffective or nervous ⟨it had a hurried evacuated look. Many houses had that. The look of the *hasty* choice made of what to take along —R.H.Newman⟩ ⟨we must, this time, have plans ready — instead of waiting to do a *hasty*, inefficient, and ill-considered job at the last moment —F.D.Roosevelt⟩ EXPEDITIOUS suggests efficient rapidity ⟨to assist me in every way in making the journey as *expeditious* as may be —Elinor Wylie⟩ ⟨if you suggested *expeditious* English methods of settling accounts he would laugh at you; he does not want his accounts settled —Norman Douglas⟩

²fast \"\ *adv* -ER/-EST [ME *faste*, fr. OE *fæste;* akin to OHG *fasto* firmly; derivative fr. the root of E ¹*fast*] **1 :** in a fast manner: as **a :** FIRMLY, FIXEDLY, SECURELY, SOUNDLY ⟨frozen ~⟩ ⟨fixed ~ in the hardened cement⟩ ⟨~ welded⟩ ⟨~ asleep⟩ **b :** LOYALLY, STAUNCHLY, UNWAVERINGLY ⟨held ~ to his belief in justice⟩ ⟨labor held ~ to its right to strike —F.L.Paxson⟩ **c :** leaving no room for play : in the manner of one caught and immovable : TIGHTLY ⟨a foot stuck ~ between the boards of the floor⟩ ⟨holding his mother's hand ~⟩; *also* **:** leaving no access or outlet ⟨a door shut ~⟩ ⟨the blinder over his eyes as ~ as ever —Mary Deasy⟩ **d :** in a rapid manner : QUICKLY, SWIFTLY ⟨run ~⟩ ⟨perils had thickened about him ~ —Charles Dickens⟩ ⟨a building ~ going to ruin⟩; *also* **:** READILY, EAGERLY ⟨complete the task ~ if paid enough⟩ **e :** in quick succession ⟨bullets coming thick and ~⟩ **f :** with speed and accuracy of mental process : with intellectual agility ⟨a man who could think ~ in a crisis⟩; *also* **:** continuously and facilely with the intent of influencing or deceiving someone or evading trouble or confusing an issue ⟨when the police caught him in the act he talked ~ to try to prove his innocence⟩ ⟨what he lacks in knowledge he can make up for by talking ~ —Stuart Chase⟩ **g :** in a wild or dissipated way ⟨living too ~ for his health⟩ **:** so as to flout the conventions, esp. sexual convention in one's behavior ⟨living ~ and free⟩ ⟨playing ~ with the ladies⟩ **h :** ahead or in advance of a correct time or posted schedule ⟨a clock that runs ~⟩ ⟨a train running two minutes ~⟩ **2** *obs* **:** with a fixity of attention : ZEALOUSLY, STEADILY **3** *archaic* **:** CLOSE, NEAR ⟨sat ~ by hell's gate —John Milton⟩ **4** *obs* **:** AT ONCE; IMMEDIATELY

³fast *vt* -ED/-ING/-S [ME *fasten, festen* fr. OE *fæstan;* akin to OHG *festen* to make fast, ON *festa* to settle, fix; derivative fr. the root of E ¹*fast*] *obs* **:** to make fast : BIND

⁴fast \"\ *interj* [²*fast*] — used as an exclamation in archery expressing a warning to one about to pass in the line of an arrow's flight

⁵fast \"\ *vb* -ED/-ING/-S [ME *fasten*, fr. OE *fæstan;* akin to OHG *fastēn* to fast, ON *fasta*, Goth *fastan;* derivative fr. the root of E ¹*fast*] *vi* **1 :** to abstain from food : omit to take nourishment in whole or in part : go hungry **2 :** to practice abstinence from food voluntarily for a time as a religious exercise or duty ⟨to counsel men to ~ and pray⟩ **3 :** to restrict one's diet by eating sparingly or by abstaining from certain foods ⟨~ in Lent⟩ **~** *vt* **:** to cause to go without food : deny food to ⟨the patient is ~*ed* and given a mild hypnotic —*Lancet*⟩ — **fast on** *or* **fast upon** *or* **fast against** *Irish law* **:** to sit fasting at the door of a defendant or debtor until the demand or debt is met or a pledge is given as is often required before the judicial seizure of property

⁶fast \"\ *n* -s [ME *faste*, fr. ON *fasta;* akin to OHG *fasta* fast; derivative fr. the root of OHG *fastēn* to fast, ON *fasta*] **1 a :** voluntary abstinence from food or from certain kinds of food for a space of time as a spiritual discipline or as a religious exercise ⟨a day for a general ~⟩ **b :** abstinence from food : the omission of or failure to take food for an unusual length of time **2 :** a time of fasting ⟨observe the ~*s* and feasts of the church⟩ ⟨went on a ~ of a month as a protest⟩

⁷fast \"\ *n* -s [alter. (influenced by ¹*fast*) of ME *fest*, fr. ON *festr* rope, mooring cable, fr. *fastr* firm — more at ¹FAST] **:** something that fastens or holds a fastening ⟨a door ~⟩ ⟨a window ~⟩: as **a :** a mooring rope or cable ⟨a stern ~⟩ ⟨a quarter ~⟩ — compare BREAST FAST **b :** a post on a pier or on shore around which hawsers are passed in mooring

fast and loose *adv* **:** RECKLESSLY, IRRESPONSIBLY **:** in a craftily deceitful way — formerly used in the phrase *to play at fast and loose;* now usu. used in the phrase *to play fast and loose* ⟨playing *fast and loose* with concepts of right and wrong to justify our own actions⟩ ⟨some dressmakers have played *fast and loose* with the original Black Watch design —*Newsweek*⟩ ⟨playing *fast and loose* with someone else's money⟩

fa station \ˈeˈfā-\ *n, usu cap F&A* **:** an aeronautical radio station

fast back *n, chiefly Brit* **:** TIGHT BACKBONE

fastball *n, Canad* **:** SOFTBALL

fast baller \ˈ=ˌbȯlə(r)\ *n* **:** a baseball pitcher who relies chiefly on a fast ball

fast break *n* **:** a basketball maneuver calculated to move the ball toward the opponents' basket for a shot as quickly as possible after gaining possession of the ball

fast-breaking \ˈ=ˈ==\ *adj, of a news story* **:** becoming news suddenly in rapidly revealed successive details

fast color salt *n, often cap F&C, sometimes cap S* **:** an azoic diazo component — see DYE table I (under *Azoic Diazo*)

fast day *n* [ME *faste day*, fr. *faste* fast + *day* — more at ⁶FAST] **:** a day appointed for fasting and prayer often as a means of invoking the favor of God: as **a** *cap* **:** a day usu. in the spring appointed by the magistrates and governors of some of the New England colonies and states as a holiday for the purpose of fasting and prayer **b :** such a legal holiday often in the summer observed in Scotland

fasted *adj* [fr. past part. of ⁵*fast*] **:** having been subjected to fasting ⟨a ~ animal⟩ **:** resulting from having been fasted ⟨the animal's ~ weight⟩

¹fas·ten \ˈfasᵊn, -aas-, -ais-, -ȧs-\ *vb* **fastened; fastened; fastening** \-s(ᵊ)niŋ\ **fastens** [ME *fastnen*, fr. OE *fæstnian* to make fast; akin to OHG *festinōn* to make fast, ON *fastna* to pledge; derivative fr. the root of E ¹*fast*] *vt* **1** *obs* **a :** to make firm or strong : RATIFY, CONFIRM **b :** to make stable or unwavering : place solidly : ESTABLISH **c :** to make fast (as a color) ⟨we ~ the dyes into the cloth first —H.I.Poleman⟩ **2 a :** to cause to hold to something else : attach esp. by pinning, tying, or nailing **b :** to cause (parts which are separate) to hold together : make fast and secure ⟨~ the ends of the rope⟩ ⟨~ my hair⟩ ⟨~ her dress⟩ **c :** to fix firmly or securely in position ⟨~ the flagpole so that it does not waver⟩ : secure against opening ⟨~ a door shut⟩ ⟨~ a window⟩; *also* **:** fix firmly by implanting (as in the memory) ⟨~*ed* firmly in my mind the main facts and principles —A.D.White⟩ **d :** to secure within limits (as within a fenced area) by fastening or enclosing — usu. used with *in* or *up* ⟨~ up the dog in the yard⟩ ⟨~ in the prisoners at nightfall⟩ **e :** to pin, nail, tie, or otherwise make immovable — usu. used with *down* ⟨~ down a flapping shutter⟩ ⟨~ down the lifeboats on deck⟩ **3 a :** to focus or direct (as the attention) intently or steadily ⟨~ his attention upon a fire in the distance⟩ : place (as one's hopes) strongly ⟨~*ed* his hopes on a quick recovery⟩ **b :** to focus or direct the attention or interest markedly upon ⟨~*ed* him with her clear blue eyes —Hamilton Basso⟩ **4** *obs* **:** to deliver (as a blow) forcefully; *also* **:** to imprint or implant (as a kiss) on the cheek **5 :** to take a firm grip with ⟨the dog ~*ed* his teeth in the man's leg⟩ **6 a :** to attach, affix, or associate (oneself) persistently and usu. objectionably or with or as if with intent to annoy or exploit or with the result of limiting the freedom of another ⟨~*ed* himself upon anyone who would listen to his sad story⟩ ⟨the con man ~*s* himself on any likely looking sucker⟩ **b :** to place forcefully : bring about the imposition of : IMPOSE ⟨too often ~*ed* the blame on the wrong man⟩ ⟨~*ed* on the community a merciless totalitarian system —J.E.Neole⟩ ⟨sought to ~ upon him the stigma of atheism —V.L.Parrington⟩ **c :** GIVE, AFFIX ⟨to which . . . later the name of "Llewellen" was ~*ed* by American breeders —W.F.Brown b.1903⟩ **~** *vi* **1 a :** to become fast or fixed ⟨where the plaster has ~*ed*, let it stick —Robert Browning⟩ **b :** to become firmly attached to a whale by means of a well placed harpoon — used of one harpooning or the boat from which the harpoon is launched **c :** to close and lock (as with catches) ⟨the lock of the bag was so damaged it would not ~⟩ **2 a :** take a firm grip or hold ⟨the stranger ~*ed* on my arm⟩ ⟨the flames ~*ed* upon the roof⟩ **b :** to focus or markedly fix attention ⟨his blue eyes ~*ed* sharply and eagerly upon the general —Kenneth Roberts⟩ ⟨the interest of the prosecution ~*ed* on one small inconsistency in the story⟩ ⟨they ~*ed* exclusively and resentfully on everything I said about power and progress —Norman Smith⟩

syn FIX, ATTACH, AFFIX: these four verbs signify in common to make to stay firmly in place. FASTEN commonly implies tying, binding, nailing, or some such process, or using a lock, catch, hook and eye, or other device, to keep a thing from moving, or it may apply to any action that suggests the use of one of these processes or devices ⟨*fasten* a sign to a post with a nail⟩ ⟨*fasten* a door by throwing a lock⟩ ⟨we will put aside the theology and *fasten* attention on the politics and the economics of the struggle —V.L.Parrington⟩ FIX is often interchangeable with FASTEN ⟨had to *fix* my collar onto my shirt with a paper clip —J.B.S.Haldane⟩ It usu. implies an attempt to keep something from falling down or losing its place and generally suggests a driving in or implanting ⟨*fix* a post in the ground⟩ ⟨he glanced about the washroom for what hooks might be *fixed* in the walls —Kay Boyle⟩ In figurative use FIX may sometimes be distinguished from FASTEN in suggesting a forthright, normal, or reasonable attitude as opposed to a devious, underhanded, or predatory one ⟨*fix* their affection upon a good person⟩ ⟨*fasten* your affection upon a mere child⟩ ⟨did not *fix* the blame on the right person⟩ ⟨*fasten* the blame upon an innocent man⟩ ATTACH suggests strongly a connection or union, a bond or link to prevent motion or keep one thing with another ⟨*attach* a cover by means of a brass hinge⟩ ⟨*attach* a card to the package⟩ ⟨guinea fowl *attach* themselves firmly to the place where they were born —F.D. Smith & Barbara Wilcox⟩ AFFIX is sometimes interchangeable with FASTEN or ATTACH ⟨*affix* a card to the package⟩ but usu. implies attachment by the imposition of one thing upon another, esp. with glue or mucilage ⟨*affix* a stamp to a letter⟩ ⟨*affix* a seal and signature to a document⟩

²fasten *n* -s [ME, fast, fr. OE *fæsten*, fr. *fæstan* to fast — more at ⁵FAST] **1** *obs* **:** a fast day **2** *obs* **:** the act of fasting

fastened *past of* FASTEN

fas·ten·er \-s(ᵊ)nə(r)\ *n* -s **:** one that fastens: as **a :** a device (as a button, hook and eye, zipper, or snap) that joins together separate parts or closes an opening (as on a garment) **b :** a device for holding shut or preventing opening ⟨attached a chain ~ to the door⟩ ⟨a catch ~ on a traveling bag⟩ **c :** a worker who fastens together the timbers, subassemblies, steel plates, and other parts in the construction of ships

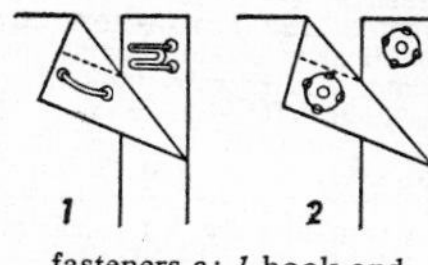

fasteners a: *1* hook and eye, *2* snap

fastening *n* -s [ME *fastninge*, fr. *fastnen* to make firm, make fast + *-inge*, *-ing* -ing — more at ¹FASTEN] **:** something that binds, holds one thing to another, or makes something fast **:** FASTENER; *specif* **:** the spikes, joint bars, bolts, and nuts used to connect rails in railroad track and affix them to ties

fastens *pres 3d sing of* FASTEN

fast·en's e'en \ˌfasᵊn'zēn\ *or* **fast·en's** \'fasᵊnz\ *n* [ME (Sc) *fastinnys evin*, fr. *fastinnys* (gen. of ME — Sc — *fastin* fast, var. of ME *fasten*) + *evin* (var. of ME *even* evening, eve) — more at ²FASTEN, ¹EVEN] *dial Brit* **:** SHROVE TUESDAY

faster *comparative of* FAST

fast·ern's e'en \ˌfasərn'zēn\ *or* **fast·ern's** \'fasərnz\ *n* [ME (Sc) *fasternis evin*, fr. *fasternis* (gen. of *fastern* fast, fr. OE — Northumbrian dial. — *fæstern*, fr. OE *fæstan* to fast) + *evin* — more at ⁵FAST] *chiefly Scot* **:** SHROVE TUESDAY

fastest *superlative of* FAST

fast green *n, often cap F&G* **:** any of several relatively fast green dyes belonging for the most part to the class of triphenylmethane dyes — see DYE table I (under *Acid Green 11*)

fast ice *n* **:** sea ice fastened to the shore

fas·tid·i·ous \fa'stidēəs *sometimes* fə'-\ *adj* [ME, haughty, disgusting, fr. MF & L; MF *fastidieux* disgusting, fr. L *fastidiosus* squeamish, haughty, disgusting, fr. *fastidium* aversion, disgust (prob. irreg. fr. *fastus* pride, arrogance + *taedium* irksomeness, disgust) + *-osus* -ose; akin to L *fastigium* top, extremity — more at ¹BRISTLE, TEDIUM] **1** *archaic* **:** SCORNFUL, HAUGHTY **2** *obs* **:** DISGUSTING, DISAGREEABLE **3 a :** overly difficult to please **:** overly nice or delicate in matters of taste ⟨grew ~ with easy living⟩ ⟨highbrow critics who are so esoteric and so ~ that they can talk only to a small circle of initiates —Granville Hicks⟩ ⟨a man falsely ~, finical, effeminate —Matthew Arnold⟩ **b :** marked by a meticulous, sensitive, or demanding attitude (as in matters of taste) ⟨an extremely stylish and ~ person⟩ ⟨~ about cleanness of the person⟩ ⟨~ attention to detail —Robert Evett⟩ ⟨a ~ aristocrat by birth and habit, he was a fine critic both of art and music —F.J.Mather⟩ **:** sensitive and particular ⟨the ~ puritanism of Virgil —John Buchan⟩ ⟨~ and well-bred and incurably polite —Elinor Wylie⟩ ⟨amahs and houseboys ~ in white jackets and black trousers —*New Yorker*⟩ **c :** reflecting a meticulous, sensitive, or demanding attitude ⟨an oar took shape with marvelous rapidity — trimmed and smoothed with a neatness almost ~ —John Burroughs⟩ ⟨Europe's intellectuals, editorial writers, and theologically ~ churchmen —*Newsweek*⟩ ⟨his ~ regard for the court's dignity —John Mason Brown⟩ **4 :** having complex nutritional requirements — used of bacteria that grow only in specially fortified artificial culture media **syn** see NICE

fas·tid·i·ous·ly *adv* **:** in a fastidious manner ⟨dressed ~ for the occasion⟩ ⟨exchanging . . . pungent plantation retorts for ~ phrased compliments of the nineties —Edmund Wilson⟩

fas·tid·i·ous·ness *n* -ES **:** the quality or state of being fastidious ⟨neatness and ~ in housekeeping⟩ ⟨a ~ of dress⟩

fas·tid·i·um \-dēəm\ *n* -s [L — more at FASTIDIOUS] **:** a mood of scornful distaste; *also* SQUEAMISHNESS

fas·tig·ial \fa'stij(ē)əl\ *adj* [*fastigium* + *-al*] **:** of or associated with the fastigium

fas·tig·i·ate \-jēət\ *or* **fas·tig·i·at·ed** \-ē,ād·əd\ *adj* [prob. fr. (assumed) NL *fastigiatus*, fr. ML *fastigiatus* lofty, fr. L *fastigium* top, extremity + *-atus* -ate] **:** narrowing toward the top: **a :** having or consisting of more or less upright clustered branches ⟨the lombardy poplar is ~⟩ ⟨the ~ cortex of the thallus of certain lichens⟩ **b** *zool* **:** united into a conical bundle — **fas·tig·i·ate·ly** \-ētlē\ *adv*

fas·tig·i·um \-jēəm\ *n* -s [L, summit, top, extremity] **:** APEX, SUMMIT, PEAK: **a :** the ridge of a house **b :** GABLE END, PEDIMENT **c** [NL, fr. L] **:** the period at which the symptoms of a disease (as a febrile disease) are most pronounced **d** [NL, fr. L] **:** the angle in the roof of the fourth ventricle

¹fasting *n* -s [ME *fastinge*, *fasting*, fr. *fasten* to fast + *-inge*, *-ing* -ing — more at ⁵FAST] **:** the act of abstaining from food esp. for an unusual time and often as a form of religious observance or for therapeutic purposes

²fasting *adj* [fr. pres. part. of ⁵*fast*] **:** of or from a fasting subject ⟨~ urine⟩ ⟨~ blood-sugar level⟩

fast·ish \'fastish, -aas-,-ais-,-äs-\ *adj* **:** rather fast

fast–joint \'=ˌ=\ *adj, of a hinge* **:** having its pin permanently secured in position ⟨a *fast-joint* butt⟩ ⟨a *fast-joint* hinge⟩

fast·land \'fast,land, 'faast-, 'faist-, 'fäst-, -,laa(ə)nd\ *n* -s [trans. of G *festland* mainland] **:** MAINLAND; *esp* **:** land that is high and dry near water **:** UPLAND

fast·ly *adv* [ME, fr. OE *fæstlīce*, fr. *fæstlīc* firm, solid, fr. *fæst* fast + *-līc* -ly (adj. suffix) — more at ¹FAST] *archaic* **:** FAST

fast–mass \'=ˌ=\ *n* **:** SHROVETIDE

fast–moving \'=ˌ==\ *adj* **1 :** moving or capable of moving rapidly usu. with sustained speed ⟨a *fast-moving* vehicle for freight transport⟩ **2** *of a dramatic or literary work* **:** full of sustained action or conflict usu. with the result of sustaining the interest

fast·nacht *also* **fas·nacht** \'fäsh(t),näkt, 'fäs(-\ *n* -s [modif. of PaG *fasnachtkuche*, fr. *fasnacht* Shrove Tuesday, festival held on Shrove Tuesday (fr. MHG *vastnaht*, *vasnaht* Shrove Tuesday, fr. *vaste* fast — fr. OHG *fasta* — + *naht* night, fr. OHG) + *kuche* cake, fr. OHG *kuocho* — more at ⁶FAST, NIGHT, CAKE] **1 :** a doughnut made of yeast-leavened dough and traditionally eaten on Shrove Tuesday **2** *usu cap* [PaG *fasnacht* & G *fastnacht* Shrove Tuesday, festival held on Shrove Tuesday, fr. MHG *vastnaht*, *vasnaht* Shrove Tuesday] **:** a festival of Christians of Germanic origin held on the last day before Lent and observed as a time of merrymaking preceding Lenten fasting

fast·ness \'fas(t)nəs, -aas-,-ais-,-äs-\ *n* -ES [ME *fastnesse*, fr. OE *fæstnes*, fr. *fæst* fast + *-nes* -ness — more at ¹FAST, -NESS] **1 :** the quality or state of being fast: as **a :** firmness or fixedness **:** fixed attachment **:** FIXITY **b** *obs* **:** SECURITY, INACCESSIBILITY **c :** SWIFTNESS, SPEED **d :** resistance to color change **:** the quality or state of being colorfast — used of dyes or dyed materials **e :** resistance to the action of certain esp. toxic substances (as that developed by some organisms) **2** *obs* **:** DENSITY, SOLIDITY **3 a :** a fortified or secure place **:** STRONGHOLD, FORT, FORTRESS, CASTLE **b :** a place of retreat or privacy ⟨visited them in their desert ~ —Simon Bourgin⟩ ⟨the poet can retire into the ~ of himself —Clifton Fadiman⟩ — often used in pl. ⟨into the ~*es* of the pine- and oak-covered hills —*Amer. Guide Series: Tenn.*⟩ ⟨down in the remote ~*es* of Staten Island —Richard Burke⟩

fast of es·ther \-'estə(r)\ *cap F&E* [after *Esther*, Jewish heroine in the Old Testament who became the queen of King Ahasuerus of Persia and successfully interceded with him for her people after three days of fasting] **:** a Jewish fast day commonly observed on the 13th of Adar, the day before Purim, in honor of Queen Esther

fast of ge·da·liah \-gə'dälyə, -,gedə'līə\ *cap F&G* **:** a Jewish fast day observed on the 3d day of Tishri and commemorating the assassination of Gedaliah, Nebuchadnezzar's governor in Judah

fast of tammuz *cap F&T* **:** a Jewish fast day observed on the 17th of Tammuz and commemorating the breach of the walls of Jerusalem by the Romans

fast of tebet *cap F&T* **:** a Jewish fast day observed on the 10th day of Tebet in commemoration of the beginning of the siege of Jerusalem by the Babylonians

fast one *n* **:** a crafty usu. dishonest or deceptive trick ⟨pulled a *fast one* on his best friend and lost his friendship⟩

fast–paced \'=ˌ=\ *adj, of a narrative* **:** FAST-MOVING ⟨an extraordinary story as *fast paced* with as much sheer narrative power as any novel of recent years —*N.Y.Times*⟩

fast pin *n* **:** a pin, screw, or nail or something resembling one of these that fastens securely or immovably; *specif* **:** the nonremovable rod that holds together the flaps on a fast-joint hinge

fast pulley *n* **:** a pulley fastened rigidly to a shaft

fast red *n, often cap F&R* **:** any of several fast red azo dyes: as **a :** a monoazo acid dye that dyes wool and silk red — called also *Fast Red A;* see DYE table I (under *Acid Red 88*) **b :** a monoazo acid dye that dyes wool and silk claret and is used chiefly as a biological stain — called also *Bordeaux B, Bordeaux red, Fast Red B;* see DYE table I (under *Acid Red 17*)

fast red base *n, often cap F&R, sometimes cap B* **:** any of several bases used as such or in the form of fast color salts in producing azoic dyes — see DYE table I (under *Azoic Diazo*)

fasts *pres 3d sing of* FAST, *pl of* FAST

fast salt *n, often cap F & sometimes cap S* **:** FAST COLOR SALT

fast scarlet R base *n, often cap F&S* **:** an orange-red crystalline amine $CH_3OC_6H_3(NO_2)NH_2$ that is often sold in the form of its stabilized diazonium complex salt with zinc chloride and is used in producing azoic dyes; 4-nitro-*ortho*-anisidine — see DYE table I (under *Azoic Diazo 13*)

fast spine *n, chiefly Brit* **:** TIGHT BACKBONE

fast–stepping \'=ˌ==\ *adj* **1** *of a horse* **:** FAST, SWIFT **2 :** notable for purposeful and usu. tireless activity or drive ⟨a *fast-stepping* businessman⟩ **3 :** characterized by a fast, active, and often wild social life

fast–talk \'=ˌ=\ *vt* [¹*fast* + *talk*, n.] *slang* **:** to influence or persuade by fluent and facile and usu. deceptive or tricky talk ⟨*fast-talked* tribal chieftains . . . out of a parcel of raindrenched, tropical real estate —*Newsweek*⟩ ⟨he's *fast-talked* you into trying to be something you're not —Martin Dibner⟩

fas·tu·ous \'faschəwəs\ *adj* [F or L; F *fastueux*, fr. L *fastuosus*, fr. *fastus* pride, arrogance + *-osus* -ose; akin to L *fastigium* top, extremity — more at BRISTLE] **1 :** HAUGHTY, ARROGANT, PRIDEFUL ⟨a ~ air of finality —Carl Van Vechten⟩ **2 :** OSTENTATIOUS, SHOWY ⟨the most ~ spectacle ever offered in the present opera house —Janet Flanner⟩ ⟨the ~ pomps and magnificence of ancient Carthage —*Times Lit. Supp.*⟩ — **fas·tu·ous·ly** *adv*

fast worker *n* **:** one who is fast and usu. smooth and shifty in his manner of gaining his personal ends (as profit, advantage, or sexual conquest)

¹fat \'fat, *usu* -ad·+V\ *n* -s [ME, fr. OE *fæt* — more at VAT] **1** *obs* **:** a large tub, cistern, or vessel **:** VAT **:** a wine cask **2** *archaic* **:** a barrel or receptacle for dry articles **3 :** a measure of quantity varying with the commodity

²fat \"\ *adj* **fatter; fattest** [ME, fr. OE *fǣtt*, past part. of *fǣtan* to cram; akin to OHG *feizit* fat (past part. of *feizen* to fatten, cram), *feiz* fat, ON *feita* to fatten, *feitr* fat, L *opimus* fat, fertile, copious, Gk *pidyein* to gush forth, *pidax* spring, *pimelē* lard, Skt *pīvan* fat, robust, *payate* he swells, grows] **1 :** notable for having an unusual amount of fat: **a :** well fed **:** PLUMP ⟨a cute ~ little baby⟩ ⟨ate a ~ capon for supper⟩ **b :** fleshy with superfluous nonmuscular flabby tissue **:** CORPULENT, OBESE ⟨a woman of medium height, a little plump but not ~ —Mary McCarthy⟩ **c** *of an animal* **:** fatted and likely to yield much red meat **d** *of food* **:** OILY, GREASY ⟨a ~, rich cheese⟩ **2 a :** well filled out **:** of sizable proportions **:** THICK ⟨a ~ letter⟩ ⟨a ~ volume of verse⟩ **:** BIG ⟨a resistor spark plug . . . permits a wider gap, thus a *fatter* hotter spark —*Newsweek*⟩ **:** unusually large ⟨he had to pay a ~ price to move his factory —Martin Turnell⟩ **:** substantial and impressive ⟨point to some ~ facts and figures to justify his claim —*Time*⟩ ⟨a ~ bank account⟩ ⟨make a mule of myself for a ~ fee on the stage —Harry Bailey⟩; *also* **:** FULL, RICH ⟨a gorgeous ~ bass voice —*Irish Digest*⟩ ⟨the ~ aroma of chocolate and coffee —Marcia Davenport⟩ **b :** well furnished, filled, or stocked ⟨a ~ refrigerator⟩ ⟨a ~ shelf⟩ ⟨this book is ~ with first-hand information —Frank Rounds⟩ **:** ABUNDANT ⟨a ~ feast⟩; *also* **:** PROSPEROUS, WEALTHY ⟨grew ~ on the war —*Time*⟩ **c** *of a type face* **:** characterized by wide letters; *also* **:** characterized by wide letters with heavy downstrokes and light upstrokes **d** *of a line of copy or type* **:** too wide to fit the measure ⟨a ~ heading⟩ **e** *of a slug* **:** cast larger than its normal body size ⟨trimming knives set to cast slugs .0015 inch ~⟩ **3 a :** richly rewarding ⟨a ~ part in a new play⟩ **:** markedly profitable or lucrative or presenting a marked opportunity of profit or advantage ⟨a nice ~ job⟩ ⟨a ~ opening in a business firm⟩ ⟨landed in the ~ post of governor of Buenos Aires —*Time*⟩ **b** *slang* **:** practically nonexistent **:** NEGLIGIBLE ⟨the depression left us with a ~ chance of making our first million⟩ ⟨a ~ lot of good it did him —Arthur Koestler⟩ **c** *archaic, of matter printed on a handpress* **:** easy and profitable **d :** making few if any demands **:** SLOTHFUL ⟨the dull, soft, ~ routine of peace —F.E.Robin⟩ **4 :** PRODUCTIVE, FERTILE, FRUITFUL ⟨growing soft on the ~ land and the easy living⟩ ⟨a ~ year for crops⟩ **5 a** *of clay or soil* **:** containing a high proportion of minerals that make clay or soil greasy to the touch, highly plastic, cohesive and compressible, difficult to work when wet, and strong when dry **b** *of beer or wine* **:** fullbodied and smooth **c** *of air or mist* **:** filled with moisture or odors **d** *of wood* **:** having a high resin content ⟨pine splinters ~ with pitch —Rebecca Caudill⟩ **e** *of coal* **:** having a high content of volatile matter **f** *of a pavement* **:** having too high a content of bitumen **g** *of mortar* **:** containing a high cement or lime content **h** *of lime* **:** pure or nearly so and slaking rapidly **6 a :** heavy, coarse, gross, or slow-witted in a way suggesting an overfed animal ⟨a foolish smile on his ~ face⟩ ⟨~ stupidity⟩ **b :** FOOLISH, EMPTY ⟨in trouble because I did not use my ~ head⟩

syn FLESHY, STOUT, CORPULENT, OBESE, CHUBBY, ROTUND, PORTLY, PLUMP: FAT suggests an abundance of flesh, esp. adipose, nonmuscular flesh; it may be uncomplimentary ⟨the unreasonably *fat* woman with legs like tree trunks —Katherine A. Porter⟩ ⟨he remained *fat*, and his round, red cheeks shone like ripe apples —W.S.Maugham⟩ FLESHY is a close synonym for FAT but may suggest an abundance of muscular flesh as well as adipose ⟨my appetite is plenty good enough, and I am about as *fleshy* as I was in Brooklyn —Walt Whitman⟩ STOUT suggests a thickset figure with abundant flesh, but is a less uncomplimentary word than FAT ⟨one very *stout* gentleman, whose body and legs looked like half a gigantic roll of flannel —Charles Dickens⟩ CORPULENT suggests a bulky excess of flesh, either graceless or burly ⟨a large burly man, gradually growing *corpulent*, with a soft oily face —Anthony Trollope⟩ OBESE suggests a graceless excess of flesh; it is often used in medical or pathological discussion and is always quite uncomplimentary ⟨a woman of robust frame . . . though stout, not *obese* —Charlotte Brontë⟩ ⟨a retarded, *obese* child who died young⟩ CHUBBY may suggest rounded ample flesh; it is often used in reference to children and suggests well-nurtured health and appeal ⟨[children] looked so fresh and pink and *chubby* —Bruce Marshall⟩ ROTUND stresses the notion of roundness and is applicable without being uncomplimentary to more-or-less short men and women of ample girth ⟨a *rotund* governor, five feet six inches in height, six feet five inches in circumference⟩ PORTLY suggests a thickset body with quite ample girth sustained with presence and carried with dignity ⟨large, imposing, *portly* people . . . with the air of grave responsibility which sometimes marks the man of large and imperious physical organism —Havelock Ellis⟩ PLUMP suggests a soft, pleasing, ample, buxom fullness with well-rounded curves and lack of sharp angularity ⟨his wife was . . . *plump* where he was spare —Dorothy Sayers⟩

³fat \"\ *vb* **fatted; fatted; fatting; fats** [ME *fatten*, fr. OE *fǣttian*, fr. *fǣtt* fat — more at ²FAT] *vi* **:** to grow fat, plump, or fleshy ⟨large *fatting* pigs —*Brit. Ministry of Agric. Advisory Leaflet*⟩ ~ *vt* **1 :** to make fat **:** FATTEN; *specif* **:** to feed (animals) with the intention of making fat for use as food — often used with *up* or *out* ⟨*fatted* out as porkers —E.W. Lloyd⟩ ⟨~ her up and kill her —Aldous Huxley⟩ **2** *archaic* **:** FERTILIZE, ENRICH **3 a :** to dress or impregnate (leather) with fat or fatty material **b :** to incorporate a fat, grease, or oil in ⟨a well-*fatted* soap⟩

⁴fat \"\ *n* -s [ME, fr. *fat*, adj. — more at ²FAT] **1 :** a part of the tissues of an animal that consists chiefly of cells distended with greasy or oily matter ⟨the ~ of meat⟩ **2 a :** the oily or greasy substance that makes up the bulk of the cell contents of adipose tissue and occurs in smaller quantities in many other parts of animals and in plants (as in seeds) **b :** any of a class of neutral solid, semisolid, or liquid chemical compounds that are insoluble in water but soluble in ether and other organic solvents, that are glycerides $C_3H_5(OOCR)_3$ of one or more fatty acids, that are obtained industrially from adipose tissues of animals, from oilseeds, and from the pulp of some fruits, and that are used chiefly in making soap, in protective coatings (as paints and varnishes), as lubricants and softening agents (as in dressing leather), and as cooking fats and a source of energy in foods by furnishing about 9.3 large calories per gram — see LIPIDE; compare OIL 1a, WAX **c :** a solid or semisolid fat (as lard, beef or mutton tallow, butterfat) obtained chiefly from land animals — distinguished from *fatty oil;* compare BUTTER 2b **3 a :** the best or richest productions **:** the best part ⟨living on the ~ of the land⟩ **b :** an effective part or effective lines or business given to an actor in a dramatic work **4 :** the condition of fatness **:** CORPULENCE, OBESITY ⟨a person somewhat inclined to ~⟩ **5 :** a meat animal that is fat and ready for market — usu. used in pl. ⟨commercial producers, all of whose pigs are being sold as ~*s* —*New Zealand Jour. of Agric.*⟩ **6 a :** something in excess or expendable **:** SUPERFLUITY ⟨slicing a little ~ off the city budget —Anthony West⟩ ⟨the new reserves would have to come from the remaining ~ of the U.S. not yet stripped for total war —*Time*⟩ **b :** resources in excess of those needed immediately **:** SAVINGS, RESERVES ⟨while the country is in a relative depression, it can still live for a time off its ~ —*Newsweek*⟩

⁵fat \(ˈ)fat, ˈfət\ *Scot var of* WHAT

⁶fat *var of* PHAT

fat acid *n* **:** FATTY ACID 2

fa·tal \'fād·ᵊl, -ātᵊl\ *adj* [ME, fr. L & MF; MF *fatal*, fr. L *fatalis*, fr. *fatum* fate + *-alis* -al — more at FATE] **1** *obs* **a :** decreed or appointed by destiny **:** FATED **b :** DOOMED, CONDEMNED **2 :** attended by or fraught with acts or a potential act of fate **:** FATEFUL ⟨a ~ hour⟩ ⟨a ~ spot⟩ **3 a :** of or belonging to fate ⟨this science sets a ~ necessity on things —H.O.Taylor⟩ **:** concerned with or dealing in fate ⟨the ~ thread of his life had nearly run out⟩ **:** resembling fate in foretelling destiny **:** PROPHETIC ⟨felt he could console himself by arguing that death was written in the ~ books⟩ **b :** like fate in proceeding according to an inevitable or fixed sequence ⟨there was always physical exercise, but that had a ~ way of coming after a time to raise more problems than it solved —Rebecca West⟩ **c** *obs* **:** OMINOUS, FOREBODING **d :** determining one's fate ⟨this ~ gift of enthusiasm, an inherited trait which determined her later life —E.S.Bates⟩ ⟨the ~ flaw in this dazzling woman: a total lack of taste —Marya Mannes⟩ **4 a :** causing death ⟨a ~ blow⟩ ⟨the ~ weapon was found by the police⟩ ⟨a ~ diabetic coma —Havelock Ellis⟩ **b :** causing or resulting in destruction or ruin **:** CALAMITOUS, DISASTROUS ⟨the ~ weekend on which he lost his total fortune in a fire⟩ ⟨the ~ eruption of the volcano that destroyed people and towns and ruined the countryside⟩ **c :** difficult to avoid and causing a harm or evil less grievous than death or ruin ⟨the ~ moment in which she accepted his proposal and began a life of boredom and frustration⟩ ⟨a ~ invitation to triviality —Mark Schorer⟩; *specif, of a woman* **:** ruinously attractive **:** being a femme fatale **syn** see DEADLY

fa·tal·ism \-,izəm\ *n* -s [prob. fr. *fatalist*, after such pairs as E *atheist: atheism*] **1 :** the doctrine that all things are subject to fate; *specif* **:** the doctrine that the occurrence of events is necessitated or is fixed in advance for all time in such a manner that human beings are powerless to change them — compare DETERMINISM **2 a :** the mental attitude of a fatalist; *specif* **:** a belief in fatalism **b :** compliance with what are believed to be the dictates of fate ⟨~ can take the form of abject submissiveness but also of heroism⟩

fa·tal·ist \-,əst\ *n* -s [prob. fr. F *fataliste*, fr. MF, fr. *fatal* + *-iste* -ist] **:** an adherent of fatalism; *specif* **:** one whose conduct is regulated by belief in fatalism

fa·tal·is·tic \ˌ=='istik, -tēk\ *adj* [*fatalist* + *-ic*] **1 :** relating to, implying, or consisting of fatalism ⟨a ~ philosophy⟩ **2 :** believing in or inclined to fatalism ⟨a ~ people⟩ — **fa·tal·is·ti·cal·ly** \-tək(ə)lē, -tēk-, -li\ *adv*

fa·tal·i·ty \fā'taləd·ē, fə'-, -lətē, -i\ *n* -ES [MF *fatalité*, fr. LL *fatalitat-*, *fatalitas*, fr. L *fatalis* decreed by destiny + *-itat-*, *-itas* -ity] **1 :** something brought about or established by fate or necessity ⟨this necessary fact and even duty of nationality is accidental; like age or sex it is a physical ~ —George Santayana⟩ **2 a :** the quality or state of causing or being likely to cause death or destruction ⟨the degree of ~ of certain diseases is higher than one imagines⟩ **b :** the quality or condition of being fated **:** subjection to fate **:** predetermination by necessity; *specif* **:** the quality or condition of being destined for disaster ⟨afraid of the ~ that seemed to mark his family's history⟩ **3 a :** invincible necessity as a principle or fact in nature **:** FATE 1 ⟨to believe in ~⟩ **b :** FATALISM **4 :** the agent or agency of fate ⟨their destiny established by an overruling ~⟩ **5 a :** a fatal outcome; *esp* **:** death resulting from a disaster ⟨a car crash that was the cause of several *fatalities*⟩ **b :** something experiencing or subject to a fatal outcome ⟨one of the *fatalities* in the drownings was a small child⟩

fa·tal·ize \'fād·ᵊl,īz\ *vt* -ED/-ING/-S *archaic* **:** to ordain or establish by or subject to fate

fa·tal·ly \'fād·ᵊlē, 'fātᵊl-, -ᵊli\ *adv* [ME, fr. *fatal* + *-ly*] **1 :** in a way established or determined by fate ⟨who would not say, with Huxley, let me be wound up every day like a watch, to go right ~, and I ask no better freedom —William James⟩ ⟨the temptation becomes more and more insidious and she is more ~ bound to yield —H.M.Parshley⟩ **2 :** in a manner suggesting fate or an act of fate **:** inevitably or implacably ⟨a man ~ stern⟩ ⟨a kind of action that brings one ~ to perdition⟩: as **a :** in a manner resulting in death **:** MORTALLY ⟨~ wounded by the accidental discharge of a gun⟩ **b :** beyond repair **:** IRREVOCABLY ⟨find himself ~ humiliated before a hard cadre of French officers because he had not pulled his chauffeur out of a burning jeep —J.W.Chase⟩ ⟨a conflict of ideals that will ~ divide the victors if they are not reconciled —F.S.Kinney⟩ **c :** in a manner resulting in ruin or evil **:** DISASTROUSLY ⟨this ~ ingenious explanation proved an obstacle for some time to a true view of the function of the arterial system —Benjamin Farrington⟩ ⟨it is ~ easy to pass off our prejudices as our opinions —W.F.Hambly⟩ **d :** IRRESISTIBLY ⟨~ attracted by vigorous, strong-willed women —*Time*⟩ ⟨thinks she is ~ attractive —J.W.Krutch⟩

fa·tal·ness \-ᵊlnəs\ *n* -ES **:** the quality or state of being fatal ⟨a poison of such ~ as to result in death⟩

fa·ta mor·ga·na \ˌfäd·ə,mȯ(r)'gänə\ *n, pl* **fata morganas** *sometimes cap F&M* [It, mirage, Morgan le Fay (sorceress of Arthurian legend)] **1 :** MIRAGE ⟨suddenly — like a *fata morgana* rising out of the desert clouds — houses, trees, and people materialized —Joseph Wechsberg⟩; *esp* **:** one with marked displacement and distortion **2 :** something insubstantial or illusory ⟨the *fata morgana* of romantic love —Anthony West⟩

fatback \'=ˌ=\ *n* [²*fat* + *back*, n.] **1 :** MENHADEN **2 :** BLUE-

FISH 1 **3 :** the strip of fat from the back of a hog carcass usu. cured by dry-salting — see PORK illustration

fatbird \ˈ=,=\ *n* **1 :** OILBIRD **2 :** PECTORAL SANDPIPER

fat body \ˈ=,=\ *n* **1 :** a lobulated mass of fatty tissue attached to each genital gland in amphibians **2 :** a fatty tissue enveloping the viscera or forming a layer under the integument and serving as a reserve of nutrition in many insects esp. in nearly mature larval stages — compare ADIPOSE TISSUE

fatcake \ˈ=,=\ *n* **:** DOUGHNUT, FRIEDCAKE

fat cat *n* **1** *slang* **a :** a wealthy contributor to a political campaign fund; *esp* **:** one who is also a political candidate **b :** a wealthy and consequently privileged person **c :** BIG SHOT **2 :** a lethargic complacent person

fat cell *n* **:** one of the constituent fat-laden cells characteristic of adipose tissue

fat-chewing \ˈ=,==\ *n* -s **:** CHATTING ⟨endless shoptalk and *fat-chewing* with many authors —Laura Z. Hobson⟩

fat-choy \ˈfatˈchȯi, ˈfät'-\ *n* -s [Chin (Cant) *faàt ts'oi*, fr. *faàt* hair + *ts'oi* vegetable] **:** an edible blue-green alga (*Nostoc commune* var. *flagelliforme*)

fat crab *n* **:** a crab that soon will shed its shell

fat dormouse *n* **:** a common dormouse (*Glis glis*) of Central Europe and Asia Minor introduced into parts of England

¹fate \ˈfāt, *usu* -ād·+V\ *n* -s [ME, fr. L or MF; MF *fate*, fr. L *fatum* prophetic declaration, oracle, what is ordained by the gods, destiny, fate, fr. neut. of *fatus*, past part. of *fari* to speak — more at BAN] **1 a :** the principle or determining cause or will by which things in general are supposed to come to be as they are or events to happen as they do **b :** foreordination by which either the universe as a whole or particular happenings are predetermined; *specif* **:** necessity as inherent in the nature of things to which the gods as well as men are in subject ⟨~ in Greek tragedy becomes the order of nature in modern thought —A.N.Whitehead⟩ — compare DETERMINISM **2 a :** whatever is destined or inevitably decreed esp. for a person **:** an appointed lot ⟨her ~ was to remain a spinster⟩ **b :** RUIN, DISASTER; *esp* **:** DEATH ⟨the villain met his ~ at the hands of the hero⟩ **c :** ultimate lot or disposition **:** final outcome **:** END ⟨the congress decided the bill's ~ by a single vote⟩ ⟨the explorer's party left no trace of the ~ that overcame them⟩ ⟨the importance of an individual thinker . . . depends upon the ~ of his ideas in the mind of his successors —A.N.Whitehead⟩ **d :** the circumstances that befall something ⟨all human beings live as members of organized groups and have their ~ inextricably bound up with that of the group to which they belong —Ralph Linton⟩ **3 :** one of the goddesses of fate or destiny esp. of classical times supposed to determine the course of human life — usu. used in pl. and then sometimes cap. ⟨waiting there, standing like a ~ in the center of the carpet, a gaunt, gray, somber woman —G.W.Brace⟩ ⟨my great-aunts, formidable ~*s* who sat in judgment on all the events of their time —Hugh Dickinson⟩ ⟨the ~*s* . . . have smiled with an astonishing kindness on his wanderings in the jungle —*Geog. Jour.*⟩

syn FATE, DESTINY, LOT, PORTION, and DOOM agree in signifying the condition or end decreed by a higher power. FATE presupposes a determining supernatural or divine agency, as the gods, God, or the law of necessity, and usu. implies inevitability, but can extend to include a human agency whose decision is finally determinative, in both applications usu. implying a more or less adverse condition or end ⟨no matter how absurd or meaningless our *fate* may be, we still must accept it and play our role —J.M.O'Brien⟩ ⟨through knowledge man can control his own *fate* —Abram Kardiner⟩ ⟨it is the *fate* of all these lakes to disappear —*Amer. Guide Series: Minn.*⟩ ⟨preparing for the end, for the final grim defense, when his men would retreat upon the one last strong fort, and there await their *fate* —Gilbert Parker⟩ ⟨the *fate* of the congressional bill was uncertain⟩ DESTINY implies an irrevocable determination, course, or appointment, as by the will of the gods, but out of context specifies neither a good nor bad course or end, more often, possibly, implying a course conceived of as good by the one destined because it is conceived of as a natural fulfillment ⟨not to impose their view of life upon any people but to inspire in all peoples an understanding of their common *destiny* —Stephen Duggan⟩ ⟨for good or ill, that clubfoot, like the mark of Jason in her life, had been his *destiny* —Ellen Glasgow⟩ ⟨always had with him, too, the special conviction of *destiny* — that his was a great age of history, and that he was born to act in and dominate these times —Henry Wallace⟩ ⟨the conception of a lordly splendid *destiny* for the human race, to which we are false when we revert to wars and other atavistic follies —Bertrand Russell⟩ LOT and PORTION imply a distribution by fate or destiny, LOT suggesting more a blind chance, PORTION implying a more or less fair apportioning of good and evil ⟨shunned extremes of passion or suffering, declaring that these were seldom the common *lot* —*Encyc. Americana*⟩ ⟨it fell to the *lot* of the U.S. to scrap thirty-two ships —C.E.Black & E.C. Helmreich⟩ ⟨poverty was his *portion* all his days —Kemp Malone⟩ ⟨a feeling of guilty remorse was her daily *portion* —Susan Ertz⟩ ⟨she is not the saint he deems it the *portion* of every creature wearing petticoats to be —George Meredith⟩ DOOM implies a final, usu. grim and calamitous, award or fate ⟨thirty-two brave men of Gonzales, who marched in even after the *doom* of the fort seemed certain —*Amer. Guide Series: Texas*⟩ ⟨lured unsuspecting ships to their *doom* on the rocks on dark and stormy nights —Richard Joseph⟩ ⟨the poor beast's ribs stood out under a coating of snow as it stood there, awaiting its *doom* —F.V.W.Mason⟩

²fate \"\ *vt* -ED/-ING/-S **:** DESTINE ⟨the two seemed *fated* for each other⟩; *also* **:** DOOM ⟨the deep antipathy . . . seeming to ~ them to antagonism —Les Savage⟩ ⟨novel about a *fated* beauty —*Newsweek*⟩

³fate \"\ *dial Brit var of* FEAT

fated *adj* [fr. past part. of ²*fate*] **1 a :** determined or controlled by fate ⟨all life is lived in a ~ field —*N.Y. Times*⟩ ⟨an ill-*fated* expedition⟩ **b :** marked by fate **:** chosen to be the locale of disastrous events ⟨the spot was ~ and narrowly escaped being the scene of a second catastrophe as frightful as the first —J.A.Froude⟩ **2 :** FATEFUL ⟨from the first there had been a ~ air about the Gallipoli expedition —Alan Moorehead⟩ ⟨the story unfolds with a tragic, ~ quietness —*Times Lit. Supp.*⟩

fate drama *n* **:** a play esp. popular in early 19th century Germany in which a malignant destiny drives the protagonist to commit a horrible crime often unsuspectingly

fate·ful \ˈfātfəl\ *adj* **1** *of an utterance* **:** OMINOUS, PROPHETIC ⟨ready at the nurse's ~ whisper to fetch whatever was needed or telephone for the physician —Ellen Glasgow⟩ **2 :** having the power of serving or accomplishing fate **:** fraught with fate **:** involving momentous consequences ⟨that ~ meeting of the U.N. when . . . it declared war on North Korea —*Saturday Rev.*⟩; *esp* **:** bringing on adverse fate **:** DEADLY, CATASTROPHIC ⟨during the ~ time the slayings occurred —*Fortnight*⟩ **3 :** controlled by fate **:** determined by irresistible and foreordained forces **syn** see OMINOUS

fate·ful·ly \-fəlē, -li\ *adv* **:** in a fateful manner

fate·ful·ness \-fəlnəs\ *n* -ES **:** the quality or state of being fateful ⟨unaware of the ~ of their meeting until it resulted in both their deaths⟩

fate line *n, sometimes cap F* **:** LINE OF FATE ⟨a double *Fate line* denotes an eventful life —Alice D. Jennings⟩

fate map *n* **:** a plan of an early embryo indicating the potentialities for development and differentiation of the various embryonic areas

fates *pl of* FATE, *pres 3d sing of* FATE

fath *abbr* fathom

fathead \ˈ=,=\ *n* **1 :** a slow-witted or stupid person **:** FOOL **2 a :** FATHEAD MINNOW **b :** SHEEPSHEAD 2c

fatheaded \ˈ=ˈ==\ *adj* **:** dull-witted **:** markedly foolish **:** STUPID, IDIOTIC

fat·head·ed·ness *n* -ES **:** the quality or state of being fatheaded

fathead minnow *also* **fatheaded minnow** *n* **:** a widely distributed No. American cyprinid fish (*Pimephales promelas*) occurring from southern Canada and New York westward down the Mississippi valley and into Mexico and in some areas esteemed as a panfish

fat hen *n* **1 :** any of several succulent or fleshy-leaved plants esp. of the genus *Chenopodium* (as lamb's-quarters) **2 :** any of certain plants of the genus *Atriplex* (esp. *A. lastata* and *A. patula*) **3 :** GROUND IVY **4 :** BUCKWHEAT 1 **5 :** SHEPHERD'S PURSE **6 :** MUGWORT 1

¹fa·ther \ˈfäthə(r), ˈfath\ə(r\ *n* -s [ME *fader*, fr. OE *fæder;* akin to OHG *fater* father, ON *fathir*, Goth *fadar*, L *pater*, Gk *patēr*, Skt *pitṛ*] **1 a :** a man who has begotten a child **:** a male parent **:** SIRE **b** *cap* (1) **:** ²GOD, DEITY 1b ⟨our *Father* who art in heaven —Mt 6:9 (RSV)⟩ (2) **:** the first person of the Trinity ⟨*Father*, Son, and Holy Ghost⟩ **2 a :** male ancestor more remote than a parent **:** FOREFATHER, ANCESTOR **3 :** one related to another in a way paralleling or suggesting the relationship of father to child: as **a :** one to whom a filial affection and respect are usu. due **:** adoptive father **:** FATHER-IN-LAW, STEPFATHER **:** a male relative who assumes the rights and obligations as well as the title of a father **b :** CONFESSOR 3 **c :** one who is the marked and usu. revered guide or most notable influence in another's spiritual, intellectual, or artistic development; *also* **:** one who is in a position of authority as guide and benefactor ⟨he had become a ~ to the village —Keith Ellis⟩ **d :** an old man — used as a respectful form of address **4** *often cap* **:** an early Christian writer accepted widely or generally as a trustworthy witness to or expositor of the early history or teachings of the church **5 a :** one that originates or institutes **:** one that first constructs, designs, or frames ⟨the ~ of modern radio⟩ ⟨~ of science fiction —D.H.Menzel⟩ ⟨the influence of Babylonian and Egyptian mathematics upon the ~*s* of Greek science, esp. Pythagoras —*Times Lit. Supp.*⟩ **b :** one of the first American colonists **:** PILGRIM FATHER **c :** an early American statesman; *esp* **:** one of the creators of the Constitution ⟨the founding ~*s*⟩ **d :** SOURCE, ORIGIN ⟨the wish is ~ to the thought⟩ ⟨such an attitude of mind may easily become the ~ of criticism —V.L.Parrington⟩ ⟨the doctrine that strife is the ~ of all things —M.R.Cohen⟩ **e :** PROTOTYPE ⟨a totem board at least fifteen feet high . . . the ~ of all totem boards —Daisy Bates⟩ **6 :** any of various ecclesiastics — used in direct address and as a title prefixed to the name (as of a priest in the Roman Catholic, Anglican, or Eastern Orthodox churches, and sometimes a deacon or a superior of a monastic house) **7 :** one of the leading men of a country, city, or council — usu. used in pl. ⟨four proposals were before the city ~*s* —Wayne Robinson⟩ ⟨surrounded by a council of the town ~*s* —Frank Yerby⟩ **8 :** the oldest or the presiding member of an associated group (as a society, a profession, or a legislative assembly) ⟨the ~ of the chapel in a printing plant⟩ ⟨the ~ of the bar⟩

²father \"\ *vt* **fathered; fathered; fathering** \-th(ə)riŋ\ **fathers** [ME *faderen*, fr. *fader* father — more at ¹FATHER] **1 a :** to make oneself the father of **:** BEGET ⟨~ three strapping sons⟩ ⟨cowards ~ cowards —Shak.⟩ **b :** to make oneself the father or author of by adoption or acknowledgment ⟨professed himself willing to have ~*ed* it —Richard Garnett †1906⟩ **c :** to be the founder, creator, or author of **:** ORIGINATE ⟨though he was no great poet he ~*ed* a school of notable poets⟩ ⟨~*ed* a plan for improving the city's schools⟩ **d :** to be at the center, base, or source of ⟨this moral fault which ~*s* democratic politics —T.V.Smith⟩ **e :** to produce by educating or training ⟨one of the most promising doctors the school had ever ~*ed*⟩ **2 a :** to fix the paternity or origin of ⟨investigation ~*ed* the child upon the lover⟩ ⟨like caterpillars . . . not to be tracked or ~*ed* —William Wordsworth⟩ **b :** to place responsibility for the origin or cause of ⟨~ a crime upon the first likely suspect⟩ **3** *archaic* **:** to care for or look after as a father might **4 :** IMPOSE, FASTEN, FOIST ⟨bent upon ~*ing* a scurrilous significance upon a perfectly innocent remark⟩ **5** *now dial Eng* **:** to bear a strong resemblance to the father of (oneself)

father christmas *n, cap F&C, chiefly Brit* **:** the Christmas spirit personified **:** SANTA CLAUS

father confessor *n* **1 :** a priest who hears confessions; *specif* **:** a priest who is one's regular spiritual guide **2 :** a person who is one's intimate spiritual guide and counselor

fa·thered \ˈ=thə(r)d\ *adj* [¹*father* + *-ed*] **:** provided with a father ⟨worse off in being fatherless than I was, ~ —Elizabeth B. Browning⟩

father family *n* **:** patrilineal family **:** patrilineal sib or gens

father figure *n* **:** one who serves as an emotional substitute for a father

fa·ther·hood \ˈ==,hu̇d\ *n* -s [ME *faderhod*, fr. *fader* + *-hod* -hood] **1 :** the quality or state of being a father **:** the character or authority of a father **:** PATERNITY **2** *usu cap* **:** Godhood in its paternal aspect

father hu·go's rose \,=ˈ(h)yü(,)gōz-\ *n, usu cap F&H* [after *Father Hugo* (Hugh Scallan) *fl* 1889 Catholic missionary who introduced it into England from China] **:** a very early blooming shrub rose (*Rosa hugonis*) with mahogany-red drooping canes, delicate leaves, and solitary but very numerous clear yellow single flowers

father image *n* **1 :** an idealization of one's father constitutive of the ego ideal and often projected onto someone to whom one then looks for guidance and protection **2 :** FATHER FIGURE

fa·ther-in-law \ˈfäthə(r)ən,lȯ, ˈfath-, -thrən-, -th(ə)rn-\ *n, pl* **fathers-in-law** \-ə(r)zən-\ [ME *fader in lawe*] **1 :** the father of one's spouse **2 :** STEPFATHER

fa·ther·land \ˈ==,land, -laa(ə)nd\ *n* **1 :** one's native land or country **:** the country to which one claims native allegiance **2 :** the native land or country of one's father or ancestors

father-lasher \ˈ=,==\ *n* [so called fr. the fact that the male guards the eggs and that it defends itself by lashing out with its tail and spines] **:** either of two small darkly mottled sculpins (*Cottus bubalis* and *C. scorpius*) found chiefly along the coasts of northwestern Europe and the British Isles

fa·ther·less \-ləs\ *adj* [ME *faderles*, fr. OE *fæderlēas*, fr. *fæder* father + *-lēas* -less — more at FATHER, -LESS] **1 a :** having no father; *esp* **:** having no father living ⟨a quiet, thoughtful little lad with the man-of-the-house air of responsibility sometimes worn by ~ only sons —Flora Thompson⟩ **b :** ILLEGITIMATE **2 :** having no known author — **fa·ther·less·ness** *n* -ES

fa·ther·li·ness \-lēnəs, -lin-\ *n* -ES **:** paternal quality **:** the kindness or benignity of or befitting a father ⟨the gentleness and ~ of the strange old man eased the young girl's fears⟩

¹fa·ther·ly \-lē, -li\ *adj* [ME *faderly*, fr. OE *fæderlīc*, fr. *fæder* + *-līc* -ly] **1 :** of, belonging to, befitting, or proper to a father ⟨unwilling to take on ~ responsibilities⟩ ⟨gave ~ counsel to the boy in the absence of a parent⟩ **2 :** like a father in affection, care, feeling, or conduct **:** paternally kind, solicitous, or benign **:** PATERNAL ⟨placed a ~ hand on his head and wished him well in his new venture⟩ ⟨noted for his ~ concern for the welfare of his company's employees —*Current Biog.*⟩

²fatherly *adv* [ME *faderly*, fr. OE *fæderlīce*, fr. *fæderlīc*, adj.] *obs* **:** in a fatherly manner

father right *n* **:** descent and inheritance in the male line

father's day *n, usu cap F&D* **:** a day (as the third Sunday in June) appointed for the special honoring of fathers by their children

fa·ther·ship \ˈfäthə(r),ship, fäthə,sh-\ *n* -s [ME *fadership*, fr. *fader* + *-ship*] **:** the quality or state of being a father; *esp* **:** the state of being the oldest member of a society or associated group (as the British House of Commons)

father-sib \ˈ=,=\ *n* **:** sib based on patrilineal descent **:** GENS

father time *n, usu cap F&T* **:** time personified esp. as an old man who is bald, bearded, and holding a scythe and water jar or sometimes an hourglass

fath·o·gram \ˈfathə,gram\ *n* -s [*fatho-* (as in *fathometer*) + *-gram*] **:** a record made by means of a sonic depth finder

¹fath·om \ˈfathəm\ *n* -s [ME *fadme*, fr. OE *fæthm* embracing or outstretched arms, fathom (unit of length); akin to OHG *fadum* thread, ON *fathmr* embracing arms, fathom (unit of length), L *patēre* to be open, *pandere* to spread, unfold, Gk *petannynai* to spread out] **1 a** *obs* **:** a full stretch of the arms in a straight line; *also* **:** GRASP, REACH **b :** intellectual grasp, penetration, or profundity **:** COMPREHENSION ⟨the themes display a newer ~ than the technical modernism of the composer's earlier works —*Newsweek*⟩ **2 a :** a unit of length equal to 6 feet based on the distance between fingertips of a man's outstretched arms and used esp. for measuring the depth of water — sometimes used in the singular when qualified by a number ⟨five ~ deep⟩ **b** *archaic* **:** any of several units of length varying around 5 and 5½ feet **c** *Brit* **:** the quantity of wood in a pile of any length measuring 6 feet square in cross section **d :** a unit of area equal to 6 square feet used by miners for measuring areas in the plane of a vein

²fathom \"\ *vb* -ED/-ING/-S [ME *fadmen*, fr. OE *fæthmian;* akin to ON *fathma* to embrace; derivative fr. the root of E ¹*fathom*] *vt* **1** *archaic* **:** to encircle (as for measuring) with outstretched arms **2 a :** to measure by a sounding line **b :** to penetrate (as a mystery) and come to understand **:** comprehend where one had not understood previously **:** get to the bottom of ⟨found the man's motives very difficult to ~⟩ ⟨trying to ~ the universe —C.S.Kilby⟩ ~ *vi* **:** to take soundings; *also* **:** PROBE, INVESTIGATE

fath·om·able \-məbəl\ *adj* **1 :** that can be sounded **2 :** capable of being comprehended

Fa·thom·e·ter \faˈthäməd·ə(r), ˈfathə(m),mēd·ə(r)\ *trademark* — used for a sonic depth finder

fath·om·less \ˈfathəmləs\ *adj* [²*fathom* + *-less*] **:** incapable of being fathomed **:** IMMEASURABLE ⟨the ~ depths of the ocean⟩ ⟨a man of wealth and ~ energy —Bruce Catton⟩ **:** INCOMPREHENSIBLE ⟨a philosophy complex and, to the ordinary thinker, quite ~⟩ — **fath·om·less·ly** *adv* — **fath·om·less·ness** *n* -ES

fathom line *also* **fathom curve** *n* **:** a usu. sinuous line on a nautical chart joining all points having the same depth of water and thereby indicating the contour of the ocean floor

fa·tid·ic \fāˈtidik, fəˈ-\ *or* **fa·tid·i·cal** \-dəkəl\ *adj* [*fatidic* fr. L *fatidicus*, fr. *fati-* (fr. *fatum* fate) + *-dicus* (fr. *dicere* to say); *fatidical* fr. L *fatidicus* + E *-al* — more at FATE, DICTION] **:** of or belonging to prophecy **:** PROPHETIC

fat·i·ga·bil·i·ty \,fad·ə̇gəˈbiləd·ē, ,fat|, |ēg-, -lətē, -i\ *also* **fa·tigu·abil·i·ty** \fə,tēgəˈb-\ *n* -ES **:** susceptibility to fatigue

fat·i·ga·ble \ˈfad·ə̇gəbəl, ˈfat|, |ēg- *also* **fa·tigu·able** \fəˈtēgəbəl\ *adj* [*fatigable* fr. LL *fatigabilis*, fr. L *fatigare* + *-abilis* -able; *fatiguable* fr. ²*fatigue* + *-able*] **:** easily tired **:** susceptible to fatigue

¹fatigate *adj* [ME *fatigat*, fr. L *fatigatus*, past part. of *fatigare*] *obs* **:** TIRED, WEARY, FATIGUED

²fatigate *vt* -ED/-ING/-S [L *fatigatus*, past part. of *fatigare*] *obs* **:** FATIGUE, TIRE

¹fa·tigue \fəˈtēg, *chiefly dial* -tig\ *n* -s [F, fr. MF, fr. *fatiguer*, v.] **1 a :** weariness from labor or exertion **:** exhaustion of strength; *also* **:** tiredness or physical or nervous exhaustion from causes other than physical or intellectual exertion (as from anoxia, motion sickness, or emotional tension) **b :** loss of power resulting from continued work but removable by rest **c :** exhaustion in productive power (as of soil) **d :** the transitory refractory state induced in a sensory receptor or motor end organ by continued or repeated stimulation — compare ADAPTATION **2 a :** a tiring duty **:** LABOR, TOIL **b** (1) **:** manual or menial work often assigned as a punishment; *esp* **:** such work (as the cleaning up of a camp area or the building of a road) performed in the course of service by a member of one of the military services other than the navy (2) **:** one such task ⟨punishments include loss of rewards or privileges, temporary loss of recreation (usu. associated with a ~ such as floor scrubbing or potato peeling) —*Lancet*⟩ **c fatigues** *pl* **:** the uniform or work clothing worn on fatigue and in the field **3 a :** the tendency of a material (as a metal) to break under repeated cyclic loading at a stress considerably less than the tensile strength in a static test **b :** the decrease of efficiency (as of a luminescent or light-sensitive material) with use

²fatigue \"\ *vb* -ED/-ING/-S [F *fatiguer*, fr. MF, fr. L *fatigare;* akin to L *affatim* sufficiently, *fatisci* to fall apart, become exhausted, and prob. to L *fames* hunger — more at DAZE] *vt* **1 :** to weary with labor or exertion **:** TIRE **2 :** to induce a condition of fatigue in (as a material or an effector organ) ~ *vi* **1 :** to undergo or suffer fatigue (as of a metal) **2 :** to perform fatigue (as in the army) **syn** see TIRE

³fatigue \"\ *adj* [¹*fatigue*] **:** consisting of, done, or used in fatigue ⟨~ detail⟩ ⟨a ~ uniform⟩ **:** belonging to fatigues ⟨a ~ cap⟩ ⟨grabbed his ~ collar and pulled him out of line⟩

fatigue call *n* **:** a bugle call warning those detailed for fatigue duty to report to a designated place

fatigue curve *n* **:** a graph showing the rate of decline of strength or speed in long-continued work

fa·tigue·less \-ləs\ *adj* **:** incapable of tiring **:** UNTIRING

fatigue limit *n* **:** the highest stress that a material can withstand for an infinite number of cycles without breaking — called also *endurance limit;* compare FATIGUE STRENGTH

fatigue ratio *n* **:** the ratio of the fatigue limit or fatigue strength to the static tensile strength of a material — called also *endurance ratio*

fa·tigue·some \fəˈtēgsəm\ *adj* **:** FATIGUING, WEARISOME

fatigue strength *n* **:** the highest stress that a material can withstand for a given number of cycles without breaking — called also *endurance strength;* compare FATIGUE LIMIT

fatigue syndrome *n* **:** COMBAT FATIGUE

fa·tigu·ing·ly *adv* [*fatiguing* (pres. part. of ²*fatigue*) + *-ly*] **:** in a manner that tires or wearies

fa·ti·ha *or* **fa·ti·hah** \ˈfätē,hä\ *n* -s *often cap* [Ar *fātiḥah* that which opens or begins] **:** the short opening sura of the Koran used by Muslims as a prayer

fa·til·o·quent \fāˈtiləkwənt, fəˈ-\ *adj* [modif. (influenced by E *eloquent*) of L *fatiloquus*, fr. *fati-* (fr. *fatum* fate) + *-loquus* (fr. *loqui* to speak) — more at FATE, LOQUACIOUS] *archaic* **:** PROPHETIC

fat·i·mid \ˈfad·əməd, -(,)mid\ *also* **fat·i·mite** \-,mīt\ *n* -s *cap, often attrib* [*Fatima* †A.D.632 daughter of Muhammad by his first wife + E *-id* or *-ite*] **:** a descendant of Fatima, a daughter of Muhammad, and Ali, the cousin of Muhammad and fourth caliph of Islam, regarded by the Shi'ites as a true heir to the caliphate; *esp* **:** a member of the Fatimid dynasty ruling portions of No. Africa during the period A.D. 909–1171

fating *pres part of* FATE

fat-kidneyed *adj, obs* **:** GROSS, CLUMSY

fat·less \ˈfatləs\ *adj, of meat* **:** LEAN

fatlike \ˈ=,=\ *adj* **:** resembling fat **:** FATTY

fat·ling \ˈfatliŋ\ *n* -s **:** a young animal (as a calf, lamb, or kid) fattened for slaughter

fat liquor *n* [⁴*fat* + *liquor*] **:** a liquor made of an emulsion of soap and fat (as castor oil or degras) or of sulfonated oil and used in tanning leather

fat-liquor \ˈ=,==\ *vt* [*fat liquor*] **:** to fill the fiber of (a leather) with oil or fat **:** treat (leather) with fat liquor

fat·ly *adv* [ME, fr. ²*fat* + *-ly*] **1 :** RICHLY, LUXURIANTLY ⟨a ~ prosperous landscape⟩ **2 :** in the manner of one that is fat ⟨walking ~ down the road —Claud Cockburn⟩ ⟨turned ~ and looked at him —William Faulkner⟩ **3 :** SMUGLY, COMPLACENTLY ⟨any of the reasons usu. given so patly and ~ —Sinclair Lewis⟩

fat mouse *n* [so called from its accumulation of oily fat before hibernation] **:** any of several silky furred tropical and southern African short-tailed mice (genus *Steatomys*) regarded as a great delicacy by the natives

fat·ness *n* -ES [ME *fatnesse*, fr. OE *fǣtnes*, fr. *fǣtt* fat + *-nes* -ness — more at FAT] **1 a :** the quality or state of being fat or rich in fats **:** fullness of flesh **:** CORPULENCE, OBESITY **b :** FERTILITY, FRUITFULNESS ⟨the ~ of the orchards⟩ ⟨a land of all but incredible ~ and beauty —Russell Lord⟩ **2** *obs* **:** greasy or oily substance found in animal or vegetable matter **:** FAT **3 :** something that makes rich or fertile ⟨let it come like the abundant ~ of the clouds upon the thirsting earth —Benjamin Fine⟩

fat paint *n* **:** FATTY PAINT

fat pine *n* **1** *chiefly Midland* **:** KINDLING WOOD **2 :** any of several trees (as the longleaf pine) abounding in pitchy heartwood

fat pork *n* **1 :** the fruit of a wild fig (*Clusia flava*) **2 :** the fruit of the coco plum

fat-rumped sheep \ˈ=,=-\ *n* **:** a coarse-wooled sheep widespread in western and central Asia that develops large accumulations of fat on the rump during periods of abundant feed

fats *pl of* FAT, *pres 3d sing of* FAT

fat scab *n* : RAIN ROT

fats·hed·era \fat'sed(ə)rə, -ts'he-\ *n* -s *sometimes cap* [*fatsia* + NL *Hedera*] : a vigorous upright ornamental foliage plant with glossy deeply lobed palmate leaves that is a hybrid between the common ivy (*Hedera helix*) and a fatsia (*Aralia elata*)

¹**fat·sia** \'fatsēə\ [NL] *syn of* ECHINOPANAX

²**fatsia** \"\ *n* -s **1** : DEVIL'S CLUB **2** : a prickly tree (*Aralia elata*) with immense leaves and large flower clusters

fat·so \'fat(,)sō\ *n* -ES [prob. fr. *Fats*, nickname of a fat person (fr. ²*fat* + -*s*, noun plural suffix used in casual nicknames such as *Whiskers* or *Cuddles* identifying a person by a characteristic feature or activity) + -*o*] *slang* : a fat person — often used as a disparaging form of address

fat-soluble \'≈¦≈≈≈\ *adj* : soluble in fats or fat solvents (as ether) : OIL-SOLUBLE — used esp. of certain vitamins ⟨*fat-soluble* vitamin A⟩ ⟨*fat-soluble* A⟩

fatstock \'≈,≈\ *n* : livestock that is fat and ready for market

fat-tailed lemur \'≈,≈-\ *n* : any of several Malagasy mouse lemurs (genus *Cheirogaleus*) with much-thickened tails sometimes regarded as constituting a separate genus (*Atililemur* or *Opolemur*)

fat-tailed sheep *n* : a coarse-wooled mutton sheep that has great quantities of fat on each side of the tail bones, that is widely distributed in southeastern Europe, No. Africa, and Asia, and that occurs in many local breeds or races

fatted *adj* [fr. past part. of ³*fat*] : FATTENED, FAT ⟨killed for him the ~ calf —Lk 15:30 (RSV)⟩

fat·ten \'fatᵊn\ *vb* **fattened; fattened; fattening** \-t(ᵊ)niŋ\ **fattens** [²*fat* + -*en*] *vt* **1 a** : to make fat, fleshy, or plump — often used with *up* ⟨attempting to ~ her children up with potatoes, spaghetti, and creamed dishes⟩ : make bigger or more substantial ⟨~ the record by making false entries⟩ ⟨~ the young author's self-esteem —E.J.Simmons⟩; *esp* : to feed (as a stock animal) for slaughter **b** (1) : to add to (a pot) in a card game esp. by an additional ante (2) : to play a high-scoring card to (a trick one's partner or a favored opponent is expected to win, as in pinochle) **2** : to make fertile and fruitful : ENRICH ~ *vi* : to grow fat, corpulent, or plump ⟨herds ~*ing* on the early clover⟩ : grow rich and prosperous ⟨early kings ~*ing* on the labor of slaves and enemy captives⟩ ⟨boulevard papers with large circulations ~*ing* on sex, crime, and scandal —*Newsweek*⟩ — often used with *out* ⟨a skinny cow ~*ing* out into a good carcass⟩

fat·ten·er \-t(ᵊ)nə(r)\ *n* -s **1** : one that fattens ⟨selling young goslings to ~*s*⟩ **2** : stock to be fattened for slaughter ⟨some of the pigs were singled out as breeders and the rest left as ~*s*⟩

fattening *adj* [fr. gerund & pres. part. of *fatten*] : used in or subject to the process of fattening up for slaughter ⟨a ~ pen⟩ ⟨a ~ hog⟩

¹**fatter** *comparative of* FAT

²**fat·ter** \'fad·ə(r), 'fatə(r)\ *n* -s [³*fat* + -*er*] **1** : FATTENER **2** [⁴*fat* + -*er*] : a worker who trims excess fat from meat or who cuts fat from intestines for rendering into lard

fattest *superlative of* FAT

fat·ti·ly \'fad·ᵊlē, -at|, |ᵊli\ *adv* : in a fatty manner

fat·ti·ness \|ēnəs, |in-\ *n* -ES : the quality or state of being fatty ⟨made ill by the excessive ~ of the meal⟩ ⟨made greasy by the ~ of the wool⟩

fatting *pres part of* FAT

fat·tish \'fad·|ish, -at|, |ēsh\ *adj* [ME, fr. ²*fat* + -*ish*] : somewhat fat ⟨a ~ girl⟩ ⟨an almost white . . . tenacious ~ clay —William Bartram⟩

fat·trels \'fa·trəlz\ *n pl* [origin unknown] *Scot* : ends of ribbons ⟨the ~ on a lady's bonnet⟩

¹**fat·ty** \'fad·|ē, -at|, |i\ *adj* -ER/-EST [ME, fr. ⁴*fat* + -*y*, adj. suffix] **1 a** : containing fat esp. in unusual amounts ⟨a rather ~ steak⟩ : ADIPOSE ⟨getting ~ around the hips⟩ : CORPULENT ⟨a short ~ woman in black —John Updike⟩ ⟨the curious ~ grace of the butcher —Josephine Johnson⟩ **b** : having the qualities of fat : GREASY ⟨a rather ~ wool⟩ ⟨the constant frying left a ~ deposit on the kitchen woodwork⟩ **c** : having or marked by too great a deposit of fat ⟨a ~ liver⟩ ⟨~ cirrhosis⟩ **d** : STICKY, COHESIVE — used of cement pastes, mortars, concretes, or clays **2** : derived from or chemically related to the fats : ALIPHATIC ⟨~ alcohols⟩

²**fatty** \"\ *n* -ES [²*fat* + -*y*, n. suffix] : one that is fat ⟨the pill would weigh almost two ounces, for a 150-pound person . . . would be . . . still bigger for a ~ —*Springfield (Mass.) Daily News*⟩

fatty acid *n* **1** : any of the series of saturated aliphatic monocarboxylic acids $C_nH_{2n+1}COOH$ (as acetic acid or lauric acid) many of which occur naturally usu. in the form of esters in fats, waxes, and essential oils **2** : any of the saturated or unsaturated monocarboxylic acids that occur naturally in the form of glycerides in fats and fatty oils, that in almost all cases contain an even number of carbon atoms most commonly 12 to 24 in the higher acids (as palmitic acid or oleic acid), that in a few cases contain a substituting group (as hydroxyl in ricinoleic acid), that are obtained by hydrolysis of fats or by synthesis, and that are used chiefly in making soap, detergents, metallic soaps, and other derivatives

fatty degeneration *n* **1** : a process of tissue degeneration marked by the deposition of fat globules in the cells **2** : moral or artistic degeneration esp. as a result of sloth or complacency, overindulgence, or luxury

fatty infiltration *n* : infiltration of the tissue of an organ with excess amounts of fat

fatty oil *n* : a fat that is liquid at ordinary temperatures and that is obtained from plants or marine animals — called also *fixed oil;* distinguished from *essential oil* and *volatile oil;* compare OIL 1a

fatty paint *n* : a liquid paint in which the oil has become unduly polymerized, oxidized, or thickened to a pasty buttery abnormal consistency

fa·tu·i·tous \fə'tüəd·əs, fə·'tyü-, -üətəs\ *adj* [*fatuity* + -*ous*] : characterized by fatuity : FATUOUS

fa·tu·i·ty \-üəd·ē, -üətē, -i\ *n* -ES [MF *fatuité* foolishness, fr. L *fatuitat-, fatuitas,* fr. *fatuus* foolish + -*itat-*, -*itas* -ity] **1 a** : something foolish, silly, absurd, or stupid (as an action) ⟨the exaggerated patience of all children dealing with the *fatuities* of all adults —*New Yorker*⟩ **b** : FOOLISHNESS, INANITY, ABSURDITY ⟨in the light of what has happened, this remark has a poisonous ~ —Anthony West⟩ ⟨refined her good manners into docility, her gentleness almost to ~ —Louis Auchincloss⟩; *also* : STUPIDITY ⟨the vessels . . . had just arrived at the landing place — and here, with incredible ~, were allowed to remain, with most of their indispensable contents still on board —Francis Parkman⟩ **2** *archaic* : IMBECILITY, IDIOCY, DEMENTIA

fat·u·oid \'fachə,wȯid\ *n* -s [NL *fatua* (specific epithet of *Avena fatua,* fr. L, fem. of *fatuus*) + E -*oid*] : an aberrant form arising in cultivated oats that is believed to be a mutation and that resembles both the parent variety and the wild oat (*Avena fatua*) — called also *false wild oats*

fat·u·ous \'fachəwəs\ *adj* [L *fatuus* foolish, silly — more at BAT] **1 a** : marked by want of intelligence and rational consideration; *esp* : marked by futile ill-founded hope or desire, by witless complacent disregard of reality, or by inane lack of consideration ⟨the ~ adorer of that dilapidated, horrible woman —Arnold Bennett⟩ ⟨men do argue about religion, and it is ~ for those who argue on one side to try also to discredit all rational arguments —M.R.Cohen⟩ : inanely foolish ⟨aware that a ~ expression was spreading like melted wax over his features —Ellen Glasgow⟩ : ABSURD ⟨one of the most ~ plans for city improvement ever devised⟩ : STUPID, SILLY ⟨a foolish woman given to ~ remarks⟩ **b** *chiefly Scots law* : DEMENTED, IMBECILE **2** *archaic* : resembling an ignis fatuus : without reality : ILLUSORY **syn** see SIMPLE

fat·u·ous·ly *adv* : in a fatuous manner : FOOLISHLY, INANELY

fat-witted \'≈¦≈≈\ *adj* : STUPID, IDIOTIC, FATHEADED

fatwood \'≈,≈\ *n, South & Midland* : LIGHTWOOD 1

fau·bourg \(')fō¦bü(ə)r, 'fō,bu̇rg, -,bərg, *F* fōbüʀ\ *n* -s [alter. (influenced by F *faubourg* suburb, fr. MF *fauxbourg*) of ME *fabour, fabor,* fr. MF *fauxbourg,* by folk etymology (influence of MF *faux* false, fr. L *falsus*) fr. *forsbourg,* fr. OF *forsborc,* fr. *fors* outside of, outside (fr. L *foris* out of doors, out) + *borc* town; akin to L *foris, fores* door — more at FALSE, DOOR, BOURG] **1** : a suburban area : SUBURB; *esp* : a suburb of a French city **2 a** : a district formerly outside a city's wall but now within the city **b** : a city quarter

¹**fau·cal** \'fȯkəl\ *adj* [L *fauces* + E -*al*] **1** : FAUCIAL **2** : formed or occurring in or near the fauces : PHARYNGEAL

²**faucal** \"\ *n* -s : a faucal sound

fau·cal·ize \-ə,līz\ *vb* -ED/-ING/-S : to modify by faucal articulation

faucal plosive *n* : a stop consonant released through the nasal cavity by sudden lowering of the velum (as the \t\ in \'kätᵊn\ *cotton*)

fau·ces \'fȯ,sēz\ *n pl* [L, pl., fauces, throat] **1** *usu sing in constr* : the narrow passage from the mouth to the pharynx situated between the soft palate and the base of the tongue and bounded laterally by two curved folds enclosing the tonsil on each side — called also *isthmus of the fauces* **2** : the throat of a gamopetalous corolla **3** : the portion of the interior of a spiral shell that can be seen by looking into the aperture

fauces ter·rae \¦fau̇,kā'ste,rī, ¦fȯ,sēz'te,rē\ *n pl* [L, gulf] : headlands or promontories enclosing an arm of the sea that under international law is territorial water and not part of the high seas

fau·cet \'fȯsət,'fä-, *archaic* 'fa-; *usu* -əd·+V\ *n* -s [ME, fr. MF *fausset,* fr. *fausser,* to damage, be false to, fr. LL *falsare* to falsify, fr. L *falsus* false — more at FALSE] **1** *now dial* : a peg used to stop a vent hole in a cask or other vessel **2** : a fixture for drawing a liquid from a pipe, cask, or other vessel : TAP, COCK **3** : HUB 5a (1)

faucet 2

fau·chard \(')fō¦shär\ *n* -s [F, fr. OF *fausart, fauchart,* fr. *faus, faux* sickle, scythe (fr. L *falx*) + -*ard*, -*art* -ard] : a long-handled medieval weapon with a long convex edge

faucht \'fäkt\ *Scot var of* FOUGHT

fau·cial \'fȯshəl\ *adj* [L *fauces* + E -*ial*] : of or involving the fauces ⟨a ~ tonsil⟩ ⟨~ diphtheria⟩

faud \'fȯd,'fäd\ *dial Brit var of* FOLD

faugh *a forcefully articulated p-sound or a forceful trilling of the lips; often read as* 'fȯ\ *interj* — used to express contempt, disgust, or abhorrence

faught \'fȯkt\ *Scot var of* FIGHT

fau·ja·site \'fōzhə,sīt,-,zīt\ *n* -s [F, fr. Barthélemy *Faujas* de Saint-Fond †1819 Fr. geologist + F -*ite*] : a mineral $(Na_2,Ca)Al_2Si_4O_{12}.6H_2O$ consisting of a colorless or white hydrous aluminosilicate of sodium and calcium (hardness 5, sp. gr. 1.92)

fauj·dar *or* **fouj·dar** \'fau̇j,där\ *n* -s [Hindi *fawjdār,* fr. Per, fr. Ar *fawj* host, troop + Per -*dār* holder — more at BHUMIDAR] **1** *India* : a petty officer (as in charge of police) **2** *India* : a criminal judge

fauj·da·ri *or* **fouj·da·ry** \-rē\ *n, pl* **faujdaris** *or* **foujdaries** [Hindi *fawjdārī,* fr. Per, fr. *fawjdār*] **1** *India* : a faujdar's jurisdiction **2** *India* : a criminal court

faul·chion *var of* FALCHION

fauld \'fȯld\ *chiefly Scot var of* FOLD

¹**fault** \'fȯlt, *archaic* 'fōt\ *n* -s [ME *faute, faulte,* fr. OF *faute,* fr. (assumed) VL *fallita,* fr. fem. of (assumed) VL *fallitus,* past part. of L *fallere* to deceive — more at FAIL] **1** *obs* **a** : LACK, SCARCITY ⟨one it pleases me, for ~ of a better, to call my friend —Shak.⟩ **b** : NEGLECT, DEFAULT **2** : a defect in quality or constitution: **a** : an imperfection in character or disposition : FAILING, WEAKNESS; *esp* : a blameworthy moral weakness less serious than a vice **b** : a physical or intellectual imperfection or impairment ⟨a theory with some serious ~*s*⟩ : FLAW, BLEMISH : a damaged part ⟨a ~ in a bolt of cloth⟩ **c** (1) : a violation of a rule in a racket game which results in loss of service or a point for the opponent or both (as a failure to serve the ball legitimately into the proper court) (2) : a service in a racket game that strikes outside the proper service court **d** : a defective point in an electric circuit due to a crossing of wires, a ground, a break in the circuit, a failure of insulation **3** : a failure to do what is right: **a** : a moral transgression : SIN ⟨fell down at the pope's feet confessing his ~ —R.W. Southern⟩ **b** : a wrongdoing of an excusable kind : MISDEMEANOR ⟨a small boy's ~*s*⟩ **c** : MISTAKE, ERROR ⟨a subtle ~, committed most . . . when we are least aware of it —S.L. Payne⟩ **d** : a failure to do something required by law or the doing of something forbidden by law — compare NEGLIGENCE **4 a** : responsibility for wrongdoing or failure ⟨it was not the driver's ~ that the car went out of control⟩ **b** : the wrongdoing or failure attributable to a particular inadequacy, flaw, or failure ⟨the accident was the ~ of a broken steering rod⟩ **5** : a fracture in the earth's crust accompanied by a displacement of one side of the fracture with respect to the other and in a direction parallel to the fracture **6** : a lost scent in hunting; *also* : the act of losing the scent : CHECK

syn FAILING, FRAILTY, FOIBLE, VICE: FAULT implies some falling short, though usu. not far, of a standard of moral perfection in disposition or action ⟨his lack of interest in theology is a weakness but not a major *fault* —C.H.Hopkins⟩ ⟨there are *faults* which are not *faults* of will, but *faults* of mere inadequacy to some unforeseen position —J.A.Froude⟩ ⟨a victim of many small *faults* of envy and spitefulness⟩ FAILING implies a shortcoming, usu. a weakness of character of which one may be unaware ⟨the one *failing* — common to all elderly observers since Adam's hair turned gray — of imagining that the entire youth of the world is going to the dogs —Douglas Stewart⟩ ⟨we should keep in mind the *failings* of resting on what seem to be our laurels and being content with an optimism grown on sheer apathy —H.A.Sosland⟩ FRAILTY stresses a general weakness of character or an instance of usu. chronic weakness deriving from such a character ⟨that shuddering relish for the horrors of conventions at their worst I grant to be a purely human *frailty*, like a fondness for detective stories —J.L. Lowes⟩ FOIBLE usu. implies a harmless weakness of character, often no more than an idiosyncrasy ⟨to indulge on occasion in a kind of willful coquettishness hardly appropriate to her age or appearance . . . was the result rather of a *foible* than of any fundamental folly —J.W.Krutch⟩ ⟨his dear father's one intellectual *foible* — that willful blindness of his to the march of time —Robert Graves⟩ ⟨it is a *foible* in most decent human beings to hope that whatever our failings, at least we are not disfigured by vulgarity of spirit —Kate O'Brien⟩ VICE usu. stresses violation of moral law but in this comparison can apply to any large or small imperfection or weakness of character ⟨the great *vices* such as mendacity, vanity —Norbert Guterman⟩ ⟨she was criminally proud. That was her *vice* —Arnold Bennett⟩ ⟨his only *vice* was . . . an insatiable lust for power —*Time*⟩ ⟨reading was his *vice.* How could he solace his inactive hours? —Sydney Greenbie⟩ ⟨the great *vice* of English drama from Kyd to Galsworthy has been that its aim of realism was unlimited —T.S.Eliot⟩

— **at fault 1 a** : unable to find the scent and continue chase **b** : in trouble or embarrassment and unable to proceed **2** *also* **in fault** : responsible or to blame for a mistake or blemish : CULPABLE ⟨looking for the person *at fault* for an inadequately constructed house⟩ ⟨if war should break out it would be difficult to determine who is really *at fault*⟩ — **for fault of** *or* **for the fault of** *obs* : in default of : through want of — **to a fault** *adv* : almost to the point of absurdity : EXCESSIVELY ⟨gentle *to a fault*⟩ ⟨meticulous *to a fault* in all matters of dress⟩ — **with all faults** *adv* : with no guarantee against defects ⟨merchandise sold *with all faults*⟩

²**fault** \"\ *vb* -ED/-ING/-S [ME *fauten,* fr. *faute,* n. — more at ¹FAULT] *vi* **1** : to commit a fault : go wrong : ERR, BLUNDER ⟨not one singer forgot a word; not a pianist ~*ed* —Hartzell Spence⟩ ⟨his tongue stammering and ~*ing* with rage —Earl of Chesterfield⟩ : fall short : FAIL **2** : to fracture so as to produce a geologic fault ~ *vt* **1 a** : to find a fault or flaw in ⟨conducted himself with such calm dignity that few could ~ him —*Newsweek*⟩ ⟨he had been ~*ed* by professional critics for the lack of music in his speaking of verse —Tyrone Guthrie⟩ ⟨his arguments were logical and hard to ~ —Anthony West⟩ ⟨I ~ this speech in three ways —J.E.Agate⟩; *specif* : to grade (a person or animal) down for imperfect performance or feature in a contest ⟨the dog was ~*ed* in stance⟩ **b** *now dial* : BLAME, SCOLD, CENSURE ⟨don't ~ him for that⟩ **2** : to produce a geologic fault in; *also* : to place in a particular position or shape by reason of such a fault ⟨sediments ~*ed* down against older rocks —Frank Dixey⟩ — used chiefly in the passive **3** : to commit an error in : BUNGLE ⟨the acrobat deliberately ~*ed* the performance once to make it look difficult⟩

fault·age \'fȯltij\ *n* -s : geologic faulting : geologic faults

fault block *n* : a body of rock bounded by faults

fault breccia *or* **fault rubble** *n* : a rock composed of angular fragments that have resulted from movement along a fault : CRUSH BRECCIA

fault cliff *n* : a cliff formed by faulting

fault conglomerate *n* : CRUSH CONGLOMERATE

fault·ed \'fȯltəd\ *adj* [¹*fault* + -*ed*] : marked by faults : FAULTY ⟨a book that is good although ~⟩

fault·er \-tər\ *n* -s [alter. (influenced by -*er*, n. suffix) of ME (Sc) *fautor, fautour* wrongdoer, fr. ME *fauten* to commit a fault + -*or*, -*our* -or] *dial Brit* : a wrongdoer esp. against the church

faultfinder \'≈,≈\ *n* : one esp. given to faultfinding

¹**faultfinding** \'≈,≈≈\ *n* -s [¹*fault* + *finding,* fr. gerund of *find*] : the tendency to unremitting petty esp. unjustified criticisms or the act of persistently finding petty flaws and inadequacies in another ⟨reviews of appreciation and not of contemptuous ~ —A.C.Benson⟩

²**faultfinding** \"\ *adj* [¹*fault* + *finding,* fr. pres. part. of *find*] : disposed to or given to faultfinding : unreasonably or perversely noticing and stressing faults ⟨his *faultfinding* critic —J.T.Field⟩ **syn** see CRITICAL

fault·ful \-fəl\ *adj* : full of faults — **fault·ful·ly** \-fəlē\ *adv*

fault gouge *n* : finely comminuted uncemented rock characteristic of fault zones

fault·i·ly \'fȯltəlē,-li\ *adv* : in a faulty or blamable manner ⟨denial of statements ~ attributed to the secretary of state —*Current Biog.*⟩

fault·i·ness \-tēnəs, -tin-\ *n* -ES : the quality or state of being faulty ⟨the notable ~ of a man's reasoning⟩

faulting *n* -s [fr. gerund of *fault*] : the act or process of fracturing so as to produce a fault; *also* : FAULT

fault·less \'fȯltləs\ *adj* [ME *fautles,* fr. *faute* fault + -*les* -less — more at FAULT] : having no fault : free from defect, imperfection, failing, blemish, or error : IRREPROACHABLE ⟨gave a ~ performance on his first appearance as a concert pianist⟩ ⟨a ~ complexion⟩ ⟨~ workmanship⟩ — **fault·less·ly** *adv* — **fault·less·ness** *n* -ES

fault line *n* : the geologic line determined by the intersection of a fault with the earth's surface or with some other plane of reference

fault-line scarp *n* : a cliff or escarpment resulting from the erosion of soft rock that has been brought against hard rock by faulting

fault-line valley *also* **fault valley** *n* : a valley that follows a fault line

fault plane *n* : a fault surface that is not notably curved

fault rock *n* : a rock that consists of fragments produced by the crushing and grinding which accompany a dislocation and is often found along the fault plane — compare CRUSH BRECCIA, CRUSH CONGLOMERATE

faults *pl of* FAULT, *pres 3d sing of* FAULT

fault scarp *n* : a cliff or escarpment directly resulting from an uplift along one side of a fault

fault slip *n* : a geologic fault

fault surface *n* : the surface along which the dislocated masses have moved in a geologic fault — see FAULT PLANE

fault terrace *n* : a topographic bench or step on a hill slope formed by displacement by two approximately parallel faults along each of which the downhill side has moved down relatively to the uphill side

fault trace *n* : a line of intersection of a fault plane with the earth's surface

fault trough *n* : a usu. long and narrow depression bounded on either side by faults — compare GRABEN

fault vent *n* : a volcanic vent situated on a fault

faulty \'fȯltē, -ti\ *adj* -ER/-EST [ME *fauty,* fr. *faute* fault + -*y*] **1 a** : marked by a fault : having a fault, blemish, or defect : IMPERFECT, UNSOUND ⟨a ~ mechanism⟩ ⟨a ~ argument⟩ ⟨~ digestion⟩ ⟨his technique was ~ and his taste was worse —J.B.Priestley⟩ **b** : prone to faults ⟨memory is often ~ among the mentally ill —Hartzell Spence⟩ : apt to do wrong ⟨this pleasant ~ world —C.E.Montague⟩ **c** : not fit for the use or result intended or desired ⟨the first mate's ~ stowage plan causes a cargo shift —E.B.Garside⟩ **2** *archaic* **a** : guilty of a fault **b** : consisting of a fault : BLAMABLE

fault zone *n* : an area in which there are several closely spaced faults

faun \'fȯn, 'fän\ *n* -s [ME, fr. L *faunus;* akin to Goth af*dauiths* maltreated, Russ *davit'* to press, crush, strangle] : an Italic deity of fields and herds represented as having human shape, with pointed ears, small horns, and sometimes a goat's tail, or as half goat and half man

faun

fau·na \'fȯnə,'fänə\ *n, pl* **fau·nas** \-nəz\ *also* **fau·nae** \-,nē\ [NL, fr. LL *Fauna,* Roman goddess connected with the fauns, fr. L *faunus*] **1** : animals in general or animal life esp. as distinguished from flora; *esp* : the animals or animal life characteristic of or peculiar to a region or locality, period, or geological stratum **2** : the animals or animal life occurring, developed, or adapted for living in a specified environment ⟨cave ~⟩ ⟨protozoal ~ of the human intestine⟩ **3** : a systematic treatise upon the animals of an area or period — compare FLORA 1

fau·nal \'fȯnᵊl, 'fän-\ *adj* [*fauna* + -*al*] : of or relating to fauna — **fau·nal·ly** \-nᵊlē\ *adv*

faunal area *n* : a region characterized by a particular kind of animal community

fau·nat·ed \'fȯ,nād·əd, 'fä,-\ *adj* [*fauna* + -*ate* + -*ed*] : possessing an extensive intestinal fauna of commensal microorganisms — used of certain animals (as termites)

faunch \'fȯnch,'fä-\ *vi* -ED/-ING/-ES [origin unknown] *dial* : to display angry excitement : rant and rave ⟨it was enough to make anybody ~⟩

fau·nist \'fȯnəst, 'fän-\ *n* -s [*fauna* + -*ist*] : a specialist on faunas

fau·nis·tic \(')fȯ¦nistik,(')fä¦-\ *or* **fau·nis·ti·cal** \-təkəl\ *adj* : of or relating to zoogeography : FAUNAL — **fau·nis·ti·cal·ly** \-tək(ə)lē\ *adv*

fau·ni·zone \'fȯnə,zōn, 'fän-\ *n* -s [*fauni-* (fr. *fauna*) + *zone*] : a group of geologic beds deposited during the life span of a particular assemblage of organisms and thus characterized by the fossils of a particular fauna

fau·nol·o·gy \fȯ'näləjē, fä'-, -ji\ *n* -s [*fauno-* (fr. *fauna*) + -*logy*] : ZOOGEOGRAPHY

faun·tle·roy \'fȯntlə,rȯi, 'fän-\ *adj, usu cap* [after Lord *Fauntleroy,* boy hero of Frances Hodgson Burnett's novel *Little Lord Fauntleroy* (1886)] : characterized by a short tailored jacket, knee-length trousers, rather frilly shirt, wide collar with rounded corners, or large loose bow ⟨dressed the boy in *Fauntleroy* clothes and kept his hair in curls —R.L.Taylor⟩ ⟨a ~ suit⟩ ⟨a ~ collar⟩

fau·nule \'fȯ,nyül, 'fä,-\ *also* **fau·nu·la** \-nyələ\ *n, pl* **faunules** \-lz\ *also* **faunu·lae** \-yə,lē\ [NL *faunula,* fr. *fauna* + -*ula*] : a diminutive fauna; *esp* : an association of animal fossils found in a single stratum or a succession of strata of limited thickness

faur \(')fōr\ *Scot var of* WHERE

faured \'fōrd\ *Scot var of* FAVORED

fause \'fȯs\ *adj* [by alter.] *chiefly Scot* : FALSE

fau·sen \'fȯsᵊn\ *n* -s [origin unknown] *archaic* : EEL — used chiefly of catadromous eels and sometimes specif. of developmental forms (as the elver or the yellow eel) in their life cycle

faustian \'fau̇stēən, 'fȯs-\ *adj, usu cap* [Johann *Faust* (name in Latinized form Johannes *Faustus*) †*ab*1540 Ger. magician and astrologer represented in several dramatic works (notably by Marlowe and Goethe) as growing dissatisfied with the limited nature of human knowledge and consequently selling his soul to the devil in exchange for worldly experience and power + E -*ian*] : of, belonging to, resembling, or befitting Faust or Faustus: as **a** : sacrificing spiritual values for material gains **b** : insatiably striving for knowledge and mastery **c** : constantly troubled and tormented by spiritual dissatisfaction or spiritual striving

faust slipper \\'faüst-\\ *n, usu cap F* **:** a high-cut house shoe having in the sides V-shaped cuts without goring — compare ROMEO

faut \\'fōt\\ *chiefly Scot var of* FAULT

¹faute de mieux \\fōtdəmyœ\\ *adv* [F, for lack of something better] **:** for lack of something better or more desirable ⟨sherry made him dopey but he drank it *faute de mieux* —F.T. Marsh⟩ ⟨we would welcome it — *faute de mieux* — even if it were only mediocre —F.B.Agard & W.G. Moulton⟩

Faust slipper

²faute de mieux \\"\\ *adj* **:** adopted or undertaken for lack of something better ⟨only the result of a *faute de mieux* formula, and not of a desired stylization —R.J.Goldwater⟩ ⟨such marriages . . . were *faute de mieux* and usually accepted because there was no other alternative —L.S.B.Leaky⟩

fau·teuil \\(ˈ)fō¦tər(·), (ˈ)fō¦tē, *F* fōtœy\\ *n, pl* **fau·teuils** \\-ərz,-ēz,-œy\\ [F, fr. OF *faudestuel* folding chair, of Gmc origin; akin to OE *fyldestōl* folding chair, OS *faldistōl*, OHG *faltistuol*; all these fr. a prehistoric WGmc compound whose first constituent is akin to OHG *faldan* to fold and whose second constituent is represented by OHG *stuol* chair — more at FOLD, STOOL] **1 :** ARMCHAIR; *esp* **:** an upholstered chair with open arms **2** *Brit* **:** a theater stall

¹fau·tor \\'fȯd·ə(r)\\ *n* -s [ME *fautour*, fr. L or MF; MF *fauteur*, fr. L *fautor*, fr. *fautus* (past part. of *favēre* to be favorable) + *-or* — more at FAVOR] *archaic* **:** one that gives support **:** PATRON, PROTECTOR, PARTISAN, ABETTOR

²fau·tor \\'fōtər\\ *Scot var of* FAULTER

fautress *or* **fautrix** *n* [*fautress* fr. *fautor* + *-ess*; *fautrix* fr. L, fem. of *fautor* — more at -TRIX] *obs* **:** a female fautor

¹fauve \\'fōv\\ *n* -s [F, lit., wild animal, fr. *fauve*, adj., wild, tawny, fr. OF, tawny, of Gmc origin; akin to OHG *falo* fallow — more at FALLOW] **1 :** a painter whose work is marked by fauvism **:** FAUVIST **2 :** a rebel or nonconformist in art

²fauve \\"\\ *adj* **:** of or relating to the fauvists or to fauves

fau·vette \\fō'vet\\ *n* -s [F, fr. OF *fauvete*, fr. *fauve* + *-ete* -ette] *archaic* **:** any of several small singing birds (as the garden warbler of Europe)

fau·vism \\'fō,vizəm\\ *n* -s *often cap* [F *fauvisme*, fr. *fauve*, n. + *-isme* -ism] **:** a movement or a practice in painting typified by the work of the French painter Henri Matisse and characterized by markedly vivid colors and the free treatment of form resulting in a marked vibrant and decorative effect

fau·vist \\-vəst\\ *n* -s *often cap* [¹*fauve* + *-ist*] **:** one who practices or advocates fauvism; *specif* **:** a member of a group of French artists who about 1906 revolted from the restrictiveness of academic and neo-impressionist art

faux·bour·don \\'fōbə(r)‚dän, ¦==¦dōⁿ\\ *n* -s [F *faux-bourdon*, fr. MF, fr. *faux* false (fr. L *falsus*) + *bourdon* bass horn — more at FALSE, BOURDON] **1 :** harmonic progressions of the 15th century characterized by parallel fourths in the upper voices and based chiefly on parallel sixth chords **2 :** a sacred homophonic choral composition

faux·bourg *like* FAUBOURG\\ *archaic var of* FAUBOURG

faux jour \\(ˈ)fō¦zhü(ə)r\\ *n, pl* **faux jours** \\-r(z)\\ [F, lit., false light] **:** a window in a partition opposite one in an outer wall that allows daylight to pass

faux pas \\(ˈ)fō¦pä\\ *n, pl* **faux pas** \\-ä(z)\\ [F, lit., false step] **:** BLUNDER; *esp* **:** a social blunder **syn** see ERROR

faux sa·ti·ne \\¦fō,sat³n'ā\\ *n* [perh. fr. F *faux* false + *satiné* — more at SATINÉ] **:** a light-tan oily wood that is obtained from cypress knees and is valued chiefly for its crotch figure which is used in ornamental veneers

fav *abbr* favorite

fa·va \\'fävə\\ *or* **fava bean** *also* **fa·ba** \\'fäbə\\ *n* -s [*fava* fr. It, fr. L *faba* bean; *faba* fr. NL (specific epithet of the broad bean *Vicia faba*), fr. L, bean — more at BEAN] **:** BROAD BEAN

fa·vel·la \\fə'velə\\ *n, pl* **favel·lae** \\-e,lē\\ [NL, fr. L *favus* honeycomb + NL *-ella*] **:** an agglomeration of spores in various red algae (family Ceramiaceae) resembling cystocarps but naked or with only a thin membrane or gelatinous envelope

fav·el·lid·i·um \\‚favə'lidēəm\\ *n, pl* **favellid·ia** \\-ēə\\ [NL, fr. *favella* + *-idium*] **:** a favella immersed in an algal frond

fa·vel·loid \\fə've,lȯid\\ *adj* [*favella* + *-oid*] **:** relating to or resembling a favella

fav·en·tine \\'favən‚tēn, -tīn\\ *adj, usu cap* [L *faventinus*, fr. *Faventia* (now Faenza, city in northern Italy) + L *-inus* -ine] **:** of or belonging to Faenza, Italy ⟨*Faventine* majolica⟩

fa·ve·o·late \\fə'vēəlǝt, -ə,lāt\\ *adj* [prob. fr. (assumed) NL *faveolatus*, fr. NL *faveolus* + L *-atus* -ate] **:** HONEYCOMBED, ALVEOLATE

fa·ve·o·lus \\-ələs\\ *n, pl* **faveo·li** \\-ə,lī\\ [NL, dim. of L *favus* honeycomb] **:** ALVEOLA 1

fav·e·rolle \\'favə,rōl, ¦==¦\\ *n* [prob. fr. *Faverolles*, northern France] **1** *usu cap* **:** a breed of general purpose fowls developed in France by intercrossing Houdan, Dorking, and Asiatic fowls and comprising moderate-sized deep-bodied birds with five toes, partially feathered shanks, a single comb, and very distinctive feather beard and muffs below the bill and on the cheeks **2** -s *often cap* **:** a bird of the Faverolle breed

favi *pl of* FAVUS

fa·vi·form \\'fāvə,fȯrm, 'fav-\\ *adj* [prob. fr. (assumed) NL *faviformis*, fr. (assumed) NL *favi-* (fr. L *favus* honeycomb) + L *-formis* -form] **:** resembling a honeycomb in structure

fa·vil·la \\fə'vilə\\ *n, pl* **favil·lae** \\-i,lē\\ [L, glowing ashes; akin to L *fovēre* to warm — more at DAY] **:** a small incandescent fragment of lava from a volcano

fa·vism \\'fä,vizəm\\ *n* -s [It *favismo*, fr. *fava* broad bean + *-ismo* -ism — more at FAVA] **:** a severe allergic reaction caused by eating the broad bean or by inhaling its pollen that is marked by hemolytic anemia, eosinophilia, jaundice, fever, and often diarrhea and is observed chiefly in southern Italy

fa·vo·ni·an \\fə'vōnēən\\ *adj* [L *favonianus*, fr. *favonius* west wind + *-anus* -an; akin to L *fovēre* to warm] **:** of or belonging to the west wind **:** MILD, BLAND

¹fa·vor \\'fāvə(r)\\ *n* -s *see -or in Explan Notes* [ME *favour*, *favor* friendly regard, attractiveness, fr. OF *favor* friendly regard, fr. L, fr. *favēre* to be favorable; akin to OHG *gouma* attention, ON *gā* to heed, OSlav *gověti* to revere] **1** *archaic* **a :** a quality that arouses approbation **:** CHARM **b :** APPEARANCE **c :** COUNTENANCE, FACE; *also* **:** a feature of the face **2 a** (1) **:** friendly regard, goodwill, or esteem shown toward another esp. by a superior ⟨a politician attempting to keep the ~ of the voters⟩ (2) **:** the act of approving or the state of being approved of **:** APPROBATION ⟨look with ~ upon an enterprise⟩ ⟨enjoy ~ in an enterprise⟩ (3) *obs* **:** the object of approval ⟨his chief delight and ~ —John Milton⟩ **b :** bias in favor **:** PARTIALITY ⟨the judge showed ~ toward the plaintiff⟩ ⟨the students naturally showed ~ toward their own team⟩ **c** *archaic* **:** LENIENCY; *also* **:** a lenient action **d** *archaic* **:** INDULGENCE, PERMISSION, LEAVE **e :** POPULARITY ⟨it was a fad, something that would lose ~ quickly⟩ **3 a :** kindness esp. when marked by benevolence in the agent or great gratification in the one benefiting ⟨enjoying the ~ of a rich and generous patron⟩; *also* **:** an act or instance of such kindness ⟨showering ~*s* on the needy and deserving⟩ **b** *archaic* **:** HELP, ASSISTANCE **c favors** *pl* **:** effort in one's behalf or interest **:** ATTENTION ⟨vying for the king's ~*s*⟩; *also* **:** the product of such effort or interest ⟨magazines paid well for the young writer's ~*s*⟩ **4 a :** an object or token of favor (as a glove or ribbon) given esp. formerly by a lady to a favored one (as a lover or a favored knight in a tournament) to be worn conspicuously **b :** appropriate knickknacks, small gifts, or amusing or decorative items (as crackers, noisemakers, corsages for the women, or souvenirs) given out at a celebration or party (as by placing at a place setting) ⟨the younger element snapped frilly ~*s* which blossomed into frivolous paper hats —Silas Spitzer⟩ **c :** EMBLEM, BADGE ⟨wore the Republican party ~⟩ **5 a :** a special privilege or right granted or conceded ⟨have the ~ of a new trial⟩ ⟨grant a ~ to a good friend⟩ ⟨dropped his sword and shouted for mercy, a ~ that the Roman was pleased to bestow —L.C.Douglas⟩ **b :** sexual privileges or sexual intercourse usu. as granted by a woman — usu. used in pl. or in the phrase *the ultimate favor* ⟨her niece, a prostitute, had been granting her ~*s* to policemen —M.R. Werner⟩ ⟨a young woman . . . worked for a publishing firm and was generally supposed to have granted the ultimate ~ to every male author on the list who sold over 20,000 copies —Clifton Fadiman⟩ **6** *archaic* **:** LETTER, COMMUNICATION **7 a :** BEHALF, INTEREST ⟨a man who acts only in his own ~⟩ **b :** a difference that favors ⟨of the speed of the two swimmers there is a slight ~ for the first⟩ — **in favor of** *prep* **1 :** to the special advantage or benefit of ⟨there shall be no discrimination *in favor of*, or to the prejudice of, either race —*Amer. Guide Series: N.C.*⟩: as **a :** in accord or sympathy with **:** on the side of ⟨*in favor of* the group working for greater sanitation⟩ **b :** for the acquittal of ⟨the jury returned *in favor of* the man accused of robbery⟩ **:** in support of ⟨the court's decision was *in favor of* the corporation that brought the suit⟩ **2 :** to the order of — used of a check or other draft — **in one's favor 1 :** in one's good graces ⟨doing extra works to get back *in the teacher's favor*⟩ **2 :** to one's advantage according to the laws of probability ⟨the odds in the gambling game were *in the bettor's favor*⟩ — **out of favor** *adv* **:** under displeasure **:** DISLIKED; *also* **:** not popular **:** NEGLECTED ⟨certain ideas . . . however much obscured and *out of favor* for a time, live on —C.I. Glicksberg⟩ — **under favor** *adv, archaic* **:** with permission (of one addressed or implied) **:** subject to being overruled

²favor \\"\\ *vt* **favored; favored; favoring** \\-v(ə)riŋ\\ **favors** *see -or in Explan Notes* [ME *favouren*, *favoren*, fr. *favour*, *favor*, n. — more at ¹FAVOR] **1 a :** to regard or treat with favor, goodwill, or approval **:** show favor to **:** treat with consideration ⟨~ any bill that cuts my taxes⟩ ⟨as a father he ~*ed* little girls⟩; *also* **:** to act in a way that encourages ⟨the board ~*ed* the protection of labor without freezing it —*Current Biog.*⟩ **b :** to do a kindness for or oblige esp. with a gift ⟨the author ~*ed* us with a copy of his latest book⟩; *also* **:** to provide with a special quality, characteristic, or possession ⟨he was ~*ed* with great intelligence and phenomenal good looks⟩ **c :** to treat gently or carefully **:** avoid overworking **:** SPARE ⟨like a hound ~*ing* a sore foot —Nelson Algren⟩ ⟨sorry to hear you had a return of your rheumatism — I do hope you will ~ yourself more —Walt Whitman⟩ **d :** to give (oneself) free course ⟨typically tends to ~ himself with special foods and laborsaving devices⟩ **2 a :** to show partiality toward ⟨the jurors clearly ~*ed* the defendant⟩ ⟨a ~*ed* class of citizens⟩ **:** side with ⟨the neutral nations seemed to ~ neither side⟩ **:** to regard above others **:** PREFER ⟨the patient said he would ~ a harder bed⟩; *esp* **:** to prefer as a matter of passing favor or temporary enthusiasm or popularity ⟨certain ~*ed* movie stars⟩ ⟨the most ~*ed* gun on the skeet field today . . . seems to be the very heavy 12-gauge autoloader —Bob Nichols⟩ **b :** to choose as a favorite in or as if in betting ⟨the Russians are ~*ed* to win —Samuel Reshevsky⟩ **c :** to tend to have as if by preference ⟨in the spring, suits ~*ed* moderately full to very wide skirt hemlines —*Collier's Yr. Bk.*⟩ **3 a :** to give support or confirmation to **:** SUSTAIN ⟨adducing facts which ~*ed* his contention⟩ **:** AID ⟨he felt that God was ~*ing* him in his efforts⟩ **b :** to afford advantages for success to **:** FACILITATE ⟨the continued good weather distinctly ~*ed* the vacation trade⟩ **:** be propitious for ⟨a wind ~*ing* their speedy return⟩ ⟨high humidity ~*ed* the incidence of disease —G.G.Weigend⟩ **4 :** to bear a resemblance to ⟨the daughter rather ~*ed* the father's side of the family⟩

syn COUNTENANCE, ENCOURAGE: FAVOR may be used in reference to a well-disposed inclination, an expressed preference, active support, or, more broadly, a circumstance or agency conducive to a result ⟨a number of wealthy and influential Newport folk *favored* dramatic performances, although a majority of their fellow citizens continued to condemn them —*Amer. Guide Series: R.I.*⟩ ⟨in general the marshmen *favor* a broad, roomy canoe —Wilfred Thesiger⟩ ⟨we had been *favored* by tail winds and would put down at Idlewild —Bennett Cerf⟩ ⟨the summer weather at Maudheim *favored* the formation of this type of snow —Valter Schytt⟩ COUNTENANCE may indicate mere toleration; it may imply more positive favoring ⟨really fail to see why you should *countenance* immorality just to please your father —Sheila Kaye-Smith⟩ ⟨her popularity had been retrieved, grievances against her silenced, her past *countenanced*, and her present irradiated by the family approval —Edith Wharton⟩ ⟨several of them appeared at the bar to *countenance* him when he was tried at the Horsham assizes —T.B.Macaulay⟩ ENCOURAGE indicates heartening stimulation, inciting or inducing esp. by expressions of approval, confidence, liking, or comfort ⟨openly *encouraged* from Germany and Italy, fascist organizations, although from time to time banned, carried on insidious and demoralizing propaganda —F.A.Ogg and Harold Zink⟩ ⟨*encouraged* her in her ambition to be an actress —*Current Biog.*⟩ **syn** see in addition OBLIGE

fa·vor·able \\'fāv(ə)rəbəl, -vrəb-\\ *adj* [ME *favourable*, *favorable*, fr. MF *favorable*, fr. L *favorabilis* popular, pleasing, fr. *favor* + *-abilis* -able — more at FAVOR] **1 a :** disposed to favor **:** FAVORING, APPROVING, PARTIAL ⟨taking a ~ attitude toward our request⟩ **:** expressing approval **:** COMMENDATORY ⟨a ~ recommendation⟩ ⟨a ~ grade on an exam⟩; *also* **:** giving a result that is in one's favor ⟨a ~ comparison⟩ **b** *obs* **:** GRACIOUS, OBLIGING **c :** granting or obliging in what is desired **:** AFFIRMATIVE ⟨gave a ~ answer to our request⟩ **2 :** winning approval **:** PLEASING, AGREEABLE ⟨made a ~ impression on his future colleagues⟩ **3 a :** tending to promote or facilitate **:** ADVANTAGEOUS ⟨a ~ wind blew us into port without a mishap⟩ ⟨a business climate ~ to almost any enterprise⟩ **b :** having the value of exports exceed that of imports ⟨a ~ balance of trade⟩ **4 a :** indicative of a successful outcome **:** affording cheer or reason for optimism **:** boding well ⟨a ~ weather for our yacht trip⟩ ⟨~ conditions for opening a new business⟩ **b :** marked by success **:** turning out in the way desired or hoped ⟨a ~ demonstration of a new invention⟩ ⟨made a ~ adjustment to the new conditions of her life⟩

syn BENIGN, AUSPICIOUS, PROPITIOUS: FAVORABLE describes persons, events, or conditions whose disposition or effect is kindly, helpful, advantageous, or encouraging and likely to presage or facilitate a happy outcome ⟨a hot dry summer, *favorable* to contemplative life out of doors —Joseph Conrad⟩ ⟨they won't take a chance of battle unless they can feel sure of most *favorable* conditions —Alexander Forbes⟩ ⟨my position in reference to them, being paternal and protective, was *favorable* to the growth of friendly sentiments —Nathaniel Hawthorne⟩ BENIGN may apply to persons or agencies that have power or position to harm, hinder, or check but whose disposition appears kindly and encouraging ⟨that *benign* friend who had previously comforted him in his misery —Anthony Trollope⟩ ⟨always *benign*, there was not a grain of ill will anywhere in him —A.N.Whitehead⟩ ⟨the *benign* and fatherly old man put his arm round her waist —Arnold Bennett⟩ AUSPICIOUS describes events or conditions pointing toward good or favorable outcomes or developments ⟨court astrologers pronounced March 2, 1949, an *auspicious* date for the coronation —*Current Biog.*⟩ ⟨at least pay the boy then; I have no pice with me, and he brought *auspicious* news —Rudyard Kipling⟩ PROPITIOUS describes, perhaps more mildly so than AUSPICIOUS, events or conditions that are favorable. PROPITIOUS may describe that which lacks any discouraging indication without having the optimistic ring of AUSPICIOUS ⟨although it was already late in the autumn, the weather was *propitious* —J.L.Motley⟩ ⟨after so *propitious* an opening it seemed that acerbities might be quelled, rivalries mitigated —S.H.Adams⟩

fa·vor·able·ness *n* -ES **:** the quality or state of being favorable ⟨pleased by the ~ of the court's decision⟩

fa·vor·ably \\-blē, -li\\ *adv* [ME *favourably*, *favourablely*, fr. *favourable* + *-ly*] **:** in a favorable manner

fa·vored \\¦fāvə(r)d\\ *adj* [fr. past part. of ²*favor*] **1 :** endowed with special advantages, good qualities, or gifts ⟨a ~ position in the firm⟩ ⟨a place ~ by nature⟩ ⟨a student clearly ~⟩ **2** [¹*favor* + *-ed*] **:** having an appearance or features of a particular kind — usu. used in combination ⟨a well-*favored* community⟩ ⟨an ill-*favored* child⟩ ⟨hard-*favored*⟩ **3 :** providing preferential treatment ⟨better management of the existing collective farms with ~ rates of credit —Jack Raymond⟩

fa·vor·er \\-vərə(r)\\ *n* -s **:** one that favors, furthers, or promotes

favoring *pres part of* FAVOR

¹fa·vor·ite \\'fāv(ə)rə̇t, -vərl, *usu* ǀd.+V\\ *n* -s [It *favorito*, past part. of *favorire* to favor, fr. *favore* favor, fr. L *favor*] **1 a :** something treated or regarded with special favor **:** something esp. liked or loved ⟨like other fertile districts, this territory was once a ~ with the Indians —*Amer. Guide Series: Mich.*⟩ ⟨of all books, the Bible was his ~⟩; *specif* **:** one unusually loved, trusted, or provided with favors by a person of high rank or authority ⟨the Duke of York . . . granted the area between the Hudson and Delaware rivers to two of his ~*s* —*Amer. Guide Series: N.J.*⟩ ⟨the political rule, by palace intrigue, of ~*s*, women, and eunuchs —W.G.Sumner⟩ ⟨committing to a wicked ~ all public cares —John Milton⟩ **b :** something having marked esp. lasting popularity ⟨approximately thirty active winter playland areas in Vermont . . . include old ~*s* of all sizes —*N.Y. Times*⟩ **2** *obs* **:** SUPPORTER, FOLLOWER, PARTISAN **3 :** a short curl at the temple fashionable in the 17th and 18th centuries — usu. used in pl. **4 :** a competitor (as a horse in a race) judged most likely to win **:** the competitor against whom the shortest odds are laid in the betting **syn** see PARASITE

²favorite \\"\\ *adj* **:** constituting a favorite ⟨a ~ picnic place⟩ **:** accorded special treatment or attention usu. loving or affectionate ⟨a ~ daughter⟩; *specif* **:** markedly popular esp. over an extended period of time ⟨~ melodies from light opera⟩ ⟨small dogs are ~ pets⟩

favorite sentence *n* **:** the most common sentence type in a language (as in English the actor-action type, as *he won*)

favorite son *n* **:** a person favored as their candidate by the delegates of his state at the presidential nominating convention of a party

fa·vor·it·ism \\'fāv(ə)rə̇d·‚izəm, -vərl, ǀ‚di-\\ *n* -s **1 :** the treating of one person, family, or class of men with special favor or partiality to the correlative neglect of others ⟨~ in federal tax legislation —C.S.Shoup⟩ ⟨the workers think that most raises are based on ~ —S.L.Payne⟩ **2 :** the state or fact of being a favorite

favorless *adj, obs* **:** showing no favor **:** UNPROPITIOUS

favors *pl of* FAVOR, *pres 3d sing of* FAVOR

fa·vose \\'fā,vōs\\ *adj* [prob. fr. (assumed) NL *favosus*, fr. L *favus* honeycomb + *-osus* -ose] **:** ALVEOLATE — **fa·vose·ly** *adv*

fav·o·site \\'favə,sīt\\ *n* -s [NL *Favosites*] **:** a fossil coral of the genus *Favosites* or a related genus

fav·o·si·tes \\‚==¦sīd·(‚)ēz\\ *n, cap* [NL, prob. fr. (assumed) NL *favosus* + NL *-ites* -ite] **:** a genus (the type of a large exclusively Paleozoic family Favositidae) of extinct corals having polygonal cells with perforated walls esp. abundant in the Silurian and Devonian rocks — **fav·o·sit·oid** \\¦==¦sīd·‚ȯid\\ *adj*

fa·vour \\'fāvə(r)\\ *Brit var of* FAVOR

fa·vous \\'fāvəs\\ *adj* [L *favus* honeycomb + E *-ous*] **:** FAVOSE

Fa·vrile \\fəv'rē(ə)l\\ *trademark* — used for glassware of delicate design and with an iridescent surface

fa·vus \\'fāvəs\\ *n* [NL, fr. L, honeycomb] **1** -ES **:** a contagious skin disease caused by a fungus (as *Achorion schoenleinii*) occurring in man on hairy surfaces that become covered with yellowish crusts and often depilated and also attacking many domestic animals and fowls **2** *pl* **fa·vi** \\-‚vī\\ **:** a tile or flagstone cut into a hexagonal shape to produce a honeycomb pattern (as in a pavement)

faw \\'fō, 'fä\\ *dial var of* FALL

¹fawn \\'fȯn, 'fän\\ *vi* -ED/-ING/-S [ME *faunen*, fr. OE *fagnian*, *fægnian* to rejoice, fr. *fagen*, *fægen* glad — more at FAIN] **1 :** to show delight or affection in such behavior as wagging the tail or licking — used esp. of dogs ⟨the puppy was ~*ing* on its master as if it understood what he suffered⟩ **2 :** to act in a sycophantic way **:** court favor by a cringing or overly flattering manner **:** GROVEL ⟨they ~ and slaver over us —Robinson Jeffers⟩ ⟨died, still ~*ing* like the coward that he had always been —Bernard Pares⟩ ⟨your knights here, who ~ on a damsel with soft words in the hall, and will kiss the dust off their queen's feet —Charles Kingsley⟩ ⟨courtiers who ~ on a master while they betray him —T.B.Macaulay⟩

²fawn *n* -s *obs* **:** the act of fawning

³fawn \\'fȯn, 'fän\\ *n* -s [ME *foun*, fr. MF *faon*, *feon* young of an animal, fr. OF, fr. (assumed) VL *feton-*, *feto*, fr. L *fetus* offspring — more at FETUS] **1 :** a young deer; *esp* **:** one still unweaned or retaining a distinctive baby coat **2 :** ¹KID 1 **3** *or* **fawn brown :** a variable color averaging a light grayish brown that is yellower, darker, and slightly stronger than Deauville sand — called also *autumn blond*, *faon* **4 :** one that is fawn colored

⁴fawn \\"\\ *vi* -ED/-ING/-S [ME *faunen*, fr. MF *faonner* to give birth to young (said of an animal), fr. OF, fr. *faon*, *feon* young of an animal] **:** to give birth to a fawn

fawning *adj* [fr. pres. part. of ¹*fawn*] **:** characteristic of one that fawns **:** servilely abject **:** SYCOPHANTIC ⟨sent the most objectionable ~ greetings⟩ — **fawn·ing·ness** *n* -ES

fawn·ing·ly *adv* **:** in a fawning manner **:** in an overly flattering, cringing, servile, or groveling manner

fawn lily *n* **:** any of several plants of the genus *Erythronium*; *esp* **:** a Californian dogtooth violet (*E. californicum*) with creamy white flowers sometimes yellow tinged

fawny \\'fȯnē, 'fänē\\ *adj* -ER/-EST [³*fawn* + *-y*] **:** of a color approximating fawn

¹fay \\'fā\\ *vb* -ED/-ING/-S [ME *feien*, fr. OE *fēgan*; akin to OS *fōgian* to fit, join, OHG *fuogen* to fit, join, L *pangere* to fasten — more at PACT] *vt, in shipbuilding* **:** to fit, fasten, or join closely or tightly ~ *vi* **1 a :** to fit closely together or nicely esp. against something else (as a surface) ⟨paint a ~*ing* surface before making an overlapping metal joint⟩ — often used with *in*, *into*, *with*, or *together* **b** *archaic* **:** AGREE, JIBE **2** *dial Eng* **:** SUCCEED, PROSPER

²fay \\"\\ *vt* -ED/-ING/-S [ME *feien*, fr. ON *fægja* to clean, polish; akin to ON *fāga* to clean, decorate — more at FAIR] *dial Brit* **:** CLEAN **:** clear away — often used with *up* or *out*

³fay \\"\\ *n* [ME *fai*, *fei*, fr. OF *fei* — more at ¹FAITH] *obs* **:** FAITH

⁴fay \\"\\ *n* -s [ME *faie*, *fei* someone or something enchanted, fr. MF *fee*, *feie* fairy — more at FAIRY] **:** FAIRY, ELF

⁵fay \\"\\ *adj* -ER/-EST [ME *faie* having magical powers, enchanted, fr. *faie*, *fei*, n.] **:** like an elf ⟨a ~ and delicate daughter⟩

⁶fay \\"\\ *n* -s [perh. by shortening] *slang* **:** OFAY

fa·yal·ite \\fə'yä,līt, fī'ä-\\ *n* -s [G *fayalit*, fr. *Fayal*, island in the Azores + G *-it* -ite] **:** a mineral Fe_2SiO_4 consisting of an iron silicate isomeric with olivine and occurring in crystals or massive (sp. gr. 4.1)

fayence *var of* FAIENCE

fay in *vb, NewEng* **:** ¹FAY

¹fa·yum·ic *or* **fay·yum·ic** \\(ˈ)fā¦yümik, (ˈ)fī¦-\\ *adj, usu cap* **1 :** of, belonging to, or situated in the Fayum, a fertile depression in Egypt south of Cairo and connected with the Nile valley by a narrow pass **2 :** of, belonging to, being, or composed in Fayumic

²fayumic *or* **fayyumic** \\"\\ *n* -s *usu cap* **:** a dialect of Coptic spoken in the early Christian period in Middle Egypt of which fragments of a New Testament translation survive

faze *also* **phase** \\'fāz\\ *vt* -ED/-ING/-S [alter. of *feeze*] **:** to disturb the composure of **:** DISCONCERT, WORRY, BOTHER, DAUNT ⟨he had never navigated a ship up the St. Lawrence before, but that didn't ~ him —James Dugan⟩ ⟨calamitous personal defeat did not seem to ~ him⟩ **syn** see EMBARRASS

fa·zen·da \\fə'zendə\\ *n* -s [Pg, fr. L *facienda* things to be done — more at HACIENDA] **1 :** a Brazilian plantation; *esp* **:** a coffee plantation **2 :** the house on a fazenda

fa·zen·dei·ro \\‚faz³n'dā(‚)rō\\ *n* -s [Pg, fr. *fazenda*] **:** a Brazilian planter or cattleman

FB *abbr* **1** fire brigade **2** flying boat **3** freight bill **4** fullback

FBI \\¦ef,bē'ī\\ *n* -s [*F*ederal *B*ureau of *I*nvestigation, a bureau of the U.S. Department of Justice that investigates violations of certain federal statutes] **:** a governmental investigating agency ⟨toying with the idea of dissolving the discredited German *FBI* —*Springfield (Mass.) Daily News*⟩

FBM *abbr* foot board measure

fc *abbr* franc

FC *abbr* **1** fideicommissum **2** fire control **3** flood control **4** follow copy **5** food control **6** football club **7** footcandle **8** free church

FC&S *abbr* free of capture and seizure

fc&s warranty *n, usu cap F&C&S* **:** a clause in a marine in-

surance policy excluding coverage if loss is caused by capture or seizure of the insured ship or by atomic fission or radioactive force
fcap *abbr* foolscap
FCC *abbr* first-class certificate
f center *n, usu cap F* **:** a point in a crystalline compound (as a silver halide) at which a negative ion missing from the crystal lattice has been replaced by an electron
fcg *abbr* facing
f clef *n, usu cap F* **:** a clef placing the F below middle C on the fourth line of the staff — called also *bass clef;* see CLEF illustration; compare C CLEF, G CLEF
fco *abbr* [It *franco*] postage free; delivered free
fcp *abbr* foolscap
FCS *abbr, often not cap* free of capture and seizure
fcst *abbr* forecast
fc station *n, usu cap F&C* **:** a coast radio station
fcty *abbr* factory
fcy *abbr* fancy
fd *abbr* **1** field **2** forced **3** ford **4** found **5** fund
FD *abbr* **1** [L *Fidei Defensor*] Defender of the Faith **2** fire department **3** first day **4** focal distance **5** forced draft **6** free delivery **7** free discharge **8** free dispatch **9** free dock
fd&c color *n, usu cap F&D & 1st C* [*Food, Drug, and Cosmetic Act* + *color*] **:** any of the synthetic dyes that in certified batches are permitted for use in foods, drugs, and cosmetics by the Federal Food, Drug, and Cosmetic Act of 1938 and subsequent legislation — compare D&C COLOR, EXT D&C COLOR; *see* DYE table II
FDC *abbr* **1** fire direction center **2** first-day cover
FDD *abbr* [F *franc de droits*] free of charge
fdg *abbr* funding
fdn *abbr* foundation
fdry *abbr* foundry
Fe *symbol* **1** [L *ferrum*] iron **2** quadragesimo-octavo
fea·ber·ry \'fē-, 'fā- — *see* BERRY\ *n* [*fea-* (perh. alter. of ME *theve-* as in *thevethorn* bramble, fr. OE *thefanthorn*) + *berry;* akin to OHG *depandorn* bramble] *dial Eng* **:** GOOSEBERRY 1a
feak *n* -s [origin unknown] *obs* **:** a lock or curl of hair
¹feal \'fē(ə)l\ *vt* [ME *felen*, fr. ON *fela;* akin to OE *fēolan* to undergo, enter, OHG *felahan* to conceal, Goth *filhan* to conceal, OE *fell* skin, hide — more at FELL] *dial Eng* **:** CONCEAL
²feal \"\ *adj* [MF, fr. OF, alter. (influenced by OF *-al*, fr. L *-alis*) of *feeil*, fr. L *fidelis* faithful, fr. *fides* faith — more at FAITH] *archaic* **:** FAITHFUL, LOYAL
feal and divot *n* [*feal* fr. ME (Sc) *faile* turf] *Scots law* **:** the right of taking turf for making fences or thatching houses
fe·al·ty \'fē(ə)ltē, -ti\ *n* -ES [alter. (influenced by MF *fealté*) of ME *feute, feaute*, fr. OF *feauté, fealté*, alter. (influenced by *feal* faithful) of *feelté*, fr. L *fidelitat-, fidelitas* fidelity, fr. *fidelis* faithful + *-itat-, -itas* -ity] **1 a :** the fidelity of a vassal or feudal tenant to his lord **b :** the obligation of such fidelity ⟨received him as king and lord of Ireland, vowing loyal obedience to him and his successors, and acknowledging ~ to them forever —Owen Wister⟩ **c :** an oath committing one to such fidelity ⟨swore ~ to his overlord⟩ **2 a :** FAITHFULNESS, ALLEGIANCE ⟨the board . . . to be appointed by the President, presumably from names submitted by the Academy or those holding strong ~ to it —M.L.Cooke⟩ ⟨~ to facts⟩; *specif* **:** faithfulness or allegiance conceived as an obligation or duty ⟨the ~ owed by a citizen to the best interest of his country⟩ **b :** an oath committing one to such fidelity or allegiance ⟨swore ~ to the Constitution with his hand resting upon a Bible —*Time*⟩ **syn** see FIDELITY
¹fear \'fi(ə)r, -iə\ *n* -s [ME *fer, fere*, fr. OE *fǣr* sudden danger, disaster; akin to OHG *fāra* ambush, danger, ON *fār* harm, misfortune, Goth *ferja* spy, L *periculum* attempt, peril, Gk *peiran* to attempt, OE *faran* to go — more at FARE] **1 a :** an unpleasant emotional state characterized by anticipation of pain or great distress and accompanied by heightened autonomic activity esp. involving the nervous system **:** agitated foreboding often of some real or specific peril — compare ANXIETY **b :** an instance or manifestation of this feeling ⟨they have created ~ of the free mind —John Mason Brown⟩ **c :** calm recognition or consideration of whatever may injure or damage **:** reasoned caution **:** intelligent foresight **2 a :** the state or habit of feeling agitation or dismay **:** a condition between anxiety and terror either natural and well-grounded or unreasoned and blind ⟨anesthetics have removed the ~ of physical pain —H.W.VanLoon⟩ ⟨the only thing we have to fear is ~ itself —F.D.Roosevelt⟩ ⟨living in ~⟩ **b :** anxious concern **:** SOLICITUDE ⟨a ~ that the boy will not make out well in his examination⟩ **3 :** profound reverence and awe ⟨the ~ of the Lord is the beginning of wisdom —Ps 111:10 (RSV)⟩ ⟨godliness and holy ~⟩ **4 :** something that is the object of apprehension or alarm **:** a ground for fear **:** DANGER ⟨starvation is still a real ~ in the minds of many peoples of the world⟩
syn DREAD, FRIGHT, ALARM, DISMAY, CONSTERNATION, PANIC, TERROR, HORROR, TREPIDATION: with the possible modified exception of DISMAY and CONSTERNATION, these nouns in one sense which they have in common signify the agitation aroused by anticipation of danger or the actual awareness of a present danger. FEAR, the most general of the terms, implies apprehension and anxiety and sometimes a loss of courage amounting to cowardice ⟨the human *fear* of death —Douglas Stewart⟩ ⟨a *fear* of failure⟩ ⟨the *fear* of the unknown⟩ ⟨tremble and grovel with *fear*⟩ DREAD is similar to FEAR but usu. adds the idea of extreme fear-inspired reluctance to face or meet a particular dreaded person or situation ⟨we face the threat —not with *dread* and confusion—but with confidence and conviction —D.D.Eisenhower⟩ ⟨though she was without definite fear, an obscure *dread* was beating against the wall of her consciousness —Ellen Glasgow⟩ FRIGHT implies the shock of sudden, startling, and short-lived fear ⟨a face to inspire *fright*⟩ ⟨the sound produces a kind of horror that is something more than mere *fright* —Ernie Pyle⟩ ⟨disquietude had developed into *fright; fright* quickly developed into terror —Emile Gaboriau⟩ ALARM suggests intense, usu. sudden, apprehension ⟨instantly the *alarm* began in her nerves; she felt the warning quiver dart through them like the vibration in a wire —Ellen Glasgow⟩ ⟨with an astonishment bordering on *alarm* —Jane Austen⟩ DISMAY, of these words the least generally associated with the idea of fear, usu. implies a sudden discouragement or loss of courage or initiative, generally accompanied by a certain mental confusion usu. induced by an unexpected turn of events ⟨view a difficult task with *dismay*⟩ ⟨when the child told her first lie her foster-mother was nearly sick with *dismay* and anxiety —Margaret Deland⟩ ⟨he is flung neck and crop into a world which he does not comprehend, and his *dismay* is hysterical —John Buchan⟩ CONSTERNATION implies fear only incidentally, stressing rather the idea of a temporary confusion or paralysis of faculties induced by something startlingly contrary to expectation or hope or something shocking ⟨he looked down on her with stirrings of tender pride which altered to *consternation* as slow tears came stealing down the nearest cheek —Mary Austin⟩ ⟨the more adventurous drivers enjoyed timing the trip down to the last second so that they could race the tide to safety, much to the *consternation* of their passengers —*Amer. Guide Series: Calif.*⟩ PANIC is overmastering and unreasoning fear or fright usu. as manifesting itself in hysterical activity ⟨thrown into a *panic* by the threat of raids by pirates —*Amer. Guide Series: Mich.*⟩ ⟨all the possible phases of that sort of anguish, beginning with instinctive *panic*, through the bewildered stage, the frozen stage, and the stage of blanched apprehension, down to the instinctive prudence of extreme terror —Joseph Conrad⟩ TERROR is extreme violent fear or dread, such as might conduce to panic ⟨his appeal was to fear, and he so impressed his hearers that frequently they fell to the floor or shrieked in *terror* —H.E. Starr⟩ ⟨in *terror*, the wild horse seems to lose possession of his senses and plunges ahead regardless of obstacles —*Amer. Guide Series: Ariz.*⟩ HORROR throws emphasis upon the idea of strong abhorrence or shuddering revulsion induced or accompanied by fear ⟨such a *horror* of his cruelty, duplicity, and power, that I could scarce conceal a shudder —R.L. Stevenson⟩ ⟨he saw, to his *horror*, that the three pairs of legs continued to parade but there seemed to be no bodies above them —*Amer. Guide Series: R.I.*⟩ TREPIDATION carries the idea of a trembling fear, born of timidity ⟨they went in *trepidation*, almost afraid that the delight of exploring this ruin might be denied them —D.H.Lawrence⟩ ⟨I should very shortly perish of *trepidation* and suspense in so sinister an environment —Elinor Wylie⟩
— for fear : by reason of an apprehension lest ⟨worried *for fear* the child will hurt himself⟩ **— without fear or favor :** in a manner uninfluenced by fear, prejudice, or partiality
²fear \"\ *vb* -ED/-ING/-S [ME *feren*, fr. OE *fǣran*, fr. *fǣr* sudden danger — more at ¹FEAR] *vt* **1** *now dial* **a :** FRIGHTEN, TERRIFY ⟨be careful not to ~ the horse by shouting⟩ **b :** to scare away ⟨~ the crows out of the corn⟩ **2** *obs* **:** DETER **3** *archaic* **:** to feel fear in (oneself) ⟨I ~ me he is slain —Christopher Marlowe⟩ **4 a :** to have a reverential awe of ⟨~ God⟩ **b :** to stand in awe of ⟨~ anyone in authority⟩ **5 a :** to be afraid of **:** consider, expect, or anticipate with feelings of alarm, foreboding, or solicitude ⟨most men ~ death⟩ ⟨~ the unexpected and unknown⟩ ⟨~ evil and misfortune⟩ **b :** to hesitate (to do something) for fear of doing wrong or causing unhappiness ⟨~ to disturb someone's thoughts⟩ **c :** to suspect or conclude regretfully ⟨I ~ I have made too many mistakes⟩ **~** *vi* **:** to be apprehensive **:** be afraid ⟨I ~ lest we commit an inexcusable blunder⟩ ⟨if the night seems cold, you need not ~ if the house is well heated⟩ **— fear·er** *n*
feared \'fi(ə)rd, -iəd\ *adj* [ME *fered*, past part. of *feren* to frighten] *chiefly dial* **:** AFRAID ⟨he was ~ to go⟩
fear·ful \'fi(ə)rfəl, -iəf-\ *adj, sometimes* -ER/-EST [ME *ferful*, fr. *fer, fere* fear + *-ful* — more at ¹FEAR] **1 a :** inspiring or likely to inspire fear, fright, or alarm **:** dangerous and alarming ⟨spent a ~ night alone in the woods⟩ ⟨won the war but at a ~ cost⟩ **b :** caused by, indicative of, or attended by fear ⟨casting ~ glances at the large dog as he passed it⟩ **2 :** full of fear, alarm, awe, concern, or apprehension: **a :** AFRAID, APPREHENSIVE ⟨Henry, ~ lest his prize should escape him at the last, was driven to offer terms —J.R.Green⟩ ⟨~ for his safety⟩ **b :** inclined to fear **:** TIMOROUS ⟨heaped scorn on all ~ people who strove only for comfort and security⟩ **c** *archaic* **:** CAUTIOUS **d :** marked by awe or reverence ⟨riveted his eyes in ~ ecstasy —Thomas Gray⟩ **3 a :** extremely bad, shocking, or revolting ⟨~ slum conditions⟩ **b :** EXTREME, LARGE, NUMEROUS — usu. used as a generalized intensifier with the force of a superlative ⟨a patron who had taken a ~ shellacking wagered every last chip —Bennett Cerf⟩ ⟨she exercises a ~ attraction —C.W.Cunnington⟩ ⟨a ~ litter of paper —Arnold Bennett⟩
syn AWFUL, DREADFUL, FRIGHTFUL, TERRIBLE, TERRIFIC, HORRIBLE, HORRIFIC, SHOCKING, APPALLING, DIRE: in loose use most of these words may be used to mean little more than *extreme*. More precisely, FEARFUL applies to what makes one feel fear, fright, alarm, agitation, or loss of courage ⟨our *fearful* trip is done, the ship has weathered every rack —Walt Whitman⟩ ⟨a *fearful* battlefield, the earth of it gaped open by shells and bombs —Ira Wolfert⟩ ⟨monsters, ghosts, spirit voices, and other *fearful* sights and sounds —*Time*⟩ AWFUL describes that which strikes one profoundly with overpowering awareness of might, power, or significance transcending the individual ⟨he looked at war and he saw through all the sham glory to the *awful* evil beneath —Edith Hamilton⟩ ⟨the *awful* impersonality of those great rock-creatures, the terrible impartiality of that cold, clinging wind which swept by, never an inch lifted above ground —John Galsworthy⟩ ⟨the *awful* arithmetic of the atomic bomb —D.D.Eisenhower⟩ DREADFUL applies to what fills one with a haunting shuddering fear or yearning to escape, often unanalyzable and persistent ⟨he perished, he and his house, struck by a thunderbolt in the midst of a *dreadful* storm —J.G.Frazer⟩ ⟨in his delirium his ravings have been *dreadful;* of wolves and poison and blood; of ghosts and demons —Bram Stoker⟩ FRIGHTFUL is applicable either to what causes consternated fright at the moment or to what is generally awful, outrageous, or enormous ⟨the Ghost of a Lady, dressed in deep mourning, a scar on her forehead, and a bloody handkerchief at her breast, *frightful* to behold —George Meredith⟩ ⟨look at what the British did in Greece — the most *frightful* military blunder, for which they are paying now —Upton Sinclair⟩ ⟨a *frightful* spectacle of poverty, barbarity, and ignorance —T.B.Macaulay⟩ TERRIBLE describes whatever inspires terror or extreme desperate dominating fear; it may describe something unendurable or excruciating to feelings or sensibilities ⟨so *terrible* was his wrath at their resistance that the Dean of St. Paul's, who stood forth to remonstrate, dropped dead of sheer terror at his feet —J.R.Green⟩ ⟨three *terrible* days in the hospital, tortured by a monster headache, a frightful thirst —Xavier Herbert⟩ ⟨one of those *terrible* women produced now and then by the Roman stock, unsexed, implacable, filled with an insane lust of power —John Buchan⟩ TERRIFIC applies to what compels terror, often by force, stunning effect, release of energy, explosive manifestation ⟨eyes starting with frantic terror at the *terrific* scene that met them —C.G.D.Roberts⟩ ⟨a *terrific* barrage of shell and bomb fragments, smoke, flame and debris from the stricken vessel —F.D.Roosevelt⟩ ⟨in 1848 a $75,000 dam was completed, and on the same day it was swept away by the *terrific* pressure, incorrectly calculated, of the water behind it —*Amer. Guide Series: Mass.*⟩ HORRIBLE describes that which instills a combination of terror and loathing or one of pure loathing at hideousness or hatefulness ⟨there came a most *horrible* yell — the most dreadful sound, Mr. Holmes, that ever I heard. It will ring in my ears as long as I live. I sat frozen with horror for a minute or two —A. Conan Doyle⟩ ⟨every *horrible* detail of Nazi atrocity —*Encounter*⟩ ⟨the most *horrible* monsters and tortures, and the most loathsome and noisome abominations, that his fervid imagination could concoct —C.W.Eliot⟩ HORRIFIC is close to HORRIBLE but may stress actual effect rather than the potential effect of the latter ⟨that *horrific* yarn "The Body-Snatcher" —C.E.Montague⟩ ⟨there was a *horrific*, splitting, tearing roar, and then I knew no more —A.C.Whitehead⟩ SHOCKING is a milder term applying to what startles, esp. as contrary to expectations, taste, sensibilities, or morality ⟨his face has been terribly mutilated, and — what seems even more *shocking* — the poor fellow's hands have been cut right off at the wrists —Dorothy Sayers⟩ ⟨the *shocking* realities of a world in which the principles of common humanity and common decency are being mowed down by the firing squads of the Gestapo —F.D.Roosevelt⟩ APPALLING describes what terrifies and also dismays or dumbfounds ⟨a huge bomb had . . . gone off with such *appalling* violence that it killed thirty people outright and injured hundreds —F.L.Allen⟩ ⟨an *appalling* exhaustion rendered her helpless —Arnold Bennett⟩ DIRE applies to the extremely fearful and dread or ominous ⟨prophets of the downfall of American democracy have seen their *dire* predictions come to naught —F.D.Roosevelt⟩ ⟨the *dire* possibilities of a head-on collision —O.S.Nock⟩ ⟨wolves ran in ferocious packs, *dire* wolves, larger than any wolf man has seen —Marjory S. Douglas⟩ **syn** see in addition AFRAID
fear·ful·ly \-f(ə)lē, -li\ *adv* [ME *ferfulli*, fr. *ferful* fearful + *-li* -ly] **:** in a fearful manner — usu. used as a generalized intensifier with the force of a superlative ⟨~ talented people —Harvey Breit⟩ ⟨a ~ difficult role —Winthrop Sargeant⟩ ⟨a ~ hot day⟩
fear·ful·ness \-fəlnəs\ *n* -ES **1 :** the quality or state of being afraid **:** TIMIDITY **2 :** the quality of causing fear or awe **:** DREADFULNESS
fear·less \'fi(ə)rləs, -iəl-\ *adj* **1 :** marked by freedom from fear and by resolution in braving dangers **:** not timid **:** BOLD ⟨a ~ soldier⟩ ⟨a less courageous man would have hesitated, but Parker was utterly ~ —V.L.Parrington⟩ **2** *obs* **:** looked upon without fear **:** HARMLESS **syn** see BRAVE
fear·less·ly *adv* **:** in a fearless manner ⟨advanced ~ upon the enemy⟩
fear·less·ness *n* -ES **:** the quality or state of being without fear **:** BRAVERY
fearnought *also* **fearnaught** \'=,=\ *n* -s [²*fear* + *nought, naught*] **1 :** a thick heavy overcoating that is made of wool often mixed with shoddy and that has a rough shaggy face; *also* **:** a garment made of this material — called also *dreadnought* **2 a :** a machine for disentangling woolen fiber prior to carding that consists usu. of one large cylinder with hooked teeth and several worker and stripper rollers **b :** a picker preceding the card
fears *pl of* FEAR, *pres 3d sing of* FEAR
fear·some \'fi(ə)rsəm, -iəs-\ *adj* **1 a :** arousing or likely to arouse fear, fright, or terror ⟨a ~ monster⟩ ⟨a ~ place it is, with a straight drop to the sea, hundreds of feet below —C.B. Nordhoff & J.N.Hall⟩ ⟨a shadowy garret; sordid, dark, and ~ —John Mason Brown⟩ **b :** AWE-INSPIRING — often used as a generalized intensifier with the force of a superlative ⟨the moment had a magical and ~ quality⟩ ⟨he had a ~ sincerity that made good manners seem false —Mary McCarthy⟩ ⟨she had acquired a perfectly ~ artificial tact —Mary M. Colum⟩ **2 :** TIMID, TIMOROUS ⟨a little ~ beast⟩ ⟨the ~ cook did not like dogs —Virginia D. Dawson & Betty D. Wilson⟩ — **fear·some·ly** *adv* — **fear·some·ness** *n*
fea·si·bil·i·ty \,fēzə'biləd-ē, -lətē, -i\ *n* -ES **:** the quality of being feasible **:** PRACTICABILITY ⟨a plan so complex its ~ was doubtful⟩ ⟨established the ~ of polar flying —*Current Biog.*⟩
fea·si·ble \'fēzəbəl\ *adj* [ME *faisible*, fr. MF, fr. *fais-* (stem of *faire* to make, do), fr. L *facere*) + *-ible* — more at DO] **1 :** capable of being done, executed, or effected **:** possible of realization ⟨irradiation of pork is simple, rapid, commercially ~ and sanitary —*Biol. Abstracts*⟩ ⟨a ~ method⟩ ⟨a ~ plan⟩ **2 :** capable of being managed, utilized, or dealt with successfully **:** SUITABLE ⟨all odd moments were spent upon the links, in any garment ~ to the opportunity —Clive Arden⟩ ⟨coal, oil, and waterfalls are the most ~ sources of power in sight at present —C.C.Furnas⟩ **3 :** REASONABLE, LIKELY ⟨gave an explanation that seemed ~ enough⟩ **syn** see POSSIBLE
fea·si·ble·ness *n* -ES **:** the quality or state of being feasible ⟨spent an hour discussing the ~ of the plan for city improvement⟩
fea·si·bly \-blē, -li\ *adv* **:** in a feasible manner
¹feast \'fēst\ *n* -s [ME *feste* festival, holiday, feast, fr. OF, festival, fr. L *festa* (neut. pl.), fr. neut. pl. of *festus* solemn, festal; akin to L *fanum* temple, *feriae* holidays, Arm *dikʻ* gods] **1 a :** an elaborate meal often accompanied by a ceremony or entertainment **:** BANQUET **b :** something partaken of or shared in with delight **:** something highly agreeable and usu. sumptuous ⟨the ~ of reason —Alexander Pope⟩ ⟨a ~ for the eyes⟩ **2 :** a religious festival of rejoicing as opposed to a fast **a :** a holy day set apart annually for solemn commemoration (as of an event in the life of Christ) ⟨the ~ of the Nativity⟩ **b :** an anniversary marked out in the church calendar for special services or devotions ⟨the ~ of Corpus Christi⟩ **3** *archaic* **:** FEASTING, FESTIVITY
²feast \"\ *vb* -ED/-ING/-S [ME *festen*, fr. *feste*, n.] *vi* **1 :** to have or take part in a feast **:** dine on rich provisions **2 :** to enjoy some unusual pleasure or delight **~** *vt* **1 :** to present a feast to **:** entertain lavishly esp. by a banquet ⟨we were ~*ed* on filet mignon and strawberry shortcake⟩ **2 :** DELIGHT, GRATIFY ⟨~*ing* our eyes on the colors and contours of the landscape in autumn⟩ **3 :** to commemorate annually and with religious ceremonies — **feast·er** *n*
feast day *n* [ME *feste day*, fr. *feste* festival + *day*] **:** a day set as a commemorative festival; *esp* **:** a periodic religious festival
feast·ful \'fēstfəl\ *adj* [ME *festful*, fr. *feste* festival + *-ful*] *archaic* **:** devoted to feasting **:** FESTIVE, FESTAL ⟨~ days —John Milton⟩
feast of booths *usu cap F&B* **:** SUKKOTH
feast of dedication *usu cap F&D* **:** HANUKKAH
feast of fools *usu cap both Fs* [trans. of ML *festum stultorum*] **:** a medieval burlesque festival held esp. in France usu. on the feast of the Circumcision (January 1), a prominent feature being mummeries such as a burlesque of the high mass conducted by the lower clergy under a leader elected for the occasion with a burlesque title
feast of ingathering *usu cap F&I* **:** SUKKOTH
feast of lanterns *usu cap F&L* **1 :** a Chinese annual festival on the 15th day of the 1st month according to the old Chinese calendar that is the concluding part of the new-year celebration **2 :** ²BON
feast of lights *usu cap F&L* **:** HANUKKAH
feast of lots *usu cap F&L* **:** PURIM
feast of orthodoxy *usu cap F&O* **:** a solemn feast of the Eastern Orthodox Church celebrated on the first Sunday of Lent and commemorating the victory over iconoclasm, the restoration of images to churches, and the victory over all heresies
feast of tabernacles *usu cap F&T* **:** SUKKOTH
feast of unleavened bread *usu cap F&U&B* **:** an ancient 7-day agricultural feast marked by the offering of new grain to the Lord which began on the 15th day of the 1st month, the day after the 1st day of the Passover, and finally became one continuous festival with the Passover
feast of weeks *usu cap F&W* **:** SHABUOTH
feast-or-famine \'=·=·'=·=\ *adj* **:** marked by extremes (as of success and failure or prosperity and depression) ⟨ski-area operators agree that theirs is uniquely a *feast-or-famine* business —William Gilman⟩ ⟨it follows . . . that mineral exploitation is a *feast-or-famine* industry —H.A.Meyerhoff⟩
¹feat \'fēt, *usu* -ēd-+V\ *n* -s [ME *fait, fet* action, act, deed, fr. MF, deed, fr. L *factum*, fr. neut. of *factus*, past part. of *facere* to make, do — more at DO] **1** *obs* **a :** TECHNIQUE, KNACK, SKILL **b :** a deed or act of a specialized kind **c :** skilled or specialized activity **:** PROFESSION **2 a :** ACT, DEED **b :** a deed notable esp. for courage **:** a heroic achievement **:** EXPLOIT ⟨a story of knights and ~s in arms⟩ ⟨the amazing ~s of ordinary foot soldiers⟩ **c :** an act or product of skill, endurance, dexterity, or ingenuity **:** ACCOMPLISHMENT ⟨~s of an acrobat⟩ ⟨~s of scholarship⟩ ⟨a difficult engineering ~⟩
²feat \"\ *adj* -ER/-EST [ME *fete, fayt*, fr. MF *fait* made (past part. of *faire* to make, do), fr. L *factus*, past part. of *facere*] **1** *now dial Eng* **:** SUITABLE, FITTING, APPROPRIATE **2** *now dial Brit* **a :** clever and graceful **b :** DEXTEROUS, ADROIT **3** *now dial Brit* **a :** attractively neat **:** TRIM **b** *of dress* **:** BECOMING **4** *obs* **:** AFFECTED, OVERNICE **syn** see DEXTEROUS
¹feath·er \'fet͟hə(r)\ *n* -s [ME *fether*, fr. OE; akin to OHG *fedara* wing, ON *fjöthr* feather, L *petere* to go to or toward, seek, Gk *petesthai* to fly, *piptein* to fall, *pteron* wing, feather, Skt *patati* he flies, falls] **1 a :** one of the light horny epidermal outgrowths that form the external covering of the body of birds and the greater part of the surface of their wings, that arise from the surface epidermis of vascular dermal papillae lying in depressed follicles, and that consist of a shaft divided into a hollow proximal quill and a distal rachis furrowed on one side, filled with a pithy substance, and bearing on each side a series of somewhat obliquely directed barbs which bear barbules which in turn bear barbicels commonly ending in hooked hamuli and interlocking with the barbules of an adjacent barb to link the barbs into a continuous vane — see AFTERSHAFT, DOWN, FILOPLUME, PINFEATHER, PTERYLA **b** *feathers pl, obs* **:** WINGS ⟨set ~s to thy heels —Shak.⟩ **c** (1) *obs* **:** PLUMAGE (2) **:** ATTIRE, DRESS, CLOTHES — usu. used in pl. **d** (1) *archaic* **:** a decorative crest or badge consisting of a feather or group of feathers **:** PLUME — often used in pl. (2) **:** a foaming crest of a wave **e** (1) *obs* **:** BIRD (2) *archaic* **:** feathered game **f :** the vane of an arrow — see ARROW illustration **2 :** a feathery tuft or fringe of hair; *specif* **:** a fringe of long hair (as that on the legs of certain dogs or horses) — see DOG illustration **3 a :** something extremely light or insignificant ⟨so frightened that he shied at ~s⟩ ⟨you could have knocked me over with a ~⟩ **b** [by shortening] **:** FEATHERWEIGHT **4 :** KIND, NATURE, SPECIES ⟨the typical tavern-keeper was a panderer, a thief, and an all-around rascal and . . . his clients were of the same ~ —L.C. Douglas⟩ **5 a :** CONDITION, TRIM, FETTLE ⟨feeling in fine ~ on the day of the race⟩ **b :** MOOD, SPIRITS ⟨woke up in good ~⟩ **6 :** a projecting strip, rib, fin, or flange: as **a :** a strength-

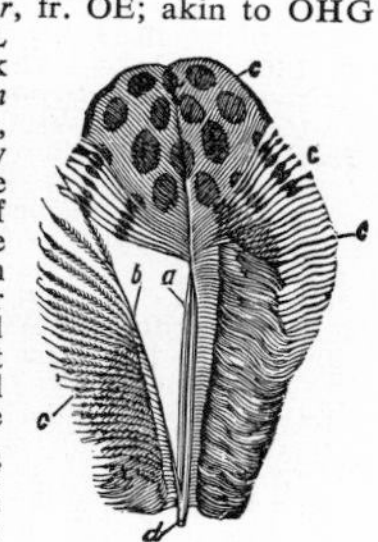

feather 1a: *a* shaft with some of the barbs cut away from the left, *b* aftershaft with barbs cut away on the right, *c* barbs, *d* quill

ening rib, web, or bracket **b** : a tongue fixed or cut (as in the edge of a board) to fit into a corresponding groove (as in another board) to make a flush joint without nails, screws, or pegs : FEATHER KEY **7** : a feathery flaw in the eye or in a precious stone **8 a** : the act of feathering an oar **b** : the angular adjustment of an oar blade as it leaves the water **9** : one of two wedge-shaped short metal rods curved at the upper end and driven into a hole drilled in rock and forced apart by another rod driven in between them in order to split the rock **10** : the wake made by the periscope of a submarine running submerged — **a feather in one's cap** : an honor, a trophy, or a mark of distinction : a notable accomplishment ⟨it was *a feather in the governor's cap* that he had stayed above corruption throughout his term⟩

²**feather** \"\ *vb* **feathered**; **feathered**; **feathering** \-t͟h(ə)riŋ\ **feathers** [ME *fetheren*, fr. OE *gefetheran*, *gefitherian*, fr. *fether*, n. — more at ¹FEATHER] *vt* **1** *obs* : to give wings to; *also* : to help to speed **2 a** : to furnish with a feather (as an arrow or a cap) **b** : to cover, clothe, or adorn with or as if with feathers ⟨birches and oaks still ~*ed* the narrow ravines —Sir Walter Scott⟩ ⟨red-*feathered* skies —Virginia Woolf⟩ **3 a** : to reduce the edge of to the fineness of a featheredge esp. by cutting, shaving, or wearing away **b** : to thin and cut (the hair) in short tapered lengths **c** : to spread out (as paint) esp. around the edges of a particular area in order to blend in with adjoining matter **4 a** (1) *of a bird* : to cut (the air) with a wing (2) *of a fish* : to cut (the water) with a fin **b** : to turn (an oar or paddle blade) parallel to the surface of the water during recovery to eliminate air resistance **c** *aeronautics* (1) : to rotate (propeller blades) so that the chords become approximately parallel to the thrust axis thus reducing drag and preventing windmilling in case of engine failure; *also* : to rotate the propeller blades of (an engine) in such a manner (2) *in a rotary-wing aircraft* : to increase and decrease periodically the angle of incidence of (a rotor blade) by rotation about the axis to equalize the lift produced by advancing and retreating blades in forward flight **5 a** : to dye (fur) by applying dye to the top hairs with a feather **b** : to apply a slip decoration to in ceramics by light brushing **6** : to join by a tongue and groove **7** : to adjust (the main light) in photographic portraiture so that the subject is illuminated by the outer part of the light beam ~ *vi* **1** : to grow or form feathers : become fledged — often used with *out* ⟨birds ~*ing out*⟩ **2** : to have or take on the appearance of a feather or something feathered : grow or spread to give the effect of something feathered **3** *of a hound* : to move the stern nervously from side to side (as in searching for a trail) **4** : to soak in and spread : BLUR — used of writing in ink or a printed impression on soft or unsized paper **5** : to feather an oar or an airplane propeller blade **6** : to produce branches or laterals **7** : to spread and thin out esp. at the edges — often used with *away* or *out* ⟨bits of smoke began to ~ away from the top of the hill —Walt Sheldon⟩ **8** : to form a shape resembling a feather in emerging ⟨the soaring white streams that ~*ed* from the nozzles of the swarming fireboats —Robert O'Brien⟩ —**feather one's nest** : to provide for oneself esp. reprehensibly while in a position of trust (as from property confided to one's care) ⟨this genius at fund raising was also able to *feather his nest* most adequately by an adroit manipulation of the nation's funds with his own —Sidney Warren⟩

³**feather** \"\ *adj* [¹*feather*] : consisting of or resembling a feather : having a feather : composed of or containing feathers ⟨a ~ edge to the board⟩ ⟨a ~ pillow⟩

feather alum *n* **1** : HALOTRICHITE **2** : ALUNOGEN

feather ball *n* : a low tuberculate Mexican cactus (*Neomammillaria plumosa*) with white feathery spines

feather bed *n* [ME *fetherbed*, fr. *fether* feather + ¹*bed* — more at FEATHER] **1 a** : a feather mattress **b** : a bed having a feather mattress **2** : a markedly easy and comfortable state or position : SINECURE **3** : a bed often formed in pools and shallow lakes by the crowded growth of stoneworts; *also* : a stonewort of the genus *Chara*

¹**featherbed** \ˈ==ˌ=\ *adj* : calling for, requiring, or sanctioning featherbedding ⟨a ~ rule⟩ : created by or resulting from featherbedding ⟨a ~ job⟩

²**featherbed** \"\ *vi* **1** : to require more workmen than are strictly needed or a placing of workmen in nonproductive or unnecessary jobs or a limiting of productive output under a featherbed rule **2** : to do featherbed work or to put in time in a featherbed job or under a featherbed rule ~ *vt* **1** : to bring under a featherbed rule ⟨many tasks are *featherbedded* to employ two craftsmen . . . where one would do —*Time*⟩ **2** : to assist or stimulate (as an industry or an economy) by government aid

featherbedding \ˈ==ˌ==\ *n* [fr. gerund of ²*featherbed*] : the requiring of an employer usu. under a union rule or by safety statute to pay more employees than are needed for a particular operation or to pay full wages for nonproductive labor or unnecessary or duplicating jobs or made-work or for output artificially restricted below normal working capacity

feather bell *n* : FEATHER-FLEECE

feather boarding *n* : featheredged boarding

featherbone \ˈ==ˌ=\ *or* **featherboning** \ˈ==ˌ==\ *n* : a corset bone made from the quills of domestic fowl or of plastic

featherbrain \ˈ==ˌ=\ *n* : a foolish scatterbrained person

featherbrained \ˈ==ˈ=\ *adj* [¹*feather* + *brained*] : not very bright : FOOLISH, FRIVOLOUS ⟨too ridiculous and ~ a man for any position of responsibility⟩

feather bunchgrass *n* : a sparingly branched feather grass (*Stipa viridula*) with a narrow erect panicle that is densely flowered from near the base

feather coral *n* [so called fr. the appearance of the septa] : TETRACORAL

feather crotch *n* : a feathery pattern in the grain of veneer cut from the crotch

feathercut \ˈ==ˌ=\ *n* : a style of cutting women's and girls' hair in short tapered lengths that shape into small curls with a feathery effect at the tips

feather dance *n*, *often cap F&D* : a ceremonial dance of eastern woodland Amerinds in which male participants orig. carried feathered wands

feather duster *n* : a dusting brush made of feathers

feathered *adj* [fr. past part. of ²*feather*] : resembling or suggesting a feather: as **a** : having feathery tufts or markings that are shaped like a feather ⟨~ asparagus⟩ **b** : shaved thin on the edge ⟨a ~ board⟩

feathered columbine *also* **feather columbine** *n* **1** : an Old World meadow rue (*Thalictrum aquilegifolium*) with foliage resembling that of the columbine **2** : EARLY MEADOW RUE

feather duster

¹**featheredge** \ˈ==ˌ=\ *n* **1 a** : a very thin sharp edge; *esp* : one that is easily broken or bent over like the edge of a feather **b** : such an edge that is bent or curled over on a cutting tool **2 a** : a thin edge of a board of triangular or trapezoidal section **b** : a board with one edge thinner than the other **3** : DECKLE EDGE **4** : the thin edge of a gravel road built on a flat subgrade, the thickness of the gravel surface being gradually increased from the edges to the center line **5** : a blurred edge (as of a written or printed character) caused by feathering **6** : a fringe of hair; *esp* : a thin narrow fringe at the nape of the neck

²**featheredge** \"\ *vt* **1 a** : to produce a featheredge upon **b** : to make into a featheredge ⟨the thin boards were *featheredged* for clapboards⟩ **2** : to smooth out one edge of as thin as possible ⟨~ the new paint along the edge of the painted area⟩ **3** : to make the edge of (a photograph) thin (as by cutting, tearing, or sandpapering) so as to match smoothly with other photographs in a mosaic

³**featheredge** \"\ *adj* **1** : FEATHEREDGED **2** : consisting of or being a featheredge

featheredge file *n* [*featheredge* fr. ³*feather* + *edge*] : a file of narrow rhomboidal or double half-round section

featheredger \ˈ==ˌ==\ *n* [*feather edge* (fr. ³*feather* + *edge*) + *-er*] : FEATHERER

feathered serpent *n* : the symbolic representation of Quetzalcoatl, one of the chief Aztec gods

feathered shot *n* : FEATHER SHOT

feath·er·er \ˈfet͟hərə(r)\ *n* -s : a worker who feathers the edges of shoe welts to leave the edge of the outsole more accessible for trimming — called also *featheredger*

feather fern *n* : a Japanese herb (*Astilbe japonica*) with feathery compound leaves and paniculate white flowers

feath·er·few \ˈfet͟hə(r),fyü\ *n* -s [ME *fetherfewe* feverfew, centaury, modif. (influenced by *fether* feather) of (assumed) AF *fevrefue*, fr. LL *febrifugia* centaury — more at FEBRIFUGE, FEATHER] *chiefly dial* : FEVERFEW

feather–fleece \ˈ==ˌ=\ *n* : a bulbous often branched leafy plant (*Stenanthium robustum*) of the family Liliaceae with linear leaves, linear lanceolate perianth segments, and winged seeds

featherfoil \ˈ==ˌ=\ *n* [¹*feather* + *foil* (leaf)] : a plant of the genus *Hottonia*

feather–footed \ˈ==ˈ==\ *adj* : moving very lightly and silently ⟨*feather-footed* dancers⟩

feather geranium *n* : JERUSALEM OAK 1

feather germ *n* : the undifferentiated feather forming a dermal papilla in the skin of a bird

feather grass *n* **1** : a grass of the genus *Stipa* (esp. the European *S. pennata*) **2** : a grass (*Leptochloa filiformis*) of the southern U.S. and tropical America

featherhead \ˈ==ˌ=\ *n* : a foolish or scatterbrained person ⟨that ultraprofound look of the pretty ~ who suddenly turns serious —J.B.Priestley⟩

featherheaded \ˈ==ˈ==\ *adj* [¹*feather* + *headed*] : being a featherhead : markedly not bright : FOOLISH, SCATTERBRAINED ⟨grown into one of the most ~ of her sex —*New Statesman & Nation*⟩

featherier *comparative of* FEATHERY

featheriest *superlative of* FEATHERY

feath·er·i·ness \ˈfet͟h(ə)rēnə̇s, -rin-\ *n* -ES : the quality or state of being feathery or extremely light

feathering *n* -s [partly fr. ¹*feather* + *-ing*, partly fr. gerund of ²*feather*] **1 a** : a covering of feathers : PLUMAGE; *collectively* : FEATHERS **b** : a style in which feathers are attached to the shafts of arrows; *also* : the feathers of an arrow **2** : a fringe of hair (as on the legs of a dog) **3** : FOLIATION 5 **4** : a shaving or small bit of cinnamon bark **5** : a process in which the fat in homogenized milk precipitates or flocculates at the surface of hot coffee or tea; *also* : the precipitate so formed **6** : photographic illumination by means of feathering

feathering screw *n* [*feathering* fr. gerund of ²*feather*] : a screw propeller on a ship the blades of which may be moved while revolving to alter the pitch, to reverse the ship, or to move edgeways through the water

feather joint *n* **1** : a joint formed by making a mating groove in each of the contiguous pieces and inserting a feather in the opening formed when the pieces are butted together **2** : one of a set of joints that are developed by shear and tension in a zone of deformation of the earth's crust (as along a fault) and that resemble in pattern the barbs and shaft of a feather

feather key *n*, *in machinery* : a sunk key without taper that is permanently fixed in one of the connected pieces and that is a sliding fit in a keyway in the other so as to permit relative longitudinal motion — called also *spline*

featherleaf cedar \ˈ==ˌ=-\ *n* : AMERICAN ARBORVITAE

feather–legged *US usu* ˈ==ˌlegə̇d, *Brit usu* -gd\ *adj* **1** *of a domestic fowl* : having feathers on the outer surface of the shank and usu. extending onto the outer or outer and middle toe **2** *South & Midland* : unwilling to fight : COWARDLY

feath·er·less \ˈfet͟h(ə)rlə̇s\ *adj* [ME *fetherles*, fr. *fether* feather + *-les* -less] : having no feathers — **feath·er·less·ness** *n* -ES

featherlight \ˈ==ˈ=\ *adj* : extremely light ⟨he hung on tenaciously, his body ~ —I.L.Idriess⟩ ⟨operated by a ~ touch —*advt.*⟩

feath·er·man \ˈ==mən, -ˌman\ *n*, *pl* **feathermen** [ME *fetherman*, fr. *fether* feather + *man* — more at FEATHER] : a tradesman or hawker of former times who dealt in feathers or plumes

feather merchant *n*, *slang* : one in a position that involves little effort or responsibility or that calculatedly evades effort or responsibility : LOAFER

feather mite *n* : any of several small mites living on the feathers and feeding on the blood of domestic and wild birds

feather mosaic *n* : FEATHERWORK

feather moss *n* [so called fr. the feathery branches] : a moss of *Hypnum* or related genera

feather ore *n* : a capillary or fibrous form of jamesonite

feather out *vi* : to end irregularly (as of a lenticular rock formation)

feather palm *n* : a palm with pinnate leaves

featherpate \ˈ==ˌ=\ *n* : FEATHERHEAD

featherpated \ˈ==ˈ==\ *adj* : FEATHERHEADED

feather picking *n* : a common vice of young chickens and turkeys involving pecking at or pulling the developing feathers of other members of the flock, a practice that is related to and may lead to cannibalism

feather poke *n* [¹*feather* + *poke* (bag)] *dial Eng* : any of several birds that line their pocket-shaped nests with feathers (as the long-tailed titmouse)

feather rot *n* : a common rot of both dead and living tree trunks caused by a fungus (*Poria subacida*) and characterized by the white stringy or spongy nature of the rotted tissue

feathers *pl of* FEATHER, *pres 3d sing of* FEATHER

feather shot *n* : copper granulated by being poured molten into cold water

feather star *n* [so called fr. the superficial resemblance of the arms to feathers] : COMATULID

¹**featherstitch** \ˈ==ˌ=\ *n* : an embroidery stitch consisting of a line of diagonal blanket stitches worked alternately to the left and right

²**featherstitch** \"\ *vb* : to embroider in featherstitch

feather tip *n* : a very thin end in lumber (as in certain grades of shingles)

feather–tongue \ˈ==ˌ=\ *vt* : to make with a tongue fitting a groove

feathertop \ˈ==ˌ=\ *or* **feathertop grass** *n* : any of several grasses having feathery panicles (as members of the genera *Pennisetum* and *Calamagrostis*)

featherstitch

feather tract *n* : PTERYLA

feather tree *n* **1** : SMOKE TREE 1a **2** : a mountain mahogany (*Cercocarpus montanus*) that is usu. a low spreading evergreen shrub, is widely distributed in interior uplands of western No. America, and is a major browse plant over much of its range

feather tye \ˈ==ˌtī\ *n* [¹*feather* + E dial. *tye* tick (of a mattress or pillow), perh. fr. ME, small box, case, fr. OE *tēag*] *dial* : FEATHER BED 1

featherweed \ˈ==ˌ=\ *n* **1** : CATFOOT **2** : a red alga of the genus *Ptilota*

¹**featherweight** \ˈ==ˌ=\ *n* **1** : a very light weight; *specif* : the lightest weight a racehorse may carry in a handicap **2** : one that is very light in weight: as **a** : a boxer or wrestler of a weight falling within a fixed class of very light body weights: (1) : a professional boxer weighing between 118 and 120 lbs — compare BANTAMWEIGHT, FLYWEIGHT, HEAVYWEIGHT, MIDDLEWEIGHT, WELTERWEIGHT (2) : an intercollegiate boxer weighing between 125 and 134 lbs (3) : a wrestler weighing between 123 and 134 lbs **b** (1) : a paper that is bulky but light in weight (as some book papers) (2) : a paper that is light in weight (as some thin writing papers) **3** : a person that is not very bright : FEATHERBRAIN ⟨a giant on the football field but a ~ in the classroom⟩

²**featherweight** \"\ *adj* **1** : constituting or being a featherweight : extremely light in weight ⟨a ~ boxer⟩ ⟨a bicycle of ~ construction⟩ **2** : very light or careful in touch or handling ⟨the book is ~ in its treatment of the incendiary theme⟩ **3** : of small significance ⟨a ~ comedy⟩ ⟨a ~ but charming novel —*New Yorker*⟩

featherwood \ˈ==ˌ=\ *n* **1** : an Australian timber tree (*Polyosma cunninghamii*) of the family Escalloniaceae **2** : the wood of the featherwood resembling hickory — called also *hickory*

featherwork \ˈ==ˌ=\ *n* **1** : a net or fabric completely covered with overlapping feathers usu. having a design — called also *feather mosaic* **2** : the art or method of making featherwork

feath·ery \ˈfet͟h(ə)rē, -ri\ *adj*, *often* -ER/-EST **1** : resembling or suggesting a feather, a bunch of feathers, or the barbs of a feather in shape, texture, quality, or weight: as **a** : light and delicate ⟨a ~ touch on the piano keys⟩ : almost weightless and delicately unsubstantial ⟨~ snow⟩ ⟨~ ash⟩ **b** : delicately marked or flecked as if with a feather or in a way resembling feather markings ⟨a ~ sky⟩ : marked by delicate tracery or extremely lightly applied decoration or decorative elements ⟨an orchestra playing with a ~ elegance⟩ **c** : light and fluffy ⟨~ pastry⟩ **d** : fanning out gracefully and delicately like feathers in a plume ⟨~ palm trees⟩ **2** : covered with or as if with feathers ⟨joined the ~ congregation of jays⟩ ⟨a ~ landscape⟩

¹**feat·ly** \ˈfētlē, -li\ *adv* [ME *fetly*, fr. *fete*, *fayt* suitable + *-ly* — more at FEAT] **1 a** : FITLY, PROPERLY **b** : neatly and beautifully ⟨a chick ~ feathered in royal scarlet —Llewelyn Powys⟩ **2** : gracefully and nimbly or dexterously ⟨foot it ~ here and there —Shak.⟩ ⟨convinced that a conductor should handle himself as ~ as his orchestra —*Time*⟩ **3** : SKILLFULLY

²**featly** \"\ *adj*, *often* -ER/-EST **1** : GRACEFUL ⟨one of the lead horses . . . lifting his forefeet in ~ fashion —Howard Taubman⟩ **2** *obs* : neat and comely; *also* : APPROPRIATE, JUST, FITTING

feat·ness *n* -ES *now dial Brit* : the quality or state of being feat

feats *pl of* FEAT

¹**fea·ture** \ˈfēchə(r)\ *n* -s [ME *feture*, fr. MF *faiture*, *feture*, fr. L *factura* act of making, formation, fr. *factus* (past part. of *facere* to make, do) + *-ura* -ure — more at DO] **1 a** : the makeup, structure, form, or outward appearance of a person or thing ⟨a man of large ~⟩ **b** *obs* : a part of the body : LIMB **c** : something that goes to make up something else : ELEMENT, PART, CONSTITUENT ⟨a ~ of English grammar is the number of periphrastic forms⟩ ⟨it is also possible to hear ~*s* of pitch and intonation —Stanley Newman⟩ ⟨this course teaches the student the ~*s*, operation, and care of darkroom equipment —*Bull. of Meharry Med. Coll.*⟩ ⟨it was a bad evening from then on, its only good ~ being its shortness —Lloyd Alexander⟩ **2 a** : the makeup or cast of the face or its parts : facial aspect or appearance ⟨stern of ~ even when he smiled⟩ **b** (1) : a part of the face : LINEAMENT ⟨a man with oriental ~*s*⟩ ⟨her head . . . seems too small for her generous ~*s* —*Time*⟩ (2) **features** *pl* : FACE, COUNTENANCE ⟨an embarrassed blush on his ~*s*⟩ **c** *obs* : physical beauty ⟨cheated of ~ by dissembling nature —Shak.⟩ **d** : distinctive outline, form, or quality ⟨could not well describe the ~*s* of the painting⟩ ⟨an experience with no special or distinctive ~⟩ **3** *archaic* : a shape or a thing with form : a visible form : APPARITION **4 a** : a marked element of something : something that is esp. prominent : PECULIARITY, CHARACTERISTIC ⟨sparse pine growth was a ~ of the landscape⟩ **b** : something offered to the public or to a clientele that is exhibited or advertised as particularly attractive : a special inducement: as (1) : a distinctive, prominent, or unusual article, story, or picture (as one with strong emotional or human-interest appeal) in a newspaper or periodical ⟨an account of the fire was a ~ of the Sunday supplement⟩; *esp* : a newspaper story that consists of background or analysis or that depends on unusual treatment as contrasted with a straight news story (2) : a special department in a newspaper or periodical ⟨detailed weather reports are a ~ of the morning paper⟩ (3) : the main presentation in a program at a motion-picture theater : a film of considerable length presented as the main attraction at a theater **5** : an evidence of human occupation (as a house floor, fire pit, or storage pit) encountered in archaeological excavation

²**feature** \"\ *vb* **featured**; **featured**; **featuring** \-ch(ə)riŋ\ **features** *vt* **1** *now dial* : to resemble in features : FAVOR **2** : to be a feature of ⟨another performance of the Haydn Mass . . . *featured* our stop in Atlanta —R.K.Leopold⟩ ⟨agricultural radicalism *featured* the period from 1880 to 1896 —C.A.M. Ewing⟩ **3** : to picture or portray in the mind : IMAGINE ⟨can you ~ wearing a necktie out here —K.M.Dodson⟩ **4 a** : to make a feature of : give special prominence to ⟨the newspaper *featured* the story of the murder⟩ ⟨the theater was *featuring* a murder-mystery film⟩ **b** : to be marked by : have as a characteristic or feature ⟨the string quartets ~ a style more characteristic of the last century than this one⟩ **c** : to provide with a special feature ⟨their annual Blossom Festival, *featured* by parades, balls, concerts —*Amer. Guide Series: Mich.*⟩ ~ *vi* : to play a significant part : comprise a feature ⟨other lesser-known figures who ~ in the book —*Times Lit. Supp.*⟩ ⟨a Ten-Year Plan in which . . . urgently needed rehousing, hydroelectric, and other development schemes were intended to ~ largely —*New Statesman & Nation*⟩

³**feature** \"\ *adj* : being a special or main attraction : constituting a feature ⟨a ~ story on candidates' wives⟩ ⟨a ~ performer⟩ ⟨a ~ picture⟩

fea·tured \-chə(r)d\ *adj* [ME *fetured*, fr. *feture* feature + *-ed* — more at ¹FEATURE] **1** *obs* : SHAPED, FASHIONED **b** : well shaped : attractive of appearance **2 a** : provided with form or lineaments (as by carving) **b** : having facial features of a particular kind — usu. used in combination ⟨a grim-*featured* man⟩ ⟨a heavy-*featured* face⟩ ⟨a sharp-*featured* woman⟩ **3** [fr. past part. of ²*feature*] : displayed, advertised, or presented as a feature ⟨a ~ attraction⟩ ⟨a ~ story⟩; *or* **b** : given special prominence : STARRING ⟨a ~ actor⟩

fea·ture·less \ˈfēchə(r)lə̇s\ *adj* **1** : having no distinct or distinctive features ⟨the top is largely ~ plateau —*London Calling*⟩ ⟨the long ~ months with no special credit or romance —Mary Webb⟩ ⟨vast tracts of ~ ocean —W.H.Dowdeswell⟩ **2** : inactive and without any material price change — used of business or market activity

fea·ture·ly \-lē,-li\ *adj* : HANDSOME ⟨~ warriors of Christian chivalry —S.T.Coleridge⟩

fea·tur·ette \ˌfēchəˈret\ *n* -s **1** : a short feature film **2** : SHORT 8e

fea·tur·ish \ˈfēch(ə)rish\ *adj* : having the quality or some of the qualities usu. marking a feature article in a newspaper : tending to use eye-catching or sensational matter or devices in the presentation of news

¹**feaze** *var of* FEEZE

²**feaze** \ˈfāz, ˈfēz\ *vi* -ED/-ING/-S [prob. fr. obs. D *vase*, *vese* fringe, frayed edge, fr. MD — more at FASH] **1** *dial Brit* : to become frayed — usu. used with *out* ⟨his coat was all *feazed* out at the edges⟩ **2** *dial Brit* : to become rough or jagged at the edges

feazings *n pl* [fr. pl. of *feazing*, gerund of ²*feaze*] : the unlaid end of a rope

febri- *comb form* [LL, fr. L *febris* — more at FEVER] : fever ⟨*febricide*⟩

fe·bric·i·ty \fə̇ˈbrisəd·ē, fēˈ-\ *n* -ES [ML *febricitat-*, *febricitas*, irreg. fr. L *febris* fever + *-itat-*, *-itas* -ity] : the quality or state of being feverish

fe·bric·u·la \-ˈbrikyələ\ *n* -s [L, dim. of *febris*] : a slight and transient fever

fe·brif·ic \-ifik\ *adj* [prob. fr. (assumed) NL *febrificus*, fr. LL *febri-* + L *-ficus* -fic] *archaic* : producing fever

fe·brif·u·gal \fə̇ˈbrif(y)əgəl, fēˈ-, ˌfebrəˈfyügəl\ *adj* [prob. fr. (assumed) NL *febrifuga*, n., febrifuge + E *-al*] : mitigating or removing fever

feb·ri·fuge \ˈfebrə̇ˌfyüj\ *n or adj* [F *fébrifuge*, prob. fr. (assumed) NL *febrifuga*, fr. LL *febrifuga*, *febrifugia* centaury, fr. *febri-* + *-fuga*, *-fugia* (fr. L *fugare* to put to flight) — more at -FUGE] : ANTIPYRETIC

fe·brif·u·gine \fə̇ˈbrifyəˌjēn, fēˈ-, -jə̇n\ *n* -s [NL *febrifuga* (specific epithet of the ch'ang shan *Dichroa febrifuga*) (fr. fem. of — assumed — NL *febrifugus*, adj., antipyretic, fr. — assumed — NL *febrifuga*, n., antipyretic) + E *-ine* — more at FEBRIFUGE] : a toxic emetic crystalline alkaloid $C_{16}H_{19}N_3O_3$ that is obtained from ch'ang shan and is a potent antimalarial

feb·rile \ˈfebrəl, ˈfēb-, -ˌbrīl\ *adj* [ML *febrilis*, fr. L *febris* fever] : of or relating to fever : marked by fever : FEVERISH ⟨a ~ reaction caused by an allergen⟩ ⟨the ~ tempo of the city's social life in winter⟩ ⟨a book obviously written by a talented, ~ intellectual —Janet Flanner⟩

fe·bril·i·ty \fə̇ˈbriləd·ē, fēˈ-, feˈ-, -ətē, -i\ *n* -ES : FEVERISHNESS

fe·bris \ˈfebrə̇s, ˈfāb-\ *n* -ES [L] : FEVER

¹**fe·bro·ni·an** \fə̇ˈbrōnēən\ *adj*, *cap* [Justinus *Febronius* (pseudonym of Johann N. von Hontheim †1790 German

Roman Catholic prelate) + E *-an*] **:** of, relating to, or advocating Febronianism

²febronian \"\ *n* -s *cap* **:** an advocate of Febronianism

fe·bro·ni·an·ism \-ē,nizəm\ *n* -s *usu cap* **:** the principle applied in 1763 to the Roman Catholic Church by Johann N. von Hontheim, suffragan bishop of Treves, that final ecclesiastical authority belongs to the whole church and not merely to the papacy, that papal power is inferior to that of the whole body of the episcopate, and that papal power is limited in matters of doctrine by general church councils and in matters of discipline by national churches

feb·ru·ary \÷'feb(y)ə,wer|ē, |i, 'febrə,wer| *also* ÷-b,wer| *or* ÷-b,rer| *sometimes* ÷-bə,rer| *or* ÷-bwər| *or* ÷-b(ə)r| *or* ÷-brər| *or* ÷-b,yer|\ *n, pl* **februaries** *or* **februarys** *usu cap* [ME *februarie*, fr. L *februarius*, fr. *februa*, pl., feast of purification held on the 15th of February + *-arius* -ary; perh. akin to L *fumus* smoke, vapor — more at FUME] **:** the second month in the Gregorian calendar — abbr. *Feb.*; see MONTH table

february daphne *n, usu cap F* **:** MEZEREON 1

february fill-dike \-'=,=\ *n, usu cap 1st F* **:** FEBRUARY; *also* **:** the period of the sun's occupation of Aquarius according to astrology

feb·ru·a·tion \,febrə'wāshən\ *n* -s [L *februation-, februatio*, fr. *februatus* (past part. of *februare* to purify, fr. *februa*) + *-ion-, -io* -ion] *archaic* **:** purification by a religious ceremony

fec *abbr* [L *fecit*] he made

fe·cal *also* **fae·cal** \'fēkəl\ *adj* [MF *fecal*, fr. L *faec-, faex* dregs, sediment + MF *-al*] **:** of, relating to, being, or involving feces ⟨a ~ mass⟩ ⟨~ egg counts⟩

fe·ca·lith *also* **fae·ca·lith** \-kə,lith\ *n* -s [*fecal* + *-lith*] **:** a concretion of dry compact feces occas. formed in the intestine or vermiform appendix

fe·cal·oid \-kə,lȯid\ *adj* [ISV *fecal* + *-oid*] **:** resembling dung

fe·ces *also* **fae·ces** \'fē(,)sēz\ *n pl* [ME *feces* (pl.), *fece* (sing.), *fex* (sing.), fr. L *faec-, faex* dregs, sediment] **1 :** the sediment formed after infusion or distillation **:** DREGS, REFUSE **2 :** bodily waste discharged through the anus **:** DUNG, MANURE

fech·ne·ri·an \(')fek¦nirēən, -ek¦-\ *adj, usu cap* [Gustav Theodor *Fechner* †1887 Ger. physicist, philosopher, & experimental psychologist + E *-ian*] **:** of, relating to, or discovered by G. T. Fechner, German physicist considered to be a founder of psychophysics and experimental psychology

fech·ner's law \'fek|nə(r)z-, -k|\ *n, usu cap F* **:** WEBER-FECHNER LAW

fecht \'fekt\ *Scot var of* FIGHT

fecial *var of* FETIAL

fe·cit \'fākət\ [L, 3d pers. sing. perf. indic. of *facere* to make, do — more at DO] **:** (he) created or executed (it) — used with the name of the executing artist or craftsman on a painting, piece of sculpture, or other art object or piece of craftsmanship

feck \'fek\ *n* [ME (Sc) *fek*, by shortening & alter. fr. ME ¹*effect*] **1** *Scot* **a :** the greater share **:** MAJORITY — usu. used with *the* ⟨the ~ of the town council didn't fancy his backers —John Buchan⟩ **b :** PART, PORTION ⟨took the best ~ of a year⟩ ⟨sold the best ~ of the litter⟩ **2** *Scot* **:** VALUE, WORTH ⟨no ~ would come from it⟩ **3** *Scot* **:** a number or quantity esp. when large ⟨a whole ~ of them came⟩

feck·et \'fekət\ *n* -s [origin unknown] *Scot* **:** VEST 2a

feck·ful \'fekfəl\ *adj* [*feck* + *-ful*] **1** *chiefly Scot* **:** EFFICIENT, EFFECTIVE **2** *chiefly Scot* **a :** STURDY, TRUSTY **b :** POWERFUL, VIGOROUS — **feck·ful·ly** \-əlē\ *adv, chiefly Scot*

feck·less \-kləs\ *adj* [*feck* + *-less*] **1 a :** weak in mind or body **:** HELPLESS, INCOMPETENT ⟨a pretty, ~ little widow who is not very good at "managing" —*New Statesman & Nation*⟩ **b :** INEFFICIENT ⟨a day of ~ house heating⟩ **2 :** having no real worth or purpose **:** MEANINGLESS, PURPOSELESS ⟨a ~ figurehead⟩ ⟨what strikes most at first, frequently turns out to be ~ —Amy Lowell⟩ ⟨three years of ~ negotiations —*Time*⟩ **3 a :** lazy and worthless ⟨here were failure and defeat visiting the energetic along with the ~, the able along with the unable —F.L.Allen⟩ **b :** indifferent to responsibility **:** UNRELIABLE **4 :** awkward and unskilled **5 :** UNTHINKING, IRRESPONSIBLE ⟨a certain childish, ~ gaiety⟩ **6 :** impractical and shiftless ⟨he was ~, a gambler, a lover of what is called low company, but he was generous —Robert Lynd⟩ — **feck·less·ly** *adv* — **feck·less·ness** *n* -ES

feck·ly \-lī\ *adv* [*feck* + *-ly*] **1** *chiefly Scot* **:** for the most part **2** *chiefly Scot* **:** ALMOST, NEARLY

fec·u·la \'fekyələ\ *n, pl* **fecu·lae** \-,lē\ [NL, fr. *feces* dung (fr. L *faeces*, pl. of *faec-, faex* dregs, sediment) + *-ula*] **:** a fecal pellet of an insect

fec·u·lence \-lən(t)s\ *n* -s [F *féculence*, fr. LL *faeculentia*, fr. *faeculentus* + *-ia* -y] **1 :** something that is feculent **:** SEDIMENT, DREGS, FECES **2 :** the state or quality of being feculent **:** MUDDINESS, FOULNESS

fec·u·len·cy \-nsē, -si\ *n* -ES [LL *faeculentia*] *archaic* **:** FECULENCE

fec·u·lent \-nt\ *adj* [ME, fr. L *faeculentus*, fr. *faec-, faex* dregs, sediment] **:** foul with impurities or excrement **:** covered with filth **:** abounding in sediment or noxious matter **:** FECAL

fe·cund \'fēkənd, 'fek-\ *adj* [ME *fecund*, *fecound*, fr. MF *fecond*, fr. L *fecundus* — more at FEMININE] **1 a :** characterized by having produced many offspring or by having yielded vegetation, fruit, or crops to a marked or satisfying degree ⟨~ pastures⟩ ⟨~ herds⟩ **b :** capable of producing **:** not sterile or barren **:** markedly fertile ⟨born into a notably ~ family⟩ **2 :** marked by noteworthy intellectual productivity and inventiveness ⟨ideas are, in Paris, so far more numerous and ~ ... that Paris has on an average some eighty odd daily papers —W.C.Brownell⟩ ⟨a good part of these inventions came to birth — or were further nourished — in the ~ mind of Leonardo da Vinci —Lewis Mumford⟩ **syn** see FERTILE

fec·un·date \'fēkən,dāt, 'fek-\ *vt* -ED/-ING/-S [L *fecundatus*, past part. of *fecundare* to fertilize, fr. *fecundus* fecund] **1 :** to make fruitful or prolific ⟨a flow of ideas *fecundating* the very atmosphere of the college⟩ **2 :** to make fertile **:** IMPREGNATE ⟨males are needed to ~ the young virgin females —W.C.Allee⟩ ⟨the sterile eggs of reason never *fecundated* by sense —P.E. More⟩ — **fec·un·da·tion** \,==ˈdāshən\ *n* -s

fe·cun·da·tive \fē'kəndəd·iv, 'fekən,dād-, 'fēk-\ *adj* **:** serving to fecundate **:** making fertile

fe·cun·da·tor \'fekən,dād·ə(r), 'fēk-\ *n* -s [LL, fr. L *fecundatus* + *-or*] **:** one that fecundates

fe·cun·da·to·ry \fē'kəndə,tōrē\ *adj* **:** of or relating to fecundation

fe·cun·di·ty \fē'kəndəd·ē, -dətē, -i\ *n* -ES [ME *fecundite*, fr. L *fecunditat-, fecunditas*, fr. *fecundus* fecund + *-itat-, -itas* -ity] **1 a :** the quality or the power of producing fruit esp. in abundance **:** FRUITFULNESS ⟨the ~ of the earth⟩ **b :** productive quality or power ⟨the ~ of the pocket-book publishers —James Rorty⟩ **c :** richness of imagination or invention ⟨the ~ of Shakespeare's genius⟩ **2 a :** the power of producing offspring esp. in large numbers or the quality that conduces to this **:** the potential reproductive capacity (as of a hen) as measured by the individual production of mature eggs and sperm **b :** the power of germinating (as in seeds) **c :** the power or quality of increasing rapidly in number or quantity or of being so increased in number or quantity **3** *archaic* **:** the power of making fruitful or fertile

¹fed \'fed\ *adj* [fr. past part. of *feed*] **1** *of poultry or stock* **:** specially nourished or fattened for market ⟨a deck of ~ lambs averaging about 95 lbs. —*Chicago Daily Drovers Jour.*⟩ **2** *slang* **:** FED UP ⟨~ with people scrounging our liquor before four o'clock —J.H.Burns⟩ — **fed to the gills** *or* **fed to the teeth :** FED UP ⟨*fed to the teeth* with this little pension that you euphemistically call a high-grade resort hotel —R.E. Sherwood⟩

²fed \"\ *n* -s *often cap* [by shortening] **1 :** FEDERAL 1 **2** *slang* **:** FEDERAL 2 ⟨so one night I stole a car and took it over the state line to sell it and the *Feds* got me —H. W. Van Couenhoven⟩

fed *abbr* federal; federated; federation

fedai *sometimes cap, var of* FIDA'I

fedarie *n* -s [alter. (influenced in meaning by L *foeder-, foedus* league) of *feodary*] *obs* **:** CONFEDERATE, ACCOMPLICE

fe·da·yee \fə,da'(y)ē, -dä-, =ˈ=,=\ *n, pl* **feda·yeen** \-ēn\ [Ar *fidā'ī* one who offers himself for his native land, fr. *fidā'* redemption] **:** a member of an Arab commando group esp. operating against Israel

fed·dan \fə'dän, -dan\ *n, pl* **feddan** *or* **feddans** [Ar *faddān* yoke of oxen, feddan] **:** an Egyptian unit of area equal to 1.038 acres

fed·der \'fedə(r)\ *dial Brit var of* FEATHER

fed·e·li·ni \,fedᵊl'ēnē\ *n* -s [It (pl.), alter. of *fidellini*, dim. of It dial. (Genoese) *fidelli* (pl.) vermicelli, prob. fr. Sp *fideos* (pl.), fr. Judeo-Spanish *fidear* to grow, fr. Ar *fāda* to abound, overflow] **:** alimentary paste smaller than vermicelli

fed·er·a·cy \'fed(ə)rəsē\ *n* -ES [prob. back-formation fr. *confederacy*] *archaic* **:** ALLIANCE, CONFEDERACY, FEDERATION

¹fed·er·al \'fed(ə)rəl\ *adj* [L *foeder-, foedus* league, compact + E *-al*; akin to L *fides* faith — more at FAITH] **1 a :** of or relating to a compact, league, or treaty; *esp* **:** of, relating to, or derived from a compact between states which by the terms of the compact surrender their general sovereignty and consolidate into a new state ⟨a ~ union⟩ **b :** of, relating to, or expressing a covenant between God and the human race or its members, esp. the covenant of works and the covenant of grace — compare FEDERAL THEOLOGY **2 a :** of or relating to a state formed by the consolidation of several states which retain limited residuary powers of government under the common sovereignty of the new state **:** being or befitting such a state ⟨some ~ states have political parties peculiar to one area⟩ **b :** of, characterized by, or constituting a form of government in which power is distributed among a number of constituent territorial units ⟨~ governments often evolved out of leagues or confederations —C.J.Friedrich⟩ ⟨a ~ system⟩ **c** *often cap* **:** of or relating to the central government of a nation having the character of a federation as distinguished from the governments of the constituent units (as states or provinces) **3** *usu cap* **:** advocating or friendly to the principle of a federal government with strong centralized powers; *esp* **:** of or relating to the American Federalists **4** *often cap* **:** of, relating to, or loyal to the federal government or the Union armies of the U.S. in the American Civil War **5** *usu cap* **:** being or belonging to a style of architecture and decoration current in the U.S. following the Revolution and before the period of Classic Revival **6** *of a British university* **:** consisting of an association of colleges that function to a very large degree as independent units — **fed·er·al·ly** \-rəlē, -li\ *adv*

²federal \"\ *n* -s *usu cap* **1 :** a supporter of the government of the U.S. in the Civil War; *specif* **:** a soldier in the federal armies ⟨*Federals* and Confederates lie buried together⟩ **2 :** a federal agent or officer

federal assembly *n, often cap F&A* **:** the two parliamentary houses constituting the legislative division of certain governments (as that of Switzerland)

federal case *n* **:** an act or activity that is or is likely to be subject to investigation by one of the criminal-investigation agencies (as the FBI) of the U.S. government

federal chancellor *n* **:** CHANCELLOR 4

federal council *n, often cap F&C* **1 :** a central legislative group or assembly in certain governments **2 :** a central executive council in certain governments (as that of Switzerland)

federal court *n* **:** a court established by authority of a federal government; *esp* **:** one established under the constitution and laws of the U.S.

federal deposit insurance *n* **:** federal insurance of bank deposits in the U.S. up to a stated limit per depositor created under the Banking Act of 1933

federal district *n* **:** a district set apart by a country as the seat of the national government (as the District of Columbia in the U.S.)

federal district court *n* **:** a district trial court of law and equity that hears cases under federal jurisdiction

fed·er·al·ese \,fed(ə)rə¦lēz, -ēs\ *n* -s *often cap, slang* **:** prose that is marked by a needlessly involved and awkwardly pretentious sentence structure and use of a jargon of polysyllabic words and that is sometimes said to characterize the documents of federal bureaus in the U.S. ⟨an enigma wrapped in ~ and tied with red tape —*Time*⟩

fed·er·al·ism \'fed(ə)rə,lizəm\ *n* -s **1 a** *often cap* **:** the federal principle of national, European, or world organization or its support **b :** the principle of federal organization of any group of more or less autonomous units or the support of such a principle **2** *usu cap* **:** the principles of the Federalists **3** *usu cap* **:** the principles of federal theology **4** *sometimes cap* **:** federal control ⟨in the lower schools the trend toward ~ is ... apparent in the proposal for Federal aid to education —Raymond Moley⟩

¹fed·er·al·ist \-ləst\ *n* -s **1 :** an advocate of federalism: as **a** *often cap* **:** an advocate of a federal union between the American colonies after the Revolution and of the formation and adoption of a constitution **b** *often cap* **:** WORLD FEDERALIST **2** *usu cap* **:** a member or adherent of the American Federalist party that in the early years of the U.S. was in favor of a strong centralized federal power as opposed to a central government of limited sovereignty and few powers and that went out of existence between 1821 and 1825

²federalist \"\ *or* **fed·er·al·is·tic** \¦fed(ə)rə¦listik, -tēk\ *adj* **:** of, relating to, or favoring federalism or federalists

fed·er·al·iza·tion \¦fed(ə)rələ'zāshən, -,lī'z-\ *n* -s **:** the state or process of federalizing or being federalized ⟨the ~ of higher education⟩ ⟨the ~ of post-office employees⟩

fed·er·al·ize \'fed(ə)rə,līz\ *vt* -ED/-ING/-S [F *fédéraliser*, fr. *fédéral* federal (prob. fr. E ¹*federal*) + *-iser* -ize] **1 :** to unite in or under a federal compact or a federal government ⟨attempting to ~ the independent states of Europe⟩ **2 :** to bring under the usu. sole jurisdiction of the federal government ⟨it does not ~ the unemployment-compensation system —H.S. Truman⟩

federal labor union *n* **:** a local labor union affiliated directly with the American Federation of Labor

federal land bank *n, usu cap F&L* **:** one of 12 regional banks established under the Federal Farm Loan Act of 1916 to facilitate the furnishing of capital to farms by making long-term loans available through subsidiary cooperative farm-loan associations or through agents on first mortgages up to one half the value of the farm plus 20 percent of the value of permanent improvements on it

federal public law *n* **:** the federal law as embodied in the rules, regulations, and decisions of public federal administrative agencies entrusted with the enforcement of various federal statutes as distinguished from the decisions of the federal courts interpreting and applying these statutes in individual cases

federal reserve agent *n, usu cap F&R* **:** the director who is designated by the board of governors of the Federal Reserve system as chairman of the board of directors of a Federal Reserve bank and who acts as official representative of the board of governors to the bank

federal reserve bank *n, usu cap F&R* **:** one of 12 banks set up under the Federal Reserve system by the Federal Reserve Act of Dec. 23, 1913, one in each of 12 districts, and serving as banks of reserve and discount for affiliated banks including all national banks and many state banks and trust companies

federal reserve district *n, usu cap F&R* **:** one of the 12 districts set up under the Federal Reserve system each of which contains a Federal Reserve bank

federal reserve note *n, usu cap F&R* **:** a currency note issued by the Federal Reserve banks and secured by a gold-certificate reserve of 25 percent and the balance of 75 percent in gold certificates, commercial paper, or U.S. government obligations

federal theology *n* **:** the theological system which rests upon the beliefs (1) that before the Fall man was under a covenant of works by which God through Adam promised man eternal blessedness if he kept his commandments and (2) that since the Fall man has been under a covenant of grace by which God by his grace promises the same blessings to all who believe in Christ — called also COVENANT THEOLOGY

federary *n* -ES [alter. (influenced in form and meaning by L *foeder-, foedus* league) of *feodary*] *obs* **:** FEDARIE

¹fed·er·ate \'fed(ə)rət\ *adj* [L *foederatus*, fr. *foeder-, foedus* league, compact + *-atus* -ate — more at ¹FEDERAL] **:** united by compact **:** forming an alliance **:** FEDERATED

²fed·er·ate \'fedə,rāt, *usu* -ād·+V\ *vb* -ED/-ING/-S *vi* **:** to unite in a league or association ⟨several nations willing to ~⟩ ~ *vt* **1 :** to organize into a federal organization ⟨~ the world⟩ ⟨a *federated* state⟩ ⟨the British provinces, then separate but now *federated* as Canada —T.H.LeDuc⟩ **2 :** to unite in a league or alliance or federation ⟨officially *federated* with Ethiopia —*Americana Annual*⟩

federated church *n* **:** a local church formed by the coming together of two or more congregations of different denominational backgrounds that unite in a common program while maintaining their separate denominational ties

fed·er·a·tion \,fedə'rāshən\ *n* -s [F *fédération* league, alliance, fr. LL *foederation-, foederatio*, fr. L *foederatus* + *-ion-, -io* -ion] **1 :** the act of uniting in a league; *esp* **:** the formation of a single sovereign power by the uniting of separate states, provinces, or colonies so that each retains the management of its own local affairs **2 :** something formed by federation: as **a :** a sovereign state formed by the union of several states that have given up certain powers to the central government while retaining for themselves control over local matters — compare CONFEDERATION 2 **b :** a union of societies or organizations ⟨a ~ of labor unions⟩ ⟨a ~ of women's clubs⟩ — **fed·er·a·tion·al** \¦==¦rāshənᵊl, -shnəl\ *adj*

fed·er·a·tive \'fedə,rād·|iv, 'fed(ə)rə|, |t|, |ēv *also* |əv\ *adj* [L *foederatus* + E *-ive*] **:** of or relating to a federation or covenant or its formation **:** based on or inclined to federation — **fed·er·a·tive·ly** \|əvlē, -li\ *adv*

fed·er·a·tor \'fedə,rād·ə(r), -ātə-\ *n* -s [²*federate* + *-or*] **:** one that forms a federation **:** one that takes part in a federation

fe·de ring \'fā(,)dā-, *It* 'fāadā\ *n* [It *fede* faith, fr. L *fides* — more at FAITH] **:** a finger ring typically bearing a device in the shape of two clasped hands and used esp. among Europeans as a token of loyalty or faith between two persons; *sometimes* **:** WEDDING RING

federita *var of* FETERITA

fedifragous *adj* [L *foedifragus*, fr. *foedi-* (fr. *foedus* league, compact) + *-fragus* (fr. *frangere* to break) — more at ¹FEDERAL, BREAK] *obs* **:** FAITHLESS, PERFIDIOUS

fedity *n* -ES [L *foeditat-, foeditas*, fr. *foedus* foul, ugly + *-itat-, -itas* -ity — more at BEBUNG] *obs* **:** FOULNESS, VILENESS, IMPURITY

fedn *abbr* federation

fe·do·ra \fə'dōrə, -dȯrə\ *n* -s *sometimes cap* [*Fédora* (1882), drama by V. Sardou †1908 Fr. playwright] **:** a soft felt hat with a low crown creased lengthwise and with or without a high roll on the side brim

fedora

fed up *adj* **:** sated to the point of disgust **:** bored beyond endurance **:** disgusted and totally out of patience ⟨a generation that is rapidly becoming *fed up* with novels about sensitive young men⟩ ⟨a great many who are *fed up* and disgusted with their jobs —*Encore*⟩ — **fed-upness** \(')=ˈ==\ *n* -ES

¹fee *n* -s [ME, fr. OE *feoh* cattle, property, money; akin to OHG *fihu* cattle, ON *fē* cattle, sheep, money, Goth *faihu* money, wealth, L *pecus* cattle, *pecunia* money, *pectere* to comb, Gk *pekein* to comb, *pokos* fleece, Skt *paśu* cattle; basic meaning: to fleece, pluck (wool)] *obs* **:** personal property **:** GOODS, LIVESTOCK, MONEY

²fee \'fē\ *n* -s [ME, fr. OF *fé, fié, fief*, of Gmc origin; akin to OHG *fihu* cattle] **1 a :** a heritable estate in land held in English feudal law of a superior lord by whom the estate was granted and who retains rights in the land or tenement and acquires rights against the tenant **b :** a feudal benefice or estate in land held of a feudal lord in feudal law; *also* **:** the interest or right of the lord in the land so held **c :** territory held in this way **d :** an estate of inheritance — see FEE SIMPLE, FEE TAIL **2 a** *obs* **:** PERQUISITE; *esp* **:** an allowance esp. of food to a cook or of game to a forester **b** *obs* **:** REWARD, PRIZE **c** *dial Brit* **:** WAGES; *esp* **:** those of a servant **d** *obs* **:** BRIBE **e** *archaic* **:** GRATUITY, TIP **3 a :** a fixed charge for admission (as to a museum) **b :** a charge fixed by law or by an institution (as a university) for certain privileges or services ⟨a license ~⟩ ⟨a toll-road ~⟩ ⟨a college-admission ~⟩ ⟨research ~*s*⟩ ⟨laboratory ~*s*⟩ ⟨tuition ~*s*⟩ **4 a :** a charge fixed by law for the services of a public officer ⟨a sheriff's ~⟩ **b :** compensation often in the form of a fixed charge for professional service or for special and requested exercise of talent or of skill (as by an artist) ⟨a doctor's ~⟩ ⟨a lawyer's retainer ~⟩ ⟨teach them this art if they shall wish to learn it, without ~ or stipulation —*Hippocratic Oath*⟩ **5** *dial Brit* **:** employment as a servant ⟨I come here to seek a ~⟩ **syn** see WAGE — **in fee 1** *also* **of fee :** as a feudal fee **2** *also* **at a fee** *or* **with fee** *obs* **:** in service **:** under obligation **3 :** in fee simple **4** *archaic* **:** as an absolute and legal possession

³fee \"\ *vt* **feed; feed; feeing; fees** [ME *feen* to enfeoff, hire, fr. ²*fee*] **1** *obs* **:** BRIBE **2 a** *chiefly Scot* **:** HIRE ⟨~ a servant⟩ **b** *now dial Brit* **:** to make use of **:** EMPLOY ⟨~ every occasion —Shak.⟩ **3 :** to reward or pay for usu. personal services rendered or to be rendered **:** give a gratuity to **:** TIP ⟨~ a waiter⟩

feeb \'fēb\ *n* -s [short for *feebleminded*] *slang* **:** a feebleminded person ⟨considered purely as playgoers, what ~*s* and addlepates they are —Russell Maloney⟩

fee bill *n* **:** a schedule of the minimum or customary fees charged by lawyers, sheriffs, or other officers of a court for specified services; *also* **:** a list of the fees taxable as costs in a particular law case

¹fee·ble \'fēbəl\ *adj, usu* **feebler** \-b(ə)lə(r)\ **feeblest** \-b(ə)ləst\ [ME *feble*, fr. OF *flebe, feble, foible*, fr. L *flebilis* lamentable, wretched, fr. *flēre* to weep — more at BLEAT] **1 a :** markedly lacking in normal strength or endurance **:** WEAK, DEBILITATED, INFIRM ⟨a ~ old man⟩ ⟨~ in mind and body⟩ **b :** unequal to strain **:** YIELDING, FRAGILE ⟨a shaky buttress providing only ~ support⟩ ⟨a flower with a ~ stem⟩ **c :** indicating weakness or infirmity ⟨taking only ~ steps⟩ ⟨gave a ~ moan⟩ **2 a :** deficient in qualities or resources that indicate or give vigor, authority, force, or efficiency **:** not strong or effective (as in character, mental ability, tone, or color) ⟨a ~ personality⟩ ⟨a ~ intelligence⟩ ⟨~ imagery⟩ ⟨a ~ attempt at a novel⟩ **b :** INADEQUATE, INFERIOR ⟨forced to deal with ~ human nature⟩ ⟨could muster only the *feeblest* of thoughts on the occasion⟩ ⟨making ~ excuses⟩ **syn** see WEAK

²feeble \"\ *vt* -ED/-ING/-S [ME *feblen*, partly fr. ME *feble*, adj., partly fr. OF *feblir, flebir* to make or become feeble, fr. *flebe, feble, foible*, adj.] *archaic* **:** to make feeble **:** ENFEEBLE

³feeble \"\ *n* -s [ME, fr. *feble*, adj.] **1** *obs* **:** a feeble person **2 a** *archaic* **:** FOIBLE 1 **b :** FOIBLE 2

feebleminded \¦==¦==\ *adj* **1** *obs* **:** irresolute and fainthearted **2 :** mentally deficient **3 :** FOOLISH, STUPID — **fee·ble·mind·ed·ly** *adv* — **fee·ble·mind·ed·ness** *n* -ES

fee·ble·ness *n* -ES [ME *feblenesse*, fr. *feble* + *-nesse* -ness] **:** the quality or state of being feeble ⟨the old man's halting steps revealed the ~ of his constitution⟩ ⟨the writing was marked by ~ of style and inanity of content⟩

feeble-wit \'==,=\ *n* **:** one that is deficient in intelligence or common sense

fee·bling \'fēb(ə)liŋ\ *n* -s [blend of ¹*feeble* and *-ling*] **:** one that is feeble in mind or body

fee·blish \-lish\ *adj* **:** somewhat feeble

fee·bly \'fēb(ə)lē, -li\ *adv* [ME *febly*, fr. *feble* feeble + *-ly* — more at ¹FEEBLE] **1 :** POORLY, SCANTILY, INSUFFICIENTLY ⟨a ~ handled newsreel talk —Gilbert Seldes⟩ **2 :** in a feeble manner **:** INEFFECTIVELY, WEAKLY ⟨a criminal only ~ prosecuted⟩ ⟨nations have ~ tried to humanize and regulate war —Vera M. Dean⟩ **:** MILDLY ⟨a ~ alcoholic wine⟩ **:** DIMLY ⟨a light shining ~ through the mist⟩

¹feed \'fēd\ *vb* **fed** \'fed\ **fed; feeding; feeds** [ME *feden*, fr. OE *fēdan*; akin to OHG *fuoten* to feed, ON *fœtha*, Goth *fodjan*; denominative fr. the root of E *food*] *vt* **1 a :** to give food to **:** supply with nourishment **:** satisfy the hunger of ⟨~ several guests⟩ ⟨~ the chickens⟩; *also* **:** SUCKLE ⟨~ a baby at the breast⟩ **b :** to convey food to the mouth of ⟨a patient so weak he had to be *fed*⟩ ⟨~*ing* a small child in a high chair⟩ **c :** to supply emotional, intellectual, or spiritual sustenance to ⟨looking for what would ~ the soul⟩ ⟨a capacity for love that found nothing to ~ it⟩ **d :** to convey to or into the mind of as if feeding a child ⟨the governed can be unknowingly *fed* with untruths —Harrison Brown⟩ ⟨thought the man was ~*ing* him all kinds of nonsense⟩ **2 a :** to furnish esp. with something that is essential or that improves or enhances ⟨~*ing* plants with fertilizer⟩ ⟨the intelligence *fed* by reading⟩ ⟨most adults do stop ~*ing* their minds —R.H.Wittcoff⟩ **b :** to supply or keep supplied esp. with something consumed ⟨lakes and rivers which ~ the Congo —Tom Marvel⟩ ⟨~*ing* a furnace with coal⟩ ⟨checks the items that are *fed* to him by the usual run of press agents —*Saturday Rev.*⟩ **c :** to pass or throw a ball or puck to (a teammate) esp. for a shot at the goal ⟨kept ~*ing* the tall center⟩ **d :** to supply (a fellow actor) with the cue lines and situations that give greater effectiveness or significance to a role; *also* **:** to supply (as cue lines) to an actor **e :** to provide a supply of (electrical energy) ⟨power is usually *fed* to the antenna —*Radio Amateur's Handbook*⟩; *also* **:** to supply electrical energy to **f** (1) **:** to supply esp. to an electronic circuit **:** send esp. through an electronic circuit — used of a signal (as in radar, radio, or telegraphy) (2) **:** to send (a radio or television program) by wire to a transmitting station for broadcast **3 a :** to produce food for ⟨the pasture *fed* the cows poorly⟩ **b :** to provide food for ⟨enough wheat to ~ the troops for a week⟩ **c :** to provide material for **:** supply (as a talent) with substance or occasion for exercise ⟨immense learning . . . drawn upon to ~ a fine sense of humor —R.M.Lovett⟩ **4 a :** SATISFY, GRATIFY ⟨*fed* his desire for revenge⟩ ⟨I will ~ fat the ancient grudge I bear him —Shak.⟩ **b :** to give support or encouragement to ⟨~*ing* false hopes⟩ **c :** AGGRAVATE, AUGMENT ⟨~ his feelings of indignation⟩ ⟨*fed* his resentment by mulling over the circumstances that aroused it⟩ ⟨vanity *fed* by flattery⟩ ⟨sensational . . . papers *fed* the public outcry with near-hysterical headlines —*Time*⟩ ⟨the public acclaim *fed* the dictator's ego⟩ **5 a :** to supply (the material to be operated upon) to a machine ⟨to ~ paper to a printing press⟩ **b :** to produce progressive operation upon or with (as in woodworking and metalworking machines) so that the work moves to the cutting tool or the tool to the work **6 a :** to give as food ⟨~ grain to chickens⟩ **b :** to furnish for use or consumption ⟨~*ing* coal to a furnace⟩ often in appropriate or convenient amounts ⟨hurried to another hospital to borrow a machine which he hoped would ~ the oxygen mechanically —Grace Reiten⟩ — often used with *out* ⟨the flatbed press *fed* out papers each afternoon about as fast as I could deal cards —C.C. Wertenbaker⟩ **7 a :** to put (cattle) to graze **b :** to cause (land or crops) to be grazed **~** *vi* **1 a** (1) **:** to consume food **:** EAT — often used with a derogatory implication when applied to a person ⟨cattle ~*ing* in a barn⟩ ⟨we determined to ~ only once a day at a restaurant —M.C.A.Henniker⟩ (2) **:** to take a meal esp. in restaurants ⟨you can ~ better here than in most other cities⟩ **b :** to satisfy the appetite **:** feed oneself **:** PREY — used with *on* or *upon* or *off* ⟨a vulture ~*ing* on carrion⟩ ⟨an animal ~*ing* off smaller animals⟩ **c :** to become nourished, strengthened, satisfied, sustained, or augmented as if by food ⟨convictions ~ . . . on many things, including items of knowledge and considerations of logic —Lucius Garvin⟩ **d :** to consume or utilize feed — used of an engine or other mechanical device ⟨a gas turbine ~*ing* on the fuel it pumps⟩ **2 :** to supply a fellow actor with the cue lines and situations that give greater effectiveness or significance to his role **3 a :** to move in or as if in supplying something with what it uses or consumes ⟨the river ~*s* into the Atlantic ocean⟩ **b :** to move into a machine or opening in order to be used or processed ⟨bullets ~ into a machine gun⟩ ⟨oil ~*s* into an engine⟩ ⟨wire ~*s* into a conduit⟩ **4 :** to load a cartridge into the chamber of a firearm esp. by the operation of the action in magazine or clip-fed arms

syn NOURISH, PASTURE, GRAZE: FEED is a general term applicable to persons, animals, and plants and anything else given material to consume or enjoy for purposes of sustaining or continuing operation ⟨to *feed* the refugees⟩ ⟨to *feed* the chickens⟩ ⟨to *feed* a furnace⟩ ⟨Hugh's growing vanity was *fed* by the thought that Clara was interested in him —Sherwood Anderson⟩ ⟨the dissatisfactions that *feed* the cause of the rebels⟩ NOURISH is applicable to supplying what furnishes elements essential to growth, well-being, and building up ⟨the humid prairie heat, so *nourishing* to wheat and corn, so exhausting to human beings —Willa Cather⟩ ⟨our press has helped to *nourish* this legend by stretching and distorting certain of the more horrendous and eccentric features —S.L.A. Marshall⟩ ⟨all writers are *nourished* by the sense of having an audience —Malcolm Cowley⟩ PASTURE suggests leading cows or sheep to grassy areas or permitting them to go to such areas ⟨*pasturing* cows in the meadow⟩ GRAZE is often synonymous with PASTURE ⟨sheep *grazing* in a field⟩ but may suggest free ranging over a less circumscribed area ⟨*grazing* cattle on the range⟩

[2]**feed** \"\ *n* -s **1 a** *obs* **:** the act of eating **b :** MEAL; *esp* **:** a sumptuous meal ⟨a bath and a shave and clean clothes and a good ~ —I.L.Idriess⟩ **2 a** *obs* **:** the right of pasture on a piece of land **b** *obs* **:** GRAZING **c** *obs* **:** pasture land **d** *dial Eng* **:** CROPS **3 a :** food esp. for livestock **:** FODDER ⟨he needed food for his family and ~ for his livestock —A.F.Gustafson⟩ **b :** a food of this kind **:** a mixture or preparation used for feeding livestock **c :** the amount given at each feeding **4 :** the fermenting wort drawn off from yeast troughs in brewing and added to the fermenting unions to keep them full and so enable the yeast to work out **5 a :** the motion or process of carrying forward the material to be operated upon (as cloth to the needle in a sewing machine) or of producing progressive operation upon any material or object in a machine (as in a lathe by moving the cutting tool along or in the work) **b** (1) **:** the degree of feeding material to a machine ⟨a fine or coarse ~⟩ (2) **:** the advance of a cutting tool at each revolution of the tool or of the work ⟨a ~ of ⅛ inch⟩; *specif* **:** the thickness of the chip cut per tooth of a milling cutter **c :** material supplied to a machine or apparatus (as lubricant to an engine, water to a steam boiler, coal to a furnace, or petroleum to a distilling column) **d :** a mechanism by which the action of feeding is produced **:** FEED MOTION **6 :** the system or surfaces of the action of a firearm that serve to move a cartridge from its magazine or clip to the chamber or act as a surface for such motion — **off one's feed 1 :** having little appetite for food **:** unwilling to eat a normal amount of food ⟨the child was *off his feed* and cried a good deal⟩ **2 :** not feeling well **:** UPSET

[3]**feed** *past of* FEE

feedback \'=,=\ *n* -s *often attrib* **1 :** the return to the input of a part of the output of a machine, system, or process: as **a :** the return to the input of a part of the output of an electronic amplifying system leading to increased amplification or decreased amplification or control of the quality of the signal — see NEGATIVE FEEDBACK, POSITIVE FEEDBACK **b :** the return to the input of a part of the output of a mechanism, this part of the input constituting information that reports discrepancies between intended and actual operation and leads to a self-correcting action that can be utilized (as in the automatic operation of machinery) ⟨~ control system⟩ **2 :** the partial reversion of the effects of a given process to its source or to a preceding stage so as to reinforce or modify it — used esp. of biological, psychological, and social systems

feed bag *n* **:** NOSE BAG — **put on the feed bag** *slang* **:** to begin eating

feedboard \'=,=\ *n* **:** a board (as on a printing press or folding machine) to hold material fed to the machine

feedbox \'=,=\ *n* **1 :** a container for feed or fodder **2 :** a casing on a machine enclosing the feed motion and the shifting mechanism

feed bunk *n* **:** [2]BUNK 3

feed case *n* **:** a detachable metal case that contains cartridges and is used in feeding certain machine guns

feed cutter *n* **:** a machine that cuts up feed or fodder (as cornstalks or alfalfa)

feed dog *n* **:** a sewing-machine device consisting of a notched piece of metal that automatically moves the material under the needle

feed efficiency *n* **:** EFFICIENCY 3d

[1]**feeder** \'fēdə(r)\ *n* -s [ME *feder, federe*, fr. *feden* to feed + *-er, -ere* -er — more at [1]FEED] **1 :** one that gives or provides food or nourishment: as **a :** one that fattens cattle for slaughter **b :** a device or apparatus for supplying food (as to an animal) ⟨an automatic poultry ~⟩ ⟨a calf ~⟩ **c :** a normal pigeon used as a foster parent for the young of short-beaked pigeons **2 :** one that eats or is notable for eating ⟨the man was a prodigious ~⟩: as **a** *obs* **:** one dependent on another for food (as a servant) **b :** an animal being fattened or one suitable for fattening — compare STOCKER **3 :** one that ministers (as to another's welfare, mind, or passions): as **a :** one that incites ⟨the ~ of . . . riots —Shak.⟩ **b** *archaic* **:** an academic tutor or crammer **4 a :** one that feeds material into or through a machine or device that operates upon it or consumes it: as (1) **:** a device that supplies crushed stone to a conveyor (2) **:** a device for supplying coal automatically to a furnace (3) **:** a worker who charges lead ore and other substances into a blast furnace (4) **:** a worker who feeds aluminum sheets into a rolling mill **b :** a strong discharge of gas from a fissure in a mine **c :** FEEDHEAD **5 :** a small lateral lode connecting with the main lode of a mine **6 a :** one that replenishes or connects with and supplies something **:** a source of supply for the maintenance or effectiveness of something else of the same general kind ⟨farm baseball teams that act as ~*s* for the major-league teams⟩ ⟨it was thought that Broadway had become a ~ for Hollywood⟩ **b :** TRIBUTARY **c** *or* **feeder line :** a branch transportation line: as (1) *also* **feeder airline :** a local-service airline connecting smaller communities with larger terminal cities and trunk lines (2) **:** a local bus line that runs into a terminal used by a trunk line **d** (1) **:** a heavy wire conductor supplying electricity at some point of any system of electric distribution (as from a substation to a distribution point) (2) **:** a conductor connecting a major unit of a radio transmitting or receiving apparatus with another; *esp* **:** the line from the aerial to the receiver or transmitter **e :** FEEDER ROAD **7 a :** a part in a play designed as a foil for one more important **b :** an actor playing such a part **:** one who feeds a fellow actor **8 :** an assorter in a garment factory **9** *chiefly Brit* **:** a baby's bib

[2]**feeder** \"\ *adj* **1 :** being, acting, or serving as a feeder ⟨a ~ root⟩ ⟨a ~ device⟩ ⟨~ air service⟩ ⟨a ~ belt⟩ ⟨a ~ cable⟩ ⟨a ~ farmer⟩ **2 :** suitable for fattening ⟨~ cattle⟩

feeder head *n* **:** FEEDHEAD

feeder man *n* **:** a workman who climbs a pole to high-tension lines and with a long insulated rod switches off the flow of current so that the lines may be repaired with safety

feeder road *n* **:** a road that serves as a traffic feeder to a more important road (as a turnpike) — compare SECONDARY ROAD

feed guide *or* **feed gauge** *n* **:** a device in a printing press for holding and releasing a sheet

feedhead \'=,=\ *n* **:** an excess of metal left above a foundry mold to supply molten metal to a solidifying casting and thus compensate for shrinkage that cannot be fed from the gate — called also *riser*

feed-in \'=,=\ *adj* **:** being or belonging to something that feeds material (as into a machine) or to the process of feeding in this way ⟨a *feed-in* device connecting the main source of power to the subsidiary outlets⟩ ⟨used the main switch box as a *feed-in* point for too many electrical outlets⟩

feeding *n* -s [ME *feding*, fr. OE *fēding*, fr. *fēdan* to feed + *-ing*] **1 a :** the act or process of one that feeds or the act or process of being fed ⟨all fruit purchased will be used to assist in relief ~ in foreign countries —*Collier's Yr. Bk.*⟩ ⟨the jamming of the mechanism stopped the ~ of the coke into the furnace⟩ **b :** an instance of feeding esp. something more or less incapable of providing its own food or of feeding itself ⟨give your lawn a late fall ~ of fertilizer⟩ ⟨gave the baby eight ounces of milk at each ~⟩ **2 :** land used for grazing

feeding board *n* **:** FEEDBOARD

feeding bottle *n* **:** NURSING BOTTLE

feeding cup *n* **:** a vessel with a spout rising near its base for use in feeding the bedfast

feeding ground *n* **:** the area in which an animal or group of animals customarily feed (as by grazing) ⟨a lion skulking about the *feeding ground* of a herd of antelope⟩ ⟨a *feeding ground* for small game⟩

feeding head *n* **:** FEEDHEAD

feeding rod *n* **:** an iron rod to keep clear the passage between riser and casting in founding

feeding station *n* **:** a central or convenient place at which food is provided (as for soldiers during a military operation); *specif* **:** a device (as a hanging platform) on which food is placed to attract birds for observation or study or for feeding birds during winter months

feedlot \'=,=\ *n* **:** a lot or plot of land on or in which livestock are fed or fattened for market — compare DRYLOT

feed mill *n* **:** a mill in which stock feeds are prepared

feed off *vt* **:** to dispose of (a crop) by turning in livestock to pasture

feed out *vt* **:** to feed or fatten (animals) to a marketable condition

feed pump *n* **:** a force pump for supplying water to a steam boiler

feed ratio *n* **:** the ratio expressing feed efficiency

feed roll *n* **1** *or* **feed roller :** a roll or one of two or more rolls by which material is drawn or fed into a machine **2 :** one of a set of small rubber rolls under the platen of a typewriter that help to roll the paper and hold it in place during typing

feeds *pres 3d sing of* FEED, *pl of* FEED

feed screw *n* **:** a screw that imparts feed motion (as in a lathe or other machine tool) — compare LEAD SCREW

feedstock \'=,=\ *n* **:** raw material supplied to a machine or processing plant (as pulpwood to a paper mill)

feedstore \'=,=\ *n* **:** a store selling livestock feeds

feedstuff \'=,=\ *or* **feedingstuff** \'==,=\ *n* **:** a feed for domestic animals; *usu* **:** any of the constituent nutrients of an animal ration ⟨cotton-seed meal has proved a useful ~ in fattening rations⟩ ⟨the basic ~*s*, carbohydrate, fat, and protein⟩

feedwater \'=,==\ *n* **:** water sometimes preheated or purified and supplied to a boiler (as for steam) or still

feedway \'=,=\ *n* **:** an aisle between rows of stalls in a barn along which feed is distributed to the mangers

feed wheat *n* **:** low-grade wheat used as stock feed

fee farm *n* [ME *fee ferme*, fr. AF *fé ferme*, fr. OF *fé* fee, fief + *ferme* lease — more at [2]FEE, [2]FARM] **:** land held of another in fee simple subject to a perpetual fixed rent without homage, fealty, or any other service than that mentioned in the feoffment; *also* **:** the estate or land so held or the rent paid

fee-faw-fum \,fē,fȯ'fəm\ *or* **fee-fo-fum** \-fō'-\ *n* -s **1 :** a bloodthirsty person **:** OGRE ⟨were all *fee-faw-fums* . . . and the sooner that was admitted, the sooner some sort of solution could be reached —William Manchester⟩ **2 :** something designed to impose upon the timid and ignorant ⟨black magic or whatever is the technical name for this sort of *fee-fo-fum* —J.C.Snaith⟩

fee gouging *n* **:** the charging of excessive fees esp. for professional services — compare FEE SPLITTING

feeing *pres part of* FEE

feeing market *also* **feeing fair** *n* [*feeing* fr. gerund of [3]*fee*] *Scot* **:** a market where servants gather to be hired for the coming season or year

[1]**feel** \'fēl, *esp before pause or consonant* -ēəl\ *vb* **felt** \'felt\ **felt; feeling; feels** [ME *felen*, fr. OE *fēlan;* akin to OHG *fuolen* to feel, ON *fālma* to fumble, grope, L *palpare* to caress, and perh. to Gk *pallein* to shake, brandish — more at POLEMIC] *vt* **1 a** (1) **:** to perceive by tactile, muscular, integumental, or other sensation excited by some physical stimulus **:** be aware of esp. on contact in the body or limbs ⟨~ a sharp blow⟩ ⟨~ a cold draft⟩ ⟨*felt* a sudden pain⟩ ⟨after an hour of climbing we began to ~ fatigue⟩ (2) *archaic* **:** to perceive by smell or taste **b** (1) **:** TOUCH, HANDLE ⟨*felt* the coat to see if it was wet⟩ (2) *slang* **:** to feel up **c :** to examine or explore by such methods as touching, lifting, or sounding **:** make a trial of **:** test by touching, lifting, or sounding ⟨*felt* the rock to see how heavy it was⟩ **2 a :** to experience or undergo passively **:** endure without taking any positive action against ⟨~ inconvenience at having to stay overnight⟩ ⟨continually *felt* the resentment of his competitors⟩ ⟨though I was tired I *felt* the music with more pleasure now —Chandler Brossard⟩ **b :** to be conscious of (a subjective state) ⟨~ a strong sense of our own pleasure in her company⟩ ⟨~ importance⟩ ⟨*felt* a mild inclination to cry —T.B.Costain⟩ **c :** to suffer from **:** have one's sensibilities markedly affected by ⟨~ the insult deeply⟩ ⟨~ his son's ingratitude as if it were a wound⟩ **d :** to experience the special or typical effect of (as a subjective experience) ⟨~ the judge's wrath⟩ **:** experience the intoxicating effect of (as an alcoholic drink) ⟨drank for a long time before they began to ~ the liquor⟩ **:** experience the emotional force of ⟨young conductors don't bother much anymore to ~ music —Virgil Thomson⟩ **3 a :** to find out by or as if by the tactile sense — used with a clause as object ⟨~ if any bones had been broken⟩ ⟨~ how the tiller worked⟩ **b :** to ascertain (as a man's attitude) by cautious trial **:** sound out ⟨by diplomatic query tried to ~ the sentiments of the neighborhood⟩ **:** discover by careful and tentative investigatory methods ⟨when the architects designed their first building they were clearly ~*ing* their way⟩ — often used with *out* ⟨~*ing* out the sentiments of their neighbors on the subject of school improvement⟩ **4 a :** to be aware of (something objective) by instinct or inference rather than through actual experience or sensation ⟨~ the presence of an intruder in the room⟩ ⟨~ trouble brewing⟩ **b :** to be persuaded or convinced of emotionally rather than intellectually **:** believe esp. on indefinite grounds ⟨*felt* that the move would be unwise although she could give no positive reason⟩ ⟨*felt* that what he said was probably true⟩ **c :** BELIEVE, THINK, HOLD — now used with a clause as object ⟨they *felt* that their own argument was as sound as that of their opponents⟩ ⟨I am a reader, so I ~ I have a right to criticize authors —Alice Hamilton⟩ ⟨we feel that he should retire⟩ **~** *vi* **1 :** to receive or be able to receive a tactile sensation **:** perceive by touching or making contact ⟨lost all ability to ~ in his fingertips⟩ **2 a :** to search for something or guide oneself using the sense of touch esp. in the fingers **:** GROPE ⟨she *felt* in her purse for her keys⟩ ⟨*felt* along the wall in the dark for an opening⟩ ⟨*felt* under the table with his foot for the spoon he had dropped⟩ **b :** to seek or search out with caution or uncertainty ⟨went quietly through the woods ~*ing* for the enemy⟩ ⟨began to explain at random while ~*ing* for an excuse⟩ **c :** to find by trial and error ⟨in the absence of a book of instructions we had to ~ for the best way to rig the mechanism⟩ **3 :** to manifest itself to the tactile sense or to physical sensation — usu. used with a specifying adjective ⟨it ~*s* cold outside⟩ ⟨how it ~*s* to be hungry⟩ **4 a :** to have sympathy or pity ⟨capable of ~*ing* for the poverty stricken and underfed⟩ **b :** to achieve or experience aesthetic identification ⟨we ~ for the hero who is in danger . . . and we unconsciously desire to realize the escape —John Erskine †1951⟩ **5 a :** to be conscious of an inward particular impression, state of mind or feeling, or physical condition **:** perceive oneself to be ⟨~ assured⟩ ⟨~ friendly⟩ ⟨~ sick⟩ ⟨~ in a happy frame of mind⟩ ⟨~ bad⟩ ⟨~ good⟩ **b :** to have a marked sentiment or opinion pro or con ⟨~ strongly about the disposition of school funds⟩ **6 :** to react emotionally or instinctively rather than as a result of rational or meditative analysis ⟨a man who ~*s* but seldom thinks⟩ — **feel in one's bones :** to feel strongly and instinctively (as that something is true or false) **:** hold a strong opinion based on no concrete evidence — **feel like :** to have an inclination for ⟨*feel like* taking a walk⟩ ⟨*feel like* being alone⟩ — **feel no pain :** to be drunk — **feel of :** to examine by touching **:** FEEL ⟨*feel of* a fabric to discover its texture⟩ ⟨*feel of* a pear to see if it is ripe⟩ — **feel one's oats : 1** *of a horse* **:** to act spirited or frisky **2 a :** to be actively exuberant ⟨the children were *feeling their oats* and running madly around the house⟩ **b :** to act in a newly self-confident and often self-important manner — **feel the helm** *of a ship* **:** to obey the helm

[2]**feel** \"\ *n* -s [ME *fele*, fr. *felen* to feel — more at [1]FEEL] **1 a :** the sense of touch ⟨a blanket soft to the ~⟩ **b** (1) **:** an instance of or opportunity of feeling by touching ⟨took a ~ of the bump on his head⟩ (2) *slang* **:** an instance or opportunity of feeling up **2 :** EXPERIENCE, SENSATION, FEELING ⟨the ~ of an insect's bite⟩ ⟨the ~ of joy⟩ ⟨learned to relish the ~ of power —A.W.Long⟩ ⟨there was a ~ of the train's being about to leave —Eudora Welty⟩ **3 a :** the quality or properties of a thing as imparted or its typical quality or properties as recognized or determined through or as if through touch or handling ⟨a greasy ~⟩ ⟨testing the ~ of the cloth⟩ ⟨the warm ~ of her flesh —Stuart Cloete⟩ **b :** typical or peculiar quality, air, or atmosphere ⟨the house had the ~ of a home⟩ ⟨the place has the ~ of an old English pub —James Cerruti⟩ **4 a :** knack, facility, or skill often deriving from an innate ability — used with *for* ⟨a good ~ for the handling of planes⟩ ⟨he will develop a ~ for words which will help to make him articulate —*Nat'l Catholic Educational Assoc. Bull.*⟩ ⟨these provincial companies have a ~ for opera that you'll find nowhere else in the world —T.H.Fielding⟩ **b :** a quality (as in an art work) resulting from such knack, facility, or skill — used with *for* ⟨a strong ~ in the artist's work for balance and proportion⟩ **5 :** an awareness of the spirit or temper of something or of its distinguishing or special qualities ⟨the ~ of the country⟩ — often used with *for* ⟨he has a sensitive ~ for the vast reaches in which his particular war took place —James Michener⟩

[3]**feel** \"\ *Scot var of* FOOL

[4]**feel** \"\ *var of* FEIL

feel·er \'fēlə(r)\ *n* -s [ME *feler* one that feels, fr. *felen* to feel + *-er, -ere* -er] **1 :** a tactile process of an animal: as **a :** a sensory tentacle **b :** ANTENNA 1 **c :** VIBRISSA **2 :** something ventured (as a proposal, remark, or tentative action) to ascertain the views or reactions of others ⟨ready to explore any peace ~*s* no matter what their origin —*Current Biog.*⟩ ⟨~*s* being put out by certain manufacturers in an effort to determine whether or not stripings and patterns are due for reacceptance in popularity —*Apparel Arts*⟩ ⟨the letter was a ~ to see how Washington would look upon such a movement —H.E.Scudder⟩ **3** *or* **feeler gage :** a thin metal strip of known thickness used as a gage or one of a set of metal strips of graduated thicknesses so used **4 :** a loom device in textile manufacturing that replaces nearly empty bobbins in shuttles

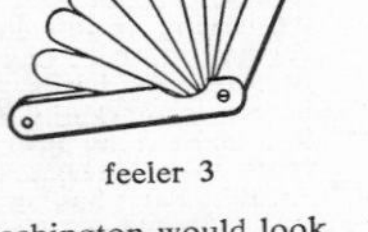

feeler 3

feeler pin *n* **:** a pin controlling a tripping mechanism on various duplicating machines that allows the printing roll or rolls to come into position for printing only while there is paper in the machine

fee·less \'fēləs\ *adj* **:** being without a fee **:** yielding no fee **:** requiring no fee

[1]**feeling** *n* -s [ME *felinge, feling*, fr. *felen* to feel + *-inge, -ing* -ing — more at [1]FEEL] **1 a :** the one of the five senses of which the skin is the chief end organ and of which the sensations of touch, contact, temperature, and pressure are characteristic **b :** a sensation experienced through this sense; *esp* **:** a sensation of touch **2 :** a sensation, a complex of sensations, or a perception belonging to the more general forms of sensibility: **a :** bodily consciousness **:** organic sensation **b :** a generalized sensation involving touch, contact, temperature, pressure, or physical pain or pleasure **c :** appreciative or responsive awareness or recognition ⟨experience a ~ of safety⟩ ⟨a ~ of injury followed the unfair decision of the court⟩ **d :** sympathetic aesthetic response **3 a :** the undifferentiated background of one's awareness considered apart from any identifiable sensation, perception, or thought **b :** the overall quality of one's awareness esp. as measured along a pleasantness-unpleasantness continuum — compare [1]AFFECT 2, EMOTION **4 a :** the condition of one that feels **:** an emotional state **:** EMOTION ⟨a kindly ~ inside him whenever he was treated decently⟩ ⟨experienced a ~ of pride at the accomplishment⟩ ⟨a ~ of reverential awe for these immemorial shelters —Norman Douglas⟩; *also* **:** a particular emotion ⟨human ~*s* — human hopes, aspirations, fears, and sorrows —H.R.Collins⟩ **b feelings** *pl* **:** SENSIBILITIES ⟨a biting remark that hurt the ~*s* of a good friend⟩ **c :** emotional reaction ⟨so unable to control her ~*s* that she broke down and wept⟩; *specif* **:** the emotional reaction of one person or group to another or the emotional relationship of one person or group to another or of two persons or groups ⟨wished to improve the ~ between the two countries⟩ ⟨bad ~ existed wherever he went and he expected an outburst of hostilities at any moment⟩ ⟨the act promoted the best ~ possible between the families⟩ **d :** a reaction consisting of or combining hostility, distrust, dislike, opposition, resentment, or hatred and usu. marked by belligerence ⟨there was ~ between the groups so we hesitated to intervene⟩ ⟨~ ran high at the proposal⟩ **e :** tender emotion **:** FONDNESS, AFFECTION, LOVE ⟨don't have any ~ anymore about you —Louis Auchincloss⟩ **5 a :** OPINION, BELIEF ⟨asked the professor what his ~*s* were on the international

crisis⟩ **b :** unreasoned opinion **:** frame of mind **:** emotional attitude **:** SENTIMENT ⟨expressing the ~*s* of an essentially irrational child⟩ ⟨impossible to imagine the ~ about so controversial a person⟩ **6 :** capacity to feel emotion **:** emotional responsiveness ⟨found out how much ~ his mother really had⟩; *esp* **:** delicate and sympathetic emotional responsiveness ⟨a man of fine ~⟩ **7 a :** a character or quality ascribed to or associated with something as a result of one's impression or emotional state **:** FEEL, ATMOSPHERE ⟨the place had the ~ of a haunted house⟩; *esp* **:** the emotional quality (as of a work of art or literature) that calls to mind a particular era, period, place, culture, or civilization ⟨a collection of scenic wallpapers that . . . have a slight Japanese ~ —*New Yorker*⟩ ⟨a Baroque ~ in the architecture⟩ ⟨the ~ of the outdoors has been realized with sky-blue ceiling and natural colors —*Playthings*⟩ **b :** the impression something gives to one observing or experiencing ⟨thoroughfares and railways alive with busy traffic . . . give the ~ of energy and power —Samuel Valkenburg & Ellsworth Huntington⟩ **c** *or* **feeling tone :** the quality of a work of art which embodies, conveys, or is calculated to convey emotion **8 :** the ability to deal with or handle something with sensitivity and facility — used with *for* ⟨he has no true ~ for words —*Geog. Jour.*⟩ ⟨a young painter with a good ~ for color⟩ **9 :** PRESENTIMENT ⟨recent attempts to combine quantum mechanics and electrodynamics have produced . . . relatively little ~ of a final result —W.V.Houston⟩ ⟨these may all be short and scattered straws on which to base my ~ of a trend —W.I.Nichols⟩

syn AFFECTION, EMOTION, SENTIMENT, PASSION: FEELING, the most general of the terms in this connection, denotes any partly mental, partly physical (but not entirely sensory) response, or the resulting state, marked by pleasure, pain, attraction, or repulsion ⟨hostile *feelings* toward strangers⟩ ⟨the sentimental song aroused no *feeling* in him at all⟩ ⟨expressions of patriotic *feeling* —D.W.Brogan⟩ ⟨she had a *feeling* that all would be well —Gilbert Parker⟩ AFFECTION is usu. applied to feelings marked by inclination toward, liking, or fondness ⟨his personality aroused the lasting *affection* of the generations of students he instructed —W.S.Rusk⟩ ⟨the authors' *affection* for the buildings they have seen in China —Jane G. Mahler⟩ ⟨without fear or favor, *affection* or ill-will —F.T.Giles⟩ EMOTION usu. suggests a condition that involves more of the total mental and physical response than does FEELING, or implies feelings marked by a certain excitement or agitation ⟨rousing the patriotic *emotions* of the citizenry —Oscar Handlin⟩ ⟨every other *emotion* — affection, tenderness, sympathy, sentiment —Ellen Glasgow⟩ ⟨the *emotions* which we ordinarily distinguish — ambition, lust, pity, pride, anger, and many others —Stuart Hampshire⟩ SENTIMENT suggests a larger intellectual element than do the other terms, applying commonly to an emotion inspired by an idea, often suggesting a refined or an affected feeling ⟨one of the centers of anti⸗slavery *sentiment* —*Amer. Guide Series: Tenn.*⟩ ⟨a considerable *sentiment* in favor of the proposition —J.H.Easterby⟩ ⟨man of liberal *sentiments* and cultivated understandings —T.B. Macaulay⟩ PASSION suggests a strong, esp. a controlling, emotion, implying urgency of desire (as for possession or revenge) ⟨the love of dancing amounts almost to a *passion* —*Amer. Guide Series: La.*⟩ ⟨this consuming *passion* for law —H.E.Scudder⟩ **syn** see in addition SENSATION

[2]**feeling** *adj* [ME *feling*, fr. *felen* to feel + *-inge*, *-ing* -ing (alter. of *-inde*, *-ende*)] **1 a :** SENTIENT, SENSITIVE ⟨not a mere lump of clay but a ~ creature⟩ **:** having the capacity to feel or respond emotionally **b :** easily affected or moved emotionally ⟨a ~ heart⟩ **2 :** expressing or evincing great sensitivity or emotional susceptibility ⟨wrote in passionate ~ language⟩ **3** *obs* **:** deeply or keenly felt ⟨a ~ grief⟩ — **feel·ing·ness** *n* -ES

feel·ing·ful \ˈfēliŋfəl, -lēŋ-\ *adj* **:** marked by strong feeling ⟨a ~ expression of his hope for peace⟩

feel·ing·less \-ŋlə̇s\ *adj* **:** having no feeling **:** devoid of a normal capacity to feel ⟨their arms got tired, then heavy and achy, then dead and ~ —H.L.Davis⟩ ⟨an unsympathetic and positively ~ man⟩ — **feel·ing·less·ly** *adv*

feel·ing·ly *adv* [ME *felingly*, fr. *feling*, adj. + *-ly*] **:** with great feeling ⟨spoke ~ of his early childhood when he had been extremely happy⟩

feeling tone *n* **1 a :** FEELING 7c **b :** a particular quality of one's awareness measured in terms of pleasantness and unpleasantness **2 a :** the overall quality of an experience esp. as attributed to the thing experienced ⟨a second translation which I think reproduces the *feeling tone* of the original —Ernest Beaglehole⟩ **b :** one of the emotional shades of an experience esp. as attributed to the thing experienced

feel out *vt* **1 :** to sound out the sentiments of ⟨*felt out* the neighbors on the subject of local political reform⟩ — compare FEEL *vt* 3b **2 :** to test the validity or practicability of by cautious investigation, trial, or application ⟨*feel out* a new idea by submitting it to a group of colleagues⟩

feels *pres 3d sing of* FEEL, *pl of* FEEL

feel up *vt*, *slang* **:** to caress the upper thighs and genital area of

fee patent *n* **:** a patent for an estate in fee simple

feer \ˈfē(ə)r\ *vi* -ED/-ING/-S [prob. fr. ME (northern dial.) *feren* to plow, fr. OE *fȳrian* to make a furrow, fr. *furh* furrow — more at FURROW] *chiefly Scot* **:** to mark off land for plowing

feerie *var of* FEIRIE

feering *n* -S [fr. gerund of *feer*] *chiefly Scot* **:** feered or furrowed land

fee·ry–fa·ry \ˌfēriˈfāri\ *n* [redupl. of obs. Sc *fary* state of confusion or excitement, fr. ME (Sc), fairyland, state of confusion or excitement, fr. ME *faierie*, *fairie* fairyland — more at FAIRY] *chiefly Scot* **:** BUSTLE, TUMULT

fees *pl of* FEE, *pres 3d sing of* FEE

fee simple *n*, *pl* **fees simple** [ME, fr. AF *fé simple*, fr. *fé* fee, fief (fr. OF) + MF *simple* — more at [2]FEE, SIMPLE] **:** a freehold estate of inheritance in land or hereditaments that may last forever and may be inherited by all classes of both lineal and collateral heirs of an individual owner or grantee — distinguished from *fee tail;* see FEE SIMPLE ABSOLUTE, FEE SIMPLE DEFEASIBLE

fee simple absolute *n*, *pl* **fees simple absolute :** a fee simple that has no limitation, qualification, or condition affecting it and is the maximum possible ownership in real estate under system of property founded on the English common law

fee simple conditional *n*, *pl* **fees simple conditional :** an estate in fee granted to a person and his issue or to a designated class of his issue that is subject to the possibility of reversion in case there is no such issue or no alternative gift to a designated person in case there is no such issue and that exists in states where the English Statute De Donis of 1285 or a similar statute converting such an estate into a fee-tail estate has not been adopted — compare FEE TAIL, REVERSION

fee simple defeasible *n*, *pl* **fees simple defeasible :** a fee⸗simple estate that may come to an end under a stipulated provision; *sometimes* **:** FEE SIMPLE DETERMINABLE

fee simple determinable *n*, *pl* **fees simple determinable :** a fee-simple estate subject by the provisions of the instrument creating it to come to an end automatically upon the occurrence of an event stated therein

fee splitter *n* **:** a physician who engages in fee splitting

fee splitting *n* **:** a dividing of a professional fee for specialist's medical services with the recommending physician

fee system *n* **:** a system by which a sheriff or warden is compensated through county, municipal, or state funds for boarding prisoners

[1]**feet** [ME *fet*, *feet*, fr. OE *fēt*] *pl of* FOOT

[2]**feet** \ˈfēt\ *n pl*, *Scot* **:** FOOTWEAR; *specif* **:** shoes and stockings ⟨you're soaking wet; sit by the stove and change your ~⟩

feet·age \ˈfēd·ij\ *n* -S [[1]*feet* + *-age*] **:** FOOTAGE — sometimes used of lumber and leather

fee tail *n*, *pl* **fees tail** [ME *fee taille*, fr. AF *fé taillé*, fr. OF *fé* fee, fief + *taillé*, *taillié*, past part of *taillier* to cut, decide, determine — more at [2]FEE, TAIL (entailed)] **:** an estate in fee granted to a person and his issue or a designated class of his issue that is subject to the possibility of reversion if there is no such issue or no alternative gift to a designated person in case there is no such issue, that is subject under modern statutes to being converted into a fee simple absolute by the owner's barring the entail by executing a deed in his lifetime or to being converted to other types of estates more in harmony with present social conditions, and that is the estate created by the English Statute De Donis of 1285 or a similar statute operating upon a grant that would otherwise create a fee simple conditional — compare REVERSION

feetfirst \ˈ⸗ˈ⸗\ *adv* **1 :** with both feet or all four feet foremost ⟨jumped into the water ~⟩ **2** *slang* **:** in a coffin **:** DEAD ⟨carried out ~⟩

feet foremost *adv* **:** FEETFIRST 2

feet of clay [so called fr. the feet (partly of iron and partly of clay) of the image in Nebuchadnezzar's dream in Dan 2:33] **1 :** a generally concealed or unobserved but marked weakness or frailty in one hitherto idolized for qualities seemingly superior to those of common humanity or feared because of formidable and seemingly unassailable command or strength **2 :** a focal weakness (as cowardice or fear) in a seemingly commanding person

[1]**feeze** *or* **feaze** \ˈfēz, ˈfāz\ *vt* -ED/-ING/-S [ME *fesen*, fr. OE *fēsian;* perh. akin to Norw *fuse* to gush, rush, ON *fjūka* to be driven by the wind — more at FOG] **1** *obs* **:** to drive away **:** put to flight **2 :** FAZE

[2]**feeze** \"\ *n* -S [ME *veze*, fr. *fesen*, *vesen* to drive away — more at [1]FEEZE] **1** *now dial* **:** a violent impact **:** RUSH **2** *dial* **:** a state of alarm or excitement

[3]**feeze** \"\ *vt* -ED/-ING/-S [obs. Sc *fize*, n., screw, fr. Flem *vize*, fr. MD *vise*, fr. MF *vis* — more at VISE] *dial Brit* **:** to tighten by turning **:** TWIST ⟨~ a fiddle string⟩

feg \ˈfeg\ *chiefly Scot var of* FIG

fe·ga·ry \fə̇ˈgāri\ *n* -ES [alter. of *vagary*] **1** *now dial Brit* **a :** WHIM **b :** an eccentric prank **2** *now dial Brit* **:** GEWGAW — usu. used in pl.

feg·a·tel·la \ˌfegəˈtelə\ [NL, fr. It, liverwort, dim. of *fegato* liver, fr. LL *ficatum* liver of an animal fattened with figs (trans. of Gk *sykōton*), fr. L *ficus* fig + *-atum* (neut. of *-atus* -ate) — more at FIG] *syn of* CONOCEPHALUM

fegs \ˈfegz, ˈfāgz\ *n* [alter. of [1]*faith*] *chiefly Scot* **:** FAITH — used interjectionally to express surprise or as a mild invocation

feh·ling solution \ˈfāliŋ-\ *or* **fehling's solution** \-ŋz-\ *n*, *usu cap F* [after Hermann *Fehling* †1885 Ger. chemist] **:** a blue solution that is made by mixing an alkaline solution of Rochelle salt with a solution of copper sulfate and that is used as a mild oxidizing agent esp. in testing for glucose and other reducing sugars and for aldehydes, being itself reduced to red cuprous oxide which precipitates

feh·me \ˈfāmə\ *n*, *pl* **fehmen** *or* **fehmes** *often cap* [G *feme*, fr. MHG (Westphalian dial.) *vēme;* akin to OFris *fēma* to outlaw, MD *veme* secret tribunal] **1 :** a late medieval German secret tribunal **2 :** a unit of a secret Nazi organization intent upon seeking out and executing those considered enemies of National Socialism

feh·mic \-mik\ *adj* **:** of or relating to the Fehme

fei \ˈfāˌē\ *n*, *pl* **feis** *or* **fei** [Tahitian] **:** a wild banana (*Musa fehi*) widely cultivated in Polynesia and distinguished by an upright fruiting stalk bearing large thick fruits that have reddish orange or yellow skin and are edible only when cooked

feif·teen \(ˈ)fefˈtēn\ *Scot var of* FIFTEEN

feign \ˈfān\ *vb* -ED/-ING/-S [ME *feinen*, *feignen*, fr. OF *feign-*, stem of *feindre*, fr. L *fingere* to shape, form, devise, feign — more at DOUGH] *vt* **1 a :** to cause (oneself) to appear ⟨~ himself to be sick⟩ ⟨~*ed* herself above such paltry activities⟩ **b :** to give a sham appearance of **:** simulate falsely ⟨~ sickness⟩ ⟨~ a limp merely to arouse sympathy⟩ ⟨one of the birds which ~*s* death when taken in the hand — lying limply with closed eyes —E.A.Armstrong⟩ **:** PRETEND ⟨~*ed* to be asleep⟩ **:** give a false impression ⟨everybody had ~*ed* . . . that his wife was as other wives —Arnold Bennett⟩ **c** *obs* **:** conceal esp. by disguising **:** DISSEMBLE **2 a :** to fashion by inventing (as a story or accusation) or by forging (as a document) **b :** to assert or relate as if true **:** ALLEGE ⟨~ that he was not feeling well so that he could leave the party early⟩ **c** *archaic* **:** to give fictional or fabled representation to **:** relate in fiction or fable **d** *archaic* **:** to give an imitation of (as a voice or manner) **:** COUNTERFEIT **3 a** *archaic* **:** to give a mental existence to or conjure up (something unreal) **:** IMAGINE **b** *obs* **:** to believe erroneously ~ *vi* **1** *obs* **:** to give false information **:** LIE **2 :** DISSEMBLE, PRETEND ⟨he told the truth because he was no good at ~*ing*⟩ **3 :** to create or invent fictional representations ⟨the ~*ing* novelist —W.V.O'Connor⟩ **syn** see ASSUME

feigned \ˈfānd\ *adj* [ME *feined*, *feigned*, past part. of *feinen*, *feignen* to feign] **1 :** FICTITIOUS, IMAGINARY ⟨an actual or ~ account of what happened⟩ **2 a :** not real or genuine **:** INSINCERE, FALSE ⟨showered him with ~ compliments⟩ **b :** PRETENDED, COUNTERFEIT ⟨he slipped into the part of the tranquil, fearless matador, and the ~ calm brought him genuine calm —Barnaby Conrad⟩ ⟨presented him with a ~ copy, not with the original⟩; *also* **:** altered to deceive **:** DISGUISED ⟨spoke in a ~ voice and a foreign accent⟩ — **feigned·ly** \ˈfān(ə̇)dlē, -li\ *adv*

feigned issue *n* **:** an issue framed often by an equity court or by arrangement of the parties in order to try before a jury a question of fact which the court either has not the power to try or is unwilling to try **:** an issue of fact that does not actually exist between the parties to litigation since it is based upon an obvious fiction

feign·er \ˈfānə(r\ *n* -S **:** one that feigns

fei·joa \fāˈyōə, fāˈhōə\ *n* [NL, fr. Juan de Silva *Feijó*, 19th cent. Span. naturalist] **1** *cap* **:** a small genus of So. American shrubs or trees (family Myrtaceae) having opposite leaves, fragrant white or purplish white flowers, and edible greenish red fruit **2** -S **:** any plant of the genus *Feijoa* **3** -S **:** the fruit of a feijoa

fei·jo·a·da \ˌfāzhəˈwäthə\ *n* -S [Pg, fr. *feijão* bean, fr. L *phaseolus* kidney bean — more at FRIJOL] **:** a thick stew that is made of black beans and preferably fatty meat (as sausage) with vegetables and that is popular in Brazil and some other So. American countries

feil \ˈfēl\ *adj* [perh. fr. [1]*feel*] *chiefly Scot* **:** neat and cosy **:** COMFORTABLE

feinne *also* **fein** \ˈfēn\ *n pl*, *usu cap* [IrGael *fianna*, *fēinne*, pl. of *fiann* band of Fenians] **:** FENIANS 1

[1]**feint** *adj* [ME — more at [1]FAINT] *archaic* **:** FEIGNED

[2]**feint** \ˈfānt\ *n* -S [F *feinte*, fr. OF *fainte* fabrication, feigning, fr. *faint*, *feint*, past part. of *faindre*, *feindre* to feign — more at FEIGN] **:** something feigned or intended to deceive esp. for an advantage **:** a false or deceptive act **:** TRICK; *specif* **:** a mock blow or attack on or toward one part in order to distract opposition while one attacks another part (as in fencing, boxing, or military strategy) **syn** see TRICK

[3]**feint** \"\ *vb* -ED/-ING/-S *vi* **:** to make a feint ⟨moved about with the grace of a ballet dancer, could counter and ~ —Nat Fleischer⟩ ~ *vt* **1 :** to lure or deceive with a feint ⟨the guard was ~*ed* out of position⟩ **2 :** to make a pretense of ⟨the assailant ~*ed* a rush, then stopped abruptly⟩

[4]**feint** \"\ *or* **faint** \"\ *adj* [*feint* alter. of [1]*faint; faint* fr. [1]*faint*] **:** being or belonging to fine pale horizontal lines produced by pen ruling (as in account books) ⟨~ lines⟩ ⟨~ ruling⟩

[5]**feint** *or* **faint** \"\ *n* -S **:** a feint line

feints *or* **faints** \ˈfān(t)s\ *n pl* [[1]*faint* + *-s*] **:** the weak and impure spirit containing fusel oil that is produced in the very first and the last part of the distillation of liquor (as whiskey) and that requires rectification

fei·rie \ˈfērē\ *adj* [ME (Sc) *fery*, fr. ME *fere* sound, strong + *-y* — more at FERE] **1** *Scot* **:** sturdy and strong **2** *Scot* **:** active and agile; *specif* **:** able to walk

[1]**feis** \ˈfesh\ *n*, *pl* **fei·sean·na** \-shənə\ *often cap* [IrGael, fr. MIr, feast; akin to OE *wist* food, feast, existence, OHG *wist* food, ON *vist* food, dwelling, Goth *wists* nature, essence, OE *wesan* to be — more at WAS] **1 :** an assembly in ancient Ireland for the promulgation of laws and for competition in artistic, intellectual, and physical prowess — compare AENACH **2 :** an Irish folk festival or convention patterned on the ancient feis and featuring games and competitions and usu. traditional Irish music and dancing — compare EISTEDDFOD

[2]**feis** *pl of* FEI

feist *or* **fice** *or* **fist** \ˈfīs(t)\ *n* -S [by shortening & alter. fr. obs. *fisting* \ˈfīstiŋ\, adj., breaking wind (in such expressions as *fisting dog*, *fisting hound*), fr. pres. part. of obs. *fist* \ˈfīst\, v., to break wind, fr. ME *fisten*, fr. *fist* flatus; akin to MHG *vist*, *vīst* flatus, emission of gas from the colon, ON *fīsa* to break wind — more at SPIRIT] **1** *chiefly dial* **:** a small dog of uncertain ancestry **:** MONGREL, CUR **2** *chiefly dial* **a :** a person of little worth **b :** someone with a bad temper

feisty \-tē\ *adj* -ER/-EST [*feist* + *-y*] **1** *chiefly South & Midland* **:** like a feist in behavior or appearance **2** *chiefly South & Midland* **:** being in a state of excitement or agitation: as **a :** full of nervous energy **:** FIDGETY **b :** touchy and quarrelsome **:** looking for trouble **c :** frisky and exuberant **3** *chiefly South & Midland* **a :** inclined to put on airs **:** AFFECTED, HAUGHTY **b :** WILFUL, PETULANT

fei ts'ui \ˈfātˈswē, ˈfāchˈwē\ *n* -S [Chin (Pek) *fei*[3] *ts'ui*[4] *yü*[4], fr. *fei*[3] *ts'ui*[4] kingfisher + *yü*[4] jade] **:** emerald-green jadeite from Burma

feke *var of* FAKE

feld·sher \ˈfel(d)shə(r)\ *n* -S [Russ *fel'dsher*, fr. G *feldscher*, *feldscherer* field surgeon, fr. *feld* field (fr. OHG) + *scherer* barber, surgeon, fr. OHG *skerāri* shearer, fr. *skeran* to shear + *-āri* -er — more at FIELD, SHEAR, -ER] **:** a practitioner of medicine in certain east European countries and esp. Russia without the full training or the status of a qualified doctor; *esp* **:** an assistant to a physician esp. on the battlefield

feld·spar \ˈfelzˌpär, -l(d)ˌsp-, -pȧ(r\ *also* **feld·spath** \-path\ *n* -S [*feldspar* part trans. of obs. G *feldspath* (now *feldspat*); *feldspath* fr. obs. G *feldspath* (now *feldspat*), fr. G *feld* field (fr. OHG) + obs. G *spath* spar (now *spat*), fr. MHG *spat*, *spāt;* akin to OHG *spān* chip of wood — more at SPOON] **:** any of a group of usu. white or nearly white, flesh-red, bluish, or greenish minerals that are closely related in crystalline form, that are all aluminum silicates with potassium, sodium, calcium, or barium, that occur in crystals and crystalline masses which are vitreous in luster and break rather easily in two directions at approximately right angles to each other, that are essential constituents of nearly all crystalline rocks (as granite, gneiss, most kinds of basalt, and trachyte), that on decomposition yield a large part of the clay of the soil and also the mineral kaolinite, and that include the monoclinic species orthoclase and celsian and the triclinic species microcline, anorthoclase, anorthite, albite, and other plagioclases (hardness 6–6.5, sp. gr. 2.5–2.9)

feld·spath·ic \(ˈ)felzˈpathik, -l(d)ˈsp-\ *also* **feld·spath·ose** \ˈ⸗ˌ⸗ˌthōs\ *adj* [*feldspathic* fr. ISV *feldspath* + *-ic; feldspathose* fr. *feldspath* + *-ose*] **:** being, belonging to, or containing feldspar — used esp. of a porcelain glaze containing feldspar

feld·spath·iza·tion \ˌ⸗ˌ⸗thə̇ˈzāshən\ *n* -S [ISV *feldspath* + *-ize* + *-ation*] **:** the process of feldspathizing or of being feldspathized

feld·spath·ize \ˈ⸗ˌ⸗ˌtīz\ *vb* -ED/-ING/-S [*feldspath* + *-ize*] **:** to develop into feldspar by metamorphism

feld·spath·oid \-ˌthȯid\ *n* -S [ISV *feldspath* + *-oid*] **:** a mineral consisting of an aluminous silicate (as leucite nepheline) that has too little silica to form feldspar — **feld·spath·oi·dal** \ˌ⸗ˌ⸗ˈthȯidᵊl\ *adj*

felf \ˈfelf\ *dial Eng var of* [1]FELLY

fe·li·bre \fāˈlēbrə, -rᵊ\ *n*, *pl* **felibres** \-rəz,-rᵊ\ *often cap* [F *félibre*, fr. Prov *felibre* felibre, any one of the learned men with whom Jesus at the age of twelve disputed in the Temple (Lk 2:46), perh. fr. LL *fellebris* being not yet weaned, fr. L *fellare*, *felare* to suck — more at FEMININE] **:** a member or supporter of the Felibrige, a literary association of Provençal writers founded near Avignon in 1854 esp. for the maintenance and purification of Provençal as a literary language

fe·li·bre·an \-rēən\ *adj*, *often cap* [F *félibréen*, fr. *félibre*] **:** of or relating to the felibres

fe·li·cia \fə̇ˈlish(ē)ə, -lēshə\ *n*, *cap* [NL, fr. L *felic-*, *felix* happy + NL *-ia*] **:** a large genus of So. African herbs or subshrubs (family Compositae) with solitary flower heads and bright blue rays — see BLUE DAISY

fe·li·cide \ˈfēləˌsīd\ *n* -S [*feli-* (fr. L *feles*, *felis* cat) + *-cide*] **:** the killing of a cat

fe·li·cif·ic \ˌfēləˈsifik\ *adj* [L *felic-*, *felix* happy + E *-i-* + *-fic*] **1 :** bringing about or designed to bring about or produce happiness ⟨conclude that the validity of ethical judgments is not determined by the ~ tendencies of actions —A.J.Ayer⟩ **2 :** measured or measuring value in terms of happiness ⟨an ethics that is ~ in character⟩

[1]**felicitate** *adj* [LL *felicitatus*, past part. of *felicitare* to make happy, fr. L *felicitas* felicity] *obs* **:** made happy

[2]**fe·lic·i·tate** \fə̇ˈlisəˌtāt, *usu* -ād·+V\ *vt* -ED/-ING/-S [LL *felicitatus*, past part. of *felicitare*] **1** *archaic* **:** to make happy or prosperous **2 a :** to reckon or consider as happy or fortunate ⟨*felicitating* himself on having so good a wife⟩ **b :** CONGRATULATE ⟨make a point of *felicitating* those you know whenever there is an occasion in their lives for rejoicing —Agnes M. Miall⟩ — **fe·lic·i·ta·tor** \-ād·ə(r), -ātə-\ *n* -S

fe·lic·i·ta·tion \⸗ˌ⸗⸗ˈtāshən\ *n* -S [F *félicitation*, fr. *féliciter* to make happy, congratulate (fr. LL *felicitare* to make happy) + *-ation*] **:** the act or an instance of felicitating **:** CONGRATULATION

fe·lic·i·tous \fə̇ˈlisəd·əs, -isətəs\ *adj* [*felicity* + *-ous*] **1 a :** happily suited to an occasion or purpose **:** expressed or applied with a fastidious appropriateness or telling effectiveness ⟨a ~ expression of affection⟩ ⟨handled the delicate matter in a most ~ manner⟩ **b :** marked by happy or fastidious appropriateness of expression or manner ⟨a ~ writer⟩ **2 a :** marked by general happiness or good fortune ⟨a ~ life⟩ ⟨a ~ country⟩ ⟨she had everything . . . life was indeed ~ —Rose Macaulay⟩ **b :** PLEASANT, CHARMING, DELIGHTFUL ⟨the ride through the countryside is a ~ journey for city people⟩ **syn** see FIT

fe·lic·i·tous·ly *adv* **:** in a felicitous manner ⟨~ translated into English⟩

fe·lic·i·tous·ness *n* -ES **:** the quality or state of being felicitous ⟨pleased by the ~ of the phrasing⟩

fe·lic·i·ty \fə̇ˈlisəd·ē, -sətē, -i\ *n* -ES [ME *felicite*, fr. MF *felicité*, fr. L *felicitat-*, *felicitas*, fr. *felic-*, *felix* happy, fruitful + *-itat-*, *-itas* -ity — more at FEMININE] **1 a :** the quality or state of being happy ⟨everlasting joy and ~ —*Bk. of Com. Prayer*⟩ ⟨no one more entitled by unpretending merit, or better prepared by habitual suffering, to receive and enjoy ~ —Jane Austen⟩ **b :** something that promotes or is the source of happiness **2** *archaic* **a :** good fortune **:** SUCCESS **b :** a fortunate achievement **:** a stroke of fortune **3 a :** a felicitous manner, faculty, or quality esp. in art or language **:** telling or elegant neatness or appropriateness **:** APTNESS, GRACE ⟨~ in the painting of children⟩ ⟨pleased by the ~ of the expression⟩ ⟨a writer of fluency and ~, of graciousness and gentleness —Saxe Commins⟩ ⟨the special *felicities* of water color as opposed to oil⟩ **b :** a felicitous turn of phrase or artistic expression **:** a happy achievement **:** an apt expression ⟨a style marked by *felicities*⟩ ⟨a poem is more than the sum of its *felicities* —*Times Lit. Supp.*⟩ **syn** see HAPPINESS

[1]**fe·lid** \ˈfēlə̇d\ *n* -S [NL *Felidae*] **:** one of the Felidae **:** CAT

[2]**felid** \"\ *adj* **:** of or relating to the Felidae

fe·li·dae \ˈfēləˌdē\ *n pl*, *cap* [NL, fr. *Felis*, type genus + *-idae*] **:** a cosmopolitan family comprising lithe-bodied digitigrade carnivorous mammals having soft and often strikingly patterned fur, comparatively short limbs with soft pads on the feet, usu. sharp curved retractile claws, a broad and somewhat rounded head with short but powerful jaws equipped with teeth suited to grasping, tearing, and shearing through flesh, erect ears, and typically eyes with narrow or elliptical pupils and esp. adapted for seeing in dim light and including the true cats (as the lion, tiger, jaguar, leopard, or cougar), the cheetah, and extinct related forms

fe·li·form \ˈfēləˌfȯrm\ *adj* [*feli-* (fr. L *feles*, *felis* cat) + *-form*] **:** resembling a cat

[1]**fe·line** \ˈfēˌlīn\ *adj* [L *felinus*, fr. *feles*, *felis* cat + *-inus* -ine] **1 :** of or relating to the genus *Felis* or the family Felidae ⟨the ~ tribe⟩ **2 :** resembling or suggesting a cat in manner or quality: **a :** sleekly graceful ⟨the women . . . were fair to look upon, ~ in movement —Douglas Carruthers⟩ **b :** SLY, TREACHEROUS ⟨a ~ old gossip⟩ **c :** STEALTHY — **fe·line·ly** *adv* — **fe·line·ness** \-īnnə̇s\ *n* -ES

[2]**feline** \"\ *n* -S **:** a feline animal **:** CAT

feline distemper *n* **1** *or* **feline enteritis :** PANLEUCOPENIA **2 :** a disease of cats closely related or identical to panleucopenia in which gastrointestinal symptoms predominate

fe·lin·i·ty \fēˈlinəd·ē\ *n* -ES **:** the quality of being feline; *also* **:** a feline characteristic ⟨those elusive *felinities* — beauty, sleekness, grace, and movement —*All-Pets Mag.*⟩

fe·lis \ˈfēlə̇s\ *n*, *cap* [NL, fr. L *feles*, *felis* cat] **:** the type genus of Felidae comprising the true or typical cats

[1]**fell** \ˈfel\ *n* -s [ME *fel* skin, fr. OE *fell;* akin to OHG *fel* skin, ON *berfjall* skin of a bear, Goth *thrūtsfill* leprosy, L *pellis* skin, Gk *pelma* sole, Russ *pelena* swaddling clothes, covering] **1 a :** an animal skin with or without the original hair or wool **:** PELT, HIDE **b :** the skin of a human being **2 :** the flesh immediately under the skin **:** a thin tough membrane covering a carcass immediately under the hide and consisting of superficial fascia more or less intermingled with fatty tissue **3 :** a heavy covering of esp. thick hair or wool **:** FLEECE

[2]**fell** \ˈ"\ *vt* -ED/-ING/-S [ME *fellen,* fr. OE *fellan, fyllan;* akin to OHG *fellen* to fell, ON *fella;* causative fr. the root of E *fall* (v.)] **1 :** to cut, beat, or knock down or bring down (as with a missile) ⟨~ a tree⟩ ⟨~ an opponent⟩ ⟨strong enough to ~ an ox⟩ ⟨~*ed* the deer with a single shot⟩ ⟨got as far as the top of the prison wall where a live electric wire ~*ed* him —*N.Y. Times*⟩; *also* **:** KILL ⟨a final attack of pneumonia ~*ed* him —*Time*⟩ **2** *chiefly Scot* **a :** SLAUGHTER ⟨~ a fat swine⟩ **b :** to bring to a state of exhaustion or prostration esp. by beating ⟨~*ed* the old mare⟩ **3 :** to sew with a flat-fell seam **:** HEM, BLINDSTITCH

[3]**fell** \ˈ"\ *n* -s **1 a :** the act of felling something (as a tree) **b :** the timber cut down in one season **2 a :** the junction of the last filling thread with unwoven warp threads when a cloth is being woven **b :** the final yard or so in weaving out a warp

[4]**fell** \ˈ"\ *past tense and dial past part of* FALL

[5]**fell** \ˈ"\ *adj* -ER/-EST [ME *fel,* fr. OF *fel* (nom. case form) cruel, fierce, fr. ML *fellon-, fello* villain, rogue — more at FELON] **1 a :** FIERCE, CRUEL, SAVAGE ⟨a ~ and barbarous enemy⟩ ⟨swoop down and massacre his relatives, carrying off two young girls for their own ~ purpose —*Time*⟩ **b :** AWESOME, SINISTER, MALEVOLENT ⟨turned on him a ~ countenance⟩ **c :** killing or markedly sickening or destroying **:** DEADLY, MURDEROUS, DIRE ⟨a ~ poison⟩ ⟨a ~ disease⟩ ⟨a murderer bent on his ~ purpose⟩ **2** *chiefly Scot* **a :** EAGER, INTENT ⟨~ on seeing him⟩ **b :** SHREWD, CLEVER ⟨~ at poetry⟩ **c :** SHARP, PUNGENT ⟨~ cheese⟩ **d :** SPIRITED, ENERGETIC **3** *chiefly Scot* **:** strange and inexplicable ⟨a ~ part of her died with him⟩ **syn** see FIERCE

[6]**fell** \ˈ"\ *adv* [ME *fel,* fr. *fel,* adj.] **1** *chiefly Scot* **:** in a fell manner: as **a :** FIERCELY, CRUELLY **b :** VIGOROUSLY, EAGERLY **2** *chiefly Scot* **:** VERY, GREATLY

[7]**fell** \ˈ"\ *n* -s [ME, fr. ON *fell, fjall;* akin to OHG *felis* rock, MIr *all* cliff, LGk *pella* stone, Skt *pāṣāṇa*] **1** *chiefly Scot* **:** MOUNTAIN, HEIGHT — now used chiefly in place names ⟨Capel Fells⟩ **2** *dial Brit* **:** an elevated wild field **:** a hill moor

fell·age \ˈfelij\ *n* -s **:** the act or process of felling (as a tree)

fel·la·gha \fəˈlägə, -lagə\ *n, pl* **fellaghas** *also* **fellagha** [Ar *fallāq* (pl. *fallāqah*) bandit, robber] **:** a member of an Algerian or Tunisian Muslim and nationalist guerrilla band

fel·lah \ˈfelə, fəˈlä\ *n, pl* **fella·hin** *or* **fella·heen** \ˌfeləˈhēn, fəˌläˈhēn\ [Ar *fallāḥ*] **1 :** a peasant or agricultural laborer in Egypt, Syria, and other Arabic-speaking countries **2 :** one of a race type in modern Egypt descended from ancient Egyptians

fel·la·ta \fəˈläd·ə\ *n, pl* **fellata** *or* **fellatas** *usu cap* **:** FULA 1

fel·la·tio \fəˈlāshē,ō, feˈ-, -lädē-\ *also* **fel·la·tion** \-lāshən\ *n* -s [NL *fellation-, fellatio,* fr. L *fellatus, felatus* (past part. of *fellare, felare* to suck) + *-ion-, -io* -ion — more at FEMININE] **:** the practice of obtaining sexual satisfaction by oral stimulation of the penis

felled *past of* FELL

fel·len \ˈfelən\ *n* -s [prob. by shortening & alter. fr. *felonwood* & *felonwort*] **:** BITTERSWEET 2a

fell·er \ˈfelə(r)\ *n* -s [ME *fellere,* fr. *fellen* to fell + *-er, -ere* -er] **:** one that fells: as **a :** FALLER 1 **b :** a worker who fells seams or binds the seams of knitted garments; *also* **:** a sewing machine attachment for flat-fell seams

fellfare *var of* FIELDFARE

fell–field \ˈ⸗,⸗\ *n* **:** a treeless rock-strewn area that is above the timberline or in the frigid zones and that is dominated by low plants or by grasses and sedges

fellies *pl of* FELLY

felling *n* -s [ME, fr. *fellen* to fell + *-inge, -ing* -ing] **1 :** FELLAGE **2 :** an area on which trees have been or are to be felled

felling ax *n* **:** an ax designed esp. for cutting down trees

felling wedge *n* **:** FALLING WEDGE

fellmonger \ˈ⸗,⸗⸗\ *n* -s *Brit* **:** one whose vocation is the removal of hair or esp. wool from hides in preparation for leather making

fellmongered \ˈ⸗,⸗⸗\ *adj* [fr. *fellmongering,* after such pairs as E *covering: covered*] *Brit, of wool* **:** removed in fellmongering

fellmongering \ˈ⸗,⸗(⸗)⸗\ *n* -s *Brit* **:** the trade or occupation of a fellmonger

fellmongery \ˈ⸗,⸗(⸗)⸗\ *n* -ES [*fellmonger* + *-y*] **1** *Brit* **:** the place of business of a fellmonger **2** *Brit* **:** fellmongering as a business

fell·ness *n* -ES [ME *felnes,* fr. *fel* fell + *-nes* -ness] **:** the quality or state of being fell **:** extreme cruelty, harshness, or destructiveness of character or effect ⟨a ~ of aspect⟩ ⟨the ~ of the blow staggered him⟩

felloe *var of* FELLY

[1]**fel·low** \ˈfe(,)lō, -lə, *often* -lə*w*+V\ *n* -s [ME *felawe,* fr. OE *fēolaga,* fr. ON *fēlagi,* fr. *fē* cattle, sheep, money + *-lagi* (akin to ON *leggja* to lay) — more at FEE, LAY] **1 a** *obs* **:** one associated with another as a sharer **:** PARTNER **b :** COMPANION, COMRADE, ASSOCIATE — used chiefly of men **c** *archaic* **:** ACCOMPLICE, HENCHMAN **2 a :** an equal in rank, power, or character **:** PEER ⟨more like a ~ than a subject⟩ ⟨the final line of seventeen syllables has no ~ —H.O.Taylor⟩ **b :** one of a pair: as (1) *obs* **:** SPOUSE (2) **:** something that matches or resembles another ⟨the vase is the exact ~ to one on the shelf⟩ **3 :** a member of a company or group having common characteristics or common interests: as **a :** a creature of the same kind **:** one of a usu. relatively homogeneous group ⟨all men are ~*s* in their need of food, clothing, and companionship⟩ **b :** CONTEMPORARY ⟨didn't like the company of his ~*s* but preferred to associate by way of reading and study with ancient Romans⟩ **c** *sometimes cap* **:** a member of an incorporated literary, scientific, and often professional society ⟨a ~ of several scholarly associations⟩ ⟨a ~ of the American College of Surgeons⟩ ⟨a ~ of the Royal Geographical Society⟩; *often* **:** such a member given a rank usu. of distinction with the title *Fellow* **d fellows** *pl* **:** a social group of usu. youngsters or teen-agers or the male members of such group **4 a** *obs* **:** a person of one of the lower social orders — used as a customary form of address to servants or those of lower social rank **b** *archaic* **:** a worthless or contemptible person **c :** MAN ⟨saw three strange ~*s* standing in a doorway⟩ — often used in phrases of familiar address ⟨no trouble at all, my dear ~⟩ ⟨I say, old ~, could you give me a lift home⟩ **d :** THING, CREATURE — used of children or animals ⟨the poor little ~ had fallen off his tricycle⟩ ⟨I fired twice but the big ~ got away and we lost his trail⟩ **e :** ONE ⟨the queer way you look at a ~ you'd think I'd committed a crime⟩ **5 a :** an incorporated member of a college or collegiate foundation esp. in a British university **b :** a member of the corporation or governing body in one of certain colleges or universities **c :** a scholar of some note who is appointed by a British university to reside and work in one of its colleges **6 :** a person appointed to one of a number of positions granting a stipend and allowing for advanced study: as **a :** a graduate student in an American university who is granted money to continue research usu. in preparation for an advanced degree and often with certain teaching duties **b :** a young physician who has completed training as intern and resident and has been granted a stipend and position allowing him to do further study and research in a specialty **c :** one who has been granted money to do research by a foundation

[2]**fellow** \ˈ"\ *vt* -ED/-ING/-S [ME *felawen* to join in partnership, fr. *felawe,* n. — more at [1]FELLOW] *archaic* **:** to produce or find an equal to **:** MATCH

[3]**fellow** \ˈ"\ *adj* [[1]*fellow*] **1 a :** belonging to the same group or class as oneself or as another — used only in attributive position ⟨a ~ creature⟩ ⟨a ~ lodge member⟩ ⟨a ~ trainee⟩ ⟨a ~ disciple⟩ ⟨a ~ pupil⟩ ⟨a ~ employee⟩ **b :** having or sharing the same occupation or avocation ⟨a ~ musician⟩ ⟨a ~ plumber⟩ ⟨a ~ golfer⟩ **c :** experiencing or suffering the same fate (as misfortune) ⟨a ~ paraplegic⟩ ⟨a ~ prisoner⟩ ⟨a ~ exile⟩ **d :** having the same weaknesses or strengths ⟨a ~ mortal⟩ ⟨a ~ sinner⟩ ⟨a ~ saint⟩ **e :** subject to the same government or political or civil obligations or having the same allegiance ⟨a ~ citizen⟩ ⟨a ~ American⟩ **2 :** accompanying one **:** accompanying another ⟨a ~ voyager⟩ **3 :** sympathetic as if one were of the same group as another or in the same circumstance ⟨the Indian's ~ feeling for wild things —*Amer. Guide Series: Tenn.*⟩

fellow commoner *n* **:** an undergraduate at Oxford, Cambridge, or Trinity College, Dublin, formerly permitted to dine at the same table as the fellows of his college

fellowcraft *n* **1 :** the second degree of Freemasonry **2 :** one who has taken the degree of fellowcraft — compare BLUE LODGE

fellow feeling *n* **1 :** SYMPATHY **2 :** a feeling of community of interest or of mutual understanding ⟨that sympathy must be more than the mere *fellow feeling* of other craftsmen —H.L.Mencken⟩

[1]**fel·low·ly** \-lōl|ē, -ləl|, |i\ *adj* [ME *felawely,* fr. *felawe* fellow + *-ly* — more at FELLOW] **:** SOCIABLE, COMPANIONABLE

[2]**fellowly** \ˈ"\ *adv* [ME *felawely,* fr. *felawely,* adj.] **:** in a fellowly manner

fel·low·man \ˈ⸗⸗ˈman, -maa(ə)n\ *n, pl* **fellowmen 1 :** a kindred human being ⟨the question of the meaning of existence is answered neither by a god nor a ~ —Karl Lowith⟩ **2 :** fellow human beings ⟨a shrewd judge of his ~⟩ ⟨trying to be of service to his ~⟩

fellow servant *n* **:** an employee working with another employee on a common enterprise of their employer under such circumstances that each employee if negligent may expose the other to harm which the employer cannot reasonably be expected to guard against or be held legally liable for

[1]**fel·low·ship** \ˈ⸗⸗,ship\ *n* -s [ME *felaweship,* fr. *felawe* fellow + *-shipe* -ship] **1 a :** the companionship of persons on equal and friendly terms **:** COMPANY, SOCIETY ⟨looking for the ~ of companionable people⟩ ⟨the inability of the individual to find satisfactory ~ in the group —N.A.Ford⟩ **b :** the state of being together or sharing (as in an activity or experience) **:** mutual participation, interest, or experience **:** common interest or experience ⟨their ~ in crime —A.J.Ayer⟩ **c :** intimate mutual personal intercourse ⟨a ~ with great men⟩ ⟨a ~ with the glorious firmament —E.J.Banfield⟩ **2 :** a company or group of equals or associates **:** UNION, ASSOCIATION ⟨he belongs to an organized ~ that circulates a devotional literary criticism —Bernard DeVoto⟩: **a** *archaic* **:** the fellows of a college or university **b** *archaic* **:** a guild or corporation **c :** BROTHERHOOD, FRATERNITY; *also* **:** a group with the intimate relationship or common purposefulness of a brotherhood or fraternity ⟨a ~ of women and girls devoted to the task of realizing in our own communities those ideals . . . to which we are committed as Christians —*Current Biog.*⟩ **d :** a local group of 10 or more Unitarians or Universalists ineligible for church status and usu. without a minister but recognized and regulated by the denomination **3 :** the quality or state of being comradely **:** FRIENDLINESS, COMRADESHIP **4 a :** the state or relationship of being an equal or an associate **b** *obs* **:** membership in a society **:** PARTNERSHIP, ALLIANCE **c :** mutual relation between members or branches of the same church **:** COMMUNION 3a **5 a :** the position or rank of a fellow (as of a university, college, or hospital) **b** (1) **:** the stipend or endowments of a fellow (as of a college or university) (2) **:** a sum of money offered or granted by an educational institution, a public or private agency, organization, or foundation for advanced study or research or for creative writing **c :** a foundation for the providing of such a stipend or sum

[2]**fellowship** \ˈ"\ *vt* **fellowshiped** *or* **fellowshipped; fellowshiped** *or* **fellowshipped; fellowshiping** *or* **fellowshipping; fellowships** [ME *felaweshipen* to join in fellowship, fr. *felaweshipe,* n.] **:** to join in fellowship or be in communion with (a church or church member)

fellow–travel \ˈ⸗⸗ˈ⸗⸗\ *vi* [back-formation fr. *fellow traveler*] **:** to be or act as a fellow traveler ⟨continued to *fellow-travel* with the Communists in various front organizations —H.L. Varney⟩

fellow traveler *n* [trans. of Russ *poputchik*] **:** one that sympathizes with and often furthers the ideals and program of an organized group (as the Communist party) without membership in the group or participation in its activities

fell pony *n* [prob. fr. [7]*fell*] **1** *usu cap F* **:** a breed of small hardy English ponies native to the regions west of the Pennine range **2** *often cap F* **:** an animal of the Fell pony breed formerly much used for pack purposes

fells *pl of* FELL, *pres 3d sing of* FELL

fell seam *n* **:** FLAT-FELL SEAM

fellside \ˈ⸗,⸗\ *n* -s **:** HILLSIDE, MOUNTAINSIDE

fell system \ˈfel-\ *n, usu cap F* [after *Fell,* 19th cent. engineer who used it in a mountain railway across Mont Cenis that was opened in 1868] **:** a system of tracking for mountain railroads that uses a central elevated double-headed rail laid sideways and gripped tightly on each side by horizontal wheels attached to the locomotive

fellup *usu cap, var of* FELUP

fellwort *var of* FELWORT

fel·ly \ˈfelē, -li\ *also* **fel·loe** \-(,)lō\ *n, pl* **fellies** *also* **felloes** [ME *fely, felive,* fr. OE *felg;* akin to OS & OHG *felga* felly, OE *fealg, fealh* piece of plowed land, Russ *polosa* strip, plot of ground, region] **:** the exterior rim or a segment of the rim of a wheel supported by the spokes

f felly

[2]**fel·ly** \ˈfel(l)ē, -)i\ *adv* [ME *felly,* fr. *fel* fell + *-ly* — more at FELL (fierce)] **:** in a fell manner: as **a :** FIERCELY, CRUELLY, BARBAROUSLY, SAVAGELY, DESTRUCTIVELY **b** *obs* **:** KEENLY, BITTERLY, TERRIBLY

felo–de–se \ˌfe(,)lōdəˈsā, -ˈsē, ˌfā-(,)lōdəˈsā, ˌfē(,)lōdəˈsē\ *n, pl* **fe·lo·nes–de–se** \fəˈlō(,)nēzd-, feˈ-\ *or* **felos–de–se** [ML *felo de se,* fr. *felo, fello* rogue, evildoer, felon + L *de* of, from + *se* (abl.) oneself — more at FELON, DE-, SUICIDE] **1 :** one that deliberately kills himself or dies from the effects of his commission of an unlawful malicious act **2 :** the act of deliberate self-destruction — compare SUICIDE

fe·loid \ˈfē,lȯid\ *adj* [NL *Feloidea*] **:** of or relating to the Aeluroidea

fe·loi·dea \fēˈlȯidēə, fəˈ-\ [NL, fr. *Felis* + *-oidea*] *syn of* AELUROIDEA

[1]**fel·on** \ˈfelən\ *adj* [ME *feloun,* fr. OF *felon* (oblique case form), fr. ML *fellon-, fello* villain, rogue, prob. fr. (assumed) OFrk *fillo* one who skins, one who whips; akin to OHG *fillen* to skin, whip, *fel* skin — more at FELL] **1** *archaic* **a :** CRUEL, FIERCE; *also* **:** MURDEROUS **b :** SAVAGE, WILD **2** *archaic* **:** WICKED, EVIL

[2]**felon** \ˈ"\ *n* -s [ME *feloun,* fr. OF *felon* (oblique case form) villain, rogue, fr. ML *fellon-, fello*] **1 :** a person who has committed a felony **2** *archaic* **:** one that is wicked **:** VILLAIN **syn** see CRIMINAL

[3]**felon** \ˈ"\ *n* -s [ME *feloun* suppurative sore, fr. OF *felon,* lit., villain] **1 :** a usu. suppurative infection involving the deep tissues on the palmar surface of a fingertip — called also *whitlow;* compare PARONYCHIA **2 :** a severe inflammation on a finger or toe esp. if involving the bone

felon de se *or* **felon of oneself** *n, pl* **felones de se** *or* **felons of oneself** [*felon de se* part trans. of ML *felo de se; felon of oneself* trans. of ML *felo de se*] *obs* **:** FELO-DE-SE

felon herb *n* **1 :** MUGWORT 1 **2 :** MOUSE-EAR 1a

fe·lo·ni·ous \fəˈlōnēəs, feˈ-\ *adj* [ME, fr. *felonie* felony + -ous] **:** of, relating to, or having the quality of a felony **:** being against the law **:** VILLAINOUS, CRIMINAL — **fe·lo·ni·ous·ly** *adv* — **fe·lo·ni·ous·ness** *n* -ES

felonious homicide *n* **:** the killing of a human being without legal justification

fel·on·ry \ˈfelənrē\ *n* -ES **:** FELONS; *specif* **:** the convict population of a penal colony

felonweed \ˈ⸗⸗,⸗\ *n* [*felon* (infection) + *weed;* fr. its use as a remedy for felons] **:** TANSY RAGWORT

felonwood \ˈ⸗⸗,⸗\ *n* **:** BITTERSWEET 2a

felonwort \ˈ⸗⸗,⸗\ *n* **1 :** BITTERSWEET 2a **2 :** CELANDINE 1 **3 :** MASTERWORT a **4 :** HERB ROBERT

fel·o·ny \ˈfelənē, -ni\ *n* -ES [ME *felonie,* fr. OF, treachery, ill will, misdeed, fr. *felon* villain, rogue] **1 :** an act on the part of a vassal involving the forfeiture of his fee or an act of a lord involving the forfeiture of his lordship in feudal law **2 :** a grave crime (as murder, manslaughter, rape, robbery, larceny, burglary, mayhem, arson, rescue of a felon, some types of prison breach, some offenses for which benefit of clergy was abolished, and sometimes treason) declared expressly as distinguished from a misdemeanor in English common law and resulting in outlawry if the offender fled and until the Forfeiture Act of 1870 resulting upon conviction in the offender's loss of his goods or lands or both and sometimes in punishment by loss of a member, whipping, death, or long imprisonment **3 a :** one of several grave crimes that are distinguished from treason or minor misdemeanors, that are expressly declared to be such by the common law or judicial decisions or statutes of a state that follows the English common law, and that sometimes include sodomy and offenses deemed serious in more modern times (as kidnapping or wilful evasion of income taxes) **b :** a crime declared a felony by statute because it may be punished by death or by imprisonment in a penitentiary or state prison regardless of the punishment actually imposed **c :** a crime declared to be a felony by statute because of the punishment actually imposed (as death or imprisonment for the length of time prescribed by the statute) **d :** any crime for which the punishment in federal law may be death or imprisonment for more than one year

felos–de–se *pl of* FELO-DE-SE

fels \ˈfels\ *also* **fals** \ˈfals\ *n, pl* **fa·lus** \fəˈlüs\ [Ar *fals* (pl. *fulūs*), fr. LGk *phollis,* a small coin, fr. LL *follis,* fr. L, bellows, leather moneybag — more at BLOW] **:** an Arabic copper coin

fel·sen·meer \ˈfelzən,me(ə)r\ *n* -s [G, fr. *felsen, fels* rock (fr. OHG *felis*) + *meer* sea (fr. OHG *meri*) — more at FELL (mountain), MARINE] **:** an assemblage of angular and subangular rock fragments completely mantling the surface and commonly present in mountainous regions above timberline where slopes are not too steep to retain the loose debris

fel·sic \ˈfelsik\ *adj* [*feldspar* + *silica* + *-ic*] **:** consisting of or chiefly consisting of feldspar or feldspathoid quartz

fel·site \ˈfel,sīt\ *n* -s [*felspar* + *-ite*] **:** a dense macrocrystalline igneous rock that is like flint in fracture and that consists almost entirely of feldspar and quartz — **fel·sit·ic** \(ˈ)felˈsid·ik\ *adj*

fel·so·phyre \ˈfelsə,fī(ə)r\ *n* -s [G *felsophyr,* fr. *felso-* (fr. *felsit* felsite, fr. E *felsite*) + *-phyr* -phyre] **:** a porphyritic rock having a felsitic groundmass — **fel·so·phyr·ic** \ˌ⸗⸗ˈfirik, -fīr-\ *adj*

fel·spar *n* -s [by alter. (influenced by G *fels* rock)] *chiefly Brit* **:** FELDSPAR

fel·spath·ic *adj* [irreg. (influenced by *felspar*) fr. ISV *feldspathic*] *chiefly Brit* **:** FELDSPATHIC

[1]**felt** \ˈfelt\ *n* -s [ME, fr. OE; akin to OS *filt* felt, OHG *filz* felt, Sw dial. *filta* to beat, L *pellere* to drive, beat, push, Gk *pelas* near] **1 a :** a cloth constructed usu. of wool and fur fibers often mixed with natural or synthetic fibers by the interlocking of the loose fibers through the action of heat, moisture, chemicals, and pressure without spinning, weaving, or knitting **b :** a firm woven cloth of wool or cotton heavily napped and shrunk to form a smooth resilient texture and used widely by manufacturers esp. of printing presses, pianos, and textiles **2 a :** an article of felt cloth; *esp* **:** a soft hat made of felt **b :** a length of felt used as protective or absorbent padding esp. in industry — see SILENCE CLOTH **3 :** any of several materials resembling felt in composition: as **a :** a heavy paper of organic or asbestos fibers impregnated with asphalt and used in building construction (as under shingling) **b :** pressed boards of rags or old paper used as insulation (as in a refrigerator) **c :** sheets of semirigid pressed fiber insulation used under the sheathing of a building or between rough and finish flooring **4 a :** a blanket of absorbent material (as wool) between pairs of which wet sheets of handmade paper are pressed in papermaking **b :** an endless belt commonly of textile material on which a web is carried (as after leaving the wire) in a papermaking machine

[2]**felt** \ˈ"\ *vb* -ED/-ING/-S [ME *felten,* fr. *felt,* n.] *vt* **1 :** to make into felt or a substance like felt **2 :** to cause to adhere and mat together (as the fibers in paper) **3 :** to cover with felt ⟨~ a cylinder⟩ ⟨a ~*ed* roof⟩ ~ *vi* **:** to become felted — sometimes used with *up* ⟨mustn't ~ up after repeated washing —*Punch*⟩

[3]**felt** *past of* FEEL

felted *adj* [fr. past part. of *felt*] **1 a :** made of or into felt ⟨~ cloth⟩ **b :** covered with felt **2 a :** MATTED — used esp. of woolen cloth that has shrunk **b :** having hairs, filaments, or hyphae closely woven or matted together

[1]**felt·er** \ˈfeltə(r)\ *vt* -ED/-ING/-S [ME *filteren, felteren,* fr. (assumed) AF *feltrer* to cover with felt, fr. (assumed) OF *feltrer* (whence OF *feutrer*), fr. OF *feltre, feutre* felt, of Gmc origin; akin to OS *filt* felt] *now dial Brit* **:** to mat together like felt **:** INTERTWINE

[2]**felter** \ˈ"\ *n* -s **:** one that makes felt or works with felt: as **a :** an operator of a machine that produces felting **b :** a worker who attaches felt weather stripping

felt fern *n* **:** TONGUE FERN

felt finish *n* **:** the finish applied at the wet press in papermaking by a felt of special weave

felt fungus *n* **:** a fungus (*Septobasidium pseudopedicellatum*) that frequently encircles the twigs and branches of various trees (as citrus in the southern U.S.)

felting *n* -s [fr. gerund of *felt*] **1 a :** the process by which fibers are made to mat together esp. in the manufacture of felt **b :** the material made by this process; *esp* **:** FELT **c :** the quality of fibers that causes them to felt **2 :** a felted mass (as of hair) **3 :** the action of shrinking into a matted state — used esp. of such shrinking in woolen cloth

feltlike \ˈ⸗,⸗\ *adj* **:** resembling felt in appearance or texture **:** soft and matted **:** having a napped somewhat fuzzy appearance or quality

felt·man \ˈ⸗mən, -,man\ *n, pl* **feltmen :** a maintenance mechanic who replaces the clothing used on papermaking machines

felt paper *n* **:** a highly porous absorbent paper used in the manufacture of some building and roofing papers

felt rust *n* **:** the telia of a rust (*Cronartium ribicola*) on currants and gooseberries — compare WHITE PINE BLISTER RUST

felt side *n* **:** the side of a sheet of machine-made paper that was not in contact with the wire of the papermaking machine during manufacture — called also *right side, top side*

feltwork \ˈ⸗,⸗\ *n* [*felt* (cloth)] **:** a fibrous network ⟨in the meshes of a loose ~ of silk, the young spiders are destined to live for some time —*Nature Mag.*⟩

feltwort \ˈ⸗,⸗\ *n* [ME, fr. OE *feltwyrt,* fr. *felt* + *wyrt* herb — more at FELT (cloth), WORT] **:** a mullein (*Verbascum thapsus*) with thick woolly leaves

felty \ˈfeltē\ *adj* -ER/-EST [*felt* + *-y*] **1 :** resembling or suggesting felt or a felted mass; *specif* **:** belonging to or having a texture that is like felt and that is produced by unoriented microlites of various minerals **2 :** FELTED

fe·luc·ca *also* **fe·lu·ca** \fəˈlükə, -ˈləkə\ *n* -s [It *feluca,* prob. fr. Sp *falúa, faluca,* perh. fr. Ar *fulūk,* pl. of *fulk* ship, fr. Gk *epholkion* small boat towed behind a ship, fr. *ephelkein* to drag along, tow, fr. *epi-* + *helkein* to drag, pull — more at SULCUS] **:** a narrow fast lateen-rigged commonly two or three-masted sailing ship chiefly of the Mediterranean area that is usu. low and decked at the ends or from stem to foremast and often has an awning and provision for the use of oars

fe·lup *or* **fel·lup** *or* **fu·lup** \fəˈlüp\ *n, pl* **felup** *or* **felups** *or* **fellup** *or* **fellups** *or* **fulup** *or* **fulups** *usu cap* **:** a member of a Negro people on the Atlantic coast of the western Sudan

fel·wort *or* **fell·wort** \ˈfel,⸗\ *n* [ME *feldwurt,* fr. OE *feldwyrt,* fr. *feld* field + *wyrt* herb — more at FIELD] **:** any of several plants of the family Gentianaceae

fem *var of* FEMME

fem *abbr* **1** female **2** feminine

[1]**fe·male** \ˈfē,māl\ *n* -s [ME, alter. (influenced by *male*) of *femel, femelle,* fr. MF & ML; MF *femelle,* fr. ML *femella,* fr. L, young woman, girl, dim. of *femina* woman — more at FEMININE] **1 :** an individual that bears young or produces eggs as distinguished from one that begets young ⟨the ~ has to carry an embryo inside her body⟩: as **a :** a female animal **b :** a woman or girl as distinguished from a man or boy

⟨74 percent of the employees were ~s⟩ ⟨when she was a few days old she became . . . the richest ~ in France —William Maxwell⟩ **2 :** WOMAN ⟨the guide perceived that the ~s could command their steeds —J.F.Cooper⟩ — now usu. used disparagingly ⟨ladies of culture and refinement or coarse common ~s⟩ ⟨the backbiting of catty ~s⟩ **3 :** a pistillate plant

²female \"\ *adj* [ME, alter. (influenced by *male*) of *femel, femelle,* fr. MF & ML; MF *femel, femelle,* fr. ML *femellus,* fr. L *femella,* n.] **1 a :** of, by, for, or being the sex that bears young or a member of that sex: as (1) **:** being a woman or girl or composed of members of the female sex ⟨a ~ heir⟩ ⟨the ~ population⟩ **:** WOMAN ⟨a ~ pilot⟩ (2) **:** belonging to, peculiar to, or characteristic of a woman ⟨a ~ name on the doorplate⟩ ⟨composed for ~ voices⟩ ⟨~ sensitiveness⟩ (3) **:** engaged in or exercised by women ⟨~ tillage of the fields⟩ ⟨~ suffrage⟩ **b :** exhibiting femaleness ⟨exceptional ~ behavior by the male bird⟩; *specif* **:** producing or capable of producing eggs ⟨the uterus is a ~ organ⟩ — symbol ♀ **2 a :** having some quality (as passiveness, gentleness, delicacy of color or sound, highness of pitch) associated with the female sex ⟨the ~ castanet . . . gives a delicate sound while the male . . . with its deeper tone plays the role of accompaniment —F.C.Schang⟩ **b** (1) **:** designed with a hollow into which a corresponding male part fits ⟨the ~ coupling of a hose⟩ ⟨the ~ molding of a table hinge⟩ (2) **:** faced with a character in intaglio ⟨a ~ stamping die⟩ ⟨a ~ typefounding matrix⟩ **3 :** FEMININE 4 **4** *of a dialect or speech form* **:** normally used only by women or by men speaking to women **5 :** of, associated with, or being the material, receptive, or productive principle of the cosmos — compare YIN

syn FEMININE, WOMANLY, WOMANLIKE, WOMANISH, EFFEMINATE, LADYLIKE: FEMALE, opposed to *male,* stresses the fact of sex and usu. lacks the rich connotation of various of the others in this set ⟨a *female* voice⟩ ⟨use of *female* labor in the mills⟩ ⟨*female* fashions⟩ ⟨the tender ministries of *female* hands —Alfred Tennyson⟩ FEMININE, opposed to *masculine,* has practically supplanted FEMALE in references to what is characteristic of or appropriate to women, esp. women's attitudes, qualities, and attributes ⟨the sweet, rich, almost *feminine* curves of his sensitive mouth —J.C.Powys⟩ ⟨the *feminine* task of mending a pair of gloves —Nathaniel Hawthorne⟩ ⟨the strangely *feminine* jealousies and religiousness —John Steinbeck⟩ ⟨the *feminine* touch of embroidery and lace —*N.Y. Times*⟩ WOMANLY, opposed to *manly* and also, from another point of view, to *girlish,* often describes qualities that befit a woman or make her particularly attractive ⟨yet more *womanly* was the purity with which she passed through the brutal warriors of a medieval camp —J.R.Green⟩ ⟨a *womanly* tenderness such as any man might prize at a sanctified hearthside —R.P.Warren⟩ WOMANLIKE may be used in reference to faults or foibles ascribed to women ⟨*womanlike,* taking revenge too deep for a transient wrong —Alfred Tennyson⟩ WOMANISH is often derogatorily used in situations in which manliness might be wanted or expected ⟨*womanish* entreaties and lamentations —T.B.Macaulay⟩ ⟨the lank and gray-haired, long-nosed, elderly poet whose head leaned with a weak, *womanish* tilt —H.V.Gregory⟩ EFFEMINATE often describes or suggests unmanly softness, delicacy, enervation, or lack of strength ⟨his manner, in spite of his rugged appearance, was oddly *effeminate* —John Buchan⟩ ⟨he saw in delicate, laborious, discriminating taste, an *effeminate* pedantry, and would, when the mood was on him, delight in all that seemed healthy, popular, and bustling —W.B.Yeats⟩ In reference to girls and young women LADYLIKE suggests decorous propriety; in references to boys and men it sarcastically suggests daintiness, delicacy, softness, primness, and lack of masculine force and strength ⟨your daughter may be better paid, better dressed, more gently spoken, more *ladylike* than you were in the old mill —G.B.Shaw⟩ ⟨that *ladylike* quality which is the curse of southern literature —Margaret Leech⟩

female complaint *n* **:** any of various ill-defined or imaginary disorders of the human female usu. associated with or attributed to the generative function

female dragon *also* **female water dragon** *n* **:** WATER ARUM

female fern *n* **1 :** LADY FERN **2 :** the common brake (*Pteridium aquilinum*)

female fluellin *n* **:** a cancerwort (*Kickxia spuria*)

female hormone *n* **:** a sex hormone (as an estrogen) primarily produced and functioning in the female

female impersonator *n* **:** a male entertainer who plays the role of a woman (as in vaudeville)

female nervine *n* **:** SHOWY LADY'S SLIPPER

fe·male·ness *n* -ES **:** the qualities (as of form, physiology, or behavior) that distinguish an individual that produces large usu. immobile gametes from one that produces spermatozoa or spermatozoids **:** FEMININITY — opposed to *maleness;* see SEX

female pronucleus *n* **:** the nucleus that remains in a female gamete after reduction and extrusion of polar bodies and that contains only one half of the number of chromosomes characteristic of its species — compare MALE PRONUCLEUS

female rhyme *n* **:** FEMININE RHYME

females *pl of* FEMALE

fem·cee \ˈfem,sē\ *n* -S [blend of *fem*ale and *emcee*] **:** a mistress of ceremonies esp. on a radio or television program

feme \ˈfem, ˈfēm\ *n* -S [AF, fr. OF, woman, wife, female, fr. L *femina* woman, female] **1** *also* **femme** \ˈfem\ **:** WIFE — used in heraldry correlatively with *baron* **2** *law* **:** WOMAN ⟨the ~ plaintiff⟩

feme cov·ert \fem'kəvərt, fēm-, -kōv-\ *also* **femme cou·verte** \,femkü'vę(ə)rt\ *n, pl* **femes covert** *also* **femmes couvertes** \-mz(')k-\ [AF] *law* **:** a married woman — distinguished from *feme sole*

fem·er·ell \ˈfem(ə)rəl, -mə,rel\ *n* -S [ME *femerell, fumerel,* fr. MF *fumeraille* & *fumeril,* modif. of LL *fumariolum* vent, smoke hole — more at FUMAROLE] **:** a small open structure on a roof (as of a medieval kitchen) for ventilation **:** LOUVER

feme sole \ˈfem'sōl, ˈfēm'-\ *n, pl* **femes sole** \-m(z)'s-\ [AF] **1** *law* **:** a woman not in the married state — distinguished from *feme covert* **2** *law* **:** a married woman acting or contracting with respect to her separate estate

fem·ic \ˈfemik, fē-\ *adj* [*fe*rro*m*agnesian + *-ic*] **1 :** belonging to or being a group of mostly ferromagnesian minerals including amphibole and pyroxene **2 :** MAFIC

fem·i·nal \ˈfemənᵊl\ *adj* [L *femina* woman + E *-al*] **:** FEMININE — **fem·i·nal·i·ty** \,==ˈnaləd·ē\ *n* -ES

fem·i·ne·i·ty \,==ˈnēəd·ē\ *n* -ES [L *femine*us womanly (fr. *femina* woman) + E *-ity*] **:** FEMININITY

fem·i·nie \ˈfemənē\ *n pl* [ME *femenie, feminie,* fr. MF, fr. OF, fr. L *femina* + OF *-ie* -y] **1 :** the world of women **:** WOMANKIND **2 :** a class of women **:** WOMEN ⟨when a man . . . wishes to go on a great duty . . . this selfishness on the part of the ~ is rather too much —Iris Origo⟩

¹fem·i·nine \ˈfemənən\ *adj* [ME *feminin, feminine,* fr. MF *feminin,* fr. L *femininus,* fr. *femina* woman, female + *-inus* -ine; akin to OE *delu* nipple, OHG *tila* female breast, ON *dilkr* sucking lamb, Goth *daddjan* to suckle, L *felare* to suck, suckle, *filius* son, *felix, fetus,* & *fecundus* fruitful, Gk *thēlys* female, *thēlē* nipple, Skt *dhayati* he sucks; basic meaning: to suck, suckle] **1 :** FEMALE 1a ⟨the ~ members of society⟩ ⟨the ~ lead in the play⟩ **2 :** characteristic of or appropriate or peculiar to women ⟨the gentler virtues which are especially ~⟩ **:** marked by or having features, attitudes, or qualities associated with women ⟨frilly ~ fashions⟩; *specif* **:** receiving or enduring action **:** PASSIVE ⟨each individual showing a mixture of masculine aggression and ~ tendencies⟩ **3 :** belonging to, connected with, or constituting the gender that ordinarily includes most words or grammatical forms referring to females ⟨the ~ gender⟩ ⟨a ~ noun⟩ ⟨a ~ form of an adjective⟩ ⟨a ~ ending⟩ — compare MASCULINE, NEUTER **4** *of a sign of the zodiac* **:** having a feminine influence ⟨beginning with Taurus alternate signs are ~⟩ **5 a :** having an unstressed and usu. hypermetric final syllable ⟨a line of iambic verse with a ~ ending⟩ **b :** having the final chord occurring on a weak beat ⟨music typified by ~ cadences⟩ **syn** see FEMALE

²feminine \"\ *n* -S [ME *feminin, feminine,* fr. *feminin, feminine,* adj.] **1 :** WOMAN ⟨sat serene, the eternal ~ of all the ages —Winston Churchill⟩ ⟨an anthology of fiction, articles, and cartoons all dealing with the ~ —Ward Moore⟩; *specif* **:** a markedly feminine woman or girl ⟨charming ~s and sloppy females⟩ **2 a :** a noun, pronoun, adjective, or inflectional form or class of the feminine gender **b :** the feminine gender

feminine caesura *n* **:** a caesura that follows an unstressed or short syllable — see EPIC CAESURA, LYRIC CAESURA

fem·i·nine·ly *adv* **:** in a feminine manner ⟨a ~ fair complexion⟩

fem·i·nine·ness \-nən(n)əs\ *n* -ES **:** the quality or state of being feminine

feminine rhyme *n* **:** double rhyme in verses with feminine endings (as *motion, ocean*)

fem·i·nin·i·ty \,femə'ninəd·ē, -ətē, -i\ *n* -ES [ME *femininite,* fr. *feminin, feminine,* adj. + *-ite* -ity] **1 :** the quality or nature of the female sex **:** WOMANLINESS ⟨disarmed by her delicate ~⟩ ⟨accused of catty ~⟩ **2 :** WOMANISHNESS, EFFEMINACY ⟨the ~ of his manner⟩ **3 :** WOMEN, WOMANKIND ⟨neither in Oriental women nor in the confident ~ of his own country⟩

fem·i·nism \ˈ===,nizəm\ *n* -S [¹*feminine* + *-ism*] **1 :** the presence of female characteristics in males **2** [prob. fr. F *féminisme,* fr. *féminin* feminine + *-isme* -ism] **a :** the theory of the political, economic, and social equality of the sexes **b :** organized activity on behalf of women's rights and interests; *specif* **:** the 19th and 20th century movement seeking to remove restrictions that discriminate against women

¹fem·i·nist \-,nəst\ *n* -S [F *féministe,* fr. *féminin* feminine + *-iste* -ist] **:** one that advocates or practices feminism

²feminist \"\ *also* **fem·i·nis·tic** \¦===¦nistik\ *adj* **:** of or relating to feminism

fe·min·i·ty \fe'minəd·ē\ *n* -ES [ME *feminite,* fr. MF *feminité,* fr. OF, fr. *feminin* feminine + *-ité* -ity] **:** FEMININITY

fem·i·ni·za·tion \,femənə'zāshən, -,nī'z-\ *n* -S **:** the process or condition of being feminized; *specif* **:** development of female secondary sex characteristics in a male or castrate

fem·i·nize \ˈfemə,nīz\ *vt* -ED/-ING/-S [F *féminiser,* fr. MF, fr. *feminin* feminine + *-iser* -ize] **1 :** to give a feminine quality to ⟨changes that ~ the hat⟩ ⟨influences that will ~ their robust morality⟩ **2 :** to cause (a male or castrate) to take on feminine characters (as by implantation of ovaries or administration of estrogenic substances) **3 :** to cause (as a population) to be made up more of females than of males **:** render preponderantly feminine in composition ⟨low salaries have *feminized* the teaching profession⟩

femino- *comb form* [L *femina* — more at FEMININE] **:** woman ⟨*femino*logy⟩

¹femme *var of* FEME

²femme *or* **fem** \ˈfem\ *n* -S [F *femme,* fr. L *femina*] *slang* **:** WOMAN 1

femme couverte *var of* FEME COVERT

femme du monde \,femdü'mänd, *F* fȧmdüemōⁿd\ *n, pl* **femmes du monde** \"\ [F, lit., woman of the world] **:** a sophisticated or worldly woman

femme fa·tale \,femfə'tal, ,fam-, fǟm-, -fə'tǟl,fȧ'tǟl, *F* fȧmfȧtȧl\ *n, pl* **femmes fatales** \-mf . . . al(z), -ǟl(z), *F* -mf . . . ȧl\ [F, lit., disastrous woman] **1 :** a seductive woman who lures men into dangerous or compromising situations **:** SIREN ⟨the glittering eye of a *femme fatale* in any Hollywood film —Katherine Anne Porter⟩ **2 :** a woman who attracts men by an aura of charm and mystery ⟨vying for the attention of a young *femme fatale* —E.D.Radin⟩

femora *pl of* FEMUR

¹fem·o·ral \ˈfemərəl\ *adj* [LL *femoralis,* fr. L *femor-, femur* thigh, femur + *-alis* -al] **:** of, relating to, or located near the femur or thigh

²femoral \"\ *n* -S **:** either of two femoral shields of the plastron of a turtle

femoral artery *n* **:** the chief artery of the thigh lying in the anterior inner part of the thigh and being undivided as far as a point about two inches below Poupart's ligament where it divides into (1) a large deep branch and (2) a smaller superficial branch — called also respectively (1) *deep femoral artery,* (2) *superficial femoral artery*

femoral canal *n* **:** the space between the femoral vein and the inner wall of the femoral sheath, being from a quarter to half an inch long and extending from the femoral ring to the saphenous opening

femoral nerve *n* **:** the largest branch of the lumbar plexus that in man comes from the 2d, 3d, and 4th lumbar nerves and supplies extensor muscles of the thigh and skin areas on the front of the thigh and medial surface of the leg and foot and that sends articular branches to the hip and knee joints — called also *anterior crural nerve*

femoral ring *n* **:** the oval upper opening of the femoral canal often the seat of a hernia — see CRURAL SEPTUM

femoral sheath *n* **:** the fascial sheath investing the femoral vessels

femoral triangle *or* **femoral trigone** *n* **:** SCARPA'S TRIANGLE

femoral vein *n* **:** the chief vein of the thigh constituting a continuation of the popliteal vein that accompanies the femoral artery in the upper part of its course and continues above Poupart's ligament as the external iliac vein

femoro- *comb form* [NL, fr. L *femor-, femur* thigh] **:** femoral ⟨*femoro*cele⟩ **:** femoral and ⟨*femoro*fibular⟩

fem·o·ro·tibial index \¦femə(,)rō+ . . . -\ *n* [*femoro-* + *tibial*] **:** the ratio of the length of the femur to the length of the tibia multiplied by 100 ⟨compared the *femorotibial indexes* of fossil men and modern anthropoids⟩

fe·mur \ˈfēmə(r)\ *n, pl* **femurs** \-ə(r)z\ *or* **fem·o·ra** \ˈfemərə\ [L] **1 :** one of the three flat narrow spaces separating the grooves of a triglyph **:** SHANK **2 a :** the proximal bone of the hind or lower limb that is in man the longest and largest bone, extending from the hip to the knee, articulating above with the acetabulum by a rounded head connected with the shaft of the bone by an oblique neck that bears a pair of trochanters for the attachment of muscles, and articulating with the tibia below by a pair of condyles — called also *thighbone* **b :** THIGH **3** [NL, fr. L] **a :** the segment of an insect's leg that is third from the body, is often enlarged, and constitutes the principle horizontal element **b :** MEROPODITE

¹fen \ˈfen\ *n* -S [ME, fr. OE *fenn* marsh, mud, dirt; akin to OHG *fenna* marsh, ON *fen,* Goth *fani* clay, Skt *paṅka* mud, mire] **:** low peaty land covered wholly or partly with water unless artificially drained

²fen \"\ *dial var of* FEND

³fen \"\ *also* **fan** \ˈfan\ *or* **fin** \ˈfin\ *or* **vents** \ˈven(t)s\ *interj* [prob. alter. of ¹*fend*] — used as a ritual call by children esp. in certain games (as marbles) to prevent certain actions by an opponent or teammate or to exempt the first caller from a task or action

⁴fen \ˈfən\ *or* **fan** \ˈfän\ *n* -S [Chin (Pek) *fên*¹] **:** CANDAREEN 1

fenagle *var of* FINAGLE

¹fence \ˈfen(t)s\ *n* -S *often attrib* [ME *fens,* short for *defens* — more at DEFENSE] **1** *archaic* **:** a means of protection or security **:** DEFENSE ⟨my whole body wanted a ~ against heat and cold —Jonathan Swift⟩ **2 a :** a barrier intended to prevent escape or intrusion or to mark a boundary ⟨large areas of range were put under ~⟩: as (1) **:** a structure of posts and boards, wire, pickets, or rails commonly used as an enclosure for a field or yard ⟨erected a ~ that was horse high, hog tight, and bull strong⟩ (2) **:** something legally constituting an enclosure around land (as a bank of earth high enough to confine livestock) **b :** something resembling a fence in appearance or function ⟨a teapot rimmed with a silver ~⟩ ⟨a ~ of mountains around the valley⟩ ⟨built a radar ~ across the continent⟩ **:** an immaterial barrier or boundary line ⟨erected legislative ~s to control the development of industrial and residential areas⟩ ⟨on the other side of the ~ in the argument⟩ **c** (1) **:** an obstacle met in fox hunting that can be jumped (as a fence, hedge, brook, or chicken coop) (2) **:** an artificial obstacle on the course of a steeplechase or horse show **:** JUMP **d :** FENCING 3 **3 :** FENCING 4 ⟨books of ~⟩ **4 a :** a receiver of stolen property **:** a dealer in stolen goods **b :** a place where stolen goods are bought and sold **5 a :** an attachment to a plane, saw bench, or woodworking machine that controls the location or extent of the cut — see BEADING PLANE illustration **b :** an attachment to a marking gauge that serves to guide the marking **6 :** a projection on a lock forming an obstruction to throwing the bolt except when the gatings of the tumblers are properly arranged (as by the key) to allow the fence to pass **7 :** a means of political support for an officeholder, candidate, or institution **:** a political interest — usu. used in pl. ⟨building his ~s for election as governor —*Springfield (Mass.) Daily News*⟩ ⟨the tedious, tricky, and often tense art of diplomatic *fence*-mending —*Newsweek*⟩ **8 :** a fixed plate that projects from the upper surface of an airplane wing and sometimes continues around the leading edge, that is substantially parallel to the airstream, and that is used to prevent spanwise flow — called also *stall fence* — **on the fence :** in a position of neutrality or indecision ⟨some who had been *on the fence* came out in favor of the plan⟩

²fence \"\ *vb* -ED/-ING/-S [ME *fensen,* fr. *fens,* n.] *vt* **1 a :** to surround, separate, or delineate with or as if with a fence **:** erect a fence around or along (as a field or boundary) ⟨he *fenced* his yard with white pickets⟩ ⟨mountains ~ in the valley⟩ ⟨~ off a corner of the sea with dikes⟩ ⟨the canonical books are those the church has *fenced* off from other writings⟩ **b :** to keep in or out with or as if with a fence: as (1) **:** to secure in an enclosure **:** CONFINE ⟨~ sheep⟩ (2) **:** to restrict the activity of ⟨minds that were *fenced* round with dogma⟩ (3) **:** to ward off **:** REPEL, EXCLUDE ⟨laws that ~ out undesirable immigrants⟩ **2 :** to provide a defense or screen for **:** give security to **:** PROTECT ⟨a motorcycle escort on each side *fenced* the celebrity's limousine⟩ **:** SHIELD ⟨she had *fenced* his tatters even from her own eyes —Mary King⟩ **:** HEDGE ⟨~s his doctrines with the specious plea that statesmen must live as the world lives —*Times Lit. Supp.*⟩ **3** *Scots law* **a :** to open the proceedings of (the parliament or a court of law) with a form of words forbidding persons to interrupt or obstruct the proceedings unnecessarily **b :** to secure or strengthen (a provision in a contract) by a condition (as by a clause imposing forfeiture) **4 :** to sell (stolen property) with criminal intent **:** dispose of (stolen goods) gainfully esp. to a fence ⟨the gang stole cars and *fenced* them themselves⟩ — compare RECEIVE **5 :** to turn aside **:** EVADE, PARRY ⟨the chairman ~s awkward questions⟩ **~** *vi* **1 a :** to practice the art of fencing ⟨he ~s daily with a skilled foilsman⟩ **b :** to use tactics of attack and defense resembling those of fencing (as thrusting, guarding, parrying) ⟨the tennis players *fenced* for an opening⟩ **c :** to baffle inquiry by equivocation or evasion **:** parry arguments by shifting ground ⟨he ~s skillfully on the witness stand⟩ **2** *obs* **:** to provide protection or security **:** guard or defend oneself — used with *against* ⟨a constant endeavor to ~ against the infirmities of ill health —Laurence Sterne⟩ **3 :** to leap a fence — used of a horse and rider or a greyhound ⟨the hunter ~s leaving a safe but not wasteful space above the jump⟩ **4 :** to build or repair a fence ⟨when farmers *fenced* with rails⟩ **syn** see DODGE, ENCLOSE — **fence the tables** *in Scottish Presbyterian churches* **:** to make a solemn address to those who present themselves to commune at the Lord's Supper on the conditions prerequisite to the service in order to hinder those who are unworthy from approaching the table

fence arbor *n* **:** an arbor connecting the spindle and tumblers of a combination lock

fence law *n* **:** one of the laws enacted by most states regulating the erection and maintenance of a fence sufficient to prevent trespass by livestock on cultivated ground ⟨two angry factions: the crop people who wanted *fence laws,* and the stock people who wanted free range —Carl Withers⟩

fence·less \-ləs\ *adj* **1 :** being without enclosure ⟨the ~ prairies of the old West⟩ **2** *archaic* **:** being without defense ⟨marked his ~ dwelling for their wrath —C.G.D.Roberts⟩ — **fence·less·ness** *n* -ES

fence lizard *n* **1 :** PINE LIZARD **2 :** AMERICAN CHAMELEON

fence month *n* **:** the closed season for deer in England lasting from June 9 to July 9

fence nail *n* **:** a heavy cut nail of tapered cross section used in building fences

fence-off \ˈ=,=\ *n* -S [²*fence* + *off* (as in *play-off*)] **:** a fencing bout for deciding a tie between individuals or teams

fenc·er \ˈfen(t)sə(r)\ *n* -S **1 :** one that fences as: **a :** one who practices the art of fencing **:** SWORDSMAN **b :** one who builds or repairs fences **c :** a horse trained to jump fences **2 :** an electric-fence controller

fence rider *n* **:** a ranch hand who inspects and repairs fences

fence·row \ˈ=,rō\ *n* [¹*fence* + *row*] **:** the land occupied by a fence including the uncultivated area on each side

fences *pl of* FENCE, *pres 3d sing of* FENCE

fence-sitter \ˈ=,==\ *n* [¹*fence* + *sitter*] **:** an undecided or neutral person ⟨whether he is a *fence-sitter* by conviction or is waiting to see which side wins⟩

fence-sitting \ˈ=,==\ *n* [¹*fence* + *sitting* (n.)] **:** a state of indecision or neutrality with respect to conflicting positions ⟨his reluctance to commit himself publicly has the appearance of *fence-sitting*⟩

fence viewer *n* **:** a local official who administers the fence laws (as by inspection of new fence and settlement of disputes arising from trespass by livestock that have escaped enclosure)

fen·chene \ˈfen,chēn\ *n* -S [G *fenchen,* fr. *fenchel* fennel (fr. OHG *fenihhal,* fr. L *feniculum*) + G *-en* -ene — more at FENNEL] **:** any of several isomeric liquid terpenes $C_{10}H_{16}$ obtained esp. by dehydration of fenchyl alcohol

fen·chol \-,chōl, -ōl\ *n* -S [ISV *fenchene* + *-ol*] **:** FENCHYL ALCOHOL

fen·chone \-,chōn\ *n* -S [G *fenchon,* fr. *fenchel* fennel + *-on* -one] **:** an oily terpenoid ketone $C_{10}H_{16}O$ that is isomeric with camphor and has a camphoraceous odor, that exists in three optically different forms, occurring as the dextrorotatory form esp. in fennel oil and as the levorotatory form in thuja oil, and that is used chiefly as a pine scent; 1,3,3-trimethyl-2-keto-norbornane

fen·chyl alcohol \-,chil-, -,chəl-\ *n* [ISV *fenchene* + *-yl*] **:** either of two stereoisomeric alcohols $C_{10}H_{17}OH$ made by hydrogenation of fenchone; *esp* **:** the solid racemic alpha-fenchyl alcohol obtained from pine oil from the stumps of southern pine

¹fen·ci·ble \ˈfen(t)səbəl\ *adj* [ME *fensable, fensible,* short for *defensable, defensible* — more at DEFENSIBLE] **1** *chiefly Scot, of a man* **a :** capable of defending or bearing arms for his country **b :** eligible for military service **2** *archaic* **:** capable of being defended ⟨this old tower . . . is ~ —Sir Walter Scott⟩ **3 :** being of the corps of fencibles ⟨~ and militia regiments⟩

²fencible \"\ *n* -S **:** a soldier in a corps enlisted only for home service and for the duration of a war esp. in Britain and the U.S. during the second half of the 18th and first half of the 19th centuries

fencing *n* -S [ME *fensing,* fr. gerund of *fensen* to protect — more at FENCE] **1 :** FENCE 2a(1) ⟨makeshift ~ blocked the gaps between the buildings⟩ **2 :** the fences of a property or region ⟨the ~ of the farm was in poor repair⟩ **3 :** material used in building a fence **4 :** the art or practice of attack and defense with foil, epee, or saber which has as its object the scoring of a touch and for which blunted weapons and usu. protective clothing and masks are used — compare PARRY

fencing patent *n* **:** a patent broader in scope than the product or process actually intended to be manufactured thereunder that is procured to hinder competitors — called also *blocking patent*

¹fend \ˈfend\ *vb* -ED/-ING/-S [ME *fenden,* short for *defenden* — more at DEFEND] *vt* **1 :** DEFEND, PROTECT ⟨~*ing* himself from her clamor —Elizabeth M. Roberts⟩ **2 a :** to keep off **:** prevent from entering or hitting **:** ward off **:** REPEL ⟨raised his arm up to ~ branches from his eyes⟩ — often used with *off* ⟨her policy of ~*ing* off her suitor was no good; she would have to rebuff him —Rex Ingamells⟩ **b :** to push or keep (a boat) from a shore, dock, or ship **:** SHOVE — often used with *off* **3** *dial Brit* **:** to provide for **:** SUPPORT **~** *vi* **1** *dial Brit* **a :** to make an effort **:** STRUGGLE **b :** to get along **:** FARE **2 a :** to look out (for oneself) **:** MANAGE ⟨parents who go out and leave their young children to ~ for themselves⟩ **b :** to supply a livelihood (as for oneself) **:** PROVIDE ⟨told at the age of 18 to ~ for himself⟩ ⟨three children to ~ for⟩

²fend \"\ *n* -S *chiefly Scot* **:** an effort or attempt esp. at self-support ⟨he makes a good ~⟩

fend·er \ˈfendə(r)\ *n* -S *often attrib* [ME *fendour,* fr. *fenden,* v. + *-our* -or] **1 :** a device attached or set up to prevent something from sustaining or inflicting damage: as **a** (1) **:** a buffer (as a camel or pudding) between a ship and wharf or between two ships that absorbs and distributes shock and prevents

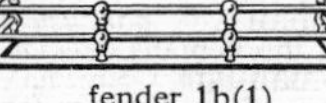

fender 1b(1)

chafing (2) **:** a pile or a row or cluster of piles placed to protect a dock or bridge pier from damage by docking ships or floating objects (3) **:** a timber or other obstruction set up to protect a scaffold base from impact or interference **b** (1) **:** a low often ornamental fence of iron or brass set before a hearth to confine coals and ashes — see CURB 5g (2) **:** FIRE SCREEN **c :** a device in front of a locomotive or streetcar that is designed to catch or throw aside an object struck **d** (1) **:** a guard or protective covering over a wheel of an automobile or other vehicle (2) *Brit* **:** ⁴BUMPER 2a **e :** a rail in a farrowing pen that prevents the sow from crushing the little pigs against the wall when she lies down **f :** a sheet temporarily inserted between the pastedown and flyleaf of a book in the course of binding to protect the pages (as from paste and pressure on the covers) **g :** an oblong or triangular shield of leather attached to the stirrup leather of a saddle to protect a rider's legs — see STOCK SADDLE illustration **2 :** a strip of stiff paper glued to the tympan of a platen press to prevent the sheets from sliding over the feed guides

fender bar *n* **:** a long fore-and-aft fender for a ship

fender beam *n* **1 :** the inclined advance piece of an icebreaker **2 :** the horizontal top beam into which the posts of a saw gate are framed

fender bolt *n* **1 :** a bolt with a projecting head designed to protect the adjacent parts **2 :** a bolt securing a fender

fender boom *n* **:** a boom used to keep floating logs in a course

fend·ered \'fendə(r)d\ *adj* [*fender* + *-ed*] **:** protected with a fender ⟨the ship should be well ~ amidships⟩

fend·er·ing \-d(ə)riŋ\ *n* -S [*fender* + *-ing*] **:** material used for fenders (as on a ship)

fen·der·less \-dələs, -dᵊl-\ *adj* **:** having no fenders

fender post *n* **:** one of the guiding stanchions of a saw gate

fender skid *n* **:** a log placed on the lower side of a skidding trail to keep the logs on the trail

fender skirt *n* **:** a panel that fits flush with the side of an automobile fender and conceals the upper part of a wheel

fender stool *n* **:** a long stool placed near or extending from a fireplace fender

fendy \'fendi\ *adj* [¹*fend* + *-y*] **1** *chiefly Scot* **:** capable and resourceful (as at managing and providing) **2** *dial Brit* **:** ECONOMICAL, THRIFTY

feneration *n* -S [L *faeneration-, faeneratio*, fr. *faeneratus, feneratus* (past part. of *faenerari, fenerari* to lend on interest, irreg. fr. *faenor-, faenus, fenor-, fenus* interest) + *-ion-, -io* -ion — more at FAENUS] *obs* **:** the act or practice of lending money on interest **:** USURY

fen·es·tel·la \,fenə'stelə\ *n* [L, small opening or window, dim. of *fenestra* window] **1** -S **a :** a niche like a window in the south wall of the sanctuary near the altar (as of a Roman Catholic church) containing the piscina and often also the credence **b :** a small window or opening like a window (as in an altar front for allowing relics within to be seen) **2** *cap* [NL, fr. L, small window] **:** a genus (the type of the family Fenestellidae) of Paleozoic bryozoans whose colonies form lacy fronds — compare LACE BRYOZOAN

fen·es·tel·lid \-eləd\ *n* -S [NL *Fenestellidae*, family of bryozoans, fr. *Fenestella*, type genus + *-idae*] **:** a bryozoan of the genus *Fenestella* or the family Fenestellidae

fen·es·tel·loid \¦==¦=,lȯid\ *adj* [NL *Fenestella* + E *-oid*] **:** resembling or related to the genus *Fenestella*

fe·nes·tra \fə'nestrə\ *n, pl* **fenes·trae** \-,strē, -,strī\ [NL, fr. L, opening in a wall for air and light, window] **1** *anat* **:** a small opening; *esp* **:** either of two membrane-covered apertures in the bone between the middle and inner ear: (1) an oval opening between the middle ear and the vestibule having the base of the stapes or columella attached to its membrane and (2) a round opening between the middle ear and the cochlea — called also respectively (1) *fenestra ova·lis* \-ō'välәs, -val-, -val-\ or *fenestra ves·ti·bu·li* \-ve'stibyə,lī\ and (2) *fenestra ro·tun·da* \-rō'təndə\ or *fenestra coch·le·ae* \-'käklē,ē, -lē,ī\ **2 a :** an opening like a window cut in bone (as in the inner ear in the fenestration operation) **b :** a window cut in a surgical instrument (as an endoscope) **3 a :** a transparent spot (as in the wings of certain moths) **b :** one of two pits covered with membrane on the head of certain cockroaches **c :** the fontanel of a termite

¹fe·nes·tral \-,strəl\ *n* -S [ME, fr. MF, fr. OF, window, opening, fr. *fenestre*, fr. L *fenestra*] **:** a casement or window sash closed with cloth or translucent paper instead of glass

²fenestral \"\ *adj* [L *fenestra* + E *-al*] **1 :** of or relating to a window **2** [NL *fenestra* + E *-al*] **:** of, relating to, or having a fenestra

fe·nes·trate \fə'ne,strāt, 'fenə,s-\ *adj* [L *fenestratus*] **:** FENESTRATED 2

fen·es·trat·ed \'fenə,strād·əd, fə'ne,s-\ *adj* [L *fenestratus* (past part. of *fenestrare* to provide with openings or windows, fr. *fenestra* opening, window) + E *-ed*] **1 :** provided with or characterized by windows ⟨symmetrically ~ buildings⟩ **2 :** having one or more openings or transparent spots **:** PERFORATED ⟨~ forceps with loops at the grasping end⟩ **:** RETICULATED ⟨part of the dress may be flimsy, ~, or transparent — P.M.Gregory⟩ ⟨the ~ leaves of some plants⟩

fenestrated membrane *n* **:** an elastic membrane of the inner coat of large arteries composed of broad elastic fibers that become fused to form a perforated sheet

fen·es·tra·tion \,fenə'strāshən\ *n* -S [L *fenestratus* + E *-ion*] **1 a :** the arrangement, proportioning, and design of windows and doors in a building **b** (1) **:** openings admitting daylight to a building ⟨classroom ~ consists of glass block panels over continuous windows⟩ (2) **:** the furnishing of a building with fenestration ⟨~ with louvered wall and continuous windows to control the amount and distribution of daylight⟩ **2 a :** an opening or break in a surface (as in a wall or membrane) ⟨the level of brightness at the ~s⟩ **b :** the presence of such openings **3** *or* **fenestration operation :** the operation of cutting an opening in the bony labyrinth between the inner ear and tympanum to replace natural fenestrae that are not functional because of sclerotic or other changes and to improve hearing impaired by such fenestrae

fen·es·tra·to \,fenə'strād·(,)ō\ *n* -S [It *finestrato*, fr. *finestrato*, adj., provided with windows, fr. L *fenestratus*, past part. of *fenestrare*] **:** a group of windows considered as a single window divided by mullions or colonnettes (as in Venetian palaces)

fe·nes·trule \fə'ne,strül\ *n* -S [L *fenestrula* small window, dim. of *fenestra* opening, window] **:** one of the small openings between intersecting branches of a lacy bryozoan colony

fen fire *n* [¹*fen*] **:** IGNIS FATUUS

fêng huang *or* **fung-hwang** \'fəŋ'(h)wäŋ\ *n* [Chin (Pek) *fêng⁴ huang²*, fr. *fêng⁴* male phoenix + *huang²* female phoenix] **1 :** the bird that in Chinese myth watches with the dragon, tortoise, and kylin over the empire and appears in times of prosperity and that is often represented in art as composite in appearance sometimes as a symbol of the empress **2 :** a bird with rich plumage and graceful form and movement domestic in the former imperial court of China, associated with the mythical fêng huang as an emblem of good fortune, and identified by some with the ocellated argus

feng·ki·eh \'fəŋjē¦ā\ *adj, usu cap* [fr. *Fengkieh* (Kweichow), city in Szechwan, central China] **:** of or from the city of Fengkieh, China **:** of the kind or style prevalent in Fengkieh

fen groundsel *n* [¹*fen*] **:** either of two European groundsels (*Senecio paludosus* and *S. palustris*) found in wet places

fêng shui \'fəŋ'shwā\ *n* [Chin (Pek) *fêng¹ shui³*, lit., wind and water, fr. *fêng¹* wind + *shui³* water] **:** a system of geomancy employed in China to bring practice into harmony with natural forces (as in determining the site of a grave or house)

¹fe·nian \'fēnēən, -nyən\ *n* -S *usu cap* [modif. (influenced by *Feni* ancient inhabitants of Ireland) of IrGael *féinne* (pl. of *fiann* band of Fenians) + E *-ian*] **1 :** one of a legendary band of warriors who defended Ireland in the 2d and 3d centuries A.D. ⟨the cycle of romance describing the battles, hunts, and rivalries of the *Fenians*⟩ **2 :** a member of a secret organization consisting mainly of Irishmen and men of Irish birth or ancestry and having for its aim the overthrow of British rule in Ireland

²fenian \"\ *adj, usu cap* **:** of, relating to, or characteristic of the Fenians ⟨*Fenian* conspirators⟩

fe·nian·ism \-ə,nizəm\ *n* -S *usu cap* **:** the principles and practices of the Fenians ⟨embers of the old *Fenianism* were quickened into flame —*Manchester Guardian Weekly*⟩

fen·land \'fen,land, -,lənd\ *n* [¹*fen* + *land*] **:** an area of low often marshy ground ⟨towns of the ~⟩ — often used in pl. ⟨undrained marsh and ~s of considerable extent —*Ecology*⟩

fen·man \-,mən\ *n, pl* **fenmen** [¹*fen* + *man*] **:** an inhabitant of a fen esp. of the lowlands of southeastern Lincolnshire and adjacent English counties known as the Fens

fen·nec \'fenik\ *n* -S [Ar *fanak*] **:** a small African fox (*Fennecus zerda*) of a pale fawn color that is remarkable for the large size of its ears; *sometimes* **:** any of various related foxes

fen·nel \'fenᵊl\ *n* -S [ME *fenel*, fr. OE *finugl, finul, finol*, fr. (assumed) VL *fenuculum*, fr. L *feniculum, faeniculum*, dim. of *fenum, faenum* hay; perh. akin to L *fetus* fruitful — more at FEMININE] **1 :** a perennial European herb (*Foeniculum vulgare*) adventive in No. America and cultivated for the aromatic flavor of its seeds **2 :** the seed of the fennel **3 :** a staminate plant of the hemp (*Cannabis sativa*)

fennel-flower \'==,=\ *n* **:** NIGELLA 2

fennel oil *n* **:** a colorless or pale yellow essential oil obtained from fennel seed and used chiefly as a flavoring material

fennel seed *n* [ME *fenel-seed*, fr. OE *finolsǣd*, fr. *finol* fennel + *sǣd* seed — more at SEED] **1 :** the seed of fennel **2 :** the seed of a fennel-flower (*Nigella sativa*) sometimes used as a condiment

fennel water *n* **:** a saturated solution of fennel oil in distilled water used as a stimulant and carminative

fen nightingale *n* **:** a croaking frog

fenno- *comb form, usu cap* [Sw, fr. L *Fenni* Finns] **1 :** Finnish and ⟨*Fenno*-German⟩ **2 :** including Finland ⟨*Fenno*-Scandinavia⟩

fen·no·man \'fenō¦män\ *n* -S *usu cap* [Sw, fr. *fenno-* + *-man* maniac, (fr. F *-mane*, back-formation fr. *manie* mania) — more at BIBLIOMANIA] **:** a partisan of the nationalist movement in Finland that began in the middle of the 19th century by advocating the use and cultivation of the Finnish language — compare SWEKOMAN

fen·no·scan·di·an \¦fe(,)nō¦skandēən\ *adj, usu cap* [*Fennoscandia*, the part of northern Europe comprising Finland, Sweden, Norway, and Denmark + E *-an*] **:** of or relating to the region of Fennoscandia ⟨the *Fennoscandian* ice cap . . . had central thickness not far from three miles —R.A.Daly⟩

fen·ny \'fenē, -ni\ *adj* [ME, fr. OE *fennig*, fr. *fenn* marsh + *-ig* -y — more at FEN] **1 :** having the characteristics of a fen **:** BOGGY ⟨the ~ ground along the lake shore⟩ **2 :** peculiar to or found in a fen ⟨long ~ grass⟩ ⟨fillet of a ~ snake, in the caldron boil and bake —Shak.⟩

fen orchid *or* **fen orchis** *n* **:** a small terrestrial orchid (*Liparis loeselii*) of eastern No. America and Europe with two nearly basal leaves and racemose irregular flowers

fen·ouil·let *or* **fen·ouil·lette** \¦fenᵊl¦et\ *n* -S [F *fenouillette*, fr. *fenouil*, small fennel, dim. of *fenouil* fennel, fr. MF *fenoil*, fr. (assumed) VL *fenuculum* — more at FENNEL] **:** a liqueur flavored with fennel seed

fens *pl of* FEN

fen·ster \'fenztə(r), -n(t)st-\ *n* -S [G, lit., window, fr. OHG; akin to OE *fenester* window, MLG & MD *venster, venstere*; all fr. a prehistoric WGmc word borrowed fr. L *fenestra*] **:** an erosional opening down through overthrust rock exposing the underlying rock — called also *window*

fent \'fent\ *n* -S [ME *fente, fent*, fr. MF *fente* — more at VENT (hole)] **1** *dial Eng* **:** a slit or opening in a garment; *esp* **:** a neck opening or placket **2 :** a remnant of cloth; *specif* **:** a short and often imperfect end or length of finished fabric

fen·u·greek \'fen(y)ə,grēk, -nē,g-\ *also* **foenn·greek** \-n,g-\ *or* **foen·u·greek** \-n(y)ə,g-, -nē,g-\ *n* [ME *fenigrek*, fr. MF *fenugrec*, fr. L *fenum Graecum, faenum Graecum*, lit., Greek hay, fr. *fenum, faenum* hay + *Graecum*, neut. of *Graecus* Greek — more at FENNEL, GREEK] **:** a leguminous annual Asiatic herb (*Trigonella foenumgraecum*) with aromatic seeds used in making curry, imitation vanilla flavoring, and some veterinary medicines

fenus *var of* FAENUS

feod \'fyüd\ *n* -S [ML *feodum*] *obs* **:** ³FEUD — **feod·al** \-dᵊl\ *adj, obs* — **feo·dal·i·ty** \fyü'daləd·ē\ *n* -ES *obs*

feo·da·ry \'fyüdərē\ *n* -ES [ME, fr. ML *feodarius*, fr. *feodum* + L *-arius* -ary] **1 a :** a feudal tenant **:** VASSAL **b :** SUBJECT, DEPENDENT, SERVANT **2 :** an officer of the ancient English Court of Wards appointed to receive rents **3** [influenced in meaning by L *foeder-, foedus* league — more at FEDERAL] *obs* **:** CONFEDERATE, ACCOMPLICE **4** [ME, fr. ML *feodarium*, fr. *feodum* + L *-arium* -ary] **:** a book compiling the details of feudal duties and services

feo·dum \'fyüdəm, 'feüd-\ *n, pl* **feo·da** \-də\ [ML *feodum, feudum* — more at FEUD] **:** ³FEUD — opposed to *alodium*

feoff \'fef, 'fēf\ *vt* -ED/-ING/-S [ME *feffen, feoffen*, fr. AF *feoffer* & OF *fieffer*, fr. *fiu, fief* fief — more at FEE (estate)] **:** to invest with a fee or feud **:** put in possession of a freehold interest in corporeal hereditament or of a leasehold **:** ENFEOFF

feoff·ee \(')fe¦fē, (')fē¦fē\ *n* -S [ME *feffe, feoffe*, fr. AF *feoffé*, past part. of *feoffer*, v.] **:** the person to whom a feoffment is made **:** the person enfeoffed; *specif* **:** a trustee in England invested with a freehold estate (as a member of certain boards holding land for public uses)

feoff·ment \'fefmənt, 'fēf-\ *n* -S [ME *feffement, feoffement*, fr. AF, fr. *feffer, feoffer*, v. + *-ment*] **1 :** the granting of a feudal fee **2 :** the act of granting a freehold estate in land by actual delivery of possession orig. by livery of seizin **3 :** a deed of enfeoffment

feof·for \'fefər, 'fēf-, (')fe¦fȯ(ə)r\ *or* **feoff·er** \'=fər\ *n* -S [ME *feoffor, feffour*, fr. AF *feoffour*, fr. *feoffer*, v. + *-our* -or] **:** one that makes a feoffment to another **:** one that enfeoffs

FEP *abbr* fore edges painted

fer \'fər(·), 'fə(r)\ *dial var of* FAR

-fer \fə(r)\ *n comb form* -S [F & L; F *-fère*, fr. L *-fer* (n. & adj. comb. form), fr. *ferre* to bear, carry — more at BEAR] **:** one that bears ⟨*aquifer*⟩ ⟨*conifer*⟩

fe·ra·cious \fə'rāshəs\ *adj* [L *ferac-, ferax* (fr. *ferre* to bear) + E *-ious*] **:** producing abundantly **:** PROLIFIC, FRUITFUL ⟨a world so ~, teeming with endless results —Thomas Carlyle⟩

fe·rae \'fe,rī; 'fe,rē, 'fi,-\ *n pl, cap* [NL, fr. L, wild animals, fr. fem. pl. of *ferus*, adj., wild — more at FIERCE] **1** *in some classifications* **:** a subdivision of Mammalia coextensive with Carnivora **2** *in some former classifications* **:** a subdivision of Mammalia comprising Carnivora together with a varied assemblage of chiefly carnivorous marsupials, bats, insectivores, rodents, and primates

ferae na·tu·rae \'fe,rīnə'tü,rē; 'fe,rēnə'tü,rē, 'fi,-\ *adj* [L, of a wild nature] *of an animal* **:** wild by nature **:** not usu. tamed — used of such animals as foxes and wild ducks in which at the common law no one can claim absolute property although a qualified property may be obtained by capturing them, by owning the land on which they are found, or by having a special privilege of hunting them

fer·a·ghan *or* **fer·e·ghan** \¦ferə¦gän\ *n* -S *usu cap* [fr. *Fergana, Ferghana*, region in west central Asia (fr. Per *Farghāna*)] **:** a usu. small heavy Persian rug chiefly of cotton having usu. a web and a fringed end, a deep blue or rose field with an allover herati sometimes guli hinnai design and a main border with a turtle design, and being highly prized if antique

¹fe·ral \'firəl, 'fer-\ *adj* [ML *feralis*, fr. L *fera* wild animal (fr. fem. of *ferus* wild) + *-alis* -al] **1 a :** suggestive of a beast of prey ⟨~ teeth⟩; *specif* **:** characterized by inhuman ferocity ⟨the ~ hostility of his fellow officers as they denounced and judged him —Albert Hubbell⟩ **b :** being, characteristic of, or suggesting an animal in the state of nature ⟨the human and ~ inhabitants of the forest⟩ ⟨as ~ in her wariness as the fierce . . . dogs that stalked the countryside —Ann F. Wolfe⟩ **c :** lacking a human personality due to being reared in isolation from all or nearly all human contacts **:** not socialized ⟨~ children who had been adopted by wolves⟩ **2 a :** existing in a state of nature **:** not domesticated or cultivated ⟨~ and semidomestic animals⟩ **b :** having escaped from domestication and become wild ⟨several species introduced by settlers soon became ~⟩ **syn** see BRUTAL

²feral \"\ *adj* [L *feralis*] **1** *archaic* **:** causing death **:** DEADLY, FATAL ⟨thence come . . . ~ diseases —Robert Burton⟩ **2 :** of or relating to the dead **:** FUNEREAL, GLOOMY ⟨in ~ order slow the slaughter barges go —F.T.Palgrave⟩

fe·ra·lia \fə'rālēə\ *n pl, usu cap* [L, fr. neut. pl. of *feralis* of the dead] **:** public religious ceremonies of ancient Rome held in honor of the dead upon the last day of the Parentalia — compare MANES

fe·rash *also* **far·rash** *or* **fer·rash** \fə'räsh\ *n* -ES [Hindi *farrāsh*, fr. Ar, spreader of carpets] **:** an Oriental servant (as in the Indian subcontinent) usu. employed in menial work

fer·bam \'fər,bam, 'fe(ə)r,-\ *n* -S [*ferric dimethyl-dithiocarbamate*] **:** a fungicide $[(CH_3)_2NCSS]_3Fe$ obtained as a black powder; ferric dimethyl-dithiocarbamate

fer·ber·ite \'fərbə,rīt, 'fer-\ *n* -S [G *ferberit*, fr. Rudolph *Ferber*, 19th cent. German + G *-it* -ite] **:** a mineral $FeWO_4$ consisting of a valuable ferrous tungstate occurring in black granular masses

fer-de-lance \¦ferdə¦lan(t)s, ¦fər-, -län-\ *n, pl* **fer-de-lance** [F, lit., lance iron, spearhead] **:** a large extremely venomous pit viper (*Bothrops atrox*) that has a horny spine terminating the tail and that is widely distributed in Central and So. America and in some of the West Indies where it infests the sugar plantations and is greatly dreaded — called also *bonetail*

fer-de-mo·line \,ferdəmō'lēn\ *or* **fer-de-mou·lin** \-mü'laⁿ\ *n, pl* **fers-de-moline** *or* **fers-de-moulin** \-rdə-\ [F *fer de moulin* mill-iron] **:** MILLRIND 2

¹fere \'fi(ə)r\ *n* [ME, fr. OE *gefēra*, derivative fr. the root of *faran* to travel — more at FARE] **1** *archaic* **a :** MATE, COMPANION ⟨the lamb . . . raceth freely with his ~ —Alfred Tennyson⟩ **b :** a wife or husband ⟨own her ~ and plighted lord —E.G.Bulwer-Lytton⟩ **2** *now dial Brit* **:** a person of the same rank or competence **:** EQUAL, PEER, MATCH

²fere \'fēr\ *adj* [ME, fr. OE *fēre* able to go, fit for military service; akin to OHG *gifuori* fit, suitable, ON *fœrr* able, strong, fit for use, OE *faran* to travel] *now chiefly Scot* **:** in good health **:** SOUND, STRONG — often used in the phrase *hale and fere*

fer·e·to·ry \'ferə,tōrē\ *n* -ES [ME *fertre, feretory, firetree*, fr. AF *fertre* & MF *fiertre*, fr. ML *feretrum*, fr. L, litter, bier, fr. Gk *pheretron*, fr. *pherein* to carry — more at BEAR] **1 :** an ornate often portable bier for the relics of a saint **2 :** a place for keeping a feretory; *esp* **:** a narrow space behind the high altar of a medieval cathedral or large church

ferfel *var of* FARFEL

fer·gha·nite *also* **fer·ga·nite** \fər'gä,nīt, 'fərgə,n-\ *n* -S [Russ *ferganit*, fr. *Fergana*, region in west central Asia + Russ *-it* -ite] **:** a mineral $U_3(VO_4)_2.6H_2O$ consisting of a hydrated uranium vanadate occurring in sulfur-yellow scales

fer·gu·son·ite \'fərgəsə,nīt\ *n* -S [Robert *Ferguson* †1865 Scot. physician + E *-ite*] **:** a brownish black mineral (Y,Er,-Ce,Fe)(Nb,Ta,Ti)O_4 consisting essentially of an oxide of yttrium, erbium, niobium, and tantalum with other metals often including uranium and isomorphous with formanite (hardness 5.5–6)

¹fe·ria \'firēə, 'fer-\ *n, pl* **feri·as** \-ēəz\ *also* **feri·ae** \'firē,ē, 'ferē,ā\ [ML, fr. LL, festal day, day of the week (as in *prima feria* Sunday, *secunda feria* Monday, etc., orig. designations for the days of Easter week) — more at FAIR] **:** a day of the Roman Catholic or Anglican church calendar other than Sunday on which no feast regularly falls often having a special commemorative office ⟨the Sundays and ~s of Lent⟩ — see GREATER FERIA

²fe·ria \'ferēə, -r(,)yä\ *n* -S [Sp, fair, market, fr. ML — more at FAIR] **:** a market festival in Spain and places affected by Spanish culture often celebrating a local religious holiday (as the day of a town's patron saint) **:** FAIR ⟨the annual bullfight at the start of a 3-day ~⟩

¹fe·ri·al \'firēəl, 'fer-\ *adj* [ME, fr. MF & ML; MF *ferial*, fr. ML *ferialis*, fr. LL *feria* + L *-alis* -al] **1 :** of, relating to, or being a feria; *esp* **:** belonging to any day of an ecclesiastical calendar that is marked by no special observance ⟨a cloth of gold vestment can be worn for festal as well as for dominical and ~ offices⟩ **2** *archaic* **:** of or being a legal holiday when labor is suspended and judicial proceedings may not be held or process served

²ferial \"\ *n* -S **:** ¹FERIA

fe·ri·a·tion \,firē'āshən, ,fer-\ *n* -S [ML *feriation-, feriatio*, fr. L *feriatus* (past part. of *feriari* to rest from work, keep holiday, fr. *feriae* days of rest, holidays) + *-ion-, -io* -ion — more at FEAST] *archaic* **:** the keeping of a holiday esp. by refraining from work

fe·rine \'fē,rīn, 'fi,-, 'fe,-\ *adj* [L *ferinus*, fr. *fera* wild animal (fr. fem. of *ferus* wild) + *-inus* -ine — more at FIERCE] **:** ¹FERAL 1a,1b

fe·rin·ghee *or* **fe·rin·ghi** *or* **fe·rin·gi** \fə'riŋgē\ *n* -S *usu cap* [Per *Firingī, Farangī*, fr. Ar *Farenjī, Ifranjī*, modif. of MF *Franc* Frank — more at FRANK] **1** *India* **:** EUROPEAN 1a **2** *India* **:** a Eurasian esp. of Portuguese-Indian blood — usu. used disparagingly

fer·i·ty \'ferəd·ē\ *n* -ES [L *feritas*, fr. *ferus* wild + *-itas* -ity] **:** the state of being feral **:** WILDNESS, BARBARITY ⟨the ~ of the animals of the deep forests⟩

ferk \'fərk, 'fe(ə)rk\ *var of* FIRK

¹fer·lie \'ferlē\ *adj* [ME *ferly, ferlich*, fr. OE *fǣrlīc* sudden, unexpected, fr. *fǣr* sudden danger or attack, calamity + *-līc* -ly — more at FEAR] *now dial* **:** STRANGE, SURPRISING ⟨gey ~ sight outside the door⟩

²fer·lie *also* **fer·ly** \"\ *n, pl* **ferlies** [ME, fr. *ferly*, adj.] **1** *Scot* **:** a strange or unusual sight **:** WONDER **2** *Scot* **:** a freakish person or animal sometimes seen in hallucinations ⟨when he was real drunk and the ~s came sniftering out of the whisky bottles at him —L.G.Gibbon⟩ **3** *Scot* **:** NEWS, GOSSIP — usu. used in pl. **4** *Scot* **:** SURPRISE, AMAZEMENT

³ferlie *also* **ferly** \"\ *vb* **ferlied; ferlying; ferlies** [ME *ferlien*, fr. *ferly*, adj.] *Scot* **:** WONDER

ferling *n* -S [ME, fr. OE *fēorthling*, fr. *fēortha* fourth + *-ling* — more at FOURTH] *obs* **:** a fourth part; *specific* **:** FARTHING

ferm \'fe(ə)rm\ *n* -S [ME *ferme* rent, lease — more at FARM] **:** ²FARM ⟨~s paid in kind or money by landowners in Anglo-Saxon and Norman times⟩

fer·mail \'fər,māl\ *n* [MF *fermail, fermaille*, fr. ML *firmaculum*, fr. L *firmare* to make fast + *-culum* -cle — more at FIRM (v.)] **:** a medieval clasp for clothing; *esp* **:** a late medieval English or French closed-ring brooch worn by both sexes (as to close a robe at the throat)

fer·man·agh \fə(r)'manə\ *adj, usu cap* [fr. *Fermanagh*, county in Northern Ireland] **:** of or from County Fermanagh, Northern Ireland **:** of the kind or style prevalent in Fermanagh

fer·ma·ta \fer'mäd·ə\ *n* -S [It, stop, pause, fr. *fermata* (fem. of *fermato*, past part. of *fermare* to stop, fr. L *firmare* to make fast), fr. L *firmata*, fem. of *firmatus*, past part. of *firmare*] **1 :** a prolongation at the discretion of the performer of a musical note, chord, or rest beyond its given time value **2 :** a sign consisting of a dot under or over a half circle placed over or under a note, chord, or rest indicating a fermata — called also *hold, pause*

fer·mat's principle \(')fer¦mäz—\ *n, usu cap F* [after Pierre de *Fermat* †1665 Fr. mathematician, its formulator] **:** a statement in optics: the path actually followed by a ray of light undergoing reflection or refraction is one of either minimum or maximum time as compared with adjacent arbitrary paths except for reflection or refraction at an aplanatic surface or passage through an aplanatic lens for which the time is constant

¹fer·ment \fə(r)'ment, ¦fər¦m-, ¦fə¦m-, ¦fəi¦m-\ *vb* -ED/-ING/-S [ME *fermenten*, fr. MF & L; MF *fermenter*, fr. L *fermentare* to cause to rise or ferment, fr. *fermentum*, n.] *vi* **1 :** to undergo fermentation **:** WORK ⟨spores survive and the fruit ~s⟩ **2 a :** to be in a state of individual or social ferment **:** be inwardly active ⟨everything ~s in him — his thoughts, sensations, and memories; nothing stays quiet —Janet Flanner⟩ **:** become mentally or emotionally agitated ⟨the squire continued ~*ing* to the highest degree of exasperation —T.L.Peacock⟩ **:** SEETHE; *also* **:** to undergo a process of ferment **:** develop by agitated inner activity ⟨but underneath things will be ~*ing*, basic decisions shaping up that will have far-reaching effects —*Kiplinger Washington Letter*⟩ ⟨still have a novel ~*ing* in my system —Virginia D. Dawson & Betty D. Wilson⟩ **b :** to act as a ferment in an individual or society **:** arouse agitation or promote change ⟨the idea of the self-rule of the people took hold and ~*ed* vigorously⟩ ~ *vt* **1 :** to cause to undergo fermentation ⟨enzymes that ~ tobacco⟩ **2 a :** to produce or bring to maturity as if by fermentation ⟨oppressive poverty ~*ed* violent discontent⟩ ⟨travel and reflection ~*ed* his already full mind⟩ **b :** to cause ferment (as of emotion) in **:** work into a state of ferment : AGITATE, EXCITE, FOMENT ⟨quick-spreading rumors ~*ed* the city and violence soon broke out⟩

²**fer·ment** \ˈfər,ment, ˈfə̄,m-, ˈfəi,m- *sometimes* ,=ˈ= *or* ,fə(r)ˈm- *or chiefly Brit* ˈ=,mənt\ *n* -s [ME, fr. L *fermentum* leaven, yeast — more at BARM] **1 a :** an agent capable of bringing about fermentation and other metabolic processes: (1) **:** a living organism (as a yeast or bacterium) that acts by virtue of its enzymes — called also *organized ferment;* used chiefly commercially; compare STARTER 3d (2) **:** ENZYME — called also *unorganized ferment* **b :** a person or thing that stimulates agitation or the active working out of change in an individual or society ⟨the possessive instinct, the most violent of ~s —Havelock Ellis⟩ ⟨the active ~ at work in China . . . was that of nationalism —*Times Lit. Supp.*⟩ **2 a :** FERMENTATION 1 **b :** a state of unrest **:** AGITATION, EXCITEMENT, TUMULT ⟨that ~ in the air which accompanies an election —John Buchan⟩ ⟨she was thrown into a ~ by his unexpected arrival⟩; *also* **:** a process of active often disorderly development in an individual life or in a society **:** the painful or disturbing transition from old to new ⟨a continent in ~, awakening to a new era after centuries of stagnation —Tad Szulc⟩ ⟨the great period of creative ~ in literature —William Barrett⟩

fer·ment·abil·i·ty \(,)=,mentəˈbiləd·ē, -lətē, -i\ *n* -ES **:** the quality or state of being fermentable

fer·ment·able \(,)=ˈmentəbəl\ *adj* **:** capable of undergoing esp. alcoholic fermentation

fer·men·tal \(ˈ)=ˈment³l\ *adj* [²*ferment* + *-al*] **:** FERMENTATIVE

fermentate *vt* -ED/-ING/-S [L *fermentatus,* past part.] *obs* **:** to cause to ferment

fer·men·ta·tion \,fərmənˈtāshən, ,fə̄m-, ,fəim-, -,men-\ *n* -s [ME *fermentacioun,* fr. LL *fermentation-, fermentatio,* fr. L *fermentatus* (past part. of *fermentare* to cause to rise or ferment) + *-ion-, -io* -ion — more at FERMENT] **1 a :** a chemical change accompanied by effervescence and suggestive of changes produced in organic materials by yeasts **b :** any of various enzymatic transformations of organic substrates (as the formation of alcohol from sugars or of vinegar from cider or the souring of milk); *esp* **:** a transformation of a carbohydrate material that yields such products as alcohols, acids, and carbon dioxide and that typically involves decomposition without the participation of oxygen — see ALCOHOLIC FERMENTATION; compare GLYCOLYSIS **c** (1) **:** any of various controlled aerobic or anaerobic processes used for the manufacture of certain products (as alcohols, acids, vitamins of the B complex, or antibiotics) by the action usu. of yeasts, molds, or bacteria (2) **:** any of various industrial processes for improving esp. flavor, aroma, or quality (as of tea, tobacco, or cheese) by means of fermentation **2 :** FERMENT 2b

fermentation tube *n* **:** a modified culture tube with an upright closed arm for collecting gas formed in broth cultures by microorganisms

fer·ment·ative \fə(r)ˈmentəd·iv\ *also* **fer·men·tive** \-entiv\ *adj* **1 :** causing or having power to cause fermentation ⟨the ~ substance in yeast⟩ **2 :** of or produced by fermentation ⟨the ~ process⟩ ⟨~ gases⟩ **3 :** FERMENTABLE

fer·ment·er *pronunc at* ¹FERMENT+ə(r)\ *n* -s **1 :** one that ferments: as **a :** a worker who attends a fermentation process (as of moistened tobacco or of mash for beer) **b :** an organism that causes fermentation **2** *or* **fer·men·tor** \"\ **a :** a vessel in which mash is fermented during the brewing process **:** a fermenting tank **b :** a laboratory apparatus for carrying out fermentation

fermentation tube

fer·men·tes·ci·ble \¦fərmən¦tesəbəl\ *or* **fer·men·tis·ci·ble** \-tis-\ *adj* [*fermentescible* fr. L *fermentescere* to swell, rise, ferment (fr. L *fermentum* leaven, yeast + *-escere,* incho. verb ending) + *-ible; fermentiscible* irreg. fr. L *fermentescere* + E *-ible* — more at BARM] **:** FERMENTABLE

fer·men·tol·o·gist \,==ˈtäləjəst\ *n* -s **:** a specialist in fermentology; *specif* **:** a chemist who experiments with ingredients and production processes of alcoholic beverages in order to control and improve taste, color, odor, and other characteristics — called also *oenologist*

fer·men·tol·o·gy \-əjē\ *n* -ES [²*ferment* + *-alogy*] **:** a science that deals with ferments and fermentation — compare ENZYMOLOGY

ferments *pres 3d sing of* FERMENT, *pl of* FERMENT

fer·me·ture \ˈfərmə,chu̇(ə)r\ *n* -s [F, lit., act of closing, apparatus for closing, fr. MF, fr. ML *firmatura* lock, clasp, fr. L *firmatus* (past part. of *firmare* to make fast) + *-ura* -ure — more at FIRM (v.)] **:** the mechanism closing the breech of a breech-loading firearm

fer·mi-di·rac distribution \¦fer(,)mēdə¦rak—\ *n, usu cap F&D* [after Enrico *Fermi* †1954 Ital. physicist and Paul A. M. *Dirac* b1902 Eng. physicist] **:** an assumed statistical distribution of speeds among the electrons responsible for thermal conduction in metals

fermi-dirac statistics *also* **fermi statistics** *n, usu cap F&D* **:** quantum-mechanical statistics according to which subatomic particles of a given class (as electrons, protons, and neutrons) have a quantum-mechanical symmetry that makes it impossible for more than one particle to occupy any particular quantum-mechanical state — compare BOSE-EINSTEIN STATISTICS

fer·miere \fermyeer\ *adj* [F (*à la*) *fermière* in the manner of the farmer's wife] *of a food* **:** prepared in plain country style

fer·mi·on \ˈfermē,än, ˈfər-\ *n* -s [Enrico *Fermi* + E *-on*] **:** a particle (as an electron, proton, or neutron) having a half-odd-integer number of quantum units of spin and conforming to the Fermi-Dirac statistics

fer·mi·um \-ēəm\ *n* -s [NL, fr. Enrico *Fermi* + NL *-ium*] **:** a radioactive metallic element artificially produced (as by bombardment of plutonium with neutrons) — symbol *Fm;* see ELEMENT table

fer·mor·ite \ˈfərmə,rīt\ *n* -s [Lewis L. *Fermor* †1954 Eng. geologist + E *-ite*] **:** a mineral $(Ca,Sr)_5[(As,P)O_4]_3$ that consists of an arsenate, phosphate, and fluoride of calcium and strontium and that is related to apatite and found in white crystalline masses

fern \ˈfərn, ˈfə̄n, ˈfəin\ *n* -s *often attrib* [ME *fern, ferne,* fr. OE *fearn;* akin to OHG *farn* fern, MIr *raith* fern, Skt *parṇa* wing, feather, leaf, and perh. to OE *faran* to travel — more at FARE] **1 a :** any of numerous nonflowering vascular plants constituting a class (Filicineae) of the division Tracheophyta; *esp* **:** a plant of the order Filicales resembling seed plants in being differentiated into root, stem, and leaflike fronds and in having vascular tissue but differing in reproducing by spores that are borne usu. in sori on fertile fronds or fertile portions of vegetative fronds and that upon germination commonly produce a flat typical thallus which produces antheridia and archegonia upon its surface, the egg of the archegonium giving rise to the sporophyte which is the conspicuous generation in the life cycle — see FROND illustration **b :** a frond of a fern **c :** a growth or quantity of ferns ⟨admiring the ~ of the park⟩ ⟨decorated with white roses banked with ~⟩ **2 :** any of various plants with fernlike foliage — usu. used in combination ⟨asparagus ~⟩ ⟨sweet ~⟩

fern ally *n* **1 a :** a pteridophyte other than a member of the order Filicales **b :** any of various pteridophytes (as horsetails or club mosses) that are not leafy in habit as distinguished from the leafy true ferns **2 :** WATER FERN 1

fer·nam·bu·co wood \,fərnam¦b(y)ü(,)kō-, ¦fernəm¦bü(,)kō-\ *n, usu cap F* [fr. *Fernambuco* (now *Pernambuco*), state of Brazil, fr. Pg] **:** PERNAMBUCO WOOD

fer·nan·de·ño \,fərnənˈdān(,)yō, ,fer-\ *n, pl* **fernandeño** *or* **fernandeños** *usu cap* [Sp *fernandeño,* fr. San *Fernando,* Franciscan mission in Los Angeles county, Calif. + Sp *-eño* (suffix added to place names to form names of inhabitants)] **1 :** a Shoshonean people of the valley of the Los Angeles river, California **2 :** a member of the Fernandeño people

fer·nan·di·nite \,fərnənˈdē,nīt\ *n* -s [Eulagio E. *Fernandini,* 20th cent. Peruvian mine owner + E *-ite*] **:** a mineral consisting of a massive dull green hydrous calcium vanadyl vanadate

fern asparagus *n* **:** ASPARAGUS FERN

fern ball *n* **:** a ball composed of the compacted rhizomes of several small drooping ferns that is usu. imported in a dry dormant condition from Japan for use in house decoration — see BALL FERN

fernbird \ˈ=,=\ *n* [*fern* + *bird*] **:** a small passerine bird (*Bowdleria punctata*) of New Zealand that frequents marshy ground and is becoming rare

fernbrake \ˈ=,=\ *n* [*fern* + *brake* (thicket)] **:** a dense growth of ferns

fern-bush \ˈ=,=\ *n* **:** a low densely branched very leafy white-flowered shrub (*Chamaebatiaria milbefolium*) of the family Rosaceae that is widely distributed in dry uplands of the western U.S. — called also *desert sweet*

fern clubmoss *n* **:** an epiphytic Australasian fern ally (*Tmesipteris tannensis*) with large lanceolate green leaves that grows on trunks of tree ferns

fern cycad *n* **:** CYCAD FERN

ferned \ˈfərnd, ˈfə̄nd, ˈfəind\ *adj* **:** abounding in or covered with ferns

fer·nent \fə(r)ˈnent\ *or* **fer·ninst** \-ˈnin(t)st, -ˈninzt\ *var of* FORNENT

fern·ery \ˈfərn(ə)rē, ˈfə̄n-, ˈfəin-, -ri\ *n* -ES **1 a :** a place where ferns are growing **b :** a planter for ferns **2 :** a collection of growing ferns

fern·flö·te \ˈfern,flœ̄tə\ *n* -s [G, fr. *fern* far (fr. OHG *ferrana* from far, fr. *ferro* far) + *flöte* flute — more at FAR, BLOCKFLÖTE] **:** a very soft organ pipe of flute tone and 8-foot or 4-foot pitch

fernery

fern fruit *n* **:** SORUS a

ferngale \ˈ=,=\ *n* [*fern* + *gale* sweet gale, fr. ME *gale, gayl,* fr. OE *gagel;* akin to MLG & MD *gagel* sweet gale] **:** SWEET FERN 1a

fern green *n* **:** a moderate yellow green that is greener and paler than average moss green, duller than average pea green, and duller and very slightly greener than apple green (sense 1)

fernleaf \ˈ=,=\ *n, pl* **fernleaf 1 :** a delicate red alga (*Callithamnion gracillimum*) with finely divided thallus **2 :** a disease of tomatoes caused by the cucumber mosaic virus and characterized by mottling and fernlike narrowing of the leaves

fernlike \ˈ=,=\ *adj* **:** resembling a fern esp. in leaf shape

fern moss *n* **:** any of various fernlike mosses esp. of the genus *Thuidium*

fern owl *n* **:** a nightjar (*Caprimulgus europaeus*)

fern palm *n* **:** any of several cycads with palmlike foliage

fern poisoning *or* **fern staggers** *n* **:** BRACKEN POISONING

ferns *pl of* FERN

fern scale *n* **:** a tropical armored scale (*Pinnaspis aspidistrae*) common on potted ferns and in greenhouses

fern seed *n* **:** the dustlike asexual spores of ferns that were formerly taken for seeds and reputed to render one invisible

fern·tick·le \ˈfern,tikəl\ *n* -s [ME *ferntikel, ferntikill,* fr. *fern* + *-tikel, -tikill,* prob. fr. L *-ticula* (as in *lenticula* lentil, group of freckles) — more at LENTIL] *n, chiefly Scot* **:** FRECKLE — **fern·tick·led** \-kəld\ *adj*

fern tree *n* **:** TREE FERN

fern weevil *n* **:** a weevil (*Syagrius fulvitarsis*) of Australia and the Pacific islands that feeds on ferns

fernwort \ˈ=,=\ *n* **:** a plant belonging to the Pteridophyta **:** FERN ALLY **:** FERN

ferny \ˈfərnē, ˈfə̄nē, ˈfəinē, -ni\ *adj, usu* -ER/-EST [ME, fr. *fern* + *-y*] **1 :** of or abounding in ferns **2 :** FERNLIKE ⟨the ~ shadows of locust leaves —W.V.T.Clark⟩

fer·o·cac·tus \,ferəˈkaktəs, ,fir-\ *n, cap* [NL, fr. *fero-* (fr. L *ferus* wild, fierce) + *cactus*] **:** a genus of nearly globular deeply ribbed cacti of Mexico and the adjacent U. S. having numerous spines, large funnel-shaped flowers, and dry fruits

fe·ro·ce \fāˈrō(,)chā\ *adj* [It, fr. L *feroc-, ferox*] **:** FIERCE, FEROCIOUS — used as a direction in music

fe·ro·cious \fəˈrōshəs\ *adj* [L *feroc-, ferox* fierce (fr. *ferus* wild, fierce + *-oc-, -ox* looking, appearing — akin to L *oculus* eye) + E *-ious* — more at FIERCE, EYE] **1 a :** characterized by wild or extreme rapacity, cruelty, acrimony, or destructiveness **:** violently aggressive **:** BLOODTHIRSTY ⟨a ~ tiger⟩ ⟨the raiders' ~ butchery of women and children⟩ **:** BITTER ⟨the ~ word battles he has had with other editors⟩ **:** DEVASTATING ⟨the ~ torrents of the flood⟩ **b :** suggesting a ferocious character or mood **:** FORMIDABLE ⟨a ~ beard⟩ ⟨a ~ smile⟩ **2 :** very great **:** EXTREME, EXCESSIVE ⟨he was a ~ bore⟩ **:** FURIOUS ⟨sought to forget his troubles through ~ activity⟩ ⟨a ~ wind swept the sea⟩ **syn** see FIERCE

fe·ro·cious·ly *adv* **:** in a ferocious manner ⟨pounces ~ on a trivial error of fact —C.W.Shumaker⟩ ⟨a ~ & logical system⟩

fe·ro·cious·ness *n* -ES **:** FEROCITY

fe·roc·i·ty \fəˈräsəd·ē, -sətē, -i\ *n* -ES [F & L; F *férocité,* fr. L *ferocitas,* fr. *feroc-, ferox* fierce + *-itas* -ity] **1 :** the quality or state of being ferocious **:** savage wildness **:** FURY ⟨turned on them with a ~ which made a savage of him on the spot —Virginia Woolf⟩ **:** extreme or furious intensity **:** ARDOR ⟨a wild ~ of joy overcame him —Liam O'Flaherty⟩ **2 :** an instance of ferocity ⟨has his great sentimentalities to compensate for his chronic *ferocities* —Edmund Wilson⟩

-fer·ous \f(ə)rəs\ *adj comb form* [ME, fr. L *-fer* & MF *-fere* (fr. L *-fer*) + E *-ous* — more at -FER] **:** bearing **:** producing **:** yielding ⟨auri*ferous*⟩ ⟨ovuli*ferous*⟩ — almost always preceded by *i* — **-fer·ous·ly** *adv comb form* — **-fer·ous·ness** *n comb form* -ES

fer·rai·o·lo·ne \fə,rīəˈlōnē\ *n* -s [It, aug. of *ferraiolo* large mantle, cloak, prob. fr. Ar *feryūl* wool cape, fr. L *palliolum* small Greek mantle, dim. of *pallium* Greek mantle — more at PALL] **:** a large full length cloak having a large flat collar, varying in color according to the wearer's rank, and forming the necessary complement of full ecclesiastical dress among Roman Catholic clergy on nonliturgical occasions (as an academic ceremony or papal audience)

fer·ra·ra \fəˈrärə\ *adj, usu cap* [fr. *Ferrara,* Italy] **:** of or from the city of Ferrara, Italy **:** of the kind or style prevalent in Ferrara

¹**fer·ra·rese** \fəˈrä,rēz, -ēs, ¦ferə¦r-\ *adj, usu cap* [It, adj. & n., fr. *Ferrara* Italy + It *-ese*] **1 :** of, relating to, or characteristic of Ferrara, a city in Italy **2 :** of, relating to, or characteristic of the people of Ferrara

²**ferrarese** \"\ *n, pl* **ferrarese** *cap* **:** a native or resident of Ferrara, Italy

ferrash *var of* FERASH

fer·rate \ˈfe,rāt\ *n* -s [ISV *ferr-* (fr. L *ferrum* iron) + *-ate*] **:** any of various classes of compounds containing iron and oxygen in the anion or regarded as so constituted: as **a :** a strongly oxidizing dark red salt analogous to the chromates and sulfates and formed in various ways (as by heating iron filings with a nitrate) ⟨potassium ~ K_2FeO_4⟩ — called also *ferrate(VI)* **b :** FERRITE

fer·rei·ro \fəˈrā(,)rō\ *n* -s [Pg, lit., blacksmith, fr. L *ferrarius,* fr. *ferrum* iron + *-arius* -ary — more at FARRIER] **:** a Brazilian tree frog (*Hyla faber*) that produces notes resembling measured beating on a copper plate

fer·rel \ˈferəl\ *archaic var of* FERRULE

fer·rel's law \ˈferəlz-\ *n, usu cap F* [after William *Ferrel* †1891 Am. meteorologist, its formulator] **:** a statement in meteorology: a wind in any direction tends to deflect to the right in the northern hemisphere and to the left in the southern with a force that is directly proportional to the mass of wind in question, its velocity, the sine of the latitude, and the angular velocity of the earth's rotation

fer·re·ous \ˈferēəs\ *adj* [L *ferreus,* fr. *ferrum* iron] **:** of, like, or containing iron

ferrer *n* -s [ME *ferrour* blacksmith who shoes horses, veterinarian — more at FARRIER] **1** *obs* **:** IRONSMITH **2** *obs* **:** FARRIER

¹**fer·ret** \ˈferət, *usu* -əd·+V\ *n* -s [ME *feret, ferret, furet,* fr. MF *furet, fuiret,* fr. (assumed) VL *furittus,* lit., small thief, dim. of L *fur* thief — more at FURTIVE] **1 a :** a semidomesticated variety of the European polecat sometimes treated as a separate species (*Mustela furo*) that is usu. albino with red eyes and is much used for hunting rodents and sometimes rabbits in Europe and occas. in the U. S. **b :** BLACK-FOOTED FERRET **2 :** a person who searches actively and persistently (as for incriminating information) ⟨German ~s who constantly spied on the Allied prisoners of war⟩ **3 :** an airplane equipped to detect a radar installation and analyze its signals

²**ferret** \"\ *vb* -ED/-ING/-S [ME *fereten, fureten,* fr. *feret, furet,* n.] *vt* **1 :** to hunt with a ferret: **a :** to hunt over ⟨they have *ferreted* the duke's fields⟩ **b :** to hunt for **:** TAKE *esp* **:** to drive esp. from covert ⟨they *ferreted* a number of rabbits⟩ **2 :** to worry or harry as with a ferret ⟨the king kept *ferreting* the rebellious baron⟩ ~ *vi* **1 :** to hunt game or drive out vermin with a ferret ⟨some U. S. states have laws against *ferreting*⟩ **2 :** to search carefully or diligently and sometimes presumptuously **:** search about **:** PRY ⟨old-fashioned . . . to go *ferreting* into people's pasts —Virginia Woolf⟩

³**ferret** \"\ *also* **fer·ret·ing** \-əd·iŋ\ *n* -s [*ferret* fr. earlier *ferret silk,* prob. modif. of It *fioretti* floss silk, fr. pl. of *fioretto* small flower, dim. of *fiore* flower, fr. L *flor-, flos; ferreting* fr. *ferret* + *-ing* — more at BLOW (blossom)] **1 :** a narrow silk tape or ribbon for trimming or decorative lacing **2 :** a strong tape of cotton or wool for binding or shoelaces

ferret-badger \ˈ==,==\ *n* **:** any of several heavy-bodied mammals (as *Helictis moschata*) of southeastern Asia that resemble the weasel — called also *pahmi*

fer·ret·er \ˈferəd·ə(r)\ *n* -s [ME *fereter, fureter,* fr. *feret, furet* ferret + *-er*] **:** one that ferrets ⟨paid a ~ to drive out the rats⟩

ferret out *vt* **:** to find or uncover with keen, diligent, crafty, or shrewd search ⟨*ferret out* the enemies of the country⟩ ⟨*ferret* the facts *out* after hours of painstaking examination of records⟩ **syn** see SEEK

ferret-polecat \¦==¦=,=\ *n* **:** an unusually vicious ferret valuable as a rodent destroyer, closely resembling the wild European polecat, and said to result from interbreeding the domestic ferret with the wild polecat

fer·rety \ˈferəd·ē\ *adj* [¹*ferret* + *-y*] **:** suggestive of a ferret ⟨into his ~ eyes there came a gentler look —Norman Douglas⟩

ferri- *comb form* [L *ferri-,* fr. *ferrum* iron] **1 :** iron ⟨*ferri*ferous⟩ **2** [*ferric*] **:** containing ferric iron ⟨ferrihemoglobin⟩

fer·ri·age *or* **fer·ry·age** \ˈferēij, -riij\ *n* -s [ME *feriage,* fr. *ferien* to ferry + *-age* — more at FERRY] **1 :** the act or business of transporting by ferry ⟨cross the larger streams by ~⟩ **2 :** the fare to be paid for a ferry passage ⟨no money to pay the ~⟩

fer·ri·an \ˈferēən\ *adj* [*ferri-* + *-an*] **:** containing ferric iron

fer·ric \-rik\ *adj* [L *ferrum* iron + E *-ic* — more at FARRIER] **:** of, relating to, or containing iron — used esp. of compounds in which this element has a higher valence, usu. three, than in the ferrous compounds or of iron with such a valence

ferric acetate *n* **:** either of two acetates of iron used chiefly in the textile industry as mordants and formerly in medicine as tonics: **a :** the normal acetate $Fe(C_2H_3O_2)_3$ known best in solution **b :** a basic acetate $Fe(OH)(C_2H_3O_2)_2$ obtained as brownish red scales or powder

ferric ammonium citrate *n* **:** a complex salt containing varying amounts of iron, one type being obtained as red crystals or a brownish yellow powder and another type as green crystals or powder and both being used in medicine for treating iron-deficiency anemia and in photography for making blueprints

ferric chloride *n* **:** a deliquescent salt $FeCl_3$ that is obtained in anhydrous form (as by heating iron in chlorine) as dark crystals appearing red by transmitted light and green by reflected light, that forms several crystalline hydrates (as the yellow hexahydrate $FeCl_3.6H_2O$), and that is used chiefly as an oxidizing agent, as a catalyst, as an etching agent in photoengraving, as a coagulant in treating industrial wastes, and in medicine in a water solution or tincture usu. as an astringent or styptic; iron trichloride

ferric hydroxide *n* **:** any of several hydrates $Fe_2O_3.nH_2O$ of ferric oxide that are capable of acting both as bases and weak acids **:** hydrated ferric oxide: as **a :** a reddish brown gelatinous precipitate obtained by adding an alkali to a ferric salt solution and often regarded as the trihydrate $Fe(OH)_3$ **b :** a red to reddish brown crystalline oxide and hydroxide FeO-(OH) occurring in nature as lepidocrocite

ferric oxide *n* **:** the red or black crystalline sesquioxide of iron Fe_2O_3 that is found in nature both as hematite and as hydrated forms (as rust and limonite) and is also obtained synthetically (as by calcining ferrous sulfate or hydrated ferric oxide) and that is used chiefly as a pigment and polishing material and in the removal of hydrogen sulfide from gases — called also *iron(III) oxide;* compare IRON OXIDE a, IRON RED, ROUGE 2

ferric sulfate *n* **:** a salt $Fe_2(SO_4)_3$ that is found in nature as the hydrated minerals coquimbite and quenstedtite and is also obtained synthetically (as by oxidation of ferrous sulfate) in the white anhydrous form and that is used chiefly in making iron alums, in pickling metals, as a mordant in dyeing, and as a coagulant in treating industrial wastes

fer·ri·cyanic acid \¦fe,rī, ¦ferē+. . .-\ *n* [*ferri-* + *cyanic*] **:** a brown crystalline unstable acid $H_3Fe(CN)_6$ obtained by treating ferricyanides with strong acids

fer·ri·cyanide \"+\ *n* -s [ISV *ferri-* + *cyanide*] **:** a salt of ferricyanic acid obtained usu. by oxidation of a ferrocyanide — see IRON BLUE ⟨cupric ~ $Cu_3[Fe(CN)_6]_2$⟩

fer·ri·did·dle \¦ferē¦did³l\ *n* -s [origin unknown] *dial* **:** CHIPMUNK

ferried *past of* FERRY

¹**fer·ri·er** \ˈferēə(r), -eriə-\ *n* -s [ME *ferier,* fr. *ferien* to ferry + *-er* — more at FERRY] **:** FERRYMAN

²**ferrier** \"\ *var of* FARRIER

ferries *pres 3d sing of* FERRY, *pl of* FERRY

fer·rif·er·ous \fəˈrif(ə)rəs, (ˈ)feˈr-\ *adj* [*ferri-* + *-ferous*] **:** containing iron **:** iron-bearing ⟨highly ~ carbonates⟩

fer·ri·hemoglobin \¦fe,rī, ¦ferē+\ *n* [*ferri-* + *hemoglobin*] **:** METHEMOGLOBIN

fer·ri·magnetic \"+\ *adj* [ISV *ferri-* + *magnetic*] **:** of or relating to a class of substances (as ferrite) characterized by magnetization in which the polarization in one group of magnetic atoms is antiparallel to the polarization in another group — **fer·ri·magnetism** \"+\ *n*

fer·ri·molybdite \"+\ *n* [ISV *ferri-* + *molybdite*] **:** a mineral $Fe_2(MoO_4)_3.8H_2O(?)$ consisting of hydrated iron molybdate

fer·ri·natrite \,fe,rīˈnā,trīt, ,ferē'-\ *n* -s [alter. (influenced by *ferri*) of *ferronatrite,* fr. *ferro-* + *natron* + *-ite*] **:** a mineral $Na_3Fe(SO_4)_3.3H_2O$ consisting of a greenish or white sodium ferric iron double sulfate usu. occurring in spherical forms

fer·ri·porphyrin \¦fe,rī, ¦ferē+\ *n* [*ferri-* + *porphyrin*] **:** a red-brown to black ferric derivative of a porphyrin that differs from a ferroporphyrin by the additional combination of a univalent anion (as chloride) with the iron atom

fer·ri·protoporphyrin \"+\ *n* [*ferri-* + *protoporphyrin*] **:** a ferriporphyrin in which the porphyrin is protoporphyrin — see HEMATIN, HEMIN

fer·ri·sicklerite \"+\ *n* [ISV *ferri-* + *sicklerite*] **:** a mineral $(Li,Fe,Mn)(PO_4)$ consisting of phosphate of lithium, ferric iron, and manganese with more iron than manganese and isomorphous with sicklerite

fer·ris wheel \ˈferəs-\ *n, usu cap F* [after George Washington Gale *Ferris* †1896 Am. engineer who designed such a wheel for the World's Columbian Exposition in Chicago in 1893] **:** an amusement device consisting of a large power-driven wheel made in two parallel sections having seats suspended between the sections, the seats maintaining a horizontal position while the wheel rotates in a vertical plane

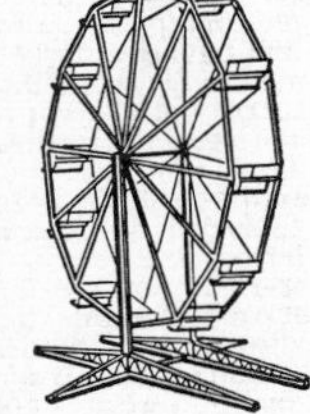
Ferris wheel

fer·rite \ˈfe,rīt\ *n* -s [L *ferrum* iron + E *-ite*] **1 :** any of several compounds formed usu. by treating hydrated ferric oxide with an alkali or by heating ferric oxide with a metallic oxide and regarded in some cases as salts of a ferric hydroxide acting in its capacity of an acid and in other cases as spinels ⟨sodium ~ $NaFeO_2$⟩ ⟨zinc ~ $ZnFe_2O_4$ has a spinel structure⟩ — called also *ferrate, ferrate(III)* **2 :** a solid solution in which alpha iron is the solvent

fer·rit·ic \fəˈridik, (ˈ)feˈr-\ *adj* **:** composed chiefly of ferrite ⟨~ stainless steel⟩

fer·ri·tin \ˈferət³n\ *n* -s [ISV *ferr-* (fr. L *ferrum* iron) + *-ite* + *-in*] **:** an amber-colored crystalline protein that contains more than 20 percent of iron in the form of a ferric hydroxide-phosphate complex with apoferritin, that is abundant esp. in the liver and spleen, and that constitutes a body mechanism for the storage of reserves of iron

fer·ri·tize \-rə,tīz\ *vt* -ED/-ING/-S **:** to convert (as steel) into ferrite

fer·ri·tungstite \ˌfe,rī, ¦ferē+\ *n* [*ferri-* + *tungstite*] **:** a mineral $Fe_2(WO_4)(OH)_4.4H_2O$ consisting of a hydrous ferric tungstate and occurring as a yellow ocherous powder

fer·riv·o·rous \fə'rivərəs, (')fe¦r-\ *adj* [*ferri-* + *-vorous*] **:** feeding on iron

ferro- *comb form* [ML *ferro-*, fr. L *ferrum* iron — more at FARRIER] **1 :** iron **:** containing iron ⟨*ferro*concrete⟩ **2 :** iron and ⟨*ferro*nickel⟩ — chiefly in names of alloys **3** [*ferrous*] **:** containing ferrous iron ⟨*ferro*ferricyanide⟩

fer·ro·alloy \¦fe(,)rō+\ *n* [*ferro-* + *alloy*] **:** a crude alloy of iron with one or more other elements, (as metals) used for deoxidizing molten steel and making alloy steels

fer·ro·aluminum \"+\ *n* [*ferro-* + *aluminum*] **:** an alloy of iron and aluminum that is sometimes added to molten steel to deoxidize the metal or to provide aluminum (as in steel for nitriding)

fer·ro·an \'ferəwən, 'fe,rōən\ *adj* [*ferro-* + *-an*] **:** containing ferrous iron

fer·ro·bacteria \¦fe(,)rō+\ *n pl* [*ferro-* + *bacteria*] **:** IRON BACTERIA

fer·ro·boron \"+\ *n* [*ferro-* + *boron*] **:** an alloy of iron and boron sometimes added to molten steel

fer·ro·car·bon titanium \¦ferō¦kärbən-\ *n* **:** a crude alloy of iron, carbon, and titanium containing 15 to 20 percent titanium and 3 to 8 percent carbon and sometimes added to molten steel

fer·ro·cene \'ferə,sēn\ *n* -s [*ferro-* + cyclopenta*diene*] **:** a crystalline very stable organometallic compound $(C_5H_5)_2Fe$ of cyclopentadiene and iron; *also* **:** any analogous compound with other heavy metals (as chromium)

fer·ro·cerium \¦fe(,)rō+\ *n* [NL, fr. *ferro-* + *cerium*] **:** a crude iron alloy containing a high percentage of cerium and used for flints in cigarette lighters

fer·ro·chromium \"+\ *or* **fer·ro·chrome** \'ferə,krōm\ *n* [NL, fr. *ferro-* + *chromium*] **:** a crude alloy of iron and chromium used chiefly to incorporate chromium in iron or steel

fer·ro·columbium \¦fe(,)rō+\ *n* [NL, fr. *ferro-* + *columbium*] **:** a crude alloy of iron and niobium used chiefly to add niobium to steel

fer·ro·concrete \"+\ *n* [*ferro-* + *concrete*] **:** REINFORCED CONCRETE

fer·ro·cyanic acid \"+. . .-\ *n* [*ferrocyanic* ISV *ferro-* + *cyanic*] **:** a white crystalline acid $H_4Fe(CN)_6$ obtained by treating ferrocyanides with acids

fer·ro·cyanide \"+\ *n* [ISV *ferrocyanic* + *-ide*] **:** a salt of ferrocyanic acid obtained usu. by reaction of a cyanide (as calcium cyanide) with ferrous sulfate or by recovery from spent oxide ⟨calcium ~ $Ca_2Fe(CN)_6$⟩ — see IRON BLUE, PRUSSIAN BLUE

fer·ro·dolomite \"+\ *n* [*ferro-* + *dolomite*] **:** a mineral component $CaFe(CO_3)_2$ consisting of calcium iron carbonate in ankerite

¹fer·ro·electric \"+\ *adj* [*ferro-* + *electric*] **:** having dielectric properties (as electric hysteresis or a saturation limit for electric polarization) ⟨~ crystals⟩ — **fer·ro·electricity** \"+\ *n*

²ferroelectric \"\ *n* **:** a ferroelectric substance

fer·ro·equi·nol·o·gist \,fe(,)rō,ēkwə'näləjəst, -ē,kwī'n-\ *n* -s [*ferroequino-* "iron horse" (fr. *ferro-* + *equino-*, fr. L *equinus* equine + *-logy* + *-ist* — more at EQUINE] **:** RAILFAN

fer·ro·gabbro \¦fe(,)rō+\ *n* [*ferro-* + *gabbro*] **:** a gabbro having pyroxene and olivine that are abnormally high in iron

fer·ro·hemoglobin \"+\ *n* [*ferro-* + *hemoglobin*] **:** HEMOGLOBIN 1b

fer·ro·magnesian \"+\ *adj* [*ferro-* + *magnesian*] **:** containing iron and magnesium

²ferromagnesian \"\ *n* -s **:** a ferromagnesian mineral

fer·ro·magnet \"+\ *n* [*ferro-* + *magnet*] **:** a magnet composed of ferromagnetic material

¹fer·ro·magnetic \"+\ *adj* [*ferro-* + *magnetic*] **:** of or relating to a class of substances characterized by abnormally high magnetic permeability, definite saturation point, and appreciable residual magnetism and hysteresis — **fer·ro·mag·netism** \"+\ *n*

²ferromagnetic \"\ *n* **:** a ferromagnetic substance (as iron, nickel, cobalt, and numerous alloys)

fer·ro·manganese \"+\ *n* [*ferro-* + *manganese*] **:** an alloy of iron and manganese containing usu. about 80 percent manganese and used in steelmaking — compare SPIEGELEISEN

fer·ro·molybdenum \"+\ *n* [*ferro-* + *molybdenum*] **:** a crude alloy of iron and molybdenum used to add molybdenum to iron or steel

fer·ro·nickel \"+\ *n* [*ferro-* + *nickel*] **:** a crude alloy of iron and nickel sometimes used in making nickel steel

fer·ron·nière *also* **fer·ro·nière** \¦feran¦ye(ə)r\ *n* -s [F *ferronnière*, after *La Belle Ferronnière*, portrait of a woman wearing such a jewel painted by Leonardo da Vinci †1519 Ital. artist] **:** a pendant jewel worn (as by women in 15th century Italy and early 19th century England) in the middle of the forehead

fer·ro·phosphorus \¦fe(,)rō+\ *n* [*ferro-* + *phosphorus*] **:** a crude alloy of iron and phosphorus

fer·ro·porphyrin \"+\ *n* [*ferro-* + *porphyrin*] **:** a red ferrous derivative of a porphyrin in which the iron atom is held by nitrogen atoms of the porphyrin

fer·ro·protoporphyrin \"+\ *n* [*ferro-* + *protoporphyrin*] **:** HEME

fer·ro·prussiate process \"+ . . . -\ *n* [*ferro-* + *prussiate*] **:** the process of making a blueprint

fer·ro·silicon \"+\ *n* [*ferro-* + *silicon*] **:** a crude alloy of iron and silicon containing 15 to 95 percent silicon and used for deoxidizing molten steel and making silicon steel and high-silicon cast iron

fer·ro·sil·ite \,ferō'si,līt\ *n* -s [*ferro-* + *silicate*] **:** a mineral component consisting of an iron silicate $FeSiO_3$ in hypersthene — compare CLINOFERROSILITE, ORTHOFERROSILITE

ferroso- *comb form* [NL *ferrosus* ferrous — more at FERROUS] **:** ferrous and ⟨*ferroso*ferric⟩

fer·ro·so·ferric oxide \fə¦rōsə, fe¦+ . . . -\ *n* [ISV *ferroso-* + *ferric*] **:** a black magnetic iron oxide Fe_3O_4 found in nature as magnetite, also obtained synthetically (as from iron by heating in steam or from a ferrous salt and an alkali by precipitation and oxidation), and used chiefly as a pigment and polishing material — called also *iron(II,III) oxide*

fer·ro·spinel \¦fe(,)rō+\ *n* [*ferro-* (fr. *ferromagnetic*) + *spinel*] **:** any of several synthetic crystalline magnetic substances of spinel structure that contain iron and are poor electrical conductors

fer·ro·titanium \"+\ *n* [*ferro-* + *titanium*] **:** an alloy of iron and titanium containing 15 to 45 percent titanium and used in steelmaking

fer·ro·tungsten \"+\ *n* [*ferro-* + *tungsten*] **:** a crude alloy of iron and tungsten used in making alloy steels

¹fer·ro·type \'ferə,tīp\ *n* [*ferro-* + *type*] **1 :** a positive photograph made by a collodion process on a thin iron plate and having a darkened surface (as of black enamel) — called also *tintype* **2 :** the process by which a ferrotype is made

²ferrotype \"\ *vt* **:** to give a gloss to (a photographic print) by squeegeeing facedown while wet upon a ferrotype plate and allowing to dry

ferrotype plate *or* **ferrotype tin** *n* **:** a highly polished black-enameled or chromium-plated metal sheet that is used in ferrotyping

fer·ro·typ·er \-pə(r)\ *n* **:** one that ferrotypes

fer·ro·uranium \¦fe(,)rō+\ *n* [*ferro-* + *uranium*] **:** a crude alloy of iron and uranium

fer·rous \'ferəs\ *adj* [NL *ferrosus*, fr. L *ferrum* iron + *-osus* -ous — more at FARRIER] **1 :** of, relating to, or containing iron — used specif. of compounds in which this element is bivalent or of bivalent iron; compare FERRIC **2** *of an alloy* **:** containing more iron than any other metal

ferrous carbonate *n* **:** a salt $FeCO_3$ occurring in nature as the mineral siderite, obtained synthetically as a white easily oxidizable precipitate, and used in medicine in treating iron-deficiency anemia

ferrous chloride *n* **:** a deliquescent salt $FeCl_2$ obtained in anhydrous form as colorless crystals (as by heating iron in hydrogen chloride) and used chiefly in the textile industry as a mordant and in metallurgy; iron dichloride

ferrous hydroxide *n* **:** a basic compound $Fe(OH)_2$ that is usu. obtained as a nearly white gelatinous precipitate by adding an alkali to a ferrous salt solution and that turns green and finally reddish brown in air on oxidation to ferric hydroxide

ferrous oxalate *n* **:** a yellow crystalline salt $FeC_2O_4.2H_2O$ found in nature as humboldtine and formerly used in potassium oxalate solution as a photographic developer

ferrous oxide *n* **:** the monoxide of iron FeO obtained as a readily oxidizable black powder (as by heating ferrous oxalate) — called also *iron(II) oxide*

ferrous sulfate *n* **:** an astringent salt $FeSO_4$ obtained usu. in the form of the pale green efflorescent crystalline heptahydrate $FeSO_4.7H_2O$ as a by-product (as in pickling iron or steel) and used chiefly in making other iron salts, pigments, and ink, in treating industrial wastes, and in medicine esp. for treating iron-deficiency anemia

ferrous sulfide *n* **:** the monosulfide of iron FeS found in nature as pyrrhotite and as troilite, obtained as brown or black metallic masses by fusing iron and sulfur or as a black precipitate by adding an alkaline sulfide to the solution of a ferrous compound, and used chiefly in making hydrogen sulfide

fer·ro·vanadium \¦fe(,)rō+\ *n* [*ferro-* + *vanadium*] **:** a crude alloy of iron and vanadium used in making steel or cast iron

fer·ro·zirconium \"+\ *n* [*ferro-* + *zirconium*] **:** a crude alloy of iron and zirconium usu. containing 12 to 40 percent zirconium

fer·ruc·cite \fə'rü,chīt\ *n* -s [It, fr. *Ferruccio* Zambonini †1932 Ital. mineralogist + It *-ite*] **:** a mineral $NaBF_4$ consisting of sodium fluoborate occurring in white orthorhombic crystals at Vesuvius

fer·ru·gi·nate \fə'rüjə,nāt, fe'-\ *vt* -ED/-ING/-S [*ferruginous* + *-ate*] **:** to charge or stain (as rock) with a compound of iron — **fer·ru·gi·na·tion** \=,==ˈnāshən\ *n* -s

¹fer·ru·gi·nous \fə'rüjənəs, fe'-\ *also* **fer·ru·gin·e·ous** \¦fer(y)ə¦jinēəs\ *adj* [L *ferruginus*, *ferrugineus*, fr. *ferrugin-*, *ferrugo* iron rust, fr. *ferrum* iron — more at FARRIER] **1 :** of or containing iron **2 :** resembling iron rust in color

²ferruginous \"\ *n* -ES **:** a dark reddish orange to strong brown that is less strong than English red (sense 2a)

ferruginous roughleg *or* **ferruginous rough-legged hawk** *n* **:** a rather large light-colored rough-legged hawk (*Buteo regalis*) that feeds chiefly on rodents and is widely distributed in western No. America

¹fer·rule \'ferəl\ *n* -s [alter. (influenced by L *ferrum* iron) of ME *virell*, *verelle*, *virole*, fr. MF *virelle*, *virole*, fr. OF *virol*, fr. L *viriola* small bracelet, dim. of *viria* armlet, bracelet, of Celt origin; akin to OIr *fiar* oblique — more at VEER] **1 a :** a band or cap usu. of metal enclosing the end of a cane, tool handle, table leg, or similar object to strengthen it or prevent splitting and wearing **b :** the protective point or knob on the far end of an umbrella **c :** the edge or corner covering of a book **2 :** a tube or bushing making a tight joint between a tube and tube plate or between two tubes or pipes (as of different metals) **3 a :** the metal band around a paint brush that binds the bristles to the head **b :** a metal or plastic band holding an eraser to a pencil **4 :** one of the complementary parts of a joint of a demountable fishing rod consisting of a sleeve and a shaft fitting into it to join the sections — called also respectively *female ferrule*, *male ferrule* **5 :** a metal band or socket in which the terminal of a wire or wire rope is secured for firm grip **6 :** a plug for a cleanout in a plumbing trap or soil pipe

²ferrule \"\ *vt* -ED/-ING/-S [alter. (influenced by L *ferrum* iron) of ME *virellen*, fr. MF *vireler*, fr. OF *viroler*, fr. *virol*, n.] **:** to supply with a ferrule

fer·rum \'ferəm\ *n* -s [L] **:** IRON — symbol *Fe*

fer·ru·mi·nate \fə'rümə,nāt\ *vt* -ED/-ING/-S [L *ferruminatus*, *feruminatus*, past part. of *ferruminare*, *feruminare*, fr. *ferrumin-*, *ferrumen*, *ferumin-*, *ferumen* solder, glue; perh. akin to L *firmus* firm — more at FIRM] **:** to join together (as metals) **:** SOLDER — **fer·ru·mi·na·tion** \=,=='nāshən\ *n* -s

¹fer·ry \'ferē, -ri\ *vb* -ED/-ING/-ES [ME *ferien*, fr. OE *ferian* to carry, bring, convey; akin to OHG *ferien*, *ferren* to transport, convey, ON *ferja* to transport, ferry, Goth *farjan* to travel in a boat; frequentatives fr. the root of OE *faran* to go, travel — more at FARE] *vt* **1 a :** to convey over a river or other body of water by boat ⟨*ferried* himself across the river⟩ ⟨~ troops from ship to shore⟩ ⟨~ supplies out to the island⟩ **b :** to cross (as a river) by a ferry ⟨whether they swim, ford, or ~ the river⟩ **2 a :** to convey from one place to another **:** TRANSPORT ⟨official cars could ~ the delegates over to the . . . reception —A.J.Liebling⟩ ⟨had to ~ a rare book across the Atlantic —Bernard Kalb⟩ **b :** to fly (an airplane) from the factory or other shipping point to the designated delivery point or from one base to another ⟨~ large planes to overseas bases⟩ **c :** to transport (as across an ocean) in an airplane ⟨our domestic airlines . . . ~ high-ranking military personnel between the United Nations —*Congressional Record*⟩ ~ *vi* **:** to pass over water in a boat or by a ferry ⟨reached Hoboken late . . . and *ferried* across to New York —G.A.Hamid⟩ ⟨~ across the river⟩

²ferry \"\ *n* -ES *often attrib* [ME *ferie*, *fery*, prob. fr. ON *ferja*, fr. *ferja*, v.] **1 :** a place where persons or things are carried across a river or other body of water in a boat ⟨rowed the traveler over the ~⟩ **2 a :** a service for carrying usu. on schedule persons, animals, vehicles, or goods across a ferry on a boat ⟨the opening of the new bridge and the termination of the ~⟩ **b :** an organized service and route for flying airplanes esp. across a sea or continent for delivery to the user ⟨the Atlantic ~ to British bases⟩ **c :** air transportation of persons or things that operates regularly between two points ⟨via the air ~ that carries tourists and their cars to the island⟩ ⟨a ~ plane⟩ **3 :** FERRYBOAT ⟨take the passenger and automobile ~ across the lake⟩ ⟨the railway ~ operating on the cross-channel route⟩ **4 :** a franchise or right to operate as a common carrier a ferry service across a body of water

ferryage *var of* FERRIAGE

ferryboat \'==,=\ *n* [ME *feryboot*, fr. *fery* ferry + *boot* boat — more at BOAT] **:** a boat used in ferry service

ferry bridge *n* **:** a floating or hanging structure hinged or movably fastened to a wharf to facilitate passing on or off a ferryboat

ferry car *n* **:** a railroad car used generally within terminal limits to distribute or collect shipments of less than a carload to or from industries on private sidings — called also *trap car*

ferry-flat \'==,=\ *n* **:** a flatboat used chiefly for ferrying (as on the Mississippi river)

ferry-house \'==,=\ *n* **1 :** the house of the keeper of a ferry **2 :** the structure on a ferry wharf usu. containing a ticket office, waiting room, and other facilities

fer·ry·man \-mən, -,man\ *n, pl* **ferrymen** [ME *feryman*, fr. *fery* + *man*] **:** a person who operates a ferry

ferry-place \'==,=\ *n* [ME *fery place*, fr. *fery* ferry + *place*] **:** a place used or usable for a ferry landing

ferry push car *n* **:** a long flatcar used as a bridge between a locomotive and the cars it is moving on or off a car ferry where the land-to-ferry incline is too steep for the locomotive to operate

fers *n* -ES [ME, fr. MF *fierce*, fr. Ar *farzan*, fr. Per *farzīn*] *obs* **:** a chess queen

-fers *pl of* -FER

fers·man·ite *also* **fers·man·nite** \'fərzmə,nīt, -rsm-\ *n* -s [Russ *fersmanit*, fr. Aleksandr E. *Fersman* †1945 Russ. mineralogist + Russ *-it* -ite] **:** a mineral $(Na,Ca)_2(Ti,Cb)\text{-}Si(O,F)_6$ consisting of a silicate fluoride of sodium, calcium, titanium, and columbium

fers·mite \-,mīt\ *n* -s [Russ *fersmit*, fr. A. E. *Fersman* + Russ *-it* -ite] **:** a mineral $(Ca,Ce)(Cb,Ti)_2(O,F)_6$ consisting of an oxide and fluoride of calcium and columbium with cerium and titanium

fer·tile \'fərd·ᵊl, fə̄l, fəil, ¦tᵊl *sometimes* ¦(,)til, *chiefly Brit* ¦,tīl\ *adj* [ME, fr. MF & L; MF *fertile*, fr. L *fertilis*, fr. *ferre* to bear, produce — more at BEAR] **1 a :** characterized by production of great quantities **:** abundant in yield **:** PRODUCTIVE ⟨prodigally ~ fields of ripening corn and oats⟩ ⟨peopled chiefly by three ~ families⟩ ⟨a ~ author with 50 books already published⟩ ⟨a philosophic tradition ~ in lucid writers⟩; *specif* **:** characterized by abundant resourcefulness of thought or imagination **:** CREATIVE, INVENTIVE ⟨his mind ~ in projects for the advancement of his fellows —H.W.H.Knott⟩ ⟨the ~ handling of folk themes in his new composition⟩ **b :** produced abundantly **:** NUMEROUS, TEEMING ⟨GI's . . . wading into the shore in numbers . . . prodigally ~ —John Mason Brown⟩ **2 a** (1) **:** capable of sustaining abundant and vigorous vegetation **:** favorable to plant growth ⟨~ fields of loam⟩ ⟨made the soil ~ again by adding the needed chemicals⟩ ⟨a ~ region awaiting the plow⟩ (2) **:** making the soil fertile **:** FERTILIZING (3) **:** affording favorable conditions or abundant possibilities for development ⟨countries where such misery exists are ~ soil for Communist infiltration —*N. Y. Times Mag.*⟩ ⟨what happens to responses during this period . . . would seem to offer a ~ field for research —Ralph Linton⟩ **b** *of a seed or egg* **:** capable of growing or developing **c** (1) **:** capable of producing fruit **:** fruit-bearing ⟨~ flowers⟩ ⟨~ trees⟩ (2) *of an anther* **:** containing pollen (3) **:** developing spores or spore-bearing organs **d** (1) **:** capable of breeding or reproducing esp. as indicated by the prior production of viable offspring ⟨a bull warranted ~⟩ (2) **:** likely to conceive or beget offspring ⟨few men over 60 are highly ~⟩ (3) **:** potentially reproductive ⟨few men of ~ age⟩ (4) *of an estrous cycle* **:** marked by the production of one or more viable eggs **e** *of a bee* **:** producing eggs **3 :** capable of being converted into fissionable material ⟨~ uranium 238⟩

syn FECUND, FRUITFUL, PROLIFIC: FERTILE may apply to a soil facilitating ready growth or to something likened to a productive seed bed; it may also apply to persons or animals able to produce young ⟨past fields where the wheat was high. Peaches grew in the orchards; it was a *fertile* country —S.V. Benét⟩ ⟨planted so deeply in *fertile* minds that even now they are sending up fresh crops —H.S.Canby⟩ ⟨India, where the people are more *fertile* than the land —*Time*⟩ FECUND may apply to whatever yields in abundance or with rapidity ⟨giving lessons to a few of the *fecund* king's offspring —E.J.Kahn⟩ ⟨a good part of these inventions came to birth — or were further nourished — in the *fecund* mind of Leonardo da Vinci —Lewis Mumford⟩ FRUITFUL may apply to anything bearing or borne in abundance or in gratifying numbers or to conditions that facilitate such bearing ⟨prefer that a coconut palm should be planted by an old woman who has many children, because they believe that a tree planted by so *fruitful* a woman will bear a plentiful crop of coconuts —J.G.Frazer⟩ ⟨rewarding land, too, much of it; rich, wide, and in years when the rains came, wonderfully *fruitful* —Russell Lord⟩ ⟨the enormously *fruitful* discovery that pitch of sound depends upon the length of the vibrating chord —Havelock Ellis⟩ PROLIFIC stresses rapidity in production or reproduction and may or may not be derogatory ⟨the defectives are appallingly *prolific:* the others have fewer children —G.B.Shaw⟩ ⟨the starling is so *prolific* that the flocks become immense —Richard Jefferies⟩ ⟨an extremely *prolific* writer whose literary output, if collected, might easily fill half-a-hundred volumes —*Encyc. Americana*⟩

fertile frond *n* **:** a frond bearing spores and often differing markedly in color, form, and size from the sterile fronds (as in sensitive fern)

fer·tile·ly \-ᵊl(l)ē, -il(l)i, -īll, ¦i\ *adv* **:** in a fertile or fruitful manner

fer·tile·ness *n* -ES **:** FERTILITY

¹fer·til·i·ty \,fər'tiləd·ē, fə̄'-, fəi'-, ,fə(r)'-, -lətē, -i\ *n* -ES [ME *fertilite*, fr. MF *fertilité*, fr. L *fertilitas*, fr. *fertilis* fertile + *-itas* -ity] **1 :** the quality or state of being fertile: **a :** an actual state of productive abundance ⟨insure the ~ of the rice crop⟩ ⟨a theme he develops with ~ and power⟩ **b :** a capacity for producing or reproducing ⟨the ~ of the theory should provoke new developments in research⟩ ⟨a high degree of ~ in one member of a childless couple and relative infertility in the other⟩ **c :** a capacity to provide the necessary nutriments or conditions for plant growth ⟨used manure to keep up the ~ of their land⟩ **d :** actual reproductive capacity as measured by production of offspring ⟨a ram of proven ~⟩ ⟨a breed noted for its high ~⟩ — compare FECUNDITY **2 :** the birthrate of a population (as of a national, religious, or ethnic group) **:** reproductive performance — opposed to *mortality*

²fertility \"\ *adj* **1 :** of or relating to fertility ⟨the serpent was a ~ symbol —A.P.Davies⟩ ⟨~ statistics⟩ **2 :** of or associated with a fertility cult ⟨~ rites practiced by the Canaanites⟩ ⟨~ gods⟩ ⟨~ myths⟩; *also* **:** believed to promote the fertility of the land and its animals and people ⟨~ dances surviving in medieval Europe⟩

fertility cult *n* **1 :** a system of nature worship involving rites and ceremonies believed to insure productiveness of plants, animals, and people and often directed toward the propitiation of a special deity **2 :** the body of followers and practitioners of such a system

fer·til·iz·abil·i·ty \,fər¦d·ᵊl,īzə'biləd·ē, ,fə̄l, ,fəil, ¦tᵊl-, -bilətē, -i\ *n* -ES **:** capability of being fertilized; *specif* **:** the period in the life of an egg during which it is able to participate effectively in fertilization ⟨the length of life of an egg and the length of its ~ —George Barth⟩

fer·til·iz·able \'==,=zəbəl, ,=='===\ *adj* **:** capable of being fertilized

fer·til·iza·tion \,==ə'zāshən, -,ī'z-\ *n* -s **1 :** the act or process of making or becoming fertile: **a** (1) **:** the application of fertilizer (2) **:** the bringing about or promoting of an intellectual or economic development **:** ENRICHMENT **b** (1) **:** the act or process of fecundation, insemination, impregnation, or pollination — not often used technically (2) **:** the process of union of two germ cells whereby the somatic chromosome number is restored and the development of a new individual is initiated in animals typically involving penetration of a large passive female cell by a smaller active male cell followed by completion of the maturation of the female cell and by fusion of the haploid gamete pronuclei to form a diploid synkaryon within a new initially unicellular zygote and in most seed plants depending upon penetration of the ovule and embryo sac containing the egg by a pollen tube that discharges the nonmotile male nucleus — compare CONJUGATION, DOUBLE FERTILIZATION, PARTHENOGENESIS, POLYSPERMY **2 :** an instance of fertilization — **fer·til·iza·tion·al** \¦==(,)=¦zāshənᵊl, -shnəl\ *adj*

fertilization cone *n* **:** ENTRANCE CONE

fertilization membrane *n* **:** a resistant membranous layer that separates from the surface of many eggs immediately after entry of a sperm and thus prevents multiple fertilization

fertilization tube *n* **:** a branch that projects from the antheridium and pierces the oogonium to provide for passage of the male nucleus in certain phycomycetous fungi

fer·til·ize \'fər¦d·ᵊl,īz, 'fə̄l, 'fəil, ¦tᵊl-\ *vb* -ED/-ING/-S *see -ize in Explan Notes* [prob. fr. F *fertilizer*, fr. MF, fr. *fertile*, adj. + *-iser* -ize] *vt* **:** to make fertile: as **a** (1) **:** to apply compost, manure, or commercial fertilizer to (a growing medium) in order to supply nutriments or make available nutriments already present ⟨~ the fishpond with commercial fertilizer to promote plankton growth⟩ (2) **:** to stimulate, supply, or enrich the development of ⟨the struggles of the war had . . . *fertilized* and quickened the thinking and feeling of the region —Van Wyck Brooks⟩ ⟨~ the country's economy with foreign capital⟩ ⟨reading that will ~ his vocabulary⟩ **b** (1) **:** to cause or tend to cause fertilization in (as by pollinating or inseminating) ⟨the wind ~s many plants⟩ — not used technically (2) **:** to participate with (a germ cell of the opposite sex) in fertilization ⟨under certain circumstances spermatozoa from one species may ~ ova from another⟩ ~ *vi* **:** to make something fertile; *specif* **:** to apply fertilizer to soil ⟨who raise grain but do not ~⟩

fer·til·iz·er \-zə(r)\ *n* -s **1 :** one that fertilizes ⟨he was not only a very distinguished writer but . . . a ~ of other talents —Lloyd Morris⟩ **2 :** a substance (as manure, lime, or commercial fertilizer) used to fertilize soil; *esp* **:** one chemically prepared that supplies nutrients (as a mixture containing varying percentages of nitrogen, available phosphate, and water-soluble potash)

fertilizer analysis *or* **fertilizer grade** *n* **:** ANALYSIS 4c

fer·til·i·zin \(,)fər'tiləzən, 'fərd·ᵊl,īz-\ *n* -s [*fertilize* + *-in*] **:** a sperm-agglutinating agent produced by an egg (as of an ascidian) that plays a part in the preliminaries of fertilization

fe·ru \fə'rü\ *n* -s [Yoruba] **:** a bast fiber derived from an African tree (*Cochlospermum tinctorium*) and used in making rope

fer·u·la \'fer(y)ələ\ *n* [NL, fr. L, giant fennel — more at FESTUCA] **1** *cap* **:** a large genus of Old World plants (family Umbelliferae) with deeply divided leaves, compound umbels of yellow flowers, and membranous-winged fruit with three threadlike ridges — see ASAFETIDA, GALBANUM **2** -s : any plant of the genus *Ferula*

1fer·ule \ˈferəl\ *also* **fer·u·la** \ˈfer(y)ələ\ *n* -s [L *ferula* giant fennel, whip, rod for punishment] **1** : any of several instruments (as a rod, switch, or ruler) used to punish school children; *specif* : a flat piece of wood like a ruler used esp. on the hands **2** : punishment with a ferule ⟨as boys that slink from ~ —Alfred Tennyson⟩ **3** : school discipline ⟨this tutelage under Miss Newcomb's ~ —Dixon Wecter⟩

2ferule \ˈ"\ *vt* -ED/-ING/-S : to punish with a ferule

fe·ru·lic acid \fəˈrülik-\ *n* [*ferula* + *-ic*] : a white crystalline acid $HO(CH_3O)C_6H_3CH{:}CHCOOH$ that is structurally related to vanillin and is obtained esp. from various resins (as asafetida or opoponax)

fer·un·gu·la·ta \ˌfer+\ *n pl, cap* [NL *Ferae* + *Ungulata*] *in some classifications* : a major division of eutherian mammals comprising the Ungulata and the Carnivora

fer·va·nite \ˈfərvəˌnīt\ *n* -s [*ferrum* + *vanadium* + *-ite*] : a mineral $Fe_4V_4O_{16}.5H_2O$ consisting of a rare hydrated iron vanadate occurring with radioactive minerals but not itself radioactive

fer·ven·cy \ˈfərvənsē, ˈfəv-,ˈfəiv-, -si\ *n* -ES [ME *fervence, fervency*, fr. MF *fervence*, fr. LL *ferventia*, fr. L *fervent-, fervens* (pres. part.) + *-ia* -y] : FERVOR ⟨calmness as opposed to ~ in everything —Fanny Butcher⟩

fer·vent \-vənt\ *adj* [ME, fr. MF & L; MF *fervent*, fr. L *fervent-, fervens*, pres. part. of *fervēre* to boil, glow — more at BURN] **1** : intensely hot ⟨the tessellated plain . . . seemed on this ~ day to be half-molten —Mary Webb⟩ **2** : of great intensity ⟨the ~ heat . . . merely communicated a genial warmth to their half-torpid systems —Nathaniel Hawthorne⟩; *specif* : characterized by often deep fervor of feeling or expression ⟨~ patriotism⟩ ⟨expressed a ~ hope⟩ ⟨the religious center . . . was the austere yet ~ meetinghouse —Ruth Suckow⟩ ⟨setting ~ kisses upon his hands —Paul Bowles⟩ ⟨~ diction —H.O.Taylor⟩ : ENTHUSIASTIC ⟨had no longer any cause to grow ~ or furious about —Edmund Wilson⟩ : EARNEST ⟨a ~ moral sense⟩ : ZEALOUS ⟨he is known as a ~ champion of the trivial detail —R.L.Taylor⟩ ⟨a moment ends the ~ din —William Wordsworth⟩ **syn** see IMPASSIONED

fer·vent·ly *adv* [ME, fr. *fervent* + *-ly*] : in a fervent manner ⟨discussed the issue ~⟩ ⟨wished ~ that he might⟩

fer·vent·ness *n* -ES [ME *ferventnes*, fr. *fervent* + *-nes* -ness] : FERVOR

fer·vid \ˈfərvəd, ˈfəv-, ˈfəiv-\ *adj* [L *fervidus*, fr. *fervēre* to boil] **1** : giving off intense heat : very hot : BURNING ⟨set out on an expedition when the ~ heat subsides —Frances Trollope⟩ **2** : characterized by often extreme fervor of feeling or expression : IMPASSIONED ⟨overcome by ~ enthusiasm⟩ : ZEALOUS ⟨the voters . . . have always taken ~ partisans somewhat humorously —G.W.Johnson⟩ : VEHEMENT ⟨~ eloquence with which he urged his proposal⟩ : EBULLIENT ⟨the most loathsome and noisome abominations that his ~ imagination could concoct —C.W.Eliot⟩ **syn** see IMPASSIONED

fer·vid·i·ty \ˌfərˈvidəd·ē, fəˈ-, fəiˈ- -dətē, -i\ *n* -ES : FERVOR ⟨writes with ~, faith, and feeling —*New Yorker*⟩

fer·vid·ly *adv* : in a fervid manner : PASSIONATELY, INTENSELY ⟨to believe not perfunctorily but ~ that the power that orders nature and history is on one's side —Brand Blanshard⟩

fer·vid·ness *n* -ES : FERVOR

fer·vor \ˈfərvər, ˈfəvə(r, ˈfəivə(r\ *n* -s *see -or in Explan Notes* [ME *fervour*, fr. MF & L; MF *ferveur*, fr. L *fervor*, fr. *fervēre* to boil, glow + *-or*] **1** : intense heat ⟨those deserts . . . whose . . . ~s scarce allowed a bird to live —P.B.Shelley⟩ **2 a** : intensity of feeling or expression : PASSION ⟨rejected communism with as much ~ as they had accepted it —Margaret Marshall⟩ ⟨she cried quietly but with ~ —Robert Murphy⟩; *specif* : deep or excited interest in or enthusiasm for something ⟨the book has been greeted by Frenchmen with a ~ that no previous book on art ever aroused —George Duthuit⟩ : EARNESTNESS ⟨the moral ~ of a reformer⟩ ⟨ages of spiritual ~ . . . in which . . . men have been unusually excited about their souls —Clive Bell⟩ : ZEAL ⟨the tackling on both sides attains the ~ of a holy war —*New Yorker*⟩ **b** : an instance of emotional fervor ⟨the almost hysterical ~s of wartime⟩ **syn** see PASSION

fer·vor·ous \-v(ə)rəs\ *adj* : full of fervor

fès *or* **fes** *usu cap, var of* FEZ

fes·cen·nine \ˈfesᵊnˌīn, -ˌēn\ *adj, usu cap* [L *fescenninus*, prob. fr. *Fescenninus* of Fescennium, fr. *Fescennium*, ancient town in Etruria, Italy, famous for such songs and verses + L *-inus* -ine] **1** : sung or read at a rural festival or a wedding in ancient Italy and marked by often obscene mockery ⟨~ songs⟩ ⟨lively ~ verses on the emperor's marriage⟩ **2** : SCURRILOUS, OBSCENE ⟨street corner idlers making ~ comments on passing girls⟩

1fes·cue \ˈfe(ˌ)skyü\ *n* -s [ME *festu*, fr. MF, fr. VL *festucum*, fr. L *festuca* — more at FESTUCA] **1** *obs* : STRAW, RUSH, TWIG **2** : a small pointer (as a straw, stick, or quill) used to point out letters to or by children learning to read **3** *also* **fescue grass** : a grass of the genus *Festuca* — see MEADOW FESCUE, SHEEP FESCUE

2fescue *vt* -ED/-ING/-S *obs* : to assist (a reader) with a fescue

fescue foot *n* : a disease of the feet of cattle resembling ergotism but considered due to feeding on certain grasses of the genus *Festuca* which contain a toxic principle similar to ergot

fesh \ˈfesh\ *Scot var of* FETCH

1fess *also* **fesse** \ˈfes\ *n, pl* **fesses** [ME *fes, fesse*, fr. MF *faisse, fesse*, fr. L *fascia* band — more at FASCIA] : a broad bar drawn horizontally across the middle of a heraldic field — **in fess** *adv* **1** : in a line in the direction of a fess — used of two or more charges; usu. used only of charges in a line across the middle of the field; compare BARWISE 2, 1BASE 5a, *in chief* at 1CHIEF **2** : FESSWISE 1, BARWISE 1 — **per fess** : divided in two by a horizontal line across the middle

fess

2fess \ˈ"\ *vb* -ED/-ING/-ES [short for *confess*] *slang* : CONFESS, OWN — usu. used with *up* ⟨~ up to having put something over on me⟩ ⟨~ up you're still carrying the torch for her —W.G.Smith⟩

3fess \ˈ"\ *adj* [perh. alter. of *fierce*] **1** *dial Eng* : LIVELY, SMART ⟨what a ~ little bonfire —Thomas Hardy⟩ **2** *dial Eng* : CONCEITED, IMPUDENT

fess point *n* : the center of a heraldic field

fesswise *also* **fesseways** *or* **fessewise** *or* **fessways** \ˈ=ˌ=\ *adv* **1** : in the direction of a fess : HORIZONTALLY, BARWISE 1 ⟨three keys ~ in pale⟩ **2** : in fess ⟨three escarbuncles ~⟩

-fest \ˌfest\ *n comb form* -s [G *fest* festival, holiday, fr. MHG *vest*, fr. L *festum*, fr. neut. of *festus* solemn, festal — more at FEAST] **1** : festive gathering esp. for competition ⟨shooting*fest*⟩ ⟨turner*fest*⟩ ⟨song*fest*⟩ **2** : session often informal or spontaneous ⟨gab*fest*⟩ : outburst of activity ⟨slug*fest*⟩

fes·ta \ˈfestə\ *n* -s [It, fr. L, festival — more at FEAST] : CELEBRATION; *specif* : an annual local celebration in Italy of the day of the patron saint

fes·tal \ˈfestᵊl\ *adj* [L *festa* or *festum* festival + E *-al*] **1** : of or belonging to a religious feast ⟨the ~ day of that saint⟩ ⟨~ celebration of the Holy Communion⟩ **2** : of, given over to, or suited to festivity ⟨~ occasions⟩ ⟨~ crowds⟩ ⟨~ garments⟩ — **fes·tal·ly** \-təlē, -li\ *adv*

festal letter *n* : PASCHAL LETTER

1fes·ter \ˈfestə(r)\ *n* -s [ME *fester, festre*, fr. MF *festre*, fr. L *fistula* pipe, tube, a kind of ulcer] **1** : a suppurating sore : PUSTULE, ABSCESS **2** : pus from an abscess

2fester \ˈ"\ *vb* **festered; festered; festering** \ˈfest(ə)riŋ\ **festers** [ME *festren*, fr. *festre*, n.] *vi* **1** : to generate pus ⟨the wound becomes inflamed and ~s⟩ **2** : to become putrid : PUTREFY, ROT ⟨a heritage of blackened ruins and ~*ing* cemeteries —G.B.Shaw⟩ **3 a** : to produce continual or progressive irritation or malignancy (as in a mind or population) : RANKLE ⟨an injustice that will ~ in their minds until the situation is corrected⟩ ⟨resentment that ~*ed* until it broke out in violence⟩ **b** : to develop by becoming increasingly virulent or malignant ⟨the quarrel . . . began to fester and quickly ~*ed* into the definitive schism of 1054 —A.J.Toynbee⟩ **c** : to undergo or exist in a state of often progressive deterioration ⟨comradeship can ~ into hatred —Merle Miller⟩ : reek with corruption ⟨the city's ~*ing* slums⟩ ~ *vt* : to exert a malignant influence on : INFLAME, CORRUPT ⟨the Argentina situation stood out as the sorest thumb of Pan-America, continuing to ~ and fever the whole system —*Annals of Amer. Acad. of Polit. & Soc. Sci.*⟩

1fes·ti·nate \ˈfestəˌnāt, -ˌnət\ *adj* [L *festinatus*, past part.] : HASTY ⟨not likely to survive the wrecker's ~ crowbar —J.C. Adams⟩ — **fes·ti·nate·ly** *adv*

2fes·ti·nate \-ˌnāt\ *vi* -ED/-ING/-S [L *festinatus*, past part. of *festinare* to hasten, make haste — more at BORZOI] : HASTEN; *specif* : to accelerate the gait involuntarily in walking (as in certain nervous diseases) ⟨a *festinating* gait⟩

fes·ti·na·tion \ˌ==ˈnāshən\ *n* -s [L *festination-, festinatio*, fr. *festinatus* (past part.) + *-ion-, -io* -ion] : an act or instance of festinating

fes·ti·no \feˈstē(ˌ)nō\ *also* **fes·tine** \feˈstēn\ *n* -s [It *festino*, dim. of *festa* feast, holiday, festival, fr. L *festa* festival — more at FEAST] *archaic* : FEAST, ENTERTAINMENT

1fes·ti·val \ˈfestəvəl\ *adj* [ME, fr. MF, fr. OF, fr. L *festivus* festive, gay + OF *-al* — more at FESTIVE] : of, belonging to, appropriate to, or set apart as a festival ⟨the ~ celebration of the Holy Communion⟩ ⟨playing ~ concerts⟩ ⟨their mood was ~⟩ ⟨on a ~ day⟩ — **fes·ti·val·ly** \-vəlē, -li\ *adv*

2festival \ˈ"\ *n* -s **1** : a time of celebration marked by special observances: **a** : an occasion observed with religious ceremonies ⟨the planting and harvest ~s of primitive peoples⟩ : FEAST ⟨the great ~s of Whitsuntide, Trinity Sunday, and Corpus Christi —S.E.Morison⟩ **b** : an occasion devoted to festive community observances often held annually to celebrate the anniversary of a notable person or event or the harvest of an important product : a program of public festivity ⟨the best known ~ at the college is Founder's Day⟩ **2 a** : a program of cultural events consisting typically of a series of performances of works in the arts sometimes devoted to a single artist or a particular genre and often held annually for a period of several days or weeks ⟨a Bach ~⟩ ⟨a Shakespeare ~⟩ ⟨a drama ~⟩ ⟨a dance ~⟩ **b** : something resembling such a festival ⟨the radio station held a ~ of books with readings, talks, and discussions⟩ ⟨a cartoon ~ for children advertised by the local theater⟩ ⟨the occasional ~s at which the square-dance clubs of the area gather⟩ **3** : CONVIVIALITY, GAIETY, CHEERFULNESS ⟨alcohol had always loosened . . . his sense of ~ but now it only dragged him down into despondency —Budd Schulberg⟩ **4 a** : 5FAIR 2 **b** : STRAWBERRY FESTIVAL

festival of freedom *usu cap both Fs* : PASSOVER 1

festival of lanterns *usu cap F&L* : FEAST OF LANTERNS

festival of lights *usu cap F&L* : HANUKKAH

festival of weeks *usu cap F&W* : SHABUOTH

fes·tive \ˈfestiv, -tēv *also* -təv\ *adj* [L *festivus*, fr. *festum* festival, feast + *-ivus* -ive — more at -FEST] **1** : of, belonging to, or befitting a feast, festival, or other celebration ⟨banqueting merrily round the ~ board⟩ ⟨raise the flag on public holidays and other ~ occasions⟩ ⟨a set of diamond . . . cuff buttons for ~ wear —Ring Lardner⟩ **2** : of or marked by gaiety, conviviality, or revelry : JOYOUS, MERRY, SPORTIVE ⟨came across the floor with a ~ stride —Theodore Dreiser⟩ ⟨a ~ party of sailors and girls at the next table⟩ — **fes·tive·ly** \-təvlē, -li\ *adv* — **fes·tive·ness** \-tivnəs, -tēv- *also* -təv-\ *n* -ES

fes·tiv·i·ty \feˈstivəd·ē, fəˈs-, -vətē, -i\ *n* -ES [ME *festivite*, fr. MF *festivité*, fr. L *festivitas*, fr. *festivus*, adj. + *-itas* -ity] **1** : FESTIVAL ⟨the Pickwickian Christmas . . . was mainly a gratuitous ~ —Aldous Huxley⟩ **2** : the quality or state of being festive : joyfulness in company (as at a social gathering) : GAIETY ⟨hung with banners which give it an air of restrained ~ —Kay Fuller⟩ **3** : festive activity : REJOICING, MERRYMAKING ⟨general ~ is to follow the parade⟩ — often used in pl. ⟨the *festivities* end with a fireworks display⟩

fes·ti·vous \ˈfestəvəs\ *adj* [L *festivus* + E *-ous*] : FESTIVE

1fes·toon \(ˈ)feˈstün\ *n* -s [F *feston*, fr. It *festone*, fr. *festa* celebration, feast — more at FESTA] **1 a** : a decorative chain (as of flowers or leaves) hanging typically in a curve between two points ⟨decorated with ~s of flowers and ivy intertwined⟩ **b** : a carved, molded, or painted ornament representing a festoon : SWAG ⟨around the mirror were carved ~s of flowers wound with ribbon⟩ **c** : a piece of fabric suspended or bound at intervals to form graceful rounded folds ⟨a fringed damask ~ for the archway⟩ **2** : a usu. hanging open loop or curve ⟨the paper is looped over these spars in long ~s —F.H.Norris⟩; *esp* : something suspended in a curve between two points ⟨between the mulberry trees swing long ~s of grapevines⟩ **3** : something resembling a pendent garland ⟨live oaks with long . . . ~s of Spanish moss —F.B. Gipson⟩ **4** : one of the somewhat quadrangular segments bordering the body of certain ticks — see TICK illustration

festoon 1a

2festoon \ˈ"\ *vt* -ED/-ING/-S **1 a** : to hang upon in a festoon (as for adornment) : drape with festoons ⟨razor grass . . . hung in emerald loops from branch to branch, ~*ing* living foliage and dead stump alike —William Beebe⟩ **b** : hang down from like a pendent garland ⟨blossoms ~ the vine⟩ ⟨bearded moss ~s the branches⟩ ⟨icicles ~ the eaves⟩ **c** : to hang upon or adorn as if comprising a festoon ⟨the old wooden carriages . . . have passengers . . . hanging from the sides; the more hardy commuters even ~ tender and locomotive —H.T. De Sa⟩ ⟨the margins of the manuscript were ~*ed* with additions and corrections⟩ **2** : to form into a festoon : suspend in festoons ⟨the telegraph wires whipped back and ~*ed* themselves round our machine —Francis Yeats-Brown⟩; *specif* : to hang (material) in festoons for drying **3** *dentistry* **a** : to shape (a crown or band) to conform to the contour of tissues with which there is to be association **b** : to mold (the plate of a denture) about the base of the teeth or facings to resemble the natural gum line

festoon cloud *n* : MAMMATOCUMULUS

festoon drier *n* : a mechanism for supporting material in loops while it is being dried by circulating air

festoon drying *n* : the drying of material (as rubber, plastic, impregnated fabric, or a web of paper) by supporting it in long loops and moving it through a drying chamber

fes·toon·er \-nə(r)\ *n* -s : a sewing-machine operator who finishes the edges of knit goods

fes·toon·ery \feˈstünərē, -ri\ *n* -ES : festoons (as of a room) considered as a group ⟨the elegant ~ of the ballroom⟩

festoon lighting *n* : lighting by festoons of electric lamps wired to a flexible cable

festoon pine *n* : a creeping evergreen plant (*Selaginella rupestris*) of eastern No. America with tufted stems

-fests *pl of* -FEST

fest·schrift \ˈfestˌshrift\ *n, pl* **fest·schrif·ten** \-ftən\ *or* **festschrifts** *often cap* [G, fr. *fest* festival + *schrift* writings, fr. OHG *scrift*, fr. *scrīban* to write — more at -FEST, SCRIBE] : a usu. miscellaneous volume of writings from several hands for a celebration; *esp* : one of learned essays contributed by students, colleagues, and admirers to honor a scholar on a special anniversary

fes·tu·ca \feˈst(y)ükə, fəˈ-\ *n, cap* [NL, fr. L, stalk, straw, rod for touching slaves in manumission; prob. akin to L *ferula* giant fennel] : a large genus of mostly tufted perennial grasses comprising the fescues and having flat leaves and panicled spikelets with acute pointed or awned flowering scales — see GREAT BUNCH GRASS, SHEEP'S FESCUE, TALL FESCUE

fes·tu·cine \ˈfest(y)əˌsīn, -ˌsēn\ *adj* [L *festuca* stalk, straw + E *-ine*] : of the color straw yellow

fet \ˈfet\ *vt* **fet; fet; fetting; fets** [ME *fetten, feten*, fr. OE *fetian* — more at FETCH] *dial Eng* : FETCH

fe·ta \ˈfed·ə\ *n* -s [NGk (*tyri*) *pheta*, fr. *tyri* cheese + *pheta*, fr. It *fetta* slice] : a white cheese made of the milk of sheep or goats and cured in brine

fe·tal *also* **foe·tal** \ˈfēd·ᵊl, -ētᵊl\ *adj* [*fetus, foetus* + *-al*] : of, relating to, characteristic of, or in the stage or condition of a fetus

fetal circulation *n* : the course of the blood in the vessels of the fetus, impure blood passing in man and the higher mammals to the placenta by the umbilical arteries, returning purified and charged with nutriment by the umbilical vein, and entering the inferior vena cava either directly by the ductus venosus or after passing through the liver

fe·tal·iza·tion *also* **foe·tal·iza·tion** \ˌ==ˌ=ˈzāshən, -ˌīˈz-\ *n* -s : a retention in the postnatal life of higher forms of conditions occurring during development of related lower forms ⟨the human skull shows ~ in comparison to the gorilla's since it resembles the simple infant gorilla skull rather than the massive specialized adult skull⟩

fetal membrane *n* : an embryonic membrane

fetal rickets *n* : ACHONDROPLASIA

fe·ta·tion *also* **foe·ta·tion** \fēˈtāshən\ *n* -s [*fetus, foetus* + *-ation*] : the formation of a fetus : PREGNANCY

1fetch \ˈfech\ *vb* -ED/-ING/-ES [ME *fecchen*, fr. OE *feccan, fetian*; akin to OE *fatian* to fetch, OHG (*sih*) *vazzōn* to climb, ascend, ON *feta* to step, find one's way, OE *fōt* foot — more at FOOT] *vt* **1 a** : to go after and bring back : go and get ⟨escaped while the guard was out to ~ their supper⟩ ⟨~ me a drink⟩ ⟨had to leave her alone while he ~*ed* the doctor from town⟩; *broadly* : to convey or conduct from one place to another : come and get ⟨inside the station as I waited for my friends to ~ me —D.L.Cohn⟩ : BRING ⟨the souvenirs he ~*ed* back from Europe⟩ ⟨come and ~ along your family⟩ : TAKE ⟨had enough money to ~ him from New York to Philadelphia⟩ **b** *now dial* : to carry off : FILCH **c** : to draw from an often remote source : DERIVE, DEDUCE ⟨~*ed* his arguments from afar⟩ ⟨~ analogies from nature⟩ **2 a** : to cause to come ⟨~ the discussion to a close⟩ ⟨one shot ~*ed* it down⟩ : draw forth : ELICIT ⟨the sound of the sob ~*ed* tears to the eyes —Arnold Bennett⟩ ⟨~ a laugh from the audience⟩ ⟨a scamper of feet ~*ed* me out of my berth and up on deck —A.T.Quiller-Couch⟩ **b** : to bring as a price or similar return : sell for ⟨the pigs ~*ed* a good price at the market⟩ : bring in : REALIZE ⟨risk capital ~*es* a higher interest rate⟩ ⟨professional skill . . . ~*es* very much smaller pay in Germany —J.A.Hobson⟩ **c** : to win the interest or admiration of : ATTRACT ⟨two of the men . . . were ~*ed* by the notion of striking it rich —*Newsweek*⟩ ⟨he doesn't ~ the girls like William —D.H.Lawrence⟩ **d** *chiefly dial* : to revive from unconsciousness : bring around — often used with *to* or *around* **e** : to bring to agreement : CONVINCE — often used with *round* ⟨his argument ~*ed* her round⟩ **3 a** : to give (a blow) by striking : DEAL ⟨~ him a clip on the chin⟩ — not often in formal use **b** *now chiefly dial* : to bring about (a movement or action) : PERFORM, ACCOMPLISH ⟨I meant to go . . . but time was short and I didn't ~ it —O.W.Holmes †1935⟩; *specif* : to take into the lungs : DRAW ⟨sat ~*ing* her breath in dry sobs —Ngaio Marsh⟩ **c** : to bring forth (a sound or speech) ⟨~ a sneeze⟩ : UTTER ⟨~ a loud whoop⟩ : HEAVE ⟨~ a sigh⟩ **d** : to make an end of (as a person) : do for : KILL ⟨got in another shot and ~*ed* him —Bret Harte⟩ — not often in formal use **4 a** : to make (a point) by sailing esp. despite adverse wind or tide ⟨~ the harbor before the storm breaks⟩ **b** : to arrive at : REACH ⟨~*ed* home after his long ride⟩ **5** : DAMN — used in an oath ⟨dad ~ it⟩ ~ *vi* **1** : to get and bring something ⟨the German housewife has to spend a lot of time ~*ing* and carrying —Marieluise Capitaine⟩; *specif* : to retrieve killed game : SEEK — often used in the imperative as a command to a dog **2** : to take a roundabout way : CIRCLE — usu. used with *about, around*, or *round* ⟨working through the parts beyond Jago Row, he ~*ed* round into Honey Lane —Arthur Morrison⟩ **3** *of a boat* : GO, COME ⟨~ about⟩ : hold a course ⟨~ to windward⟩ **4** *chiefly Scot* : to breathe with difficulty ⟨she ~*es* and fights for breath —Robert Burns⟩ **5** *dial* : to recover consciousness, health, or weight : REVIVE — often used with *up* ⟨give him another glass — then he'll ~ up —Thomas Hardy⟩ — **fetch about** *obs* : to effect a change in ⟨*fetch about* this form of speech —2 Sam 14:20 (AV)⟩ — **fetch a compass** : to circle around ⟨from thence we *fetched a compass* —Acts 28:13 (AV)⟩ — **fetch a pump** : to prime a pump — **fetch off** *obs* : to get the better of ⟨as I return I will *fetch off* these justices —Shak.⟩

2fetch \ˈ"\ *n* -ES [1*fetch*] **1** : an act or instance of fetching ⟨in the trial for two sheep dogs each must keep its own side till the ~ is finished⟩ **2** : a stratagem contrived in a far-fetched, ingenious, or devious way : ARTIFICE, SOPHISM ⟨the mere ~ of a debater at a loss for arguments⟩ : TRICK ⟨one of the cunningest ~*es* of Satan that he . . . dodging behind this neighbor or that acquaintance compels us to wound him through them —J.R.Lowell⟩ **3** *dial Eng* : a catch in the throat or voice; *specif* : a dying gasp **4** : the distance along open water or land over which the wind blows : SWEEP ⟨wind coming from the . . . deserts with a clear ~ of a thousand miles —Joseph Furphy⟩; *specif* : the distance traversed by waves without obstruction (as when caused by steady winds)

3fetch \ˈ"\ *n* -ES [origin unknown] **1 a** : the phantom double of a living person appearing as an omen of the death of the person : WRAITH **b** : something that looks or acts exactly like another : COUNTERPART ⟨the muddy field before them which was the exact ~ of the muddy field behind —*Strand Mag.*⟩ **2** : GHOST, APPARITION ⟨a harrowing graveyard with . . . a ~ —*Saturday Rev.*⟩

4fetch *var of* FITCH

fetch away *or* **fetch way** *vi* : to move from place as a result of a ship's rolling or pitching : SHIFT, SLIDE ⟨some of the cargo had been loosely stowed and *fetched away* a little when the storm hit⟩

fetch candle *n* [perh. fr. 1*fetch*] : a corpse candle supposed to pass between the home and the grave of the beholder

fetching *adj* [fr. pres. part. of 1*fetch*] : tending to win interest or admiration : ATTRACTIVE ⟨a memoir that must be one of the most ~ tourist baits in all the state —S.H.Holbrook⟩ ⟨a ~ gown⟩ — **fetch·ing·ly** *adv*

fetch up *vt* **1** : to bring up or out : PRODUCE ⟨a tyrant *fetched up* by frightened capitalists —H.J.Muller⟩ : RECALL ⟨can *fetch up* anecdotes on almost any phase of straits historic lore —R.M.Dorson⟩ **2** : to make up (as leeway or lost time) **3** *chiefly dial* : to bring up : RAISE, REAR ⟨she *fetched up* three boys⟩ **4** : to bring to a stop ⟨he was *fetched up* short by a stop light⟩ ~ *vi* : to come to a standstill, stopping place, or result : end up : STOP ⟨*fetched up* suddenly against the wall⟩ : ARRIVE ⟨it was enough to make the voyage at all, and indeed he should have *fetched up* in Virginia —Alan Villiers⟩ : CONCLUDE ⟨sorted the wooden boxes . . . and *fetched up* with fourteen —Frederick Way⟩

fetch-up \ˈ=ˌ=\ *n* -s [*fetch up*] : an abrupt stop (as at the end of a fall) ⟨injured in the *fetch-up* of the toboggan against the tree⟩

1fete *or* **fête** \ˈfāt, *usu* -ād·+V\ *n* -s [F *fête*, fr. MF *feste*, fr. OF — more at FEAST] : a festive celebration or entertainment : FESTIVAL ⟨the ~ of the Assumption of the Virgin in Paris⟩ ⟨the village ~s go on, as English as a cowslip —C.G.Glover⟩ ⟨Class Day, the great ~ of the year —Catherine D. Bowen⟩; *specif* : an often outdoor entertainment on a lavish scale ⟨~s in the park of the Château of Versailles with sky, water, and sylvan illuminations and amplified music and discourses —Janet Flanner⟩

2fete *or* **fête** \ˈ"\ *vt* -ED/-ING/-S [F *fêter*, fr. MF *fester*, fr. OF, fr. *feste*, n.] : to honor (a person) or commemorate (an event) with a fete ⟨*feted* the royal visitors with banquets and parades⟩ : ENTERTAIN ⟨when the circus came to town . . . he would welcome the train in the railway yards, ~ the performers —Green Peyton⟩ : CELEBRATE ⟨*feted* his recovery with ice cream and cake⟩ ⟨literary weeklies here all *feted* her with photographs of herself and with the compliments of others —*New Yorker*⟩ : EXTOL ⟨Sade has been *feted* as a great thinker —François Bondy⟩

fête cham·pê·tre \ˌfāt,shäⁿˈpetr(ᵊ), -shäⁿˈp-, -pāt-, -t(rə)\ *n, pl* **fêtes champêtres** \-t,sh. . .tr(ᵊ), . . .tra(z), . . .t(s)\ [F, lit., rural festival] **1** : a gathering for amusements in a rural setting of 18th century French courtiers costumed as shepherds and shepherdesses **2** : an outdoor entertainment : a large garden party

fête ga·lante \-gəˈläⁿt\ *n, pl* **fêtes galantes** \-tg. . .nt(s)\ [F, lit., gay festival] : FÊTE CHAMPÊTRE 1

fet·er·i·ta *also* **fed·er·i·ta** \ˌfed(·)əˈrēd·ə\ *n* -s [Sudanese Ar; akin to Ar *fatīrah* unleavened bread] : any of various grain sorghums that are derived from a Sudanese sorghum (*Sorghum vulgare* var. *caudatum*) and are characterized by compact oval heads of exceptionally large soft white seeds

feth \ˈfeth\ *Scot var of* FAITH

feth·er *dial var of* FEATHER

feti- — see FETO-

fe·tial *or* **fe·cial** \ˈfēshəl\ *n, pl* **fetials** \-lz\ *or* **fe·ti·a·les** \ˌfād·ēˈäˌlās\ *or* **fecials** [L *fetialis*, prob. fr. (assumed)

OL *fetis* statute, treaty (akin to Goth *gadeths* deed) + L *-alis* -al — more at DEED] **:** a member of a priestly board in ancient Rome responsible for overseeing diplomatic negotiations

²**fetial** *or* **fecial** \"\ *adj* [L *fetialis* of a fetial, fr. *fetialis*, n.] **:** dealing with matters (as a treaty or declaration and rules of war) affecting relations between nations ⟨the ~ law of Rome⟩ **:** DIPLOMATIC ⟨a member of the ~ profession⟩

fe·ti·ci·dal *also* **foe·ti·ci·dal** \ˌfēd·əˌsīdᵊl\ *adj* **:** of or relating to feticide **:** tending to cause intrauterine death of a fetus ⟨a ~ infection⟩

fe·ti·cide *also* **foe·ti·cide** \ˈfēd·əˌsīd\ *n* -s [*feti-, foeti-* + *-cide*] **:** the act of killing a fetus **:** ILLEGAL ABORTION

fet·id *also* **foet·id** \ˈfe|d·əd, |təd *sometimes* ˈfē|\ *adj* [ME *fetid*, fr. L *fetidus, foetidus*, fr. *fetēre, foetēre* to have an offensive smell, stink; akin to L *fumus* smoke — more at FUME] **1 :** having an offensive smell **:** STINKING, RANK ⟨store fronts ~ with the smell of old vegetables —A.J.Liebling⟩ ⟨the air of the room was ~ with stale tobacco smoke —A. Conan Doyle⟩ **2 :** containing the volatile constituents of asafetida — **fet·id·ly** *adv* — **fet·id·ness** *n* -ES

fetid aloe *n* **1 :** GIANT CABUYA **2 fetid aloes** *pl* **:** CABALLINE ALOES

fetid buckeye *n* **:** OHIO BUCKEYE

fetid cassia *n* **:** SICKLEPOD 2

fetid chamomile *n* **:** MAYWEED 1

fetid cress *n* **:** a European peppergrass (*Lepidium ruderale*) adventive in No. America

fetid currant *n* **:** SKUNK CURRANT

fetid hellebore *n* **1 :** BEAR'S-FOOT **2 :** SKUNK CABBAGE 1a

fetid horehound *n* **:** BLACK HOREHOUND

fe·tid·i·ty \feˈtidəd·ē, fēˈ-, -idətē, -i\ *n* -ES **:** FETIDNESS

fetid marigold *n* **:** a prairie weed (*Dyssodia papposa*) of the western U. S. with ill-smelling herbage

fetid marsh fleabane *n* **:** a marsh fleabane (*Pluchea foetida*) with fetid foliage

fetid nightshade *n* **:** HENBANE

fetids *n pl, obs* **:** fetid drugs

fetid shrub *n* **:** a papaw (*Asimina triloba*)

fetid wood witch *n* **:** STINKHORN

fetid yew *n* **:** STINKING CEDAR 1

fe·tii \fəˈtēˌē\ *n, pl* **fetii** [Tahitian *feti'i*] *in French Oceania* **:** a member of one's extended family **:** RELATION

feting *pres part of* FETE

fe·tip·a·rous *or* **foe·tip·a·rous** \fēˈtipərəs\ *adj* [*feti-, foeti-* + *-parous*] **:** that bear young very incompletely developed ⟨~ marsupials⟩

fet·ish *also* **fet·ich** \ˈfe|d·|ish, |t|, |ēsh *also* ˈfē| *or* ˈfā|\ *n* -ES *often attrib* [F & Pg; F *fétiche*, fr. Pg *feitiço*, fr. *feitiço*, adj., artificial, false, fr. L *facticius* factitious — more at FACTITIOUS] **1 a :** a natural or artificial object (as an animal tooth or a wood carving) believed among a primitive people to have a preternatural power to protect or aid its owner often because of ritual consecration or animation by a spirit; *broadly* **:** any material object regarded with superstitious or extravagant trust or reverence ⟨all our ~*es* . . . Sunday school cards, a silver cross that I had for my baptism, a Bible —*Amer. Mercury*⟩ **b :** an object of extreme or irrational reverence or devotion **:** PREPOSSESSION ⟨security . . . may be sought excessively and become a ~ —Bertrand Russell⟩ ⟨a goose-stepping army which makes a ~ of discipline —*Scribner's*⟩ ⟨accept the ~ that birth and station presuppose any innate superiority —Theodore Dreiser⟩ **c :** an object (as a shoe or glove) or a part of the body that arouses libidinal interest often to the exclusion of genital impulses **2 :** a rite or incantation or cult of fetish worshipers ⟨their tribal custom and ~⟩ **3 :** irrational reverence or attachment **:** FIXATION ⟨had a ~ for red hair and so married a redhead⟩

fet·ish·ism *also* **fet·ich·ism** \-ˌshizəm\ *n* -s **1 :** belief in and use of magical fetishes ⟨tribes that still practice ~⟩ **:** a religion marked by the use of fetishes **2 :** extravagant irrational devotion to some object, idea, or practice **:** WORSHIP ⟨~ of the Bible as a material object⟩ ⟨a ~ of luxury goods⟩ ⟨suffers from ~ of weekly housecleaning⟩ **3 :** the often pathological displacement of erotic or libidinal interest and satisfaction to a fetish (as an inanimate object) — compare PARTIALISM

fet·ish·ist *also* **fet·ich·ist** \-ˌshəst\ *n* -s **1 :** a believer in magical fetishes **2 :** one addicted to a fetish ⟨a ~ about gadgets⟩ ⟨a shoe ~ and other sex deviants⟩

fet·ish·is·tic *also* **fet·ich·is·tic** \ˌfe|d·|iˈshistik, |t|, |ēˈsh-, -istēk *also* |fē| *or* |fā| *also* **fe·tish·ic** \feˈtishik, fēˈ-,fāˈ-, -shēk\ *adj* **1 :** of, belonging to, or characterized by fetishism **2 a :** invested with extraphysical or symbolic significance ⟨~ objects gathered in shrines⟩ ⟨the injection had become a ~ symbol —Wenzell Brown⟩ **b :** marked by fixed irrational regard ⟨its ~ veneration for education —D.S.Savage⟩ ⟨a ~ response to women's shoes⟩ — **fet·ish·is·ti·cal·ly** \ˌ≈≈ˈstək(ə)lē, -stēk-, -li\ *adv*

fet·ish·ize \ˈfe|d·|iˌshīz, |t|, |ēˌsh- *also* ˈfē| *or* ˈfā|\ *vt* -ED/-ING/-S **:** to make a fetish of **:** treat or regard as a fetish ⟨an Australian *fetishizes* a piece of wood; a devout believer, an ikon or the name of a saint . . .; a Communist, the portrait of Lenin or Stalin —P.A.Sorokin⟩

¹**fet·lock** \ˈfetˌläk\ *n* -s [ME *fitlok, fetlak;* akin to MHG *vizzelach, vizlach, vizloch* fetlock, *vezzel, vizzel* pastern, OE *fōt* foot — more at FOOT] **1 :** a projection like a cushion bearing a tuft of long hair on the back side of the leg above the hoof of the horse and similar animals **2 :** the tuft of hair itself **3** *or* **fetlock joint :** the joint of the limb at the fetlock between the great pastern bone and the metatarsal or metacarpal

1 fetlock 1

²**fetlock** \"\ *n* -s [by alter. (influence of ¹*fetlock*)] **:** ¹FETTERLOCK

fet·low \ˈfetˌlō\ *n* -s [perh. alter. (influenced by ³*felon*) of *whitlow*] **:** a felon in cattle

feto- *or* **feti-** *also* **foeto-** *or* **foeti-** *comb form* [*feto-, foeto-* fr. L *fetus, foetus; feti-, foeti-* fr. L, fr. *fetus, foetus*] **:** fetus ⟨*fetometry*⟩ ⟨*feticide*⟩ **:** fetal and ⟨*fetoplacental*⟩

fe·tor *also* **foe·tor** \ˈfēd·ə(r)\ *n* -s [ME *fetour*, fr. L *fetor*, fr. *fetēre, foetēre* to have an offensive smell, stink + *-or* — more at FETID] **:** a usu. strong offensive smell **:** STENCH, FETIDNESS ⟨burned sugar to dispel the ~ of the sickroom —Jean Stafford⟩ ⟨~ of breath⟩

fets *pres 3d sing of* FET

¹**fet·ter** \ˈfed·ə(r), -etə-\ *n* -s [ME *feter*, fr. OE *feter, fetor;* akin to OHG *fezzera* fetter, MD *veter*, ON *fjǫturr* fetter, OE *fōt* foot — more at FOOT] **1 :** a chain or shackle for the feet **:** BOND ⟨a cow dragging her ~ chain and picket⟩ — used chiefly in the pl. ⟨the ~*s* of the galley slave⟩ **2 :** something that confines or restrains **:** RESTRAINT ⟨world trade free of political ~*s*⟩ **3 :** a long link in an ornamental chain

²**fetter** \"\ *vt* **fettered; fettered; fettering; fetters** [ME *feteren*, fr. OE *gefeterian*, fr. *feter, fetor*, n.] **1 :** to put fetters upon **:** shackle the feet of with a chain **2 :** to bind (one thing or person) to another as if with a chain ⟨God who has ~*ed* our everyday senses to an understanding of nothing but the things immediately around us —T.B.Costain⟩ **3 a :** to restrain from free action **:** deprive of freedom ⟨we reverence tradition but we will not be ~*ed* by it —W.R. Inge⟩ **b :** to render helpless or impotent ⟨deafness, by ~*ing* the powers of utterance, cheats many of their birthright of knowledge —Malachy Hynes⟩ **syn** see HAMPER

fetterbush \ˈ≈≈ˌ≈\ *n* **1 :** a showy shrub (*Lyonia lucida*) of the southern U.S. with persistent leaves and angled branchlets **2 :** MOUNTAIN FETTERBUSH **3 :** a plant of the genus *Leucothoe*

fettered cat *n* **:** KAFFIR CAT

fet·ter·less \-ərləs, *-R* -əl- *or* -ᵊl-\ *adj* **:** having no fetters **:** FREE, UNBOUND

¹**fetterlock** \ˈ≈≈ˌ≈\ *n* [ME *feterlok*, fr. *feter* fetter + *lok* lock — more at LOCK (fastening)] **1 :** a device formerly attached to a horse's leg to hamper running away **:** CLOG — called also *fetlock* **2 :** an armorial representation of a fetterlock

²**fetterlock** \"\ *n* [by alter. (influence of ¹*fetterlock*)] **:** ¹FETLOCK

fet·ti·cus \ˈfed·əkəs\ *n* -ES [modif. of D *vettekous*, fr. *vet* fat (fr. MD) + *kous* stocking, fr. MD *couse*, fr. OF (Picardy dial.) *cauce*, fr. ML *calcea;* akin to OE *fætt* fat — more at FAT, CHAUSSES] **:** CORN SALAD

fetting *pres part of* FET

¹**fet·tle** \ˈfed·ᵊl, -etᵊl\ *n* -s [fr. (assumed) ME *fetel*, fr. OE, belt; akin to OHG *fezzil* sword belt, ON *fetill*, and prob. to OE *fæt* vessel — more at VAT] *dial Brit* **:** straw or hay esp. when used as a basket handle

²**fettle** \"\ *vb* **fettled; fettled; fettling** \ˈfed·ᵊliŋ, -t(ᵊ)l-\ **fettles** [ME *fetlen, fetelen* to shape, prepare, get ready; prob. akin to OE *fæt* vessel] *vt* **1** *chiefly Brit* **:** to set in working order **:** MEND, REPAIR ⟨~ a gun⟩ **2** *dial Brit* **:** to make neat or orderly **:** ARRANGE ⟨~ up the house⟩ **3** *dial Brit* **a :** to feed and care for (a domestic animal) **b :** to groom and harness (a horse) **c :** to dress up **:** ARRAY **4** *dial Eng* **:** MULL ⟨~ a beverage⟩ **5 :** to cover or line the hearth of (a reverberatory furnace) with fettling **6 a :** to clean and smooth (as a metal or plastic) after casting or molding **:** DRESS **b :** to trim off excess clay at the seams of (cast and partly dried pottery ware) **c :** to remove excess dried glaze from (tile) before firing **7 :** to clean accumulated fibers from the card clothing of (a woolen or worsted carding machine) ~ *vi* **1** *dial Eng* **:** to make preparations **:** get ready **2** *dial Eng* **:** to fuss esp. over trifles **3** *dial Eng* **:** to get along **:** FARE

³**fettle** \"\ *n* -s **1 a :** a state of fitness or order **:** CONDITION, TRIM ⟨in pretty good ~ for a man of his years —R.L.Duffus⟩ **b :** state of mind **:** SPIRITS ⟨the good news put him in fine ~⟩ **2 :** FETTLING

fet·tler \ˈfed·ᵊlə(r), -et(ᵊ)l-\ *n* -s [²*fettle* + *-er*] **:** one that fettles: as **a** *chiefly Brit* **:** a repairman or maintenance man (as on a railway) **b :** a pottery worker who smooths greenware with a knife, felt, emery, and a wet sponge **c :** a worker who cleans or cuts excess glaze from tile

fettling *n* -s [fr. gerund of ²*fettle*] **:** loose material (as ore or sand) that is thrown on the hearth of a furnace esp. to protect it

fet·tu·cel·le \ˌfed·əˈchelē\ *n* -s [It *fettuccelle*, pl. of *fettuccella*, dim. of *fettuccia* small slice, ribbon, dim. of *fetta* slice] **:** alimentary paste in ribbon shape

fet·tu·ci·ni \-ˈchēnē\ *also* **fet·tu·ci·ne** \", -ˌnā\ *n pl but sing or pl in constr* [It *fettuccine*, pl. of *fettuccina*, dim. of *fettuccia*] **:** alimentary paste in narrow strips **:** NOODLES

fe·tus *also* **foe·tus** \ˈfēd·əs, -ētəs\ *n* -ES [L, action of bearing young, offspring, fetus, fr. *fetus, foetus*, adj., pregnant, fruitful, newly delivered — more at FEMININE] **:** an unborn or unhatched young vertebrate esp. after passing through the earliest developmental stages and attaining the basic structural plan of its kind; *specif* **:** a developing human from usu. three months after conception to birth — compare EMBRYO

¹**feu** *or* **few** \ˈfyü\ *n* -s [ME (Sc dial.) *feu*, fr. MF *fé, fié, fief, fieu* — more at FEE] **1** *Scots law* **:** a feudal benefice **:** FEE **2** *Scots law* **a :** a tenure where the vassal in place of military services makes a return in grain or in money — compare BLANCH, WARDHOLDING **b :** a grant of land to be so held **c :** a perpetual lease for a fixed rent — compare EMPHYTEUSIS **3** *Scots law* **:** a piece of land held under one of these tenures

²**feu** \"\ *vt* **feued; feued; feuing; feus** *Scots law* **:** to grant (land) upon feu

feu·ar \ˈfyüər\ *n* -s [¹*feu* + *-ar* (Sc var. of *-er*)] *Scots law* **:** one who holds a feu

feu charter *n, Scots law* **:** the charter securing a feu

feucht \ˈfyükt\ *Scot past of* FIGHT

¹**feud** \ˈfyüd\ *n* -s [alter. of ME *fede, feide*, fr. MF *faide, feide*, fr. OHG *fēhida*, of Gmc origin; akin to OE *fǣhth* enmity, hostility, feud, *fede*, OFris *feithe, faithe;* derivatives fr. the root of OE *fāh* hostile — more at FOE] **:** a prolonged or inveterate mutual enmity marked by bitter and often violent conflicts **:** a war of revenge or rivalry between individuals or factions **:** a relationship of aggressive hostility **:** STRIFE, QUARREL ⟨a political ~ of long standing⟩ ⟨a new outbreak of the virulent ~ between labor and management⟩ ⟨had they been united, they might have prevailed; but they were always at ~ with each other —Goldwin Smith⟩; *specif* **:** an inveterate strife between families or clans marked by bloodshed and by alternate attacks to take revenge for former injuries

²**feud** \"\ *vi* -ED/-ING/-S **:** to carry on a feud **:** BATTLE ⟨is currently ~*ing* with the Treasury over her refusal to withhold employees' taxes —*Newsweek*⟩ ⟨the two families of the valley have ~*ed* for generations⟩

³**feud** \"\ *n* -s [ML *feodum, feudum*, of Gmc origin; akin to OHG *fihu* cattle — more at FEE] **:** an estate in land held of a lord or superior by a tenant or vassal on condition he render certain services to the lord or superior **:** a feudal benefice **:** FEE, FIEF — compare ALODIUM

feuda *pl of* FEUDUM

¹**feu·dal** \ˈfyüdᵊl\ *adj* [ML *feodalis, feudalis*, fr. *feodum, feudum* + L *-alis* -al] **1 a :** of, relating to, or having the characteristics of a feud or fief **:** founded upon or involving the relation of lord and vassal with tenure of land in feud ⟨~ rights and services⟩ ⟨~ tenure⟩ ⟨~ polity⟩ — distinguished from *domanial* **b :** of, existing in, characterized by, or relating to the feudal system ⟨the ~ era⟩ ⟨his ~ lord⟩ ⟨the ~ states of medieval Europe⟩ ⟨a volume of ~ studies⟩ **c :** of feudal times ⟨ruins of a ~ castle⟩ ⟨a map of ~ England⟩ **2 :** resembling that of a medieval lord in imperiousness or impressiveness **:** characterized by a grand style or manner ⟨lived in almost ~ ease among devoted retainers and entertained with a lavish hand —A.C.Cole⟩ **:** IMPOSING ⟨owner of the . . . railroad had built his ~ castle —Harrison Smith⟩ **3 a :** marked by or upholding the domination of a privileged class **:** OLIGARCHIC ⟨replace the ~ bureaucracy with an equitable civil service⟩ ⟨strongly ~ by instinct, he led the opposition to . . . demands for equal electoral privileges —Andrew Boyle⟩; *specif* **:** controlled absolutely by and for the benefit of an individual or small group (as of landowners) ⟨the Arab governments, representing largely ~ societies in which the masses are incredibly poor —Peter Allen⟩ ⟨textile-mill towns are ~ empires with their own stores . . . courts . . . police, and jails —Lawrence Lader⟩ **b :** of, belonging to, or constituting a ruling class ⟨the ~ bourgeois type . . . represented a coalition of the army, the bureaucracy, and the owners of the large estates and factories for the joint exploitation of the state —Franz Neumann⟩; *specif* **:** ruling absolutely within a limited domain ⟨the last survivor of the ~ tribal chieftains —Robert Payne⟩ **4 :** of or marked by division into independent often absolutely ruled domains ⟨where no central government has replaced the ~ structure of tribal society⟩ **5 :** characterized by reciprocal and contractual relations between members (as of a society) ⟨monarchical and democratic societies, ~ or caste — divided ones, priest-ridden and relatively irreligious ones . . . evolve —A.L.Kroeber⟩

²**feudal** \"\ *adj* [¹*feud* + *-al*] **:** of, associated with, or engaged in a retaliatory or competitive feud ⟨~ hatred⟩ ⟨the man who rescued a ~ enemy —*Emporia (Kans.) Gazette*⟩

feu·dal·ism \-dᵊlˌizəm\ *n* -s [¹*feudal* + *-ism*] **1 a :** the system of polity flourishing in Europe from the 9th to about the 15th centuries, based upon the relation of lord to vassal with the holding of all land in fee (as of the king), and having as its principal incidents homage, service of tenants under arms and in court, wardship, and forfeiture **b :** the principles or relations and usages on which the feudal system was based — compare COMMENDATION, FEUD, LIEGE, LORD, PRECARIUM, VASSAL **2 :** any social system in which great landowners or hereditary overlords exact revenue from the land and also exercise the functions of government in their domains **3 :** control by an entrenched minority esp. for its own benefit **:** social, political, or economic oligarchy ⟨he was a pioneer of industrial ~, a benevolent despot —F.W.Coburn⟩

feu·dal·ist \-dᵊləst\ *n* -s **1 :** a representative or upholder of feudalism **2 :** a specialist in medieval feudalism

feu·dal·is·tic \ˌ≈≈ˈistik, -tēk\ *adj* **:** of or having the character of feudalism or feudalists ⟨~ institutions⟩; *esp* **:** characterized by control by and for an entrenched minority ⟨~ and vested economic interests⟩ ⟨a reactionary and ~ regime⟩

feu·dal·i·ty \fyüˈdaləd·ē, -lətē, -i\ *n* -ES [modif. of F *féodalité*, fr. *féodal* feudal (fr. ML *feodalis*) + *-ité* -ity] **1 :** the quality or state of being feudal **:** feudal principles or practice ⟨the trend to ~ dissolved the empire into many independent domains⟩ **2 :** a feudal holding, domain, or concentration of power ⟨a league of Greek *feudalities* led by Agamemnon —*Time*⟩ ⟨the eviction of the great economic . . . *feudalities* and the return to the nation of . . . the sources of mineral wealth —C.J.Friedrich⟩ **3 :** the feudal aristocracy or ruling group ⟨the ~, scornful and fearful of the new men . . . were ready to rally to her banner —Basil Henning⟩

feu·dal·iza·tion \ˌfyüdᵊləˈzāshən, -dᵊlˌīˈz-\ *n* -s **:** the act or process of feudalizing ⟨the Norman Conquest brought only partial ~ to England⟩

feu·dal·ize \ˈfyüdᵊlˌīz\ *vt* -ED/-ING/-S **:** to make feudal **:** reduce to feudal tenure or dependence ⟨~ alodial lands⟩ ⟨*feudalized* the bourgeoisie⟩

feu·dal·ly \-dᵊlē, -dᵊli\ *adv* **:** in a feudal manner

feudal system *n* **:** a feudal system of polity **:** FEUDALISM

¹**feu·da·tary** \ˈfyüdəˌterē\ *n* -ES [ML *feudatarius*, fr. *feudatarius*, adj.] *archaic* **:** ²FEUDATORY 1

²**feudatary** *adj* [ML *feudatarius*, fr. *feudatus* (past part. of *feudare* to enfeoff, fr. *feudum* fief, feud) + L *-arius* -ary — more at FEUD] *obs* **:** ¹FEUDATORY

feu·da·to·ri·al \ˌ≈≈ˈtōrēəl, -tȯr-\ *adj* **:** FEUDAL

¹**feu·da·to·ry** \ˈfyüdəˌtōrē, -tȯrē, -ri\ *adj* [ML *feudatorius*, fr. *feudatus* + L *-orius* -ory] **1 :** standing in or belonging to the relation of a feudal vassal to his lord **2** *of a kingdom or state* **:** under the overlordship of a foreign state

²**feudatory** \"\ *n* -ES [ML *feudatorius*, fr. *feudatorius*, adj.] **1 a :** one holding lands by feudal tenure **:** the tenant of a feud; *esp* **:** a feudal lord **b :** a prince or ruler subject to the overlordship of a foreign ruler **2 a :** a dependent lordship **:** FEUD **b :** a feudatory state

feu de joie \ˌfœdəzhwä\ *n, pl* **feux de joie** \"\ [F, lit., fire of joy] **1 :** BONFIRE **2 2 :** a salute fired by rifles in rapid succession along a line of troops (as to celebrate a victory)

feuding *pres part of* FEUD

¹**feud·ist** \ˈfyüdəst\ *n* -s [³*feud* + *-ist*] **:** a specialist in feudal law

²**feudist** \"\ *n* -s [¹*feud* + *-ist*] **:** one who is party to a hostile feud

feuds *pl of* FEUD, *pres 3d sing of* FEUD

feu·dum \ˈfyüdəm\ *n, pl* **feu·da** \-də\ *or* **feudums** [ML — more at FEUD] **:** ³FEUD

feu-duty \ˈ≈ˌ≈\ *n, Scots law* **:** the annual rent paid by the tenant of a feu

feued *past of* FEU

feu·er·bach·i·an \ˌfȯiə(r)ˈbäkēən, -äkē-\ *adj, usu cap* [Ludwig A. *Feuerbach* †1872 Ger. philosopher + E *-ian*] **:** of or relating to the sensationalistic and materialistic theories of Ludwig Feuerbach

feuil·lage \fœyäzh\ *n* -s [F, fr. MF *fuellage* — more at FOLIAGE] **:** FOLIAGE

feuille \fœy\ *n, pl* **feuilles** \"\ [F, lit., leaf, fr. OF *fuelle, fueille, foille* — more at FOIL] **:** TERRAPIN 2

feuille morte \-ˈmȯrt\ *n* [F, lit., dead leaf] **:** a brownish orange that is deeper and slightly redder than leather, yellower and deeper than spice, and yellower and deeper than gold pheasant — called also *autumn leaf, dead leaf, foliage brown, leather lake, oakleaf brown, philamot, withered leaf*

feuil·le·ton \ˌfər·əˈtōⁿ, ˌfəē-, F fœytōⁿ\ *n* -s [F, fr. *feuillet* sheet of paper, folio, fr. OF *fuellet, foillet* small leaf, sheet of paper, dim. of *fuel, fueil, foil* leaf — more at FOIL] **1 :** a part of a European newspaper or magazine devoted to material designed to entertain the general reader **:** a feature section **2 :** a writing printed in a feuilleton (as an installment of a serialized novel) **3 a :** a novel printed in installments **:** SERIAL **b :** a work of fiction catering to popular taste **:** THRILLER **4 :** a short literary composition often having a familiar tone and reminiscent content **:** SKETCH ⟨these ~*s* are self-analytical studies and personal confessions, memories, scenes of animal life, symbolic stories dealing with personal and national problems —Izidor Cankar⟩ — **feuil·le·ton·ism** \ˈfər·ətəˌnizəm, ˈfəē-\ *n* -s

feuil·le·ton·ist \ˈfər·ətənəst, ˈfəē-, -ˌnist\ *n* -s [F *feuilletoniste*, fr. *feuilleton* + *-iste* -ist] **:** a writer of feuilletons; *esp* **:** a writer of regularly appearing critical or familiar essays or of a column

feuing *pres part of* FEU

feul·gen reaction \ˈfȯilgən-\ *n, usu cap F* [after Robert *Feulgen* b1884 Ger. physiologist] **:** the development of a purplish color in a microscopic preparation hydrolyzed and stained with a modified Schiff reagent that is considered to indicate the presence of chromatin and used to identify chromatinic structures in cells or as an aid in distinguishing nuclei in various microorganisms

feus *pl of* FEU, *pres 3d sing of* FEU

¹**fe·ver** \ˈfēvə(r)\ *n* -s *often attrib* [ME, fr. OE *fēfer, fēfor*, fr. L *febris;* akin to L *fovēre* to warm — more at DAY] **1 a :** a rise of body temperature above the normal whether a natural response (as to infection) or artificially induced for therapeutic reasons **b :** an abnormal bodily state characterized by increased production of heat, accelerated heart action and pulse, and systemic debility with weakness, loss of appetite, and thirst **c :** any of various diseases of which fever is a prominent symptom ⟨typhoid ~⟩ ⟨yellow ~⟩ ⟨quartan ~⟩ **2 a :** a state of heightened or intense emotion (as of excitement, anxiety, or desire) **:** abnormal intensity ⟨in a fervor and ~ of resentment colonists all over the land voluntarily carried their tea to public bonfires —C.G.Bowers⟩ ⟨terror hung over the West, the frontier was in a ~, forts and blockhouses were hastily constructed —*Amer. Guide Series: Ind.*⟩ ⟨a ~ of passionate love —T.L.Peacock⟩ **b :** a widely contagious usu. transient enthusiasm (as for gold prospecting, migration to the West, or stock speculation) **:** CRAZE ⟨caught uranium ~⟩ ⟨football ~ raged in the university⟩ ⟨gripped by a ~ for emigration⟩ **3 :** a state of agitated or intense activity **:** urgent haste ⟨what a ~ of preparation seized the fort on the afternoon before that great day —Walter O'Meara⟩ ⟨worked at a ~ pitch⟩ **4 :** an abnormal often unstable condition of mind or society ⟨the ~ is over; already unemployment . . . has started to drop —*Economist*⟩

²**fever** \"\ *vb* **fevered; fevered; fevering** \-v(ə)riŋ\ **fevers** *vt* **:** to throw into a fever **:** affect with fever **:** HEAT, AGITATE ⟨the gold coin, clutched deep in his trouser pocket, ~*ed* him —A.J. Cronin⟩ ~ *vi* **1 :** to contract or be in a fever **:** be or become feverish ⟨the malaria victim ~*s* intermittently⟩ ⟨he ~*ed* for his far-off home⟩ **2 :** to move or live feverishly ⟨Germany has not experienced a revolution; she has only ~*ed* through a convulsion caused by overexertion and fright —Maximillian Harden⟩

fever and ague *n* **:** MALARIA 2

fever bark *n* **:** any bark used in the treatment of fevers: as **a :** CINCHONA BARK **b :** bark of the bitterbark (*Alstonia constricta*)

fever blister *also* **fever sore** *n* **:** COLD SORE

feverbush \ˈ≈≈ˌ≈\ *n* **1 :** SPICEBUSH 1 **2 :** BLACK ALDER 1

fever cabinet *also* **fever box** *n* **:** an electric apparatus used in fever therapy to raise the body temperature of a patient above the normal level

fever chart *n* **1 :** a chart indicating the course of a patient's fever **2 :** the rising and falling course of conditions (as in politics or business)

fevercup \ˈ≈≈ˌ≈\ *n* **:** PITCHER PLANT a

fe·ver·few \ˈfēvə(r)ˌfyü\ *n* -s [ME *feverfew, feverfu*, fr. (assumed) AF *fevrefue*, feverfew, centaury, fr. LL *febrifugia* centaury — more at FEBRIFUGE] **:** a perennial European herb (*Chrysanthemum parthenium*)

fevergum \ˈ≈≈ˌ≈\ *n* **:** a blue gum (*Eucalyptus globulus*)

fever heat *n* **1 :** the state of a human body when the oral temperature exceeds 98.6° Fahrenheit **2 :** FEVER PITCH

fe·ver·ish \ˈfēv(ə)rish, -rēsh\ *adj* [ME, fr. *fever* + *-ish*] **1 a :** showing symptoms indicating fever (as increased heat and thirst, delirium) **:** having a fever ⟨the patient is ~⟩; *specif* **:** abnormally hot ⟨the child's forehead felt ~⟩ **b :** of or indicating fever ⟨a ~ condition⟩ ⟨a ~ spot burned on each cheek⟩ **c :** infected with or tending to cause fever ⟨a damp, ~, unhealthy spot —R.L.Stevenson⟩ **2 a :** marked by aroused or intense feeling or activity or by irregular variations **:** characterized by fever **:** AGITATED ⟨lay sleepless while his ~ mind went over the catastrophes of the day⟩ **:** ARDENT ⟨novels . . . in which every young man is sleek and ~ for an unattainable success —Marjory S. Douglas⟩ **:** HECTIC ⟨a burst of ~ activity just before sailing time⟩ **:** UNSTABLE ⟨a ~ condition of the stock market with extreme fluctuations between gains and losses) **b** : suggesting in appearance the delirium of a fever ⟨a wallpaper with a ~ contemporary design⟩ **3** : uncomfortably hot : SULTRY ⟨the afternoon was ~ for so temperate a seacoast —Robinson Jeffers⟩ — **fe·ver·ish·ly** *adv* — **fe·ver·ish·ness** *n* -ES

fe·ver·less \'fēvə(r)ləs\ *adj* : having no fever

fe·ver·ous \'fēv(ə)rəs\ *adj* [ME, fr. *fever* + *-ous*] : FEVERISH

fever pitch *n* : a degree of abnormal excitement that usu. develops rapidly among a number of people and sometimes leads to impulsive violence ⟨worked themselves to *fever pitch* while watching their team lose —*N.Y.Times*⟩ ⟨when at last the hour of the full-dress trial drew near, popular excitement rose to *fever pitch* —E.M.Lustgarten⟩ ⟨fanned his wrath to *fever pitch* —Jack London⟩

fever plant *n* **1** : an evening primrose (*Oenothera biennis*) **2** : an African shrub (*Ocimum viride*)

feverroot \'≈,≈\ *n* ['*fever* + *root*] : a coarse American herb (*Triosteum perfoliatum*) — called also *horse gentian, tinker's root*

fevers *pl of* FEVER, *pres 3d sing of* FEVER

fever therapy *n* : a treatment of disease by fever induced by various artificial means

fever thermometer *n* : CLINICAL THERMOMETER

fever tick *n* : a tick that transmits the causative agent of a fever; *specif* : a cattle tick of the genus *Boophilus* that transmits piroplasmosis or anaplasmosis

fever tree *n* : any of several usu. tropical or subtropical shrubs or trees thought to indicate regions free from fever or planted because they yield remedies for fever: as **a** : a blue gum (*Eucalyptus globulus*) **b** : an ornamental tree (*Pinckneya pubens*) of the southeastern U.S. that yields Georgia bark **c** : an African tree (*Acacia xanthophloea*) supposed to mark healthful regions **d** : FEVER PLANT 2

fevertwig \'≈,≈\ *also* **fevertwitch** \'≈,≈\ *n* : BITTERSWEET 2b

feverweed \'≈,≈\ *n* **1** : any of several plants of the genus *Eryngium* (as *E. aquaticum* of the southern U.S. or *E. campestre* of Europe) **2** : an American false foxglove (*Gerardia pedicularia*) **3** : a verbena (*Verbena stricta*) of the southwestern U.S.

feverwort \'≈,≈\ *n* **1** : FEVERROOT **2** : BONESET

¹few \'fyü\ *pron, pl in constr* [ME *fewe*, pron. & adj., fr. OE *fēawa, fēa;* akin to OHG *fao, fō, fōh* little, ON *fār* little, taciturn, Goth *fawai* few, L *paucus* little, *pauper* poor, Gk *pauros* small, slight, *paid-, pais* child, Skt *putra* son, child] : not many persons or things ⟨many are called but ~ are chosen —Mt 22:14 (RSV)⟩ ⟨~ of the statements are true⟩

²few \"\ *adj* **fewer** \'fyüə(r); -ü(ə)r, -üə\ **fewest** \-üəst\ [ME *fewe*] **1** : consisting of or amounting to a small number : not many ⟨one of his ~ pleasures⟩ ⟨has relatively ~ friends⟩ ⟨less construction means ~*er* jobs⟩ ⟨holidays were ~ and far between⟩ ⟨was applauded by the ~ people present⟩ **2** : some at least : not many but some — used with a preceding *a* to designate being some rather than none ⟨caught a ~ fish⟩ ⟨leave a ~ flowers for the next person⟩; see ²A 1 **3** *dial* : LITTLE ⟨a piece of salt jowl meat and a ~ syrup —G.S. Perry⟩

³few \"\ *n, pl in constr* [ME *fewe*, fr. *fewe*, pron. & adj.] **1** : a small number of units or individuals — used with preceding *a* ⟨sold a ~ of the old books⟩ ⟨a ~ of the soldiers were wounded⟩ **2** : a special limited number : MINORITY — used with preceding *the* ⟨a society based on privileges for the ~⟩ ⟨a car built for the discriminating ~⟩ **3** : an indefinite but not very large number of drinks — used with preceding *a* ⟨went into a crummy-looking beer joint and had a ~ —Len Zinberg⟩ — **a few** *chiefly dial* : to some degree or extent : a little ⟨we'd already made out that he could ride *a few* —*Smart Set*⟩ — **a good few** *dial chiefly Eng* : quite a few — **in few** *archaic* : in short : BRIEFLY ⟨the firm resolve I here *in few* disclose —Alexander Pope⟩ — **not a few** : quite a few ⟨*not a few* of the members were absent⟩ ⟨a custom followed in *not a few* countries⟩ — **quite a few** : a considerable number : a good many ⟨*quite a few* of the merchants cut prices⟩ ⟨owns *quite a few* horses⟩ ⟨maybe not a hundred but *quite a few*⟩

⁴few \"\ *var of* FEU

fewer *pron, pl in constr* [ME *fewere*, fr. OE *fēawran*, fr. compar. of *fēawa*, adj, few — more at FEW] : a smaller number of persons or things ⟨few know and ~ care⟩ ⟨~ are here than had been expected⟩ ⟨to the more ye shall give the more inheritance, and to the ~ ye shall give the less inheritance —Num 33:54 (AV)⟩

fewmet *var of* ¹FUMET

few·ness *n* -ES [ME *fewenesse*, fr. OE *fēawnes, fēanes*, fr. *fēawa, fēa* few + *-nes* -ness] **1** : the state of being few : PAUCITY **2** : smallness in amount or quantity ⟨according to the ~ of years —Lev 25:16 (AV)⟩

fewterer *n* -S [ME *vewter, feutrere, fewterer*, fr. MF *veltrier, veautrier*, fr. *veltre, veautre* greyhound, fr. LL *vertragus*, fr. Gaulish] *obs* : a keeper of dogs (as greyhounds) : SLIPPER

few·trils \'fyü·trəlz\ *n pl* [origin unknown] *dial Eng* : odds and ends : TRIFLES

¹fey \'fā\ *adj* -ER/-EST [ME *feie, feye, fay*, fr. OE *fǣge;* akin to OS *fēgi, fēg* doomed to die, OHG *feigi*, ON *feigr*, and perh. to OE *fāh* hostile, outlawed — more at FOE] **1 a** *now chiefly Scot* : fated to die : DOOMED ⟨they dashed and hewed and smashed till ~ men died away —Robert Burns⟩ **b** : marked or disturbed by an apprehension of death or calamity ⟨another and lesser man . . . gave a ~ lonely warning —Hodding Carter⟩ **2 a** : being in a wild or elated state of mind formerly believed to portend death : behaving in an excited irresponsible manner : beside oneself ⟨she must be ~ and in that case has not long to live —Sir Walter Scott⟩ ⟨was ~ that night, with a kind of febrile gaiety, because the favored lover of the moment was home —Frances Towers⟩ **b** : out of one's mind : MAD ⟨he went ~⟩ : TOUCHED ⟨the apparently ~ but sharply pointed eccentricities —Louis Untermeyer⟩ **3** [prob. influenced in meaning by ⁴*fay*] **a** : able to see fairies or to have intuitions about the future : possessing a sixth sense : CLAIRVOYANT ⟨what qualifications have I to discuss fairies; am I ~ —O.S.J. Gogarty⟩ ⟨not being ~ he never suspected what it would lead to⟩ **b** : characterized by an unworldly air or attitude : ELFIN ⟨she has that half shy, half ~ smile and that birdlike perkiness —A.G.Ogden⟩ ⟨the ~ quality was there, the ability to see the moon at midday —John Mason Brown⟩ : VISIONARY ⟨a Celtic penchant for ~ fancies that contrasted with the other's stolid matter-of-factness⟩

²fey \"\ *var of* ²FAY

fey·ther \'fāthə(r)\ *dial Brit var of* FATHER

¹fez *or* **fès** *or* **fes** \'fez\ *adj, usu cap* [fr. *Fez* (*Fès*), Morocco] : of or from the city of Fez, Morocco : of the kind or style prevalent in Fez

²fez \'fez\ *n, pl* **fezzes** *also* **fezes** [F, fr. *Fez* (*Fès*), Morocco] : a brimless cone-shaped hat that has a flat crown usu. with a long tassel attached, is usu. made of red felt, is worn by men in eastern Mediterranean countries (as Turkey), and has been adapted for women's hats in Europe and America

fez

fez·zani \fe'zanē, fə'z-, -zänē\ *n, pl* **fezzani** *or* **fezzanis** *cap* [fr. *Fezzan*, region in southwestern Libya] **1** : a people in Fezzan, Libya, of mixed Negroid and Arab ancestry **2** : a member of the Fezzani people

fez·zi \'fezē\ *n* -S *cap* [fr. *Fez*, Morocco] : a native or resident of Fez, Morocco

ff *abbr* **1** [L *fecerunt*] they made **2** folios **3** following **4** fortissimo

FF \(')e'fef\ *n* -S **1** : FIRST FAMILY **2** : a member of a first family ⟨a snobbish *FF*⟩

FF *abbr* **1** first family **2** fixed focus **3** thick fog **4** folded flat **5** [L *fratres*] brothers **6** freight forwarder **7** French fried **8** full-fashioned

FFA *abbr* **1** foreign freight agent **2** for further assignment **3** free foreign agency **4** free from alongside **5** free from average

fff *abbr* [It *fortississimo*] as loud as possible

FFI *abbr* free from infection

f flat *n, usu cap 1st F* : the tone a half step below F and sounding enharmonically the same as E in the tempered scale

FFT *abbr* for further transfer

FFV *abbr* first families of Virginia

ffy *abbr* faithfully

FG *abbr* **1** fine grain **2** flat grain **3** friction glaze **4** fuel gas **5** fully good

FGA *abbr* **1** foreign general agent **2** free of general average **3** free of general average

fgn *abbr* foreign

fgt *abbr* freight

f-head \'≈,≈\ *adj, cap F* : having one valve in the head and the other on the side of the engine cylinder ⟨an *F-head* engine⟩

f-hole \'≈,≈\ *n* : one of the two *f*-shaped sound holes in the top of a violin or other bowed stringed instrument

f horn *n, usu cap F* : a French horn in F

f i *abbr* for instance

FIA *abbr* full interest admitted

fi·a·cre \fē'äkr(ᵊ), ,k(rə), F fyäk\ *n, pl* **fiacres** \kr(ᵊ), ,krə(z), ,k(s)\ [F, fr. the Hotel St. *Fiacre*, Paris, where such vehicles were first hired out] : a small hackney coach

fi·a·dor \,fēə'dō(ə)r\ *n* -S [Sp, lit., guarantor, fr. *fiado* (past part. of *fiar* to trust, guarantee, fr. — assumed — VL *fidare*, alter. of L *fidere* to trust) + *-or* — more at BIDE] : a cord fastened to a hackamore and acting as a throatlatch

fi·an·cé \,fē,än'sā, fē¦, ,äⁿ ¦-, ,än¦-\ *n* -S [F, fr. MF, fr. past part. of *fiancer* to vow, promise, betroth, fr. OF *fiancier*, fr. *fiance* vow, promise, trust, fr. *fier* to trust (fr. — assumed — VL *fidare*) + *-ance*] : a man engaged to be married — usu. used with preceding possessive

fi·an·cée \"\ *n* -S [F, fem. of *fiancé*] : a woman engaged to be married — usu. used with preceding possessive

¹fi·an·chet·to \÷,fēən'ched·(,)ō, -n'ke-\ *n, pl* **fianchet·ti** \-d·(,)ē\ [It, dim. of *fianco* flank, side, fr. OIt, fr. OF *flanc* — more at FLANK] : a position or opening in chess with one or both pawns at Kt3 to make room for the bishop on Kt2

²fianchetto \"\ *vb* -ED/-ING/-ES : to develop (a bishop) in a chess game to Kt2

fi·an·na \'fēənə\ *n pl, usu cap* [IrGael *fianna, fēinne*, pl. of *fiann* band of Fenians] : FENIANS

fiants *n pl but sing or pl in constr* [MF *fientes*, pl. of *fiente* dung, fr. (assumed) VL *femita*, fr. LL *femus*, alter. of L *fimus;* prob. akin to L *fumus* smoke — more at FUME] *obs* : the dung of the fox, wolf, boar, or badger

¹fi·ar \'fēər\ *n* -S [ME (Sc dial.) *fiar, fear*, fr. *fe* fee + *-ar* -er — more at FEE] *Scots law* : one in whom the fee simple of an estate is vested subject to a liferent

²fiar \"\ *n* -S [ME *feor*, fr. OF *fuer, feor* market price, price, fr. L *forum* market — more at FORUM] **1** *Scot* : PRICE, STANDARD **2 fiars** *also* **fiars prices** *pl* : prices of grain in Scotland fixed for the year by law

fiard \fē'ärd, 'fyä-\ *n* -S [Sw *fjärd, fjord*, fr. OSw *fiordher, fiærdher;* akin to ON *fjörthr* fjord — more at FORD] : FJORD

fi·as·co \fē'a(,)skō, -'aa-, -'ai-, *in sense 1 & sometimes in sense 2* -'ä- *or* -'à-\ *n, pl* **fiascoes** *also* **fiascos** \-kōz\ *see sense 1* [It, of Gmc origin; akin to OHG *flaska* bottle — more at FLASK] **1** *pl* **fias·chi** \-kē\ : BOTTLE, FLASK; *specif* : a bottle of wine **2** : an utter and often ridiculous failure esp. of an ambitious or pretentious undertaking ⟨the campaign to abolish the sales tax ended in a ~⟩

¹fi·at \'fī,at, -īəl; 'fē,al, 'fēəl, 'fē,äl, 'fē,äl; *usu* |d·+V\ *n* -S [L, let it be done, 3d sing. pres. subj. of *fieri* to become (used as passive of *facere* to do) — more at BE, DO] **1** : official endorsement or sanction : PERMISSION ⟨a colonial governor acting under the ~ of the king⟩ **2** : a command or act of will that creates something without or as if without further effort **3** : an authoritative decision of consciousness : mental determination of one of two or more alternatives ⟨the ~ of will⟩ ⟨a ~ of conscience⟩ **4** : an arbitrary edict : a summary judicial or executive pronouncement ⟨the question of what conduct shall be made criminal . . . should never be determined by police ~ —*Harvard Law Rev.*⟩

²fiat \"\ *adj* : established, sanctioned, or created by or as if by fiat ⟨~ value⟩

fiat money *n* : money (as paper currency) that is not convertible into coin or specie of equivalent value and thus is dependent for its value on the decree of government

¹fib \'fib\ *n* -S [perh. by shortening & alter. fr. *fable*] : a trivial falsehood : an innocuous lie ⟨a child who tells ~*s*⟩

²fib \"\ *vi* **fibbed; fibbed; fibbing; fibs** : to tell a fib **syn** see LIE

³fib \"\ *vb* **fibbed; fibbed; fibbing; fibs** [origin unknown] *Brit* : BEAT, PUMMEL ⟨*fibbing* him on the ear —David Garnett⟩

FIB *abbr* **1** free into barge **2** free into bunker

fib·ber \'fibə(r)\ *n* -S : one that tells fibs

fib·bery \-b(ə)rē\ *n* -ES : the practice of fibbing : FALSEHOOD

¹fi·ber *or* **fi·bre** \'fībə(r)\ *n* -S [F *fibre*, fr. L *fibra*] **1** : a thread or a structure or object resembling a thread: as **a** (1) : a slender root (as of a grass) (2) : an elongate tapering cell that has at maturity a small lumen and no protoplasm content, that is found in many plant organs and is esp. well developed in the xylem and phloem of the vascular system, and that imparts elasticity, flexibility, and tensile strength to the plant or organ — compare SCLEREID **b** (1) : the axis cylinder of a nerve cell with its sheath (2) : one of the structures composing most of the intercellular matrix of ordinary and elastic connective tissues (3) : one of the elongated contractile cells constituting muscular tissue **c** : a natural or man-made object that has a length usu. many hundred or thousand times greater than its width, that possesses considerable tensile strength, pliability, and resistance esp. against heat, light, some chemicals, and mechanical abrasion, that is obtained from animals (as wool, hair, silk, fur), vegetable matter (as cotton, flax, hemp, straw), or minerals or metals (as asbestos, aluminum, gold) or that is synthesized industrially (as rayon, nylon, glass fiber), and that may be wholly crystalline like asbestos and metal wires, wholly amorphous like glass, or in the case of the most widely used fibers, which are high polymers, partly crystalline and partly amorphous with elongated crystalline domains embedded in an amorphous matrix consisting of the same chemical substance; *specif* : a fiber sufficiently long, pliable, cohesive, and strong to be spun into a yarn made into a fabric or cordage or used in loose masses for stuffing (as in pillows or mattresses) — see FIBRIL c, MICELLE; compare FILAMENT a(3) **2** : a material made of or from fibers: as **a** : a durable material resembling straw that is woven of prepared paper and used esp. for suitcases, furniture, mats, and caps **b** : the vegetable tissues constituting the major raw material of most papers **c** : VULCANIZED FIBER **3 a** : an element that imparts strength, body, or substance ⟨his objectivity gave ~ to his point of view⟩ **b** : basic toughness : DURABILITY, FORTITUDE, STRENGTH ⟨hurdles that might have seemed insurmountable to persons of lesser ~ —R.L.Taylor⟩ **c** : essential structure or makeup : ESSENCE ⟨the very ~ of a person's thought⟩ **4** : CRUDE FIBER **5** : the pattern of directional structure in a wrought metal (as wire)

²fi·ber \'fē,bi(ə)r, ,beə, 'fībə(r)\ [NL, fr. L, beaver — more at BEAVER] *syn of* ONDATRA

fiberboard \'≈,≈\ *n* : a material made by compressing fibers (as of wood) into thick stiff sheets; *also* : a board or a sheet of this material

fiber box *also* **fiberboard box** *n* : a shipping container made from corrugated or solid paperboard by slotting, scoring, joining, folding, and sealing

fiber can *n* : a rigid multi-ply paperboard container generally cylindrical but sometimes oval or rectangular with rounded corners having inserted or formed paper ends

fi·bered \'fībə(r)d\ *adj* **1** : having or made up of fibers **2** : possessing fiber ⟨the tough-*fibered* spirit of our times —Dana Burnet⟩

fiber glass *n* : glass in fibrous form used in making various products (as glass wool, yarns, textiles) ⟨*fiber glass* insulation⟩ ⟨a *fiber glass* boat⟩ — called also *fibrous glass, spun glass*

fiber grease *n* : a lubricating grease having a fibrous consistency

fi·ber·iza·tion \,fībərə'zāshən, -,rī'z-\ *n* -S : the process of fiberizing

fi·ber·ize \'fībə,rīz\ *vt* -ED/-ING/-S : to reduce to fibers : separate into fibers by crushing or beating : DEFIBRATE; *also* : to treat or mix with fibers (as in the manufacture of rubber fabric)

fi·ber·iz·er \-zə(r)\ *n* -S : one that fiberizes

fi·ber·less \'fībə(r)ləs\ *adj* : lacking fiber : devoid of fibers

fiber of corti *usu cap C* : ROD OF CORTI

fiber of mül·ler \-'myülə(r), -'mil-,-'mül-,-'məl-, G 'mʊel-\ *usu cap M* [after Heinrich M. *Müller* †1864 Ger. anatomist] : any of certain neuroglia fibers that extend through the entire thickness of the retina and act as a support for the other structures

fiber of re·mak \-'rā,mäk\ *usu cap R* [after Robert *Remak* †1865 Ger. physiologist] : an unmedullated nerve fiber

fiber of shar·pey \-'shärpē\ *usu cap S* [after William *Sharpey* †1880 Scot. anatomist] : any of the thready processes of the periosteum that penetrate the tissue of the superficial lamellae of bones

fiber plant *n* : a plant yielding a useful fiber (as hemp, flax)

fiber plaster *n* : a gypsum plaster used in building to which hair fiber or wood fiber has been added as a binder

fiber-reactive dye *n* : a dye that combines chemically with fibers, esp. cellulose — see DYE table I

fiber saturation point *n* : the point in drying wood at which all free moisture has been removed from the cell itself while the cell wall remains saturated with absorbed moisture

fiber tracheid *n* : a tracheid having pointed ends, a relatively thick wall, and a narrow lumen as in a fiber but with small bordered pits and prob. functioning in support rather than conduction

fiber tract *n* : TRACT

fibr- *or* **fibro-** *comb form* [L *fibra*] **1 a** : fiber : fibrous and : fibrous tissue ⟨*fibro*genic⟩ ⟨*fibr*osis⟩ **b** : of or containing fibrous tissue ⟨*fibro*caseous⟩ ⟨*fibro*cartilage⟩ ⟨*fibro*angioma⟩ ⟨*fibro*carcinoma⟩ **2** : fibrotic ⟨*fibro*bronchitis⟩ **3 a** : fibroma and : fibromatous ⟨*fibro*myxoma⟩ ⟨*fibro*chondroma⟩ **b** : a fibroma containing ⟨*fibro*cyst⟩ **4** : fibrin ⟨*fibro*hemorrhagic⟩ ⟨*fibro*purulent⟩

fi·brat·ed \'fī,brād·əd\ *adj* [L *fibratus* (fr. *fibra* fiber + *-atus* -ate) + E *-ed*] : containing fibers or fibrous material

fi·bra·tion \fī'brāshən\ *n* -S [prob. fr. F, fr. *fibr-* + *-ation*] : the arrangement or formation of fibers or fibrous structure

fibre *var of* FIBER

fi·bril \'fībrəl, 'fib-, -(,)bril\ *n* -S [NL *fibrilla*, dim. of L *fibra* fiber] : a small thread or small fiber: as **a** (1) : a filamentous outgrowth of the thallus in lichens (2) : ROOT HAIR **b** (1) : one of the fine threads into which a striated muscle fiber may be longitudinally split after treatment with alcohol — compare MYOFIBRIL (2) : NEUROFIBRIL **c** : one of the minute elongated elements that make up the structure of fibers of certain natural and synthetic materials (as textile fibers, wood, or fibrous proteins) and that are held to be made up ultimately of long-chain molecules oriented in a bundle in one direction — compare CRYSTALLITE 2

fi·bril·la \fī'brilə, fə'-\ *n, pl* **fibril·lae** \-,lē\ [NL] : FIBRIL c

fi·bril·lar \'fībrələ(r), 'fib-; fī'bril-,fə'bril-\ *adj* [NL *fibrilla* + E *-ar*] **1** : of or like fibrils or fibers ⟨a ~ network⟩ **2** : of or exhibiting fibrillation ⟨~ twitchings⟩

fibrillar theory *n* : a theory of protoplasmic structure: protoplasm is essentially composed of fine sometimes branched fibrils that interlace but do not form a continuous network and are bathed in a fluid matrix

fi·bril·lary \'fībrə,lerē, 'fib-; fī'brilərē, fə'b-\ *adj* [NL *fibrilla* + E *-ary*] **1** : of or relating to fibrils or fibers ⟨~ overgrowth⟩ **2** : of, relating to, or marked by fibrillation ⟨~ chorea⟩

¹fi·bril·late \'fībrə,lāt, 'fib-\ *vb* -ED/-ING/-S [NL *fibrilla* + E *-ate* (v. suffix)] *vi* : to undergo or exhibit fibrillation ~ *vt* : to cause to undergo or exhibit fibrillation; *specif* : to cause (the heart) to fibrillate

²fi·bril·late \'fībrə,lāt, 'fib-; fī'brilət, fə'b-\ *or* **fi·bril·lat·ed.** \'fībrə,lād·əd, 'fib-\ *adj* [*fibrillate* fr. NL *fibrilla* + E *-ate*, adj suffix; *fibrillated* fr. past. part. of ¹*fibrillate*] : having a fibrous structure : furnished with fibrils : FRINGED

fi·bril·la·tion \,fibrə'lāshən, ,fīb-\ *n* -S **1** : the act or process of forming fibrils or the state of being fibrillate **2 a** : muscular twitching involving individual muscle fibers acting without coordination — compare FASCICULATION **b** : very rapid irregular contractions of the muscle fibers of the heart resulting in a lack of synchronism between heartbeat and pulse beat — see AURICULAR FIBRILLATION, VENTRICULAR FIBRILLATION **3** : the breaking down of fibers such as occurs in beating paper pulp

fi·brilled \'fībrəld, 'fib-, -(,)brild\ *adj* [*fibril* + *-ed*] : FIBRILLATE

fi·bril·li·form \fī'brilə,fȯrm, fə'b-\ *adj* [NL *fibrilla* + E *-iform*] : resembling a fibril

fi·bril·lo·gen·ic \,fībrəlō¦jenik, ,fib-; fī¦brilə¦j-, fə¦b-\ *adj* [NL *fibrilla* + E *-o-* + *-genic*] : inducing fibrillation esp. of the heart — **fi·bril·lo·gen·i·cal·ly** \-nək(ə)lē\ *adv*

fi·bril·lose \'fībrə,lōs, 'fib-\ *adj* [NL *fibrilla* + E *-ose*] : furnished with or composed of fibril

fi·bril·lous \-ləs\ *adj* [NL *fibrilla* + E *-ous*] : belonging to or composed of fibrils

fi·brin \'fībrən\ *n* -S [ISV *fibr-* + *-in*] : a white insoluble fibrous protein formed from fibrinogen by the action of thrombin esp. in the clotting of blood but capable of being solubilized by certain enzymes (as plasmin, pepsin, or trypsin)

fibrin film *n* : a pliable translucent film prepared from fibrinogen and thrombin from human blood plasma and used in the surgical repair of defects

fibrin foam *n* : a spongy substance prepared from fibrinogen and thrombin from human blood plasma and used esp. after saturation with thrombin as an absorbable clotting agent in surgical wounds

fi·brin·o·gen \fī'brinəjən, -,jen\ *n* -S [ISV *fibrin* + *-o-* + *-gen;* orig. formed in G] : a globulin that is produced in the liver, is present esp. in blood plasma, and is converted into fibrin normally by the action of thrombin during clotting of blood

fi·brin·o·gen·o·pe·nia \(,)fī,brinə,jenə'pēnēə, -nyə\ *n* -S [NL, fr. ISV *fibrinogen* + NL *-o-* + *-penia*] : a deficiency of fibrin or fibrinogen or both in the blood

fi·brin·oid \'fībrə,nȯid\ *n* -S *often attrib* : a material that somewhat resembles fibrin and is derived from connective tissue which occurs in the normal placenta and in certain pathological processes (as caseous necrosis) postnatally

fi·bri·nol·y·sin \,fībrə'nälәsən\ *n* -S [ISV *fibrin* + *-o-* + *lysin*] **1** : PLASMIN **2** : STREPTOKINASE

fi·bri·nol·y·sis \-səs\ *n* -ES [NL, fr. ISV *fibrin* + NL *-o-* + *-lysis*] : the breakdown of fibrin to soluble products usu. through enzymatic action — **fi·bri·no·lyt·ic** \,fībrənō¦lid·ik, fī¦brinə¦l-\ *adj*

fi·bri·no·pe·nia \,fībrənō'pēnēə, -nyə\ *n* -S [NL, fr. ISV *fibrin* + NL *-o-* + *-penia*] : FIBRINOGENOPENIA

fi·bri·no·purulent \,fībrə(,)nō, fī,brinə+\ *adj* [*fibrin-* + *-o-* + *purulent*] : containing, characterized by, or exuding fibrin and pus (as in certain inflammations)

fi·brin·ous \'fībrənəs\ *adj* [ISV *fibrin* + *-ous*] : marked by the presence of fibrin ⟨~ pericarditis⟩ ⟨~ exudate⟩

fibro- — see FIBR-

fi·bro·adenoma \,fī(,)brō+\ *n* [NL, fr. *fibr-* + *adenoma*] : adenoma with a large amount of fibrous tissue

fi·bro·blast \'fībrə,blast\ *n* [ISV *fibr-* + *-blast*] : an undifferentiated mesenchyme cell giving rise to connective tissue — **fi·bro·blas·tic** \¦≈¦blastik\ *adj*

fi·bro·cartilage \¦fī(,)brō+\ *n* [ISV *fibr-* + *cartilage*] : cartilage in which the matrix except immediately about the cells is largely composed of fibers like those of ordinary connective tissue; *also* : a structure or part composed of such cartilage — **fi·bro·cartilaginous** \"+\ *adj*

fi·bro·cement \"+\ *n* [*fibr-* + *cement*] *Brit* : ASBESTOS CEMENT

fi·bro·crystalline \"+\ *adj* [*fibr-* + *crystalline*] : composed of or characterized by fibrous crystals

fi·bro·cyte \'fībrə,sīt\ *n* -S [ISV *fibr-* + *-cyte*] : FIBROBLAST; *specif* : a spindle-shaped connective-tissue cell characteristic of fibrous tissue — **fi·bro·cyt·ic** \¦≈¦sid·ik\ *adj*

fi·bro·elastic \¦fī(,)brō+\ *adj* [*fibr-* + *elastic*] : consisting of both fibrous and elastic elements

fi·bro·fer·rite \,fībrō'fe,rīt\ *n* [G *fibroferrit*, fr. *fibr-* + L *ferrum* iron + G *-it* -ite — more at FARRIER] : a mineral $Fe(SO_4)(OH).5H_2O$ consisting of a fibrous hydrated basic ferric sulfate

¹fi·broid \'fī,brȯid\ *adj* [*fibr-* + *-oid*] : like, forming, or composed of fibrous tissue

²fibroid \"\ *n* -S : a benign fibromyoma of the uterine wall

fi·bro·in \'fībrəwən\ *n* -S [F *fibroïne*, fr. *fibr-* + *-ine*] : the insoluble protein of silk comprising the filaments of the raw fiber held together by sericin

fi·bro·lite \ˈfībrə,līt\ *n* -s [*fibr-* + *-lite*] : SILLIMANITE — **fi·bro·lit·ic** \ˌ≡≡ˈlidik\ *adj*

fi·bro·ma \fīˈbrōmə\ *n, pl* **fibromas** \-məz\ *also* **fibroma·ta** \-məd·ə\ [NL, fr. *fibr-* + *-oma*] : a benign tumor consisting mainly of fibrous tissue — **fi·brom·a·tous** \(ˈ)fīˈbrämədəs, -rōm-\ *adj*

fi·bro·ma·to·gen·ic \fīˈbrōmədˌōˈjenik\ *adj* [NL *fibromat-, fibroma* + E *-genic*] : inducing or tending to induce the development of fibromas

fi·bro·ma·toid \fīˈbrōmə,tȯid\ *adj* [NL *fibromat-, fibroma* + E *-oid*] : resembling a fibroma

fi·bro·ma·to·sis \(ˌ)fī,brōməˈtōsəs\ *n, pl* **fibromato·ses** \-ō,sēz\ [NL, fr. *fibromat-, fibroma* + *-osis*] : a condition marked by the presence of or a tendency to develop multiple fibromas

fi·bro·myoma \ˌfī(ˌ)brō+\ *n, pl* **fibromyomas** *also* **fibro·myomata** [NL, fr. *fibr-* + *myoma*] : a mixed tumor containing both fibrous and muscle tissue — **fi·bro·myomatous** \"+\ *adj*

fibromyositis \"+\ *n* [NL, fr. *fibr-* + *myositis*] : inflammation of fibrous and muscle tissue

fi·bro·pla·sia \ˌfībrəˈplāzh(ē)ə\ *n* -s [NL, fr. *fibr-* + *-plasia*] : the process of forming fibrous tissue (as in wound healing) — **fi·bro·plas·tic** \ˌ≡≡ˈplastik\ *adj*

fi·bro·plaster \ˈfībrō+,-\ *n* [*fibr-* + *plaster*] : FIBROUS PLASTER

fi·bro·sarcoma \ˌfī(ˌ)brō+\ *n* [NL, fr. *fibr-* + *sarcoma*] : a sarcoma of relatively low malignancy made up chiefly of spindle-shaped cells that tend to form collagenous fibrils — called also *spindle-cell sarcoma*

¹fi·brose \ˈfī,brōs\ *adj* [L *fibra* fiber + E *-ose*] : FIBROUS

²fibrose \"\ *vi* -ED/-ING/-S : to form fibrous tissue ⟨a *fibrosed* wound⟩

fi·bro·sis \fīˈbrōsəs\ *n, pl* **fibro·ses** \-ō,sēz\ [NL, fr. *fibr-* + *-osis*] : a condition marked by a relative increase in the formation of interstitial fibrous tissue in any organ or region of the body : fibrous degeneration — **fi·brot·ic** \(ˈ)fīˈbräd·ik\ *adj*

fi·bro·sit·ic \ˌfībrəˈsid·ik\ *adj* [NL *fibrositis* + E *-ic*] : of, relating to, or characteristic of fibrositis

fi·bro·si·tis \ˌ≡≡ˈsīd·əs\ *n* -ES [NL, fr. *fibrosus* fibrous (fr. ISV *fibrous*) + *-itis*] : a painful muscular condition that is believed to originate in the connective tissue associated with muscles and joints and in some instances to involve a psychosomatic factor and that is commonly accompanied by the formation of painful subcutaneous nodules

fi·bro·spon·gi·ae \ˌfībrəˈspənjē,ē, -pän-\ *n pl, cap* [NL, fr. *fibr-* + *-spongiae*] *in former classifications* : an order of Porifera comprising sponges with fibrous skeletons and including all forms not placed in Calcispongiae

fi·brous \ˈfībrəs\ *adj* [F *fibreux*, fr. *fibre* fiber (fr. L *fibra*) + *-eux* -ous] **1 a** : containing, consisting of, or like fibers ⟨~ roots⟩ ⟨the ~ husk of a coconut⟩ ⟨~ proteins⟩ **b** : characterized by fibrosis **c** : capable of being separated into fibers ⟨a ~ mineral⟩; *also* : breaking in a manner that exposes needlelike grains **2** : possessing body, strength, or toughness : SINEWY, HARDENED — **fi·brous·ly** *adv* — **fi·brous·ness** *n* -ES

fibrous glass *n* : FIBER GLASS

fibrous plaster *n* : plastering reinforced with fiber (as Manila hemp or sisal) or provided with a cloth backing and used chiefly as sheeting, cornice molding, and cover strips

fibrous ring *n* : a strong laminated ring of fibrous tissue that forms the outer part of an intervertebral disk — see PULPY NUCLEUS

fibrous root *n* : a root (as in most grasses) that has no prominent central axis and that branches in all directions — distinguished from *taproot* and *tuberous root* — see ROOT illustration

fibrous-rooted begonia \ˌ≡≡-≡-\ *n* : a begonia with fibrous rather than rhizomatous or tuberous roots; *esp* : any of numerous rather small bushy free-flowering begonias with white, pink, or red single or double flowers that have been developed in cultivation from a Brazilian wild plant (*Begonia semperflorens*) — compare RHIZOMATOUS BEGONIA, TUBEROUS BEGONIA

fi·bro·vascular \ˌfī(ˌ)brō+\ *adj* [*fibr-* + *vascular*] : having or consisting of fibers and conducting cells (as vessels) — compare VASCULAR

fibrovascular bundle *n* : VASCULAR BUNDLE

fibs *pl of* FIB, *pres 3d sing of* FIB

fib·ster \ˈfibztə(r), -bst-\ *n* -s [¹*fib* + *-ster*] : FIBBER

fib·u·la \ˈfibyələ\ *n, pl* **fibu·lae** \-,lē\ *or* **fibulas** [L, prob. fr. *figere, fivere* to fasten, pierce — more at DIKE] **1** : a clasp somewhat resembling a safety pin used by the ancient Greeks and Romans **2** [NL, fr. L] **a** : the outer or postaxial and usu. the smaller of the two bones of the hind limb below the knee that is rudimentary and often ankylosed with the tibia in most birds and many mammals (as the horse and the ruminants) and in man the slenderest bone of the body in proportion to its length and that articulates above with the external tuberosity of the tibia and below with the talus, its lower end forming the external malleolus of the ankle **b** : JUGUM 2

fibulae 1

fib·u·lar \-lə(r)\ *adj* [NL *fibula* + E *-ar*] : of, relating to, or lying in the direction of the fibula

fib·u·la·re \ˌfibyəˈlārē, -la(a)rē\ *n, pl* **fibula·ria** \-rēə\ [NL, fr. *fibula* + L *-are* (neut. of *-aris* -ar)] : the outer or postaxial element or bone of the proximal row of the tarsus; *specif, in higher vertebrates* : CALCANEUM

fib·u·lo·calcaneal \ˌfibyə(ˌ)lō+\ *adj* [NL *fibula* + E *-o-* + *calcaneal*] : belonging to the fibula and the calcaneum

-fic \fik, fēk\ *adj suffix* [MF & L; MF *-fique*, fr. L *-ficus*, fr. *facere* make, do — more at DO] : making : causing : bringing about ⟨acidi*fic*⟩ ⟨proli*fic*⟩

fi·car·ia \fīˈka(a)rēə\ *n, cap* [NL, fr. L *ficus* fig + NL *-aria*; fr. the appearance of the roots — more at FIG] : a small genus of European herbs (family Ranunculaceae) closely related to the buttercups but having three sepals and swollen smooth achenes

fic·a·ry \ˈfikərē\ *n* -ES [NL *Ficaria*] : LESSER CELANDINE

-fi·ca·tion \fəˈkāshən\ *n comb form* -s [ME *-ficacioun*, fr. MF & L; MF *-fication*, fr. L *-fication-, -ficatio*, fr. *-ficatus* (past part. ending of verbs ending in *-ficare* to make, fr. *-ficus* -fic) + *-ion-, -io* -ion] : making : production ⟨paci*fication*⟩ ⟨vini*fication*⟩ ⟨russi*fication*⟩ — compare -FACTION; -FY

fice *var of* FEIST

fice dog *n* : FEIST 1

¹fich·te·an \ˈfiktēən, -ikt-\ *adj, usu cap* [Johann Gottlieb *Fichte* †1814 Ger. philosopher + E *-an*] : of or having to do with Johann Gottlieb Fichte or his idealist philosophy

²fichtean \"\ *n* -s *usu cap* : an adherent of Fichteanism

fich·te·an·ism \-,nizəm\ *n* -s *usu cap* : a post-Kantian idealist philosophy in which an attempt is made to perfect the Kantian system by connecting practical reason with pure reason through deducing a priori from the ego not only the categories of our knowledge of nature but also the doctrines of ethical and legal obligations and thereby uniting these two critiques in one system — compare ABSOLUTE EGO

fichu \ˈfi(ˌ)shü *sometimes* (ˈ)fēˈshü\ *n* -s [F, neckerchief, small shawl, fr. past part. of *ficher* to drive in, pin, fasten, fr. (assumed) VL *figicare*, fr. L *figere* to fasten, pierce — more at DIKE] : a woman's scarf often of sheer white fabric in a triangular shape that is draped over the shoulders and fastened in front or worn to fill in a low neckline

fichu

fic·i·dae \ˈfisə,dē\ *n pl, cap* [NL, fr. *Ficus*, type genus + *-idae*] : a family of chiefly tropical marine gastropod mollusks (suborder Taenioglossa) — see FICUS 2, FIGSHELL

fi·cin \ˈfīsᵊn\ *n* -s [NL *Ficus* (genus name of *Ficus doliaria*, species that produces it) + E *-in*] : a proteinase obtained usu. as a pale tan powder from the latex of fig trees and used as an anthelmintic and protein digestant (as for curdling milk)

¹fick·le \ˈfikəl\ *adj, often* **fickler** \-k(ə)lə(r)\ *often* **ficklest** \-k(ə)ləst\ [ME *fikel* false, deceitful, inconstant, fr. OE *ficol* guileful, deceitful; akin to OE *befician* to deceive, *fācen* deceit, fraud, OHG *feihhan* deceit, guile, ON *feikn* terror, misfortune, L *piget* it irks, disgusts, and prob. to OE *fāh* hostile — more at FOE] : marked by lack of steadfastness, constancy, stability : given to ready change, inconstancy, whimsical choice, or unpredictable variability ⟨the conventionally ~ woman —J.L. Lowes⟩ ⟨because the people are so easily misled, and so ~ in their views —Will Durant⟩ **syn** see INCONSTANT

²fickle \"\ *vt* -ED/-ING/-S [perh. fr. ME *fikelen* to deceive, beguile, fr. *fikel*, adj.] **1** *chiefly Scot* : PERPLEX, BAFFLE **2** *chiefly Scot* : OUTWIT

fick·le·ness *n* -ES : the quality or state of being fickle

fick's law \ˈfiks-\ *n, usu cap F* [after Adolf *Fick* †1901 Ger. physiologist] : a law of chemistry and physics: the rate of diffusion of one material in another is proportional to the negative of the gradient of the concentration of the first material

fi·co \ˈfē(ˌ)kō\ *n* -ES [modif. of It *fica*, fr. (assumed) VL — more at FIG] : FIG 6b

¹fi·coid \ˈfī,kȯid\ *adj* [NL *Ficus* + E *-oid*] **1** : resembling a fig or a plant of the genus *Ficus* **2** [NL *Ficoideae*] : of or relating to the Aizoaceae

²ficoid \"\ *also* **fi·coi·dal** \(ˌ)fīˈkȯidᵊl\ *n* -s : a plant of the family Aizoaceae

fi·coi·de·ae \fīˈkȯidē,ē\ [NL, fr. *Ficoides* (syn. of *Mesembryanthemum*) (fr. *Ficus* + L *-oides* -oid) + *-eae*] *syn of* AIZOACEAE

fict *abbr* **1** [L *fictilis*] earthen **2** fiction **3** fictitious

¹fic·tile \ˈfiktᵊl, -(ˌ)til, -,tīl\ *adj* [L *fictilis*, fr. *fictus* (past part. of *fingere* to shape, form, devise, feign) + *-ilis* -ile — more at DOUGH] **1** : molded or capable of being molded into the form of an art work or artifact **2 a** *of an art work or artifact* : molded of earth, clay, or other soft material **b** : of or belonging to pottery or earthenware **3** : capable of being led or directed : PLIABLE ⟨~ masses of people ripe for propaganda⟩

²fictile \"\ *n* -s [L, fr. neut. of *fictilis*] : a piece of fictile ware

fic·tion \ˈfikshən\ *n* -s [ME *ficcioun*, fr. MF *fiction*, fr. L *fiction-, fictio*, fr. *fictus* + *-ion-, -io* -ion] **1** : the act of creating something imaginary : a fabrication of the mind **2 a** : an overintentional fabrication : a convenient assumption that overlooks known facts in order to achieve an immediate goal **b** : an unfounded, invented, or deceitful statement ⟨the ~s on a bottle of patent medicine⟩ **3 a** : fictitious literature (as novels, tales, romances) **b** : a work of fiction; *esp* : NOVEL **4 a** : an assumption of a possible thing as a fact irrespective of the question of its truth; *specif* : an allegation or supposition in law of a state of facts assumed to exist which the practice of the courts allows to be made in pleading and refuses to allow the adverse party to disprove — distinguished from *presumption* **b** : an assumption concealing or affecting to conceal that a law has undergone an alteration by which its operation it is modified while in its letter it remains unchanged **5** *archaic* : the act of fashioning or inventing **6 a** : unfounded belief : ASSUMPTION ⟨all the ~s that go to make up a man's public reputation⟩ **b** : a practical or useful illusion or pretense ⟨it was only a ~ of independence his mother gave him; he was almost totally under her power —G.A.Wagner⟩ **c** : an imaginary, ideal, logical, or hypothetical construct without a known counterpart in reality or a conception of assumed validity or actuality that serves heuristic purposes esp. in the guidance of practical affairs ⟨the average man is a ~⟩

syn FIGMENT, FABRICATION, FABLE: FICTION may refer to any composition wholly an invention of the imagination or noticeably more the product of the imagination than of factual reporting ⟨when we call a piece of literature a work of *fiction* we mean no more than that the characters could not be identified with any persons who have lived in the flesh, nor the incidents with any particular events that have actually taken place —A.J.Toynbee⟩ ⟨at a loss what to invent to detain him, beyond the stale *fiction* that his father was coming tomorrow —George Meredith⟩ FIGMENT may suggest a product of unrestrained fancy or quite free imagination ⟨a gigantic fancy of his own! And all these figures were *figments* of his brain —John Galsworthy⟩ ⟨the metaphysical *figments* of our own creation —Havelock Ellis⟩ FABRICATION may apply to an account made up with artifice, deft or clumsy, and with specific intent to deceive ⟨the doctor was a great liar, but a valuable liar. His *fabrications* seemed to be the framework of a forgotten but imposing plan —Djuna Barnes⟩ ⟨the government story was not a complete *fabrication* but a careful distortion—Christopher Devlin⟩ FABLE may apply to an obviously fictitious narrative in which the impossible, marvelous, and incredible are employed, often to suggest some moral ⟨the *fables* of Aesop⟩ ⟨whispered suspicions, old wives' tales, *fables* invented by men who had nothing to do but loaf in the drugstore and make up stories —Sherwood Anderson⟩ ⟨witchcraft and diabolical possession and diabolical disease have long since passed into the region of *fables* —W.E.H.Lecky⟩

fic·tion·al \-shənᵊl, -shnəl\ *adj* : of, relating to, characterized by, or suggestive of fiction — **fic·tion·al·ly** \-ē, -əlē, -i\ *adv*

fic·tion·al·ism \-shənᵊl,izəm, -shnə,li-\ *also* **fic·tion·ism** \-shə,nizəm\ *n* -s : a theory describing or advocating the use of fictions (sense 6c)

fic·tion·al·is·tic \ˌfikshənᵊlˈistik, -shnəˈli-\ *adj* : FICTIONAL

fic·tion·al·iza·tion \ˌfikshənᵊləˈzāshən, -shnələˈ-, -ᵊl,īˈz-, -ə,līˈz-\ *or* **fic·tion·iza·tion** \ˌfiksh(ə)nəˈz-, -shə,nīˈz-\ *n* -s : an act, process, or product of fictionalizing; *esp* : a fictionalized version (as of a summer vacation)

fic·tion·al·ize \ˈfikshənᵊl,īz, -shnə,līz\ *or* **fic·tion·ize** \ˈfikshə,nīz\ *vt* -ED/-ING/-S : to make into, treat in the manner of, or regard as fiction ⟨~ the diary he kept in prison⟩

fic·tion·eer \ˌfikshəˈni(ə)r\ *n* -s : one who writes fiction esp. in quantity ⟨the strident din of the popular ~s — E.A.Boyd⟩

fictioneering *n* -s : the production of or practice of writing fiction in quantity or of commonplace quality ⟨she never quite goes over the limit into blatant ~ —G.W.Johnson⟩

fic·tion·er \ˈfiksh(ə)nə(r)\ *n* -s : FICTIONIST

fic·tion·ist \-nəst\ *n* -s : a writer of fiction; *esp* : NOVELIST

fic·tious \ˈfikshəs\ *adj* [*fiction* + *-ous*] *archaic* : given to fiction : FICTITIOUS

fic·ti·tious \(ˈ)fikˈtishəs\ *adj* [L *fictitius, ficticius*, fr. *fictus* (past part. of *fingere* to shape, form, devise, feign) + *-itius, -icius* -itious — more at DOUGH] **1** : of, relating to, or suggestive of fiction or a fiction ⟨~ value⟩ : IMAGINARY **2 a** (1) : conventionally or hypothetically assumed ⟨a ~ entity⟩ ⟨a ~ concept⟩ (2) : accepted although known to be untrue, unnatural, or unreal : arbitrarily accepted as genuine ⟨like a jealous stepmother . . . wary of the favors she bestows on her ~ offspring —J.F.Cooper⟩ **b** *of a name* : ASSUMED **c** *of a celestial object* : assumed at a given time to be in the position that would be occupied if the apparent motion were perfectly uniform ⟨the ~ sun⟩ **3** : FEIGNED, SIMULATED : not genuinely felt ⟨sure that his equanimity was ~ —George Meredith⟩

syn FABULOUS, LEGENDARY, MYTHICAL, APOCRYPHAL: FICTITIOUS applies to fabrication or contrivance, often artful, without necessary intent to deceive, or to false evaluation ⟨a *fictitious* reconstruction of primitive life before the coming of the white man —*Amer. Guide Series: Oregon*⟩ ⟨he was a novelist: his amours, and his characters, were *fictitious* —O.S. J.Gogarty⟩ ⟨a *fictitious* expansion of expenditure creating a morbid speculation —Norman Angell⟩ FABULOUS applies to the marvelous or incredible; it describes that which, existent or not, transcends accustomed sober reality ⟨*fabulous* atomic weapons⟩ ⟨the *fabulous* pirate treasures of Captain Kidd⟩ ⟨out in Montana in the 1860s *fabulous* mining strikes made boom towns overnight —*Saturday Rev.*⟩ ⟨the mouth of the converter belched fire like some *fabulous* dragon, its flames leaping forty or fifty feet into the air —Allan Nevins & H.S.Commager⟩ LEGENDARY may apply to that which undergoes distortion, elaboration, or exaggeration by popular tradition ⟨*legendary* wonders, such as the Seven Cities which, situated on great heights, had jewel-studded doorways and whole streets of busy goldsmiths —Allan Nevins & H.S.Commager⟩ ⟨*legendary* history reported in the next generation that the elements had been pregnant with auguries: images had sweated; the sky had blazed with meteors —J.A.Froude⟩ MYTHICAL suggests quite fanciful or imaginative creation, embellishment, or explanation and implies nonexistence ⟨these ancestors are not creations of the *mythical* fancy but were once men of flesh and blood —J.G.Frazer⟩ ⟨the *mythical* islands, Antilia, St. Brendan, and the rest, with which map makers had for centuries decorated their maps —G.C.Sellery⟩ APOCRYPHAL suggests lack of known authentic source and implies spuriousness or dubiousness about what is described ⟨it is not possible to attach much weight to the Sanson memoirs — they are so plainly *apocryphal* —Agnes Repplier⟩ ⟨tales, possibly *apocryphal* and certainly embroidered, of his feats of intelligence work in the eastern Mediterranean —R.W.Firth⟩

fic·ti·tious·ly *adv* : in a fictitious manner

fic·ti·tious·ness *n* -ES : the quality or state of being fictitious

fictitious person *n* **1** : a supposed but in fact nonexistent person referred to in some legal documents or proceedings (as the "Richard Roe" in English ejectment cases or the payee "Cash" in a check) **2** : JURISTIC PERSON

fic·tive \ˈfiktiv\ *adj* [*fiction* + *-ive*] **1** : of, relating to, or capable of imaginative creation ⟨~ art⟩ ⟨~ talent⟩ **2** : not genuine : IMAGINARY, FEIGNED ⟨~ sympathy⟩ — **fic·tive·ly** \-tə̇vlē\ *adv*

fi·cus \ˈfīkəs\ *n, cap* [NL, fr. L, fig — more at FIG] **1** : a large genus of tropical trees or shrubs (family Moraceae) distinguished usu. by their leaves and by their fruit which consists of a pear-shaped or globose receptacle enclosing numerous minute diclinous flowers — see BANYAN, FIG 2a, PIPAL, RUBBER PLANT **2** : the type genus of Ficidae comprising gastropods with light thin spirally ribbed and sculptured shells that are more or less pear-shaped or fig-shaped — compare FIGSHELL

¹fid \ˈfid\ *n* -s [origin unknown] **1** : a wooden or metal bar or pin: as **a** : a square bar of wood or iron used to support the topmast or a topgallant mast and passed through a hole or mortise at its heel and resting on the trestletrees **b** : a pin usu. of hard wood that tapers to a point and is used in opening the strands of a rope (as in splicing) or in stretching eyes — compare MARLINESPIKE **2 a** *obs* : a plug of oakum to stop the vent of a cannon **b** *dial Eng* : CHUNK, LUMP ⟨a ~ of tobacco⟩

fid 1b

²fid \"\ *vt* **fidded; fidded; fidding; fids** : to secure (as a topmast) and support in place with a fid

fid *abbr* **1** fidelity **2** fiduciary

-fid \fəd, ˌfid\ *adj comb form* [L *-fidus*, fr. the root of *findere* to split — more at BITE] : divided into (so many) parts ⟨sexi*fid*⟩ or (such) parts ⟨pinnati*fid*⟩

fi·da'i *or* **fi·da'i** *or* **fi·dai** \fiˈdäˌē\ *also* **fi·da·wi** \-äwē\ *or* **fe·dai** \-äˌē\ *n, pl* **fida'is** *or* **fida'is** *or* **fidai** *or* **fidais** *also* **fidawi** *or* **fidawis** *or* **fedai** *or* **fedais** *sometimes cap* [Per *fidā'ī*] : a member of an Ismaili order of assassins known for their willingness to offer up their lives in order to carry out delegated assignments of murdering appointed victims

fidate *vt* -ED/-ING/-S [prob. fr. L *fidus* trusty, safe + E *-ate*; akin to L *fidere* to trust — more at BIDE] : to exempt in chess from capture (as in problems) — **fi·da·tion** \fīˈdāshən, fəˈ-\ *n* -s

-fi·date \fədə̇t, fə,dāt, *usu* |d·+V\ *adj comb form* [L *-fidatus*, fr. *-fidus* -fid + *-atus* -ate] : -FID

¹fid·dle \ˈfidᵊl\ *n* -s [ME *fithele, fidel*, fr. OE *fithele*, prob. fr. ML *vitula*, perh. fr. L *vitulari* to celebrate, be joyful] **1** : a bowed stringed instrument: **a** : a folk instrument used esp. to accompany dancing ⟨the sound of the ~ on the village green⟩ **b** : VIOLIN **c** : an instrument that resembles the violin ⟨a gourd ~⟩ **2** : FIDDLER **3** : a flat restraining surface (as a slat, rack, or light railing of cords on shipboard to keep dishes from sliding off a cabin table during rough weather) **4** : FIDDLESTICKS

²fiddle \"\ *vb* **fiddled; fiddled; fiddling** \-d(ᵊ)liŋ\ **fiddles** [ME *fithelen, fidelen*, fr. *fithele, fidel*, n.] *vi* **1** : to play on a fiddle **2 a** : to keep the hands or fingers moving nervously — usu. used with *with* ⟨~ about with his tie⟩ **b** : to work aimlessly, fruitlessly, or pointlessly : TINKER — usu. used with *with* ⟨*fiddled* around with the engine for hours⟩ **c** : MEDDLE, TAMPER — usu. used with *with* ⟨a back window broken out or a door lock *fiddled* with —MacKinlay Kantor⟩ ~ *vt* **1** : to play (as a tune) on a fiddle **2** : CHEAT, SWINDLE

fiddle away *vt* : to waste or fritter away ⟨he *fiddled away* his time and strength⟩

fiddleback \ˈ≡≡,≡\ *n, often attrib* : something resembling a fiddle: as **a** *or* **fiddleback chasuble** : a chasuble with a wavy broad backpiece — see CHASUBLE illustration **b** : a wavy grain in wood due to an irregular arrangement of the fibers that gives an undulating appearance to a smooth surface **c** : an Australian beetle (*Eupoecila australasiae*) related to the goliath beetles

fiddleback chair *n* : a chair usu. in Queen Anne style having a splat resembling the outline of a violin

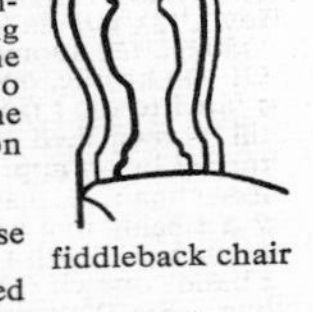
fiddleback chair

fiddle beetle *n* : any of several large flat-tened long-legged Oriental ground beetles of the genus *Mormolyce* having an elongated head and thorax and expanded wing cases and resembling a violin in outline

fiddle block *n* : a tackle block having two sheaves of different diameters one above the other instead of side by side as in a common double block

fiddle bow *n* : FIDDLESTICK

fiddle case *n* : the fruit of the rattle (sense 3a)

fid·dle-dee-dee \ˌfidᵊldēˈdē\ *interj* — used to express impatience, disbelief, or scorn

fiddle dock *n* : a dock (*Rumex pulcher*) with fiddle-shaped leaves

fiddle drill *n* : BOW DRILL

¹fid·dle-fad·dle \ˈfidᵊl,fadᵊl\ *n* [redupl. of ¹*fiddle*] : trifling or foolish talk, comment, or action : NONSENSE — often used interjectionally

²fiddle-faddle \"\ *vb* **fiddle-faddled; fiddle-faddled; fiddle-faddling** \-d(ᵊ)liŋ\ **fiddle-faddles** : TRIFLE, MEDDLE, FIDDLE — **fid·dle-fad·dler** \-d(ᵊ)lə(r)\ *n* -s

fiddle flower *n* : a bleeding heart (*Dicentra spectabilis*)

fiddle-footed \ˈ≡≡ˈ≡≡\ *adj* **1** : SKITTISH, JUMPY ⟨a *fiddle-footed* horse⟩ **2** : prone to wander or drift ⟨*fiddle-footed* cowboys⟩

fiddlehead \ˈ≡≡,≡\ *n* **1** : an ornament on a ship's bow curved like the scroll at the head of a violin **2** : one of the young unfurling fronds of certain ferns (as the cinnamon fern and ostrich fern) that are often eaten as greens

fiddleheaded \ˈ≡≡ˈ≡≡\ *adj* : having a head shaped like a violin ⟨a ~ spoon⟩

fiddle-leaf fig *n* : an African fig tree (*Ficus lyrata*) that has very large violin-shaped or guitar-shaped leaves and that is often cultivated as a pot or tub plant

fiddle-neck \ˈ≡≡,≡\ *n* [so called fr. the shape of the flower racemes] **1** : a hairy annual Californian herb (*Phacelia tanacetifolia*) with large pinnately divided leaves and bluish flowers **2** : a plant of the genus *Amsinckia*

fid·dler \ˈfid(ᵊ)lə(r)\ *n* -s [ME *fitheler, fideler*, fr. OE *fithelere*, fr. *fithele* fiddle + *-ere* -er — more at FIDDLE] **1** : one that fiddles **b** : VIOLINIST **2 a** *also* **fiddlerfish** \ˈ≡(≡)≡,≡\ : any of several rays of the family Rhinobatidae that resemble a violin in outline — called also *fiddlefish, fiddle shark* **b** *also*

fiddler cat *or* **fiddler catfish** : SPOTTED CAT

fiddler beetle *n* : any of certain beetles: as **a** : FIDDLEBACK **b** : a root-girdling beetle (*Prepodes vittatus* or a related species) destructive to citrus in Jamaica

fiddler crab *also* **fiddler** *n* **1** : any of numerous burrowing crabs of the genus *Uca* widely distributed in salt marshes and along sandy or muddy shores of No. and So. America, the Indian ocean, and other areas and having in the male one claw much enlarged and often held in a position suggesting that in which a fiddle is held — called also *beckoning crab, fighting crab* **2** : any of several crabs structurally similar to the fiddler crab

fiddler crab 1

fiddler's green *n, usu cap F&G* : a heaven reserved for sailors or soldiers, esp. cavalrymen

fiddles *pl of* FIDDLE, *pres 3d sing of* FIDDLE

fiddlestick \'==,=\ *n* [ME *fidel stik*] **1 a :** the bow usu. strung with horsehair that is used in playing the fiddle **b :** a stick on a seeding machine that is worked back and forth to broadcast seed **2 a :** TRIFLE ⟨she didn't care a ~ for that⟩ **b :** NONSENSE — usu. used in the pl. ⟨nothing but utter ~*s*⟩ **c** — used in the pl. interjectionally to express disapproval, disbelief, or derision

fiddle waist *n* **:** an extremely narrow shank on a shoe

fiddlewood \'==,=\ *n* **1 :** any of several trees of the family Verbenaceae esp. of the genus *Citharexylum* **2 :** the hard wood of a fiddlewood

fid·dley *or* **fid·ley** \'fid(ᵊ)lē\ *n* -s [origin unknown] **:** the uppermost part of the stokehole of a steamship or an alleyway across this on a level with the between decks and roofed usu. with a grating for ventilation

fiddley hatch *n* **:** a hatch around the smokestack and uptake on the weather deck of a ship for ventilation of the boiler room

[1]**fiddling** *adj* [fr. pres. part. of [2]*fiddle*] **:** TRIFLING, PETTY

[2]**fiddling** *n* [fr. gerund of [2]*fiddle*] **:** the process of sewing book sections together by hand with cross-stitch or overcast stitch from one section or group of leaves to the next in alternation often for use in books having a number of single leaves and having cords or bands in sawed-in grooves

[1]**fi·dei·com·mis·sary** \¦fīdē,ī'kämə,serē, -dē,īkə'misərē\ *n* -ES [LL *fideicommissarius*, fr. *fideicommissum* + L *-arius* -ary (n. suffix)] **:** a person who is the beneficiary under civil law of a fideicommissum and who is nearly equivalent to a cestui que trust of common law

[2]**fideicommissary** \¦==,=¦==,==, ¦==,==¦===\ *adj* [LL *fideicommissarius*, fr. *fideicommissum* + L *-arius* -ary (adj. suffix)] **:** of, having to do with, or of the nature of a fideicommissum

fideicommissary heir *n* **:** one that receives property from a fiduciary heir

fideicommissary substitution *n* **1 :** the substitution under Roman and civil law of another heir or donee by a fideicommissum or direction that the original heir or donee at his death or upon some stated event or condition transfer the inheritance or gift or a part thereof to the substituted heir or donee **2 :** a gift of property under Roman and civil law by will or gift inter vivos wherein the donee (as an heir of the testator or an heir of such person) is directed and under a duty to transfer the property to another or other persons designated as donees

fi·dei·com·mis·sion \¦fīdē,īkə'mishən\ *n* [*fideicommissum* + *-ion*] **:** the making of a fideicommissum

fi·dei·com·mis·sion·er \-sh(ə)nə(r)\ *n* **:** the fiduciary of a fideicommissum

fi·dei·com·mis·sor \-kə'misər, -'kämə,sȯ(ə)r\ *n* -s [*fideicommissum* + *-or*] **:** the grantor of a fideicommissum

fi·dei·com·mis·sum \-,kə'misəm\ *n, pl* **fideicommis·sa** \-sə\ [LL, fr. neut. of *fideicommissus*, past part. of *fideicommittere* to bequeath in trust, fr. *fidei* (gen. of *fides* faith, trust) + *committere* to connect, entrust — more at FAITH, COMMIT] **1 :** a gift under Roman law of property stipulated by the donor to be transferred by the donee at a given time or upon a stated condition to a third person for his benefit and made between living persons in contemplation of death or by will **2 :** the substantial equivalent of a gift to a donee under civil law upon a trust created to transfer the property to another — compare SUBSTITUTION

fi·de·ism \'fē(,)dā,izəm, 'fīdē,-\ *n* -s [prob. fr. F *fidéisme*, fr. L *fides* faith + F *-isme* -ism — more at FAITH] **:** exclusive or basic reliance upon faith alone accompanied by a consequent disparagement of reason and utilized esp. in the pursuit of philosophical or religious truth — **fi·de·ist** \-ēəst\ *n* -s — **fi·de·is·tic** \¦fīdē¦istik\ *adj*

fi·de·jus·sio \,fīdē'jəsē,ō\ *n, pl* **fidejussi·o·nes** \,==,==-'ō(,)nēz\ [LL] **:** FIDEJUSSION

fi·de·jus·sion \,fīdē'jəshən\ *n* -s [LL *fidejussion-*, *fidejussio*, fr. *fidejussus* (past part. of *fidejubēre* to give surety, fr. L *fide* — abl. of *fides* — + *jubēre* to order) + L *-ion-*, *-io* -ion — more at JUSSIVE] **1 :** the contract of guaranty or suretyship under Roman and civil law made by stipulation accessory to an existing contract — compare INTERCESSION **2 :** the contract or obligation (as under Scots law) of guaranty or suretyship — **fi·de·jus·sion·ary** \-shə,nerē\ *adj*

fi·de·jus·sor \-'jəsə(r)\ *n* -s [LL, fr. *fidejussus* + L *-or*] **:** one under Roman and civil law who enters into or authorizes a fidejussion, a guarantor, or surety

fi·del·i·ty \fə'delәd·ē, fī'-, -lәtē, -i\ *n* -ES [ME *fidelite*, fr. MF *fidelité*, fr. L *fidelitat-*, *fidelitas* — more at FEALTY] **1 a :** the quality or state of being faithful or loyal (as to a person, cause, party, or nation) **:** LOYALTY; *specif* **:** adherence to the marriage contract **:** conjugal loyalty **b :** accuracy in details (as in the reproduction of a manuscript, the reporting of an event, the performance of a duty) **:** EXACTNESS **2** *obs* **:** WORD OF HONOR **3 a :** the degree to which an electronic device (as a radio receiving set, phonograph, or recording device) accurately reproduces at its output end the signal or wave form received at its input end **b :** the relative tendency of a kind of organism (as a species) to be restricted to the ecological community to which it is most perfectly adapted — often used with a percentage expressing the degree to which such a tendency has developed ⟨a substory plant of the beech-maple community with a 90 percent ~⟩ — compare EXCLUSIVE 1b

syn ALLEGIANCE, FEALTY, LOYALTY, DEVOTION, PIETY: FIDELITY implies strict and continuing faithfulness as to an obligation, trust, or duty ⟨a profound reverence for and *fidelity* to the truth, sometimes almost amounting to fanaticism —H.L.Mencken⟩ ⟨the oath which might be exacted — that of *fidelity* to the constitution — is prescribed —John Marshall⟩ ⟨it is equally certain, without any groundless aspersion of Harriet's conjugal *fidelity*, that the fault was not Shelley's —Richard Garnett †1906⟩ ALLEGIANCE suggests adherence as that of medieval vassal to his lord or of a modern free citizen to his country ⟨I pledge *allegiance* to the Flag of the United States of America and to the Republic for which it stands —Francis Bellamy⟩ ⟨to exclude unnaturalized foreigners; the latter forming no part of the sovereignty, owing it no *allegiance*, and therefore under no obligation to defend it —R.B.Taney⟩ ⟨he claims no political *allegiance*, is a member of the bipartisan National Committee on Strengthening Congress —*Current Biog.*⟩ FEALTY implies a strict fidelity acknowledged and cherished by the individual ⟨abolitionism, to which I swore *fealty* —J.R.Lowell⟩ ⟨constant in *fealty* to his faith, extracting fresh allegiance —W.O. Clough⟩ ⟨profoundly grateful and emboldened by their comradeship and their *fealty* —A.E.Stevenson †1965⟩ LOYALTY may imply steadfast and reliable personal attachment; in today's English it is taken to indicate absence of anything treasonable or subversive ⟨the *loyalties* which lead men to go to war —Virginia Woolf⟩ ⟨western man subordinated religious *loyalties* to national ones —Isaac Deutscher⟩ ⟨*loyalty* in these terms is allegiance to the democratic way of life, to the process or system that welcomes into free competition even the most loathsome ideas —*New Republic*⟩ DEVOTION may indicate zealous self-dedication and ardent attachment ⟨in the Declaration of the Rights of Man adopted amid swirling revolution in 1789, France rose to a height of *devotion* to human liberties from which she has never receded —F.A. Ogg & Harold Zink⟩ ⟨he loved with a passionate intensity of *devotion* the greatness of Roman traditions, and the memory of the mighty dead —Agnes Repplier⟩ ⟨a *devotion* to the welfare of children, a complete absorption in the business of parenthood, and a willingness not only to subordinate all other interests to those of the offspring, but, if necessary, to lay down life itself upon the altar of family duty —J.W. Krutch⟩ PIETY applies to fidelity to spiritual or natural obligations ⟨*piety* is the knowledge and worship of the gods: it consists in forming an adequate conception of them and imitating their perfection —Frank Thilly⟩ ⟨the principle of filial *piety*, which has existed throughout the world and is embodied in the Fifth Commandment —Bertrand Russell⟩

fidelity bond *n* **:** a bond or other form of contract for indemnifying an employer against financial loss due to the dishonesty of an employee — see INSURANCE

fidelity insurance *n* **:** insurance against loss by reason of the dishonesty or nonperformance of an employee of the insured

fi·de·pro·mis·sion \,fīdēprō'mishən\ *n* -s [LL *fidepromission-*, *fidepromissio*, fr. *fidepromissus* (past part. of *fidepromittere* to give surety, fr. L *fide* — abl. of *fides* faith, trust — + *promittere* to promise) + L *-ion-*, *-io* -ion] **:** contract of guaranty or suretyship under Roman law by stipulation — **fi·de·pro·mis·sor** \-prō'misər, -'prämə,sȯ(ə)r\ *n* -s

fi·des fac·ta \,fē,dā'sfäktə\ *n* [ML, lit., assurance given] **:** a ceremony in Teutonic law required for the making of a binding contract except in cases of bailment and consisting of making faith with a gage and pledge

fidge \'fij\ *n or vb* [prob. alter. of [3]*fitch*] *dial* **:** FIDGET

[1]**fid·get** \'fijət, *usu* -əd·+V\ *n* -s [irreg. fr. *fidge*] **1 :** the quality or state of being restless **:** a condition marked by incessant changes of position or nervous movement **:** DYSPHORIA ⟨in a terrible ~ over unpaid bills⟩ — often used in pl. ⟨a person suffering from the ~*s*⟩ **2** [[2]*fidget*] **:** one that exhibits or suffers from the fidgets ⟨his aunt being a regular old ~⟩

[2]**fidget** \"\ *vb* -ED/-ING/-S *vi* **1 :** to move uneasily one way and the other **:** act nervously or impatiently ⟨the speaker kept ~*ing* and clearing his throat⟩ **2 :** to be nervously uneasy **:** WORRY ⟨always ~*ing* about her health⟩ **3 :** to tinker or play nervously or absently — used with *with* ⟨~*s* with his tie⟩ ~ *vt* **1 :** to cause physical uneasiness in **:** make nervous ⟨a pitcher ~*ed* by the constant movement of a batter⟩ **2 :** to move or play with restlessly ⟨a policeman eyeing traffic and ~*ing* his whistle⟩

fid·get·er \-əd·ə(r), -ətə-\ *n* -s **:** one that fidgets

fid·get·i·ness \-d·|ēnəs, -t|, |in-\ *n* -ES **:** the quality or state of being fidgety

fid·get·ing·ly *adv* **:** in a fidgety manner

fid·gety \'fijəd·ē, -ətē, -i\ *adj* **1 a :** inclined to fidget ⟨a ~ person⟩ **b :** exhibiting nervous jumpy movements ⟨~ hands⟩ **2 a :** making unnecessary ado **:** FUSSY ⟨a ~ old man⟩ **b :** showing overmuch care or attention to detail ⟨~ ornamentation⟩

fidg·in fain \'fijən,fān\ *adj* [*fidgin* fr. pres. part. of *fidge*] *chiefly Scot* **:** restless with curiosity or excitement

fid hole *n* **:** a hole in the heel of a topmast or topgallant mast through which the fid or other spar passes

fid hook *n* **:** a stout steel hook with a slot in the flattened end for connecting chains (as in lumbering)

fid·ia \'fidēə\ *n* [NL] **1** *cap* **:** a genus of small beetles (family Chrysomelidae) including the grape rootworm (*F. viticida*) and being very injurious to vines in America **2** -s **:** any beetle of the genus *Fidia*

fid·i·bus \'fidəbəs\ *n, pl* **fidibuses** *or* **fidibus** [G (orig. student slang), fr. L. dat. pl. of *fides* lyre (a jocular allusion to a line of Horace); akin to Gk *sphides* sausage] **:** a paper spill for lighting pipes

fidley *var of* FIDDLEY

FIDO \'fī(,)dō\ *abbr or n* -s [*F*og *I*nvestigation *D*ispersal *O*perations] **:** a system in which fog above runways is evaporated by the heat from liquid-fuel burners at their sides to permit aircraft to operate

fids *pl of* FID, *pres 3d sing of* FID

fi·du·cia \fə'd(y)üsh(ē)ə, fī'-\ *n, pl* **fiduci·ae** \-shē,ē\ [L, lit., trust, confidence, fr. *fidere* to trust — more at BIDE] **:** a contract used under Roman and civil law (as in the emancipation of children, in connection with testamentary gifts, and in pledges) and constituting essentially a contract of sale to a person usu. by mancipation coupled with an agreement that the purchaser should sell the property back upon the fulfillment of certain conditions — called also *contractus fiduciae*

fi·du·cial \fə'd(y)üshəl, fī'-\ *adj* [LL *fiducialis*, fr. L *fiducia* + *-alis* -al] **1 :** founded on faith or trust ⟨his ~ reliance on certain religious beliefs⟩ **2 :** having the nature of a trust **:** FIDUCIARY ⟨a ~ power⟩ **3 :** taken as an origin or zero of reference ⟨a ~ point on a scale⟩ — **fi·du·cial·ly** \-əlē\ *adv*

fi·du·ci·ar·i·ly \fə¦d(y)üshē¦erəlē, fī¦-, ,fī,=='===\ *adv* **:** in a fiduciary manner

[1]**fi·du·ci·ary** \fə'd(y)üshē,erē, fī'-, -ri\ *adj* [L *fiduciarius*, fr. *fiducia* trust + *-arius* -ary] **1 :** holding, held, or founded in trust or confidence **2 :** of, having to do with, or involving a confidence or trust **:** of the nature of a trust ⟨a ~ capacity⟩ ⟨a ~ relation⟩ **3 :** resting upon public confidence for value or currency ⟨~ fiat money⟩

[2]**fiduciary** \"\ *n* -ES **:** one (as a corporate trust company or the trust department of a bank) that holds a fiduciary relation or acts in a fiduciary capacity to another (as one whose funds are entrusted to it for investment)

fiduciary bond *n* **:** a surety bond filed by a fiduciary (as the administrator of an estate) to guarantee faithful performance of his duties

fiduciary coemption *n* **:** a fictitious sale under Roman law by which a woman can change her guardian or gain legal capacity to make a will — compare COEMPTIO

fiduciary contract *n* **:** FIDUCIA

fiduciary heir *n* **:** an heir in Roman Dutch law who takes the property subject to its passing to another (as the fideicommissary heir) on fulfillment of certain conditions

fiduciary relation *n* **1 :** the relation that is declared by a court to exist between parties to a transaction when the court desires to hold the offending party responsible to prevent unjust enrichment as though he were in fact a trustee for the other **2 :** the relation existing when one person justifiably reposes confidence, faith, and reliance in another whose aid, advice, or protection is sought in some matter **:** the relation existing when good conscience requires one to act at all times for the sole benefit and interests of another with loyalty to those interests **:** the relation by law existing between certain classes of persons (as confidential advisor and the one advised; executors or administrators and legatees or heirs; conservators and wards, trustees, or beneficiaries; partners, joint adventurers, corporate directors or officers and stockholders; majority and minority stockholders; factors, agents, or brokers and principals; attorneys and clients; promoters and stock subscribers; mutual savings banks or investment corporations and their depositors or investors; receivers, trustees in bankruptcy, or assignees in insolvency and creditors)

fie \'fī\ *interj* [ME *fi*, *fy*, fr. OF] — used to express disgust, dislike, or the affectation of being shocked

-fied *past of* -FY

fied·ler·ite \'fēdlə,rīt\ *n* -s [G *fiedlerit*, fr. Karl G. *Fiedler* †1853 Ger. mine commissioner + G *-it* -ite] **:** a lead mineral $Pb_3(OH)_2Cl_4$ that is prob. a hydroxychloride and occurs in colorless monoclinic crystals

fief \'fēf\ *n* -s [F, fr. OF *fief*, *fié*] **1 :** a feudal estate **:** FEE **2 :** something over which one has rights or exercises control

fief·dom \-dəm\ *n* -s [*fief* + *-dom*] **:** an area over which one exercises control

[1]**field** \'fēld, *chiefly before pause or consonant* -ēəld\ *n* -s [ME *feld*, *fild*, *field*, fr. OE *feld*; akin to OFris, OS, & OHG *feld* field, OE *fold* earth, OS *folda*, ON *fold*; akin to OE *flōr* floor — more at FLOOR] **1 a** (1) **:** a land area free of woodland, cities, and towns **:** open country (2) **:** the open country near or belonging to a city — usu. used in pl. **b** (1) **:** an area of cleared enclosed land used for cultivation or pasture ⟨a ~ of wheat⟩ ⟨a ~ of cattle⟩ (2) **:** an area of land containing, yielding, or worked for a natural resource ⟨a coal*field*⟩ ⟨oil ~*s*⟩ ⟨diamond ~*s*⟩ **c :** the place where a battle is fought **:** BATTLEGROUND **d :** a large unbroken expanse of sea ice **2 a :** an area, category, or division wherein a particular activity or pursuit is carried out ⟨a lawyer eminent in his ~⟩ ⟨a wide ~ of speculation⟩ ⟨the ~ of analytical chemistry⟩ **b** (1) **:** the sphere of practical operation of an organization or enterprise; *specif* **:** the place or territory where direct contacts (as with customers) may be made or firsthand knowledge obtained ⟨salesmen in the ~⟩ (2) **:** the scene of observation (as of actual phenomena) outside of a laboratory ⟨geologists working in the ~⟩ **c :** an area outside of a military post where exercises or maneuvers are carried out ⟨new equipment being tested in the ~⟩ **d** (1) **:** an athletic or sports area or space (as an outdoor enclosure for baseball, cricket, football) (2) **:** the portion enclosed by the racing track of an indoor or outdoor sports area on which are contested events of a track-and-field meet **3 :** a space or ground on which something is drawn or projected: as **a :** the space on either surface of a coin, token, or medal that does not contain the central figure of the design, the inscription, or the exergue **b :** the ground of each division in a flag **c** *heraldry* (1) **:** the whole surface of an escutcheon (2) **:** so much of an escutcheon as is shown unconcealed by the different bearings upon it **d :** the area of a seal inside the inscription or other device about the circumference **4 :** BATTLE ⟨an extremely costly ~⟩ **5 :** the persons, participants, or elements that make up all or part of a sports activity: **a :** all the participants with the exception usu. of the favorite in an athletic contest or sporting event where more than two are entered; *esp* **:** the horses or dogs that are for purposes of pari-mutuel betting grouped together usu. as the 12th betting unit when the number of entries exceeds 12 **b :** all the players that are in action esp. in football ⟨ran through a broken ~⟩ **c :** the side of a team not at bat **d :** a fielder in cricket; *collectively* **:** the members of the fielding side **e :** the group of numbers 2, 3, 5, 9, 10, 11, and 12 or 2, 3, 4, 9, 10, 11, and 12 on which a bet in craps pays even money **6 a :** a continuously distributed entity in space that accounts for actions at a distance ⟨electric ~⟩ ⟨gravitational ~⟩ **b :** FIELD INTENSITY **c :** a complex of coexistent forces (as biological, psychological, and social or interpersonal) which serve as causative agents or as a frame of reference in human experience and behavior **7 a** *math* **:** a domain or aggregate of elements or magnitudes that when combined by addition, subtraction, multiplication, and division, the divisor 0 being excluded, always produce an element of the aggregate **b :** a region of embryonic tissue potentially capable of a particular type of differentiation ⟨a neural ~⟩ ⟨an ear ~⟩ **c :** a region of space in which a given effect (as gravity, magnetism, or electricity) exists and has a definite value at each point **8 a** (1) **:** the usu. circular area visible through the lens system of an optical instrument (as a microscope or telescope) (2) **:** the whole area of a television image **b :** the site of a surgical operation **c :** the total range of meanings associated with a set of words which are related but not identical in meaning (as *mind*, *thought*, *intellect*, *spirit*, *intelligence*, *insight*) — called also *semantic field*, *word field* **d :** CARD FIELD **9 a :** the field magnet of a generator — see DYNAMO illustration **b :** a series of open-joint drain tiles that leads off septic-tank overflow to its absorption area

syn DOMAIN, PROVINCE, SPHERE, TERRITORY, BAILIWICK: FIELD denotes a limited and demarcated area of knowledge or endeavor to which pursuits, activities, and interests are confined, often one determinedly chosen at a certain time or by the necessities of a situation ⟨the provincial governments and the federal government in Ottawa share some *fields* of government business —*Canadian Citizenship Series*⟩ ⟨organizations functioning in the *field* of cartography —*Americana Annual*⟩ ⟨a writer whose reputation . . . has been pretty much confined to the whodunit *field* —James Kelly⟩ DOMAIN may apply to a clearly defined area of activity marked by a degree of exclusive mastery and control discouraging outside interference or unwarranted intrusion ⟨advances in the *domain* of the history of ideas —Benjamin Farrington⟩ ⟨the *domain* of artifact typology or cultural taxonomy —Philip Phillips & G.R.Willey⟩ ⟨great work in the *domain* of physiological chemistry of the cornea —*Americana Annual*⟩ PROVINCE indicates an area of special jurisdiction, responsibility, competence, power, or influence ⟨economic theory is not the *province* of the lawyer or courts of law —C.A.Cooke⟩ ⟨the almost impertinently realistic explorations into behavior which are the *province* of the psychiatrist —Edward Sapir⟩ ⟨a decision that, in any case, was not within the *province* of the F.B.I. —*New Statesman & Nation*⟩ SPHERE may more strongly imply circumscribed limits setting apart activities and interests ⟨a long and profound process of social change . . . but this time in the economic *sphere* —John Strachey⟩ ⟨the congress and the president, acting in their proper *spheres*, must perform their duties to the American people in support of our highest traditions —D.D.Eisenhower⟩ ⟨composing, in which *sphere* he is a prolific worker —*London Calling*⟩ TERRITORY is close to DOMAIN but lacks its suggestions of inviolability ⟨prose has preempted a lion's share of the *territory* once held, either in sovereignty or on equal terms, by poetry —J.B.Lowes⟩ BAILIWICK may suggest a petty area of individual power and authority ⟨love the Romantics, and feel that lyric poetry and impassioned prose are their proper *bailiwick* —Katharine F. Gerould⟩ ⟨to achieve an authoritative position within your own little *bailiwick* —W.J.Reilly⟩

[2]**field** \"\ *vb* -ED/-ING/-S *vt* **1 :** to expose (as grain, malt, or fiber) to the action of the air and sun in the field **2 :** to handle (as a batted ball) while playing in the field **3 a :** to put (a team or designated players) into the field for actual play ⟨~ a weak team⟩ **b :** to put into the field ⟨the greatest army any nation ever ~*ed*⟩ ~ *vi* **1** *obs* **:** to take to the battlefield **:** engage in battle **2 :** to play as a fielder

[3]**field** \"\ *adj* **1 :** of or having to do with a field: as **a :** growing in or inhabiting the fields or open country or cleared land **b :** made, conducted, or used in the field ⟨~ operations⟩ ⟨~ equipment⟩ **c :** operating or active in or assigned to the field ⟨a ~ agent⟩ ⟨a ~ worker for a benevolent society⟩ **2 :** of, relating to, or contested on the field and not on the track — see FIELD EVENT

field ambulance *n* **:** AMBULANCE 1

field archery *n* **:** competitive archery in which shooting is done at a simulated hunting ground

field army *n* **:** a military unit organized to be capable of independent action and consisting conventionally of a headquarters, two or more corps, and auxiliary troops

field arrow *n* **:** a hunting arrow

field artillery *n* **:** artillery other than antiaircraft artillery used with armies in the field and classified according to the weight and caliber of its cannon as light, medium, or heavy

fieldball \'=,=\ *n* **:** a game played on a soccer field with a soccer ball or basketball by two teams of 11 members each and combining many of the techniques of basketball and soccer with the object being to score by throwing the ball under the crossbar between the uprights of the opponents' goal

field balm *n* **1 :** a European perennial savory (*Satureia nepeta*) naturalized in the U. S. and having stiff branches and axillary clusters of lilac or violet flowers **2 :** GROUND IVY

field basil *n* **:** WILD BASIL

field bean *n* **1 :** BROAD BEAN **2 :** a bean grown primarily for its ripe edible seeds ⟨always put in a plot of *field beans* for our own winter baked beans⟩

field bed *n* **1 :** a bed used in the field **2 :** a four-poster of moderate height with a canopy supported on a frame that is strongly arched so as to give greater height at the center than at the ends

field bed 2

field bee *n* **:** a honey-gathering worker bee

field beet *n* **:** MANGEL-WURZEL

field betony *n* **:** a bristly annual European hedge nettle (*Stachys arvensis*) with purplish flowers

field bindweed *n* **:** a prostrate or weakly climbing European perennial plant (*Convolvulus arvensis*) established in No. America where it often becomes a serious weed — called also *wild morning glory*

fieldbird \'=,=\ *n* **:** PLOVER: as **a :** GOLDEN PLOVER **b :** UPLAND PLOVER

field book *n* **:** a notebook used for keeping field notes in surveying

field brome *n* **:** an annual or biennial weed grass (*Bromus arvensis*) with soft pubescent leaf sheaths and an open panicle — called also *bromegrass*

field capacity *n* **:** the water-retaining capacity of a soil usu. including both the hygroscopic and capillary water of the soil and being expressed as a percentage of the dry weight of the soil ⟨a silty loam with a *field capacity* of 35 percent⟩ — called also *field moisture capacity*

field captain *n* **1 a :** the official in charge of the men's division of an archery tournament **b :** the chief official in an all-men's archery tournament **2 :** a player on the field esp. in football who acts as representative of the team (as in accepting or refusing penalties of the opposing team)

field chamomile *n* **:** a European white-flowered weed (*Anthemis arvensis*) naturalized in No. America — called also *corn chamomile*

field chickweed *n* **:** a densely tufted perennial chickweed (*Cerastium arvense*) of the north temperate zone

field chopper *n* **:** an implement that while moving across a field mows the standing crop and chops and loads it as silage

field code *n* **:** a code book for use in combat areas

field coil *n* **:** a current-bearing coil used to excite a field (as of a generator, motor, or loudspeaker)

field conventicle *n* **:** a religious meeting held out of doors

field corn *n* **:** an Indian corn (as dent corn, flint corn, or soft corn) grown for feeding stock or for market grain and having kernels that are usu. white or yellow and not sweet

field-cor·net \ˈ=,kȯrˈnet, =ˈkȯrnət\ *n* -s [trans. of Afrik *veldkornet*] **1 :** a commander of the burghers in Cape Province during the former native risings **2 :** a minor magistrate similar to a justice of the peace who represents the government in a rural district in Cape Province — **field-cor·net·cy** \-sē\ *n* -ES

field crane's-bill *n* **:** ALFILARIA

field cress *n* **:** a wild European peppergrass (*Lepidium campestre*) naturalized in America — called also *cow cress, crowdweed, field peppergrass*

field cricket *n* **:** any of several crickets of *Gryllus* and related genera; *esp* **:** a common American cricket (*Acheta assimilis*) sometimes destructive to crops

field crop *n* **:** a crop (as hay, grain, or cotton) grown for agricultural purposes covering a large area but excluding fruits, vegetables, and ornamental plants

field crowfoot *n* **:** CORN CROWFOOT

field current *n* **:** the current supplied to the field windings of a generator or motor to establish the magnetic field for its operation

field cypress *n* **:** GROUND PINE 1

field daisy *n* **:** DAISY 1b

field day *n* **1 a :** a day when troops are given exercises or maneuvers in the field **b :** an outdoor get-together held for entertainment and relaxation ⟨the annual *field day* of a company union⟩ **c :** a day of open-air sports and athletic competition (as in schools) **2 :** a thorough general cleaning in the navy **3 a :** an occasion marked usu. by extreme fun or hilarity ⟨the children had a *field day* when the teacher left the room⟩ **b :** an occasion or opportunity for unrestrained ridicule ⟨the newspapers had a *field day* with the scandal⟩ **c :** a period when full opportunity suddenly, unexpectedly, or finally appears to unleash and satisfy natural powers, thwarted ability, or restrained desire ⟨the artillery had a *field day* with the retreating infantry⟩

field dodder *n* **:** a very widespread annual (*Cuscuta pentagona*) parasitic on various herbaceous plants

field dog *n* **:** a dog (as a pointer) used for hunting in the field

field driver *n* **:** a town officer esp. in early New England authorized to round up and impound domestic farm animals roaming at large

fielded *adj* [fr. pres. part. of ²*field*] *obs* **:** fighting in the battlefield and not in a fort

fielded panel *n* **:** a raised or recessed panel with a wide flat surface surrounded by moldings; *also* **:** such a panel divided into smaller panels

field emission *n* **:** the emission of electrons from a metallic conductor due solely to the action of an electric field — compare PHOTOEMISSION, THERMIONIC EMISSION

fielden *adj, obs* **:** of or having to do with fields **:** RUSTIC

field·er \ˈfēldə(r)\ *n* -s **:** one that fields: as **a :** a player stationed in the field (as in baseball or cricket) **b :** a player considered as to his ability at fielding

fielder's choice *n* **:** an attempt by a fielder handling a batted baseball to retire a base runner other than the batter when a play to first base would probably retire the batter

field event *n* **:** an athletic contest involving the broad jump, high jump, pole vault, shot put, and the discus, javelin, and hammer throws — compare TRACK

field exercise *n* **:** a military training exercise simulating war conditions in the field with one side fully or partly equipped and manned and the other represented only on paper or by token forces — compare MANEUVER, WAR GAME

field·fare \ˈ=,fa(a)(ə)r, -,fe|\ *also* **fell·fare** \ˈfel,-\ *n* -s [ME *fildefare, feldefare*, fr. OE *feldeware*, fr. *feld* field + *-ware* dweller — more at FIELD] **1 :** a medium-sized thrush (*Turdus pilaris*) that breeds in northern Europe and western Asia and winters in Britain, central and southern Europe, and parts of Africa and Asia and that has the head, nape, and lower part of the back ash-colored and the upper part of the back and wing coverts chestnut **2 :** ROBIN 1c

field fever *n* **:** a European leptospirosis of man

field fortification *n* **:** fortification for more or less temporary use constructed in the field

field frame *n* **:** the principal magnetic structure of a motor or generator including the poles if they are an integral part — called also *yoke*

field garlic *n* **:** CROW GARLIC

field glass *n* **:** a hand-held optical instrument for use outdoors usu. consisting of two telescopes on a single frame with a focusing device — usu. used in pl.

field glasses

field goal *n* **1 :** a score in football made by drop-kicking or place-kicking the ball over the crossbar from ordinary play — compare EXTRA POINT **2 :** a basket in the game of basketball made while the ball is in play

field grade *n* **:** the grade of a field officer

field gray *n* **:** a dark gray (as of some military field uniforms)

field gromwell *n* **:** CORN GROMWELL

field guide *n* **:** a manual that identifies objects in a class and esp. natural objects and that is suitable for carrying into the field ⟨a *field guide* to birds⟩

field hand *n* **:** an outdoor farm laborer; *specif* **:** a Negro slave in America before 1865 who worked in the fields in distinction from one employed about the house of the master

field-handball \(ˈ)=ˈ=,=\ *n* **:** FIELDBALL

field hockey *n* **:** a game played on a turfed field between teams of 11 players each whose object is to hit a hard leather or plastic ball into the goal cage by the use of curved sticks that have a blade flattened on the left side and rounded on the right

100 yd. E F G C A C G E F 25 50 25

diagram of hockey field: *A*, point for initial bully; *C,C*, striking circles; *EF, EF*, sidelines; *EE, FF*, goal lines; *G,G*, goals

field horsetail *n* **:** a horsetail (*Equisetum arvense*) of the U.S. and Canada that produces from the same rhizomes brownish reproductive shoots in early summer and greenish chlorophyll-bearing vegetative shoots usu. after the former have shed their spores

field hospital *n* **:** a military organization of surgeons, nurses, and orderlies with equipment for establishing a temporary hospital in the field

field house *n* **1 :** a building on or near an athletic field for housing equipment and providing dressing facilities **2 :** a building enclosing a stadium or arena suitable for track events, basketball, and gymnastics

field ice *n* **:** floating ice in large comparatively flat tracts

fielding *pres part of* FIELD

fielding average *n* **:** a ratio in baseball obtained by dividing the number of total chances into the total of putouts and assists

field intensity *n* **1 :** the attribute of a magnetic, electric, gravitational, or other field of force that at any point is measured by the force which the field exerts upon a unit pole, unit charge, or unit mass placed at that point — called also *field strength* **2 :** the intensity of radiation at any point in a radiation field

field jacket *n* **:** a military jacket issued for wear in the field

field kale *n* **:** CHARLOCK

field kitchen *n* **:** the place where food for a military unit in the field is prepared; *also* **:** the portable cooking apparatus used in such a place

field lark *n, South & Midland* **:** MEADOWLARK

field larkspur *n* **:** an annual European larkspur (*Delphinium consolida*) naturalized in No. America having flowers with two petals succeeded by smooth follicles

field lens *n* **1 :** a lens located at or near the plane of a real image whose function is to collect and redirect the rays into some other element of the optical system **2 :** the one of two lenses forming the eyepiece of a telescope or compound microscope that is nearer the object glass and that directs the rays into the eye lens

field line *n* **:** any one of a system of nonintersecting lines so drawn in mapping a vector field that the direction of the tangent to it at any point is that of the vector at that point

field madder *n* **:** an annual European weed (*Sherardia arvensis*) of the family Rubiaceae with square stems, whorled leaves, and heads of blue or pink flowers — called also *blue field madder*

field magnet *n* **:** a magnet for producing and maintaining a magnetic field esp. in a generator or electric motor

field·man \ˈfē(ə)l(d)mən, -,man, -,maa(ə)n\ *n, pl* **fieldmen** **:** one that works in the field: as **a :** a traveling representative of a business organization (as a man who negotiates with farmers for the raising of crops under contract for a food-processing company) **b :** an investigator or advisor who works outdoors or away from the center of administration or activity (as a man who conducts educational programs for milk producers in an assigned territory)

field maneuver *n* **:** a maneuver in which troops in training oppose each other in given military situations

field marigold *n* **:** CORN MARIGOLD

field mark *n* **:** a marking (as of a bird) useful for identification from a distance

field marshal *n* **:** an officer (as in the British and several other armies) of the highest rank who corresponds in rank to a general of the army in the U.S. Army

field martin *n* **:** KINGBIRD

field milkwort *n* **:** PURPLE MILKWORT

field mint *n* **1 :** CATNIP **2 :** CORN MINT

field moisture *n* **:** the water in the ground above the water table

field moisture capacity *n* **:** FIELD CAPACITY

field mouse *n* **:** any of various mice that inhabit open fields: as **a :** any mouse of the New World genus *Microtus* **b :** any mouse of the Old World genus *Apodemus*

field mushroom *n* **1 :** MEADOW MUSHROOM **2 :** HORSE MUSHROOM

field music *n* **:** the drummers, fifers, buglers, and pipers attached to military companies who sound the various calls for the troops and play for marching in the absence of the band; *also* **:** the music produced by drummers, fifers, pipers, or buglers

field mustard *n* **:** CHARLOCK

field name *n* **:** a name that can be applied to a rock without critical microscopic or chemical analysis in a laboratory

field negro *n, cap N* **:** a Negro field hand

field note *n* **:** an item in a systematic record of the measurements made by a surveyor or the observations of a researcher in the field

field of consciousness : the totality of consciousness at any one time

field officer *n* **1 :** a military officer of the rank of colonel, lieutenant colonel, or major — compare GENERAL OFFICER **2 :** a member of the Salvation Army responsible for administration of a corps center

field of fire : the area that can be covered by the fire from a weapon or a group of weapons from a given position

field of force : a vector field in which the vector associated with each point is measurable by a force

field of honor 1 : a place where a duel is fought **2 :** BATTLEFIELD

field of vision : VISUAL FIELD

field order *n* **:** a combat order of prescribed form giving instructions for a specific operation

field pea *n* **:** a pea (*Pisum sativum* var. *arvense*) native to the Mediterranean region and northern Africa that is widely grown esp. in the U. S. and Canada for forage and food and has short flower stalks a little longer than the stipules, colored flowers, and small pods and seeds — called also *Austrian winter pea*

field pennycress *n* **:** PENNYCRESS

field peppergrass *n* **:** FIELD CRESS

fieldpiece \ˈ=,=\ *n* **:** a gun or howitzer for use in the field **:** a piece of field artillery

field pine *n* **:** BEACH HEATHER

field plover *n* **:** any of certain plovers: as **a :** GOLDEN PLOVER **b :** UPLAND PLOVER

field poppy *n* **:** CORN POPPY

field pumpkin *n* **:** PUMPKIN 1a(1)

field ration *n* **:** any of the various types of rations provided when troops are actually issued food in distinction from a money allowance

field rheostat *n* **:** a rheostat for regulating the current supplied to the field winding of a generator or motor

field rivet *n* **:** a rivet driven in place on work in the field — opposed to *shop rivet*

field run *n* **:** a crop product that has not been graded or sorted

field rush *n* **:** the common wood rush

fields *pl of* FIELD, *pres 3d sing of* FIELD

field scabious *n* **:** a perennial European scabious (*Scabiosa arvensis*) introduced in eastern U.S. and having bluish lilac flowers

field scorpion grass *n* **:** a common forget-me-not (*Myosotis arvensis*) of Europe and No. America with small blue or white flowers in one-sided racemes

field service *n* **1 :** service (as of troops, company agents, social-service workers) in the field **2 :** labor in the fields performed by Negro slaves in America before 1865

field slave *n* **:** a slave field hand

fields·man \ˈfēl(d)zmən\ *n, pl* **fieldsmen** **:** FIELDER

field sorrel *n* **:** SHEEP SORREL 1

field sow thistle *n* **:** PERENNIAL EUROPEAN SOW THISTLE

field spaniel *n* **:** a large usu. black hunting and retrieving spaniel that has a dense flat or slightly waved coat and that is now nearly extinct as a separate breed

field sparrow *n* **:** a sparrow that frequents fields: **a :** a small American sparrow (*Spizella pusilla*) closely related to the chipping sparrow but paler colored **b :** HEDGE SPARROW

field speedwell *n* **:** an annual speedwell (*Veronica agrestis*) of Europe widely naturalized in No. America having oval stalked leaves and minute blue axillary flowers on long stalks

field spider *n* **:** SPIDER 5e

field spool *n* **:** SPOOL 1a(3)

field station *n* **:** EXPERIMENT STATION

fieldstone \ˈ=,=\ *n* **:** stone used as taken from the field (as in building) ⟨the clay-daubed ~ chimney —William Faulkner⟩

field stop *n* **:** a diaphragm that determines the size of the field of an optical instrument

field strength *n* **:** FIELD INTENSITY

field-strip \ˈ=,=\ *vt* **:** to take apart (a weapon) to the extent authorized for routine cleaning, lubrication, and minor repairs

field system *n* **:** the prevailing system of husbandry in medieval times in England and parts of western Europe whereby the arable land of a village unit was composed of unenclosed strips held by the different owners or cultivators subject to use as a common for pasture during a certain period of each year

field theory *n* **1 a :** a theory in physics: the interaction of two separated physical systems is attributed to the intermediary of a field that propagates or extends from one to the other **b :** a theory in physics: particles are assumed to be the manifestation of quantum fields **2 :** a method of analysis in behavioral science that describes actions or events as the resultant of dynamic interplay among sociocultural, biomechanical, and motivational forces

field thistle *n* **:** a prickly stout No. American thistle (*Cirsium discolor*) with heads of purplish pink flowers

field thyme *n* **:** FIELD BALM 1

field tile *n* **:** unglazed clay drain tile without bell ends

field train *n* **:** the portion of the transportation including personnel of military units lower than a division that carries reserve stocks of supplies of all kinds not immediately required during combat

field trial *n* **:** a trial of sporting dogs in actual performance — compare BENCH SHOW

field trip *n* **:** a visit made by students and usu. a teacher for purposes of firsthand observation (as to a factory, farm, clinic, museum)

field vole *n* **:** a small European vole (*Microtus agrestis*) often troublesome in grainfields

field winding *n* **:** the winding of the field magnet of a dynamo or motor

fieldwork \ˈ=,=\ *n* **1 :** a temporary fortification thrown up by an army in the field **2 a :** work done in the field (as by students) to gain practical experience through firsthand observation **b :** the gathering of anthropological or sociological data through the interviewing of subjects in the field

field wormwood *n* **:** a European wormwood (*Artemisia campestris*) that is similar to common wormwood in its properties

fieldwort \ˈ=,=\ *n* **:** a bastard gentian (*Gentiana acuta*) or its European relative (*G. amarella*)

field woundwort *n* **:** FIELD BETONY

field-wren \ˈ=,=\ *n* **:** any of several more or less streaked brown Australian warblers (genus *Calamanthus*) chiefly of open fields and scrubby areas

field yam-root \=ˈ=,=, ˈ=,=,=\ *n* **:** the root of a carrion flower (*Smilax herbacea*)

fiend \ˈfēnd\ *n* -s [ME *feend, fiend* enemy, devil, demon, fr. OE *fēond, fiend;* akin to OHG *fiant* enemy, ON *fjāndi*, Goth *fijands*, all fr. the pres. part. of a Gmc verb represented by OE *fēon, fēogan* to hate, OHG *fiēn, fijēn*, ON *fjā*, Goth *fijan;* akin to Goth *faian* to scorn, Skt *pīyati* he scorns] **1 a :** the arch enemy of man **:** DEVIL, SATAN **b :** an infernal being **:** DEMON **c :** a person of great wickedness or maliciousness **2 :** a person excessively devoted to or captivated by a pursuit, practice, or object of study **:** FANATIC, BUG ⟨a golf ~⟩ ⟨a target-shooting ~⟩ **3 :** a person who uses or consumes immoderate or excessive quantities ⟨an aspirin ~⟩ ⟨a cigar ~⟩ ⟨a ~ for ice cream⟩ **4 :** a person remarkably clever at some skill or study ⟨a ~ at mathematics⟩

fiend·ish \-dish,-dēsh\ *adj* **1 :** perversely diabolical **:** HIDEOUS ⟨a ~ pleasure in hurting people⟩ **2 :** extremely cruel or wicked ⟨a ~ old man⟩ **3 :** excessively bad, unpleasant, or difficult ⟨~ weather⟩ ⟨a ~ punishment⟩ — **fiend·ish·ly** *adv* — **fiend·ish·ness** *n* -ES

fiend·ly \-dlē,-dli\ *adj* -ER/-EST [ME *feendly, fiendly*, fr. OE *fēondlic, fiendlic*, fr. *fēond, fiend* fiend + *-lic* -ly] *archaic* **:** of, relating to, or befitting a fiend **:** FIENDISH

fient \ˈfēnt, ˈfint\ *n* -s [alter. of *fiend*] *Scot* **:** FIEND, DEVIL — often used in imprecations

fier \ˈfēr\ *Scot var of* FERE

¹fi·e·ras·fer \,fīəˈrasfə(r) ,fēə-\ [NL, fr. Prov *fielat-fèr, fierasfèr*, fr. *fielat, fieras* net, moray (fr. OProv *filat*, fr. *fil* thread, fr. L *filum*) + *fèr* fierce, wild, fr. L *ferus* — more at FILE] *syn of* CARAPUS

²fierasfer \ˈ"\ *n* -s **:** any of the small inquiline fishes of the genus *Carapus* — **fi·e·ras·fer·oid** \ˌ==ˈ=fə,rȯid\ *n or adj*

fi·e·ras·fer·id \ˌ==ˈ=fərəd\ *n* -s [NL *Fierasferidae*] **:** FIERASFER, PEARL FISH

fi·e·ras·fer·i·dae \ˌ==,raˈsferə,dē\ [NL, fr. *Fierasfer* + *-idae*] *syn of* CARAPIDAE

¹fierce \ˈfi(ə)rs, ˈfiəs\ *adj* -ER/-EST [ME *fers, fiers*, fr. OF, fr. L *ferus* wild, savage, cruel; akin to Gk *thēr* wild animal, OSlav *zvěrĭ*] **1 a :** marked by grim, pugnacious, or wild hostility **:** MERCILESS ⟨~ fighting⟩ **b :** given to fighting or killing **:** savagely intractable and likely to attack ⟨~ native tribes⟩ **2 a :** marked by furious unrestrained zeal or vehemence ⟨a ~ argument⟩ **:** heated or violent in nature **:** without moderation, restraint, or control ⟨a ~ temper⟩ **b** (1) **:** extremely vexatious, disappointing, or hard to bear **:** CRUSHING ⟨~ pain⟩ (2) **:** unpleasantly or uncomfortably intense or extreme ⟨a ~ light⟩ ⟨a ~ silence⟩ **3 a** *obs* **:** PROUD, ARROGANT **b :** wild, unfriendly, or menacing in aspect or appearance ⟨a ~ old hermit⟩ ⟨~ and barren moors⟩ **4 a :** furiously active **:** extremely eager ⟨a ~ effort⟩ **:** VIOLENT ⟨a ~ dash up the mountainside⟩ **b** *dial Eng* **:** in vigorous health or spirits **:** CHIPPER

syn FEROCIOUS, FELL, SAVAGE, CRUEL, INHUMAN, BARBAROUS are applied to persons and their actions. FIERCE may connote wild menacing demonstration, grim, invincible determination, or feral combativeness ⟨the treaty was received with a *fierce* outburst of indignation. Jay was burned in effigy by wild mobs; angry orators and editors heaped execration upon Washington —Allan Nevins & H.S.Commager⟩ ⟨the *fiercest* and most treacherous of foes, whose way is to dash upon their prey amid the tempest —H.O.Taylor⟩ ⟨a *fierce* tiger of crime, which could only be taken fighting hard with flashing fang and claw —A. Conan Doyle⟩ FEROCIOUS may indicate a complete insensible lack of mercy, a wild bloodthirstiness ⟨the *ferocious* slaughters instituted . . . by barbarian conquerers —Lewis Mumford⟩ ⟨*ferocious* countenances which had been glaring at the prisoner a moment before, as if with impatience to pluck him out into the streets and kill him —Charles Dickens⟩ FELL may combine notions of direness, malignancy, murderousness, or wasting enervation ⟨murdered by his cruel uncle's mandate *fell* —S.T.Coleridge⟩ ⟨like a famine or plague or aught more *fell* —P.B.Shelley⟩ ⟨we cannot tell what the course of this *fell* war will be as it spreads, remorseless —Sir Winston Churchill⟩ SAVAGE may indicate the wild mercilessness of uncivilized tribal society or an utter, nearly animal lack of compunction or inhibition ⟨the son . . . had been trained in *savage* Sicilian loyalty and lived only to avenge his father —G.K.Chesterton⟩ CRUEL indicates pleasure in or callous indifference to pain inflicted on or anticipated or wished for another ⟨he became haughty, tyrannical, and *cruel.* You must have heard tales in Tahiti of how he punished his men by whipping them till the blood ran down their backs —C.B.Nordhoff & J.N.Hall⟩ ⟨*cruel*, and full of hate and malice and a petty rage —G.D. Brown⟩ INHUMAN indicates a nonhuman insensateness to pain or suffering or, occas., to concern, vexation, or chagrin ⟨there an *inhuman* and uncultured race . . . rushed to war, tore from the mother's womb the unborn child —P.B.Shelley⟩ ⟨there were few *inhuman* barbarities aside from the custom of scalping —*Amer. Guide Series: Maine*⟩ BARBAROUS suggests the cruelty or indifference to suffering and pain of the uncivilized ⟨you have been wantonly attacked by a ruthless and *barbarous* aggressor. Your capital has been bombed, your women and children brutally murdered —Sir Winston Churchill⟩ ⟨he required as a condition of peace that they should sacrifice their children to Baal no longer. But the *barbarous* custom was too inveterate and too agreeable to Semitic modes of thought to be so easily eradicated —J.G.Frazer⟩

²fierce \ˈ"\ *adv* [ME *fers, fiers*, fr. *fers, fiers* adj.] **:** FIERCELY, TERRIBLY, AWFULLY

fierce·ly *adv* [ME *fersly, fiersly*, fr. *fers, fiers* + *-ly*] **:** in a fierce manner

fierc·en \ˈfirsᵊn, -iəs-\ *vi* -ED/-ING/-S **:** to become fierce or fiercer ⟨the storm ~*ed* hour by hour⟩

fierce·ness \-snəs\ *n* -ES [ME *fersnesse, fiersnesse*, fr. *fers, fiers* + *-nesse* -ness] **:** the quality or state of being fierce **:** FEROCITY

fi·eri fa·ci·as \ˌfēərēˈfākē,äs\ *n* [ME, fr. L, cause (it) to be done!] **:** a common-law writ lying for one who has recovered judgment in debt or damages commanding the sheriff that he cause satisfaction to be made of the goods and chattels of the defendant in the sum claimed — compare CAPIAS, ELEGIT, EXECUTION, LEVARI FACIAS

fi·er·i·ly \ˈfī(ə)rəlē, -li\ *adv* **:** in a fiery manner ⟨a book that is ~ opinionated⟩

fi·eri·ness \-rēnəs, -rin-\ *n* -ES **:** the quality or state of being fiery ⟨impressed by the ~ of the man's speech⟩ ⟨there was ~ in her glance⟩

¹fi·ery \ˈfī(ə)rē, -ri\ *adj, often* -ER/-EST [ME *firy, fiery*, fr. *fir, fire, fier* fire + *-y* — more at FIRE] **1 a :** made up of fire ⟨~ tongues playing about the roof of a burning building⟩ **b** (1) **:** BURNING, BLAZING ⟨the ~ interior of a furnace⟩ (2)

heraldry : vomiting flames ⟨a ~ lynx⟩ c : using fire ⟨the ~ experiments of the ancient alchemists⟩ d : liable to catch fire or explode ⟨a ~ vapor⟩ e : containing flammable substances ⟨a ~ mine⟩ 2 a : hot like a fire ⟨savoring the ~ taste of red pepper⟩ b (1) : INFLAMED ⟨a raw, ~ throat⟩ ⟨a ~ boil⟩ (2) : hot and dry and often reddened : feverish and flushed ⟨his forehead was ~ to the touch⟩ c *of a sign of the zodiac* : having a hot and dry complexion 3 a : of the color of fire : RED ⟨a ~ sunset⟩ b : intensely or unnaturally red ⟨~ lips and fingernails⟩ 4 a : full of, charged with, or exuding emotion, spirit, or passion ⟨a ~ speech⟩ ⟨a ~ love affair⟩ ⟨a ~ horse⟩ b : easily provoked : IRRITABLE ⟨a ~ personality⟩ 5 : in such a condition as to cause a bowled ball in cricket to rise high and fast after landing — used of a cricket; compare FAST

2fiery \"\ *adv* : in a fiery manner : FIERILY

fiery azalea *n* : FLAME AZALEA

fiery cross *n* 1 : a cross of wood partly charred and sometimes stained with blood formerly carried from clan to clan as a rallying signal in the Highlands of Scotland — called also *crostarie* 2 : a burning cross; *esp* : a burning cross used as a symbol of the Ku Klux Klan

fiery red *n* : a strong reddish orange that is paler and slightly yellower than poppy, redder and paler than paprika, and redder and darker than fire red — called also *firecracker, minium, red lead;* compare FLAME, FLAME RED

-fies *pres 3d sing of* -FY

fi·es·ta \fē'estə\ *n* -s [Sp, fr. L *festa* — more at FEAST] 1 : FESTIVAL; *specif* : a religious celebration (as in Spain and Latin America) featuring processions and dances of pagan heritage addressed to Christian saints 2 : a deep pink that is bluer, lighter, and stronger than average coral (sense 3b), yellower than begonia, and stronger than sweet william

fiesta flower *n* : a straggling annual Californian herb (*Nemophila aurita*) with deep purple or violet flowers

fi·este·ro \,fēə'ste(,)rō\ *n* -s [MexSp, fr. Sp *fiesta* + *-ero* -er (fr. L *-arius*)] : one of a group of persons among the Cahita, Mayo, and Yaqui responsible for the conduct of a fiesta

fi fa *abbr* fieri facias

1fife \'fīf\ *n* -s [G *pfeife* fife, whistle, pipe, fr. OHG *pfīfa* — more at PIPE] 1 : a small transverse flute with shrill tone used chiefly to accompany the drum 2 : a shrill flute stop in a pipe organ of 1-foot or 2-foot pitch

fife 1, with raised finger holes and gutta-percha embouchure

2fife \"\ *vb* -ED/-ING/-S *vi* : to play a fife ~ *vt* : to play (a tune) on a fife

fif·er \'fīfə(r)\ *n* -s : one that plays a fife

fife rail *n* 1 : a railing around the bulwarks of a quarterdeck 2 : a rail about the mast near the deck to which running rigging is belayed

fife·shire \'fīf,shi(ə)r, -iə, -,shə(r)\ *or* **fife** *adj, usu cap* [fr. *Fifeshire* or *Fife* county, Scotland] : of or from the county of Fife, Scotland : of the kind or style prevalent in Fife

fif·ie \'fīfē\ *n* -s [*Fife* county, Scotland + E *-ie*] : a Scottish fishing lugger with straight stem and sternposts

FIFO \'fī(,)fō\ *abbr* first in, first out

1fif·teen \(')fif¦tēn\ *adj* [ME *fiftene*, fr. OE *fīftēne, fīftȳne, fīftēne* (akin to OHG *finfzehan*, ON *fimmtān*, Goth *fimftaihunim*, dat.), fr. *fīf* five + *-tīene, -tȳne, -tēne* (fr. *tīen, tȳn, tēn* ten) — more at FIVE, TEN] : being one more than 14 in number ⟨~ years⟩ — see NUMBER table; used prepositively to designate various years of the 16th century ⟨the *fifteen-eighties*⟩ ⟨the early *fifteen*-hundreds⟩

2fifteen \"\ *pron, pl in constr* [ME *fiftene*, fr. OE *fīftīene, fīftȳne, fīftēne*, fr. *fīftīene, fīftȳne, fīftēne*, adj.] : 15 countable persons or things not specified but under consideration and being enumerated ⟨~ are here⟩ ⟨~ were found⟩

3fifteen \"\ *n* -s 1 : 10 and five : three times five 2 a : 15 units or objects ⟨a total of ~⟩ b : a group or set of 15 ⟨arranged by ~*s*⟩ 3 : the numerable quantity symbolized by the arabic numerals 15 4 : the 15th in a set or series; *esp* : an article of clothing of the 15th size ⟨wears a ~⟩ 5 : a combination of cards in cribbage whose total value is 15, each such combination counting two points 6 : the first score in a game of tennis — called also *five*

fifteen ball *n* : a pool game using a cue ball and 15 numbered balls racked in order with the highest at the apex of the triangle and in which players are credited with points corresponding to the number on the pocketed ball, the first to score 61 points being the winner

fif·teen·er \-nə(r)\ *n* -s : a line of verse of 15 syllables

fifteen-pounder \¦=,=¦==\ *n* : a gun whose missile weighs 15 pounds

fifteen-spined stickleback \¦=,=¦-=-\ *n* : a large European marine stickleback (*Spinachia spinachia*) with 15 spines

1fif·teenth \(')fif¦tēn(t)th\ *adj* [ME *fiftenthe*, adj. & n., alter. (influenced by *fiftene*) of *fiftethe*, fr. OE *fīftēotha* (akin to ON *fimmtāndi* fifteenth, Goth *fimftataihundin*, dat. sing. neut.), fr. *fīftīene, fīftȳne, fīftēne* + *-otha, -tha* -th] 1 : being number 15 in a countable series ⟨the ~ day⟩ — see NUMBER table 2 : being one of 15 equal parts into which something is divisible ⟨a ~ share of the money⟩

2fifteenth \"\ *n, pl* **fifteenths** \-n(t)s,-n(t)ths\ [ME *fiftenthe*] 1 : number 15 in a countable series ⟨the ~ of the month⟩ 2 : the quotient of a unit divided by 15 : one of 15 equal parts of something ⟨one ~ of the total⟩ 3 : a tax of one fifteenth on personal property that formed a part of a grant to the English king from 1272 to 1624 4 a : a 2-foot stop in a pipe organ b : an interval or compass of a double octave

1fifth \'fif(t)th, 'fift, *rapid or substand* 'fith\ *adj* [ME *fifte, fifthe*, adj. & n., fr. OE *fīfta* (akin to OHG *fimfto, finfto*, ON *fimmti*), fr. *fīf* five + *-ta* (fr. *-otha, -tha* -th) — more at FIVE] 1 : being number five in a countable series ⟨the ~ day⟩ — see NUMBER table 2 : being one of five equal parts into which something is divisible ⟨a ~ share of the money⟩

2fifth \"\ *n, pl* **fifths** \'fif(t)ths, 'fif(t)s, *rapid or substand* 'fiths\ [ME *fifte, fifthe*] 1 : number five in a countable series ⟨the ~ of the month⟩ 2 : the quotient of a unit divided by five : one of five equal parts of something ⟨one ~ of the total⟩ 3 a : the musical interval embracing five diatonic degrees b : the tone at this interval; *specif* : DOMINANT 2b c : the harmonic combination of two tones at this interval 4 : a unit of capacity for liquor equal to one fifth of a U. S. gallon; *also* : a bottle holding this quantity of liquor 5 : QUINTE

3fifth \"\ *adv* [1fifth] 1 : in the fifth place 2 : with four exceptions ⟨the nation's ~ largest city⟩

fifth column *n* [trans. of Sp *quinta columna;* fr. the fact that during the Spanish Civil War rebel sympathizers in Madrid were so called when in 1936 four rebel columns advanced against this city] : a group of secret sympathizers or supporters of an enemy that engage in espionage, sabotage, and other subversive activities within the defense lines or borders of a nation — **fifth columnism** *n* — **fifth columnist** *n*

fifth cranial nerve *or* **fifth nerve** *n* : TRIGEMINAL NERVE

fifth day *n, usu cap F* : THURSDAY — used chiefly by the Friends

fifth estate *n* : a class or group existing in addition to the traditional four ⟨scientists who today make up a *fifth estate*⟩

fifth freedom *n* : the right of an international airline to pick up and deliver at intermediate points along a route

fifth·ly \'fif(t)thlē, 'fiftlē, -li\ *adv* : in the fifth place

fifth monarchy *n* : a universal monarchy supposed to be prophesied in Daniel 2 and to follow the monarchies of the Assyrians, Persians, Greco-Macedonians, and Romans

fifth monarchy man *n, usu cap F & both Ms* : a member of a fanatical sect in England at the time of the Commonwealth who believed that the fifth monarchy during which Christ would reign on earth a thousand years was near at hand and that they must assist to establish it by force

fifth quarter *n* : the parts of a slaughtered animal other than offal that supplement the four quarters (as the giblets in poultry and the head, tail, hide, horns, hoofs, fat, tallow, tongue, heart, and liver in cattle and sheep)

fifth wheel *n* 1 a : a horizontal wheel or segment of a wheel that consists of two parts rotating on each other above the kingbolt above the fore axle of a carriage or wagon and beneath the body and that forms an extended support to prevent tipping b : a coupling in the form of two disks rotating on each other for attaching a vehicle body to the front axle so as to support it in turning c : a similar coupling between tractor and trailer of a semitrailer 2 a : a spare wheel b : a light wheel trailed behind an automobile for measuring speed or distance 3 : one that is superfluous or burdensome ⟨committees without authority to act are *fifth wheels* —F.L.Allen⟩

1fif·ti·eth \'fiftēəth, -tiəth\ *adj* [ME *fiftithe*, adj. & n., fr. OE *fīftigotha* (akin to ON *fimmtugandi*), fr. *fīftig* fifty + *-otha, -tha*, -th] 1 : being number 50 in a countable series ⟨the ~ day⟩ — see NUMBER table 2 : being one of 50 equal parts into which something is divisible ⟨a ~ share⟩

2fiftieth \"\ *n* -s [ME *fiftithe*] 1 : number 50 in a countable series 2 : the quotient of a unit divided by 50 : one of 50 equal parts of something ⟨one ~ of the total⟩

1fif·ty \'fiftē, -ti\ *adj* [ME *fifty*, fr. OE *fīftig*, fr. *fīftig*, n., group of 50, fr. *fīf* five + *-tig* group of ten — more at FIVE, EIGHTY] : being one more than 49 in number ⟨~ years⟩ — see NUMBER table

2fifty \"\ *pron, pl in constr* [ME, fr. *fifty*, adj.] : 50 countable persons or things not specified but under consideration and being enumerated ⟨~ are here⟩ ⟨~ were found⟩

3fifty \"\ *n* -ES [ME] 1 : five tens : twice 25 : 10 fives 2 a : 50 units or objects ⟨a total of ~⟩ b : a group or set of 50 ⟨arranged by *fifties*⟩ 3 a : the numerable quantity symbolized by the arabic numerals 50 b : the letter L 4 : the 50th in a set or series; *esp* : an article of clothing of the 50th size ⟨a ~ is too big⟩ 5 : something having as an essential feature 50 units or members 6 **fifties** *pl* a : the numbers 50 to 59 inclusive ⟨a score in the *fifties*⟩ ⟨low grades in the *fifties*⟩ b : the members of a series or set of successive numbers that end in 50 to 59 inclusive ⟨the *fifties* of the preceding century⟩ ⟨lives in the *fifties* in the next block⟩ c : the portion of a continuum lying between 50 and 60 on a scale of measurement or segmentation ⟨temperatures in the *fifties* tomorrow⟩ ⟨a man in his *fifties*⟩ ⟨dresses selling in the *fifties*⟩ ⟨in the latitude of the *fifties*⟩ 7 a : a fifty-pound note b : a fifty-dollar bill 8 : a 50 caliber gun — usu. written .50

1fifty-eight \¦==¦=\ *adj* : being one more than 57 in number ⟨*fifty-eight* years⟩ — see NUMBER table

2fifty-eight \"\ *pron, pl in constr* : 58 countable persons or things not specified but under consideration and being enumerated ⟨*fifty-eight* are here⟩ ⟨*fifty-eight* were found⟩

3fifty-eight \"\ *n* 1 : eight and 50 : 29 times two 2 a : 58 units or objects ⟨a total of *fifty-eight*⟩ b : a group or set of 58 3 : the numerable quantity symbolized by the arabic numerals 58 4 : the 58th in a set or series

1fifty-eighth \¦==¦=\ *adj* 1 : being number 58 in a countable series ⟨the *fifty-eighth* day⟩ — see NUMBER table 2 : being one of 58 equal parts into which something is divisible ⟨a *fifty-eighth* share of the money⟩

2fifty-eighth \"\ *n* 1 : number 58 in a countable series 2 : the quotient of a unit divided by 58 : one of 58 equal parts of something ⟨one *fifty-eighth* of the total⟩

1fifty-fifth \¦==¦=\ *adj* 1 : being number 55 in a countable series ⟨the *fifty-fifth* day⟩ — see NUMBER table 2 : being one of 55 equal parts into which something is divisible ⟨a *fifty-fifth* share of the money⟩

2fifty-fifth \"\ *n* 1 : number 55 in a countable series 2 : the quotient of a unit divided by 55 : one of 55 equal parts of something ⟨one *fifty-fifth* of the total⟩

1fifty-fifty \¦==¦==\ *adv* : EQUALLY ⟨profits shared *fifty-fifty*⟩

2fifty-fifty \"\ *adj* 1 : shared, assumed, or borne equally (as by two people) ⟨a *fifty-fifty* proposition⟩ 2 : half favorable and half unfavorable ⟨a *fifty-fifty* chance to live⟩ : half pro and half con ⟨a *fifty-fifty* decision⟩

1fifty-first \¦==¦=\ *adj* 1 : being number 51 in a countable series ⟨the *fifty-first* day⟩ — see NUMBER table 2 : being one of 51 equal parts into which something is divisible ⟨a *fifty-first* share of the money⟩

2fifty-first \"\ *n* 1 : number 51 in a countable series 2 : the quotient of a unit divided by 51 : one of 51 equal parts of something ⟨one *fifty-first* of the total⟩

1fifty-five \¦==¦=\ *adj* : being one more than 54 in number ⟨*fifty-five* years⟩ — see NUMBER table

2fifty-five \"\ *pron, pl in constr* : 55 countable persons or things not specified but under consideration and being enumerated ⟨*fifty-five* are here⟩ ⟨*fifty-five* were found⟩

3fifty-five \"\ *n* 1 : five and 50 : five times 11 : 11 fives 2 a : 55 units or objects ⟨a total of *fifty-five*⟩ b : a group or set of 55 3 : the numerable quantity symbolized by the arabic numerals 55 4 : the 55th in a set or series

1fifty-four \¦==¦=\ *adj* : being one more than 53 in number ⟨*fifty-four* years⟩ — see NUMBER table

2fifty-four \"\ *pron, pl in constr* : 54 countable persons or things not specified but under consideration and being enumerated ⟨*fifty-four* are here⟩ ⟨*fifty-four* were found⟩

3fifty-four \"\ *n* 1 : four and 50 : three times 18 : six times nine 2 a : 54 units or objects ⟨a total of *fifty-four*⟩ b : a group or set of 54 3 : the numerable quantity symbolized by the arabic numerals 54 4 : the 54th in a set or series

1fifty-fourth \¦==¦=\ *adj* 1 : being number 54 in a countable series ⟨the *fifty-fourth* day⟩ — see NUMBER table 2 : being one of 54 equal parts into which something is divisible ⟨a *fifty-fourth* share of the money⟩

2fifty-fourth \"\ *n* 1 : number 54 in a countable series 2 : the quotient of a unit divided by 54 : one of 54 equal parts of something ⟨one *fifty-fourth* of the total⟩

1fifty-nine \¦==¦=\ *adj* : being one more than 58 in number ⟨*fifty-nine* years⟩ — see NUMBER table

2fifty-nine \"\ *pron, pl in constr* : 59 countable persons or things not specified but under consideration and being enumerated ⟨*fifty-nine* are here⟩ ⟨*fifty-nine* were found⟩

3fifty-nine \"\ *n* 1 : nine and 50 2 a : 59 units or objects ⟨a total of *fifty-nine*⟩ b : a group or set of 59 3 : the numerable quantity symbolized by the arabic numerals 59 4 : the 59th of a set or series

1fifty-ninth \¦==¦=\ *adj* 1 : being number 59 in a countable series ⟨the *fifty-ninth* day⟩ — see NUMBER table 2 : being one of 59 equal parts into which something is divisible ⟨a *fifty-ninth* share of the money⟩

2fifty-ninth \"\ *n* 1 : number 59 in a countable series 2 : the quotient of a unit divided by 59 : one of 59 equal parts of something ⟨one *fifty-ninth* of the total⟩

1fifty-one \¦==¦=\ *adj* : being one more than 50 in number ⟨*fifty-one* years⟩ — see NUMBER table

2fifty-one \"\ *pron, pl in constr* : 51 countable persons or things not specified but under consideration and being enumerated ⟨*fifty-one* are here⟩ ⟨*fifty-one* were found⟩

3fifty-one \"\ *n* 1 : one and 50 : three times 17 2 a : 51 units or objects ⟨a total of *fifty-one*⟩ b : a group or set of 51 3 : the numerable quantity symbolized by the arabic numerals 51 4 : the 51st in a set or series

1fifty-second \¦==¦=\ *adj* 1 : being number 52 in a countable series ⟨the *fifty-second* day⟩ — see NUMBER table 2 : being one of 52 equal parts into which something is divisible ⟨a *fifty-second* share of the money⟩

2fifty-second \"\ *n* 1 : number 52 in a countable series 2 : the quotient of a unit divided by 52 : one of 52 equal parts of something ⟨one *fifty-second* of the total⟩

1fifty-seven \¦==¦=\ *adj* : being one more than 56 in number ⟨*fifty-seven* years⟩ — see NUMBER table

2fifty-seven \"\ *pron, pl in constr* : 57 countable persons or things not specified but under consideration and being enumerated ⟨*fifty-seven* are here⟩ ⟨*fifty-seven* were found⟩

3fifty-seven \"\ *n* 1 : seven and 50 : three times 19 2 a : 57 units or objects ⟨a total of *fifty-seven*⟩ b : a group or set of 57 3 : the numerable quantity symbolized by the arabic numerals 57 4 : the 57th in a set or series

1fifty-seventh \¦==¦=\ *adj* 1 : being number 57 in a countable series ⟨the *fifty-seventh* day⟩ — see NUMBER table 2 : being one of 57 equal parts into which something is divisible ⟨a *fifty-seventh* share of the money⟩

2fifty-seventh \"\ *n* 1 : number 57 in a countable series 2 : the quotient of a unit divided by 57 : one of 57 equal parts of something ⟨one *fifty-seventh* of the total⟩

1fifty-six \¦==¦=\ *adj* : being one more than 55 in number ⟨*fifty-six* years⟩ — see NUMBER table

2fifty-six \"\ *pron, pl in constr* : 56 countable persons or things not specified but under consideration and being enumerated ⟨*fifty-six* are here⟩ ⟨*fifty-six* were found⟩

3fifty-six \"\ *n* 1 : six and 50 : four times 14 : seven times eight 2 a : 56 units or objects ⟨a total of *fifty-six*⟩ b : a group or set of 56 3 : the numerable quantity symbolized by the arabic numerals 56 4 : the 56th in a set or series

1fifty-sixth \¦==¦=\ *adj* 1 : being number 56 in a countable series ⟨the *fifty-sixth* day⟩ — see NUMBER table 2 : being one of 56 equal parts into which something is divisible ⟨a *fifty-sixth* share of the money⟩

2fifty-sixth \"\ *n* 1 : number 56 in a countable series 2 : the quotient of a unit divided by 56 : one of 56 equal parts of something ⟨one *fifty-sixth* of the total⟩

1fifty-third \¦==¦=\ *adj* 1 : being number 53 in a countable series ⟨the *fifty-third* day⟩ — see NUMBER table 2 : being one of 53 equal parts into which something is divisible ⟨a *fifty-third* share of the money⟩

2fifty-third \"\ *n* 1 : number 53 in a countable series 2 : the quotient of a unit divided by 53 : one of 53 equal parts of something ⟨one *fifty-third* of the total⟩

1fifty-three \¦==¦=\ *adj* : being one more than 52 in number ⟨*fifty-three* years⟩ — see NUMBER table

2fifty-three \"\ *pron, pl in constr* : 53 countable persons or things not specified but under consideration and being enumerated ⟨*fifty-three* are here⟩ ⟨*fifty-three* were found⟩

3fifty-three \"\ *n* 1 : three and 50 2 a : 53 units or objects ⟨a total of *fifty-three*⟩ b : a group or set of 53 3 : the numerable quantity symbolized by the arabic numerals 53 4 : the 53d in a set or series

1fifty-two \¦==¦=\ *adj* : being one more than 51 in number ⟨*fifty-two* years⟩ — see NUMBER table

2fifty-two \"\ *pron, pl in constr* : 52 countable persons or things not specified but under consideration and being enumerated ⟨*fifty-two* are here⟩ ⟨*fifty-two* were found⟩

3fifty-two \"\ *n* 1 : two and fifty : four times 13 2 a : 52 units or objects ⟨a total of *fifty-two*⟩ b : a group or set of 52 3 : the numerable quantity symbolized by the arabic numerals 52 4 : the 52d in a set or series

1fig \'fig\ *n* -s [ME *fige, figue*, fr. OF *fige, figue*, fr. OProv *figa*, fr. (assumed) VL *fica*, fr. L *ficus* fig tree, fig, of non-IE origin; akin to the source of Gk *sykon* fig, Arm *t'uz*] 1 a : an oblong to pear-shaped or nearly globose edible fruit of warm regions that is greenish, yellowish to orange, or purple when ripe, that has a thick soft skin enclosing a sweet pulp full of tiny seeds, and that is available commercially chiefly dried — see COMMON FIG, SMYRNA FIG, SYCONIUM b *obs* : poison given in a fig 2 *or* **fig tree** : a tree of the genus *Ficus; usu* : any of the cultivated or escaped trees derived from a tree (*F. carica*) native to southwestern Asia but extensively grown in several varieties in warm regions of the New and Old Worlds for the edible figs that are their fruit — see CAPRIFIG 3 a *Austral* : any of several woody plants that resemble fig trees or produce fruits resembling figs: as (1) : BLUEBERRY ASH (2) : a slender twining xerophytic vine (*Marsdenia australis*) that produces pear-shaped fruits sometimes eaten by the aborigines b : FIG BANANA c : COCHINEAL FIG d *dial chiefly Eng* : RAISIN 4 : something resembling the fruit of the fig tree (as piles or a warty excrescence on the frog of a horse's hoof) 5 : a small piece of tobacco 6 a [MF *figue* (in *faire la figue* make a fig), fr. It *fica* (in *far la fica*), fr. *fica* fig, vulva, fr. (assumed) VL *fica* fig] : a gesture or sign of contempt (as thrusting a thumb between two fingers) b : the least bit : the merest trifle : PARTICLE ⟨he doesn't give a ~ for his appearance⟩ ⟨who cares a ~ for widows swindled in the . . . real-estate boom —Lee Rogow⟩ — often used interjectionally to express scorn or contempt ⟨a ~ for housework! she said to herself —Glenway Wescott⟩

2fig \"\ *vt* **figged; figged; figging; figs** *obs* : to insult by giving the sign of the fig to

3fig \"\ *vi* [perh. alter. of ME *fiken* — more at FIKE] *now dial Eng* : to move about restlessly : pace back and forth

4fig \"\ *vt* **figged; figged; figging; figs** [origin unknown] 1 : to dress or adorn — used with *out* or *up* ⟨a richly *figged* out dowager⟩ 2 : to put ginger or pepper in the anus or vagina of (a horse) to stimulate action or improve carriage

5fig \"\ *n* -s 1 : DRESS, ARRAY ⟨the appealing figure of a young woman in dazzling royal full ~ —Mollie Panter-Downes⟩ 2 : CONDITION, FORM ⟨in fine ~ for a race⟩

fig *abbr* 1 figurative 2 figure

figa·ro sauce \'figə,rō-, 'feg\ *n* [prob. after *Figaro*, the hero of *Le Barbier de Séville* (1775) and *Le Mariage de Figaro* (1784), comedies by P. A. Caron de Beaumarchais †1799 Fr. playwright] : hollandaise sauce with tomato puree added

figary *var of* FEGARY

fig banana *n* : a small plump tropical American banana having a flavor somewhat like a fig

fig bar *n* 1 : a bar-shaped form of pressed figs 2 : a bar-shaped cookie with a fig filling

fig-bird \'=,=\ *n* : any of several largely greenish yellow Australian orioles (genus *Sphecotheres*) that feed chiefly on figs and other fruits

figeater \'=,==\ *n* 1 : GREEN JUNE BEETLE 2 : BECCAFICO

figent *adj* [alter. of *fidge* + *-ent*] *obs* : FIDGETY, VOLATILE

fig family *n* : MORACEAE

fig faun *n* : one of a class of rural deities or monsters supposed to live on figs and referred to in Jer 50 : 39 (DV)

figged \'figd\ *adj* 1 *dial chiefly Eng* : made with figs or raisins ⟨a ~ pudding⟩ 2 *dial chiefly Eng* : SPECKLED, SPOTTED

fig·ging \'figiŋ\ *n* -s : a granular appearance in soft soap that resembles the seeds of a fig, that is held to be due to the crystallization of a harder soap, and that is sometimes considered an indication of superior quality

fig·gy \'figē\ *adj* -ER/-EST : containing or resembling figs

1fight \'fīt, *usu* -īd.+V\ *vb* **fought** \'fȯt, *usu* -ȯd.+V\ *or dial* **fit** \'fit, *usu* -id.+V\ *or* **fout** \'fōt, 'fau̇, *usu* |d.+V\ **fought** *or dial* **fit** *or* **fought·en** \'fȯtᵊn\ *or* **fout; fighting; fights** [ME *fighten*, fr. OE *feohtan;* akin to OFris *fiuchta* to fight, OS & OHG *fehtan* to fight, L *pectere* to comb — more at FEE] *vi* 1 a : to contend physically for victory with vigor, fierceness, and determination ⟨*fought* on the ridge until nightfall⟩ : strive to overcome or destroy a person, animal, or thing esp. by blows or weapons — often used with *against* or *with* ⟨brother ~*ing* against brother⟩ b : to engage in prize-fighting esp. as a profession or career : BOX 2 a : to put forth a grim, determined, or dogged effort (as for the achievement of a goal or purpose) — often used with *for* ⟨~ for freedom⟩ or *to* ⟨~ to bring about some needed changes⟩ b *of a Salvationist* : to war aggressively against evil and for the cause of God ~ *vt* 1 a (1) : to contend against in or as if in battle or physical combat esp. with determination to cease only upon achieving victory or sustaining defeat ⟨~ the invaders of his homeland⟩ (2) : to box against in the prize ring ⟨*fought* several strong challengers⟩ b (1) : to attempt to prevent the success, fruition, or effectiveness of ⟨the company *fought* the strike for months⟩ (2) : to oppose the passage, development, or appearance of ⟨the northern senators *fought* the bill bitterly⟩ ⟨~ a bad habit⟩ 2 a : to carry on : WAGE ⟨~ a war⟩ ⟨~ a battle⟩ b : to take part in (as a boxing match) ⟨*fought* a dozen professional matches before he was 20 years old⟩ 3 a : to struggle with the inconvenience, discomfort, or hardship of ⟨~ a leaky roof all year⟩ b : to struggle to endure or surmount — used with *out* ⟨a ship ~*ing* out a storm at sea⟩ 4 a : to win or gain by struggle ⟨*fought* his way through the underbrush⟩ b : to resolve or surmount by struggle — used with *out* ⟨the two men *fought* out their differences in court⟩ or *down* ⟨*fought* down his fear⟩ 5 a (1) : to manage (a ship) in a battle or storm (2) : to cause to fight or contend ⟨~ cocks⟩ b : to handle, treat, or manage in an unnecessarily rough or overly deliberate manner ⟨she always *fought* the shift and could wear a transmission out in six months⟩ 6 : to become unnecessarily or unnaturally difficult for ⟨the minute your work starts ~*ing* you, give up —Marian Corey⟩ **syn** see CONTEND, CONTEST — **fight shy of** : to avoid meeting : refuse to face up to

2fight \"\ *n* -s [ME, fr. OE *feoht;* akin to OFris *fiucht* fight, OHG *gifeht;* derivative fr. the root of OE *feohtan* to fight] 1 *archaic* : the act of fighting 2 a : a hostile encounter between opposing forces or individuals : BATTLE, COMBAT b : a boxing match c : a verbal disagreement 3 : a struggle to achieve a goal or an objective ⟨an uphill ~ for reelection⟩ 4 *obs* : a screen put up to protect combatants on a naval vessel 5 : strength or disposition for fighting : PUGNACITY ⟨he still has a lot of ~ in him⟩ **syn** see CONTEST

fight·able \'fīd·əbəl, -ītə-\ *adj* **1 :** fit for fighting ⟨a ~ ship⟩ **2 :** eager to fight ⟨an opponent still excited and ~⟩
fight·er \'fīd·ə(r), -ītə-\ *n* -s [ME, fr. OE *feohtere*, fr. *feohtan* + *-ere* -er] **:** one that fights: as **a** (1) **:** WARRIOR, SOLDIER (2) **:** a pugnacious or game individual (3) **:** PRIZEFIGHTER, BOXER **b** *or* **fighter plane :** a military or naval airplane of high speed, high rate of climb, excellent maneuverability, and armament designed to destroy enemy aircraft in the air
fighter-bomber \'⸗⸗'⸗⸗\ *n* **:** a fighter aircraft fitted to carry bombs, rockets, or napalm tanks in addition to its normal armament and used to support friendly ground troops and to cut enemy supply lines so as to isolate the battlefield and also to engage enemy aircraft
fighter-interceptor \'⸗⸗,⸗⸗'⸗⸗\ *n* **:** a fighter aircraft designed to intercept and destroy enemy aircraft in the air
fighting *adj* [ME, fr. pres. part. of *fighten* to fight] **1 :** designed or intended to fight ⟨a ~ ship⟩ **2 a :** fit to fight ⟨a boxer in ~ condition⟩ **b :** that qualifies to fight ⟨a boxer at ~ weight⟩ **3 a** (1) **:** prone to fight **:** WARLIKE ⟨a ~ tribe⟩ (2) **:** liable to provoke a fight ⟨those are ~ words⟩ **b :** showing a readiness to fight **:** GAME, PLUCKY ⟨a ~ spirit⟩ — **fight·ing·ly** *adv*
fighting chair *n* **:** a chair from which a salt-water angler plays a hooked fish
fighting chance *n* **:** a chance that may be realized by a struggle **:** a possible but not easy chance ⟨the patient had a *fighting chance* to live⟩
fighting cock *n* **:** GAMECOCK
fighting crab *n* **:** FIDDLER CRAB
fighting fish *n* **:** BETTA
fighting top *n* **:** the top (sense 4b) on a warship
fight-off \'⸗,⸗\ *n* -s [²*fight* + *-off* (as in *play-off*)] **:** a prizefight to decide a tie or to determine a single winner in a class — compare PLAY-OFF
fights *pres 3d sing of* FIGHT, *pl of* FIGHT
fight talk *n* **:** a pregame or intermission talk made (as by a football coach) to inspire the players and spur them to their best possible efforts **:** PEP TALK
fig leaf *n* **1 :** the leaf of a fig tree **2 :** something that conceals, masks, or camouflages usu. inadequately, prudishly, or dishonestly ⟨the rhetorical *fig leaves* by which the pursuit of wealth and power hid itself from the public gaze —H.J.Laski⟩
fig marigold *n* **:** any of several plants of the genus *Mesembryanthemum* cultivated for their showy white or pink flowers — see AIZOACEAE
fig·ment \'figmənt\ *n* -s [ME, fr. L *figmentum*, fr. *fig-* (stem of *fingere* to shape, form, devise, feign) + *-mentum* -ment — more at DOUGH] **:** something made up, fabricated, or contrived ⟨uses this dim ~ of the chronicles as an excuse to present the doubts and indecisions of a humanistic age —Herbert Read⟩ ⟨a ~ of an author's imagination⟩ **syn** see FICTION
fig mite *n* **:** a minute blister mite (*Aceria ficus*) that feeds on the leaves of figs causing rusting
fig moth *n* **:** ALMOND MOTH
Fig New·tons \fig'n(y)üt°nz\ *trademark* — used for bar-shaped cookies having fig filling
figo *n* -s [modif. of OSp or Pg *figa* fig, vulva, fr. (assumed) VL *fica* fig — more at FIG] *obs* **:** FICO
fig parrot *n* **:** LORILET
figpecker \'⸗,⸗⸗\ *n* **:** BECCAFICO
fig rust *n* **:** a rust disease of figs that is troublesome in the southeastern U.S. and is caused by a fungus (*Physopella fici*)
figs *pl of* FIG, *pres 3d sing of* FIG
fig scale *n* **:** an elongate armored scale (*Lepidosaphes ficus*) that is related to the typical oystershell scale and that feeds on fig trees
figshell \'⸗,⸗\ *n* **1 :** a gastropod mollusk of the family Ficidae that has a fig-shaped shell; *also* **:** the shell of one of these mollusks **2 :** any of several mollusks of the family Tonnidae
fig soap *n* **:** a soft soap showing figging
fig sunday *n, usu cap F&S* [so called fr. the custom of eating figs on this day] **:** PALM SUNDAY
fig tree *n* **:** ¹FIG 2
fig·ur·able \'fig(y)ərəbəl\ *adj* **1 :** capable of being figured **2 :** capable of being brought to a fixed form or shape
fig·ur·al \-rəl\ *adj* [ME, fr. LL *figuralis*, fr. L *figura* figure + *-alis* -al — more at FIGURE] **1** *obs* **:** FIGURATIVE 1 **2 :** FIGURATIVE 2 **3 :** FIGURATE 2 **4 :** relating to or consisting wholly or for the most part of human or animal figures ⟨a ~ composition⟩ ⟨finely etched with bands of floral and ~ subjects⟩ — **fig·ur·al·ly** \-rəlē\ *adv*
fig·u·rant \'figyə,ränt, -räⁿ-,rant, ,⸗⸗'⸗; 'figyərənt\ *n* -s [F *figurant*, fr. pres. part. of *figurer* to figure, represent, appear — more at FIGURE] **1 :** a member of a dance troupe who dances only in groups or figures **2 :** one that figures in a scene without speaking or without taking a prominent part
fig·u·rante \'figyə,ränt, -rant, ,⸗⸗'⸗; 'figyərənt\ *n* -s [F, fem. of *figurant*] **:** a female figurant; *esp* **:** a member of a ballet troupe
fig·u·rate \'figyərə̇t, -,rāt\ *adj* [L *figuratus*, past part. of *figurare* to form — more at FIGURE] **1 :** relating to, composed of, or suggestive of a figure **2 :** involving passing discords by the freer melodic movement of one or more voice parts **:** FLORID ⟨~ counterpoint⟩ — contrasted with *simple* — **fig·u·rate·ly** *adv*
figurate number *n* **:** any of a progression of numbers formed from an arithmetical progression in which the first term is 1 and the difference an integer by taking the first term, and the sums of the first two, first three, first four, and so on as the successive terms of a new progression and by operating on this in the same way, and so on, the numbers in each sequence being such that points representing them are capable of arrangement in geometrical figures
fig·u·ra·tion \,figyə'rāshən\ *n* -s [ME *figuracioun*, fr. MF or L; MF *figuration*, fr. L *figuration-, figuratio*, fr. *figuratus* (past part. of *figurare* to figure) + *-ion-, -io* -ion — more at FIGURE] **1 :** the act or action of creating or providing a figure ⟨Dante's unique ~ of the underworld⟩ **2 :** FORM, SHAPE, OUTLINE ⟨he studied words and ~s on pieces of money —Carl Sandburg⟩ **3 :** the act or action of representation in figures and shapes **:** emblematic or typical representation; *also* **:** the result of such an act or action ⟨the new cubism was explained as a synthesis of colored ~s of objects —Janet Flanner⟩ **4 :** the ornamental treatment of a musical passage by the use of decorative and usu. repetitive figures specif. in variations of a theme ⟨brilliant string ~s first for violins and then for cellos and basses —Cecil Gray⟩
fig·u·ra·tive \'fig(y)ərəd·iv, -grə|, |tiv\ *adj* [ME, fr. MF or LL; MF *figuratif*, fr. LL *figurativus*, fr. L *figuratus* + *-ivus* -ive] **1 :** representing or represented by a figure or resemblance ⟨the ~ art of the humanistic tradition —Herbert Read⟩ **2 :** transferred in sense from literal or plain to abstract or hypothetical (as by the expression of one thing in terms of another with which it can be regarded as analogous) **:** METAPHORICAL ⟨~ language⟩ ⟨in a ~ sense, civilization marches up and down —Lewis Mumford⟩ **3 :** characterized by figures of speech or elaborate expression ⟨a ~ description⟩ ⟨a ~ author⟩ — **fig·u·ra·tive·ly** \|d·ə̇vlē, |tə̇v-, -li; 'figər|\ *adv* — **fig·u·ra·tive·ness** \-ivnə̇s\ *n* -ES
¹fig·ure \'figyə(r), *usual in Brit speech & frequent in US speech but regarded by many in the US as substand* -gə(r); *"figur-" followed by a vowel other than "e" is usually or often pronounced with y in Brit speech*\ *n* -s [ME, fr. OF, fr. L *figura*, fr. *fig-* (stem of *fingere* to shape, form, devise, feign) + *-ura* -ure — more at DOUGH] **1 a :** a number symbol (as one of the arabic numerals) **:** NUMERAL, DIGIT **b figures** *pl* **:** figures used in arithmetical calculating ⟨~s can be made to prove anything⟩ **:** arithmetical calculations ⟨he is good at ~s⟩ **c :** a written or printed character (as a letter, mathematical symbol, or cipher) **d :** value esp. as expressed in numbers **:** PRICE, AMOUNT, SUM ⟨the house sold at a low ~⟩ **e :** a numeral of a continuo in music **2 a :** a body apparent chiefly in outline **:** an object significant or noticeable only in its form ⟨a ~ moving slowly in the dusk⟩ **b :** a surface shape in a work of art visually appreciable and separable from its surroundings ⟨*figure*-ground relationship⟩ **c :** the part of a total stimulus situation which is most clearly perceived by an observer and to which he responds **3 a :** the representation of a form (as by drawing, painting, modeling, carving, embroidering); *specif* **:** a representation of the human form esp. in the nude **b :** a diagram or pictorial illustration (as a linecut or photoreproduction) augmenting text matter (as of a book) — abbr. *fig.* **4 :** a person, thing, or action conceived of as analogous to another person, thing, or action of which it is a type or representative ⟨Adam . . . who is the ~ of him that was to come —Rom 5:14 (AV)⟩ **5 :** a diagram made to represent any definite combination of geometric elements **6 :** an imagined form **:** PHANTASM ⟨a ~ of idle dreaming⟩ **7 a :** a figure of speech: as (1) **:** METAPHOR (2) **:** SIMILE **b :** an intentional deviation from the ordinary form or syntactical relation of words (as in syncope) **8 a :** the two-dimensional proportions of a body or object ⟨the ~ of a ship on the horizon⟩ **b :** the shape of the human body ⟨a woman with a good ~⟩ **9 :** a diagram or scheme representing the heavens at a given moment (as at the moment of birth) **:** HOROSCOPE **10 :** the form of a syllogism with respect to the relative position of the middle term — compare MOOD **11 a :** a pattern or design (as in nature or in a cloth, paper, or other manufactured article) wrought out often repetitively in systematic arrangement ⟨the beautiful ~s of crystals⟩ ⟨a polka-dot ~⟩ **b :** the pattern produced on a wood surface by irregular coloration and by sawing through growth rings, knots, burls, and other deviations from regular grain; *esp* **:** any such wood surface of decorative value **12 a :** consequence in station or mode of living **:** RANK, GRANDEUR ⟨a person of ~⟩ **b :** conspicuous part or appearance **:** impressive effect — often used with *cut* or *make* ⟨the couple cut quite a ~⟩ **c :** appearance made or impression produced ⟨a person who always presented a sorry ~⟩ **13 a :** a series of movements that form one unit of a dance (as bowing to partners in a square dance) **b :** an outline representation of a form traced by means of a series of evolutions (as with skates on an ice surface or by an airplane in the air) **14 :** a prominent personality **:** PERSONAGE ⟨whether people are impressed with you as a ~ or a person —Anthony Perkins⟩ **15 :** a short coherent group of notes or tones or chords constituting a germ which by varied repetition and association with other figures may grow into a phrase, theme, or accompaniment or entire musical composition — compare MOTIVE **syn** see FORM, NUMBER

THE FOUR SYLLOGISTIC FIGURES*

S=SUBJECT M=MIDDLE TERM P=PREDICATE

(1)	(2)	(3)	(4)
M is P	P is M	M is P	P is M
S is M	S is M	M is S	M is S
∴ S is P	∴ S is P	∴ S is P	∴ S is P

*The first three figures were formulated by Aristotle, the fourth reputedly by Galen

²figure \"\ *vb* **figured; figured; figuring** \-gyəriŋ,-g(ə)riŋ\ **figures** [ME *figuren*, fr. MF *figurer*, fr. L *figurare*, fr. *figura*] *vt* **1 a :** to represent by or as if by a figure **:** PORTRAY ⟨an emblem wherein the apostles were *figured*⟩ **b** *archaic* **:** to represent or express by a metaphor **:** SYMBOLIZE **c** *obs* **:** FORESHADOW **2 a :** to adorn or embellish with a pattern or design ⟨*figured* cloth⟩ **b** (1) **:** to write figures over or under (the bass) in order to indicate the accompanying chords of a musical composition (2) **:** to embellish in music with passing notes or figures **3 a :** to indicate or represent by numerals ⟨water depth *figured* along a wharf piling⟩ **b :** to provide with numerals ⟨a watch dial *figured* in luminescent green⟩ **4 :** to give the requisite shape to (as a mirror, lens, or prism) **5 a** (1) **:** COMPUTE, RECKON ⟨~ expenses⟩; *specif* **:** ADD — usu. used with *up* ⟨~ up an account⟩ (2) **:** to determine or ascertain — usu. used with *out* ⟨~ a way out of a difficulty⟩ **b** (1) **:** SOLVE — usu. used with *out* ⟨~ a problem out⟩ (2) **:** CONCLUDE, DECIDE ⟨he *figured* there was no use in further effort⟩ (3) *slang* **:** to perceive the true makeup of **:** UNDERSTAND ⟨he *figured* the whole scheme right away⟩ **6 a :** REGARD, CONSIDER ⟨~ himself a good candidate⟩ **b :** THINK, ASSUME ~ *vi* **1 :** to make a figure **:** be or appear important ⟨the vice-president really *figured* in the company⟩ **2 :** to perform a figure in dancing **3 :** COMPUTE, CALCULATE ⟨a carpenter *figuring* on a board with a stub of pencil⟩ **4** *slang* **:** to seem rational, normal, or expected **:** be understandable ⟨sure, that ~*s*⟩ — **figure on 1 :** to take into consideration (as in planning or reckoning) ⟨*figuring on* $50 a month extra income⟩ **2 :** to rely on ⟨a person you can always *figure on* to pay his bills⟩ **3 :** PLAN ⟨I *figure on* going over to town to buy us some stores —Helen Eustis⟩
figure caster *n, obs* **:** ASTROLOGER
figured *adj* [ME, fr. past part. of *figuren*] **1 :** REPRESENTED, PORTRAYED ⟨a lion ~ on a coin⟩ **2 :** adorned with, formed into, or marked with a figure ⟨~ muslin⟩ **3 :** FIGURATIVE ⟨~ language⟩ **4 a :** FIGURATE 2 **b :** indicated in music by figures **5 :** expressed in logic in the form of a figure ⟨a ~ syllogism⟩
figured bass *n* **:** CONTINUO; *esp* **:** the system or practice of indicating harmonic progression by numerals placed under the bass notes
figured glass *n* **:** sheet glass that is rolled with an intaglio figure or pattern on one side and that has powerful light-diffusing properties but is not transparent
figure eight *also* **figure of eight** *n* **:** something felt to resemble the arabic numeral eight in form or shape: as **a :** a small stopper knot **b :** a stitch used in embroidery **c :** a weave used in basketry **d :** a dance pattern; *esp* **:** a square-dance figure in which a couple passes between the partners of an adjacent couple and around each **e :** a figure executed by a skater in any of several prescribed ways

figure eight a

figure-four scissors *n* **:** a wrestling hold secured from a rear position by wrapping one leg around the opponent's waist and hooking the foot of this leg beneath the knee of the holder's other leg
figure-four trap *n* **:** a trap in which the trigger and support are fixed in the shape of the figure four and which when sprung causes a box or heavy lid to fall upon the game
figurehead \'⸗⸗,⸗\ *n* **1 :** the figure, statue, or bust on the bow of a ship at the stemhead **2 :** a nominal but not real head or chief; *esp* **:** one who allows his name to be used to give standing to enterprises in which he has no responsible interest or duties
figure in *vt* **1 :** to include esp. in a reckoning ⟨forgetting to *figure in* occasional expenses in a budget⟩ **2 :** to be a part of **:** be implicated in ⟨persons who *figured in* a robbery⟩
fig·ure·less \'fig(y)ə(r)lə̇s\ *adj* **:** lacking or devoid of a figure **:** SHAPELESS
figure-of-eight bandage *n* **:** a bandage in which the successive turns cross each other as in the figure eight — see BANDAGE illustration

figurehead 1

figure of merit : a numerical quantity based on one or more characteristics (as of a device or solution) under specified conditions and used for indicating comparative efficiency or effectiveness; *specif* **:** the current in amperes that must flow through a galvanometer to produce a deflection of one scale division
figure of speech : an expression (as a metaphor or euphemism) that substitutes a variation in point of view by which one thing or notion is referred to as if it were different in some way (as in identity, degree, shape) from what it actually is or seems to be but so related that the expression successfully implies an intended meaning or effect either slightly or greatly different from what is literally said (as "the apple of my eye", "forever chasing rainbows", "she didn't go to the party because she had nothing to wear", "a pretty pickle")
figure of the earth : the precise geometric shape of the planet — compare GEOID
fig·ur·er \'fig(y)ərə(r)\ *n* -s **:** one that figures; *specif* **:** a molder of figures for pottery
figures *pl of* FIGURE, *pres 3d sing of* FIGURE
figure skate *n* **:** a skate used for figure skating and having a hollow-ground blade slightly curved from heel to toe with a row of jagged points on the forepart of the blade

figure skate

figure skating *n* **:** skating in which the skater describes or outlines prescribed figures
figure stone *n* **:** AGALMATOLITE
fig·u·rine \,fig(y)ə'rēn\ *n* -s [F, fr. It *figurina*, dim. of *figura* figure, fr. L — more at FIGURE] **:** a small carved or molded figure; *esp* **:** a statuette in terracotta or similar material that is often adorned with painting or gilding and that is found in ancient tombs and ruins — compare TANAGRA
figuring *pres part of* FIGURE
figurist *n* -s *obs* **:** one that believes in the figurative presence of Christ in the Eucharist
fig wasp *n* **:** a minute insect (*Blastophaga psenes*) of the family Agaontidae that breeds in the caprifig and is important as the agent in the process of caprification; *broadly* **:** an insect of the family Agaontidae
fig wax *n* **:** GONDANG WAX
figwort \'⸗,⸗\ *n* **:** a plant of the family Scrophulariaceae esp. of the genus *Scrophularia* **:** PILEWORT 2
figwort family *n* **:** SCROPHULARIACEAE
¹fi·ji \'fē(,)jē, -ji, *chiefly Brit* (')fē'jē\ *n, pl* **fiji** *or* **fijis** *usu cap* [Fiji *Viti*] **1 a :** a Melanesian people of the Fiji islands **b :** a member of this people **2 :** the Austronesian language of the Fiji people
²fiji \"\ *adj, usu cap* **:** FIJIAN
¹fi·ji·an \'fē(,)jēən, -jiən, *chiefly Brit* (')fē'jēən\ *adj, usu cap* [*Fiji* islands, southwest Pacific + E *-an*] **1 :** of or relating to the Fiji islands **2 :** of or relating to the Fijian people **3 :** of or relating to the Fijian language
²fijian \"\ *n* -s *cap* **:** FIJI
fiji disease *n, usu cap F* **:** a virus disease of sugarcane first reported from the Fiji islands and characterized by elongated white to brown swellings on the underside of the leaves followed by stunting and death
¹fike \'fīk\ *vb* -ED/-ING/-S [ME *fiken*, prob. of Scand origin; akin to ON *fīkjask* to desire eagerly, *fīkenn* eager, Norw *fika* to strive, hurry, Dan *fige*; akin to OE *fācian* to try to obtain, to get] *vi* **1** *dial Brit* **:** to move restlessly **:** FIDGET **2** *dial Brit* **:** WORRY, FUSS ⟨don't ~ about it⟩ **3** *dial Brit* **:** to bustle about **:** create a fuss over nothing **~** *vt, chiefly Scot* **:** to bring pain to **:** HURT
²fike \"\ *n* -s **1** *dial Brit* **:** FIDGET, WORRY **2** *dial Brit* **:** a passing fancy **:** FAD, WHIM
³fike *var of* FYKE
fik·ery \'fīk(ə)ri\ *n* -ES *chiefly Scot* **:** FUSSINESS
fik·ie \'fīkē\ *adj* **1** *chiefly Scot* **:** FIDGETY, RESTLESS **2** *chiefly Scot* **:** tricky and troublesome ⟨a ~ task⟩ **3** *chiefly Scot* **:** elaborate and decorative ⟨a ~ gown⟩
fil \'fil\ *n* -s [back-formation from *fils* (taken as pl.)] **:** a coin in the currency of Iraq equal to $1/1000$ dinar
fil *abbr* **1** filament **2** fillet **3** fillister **4** filter
fila *pl of* FILUM
filabeg *var of* FILLEBEG
fi·la·go \fə'lā(,)gō, -lä(-\ *n* [NL, fr. ML, a plant, prob. cudweed, fr. L *filum* thread + *-ago* (as in *plantago* plantain) — more at FILE, PLANTAIN] **1** *cap* **:** a genus of small woolly herbs (family Compositae) with entire leaves and small flower heads in capitate clusters **2** -s **:** any plant of the genus *Filago* — see COTTON ROSE
filagree *var of* FILIGREE
fil·a·ment \'filəmənt\ *n* -s [MF, fr. ML *filamentum*, fr. LL *filare* to spin + L *-mentum* -ment — more at FILE] **:** a long thin flexible object that has a small cross section **:** a fiber of great or indefinite length: as **a** (1) **:** the fine tenuous material of a spider web (2) **:** one of the two continuous cores of the fiber of silk; *also* **:** the whole fiber (3) **:** a single continuous man-made fiber produced from a liquid bath (as by extrusion through a small orifice) and used either in the form of a monofilament or in groups for textile yarns with little or no twist or for cordage — often distinguished from *staple* (4) **:** a slender barb of a down feather **b** (1) **:** a metal wire drawn very fine ⟨tungsten ~s⟩ (2) **:** a fine conductor (as of carbon or metal) that is rendered incandescent by the passage of an electric current; *specif* **:** a cathode in the form of a metal wire in an electron tube heated by current passing through — see INCANDESCENT LAMP illustration **c** (1) **:** a thin and fine elongated constituent part of a gill (2) **:** an elongated thin series of cells attached one to another or a very long cylindrical single cell (as of certain algae, fungi, and bacteria) **d :** the anther-bearing stalk of a stamen — see FLOWER illustration **e :** a body in mathematics whose transverse dimensions are negligible compared with its length
fil·a·men·ta·ry \,filə'mentərē, -n·trē, -ri\ *adj* **:** having the characteristics of a filament **:** formed by or consisting of filaments ⟨~ crystals⟩ ⟨a ~ structure⟩
filament battery *n* **:** A BATTERY
fil·a·ment·ed \'filə mentə̇d\ *adj* **:** having or provided with one or more filaments
filament lamp *n* **:** a lamp containing a filament heated to incandescence
fil·a·men·tous \,filə'mentəs\ *also* **fil·a·men·tose** \,⸗⸗'men-,tōs, '⸗⸗mən-\ *adj* [*filamentous* fr. F *filamenteux*, fr. MF, fr. *filament* + *-eux* -ous; *filamentose* fr. *filament* + *-ose*] **:** resembling a filament **:** composed of filaments **:** THREADY ⟨~ algae⟩ ⟨~ fibers⟩
¹fil-american \'fil+\ *adj, usu cap* [*Filipino* + *American*] **:** being Filamerican ⟨a *Filamerican* soldier⟩ **:** consisting of Filamericans ⟨the *Filamerican* troops⟩
²filamerican \"\ *n, cap* **:** a Filipino with sympathetic or loyal feelings toward America
fi·lan·der \fə'landə(r)\ *n* -s [D, after Kornelis *Philander* de Bruyn †1726? Dutch traveler] **:** a kangaroo (*Macropus brunii*) native to the Aru islands
fi·la·ni \fə'länē\ *or* **fil·la·nin** \-nən\ *n, pl* **filani** *or* **filanis** *or* **fillanin** *or* **fillanins** *usu cap* **:** FULA
fi·lao \'fēlaů, -lä(,)ō\ *n* -s [Sp, fr. Malagasy] **:** a beefwood (*Casuarina equisetifolia*) with very pendulous branches
fi·lar \'fīlə(r)\ *adj* [L *filum* thread + E *-ar* — more at FILE] **:** of or relating to a thread or line; *esp* **:** possessing threads across the field of view ⟨a ~ eyepiece⟩ ⟨a ~ microscope⟩
fil·a·ree \'filə,rē, ,⸗⸗'⸗\ *or* **fil·a·ria** \,⸗⸗'rēə\ *n* -s [modif. of AmerSp *alfilerillo* — more at ALFILARIA] **:** ALFILARIA
fi·lar·ia \fə'la(a)rēə\ *n* [NL, fr. L *filum* + NL *-aria*] **1** *pl* **fi·lar·i·ae** \-ē,ē, -,ī\ **:** any of an important group of slender filamentous nematodes that as adults are parasites in the blood or tissues of mammals and as larvae usu. develop in biting insects, that belong to the Filariidae and related families, and that for the most part were once included in the genus *Filaria* and are now divided among various genera (as *Wuchereria* and *Onchocerca*) **2** *cap* **:** the type genus of Filariidae
fi·lar·i·al \fə'la(a)rēəl\ *adj* [NL *filaria* + E *-al*] **:** of, relating to, infested with, transmitting, or caused by filariae or related parasitic worms
fil·a·ri·a·sis \,filə'rīəsə̇s\ *also* **fi·lar·i·o·sis** \fə,la(a)rē'ōsə̇s\ *n, pl* **filaria·ses** \-ī,sēz\ *also* **filario·ses** \-ō,sēz\ [NL, fr. *filaria* + *-iasis* or *-osis*] **:** infestation with or disease caused by filariae — compare BANCROFTIAN FILARIASIS, ELEPHANTIASIS
fi·lar·i·at·ed \fə'la(a)rē,ād·ə̇d\ *adj* [NL *filaria* + E *-ate* + *-ed*] **:** marked by the presence of filariae ⟨a ~ person⟩
fi·lar·i·ci·dal \fə¦la(a)rə'sīd°l\ *adj* [NL *filaria* + E *-cidal*] **:** destructive to filariae
fi·lar·i·cide \-⸗'⸗,sīd\ *n* -s [NL *filaria* + E *-cide*] **:** a filaricidal agent
fi·lar·i·form \-,fȯrm\ *adj* [NL *filaria* + E *-form*] *of a larval nematode* **:** resembling a filaria esp. in having a slender elongated form and in possessing a delicate capillary esophagus
¹fi·lar·i·id \fə'la(a)rēəd\ *or* **fi·lar·id** \-rəd, 'filərəd\ *adj* [NL *Filariidae*] **:** of or relating to Filarioidea, Filariidae, or filariae
²filariid \"\ *or* **filarid** \"\ *n* -s **:** FILARIA 1
fil·a·ri·idae \,filə'rīə,dē\ *n pl, cap* [NL, fr. *Filaria*, type genus + *-idae*] **:** a family of nematode worms formerly

coextensive with Filarioidea and now usu. restricted to a few forms not of medical importance
fi·lar·i·oid \fə'la(a)rē,ȯid\ *adj* [NL *Filarioidea*] **:** of or relating to the Filarioidea
fi·lar·i·oi·dea \fə,la(a)rē'ȯidēə\ *n pl, cap* [NL, fr. *Filaria* + *-oidea*] **:** a large superfamily of the nematode order Spirurida comprising the medically important filarial worms and related forms and having a slender thready body, a simple anterior end with the oral lips inconspicuous, a cylindrical esophagus lacking a bulbus, and often unequal and dissimilar copulatory spicules in the male
filar micrometer *n* **:** an instrument for accurately measuring small distances or angles usu. consisting of two parallel fine platinum wires mounted in the focal plane of a microscope or telescope, one wire being fixed and the other movable by means of a finely threaded screw
fi·lasse \fə'las\ *n* -s [F, fr. OF *filace*, fr. (assumed) VL *filacea*, fr. L *filum* thread + *-acea* (fr. fem. of *-aceus* -aceous) — more at FILE] **:** vegetable fiber (as jute or ramie) prepared for manufacture
fi·late \'fī,lāt\ *adj* [L *filum* + E *-ate*] **:** slender and without appendages **:** THREADY
fil·a·ture \'filə,chu̇(ə)r, -,chər\ *n* -s [F, fr. LL *filatus* (past part. of *filare* to spin) + F *-ure* — more at FILE] **1 :** the reeling of silk from cocoons **2 :** a reel for drawing off silk from cocoons **3 :** a factory where silk is reeled
fil·beard \'fil,bird\ *dial Eng var of* FILBERT
fil·bert \'filbə(r)t, *usu* -d.+V\ *n* -s [ME *filberd, filbert*, fr. AF *philber*, after St. *Philibert* †684 Frankish abbot whose feast day (Aug. 20) falls in the nutting season] **1 a :** either of two European hazels (*Corylus avellana pontica* and *C. maxima*) **b :** the thick-shelled and sweet-flavored nut produced by the filberts and for which they are frequently cultivated **c :** HAZELNUT **2** *or* **filbert brown :** HAZEL 4 **3** *slang* **:** a person who presumes to be an expert analyst ⟨a football ~⟩
filbert blight *n* **:** a blight of the filbert caused by a bacterium (*Xanthomonas corylina*) and characterized esp. by the formation on the trunk of cankers which often girdle and kill the tree
filbert worm *n* **:** the pink or whitish larva of an olethreutid moth (*Melissopus latiferreanus*) that is a destructive borer in acorns, filberts, chestnuts, and various other nuts and fruits throughout the U.S.
¹filch \'filch\ *vt* -ED/-ING/-ES [ME *filchen* to attack, steal, perh. fr. OE *gefylce* band of men, troop, army; akin to ON *fylki* band of men, shire, OE *folc* folk — more at FOLK] **:** to steal furtively **:** PILFER ⟨~*ed* some cigarettes⟩ **syn** see STEAL
²filch \"\ *n* -ES *obs* **:** a hooked staff used by thieves to snatch articles (as from windows)
¹file \'fīl, *esp before pause or consonant* -īəl\ *n* -s [ME, fr. OE *fēol, fīl;* akin to OHG & OS *fīla* file, ON *thēl*, and prob. to Skt *piṁśati* he cuts or hacks out — more at PAINT] **1 a :** a hardened steel tool in the form of a bar or rod that has cutting ridges on its surface made by chisel cuts and that is used for forming or smoothing surfaces esp. of metal by means of the cutting or abrading action of the ridges — see BLUNT FILE, DOUBLE-CUT FILE, FLOAT-CUT FILE, MACHINE FILE, RASP, ROTARY FILE, SINGLE-CUT FILE, TAPER FILE **b :** a narrow instrument for shaping fingernails with a fine rough metal or emery surface **2 :** the corrugated part of the stridulating organ of an insect that produces sound when rubbed **3 :** a shrewd or crafty person ⟨an old ~ of a storekeeper⟩

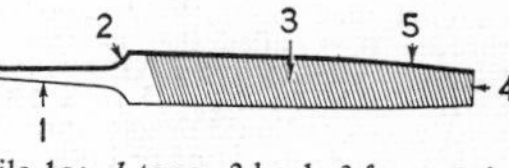

file 1a: *1* tang, *2* heel, *3* face, *4* tip, *5* edge

²file \"\ *vb* -ED/-ING/-S [ME *filen*, fr. OE *fēolian, filian;* akin to OHG *fīlōn* to file, ON *thēla;* derivative fr. the root of OE *fēol, fīl*] *vt* **1 a :** to rub, smooth, or cut with a file ⟨~ a piece of stock⟩ ⟨*filed* away the rough edges⟩ **b :** to sharpen with a file ⟨~ a saw⟩ **2 :** to refine esp. by careful revision ⟨a prose style with all ineptitudes *filed* away⟩ **~ *vi* :** to use or work with or as if with a file
³file \"\ *vt* -ED/-ING/-S [ME *filen*, fr. OE *fȳlan*, fr. *fūl* foul — more at FOUL] **1** *chiefly dial* **:** DEFILE, BEFOUL **2** *chiefly dial* **:** DEBAUCH, DISHONOR
⁴file \"\ *vb* -ED/-ING/-S [ME *filen*, fr. MF *filer* to string documents on a string or wire, fr. *fil* thread, string, fr. L *filum;* akin to W *gewyn* sinew, nerve, Lith *gija* thread, *gysla* vein, sinew, Arm *jil* sinew, cord] *vt* **1 :** to arrange (as papers, cards, or letters) in a particular order for preservation and reference **2** *obs* **:** THREAD, STRING **3 a** (1) **:** to deliver (as a legal paper or instrument) after complying with any condition precedent (as the payment of a fee) to the proper officer for keeping on file or among the records of his office (2) **:** to send (newspaper copy) to a newspaper or news agency by telephone, telegraph, or cable ⟨*filed* a good story⟩ **b :** to place (as a paper or instrument) on file among the legal or official records of an office esp. by formally receiving, endorsing, and entering **c :** to return (a law case) to the office of the clerk of a court without action on the merits **4 :** to perform the first act of (as a lawsuit) **:** COMMENCE **~ *vi* :** to register as a candidate esp. in a primary election ⟨~ for county attorney⟩
⁵file \"\ *n* -s [MF *fil*] **1 a :** a wire or cord that documents are strung from esp. in an order devised to facilitate reference **b :** a container (as a folder or a metal cabinet) in which papers are kept usu. in chronological or alphabetical order for ready reference **2** *obs* **:** THREAD **3 a** *obs* **:** ROLL, LIST **b :** a collection of cards or papers usu. arranged or classified ⟨a ~ of newspapers⟩ ⟨a letter ~⟩ **4 :** LABEL 3
⁶file \"\ *n* -s [MF *file* row, fr. *filer* to spin, fr. LL *filare*, fr. L *filum* thread] **1 a :** a row of persons, animals, or things arranged one behind the other ⟨a ~ of infantrymen⟩ ⟨to pass in ~⟩ — compare RANK **b :** a row of squares extending vertically across a chessboard ⟨a knight's pawn may capture on the rook's or the bishop's ~⟩ **2 a :** a man in a military formation who occupies a position in a single rank **b :** a number or numerical position on the lineal list for promotion ⟨a navy ~⟩
⁷file \"\ *vi* -ED/-ING/-S [MF *filer*, fr. *file*, n.] **:** to march in a line not abreast but one after another
⁸fi·lé \fə'lā, (')fi¦lā, (')fē¦lā\ *n* -s [AmerF (Louisiana) fr. F, past part. of *filer* to twist, spin] **:** powdered young leaves of sassafras used to thicken soups or stews
⁹file \'fī(ə)l\ *n* -s [ME, perh. of Celt origin; akin to OIr *fȳla* dirty fellow] *dial Eng* **:** RASCAL
¹⁰file *n* -s [fr. obs. slang *file* to steal, of unknown origin] *obs* **:** PICKPOCKET
¹¹file \(')fī(ə)l\ *Scot var of* WHILE
¹²file \"\ *n* -s [D *feil*] *dial* **:** a cloth esp. for wiping a floor or table
¹file card *n* [¹*file*] **:** a wire brush for cleaning files
²file card *n* [⁵*file*] **:** a card of a size and shape suitable to be used in a file
file case *n* [⁵*file*] **:** an attaché case with a file for papers in the lid
file clerk *n* [⁵*file*] **:** a clerk who works on files: *esp* **:** a clerk who arranges materials or records in accordance with a particular filing system
file closer *n* [⁶*file*] **:** a commissioned or noncommissioned officer in the rear of a line or on the flank of a column who rectifies mistakes and ensures steadiness in the ranks
filefish \'ˌ=,=\ *n* [¹*file* + *fish*] **:** any of certain fishes with rough granulated leathery skins: as **a :** TRIGGERFISH **b :** any of numerous closely related oddly shaped fishes (family Monocanthidae) differing from the triggerfishes in having the scales reduced to prickles like those of shagreen and the first dorsal fin to a single long spine
file-hard \'=¦=\ *adj* [¹*file*] **:** so hard as not to be cut by a file
file holder *n* [¹*file*] **:** a handle sometimes used in benchwork with clamps for attaching to the heel and point of a file and provision for springing the center of the file downward
file meristem *n* [⁵*file*] **:** RIB MERISTEM
file off *vi* [⁷*file*] **:** to march in a single file from some other formation
¹fil·er \'fīlə(r)\ *n* -s [²*file* + *-er*] **:** one that files; *specif* **:** a worker who smooths, shapes, or sharpens with a file
²filer \"\ *n* -s [⁴*file* + *-er*] **:** one that files; *specif* **:** FILE CLERK
files *pl of* FILE, *pres 3d sing of* FILE
file shell *n* [¹*file*] **:** any of a family (Limidae) of small equivalve bivalve mollusks with the yellowish or white valves closely ribbed and covered with spiny scales suggesting a rasp or file
file signal *n* [⁵*file*] **:** a small movable colored tab attached to a filed card or folder as a temporary indicator
file snake *n* [¹*file*] **:** any of several large harmless African colubrid snakes of the genus *Mehelya* that have a steeply ridged back making them resemble a 3-cornered file
file-soft \'=¦=\ *adj* [¹*file*] **:** soft enough to be readily cut by a file
¹filet *var of* FILLET
²fi·let \fə'lā, 'fi(,)lā\ *also* **filet lace** *n* -s [F *filet*, lit., net, fr. OF *filé*, fr. OProv *filat* — more at FIERASFER] **:** a lace with geometric designs made by darning patterns on a square-mesh ground or by crocheting ⟨a tablecloth of fine damask and the frilly cloth of ~ —*Amer. Cookery*⟩
file-tailed rat \'=,=-\ *n* [¹*file*] **:** ROUND-TAILED MUSKRAT
file-tail shark *n* [¹*file*] **:** a small dark brown shark (*Parmaturus xaniurus*) of the coast of southern and Lower California having a broad crowded band of enlarged scales on the upper edge of the tail
file 13 *n* **:** WASTEBASKET
fi·let mi·gnon \ˌfi(,)lā(,)mēn'yōⁿ, fə,lā-, -'mēn,-\ *n, pl* **filets mignons** [F, lit., dainty fillet] **:** a fillet of beef cut from the thick end of a beef tenderloin — compare TOURNEDOS
file wrapper *n* [⁵*file*] **:** the written record in the patent office of negotiations between an applicant and that office preceding the issuance or rejection of a patent
file wrapper estoppel *n* **:** a doctrine in patent law that one who has acquiesced in the rejection of a broad claim in his application for a patent may not later assert that a claim deliberately more restricted is equivalent to the original claim
fi·li \'fil(y)ə\ *n, pl* **fi·li** \'fi'lē\ [OIr, lit., seer; akin to W *gweled* to see — more at BULTO] **:** a poet in ancient Ireland of higher rank than the bard and belonging to a class who were also lawyers, historians, genealogists, and storytellers
fili- *comb form* [L *filum* — more at FILE] **:** thread or threads **:** something resembling thread or threads ⟨*fili*cauline⟩ ⟨*fili*ferous⟩
fil·ial \'filēəl *also* -lyəl\ *adj* [ME, fr. LL *filialis*, fr. L *filius* son + *-alis* -al — more at FEMININE] **1 :** of or relating to a son or daughter; *esp* **:** becoming to a child in relation to his parents ⟨~ obedience⟩ **2 :** bearing or assuming the relation of a child or offspring — **fil·ial·ly** \-ēəlē, -yəlē, -li\ *adv* — **fil·ial·ness** \-əlnəs\ *n* -ES
filial generation *n* **:** a generation in a cross successive to a parental generation — symbol F_1 for the first, F_2 for the second, etc.
fil·i·al·i·ty \ˌfilē'aləd·ē, fil'ya-\ *n* -ES [LL *filialitas*, fr. *filialis* + L *-itas* -ity] **:** the relation or attitude of a child to a parent
filial piety *n* [trans. of Chin (Pek) *hsiao⁴*] **:** reverence for parents considered in Chinese ethics the prime virtue and the basis of all right human relations
fil·i·ate \'filē,āt, *usu* -ād.+V\ *vt* -ED/-ING/-S [ML *filiatus*, past part. of *filiare*, fr. L *filius* son] **:** to declare (an illegitimate child) the offspring of a particular father **:** AFFILIATE
fil·i·a·tion \ˌfilē'āshən\ *n* -S [ME *filiacioun*, fr. LL *filiation-, filiatio*, fr. L *filius* + *-ation-, -atio* -ation] **1 a :** relationship esp. of a son to his father **b :** the relationship between a parent and a child whether legitimate or illegitimate **2 :** one that is derived from a parent or source **:** OFFSHOOT ⟨~*s* from a common stock⟩ **3 a :** the act or action of determining relationship ⟨a scholar's careful ~ of manuscripts⟩ **b :** adjudication of paternity **:** AFFILIATION **4 :** descent from or as if from a parent ⟨to determine the ~ of a language⟩ **5 :** the formation of branches or offshoots
filibeg *var of* FILLEBEG
fil·i·bran·chia \ˌfilə'braŋkēə\ *n pl, cap* [NL *fili-* + *-branchia*] **:** an order of Lamellibranchia that comprise marine bivalve mollusks having two pairs of laminated gills formed of distinct V-shaped filaments with interfilamentary junctions either absent or formed by groups of interlocking cilia and nonvascular and that include mussels, ark shells, and scallops — **fil·i·bran·chi·ate** \ˌ=;=¦=kēət, -ē āt\ *adj*
fil·i·branchiata \ˌfilə+\ [NL *fili-* + *Branchiata*] *syn of* FILIBRANCHIA
¹fil·i·bus·ter \'filəbəstə(r)\ *n* -s [Sp *filibustero*, lit., freebooter, prob. fr. F *flibustier, fribustier*, fr. E *fleebooter, freebooter* — more at FREEBOOTER] **1 a :** an American who in the mid-19th century took part in fomenting revolutions and insurrections in a Latin-American country **b :** an irregular military adventurer; *specif* **:** an organizer or member of a hostile expedition to a country with which his own is at peace **2** [²*filibuster*] **a :** the use of extreme dilatory tactics (as speaking merely to consume time) by an individual or group in an attempt to delay or prevent action by the majority in a legislative or deliberative assembly; *also* **:** an instance of this ⟨~*s* are most often associated . . . with proceedings in the U.S. Senate —H.D.Scott⟩ ⟨a Communist ~ designed to prevent passage of a new Italian electoral law —*Springfield (Mass.) Union*⟩ **b :** FILIBUSTERER
²filibuster \", ˌ=ˈ=ˌ=\ *vb* **filibustered; filibustered; filibustering** \-t(ə)riŋ\ **filibusters** *vi* **1 :** to carry out insurrectionist or revolutionary activities esp. in a foreign country **2 :** to engage in a filibuster ⟨he had ~*ed* for 22 hours and 26 minutes without leaving the Senate floor —*Time*⟩ **~ *vt* :** to subject to filibustering ⟨any . . . proposal to alter the rules could be ~*ed* —P.H.Douglas⟩
fil·i·bus·ter·er \-tərə(r)\ *n* -s **:** one that filibusters
fil·i·bus·ter·ism \-tə,rizəm, ˌ=ˈ=ˌ=ˌ=\ *n* -s **:** the practice of filibustering
fil·i·cal \'filəkəl\ *adj* [NL *Filicales*] **:** of or relating to the order Filicales
fil·i·ca·les \ˌfilə'kā(,)lēz\ *n pl, cap* [NL, fr. *Filic-, Filix* + *-ales*] **:** an order of herbaceous, arborescent, or occas. climbing plants (class Filicineae) that comprise the true ferns, that are characterized by exstipulate fronds, leptosporangiate sporangial development, and small thin-walled sporangia which are usu. borne in sori on the undersides of the fronds, and that have a characteristic ring of thick-walled cells which assists in dehiscence of the spores — compare FERN ALLY, PTERIDOPHYTA
fili·cauline \ˌfilə, ¦fīlə+\ *adj* [*fili-* + *cauline*] **:** having a filamentous stem
fil·i·ces \'filə,sēz\ [NL, fr. *Filic-, Filix*] *syn of* FILICALES
fi·lic·ic acid \fə'lisik-\ *n* [ISV *filic-* (fr. NL *Filic-, Filix*) + *-ic*] **:** a phenolic anthelmintic substance that is obtained as a colorless powder from the rhizome of the common male fern
fil·i·ci·dal \ˌfilə'sīdᵊl\ *adj* **:** of or relating to filicide
fil·i·cide \'filə,sīd\ *n* -s [L *filius* son & *filia* daughter + E *-cide* — more at FEMININE] **:** the murdering of a son or daughter; *also* **:** the parent who commits such a murder
fi·lic·i·form \fə'lisə,fȯrm\ *adj* [L *filic-, filix* fern + E *-iform*] **:** shaped like a fern or fern frond
fil·i·cin \'filəsən\ *n* -s [ISV *filic-* (fr. NL *Filic-, Filix*) + *-in*] **:** FILICIC ACID; *also* **:** the mixture of active principles obtained in the chemical assay of the male fern
fil·i·ci·nae \ˌfilə'sī,nē\ [NL] *syn of* FILICINEAE
fil·i·cin·e·ae \ˌfilə'sinē,ē\ *n pl, cap* [NL, fr. *Filic-, Filix* + *-ineae*] **1 :** a class of Pteropsida comprising plants (as the typical ferns) that produce no seeds and have large often complex leaves, sperms which must be transported by water, and well-developed alternation of generation usu. with independent gametophytes and sporophytes which often differ radically in size and form and including the orders Marattiales, Ophioglossales, and Filicales with living representatives and the extinct order Coenopteridales — compare ANGIOSPERMAE, GYMNOSPERMAE **2** *in some classifications* **:** a class or other group coextensive with Filicales — **fil·i·cin·e·an** \ˌfilə-¦sinēən\ *adj*
fil·i·cite \'filə,sīt\ *n* -s [ISV *filic-* (fr. L *filic-, filix* fern) + *-ite*] **:** a fossil fern
fil·i·ci·tes \ˌ=ˌ='sīd·(,)ēz\ *n pl, cap* [NL, fr. ISV *filicite*] *in former classifications* **:** a group including all fossil ferns
fil·i·col·o·gy \ˌfilə'käləjē\ *n* -ES [L *filic-, filix* fern + E *-o-* + *-logy*] **:** PTERIDOLOGY
fil·i·cor·nia \-'kȯ(r)nēə\ [NL, fr. *fili-* + L *cornu* horn + NL *-ia* — more at HORN] *syn of* ADEPHAGA
fi·lif·er·ous \(')fī¦lif(ə)rəs, fə'l-\ *adj* [*fili-* + *-ferous*] **:** bearing threads
¹fili·form \'filə,fȯrm, 'fīl-\ *adj* [*fili-* + *-form*] **:** having the shape of a thread or filament ⟨a ~ peduncle⟩ — see ANTENNA illustration
²filiform \"\ *n* -s **:** an extremely slender bougie
filiform apparatus *n* **:** a prolongation of the synergids beyond the summit of the embryo sac
fili·formed \-md\ *adj* [*fili-* + *formed*] **:** FILIFORM
filiform papilla *n* **:** any of numerous minute pointed papillae on the tongue
fi·lig·er·ous \(')fī¦lijərəs, fə'l-\ *adj* [*fili-* + *-gerous*] **:** FLAGELLATE
fil·i·grain *also* **fil·i·grane** \'filə,grān\ *n* -s [F *filigrane*] **:** FILIGREE — **fil·i·grained** \-nd\ *adj*
¹fil·i·gree *also* **fil·a·gree** \'filə,grē\ *n* -s *often attrib* [short for earlier *filigreen, filagreen*, modif. of F *filigrane*, fr. It *filigrana*, fr. *fili-* (fr. L *filum* thread) + *grana* grain, fr. L, pl. of *granum* grain — more at FILE, CORN] **1 :** ornamental work formerly with grains or beads but now esp. of fine wire of gold, silver, or copper that is used chiefly to decorate gold and silver surfaces **2 a :** ornamental openwork of delicate or intricate design **b :** a pattern or design resembling such openwork

filigree 1

²filigree \"\ *vt* **filigreed; filigreed; filigreeing; filigrees** **:** to adorn with or as if with filigree
¹filing *n* -s [ME, fr. gerund of *filen* to file — more at FILE] **1 :** an act or instance of using a file (as for abrading or smoothing) **2 :** a fragment or particle rubbed off in filing ⟨iron ~*s*⟩
²filing *n* -s [fr. gerund of ⁴*file*] **:** preservation and methodical arrangement (as of documents, papers, letters) ⟨a ~ system⟩ ⟨a ~ card⟩ ⟨have some ~ to do⟩
fil·io·pietistic \ˌfilē(,)ō+\ *adj* [L *filius* son + E *-o-* + *pietistic* — more at FEMININE] **:** of or relating to an often excessive veneration of ancestors or tradition
filip *var of* FILLIP
fil·i·pen·du·la \ˌfilə'penjələ, -nd(y)ələ\ *n* [NL, fr. *fili-* + L *pendula*, fem. of *pendulus* hanging — more at PENDULOUS] **1** *cap* **:** a small genus of perennial herbs (family Rosaceae) of north temperate regions with pinnately divided leaves and small white or pink flowers in cymose panicles **2** -s **:** any plant of the genus *Filipendula*
fil·i·pen·du·lous \ˌ=ˌ='=ləs\ *adj* [*fili-* + *pendulous*] **:** suspended by or strung upon a thread
fil·i·pi·na \ˌfilə'pēnə\ *n* -s *cap* [Sp. fem. of *filipino*] **:** a female Filipino
fil·i·pi·ni·za·tion \ˌfilə,pēnə'zāshən\ *n* -s *usu cap* **:** the act of Filipinizing **:** the condition of being Filipinized
fil·i·pi·nize \ˌ=ˌ='pē,nīz, 'ˌ=ˌ=ˌ=\ *vt* -ED/-ING/-S *usu cap* **:** to provide with personnel preponderantly or totally Filipino ⟨*Filipinized* the police force⟩
¹fil·i·pi·no \ˌfilə'pē(,)nō\ *n* -s *cap* [Sp, adj. & n., fr. (*Islas*) *Filipinas* Philippine islands] **1 :** a native of the Philippine islands; *specif* **:** a member of a Christianized Philippine people as distinguished from a member of a people predominantly pagan or Muslim **2 :** a citizen of the Republic of the Philippines
²filipino \ˌ=ˌ=¦(,)=\ *adj, usu cap* [Sp] **1 :** of, relating to, or characteristic of the Filipinos **2 :** of, relating to, or characteristic of the Philippines **:** PHILIPPINE
filipino language *n, cap F* **:** TAGALOG 2
fi·li·us nul·li·us \ˌfēlēəs'nəlēəs, -'su̇lēəs\ *n, pl* **fi·lii nullius** \ˌfēlē,ēnə'l-, -ē,ē'nu̇l-\ [L, nobody's son] **:** an illegitimate child **:** BASTARD
filius po·pu·li \ˌfēlēə'spȯpə,lē\ *n, pl* **fi·lii populi** \ˌfēlē,ē'pȯ-\ [L, son of the people] **:** FILIUS NULLIUS
fi·lix \'fīliks, 'fil-\ [NL, fr. L, fern] *syn of* CYSTOPTERIS
fi·lix·mas \'fīlik'smas, 'filik'smas\ *n* -ES [NL *filix mas* male fern] **:** ASPIDIUM 2
¹fill \'fil\ *vb* -ED/-ING/-S [ME *fillen*, fr. OE *fyllan;* akin to OHG *fullen* to fill, ON *fylla*, Goth *fulljan;* causative fr. the root of E ¹*full*] *vt* **1 a** (1) **:** to supply with as much as can be held or contained ⟨*filling* the holes in the road⟩ (2) **:** to place or put as much material in as can be often conveniently contained ⟨~ a box⟩ **:** pour as much of a substance into as can be often conveniently held ⟨~ a cup⟩ ⟨~ a barrel with apples⟩ (3) **:** to furnish (as a container) esp. in proportion **:** PROVIDE ⟨~ a glass with water⟩ ⟨~ a page with print⟩ (4) **:** POUR ⟨~ wine into bottles⟩ **:** LOAD, PUT ⟨~ coal into bins⟩ (5) **:** to make full or complete (as a partly empty line or an incomplete column in printed matter) by respacing the existing printed matter or by adding matter (6) **:** to give a pleasingly full form to (as a dress) in wearing — often used with *out* ⟨she ~*ed* the dress nicely⟩ ⟨he began to ~ his suits out well as he grew older⟩ **b** (1) **:** to stop up **:** OBSTRUCT ⟨wreckage ~*ed* the channel⟩ — often used with *up* ⟨the traffic jam *filled* the street up completely⟩ (2) **:** to make an embankment in or raise the level of (a low place) with earth, gravel, or rock **c** (1) **:** PLUG ⟨~ a chink⟩ **:** CAULK ⟨~ the seams with oakum⟩ (2) **:** to stop up the interstices, crevices, or pores of (as cloth, wood, leather) with some foreign substance for the sake of hardening, dressing, or adulterating (3) **:** LOAD 3c(1) (4) **:** to close up (a cavity in a tooth) with gold, silver, or other comparatively inert material **d** *obs* **:** IMPREGNATE **e** (1) **:** to feed and water (livestock) immediately before sale to increase the apparent weight (2) **:** to stuff (a food) with a filling ⟨~*ed* rolls⟩ **2 a :** to occupy the whole of ⟨his huge bulk ~*ed* the chair⟩ **b :** to swarm in **:** PERVADE ⟨shoppers ~*ed* the city⟩ **c** (1) **:** PACK, LOAD, SURFEIT ⟨her presence ~*ed* his heart with joy⟩ ⟨~*ed* his head with foolish ideas⟩ (2) **:** SATISFY, SATIATE ⟨~ their guest with good food⟩ (3) **:** to belly out **:** DISTEND — often used with *out* ⟨the wind ~*ed* the sails out⟩ **d** (1) **:** to supply fully or completely **:** MEET ⟨~ a longfelt want⟩ (2) **:** STOCK ⟨~ a stream with trout⟩ **3 a :** to execute or fulfill the requirements of (a business order) **b :** to complete or make out — often used with *out* ⟨~ out a check⟩ or *up* ⟨~ up the blanks in a questionnaire⟩ or *in* ⟨~ in the tax form⟩ **c :** to make up (a prescription) **4 a :** OCCUPY, HOLD ⟨~ a throne⟩ **b :** to provide with incumbents ⟨~ vacancies left by retirements⟩ — often used with *up* **c :** to possess and perform the duties of ⟨~ an office⟩ **5 :** to trim (a sail) so that the wind will blow on the after side **6 :** to cover the surface of with a layer of precious metal — used chiefly as a past participle ⟨a gold-*filled* watch⟩ **7 :** to draw the cards in poker necessary to complete (a full house, a flush, or a straight) **~ *vi* 1 a** (1) **:** to become full ⟨the rivers ~*ed*⟩ (2) *of the eyes* **:** to become full with tears (3) **:** to become so suffused with ink (as of the bowl of a letter or the space between the dots of a halftone) as to print improperly — often used with *in* or *up* **b :** to have the whole capacity occupied ⟨the stadium ~*ed* and overflowed⟩ **c :** to fill a cup or glass for drinking **2 a :** to become blocked, burdened, or obstructed by or as if by accumulations — often used with *in* ⟨the harbor gradually ~*ed* in⟩ or *up* ⟨the channel ~*ed* up⟩ **b** (1) **:** to become heavy, choked, or fraught ⟨his heart ~*ed* at the words⟩ ⟨their expressions ~*ed* with grief⟩ (2) **:** to swell out in or as if in fullness ⟨the sails ~*ed* with wind⟩ ⟨her body began to ~ out⟩ ⟨the balloon ~*ed* up⟩ **3 :** to complete a full house, flush, or straight in poker — **fill one's shoes :** to take one's place **:** take over one's job or position and fulfill its duties or responsibilities satisfactorily — **fill the bill :** to answer a need **:** serve the purpose usu. satisfactorily
²fill \"\ *n* -s [ME *fille*, fr. OE *fyllo;* akin to OHG *fulli* fill, abundance, ON *fyllr*, Goth *ufarfullei* great abundance; derivative fr. the root of E ¹*full*] **1 :** a full supply; *esp* **:** a quantity that satisfies or satiates — usu. used with a possessive ⟨eat your ~⟩ ⟨she wept her ~⟩ **2 a** (1) **:** material used to fill a receptacle, cavity, or passage ⟨a ~ for a trench⟩ — see BACKFILL; compare GOB (2) **:** an embankment (as in railroad construction) to fill a hollow or ravine or the place filled by such an embankment; *also* **:** the depth of the filling material when in place (3) **:** material that is used to take up unused or vacant periods (as in a radio or television schedule) **b :** the

contents of the digestive tract of an animal **3 :** the maximum width of the paper producible by a particular papermaking machine
³fill \"\ *n* -s [by alter.] *chiefly dial* **:** THILL
fillanin *usu cap, var of* FILANI
fill away *vi* **1 :** to trim a sail so that it will catch the wind full **2 :** to proceed on the course esp. after being brought up in the wind ⟨the fleet had . . . begun to *fill away* on a northerly course —S.E.Morison⟩
fill cap *n* **:** a metal cap screwed on the top of the pipe through which a fuel-oil tank is filled
fill-dike \ˈ=,=\ *n* **:** FEBRUARY FILL-DIKE
fil·le·beg *or* **fil·i·beg** *or* **fil·a·beg** *or* **phil·a·beg** *or* **phil·i·beg** \ˈfilə,beg, ˈfēl-\ *n* -s [ScGael *fēile-beag,* fr. *fēileadh* kilt + *beag* little; akin to OIr *becc, bec* small, W *bach*] **:** KILT
filled *past of* FILL
filled board *n* **:** a board or paper made on a cylinder machine in which the inner layers differ in material from the outer layers
filled cheese *n* **:** a product made from whole or skim milk enriched by the addition of foreign fatty material
fille de joie \ˌfēdə'zhwä\ *n, pl* **filles de joie** \"\ [F, lit., pleasure girl] **:** PROSTITUTE
filled milk *n* **:** skim milk enriched in fat content by the addition of vegetable oils
filled soap *n* **:** a soap from which the water and glycerol have not been removed by salting out or to which an adulterant that is not necessarily an inactive one has been added
¹fill·er \ˈfilə(r)\ *n* -s [¹*fill* + *-er*] **1 a :** something that fills: as (1) **:** a substance added to a product to increase the bulk or weight of the product (as in the case of wood flour added to a plastic) or to dilute expensive materials and often also to improve the product (as in its mechanical or electrical properties) **:** EXTENDER — compare DILUENT (2) **:** any inert material or one containing little plant food that is added to commercial fertilizers or pest-control chemicals to secure the weight or bulk needed to give the desired composition or physical condition (3) **:** a composition (as of powdered silica and oil) used to fill the pores and grain of a wood or other surface before paint or varnish is applied (4) **:** mineral matter (as clay, talc, or titanium dioxide) that is added to paper in papermaking (as in the beater) to increase opacity and improve printing quality (5) **:** asphalt, cement, or coal-tar pitch used to fill the joints of brick and stone-block pavements (6) **:** dry limestone dust, dust from another appropriate stone, or portland cement used in the surface mixture of sheet-asphalt pavement (7) **:** a plate or other piece used to cover or fill in a space between two parts of a structure **b** (1) **:** a standing tree or standard higher than the surrounding coppice — usu. used in pl. (2) **:** any rapidly growing plant used to occupy idle space in a permanent planting; *esp* **:** an early maturing variety in orcharding planted between the regular units (3) **:** a stream that fills a lake **c** (1) **:** tobacco used to add bulk to cigarettes without modifying their flavor or to form the bulk of plugs and twists; *esp* **:** tobacco used to form the core of a cigar — compare BINDER, WRAPPER (2) **:** filling for a pie or a layer cake **d** (1) **:** copy used primarily to fill extra space in a column or page of a newspaper or periodical; *esp* **:** a brief item of fact (as from a reference book) appearing in a newspaper ⟨a ~ from an encyclopedia⟩ (2) **:** paper used in a loose-leaf notebook (3) **:** the inner layer or layers of a filled board **e** (1) **:** a worker who fills pillows, comforters, cushions (2) **:** a worker who puts rags and chemicals into a boiler that will clean and bleach the rags for use in papermaking (3) **:** BACKFILLER (4) **:** a worker who fills and tests aircraft inclinometers **f** (1) **:** a light form made often of wood and placed in a shoe to maintain its shape while on display **:** material used to fill the space between the outsole and the insole of a shoe (2) **:** a device or implement (as a funnel, pipe, or syringe) that supplies or conducts the filling material to its receptacle ⟨a fountain pen ~⟩ **g :** a card (as a ten or nine) that adds to the strength of a hand in bridge but is not recognized by a given method of evaluating the hand's strength **:** INTERMEDIATE **2 :** a worker who measures marble blocks, marks them for cutting, and verifies their measurements after cutting
²fill·er \"\ *n* -s [³*fill* + *-er*] *now dial* **:** THILL HORSE
³fil·ler \ˈfi,le(ə)r, -eə\ *n, pl* **fillers** *or* **filler** [Hung *fillér*] **1 :** a Hungarian unit of value worth before 1925 $\frac{1}{100}$ korona, from 1925 to 1946 $\frac{1}{100}$ pengő, after 1946 $\frac{1}{100}$ forint — see MONEY table **2 :** a coin representing one filler
filler-in \ˌ==ˈ=\ *n, pl* **fillers-in** [*fill in* + *-er*] **1 :** one that fills in (as colors, designs, materials); *specif* **:** one that paints designs on pottery or porcelain by hand **2 :** one that substitutes
filler man *n* **:** a tobacco worker who places filler leaves on trays so that air can circulate among them and dry them to the proper moisture content for use in cigars
filler vase *n* **:** a funnel-shaped vase with a small handle near the top esp. characteristic of Minoan potters
¹fil·let \ˈfilət, *usu* -əd.+V; *in sense 2e* " *or like* FILET\ *also* **fi·let** \fəˈlā, ˈfi(,)lā\ *n* -s [ME *filet,* fr. MF *filet,* dim. of *fil* thread — more at FILE] **1 :** a narrow strip of ornamental material (as a ribbon for a woman's hair or a border or edging of a painting) **2 :** a thin narrow strip of any material: as **a :** a narrow strip of card clothing **b :** a strip of metal from which coin blanks are punched **c :** a scantling smaller than a batten **d :** a band of fibers; *specif* **:** LEMNISCUS **e** [F *filet,* fr. MF] **:** a piece or slice of boneless meat or fish; *specif* **:** the tenderloin of beef — compare FILET MIGNON **3 a :** a concavely curved section at the angle formed by the junction of two surfaces **:** a rounded inside corner; *also* **:** a strip fitted into the angle of such a junction or corner to form a concave section **b :** a fairing member of metal, wood, or fabric employed to promote smooth airflow at an internal angle produced by the juncture of two surfaces on an aircraft **c :** a bead of cementing material placed along a joint formed by two parts or pieces to strengthen the joint or make it watertight **4 :** a narrow flat member: **a :** a flat molding separating other moldings **:** REGLET — see BASE illustration **b :** the space between two flutings in a shaft **5 a :** a metal wheel for impressing designs on book covers — called also *roulette* **b :** the plain line or repetitive design in blind or gold rolled on a book by a fillet

fillet 1

²fillet \"\ *vt* -ED/-ING/-S **1 :** to bind, furnish, or adorn with or as if with a fillet **2 :** to round off (a corner, hollow, or reentrant angle) with a fillet **3 a :** to cut into fillets **b :** to treat as a fillet
fil·let·er \ˈfiləd·ə(r), fəˈlāə(r)\ *n* -s **:** one that fillets; *specif* **:** one that slices fillets from the sides of fish
fillet gauge *n* **:** a gauge for gauging convex or concave surfaces
filleting *n* -s **1 :** the protecting of a joint (as between roof and parapet wall) with mortar or cement where flashing is sometimes used **2 :** FILLETS; *also* **:** the material used for fillets
fillet weld *n* **:** a weld of approximately triangular section external to the pieces being welded
fill in *vt* **1 :** INSERT ⟨*fill in* figures⟩ **2 :** to enrich (as a design) with detail **3 :** to give (a person) lacking, necessary, or recently acquired information — often used with *on* ⟨his friend *filled* him *in* on the details⟩ ~ *vi* **:** to fill a vacancy usu. temporarily **:** SUBSTITUTE ⟨when I am called on to *fill in* in an emergency —Milton Cross⟩
fill-in \ˈ=,=\ *n* -s [*fill in*] **1 :** something that fills in: as **a** (1) **:** an insert esp. in the low neckline of a woman's dress or blouse (2) **:** an insertion made of a name, address, date, or salutation in a form or letter already printed **b** (1) **:** goods purchased to replenish stock **:** REPLACEMENTS (2) **:** mechandise purchased to supplement a line or assortment of goods in stock or substituted for an advertised article that is out of stock (3) **:** an order to replenish or complete stock or an assortment on hand **c :** written or typewritten matter inserted in blank spaces left for the purpose (as in printed or mimeographed forms or form letters) **2 :** a person who fills another's place
filling *n* -s [ME, fr. gerund of *fillen* to fill — more at FILL] **1 :** an act or instance of filling ⟨the ~ of bottles⟩ ⟨the ~ of an order⟩ **2 :** something used to fill a cavity, container, or depression **:** FILLER, FILL **3 :** something that completes or rounds off: as **a** (1) **:** the yarn interlacing the warp at right angles in the weaving of fabrics; *also* **:** yarn for the shuttle (2) **:** a pattern of fancy stitches used to cover or complete the open spaces in embroidery and lace designs **b :** a sweet or savory food mixture used to fill pastry, cake, or sandwiches **c :** ¹FILLER 1a(4) **4 :** simple sporadic lymphangitis of the leg of a horse commonly due to overfeeding and underexercising
filling fork *n* **:** a loom feeler that actuates a stop motion when filling yarn breaks or is not properly laid
filling knitting *n* **:** WEFT KNITTING
filling notch *or* **filling slot** *n* **:** an opening cut into the shoulders of a ball bearing to permit introduction of the balls
filling point *n* **:** the level in a liquid container (as a bottle) up to which it is usu. filled or at which it has its nominal capacity
filling station *n* **:** a retail station for servicing automobiles and other motor vehicles esp. with gasoline and oil
fill-in light *also* **fill light** *n* **:** a light used in photography to illuminate the deep shadows caused by the main light
fill-in test *n* **:** COMPLETION TEST
¹fil·lip *also* **fil·ip** \ˈfiləp\ *n* -s [prob. of imit. origin] **1 a :** a blow or gesture made by the sudden forcible straightening of a finger curled up against the thumb **b :** a short smart blow **:** BUFFET ⟨giving her a . . . ~ on the shoulder with his heavy gloves —Glenway Wescott⟩ **2 a :** something added that tends to arouse or excite ⟨the Declaration of Independence gave a brief ~ to patriotism but only for a short period —S.E.Morison & H.S.Commager⟩ **b :** a stimulating or rousing agent ⟨businessmen . . . cannot see where the next big ~ for business will come from —*Newsweek*⟩ **3 :** a trivial addition **:** a minor embellishment ⟨quite necessary adjuncts instead of merely extra ~*s* —Lois Long⟩
²fillip \"\ *vt* -ED/-ING/-S **1 a :** to strike by holding the nail of a finger against the ball of the thumb and then suddenly releasing it from that position **b :** to make a filliping motion with ⟨the man ~*ed* his fingers toward his accuser —S.H. Adams⟩ **2 :** to project quickly by or as if by a fillip **:** SNAP ⟨~*ed* crumbs off the table⟩ **3 :** to urge on **:** STIMULATE ⟨with this to ~ his spirits —Robert Westerby⟩
fil·li·peen \ˈfilə,pēn, ,==ˈ=\ *or* **fil·li·peen·er** \-nə(r)\ *n* -s [by alter.] **:** PHILOPENA
fil·lis·ter \ˈfiləstə(r)\ *n* -s [origin unknown] **:** an adjustable rabbet plane; *also* **:** a rabbet esp. on the outer edge of a window-sash bar)
fillister head *or* **fillister screwhead** *n* **:** a slotted cylindrical screwhead with a convex or flat top
fillmass \ˈ=,=\ *n* [¹*fill* + *mass;* trans. of G *füllmasse*] **:** massecuite used esp. in beet-sugar making
fill out *vt* **:** to make (as an account or report) more complete or more substantial by amplifying or expanding matter already touched on or by giving additional pertinent details ⟨*filled* his story of the battle *out* by reporting the reactions of both officers and men⟩
fil·low·ite \ˈfilə,wīt\ *n* -s [A. N. *Fillow,* 19th cent. Am. mine owner + E *-ite*] **:** a mineral $H_2Na_6(Mn,Fe,Ca)_{14}(PO_4)_{12}$. $H_2O(?)$ consisting of a brown, yellow, or colorless hydrous phosphate of manganese, iron, sodium, and other metals
fills *pres 3d sing of* FILL, *pl of* FILL
fill-up \ˈ=,=\ *n* -s [fr. *fill up,* v.] **:** something that fills up **:** FILLER, FILL
fil·ly \ˈfilē, -li\ *n* -ES [ME *fyly,* fr. ON *fylja;* akin to OHG *fuli* foal, ON *foli* — more at FOAL] **1 :** a young female horse usu. of less than four years **2 :** a young woman **:** GIRL ⟨the attempts of a middle-aged gentleman to keep up with a ~ half his age —John McCarten⟩
¹film \ˈfilm, ˈfium, *dial or substand* ˈfiləm\ *n* -s *often attrib* [ME *filme,* fr. OE *filmen, fylmen;* akin to OFris *filmene* skin, Gk *pelma* sole of the foot, OE *fell* skin — more at FELL] **1 a :** a thin skin **:** a membranous covering **:** PELLICLE **b :** a pathological growth on or in the eye **2 a :** HAZE, MIST **b :** a thin covering or coating or veil **3 a** (1) **:** an exceedingly thin layer **:** LAMINA ⟨a ~ of soil⟩ ⟨a coal ~⟩ (2) **:** a split sheet of mica 0.001 to 0.009 inch thick — usu. used in pl. **b** (1) **:** a thin often flexible transparent sheet (as of cellophane, polyethylene, rubber, or an adhesive) used esp. as a wrapping or packaging material (2) **:** a thin flexible transparent sheet of cellulose acetate, cellulose nitrate, or other plastic material that is used for taking photographs and that is coated with a light-sensitive emulsion which when exposed and developed contains negative or positive images in black silver or in color **4 :** MOTION PICTURE ⟨a ~ of the life of our first president⟩ ⟨~ coverage of a sports event⟩ **5 :** FILM COLOR
²film \"\ *vb* -ED/-ING/-S *vt* **1 :** to cover with or as if with a film **2 a :** to make a motion picture of ⟨~ a scene⟩ **b :** to make a motion picture from a scenario based upon ⟨~ a novel⟩ ~ *vi* **1 :** to become covered or obscured with or as if with a film **2 a :** to be suitable for photographing ⟨she ~*s* well⟩ **b :** to make a motion picture
film·able \-məbəl\ *adj* **:** suitable for being filmed or adapted to motion pictures ⟨~ novels and plays —Andrew Buchanan⟩ ⟨of all the novelists of his day . . . the most ~ —Stanley Kauffmann⟩
film badge *n* **:** a dosimeter of photographic film
film base *n* **:** BASE 2d(1)
film clip *n* **:** a strip of motion-picture film; *specif* **:** one inserted in a live telecast
film color *n* **:** a vague soft smooth expanse of color (as seen when the eyes are closed or when looking at certain kinds of sky) that appears as nontransparent, not on the surface of an object, and at no definite distance; *broadly* **:** a colored expanse of soft texture
film cutout *n* **:** a thin insulating film that breaks down when a series filament street lamp fails and that short-circuits the lamp so as not to interrupt the service elsewhere
film·dom \ˈfilmdəm, ˈfiumd-\ *n* -s **1 :** the motion-picture industry **2 :** the personnel of the motion-picture industry
film·er \-mə(r)\ *n* -s **:** one that films
film gate *n* **:** a portion of a motion-picture mechanism which positions the film while it remains stationary or passes before the aperture
filmgoer \ˈ=,==\ *n* **:** one that goes to see motion pictures ⟨weekly ~*s* —*Irish Digest*⟩ ⟨inveterate ~*s* —George Woodcock⟩
film holder *n* **:** a lighttight container for photographic film
film·ic \-mik\ *adj* **:** of, relating to, resembling, or having the characteristics of motion pictures — **film·i·cal·ly** *adv*
film·i·ly \-məlē, -li\ *adv* **:** in a filmy manner
film·i·ness \-mēnəs, -min-\ *n* -ES **:** the quality or state of being filmy ⟨pleased by the ~ of the dress material⟩
film·iza·tion \,filməˈzāshən, ,fium-\ *n* -s **:** an adaptation (as of a novel or play) for motion pictures
film·ize \ˈfil,mīz, ˈfiu,-\ *vt* -ED/-ING/-S **:** CINEMATIZE
filmland \ˈ=,=\ *n* **:** FILMDOM
filmlike \ˈ=,=\ *adj* **:** FILMY
film pack *n* **:** a flat package of sheet films for daylight loading with each film being attached to a paper tab by which after exposure it is withdrawn from the front and moved to the back of the package
film phonograph *n* **:** a phonograph for playing only the sound recording on a photographic or magnetic film
film pickup *n* **:** the transmission by television of events outside the studio or of motion pictures
film play *n* **:** MOTION PICTURE
film recorder *n* **:** a recorder of sound on a photographic or magnetic film
filmslide \ˈ=,=\ *n* **:** a photographic transparency for projection consisting of a small piece of film mounted between two clear glass plates or cardboard masks
filmstrip \ˈ=,=\ *n* **:** a strip of film usu. 35 millimeters wide bearing photographs, diagrams, or printed or other graphic matter intended for still projection ⟨~*s,* recordings, maps . . . were used —Joeseph Alessandro⟩ — called also *slidefilm, stripfilm*
filmwright \ˈ=,=\ *n* **:** one who writes the script for a motion picture
filmy \ˈfilmē, ˈfiumē, -mi\ *adj* -ER/-EST **1 a :** light, transparent, and fluffy ⟨the ~ seeds of dandelions⟩ **:** GAUZY ⟨~ curtains⟩ **b :** TENUOUS, SLIGHT ⟨a ~ vesture of rhythm —*Sewanee Rev.*⟩ **2 a :** covered with haze **:** slightly misty ⟨a ~ sky⟩ **b :** GLAZED, GLASSY ⟨~ eyes⟩
film yeast *n* **:** FLOR
filmy fern *or* **film fern** *n* **1 :** a fern of the family Hymenophyllaceae **2 :** BRISTLE FERN
filo·plume \ˈfilə,plüm, ˈfīl-\ *n* [L *filum* thread + E *-o-* + *plume* — more at FILE] **:** a hairlike feather; *specif* **:** a feather with a slender scape and with but few barbs
fil·o·po·di·um \,==ˈpōdēəm\ *also* **fil·o·pod** \ˈ==,päd\ *n, pl* **filopo·dia** \-ōdēə\ *also* **filopods** [NL, fr. *filo-* (fr. L *filum*) + *-podium*] *zool* **:** a filamentous chiefly ectoplasmic pseudopodium typical of testaceous rhizopods
fi·lose \ˈfī,lōs\ *adj* [L *filum* + E *-ose*] **1 :** FILAMENTOUS **2 :** terminating in a threadlike process
fil·o·selle \ˌfiləˈsel, -ˈzel\ *n* -s [F, silk floss, filoselle, fr. MF, fr. OIt (dial.) *filosello* silkworm cocoon, silk floss, modif. (influenced by *filo* thread, fr. L *filum*) of (assumed) VL *follicellus,* alter. of L *folliculus* small bag, husk, pod — more at FILE, FOLLICLE] **:** soft silk thread for embroidery
filo silk \ˈfī(,)lō-, ˈfē\ *n* [*filoselle* + *silk*] **:** FILOSELLE
fils \ˈfils, ˈfēls\ *n, pl* **fils** [Ar *fils, fals*] **1 :** a monetary unit in Iraq and Jordan equal to $\frac{1}{1000}$ dinar — see MONEY table **2 :** a coin representing one fils
¹fil·ter \ˈfiltə(r)\ *n* -s *often attrib* [ME *filtre,* fr. ML *filtrum* felt, piece of felt used for straining liquids, of Gmc origin; akin to OS *filt* felt — more at FELT] **1 :** a porous article or mass (as of cloth, paper, or sand) that serves as a medium for separating from a liquid or gas passed through it matter held in suspension or dissolved impurities or coloring matter: as **a :** a circular piece of filter paper folded twice or fluted to fit a conical funnel or used flat (as in a Büchner funnel) esp. for laboratory filtrations **b** *also* **filter candle :** a candle-shaped hollow cylinder closed at one end and made of diatomite or unglazed porcelain with minute pores that prevent the passage of cells or bacteria and other microscopic organisms but not of ultramicroscopic bodies (as the filterable viruses) **2 a :** an apparatus (as a tube or tank) containing a filter medium and operating by gravity, pressure, or vacuum **b :** TRICKLING FILTER **3 :** a device or material for suppressing or minimizing waves or oscillations of certain frequencies passing through it without greatly altering the intensity of others: **a :** a combination of capacitors and inductors in an electric circuit that transmits only frequencies within a selected band — called also *band-pass filter;* see HIGH-PASS FILTER, LOW-PASS FILTER **b :** a transparent material (as glass or gelatin) that usu. transmits radiant energy of some wavelengths more freely than others, interference and polarization effects being used in some types **:** COLOR FILTER **c :** a tube or a combination of tubes, branch tubes, orifices, and resonant cavities in a sound channel that limits the frequency range of sounds passing through it — called also *acoustic filter*

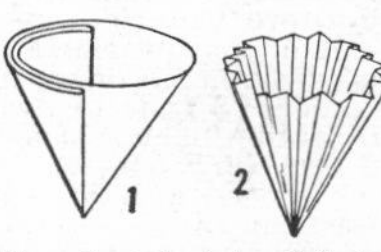

filters 1a: *1* plain, *2* fluted

²filter \"\ *vb* **filtered; filtered; filtering** \-t(ə)riŋ\ **filters** [ML *filtrare,* fr. *filtrum*] *vt* **1 :** to subject to the action of a filter **:** pass (a liquid or gas) through a filter for the purpose of purifying or separating or both **:** STRAIN; *also* **:** to act as a filter toward **2 :** to remove from a fluid by means of a filter — usu. used with *off* or *out* ⟨~ off impurities⟩ ~ *vi* **1 a :** to pass through or as if through a filter **:** PERCOLATE **b** *of light* **:** to pass through something that partially obstructs ⟨daylight ~*ing* through thick clouds —Francis Stuart⟩ ⟨sunlight ~*ing* through the shutters —T.B.Costain⟩ **2 a :** INFILTRATE 2 ⟨~ through the front lines⟩ **b :** to enter or cross over in small units over a period of time ⟨races which ~*ed* into Europe toward the end of the old stone age —Emma Hawkridge⟩
fil·ter·abil·i·ty \,filt(ə)rəˈbiləd·ē, -lətē, -i\ *n* -ES **:** the quality or state of being filterable
fil·ter·able *or* **fil·tra·ble** \ˈfilt(ə)rəbəl\ *adj* **:** capable of being filtered or of passing through a filter
filterable virus *or* **filtrable virus** *n* **:** an infective agent having essential constituent elements that are so small or in such physical state that a fluid containing it retains its infectivity after passing through a filter of diatomite or unglazed porcelain with pores too minute to permit the passage of bacteria — see VIRUS 2b
filter aid *n* **:** an agent consisting of solid particles (as of diatomite) that improves filtering efficiency (as by increasing the permeability of the filter cake) and that is either added to the suspension to be filtered or placed on the filter as a layer through which the liquid must pass
filter alum *n* **:** ALUMINUM SULFATE ⟨use of *filter alum* as a coagulant in water purification⟩
filter bed *n* **:** a bed of sand, gravel, or similar matter used for filtering large quantities of water or sewage
filter-bottom block *n* **:** a hollow vitrified salt-glazed clay block used in the floors of trickling filters in sewage-treatment plants
filter cake *n* **:** the solid mass remaining on a filter after the liquid that contained it has passed through; *specif* **:** the residue of impurities filtered from clarified juice of sugarcane that is used as a fertilizer
filter center *n* **:** a station in a military aircraft warning net that receives reports on aircraft sighted at observation posts and relays this information to stations where it is evaluated for action
fil·ter·er \ˈfiltərə(r)\ *n* -s **:** a worker who tends a filtration process in any of various capacities (as by operating a filter press) — called also *filterman*
filter factor *n* **:** a number by which the normal exposure time must be multiplied to compensate for the use of a color filter with a given photographic material and source of illumination
filter feeder *n* **:** an animal that obtains its food by filtering organic matter or minute organisms from a current of water that passes through some part of its system
filter flask *or* **filtering flask** *n* **:** a flask that is used for receiving a filtering liquid and that is usu. of heavy-walled glass and is often provided with a side tube to connect with a suction pump
filter fly *n* **:** any of a number of long-legged hairy-bodied two-winged flies (family Psychodidae) common about sewage filters
fil·ter·man \ˈfiltə(r)mən\ *n, pl* **filtermen 1 :** FILTERER **2 :** DECKER MAN
filter paper *n* **:** porous unsized paper used esp. for filtering; *specif* **:** such a paper chemically treated for use in quantitative analysis
filter press *n* **:** a filter consisting usu. of a series of rigid corrugated plates with intervening filter medium (as cloth) assembled in a framework so that the suspension to be filtered can be forced under pressure into the assembled press and the solids can collect as cake between the plates — see PLATE-AND-FRAME FILTER

filter flask with side tube

filter-press \ˈ=ˌ=\ *vt* [*filter press*] **:** to pass through a filter press
filter stick *n* **:** a short tube (as of glass or porcelain) provided with a filter plate or filter medium at one end and used esp. in microanalysis for siphoning off liquid above a precipitate
filter tip *n* **:** a cigar or cigarette tip of cotton, crepe paper, asbestos fiber, alpha cellulose, or cellulose acetate designed to filter the smoke before it enters the smoker's mouth; *also* **:** a cigar or cigarette provided with such a tip — **filter-tipped** \ˈ==ˈ=\ *adj*
filth \ˈfilth *also* -lth\ *n* -s [ME, fr. OE *fȳlth* (akin to OHG *fūlida* foulness, OS *fūlitha*) fr. OE *fūl* foul + *-th* — more at FOUL] **1 :** the quality or state of being dirty ⟨moral ~⟩ ⟨the faded aristocrat who lives in drunkenness and ~ —William Peden⟩ **2 :** something that tends to corrupt or disgust ⟨literature full of ~ and perversion⟩ **3** *now dial Eng* **a :** RASCAL, SCOUNDREL **b :** WHORE, SLUT **4 a :** rotten, foul, or unhealthy matter ⟨the ~ of a slaughterhouse⟩ **b** *chiefly Midland* (1) **:** underbrush and unwanted vegetation ⟨to cut ~⟩ (2) **:** WEEDS, TARES ⟨the hay bales were full of ~⟩
filth disease *n* **:** a disease due to pollution of the soil or water or to insanitary and filthy surroundings and habits
filth·i·ly \-thəlē, -li\ *adv* **:** in a filthy manner
filth·i·ness \-thēnəs, -thi-\ *n* -ES **:** the quality or state of being filthy ⟨saw only the disorder of his hair and the ~ of his clothes and person⟩

filthy \-thē,-thi\ *adj* -ER/-EST [ME, fr. *filth* + *-y*] **1 :** covered with, having the appearance of, or containing filth : very dirty ⟨~ clothes⟩ ⟨~ streets⟩ **2 a :** UNDERHANDED, VILE ⟨~ politics⟩ **b :** OBSCENE ⟨a ~ joke⟩ **syn** see DIRTY

filthy lucre *n* **1** *obs* : shameful gain **2 :** MONEY

filtrable *var of* FILTERABLE

1fil·trate \ˈfil·ˌtrāt, *usu* -ād·+V\ *vb* -ED/-ING/-S [ML *filtratus*, past part. of *filtrare* to filter — more at FILTER] : FILTER

2filtrate \"\ *n* -S : something that has been filtered (as the fluid that has passed through a filter)

fil·tra·tion \fil·ˈtrāshən\ *n* -S **1 :** the process of filtering **2 :** the process of passing through or as if through a filter : PERCOLATION; *also* : DIFFUSION

fi·lum \ˈfīləm\ *n, pl* **fi·la** \-lə\ [NL, fr. L, thread — more at FILE] : a filament or threadlike structure

fi·lum aquae \ˌfīləˈmä,kwē, ˌfēləˈmä,kwī\ *n, pl* **fi·la aqua·rum** \ˌfīlə·əˈkwa(a)rəm, ˌfēlə·əˈkwärəm\ [ML, lit., thread of water] : the thread of a stream

fi·lum ter·mi·na·le \ˈfīləm,tərməˈnā(ˌ)lē, ˈfēləm,tərməˈnäˌlā\ *n, pl* **fila termina·lia** \ˈfīlə,tərməˈnālēə, ˈfēlə,tərməˈnälēə\ [NL, lit., terminal thread] : the slender threadlike prolongation of the spinal cord below the origin of the lumbar nerves : the last portion of the pia mater

fim·ble \ˈfimbəl\ *or* **fimble hemp** *n* -S [MD *femeel, fimele*, fr. OF (*chanvre*) *femelle*, fr. *chanvre* hemp + *femelle* female — more at FEMALE] : a male hemp plant; *also* : the fiber of this plant

fim·bria \ˈfimbrēə\ *n, pl* **fimbri·ae** \-rē,ē, -ē,ī\ [NL, fr. L, fringe] **1 a** *fimbriae, pl* : a bordering fringe; *esp* : such a fringe at the entrance of the fallopian tubes **b :** a band of nerve fibers bordering the hippocampus and joining the fornix **2 :** a border that resembles a fringe (as the peristome of a moss)

fim·bri·al \-rēəl\ *adj* [NL *fimbria* + E *-al*] : of, relating to, or marked by fimbriae

1fim·bri·ate \-rē,āt\ *vt* -ED/-ING/-S [L *fimbria* + E *-ate* (v. suffix)] : to furnish with a fimbriation

2fim·bri·ate \-rēət, -rē,āt\ *adj* [L *fimbriatus* fringed, fr. *fimbria* + *-atus* -ate (adj. suffix)] **1 :** having the edge or extremity bordered by slender processes : FRINGED ⟨~ petals⟩ **2 :** FIMBRIATED

fim·bri·at·ed \-ē,ād·əd\ *adj* [L *fimbriatus* + E *-ed*] **1 :** FIMBRIATE **2 :** having a narrow border of specified tincture

fim·bri·a·tion \ˌ==ˈāshən\ *n* -S [ML *fimbriation-, fimbriatio*, fr. L *fimbriatus* + *-ion-, -io* -ion] **1 :** FRINGE, BORDER **2** *heraldry* : a narrow border to an ordinary

fim·bril·late \ˈfimbrə,lāt, (ˈ)fimˈbrilət\ *also* **fim·bril·lose** \ˈfimbrə,lōs\ *adj* [NL *fimbrilla* minute fringe (dim. of L *fimbria* fringe) + E *-ate* or *-ose*] : bordered with a minute fringe

fim·bri·sty·lis \ˌfimbrəˈstīləs\ *n, cap* [NL, fr. L *fimbria* + *-stylis* (fr. *stylus*)] : a genus of sedges (family Cyperaceae) having small usu. brownish flowers in loose umbels

fi·mic·o·lous \(ˈ)fīˈmikələs, fəˈm-\ *adj* [ISV *fimi-* (fr. L *fimus* dung) + *-colous* — more at FIANTS] : inhabiting or growing on dung

1fin \ˈfin\ *n* -S [ME *finne, finn*, fr. OE *finn*; akin to MLG & MD *vinne* fin, MHG *vinne* nail, OSw *fina* fin, L *spina* thorn, spine — more at SPINE] **1 :** a membranous process resembling a wing or a paddle in fishes and certain other aquatic animals that is used in propelling, balancing, or guiding the body **2 :** something resembling a fin esp. in appearance or function: **a :** a sharp plate or projection used as the colter of a plow **b :** HAND, ARM **c (1) :** an appendage of a boat (as a submarine); *also* : FIN KEEL **(2) :** a fixed or adjustable airfoil attached to an airplane approximately parallel to the vertical plane of symmetry to afford directional stability **(3) :** one of a pair of usu. slender projections at the rear of an automobile or other vehicle usu. consisting of an extension of the fender line or an upsweep above the fender line and intended to ornament or to provide added stability in motion — called also *tail fin* **d :** FLIPPER 1b — usu. used in pl. **e :** a ridge or piece of excess metal left along the edge of a casting where metal overflows the mold, at the edges of the groove when rolling with grooved rolls, around the parting line of a drop forging, or on a welded joint; *also* : a piece of excess material (as plastic or glass) left along the edge of a casting where the material overflows the mold **f (1) :** a thin sheet of metal squeezed out between the collars of the rolls in rolling or through the joints of a mold **(2) :** any of the projecting ribs on a radiator or internal-combustion engine cylinder **g :** FEATHER KEY, SPLINE **h :** a thin wall or panel used for screening of light or interruption of a view

2fin \"\ *vb* **finned; finned; finning; fins** *vi* **1 :** to show the fins above the water : break water — used of fish ⟨the fish is often sighted *finning* near the surface —I.N.Gabrielson⟩ **2 :** to propel oneself through the water on the back using the hands alone in a finning motion while the arms remain at the sides ~ *vt* : to construct or equip with fins — usu. used as past participle ⟨the cylinder head and barrel are heavily *finned* for strength —*Principles of Automotive Vehicles*⟩ ⟨*short-finned*⟩ ⟨steam is condensed in a *finned* coil —*Mech. Engineering*⟩

3fin \"\ *adj* : relating to a plow colter shaped like a fin

4fin *var of* FEN

5fin \ˈfin\ *n* -S [Yiddish *finf* five, fr. MHG *vumf, vimf*, fr. OHG *funf, finf* — more at FIVE] *slang* : a five-dollar bill ⟨you owe me a ~ already —Chandler Brossard⟩

fin *abbr* **1** finance; financial **2** finis **3** finish; finished

fin·able *or* **fine·able** \ˈfīnəbəl\ *adj* [ME *finable*, fr. *finen* to pay, pay a fine (fr. MF *finer*) + *-able* — more at FINE] : subject to the payment of a fine or liable to a fine

fi·na·gle *also* **fe·na·gle** \fəˈnāgəl\ *vb* **finagled** *also* **fenagled; finagled** *also* **fenagled; finagling** *also* **fenagling** \-g(ə)liŋ\ **finagles** *also* **fenagles** [perh. alter. of *fainaigue*] *vt* **1 :** to arrange for : WANGLE, MANAGE ⟨~ a 10-day leave⟩ **2 :** to obtain by chicanery or trickery : SWINDLE ⟨he bluffed and *finagled* his way into a fortune⟩ ~ *vi* : to use devious or questionable methods to achieve one's ends : MANEUVER

fi·na·gler \-g(ə)lə(r)\ *n* -S : one that finagles : CHEATER, SWINDLER

finagling *n* -S : maneuvering or manipulation esp. of a political or financial nature and sometimes of a dishonest character ⟨trying to cover up his financial ~*s*⟩ ⟨a master of backstairs ~⟩

1fi·nal \ˈfīnᵊl\ *adj* [ME, fr. MF *final, finel*, fr. L *finalis*, fr. *finis* boundary, limit, end + *-alis* -al; perh. akin to L *figere* to pierce, fasten — more at DIKE] **1 a (1) :** not to be altered or undone : CONCLUSIVE, DECISIVE ⟨a genuinely popular ballad can have no fixed and ~ form, no sole authentic version —F.J.Child⟩ ⟨all sales are ~⟩ ⟨the industry was heading toward its ~ decline —R.H.Brown⟩ ⟨in all free states the Constitution is ~ —John Adams⟩ **(2) :** constituting the ultimate in degree, achievement, or utilization : approaching perfection : PERFECT : not to be done again : DEFINITIVE ⟨a concept of art as disinterested, digested, measured, disciplined, and ~ —S.E.Hyman⟩ ⟨line, color, and tonal relations coalesce with ~ surety —Bernard Smith⟩ ⟨they have succumbed to the ~ sin, despair —*The Reporter*⟩ ⟨a meticulously detailed, authentic, and one would imagine ~ biography —Evelyn Eaton⟩ **b (1) :** ending a court action or proceeding leaving nothing further to be determined by the court or to be done except the administrative execution of the court's finding but not precluding an appeal — used of a court order, decision, judgment, decree, or sentence; compare INTERLOCUTORY **(2) :** being a court finding that is conclusive as to jurisdiction and precluding the right to appeal to or continue the case in any other court upon the merits ⟨in some minor matters the decisions of the lower courts are usu. made ~⟩ — often used in the phrase *final and conclusive* **(3) :** being a judgment or decree of the Supreme Court of the U.S. given under the provisions of the statutes giving it jurisdiction over appeals and writs of error that eliminates the litigation between the parties on the merits and leaves nothing for the inferior court to do in case of an affirmance except to execute the judgment or decree **(4)** *of a court hearing* : being the last at which evidence may be presented or the last at which argument may be made **2 a :** relating to or occurring at the end or conclusion : LAST, TERMINATING ⟨~ illness⟩ ⟨the ~ day of a school term⟩ ⟨one ~ comment is necessary⟩ ⟨in the ~ analysis, this is a second-rate work⟩ **b (1) :** last in a series of economic increments — compare MARGINAL **(2) :** not to be processed further but consumed or utilized as is : ULTIMATE — used of a commodity **c :** of that form regularly employed only at the end of a word — used of a letter in any of a number of alphabets (as the Hebrew and Arabic) that has two or more positional forms ⟨writing a ~ letter in medial position⟩ **3 a :** relating to an end or object to be gained : related to the purpose or ultimate end in view **b :** expressive of purpose — used of a subordinate clause, sometimes also of a conjunction (*that, in order that, lest*) introducing it **syn** see LAST

2final \"\ *n* -S : something that is final: as **a :** a deciding match, game, heat, or trial — usu. used in pl. ⟨qualified to play in the ~*s*⟩ **b :** the last examination in a course — usu. used in the pl. with *the* ⟨busily preparing for the ~*s*⟩; *also* : the last examination or set of examinations taken by a candidate for an advanced degree ⟨after his thesis was accepted, he'd come down . . . and take his ~ —G.R.Stewart⟩ **c** [ML *finalis*, fr. L, adj.] : the keynote of an ecclesiastical mode ⟨the ~ is *d* in Dorian mode⟩ **d :** the final sound or letter of a syllable, morpheme, or word **e :** a form of an alphabetical letter (as in the Hebrew and Arabic alphabets) that regularly is used only at the end of a word **f :** FINAL EDITION

final cause *n* [ME] : something that is the end or purpose of a process — used in Aristotelianism and some other teleological doctrines

final common path *also* **final common pathway** *n* : a motoneuron that forms the terminal step of one or more reflex circuits transmitting their stimuli to an effector end organ

final drive *n* : the means for transmitting power from the propeller shaft to the rear axle in an automotive vehicle

fi·nale \fəˈnalē, fēˈ-, -näl-,-nāl-, -li\ *n* -S [It, fr. *finale*, adj., final, fr. L *finalis* — more at FINAL] : the close or termination of something: as **a (1) :** the last section or movement of an instrumental musical composition **(2) :** the last section or piece in any act of an opera usu. arranged for a large ensemble **b :** the closing part, piece, scene, or number in any public performance ⟨the ~ of a ballet⟩ **c :** the close or conclusion of any sequence, series, or action : the last and often climactic event or item in a series ⟨this was the sad ~ of every reflection —Jane Austen⟩ ⟨the novel has its ~ at a cocktail bar⟩ ⟨drop over a high cliff as a ~ to a succession of cascades —*Amer. Guide Series: Oregon*⟩ ⟨the ~ is cut-up fresh fruit —Jane Nickerson⟩

final edition *n* : the last edition of a morning, afternoon, or evening newspaper issued on any one day

fi·na·lis \fēˈnäləs\ *n, pl* **fina·les** \-,lās\ [ML, fr. L, adj., final] : FINAL c

fi·nal·ism \ˈfīnᵊl,izəm\ *n* -S : a belief in final causes : teleological doctrine — compare TELEOLOGY

1fi·nal·ist \-ᵊləst\ *n* -S [F *finaliste*, fr. *final* + *-iste* -ist] **1 :** a believer in or advocate of finalism **2 :** any of the contestants who meet in the final round of a competition

2finalist \"\ *or* **fi·nal·is·tic** \ˌ==ˈistik\ *adj* : TELEOLOGICAL

fi·nal·i·ty \fīˈnaləd·ē, fəˈ-, -lətē, -i\ *n* -ES **1 a :** the character or condition of being final, finished, conclusive, irrevocable, or complete : CONCLUSION ⟨there is a ~ to a diplomatic defeat that cannot be overcome —*New Republic*⟩ ⟨has not been able to bring to ~ many of the interesting ideas . . . generated by his fertile mind —W.E.L.Clark⟩ ⟨there appears to be a disposition not to accept the ~ of the revolution in China —Aneurin Bevan⟩ **b :** the quality, manner, or air of being final or decisive ⟨walked across the court with a kind of ~ in his stride —R.P.Warren⟩ ⟨spoke with curt ~⟩ ⟨certitude and ~ mark their assertions —Paul Radin⟩ **2 :** the condition of being so perfect or finished as to be incapable of improvement : the condition of being the ultimate authority or the last word : PERFECTION, INEVITABILITY ⟨in the work of the great classical writers a ~ of effect which places certain of their scenes beyond the reach of change —Virginia Woolf⟩ ⟨we cannot claim ~ of judgment —Herbert Reade⟩ ⟨the authentic ~ of his autobiography —W.T.Scott⟩ **3 :** the categorial or causal relation of end or purpose to its means : TELEOLOGY 1 **4 :** something that is final : a final, ultimate, or fundamental fact, action, detail, condition, or belief ⟨a code of *finalities* is a necessary condition of profitable talk between two persons —O.W. Holmes †1935⟩ **5 :** 1CLOSURE 11

fi·nal·iza·tion \ˌfīnᵊləˈzāshən, -ᵊl,īˈz-\ *n* -S : the act, process, or an instance of finalizing ⟨the ~ of a sound doctrine set forth in service manuals for use and guidance in future maneuvers —Kalman Siegel⟩

fi·nal·ize \ˈfīnᵊl,īz\ *vb* -ED/-ING/-S *vt* : to put in final or finished form : FINISH, COMPLETE, CLOSE ⟨soon my conclusions will be *finalized* —D.D.Eisenhower⟩ ⟨the couple ~ plans to marry at once —S.J.Perelman⟩ ⟨empowered to . . . ~ the deal —James Joseph⟩ : give final approval to ⟨the list has not been *finalized* by the deputy, but it won't be changed now —Robertson Davies⟩ ⟨ties up the day's loose ends, *finalizing* the papers prepared and presented by his staff —*Newsweek*⟩ ~ *vi* : to bring something to completion ⟨if we don't ~ tonight, those two . . . will get suspicious and sell to someone else —I.L. Idriess⟩

fi·nal·ly \ˈfīn(ᵊ)lē, -li\ *adv* [ME, fr. 1*final* + *-ly*] **1 a :** after a certain space of time : as the last act or occurrence in a series : in the end : at last : EVENTUALLY ⟨he carefully adjusted his tie, took one last look about the room, and ~ walked out the door⟩ ⟨the theologians . . . ~ adjusted theology to the new conceptions —G.C.Sellery⟩ ⟨pressure falls steadily and may ~ reach a point at which shock occurs —Morris Fishbein⟩ **b :** in the last analysis : ULTIMATELY ⟨the creation of the work of art is what ~ concerns us —Michael Kitson⟩ ⟨the generality and heartiness of assent on which laws ~ depend for effectiveness —*Modern Churchman*⟩ ⟨can positively and ~ depend upon him —Walter de la Mare⟩ **c :** by way of conclusion : as the last point ⟨~, I wish to thank all who cooperated in this important project⟩ ⟨~, the essayist considers the vexing problem of free will⟩ **2 :** for all time : beyond change : IRREVOCABLY, CONCLUSIVELY, DECISIVELY ⟨this question which you have answered so ~ —Willa Cather⟩ ⟨reluctance to commit himself ~ to one extreme or the other —E.D.H.Johnson⟩

final process *n* : EXECUTION 3b

final record *n* **1 :** the court record corresponding to the common-law judgment record **2 :** the record of a case in its final form as shown by the permanent docket entries made by the recording officer of the court

final recovery *n* : the ultimate judgment or decree of a court on the merits; *sometimes* : the verdict rendered by a jury

final utility *n* : MARGINAL UTILITY

1fi·nance \fəˈnan(t)s, ˈfī,n-, -naa(ə)n- *also* fīˈn-\ *n* -S [ME *finaunce* ending, settlement, payment, ransom, fr. MF *finance*, fr. *finer* to end, pay + *-ance* — more at FINE] **1 finances** *pl* : the pecuniary affairs or resources of a state, company, or individual ⟨school had to close for lack of ~*s*⟩ ⟨his ~*s* were in bad shape⟩ ⟨company with ample ~*s*⟩ **2 :** the obtaining of funds or capital : FINANCING ⟨productive business expansion for which ~ would otherwise be unavailable —F.D.Roosevelt⟩ **3 :** the system that includes the circulation of money, the granting of credit, the making of investments, and the provision of banking facilities ⟨people employed in . . . trade, ~, personal services, and government —P.H. Landis⟩

2finance \"\ *vb* -ED/-ING/-S [ME *finauncen*, fr. *finaunce*, n.] *vt* **1 :** to raise or provide funds or capital for ⟨~ a war⟩ ⟨~ a new home⟩ ⟨encouraged and *financed* a career⟩ ⟨~ a new venture⟩ **2 :** to provide with necessary funds in order to achieve a desired end ⟨~ a son through school⟩ ⟨~*ed* the government through this emergency⟩ **3 :** to sell on credit : to supply on credit ⟨the early motor-vehicle producers were not in a position to ~ . . . the automobile distributors and dealers who wished to obtain cars for resale to consumers —C.W. Phelps⟩ ⟨your store bill is too high, we just can't ~ you any longer⟩ ~ *vi* : to secure needed funds or capital ⟨governments and individuals ~ through borrowing⟩ — **fin·ance·able** *adj*

finance bill *n* **1 :** a bill of exchange drawn usu. by one bank on another bank for the purpose of transferring funds as a result of loans or for temporarily procuring money by discounting the bill **2 :** a legislative act to provide the necessary funds for the public treasury : a revenue bill — compare MONEY BILL

finance capitalism *n* : a stage of capitalism in which economic and political domination is exercised by financial institutions or financiers rather than by industrial capitalists

finance company *n* : a company that buys accounts receivable from business usu. in the form of installment notes covering the purchase of durable goods (as automobiles)

fi·nan·cial \fəˈnanchəl, (ˈ)fīˈn-, -naan-\ *adj* [1*finance* + *-ial*] **1 :** relating to finance or financiers ⟨rumors heard in high ~ circles⟩ ⟨found himself in severe ~ difficulties⟩ ⟨the ~ aspect of a college education⟩ **2 :** in good standing as to payment of dues : paying dues : not honorary — used of a member of a society, trade union, or other association

financial institution *n* : an enterprise specializing in the handling and investment of funds (as a bank, trust company, insurance company, savings and loan association, or investment company)

fi·nan·cial·ly \-ch(ə)lē, -li\ *adv* : in respect to finance : from a financial point of view ⟨~ Constantinople was the center of an area much more extensive than the Empire —R.W. Southern⟩ ⟨the project is ~ unsound⟩

financial year *n* : FISCAL YEAR

1fin·an·cier \ˌfinənˈsi(ə)r, fəˌnanˈ-, fəˌnaanˈ-, -ˈsiə *also* ˌfīˌna(a)n- *or* ˌfiˌna(a)nˈ- *or* ˌfīnən-, *chiefly Brit* fīˈnansiə(r) *or* fiˈnansiə(r)\ *n* -S [F, fr. MF, fr. *finance* + *-ier* -er] **1 a** *obs* : an officer who administers the public revenues **b :** a large-scale investor : CAPITALIST **c :** a person who undertakes to secure large funds for a government or business : INVESTMENT BANKER **2** *obs* : a receiver, farmer, or administrator of public taxes in France before the Revolution

2financier \"\ *vi* -ED/-ING/-S : to conduct financial operations often by sharp, ruthless, or reprehensible practices ⟨put an end to such ~*ing* and unhallowed practices —Hartley Withers⟩ ⟨cold-eyed ~*ing* —Carlos Baker⟩

fi·nan·cière \fēnäⁿsyeer\ *adj* [F (*à la*) *financière*, lit., in the manner of a financier] : having or being a garnish or a sauce the principal ingredients of which are truffles, mushrooms, olives, Madeira wine, and sometimes balls of forcemeat ⟨sweetbreads ~⟩

financing *n* -S : the act, process, or an instance of raising or providing funds ⟨announcement of new ~ has almost invariably been followed by a drop in the stock of the company concerned —*Time*⟩; *also* : the funds thus raised or provided ⟨new ~ will consist of $34,000,000 additional first mortgage bonds —*Barron's*⟩

finback \ˈ=,=\ *n* [so called fr. the prominent dorsal fin] : a whalebone whale of the genus *Balaenoptera* : RORQUAL; *esp* : a common whale of the Atlantic coast of the U. S. (*B. physalus*) attaining a length of over 60 feet and now the commonest large whale of the region

fin boom *n* : an adjustable boom used in logging on navigable streams where permanent booms are not allowed

fin·ca \ˈfēŋkə, ˈfiŋ-\ *n* -S [Sp, fr. *fincar* to remain, fr. (assumed) VL *figicare*, fr. L *figere* to pierce, fasten — more at DIKE] : a rural property, ranch, or estate in Spain or Spanish America; *esp* : a landed estate in Spanish America devoted to the cultivation of tropical crops

finch \ˈfinch\ *n* -ES [ME, fr. OE *finc*; akin to OHG *fincho* finch, MD *vinke* finch, Sw *spink* small bird, sparrow, Gk *spingos, spiza, spinos* chaffinch, *spizein* to chirp, Skt *phingaka* drongo] **1 :** a bird of the family Fringillidae including the sparrows, grosbeaks, crossbills, goldfinches, linnets, buntings, and related birds, being of small or moderate size and rather stout build, having generally a short stout conical bill adapted for crushing seeds, being often very beneficial to agriculture by destroying the seeds of weeds, and being sometimes fine singers (as the canary) — used often in combination ⟨bull*finch*⟩ ⟨chaf*finch*⟩ ⟨gold*finch*⟩; see BILL illustration **2 :** any of various African and Australian weaverbirds (family Ploceidae) — see FIRE FINCH, GOULDIAN FINCH

finch falcon *n* : FALCONET 2

fin colter *n* : a colter having a fin-shaped hanging knife

1find \ˈfīnd\ *vb* **found** \ˈfau̇nd\ **found; finding; finds** [ME *finden*, fr. OE *findan*; akin to OE *fētha* foot soldier, troop of foot soldiers, OS *findan, fithan* to find, *fāthi* act of going, OHG *findan* to find, *fendo, fendeo* one that walks, ON *finna* to find, Goth *finthan* to find, find out, L *pont-, pons* bridge, Gk *pontos* sea, *patos* path, Skt *patha* way, path, course; basic meaning: going, stepping] *vt* **1 a (1) :** to come upon accidentally : gain the first sight of (as something new or unknown) ⟨*found* the tracks of some unknown animal⟩ ⟨*found* a large stone blocking the way⟩ ⟨the child *found* a coin in the street⟩ ⟨the well diggers *found* a number of Indian artifacts⟩ **(2) :** to fall in with (a person) : ENCOUNTER ⟨~*s* interesting people wherever he goes⟩ **b (1) :** to meet with (a particular kind of reception or treatment) ⟨he hoped to ~ favor in her sight⟩ ⟨his doctrines *found* no acceptance among scholars⟩ **(2) :** to obtain or come to have (something desirable) as if without effort ⟨the book *found* a host of readers⟩ ⟨the new product *found* few buyers⟩ **2 a :** to come upon (a material object) by searching or effort ⟨they *found* water at a depth of 10 feet⟩ ⟨the committee must ~ a suitable man for the job⟩ ⟨*found* his missing brother at last⟩ **b :** to discover by study or experience directed to an object or end ⟨~ the answer to a complex mathematical problem⟩ ⟨scientific research is ~*ing* important new principles nearly every day —C.E.Kellogg⟩ ⟨~*s* that . . . the volumes of the other gas . . . are in the ratio 1:2 —L.K.Nash⟩ **c :** to hit upon : DEVISE, INVENT, CONTRIVE ⟨*found* a more modern method of treating the processed material⟩ **d :** to secure or obtain (something needed or desirable) by effort or management : summon up : PROCURE ⟨*found* the time to continue his studies⟩ ⟨~ bail for a prisoner⟩ ⟨~ the courage to address a large audience⟩ **e :** to attain to : arrive at : REACH ⟨the bullet *found* its mark⟩ **f :** to discover by sounding ⟨preliminary surveys failed to ~ any solid bottom —O.S.Nock⟩ **g :** to obtain as if by effort ⟨the spirit of adventure . . . *found* vent in the life of the explorer —B.K.Sandwell⟩ ⟨authors whose textbooks ~ publication —James Britton⟩ ⟨the new system has *found* its first codification —*Reporter*⟩ **3** *dial* : to perceive or detect by or as if by the senses; *specif* : FEEL, SUFFER ⟨~ pain⟩ ⟨~ punishment⟩ ⟨grandpa *found* his rheumatism again this morning⟩ **4 a :** to learn by experience or trial : discover by the intellect or the feelings : PERCEIVE, EXPERIENCE, DETECT, REGARD, FEEL ⟨*found* him a very sensible and tactful man⟩ ⟨~ much pleasure in his company⟩ ⟨*found* something repellent about the man⟩ ⟨~ no logic in his argument⟩ ⟨*found* a strange odor in the room⟩ **b (1) :** to perceive (oneself) to be in a certain place or condition ⟨when he awoke, he *found* himself in a luxuriously furnished apartment⟩ ⟨~ herself in a dilemma⟩ ⟨*found* themselves in the presence of the sovereigns⟩ **(2) :** to perceive (oneself) to be in a certain condition with respect to health — usu. used in a question ⟨how do you ~ yourself to-day? —Winston Churchill⟩ **c (1) :** to gain or regain the use or power of ⟨after a second's pause, he *found* broken speech —Arthur Morrison⟩ ⟨a baby just beginning to ~ her feet⟩ **(2) :** to attain to (the exercise of one's inherent powers) : establish (a place or footing) in a profession or career : recover from (a financial, moral, or other downfall) — often used in such phrases as *find one's wings, find one's feet* ⟨the youthful poet had just begun to ~ his wings⟩ ⟨continue a small unearned allowance while his son *found* his feet at the bar —Geoffrey Gorer⟩ ⟨when he *found* his feet the army . . . decided to overlook the prison record and accept his reform —Gordon Harrison⟩ **d :** to bring (oneself) to a consciousness of one's powers, capacities, or of one's proper sphere of activity : raise (oneself) to that point of efficiency, effectiveness, achievement or to that mode of life of which one is inherently capable ⟨it was an army that had *found* itself —F.V.W. Mason⟩ ⟨must help the student to ~ himself as an individual —N.M.Pusey⟩ ⟨she suddenly ~*s* herself, and becomes the acknowledged leader of all the women of the neighborhood —Vernon Jarratt⟩ **5 a (1) :** to provide for the use of : provide with : SUPPLY ⟨for selected children the church ~*s* half of this sum, leaving the parent to ~ the rest —Ernest & Pearl Beaglehole⟩ — often used with *in* ⟨there'd be all the neighbors to ~ in victuals and drink —Mary Webb⟩ ⟨we are *found* in everything—house, servants, food —Rachel Henning⟩ **(2) :** to provide (room and board) esp. as a condition of employment : MAINTAIN ⟨he was chopping by day's work—75 cents a day—and *found* himself —Herman Melville⟩ — often used in the phrases *everything found, all found* ⟨combining business and pleasure in a new kind of holiday camp with all *found* —Fred Majdalany⟩ ⟨no worries, everything *found,* and lots of Saturday-night spirits —Lionel Shapiro⟩ ⟨why should you go to the workhouse? I offer you 14 pounds and everything *found* —George Moore⟩ **b :** to equip with what is needful or necessary ⟨the boat comes fully *found,* ready to go —*Holiday*⟩ **6 :** to arrive at (a conclusion) **:** come to (a finding) **:** determine and declare (as a verdict in a judicial proceeding) **:** agree or settle upon and deliver ⟨he was *found* guilty⟩ ⟨~ a verdict⟩ ⟨~ a true bill of indictment against an accused person⟩ **7** *chiefly Midland* **:** to give birth to — used of animals ⟨about February . . . the mother bears ~ their cubs —Mary Sloop⟩ ~ *vi* **1 :** to discover the game or scent — used chiefly of hunting dogs ⟨when the hounds *found,* they went off at a very fast clip —*Scientific Monthly*⟩ ⟨harked back to the famous runs of his youth, telling me where they had *found,* where killed, and hazards in between —Adrian Bell⟩ **2 :** to determine a case judicially or quasi-judicially by a verdict or decision — used of a court, jury, or a quasi-judicial administrative body — **find fault :** to discover and proclaim some defect or censurable action or quality **:** criticize unfavorably ⟨he is chronically *finding fault*⟩ — often used with *with* ⟨at times *found fault* with interpretation, balance, tone quality —*Current Biog.*⟩ — **find in one's heart** *archaic* **:** to be willing or disposed ⟨I could *find in my heart* to ask your pardon —Philip Sidney⟩ — **find one's way 1 a :** to make one's way by searching, inquiry, or trial and error **:** manage to reach some destination ⟨could not *find his way* to my house⟩ ⟨*found his way* to the pantry in total darkness⟩ **b :** to go to or reach some place by or as if by chance or after an interval of wandering ⟨maybe fur traders *found their way* to California —R.A.Billington⟩ ⟨when the white men first *found their way* to this continent⟩ **:** move along a certain route or path ⟨the waters *find their way* . . . through the lake's outlet —Tom Marvel⟩ **2 :** to be carried or brought to some place ⟨the tapestry was cut into three sections . . . and the various parts *found their* separate *ways* to the U.S. —*Time*⟩ **:** obtain entrance **:** ENTER ⟨dozens of curious little crackpot movements *found their way* into the curriculum —Martin Gardner⟩ **3 :** to end up ⟨a considerable portion of . . . the land grants . . . *found its way* into the hands of private speculators —*Amer. Guide Series: Oregon*⟩

²find \"\ *n* -s **1 :** the act or an instance of finding esp. something valuable **:** DISCOVERY ⟨announced the ~ of an important manuscript⟩ ⟨a ~ of high-quality ore deposits⟩; *specif* **:** discovery of game or a scent by a hunting dog ⟨his first ~ was at the far end of one of the stubble fields —*Popular Dogs*⟩ **2 a :** something that is found ⟨any small archaeological ~ may provide valuable historical evidence⟩; *esp* **:** a valuable discovery ⟨these letters constitute a real ~⟩ ⟨an important uranium ~⟩ **b :** a person whose ability or value proves to be surprisingly or unexpectedly great ⟨the boy . . ., not yet 24 years old, was a ~ —Will Irwin⟩ ⟨the young actress was the theatrical ~ of the year⟩

find·er \ˈfīndə(r)\ *n* -s [ME, fr. *finden* + *-er*] **1 :** one that finds **2 :** one that deals in findings (as of a shoemaker) **3 :** a small astronomical telescope of low power and wide field attached to a larger telescope parallel to its axis for the purpose of finding an object more readily **4 :** a device sometimes used by artists to aid in the selection or arrangement of a subject and usu. made of a card with a rectangular opening through which the object may be viewed as if within a picture frame **5 :** a device attached to or forming a part of a camera for showing the area of the subject that will be included in the picture (as by reflecting upon a viewing lens an image formed by a lens of short focus or by viewing directly with a sight held at eye level) **6 :** a person (as an investment banker) who originates a financial operation (as public financing for a corporation) for a fee

finders' leather *n* **:** sole leather specially processed for use by shoe repairers

finder switch *n* **:** an electric switch that automatically finds a circuit out of a large number of circuits from which a signal comes — used esp. in telephone circuits

fin-de-siè·cle \ˌfaⁿdəˌsyekl(ᵊ), -sēˌek-, -k(lə)\ *adj* [F *fin de siècle* end of the century] **1 a :** of or relating to the close of the 19th century ⟨recreated in its *fin-de-siècle* splendor on a sound stage in London —T.F.Brady⟩ **b :** of, relating to, characterized by, or resembling in one or another respect the late 19th century literary and artistic climate of sophistication, escapism, extreme aestheticism, world-weariness, and fashionable despair **:** DECADENT 2a ⟨this attitude grew into a *fin-de-siècle* one of cultivated fatigue and bored aestheticism —Peter De Vries⟩ ⟨queer that in 1917 a man of 29 should be writing in so adolescent and *fin-de-siècle* a manner —Jacob Isaacs⟩ ⟨early dabblings in the mood of the *fin-de-siècle* aesthetes —R.D.Jacobs⟩ **2 :** of or relating to the end of an era

findfault \ˈ=ˌ=\ *n* [¹*find* + *fault*] *dial Eng* **:** FAULTFINDER

finding *n* -s [ME, fr. gerund of *finden* to find — more at FIND] **1 :** FIND 2a ⟨archaeological ~*s* along the route . . . led some authorities to conclude that the district was once the home of the mound builders —*Amer. Guide Series: Mich.*⟩ **2 findings** *pl* **a :** the small parts and the materials other than leather that enter into the making of a shoe (as nails, eyelets, laces, buckles) **b :** small articles used in various trades (as buttons, thread, zippers for dressmakers, or catches, swivels, clasps, wire for jewelers) **3 a :** the result of a judicial or quasi-judicial examination or inquiry esp. into matters of fact as embodied in the verdict of a jury or decision of a court, referee, or administrative body **b :** the result or conclusion of any inquiry or investigation — usu. used in pl. ⟨the ~*s* of natural science⟩ ⟨published his ~*s* in scholarly journals⟩

finding list *n* **:** an index, catalog, or list (as of books or rare coins) usu. without brief description and annotation **:** CHECKLIST

fin·don haddock \ˌfin(d)ən-\ *n, cap F* [*Findon,* village near Aberdeen, Scotland, noted for its smoked fish] **:** FINNAN HADDIE

find out *vt* **1 a :** to catch in a theft or offense of any kind ⟨the Indian ate one of the loaves, and was . . . *found out* —Edward Clodd⟩ **b :** DETECT, DISCOVER ⟨*found out* that he was divorced⟩ **:** LEARN ⟨the press *found out* and proclaimed his youthful sins⟩ ⟨vainly tried to *find out* his name and occupation⟩ **2 a :** to penetrate to the true character or identity of **:** penetrate the disguise of **:** UNMASK ⟨if I tried to wear a halo and faked it, I'd be *found out* for sure —Jackie Gleason⟩ ⟨afraid the truth would *find* them *out* —H.S.Reuss⟩ **b :** to bring retribution upon **:** visit with retribution ⟨his sins have *found* him *out*⟩ ⟨the fallacies in their doctrine and their own imperfect abilities have *found* them *out* —*Time & Tide*⟩ ~ *vi* **:** to discover, learn, or verify something secret, unknown, or uncertain ⟨you don't know for sure, and how are you going to *find out*⟩

finds *pres 3d sing of* FIND, *pl of* FIND

findspot \ˈ=ˌ=\ *n* [²*find* + *spot*] **:** the place where an archaeological object has been found

¹fine \ˈfīn\ *n* -s [ME *fin, fine,* fr. OF *fin,* fr. L *finis* boundary, limit, end — more at FINAL] **1** *obs* **:** END, CONCLUSION, CLOSE **2 a :** a sum formerly paid as compensation or for exemption from punishment but now imposed as punishment for a crime — distinguished from *forfeiture* and *penalty* **b :** a forfeiture or penalty paid to an injured party in a civil action **c :** a sum of money ordered paid by one in contempt of court to vindicate the court's authority **d** (1) **:** a sum paid to a library as a penalty for keeping a book beyond the date due (2) **:** the monetary penalty imposed for infraction of a rule or obligation ⟨club members who were late had to pay a 25-cent ~⟩ **3 a** *feudal law* (1) **:** a money payment made by a tenant to his lord on a particular occasion (as a transfer of the tenant right) (2) **:** an endowment whereby a tenant's widow was permitted to claim her dower **b** (1) **:** a final amicable agreement or compromise of an actual or fictitious controversy or suit formerly made in England by leave of the king or his justices (2) **:** a settlement giving exemption or release; *esp* **:** one obtained by a payment of money **c** *or* **fine of lands :** a compromise of a fictitious suit used as a form of conveyance of lands where ordinary conveyances were less efficacious (as in cases involving married women or entailed estates) **d** *English & early American law* **:** an agreement effecting a conveyance of estates in land by entering into a friendly lawsuit whereby one party's claim of title was formally recognized by the other, putting an end to all litigation between them **e** *English law* **:** a sum of money charged for any benefit, favor, or privilege (as obtaining or renewing a lease) — **in fine :** in conclusion **:** in short ⟨it is shorn of all pathos, sympathy, understanding, and romance—of everything human, *in fine* —O.S.J.Gogarty⟩

²fine \"\ *vb* -ED/-ING/-S [ME *finen,* fr. MF *finer* to end, pay (as a fine), fr. *fin,* n., end] *vt* **1 :** to pay by way of fine or composition **2** [¹*fine*] **:** to set a fine on by judgment of a court esp. as a punishment **:** punish by fine ~ *vi, archaic* **:** to pay a fine, penalty, composition, ransom, or consideration for any special privilege or exemption; *esp* **:** to pay for release from accepting the duties of an office — often used with *for, off,* or *down*

³fine \"\ *adj* -ER/-EST [ME *fin, fine,* fr. OF *fin,* fr. L *finis,* n., boundary, limit, end (as in such phrases as *finis honorum* the height of honor, the highest honor; trans. of Gk *telos,* lit., end) — more at FINAL, WHEEL] **1 a :** free from impurity **:** brought to perfection **:** highly purified **:** REFINED, SUPERIOR, PURE ⟨~ gold and silver⟩ **b** *of a metal* **:** having a stated proportion of pure metal in the composition ⟨gold 23 karats ~⟩ — compare FINENESS 2b **c** *of glass* **:** freed from bubbles **2 a** (1) **:** very small **:** MINUTE ⟨~ print⟩ (2) **:** marked by subtlety, refinement, or intricacy of thought or expression **:** HAIRSPLITTING ⟨very ~ legal points were involved⟩ ⟨I cannot follow these ~ distinctions⟩ (3) **:** performed with extreme care and accuracy ⟨~ measurement⟩ ⟨~ adjustment⟩ (4) *of bodily tremors* **:** of slight excursion **b :** not coarse **:** constituting small particles ⟨~ sand⟩ ⟨~ flour⟩ **c** (1) **:** not thick or clumsy **:** SLENDER, FILMY ⟨~ thread⟩ ⟨~ chiffon⟩ ⟨a fine-boned hand⟩ (2) *of wool* **:** having a diameter similar to that of merino wool (3) *of paper* **:** of a grade suitable for writing, printing, or drawing **d :** THIN, KEEN, ATTENUATED ⟨a sword with a ~ edge⟩ **e** (1) **:** made of delicate materials **:** delicately fashioned or proportioned **:** exquisite in texture **:** LIGHT, CLEAR, FAIR, FRAGILE ⟨he was ~ in profile, in the texture of his fair skin —Osbert Sitwell⟩ ⟨many of the present inhabitants have ~ skins, fair hair, and florid complexions —Tobias Smollett⟩ ⟨~ linen⟩ ⟨~ china⟩ (2) **:** sharp forward or aft — used of a ship **f** (1) **:** trained to a point of weight and muscular activity close to the limit of efficiency — used of an athlete or animal (2) *cricket* **:** being to the rear of the defending batsman and nearer than usual to the line of flight of a bowled ball ⟨caught at ~ leg⟩ — compare SQUARE **g :** having a delicate or subtle quality ⟨the ~ scent of burning wax —Vicki Baum⟩ ⟨the ~ bouquet of a vintage wine⟩ ⟨the ~ irony of it all⟩ ⟨~, rapier-edged humor⟩ **3 a** *obs* **:** CLEVER, INGENIOUS, CUNNING, CRAFTY **b :** subtle, sensitive, or acute in perception or feeling ⟨he has a ~ ear for the . . . idiomatic English that passes for conversation among the youths of the day —Max Wilk⟩ **4 a :** superior in character, nature, ability, or prospects **:** NOBLE, SKILLFUL, EXCELLENT ⟨a ~ man⟩ ⟨a ~ ship⟩ ⟨a ~ musician⟩ ⟨you have a ~ future before you⟩ **b :** superior in construction, execution, design, or expression ⟨a ~ work of art⟩ ⟨a ~ orchestra was playing⟩ **c :** of noble or attractive appearance **:** BEAUTIFUL, HANDSOME, PLEASANT, BRIGHT ⟨a ~ view⟩ ⟨a ~ morning⟩ ⟨a very ~ garden⟩ **d** (1) **:** ORNATE, SHOWY **:** ELEGANT ⟨~ feathers make ~ birds⟩ ⟨wore a ~ new dress⟩ (2) *of writing* **:** excessively ornate **:** affectedly elegant **:** FLORID, RHETORICAL ⟨this last sentence is so ~ I am quite ashamed —Thomas Gray⟩ (3) **:** marked by or displaying elegance or refinement often affected or excessive **:** FASTIDIOUS, DAINTY ⟨our ~ neighbors wouldn't speak to the likes of us⟩ ⟨sneered at the stranger's ~ ways⟩ **5 a :** SPLENDID, NOTABLE, ADMIRABLE ⟨spoke with ~ enthusiasm⟩ ⟨his terrible slashing wit, his ~ scorn of stupidity and cowardice —John Reed⟩ ⟨what a ~ darling baby⟩ **b :** GREAT, TERRIFIC, AWFUL — used as an intensive ⟨had come running in a ~ embarrassment —Glenway Wescott⟩ ⟨you make a ~ mistake if you think I'm out for quarreling —Mrs. Patrick Campbell⟩ **c :** very well **:** EXCELLENT ⟨I feel ~⟩

⁴fine \"\ *adv* [ME *fin, fine,* fr. *fin, fine,* adj.] **1 :** FINELY: as **a :** ELEGANTLY, MINCINGLY ⟨talks and walks so ~, just like a great lady⟩ **b :** SPLENDIDLY, WELL ⟨you did ~⟩ ⟨he made out ~⟩ ⟨I liked it ~⟩ **c :** SUBTLY, DELICATELY, MINUTELY ⟨the line between victory and defeat . . . will be ~ drawn⟩ **2** *Scot* **:** SURELY **:** for certain ⟨~ I know him though I haven't seen him for years —John Buchan⟩ **3 :** with a very narrow margin of time or space — often used with *cut* or *run* ⟨close thing . . . mustn't run it so ~ another time —P.G.Wodehouse⟩

⁵fine \"\ *vb* -ED/-ING/-S [ME *finen,* fr. *fin, fine,* adj.] *vt* **1 :** REFINE, PURIFY, CLARIFY ⟨~ and filter wine⟩ ⟨beer is sometimes *fined* before bottling —B.M.Brown⟩ ⟨~ gold⟩ ⟨the glass will be fully *fined* before being admitted to the working chamber —*Glass Industry*⟩ **2 :** to make finer or less coarse or dull in quality, size, bulk, texture, or appearance ⟨~ his wits⟩ **:** SHARPEN, PULVERIZE — often used with *down* ⟨the one-way disc plow . . . ~*s* the soil to the extent of increasing losses from blowing —*Soils & Men*⟩ ⟨the women, except . . . where Italian influence has *fined* down the bone structure, are . . . well built —Don Smith⟩ ⟨material *fined* and refined until every . . . word . . . has its place in an artistic whole —*Times Lit. Supp.*⟩ ⟨*fined* his tuning, eliminating the interference —Rayne Kruger⟩ ⟨in this story . . . human beings are *fined* down to bee size —*N.Y. Herald Tribune*⟩ **3 :** to make less or finer by graduations — used with *away* or *down* ⟨~ down a ship's lines⟩ ~ *vi* **1 :** to become fine, pure, or clear ⟨the weather gradually *fined*⟩ ⟨the ale will ~⟩ — often used with *off* **2 :** to become fine in lines or proportions **:** DIMINISH, DWINDLE — often used with *away* or *down* ⟨even her fatness seemed puppy fat . . . that must ~ down before very long —Mollie Panter-Downes⟩

⁶fi·ne \ˈfē(ˌ)nā\ *n* [It, fr. L *finis* boundary, limit, end — more at FINAL] **:** END — used as a direction in music to mark the closing point after a repeat

⁷fine \fēn\ *n* -s [F, short for *fine champagne*] **:** ordinary French brandy; *esp* **:** one of undisclosed origin sold in French restaurants

fineable *var of* FINABLE

fine aggregate *n* **:** that portion of the aggregate used in concrete that is smaller than about $\frac{3}{16}$ inch

fine art \ˈ=ˈ=\ *n* [back-formation fr. *fine arts,* pl., trans. of F *beaux-arts*] **1 a :** art that is concerned primarily with the creation of beautiful objects **:** art for which aesthetic purposes are primary or uppermost **b :** the objects themselves ⟨the fetishes of the Negro sculptor . . . are *fine art* —John Dewey⟩ **2 :** any art (as painting, drawing, architecture, sculpture, music, ceramics, or landscape architecture) for which aesthetic purposes are primary or uppermost — usu. used in pl.

finebent \ˈ=ˌ=\ *n* **:** any of several grasses of the genus *Agrostis; esp* **:** RHODE ISLAND BENT

fine-bore \ˈ=ˌ=\ *vt* **:** to bore accurately (a gun or gun barrel) so as to give a fine finish

fine cham·pagne \fēnshäⁿpänʸ\ *n* [F] **:** a French brandy designated by French law as one distilled from wine made from grapes grown in the vineyards Grande Champagne and Petite Champagne in Charente department, France — called also *grande champagne*

fine chemical *n* **:** a chemical (as a photographic chemical, a perfume, or a pharmaceutical) produced and handled in relatively small amounts and usu. in a more or less pure state — compare HEAVY CHEMICAL

finecomb \ˈ=ˌ=\ *vt* **:** to search thoroughly ⟨technicians ~*ed* the liquor stores for clues —Al Spiers⟩

fine cut *n* **:** tobacco cut into small shreds for chewing or smoking

fined *past of* FINE

fine-draw \ˈ=ˈ=\ *vt* **:** to make a concealed joining of; *esp* **:** to mend (torn edges) by drawing together with invisible stitches

fine-drawn \ˈ=ˈ=\ *adj* **:** drawn out to extreme subtlety ⟨I don't follow his *fine-drawn* speculations⟩

fine frame *n* **:** SPEEDER 1b

fine-grain \ˈ=ˈ=\ *adj* **1 :** producing images of low graininess so that considerable enlargement without undue coarseness is permitted — used of a photographic developer **2** *also* **fine-grained** \ˈ=ˈ=\ **:** characterized by comparatively fine graininess — used of a photographic image or photographic emulsion

fine gravel *n* **:** gravel having particles ranging between 1 and 2 mm in diameter

fine harness *n* **:** a show class of light harness horses; *also* **:** a horse trained to participate in such a class

fine herbs \ˈfīˈnərbz, ˈfīnˈhər- — *see* HERB\ *n pl* [trans. of F *fines herbes*] **:** FINES HERBES

fine-leaved heath \ˈ=ˈ=-\ *n* **:** a common European heath (*Erica cinerea*) with very slender leaves in whorls of three

fine·less \ˈfīnləs\ *adj* [¹*fine* (end) + *-less*] *archaic* **:** ENDLESS

fine·ly *adv* [ME, fr. *fin, fine* + *-ly*] **:** in a fine manner: as **a :** EXCELLENTLY, SPLENDIDLY, ADMIRABLY ⟨the house has been ~ restored⟩ ⟨a large modern plant ~ housed and staffed —*Amer. Guide Series: N.H.*⟩ **b :** with nice or close discrimination **:** to a fine point **:** DISCRIMINATINGLY, PRECISELY ⟨with color lines so ~ drawn that a contemporary record recognized 250 different blood combinations —*Time*⟩ ⟨~ detailed maps and guide books —E.W.Smith⟩ **c :** with delicacy or subtlety (as in action, expression, or feeling) **:** SENSITIVELY ⟨you play a little too ~ . . . I want some roughness here —*Time*⟩ ⟨~ modulated thought —Cecil Sprigge⟩ ⟨he was a deeply and ~ feeling man —T.W.Beach⟩ **d :** in small particles **:** MINUTELY ⟨~ divided nickel⟩ **e :** in an impressive or elegant manner **:** BRAVELY ⟨she moves ~, with a slow steady elegance —Kenneth Tynan⟩ **f :** GREATLY, REALLY — used as an intensive ⟨had his temper ~ up now—Mary Deasy⟩

fine·ness \ˈfīnnəs\ *n* -ES [ME *finenesse,* fr. *fin, fine* + *-nesse* -ness] **1 :** exquisite perfection or elaborateness of form, texture, or construction **:** superior quality ⟨this material surpasses all others in ~⟩ **2 a :** freedom from foreign matter or alloy **:** CLEARNESS, PURITY ⟨the ~ of the gold⟩ **b :** the proportion of pure silver or gold in jewelry, bullion, or coins often expressed in parts per thousand and being in U. S. silver coin $\frac{9}{10}$ or .900 fine and in English gold coin $11\frac{1}{2}$ or .9166 fine — compare KARAT **3 a** (1) **:** brave or striking appearance **:** ELEGANCE, DELICACY ⟨he was struck by the ease, the poise, the ~ of every motion —S.H.Adams⟩ ⟨the ~, the perfection, the chiseled quality of her features⟩ (2) **:** sensitivity or delicacy of touch or manipulation ⟨the pianist's notable ~ of rendition⟩ ⟨the ~ of the surgeon's technique⟩ **b :** SUBTLETY, SENSITIVITY, ACUITY ⟨not in the name of some high-flown ~ of feeling but in the name of simple social practicality —Lionel Trilling⟩ ⟨this does not mean that there is no ~ of discrimination in his handling of its themes —T.W.Beach⟩ **4 :** the condition or degree of slenderness, thinness, or sharpness ⟨the ~ of wire⟩ ⟨the ~ of a knife's edge determines its cutting power⟩ **5 a :** the condition of being finely divided **:** the condition of being finely composed (as of particles, threads, or fibers) ⟨marveled at the ~ of the sand⟩ **b :** the extent of subdivision of a substance as indicated under prescribed conditions (as of cement, sand, gravel, or pigments) **c :** the relative width, diameter, linear density, or weight per unit length (as of fibers or yarns) expressed in a number of units

fineness ratio *n* **:** the ratio of the length of a streamlined body (as a fuselage) to its maximum diameter

fine of lands : ¹FINE 3c

fine print *n* **:** a part of a contract (as an insurance policy) or a certificate of ownership (as of stock) printed in type of small size or in footnotes that contains qualifications, limitations, or exceptions which make a contractual agreement less favorable ⟨be sure to read the *fine print*⟩ — called also *small print*

¹finer *comparative of* FINE

²fin·er \ˈfīnə(r)\ *n* -s [ME *finour, finer,* fr. *finen* to refine + *-our* -or or *-er* — more at FINE] **1 :** a workman who refines **:** ROLLER, TRIMMER **2 :** one who puts the mainspring assembly into clocks

¹fin·ery \ˈfīn(ə)rē, -ri\ *n* -ES [⁵*fine* + *-ery*] **:** REFINERY

²finery \"\ *n* -ES [³*fine* + *-ery*] **1** *obs* **:** FINENESS **:** BEAUTY, ELEGANCE; *esp* **:** ostentatious luxury or lavishness **2 a :** ornament or decoration esp. in excessive amounts **b :** showy clothing and jewels; *also* **:** an individual's best or dressy clothing ⟨a modest woman, dressed out in all her ~ —Oliver Goldsmith⟩

fines \ˈfīnz\ *n pl* [³*fine* + *-s*] **1 :** finely crushed or powdered material (as ore); *esp* **:** material finer than the minimum for any specified grade or passing through a screen on which the coarser material is retained **2 :** very small particles; *esp* **:** those smaller than average in a mixture of particles of various sizes ⟨the ~ in glacial drift⟩ **3 :** very small fragments of fiber

fine sand *n* **:** sand composed of grains ranging from 0.10 to 0.25 mm in diameter

fines herbes \fēnzerb\ *n pl* [F, lit., fine herbs] **:** a mixture of culinary herbs (as parsley, chervil, chives, tarragon, thyme) in various combinations used as a seasoning when chopped or as a garnish when whole

fine sight *n* **:** disposition of the gunsight in firing so that only the tip of the front sight is seen through the notch of the rear sight

finespun \ˈ=ˈ=\ *adj* **1 :** developed or elaborated with extreme care, skill, delicacy, ingenuity ⟨the satire touches also, with ~ ridicule, every kind of human pretense or affectation —Carl van Doren⟩ ⟨a ~ novel⟩ **2 :** too subtle, tenuous, or refined **:** engrossed or concerned with narrow or minute detail **:** developed in excessively fine or hairsplitting detail ⟨the emergency . . . does not permit of ~ distinctions and long arguments —*Newsweek*⟩ ⟨~ theories⟩ ⟨economics has long enjoyed the reputation of being the most ~ . . . of the social sciences —R.A.Lester⟩

¹fi·nesse \fəˈnes\ *n* -s [ME, fr. MF, fr. *fin* fine — more at FINE] **1 :** fineness or delicacy esp. of workmanship, structure, texture, or flavor ⟨trinkets of an extreme ~ —Arnold Rosin⟩ ⟨the wines . . . make up in richness and bigness what they lack in ~ —H.T.Grossman⟩ **2 :** delicate skill **:** exquisite grace **:** SUBTLETY, REFINEMENT ⟨it is no surprise to find him playing with persuasion and ~ —Howard Barnes⟩ **3 a :** adroit maneuvering **:** CUNNING, STRATEGY ⟨Danish ~, which consists of a fine balance of imagination and horse sense —*Atlantic*⟩ **b :** TRICK, STRATAGEM ⟨it is a frequently available ~, in such positions, not to capture hostile pawns, but to pass them by —C.T.S.Purdy⟩ **4 :** deliberate omission to play one's highest card in a suit in bridge or deliberate omission to trump in the hope or assurance that a lower card played from one's own or one's partner's hand will take the trick because the only higher opposing card is in the hand of an opponent who has already played to the trick

²finesse \"\ *vb* -ED/-ING/-S *vi* **:** to make a finesse in playing cards — sometimes used with *for* ⟨~ for the jack⟩ or *against* ⟨~ against opponent on the right⟩ ~ *vt* **1 a :** to play (a card) as a finesse ⟨can ~ the jack if the queen lies on the right⟩ **b :** to play a card one lower than (the middle card of a three-card sequence) ⟨hoped by playing the jack to ~ the queen⟩ **c :** to refrain from topping the lead of (one's partner) with a card two points higher in hope that the intervening card is not in the fourth hand and therefore cannot win the trick **2 :** to bring about or manage by adroit maneuvering **:** MANEUVER ⟨the man who *finessed* the entry of American troops into New Caledonia without firing a shot —Joseph Driscoll⟩ ⟨~ his way through tight places where the flick of an eyelash might mean death —Marquis James⟩ **:** get the better of by adroit maneuvering **:** get around **:** EVADE, TRICK ⟨trying to ~ an eagle-eyed editor who's on to all the tricks —J.C.G.Conniff⟩ ⟨*finessed* rather than faced the hottest critical barrage of his prime-ministership —*Time*⟩ ⟨felt that in some way he had been *finessed,* and was trying to figure out where —Robertson Davies⟩ **3 :** to play (a croquet ball) into a position where it will be of the least use to an opponent

¹finest *superlative of* FINE

²fin·est \ˈfīnəst\ *n, pl in constr* [¹*finest*] **:** POLICEMEN — usu. qualified and localized explicitly or implicitly by the possessive form of a city ⟨a dozen of the city's ~⟩

fine stuff *n* **:** the material (as plasterer's putty or a mixture of fine sand with plasterer's putty) used for the final coat of a plastered wall

fine-tooth comb *n* **1 :** a comb with teeth set close together used esp. for cleaning lice, nits, and other matter from the hair **2 :** an attitude or system of thoroughly searching or scrutinizing ⟨went through that house with a *fine-tooth comb* —Merle Miller⟩

fine-tooth-comb \ˈ=ˈ=ˈ=\ *vt* [*fine-tooth comb*] **:** to search or scrutinize intensively or minutely ⟨I *fine-tooth-combed* that patch of roadside, inch by inch —*True Crime Cases*⟩ ⟨scientists have gone to *fine-tooth-comb* the Urals and mid-Asia for new raw materials and power resources —Joseph Prescott⟩

finetop \ˈ=ˌ=\ *n* **:** RHODE ISLAND BENT

fine-top salt grass *n* **:** a perennial dropseed grass (*Sporobolus airoides*) that forms dense clumps and has open panicles

fine-wool \'⸗¦⸗\ *adj* **:** having or producing wool similar to that of the merino in fineness ⟨a *fine-wool* sheep⟩ ⟨*fine-wool* breeding⟩

finfish \'⸗,⸗\ *n pl* **:** true fish — distinguished from *shellfish*

fin fold *n* **:** a median fold of integument which extends along the body of an embryo fish and from which the dorsal, caudal, and anal fins are developed

finfoot \'⸗,⸗\ *n, pl* **finfoots :** SUN-GREBE

fin·gent \'finjənt\ *adj* [L *fingent-, fingens,* pres. part. of *fingere* to shape, form — more at DOUGH] **:** PLIABLE, FLEXIBLE, YIELDING ⟨showing a somewhat more ~ mood —C.L.Sulzberger⟩

[1]**fin·ger** \'fiŋgə(r)\ *n* -s [ME, fr. OE; akin to OHG *fingar* finger, ON *fingr,* Goth *figgrs,* and perh. to OE *fīf* five — more at FIVE] **1 :** one of the five terminating members of the hand **:** a digit of the forelimb; *specif* **:** one of the four extremities of the hand other than the thumb **2 a :** something that resembles or does the work of a finger ⟨a ~ of toast⟩ ⟨a ~ of land extending into the sea⟩ ⟨the ~ of a clock⟩ **b :** a part of a glove into which a finger is inserted **c :** one of the bananas or plantains in a hand **d :** a vegetable drug cut or compressed into the size and shape of a finger ⟨a ~ of rhubarb⟩ **e :** a projecting rod, wire, or piece (as a pawl for a ratchet) that is brought into contact with an object to effect, direct, or restrain a motion **3 a :** FINGERBREADTH **b :** an amount of liquor equal to the quantity in a glass filled up to one fingerbreadth **4 a :** CONCERN, INTEREST, PART, SHARE ⟨he seems always to have a ~ in some magisterial affair —V.L.Parrington⟩ — often used in the phrase *to have a finger in the pie* ⟨has a ~ in every political pie⟩ **b fingers** *pl* **:** POSSESSION ⟨marries the boss's daughter, and gets his ~s on the armament industry —Sherwood Anderson⟩ **5** *slang* **:** one who keeps tabs on or reports on a person **:** FINGER MAN, INFORMER ⟨first they get a ~ on him —J.M.Cain⟩ — **lift a finger :** to make an effort **:** WORK

[2]**finger** \"\ *vb* **fingered; fingered; fingering** \-ŋg(ə)riŋ\ **fingers** [ME *fingeren,* fr. *finger,* n.] *vt* **1 :** to touch or feel with the fingers **:** toy with **:** HANDLE ⟨eyeing her . . . as a broker buys a diamond . . . as a country woman ~s a bolt of tweed —Francis Hackett⟩ ⟨~*ed* his scraggy chin before he answered —C.G.D.Roberts⟩ ⟨~*ed* his heavy underlip as if probing it for a cold sore —Kenneth Roberts⟩ **2** *obs* **:** STEAL, PILFER, PURLOIN **3 a :** to play (a musical instrument) with the fingers **b :** to play with a specific fingering **c :** to mark the notes of (a music score) as a guide in playing **4 :** to extend into or penetrate in the shape of a finger ⟨the long beams of the searchlights ~*ing* the sky —R.H.Newman⟩ ⟨new roads ~*ing* once trackless plains⟩ **5 :** to point out **:** IDENTIFY, INDICATE, DESIGNATE ⟨far be it from me to ~ any individual to be blasted by the presidential wrath —G.W.Johnson⟩ ⟨the man he ~*ed* for the mayor's job was an old-time politician⟩ ⟨practically all of them had been ~*ed* by the more reliable ex-Communists —Elmer Davis⟩: as **a :** to point out, name, or identify to the police esp. in a police lineup ⟨she ~*ed* a boy friend . . . as one of the killers —Lew Arthur⟩ **b :** to indicate to a criminal (as the intended victims or the place or object to be robbed) ⟨in those days you merely ~*ed* the victim . . . and in a few days your enemy's body was discovered in the gutter —Danny Ahearn⟩ ⟨sometimes the dock boss . . . ~s the load to be stolen —Malcolm Johnson⟩ **c** *slang* **:** to keep tabs on **:** report on **:** SHADOW ⟨we've been ~*ing* him for months —L.A.Norris⟩ ~ *vi* **1 :** to touch or handle something ⟨the rosaries, the strings of round bells . . . brought them toward him . . . snatching and ~*ing* —Marjory S. Douglas⟩ **2 a :** to use the fingers in playing a musical instrument **b :** to have a certain fingering (as of a musical instrument) ⟨it ~s like a cornet⟩ **3 :** to extend in the shape or manner of a finger ⟨the docks ~*ed* out into the water —R.P.Warren⟩ ⟨forests, farms, industries . . . ~*ing* through great river valleys —Betty F. Martin⟩ ⟨searchlights ~*ed* across the black water —*Time*⟩

finger alphabet *n* **:** MANUAL ALPHABET

finger and toe *also* **finger-and-toe disease** *n* **:** CLUBROOT

finger bar *n* **:** CUTTER BAR

fingerboard \'⸗⸗,⸗\ *n* **1 a :** the part of a stringed instrument against which the fingers press the strings to vary the pitch — see VIOLIN illustration **b :** the keyboard of a piano or organ **:** MANUAL **2 a :** FINGERPOST **b :** a pointed guideboard often bearing a symbol representing a hand with extended index finger ⟨weather-beaten ~s —F.V.W.Mason⟩

finger bowl *n* **1 :** a bowl or basin to hold water for rinsing the fingers at table **2** *biol* **:** a round shallow bowl of heavy glass used esp. for culturing aquatic organisms

fingerbreadth \'⸗⸗,⸗\ *n* **:** a unit of length based on the breadth of a finger **:** DIGIT 2

finger brush *n* **:** a brush for applying size to book covers

finger clamp *n* **:** a flat clamp of which the end that holds the work is shaped to fit into a hole in the work

finger-cone pine *n* **:** WESTERN WHITE PINE 1

finger coral *n* **:** SEA GINGER

finger cymbal *n* **:** CASTANET

fin·gered \¦fiŋgə(r)d\ *adj* **1 :** having fingers ⟨the ~ roots of giant trees⟩ **2 :** DIGITATE 2

fingered citron *also* **fingered lemon** *n* **:** BUDDHA'S-HAND

fingered kelp *n* **:** DEADMAN'S HAND 1c

fin·ger·er \'fiŋgərə(r)\ *n* -s [[1]*finger* + *-er*] **:** one that makes the fingers of gloves

finger fern *n* **1 :** SCALE FERN **2 :** any fern of the genus *Asplenium* **3 :** HART'S-TONGUE 1

fingerfish \'⸗⸗,⸗\ *n* **:** STARFISH

fingerflower \'⸗⸗,⸗⸗\ *n* **:** FOXGLOVE 1

finger-foxed \¦⸗⸗¦⸗\ *adj* **:** having a quarter or foxing so designed that the upper portion extends forward to the throat of a shoe in a narrow strip below the upper part of the quarter

finger fracture *n, med* **:** a breaking of the fibers of the mitral commissure to relieve stenosis of the mitral valve that is performed by a finger thrust through the valve — compare COMMISSUROTOMY

finger grass *n* **1 :** CRABGRASS 1a **2 :** any grass of the genus *Chloris* **3 :** YARD GRASS

finger guard *n* **:** a metal piece attached to the shaft of a carving fork for protecting the fingers from the carving knife

fingerhold \'⸗⸗,⸗\ *n* **1 :** a hold or grasp by the fingers **2 :** any weak hold or support ⟨it gave a ~ to her theories and suspicions —Victor Canning⟩

finger hole *n* **1 :** a hole in a wind instrument for changing the pitch of the tone according as it is left open or closed by the finger **2 :** either of two holes bored in a large bowling ball to provide a grip **3 :** any of the small holes in the disk of a dial telephone by which the number desired is dialed

[1]**fingering** *n* -s [ME, fr. gerund of *fingeren* to finger] **1 a :** the act or method of using the fingers (as in playing a musical instrument or typing) **b :** the marking of the method of fingering (as by figures on a music score) **2 :** the controlling of the depletion of a fencing foil by the action of the fingers only

[2]**fin·ger·ing** \'fiŋg(ə)riŋ\ *or* **fingering yarn** *n* -s [fr. earlier *fingram,* prob. fr. F *fin grain* fine grain] **:** a plied worsted yarn for hand knitting

finger joint *n* **:** a joint in cabinetmaking formed by cutting two board ends into matching fingerlike projections that fit together

finger lake *n* **:** any of several long relatively narrow lakes in central New York state; *also* **:** a lake of similar shape elsewhere

fin·ger·less \'fiŋgə(r)ləs\ *adj* **:** having no fingers **:** having lost the fingers

fingerlike \'⸗⸗,⸗\ *adj* **:** resembling a finger esp. in slender elongated form and flexibility **:** DIGITATE 2 ⟨~ projections of the margin of the ostium of a fallopian tube⟩ ⟨~ tendrils by which the vine clings⟩

finger lime *n* **:** a spiny Australian citrus shrub or tree (*Microcitrus australasica*) with smooth slender elongated fruits

fin·ger·ling \'fiŋgə(r)liŋ\ *n* -s [[1]*finger* + *-ling*] **:** a small fish no longer than a finger; *esp* **:** a young fish from two weeks after complete absorption of the yolk sac up to one year of age

finger man *n* **:** one who fingers (as for a gangster) ⟨Chicago gangster methods, with *finger men* pointing out unreliables for the triggermen to kill —*Newsweek*⟩ ⟨the miraculous finder of lost boys and girls, the brilliant *finger man* of thousands of sheriff's posses and private trailers —James Thurber⟩

finger millet *n* **:** RAGGEE

fingernail \'⸗⸗,⸗⸗'⸗\ *n* [ME *finger neil*] **:** the nail of a finger

fingernail clam *also* **fingernail shell** *n* **:** a small freshwater bivalve mollusk of a cosmopolitan genus (*Sphaerium*)

finger nut *n* **:** WING NUT

finger of apollo *usu cap A* [after *Apollo,* Greco-Roman god of the sun] **:** the third finger that when long and prominent is usu. held by palmists to indicate predominance of qualities characterizing an Apollonian

finger of jupiter *usu cap J* [after *Jupiter,* Roman god of the sky, fr. L *Juppiter* — more at DEITY] **:** the first finger that when long and prominent is usu. held by palmists to indicate predominance of qualities characterizing a Jupiterian

finger of mercury *usu cap M* [fr. *Mercury* (planet)] **:** the little finger that when long and straight is often held by palmists to indicate mental capacity for making use of talents and opportunities and power of expression esp. in speaking

finger of saturn *usu cap S* [after *Saturn,* Roman god connected with the sowing of seeds, fr. L *Saturnus*] **:** the second finger that when long and prominent is usu. held by palmists to indicate predominance of qualities characterizing a Saturnian

finger paint *n* **:** a pigment of the consistency of jelly

finger-paint \'⸗⸗,⸗\ *vi* **:** to apply finger paint in splotches to wet paper and spread it mainly with the fingers ~ *vt* **:** to form (a design) with finger paint

finger painting *n* **1 :** the technique of using finger paint **2 :** a picture or design made with finger paint

fingerparted \¦⸗⸗¦⸗⸗\ *adj* **:** DIGITATE

finger plate *n* **:** a protective plate (as of metal, glass, or plastic) used to prevent soiling of a surface (as of a door) by finger marks

fingerpost \'⸗⸗,⸗\ *n* **1 :** a guidepost bearing one or more index fingers **2 :** something that serves as a clue, indication, or aid to understanding or knowledge ⟨many admirable ~s to the study of old London have been written —Elizabeth Montizambert⟩ ⟨despite these significant ~s to her intention, the book has been somewhat inexplicably assigned a literal exactness —John McKellar⟩

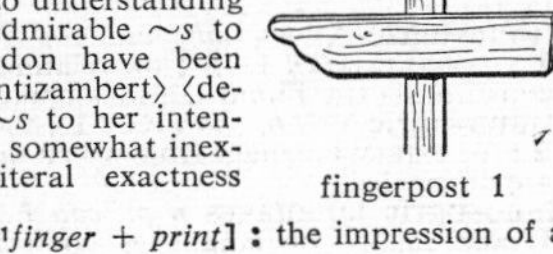
fingerpost 1

[1]**fingerprint** \'⸗⸗,⸗\ *n* [[1]*finger* + *print*] **:** the impression of a fingertip on any surface (as upon glass or polished metal); *esp* **:** an impression of the lines upon the finger taken in ink for purpose of identification

[2]**fingerprint** \"\ *vt* **:** to take fingerprints of ⟨hustled him into the sheriff's office, where he was ~*ed* . . . and locked in the bullpen to await bond —H.H.Martin⟩

fingerprints: *1* arch, *2* loop, *3* whorl, *4* composite

finger ring *n* **:** a metal ring worn on the finger as an ornament or as a token of marriage or betrothal

finger roll *n* **1 :** bread shaped in long slender rolls **2 :** an Italian breadstick

fingerroot \'⸗⸗,⸗\ *n* **:** FOXGLOVE 1

fingers *pl of* FINGER, *pres 3d sing of* FINGER

finger spelling *n* **:** communication by means of one of the manual alphabets **:** DACTYLOLOGY

finger sponge *n* **:** a sponge having finger-shaped lobes; *esp* **:** a common red or orange sponge (*Chalina oculata*) related to the important commercial sponges and widely distributed in shallow waters on both coasts of the Atlantic ocean

fingerstall \'⸗⸗,⸗\ *n* [ME, fr. [1]*finger* + *stall*] **:** [1]COT 3b

finger-tame \'⸗⸗,⸗\ *adj, of a pet bird* **:** trained to perch on a finger

[1]**fingertip** \'⸗⸗,⸗\ *n* [[1]*finger* + *tip*] **1 :** the tip of a finger **2 :** a protective covering for the end joint of a finger **3 :** a southern California succulent herb (*Stylophyllum edule*) of the family Crassulaceae with pencil-shaped leaves — **at one's fingertips 1 :** within easy reach ⟨thanks to an excellent filing system, he has all the figures *at his fingertips*⟩ **2 :** instantly or readily produced or available as a result of thorough familiarity with the subject ⟨he had the whole answer *at his fingertips*⟩ — **to one's fingertips :** COMPLETELY, THOROUGHLY ⟨a gentleman *to his fingertips*⟩

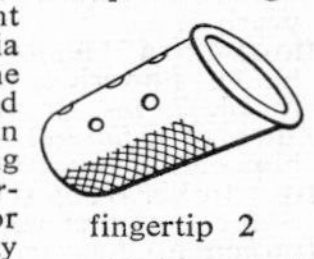
fingertip 2

[2]**fingertip** \"\ *adj* **:** extending from the shoulder to mid-thigh — used of coats, veils, and similar clothing

finger wave *n* **:** a method or style of setting hair by dampening with water or wave solution and forming waves with fingers and a comb and shaping curls by winding strands of hair around the operator's finger

finger weaving *n* **:** the intertwisting or weaving of threads without a shuttle; *esp* **:** BRAIDING

fin·gery \'fiŋg(ə)rē, -ri\ *adj* **:** branching like or resembling fingers ⟨the chestnuts . . . with their interknit ~ leaves —Elizabeth Bowen⟩

fin·go \'fiŋ(,)gō\ *n, pl* **fingo** *or* **fingos** *or* **fingoes** *usu cap* **1 a :** a So. African people descended from a group of Negro refugees who were driven southward in native wars and later settled east of Great Fish river, Union of So. Africa **b :** a member of this people **2 :** the Bantu language of the Fingo people

fin·i·al \'finēəl, *chiefly Brit* 'fīn-\ *n* -s [ME, fr. *finial,* adj., final, alter. of *final* — more at FINAL] **1 :** a usu. foliated ornament forming the upper extremity (as of a pinnacle, canopy, or gable) esp. in Gothic architecture; *sometimes* **:** the pinnacle itself **2 :** any terminating or capping ornament or detail (as a vase in a broken pediment or an ornament on an automobile instrument panel or topping a lampshade)

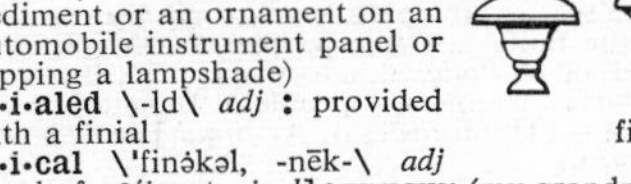
finials 1

fin·i·aled \-ld\ *adj* **:** provided with a finial

fin·i·cal \'finəkəl, -nēk-\ *adj* [prob. fr. [3]*fine* + *-ical*] **:** FINICKY ⟨my grandmother's voracity, so ~, so selective, chilled me with its mature sensuality —Mary McCarthy⟩ ⟨one novel . . . was planned with ~ care —Robert Molloy⟩ **syn** see NICE

fin·i·cal·i·ty \,finə'kaləd·ē\ *n* -ES **:** FINICALNESS

fin·i·cal·ly \-k(ə)lē, -li\ *adv* **:** in a finical manner ⟨~ tasting the unaccustomed dishes⟩

fin·i·cal·ness \-kəlnəs\ *n* -ES **:** the quality or state of being finical

fin·ick *also* **fin·nick** \'finik, -nēk\ *vi* -ED/-ING/-S [back-formation fr. *finicking*] **1 :** to become excessively or affectedly dainty or refined in speech or manner **:** put on airs **2 :** to dawdle about ⟨~*ed* with her food —Elizabeth Taylor⟩ ⟨she was not one who had time to ~ about snipping at blossoms —Adrian Bell⟩

fin·ick·i·ness \-nəkēnəs, -nēk-, -kin-\ *n* -ES **:** the quality or state of being finicky ⟨instability, irritability, — and above all, a tendency to sudden whims and . . . fancies —Margaret Mead⟩ ⟨the gourmet's ~ with his appetite —William Becker⟩

fin·ick·ing \-kiŋ,-kən\ *or* **fin·i·kin** \-kən\ *adj* [alter. of *finical*] **:** FINICKY ⟨they seem to have approached the usually ~ processes involved . . . in a singularly carefree manner —R.M.Coates⟩

fin·ick·ing·ly *adv* **:** in a finicking manner

fin·ick·ing·ness \-kiŋnəs,kən(n)əs\ *n* -ES **:** the quality or state of being finicking

fin·icky *also* **fin·nicky** \'finəkē, -ki\ *adj, sometimes* -ER/-EST [alter. of *finicking*] **:** excessively nice, dainty, or exacting in taste or standards **:** marked by or displaying too much concern with trifles or details **:** hard to please **:** overly scrupulous **:** OVERNICE, METICULOUS, FUSSY, PARTICULAR ⟨his ~ concern for the detailed order of his existence —Jack Richmond⟩ ⟨very ~ about his food⟩ ⟨of all fruits, strawberries are most ~ about soil and climate —*House Beautiful*⟩

fin·i·fy \'finə,fī, 'fīn-\ *vt* -ED/-ING/-ES [[3]*fine* + *-ify*] *now dial* **:** to deck out **:** make fine in appearance **:** ADORN ⟨ladies minced about, *finified* in their gala best —S.H.Adams⟩

fining *n* -s [fr. gerund of [5]*fine*] **1 :** the act or process of fining: as **a :** the conversion of pig iron into wrought iron in a hearth or charcoal fire, a process now superseded by puddling **b :** the process of freeing molten glass of bubbles usu. by the addition of certain chemical agents **c :** the operation or process by which a beverage (as wine or beer) is clarified (as by bringing suspended matter to the bottom) **2 :** material (as isinglass, gelatin, egg white) used for clarifying a liquid (as a beverage) — often used in pl. ⟨when ~s are poured into a cask . . . they should reach every part of the wine —A.L. Simon⟩

fin·is \'finəs, 'fīn- *also* 'fēn-\ *n* -ES [ME, fr. L — more at FINAL] **:** END, CONCLUSION ⟨white settlers poured onto the prairies . . . and wrote ~ to their carefree existence —D.F.Symington⟩ ⟨the story . . . is far from complete because ~ is not yet written —R.G.Whalen⟩

[1]**fin·ish** \'finish, -nēsh, *chiefly in pres part* -nəsh\ *vb* -ED/-ING/-ES [ME *finisshen,* fr. MF *feniss-, finiss-,* stem of *fenir, finir,* fr. L *finire* to limit, finish, end, fr. *finis* boundary, limit, end — more at FINAL] *vt* **1 a :** to bring to an end **:** arrive at the end of **:** TERMINATE, COMPLETE ⟨he ~*ed* speaking, and a long silence fell⟩ ⟨he ~*ed* his days in poverty and loneliness⟩ ⟨a rapid reader, he can ~ a chapter in a few minutes⟩ **b :** to use, consume, or dispose of entirely ⟨he ~*ed* the meal to the last crumb —Louis Bromfield⟩ — often used with *off* ⟨the sailors lounging in the bar began to ~ off their drinks —Allen Upward⟩ **c :** to serve as the close or last item of ⟨a pleasant wine ~*es* the meal, nicely accenting the dessert⟩ ⟨a thrilling 100-yard dash ~*ed* the meet⟩ **2 a :** to expend the final labors on **:** bring to completion or issue ⟨tried to ~ the work his illustrious predecessor had started⟩ **b :** to perform completely **:** perfect with all possible labor and attention **:** give the ultimate touches to ⟨he always spoke in completed sentences . . . he ~*ed* his thought —W.A.White⟩ — often used with *up* ⟨advised him to ~ up the painting a little before exhibiting⟩ **c :** to complete the education of; *esp* **:** to prepare (a young woman) for entrance into society ⟨she received her ~*ing* in Paris⟩ **d :** to fatten (an animal) esp. for the market **e :** to put on as a finish ⟨all interior walls are ~*ed* with lime plaster —*Amer. Guide Series: Minn.*⟩ **f :** to cut, sort, trim, count, and pack (paper after it leaves the paper machine) **g :** to tool the title and decoration on (a hand-bound book) **h** (1) **:** to give (as cloth) special characteristics that improve appearance and usefulness by processing (as mercerizing, fulling, calendering, embossing) (2) **:** to complete work on (a garment); *esp* **:** to finish (a raw edge) by hemming, pinking, overcasting, facing **i :** to subject (newly formed soap or a kettle of soap) to the processes of fitting and settling **3 a :** to bring to an end the significance, usefulness, or effectiveness of **:** exhaust the power, worth, or vitality of **:** deal a mortal blow to ⟨the combination of . . . unfamiliar car, narrow streets, and strange town will just about ~ you —Richard Joseph⟩ ⟨his stunning defeat ~*ed* the young congressman as a political force⟩ — often used with *off* ⟨the romance of chivalry was already moribund and the new economic and social trends ~*ed* it off⟩ **b** (1) **:** to bring about the death of **:** KILL ⟨after wounding me with his spear he was about to ~ me with his knife —W.H.Hudson †1922⟩ — often used with *off* ⟨his woman ~*ed* him off . . . with a skinning knife —Walter O'Meara⟩ (2) **:** to bring about the decisive or final defeat of ⟨the cavalry charge ~*ed* the enemy; they broke and ran⟩ ~ *vi* **1 a :** to come to an end **:** TERMINATE, END ⟨the Civil War ~*ed* in 1865⟩ ⟨until British rule ~*ed* one had to obtain a visa from the British Foreign Office —W.B.Fisher⟩ **b** (1) **:** to come to the end of a course, task, or undertaking **:** complete a task or assignment ⟨it was noon, and he still had not ~*ed*⟩ ⟨he ~*ed* by reciting a cycle of sonnets⟩ ⟨I shall ~ with a Chopin nocturne —Lillian Hellman⟩ — often used with *up* ⟨you can ~ up now⟩ (2) **:** to finish a race or other competition in a certain manner or position ⟨the gelding ~*ed* strong and lost only by a nose⟩ ⟨he ~*ed* third in the oratorical contest⟩ **c :** to have a certain issue or outcome **:** RESULT ⟨any illness must ~ fatally for him —Osbert Sitwell⟩ **2 :** to become smooth (as of lumber) **3 :** to attend a finishing school **4** *of an animal* **:** to become suitably fat for marketing **syn** see CLOSE — **finish with 1 :** to have done with **:** cease to have relations with ⟨she decided to *finish with* him for good⟩ **2 :** to complete work upon ⟨as soon as he had *finished with* the statue he went on to a more ambitious project⟩

[2]**fin·ish** \"\ *n* -ES **1 a :** the final stage **:** CONCLUSION, END ⟨a fight to the ~⟩ ⟨flaunted the riskiest of their stunts and then . . . broke into their whirlwind ~ —Winifred Bambrick⟩ ⟨turned a slow start into a fast ~⟩ **b :** the cause of one's ruin **:** DOWNFALL ⟨his taste for gambling was his ~⟩ **2 :** something that finishes, completes, or perfects: as **a** (1) **:** the joiner work and other fine work required for the completion of a building esp. of the interior — see INSIDE FINISH, OUTSIDE FINISH (2) **:** the higher grade of lumber used for this work — called also *uppers* (3) **:** decorative surface treatment (as on paper, wood, stone, brick, plaster, or stucco) (4) **:** a finishing material used in painting ⟨oil ~⟩ — see FINISHING COAT **b :** the labor required for the last stage (as of a work of art) ⟨the sculptor is now doing the ~ on this splendid head⟩ **c :** a plain or decorative method of completing a part or an edge of a garment by use of a hem, binding, arrowhead, edging **d :** FAT; *esp* **:** the layer of fat lying beneath the skin of an animal well fattened for market or show **e :** the top or closure part of a glass container including the pouring lip and the threads or other means of attaching or inserting a closure **f :** the final treatment or coating of a surface **3 a :** the result or product of a finishing process esp. with regard to its quality, appearance, or characteristics ⟨a fabric with a water-resistant ~⟩ ⟨a cloth with a glazed ~⟩ ⟨paper with a glossy ~⟩; *specif* **:** the state of a surface (as of furniture or pottery) after the tool marks have been obliterated **b :** [6]FIT 3 **c :** the quality or state of being perfected or minutely elaborated **:** impeccable, finished, or flawless quality **:** PERFECTION ⟨the exquisite ~ of this artist's work⟩ ⟨the machine . . . worked with neither the accuracy nor the ~ of these girls —Sam Pollock⟩ ⟨his novels have a ~, a flavor, that the cultivated recognize and relish⟩ ⟨at the age of 60 he danced . . . and still displayed great ~ and fine style —Anatole Chujoy⟩ **d :** cultivation in manners and speech **:** social polish

finished *adj* **1 :** brought to conclusion **:** ENDED, COMPLETED ⟨typing the ~ letters on company letterheads —J.R.Gregg⟩ ⟨gave me the ~ manuscript to read⟩: as **a :** ready for packing, shipment, or sale — used of materials or goods **b :** PROCESSED ⟨storage facilities for both raw and ~ water —*U. S. Geol. Survey List*⟩ **c** *of an animal* **:** fattened esp. for the market **d :** in a hopeless condition **:** defeated, wounded, or ailing beyond hope of recovery **:** done for **:** DOOMED ⟨about that time I was feeling very feeble and ~ —O.W.Holmes †1935⟩ ⟨so the press telegrapher was ~, or practically so —C.B. Davis⟩ ⟨a lot of wishful thinkers assume that the enemy is ~⟩ ⟨their class, the upper middle, was ~ politically and economically —Mary McCarthy⟩ **2 :** possessed of, brought to, or displaying the highest degree of skill, polish, or excellence **:** marked by the highest quality **:** CONSUMMATE, PERFECTED ⟨written with the ~ workmanship which always delights us —Edward Sackville-West⟩ ⟨the texture of his writing is even and ~ —*Times Lit. Supp.*⟩ ⟨a group of gentle, highly ~, memorable stories —Paul Pickrel⟩ ⟨a glitteringly ~ troupe from the start —Wilder Hobson⟩ ⟨he's the most ~ blackmailer in America —Donn Byrne⟩

fin·ish·er \-shə(r)\ *n* -s **1 :** one that finishes: as **a :** a worker who performs the finishing steps of shaping, assembling, adjusting, smoothing, painting, polishing, cleaning, or decorating an item of manufacture **b :** a machine that performs the finishing steps in a processing, manufacturing, or similar operation **2 :** something that finishes or settles a matter decisively ⟨I looked to have a knife through me forthwith as a ~ —J.H.Wheelwright⟩

finisher card *n* **:** the last and finest of three cards used in producing wool sliver — compare BREAKER CARD

finish hardware *n* **:** visible or exposed hardware fittings (as locks, hinges, handles, plates) used in building construction

finishing *n* -s [ME *finisshing*, fr. gerund of *finisshen* to finish — more at FINISH] **:** the act or process of completing **:** the final work upon or ornamentation of a thing; *specif* **:** the processing applied to cloth after it is taken from the loom

finishing coat *also* **finish coat** *n* **1 :** the final usu. white coat of plastering applied to walls and ceilings **2 :** the final coat of paint

finishing hydrate *n* **:** hydrated lime used in the finishing coat for plastered walls

finishing machine *n* **:** a mechanical device running on forms that is used to strike off and shape concrete surfaces (as highway and airfield pavements)

finishing nail *n* **:** a wire nail used for finishing whose small cylindrical head is easily countersunk and the resulting hole concealed by a filler

finishing powder *n* **:** a dry sizing for making gold adhere to book covers while finishing

finishing room *n* **:** a room or department where the last steps of a manufacturing, processing, or assembling operation are performed; *specif* **:** a part of the plant in a paper mill where the paper is cut, sorted, trimmed, counted, and packed for shipment

finishing school *n* **:** a private school that prepares young women for social life (as by emphasizing cultural accomplishments and social graces) rather than for a vocational or professional career

finishing stove *n* **:** a small rack-topped stove for heating a bookbinder's finishing tools

finish line *n* **:** a line marking the end of a racecourse

fi·ni·tary \'fīnə,terē, 'fin-\ *adj* [*finite* + *-ary*] **:** having a finite character; *specif* **:** capable of being completed in a finite number of steps — used of a proof or other logical procedure

[1]**fi·nite** \'fī,nīt, *usu* -nīd.+V\ *adj* [ME *finit*, fr. L *finitus*, past part. of *finire* to limit, finish, end — more at FINISH] **1 a :** having definite or definable limits or boundaries **:** not illimitable **:** LIMITED, BOUNDED ⟨a ~, although not very definite, thickness will reduce the intensity to a point where it is relatively insignificant —Samuel Glasstone⟩ ⟨the power of credence, of imaginatively realizing a supreme event . . . is ridiculously ~ —Arnold Bennett⟩ ⟨the absorption of all peoples into a ~, small community —C.E.Odegaard⟩ ⟨a universal theory cannot be induced from a ~ number of facts —Maurice Cranston & J.W.N.Watkins⟩ **b :** having a nature, character, or existence subject to limitations or marked by imperfections **:** limited in power **:** not absolute **:** HUMAN, MORTAL ⟨a ~ God who struggles in his great and comprehensive way as we struggle in our weak and silly way —H.G.Wells⟩ ⟨the impossible gulf between the ~ Easterner and the infinite, pure virtue of the cowboy —D.B.Davis⟩ ⟨incurable ills such as death, destruction . . . and ignorance . . . will always be characteristic of ~ beings —M.R.Cohen⟩ ⟨fate was inhuman, it was cruel, it excited and crushed every ~ wish —F.R.Leavis⟩ ⟨have pity on ~ us —Don May⟩ **2 a :** having a character or being completely determinable in theory or in fact either as an object of thought or as susceptible of complete enumeration or of physical measurement **b :** subject to experience **c :** neither infinite nor infinitesimal **3 :** expressible by a number less than some positive integer (as 25) and greater than the negative of that integer (−25) — used of a quantity, magnitude, or number ⟨the area of a circle with radius 4 is ~ because expressible by the number 16π that is less than the positive integer 64 and greater than −64⟩ **4** *of a verb or verb form* **:** showing distinction of grammatical person and number esp. in agreement with a subject form ⟨the ~ verb *runs* in *he runs fast*⟩ — **fi·nite·ly** *adv*

[2]**finite** \"\ *n* -s **:** a finite thing or being **:** something that is finite

[3]**finite** *vt* -ED/-ING/-s **:** to make finite **:** LIMIT

finite canon *n* **:** a musical canon that comes to a definite end with its theme — contrasted with *circular canon*

fi·nite·ness *n* -ES **:** the quality or state of being finite ⟨recoiled at the thought that the quality of ~ was not foreign to Eden —Thomas Hardy⟩

finite proposition *n* **:** a logical proposition with a limited or definite predicate (as *is white* or *is human*) as contrasted with one whose predicate is an indefinite negative (as *not white* or *not man*)

finite set *n, math* **:** a set consisting of a finite number of elements

fi·nit·ism \'fī,nīd.,izəm\ *n* -s **:** a theory or belief holding that a particular entity or domain (as the world, God, or knowledge) is finite ⟨cosmological ~⟩ ⟨a theistic ~⟩

fi·nit·ist \-d.əst\ *or* **fi·nit·is·tic** \;=,=;istik\ *adj* **:** relating to or being finitism ⟨a ~ system⟩

fin·i·tive \'finəd.iv, -ativ\ *adj* [L *finitus* (past part. of *finire* to limit, finish, end) + E *-ive* — more at FINITE] **:** TERMINATIVE

fin·i·tude \'finə,tüd, 'fīn-, -nə-,tyüd\ *n* -s [blend of [1]*finite* and *-tude*] **:** the quality or state of being finite ⟨human ~⟩

fin·i·ty \'finəd.ē, -natē, -i\ *n* -ES [[1]*finite* + *-y*] **:** FINITUDE

[1]**fink** \'fiŋk\ *n* -s [origin unknown] **1** *slang* **:** INFORMER, SQUEALER **2** *slang* **:** STRIKEBREAKER ⟨couple of minutes ago I saw a guy I recognized for a company ~ —Alexander Saxton⟩

[2]**fink** \"\ *vi* -ED/-ING/-s **1** *slang* **:** SQUEAL, INFORM ⟨you have to ~ on somebody . . . to get a parole —*Police Dragnet*⟩ **2** *slang* **:** to act as a strikebreaker ⟨he ~*ed* back in the 1934 and 1936 strikes —R.F.Mirvish⟩

[3]**fink** \"\ *n* -s [Afrik *vink*, fr. MD *vinke* — more at FINCH] *Africa* **:** FINCH

fin keel *n* **1 :** a plate of metal fixed to the keel of a shallow boat to provide lateral resistance usu. supplemented by a cigar-shaped bulb of lead to provide stability **2 :** a long narrow and shallow ship (as a yacht) fitted with a fin keel and lead bulb **3 :** a yacht with shallow body carried down in an extension of wood or metal which in turn carries a metal keel

fin·land \'finlənd\ *adj, usu cap* [fr. *Finland*, country in northern Europe, fr. Sw, fr. *finne* Finn (fr. OSw) + *land* country, fr. OSw; akin to ON *land* — more at LAND] **:** of or from Finland **:** of the kind or style prevalent in Finland **:** FINNISH

fin·land·er \-,landə(r), -lən-\ *n* -s *cap* **:** FINN 2

fin·lay process \'finlē-, -(,)lā-\ *n, usu cap F* [after Clare L. *Finlay*, 20th cent. Brit. photography expert] **:** an additive process of color photography in which exposure is made on a panchromatic plate behind a regular mosaic three-color screen — called also *Paget process*

fin·less \'finləs\ *adj* **:** having no fin **:** devoid of fins ⟨a ~ animal⟩

fin·let \'finlət\ *n* -s [*fin* + *-let*] **:** a little fin **:** one of the parts of a divided fin

[1]**finn** \'fin\ *n* -s *cap* [Sw *finne*, fr. OSw; akin to ON *finnr* Finn, OE *Finnas*, pl.] **1 a :** a member of a people speaking Finnish **b :** a member of a people speaking a language akin to Finnish **c :** a member of a people speaking or formerly speaking a Uralic language **2 a :** a native or inhabitant of Finland **b :** one that is of Finnish descent

[2]**finn** \"\ *adj, usu cap* **:** FINNISH

fin·nage \'finij\ *n* -s [*fin* + *-age*] **:** the whole set of fins of a fish

fin·nan had·die \,finən'hadē, -di\ *or* **finnan haddock** *n* [alter. of *findon haddock*] **:** smoked haddock

finned *past of* FIN

fin·ne·man·ite \'finəmə,nīt\ *n* -s [K. J. *Finneman*, 20th cent. Swede who discovered it + E *-ite*] **:** a mineral $Pb_5(AsO_3)_3Cl$ consisting of arsenite and chloride of lead

fin·ner \'finə(r)\ *n* -s [[1]*fin* + *-er*] **:** FINBACK

finnes·ko *also* **finnes·koe** \'finz,kō, -n(ə),skō, -kü\ *n, pl* **finnesko** *also* **finneskoe** [Norw *finnsko*, fr. *finn* Finn, Lapp (fr. ON *finnr*) + *sko* shoe, fr. ON *skōr* — more at FINN, SHOE] **:** a boot made of tanned reindeer skin with the fur outside

[1]**fin·nic** \'finik\ *adj, usu cap* [[1]*Finn* + *-ic*] **1 :** of or relating to the Finns (sense 1) **2 :** of, relating to, or constituting the branch of the Finno-Ugric subfamily of the Uralic family of languages that includes Finnish, Estonian, Lapp, Cheremis, Mordvin, Votyak, Permian, and various other languages — see URALIC LANGUAGES table

[2]**finnic** \"\ *n* -s *cap* **:** the Finnic languages

finnick *var of* FINICK

finnicky *var of* FINICKY

finning *pres part of* FIN

[1]**finn·ish** \'finish, -nēsh\ *adj, usu cap* [[1]*Finn* + *-ish*] **1 :** of or relating to the Finns (sense 1) **2 :** of, relating to, characteristic of, or composed in the Finnish language **3 :** of or relating to Finland or its inhabitants

[2]**finnish** \"\ *n* -ES *cap* **1 :** a Finno-Ugric language spoken in Finland, Karelia, and small areas of Sweden and Norway — see URALIC LANGUAGES table **2 :** the form of the Finnish language spoken in Finland and adopted as the official language of that nation

finn·mark *or* **fin·mark** \'fin,märk\ *n* [Sw *finmark*, fr. *finne* Finn + *mark* (coin), fr. OSw; akin to ON *mörk* mark (coin and weight) — more at FINN, MARK] **:** a Finnish mark — compare MARKKA

fin·nock *also* **fin·noc** \'finək\ *n* -s [ScGael *fionnag* whiting, fr. *fionn* white; akin to OIr *find* white, W *gwyn*, Corn *guyn*, Bret *gwenn* white, L *vidēre* to see — more at WIT] **:** a European sea trout: as **a :** a pale or whitish Scottish sea trout **b :** a young or grilse sea trout

[1]**finno-ugrian** \;fi(,)nō +\ *adj, usu cap F&U* [*Finno-* (fr. [1]*Finn* + *-o-*) + *Ugrian*] **1 :** of or relating to the Finno-Ugrians **2 :** FINNO-UGRIC 2

[2]**finno-ugrian** \"\ *n, cap F&U* **1 :** a member of any of various peoples of north and east Europe and western Siberia speaking related languages and historically antecedent to the Slavic expansion in those regions, including the ancestors and present members of the Finnish, Hungarian, Bulgarian, Ostyak and Vogul peoples, the Lapps, Estonians, and others **2 :** FINNO-UGRIC

[1]**finno-ugric** \"+\ *adj, usu cap F&U* [*Finno-* + *Ugric*] **1 :** FINNO-UGRIAN 1 **2 :** of, relating to, characteristic of, or constituting the Finno-Ugric languages

[2]**finno-ugric** \"\ *n, cap F&U* **1 :** the Finno-Ugric languages **2 :** the extinct language from which the Finno-Ugric languages are descended

finno-ugric languages *n pl, cap F&U* **:** a subfamily of the Uralic family of languages comprising various languages spoken in Hungary, Lapland, Finland, Estonia, and in Russia north and east of the Volga as far as the Ob river in Siberia — see URALIC LANGUAGES table

finno-ugrist \,fi(,)nō'(y)ügrəst\ *also* **finno-ugri·cist** \-grəsəst\ *n* -s *usu cap F&U* [[2]*Finno-Ugric* + *-ist*] **:** a specialist in the Finno-Ugric languages

fin·ny \'finē, -ni\ *adj* -ER/-EST [*fin* + *-y*] **1 :** having or characterized by fins **2 :** relating to or being fish ⟨toothsome food of the ~ tribe —*Quartermaster Rev.*⟩ ⟨these would . . . complete the list of our ~ contemporaries —H.D.Thoreau⟩

finny whale *n* **:** FINBACK

fi·no \'fē(,)nō\ *n* -ES [Sp, fr. *fino* fine, fr. L *finis*, n., boundary, limit, end — more at FINE (adj.)] **:** the driest Spanish sherry

fi·noc·chio *also* **fi·no·chio** \fə'nōkē,ō, -nók-\ *n* -s [It *finocchio* fennel, fr. (assumed) VL *fenuculum* — more at FENNEL] **:** FLORENCE FENNEL

fin ray *n* **:** one of the horny dermal rods that form the projecting part of the skeleton of the fins of fishes

fin rot *n* **:** a common disease of hatchery fishes in which the fin tissues become eroded and necrotic and which is believed to result from bacterial infection esp. in the presence of an inadequate diet

fins *pl of* FIN, *pres 3d sing of* FIN

fin·sen light \'fin(t)sən-, -nzən-\ *n, usu cap F* [after Niels R. *Finsen* †1904 Danish physician] **:** a mixture of blue, violet, and near ultraviolet light that is produced by a lamp using a high-temperature carbon arc or a mercury arc and that is used in the treatment of lupus and certain other skin conditions and in testing paints and other protective coatings

fin whale *n* **:** FINBACK

FIO *abbr* free in and out

fiord *var of* FJORD

fior dell'al·pi \(,)fē,órde'lal(,)pē\ *also* **fior di alpi** \-dē'al(-\ *n* [It, lit., flower of the alps] **:** a yellow colored Italian liqueur containing a twig encrusted with crystallized sugar inside its bottle

fi·o·rin \'fīərən, 'fēə-\ *n* -s [IrGael *fiorthann* wheat grass] **:** REDTOP 1

fi·o·rite \fē'ōr,īt\ *n* -s [Santa *Fiora*, Tuscany, Italy, its locality + E *-ite*] **:** an opal occurring near hot springs in grayish or whitish incrustations that sometimes are fibrous and pearly

fio·ri·tu·ra \fē,ōrə'türə\ *n, pl* **fioritu·re** \-rā\ [It, lit., bloom, flowering, fr. *fiorito* (past part. of *fiorire* to bloom, fr. LL *florire*) (fr. LL *floritus*, past part. of *florire* to bloom, alter. of L *florēre*) + *-ura* -ure — more at BLOW (to cause to blossom)] **:** ORNAMENT 5 — usu. used in pl.

fip \'fip\ *n* -s [by shortening] **:** FIPPENNY BIT ⟨wouldn't give a ~ for any other way of travel —S.H.Adams⟩

fip·pence \'fipən(t)s\ *n* [by alter.] *Brit* **:** FIVEPENCE

fip·pen·ny \'fip(ə)nē\ *n* [by alter.] *dial* **:** FIVEPENCE

fippenny bit *n* **:** a Spanish half real piece **:** a silver coin worth 1/16 of a Spanish dollar that circulated in the eastern U.S. before 1857 and passed current for about six cents — called also *fip*, *fourpence ha'penny*, *sixpence*

fip·ple \'fipəl\ *n* -s [origin unknown] **:** a block containing a flue and a lip-stopping end of a whistle, flute, or organ pipe

fipple flute *n* **:** a wind instrument (as the recorder and flageolet) in which the air blown into the mouthpiece strikes a flat sharp lip, producing the sound waves within the body of the instrument

fi·que \'fē(,)kā\ *n* -s [AmerSp, prob. fr. Quechua *ppiqui*, *phiqui* thread, fiber, vein] **:** MAURITIUS HEMP

[1]**fir** *R* 'fər, +V 'fər·; *-R* 'fə̄, + *suffixal vowel* 'fər· *also* 'fər, + *vowel in a following word* 'fər· *or* 'fə̄ *also* 'fər\ *n* -s [ME *firre*, *fir*, fr. OE *fyrh*, *furh*; akin to OHG *forha*, *foraha* fir, ON *fȳri* fir forest, *fura* fir, Goth *fairguni* mountain, L *quercus* oak] **1 :** any of several evergreen trees: as **a :** a tree of the genus *Abies* typically large and attractive in appearance and valued for its wood or resin — see BALSAM FIR **b :** any of various related coniferous trees — usu. used in combination ⟨Douglas ~⟩ ⟨Scotch ~⟩ **2 a :** the wood of any tree of the genus *Abies* distinguished from that of pine, spruce, or larch by the absence of resin ducts **b :** the wood from any of various other conifers: as (1) **:** SPRUCE 1b (2) *Brit* **:** PINE 2a **3** *or* **fir green :** a dark grayish green that is yellower and stronger than average ivy, yellower and deeper than Persian green, and yellower, lighter, and stronger than hemlock green

fir *abbr* firkin

fir balsam *n* **:** BALSAM FIR 1

fir·bolg \'fi(ə)r bəlag\ *or* **fir·bolgs** \-gz\ *n pl, usu cap* [OIr *Fir Bolg* men of the Builg (a Celtic people), fr. *fir* (pl. of *fer* man) + *Bolg*, gen. pl. of *Builg*; akin to W *gwr* man, Bret *gour*, L *vir* — more at VIRILE] **:** an early people of Ireland

fir·ca \'fi(ə)rkə\ *n* -s [Hindi *firqa*, fr. Ar *firqah*] *India* **:** COMMUNITY, TRIBE, GROUP

fir club moss *n* **:** a club moss (*Lycopodium selago*) of northern Europe and America having the appearance of a miniature fir

[1]**fire** \'fī(ə)r, -īə\ *n* -s [ME *fir*, *fire*, fr. OE *fȳr*; akin to OHG *fiur* fire, ON *fȳrr*, *fūrr*, *funi*, Goth *fon*, Umbrian *pir*, Gk *pyr*, Arm *hur* fire, torch] **1 a :** the phenomenon of combustion as manifested in light, flame, and heat and in heating, destroying, and altering effects **:** IGNITION **b :** one of the four elements of the alchemists **c fires** *pl* **:** the heat, flame, or burning material of a specified place or thing ⟨the deep internal ~s of the volcanic region⟩ ⟨the ~s of hell⟩ **d** (1) **:** intense love or hate **:** PASSION ⟨the younger men, the warriors, the new leaders who had ~ in their hearts —Marjorie S. Douglas⟩ (2) **:** ardor of spirit or temperament **:** DRIVE, COURAGE, ZEAL, ENTHUSIASM, FERVOR ⟨the glow and ~ of a faith that was content to bide its hour —B.N.Cardozo⟩ (3) **:** liveliness of imagination or fancy **:** GENIUS, INSPIRATION, VIVACITY ⟨color and ~ were imparted to the works of the classic master —A.E.Wier⟩ ⟨the force and ~ of his oratory⟩ **2 a :** fuel in a state of combustion (as on a hearth or in a stove or furnace) ⟨warmed his hands at the crackling ~⟩ ⟨stirred up the ~ with a poker⟩ — compare OPEN FIRE **b** *Brit* **:** a small gas or electric space heater ⟨electric ~s designed for efficiency —*Punch*⟩ **3 a :** a destructive burning (as of a house, town, or forest) ⟨engines clanging their way to the ~⟩ **b :** purposive destruction by burning — often used in the phrase *by fire and sword* ⟨he was going back . . . to carry the city by ~ and sword —Frank Yerby⟩ **c** (1) **:** death or torture by fire; *specif* **:** burning at the stake — used with *the* ⟨forced the shocked prelate, under threat of the ~, to confess heresies he was not guilty of —G.C.Sellery⟩ (2) **:** an experience that tests or tempers quality or character **:** a severe trial or ordeal ⟨he had proved himself in the ~ of battle⟩ — often used in pl. ⟨workers whose ideas have been tested in the ~s of performance —G.T.Trewartha⟩ **4 a** *dial Brit* **:** FUEL, FIREWOOD; *specif* **:** KINDLING **b** *archaic* **:** an inflammable composition or a device for producing a fiery display **:** FIREWORKS **5 a :** fever or inflammation esp. from a disease **b :** a plant disease producing a burnt appearance — see TULIP FIRE **6 :** BRILLIANCY, LUMINOSITY; *specif* **:** the play of prismatic colors in light flashes from a gemstone **7 a :** the discharge of firearms **:** FIRING ⟨troops rent by a heavy ~⟩ **b :** intense and usu. continuing criticism **:** verbal attack ⟨atomism had come under the ~ of the Socratic schools —Benjamin Farrington⟩ ⟨the ~ of his article is concentrated on the two hapless institutions —Nicolas Slonimsky⟩ **c :** a series (as of remarks) usu. following closely one upon the other ⟨they fell to, a running ~ of comments going on all the time —Robert Keable⟩ **8 :** the heating powers of a substance (as liquor) ⟨with the ~ of the drink melting the cold that was in the marrow of our bones —Mary Deasy⟩ — **on fire :** BURNING, EAGER

[2]**fire** \"\ *vb* -ED/-ING/-s [ME *firen*, fr. *fir*, *fire*, n.] *vt* **1 a :** to set on fire **:** set fire to ⟨*fired* the house⟩ **b** (1) **:** KINDLE, LIGHT, IGNITE ⟨the oven holds sufficient heat to ~ a fresh charge of coal —*Amer. Guide Series: Pa.*⟩ — often used with *up* ⟨he *fired* up a cigar —Gilbert Millstein⟩ (2) **:** to cause to explode by lighting or igniting ⟨*fired* the train of powder⟩ ⟨~ a mine⟩ (3) **:** to cause (an internal-combustion engine) to start operation (4) **:** to cause (an electron tube) to begin conducting a gas discharge **c** (1) **:** to give life or spirit to **:** ANIMATE, INSPIRE ⟨his description *fired* my imagination⟩ ⟨*fired* his ambition for a college education⟩ (2) **:** to fill with passion **:** INFLAME, AROUSE ⟨he was *fired* by her fresh young beauty⟩ **d :** to light up as if by fire **:** ILLUMINATE ⟨his eye had caught the flash of larkspur and snapdragons that *fired* the lawn —G.M. Smith⟩ **2 a :** to expel, purge, drive out, or drive away by or as if by fire ⟨such surrender is above all things delightful . . . it ~*s* the cold skepticism out of us —Virginia Woolf⟩ **b :** to dismiss from employ or service usu. peremptorily or summarily ⟨*fired* him with one week's notice⟩; *also* **:** to throw out or eject forcibly **3 a** (1) **:** DETONATE ⟨~ a charge of dynamite⟩ (2) **:** to propel from or as if from a gun ⟨~ cannonballs⟩ ⟨~ an arrow⟩ ⟨~ a rocket⟩ **:** DISCHARGE ⟨~ a musket⟩ (3) **:** to score (a certain number) in a game or contest (as golf or target shooting) ⟨*fired* a 68⟩ **b :** to throw with speed or force **:** HURL ⟨stripped to his shorts and *fired* the wet clothes into the corner of the closet —Charles Jackson⟩ ⟨throwing clods at me by way of contempt and derision, and I *fired* back rocks —W.A. White⟩ ⟨*fired* a long pass to the left end⟩ **c :** to utter with force and rapidity ⟨*fired* questions at the prisoner⟩ **4 :** to apply fire, heat, or fuel to: as **a :** to prepare (as ceramics) by applying heat **:** burn in a kiln ⟨~ pottery⟩ **b :** to sear (the leg of a horse) with a hot iron in order to convert a crippling chronic inflammation into an acute inflammation that will stimulate the natural healing responses of the body **c :** to feed or serve the fire of ⟨~ a boiler⟩ **:** build a fire under in order to heat ⟨unless you have lived by lamplight or *fired* a washpot in the back yard, you'll never know what electricity means —James Street⟩ **d :** to heat gently in order to dry ⟨~ tea leaves⟩ **e :** to subject (a barn full of tobacco) to the drying and heating and combustion products of a charcoal fire for curing purposes **f :** to protect against freezing by the use of smudge pots ⟨a freeze comes in and I must ~ my young orange grove —Marjorie K. Rawlings⟩ **~** *vi* **1 a :** to take fire **:** KINDLE, IGNITE ⟨damp gunpowder will not ~⟩ **b :** to have the explosive charge ignite at the proper time — used of an internal-combustion engine **c :** GLOW, REDDEN ⟨her features *fired* at the thought; she clenched her hands in anger⟩ **d** (1) *of flax* **:** to become covered with dark blotches (2) **:** to turn yellow prematurely (as from drought) — used of corn or grain **2 :** to become irritated **:** become angry or inflamed with passion ⟨*fired* inwardly at these sarcasms —Tobias Smollett⟩ — often used with *up* ⟨*fired* up with a superb indignation —H.J. Laski⟩ **3 a :** to discharge artillery or firearms ⟨~ at point-blank range⟩ **b :** to emit forcefully or let fly an object ⟨as long as the tail is lowered, the skunk will not ~ —*Animal Trap Co. of Amer.*⟩ ⟨the archers raised their bows but did not ~⟩ **4 :** to undergo a change by the action of fire (as in the making of pottery) ⟨iron-bearing clays ~ to a red color⟩ **5 :** to light or tend a fire (as in a furnace) ⟨the ship's firemen went on strike, and there was no one to ~⟩ **6 :** to ring all the bells in a chime at once **syn** see DISMISS

[3]**fire** \"\ *adj* **1 :** involved in burning or the use of fire ⟨~ building⟩ ⟨~ floor⟩ **2 :** relating to, used in, or concerned with fire fighting ⟨~ bucket⟩ ⟨~ district⟩ ⟨~ hydrant⟩ **3 :** FIERY

fire agriculture *n* **:** the growing of crops by burning a forest and planting among the charred stumps

fire alarm *n* **:** a signal given on the breaking out of a fire; *also* **:** an apparatus for giving such a signal

fire and brimstone *n* [fr. *fire and brimstone*, a phrase used often in the Bible (esp. Rev 20 : 10) to designate God's means of destroying sinners] **:** eternal damnation and the torments of hell for sinners ⟨sermons full of *fire and brimstone*⟩

fire-and-brimstone \,==='=(,)=\ *adj* [*fire and brimstone*] **:** of or relating to an ultimate day of violent reckoning and retribution **:** APOCALYPTIC ⟨a hive of revivalism, hymn singing, and *fire-and-brimstone* auguries from self-appointed minor prophets —Peter Ustinov⟩

fire ant *n* **:** a stinging ant; *specif* **:** any of numerous small fiercely stinging omnivorous ants constituting a genus (*Solenopsis*) now nearly cosmopolitan in warm regions

fire apparatus *n* **:** apparatus for fighting or extinguishing fire (as automobile fire engines or ladder trucks)

fire area *n* **:** one of various sections of a building that are separated from each other by fire-resistant walls

firearm \'=,=\ *n* **:** a weapon from which a shot is discharged by gunpowder — usu. used only of small arms

fire arrow *n* **:** an arrow bearing a flaming substance to set its mark afire

fire assay *n* **:** an assay in which the material is subjected to high heat (as in fusion, scorifying, and cupellation)

fire away *vi* **:** to begin speech and proceed with it rapidly ⟨useless to *fire away* with a lot of details —F.L.Mott⟩

fireback \'=,=\ *n* **1** *or* **fire-backed pheasant** \'=,=-\ **:** any of several pheasants (genus *Lophura*) of southern Asia and the East Indies having the lower back of the male a bright coppery or fiery maroon **2 :** the back wall or back lining of a fireplace or furnace; *also* **:** a decorated cast-iron plate to fit into the back of an open fireplace

fireball \'=,=\ *n* **1 :** a ball of fire or something resembling such a ball: as **a :** a brilliant meteor that may trail bright sparks — compare BOLIDE **b :** BALL LIGHTNING **c :** a ball filled with powder or other combustibles formerly used as a projectile to be thrown among the enemy **d** *heraldry* **:** a grenade or bomb fired proper **e :** the highly luminous cloud of vapor and dust created by a nuclear explosion **f** (1) **:** MALTESE CROSS 2 (2) **:** SUMMER CYPRESS **g :** a fast ball in baseball **2 :** a highly energetic indefatigable person **:** HUSTLER ⟨the British production ~ had one simple mission: get more of everything for the British —Time⟩

fire balloon *n* **1 :** a balloon raised by the buoyancy of air heated by a fire placed in the lower part **2 :** a balloon sent up at night with fireworks that ignite at a regulated height

fire-baptized \';=,=;=, ='=,=;=\ *adj* **:** of or having experienced a baptism of fire

fire bar *n* **:** a bar of a grate or boiler furnace

fire bean *n* **:** SCARLET RUNNER

firebed \'=,=\ *n* **:** a layer of burning fuel (as that in the furnace under a boiler)

fire beetle *n* **1 :** a tropical American beetle of the genus *Pyrophorus*; *esp* **:** a common large beetle (*P. noctilucus*) having powerful luminous organs on the sides of the thorax and base of the abdomen — compare FIREFLY **2** *Austral* **:** any of several beetles attracted to firelight

fire-bellied toad \'⸗,⸗⸗-\ *n* **:** a toad (*Bombina bombina*) of central and eastern Europe with red or orange patches marbled with black on its underparts

firebird \'⸗,⸗\ *n* **:** any of several small birds having brilliant orange or red plumage (as the Baltimore oriole, the scarlet tanager, or the vermilion flycatcher)

fire blanket *n* **:** a blanket of fireproof or flameproof material for use in smothering small fires

fire blast *n* **:** a disease of plants (as hops) causing them to appear scorched

fire·blende \'fī(ə)r,blend, -īə,b-\ *n* [trans. of G *feuerblende*, fr. *feuer* fire + *blende*] **:** PYROSTILPNITE

fire blight *n* **1 :** a destructive highly infectious disease of apples, pears, and related fruits that is caused by a bacterium (*Erwinia amylovora*) and that produces a scorched or blackened appearance of the leaves and twigs, cankers on the trunk, or discoloration of flowers and fruit **2 :** the organism causing fire blight

fire blocks *n pl* **:** pieces of wood nailed horizontally between studs or joists to prevent the spread of fire and hot gases

fireboard \'⸗,⸗\ *n* **1 :** a screen or panel often painted or otherwise decorated to close a fireplace when not in use **2** *Midland* **:** MANTELPIECE

fireboat \'⸗,⸗\ *n* **:** a boat equipped with pumps and other apparatus for fighting fire on or from the water

firebolt \'⸗,⸗\ *n* **:** THUNDERBOLT, LIGHTNING

fire bomb *n* **:** INCENDIARY BOMB

fire boss *n* **:** one who examines a coal mine to determine whether firedamp is present, to search for fires caused by blasting, and to check on the general safety of the mine — called also *fireman, gasman*

fire·bote \'⸗,bōt\ *or* **fire·boot** \'⸗,büt\ *n* -s [ME *firbote*, fr. *fir, fire* + *bote* boot (profit) — more at BOOT] **:** the right of a tenant to take from the land occupied by him a reasonable amount of wood for maintaining fires in his house and in the houses of his servants; *also* **:** the wood or fuel used for this purpose

firebox \'⸗,⸗\ *n* **1 :** a chamber (as of a furnace or steam boiler) that contains a fire; *specif* **:** the compartment of a steam locomotive in which the fuel is burned **2 :** FIRE ALARM

firebrand \'⸗,⸗\ *n* [ME *firbrond, firbrand*, fr. *fir, fire* + *brond, brand* — more at FIRE, BRAND] **1 :** a piece of burning wood **2 :** a person who creates unrest, disaffection, or strife by noisy or violent agitation **:** TROUBLEMAKER, HOTHEAD, AGITATOR, INCENDIARY ⟨far from being considered ~*s*, young people of today are accused of being too quiet —*Harper's*⟩ ⟨a political ~⟩

firebrat \'⸗,⸗\ *n* **:** an insect (*Thermobia domestica*) of the family Lepismatidae of Europe and America that lives in warm moist places (as in buildings)

firebreak \'⸗,⸗\ *n* **:** a barrier of cleared or plowed land intended to check a forest fire or prairie fire

firebrick \'⸗,⸗\ *n* **:** a refractory brick (as of fireclay) capable of sustaining high temperature without fusion and used esp. for lining furnaces, fireplaces, and tall chimneys

fire bridge *n* **:** a low separating wall usu. of firebrick between the hearth and the grate in a reverberatory furnace

fire brigade *n* **:** a body of fire fighters: as **a :** a private, institutional, or temporary fire-fighting organization **b** *Brit* **:** FIRE DEPARTMENT

firebug \'⸗,⸗\ *n* **1 :** INCENDIARY, PYROMANIAC **2 :** one who patrols a metal mine looking for fire hazards and other dangers **3** *dial* **:** FIREFLY **4 :** an insect of the family Pyrrhocoridae

fireburn bush \'⸗,⸗-\ *n* **:** a West Indian woody vine (*Triopteris jamaicensis*) of the family Malpighiaceae with violet flowers and linear leaves

fire bush *n* **1 :** FIRE THORN **2 :** a low West Indian shrub (*Croton lucidus*) having small flowers in terminal racemes **3 :** SPINDLE TREE **4 :** SUMMER CYPRESS

fire chaser *n* **:** SMOKECHASER

fire check *n* **:** a fine shallow crack in an unglazed ceramic body or a glass article caused by sudden heating

fire cherry *n* **:** PIN CHERRY

fire chief *n* **1 :** the head of a fire department **2 :** FIRE MARSHAL

fireclay \'⸗,⸗\ *n* **:** clay that will withstand high temperatures without deforming, that is used for firebrick, crucibles, and many refractory shapes, and that approaches kaolin in composition, the better grades containing at least 35 percent alumina when fired

fire cock *n* **:** a cock to furnish water for extinguishing fires

fire company *n* **:** a body of men organized and equipped to extinguish fires

fire control *n* **1 :** all operations connected with the planning, preparation, and delivery of fire on targets **2 :** fire protection or extinction

firecracker \'⸗,⸗⸗\ *n* **1 :** a cylinder that is usu. of thick paper, contains an explosive and a fuse, and is usu. discharged for amusement to make a noise **2** *California* **:** a young sardine **3 :** FIERY RED **4** *also* **firecracker flower :** a Californian herb (*Brodiaea coccinea*) with scarlet tubular flowers

firecrest \'⸗,⸗\ *also* **fire-crested wren** \'⸗,⸗⸗-\ *n* **:** a small European kinglet (*Regulus ignicapillus*) with a bright red crest

fire-cure \'⸗¦⸗\ *vt* **:** to cure (tobacco) over open fires in direct contact with the smoke — compare FLUE-CURE

fire curtain *n* **:** CURTAIN BOARD

fire cut *n* **:** a slanted cut in the end of a wood beam or joist resting in a masonry wall that in case of fire allows the wood to fall out without wrecking the wall

fired \'fī(ə)rd, -īəd\ *adj, heraldry* **:** represented as on fire — used of a fireball

firedamp \'⸗,⸗\ *n* **:** a combustible gas that is formed in mines by decomposition of coal or other carbonaceous matter and that consists chiefly of methane; *also* **:** the explosive mixture formed by this gas with air

fire department *n* **1 a :** a permanent organization for preventing or putting out fires; *esp* **:** a government division (as in a municipality) having these duties **b :** FIRE COMPANY **2 :** the members of a fire department ⟨the . . . *fire department* . . . dashed up in three splendid long scarlet wagons —Nathaniel Burt⟩

fire direction *n* **:** tactical employment of firepower including the selection of targets and the massing of fires

fire direction center *n* **:** an element of an artillery command post consisting of gunnery and communication personnel and equipment by which the commander exercises fire direction and fire control

fire division wall *n* **:** a wall that subdivides a fire-resistive building to restrict the spread of fire

firedog \'⸗,⸗\ *n* **:** ANDIRON

fired-on \'⸗¦⸗\ *adj, ceramics* **:** made a part of the ware by firing or fusing ⟨a *fired-on* enamel⟩

fire door *n* **1 :** the door or opening through which fuel is supplied to a furnace or stove **2 :** a fire-resistive door; *specif* **:** an automatic door secured in the open position by a fusible link or thermostatically operated device designed to release the door under the influence of heat and permit its closing by gravity or by weights or other contrivances

firedrake \'⸗,⸗\ *also* **firedragon** \'⸗,⸗⸗\ *n* [ME *firdrake*, fr. OE *fȳrdraca*, fr. *fȳr* fire + *draca* dragon — more at FIRE, DRAKE] **:** a dragon breathing fire esp. in Teutonic mythology as the guardian of a treasure and in folk tales as the abductor or guardian of maidens

fire drill *n* **1 :** a primitive device for kindling fire consisting of a stick that is revolved rapidly between the hands or by means of a bow or thong with the stick's lower end being pressed into a hole made in a piece of wood **2 :** a practice drill with fire-extinguishing apparatus or in the conduct and manner of exit to be followed in case of fire

fire-eater \'⸗,⸗⸗\ *n* **1 :** a performer who pretends to eat fire **2 a :** a person of violent, pugnacious, or swaggering disposition **:** BULLY ⟨another *fire-eater* . . . , mighty fighter and hunter whose deeds were already epic along the moving frontier —*Amer. Guide Series: Texas*⟩ **b :** a person who displays very militant or aggressive partisanship (as in political questions) ⟨inside all parties there are moderates and extremists . . . ; the pacific and the *fire-eaters* —Barbara & Robert North⟩; *specif* **:** a violent Southern proslavery partisan before the Civil War ⟨Southern *fire-eaters* . . . held the government had no power to ban slavery in the West —R.A.Billington⟩ — used chiefly by northern opponents

fire-eating \'⸗,⸗⸗\ *adj* **:** violent, aggressive, belligerent, or highly militant in disposition, bearing, or policy ⟨a *fire-eating* radical⟩ ⟨the *fire-eating* partisans of immediate war⟩ ⟨a *fire-eating*, hectoring, swashbuckling bully⟩

fire engine *n* **:** an apparatus for throwing an extinguishing agent (as a jet of water) upon a fire: as **a :** a force pump with an air chamber to ensure a steady flow or an arrangement of two pumps working alternately or a direct-coupled steam engine and pump on wheels **b :** an automotive truck equipped with a motor-driven pump and hose and sometimes with a chemical fire-extinguishing unit **c :** any usu. mobile apparatus (as a ladder truck) used in connection with the extinguishing of fires

fire escape *n* **:** a device for facilitating escape from a burning building: as **a :** a stairway usu. of steel attached to the outside of a building **b** *Brit* **:** a wheeled extension ladder

fire-exit bolt *n* **:** a locking device for the exit doors of public buildings so designed that it is released by pressure applied from the inside of the building

fire extinguisher *n* **:** a portable or wheeled apparatus for putting out small fires by ejecting fire-extinguishing agents that may consist of water alone, water and chemicals (as soda-acid solutions or foam), or chemicals alone (as carbon tetrachloride, carbon dioxide, or dry chemicals)

portable fire extinguishers

fire-eyed \'⸗¦⸗\ *adj, archaic* **:** having glowing eyes

firefall \'⸗,⸗\ *n* **:** a tree whose fall is caused by the partial destruction of its roots in a ground fire

firefang \'⸗,⸗\ *vi* [fr. obs. E *firefang*, v.t., to singe, scorch, fr. [1]*fire* + [1]*fang*] **:** to become overheated, excessively dry, and damaged as a result of slow oxidative decomposition of organic matter — used esp. of manure or grain

fire fight *n* **:** an exchange of fire between opposing military units as distinct from the fighting when the two forces close with each other (as during an assault)

fire fighter *n* **:** one who fights fires: as **a :** a member of a municipal fire department **b :** one of a crew that combats forest fires **c :** one who fights mine fires

fire fighting *n* **:** the activity of a fire fighter; *specif* **:** the effort to extinguish or to check the spread of a fire

fire finch *n* **:** any of several small African weaverbirds often kept as cage birds or in aviaries and noted for the brilliant largely red plumage of the male

firefinder \'⸗,⸗⸗\ *n* **:** a device consisting of a map and a sighting instrument for determining (as from a fire tower) the location of a forest fire

fire-fish \'⸗,⸗\ *n* **:** a small scarlet and orange banded coral fish (*Pterois volitans*) of the Indo-Pacific region having the pectoral fin rays greatly prolonged into slender projections and the sharp dorsal spines equipped with venom and capable of causing painful injury

fireflaught \'⸗,⸗\ *n* **1** *chiefly Scot* **a :** SHEET LIGHTNING **b :** SHOOTING STAR **c :** WILL-O'-THE-WISP **d :** AURORA BOREALIS **2** *chiefly Scot* **:** a quick-tempered person

fire-float \'⸗,⸗\ *n* **:** a boat used to aid ships afire

fire flow *n* **:** the quantity of water available (as in a city) for fire-protection purposes in excess of that required for other purposes

fireflower \'⸗,⸗⸗\ *n* **:** MEXICAN FIRE PLANT 1

firefly \'⸗,⸗\ *n* **1 :** a winged nocturnal light-producing insect usu. producing a bright soft intermittent light without sensible heat by oxidation of luciferin: as **a :** the male of various elongated flattened beetles of the family Lampyridae — compare GLOWWORM **b :** any of several tropical click beetles **2 :** a moderate to strong red that is bluer and lighter than blood red and yellower and very slightly darker than camellia

firefly squid *n* **:** a brilliantly luminescent squid (*Watseonia scintillans*) caught in great quantities off the western coast of Japan where it is used for fertilizer

fire-form \'⸗¦⸗\ *vt* **:** to reshape a rifle cartridge case by loading and firing it until it conforms to the chamber of the rifle for which the case is being prepared ⟨using the new ammunition to *fire-form* to fit the large chamber —P.B.Sharpe⟩

fire frame *n* **:** a cast-iron frame made to be permanently set into a large fireplace to reduce its size

fire fungus *n* **1 :** any of various fungi (as those of the order Sphaeriales) that form dark or nearly black stromata or perithecia — called also *black fungus* **2 :** any fungus (as of the genus *Pyronema*) appearing esp. on burned areas or soil

fire gilding *n* **:** a mode of gilding with an amalgam of gold and quicksilver, the latter metal being driven off by heat

fire grass *n* [so called fr. its growing on burned land] **:** PARSLEY PIERT 1

fireground \'⸗,⸗\ *n* **:** an area in which fire-fighting operations are carried on

fireguard \'⸗,⸗\ *n* **1 :** FIRE SCREEN **2 :** FIREBREAK **3 :** one who watches for the outbreak of fire (as in a forest region); *also* **:** one whose duty is to extinguish small fires

fire gun *n* **1 :** a fire-hose nozzle having a handle shaped somewhat like a pistol grip **2 :** BLOWTORCH

firehall \'⸗,⸗\ *n, North & Canad* **:** FIRE STATION

fire hangbird *n* **:** BALTIMORE ORIOLE

fire hat *n* **:** a fireman's protective hat having a high domed crown and a brim extended at the rear as a neck guard

fire hook *n* [ME, fr. *fire* + *hook*] **1 :** a stout pole having a hooked metal head and used esp. in fire fighting for tearing down walls or ceilings **2 :** a hook for raking a furnace fire

firehorse \'⸗,⸗\ *n* **:** a horse specially trained for hauling a fire engine

firehouse \'⸗,⸗\ *n* [ME *firhous*, fr. OE *fȳrhūs*, fr. *fȳr* fire + *hūs* house — more at FIRE, HOUSE] **1** *dial Brit* **:** a dwelling house or unit having a fireplace — often contrasted with *outhouse* **2 :** FIRE STATION

firehouse pinochle *n* **:** pinochle played by four players in two partnerships

fire hunt *n* **1 :** a night hunt in which torches or other lights are used **2 :** a hunt in which fire is set to the woods in an area and the animals are killed as they attempt to escape

fire-hunt \'⸗,⸗\ *vt* **1 :** to hunt (animals) at night with the aid of a torch or light **2 :** to hunt by driving (animals) from the woods with a fire

fire insurance *n* **:** insurance against loss from damage or destruction of specified property by fire

fire iron *n* [ME *firiren*, fr. *fir, fire* + *iren* iron — more at IRON] **1 fire irons** *pl* **:** utensils for a fireplace or grate (as tongs, poker, and shovel) — compare SLICE BAR **2 :** ANDIRON — usu. used in pl.

fire laddie *n* **:** FIREMAN

fire lane *n* **:** FIREBREAK

fire·less \'fī(ə)rləs, -īəl-\ *adj* **:** having no fire

fireless cooker *n* **:** an insulated chamber that when heated to a cooking temperature by any of several means can maintain that temperature without the addition of further heat

fireless locomotive *n* **:** a steam locomotive of conventional design except that it has no firebox, its steam being obtained from an outside source, stored, and admitted to the cylinders at reduced pressure as required — called also *steam storage locomotive*

firelight \'⸗,⸗\ *n* **:** the light of a domestic fire or campfire

fire limits *n pl* **:** the limits fixed by a town or city government within which only structures meeting certain specifications with respect to fire resistance are permitted, there being sometimes two or three such zones with varying requirements

fire line *n* **1 a :** a police barrier or line about a burning building — usu. used in pl. **b :** a line of fire hose **2 a :** FIREBREAK **b :** a line of hardwood seedlings planted along abandoned railway grades for the protection of young conifers **c :** the gutter or strip dug or scraped in a forest-fire control line **d :** the front line of an advancing prairie or forest fire

firelit \'⸗,⸗\ *adj* **:** illuminated by an open flame

fire load *or* **fire loading** *n* **:** the weight of combustible material per square foot of floor space

firelock \'⸗,⸗\ *n* **1 :** a gunlock employing a slow match to ignite the powder charge; *also* **:** a gun having such a lock **2 a :** FLINTLOCK **b :** WHEEL LOCK

fire lookout *n* **:** a lookout stationed in a fire tower who keeps watch over a large area of forest and on sighting a fire notifies a dispatcher of its location — called also *towerman*

fire main *n* **:** a pipe for water to be used in putting out fire

fire maker *n* **1 :** a device formerly used for making fire that consists of a piece of flint which is held immovably in place by metal prongs and which is struck by a hammer like that of a musket by cocking the hammer and pulling a trigger, the spark thus produced falling into a metal box filled with wood shavings or other flammable material **2** *usu cap F&M* **:** the third of four ranks attained by camp fire girls — compare TORCH BEARER, TRAIL SEEKER, WOOD GATHERER

fire·man \'⸗mən\ *n, pl* **firemen 1** *obs* **:** GUNNER **2 :** one who fights fires; *esp* **:** a member of a fire department below the rank of lieutenant **3 :** one who tends or feeds fires **:** STOKER; *specif* **:** the crew member of a locomotive whose principal duties include firing and operating the boiler if the locomotive is steam operated or servicing the motors if it is other than steam and assisting the locomotive engineer by watching for signals or track obstructions **4 :** an enlisted man in the U.S. Navy who performs general duties concerned with the operation of engineering machinery **5 :** FIRE BOSS **6 :** a relief pitcher in baseball

fire·man·ic \(')fī(ə)r¦manik\ *adj* **:** of or relating to fire fighters or to fire fighting

fire·man·ship \'fī(ə)rmən,ship\ *n* -s **:** the practice, skill, or occupation of fire fighting

fireman's red *n* **:** a vivid red commonly used for fire apparatus

fire mark *n* **:** a metal plate attached to a building to mark it as insured used by 18th century fire-insurance companies

fire marshal *n* **1 :** the head of a city, county, state, or provincial fire-prevention or fire-investigation bureau **2 :** one who is in charge of the fire-fighting personnel and equipment of an industrial establishment — called also *fire chief*

fire medusa *n* **:** a scyphozoan jellyfish (genus *Chiropsalmus*) of the tropical Pacific ocean having a severe sting that may cause serious injury or even death

fire mission *n* **:** the assignment of a specific target usu. including orders as to when to fire the amount of ammunition to be used

firemouth \'⸗,⸗\ *n* **:** a small cichlid fish (*Cichlasoma meeki*) that is fiery red along the belly and mouth with a metallic green blotch on the gill cover and that is often kept in tropical aquariums

fire-new \'⸗¦⸗\ *adj* **:** BRAND-NEW ⟨it may be considered a *fire-new* cross section of these lexicons —Paul Rosenfeld⟩

fir engraver *n* **:** an engraver beetle (*Scolytus ventralis*) very destructive to fir trees in western No. America

fire off *vt* **:** to complete the firing of (a kiln)

fire-on-the-mountain \¦⸗⸗¦⸗⸗\ *n, pl* **fires-on-the-mountain :** MEXICAN FIRE PLANT 1

fire opal *n* **:** GIRASOL 2

fire partition *n* **:** a fire-resistant interior wall intended to retard the spread of fire or to provide protection to occupants during the evacuation of a burning building

fire patrol *n* **:** SALVAGE CORPS

fire patrolman *n* **1 :** a member of a salvage corps who accompanies municipal fire trucks to protect property at the scene of the fire from unnecessary damage **2 :** one who patrols a certain area (as a mine, factory, or national forest) watching for fires or fire hazards

fire pink *n* **:** a scarlet-flowered sticky catchfly (*Silene virginica*) of the eastern U.S.

fire pit *n* **:** a pit whose floor is wholly or partly incandescent lava ⟨the *fire pit* of a crater⟩

fireplace \'⸗,⸗\ *n* **1 :** a square or rectangular opening made at the base of a chimney in or against the wall of a room and surrounded with brick, stone, or metal to hold an open fire for heating and formerly for cooking **:** HEARTH **2 :** an outdoor place made for cooking over an open fire contained within a low structure of stone, brick, or metal

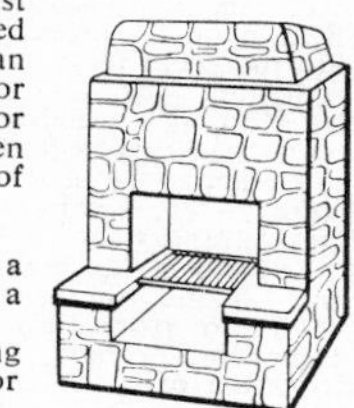
fireplace 2

fire plant *n* **:** SUMMER CYPRESS

fire-plow *also* **fire-plough** \'⸗,⸗\ *n* **:** a stick which is rubbed in a groove of a board to produce fire

fireplug \'⸗,⸗\ *n* **:** a hydrant for drawing water from the mains (as in a street or building) for extinguishing fires

fire point *n* **:** the lowest temperature at which a volatile combustible substance continues to burn in air after its vapors have been ignited (as when heating is continued after the flash point has been determined) — compare IGNITION TEMPERATURE

fire-polish \'⸗¦⸗⸗\ *vt* **:** to make (glassware) smooth, gloss, or brilliant in appearance by reheating in the process of manufacture

fire polish \"\ *n* **:** the smoothness or brilliancy of surface imparted to glassware by fire polishing

fire polishing *n* **:** the process of reheating glassware in order to impart a smooth or brilliant surface

firepot \'⸗,⸗\ *n* **:** a pot that holds fire: as **a :** a small earthen pot filled with combustibles formerly used as a missile in war **b :** the vessel that holds the fuel or fire in a furnace **c :** a solderer's furnace

firepower \'⸗,⸗⸗\ *n* **:** the capacity (as of a military unit, a tank, a ship) to deliver prompt and effective fire on a specific target; *specif* **:** the aggregate of effective shells and missiles that can be placed upon a target

fire prevention *n* **:** measures and practices directed toward the prevention and suppression of destructive fires — **fire preventionist** *n*

[1]**fireproof** \'⸗¦⸗\ *adj* [*fire* + *proof*] **:** proof against fire **:** relatively noncombustible: as **a** *of a building* **:** having all parts that carry weights or resist stresses and also all exterior and interior walls and stairways made of noncombustible materials and having all structural members that are made of steel and iron, which are injuriously affected by heat, protected effectively by other materials not so affected — compare FIRE-RESISTIVE, FIRE-RETARDANT, FLAMEPROOF **b** *of paper* **:** so treated that it will char but not burn on exposure to a flame — **fire·proof·ness** *n* -ES

[2]**fireproof** \"\ *vt* **:** to make fireproof

fireproofing *n* **1 :** the act or process of making a thing fireproof **2 :** the materials used in the process of fireproofing

fireproofing tile *n* **:** tile for use as a protection against fire for structural members

fire protection *n* **1 :** measures and practices for preventing or reducing injury and loss of life or property by fire **2 :** activities relating to the extinguishment of fire

fir·er \'fīrə(r)\ *n* -s **1 :** one that fires **:** one that lights, replenishes, and attends to a fire (as for a brickkiln) **2 :** a worker who bakes enameled jewelry settings to cause fusion of the enamel to the setting — called also *baker*

fire raft *n* **:** a raft loaded with combustibles for setting fire to an enemy's ships or waterfront

fire-raising \'⸗,⸗⸗\ *n, Brit* **:** the crime of willfully or recklessly burning buildings or such property as stored cereals or growing woods

fire red *n* **1 :** a strong reddish orange that is yellower and paler than poppy or paprika, yellower and lighter than fiery red, and yellower and paler than average coral red — called also *mineral orange, Paris red;* compare FLAME, FLAME RED **2** *also* **fire red toner :** a brilliant orange-red azo dye that has good resistance to light and heat, is made from diazotized 2-chloro-4-nitroaniline, and is used as a pigment for paint and for lithographic and offset inks; chlorinated para red — called also *Permanent Red R;* see DYE table I (under *Pigment Red 4*)

fire resistance *n* **:** degree of resistance of material to fire often measured in terms of time of withstanding a standard test fire

fire-resistant *adj, of a structural element* **:** so resistant to fire that for a specified time and under conditions of a standard heat intensity it will not fail structurally or allow transit of heat and will not permit the side away from the fire to become hotter than a specified temperature

fire-resistive *or* **fire-resisting** \¦⸗⸗¦⸗⸗\ *adj* **:** immune to the effects of exposure to fire of a certain specified severity and duration — compare FIREPROOF

fire-retardant \ˌ═ˌ═ˈ══\ *adj* **:** having the ability or tendency to slow up or halt the spread of fire (as by providing insulation) ⟨*fire-retardant* preservatives⟩ ⟨*fire-retardant* construction⟩

fire retardant *n* **:** a substance that is fire-retardant

fire-retarded \ˈ═ˌ═ˈ══\ *adj* **:** protected with a fire-retardant material

fireroom \ˈ═ˌ═\ *n* **1 :** STOKEHOLD **2** *obs* **:** a room heated by a fireplace

fire runner *n* **:** one who goes into a mine after the blasting to search for fires and to replace damaged brattices

fires *pl of* FIRE, *pres 3d sing of* FIRE

firesafe \ˈ═ˌ═\ *adj* **:** offering protection or protected against fire — **firesafety** \ˈ═ˌ══\ *n*

fire salamander *n* **:** SPOTTED SALAMANDER a

fire sale *n* **:** a sale of merchandise damaged or believed to be damaged as the result of a fire

fire sand *n* **1 :** a highly refractory sand that consists mainly of coarse quartz grains with alumina or clayey sand and that is used esp. for foundry purposes **2 :** a grayish green powder or granular refractory material obtained as a by-product in the manufacture of silicon carbide

fire saw *n* **:** an implement for producing fire by friction consisting of a piece of wood (as bamboo or rattan) that is sawed or rubbed against the grain of another

fire scarlet *n* **:** CASTILIAN RED

fire screen *n* **:** a protecting wire screen or grating placed before or fitting over the front of an open fireplace — compare FENDER 1b(1)

fire service *n* **:** an organized fire-fighting and fire-preventing service (as of a city); *also* **:** the occupation of fire fighting

fireset \ˈ═ˌ═\ *n* **:** a set of fire irons (as tongs, shovel, brush, and poker)

fire setting *n* **:** the process of softening or cracking the working face of a lode by the action of fire

fire ship *n* **:** a ship carrying combustibles or explosives sent among the enemy's ships or works to set them on fire

fire shutter *n* **:** a metal shutter constructed to resist fire for a period often specified as one hour

fireset

¹fireside \ˈ═ˌ═\ *n* [¹*fire* + *side*] **1 :** a place near the fire or hearth; *esp* **:** the sides of the fireplace where seats were formerly placed **2 a :** HOME ⟨shiploads of excellent gentlemen . . . were driven from their ~*s* —V.L.Parrington⟩ ⟨a virtuous people, fighting in defense of their altars and ~*s* —W.E.Channing⟩ **b** *archaic* **:** one's household **:** FAMILY ⟨by so doing she would bring comfort and relief to an anxious ~ —S.H.Adams⟩

²fireside \"\ *adj* **:** having an informal or intimate quality ⟨a report . . . written in ~ language —H.M.Baus⟩ ⟨a ~ chat⟩ ⟨~ commentator to musical America —R.D.Welch⟩

fire station *n* **:** a building housing fire apparatus and usu. firemen

fire step *n* **:** FIRING STEP

fire stick *n* [ME *fir sticke*, fr. *fir, fire* + *sticke* stick — more at STICK] **1 :** a hardwood stick that is rubbed or twirled to make fire by friction — compare FIRE DRILL 1 **2 :** FIREBRAND **3 a fire sticks** *pl* **:** primitive fire tongs made of two sticks **b :** POKER 1

firestone \ˈ═ˌ═\ *n* [ME *firston*, fr. OE *fȳrstān*, fr. *fȳr* fire + *stān* stone — more at FIRE, STONE] **1 :** pyrite formerly used for striking fire; *also* **:** FLINT **2 :** a stone that will endure high heat and is used esp. for lining furnaces and kilns — used esp. of a sandstone occurring in the south of England **3 :** a plate of iron covering the front of the furnace in a slag hearth except for a few inches of space between it and the bedplate

fire stop *n* **:** a member or material used to fill or close open parts of a structure for preventing the spread of fire and smoke — compare FIRE BLOCKS

fire-stop \ˈ═ˌ═\ *vt* [*fire stop*] **:** to provide with a fire stop

firestopping \ˈ═ˌ══\ *n* **:** a system of fire stops

fire storm *n* **:** an atmospheric disturbance caused by a large fire (as after the bombing of a city) in which the central column of rising heated air induces a strong wind often accompanied by rain

fire superiority *n* **:** fire superior in effect to that of the enemy; *also* **:** the degree of such superiority

fire support *n* **:** assistance to infantry and armored units by artillery fire, naval gunfire, and airplane strafing and bombing

firetail \ˈ═ˌ═\ *n* **:** any of several birds with red or reddish tails: as **a** *dial Eng* **:** REDSTART 1 **b :** DIAMOND SPARROW 1

fire test *n* **:** a test by fire (as one to determine the burning point of an oil or one to determine the resistance of porcelain or concrete to heat) — see TIME-TEMPERATURE CURVE

firetest \ˈ═ˌ═\ *vt* **:** to subject to a fire test

fire thorn *n* **:** a plant of the genus *Pyracantha; specif;* a European partly evergreen tree (*P. coccinea*) with white flowers and orange-red fruits

firetop \ˈ═ˌ═\ *n* **:** FIREWEED b

fire tower *n* **1 :** a tower from which a watch for fires is maintained **2 :** a fireproof and smokeproof compartment running vertically through or attached to a building and containing a fireproof stairway **3 :** WATER TOWER 2 **4 :** DRILL TOWER

firetrap \ˈ═ˌ═\ *n* **:** a building or other place so constructed as to make egress hazardous in case of fire; *also* **:** combustible rubbish creating a fire hazard

fire tree *n* **1 :** a New Zealand tree (*Metrosideros tomentosa*) with hard wood **2 :** SUN TREE

fire trench *n* **:** a trench constructed to facilitate the delivery of small-arms fire

fire truck *n* **:** an automotive vehicle equipped with fire-fighting apparatus

fire tube *n* **:** ³FLUE d

fire-tube boiler *n* **:** a boiler in which water surrounds the tubes through which hot gases pass from the furnace to the stack

fire wagon *n* **:** FIRE ENGINE

fire walking *n* **:** the ceremony or ordeal of walking barefooted through fire, over a bed of embers, or over hot stones

fire wall *n* **1 :** a wall to prevent the spread of fire usu. made of noncombustible materials; *esp* **:** a wall completely separating two parts of a building from the basement to three feet above the roof and consisting of fire-resistive material and having all openings protected by automatically closing fire doors **2 :** a wall to retain oil in case of its escape from a tank or to prevent the spread of burning oil

fire ward *n, archaic* **:** FIRE WARDEN

fire warden *n* **:** an officer who has responsibility for fire control in a particular area: as **a :** one who directs a crew in the suppression of forest fires **b :** a fire patrolman in a logging area

firewater \ˈ═ˌ══\ *n* [prob trans. of an AmerInd expression like Algonquian *scoutiouabou* firewater] **:** strong alcoholic beverage

fireweed \ˈ═ˌ═\ *n* **:** any of several weeds troublesome in clearings or burned districts: as **a :** a plant of the genus *Erechtites; esp* **:** an American weed (*E. hieracifolia*) **b :** a tall perennial (*Epilobium angustifolium*) with creeping rootstocks, lanceolate leaves, and long spikes of pinkish purple flowers that tends to occur in great abundance in burned over areas or recent clearings and is an important honey plant in parts of No. America **c :** JIMSONWEED **d :** HORSEWEED 1 **e :** HOARY PLANTAIN 1 **f :** a wild lettuce (*Lactuca canadensis*) **g :** ORANGE HAWKWEED

fire wheel *n* **1 :** INDIAN BLANKET **2 :** a wheel of fireworks

fire willow *n* **:** an erect willow (*Salix scouleriana*) of western No. America appearing soon on burned over areas

fire wind *n* **:** a wind caused by a fire storm

fire window *n* **:** a window constructed to resist a fire of known standard intensity for a specified time (as 20 minutes or one hour)

firewoman \ˈ═ˌ══\ *n, pl* **firewomen :** a female fire fighter

firewood \ˈ═ˌ═\ *n* [ME *firwode*, fr. *fir, fire* + *wode* wood — more at WOOD] **1 :** wood for fuel **2 :** LEATHERWOOD 1b

firework \ˈ═ˌ═\ *n, often attrib* **1 :** a device for producing a striking display (as of light, noise, or smoke) by the combustion of explosive or flammable compositions esp. for exhibition, signaling, or illumination and typically consisting of a paper case containing combustible material (as charcoal, sulfur, or a metal powder), an oxidizing agent (as a nitrate or chlorate), and a metal salt as coloring agent if color is desired **:** PYROTECHNIC ⟨the sodium rocket was not merely a beautiful . . . ~ —*Time*⟩ **2 fireworks** *pl* **:** a display of fireworks ⟨the celebration was marked by ~*s* and much oratory⟩ **3 a fireworks** *pl but sometimes sing in constr* **:** a display of fiery temper, great excitement, or intense activity ⟨whenever those two get together there were sure to be ~*s*⟩ ⟨political ~*s*⟩ ⟨a ~*s* of rage —W.A.White⟩ **b :** a spectacular display (as of musical or verbal brilliance ⟨a natural ~ of . . . wit too good to print —Winthrop Sargeant⟩ — usu. used in pl. ⟨many Spanish dancers tend to overdo the ~*s* —*Dance Observer*⟩

fireworm \ˈ═ˌ═\ *n* **1 :** the larva of various small tortricid moths that eats the leaves of the cranberry giving the vines a scorched look **2 :** GLOWWORM

fire worship *n* **:** religious homage to fire or to a deity symbolized by fire

fir green *n* **:** FIR 3

¹firing *n* -s [ME, fr. gerund of *firen* to fire — more at FIRE] **1 :** the act or an instance of treating, preparing, or curing by heat; *specif* **:** the process of maturing ceramic products by the application of heat **2 :** FIREWOOD, COAL, FUEL **3 :** the burning or scorching of plants esp. by unfavorable soil conditions or other environmental conditions

²firing *adj* [fr. pres. part. of ²*fire*] **:** of or relating to the operation or operating parts of a firearm ⟨~ cycle⟩ ⟨~ mechanism⟩

firing data *n pl* **:** the commands necessary for the settings (as of instruments or fuzes) in the firing of a weapon esp. in the artillery

firing iron *n* **:** an iron used by veterinarians in cauterizing or firing a horse

firing line *n* **1 a :** a line from which fire is delivered against the enemy **:** FRONT LINE **b :** a line from which target practice is conducted **2 :** the forefront of any activity — used esp. in the phrase *on the firing line* ⟨the man or woman engaged in advertising production must know what he must do when he is on the *firing line* —Ben Dalgin⟩

firing order *n* **:** the order in which the several cylinders of an internal-combustion engine are sparked and fired

firing pin *n* **:** the pin that strikes the primer of the cartridge in the breech mechanism of a firearm

firing point *n* **:** a position (as on a firing line) from which a weapon is fired

firing ring *n* **:** one of various flat clay rings so placed in a pottery kiln that they may be withdrawn successively as the firing proceeds, the amount of shrinkage of the ring indicating the intensity of the fire

firing squad *also* **firing party** *n* **1 :** a detachment detailed to fire volleys over the grave of one buried with military honors **2 :** a detachment detailed to carry out a sentence of death by shooting

firing step *n* **:** a ledge or board along the front wall of a trench used to stand on when firing

firing table *n* **:** a table giving the elements of standard trajectories for a particular gun and type of ammunition and for effects produced by conditions (as of temperature or wind) that are not standard

firing tread *n* **:** BANQUETTE TREAD

firk \ˈfərk, ˈfi(ə)rk\ *vb* -ED/-ING/-S [ME *ferken*, fr. OE *fercian* to convey, bring, proceed; akin to OE *faran* to go, travel — more at FARE] *vi* **1** *dial Brit* **:** to move quickly **:** HASTEN; *also* **:** to be lively or frisky **2** *dial Brit* **a :** JERK, TWITCH **b :** FIDGET, FUSS ~ *vt* **1** *archaic* **:** BEAT, STRIKE, CHASTISE, CONQUER ⟨I'll ~ you, I'll rattle you —Thomas Gray⟩ **2** *obs* **:** to get dishonestly **:** CONTRIVE, CHEAT

fir·kin \ˈfərkən, -ə̄k-,-əik-\ *n* -S [ME *ferdkyn, firdekyn, fyrkyn*, fr. (assumed) MD *veerdelkijn, vierdelkijn*, dim. of MD *veerdel, vierdel* fourth, fr. *veerde, vierde* fourth (adj.) + *-del* (fr. *deel* part); akin to OE *fēortha* fourth and *dǣl* part — more at FOURTH, DEAL] **1 :** a small wooden vessel or cask of indeterminate size **2 :** any of various British units of capacity usu. equal to ¼ barrel: as **a :** a unit equal to 9 imperial gallons **b :** an old unit for ale equal to 8 ale gallons **3 :** any of various British units of weight; *specif* **:** a unit for butter equal to 56 pounds

firkin 1

fir·lot \ˈfi(ə)rlət, ˈfər-\ *n* -S [ME *ferlot*, fr. ON *fjōrthi hlotr* fourth part, fr. *fjōrthi* fourth + *hlotr* part; akin to OE *fēortha* fourth and OE *hlot* lot — more at FOURTH, LOT] **1 :** any of various old Scottish units of dry capacity equal to ¼ boll or from ½ to 1½ Winchester bushels **2 :** a container of one firlot capacity

¹firm \ˈfərm, -ə̄m,-əim\ *adj* -ER/-EST [alter. (influenced by L *firmus*) of ME *ferm, ferme*, fr. MF *ferm*, fr. L *firmus;* akin to L *fretus* trusting, daring, Gk *thrēsasthai* to sit down, *thronos* chair, throne, Skt *dhārayati* he holds, carries, keeps; basic meaning: holding, supporting] **1 a :** securely or solidly fixed in place **:** not loose **:** IMMOVABLE ⟨his teeth were ~ —D.B. Chidsey⟩ ⟨~ in the saddle⟩ ⟨the gate and its pillars were ~, but at one side the fence had fallen —John Glassco⟩ **b** (1) **:** not weak, wavering, or uncertain **:** SOLID, ROBUST ⟨walked with a ~ tread⟩ ⟨a ~ handshake⟩ ⟨a ~ steady touch on the piano⟩ (2) **:** SOUND, HEALTHY ⟨her mind was still ~; but her limbs trembled . . . violently —Ellen Glasgow⟩ **c :** having a solid or compact structure or texture **:** withstanding stress or pressure **:** not flabby or soft ⟨~ flesh⟩ ⟨~ muscles⟩ ⟨the snow was ~, not powdery⟩ ⟨the creek has a ~ bottom⟩ **2 a** (1) **:** not subject to change, revision, or withdrawal **:** FIXED, SETTLED, DEFINITE, ESTABLISHED ⟨at this meeting . . . two ~ decisions were taken —*N.Y. Times*⟩ ⟨I cannot quote you a ~ price⟩ ⟨is this a ~ offer⟩ ⟨like a mother with no baby-sitter and a ~ date at the theater —E.B.White⟩ (2) **:** not subject to price weakness on an increase in offerings **:** STEADY — used esp. of commodities, securities, and interest rates (3) *of electric power* **:** dependable or flowing steadily because supplemented by a reserve source **b** (1) **:** not easily moved, shaken, excited, or disturbed **:** UNSHAKEN, CONVINCED, DETERMINED ⟨~ nerves⟩ ⟨a ~ believer in democracy⟩ ⟨~ confidence in his own ability⟩ (2) **:** not fickle or vacillating **:** STEADFAST, LOYAL, CONSTANT ⟨a ~ friend⟩ ⟨~ in his devotion⟩ (3) **:** making no concessions **:** showing no weakness **:** UNYIELDING, RIGOROUS, INFLEXIBLE, SEVERE, HARD ⟨a ~ and even tough diplomacy —Hugh Gaitskell⟩ ⟨when a strong hand must be used, be impersonal but ~ —Dorothy Barclay⟩ ⟨~ discipline —L.C.Douglas⟩ **c** (1) **:** not easily challenged or undone **:** ASSURED, SECURE, STRONG ⟨took ~ possession of the enemy's trenches⟩ ⟨holds a ~ position as the country's leading poet⟩ ⟨this horse is a ~ favorite for the big race⟩ (2) **:** WELL-FOUNDED, CERTAIN ⟨the fuller and ~*er* account would have set several facts in clearer . . . perspective —A.S.P.Woodhouse⟩ **:** THOROUGH ⟨he has a ~ knowledge of the subject⟩ (3) **:** marked by solidity, precision, or clarity **:** convincingly, realistically, or solidly drawn ⟨the plot is thin, but the atmosphere is ~ —Nicola Chiaromonte⟩ ⟨the deep richness of the book . . . and its ~ design —W.T. Scott⟩ **3 :** indicating firmness or resolution ⟨the ~ almost arrogant voice of a vigorous young man —E.K.Genn⟩ ⟨a ~ mouth⟩

syn HARD, SOLID: FIRM may apply to a resistant tight compactness or resilient consistency of substance withstanding strain, stress, or pressure; it may imply stability or resolution ⟨a *firm* weave⟩ ⟨a *firm* foundation⟩ ⟨the snow, far from being soft and powdery, was *firm* and hard —John Hunt & Edmund Hillary⟩ ⟨only the pier actually hit was demolished; the adjoining piers stood *firm* —O.S.Nock⟩ ⟨he stood *firm* on recommendations he believed were to the city's benefit, often in the face of popular opposition —*Current Biog.*⟩ ⟨she was *firm* and determined with a firmness that was impervious to assault⟩ HARD may apply to a strong and rigid resistance to pressure or a sound unyielding stability; it may imply unyielding or harsh obduracy ⟨*hard* coal⟩ ⟨*hard* wood⟩ ⟨*hard* cash⟩ ⟨a *hard* man to deal with⟩ ⟨the oppressive conflict between esthetic values and a *hard* materialistic view of nature and human nature —Victor Lowe⟩ SOLID, as opposed to *fluid*, indicates a density and coherence giving fixed form; as opposed to *flimsy* or *unsubstantial*, it indicates strong sound stability; in reference to persons, it may imply complete reliability or sobriety ⟨a *solid* substance⟩ ⟨the bungalow was a very *solid* one —Rudyard Kipling⟩ ⟨courses that are *solid* in purpose and preparation and that are backed up with a maximum of good scholarship —Elizabeth Jacobs⟩ ⟨all we knew was that there was something of force and majesty and authority, *solid*, consistent, and beautiful —R.A.Cram⟩

²firm \"\ *adv* -ER/-EST [ME *ferm, ferme*, fr. *ferm, ferme*, adj.] **:** FIXEDLY, STEADFASTLY, SOLIDLY, FIRMLY — used chiefly in the phrases *stand firm* and *hold firm* ⟨if England had not stood ~ . . . our way of life would have gone up the flue —Richard Joseph⟩ ⟨begged his men to hold ~ till relief came⟩

³firm \"\ *vb* -ED/-ING/-S [ME *fermen, firmen*, fr. MF & L; MF *fermer*, fr. L *firmare*, fr. *firmus*] *vt* **1 a** (1) **:** to cause to become firm in texture or consistency **:** make solid or compact ⟨~ cheese⟩ ⟨~*ing* a light soil by rolling or harrowing —F.D. Smith & Barbara Wilcox⟩ ⟨a new face cream that ~*s* your skin⟩ (2) **:** to make fast or secure **:** set firmly **:** TIGHTEN ⟨~ a post in the ground⟩ ⟨~*ing* the grip on the sword —Tom Lea⟩ **b :** to bolster the courage or resources of **:** strengthen in some way **:** ENCOURAGE ⟨~*ed* herself with great care for the day —R.O. Bowen⟩ — often used with *up* ⟨voted a state of siege to ~ up his government —*Time*⟩ ⟨unless other factors ~ up the . . . price index substantially, it goes down —*Wall Street Jour.*⟩ ⟨his failure to ~ up his materialism . . . with data from the natural and social sciences —P.B.Rice⟩ **c :** SETTLE ⟨~ a contract⟩ **:** CONFIRM, ESTABLISH **2** *obs* **:** SIGN, VALIDATE ~ *vi* **1 :** to become firm in some way **:** take clear, definite, or fixed shape **:** HARDEN, CRYSTALLIZE, JELL ⟨his face ~*ed* and he spoke with restrained anger⟩ ⟨confidence is ~*ing* that the slump will be of short duration⟩ — often used with *up* ⟨opinion on this is ~*ing* up, and it's more optimistic than it was —*Kiplinger Washington Letter*⟩ ⟨the cheese is ~*ing*⟩ ⟨diplomats said more informal soundings must take place before things ~ up —*N.Y. Herald Tribune*⟩ **2 :** to recover from a decline **:** expand or rise after a contraction or fall ⟨after a long decline prices are ~*ing* again⟩ — often used with *up* ⟨cattle prices are ~*ing* up⟩ ⟨the market ~*ed* up a bit⟩

⁴firm \"\ *n* -S [Sp *firma*, fr. *firmar* to affirm, confirm, sign, fr. L *firmare*] **1** *obs* **:** SIGNATURE; *esp* **:** official signature of state papers **2** [G *firma*, fr. obs. G, signature, fr. It, fr. *firmare* to sign, fr. L *firmare* to make firm, confirm] **a :** the name, title, or style under which a company transacts business **:** the firm name **b :** a partnership of two or more persons not recognized as a legal person distinct from the members composing it — compare COMPANY 3 **c :** a business unit or enterprise ⟨the organizational framework within which the Soviet ~ operates —Holland Hunter⟩

fir·ma·ment \ˈfərməmənt, ˈfə̄m-,ˈfəim-\ *n* -S [ME, fr. LL & L; LL *firmamentum* vault of the sky (trans. of Gk *stereōma*, lit., solid body, foundation, trans. of Heb *rāqīa'*), fr. L, strengthening, support, fr. *firmare* to make firm + *-mentum* -ment — more at FIRM] **1 :** the vault or arch of the sky **:** HEAVENS **2** *in ancient astronomy* **:** the orb of the fixed stars **:** the 8th and outermost celestial sphere; *sometimes* **:** any of the crystalline heavens ⟨the first ~ or primum mobile⟩ **3** *obs* **:** fixed foundation **:** established basis

fir·ma·men·tal \ˌ═ˌ═ˈmentᵊl\ *adj* **:** relating to the firmament **:** being of the upper regions **:** CELESTIAL

firmament blue *n* **:** a pale blue to light greenish blue that is bluer than aquamarine

fir·man \fərˈmän, ˌfərˈmän, ˈfərmən\ *n* -S [Turk *ferman*, fr. Per *fermān*, fr. OPer *framānā*] **:** a decree or mandate, order, license, or grant issued by the ruler of an Oriental country

firmer *comparative of* FIRM

fir·mer chisel \ˈfərmər-\ *n* [modif. of F *fermoir*, alter. of MF *formoir* chisel, fr. *former* to form — more at FORM] **:** a woodworker's hand chisel having a thin flat blade usu. at least 6 inches long and ⅛ to 2 inches wide — see CHISEL illustration

fir·mer gouge \"-\ *n* [*firmer* (*chisel*)] **:** a woodworking gouge similar in length and thickness to the firmer chisel

firmest *superlative of* FIRM

fir·mi·ster·nal \ˌfərməˈstərnᵊl\ *adj* [NL *Firmisternia* + E *-al*] **1 :** having the epicoracoids meet in the median neutral line **2 :** of or relating to the Firmisternia

fir·mi·ster·nia \ˌ═ˌ═ˈ═nēə\ *n pl, cap* [NL, fr. L *firmus* strong, firm + NL *sternum* + -ia — more at FIRM, STERNUM] *in some classifications* **:** a division of the amphibian suborder Linguata in which in the adult state the epicoracoids of the two sides meet in the median ventral line — compare ARCIFERA

firmland *n* [¹*firm* + *land*] *obs* **:** TERRA FIRMA

firm·ly *adv* [ME *fermely, firmely*, fr. *ferm, ferme* firm + *-ly* — more at FIRM] **:** in a firm manner **:** STEADFASTLY, RESOLUTELY, SOUNDLY, SOLIDLY, STRONGLY ⟨~ entrenched in the mountainous parts along the northern border —*Collier's Yr. Bk.*⟩ ⟨a group of staid brownstone and brick dwellings stands ~ against time —*Amer. Guide Series: N.Y. City*⟩

firm·ness *n* -ES **:** the quality or state of being firm

fir moss *n* **:** FIR CLUB MOSS

firm red heart *n* **:** an incipient decay of heartwood characterized by a reddish color

firm up *vt* **:** to assure a steady flow of (as hydroelectric power) by means of a reserve supplementary source of electric power

firn *or* **firn snow** \ˈfi(ə)rn\ *n* -S [G, fr. G dial. (Switzerland) *firn* of or relating to the previous year, fr. OHG *firni* old; akin to OE *fyrn, firn* former, ancient, Goth *fairneis* old, ON *fyrnd* age, antiquity, *forn* old, OE *faran* to go — more at FARE] **:** NÉVÉ

firn·ifi·ca·tion \ˌfirnəfəˈkāshən\ *n* -S [*firn* + *-i-* + *-fication*] **:** the process whereby snow is changed to névé

firn line *n* **:** NÉVÉ LINE

fir pine *n* **:** BALSAM FIR 1

fir·ring *n* -S [by alter.] **:** FURRING 3b(1)

fir·ry \ˈfər·ē, -r·i *also* ˈfərē *or* -ri\ *adj* [*fir* + *-y*] **:** made of fir **:** abounding in firs

¹first \ˈfərst, ˈfə̄st, ˈfəist\ *adj* [ME, fr. OE *fyrst;* akin to OHG & OS *furist* first, ON *fyrstr;* superlative fr. the root of OHG & OS *furi* before, for, ON *fyr;* akin to OE *faran* to go — more at FARE] **1 a** (1) **:** being number one in a countable series ⟨the ~ day⟩ **:** beginning a series — see NUMBER table ⟨the ~ volume⟩ ⟨my ~ voyage⟩ (2) **:** being a type of grammatical declension or conjugation conventionally placed first in a standard arrangement of the types (3) **:** being the lowest forward gear or speed in an automotive vehicle **b :** preceding all others **:** earliest in time ⟨the ~ to come⟩ ⟨the ~ train leaves at noon⟩ **c :** foremost in position **:** being in front of all others ⟨~ in the race⟩ **d** (1) **:** foremost in rank, importance, or worth **:** CHIEF ⟨of ~ importance⟩ ⟨~ in the hearts of his countrymen —Henry Lee⟩ ⟨your ~ concern is to get well⟩ ⟨the ~ American actor of our day —Lee Rogow⟩ (2) **:** highest or most prominent in carrying the melody among several voices or instruments of the same class ⟨~ soprano⟩ ⟨~ violin⟩ (3) **:** having primary jurisdiction in the Mormon Church; *esp* **:** having jurisdiction throughout the church ⟨the ~ presidency⟩ **e :** having precedence over colleagues of the same general grade or duties — used in titles ⟨~ mate⟩ ⟨~ ballerina⟩ **2 :** smallest, slightest, or most rudimentary ⟨I haven't the ~ idea of what you mean⟩ **3 a** *North* **:** EAGER, ANXIOUS ⟨he was so ~ to hear about it⟩ **b** *dial Brit* **:** NEXT, FOLLOWING — often used postpositively with expressions of time ⟨I'll come to see him Sunday ~⟩ **4 a :** being between 0.51 and 1.50 on the magnitude scale — used of the magnitude of a star **b :** being 1.50 or brighter on the magnitude scale — used of the apparent visual magnitude of any of the 22 brightest stars in the sky

²first \"\ *adv* [ME, fr. OE *fyrst*, fr. *fyrst*, adj.] **1 :** before any or some other person or thing (as in time, space, rank, or importance) **:** as the first thing to be mentioned **:** to begin with ⟨I will pay you ~, and then the others⟩ ⟨~, I wish to consider the economic problem⟩ ⟨~ of all, let me say that I regard my opponent with great respect⟩ — often used with *off* ⟨~ off, he was likely to get a shave and a haircut —S.E.Fletcher⟩ ⟨~ off, we heard a splendid performance of Haydn's Symphony —Philip Hamburger⟩ **2 :** for the first time ⟨we ~ met at a formal party⟩ **3 :** in preference to anything else **:** rather than do, be, or bear something **:** SOONER ⟨surrender? we will die ~⟩ **4** *North* **:** JUST, ONLY ⟨are you back already or are you ~ leaving⟩

FISHES

MUSKELLUNGE
BLACK BASS
YELLOWBELLY SUNFISH
WHITEFISH
GARFISH
BROOK TROUT
CATFISH
CARP
EEL
ATLANTIC SALMON
PACIFIC SALMON
MAKO
DOGFISH
TUNA
MACKEREL
FLOUNDER
DOLPHIN
SAILFISH
SWORDFISH
TARPON
BLUE ANGELFISH
STRIPED BASS
RED SNAPPER
HALIBUT
COD

[3]**first** \"\ *n* -s [ME, fr. *first*, adj.] **1 a :** number one in a countable series ⟨the ~ of the month⟩ **b :** the first part **:** BEGINNING, OUTSET ⟨the last of life for which the ~ was made —Robert Browning⟩ ⟨from the ~ I disliked the man⟩ ⟨at ~ I didn't know what to make of it⟩ **c :** the first thing ⟨the ~ I knew, the fire had spread to the bedroom⟩ **2 :** the first occurrence or item of its kind ⟨out of doors marked "restricted" today flow the aviation ~s of tomorrow —*First in Flight*⟩ ⟨Vermont has several educational ~s —*Amer. Guide Series: Vt.*⟩; *specif* **:** a first edition (as of a book) **3 a :** the first gear or speed in an automotive vehicle **b :** FIRST BASE **c :** UNISON **:** PRIME 8c **d :** PRIME 7 **4 a :** an article of commerce of the finest grade — usu. used in pl. ⟨clear unspotted skins graded as ~s⟩ **b :** FIRST CLASS ⟨he took a ~ in classics⟩ **c :** the winning place in a race or other sports contest

first aid *n* **:** emergency and sometimes makeshift treatment given to someone (as a victim of an accident) requiring immediate attention where regular medical or surgical care is not available

first-aid·er \ˌfər'stādər; fə̄'stādə(r, fəi's-\ *n* **:** one trained in giving first aid

first and last *adv* **:** taking everything together **:** all in all **:** in the last analysis **:** ALTOGETHER ⟨she holds that he was *first and last* a poet —*Times Lit. Supp.*⟩

first angle *n* **:** an angle of the Great Triangle formed on the palm by the intersection of the lines of Head and Life and when clear, well pointed, and even usu. held by palmists to indicate diplomacy and refinement of thought and conduct — called also *upper angle;* compare SECOND ANGLE, THIRD ANGLE

first approximation *n* **:** a roughly approximate value of a quantity often preliminary to more precise determination ⟨the value of pi to a *first approximation* is 22/7⟩

first attack *n* **:** a member of the offense on a men's lacrosse team

first base *n* **1 a :** the base that must be touched first by a base runner in baseball **b :** the player position for defending the area around first base **2 :** the first step or stage in a course usu. involving several steps or stages ⟨the widely advertised romance never got to *first base* —Bennett Cerf⟩

first baseman *n, pl* **first basemen :** the baseball player stationed at the first-base position — see BASEBALL illustration

first bass *n* **:** the principal contrabass player of an orchestra

first bite *n, in line engraving* **:** the first etch or action of the acid upon the plate before the application of dragon's blood

first border *n* **:** a row of lights over the front of the stage parallel to the proscenium — called also *concert border*

[1]**firstborn** \'=,=\ *adj* [ME, fr. *first* + *born* born] **:** first brought forth **:** first in the order of nativity **:** ELDEST

[2]**firstborn** \"\ *n, pl* **firstborn** *also* **firstborns** [ME, fr. [1]*firstborn*] **:** one that is firstborn; *esp* **:** a firstborn son

first bottom *n* **:** the floodplain of a river **:** low-lying flatland along a stream that may be inundated at flood stage

first call *n* **:** a warning bugle call usu. played 15 minutes before assembly (as for reveille or retreat)

first captain *n* **:** the highest ranking cadet officer of a cadet corps or a military school

first cause *n* **1** *in some philosophies* **:** the self-created being to which every chain of causes must ultimately go back **2** *usu cap F&C* **:** GOD — compare PRIME MOVER

first-chop \'=,=\ *adj* [[1]*first* + *chop* (quality, class)] **:** FIRST-CLASS ⟨I believe London is simply teeming with *first-chop* unwritten plays —Katherine Mansfield⟩

first class *n* **1 a :** the first and usu. highest group in a classification; *specif* **:** the group of persons who have obtained highest distinction in an honors course at a British university **b :** a place in or a member of such a group **2 :** the highest of usu. three classes of accommodations (as on a passenger ship) — compare CABIN CLASS **3 :** a class of mail that comprises letters, postcards, any matter wholly or partly in handwriting or typewriting, and any matter sealed against inspection, that requires the highest rate of postage, and that is accorded privileged treatment such as free forwarding or return to sender in case of nondelivery to addressee **4 :** the third rank in the rising scale of ranks in the Boy Scouts of America or the Girl Scouts of America — compare SECOND CLASS, TENDERFOOT

[1]**first-class** \'=,=\ *adj* [*first class*] **1 :** of or relating to the highest grade in a series ⟨a *first-class* railway carriage⟩ ⟨a *first-class* honors degree⟩ **2 :** of the best quality **:** of the highest excellence ⟨a *first-class* telescope⟩ ⟨*first-class* work⟩

[2]**first-class** \"\ *adv* **:** by a first-class conveyance **:** with first-class accommodations ⟨they travel *first-class*⟩

first class·man \'=,=mən\ *n, pl* **first classmen :** a fourth-year student in a military school (as Annapolis or West Point)

first-class saloon *n, Brit* **:** a railroad car whose facilities are adaptable for day or night occupancy

first coat *n* **1 :** SCRATCH COAT **2 :** the first layer of paint

firstcomer \'=,==\ *n* **:** one that comes first ⟨the ~s to the New World did not possess boats —W.T.Corlett⟩

first cousin *n* **:** COUSIN 1b

first cranial nerve *n* **:** OLFACTORY NERVE

first cross *n* **:** an animal produced by interbreeding members of two pure breeds — contrasted with *mongrel* and *purebred*

first day *n* **1** *usu cap F* **:** SUNDAY — used chiefly by the Friends **2 a :** a day when the postage stamps of a new issue are first placed on sale; *esp* **:** one on which recognition of the event is made by special cancellations and often by cachets on mail bearing the stamps **b :** FIRST-DAY COVER

first-day city *n* **:** a city officially chosen for the first-day sale of a new postage stamp

first-day cover *n* **:** a philatelic cover bearing postal markings showing that it was mailed on a first day at a first-day city and that its stamp belongs to the new issue of that first day

first defense *n* **:** a lacrosse player whose defensive position is in front of the goal

first-degree \'==,=\ *adj* [fr. *first degree* (as in such phrases as *of the first degree, to the first degree*)] **1 :** of the lowest or mildest in a series ⟨*first-degree* initiation⟩ ⟨*first-degree* laceration⟩ **2 :** of the highest or most serious in a series ⟨*first-degree* murder⟩

first-degree burn *n* **:** a mild burn characterized by heat, pain, and reddening of the burned surface but not exhibiting blistering or charring of tissues

first derivative *n, math* **:** the derivative of a function

first-desk \'=,=\ *adj* **:** first in rank among players of the same instrument in an orchestra ⟨the *first-desk* players of the string section⟩

first division *n* **:** the highest ranking half of a sports league; *specif* **:** the five leading baseball teams in each of the major leagues

first down *n* **:** the first in a series of four downs in which a football team must net a 10-yard gain to retain possession of the ball; *also* **:** the right to start such a series

first edition *n* **1 a :** the copies of a literary work first printed from the same type and issued at the same time **b :** the first pressrun of a newspaper for a given date **2 :** a single copy from a first edition

first family *n, sometimes cap both Fs* **1 :** a family of high social rank or pretensions esp. due to descent from the first settlers of a place ⟨those few inhabitants of Boston who regard themselves as the . . . end-all of American civilization — the thirty or forty *first families* —Katharine Rosin⟩ — abbr. *FF* **2 :** the family enjoying preeminent status in some place ⟨the closest relatives of the young god-king automatically became the nation's *first family* —Heinrich Harrer⟩

first filial generation *n* **:** the first generation produced by a cross with all members heterozygous for characters in which the parents differ

first flight *n* **1 :** a first flight in which airmail is carried over a newly established route **2 :** FIRST-FLIGHT COVER

first-flight cover *n* **:** a philatelic airmail cover bearing postal markings such as special cancellation and often a cachet showing that it was carried on a first flight

first floor *n* **1 :** GROUND FLOOR **2** *Brit* **:** the floor next above the ground floor

[1]**firstfoot** \'=,=\ *n* -s [[1]*first* + *foot*] **1** *Brit* **:** the first person entering a house on New Year's day, such a person being popularly believed to bring good luck to the household if brunet and bad luck if blond **2** *Brit* **:** the first person met on the way to a special event (as a christening or wedding)

[2]**firstfoot** \"\ *vt, Brit* **:** to enter (a household) as a firstfoot ~ *vi* **1** *Brit* **:** to be a firstfoot — usu. used with *it* **2** *Brit* **:** to go about to various houses intending to be firstfoot

first-foot·er \-ə(r)\ *n* **:** FIRSTFOOT 1

firstfruits \'=,=\ *n pl* [ME *first fruites*] **1 :** the earliest gathered fruits of the season; *specif* **:** those offered by the ancient Hebrews and other ancient nations to the Deity in acknowledgment of the gift of fruitfulness **2 :** the income for the first year formerly payable to a superior by every holder of a feudal or ecclesiastical benefice or an office of profit **3 :** the earliest products, effects, or results of any work, endeavor, or process

first-generation \ˌ=,==,==\ *adj* **1 :** born in the U. S. — used of an American of immigrant parentage **2 :** FOREIGN-BORN — used of a naturalized American

[1]**firsthand** \'=,=\ *adv* [fr. *(at) first hand*] **:** directly from the original source **:** by direct observation or experience ⟨they will learn them ~ — and they will not like them —H.S.Truman⟩ ⟨individual citizens should know ~ what goes on in the courts —Dorothy Barclay⟩

[2]**firsthand** \"\ *adj* **:** obtained or coming directly from the original source **:** obtained by or based on direct observation or experience **:** DIRECT, IMMEDIATE ⟨authentic ~ facts about business properties and market conditions —*advt*⟩ ⟨keep in ~ touch with the changing . . . situation —*Current Biog.*⟩ ⟨~ information⟩ ⟨a ~ account, written by the doctor of a small merchant ship —H.R.Viets⟩

first in, first out *adj* **:** being or relating to a method of valuing inventories by which items in the lot first received are assumed to be issued or sold first and requisitions are priced at the cost per item of the oldest lot on hand — compare LAST IN, FIRST OUT

first intention *n* **1 :** the healing of an incised wound by the direct union of skin edges without granulations — compare SECOND INTENTION **2 :** a conception of a thing (as man, stone) formed by the direct or primary application of the mind to an individual object — compare SECOND INTENTION

first inversion *n* **:** a triad in music with its third in the bass — see TRIAD illustration

first lady *n, often cap F&L* **1 a :** the wife of the president of the U. S. or if he has no wife the woman whom he chooses to act as hostess at the White House **b :** the wife or hostess of the chief executive of any other country or jurisdiction ⟨one of the daughters will serve as father's hostess and thus be the new *first lady* of California —*Time*⟩ ⟨cabinet ministers had gathered . . . as the . . . bulletins indicated that the *First Lady* lay dying —*N.Y.Times*⟩ **2 :** the leading woman representative or practitioner of any art or profession ⟨the *first lady* of French letters⟩ ⟨the *first lady* of the dance⟩

first law of thermodynamics : LAW OF THERMODYNAMICS 1

first lien *n* **:** a lien taking precedence over all other claims, charges, or encumbrances of the same general category but not necessarily over those imposed by the sanction of government (as taxes or costs of administration or other preferred claims given priority by law)

first lieutenant *n* **1 a :** a commissioned officer in the army, air force, or marine corps ranking below a captain and above a second lieutenant **b :** the naval officer responsible for the upkeep and cleanliness of a ship or station **2 :** a Salvation Army officer ranking above a second lieutenant and below a captain

first-line \'=,=\ *adj* **1 :** available for immediate effective combat service ⟨*first-line* troops⟩ ⟨*first-line* ships⟩ **2 :** of the first quality or importance ⟨there are in the area no potential *first-line* industrial centers —S.G.Hanson⟩ ⟨a *first-line* tire⟩ ⟨attended by 50 *first-line* business executives —*Amer. Standards Assoc.*⟩

first·ling \'=liŋ, -lēŋ\ *n* -s **1 :** the first of a class or kind ⟨the ~s of my tiny library —C.E.Montague⟩ **2 :** the first produce, offspring, or result of something ⟨an offering of lambs, all ~s, laid on his altar —W.B.Smith & Walter Miller⟩

first lord of the treasury : the principal lord commissioner of the treasury whose office has only nominal official duties but is usu. held by the British prime minister

first·ly *adv* [[1]*first* + *-ly*] **:** in the first place (as in a series of topics) **:** before anything else **:** FIRST

first man *n* **:** FIRST SLIP

first mean line *n* **:** ACUTE BISECTRIX

first meridian *n* **:** PRIME MERIDIAN

first mortgage *n* **:** a mortgage that has priority as a lien over all mortgages and liens except those imposed by paramount authority of law (as taxes, betterments, and public water charges); *sometimes* **:** a mortgage that has priority over other mortgages only

first-movement form *n, chiefly Brit* **:** SONATA FORM

first mover *n* **:** FIRST CAUSE

first name *n* **:** the name that stands first in one's full name **:** CHRISTIAN NAME, FORENAME ⟨called him by one of his *first names* —Thomas Wolfe⟩ — contrasted with *last name*

[1]**first-name** \'=,=\ *vt* [*first name*] **:** to address by the first name ⟨the doctor's son from Edinburgh and the boy from Abilene were soon *first-naming* each other —T.C.Mendenhall †1924⟩

[2]**first-name** \'=,=\ *adj* [*first name*] **:** familiar enough to speak and be spoken to by a first name or nickname ⟨on *first-name* terms with almost everyone —Keith Ellis⟩ ⟨on a *first-name* basis with scores of the neighborhood children —*Lamp*⟩

first nerve *n* **:** OLFACTORY NERVE

first·ness *n* -ES **:** a fundamental category in Peircean philosophy comprising qualities like redness, hardness, bitterness, and nobility and expressive of possibility, spontaneity, and chance — compare SECONDNESS, THIRDNESS

first night *n* **1 :** the night on which a theatrical production is first performed at a given place **2 :** the performance given on a first night

first-night·er \'='=ə(r)\ *n* -s [*first night* + *-er*] **:** a spectator habitually present at first-night performances

first of aries *usu cap A, astron* **:** the first point of Aries

first off *adv* [[2]*first*] **:** right away ⟨won't want to have to see people *first off* —B.A.Williams⟩

first offender *n* **:** one legally convicted of an offense for the first time

first officer *n* **1 :** a first mate in the merchant service **2 :** COPILOT

first-order reaction *n* **:** a chemical reaction in which the rate of reaction is directly proportional to the concentration of the reacting substance — compare ORDER OF A REACTION

first or last *adv* **:** at one time or another **:** at the beginning or end ⟨and all are fools and lovers *first or last* —John Dryden⟩

first-page \'=,=\ *adj* **:** FRONT-PAGE

first papers *n pl* **:** papers declaring intention that are filed by an applicant for citizenship as the first step in the process of naturalization — compare SECOND PAPERS

first person *n* **1 a :** a set of linguistic forms (as verb forms, pronouns, and inflectional affixes) referring to the speaker or writer of the utterance in which they occur ⟨Latin *videmus* "we see" is in the *first person* plural⟩ ⟨English *me* is an objective singular pronoun of the *first person*⟩ ⟨in Sanskrit verbs *-mi* is a much-used ending of the *first person* singular⟩ **b :** a linguistic form belonging to such a set ⟨Latin *video* "I see" and *eo* "I go" are *first persons*⟩ **c :** reference of a linguistic form to the speaker or writer of the utterance in which it occurs ⟨the Latin verb ending *-o* that marks the *first person*⟩ **2 :** a style of discourse characterized by the use of verbs and pronouns of the first person in the most essential statements ⟨fictitious narratives are sometimes put into the *first person* for greater vividness⟩

first personal *adj* **:** of or relating to the first person ⟨a *first personal* pronoun⟩

first philosophy *n, usu cap F&P* **1** *Aristotelianism* **:** a study of being as being dealing with the fundamental type of being or substance upon which all others depend and with the most fundamental causes — distinguished from *second philosophy;* compare METAPHYSICS **2** *Aristotelianism* **:** a study of supersensible immutable being — compare THEOLOGY

first point *n* **:** the westernmost point of a zodiacal sign

first presidency *n, usu cap F&P* **:** the presiding body in the Mormon Church comprising the president and two counselors

first principles *n pl* **:** principles that are basic or self-evident

first public examination *n* **:** an examination taken after a certain period of residence by every candidate for the B.A. degree (as at Oxford University) — see MODERATION 3

[1]**first-rate** \'=,=\ *adj* [[1]*first* + *rate*] **1 :** of the first order of size or importance ⟨a *first-rate* blunder⟩ ⟨the temptation to rush into print . . . resulted in a *first-rate* headache —*Newsweek*⟩ ⟨a *first-rate* power⟩ ⟨a book of *first-rate* significance⟩ **2 :** of the first order of quality **:** extremely good **:** EXCELLENT, ADMIRABLE ⟨none of those ancestors of his was ever *first-rate*, not one —Hamilton Basso⟩ ⟨*first-rate* entertainment⟩ ⟨a *first-rate* book⟩ — **first-rate·ly** *adv* — **first-rate·ness** *n* -ES

[2]**first-rate** \"\ *adv* **:** very well **:** quite well ⟨have not felt *first-rate* myself —Walt Whitman⟩ ⟨the fan worked *first-rate* —Marquis James⟩

first-rat·er \(ˌ)='rād·ər, -ātə-\ *n* **:** one that is first-rate ⟨in all reports a *first-rater* —Charles Dickens⟩

first reader *n, usu cap F&R* **:** a member of a Christian Science church or society chosen to conduct services and meetings for a specified time and specif. to read aloud from the writings of Mary Baker Eddy — see SECOND READER

first reading *n* **:** the first reading of a measure before a quorum of a legislative assembly typically of the title or number only and usu. either upon its introduction or before its reference to a committee

first run *n* **1 :** the earliest and richest sap flow in the sugar maple **2** [*first-run*] **:** the first showing of a new motion picture ⟨a house that had specialized in *first runs* of distinguished British productions —Arthur Knight⟩ ⟨a *first run* . . . cost the exhibitor twenty times as much as a twentieth run —Lewis Jacobs⟩

first-run \'=,=\ *adj* **:** relating to or specializing in the first showings of new motion pictures ⟨a *first-run* movie⟩ ⟨a deluxe *first-run* theater⟩

firsts *pl of* FIRST

first sergeant *n* **1 :** the chief enlisted assistant to the commander of a company or equivalent unit esp. in the army or marine corps **2 :** MASTER SERGEANT

first slip *n* **:** the slip positioned nearest to the wicketkeeper — see CRICKET illustration

first sound shift *n* **:** CONSONANT SHIFT 1

first speed *n* **:** the forward transmission gear ratio in an automotive vehicle giving the lowest ratio of propeller-shaft to engine-shaft speed and the highest multiplication of torque

first story *n* **:** FIRST FLOOR

first-string \'=,=\ *adj* **1 :** being a regular as distinguished from a substitute (as on a football team) ⟨*first-string* quarterback⟩ **2 :** being of the first order of quality or importance ⟨drew highly favorable notices from nearly all the *first-string* critics —*Current Biog.*⟩ ⟨almost the only *first-string* American statesman who managed to combine high office with humor —A.J.Liebling⟩

first watch *n* **:** the watch on a ship from 8 p.m. to midnight

first water *n* **1 :** the highest quality or purest luster — used of gems (as diamonds and pearls) **2 :** the highest grade or excellence **:** the highest degree **:** the first quality ⟨this is choral music of the *first water* —P.H.Lang⟩ ⟨a fool of the *first water* —Thomas Wolfe⟩ ⟨an alarmist of the *first water* —Katherine Mansfield⟩

firth \'fərth\ *n* -s [ME, fr. ON *firth-, fjörthr* — more at FORD] **:** a narrow arm of the sea **:** the opening of a river into the sea

fisc \'fisk\ *n* -s [MF & L; MF, fr. L *fiscus*] **1 :** FISCUS **2 :** a state or royal treasury **3** *or* **fisk** \"\ *Scots law* **a :** the public or crown treasury to which estates escheat — used chiefly in the phrase *as to the fisk* **b :** the estate of a rebel or the crown's right to it

[1]**fis·cal** \'fiskəl\ *n* -s [Sp, fr. *fiscal*, adj., fr. L *fiscalis*] **1 :** a public officer (as a prosecutor or policeman) or colonial magistrate usu. concerned with law enforcement or revenue **2 :** a prosecuting attorney in the Philippines **3** [[2]*fiscal*] **:** REVENUE STAMP **4** *also* **fiscal shrike** [Afrik *fiskaal*, a government official, fiscal shrike, fr. *fiskaal*, adj., fiscal, fr. L *fiscalis*] **:** a common black-and-white African shrike (*Lanius collaris*)

[2]**fiscal** \"\ *adj* [L *fiscalis*, fr. *fiscus* rush basket, money basket, treasury + *-alis* -al; akin to L *fidelia* earthen vessel, Gk *pithos* wine jar, and perh. to Icel *bitha* milk jug, Norw *bide* butter tub] **1 :** of or relating to taxation, public revenues, or public debt management and policies **2 :** of or relating to financial matters generally — **fis·cal·ly** \-əlē, -əli\ *adv*

fiscal agent *n* **:** a bank or trust company acting as the financial representative of a corporation or service organization

fiscal cancellation *n* **:** a cancellation of a revenue stamp or a cancellation on a postage stamp showing that it was used as a revenue stamp

fis·cal·i·ty \fi'skaləd·ē\ *n* -ES **:** excessive regard for financial considerations **:** spirit of gain; *also* **:** fiscal policy or question

fiscal period *n* **:** a uniform period by or for which accounts are reckoned (as one year)

fiscal policy *n* **:** the financial policy of a government particularly as regards the budget and the method and timing of borrowings and esp. in relation to central-bank credit policy

fiscal shrike *n* **:** FISCAL 4

fiscal stamp *n* **:** REVENUE STAMP

fiscal year *n* **:** the year by or for which accounts are reckoned **:** the year between one annual time of settlement or balancing of accounts and another, ending regularly on December 31 for private individuals and institutions and on June 30 for the U. S. government

fisch·er·ite \'fishə,rīt\ *n* -s [G *fischerit*, fr. Gotthelf *Fischer* von Waldheim †1853 Ger. naturalist + G *-it* -ite] **:** a mineral $AlPO_4.Al(OH)_3+2\frac{1}{2}H_2O$ consisting of a green basic aluminum phosphate perhaps identical with wavellite

fischer-tropsch process *also* **fischer-tropsch synthesis** \'fishə(r)'trōp|sh-, -rōp|, -räp|\ *n, usu cap F&T* [after Franz *Fischer* †1948 Ger. chemist and Hans *Tropsch* †1935 Ger. chemist born in Czechoslovakia] **:** a process originated in Germany esp. for producing liquid and gaseous hydrocarbon fuels (as gasoline or gas oil) by passing a mixture of carbon monoxide and hydrogen over metal or other catalysts at elevated temperatures and at normal or higher pressures — see OXYL PROCESS, SYNTHESIS GAS

fis·cus \'fiskəs\ *n, pl* **fis·ci** \-,s(k)ī, -,skē\ [L, rush basket, money basket, treasury — more at FISCAL] **:** the one of the three branches of the public treasury under the Roman Empire that was most under imperial control

fi·set·in \fə'zet°n\ *n* -s [G, fr. *fiset-* (in *fisetholz*, wood from a species of fustic) + *-in*] **:** a yellow crystalline flavone pigment $C_{15}H_{10}O_6$ obtained from the wood of various trees or shrubs (as fustet or sumac)

[1]**fish** \'fish\ *n, pl* **fish** *or* **fishes** [ME, fr. OE *fisc;* akin to OHG *fisc* fish, ON *fiskr*, Goth *fisks*, L *piscis*, OIr *īasc*] **1 :** an exclusively aquatic vertebrate or invertebrate animal — usu. used in combination ⟨star*fish*⟩ ⟨cuttle*fish*⟩ ⟨jelly*fish*⟩ **2 a :** any of numerous cold-blooded strictly aquatic water-breathing craniate vertebrates that include the cyclostomes, elasmobranchs, and higher gilled aquatic vertebrates with cartilaginous or bony skeletons or sometimes only the last of these groups, being on the one hand nearly coextensive with Pisces in its broadest use, on the other coextensive with Teleostomi, usu. with the addition of Choanichthyes, that

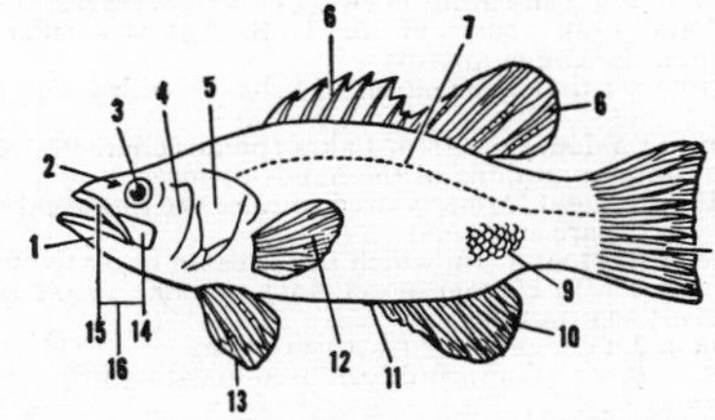

diagram of a fish: *1* mandible, *2* external naris, *3* eye, *4* cheek, *5* operculum, *6, 6* dorsal fins, *7* lateral line, *8* caudal fin, *9* scales, *10* anal fin, *11* anus, *12* pectoral fin, *13* pelvic fin, *14* maxilla, *15* premaxilla, *16* upper jaw

have typically an elongated somewhat spindle-shaped body terminating in a broad caudal fin, limbs in the form of fins when present at all, and a 2-chambered heart by which blood is sent through the thoracic gills to be oxygenated before passing to the organs and tissues of the body and returning in venous condition to the heart, that are usu. oviparous, often producing great numbers of eggs which are fertilized in the water after they are laid, and that are important to man esp. as a source of food, fertilizers, and oils and for sport **b :** a particular kind of fish: as (1) *Brit* **:** SALMON (2) **:** COD (3) *Africa* **:** a dogfish served as food **3 :** the flesh of fish used as food **4 a :** PERSON — often used with a disparaging qualifier ⟨regarded him as . . . a queer ~ —Nevil Shute⟩ ⟨as cold a ~ as you'd care to meet —*Saturday Rev.*⟩ ⟨a handful of poets, philosophers and other odd ~ —G.W. Johnson⟩ **b :** a person who is easily taken in **:** SUCKER ⟨I feel sorry for the poor ~⟩ **5 :** something that resembles a fish: as **a** (1) **:** a purchase used to fish the anchor (2) **:** a piece of timber that is shaped like a fish and that is used to strengthen a mast or yard **b :** FISHPLATE **c :** FISH JOINT 1 **d** *slang* **:** TORPEDO 3 **e :** tools or other equipment lost down a drilled well and recoverable only by fishing **6 a :** a simplified form of the game of authors usu. played by children **b :** a fish counter (as in a game of chance) sometimes shaped like a fish **7** *slang* **a** *pl fish* **:** DOLLAR ⟨got over a thousand ~ apiece in back pay —Frederic Wakeman⟩ **b :** a new prison inmate ⟨three days after my arrival in Sing Sing prison as a new ~ in the teen-age bracket —Frank O'Leary⟩ **8 :** a ballroom dance in which the partners move in close embrace — **fish out of water :** a person that is out of his proper sphere or element — **neither fish nor fowl :** one that does not belong to a definite class, party, or category **:** a nondescript person or thing; *also* **:** a person without convictions **:** TRIMMER — often used in the phrase *neither fish nor fowl nor good red herring* — **other fish to fry :** other affairs of interest or concern ⟨was asked to the party but had *other fish to fry*⟩

²fish \"\ *vb* -ED/-ING/-ES [ME *fisshen*, fr. OE *fiscian*; akin to OHG *fiscōn* to fish, ON *fiska*, Goth *fiskon*; denominative fr. the root of E ¹*fish*] *vi* **1 a** (1) **:** to attempt to catch fish ⟨~ for by any means or for any purpose ⟨~ from a boat⟩ ⟨~ for cod⟩ (2) **:** to catch fish ⟨leaders a few inches long or too short . . . — there were always a hundred little things which could cause a boat not to ~ —E.K.Gann⟩ **b** (1) **:** to search for anything that is under water (as with a hook or dredge) ⟨~ for pearls⟩ (2) **:** to recover or attempt to recover tools or other equipment lost down a drilled well **c :** to engage in a search of any kind by or as if by groping or feeling ⟨~*ing* in the subconscious . . . brings to light . . . wayward associations —D.L.Bolinger⟩ ⟨for ten minutes or so this trio was busily engaged ~*ing* in the grass, for a lost token is a serious matter —O.S.Nock⟩ ⟨~*ing* in an inside pocket he handed me a square white envelope —Hartley Howard⟩ — often used with *for* ⟨he started to ~ around for a match —L.C.Stevens⟩ ⟨~*ing* for other applications the industry has produced a novel parade of articles —*Monsanto Mag.*⟩ **d :** to seek to elicit or draw forth by hinting or other roundabout means — often used with *for* ⟨~*ing* for praise of his ability —Arnold Bennett⟩ ⟨~*ing* for compliments⟩ **2 :** to be in adjustment for catching fish — used of a net or other fishing device **3 :** to be fishable ⟨this stream ~*es* well⟩ **4** *of a Salvationist* **:** to speak with individuals to help them make the decision to follow Christ **:** engage in personal evangelism ~ *vt* **1 a :** to catch or try to catch (as salmon); *also* **:** to collect (as coral) from the sea bottom **b :** to draw as if fishing ⟨he ~*ed* his one crutch from under the bed —Earle Birney⟩ ⟨~*ed* some cigarettes out of his shirt pocket —R.O.Bowen⟩ ⟨the ammunition also sank but was ~*ed* up —Frank Sebenham⟩ **2 a :** to fish in ⟨~*ed* the stream all morning⟩ **b :** to fish with **:** use in fishing (as a boat, net, or lure) **3 :** to draw or pull (electric wires) through a conduit or between floors or walls with a hook and line or wire **4 :** to hoist the flukes of (an anchor) — **fish or cut bait :** to make a choice between alternatives **:** cease temporizing or procrastinating; *specif* **:** to choose either to engage wholeheartedly or actively in some work or scheme or to withdraw from it completely

fish·abil·i·ty \ˌfishə'biləd·ē\ *n* -ES **:** the quality or state of being fishable

fish·able \'fishəbəl\ *adj* **:** suitable, promising, or legally open for fishing ⟨a ~ brook⟩

fish-and-chips \ˌ=ˌ=='=\ *n pl* **:** fried fish and French fried potatoes

fish ball *n* **:** a globular cake made of fish (as salted codfish) shredded, mixed with mashed potato, and fried

fish basket *n* **:** a fishing device made of wooden slats usu. set in a running stream to trap fish moving downstream

fish beam *n* **:** a beam one of whose sides swells out like the belly of a fish

fishbed \'=ˌ=\ *n* **:** a sedimentary stratum rich in fossil remains of fish

fish begonia *n* **:** an ornamental Brazilian herb (*Begonia maculata*) that is often cultivated and has showy spotted fishtail-shaped leaves

fish-bellied \'=ˌ==\ *adj* **:** bellying out on the underside; *specif* **:** bent downward in the middle and usu. also bent upward correspondingly — used of joists, beams, and similar structural members

fish belly rail *n, Brit* **:** a short-span rail supported on chairs and curved on the underside so as to be deeper at the middle than at the ends of the span

fish belly sill *n* **:** a side or center sill shaped like a fish and used in railroad car construction

fish·ber·ry \'fish-— *see* BERRY\ *n* **:** FISH POISON; *specif* **:** ²COCCULUS

fish blanket *n* **:** HORNWORT

fish-blooded \'=ˌ==\ *adj* **:** COLD-BLOODED ⟨one of those brittle *fish-blooded* aristocrats who stand firm for kindness to animals and discipline for the lower classes —Leslie Charteris⟩

fish boat *n* [ME *fishboot*, fr. *fish* + *boot* boat — more at BOAT] **:** a boat from which fish are caught

fishbolt \'=ˌ=\ *n, Brit* **:** a bolt for securing a fishplate; *specif* **:** a bolt joining two opposite fishplates

fishbowl \'=ˌ=\ *n* **1 :** a bowl for the keeping of live fish **2 :** something that is open to inspection from all sides ⟨in the ~ of so small a town . . . it would have been impossible for . . . a secret to be kept —Robert Benton⟩

fish cake *n* **:** a flattened fish ball

fish car *n* **:** a railroad car equipped with water tanks for the transportation of live fish and also provided with quarters for the operators in charge of the car

fish crow *n* **:** a fish-eating crow (*Corvus ossifragus*) of the Atlantic and Gulf coasts of the U. S. that is smaller and quieter than the common crow

fish culture *n* **:** the propagation of fishes — called also *pisciculture*

fish dance *n* **:** a dance of Great Lakes Indians characterized by imitative flipping motions of the hands or feet

fish davit *n* **:** a davit formerly used to raise the fluke end of an anchor — compare CAT DAVIT

fish day *n* [ME] **:** a day on which fish is eaten in place of flesh in accordance with custom or religious practice **:** FAST DAY

fish duck *n* **:** MERGANSER

fish eagle *n* **1 :** OSPREY **2 :** EAGLE VULTURE

fish eater *n, Brit* **:** a knife and fork used in eating fish

fished *past of* FISH

fish·er \'fishə(r)\ *n* -S *see sense 2* [ME *fissher*, fr. OE *fiscere*, fr. *fisc* fish + *-ere* -er — more at FISH] **1 :** one that fishes; *esp* **:** a person, animal, or boat that is engaged or is employed in fishing **2** *pl also* **fisher a :** a large dark brown somewhat vulpine arboreal carnivorous mammal (*Martes pennanti*) that is related to the marten and the weasels and that is native to much of the forested northern half of No. America but is now extinct over much of its former range due to excessive hunting because of its valuable pelt **b :** the fur or pelt of this animal

fisher-cat \'=ˌ=\ *n* **:** FISHER 2a

fisherfolk \'==ˌ=\ *n, pl in constr* **:** people whose occupation is fishing, esp. deep-sea fishing

fish·er·man \'fishə(r)mən\ *n, pl* **fishermen** [ME, fr. *fisher* + *man* man] **1 :** one who engages in fishing as an occupation or for pleasure **2 :** a ship used in commercial fishing

fisherman's bend *n* **:** a knot for tying a line to a spar or ring that is made by passing the end twice round the spar or through the ring and then back under both turns — called also *anchor bend*

fisherman's bend

fisherman's knot *n* **:** a knot for tying the ends of two lines together that is made by tying overhand knots in the ends around the opposite standing parts — called also *Englishman's knot, true lover's knot, waterman's knot*

fisherman's staysail *n* **:** a triangular or quadrilateral sail between the foremast and mainmast of a fishing schooner

fish·ery \'fish(ə)rē, -ri\ *n* -ES [²*fish* + *-ery*] **1 :** the act, process, occupation, or season of taking fish or other sea products **:** FISHING ⟨the golden age of the whale ~⟩; *also* **:** the catch of a specified fish or sea product ⟨the menhaden ~ for the year⟩ **2 :** a place for catching fish or taking other sea products ⟨an oyster ~⟩ ⟨a salmon ~⟩ **3 :** a fishing establishment; *also* **:** its group of fishermen **4 :** the legal right to take fish at a certain place or in particular waters esp. by drawing a seine or net — see COMMON FISHERY, FREE FISHERY, SEVERAL FISHERY **5 :** the technology of fishery **:** a branch of knowledge concerned with the methods and economics of fishery and the utilization and preservation of fish resources — usu. used in pl. **:** a number of schools of *fisheries* have been established⟩

fishery salt *n* **:** a coarse grade of common salt used in curing fish

fishes *pl of* FISH, *pres 3d sing of* FISH

fisheye \'=ˌ=\ *n* **1 :** a diamond or other gemstone cut too thin for proper brilliancy **2 :** a large translucent globule of cooked tapioca — usu. used in pl. **3 :** a small blemish in finished paper caused by the crushing and glazing of an adventitious particle by the calender **4 :** ocular lymphomatosis of the fowl — compare LEUKOSIS **5 :** a cold or suspicious stare ⟨I saw you guys giving me the ~ . . . so I ran —Eddie Krell⟩

fishfall \'=ˌ=\ *n* **:** the tackle on a fish davit

fish-farming \'=ˌ==\ *n* **:** the rearing of fishes esp. in ponds for food

fish-finder \'=ˌ==\ *n* **:** a sonic depth finder used to determine the position of schools of fish in the sea

fish flake *n* **:** a frame on which fish are dried

fish flop *n* **1 :** a semiaerial tumbling stunt consisting of a backward roll into a headstand followed immediately by the easing of the body down onto the chest, belly, and thighs and finishing in a stand **2 :** a somersault with flipping of the feet in the air

fish flour *n* **:** flour made of pulverized dried fish

fish fly *n* **:** any of various insects (family Corydalidae) resembling but smaller than the dobsonfly

fish fork *n* **1 :** a large short-handled fork used in loading and unloading fish **2 a :** an individual 4-tined fork larger than a salad fork that is used with an individual fish knife in eating fish **b :** a large broad 4-tined fork that is used with a broad serving knife in serving fish

fish fry *n* **1 :** a picnic at which fish are caught, fried, and eaten; *also* **:** an indoor supper at which fish are fried and eaten **2 :** fried fish

fish fungus *n* **1 :** a water mold (*Saprolegnia ferax*) that attacks living fish esp. when crowded in hatcheries or aquariums **2 :** a reddish fungus (*Clathrocystis roseopersicina*) sometimes appearing on salted codfish

fishgarth \'=ˌ=\ *n* [ME, fr ¹*fish* + *garth*] **:** a dam or weir in a river or on the seashore for keeping fish or taking them

fish gelatin *n* **:** ISINGLASS

fish geranium *n* **:** an upright herb (*Pelargonium hortorum*) often cultivated for its scalloped crenate-toothed leaves with a broad color zone inside the margin

fish·gig \'fish,gig\ *n* [by folk etymology fr. *fizgig*] **:** a fish spear having two or more barbed prongs

fish glue *n* **:** either of two gelatinous substances obtained from fish waste products: **a :** ISINGLASS **b :** a strong adhesive obtained by heating with water esp. the skins, fins, and bones of fish (as cod, haddock, or hake) and used chiefly in liquid form in the cold

fish grass *n* **:** WATER SHIELD 2

fish guano *n* **:** a fertilizer prepared from fish **:** FISH MEAL

fish-handler's disease *n* **:** ERYSIPELOID

fish hatchery *n* **:** an establishment in which young fish are produced and reared esp. for later release in natural waters

fish hawk *n* **:** OSPREY

fish hoek skull \'fish,hu̇k-, 'fi,shu̇k-\ *n, usu cap F&H* [fr. *Fish Hoek* (Vishoek), town in Cape Province, Union of So. Africa, where it was discovered] **:** a southern African fossil skull that resembles that of a Bushman and that is found in association with artifacts suggesting an advanced type of the European Mousterian

fishhold \'=ˌ=\ *n* **:** the hold in a fish boat for keeping fish

fish·hook \'fish,hu̇k, 'fi,shu̇k\ *n* [ME *fishhok*, fr. *fish* + *hok* hook — more at HOOK] **1 :** a hook for catching fish **2 :** a large hook with a pendant to the end of which the fish tackle is hooked in fishing an anchor

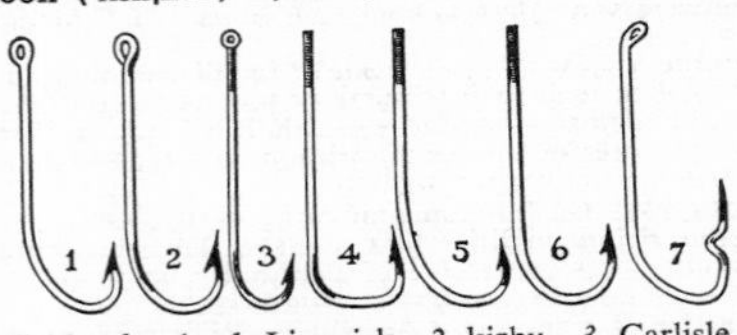

fishhooks 1: *1* Limerick, *2* kirby, *3* Carlisle, *4* Kendal sneck bent, *5* sproat, *6* Aberdeen, *7* barbless

fishhook cactus *n* **1 :** CHOLLA **2 :** a low cactus (*Ferocactus wislizenii*) of southwestern U. S. and adjacent Mexico

fishhook money *n* **:** Persian larin money

fish house *n* **:** BOB-HOUSE

fish house punch *n* **:** a punch usu. consisting of lemon juice, rum, peach liqueur, brandy, sugar, bitters, and carbonated or plain water

fishier *comparative of* FISHY

fishiest *superlative of* FISHY

fish·ify \'fishə,fī\ *vt* -ED/-ING/-ES **:** to change to fish

fish·i·ly \'fishəlē, -li\ *adv* **:** in a fishy manner ⟨looked at me ~⟩

fishing *n* -S [ME *fisshing*, fr. gerund of *fisshen* to fish — more at FISH] **1 a :** the act of one that fishes **b :** the occupation or pastime of catching fish **2 a :** a place for catching fish ⟨a descriptive list of the free and open mainland Scottish ~*s* —*Times Lit. Supp.*⟩ **b :** the right of taking fish

fishing banks *n pl* **:** a plateau under the sea at a comparatively small depth where fish frequently gather in schools

fishing bear *n* **:** a bear of northeastern Asia that constitutes a race (*Ursus arctos beringianus*) of the Eurasian brown bear and that lives largely on fish

fishing cat *n* **:** a spotted swamp-dwelling wildcat (*Felis viverrina*) of southeastern Asia that feeds mainly on fish and mollusks

fishing duck *n* **:** MERGANSER

fishing eagle *n* **:** any of several rather large birds of prey that commonly feed on fishes: as **a :** OSPREY **b :** a large eagle (*Ichthyophaga ichthyaetus*) of tropical Asia that resembles the osprey in habits **c :** a large eagle (*Haliaeetus leucoryphus*) of southeast Europe and central Asia that ranges southward to northern India and Burma **d :** EAGLE VULTURE

fishing expedition *n* **1 :** a legal proceeding carried on for the primary purpose of interrogating an adversary or examining his property or books, papers, and records in order to discover information essential to and to be used as a basis for a later proceeding or defense **2 :** an investigation that has no clearly defined objective or that does not stick to its stated or authorized objective and that engages in expedients of doubtful propriety or legality (as the irrelevant questioning of witnesses) in the hope of turning up incriminating or newsworthy evidence ⟨promised at the outset of the investigation that it would not . . . degenerate into a witch-hunt or a *fishing expedition* —Tom Fitzsimmons⟩

fishing float *n* **:** a scow used in seine fishing and designed to be moved from one fishing ground to another

fishing frog *n* **:** ANGLER 2

fishing ground *n* **:** an area in a body of water where fishes congregate and fishing is usu. good

fishing pole *n* **:** a slender tapering pole with a line attached to the tip used in fishing — compare FISHING ROD

fishing rod *n* **:** a springy tapering often jointed rod (as of wood, split bamboo, or steel) equipped with hand grip and line guides and used with fishing line and reel for catching fish

fishing space *n* **:** the space between the head and base of a railroad rail for seating the fishplate

fishing tool *n* **:** a tool for recovering objects from inaccessible places

fishing wand *n, Scot* **:** FISHING ROD

fishing worm *n* **:** FISHWORM 1

fish joint *n* **1 :** a joint for forming separate limbs into a bow or bowstave by fitting a wedge end into a V slot or a double wedge into a W slot **2 :** a butt joint in which the two abutting members are held in alignment by one or more fishplates

fish-joint \'=ˌ=\ *vt* **:** to fasten with a fish joint

fish kettle *n* **:** a long kettle for boiling fish whole that is usu. provided with a rack and handle

fish killer *n* **:** GIANT WATER BUG

fish knife *n* [ME *fishknif*, fr. ¹*fish* + *knif* knife — more at KNIFE] **1 :** a small knife with an ornamental upper edge that is used with a fork in eating fish **2 :** a large knife with broad blade and decorative upper edge that is used with a large 4-tined fork in serving fish

fish ladder *n* **:** a series of pools arranged like steps by which fishes can pass over a dam in going upstream

fish leaves *n pl* **:** the floating leaves of the common pondweed (*Potamogeton natans*)

fishline \'=ˌ=\ *n* **:** a line used in fishing

fish-liver oil *n* **:** a fatty oil from the livers of various fishes (as cod, halibut, or sharks) used chiefly as a source of vitamin A and formerly also of vitamin D

fish louse *n* **:** any of various small crustaceans (as the carp louse) parasitic on fishes; *esp* **:** any of various true copepods that are found on the skin or gills or in the mouth of fishes and that exhibit varying degrees of degeneration in the adult state due to their parasitic habits — see LERNAEA

fish·man \'fishmən\ *n, pl* **fishmen** [ME, fr. ¹*fish* + *man*] **1 :** one who cleans fish in preparation for cooking **2 :** one who sells fish and other seafood

fish maw *n* **:** the air bladder of a fish

fish meal *n* **:** ground dried fish and fish waste used as fertilizer and in animal feeds

fish mint *n* **:** either of the two mints (*Mentha aquatica* and *M. longifolia*) that usu. grow in moist places

fish mold *n* **:** a water mold growing on fish — compare SAPROLEGNIALES

fishmonger \'=ˌ==\ *n* [ME, fr. ¹*fish* + *monger*] *chiefly Brit* **:** a fish dealer

fish moth *n* **1 :** SILVERFISH **2 :** FIREBRAT

fishmouth \'=ˌ=\ *n* **:** TURTLEHEAD

fishnet \'=ˌ=\ *n* [ME, fr. OE *fiscnett*, fr. *fisc* fish + *nett* net — more at FISH, NET] **:** netting fitted with floats and weights or with a supporting frame often oval for catching fish

fish oil *n* **:** a fatty oil from the bodies of fishes or marine mammals (as menhaden, sardines, or whales) used chiefly as a drying oil in paint and varnish and usu. after being hydrogenated for soapmaking

fish out *vt* **:** to exhaust the supply of fish in by fishing ⟨this lake has been *fished out*⟩

fish owl *or* **fishing owl** *n* **:** any of various fish-eating owls of the Old World genera *Scotopelia* and *Ketupa*

fish paper *n* **:** a tough flexible paper or board used for electrical insulation made largely from cotton fiber and vulcanized

fish pearl *n* **:** a glass bead lined or coated with essence d'orient to simulate a pearl

fish pier *n* **:** a pier for fish boats to tie up to

fish·plate \'=ˌ=\ *n* **:** a steel plate lapping a joint of heavy timbers or railroad rails and secured to the sides so as to connect the members end to end

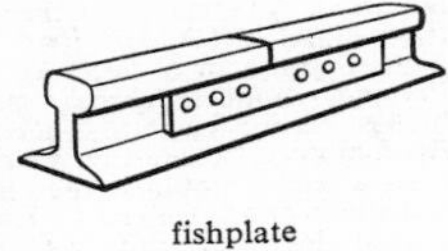
fishplate

fish poison *n* **:** any of numerous plants or drugs used to kill or stupefy fish by placing the drug or an extract of it in the water: as **a :** JAMAICA DOGWOOD **b :** RED BUCKEYE **c :** ²COCCULUS

fish poisoning *n* **1 :** acute illness resulting from the consumption of fish: **a :** illness due to eating fish that normally contain neurotoxins in their flesh **b :** illness due to eating stale fish: (1) **:** a histamine intoxication (2) **:** a bacterial food poisoning **2 :** ERYSIPELOID

fish pole *n* **:** FISHING POLE

fish pomace *or* **fish scrap** *n* **:** refuse of fish after the oil is expressed that is used for fertilizer

fishpond \'=ˌ=\ *n* [ME, fr. ¹*fish* + *pond*] **1 :** a pond stocked with edible fish **2 :** a grab bag from which articles are extracted by means of a pole and line

fish pot *n* **1 :** a structure built in a stream for catching fish ⟨in the construction of any such *fish pot* necessary portable slats, tilts, slides or escapes shall be installed —*Md. House Bill*⟩ — compare WEIR **2 :** a receptacle for catching fish or shellfish — compare CRAB POT, LOBSTER POT

fishpound \'=ˌ=\ *n* **:** a net attached to stakes that is used for catching fish **:** WEIR

fish scale *n* **1 :** the scale of fish; *also* **:** something resembling it **2 :** a defect in enamel on sheet iron characterized by blistering and the detachment of small flakes of enamel

fish screen *n* **:** a sometimes electrified screen designed to exclude fishes from an intake (as of a power plant or waterworks)

fish service *n* **:** a china service for fish consisting of a platter, sauce boat, and a specified number of plates

fishskin disease *or* **fish-scale disease** \'=ˌ=-\ *n* **:** ICHTHYOSIS

fish stick *n* **1 a** *also* **fish water :** a by-product of fish processing containing considerable quantities of amino acids, animal protein factor, and other vitamins and minerals **b :** the product of its dehydration used chiefly in animal feeds **2 :** a stick of fish ⟨*fish sticks* and French fried potatoes⟩

fish story *n* **:** an extravagant or incredible story

fish tackle *n* **:** a tackle or purchase used to raise the flukes of an anchor up to the gunwale

¹fishtail \'=ˌ=\ *n* [ME *fish tail*] **1 :** something suggesting the tail of a fish esp. in being somewhat triangular with a median notch: as **a :** an arrow that wobbles in flight **b :** a railroad semaphore the arm of which is notched at the end and which is used as an advance warning signal **2 :** a turning ballroom step **3 :** the aeronautical maneuver of fishtailing

²fishtail \"\ *also* **fishtailed** \'=ˌ=\ *adj* **:** having a shape that imitates or resembles the shape of a fish's tail ⟨a gardener's knife with a sharp ~ blade —*New Yorker*⟩ ⟨the ~ gas jets in the square-sided station lamps —Anthony West⟩ ⟨some of the women were wound up in ~ skirts which defy description —G.H.Reed b.1887⟩

³fishtail \"\ *vi* **1 :** to swing the tail of an airplane from side to side during a glide without altering the flight path in order to reduce speed in approaching the ground for a landing **2** *of a ship* **:** to move through the water with a side-to-side or whipping motion of the stern ⟨the short-ranged sleek destroyer ~*ing* alongside —K.M.Dodson⟩

fishtail bit *also* **fishtail** *n* **:** a drilling bit shaped like a fish's tail

fishtail burner *n* **:** a gas burner in which two jets of gas issuing from two holes inclined toward each other impinge and form a fan-shaped flame

fishtail cutter *n* **:** a flat milling cutter for milling (as slots, keyways)

fishtail palm *n* **:** a palm of the genus *Caryota*

fishtail wind *n* **:** a variable wind that blows toward the targets on a rifle range

fish tape *or* **fish wire** *n* **:** a flat tempered spring-steel tape or wire used in pulling electric wires and cables (as into conduit runs) — called also *snake wire*

fish tapeworm *n* **:** a large pseudophyllidean tapeworm (*Diphyl-*

lobothrium latum) as an adult infesting the human intestine and sometimes associated with a peculiar macrocytic anemia resembling pernicious anemia and having its early development in a copepod and intermediate stages in freshwater fishes, from which it is transmitted to man or other fish-eating mammals when raw fish is eaten

fish trap *n* **:** a device for catching fish that consists of a net or other structure which diverts the fish into an enclosure so arranged that egress is more difficult than ingress

fishway \ˈ=,=\ *n* **:** a contrivance for enabling fish to pass around a fall or dam in a stream; *specif* **:** FISH LADDER

fishweed \ˈ=,=\ *n* **1 :** MEXICAN TEA **2 :** PONDWEED

fishweir \ˈ=,=\ *n* [ME *fishwer*, fr. OE *fiscwer*, fr. *fisc* fish + *wer* weir — more at FISH, WEIR] **:** FISHGARTH

fish well *n* **:** a well for fish on a fish boat

fish wheel *n* **:** SALMON WHEEL

fishwife \ˈ=,=\ *n* [ME, fr. *fish* + *wife*] **1 :** a woman who sells fish at retail **2 :** a scurrilously abusive woman ⟨began to berate them in the coarse language of a ~ —Louis Bromfield⟩

fishwood \ˈ=,=\ *n* **1 :** STRAWBERRY BUSH 1a **2 :** JAMAICA DOGWOOD

fishworm \ˈ=,=\ *n* **1 :** an earthworm used as bait **2 :** a worm parasitic in or on fishes

fishy \ˈfishē, -shi\ *adj* -ER/-EST [ME, fr. ¹*fish* + -*y*] **1 :** of or relating to a fish **:** like a fish **:** abounding in fish ⟨the ~ deep⟩ ⟨a ~ odor⟩ ⟨a ~ taste⟩ **2 a :** inspiring doubt or suspicion **:** DUBIOUS, QUESTIONABLE, UNCONVINCING ⟨he could not help scenting something ~ about an Englishman who chose to live abroad —Margery Sharp⟩ ⟨that story sounds very very ~ to me —Erle Stanley Gardner⟩ ⟨there is something of a ~ nature going on in the office —Dorothy Sayers⟩ ⟨using his position to line his pocket through ~ and degrading commercial deals —*Time*⟩ **b :** lacking warmth or passion **:** FRIGID, COLD, SUSPICIOUS, LACKLUSTER, DULL ⟨they remembered his ~ handclasp and downcast eyes —H.S.Canby⟩ ⟨a fervent urge . . . to hit him between his damnable cold, ~, evasive eyes —Vicki Baum⟩ ⟨she looked with a ~ eye on the glamorous scenes that we loved —W.A.White⟩ ⟨drawled . . . in his usual cautious, ~ tone —Frank O'Connor⟩

fishy-back \ˈ=,=,=\ *n* **:** the movement of truck trailers or freight containers by barge or ship — compare PIGGYBACK

fisk *var of* FISC

fissi- *comb form* [LL, fr. L *fissus*, past part. of *findere* to split — more at BITE] **1 :** divided **:** cleft ⟨*fissi*lingual⟩ **2 :** fission ⟨*fissi*parous⟩

fis·si·den·ta·ce·ae \ˌfisəden'tāsē,ē\ *n pl, cap* [NL, fr. *Fissident-, Fissidens*, type genus (fr. *fissi-* + L *dent-, dens* tooth) + -*aceae* — more at TOOTH] **:** a family of chiefly tropical acrocarpous mosses (order Fissidentales) characterized by 2-ranked clasping vertically placed leaves — **fis·si·den·ta·ceous** \ˌ=====ˈtāshəs\ *adj*

fis·si·den·ta·les \ˌ=====ˈtā(ˌ)lēs\ *n pl, cap* [NL, fr. *Fissident-, Fissidens* + -*ales*] **:** a small order of Musci coextensive with the family Fissidentaceae

fis·sile \ˈfisəl, -(ˌ)sil, -ˌsīl\ *adj* [L *fissilis*, fr. *fissus* + -*ilis* -ile] **1 :** capable of being split, cleft, or divided in the direction of the grain ⟨~ wood⟩ or along natural planes of cleavage ⟨~ crystals⟩ **2 :** FISSIONABLE

fis·si·lin·gual \ˌfisəˈliŋgwəl\ *adj* [*fissi-* + *lingual*] **:** of or relating to the Fissilinguia

fis·si·lin·guia \ˌ==ˈ=gwēə\ *n pl, cap* [NL, fr. *fissi-* + L *lingua* tongue + NL -*ia* — more at TONGUE] *in some classifications* **:** a group of lizards having the tongue forked (as members of the family Lacertilidae)

fis·sil·i·ty \fiˈsiləd·ē\ *n* **:** the quality of being fissile

¹fis·sion \ˈfishən *also* -izh-\ *n* -S [L *fission-, fissio*, fr. *fissus* (past part. of *findere* to split) + -*ion-, -io* -ion — more at BITE] **1 :** the process or an instance of cleaving, splitting, or breaking up into parts ⟨cites the ~ of many families during the civil strife —Boyd Keenan⟩ ⟨our diplomacy will have to be resourceful . . . to avert disastrous ~*s* in the free world during the next few weeks —E.K.Lindley⟩ **2 :** reproduction by spontaneous division of the body into two or more parts each of which grows into a complete organism, being the common mode of reproduction among the bacteria, fission algae, and protozoa — see BINARY FISSION, MULTIPLE FISSION **3 :** CLEAVAGE 5 **4 :** the splitting of an atomic nucleus (as by bombardment with neutrons) esp. into approximately equal parts resulting in the release of enormous quantities of energy when certain heavy elements (as uranium and plutonium) are split — called also *nuclear fission;* contrasted with *fusion;* distinguished from *spallation*

²fission \"\ *vb* **fissioned; fissioned; fissioning** \-sh(ə)niŋ, \-zh(-\ **fissions** *vt* **:** to cause to undergo fission ⟨an element ~*ed* by high energy particles⟩ ~ *vi* **:** to undergo fission ⟨the number of free atoms released when a U-235 atom ~*s* —*Scientific American*⟩

fis·sion·abil·i·ty \ˌfish(ə)nəˈbiləd·ē, -lətē, -i *also* ˌfizh-\ *n* -ES **:** the property of being fissionable — used esp. of chemical elements and materials

¹fis·sion·able \ˈfish(ə)nəbəl *also* ˈfizh-\ *adj* [²*fission* + -*able*] **:** capable of undergoing fission ⟨~ nuclei⟩ — **fissionable**

²fissionable \"\ *n* -S **:** fissionable material — usu. used in pl. ⟨large units capable of generating the volume required for production of ~*s* on a significant scale —*New Republic*⟩

fis·sion·al \-ənᵊl\ *adj* [¹*fission* + -*al*] **:** occurring in or by means of or involving division usu. of a cell ⟨~ reproduction⟩ ⟨~ irregularities⟩

fission alga *n* **:** BLUE-GREEN ALGA

fission bomb *n* **:** ATOM BOMB 1 — compare FUSION BOMB

fission fungus *n* **:** SCHIZOMYCETE, BACTERIUM

fission yeast *n* **:** a yeast that reproduces by division of each cell into two daughter cells of equal size (as members of the genus *Schizosaccharomyces*) — compare BUDDING YEAST

fis·sip·a·rous \(ˈ)fiˈsipərəs, fəˈs-\ *adj* [*fissi-* + -*parous*] **1 :** producing new biological units or individuals by fission **2 :** tending to break up into parts or to disintegrate **:** DIVISIVE, FACTIONAL, SEPARATIVE, DISINTEGRATIVE ⟨~ tenderness⟩ ⟨the problem of erecting a government on the shifting sands of the ~ center parties —*Newsweek*⟩ ⟨he knows how to reconcile ~ elements in his party —W.H.Stevenson⟩ — **fis·sip·a·rous·ly** *adv* — **fis·sip·a·rous·ness** *n* -ES

¹fis·si·ped \ˈfisəˌped\ *adj* [LL *fissiped-, fissipes*, fr. *fissi-* fr. L *fissus*, past part. of *findere* to split) + *ped-, pes* foot — more at BITE, FOOT] **1 :** having the toes separated to the base **:** cloven-footed **2** [NL *Fissipeda*] **:** of or relating to the Fissipeda

²fissiped \"\ *n* -S **:** one of the Fissipeda

fis·sip·e·da \fəˈsipədə\ *n pl, cap* [NL, irreg. fr. LL *fissiped-, fissipes*] **:** a suborder of Carnivora that includes recent land carnivores (as cats, dogs, bears) and extinct related forms

fis·sip·e·dal \(ˈ)fiˈsipədᵊl, fəˈs-; ˌfisəˈpedᵊl, -ˈpēd-\ *also* **fis·sip·e·date** \fəˈsipəˌdāt, -ˌdət\ *adj* [LL *fissiped-, fissipes* + E -*al* or -*ate*] **:** FISSIPED

fis·si·pe·dia \ˌfisəˈpēdēə\ *n pl, cap* [NL, alter. of *Fissipeda*] *syn of* FISSIPEDA

fis·si·pe·di·al \ˌ==ˈ=dēəl\ *adj* [NL *Fissipedia* + E -*al*] **:** FISSIPED

fis·si·ros·tres \ˌfisəˈräˌstrēz\ *n pl, cap* [NL, fr. *fissi-* + -*rostres* (fr. L *rostrum* beak) — more at ROSTRUM] *in former classifications* **:** a group of birds having the bill deeply cleft, including the swifts, goatsuckers, swallows, and others, and not representing natural relationships

fis·sive \ˈfisiv\ *adj* [L *fissus* (past part. of *findere* to split) + E -*ive* — more at BITE] **:** relating or tending to fission

¹fis·sle *or* **fis·tle** \ˈfisəl\ *vi* -ED/-ING/-S [prob. of imit. origin] **1** *chiefly Scot* **:** to make a rustling sound **2** *chiefly Scot* **a :** to bustle about **b :** FIDGET

²fissle *or* **fistle** \"\ *n* -S **1** *chiefly Scot* **:** a rustling sound **2** *chiefly Scot* **:** COMMOTION, FUSS

fis·su·ra \fəˈs(h)u̇rə\ *n, pl* **fissu·rae** \-ˌrē, -ˌrī\ [NL] **:** FISSURE 2

fis·sur·al \ˈfishərəl\ *adj* [*fissure* + -*al*] **:** of or relating to a fissure

fis·su·ra·tion \ˌfishəˈrāshən\ *n* -S [ISV *fissure* + -*ation*] **1 :** the act of fissuring **2 :** the state of being fissured

¹fis·sure \ˈfishə(r)\ *n* -S [ME, fr. MF, fr. L *fissura*, fr. *fissus* (past part. of *findere* to split) + -*ura* -ure — more at BITE] **1 a :** a narrow opening, chasm, or crack of some length and considerable depth usu. occurring from some breaking, rending, or parting **:** CLEAVAGE ⟨one of those abrupt ~*s* with which the earth in the Southwest is riddled —Willa Cather⟩ **b** (1) **:** a usu. profound disagreement or discord portending or making for total disruption or breakup **:** DIVISION ⟨the serious ~ in the Labor Party —Felix Morley⟩ (2) **:** a serious weakness or flaw ⟨the traders of the English colonies were eating their way into the French colonial system, exploring its ~*s* systematically —O.G.Creighton⟩ **2** [NL *fissura*, fr. L] **a :** one of the clefts separating the lobes of the liver and lodging peritoneal folds, ligaments, blood and lymph vessels, and other structures — called also *fossa* **b :** any of certain clefts between bones or parts of bones in the skull **c :** any of the deep clefts of the brain; *esp* **:** one of those collocated with elevations in the walls of the ventricles ⟨the dentate ~⟩ — compare SULCUS **d :** the cleft in the anterior or ventral part of the spinal cord; *also* **:** the posterior septum of the spinal cord **3 :** a slit in tissue usu. at the junction of skin and mucous membrane ⟨~ of the lip⟩ ⟨anal ~⟩ **syn** see CRACK

²fissure \"\ *vb* **fissured; fissured; fissuring** \-sh(ə)riŋ\ **fissures** *vt* **:** to break into fissures **:** CLEAVE ⟨sudden canyons deeply *fissured* the earth —Dan Wickenden⟩ ~ *vi* **:** CRACK, FRACTURE, DIVIDE ⟨the main castes *fissured* into scores, even hundreds, of subcastes —J.B.Noss⟩

fis·sure·less \-lə̇s\ *adj* **:** devoid of fissures ⟨a completely ~ large rock⟩

fis·su·rel·la \ˌfishəˈrelə\ *n, cap* [NL, dim. of L *fissura*] **:** a genus (the type of a cosmopolitan family Fissurellidae) of marine gastropods (suborder Rhipidoglossa) comprising the keyhole limpets and having a conical shell with an opening at the apex

fissure of ro·lan·do \-rōˈlan(ˌ)dō, -län-\ *usu cap R* [after Luigi *Rolando* †1831 Ital. anatomist] **:** CENTRAL SULCUS

fissure of syl·vi·us \-ˈsilvēəs\ *usu cap S* [after Franciscus *Sylvius* (Franz de la Boë) †1672 Ger. anatomist] **:** LATERAL FISSURE

fissure vein *n* **:** a crack in the earth's crust filled with minerals deposited from aqueous solution including sometimes such adjacent rock as has been sufficiently mineralized to be mined as ore

fis·sur·iform \ˈfishərəˌfȯrm, fiˈshu̇r-\ *adj* [¹*fissure* + -*iform*] **:** resembling a fissure

fis·sury \ˈfishərē, -ri\ *adj* [¹*fissure* + -*y*] **:** abounding in fissures

¹fist \ˈfist\ *n* -S [ME, fr. OE *fȳst;* akin to OFris *fest* fist, OS & OHG *fūst*, OSlav *pęstĭ*] **1 :** a hand with fingers doubled into the palm **:** a clenched hand **2 a :** a hand whether closed as if to grasp or grip **:** CLUTCH, GRASP ⟨once he gets his ~ on something he never lets go of it⟩ **b :** a hand whether closed or not ⟨let's make up; give me your ~⟩ **c :** HANDWRITING ⟨you wrote an exquisite ~ —J.E.Agate⟩ **d :** the manner of tapping out a message that is peculiar to a particular telegraph operator **3 a :** a piece of work performed in a specified manner or with a specified degree of success **:** ATTEMPT, EFFORT, JOB ⟨all make a fair ~ at criticizing what they call the capitalist system —A.J.Nock⟩ **b** *dial* **:** a poor job of work **:** MESS ⟨made a ~ of doing that painting⟩ **4 :** INDEX 9

²fist \"\ *vt* -ED/-ING/-S **1 :** to clench (one's hand) into a fist ⟨I'd ~*ed* my hands inside their mittens to keep the fingers warm —C.A.Lindbergh b. 1902⟩ **2 :** to grip with the fist **:** HANDLE ⟨he did his best at ~*ing* frozen canvas with the rest of us —Raymond McFarland⟩ ⟨the crack jehu ~*s* the ribbons above the capering leaders and snorting bays—*Saturday Rev.*⟩

³fist *var of* FEIST

fist cods *n pl but sing or pl in constr* [²*fist* + *cods* (testes)] **:** a slaughterhouse worker who removes the hide from the rear legs of lambs and calves and curries calf carcasses

fist·ed \ˈfistə̇d\ *adj* [¹*fist* + -*ed*] **1 :** having fists **2** *of the hand* **:** clenched into a fist ⟨turned and beat ~ hands upon the mantelpiece —*Chatelaine*⟩

fistfight \ˈ=,=\ *n* **:** a usu. spontaneous fight with bare fists ⟨anger provides that No. 1 difference between a ~ and a boxing bout —Jack Dempsey⟩

fist·ful \ˈfistˌfu̇l\ *n* -S **1 :** HANDFUL ⟨a ~ of silver⟩ **2 :** a considerable number **:** COLLECTION ⟨a ~ of tired, outworn slogans —Bradford Smith⟩ ⟨last night a whole ~ of Chopin's greatest works were played —Virgil Thomson⟩

fist hatchet *also* **fist ax** *n* **:** HAND AX

fist·i·ana \ˌfistēˈanə, -ˈä-, -ˈā- *also* -ˈā-\ *n* -S [¹*fist* + -*i-* + -*ana*] **:** the world of boxing ⟨one of ~'s most famous championship bouts⟩

fist·ic \ˈfistik, -tēk\ *adj* **:** relating to boxing or to fighting with the fists **:** PUGILISTIC ⟨she immediately became a ~ authority —Mickey Walker⟩

fist·i·cuff \ˈfistə̇ˌkəf, -tē,-\ *n* -S [alter. of earlier *fisty cuff*, fr. *fisty* + *cuff*] **1 :** a blow with the fist or hand **2 fisticuffs** *pl but sing or pl in constr* **:** a fight with the fists **:** BOXING ⟨intervillage or camp disputes were settled by ~*s* — R.P.Schaedel⟩

fist·i·cuff·er \-fə(r)\ *n* -S **:** BOXER

fistle *var of* FISSLE

fist·mele \ˈfistˌmēl\ *n* -S [¹*fist* + *mele*, obs. var. of *meal* (measure)] **:** the breadth of a fist with thumb stuck out used esp. in archery to give the correct height of a string from a braced bow **:** about 7 inches

fistmele

fistnote \ˈ=,=\ *n* **:** a usu. important note (as in a book) preceded by a printing character in the shape of a fist with pointed index finger — symbol ☞

fis·tu·la \ˈfis(h)chələ\ *n, pl* **fistulas** \-ləz\ *or* **fistu·lae** -\ˌlē, -ˌlī\ [ME, fr. L] **1** *obs* **:** a reed instrument or pipe; *esp* **:** MUSETTE 1b **2 :** an abnormal congenital or acquired passage leading from an abscess or hollow organ to the body surface or from one hollow organ to another and permitting passage of fluids (as pus) or secretions ⟨a salivary ~⟩ — compare SINUS **3 :** FISTULOUS WITHERS

fistula of the withers : FISTULOUS WITHERS

fis·tu·lar \-lə(r)\ *adj* [LL *fistularis*, fr. L *fistula* + -*aris* -ar] **:** FISTULOUS

fis·tu·la·ri·idae \ˌfis(h)chələˈrīəˌdē\ *n pl, cap* [NL, fr. *Fistularia*, type genus (fr. L *fistula* + NL -*aria*) + -*idae*] **:** a family (type genus *Fistularia*) of hemibranchiate fishes of warm seas that have the head prolonged into a tube with the mouth terminal, that are otherwise structurally similar to the sticklebacks, and that comprise the cornetfishes

¹fis·tu·lar·i·oid \ˌ==ˈ=la(a)rēˌȯid\ *adj* [NL *Fistularia* + E -*oid*] **:** related to or resembling the family Fistulariidae

²fistularioid \"\ *n* -S **:** a fistularioid fish

fis·tu·lat·ed \-ˌlād·ə̇d\ *adj* [*fistula* + -*ate* + -*ed*] **:** having a fistula; *esp* **:** having an artificial fistula used for experiment (as on the digestive process)

fis·tu·li·na \ˌ==ˈlīnə, -ˈlēnə\ *n, cap* [NL, fr. L *fistula* + NL -*ina*] **:** a genus of basidiomycetous fungi (family Polyporaceae) related to *Boletus* but having each of the pores separate although crowded

fis·tu·li·za·tion \-lə̇ˈzāshən, -ˌlīˈz-\ *n* -S **:** the condition of being fistulized or having fistulas

fis·tu·lize \ˈ==ˌlīz\ *vb* -ED/-ING/-S *see -ize in Explan Notes*, *vt* **:** to produce (an artificial channel) by surgical means (as for relieving pressure in glaucoma) ~ *vi* **:** to develop a fistula ⟨a *fistulizing* bone lesion⟩

fis·tu·lose \ˈfis(h)chəˌlōs\ *adj* [L *fistulosus*] **:** FISTULOUS

fis·tu·lous \-ləs\ *adj* [ME, fr. L *fistulosus*, fr. *fistula* + -*osus* -ous] **1 :** having the form or nature of a fistula **:** relating to or having a fistula ⟨a ~ ulcer⟩ — compare FISTULOUS WITHERS **2 :** hollow like a pipe or reed

fistulous withers *n pl but usu sing in constr* **:** a deep-seated chronic inflammation of the withers of the horse usu. involving the cervical ligaments and the bursas of the vertebral spines and discharging seropurulent or bloody fluid through one or more openings which may be initiated by mechanical injury but of which the development depends on infection esp. with the bacterium (*Brucella abortus*) that causes bovine contagious abortion

fist wedge *n* **:** HAND AX

fisty \ˈfistē, -ti\ *adj* **:** FISTIC

¹fit \ˈfit, *usu* -id·+V\ *n* -S [ME, fr. OE *fitt;* akin to OS *fittea* division of a poem, text, OHG *fizza* skein, yarn, ON *fit* web (of an animal's foot), and perh. to OE *fōt* foot — more at FOOT] **1** *archaic* **:** a division of a poem or song **:** a canto or a similar division **2** *obs* **:** a strain of music

²fit \"\ *n* -S [ME, fr. OE *fitt* strife, conflict] **1** *obs* **:** a painful, dangerous, exciting, or mortal crisis or experience **2 a** *archaic* **:** a spell or bout of illness or of some specified disease **b :** a stroke of some disease (as epilepsy or apoplexy) that produces convulsions or unconsciousness **:** SEIZURE, PAROXYSM ⟨he was seized with a ~ which was repeated about every two hours until his death —D.D.Martin⟩ **c :** a sudden, severe, but transient attack of any physical disturbance ⟨~*s* of shivering that weaken knees and set teeth to chattering —Kenneth Roberts⟩ **3 :** a sudden often unaccountable burst or flurry (as of activity or emotion) **:** a brief period **:** SPELL, MOOD, IMPULSE ⟨a ~ of jealousy⟩ ⟨a ~ of idleness⟩ ⟨there is much praise or ridicule, as the ~ takes the onlookers —C.P.Conigrave⟩ ⟨something that grandpa threw together in a ~ of tinkering —*Car Life*⟩ ⟨he may have ~*s* of deep depression following ~*s* of anger —H.A.Overstreet⟩ ⟨went off into a quiet ~ of laughter —M.V.Reidy⟩ **4 :** an outburst of anger, chagrin, or intense excitement ⟨she simply had a ~ when she learned what had happened⟩ — **by fits** *or* **by fits and starts** *adv* **:** at intervals **:** impulsively and irregularly **:** FITFULLY, INTERMITTENTLY ⟨slow wandering footsteps that halted and came on *by fits* —Pearl Buck⟩ ⟨Japanese expansion proceeded not according to any coldly calculated master plan but rather *by fits and starts* —O.D.Tolischus⟩

³fit \"\ *adj* **fitter; fittest** [ME; akin to ME *fitten* to be suitable for] **1 a :** adapted to an end, object, or design **:** suitable by nature or by art **:** SUITED, QUALIFIED, APPROPRIATE ⟨found him a ~ officer and gentleman —*Time*⟩ ⟨soft water ~ for manufacturing is restricted to the central part of the district⟩; *specif* **:** so adapted to the environment as to be capable of surviving — often used in the phrase *the survival of the fittest* **b :** becoming from the viewpoint of propriety, convenience, or morality **:** SEEMLY, PROPER, MEET, PRUDENT, EXPEDIENT ⟨pictures . . . not ~ for young people to see —D.M.Davin⟩ ⟨it is not ~ for us to inquire into sacred things⟩ ⟨he gave credit where he thought ~ —Adrian Bell⟩ ⟨one can wish that the editors had seen ~ to include a few more illustrations —Stuart Preston⟩ **2 a** *obs* **:** made to fit **:** of the right dimensions **:** CLOSE-FITTING **b :** made or put in a suitable condition **:** READY, PREPARED ⟨corn . . . must be passed through a grain drier before it is ~ to store —F.D.Smith & Barbara Wilcox⟩ ⟨the work of getting the ship ~ for sea —Nevil Shute⟩ **c :** so affected as to be ready to do or suffer something **:** DISPOSED ⟨fair ~ to cry I was —Bryan MacMahon⟩ ⟨shivering and shaking ~ to die with cold —*Time*⟩ **3 :** sound physically and mentally **:** qualified from the viewpoint of health **:** HEALTHY ⟨he keeps ~ by playing tennis and squash —*Current Biog.*⟩ ⟨you aren't ~ to get breakfast —Ellen Glasgow⟩ ⟨if you are young, ~, and keen you can be . . . an officer in the Royal Air Force —*Punch*⟩ ⟨the best prescription for a ~ old age is a bad illness in middle life —John Buchan⟩

syn SUITABLE, MEET, PROPER, APPROPRIATE, FITTING, APT, HAPPY, FELICITOUS: FIT suggests being adapted or adaptable to an end in view, situation, or occasion, sometimes an especial readiness for use ⟨a wooden image, movable and *fit* to be carried in procession —George Santayana⟩ ⟨the magnificent hall which seemed only a *fit* setting for her beauty —Nathaniel Hawthorne⟩ ⟨a ship *fit* for service⟩ SUITABLE applies to whatever answers demands or requirements smoothly, without difficulty, doubt, or objection ⟨the plain walls of the interior provide a *suitable* foil for the decorative color and woodwork —*Amer. Guide Series: Minn.*⟩ ⟨large tracts of land *suitable* for vineyards —Robert Hichens⟩ ⟨because of its proscribed theme, the play was not considered *suitable* movie material —*Current Biog.*⟩ ⟨after a *suitable* interval, not to seem importunate —Mary Austin⟩ MEET describes what is nicely adapted or rightly or justly applicable; it may be somewhat stronger and more complimentary than SUITABLE ⟨now that death has shut the door behind Kipling, leaving his completed work here with us, ready for the passionless estimate of posterity, it is *meet* for critics to weigh that work in their delicate scale —Katharine F. Gerould⟩ ⟨Sabbath was made a solemn day, *meet* only for preaching, praying, and Bible reading —C.A. & Mary Beard⟩ ⟨is it *meet* that an utter stranger should thus express himself? —W.S.Gilbert⟩ PROPER may suggest a fitness by nature or by right reason, good judgment, or social sanction ⟨water, the *proper* element for fish⟩ ⟨a few Yankees of the swindling kind who found their *proper* sphere in the peddling business —Van Wyck Brooks⟩ ⟨when a child has mastered a difficulty after persistent efforts, praise is a *proper* reward —Bertrand Russell⟩ ⟨the education *proper* to a hero —*Encyc. Americana*⟩ APPROPRIATE may suggest distinctive, peculiar, or distinguishing fitness ⟨the magician does not doubt that . . . the performance of the proper ceremony, accompanied by the *appropriate* spell, will inevitably be attended by the desired results —J.G. Frazer⟩ ⟨we have agreed that our writing should be *appropriate:* that it should fit the occasion —A.T.Quiller-Couch⟩ FITTING may suggest an especial harmony or congruousness ⟨the *fitting* expression for the deeds they do —G.W.Russell⟩ ⟨a *fitting* occasion to reassess the validity of the mechanical conception of the universe of which he was unwittingly the prime author —*Times Lit. Supp.*⟩ APT connotes a fitness marked by nicety and discrimination ⟨had shown that essential objectives could be gained by an *apt* combination of blackmail and negotiation —*Times Lit. Supp.*⟩ ⟨the *apt* and telling turns of expression, the phrases of homely vigor or happy pregnancy which have become a part of our linguistic stock in trade —J.L.Lowes⟩ ⟨what time so *apt* for inculcating obedience and other Christian virtues as this solemn hour —H.O.Taylor⟩ HAPPY applies to whatever is quite successfully, effectively, or pleasingly fit ⟨our ideal should be to make our battle a series of single combats, our ranks a *happy* alliance of agile commanders-in-chief —T.E. Lawrence⟩ ⟨of all writers he perhaps best combines in his style a felicitous elegance with a *happy* vernacular, the grace of philosophers and wits and the wit of the people —Carl Van Doren⟩ FELICITOUS suggests the opportunely or strikingly happy ⟨had a way of illuminating an array of factual data with *felicitous* theoretical insights —D.G.Mandelbaum⟩ ⟨some of the most *felicitous* turns of thought and phrase in poetry are the result of a flash of inspiration —J.L.Lowes⟩ — **fit to be tied :** angry or irritated to an extreme **:** ready to explode with wrath ⟨the hardheaded businessman looks *fit to be tied* —*New Republic*⟩ ⟨*fit to be tied* when she came home late⟩ — **fit to kill :** to an extreme ⟨dressed up *fit to kill*⟩ **:** at a great rate ⟨they were so happy that they blubbered *fit to kill* —S.J.Perelman⟩

⁴fit \"\ *adv* [ME, fr. *fit*, adj.] *archaic* **:** FITLY

⁵fit \"\ *vb* **fitted** *or* **fit; fitted** *or* **fit; fitting; fits** [ME *fitten*, fr. or akin to MD *vitten* to be suitable; akin to ON *fitja* to knit, OHG *fizzōn* to surround, *fizza* skein, yarn — more at ¹FIT] *vt* **1 a** (1) **:** to be suitable for or to **:** answer the requirements of **:** harmonize with **:** BEFIT, SUIT ⟨for all that it is a good constitution — a constitution that ~*s* us —Elmer Davis⟩ ⟨these fashions ~ the life of the sport car, the penthouse, modern furniture —*Women's Wear Daily*⟩ ⟨a girl that *fitted* you perfectly —Bob Nichols⟩ ⟨in appearance he *fitted* his job to perfection —S.H.Adams⟩ ⟨no program of work will ~ every community —Beatrice S. Rossell⟩ ⟨the name *fit* him to perfection —*Deerfield (Wis.) Republican*⟩ (2) *archaic* **:** to be seemly or proper for **:** become from the viewpoint of propriety, convenience, or morality — often used with impersonal *it* as subject ⟨it ~*s* us then to be as provident as fear may teach us —Shak.⟩ **b** (1) **:** to be correctly adjusted to or shaped for **:** conform to the contours of ⟨the coat ~*s* him beautifully⟩ ⟨the key ~*s* the lock⟩ ⟨I had grown tall enough to ~ my coffin —Sacheverell Sitwell⟩ (2) **:** to insert, apply, or adjust until snugly or correctly in place **:** cause to conform to the outlines or contours of a receptacle ⟨students are taught to ~ braces of different types⟩ ⟨~ a stopper into a bottle⟩ (3) **:** to make a place or room for (as by adjusting, maneuvering) **:** ACCOMMODATE ⟨he was *fitting* many concert appearances into a crowded schedule —*Current Biog.*⟩ ⟨always came in as though he . . . was *fitting* you in at great inconvenience —Fred Majdalany⟩ ⟨~ three or four men into a single turret —Tom Wintringham⟩ ⟨most of his library had been *fitted* in here —Lucien Price⟩ **c :** to be in agreement with or accord with ⟨this theory ~*s* all the known facts⟩ ⟨does not quite ~ the assumption that the sole cause of the business slowdown is an attempt to cut inventories —George Shea⟩ **2 a :** to make fit or suitable : adapt to the purpose intended : put into a condition of readiness : PREPARE, QUALIFY ⟨a comfortable stall was *fitted* for the horse —*Irish Digest*⟩ ⟨each ant is *fitted* to his place in the community by a combination of structural specialization and instincts —Ralph Linton⟩ ⟨vigorous training ~*s* men for the ordeals of battle⟩ ⟨his temperament *fitted* him to understand an age of courageous exploits —Van Wyck Brooks⟩ **b :** to prepare for college ⟨he was *fitted* for college by his own father⟩ **c :** to till (land) in preparation for planting ⟨came up with the team and drag from the field . . . where he had been *fitting* the bean ground —Gordon Webber⟩ **d** (1) **:** to bring to a required form and size : shape rightly : adapt to a model : ADJUST ⟨*fitted* the garment to the client's specifications⟩ (2) **:** to cause to conform to or suit something else ⟨you must ~ the words to the music⟩ ⟨tried to ~ his spending to his income⟩ ⟨~ your conduct to your circumstances⟩ (3) **:** to determine the required specifications of something for : MEASURE ⟨came to the house and *fitted* you for handmade French lingerie —Margaret A. Barnes⟩ ⟨*fitted* me for glasses⟩ : determine the fit of a garment on ⟨*fitted* her with the dress and found that it needed alterations⟩ (4) **:** to supply with something that is shaped, adjusted, or designed for the use required : PROVIDE, EQUIP ⟨*fitted* the ship with new engines⟩ ⟨its many and diversified laboratories are *fitted* with the latest in equipment —*Investor's Reader*⟩ (5) **:** to finish (animals) for the show ring; *also* : to dress and prepare (animals) for showing (6) **:** to subject (newly formed soap) before settling to a process of boiling with steam or water and additional alkali as needed until the desired texture is attained (7) **:** to adjust (a smooth curve of specified type) to a given set of points in such a way as to minimize the sum of the squares of the distances measured parallel to the axis of ordinates from the given points to the curve (8) **:** to design (a character in a font) so that the apparent distance to any close-set adjacent character will be as nearly uniform as the shape of the individual characters allows (9) *of a hand or suit in bridge* **:** to contain cards that increase the trick-winning capacity of (a partner's hand) **~ *vi* 1** *archaic* **:** to be seemly, proper, or suitable **2 a :** to become adjusted to a particular shape or size : conform in contour when applied or assumed ⟨his coat ~*s* beautifully⟩ **b :** to be in harmony or accord : make the proper adjustment : meet the needs : become suited : COINCIDE, AGREE, CONFORM, BELONG, ADJUST ⟨a conservative in a semiliberal setting . . . doesn't seem to ~ —*Kiplinger Washington Letter*⟩ ⟨I'm glad that your new secretary seems likely to ~ —H.J.Laski⟩ ⟨none of the familiar labels . . . seems to ~ quite so well —J.W.Krutch⟩ — often used with *in, into,* or *with* ⟨where does the wife ~ into all this —W.H.Whyte⟩ ⟨his somber pessimism *fitted* in with her own mood⟩ ⟨many of them have been able to ~ into the white man's life without giving up the ancient ways —H.A.Overstreet⟩ ⟨we should have to determine where you would ~ in —C.B.Kelland⟩ ⟨employers were likely to select . . . those . . . who would ~ easily and docilely with the rest of the workers —Oscar Handlin⟩ **c** *of the hands of two partners* **:** to constitute a fit (sense 4) **3 :** to prepare for college esp. by attending a college-preparatory school **syn** see PREPARE

⁶**fit** \"\ *n* -s **1 a :** the quality or state of being fitted or adapted : the manner in which or the degree to which something fits or conforms to some standard : AGREEMENT, ACCORD, ADJUSTMENT ⟨yearning for the good old days and the job and the comfortable ~ of old ways —Dixon Wecter⟩ ⟨a qualitative verbal assessment of the degree of ~ between the interpretations —*Amer. Anthropologist*⟩ ⟨I believe the average American's notions about the average Briton are at least as bad a ~ —Richard Joseph⟩ **b :** the manner in which clothing fits a wearer ⟨advising me about the ~ of my corsets —Mary Austin⟩ ⟨the ~ of the dress is snug⟩ ⟨American man-produced fashions are the envy of all Europe because of their crisp styling and ~ —*Wall Street Jour.*⟩ **c :** the degree of closeness with which surfaces are brought together in an assembly of parts (as a shaft in a hole or a nut on a screw) **d :** the conformity of a set of statistical observations to a corresponding set of values or of a curve that represents observations to a corresponding curve that serves as a standard **2 :** a piece of clothing that fits ⟨the gown was an excellent ~⟩ **3 :** the texture attained in fitting soap — called also *finish* ⟨a close (soft) ~ is used on large kettles —G.W.Busby⟩ **4 :** such distribution of cards in the two hands of a bridge partnership that each can help the other to win tricks in every or nearly every suit

⁷**fit** \"\ *Scot var of* FOOT

⁸**fit** \"\ *dial past of* FIGHT

FIT *abbr* 1 free in truck 2 free of income tax

¹**fitch** \'fich\ *n* -ES [ME *ficche, fecche, vecche* — more at VETCH] **1** *dial* **:** VETCH **2 fitches** *pl* **:** SPELT ⟨lentiles, and millet, and ~*es* —Ezek 4:9 (AV)⟩ **3 fitches** *pl* **:** a forage herb (as tares) ⟨the ~*es* are beaten out with a staff —Isa 28:27 (AV)⟩

²**fitch** \"\ *or* **fitch·ew** \'fi(,)chü\ *n, pl* **fitches** *or* **fitchews** [ME *fiche, ficheux, fitchewes,* fr. MF or MD; MF *fichau,* fr. MD *vitsau, fitsau, visse*] **1 a :** POLECAT 1a **b :** the fur or pelt of the fitch **2** *also* **fitch brush :** a small brush made of the hair of a fitch, skunk, or hog

³**fitch** \"\ *vi* -ED/-ING/-ES [ME *fichen,* prob. alter. of *fiken* — more at FIKE] *dial Brit* **:** FIDGET

⁴**fitch** \"\ *also* **fetch** \'fech\ *n* -ES [origin unknown] **:** a plait in which two canes or osiers are intertwined so as to bind the stakes and by-stakes in successive or alternate loops — see BASKET illustration

fitched \'ficht\ *adj* [MF *fiché* + E *-ed*] **:** FITCHÉE

fitch·ée *or* **fitchy** *also* **fitché** \'fichē, (')fi¦chā\ *adj* [MF *fiché,* past part. of *ficher* to drive in, pin, fasten — more at FICHU] *of a cross* **:** having the lower extremity pointed instead of ending in the form characteristic of the kind of cross in question ⟨a cross botonée ~⟩ ⟨a crosslet ~⟩ — **fitchée at the foot :** having a point descending from the lower extremity, the shape of which is not modified — used of a cross the outer aspects of whose arms are flat ⟨a cross formée ~⟩

fitch·et \'fichət\ *or* **fitchet weasel** *n* -s [²*fitch* + *-et*] **:** POLECAT 1a

fitching *n* -s [⁴*fitch* + *-ing*] **1 :** ⁴FITCH **2 :** the act of plaiting a fitch

fite \'fīt\ *Scot var of* WHITE

fit·ful \'fitfəl\ *adj* [²*fit* + *-ful*] **1** *obs* **:** characterized by fits or paroxysms ⟨life's ~ fever —Shak.⟩ **2 :** having a spasmodic, irregular, or intermittent character : changeable or uncertain in mood : occurring in fits or spurts : coming and going : VARIABLE, CAPRICIOUS, UNSTABLE, IMPULSIVE ⟨his education must have been ~, to say the most of it —Osbert Sitwell⟩ ⟨there was a ~ cannonade far away in the southwest —H.G. Wells⟩ ⟨one of the most constant complaints is of insomnia or . . . ~ sleep —H.G.Armstrong⟩ ⟨hitherto I've been gloomy, moody, ~ —W.S.Gilbert⟩ — **fit·ful·ly** \-fəlē, -li\ *adv* — **fit·ful·ness** *n* -ES

fit·i·fied \'fid·ə,fīd\ *adj* [²*fit* + *-ify* + *-ed*] **1** *Midland* **:** tending to have or be afflicted with fits; *specif* **:** EPILEPTIC **2** *Midland* **:** erratic and eccentric in behavior : TEMPERAMENTAL

fit·ly *adv* [³*fit* adj + *-ly*] **:** in a fit manner or at a fit time : SUITABLY, PROPERLY, DECOROUSLY ⟨his last book ~ presents his seasoned theological convictions⟩ ⟨the author may ~ regard it as the crown of an arduous . . . life's work —*Times Lit. Supp.*⟩

fit·ment \'fitmənt\ *n* -s [⁵*fit* + *-ment*] **1 a :** EQUIPMENT, FURNISHING, FURNITURE — used esp. of built-in furniture **b fitments** *pl* **:** FITTINGS **2 :** a dispensing or pouring device used with or as part of the closure of a bottle

fit·ness *n* -ES [³*fit* + *-ness*] **1 :** the quality or state of being fit or fitted ⟨the physical ~ . . . of large numbers of people had been impaired by poverty —F.A.Ogg & P.O.Ray⟩ **2 :** the condition of being qualified or suitable : ELIGIBILITY, SOUNDNESS, CAPACITY ⟨subjected to endurance tests to prove their ~ . . . for the status of manhood —Francis Birtles⟩ ⟨the law prescribed that the ordaining bishop should assure himself . . . of the candidate's ~ in education and morals —G.G. Coulton⟩ ⟨officials . . . should be chosen for their ~ to understand intellectual questions —Zechariah Chafee⟩ **3 :** essential rightness or reasonableness : PROPRIETY, CORRECTNESS, APPROPRIATENESS ⟨one observes a nice historical ~ in the fact —H.O.Taylor⟩ ⟨no one with a sense of ~ ever docked the tail of a Shetland pony —Ben Riker⟩ — often used in the phrase *fitness of things* ⟨the sheep . . . lay quiet enough, having an inborn sense of the ~ of things —John Galsworthy⟩ ⟨it does appear to be . . . inherent in the eternal ~ of things —T.L.Peacock⟩

fit out *vt* **:** to supply with necessaries or means : FURNISH, EQUIP, OUTFIT, PREPARE ⟨friends *fitted* him *out* with a new suit and new shoes⟩ ⟨*fit out* a privateer⟩ ~ *vi* **:** OUTFIT ⟨the ship, a former merchantman, was *fitting out* as a privateer⟩

fit plant *n* [²*fit*] **:** INDIAN PIPE

fitroot \'ˌ=ˌ=\ *also* **fits·root** \'fits,=\ *n* [²*fit* + *root*] **:** INDIAN PIPE

fits *pl of* FIT, *pres 3d sing of* FIT

fitted *adj* [fr. past part. of ⁵*fit*] **1 a :** shaped to conform to the lines of something else ⟨~ sheets⟩ ⟨~ closets⟩; *specif* **:** shaped to conform to the lines of the body ⟨a ~ coat⟩ ⟨a ~ sleeve⟩ **b :** equipped with accessories ⟨a genuine leather ~ case⟩ **2 :** ADAPTED, QUALIFIED ⟨for the accomplishments of the task . . . his energy and enthusiasm . . . make him peculiarly ~ —Arthur Fisher⟩

fit·ted·ness *n* -ES **:** FITNESS ⟨worried about his own ~ to carry on the work⟩

fit·ten \'fitᵊn\ *adj* [alter. of ¹*fitting*] *dial* **:** qualified or suited for : FIT ⟨a ~ place to live⟩

¹**fitter** *comparative of* FIT

²**fit·ter** \'fid·ə(r), -itə-\ *n* -s **:** one that fits or makes to fit: as **a :** a person who tries on, adjusts, or alters articles of clothing for a customer **b :** a worker who uses hand and machine tools to fit parts together and to assemble machinery and other equipment **c :** SHIPFITTER **d :** an upfitter of furniture or caskets **e :** one that sharpens and repairs saws **f :** one that selects trees to be felled for tanbark and after they have been felled cuts rings through the bark to prepare them for the peelers **g :** one that makes plaster casts of stumps, prepares them for use in making artificial limbs, and fits the assembled limbs to the wearers **h :** a finish carpenter who installs prefabricated window frames and sash

fit·ters \'fitə(r)z\ *n pl* [ME *fiteres;* akin to OHG *vetze* rag, ON *fat* vessel, dress — more at VAT] *now dial Eng* **:** RAGS, TATTERS, FRAGMENTS

fittest *superlative of* FIT

fittig reaction *or* **fittig synthesis** *n, usu cap F* [after Rudolf *Fittig* †1910 Ger. chemist] **:** the Wurtz-Fittig reaction applied to the synthesis of aromatic hydrocarbons

¹**fitting** *adj* [ME, fr. pres. part. of *fitten* to fit — more at FIT] **:** APPROPRIATE, SUITABLE, PROPER ⟨the ~ expression for the deeds they do —G.W.Russell⟩ ⟨a ~ rebuke for his rudeness⟩ **syn** see FIT

²**fitting** *n* -s [fr. gerund of ⁵*fit*] **1 a :** something used in fitting up : ACCESSORY, ADJUNCT, ATTACHMENT ⟨living quarters with splendid ~*s* — marble pavements, ivory doors, crystal chandeliers —Christopher Rand⟩ ⟨an unusual ~ in these days is a hand throttle, fitted to the instrument panel —*Country Life*⟩ ⟨the ~*s* of the violin have been considerably altered since the greatest period of violin making —Robert Donington⟩ **b :** a small often standardized part (as a coupling, valve, gauge) entering into the construction of a boiler, steam, water, or gas supply installation or other apparatus — usu. used in pl.; see GAS FITTING, PIPE FITTING **2 :** a trying-on of tailor-made clothes (as a suit or dress) in the process of completion **3** *Brit* **:** SIZE ⟨nylons are also being made in three ~*s* — for the slim, stocky, and oversize leg —*Irish Digest*⟩ ⟨~*s* for every foot —*Melbourne (Australia) Weekly Times*⟩

fit·ting·ly *adv* **:** in a fitting manner

fit·ting·ness *n* -ES **:** the quality or state of being fit

fit·tit \'fitət\ *Scot var of* FOOTED

fit·to·nia \fə'tōnēə\ *n, cap* [NL, fr. Elizabeth and Sarah Margaret *Fitton,* 19th cent. Irish writers on botany + NL *-ia*] **:** a small genus of Peruvian trailing herbs (family Acanthaceae) that are cultivated as foliage plants and that have leaves with showy red or white venation and inconspicuous flowers in bracted terminal spikes

fit·ty \'fitī\ *adj* [³*fit* + *-y*] **1** *dial chiefly Eng* **:** suitable and becoming : APPROPRIATE **2** *dial chiefly Eng* **a :** being in good order : TRIM **b :** HANDSOME, STRIKING

fit up *vt* **:** to furnish with things suitable : make proper for use : EQUIP ⟨he *fitted up* one courtyard of the homestead and taught science to all . . . whom he could interest —Nora Waln⟩

¹**fit-up** \'=,=\ *n* -s [*fit up*] **1** *Brit* **a :** a place (as an inn or hall) fitted up as a temporary theater or stage ⟨meager productions in village *fit-ups* —*Country Life*⟩; *also* **:** the makeshift or improvised scenery and properties used or carried by a traveling theatrical company **b** *or* **fit-up company :** a traveling theatrical group that carries its own scenery and properties ⟨I started my stage training . . . in a *fit-up company* —*Listener*⟩ **2 :** ⁶FIT 1c

²**fit-up** \"\ *adj* **:** of or relating to a fit-up ⟨having played much in inns and similar *fit-up* places —Arnold Bennett⟩

fit-up man *n* [*fit up*] **:** one who does the initial fitting together of parts of tanks, boilers, and other vessels in preparation for final assembly by the boilermaker

fitweed \'=,=\ *n* [²*fit* + *weed*] **:** a tropical American herbaceous feverweed (*Eryngium foetidum*) with fetid prickly leaves

fitz·ger·ald contraction \(')fits¦jerəld-\ *n, usu cap F&G* [after George F. *FitzGerald* †1901 Irish physicist] **:** a longitudinal contraction that according to relativity theory every moving body is believed to undergo in the dimension parallel to the direction of motion

fitz·hugh \'fits,(h)yü *sometimes* =¦=\ *n* -s *usu cap* [perh. alter. of *Foochow* (Minhow), city in southeastern China] **:** a pattern (as of pomegranates or butterflies) appearing on Chinese export porcelain of the 18th and earlier 19th centuries

fitz·roya \fits'rōi(y)ə ˌ=ˌ==\ *n, cap* [NL, after Robert *Fitzroy* †1865 Eng. naval commander & meteorologist] **:** a genus of commercially important evergreen timber trees (family Pinaceae) of Chile and Tasmania with irregular branching, ternate decurrent scalelike leaves, and small globose cones

¹**five** \'fīv\ *adj* [ME, adj. & pron., fr. OE *fīf;* akin to OHG *funf, finf* five, ON *fimm,* Goth *fimf,* L *quinque,* Gk *pente,* Skt *pañca*] **:** being one more than four in number ⟨~ years⟩ — see NUMBER table

²**five** \"\ *pron, pl in constr* [ME] **:** five countable persons or things not specified but under consideration and being enumerated ⟨~ are here⟩ ⟨~ were found⟩

³**five** \"\ *n* -s [ME, fr. *five,* pron. & adj.] **1 :** one more than four **2 a :** five units or objects ⟨a total of ~⟩ **b :** a group or set of five ⟨arranged by ~*s*⟩ **3 a :** the numerable quantity symbolized by the arabic numeral 5 **b :** the figure 5 **c :** the letter V **4 :** five o'clock — compare BELL table, TIME illustration **5 a :** a playing card marked to show that it is fifth in a suit **b :** a domino with five spots on one of its halves **c :** a die with five spots on the uppermost side **d :** an article of clothing of the fifth size ⟨wears a ~⟩ **6 a :** a five-pound note **b :** a five-dollar bill **7 :** a playing team of five members; *esp* **:** a basketball team **8 :** FIFTEEN 6

five-and-dime \¦=ˌ=¦=\ *n* **:** FIVE-AND-TEN

five-and-ten \¦==¦=\ *n* **1 :** a store selling articles priced at 5 or 10 cents **2 :** a variety store selling inexpensive articles of merchandise

five back *n* **:** a bowling game in which four pins are spotted on the back line and one at the end of the line next in front and in which three balls not exceeding six inches in diameter are rolled in each inning — called also *fivepins*

five-centered arch \'=ˌ==-\ *n* **:** an arch whose intrados curve is described from five centers

five-corners \'=¦==\ *n pl but usu sing in constr* **:** the pentagonal fruit of any Australian shrub of the genus *Styphelia* (esp. *S. triflora*)

five-corns \'=¦=\ *n pl* **:** the fruits of the cupseed

five-day week *n* **:** a week having five working days

five-eighth *or* **five-eighths** \(')=¦=\ *n* **:** a rugby player whose position is between the halfbacks and the three-quarter backs; *also* **:** the position of this player

five-em space *n* [contr. of *five-to-em space*] **:** a space in printing that is ⅕ of an em in thickness

five-figure \'=¦==\ *adj* **:** containing five numerical figures : rated at an annual salary of $10,000 or more

five-finger \'=ˌ==\ *n* **1 a :** CINQUEFOIL 1 **b :** OXLIP 2 **c :** BIRD'S-FOOT TREFOIL 1 **d :** VIRGINIA CREEPER **2 :** a 5-rayed starfish

five-fingered creeper \'=ˌ==-\ *or* **five-fingered ivy** *n* **:** VIRGINIA CREEPER

five-fingered jack *n, usu cap J* **:** a common cinquefoil (*Potentilla canadensis*) of eastern No. America

five-fingered root *n* **:** the root of a water dropwort (*Oenanthe crocata*)

five-fingers \'=ˌ==\ *n pl but sing in constr* **1 :** FIVE-FINGER 1 **2 :** GINSENG 2

five-flowered gentian \'=ˌ=-\ *n* **:** an annual gentian (*Gentiana quinquefolia*) of eastern No. America

¹**five·fold** \'fīv¦fōld\ *adj* [ME *fiffold,* fr. OE *fīffeald,* fr. *fīf* five + *-feald* -fold] **1 :** having five parts or aspects **2 :** being five times as large, as great, or as many as some understood size, degree, or amount ⟨a ~ increase⟩

²**fivefold** \"\ *adv* **:** to five times as much or as many : by five times ⟨increased ~⟩

five hundred *n* **1 a :** the numerable quantity symbolized by the arabic numerals 500 — see NUMBER table **b :** the letter D **2 a :** a card game developed from euchre and played with a pack of cards varying from 24 to 62 cards and often including a joker in which 2 to 6 players bid for the right to name the trump suit or no trump and the first to score 500 points wins **b :** any of various games in which the objective is 500 points

five hundred rum *or* **five hundred rummy** *n* **:** a variety of rummy for from 2 to 4 players in which the object is to lay down 500 or more points in melds — called also *pinochle rummy*

five-leaf \'=ˌ=\ *n* [ME *fivelef, fiflef,* fr. OE *fīflēaf,* fr. *fīf* + *lēaf* leaf — more at FIVE, LEAF] **:** CINQUEFOIL

five-leaved chaste tree \'=ˌ=-\ *n* **:** an Asiatic shrub or small tree (*Vitex negundo*) with showy lilac panicled flowers

five-leaved ivy *n* **:** VIRGINIA CREEPER

five-leaved pine *n* **1 :** SWISS PINE **2 :** any of several pines with five needles; *esp* **:** WHITE PINE 1a

five-lined lizard \'=ˌ=-\ *n* **:** BLUE-TAILED SKINK

five·ling \'fīvliŋ\ *n* -s **:** a twin crystal consisting of five individuals

five·pence *Brit* 'fīvpən(t)s *or* 'fī(f)pə- *or* 'fipə-, *US* " *or* -īv-,pen-\ *n, pl* **fivepence** *or* **fivepences 1 :** the sum of five usu. British pennies **2 a :** five U.S. cents **b :** a five-cent piece

five·pen·ny morris \-nē-,-ni-, *or* 'fipnē- *or* 'fipni-\ *n* **:** morris played with five counters

five-per·cent·er \,fīvpə(r)'sentə(r)\ *n* -s **:** one that for a fee of five percent helps businessmen obtain government contracts or do other business with the government

fivepins \'=ˌ=\ *n pl* **:** FIVE BACK

fiv·er \'fīvə(r)\ *n* -s **1** *slang* **:** a five-dollar bill **2** *slang* **:** a five-pound note

fives \'fīvz\ *n pl but sing in constr* [fr. pl. of ³*five*] **:** a game similar to handball for two or four players — see ETON GAME, RUGBY GAME

fivescore \'=¦=\ *adj* **:** being 100 in number

five-shooter \'=¦==\ *n* **:** a revolver with a five-round capacity

five-sisters \'=¦==\ *n pl but sing in constr* **:** WHORLED LOOSESTRIFE

five·some \'fīvsəm\ *n* -s [²*five* + *-some*] **1 :** a group of five persons playing together **2 :** any group of five persons or things

five-spot \'=ˌ=\ *n* **1 :** a California annual herb (*Nemophila maculata*) with showy flowers having a conspicuous purple blotch at the end of each corolla lobe **2 :** an oil well made to produce copiously by pumping water under pressure into four other holes surrounding it **3 a :** ³FIVE 5a **b** *slang* **:** a five-dollar bill

five-star \'=ˌ=\ *adj* **1 :** being of five-star rank ⟨was made a *five-star* general⟩ **2** [so called fr. the use of multiple asterisks in the literary or dramatic reviews of some publications to symbolize degrees of merit] **:** being of the first class or quality ⟨there are not enough *five-star* works of art to go around —J.T.Soby⟩ ⟨a *five-star* book for those interested in the creation of our republic —J.R.Chamberlain⟩

five-star rank *n* [so called fr. the insignia on the uniform] **:** the rank of general of the army, general of the air force, or fleet admiral

fivestones \'=ˌ=\ *n pl but sing in constr, Brit* **:** jacks played with five stones

five-ten limits \'=¦=-\ *n pl* **:** limitations fixing the maximum liability of an insurer at $5000 for the bodily injury or death of any one person and subject to the same limit per person at $10,000 for any one accident irrespective of how many persons are killed or injured

five-toed jerboa \'=ˌ=-\ *n* **:** any of several large active long-eared jerboas (genus *Allactaga*) of eastern Europe and Asia (as *A. sibirica*)

five-year cure \'=ˌ=-\ *n* **:** survival without clinically evident recurrence for five years after treatment for certain diseases (as cancer)

five-year plan \'=¦=-\ *n, often cap F&Y&P* [trans. of Russ *pyatiletka*] **1 :** one of a continuing series of Soviet governmental programs designed to achieve usu. specified goals in the planned, coordinated, and cumulative development of the Soviet economy and other sectors of Soviet life (as education and science) over a period of five years **2 :** a national governmental program of planned, coordinated, and cumulative economic and social development over a period of five years

FIW *abbr* free in wagon

¹**fix** \'fiks\ *vb* -ED/-ING/-ES [ME *fixen,* fr. L *fixus,* past part. of *figere* to fasten, pierce — more at DIKE] *vt* **1 a** (1) **:** to make (a material object) firm, stable, or stationary : make fast ⟨~ a post in the ground⟩ ⟨the internal passport system introduced . . . to ~ the population —Bernard Pares⟩ (2) **:** to implant firmly (as an idea or institution) : make permanent ⟨intent on ~*ing* a way of life outmoded in the home country —D.M. Friedenberg⟩ ⟨harsh words, threats . . . only ~ the habit deeper —H.R.Litchfield & L.H.Dembo⟩ (3) **:** to give a final or permanent form to : make definite and settled : CRYSTALLIZE ⟨~*ed* the cultural pattern that dominates the contemporary scene —*Amer. Guide Series: Minn.*⟩ ⟨Greene and his fellows evolved the style of what was to become Shakespearean drama, and . . . Marlowe ~*ed* it —W.B.Adams⟩ (4) **:** to give definite, visible, or fixed form to (something that is intangible, fleeting, or elusive) : CAPTURE, EVOKE ⟨that other aspect of truth which the scientist tries to catch and ~ —J.L.Lowes⟩ ⟨~*ed* their fears . . . in ebony images —F.J.Mather⟩ ⟨a voyage of speculation that aimed rather to survey the world than to ~ a convincing vision —Edmund Wilson⟩ ⟨~ in words, before time blurs them, the clear lineaments of genius —*Dock Leaves*⟩ **b** (1) **:** to make nonvolatile or solid : cause to form a nonvolatile or solid compound ⟨~ ammonia⟩; *also* **:** COMBINE ⟨~ nitrogen to form ammonia⟩ ⟨leaves of many plants take up carbon dioxide and ~ it in organic acids⟩ (2) **:** to make (a fertilizer element or a trace element) insoluble by combination with soil minerals and thus often unavailable or only slowly available to plants (3) **:** to make (a perfume) more lasting by adding a substance that reduces the rate of evaporation (4) **:** to treat so as to make some condition permanent ⟨~ an oil in the vapor state by mixing it with a gas⟩ (5) **:** to make the image of (a photographic negative or positive) more permanent by changing the unused silver salts to a soluble form that can be removed by washing (6) **:** to kill, harden, and preserve (as organisms or fresh tissues) for microscopic study or other purposes usu. by immersion in dilute acids, alcohol, or solutions of substances that quickly coagulate living tissue (7) **:** to establish or make (as a trait, quality, peculiarity) permanent by selective breeding **c** (1) **:** FASTEN, ATTACH, AFFIX ⟨once the toxin has been combined with our tissues, it remains firmly ~*ed* to them —Justina Hill⟩ ⟨the old-fashioned scythe blade . . . usually works loose, unless skillfully ~*ed* —F.D.Smith & Barbara Wilcox⟩ ⟨will be able to ~ a silver and red badge to their vehicles —*N.Y. Times*⟩ (2) **:** to direct in an unwavering or concentrated manner : CONCENTRATE ⟨~*ed* his ambition upon orthopedic surgery as his lifework —J.M.Phalen⟩; *specif*

: to direct an unwavering gaze upon ⟨his mother ~es him icily —Samuel Taylor⟩ ⟨~ed her with his eye —Agnes S. Turnbull⟩ (3) : to hold fast : CAPTURE ⟨tried to ~ her eyes with his, but she was . . . looking away —Marcia Davenport⟩ ⟨seemed capable of being . . . attractive without wanting to ~ the attention of every man near her —Jane Austen⟩ **2 a :** to set or place definitely : STATION, SETTLE ⟨~ed his residence in the city⟩ ⟨~ed himself in New York⟩ **b :** to assign precisely : settle on : DETERMINE, DEFINE ⟨federal and state courts ~ not only wages but hours and working conditions as well —Nathaniel Peffer⟩ ⟨~ the limits of a debate⟩ ⟨wonder why such a lonely spot was ~ed in the first place —Sydney Moorhouse⟩ ⟨difficult to ~ the place of this remarkable statesman in history⟩ ⟨no time or place has yet been ~ed —Jess Whitworth⟩ **c :** ASSIGN, PLACE ⟨~ responsibility⟩ ⟨~ the guilt⟩ ⟨so many mistakes were made . . . that it was difficult to ~ the blame —Isaac Rosenfeld⟩ **3 a :** to set or place in order or in a certain pattern : adjust or settle properly or for a desired end ⟨~ed his face in an expression of mock disgust —C.B.Flood⟩ ⟨~ed his spectacles and read aloud —George Meredith⟩ ⟨~ed its door so that it couldn't be opened from the outside —Raymond Chandler⟩ **b :** to line the hearth of (a furnace) with fettling **4 a** (1) **:** to put in neat-appearing order : ARRANGE, PREPARE ⟨~ed the same room for you —Ellen Glasgow⟩ ⟨~ed their hair in the Hollywood manner —Norman Cousins⟩ ⟨asked me to ~ the table for the family dinner⟩; *specif* : to get (food) ready ⟨~es lunches for the children to take to school —*N.Y. Times*⟩ ⟨coffee ~ed with milk —Lorraine Calhoun⟩ ⟨~ed himself a drink⟩ (2) : REPAIR, MEND ⟨they know how to ~ their cars —Feliks Gross⟩ ⟨called in a plumber to ~ the drain⟩; *also* : to improve the physical condition of : RESTORE, CURE — often used with *up* ⟨that doctor ~ed up my son fine⟩ ⟨told her that food would ~ her up —E.D.Radin⟩ (3) : to take care of : see to : SOLVE ⟨getting your name in the society columns won't ~ anything —*Better Homes & Gardens*⟩ ⟨anything that's wrong with our life today, people expect the schools to ~ —Hannah Lees⟩ — often used with impersonal *it* as object ⟨the battalion surgeon ~ed it so I didn't have to go to the hospital —P.B.Kyne⟩ (4) : CASTRATE, SPAY (5) : to remove a principal means of defense from (as a pet skunk) **b :** to do for (someone) : get even with : PUNISH ⟨wish I could ~ them —P.G.Wodehouse⟩ ⟨God'll ~ you —Dan Browne⟩ ⟨the vigilante committee warned sheepmen away . . . on the threat of ~ing them up —*Amer. Guide Series: Oregon*⟩ **c** (1) **:** to determine the outcome of (a contest) by bribery or other improper methods ⟨all his fights have been ~ed —Budd Schulberg⟩ ⟨arrested for ~ing games —*Sports Illustrated*⟩ ⟨he can ~ an election so that one of his stooges becomes a key official —Malcolm Johnson⟩ : tamper with in advance ⟨a horse ~ed to lose a race⟩ ⟨a ~ed slot machine⟩ (2) : to induce by bribery or influence to give a favorable decision ⟨the jury had been ~ed⟩ : obtain the quashing or disposal of by tampering or other arrangement ⟨~es a traffic ticket or bribes a building inspector —Herman Kogan⟩ **5** *slang* **:** to give (someone) a narcotic ~ *vi* **1 :** to become fixed; *esp* : to become firm or stable **2 a :** to settle or remain permanently : cease from wandering **b :** to direct the gaze or attention : FOCUS, FIXATE ⟨her eyes ~ed sideways for an instant⟩ — often used with *on* or *upon* ⟨the examinee is then directed to ~ on the examiner's right eye —H.G.Armstrong⟩ **c :** ARRANGE, DETERMINE, AGREE, DECIDE ⟨the general had ~ed to be out by that hour —Jane Austen⟩ — usu. used with *on* or *upon* ⟨~ with a contractor on a sum to be paid for the job —*Glasgow Sunday Post*⟩ ⟨had ~ed on the first week in November —Edna Ferber⟩ ⟨~ed on a cabin by the lake to spend vacation⟩ **3 :** to get set : be about to : PREPARE, INTEND — used chiefly in the present participle ⟨are ~ing to ship some cattle —F.B.Gipson⟩ ⟨~ing to cop the first postwar contract in the shipbuilding industry —*Time*⟩ ⟨~ing to leave town for good —Erskine Caldwell⟩ ⟨~ing to rain⟩ **syn** see FASTEN, SET — **fix bayonets 1 :** to attach a bayonet to a rifle — used as a command **2 :** to raise the right hand in a mass swearing-in ceremony — used of Salvationists

2fix \"\ *n* -ES **1 a :** a position of difficulty or embarrassment : PREDICAMENT, DILEMMA ⟨found himself in an awful ~⟩ **b :** the position (as of a ship or airplane) obtained by bearings of fixed objects, by observations of heavenly bodies, or by radio means; *also* : a determination of one's position **2 :** FETTLING **3 a** (1) **:** an arrangment whereby relative immunity from application of the law is obtained through the employment of economic, political, or social influence and esp. through the payment of money to law-enforcement officers or other authorities ⟨collusion between state party officials and the local collector of internal revenue led to tax ~es for gamblers, racketeers, and businessmen —*New Republic*⟩ (2) : the money paid (as by the owner of a gambling house) to a law-enforcement officer or other person wielding influence or authority for protection from the law : BRIBE **b :** an instance of collusion or private agreement that gives special or unfair advantage to one of the parties ⟨in the dream life of the little businessman the sure ~ is replacing the open market —C.W. Mills⟩; *specif* : a sports contest whose outcome is prearranged ⟨virtually impossible for a spectator to recognize a ~ even if he is told —O.R.Cohen⟩ **4** *slang* **:** a shot of a narcotic **5 :** a tall drink made with alcoholic liquor, lemon juice, and sweetening, served in cracked ice, and decorated with fruit ⟨brandy ~⟩ ⟨gin ~⟩ **syn** see PREDICAMENT

fix·able \'fiksəbəl\ *adj* : capable of being fixed

fix·ate \'fik,sāt, *usu* -ād·+V\ *vb* -ED/-ING/-S [L *fixus* (past part. of *figere* to fasten, pierce) + E *-ate* — more at DIKE] *vt* **1 :** to make fixed, stationary, or unchanging : FIX ⟨it is the groups that become *fixated* by orthodoxy that decline —D.F. Fleming⟩ ⟨Protestants have been *fixated* in defending the thought of the reforming sixteenth century —J.W.Nixon⟩ **2 :** to focus one's eyes upon : concentrate one's gaze on ⟨~ a word on the moving sheet —R.S.Woodworth⟩ **3 :** to direct (the libido) toward a pregenital form of gratification ~ *vi* **1 :** to focus or concentrate one's gaze or attention — usu. used with *on* or *upon* ⟨an infant with normal vision . . . will ~ on a light held before him —*Jour. Amer. Med. Assoc.*⟩ **2 :** to undergo arrestment at a certain stage of development ⟨men and women of a certain caliber ~ in any job —H.A.Overstreet⟩; *specif* : to undergo arrestment at a certain stage of psychosexual development

fixated *adj* [*fixate* + *-ed*] : arrested at a certain phase of adjustment or development; *esp* : arrested at a pregenital level of psychosexual development

fix·a·tif *like* FIXATIVE, *or* ¦fiksə¦tēf\ *n* -S [F, prob. fr. E *fixative*] : FIXATIVE

fix·a·tion \fik'sāshən\ *n* -S [ME *fixacioun*, fr. ML *fixation-*, *fixatio*, fr. L *fixus* + *-ation-*, *-atio* -ation] **1 :** the act of fixing or fixating : the state of being fixated ⟨~ of the kidney by operative means⟩ ⟨would entail the ~ of their present condition of inferiority —*New Republic*⟩ ⟨a marketing board should concentrate . . . on distribution and not on price ~ —*Farmer's Weekly* (*So. Africa*)⟩ **2 :** the act or an instance of focusing the eyes upon an object **3 a :** a habit formation : persistent, obsessive, or compulsive behavior **b :** an excessive, obsessive, or unhealthy preoccupation or attachment : OBSESSION ⟨public ~ on the rising tide of juvenile delinquency —*Nervous Child*⟩ ⟨~s about cleanliness⟩ ⟨isn't really love, it's just a ~ —Malcolm Cowley⟩ **4 :** a persistent concentration of libidinal energies upon pregenital zones, objects, persons, or substitute figures and consequent arrest of libidinal development at an immature level **5 :** the immobilization of the parts of a fractured bone esp. by the use of various metal attachments **6 :** NITROGEN FIXATION

fix·a·tive \'fiksəd·iv, -ətiv\ *n* -S [fr. *fixative*, adj., "tending to fix", fr. 1*fix* + *-ative*] : something that fixes or sets: as **a :** a substance (as musk or benzoin) added to a perfume esp. for preventing the more volatile ingredients from evaporating too rapidly **b :** a varnish usu. applied by spraying and used esp. for the protection of crayon drawings **c :** a substance or mixture of substances used to fix living tissue

fixed \'fikst\ *adj* [ME, fr. past part. of *fixen* to fix — more at FIX] **1 a :** securely placed or fastened ⟨a ~ piece of wood⟩ : not adjustable ⟨a ~ resistor⟩ : permanently and definitely located : STATIONARY, IMMOVABLE ⟨there were no ~ theaters in the provinces —G.M.Trevelyan⟩ **b** (1) **:** NONVOLATILE ⟨a ~ acid⟩ ⟨~ carbon⟩ (2) : COMBINED 1b, BOUND 6 ⟨~ nitrogen⟩ (3) : slowly soluble as a result of combination ⟨~ copper fungicides⟩ **c** (1) **:** not subject to change or fluctuation : ABSOLUTE, SETTLED, DEFINITE ⟨revolution . . . could never be a ~ right —S.W.Chapman⟩ ⟨urged the assembly to grant him a ~ salary⟩ ⟨a ~ rate pays for transportation . . . and food on tours —*Current Biog.*⟩ (2) : held to tenaciously and often blindly or obsessively : UNSWERVING, SET ⟨is very ~ in his ways and thought⟩ ⟨the man of ~ ideas . . . is today a public danger —*Nation*⟩ (3) : having a final or crystallized form or character : incapable of further development : FROZEN ⟨America is not yet a ~ and settled land —Barbara Ward⟩ ⟨the respect of the eighteenth century for ~ forms —R.B. West⟩ ⟨animal species are ~ and it is possible to define them in static terms —H.M.Parshley⟩ (4) : recurring on the same date from year to year ⟨~ feast⟩ **d :** RIGID, IMMOBILE, CONCENTRATED ⟨sat with a look of ~ attention on his face⟩ ⟨her thick glasses gave her eyes a ~ stare —Allen Tate⟩ **2 :** supplied with a definite amount of something needed or desirable : PROVIDED ⟨how are we ~ for seamen —*Argosy*⟩; *esp* : supplied with money ⟨began to feel . . . that I was well ~ —W.A. White⟩

fixed accent *n* **1 :** word accent occurring regularly on a specified syllable of a word or on a syllable which is specified in terms of vowel length or consonant combinations in the word **2 :** word accent occurring on the same syllable in derivative and inflectional forms of a root or stem

fixed ammunition *n* : ammunition in which the projectile is permanently attached to a case that contains the primer and the propellant in distinction from separate-loading ammunition

fixed arch *n* : an arch without hinges

fixed armament *n* : guns or weapons that are permanently emplaced

fixed assets *n pl* : tangible assets (as land, buildings, machinery, equipment) of a permanent or long-term nature — compare CAPITAL ASSETS

fixed bayonet *n* : a bayonet when fitted in its place on the end of a rifle

fixed beam *n* : a restrained or built-in beam

fixed block *n* **1 :** a tackle block that is immovable **2 :** one of the sheaves in a ship's chesstree

fixed capital *n* : capital that is durable in character (as buildings and machinery) and can be used over an extended period of time without replacement

fixed cell *n* : a usu. large, irregular, and branching phagocytic cell existing in certain tissues (as connective tissue), lymph nodes, or spleen but sometimes becoming amoeboid and moving through the tissues — compare WANDERING CELL

fixed charge *n* : a recurring expense (as rent, insurance, depreciation, interest on funded debt, taxes on real estate) that is constant and does not fluctuate with business volume

fixed cost *n* : cost that remains constant and does not vary with short-term changes in production

fixed–do system \'fiks(t)'dō-\ *n* : the system of solmization in which a certain syllable (as *do* for C, C♯, C♭) is used for a given tone and its chromatic derivatives without regard to its key relation

fixed exchange *n* : a system of foreign exchange that quotes the value of a foreign unit of currency in terms of the money of the home country — called also *direct exchange;* compare INDIRECT EXCHANGE

fixed–focus \'=¦==\ *adj* : not provided with a focusing adjustment — used of a camera having a lens of small aperture focused at about 8 to 15 feet

fixed gunnery *n* : the firing of a gun having no traverse so that the entire gun platform or aircraft must be maneuvered for aiming — compare FLEXIBLE GUNNERY

fixed idea *n* [prob. trans. of F *idée fixe*] **1 :** a preconceived belief : PREPOSSESSION **2 :** a usu. delusional idea that dominates the whole mental life during a prolonged period (as in certain mental disorders)

fixed–income \'=¦=(,)=\ *adj* : having a uniform or relatively uniform annual income or yield ⟨bonds and preferred stocks are *fixed-income* securities⟩ ⟨white-collar workers form a *fixed-income* group⟩

fixed liability *n* : a liability (as a bond or mortgage) that does not mature for at least one year from the date incurred or from a given balance-sheet date — called also *funded debt*

fixed light *n* **1 :** a light that emits constant beams — compare LIGHTHOUSE **2 :** a circular port with a fixed glass and cover used on a ship (as in a deckhouse or skylight)

fixed·ly \-sədlē, -stl-, -li\ *adv* : in a fixed manner ⟨staring ~ into the empty fireplace —Aldous Huxley⟩ ⟨smiling ~ in a travesty of carefree good nature —Erle Stanley Gardner⟩

fixed·ness \-sədnəs, ·s(t)n-\ *n* -ES : the quality or state of being fixed

fixed oil *n* : a nonvolatile oil; *esp* : FATTY OIL — distinguished from *essential oil*

fixed point *n* : any one of several definite temperatures determined by natural phenomena (as the freezing point of water) and used as reference points in the calibrating of thermometers

fixed price *n* **1 :** a uniform price for all customers as opposed to a price obtained by bargaining **2 :** a price fixed by international agreement or by a governmental price-fixing agency **3 :** a price established by a contract and not subject to subsequent change

fixed service *n* : communication service carried on among fixed stations

fixed sign *n* : one of the four zodiacal signs Taurus, Leo, Scorpio, and Aquarius

fixed signal *n* : a signal of fixed location used to indicate a condition affecting the movement of a train or engine

fixed spool *n* : a fishing spool that remains stationary when line is wound onto it or cast off it

fixed–spool fishing *n* : SPINNING

fixed star *n* : a true star at such great distance that its motion can be measured only by very precise observations over long periods as distinguished from a planet or other obviously moving body

fixed station *n* : a permanently located radio transmitting station used for communicating with similar stations

fixed virus *n* : a virus made constant in its reactions by repeated passage through a host other than the usual host

fixed weight *n* : the weight of the hull, machinery, and all the fittings and parts of an airplane which are fixed in position and nonconsumable

fixed year *n* : a calendar year remaining constant in relation to the seasons

fix·er \'fiksə(r)\ *n* -S **1 :** one that fixes: as **a :** a worker who sets up and adjusts knitting and sewing machines for specific operations **b :** LOOMFIXER **c :** one that is employed in industry to make parts for or to make repairs upon machinery **2 a :** one that intervenes with police officials or other authorities for a person in legal difficulty or with government officials for a person seeking a political favor often with use of corrupt methods and for a fee or other consideration : an influence peddler ⟨a big politico, a ~ you have to see if you want to open a gambling hall —Raymond Chandler⟩ **b :** a go-between (as a lawyer) employed by a circus to make arrangements with officials in advance of performance **c :** one that adjusts matters and esp. smooths over disputes (as between factions of a party) by negotiation : TROUBLESHOOTER ⟨party ~s hustled around to put the pressure on deviating Democrats —*Time*⟩ **d :** PLAY DOCTOR **3 :** FIXATIVE; *specif* : a fixing bath in photographic work **4** *slang* : a peddler of dope

fixer mason *n* : a mason whose main occupation consists in placing the great blocks of stone accurately into position in a building

fixes *pres 3d sing of* FIX, *pl of* FIX

fixing *in sense 1 often* -ən *by persons who ordinarily pronounce the ending "-ing"* iŋ *or* ēŋ\ *n* -S [fr. gerund of 1*fix*] **1 fixings** *pl* : TRIMMINGS, EMBELLISHMENTS, ACCESSORIES; *esp* : the accessories or supplements of a meal ⟨turkey with all the ~s, including mince pie⟩ **2 :** FETTLING

fix·i·ty \'fiksəd·ē, -sətē, -i\ *n* -ES [ML *fixitas*, fr. L *fixus* (past part. of *figere* to fasten, pierce) + *-itas* -ity — more at DIKE] **1 :** the quality or state of being fixed or stable ⟨the idea of the ~ of species —M.F.A.Montagu⟩ ⟨all grammars have the same degree of ~ —Edward Sapir⟩ **2 :** something that is fixed ⟨the so-called *fixities* such as atoms or God —Frank Thilly⟩ ⟨now inventing rules, the unfixing of *fixities* —H.A.Overstreet⟩

fix·ture \'fikschə(r)\ *n* -S [modif. (influenced by *mixture*) of LL *fixura*, fr. L *fixus* + *-ura* -ure] **1 :** the act of fixing : the state of being fixed ⟨its final definite ~ for the 25th was probably due to an attempt to harmonize it with the pre-Christian Roman calendar —G.G.Coulton⟩ **2 a :** something that is fixed or attached as a permanent appendage or a structural part ⟨hanging glass ~s⟩ ⟨a plumbing ~⟩; *specif* : an electric lighting device usu. ornamental and permanently mounted in place ⟨~s providing semi-direct light —*advt*⟩ **b** (1) **:** a device for supporting work during machining without guiding the cutting tools (2) : a similar device for holding parts in the correct position during assembly or testing **c** (1) **:** a chattel that has been so wrought into or annexed to realty (as a house) that it may be regarded as legally a part of it usu. depending upon such considerations as whether it may be removed without irreparable damage, whether the parties (as landlord and tenant) regarded or are presumed by law to have regarded it as removable, whether its annexation was intended to be permanent and to further the purposes for which the structure is designed, or whether its annexation is really necessary to the contemplated use of the structure or only ornamental or convenient — called also *immovable fixture;* opposed to *fitting* (2) : such a chattel still legally the property of the annexer — called also *movable fixture* (3) : a chattel (as shelving or machinery) annexed to realty for purposes of trade or manufacture and legally still the property of the annexer — called also *trade fixture* **d :** an accessory or article that serves a special purpose ⟨an efficient cooking stove . . . alone represented the twentieth century in the ~s of the house —Arnold Bennett⟩ ⟨this new display ~ has been carefully designed to build you year-round sales —*Circle & Monogram*⟩ **3 a** (1) **:** one of a scheduled series of sporting events (as a game, contest, race) ⟨the winner will then meet the leader of the western section, where several ~s have still to be played —*Weekly Scotsman*⟩ (2) : a regularly scheduled event (as a festival or exhibition) ⟨a three-monthly classified calendar of ~s —*Britain: Information & Events*⟩ ⟨submitting a fairly large team of 2½-year-old rams at this ~ —*Westralian Farmers Co-op. Gazette*⟩ ⟨racegoers feel there should be more ~s there —*Sydney* (*Australia*) *Bull.*⟩ **b :** a familiar, invariably present, or permanent item, element, or feature in some particular setting ⟨a simile so vivid that it has become a ~ in anthologies —Bernard DeVoto⟩ ⟨resolved to make foreign economic aid a budget ~ as long as the cold war lasts —*Newsweek*⟩; *esp* : a person of long and continued association (as through residence or employment) with some place, activity, or other setting ⟨now a ~ in the stock department, being a member of the office force there —*Nightmare*⟩ ⟨the year in which he became a ~ at second base —*Current Biog.*⟩ ⟨a ~ in most rosters of the world's best-dressed women —*Time*⟩

fix up *vt* **1 a :** to arrange a settlement of : bring to a conclusion ⟨*fix up* a dispute⟩ ⟨today a contract was definitely *fixed up* —Arnold Bennett⟩ **b :** CONTRIVE, DEVISE ⟨*fixed up* an emergency mast⟩ **c :** FURNISH, EQUIP ⟨*fixed* the room *up* as a study⟩ **2 :** to provide with something needed or desirable : SUPPLY, ACCOMMODATE ⟨*fix up* a small loan⟩ — often used with *with* ⟨*fixed up* his relations with positions —*N.Y. Times*⟩ ⟨can sew up a client merely by *fixing* him *up* with a memorable game at his club —*Time*⟩ **3 :** to dress up : spruce up ⟨*fixed* myself *up* as well as I could —J.B.Benefield⟩

fix·ure \'fikshə(r)\ *n* -S [LL *fixura* — more at FIXTURE] *archaic* : fixed position : FIRMNESS

fixy \'fiksē\ *adj* [1*fix* + *-y*] *dial* : FUSSY, PARTICULAR, ELEGANT

fi·ze·ly·ite \fə'zālē,īt\ *n* -S [Hung *fizélyite*, fr. Sandor *Fizély*, 20th cent. Hung. mining engineer, its discoverer + Hung *-it* -ite] : a mineral $Pb_5Ag_2Sb_8S_{18}$(?) consisting of a lead silver antimony sulfide occurring as a metallic lead-gray prism

fiz·gig \'fiz,gig\ *n* -S [alter. of earlier *fisgig*, perh. fr. *fise* flatus (fr. ME) + *gig* (girl); akin to ME *fist* flatus — more at FEIST] **1** *archaic* **:** a gadding flirting girl or woman **2 :** a firework of damp powder that fizzes or hisses when it explodes **3 :** WHIRLIGIG 1 **4 :** FISHGIG

1fizz \'fiz\ *vi* -ED/-ING/-ES [prob. of imit. origin] **1 :** to make a hissing or sputtering sound (as of a freshly poured effervescent beverage or a burning fuse) : EFFERVESCE **2 :** to exhibit strong excitement or exhilaration ⟨~ing with the desire to learn the latest hot news —P.G.Wodehouse⟩ ⟨letters home ~ed with high spirits —*Time*⟩

2fizz \"\ *n* -ES **1 a :** a hissing sound ⟨the ~ of champagne⟩ **b :** LIVELINESS, ACTIVITY **2 :** an effervescent beverage (as ginger ale or champagne); *specif* : a tall drink variously made of spirituous liquor, carbonated water, and lemon juice often with the yolk or the white of an egg or both, sweetened, and chilled ⟨sloe-gin ~⟩ ⟨brandy ~⟩

fizz·er \-zə(r)\ *n* -S [1*fizz* + *-er*] : a very fast ball in cricket

1fiz·zle \'fizəl\ *vi* **fizzled; fizzled; fizzling** \-z(ə)liŋ\ **fizzles** [prob. alter. of *fist* to break wind (fr. ME *fisten*) + *-le* — more at FEIST] **1** *obs* **:** to break wind quietly **2 :** to make a hissing or sputtering sound ⟨had to drink it hot while it *fizzled* —C.T.Jackson⟩ **3 :** to fail or peter out esp. after a promising start : end feebly or lamely ⟨the attempt at surrender having *fizzled* —P.W.Thompson⟩ ⟨every coach knows the agony of watching a . . . rally ~ —W.L.Myers⟩ — often used with *out* ⟨all attempts at friendliness seemed to ~ out —Clive Arden⟩

2fizzle \"\ *n* -S **1** *archaic* **:** the act of breaking wind quietly **2 :** HISS, SPUTTER, FIZZ **3 :** an abortive effort : FAILURE, FIASCO ⟨the store was a ghastly ~ —E.J.Kahn⟩

fizzwater \'=,==\ *n* : SODA WATER 2a

fizzy \'fizē, -zi\ *adj* -ER/-EST : EFFERVESCENT, FIZZING ⟨poured out the ~ liquid —G.A.Wagner⟩

fjäll \fē'el, 'fyel\ *n* -S *usu cap* [Sw, lit., mountain, fr. OSw *fiæll;* akin to ON *fjall* mountain, fell — more at FELL] : a Swedish breed of small white polled dairy cattle with red or black points and flecking on the sides

fjeld \fē'el, 'fyel\ *n* -S [Dan; akin to ON *fjall* mountain] : a barren plateau of the Scandinavian upland

fjord *or* **fiord** \fē'ȯ|(ə)rd, 'fyȯ|, |(ə)d\ *n* -S [Norw *fjord*, fr. ON *fjörthr* — more at FORD] : a narrow generally deep inlet of the sea between high cliffs or steep slopes (as on the coasts of Norway and Alaska); *also* : an embayment of the coast in a Scandinavian country regardless of the adjacent topography

fjord·ed \-ȯrdəd,-ȯ(ə)dəd\ *adj* : cleft by fjords

fjord shoreline *n* : a shoreline of submergence characterized by the presence of many fjords

fl *abbr* **1** flange **2** flash; flashing **3** flood **4** floor **5** [L *flores*] flowers **6** florin **7** [L *floruit*] he flourished **8** flour **9** fluid **10** flush **11** flute

FL *abbr* **1** [L *falsa lectio*] false reading **2** flag lieutenant **3** flight lieutenant **4** focal length **5** footlambert **6** foreign language

flab \'flab\ *n* -S [back-formation fr. *flabby*] : soft flabby body tissue

flab·ber·gast \'flabə(r),gast, -gaa(ə)st, -gaist,-gåst\ *vt* -ED/-ING/-S [origin unknown] : to overwhelm with shock, surprise, or wonder (as by extraordinary statements or unexpected news) **syn** see SURPRISE

flab·ber·gast·ing·ly \'==,===, ,=='===\ *adv* [*flabbergasting* (pres. part. of *flabbergast*) + *-ly*] : to a flabbergasting degree ⟨a ~ precise young man⟩

flab·bi·ly \'flabəlē, -li\ *adv* : in a flabby manner

flab·bi·ness \-bēnəs, -bin-\ *n* -ES : the quality or state of being flabby ⟨the ~ of wasted unused muscles⟩ ⟨moral ~⟩

flab·by \'flabē, -bi\ *adj* -ER/-EST [alter. of *flappy*] **1** *of body tissues* **a :** slack and flaccid : yielding to the touch and easily moved or shaken : lacking tone and resilience or firmness ⟨a sagging ~ belly hanging over his belt⟩ **b :** weak and enfeebled ⟨muscles ~ from disuse⟩ **2 :** weak and ineffective : FEEBLE ⟨~ liberals⟩ ⟨dull ~ writings⟩; *sometimes* : tending to cause a flabby state (as of the mind or will) ⟨roused from his ~ despondency⟩

flabel *n or vb* [*flabel*, n., fr. L *flabellum* fan; *flabel*, v., fr. *flabel*, n.] *obs* : FAN

flab·el·lar·i·um \,flabə'la(a)rēəm\ *n, pl* **flabellar·ia** \-rēə\ [NL, fr. L *flabellum*] : VIBRACULUM

fla·bel·late \flə'belət, 'flabə,lāt\ *also* **fla·bel·li·form** \flə'belə,fȯrm\ *adj* [*flabellate* prob. fr. (assumed) NL *flabellatus*, fr. L *flabellum* fan + *-atus* -ate; *flabelliform* prob. fr. (assumed)

NL *flabelliformis*, fr. L *flabelli-* + *-formis* -form] : resembling a fan in shape

flabelli- *comb form* [L, fan, fr. *flabellum*] : fan ⟨*flabelliform*⟩ ⟨*flabellinerved*⟩

fla·bel·li·nerved \flə'belə +,-\ *adj, of a leaf* : having the veins radiating like the spokes of a fan ⟨the ginkgo has ~ leaves⟩

fla·bel·lum \flə'beləm\ *n, pl* **flabel·la** \-elə\ [LL, fr. L, fan, dim. of *flabrum* breeze, fr. *flare* to blow — more at BLOW] **1** : a ceremonial fan: **a** : a fan used in religious ceremonies **b** : a fan displayed on state occasions among the appurtenances of certain dignitaries (as a pope or formerly a bishop or royal personage) **2** [NL, fr. L] : a body organ or part that resembles a fan: as **a** : the epipodite of certain limbs of crustaceans **b** : the proximal exite of the limb of a branchiopod

flac·cid \'flaksəd, ÷'flasəd, ÷'flaasəd\ *adj* [L *flaccidus*, fr. *flaccus* flabby] **1 a** : yielding to pressure for want of firmness and stiffness : FLABBY ⟨a ~ muscle⟩ **b** *of a plant cell or tissue* : deficient in turgor **2** : weak and ineffective : lacking vigor or force ⟨~ leadership⟩ ⟨~ opinions drably expressed⟩ — **flac·cid·ly** *adv*

flabella 1b

flac·cid·i·ty \flak'sidəd·ē, ÷fla(a)'si-, -idətē, -i\ *also* **flac·cid·ness** \'flaksədnəs, ÷'fla(a)səd-\ *n* -ES : the quality or state of being flaccid

flaccid paralysis *n* : paralysis in which muscle tone is lacking in the affected muscles and in which tendon reflexes are decreased or absent

fla·che·rie \,flashə'rē, fla'shrē, -lā-\ *also* **flach·ery** \'flashərē\ *n, pl* **flacheries** [F *flacherie*, fr. F dial. (Dauphiné) *flacharié*, fr. Prov *flacarié* flaccidity, flacherie, fr. *flac* flaccid, soft, fr. L *flaccus* flabby] : a disease of silkworms and other caterpillars marked by loss of appetite, sluggishness, dysentery, and flaccidity of the body, terminating fatally with rapid darkening and liquefaction of the body, and caused by an infective agent not certainly identified

1**fla·cian** \'flāsh(ē)ən\ *n* -S *usu cap* [Matthias *Flacius* Illyricus †1575 Ger. Protestant theologian + E *-an*] : an adherent to Flacian doctrines or views

2**flacian** \"\ *adj, usu cap* : relating to or in accordance with the Lutheran teaching of Matthias Flacius Illyricus who accused Melanchthon and the adiaphorists of falsifying Luther's views

1**flack** \'flak\ *vb* -ED/-ING/-S [ME *flacken*, perh. alter. of *flakeren* to flutter] *vi, now dial* : FLAP, FLUTTER ⟨clothes ~*ing* on the line⟩ ~ *vt, now dial* : FLICK ⟨~ the dust from your collar⟩

2**flack** \"\ *n* -S [imit.] **1** *dial Eng* : STROKE, BLOW, FLAP **2** : a recurrent sound of striking (as of a loose tire chain on a frozen road)

3**flack** \"\ *n* -S [origin unknown] : PRESS AGENT

4**flack** *var of* FLAK

flack·er \'flakə(r)\ *vi* -ED/-ING/-S [ME *flakeren*; akin to MD *flackeren* to flutter, MHG *vlackern* to flicker, ON *flökra* to roam around, and perh. to L *plangere* to beat — more at PLAINT] *dial Eng* : FLUTTER, PALPITATE

flac·on \'flakən\ *n* -S [F, fr. MF *flacon*, *flascon* — more at FLAGON] : a small usu. ornamental bottle with a tight cap

fla·cour·tia \flə'kůrd·ēə, fla'-, -kōr-\ *n, cap* [NL, fr. Étienne de *Flacourt* †1660 Fr. colonizer + NL *-ia*] : a small genus of often spiny trees or shrubs (family Flacourtiaceae) of tropical Asia and Africa with leaves pinnately veined, flowers in small axillary racemes or clusters, sepals imbricated, and seed enclosed in a stony covering which is surrounded by an edible pulp — see GOVERNOR'S PLUM

fla·cour·ti·a·ce·ae \=,==ˈāsē,ē\ *n pl, cap* [NL, fr. *Flacourtia*, type genus + *-aceae*] : a family of chiefly tropical trees and shrubs (order Parietales) having flowers with numerous stamens and often with enlarged receptacle and undifferentiated perianth and including the chaulmoogras — see FLACOURTIA — **fla·cour·ti·a·ceous** \=;==;āshəs\ *adj*

1**flae** \'flā\ *chiefly Scot var of* FLAY

2**flae** \"\ *chiefly Scot var of* FLEA

1**flaff** \'flaf\ *vb* -ED/-ING/-S [*flaff* fr. ME (Sc) *flaffen*, of imit. origin; *flaffer* freq. of *flaff*] *vi or* **flaf·fer** \-afər\ *chiefly Scot* : FLAP, FLUTTER ⟨~ in the wind⟩ ~ *vt, chiefly Scot* : to cause to flutter or flap ⟨the bird ~*s* his wings⟩

2**flaff** \"\ *n* -S **1** *chiefly Scot* : a movement made by flapping or fluttering **2** *chiefly Scot* : a burst or gust esp. of wind

1**flag** \'flag, -aa(ə)-,-ai-\ *n* -S [ME *flagge* reed, rush] **1** : any of various monocotyledonous plants with long ensiform leaves: as **a** : a plant of the genus *Iris*: as (1) : the common yellow-flowered iris (*I. pseudacorus*) of Europe (2) : either of two blue-flowered No. American irises (*I. versicolor* and *I. prismatica*) **b** : SWEET FLAG **c** : CATTAIL 1 **2** : a leaf of a flag or of a cereal grass

2**flag** \"\ *vt* **flagged; flagged; flagging; flags** : to caulk (as the joints of a barrel) with cattails or other flags

3**flag** \"\ *n* -S [ME *flagge* piece of turf, flagstone, fr. ON *flaga* slab; akin to ON *flag* spot where the turf has been cut, OE *flēan* to skin — more at FLAY] **1** *dial Brit* : a piece of sod or turf **2** *dial Brit* : a slice of earth turned over in plowing **3 a** : a hard evenly stratified stone (as fine-grained sandstone or firm shale) that splits into flat pieces suitable for paving ⟨a valuable ~ quarry⟩ **b** : a piece of such stone; *esp* : a thin piece split from such stone ⟨looked down at the cracked ~*s* beneath which the roots spread —Virginia Woolf⟩ **c** : a surface of such stone ⟨scrubbed down the ~ of the terrace each morning⟩

walk paved with flags

4**flag** \"\ *vt* **flagged; flagged; flagging; flags** [ME *flaggen*, fr. *flagge*, n. — more at 3FLAG] : to lay (as a pavement) with flags : cover (as an earthen surface) with flat stones

5**flag** \"\ *n* -S [perh. fr. 1*flag*] **1 a** : a usu. rectangular piece of fabric (as light flexible cloth) of distinctive design that is used as a symbol (as of a nation) or as a signaling device and is usu. displayed hanging free from a staff or halyard to which it is attached by one edge — see 2FLY 6c, HOIST; compare BANNER, ENSIGN, PENNANT, PENNON, STANDARD **b** : a flag that is the personal symbol of an admiral and is hoisted on a ship on which he is present and in command **c** : a representation of a flag ⟨embroidered a ~ on the cushion⟩ ⟨little ~*s* stenciled on the boxes⟩ ⟨a ~ of growing flowers⟩ **d** : something that is used like a flag to signal or attract attention **2 a flags** *pl, archaic* : the secondaries of a bird's wing **b** : the tail of certain dogs (as setters and hounds); *also* : the long hairs fringing a setter's tail **c** : the tail of a deer **3** : any of certain signaling devices: as **a** : one of the cross strokes on a musical note of less than a quarter-note time value ⟨the eighth note has one ~, the sixteenth two⟩ — called also *hook* **b** : a marker (as a piece of cardboard or a turned rule) inserted between lines of type to remind the compositor that an addition or correction must be made at that place — called also *watchman* **c** : RANGE POLE **d** : a thin oblong piece (as of metal or plastic) projecting from a movable rod by which it may be raised or lowered that is used for signaling (as of the availability of a taxi or the presence of mail in a rural delivery box) **e** : MASTHEAD 2a **f** : a usu. colored metal or plastic clip that may be attached to a card or sheet of paper as a reminder of some future attention required **g** : a marker (as a small strip of colored paper) placed to protrude from a roll of paper at a place where it has broken and been spliced **4** : the end of a bristle for use in brushes that is farthest from the root, is relatively soft and flexible and often somewhat frayed, and is usu. the free end in the finished brush **5** : something usu. or properly symbolized by the display of a particular flag: as **a** : FLAGSHIP **b** : an admiral functioning in his office of command **c** : NATIONALITY; *esp* : the nationality of registration of a ship or airplane — called also *registry* **6** : FEATHER 7 **7** [7*flag*] : a wilted or dead leaf or a branch with such leaves on an otherwise healthy plant (as a tree) that is frequently indicative of an interference with the water supply to the leaves

flag 1a

syn ENSIGN, BANNER, STANDARD, COLORS, JACK, PENNANT, PENDANT, PENNON, STREAMER: FLAG is a very general term; in most situations it lends itself readily to substitutions for the more specific words following. ENSIGN, commonly used in naval or nautical affairs, often indicates a flag showing nationality or nation. BANNER, often a romantic and literary synonym for FLAG, is frequently used in situations involving emotional ties and appeals ⟨the star-spangled *banner*, oh! long may it wave —F.S.Key⟩ STANDARD is often used in reference to the flag, often an elongated one, of an individual, a cause or party, or a mounted or motorized unit, esp. when serving as a rallying point ⟨with the *standards* of the peoples plunging through the thunderstorm —Alfred Tennyson⟩ ⟨after the execution of Charles I, the royal *standard* was replaced by the Commonwealth *standard* —W.G.Perrin⟩ COLORS — the form more common than the singular COLOR — may refer to national flags, flags emblematic of affiliation or partisanship, flags of most military units ⟨the call to the *colors*⟩ ⟨to join the *colors*⟩ ⟨a ship carrying French *colors*⟩ ⟨afraid to show his *colors*⟩ ⟨the British *colors* were planted on the summit of the breach —Duke of Wellington †1852⟩ The following words are more specific and limited in use: JACK typically designates a small oblong flag indicating nationality and is used on the bowsprits of ships. PENNANT and PENDANT, the latter more English than American, typically refer to flags more or less triangular in shape used to identify individual units or to signal. PENNON may apply to a narrower flag, one suitable to hanging from a lance ⟨that squadron swung around . . . with a wicked whistling of wind in the *pennons* of its lances —Rudyard Kipling⟩ STREAMER is likely to refer to a long narrow flag capable of streaming in the wind.

6**flag** \"\ *vb* **flagged; flagged; flagging; flags** *vt* **1 a** : to put a flag on (as for decoration or identification) ⟨the course will be *flagged* at regular intervals⟩ ⟨he *flagged* the important pages with bright red tabs clipped to the margins⟩ **b** : to cause (a horse) to be docked **2 a** : to catch the attention of by or as if by signaling with a flag; *esp* : to signal to stop (as by waving the hand or a flag) ⟨hurry and ~ me a taxi or I'll miss my train⟩ — often used with *down* ⟨the watchman *flagged* down the truck⟩ **b** : to decoy (game) by waving a flag, handkerchief, or other object to arouse curiosity **c** : to convey (as a message) by means of flag signals ⟨*flagging* his orders to the other ships⟩ ~ *vi* **1** : to wave or signal with a flag **2** *of a pointing dog* : to wag the tail slightly when uncertain as to the exact position of birds

7**flag** \"\ *vb* **flagged; flagged; flagging; flags** [origin unknown] *vi* **1 a** *of flexible bodies* : to hang loose without stiffness : bend down : be loose, yielding, or limp **b** *of a plant* : to droop esp. from lack of water; *often* : to produce flags **2** *obs* : to move weakly — used chiefly of wings **3 a** : to become unsteady or feeble : slacken and decline : fall away ⟨his interest *flagged* as their lack of success continued⟩ ⟨the men get impatient and the morale ~*s* —Michael Gladych⟩ **b** : to grow spiritless and dull ⟨his wit *flagged* under such constant strain⟩ **c** : to decline in interest or attraction ⟨when everyone had had a say, the topic *flagged*⟩ ⟨such self-indulgent pleasures soon ~⟩ ~ *vt* **1** *archaic* **a** : to cease to use (as wings) vigorously : allow to move weakly **b** : to permit to droop or to fall into feebleness **2** : to exhaust the vigor or vitality of : ENERVATE ⟨such sorrow *flags* the strongest spirit⟩

syn see DROOP

8**flag** \"\ *adj, archaic* : PENDULOUS, DROOPING

9**flag** \"\ *n* -S [perh. modif. of (assumed) LG *vleger*, a Frisian coin, fr. MLG *vleger*] *Brit* : GROAT, FOURPENCE

10**flag** \"\ *n* -S [prob. alter. of *flake*] *chiefly Scot* : a large snowflake

flag alarm *n* [5*flag*] : a signal made by a small flag that appears on the indicator of an instrument which begins giving unreliable readings

flag badge *n* : a badge or cognizance used for distinction on a flag whose design except for the badge is used in common by two or more dominions, colonies, or territories within an empire

flag bag *n* : a metal or wooden locker or other container in which the signal flags of a ship are stored

flag blue *n* : a grayish to dark purplish blue that is bluer and less strong than independence

flag bottom *n* [1*flag*] : a rush seat of a chair or settee — called also *flag seat*

flag bridge *n* [5*flag*] : the first bridge above the flight deck on an aircraft carrier : the admiral's bridge

flag captain *n* : the commanding officer of a flagship

flag carrier *n* : an air or sea transport line flying the flag of the country to which it belongs

flag country *n* : the part of a flagship set aside for the use of its flag officer

flag day *n* **1** *usu cap F&D* : an annual celebration or holiday (as June 14 in the U.S.) for commemorating the origin of or for honoring a national flag **2** *Brit* : a day on which contributions (as to a charity) are solicited and small flags are given to contributors — compare TAG DAY

flag discrimination *n* : preferential treatment of ships of a particular registry in the assignment of cargo

flagella *pl of* FLAGELLUM

1**flag·el·lant** \'flajələnt, flə'jel-\ *n* -S [L *flagellant-*, *flagellans*, pres. part. of *flagellare* to whip] : one that whips: as **a** *usu cap* : a member of one of the organized groups that since the 12th century have practiced self-castigation as a religious rite **b** : a person who responds sexually to being beaten by or to beating another person — **flag·el·lant·ism** \-ən,tizəm\ *n* -S

2**flagellant** \"\ *adj* [L *flagellant-*, *flagellans*] **1** : FLAGELLATING, LASHING ⟨a vicious ~ speech⟩ **2** : believing in or practicing flagellation

fla·gel·lar \flə'jelə(r), 'flajəl-\ *adj* [*flagellum* + *-ar*] : of or relating to a flagellum

flagellar antigen *n* : any of various antigens associated with the flagella of motile bacteria and used in serological identification of various bacteria — distinguished from *somatic antigen*; called also *H antigen*

flag·el·lar·ia \,flajə'la(a)rēə\ *n, cap* [NL, fr. L *flagellum* whip, shoot of a plant + NL *-aria*] : a small genus (the type of the family Flagellariaceae) of tropical or subtropical monocotyledonous herbs with sheathing leaves terminating in a cirrhus and small persistent flowers in panicles — **flag·el·lar·i·a·ceous** \=;==,==;āshəs\ *adj*

1**flag·el·la·ta** \,flajə'lād·ə, -lād·ə\ [NL, fr. *flagellum* + *-ata*] *syn of* MASTIGOPHORA

2**flagellata** \"\ [NL, fr. *flagellum* + *-ata*] *syn of* FLAGELLATAE

flag·el·la·tae \-lād·,ē, -lād·,ē\ *n pl, cap* [NL, fr. *flagellum* + *-atae* (fr. L, fem. pl. of *-atus* -ate)] *in some classifications* : a class of flagellated unicellular organisms comprising the Chrysomonadina, Cryptomonadina, Euglenoidina, and closely related flagellate and algal organisms and being nearly equivalent in scope to Phytomastigina of other classifications

1**flag·el·late** \'flajə,lāt, *usu* -ād.+V\ *vt* -ED/-ING/-S [L *flagellatus*, past part. of *flagellare*, fr. *flagellum* whip, dim. of *flagrum* whip; akin to MD *blaken* to blow, wave, ON *blaka* to wave, flutter, Lith *blaškyti* to throw back and forth] **1** : WHIP, SCOURGE, FLOG **2** : to drive, punish, or stigmatize by or as if by whipping ⟨the papers *flagellated* the levity of his conduct⟩ ⟨*flagellating* herself to her daily task⟩

2**flag·el·late** \-,lə̇t, -,lāt, flə'jelə̇t, *usu* |d.+V\ *adj* [NL *flagellatus*, fr. *flagellum* + L *-atus* -ate] **1 a** : having or bearing flagella **b** : shaped like a flagellum **2** [3*flagellate*] : of, relating to, or caused by flagellates ⟨~ dysentery⟩

3**flagellate** \"\ *n* -S [NL *Flagellata* & *Flagellatae*] : a flagellate protozoan or alga

4**flag·el·late** \'flajə,lāt, *usu* -ād.+V\ *vi* -ED/-ING/-S [back-formation fr. 2*flagellation*] : to develop a flagellum

flag·el·lat·ed \'flajə,lād·əd\ *adj* [2*flagellate* + *-ed*] : FLAGELLATE 1 ⟨~ organisms⟩

flagellated chamber *n* : one of the outpouchings of the wall of the central cavity of a sponge that is lined with choanocytes and connects with incurrent canals through prosopyles

1**flag·el·la·tion** \,flajə'lāshən\ *n* -S [ME *flagellacion*, fr. L *flagellation-*, *flagellatio*, fr. *flagellatus* (past part. of *flagellare* to whip) + *-ion-*, *-io* -ion] : an act or instance of flagellating : BEATING, FLOGGING, SCOURGING; *esp* : the practice of a flagellant

2**flagellation** \"\ *n* -S [*flagellum* + *-ation*] : the formation of flagella; *also* : the flagella or the arrangement of flagella on an organism or surface

flag·el·la·tor \'==,lād·ə(r)\ *n* -S [ML, fr. L *flagellatus* + *-or*] : one that flagellates : SCOURGER, FLAGELLANT

flag·el·la·to·ry \'flajələ,tōrē, flə'jel-\ *adj* [1*flagellate* + *-ory*] : relating to flagellation

flag·el·lif·er·ous \,flajə'lif(ə)rəs\ *adj* [prob. fr. F *flagellifère* flagelliferous (fr. *flagelli-* — fr. NL *flagellum* — + *-fère* -ferous — fr. L *-fer*) + E *-ous* — more at -FEROUS] : having flagella : FLAGELLATE

fla·gel·li·form \flə'jelə,fȯrm\ *adj* [ISV *flagelli-* (fr. NL *flagellum*) + *-form*] : elongated, slender, and tapering like a flagellum

flag·el·lo·sis \,flajə'lōsə̇s\ *n, pl* **flagello·ses** \-ō,sēz\ [NL, fr. *flagell-* (fr. *Flagellata*) + *-osis*] : infestation with or disease caused by flagellate protozoans

fla·gel·lum \flə'jeləm\ *n, pl* **flagel·la** \-elə\ *also* **flagellums** [L, whip, shoot of a plant] **1** : WHIP, SCOURGE **2** [NL, fr. L] : any of various elongated filiform appendages of animals: as **a** : the slender distal part of some antennae **b** : a sensory organ that suggests a comb on the chelicerae of most solpugids and pseudoscorpions **3** [NL, fr. L] : a long tapering process that projects singly or in groups from a cell or microorganism, is possibly equivalent to a much enlarged cilium, and is the primary organ of motion of flagellated protozoans and many algae, bacteria, and zoospores **4** : a long slender shoot (as a stolon or runner) of a plant

1**fla·geo·let** \,flajə'let, -lā\ *n* -S [F, fr. OF *flajolet*, fr. *flajol* flute (fr. assumed VL *flabeolum*, fr. L *flare* to blow) + *-et* — more at BLOW] **1** : a small fipple flute resembling the treble recorder but having usu. four finger holes and two thumbholes and a cylindrical mouthpiece **2** : a labial 2-foot pipe-organ stop with a flute quality

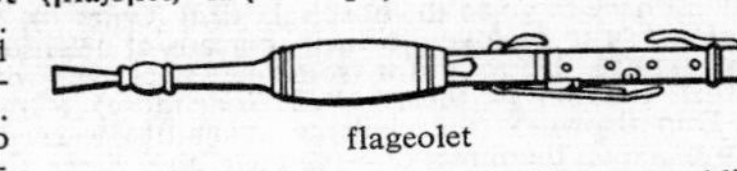

flageolet

2**fla·geo·let** \flȧzhȯlā\ *n, pl* **flageolets** \"\ [F, modif. (influenced by *flageolet* flute) of Prov *faioulet*, fr. OProv *faiolet*, dim. of (assumed) OProv *faiol* kidney bean (whence Prov *faiou*), fr. (assumed) VL *fabeolus*, alter. (influenced by L *faba* bean) of L *phaseolus* kidney bean — more at FRIJOL, BEAN] : a green kidney bean of France

flageolet tone *n* : 2HARMONIC 1b

flagfish \'=,=\ *n* : any of several brilliantly colored fishes chiefly of tropical seas

flag flower *n* : an iris flower

flagged *past of* FLAG

flag·ger \'flagə(r), -laag-,-laig-\ *n* -S [1*flag* + *-er*] *dial* : a wild iris

1**flag·ging** \'flagiŋ, -laag-,-laig-, -gēŋ\ *adj* [fr. pres. part. of 7*flag*] **1** : LANGUID, WEAK **2** : DWINDLING, DIMINISHING, WEAKENING ⟨~ hopes⟩ ⟨~ demands for farm products⟩ — **flag·ging·ly** *adv*

2**flagging** \"\ *n* -S [3*flag* + *-ing*] **1** : flagstones for paving **2** : a pavement or walk of flagstones

flagging iron *n* [*flagging* fr. gerund of 2*flag*] : a prying tool with a double-hooked head used in caulking barrels with flags or for removing barrelheads

1**flag·gy** \'flagē, -aag-,-aig-, -gi\ *adj* [ME *flaggi*, fr. *flagge* reed, rush + *-i*, -y -y] **1** : abounding with flags or other reedy plants ⟨a ~ marsh⟩ **2** *obs* : like an iris or other flag

2**flaggy** \"\ *adj* [7*flag* + *-y*] **1** *archaic* : soft and flabby **2** *archaic* : hanging limply : DROOPING

3**flaggy** \"\ *adj* [3*flag* + *-y*] **1** *of rock* : splitting or tending to split into layers of suitable thickness for use as flagstones : formed of laminated strata from 10 to 100 millimeters in thickness **2** *of soil* : full of pieces of flagstone

4**flaggy** \"\ *adj* [prob. fr. 5*flag* + *-y*] : split and frayed ⟨the ~ end of a bristle⟩ — compare 5FLAG 4

flag·i·tate \'flajə,tāt\ *vt* -ED/-ING/-S [L *flagitatus*, past part. of *flagitare*; akin to L *flagrum* whip] : IMPORTUNE — **flag·i·ta·tion** \,==ˈtāshən\ *n* -S

fla·gi·tious \flə'jishəs\ *adj* [ME *flagicious*, fr. L *flagitiosus*, fr. *flagitium* shameful or disgraceful thing + *-osus* -ose; akin to L *flagrum* whip — more at FLAGELLATE] **1** : disgracefully or shamefully criminal : grossly wicked : SCANDALOUS **2** : guilty of or characterized by enormous crimes or scandalous vices : VILLAINOUS, CORRUPT **syn** see VICIOUS

fla·gi·tious·ly *adv* : in a flagitious manner : VICIOUSLY, WICKEDLY

fla·gi·tious·ness *n* -ES : the quality or state of being flagitious : CORRUPTION, VICE, VILLAINY

flag law *n* : a law that prescribes rules concerning the use and display of the flag of a sovereign body (as a nation)

flag lieutenant *n* : an officer on an admiral's staff who acts as his personal aide

flag lily *n* : 1FLAG 1a

flag line *n* : a sea or sometimes air transport line under a particular national registry ⟨American *flag lines* in the Pacific⟩; *often* : FLAG CARRIER

flag list *n* : a list of admirals of a particular navy

flag·man \'=mən\ *n, pl* **flagmen** **1** *obs* : ADMIRAL **2** : a person who signals with or as if with a flag esp. to warn of danger (as on a highway) or to direct some operation (as the use of hoisting equipment or the maneuvering of heavy machinery) **3** : a member of a surveying party who carries a range pole

flag of convenience : registry of a merchant ship under a foreign flag in order to compete with ships of foreign nations ⟨must operate under a *flag of convenience* or go out of business —Walter Hamshar⟩

flag officer *n* **1** : a naval officer entitled to display a flag with one or more stars that indicate his command rank ⟨in the U. S. Navy a *flag officer* with two stars is a rear admiral⟩ — compare GENERAL OFFICER **2** : a person (as the president of a yachting club) entitled to display a special identifying flag on his boat

flag of truce : a white flag carried or displayed to an enemy as an invitation to conference or parley or to signify a desire of making some communication not hostile; *sometimes* : the bearer of such a flag

flag·on \'flagən, -laig-\ *n* -S [ME *flagon*, *flakon*, fr. MF *flacon*, *flascon*, fr. LL *flascon-*, *flasco* bottle — more at FLASK] **1** : a vessel for liquid (as wine or liquor): as **a** : a large usu. metal or pottery vessel with handle and spout and often a lid **b** : a vessel used to hold eucharistic wine **c** : a large bulging short-necked bottle; *sometimes* : a glass flacon **2 a** : the contents of a flagon ⟨a ~ of wine⟩ **b** : a measure usu. of about two quarts

flagon 1b

flag plot *n* : the admiral's tactical and navigational control room aboard a flagship

flagpole \'=,=\ *n* **1** : a pole to raise a flag on **2** : RANGE POLE

fla·gran·cy \'flāgrənsē, -si *also* -la(i)g-\ *also* **fla·grance** \-n(t)s\ *n, pl* **flagrancies** *also* **flagrances** [L *flagrantia* glowing heat, fr. *flagrant-*, *flagrans* + *-ia* -y] **1** : the quality or state of being flagrant : ATROCITY ⟨the ~ of his vicious conduct⟩ **2** *obs* : a burning or heated state

flag rank *n* : any of the naval grades senior to that of captain — compare RANK table

1**fla·grant** \'flāgrənt *also* -la(i)g-\ *adj* [ME, fr. ML *flagrant-*, *flagrans*, alter. of L *fragrant-*, *fragrans* — more at FRAGRANT] *dial* : FRAGRANT

2**flagrant** \"\ *adj* [L *flagrant-*, *flagrans*, pres. part. of *flagrare* to flame, burn — more at BLACK] **1** *archaic* : FLAMING, GLOWING, BURNING **2** *archaic, of a war or other contest* : carried on hotly : RAGING **3** : extremely, flauntingly, or purposefully conspicuous usu. because of uncommon evil, unworthiness, unpleasantness, or truculence : glaringly evident : NOTORIOUS ⟨~ neglect of duty⟩ ⟨even in the most ~ crimes had denied the justice and righteousness of capital punishment —Jack London⟩

syn GLARING, GROSS, RANK: FLAGRANT may describe offenses or errors so conspicuously or outstandingly bad that it is impossible not to notice them ⟨ended their sinful career by open and *flagrant* mutiny and were shot for it —Rudyard Kipling⟩ ⟨the extremes of wealth and poverty were most *flagrant*, slums crowding the marble palaces of the rich —Allan Nevins & H.S.Commager⟩ GLARING applies to the obtrusively conspicuous; it may suggest the painfully and harshly vivid ⟨this evil is so *glaring*, so inexcusable by any sophistry that the cleverest landlord can devise —G.B.Shaw⟩ ⟨*glaring* imperfections which go far beyond a mere lack of verbal felicity —J.W.Krutch⟩ GROSS may refer to inexcusable faults or offenses displayed blatantly, callously, coarsely, and without mitigation or palliation ⟨my anger and disgust at his *gross* earthy egoism had vanished —W.H.Hudson †1922⟩ ⟨an ordinary Fascist type of state, *gross*, brutal, and violent —William Empson⟩ RANK may apply to what is openly objectionable in the extreme and utterly stigmatized ⟨*rank* heresy⟩ ⟨it was hatred, simple hatred, that *rank* poison fatal to Mr. Hazard's health, which now plagued his veins —Elinor Wylie⟩

fla·gran·te de·lic·to \flə¦grantēdə'lik(,)tō, flä¦-\ *or in* **flagrante delicto** \,inf-\ *adv* [ML, lit., while the crime is blazing] : in the very act of committing a misdeed ⟨caught the thief *flagrante delicto*⟩ — sometimes used substantively usu. without *in*

fla·grant·ly *adv* [[2]*flagrant* + *-ly*] : in a flagrant manner : NOTORIOUSLY

fla·grant·ness *n* -ES : the quality or state of being flagrant ⟨punishment was according to the ~ of the crime⟩

flagration *n* -S [prob. back-formation fr. *conflagration*] *obs* : CONFLAGRATION, FIRE

flagroot \'=,=\ *n* : the root of the sweet flag

flags \'flagz, -aa(ə)gz,-aigz\ *n pl but sing or pl in constr, slang* : a naval signalman

flag seat \'=¦=\ *n* [[1]*flag*] : FLAG BOTTOM

flag secretary *n* : an admiral's aide who is usu. senior to the flag lieutenant and handles the correspondence

flagsetter \'=,==\ *n* : one that lays flagstones

flagship \'=,=\ *n* **1** : the ship that carries the flag officer or the commander of a fleet or subdivision thereof and flies his flag **2** : the finest or largest ship of a shipping line

flag–signal \'=¦==\ *vt* : to signal by flagging

flag smut *n* [[1]*flag*] **1** : a smut of cereal and other grasses that chiefly affects the leaves and stems and is characterized by formation of linear chains of sori within the plant tissues which later rupture releasing black masses of spores and causing fraying of affected areas; *esp* : such a disease of wheat caused by a smut fungus (*Urocystis tritici*) **2** : a smut fungus causing flag smut

flagstaff \'=,=\ *n* : a staff on which a flag is hoisted

flag station *n* : a flag stop on a railroad

[1]**flagstone** \'=,=\ *n, often attrib* [[3]*flag* + *stone*] : [3]FLAG 3 ⟨a large room with a ~ floor —Flora Thompson⟩

[2]**flagstone** \"\ *vt* : to lay flagstone upon

flag stop *n* : a point at which a vehicle engaged in public transportation stops only on prearrangement or signal (as by display of a flag)

flag–wagger \'=,==\ *n, chiefly Austral* : FLAG-WAVER

flag–waver \'=,==\ *n* **1** : one that waves a flag (as in signaling) **2 a** : a chauvinistic patriot **b** : a vociferous partisan (as of a class or a political movement) **3** : something (as a song) that tends to rouse patriotic sentiment

flag–waving \'=,==\ *n* -S : ardently or violently emotional appeal to or expression of patriotic or partisan sentiment

[1]**flail** \'flāl, *esp before pause or consonant* -āəl\ *n* -S [ME *fleil, flail* flail, whip, partly fr. (assumed) OE *flegel* flail (whence OE *fligel*) & partly fr. MF *flaiel, flael* flail, whip; (assumed) OE *flegel* akin to OHG *flegil* flail; both fr. a prehistoric WGmc word borrowed fr. LL *flagellum* flail, fr. L *flagellum* whip; MF *flaiel, flael* fr. LL *flagellum* flail & L *flagellum* whip — more at FLAGELLATE] **1** : an instrument for threshing grain from the ear by hand consisting of a wooden handle at the end of which a stouter and shorter stick is so hung as to swing freely — see SWIPLE **2 a** : a primitive weapon (as a morning star) that resembles the agricultural flail in basic structure **b** : any of certain devices used to detonate mines; *sometimes* : a vehicle (as a tank) by which such a flail is propelled **3** *obs* : a swinging part (as a gate bar or a lever of a press)

[2]**flail** \"\ *vb* -ED/-ING/-S [ME *flailen*, fr. *fleil, flail*, n.] *vt* **1** : SCOURGE, WHIP; *sometimes* : to drive by beating ⟨~*ed* the pig back to his sty⟩ **2 a** : to strike with or as if with a flail ⟨~*ing* his opponent about the head and shoulders⟩ ⟨startled wings ~*ed* the water⟩ **b** : to move, swing, or beat as though wielding a flail ⟨~*ed* his arms in front of his face to drive away the insects⟩ **3** : to thresh (grain) with a flail ~ *vi* **1** : to engage or participate in flailing ⟨propellers ~*ing* futilely⟩ ⟨they ~*ed* away at each other⟩ **2** : to progress erratically as though along a path through which a flail moves in beating grain ⟨~*ed* up the slope with a rush⟩ ⟨~*ed* around for several months trying to decide to get a job⟩

[3]**flail** \"\ *adj* : exhibiting abnormal mobility and loss of response to normal controls — used of body parts (as joints) damaged by paralysis, accident, or surgery ⟨~ foot⟩ ⟨the arm remained ~ at the shoulder⟩

flail tank *n* : a tank equipped with chain flails to detonate mines

[1]**flair** *var of* FLARE

[2]**flair** \'fla(a)(ə)r, 'fle|, |ə\ *n* -S [F, lit., sense of smell, fr. OF, odor, fr. *flairier* to give off an odor, fr. LL *flagrare*, alter. of L *fragrare* to give off an odor, be fragrant — more at FRAGRANT] **1** : discriminating sense : instinctive discernment ⟨an analysis with more ~ than penetration⟩ ⟨relying too much on taste and ~⟩ **2** : natural ability or capacity ⟨a ~ for hospitality⟩ ⟨developed his ~ for cartooning⟩; *often* : an active liking commonly involving use or participation : BENT ⟨his ~ for the dramatic⟩ ⟨developed a ~ for the picturesque⟩ **syn** see LEANING

flaith \'flä\ *n* -S [IrGael] : an Irish chief or noble of one of several grades holding rent-free land

flaj·o·lo·tite \,flajə'lō,tīt\ *n* -S [F, fr. *Flajolot fl*1871 Fr. mineralogist who analyzed it + F *-ite*] : a mineral $4FeSbO_4 \cdot 3H_2O$ occurring as a hydrous iron antimonate in lemon-yellow nodular masses resembling clay

flak *also* **flack** \'flak\ *n, pl* **flak** [G *flak*, fr. *fliegerabwehrkanone* antiaircraft gun, fr. *fliegerabwehr* defense against air attack (fr. *flieger* aviator — fr. *fliegen* to fly, fr. OHG *fliogan* — + *abwehr* defense, fr. *abwehren* to ward off, fr. *ab* off, away — fr. OHG *aba* — + *wehren* to restrain, forbid, fr. OHG *werren* to defend) + *kanone* cannon, fr. It *cannone* — more at FLY, OF, WEIR, CANNON] **1** : antiaircraft guns ⟨~ battery⟩ ⟨~ ship⟩ **2** : the bursting shells fired from flak ⟨despite heavy ~ damage made a safe landing⟩

flak curtain *n* : flexible steel mesh or plates covered with canvas and used in military aircraft to protect vulnerable areas from enemy gunfire

[1]**flake** \'flāk\ *n* -S [ME *flake, fleke*, fr. ON *flaki, fleki* hurdle; akin to OE *flōc* flounder, MD *vlac* flat, smooth, OS *flaka* sole of the foot, OHG *flah* smooth, Norw *flak* disk, floe, L *plaga* region, Gk *pelagos* sea, L *placēre* to please — more at PLEASE] **1** *now dial* : a movable section of fence (as a paling or hurdle) **2 a** : a rack for storing provisions **b** : a stage, platform, or tray for drying fish or produce **3** : a sheltering framework in a mine

[2]**flake** \"\ *n* -S [ME, of Scand origin; akin to Norw *flak* disk, floe] **1 a** : one of the small flocculent masses of ice crystals in which snow falls; *broadly* : any small loose mass or bit ⟨~*s* of froth on the horse's chest⟩ ⟨bright ~*s* of cloud⟩ **b** : a particle of incandescent or burning matter thrown off from a fire ⟨~*s* of flame⟩ **2 a** : a thin flattened piece or layer : CHIP, LAMINA, SCALE ⟨~*s* of flint detached by pressure were among early man's best tools⟩ ⟨slice the potatoes into ~*s*⟩; *often* : something flattened to resemble such a flake ⟨cereal ~*s*⟩ **b** : a lock of hair **c** : MYOCOMMA 1 **d** : MEDULLARY RAY; *also* : FLAKE FIGURE **3** : a carnation with only two colors in the flower which has petals with large stripes **4** : an internal fissure in ferrous metal

[3]**flake** \"\ *vb* -ED/-ING/-S [ME *flaken*, fr. *flake*, n.] *vi* **1** : to fall as or like flakes of snow ⟨petals *flaking* down in the light breeze⟩ **2 a** : to separate into flakes ⟨sandstone ~*s* readily in heat⟩ **b** : to peel or scale off ⟨look how the paint has *flaked*⟩ ~ *vt* **1** : to form or separate into flakes ⟨~ the fish for the salad⟩ **2** : to cover with or as if with flakes (as of snow) ⟨her hair *flaked* with white⟩ ⟨shavings *flaked* the floor⟩ **3 a** : to remove flakes from (as a stone) : work (as flint) by pressing off flakes; *also* : to form (as an arrowhead) by flaking stone **b** : to remove (as worn paint) in flakes

[4]**flake** *var of* FAKE

[5]**flake** \'flāk\ *n* -S [perh. fr. [2]*flake*] *Brit* : a dogfish esp. when used as food

flake figure *n* : a figure in lumber or veneer produced by sawing through the medullary rays

flake ice *n* : ice in the form of thin scales made usu. by freezing a thin film on a metal plate and scraping it off

flake·less \'flākləs\ *adj* : having no flakes : not tending to flake off ⟨a ~ paint⟩

flake·let \-lət\ *n* -S : a small flake (as of snow)

flake out *vi* [prob. fr. [4]*flake*] *slang* : to fall asleep : collapse from exhaustion

flak·er \'flākə(r)\ *n* -S : one that flakes: as **a** : a person that produces flint flakes for striking fire or that manufactures flaked stone implements **b** : a worker who places cleaned fish on flakes for drying **c** *or* **flaking mill** : a machine for reducing material (as cereal grain, fish, soap, ice) to flakes **d** : a prehistoric implement of bone or other material used to press off flakes of stone in making stone implements

flake stand *n* [[2]*flake*] : the vessel in which the worm of a still is cooled

flake tool *n* : a Stone-Age tool that is a flake of stone struck off from a larger piece and sometimes retouched — compare CORE TOOL

flake white *n* [[2]*flake*] : white lead selected for whiteness and fine texture esp. for artists' use

flak·i·ly \'flākəlē, -li\ *adv* : in a flaky manner

flak·i·ness \'flākēnəs, -kin-\ *n* -ES : the quality or state of being flaky

flak suit *or* **flak vest** *n* : body armor made of overlapping steel plates in a padded cover and worn by aircrewmen to protect them from shrapnel

flaky \'flākē, -ki\ *adj* -ER/-EST [[2]*flake* + *-y*] **1** : consisting of flakes or full of small loose masses : not firmly united into a whole ⟨~ mica-filled sand⟩ **2** : cleaving off in flakes or layers : FRIABLE ⟨a crisp ~ piecrust⟩

flaky fir *n* : a Chinese evergreen tree (*Abies squamata*) having shaggy purplish bark that comes off in thin papery layers and being sometimes cultivated as an ornamental

[1]**flam** \'flam, -aa(ə)m\ *n* -S [prob. short for *flimflam*] **1 a** : FALSEHOOD, TRICK, DECEPTION **b** *obs* : a fanciful bit of writing **2** : HUMBUG, NONSENSE, RUBBISH

[2]**flam** \"\ *vb* **flammed; flammed; flamming; flams** : DECEIVE, TRICK, CHEAT

[3]**flam** \"\ *var of* [1]FLAN

[4]**flam** \"\ *n* -S [prob. imit.] : a drumbeat of two strokes of which the first is a very quick grace note

flam·ant \'flamənt, -lām-\ *adj* [MF, pres. part. of *flamer* to flame, fr. OF — more at FLAME] *heraldry* : FLAMING; *esp* : having flames rising from the top

flamb \'flam\ *vt* -ED/-ING/-S [ME *flaumen, flamben* to flame, shine, baste — more at FLAME] *Scot* : [2]BASTE

flam·bé \(')fläm¦bā\ *adj* [F, singed, passed through a flame, past part. of *flamber* to flame, singe, fr. OF, to flame, fr. *flambe* flame] **1** : being or decorated with an irregularly applied or splashed pottery glaze that is usu. red and somewhat iridescent ⟨two Chinese ~ vases⟩ ⟨a fine ~ glaze⟩ **2** *also* **flam·béed** \-ād\ *of a food* : dressed or served covered with flaming brandy or other flaming liquor ⟨a perfectly browned ~ crepe suzette⟩

flam·beau \'flam,bō\ *n, pl* **flam·beaux** \-ōz\ *or* **flambeaus** [F, fr. MF, fr. *flambe* flame, fr. OF, alter. of *flamble* — more at FLAME] **1** : a flaming torch usu. made by combining thick wicks saturated with a quick-burning substance (as pitch); *broadly* : TORCH **2** : an ornamental candlestick **3** : one of a group of kettles used in boiling sugar **4** : ROYAL POINCIANA

flam·bor·ough \'flam,bərə\ *n* -S *usu cap* [prob. fr. *Flamborough* Head, promontory on east coast of Yorkshire, northern England] : an old English sword dance

flam·boy·ance \flam'bòi(y)ən(t)s\ *also* **flam·boy·an·cy** \-nsē, -si\ *n, pl* **flamboyances** *also* **flamboyancies** [*flamboyance* fr. *flamboyant*, after such pairs as E *compliant*: *compliance*; *flamboyancy* fr. *flamboyant* + *-cy*] : the quality or state of being flamboyant

[1]**flam·boy·ant** \(')¦bòi(y)ənt\ *adj* [F, lit., flaming, pres. part. of *flamboyer* to flame, blaze, fr. OF *flamboier*, fr. *flambe* flame] **1** *often cap, of architecture* : characterized by waving curves suggesting flames ⟨the ~ tracery of windows in the later French Gothic style⟩; *broadly* : belonging to the florid French Gothic school of architecture **2 a** : resembling a flame in form or color **b** : FLORID, ORNATE; *also* : RESPLENDENT **3** : given to show or ostentation : SHOWY, UNRESTRAINED ⟨~ advertising⟩ **syn** see ORNATE

[2]**flamboyant** \"\ *n* -S : ROYAL POINCIANA

flam·boy·ant·ly *adv* : in a flamboyant manner : with flamboyance

flam·doo·dle \'flam¦düdᵊl\ *n* [alter. (prob. influenced by [1]*flam*) of *flapdoodle*] *dial* : NONSENSE; *esp* : pretentious nonsense

[1]**flame** \'flām\ *n* -S [ME *flaume, flambe*, fr. MF *flame, flamme* (fr. OF, fr. L *flamma*) & MF *flambe*, fr. OF, alter. of *flamble*, fr. L *flammula* small flame, dim. of L *flamma* flame; akin to L *flagrare* to burn — more at BLACK] **1** : the glowing gaseous part of a fire : a body of gas or vapor that gives off energy usu. in the form of light and heat as a result of a rapid chemical reaction between a combustible material and air, oxygen or other oxidizing agent, that may be luminous, yellow, and smoky if it contains suspended incandescent particles (as of carbon in the case of a candle) or variously colored if certain elements or their compounds are present or predominantly nonluminous, bluish, and hotter as the proportion of air or oxygen in the burning mixture is increased, and that when nonluminous (as produced by a Bunsen burner) typically shows a bright inner cone constituting the flame front where the combustion starts and separating the incoming premixed fuel gas and air from a pale outer cone where the excess of fuel gas reacts with the oxygen of the surrounding air ⟨the ~ of a gas stove⟩ ⟨~*s* from the burning log⟩ ⟨the ~ in a rocket motor⟩ — see OXIDIZING FLAME, REDUCING FLAME **2 a** : a state of blazing combustion ⟨burst into ~⟩ **b** : a condition or appearance suggesting a flame (as a light ray) **c** : BRILLIANCE, LUMINESCENCE ⟨the full moon's ~ brightened the frosty meadow⟩ **3** : burning zeal or passion : elevated and noble enthusiasm ⟨a ~ of righteous indignation filled him with zeal⟩ **4** : a person beloved : SWEETHEART **5** : something (as an ornament, streak, or patch) resembling a flame in shape or color **6** : a strong reddish orange that is yellower and paler than poppy or paprika and yellower and lighter than flame red — compare FIERY RED, FIRE RED

1
2
3

nonluminous flame produced by a Bunsen burner: *1* outer cone, *2* inner cone, *3* incoming premixed fuel gas and air

[2]**flame** \"\ *vb* -ED/-ING/-S [ME *flaumen, flamben* to flame, shine, baste, fr. MF *flamer, flammer* to flame (fr. OF, fr. L *flammare*, fr. *flamma* flame) & MF *flamber* to flame, fr. OF, fr. *flambe* flame — more at FLAME (n.)] *vi* **1** : to burn with a flame or blaze : burn like gas emitted from bodies in combustion : burst into flame : BLAZE ⟨the overheated fat *flamed* up suddenly⟩ **2** : to burst forth like flame : break out in violence of passion ⟨he *flamed* with indignation —T.B.Macaulay⟩ **3 a** : to seem or move like a flame : shine brightly ⟨the sun's rays *flamed* in the window⟩ **b** : to dart or flicker like a flame ⟨eyes *flaming* furiously⟩ ~ *vt* **1** : to send or convey by means of flame ⟨the comet *flamed* a warning of the divine portent⟩ ⟨a message could be *flamed* by signal fires from one village to the next⟩ **2** *obs* **a** : to consume by burning : BURN **b** : KINDLE, INFLAME, EXCITE **3** : to treat or affect with flame: as **a** : to cleanse with or sterilize by fire ⟨~ the lip of each culture tube⟩ **b** : to dress food with flaming brandy or other liquor **c** : to sear and destroy (as weeds) with flame (as by use of a flamethrower) **4** : to brighten with or as if with flame ⟨the fireplace *flamed* the opposite wall⟩ : give a burning appearance to ⟨the setting sun *flamed* the western sky⟩ **syn** see BLAZE

flame anneal *vt* : to soften (metal) by heating with a gas flame

flame azalea *n* : an azalea (*Rhododendron calendulaceum*) of the eastern U. S. with showy orange or yellow flowers — called also *fiery azalea, yellow azalea*

flame blue *n* : DARK WEDGWOOD

flame cell *n* : a large hollow cell containing a tuft of vibratile cilia and terminating the branches of the excretory vessels of many flatworms and rotifers and some other lower invertebrates

flame characin *or* **flame fish** *n* : a small orange-red So. American freshwater fish (*Hyphessobrycon flammeus*) with black-tipped fins that is frequently kept in the tropical aquarium

flame cultivator *n* : an agricultural device employing one or more flamethrowers to destroy small weeds between row crops by fire — called also *flame weeder*

flame–cut \'=,=\ *vt* : to cut (a metal) with a gas flame

flamed \'flāmd\ *adj* [[1]*flame* + *-ed*] : having markings suggesting flames ⟨a ~ maple veneer⟩; *esp, of a tulip* : having a broad irregular mark up the center of each petal

flameflower \'=,=\ *n* : KNIPHOFIA 2

flame–harden \'=,==\ *vt* : to harden (a ferrous alloy) by heating above the transformation temperature and then cooling as rapidly as necessary

flameholder \'=,==\ *n* : a device used to maintain continuous combustion in a flowing mixture in the combustion chamber of certain jet engines

flame·less \'flāmləs\ *adj* : having or producing no flame ⟨~ fuels⟩ — **flame·less·ly** *adv*

flame·let \'flāmlət\ *n* -S : a small or feeble flame

flame lily *n* **1** : WOOD LILY 1b **2** : ATAMASCO LILY

flame lousewort *n* : a lousewort (*Pedicularis flammea*) of arctic America and Europe with crimson-purple flowers

fla·men \'flāmən, -lām-\ *n, pl* **fla·mens** \-nz\ *or* **flam·i·nes** \'flamə,nēz, -läm-\ [ME *flamin*, fr. L *flamin-, flamen*; perh. akin to OE *blōtan* to sacrifice, OHG *bluozan*, ON *blōta* to sacrifice, Goth *blotan* to worship] : a priest devoted to the service of a particular god of the Roman pantheon

fla·men·co \flə'meŋ(,)kō\ *n* -S [Sp, flamingo, Fleming, Flemish, buxom and ruddy, resembling a gypsy, being in gypsy style, fr. MD *Vlaminc* Fleming] **1 a** : a vigorous rhythmic dance style of the Andalusian gypsies; *also* : a dance in this style **b** : music or song accompanying or suitable to accompany such a dance which is often more or less impromptu and shows distinct Arab influence; *also* : a piece of such music **2** : a Spanish gypsy; *sometimes* : Spanish gypsy custom or style **3** : a brightly colored snapper (*Lutjanus guttatus*) of the Pacific coast from Mexico to Ecuador having the sides bright red, the back green, and the undersurface silvery and bearing red dorsal and caudal fins and yellowish anal and ventral fins

flame nettle *n* : a plant of the genus *Coleus*

flame–of–the–woods \¦===¦=\ *n, pl* **flames–of–the–woods** : an East Indian shrub (*Ixora coccinea*) with showy scarlet flowers

flame orange *n* : a strong orange that is deeper and slightly redder than pumpkin and redder and deeper than cadmium orange

flameout \'=,=\ *n* -S [[2]*flame* + *out*] : the cessation of operation of a jet aircraft engine (as through improper combustion or exhaustion of the fuel supply) — called also *blowout*

flame peeling *n* : the exposure of fruit or vegetables to intense heat to char the peel and facilitate its rapid removal by a powerful stream of water

flame photometer *n* : a spectrophotometer in which a spray of metallic salts in solution is vaporized in a very hot flame and subjected to quantitative analysis by measuring the intensities of the spectrum lines of the metals present — **flame photometry** *n*

flame projector *n* : FLAMETHROWER

[1]**flameproof** \'=,=\ *adj* **1** : resistant to the action of flame : not burning on contact with flame; *esp* : not tending to propagate fire if ignited **2** : safeguarded against causing destructive explosion (as by generating sparks) — used esp. of machinery in mines, oil refineries, cereal mills

[2]**flameproof** \"\ *vt* : to make flameproof

flam·er \'flāmə(r)\ *n* -S : one that flames

flame reaction *n* : the characteristic coloration that certain chemical elements or their compounds impart to a nonluminous flame (as yellow from sodium or green from copper)

flame red *n* : a strong reddish orange that is redder and slightly duller than poppy, redder and slightly paler than paprika, redder and deeper than flame, and redder and deeper than average coral red — compare FIERY RED, FIRE RED, FLAME

flames *pres 3d sing of* FLAME, *pl of* FLAME

flame scarlet *n* : a strong reddish orange that is yellower and lighter than fire red and yellower and paler than flame red, poppy, or flame — called also *Florentine*

flame spectrum *n* : the spectrum obtained by volatilizing substances in a nonluminous flame

flamethrower \'=,==\ *n* : a device that expels from a nozzle a burning stream of liquid or semiliquid fuel under pressure and is used in war esp. to penetrate enclosures (as tanks or pillboxes) or in agriculture to kill insects or weeds

flame trap *n* : a device (as a wire gauze across a nozzle inlet) for preventing the flame of burning gas from backing up into the supply pipe and causing an explosion

flame tree *n* : any of several trees or shrubs with showy scarlet or yellow flowers: as **a** : either of two Australian trees: (1) : a bottle tree (*Brachychiton acerifolius*) of southern Australia with panicles of brilliant scarlet flowers (2) : a small evergreen tree (*Nuytsia floribunda*) of the family Loranthaceae that is restricted to western Australia and is distinguished by axillary racemes of yellow-orange flowers **b** : ROYAL POINCIANA **c** : HUISACHE

flame tube *n* : a heat-resistant ceramic or metal tube inside the combustion chamber of a jet engine in which the actual combustion takes place

flame vine *n* : a Brazilian woody vine (*Pyrostegia ignea*) of the family Bignoniaceae that has tendril-bearing compound leaves and orange-red tubular flowers in clusters and that is widely cultivated in warm regions

flameware \'=,=\ *n* : cooking ware (as of glass) that can be used over an open flame without breaking

flame weeder *n* : FLAME CULTIVATOR

flam·few \'flam,fyü\ *n* -S [modif. of MF *fanfelue* trifle, silliness, fr. ML *famfaluca* bubble, modif. of Gk *pompholyg-, pompholyx*] : GEWGAW

flamines *pl of* FLAMEN

[1]**flaming** *adj* [fr. pres. part. of [2]*flame*] **1** : emitting flames : BLAZING ⟨a ~ crackling fire⟩ **2 a** : of the color of flame; *usu* : of the color flame scarlet, flame red, flame, or fire red ⟨her ~ hat clashed madly with a purple coat and orange scarf⟩ **b** : highly chromatic : brilliantly colored ⟨the ~ sunset sky⟩ **3** : suggesting a flame in having a wavy outline **4 a** : ARDENT, PASSIONATE ⟨a ~ devotion⟩ **b** : burning with zeal : irrepressibly earnest ⟨a ~ speaker kindling in his hearers a love of righteousness⟩ **c** : extravagant or monstrous ⟨repeated some of the most ~ tales⟩ **5** *slang Austral* — used as a generalized intensive; compare [1]BLOODY 6 — **flam·ing·ly** *adv*

[2]**flaming** *n* -S [fr. gerund of [2]*flame*] : the process of reheating glass in a reducing flame to bring out the color imparted by a metallic base

fla·min·gant \flämaⁿgäⁿ\ *n, pl* **flamingants** \-äⁿ(z)\ *usu cap* [F, Flemish-speaking, fr. pres. part. of F dial. (Walloon) *flaminguer* to speak Flemish, fr. Flem *Vlaming* Fleming, fr. MD *Vlaminc*] : one of the party among the Flemings of Belgium that seeks to revive Flemish to the exclusion of French

fla·min·go \flə'miŋ(,)gō\ *n, pl* **flamingos** *also* **flamingoes** [obs. Sp *flamengo* (now *flamenco*) flamingo, Fleming, fr. MD *Vlaminc* Fleming] **1** : any of several aquatic birds that constitute the family Phoenicopteridae and with related extinct birds the suborder Phoenicopteri of the order Ciconiiformes, that have remarkably long legs and neck, webbed feet, a broad lamellated bill resembling that of a duck but abruptly bent downward, and usu. rosy-white plumage with scarlet wing coverts and black wing quills, and that are gregarious, breeding in colonies and building nests of mud in swamps and shallow lagoons and laying but one or two eggs **2 :** a moderate reddish orange that is duller and slightly redder than crab apple and redder and lighter than burnt ocher **3 :** a synchronized swimming stunt executed from a back layout position in which the legs are brought successively to the vertical and held in such position while the upper trunk drops backward to a head-down position after which the body is submerged

flamingo flower *or* **flamingo plant** *n* **:** either of two commonly cultivated anthuriums (*Anthurium scherzerianum* and *A. andraeanum*) with bright scarlet spathe and spadix

flaming pinkster *n* [*flaming* (pres. part. of ²*flame*) + *pinkster* (as in *pinkster flower*)] **:** FLAME AZALEA

flaming poppy *n* **:** WIND POPPY

fla·min·i·an \flə'minēən\ *adj, usu cap* [L *flaminianus*, fr. Gaius *Flaminius* †217 B.C. Roman general and statesman + L *-anus* -an] **:** of or relating to the Roman censor Gaius Flaminius or the public works which he executed ⟨the *Flaminian* Way led northward from Rome⟩

fla·min·i·ca \flə'minəkə\ *n* -s [L, fr. *flamin-*, *flamen* flamen] **:** the wife of a flamen

flam·ma·bil·i·ty \ˌflamə'bilәd·ē, -lәtē, -i\ *n* -ES **:** ability to support combustion **:** burning rate ⟨few materials completely lack ~⟩; *usu* **:** high capacity for combustion ⟨the dangerous ~ of certain otherwise valuable organic solvents⟩

¹**flam·ma·ble** \'flaməbəl\ *adj* [L *flammare* to flame, set on fire + E *-able* — more at FLAME] **:** capable of being easily ignited and of burning with extreme rapidity — now used technically in preference to *inflammable;* compare COMBUSTIBLE, EXPLOSIVE ⟨cannot be used for safety reasons in coal mines in which ~ gases are present —A.C.Morrison⟩

²**flammable** \"\ *n* -s **:** a flammable substance

flam·ma·tion \flə'māshən, flа'-\ *n* -s [L *flammare* + E *-ation*] **:** an act of setting afire **:** IGNITING

flammed *past of* FLAM

flam·me·ous \'flamēəs\ *adj* [L *flammeus*, fr. *flamma* flame — more at FLAME] **:** consisting of or resembling the color of flame ⟨a ~ flycatcher⟩

flam·mif·er·ous \(ˈ)fla¦mif(ə)rəs, flə'm-\ *adj* [L *flammifer* flammiferous (*fr. flammi-* — fr. *flamma* flame — + *-fer*) + E *-ous*] **:** producing or bright with flame

flamming *pres part of* FLAM

flam·mu·lat·ed \'flamyə,lād·əd\ *adj* [L *flammula* small flame + E *-ate* + *-ed* — more at FLAME] **:** having flame-shaped markings — used of the plumage of certain birds — **flam·mu·la·tion** \ˌ==ˈlāshən\ *n* -s

flam·mule \'fla,myül\ *n* -s [L *flammula*] **:** a small flame; *esp* **:** one shown in a picture of a Chinese or Japanese god

flams *pres 3d sing of* FLAM, *pl of* FLAM

flamy \'flāmē, -mi\ *adj* [ME *flaumy*, fr. *flaume* flame + *-y* — more at FLAME] **1 :** composed of flame **:** FLAMING, BLAZING **2 a :** resembling flame esp. in color **b :** of the color flame

¹**flan** \'flan\ *n* -s [ME (Sc), fr. ON, rush, fr. *flana* to rush heedlessly; akin to Gk *planasthai* to wander — more at PLANET] *Scot* **:** a sudden gust of wind

²**flan** \"\ *vi* **flanned; flanned; flanning; flans** [perh. alter. (influenced by obs. *flan*, adj., spreading and shallow) of *flanch*, v.] *dial* **:** to expand or widen toward the top

³**flan** \'flan, 'flän, 'flänⁿ\ *n* -s [F, fr. OF *flaon*, fr. LL *fladon-*, *flado* flat cake, of Gmc origin; akin to OHG *flado* sacrificial cake; akin to Gk *platys* flat, broad — more at PLACE] **1 :** a large open pie usu. with straight sides filled with custard, cheese, jam, or fruit and often glazed with fruit syrup **2 :** the metal disk of a coin, token, or medal as distinguished from the design and lettering stamped on it

flan·card *or* **flan·chard** \'flaŋkə(r)d\ *n* -s [MF *flancard*, fr. *flanc* flank + *-ard*] *archaic* **:** a piece of armor for the thigh or flank

¹**flanch** *also* **flanche** \'flanch, -å-\ *or* **flaunch** *or* **flaunche** \-ȯ-,-ä-\ *n* -ES [ME *flaunche*, prob. fr. MF *flanche* flank, fr. *flanc*] **:** either of two curved segments encroaching on a heraldic field one from each side

flanches

²**flanch** \'flànch\ *n* -ES [perh. fr. ¹*flanch*] *Brit* **:** a flange esp. of a wheel

³**flanch** \"\ *vb* -ED/-ING/-ES *vi* **:** to slant outward **:** FLARE ~ *vt* **:** draw in toward the top — used with *up* and esp. of a chimney ⟨~ up the chimney so that it will shed rain⟩

flanched \-cht\ *adj* [¹*flanch* + *-ed*] **:** having flanches

flan·con·nade *also* **flan·co·nade** \ˌflaŋkə¦nād, -näd\ *n* -s [F, irreg. fr. *flanc* flank] **:** a bind in fencing that terminates in a thrust under the adversary's arm

flan·dan \'flan,dan\ *n* -s [origin unknown] **:** a woman's pinner of a style used in the 17th century

flan·der·kin \'flandə(r)kən\ *n* -s *usu cap* [*Flanders* + E *-kin*] *archaic* **:** FLEMING

flan·ders baby \'flan|də(r)z-, 'flaan|, 'flàn|\ *n, usu cap F* [*Flanders*, region in western Belgium and the adjacent part of northern France + E *baby*] **:** a wooden doll produced in the Netherlands and popular in England in the 18th and 19th centuries

flanders brick *n, usu cap F* **:** BATH BRICK

flanders poppy *n, usu cap F* **:** CORN POPPY

flane *n* -s [ME (Sc & dial. of northern England) *flan, flane*, fr. OE *flān;* akin to ON *fleinn* dart and perh. to OE *flint* — more at FLINT] *obs* **:** ARROW

flâ·ne·rie \(ˈ)flän¦rē\ *n* -s [F, fr. MF *flanerie*, fr. (assumed) MF dial. (Normandy) *flaner* to saunter aimlessly (whence F *flâner*) + MF *-erie* -ery] **:** aimless or idle quality or state

fla·neur \(ˈ)flä¦nər(·)\ *n* -s [F *flâneur* idler, fr. MF *flaneur*, fr. (assumed) MF dial. (Normandy) *flaner* to saunter aimlessly (fr. ON *flana* to wander about) + MF *-eur* -or (fr. L *-or*) — more at FLAN] **:** an aimless and usu. self-centered and superficial person: as **a :** MAN-ABOUT-TOWN, BON VIVEUR **b :** an intellectual trifler

fla·neuse \-¦nərz, -¦nœz\ *n* -s [F *flâneuse*, fem. of *flâneur*] **:** a woman who is or who behaves like a flaneur

flang *dial past of* FLING

²**flang** \'flaŋ, -aiŋ\ *n* -s [origin unknown] **:** a miner's pick with two points

¹**flange** \'flanj, -aa(ə)nj\ *n* -s [perh. alter. of ¹*flanch*] **1 :** a spreading out (as of a vein of ore) **2 a :** a rim or edge (as on a shaft or a pipe fitting) projecting at right angles to provide strength or means of attachment to another part **b :** a projecting edge around the inside rim of a car or locomotive wheel to guide and keep it on the track **c :** the wide portion at the top and bottom of an I beam, channel, or plate girder — compare WEB **d :** a projecting edge, tuck, or insert of cloth used for decoration on clothing **3 :** a foundry molder's tool for forming flanges

flange 2d

²**flange** \"\ *vb* -ED/-ING/-S *vt* **:** to make a flange on **:** furnish with a flange ⟨*flanging* the lead to make a joint⟩ ~ *vi* **1 :** to widen or spread — used with *out* ⟨the swollen stream *flanged* out over the lowlands **2 :** to shape flanges ⟨it is easier to ~ by machine than by hand⟩

flange·less \-ləs\ *adj* **:** lacking a flange

flangeless tire *n* **:** BALD TIRE

flange nut *n* **:** a nut with an enlarged base that obviates the need for a washer

flange plate *n* **:** COVER PLATE 2

flang·er \-jə(r)\ *n* -s **1 :** one that makes or repairs flanges: as **a :** a worker who flanges the tops of glass flasks **b :** a worker who prepares or adjusts flanges on metal plates (as in ship-building) **c :** a worker who forms the flanges of glass tubes used for hypodermic syringe cylinders **d :** a worker who shapes hat brims by pressing **e :** a tool or machine for forming flanges **2 :** a scraper for clearing ice and snow from the inside of railroad rails to provide clearance for the wheel flanges

flange rail *n* **1 :** a railroad rail with a flange on one side formerly used to keep wheels from running off the track and now replaced by the T rail **2 :** T RAIL — compare BULLHEADED 3b

flange steel *n* **:** steel ductile enough to be flanged esp. for the heads of steam boilers

flange turner *n* **:** a worker who performs any or all machine and hand operations necessary to form flanges on heavy steel plates used in boilermaking or automobile, locomotive, or ship building **:** FLANGER

flange union *n* **:** a pair of companion flanges for bolting or welding together

flangeway \'=ˌ=\ *n* **:** the passageway for the flange of a wheel running on rails

¹**flank** \'flaŋk, -aiŋk\ *n* -s *often attrib* [ME, fr. OF *flanc*, of Gmc origin; akin to OHG *hlanca* loin, flank — more at LANK] **1 a :** the fleshy part of the side between the ribs and the hip; *broadly* **:** the side of a quadruped ⟨the horse stood with quivering ~s⟩ — see COW illustration **b :** a cut of meat from this part of an animal — see BEEF illustration **c :** hide or leather from the flank or belly of an animal **2 a :** SIDE ⟨sheltering on the ~ of the hill⟩ **b :** the right or left of a formation (as a line of battle, a line of scrimmage, a marching column) ⟨attacked the enemy on both ~s⟩ **c :** the part of a bastion that reaches from the curtain to the face and defends the curtain and the flank and face of the opposite bastion **d :** either side of a fortification — see BASTION illustration **3 a :** the area along either side of an escutcheon — see POINT illustration **b :** the central part of this area **4 a :** the profile of the root of a gear tooth or the portion of a gear tooth between the root and the pitch circle **b :** the contacting face of a screw thread **c :** either side of a cutting tool (as a chisel) intersecting the cutting edge and adjacent to the face

²**flank** \"\ *vb* -ED/-ING/-S *vt* **1 :** to shelter or protect a side of ⟨used cavalry to stabilize and ~ the infantry during an attack⟩ ⟨a wall ~*ed* with tall towers⟩ **2 a :** to attack or threaten the flank of (as a body of troops) **b :** to turn the flank of ⟨the reserve forces were unexpectedly ~*ed* and immobilized by a detachment of tanks⟩ **3 a :** to stand or be situated at the side of **:** border esp. on each side ⟨a long avenue ~*ed* with lindens and oaks⟩ **b :** to place on each side of ⟨by ~*ing* the mirror with tall candelabra⟩ **4** *archaic* **:** ESCAPE, EVADE ⟨successfully ~*ed* his pursuers⟩ ⟨the recruits ~*ed* drill whenever possible⟩ ~ *vi* **1 :** to be placed or move to, toward, or along a side ⟨at the wave of his handler's hand the dog ~*ed* off and turned the straggling sheep⟩ **2 :** to present the flank — used with *on* ⟨the fort ~*ed* on a swamp⟩

³**flank** \"\ *vt* -ED/-ING/-S [prob. imit.] **:** FLICK, FLIP

flank angle *n* **:** the angle between the flank of a screw thread and the perpendicular to the axis of the screw

¹**flank·er** \-kə(r)\ *n* -s **:** one that flanks: as **a :** something that adjoins on the side (as a fort commanding the flank of an assailing force); *esp* **:** a lateral wing of a building ⟨the great kitchen took up most of the long west ~⟩ **b :** men so posted or marched as to protect the flank of a column on the march **c** *chiefly Brit* **:** a driver posted on the flank of the line of a grouse drive to turn birds that tend to break away **d** *West* **:** a cowhand who throws a roped calf on its side for branding **e :** an animal (as a sheep) that stays off to one side of a grazing herd **f :** a football player who takes a place on the line to the right of the right end or to the left of the left end

²**flank·er** \"\ *vt* -ED/-ING/-S *obs* **:** to defend or support by flankers

³**flan·ker** \"\ *n* -s [obs. *flanker*, v., to sparkle] **:** a large spark thrown off by a wood fire esp. up a chimney

flank guard *n* **:** a detachment charged with the protection of a flank of a marching force

flanking *n* -s [fr. gerund of ²*flank*] **:** the maneuvering of towed barges around a bend in a river by means of a towboat at the rear which is backed as a brake so that the barges are controlled but brought around the bend primarily by the current of the river

flanking fire *also* **flank fire** *n* **:** fire delivered on an enemy flank from a position to the side of that enemy

flank speed *n* **:** the full speed of which a ship is capable ⟨proceeding at *flank speed*⟩

flank steak *n* **:** the triangular internal oblique muscle of the beef flank — see BEEF illustration

flank vault *n* **:** a vault made with one supporting hand, both legs extended to one side, and the body facing ahead throughout

flankwise \'=ˌ=\ *adv (or adj)* **:** on, along, about, or by way of the flank ⟨a ~ movement of cavalry⟩ ⟨charged the enemy ~⟩

flanky \'flaŋkē, -aiŋ-, -ki\ *adj* [¹*flank* + *-y*] **1** *of leather* **:** having a loose coarse texture **2** *of a body* **:** well-developed in the flank region ⟨a soft ~ torso⟩

flanned *past of* FLAN

¹**flan·nel** \'flanᵊl\ *n* -s *often attrib* [ME *flaunneol*, a woolen cloth or garment, *flanyn*, a penitential garment, prob. fr. (assumed) MW *gwlanen* flannel (whence W *gwlanen*), fr. (assumed) MW *gwlân* wool (whence W *gwlân*); akin to L *lana* wool — more at WOOL] **1 a :** a soft twilled fabric with a loose texture and a slightly napped surface made in various weights of wool or worsted yarns and often in combination with cotton or synthetic yarns **b :** a napped cotton fabric of soft yarns simulating the texture of wool flannel: (1) **:** FLANNELETTE (2) **:** a stout cotton fabric usu. softly napped on one side and twilled on the other and used esp. for work gloves, filters, polishing cloths (as for shoes), and linings — called also *Canton flannel* (3) **:** OUTING FLANNEL **2 flannels** *pl* **a :** warm undergarments of flannel or sometimes of knit fabric; *esp* **:** men's long underdrawers **b :** outer garments of flannel; *esp* **:** men's trousers **c :** flannel garments forming a uniform (as of a club or team) **d** *Brit* **:** the place on a team represented by the wearing of such flannels or an individual holding such a place **3** *Brit* **:** WASHCLOTH

²**flannel** \"\ *vt* **flanneled** *or* **flannelled; flanneled** *or* **flannelled; flanneling** *or* **flannelling; flannels :** to clothe or enclose in or rub with flannel

flannel board *n* **:** a display board covered with flannel or felt to which suitably backed matter (as for the illustration of a lesson or lecture) adheres when pressed firmly in contact

flannelbush \'==ˌ=\ *n* **:** a Californian and Mexican shrub (*Fremontia californicum*) having a felty covering on the lower leaf surfaces

flannel cake *n, chiefly East & Midland* **:** a griddlecake esp. of wheat flour

flan·nel·ette \ˌflanᵊl¦et, *usu* -ed·+V\ *n* -s **:** a cotton flannel napped on one or both sides and used esp. for undergarments and nightwear

flannelflower \'==ˌ==\ *n* **1 :** MULLEIN **2 :** a Brazilian vine (*Macrosiphonia longiflora*) of the family Apocynaceae having woolly leaves **3 :** an Australian plant (*Actinotus helianthi*) of the family Umbelliferae of which the umbels have a white velvety involucre — called also *satinflower*

flannelgraph \'==ˌ=\ *n* **:** one of the figures used on a flannel board (as for illustrating a story or lecture) ⟨developed the idea with ~s against a pictorial background⟩

flannelleaf \'==ˌ=\ *also* **flannel plant** *n* **:** a mullein (*Verbascum thapsus*)

flan·nel·ly \'flanᵊlē, -ᵊli\ *adj* [¹*flannel* + *-y*] **1** *of the voice* **:** blurred and muted as if heard through flannel **2 :** resembling flannel esp. in soft fluffy texture or appearance ⟨the sky full of ~ little clouds⟩

flannel moth *n* **:** a moth of the family Megalopygidae most of which have very hairy larvae

flannelmouth \'==ˌ=\ *n* **:** a flannelmouthed person

flannelmouthed \'==ˌ=\ *adj* **1 :** talking thickly with or as if with a brogue ⟨a ~ immigrant right off the boat⟩ **2 :** SMOOTH-SPOKEN **:** oily or tricky in speech

flannelmouthed sucker *n* **:** a large fish (*Catostomus latipinnis*) formerly used as food by Indians of the Colorado river region

flan·nen \'flanən\ *n* -s [ME *flanyn*, a penitential garment] *dial* **:** FLANNEL

flanning *pres part of* FLAN

flans *pres 3d sing of* FLAN, *pl of* FLAN

¹**flap** \'flap\ *n* -s [ME *flappe*, prob. of imit. origin; in senses 5, 6, and 7, prob. fr. ²*flap*] **1** *obs* **:** STROKE, BLOW; *often* **:** a stroke with something broad (as the open hand) **:** SLAP **2** *obs* **:** something broad and flat (as a flyswatter) used for striking **3 :** something that is broad, limber, or flat and usu. thin and that hangs loose or projects freely: as **a :** a hinged leaf or fold (as of a table, door, or shutter) **b :** half of a hinge having two broad leaves through which screw holes are pierced esp. when one of them is to be screwed to the face of a door or shutter instead of to the edge — see STRAP HINGE **c** (1) **:** a piece on a garment that hangs free ⟨double ~s set off the pockets⟩ or can be adjusted to hang free ⟨a storm cap with a wool-lined ~ that can be pulled down to protect the ears⟩ (2) **:** a tongue of a shoe (3) **:** a brim of a hat **d** (1) **:** a projecting edge of a flexible book cover (as in a divinity circuit binding) (2) **:** a part of a book jacket that folds under the book's cover **e :** a piece of tissue partly severed from its place of origin for use in surgical grafting and repair of bodily defects **f :** an extended part that forms the closure of a bag, envelope, carton, or fiberboard case **g :** a cloth or rubber strip inserted between the tube and the beads of an automobile tire to protect the tube from contact with the rim **h :** a movable auxiliary airfoil usu. attached to the trailing edge of an airplane wing to increase wing resistance **4 :** a flat piece, slice, or layer ⟨a ~ of bread⟩ **5 a :** the motion of something broad and limber (as a sail or wing) ⟨the steady ~ of northbound wings⟩; *also* **:** a single stroke of such motion ⟨the sail gave a ~ as the breeze died⟩ **b :** the sound of such motion ⟨startled by the sudden ~ of a loose shutter⟩ **c :** a brush followed by a step on the same foot in tap dancing **6 :** an energetic single bouncing of the tip of the tongue against the hard palate (as in a frequent American articulation of the *tt* in *Betty* or a frequent southern British articulation of the *rr* in *berry*) **7 a :** a state of excitement or panicky confusion **:** HULLABALOO ⟨the president's statement had everybody in a ~⟩ **b :** CRISIS ⟨when there was a ~ abroad —Thomas Braden⟩

²**flap** \"\ *vb* **flapped; flapped; flapping; flaps** [ME *flappen*, fr. *flappe*, n.] *vt* **1 a** *obs* **:** STRIKE, CLAP **b :** to beat with or as if with a flap **:** strike with a surface (as of a bird's wing or of a flyswatter) ⟨the loose scarf *flapped* his face⟩ **2 a :** to toss sharply **:** FLING — usu. used with *down* ⟨*flapped* the paper down angrily⟩ **b :** to turn (as a pancake) by tossing **3 :** to move or cause to move in flaps ⟨a bird *flapping* its wings⟩ ⟨the uncertain breezes ~ the sails⟩ **4 :** to arouse the attention of by or as if by striking with a flap ⟨sent an emissary to ~ the local agents⟩ **5 :** to lower the flap of (as a hat or cap) **6 :** to break (the surface of the slag) in the fire-refining of copper by striking with a rabble, exposing the molten metal to the air, and hastening oxidation **7 :** to utter with a flap articulation ⟨a *flapped r*⟩ ~ *vi* **1 :** to give a quick blow (as with the hand) **:** CLAP **2 :** to sway loosely usu. with a noise of striking and esp. when moved by wind ⟨the tent *flapped* in the rising breeze⟩ **3 a :** to beat or pulsate wings or something suggesting wings ⟨the children *flapped* with their arms as they scurried down the hill⟩ **b :** to progress by flapping ⟨early ideas of airplanes that would ~ like birds⟩ **c** *of a rotor blade* **:** to move up and down while rotating at the center **4 a :** to flutter ineffectively (as by beating of wings) ⟨the bird *flapping* helplessly against the screen⟩ **b :** to act or move erratically or to little effect ⟨such childish *flapping* to and fro will get you nowhere⟩ **5 :** to talk foolishly or to no purpose — usu. used with *about* ⟨the thing's settled, there's no use *flapping* about it now⟩ ⟨all he does is ~ about his own importance⟩

flapdock \'=ˌ=\ *n* **:** a foxglove (*Digitalis purpurea*)

flap·doo·dle \'flap,düdᵊl\ *n* -s [origin unknown] **:** foolish, empty, and often specious talk, writing, ideas, or opinions **:** NONSENSE ⟨his book contains a number of good pieces and a quantity of ~ as well —John Lardner⟩

flapdragon \'=ˌ==\ *n* **1 :** SNAPDRAGON 3 **2** *obs* **:** GERMAN, DUTCHMAN — usu. used disparagingly

flap-eared \'=¦=\ *adj* **1** *of a human* **:** having large ears standing well out from the head **2** *of a quadruped* **:** having large flexible or pendent ears

flap gate *n* **:** a gate hinged at the top and opening one way only and placed in a channel to close automatically on reversal of flow — compare FLAP VALVE

flap hinge *n* **:** STRAP HINGE

flapjack \'=ˌ=\ *n* [²*flap* + *Jack* (the name)] **1 :** GRIDDLE CAKE **2** *chiefly dial* **:** a fruit turnover **3** *also* **flapjack terrapin** *or* **flapjack turtle :** a No. American soft-shelled turtle **4** *chiefly Brit* **:** a large flat circular compact for face powder

flap-jawed \'=¦=\ *adj* **:** inclined to talk excessively and often indiscreetly ⟨fed up at the *flap-jawed* way some . . . columnists were talking —*Time*⟩

flapmouthed \'=ˌ=\ *adj* **:** FLAP-JAWED

flapped \'flapt\ *adj* [¹*flap* + *-ed*] **:** fitted or adorned with flaps ⟨a ~ pocket⟩

¹**flap·per** \'flapə(r)\ *n* -s **1 :** one that flaps: as **a :** a person or thing that reminds or warns one of something likely to be overlooked ⟨a spring ~ can be built into the clutch to sound a warning —A.F.Cragne⟩ **:** one that jogs the memory ⟨till their memories were again roused by their ~s —Jonathan Swift⟩ **b :** something for use in flapping or striking (as a flyswatter) **c :** a part that hangs or droops (as the swingle of a flail) **d :** FLIPPER 1 **e** *Brit* **:** a game bird; *esp* **:** a young wild duck not yet able to fly well **f** *slang* **:** HAND 1a(1) **g :** a worker who strikes the surface of molten metal with a rabble in copper refining **2 :** a young woman: **a** *archaic* **:** an immoral or dissolute young woman **b** *chiefly Brit* **:** a young girl not yet introduced to society — compare BUD **c :** a young woman who aggressively manifests freedom from constraint and conventions in conduct and dress — used esp. during the period of World War I and the following decade **d** *Brit* **:** a woman between 21 and 30 years of age — used disparagingly during the period that the vote was withheld from women below 30 years of age in Britain

²**flapper** \"\ *vi* **flappered; flappered; flappering** \-p(ə)riŋ\ **flappers :** to move in a flapping way

flapping *pres part of* FLAP

flapping meeting *also* **flapper meeting** *n, Brit* **:** an irregular horse race or series of horse races not under the supervision of any authoritative body

flap·py \'flapē, -pi\ *adj* -ER/-EST [²*flap* + *-y*] **1 :** SLACK, FLABBY ⟨~ skin⟩ **2 :** flapping or likely to flap ⟨long ~ hound ears⟩ ⟨loose ~ trousers⟩

flaps *pl of* FLAP, *pres 3d sing of* FLAP

flap table *n* **:** a drop-leaf table

flap tile *n* **:** a tile with a bent-up portion (as at a corner)

flap valve *also* **flapper valve** *n* **:** a valve (as in a pump) composed of a disk hinged on one edge and swinging one way only

¹**flare** \'fla(ə)|(ə)r, 'fle|, |ə\ *vb* -ED/-ING/-S [origin unknown] *vi* **1 a :** to stream or flutter in or as if in a current of air ⟨her coat *flared* behind her as she ran⟩ **b :** to burn with an unsteady or wavering flame ⟨the candle *flared* in the breeze as the door opened⟩ **2 a :** to shine with a sudden light **:** flame up brightly ⟨the fire *flared* brightly when the log crumbled into coals⟩; *often* **:** to emit a dazzling or painfully bright light ⟨the new snow *flaring* under the spring sun⟩ ⟨arc lights *flared*⟩ **b :** to become suddenly excited or angry **:** get in a passion (as of rage) — usu. used with *up* ⟨she ~s up at the slightest thing⟩ **c :** to express anger, passion, or vehement disapproval — usu. used with *out* ⟨she *flared* out at him furiously⟩ ⟨*flaring* out at such abuses⟩ **3 :** to open or spread outward **:** project beyond the perpendicular **:** have a flare usu. in a specified direction ⟨her skirt *flaring* about her legs⟩ ⟨a boat of shallow draft with the gunwales *flaring* out⟩ ~ *vt* **1 a :** to make to stream or flutter in or as if in a breeze ⟨the wind *flared* her skirts⟩ **b :** to display flaringly ⟨*flaring* a scarf from side to side to catch their eye⟩ **2 a :** to cause to flare ⟨the breeze *flared* the candle⟩ **b :** to give the appearance of a flaring flame ⟨sunset *flared* the western sky⟩ **c :** to signal with a flare or by flaring ⟨torches *flaring* the alarm⟩ **d :** to burn (a jet of waste gas) in the open air **3 :** to shape with a flare **:** spread gradually outward in shaping ⟨*flared* the coat with inset panels⟩ ⟨as the potter *flares* the neck of a jar⟩ ⟨gloved hands folded on a *flared* umbrella —Alan Brien⟩ **4 :** to level the flight path of (an airplane) just before making contact with the ground in landing so as to achieve a smooth transition from the steady glide to the ground run

syn see BLAZE

²**flare** \"\ *n* -s **1 :** an unsteady glaring light **2 :** a strong or flaring fire or blaze of light: as **a** *or* **flare light :** such a flare used to illuminate or attract attention (as on an airfield or battleground at night or as a prearranged signal); *also* **:** a device or composition (as a torch, Very light, or mag-

nesium ribbon) used to produce such a flare **b :** SOLAR FLARE **c :** the flame of a jet of waste gas (as from a sewage-disposal plant or coke oven) burned in open air for disposal **3 :** a sudden outburst (as of sound, excitement, or anger) ⟨a harsh ~ of trumpets⟩ ⟨a ~ of temper⟩ **4** *sometimes* **flair :** a spreading outward or a place or part that spreads ⟨the ~ of a fireplace⟩ ⟨the ~ of an urn⟩: as **a :** the upward and outward curve of the bow of a ship that throws aside spray when in motion **b :** fullness produced by gradually increasing the width towards the edge of a garment (as a gored skirt) **c :** an area of skin flush resulting from and spreading out from a local center of vascular dilation and hyperemia ⟨urticaria ~⟩ **d** *usu* **flair :** a tapered widening of the flangeway at the end of the guard line of a railroad track structure (as at the end of a guardrail or at the end of a frog or crossing wing rail) **5 :** light resulting from interreflection (as between lens surfaces) or an effect of this light: **a :** non-image-forming light that reaches the sensitive film in a camera **b** *or* **flare spot :** the resulting fogged or dense area in a photographic negative

³flare \"\ *n* -S [perh. alter. of ⁴*fleck*] *Brit* **:** LEAF FAT

flareback \ˈ≈,≈\ *n* -S [¹*flare* + *back*, adv.] **1 :** a burst of flame back or out from a furnace or similar space in opposition to the normal direction of the draft **2 :** an outburst (as of protest or angry rebuke) in response to a previous statement, criticism, or other cause **3 :** a burst of flame from the breech of a heavy gun that sometimes occurs on the opening of the breech when the gun has been fired and is due to gases left in the gun which ignite on admission of the air if a spark is present

flareboard \ˈ≈,≈\ *n* **:** a slanting extension of either side of an open box or frame (as on a wagon or motortruck) that increases the capacity

flare gun *or* **flare pistol** *n* **:** a handgun for firing signal rockets

flare kiln *n* **:** a kiln built of brick, shaped like the top and neck of a bottle, and formerly used to burn chalk and limestone into quicklime

flare·less \-ləs\ *adj* **:** free from flare: as **a** *of an explosive* **:** exploding without flame **b** *of a garment* **:** having straight lines without flared fullness

flare–out \ˈ≈,≈\ *n* -S [¹*flare* + *out*] **:** a leveling of the approach glide of an airplane made in such a way that the gliding angle is rapidly decreased by nosing up the airplane as it makes contact with the ground

flare path *n* **:** a path outlined by lights (as flares or electric lamps) on the ground to guide an airplane pilot in landing

flar·er \-a(a)rə(r), -erə-\ *n* -S **1 :** an operator of a machine that coils and flares strips of hoop steel for barrels — called also *coiler* **2 :** an operator of a machine that shapes riveted barrel hoops by alternate expansion and contraction

flare star *n* **:** a star (as a faint red dwarf) that undergoes sudden and unpredicted increases in brightness amounting often to several magnitudes in only a few minutes and fades as quickly

flare–up \ˈ≈,≈\ *n* -S [fr. *flare up* (verb phrase), fr. ¹*flare* + *up*] **1 a :** a sudden bursting into flame or light **:** FLARING ⟨a sharp *flare-up* of the dying fire⟩ ⟨excessive head lamp *flare-up* when engine speed is increased —H.F.Blanchard & Ralph Ritchen⟩ **b** *or* **flare–up light :** a brilliantly flammable torch or flare used for signaling or emergency illumination (as on a fishing boat) **2 :** a sudden outburst: as **a :** an outburst of anger, discontent, or antagonism usu. leading to heated words or violent action ⟨struck his brother in a *flare-up* of fury⟩ **b :** a sudden intensification of something previously mild or quiescent ⟨a *flare-up* of labor disputes⟩ ⟨a new *flare-up* of border disorders⟩; *esp* **:** a sudden increase in the symptoms of a latent or subsiding disease ⟨a *flare-up* of malaria⟩

flaring *adj* [fr. pres. part. of ¹*flare*] **1 a :** flaming or blazing brightly or unsteadily; *often* **:** DAZZLING **b :** gaudy and glaring ⟨a ~ resort hotel⟩ **2 a :** opening or spreading outward ⟨a ~ neckline⟩ **b :** having flare ⟨a graceful boat with a ~ bow⟩ — **flar·ing·ly** *adv*

flary \-a(a)rē, -erē, -ri\ *adj* [²*flare* + -*y*] **:** showy and bright **:** GAUDY

fla·ser \ˈfläzə(r)\ *n* -S [G, vein in wood or rock, prob. dial. modif. of *flader* vein in wood, veined wood, maple tree, fr. MHG *vlader* vein in wood, veined wood; perh. akin to Gk *platys* flat, broad — more at PLACE] **:** an irregular usu. streaked lens of granular texture found in a micaceous interstitial mass of rock and produced by shearing and pressure during metamorphism

¹flash \ˈflash, -aa(ə)-,-ai-\ *vb* -ED/-ING/-ES [ME *flaschen*, of imit. origin] *vi* **1 :** RUSH, DASH, SPLASH — used of flowing or tidal water ⟨flood waters ~*ing* over the rocky stream bed⟩ **2 a :** to break forth in or like a sudden flame **:** appear as a momentary flare ⟨the steel ~*ed*⟩ ⟨lightning ~*ing* in the sky⟩ ⟨the light ~*ed* on⟩ **b** *of a combustible* **:** to ignite with a flare ⟨the powder ~*ed*⟩ **c** *of a gun* **:** to give forth flame in the discharge **3 a :** to appear as suddenly as a flash ⟨an explanation ~*ed* into her mind⟩ **b :** to move with great speed **:** come, go, or pass like a flash ⟨the squirrel ~*ed* up a tree⟩ ⟨time ~*ed* by and we had to leave⟩ **4** *archaic* **:** to make a good showing **:** put one's best foot forward **:** show off **5 a :** to enter suddenly into another state (as of action or consciousness) ⟨he ~*ed* awake at the sound⟩ ⟨~*ing* into action as the starter's flag fell⟩ **b :** to break forth or out so as to make a sudden or unexpected display ⟨the sun ~*ed* from behind a cloud⟩ **c :** to act or speak vehemently and suddenly esp. in anger or disagreement — usu. used with *out* ⟨~*ing* out against such abuses⟩ ⟨sometimes she ~*es* out furiously before she thinks⟩ **6 a :** to light up or glow suddenly or intermittently ⟨fireflies ~*ing* in the meadow⟩ ⟨sunlight ~*ing* on the water⟩ **b :** to reflect light brilliantly or intermittently ⟨her diamonds ~*ed* and twinkled under the candles⟩ ⟨the windows ~*ed* with the setting sun⟩ **c** *of the eyes* **:** to glow or gleam esp. with animation or passion **:** SPARKLE ⟨eyes ~*ing* with delight⟩ **7** *in glass manuf* **:** to expand or open out into a sheet — used of a blown globe of glass **8** *of a liquid* **:** to change suddenly or violently into vapor ⟨when released from pressure the oil ~*es* into vapor⟩ **~** *vt* **1 a** *archaic* **:** to cause (water) to splash **b :** to fill (as a channel) or pass (as a boat) over an obstacle by means of a sudden inflow of water **2 a :** to cause the sudden appearance of (light or a source of illumination) **:** EMIT ⟨the oars ~*ed* cold greenish light⟩ — often used with *on* ⟨he ~*ed* on the light⟩ **b :** to cause to burst violently into fire ⟨a lighted match probably ~*ed* the escaping gas⟩ **c :** to cause (light) to reflect or cause (as a mirror) to reflect light ⟨~*ing* spots of light on the ceiling with a mirror⟩ ⟨~*ing* a mirror in the sunlight⟩; *often* **:** to convey or communicate (information or a message) by means of flashes of light ⟨~*ed* his position with a torch⟩ ⟨the general's answer was ~*ed* by heliograph⟩ **d :** to cause to glow or gleam usu. suddenly or transiently ⟨~*ed* her bright eyes at the boy⟩ **e :** to burn (as a sample of explosive) under controlled conditions in order to determine the character and amount of residue **3 a :** to convey, make known, or cause to appear with great speed or instantaneously ⟨the news of the surrender was ~*ed* around the world by radio and telegraph⟩ ⟨the operator ~*ed* a message on the screen⟩ **b :** to show off **:** display obtrusively or ostentatiously ⟨only a fool would ~ a fat wallet in such company⟩ **c :** to expose to view suddenly and usu. briefly ⟨the detective ~*ed* his badge⟩ ⟨~*ing* a shy smile⟩; *esp* **:** to expose (the face of a playing card) momentarily whether by accident (as in dealing) or by design (as in certain card tricks) **d :** to type (a word or phrase) as a unit without thinking of the individual letters as they are struck **4 :** to cover with or form into a thin layer: as **a :** to protect (as the valley, hip, or edge of a roof) against rain by covering with sheet metal or a substitute laid over or under the edge of the roofing **b :** to coat (as plain glass) with a thin layer (as of colored glass or metal; *also* **:** to apply (as a layer of colored glass) to — often used with *on* **c :** to pass a blowtorch flame over the surface of a layer of melted wax of (an electrotype case) to remove air bubbles prior to use in an electrotype mold **5 a :** to cause (glass) to flash **b :** to reheat (glass) to intensify the color esp. when red or yellow **6 :** to subject (an exposed photographic negative or positive) to a supplementary uniform exposure to light before development in order to modify detail or tone **7 a :** to convert (a liquid) quickly into vapor (as in a flash boiler) **b :** to eliminate in the form of vapor esp. by exposure to intense or sudden heating — usu. used with off ⟨~*ing* off the turpentine in purifying gum⟩ **c :** to vaporize (a getter) by heating the vacuum-tube filament in order to clear the tube of residual gas **d :** to reduce the pressure of suddenly (as by releasing into a vaporizing chamber or tower under lower pressure) ⟨the hot tar is ~*ed* into a vacuum chamber⟩

²flash \"\ *n* -ES **1 a :** a sudden burst of light **:** a light instantaneously appearing and disappearing ⟨a ~ of lightning⟩ **b :** a transient light (as from a lantern or torch) displayed as a signal; *also* **:** a movement of a flag in signaling **2 :** a sudden and brilliant burst (as of wit or genius) **:** a momentary and sudden show ⟨occasional ~*es* of industry⟩ **3 :** the duration of a flash **:** a brief time ⟨answered in a ~⟩ ⟨for a ~ we thought we saw them⟩ **4 a :** SHOW, DISPLAY; *esp* **:** a vulgar ostentatious display **b** *archaic* **:** a showy ostentatious person **:** SWELL, FOP **c :** something or someone that attracts notice (as by gaudiness or excellence); *esp* **:** an outstanding athlete **d :** brightness of color in flue-cured tobacco **5** *obs* **a :** ostentatious or bombastic talk or phrasing **b** [perh. fr. ³*flash*] **:** SLANG, CANT **6 a** *obs* **:** a splash or wave of water **b** *archaic* **:** a sudden stream of water released (as at a shoal or weir) to permit passage of a boat **7 :** something flashed: as **a :** GLIMPSE, LOOK ⟨caught a ~ of the scene as he hurried by⟩ **b :** SMILE **c :** a first brief news report; *usu* **:** one of an esp. newsworthy event sent to a newspaper or news broadcaster by wire — compare BULLETIN **d :** FLASHLIGHT c, d **e :** the quick-spreading flame or momentary intense outburst of radiant heat from the burst of a bomb, bazooka, or other explosive blast or from a flamethrower or welding arc **f** *Brit* **:** a bright tab worn as part of the insignia of a military uniform: (1) **:** a red shoulder patch — called also *shoulder flash* (2) **:** a red tab attached to a kilt garter as part of the uniform of certain Scottish units **g :** the body exposure at the end of a striptease **8 a :** FIN 2 c **b :** the recesses in a set of dies that receive the fin **9 :** a thin layer: as **a :** a layer of glass flashed on **b :** a very thin electroplated coating usu. less than ¹⁄₁₀₀,₀₀₀ inch thick **c :** a surface coloration on brick or pottery produced in the kiln by metallic oxides, manipulation of flame, or accidentally **10 :** a strong red that is yellower, darker, and slightly less strong than geranium (sense 3a) and yellower and slightly lighter than Goya **11 :** the rapid conversion of a liquid into vapor **12 :** FLASHING 4

³flash \"\ *adj* [²*flash*] **1 a** *of a thing* **:** showy but counterfeit **:** cheap, pretentious, and vulgar ⟨~ finery⟩; *sometimes* **:** such as appeals to the uncritically fashionable **:** SMART ⟨a ~ hotel⟩ **b** *of a person* (1) **:** vulgarly pretentious **:** given to showy display (2) **:** belonging to a sporting set; *often* **:** SPORTY, FAST (3) **:** being a thief, tramp, or a member of some other class that is considered beyond the bounds of normal society **c :** of, relating to, or characteristic of flash things or people ⟨a ~ appearance⟩ ⟨~ behavior⟩ **2 a :** of sudden origin, swift advance, and usu. short duration ⟨a ~ fire⟩ ⟨a valley subject to ~ flooding⟩ **b** *of a food-processing method* **:** involving extremely brief exposure to some very intense altering agent (as heat or cold) ⟨~ drying of milk⟩ ⟨processed by ~ freezing⟩ **3 :** caused by or used to protect against flash ⟨~ injury⟩ ⟨~ gear⟩ — see FLASH BURN

⁴flash *adj* [ME *flasch* tepid, fr. MF *flache*, fem. of *flac* weak, feeble, slack, fr. L *flaccus* flabby] **1** *obs, of food* **:** lacking in savor **:** INSIPID, FLAT, TASTELESS **2** *obs* **:** lacking meaning or validity **:** TRASHY **:** weak and worthless — used esp. of essentially mental matters (as speech or reasoning)

⁵flash *n* [ME (Sc) *flasche*] *obs* **:** a sheaf of arrows

¹flashback \ˈ≈,≈\ *n* -S, *often attrib* [¹*flash* + *back*, adv.] **1 a :** a literary or theatrical technique used esp. in motion pictures and television that involves interruption of the chronological sequence of events by interjection of events or scenes of earlier occurrence often in the form of projected reminiscence **b :** a piece or instance of literary or theatrical flashback ⟨we got to the movie at the beginning of the ~ to the hero's school days⟩ — called also *backflash* **c :** a past incident recurring vividly in the mind ⟨he saw his whole life in a series of ~*s*⟩ **2 a :** a recession of flame to a position where it is not expected or not wanted (as into a blowpipe); *esp* **:** BACK DRAFT **b :** ARC-BACK

²flashback \"\ *vi* **1 :** to appear or become introduced as flashbacks ⟨his life ~*ed* before his eyes⟩ **2 :** to employ flashbacks ⟨the play ~*s* to the hero's childhood⟩ ⟨a writer who ~*s* in a masterly way to impart a feeling of vitality to his characters⟩

flashboard \ˈ≈,≈\ *n* [¹*flash* + *board*] **:** a board or one of a series of boards projecting above the top of a dam to increase the depth of the water — called also *flushboard*

flash boiler *n* **:** a steam boiler that has very strong tubes with little water space which are kept nearly red-hot so that the water coming to them in small amounts is flashed into steam and superheated

flash bomb *n* **:** an aerial bomb that explodes in the air to provide brilliant illumination for aerial photography of the ground at night

flashbulb \ˈ≈,≈\ *n* **:** an electric flash lamp in which metal foil or wire is burned

flash burn *n* **:** tissue injury caused by exposure to radiant heat of high intensity (as from electrical discharges or explosions)

flash card *n* **1 :** a card bearing words, numbers, or pictures briefly displayed by a teacher to a class during drills (as in reading, spelling, or arithmetic) **2 :** a card displayed by a judge to make known his scoring of a performance (as in diving or gymnastics)

flash color *n* **:** a patch of bright color that is apparent only during motion on an otherwise neutrally tinted animal and that is believed to distract the attention of pursuers who lose sight of the prey when it comes to rest and the bright patch is obscured — compare WARNING COLORATION

flash defilade *n* **:** a condition in which the flash of a gun when fired is concealed from enemy observation by an intervening obstacle (as a ridge)

flash–dry \ˈ≈,≈\ *vt* **:** to dry (as a granular material) quickly (as by placing in an up-current of hot air)

flashed *adj* of FLASH

flash·er \-shə(r)\ *n* -S **:** one that flashes: as **a** *archaic* **:** a flashy or showy person **b :** TRIPLETAIL 1a **c :** a worker who flashes glass **d :** a device (as a traffic signal) that catches the attention by flashing **:** BLINKER **e :** a device for automatically lighting and extinguishing electric lamps by mechanical, thermal, or other means (as by regulating the flow of current through the lamps composing a display sign)

flashes *pres 3d sing of* FLASH, *pl of* FLASH

flash factor *n* **:** a number characteristic of a given photoflash lamp and a given film speed that when divided by the distance in feet between the lamp and the subject indicates the correct f-number for that distance

flash flood *n* **:** a local flood of relatively great volume and short duration that generally results from heavy rainfall in the immediate vicinity

flashflood \ˈ≈,≈\ *vt* [*flash flood*] **:** to flood suddenly **:** cause a flash flood in ⟨heavy rains ~*ed* the valley⟩

flashgun \ˈ≈,≈\ *n* **1 :** a device for holding and igniting flashlight powder **2 :** a device including a battery case, a lamp socket, and a reflector that is used for holding and operating a flashbulb

flashgun 2

flash hider *n* **:** a tubular device fitted to the muzzle of a firearm to conceal the flash of the burning powder gases

flash hole *n* **:** a hole in the bottom of the primer recess in the base of a cartridge case for admitting the flash of the ignited primer to the propelling charge

flashier *comparative of* FLASHY

flashiest *superlative of* FLASHY

flash·i·ly \-shəlē, -li\ *adv* **:** in a flashy manner or style ⟨a ~ dressed man⟩

flash in *vt* **:** to alter (details or tone) by flashing a photographic negative or positive

flash·i·ness \-shēnəs, -shin-\ *n* -ES **:** the quality or state of being flashy

flashing *n* -S [fr. gerund of ¹*flash*] **1 :** the reheating of an article of glass at the furnace aperture to restore its plastic condition; *esp* **:** the reheating of a globe of crown glass to allow it to flash **2 :** strips of sheet metal (as copper or galvanized iron) bent to fit in the interior angle between a wall and a roof surface or in the valley between two intersecting roof surfaces in order to make a watertight joint — compare COUNTERFLASHING, FILLETING **3 :** a lap joint (as a bell-and-spigot joint) in plumber's leadwork **4 :** the small-stop exposure to white paper of the photographic emulsion as a preliminary step in making a halftone

flashing block *n* **:** a terracotta block built into a parapet wall and containing a groove to receive the upper end of roof flashing in order to avoid the use of counterflashing

flash·ing·ly *adv* [*flashing* (pres. part. of ¹*flash*) + -*ly*] **:** in a flashing manner or style **:** SPARKLINGLY

flashing ring *n* **:** a ferrule around a pipe (as a drain) for holding it firm where it passes through a floor, wall, or ceiling

flashing tile *n* **:** a structural clay tile made with a recess to receive the flashing from a roof and used in a wall just above the junction of a flat roof with the wall — compare FLASHING BLOCK

flash in the pan 1 : the firing of the priming in the pan of a flintlock musket without discharging the piece **2 a :** a sudden spasmodic effort that accomplishes nothing **b :** a person of brilliant promise but little ultimate performance or worth

flash lamp *n* **:** a lamp for producing a brief but intense flash of light for taking photographs

flashlight \ˈ≈,≈\ *n, often attrib* **:** a flash of light or a light that flashes on and off: as **a** (1) **:** a scintillating light sometimes used in lighthouses (2) **:** a light shown by some lighthouses produced by revolution of reflectors or prismatic lenses so arranged as to show a bright light at regular intervals alternating with periods of dimness — called also *revolving light* **b :** a clear, sudden, or intermittent light used to signal (as on a ship) or illuminate (as an advertising sign) **c** (1) **:** a sudden bright artificial light used in taking photographic pictures (2) **:** metallic powder or other material to produce such a light (3) **:** a photograph taken by such a light **d :** a small battery-operated portable electric light

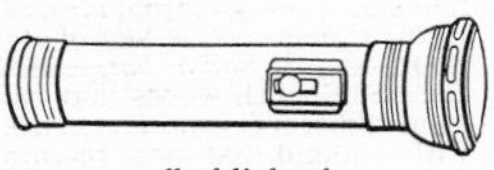

flashlight d

flashmeter \ˈ≈,≈≈\ *n* **:** TACHISTOSCOPE

flash·ness *n* -ES **:** the quality or state of being flash **:** FLASHINESS

flashold·er \ˈfla|,shōldə(r), -laa|, -lai|, |sh,hō-\ *n* [²*flash* (as in *flashbulb*) + *holder*] **:** FLASHGUN 2

flashover \ˈ≈,≈≈\ *n* -S *often attrib* [¹*flash* + *over*] **1 :** an electrical discharge or arc through the air to the ground from a high potential source or between two conducting portions of a machine or structure **2 :** the sudden spread of flame over an area when it becomes heated to the flash point

flashover voltage *n* **:** the voltage at which a current flashes from electrode to electrode or ground with the formation of a sustained arc

flashpan \ˈ≈,≈\ *n* **:** a pan for priming in a flintlock

flash paper *n* **:** thin paper (as tissue) treated with acid so that it will vanish in a flash when ignited

flash pasteurization *n* **:** pasteurization in which a fluid (as milk or fruit juice) is subjected very briefly to a relatively high temperature

flash photography *n* **:** photography by means of flashlight

flash plate *n* **:** a steel plate that protects the deck of a ship from the anchor chain

flash point *n* **1** *also* **flashing point :** the lowest temperature at which the vapors above a volatile combustible substance (as a petroleum product) ignite momentarily in air when tested usu. by applying a small flame under specified conditions ⟨the degree of flammability of a liquid is expressed mainly by means of its *flash point* —*Dict. of Fire Technology*⟩ **2 :** a point (as of interest or tension) at which someone or something bursts suddenly into action or being ⟨near the *flash point* of war⟩

flash ranging *n* **:** the locating of enemy weapons and the adjusting of friendly fire by observation of flashes from at least two observation posts — compare SOUND RANGING

flash spectrum *n* **:** a bright-line spectrum produced by the sun's reversing layer and observable for a few seconds at the beginning and end of a total solar eclipse

flashtube \ˈ≈,≈\ *n* **:** an electric flash lamp in which light can be obtained repeatedly by passing pulses of electric current through a gas **:** STROBE

flash–type \ˈ≈,≈\ *vt* **:** ¹FLASH 3d

flash weld *n* **:** a weld made by flash welding

flash welding *n* **:** butt welding in which a light initial pressure on the parts is quickly relieved and followed by a period of arcing and finally by heavy pressure

flashy \ˈflashē, -aash-,-aish-, -shi\ *adj* -ER/-EST [in sense 1, fr. ⁴*flash* + -*y*; in other senses, fr. ¹*flash* & ²*flash* + -*y*] **1** *now chiefly dial* **:** flat and watery **:** INSIPID ⟨the heavy rains have brought on a crop of soft ~ grass that does not cure well⟩ **2 :** momentarily dazzling **:** transitorily or superficially bright or pleasing **3 :** FIERY, IMPETUOUS ⟨a ~ temper⟩ **4 a :** superficially attractive **:** BRIGHT; *often* **:** ostentatious or showy beyond the bounds of good taste ⟨~ manners⟩ **:** GAUDY ⟨~ dress⟩ **b** *of an animal* **:** noticeable by reason of excellent conformation and finish ⟨a ~ boxer bitch⟩ **syn** see GAUDY

¹flask \ˈflask, -aa(ə)-,-ai-,-à-\ *n* -S *often attrib* [MF *flasque* powder flask, prob. modif. of OSp *frasco* powder flask, flask for liquids, modif. of LL *flascon-*, *flasco* bottle, prob. of Gmc origin; akin to OE *flasce*, *flaxe* bottle, OHG & ON *flaska*; perh. derivative fr. the root of OHG *flehtan* to braid, plait — more at PLY] **1 :** a vessel (as of metal, glass, skin) somewhat narrowed or necked toward the outlet, often fitted with a stopper, cap, or other closure, and used as a container: as **a :** a container usu. of horn, metal, or leather used to carry powder for a muzzle-loading firearm **b :** a necked vessel for holding liquids; *esp* **:** a broad flattened vessel of metal or sometimes glass curved to fit a pocket and used esp. to carry alcoholic beverages on the person **c :** a standard iron container in which 76 pounds of mercury is sold; *also* **:** a unit of weight for mercury equal to 76 pounds **d :** any of various usu. blown-glass vessels used for technical purposes in a laboratory **2 :** a wooden or metal frame that holds the sand forming the mold used in a foundry

²flask \"\ *vt* -ED/-ING/-S **:** to enclose in a flask; *esp* **:** to place (a denture) in a flask for processing

flas·ker \-kə(r)\ *vb* -ED/-ING/-S [prob. imit.] *dial Eng* **:** FLUTTER

flask·et \-kət\ *n* -S [ME, a container, fr. (assumed) ONF *flasket* small bottle (OF *flaschet*), dim. of ONF *flaske* bottle (OF *flasche*), fr. (assumed) VL *flasca* bottle (whence ML *flasca*), prob. of Gmc origin; akin to OE *flasce*, *flaxe* bottle, OHG & ON *flaska* — more at FLASK] **1** *now dial Eng* **:** a long shallow basket **2 :** a small flask

flask–shaped \ˈ≈,≈\ *adj* **:** resembling a typical flask in shape; *usu* **:** necked and either globular or flattened in body

flasque \ˈflask, -aa(ə)-,-ai-,-à-\ *n* -S [perh. fr. F, cheek of a gun carriage] **:** a heraldic bearing similar to a flanch but narrower

¹flat \ˈflat, *usu* -ad·+V\ *adj* **flatter**; **flattest** [ME, fr. ON *flatr*; akin to OS *flat* shallow, OHG *flaz* flat, Latvian *plañdīt* to make broad, Gk *platys* flat, broad — more at PLACE] **1 :** having or marked by a continuous surface that is horizontal or nearly so without significant curvature or inclination and without noteworthy elevations or depression ⟨a ~ top⟩ ⟨a ~ plateau⟩ ⟨a ~ deck⟩ **2 a :** lying at full length or spread out upon the ground **:** level with the ground or earth ⟨urged the pony ~ out and belly to the ground —Alan LeMay⟩ **:** PROSTRATE ⟨grass ~ after the storm⟩ **b :** utterly ruined, incapacitated, or destroyed **:** laid low ⟨buildings ~ from the blast⟩ ⟨was ~ with diphtheria⟩ ⟨my hopes all ~ —John Milton⟩ **c :** resting with a surface against or immediately adjoining something ⟨push the chairs ~ against the wall⟩ ⟨is ~ on his back in bed⟩ **3 a :** having a smooth or even surface whether horizontal or not ⟨use the *flatter* side for the face⟩ ⟨a ~ slab of rock⟩ **b :** smooth or even by comparison with something usu. implied ⟨a broad ~ face⟩ ⟨a design worked in ~ relief⟩ **c** *of a fur* **:** having a smooth sleek surface due to hairs lying strongly inclined to the surface; *sometimes* **:** having the hairs sparse and short **d** *of a knit fabric* **:** lacking ribs **:** FLATKNIT **4 :** arranged or laid out so as to be level, smooth, or even ⟨maps ~ on the desk⟩ **5 a :** having the major surfaces essentially parallel and distinctly greater than the minor surfaces ⟨a ~ piece of wood⟩ ⟨coins are usually round and ~⟩

b *of a shoe heel* : very low and broad; *also, of a shoe* : having a flat heel or no heel ⟨~ shoes for ballet⟩ **6 a** : clear and unmistakable : DOWNRIGHT, POSITIVE ⟨a ~ contradiction of his sister's statement⟩ ⟨a ~ failure⟩; *sometimes* : PEREMPTORY ⟨a ~ denial of responsibility⟩ **b** : not varied or varying (as from a fixed or normal amount or standard) : ABSOLUTE, FIXED ⟨a ~ service charge⟩ ⟨a ~ rate⟩; *also* : having no fraction either lacking or in excess : EXACT, PRECISE ⟨made the bus in a ~ 10 seconds⟩ ⟨ran the mile in four minutes ~⟩ **7 a** : weak or lacking in animation, spirit, zest, or vigor : devoid of qualities that please, interest, or stimulate : DULL, LIFELESS ⟨a ~ drab deadly round of work, eat, sleep⟩ ⟨~ puerile writing lacking both substance and style⟩ ⟨plays whose composition is neither lifelike nor unlifelike but just ~ —Marston Balch⟩ **b** : lacking mental alertness or vigor : dull and stupid ⟨~ cloddish minds⟩ **c** : lacking savor : INSIPID, TASTELESS ⟨the stew is too ~⟩ **d** *of an effervescent drink* : having given off the included gas and become still : lacking effervescence or sparkle ⟨beer goes ~ on standing⟩ **e** : commercially inactive : dull and depressed ⟨the market is very ~ for this time of year⟩ **f** : DEFLATED — used chiefly of pneumatic tires **g** : lacking funds : having no money **8 a** : characterized by lack of clearness, sharpness, accuracy of pitch, or sonority — used esp. of the tone quality of a musical instrument or voice ⟨the bell has a ~ sound as if cracked⟩ **b** *of a musical note or tone* : minor or lower by a half step ⟨a ~ seventh⟩; *also, of a key or tonality* : having a flat in the signature ⟨the key of B ~⟩ **c** *of the vowel a* (1) : pronounced as in *bad* or *bat* — used esp. when so pronounced in a class of English words that have the vowel of *palm* or *par* in some dialects ⟨pronouncing *ask* with a ~ *a*⟩ (2) : pronounced with a sound that more resembles in quality the *a* of *bat* than the *o* of *bother* without actually being the *a* of *bat* — used of the *a* of such words as *part, palm, father* as often pronounced in eastern New England **9 a** : having a low trajectory ⟨the bow shoots a ~ arrow⟩ ⟨made a ~ pass that was intercepted⟩ **b** *of a tennis ball* : hit squarely without being spun by the racket ⟨a ~ drive⟩ **10** : not having an inflectional ending or sign — used esp. of an adherent noun, an infinitive without the sign *to*, or an adverb with no adverbial ending **11** *of a curve or angle* : GRADUAL, SHALLOW : not sharp or steep ⟨~ dive⟩ ⟨~ glide⟩ **12 a** *of a weather map* : showing little regional variation in barometric pressure **b** *of weather* : having not much wind or pressure variation : CALM **13** *of a sail* : made taut so as to prevent or reduce bellying ⟨eased before the wind with all sheets ~⟩ **14 a** : uniform in hue or shade ⟨figures standing out against a background of ~ wash⟩ **b** *of a painting* : having little or no illusion of depth, interest being concentrated on the surface treatment **c** *of a photograph or negative* : lacking contrast **d** *of a lighting arrangement* : not emphasizing shadows or contours — used esp. of an arrangement for photography in which light comes from a point that is in front of the subject and in line with the camera **e** : free from gloss ⟨a ~ paint⟩ **f** *of a proof* : made from an unfinished printing surface ⟨took a ~ proof from a form on the press but not yet made ready⟩ **15** : having no bevel — used of ship timbers **16** : being or relating to a transducer response or output that is in constant ratio to the input as the frequency varies so that there is distortionless reproduction over a specified frequency range **syn** see INSIPID, LEVEL

2flat \"\ *n* -s [ME, fr. *flat*, adj. — more at 1FLAT] **1 a** (1) : a level surface of land with little or no relief : PLAIN (2) : a level tract lying at little depth below the surface of water or alternately covered and left bare by the tide : SHOAL, SHALLOW, STRAND (3) : a tract of wet low-lying level land : MARSH, SWAMP (4) *chiefly North & Midland* : BOTTOM 6 **b** (1) : one of the divisions of cropland used in common (2) *dial* : a field growing a crop **c** : a horizontal extension of a mineral vein; *also* : a flat horizontal deposit (as of ore) **d** : a running track or other course for a flat race ⟨a race for three-year-old trotters on the ~⟩ **e** : the part of a football field immediately adjacent to the flanks of either team **2** : a flat part or surface: as **a** : one of the larger essentially parallel surfaces of something characterized by great disparity in the size of its surfaces — often opposed to *edge* ⟨struck the boy with the ~ of the ruler⟩ ⟨drive the stake with the ~ of your ax⟩ **b** : the palm of the hand sometimes together with the palmar surface of the fingers ⟨pat out the dough with the ~ of your hand⟩ **3** : an improper die that because of imperfectly cubical form tends to present a particular face more frequently than a perfect die **4 a** : a musical note or tone one half step lower than a specified note or tone ⟨A flat is the ~ of A⟩ **b** : a character ♭ on a line or space of the musical staff indicating a pitch a half step lower than the line or space would otherwise indicate without it **5** : something of broad shallow form: as **a** : a shallow basket, crate, or other container in which produce is shipped to market **b** : a broad-brimmed low-crowned straw hat **c** : a platform on wheels upon which displays (as of emblematic designs) are drawn in processions — compare FLOAT **d** : a shallow box in which seedlings are started **e** : a flat-bottomed boat with a shallow draft and without keel **f** : a flatcar or other draft vehicle (as a motortruck or handcart) without raised sides **g** : a pressed paper divider having shallow depressions in which eggs are placed to fill a single layer of an egg case **h** : a flat piece of theatrical scenery typically consisting of a wood frame covered with painted cloth and used to form a section of a set wall or ceiling or to mask a door or window **i** : one of the slats with teeth that are mounted on an endless chain above the cylinder of a carding machine and that assist in ordering the textile fiber being carded **6** : something of broad and thin or flat form: as **a** : a plane mirror or reflector; *also* : a transparent disk with one or both surfaces accurately plane — called also *optical flat* **b** : a mature mushroom with a fully expanded cap — compare BUTTON 2d **c** : a picture-frame mat **d** : a level deck on a ship; *esp* : one onto which cabins open **e** : a shoe or slipper having a flat heel or no heel **f** : an architectural member having the form of a platform of generally horizontal character (as the deck of a roof with steep sides or any roof of which the slope does not much exceed one in twenty) **g** : a long flat square-edged artist's brush — compare BRIGHT, ROUND **h** : a collapsed or knocked down container as sent in bulk to the purchaser **i** : the straight part of the cutting edge of a machine tool **7** : a punctured tire : a pneumatic tire with no air pressure **8 a** : a rolled metal bar of uniform rectangular cross section **b** : the cylindrical portion of the contour at either root or crest of certain screw threads **9** : EUCLIDEAN SPACE **10** : a surface (as of paint) that is not glossy **11 a** : an unfolded sheet of paper **b flats** *pl* : writing paper with a flat smooth surface **12** : the thick glass on which negative films are laid close together for printing on sensitized metal in making a photoengraving; *also* : an assemblage of negative or positive films from which a photo-offset plate is made **13** : an inferior grade of rough diamonds **14 a** : a dance step with the full surface of the foot **b** : the act of gliding upright on both edges of a skate blade during a curve where the single edge position is correct; *also* : the double track that shows on the ice when a flat occurs — called also *double edge*

3flat \"\ *adv* [1*flat*] **1** : in a flat manner : DIRECTLY, POSITIVELY ⟨came out ~ for less work and higher pay⟩ **2 a** : at full length ⟨fell ~ on his face⟩ **b** : on or against a flat surface ⟨lying ~ on his back⟩ ⟨spread out ~ on the ground⟩ **3** : WHOLLY, COMPLETELY ⟨~ broke⟩ **4** : without charging or without paying interest (as when giving or receiving credit); *esp* : without allowance or charge for accrued interest — used of the selling or quoting of bonds **5** : below the proper musical pitch ⟨he sang slightly ~⟩ **6** : with flat sail ⟨sailing ~ in a high wind⟩

4flat \"\ *vb* **flatted; flatted; flatting; flats** [1*flat*] *vt* **1** *obs* : to lay flat : LEVEL, RAZE **2** *archaic* : to make flat or level : FLATTEN **3** *obs* : to make dull, insipid, or spiritless ⟨passions are allayed, appetites are *flatted* —Isaac Barrow⟩ **4 a** : to depress (a musical tone) in pitch **b** : to lower in pitch by a half step ⟨a *flatted* fifth⟩ **5 a** : to cover (a surface) with a flat coat (as of paint) **b** : to remove the gloss from (a painted or varnished surface) esp. by sanding **c** : to free (a paint) from the tendency to set with a glossy surface (as by the addition of turpentine) **6** : to plant (as bulbs) in or transplant (as seedlings) into a flat ~ *vi* **1** *obs* : to become flat or flattened : sink or fall to an even surface **2** *of a musical tone* : to fall from the true or intended pitch ⟨could tell the approach of the milkman by the whistled notes that somehow always *flatted*⟩

5flat \"\ *n* -s [1*flat*] **1** : a floor, loft, or story in a building **2 a** *chiefly Brit* : an apartment or suite of rooms occupying or forming part of one floor of a building — compare MAISONETTE **b** *chiefly North* : an apartment on one floor usu. with separate outdoor entry and sometimes lacking amenities ⟨a cold-water ~⟩ — compare TENEMENT; see RAILROAD FLAT **3** : a building divided into flats — often used in pl.

flat advertising rate *n* : a uniform rate of charge per unit of advertising space that is applicable irrespective of the amount of space contracted for

flat arch *n* : a spanning member constructed of mutually supporting voussoirs and having a straight or almost straight horizontal intrados and extrados

flat back *n* : a book backbone made without rounding and sometimes without backing; *also* : a book so bound or the style of binding featuring this construction

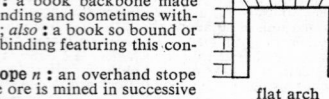

flat-back stope *n* : an overhand stope in which the ore is mined in successive horizontal cuts

flat arch

1flatbed \ˈ⸗,⸗\ *adj* [1*flat* + *bed*] : having a horizontal bed on which a horizontal printing surface rests — usu. used of a cylinder press; compare ROTARY PRESS

2flatbed \"\ *n* [in sense 1, fr. 1*flatbed*; in sense 2, fr. 1*flat* + *bed*] **1** : a flatbed printing press **2** : a motortruck or trailer with a body in the form of a platform or shallow box

flat bet *n* : a bet at even money (as in craps)

1flatboat \ˈ⸗,⸗\ *n* : a boat with a flat bottom and square ends used for transportation of bulky freight esp. in shallow waters

2flatboat \"\ *vi* : to engage in the management of or labor or travel on a flatboat ~ *vt* : to transport (as supplies or passengers) by flatboat ⟨~*ed* his fruit to the city⟩

flat·boat·man \-mən\ *n, pl* **flatboatmen** : a member of the crew of a flatboat

flat-bodied \ˈ⸗ˈ⸗⸗\ *also* **flat-body** \ˈ⸗ˈ⸗⸗\ *adj* : having the body dorsoventrally flattened — used esp. of insects

flat bone *n* : any of various bones (as of the skull, the jaw, the pelvis, or the rib cage) not rounded in cross section

flat bow *n, archery* : a bow of uniform thickness that differs only in dimension from the longbow

flatbread \ˈ⸗,⸗\ *or* **flat·brod** \ˈ⸗,brōd\ *n* [*flatbread* trans. of Norw *flatbrød*; *flatbrod* modif. of Norw *flatbrød*, fr. *flat* (fr. ON *flatr*) + *brød* bread, fr. ON *brauth* — more at FLAT, BREAD] : a thin dry wafer made of rye flour dough and used esp. among Scandinavian peoples

flat bug *n* : an insect of the family Aradidae

flatcap \ˈ⸗,⸗\ *n* **1** : a round low-crowned cap worn in 16th and 17th century England esp. in London **2** : a wearer of a flatcap; *esp* : LONDONER

flatcar \ˈ⸗,⸗\ *n* : a railroad freight car without permanent raised sides, ends, or covering

flat carving *n* : carving (as on furniture) consisting of flat surfaces thrown into relief by cutting back the spaces around and between them

flatcatcher \ˈ⸗,⸗⸗\ *n* [E slang *flat* dupe, fool (fr. E 1*flat*) + E *catcher*] **1** *Brit* : SWINDLER **2** *Brit* : a horse that looks good but is not

flat chisel *n* : a chisel (as a cold chisel) of hardened and tempered steel used to obtain a flat and finished surface (as on wood or stone)

flat-coated retriever \ˈ⸗,⸗⸗-\ *n* : an active medium-sized sporting dog of a breed of English origin characterized by a black or liver-colored dense close smooth coat and a rather long head

flat-compound \,⸗⸗ˈ⸗, ⸗ˈ⸗,⸗\ *vt* : to add to (the ordinary winding of a dynamo) a series field winding with the requisite number of turns to make the terminal voltage of a generator or the speed of a motor nearly independent of its load

flat cost *n* : the part of the cost (as of a building) representing direct outlay for labor and material

flat countersink *n* : a tool for countersinking in metal — see COUNTERSINK illustration

flat crab *n* : PORCELAIN CRAB

flat crepe *n* : a silk or rayon crepe similar to crepe de chine but with a flatter surface and a duller finish

flatcrown \ˈ⸗,⸗\ *also* **flatcrown tree** *n* : a deciduous African tree (*Albizzia gummifera*) with hairy foliage, flowers in globular heads, and moderately heavy yellowish to grayish or brown wood used locally for carving

flat-earth·er \ˈ⸗ˈərthər\ *n* -s [*flat earth* + *-er*] : a person who maintains the earth to be a flat body

flat engine *n* : an internal-combustion engine having cylinders arranged by pairs on opposite sides of the crankshaft and in one horizontal plane

flat envelope *n* : a piece of paper cut ready to make into an envelope

flat etch *n* : FIRST BITE

flat-fell seam \ˈ⸗,fel-\ *n* [obs. E *flat fell* (fr. E 1*flat* + obs. E *fell*, n., action of felling a seam, felled seam, fr. E 2*fell*) + E *seam*] : a strong seam with two lines of stitching showing on the right side that is produced by folding one raw edge under the other and stitching it flat or slip-stitching it on the wrong side

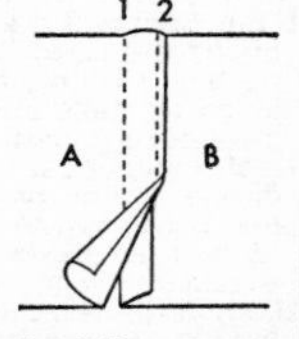

flat-fell seam: *1* first stitching, joining pieces *A* and *B*; *2* second stitching

flat file *n* : a file of rectangular section about four times as wide as thick at the heel and tapering toward the point

flatfish \ˈ⸗,⸗\ *n* **1** : any of numerous marine teleost fishes that are usu. considered to constitute an order Heterosomata, that are distinguished as adults by swimming on one side of a laterally compressed body and by having both eyes on the upper side due to gradual twisting of the skull and the lower side blind and largely devoid of color, and that include important food fishes (as the halibuts, flounders, turbots, and soles) **2** : any of various fishes with laterally compressed bodies that do not habitually swim on one side: as **a** : GIZZARD SHAD **b** : PUMPKINSEED **c** : INDIAN FISH 1a

1flatfoot \ˈ⸗,⸗, *in sense 3* ˈ⸗,⸗\ *n, pl* **flatfeet** \ˈ⸗ˈ⸗\ **1 a** : a condition in which the arch of the instep is flattened so that the entire sole rests upon the ground **b** : a condition in horses in which the hoof is very large and sloping and the frog is excessively prominent **2** : a foot affected with flatfoot **3** : a person having or held likely to have flatfeet: as **a** *pl often* **flatfoots** *slang* : POLICEMAN; *esp* : a patrolman that walks a regular beat **b** *slang* : SAILOR

2flatfoot \ˈ⸗ˈ⸗\ *vi* : to walk in a flat-footed manner or style

1flat-footed \ˈ⸗ˈ⸗⸗\ *adj* [1*flat* + *footed*] **1** : affected with flatfoot; *broadly* : walking with the somewhat dragging or shambling gait characteristic of a person with severe flatfeet **2** : having a flat base ⟨a *flat-footed* rail⟩ **3 a** : firm and well balanced on the feet ⟨a *flat-footed* stance⟩ **b** : free from reservation : complete and determined : FORTHRIGHT ⟨*flat-footed* support for an idea⟩ **4** : found in an unprepared state : UNREADY — used chiefly in the phrase *catch one flat-footed* — **flat-foot·ed·ly** *adv* — **flat-foot·ed·ness** *n* -ES

2flat-footed \"\ *adv* : openly and determinedly : FLATLY

flatfoot walk *also* **flat-footed walk** *n* : a slow 4-beat gait in which the horse's hooves touch the ground in the order right fore, left rear, left fore, right rear

flat glass *n* : a drawn sheet glass or rolled glass

flat grain *n* : a grain in lumber parallel or nearly parallel with the face of the piece (as of veneering stock) that is produced by sawing nearly at right angles to the annual rings

flat grain beetle *n* : a minute flattened oblong reddish brown cucujid beetle (*Cryptolestes pusillus*) common in stored grain where it feeds chiefly on damaged grains and debris

flat-hat \ˈ⸗ˈ⸗\ *vi* [1*flat* + *hat*, n.; fr. an alleged incident in which a pedestrian's hat was crushed by the undercarriage of a low-flying plane] **1** : to fly low in an airplane in an unnecessarily dangerous or reckless manner : HEDGEHOP **2** : to show off — **flat-hatter** \ˈ⸗ˈ⸗⸗\ *n*

flat·head \ˈ⸗,⸗\ *n, pl* **flatheads** *or* **flathead** **1** *usu cap* **a** : any of several Indian peoples (as the Chinook, Catawba, Choctaw, and Waxhaw) of No. America that formerly practiced head-flattening **b** : a member of any of such peoples **2** *usu cap* **a** : a Salish people that formerly occupied most of western Montana **b** : a member of such people **3 a** : HOGNOSE SNAKE **b** : any of various fishes with more or less flat heads: as (1) : any of a family (Platycephalidae) of chiefly Indo-Pacific marine food fishes that resemble sculpins (2) : BARRAMUNDA a (3) : a large minnow (*Platygobio gracilis*) of rivers of the Rocky mountain area (4) : FLATHEAD CATFISH **4 a** : a flattened head of a rivet or bolt; *also* : a rivet or bolt with such a head **b** : a screw with a head flat on top and tapering to the shaft so that it can be countersunk **5** : a stupid or gullible person : SIMPLETON **6** *South* : FALLER 1

flathead catfish *or* **flathead cat** *n* : a large yellowish brown-mottled catfish (*Pylodictis olivaris*) of the Mississippi drainage, the Gulf states, and westward to the Rio Grande

flat·head·ed \ˈ⸗ˈ⸗⸗\ *also* **flat·head** \ˈ⸗ˈ⸗\ *adj* : having a flat or flattened head ⟨a ~ nail⟩ ⟨~ snakes⟩

flatheaded adder *n* [so called fr. its habit of flattening its head when disturbed] : HOGNOSE SNAKE

flatheaded apple tree borer *n* : a flattened elongate-oval beetle (*Chrysobothris femorata*) bronze above and bright and brassy beneath that is widespread in hardwoods — called also *apple tree borer*

flatheaded borer *or* **flathead borer** *n* [so called fr. its much enlarged and flattened thorax] : any of numerous beetle larvae of the family Buprestidae that bore beneath the bark or in the sapwood of trees

flatheaded cat *n* : a wildcat (*Felis planiceps*) of southeastern Asia

flat hoop *n* : a wooden hoop dressed flat on both sides

flatiron \ˈ⸗,⸗(⸗)\ *n* **1** : an iron that has a flat smooth surface for ironing clothes and that typically has a base with the general contour of an isosceles triangle — compare BOX IRON, SADIRON **2** *geol* : a short triangular hogback that when viewed from the side resembles a huge flatiron standing on its heel **3** *also* **flatiron collier** *Brit* : a coal carrier with hinged funnels and masts used on the Thames river

flat·ite \ˈflad,īt\ *n* -s *Austral* : a person who lives in a flat

flat joint *n* [prob. so called fr. the flat surface on which a shell game is played] **1** *slang* : a confidence game (as the shell game) carried out by an organized mob **2** *slang* : a gambling game or wheel usu. connected with a circus or carnival that can be manipulated at the will of the operator

flatiron 1

flat-joint pointing *n* [*flat joint* (fr. 1*flat* + *joint*) + *pointing*] : the making of a masonry joint that is flush with the wall surface

flat keel *n* : a ship's keel consisting of a heavy strake of plating stiffened by an upright vertical keel — called also *flat-plate keel*

flat key *n* : a rectangular key set upon a flat on a shaft and used for transmitting small torques

flat-knit \ˈ⸗ˈ⸗\ *adj* : knitted on a flat machine with needles arranged in a straight line — contrasted with *circular-knit*

flat knot *n* : REEF KNOT

flatland \ˈ⸗,⸗\ *n* **1 a** : land that lacks significant variation in elevation ⟨the farm includes a valuable stretch of ~ along the river⟩ **b** : a region in which the land is predominantly flat — usu. used in pl. ⟨coastal ~*s*⟩ **2** : a hypothetical two-dimensional world — **flat·land·er** \-də(r)\ *n* -s

flat·let \ˈflatlət\ *n* -s *Brit* : a small compact flat typically consisting of a single dwelling room with kitchenette and bath

1flat·ling \-liŋ,-lən\ *or* **flat·lings** \-ŋz,-nz\ *or* **flat·lins** \-nz\ *adv* [ME *flatling, flatlinges*, fr. 1*flat* + *-ling, -linges* -ling, -lings] **1** *now dial Brit* : in a flat or horizontal position ⟨had stumbled backwards and fallen *flatlings* into the ditch —J.H. McCarthy⟩ **2** *now dial Brit* : with a flat side or edge ⟨smote him ~ with his sheathed sword —William Morris⟩

2flat·ling \-liŋ\ *adj* **1** *obs, of a blow* : dealt with the flat side of a weapon **2** : falling or pressing down on one ⟨we lift the weight of ~ years —Rudyard Kipling⟩

flatlock \ˈ⸗ˈ⸗\ *adj, of a seam* : made by bringing two raw edges together and covering them with machine stitching

flat·ly *adv* [ME (Sc), fr. ME 1*flat* + *-ly*] **1** *obs* : into a flat position : PROSTRATE **2 a** : BLUNTLY, CATEGORICALLY, PLAINLY ⟨he ~ denied the charges⟩; *sometimes* : EMPHATICALLY, PEREMPTORILY ⟨presenting the case ~ and sternly⟩ ⟨~ challenged the truth of the statement⟩ **b** : ABSOLUTELY, WHOLLY ⟨acting ~ against his convictions⟩ **3** : in a flat manner ⟨sagging ~ in his arms⟩: as **a** : without zest or spirit : in a dull and uninterested manner ⟨droned on ~ about her troubles⟩ **b** : without indication or development of a third dimension ⟨roses stenciled ~ on the chair backs⟩

flat machine *n* : a knitting machine with needles arranged on a horizontal flat bed

flat·ness *n* -ES [ME *flatnesse* flat surface, fr. 1*flat* + *-nesse* -ness] : the quality or state of being flat

1flat-out \ˈ⸗ˈ⸗\ *adj* **1** *chiefly dial* : frank and open : ALL-OUT, DOWNRIGHT **2** : MAXIMUM, TOP ⟨no technical understanding of driving skill, and anything but *flat-out* speed is lost on them —Ken Purdy⟩

2flat-out \"\ *adv* **1** *chiefly dial* : bluntly and directly : OPENLY ⟨told him *flat-out* what I thought⟩ **2** : at top speed

flat pass *n* : a forward pass in football thrown nearly level toward the sidelines

flat pea *n* **1 a** : a European perennial pea (*Lathyrus sylvestris*) sometimes cultivated for fodder or as a green-manure crop **b** : the seed of the flat pea **2** : any of several Australian evergreen leguminous shrubs that constitute a small genus (*Platylobium*) and are sometimes cultivated in warm regions for their bright yellow pealike flowers

flat peach *n* [trans. of Chin (Pek) *pien3 t'ao2*] : PEEN-TO

flat-plate keel *n, Brit* : FLAT KEEL

flat point *or* **flat-point lace** *n* **1** : needle-point lace with flat designs instead of raised or padded designs **2** : bobbin-made lace in contrast to needlepoint lace

flat race *n* : a race on a level course without hurdles or other obstacles

flat racing *n* : the sport of riding in flat races

flat reinsurance *n* : a reinsurance agreement (as in marine insurance) that is not subject to cancellation or change

flat relief *n* : bas-relief in which projected parts have little or no modeling and the details are frequently marked by incised lines

flat-ring \ˈ⸗ˈ⸗\ *adj* : having or employing a flat ring : DISCOIDAL ⟨*flat-ring* winding of an induction coil⟩

flat-rolled \ˈ⸗ˈ⸗\ *adj* : formed by rolling between plain cylindrical rolls — used of metal sheet, strip, plate, and some bars

flat roof *n* : a nearly horizontal roof pitched for water drainage only

flat rope *n* : a rope of metal or fiber having a flat cross section and usu. formed by braiding or sewing rather than by twisting

flats *pl of* FLAT, *pres 3d sing of* FLAT

flat sage *n* : SPART GRASS

flat-sawn \ˈ⸗ˈ⸗\ *adj, of lumber* : sawed so as to produce a flat-grain surface

flat seizing *n* : a seizing in which the lines seized are parallel to each other and a single binding layer is used — compare ROUND SEIZING

flat silver *n* : knives, forks, spoons, and other eating or serving utensils made of or plated with silver

flat-slab construction *n* : reinforced-concrete floor construction not requiring beams and girders to transmit the floor load to supporting columns

flat sour *n* : fermentation of canned products (as peas or corn) that is caused by thermoduric microorganisms which survive the canning process and that is characterized by the formation of acid without gas; *sometimes* : the off-flavor produced by such fermentation

flat spin *n* **1** : a spin in which the longitudinal axis of an airplane inclines downward at a smaller angle than 45 degrees **2** *slang* : a state of mental confusion

flat·tail mullet \ˈ⸗ˈ⸗-\ *also* **flat tail** \ˈ⸗ˈ⸗\ *n* : an Australian mullet (*Liza argentia*) that is an important food fish

flat·ted \ˈflatəd\ *adj* [5*flat* + *-ed*] *Brit, of a building* : divided into flats

flat·ten \'flat°n\ *vb* **flattened; flattened; flattening** \-t(°)niŋ\ **flattens** [¹*flat* + -*en*] *vt* **1 :** to reduce to an even or more nearly even surface **:** make flat **:** LEVEL, SMOOTH ⟨~ the seams with a steam iron⟩ ⟨time ~*s* the mountains⟩ **2 a :** to throw down **:** bring to the ground **:** PROSTRATE ⟨the hurricane ~*ed* the forest⟩ **b :** DEPRESS, DEJECT, DISPIRIT ⟨was ~*ed* by grief⟩ **c :** to completely overwhelm ⟨the senator ~*ed* his opposition⟩: as (1) **:** to ruin financially ⟨the depression ~*ed* many young or small businesses⟩ (2) *slang* **:** to knock out ⟨the boxer was ~*ed* in the seventh round⟩; *sometimes* **:** to defeat decisively in any contest (3) **:** to kill or destroy by or as if by crushing ⟨the car ~*ed* the farmer's hen⟩ (4) **:** to make (as oneself) helplessly drunk **3** *archaic* **:** to make vapid or insipid **4 a :** to make (as paint) lusterless **b :** to cover (a surface) with a priming coat or a coat of flat paint **5** *Brit* **:** FLAT 4 **6 :** to adjust (a sail) by hauling in the aftermost clew to help turn a sailboat — often used with *in* ~ *vi* **1 :** to become flat or flatter: as **a :** to become dull, savorless, or lacking in spirit **b :** to get, move, or extend in or into a flat position or form — often used with *out* ⟨hills ~*ing* into coastal plains⟩ ⟨the ruts ~*ed* out under the pressure of wheels⟩ **c :** to become uniform or stabilized often at a new higher or lower level — usu. used with *out* ⟨prices are expected to ~ out after the holiday buying⟩ ⟨performance tended to ~ out after an initial period of improvement⟩ **d** (1) **:** to manipulate an airplane so as to bring its longitudinal axis parallel with the ground (as after a climb or a dive) — used with *out* (2) *of an airplane* **:** to assume such a position — used with *out* **2 :** to extend oneself in making an effort ⟨the horses ~*ed* into their collars⟩ ⟨rose refreshed and ~*ed* to the task of grubbing roots⟩

flattened–strand rope *n* **:** a wire rope having the wires in each strand arranged so as to form flat surfaces on the strands

flat·ten·er \'flat(°)nə(r)\ *n* -S **:** one that flattens: as **a :** a worker who flattens materials (as metal, leather, paper, or glass) **b :** a machine for flattening or straightening plates or sheets

flattening oven *n* [*flattening* fr. gerund of *flatten*] **:** a heating chamber in which split glass cylinders are flattened and annealed

flattening stone *n* **:** a stone used in a flattening oven

¹**flat·ter** \'fladə(r), -atə-\ *vb* -ED/-ING/-S [ME *flateren*, irreg. fr. OF *flater* to lick, flatter, fr. (assumed) OFrk *flat*, adj., flat; akin to OHG *flaz* flat — more at FLAT] *vt* **1 :** to praise excessively or fulsomely esp. from motives of self-interest **:** gratify or appeal to the self-love or vanity of usu. by artful and interested commendation or attentions **2 a** *archaic* **:** to make more pleasant or less oppressive **:** BEGUILE, SOOTHE **b :** to encourage (as a person or his hopes) esp. by false or specious representations ⟨~*ed* the old man by asking him to climb the mountain⟩ **c :** to please or gratify (as oneself) usu. with the assurance that something (as a view or procedure) is right or acceptable ⟨~ myself that only the most caviling critics can take exception to my interpretation⟩ ⟨~*ed* himself that the young people wanted his company for its own sake, not the luxuries he provided⟩; *also* **:** to congratulate (oneself) in respect to something ⟨suppose I may ~ myself that I am not a fool⟩ **d :** GRATIFY ⟨balmy breezes ~*ed* his skin⟩ **3 a :** to portray too favorably ⟨that picture ~*s* him⟩ **b :** to display or set off to advantage **:** make the most of the good points of ⟨a draped neckline designed to ~ the stylish stout⟩ ⟨soft rosy light that ~*s* tired skins⟩ **4** *obs* **:** to touch caressingly **:** FONDLE ~ *vi* **1** *obs, of an animal* **:** to show fondness (as by fawning or cries) **2 :** to use flattery

²**flatter** *vi* -ED/-ING/-S [ME *flateren*, alter. of *floteren* to float, flutter — more at FLUTTER] *obs* **:** FLUTTER, FLOAT

³**flatter** *comparative of* ¹FLAT

⁴**flat·ter** \'fladə(r), -atə-\ *n* -S [⁴*flat* + -*er*] **:** one that flattens: as **a :** a drawplate with a narrow rectangular orifice for drawing flat strips (as watch springs) **b :** a flat-faced swage used in smithing

flatter b

flat·ter·er \-adərə(r), -atə-\ *n* -S [ME *flaterer*, fr. *flateren* to flatter + -*er*] **:** one that flatters

flattering *adj* [fr. pres. part. of ¹*flatter*] **:** marked by flattery; *esp* **:** tending to display to advantage or to enhance the good points of something ⟨a ~ new shade of rose⟩ — **flat·ter·ing·ly** *adv*

flat·tery \'fladəre, -atə-, -ri\ *n* -ES [ME *flaterie*, fr. MF, fr. OF, fr. *flater* to flatter + -*erie* -ery] **1 a :** the act or practice of flattering **:** the act of pleasing by artful commendation **:** ADULATION **b :** something that flatters or is felt flatteringly; *often* **:** false, insincere, or excessive praise ⟨just praise is only a debt but ~ is a present —Samuel Johnson⟩ **2** *obs* **:** a pleasing self-deception

flattest *superlative of* FLAT

flat·tie *also* **flat·ty** \'fladē\ *n, pl* **flatties** [¹*flat* + -*ie*, -*y*] **:** something characterized by flatness: as **a :** a small working boat peculiar to Chesapeake Bay and more southern waters of the eastern U.S. that is sloop-rigged and that has a flat bottom, straight sides, and a centerboard **b :** FLAT 6e **c** *slang* **:** POLICEMAN

flatting *pres part of* FLAT

flatting agent *n* [*flatting* fr. gerund of ⁴*flat*] **:** a material added to a coating (as a paint or varnish) to cause it to set with a matte surface

flatting mill *n* **:** a rolling mill producing sheet metal (as ribbon for the planchets of a mint)

flatting oil *n* **:** a liquid that when added to pigment-oil paste produces a paint which dries with a flat appearance

flat·tish \'flad·|ish, -at|, |ēsh\ *adj* **:** somewhat flat

flattop \'=,=\ *n, often attrib* **:** something with a flat or flattened upper surface: as **a :** a plant of the genus *Eriogonum* **b :** a building with a flat roof **c :** AIRCRAFT CARRIER **d** *slang* **:** CREW CUT

flat-topped crab \'=,=-\ *n* **:** a porcelain crab (*Petrolisthes eriomerus*) of rocky shores along the Pacific coast of No. America

flat tuning *n* **:** tuning of a radio such that the current in the receiving apparatus is but slightly affected by a change in the frequency of the received waves — compare SHARP TUNING

flat turn *n* **:** a turn of an airplane made without banking

flat–turret lathe *n* **:** a turret lathe having a low flat turret and a cross-sliding headstock with power feed

flat·u·len·cy \'flachələn(t)s\ *also* **flat·u·len·cy** \-lənsē, -si\ *n, pl* **flatulences** *also* **flatulencies** [*flatulence* fr. *flatulency*, after such pairs as E *abstinency: abstinence; flatulency* fr. *flatulent* + -*cy*] **:** the quality or state of being flatulent

flat·u·lent \-nt\ *adj* [MF, irreg. fr. L *flatus* act of blowing, act of breaking wind, fr. *flatus*, past part. of *flare* to blow — more at BLOW] **1 :** full of air or other gas ⟨the burner content was very ~⟩ **2 :** marked by or affected with gases generated in the intestine or stomach ⟨~ dyspepsia⟩ ⟨feeling somewhat ~ after a heavy meal⟩ **3 :** causing or likely to cause flatulence of the intestine or stomach ⟨dried beans are popularly considered very ~ food⟩ **4 :** pretentious without real worth or substance ⟨the barren and ~ gods served by his countryman —V.L.Parrington⟩ **:** swollen and empty ⟨~ rhetoric⟩ **:** TURGID **syn** see INFLATED

flat·u·lent·ly *adv* **:** in a flatulent manner **:** with flatulence

flat·u·os·i·ty \,flachə'wäsədē\ *n* -ES [*flatuous* + -*ity*] *archaic* **:** FLATULENCE

flat·u·ous \'flachəwəs\ *adj* [MF *flatueux*, fr. L *flatus* + MF -*eux* -ous] *archaic* **:** FLATULENT

fla·tus \'flādəs, -ātəs\ *n* -ES [L, act of blowing, act of breaking wind] **1 :** a puff of wind **:** BREATH **2 :** gas generated in the stomach or bowels

fla·tus vo·cis \,flād·əs'vōkəs, -d·ə'swō-\ *n, pl* **flatus vocis** [ML, lit., breath of the voice] **:** a mere name, word, or sound without a corresponding objective reality — used by the nominalists of universals

flatware \'=,=\ *n* **:** tableware that is more or less flat and usu. formed or cast in a single piece: **a :** dishes (as plates, platters) that are flat or shallow as distinguished from deeper vessels (as tureens or pitchers) — compare HOLLOW WARE **b :** table knives, forks, spoons, and other eating or serving utensils — compare FLAT SILVER

flat warehouse *n* **:** a one-story building or room used for storing bagged grain

flat wash *n* **:** FLATWORK

flatweed \'=,=\ *n* **:** CAT'S-EAR 1

flat wheel *n* **:** a railroad wheel which has flat spots on the tread (as from skidding on the rail)

flatwise *or* **flatways** \'=,=\ *adv* **:** with the flat side downward or next to another object

flatwoods \'=,=\ *n pl* **:** low-lying dry timber land; *specif* **:** level pineland occupying most of the Florida peninsula and producing typically the longleaf pine

flatwork \'=,=\ *n* **:** articles (as sheets, towels, tablecloths) that in laundering can be finished mechanically as distinguished from those requiring hand ironing

flatwork ironer *n* **:** MANGLE

flatworm \'=,=\ *n* **:** a worm of the phylum Platyhelminthes; *esp* **:** TURBELLARIAN

flat wrack *n* **:** any of various seaweeds of the genus *Fucus* (esp. *F. spiralis*) with broad fronds

flat yard *n* **:** a railroad switchyard in which cars are moved by means of locomotives instead of by gravity

flau·ber·tian \flō'bərshən, flō'-, -'bərd·ēən; flō'bershən, -ō-'berd·ēən\ *adj, usu cap* [Gustave *Flaubert* †1880 Fr. novelist + E -*ian*] **:** relating to or characteristic of the writer Flaubert or his realistic novels ⟨*Flaubertian* realism⟩

flaucht *or* **flaught** \'flakt, -ō-\ *n* -S [ME *flaght, flawght;* prob. akin to OE *flēan* to skin — more at FLAY] **1** *chiefly Scot* **:** FLAKE; *esp* **:** SNOWFLAKE **2** *chiefly Scot* **:** a flash esp. of fire or lightning

flaucht·bred \-,bred\ *adv* [Sc *flocht* flutter, bustle, excitement (fr. ME — Sc — *flocht*) + *braid* (broad); ME (Sc) *flocht* prob. of Scand origin; akin to ON *flōtti* flight — more at FLIGHT (running away)] **1** *Scot* **:** with limbs outstretched **:** SPREAD-EAGLED **2** *Scot* **:** EAGERLY, ENTHUSIASTICALLY

¹**flauch·ter** *or* **flaugh·ter** \'flȯkər, -läk-\ *vb* -ED/-ING/-S [Sc *flocht* flutter, bustle, excitement + E -*er* (freq. suffix)] *vi, chiefly Scot* **:** FLUTTER, FLICKER ⟨the candle ~*s* in the draft⟩ ~ *vt, chiefly Scot* **:** EXCITE, FLUSTER ⟨a little whiskey had ~*ed* him⟩

²**flauchter** *or* **flaughter** \"\ *n* -S *chiefly Scot* **:** FLICKERING

flaunch *or* **flaunche** *var of* FLANCH

¹**flaunt** \'flȯnt, -ä-, -ȧ-\ *vb* -ED/-ING/-S [prob. of Scand origin; akin to Norw dial. *flanta* to gad about; akin to ON *flana* to rush heedlessly, Gk *planasthai* to wander — more at PLANET] *vi* **1 :** to wave or flutter showily ⟨their flag ~*s* in the breeze⟩ ⟨scarlet tulips ~*ing* in the spring sun⟩ **2 a :** to display or obtrude oneself to public notice esp. by reason of excessive or gaudy finery or impropriety of behavior **:** seek to attract attention esp. by appearing or acting brash and brazen ⟨a pair of pretty girls giggling and ~*ing* on the street corner⟩ **b :** to make a showy appearance **:** stand out brightly or distinctly ⟨warm short days ~*ing* with dahlia and marigold —C.G.Glover⟩ ~ *vt* **1 :** to display ostentatiously ⟨the winners ~*ing* their victory⟩ **:** make an impudent show of **:** PARADE **2 :** to treat contemptuously **:** FLOUT ⟨~ army regulations⟩ **syn** see SHOW

²**flaunt** \"\ *n* -S **1 :** act of flaunting **:** DISPLAY **2** *obs* **:** something displayed for vain show ⟨in these my borrowed ~*s* — Shak.⟩

flaunt·er \-tə(r)\ *n* -S **:** one that flaunts

flaunt·ing·ly *adv* **:** in a flaunting manner

flaunty \-tē,-ti\ *adj* -ER/-EST [¹*flaunt* + -*y*] **:** given to or characterized by flaunting **:** OSTENTATIOUS ⟨a ~ display of newly acquired possessions⟩

flau·tan·do \flaů'tän(,)dō\ *also* **flau·ta·to** \-äd·(,)ō\ *adv* (*or adj*) [*flautando* fr. It, sounding like a flute, verbal of (assumed) It *flautare* to sound like a flute, fr. It *flauto* flute; *flautato* fr. It, sounded like a flute, past part. of (assumed) It *flautare*] **:** in the manner of a flute; *specif* **:** over the fingerboard — used as a direction in stringed-instrument playing

flau·ti·no \-'tē(,)nō\ *n* -S [It, dim. of *flauto* flute] **1 :** a small flute **:** PICCOLO **2 :** a small accordion **3 :** a labial pipe organ stop usu. of 4-foot pitch

flau·tist \'flȯd·əst, -laůd-\ *n* -S [It *flautista*, fr. *flauto* flute + -*ista* -ist] **:** FLUTIST

flau·to \'flaů,tō\ *n, pl* **flau·ti** \-,tē\ [It, fr. OProv *flaut* — more at FLUTE] **1 :** FLUTE **2** *archaic* **:** RECORDER 3a

flauto ama·bi·le \-ä'mäbē,lā\ *n* [It, pleasing flute] **:** a sweet-toned labial pipe organ stop of 4-foot or 8-foot pitch

flauto dol·ce \-'dōl,chā\ *n* [It, sweet flute] **:** FLUTE-DOUCE

flauto piccolo *n* [It, small flute] **:** PICCOLO

flauto tra·ver·so \-trə'vər(,)sō, -ver-\ *n* [It, lit., transverse flute] **1 :** FLUTE 1b **2 :** a 4-foot or 8-foot organ stop of quality like that of the flute

flav- *or* **flavo-** *comb form* [L *flavus* — more at BLUE] **1 :** yellow ⟨*flav*in⟩ ⟨*flavo*-virescent⟩ **2 :** flavin ⟨*flavo*enzyme⟩

flav·a·none \'flavə,nōn, 'flāv-\ *n* -S [ISV *flav-* + -*ane* + -*one*] **:** a colorless crystalline ketone $C_{15}H_{12}O_2$; 2,3-dihydroflavone; *also* **:** any of the derivatives of this ketone many of which (as eriodictyol) occur in plants often in the form of glycosides (as hesperidin)

fla·van·throne \flā'van,thrōn, fla'-, |=,=|=\ *also* **fla·van·threne** \-rēn\ *n* -S [*flavanthrone* fr. *flavanthrene* + -*one;* *flavanthrene* ISV *flav-* + -*anthrene*] **:** a yellow vat dye $C_{28}H_{12}N_2O_2$ related to anthraquinone

fla·ve·do \flə'vē(,)dō, flā'-\ *n* -S [NL, fr. L *flavus* yellow] **:** the outer colored layer of the mesocarp of a citrus fruit — compare ALBEDO

fla·ve·ria \-'virēə\ *n, cap* [NL, perh. irreg. fr. L *flavus* yellow] **:** a genus of chiefly tropical American herbs (family Compositae) with opposite leaves and small yellow flowers in clustered heads

fla·ves·cence \-'ves°n(t)s\ *n* -S [fr. *flavescent*, after such pairs as E *abstinent: abstinence*] **:** a yellowing or blanching of normally green plant parts that accompanies peach yellows, mosaic mottling, and certain other virus diseases and is due to diminution of chlorophyll

fla·ves·cent \-°nt\ *adj* [L *flavescent-, flavescens*, pres. part. of *flavescere* to turn yellow, fr. *flavus* yellow] **:** turning yellow **:** YELLOWISH

fla·vi·an \'flāvēən\ *adj, usu cap* [L *flavianus*, fr. *Flavius* (name borne by members of a particular Roman gens) + L -*anus* -an] **:** of or relating to the ancient Roman gens bearing the name Flavius and esp. to the three Roman emperors Vespasian, Titus, and Domitian who belonged to this gens

fla·vi·a·nate \'flāvēə,nāt, 'flav-\ *n* -S [ISV *flavian-* (as in *flavianic acid*) + -*ate*] **:** a salt of flavianic acid

fla·vi·an·ic acid \|=|=|anik-\ *n* [*flavianic* prob. ISV *flav-* + -*ian* + -*ic*] **:** a yellow crystalline acid $C_{10}H_6N_2O_8S$ used chiefly in precipitating arginine, tyrosine, or organic bases (as insoluble salts)

fla·vid \'flavəd, -lav-\ *adj* [L *flavidus*, fr. *flavus* yellow] **:** YELLOW ⟨a ~ gold coin⟩

fla·vin \'flāvən *also* -lav-\ *or* **fla·vine** \", -,vēn\ *n* -S [ISV *flav-* + -*in*, -*ine*] **1 :** a yellow dye obtained by extracting quercitron bark — see DYE table I (under *Natural Yellow 10*) **2 :** any of the yellow acridine dyes used in medicine for their antiseptic properties; *esp* **:** ACRIFLAVINE **3 :** any of a class of yellow water-soluble nitrogenous pigments derived from isoalloxazine and occurring in the form of nucleotides as coenzymes of flavoproteins; *esp* **:** RIBOFLAVIN

flavin adenine dinucleotide *n* **:** a coenzyme $C_{27}H_{33}N_9O_{15}P_2$ of certain flavoproteins (as xanthine oxidase); riboflavin 5'-adenosine-diphosphate — called also *FAD*

flavin enzyme *n* **:** FLAVOPROTEIN

flavin mononucleotide *n* **:** RIBOFLAVIN PHOSPHATE

flavo·bacterium \¦flā(,)vō, ¦fla(-+\ *n, cap* [NL, fr. *flav-* + *bacterium*] **:** a genus of bacteria related to *Achromobacter* and comprising soil or water bacteria that produce yellow or orange pigments and often reduce nitrates to nitrites

fla·vone \'flā,vōn, 'fla,-, =¦=\ *n* -S [ISV *flav-* + -*one;* orig. formed as G *flavon*] **:** a colorless crystalline ketone $C_{15}H_{10}O_2$ found as a dust on the leaves, stems, and seed capsules of many primroses, and also prepared synthetically; 2-phenylchromone; *also* **:** any of the derivatives of this ketone many of which (as chrysin) occur as yellow plant pigments often in the form of glycosides (as apiin) — compare FLAVANONE, ISOFLAVONE

¹**fla·vo·noid** \'flāvə,nȯid, 'flav-\ *adj* [*flavone* + -*oid*] **:** of, relating to, or like flavone or isoflavone in chemical structure

²**flavonoid** \"\ *n* -S **:** a flavonoid compound (as a plant pigment) — see BIOFLAVONOID; compare ANTHOCYANIDIN, ANTHOXANTHIN, CHALCONE

fla·vo·nol \-nōl,-nōl\ *n* -S [ISV *flavone* + -*ol;* orig. formed in G] **:** any of various hydroxy derivatives of flavone; *esp* **:** the colorless crystalline 3-hydroxy compound $C_{15}H_9O_2(OH)$ many of whose derivatives occur as yellow plant pigments often in the form of glycosides (as quercetin, morin)

fla·vo·protein \¦flā(,)vō, ¦fla(-+\ *n* [ISV *flav-* + *protein*] **:** any of a class of dehydrogenases that contain a flavin and in some cases also a metal, that occur in animal and plant cells, and that play a major role in biological oxidations by oxidizing metabolites directly or through the agency of pyridine nucleotides and by being in turn oxidized usu. by cytochromes — called also *flavin enzyme;* compare YELLOW ENZYME

fla·vo·purpurin \"+\ *n* [ISV *flav-* + *purpurin;* orig. formed in G] **:** a yellow crystalline compound $C_{14}H_5O_2(OH)_3$ found in commercial synthetic alizarin and also made separately; 1,2,6-trihydroxy-anthraquinone

¹**fla·vor** \'flāvə(r)\ *n* -S *see -or in Explan Notes* [ME *flavour*, fr. (assumed) MF *flavour*, fr. OF *flavor*, alter. (influenced by OF *savor*) of *flaor, flaur*, fr. (assumed) VL *flator*, fr. L *flare* to blow — more at BLOW] **1 a** *archaic* **:** that quality of something which affects the sense of smell **:** ODOR, FRAGRANCE, AROMA **b :** that quality of something which affects the sense of taste or gratifies the palate **:** SAVOR ⟨condiments impart ~ to food⟩ **c :** the blend of taste and smell sensations evoked by a substance (as a portion of food or drink) in the mouth ⟨a pungent bitter ~⟩ **2 :** any agent (as a spice or extract) designed to impart flavor to or alter the flavor of something ⟨kept cinnamon, vanilla, and other ~*s* and extracts on a special shelf⟩ **3 :** characteristic or predominant quality ⟨the full ~ of English country life⟩; *often* **:** characteristic style (as of a school or individual) in literature or art ⟨the acrid ~ of his prose⟩ **syn** see TASTE

²**flavor** \"\ *vb* **flavored; flavored; flavoring** \-v(ə)riŋ\ **flavors** *see -or in Explan Notes* [ME *flavren* to give off an odor, fr. *flavour*, n.] *vt* **:** to give or add flavor to ⟨~*ed* the salad with herbs and vinegar⟩; *often* **:** to give character or zest to ⟨his witty ad libs ~ the whole performance⟩ ~ *vi* **:** to have a flavor **:** SMACK — used with *of* ⟨this ~*s* of treason⟩

flavored *adj* [fr. past part. of ²*flavor*] **:** having or indicating a particular flavor ⟨high-*flavored* cordials⟩ ⟨a hate-*flavored* and acrimonious discussion⟩

fla·vor·ful \-və(r)fəl\ *adj* **:** full of flavor **:** SAVORY, TASTEFUL — **fla·vor·ful·ly** \-əlē,-əli\ *adv*

flavoring *n* -S [fr. gerund of ²*flavor*] **:** FLAVOR 2 ⟨~ essences⟩

fla·vor·less \-və(r)ləs\ *adj* **:** lacking in flavor **:** FLAT, DRAB ⟨~ platitudes⟩ ⟨I cultivated her ~ friends with the object of getting asked to their parties —Edmund Wilson⟩

fla·vor·ous \-v(ə)rəs\ *adj* **:** FLAVORSOME ⟨a carefully wrought, ~ reminiscence —*N.Y. Herald Tribune*⟩

fla·vor·some \-və(r)səm\ *adj* **:** richly and usu. pleasingly flavored **:** FLAVORFUL, PALATABLE, TASTY; *often* **:** characterized by or tending to impart a particular flavor ⟨~ dialogue —John Gassner⟩ ⟨folksy, ~ yarns —Jay Walz⟩ **syn** see PALATABLE

fla·vory \-v(ə)rē, -ri\ *adj* [¹*flavor* + -*y*] **:** rich in flavor — used esp. of teas ⟨a ~ tea with a good bouquet⟩

fla·vous \'flāvəs, -lav-\ *adj* [L *flavus* yellow — more at BLUE] **:** YELLOW 1a; *esp* **:** of a clear pure yellow — used chiefly in technical descriptions in taxonomy and usu. postpositively ⟨elytra and antennae ~⟩; compare LUTEOUS

¹**flaw** \'flȯ\ *n* -S [ME *flaw, flawe*, prob. of Scand origin; akin to Sw *flaga* flaw, flake, ON *flaga* slab; akin to OE *flēan* to skin — more at FLAY] **1** *obs* **:** FLAKE, FRAGMENT, BIT ⟨this heart shall break into a hundred thousand ~*s* —Shak.⟩ **2 :** a faulty part **:** CRACK, BREACH, GAP, FISSURE ⟨a ~ in a gem or a vase⟩ ⟨a ~ in a bar of steel⟩ **3 :** a fault or defect esp. in a character or a piece of work ⟨the greatest ~ in his plan was failure to anticipate costs⟩ ⟨a complexion without a ~⟩; *esp* **:** a fault in a legal paper that may nullify it ⟨a ~ in a will⟩ ⟨found a ~ in the statute⟩ **4** *Scot* **:** LIE, FIB **5** *chiefly Scot* **:** a thin layer of turf or peat **6 :** a nearly vertical geological fault transverse to the strike of the rocks and characterized by horizontal displacement **syn** see BLEMISH

²**flaw** \"\ *vb* -ED/-ING/-S *vt* **1 :** to make flaws in **:** CRACK ⟨a ~*ed* diamond⟩ ⟨the brazen caldrons with the frosts are ~*ed* —John Dryden⟩ **2 :** to make a breach or defect in **:** VIOLATE, NULLIFY ⟨~ an agreement⟩ ⟨France hath ~*ed* the league —Shak.⟩ ~ *vi* **:** to become defective **:** CRACK, BREAK ⟨pavements warping and ~*ing* in the heat⟩ ⟨columns of smoke that . . . ~*ed* suddenly in the canyon wind —W.V.T.Clark⟩

³**flaw** \"\ *n* -S [of Scand origin; akin to Norw *flaga* gust, squall; akin to MHG & MLG *vlage* gust, attack, Lith *plakti* to beat, L *plangere* to beat — more at PLAINT] **1 :** a sudden burst of wind of short duration with or without rain or snow ⟨the wind changed with ~*s* from westward —Archibald MacLeish⟩; *also* **:** a spell of stormy weather **2** *obs* **:** an outburst esp. of passion or anger **:** a sudden tumult or disorder

flawed *adj* [fr. past part. of ²*flaw*] **:** having a flaw **:** DEFECTIVE, FAULTY

flaw·less \-ōləs\ *adj* **1 :** lacking flaw or imperfection **:** PERFECT ⟨~ diction⟩ **2** *of a gemstone* **:** having no internal flaws — **flaw·less·ly** *adv* — **flaw·less·ness** *n* -ES

flawn \'flȯn, 'flän\ *n* -S [origin unknown] **:** MANILA GRASS

¹**flawy** \'flȯi, -ōē\ *adj, often* -ER/-EST [¹*flaw* + -*y*] **:** full of flaws (as cracks) **:** DEFECTIVE ⟨a ~ lot of pottery⟩

²**flawy** \"\ *adj, often* -ER/-EST [³*flaw* + -*y*] **:** subject to or characterized by sudden gusts of wind

flax \'flaks\ *n* -ES *often attrib* [ME *flax, flex*, fr. OE *fleax*, akin to OFris *flax*, OHG *flahs* flax, L *plectere* to plait, braid — more at PLY] **1 a :** a plant of the genus *Linum;* *esp* **:** a slender erect annual (*L. usitatissimum*) with linear leaves and blue flowers that is widely cultivated for (1) its long silky bast fibers which when freed from the stem by retting and mechanical processes are used in textile manufacture and are the source of linen and (2) its seeds which yield a valuable oil and a meal used esp. for cattle feed — see FLAXSEED **b :** the bast fiber of the flax plant esp. when cleaned and prepared for spinning **2 :** any of several plants resembling flax — usu. used with a qualifying term ⟨white ~⟩ ⟨several toad*flaxes*⟩ **3 :** a grayish yellow that is less strong and slightly greener than chamois, lighter and very slightly redder than old ivory, and redder and slightly lighter and stronger than crash — called also *peanut, pebble*

flax bellflower *n* **:** HAREBELL 1

flaxbird \'=,=\ *n* [so called fr. its habit of feeding on the seeds of flax] **:** GOLDFINCH 3

flax bollworm *n* **:** a grub that is the larva of a moth (*Heliothis ononis*) and is closely related to the cotton bollworm but feeds chiefly in the seedpods of flax

flax brake *also* **flaxbreak** *or* **flax breaker** *n* [*flax brake* fr. *flax* + *brake* (machine); *flax break* & *flax breaker* by folk etymology fr. *flax brake*] **:** a machine for separating the woody stem tissues from the fiber in flax

flax buncher *n* **:** a grain-binder attachment used to cut flax in unbound bunches

flax canker *n* **1 :** heat canker of flax **2** *or* **flax anthracnose** **:** a cankered condition of flax caused by a fungus (*Colletotrichum linicolum*)

flax comb *n* **:** HACKLE 1

flax dodder *n* **:** a dodder (*Cuscuta epilinum*) infesting cultivated flax — called also *flax vine*

flaxdrop \'=,=\ *n* **:** FLAX DODDER

Flax·e·dil \'flaksə,dil\ *trademark* — used for gallamine triethiodide

flax·en \'flaksən\ *adj* [ME *flaxen, flexen*, fr. *flax, flex* flax + -*en*] **1 a :** made of flax ⟨~ linens⟩ **b :** resembling flax esp. in being of pale soft strawy color — used chiefly of the hair ⟨~ curls⟩ **2** *archaic* **:** of or relating to flax

flax family *n* **:** LINACEAE

flaxflower blue \'=,=-\ *n* **:** a moderate blue to light purplish blue

flaxlike \'=,=\ *adj* **:** resembling flax ⟨a slender ~ herb⟩ ⟨soft but tough ~ fiber⟩

flax lily *n* **1 :** NEW ZEALAND FLAX **2 :** any of several plants constituting a genus (*Dianella*) of the family Liliaceae; *esp* **:** an Australian plant (*D. laevis*) that yields a long silky fiber formerly used by the aborigines for making baskets

flax-polled \'=,=\ *adj* **:** having flaxen hair

flax ripple *n* **:** a comb for removing bolls or seeds from flax

flax rust *n* **1 :** a disease of flax caused by a rust fungus (*Melampsora lini*) **2 :** the fungus causing flax rust
flax·seed \ˈflak,sēd *sometimes* -ks,sēd\ *n* **1 a :** a seed of the flax plant **b :** seeds of flax in bulk; *esp* **:** the commercial product consisting of these seeds that is used as a demulcent and emollient in inflammatory conditions of the respiratory, intestinal, and urinary passages and that yields linseed oil **2 :** a minute annual allseed (*Millegrana radiola*) that is closely related to true flax and is native to parts of Europe and Africa **3 :** the brown-shelled pupa of the Hessian fly resembling a flaxseed in size and appearance
flax-sick \ˈ=,=\ *adj, of soil* **:** so infested with fungi (as *Fusarium lini*) that flax cannot be grown
flax star *n* **:** a low annual Mediterranean herb (*Asterolinon linumstellatum*) of the family Primulaceae bearing solitary greenish flowers
flax straw *n* **1 :** the whole flax plant after pulling and drying **2 :** the fiber flax retted and broken but not scutched
flax vine *n* **:** FLAX DODDER
flaxweed \ˈ=,=\ *n* **:** TOADFLAX 1
flax wheel *n* **:** SAXON WHEEL
flax wilt *n* **:** a destructive disease of flax due to a fungus (*Fusarium lini*) which causes damping-off of young seedlings and wilting, yellowing, and death of older plants — compare FLAX-SICK
flaxy \ˈflaksē\ *adj* -ER/-EST [*flax* + *-y*] **:** resembling flax esp. in texture **:** FLAXEN
flay \ˈflā\ *vt* -ED/-ING/-S [ME *flen*, fr. OE *flēan*; akin to MD *vlaen* to skin, ON *flā* to skin, Lith *plėšti* to tear] **1 :** to strip off the skin or surface of **:** SKIN ⟨~ an ox⟩ ⟨~*ed* him with a lash⟩ ⟨with her nails she'll ~ thy wolfish visage —Shak.⟩ **2 :** to subject to treatment like or likened to skinning: as **a :** to strip of possessions ⟨the people ~*ed* by excessive taxes⟩ **b :** to reprove harshly **:** criticize severely **:** CENSURE, EXCORIATE ⟨his wife ~*ed* him when she heard where he had been⟩ **syn** see SKIN — **flay a flint :** to exact all possible gain
flay·er \ˈflā(ə)r, -le(ə)r, -leə\ *n* -S [ME *flear*, fr. *flen* to flay + *-ar, -er, -ere* -er] **:** one that flays
f layer *n, cap F* **1 :** the highest known and most densely ionized regular layer of the ionosphere occurring at night within the F region and resulting from the merger of the F_1 layer and F_2 layer **2 :** the zone in a forest soil characterized by abundant presence of plant remains actively undergoing decay
flayflint \ˈ=,=\ *n, archaic* **:** SKINFLINT, MISER
fld *abbr* **1** field **2** fluid
[1]**flea** \ˈflē\ *n* -S [ME *fle, flee*, fr. OE *flēah, flēa*; akin to OHG *flōh* flea, ON *flō*; prob. derivative fr. the root of E *flee*] **1 :** any of an order (Siphonaptera) of wingless bloodsucking insects that have a hard laterally compressed body, long legs adapted to leaping, and free-living larvae, feed on warm-blooded animals, that include important pests of man and domestic animals — see DOG FLEA, PULEX, STICKTIGHT FLEA **2 :** FLEA BEETLE **3 :** PUCE — **flea in one's ear :** an unwelcome and usu. unexpected hint or warning **:** an irritating rebuke ⟨I'll put a *flea in his ear* if he comes nosing around here⟩ ⟨sent the boy about his business with a *flea in his ear*⟩
[2]**flea** \"\ *vt* -ED/-ING/-S **:** to rid of fleas ⟨don't forget to ~ the dog⟩
fleabag \ˈ=,=\ *n* **1 a :** BED; *often* **:** SLEEPING BAG ⟨he thrust one of his legs cumbrously out of the top of his ~ —F.M. Ford⟩ **b :** an inferior hotel or rooming house ⟨three dollars for a room in a handy ~ —Jack Lait & Lee Mortimer⟩ **2 a :** a flea-ridden animal **3 :** a slatternly old woman
fleabane \ˈ=,=\ *n* **:** any of various plants of the family Compositae that are supposed to drive away fleas: as **a** *also* **fleabane mullet :** a hairy perennial herb (*Pulicaria dysenterica*) with yellow ray flowers that is native to Europe but widely naturalized **b :** any of several plants of the genera *Erigeron* and *Artemisia* — see DAISY FLEABANE
flea beetle *n* **:** any of various small chrysomelid beetles that have the thighs of the hind legs thickened and adapted for leaping, that constitute *Altica, Epitrix*, and numerous other genera, that feed on the leaves and tender new growth of plants, and that sometimes serve as vectors of virus diseases of plants — see POTATO FLEA BEETLE
fleabite \ˈ=,=\ *n* **1 :** the bite of a flea; *also* **:** the red spot caused by such a bite **2 a :** a trifling wound or pain suggesting that of the bite of a flea **b :** a small irritation **:** a trifling annoyance **3 :** a minute amount
fleabiting *n* -S [*biting* fr. gerund of *bite*] *obs* **:** FLEABITE
flea-bitten \ˈ=,==\ *adj* **1 :** bitten by or infested with fleas ⟨a *flea-bitten* old hound⟩ ⟨*flea-bitten* lodgings⟩ **2** *of a horse* **:** having a white or gray coat flecked with minute dots of bay or sorrel ⟨a rangy *flea-bitten* gray⟩
flea bug *n* **1 :** FLEAHOPPER **2 :** TOBACCO FLEA BEETLE
flead \ˈflēd\ *n* -S [perh. alter. of [4]*fleck*] *dial Brit* **:** unrendered leaf fat of the hog
fleadock \ˈ=,=\ *n* -S **:** BUTTERBUR
fleahopper \ˈ=,==\ *n* **:** any of various small jumping bugs several of which feed on cultivated plants — see COTTON FLEAHOPPER, GARDEN FLEAHOPPER
fleam \ˈflēm\ *n* -S [ME *fleme*, fr. MF *flieme*, fr. LL *phlebotomus*, modif. of Gk *phlebotomon*, fr. *phleb-* + *-tomon* (fr. *temnein* to cut) — more at TOME] **1 :** a sharp lancet formerly much used for bloodletting **2 :** angle of bevel of the edge of a sawtooth with respect to the plane of the blade
flea market *also* **flea fair** *n* **:** an outdoor market at which antiques and secondhand articles (as furniture, pottery, or jewelry) are sold esp. from parked vehicles
flea mint *n* **:** PENNYROYAL 1
fleam tooth *n* **:** a sawtooth shaped like an isosceles triangle
fleaseed \ˈ=,=\ *n* [so called fr. the resemblance of its seeds to fleas] **1 :** the seed of the fleawort **2 :** an oak-leaf gall of the southwestern U.S. that becomes detached and moves about independently due to the activity of the enclosed insect larva
flea soap *n* **:** soap to remove or kill fleas while cleansing
flea·some \ˈflēsəm\ *adj* **:** full of fleas
fleaweed \ˈ=,=\ *n* [so called fr. the alleged power of its smell to drive off fleas] **1** *dial Eng* **:** YELLOW BEDSTRAW **2 :** BLUE CURLS 1
flea weevil *n* **:** any of various small broad weevils that have large eyes and hind legs adapted for leaping and that include some with larvae which are leaf miners on cultivated plants — see APPLE FLEA WEEVIL
fleawort \ˈ=,=\ *n* [ME *flewort*, fr. OE *flēawyrt*, fr. *flēah, flēa* flea + *wyrt* herb, root — more at FLEA, WORT] **1 :** an Old World plantain (*Plantago psyllium*) having seeds that swell and become gelatinous when moist and that are used as a mild laxative — called also *psyllium* **2 :** any of various plants supposedly efficacious as destroyers of fleas
fleb·ile \ˈflebəl, ˈfleb-\ *adj* [L *flebilis* lamentable, wretched — more at FEEBLE] **:** TEARFUL, DOLEFUL
flebotomus [NL, fr. LL *flebotomus, phlebotomus* lancet] *syn of* PHLEBOTOMUS — a prior name made unavailable by action of the International Commission on Zoological Nomenclature
flech \ˈflek\ *Scot var of* FLEA
flèche \ˈflāsh, -lesh\ *n* -S [F, lit., arrow, fr. OF *fleche*, of Gmc origin; akin to MD *vlieke* arrow, MLG *flieke* long arrow; akin to OHG *fliogan* to fly — more at FLY] **1 :** SPIRE; *esp* **:** a slender spire above the intersection of the nave and transepts of a church or cathedral and commonly carrying the Sanctus bell **2 :** a method of reaching the opponent that is used esp. in fencing with saber or épée and that consists of one or more rapid steps forward beginning with the rear foot

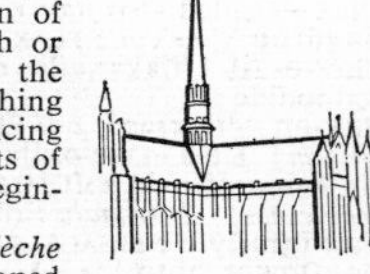
flèche 1

flé·chette \flāˈshet\ *n* -S [F, fr. *flèche* arrow + *-ette*] **:** a small dart-shaped projectile clustered in an explosive warhead, dropped from an airplane, or fired from a hand-held gun
[1]**fleck** \ˈflek\ *vt* -ED/-ING/-S [back-formation fr. *flecked*, adj., spotted, dappled (taken as a past part.), fr. ME, prob. modif. (influenced by ME [1]-*ed*) of ON *flekkōttr*, fr. *flekkr* spot; akin to MD *vlecke* spot, stain, OHG *flec, fleccho* spot, piece of land, and perh. to L *plaga* region — more at FLAKE] **:** STREAK, STRIPE **:** VARIEGATE, DAPPLE, SPOT ⟨blood ~*ed* the snow⟩
[2]**fleck** \"\ *n* -S **1 :** SPOT, MARK: as **a :** a blemish (as a freckle) on the skin **b :** a spot of color or brightness ⟨~*s* of fire rose from the embers⟩ ⟨a tweed brightened with ~*s* and nubs of bright wool⟩ **2 :** FLAKE, PARTICLE ⟨a ~ of soot on her nose⟩ ⟨scattered ~*s* of snow⟩ **3 :** any of various plant diseases of which the characteristic injury takes the form of small usu. elongated discolored lesions of the foliage ⟨~ in lilies appears to be a virus disease though similar conditions in other plants may be caused by fungi⟩
[3]**fleck** \"\ *vi* [perh. alter. of [1]*flack*] *now dial Brit* **:** FLIT, FLUTTER
[4]**fleck** \"\ *n* -S [alter. of [2]*flick*] *dial Eng* **:** LEAF FAT
[5]**fleck** \"\ *n* -S [irreg. fr. *flea*] *Scot* **:** FLEA
fleck·er \-kə(r)\ *vt* -ED/-ING/-S [freq. of [1]*fleck*] **:** SPOT, STREAK — used chiefly as a participial adjective ⟨a quiet sun-*fleckered* spot beneath a tall elm⟩
fleck·less \-kləs\ *adj* **:** free from flecks; *esp* **:** FLAWLESS — **fleck·less·ly** *adv*
flec·tion *or* **flex·ion** \ˈflekshən\ *n* -S [*flection* alter. (influenced by such words as *correction*) of *flexion*, fr. L *flexion-, flexio* bend, turn, curve, fr. *flexus* (past part. of *flectere* to bend) + *-ion-, -io* -ion] **1 :** the act of flexing or bending **:** TURNING ⟨twisting and ~ of the vines by the wind⟩ **2 :** a part bent **:** BEND, FOLD, TURN ⟨an oxbow is a broad ~ of a stream⟩ **3 :** INFLECTION 4 **4** *usu flexion* **a :** a movement involving the bending of a joint esp. between the bones of a limb by which the angle between the bones is diminished **b :** a forward raising of the arm or leg by a movement at the shoulder or hip joint — opposed to *extension* **c :** the yielding of a horse to the pressure of the bit resulting in bending the head at the poll
flec·tion·al *or* **flex·ion·al** \-shənᵊl,-shnəl\ *adj* **:** capable of or relating to flection esp. of words
flec·tor \ˈflektə(r)\ *n* -S [obs. E *flect*, v., to bend (fr. L *flectere*) + E *-or*] **:** something used in bending; *esp* **:** FLEXOR
[1]**fledge** \ˈflej\ *adj* [ME *flegge, flygge*, fr. OE *-flycge* (in *unflycge* not yet fledged); akin to MD *vlugge* able to fly, OHG *flucki*; derivative fr. the root of E *fly*] *archaic* **:** capable of or fitted for flying **:** FEATHERED, FLEDGED
[2]**fledge** \"\ *vb* -ED/-ING/-S *vi* **1 a** *of a bird* **:** to acquire the feathers necessary for flight **b** *of an insect* **:** to attain the winged adult stage (as by metamorphosis) **2 :** to attain the state of independence or competence characteristic of maturity ⟨the newly *fledged* dancer⟩ ~ *vt* **1 :** to rear or care for (a young bird) until plumage is developed enough for flying **2 a :** to cover with or as if with feathers or a feathery growth ⟨your master, whose chin is not yet *fledged* —Shak.⟩ **b :** to furnish (as a nest) with a feathery covering **3 :** to furnish (as an arrow) with feathers for flying
fledge·less \-ləs\ *adj* **:** UNFLEDGED
fledg·ling *also* **fledge·ling** \-jliŋ,-jlēŋ\ *n* -S *often attrib* **1 a :** a young bird just fledged **b :** a young bird capable of leaving the nest and surviving **2 :** something or someone characterized by immaturity; *esp* **:** a person not fully experienced in some activity ⟨~ dramatists⟩
fledgy \ˈflejē, -ji-\ *adj, often* -ER/-EST [[1]*fledge* + *-y*] **:** FEATHERED, DOWNY, FEATHERY ⟨a ~ sea-bird choir —John Keats⟩
[1]**flee** \ˈflē\ *vb* **fled** \ˈfled\ **fled; fleeing; flees** [ME *fleen*, fr. OE *flēon*; akin to OHG *fliohan* to flee, ON *flȳja*, Goth *thliuhan* to flee, and prob. to OE *flēogan* to fly — more at FLY] *vi* **1 a :** to run away from or as if from danger or evil **:** hasten off ⟨cowards ~*ing* before a revolution —R.W.Emerson⟩ ⟨a person . . . who shall ~ from justice —*U.S.Constitution*⟩ **b :** to hurry toward a source of security or protection — used with *to* or *into* ⟨he *fled* back to the shelter of his cab —Osbert Sitwell⟩ ⟨the survivors *fled* into the wilderness⟩ **2 :** to pass away swiftly **:** VANISH ⟨mists ~*ing* before the rising sun⟩ ⟨the truck was gathering speed . . . and the fields were ~*ing* past in the twilight —Kay Boyle⟩ **3** *archaic* **:** FLY, SPEED ⟨the arrow *fled* from the bow⟩ ~ *vt* **1 a :** to run away from **:** endeavor to avoid (as a threatened danger) or escape from (as an adversary) ⟨heard her ~*ing* his approach —T.B.Costain⟩ ⟨the lowlanders were ~*ing* the rising waters⟩ **b :** SHUN, AVOID, EVADE ⟨governments long in office are not inclined to ~ party and political considerations —S.L.A.Marshall⟩ **2 :** to leave abruptly **:** depart from suddenly or unexpectedly **:** ABANDON, FORSAKE ⟨when fortune *fled* her spoiled and favorite child —Lord Byron⟩ ⟨~*ing* the city for the hot months —Jerome Weidman⟩ **syn** see ESCAPE
[2]**flee** \"\ *chiefly Scot var of* FLY
[3]**flee** \"\ *dial Brit var of* FLAY
[1]**fleece** \ˈflēs\ *n* -S [ME *flees*, fr. OE *flēos, flȳs*; akin to MD *vlies* fleece, MHG *vlius* fleece, L *pluma* down, small soft feather, Lith *pluskos* (pl.) tufts of hair] **1 a :** the coat of wool that covers a sheep or similar animal ⟨the ~ of the vicuna is very soft⟩ **b :** the wool obtained from a sheep at one shearing ⟨a ~ of over 16 pounds⟩ **c :** a heraldic representation of the fleece of a ram depicted complete with head and feet as if stuffed and suspended by a belt about its middle **2 :** any of various coverings resembling a fleece esp. in soft or woolly quality ⟨a heavy ~ of snow⟩ ⟨a cloud ~ half covered the sky⟩: as **a :** a covering of vegetation **b :** a head of hair **c :** a soft bulky knitted or woven fabric that has a deep pile or long nap and that is made usu. of wool or synthetic fibers and used chiefly for clothing **3 :** meat taken from either side of the hump of the buffalo **4** *obs* **a :** booty from the fleecing of a victim **b :** the act of fleecing a victim **5 :** a web of cotton or wool fiber during the carding process

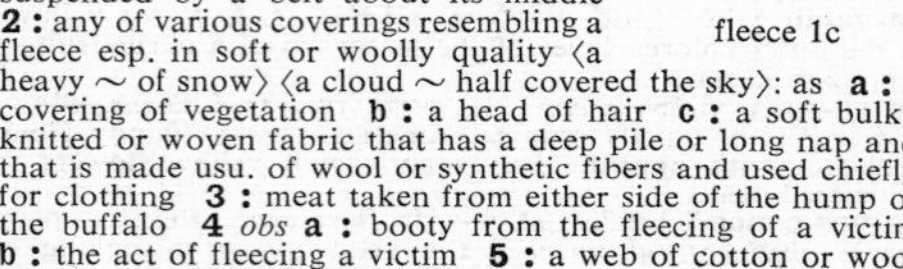
fleece 1c

[2]**fleece** \"\ *vt* -ED/-ING/-S **1 a :** to shear the fleece from (as a sheep) **b :** to remove (as wool) by shearing or plucking **2 a :** to strip (as a person) of property by fraud or extortion **:** DESPOIL, PLUNDER ⟨*fleeced* the church to build an estate for his sons⟩; *sometimes* **:** to charge excessively for service or goods ⟨garish roadhouses where the customer knew he would be *fleeced*⟩ **b :** to obtain by rapacious or improper means ⟨never hesitated to ~ a fee from a poor widow⟩ **3 :** to cover or fleck with (fleecy masses) ⟨a blue sky *fleeced* with little clouds⟩
fleece·able \-səbəl\ *adj* **:** capable of being or likely to be fleeced **:** GULLIBLE
fleeced \ˈflēst\ *adj* [[1]*fleece* + *-ed*] **1 :** covered with or as if with a fleece ⟨long-*fleeced* sheep⟩ **2** *of textiles* **:** having a soft nap
fleeceflower *or* **fleecevine** \ˈ=,=\ *n* **:** SILVER-LACE VINE
fleece·less \ˈflēsləs\ *adj* **:** having no fleece
fleece-lined \ˈ=ˈ=\ *adj* **1 :** lined with fleece **2** *of knit goods* **:** having a heavily fleeced inner surface
fleec·er \ˈflēsə(r)\ *n* -S **:** one that fleeces
fleece wool *n* **:** wool sheared in a continuous fleece that is usu. dagged, folded, and tied individually
fleece worm *n* **:** any of various blowfly maggots developing in the wool of sheep; *esp* **:** the maggot of the black blowfly (*Phormia regina*)
fleech \ˈflēch\ *vb* -ED/-ING/-ES [ME (Sc) *flechen*] *dial* **:** to coax or wheedle esp. by flattery
fleec·i·ness \ˈflēsēnəs, -sin-\ *n* -ES **:** the quality or state of being fleecy
fleecy \-sē,-si\ *adj* -ER/-EST [[1]*fleece* + *-y*] **:** covered with, made of, or resembling fleece or a fleece ⟨~ white clouds⟩ ⟨winter coats are getting *fleecier* —Lois Long⟩ ⟨stems ~ with soft hairs⟩
fleed \ˈflēd\ *var of* FLEAD
fleeing *pres part of* FLEE
fleem *chiefly dial var of* FLEAM
[1]**fle·er** \ˈflēə(r), -li(ə)r, -liə\ *n* -S [ME, fr. *flen* to flee + *-er, -ere -er*] **:** one that flees
[2]**fleer** \ˈfli(ə)r, -iə\ *vb* -ED/-ING/-S [ME *fleryen*, of Scand origin; akin to Norw *flire* to giggle, Sw (dial.) *flira* — more at FLIMFLAM] *vi* **1 a :** to laugh, grin, or grimace in a coarse manner **b :** to make a wry face in contempt or grin in scorn **:** SNEER, MOCK, GIBE **2** *obs* **:** to grin or smile with an often affected or artful air of civility ~ *vt* **:** to laugh at contemptuously **:** make a mock of **:** hold up to contempt **syn** see SCOFF
[3]**fleer** \"\ *n* -S **1 :** a word or look of derision or mockery ⟨mark the ~*s*, the gibes, and notable scorns —Shak.⟩ **2 :** a grin simulating civility **:** LEER
fleer·er \ˈfliərə(r)\ *n* -S **:** one that fleers
fleer·ing·ly *adv* **:** in a fleering manner **:** with a fleer
flee·rish \ˈflērish\ *n* -ES [alter. (influenced by *flint*) of earlier Sc *furisine*, prob. fr. (assumed) ME (Sc) *furisen*, prob. fr. MLG *vūrīsern*, fr. *vūr* fire + *īsern* iron; akin to OHG *fiur* fire and to OHG *īsan, īsarn* iron — more at FIRE, IRON] *Scot* **:** STEEL 3c
flees *pres 3d sing of* FLEE
fleesh \ˈflēsh\ *chiefly Scot var of* FLEECE
[1]**fleet** \ˈflēt, *usu* -ēd.+V\ *vb* -ED/-ING/-S [ME *fleten*, fr. OE *flēotan*; akin to OHG *fliozzan* to flow, float, ON *fljōta* to flow, float, Lith *plausti* to wash, OE *flōwan* to flow] *vi* **1** *now dial Brit* **:** FLOAT **2 a** *obs* **:** FLOAT, DRIFT ⟨clouds and mist ~*ing*⟩ **b :** to move waveringly **:** FLUCTUATE **3 a** *archaic* **:** to glide along or away **:** FLOW **b :** to fade away **:** DISSOLVE, VANISH **4** *obs* **:** to become filled **:** ABOUND **5 :** to fly swiftly **:** pass over quickly **:** HASTEN, FLIT ⟨clouds ~*ing* across the sky⟩ ~ *vt* **1 :** to cause (time) to pass **:** while away ⟨many young gentlemen . . . ~ the time carelessly —Shak.⟩ **2** *obs* **:** to pass over rapidly **:** skim the surface of **3** [alter. of [1]*flit*] **a :** to move or change in position — used only in certain nautical phrases ⟨~ aft the crew⟩ **b :** to draw apart the blocks of (a tackle) in order to shift the moving block **c :** to cause (as a cable or hawser) to slip down the barrel of a capstan or windlass
[2]**fleet** \"\ *n* -S [ME *flet, flete*, fr. OE *flēot* estuary, river; akin to MHG *vliez, vlieze* river, brook, ON *fljōt* river; derivative fr. the root of OE *flēotan* to float] **1** *now dial Eng* **:** a shallow inlet or estuary **:** a small creek **2** *now dial Eng* **:** SEWER, DRAIN
[3]**fleet** \"\ *n* -S [ME *flet, flete*, fr. OE *flēot* ship, fr. *flēotan* to float] **1 :** a number of warships under a single command **:** a naval force: **a :** an organization of ships and airplanes under a flag officer and suitable for undertaking major naval operations **b :** the whole naval forces afloat of a particular country **2 :** a group of boats in company or engaged in the same business ⟨the whaling ~⟩ ⟨the ~ of small craft now in the harbor⟩ **3** *now chiefly dial* **:** a group (as of birds) moving or acting together ⟨a ~ of crows pulling at the corn⟩ **4 a** *Brit* **:** a line of fishing nets joined together **b :** a fishing line having a hundred hooks **5 :** a group (as of airplanes or trucks) comparable to a fleet of ships ⟨a ~ of clouds overhead⟩; *esp* **:** such a group operated under unified control (as by a commercial or military organization) ⟨three separate taxi ~*s* operating in one area⟩ ⟨a ~ of 500 haulage units⟩ **6 :** a group of affiliated insurance companies esp. when handling fire insurance
[4]**fleet** \"\ *vt* -ED/-ING/-S [ME *fleten*, fr. OE *flēotan* to skim, fr. *flēotan* to float] *dial Eng* **:** to take the cream from (milk) **:** SKIM
[5]**fleet** \"\ *adj* -ER/-EST [prob. fr. [1]*fleet*] **1 :** swift in motion **:** moving or able to move with velocity ⟨the antelope is very ~⟩; *often* **:** light and quick in going from place to place **:** NIMBLE, AGILE ⟨the ~ scurryings of squirrels⟩ ⟨in mail their horses clad, yet ~ and strong —John Milton⟩ **2 :** lacking permanence or substance **:** EVANESCENT, FLEETING **syn** see FAST
[6]**fleet** \"\ *adv (or adj)* [prob. fr. [2]*fleet*] **1** *now chiefly dial* **:** LIGHT, SHALLOW ⟨a ~ soil⟩ ⟨cream rising in ~ dishes⟩ **2** *now chiefly dial* **:** near the surface **:** SUPERFICIALLY ⟨potatoes with ~ eyes⟩ ⟨some soils should be plowed ~⟩
[7]**fleet** \"\ *n* -S [prob. fr. [1]*fleet*] **1 :** a long straight fake of a stowed rope **2 :** the act of fleeting **:** a change in position
fleet admiral *n* **:** a naval officer of the highest rank whose insignia is five stars
fleet-book evidence \ˈflēt-\ *n, usu cap F* [so called fr. the fact that books recording clandestine marriages in Fleet prison chapel, London, England, and in nearby houses were declared inadmissible as evidence in British courts] *Brit* **:** evidence usu. documentary that is inadmissible because inherently unreliable
fleet-foot \ˈ=,=\ *also* **fleet-footed** \ˈ=ˈ==\ *adj* **:** swift of foot — **fleet-foot·ed·ness** *n*
fleet·ful \ˈflēt,fu̇l\ *n* -S **:** as many as would fill or make up a fleet ⟨whole ~*s* of students from distant lands⟩
fle·eth \ˈflēəth\ *archaic pres 3d sing of* FLEE
fleet in being : a fleet of naval vessels that because of its mere existence is a factor in the calculations of opposing strategists even though it is inactive or appears to be immobilized
fleeting *adj* [fr. pres. part. of [1]*fleet*] **:** passing swiftly **:** TRANSITORY, PASSING, BRIEF ⟨a ~ glimpse⟩ ⟨autumn's ~ beauty⟩ **syn** see TRANSIENT
fleet·ing·ly *adv* **:** for an instant **:** BRIEFLY
fleet·ing·ness *n* -ES **:** the quality or state of being fleeting
fleet·ings \ˈflētiŋz\ *n pl* [pl. of E dial. *fleeting* action of skimming, fr. ME *fletinge*, fr. *fleten* to skim + *-inge, -ing* -ing] *dial Eng* **:** milk curds (as for the making of cheese)
fleet insurance *n* **:** insurance by which a number of ships, automobiles, or airplanes are covered under one contract
fleet·ly *adv* **:** in a fleet manner **:** RAPIDLY
fleet marriage *n, usu cap F* **:** a marriage performed during the late 17th and early 18th centuries in or near the Fleet prison in London without public notice, witnesses, or consent of parents
fleet·ness *n* -ES **:** the quality or state of being fleet
fleet parson *n, usu cap F* **:** a disreputable clergyman who performed Fleet marriages
fleets *pres 3d sing of* FLEET, *pl of* FLEET
fleet street *n, usu cap F&S* [after *Fleet Street* (running from Ludgate Circus to the Strand), London, England, that has become the center of the London newspaper district] **:** the London press
[1]**fleg** \ˈfleg\ *vt* [prob. alter. of *fley*] *Scot* **:** to scare out **:** FRIGHTEN
[2]**fleg** \"\ *n* -S *Scot* **:** FRIGHT, SCARE ⟨got a ~ and was ready to jump out of my skin —Sir Walter Scott⟩
[3]**fleg** \"\ *n* -S [origin unknown] *Scot* **:** BLOW; *esp* **:** KICK ⟨fortune gave him many a ~⟩
[4]**fleg** \"\ *vi* **flegged; flegged; flegging; flegs** [origin unknown] *Scot* **:** to rush around or away **:** FLEE
flegm *obs var of* PHLEGM
fleid \ˈflēd, -lād\ *var of* FLEYED
flei·shig *or* **flei·schig** \ˈflāshik, -lish-\ *adj* [Yiddish *fleyshig*, fr. MHG *vleischic* of meat, meaty, fat, fr. *vleisch* meat (fr. OHG *fleisk*) + *-ic* -y (fr. OHG *-ig*) — more at FLESH] *Jewish cookery* **:** made of, prepared with, or used for meat or meat products ⟨a ~ menu⟩ ⟨~ puddings made with chicken fat instead of butter⟩
flei·shigs *or* **flei·schigs** \-ks\ *n pl, Jewish cookery* **:** meat or meat products or dishes prepared with meat products rather than dairy products
fleiss·ner grille \ˈflīsnə(r)-\ *n, usu cap F* [after Eduard *Fleissner* von Wostrowitz, Austrian cryptographer] **:** a square grille designed to be reconstructed from a key word and used for cryptographic transposition without cover text and to be rotated 90 degrees on the paper whenever the spaces are exhausted so that a solid block of transposed ciphertext is produced after four successive turns or sometimes when reversal of the grille is provided for after eight turns
fleme \ˈflēm\ *vt* -ED/-ING/-S [ME *flemen*, fr. OE *flēman, flȳman*, fr. *flēam* flight; akin to OE *flēon* to flee — more at FLEE] *archaic, chiefly Scot* **:** to drive away **:** BANISH
flem·ing \ˈflemiŋ, -mēŋ\ *n* -S *cap* [ME, fr. MD *Vlaminc, Vleminc*, fr. *Vlam-* (as in *Vlamland* Flanders) + *-inc -ing*; akin to OHG *-ing* one belonging to — more at -ING] **:** a member of the Germanic people inhabiting northern Belgium (as Flanders, Antwerp, Brabant, and Limburg) and the Nord department of France — compare WALLOON
fleming valve \"-\ *n, usu cap F* [after Sir John Ambrose *Fleming* †1945 Eng. electrical engineer, its inventor] **:** DIODE
[1]**flem·ish** \ˈflemish, -mēsh\ *adj, usu cap* [ME, fr. MD *vlamesch, vlemesch*, fr. *vlam-* (as in *Vlamland* Flanders) + *-esch* -ish; akin to OHG *-isk, -isc* -ish — more at -ISH] **1 :** relating to Flanders or to the Flemings **2 :** of, relating to, or in the Flemish language **3 :** of, relating to, or being a style of furniture developed in Flanders esp. in the 17th century when it was similar to and greatly influenced the Jacobean style
[2]**flemish** \"\ *n* -ES [ME, fr. *flemish*, adj.] **1** *cap* **:** the West Germanic language used by the Flemings and made up of dialects of Dutch — see INDO-EUROPEAN LANGUAGES table **2 flemish** *pl, cap* **:** the Flemings **3** *usu cap* **:** FLEMISH GIANT
[3]**flemish** \"\ *vt* -ED/-ING/-ES *often cap* [[1]*flemish*] **:** to lay (a ship's line) in a flemish coil — usu. used with *down*
flemish blue *n, often cap F* **:** a dark blue that is less strong and slightly redder than Peking blue, greener and paler than Japan

blue, and greener, lighter, and stronger than Majolica blue (sense 1)

flemish bond *n, often cap F* **:** a masonry bond in which each course consists of headers and stretchers alternately so laid as to always break joints

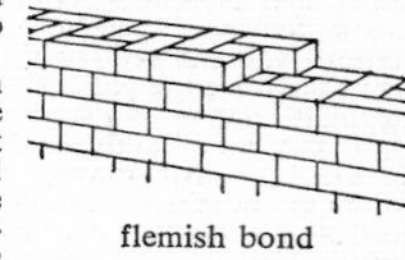
flemish bond

flemish coil *n, sometimes cap F* **:** a flat coil of rope with the end in the center and the turns lying against each other used esp. on shipboard

flemish eye *n, often cap F* **:** an eye formed at the end of a rope without splicing by dividing the strands and laying them over each other

flemish foot *n, often cap 1st F* **:** a furniture bun foot with a C-shaped or S-shaped scroll

flemish garden wall bond *n, often cap F* **:** a masonry bond in which all courses consist of one header to three or four stretchers, the courses breaking joints in a variety of patterns

flemish giant *n, usu cap F* **:** a rabbit of a breed prob. of Belgian origin that is characterized by large size, vigor, and solid coat color in black, white, or various grays

flemish horse *n, usu cap F* **:** a short footrope at the outer end of a yard on a ship — see SAIL illustration

flemish knot *n, usu cap F* **:** FIGURE EIGHT a

flemish scroll *n, often cap F* **:** a double scroll on furniture formed of two C-scrolls in opposite directions joined by an angle

flemish scroll

flem·ming's fluid *or* **flemming's solution** \ˈflemiŋz-, -mēŋz-\ *n, usu cap F* [after Walther *Flemming* †1905 Ger. anatomist and cytologist] **:** a fixing fluid composed of osmium tetroxide, chromic anhydride, and acetic acid in aqueous solution and used in microscopy chiefly for preserving details of cells

flens·burg \ˈflenz,bərg, -n(t)s,bu̇(ə)rk\ *adj, usu cap* [fr. *Flensburg*, Germany] **:** of or from the city of Flensburg, Germany **:** of the kind or style prevalent in Flensburg

flense \ˈflen(t)s\ *also* **flench** \-nch\ *or* **flinch** \-linch\ *vt* **flensed** *also* **flenched** *or* **flinched; flensed** *also* **flenched** *or* **flinched; flensing** *also* **flenching** *or* **flinching; flenses** *also* **flenches** *or* **flinches** [D *flensen* or Dan & Norw *flense;* akin to MHG *vlans* large mouth, mouth of an animal, Norw *flans* horse's pizzle, Icel *flanni* penis] **:** to strip (as a whale or seal) of blubber or skin

flens·er \ˈflen(t)sə(r)\ *n* -s **:** one that flenses animals; *esp* **:** one that cuts free whale blubber as an occupation — compare LEMMER

¹flesh \ˈflesh\ *n* -ES *often attrib* [ME, fr. OE *flǣsc;* akin to OHG *fleisk* flesh, meat, ON *flesk* bacon, ham, *flīs* slice, splinter, and prob. to ON *flā* to flay — more at FLAY] **1 a :** the soft parts of the body of man or a lower animal (as a vertebrate) usu. excluding the integument **b :** the body parts composed chiefly of skeletal muscle with accompanying fat and connective tissues as distinguished from visceral structures and bone — called also *meat* **c :** sleek well-fatted condition of body **:** FAT ⟨the steer was in excellent ~ when shown⟩ ⟨lost ~ during his illness⟩ **d :** the surface or external appearance of the body — used esp. with reference to color ⟨sun-tanned ~⟩ **2 a :** food of animal origin comprising edible parts of any animal used as food ⟨*flesh*-eating mammals⟩ **b :** flesh of mammals or sometimes of mammals and birds as an article of diet ⟨abstain from ~ during religious fasts⟩ — distinguished from *fish* and often from edible organs (as liver or brains) or from foods of vegetable origin **3 a :** the physical being of man — distinguished from *soul* **b :** HUMAN NATURE: (1) **:** tender sensitivity (2) **:** carnal weakness **:** tendency to transient or physical pleasure **:** desire for sensual gratification ⟨indulgence of the ~⟩ **4 a :** human beings **:** MANKIND, HUMANITY **b :** living beings **:** animal life ⟨inconceivable that all ~ should be swept from the earth⟩ **c :** a stock, kindred, or race constituting a unified whole ⟨this English ~⟩ ⟨men of my own ~ and kin⟩ **5 a :** a fleshy mesocarp (as of an apple or stone fruit) **:** the sarcocarp of a fleshy fruit; *broadly* **:** the fleshy part of any fruit (as an aggregate or composite fruit) **b :** the part of an edible plant suitable for or actually consumed as food usu. excluding integuments and seeds even if these are also consumed ⟨a new tomato with splendid firm ~⟩ — used chiefly of parts (as fruits, fruiting bodies, or roots) that are more or less fleshy in structure **6 :** a pale orange yellow to yellowish gray — called also *moonlight* **7** *or* **flesh side :** the inner side of a hide — compare GRAIN 4b(1) **8** *Christian Science* **:** an illusion that matter has sensation — **after the flesh :** in a natural, earthly, or gross manner or relationship — **in the flesh :** in person and alive ⟨saw him *in the flesh* not three days ago⟩ ⟨in movies . . . but never *in the flesh* —W.R.Inge⟩

²flesh \"\ *vb* -ED/-ING/-ES *vt* **1 a :** to feed (as a hawk or hound) with flesh from the kill to encourage interest in the chase — compare BLOOD *vt* 3a **b :** BLOOD *vt* 3b, 3c **c** *obs* **:** to arouse or habituate (as a person) to some emotion or response (as of lust, cupidity, or hate) esp. by experience **2 :** to drive or thrust (as a weapon) into flesh ⟨the dog ~*ed* his fangs in the deer's leg⟩ **3** *archaic* **:** GRATIFY, SATIATE ⟨~ his cupidity⟩ **4 a :** to clothe or cover with or as if with flesh ⟨the modeler builds up his figure by ~*ing* a wire frame with clay⟩; *broadly* **:** to give substance or a feeling of reality to — usu. used with *out* ⟨they ~*ed* out the president's plan with statistics and procedural details⟩ ⟨the duchess was not as well ~*ed* out as the other characters in the play⟩ **b :** to cause to grow **:** FATTEN ⟨a garden ~*ed* by rain and sun⟩ — often used with *up* ⟨you'll have to ~ those steers up if you expect them to bring top prices⟩ **5 :** to free from flesh; *esp* **:** to scrape (a skin) free of fat, membrane, or other adherent tissue ~ *vi* **:** to put on weight or substance **:** become fleshy — often used with *up* or *out* ⟨on a better diet the children soon began to ~ up⟩ ⟨that steer is ~*ing* out well⟩

flesh and blood *n* [ME *flesh and blod*] **1 :** corporeal nature as composed of flesh and of blood with their infirmities and proclivities ⟨such neglect was more than *flesh and blood* could stand⟩ **2 :** near kindred — used chiefly in the phrase *one's own flesh and blood* **3 :** substance and reality ⟨attempting to give *flesh and blood* to nebulous ideas⟩

fleshburn \ˈ=,=\ *n* **:** a brush with which to rub or cleanse the flesh of the body

flesh crow *n* **:** CARRION CROW

flesh·en \ˈfleshən\ *adj* [ME, fr. OE *flǣscen*, fr. *flǣsc* flesh + -*en*] **:** consisting of flesh

flesh·er \-shə(r)\ *n* -s [ME, fr. *flesh* + -*er*] **1** *Scot* **:** a meat seller **:** BUTCHER **2 a :** a primitive implement (as of bone or stone often with serrated edges) for fleshing hides **b :** a curved knife or other device used for fleshing skins or hides **3 :** a worker who fleshes hides or pelts with a fleshing knife or a fleshing machine **4 :** the inner layer of a split sheepskin generally tanned for chamois

flesh-fallen \ˈ=,=(=)\ *adj* **:** become thin **:** EMACIATED

flesh fly *n* [ME *flesh-flie*, fr. *flesh* + *flie* fly] **:** any of numerous flies (superfamily Muscoidea) whose maggots feed on flesh (as a bluebottle or a blowfly); *esp* **:** any of various viviparous flies that deposit living larvae on fresh meat and that constitute the genus *Sarcophaga* — called also *meat fly*

flesh fork *n* **:** a large long-handled fork used to lift meat (as from the pot in which it was cooked)

fleshhook \ˈ=,=\ *n* [ME, fr. *flesh* + *hook*] **1 :** a hook for lifting pieces of flesh (as from a pot) **2 :** a hook on which to hang meat (as in a butcher shop)

flesh hoop *n* **:** the hoop on which a drumhead is mounted — compare COUNTER HOOP

fleshier *comparative of* FLESHY

fleshiest *superlative of* FLESHY

flesh·i·ness \ˈfleshēnəs, -shin-\ *n* -ES [ME *fleshines*, fr. *fleshy* + -*nes* -ness] **:** the state of being fleshy **:** stout or plump habit of body **:** CORPULENCE

flesh·ing \ˈfleshiŋ, -shēŋ\ *n* -s [¹*flesh* + -*ing*] **1 fleshings** *pl* **:** close-fitting usu. flesh-colored tights **2 fleshings** *pl* **:** material removed in fleshing a hide or skin **3** [fr. pres. part. of ²*flesh*] **a :** the distribution of the lean and fat on an animal ⟨note the excellent ~ of the rump⟩ **b :** the capacity of an animal to put on flesh or finish ⟨easy ~ is important in the beef herd⟩

fleshing knife *or* **fleshing tool** *n* **:** a blunt concave knife or a flexible wire tool used to flesh a skin or hide

fleshing machine *n* **:** a machine used in tanneries for removing excess fat and flesh from hides and skins

flesh·less \-shləs\ *adj* [ME *fleshles*, fr. *flesh* + -*les* -less] **1 :** lean and gaunt **:** EMACIATED ⟨a pale ~ face⟩ **2 :** being without substance or body **:** DISEMBODIED ⟨~ ghosts⟩

fleshlike \ˈ=,=\ *adj* **:** resembling flesh esp. in texture or appearance

flesh·li·ly \-shləlē, -əli\ *adv* [*fleshly* + -*ly*] **:** in a fleshly manner

flesh·li·ness \-shlēnəs, -lin-\ *n* -ES [ME, fr. OE *flǣsclicnes*, fr. *flǣsclic* fleshly + -*nes* -ness] **:** preoccupation with carnal matters

flesh·ly \-lē,-li\ *adj, often* -ER/-EST [ME, fr. OE *flǣsclic*, fr. *flǣsc* flesh + -*lic* -ly] **1 a :** of or relating to the flesh or body **:** CORPOREAL, BODILY ⟨~ strength⟩ ⟨the ~ eye⟩ **b :** of or relating to bodily appetites **:** CARNAL, SENSUAL; *esp* **:** LASCIVIOUS, LIBIDINOUS ⟨~ indulgences⟩ **c :** relating to or characteristic of the bodily life **:** not spiritual ⟨~ views of life⟩ **:** WORLDLY **2 a :** having or composed of flesh **:** FLESHY **b** *obs* **:** having much flesh **:** FAT **3** *of the heart* **:** easily moved (as to compassion) **:** kind and tender **:** SOFT ⟨can there be such deceit in Christians, or treason in the ~ heart of man?— Christopher Marlowe⟩ **4 :** exhibiting or characterized by sensuous quality ⟨~ art⟩ ⟨a ~ poet⟩ **syn** see CARNAL

flesh–meat \ˈ=,=\ *n* [ME *fleshmete*, fr. OE *flǣscmete*, fr. *flǣsc* flesh + *mete* food — more at FLESH, MEAT] **:** FLESH 2b — usu. distinguished from *fish*

fleshment *n* -s *obs* **:** excitement attending a successful beginning

fleshmonger \ˈ=,==\ *n* [ME *fleshmonger, fleshmanger*, fr. OE *flǣscmangere*, fr. *flǣsc* flesh + *mangere* monger — more at MONGER] **1** *obs* **:** BUTCHER **2 a** *obs* **:** PANDER **b :** a dealer in slaves

flesh ocher *n* **:** a strong yellowish pink that is yellower and duller than salmon pink, yellower and darker than melon, and yellower and less strong than peach red

flesh–out \ˈ=ˌ=\ *adj, of shoe upper leather* **:** used with the grain side against the foot

flesh peddler *n, slang* **:** a theatrical agent

flesh pink *or* **flesh red** *n* **1 :** a variable color that is pale and light yellowish pink **2** *of textiles* **:** a pale yellowish pink

fleshpot \ˈ=,=\ *n* **1 fleshpots** *pl* **:** luxurious plenty **:** high living — used with *the* ⟨those who wallow heedlessly in the ~*s*⟩ **2 :** an establishment catering to luxurious and usu. licentious tastes — usu. used in pl. ⟨elaborate urban ~*s* contain up to five distinct drinking areas —David Dodge⟩

flesh side *n* **:** FLESH 7

flesh wound *n* **:** an injury involving penetration of the body musculature without damage to skeletal or visceral structures

fleshy \ˈfleshē, -shi\ *adj* -ER/-EST [ME, fr. *flesh* + -*y*] **1 a :** marked by, characteristic of, or resembling flesh ⟨we lived ere yet this ~ robe we wore —S.T.Coleridge⟩ **b :** having or marked by ample or excess flesh whether merely adipose or muscular and sinewy ⟨bold ~ curves [of his face] had . . . far extended beyond the limits originally assigned them —Charles Dickens⟩; *usu* **:** PLUMP, CORPULENT, FAT ⟨a ~ woman⟩ **c :** composed of flesh only rather than bone or sinew ⟨he'd been shot through the ~ part of the leg and had lost a good deal of blood —C.B.Nordhoff & J.N.Hall⟩ **2 :** FLESHLY; *esp* **:** sensual and libidinous ⟨enjoying a girly show and other ~ pleasures of life —Alan Levy⟩ **3 a :** SUCCULENT, PULPY ⟨soft ~ fruits⟩ **b :** having body or substance **:** not thin, dry, or membranaceous ⟨a ~ fungus⟩ **syn** see FAT

fleshy fruit *n* **:** a fruit consisting largely of soft succulent tissue (as a berry, drupe, or pome) — see FRUIT illustration

fleshy sponge *n* **:** a sponge (class Demospongiae) lacking a definite skeleton

¹flet \ˈflet\ *Scot var of* FLAT

²flet \"\ *adj* [fr. obs. past part. of ⁴*fleet*] *dial Eng* **:** made with skimmed milk **:** SKIMMED ⟨~ cheese⟩ ⟨~ milk⟩

fletch \ˈflech\ *vt* -ED/-ING/-ES [back-formation fr. *fletcher*] **:** FEATHER ⟨~ an arrow⟩ ⟨nursed a sharpened grudge . . . keeping it barbed and ~*ed* against the time when he might let fly with it —I.S.Cobb⟩

fletch·er \ˈflechə(r)\ *n* -s [ME *flecchere*, fr. OF *flechier*, fr. *fleche* arrow + -*ier* -er — more at FLÈCHE] **:** a maker of arrows

fletch·er·ism \-chə,rizəm\ *n* -s *usu cap* [Horace *Fletcher* †1919 Am. nutritionist + E -*ism*] **:** the practice of eating in small amounts and only when hungry and of chewing one's food thoroughly

fletch·er·ite \-,rīt\ *n* -s *usu cap* [Horace *Fletcher* + E -*ite*] **:** a believer in or practicer of Fletcherism

fletch·er·ize \-,rīz\ *vt* -ED/-ING/-S *often cap* [Horace *Fletcher* + E -*ize*] **:** to reduce (food) to tiny particles esp. by prolonged chewing

fletch·er radial burner \ˈflechə(r)-\ *n, usu cap F* [fr. the name *Fletcher*] **:** a low flat gas burner with a number of jets arranged in a radial pattern designed to heat a large container resting on it

fletcher scale *n, usu cap F* [James *Fletcher* †1908 Canadian entomologist] **:** an unarmored scale (*Lecanium fletcheri*) that is related to the brown soft scale and that is a widespread pest on ornamental evergreens

fletching *n* -s [fr. gerund of ¹*fletch*] **:** the feathers on an arrow; *also* **:** the particular arrangement in which such feathers are placed ⟨all arrows of a set should have similar ~⟩

¹fleth·er \ˈfleth̲ər\ *vi* -ED/-ING/-S [perh. blend of ¹*flatter* and ¹*blether*] *Scot* **:** to fawn and flatter

²flether \"\ *n* -s *Scot* **:** FLATTERY, FAWNING

flett·ner control \ˈfletnə(r)-\ *n, usu cap F* [after Anton *Flettner* *b*1885 Ger. engineer and inventor] **:** SERVO CONTROL

flet·ton \ˈfletᵊn\ *n* -s [fr. *Fletton*, urban district in Huntingdonshire, England, center of the brickmaking industry employing this process] **:** a yellowish red brick made by compressing moist ground clay in a steel mold

fleuk \ˈfl(y)ük, -lœk\ *chiefly Scot var of* FLUKE

fleur *n* -s [by shortening] **:** FLEUR-DE-LIS 2

fleur d'a·mour \ˌflərdə'mu̇(ə)r, ˌflür-\ *n, pl* **fleur d'amour** \"\ *or* **fleurs d'amour** \"\ [F, lit., flower of love] **:** TABERNAEMONTANA 2

fleur-de-lis *or* **fleur-de-lys** \ˌflərdᵊlˈē, ˌflə̄d-, ˌflə̇id- *also* ˌflürd- *or* -üəd- *sometimes* -ˈēs\ *also* **fleur-de-luce** \-ˈlüs\ *n, pl* **fleurs-de-lis** *or* **fleur-de-lis** *or* **fleurs-de-lys** *or* **fleur-de-lys** \-ərdᵊlˈē(z), -ə̄d-, -ə̇id- *also* -u̇rd- *or* -üəd- *sometimes* -ˈēs\ *also* **fleurs-de-luce** \-ˈlüs\ *or* **fleur-de-luc·es** \-ˈlüsəz\ [alter. (influenced by F *fleur de lis*) of ME *flourdelis*, fr. MF *flor de lis, flour de lis*, lit., lily flower] **1 :** ²IRIS 2; *esp* **:** the iris chosen for the royal emblem of France by Charles V which prob. belonged to a white-flowered variety (*Iris germanica florentina*) of the German iris **2 :** a device common in artistic design and heraldry that is commonly supposed to be a conventionalized representation of an iris and that typically consists of oppositely posed C-scrolls on each side of an elongate lyrate figure, the three being closely juxtaposed or linked across the narrowest part of the scrolls by a horizontal ligature

fleur-de-lis 2

fleur·de·li·sé \ˌ==(,)ē'zā\ *adj* [F, fr. past part. of *fleurdeliser* to mark with fleurs-de-lis, fr. *fleur de lis*, fr. OF *flor de lis, flour de lis*] **:** marked or ornamented with fleurs-de-lis

fleur-de-li·sée \"\ *adj* [F *fleurdelisée*, fem. of *fleurdelisé*] **:** FLEURETTEE 1

fleur du mal \flœrdüˈmäl\ *n, pl* **fleurs du mal** \"\ [F, lit., flower of evil; fr. *Les fleurs du mal* (1857), volume of decadent poetry by Pierre-Charles Baudelaire †1867 Fr. poet] **:** a morbid or scandalous creation in literature or art

fleu·ret \ˈflər·ət, (ˈ)flü'ret\ *n* -s [F, fr. MF *floret*, modif. of OIt *fioretto* lit., little flower, dim of *fiore* flower, fr. L *flor-, flos;* fr. the resemblance of the button at the end of its foil to a flower — more at BLOW (to bloom)] **:** a light fencing foil or small sword

fleu·rette \"\ *n* -s [F, lit., little flower, fr. OF *florete, flourete, flurete* — more at FLOWERET] **:** a decorative motif in the form of a small conventionalized flower

fleu·ret·tée *also* **fleu·ret·té** \ˌflər·ə'tā, ˌflürə'-\ *or* **flo·ret·tée** \ˌflōrə'-\ *or* **flo·ret·ty** \ˈflō'red·ē\ *adj* [ME *florette, flourte, flortee*, fr. MF *flouret*é ornamented with flowery designs, fr. *flourete* small flower] **1** *also* **fleur·ty** \ˈflərd·ē, ˈflü(ə)r-\ *of a cross* **:** having each arm terminated by the head of a fleur-de-lis which has the appearance of being attached to the end of the arm rather than constituting a part of it — see CROSS illustration **2 :** FLEURY 2 **3 :** SEMÉE-DE-LIS

fleu·ron \ˈflər·,än, ˈflü,rän\ *n* -s [F, fr. MF *floron*, fr. *flor, flour, flur* flower — more at FLOWER] **1 :** a flower-shaped ornament esp. when terminating an object or forming one of a series **2 :** a printers' type ornament of floral motif often cast in units that may be combined to form borders

fleur vo·lante \ˌflərvō'länt, ˌflür-\ *n* [F, lit., flying flower] **:** a loop added in the body of the pattern of point lace

fleu·ry \ˈflər·ē, ˈflürē\ *adj* [alter. (influenced by F *fleur* flower) of ME *floury, flory*, fr. OF *floré*, fr. *flor, flour, flur* flower — more at FLOWER] **1 :** semé with fleurs-de-lis — used of a heraldic field **2** *of a cross* **:** having the ends of the arms broadening out into the heads of fleurs-de-lis — compare FLEURETTÉE 1, PATONCE, PATY — see CROSS illustration **3** *of a heraldic ordinary* **:** having the heads of fleurs-de-lis projecting out from the edge

fleury counterfleury \ˈ==ˈ==,==\ *n* **:** FLORY COUNTERFLORY

flew *past of* FLY

flewed \ˈflüd\ *adj* **:** having flews usu. of an indicated kind ⟨a deep-*flewed* hound⟩

flew·it \ˈflüət\ *n* -s [origin unknown] *chiefly Scot* **:** a sharp blow **:** BUFFET

flews \ˈflüz\ *n pl* [origin unknown] **:** the pendulous lateral parts of the upper lip of a dog, esp. a hound — see DOG illustration

¹flex \ˈfleks\ *vb* -ED/-ING/-ES [L *flexus*, past part. of *flectere* to bend] *vt* **1 :** to bend esp. repeatedly so as to form folds in ⟨sat ~*ing* the strap as he talked⟩ **2 a :** to move muscles so as to cause flexion of (a joint) ⟨stretching and ~*ing* his knees⟩ — compare EXTEND **b :** to move (a muscle or muscles) so as to flex a joint ⟨~*ed* their biceps and went to work⟩ ~ *vi* **:** to bend esp. so as to form a fold or to clasp ⟨the old man's hands ~*ed* on the head of his cane⟩ ⟨such a spring must ~ repeatedly without weakening or deforming permanently⟩

²flex \"\ *n* -ES **1 :** an act or instance of flexing ⟨gave his muscles a ~ and heaved on the bar⟩ **2** [short for ²*flexible*] *chiefly Brit* **:** electric cord

flex-crack \ˈ=,=\ *vi* **:** to develop cracks on the surface (as of rubber) as a result of repeated flexing

flexed *adj* **:** with knees drawn up to chin — used chiefly of the arrangement of the corpse for burial among certain primitive peoples ⟨buried in ~ position⟩ ⟨a ~ skeleton⟩

flex·i·bil·i·ty \ˌfleksə'biləd·ē, -lətē, -i\ *n* -ES [F *flexibilité*, fr. MF, fr. LL *flexibilitat-, flexibilitas*, fr. L *flexibilis* flexible + -*itat-, -itas* -ity] **:** the quality or state of being flexible ⟨balance and ~ in the armed forces —T.R.Phillips⟩ ⟨the ~ and spontaneity of performances —Brooks Atkinson⟩ ⟨the face of the mother, for all its amazing ~ —Thomas Wolfe⟩

flex·i·bi·lize \ˈfleksəbə,līz\ *vt* -ED/-ING/-S [L *flexibilis* + E -*ize*] **:** to render flexible **:** PLASTICIZE

¹flex·i·ble \ˈfleksəbəl\ *adj* [ME, fr. MF, fr. L *flexibilis*, fr. *flexus* + -*ibilis* -ible] **1 :** capable of being flexed **:** capable of being turned, bowed, or twisted without breaking **:** PLIABLE ⟨using ointments to keep the healing surface ~⟩ ⟨slim ~ birches bowing in the wind⟩ **2 :** willing or ready to yield to the influence of others **:** not invincibly rigid or obstinate **:** TRACTABLE, MANAGEABLE ⟨a ~ character, pleasant and cooperative but without strong convictions⟩ **3 :** characterized by ready capability for modification or change, by plasticity, pliancy, variability, and often by consequent adaptability to new situations ⟨a highly ~ curriculum⟩ ⟨a living and ~ and growing morality —Havelock Ellis⟩ ⟨a ~ schedule of rates⟩ **4 :** featuring flexible binding or flexible sewing ⟨a ~ edition⟩ — see SPINE illustration

syn ELASTIC, RESILIENT, SPRINGY, SUPPLE: FLEXIBLE is applicable to anything capable of being bent, turned, or twisted without being broken and with or without returning of itself to its former shape ⟨plumbing is easier with *flexible* copper tubing⟩ ⟨a *flexible* thin steel runner⟩ ELASTIC indicates ability to stretch, expand, or take on new shape under pressure, usu. with return to an original shape or position after pressure is withdrawn ⟨a body . . . is *elastic* when, and only when, it tends to recover its initial condition when the distorting force is removed. For example, lead, putty, and chewing gum are not elastic. Steel, rubber, air, most substances in fact, are more or less elastic —A.L.Foley⟩ RESILIENT stresses an ability to spring back and recover shape with the removal of pressure ⟨*resilient* natural rubber⟩ ⟨the *resilient* qualities of a tennis ball⟩ ⟨*resilient* mattresses and cushions⟩ SPRINGY is a nontechnical word with meanings and suggestions of both ELASTIC and RESILIENT ⟨a *springy* turf⟩ ⟨a bed of *springy* pine needles —S.E.White⟩ ⟨her bright brown hair rose in *springy* waves from her forehead, piled high on her head —Marcia Davenport⟩ SUPPLE applies to whatever bends, flexes, or folds with reasonable ease and shows resistance to cracking, breaking, or splitting ⟨*supplest* calfskin⟩ ⟨a pullover of *supple* chamois⟩

²flexible \"\ *n* -s **:** something that is flexible

flexible binding *n* **1 :** bookbinding in which flexible sewing is used **2 :** a book cover made of flexible rather than rigid boards

flexible collodion *n* **:** collodion to which small amounts of other ingredients (as camphor and castor oil) have been added to render the film left on evaporation pliable

flexible constitution *n* **:** a constitution that may be amended by the ordinary process of legislation and is therefore relatively easy to amend

flexible glue *n* **:** a mixture of glue, water, and a softening agent (as glycerol or sorbitol) used esp. in printers' rollers, bookbinding, and gasket binders

flexible gunnery *n* **:** the firing of swivel guns (as in an airplane) — compare FIXED GUNNERY

flex·i·ble·ness *n* -ES **:** FLEXIBILITY

flexible sandstone *n* **:** itacolumite in thin flexible layers

flexible sewing *n, bookbinding* **:** hand sewing in which the thread is passed through each section and over raised cords

flexible shaft *n* **1 :** a shaft or shafting made of a flexible material (as wire wrapped around a core in alternately directed layers) or composed of a series of jointed links **2 :** a high-speed rotating shaft so supported in its bearings (as by oil pressure or spring action) that a small lateral movement is possible

flexible tariff *n* **:** a tariff (as that established in the U. S. by the Fordney-McCumber Act of 1922) by which the executive under specified conditions may by proclamation modify any rate of duty by not more than a stipulated percent of the amount provided therefor

flexible wheelbase *n* **:** a wheelbase in a vehicle running on two or more pairs of wheels that is adjustable so that in rounding a curve the axles shift so as to be radial to the curve

flex·i·bly \ˈfleksəblē, -li\ *adv* **:** in a flexible manner **:** with flexibility

flex·ile \ˈfleksəl, -k,sīl, -k(,)sil\ *adj* [L *flexilis*, fr. *flexus* (past part. of *flectere* to bend) + -*ilis* -ile] **:** FLEXIBLE

flexing *pres part of* FLEX

flexion *var of* FLECTION

flex·ive \ˈfleksiv\ *adj* [L *flexus* (past part. of *flectere* to bend) + E -*ive*] *archaic* **:** FLEXIBLE

flex life *n* **:** the capability of a material (as nylon or rubber) to withstand repeated bending without fracture

flex·o·graph·ic printing \ˌfleksəˌgrafik-\ *n* [*flexo-* (fr. L *flexus*) + -*graphic*] **:** ANILINE PRINTING

flex·og·ra·phy \flek'sägrəfē\ *n* -ES [*flexo-* + -*graphy*] **:** ANILINE PRINTING

flex·om·e·ter \flek'sämәd·ə(r)\ *n* [*flexo-* + -*meter*] **:** an instrument for testing the flexibility of materials (as textiles or rubber)

flex·or \ˈfleksər, -,sȯ(ə)r\ *n* -s [NL, fr. L *flexus* (past part. of *flectere* to bend) + -*or*] **:** a muscle that serves to bend a limb or part — opposed to *extensor*

flex·u·os·i·ty \ˌflekshə'wäsəd·ē\ *n* -ES [LL *flexuositas*, fr. L *flexuosus* + -*itas* -ity] **1 :** the quality or state of being flexuous ⟨the ~ of the ureter⟩ **2 :** a winding part ⟨a little ~ running along the base of the membrane⟩

flex·u·ous \ˈflekshəwəs\ *also* **flex·u·ose** \-,wōs\ *adj* [L *flexuosus*, fr. *flexus* + -*osus* -ous, -ose] **1 a :** having turns or windings ⟨the ~ bed of the stream⟩ **b** *bot* **:** having alternate opposite curvatures **:** ZIGZAG, WAVY ⟨leaves with ~ margins⟩ **2 :** lacking rigidity in structure or action **:** FLEXIBLE: as **a :** ADAPTABLE **b :** FLICKERING, UNDULATING ⟨~ shadows⟩ — **flex·u·ous·ly** *adv*

flex·ur·al \'fleksh(ə)rəl\ *adj* **1 :** of, relating to, or resulting from flexure ⟨~ strength of wood⟩ **2 :** being or characterized by flexure ⟨~ elasticity⟩

flex·ure \'flekshə(r)\ *n* -s [L *flexura*, fr. *flexus* + *-ura* -ure] **1 :** the quality or state of being flexed **:** TURNING, FLECTION **2 :** TURN, BEND, FOLD ⟨a ~ in a rock stratum⟩ ⟨the ~ between thigh and abdomen⟩ **3** *obs* **:** ability or tendency to bend **:** PLIANCY **4 :** the last joint of a bird's wing **5 :** the slight bending of an astronomical observing instrument caused by the weight of its parts; *also* **:** the correction of the observed readings necessitated by this bending **6 :** a deformation of an elastic body wherein all points orig. in a straight line are displaced in the same plane to form a curve **7 :** one of three sharp bends of the anterior part of the primary axis of the vertebrate embryo that serve to establish the relationship of the parts of the developing brain — called also in order of occurrence *cephalic flexure*, *cranial flexure*, and *pontine flexure*

flexy \'fleksē\ *adj*, *often* -ER/-EST [¹*flex* + *-y*] **:** tending to flex freely — used esp. of clothing ⟨soft ~ moccasins⟩

fley \'fləi, 'flā\ *vb* **fleyed; fleyed; fleying; fleys** [ME *flayen*, fr. OE *āflēgan*, *āflȳgan*, fr. *ā-*, *ar-*, perfective prefix + *-flēgan*, *-flȳgan*, causative fr. the root of E *flee* — more at ABEAR, FLEE] *vt* **1** *Scot* **:** to terrify or frighten esp. by startling **2** *Scot* **:** to frighten off — usu. used with *away* **~** *vi*, *Scot* **:** to become afraid

fley·some \-səm\ *adj*, *dial Brit* **:** TERRIFYING, FRIGHTENING

flg *abbr* **1** flange **2** flooring

flib·ber·ti·gib·bet \'flibə(r)d·ē|jibət, -t|, |i|-, *usu* -jibəd·+V\ *n* -s [alter. of ME *flepergebet*, *flypyrgebet*] **1** *archaic* **:** GOSSIP, CHATTERER **2 :** a light-minded or silly restless person; *esp* **:** a pert young woman with such qualities — **flib·ber·ti·gib·bety** \-əd·|ē, -ət|, |i\ *adj*

fli·bus·tier \'flēbə,sti(ə)r, 'flib-\ *n* -s [F — more at FILIBUSTER] **1** *archaic* **:** FREEBOOTER **2** *archaic* **:** FILIBUSTER 1

flic \'flēk, 'flik\ *n* -s [F] **:** a Parisian policeman

flic-flac \'flik,flak\ *n* -s [F, of imit. origin] **:** a brushing movement of the foot used in ballet as a connecting step ⟨he teaches pirouettes and ~s —W.M.Thackeray⟩

flicht \'flikt\ *Scot var of* FLIGHT

¹**flich·ter** \-tər\ *vi* -ED/-ING/-S [ME (northern dial.) *flichteren*, fr. *flicht*, *flight*, n. + *-eren* (freq. suffix) — more at FLIGHT] **1** *chiefly Scot* **:** to fly clumsily or ineptly **:** FLUTTER **2** *Scot* **:** QUIVER, THROB, PALPITATE **3** *Scot* **:** FLICKER

²**flichter** \"\ *n* -s *Scot* **:** FLICKER

flichtered *adj* [fr. past part. of ¹*flichter*] **1** *Scot* **:** CONFUSED, FLUSTERED **2** *Scot* **:** FRIGHTENED

¹**flick** \'flik\ *n* -s [ME *flik* pelt] *dial Eng* **:** fur esp. of a rabbit or hare

²**flick** \"\ *n* -s [ME *flicke*, fr. ON *flikki* — more at FLITCH] **1** *dial* **:** FLITCH **2** *dial Eng* **:** LEAF FAT

³**flick** \"\ *n* -s [imit.] **1 a :** a light sharp stroke, movement, or blow often with something flexible ⟨just a ~ or two with a light switch is enough to teach a puppy manners⟩ ⟨test the glass with the ~ of a finger⟩ **b :** a quick and usu. sudden movement (as of the wrist) made by angular or rotary flexion and used esp. in stroking a ball or shuttlecock **2 :** a light sound comparable to that produced by the flick of a whip ⟨the ~ of cards on polished wood⟩ ⟨the busy ~ and chatter of typewriter keys⟩ **3 a :** a splash or splotch esp. of mud or water **b :** FLICKER 1

⁴**flick** \"\ *vb* -ED/-ING/-S *vt* **1 a :** to strike lightly with a quick sharp motion ⟨~*ed* him in the face with his open hand⟩ ⟨~*ing* the old horse from time to time with his whip⟩ **b :** to remove with a light blow or a series of light blows ⟨~*ed* the dust from his boots with a handkerchief⟩ **2 a :** to move or cause to move with a jerk or a sharp light blow ⟨~*ing* the ashes from his cigar⟩ ⟨~*ed* a fly from the horse's rump⟩ **b :** to propel (as a ball) with a flick **~** *vi* **1 a :** to flutter or flit **b** *of an arrow in flight* **:** to suddenly deviate from the line of flight **2 :** to use flicks ⟨~*ing* away at his rival⟩; *esp* **:** to direct flicks at something ⟨he ~*ed* at the spot with a napkin⟩ ⟨~*ing* ineffectually at the mosquitoes⟩

⁵**flick** \"\ *vt* -ED/-ING/-S [origin unknown] *archaic* **:** CUT

⁶**flick** \"\ *n* -s [short for ²*flicker*] **:** MOVIE — usu. used in pl. ⟨take his girl to the ~s⟩

¹**flick·er** \'flikə(r)\ *vb* **flickered; flickered; flickering** \-k(ə)riŋ\ **flickers** [ME *flikeren*, fr. OE *flicorian*; akin to OE *flacor* flying, MHG *vlackern* to flicker, ON *flökra* to flutter, *flakka* to flicker, flutter, L *plangere* to strike — more at PLAINT] *vi* **1 :** to flap the wings without flying **:** FLUTTER ⟨and ~*ing* on her nest made short essays to sing —John Dryden⟩ **2** *obs* **:** to make caressing motions or advances **3 a :** to waver unsteadily **:** wave or undulate like a flame in a current of air ⟨the embers ~*ed* into flame⟩; *sometimes* **:** to give a final flicker (as of light while expiring) ⟨shadows ~ on the wall⟩ — often used with *out* ⟨the light ~*ed* out⟩ **b** *of a fire or flame* **:** to burn fitfully **c :** to engage in brief and often surreptitious glances ⟨her glance ~*ed* at him⟩; *often* **:** to make an examination in brief glances ⟨the teacher's eyes ~*ed* doubtfully over the rapt pupils⟩ **~** *vt* **1 :** to cause to flicker **2 a :** to produce by flickering ⟨fitful flames ~*ing* dark horrors on the wall⟩ **b :** to make apparent or convey by some slight gesture ⟨~*ed* a warning with a lifted brow⟩

²**flicker** \"\ *n* -s **1 a :** an act of flickering ⟨the ~ of shadow on the wall⟩ **b :** a sudden brief movement or gesture ⟨a ~ of an eyelash⟩ **c :** a momentary quickening (as of interest or emotion) ⟨felt a ~ of renewed desire⟩ **d :** a tailspin of an iceboat traveling at high speed **2 :** a product of flickering: as **a :** a brief interval of brightness ⟨the final ~ of a dying fire⟩ **b :** an uncertain wavering or intermittent light ⟨the uncertain ~ of a tallow dip⟩ **c :** the wavering or fluttering visual sensation produced by intermittent light when the rate of intermittence is not rapid enough to produce complete fusion of the individual impressions — contrasted with *fusion*; see CRITICAL FLICKER FREQUENCY **d** *slang* **:** MOTION PICTURE — usu. used in pl.

³**flicker** \"\ *n* -s [prob. fr. ⁴*flick* + *-er*] **:** YELLOW-SHAFTED FLICKER; *broadly* **:** any of various large No. American woodpeckers (genus *Colaptes*) widely distributed in the southern and western U. S. and often more or less brightly marked with red or reddish color esp. about the nape and usu. speckled underparts — usu. used in combination; see GILDED FLICKER, RED-SHAFTED FLICKER

flicker fusion *n* **:** FUSION 2d(2)

¹**flickering** *adj* [ME *flikering*, fr. pres. part. of *flikeren*] **:** wavering and unsteady ⟨a ~ light⟩; *often* **:** uncertain and feeble **:** nearly extinguished ⟨held but a ~ hope of success⟩ — **flick·er·ing·ly** *adv*

²**flickering** *n* -s [ME *flikering*, fr. gerund of *flikeren*] **1 :** a wavering or uncertain movement or appearance (as of light) ⟨the ~ of gentle fingers over his face⟩ **2 :** a slight movement or trend **:** BEGINNING — often used in pl. ⟨there were ~s of unrest⟩ ⟨recurrent ~s of revolt⟩

flicker photometer *n* **:** a photometer for comparing the brightness of two lights based upon the principle that flicker between two alternating lights of different color is at a minimum when the brightness of the two is equal

flickertail \'≈,≈\ *n* **1 :** a ground squirrel (*Citellus richardsoni*) chiefly of the north-central U. S. and adjacent Canada **2** *usu cap* **:** NORTH DAKOTAN — used as a nickname

flick·ery \'flik(ə)rē, -ri\ *adj* **:** showing or moving with flickers **:** uncertain and wavering ⟨a ~ light⟩ ⟨flitted about like ~ black shadows —I.S.Cobb⟩

flick-flack \'flik,flak\ *n* -s [imit.] **:** the noise of repeated light blows ⟨the milk in the . . . churn . . . changed its squashing to a decided *flick-flack* —Thomas Hardy⟩

flicky \'flikē\ *adj*, *usu* -ER/-EST [fr. ⁴*flick* + *-y*] **:** jerky and brisk

flics *pl of* FLIC

flied *past of* FLY

fli·er *or* **fly·er** \'flī(ə)r, -īə\ *n* -s [ME, fr. *flien* to fly + *-er* — more at FLY] **1 :** one that flies with wings (as a bird or insect) or as if with wings: as **a :** FUGITIVE **b :** AERIALIST **c :** AIRCRAFT **d :** AIRMAN **2** *usu flyer* **:** one that moves with uncommon speed (as a fast coach or train) — often used in proper names ⟨the Western *Flyer*⟩ **3 :** a small dark-spotted greenish sunfish (*Centrarchus macropterus*) found in clear fresh waters near the coast from Virginia southward and in the lower Mississippi valley **4 :** a swift kangaroo; *specif* **:** BLUE DOE **5 :** any of various mechanical appliances of swift motion: as **a :** a vaned wheel that rotates the cap of a windmill as the wind veers **b :** a windmill sail **6 :** something entered into or undertaken without normal backing or reasonable grounds for assurance **:** a reckless or speculative venture ⟨took a ~ in politics soon after getting his degree⟩; *often* **:** a financial investment made with little knowledge of the facts or by one inexperienced in business in the expectation of realizing large profits **7** *usu flyer* **a :** a handbill or circular for mass distribution (as one bearing a political advertisement or the announcement of a coming sale) **b :** a supplementary catalog (as of a mail-order house) **8 :** a step in a straight flight made up of identically rectangular steps — compare WINDER **9** *usu* **flyers** *pl* **:** small floating particles; *esp* **:** hop particles in suspension in beer **10** *usu flyer*, *chiefly Brit* **:** DELIVERY 9 — often used in pl. but sing. in constr. **11** *usu flyer* **:** a device revolving above a spindle to guide and insert twist in slubbing, roving, or yarn and being usu. one of a series on a fly frame **12 :** a leaf or slip attached at one edge to another usu. larger leaf (as of printer's copy or a book) and typically containing an addition or correction **13 :** a shot that strikes a target well outside the area in which other shots of the same round have hit

flies *pres 3d sing of* FLY, *pl of* FLY

flif·fis *or* **flif·fus** \'flifəs\ *n* -ES [origin unknown] **:** a twisting double somersault performed on the trampoline

fligged \'fligd\ *dial Eng var of* FLEDGED

¹**flight** \'flīt, *usu* -īd·+V\ *n* -s *often attrib* [ME, fr. OE *flyht*; akin to MD *vlucht* flight, OE *flēogan* to fly — more at FLY] **1 a :** the act or mode of passing through the air by the use of wings ⟨the ~ of a bee⟩ ⟨the ~ of bats⟩ **b :** ability to fly ⟨~ is natural to birds⟩ **c :** the extent of a flight ⟨a ~ of many hours⟩ ⟨a ~ of 100 miles⟩; *sometimes* **:** an instance of the flying of a hawk or falcon in pursuit of game **2 a :** a passing or mode of passing through the air analogous (as in duration or distance) to that of a winged creature **:** a journey or voyage through the air ⟨the ~ of a balloon⟩ ⟨an arrow's swift ~⟩; *also* **:** a passing through space beyond the earth's atmosphere ⟨~ of a rocket⟩ **b :** a swift passage (as of time) **3 a** *obs* **:** a bird's wing **b :** FLIGHT FEATHER — usu. used in pl. **4 :** a scheduled trip of an airplane ⟨on a 9 o'clock ~ to St. Louis⟩ **5 :** a number of similar beings or things passing through or capable of passing through the air together: as **a** (1) **:** a flock of birds esp. when flying or migrating together; *broadly* **:** the birds engaging in a particular migration ⟨the spring ~ of geese on the eastern flyway was unusually large⟩ (2) **:** the young birds produced by a nesting colony in one season esp. when about to fledge or newly fledged **b :** a swarm of insects **c :** a volley of arrows or other missiles ⟨loosed a swift ~ of arrows⟩ **d :** a group of angels **e :** a number of competitors (as in a sport) grouped together on the basis of demonstrated skill or ability or for purposes of elimination contests prior to a final test **f** (1) **:** a flight formation usu. made up of at least four airplanes; *also* **:** a larger formation made up of two or more such formations (2) **:** a parade formation made up of two or more squads **6 :** an act or instance of passing above or beyond ordinary bounds **:** a mounting or soaring esp. of mind or spirit ⟨~s of fancy⟩ ⟨soaring ~s of intellect⟩ **7 a** (1) **:** a continuous series of stairs from one landing to the next (2) **:** one or more of such series making the whole ascent from one floor to another (3) **:** FLOOR, STORY **b :** a series (as of canal locks, terraces, or hurdles) resembling a flight of stairs **8 :** the tail of the clapper of a bell **9 :** the range of an arrow **10 :** a vane or flat plate on an endless belt or chain in a conveyor or elevator **11 a :** FLYBOAT **b :** a sudden sharp rise in the lines of a vessel or any of its parts **12 :** a pen or cage large enough for birds to fly freely in **13** *cricket* **:** ability to flight

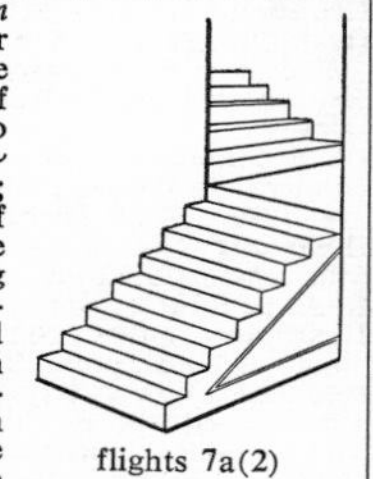
flights 7a(2)

²**flight** *adj*, *obs* **:** FLEET

³**flight** \'flīt, *usu* -īd·+V\ *vb* -ED/-ING/-S *vi* **1** *of birds, esp waterfowl* **:** to rise from or settle on resting or feeding grounds in a flock ⟨every evening the geese ~ on the marsh⟩ **2** *of birds* **:** to fly in flocks (as in migrating) ⟨hundreds of starlings ~*ed* toward the town⟩ **~** *vt* **1 :** to cause (waterfowl) to fly up from resting or feeding grounds or to shoot (waterfowl) while rising from such places **2 :** to put feathers on (an arrow) **:** FLETCH **3 :** to impart to (a cricket ball) a trajectory intended to make difficult a batsman's judgment of length

⁴**flight** \"\ *n* -s [ME, *fluht*, *fliht*; akin to OFris *flecht* flight (act of fleeing), OS & OHG *fluht*, ON *flōtti*, Goth *thlauhs*; derivatives fr. the root of OE *flēon* to flee — more at FLEE] **1 a :** an act or instance of running away (as to escape danger) ⟨fain by ~ to save themselves —Shak.⟩ ⟨his ~ was not discovered until the next day⟩ **b :** withdrawal or sudden transfer of capital (as from an enterprise or from one currency to another) to avoid risk or loss ⟨the ~ of capital that results from an unstable currency⟩ **2 :** means of escape

⁵**flight** \"\ *vt* -ED/-ING/-S **1** *obs* **:** to put to flight: ROUT **2** *archaic* **:** FRIGHTEN

flight arrow *n* **:** a light low-feathered arrow for long-distance shooting

flight bow *n* **:** a bow designed for distance shooting

flight check *n* **1 :** a test of the proficiency in flight of a member of an aircrew **2 :** a test in flight of an airplane or equipment on it

flight control *n* **1 :** the control from ground stations of airplanes in flight by means of information transmitted to the pilot by radio and other electronic devices; *also* **:** the office or system that provides this control **2 :** the system (as of levers, cables, and movable surfaces) that controls the movement of an airplane

flight cover *n* **:** FLOWN COVER

flight deck *n* **1 :** the uppermost complete deck of an aircraft carrier serving primarily as landing and takeoff area for airplanes **2 :** the forward compartment in some airplanes used by the pilot, copilot, and flight engineer

flight·ed \'flīd·əd\ *adj* [¹*flight* + *-ed*] **1 :** FEATHERED — used chiefly of heraldic representations of arrows and usu. postpositively ⟨arrows ~ argent⟩ **2** *of steps* **:** arranged in flights often of a specified kind ⟨steep-*flighted* stairs⟩

flight engineer *n* **:** the member of the flight crew of an airplane responsible for its mechanical operation

flight·er \'flīd·ə(r)\ *n* -s *in brewing* **:** a horizontal vane revolving over the surface of wort in a cooler to hasten the cooling

flight feather *n* **:** one of the quills of a bird's wing or tail that support it in flight — compare CONTOUR FEATHER; see GOOSE illustration

flight formation *n* **:** two or more airplanes flying close to each other in a predetermined arrangement

flight·i·ly \'flīd·ᵊlē, -īt|, |əl-\ *adv* **:** in a flighty manner

flight·i·ness \|ēnəs, |in-\ *n* -ES **:** the quality or state of being flighty ⟨the ~ of her temper —Nathaniel Hawthorne⟩

flight·ing \'flīd·iŋ\ *n* -s [¹*flight* + *-ing*] **:** a system of flights (as on a conveyor belt)

flight leader *n* **:** the pilot in command of a flight of military airplanes

flight·less \'flītləs\ *adj*, *of a bird* **:** lacking the ability to fly ⟨~ downy young⟩; *esp* **:** permanently unable to fly because of wing reduction accompanying evolutionary adaptation to certain specialized terrestrial habitats — used chiefly of ratite birds

flight lieutenant *n* **:** an aviation officer (as in the British Royal Air Force) equivalent in rank to a captain in the army

flight line *n* **:** the ground parking and servicing area for airplanes including hangars, operations building, and ramps but not runways or taxiways

flight nurse *n* **:** a registered nurse (as in the U. S. Air Force) who has had special training in aeromedicine and is assigned to care for patients being evacuated or transferred by air

flight officer *n* **:** an aviation officer (as in the U.S. Army Air Forces) having a rank equivalent to that of warrant officer junior grade

flight of ideas : a rambling from subject to subject with only superficial associative connections esp. in the manic phase of manic-depressive psychosis ⟨had visual and auditory hallucinations and showed *flight of ideas* —L.V.Der Horst⟩

flight path *n* **:** the path of the center of gravity of an airplane in flight relative to a stationary frame of reference

flight pay *n* **:** an additional pay allowance for hazard paid (as in the U. S. Air Force) to qualified aircrewmen who fly a minimum number of hours per month — called also *flying pay*

flights *pl of* FLIGHT, *pres 3d sing of* FLIGHT

flight shooting *n* **:** competitive shooting for distance with bow and arrow

flightshot \'≈,≈\ *n* **:** the distance to which an arrow may be shot **:** BOWSHOT

flight simulator *n* **:** an airplane pilot-training device in which the cockpit and instruments of an airplane are duplicated and the conditions of actual flight are simulated

flight song *n* **:** a song that is uttered by a bird while flying and that is often different in form from the song given while perched

flight strip *n* **1 :** an auxiliary or emergency landing field alongside a highway **2 :** a series of overlapping aerial photographs taken along a single course of flight

flight surgeon *n* **:** a medical officer (as in the U. S. Air Force) who has had additional training in the specialty of aeromedicine and who looks after the general health of the aircrewmen including the mental and physical problems associated with flying

flight-test \'≈,≈\ *vt* **:** to test (an airplane) in flight

flighty \'flīd·|ē, -īt|, |i\ *adj* -ER/-EST [¹*flight* + *-y*] **1 :** FLEETING, SWIFT, TRANSIENT ⟨the ~ purpose never is o'ertook unless the deed go with it —Shak.⟩ **2 a :** indulging in or characterized by wild and unrestrained sallies (as of imagination, humor, caprice) **:** VOLATILE ⟨proofs of my ~ and paradoxical turn of mind —S.T.Coleridge⟩ ⟨~ young girls⟩ **b** *of a horse* **:** restless and mettlesome **:** SKITTISH **3** *archaic* **:** of disordered mind **:** mildly or transitorily insane

¹**flim-flam** \'flim,flam, -aa(ə)m\ *n* -s [prob. of Scand origin; akin to ON *flim*, *flīm* mockery; akin to Norw *flire* to giggle, Sw (dial.) *flira*] **1 a :** FREAK, TRIFLE, CONCEIT **b :** DECEPTION, TRICK; *esp* **:** a trick (as in making change) by which one is swindled **2 :** TRIFLING, NONSENSE **:** deceptive humbug

²**flimflam** \"\ *vt* **flimflammed; flimflammed; flimflamming; flimflams :** to subject to a flimflam **:** TRICK; *sometimes* **:** SWINDLE

flim·flam·mer \-mə(r)\ *n* -s **:** one that gains his way by trickery and expedients **:** a user of flimflams esp. to get the better of another — **flim·flam·mery** \-m(ə)rē\ *n* -ES

¹**flim·mer** \'flimə(r)\ *vi* -ED/-ING/-S [G *flimmern*] **:** GLIMMER, FLICKER

²**flimmer** \"\ *n* -s [G, lit., glitter, tinsel, fr. *flimmern*] **:** one of the delicate lateral filaments typical of some flagella — called also *mastigoneme*

flimp \'flimp\ *vt* -ED/-ING/-S [perh. fr. Flem *flimpen* to spirit away, make disappear] *slang Brit* **:** to rob (a person) esp. with the aid of a partner who provides a distraction; *also* **:** to steal (as a watch) from another's person

flim·si·ly \'flimzəlē, -li\ *adv* **:** in a flimsy manner

flim·si·ness \-zēnəs, -zin-\ *n* -ES **:** the quality or state of being flimsy

¹**flim·sy** \'flimzē, -zi\ *adj* -ER/-EST [perh. alter. of ¹*film* + *-sy* (as in *tipsy*)] **1 :** lacking in physical strength or substance ⟨a soft ~ silk⟩; *often* **:** of inferior materials and workmanship ⟨~ shacks⟩ **2 :** having little real worth ⟨could offer only very ~ security⟩; *often* **:** lacking real worth or plausibility ⟨making ~ pretenses at elegance⟩ **3** *of persons* **a :** frail and delicate **:** ENFEEBLED, WEAK **b :** frivolous and superficial **:** making a great show based on small attainments or accomplishments **:** TRIFLING ⟨faddish ~ rogues⟩

²**flimsy** \"\ *n* -ES **1 :** something thin, frail, or unsubstantial: as **a :** a sheet of manifold paper or other very thin paper **b flimsies** *pl* **:** women's sheer lightweight clothing; *esp* **:** sheer undergarments **2 :** manuscript or copy on flimsy: as **a :** a duplicate of a wire news story **b :** one of a number of manifolded copies of a news story supplied by a news agency **c :** a train order written on thin paper to permit making several carbon copies **d :** TELEGRAM, RADIOGRAM

¹**flinch** \'flinch\ *vb* -ED/-ING/-S [MF *flenchir*, *flainchir*, prob. of Gmc origin; akin to MHG *lenken* to bend — more at LANK] *vi* **1 a :** to withdraw or shrink (as from an enterprise or responsibility) usu. because of danger, difficulties, or distress involved or foreseen ⟨~ at the thought of their own participation in partisan politics —John Lodge⟩ ⟨perilous to ~ from making the attempt —A.J.Toynbee⟩ **b :** to shrink from or as if from physical pain **:** WINCE, START ⟨~*ing* from the vile air —Marcia Davenport⟩ ⟨~*ing* from a dart of neuralgia —Ellen Glasgow⟩; *often* **:** to tense the muscles suddenly and involuntarily in anticipation of some startling unpleasant event ⟨many young shooters spoil their scores by ~*ing* just before they pull the trigger⟩ ⟨I cannot help ~*ing* when I hear the dentist's drill⟩ **2** *obs* **:** to slink off or away **~** *vt*, *archaic* **:** to draw back or hold back from (as some indulgence) **syn** see RECOIL

²**flinch** \"\ *n* -ES **:** an act or instance of flinching

³**flinch** *var of* FLENSE

¹**flinch·er** \-chə(r)\ *n* -s [¹*flinch* + *-er*] **1 :** one that flinches **2** *archaic* **:** a person who drinks sparingly

²**flin·cher** \"\ *n* -s [by alter.] **:** VELLINCH

flinch·ing·ly *adv* **:** in a flinching manner **:** as though shrinking from anticipated distress or discomfort

flin·ders \'flində(r)z\ *n pl* [ME *flenderis*, prob. of Scand origin; akin to Norw *flindra* thin piece or splinter of stone, *flinter* little piece; akin to D *flenter* piece of rag, tatter, thin piece, Fris *flanter* thin slice, dangling rag or rope, and prob. to OE *flint* flint, rock — more at FLINT] **:** pieces, splinters, or fragments ⟨broke the vase to ~⟩

flinders bar \'≈-\ *n*, *usu cap F* [after Matthew *Flinders* †1814 Eng. mariner] **:** a soft-iron bar or bundle of soft-iron rods placed vertically near a ship's compass to counteract deviation due to magnetic induction from the earth in surrounding vertical ironwork

flinders grass *n*, *usu cap F* [after Matthew *Flinders*] **:** an Australian arid-land grass (*Iseilema membranacea*) valuable for pasture and forage

flin·der·sia \flin'dərzēə\ *n* [NL, fr. Matthew *Flinders* + NL *-ia*] **1** *cap* **:** a small genus of pinnate-leaved Australasian trees (family Meliaceae) having white flowers followed by woody capsular fruits and yielding strong hardwood lumber, often with an excellent figure, that is used in cabinetmaking and construction — see FLINDOSA **2** -s **:** any tree of the genus *Flindersia*

flin·do·sa \flin'dōzə\ *also* **flin·do·sy** \-zē\ *n*, *pl* **flindosas** *also* **flindosies** [modif. of NL *Flindersia*] **:** a tall Australian timber tree (*Flindersia australis*) with tough hard wood much used for hoops, staves, and similar items — called also *native beech*

¹**fling** \'fliŋ\ *vb* **flung** \'fləŋ\ *also dial* **flang** \'flaŋ, -aiŋ\ **flung; flinging; flings** [ME *flingen*, *flengen* (also, to strike, lash out), of Scand origin; akin to ON *flengja* whip, throw, Norw, to tear loose, hurry; akin to ON *flā* to flay — more at FLAY] *vi* **1 :** to move hastily, brusquely, or violently often as an expression of mental or emotional turmoil ⟨she *flung* away from her brother's restraining hand⟩ ⟨~*ing* out of the room in a rage⟩ **2 a** *of an animal* **:** to kick or plunge wildly **:** aim a kick — now usu. used with *out* ⟨the mule *flung* out at him as he passed⟩ **b** *obs*, *of a person* **:** to struggle or fling oneself about (as in attempting to escape) **3** *Scot* **a :** to caper about **b :** to dance a fling **~** *vt* **1 a :** to throw esp. with force, violence, recklessness, or abandon **:** HURL ⟨as if a resistless flood had torn them loose from their foundations . . . ~*ing* them here and there —O.E.Rölvaag⟩ ⟨*flung* his books on the table⟩ — often used with an adverb of direction ⟨*flung* the report down in disgust⟩ ⟨*flung* up his hands in despair⟩ **b :** to cast aside by or as if by throwing forcibly **:** DISCARD, DISREGARD ⟨they *flung* off all restraint⟩ — often used with *away* ⟨~ away that dirty old cloth⟩ **2 a :** to bring, send, or put (a person) suddenly, violently, or unexpectedly into a different and usu. worse state or position — used with *into* ⟨the enemy was *flung* into

confusion⟩ ⟨the new king *flung* his brothers into prison⟩ **b** : to throw off (as a rider) or down (as a wrestling opponent) **c** *archaic* : to get the better of : OVERTHROW **d** *archaic* : SWINDLE, CHEAT **3** : to move (as a body part) suddenly or impetuously — usu. used with an adverb of direction ⟨*flung* her arms wide in greeting⟩ ⟨angrily ~*ing* up his head⟩ **4 a** : to give off or send forth : EMIT ⟨the sun ~*ing* its warm rays on the soil⟩ ⟨the massed roses *flung* their heady scent into the evening breeze⟩ **b** : to ejaculate or utter vigorously, curtly, or with strong emotion ⟨he *flung* a sharp reply as he left⟩ ⟨~*ing* a hasty word of consolation⟩ — see FLING OFF **5** : to throw (as one's efforts) into something ⟨*flung* all their resources into the revolution⟩ : address (as oneself) to something usu. with vigor or strong emotional response ⟨she *flung* herself into her new tasks gratefully⟩ **syn** see THROW — **fling oneself at someone's head** *of a woman* : to make conspicuous efforts to win the attentions of as a possible suitor

²**fling** \"\ *n* -S [ME, fr. *flingen*, v.] **1** : a sharp cast (as from the hand) : a hard throw ⟨give the thing a ~ and get rid of it for good⟩ **2 a** : a casual try : an effort not based on deep or sustained interest ⟨I'm willing to take a ~ at almost any job⟩ **b** : a usu. impulsive utterance indicative of contempt : GIBE, SARCASM ⟨not above taking an occasional sharp ~ at their folly⟩ **c** *archaic* : a hasty, impulsive, or impromptu act (as a journey) **3** : lively and unconstrained action or activity: as **a** : a plunging or kicking esp. of a horse **b** : an affair or a period marked by uninhibited gaiety, self-indulgence, or dissipation ⟨determined to have one last ~ before he sailed⟩

fling·er \-ŋə(r)\ *n* -S : one that flings; *esp* : a baseball pitcher

flinging–tree \ˈ==,=\ *n, chiefly Scot* : FLAIL

fling off *vt* : to give utterance or expression to usu. casually or carelessly ⟨*flung off* a hasty rhyme⟩ ⟨gracefully *flinging off* the proper compliments⟩ ~ *vi* : to depart hastily or brusquely ⟨*flung off* in a rage⟩ ⟨slammed the door and *flung off* to school⟩

flingy \ˈfliŋē\ *adj, often* -ER/-EST : given to or characterized by flinging : JERKY ⟨a loose ~ walk⟩

flink·ite \ˈfliŋ,kīt\ *n* -S [G or Sw *flinkit*, fr. Gustaf *Flink* †1931 Sw. mineralogist + G or Sw *-it* -ite] : a mineral $Mn_3(AsO_4)(OH)_4$ consisting of a greenish brown basic manganese arsenate in feathery forms (sp. gr. 3.87)

¹**flint** \ˈflint\ *n* -S *often attrib* [ME, fr. OE, flint, rock; akin to OHG *flins* pebble, hard stone, ON *flettugrjōt* slate, OSw *flinta* splinter of stone, and prob. to OHG *spaltan* to split — more at SPILL] **1 a** : a massive somewhat impure variety of quartz usu. gray to brown or nearly black in color, breaking with a conchoidal fracture and sharp edge, being very hard, and striking fire with steel **b** : a concretion or nodule of flint usu. embedded in other softer rock ⟨in certain areas the primitive nomads mined ~*s* from the soft chalk⟩ **c** : powdered quartz : POTTER'S FLINT **2** : an implement of flint used by primitive man **3 a** : a piece of flint for striking fire formerly used for kindling fires or igniting material (as in a flintlock gun) **b** : a material used for striking fire; *esp* : an alloy of iron and cerium commonly used in cigarette lighters **4** : something likened to flint in hardness or unyielding quality ⟨the ground was frozen to ~⟩ ⟨her heart became ~, she could only resist and deny⟩: as **a** : FLINT CORN **b** : FLINT GLASS

²**flint** \"\ *vt* -ED/-ING/-S *archaic* : to supply (as a gun) with flint

³**flint** \"\ *adj, usu cap* [fr. *Flint*, Michigan] : of or from the city of Flint, Mich. ⟨a *Flint* physician⟩ : of the kind or style prevalent in Flint

⁴**flint** *usu cap, var of* FLINTSHIRE

flint clay *n* : a hard flinty fireclay

flint corn *also* **flint maize** *n* : an Indian corn (*Zea mays indurata*) having hard, horny, rounded or short and flat kernels with the soft and starchy endosperm completely enclosed by a hard outer layer — called also *Yankee corn;* compare DENT CORN

flint–dried *also* **flint–dry** \ˈ=;=\ *adj* : dried to flinty hardness — used chiefly of unsalted hides

flint glass *n* **1** : glass formerly made using calcined flints as a source of silica **2** : heavy brilliant glass that contains lead oxide, that has a relatively high refractive index and dispersion value, and that now is used chiefly for optical structures (as lenses or prisms) — compare CROWN GLASS **3** : a clear colorless glass

flint–glazed \ˈ=;=\ *adj, of paper* : given a hard glossy surface by rolling or rubbing esp. with a flint — compare FRICTION-GLAZED

flint gray *n* : a nearly neutral slightly yellowish medium gray that is darker than gull (sense 2a) or agate gray and very slightly greener than old silver

flint·head \ˈ=,=\ *n* : WOOD IBIS 1

flinthearted \ˈ=;==\ *adj* : HARDHEARTED

flint hide *n* : a flint-dried hide

flint·ify \ˈflintə,fī\ *vt* -ED/-ING/-ES [¹*flint* + *-ify*] : to convert into or make like flint

flint·i·ly \-tᵊlē,-tᵊli, -tᵊl-\ *adv* : in a flinty manner

flint·i·ness \-tēnəs, -tin-\ *n* -ES : the quality or state of being flinty; *often* : hardness esp. of heart

flintlike \ˈ=,=\ *adj* : resembling flint : hard and resistant ⟨~ determination⟩

flintlock \ˈ=,=\ *n* **1** : a lock for an old-fashioned gun or pistol used chiefly in the 17th and 18th centuries having a flint fixed in the hammer that on striking the battery of the pan ignited the priming which communicated its fire to the charge through the touchhole — compare PERCUSSION LOCK, WHEEL LOCK **2** : a firearm fitted with a flintlock; *esp* : an old-fashioned military musket so equipped

flintlock: *1* flint, *2* pan, *3* battery

flint mill *n* **1** : TUBE MILL **2** : a revolving cylinder containing flint pebbles used for grinding materials in the manufacture of portland cement

flint paper *n* : paper that has a surface of pulverized flint or quartz and that is used like sandpaper

flints *pl of* FLINT, *pres 3d sing of* FLINT

flint·shire \ˈflint,shi(ə)r, -,shiə, -,shə(r)\ *or* **flint** *adj, usu cap* [fr. *Flintshire* or *Flint* county, Wales] : of or from the county of Flint, Wales : of the kind or style prevalent in the county of Flint

flint wheat *n* : HARD WHEAT

flintwood \ˈ=,=\ *n* : the very hard wood of an Australian tree (*Eucalyptus pilularis*)

flintwork \ˈ=,=\ *n* : work in or with flint; *esp* : masonry in which flint forms a major structural or decorative element

flintworker \ˈ=,==\ *n* : one that works with flint; *specif* : a maker of flint artifacts esp. by flaking

flinty \ˈflintē, -ti\ *adj* -ER/-EST **1** : composed of, consisting of, or abounding in flint ⟨a ~ hillside⟩ ⟨poor ~ fields⟩ **2** : resembling flint ⟨a ~ composition for driveways and walks⟩: as **a** : notably hard ⟨the bread was stale and ~⟩ ⟨~ coffee beans⟩ **b** : harsh and unyielding : rigorous and stern ⟨a ~ pride⟩ ⟨a strong ~ character yielding to no pressures⟩ **3** : having a distinctive metallic taste — used of some European white wines

¹**flip** \ˈflip\ *vb* **flipped; flipped; flipping; flips** [prob. of imit. origin] *vt* **1** : to put into motion with a small sharp impulse esp. so as to cause to turn over in the air ⟨*flipped* a coin to decide who should go⟩ ⟨boys *flipping* hazelnuts at one another⟩ **2** : to touch or move with a flip : FLICK ⟨~ the dust from your feet⟩ ⟨*flipped* him on the ear with a peashooter⟩ **3** : to propel (as oneself) with or as if with flippers ⟨various small creatures *flipping* themselves over the mud flats⟩ **4** *slang* : to get aboard (a vehicle in motion) ⟨beat his way west, *flipping* freights and hooking truck rides⟩ **5** : FLAP 7 **6** : to turn over (as a card in poker) ~ *vi* **1** : to make a small sharp darting or twitching movement (as of the fingers) as though flipping something : strike at something with such a movement ⟨*flipping* at the daisy heads with a switch⟩ **2** : to move jerkily or with or as if with flippers ⟨met a seal *flipping* over the rocks⟩ ⟨a small bird balancing and *flipping* on a twig⟩ — **flip one's lid** *also* **flip one's stack** *or* **flip one's top** *slang* : to lose self-control : become furiously angry

²**flip** \"\ *n* -S **1** : an act, instance, or result of flipping: **a** : a smart quick blow or stroke ⟨give him a ~ on the ear and come on⟩ **b** : the motion used in flipping something ⟨anyone can make a stone skip; it's all in the ~ of the wrist⟩ **c** : a somersault esp. as performed in the air in certain gymnastic and diving exercises **d** : FLAP 6 **e** : a short quick football pass **f** : vibration of the barrel of a firearm that is caused by burning powder and movement of the projectile or shot load and that is distinct from motion of the barrel in the functioning of the action, recoil of the piece, or movement by the firer **g** : stud poker in which all cards are dealt face down **2 a** : a drink popular in 18th century England and colonial America consisting of rum and beer or ale sweetened and heated often with a hot poker or loggerhead **b** : an iced drink that consists of wine, brandy, rum, or a liqueur, sugar, and egg and that is shaken and dusted with nutmeg when served ⟨brandy ~⟩ ⟨sherry ~⟩ **c** : a hot drink of sweetened liquor usu. spiced and containing beaten egg

³**flip** \"\ *adj* **flipper; flippest 1** *dial* : SUPPLE, LIMBER; *esp* : NIMBLE **2** : glib or pert in speech : FLIPPANT; *broadly* : violating good taste : fresh or smart in manner or conduct : SMART-ALECKY

⁴**flip** \"\ *n* -S [³*flip*] : a flip person : SMART ALECK

flip–book \ˈ=,=\ *n* : a series of illustrations of an animated scene bound together in sequence so that an illusion of movement can be imparted by flipping them rapidly

flip coil *n* : a small coil of wire used to determine magnetic field intensity by suddenly rotating the coil through 180 degrees and measuring the resulting current surge with a ballistic galvanometer — called also *exploring coil, search coil*

flipe *var of* FLYPE

¹**flip–flap** \ˈflip,flap\ *adv* [¹*flip* + *flap* (v.)] : with repeated strokes and noise ⟨something going *flip-flap* in the dark⟩

²**flip–flap** \"\ *or* **flip–flop** \-,fläp\ *n* **1** : the repeated sound and motion of something loose that is moved by recurrent impulses ⟨the *flip-flap* of the awning in the gusty wind⟩ **2** : a backward somersault **3** *flip-flap* : a device used esp. in amusement parks that consists of a horizontal rotating arm pivoted at its center and supporting a passenger car at each end **4** *flip-flop* : FLIP-FLOP CIRCUIT

³**flip–flap** \"\ *vi* : to move flip-flap

flip–flop circuit *n* : an electronic circuit with two permanently stable conditions (as when one electron tube is conducting while the other is cut off) so that conduction is switched from one to the other by successive pulses

flip glass *n* : a large flaring often engraved glass vessel used esp. in the 18th and early 19th centuries for heating flip; *sometimes* : a smaller glass tumbler or goblet from which flip was drunk

flip jump *n* : a toe jump in figure skating executed at the finish of a three from an inside back edge landing on the outside back edge of the opposite foot after a full turn in the air

flip·ly *adv* : in a flip manner : PERTLY

flip·ness *n* -ES : FLIPPANCY

flip·pan·cy \ˈflipənsē, -si\ *n* -ES : the quality or state of being flippant

flip·pant \-nt\ *adj* [prob. fr. ¹*flip* + *-ant*] **1** *now dial* : NIMBLE, LIMBER **2** *archaic* : being of smooth, fluent, and easy speech : speaking with readiness and ease : having a voluble tongue : TALKATIVE ⟨it becometh good men, in such cases, to be ~ —Isaac Barrow⟩ **3** : treating or tending to treat with unsuitable levity that which is serious or to which respect is due : PERT — **flip·pant·ly** *adv* — **flip·pant·ness** *n* -ES

¹**flip·per** \ˈflipə(r)\ *n* -S [¹*flip* + *-er*] **1 a** : a broad flat limb adapted for swimming (as those of seals, whales, or sea turtles) **b** : a broad flat usu. rubber shoe with the front expanded into a paddle used in skin diving and some other aquatic sports — called also *fin* **2** : one that flips or is used in flipping: as **a** *slang* : ARM **b** (1) : GRIDDLE CAKE (2) : a utensil used to turn griddle cakes **c** : a device that is essentially a lever actuated by a small steam engine and that is used for moving lumber in a sawmill **d** : a sealed can (as of processed food) in which internal pressure causes the ends to bulge **3** : a narrow flat hinged to a larger piece of theatrical scenery **4** : a strip of rubberized fabric used to strengthen the union between the wire-cored bead and the sidewall of a pneumatic tire

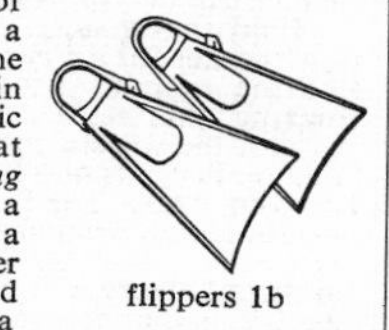

flippers 1b

²**flipper** \"\ *vb* -ED/-ING/-S *vi* : to progress by means of flippers ~ *vt* **1** : to equip with flippers **2** : to move like a flipper ⟨languidly ~*ing* a washcloth to and fro —Christopher Morley⟩

flip·per·ling \-(r)liŋ\ *n* -S [¹*flipper* + *-ling*] : a small animal with flippers (as a baby seal)

flip·per·ty–flop·per·ty \¦flipə(r)d·ē¦fläpə(r)d·ē\ *adj* [irreg. fr. *flip-flop*] : loose and floppy ⟨a *flipperty-flopperty* hat⟩

¹**flip·pery** \ˈflip(ə)rē\ *n* -ES [by alter.] : FRIPPERY

²**flippery** \"\ *n* -ES [*flippant* + *-ery*] : FLIPPANCY

flippest *superlative of* FLIP

flipping *pres part of* FLIP

flip·pi·ty–flop \¦flipəd·ē¦fläp\ *adv* (*or adj*) [irreg. fr. *flip-flop*] : with a flip and a flop : FLIP-FLAP ⟨took a *flippity-flop* tumble on the stairs⟩

flips *pres 3d sing of* FLIP, *pl of* FLIP

flip–top table *n* : a table with a hinged leaf which lies on the top and folds outward to double the size

flip–up \ˈ=,=\ *n* [fr. *flip up*, v.] : something designed to function by flipping up

¹**flird** \ˈflird\ *vi* -ED/-ING/-S [origin unknown] *Scot* : FLIRT *vi* 3a

²**flird** \"\ *n* -S **1** *Scot* : an object that is flimsy, gaudy, or unsubstantial **2** *Scot* : ²FLIRT 3

¹**flirt** \ˈflər|t, -lə̄|, -ləi|, *usu* |d·+V\ *vb* -ED/-ING/-S [origin unknown] *vt* **1** : to throw with a jerk or quick effort : fling suddenly : FLIP, FLICK ⟨they ~ water in each other's faces⟩ ⟨~*ed* the ball from his left hand⟩ **2** *obs* : to tap smartly **3** : to toss or throw about jerkily : open out or close briskly ⟨~ a fan⟩ ⟨a bird ~*s* its tail⟩ **4** *obs* : to jeer at : treat with contempt : MOCK ~ *vi* **1** *obs* : to turn up the nose (as in contempt) **2 a** : to move jerkily or by fits and starts : DART, FLIT ⟨butterflies ~*ing* among the flowers⟩ **b** *of an arrow* : to move suddenly out of the line of flight **3 a** *obs* : to turn inconstantly from one thing to another **b** : to play at courtship : act the lover without serious intent : COQUET; *often* : to trifle amorously esp. in discourse **c** : to evince superficial interest or liking : pay casual or spurious attention — used with *with* ⟨~*ing* with the idea⟩ ⟨a man who ~*ed* with all the arts but mastered none⟩ ⟨reactionary right-wing groups that ~*ed* with the fascists⟩

²**flirt** \"\ *n* -S **1 a** *now dial* : a quick blow : FLICK, TAP **b** *obs* : a turn or stroke of wit esp. when sharp or mocking : a witty jeer or gibe **2** : a sudden sharp or darting movement ⟨dusted the table with a ~ of the cloth⟩; *sometimes* : a quick throw or throwing movement : TOSS ⟨released the ball with a ~ of his wrist⟩ **3 a** *archaic* : an inconstant, giddy, pert, or wanton person **b** : a person that flirts amorously : COQUETTE **4** : a device (as a lever) for causing sudden or intermittent motion: as **a** : a lever used in some chime clocks to knock up the quarter-rack hook **b** : a lever that stops the balance in a chronograph

flirt·able \-əbəl\ *adj* : ready for flirtation

flir·ta·tion \,flərˈtāshən, flə̄-,fləi-\ *n* -S : an act or instance of flirting: as **a** : a playing at courtship : COQUETRY **b** : a transitory or coquettish love affair **c** : superficial or spurious indication of liking or approval esp. between parties normally or usu. opposed

flir·ta·tious \¦flər¦tāshəs, (ˈ)flə̄-, (ˈ)fləi¦-\ *adj* : inclined to flirt : COQUETTISH — **flir·ta·tious·ly** *adv*

flir·ta·tious·ness *n* -ES : flirtatious quality or manner ⟨the ~ of her walk⟩ ⟨her inherent ~ was always getting her in trouble⟩

flirt·er \ˈflər|d·ər, -lə̄|d·ə(r, -ləi|d·ə(r, |tə-\ *n* -S : one that flirts

flirt–gill *or* **flirt–gillian** *n* [²*flirt* + *gill* (girl)] *obs* : a pert or wanton woman

flirt·i·gig \ˈflirti,gig, ˈflər-\ *n* -S [*flirty* + *gig* (girl)] *dial Eng* : a giddy girl

flirt·ing·ly *adv* **1** : with a flirt ⟨the bird settled ~ on the swaying branch⟩ **2** : COQUETTISHLY

flirt·ish \ˈflərd·ish\ *adj* : FLIRTATIOUS

flirty \-d·ē\ *adj* -ER/-EST **1** : relating to or characterized by flirting ⟨a crisp ~ ruffle⟩ **2** : FLIRTATIOUS

¹**flisk** \ˈflisk\ *vb* -ED/-ING/-S [prob. of imit. origin] *vt, chiefly Scot* : FLICK, WHISK ⟨a horse ~*ing* flies with his tail⟩ ~ *vi, chiefly Scot* : FRISK, CAPER

²**flisk** \"\ *n* -S *Scot* : a sudden action : WHIM

flisk·ma·hoy \¦fliskma¦hȯi\ *n* -S [²*flisk* + *-mahoy* (perh. fr. *Dalmahoy*, town in Midlothian county, Scotland)] *Scot* : a flighty woman

¹**flit** \ˈflit, *usu* -id·+V\ *vb* **flitted; flitted; flitting; flits** [ME *flitten*, of Scand origin; akin to ON *flytja* to carry, convey, *flytjask* to move, migrate; akin to ON *fljōta* to flow — more at FLEET] *vi* **1** : to pass usu. quickly or abruptly from one place to another **2** *now dial* : to change one's residence : move from one place to another ⟨we *flitted* last week to our new house⟩ **3 a** : to move swiftly or briskly : pass with a rapid motion : FLEET ⟨clouds *flitting* across the sky⟩ **b** : to move briskly, irregularly, or intermittently usu. from place to place ⟨butterflies *flitting* about the garden⟩ ⟨the hummingbird ~*s* from flower to flower⟩ **4 a** *archaic* : to shift esp. in direction, attention, or condition : be unstable or shifting **b** *of a flame* : to die down : flicker nearly out ⟨candles *flitting* and flaring in the light evening breeze⟩ **5** *of time* : PASS ~ *vt, now chiefly Scot* : to transfer from one residence to another : MOVE ⟨three wagons to ~ them and their furniture⟩

²**flit** \"\ *n* -S : an act or instance of the motion of flitting : FLUTTER ⟨the sleepy world that lies beneath the mind's restless ~ —Christopher Morley⟩

³**flit** \"\ *adj* [alter. (influenced by ¹*flit*) of ⁵*fleet*] *obs* : NIMBLE, QUICK, SWIFT

Flit \"\ *trademark* — used for an insecticide

¹**flitch** \ˈflich\ *n* -ES [ME *flicche*, fr. OE *flicce;* akin to MLG *vlicke* flitch, ON *flikki*, and prob. to ON *flā* to flay — more at FLAY] **1 a** *obs* : the side of any meat animal salted and cured **b** : a side of pork cured and smoked; *often* : the side meat of a hog after removal of shoulder, loin, ham, and bones cured and smoked as bacon **c** : a strip or steak of fish (as halibut) suitable for or prepared by smoking **2 a** : a longitudinal section of a log: as (1) : an outer slab cut off in shaping a timber (2) : a thick and often specially selected length of timber for further processing (as by cutting into veneer or turning) (3) : a thick cut of timber with bark on one or more edges (4) : a lengthwise half of a balk **b** : a complete package of thin sheets of veneer laid together in sequence as they are sawed or sliced **3** : one of several elements (as planks or iron plates) that are secured together side by side to make a large girder or laminated beam

²**flitch** \"\ *vt* -ED/-ING/-ES : to cut into flitches (as fish) or cut flitches from (as logs)

flitch beam *or* **flitched beam** *n* : a beam built up of flitches between two of which a metal plate is sandwiched for reinforcement

flitch girder *n* : a girder that is built up in the manner of a flitch beam

flitch plate *n* : a metal plate sandwiched between planks in forming a flitch beam or girder

flite \ˈflīt\ *vi* -ED/-ING/-S [ME *fliten*, fr. OE *flītan* to contend, strive, wrangle; akin to OE, OFris & OS *flīt* strife, dispute, contention, OHG *flīz* strife, zeal, *flīzan* to contend, strive] **1** *now dial* **a** : CONTEND, QUARREL, WRANGLE **b** : to engage in sharp debate **2** *obs* : to make or utter complaint

flit–gun \ˈ=,=\ *n* [⁴*flit*] : a small hand insecticide sprayer chiefly for domestic use

flit·ing \ˈflīd·iŋ\ *n* -S [ME *fliting*, fr. gerund of *fliten* to quarrel] *archaic* : SCOLDING, BRAWLING, FLOUTING

¹**flit·ter** \ˈflid·ə(r), -itə-\ *vb* -ED/-ING/-S [freq. of ¹*flit*] *vi* **1** : FLUTTER, FLICKER ⟨birds ~*ing* above the water⟩ ⟨boyish plans for the summer ~*ed* into his mind⟩ **2** *obs* : to burst into fragments, dust, or foam **3** *archaic* : WAVER, DROOP ~ *vt* : to cause to move rapidly to and fro ⟨the way a skilled shuffler ~*s* the cards⟩ ⟨a fledgling ~*ing* his wings preparatory to flight⟩

²**flitter** \"\ *n* -S [¹*flit* + *-er*] : one that flits; *esp, Brit* : a workman who moves a coal conveyor or cutting machine

³**flitter** \"\ *n* -S [G; akin to MHG *vlittern* to whisper, giggle, OHG *flitarezzen* to flatter, caress, OE *floterian* to flutter — more at FLUTTER] **1** : a small bit or flake of metal **2** : fine metal fragments usu. coarser than bronze powder that are used for ornamentation and often applied in a volatile vehicle or on an adhesive base (as of size)

⁴**flitter** \"\ *dial var of* ²FRITTER

flittermouse \ˈ==,=\ *n, pl* **flittermice** [¹*flitter* + *mouse;* trans. of G *fledermaus*] : ³BAT 1

flit·tern \ˈflid·ə(r)n\ *n* -S [origin unknown] : a young oak ⟨~ bark is preferred by tanners⟩

flit·ters \ˈflid·ə(r)z\ *n pl* [alter. (influenced by ¹*flitter*) of *fitters*] : RAGS, TATTERS, FRAGMENTS ⟨fell all to ~ when he touched it⟩

¹**flitting** *n* -S [ME, fr. gerund of *flitten* to flit — more at FLIT] *dial* : the moving of an establishment from one place to another; *specif* : a household moving

²**flitting** *adj* [ME, fr. pres. part. of *flitten* to flit] : characterized by flitting; *broadly* : TRANSITORY, BRIEF, EVANESCENT ⟨a ~ touch of color⟩ ⟨~ moments⟩ — **flit·ting·ly** *adv*

¹**fliv·ver** \ˈflivə(r)\ *vi* -ED/-ING/-S [origin unknown] **1** *slang* : to be or become a failure : fall flat : FIZZLE **2** [²*flivver*] *slang* : to motor or tour in a flivver

²**flivver** \"\ *n* -S [perh. fr. ¹*flivver*] **1** *slang* **a** : a small and relatively inexpensive automobile **b** : a small airplane designed for private or personal use **c** : a small naval vessel; *esp* : a destroyer of minimal tonnage **2** *slang* : FAILURE, FRAUD, HOAX

¹**flix** \ˈfliks\ *n* -ES [perh. alter. of ¹*flick*] *archaic* : DOWN, FUR

²**flix** \"\ *n* -ES [ME *flex, flax* — more at FLAX] : FLAX 1a

flixweed \ˈ=,=\ *n* [²*flix* + *weed*] **1** : a branching annual tansy mustard (*Descurainia sophia*) that is native to Europe but widely naturalized in No. America **2** : SAND ROCKET

¹**float** \ˈflōt, *usu* -ōd·+V\ *n* -S *often attrib* [partly fr. ME *flote* boat, fleet, float, act of floating, fr. OE *flota* ship & OE *flot* sea (as in *on flote* on the sea, afloat); partly fr. ²*float;* akin to OHG *flōz* raft, stream, MLG *vlote* raft, fleet, MD, stream, fleet, ON *flot* action of flowing, fat, *floti* raft, fleet; derivatives fr. the root of OE *flēotan* to flow — more at FLEET] **1 a** : the act or state of floating ⟨every ~ of her wide skirt —Christopher Morley⟩ **b** : a slight displacement of the axis of a rotating body (as of the armature of a generator) **c** : a floating movement ⟨the slow ~ of clouds across the sky⟩; *esp* : an easy loping stride used by distance runners in the intermediate part of a race **2** : something broad and shallow and flat: as **a** *obs* : a brewing vat **b** : FLOATBOARD **c** : a floating tray for keeping shellfish (as crabs during shedding) in good condition until ready for marketing **3** *obs* **a** : a flowing or overflowing esp. of the tide or a river in flood **b** : something that flows (as the sea or a wave) **4** : something that floats in or rests on the surface of a fluid (as to sustain a weight, mark the location of something submerged, or regulate a flow): as **a** (1) : a cork or bob used to buoy up the baited end of a fishline and keep it at a desired depth (2) : one of the cork, glass, or other floating devices attached to the edge of a fishnet to buoy it up (3) : a floating indicator marking the position of something (as a lobster pot) beneath the surface of a body of water **b** : a flat-bottomed boat : RAFT **c** (1) : a platform that floats and is anchored at or near the shore and used esp. for landing or the convenience of swimmers (2) : a support projected from each side of a small boat (as a canoe) **d** : a hollow metallic ball or similar object that floats usu. at the end of a lever in a cistern, tank, or boiler and regulates by its elevation or depression the level of the liquid; *also* : a similar often horseshoe-shaped device in a carburetor of a gasoline engine **e** : an inflated bag or pillow used to support on a water surface the head or other part of the body (as of a person learning to swim) : LIFE PRESERVER **f** : an air-filled glass

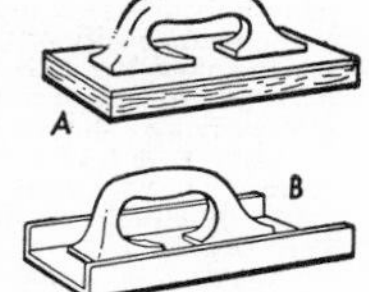

plasterer's floats: *A* regular; *B* angle

bulb used in a burette as an aid in measuring differences in the level of a liquid **g :** an air sac or other light structure containing air or gas serving to buoy up the body of a pelagic animal **:** PNEUMATOPHORE 1 **h :** a hollow vesicle found in certain algae (as of the genus *Fucus*) containing gases (as carbon dioxide) and serving to buoy up the plant **i :** a completely enclosed watertight structure fitted to an airplane to give it buoyancy and stability when in contact with a surface of water **5 :** any of several devices used in dressing, finishing, or smoothing surfaces: as **a :** a flat-faced tool for smoothing and finishing a plastic surface (as of unset concrete, plaster, or stucco) that is either rectangular with a handle on the back by which it is hand manipulated or disklike for mechanical rotation **b :** FLOAT-CUT FILE **c :** a usu. handled block used for polishing dressed stone **d** (1) **:** a platform of heavy overlapping planks cleated together that is drawn over soil to compact and smooth its surface, to improve its condition, or to crush clods — called also *clod smasher, drag, planker, slicker* (2) **:** a frame of heavy planks used for leveling land for irrigation **6 :** a trench for irrigation **7 a :** loose fragmentary rock, mineral, or ore detached from an outcrop or vein by natural forces (as weathering or the action of water) and deposited downslope often at a considerable distance from the source **b** *or* **floats** *pl but sing or pl in constr* **:** finely divided mineral material (as pulverized rock phosphate or flaky ores) that tends to remain in suspension in water ⟨~s is often used as a filler in mixed fertilizer⟩ ⟨~ gold⟩ ⟨asbestos ~s⟩ **8 :** a grant by the government of a fixed quantity of land that is not yet located by survey out of a larger specific tract of land and that will be later located with certainty in accordance with law **9 floats** *pl* **:** FOOTLIGHTS **10 a :** a portion of filling thread that passes over two or more warp threads or of warp thread that passes over two or more filling threads before interweaving; *also* **:** the passage of such thread **b :** a defective place in a fabric where warp and filling threads are not properly interlaced **c :** a portion of yarn that passes over several needles without interlacing and is usu. brought to the front at intervals to make colored patterns in knitting; *also* **:** the passage of such thread **11 a** *chiefly Brit* **:** a low underslung cart or platform on wheels used for drawing heavy loads **b :** a platform on wheels or a vehicle with a platform used as a base for a tableau or other exhibit in a procession; *broadly* **:** the entire unit of base and exhibit **12 :** a contrivance for supplying a copious stream of water to the heated surface of an object of large bulk (as an anvil or die) that is undergoing tempering **13 :** an amount of money represented at any one time by checks outstanding and in process of collection; *esp* **:** the amount of checks credited in a weekly statement to member banks of a system (as the Federal Reserve) but not yet collected by the crediting bank **14 :** a drink consisting of ice cream suspended in a liquid (as root beer)

²float \"\ *vb* -ED/-ING/-S [ME *floten,* fr. OE *flotian;* akin to ON *flota* to float; derivatives fr. the root of OE *flēotan* to flow — more at FLEET] *vi* **1 :** to become buoyed up by a fluid: as **a :** to rest on the surface of or partly submerged in a liquid ⟨a needle will ~ on water⟩ ⟨the boat ~*ed* away⟩; *esp* **:** to rest on one's back in water so that the face remains above the surface — often contrasted with *swim* ⟨he was a poor swimmer but could ~ for hours on quiet water⟩ **b :** to become waterborne by the action of rising water ⟨the logs will ~ when the river rises⟩ — often used with *off* ⟨their boat ~*ed off* as the tide came in⟩ **c :** to become suspended within the body of a fluid ⟨stars ~*ing* in the sky⟩ **2 a :** to move quietly and gently on, through, or as if on or through water or other fluid impelled by some external agent (as currents of the medium or gravity) ⟨the boat ~*ed* by⟩ ⟨yellow leaves ~*ing* down⟩ ⟨a flag ~*ing* in the breeze⟩ ⟨rumors ~*ed* about⟩ **b :** to move easily and smoothly as if floating in fluid ⟨she ~*ed* down the walk⟩ **c** *of a runner* **:** to run easily and at less than top speed ⟨a distance runner learns to spell himself by ~*ing* in the midstretch⟩ **d** *of a tool or mechanical part* **:** to remain virtually suspended in neutral position between contacts or limits set for motion **:** be free to move within limits **3 a** *obs* **:** to seem to waver **:** move uncertainly to and fro **:** WAVER — often used with *between* **b :** to be unstable (as in political affiliation or morals) **:** lack fixity of purpose or determination **c :** to make frequent changes (as of one's abode or occupation) **d :** to drift often aimlessly or heedlessly **4 a :** to fish with a float **b** *archaic* **:** to hunt deer at night from shallow boats **5 :** to become connected but adjusted so as not to share in output — used of a storage battery on the line or of an idle grid in an electron tube **6 :** to pass over or under two or more threads before interweaving **7** *of a defensive end in football* **:** to hang back to prevent the ball carrier from getting around the flank **~** *vt* **1 :** to cause to float: as **a :** to cause to rest on the surface of a fluid or to be suspended in and buoyed up by fluid ⟨the tide ~*ed* the ships⟩ **b :** to move or cause to move through the surface of water usu. by the action of an external agent (as a current) ⟨the stream ~*ed* the logs onto a sandbar⟩; *esp* **:** to convey to market by floating usu. down a river or stream ⟨the upriver farmers ~ their produce down on flatboats⟩ **c :** to cause to spread out on the surface of a liquid ⟨~ the liqueur on the surface of the coffee⟩ ⟨they ~ oil over the swamp to destroy mosquitoes⟩ **d :** to support (a building or structure) on a mat or raft foundation when the ground has low supporting value **e :** to arrange (a mechanical part) to operate smoothly by floating or as if by floating in a liquid **f :** to mount (a mechanical part) esp. in rubber so that vibration is not transmitted — see FLOATING POWER **2 :** to overflow with or as if with water **:** FLOOD — used both of natural flooding and that undertaken for military or agricultural purposes **3 :** to smooth or dress with a float: as **a :** to finish (as plaster or cement) with a float **b :** to work (land) with a float **c :** to smooth down (the teeth of an old horse) with a float **4 a :** to obtain popular support or acceptance of (as a scheme or idea) ⟨careful publicity is often required to ~ a really novel plan⟩ **b :** to offer (an issue of stocks or bonds) for sale in order to raise capital (as for beginning or expanding a business); *also* **:** to establish (as a company or enterprise) by floating securities ⟨hoped to raise enough money to ~ the company⟩ **c :** NEGOTIATE ⟨the company hoped to ~ a loan at lower interest rates⟩ **5 :** to grind (as a pigment in water) as a refining or levigating process **6 :** to solder the ends of (a tin can) — used with *up* **7 a :** to pass (a thread) over or under two or more threads before interweaving **b :** to form (a figure in textiles) by floating threads **8 a :** to connect (a storage battery) as a floating battery **b :** to join (electrical apparatus) at approximately equal potentials so that negligible current flows **9 a :** to keep in a float (sense 2c) **b :** to bloat (as oysters or scallops) by soaking in water fresher than that in the native habitat in order to give an abnormal appearance of plumpness **10** *slang* **:** to cause (a petty offender or vagrant who may become a financial burden) to move out of a community esp. by threats of legal action

float·abil·i·ty \ˌflōd·əˈbiləd·ē\ *n* -ES **:** ability to float **:** floatable quality or state

float·able \ˈflōd·əbəl\ *adj* **1 a :** able to float **b** *of an ore or mineral* **:** suitable for treatment by a flotation process **2** *of a waterway* **:** suitable for the transport of floating objects (as logs)

floatage *var of* FLOTAGE

floatation *var of* FLOTATION

floatboard \ˈ=ˌ=\ *n* **:** any of the radial rim boards of an undershot waterwheel or paddle wheel **:** VANE

float boat *n* **:** a shallow boat driven by an airplane engine and used on shallow waters and swamps esp. in Florida

float bowl *n* **:** FLOAT CHAMBER

float bridge *n* **:** a structure with tracks on an adjustable apron for transferring railroad cars to or from car floats at varying water levels

float chamber *n* **:** a chamber (as in a carburetor) having a float to regulate the level of the contained liquid

float coat *n* **:** a thin layer of mortar applied to a surface (as of concrete) and given a float finish

float-cut file \ˈ=ˌ=-\ *n* **:** a coarse single-cut file usu. for filing soft materials

floated *past of* FLOAT

float·er \ˈflōd·ə(r), -ōtə-\ *n* -S **1 :** something that rests or drifts along on or in a fluid or is free or loose from its usual attachment: as **a :** a fired clay shape floating on molten glass in a tank to hold back scum **b floaters** *pl* **:** small particles in suspension in beer **c :** a plant (as a water hyacinth) that grows on the surface of water **d :** DRIFT BOTTLE **e :** a corpse found floating in the water **2 :** a person who floats something (as a company or a loan) or who works with a float ⟨a cement ~⟩ **3 a :** a person who votes illegally in various polling places either under false registration or under the name of a properly registered person who has not already voted **b :** a person (as a delegate to a convention or a member of a legislature) who represents an irregular constituency (as made up of the voters of two counties neither of which has sufficient population to entitle it to a separate representative) **4 :** a person who floats or drifts: as **a :** a person without fixed abode or regular employment **:** VAGRANT, TRAMP **b :** a person who tends to shift from job to job often within a particular industry for other than economic reasons ⟨~s increase the expense of handling a retirement system⟩ **:** BOOMER **c :** a person without fixed political or religious affiliations or convictions **d :** a worker without regular fixed duties who is available for assignment wherever extra help is needed ⟨larger hospitals usu. have a few nurses on the staff who act as ~s or substitutes⟩ **5** *slang Brit* **:** BLUNDER **6 a :** a slowly pitched baseball with little or no spin **b :** a soft pass in football that is long and high **7** *Brit* **:** a bearer security; *esp* **:** one unlisted but acceptable as collateral **8 :** a policy of insurance to protect against loss or damage of goods in transit or goods (as furs or jewels) naturally subject to use in various places — compare INLAND MARINE INSURANCE **9 :** an order (as by a court or police official) to a person considered an undesirable citizen to leave a town or locality; *usu* **:** a heavy sentence on a petty offender that is suspended on condition that he leave the jurisdiction of the court permanently

float finish *n* **:** a finish produced on plaster, mortar, or concrete surfaces by use of a float

float grass *n* **:** FLOATING GRASS

¹floating *n* -S [fr. gerund of ²*float*] **1 :** the act or action of one that floats **2 :** spotty or irregular flooding of paint; *sometimes* **:** separation of a pigment from a mixture whether in bulk or a film **3 a :** the act or process of spreading or smoothing a surface (as of concrete, mortar, plaster, or stucco) with a float **b :** the second coat of three-coat plastering

²floating *adj* [fr. pres. part. of ²*float*] **1 :** buoyed upon or in a fluid ⟨the ~ timbers of a wreck⟩ ⟨~ motes in the air⟩ ⟨~ aquatic vegetation made the canal unusable⟩ **2 a :** free from or lacking the usual attachment — used esp. of ribs that join the sternum by a cartilaginous rather than a bony union **b :** being out of the normal position; *esp* **:** abnormally movable and displaced downward or away from normal attachments — used esp. of the kidney **3 :** continually changing **:** characterized by shifting or drifting (as from one abode or occupation to another) ⟨the ~ population⟩: as **a :** shifting or variable in form, incidence, or subject matter ⟨~ rumors⟩ **b** *of funds or capital* **:** not presently committed or invested **c** *of a debt* **:** falling due within the year; *sometimes* **:** short-term and usu. not funded **d :** enforceable in equity as a lien against whatever assets a person may have from time to time leaving him meanwhile more or less free to dispose of or encumber his assets as if no lien existed ⟨a ~ charge⟩ ⟨~ security⟩ **e :** frequently shifted in location to evade detection and arrest of participants ⟨a ~ crap game⟩ **4 a :** connected or constructed so as to operate and adjust smoothly (as if floating) **b :** of, relating to, or having mechanical parts connected or constructed in this way ⟨a ~ transmission⟩ — **float·ing·ly** *adv*

floating accent *n* **:** PIECE ACCENT

floating anchor *n* **:** SEA ANCHOR

floating axle *n* **:** a live axle used in a self-propelled vehicle to turn the wheels, the dead weight of the vehicle being carried on the ends of a fixed axle housing or casing

floating bag *n* **:** a flexible tightly sealed protective barrier placed loosely around an object (as a metal part) in a shipping box

floating battery *n* **1 :** a storage battery connected across an electric line or feeder to equalize the load and maintain the voltage constant **2 :** a battery erected on a raft or the hull of a ship or a ship carrying heavy guns and designed as a gun platform rather than for navigation formerly used in coast defense and in attacking fortifications

floating bridge *n* **1 :** a temporary bridge supported by low flat-bottomed boats or pontoons **2 :** a double bridge that has the upper level projecting beyond the lower and capable of being moved forward by pulleys and was used formerly for carrying troops over narrow moats in attacking the outworks of a fort **3 :** a ferryboat drawn and guided by chains that are anchored on the sides of a stream and that mesh with wheels on the boat

floating dock *or* **floating dry dock** *n* **1 :** a dock that floats on the water and can be partly submerged to permit a ship to enter it and afterward floated to raise the ship high and dry as in a dry dock **2 :** a flatboat or barge used as a wharf adjustable to the stage of water

floating dock 1

floating fern *n* **1 :** any of several aquatic ferns of the genus *Ceratopteris* (esp. *C. thalictroides* and *C. pteridoides*) often used in aquariums — called also *water sprite* **2 :** FLOATING MOSS; *also* **:** a related plant (*Azolla caroliniana*)

floating floor *n* **:** a floor separated from its structural support by a layer of sand, building paper, or a sound-reducing blanket

floating foundation *n* **:** a building support on soft soil that consists of a stiff reinforced concrete slab which distributes the concentrated loads by columns to the soil so that the pressure intensity on the soil is nowhere more than the acceptable amount

floating gang *n* **:** a specially organized railroad track repair group that moves over various sections of the line

floating garden *n* **:** a planting on soil buoyed up (as on the surface of a lake) by rafts of interlaced branches or other floating support found chiefly in the Mexico City area and parts of Kashmir

floating grass *n* **:** any of several marsh or semiaquatic grasses: as **a :** FLOATING MANNA GRASS **b :** MARSH FOXTAIL

floating head *n* **:** a flesh hoop of a drum entirely free from the shell

floating heart *n* **:** a plant of the genus *Nymphoides; esp* **:** a small white-flowered aquatic (*N. cordata*) with heart-shaped floating leaves

floating holder *n* **:** a holder (as for a tap) that allows a certain amount of play or freedom to enable the tool to maintain the proper path relative to the work

floating inspector *n* **:** an inspector who inspects manufacturing operations as he chooses at various points in the process

floating island *n* **1 a :** FLOATING GARDEN **b :** a floating mass of vegetation with little or no soil (as in a lake or quiet tropical sea) usu. due to detachment of matted vegetation from a marshy shore **2 :** a dessert consisting of custard with floating masses of whipped whites of egg

floating lever *n* **:** a horizontal brake lever beneath a railroad car body having its fulcrum at the end of a rod that leads from another lever and thus is movable

floating liability *n* **:** CURRENT LIABILITY

floating light *n* **:** a light shown at the masthead of a ship moored over dangerous waters (as those above sunken rocks or shoals) to warn mariners **:** LIGHTSHIP; *also* **:** a light on a buoy

floating manna grass *n* **:** any of several aquatic grasses of the genus *Glyceria* (esp. *G. fluitans* and *G. septentrionalis*)

floating moss *n* **:** an aquatic plant (*Salvinia rotundifolia*) introduced from Mexico or So. America and locally established in the U.S.

floating policy *n* **1 :** a marine insurance policy designating the general nature of insured material but leaving the exact amount and kind, name of ship, and value to be fixed at a later date **2 :** FLOATER 8

floating power *n* **:** an arrangement of an automotive power plant such that a minimum of engine vibration is transmitted to the supporting chassis

floating primrose willow *n* **:** a widely distributed primrose willow (*Jussiaea repens glabrescens*) with creeping or floating stems

floating rib *n* **:** a rib not connected with the sternum or cartilages of other ribs ventrally, in man being the 11th and 12th on each side

floating screed *n* **:** a strip of plaster first laid on to serve as a guide for the thickness of the coat of plaster to be applied (as to a wall)

floating star *n* **:** FROST FLOWER 1a

floating supply *n* **:** the quantity of something (as a commodity, money, or securities) available immediately (as for purchase, loan, or delivery)

float·less \ˈflōtləs\ *adj* **:** not having a float **:** lacking in buoyancy

float master *n* **:** one that supervises the movement of freight by barge and lighter between a railroad yard and a ship — called also *boat dispatcher*

float·o·blast \ˈflōd·əˌblast\ *n* [²*float* + *-o-* + *-blast*] **:** a pelagic statoblast of certain bryozoans that lacks hooks or spines and has a specialized capsule containing air cells

float ore *n* **:** ore so finely divided as to be held in suspension by water for prolonged periods resulting in loss of mineral during refining or in movement of ore by water to considerable distances from its point of origin

floatplane \ˈ=ˌ=\ *n* **:** a seaplane supported on the water by one or more floats — compare FLYING BOAT

float road *n* **:** a forest path (as in a swamp) cleared so that high water will take logs through

floats *pl of* FLOAT, *pres 3d sing of* FLOAT

float·sam \ˈflōtsəm\ *archaic var of* FLOTSAM

float seaplane *n* **:** FLOATPLANE

floats·man \ˈflōtsmən\ *n, pl* **floatsmen :** a worker who smooths stone (as marble or slate) usu. by holding it on a rotating sanding table

float·stone \ˈ=ˌ=\ *n* **1 :** a light porous variety of opal occurring in concretionary masses **2 :** a bricklayer's rubstone for smoothing gauged brickwork

float switch *n* **:** an electric switch operated by a float on a liquid

float valve *n* **:** an automatic valve whose opening and closing are controlled by a float at the end of a lever

float-wing seaplane *n* **:** a seaplane that receives a substantial part of its support when on the water from buoyant forces acting on its wings

floaty \ˈflōd·ē\ *adj* -ER/-EST **:** tending to float **:** floating readily **:** BUOYANT, LIGHT

flob \ˈfläb\ *vi* **flobbed; flobbed; flobbing; flobs** [perh. alter. of ¹*flop*] **:** to be clumsy or aimless in moving

¹floc \ˈfläk\ *n* -S [L *floccus* flock of wool — more at FLOCCUS] **1 :** a flocculent mass formed by the aggregation of a number of fine suspended particles (as in a precipitate or in smoke) **2 :** ³FLOCK 1,2,3

²floc \"\ *vb* **flocced** \-kt\ **flocced** \"\ **floccing** \-kiŋ\ **flocs** *vi* **:** to aggregate into flocs **:** FLOCCULATE **~** *vt* **:** to cause (as a slime) to floc

flocci *pl of* FLOCCUS

floc·cil·la·tion \ˌfläksəˈlāshən\ *n* -S [L *floccus* + *-illus* dim. ending + E *-ation*] **:** CARPHOLOGY

floc·cose \ˈfläˌkōs\ *adj* [LL *floccosus,* fr. L *floccus* + *-osus* -ose] **:** having or covered with tufts of soft woolly hairs that are often deciduous — used esp. of plants — **floc·cose·ly** \-lē\ *adv* — **floc·cos·i·ty** \fläˈkäsəd·ē\ *n* -ES

floc·cu·la·ble \ˈfläkyələbəl\ *adj* [*flocculate* + *-able*] **:** capable of being flocculated ⟨~ clays⟩

floc·cu·lant \-lənt\ *n* -S [*floccule* + *-ant*] **:** an agent that produces floccule or other aggregate formation esp. in soil ⟨lime alters soil pH and acts as a ~ in clay soils⟩; *esp* **:** a usu. acid reagent used in ceramic manufacture to increase the viscosity of a clay slip or the plasticity of tempered clay

floc·cu·lar \-lə(r)\ *adj* [NL *flocculus* + E *-ar*] **:** of or relating to a flocculus

¹floc·cu·late \-lət, -ˌlāt\ *adj* [LL *flocculus* + E *-ate* (adj. suffix)] **:** bearing small tufts of hairs — often used postpositively ⟨a heavy-bodied bee with the dorsum of the thorax ~⟩

²floc·cu·late \-ˌlāt\ *vb* -ED/-ING/-S [NL *flocculus* + E *-ate* (v. suffix)] *vt* **:** to cause to aggregate or coalesce into small lumps or loose clusters or into a flocculent mass or deposit ⟨calcium ion tends to ~ clays⟩ ⟨essential to avoid *flocculating* the pulp fibers in early stages of paper manufacture⟩ — compare COAGULATE **~** *vi* **:** to aggregate or coalesce into small lumps or loose clusters or into a flocculent mass or deposit ⟨certain clays ~ readily⟩ ⟨the bacteria of a hay infusion tend to ~ with their products into a thick zooglea⟩

³floc·cu·late \-lət, -ˌlāt\ *n* -S **:** something that has flocculated **:** a flocculent particle or mass **:** FLOC

floc·cu·la·tion \ˌfläkyəˈlāshən\ *n* -S **1 :** the act or process of flocculating **2 :** a product of flocculating; *broadly* **:** a cluster, conglomeration, or aggregate esp. of cultural traits

floc·cu·la·tor \ˈfläkyəˌlād·ə(r)\ *n* -S **:** something that induces flocculation; *esp* **:** an apparatus in which material (as water or sewage) flocculates certain suspended or dissolved constituents

floc·cule \ˈfläˌkyül\ *n* -S [LL *flocculus* small flock of wool, dim. of L *floccus* flock of wool — more at FLOCCUS] **:** a small loosely aggregated mass of material suspended in or precipitated from a liquid **:** FLOC; *often* **:** one of the flakes of a flocculent precipitate

floc·cu·lence \ˈfläkyələn(t)s\ *also* **floc·cu·len·cy** \-nsē\ *n, pl* **flocculences** *also* **flocculencies 1 :** a flocculent state **2 :** something that gives a flocculent material or surface its character (as the waxy secretion of flocculent insects)

¹floc·cu·lent \-nt\ *adj* [NL *flocculus* + E *-ent*] **1 :** of the appearance of wool; WOOLLY, FLOCKY ⟨~ cloud masses⟩ **2 :** containing, consisting of, or occurring in the form of loosely aggregated particles or soft flakes **:** made up of flocs ⟨a ~ white precipitate⟩ **3 :** covered with tufts of woolly material; *specif* **:** covered with a soft waxy substance often resembling wool — used chiefly of aphids and scales — **floc·cu·lent·ly** *adv*

²flocculent \"\ *n* -S **:** a flocculating agent **:** FLOCCULANT

floc·cu·lose \ˌlōs\ *also* **floc·cu·lous** \-ləs\ *adj* [LL *flocculus* + E *-ose* or *-ous*] **:** minutely floccose

floc·cu·lus \-ləs\ *n, pl* **floccu·li** \-ˌlī\ [LL *flocculus* — more at FLOCCULE] **1 :** a small loosely aggregated mass (as of wool) **:** FLAKE, FLOCCULE, FLOC **2** [NL, fr. LL] **:** a small irregular lobe on the under surface of each hemisphere of the cerebellum that is linked with the corresponding side of the nodulus by a peduncle **3** [NL, fr. LL] **:** a bright or dark patch on the sun seen in the light of calcium or hydrogen usu. in the vicinity of sunspots or other active regions — compare PLAGE

floc·cus \ˈfläkəs\ *n, pl* **floc·ci** \-äˌkī, -äˌkē, -äkˌsī, -äkˌsē\ [L, akin to OHG *blaha* coarse linen, OSw *blā, blār* oakum, ON *blæja* cloth, bed sheet] **1 :** a tuft of woolly hairs on a plant; *specif* **:** a mass of hyphal filaments or portion of mycelium of a fungus **2** [NL, fr. L] **:** one of the small masses or tufts making up certain cloud formations

¹flock \ˈfläk\ *n* -S [ME, fr. OE *flocc;* akin to MLG *vlocke* crowd, herd of sheep, ON *flokkr* crowd, band, troop] **1 a** *archaic* **:** a band or company of people **b flocks** *pl* **:** great numbers **:** MULTITUDES ⟨the ~s of foreign students⟩ ⟨found ~s of witnesses willing to testify⟩ **2 a :** a natural assemblage of animals (as of gregarious birds or mammals) ⟨a ~ of wild geese⟩ **b :** a company of domestic mammals (as sheep or goats) herded together **c flocks** *pl* **:** holdings (as of a person) in sheep and goats — sometimes contrasted with *herds* ⟨immensely rich in ~s and herds⟩ **d :** a company of domestic poultry ⟨a small ~ of hens feeding on the lawn⟩ ⟨making the farm ~ pay⟩ **3 a :** all Christians in their relation to Christ **b :** a Christian church or congregation in their relation to the pastor or minister in charge **c :** a company in relation to one in charge; *esp* **:** the members of a family in relation to one member (as a father) who is responsible and in charge ⟨a father worrying over the future of his little ~⟩ **4 :** an aggregation, collection, or group of anything esp. when large ⟨returned with a ~ of new ideas⟩ ⟨the latest ~ of annual reports makes depressing reading⟩ ⟨drank a ~ of martinis⟩

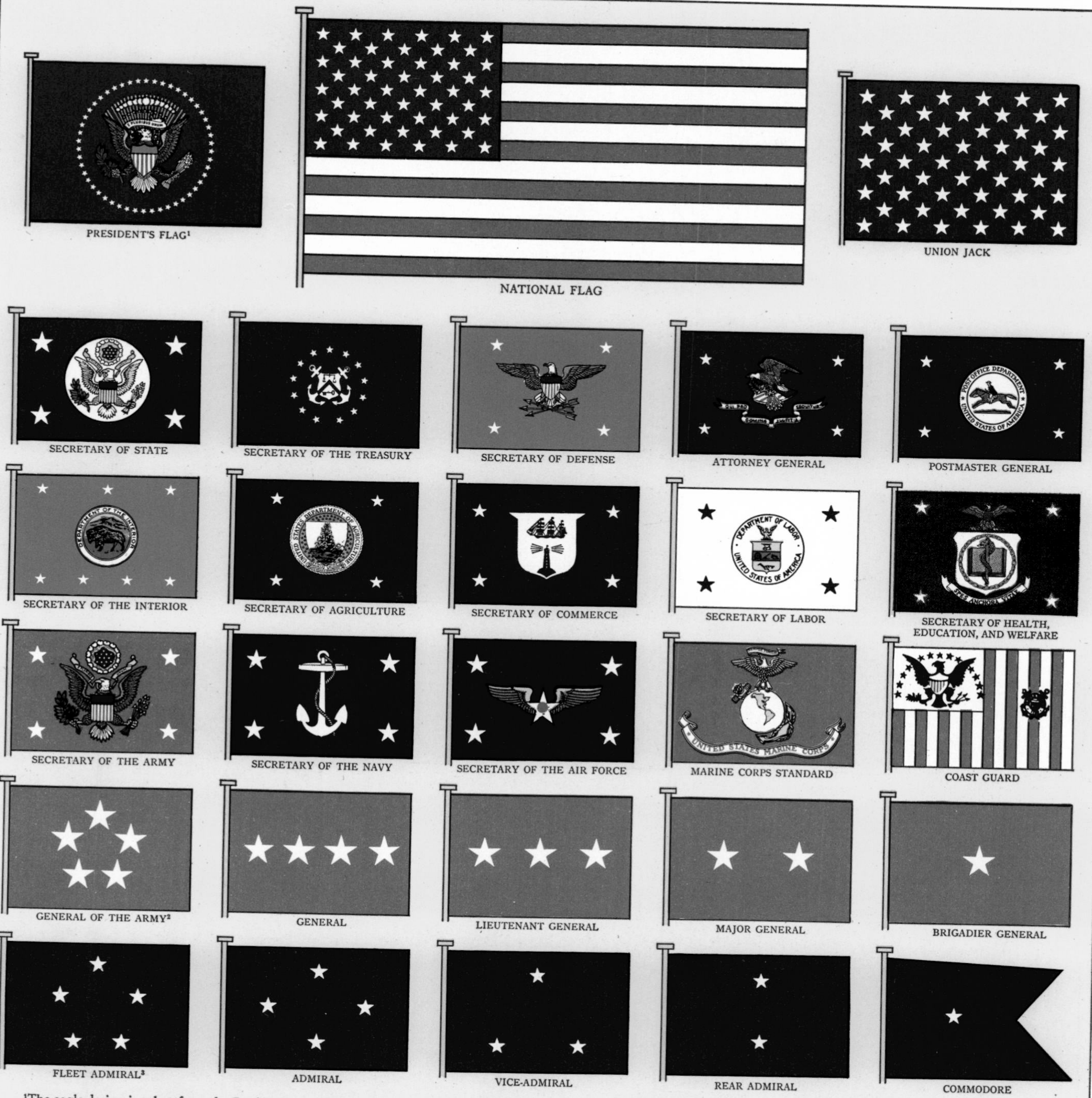

OFFICIAL FLAGS OF THE UNITED STATES

PRESIDENT'S FLAG[1]

NATIONAL FLAG

UNION JACK

SECRETARY OF STATE

SECRETARY OF THE TREASURY

SECRETARY OF DEFENSE

ATTORNEY GENERAL

POSTMASTER GENERAL

SECRETARY OF THE INTERIOR

SECRETARY OF AGRICULTURE

SECRETARY OF COMMERCE

SECRETARY OF LABOR

SECRETARY OF HEALTH, EDUCATION, AND WELFARE

SECRETARY OF THE ARMY

SECRETARY OF THE NAVY

SECRETARY OF THE AIR FORCE

MARINE CORPS STANDARD

COAST GUARD

GENERAL OF THE ARMY[2]

GENERAL

LIEUTENANT GENERAL

MAJOR GENERAL

BRIGADIER GENERAL

FLEET ADMIRAL[3]

ADMIRAL

VICE-ADMIRAL

REAR ADMIRAL

COMMODORE

[1]The eagle design is taken from the President's seal, not from the great seal of the United States, and is here correctly depicted. [2]General officers of the Air Force have personal flags with a field of ultramarine blue with arrangement of white stars similar in position and number to that of Army general officers of relative rank. [3]General officers of the Marine Corps have personal flags with a field of scarlet with arrangement of white stars similar in position and number to that of Navy flag officers of relative rank.

HISTORIC FLAGS OF THE UNITED STATES

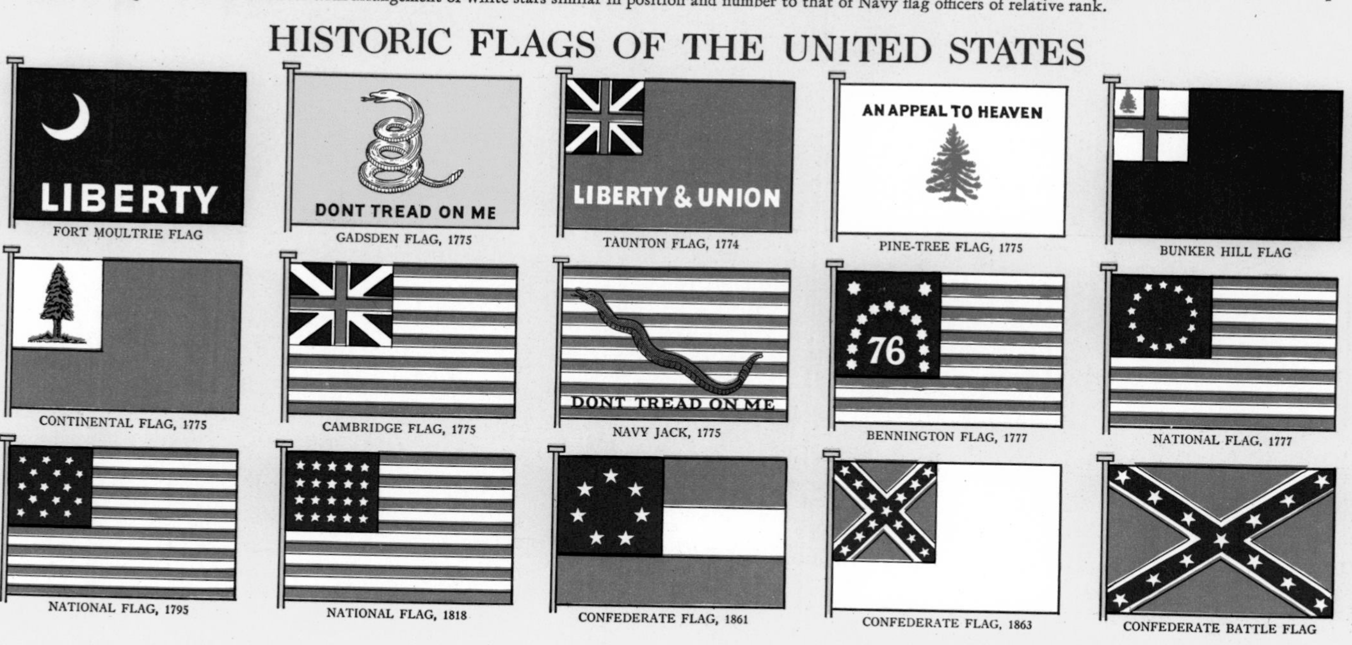

FORT MOULTRIE FLAG

GADSDEN FLAG, 1775

TAUNTON FLAG, 1774

PINE-TREE FLAG, 1775

BUNKER HILL FLAG

CONTINENTAL FLAG, 1775

CAMBRIDGE FLAG, 1775

NAVY JACK, 1775

BENNINGTON FLAG, 1777

NATIONAL FLAG, 1777

NATIONAL FLAG, 1795

NATIONAL FLAG, 1818

CONFEDERATE FLAG, 1861

CONFEDERATE FLAG, 1863

CONFEDERATE BATTLE FLAG

Plate II **GREAT SEALS OF THE UNITED STATES**

THE GREAT SEAL OF THE UNITED STATES

The design of the Great Seal of the United States was adopted by the Continental Congress June 20, 1782. The designs of the original die (cut in 1782) and the second die (cut in 1841) differ somewhat, in detail and arrangement, from the design of the later dies (cut in 1884 and 1902 respectively) shown above. The original design included both obverse and reverse. The reverse has never been cut.

*The Great Seals of Georgia, Pennsylvania, Virginia, and West Virginia have a reverse, as well as the obverse shown in this plate.
**Reverse; the obverse of the Great Seal of Maryland has never been cut.

STATE FLAGS OF THE UNITED STATES *Plate III*

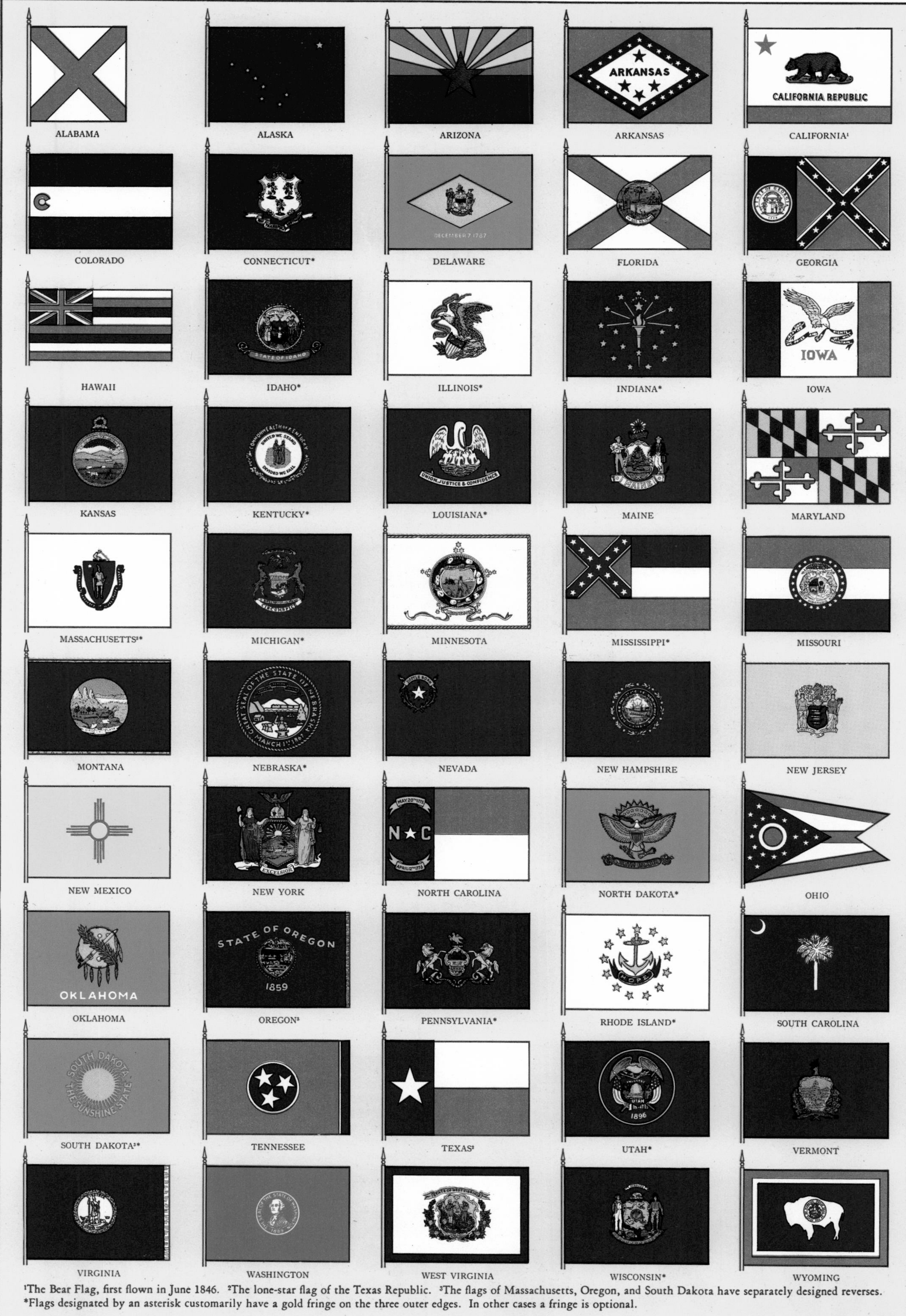

ALABAMA ALASKA ARIZONA ARKANSAS CALIFORNIA[1]
COLORADO CONNECTICUT* DELAWARE FLORIDA GEORGIA
HAWAII IDAHO* ILLINOIS* INDIANA* IOWA
KANSAS KENTUCKY* LOUISIANA* MAINE MARYLAND
MASSACHUSETTS[3]* MICHIGAN* MINNESOTA MISSISSIPPI* MISSOURI
MONTANA NEBRASKA* NEVADA NEW HAMPSHIRE NEW JERSEY
NEW MEXICO NEW YORK NORTH CAROLINA NORTH DAKOTA* OHIO
OKLAHOMA OREGON[3] PENNSYLVANIA* RHODE ISLAND* SOUTH CAROLINA
SOUTH DAKOTA[3]* TENNESSEE TEXAS[2] UTAH* VERMONT
VIRGINIA WASHINGTON WEST VIRGINIA WISCONSIN* WYOMING

[1]The Bear Flag, first flown in June 1846. [2]The lone-star flag of the Texas Republic. [3]The flags of Massachusetts, Oregon, and South Dakota have separately designed reverses.
*Flags designated by an asterisk customarily have a gold fringe on the three outer edges. In other cases a fringe is optional.

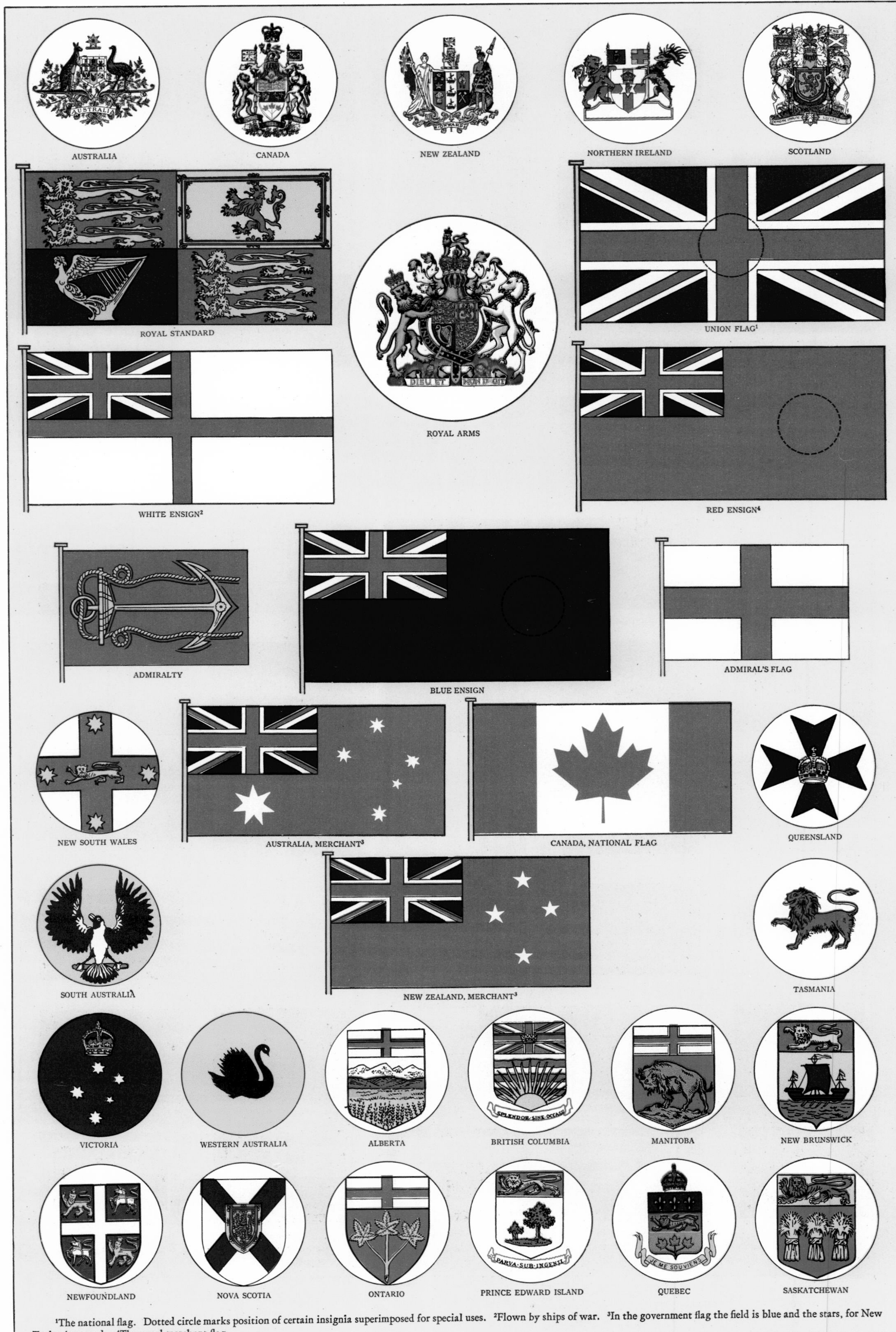

[1]The national flag. Dotted circle marks position of certain insignia superimposed for special uses. [2]Flown by ships of war. [3]In the government flag the field is blue and the stars, for New Zealand, are red. [4]The usual merchant flag.

²flock \"\ *vb* -ED/-ING/-S [ME *flocken*, fr. *flock*, n.] *vt* **1** *obs* **:** to assemble into a flock or company **2 a** *obs* **:** to crowd about (as a person) **b :** CROWD, THRONG ⟨vacationers ~*ed* the shore⟩ ~ *vi* **:** to gather into or move in bands or crowds ⟨~*ing* about the speaker⟩ ⟨people ~*ed* to the country for the weekend⟩

³flock \"\ *n* -S *often attrib* [ME; prob. akin to MHG *vlocke* snowflake, down, flock of wool (fr. OHG *floccho, flocko* down), MLG *vlocke* snowflake, flock of wool, Norw *flugsa, flygsa* snowflake, Latvian *plauki* snowflakes, *plaũkas* tufts of wool, fibers] **1 :** a lock or tuft of wool or other fiber (as cotton or hair) ⟨gleaning ~*s* from the bushes through which the sheep had passed⟩ **2 :** woolen or cotton refuse (as processing waste or old rags) reduced usu. by machinery and used esp. for stuffing furniture and mattresses ⟨cut into fragments to make ~*s* to stuff bedding —Flora Thompson⟩ **3 :** very short or pulverized fiber (as of wool, cotton, rayon, or silk) obtained often from the textile processes of shearing or napping, used esp. to form velvety patterns on cloth or paper or a soft protective covering on metal, and applied by blowing or shaking on a surface spread with adhesive **4 :** FLOC

⁴flock \"\ *vb* -ED/-ING/-S *vt* **1 :** to fill (as a mattress) with flock **2 a :** to coat (as an adhesive surface) or cover (as an evergreen bough) with flock **b :** to weight (woolen cloths) by blowing in short waste fibers and shrinking and pressing **c :** to decorate (as wallpaper) with raised patterns of flock ⟨finished with ~*ed* red wallpaper to look like velvet —Alice Griffin⟩ **3** [trans. of L *flocci facere*, lit., to make flocks] *obs* **:** to treat contemptuously ~ *vi* **:** FLOC

flock bed *n* [³*flock*] **:** a bed having or consisting of a mattress stuffed with flock

flock book *n* [¹*flock*] **:** a book containing the records and pedigrees of breeds of sheep or of a particular flock of sheep

flock duck *n* [¹*flock*] **:** SCAUP DUCK

flock·ing \ˈfläkiŋ\ *n* -S [³*flock* + *-ing*] **1 :** decorative work or a design in flock **2 :** ³FLOCK 3

flockmaster \ˈ=,==\ *n* **:** an owner or overseer of a flock (as of sheep)

flock–mate \ˈ=,=\ *vt* **:** to allow (poultry) to breed at random within a selected population — compare PEN-MATE

flockowner \ˈ=,==\ *n* **:** an owner of a flock of sheep

flock pigeon *n* **:** an Australian pigeon (*Histriophaps histrionica*) often seen in very large flocks

flock printing *n* [³*flock*] **:** a process in which material (as flock or metallic powder) is dusted or sprayed over matter (as Christmas cards or wallpaper) previously printed with an adhesive (as glue or varnish)

flockwise \ˈ=,=\ *adv* [¹*flock* + *-wise*] **:** in a flock

flocky \ˈfläkē\ *adj* -ER/-EST [ME, fr. ³*flock* + *-y*] **:** resembling or full of flock ⟨a ~ surface⟩ ⟨coarse ~ wool⟩

flocs *pl of* FLOC, *pres 3d sing of* FLOC

flodge \ˈfläj\ *n* -S [alter. of ME *floshe, flashe* swamp, pool, puddle, prob. fr. MF *flache*] *dial Eng* **:** POOL, PUDDLE

floe \ˈflō\ *also* **floe ice** *n* -S [prob. fr. Norw *flo* flat layer, fr. ON *flō* layer — more at PLEASE] **1 :** floating ice formed in a large sheet on the surface of the sea or other body of water **2 :** ICE FLOE

floeberg \ˈ=,=\ *n* **:** a mass of hummocky floe ice resembling an iceberg

floe rat *n* **:** RINGED SEAL

floer·kea \ˈflərkēə, ˈflȯr-,ˈfler-\ *n, cap* [NL, after Heinrich G. *Floerke* †1835 Ger. botanist] **:** a small genus of aquatic or marsh herbs (family Limnanthaceae) having pinnately divided leaves and small solitary flowers with three sepals and three petals — see FALSE MERMAID

flog \ˈfläg *also* ˈflȯg\ *vb* **flogged; flogged; flogging; flogs** [perh. modif. of L *flagellare* — more at FLAGELLATE] *vt* **1 :** to beat or strike with a rod or whip **:** WHIP, LASH **2 :** to strike repeatedly as if beating ⟨wind-swept branches *flogging* the ground⟩; *often* **:** to cast a fishline repeatedly into ⟨*flogged* the stream for trout⟩ **3 a :** PUNISH 3 **b :** to criticize harshly or scathingly ⟨the opposition papers continue to ~ the government over the economic crisis⟩ **4** *chiefly Brit* **a :** DRIVE, PUSH **:** force into attention or action ⟨*flogging* his keen retentive memory —Nevil Shute⟩ ⟨*flogging* herself into a rage⟩ ⟨*flogged* his new car up to town⟩ **b :** to wear out **:** EXHAUST ⟨completely *flogged* when he got to the top⟩ ⟨pastures *flogged* by overgrazing⟩ **5** *slang* **:** to take (as government property) for purposes of resale ⟨*flogging* blankets from the army depot⟩ ~ *vi* **1 :** to flap or move violently or vigorously ⟨awnings *flogging* in the wind⟩ ⟨lambs racing to their mothers with their tails *flogging*⟩ **2 :** to progress or function by a repeated sequence of movements ⟨*flogging* down the road toward his home⟩ ⟨the idling motor *flogged* away quietly⟩ — **flog a dead horse :** to attempt to revive interest in a worn-out or forgotten subject

flog·ga·ble \-gəbəl\ *adj* **:** meriting a flogging ⟨a ~ offence⟩

flog·ger \-gə(r)\ *n* -S **:** one that flogs: as **a :** BUNG STARTER **b :** a foundry worker who knocks the loose sand from a casting just taken from the mold

flogging chisel *n* **:** a large cold chisel for chipping castings

flogging hammer *n* **:** a small sledgehammer used for driving a flogging chisel or for beating metal

flo·kite \ˈflō,kīt, -lä,-\ *n* -S [Dan *flokit*, fr. *Floki* Vilgerdarson, 9th cent. viking + Dan *-it* -ite] **:** a zeolitic mineral from Iceland occurring in slender colorless or yellowish green prismatic crystals

flong \ˈfläŋ, ˈflȯŋ\ *n* -S [F *flan* flan, flong — more at FLAN] **:** a sheet (as of several layers of tissue paper superposed on a sheet of heavier paper) used for making a stereotype matrix

flong paper *n* **:** MATRIX PAPER

¹flood \ˈfləd\ *n* -S *often attrib* [ME *flood, flod*, fr. OE *flōd*; akin to OHG *fluot* flood, ON *flōth*, Goth *flodus*; derivatives fr. the root of E *flow*] **1** *archaic* **:** a body of moving water (as a river or stream) esp. when large **2 a :** the flowing in of the tide **:** the semidiurnal swell or rise of water in the ocean ⟨there is a tide in the affairs of men which, taken at the ~, leads on to fortune —Shak.⟩ — opposed to *ebb* **b :** the highest point of a tide ⟨the tide is nearly at the ~⟩ **3 a :** a rising and overflowing of a body of water that covers land not usu. under water **:** DELUGE, FRESHET ⟨a covenant never to destroy the earth again by ~ —John Milton⟩ — used with *the* to identify a flood of esp. severity or local interest ⟨still date things around here from the ~, which was about the biggest excitement we ever had⟩ or, usu. cap., the worldwide deluge reported in Gen 7 ⟨the *Flood* in the days of Noah⟩ **b (1) :** an outpouring of considerable extent ⟨gave way in a ~ of tears⟩ **(2) :** a great downpour ⟨raining in ~*s*⟩ **4 :** the element water ⟨the rocky shore that forms a barrier between earth and ~⟩ ⟨willing to go through fire and ~ to gain his objective⟩ **5 a :** a great stream of something (as light or lava) that flows in a steady course **b :** a large quantity widely diffused **:** SUPERABUNDANCE ⟨a ~ of spurious bank notes⟩ ⟨soon had a ~ of invitations⟩ **6 :** FLOODLIGHT **syn** see FLOW

²flood \"\ *vb* -ED/-ING/-S *vt* **1 a :** to cover or overwhelm with a flood **:** INUNDATE, DELUGE ⟨the river ~*ed* the lowlands⟩ **b :** to cover or cause to be covered with water or other fluid ⟨in some places it is economical to irrigate by ~*ing* the fields at regular intervals⟩ ⟨~ the bearings with oil⟩ **2 :** to fill more or less completely with water or other fluid **:** as **a :** to increase the elevation of the water in (a channel) esp. in splashing logs or in nullifying the effectiveness of a fall over a dam; *also* **:** SPLASH **b :** to supply to (the carburetor of an internal-combustion engine) an excess of fuel sufficient to raise the fuel level in the float chamber above the fuel nozzle **c :** to fill (as a compartment of a submarine) with water admitted from the sea **d :** to fill (an oil sand) with water to expel the oil **e :** to apply excessive ink to in printing ⟨the form was ~*ed* and the halftones are too heavy and dark⟩ **3 a :** to fill to full capacity or to excess ⟨shoppers ~*ed* the streets⟩ ⟨afferent impulses ~ the brain in certain hysteric states⟩ ⟨~*ing* the mails with circulars⟩ **b :** to distribute something in or provide with something in large quantities ⟨~*ing* the country with ads⟩ ⟨the room was ~*ed* with light⟩ ~ *vi* **1 a :** to pour or issue like a flood ⟨the milk ~*ed* over the table⟩ **:** OVERFLOW ⟨wine ~*ing* from the glass as her hand shook⟩ **b :** to become filled to excess with some fluid ⟨our cellar ~*s* after every heavy rain⟩ **c** *of a tide* **:** to run high ⟨could tell how the tide was ~*ing* —G.W.Brace⟩ **2 :** to have an excessive menstrual flow or a uterine hemorrhage after childbirth

flood·able \-dəbəl\ *adj* **:** capable of or subject to flooding

flood·age \-dij\ *n* -S **:** flooded state **:** INUNDATION

floodboard \ˈ=,=\ *n* **:** FLASHBOARD

flood bulb *n* **:** PHOTOFLOOD

floodcock \ˈ=,=\ *n* **:** a cock by which sea water can be admitted to flood part of a ship (as a powder magazine)

flood current *n* **:** a tidal current that moves toward a shore or up a tidal river

flood dam *also* **flooding dam** *n* **:** a dam to store floodwaters temporarily or to supply a surge of water (as for clearing a channel or splashing logs) — compare SPLASH DAM

flooded *adj* **:** covered or overfilled with water or other liquid ⟨~ fields⟩ ⟨a ~ carburetor⟩

flooded box *n* **:** an Australian tree (*Eucalyptus bicolor*) common on alluvial soils

flooded gum *n* **:** any one of several Australian gum trees (as *Eucalyptus tereticornis, E. grandis,* and *E. gunnii*) that grow on moist or alluvial soil

flood·er \-də(r)\ *n* -S **:** one that floods

flood fallowing *n* **:** a method of suppressing or eradicating soil-borne pathogens by flooding the land while it lies fallow

floodgate \ˈ=,=\ *n* [ME, fr. *flood* + *gate*] **1 a :** a gate for shutting out, admitting, or releasing a body of water **:** a sluice gate **:** SLUICE; *specif* **:** the lower gate of a lock **b :** something that acts to restrain an outburst ⟨tears do stop the ~*s* of her eyes —Shak.⟩ **2 :** the stream stopped by or allowed to pass by a floodgate **:** FLOOD ⟨a whole ~ of facts —John Ward⟩

flood gull *n* **:** BLACK SKIMMER

flooding *n* -S [fr. gerund of ²*flood*] **1 :** a filling or becoming full with or as if with some fluid esp. to excess **2 :** something produced by flooding: as **a :** a concentration at the surface of a paint film of one of the ingredients of the pigment portion giving rise to a uniform change of color of the surface — compare FLOATING **b :** a coating (as of an adhesive) applied by flooding

flood insurance *n* **:** insurance against loss resulting from flood, tidal wave, and rising water

flood lamp *n* **:** FLOODLIGHT

floodland \ˈ=,=\ *n* **:** FLOODPLAIN 1

flood·less \ˈ=ləs\ *adj* **:** having no floods **:** devoid of floods ⟨a ~ year⟩ ⟨a ~ area⟩

¹floodlight \ˈ=,=\ *n* [¹*flood* + *light*] **1 :** artificial illumination in a broad beam; *also* **:** a source of such illumination **2** *also* **floodlight projector :** a lighting unit with a parabolic or other specially shaped reflector for projecting a beam of light for illumination (as of a show window, an athletic field, an airstrip)

floodlight 2

²floodlight \"\ *vt* **:** to illuminate by means of one or more floodlights

floodmark \ˈ=,=\ *n* [ME, fr. *flood* + *mark*] **:** the mark or line to which the tide or a flood rises **:** HIGH-WATER MARK

flood·om·e·ter \,fləˈdäməd·ə(r)\ *n* [¹*flood* + *-o-* + *-meter*] **:** an instrument for measuring the height of a flood

floodplain \ˈ=,=\ *n* **1 :** a flat or nearly flat surface that may be submerged by floodwaters **2 :** a plain built up or in the process of being built up by stream deposition

floods *pl of* FLOOD, *pres 3d sing of* FLOOD

flood stage *n* **:** the stage at which a stream will overflow its banks

flood tide *n* **1 a :** the rising tide — opposed to *ebb tide* **b :** a tide at its greatest height — compare SPRING TIDE **2 :** something felt to resemble a rising tide: as **a :** a moving mass of people ⟨a *flood tide* of laughing children burst from the school⟩ **b :** something overwhelming or overspreading ⟨the *flood tide* of recurrent barbarism⟩ **c :** a high point **:** PEAK, CLIMAX ⟨the army . . . which at its *flood tide* numbered 89 combat divisions —*Life*⟩ **d :** a great and usu. increasing quantity or number ⟨a *flood tide* of shoddy novels⟩ ⟨an effort to stem the *flood tide* of wheat that threatens to overrun the already jammed federal storehouses —*N.Y.Times*⟩

floodtime \ˈ=,=\ *n* **:** the season of floods

floodwall \ˈ=,=\ *n* **:** a wall (as a levee) built to prevent inundation by high water

floodwater \ˈ=,==\ *n* **:** the water of a flood

floodway \ˈ=,=\ *n* **:** an area or channel provided as an emergency course to divert floodwaters (as from more populous regions)

floodwood \ˈ=,=\ *n* **:** wood drifting on a stream or left stranded by a flood

floo·ey \ˈflüē, -üi\ *adv (or adj)* [origin unknown] **:** AWRY — usu. used in the phrase *go flooey* ⟨if I have to leave her it will all go ~ —Theodore Dreiser⟩ ⟨with my knees going ~ and an ache in my chest —Herbert Gold⟩ ⟨something went ~ with the time and all of a sudden it was a quarter of eight —Dorothy Baker⟩

¹floor \ˈflō(ə)r, -ȯ(ə)r,-ōə,-ȯ(ə)\ *n* -S *often attrib* [ME *flor*, fr. OE *flōr*; akin to OHG *fluor* cultivated field, meadow, ON *flōrr* floor of a cow stall, OIr *lār* floor, L *planus* level, flat, Gk *planan* to cause to wander, *planasthai* to wander, OSlav *polje* field; basic meaning: broad and flat] **1 :** the bottom or lower part of any room **:** the part of a room upon which one stands **2 a :** the lower inside surface of any hollow structure ⟨the ~ of a cave⟩ ⟨the ~ of the pelvis⟩ **b :** a lower ground surface (as the bottom of the sea or the invert of the chamber of a canal lock) ⟨the ~ of the valley⟩ **3 :** the structure of supporting beams, girders, and covering that divides a building horizontally; *broadly* **:** a story of a building **4 :** the surface or the platform of a structure on which to walk, work, or travel ⟨the ~ of a bridge⟩ ⟨the ~ of a prize ring⟩ **5 a :** the main level space in a room distinguished from a platform or gallery: as **(1) :** the part of a securities or commodity exchange on which trading takes place ⟨~ traders⟩ **(2) :** the part of a legislative chamber or meeting room occupied by the members **(3) :** an inside area (as in a restaurant or nightclub) used and usu. specially dressed and prepared for dancing — called also *dance floor* **(4) :** an area often specially prepared or marked on which an indoor sports event takes place ⟨the coach sent a substitute onto the ~⟩ **b :** the occupants of a floor ⟨the whole third ~ is furious over the situation⟩: as **(1) :** the members of an assembly **:** AUDIENCE ⟨the chairman appealed to the ~⟩ ⟨questions from the ~⟩ **(2) :** the dancers participating in a square dance **c :** the attention of an audience; *broadly* **:** the right esp. of a member to address an assembly **6 a :** the athwartship vertical plate connecting the frame and reverse frame of a steel ship — see SHIP illustration **b :** an athwartship member in a wood ship attached to a wood frame **7 :** the rock underlying an unconsolidated or stratified deposit **:** BASEMENT COMPLEX **8 a :** a nearly horizontal flat surface (as the top of a hard bed or stratum) that is utilized in mining operations **b :** the bottom of any nearly horizontal mine working (as a drift, level, flat stope, or slope); *sometimes* **:** a rock stratum **c :** one of the horizontal divisions of a stope that esp. in square-set stoping are generally spaced at regular intervals between levels **9 :** the layer of organic matter covering the soil of a forest **:** DUFF **10** *in malting* **:** a batch of grain spread out for germination **11 :** a lower limit or base: as **a :** one imposed by an authoritative ruling below which a given quantity or rate is not to be allowed to fall ⟨the right of the government to establish ~*s*⟩ ⟨a ~ under prices or wages⟩ **b :** a bottom level determined by economic factors ⟨increases in wages or freight rates raise the cost ~⟩

²floor \"\ *vt* -ED/-ING/-S [ME *floren*, fr. *flor*, n.] **1 a :** to cover with a floor **:** furnish with flooring ⟨will ~ the camp next weekend⟩ **b :** to form the floor of ⟨soft herbage ~*ed* the valley⟩ **2 :** to strike down or lay level with the floor **:** knock down; *broadly* **:** SILENCE, DEFEAT ⟨his answer ~*ed* me completely⟩ **3 :** to put, send, force, or display on or toward the floor ⟨the coach ~*ed* a whole new team⟩ ⟨he ~*ed* the accelerator and the car surged ahead⟩

³floor \ˈflü(ə)r\ *Scot var of* FLOWER

⁴floor \"\ *Scot var of* FLOUR

floor·age \ˈflōrij, -lȯr-\ *n* -S **:** floor space (as of a building) ⟨total ~ 21,000 square feet⟩

floor arch *n* **1 :** an arch having a flat extrados **:** a flat or segmental arch between floor beams **2 :** a flat concrete slab between beams

¹floorboard \ˈ=,=\ *n* [¹*floor* + *board*] **1** *also* **floorboarding** \ˈ=,==\ **:** board used for or suitable for floors **:** FLOORING ⟨seasoned oak ~⟩ **2 :** a board in a floor ⟨squeaky ~*s*⟩; *often* **:** one that can be removed to give access to something beneath it (as in a boat) ⟨raise the ~ to reach the battery⟩

²floorboard \"\ *vt, slang* **:** to press (the accelerator of a car) to the floor ~ *vi, slang* **:** to drive a car at full or excessive speed

floor box *n* **:** an electrical outlet set flush with a floor

floor boy *n* **:** a boy employed in a business concern to do errands and miscellaneous jobs

floor broker *n* **:** a broker who trades on the floor of an exchange for the account and risk of others — compare FLOOR TRADER

floor chisel *n* **1 :** a caulking iron for decks and floors **2 :** a chisel with a broad edge and long shank used for ripping out floorboards — see CHISEL illustration

floor clamp *or* **floor cramp** *or* **floor dog** *n* **:** a tool used to tighten seams of floorboards before nailing them in position

floorcloth \ˈ=,=\ *n* **:** cloth covering for a floor: **a** *obs* **:** a rug or carpet **b :** heavy cloth (as canvas) usu. oiled, painted with designs, and varnished that was formerly used for a floor covering — compare LINOLEUM **c :** canvas flooring (as for a tent or a theatrical stage)

floor·er \ˈflōrə(r), -lȯrə-\ *n* -S **:** one that floors: as **a :** a workman who lays floors **b :** something that discomfits or confuses one

floor furnace *n* **:** a small pipeless furnace located close below the floor and used esp. in houses having no basement

floor girl *n* **:** a girl or woman esp. in the needle trades to run errands and do odd jobs about a shop

floor hanger *n* **:** a stirrup iron to support a floor joist

floorhead \ˈ=,=\ *n* **:** an upper extremity of the floor timbers of a wooden ship

floor hinge *n* **:** a usu. double-acting hinge placed between the bottom of a door and the floor

floor·ing \ˈflōriŋ, -lȯr-, -rēŋ\ *n* -S [fr. ¹*floor* + *-ing*] **1 :** PLATFORM, FLOOR, PAVEMENT **2 :** material (as tongue-and-groove lumber) for floors ⟨the disadvantages of softwood ~*s*⟩

flooring saw *n* **:** a handsaw that has teeth on both edges, comes to a point, is used to cut out sections (as from a floor), and cuts its own entrance into the material

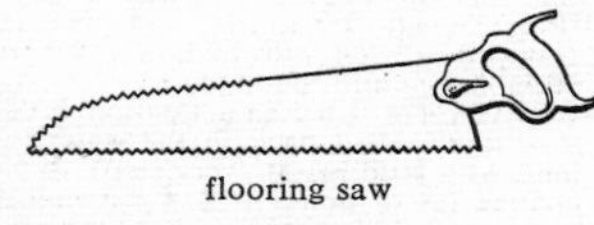

flooring saw

floor key *n* **:** a key that operates only a portion of the locks (as on one floor of a hotel) in a master-keyed system

floor knob *n* **:** a usu. rubber-ringed knob attached to a floor to prevent a door from striking the wall

floorlady \ˈ=,==\ *n* **:** FORELADY

floor lamp *n* **:** a tall usu. portable shaded lamp that stands on the floor

floor leader *n* **:** a member of a legislative body chosen by caucus of his party to have charge of its organization on the floor (as by making formal motions, opening debate, allotting time to other members of his party, and generally directing its strategy) — compare WHIP

floor–length \ˈ=ˈ=\ *adj* **:** reaching to the floor ⟨*floor-length* draperies⟩

floor·less \-ləs\ *adj* **:** having no floor

floor light *n* **:** a window in the floor that is suitable for walking on and that admits light to space below

floor load *n* **:** the load that a floor (as of a building) may be expected to carry safely if uniformly distributed usu. calculated in pounds per square foot of area **:** the live load of a floor

floor machine *n* **:** a portable machine that removes the surface layer from rough or soiled wooden floors

floor·man \ˈ=mən\ *n, pl* **floormen 1 :** any of various laborers: as **a :** a horseshoer's helper who removes old shoes, trims hoofs, and makes himself useful about the shop **b :** a worker who stacks green bricks, tile, or ceramic pipe in a drying room — called also *set-off man* **c :** a worker performing labor (as hoisting, cleaning, polishing) concerned with the maintenance of a particular floor (as of an office building) **d :** one of a crew of men who assist in the drilling of oil wells (as in running drill pipe and casing in and out of wells) — called also *roustabout* **2 :** an employee who is to some degree a representative of his employer before the public: as **a :** FLOORWALKER **b :** an employee of a bowling establishment who assigns alleys, collects fees, and supervises pinsetters **c :** a supervisor who assigns taxicabs to drivers and approves reports of meter readings **d :** a supervisory employee in a gambling house not assigned to any one table and usu. superior to the head dealers of two or more tables **e :** CALLER d

floor lamp

floor manager *n* **1 :** FLOORWALKER **2 :** a person who directs something (as the maneuverings in favor of a candidate at a convention, the progress of a bill in a legislative assembly, or the handling of material in a warehouse) from the floor **3 :** the stage manager of a television show

floor panel *n* **:** a preassembled unit of floor joists, subflooring, finished flooring, and sometimes ceiling below supported by walls, columns, or beams

floor pattern *n* **:** the design described on the floor by the steps of a dancer

floor pit *n* **:** a pit or recess below a floor line provided to facilitate the reaching of parts beneath a machine

floor plan *n* **:** a diagrammatic representation of a floor and usu. its relation to other features (as openings in adjoining walls): as **a :** a scale diagram of a room or suite of rooms viewed from above and used esp. for planning effective use and arrangement of furnishings **b :** a similar diagram of a theatrical stage **:** a staging plan **c :** a diagram of positions to be taken or of patterns to be made by ballet dancers on a floor or stage

floor planning *n* **:** a system of financed wholesale purchasing of expensive items (as automobiles or major electrical appliances) whereby a retailer stocks his sales floor with a minimal outlay of cash

floor plate *n* **1 :** a plate (as of steel or iron) set in or forming part of a floor and sometimes provided with T slots to which heavy work and portable machine tools can be bolted to facilitate machining and erection **2 :** a wooden board lying flat on the floor and supporting the studs of a wall **3 :** a plate closing the bottom of the magazine recess in a bolt-action rifle having a clip-loaded magazine

floor plug *n* **:** an electrical receptacle with its face flush with or recessed in a floor

floor pocket *n* **:** a metal box containing one or more electrical outlets set into the floor of a theatrical stage

floors *pl of* FLOOR, *pres 3d sing of* FLOOR

floor sample *n* **:** an article (as a radio or kitchen cabinet) offered for sale at a reduced price because it has been used for display or demonstration

floor show *n* **:** an entertainment (as in a nightclub or cabaret) presented from the floor rather than an elevated stage and usu. consisting of singing and dancing and sometimes of comedy and burlesque without continuity

floor slab *n* **1 :** a paving slab **2 :** the slab forming the floor of a usu. reinforced-concrete structure

floor switch *n* **:** a switch in the shaft of an electric elevator at a height corresponding to a floor level and operated by a projection on the car

floor trader *n* **:** a trader who buys and sells on the floor of an exchange for his own account and risk — compare FLOOR BROKER

floor truck *n* **:** a hand-operated conveyance typically in the form of a box or basket on wheels or casters for indoor use (as in a factory or store)

floorwalker \ˈ=,==\ *n* **1 :** a retail-store employee who supervises the salespeople of a particular section of the store and is at hand to help with customers' problems and to handle returned goods — called also *floor manager, section manager* **2 :** FLOORMAN 2d

floor·ward \ˈ⸗ wə(r)d\ *or* **floor·wards** \-dz\ *adv* **:** toward the floor ⟨pointing the stick ~⟩

floor wax *n* **:** a preparation made typically of a mixture of beeswax and vegetable waxes in a suitable vehicle and used for polishing and preserving the finish of floors

floorway \ˈ⸗,⸗\ *n* **:** the floor system of a bridge including the floor and supporting members

floorwoman \ˈ⸗,⸗⸗\ *n, pl* **floorwomen :** FORELADY

floor work *n* **:** ritual circumambulation

floo·zy *or* **floo·zie** *or* **floo·sie** *also* **floo·sy** \ˈflüzē, -zi\ *n, pl* **floozies** *or* **floosies** [origin unknown] **1 :** an attractive young woman of loose morals ⟨fool enough to become entangled with a ~ —Richard Church⟩ ⟨frontier *floozies* —Lisle Bell⟩ ⟨a tight-gowned ~ smirking at a saloon bar —Walter Goodman⟩ **2** *slang* **:** a dissolute and sometimes slovenly woman

¹flop \ˈfläp\ *vb* **flopped; flopped; flopping; flops** [alter. of ²*flap*] *vi* **1 a :** to move irregularly to and fro or up and down **:** FLAP ⟨scarf *flopping* about her ears⟩ ⟨the fledgling's wings *flopped* again and again but it could not get off the ground⟩ **b :** to move or drop with heavy clumsiness as if inert ⟨*flopped* over on his other side for a last nap⟩ **c :** to strike about with something broad and flat ⟨the fish *flopped* helplessly on the bank⟩ **d :** to progress by flopping ⟨pelicans *flopping* across the sky⟩ **2 a :** to throw oneself down heavily, clumsily, or in a completely relaxed manner ⟨so tired that I *flopped* into the hammock without another word⟩ **b** *slang* **:** to dispose oneself for rest or sleep; *specif* **:** to go to bed ⟨it's time to ~⟩ **3 :** to change or turn suddenly (as from one course to another) **4 :** to fail abysmally ⟨anyone may ~ once without disgrace⟩ ⟨in spite of good reviews the show *flopped*⟩ ~ *vt* **1** *slang Brit* **:** to strike esp. heavily ⟨*flopped* his rival on the head⟩ **2 a :** to turn or drop suddenly and usu. heavily or noisily ⟨sat *flopping* the pages of the book⟩ ⟨*flopped* her bundles on the table⟩ **b :** to settle (oneself) with a heavy clumsy movement **:** PLUMP ⟨*flopped* himself into a chair⟩ ⟨*flopped* himself over without awaking⟩ **3 a :** to make (as a photoengraving) or print (as a picture) so that an image appears with right and left sides transposed **b :** to reverse (as a two-color form) so that the colors are transposed

²flop \"\ *adv* **1 :** RIGHT, JUST, EXACTLY ⟨fell ~ on his face⟩ ⟨jumped ~ back into the hole⟩ **2 :** with a sound of flopping ⟨tumbled ~ into the mud⟩

³flop \"\ *n* -s **1 a :** an act or sound of flopping ⟨the fish gave a ~ and landed back in the water⟩ ⟨squelched through the mud with loud ~*s* at every step⟩ **b :** ABOUT-FACE **:** a sudden change (as of policy) **2 a :** a sudden decline ⟨stocks took a ~ yesterday⟩ **:** FALL, COLLAPSE **b :** something that falls flat **:** FIZZLE, DUD ⟨everyone expected his new play to be a ~⟩ **c :** something or someone lacking success, effectiveness, or adequacy **:** FAILURE ⟨was a ~ as a reporter⟩ ⟨the new economic plan was a ~ from the very beginning⟩ **3** *slang* **:** a place to sleep; *usu* **:** a cheap rooming house or hotel catering to impoverished men or a bed in such a place — compare FLOPHOUSE

flop–eared \ˈ⸗¦⸗\ *adj* **:** having long pendulous ears ⟨a *flop-eared* puppy⟩

flop·er·oo *also* **flop·per·oo** \¦fläpə¦rü\ *n* -s *slang* **:** a notable flop **:** complete failure

flophouse \ˈ⸗,⸗\ *n* **:** a cheap low-grade rooming house or hotel usu. catering chiefly to indigent men

flopover \ˈ⸗,⸗⸗\ *n* -s [fr. *flop over,* v.] **:** a defect in television reception in which a succession of frames appear to traverse the screen vertically due to a temporary maladjustment of the relative horizontal and vertical sweep frequencies

flop·per \-pə(r)\ *n* -s **:** one that flops: as **a :** FLAPPER 1e **b** *slang* **:** a person who fakes an accident in order to collect money (as from insurance)

flop·pers \-(r)z\ *n pl but sing or pl in constr* **:** AIR PLANT 2

flop·pe·ty \ˈfläpəd·ē\ *adj* **:** tending to flop **:** FLOPPY ⟨a soft ~ straw hat⟩

flop·pi·ly \ˈfläpəlē, -əli\ *adv* **:** in a floppy manner

flop·pi·ness \-pēnəs, -pin-\ *n* -ES **:** the quality or state of being floppy

flop·py \-pē, -pi\ *adj* -ER/-EST **:** soft and flexible **:** tending to flop

flor \ˈflō(ə)r\ *n* -s [Sp, mold, flower, fr. L *flor-, flos* flower — more at BLOW] **:** a coating of microorganisms probably including both yeasts and bacteria that is allowed to form on the surface of some sherry wines to which products of its fermentative activity impart a characteristic nutty flavor — called also *film yeast;* see MYCODERMA

flor *abbr* [L *floruit*] he flourished

flo·ra \ˈflōrə\ *n, pl* **floras** \-rəz\ *also* **flo·rae** \-r,ē\ [NL, after *Flora,* Roman goddess of flowers, fr. L, fr. *flor-, flos*] **1 :** a systematic treatise on or a list of the plants of an area, habitat, or period ⟨a ~ of No. America⟩ ⟨prepared a new ~ of the western mountains⟩ — compare FAUNA 3 **2 a :** plant life **:** PLANTS ⟨recent ~ exhibits many adaptations to habitat⟩ — often contrasted with *fauna* **b :** the plants or plant life characteristic of, peculiar to, or adapted for living in a particular situation (as a geological stratum, period, habitat, or region) ⟨the Devonian fossil ~⟩ ⟨postglacial ~*s*⟩ ⟨a lacustrine ~⟩ ⟨the intestinal ~⟩ **c :** plants or plant life of a particular kind or having some common characteristic ⟨the gram-negative ~ of the soil⟩ ⟨a large parasitic ~⟩ ⟨interesting moss ~⟩ — see VEGETATION 3

flo·ra del·le al·pi \¦flōrə,delə'al(,)pē\ *n* [by alter.] **:** FIOR DELL'ALPI

flo·rai·son \flȯrāzō^n\ *n* -s [F, fr. *fleur* flower, fr. L *flor-, flos*] **:** FLOWERING, BLOSSOMING ⟨the ~ of the folk dance in the mid thirties⟩

¹flo·ral \ˈflōrəl, -lȯr-\ *adj* [L *Floralis* of Flora, fr. *Flora* + L *-alis* -al] **1 a :** of, relating to, or associated with a flower ⟨~ organs⟩ **b :** resembling, made of, or based on flowers ⟨~ decorations⟩ ⟨an unusual ~ design⟩ **2 :** of, relating to, or concerned with a flora or floras ⟨characteristic alpine ~ elements⟩ ⟨isolated ~ relicts⟩ — **flo·ral·ly** \-rəlē, -li\ *adv*

²floral \"\ *n* -s **1 :** a design or pattern in which flowers predominate **2 :** something (as a fabric) with a floral design

floral element *n* **:** a group of plants forming one of the constituents of a flora and composed of plants geographically or habitally related

floral emblem *n* **:** a plant or flower recognized as symbolic of a group, organization, or sovereignty (as a club, school, or state) — see STATE FLOWER

floral envelope *n* **:** PERIANTH 1

flo·ra·lia \flōˈrālēə\ *n pl, cap* [L, fr. neut. pl. of *Floralis*] **:** an ancient Roman festival celebrated on April 28 in honor of the goddess Flora and marked esp. by nude dancing of courtesans

floral leaf *n* **1 :** any of the modified leaves (as a sepal or petal) forming the perianth of a flower **2 :** BRACT

floral organ *n* **:** any of the modified leaves comprising the calyx, corolla, androecium, and gynoecium of a flower **:** FLORAL LEAF 1

floral water *n* **:** distilled water obtained by the steam distillation of flowers (as orange flowers, roses) and used as a perfume for lotions

flo·ra's–paintbrush \,flōrəz'⸗,⸗, -ōr-\ *n, pl* **flora's–paintbrushes** *usu cap F* [prob. after the goddess *Flora*] **1 :** ORANGE HAWKWEED **2 :** TASSEL FLOWER 1

-flo·rate \¦flōr,āt, -ōrāl, -,rəl, *usu* |d·+V\ *adj comb form* [L *flor-, flos* + E *-ate*] **:** flowered ⟨bi*florate*⟩

flo·re·at·ed *adj* [by alter.] **:** FLORIATED

floren *obs var of* FLORIN

¹florence *n* -s *sometimes cap* [ME, fr. MF, fr. *Florence,* Italy] **1** *obs* **:** a gold florin **2** *obs* **:** CHIANTI

²flor·ence \ˈflȯrən(t)s, -lär-\ *adj, usu cap* [fr. *Florence,* Italy] **:** of or from the city of Florence, Italy **:** of the kind or style prevalent in Florence **:** FLORENTINE

florence brown *n, often cap F* **:** VANDYKE RED 1

flo·ren·cée \¦flȯrən¦sā, flə'ren(t)sē\ *adj* [F, fem. of *florencé,* fr. *Florence,* Italy + *-é* (fr. L *-atus* -ate); fr. the form of the lily in the arms of the city of Florence] *of a fleur-de-lis in art or heraldry* **:** having a figure in the form of a stem often seeded or flowered at the tip or leaflike or petallike in form arising between each C-scroll and the central lyrate figure ⟨the familiar fleur-de-lis ~ of the city of Florence⟩ — see FLORENTINE LILY 1

florence fennel *n, usu cap 1st F* **:** a fennel (*Foeniculum dulce*) with enlarged leaf bases used as a potherb and in salads — called also *finocchio*

florence flask *n, usu cap 1st F* **1 :** a round or pear-shaped glass flask with a long neck and often a covering of plaited raffia or straw in which olive oil or wine is shipped **2 :** a round usu. flat-bottomed glass laboratory vessel shaped like a Florence flask and usu. heat-resistant — called also *boiling flask*

Florence flask 2

florence leaf *n, usu cap F* **:** a yellow alloy or metal leaf or foil used for decorating

flor·enc·ite \-n,sīt\ *n* -s [Dr. W. *Florence,* 20th cent. scientist + E *-ite*] **:** a mineral $CeAl_3(PO_4)_2(OH)_6$ composed of basic phosphate of cerium and aluminum found in placer sands in Brazil

¹flor·en·tine \ˈflȯrən,tēn, -lär- *sometimes* -tīn\ *n* -s [L *Florentinus,* of Florentia (Florence), fr. *Florentia* + *-inus* -ine] **1** *cap* **:** a native or resident of Florence **2** *often cap* **:** FLAME SCARLET

²florentine \"\ *adj, usu cap* [L *Florentinus*] **:** FLORENCE: as **a :** in or following a style of art originated in Florence during the Renaissance and noted for fine drawing, idealized portrayal, and humanist content — compare SIENESE **b :** served or dressed with spinach — usu. used postpositively ⟨eggs *Florentine*⟩

florentine flask *or* **florentine receiver** *n, usu cap 1st F* **:** a receiver of glass or metal having an outlet near the top and one near the bottom for separating the layers of two immiscible distillates (as oil and water in the steam distillation of essential oils)

florentine glass *n, usu cap F* **:** glass ornamented with embossed figures impressed (as by a roll) while the glass is still plastic

florentine iris *n, usu cap F* **:** a European iris (*Iris florentina*) having large white flowers with lavender-tinged falls and a rhizome that yields orris

florentine lake *n, usu cap F* **:** CRIMSON LAKE 1a

florentine lily *n, usu cap F* **1 :** a fleur-de-lis florencée **2 :** GIGLIO

florentine marble *n, usu cap F* **:** a vase, statuette, or other ornament cut from a nearly white Italian alabaster

florentine mosaic *n, usu cap F* **:** a mosaic of hard or semiprecious stones chosen and arranged so that their natural colors represent figures (as of leaves or flowers) and inlaid in a background usu. of black or white marble

florentine orris *n, usu cap F* **:** ¹ORRIS

flo·res \ˈflōr(,)ēz\ *n pl* [NL, fr. L, pl. of *flor-, flos* flower — more at BLOW (to bloom)] **:** a flaky or pulverulent form of an element or chemical compound obtained by sublimation

flo·res·cence \flō'res^n(t)s, flȯ'-,flə'-\ *n* -s [NL *florescentia,* fr. L *florescent-, florescens* (pres. part. of *florescere* to begin to bloom, incho. of *florēre* to bloom) + *-ia* -y — more at FLOURISH] **1 :** a state or period of being in bloom or of flourishing ⟨the highest ~ of a civilization⟩ **2 :** an act of unfolding into or as if into the open flower **:** ANTHESIS, BLOSSOMING

flo·res·cent \-nt\ *adj* [L *florescent-, florescens,* pres. part.] **1 :** being in the stage or at the point of florescence **2** *of a cultural level or period* **:** representing the attainment of the highest development of a particular society — used esp. of prehistoric Amerind groups

flo·ret \ˈflōrət, -lȯr-\ *n* -s [alter. (influenced by L *flor-, flos* flower) of ME *flourette* — more at FLOWERET, BLOW (to bloom)] **1 a :** a small flower ⟨dainty ~*s* of the bluet⟩ **b :** a single flower of a multiple-flowered inflorescence; *esp* **:** one of the small individual flowers that make up the head of a composite plant — compare DISK FLOWER, RAY FLOWER **2 :** FLEURON **3 :** yarn spun from floss silk

flo·ret·ed \-rəd·əd\ *adj* **:** decorated with small flowers

floretté *or* **floretty** *var of* FLEURETTÉE

flori- *comb form* [L, fr. *flor-, flos* — more at BLOW (to bloom)] **:** flower or flowers ⟨*flori*culture⟩ **:** something resembling a flower or flowers ⟨*flori*ated⟩

flo·ri·at·ed \ˈflōrē,ād·əd\ *also* **flo·ri·ate** \-rēət, -rē,āt\ *adj* [*flori-* + *-ated* (fr. *-ate* + *-ed*) or *-ate*] **:** having floral ornaments or a floral form ⟨~ lace⟩ ⟨a ~ pattern⟩

flo·ri·a·tion \,flōrē'āshən\ *n* -s [*flori-* + *-ation*] **:** floral ornamentation or a floral ornament

flo·ri·bun·da \,flōrə'bəndə\ *or* **floribunda rose** \¦⸗⸗¦⸗-\ *n* -s [NL *floribunda,* fem. of *floribundus* flowering freely, fr. L *flori-* + *-bundus,* adj. suffix (as in *moribundus* moribund, but influenced in meaning by L *abundare* to abound)] **:** any of various bush roses derived from crosses of polyantha and tea roses and characterized by large seldom fragrant flowers in open clusters — called also *hybrid polyantha*

flo·ri·can \ˈflōrəkən\ *n* -s [origin unknown] **:** either of two bustards of India (*Houbaropsis bengalensis* and *Sypheotides indica*)

flo·ri·cul·tur·al \¦flōrə¦kəlch(ə)rəl\ *adj* **:** of, relating to, or concerned with floriculture — **flo·ri·cul·tur·al·ly** \-rəlē\ *adv*

flo·ri·cul·ture \ˈflōrə,kəlchə(r) *also* ,⸗'⸗⸗\ *n* [*flori-* + *culture*] **:** the cultivation and management usu. on a commercial scale of ornamental and flowering plants — compare HORTICULTURE

flo·ri·cul·tur·ist \¦flōrə¦kəlch(ə)rəst\ *n* **:** a specialist in floriculture

flor·id \ˈflȯrəd, -lär-\ *adj* [L *floridus,* fr. *flor-, flos* flower — more at BLOW (to bloom)] **1 a** *obs* **:** covered with or abounding in flowers **:** FLOWERY **b :** embellished with flowers of rhetoric **:** excessively ornate **:** enriched to excess with or as if with figures ⟨a ~ literary style⟩ ⟨~ baroque architecture⟩ **c** *of music or counterpoint* **:** ornate and embellished **:** full of elaboration **:** FIGURATE **d :** showy and gaudy and usu. without solid worth or justification **2 :** flushed or tinged with red **:** RUDDY **:** of a lively reddish color ⟨a ~ complexion⟩ **3 :** marked by health and vigor ⟨a ~ old age⟩ **:** vigorous and flourishing ⟨she was a picture of ~ health⟩ **4** *of a disease* **:** fully developed **:** manifesting a complete and typical clinical syndrome ⟨~ rickets⟩ **syn** see ORNATE

¹flor·i·da \ˈflȯrədə, -lär-\ *adj, usu cap* [*Florida,* state in the southeastern U. S., Sp, fr. (*Pascua*) *florida* Easter, fr. *Pascua* Easter, Pentecost, Twelfth Night, Christmas + *florida,* fem. of *florido* flowery, florid, fr. L *floridus;* fr. its having been discovered (on April 2, 1513) during the Easter season and fr. the blooming appearance of the land] **:** of or from the state of Florida ⟨*Florida* potatoes⟩ **:** of the kind or style prevalent in Florida **:** FLORIDIAN

²florida \"\ *n* -s *usu cap* **:** FLORIDA ORANGE

florida allspice *n, usu cap F* **:** a Carolina allspice (esp. *Calycanthus floridus*)

florida arrowroot *n, usu cap F* **1 :** an arrowroot obtained in Florida from the coontie **2 :** COONTIE

florida bayberry *n, usu cap F* **:** a white-barked evergreen shrub or small tree (*Myrica inodora*) of the Florida coast

florida bean *n, usu cap F* **:** the large seed of any of several West Indian leguminous plants (as that of cowage or the snuffbox bean) often polished and made into ornaments

florida beggarweed *n, usu cap F* **:** an annual upright tick trefoil (*Desmodium tortuosum*) of the southern U.S. and tropical America used for green manure

florida boxwood *or* **florida box** *n, usu cap F* **:** a small tree or shrub (*Schaefferia frutescens*) of southern Florida having very hard wood

florida caper *n, usu cap F* **:** a shrub or small tree (*Capparis cynophallophora*) of tropical America and Florida

florida cat's–claw *n, usu cap F* **:** CAT'S-CLAW 1b

florida cherry *n, usu cap F* **:** SURINAM CHERRY 2

florida clover *n, usu cap F* **:** MEXICAN CLOVER

florida cranberry *n, usu cap F* **:** ROSELLE

florida dogwood *or* **florida cornel** *n, usu cap F* **:** FLOWERING DOGWOOD

florida duck *n, usu cap F* **:** a duck (*Anas fulvigula fulvigula*) of Florida resembling the black duck

florida earth *n, usu cap F* **:** fuller's earth from or like that from Florida

florida gallinule *n, usu cap F* **:** a nearly cosmopolitan gallinule (*Gallinula chloropus*); *esp* **:** a dark bluish gray bird of the No. American subspecies (*G. c. cachinnans*) with white on the sides and beneath the tail, a whitish abdomen, and bright red on the bare forehead, bill, and tibias

florida gold *n, often cap F* **:** DUTCH ORANGE

florida grackle *n, usu cap F* **:** a small purple grackle (*Quiscalus quiscula quiscula*) of the southeastern U.S.

florida jay *n, usu cap F* **:** a gregarious crestless jay (*Aphelocoma coerulescens coerulescens*) of the Florida peninsula largely bluish gray in color

florida laurel *n, usu cap F* **:** SWEETLEAF

florida mahogany *n, usu cap F* **:** RED BAY

florida moss *n, usu cap F* **:** SPANISH MOSS 1

floridan *usu cap, var of* FLORIDIAN

florida orange *n, usu cap F* **:** an orange grown in Florida; *sometimes* **:** any orange other than a navel orange

florida pine *or* **florida yellow pine** *n, usu cap F* **:** LONGLEAF PINE

florida plum *n, usu cap F* **:** GUIANA PLUM

florida quinine *n, usu cap F* **:** GEORGIA BARK

florida red scale *n, usu cap F* **:** a rounded reddish armored scale (*Chrysomphalus aonidum*) that is a major pest of citrus in Florida and sometimes troublesome in greenhouses elsewhere

florida spruce pine *n, usu cap F* **:** SAND PINE 1

florida velvet bean *n, usu cap F* **:** VELVET BEAN

florida water *n, usu cap F* [fr. *Florida Water,* a trademark] **:** a light aromatic toilet water or perfume often containing orange-flower water and cinnamaldehyde or bergamot oil usu. in an alcoholic base

florida wax scale *n, usu cap F* **:** a wax scale (*Ceroplastes floridensis*) having a red body and a white waxy covering and sometimes becoming a destructive pest on cultivated plants in the southeastern U.S.

florida yew *n, usu cap F* **1 :** STINKING CEDAR 1 **2 :** a rather rare bushy upright yew (*Taxus floridana*) of Florida with spreading branches and very narrow leaves

flo·rid·e·ae \flə'ridē,ē\ *n pl, cap* [NL, fr. L *floridus* flowery + NL *-eae* — more at FLORID] **1 :** a subclass of Rhodophyceae comprising red algae that have the cells connected by evident cytoplasmic strands, growth restricted to apical cells, and the carpogonium borne terminally on a special branch — compare BANGIOIDEAE **2** *in some classifications* **:** a group coextensive with Rhodophyceae — **flo·rid·e·an** \-dēən\ *adj*

¹flo·rid·i·an \flə'ridēən, -lȯ'-,-lä'-,-lō'-\ *or* **flor·i·dan** \ˈflȯrəd^n, -lär-, -dən\ *adj, usu cap* [*Florida* + E *-ian* or *-an*] **1 :** of, relating to, or characteristic of the state of Florida **2 :** of, relating to, or characteristic of the people of Florida

²floridian \"\ *or* **floridan** \"\ *n* -s *cap* **:** a native or resident of Florida

flo·rid·i·ana \flə,ridē'anə, -lȯ,-, -lä,-, -lō,-, -'ä,-,-'ā- *also* -'ā-\ *n pl, usu cap* [*Florida* + E *-i-* + *-ana*] **:** material (as documents, anecdotes, or artifacts) distinctively bearing on or characteristic of Florida or its people or culture

floridian starch *n, often cap F* [NL *Florideae* + E *-an*] **:** a granular carbohydrate reserve in red algae that is not formed in plastids and that in several respects resembles glycogen rather than starch

flo·rid·i·ty \-'ridəd·ē\ *n* -ES **:** the quality or state of being florid ⟨the ~ of his prose⟩ ⟨a marked ~ of face⟩

flor·id·ly *adv* **:** in a florid manner **:** with floridity ⟨~ figurative prose —E.R.Bentley⟩

flor·id·ness *n* -ES **:** FLORIDITY

flo·rif·er·ous \flō'rif(ə)rəs\ *adj* [L *florifer* (fr. *flori-* + *-fer* -ferous) + E *-ous*] **1 :** bearing flowers; *esp* **:** blooming freely — used chiefly of ornamental plants **2 :** FLOWERY ⟨~ language⟩ — **flo·rif·er·ous·ly** *adv*

flo·rif·er·ous·ness *n* -ES **:** the quality or state of being floriferous; *esp* **:** a tendency or capacity to bear unusual quantities of flowers ⟨a new rose of outstanding ~⟩

flo·ri·form \ˈflōrə,fȯrm\ *adj* [*flori-* + *-form*] **:** having the form of a flower

flo·ri·gen \ˈflōrəjən, -,jen\ *n* -s [ISV *flori-* + *-gen*] **:** a hormone or hormonal agent that induces or promotes flowering — **flo·ri·gen·ic** \¦flōrə¦jenik\ *adj*

flo·ri·le·gi·um \,flōrə'lējēəm\ *n, pl* **florile·gia** \-jēə\ [NL, fr. L *florilegus* flower-culling (fr. *flori-* + *-legus,* fr. *legere* to gather) + *-ium* (as in *spicilegium* act of gleaning ears of grain) — more at LEGEND] **1** *archaic* **:** a usu. extravagantly illustrated book about flowers **2** [trans. of MGk *anthologia* — more at ANTHOLOGY] **:** a volume or collection of brief extracts or writings **:** ANTHOLOGY

flor·in \ˈflȯrən, -lär-,-lōr-\ *n* -s [ME, fr. MF, fr. OIt *fiorino,* fr. *fiore* flower (fr. L *flor-, flos*) + *-ino* -ine (fr. L *-inus*); fr. the Florentine lily on the reverse of the first florins — more at BLOW (to bloom)] **1 a :** an old gold coin first struck at Florence in 1252 weighing about 54 grains and noted for the purity of its gold **b :** any of certain gold coins of European countries patterned after the Florentine florin; *esp* **:** an English coin worth about 6 shillings issued by Edward III **2 a :** a British silver coin worth two shillings first issued in 1849; *also* **:** any one of several similar coins issued in British Commonwealth countries (as Australia and the Union of So. Africa) **3 :** GULDEN **4 :** FORINT

flo·rip·a·rous \flō'ripərəs\ *adj* [LL *floriparus,* fr. L *flori-* + *-parus* -parous] *of a plant structure normally bearing fruits* **:** producing secondary or supplementary flowers rather than fruits

flor·i·pon·dio \,flȯrə'pändē,ō\ *n* -s [Sp, perh. modif. of NL *floribundus* flowering freely — more at FLORIBUNDA] **:** any of several tropical American shrubs or trees of the genus *Datura* (esp. *D. candida*) that have narcotic seeds from which an intoxicant is prepared and that are sometimes cultivated in warm regions esp. for their very large commonly white flowers

flo·ris·bad man \ˈflȯrəs,bät-, -bad-\ *n, usu cap F* [fr. *Florisbad,* village near Bloemfontein, Union of So. Africa] **:** a primitive So. African man (*Homo helmei* or *Africanthropus helmei* syn. *Africanthropus florisbadensis*) that resembles Rhodesian man, is sometimes regarded as ancestral to certain living African races, and is based on a single skull of possibly mid-Pleistocene age, large and thick-boned, with prominent brow ridge, prognathous jaw, and flattened dorsal cranium which was found associated with artifacts suggesting those of the European Acheulean

flo·rist \ˈflōrəst, -lȯr-,-lär-\ *n* -s [L *flor-, flos* flower + E *-ist* — more at BLOW (to bloom)] **:** one whose business is the raising of flowers and ornamental plants in a nursery or greenhouse or the selling of flowers and plants so raised

flo·ris·tic \flō'ristik\ *adj* **1 :** concerned with or relating to flowers, floral emblems, or a flora **2 :** of or relating to floristics — **flo·ris·ti·cal·ly** \-tək(ə)lē\ *adv*

flo·ris·tics \-ks\ *n pl but sing or pl in constr* **:** a branch of phytogeography that deals with plants and plant groups from the numerical standpoint

flo·rist·ry \ˈflōrəstrē, -lȯr-, -lär-, -tri\ *n* -ES **:** the florist's art or skill ⟨an expert at ~⟩ ⟨classes in ~⟩

florist's chrysanthemum *n* **:** any of certain large-flowered frost-susceptible chrysanthemums largely grown under glass for the cut-flower trade and derived chiefly by selection from and hybridizing of two perennial Chinese wild chrysanthemums (*Chrysanthemum morifolium* and *C. indicum*)

florists' flower *n* **:** a flower or plant commonly cultivated and sold by florists: **a** *Brit* **:** a cultigen grown primarily for its flowers **b :** a flower raised to be cut from the plant for sale (as the rose or carnation)

flo·ri·su·gent \¦flōrə¦süjənt\ *adj* [*flori-* + L *sugent-, sugens,* pres. part. of *sugere* to suck — more at SUCK] **:** sucking nectar from flowers — used of birds (as hummingbirds) that so feed

flo·riv·o·rous \flō'rivərəs\ *adj* [*flori-* + *-vorous*] **:** feeding on flowers **:** ANTHOPHAGOUS — used esp. of insects

-flo·rous \¦flōrəs, -ōr-\ *adj comb form* [LL *-florus,* fr. L *flor-, flos* flower — more at BLOW (to bloom)] **:** having or bearing (such or so many) flowers **:** -flowered **2** -ANTHOUS — in words whose first constituent ends in *i* ⟨nocti*florous*⟩ ⟨uni*florous*⟩

flo·ru·it \ˈflȯr(y)əwət, -är-,-ōr-, *usu* -əd·+V\ *n* -s [L, (he) flourished, 3d sing. perf. indic. of *florēre* to flower, flourish — more at FLOURISH] **:** a period during which something (as a person, movement, or school) flourished most

flo·rule \ˈflōr,(y)ül, 'flȯr-\ *or* **florula** \-r(y)ələ\ *n, pl* **florules** \-r,(y)ülz\ *or* **floru·lae** \-r(y)ə,lē, -lī\ *also* **florulas** [NL *florula,* dim. of *flora*] **:** a small flora; *esp* **:** a fossil flora comparable to a faunule

flor·u·lent \ˈflȯr(y)ələnt, -rəl-\ *adj* [L *florulentus,* fr. *flor-, flos* flower] **:** FLOWERY, BLOSSOMING, FLORIATED

¹flo·ry \ˈflōrē\ *adj* [ME *floury, flory* — more at FLEURY] **1 :** FLEURY **2 :** FLEURETTÉE 1

²flory \"\ *adj* [origin unknown] *Scot* **:** VAIN, CONCEITED

flory counterflory \¦⸗⸗¦⸗⸗,⸗⸗\ *or* **flory and counterflory** *adj* [¹*flory*] **:** COUNTERFLORY

flos·cu·lar \ˈfläskyələ(r)\ *adj* [L *flosculus* small flower (dim. of *flos* flower) + E *-ar* — more at BLOW (to bloom)] **:** FLOSCULOUS

flos·cu·lar·ia \ˌfläskyə'la(a)rēə\ *n, cap* [NL, fr. L *flosculus* + NL *-aria*] : the type genus of Flosculariidae comprising rotifers in which the female is attached and tubicolous with a lobed disk bearing long setae — **flos·cu·lar·i·an** \ˌ≈≈'≈≈ən\ *adj or n*

flos·cu·la·ri·idae \ˌfläskyələ'rīəˌdē\ *n pl, cap* [NL, fr. *Floscularia*, type genus + *-idae*] : a family of rotifers (order Monogononta) with the male small in size and free-swimming and the adult female larger and tubicolous and usu. attached by a stalk derived from the modified foot

flos·cu·lous \'fläskyələs\ *also* **flos·cu·lose** \-ˌlōs\ *adj* [L *flosculus* + E *-ous* or *-ose*] **1 :** composed of florets **2** *of a floret* : tubular in form — used esp. of the disk flowers of a composite

flos fer·ri \flä'sfeˌrī\ *n* [NL, lit., flower of iron] : an aragonite that occurs in delicate white coralloid forms and is common in beds of iron ore

¹floss \'fläs, 'flȯs\ *n* -ES [fr. or akin to D *vlos*; akin to MLG *vlūs* fleece, flock of wool, MHG *vlus, vlius* fleece, Dan *flos* floss, Sw dial. *floss* long flock of wool — more at FLEECE] **1 :** waste or short silk fibers that cannot be reeled; *esp* : the short loose threads that form the outer part of the silkworm's cocoon **2 a :** soft loosely twisted thread of silk or mercerized cotton used chiefly for embroidery **b :** DENTAL FLOSS **c :** a lightweight loosely twisted wool knitting yarn **3 :** a fluffy fibrous mass of material ⟨~ candy⟩: as **a :** SILK COTTON; *esp* : KAPOK **b :** VEGETABLE SILK **c :** CORN SILK **d :** cotton staple **4 a :** something or someone showy or stylish **b :** people of fashion ⟨follow the ~ to the winter resorts⟩

²floss \"\ *n* -ES [G, lit., raft, fr. OHG *flōz* — more at FLOAT] **1 :** vitrified oxide or earth floating in a fluid state on the iron in the puddling furnace **2 :** FLOSS HOLE

³floss \"\ *n* -ES *Brit* : STREAM

flos·sa \'fläsə, 'flȯsə\ *n* -s *sometimes cap* [Sw, short for *flossamatta*, fr. Sw dial. *floss* long flock of wool + *matta* rug, carpet] : a Scandinavian handwoven carpet; *also* : the weave typical of such carpets

floss·er \-sə(r)\ *n* -s [¹*floss* + *-er*] **1 :** a worker who stitches boning into corsets and girdles **2 :** a machine for spraying out fertilizer, water, and grass seed in one operation used esp. for seeding roadsides

flossflower \'≈ˌ≈\ *n* : a plant or flower of the genus *Ageratum* : AGERATUM 2

flossflower blue *n* : a pale purple that is redder and paler than average lavender, redder and duller than mauvette or wistaria (sense 2a), and bluer and less strong than phlox pink — called also *ageratum blue*

floss hole *n* [²*floss*] **1 :** a hole at the back of a metallurgical furnace through which slag passes out **2 :** the taphole of a melting furnace

floss silk *n* : ¹FLOSS 1; *also* : floss (as for embroidery) of silk

floss-silk tree *n* : a thorny deciduous tree (*Chorisia speciosa*) of the family Bombacaceae that is native to Brazil and Argentina but often cultivated in warm regions for its large solitary pink flowers which appear while the tree is leafless and that is the chief source of vegetable silk — called also *samohu*

flossy \'fläsē, -lȯs-, -si\ *adj* -ER/-EST **1 :** relating to, made of, or resembling floss; *often* : light and soft : DOWNY ⟨~ baby hair⟩ **2 :** stylish or showy esp. in appearance : making a good superficial impression; *often* : ORNATE, FLASHY

flot \'flät\ *n* -s [by alter.] : FLAT 1c

flo·ta \'flōd·ə, -ōˌtä\ *n* -s [Sp — more at FLOTILLA] : FLEET; *esp* : a fleet of Spanish ships that formerly sailed every year from Cádiz to Vera Cruz in Mexico to obtain and transport to Spain the products of the Spanish colonies

flo·tage *also* **float·age** \'flōd·ij, -ōt|, |ēj\ *n* -s [*flotage* alter. of *floatage; floatage* fr. ²*float* + *-age*] **1 :** the act or state of floating : ability to float **2 :** material that floats on the sea or on bodies of fresh water : FLOTSAM **3** *usu floatage* : the charge for transferring railroad cars on a car float

flo·tant \'flōtᵊnt\ *adj* [F *flottant* floating, fr. pres. part. of *flotter* to float, fr. OF *floter*, of Gmc origin; akin to OE *flotian* to float — more at FLOAT] *heraldry* : flying in air ⟨a galley, sails furled, pennon ~⟩

flo·ta·tion *also* **floa·ta·tion** \flō'tāshən\ *n* -s [*flotation* alter. of *floatation; floatation* fr. ²*float* + *-ation*] **1 :** the act, process, or state of floating **2 :** an act or instance of financing (as a commercial venture, an issue of stock, or a loan) ⟨their last ~ of stock was successful⟩ ⟨the ~ of new securities is a specialized business⟩ **3 a :** the separation of the particles of a mass of finely pulverized ore according to their relative capacity for floating by virtue of the surface tension on a given liquid instead of according to their specific gravities **b :** any of various similar processes involving the relative capacity of materials for floating (as for separating oils from industrial wastes, pigments from impurities, or coal from slate) — see FROTH FLOTATION **4 :** the collection (as in sewage treatment) of substances immersed in a liquid by taking advantage of differences in specific gravities or of the buoyancy produced by the evolution of gas by chemicals or heat **5 :** the ability (as of a tire, crawler tread, platform, or vehicle) to stay on the surface of soft ground or snow

flotation gear *n* : emergency gear carried by a landplane to provide buoyancy in case of a forced landing on water

flo·ta·tive *also* **float·a·tive** \'flōd·əd·iv\ *adj* [*flotation, floatation* + *-ive*] : of, relating to, used in, or aiding flotation

flo·til·la \flō'tilə, flə'-\ *n* -s [Sp, dim. of *flota* fleet, fr. OSp, fr. OF *flote*, fr. ON *floti* raft, fleet — more at FLOAT] **1 :** a small fleet or a fleet of small watercraft: as **a :** a subdivision of a naval fleet consisting of two or more squadrons of destroyers or other small warships sometimes with supplementary ships and air support **b :** a group of ships (as canoes, rafts, or windjammers) with a common objective and sometimes a definite leader **c :** an organization of military landing craft consisting of two or more boat groups **2 :** a group (as of persons, planes, or tractors) resembling a fleet

flo·to·ri·al \(ˈ)flō'tōrēəl\ *or* **flo·te·ri·al** \-tir-\ *adj* [irreg. fr. *floater* + *-ial*] **1 :** running for or elected to office as a floater ⟨a ~ representative⟩ **2 :** represented by or entitled to be represented by a floater ⟨a ~ district⟩; *sometimes* : held by a floater ⟨a ~ post⟩

flot·sam *sometimes* **-lōt-**\ *n* -s [alter. of earlier *flotsen*, fr. AF *floteson*, fr. *floter* to float, fr. OF — more at FLOTANT] **1 :** wreckage of a ship or its cargo found floating on the sea — distinguished esp. in legal usage from *jetsam* and *lagan* **2 :** something floating or drifting about on or as if on the surface of a body of water: as **a :** a floating population (as of useless, vagrant, or worthless people) ⟨the skid row ~⟩ **b :** an accumulation of unimportant, miscellaneous, and often disordered trifles

flot·ter \'flätər\ *vi* -ED/-ING/-S [ME *floteren* to be tossed by waves, float, flutter — more at FLUTTER] *Scot* : FLOAT

¹flounce \'flaůn(t)s\ *vb* -ED/-ING/-S [perh. of Scand origin; akin to Norw *flunsa* to hurry, Sw dial. *flunsa* to plunge] *vi* **1 a :** to move suddenly and usu. clumsily and jerkily in or as if in a state of emotional turmoil ⟨*flounced* away in a rage⟩ **b :** to move with a conscious awareness of self and usu. in a manner to draw attention to one's person ⟨*flouncing* across the hotel lobby⟩ **2 :** to spring, turn, or twist with sudden effort or violence : FLOUNDER, STRUGGLE ⟨the horse *flounced* wildly on the slippery paving⟩ **3 :** to enter or leave with an effect of flouncing ⟨*flounced* out of the room⟩ ⟨*flouncing* into the discussion⟩; *often* : to walk out : drop out — usu. used with *off* or *out* ⟨an actress who *flounces* out on her contract⟩ ⟨the seamstresses *flounced* off on strike⟩ ~ *vt, archaic* : to move or cause to move suddenly, violently, or jerkily (as in flinging, splashing, or slamming)

²flounce \"\ *n* -s : an act or instance of flouncing : a sudden or sharp jerk (as of the body) ⟨moved with a ~ to open the door⟩ ⟨giving the pillows a quick ~ to straighten and smooth them⟩

³flounce \"\ *adv* : with a flouncing motion

⁴flounce \"\ *n* -s [irreg. fr. *frounce*] : a strip of fabric that is straight, gathered, pleated, or circular-cut and is attached by one edge (as in finishing or trimming) so that the free edge will have maximum fullness ⟨a vanity with a chintz ~⟩; *often* : a wide ruffle

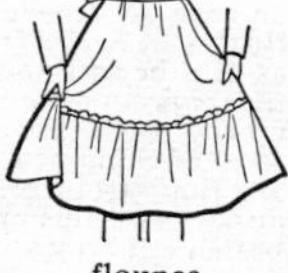

flounce

⁵flounce \"\ *vt* -ED/-ING/-S : to trim or finish with or as if with flounces

flounc·ing \'flaůn(t)siŋ\ *n* -s [⁴*flounce* + *-ing*] : material suitable for or made up into flounces; *esp* : yard goods of lace or embroidery with one plain straight edge and one fancy or ornamented edge

¹flouncy *also* **flounc·ey** \-sē\ *adj* **flouncier; flounciest** [⁴*flounce* + *-y*] : ornamented or finished with flounces ⟨a ~ girlish evening dress⟩

²flouncy \"\ *adj* -ER/-EST [¹*flounce* + *-y*] : marked by flouncing; *often* : jerky and self-conscious

¹floun·der \'flaůndə(r)\ *n, pl* **flounder** *or* **flounders** *see sense 3* [ME *flundre, flounder*, of Scand origin; akin to Sw *flundra* flounder, Norw *flundra* flounder, flat stone, ON *flythra* flounder; akin to MHG *vluoder* flounder, ON *flatr* flat — more at FLAT] **1 :** any of numerous flattened fishes constituting the order Heterosomata : FLATFISH; *usu* : any of various fishes of the families Pleuronectidae and Bothidae which include a number of important marine food fishes — see SOUTHERN FLOUNDER, SUMMER FLOUNDER, WINTER FLOUNDER; compare SOLE **2 :** PUMPKINSEED **3** *pl flounders* : something (as a metal plate, a liver fluke, or a tool formerly used in crimping boot fronts) resembling a flounder in shape

²flounder \"\ *vi* **floundered; floundered; floundering** \-d(ə)riŋ\ **flounders** [prob. alter. (influenced by ¹*flounder*) of *founder*] **1** *obs* : STUMBLE **2 a :** to fling the limbs and body (as in making efforts to move) : struggle to move or obtain footing **b :** to proceed clumsily and often self-consciously : MUDDLE ⟨they ~*ed* on from blunder to blunder —William Hamilton †1856⟩ **syn** see WALLOW

³flounder \"\ *n* -s : an act or instance of floundering

floun·der·ing·ly *adv* : in a floundering manner

¹flour \'flaů(ə)r, -aůə, *esp in the South* -aůwə(r\ *n* -s *often attrib* [ME, flower, best of anything, flour — more at FLOWER] **1 a :** finely ground meal of wheat; *esp* : a commercial product that is obtained by milling and blending wheat more or less completely freed of bran and that consists essentially of starch and gluten of the endosperm — see WHOLE WHEAT FLOUR **b :** finely ground meal of other cereal grains or seeds (as rye, barley, buckwheat, rice, or bean) **c :** finely ground meal obtained from dried food products other than cereals (as potato, banana, or cassava) **2 :** a fine soft powder (as of mineral or plant matter) usu. obtained by grinding ⟨silica ~⟩ ⟨rock ~⟩ ⟨wood ~ production utilizes waste by-products and provides fuel for power⟩ **3 :** FINES

²flour \"\ *vb* -ED/-ING/-S *vt* **1 :** to convert (as wheat or wood) into flour : grind and bolt : MILL, PULVERIZE **2 :** to sprinkle or coat with or as if with flour ⟨his coat ~*ed* with snow⟩ **3 :** to break up (mercury) into fine particles — compare DEADEN 2e ~ *vi* : to break up into particles: as **a** *of mercury* : to break into particles and become coated with sulfides so as to become useless for amalgam formation **b** *of paint* : CHALK

flour beetle *n* : any of various beetles that breed in flour, meal, and similar substances and often render them unfit for food; *specif* : a rather elongated flattened brown beetle of the family Tenebrionidae and esp. of the genus *Tribolium* — see CONFUSED FLOUR BEETLE

flour copper *n* : fine copper occurring as float

flour corn *n* : SOFT CORN 1

flour gold *n* : fine gold occurring as float

flour gravy *n* : gravy of milk, water, or stock and fat and seasoning thickened with flour

¹flour·ish \'flər·ish, 'flə·r|, |ēsh, *chiefly in pres part* |əsh\ *vb* -ED/-ING/-ES [ME *florisshen*, fr. MF *floriss-*, stem of *florir*, fr. (assumed) VL *florire*, alter. of L *florēre*, fr. *flor-, flos* flower — more at BLOW (to bloom)] *vi* **1** *chiefly Scot* : to bear flowers : BLOSSOM **2 :** to grow luxuriantly : increase and enlarge : THRIVE — used chiefly of plants and animals ⟨blueberries ~ best on an acid soil⟩ **3 a :** to be prosperous : increase in wealth, honor, comfort, happiness, or whatever is desirable : PROSPER **b :** to be in a state of activity or production — used chiefly of creative workers (as painters or writers) **c :** to reach a height of development or influence — used chiefly of technical, artistic, or philosophic schools of thought **4 a :** to play a fanciful or improvised bit of music by way of ornament or prelude **b :** to play a fanfare on trumpets **c :** to play with a flourish **5 :** BOAST, BRAG ⟨spent the evening ~*ing* over a bottle or two⟩ **6 :** to use florid language : be flowery in speech or writing **7 :** to make bold and sweeping movements or gestures esp. by way of show or in bravado ⟨~*ing* about the streets⟩ ~ *vt* **1 :** to adorn or decorate esp. with flowers or figures : ORNAMENT ⟨the corners ~*ed* with little silver cherubs⟩ **2 :** to move about in bold and sweeping figures ⟨~*ed* his cane angrily at the children⟩ **3** *obs* : to embellish with rhetorical figures or ostentatious eloquence **b :** to illuminate (a manuscript) with color or decorative figures **syn** see SUCCEED, SWING

²flourish \"\ *n* -ES **1** *chiefly Scot* : bloom or blossom esp. on a fruit tree ⟨the ~ of the apple trees⟩ **2** *obs* : blooming state or luxuriant growth usu. of plants or vegetation **3 a** *obs* : showy decoration or embellishment **b :** a florid bit of writing or speech (as a complicated figure or an ornate metaphor) **c :** a purely ornamental stroke usu. attached to or enveloping a letter or meaningful figure in a writing or engraving **4 a :** FANFARE **b :** a florid musical passage **5 :** the waving of a weapon or other thing ⟨with a last ~ of her handkerchief⟩ ⟨gave his cloak a ~ as he stepped from the coach⟩ : a brandishing esp. in salute or signal ⟨greeted him with a ~ of his cane⟩ ⟨caught the auctioneer's eye with a ~ of his catalog⟩ **6 :** a showiness or ostentation in the performance of something often intended to call forth or fix attention or admiration ⟨introduced his guest with a ~⟩ ⟨if I've got to give her a debut I'll do it with a ~⟩

flour·ish·er \-shə(r)\ *n* -s [ME *florissher*, fr. *florisshen* + *-er*] : one that flourishes

flourishing *adj* : increasing and growing : progressing well ⟨a ~ economy⟩ ⟨~ chicks⟩ — **flour·ish·ing·ly** *adv*

flour·ishy \-shē\ *adj* : characterized by flourishes : SHOWY

flour mite *n* : any of various mites that sometimes infest flour; *specif* : a small sarcoptoid mite (*Tyroglyphus farinae*) that is common in stored food products and may cause grocer's itch in persons handling infested materials

flour moth *n* : MEDITERRANEAN FLOUR MOTH

flour sulfur *n* : SULFUR FLOUR

flour worm *n* : the larva of any of various insects that breed in flour or meal; *esp* : the larva of the Mediterranean flour moth

floury \'flaů(ə)rē, -ri\ *adj* **1 :** of or resembling flour esp. in fine powdery texture ⟨a ~ clay⟩ **2 :** covered with flour ⟨wiped her ~ hands on her apron⟩

floury miller *n, Austral* : a large reddish brown cicada (*Abricta curvicosta*) having a whitish pubescence on the abdomen

¹flout \'flaůt, *usu* -aůd·+V\ *vb* -ED/-ING/-S [prob. fr. ME *flouten* to play the flute — more at FLUTE] *vt* **1 :** to treat with contempt : MOCK, INSULT **2** *obs* : to quote or say sarcastically or by way of mockery ~ *vi* : to engage in or practice mocking : SNEER, FLEER **syn** see SCOFF

²flout \"\ *n* -s : INSULT, JEER, MOCK, SCOFF; *sometimes* : MOCKERY, JEERING

flout·er \-ə(r)\ *n* -s : one that flouts

flout·ing·ly *adv* : in a mocking or contemptuous manner

floutingstock *n, obs* : an object of mockery or contempt

¹flow \'flō\ *vb* **flowed** \-ōd\ **flowed** \"\ *also archaic* **flown** \-ōn\ **flowing; flows** [ME *flowen*, fr. OE *flōwan*; akin to OHG *flouwen* to rinse, wash, ON *flōa* to flow, L *pluere* to rain, Gk *plein* to sail, float, Skt *plavate* he swims] *vi* **1 a :** to issue in a stream : GUSH, SPRING, WELL **b :** to move with a continual change of place among the constituent particles or parts : RUN, STREAM — used of liquids and of plastic or particulate bodies that move like fluids ⟨the grain ~*ed* smoothly down the elevator chute⟩ ⟨water ~*ing* over a dam⟩ ⟨molasses ~*s* slowly in cold weather⟩ **c** *of paint or other coatings* : to spread out in a uniform layer without holding brush or other applicator marks ⟨this paint ~*s* very well with a roller⟩ **2 a** *obs* : to become liquid : FUSE, MELT **b :** to deform under stress without cracking, breaking, or rupturing — used of certain solids (as metals or rocks) **3** *of water* : to rise esp. in the influx of a tide — often opposed to *ebb* ⟨the tide ~*s* twice and ebbs twice in each 24 hours⟩ **4 a :** to issue forth : ARISE, PROCEED — usu. used with *from* ⟨his authority does not ~ from his office alone⟩ ⟨wealth continues to ~ from our commerce and industry⟩ **b :** to move in or as if in a stream — usu. used with adverbs of direction ⟨money continued to ~ in⟩ **5 a :** to be in abundance or excess : ABOUND ⟨a land ~*ing* with natural resources⟩ ⟨wine ~*ed* freely all evening⟩ ⟨rivers ~*ing* with fish⟩ **b :** to fill to overflowing ⟨her heart ~*ed* with gratitude⟩ **6 a :** to move or proceed smoothly and without harshness or asperities ⟨his speech ~*ed* on to a summation⟩ : issue easily or freely ⟨words ~*ed* from him as if from a faucet⟩ **b :** to have such a contour as to suggest a graceful unimpeded uninterrupted movement ⟨the *flowing* lines of the car⟩ ⟨the dress ~*ed* and shimmered⟩ **7 :** to hang loose and floating ⟨his cloak ~*ed* from his shoulders⟩ ⟨fair hair ~*ing* in the light air⟩ **8 :** to menstruate esp. profusely ~ *vt* **1 a :** to cause to flow ⟨~*ing* oil over the swamp to kill mosquito larvae⟩ **b :** to spread (as paint) in a thick layer without brushing out thinly in the usual manner **c :** to cause or permit (an oil or gas well) to produce **2 :** to cover (as land) with water or other liquid : FLOOD, INUNDATE ⟨~ land for irrigation⟩ **3 :** to discharge (something) in a flow ⟨brought in a new oil well that ~*ed* 100 barrels a day⟩ ⟨the cut ~*ed* blood for some time⟩ **4 :** to run (molten metal) through a foundry mold to carry off bubbles, slag, and dross **5 :** to slack the sheet of (a sail) to spill the wind **syn** see SPRING — **flow by heads :** to flow intermittently — used esp. of oil wells

²flow \"\ *n* -s [ME, fr. *flowen*, v.] **1 :** the act or manner of flowing (as of a liquid) ⟨a sudden ~ of tears⟩ ⟨the chuckling ~ of rills and brooklets⟩ **2 a :** the regular inflowing of tidal waters towards the shore **b :** OVERFLOWING, INUNDATION; *esp* : one regularly recurring (as along the course of the Nile) **3 a :** an easy smooth and uninterrupted progress or movement (as of thought, music, traffic) suggesting the steady flow of water in a river ⟨ideas arose in a steady ~ as he worked⟩ ⟨a pleasing ~ of distant melody⟩ ⟨there has been a satisfactory ~ of capital to new enterprises⟩ **b :** the progressive travel of material for manufacture or of semifinished or of finished product from place to place or from operation to operation **4 :** a stream of water or other fluid or a mass of matter (as lava) that has flowed when molten ⟨a rubble ~⟩; *broadly* : STREAM **5 a :** the quantity (as of water) that flows in a certain time under specified conditions ⟨a system able to handle a ~ of 100 gallons a second⟩ **b :** the percentage increase in diameter of a mass of concrete or mortar when subjected to a standardized flow-test procedure including a prescribed flow table **6 :** form or arrangement suggesting a gentle unbroken movement ⟨the ~ of her hair over her shoulders⟩ ⟨the draperies forming a continuous graceful ~ across the three windows⟩ **7 :** the ability of a paint, varnish, or other coating to flow out to a smooth film **8 a :** menstrual discharge : MENSTRUATION **b :** production of a fluid or an instance of such production ⟨a good ~ of milk⟩ ⟨the fall ~ of honey⟩ ⟨a good sap ~ last spring⟩ **9 a :** the motion characteristic of gases, liquids, and viscous solids in which there is freedom of motion among constituent particles and change of form under the action of forces — see LAMINAR FLOW, STREAMLINE FLOW, TURBULENT FLOW **b :** a continuous transfer of energy (as of electricity or heat)

syn STREAM, CURRENT, FLOOD, TIDE, FLUX: FLOW designates the characteristic movement of a fluid, gentle or rapid, copious or meager, showing unbroken continuity ⟨the *flow* of water from the pipe⟩ ⟨the *flow* of lava from the volcano⟩ ⟨the steady *flow* of casualties from the front⟩ ⟨she helped Ruth into her coat, keeping up a cheerful *flow* of conversation —B.A. Williams⟩ STREAM may focus attention on constant succession of individual units or on their volume or speed ⟨a *stream* of water through the cellar wall⟩ ⟨a continuous *stream* of messages came in by courier —Irving Stone⟩ ⟨the *stream* of immigration turned toward middle and west Tennessee, where soils were deep and rich —*Amer. Guide Series: Tenn.*⟩ ⟨Riverside Drive and the Henry Hudson Parkway with their constant *stream* of cars —*Amer. Guide Series: N.Y. City*⟩ CURRENT strongly suggests the fact of running or flowing in a set direction with noticeable force ⟨the main *current* of the stream⟩ ⟨the Labrador *current* in the Atlantic⟩ ⟨the *current* of air from the ventilator⟩ ⟨there are thus indications in the New Testament of several cross *currents* of thought, political and social, in the early Christian church —C.H.McIlwain⟩ FLOOD suggests abundant copiousness or torrential power ⟨the trickle became a stream and then a *flood* —*Amer. Guide Series: Oregon*⟩ ⟨the rising *flood* of students is very much like the barbarian invasions —Douglas Bush⟩ ⟨a *flood* of war orders that strained the capacity of factories long idle —Oscar Handlin⟩ TIDE may suggest either surging power or periodic alternation of direction ⟨the deadly glittering *tide* of Spanish conquest surged into Central and So. America —Marjory S. Douglas⟩ ⟨the *tide* of traffic flow recedes very rapidly and the movement of people out of doors after midnight is almost negligible —H.E.Agnew⟩ ⟨she was on the threshold of womanhood, borne this way and that by conflicting *tides* of feeling —Ruth Park⟩ FLUX stresses constant change, sometimes in components, sometimes in direction ⟨a brief illusion of stability in the eternal *flux* —P.E.More⟩ ⟨as far as nature is to us more than a *flux* lacking order in its mutable changes, as far as it is more than a whirlpool of confusions, it is marked by rhythms —John Dewey⟩

³flow \'flaů\ *n* -s [of Scand origin; akin to ON *flōi* wide mouth of a river, swampy place, Dan *flo* marsh; derivatives fr. the root of ON *flōa* to flow — more at ¹FLOW] **1** *chiefly Scot* : a wet swamp or bog : MORASS **2** *chiefly Scot* : an arm or basin of the sea — used chiefly in place names ⟨Scapa Flow⟩ **3** *Scot* : a small amount

flow·abil·i·ty \ˌflōə'biləd·ē\ *n* -ES : the capacity to move by flow that characterizes fluids and loose particulate solids

flow·able \'flōəbəl\ *adj* : capable of flowing or being flowed ⟨a good ~ paint⟩

flow·age \'flōij, -ōēj\ *n* -s **1 a :** an overflowing (as of a stream or impoundment) onto adjacent land : FLOODING **b :** a body of water formed by flowage or sometimes by damming **c :** floodwater esp. of a stream **2 :** gradual deformation of a body of plastic solid (as certain rocks) caused by intermolecular shear — sometimes distinguished from *fracture*

flowage line *n* : a contour line at the edge of a body of water (as a storage reservoir or lake) that corresponds to some particular water level

flowage texture *n* : FLUIDAL TEXTURE

flow bean *n* : FLOW NIPPLE

flow birefringence *n* : an anisotropic state of a liquid resulting from shear

flow-blue \'≈ˌ≈\ *n* : an underglaze blue that was popular esp. in the early 19th century on pottery ware, that is generally printed, and that is caused to spread in firing by the use of a powder placed in the sagger

flow box *n* : a mechanical reservoir that feeds beaten paper pulp onto the wire of a papermaking machine

flow chart *also* **flow diagram** *n* : a schematic diagram or expository outline showing the progress of material through the various steps of a manufacturing process or the succession of operations in a complicated activity

flow cleavage *n* : cleavage that results from flow in hard rock and that is characterized by more or less slaty structure and reorientation or recrystallization of certain included minerals into a platy form

flow counter *n* : a device for detecting low-level radiation involving essentially transport of emanations to a Geiger counter in a stream of inert gas

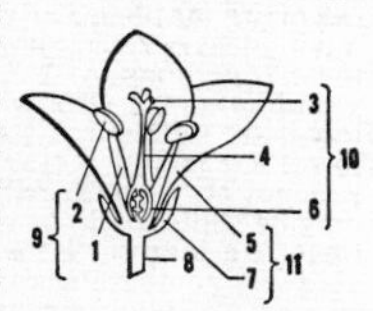

a flower in section: *1* filament, *2* anther, *3* stigma, *4* style, *5* petal, *6* ovary, *7* sepal, *8* pedicel, *9* stamen, *10* pistil, *11* perianth

flowed *past of* FLOW

¹flow·er \'flaů(ə)r, -aůə, *esp in the South* -aůwə(r\ *n* -s *often attrib* [ME *flour* flower, best of anything, flour, fr. OF *flor, flour, flur*, fr. L *flor-, flos* — more at BLOW (to bloom)] **1 a :** the part of a seed plant that normally bears reproductive organs esp. when some or all of its parts are conspicuous or brightly colored : BLOSSOM, INFLORESCENCE — not used technically **b** : a shoot of the sporophyte of a higher plant modified for reproductive purposes and consisting of a shortened axis bearing one or more series of floral leaves some or all of which are sporophylls; *esp* : such a shoot of a seed plant possessing an obvious external protective perianth often differentiated into calyx and corolla, an androecium of one or more stamens, and a gynoecium of one or more carpels **c** : BLOOM ⟨the tulips were in full ~⟩ **2 a** : the best, fairest, freshest, or choicest part, sample, or example of something ⟨she was the ~ of her family⟩ ⟨the ~ of chivalry⟩ **b** : the state or time of fresh vigor or bloom : PRIME ⟨in the ~ of youth and ardor⟩ **3** : a very finely divided powder (as one that will pass through a screen of 400 meshes to the inch); *esp* : one produced by condensation or sublimation — usu. used in pl.; see FLOWERS OF SULFUR **4 flowers** *pl, archaic* : menstrual discharges **5** : a plant cultivated or esteemed primarily for its blossoms ⟨we have separate ~ garden and kitchen garden⟩ **6 a** : an ornamental representation of a flower ⟨a skirt covered with little embroidered ~s⟩ : a floral design or artificial flower; *esp* : a printer's fleuron **b** : a flowery insertion or interpellation; *usu* : a figure of speech or other ornament of literary style **7** : SEASON 6

²**flower** \"\ *vb* **flowered; flowered; flowering** \-au̇(ə)riŋ, -au̇wər-\ **flowers** [ME *flouren*, fr. *flour*, n.] *vi* **1 a** : to produce flowers : BLOOM, BLOSSOM ⟨some roses ~ throughout the growing season⟩ **b** : to arise and develop — often used with *out* ⟨quarrels that *~ed* out as the community enlarged⟩ **2** : to come into the finest or fairest condition ⟨girls tend to ~ early in the tropics⟩ **3** *obs, of an effervescent liquid* : to froth or foam — used esp. of beer ~ *vt* **1** : to cause to bear flowers : grow until the bloom appears ⟨*~ing* azaleas under glass⟩ ⟨a rare tropical orchid that has never been *~ed* in cultivation⟩ **2** : to cover or decorate with floral designs or representations of flowers ⟨frost *~ing* the window⟩ ⟨a gay vestee *~ed* with silk⟩

flow·er·age \-au̇(ə)rij, -au̇wər-, -rēj\ *n* -s : flowers or flowering state

flower beetle *n* : a beetle that feeds upon flowers (as members of the family Cetoniidae)

flower box *n* : a usu. elongated box containing soil and used for growing ornamental plants

flower bud *n* : a plant bud that produces only a flower or flowers — compare LEAF BUD, MIXED BUD

flower cup *n* **1** : CALYX **2** : the cup-shaped interior of some flowers

flower-cup fern *n* : ALPINE WOODSIA

flower-de-luce \ˈ≈də̇ˌlüs\ *n, pl* **flowers-de-luce** [ME *flour de luce*, fr. AF, alter. of MF *flor de lis, flour de lis*, lit., lily flower] : ²IRIS 2 — compare FLEUR-DE-LIS

flow·ered \ˈflau̇(ə)rd, -au̇(w)ərd\ *adj* [ME *floured*, fr. *flour*, n. + *-ed*] **1** : having or bearing flowers ⟨a ~ lawn⟩ **2** : adorned or covered with flowers or floral figures or patterns ⟨a ~ carpet⟩ **3** : made with or partly with petals or leaves of flowers ⟨~ tea⟩

flow·er·er \-au̇rə(r), -au̇wərə(r\ *n* -s **1** : a plant that flowers esp. in some specified manner or season ⟨one of the best *~s* among the miniatures⟩ ⟨tulips are among the showiest spring *~s*⟩ **2** : a person who makes representations of flowers (as on pottery or in embroidery) usu. as a trade

flow·er·et \-au̇(ə)rət, -au̇wər-, *usu* -əd+V\ *n* -s [ME *flourette*, fr. MF *florete, flourete, flurete*, dim. of *flor, flour, flur* flower — more at FLOWER] : FLORET; *sometimes* : one of the segments into which a head of cauliflower is divisible

flower fence *n* : PRIDE OF BARBADOS

flowerfly \ˈ≈,≈\ *n* : a syrphid fly

flower girl *n* **1** : a girl peddling flowers in the street **2** : a little girl generally carrying or strewing flowers before the bride at a formal wedding

flower head *n* : a compact shortened inflorescence; *esp* : the capitulum of a composite or other plant in which the individual flowers are sessile and so arranged that the whole inflorescence gives the effect of a single flower — see COMPOSITE illustration

flow·er·i·ly \ˈflau̇(ə)rəlē, -au̇wər-\ *adv* : in a flowery manner

flow·er·i·ness \-rēnəs, -rin-\ *n* -ES : the quality or state of being flowery esp. in the use of language

¹**flowering** *adj* [ME *flouring*, fr. pres. part. of *flouren* to flower, flourish — more at FLOWER] **1** *obs* : FLOURISHING **2 a** : bearing flowers esp. in the blooming stage ⟨a ~ branch⟩ **b** : covered with or full of flowers ⟨a ~ meadow⟩ **3** : having conspicuous flowers : being of a kind grown primarily for its blossom — used chiefly in vernacular names of plants, the combination sometimes designating a plant that does not belong to the natural group indicated by the noun ⟨the fringe tree is sometimes called ~ ash⟩

²**flowering** *n* -s [ME *flouring*, fr. gerund of *flouren*] **1 a** : the act or state of producing flowers : ANTHESIS, FLORESCENCE ⟨have you ever watched the ~ of the cereus?⟩ **b** : the season when plants bloom ⟨~ will be late this year⟩ **2** : something (as ornamentation) of floral form or suggesting a blooming **3** : an unfolding or development ⟨the gradual ~ of his talent⟩ **4** : the secondary fermentation with flor formation in the production of superior sherry wines; *sometimes* : FLOR

flowering almond *n* : any of three woody plants of the genus *Prunus* grown for their showy flowers : **a** : a Chinese shrub or small tree (*P. triloba*) with fruit furrowed and hairy but becoming smooth **b** : a low Chinese shrub (*P. glandulosa*) or a similar Japanese shrub (*P. japonica*) with smooth unfurrowed fruit

flowering ash *n* **1** : any of three plants of the genus *Fraxinus*: **a** : MANNA ASH **b** : a large shrub or shrubby tree (*F. cuspidata*) of the southwestern U.S. that has fragrant white flowers **c** : a large shrub (*F. dipetala*) of the Pacific coast and coastal mountain ranges of the U.S. **2** : FRINGE TREE

flowering box *or* **flowering boxberry** *n* : MOUNTAIN CRANBERRY

flowering cherry *n* : any of several shrubs or trees of the genus *Prunus* cultivated as ornamentals for their showy bloom — see JAPANESE FLOWERING CHERRY

flowering crab *or* **flowering crab apple** *or* **flowering apple** *n* : any of various crab apples mostly of Asiatic origin that are widely cultivated for their showy single or double white to rosy red flowers — see BECHTEL CRAB

flowering currant *n* **1** : GOLDEN CURRANT **2** : WILD BLACK CURRANT

flowering cypress *n* : TAMARIX 2

flowering dogwood *also* **flowering cornel** *n* : a common spring-flowering white-bracted dogwood (*Cornus florida*)

flowering fern *n* : a fern of the genus *Osmunda* in which the naked sporangia are on modified fronds that resemble flower clusters

flowering flag *n* : ²IRIS 2

flowering flax *n* : an erect leafy branching annual herb (*Linum grandiflorum*) of northern Africa cultivated for its red flowers

flowering glume *n* : LEMMA

flowering hazel *n* : WINTER HAZEL; *esp* : a widely cultivated Japanese shrub (*Corylopsis pauciflora*) with somewhat glaucous foliage

flowering hormone *n* : FLORIGEN

flowering maple *n* : an ornamental plant of the genus *Abutilon* having leaves resembling those of maples

flowering moss *n* **1** : PYXIE **2** : a portulaca (*Portulaca grandiflora*) **3** : WIDOW'S CROSS

flowering nettle *n* **1** : HEMP NETTLE **2** : WHITE DEAD NETTLE

flowering peach *n* : any of various often dwarf or shrubby peaches grown primarily for their ornamental flowers which may be white, pink, or red and are often double

flowering plant *n* **1** : a plant that produces flowers, fruit, and seeds — compare SEED PLANT **2** : a plant notable or cultivated for its ornamental flowers

flowering plum *n* : any of several trees or shrubs of the genus *Prunus* cultivated chiefly for their blossom

flowering quince *n* : a shrub of the genus *Chaenomeles*; *esp* : JAPANESE QUINCE 2

flowering raspberry *n* : a shrubby bramble (*Rubus odoratus*) of eastern No. America having bristly stems, lobed leaves, showy rose to purplish flowers, and red edible fruit

flowering rush *n* : an aquatic or marsh plant (*Butomus umbellatus*) with sharp 3-cornered linear leaves and an umbel of rosy blossoms that is native to Europe but naturalized in waters adjacent to the St. Lawrence river

flowering shot *n* : INDIAN SHOT

flowering spurge *n* : a common spurge (*Euphorbia corollata*) of the eastern U.S. with showy white involucral appendages resembling petals

flowering straw *n* **1** : any of several skeleton weeds of the southern U.S. **2** : any of various branching leafy-stemmed composite herbs having small heads of pink or white flowers and constituting a genus *Stephanomeria* of western No. America

flowering thistle *n* : PRICKLY POPPY

flowering tobacco *n* : an ornamental plant of the genus *Nicotiana*

flowering willow *n* : DESERT WILLOW

flowering wintergreen *n* : GAYWINGS

flowering wood *n* : the portion of a woody plant that produces flower buds or mixed buds

flow·er·less \ˈflau̇(ə)rləs-, -au̇(w)əl\ *adj* : having no flowers — **flow·er·less·ness** *n* -ES

flowerless plant *n* **1** : a plant that produces no flowers **2** : a plant that produces flowers that are not noticeable (as grasses or rushes) — not used technically

flow·er·let \-lət\ *n* -s : FLORET

flowerlike \ˈ≈,≈\ *adj* : like or having the characteristics of a flower ⟨a ~ simplicity —Max Beerbohm⟩ : resembling a flower esp. in beauty or grace ⟨~ hands —Oscar Wilde⟩

flower-of-an-hour *n, pl* **flowers-of-an-hour** : an annual weedy plant (*Hibiscus trionum*) with ephemeral yellow purple-eyed flowers

flower of jove \-ˈjōv\ *usu cap J* [after *Jove* (Jupiter), chief god of the ancient Romans, fr. L *Jov-, Jupiter*; trans. of NL *flos jovis*, specific epithet of *Lychnis flos-jovis*] : a European campion (*Lychnis flos-jovis*) with white-tomentose foliage and pink flowers

flower of the winds : the figure of a compass printed on old charts that is represented with a rose in the center

flower-pecker \ˈ≈,≈≈\ *n* : any of numerous small short-tailed passerine birds of southeast Asia, the Pacific islands, and Australia that feed on the berries of tropical mistletoes and on insects and that constitute the family Dicaeidae

flower piece *n* **1** : an ornamental arrangement of flowers **2** : an ornament (as a painting) representing flowers

flowerpot \ˈ≈,≈\ *n* **1 a** : a container (as of earthenware or plastic) for earth in which plants are grown **b** *dial* : VASE; *also* : BOUQUET **2** : a firework that sends up sparks in fountains or showers

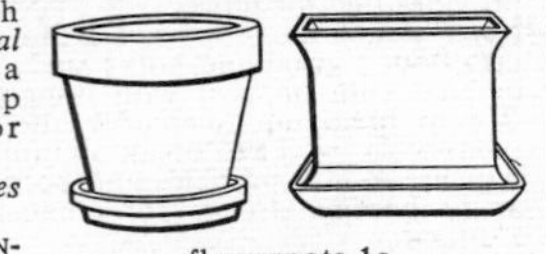

flowerpots 1a

flowers *pl of* FLOWER, *pres 3d sing of* FLOWER

flowers of antimony : ANTIMONY TRIOXIDE

flowers of madder : the macerated ground root of madder

flowers of sulfur : sublimed sulfur in the form of a fine yellow powder used esp. in agriculture and in medicine

flowers of tan : a slime mold (*Fuligo septica*) forming yellowish brown crustose compound fructifications on dead wood, leaves, and bark (as on spent tanbark)

flowers of wine : a scum formed on wine in fermentation by certain yeasts; *sometimes* : a yeast producing such a scum

flowers of zinc : zinc oxide esp. as obtained as a light white powder by burning zinc for use in pharmaceutical and cosmetic preparations

flower spike *n* : SPIKE 2

flower stalk *n* : PEDUNCLE 1a

flower thrips *n* : a yellow and orange thrips (*Frankliniella tritici*) living and feeding chiefly on flowers and causing sterility in oats and other crop plants

flower way *n* : an elevated passage from the back of a traditional Japanese theater to the stage by which actors make their entrances and exits

flow·ery \ˈflau̇(ə)rē, -ri, *esp in the South* -au̇wər-\ *adj* [ME *floury*, fr. *flour* flower + *-y* — more at FLOWER] **1 a** : relating to or covered with flowers ⟨a ~ field⟩ **b** : suggesting or like that of a flower ⟨a ~ odor⟩ ⟨a light ~ wine⟩ **2 a** *of language* : ornate and florid : characterized by much use of figures ⟨a ~ farewell speech⟩ **b** : inclined to the use of flowery language ⟨a ~ speaker⟩

flowery pekoe *also* **flowery orange pekoe** *n* : high quality tea consisting essentially of the small unbroken terminal leaves and buds

flow gauge *n* : FLOWMETER 1

flow gun *n* : a nozzle with finger-controlled flow for applying liquids (as adhesives, lubricants, or caulking)

flowing *pres part of* FLOW

flowing furnace *n* : a furnace from which molten metal can be drawn (as through a taphole) : a foundry cupola

flow·ing·ly *adv* : so as to flow or seem to flow ⟨draperies arranged ~⟩

flow·ing·ness *n* -ES : the quality or state of being flowing

flowing sheet *n* : a sheet on a sailing ship when eased off (as when the wind is aft or abeam)

flowing tracery *n* : tracery characterized by waving or flame-shaped curves that is found in English architecture of the 14th century and in the French flamboyant

flowing well *n* : an oil or water well from which the product flows without pumping due to natural or artificially supplied subterranean pressure from air or other gas

flow line *n* **1** : distinguishable differences (as of color, texture, or arrangement of crystals) indicative of flow having taken place in a plastic solid (as an igneous rock formation or wrought metal) **2** : a pipe or gutter carrying a flow of liquid esp. at zero pressure head

flow·me·ter \ˈflō,mēd·ə(r)\ *n* **1** : an instrument for measuring the velocity of flow of a liquid in a pipe **2 a** : an instrument for indicating pressure, velocity of flow, and rate of discharge of a gas or vapor flowing in a pipe ⟨a steam ~⟩ **b** : an apparatus for determining the flowing properties of materials (as paints or other coatings)

flow moss *n* [²*flow*] *dial Brit* : a wet peat bog

¹**flown** *past part of* FLY

²**flown** *adj* [fr. archaic past part of ¹*flow*] : filled esp. to excess or repletion ⟨~ with anger —Francis Hackett⟩ ⟨well ~ with wine⟩

flown cover *n* : a cover (as an envelope) that has been carried by airmail

flow nipple *n* : a nipple placed in a pipe line to regulate the flow of oil from a well — called also *flow bean*

flow nozzle *n* : a tapered length of tube that causes a fall of pressure head in a liquid flowing through it from which the rate can be calculated

flowoff \ˈ≈,≈\ *n* -s [fr. *flow off*, v.] : RUNOFF 1a

flows *pres 3d sing of* FLOW, *pl of* FLOW

flow sheet *n* : FLOW CHART; *esp* : one used of metallurgical or chemical processing

flowstone \ˈ≈,≈\ *n* : a deposit of travertine found where water flowing in a very thin sheet over rocks has deposited mineral matter — used chiefly of such deposits in caves

flow structure *n* : oriented structure developed in rock during flow

flow table *n* : a device for measuring the consistency of freshly made concrete or mortar consisting of a table top that can be raised and dropped and a mold for shaping the test specimen — compare ²FLOW 5b

flow tank *n* : a settling tank in which crude oil direct from the wells is stored for a time to free it from sediment before passing it on to the refineries

flow test *n* : a test to determine the consistency of freshly mixed concrete by measuring its spread on a flat surface under jarring

flow texture *n* : FLUIDAL TEXTURE

flow valve *n* : a valve that closes when the velocity or the pressure gradient of the fluid passing through it reaches a certain value

flr *abbr* **1** floor **2** florin

flt *abbr* **1** fleet **2** flight **3** float

fltg *abbr* flotage; floating

flu \ˈflü\ *n* -s [short for *influenza*] **1** : INFLUENZA **2** : any of certain ill-defined transitory virus diseases marked by respiratory and usu. gastrointestinal symptoms — used often with a qualifying term ⟨intestinal ~⟩

flu·ate \ˈflü,āt\ *n* -s [by contr.] : FLUOSILICATE — used esp. of solutions for waterproofing building stone or concrete

flu·a·vil \ˈflüə,vil\ *n* -s [F *fluavile*] : an amorphous yellow resin extracted from gutta-percha and balata

¹**flub** \ˈfləb\ *vb* **flubbed; flubbed; flubbing; flubs** [origin unknown] *vt* : to perform or deal with in a blundering manner : make a botch of : fail at ⟨was always *flubbing* her lines⟩ ~ *vi* : to act in a blundering manner : do something poorly or inefficiently

²**flub** \"\ *n* -s : a clumsy or stupid failure : BLUNDER, BONER

flub·dub \ˈfləb,dəb\ *also* **flub·dub·bery** \-,dəb(ə)rē\ *n, pl* **flubdubs** *also* **flubdubberies** [origin unknown] *slang* : ornate show designed to deceive; *usu* : showy bombastic argument or language : BALDERDASH

fluc·tu·ant \ˈfləkchəwənt, -ksh-\ *adj* [L *fluctuant-, fluctuans*, pres. part. of *fluctuare*] : moving like a wave : **a** : wavering or fluctuating ⟨the ~ drift of mist —Arthur Foff⟩ **b** : varying and unstable : not fixed ⟨a ~ foreign exchange rate⟩ ⟨~ populations⟩ **c** : movable and compressible — used of abnormal body structures (as certain abscesses or tumors) ⟨a ~ mass⟩ ⟨the involved nodes became ~ and were removed surgically —*Biol. Abstracts*⟩

fluc·tu·ate \-,wāt, *usu* -ād·+V\ *vb* -ED/-ING/-S [L *fluctuatus*, past part. of *fluctuare*, fr. *fluctus* action of flowing, flood, wave, fr. *fluctus*, past part. of *fluere* to flow — more at FLUID] *vi* **1** : to become wavering, unsteady, irresolute, or undetermined : VACILLATE **2 a** : to move like a wave : roll hither and thither : WAVE **b** : to drift or float backward and forward as if on waves ⟨a *fluctuating* field of air⟩ ~ *vt* : to cause to move like a wave : put in motion **syn** see SWING

fluc·tu·at·ing·ly \ˈ≈≈,≈≈≈, ,≈≈ˈ≈≈≈\ *adv* : with fluctuation : in a fluctuating manner

fluc·tu·a·tion \,fləkchəˈwāshən, -ksh-\ *n* -s [ME *fluctuacioun*, fr. L *fluctuation-, fluctuatio*, fr. *fluctuatus* + *-ion-, -io* -ion] **1** : a wavering or unsteadiness (as of opinion or prices) **2** : a motion like that of waves : a moving in this and that direction ⟨the ~s of the sea⟩ **3 a** : a slight and nonheritable variation; *esp* : such a variation occurring in response to environmental factors **b** : recurrent and often more or less cyclic alteration (as of form, size, or color of a bodily part) **4** : the wavelike motion of a fluid collected in a natural or artificial cavity of the body observed by palpation or percussion

fluc·tu·a·tion·al \ˈ≈≈ˈwāshənᵊl, -shnəl\ *adj* : relating to or subject to fluctuation ⟨~ factors in the economy⟩

¹**flue** \ˈflü\ *n* -s [ME *flue, flowe, flew*, fr. MD *vlūwe, vlouwe*; akin to OE *flōwan* to flow — more at FLOW] : FISHNET; *esp* : DRAGNET

²**flue** \"\ *adj* [ME *flew*] *dial Eng* : SHALLOW, OPEN, FLARING

³**flue** \"\ *n* -s *often attrib* [origin unknown] : an enclosed passageway for establishing and directing a current of gas (as air): as **a** (1) *now dial* : CHIMNEY (2) : a channel in a chimney for conveying flame and smoke to the outer air ⟨a big 4-flue chimney⟩ **b** : a passageway for carrying a current of air from one place to another (as for heating, cooling, or ventilating) ⟨warmed air is forced through ~s between the studs⟩ **c** (1) : an air channel to the lip of a wind instrument (as a recorder) (2) : an organ flue pipe (3) : the opening in an organ flue pipe between the lower lip and the languet **d** : a passage for conveying flame and hot gases around or through water in a steam boiler

⁴**flue** \"\ *n* -s [Flem *vluwe*, fr. F *velu* shaggy — more at VELVET] : soft downy material: as **a** : soft fluffy lint or debris ⟨swept the ~ from under the beds⟩ **b** : feather vane freed from quill and shaft; *esp* : one of soft fluffy feathers (as of the ostrich) ⟨a dainty cap trimmed with curled ostrich ~⟩

⁵**flue** \"\ *adj* [origin unknown] *dial Eng* : thin and sickly : FEEBLE

flue-cure \ˈ≈,≈\ *vt* [³*flue*] : to cure (tobacco) by means of heat transmitted through a flue without exposure to smoke or fumes — compare FIRE-CURE

flued \ˈflüd\ *adj* : having a flue

flue dust *n* : finely divided metal or metallic compounds escaping with the flue gases of a smelter or metallurgical furnace; *broadly* : such matter with accompanying fumes

flue gas *n* : the mixture of gases resulting from combustion and other reactions in a furnace, passing off through the smoke flue, composed largely of nitrogen, carbon dioxide, carbon monoxide, water vapor, and often sulfur dioxide, and sometimes serving as a source from which carbon dioxide or other compounds are recovered

fluegelhorn *var of* FLÜGELHORN

flue·less \ˈflüləs\ *adj, of a fire or combustion device* : having no flue : discharging by-products of combustion into the surrounding atmosphere ⟨a ~ oil heater⟩

flue lining *n* : a lining for chimney flues that consists of successive hollow sections of rectangular or circular hard burned clay and serves to protect the house against escape of gases or fire from the flue, the brick of the chimney usu. being built around the lining

flu·el·lin *also* **flu·el·len** \flüˈelən\ *n* -s [W *llysiau Llywelyn*, lit., Llewelyn's herbs, prob. after *Llywelyn* ab Iorwerth (Llewelyn the Great) †1240 or *Llywelyn* ab Gruffydd †1282 princes of Wales] **1** : either of two speedwells (*Veronica officinalis* and *V. chamaedrys*) **2** : TOADFLAX **3** : CANCERWORT **4** : MOUNTAIN PARSLEY

flu·el·lite \ˈflüə,līt, flüˈe,l-\ *n* -s [*fluorine* + *wavellite*] : a mineral $AlF_3.H_2O$ consisting of aluminum fluoride in colorless or white crystals

flue·man \ˈflümən, -,man\ *n, pl* **fluemen** : a worker who cleans boiler flues

flu·en·cy \ˈflüənsē, -si\ *n* -ES [LL *fluentia* action of flowing, fr. L *fluent-, fluens* + *-ia* -y] **1** *obs* : ABUNDANCE, PROFUSION **2** : fluent quality : smoothness, ease, and readiness esp. of utterance ⟨spoke with great poise and ~⟩; *sometimes* : VOLUBILITY ⟨her ~ was like the insistent chatter of a stream⟩

¹**flu·ent** \ˈflüənt\ *adj* [L *fluent-, fluens*, pres. part. of *fluere* to flow — more at FLUID] **1** : flowing or capable of flowing esp. with ease or freedom : LIQUID, FLUID ⟨a ~ stream⟩ ⟨~ metal in a crucible⟩ **2** : FREE, EASY, SMOOTH ⟨a ~ technique⟩ ⟨the Moon upon her ~ route defiant of a road —Emily Dickinson⟩: as **a** : versed in the use of language : ready with words ⟨a speaker ~ in Japanese⟩; *sometimes* : noted for or addicted to the use of profanity ⟨George Washington, who was ~ himself . . . issued . . . orders against swearing in the ranks —Burges Johnson⟩ **b** *of language* : easy and flowing : pleasingly graceful ⟨~ speech⟩ **c** *of a performance* : smooth and finished : giving an effect of ease and accurate rendition ⟨a ~ reading of the part⟩ ⟨his versification is ~ —*Brit. Book News*⟩ **syn** see VOCAL

²**fluent** *n* -s [L *fluentum*, fr. *fluent-, fluens*] *obs* : a current of water : STREAM

flu·ent·ly *adv* : in a fluent manner : with fluency

flu·ent·ness *n* -ES : the quality or state of being fluent

flue pipe *n* **1** : a pipe (as of an organ) whose tone is produced by the striking of a current of air upon an edge causing a wave motion in the air within — compare REED PIPE **2** : a pipe connecting the smoke outlet of a furnace or stove with the flue of a chimney

flues *pl of* FLUE

flue stop *n* **1** : a pipe-organ stop made up of flue pipes **2** *or* **flue stopper** : a stop for a flue opening

flue surface *n* : the aggregate surface area of boiler flues exposed to flame or hot gases

fluework \ˈ≈,≈\ *n* : pipe-organ stops in which the sound is caused by wind passing through a flue or fissure and striking an edge above — compare REEDWORK

¹**fluff** \ˈfləf\ *n* -s [prob. alter. of ⁴*flue*] **1** : NAP, DOWN, FLUE: as **a** : the soft downy plumage on the abdomen and between the thighs of most birds — see GOOSE illustration **b** : the basal downy part of a feather **2** : something fluffy : a fluffy mass ⟨a ~ of cloud near the horizon⟩: as **a** : a food rendered light and fluffy by incorporating air through beating — used esp. of dishes (as whips or soufflés) of which the texture depends on beaten egg whites **b** : something essentially trivial and lacking importance or solid worth; *esp* : a light amusing theatrical offering without real message or significance ⟨his latest is an amusing little ~ well suited to the summer theater⟩ **c** *slang* : a

young woman — used chiefly in the phrase *bit of fluff* **3 :** an error, fault, or blunder ⟨the senator made a ~ when he called attention to his party's record on this issue⟩: as **a :** a forgetting or bungling of lines (as in a theatrical performance); *sometimes* **:** the missing of a cue **b :** a misplay in a sport or game

²fluff \"\ *vb* -ED/-ING/-S *vi* **1 a :** to become fluffy ⟨the omelet ~*ed* beautifully⟩ **b :** to move lightly like fluff ⟨streaks of cloud ~*ed* in from the water⟩ **2 :** to make a mistake **:** FAIL, BUNGLE: as **a :** to play a theatrical role blunderingly **:** forget one's lines or deliver them badly **b :** to misplay in a sport ⟨he was doing well until he ~*ed* at the seventh hole⟩ ~ *vt* **1 :** to make fluffy ⟨~ out your hair⟩ ⟨~*ing* up the pillows⟩ **2 :** to wheel (a skin) usu. to produce a smoothly napped or uniform surface **3 :** to make a mistake in **:** BUNGLE: as **a :** to play (a theatrical role) blunderingly **:** forget or deliver badly (one's lines) **b :** MISPLAY ⟨~*ed* his stroke and missed the green⟩ **:** BOTCH ⟨the quarterback ~*ed* the play and lost his side control of the ball⟩

³fluff \"\ *n* -S [prob. of imit. origin] *chiefly Scot* **:** a puff or whiff ⟨a ~ of smoke⟩

fluff·er \'fləfə(r)\ *n* -S **:** one that fluffs ⟨a constant pillow ~⟩

fluff–gib \'=,gib\ *n* [³*fluff* + *gib* (cat)] *Scot* **:** a gunpowder squib

fluff·i·ly \'fləfəlē, -li\ *adv* **:** in a fluffy manner

fluff·i·ness \-fēnəs, -fin-\ *n* -ES **:** the quality or state of being fluffy

fluff louse *n* **:** a small broad biting louse (*Goniocotes gallinae*) that lives and feeds on the fluff at the base of the feathers on domestic poultry and some other birds

fluff·ment \-fmənt\ *n* -S [¹*fluff* + *-ment*] **:** something light, loose, or showy ⟨a ~ of talk⟩ ⟨soft ~*s* of material flowing from the shoulder⟩

fluffy \-fē,-fi\ *adj* -ER/-EST [¹*fluff* + *-y*] **1 :** having, covered with, or resembling fluff or down ⟨a ~ young chick⟩ ⟨~ whiskers⟩: **a :** light and soft or airy ⟨a ~ omelet⟩ ⟨big ~ cushions⟩ **b** *of soil* **:** loose and friable **c** *of snow* **:** consisting of large loose flakes with little tendency to cohere **d** *of clothing* **:** light and full ⟨a ~ summer dress⟩ **2 :** light in mind or intellectual content **:** lacking in brilliance or decisive quality ⟨a pleasant ~ little woman⟩ ⟨soft, vague, ~, uncertain policies —Geoffrey Crowther⟩ ⟨a ~ comedy⟩

fluffy–ruffle \'==,==\ *adj* **:** having a fluffy ruffled margin ⟨large *fluffy-ruffle* blossoms⟩

flü·gel *or* **flu·gel** \'flügəl\ *n* -S [G *flügel* lit., wing, fr. MHG *vlügel*; fr. the shape; akin to MLG *vlögel* wing, MD *vlōgel, vleugel*; derivatives fr. the root of E *fly*] **:** the grand piano or its predecessor

flü·gel·horn *or* **flue·gel·horn** *also* **flu·gel·horn** \-,hȯrn\ *n* -S [G *flügelhorn*, fr. *flügel* wing, flank + *horn*, fr. OHG; fr. its use to signal the flanking drivers in a battue — more at HORN] **1 :** a bugle with valves that differs from the cornet only in having a larger bore **2 :** one of the bugle family of brass instruments similar to the saxhorn

flugelman *var of* FUGLEMAN

fluible *adj* [L *fluere* to flow + E *-ible*] *obs* **:** FLUID

¹flu·id \'flüəd\ *adj* [F or L; F *fluide*, fr. L *fluidus*, fr. *fluere* to flow; akin to Gk *phlyein, phlyzein* to boil over, chatter, L *flare* to blow — more at BLOW] **1 :** having particles that easily move and change their relative position without a separation of the mass and that easily yield to pressure **:** capable of flowing **2 a :** likely to change or move **:** not fixed or rigid ⟨a ~ military situation⟩ **b :** characterized by or employing a smooth easy style or producing such an effect esp. in literature or art ⟨a ~ style⟩ ⟨~ restful lines⟩ **c :** free or tending to alter in form or content ⟨~ consciousness⟩ **d :** available for a different use or application **:** not currently pledged or firmly engaged ⟨~ capital⟩; *esp* **:** such as may be rapidly or immediately converted into cash ⟨~ assets⟩ **e :** shifting from place to place **:** MOBILE ⟨the ~ population of large cities⟩ **3 a :** of, relating to, or like a fluid **b :** characteristic of a fluid ⟨the ~ state⟩ **c :** employing, based on, or acting through or like a fluid or the fluid state ⟨~ power⟩ ⟨~ catalytic cracking of oil⟩ — compare FLUIDIZE; see FLUID CATALYST **syn** see LIQUID

²fluid \"\ *n* -S **1 :** a substance that alters its shape in response to any force however small, that tends to flow or to conform to the outline of its container, and that includes gases and liquids and in strictly technical use certain plastic solids and mixtures of solids and liquids capable of flow **2 :** a nonsolid substance in the body of an animal or a plant ⟨cerebrospinal ~⟩ ⟨body ~*s*⟩ **3 :** a hypothetical substance to which a particular phenomenon (as heat or electricity) was formerly attributed

flu·id·al \-dᵊl\ *adj* [²*fluid* + *-al*] **:** relating to or characteristic of a fluid or to flowing motion ⟨~ arrangement of components of metamorphic rock⟩ — **flu·id·al·ly** \-ᵊlē\ *adv*

fluidal texture *n* **:** texture of rock in which the arrangement of the minute crystals shows the lines of flow of the material while molten

fluid catalyst *n* **:** a solid catalyst in a finely divided state that is kept in constant motion in a stream of gas (as in the cracking of petroleum) **:** a fluidized catalyst

fluid coal *or* **fluidized coal** *n* **:** pulverized coal that is mixed with air and that is capable of being forced through pipes

fluid–compressed \'==,=\ *adj, of steel* **:** compressed while in a fluid state so as to eliminate all gases and increase structural homogeneity

fluid coupling *also* **fluid flywheel** *n* **:** a coupling (as a fluid drive) in which fluid (as oil) intervenes between moving members to transmit pressure and torque

fluid die *n* **:** one of a set of shaping dies in which a plunger descends upon a liquid previously placed in the shell to be shaped and causes the liquid to force the shell into the design in the dies

fluid dram *or* **fluid drachm** *n* **:** FLUIDRAM

fluid drive *or* **fluid clutch** *n* **:** an automotive power coupling that operates on a hydraulic turbine principle, the flywheel of the engine having a set of turbine blades connected directly to it and driving them in oil thereby turning another set of turbine blades attached to the transmission gears of the automobile

fluid dynamics *n pl but sing or pl in constr* **:** a branch of fluid mechanics that deals with fluid motion (as flow and wave motion)

fluidextract \'==,=\ *n* **:** a liquid preparation of a vegetable drug containing alcohol as a solvent or as a preservative or both with the therapeutic constituents of one gram of the standard drug in each milliliter — called also *liquid extract*

flu·id·glycerate \'==+\ *n* **:** a concentrated liquid preparation made by extracting a vegetable drug with a menstruum consisting of one volume of glycerol and three volumes of water to produce a drug strength equivalent to that of a fluidextract

flu·id·ible \'flüədəbəl, (')flü'id-\ *adj* **:** capable of flow under pressure ⟨the ~ state of metamorphic rock⟩

flu·id·ic \(')flü'idik\ *adj* **:** of, relating to, or having the characteristics of a fluid — used esp. by spiritualists

flu·id·i·form \-də,fȯrm\ *adj* [²*fluid* + *-iform*] **:** occurring in the form of or appearing to be a fluid **:** ethereal or intangible **:** FLUIDIC

flu·id·i·fy \flü'idə,fī\ *vb* -ED/-ING/-ES [¹*fluid* + *-ify*] *vt* **:** to make fluid or flowing ⟨rocks that have been *fluidified*⟩ ~ *vi* **:** to become fluid **:** accumulate fluid ⟨ore ~*ing* in the smelter⟩ ⟨the valley *fluidifies* each spring into a shallow lake as snow melts in the mountains⟩

flu·id·i·ty \-dəd.ē, -dətē, -i\ *n* -ES [prob. fr. F *fluidité*, fr. MF, fr. *fluide* fluid + *-ité* -ity — more at FLUID] **1 a :** the quality, state, or degree of being fluid **:** a liquid or gaseous state **b :** the physical property of a substance that enables it to flow and that is a measure of the rate at which it is deformed by a shearing stress as contrasted with viscosity **:** the reciprocal of viscosity **2 :** changeable or unstable quality: as **a :** easy adaptability **:** FLEXIBILITY ⟨showed the ~ of his mind by changing it frequently⟩ **b :** smooth flowing quality (as of language) ⟨the graceful ~ of the rhythm⟩ **c :** tendency to movement of population into or out of an area; *often* **:** the recurrent ebb and flow of population (as between an urban industrial and a suburban residential area)

flu·id·iza·tion \,flüədə'zāshən, -,dī'z-\ *n* -S **:** the process of fluidizing or the state of being fluidized ⟨~ of a catalyst⟩

flu·id·ize \'flüə,dīz\ *vt* -ED/-ING/-S **:** to cause to behave like a fluid; *specif* **:** to suspend (a finely divided solid) in a rapidly moving stream of gas or vapor so as to induce flowing movement of the whole (as in the transport of flour by air blast or in the catalytic cracking of petroleum) — **flu·id·iz·er** \-zə(r)\ *n* -S

flu·id·ly *adv* **:** in a fluid manner **:** with fluidity

fluid mechanics *n pl but sing or pl in constr* **:** a branch of mechanics that deals with the special properties of liquids and gases

fluid motor *n* **:** a motor commonly of the turbine type that is driven by water or compressed air

flu·id·ness *n* -ES **:** the quality or state of being fluid **:** FLUIDITY

fluidounce \'==;=\ *n* **:** either of two units of liquid capacity: **a :** a U.S. unit equivalent to $\frac{1}{16}$ pint or 1.804 cubic inches **b :** a British unit equivalent to $\frac{1}{20}$ pint or 1.7339 cubic inches — see MEASURE table

flu·idram *or* **flu·idrachm** \'flüə(d)'dram, -raa(ə)m\ *n* [¹*fluid* + *dram* or *drachm*] **:** either of two units of liquid capacity equal to ⅛ fluid ounce: **a :** a U.S. unit equivalent to 0.225 cubic inches **b :** a British unit equal to 0.2167 cubic inches — see MEASURE table

fluid stress *n* **:** stress associated with plastic flow in a solid

fluid transmission *n* **:** automotive transmission that incorporates a fluid drive

flu·i·gram *or* **flu·i·gramme** \'flüə,gram, -raa(ə)m\ *n* [¹*fluid* + *gram* or *gramme*] **:** a cubic centimeter of liquid

flu·ish \'flüish\ *adj* [*flu* + *-ish*] **:** mildly affected with influenza

¹fluke \'flük\ *n* -S [ME *fluke, floke*, fr. OE *flōc*; akin to ON *flōki* flounder, OHG *flah* smooth — more at FLAKE] **1 :** FLATFISH; *esp* **:** SUMMER FLOUNDER **2 :** a flattened, leaf-shaped or lanceolate digenetic trematode worm; *sometimes* **:** TREMATODE — see LIVER FLUKE

²fluke \"\ *n* -S [perh. fr. ¹*fluke*; fr. the flat shape, resembling a flounder] **1 :** the part of an anchor that fastens in the ground; *esp* **:** the broad end of each arm — see ANCHOR illustration **2 :** something shaped like the broad end of the arm of an anchor: as **a :** the barbed head or one of the barbs of a harpoon, whaling lance, arrow, or similar weapon **b :** one of the lobes of a whale's tail **c :** an instrument used to clean a hole in rock preparatory to blasting

³fluke \"\ *vt* -ED/-ING/-S **:** to make (a dead whale) fast by the tail (as for removing and processing blubber)

⁴fluke \"\ *n* -S [origin unknown] **1 :** an accidentally successful stroke at billiards or pool **2 :** an accidental advantage or result of an action **:** an extraordinary stroke of good or bad luck ⟨he won by a ~⟩ ⟨such a fall was a pure ~⟩

⁵fluke \"\ *vb* -ED/-ING/-S *vt* **:** to get, make, do, or succeed in by chance or accident ~ *vi* **:** to succeed or fail by chance

fluked \-kt\ *adj* [¹*fluke* + *-ed*] *of an animal* **:** infested with flukes

¹fluke·less \-kləs\ *adj* [¹*fluke* + *-less*] **:** free from flukes ⟨keep the flock as nearly ~ as possible⟩

²flukeless \"\ *adj* [²*fluke* + *-less*] **:** lacking a fluke

flukeworm \'=,=\ *n* [¹*fluke* + *worm*] **:** ¹FLUKE 2

¹fluky *also* **fluk·ey** \'flükē, -ki\ *adj* **flukier; flukiest** [¹*fluke* + *-y*] **:** infested with flukes ⟨~ meadows⟩ ⟨~ sheep⟩

²fluky \"\ *adj* -ER/-EST [⁴*fluke* + *-y*] **1 :** happening or depending on chance rather than skill **2 :** light and uncertain **:** UNSTEADY, CAPRICIOUS — used esp. of wind

flum \'fləm\ *Scot var of* FLAM

¹flume \'flüm\ *n* -S [prob. fr. obs. E, river, fr. ME *flum*, fr. OF *flum, flun*, fr. L *flumen*, fr. *fluere* to flow — more at FLUID] **1 :** a ravine or gorge with a stream running through **2 a :** an inclined channel for conveying water usu. from a distance for various uses (as power production, transportation, or irrigation) **b :** a channel (as of metal) placed in a stream of water to measure the volume or rate of flow **c :** a channel for admitting water to a water turbine

²flume \"\ *vb* -ED/-ING/-S *vt* **1 :** to divert the water of (a stream) by means of a flume; *also* **:** to divert (water) by means of a flume **2 :** to transport (as fish to a cannery or logs to a mill) by way of a flume ~ *vi* **:** to construct or use a flume ⟨*fluming* along the edge of the slope⟩

flu·mer·in \'flümərən, flü'mər·ən\ *n* -S [*fluorescein* + *mercury* + *-in*] **:** a dark red powder $C_{20}H_{10}O_6Na_2Hg$ with a greenish fluorescence that is the disodium salt of hydroxy-mercuri-fluorescein

flume runner *n* **:** a worker who prevents or releases log jams in a flume by moving logs with a cant hook or peavey — called also *herder*

flum·ma·did·dle *also* **flum·a·did·dle** \'fləmə'did'ᵊl\ *or* **flum·did·dle** \-m'-\ *or* **flum·mer·did·dle** \-mə(r)'-\ *or* **flum·my·did·dle** \-mē'-\ *or* **fum·a·did·dle** \'fəmə'-\ *n* -S [perh. alter. of *flummery*] **1 :** something foolish or worthless **:** NONSENSE, TRASH **2 :** BAUBLE, FRILL

flum·mer \'fləmə(r)\ *vt* -ED/-ING/-S [back-formation fr. *flummery*] *archaic* **:** to get around (a person) esp. by coaxing or flattery **:** BEGUILE, HUMBUG

flum·mery \-m(ə)rē, -ri\ *n* -ES [W *llymru*] **1 a :** a soft jelly or porridge made of flour or meal — compare SOWENS **b :** any of several sweet dishes chiefly for dessert; *esp* **:** a molded cold sweet of cereal with fruit or nuts **2 a :** something poor, trashy, or not worth having **b :** empty compliment or foolish deceptive language **:** HUMBUG; *sometimes* **:** an instance or the use of this ⟨greatly addicted to ~⟩

¹flum·mox *also* **flum·mix** *or* **flum·mux** \'fləməks, -mēks\ *vb* -ED/-ING/-ES [origin unknown] *vt* **:** to throw into perplexity **:** embarrass greatly **:** CONFOUND, DISCONCERT ~ *vi* **:** to fail or give up **:** COLLAPSE ⟨his scheme ~*ed* and left him high and dry⟩

²flummox *also* **flummix** *or* **flummux** \"\ *n* -ES **:** FAILURE; *also* **:** a state of confusion, perplexity, or embarrassment

¹flump \'fləmp\ *n* -S [imit.] **:** a dull heavy sound (as of a fall); *also* **:** a movement producing such a sound ⟨dropped into the chair with a ~⟩

²flump \"\ *vb* -ED/-ING/-S *vi* **:** to move or fall suddenly and heavily **:** PLUMP, PLOP ⟨~*ed* down into his chair with a sigh⟩ ~ *vt* **:** to place or drop with a flump ⟨~*ing* his books on the table⟩

flung *past of* FLING

¹flunk \'fləŋk\ *vb* -ED/-ING/-S [perh. blend of *flinch* and *funk*] *vi* **1 :** to fail esp. in a recitation or examination **2 :** to back out (as from an undertaking) through fear ~ *vt* **1 :** to fail or dismiss (a student) for deficiency or incompetence ⟨the professor ~*ed* him out after the midyear examination⟩ **2 :** FAIL ⟨~*ed* history⟩ ⟨expected to ~ his chemistry examination⟩ — **flunk·er** \-kə(r)\ *n* -S

²flunk \"\ *n* -S **:** an instance of a failure; *specif* **:** a failure in a recitation or examination

flun·ky *or* **flun·key** \'fləŋkē, -ki\ *n, pl* **flunkies** *or* **flunkeys** [fr. Sc dial., of unknown origin] **1 a :** a usu. liveried servant; *esp* **:** FOOTMAN — often used derogatorily **b :** any of various minor functionaries: as (1) **:** a ship's steward (2) **:** BULL COOK (3) **:** an engineer's helper in a logging camp (4) **:** an unskilled or general laborer **2 a :** an obsequious or cringing person **:** TOADY **b :** an unimportant or subordinate person

flun·ky·dom \-dəm\ *n* -S **:** FLUNKIES

flun·ky·hood \-,hüd\ *n* -S **:** the state of being a flunky

flun·ky·ish \-kēish, -ki·ish\ *adj* **:** resembling or suitable to a flunky

flun·ky·ism \-kē,izəm, -ki,-\ *n* -S **:** the quality or characteristics of a flunky

fluo– *comb form* [ISV, prob. by shortening] **:** FLUOR- 1 ⟨*fluoberyllate*⟩

fluo·aluminate \'flü(,)ō+\ *n* [*fluo-* + *aluminate*] **:** a complex salt (as cryolite) characterized by the anion AlF_6^{---} containing fluorine and aluminum

fluo·borate \'flüə+\ *n* [*fluo* + *-borate*] **:** a salt or ester of fluoboric acid — called also *borofluoride*

fluo·boric acid \"+...\ *n* [*fluo-* + *boric*] **:** a poisonous strong acid HBF_4 made in solution by dissolving boron trifluoride in water or by adding boric acid to concentrated hydrofluoric acid and used in solution or in the form of salts chiefly in electroplating baths — called also *borofluoric acid*

fluo·bo·rite \,flüə'bōr,īt, -bȯr-\ *n* -S [*fluoborate* + *-ite*] **:** a mineral $Mg_3(BO_3)(F,OH)_3$ consisting of magnesium fluoborate occurring in hexagonal prisms

fluo·cerite *also* **fluo·cerine** \'flüə+\ *n* -S [*fluocerite* fr. G *fluozerit*, modif. (influenced by *-it* -ite) of F *fluocérine*, fr. *fluo-* + *cérine* cerine; *fluocerine* fr. F *fluocérine*] **:** a mineral (Ce,La, Nd)F_3 consisting of reddish yellow fluoride of cerium and related metals

flu·on·o·mist \flü'änəməst\ *n* -S [³*flue* + *-onomist* (as in *economist*)] *Brit* **:** CHIMNEY SWEEP 1

fluo·phosphate \'flüə+\ *n* [*fluo-* + *phosphate*] **:** FLUOROPHOSPHATE

flu·or \'flü,ȯ(ə)r, 'flü(ə)r\ *n* -S [in sense 1a, fr. L, fr. *fluere* to flow; in other senses, fr. NL, fr. L — more at FLUID] **1** *obs* **:** STREAM, FLOWING **b :** MENSTRUATION **2** *obs* **a :** the fluid state **b :** FLUID **:** a fluid mass **3 a** [trans. of G *fluss*] *obs* **:** a mineral belonging to a group including fluorite and characterized by the alchemists as resembling gems and usable as metallurgical fluxes **b** *chiefly Brit* **:** FLUORITE

fluor– *or* **fluoro–** *comb form* [F *fluor-*, fr. NL *fluor* (mineral belonging to a group including fluorite)] **1 a :** fluorine ⟨*fluorhydric*⟩ ⟨*fluoroform*⟩ **b** *now usu fluoro-* **:** containing fluorine in place of hydrogen — in names of organic compounds ⟨*fluorobenzene*⟩ **c** *now usu fluoro-* **:** containing fluorine regarded as replacing hydroxyl or oxygen or as coordinated to a central atom — in names of inorganic acids and salts ⟨*fluoromolybdate*⟩ **d :** containing fluorine as fluoride sometimes replacing another element or group — in names of minerals and salts ⟨*fluorapatite*⟩ ⟨*fluorochloride*⟩ **2** *also* **fluori–** **:** fluorescence ⟨*fluorene*⟩ ⟨*fluoroscope*⟩ ⟨*fluorimeter*⟩

flu·o·ran·thene \flü(ə)'ran,thēn, flō'-,flȯ'-\ *n* -S [ISV *fluor-* + *anthracene*; orig. formed as G *fluoranthen*] **:** a white crystalline hydrocarbon $C_{16}H_{10}$ obtained esp. from the coal-tar distillates having the highest boiling points and from petroleum; 1,8-*ortho*-phenylene-naphthalene

flu·or·apatite \'flü(ə)'r, flō'r, flȯ'r + ,-\ *n* [G *fluorapatit*, fr. *fluor-* + *apatit* apatite] **:** an apatite containing fluorine: as **a :** apatite in which fluorine predominates over chlorine, hydroxyl, and carbonate **b :** calcium phosphate fluoride $Ca_5F(PO_4)_3$

fluor crown *n* [*fluor-*] **:** a crown glass that contains fluorine, that has a low refractive index, and that is used esp. for optical equipment

flu·o·rene \'flü(ə),rēn, 'flōr,ēn, 'flȯ,rēn\ *n* -S [ISV *fluor-* + *-ene*; orig. formed as F *fluorène*] **:** a colorless crystalline cyclic hydrocarbon $C_{13}H_{10}$ that has a violet fluorescence and that is obtained usu. from the coal-tar distillate which boils between naphthalene and anthracene; *ortho*-diphenylene-methane

flu·o·resce \(')flü(ə)'res, (')flōr,es, (')flȯ'res\ *vb* -ED/-ING/-S [back-formation fr. *fluorescence* & *fluorescent*] *vi* **:** to produce, undergo, or exhibit fluorescence ~ *vt* **:** to produce (color) in fluorescing ⟨~*s* a dark red color under ultraviolet irradiation⟩

flu·o·res·ce·in \flü(ə)'resēən, flō'-,flȯ'-\ *n* -S [*fluoresce* + *-in*] **:** a yellow granular or red crystalline phthalein dye $C_{20}H_{12}O_5$ giving a brilliant yellow-green fluorescence in alkaline solution and having a number of applications based chiefly on its visibility at high dilution or its ready conversion to eosin and related dyes — see DYE table I (under *Acid Yellow 73*)

fluorescein sodium *n* **:** URANIN

flu·o·res·cence \flü(ə)'resᵊn(t)s, flō'-, flȯ'-\ *n* -S [*fluor* (fluorite) + *-escence*] **1 :** the emission by a substance of electromagnetic radiation esp. in the form of visible light as the immediate result of and only during the absorption of radiation from some other source; *also* **:** the property of emitting such radiation **2 :** the radiation emitted during fluorescence — compare LUMINESCENCE

fluorescence microscope *n* **:** a microscope equipped to irradiate material under examination with ultraviolet in order to detect or study fluorescent components — called also *ultraviolet microscope*

flu·o·res·cent \(')flü(ə)'resᵊnt, (')flōr'e-, (')flȯ're-\ *adj* [*fluor* (fluorite) + *-escent*] **:** having, characterized by, or showing fluorescence; *also* **:** caused by fluorescence

fluorescent brightener *n* **:** a chemical agent used for its fluorescent brightening effect — see DYE table I

fluorescent lamp *n* **:** a tubular electric lamp that is coated on its inner surface with a phosphor and that contains mercury vapor whose bombardment by electrons from the cathode provides ultraviolet light which causes the phosphor to emit visible light either of a selected color or closely approximating daylight

fluorescent screen *n* **:** a screen (as of cardboard or glass) one face of which is coated with a salt (as calcium tungstate) that emits light under the action of X rays or cathode rays

fluoresci– *comb form* [*fluorescence*] **:** fluorescence ⟨*fluorescigenic*⟩

fluori– — see FLUOR-

flu·o·ri·date \'flürə,dāt, 'flōr-, 'flȯr- *usu* -ād.+V\ *vt* -ED/-ING/-S [back-formation fr. *fluoridation*] **:** to add a fluoride to (as drinking water) — compare FLUORIDIZE, FLUORINATE

flu·o·ri·da·tion \,flürə'dāshən, ,flōr-, ,flȯr-\ *n* -S [*fluoride* + *-ation*] **:** the addition of fluorine usu. as a fluoride to something: as **a :** the introduction of fluorine into rocks as indicated by the formation of such minerals as fluorite and topaz **b :** the adding of a fluoride to drinking water ⟨~ of public water supplies for prevention of tooth decay in children⟩

flu·o·ri·da·tion·ist \-sh(ə)nəst\ *n* -S **:** an advocate of the fluoridation of public water supplies

flu·o·ride \'flü(ə),rīd, 'flōr,īd, 'flȯ,rīd, -rəd\ *n* -S [*fluor-* + *-ide*] **:** a binary compound of fluorine usu. with a more electropositive element or radical **:** a salt or ester of hydrofluoric acid

flu·o·ri·di·za·tion \,flürədə'zāshən, ,flōr-, ,flȯr-, -,dī'z-\ *n* -S **:** the act or process of fluoridizing

flu·o·ri·dize \'==,dīz\ *vt* -ED/-ING/-S [*fluoride* + *-ize*] **:** to treat (as the teeth) with a fluoride — compare FLUORIDATE

fluorimeter *var of* FLUOROMETER

flu·o·ri·nate \'flürə,nāt, 'flōr-,'flȯr-, *usu* -ād.+V\ *vt* -ED/-ING/-S [*fluorine* + *-ate*] **:** to treat or cause to combine with fluorine or any of certain compounds of fluorine **:** introduce fluorine into (as an organic compound) — compare FLUORIDATE

flu·o·ri·na·tion \,=='nāshən\ *n* -S **:** the act or process of fluorinating

flu·o·rine \'flü(ə),rēn, 'flōr,ēn, 'flȯ,rēn, -rən\ *n* -S [F, fr. NL *fluor* (mineral belonging to a group including fluorite) + F *-ine*] **:** a nonmetallic univalent element belonging to the halogens that is normally a pale yellowish flammable irritating toxic gas, that is one of the most powerful oxidizing agents known, attacking water, most metals, and organic compounds, that occurs naturally only in combination in the form of minerals (as fluorite, cryolite, or fluorapatite) and in small amounts in several other minerals, in mineral waters, and in bones and teeth, that is best isolated by electrolysis of a molten mixture of hydrogen fluoride and potassium fluoride, and that is used chiefly in making fluorine compounds — symbol *F*; see ELEMENT table

fluorine test *n* **:** a determination of the relative age of fossil and subfossil bones that is based on the fact that the fluorine content of bones in contact with earth tends to increase through the ages and that is used chiefly in dating anthropological specimens

flu·o·rite \'flü(ə),rīt, 'flōr,īt, 'flȯ,rīt, *usu* -īd.+V\ *n* -S [It, fr. NL *fluor* + It *-ite*] **:** a transparent or translucent mineral of many different colors consisting of calcium fluoride, occurring commonly in crystalline cubes with perfect octahedral cleavage or in massive form, and being used as a flux, as a source of fluorine compounds, and in preparation of opalescent and opaque glasses and of enamel for cooking utensils

fluorite green *n* **:** a moderate yellowish green that is greener, lighter, and stronger than tarragon, yellower, lighter, and slightly stronger than malachite green, and yellower, stronger, and slightly lighter than verdigris

fluorite violet *n* **:** a dark to very dark purple

flu·o·ro \'flü(ə)(,)rō, 'flōr(,)ō, 'flȯ(,)rō\ *adj* [*fluor-*] **:** containing fluorine — used esp. of organic compounds; compare FLUOR- 1

fluoro– — see FLUOR-

flu·o·ro·acetate \'flü(ə)(,)rō, 'flōr(,)ō, 'flȯ(,)rō +\ *n* [*fluor-* + *acetate*] **:** a salt or ester of fluoroacetic acid; *esp* **:** SODIUM FLUOROACETATE

flu·o·ro·acetic acid \"+...\ *n* [*fluor-* + *acetic*] **:** a poisonous crystalline acid FCH_2COOH obtained from the gifblaar of southern Africa or made from chloroacetic acid

flu·o·ro·carbon \"+\ *n* [ISV *fluor-* + *carbon*] **:** any of a class of chemically inert compounds (as tetrafluoroethylene) composed entirely of carbon and fluorine and used chiefly as lubricants and in making resins and plastics **:** a perfluorinated hydrocarbon

flu·o·ro·chemical \"+\ *n* [*fluor-* + *chemical*] **:** any of various chemical compounds containing fluorine; *esp* **:** an organic compound (as a fluorocarbon) in which fluorine has replaced a large proportion of the hydrogen attached to carbon

flu·o·ro·chrome \ˈ=(=)(ˌ)=+ˌ-\ *n* [ISV *fluor-* + *chrome*] **:** any of various fluorescent substances (as the alkaloid berberine or the dye auramine) used in biological staining to produce secondary fluorescence in the specimen

flu·o·ro·form \"+ˌ-\ *n* [ISV *fluor-* + *-form* (as in *chloroform*)] **:** a colorless gas CHF_3 similar to chloroform; trifluoro= methane

flu·o·rog·ra·phy \flu̇(ə)ˈrägrəfē, flō'-,flȯ'-\ *n* -ES [*fluor-* + *-graphy*] **1 :** the art or process of etching on glass with hydrofluoric acid **2 a :** PHOTOFLUOROGRAPHY **b :** the photography of a fluorescing body

flu·o·roid \ˈflü(ə),rȯid, ˈflōr,ȯid, ˈflȯ,rȯid\ *n* -S [ISV *fluor-* + *-oid*] **:** TETRAHEXAHEDRON

Flu·o·rol \ˈflu̇(ə),rōl, ˈflōr,ōl, ˈflȯ,rōl, -rōl\ *trademark* — used for a fluorescent brightener; see DYE table I (under *Fluorescent Brightener 74*)

flu·o·rom·e·ter \flu̇(ə)ˈräməd·ə(r), flō'-,flȯ'-\ *or* **flu·o·rim·e·ter** \-rim-\ *n* [*fluor-* + *-meter*] **:** an instrument that measures fluorescence and is used esp. to determine intensities of radiations (as X rays) from the fluorescence they produce or concentrations of substances (as uranium or vitamins of the B complex) capable of forming fluorescent compounds — **flu·o·ro·met·ric** \ˌflu̇(ə)rə¦me·trik, ¦flōr-, ¦flȯr-\ *adj* — **flu·o·ro·met·ri·cal·ly** \-trək(ə)lē\ *adv* — **flu·o·rom·e·try** \flu̇(ə)ˈrämə·trē, flō'-,flȯ'-\ *n* -ES

flu·o·ro·phosphate \¦flü(ə)(ˌ)rō, ¦flōr(ˌ)ō, ¦flȯ(ˌ)rō+\ *n* [ISV *fluor-* + *phosphate*] **:** a salt or ester of a fluorophosphoric acid (as mono-fluorophosphoric acid)

flu·o·ro·phosphoric acid \"+...-\ *n* [*fluor-* + *phosphoric*] **:** any of three acids made by reaction of phosphorus pentoxide with hydrogen fluoride; *esp* **:** the mono-fluoro acid H_2PO_3F obtained as a colorless viscous liquid and as salts and esters some of which are nerve gases

flu·o·ro·photometer \"+\ *n* [*fluor-* + *photometer*] **:** FLUOROMETER — **flu·o·ro·photometric** \"+\ *adj* — **flu·o·ro·photometry** \"+\ *n*

flu·o·ro·radiography \"+\ *n* [*fluor-* + *radiography*] **:** PHOTOFLUOROGRAPHY

flu·o·ro·roentgenography \"+\ *n* [*fluor-* + *roentgenography*] **:** PHOTOFLUOROGRAPHY

[1]**flu·o·ro·scope** \ˈflu̇rə,skōp, ˈflōr-,ˈflȯr-\ *n* [ISV *fluor-* + *-scope*] **:** an instrument used chiefly in industry and in medical diagnosis for observing the internal structure of opaque objects (as metals or the living body) by means of the shadow cast by the object examined upon a fluorescent screen when placed between the screen and a source of X rays — **flu·o·ro·scop·ic** \¦==¦skäpik, -pēk\ *adj* — **flu·o·ro·scop·i·cal·ly** \-pək(ə)lē, -pēk-, -li\ *adv*

[2]**fluoroscope** \"\ *vt* -ED/-ING/-S **:** to examine by fluoroscopy

flu·o·ros·co·pist \flu̇(ə)ˈräskəpəst, flō'-,flȯ'-\ *n* -S **:** one who specializes in the use of the fluoroscope

flu·o·ros·co·py \-pē,-pi\ *n* -ES [ISV *fluor-* + *-scopy*] **:** observation or examination by means of a fluoroscope

flu·o·ro·sis \flu̇(ə)ˈrōsəs, flō'-,flȯ'-\ *n* -ES [NL, fr. *fluor-* + *-osis*] **:** an abnormal or poisoned condition (as mottled enamel on human teeth or a condition resembling osteopetrosis in Indian cattle) caused by fluorine or its compounds — **flu·o·rot·ic** \(ˈ)flü(ə)¦räd·ik, (ˈ)flō¦r-, (ˈ)flȯ¦rä-\ *adj*

flu·o·ro·thene \ˈflu̇rə,thēn, ˈflōr-,ˈflȯr-\ *n* -S [*fluor-* + *-thene* (fr. *ethylene*)] **:** any of various chemically inert insoluble plastics and resins made by polymerizing a derivative CF_2:CF-Cl of ethylene containing three atoms of fluorine and one of chlorine

fluor·spar \ˈflü(ə)r,=, ˈflōr,-, ˈflȯr,-, -üə,-, -ōə,-, -ō(ə),-\ *n* [*fluor-* + *spar*] **:** FLUORITE

fluo·silicate \¦flüə+\ *n* [ISV *fluo-* + *silicate*] **:** a salt of fluosilicic acid — called also *silicofluoride*

fluo·silicic acid \"+ . . . -\ *n* [ISV *fluo-* + *silicic*] **:** an unstable corrosive poisonous acid H_2SiF_6 that is known chiefly in aqueous solution and in the form of its salts, that is made usu. by the reaction of silicon tetrafluoride with water (as in the manufacture of superphosphate), and that is used esp. as a hardening and waterproofing agent for building materials and ceramic products, as a disinfectant, and in some electrochemical processes — called also *hydrofluosilicic acid*

fluo·sulfonic acid \"+ . . . -\ *n* [ISV *fluo-* + *sulfonic*] **:** a fuming corrosive liquid acid FSO_3H that has an irritating odor, that is made by treating hydrogen fluoride with sulfur trioxide, and that is used chiefly as a catalyst in alkylation and polymerization reactions and as a reagent in organic synthesis

flure \ˈflü(ə)r, -üə\ *dial var of* FLOOR

[1]**flurr** \ˈflər(·)\ *vb* -ED/-ING/-S [prob. of imit. origin] *vt* **:** to throw scatteringly **~** *vi* **1 :** to fly or dash up **2** *of a bird* **:** to rise or pass with a whirring of wings

[2]**flurr** \"\ *n* -S **:** a splashing or whirring sound

flurried *adj* **:** disturbed by conflicting claims for attention **:** excited, confused, or embarrassed by a press of activities ⟨the ~ cook tried to hasten dinner⟩; *broadly* **:** agitated or disordered ⟨spoke in a ~ voice⟩ — **flur·ried·ly** \-ədlē, -ēd-, -li\ *adv*

flur·ri·ment \ˈflərēmənt\ *n* -S **:** a flurried state

[1]**flur·ry** \ˈflər·ē, ˈflə·rē, |i\ *n* -ES [prob. fr. [1]*flurr* + *-y*] **1 a :** a sudden and brief commotion of the air ⟨a ~ of wind⟩ **b :** a sudden shower or snowfall with a gust of wind **2 :** spasmodic agitation **:** nervous commotion **:** FLUTTER ⟨the racket and ~ of London life —*Blackwood's*⟩ **3 :** a sudden short-lived advance or decline in prices or outburst of trading activity on the stock exchange **4 :** the violent spasms of a whale dying after being harpooned **syn** see STIR

[2]**flurry** \"\ *vb* -ED/-ING/-ES *vt* **:** to cause to become agitated and confused **:** EXCITE **~** *vi* **:** to become flurried ⟨her heart *flurried* round within her breast —John Galsworthy⟩; *usu* **:** to move or function in a flurry ⟨*flurried* about her tasks⟩ **syn** see DISCOMPOSE

flus *pl of* FLU

[1]**flush** \ˈfləsh\ *vb* -ED/-ING/-ES [ME *flusshen*, perh. of imit. origin] *vi* **1 a** *of a bird* **:** to take to wing suddenly **:** fly up (as from a place of concealment) **b** *obs, of persons* **:** to rush abroad or swarm together like a flock of birds **2 :** to cause a bird to flush **~** *vt* **:** to cause (a bird) to flush **:** put up (as a game bird)

[2]**flush** \"\ *n* -ES **1 :** a flight of flushed birds **2 :** the act of flushing birds

[3]**flush** \"\ *n* -ES [ME *floshe* — more at FLODGE] *dial Brit* **:** a low swampy place **:** a pool of standing water (as in a road)

[4]**flush** \"\ *n* -ES [perh. alter. (influenced by [1]*flush*) of [1]*flux*] **1 a :** a sudden flow (as of water) **:** a rush of liquid that fills or overflows whether naturally occurring or produced for a particular purpose ⟨the dam burst and sent a great ~ of water scouring down the valley⟩ ⟨a ~ of blood brightened her cheeks⟩ **b :** a cleansing or rinsing with or as if with water ⟨give the pot a ~ with boiling water before making the tea⟩ **2 :** a sudden increase or expansion: as **a :** a sudden and usu. abundant growth of vegetation ⟨the spring ~ of grass⟩ or of a particular plant part ⟨a second ~ of bloom⟩; *sometimes* **:** a tender young shoot (as of a tea plant) **b :** a sharp increase in milk production (as when cattle are first put out on good pasture) **c :** a sudden flood or rush of emotion ⟨a quick ~ of anger⟩ **:** THRILL **3 a :** a tinge of red or ruddy light or color (as produced on the cheeks by a sudden rush of blood) ⟨the healthy ~ of the child's face⟩ ⟨the ~ brightening a perfectly ripe peach⟩ **b :** a glowing, vigorous, or fresh state or quality ⟨a ~ of youthful ardor⟩ ⟨the first ~ of success⟩ **4 :** a transitory attack or sensation of extreme heat (as in response to certain drugs or in certain physiological states) ⟨harassed by the ~*es* natural to a woman of her age⟩ **5 :** a feed (as molasses or milk) used to stimulate the intestinal motility of domestic animals (as poultry)

[5]**flush** \"\ *vb* -ED/-ING/-ES *vi* **1 :** to flow and spread suddenly and freely **:** RUSH ⟨the tide ~*ed* through the narrow inlet⟩ ⟨as the blood ~*es* back to the extremities⟩ **2 a :** to glow suddenly, brightly, or with rich or ruddy color ⟨dawn was already ~*ing* beyond the line of hills⟩ ⟨the aurora ~*ed* far into the sky⟩ **b :** to become suddenly suffused (as with color); *esp* **:** BLUSH ⟨~*ed* hotly and denied everything⟩ **3** *of plants* **:** to start into growth **:** throw out shoots **4 :** to operate a placer mine where the continuous supply of water is insufficient by holding back water and releasing it periodically in a flood — compare BOOMING **5** *of sheep* **:** to come into breeding condition **~** *vt* **1 a :** to cause (as water) to flow ⟨~*ed* the water away⟩ **b :** to pour or cause water or other liquid to pour over or through (as a surface or a channel) ⟨~*ing* the meadow in the early fall⟩ ⟨~ the teapot with boiling water⟩; *usu* **:** to cleanse or wash out by means of a rush of liquid ⟨~ the stable floor with a hose⟩ ⟨~ the toilet⟩ **2 :** to fill with or inflame by **:** EXCITE, ANIMATE — now usu. used passively ⟨~*ed* with pride at his son's success⟩ ⟨~*ed* by a few minor successes⟩ **3 :** to make suddenly or temporarily red, rosy, or glowing as if suffused with blood or flooded with color **:** cause to blush ⟨the story ~*ed* her cheeks with shame⟩ **4 :** to prepare (sheep) for breeding by improving the ration for a time before turning the rams and ewes together **5 :** to transfer (pigment) directly from a water slurry to a dispersion in an oil or resinous base

[6]**flush** \"\ *adj* -ER/-EST **1 a :** filled to overflowing ⟨streams ~ with the spring runoff⟩ **b :** fully or generously supplied usu. with money **:** AFFLUENT ⟨particularly ~ this week⟩ **2 a** *archaic* **:** full of life and vigor **:** LUSTY, SPIRITED; *sometimes* **:** self-confident and assured **b :** of a ruddy or healthy color **:** FLUSHED **3 a** *of money or credit* **:** readily available **:** ABUNDANT ⟨money is so ~ just now that the poorest trash is bid up to ridiculous levels at the auctions⟩ **b :** prodigal or lavish esp. in expenditure ⟨so ~ you might buy your sister a trinket⟩ **4 a :** having or forming a continuous plane or unbroken surface ⟨~ paneling under the windows⟩ ⟨the river is ~ with its banks⟩; *also, of a boat* **:** having a flush deck **b :** directly abutting on or immediately adjacent to ⟨the windows of the overhang were ~ with the street⟩: as (1) *of printed matter* **:** set even with an edge or esp. with the left edge of a type page or column **:** having no indention (2) *of a cut* **:** trimmed to bleed the printing surface (3) *of a book cover* **:** trimmed even with the leaves (4) **:** arranged edge to edge so as to fit snugly ⟨be sure that the door is ~ with the casing⟩ ⟨~ wallpaper⟩ **5** *of a blow* **:** precisely delivered **:** ACCURATE, DIRECT ⟨floored his opponent with ~ shots to the chin⟩ **syn** see LEVEL

[7]**flush** \"\ *adv* [[6]*flush*] **:** without interruption: as **a :** STRAIGHT, SQUARELY ⟨caught his opponent ~ on the chin⟩ ⟨went ~ from school into politics⟩ ⟨the door came ~ with the threshold⟩ **b :** with a flush edge, cover, margin, or joining ⟨a line set ~⟩ ⟨books cut ~⟩ ⟨the timber butted ~ with the masonry⟩

[8]**flush** \"\ *vb* -ED/-ING/-ES [[6]*flush*] *vt* **:** to make, set, or trim flush ⟨~ all exposed joints in the wall⟩ ⟨often desirable to ~ a mounted stereotype⟩ ⟨~ all headings on the next three pages⟩ **~** *vi* **:** FLOAT 6

[9]**flush** \"\ *n* -ES [MF *flus, fluz*, fr. L *fluxus* flow — more at FLUX] **1 :** a hand of playing cards all of the same suit: as **a :** a poker hand with all five cards of the same suit but not in sequence — see STRAIGHT FLUSH; POKER illustration **b :** the five highest cards of the trump suit in pinochle scoring 150 points when melded **2** *or* **flush gate :** a series of three or more slalom gates set vertically on a slope

[10]**flush** \"\ *adj* [prob. alter. of [1]*fledge*] *archaic* **:** FLEDGED

[11]**flush** \"\ *vi* -ED/-ING/-ES [perh. irreg. of [2]*frush*] **1** *of a stone in a wall* **:** to break away at the edges through excess loading **2** *of mortar* **:** to become forced out to or from the joints through pressure

flushboard \ˈ=ˌ=\ *n* [[4]*flush* + *board*] **:** FLASHBOARD

flush box *n* [[5]*flush*] **:** FLUSH TANK

flush coat *n* [[5]*flush*] **:** a final coat of bituminous material spread, flushed, or sprayed on a surface to make a waterproof pavement

flush color *or* **flushed color** *n* [[5]*flush*] **:** a pigment dispersed in oil or varnish (as for use in printing ink) — compare DRY COLOR, PULP COLOR

flush deck *n* [[6]*flush*] **:** a deck on a boat continuous from bow to stern and usu. with no structure above

flush–decker \ˈ=ˌ==\ *n* -S **:** a boat with flush deck

flush door *n* [[6]*flush*] **:** a door with a flush surface that is not divided into panels and moldings — compare PANEL DOOR

flushed *past of* FLUSH

flush·er \ˈfləshə(r)\ *n* -S [[5]*flush* + *-er*] **:** one that flushes something; *usu* **:** a tank mounted on a vehicle and equipped with a battery of nozzles used for laying the dust on or flushing dirt from streets and roadways with a spray of water

flushes *pres 3d sing of* FLUSH, *pl of* FLUSH

flushgate \ˈ=ˌ=\ *n* [[5]*flush* + *gate*] **:** a gate or sluice used for flushing a channel below the gate in a dam or reservoir

flush gate *n* [[9]*flush*] **:** [9]FLUSH 2

flush–head rivet *n* [[6]*flush*] **:** a rivet with a countersunk head

flush hydrant *n* [[5]*flush*] **:** CHUCK HYDRANT

[1]**flushing** *adj* [fr. pres. part. of [5]*flush*] **1 :** serving to flush ⟨a ~ mechanism⟩ **:** used in or concerned with flushing **2 :** of, relating to, or characterized by flushing; *often* **:** BLUSHING — **flush·ing·ly** *adv*

[2]**flushing** *n* -S [fr. gerund of [5]*flush*] **:** transient reddening of the skin; *sometimes* **:** HOT FLASH

flushing bar *also* **flushing rod** *n* [fr. pres. part. of [1]*flush*] **:** a device attached in front of a mowing machine to flush ground= nesting game birds ahead of the cutter bar

flush joint *n* [[6]*flush*] **:** a joint in masonry in which the mortar is finished flush at the surface — see JOINT illustration

flush·ness *n* -ES [[6]*flush* + *-ness*] **:** the quality or state of being flush; *esp* **:** possession of abundant funds

flush·om·e·ter \ˌfləˈshäməd·ə(r)\ *n* [fr. *Flushometer*, a trademark] **:** a valve for flushing toilets or urinals by operation of a handle that discharges a definite quantity of water under pressure directly into the fixture — called also *flush valve*

flush out *vt* [[1]*flush*] **:** to bring to light **:** make public or available ⟨hoping to *flush out* some millions of hoarded dollars⟩ ⟨succeeded in *flushing out* many additional tax evaders⟩

flush plate *n* [[6]*flush*] **:** a small rectangular plate of metal or plastic that is used to cover a flush electrical switch or receptacle

flush plating *n* [[6]*flush*] **:** outside plating in steel ships joined edge to edge by edge strips and butt straps inside the plating or by welding

flush production *n* [[4]*flush*] **:** the yield of oil from a spontaneously flowing well

flush rim *or* **flushing rim** *n* [[1]*flush*] **:** the rim of a water-closet bowl having a channel or perforated tube by which the bowl is flushed simultaneously from all sides

flush ring *n* [[6]*flush*] **:** a pull ring that when not in use drops flush into an opening in its supporting surface

flush switch *n* [[6]*flush*] **:** an electrical switch mounted with only its face exposed and with its sides surrounded by a box or case that is not a part of the switch

flush tank *n* [[5]*flush*] **1 :** a tank holding a supply of water or sewage for periodically flushing out a sewer **2 :** a small tank equipped with a float and ball valve for flushing a water closet

flush toilet *n* [[5]*flush*] **:** WATER CLOSET

flush valve *n* [[5]*flush*] **1 :** FLUSHOMETER **2 :** a ball valve in a water-closet flush tank

flushy \ˈfləshē\ *adj* -ER/-EST [[4]*flush* + *-y*] **:** somewhat flushed **:** REDDISH

[1]**flus·ker** \ˈfləskə(r)\ *vi* -ED/-ING/-S [freq. of E dial. *flusk* to ruffle the feathers] **:** FLUTTER

[2]**flusker** \"\ *vt* -ED/-ING/-S [by alter.] *dial* **:** FLUSTER

[1]**flus·ter** \ˈfləstə(r)\ *vb* **flustered; flustered; flustering** \-t(ə)riŋ\ **flusters** [ME *flostren*, prob. of Scand origin; akin to Icel *flaustur* hurry, *flaustra* to deal superficially (with); prob. akin to ON *flaustr* ship, *fljōta* to flow — more at FLEET] *vt* **1 :** to heat or inflame with or as if with drinking **:** make tipsy **:** BEFUDDLE **2 :** to put into a state of disorder or confusion **:** CONFUSE, MUDDLE **3 :** to utter in a confused or incoherent manner **~** *vi* **:** to move or behave in an agitated, confused, or excited manner ⟨~*ed* down the aisle to her seat⟩ **syn** see DISCOMPOSE

[2]**fluster** \"\ *n* -S **1** *obs* **:** a state of excitement or glow (as from intoxication) **2 :** agitation mingled with confusion **:** TO-DO ⟨took it all pretty coolly: no ~, no flood of tears or questions —C.D.Lewis⟩

flus·ter·er \-tərə(r)\ *n* -S **:** AMERICAN COOT

flus·tra \ˈflə̇strə, ˈflüs-\ *n, cap* [NL] **:** a genus (the type of a widely distributed family Flustridae) of marine bryozoans (class Gymnolaemata) that form broad flattened branching colonies — see SEA MAT

flus·trat·ed \ˈflə,strād·əd\ *or* **flus·ter·at·ed** \ˈfləstə,r-\ *adj* [[1]*fluster* + *-ated* (as in *frustrated*)] **:** FLUSTERED

flus·tra·tion \ˌfləˈstrāshən\ *also* **flus·ter·a·tion** \ˌfləstəˈr-\ *n* -S [[1]*fluster* + *-ation* (as in *frustration*)] **:** the quality or state of being flustered

[1]**flute** \ˈflüt, *usu* -üd.+V\ *n* -S [ME *floute*, fr. MF *flaute*,

flute 1b

flahute, fleute, fr. OProv *flaut*, perh. alter. (influenced by *laut* lute) of *flaujol, flauja*, fr. (assumed) VL *flabeolum* — more at LUTE, FLAGEOLET] **1 :** a wind instrument stopped at one end with a vibrating air column used as a means of tone production: **a :** RECORDER **b :** an orchestral instrument consisting of a hollow cylinder with finger holes along its length, with a lateral hole for blowing into, and with a compass of three octaves up from middle C — called also *transverse flute* **2 :** FLUTIST; *usu* **:** a flute player in a band or orchestra **3 :** any of various flute-shaped things: as **a :** a long French breakfast roll **b** *or* **flute glass :** a tall slender wineglass **c :** a long shuttle used in weaving tapestry **d :** a grooved or ridged pleat used esp. in ruffles, edgings, or hat brims **e :** a groove (as in a reamer, twist drill, or tap) parallel or nearly parallel to the axis of a cylindrical piece **4 :** a groove of curved section: as **a :** any of a series of vertical grooves used to decorate columns and pilasters in classical architecture **b :** any of various similar ornamental grooves (as on furniture or silverware) **c :** one of the parallel grooves in corrugated board or glass (as in the lens of a headlight) **d** (1) **:** a natural groove or channel on a rock surface (as in a cave) (2) **: flutes** *pl* **:** scalloped or rippled rock surfaces — called also *fluting* **5 :** a molder's tool for forming grooves **6** *or* **flute stop :** a flue pipe-organ stop of flute quality and of 8-foot or 4-foot pitch

[2]**flute** \"\ *vb* -ED/-ING/-S [ME *flouten*, fr. MF *flauter*, fr. *flaute*] *vi* **:** to play on or as if on a flute **:** make a sound like that of a flute **~** *vt* **1 :** to play, whistle, or sing with a clear soft note like that of a flute **2 :** to form flutes in (as the shaft of a column or the crust of a pie)

[3]**flute** \"\ *n* -S [D *fluit*, lit., flute, fr. MD *flūte, fleute, floite*, fr. OF *flaute, flahute, fleute* — more at [1]FLUTE] **1 :** a flyboat usu. with a narrow cabin not projecting beyond the rudderhead **2 :** a former partially armed naval transport

flûte à bec \¦flüd·|ə¦bek, |(ˌ)ä¦b-\ *n, pl* **flûtes à bec** \", -üts|\ [F, lit., flute with a beak] **:** FIPPLE FLUTE, RECORDER 3a

flute budding *n* **:** patch budding in which the stock is nearly girdled

flute co·nique \¦flütkōˈnēk, -kä¦-\ *n, pl* **flutes coniques** \-t(s)k-\ [F *flûte conique*, lit., conical flute] **:** a tapered pipe= organ flute stop yielding a tone similar to the Spitzflöte of 16-, 8-, 4-, and 2-foot pitches

fluted *adj* **1 :** formed or decorated with or as if with flutes **:** CHANNELED, GROOVED — see LEG illustration **2** *of a sound* **:** high, thin, and clear as if produced by a flute

flûte d'a·mour \ˌflütdə¦mu̇(ə)r\ *n, pl* **flûtes d'amour** \-t(s)d-\ [F, lit., flute of love] **1 :** a flute ranging a minor third lower than the modern instrument **2 :** a labial pipe= organ stop usu. of 4-foot pitch and of delicate quality

flute-douce \(ˈ)flüt¦düs\ *n* -S [F *flûte douce*, lit., sweet flute] **1 :** RECORDER **2 :** a pipe-organ stop having a tone similar to that of a recorder

fluted scale *n* **:** COTTONY-CUSHION SCALE

flute glass *n* **:** [1]FLUTE 3b

flûte har·mo·nique \ˌflüt,härməˈnēk\ *n, pl* **flûtes harmoniques** \-t(s),h-\ [F, lit., harmonic flute] **:** an open flute organ pipe blown to yield the first harmonic instead of the fundamental

flutelike \ˈ=ˌ=\ *adj* **:** resembling a flute esp. in light clear sharp tone quality

flutemouth \ˈ=ˌ=\ *n* **:** CORNETFISH

flûte oc·ta·vi·ante \ˌflüd·ˌäk,tavēˈänt, -tāv-\ *n, pl* **flûtes octaviantes** \", -üt,sä-\ [F, lit., octave flute] **:** FLÛTE HARMONIQUE

flûte ou·verte \-d·ü¦ve(ə)rt\ *n, pl* **flûtes ouvertes** \", -üts-\ [F, lit., open flute] **:** an open flute organ pipe of various pitches

flut·er \ˈflüd·ə(r), -ütə-\ *n* -S [ME *flauter, flautour*, fr. OF *flouteor*, fr. *flouter* to play the flute + *-eor* —or — more at [1]FLUTE] **1** *archaic* **:** FLUTIST **2** [[2]*flute* + *-er*] **a :** a worker who flutes (as furniture parts or curtain ruffles) by hand or by machine **b :** a tool or implement for making flutings

flute stop *n* **:** [1]FLUTE 6

flûte tri·an·gu·laire \¦flüt,trīˌangyə¦la(a)(ə)r\ *n, pl* **flûtes triangulaires** \-üt(s),tl-\ [F, lit., triangular flute] **:** a 3= sided wooden flute organ pipe used to produce orchestral flute tone quality

flutey *var of* FLUTY

flutier *comparative of* FLUTY

flutiest *superlative of* FLUTY

fluting *n* -S [fr. gerund of [2]*flute*] **1 a :** a flute or series of flutes esp. as ornamentation **:** a finish of flutes ⟨a narrow band of ~ sets off the margin of the table leaves⟩ ⟨decked with ~*s* and pipings⟩ **b :** fluted material ⟨need two yards of net ~ to finish the neck and cuffs⟩ **2 :** kinking or breaking of metal strip when bent on a small radius **3 :** [1]FLUTE 4d(2)

flut·ist \ˈflüd·əst, -ütə-\ *n* -S [[1]*flute* + *-ist*] **:** a flute player

flut·o·phone \ˈflüd·ə,fōn, -ütə-\ *n* [[1]*flute* + *-o-* + *-phone*] **:** a simple wind instrument resembling a tonette but with the lower end flared like a clarinet

[1]**flut·ter** \ˈfləd·ə(r), -ətə-\ *vb* -ED/-ING/-S [ME *floteren* to float, flutter, fr. OE *floterian* to be tossed by the waves, float to and fro, freq. of *flotian* to float — more at FLOAT] *vi* **1 :** to move or flap the wings rapidly without flying or with short flights ⟨butterflies ~*ing* among the flowers⟩ **2 :** to move with quick vibrations or undulations ⟨a sail ~*s* in the wind⟩ ⟨a ~*ing* fan⟩ ⟨his pulse ~*s*⟩ **3 a :** to move about agitatedly, irregularly, or with great bustle and show without much result **:** FLIT ⟨she ~*ed* through her chores, pausing often to chat⟩ **b :** to be in a state of trembling agitation (as from fear, hope, or anticipation) **:** QUAKE, QUIVER ⟨~*ed* at the sight of her escort⟩ **~** *vt* **1 :** to move or vibrate rapidly and often irregularly ⟨the young bird ~*ed* its wings but could not get off the ground⟩ **2 :** to throw into confusion or agitation ⟨a man to ~ girlish hearts⟩ **3 :** to utter with agitation or confusion ⟨~*ed* a few words of congratulation⟩

[2]**flutter** \"\ *n* -S **1 :** an act of fluttering **:** quick and irregular motion **:** FLICKERING, VIBRATION ⟨a ~ of flame⟩ ⟨the ~ of a fan⟩ **2 :** nervous or aimless activity or state **:** AGITATION, CONFUSION, DISORDER ⟨was in a ~ until he got home⟩: as **a :** a brief run or burst of speed **b :** a sudden but usu. slight stir (as of excitement or activity in the stock market) **:** FLURRY ⟨a ~ of buying of better-class bonds⟩ ⟨a ~ of indignation followed his remarks⟩ **c** *chiefly Brit* **:** a small speculative venture or gamble ⟨took a ~ on the ponies⟩ ⟨had a little ~ in grain futures that did well⟩ **d :** an abnormal state characterized by rapid spasmodic and usu. rhythmic motion of a body part ⟨diaphragmatic ~⟩ ⟨affected with a serious ventricular ~⟩ **3 a** *obs* **:** STIR, OSTENTATION, DISPLAY **b :** delicate fluffy daintiness (as of manner or dress) ⟨all femininity and ~⟩ **4 a :** a distortion in reproduced sound similar to wow in origin but of higher pitch **b :** fluctuation in the brightness of a television receiver image **5** *or* **flutter kick :** an alternating whipping motion of the legs used in swimming (as in the crawl and backstroke) **6 :** an oscillation of definite period but unstable character set up in a part (as an aileron) of an aircraft at a definite critical speed and maintained by a combination of aerodynamic, inertial, and elastic forces; *also* **:** such an oscillation occurring in other structures (as a bridge) **7 :** a group or collection of fluttering things ⟨a ~ of pretty girls⟩

flut·ter·a·tion \ˌfləd·əˈrāshən\ *n* -S [[1]*flutter* + *-ation*] **:** a state of confusion or disorderly movement; *sometimes* **:** sound resulting from a flutteration ⟨heard the ~ of the mob⟩

flutterboard \ˈ=ˌ=ˌ=\ *n* **:** a small rectangular board rounded at one end, made of cork, plastic, or wood, and used chiefly by swimmers to support the head and upper trunk when learning or practicing leg strokes

flutter echo *n* **:** a rapid series of echoes (as in broadcast and recording studios) originating in reflection between two parallel surfaces

flut·ter·er \ˈfləd·ərə(r), -lətə-\ *n* -S **:** one that flutters

flut·ter·ing·ly *adv* : with a flutter : in the manner of one that flutters

flutter kick *n* : [2]FLUTTER 5

flut·ter·ment \-d·ə(r)mənt\ *n* -s : fluttered or disturbed state ⟨gets into such a ~ when dinner is late⟩

fluttermill \ˈ==,=\ *n*, *South & Midland* : a toy waterwheel

fluttermouse \ˈ==,=\ *n* [alter. of *flittermouse*] : [3]BAT 1

flut·ter·some \-ə(r)səm\ *adj* [[1]*flutter* + *-some*] : FLUTTERY

flutter–tonguing \ˈ==,==\ *n* : a vibratory action of the tongue produced by rolling or trilling an *r* while playing on a wind instrument (as a trumpet)

flutter valve *n* : a valve (as in an engine carburetor) actuated by fluctuations of pressure in the fluid surrounding it rather than by any external control

flutter wheel *n* : a waterwheel of moderate diameter having radial floats and placed at the bottom of a chute so as to work by impact

flut·tery \ˈfləd·ərē, -ətə-, -ri\ *adj* : given to or characterized by fluttering ⟨a light full ~ skirt⟩ ⟨~ mannerisms⟩

fluty *or* **flut·ey** \ˈflüd·ē\ *adj* **flutier**; **flutiest** : having a tone like that of a flute : resembling a flute esp. in sound

fluvi- *or* **fluvio-** *comb form* [L *fluvi-*, fr. *fluvius* — more at FLUVIAL] **1** : river, stream ⟨*fluvi*coline⟩ ⟨*fluvio*logy⟩ **2** : fluvial and ⟨*fluvio*volcanic⟩

flu·vi·al \ˈflüvēəl, -vyəl\ *adj* [L *fluvialis*, fr. *fluvius* river (fr. *fluere* to flow) + *-alis* -al — more at FLUID] **1 a** : of or relating to rivers ⟨~ law⟩ **b** : conforming to the changing course of a stream ⟨a ~ boundary⟩ **2** : growing or living in streams ⟨~ vegetation⟩ **3** : produced by river action ⟨a ~ plain⟩

flu·vi·a·les \,flüvēˈā(,)lēz\ [NL, fr. L, masc. & fem. pl. of *fluvialis*] *syn of* NAIADALES

flu·vi·al·ist \-ləst\ *n* -s : one who emphasizes the action of streams in explanation of geological phenomena

flu·vi·at·ic \¦flüvē¦ad·ik\ *adj* [L *fluviaticus*, fr. *fluvius* river + *-aticus* (as in *aquaticus* aquatic)] : FLUVIATILE

flu·vi·a·tile \ˈflüvēə,tīl\ *adj* [MF, fr. L *fluviatilis*, fr. *fluvius* river + *-atilis* (as in *aquatilis* aquatile)] : belonging to, existing in or about, or produced by the action of streams or rivers

flu·vi·a·tion \,flüvēˈāshən\ *n* -s [L *fluvi-* + E *-ation*] : the action of streams

flu·vic·o·line \(ˈ)flü¦vikə,līn, -,lən\ *adj* [ISV *fluvi-* + *-coline*] : inhabiting or frequenting rivers or streams — used of animals

flu·vio–aeolian \¦flüvē(,)ō+\ *adj* [*fluvi-* + *aeolian*] : produced or caused by action of streams and wind ⟨*fluvio-aeolian* geologic formations⟩

flu·vio·glacial \"+\ *adj* [ISV *fluvi-* + *glacial*] : GLACIOFLUVIAL

fluvioglacial drift *n* : drift transported by waters emanating from a glacier

flu·vi·o·graph \ˈflüvēə,graf, -ràf\ *n* [ISV *fluvi-* + *-graph*] : an instrument for measuring and recording automatically the rise and fall of a river

fluv·io·lacustrine \¦flüvē(,)ō+\ *adj* [*fluvi-* + *lacustrine*] : of or relating to sedimentation partly in lake and partly in stream waters or to deposits laid down under alternating or overlapping lacustrine and fluviatile conditions

flu·vi·ol·o·gy \,flüvēˈäləjē\ *n* -ES [*fluvi-* + *-logy*] : a science dealing with watercourses

flu·vio·marine \¦flüvē(,)ō+\ *adj* [*fluvi-* + *marine*] : formed by the joint action of river and sea ⟨~ deposits at the mouths of rivers⟩ : ESTUARINE

flu·vi·om·e·ter \,flüvēˈämәd·ə(r)\ *n* [ISV *fluvi-* + *-meter*] : FLUVIOGRAPH

flu·vio·terrestrial \¦flüvē(,)ō+\ *adj* [*fluvi-* + *terrestrial*] : relating to the land and its streams ⟨~ shells⟩

flu·vio·volcanic \"+\ *adj* [*fluvi-* + *volcanic*] : of or relating to combined action of volcanoes and streams ⟨beds of ~ ash⟩

[1]**flux** \ˈfləks\ *n* -ES [ME, fr. MF & ML; MF, fr. ML *fluxus*, fr. L, flow, action of flowing, fr. *fluxus*, past part. of *fluere* to flow — more at FLUID] **1 a** : a flowing or discharge of fluid from the body; *usu* : an excessive and abnormal discharge from the bowels : DIARRHEA, DYSENTERY **b** : the matter discharged in a flux **2** : an act of flowing: as **a** : a continuous moving on or passing by (as of a flowing stream) **b** : a continuing succession of changes ⟨language is subject to constant ~⟩ **3** : a running stream (as of water) : a continued flow : FLOOD, OUTFLOW ⟨a ~ of words⟩ **4 a** : the setting in of the tide toward shore — compare REFLUX **b** : a state of uncertainty or absence of clearly directed action following or accompanying some event of moment and usu. preceding the establishment of a new course of action ⟨the ~ following the death of the emperor⟩ **5 a** : a substance used to promote fusion (as by removing impurities) esp. of metals or minerals **b** : a substance (as rosin or borax) applied to surfaces to be joined by soldering, brazing, or welding just prior to or during the operation to clean and free them from oxide and promote their union **c** : a substance (as borax) added in glassmaking for promoting vitrification **d** *or* **flux oil** : a viscous nonvolatile petroleum fraction used to soften asphalt **6** : a fusible glass used as a base for enamels; *also* : an easily fusible enamel used as a ground for enamel painting **7 a** : the rate of transfer of fluid, particles, or energy (as radiant energy) across a given surface ⟨neutron ~⟩ ⟨light ~⟩ **b** : the surface integral of the normal component of field intensity over a given surface ⟨measurement of electric ~⟩ — see MAGNETIC FLUX **8** : SLIME FLUX **syn** see FLOW

[2]**flux** \"\ *vb* -ED/-ING/-ES [ME *fluxen*, fr. *flux*, n.] *vt* **1** : to cause to become fluid ⟨the intense heat ~*ed* the glass⟩ **2** : to treat with a flux esp. in order to promote fusion or softening ⟨~ the edges to be joined with solder⟩ **3** *obs* : to treat (a patient or disease) so as to cause a discharge from an affected part; *often* : PURGE ~ *vi* **1** : to flow freely **2** : to become fluid : FUSE, MELT ⟨materials that soften and ~ under the influence of heat and pressure⟩ **3** *obs* : to undergo a flux; *specif* : to bleed copiously

[3]**flux** \"\ *adj* [L *fluxus*, fr. past part. of *fluere*] *archaic* : being in or characterized by a state of flux : VARIABLE, UNSTABLE

flux density *n* : magnetic, electric, or radiant flux per unit area normal to the direction of the flux

flux·er \-sə(r)\ *n* -s : a worker who fluxes seams of tin cans for soldering

flux gate *or* **flux valve** *n* : a device based on the earth-inductor principle and used to indicate the direction of the terrestrial magnetic field

flux·ible \-səbəl\ *adj* [ME, fr. MF, fr. LL *fluxibilis* fluid, fr. L *fluxus* (past part. of *fluere* to flow) + *-ibilis* -ible — more at FLUID] **1** *archaic* : capable of being fluxed **2** *obs* : flowing freely : FLUID **3** *archaic* : INCONSTANT, VARIABLE

flux·ile \-səl, -,sīl, -(,)sil\ *adj* [LL *fluxilis*, fr. L *fluxus* (past part.) + *-ilis* -ile] **1** *obs* : FLUID **2** *archaic* : INCONSTANT, VARIABLE

flux·il·i·ty \,flək'siləd·ē\ *n* -ES : the quality or state of being fluxile

flux·ion \ˈflәkshən\ *n* -s [MF, fr. L *fluxion-*, *fluxio*, fr. *fluxus* (past part.) + *-ion-*, *-io* -ion] **1** : the action of flowing **2** : something that flows; *sometimes* : continuing motion or change **3** *obs* : an unnatural or excessive flow of blood or fluid toward a body organ **4** *obs* : the derivative of a mathematical function

flux·ion·al \-shənᵊl,-shnəl\ *adj* **1** : relating to or being a fluxion **2** : subject to fluxion : VARIABLE, INCONSTANT — **flux·ion·al·ly** \-ᵊlē,-əlē\ *adv*

fluxional texture *n* : FLUIDAL TEXTURE

flux·ion·ary \-shə,nerē\ *archaic var of* FLUXIONAL

flux·ion·ist \-sh(ə)nəst\ *n* -s : one skilled in or using fluxions esp. in mathematics

flux·ive \ˈflәksiv\ *adj* [L *flux*us (past part.) + E *-ive*] *archaic* : FLOWING, FLUID, FLUCTUATING

flux man *n* : a worker who mixes flux and supplies can-soldering machines with flux and solder

flux·me·ter \ˈflək,smēd·ə(r)\ *n* [ISV *flux* + *-meter*] : an instrument for measuring magnetic-flux density usu. by electromagnetic induction

fluxweed \ˈ=,=\ *n* [[1]*flux* (dysentery) + *weed*] **1** : a tansy mustard (*Descurainia sophia*) with spreading fruiting pedicels **2** : SPOTTED CRANESBILL **3** : SPOTTED SPURGE

flx *abbr* flexible

[1]**fly** \ˈflī\ *vb* **flew** \ˈflü\ **flown** \ˈflōn\ **flying**; **flies** [ME *fligen*, *flien*, *fleon*, fr. OE *flēogan*; akin to OHG *fliogan* to fly, ON *fljūga*, Lith *plaukti* to swim, OE *flōwan* to flow — more at FLOW] *vi* **1 a** *of a winged being* : to move in or pass through the air with wings ⟨insects ~*ing* over the water⟩ **b** : to move through the air or before the wind ⟨bullets *flew* in all directions⟩ ⟨the wind freshened and the schooner *flew* toward port⟩ ⟨clouds ~*ing* across the sky⟩ ⟨the plane *flew* south⟩ **c** : to float, wave, or soar in the air ⟨a flag *flies* from the tall staff⟩ ⟨the kite caught an updraft and *flew* up and up⟩ ⟨bright hair ~*ing* about her shoulders⟩ **2 a** : to take to flight : flee esp. from danger : run away ⟨forced to ~ for his life when his enemies came into power⟩ **b** : to fade and disappear : VANISH ⟨mists ~*ing* before the morning sun⟩ ⟨the hovering shadows had *flown* when the light went on⟩ **3** : to move, pass, or act swiftly ⟨the horses *flew* down the stretch⟩ ⟨how such rumors do ~⟩ ⟨~*ing* to his sister's assistance⟩: as **a** : to spring or rush esp. suddenly or violently ⟨the rumor brought the citizens ~*ing* to arms⟩ — often used with *into* ⟨*flew* into a rage⟩ ⟨~ into tantrums —Gertrude Samuels⟩ **b** : to become suddenly or violently disordered, broken to bits, or forced apart or off : BURST ⟨the door *flew* open⟩ ⟨the glass *flew* to bits at the impact⟩ **c** : to become expended or dissipated rapidly — used esp. of money or property ⟨after he had become established in town his inheritance *flew*⟩ **d** : to seem to pass quickly ⟨our vacation had simply *flown*⟩ ⟨the hours *flew* as she busied herself about the house⟩ **4 a** : to hunt with a hawk — usu. used with *at* ⟨*flew* unsuccessfully at a low-flying duck⟩ **b** : to pursue or attack in or as if in flight ⟨hoped yet to ~ at higher game⟩ **5** *past or past part* **flied** : to hit a fly ball in baseball ⟨*flied* to left field⟩ **6 a** : to operate an airplane **b** : to travel in an airplane ~ *vt* **1 a** : to cause to fly or float in the air (as a bird, a flag) ⟨little boys ~*ing* their kites⟩ ⟨the club *flew* its pigeons every pleasant Saturday⟩ **b** : to operate (an airplane) in flight **2 a** : to flee or escape from ⟨the bird had *flown* its cage⟩ **b** : to avoid or shun ⟨sleep *flies* the wretch —John Dryden⟩ ⟨~ such a talkative woman⟩ **3 a** : to perform by flying ⟨the bat has *flown* his nightly flight⟩ : conform to in flying ⟨birds usually ~ the same flyway in both northward and southward migration⟩ : provide by flying ⟨fighters ~*ing* close escort for the transports⟩ **b** : to operate an airplane over ⟨~ the Atlantic⟩ **4** : to fly (a hawk) at game **5** : to transport by airplane **6** *past or past part usu* **flied** : to raise (as scenery not in use) to the flies of a theater stage **syn** see ESCAPE — **fly a kite** *or* **fly one's kite** *slang* : to cease importuning or troubling — usu. used with *go* in the imperative — **fly at one's throat 1** : to attack by or as if by biting the throat ⟨the dog snapped the chain and *flew at his throat*⟩ **2** : to assail suddenly and violently — **fly blind** : to fly an airplane solely by the aid of instruments — **fly by the seat of one's pants** *slang* : to fly an airplane by a sense of feeling without the aid of instruments — **fly contact** : to fly an airplane with the aid of visible landmarks or reference points — **fly high** : to be exuberantly ambitious : be elated — **fly in the face of** *or* **fly in the teeth of** : to act forthrightly or brazenly in a way that shows small respect and usu. contempt for ⟨*flying in the face of* convention⟩ ⟨*flying in the face of* other people's rights⟩ ⟨*flying in the teeth of* accepted opinion —F.L.Allen⟩ — **fly the coop** *slang* : to depart suddenly or surreptitiously : ESCAPE, FLEE

[2]**fly** \"\ *n* -ES [ME *flye*, fr. OE *flyge* — more at FLIGHT] **1** : the action or process of flying : FLIGHT **2** : the part of a compass on which the points are marked : COMPASS CARD **3 a** : a device consisting of two or more radial vanes capable of rotating on a spindle to act as a fan or to govern the speed of clockwork or very light machinery by the resistance of the air **b** : FLYWHEEL **c** : the arrangement consisting of a lever with end weights used to operate fly presses by its momentum when turned rapidly at the end of the screw; *also* : FLY PRESS **4 a** : a horse-drawn public coach or delivery wagon **b** *chiefly Brit* : a light covered vehicle (as a single-horse pleasure carriage or a hansom cab) **5 flies** *pl* : the space over the stage of a theater where scenery and equipment can be hung out of sight until needed **6** : something attached by one edge: as **a** : a garment closing concealed by a fold of cloth extending over the fastener; *esp* : such a closing at the front of men's trousers — see FLY FRONT **b** : the outer canvas of a tent with double top usu. drawn over the ridgepole but so extended as to touch the roof of the tent at no other place; *often* : a piece of canvas suitable for such use **c** (1) : the length of an extended flag from its staff or support (2) : the outer or loose end of a flag **7** *textile manuf* **a** : FLIER 11 **b** : LATCH 3 **c** : FLY SHUTTLE **d** : airborne lint in a mill room; *specif* : short light waste fiber produced during carding, spinning, or napping **8** : the course of something projected through the air ⟨the golf ball rose in a good straight ~ right down the fairway⟩; *often* : FLY BALL **9** : FLYLEAF **10 a** : the fore flap of a bootee **b** : the overlapping part of a shoe upper **11** *or* **fly ladder** : the top section of an aerial ladder — **on the fly** : in motion: as **a** : continuously active : very busy ⟨*on the fly* all day long⟩ **b** : on the point of or in the course of departure ⟨answered *on the fly*⟩ **c** : while still in the air : before striking the ground ⟨caught the ball *on the fly*⟩

[3]**fly** \"\ *adj* [prob. fr. [1]*fly*] *slang chiefly Brit* : KEEN, ARTFUL

[4]**fly** \"\ *vb* **flied** *or* **flyed**; **flied** *or* **flyed**; **flying**; **flies** [[2]*fly* (carriage)] *vt*, *archaic* : to convey in a horse-drawn fly ~ *vi*, *archaic* : to travel in a fly

[5]**fly** \"\ *n* -ES [ME *flie*, fr. OE *flēoge*, *flȳge*; akin to OHG *flioga* fly, ON *fluga*, derivatives fr. the root of E [1]*fly*] **1** : a winged insect — now used chiefly in combination ⟨emerging may*flies*⟩ ⟨an outbreak of turnip *flies*⟩ ⟨a large caddis ~⟩ ⟨beautiful butter*flies*⟩; *collectively* : winged insects of a particular kind or in a specified relationship ⟨~ is bad on turnip this season⟩ ⟨had a lot of trouble with ~ on the sheep in this wet weather⟩ **2 a** : an insect of the order Diptera : TWO-WINGED FLY — called also *true fly* **b** : any of various rather large and stout-bodied two-winged flies (as horseflies or houseflies) as distinguished from typically smaller and slenderer two-winged flies (as mosquitoes or midges) — not used technically **c** : TSETSE FLY ⟨~ is present in much of eastern Africa⟩ **3** *obs* **a** : a demon associate (as of a witch) : FAMILIAR **b** : SPY **c** : PARASITE **4** : a fishhook dressed (as with feathers or tinsel) to suggest an insect for use as a lure in angling **5 a** *archaic* : FLYBOY **b** : DELIVERY 9 — **flies on** : lack of alertness about — used in negative expressions ⟨there's no *flies on* him⟩ ⟨he hasn't any *flies on* him⟩ — **fly in the ointment** : a detracting factor or element : an agent that spoils something that is otherwise pleasing

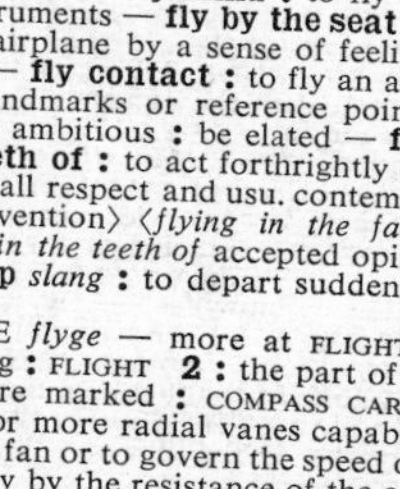

fly 4: *1* tag, *2* butt, *3* tail, *4* joint, *5* hackle, *6* body, *7* ribbing, *8* wing, *9* cheek, *10* topping, *11* horns, *12* head, *13* eye, *14* hook

[6]**fly** \"\ *adj* [*fly*-fishing] : used in or relating to fly-fishing ⟨improving his ~ technique⟩

fly·abil·i·ty \,flīəˈbiləd·ē\ *n* -ES : the quality or state of being flyable

fly·able \ˈflīəbəl\ *adj* : suitable for flying : fit to be flown ⟨~ weather⟩ ⟨a barely ~ airplane⟩

fly–about \ˈ==,=\ *adj* [fr. *fly about*, v.] **1** : given to or characterized by irregular, casual, or aimless activity or motion ⟨soft *fly-about* hair⟩ ⟨a *fly-about* boy⟩ **2** *of a horse* : SKITTISH

fly agaric *or* **fly amanita** *n* : a poisonous mushroom (*Amanita muscaria*) that has a variably colored but typically bright-red pileus with a warty white scurf on the surface and a prominent bulb at the base of the stipe, that with the related death cup is responsible for most cases of severe mushroom poisoning, that has been used as a source of poison for flypaper, and that is extensively used chiefly in northeastern Asia as an intoxicant esp. for the hallucinatory effects that it produces — called also *fly mushroom*

fly anchor *n* : SEA ANCHOR, DRAG

fly ash *n* : fine solid particles of noncombustible ash with or without accompanying combustible particles carried out of a bed of solid fuel by the draft and deposited in quiet spots within a furnace and flues or within a boiler setting or carried out of a chimney with the waste gases and often recovered for use as a constituent in commercial products (as phonograph records, cements, and bricks)

[1]**flyaway** \ˈ==,=\ *adj* [fr. *fly away*, v.] **1** *of a person* : volatile and flighty : lacking in order and practical sense ⟨a pretty ~ sort of woman⟩ **2 a** *of clothing* : loose and floating : having unconfined fullness esp. at the back ⟨a trim ~ jacket⟩ **b** : having a pointed form suggestive of a wing ⟨~ eyebrows⟩ ⟨a ~ cuff⟩ **3 a** : ready to fly — used of aircraft esp. at the factory **b** : packaged or designed to be transported in an airplane — used of supplies to be carried by military aircraft of the units that will use them **c** : relating to or involving flyaway aircraft or supplies ⟨~ price⟩ ⟨~ delivery⟩ ⟨a ~ bin⟩

[2]**flyaway** \"\ *n* -s [partly fr. [1]*flyaway*; partly fr. *fly away*, v.] **1** : a flyaway person or thing **2** : a mirage of land seen at sea **3** : a dismount from a horizontal bar consisting of a somersault executed at the front or back end of an arm swing **4** : an airplane flown (as from the factory) instead of being shipped

[3]**flyaway** \"\ *adv* [[1]*flyaway*] : as ready to fly away — used of aircraft ⟨a light plane priced $8400 ~⟩

flyaway grass *n* : ROUGH BENT

[1]**flyback** \ˈ=,=\ *adj* [fr. *fly back*, v.] : tending to fly back or capable of flying back: as **a** *of a stopwatch or chronograph* : having a sweep second hand that may be made to fly back to zero **b** *of fur, hair, or feathers* : having a tendency to fall back into position when brushed the wrong way

[2]**flyback** \"\ *n* [fr. *fly back*, v.] **1** : the return to zero of the second hand or the split-second hand of a stopwatch or chronograph **2** : the return of a cathode-ray beam in a television picture tube after it has traced one picture before it traces the next

fly ball \ˈ=ˈ=\ *n* : a ball hit in baseball into the air at least high enough to be caught by a fielder before touching the ground — compare GROUNDER

flyball \ˈ=,=\ *adj* : relating to or having ball weights that tend to fly outward when revolving and exert an effect through centrifugal force ⟨a ~ governor⟩

flybane \ˈ=,=\ *n* : any of several plants considered to be destructive to houseflies (as a catchfly or the fly agaric)

flybelt \ˈ=,=\ *n* : an area infested with tsetse fly

fly–bitten \ˈ=,==\ *adj* : marked by or as if by the bite of flies

fly block *n* : a block whose position shifts to suit the working of the tackle with which it is connected; *esp* : the double upper block of the topsail halyards of a sailing ship

[1]**flyblow** \ˈ=,=\ *n* [[5]*fly* + *blow* (deposit of insect eggs)] **1** : one of the eggs or young larvae deposited by a flesh fly or blowfly **2** : FLY-STRIKE

[2]**flyblow** \"\ *vt* **1** : to deposit flyblows in **2** : to cause (as a reputation) to be contaminated : TAINT

flyblown \ˈ=,=\ *adj* [[5]*fly* + *blown*, past part. of *blow*] **1 a** : infested with flyblows ⟨a ~ sheep⟩ **b** : covered with flyspecks ⟨dirty ~ walls⟩ **2** : TAINTED, IMPAIRED ⟨a ~ reputation⟩ **3** *often* **flyblowed** \ˈ=,=\ *slang Austral* : having no money

fly·boat \ˈflī,=\ *n* [part modif., part trans. of D *vlieboot*, fr. *Vlie*, channel between the North sea and the Zuider Zee + *boot* boat] **1** : a large flat-bottomed coasting boat formerly widely used but now chiefly Dutch **2** : any of various fast boats (as a fishing boat, a ship's boat)

fly bomb *var of* FLYING BOMB

fly book *n* : a case usu. in the form of a book for storing anglers' flies

flyboy \ˈ=,=\ *n* [[5]*fly* + *boy*] **1** : a worker who removes printed sheets from a handpress **2** : a printshop worker whose chief duty is to load and unload presses

fly–boy \"\ *n* [[1]*fly* + *boy*] *slang* : AIRCREWMAN; *esp* : a pilot in an air force

flybrush \ˈ=,=\ *n* : a device (as of feathers) formerly used to drive away houseflies

flyby \ˈ=,=\ *n* -s [fr. *fly by*, v.] : a usu. near passage past a predesignated point by an aircraft or space vehicle ⟨a ~ of Mars⟩

[1]**fly–by–night** \ˈflībə,nīt, *usu* -nīd·+V\ *n* **1** : one given to being abroad at night **2** *also* **fly–by–night·er** \¦flībə¦nīd·ə(r), -nītə-\ **a** : one that escapes at night from his creditors **b** : one without established reputation or standing and therefore regarded as a poor risk (as for credit or future productivity) **3** : a square sail sometimes spread on fore-and-aft-rigged ships when running before the wind

[2]**fly–by–night** \"\ *adj* **1** *of a business enterprise or promoter* : established or prepared to take advantage of an opportunity for immediate profit and often shady or irresponsible and inadequately financed for stability ⟨a *fly-by-night* salesman⟩ ⟨*fly-by-night* insurance plans⟩ ⟨a *fly-by-night* cut-rate drugstore⟩ **2** : TRANSITORY, PASSING ⟨a *fly-by-night* political disorder⟩ : UNRELIABLE, UNSTABLE ⟨the symphony was no *fly-by-night* venture —Green Peyton⟩

fly camp *n* : a temporary advanced camp at a distance from a base camp

fly cap *n* : a woman's cap with sides resembling wings and worn in the 17th and 18th centuries

fly–cast \ˈ=,=\ *vb* : FLY-FISH

flycaster \ˈ=,==\ *n* : an angler preferring or specializing in fly-fishing

fly casting *n* : the action of throwing the lure when fly-fishing

flycatcher \ˈ=,==\ *n* **1** : any of numerous birds (order Passeriformes) that feed upon insects taken on the wing: **a** : a member of the Old World passerine family Muscicapidae (as the spotted flycatcher) **b** : any of numerous New World birds of the family Tyrannidae (as the kingbird, peewee, and least flycatcher) — called also *tyrant flycatcher* **2** : DROSOPHYLLUM 2

fly–catching \ˈ=,==\ *adj*, *of a bird* : having the habit of catching insects on the wing

fly–catching warbler *n* : any of numerous American wood warblers having strong rictal bristles at the base of the bill and customarily feeding on insects caught on the wing

fly cop *n* [prob. fr. [3]*fly*] *slang* : PLAINCLOTHESMAN : DETECTIVE

fly cutter *n* [[2]*fly*] : a cutting tool set transversely to and revolving with the arbor of a lathe and acting upon work fed into its circular path

fly dope *n* **1** : a dressing that makes angling flies water-resistant so that they will float **2** : an insect repellent

fly dresser *n* : a maker of artificial flies for angling

flyed *past of* FLY

flyer *var of* FLIER

fly–fish \ˈ=,=\ *vi* : to angle with artificial flies ~ *vt* : to fly-fish in

fly–fisher \ˈ=,==\ *also* **fly–fisherman** \ˈ=,===\ *n*, *pl* **fly–fishers** *also* **fly–fishermen** : an angler who uses or prefers the technique of fly-fishing

fly–fishing \ˈ=,==\ *n* : the technique or act of angling by casting an artificial fly as lure

[1]**flyflap** \ˈ=,=\ *n* [ME *flieflappe*, fr. *flie* fly + *flappe* flap — more at FLY, FLAP] : a device (as a fan) for driving away or killing flies

[2]**flyflap** \"\ *vt*, *archaic* : to strike with or as if with a flyflap; *broadly* : BEAT, LASH ~ *vi* : to drive away flies with a flyflap — **flyflapper** \ˈ=,==\ *n*

flyflower \ˈ=,=\ *n* : DUTCHMAN'S-BREECHES

fly frame *n* **1** *in textile manuf* : any of various slubbing, roving, intermediate, and other frames on which flyers are used **2** *in glass manuf* : a grinding and polishing machine

fly front *n* : a concealed closing on the front of coats, skirts, shirts, dresses — compare [2]FLY 6a

fly fungus *n* **1** : FLY AGARIC **2** : a fungus (*Entomophthora muscae*) that is parasitic on flies — called also *fly mold*

fly gallery *or* **fly floor** *n* : a narrow raised platform at the side of a theatrical stage from which the lines for flying scenery are manipulated

fly governor *n* : [2]FLY 3a

fly half *n* : STANDOFF HALF

fly honeysuckle *n* **1** : any of several shrubs of the genus *Lonicera*: as **a** : EUROPEAN FLY HONEYSUCKLE **b** : a straggling shrub (*L. canadensis*) with leaf margins and petioles ciliate — called also *American fly honeysuckle* **c** : TARTARIAN HONEYSUCKLE **2** : an African shrub (*Halleria lucida*) of the family Scrophulariaceae

fly in *vt* : to switch (a railroad car) by a flying switch

fly–in \ˈ=,=\ *n* [fr. *fly in*, v.] **1** : an act of flying to a destination ⟨planned the *fly-in* of the rescue planes⟩ **2** : an outdoor theater planned for the patronage of persons remaining in their private planes — compare DRIVE-IN

[1]**flying** *adj* [ME, fr. pres. part. of *flien* to fly — more at FLY] **1** : moving or capable of moving in the air with or as if with wings ⟨~ clouds⟩ **2** : moving or made by moving lightly or

rapidly ⟨sped on ~ feet⟩ ⟨made a ~ start⟩ **:** intended for rapid movement or action ⟨a ~ coach⟩ ⟨a police ~ squad⟩ **3 :** passing about freely and usu. without evident authority ⟨~ rumors⟩ **4 :** FLEETING, TRANSITORY, BRIEF ⟨a ~ impression⟩ ⟨a ~ visit⟩ **5 :** having stylized wings — see BRAND illustration **6** *of stairs* **:** ascending without a turn

[2]**flying** *n* -s [ME, fr. gerund of *flien*] **1 flyings** *pl* **:** [2]FLY 7d **2 flyings** *pl, South & Midland* **:** the lower leaves of the tobacco plant **3 :** locomotion by air

flying bent *n* **:** MOOR GRASS 2

flying boat *n* **:** a seaplane whose hull is the means of support on water — compare FLOATPLANE

flying bomb *or* **fly bomb** *n* **:** ROBOT BOMB

flying bond *n* **:** a bond in masonry formed by inserting headers at considerable intervals only

flying boom *n* **:** a rigid fuel pipe flexibly joined to the tail of a tanker airplane and fitted at its after end with movable airfoils which are controllable from the tanker and which permit it to be guided into proper contact with an airplane being refueled in flight

flying bridge *n* **1 :** a suspended or floating usu. temporary bridge (as a pontoon bridge) **2 :** FLYING FERRY **3 :** the highest bridge on a ship having more than one

flying buttress *n* **:** a masonry structure typically consisting of a straight inclined bar carried on an arch and a solid pier or buttress against which it abuts that is used to take up the thrust of a roof or vault which cannot be supported by ordinary buttresses

flying buttress

flying camp *n* **1 :** a temporary military camp **2 :** a company, squadron, or other body of troops formed for rapid movement from place to place

flying cat *n* **1 :** FLYING MARMOT **2 :** FLYING LEMUR

flying circus *n* **1 :** a rotary echelon formation of airplanes in action **2 :** an organized group of pilots engaged in public exhibition flying

flying coachman *n* **:** a black-and-yellow honey eater (*Zanthomiza phrygia*) of Australia — called also *regent honey eater*

flying colors *n pl* **:** complete success ⟨passed his exams with *flying colors*⟩

flying column *n* **:** a strong military detachment that operates at a distance from the main force

flying deck *n* **:** a deck on a ship supported at the side by railings, stanchions, or other open framing

flying disk *n* **:** FLYING SAUCER

flying doe *n* **:** a female red kangaroo of Australia

flying dragon *n* **1 :** DRAGON 7a **2 :** DRAGONFLY

flying facade *n* **:** a front wall of a building when extended up above the roof **:** FALSE FRONT

flying fence *n* **:** a fence that in the hunting field can be cleared at a gallop

flying ferry *n* **:** a raft used as a ferry and held by an anchor cable fastened upstream from the ferry site

flying field *n* **:** a field with a graded portion for the taking off and landing of airplanes and sometimes with buildings for their shelter and maintenance

flying fish *n* **1 :** any of numerous fishes chiefly of tropical and warm seas that have long pectoral fins suggesting wings, that are capable of leaving the water and moving some distance through the air chiefly by the motion of the tail before they entirely leave the water, and that constitute the family Exocoetidae **2 :** BUTTERFLY FISH 1e; *broadly* **:** any of various related So. American fishes reputed to skim over the surface of the water **3 :** a sea robin of the genus *Prionotus* **4 :** FLYING GURNARD

flying fox *n* **1 :** FRUIT BAT **2** *Austral* **:** a carrier (as for mining material or produce) operating on cables over a gorge or other obstacle

flying frog *n* **:** any of several East Indian tree frogs of the genus *Polypedates* having very large and broadly webbed feet that serve as parachutes and enable the frogs to make very long leaps

flying gecko *n* **:** a gecko (*Ptychozoon homalocephalum*) having membranous expansions along the sides of the body, head, limbs, and tail — called also *fringed gecko*

flying gurnard *n* **:** any of several marine fishes that resemble gurnards, constitute the family Dactylopteridae, and have very large pectoral fins which allow them to glide above the water for short distances — called also *flying robin*

flying herd *n, Brit* **:** a dairy herd kept only for milk production, all calves being sold or discarded and all replacements being brought in from other sources

flying horse *n* **1 :** HIPPOGRIFF **2 :** a mechanized seat in the shape of a horse (as on a merry-go-round)

flying jen·ny \ˌ==ˈjenē\ *or* **flying jin·ny** \-ˈjinē\ *n, chiefly South & Midland* **:** a usu. simple homemade merry-go-round

flying jib *n* **:** a sail set outside of the jib and on the flying jibboom — see SAIL illustration

flying jibboom *n* **:** an extension of a jibboom — see SHIP illustration

flying lemur *n* **:** either of two arboreal nocturnal mammals that are about the size of a cat, that have a broad fold of skin extending from the neck to the tail on each side so as to embrace the limbs and form a parachute used in making long sailing leaps, very fine soft fur, and largely frugivorous habits, and that are usu. considered to constitute a distinct order (Dermoptera) although they have sometimes been placed with the insectivores or primates or even included among the bats: **a :** an East Indian mammal (*Cynocephalus volans*) that somewhat suggests a large squirrel **b :** a very similar Philippine mammal (*C. philippinensis*)

flying level *n* **:** a hand level used by civil engineers for reconnaissance over a course (as of a projected road or canal)

flying lizard *n* **:** DRAGON 7a

fly·ing·ly *adv* **:** with flying colors

flying machine *n* **:** an apparatus for navigating the air ⟨began to look anxiously for a level place on which to land his *flying machine* —Tudor David⟩

flying mare *n* **:** a wrestling maneuver in which the aggressor seizes an opponent's wrist, turns about, and jerks him over his back

flying marmot *n* **:** TAGUAN; *broadly* **:** any of various large flying squirrels of the genus *Petaurista*

flying moor *n* **:** a mooring in which the first anchor is let go while the ship has enough way to carry it at least to the point for dropping the second anchor

flying mouse *n* **:** any of several tiny flying phalangers of the genus *Acrobates*

flying officer *n* **:** an air force officer (as in the British Royal Air Force) equivalent in rank to a lieutenant in the army

flying parry *n, in fencing* **:** a backward glide on an opponent's blade in the high line followed by a cutover return made to either the high or low line

flying pay *n* **:** FLIGHT PAY

flying phalanger *or* **flying opossum** *n* **:** any of various small phalangers of the Australian region (esp. of the genera *Petaurus* and *Acrobates*) that have a wide membrane like that of the flying squirrels connecting the forelegs and hind legs and similarly used — called also *flying squirrel, squirrel;* compare SUGAR SQUIRREL

flying ring *n* **:** one of a pair of metal rings covered with leather or rubber and suspended at the ends of swinging ropes for use in gymnastic exercises

flying robin *n* **:** FLYING GURNARD

flying sap *n* **:** a sap constructed well to the front under enemy fire and covered by using two gabions filled with earth and pushed forward side by side

flying saucer *n* **:** any of various unidentified moving objects repeatedly reported as seen in the air and usu. alleged to be saucer-shaped or disk-shaped — called also *flying disk*

flying shear *n* **:** blades that cut off hot strip steel while it is being rolled by moving with the strip at the moment of severing

flying shore *n* **:** a horizontal supporting shore

flying skip *n* **:** a skip (as in dancing) covering distance while in the air

flying snail *n* **:** PTEROPOD

flying snake *n* **:** a brilliant gold-and-black tree snake (*Chrysopelea ornata*) of the family Boigidae that is able to leap clear of the ground when striking and often planes from tree to tree in the manner of a flying squirrel for distances as great as eight feet

flying speed *n* **:** an airspeed sufficient to provide the lift necessary to support an airplane in level flight

flying spider *n* **:** a ballooning spider

flying spot *n* **:** a spot of light that is moved over an image so that light reflected from or transmitted by different parts of the image is translated into electrical signals for transmission (as in television)

flying squadron *n* **1 :** a naval squadron moving rapidly from place to place at a distance from the main command **2 :** a mobile unit of workers specially trained (as for performing a variety of tasks) and available for assignment wherever needed (as to meet an emergency or maintain a steady production level) **3 :** a mobile strong-arm squad; *esp* **:** one active in a strike or in labor organizational proceedings

flying squid *n* **:** any of various squids that are able to leap out of the water

flying squirrel *n* **1 :** any of various squirrels distinguished by folds of skin connecting the forelegs and hind legs that enable them to make very long gliding leaps; *esp* **:** a small large-eyed nocturnal No. American squirrel (*Glaucomys volans*) with very soft fur that is gray or brownish above and pure white below — see PETAURISTIDAE, TAGUAN **2** *Austral* **:** FLYING PHALANGER **3 :** an African scaletail

flying start *n* **:** a start in racing in which the signal is given while the competitors are in motion

flying switch *n* **:** a maneuver in which one or more railroad cars are disconnected from a locomotive while moving and as the locomotive pulls away are switched to another track to roll to a desired position under their own momentum

flying tackle *n* **1 :** a tackle in football in which the tackler dives or throws his body through the air at the ballcarrier **2 :** a professional wrestling maneuver in which a contestant lunges at his opponent from a distance and hits him with his shoulder at or near the waist

flying tail *n* **:** a horizontal stabilizer on a high-speed airplane that has its entire surface adjustable to correct longitudinal trim

flying wedge *n* **1 :** an offensive formation in football in which the players form up in a wedge with the ballcarrier at the center **2 a :** a formation (as of guards or police) resembling the football flying wedge **b :** something notably vigorous and determined in action

flying windmill *n, slang* **:** HELICOPTER

fly kick *n* **:** the act or an instance of fly-kicking in rugby

fly–kick \ˈ=ˌ=\ *vi* **:** to kick the ball in rugby without first catching it with the hands

fly ladder *n* **:** [2]FLY 11

flyleaf \ˈ=ˌ=\ *n* [fr. [2]*fly* + *leaf*] **1 :** a blank leaf at the beginning or end of a book or similar work; *specif* **:** the free endpaper **2 :** paper attached to the inner edge of a paper box to cover the contents or for decoration

fly·less \ˈflīləs\ *adj* **:** free from infestation with flies (as houseflies or blowflies) — **fly·less·ness** *n* -ES

fly line *n* **1 :** the habitual line of flight of a bird group in its migrations — compare FLYWAY **2 :** line for use in fly-fishing

fly loft *n* **:** the flies of a theater

fly·man \ˈflīmən\ *n, pl* **flymen 1 :** the driver of a fly **2 :** a worker in the flies of a theater who manipulates curtains and scenery

fly mold *n* **:** FLY FUNGUS 2

fly mushroom *n* **:** FLY AGARIC

fly·ness *n* -ES [[3]*fly* + *-ness*] **:** the quality or state of being knowing, wide-awake, or crafty ⟨the ~ of his approach to the topic⟩

fly net *n* **:** a net to exclude or keep off insects (as from a harness horse)

fly netting *n* **:** fine cotton mesh formerly used for window screens

fly nut *n* **:** WING NUT

fly orchid *n* **:** a European orchid (*Listera muscifera*) whose flowers resemble flies

fly out *vi* **:** to be put out in baseball by hitting a fly ball that is caught ⟨*flied out* to left field⟩ ⟨*flied out* to the shortstop⟩

flyover \ˈ=ˌ==\ *n* -s [fr. *fly over*, v.] **1 :** a prearranged and usu. low-altitude flight over a public gathering or place by one or more airplanes **2** *Brit* **:** OVERPASS

fly page *n* [[2]*fly*] **:** one side of a flyleaf

flypaper \ˈ=ˌ==\ *n* **:** paper poisoned or coated with a sticky substance for killing flies

flypast \ˈ=ˌ=\ *n* -s [fr. *fly past*, v.] *Brit* **:** FLYBY

[1]**flype** \ˈflīp\ *vt* -ED/-ING/-S [ME *flipen*, prob. of Scand origin like [2]*flype*] **1** *chiefly Scot* **:** to strip off by or as if by peeling **2** *chiefly Scot* **:** to turn or fold back ⟨~ a stocking⟩

[2]**flype** \ˈ"\ *n* -s [of Scand origin; akin to Icel *flipi* lip of a horse, piece of skin or leather, *flipa* to wound, ON *fleipa* to gossip, OSw *flipa* to whimper and perh. to ON *flā* to flay — more at FLAY] *chiefly Scot* **:** a fold or flap (as of something turned back)

fly poison *n* **1 :** a bulbous herb (*Amianthium muscaetoxicum*) of the family Liliaceae of which the pounded bulb has been used as a poison for flies **2 :** any of several plants of the genus *Zigadenus* (esp. *Z. densus*)

fly press *n* **:** a fly-operated hand-screw press (as for embossing)

flyproof \ˈ=ˌ=\ *adj* **:** made tight or close enough to keep houseflies out

fly rail *n* **1 :** a bracket that turns out to support the hinged leaf of a table **2 :** a railing above the fly gallery of a theatrical stage bearing cleats or pins by which ropes may be made fast

fly reel *n* **:** a narrow-spool single-action fly-fishing reel

fly rod *n* **:** a light springy rod used with a reel and a heavily oiled or treated line in fly-casting

fly rollway *n* **:** a steep logging skidway on a slope

flysch \ˈflish\ *n* -ES *sometimes cap* [G dial. (Switzerland), lit., something that slides or flows; derivative fr. the root of OHG *fliozzan* to flow — more at FLEET] **:** a thick and extensive deposit largely of sandstone that is formed in a geosyncline adjacent to a rising mountain belt and is esp. common in the Alpine region of Europe

fly sheet *n* [[2]*fly*] **1 :** a small loose advertising sheet **:** HANDBILL **2 :** a sheet of a folder, booklet, or catalog giving directions for the use of or information about the material that follows

fly shuttle *n* [[1]*fly*] **:** a handloom shuttle operated by a cord or picker stick

[1]**flyspeck** \ˈ=ˌ=\ *n* [[5]*fly* + *speck*] **1 :** a speck or stain made by the excrement of a fly; *broadly* **:** any insignificant dot **2 :** a disease of pome fruits caused by a fungus (*Leptothyrium pomi*) and marked by clusters of small black specks on the fruit

[2]**flyspeck** \ˈ"\ *vt* **:** to soil with flyspecks

fly stone *n* **:** native cobalt arsenide used esp. formerly as a fly poison by being ground and added to sweetened water

fly–strike \ˈ=ˌ=\ *n* **:** infestation (as of the skin of sheep) with fly maggots (as of blowflies)

fly–struck \ˈ=ˌ=\ *adj* **:** infested with fly maggots

flyswatter \ˈ=ˌ==\ *also* **flyswat** \ˈ=ˌ=\ *n* **:** SWATTER

fly table *n* **:** BUTTERFLY TABLE

flyte \ˈflīt\ *var of* FLITE

fly tent *n* **:** a tent with a fly

fly·ti·er \ˈflīˌtī(ə)r, -īə\ *n* -s **:** a maker of flies for angling

flytime \ˈ=ˌ=\ *n* **:** the season of year during which a particular kind of fly (as the housefly or blowfly) is esp. troublesome

[1]**flyt·ing** *var of* FLITING

[2]**flyt·ing** \ˈflīdiŋ\ *n* -s [[1]*flyting*] **:** a dispute or exchange of personal abuse or ridicule in verse form between two characters in a poem (as an early epic) or between two poets (as of 16th century Scotland)

fly title *n* [[2]*fly*] *Brit* **:** HALF TITLE 1

flytrap \ˈ=ˌ=\ *n* **1 :** a trap for catching flies often having the form of a wire or glass cylinder with a conical cover and bottom in which is a small opening **2 a :** PITCHER PLANT **b :** DOGBANE 1 **c :** VENUS'S-FLYTRAP

[1]**fly–up** \ˈ=ˌ=\ *adj* **1 :** arranged to open by flying upward ⟨a *fly-up* lid⟩ **2 :** arranged to be reached by flying ⟨the advantages of *fly-up* waterers in the poultry house⟩

[2]**fly–up** \ˈ"\ *n* -s **:** a ceremony at which a brownie scout formally leaves her brownie troop and becomes a member of an intermediate girl scout troop

fly up *vi* [[1]*fly* + *up*] **:** to become a member of an intermediate girl scout troop on leaving a brownie scout troop

fly–up–the–creek \ˌ=(ˌ)==ˈ=\ *n* **1 :** GREEN HERON **2** *chiefly South & Midland* **:** a flighty person **3** *usu cap F&C* **:** FLORIDIAN — used as a nickname

flyway \ˈ=ˌ=\ *n* [[2]*fly* + *way*] **:** a geographic course along which birds customarily migrate between breeding and wintering areas; *broadly* **:** such a migration route together with the breeding and wintering areas that it connects

flyweight \ˈ=ˌ=\ *n* [[5]*fly* + *weight*] **1 a :** a boxer whose weight does not exceed 112 pounds — compare FEATHERWEIGHT **b :** something small or trivial of its kind **2 :** a weight (as on a closure or governor) having a flyball action

flywheel \ˈ=ˌ=\ *n* [[2]*fly* + *wheel*] **:** a heavy metal wheel for opposing and moderating by its inertia any fluctuation of speed in the machinery with which it revolves; *esp* **:** one on an engine crankshaft to counteract variable torque during the stroke and carry the engine over the dead centers

fly whisk *n* **:** a device that consists of a bundle of flexible fibers (as horsehairs) mounted in a handle, that is used primarily to brush away flies (as from a person or a horse), and that has often served as a symbol of high position or authority

flywire \ˈ=ˌ=\ *n* [[5]*fly* + *wire*] *Austral* **:** SCREEN 11

fm *abbr* **1** farm **2** fathom **3** form **4** from

FM *abbr* **1** face measurement **2** fan marker **3** field manual **4** field marshal **5** fine measurement **6** foreign mission **7** foundation member **8** frequency modulation

Fm *symbol* fermium

f major *n, usu cap F* **:** the major musical key having a signature of one flat

f minor *n, usu cap F* **:** the minor musical key having a signature of four flats

fmr *abbr* former

fn *abbr* **1** footnote **2** fusion

fnd *abbr* found

fndd *abbr* founded

fndg *abbr* founding

fndn *abbr* foundation

fndr *abbr* founder

f–number \ˈ=ˌ==\ *n* [*f*, symbol for *focal length*] **:** the ratio of the focal length to the entrance pupil diameter in an optical system or the objective of such a system; *specif* **:** a number following the symbol f/ that expresses the relative aperture of a camera lens, the smaller the number the brighter the image and therefore the shorter the exposure required ⟨the *f-number* of a lens with an f/8 relative aperture is 8⟩

fo *abbr* folio

FO *abbr* **1** field officer **2** firm offer **3** flag officer **4** flight officer **5** flying officer **6** foreign office **7** for orders **8** forward observer **9** free overside **10** fuel oil **11** full organ **12** full out

[1]**foal** \ˈfōl\ *n* -s [ME *fole*, fr. OE *fola*; akin to OHG *folo* foal, ON *foli*, Goth *fula* foal, L *pullus* young of an animal, Gk *pōlos* foal, young of an animal, girl, Gk *paid-, pais* child — more at FEW] **1 :** the young of an animal of the horse family; *esp* **:** one under one year — compare COLT, FILLY **2** *obs* **:** the young of various animals — **in foal** *or* **with foal :** PREGNANT — used of a mare

[2]**foal** \ˈ"\ *vb* -ED/-ING/-S [ME *folen*, fr. *fole*, n.] *vt* **:** to bring forth (a foal) ~ *vi* **:** to bring forth young — used of an animal of the horse family; often used with *down*

foalfoot \ˈ=ˌ=\ *n, pl* **foalfoots** [ME *folefot*, fr. *fole* + *fot*, *foot* foot; fr. the shape of the leaves] **:** COLTSFOOT a

foal·hood \ˈ=ˌhu̇d\ *n* **:** the period or state of being a foal

[1]**foam** \ˈfōm\ *n* -s [ME *fom, fome, foom*, fr. OE *fām*; akin to OHG *feim* foam, Norw *feim* coating, L *spuma* foam, *pumex* pumice, Skt *phena* foam] **1 :** a light whitish mass of fine bubbles that is formed in or on the surface of a liquid by agitation (as of ocean waves) or fermentation or effervescence **:** a dispersion of a gas in a liquid **:** FROTH, SPUME — compare EMULSION 2a **2 :** the froth formed in the mouth of an animal by salivation or on the skin (as of a horse) by sweating **3 :** SEA **4 :** something like foam ⟨a fine ~ of lace at his wrists and throat —Max Peacock⟩ **5 :** a stabilized frothy substance generated either by a chemical reaction or by mechanical agitation for use in fighting esp. gasoline and oil fires by blanketing and smothering them **6 :** material in a lightweight cellular spongy or rigid form produced by foaming: as **a :** FOAM RUBBER **b :** EXPANDED PLASTIC

[2]**foam** \ˈ"\ *vb* -ED/-ING/-S [ME *fomen*, fr. *fom, fome*, n.] *vi* **1 :** to gather or form foam **2 :** to froth at the mouth in anger **:** be angry **:** RAGE ⟨he ~*ed* and stormed and threatened⟩ **3 :** to gush out in foam ⟨blood ~*ing* from his mouth⟩ **4 :** to form a froth or scum on the water surface that entrains solids and prevents the liberation of steam — used of a steam boiler ~ *vt* **1 :** to cause to foam **:** cover with foam; *specif* **:** to cause air bubbles to form in (as concrete, mortar, or plaster) **2 :** to introduce gas bubbles into (as a plastic or resin) for the purpose of forming a lightweight cellular material **:** EXPAND, WHIP ⟨the plastic can be ~*ed* in place in a sandwich construction⟩

foam cell *n* **:** a swollen vacuolated reticuloendothelial cell filled with lipide inclusions and characteristic of certain conditions involving disturbance of lipide metabolism

foam concrete *or* **foamed concrete** *n* **:** concrete in which air bubbles have been formed primarily to reduce the weight

foamed plastic *also* **foam plastic** *n* **:** EXPANDED PLASTIC

foam·er \ˈfōmə(r)\ *n* -s **:** one that foams ⟨~*s* crashing on the shore⟩

foamflower \ˈ=ˌ==\ *n* **:** FALSE MITERWORT

foam glass *n* **:** a black opaque cellular glass material 1/15 the weight of glass that is made by firing crushed glass with powdered carbon and is used as a substitute for cork, balsa wood, or kapok in life preservers and as an insulating material

foam·i·ly \ˈfōməlē, -li\ *adv* **:** in a foamy manner

foam·i·ness \-mēnəs, -min-\ *n* -ES **:** the quality or state of being foamy

foam·ing \ˈfōmiŋ\ *adj* [ME *foming*, fr. pres. part. of *fomen* to foam — more at FOAM] **:** covered with foam **:** producing foam — **foam·ing·ly** *adv*

foaming agent *n* **:** a material used to produce foaming (as in concrete, mortar, plaster)

Foam·ite \ˈfōˌmīt\ *trademark* — used for a preparation consisting of two chemical solutions that on mixture generate a tough foam of carbon dioxide for extinguishing fires

foam·less \ˈ=ləs\ *adj* **:** having no foam **:** free from foam ⟨the blue line of a ~ sea —D.G.Rossetti⟩

foamlike \ˈ=ˌ=\ *adj* **:** having the appearance and texture of foam ⟨~ dresses⟩

foam rubber *n* **:** spongy rubber of fine texture made from latex by foaming (as by whipping) before vulcanization and used esp. in mattresses, cushions, and upholstery

foamy \ˈfōmē, -mi\ *adj* -ER/-EST [ME *fomy*, fr. OE *fāmig*, fr. *fām* foam + *-ig* -y — more at FOAM] **1 :** covered with foam **:** FROTHY **2 :** full of, consisting of, or resembling foam

[1]**fob** \ˈfäb\ *vt* **fobbed; fobbed; fobbing; fobs** [ME *fobben* — more at FOP] **1** *archaic* **:** to impose on **:** DECEIVE, CHEAT **2** *archaic* **:** to obtain or to introduce by fraud or deceit **:** palm off **3 :** to fob off

[2]**fob** \ˈ"\ *n* -s [ME] *archaic* **:** TRICK, SHAM

[3]**fob** \ˈ"\ *n* -s [perh. akin to G dial. *fuppe* pocket, *fuppen* to pocket stealthily] **1** *also* **fob pocket :** a small pocket just below the front waistband of men's trousers **2** *also* **fob chain :** a short chain or ribbon connecting a watch carried in a fob pocket and an ornament hanging outside **3 a** (1) **:** an ornament (as a seal) attached to a fob chain (2) **:** a decorative device attached to a zipper, pin, or belt **b :** the watch carried in a fob pocket

[4]**fob** \ˈ"\ *vt* **fobbed; fobbed; fobbing; fobs :** to put into one's fob **:** POCKET

fob 2

FOB *abbr, often not cap* free on board

fob off *vt* [[1]*fob*] **1 :** to put off with a deceit or with an inferior substitute for what is needed or expected ⟨the . . . patient thus denied effective examination is *fobbed off* with a bottle of medicine —*Spectator*⟩ **2 :** to pass or offer (something spurious) as genuine **:** palm off ⟨the pretentious phraseology with which they *fobbed off* their prophecies on the laity —Lancelot Hogben⟩ **3 :** to put aside

: fend off ⟨a pleasant . . . gift of humor which he used to *fob off* laymen who wanted a simple explanation of relativity —G.R.Harrison⟩ **:** thrust away ⟨why do they now *fob off* what once they would have welcomed eagerly —Walter Lippmann⟩

FOC *abbr* **1** free of charge **2** free on car

fo·cal \ˈfōkəl\ *adj* [*focus* + *-al*] **:** of, relating to, or having a focus — **fo·cal·ly** \-kəlē, -li\ *adv*

focal area *n* **:** a region whose characteristic speech features are imitated in neighboring regions **:** a center from which linguistic changes spread — compare GRADED AREA, RELIC AREA

focal infection *n* **:** a persistent bacterial infection of some organ or region (as a tonsil or the root of a tooth); *esp* **:** one causing symptoms elsewhere in the body

fo·cal·iza·tion \ˌfōkələˈzāshən, -ˌlīˈz-\ *n* -S **:** the act of focalizing or the state of being focalized

fo·cal·ize \ˈfōkəˌlīz\ *vb* -ED/-ING/-S *vt* **1 :** to bring to a focus **:** FOCUS **2 :** to adjust the focus of (as a lens or the eye) **3** *med* **:** to confine to a limited area ⟨∼ an infection⟩ ∼ *vi* **1 :** to come to a focus **:** CONVERGE, CONCENTRATE **2** *med* **:** to become confined to a limited area ⟨pullorum disease commonly ∼*s* in the ovary of the adult bird⟩

focal length *n* **:** the distance from the principal point of a lens or concave mirror to the principal focus

focal plane *n* **:** a plane that is parallel to the plane of a lens or mirror and that passes through a principal focus

focal–plane shutter *n* **:** a camera shutter used chiefly for instantaneous exposures in which a slit in an opaque curtain is passed directly across and in front of the film near the focal plane, the width of the slit and the speed of its movement determining the duration of the exposure

focal point *n* **1 :** PRINCIPAL FOCUS **2 :** a center of activity or of interest **:** the point of convergence of lines of action or of argument ⟨the producer . . . is the *focal point*, the coordinator of all these creative forces —Rebecca Franklin⟩

focal spot *n* **:** the small area of the target of an X-ray tube on which the cathode rays are focused

focht \ˈfäkt\ *Scot var of* FOUGHT

fo·com·e·ter \fōˈkäməd·ə(r)\ *also* **fo·cim·e·ter** \-ˈsim-\ *n* [F *focomètre, focimètre*, fr. *foco-, foci-* (fr. NL *focus*) + *-mètre* -meter] **:** an instrument for measuring either the visual or the photographic focal length of an objective or of another optical system

fo'c'sle *var of* FORECASTLE

¹fo·cus \ˈfōkəs\ *n, pl* **focuses** \-ōkəsəz\ *or* **fo·ci** \-ōˌsī\ [NL, fr. L, fireplace, hearth; perh. akin to Arm *bosor* red, *bots* flame] **1 :** a point at which rays (as of light, heat, sound) converge or from which they diverge or appear to diverge; *specif* **:** the point where the geometrical lines or their prolongations conforming to the rays diverging from or converging toward another point intersect and give rise to an image after reflection by a mirror or refraction by a lens or optical system **2 a :** FOCAL LENGTH ⟨a telescope of twenty-feet ∼⟩ **b :** adjustment (as of the eye or an eyepiece) for distinct vision ⟨a telescope or microscope comes sharply to ∼⟩ **c :** the position in which something must be placed (as in relation to a camera lens) for clearness of image or clarity of mental perception ⟨the whole scene was difficult to bring into ∼⟩ ⟨brought into immediate ∼ the meaning of the war⟩ **d :** the area that may be seen distinctly by the eye or resolved into a clear image by a lens ⟨wide-*focus* lens camera⟩ **3 :** one of the points that with the corresponding directrix defines a conic section ⟨conic *foci*⟩ **4 :** a localized area of disease or the chief site of a generalized disease or infection ⟨a tuberculous ∼ in the lungs⟩ **5** [L] *archaic* **:** HEARTH, FIREPLACE **6 :** a central point: as **a :** a center of activity or attraction or one drawing the greatest attention and interest ⟨Whitehall . . . was the ∼ of political intrigue and of fashionable gaiety —T.B.Macaulay⟩ **b :** a point of concentration or of emanation ⟨a happy man or woman is . . . a radiating ∼ of goodwill —R.L.Stevenson⟩ **c :** one aspect or area of a culture that is more complex and extensively elaborated than others **d :** FOCAL AREA **7 :** the place of origin of an earthquake being a rather indefinite region that approaches nearest to a point in some volcanic earthquakes and nearest to a line or plane in some tectonic earthquakes **8 :** the first-formed usu. central part of a fish scale **9 :** a unit of classification in the Midwestern system for American archaeology constituting a group of components yielding artifacts almost identical in those features determinative of type — see ASPECT; compare PATTERN, PHASE **syn** see CENTER — **in focus :** having or giving the proper sharpness of outline due to good focalization — used of an optical instrument or its parts or of an image — **out of focus :** not in focus

²focus \ˈ"\ *vb* **focused** *also* **focussed; focused** *also* **focussed; focusing** *also* **focussing; focuses** *also* **focusses** *vt* **1 a :** to bring (as light rays) to a focus **:** CONCENTRATE **b :** to cause (an electron beam esp. in a television tube) to converge and give a small bright spot **2 :** to cause to be concentrated ⟨the crime ∼*ed* public attention on the problem of parole⟩ **3 :** to adjust the focus of (as the eye or a lens) ⟨∼*ing* the glasses on a distant ship⟩ **4 :** to bring (as an image) into focus ⟨the most clearly ∼*ed* picture yet available of the American conservative mind at work —Eric Goldman⟩ ∼ *vi* **1 :** to come to a focus **:** CONVERGE **2 :** to adjust one's eye or a camera to a certain range ⟨newborn babies cannot ∼ for several months⟩

fo·cus·able \-səbəl\ *adj* **:** capable of being focused or brought into focus

fo·cus·er \-sə(r)\ *n* -S **:** one that focuses or aids in focusing

focusing cloth *n* **:** an opaque dark cloth used to cover the rear of the camera and the head and shoulders of the photographer in order to exclude most of the light except that coming through the lens

focusing coil *n* **:** a coil that focuses an electron beam (as in a cathode-ray tube) by means of a magnetic field

focusing glass *n* **:** a small magnifying glass used for enlarging the image thrown on the ground glass of a camera as an aid in exact focusing

focus lamp *n* **1 :** an incandescent lamp having a filament coiled or crumpled into a spiral or zigzag form so that the light, being concentrated in a small space, can be brought into the focus of a lens or mirror **2 :** an arc lamp with feeding mechanism so constructed as to keep the arc in a constant position with reference to the optical system by means of which its rays are focused

fo·cus·less \ˈ==ləs\ *adj* **:** having no focus **:** not focusing

FOD *abbr* free of damage

¹fod·der \ˈfädə(r)\ *n* -S *often attrib* [ME, fr. OE *fōdor, foddor* — more at FOOD] **1 :** FOOD, PROVISION — not now in formal use **2 :** something fed to domestic animals; *esp* **:** coarse food (as hay, vegetables, corn fodder) for cattle, horses, and sheep ⟨∼ plants⟩ ⟨∼ trees⟩ — compare CONCENTRATE, ROUGHAGE **3 :** something that is used to supply a constant demand **:** something to be consumed: as **a** *slang* **:** AMMUNITION **b :** raw material for artistic creation ⟨burlesques of animals, babies, and females are perennial clown ∼ —Bill Ballantine⟩ ⟨the ∼ of the middlebrow novelist —V.S. Pritchett⟩ **c :** human beings regarded for a certain purpose as an undifferentiated mass ⟨labor ∼⟩ ⟨cannon ∼⟩ ⟨factory ∼⟩

²fodder \ˈ"\ *vt* **foddered; foddered; foddering** \-d(ə)riŋ\ **fodders** [ME *fodderen*, fr. ¹*fodder*, n.] **1 :** to feed with or as if with fodder **2** *obs* **:** GRAZE

³fodder *var of* FOTHER

fodder beet *n* **:** a sugar beet used or grown for fodder

foddering *n* -S [¹*fodder* + *-ing*] **:** a portion or allowance of fodder

fod·der·less \ˈfädə(r)ləs\ *adj* **:** having no fodder ⟨∼ and starving cattle⟩

fodg·el \ˈfäjəl\ *adj* [prob. fr. *fodge*, var. of ¹*fadge*] *Scot* **:** plump and well-built **:** BUXOM

fo·di·ent \ˈfōdēənt\ *adj* [L *fodient-, fodiens*, pres. part. of *fodere* to dig — more at BED] **:** fitted for digging or burrowing ⟨a ∼ animal⟩

foe \ˈfō\ *n* -S [ME *fo, fa*, fr. OE *fāh, fā*, fr. *fāh, fā* adj., hostile, outlawed; akin to OHG *gifēh* hostile, *fēhan* to hate, ON *feikn* terrible, horrible, Goth *bifaih* greediness, L *piget* it annoys, Skt *piśuna* malicious, treacherous] **1 :** one who holds a grudge or personal enmity, hatred, or malice against another **:** ENEMY ⟨a political ∼ of long standing⟩ **2 :** an enemy in war **:** a hostile army or a member of a hostile force **:** ADVERSARY ⟨whispering, with white lips, "the ∼! They come! they come!" —Lord Byron⟩ **3 :** one who opposes on principle ⟨a ∼ to religion⟩ ⟨a ∼ of speculative theories⟩ **4 :** something prejudicial or injurious ⟨a ∼ to health⟩ **syn** see ENEMY

foe·de·ra·tus \ˌfedəˈrād·əs\ *n, pl* **foedera·ti** \-ˈād·ˌī\ [L, fr. *foederatus*, adj., allied, federated — more at FEDERATE] **:** an auxiliary soldier serving the Roman Empire

foehn *or* **föhn** \ˈfərn, ˈfen, *Ger* fœːn\ *n* -S [G *föhn*, fr. OHG *phōnno*, fr. (assumed) VL *faonius*, fr. L *favonius* warm west wind; akin to L *fovēre* to warm — more at DAY] **:** a warm dry wind blowing down the side of a mountain — compare CHINOOK 3b

foehnlike \ˈ==ˌ=\ *adj* **:** having the characteristics of a foehn

foe·less \ˈfōləs\ *adj* **:** having no enemy

foe·man \ˈfōmən\ *n, pl* **foemen** [ME *foman*, fr. OE *fāhman*, fr. *fāh* hostile + *man* — more at FOE, MAN] **:** an enemy in war **:** FOE ⟨and the stern joy which warriors feel in *foemen* worthy of their steel —Sir Walter Scott⟩

foe·nic·u·lum \fēˈnikyələm\ *n, cap* [NL, fr. L *foeniculum, faeniculum, feniculum* fennel — more at FENNEL] **:** a small genus of Eurasian herbs (family Umbelliferae) with pinnately compound leaves and yellow flowers — see FENNEL

foenngreek *or* **foenugreek** *var of* FENUGREEK

foenus *var of* FAENUS

foetid *var of* FETID

foeto- *or* **foeti-** — see FETO-

foetus *var of* FETUS

fo·far·raw \ˈfōfəˌrȯ\ *var of* FOOFARAW

¹fog \ˈfôg, ˈfäg\ *n* -S [ME *fogge, fog* rank grass, winter grass, perh. of Scand origin; akin to Norw *fogg* tall, worthless grass, ON *fugga* mold, *füll* rotten — more at FOUL] **1** *dial* **a :** dead or decaying grass on land in the winter **b :** a second growth of grass **:** AFTERMATH **2** *dial* **a :** MOSS **b :** VELVET GRASS

²fog \ˈ"\ *vb* **fogged; fogged; fogs** *vt* **1** *Brit* **a :** to pasture (animals) on fog **b :** to feed (cattle) with fog **2** *dial* **:** to leave (land) under fog ∼ *vi, dial* **:** to become overgrown with fog

³fog \ˈ"\ *n* -S [prob. of Scand origin; akin to Shetland Norse *fjog, fjug* thin layer of cloud, dust, Dan *fog* spray, shower, driving rain, ON *fjūk* snowstorm, *fjūka* to be driven by the wind (used of snow), to snow violently; akin to MHG *fochen* to blow, L *pussula, pustula* blister, pimple, Gk *physan* to blow, inflate, *pygē* buttocks, Skt *puṣyati* he thrives, flourishes, nourishes, promotes; basic meaning: blowing, inflating] **1 :** vapor condensed to fine particles of water suspended in the lower atmosphere that differs from cloud only in being near the ground and is sometimes distinguished from mist in being less transparent **2 a :** a murky or thick condition of the atmosphere **b :** a substance so diffused as to lessen the transparency of the atmosphere **c :** a suspension of fine droplets in a gas ⟨tar ∼ in manufactured gas⟩ **3 a :** a fine spray of water or foam discharged from a fog nozzle used in fire fighting **b :** a fine spray of any substance (as an insecticide) **4 :** a state of mental confusion, uncertainty, or obscurity **:** BEWILDERMENT ⟨I am in a complete ∼ as to what to do next⟩ ⟨the subject is wrapped in ∼*s* of vague thinking —H.A. Overstreet⟩ **5** *or* **fog blue a :** a variable color averaging a grayish blue that is redder and paler than electric, greener and paler than copenhagen, and redder, lighter, and stronger than Gobelin **b :** a nearly neutral slightly bluish light gray **6 :** a general or local density in a developed photographic image that is not associated with the image-forming exposure and is caused by chemical action or stray radiation

⁴fog \ˈ"\ *vb* **fogged; fogged; fogging; fogs** *vt* **1 a :** to cover or envelop with or as if with fog ⟨a *fogged* landscape⟩ **b :** to obscure (as a view) with or as if with fog ⟨a heavy smoke *fogged* our view of the city⟩ — often used with *up* ⟨the smoke *fogged* up the road ahead⟩ **c :** to make blurred ⟨his eyes were still *fogged* with sleep⟩ **d :** to make fogbound — often used with *in* ⟨the airport was *fogged* in for two days⟩ **e :** to cover or treat with a substance (as insecticide or pesticide) in the form of spray ⟨thoroughly *fogged* the area with insecticide⟩ **2 :** to make obscure or confusing to the intelligence or understanding ⟨∼ an issue with too much talk⟩ ⟨a text *fogged* by generalities⟩ — often used with *up* ⟨the issue was *fogged* up during the debate⟩ **3 :** to make confused (as a person or the mind) ⟨*fogged* by the examination⟩ ⟨arguments that only ∼ the understanding⟩ **4** *dial* **:** DRIVE, CHASE **5 :** to blur (a field of vision) with lenses that prevent a sharp focus in order to relax accommodation before testing vision **6 :** to produce fog on (a photographic film or plate) during development ∼ *vi* **1 :** to become covered or thick with fog — often used with *up* ⟨the pilot could not return because the airfield had *fogged* up behind him⟩ **2 a :** to become blurred or beclouded by a covering of fog or mist ⟨his glasses *fogged* when he entered the warm room⟩ — often used with *up* ⟨the mirror *fogged* up with the steam⟩ **b :** to become indistinct through exposure to light or radiation **3** *chiefly West* **:** RUSH, HURRY, RUN, GALLOP ⟨cattle came *fogging* down the road⟩ **4** *Brit* **:** to put fog signals in place on a railway line **syn** see OBSCURE

fo·gas \ˈfōˌgäsh\ *n, pl* **fogas** [Hung] **:** an eastern European fish (*Lucioperca sandra*) resembling a perch; *esp* **:** one from Lake Balaton in Hungary that is highly esteemed as food

fogbank \ˈ=ˌ=\ *n* **:** a mass of fog resting upon the sea

fog belt *n* **:** a region where fogs are frequent

fogbound \ˈ=ˌ=\ *adj* **1 :** covered with or surrounded by fog ⟨∼ coast⟩ **2 :** unable to move because of fog ⟨∼ ship⟩ ⟨∼ air passengers at an airport⟩

fog·bow \ˈ=ˌbō\ *n* **:** a nebulous arc or circle of white or yellowish light sometimes seen in a fogbank — called also *fogdog, fogeater, seadog*

fog buoy *n* **1 :** a buoy bearing a warning bell or whistle **2 :** a buoy towed by a ship in formation to indicate to the next astern her proper position — called also *position buoy, towing spar*

fogdog \ˈ=ˌ=\ *n* **:** FOGBOW

fogeater \ˈ=ˌ==\ *n* **1 :** FOGBOW **2 :** the full moon when rising in a fog

fogey *var of* FOGY

fog fever *n, Brit* **:** an acute pulmonary emphysema of cattle grazing on aftermath

fogfruit \ˈ=ˌ=\ *n* **:** a plant of the genus *Lippia* (as *L. lanceolata* and *L. nodiflora*)

fog·gage \ˈfôgij, ˈfäg-\ *n* -S [ME (Sc dial.) *fogage* winter grass, winter grazing, fr. *fog* winter grass + *-age* — more at FOG] *chiefly Scot* **:** ¹FOG 1a

fog·ga·ra \ˈfägərə\ *n* -S [Ar] **:** an underground conduit for water in desert country (as in the Sahara)

¹fog·ger \ˈfôgə(r), ˈfäg-\ *n* -S [²*fog* + *-er*] *dial Eng* **:** a farm laborer chiefly engaged in caring for cattle

²fogger \ˈ"\ *n* -S [⁴*fog* + *-er*] **:** one that fogs: *esp* **:** an apparatus for spreading a fog of pesticide

fog·gie \ˈfägi\ *Scot var of* FOGY

fog·gi·ly \ˈfôgəlē, ˈfäg-, -li\ *adv* **:** in a foggy manner **:** MISTILY

fog·gi·ness \-gēnəs, -gin-\ *n* -ES **:** the quality or state of being foggy

fogging *pres part of* FOG

fog grass *n* **:** ¹FOG 1

fog gun *n* **:** FIRE GUN 1

¹fog·gy \ˈfôgē, ˈfägē, -gi\ *adj* -ER/-EST [¹*fog* + *-y*] **1** *dial Brit* **:** of, covered with, or resembling coarse grass **2** *chiefly Scot* **:** MOSSY

²foggy \ˈ"\ *adj* -ER/-EST [³*fog* + *-y*] **1** *obs* **:** BLOATED, FLABBY **2** *obs* **:** MARSHY, BOGGY **3 a :** filled or abounding with fog ⟨∼ coast⟩ ⟨a ∼ morning⟩ **b :** covered or made opaque by moisture or grime ⟨a ∼ skylight⟩ **c :** FOGGED ⟨a ∼ old snapshot⟩ **4 :** not clear: as **a :** slightly hoarse or husky in tone ⟨her ∼, appealing voice —*Time*⟩ **b :** VAGUE, MUDDLED, CONFUSED ⟨the ∼ language of prophecy⟩ **c :** TENUOUS — used esp. in negative statements ⟨they haven't the *foggiest* notion of what they are voting for⟩

¹foghorn \ˈ=ˌ=\ *n* [³*fog* + *horn*] **1 :** a horn sounded as a fog signal **2 :** a loud hoarse or insistent voice

²foghorn \ˈ"\ *vt* **:** to sound by or as if by a foghorn ⟨personal faults . . . we hear ∼*ed* over the radio —Kay Hardy⟩

fogie *var of* FOGY

fo·gle \ˈfōgəl\ *n* -S [origin unknown] *slang* **:** a silk handkerchief or neckerchief

fogle hunter *or* **fogle heister** *n, slang* **:** PICKPOCKET

fog·less \ˈfôgləs, ˈfäg-\ *adj* **:** marked by the absence of fog ⟨the first ∼ morning in a week⟩

fog light *or* **fog lamp** *n* **:** a lamp or automotive headlight often yellow in color and specially designed to penetrate fog, dust, or smoke

fog nozzle *n* **:** a fire-hose nozzle that discharges a fine spray of water or foam

fo·go \ˈfō(ˌ)gō\ *n* -S [prob. alter. of *hogo*] *dial* **:** STENCH, STINK

fo·gón \fōˈgōn\ *n, pl* **fogo·nes** \-ˈgō(ˌ)nās\ [Sp, hearth, fireplace, prob. fr. Catal *fogó*, fr. *foc* fire, fr. L *focus* hearth, fireplace, fire — more at FOCUS] **:** a corner-set fireplace found in Indian and Spanish American architecture in southwestern U.S.

fo·gou \ˈfō(ˌ)gō\ *n* -S [Corn *fogo, fougo, ogo*; akin to W *gogof* cave, Bret *kougoñ*] *dial Eng* **:** CAVE

fo·gram *or* **fo·grum** \ˈfōgrəm\ *n* -S [origin unknown] **:** an antiquated person **:** FOGY

fog room *n* **:** a room for the curing of concrete into which water is sprayed in a fine mist

fogs *pres 3d sing of* FOG, *pl of* FOG

fo·gy *also* **fo·gey** *or* **fo·gie** \ˈfōgē, -gi\ *n, pl* **fogies** *also* **fogeys** [origin unknown] **1 :** a person who is behind the times, overconservative, or slow — usu. used with *old* ⟨notorious old bore; regular old ∼ —W.M.Thackeray⟩ **2 :** one of the increases over base pay that are given after specified periods of military service

fo·gy·ish \-gēish\ *adj* **:** having old-fashioned views **:** OUT-OF-DATE **:** ANTIQUATED ⟨∼ educators⟩ ⟨∼ opinions⟩

fo·gy·ism \-gēˌizəm\ *n* -S **:** conservative or old-fashioned ideas or behavior

foh \ˈfō\ *archaic var of* FAUGH

föhn *var of* FOEHN

foi·ble \ˈfȯibəl\ *n* -S [obs. F (now *faible*), fr. obs. *foible*, adj. (now *faible*), weak, fr. OF *fleble, feble, foible* — more at FEEBLE] **1 :** the part of a sword blade or foil blade between the middle and point — opposed to *forte* **2 :** a minor flaw or shortcoming in personal character or behavior **:** FAILING, WEAKNESS ⟨longing for past ages is a human ∼⟩ **3 :** an eccentric or whimsical liking for or interest in something **:** FAD ⟨hi-fi looked like the private ∼ of experts —Brooks Atkinson⟩ **syn** see FAULT

foie gras \fwäˈgrä\ *n* [F] **:** fat liver esp. of a goose usu. in the form of a pâté, puree, or terrine

¹foil \ˈfȯil, *esp before pause or consonant* -ȯiəl\ *vt* -ED/-ING/-S [ME *foilen* to trample, full (cloth), modif. of MF *fouler* — more at FULL] **1** *obs* **:** to tread under foot **:** TRAMPLE **2 :** to spoil (a trail or scent) by crossing or retracing **3 a :** to prevent (a person) from attaining a desired end **:** keep from achieving a goal **:** DEFEAT, REPULSE ⟨∼*ed* at Council Bluffs . . . they turned toward the southwest —R.A.Billington⟩ **b :** to bring (as a scheme, an effort, an attack) to naught **:** make vain and ineffectual **:** BAFFLE ⟨intelligence as a means to ∼ brute force —Lafcadio Hearn⟩ **syn** see FRUSTRATE

²foil \ˈ"\ *n* -S [ME *foyle*, fr. *foilen*, v.] **1** *archaic* **:** DEFEAT, CHECK, FRUSTRATION **2** *obs* **:** an incomplete fall in wrestling **3** *also* **foil·ing** \ˈfȯiliŋ\ *archaic* **:** the track or trail of an animal **4 a :** a fencing weapon that resembles an épée but has a flat guard which may be round, oval, rectangular, or figure-eight in outline and a lighter and more flexible blade of rectangular or square cross section tapering to a blunt point **b foils** *pl* **:** the art or practice of fencing with foils that limits the target to the trunk

³foil \ˈ"\ *n* -S [ME *foile, foil*, fr. MF *fuelle, fueille, foille* (fr. L *folia*, pl. of *folium*) & *fuel, fueil, foil*, fr. L *folium* — more at BLADE] **1 :** a plant leaf — now used chiefly in compounds; compare SEXFOIL, TREFOIL **2 a :** one of several small curved indentations that meet and form points or cusps; *specif* **:** an indentation between cusps in Gothic tracery **b :** one of several arcs that enclose a complex figure ⟨the rim of a tray having eight ∼*s*⟩ **3** *obs* **a :** a leaf of paper **b :** COUNTERFOIL **4 a :** a paper-thin material **:** TISSUE; *esp* **:** very thin metal for such purposes as providing decorative covering or moistureproof lining or wrapping **b :** a thin coat of tin or silver laid on the back of a looking glass to cause reflection **c** *or* **foil paper :** METALLIC PAPER 3 **5 a** *obs* **:** the setting of a jewel **b :** a thin piece of metal or other material put under a paste or inferior stone to add color or brilliancy **6 :** something that serves by contrast of color or quality to set off another to advantage or sometimes to disadvantage ⟨everything was animated and gay . . . the men in their black coats were an admirable ∼ —Victoria Sackville-West⟩ ⟨an artist and an intellectual, a ∼ for her sentimental mother —B.R.Redman⟩ ⟨acting as a ∼ for a stage comedian⟩

foils 2a

⁴foil \ˈ"\ *vt* -ED/-ING/-S **1 :** to back or cover with foil **2 :** to enhance or set off by contrast

foiled \ˈfȯi(ə)ld\ *adj* [³*foil* + *-ed*] *of an arch or window* **:** ornamented with foils **:** having curved indentations

foil·ing \ˈfȯiliŋ\ *n* -S [³*foil* + *-ing*] **:** ornamentation with foils

foils·man \ˈfȯilzmən\ *n, pl* **foilsmen :** one who fences with a foil **:** FENCER

¹foin \ˈfȯin\ *vi* -ED/-ING/-S [ME *foinen*, fr. *foin* fork for spearing fish, fr. MF *foisne, foine*, fr. L *fuscina*] *archaic* **:** to thrust with a sword or spear **:** LUNGE

²foin \ˈ"\ *n* -S [ME, fr. *foinen*, v.] **1 a :** a pass in fencing **:** LUNGE **b :** a wound made by a thrust **2** *archaic* **:** ²FOIL 4

³foin *n* -S [ME *foine, foin, fune*, fr. OF *foine, faine*, fr. (assumed) VL *fagina*, fr. L *fagus* beech + *-ina* (fr. fem. of *-inus* -ine) — more at BEECH] *obs* **:** the stone marten or its fur

foi·son \ˈfȯizᵊn\ *n* -S [ME *foisoun*, fr. MF *foison*, fr. L *fusion-, fusio* action of pouring, founding, melting, effusion — more at FUSION] **1** *archaic* **:** rich harvest **:** PLENTY, ABUNDANCE ⟨that from the seedness the bare fallow brings to teeming ∼ —Shak.⟩ **2** *chiefly Scot* **a :** nourishment or sustenance esp. from food or drink **b :** physical energy or strength **c :** strength of mind or character

foi·son·less \-ləs\ *adj, dial Brit* **:** FUSHIONLESS

¹foist *n* -S [fr. earlier *fuste*, fr. MF, fr. *fust* wood, stick, beam, barrel, fr. L *fustis* cudgel] **1** *obs* **:** a light galley **2** *obs* **:** RIVERBOAT **:** BARGE

²foist \ˈfȯist\ *vb* -ED/-ING/-S [prob. fr. obs D *vuisten* to take into one's hand, fr. MD *vūsten, vuisten*, fr. *vūst, vuist* fist; akin to OE *fȳst* fist — more at FIST] *vt* **1** *obs* **:** to introduce when palmed **:** PALM — used of dice **2 a :** to introduce or insert surreptitiously or without warrant ⟨the comments of men . . . had been ∼*ed* into Christian religion —Matthew Arnold⟩ **b :** to force another to accept esp. by stealth or deceit ⟨there are two nestlings unless a cowbird has ∼*ed* its brat upon them —D.C.Peattie⟩ ⟨when the states . . . ∼ unnecessary expenses on local taxpayers —T.C.Desmond⟩ **c :** to attribute wrongfully ⟨an author may try out a theory on paper and be dissatisfied with it. If by chance the document survives him it is unfair to ∼ the doctrine upon him —R.I. Aaron⟩ ⟨a purely imaginary characteristic is ∼*ed* on the universe and presented as an axiom of science —Herbert Dengle⟩ **3 :** to pass off (something spurious) as genuine or worthy ⟨her novel is better written than many ∼*ed* on the reading public —Harry Hansen⟩ ∼ *vi* **1** *obs* **:** to practice cheating **2** *obs* **:** to pick pockets

³foist *n* -S **1** *obs* **:** FOISTER **2** *obs* **:** RASCALITY, SWINDLE

foist·er \ˈfȯistə(r)\ *n* -S [²*foist* + *-er*] **1** *archaic* **:** PICKPOCKET **2** *obs* **:** a palmer of dice **:** CHEAT, ROGUE

foisty \ˈfȯistē\ *adj* -ER/-EST [alter. of *fusty*] *dial Brit* **:** MUSTY, MOULDY

FOK *abbr* free of knots

fol *abbr* **1** folio **2** following

fo·la·cin \ˈfōləsən, ˈfälə-\ *n* -S [*folic acid* + *-in*] **:** FOLIC ACID 1

¹fold \ˈfōld\ *n* -S [ME *fold, fald*, fr. OE *falod, falud, fald*; akin to OS *faled* pen, enclosure, MLG *valt* pen, enclosure, manure heap, MD *vaelt, vaelde*, and perh. to ON *fjöl* plank, OHG *spaltan* to split — more at SPILL] **1 a :** an enclosure for sheep **:** PEN **b** *Brit* **:** a small portable wire enclosure that is commonly attached to a coop or hutch for moving poultry or rabbits about onto fresh grass **2 a :** a flock of sheep **b :** a group, institution, or organization providing spiritual salvation or paternal guidance, care, and protection **:** the company of the faithful or of the righteous **:** the adherents of a common religious or political belief ⟨the ∼ of Protestantism⟩ ⟨a drift into the Republican ∼⟩ **3** *dial Eng* **:** an enclosed area or yard adjoining or surrounding a house

²fold \"\ *vt* -ED/-ING/-S [ME *folden,* fr. ¹*fold,* n.] **1 :** to pen up or confine (as sheep) in a fold or on a crop to be grazed **2 a :** to pen sheep for the fertilization of (land) **b :** to pen grazing animals for the harvesting of (a crop)

³fold \"\ *vb* -ED/-ING/-S [ME *folden, falden,* fr. OE *fealdan;* akin to OHG *faldan* to fold, ON *falda* to fold, cover the head, Goth *falthan* to roll up, fold, L *duplus* double, Gk *diplasios* twofold, Skt *puṭati* he covers with, *puṭa* fold] *vt* **1 :** to lay one part over another part of **:** double upon itself **:** lay in pleats ⟨~ a length of cloth⟩ ⟨~ a letter⟩ ⟨~ printed sheets for binding⟩ ⟨~ over the edge to make a hem⟩ **2 :** to reduce the length or bulk of by doubling over or lapping over ⟨~ a tent⟩ ⟨~*ed* his long legs under the chair⟩ — often used with *up* ⟨the bedding was ~*ed* up and stowed away⟩ **3 :** to clasp together (as the hands) **:** ENTWINE ⟨~ your arms⟩ ⟨the bird ~*s* its wings⟩ **4 :** to clasp or enwrap closely **:** ENVELOP, EMBRACE, SURROUND ⟨~*ing* her son to her breast⟩ ⟨a village ~*ed* away in the hills⟩ **5 :** to bend (a surface or stratum) into folds **6 a :** to incorporate (a food ingredient) into a mixture by repeated overturnings without stirring or beating ⟨~ beaten egg whites into cake mix⟩ ⟨~ raisins into batter⟩ **b :** to incorporate closely **:** make a part of something (as by enveloping) ⟨all sorts of persons, places, and animals have been ~*ed* into this version of Tolstoy's vision —Philip Hamburger⟩ **7 :** ¹PLY 1b **8 a :** to turn (one's cards) facedown to concede defeat or indicate dropping **b :** to bring (as a business venture) to an end **:** close up ⟨after a few months he decided to ~ the magazine⟩ ~ *vi* **1 :** to become doubled or pleated **:** become flatter or smaller by doubling ⟨the bed ~*s* into a recess in the wall⟩ — often used with *up* ⟨watched him ~ up into the seat⟩ ⟨the map ~*s* up into a handy case⟩ **2 :** to fold up

⁴fold \"\ *n* -S [ME *fold, folde,* fr. *folden,* v.] **1 :** a doubling or folding over esp. of a flexible substance **:** the manner in which something is folded ⟨an accordion ~ is used for maps⟩ **2 :** a part doubled or laid over another part **:** PLEAT, BEND, PLICATION ⟨hidden in the ~*s* of the curtain⟩ ⟨~*s* of a banner⟩ **:** LAYER, COAT **3 :** a coil of a snake **4** *archaic* **:** one side of a double door or gate **:** LEAF **5 :** the pages or leaves of a book formed by folding one sheet of paper **6 a :** a bend or flexure into an arch or a trough produced in rock by forces operative after the depositing or consolidation of the rock — see ANTICLINE, SYNCLINE **b** *chiefly Brit* **:** an undulation in the landscape either upward (as a low rounded hill) or downward (as a hollow) **7** *anat* **:** a margin apparently formed by the doubling upon itself of a membrane or other flat structure **:** PLICA, RUGA ⟨neural ~*s*⟩ ⟨vocal ~*s*⟩ **8 :** PLY 2a **9 :** the crease made by folding a newspaper in half ⟨a headline should not be placed across the ~⟩ **10 :** FOLDER 2

-fold \ˌfōld\ *suffix* [ME *-fold, -fald,* fr. OE *-feald;* akin to OHG *-falt -fald,* ON *-faldr,* Goth *-falths;* derivatives fr. the root of E ³*fold*] **1 :** multiplied by (a specified number) **:** times — in adjectives ⟨a twelve*fold* increase⟩ and adverbs ⟨it will repay you ten*fold*⟩ **2 :** having (so many) laps, layers, or parts ⟨the three*fold* aspect of the problem⟩

fold·able \ˈfōldəbəl\ *adj* **:** that can be folded **:** FOLDING

fold·age \ˈfōldij\ *or* **fald·age** \ˈfōldij, ˈfal-\ *n* -S [ME *faldage,* fr. *fold, fald* + *-age*] *old English law* **:** the right of the lord of a manor to have his tenant's sheep graze on his land so as to manure it

foldaway \ˈ=ˌ=ˌ=\ *adj* [fr. *fold away,* v.] **:** designed to fold out of the way or out of sight ⟨~ doors⟩ ⟨~ bed⟩

foldboat \ˈ=ˌ=\ *n* [trans. of G *faltboot*] **:** FALTBOAT

foldboater \ˈ=ˌ==\ *n* **:** a person operating a faltboat

foldboating \ˈ=ˌ==\ *n* **:** traveling in a faltboat; *esp* **:** the sport of shooting rapids and cruising on swift water in a faltboat

fold breccia *n* **:** a breccia resulting from the folding of brittle rock strata

foldcourse \ˈ=ˌ=\ *n* [¹*fold* + *course*] **1** *English law* **a :** land to which foldage is incident **b :** the right of foldage **2 :** SHEEPWALK

folded dipole *n* **:** an antenna in the form of an elongated horizontal loop resembling a dipole in appearance with connections at the middle of one or both of the two parallel sides

folden *archaic past part of* FOLD

fold·er \ˈfōldə(r)\ *n* -S [fr. ³*fold* + *-er*] **1 :** one that folds: as **a :** an instrument or machine for folding paper, leather, or other flexible material **b :** a worker who folds or who operates a folding machine **c :** CLEANER 1e **2 :** a printed circular folded usu. so that the printed matter does not cross the fold ⟨advertising ~⟩ ⟨railroad timetable ~⟩ — compare BROADSIDE **3 :** a folded cover or large envelope for holding or filing loose papers **4 :** a cut and creased flat piece of paperboard or corrugated board designed to be folded and secured as a shipping case (as for a book)

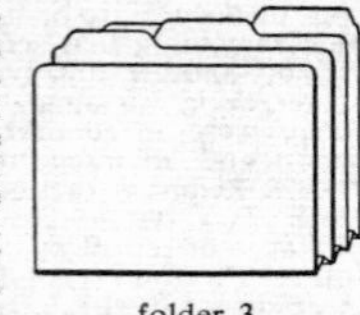
folder 3

fol·de·rol \ˈfäldəˌräl\ *also* **fal·de·ral** \ˈfaldəˌral\ *n* -S [fr. *fol-de-rol, fal-deral,* a refrain in old songs] **1 :** impractical, unnecessary, or excessive trimming, finery, or effects **:** pretty but flimsy or useless ornament **:** something that is unnecessary **:** TRIFLE, GEWGAW ⟨a gas or electric range and other ~*s* of an effete generation —Della Lutes⟩ ⟨the new collections of custom furs around town reveal plenty of ~, but there are practical things too —Lois Long⟩ **2 :** nonsensical talk or action **:** PIFFLE, NONSENSE ⟨the rest of the play . . . is a windy collection of improbable motives and costumed ~ —*Newsweek*⟩

¹folding *adj* [ME, fr. pres. part. of *folden* to fold — more at FOLD (to bend)] **1 :** capable of being folded up **:** COLLAPSIBLE ⟨~ chair⟩ ⟨~ table⟩ ⟨~ screen⟩ ⟨~ camera⟩ **2** *of paper and boards* **a :** safely foldable **b :** designed to be folded

²folding *n* -S [ME, action of penning livestock, fr. gerund of *folden* to fold — more at FOLD (to pen)] *Brit* **:** rotation grazing; *specif* **:** short-time intensive grazing of small areas of arable crops on which animals are confined by a portable fence

folding box *or* **folding carton** *n* **:** a container or carrier of paperboard that can be folded flat for shipment to the user

folding brake *n* **:** a device for folding over an edge on thin sheet metal

folding door *n* **1 :** a door in sections that can be folded back **:** an accordion door **:** DOUBLE DOOR **2 :** either of a pair of sliding doors between two rooms en suite

folding door 1

folding money *n* **:** ready or plentiful cash **:** money in sizable amounts **:** PAPER MONEY, BILLS — contrasted with *small change*

folding stair *n* **:** a movable stair (as to an attic) that can be folded or retracted out of the way

folding star *n* [²*folding;* fr. its rising at the time sheep were put into the fold] **:** EVENING STAR 1

folding strength *n* **:** the capacity of paper to withstand repeated folding without rupture

fold·less \ˈfōldləs\ *adj* [⁴*fold* + *-less*] **:** having no fold or crease

fold mountain *n* **:** a mountain whose rocks are predominantly folded

foldout \ˈ=ˌ=\ *n* -S [fr. *fold out,* v.] **:** an extra die-cut or folded leaf in a book, magazine, or other printed work

folds *pres 3d sing of* FOLD, *pl of* FOLD

fold soke *n* [ME *faldsok, faldsoken,* fr. *fald, fold* + *sok, soken* soke] **:** FOLDAGE

fold up *vi* **1 :** to give way **:** COLLAPSE, CRUMPLE ⟨at the first shot the deer stopped short, then suddenly *folded up*⟩ ⟨the old chair suddenly *folded up* under him⟩ **2 a :** to cease resistance or exertion **:** give up **:** FAIL, QUIT ⟨the horse *folded up* in the homestretch⟩ ⟨the defense *folded up* under the savage attack⟩ ⟨the weak just get crushed; you can't blame them for *folding up* —K.M.Dodson⟩ **b :** to stop production or operation for lack of funds, support, or business success **:** go bankrupt **:** close up **:** CLOSE ⟨small businesses were *folding up* right and left⟩

fold yard *n* [¹*fold*] *Brit* **:** an enclosure for sheep or cattle

fol·ger·ite \ˈfōljəˌrīt\ *n* -S [W.M.*Folger* †1928 Am. naval officer + E *-ite*] **:** PENTLANDITE

¹folia *pl of* FOLIUM

²fo·lia \fōˈlēə\ *n* -S [Pg, lit., folly, madness, fr. OPg, fr. OProv, fr. *fol* foolish, mad (fr. LL *follus*) + *-ia -y* (fr. L) — more at FOOL] **:** a noisy carnival dance of Portuguese origin

fo·li·a·ceous \ˌfōlēˈāshəs\ *adj* [L *foliaceus,* fr. *folium* leaf + *-aceus* -aceous — more at BLADE] **1 :** belonging to, consisting of, or having the texture or form of a foliage leaf ⟨~ sepal⟩ ⟨~ thallus⟩ ⟨~ inflorescence⟩ **2** *zool* **:** resembling a leaf in form or mode of growth **3 :** consisting of thin laminae of a mineral substance **:** having the form of a leaf or plate ⟨~ spar⟩

fo·li·a·ceous·ness *n* -ES **:** the quality or state of being foliaceous

fo·li·age \ˈfōl(ē)ij, -lyij\ *n* -S [alter. (influenced by L *folium*) of earlier *fuellage, foillage,* fr. MF *fuellage,* fr. *fuelle, fueille, foille* leaf + *-age* — more at FOIL] **1 :** the mass of leaves of a plant as produced in nature **:** LEAFAGE ⟨a tree with handsome ~⟩ **2 :** a cluster of leaves, flowers, and branches **3 :** a carved representation of leaves, flowers, and branches used for architectural ornamentation (as of capitals, friezes)

foliage brown *n* **:** FEUILLE MORTE

fo·li·aged \-jd\ *adj* **:** furnished or decorated with foliage **:** LEAVED ⟨the variously ~ mulberry⟩

foliage green *n* **:** a moderate yellow green that is greener and duller than average moss green and yellower and duller than average pea green or average apple green

foliage leaf *n* **:** an ordinary green leaf as distinguished from floral leaves, scales, and bracts

fo·li·a·geous \ˌfōlēˈājəs\ *adj* **:** containing representations of foliage

foliage plant *n* **:** a plant grown primarily for its decorative foliage (as members of the genera *Coleus* and *Philodendron*)

fo·li·al \ˈfōlēəl\ *adj* [L *folium* leaf + *-al*] **:** FOLIAR

fo·li·ar \ˈfōlēə(r)\ *adj* [F *foliaire,* fr. L *folium* leaf + F *-aire* -ar] **:** consisting of or relating to leaves

foliar bundle *n* **:** LEAF TRACE

foliar feeding *n* **:** the feeding of plants through leaves by spraying plant food on them

foliar gap *n* **:** LEAF GAP

foliar trace *n* **:** LEAF TRACE

¹fo·li·ate \ˈfōlēət, -ēˌāt, *usu* -ăd·+V\ *adj* [L *foliatus* leaved, fr. *folium* leaf + *-atus* -ate — more at BLADE] **1 :** shaped like a leaf ⟨~ sponge⟩ ⟨~ spearhead⟩ **2 :** furnished with or composed of leaves or leaflets **:** LAMINATED, FOLIATED, LEAFY ⟨~ stalk⟩ — used in combination ⟨3-*foliate*⟩ **3 :** FOLIOLATE

²foliate \"\ *n* -S **:** a rock displaying foliation

³foliate \-ēˌāt, *usu* -ăd·+V\ *vb* -ED/-ING/-S [L *folium* + E *-ate* (v. suffix)] *vt* **1 :** to beat into a leaf or thin foil **2 :** to spread over (glass) with a thin coat of tin amalgam ⟨~ a mirror⟩ **:** FOIL **3 :** to number the leaves of (as a manuscript) — compare FOLIO, PAGE **4 a :** to form (as an arch) into foils **b :** to ornament (as a pedestal) with foliage ~ *vi* **1 :** to divide into laminae or leaves **2 :** to put forth leaves

fo·li·at·ed \ˈfōlēˌād·əd\ *adj* [L *foliatus* + E *-ed*] **1 :** produced or formed by foliating **:** characterized by foliation **:** ornamented with foils or with foliage **2 :** FOLIATE ⟨where weeds were as high and ~ as trees —Peggy Bennett⟩ **3 :** characterized by being separable into thin plates or folia ⟨graphite has a ~ structure⟩ **4** *of a joint in carpentry* **:** LAPPED, RABBETED

foliate papilla *n* **:** any of certain paired oval papillae of the lateral aspect of the posterior part of the tongue that are rudimentary in man but form the chief organs of taste of certain other mammals (as rabbits)

fo·li·a·tion \ˌfōlēˈāshən\ *n* -S [L *folium* + E *-ation*] **1 a :** the process of forming into a leaf **b :** the state of being in leaf **c :** VERNATION **2 a :** the act of foliating the leaves of a book or manuscript **b :** foliated numbers **3 :** the act of coating with tin amalgam (as in making mirrors) **4 a :** ornamentation with naturalistic or conventionalized foliage **b :** an ornament or decoration resembling a leaf **5 :** the enrichment of an opening by means of foils formed by cusps — compare TRACERY **6 :** the act of beating a metal into a thin plate, leaf, or foil **7 :** foliated texture **:** the process or property of dividing into plates or slabs due to the parallel arrangement or cleavage of the minerals **:** BANDED STRUCTURE

fo·lic acid \ˈfōlik-, ˈfäl-\ *n* [L *fo*lium leaf + E *-ic;* fr. its presence in green leaves] **1 :** a yellow or yellowish orange crystalline vitamin $C_{19}H_{19}N_7O_6$ of the vitamin B complex obtained esp. from leaves and from liver and also made synthetically and used chiefly in the treatment of nutritional megaloblastic anemia and sprue — called also *folacin, PGA, pteroylglutamic acid, pteroylmonoglutamic acid, vitamin* B_c **2 :** PTEROYLGLUTAMIC ACID 2

fo·lie à deux \(ˌ)fōˌlē(ˌ)äˈdə(r·), -dȯ\ *n, pl* **folies à deux** \-ē(ˌ)(z)ä-\ [F, lit., double madness] **:** the presence of the same or similar delusional ideas in two persons closely associated with one another; *esp* **:** the result of transmission of delusional ideas from one person to another

folie du doute \-ēdəˈdüt\ *n, pl* **folies du doute** \-ē(z)də-\ [F, lit., madness of doubt] **:** pathological indecisiveness esp. when extended to ordinarily simple choice situations

fo·lif·er·ous \fōˈlif(ə)rəs\ *also* **fo·li·if·er·ous** \ˌfōlēˈif(ə)rəs\ *adj* [L *folium* leaf + E *-ferous*] **:** producing leaves

fo·li·ic·o·lous \ˌfōlēˈikələs\ *adj* [ISV *folii-* (fr. L *folium* leaf) + *-colous*] **1 :** growing upon leaves ⟨~ liverworts⟩ **2 :** parasitic upon leaves ⟨~ fungi⟩

fo·li·i·form \ˈfōlēəˌfȯrm\ *adj* [ISV *folii-* + *-form;* prob. orig. formed as F *foliiforme*] **:** having the shape of a leaf

fo·lin·ic acid \fōˈlinik-\ *n* [*folic* + *-in* + *-ic*] **:** any of several natural or synthetic acids (as leucovorin) that are metabolically active forms of folic acids and that support the growth of certain bacteria (as *Leuconostoc citrovorum*) — called also *citrovorum factor*

¹fo·lio \ˈfōlē,ō, -ōl,yō\ *n* -S [ME, fr. L, abl. of *folium* leaf of a tree, leaf of paper — more at BLADE] **1 a :** a leaf esp. of a manuscript or book **b :** a leaf number ⟨a school workbook in which writing is to appear on only one side of the leaf often has ~*s* on the right-hand pages⟩ **c :** a page number ⟨in books the even ~*s* are on the left-hand pages and the odd ~*s* on the right-hand pages⟩ **d :** an identifying reference in accounting used in posting to indicate source of entry and account to which entered **2 a :** a sheet of paper folded once **b :** a case or folder for loose papers **3 a :** the size or form of a folio book ⟨books in ~⟩ **b :** a folio book or publication **c :** a book of the largest size — see BOOK tables **d :** the size of a piece of paper cut two from a sheet; *also* **:** paper or a page of this size — abbr. *fo* or *f;* symbol *F;* see BOOK tables **4 :** a certain number of words taken as a unit or division in a document for purposes of measurement or reference (as in Great Britain and Ireland 72 or 90 and in the U.S. generally 100 by statutory provision) **5** *also* **folio post :** a certain size (as 17 x 22 inches) of a sheet of esp. writing or ledger paper

²folio \"\ *adj* **1 :** formed of sheets each folded once into two leaves or four pages ⟨a ~ edition⟩ ⟨a work in five volumes ~⟩ **2 a :** of the size of a folio book ⟨a ~ case⟩ ⟨a huge ~ atlas⟩ **b :** produced in folio ⟨to the bibliographer . . . a book made up in octavo format may be the same size as one in ~ format, depending on the size of the sheet used for the text —Edith Diehl⟩ **3 :** of full size and not folded — used of sheets and reams of paper

³folio \"\ *vt* -ED/-ING/-S **1 :** to put a serial number on each leaf or each page of (a manuscript or a book) — compare FOLIATE, PAGE **2** *law* **:** to mark with its number each folio in (as a pleading, brief, affidavit)

fo·lio·branch \ˈfōlēōˌbraŋk, -aiŋk\ *also* **fo·lio·bran·chi·ate** \ˌ===ˈbraŋkēət, -ēˌāt\ *adj* [*folio-* (fr. L *folium* leaf) + *-branch* or *branchiate*] **:** having gills that resemble leaves

fo·lio·cel·lo·sis \ˌfōlēōsəˈlōsəs\ *n, pl* **foliocello·ses** \-ōˌsēz\ [NL, fr. *folio-* + ISV *cell* + NL *-osis*] **:** MOTTLE-LEAF

fo·li·o·late \ˈfōlēəˌlāt, *usu* -ăd·+V\ *adj* [*foliole* + *-ate*] **:** having leaflets **:** relating to or consisting of leaflets — usu. used in combination ⟨bi*foliolate*⟩

fo·li·ole \ˈfōlēˌōl\ *n* -S [F, fr. LL *foliolum,* dim. of *folium* leaf — more at BLADE] **1 :** LEAFLET **2 :** a small leaf-shaped organ or a part resembling a leaf

fo·li·o·lif·er·ous \ˌ===ˈlif(ə)rəs\ *adj* [*foliole* + *-i-* + *-ferous*] **:** bearing leaflets

fo·li·o·lose \ˈ===ˌlōs\ *adj* [*foliole* + *-ose*] **:** FOLIOLATE

fo·li·ose \ˈfōlēˌōs\ *or* **fo·li·ous** \-ēəs\ *adj* [L *foliosus,* fr. *folium* + *-osus* -ous, -ose] **1 :** LEAFY **2 :** resembling a leaf ⟨the ~ lichens are flat and thin —E.A.Bessy⟩

fo·li·ot \ˈfōlēət\ *n* -S [F, fr. MF, prob. fr. *folier* to play the fool, fr. *fol* foolish, mad — more at FOOL] **:** the earliest form of mechanical-clock escapement consisting of a crossbar with adjustable weights for regulating the rate of oscillation of a verge or vertical spindle

-folious \ˌfōlēəs\ *adj comb form* [L *foliosus*] **:** having (such or so many) leaves ⟨centi*folious*⟩

fo·li·um \ˈfōlēəm\ *n, pl* **fo·lia** \-ēə\ [NL, fr. L, leaf — more at BLADE] **1 :** one of the lamellae of the cerebellar cortex **2 :** a thin layer occurring esp. in metamorphic rocks **3 :** FOLIO 1

¹folk \ˈfōk\ *n, pl* **folk** *or* **folks** [ME, fr. OE *folc;* akin to OHG *folc* people, band of warriors, ON *folk* and perh. to Alb *plok, plogn* heap, OE *full* — more at FULL] **1** *pl folks, archaic* **a :** a group of kindred tribes forming a nation **:** PEOPLE ⟨the organization of each ~ . . . sprang mainly from war —J.R. Green⟩ **b :** an animal kind or species ⟨the conies are but a feeble ~ —Prov 30:26 (AV)⟩ **2** *pl folk* **:** the masses of people in a homogeneous social group as contrasted with the individual or with a selected class **:** the great proportion of the members of a people that determines the group character and that tends to preserve its characteristic form of civilization and its customs, arts and crafts, legends, traditions, and superstitions from generation to generation **3** *pl folk, archaic* **:** a mass or group of people in relation to a superior: as **a :** the subjects of a king **b :** the lay members of the church **:** LAITY **c :** the followers or retainers of a lord **d :** the domestics of a household **4** *folk or folks pl* **:** a certain kind or class of people — used with a qualifying adjective or phrase ⟨fine ~*s*⟩ ⟨parties for the young ~*s*⟩ ⟨protecting their women*folk*⟩ ⟨always ready to help ~*s* in trouble⟩ **5** *folks pl* **:** people indefinitely ⟨~*s* say the house is haunted⟩ **6** *folks pl* **a :** the persons of one's own family **:** RELATIVES **b :** persons without pretensions or free from formality of manner ⟨they like best the actors that they can feel easy with, that are just ~*s* —*Yale Rev.*⟩

²folk \"\ *adj* [trans. of G *volks-* (as in *volkslied* folk song), fr. gen. of *volk* people, common people, nation, fr. OHG *folc*] **1 :** originated or widely used among the common people as distinguished from the academic, the cosmopolitan, the modern and professional, or the sophisticated ⟨~ belief⟩ ⟨~ hero⟩ ⟨~ music⟩ ⟨~ remedy⟩ ⟨~ speech⟩ **2 :** of or relating to the common people or to the study of the common people ⟨~ sociology⟩

folk art *n* [prob. trans. of G *volkskunst*] **:** the traditional typically anonymous art of the people that is an expression of community life and is distinguished from academic or self-conscious or cosmopolitan expression — compare COURT ART

folkcraft \ˈ=ˌ=\ *n* **1 :** the art and tradition of management of public affairs by the common people — distinguished from *statecraft* **2 :** artisanship and artistry carried on by the common people

folk dance *n* [trans. of G *volkstanz*] **:** a dance that originates as ritual among and is characteristic of the common people of a country and that is transmitted from generation to generation with increasing secularization — distinguished from *court dance*

folk etymology *n* [trans. of G *volksetymologie*] **:** the transformation of words so as to give them an apparent relationship to other better-known or better-understood words (as the change of *asparagus* to *sparrowgrass* or the change of *chaise longue* to *chaise lounge*) — called also *popular etymology*

folkfree \ˈ=ˌ=\ *adj* [trans. of OE *folcfrī*] **:** having a free man's rights **:** having folkright

folk high school *n* [trans. of Dan *folkehøjskole*] **:** a school established in Denmark and elsewhere in the Scandinavian countries for liberal education for working adults

folk·ish \ˈfōkish\ *adj* **:** having a folk character ⟨a ~ orchestral suite⟩ ⟨~ comedy⟩ — **folk·ish·ness** *n* -ES

folkland \ˈ=ˌ=\ *n* [alter. of OE *folcland,* fr. *folc* folk, people, band of warriors + *land* — more at FOLK, LAND] **:** land held in early England by customary law without written title — opposed to *bookland*

folklike \ˈ=ˌ=\ *adj* **:** having the character of anonymous tradition **:** FOLKISH

folklore \ˈ=ˌ=\ *n* [trans. of G *volkskunde*] **1 :** traditional customs, beliefs, dances, songs, tales, or sayings preserved orally and unreflectively among a people or group **2 :** a comparative science that investigates the life and spirit of a people or of peoples as revealed in their traditional customs and tales — compare MYTHOLOGY **3 :** a widely held unsupported specious notion or body of notions

folk·lor·ic \ˈ=ˌlȯrik, -lōr-, -rēk\ *adj* **:** of, resembling, or characteristic of folklore ⟨a ~ competition in which nearly a hundred couples dance the fandango —*Holiday*⟩ ⟨~ music⟩

folk·lor·ish \-rish, -rēsh\ *adj* **:** FOLKISH

folk·lor·ism \-ˌrizəm\ *n* -S **:** the study of folklore

folk·lor·ist \-rəst\ *n* -S **:** a student of folklore — **folk·lor·is·tic** \ˌ=ˌ=ˈistik, -tēk\ *adj*

folk medicine *n* **:** traditional medicine as practiced nonprofessionally by people isolated from modern medical services and involving esp. the use of vegetable remedies on an empirical basis and the retention of outmoded theories

folk·moot \ˈfōkˌmüt\ *or* **folk·mote** \-ˌmōt\ *n* -S [alter. of OE *folcmōt, folcgemōt,* fr. *folc* people + *mōt, gemōt* meeting — more at FOLK, MOOT] **:** an assembly of the people; *esp* **:** a general assembly, court, or council (as of a town, city, or shire) in early England — compare MOOT

folk nation *n* **:** a political unity of related tribes ⟨the Iroquois Confederacy was a *folk nation*⟩

folk psychology *n* [trans. of G *völkerpsychologie*] **1 :** the study of the mind and behavior esp. of primitive peoples through analysis of the human factors involved in their cultural and technological development **2 :** the mental traits common to or characteristic of a people

folkright \ˈ=ˌ=\ *n* [trans. of OE *folcriht*] **:** the right of the people under the customary laws and usages esp. in early England

folks *pl of* FOLK

folk's-glove \ˈ=ˌ=\ *n, pl* **folk's-gloves** [by folk etymology] **:** FOXGLOVE 1

folks·i·ly \ˈfōksəlē, -li\ *adv* **:** in a folksy manner

folks·i·ness \-sēnəs, -sin-\ *n* -ES **:** the quality of being folksy ⟨the ~ is exaggerated to an excruciating degree —Quentin Anderson⟩

folk singer *n* **:** a singer of folk songs

folk society *n* **:** a usu. small isolated illiterate society characterized as homogeneous in cultural tradition, as having a sacred rather than secular orientation, and as possessing a high degree of internal integration and group solidarity — contrasted with *urban society*

folk song *n* [trans. of G *volkslied,* trans. of E *popular song*] **1 :** a song originating in or traditional among the common people of a country or region and forming part of their characteristic culture — compare LIED, POPULAR SONG **2 :** a song having such qualities of folk song as stanzaic form, choral refrain, and simplicity of melody and accompaniment but written by a known composer — compare ART SONG

folk state *n* [trans. of G *volksstaat*] **:** a state embracing a racially homogeneous population **:** a state having ethnic unity

folk story *n* **:** FOLKTALE

folksy *also* **folks·ey** \ˈfōksē, -si\ *adj* **folksier; folksiest** [*folks* (pl. of ¹*folk*) + *-y*] **1 :** SOCIABLE, FRIENDLY, NEIGHBORLY ⟨find it hard to be ~ just after prayer —Christopher Morley⟩ **2 :** informal, casual, or familiar often artificially or excessively ⟨~ radio commentator —*Newsweek*⟩ ⟨~, saccharine radio programs —*Time*⟩ **3 :** relating to or having the character of folk arts or crafts or other aspects of popular culture ⟨~ musical composition⟩

folktale \ˈ=ˌ=\ *n* **:** a tale circulated by word of mouth among the common people; *esp* **:** a tale traditional among a people and characteristically anonymous, timeless, and placeless

folk tune *n* **:** a traditional popular vocal or instrumental melody; *specif* **:** the melody of a folk song

folkway \ˈ=ˌ=\ *n* **:** a mode of thinking, feeling, or acting common to a people or to a social group; *esp* **:** a social habit that has not been rationalized or given ethical force

foll *abbr* following
fol·ler \'fälər\ *dial var of* FOLLOW
folles *pl of* FOLLIS
fol·let·to \fə'led·(,)ō\ *n, pl* **follet·ti** \-(,)ē\ [It, fr. OIt, fr. OF *folet* fool, goblin, fr. *fol* foolish, mad — more at FOOL] : IMP, GOBLIN, FAIRY; *esp* : a supernatural being who is a survival in popular form of an ancient Etruscan or Roman deity
fol·li·cle \'fäləkəl, -lēk-\ *n* -S [NL *folliculus,* fr. L, small bag, husk, pod, dim. of *follis* bag, sack — more at FOOL] **1 a :** a small cavity or deep narrow-mouthed depression ⟨a hair ~⟩; *esp* : a small simple or slightly branched gland : CRYPT **b :** a small lymph node — see GRAAFIAN FOLLICLE **2 :** a dry dehiscent one-celled, many-seeded, and monocarpellary fruit (as that of the peony, larkspur, or milkweed) differing from a pod or legume in opening along only one (as the inner or ventral) suture — see FRUIT illustration **3 :** an air sac (as on a sea plant)
follicle mite *n* : any of several minute mites of the genus *Demodex* that are parasitic in the hair follicles
follicle–stimulating hormone *n* : a hormone of protein-carbohydrate composition obtained from the anterior lobe of the pituitary body that stimulates the growth of Graafian follicles in the female and activates the sperm-forming cells in the male —abbr. *FSH;* see LUTEINIZING HORMONE
fol·lic·u·lar \fə'likyələ(r), (')fä¦l-\ *adj* [NL *folliculus* + E *-ar*] **1 :** like, belonging to, or provided with follicles : consisting of or involving follicles **2 :** affecting follicles ⟨~ tonsillitis⟩
follicular hormone *n* : ESTRONE
follicular mange *n* : DEMODECTIC MANGE
fol·lic·u·late \fə'likyələt, (')fä¦l-, -,lāt\ *also* **fol·lic·u·lat·ed** \-,lād·əd\ *adj* [*follicule* + *-ate, -ated*] : having or consisting of follicles
fol·li·cule \'fälə,kyül\ *n* -S [NL *folliculus* — more at FOLLICLE] : FOLLICLE
fol·lic·u·lin \fə'likyələn, fä'-\ *n* -S [NL *folliculus* + E *-in*] : ESTROGEN; *esp* : ESTRONE
fol·lic·u·li·na \=,==ˈlīnə, -ˈlēnə\ *n, cap* [NL, fr. L *folliculus* + NL *-ina*] : a genus (the type of the family Folliculinidae) of spirotrichous trumpet-shaped tube-dwelling chiefly marine ciliates related to *Stentor*
¹fol·lic·u·li·nid \=¦==ˈlīnəd, -ˈlin-\ *adj* [NL *Folliculinidae,* fr. *Folliculina,* type genus + *-idae*] : of or relating to the genus *Folliculina* or the family Folliculinidae
²folliculinid \"\ *n* -S : a ciliate of the genus *Folliculina* or the family Folliculinidae
fol·lic·u·li·tis \=,==ˈlīd·əs\ *n* -ES [NL, fr. *folliculus* + *-itis*] : inflammation of one or more follicles
fol·lic·u·lose \fə'likyə,lōs, (')fä¦l-\ *adj* [NL *folliculus* + E *-ose*] **1 :** containing follicles **2 :** resembling a follicle
fol·lic·u·lus \=ˈ==ləs\ *n, pl* **follicu·li** \-,lī, -,lē\ [NL — more at FOLLICLE] : FOLLICLE
follies *pl of* FOLLY
fol·lis \'fäləs, 'fōl-\ *n, pl* **fol·les** \-ä,lēz, -ō,lās\ [LL, fr. L *follis* bag — more at FOOL] **1 :** a Roman bronze coin of the late Empire having a silver coating and a very small value **2 :** a large bronze coin current in the Byzantine Empire under Anastasius (A.D. 491-518) that was marked with a large M
¹fol·low \'fä(,)lō, -lə, *often* -ləw+V\ *vb* -ED/-ING/-S [ME *folwen, folowen,* fr. OE *folgian;* akin to OE *fylgan* to follow, OFris *folgia, fulgia,* OS *folgōn,* OHG *folgēn,* ON *fylgja,* and perh. to W *ôl* mark, track, *olaf* last, Corn *ōl* mark, trace, track] *vt* **1 :** to go, proceed, or come after : move behind over the same path or course often as an attendant or retainer ⟨the bravest man I ever knew ~*ed* me up San Juan Hill —Theodore Roosevelt⟩ **2 a :** to go after in pursuit or in an effort to overtake ⟨fraud statutes, the principle of which is to ~ and punish the security swindler under the criminal law —Frank Parker⟩ **b :** to seek to attain : strive after ⟨yearning in desire to ~ knowledge —Alfred Tennyson⟩ **3 a :** to accept as authority : take as leader or master ⟨we have forsaken all, and ~*ed* thee —Mt 19:27 (AV)⟩ **b :** to act in accordance with : OBEY ⟨~ directions⟩ ⟨~ a policy⟩ **c :** to yield to and obey (the guidance of a dancing partner) ⟨the girl must learn to ~ the man's lead⟩ **4 a :** to copy after : take as an example : take after : IMITATE ⟨the new building ~*s* the facades and roof lines of the original buildings —Maxwell Mays⟩ **b :** to move or change in constant relation to : correlate with ⟨school enrollment ~*s* the birthrate⟩ ⟨the condition of the ionosphere has ~*ed* the course of the sun's activity —*London Calling*⟩ **5 a :** to walk or proceed along (as a road or course) ⟨~ a path through the woods⟩ **b :** to engage in (a profession, trade, or calling) : PURSUE ⟨those who ~ the sea⟩ ⟨a district where cotton raising is widely ~*ed*⟩ **6 a :** to attend the funeral of ⟨~*ed* his poor body to the grave⟩ **b** *dial* : ESCORT, ACCOMPANY ⟨he ~*ed* her home from the party⟩ **7 a :** to come or take place after in time, sequence, or order ⟨a juggling act ~*ed* the singer⟩ **b :** to cause to be followed : place in sequence : furnish with a successor ⟨~*ed* dinner with a liqueur⟩ ⟨~*ed* a fine first novel with an even finer one⟩ **8 a :** to come about or take place as a result, effect, or natural consequence of : ensue after ⟨the Nemesis that attends upon human pride, the vengeance that ~*s* crime —G.L.Dickinson⟩ **b :** to come to be existent or present at a place in consequence or as a result of ⟨the flag often ~*s* trade⟩ ⟨houses ~*ed* the factories⟩ **9 a :** to watch steadily (as a receding object) : keep the eyes fixed upon (something in motion) ⟨~*ed* the ball over the fence⟩ **b :** to keep the mind upon (something in progress) ⟨~ a speech⟩ ⟨~ a play⟩ **c :** to attend to the successive members or stages of ⟨~ a magazine serial⟩ : keep abreast of ⟨~*ed* the developments in his field⟩ ⟨his friends ~*ed* his career with interest⟩ **d :** to understand the logical force of (as an argument or line of thought) : keep up with ⟨I don't quite ~ you⟩ ~ *vi* **1 :** to go or come after a person or thing in place, time, or sequence ⟨if one sheep goes through the gate the rest will ~⟩ **2 :** to result or occur as a consequence, an effect from a cause, or as valid inference from a premise ⟨as they were rich but it did not ~ that they had not made their money honestly —Margaret Deland⟩
syn SUCCEED, ENSUE, SUPERVENE: FOLLOW is a general term often interchangeable with SUCCEED or ENSUE. SUCCEED suggests following another in an office, rank, title, position, or role ⟨George III *succeeded* George II⟩ ⟨George III *succeeded* to the throne after George II⟩ It is likely to suggest a fixed, predictable, or likely order, although it does not always do so ⟨simplicity of concept *succeeds* complexity of calculation —E.T.Bell⟩ ⟨the anxieties of common life began soon to *succeed* to the alarms of romance —Jane Austen⟩ ENSUE means to follow; it is likely to indicate following as a consequence or plausible concomitant and is unlikely to be used with completely unusual or unexpected developments ⟨the riot which *ensued* on that damp evening —T.B.Costain⟩ ⟨if a leech is pulled off . . . he is liable to leave his jaws in the wound, and blood poisoning may *ensue* —C.S.Forester⟩ SUPERVENE indicates a taking place after or during something else of an additional, unlooked-for, unpredictable development which may change or counter expectations ⟨two worlds, two antagonistic ideals, here in evidence before him. Could a third condition *supervene,* to mend their discord —Walter Pater⟩ ⟨with this undue elevation of spirits had *supervened* an entire oblivion or contempt of those undefined apprehensions —Sheridan Le Fanu⟩
syn PURSUE, CHASE, TAG, TRAIL, TAIL: FOLLOW is the general term meaning to come behind after one in his path. It may be used to indicate performance of this action in any way or with any motive from loyal devotion of a retainer to a leader to malevolent intent to harm ⟨what was it that made men *follow* Oliver Cromwell and take at his hands that which they would not receive from any of his contemporaries —S.M.Crothers⟩ ⟨my man that shall . . . do all a hunter can to trace and *follow* and find and catch and crucify . . . all your crew —Robert Browning⟩ PURSUE indicates a persistent, determined, continuing following after in order to overtake or attain ⟨as lean dogs *pursue* some struck and sobbing fawn —P.B.Shelley⟩ ⟨he *pursues* his object with a pertinacity and ingenuity that does credit to his understanding —S.M.Crothers⟩ ⟨to *pursue* every tangle of thought to its final unravelment —A.N.Whitehead⟩ CHASE implies a rapid, active quest after something in flight or, sometimes, activity designed to put to flight ⟨and watch the fearless chamois-hunter *chase* his prey through tracts abrupt of desolate space —William Wordsworth⟩ ⟨the last defeated warrior was *chased* upon a reservation —R.A.Billington⟩ TAG, an informal word, may suggest close following, usu. without any intention, esp. malevolent intention, to overtake or injure ⟨they *tagged* happily after the mayor's secretary down the city-hall corridors —*Time*⟩ TRAIL indicates a close following of another's footsteps or track ⟨I tracked him, as I have *trailed* Coleridge, into almost every section of eight floors of a great library —J.L.Lowes⟩ In intransitive uses it may lack suggestions of intentness and connote aimless or casual following ⟨watch the miners troop home — small black figures *trailing* slowly in gangs across the white field —D.H.Lawrence⟩ TAIL, an informal term, suggests intent, stealthy following in order to observe but usu. not to overtake or capture ⟨sometimes *tailed* . . . by Army, Navy, or FBI cars —*Time*⟩ — **as follows :** as comes next — used impersonally ⟨their names are *as follows*⟩ — **follow copy :** to reproduce matter (as by typesetting or typewriting) exactly as it appears in copy — **follow one's nose 1 :** to go in a straight or obvious course ⟨just *follow your nose* until you get there; you can't miss it⟩ **2 :** to proceed without plan or reflection : to obey one's instincts — **follow suit 1 :** to play a card of the same suit as the card led **2 :** to follow an example set — **follow the hounds :** to hunt on horseback with hounds — **follow the string** *of an archery bow* : to become curved from use
²follow \"\ *n* -S **1 :** the act or process of following **2 a :** a stroking technique used by a billiard player consisting of striking the cue ball above its center; *also* : the forward spin so imparted to the ball **b :** FOLLOW SHOT **3 :** FOLLOW-UP 4
follow block *n* **1 :** a circular wooden block used in spinning sheet metal on a lathe **2 :** an adjustable block or plate used in a card file to keep the cards in upright position
followed *past of* FOLLOW
fol·low·er \'fäləwə(r), -lōə-\ *n* -S [ME *folwer, folower,* fr. OE *folgere,* fr. *folgian* to follow + *-ere* -er — more at FOLLOW] **1 a :** one in the service of another : RETAINER, ATTENDANT, SERVANT **b :** one that follows the opinions or teachings of another : ADHERENT, DISCIPLE **c :** one that imitates another **d :** a beau or admirer esp. of a maidservant **2** *archaic* : one that chases : PURSUER **3** *Brit* : a young domestic animal ⟨a herd of 34 Ayrshire cows and 36 ~*s*⟩ **4 a :** a disk of wood used to apply pressure to hooped cheese **b :** a short wooden piece placed on top of a pile so that the pile may be driven below the bottom limit of a pile driver or below a water surface **c** (1) **:** a short metal cylinder in the tubular magazine of a firearm between the spiral spring and the column of cartridges (2) **:** the short metal arm in a box magazine between the magazine spring and the cartridges **d :** the movable plate of a screw press **e :** a flange for holding piston rings in position **f :** a gland in a stuffing box **g** *or* **follower block :** FOLLOW BLOCK **h** *or* **follower plate :** the metal plate bearing against either end of a railroad-car draft gear and transmitting the stresses from the coupler to the draft gear and from the draft gear to the draft sill **5 :** a sheet of parchment or paper added to the first sheet of an indenture or other deed **6 :** a machine part (as a cogwheel) that receives motion from another part — see WHITWORTH'S QUICK RETURN illustration **7 :** a tool used during disassembly of a cylinder lock to keep the springs and drivers in place
follower rest *n* : FOLLOW REST
fol·low·er·ship \-,ship\ *n* **1 :** the body of followers of a leader : FOLLOWING **2 :** the capability of following a leader or obeying authority ⟨statesmanship gives way to demagogy and leadership degenerates into ~ —L.J.Halle⟩
¹following *adj* [ME *folwing, folowing,* fr. pres. part. of *folwen, folowen* to follow — more at FOLLOW] **1 :** next after : SUCCEEDING, ENSUING ⟨the meeting was held on the ~ day⟩ **2 :** that immediately follows ⟨the ~ table shows the rate of increase⟩ ⟨trains will leave at the ~ times⟩ **3** *of a wind* : blowing or running in the direction in which a ship is moving **4 :** east of or having a greater right ascension than so as to follow in the field of a telescope by reason of diurnal motion — compare PRECEDING
²following *n* -S [ME *folwing, folowing,* fr. gerund of *folwen, folowen*] **1 :** the followers, adherents or partisans of one **2 a :** the regular readers of an author or publication **b :** the patrons of a sport or entertainment **c :** the admirers or supporters of a performer in the arts, sports, or entertainment : FANS
³following *prep* [¹*following*] : subsequent to : after in time ⟨~ the lecture the meeting was open to discussion⟩
following sea *n* : a sea moving in about the direction of a ship's heading — compare HEAD SEA, QUARTERING SEA
¹follow on *vi* **1** *of a batting side in cricket* : to go in for a second innings immediately after its first at the option of the opposing side and when behind by a certain number of runs (as 200 or 150) **2 :** to move on in the direction of a body going before (as of a billiard ball in a follow shot) ~ *vt* : to come after : SUCCEED
²follow on *n, pl* **follow ons** [¹*follow on*] : the act or an instance of following on
follow out *vt* **1 :** to follow to the end or to a conclusion ⟨*followed out* all the cross references⟩ **2 :** EXECUTE : carry out ⟨faithfully *followed out* his instructions⟩
follow rest *n* **1 :** a tool rest that travels with the slide rest of a lathe **2 :** a rest that is fixed as to position relative to a grinding wheel and used for supporting cylindrical work
follows *pres 3d sing of* FOLLOW, *pl of* FOLLOW
follow shot *n* : a billiard shot made by hitting the cue ball above the center that causes the cue ball to roll forward after contact with the object ball — compare DRAW SHOT
follow spot *n* : a spotlight for following a performer moving about a stage
follow–the–leader \,==ˈ=ˈ==\ *also* **follow–my–leader** \,==(,)=ˈ==\ *n* : a game in which the players in single file must imitate all the actions of the leader
follow through *vi* **1 :** to continue a stroke or motion (as the swing of a bat, club, or racket) to the end of its arc : complete the swing **2 :** to press on in an activity or process beyond the initial or preparatory stages esp. to a conclusion ⟨after a bombardment the infantry failed to *follow through*⟩
follow–through \'==,= ,==ˈ=\ *n* -S [*follow through*] **1 :** the act of following through (as in the swing of a bat, club, or racket); *also* : the part of the stroke following the striking of the ball **2 :** the act of carrying out a planned or initiated activity to a conclusion ⟨reports and recommendations will be submitted to the director of purchases for *follow-through* —*Management Rev.*⟩
follow up *vt* **1 :** to pursue closely and steadily ⟨*followed up* the wounded deer⟩ **2 a :** to follow (an act or achievement) with a similar or related act **b :** to strengthen the effect of by further action ⟨*follow up* victory with rapid advance⟩ : PURSUE, EXPLOIT ⟨*followed up* his initial effort⟩ ⟨*follow up* an early advantage⟩ **3 :** to seek further details about (a news story already printed or broadcast); *also* : to print or broadcast usu. on subsequent days one or more stories other than the first on (a news event) **4 :** to maintain constant or intermittent contact with (as a case) after diagnosis or therapy
¹follow–up \'==,=\ *adj* [*follow up*] : of or relating to renewed or repeated action: as **a :** relating to a second or subsequent offer or proposal (as to a possible customer) ⟨a *follow-up* letter⟩ ⟨a *follow-up* order⟩ **b :** serving to test or reinforce the effectiveness of previous action ⟨*follow-up* instruction⟩ **c :** relating to the study or treatment of persons after institutionalization ⟨*follow-up* care of the mentally ill⟩ ⟨*follow-up* survey of delinquent children⟩ ⟨*follow-up* study of the results of surgery⟩
²follow–up \"\ *n* -S [*follow up*] **1 :** a system of pursuing an initial effort (as in advertising or in the activity of a salesman) by supplementary action **2 :** a system of recording the steps taken in the collection of an overdue account **3 a :** reexamination of or maintenance of contact with a patient at a prescribed interval or intervals following a basic examination, a course of treatment, or surgery **b :** a patient or case so followed up **4 :** a news story presenting new information on or a new handling of a story printed or broadcast earlier; *also* : a news story of minor significance related and usu. attached to one of major significance
fol·ly \'fälē, -li\ *n* -ES [ME *folie,* fr. OF, fr. *fol* foolish, mad + *-ie* -y — more at FOOL] **1 :** lack of good sense or of normal prudence and foresight : weakness or triviality of intellect ⟨answer not a fool according to his ~ —Prov 26:4 (AV)⟩ ⟨~ has a louder voice than common sense —C.H.Grandgent⟩ **2 :** inability or refusal to accept existing reality or to foresee inevitable consequence ⟨the ~ of passing on hills and blind curves⟩ ⟨reformers . . . are prone to regard the existing order as sheer ~ or evil —H.J.Muller⟩ **3 :** a thoughtless act or irrational idea : an unconsidered or unwise procedure ⟨she had been guilty of the capital ~ of cutting herself off from her family —Arnold Bennett⟩ **4 a** *obs* : EVIL, WICKEDNESS; *esp* : LEWDNESS **b :** actions or conduct so misguided as to result in destruction or tragic consequence ⟨saints have preached . . . the ~ of human strife —M.R.Cohen⟩ **5 :** an excessively costly or unprofitable undertaking; *esp* : a ruinously costly often unfinished building **6 a :** a lapse from strict propriety or sobriety : INDULGENCE, WHIM, VANITY, FOOLERY ⟨let us go while we are in our prime; and take the harmless ~ of the time —Robert Herrick †1674⟩ ⟨*follies* of fashion⟩ **b :** a summer-house or pavilion designed for picturesque effect or to suit a fanciful taste **7 follies** *pl* : a stage revue
fol·ly·er \'fälēə(r)\ *or* **vol·y·er** \'välēə(r)\ *n* -S [fr. E dial. var. of *follower*] : a small lug-rigged often British boat used in seine fishing
folo *like* FOLLOW\ *n* -S [alter. of ²*follow*] : FOLLOW-UP 4
fol·som \'fōlsəm *also* -lts-\ *adj, usu cap* [fr. *Folsom,* N.M., its type station] : of or relating to a prehistoric culture of No. America on the east side of the Rocky mountains from Alberta, Canada, to southern New Mexico that is characterized esp. by a leaf-shaped flint projectile point having a concave base with side projections and a longitudinal groove on each face ⟨*Folsom* man⟩
fol·som·oid \-sə,mȯid\ *adj, usu cap* : resembling a Folsom projectile point
¹fo·ment \'fō,ment\ *n* -S [ME, fr. L *fomentum,* fr. (assumed) OL *fovementum,* fr. *fovēre* to warm + *-mentum* -ment — more at DAY] **1 :** FOMENTATION **2 :** a state of excitation : FERMENT
²foment \(')=¦=\ *vt* -ED/-ING/-S [ME *fomenten,* fr. LL *fomentare,* fr. L *fomentum*] **1 :** to apply hot moist cloths to (the body) : treat with moist heat **2 :** to nurse to life or activity : promote the growth of : ROUSE, INCITE, ENCOURAGE, INSTIGATE ⟨a special need for ~*ing* exchanges of professors, students, and publications —D.D.Brand⟩ — usu. used in an unfavorable sense ⟨~ revolution⟩ ⟨~ riots⟩ **3** *obs* : EXCITE **syn** see INCITE
fo·men·ta·tion \,fōmən'tāshən, -,men-\ *n* -S [ME *fomentacioun,* fr. LL *fomentation-, fomentatio,* fr. *fomentatus* (past part. of *fomentare*) + L *-ion-, -io* -ion] **1 :** the act of fomenting : EXCITATION, INSTIGATION, ENCOURAGEMENT **2 a :** the application of hot moist substances (as wet cloths) to the body for the purpose of easing pain **b :** the material thus applied **c :** POULTICE
fo·ment·er \(')fō¦mentə(r)\ *n* -S : one that foments ⟨a ~ of class antagonisms —D.M.Potter⟩
fo·mes \'fō(,)mēz\ *n, cap* [NL, fr. L, touchwood, tinder; akin to L *fovēre* to warm] : a genus of bracket fungi (family Polyporaceae) usu. forming corky or woody perennial sporophores often of large size and including some fungi that cause destructive heartrots of timber and other trees
fomi·tes \'fämə,tēz, 'fōm-\ *n pl* [NL, fr. L, pl. of *fomes*] : inanimate objects (as clothing, dishes, toys, books) that may be contaminated with infectious organisms and serve in their transmission
fo·mor \'fō,mȯ(ə)r, -ō,wȯ-\ *n* -S *cap* [obs. IrGael *fomór, fomorach* (now *fomhuireach*), fr. IrGael *fo* under (fr. OIr) + *muir* sea (fr. OIr); akin to L *sub* under and *mare* sea — more at OVER, MARINE] : FOMORIAN
fo·mor·i·an \(')fō¦mōrēən, -ō¦wō-\ *n* -S *cap* [obs. IrGael *fomor* + E *-ian*] : one of a race of sea robbers in Celtic legend who were prob. orig. gods representing the powers of evil and darkness
fon \'fän\ *n, pl* **fon** *or* **fons** *usu cap* **1 a :** a Negro people of Dahomey esp. in the region of Abomey in West Africa **b :** a member of such people **2 :** the language of the Fon people that is closely related to or a dialect of Ewe
fonc·tion·naire \,fəŋ(k)shə¦na(a)(ə)r, F fōⁿksyȯneer\ *n, pl* **fonctionnaires** \-na(a)(ə)rz, -neer\ [F, fr. *fonction* function, office + *-aire* -ary — more at FUNCTION] : a French or French colonial government official
¹fond \'fänd\ *adj* -ER/-EST [ME *fonned, fond,* fr. *fonne* fool, dupe, buffoon + *-ed*] **1 :** FOOLISH, SILLY, INFATUATED ⟨~ scheme⟩ ⟨~ pride⟩ — used of persons now chiefly in dial. ⟨our John be right ~ about her⟩ **2 :** hopeful and credulous to an absurd degree ⟨a ~ promoter of visionary schemes⟩ ⟨grant I may never prove so ~ to trust man on his oath and bond —Shak.⟩ **3** *chiefly Scot* : EAGER, ANXIOUS — used with *to* ⟨very ~ to get the hay in before the fair⟩ **4 a :** having an affection or liking — used with *of* ⟨~ of his nephew⟩ ⟨~ of skating⟩ ⟨~ of music⟩ **b :** having a tendency or predisposition — used with *of* ⟨historians and biographers . . . are ~ of explaining him as "a man of his age" —Irving Kristal⟩ ⟨~ of painting big pictures —David Sylvester⟩ **5 a :** foolishly tender : weakly indulgent ⟨hopelessly spoiled by a ~ mother⟩ **b :** LOVING, AFFECTIONATE ⟨a ~ wife⟩ ⟨a ~ kiss⟩ **6 :** doted on : regarded with unreasoning affection : DEAR ⟨his ~*est* hopes fulfilled⟩ : clung to with strong attachment ⟨how are we to rid ourselves of our ~ prejudices and open our minds —James Ford⟩
²fond *vb* -ED/-ING/-S *vi, obs* : to be foolish : be fond : DOTE ~ *vt* **1** *obs* : BEFOOL, BEGUILE **2** *obs* : FONDLE, CARESS
³fond \'fänd\ *n* -S [F — more at FUND] **1 :** a background or foundation for added characteristics or aspects : GROUNDWORK, BASIS **2** *obs* : FUND **3 :** the ground of a lace usu. forming the background for a design
fon·da \'fändə\ *n* -S [Sp, prob. fr. Lingua Franca, fr. Ar *funduq* — more at FONDUK] *Southwest* : BOARDINGHOUSE, INN
fon·dant \'fändənt\ *n* -S [F, fr. pres. part. of *fondre* to melt — more at FOUND] **1 :** a creamy plastic mass of cooked or uncooked sugar used as a basis for candies or icings **2 :** a candy consisting chiefly of fondant
fon·dante potatoes \'fän,dant-\ *n pl* [F *fondante,* fem. of *fondant,* pres. part. of *fondre*] : potato balls or ovals that are first half cooked in water and then braised in butter
fond·ish \'fändish\ *adj* : somewhat fond
fon·dle \'fänd³l\ *vb* **fondled; fondled; fondling** \-nd(³)liŋ, -lēŋ, ÷-nl-\ **fondles** [²*fond* + *-le*] *vt* **1** *obs* : to treat with doting indulgence : PAMPER, CODDLE **2 :** to handle tenderly, lovingly, or lingeringly : treat caressingly : CARESS ⟨the nurse *fondled* the child⟩ ⟨*fondled* her jewels⟩ ⟨*fondling* his favorite phrase⟩ ⟨*fondling* the memory of her past goodness to him —Liam O'Flaherty⟩ ~ *vi* : to show affection or desire by caressing
fon·dler \-d(³)lə(r)\ *n* -S : one that fondles
fond·ling \'fändliŋ, -lēŋ\ *n* -S [¹*fond* + *-ling*] **1** *obs* : FOOL, SIMPLETON, NINNY **2 :** a person or thing fondled or caressed : PET
fon·dling·ly \'fänd(³)liŋlē, -lēŋ-, -li\ *adv* : in a fondling manner : CARESSINGLY, AFFECTIONATELY
fond·ly \'fändlē, -li\ *adv* [ME *fonnedly, fondly,* fr. *fonned, fond* foolish + *-ly* — more at FOND] **1** *archaic* : FOOLISHLY ⟨make him speak ~ like a frantic man —Shak.⟩ **2 :** in a fond manner : AFFECTIONATELY, TENDERLY ⟨he was often spoken of ~ as "the old man"⟩ **3 :** in a willingly credulous manner ⟨the result was not what we ~ hoped⟩
fond·ness \'fän(d)nəs\ *n* -ES [ME *fonnednesse, fondnesse,* fr. *fonned, fond* foolish + *-nesse* -ness] **1** *obs* : FOOLISHNESS, FOLLY **2 :** doting affection : tender liking **3 :** APPETITE, PROPENSITY, RELISH ⟨he had a ~ for truffles⟩ ⟨~ for argument⟩
¹fon·du \(')fän¦d(y)ü\ *adj* [F, fr. past part. of *fondre* to melt — more at FOUND] **1 :** passing into each other by subtle gradations : BLENDED — used of colors or of the surface or material on which the colors are laid **2 :** MELTED — used of foods
²fon·du \(')fän¦d(y)ü, F fōⁿdüe\ *n* -S [F, fr. past part. of *fondre*] : a lowering or sinking down of the body in ballet dancing by bending the knee of the supporting leg
fon·due *also* **fon·du** \(')fän¦d(y)ü\ *n* -S [F *fondue,* fr. fem. of *fondu,* past part. of *fondre*] **1 :** a preparation of melted cheese usu. flavored with wine or brandy : cooked cheese **2 :** a soufflé made with bread crumbs
fon·duk *or* **fon·douk** *or* **fun·duck** \'fän(,)dək, 'fən-, -,dük, -,dük\ *n* -S [Ar *funduq,* fr. Gk *pandokeion, pandocheion* inn, fr. *pandokos* all-receiving, common to all, fr. *pan-* + *-dokos*

(fr. *dekesthai, dechesthai* to accept, receive, welcome); akin to Gk *dokein* to seem good, seem, think — more at DECENT] **1 :** a business establishment or commercial warehouse in northern Africa **2 :** an inn or hotel in northern Africa

f_1 layer \ˈef¦wən-\ *n, usu cap F* **:** the lower and usu. less densely ionized of the two layers into which the F region of the ionosphere splits in the daytime occurring at varying heights from about 90 to 150 miles above the earth's surface and being more densely ionized than the E layer

fo·nio \ˈfōnē,ō\ *n* -s [F, fr. a native name in northern Africa] **:** a crabgrass (*Digitaria exilis*) of northern Africa with seeds that are used as a cereal

fo·no \ˈfō(,)nō\ *n* -s [Samoan & Tongan] **:** a Samoan council of faipules constituting the central political structure of a village, district, or island

fons \ˈfänz, ˈfōn(t)s\ *n, pl* **fon·tes** \-än·,tēz, -ōn·,tās\ [L — more at FOUNT] **:** FOUNT, SOURCE

fons et ori·go \,fōn(t),sed·əˈrē(,)gō\ *n* [LL] **:** source and origin ⟨western Europe, which . . . is always dimly assumed as the *fons et origo* of all social forces —Donald Davidson⟩ **:** original cause ⟨that this survival of the family god was the *fons et origo* of Hebrew monolatry —*Times Lit. Supp.*⟩

¹font \ˈfänt\ *n* -s [ME *fant, font, funt,* fr. OE *fant, font,* fr. LL *font-, fons,* fr. L, fountain, spring, source — more at FOUNT] **1 :** a basin or vessel often mounted on a pedestal in which water is contained for baptizing ⟨that name was given me at the ~ —Shak.⟩ **2** *archaic* **:** FOUNTAIN, SPRING, SOURCE **3 :** a receptacle for holy water **4 :** the oil reservoir of a lamp

font 1

²font \"\ *n* -s [MF *fonte,* fr. (assumed) VL *fundita,* fem. of (assumed) VL *funditus,* past part. of L *fundere* to found, pour — more at FOUND] **1 a :** the act or process of casting or founding **b :** a chamber for holding molten glass that is forced into a mold by pressure from a plunger **2 a :** an assortment of type, matrices, or characters of one size and style including a due proportion of all the letters in the alphabet, points, accents, and figures **b :** a set of any one sort of typographical material ⟨a ~ of brass rules⟩ ⟨a ~ of wood furniture⟩

³font \"\ *vt* -ED/-ING/-S **:** to arrange or make up (as type) into fonts **:** equip (as a type case or cabinet) with a font or fonts — often used with *up*

fon·tai·nea \fän·ˈtānēə\ *n, cap* [NL, after William M. *Fontaine* †1913 Am. geologist] **:** a genus of fossil dicotyledonous plants from the Cretaceous of No. America

font·al \ˈfäntᵊl\ *adj* [LL & L; LL *fontalis* baptismal, fr. L, of a fountain, spring or source, fr. *font-, fons* + *-alis* -al] **1 :** relating to a font, fountain, source, or origin **:** ORIGINAL, PRIMARY ⟨from the ~ light of ideas only can a man draw intellectual power —S.T.Coleridge⟩ **2 :** BAPTISMAL

fon·ta·nel *also* **fon·ta·nelle** \¦fäntᵊn¦el\ *n* -s [ME *fontinelle,* fr. MF *fontenele* little spring, fontanel, dim. of *fontaine* spring — more at FOUNTAIN] **1** *obs* **a :** an opening for the discharge of bodily secretions **b :** an ulcer or vent discharging secretions from the body **2 :** a membrane-covered opening in bone or between bones; *specif* **:** one of the intervals closed by membranous structures between the uncompleted angles of the parietal bones and the neighboring bones of a fetal or young skull

fon·tange *or* **fon·tanges** \fōⁿtäⁿzh\ *n, pl* **fontanges** \"\ [F *fontange,* after Marie Angélique de Scorraille de Roussilles, duchess of *Fontanges* †1681 Fr. mistress of Louis XIV] **:** COMMODE 1

fontes *pl of* FONS

fon·ti·na \fän·ˈtēnə, fōn-·-\ *n* -s [It] **:** a soft cooked ripened cheese of creamy texture and mild flavor

fon·ti·nal \ˈfäntᵊnəl\ *adj* [L *fontinalis* of or from a spring, irreg. fr. *font-, fons* spring + *-alis* -al] **:** growing in or near springs

fon·ti·na·la·ce·ae \,fäntᵊnəˈlāsē,ē\ *n pl, cap* [NL, fr. *Fontinalis,* type genus + *-aceae*] **:** a small family of aquatic mosses (order Isobryales) having long floating stems and capsules nearly covered by the surrounding leaf clusters — see DICHELYMA, FONTINALIS

fon·ti·nal·is \-ᵊnˈaləs, -ˈäl-,-ˈäl-\ *n* [NL, fr. L] **1** *cap* **:** the type genus of Fontinalaceae **2** -ES **:** any water moss of the genus *Fontinalis*

font name *n* **:** FIRST NAME, FORENAME

foo \(ˈ)fü\ *Scot var of* HOW

¹foo·chow \ˈfü¦jō, -¦chaů\ *n* -s *cap* [fr. *Foochow* (Minhow), China] **:** a dialect of Chinese spoken in and near Foochow in southeastern China

²foochow \"\ *adj, usu cap* [fr. *Foochow* (Minhow), China] **:** of or from the city of Foochow (now Minhow), China **:** of the kind or style prevalent in Foochow

food \ˈfüd *sometimes* ˈfůd\ *n* -s *often attrib* [ME *fode,* fr. OE *fōda;* akin to OE *fōdor, foddor* food, fodder, OHG *fuotar* food, fodder, ON *fæða, fæthi* food, *fōthr* fodder, Goth *fodeins* food, L *pabulum* food, fodder, *panis* bread, *pascere* to pasture, feed, graze, Gk *pateisthai* to eat, OSlav *pasti* to graze] **1 a :** material consisting of carbohydrates, fats, proteins, and supplementary substances (as minerals, vitamins) that is taken or absorbed into the body of an organism in order to sustain growth, repair, and all vital processes and to furnish energy for all activity of the organism ⟨any population is limited by the available supply of ~⟩; *esp* **:** parts of the bodies of animals and plants consumed by animals **:** PROVENDER, PROVISIONS, VIANDS ⟨acres devoted to growing ~⟩ ⟨longing for the ~s of her homeland⟩ — compare METABOLISM, NUTRITION **b :** simple inorganic substances that are absorbed by plants in gaseous form (as carbon dioxide) or in solution in water (as nitrates, phosphates) **:** plant nutrients **c :** complex organic substances constructed within the bodies of green plants by photosynthesis or other processes for use directly as building material and as source of energy for growth and reproduction **2 a :** nutriment in solid form — opposed to *drink* **b :** the chief substance of regularly taken meals as distinguished from candy, appetizers, or condiments **3 a :** something that nourishes or develops ⟨spiritual ~⟩ ⟨intellectual ~⟩ or sustains ⟨praise was her favorite ~ —Eden Phillpotts⟩ **b :** something that supplies a process or activity ⟨~ for thought⟩ **4** *obs* **:** the act of eating **5 foods** *pl* **:** stocks or bonds of food companies

food ball *n* **:** HAIR BALL

food canal *n* **:** ALIMENTARY CANAL

food chain *n* **:** a sequence of organisms in a community each of which uses the next usu. lower member of the sequence as a food source, plants being the ultimate basis of the sequence

food chopper *n* **:** a machine or implement that chops or grinds food

food color *n* **:** a dye or pigment permitted for use in foods — see DYE tables I and II

food conversion *n* **:** the rate at which an animal converts food into tissue usu. expressed as pounds of food consumed per pound of liveweight gained

food cycle *n* **:** a group of food chains constituting all or a significant part of the food relations that enable survival of the population of a community

food fish *n* **:** a fish used as human food — often distinguished from *game fish;* compare PANFISH

food-gatherer \ˈ=,===\ *n* **:** one that lives upon food procured by hunting, fishing, and gathering rather than through agriculture or animal husbandry

food grain *n* **:** a grain (as wheat, rice, rye, or buckwheat) grown for human food

food·less \ˈ=ləs\ *adj* [ME *fodeles,* fr. *fode* food + *-les* — more at FOOD] **:** lacking food **:** barren of food — **food·less·ness** *n* -ES

food mill *n* **:** a heavy colander through which food is pressed by means of a flat plate attached to a rotating handle

food mill

foo dog *usu cap F, var of* FU DOG

food plant *n* **:** a plant (as wheat, potato, cabbage) some part of which provides food for human consumption

food poisoning *n* **1 :** either of two acute gastrointestinal disorders caused by bacteria or their toxic products: **a :** a rapidly developing intoxication marked by nausea, vomiting, prostration, and often severe diarrhea and caused by the presence in food of toxic products produced by bacteria (as certain staphylococci) **b :** a less rapidly developing infection esp. with salmonellas that has generally similar symptoms and that results from multiplication of bacteria ingested with contaminated food — called also *bacterial food poisoning;* compare BOTULISM, MUSSEL POISONING, SALMONELLOSIS **2 :** a gastrointestinal disturbance occurring after consumption of food which is contaminated with chemical residues (as from sprays) or food (as certain fungi) which is inherently unsuitable for human consumption

food press *n* **:** a perforated metal cone through which food is pressed by means of a wooden pestle

foodstuff \ˈ=,=\ *n* **:** a substance with food value: as **a :** the raw material of food before or after processing ⟨a bountiful crop of cereal ~s⟩ ⟨a basket of ~s including flour⟩ ⟨green ~s from the garden⟩ **b :** an element of nutrition (as protein, carbohydrate, vitamin) ⟨the sponge obtains its necessary ~s from the plankton⟩

food tube *n* **:** ALIMENTARY CANAL

food unit *n* **:** a unit of 1701 calories that is used in nutritional research

food vacuole *n* **:** one of the usu. transitory vacuoles in the protoplasm of a protozoan in which digestion takes place — see AMOEBA illustration

food web *n* **:** FOOD CYCLE

foo·fa·raw \ˈfüfə,rȯ\ *also* **foo·foo·rah** \-fə,rä, -rȯ\ *or* **fo·far·raw** \ˈfō-\ *n* -s [origin unknown] **1 :** frills and flashy finery ⟨too much ~ on that dress to suit me⟩ **2 :** a disturbance or to-do over a trifle **:** FUSS ⟨what's the occasion for all this ~⟩

¹foo-foo \ˈfü(,)fü\ *n* -s [perh. by alter. & redupl. fr. ¹*fool*] *slang* **:** FOOL, NINNY

²foo-foo \"\ *n* -s [of African origin; akin to Ewe *fuˈfuˈ* food made from boiled and pounded yam, cassava, and coco, Wolof *fufu* food made from cassava meal] **:** a dough made from boiled and mashed plantains

¹fool \ˈfül\ *n* -s [ME *fol, fool,* fr. OF *fol,* fr. LL *follis,* fr. L, bellows, bag; akin to L *flare* to blow — more at BLOW] **1 :** a person lacking in judgment or prudence ⟨a ~ and his money are soon parted⟩ **:** one that acts stupidly or recklessly ⟨fortune favors ~s⟩ **2 a :** a retainer formerly kept in great households to provide casual entertainment and commonly dressed in motley with cap, bells, and bauble — called also *jester* **b :** one that is victimized or that is made to appear foolish **:** GULL, DUPE, BUTT ⟨a ~ of circumstances⟩ ⟨history has made ~s of many rash prophets⟩ ⟨he doesn't look very bright but he's nobody's ~⟩ **3 a :** a harmlessly deranged person or one lacking in common powers of understanding **:** NATURAL, IDIOT — now used chiefly in the phrase *born fool* **b :** one having a special weakness ⟨a ~ for women⟩ or fondness ⟨a ~ for candy⟩ **c :** one with a marked propensity or talent for a certain activity ⟨a letter-writing ~⟩ ⟨that horse is a running ~⟩ ⟨a ~ for luck⟩ **4 :** one that cannot stand comparison with another ⟨home's a ~ beside this-here place . . . let's dance another round —Elizabeth M. Roberts⟩ **5 a :** mashed fruit and cream **b :** a dessert made of pulped fruit covered with a custard and cream ⟨gooseberry ~⟩ **6 :** PLUM POCKET

syn FOOL, IDIOT, IMBECILE, MORON, SIMPLETON, and NATURAL are often applied popularly and interchangeably to anyone regarded as lacking sense or good judgment but can be more strictly applied to someone mentally deficient in a given degree. FOOL, the most general, can apply to anyone mentally deranged as well as mentally deficient, implying lack or loss of reason or intelligence; it may be used as an extremely offensive term of contempt ⟨*fools* rush in where angels fear to tread —Alexander Pope⟩ ⟨he was a *fool* and liable, as such, under the stress of bodily or mental disturbance, to spasmodic fits of abject fright which he mistook for religion —Norman Douglas⟩ ⟨I was a *fool,* if you like, and certainly I was going to do a foolish, overbold act —R.L.Stevenson⟩ ⟨to act like a *fool*⟩ IDIOT, IMBECILE, and MORON are technical designations for one mentally deficient. An IDIOT is incapable of connected speech or of avoiding the common dangers of life and needs constant attendance. An IMBECILE is incapable of earning a living but can be educated to attend to simple wants or avoid most ordinary dangers. A MORON can learn a simple trade but requires constant supervision in his work or recreation. In nontechnical use, IDIOT implies utter feeblemindedness; IMBECILE implies half-wittedness; MORON implies general stupidity ⟨comes like an *idiot,* babbling and strewing flowers —Edna S. V. Millay⟩ ⟨actually there never is a status quo, except in the minds of political *imbeciles* —Henry Miller⟩ ⟨even *morons* get college degrees —H.R.Warfel⟩ SIMPLETON, a term of indulgent contempt, implies silliness or lack of sophistication ⟨a sweet-natured *simpleton* who wrote lovely songs for children —S.F. Damon⟩ ⟨in spite of her experience of his lying, she had never suspected that that particular statement was a lie. What a *simpleton* she was! —Arnold Bennett⟩ NATURAL, now rare, once designated any congenitally feebleminded person ⟨the man is not a *natural;* he has a very quick sense, though very slow understanding —Richard Steele⟩

²fool \"\ *vb* -ED/-ING/-S [ME *folen,* fr. MF *foler,* fr. *fol* foolish] *vi* **1 a :** to spend time idly or aimlessly **:** waste time ⟨is this a time for ~*ing* —John Dryden⟩ — often used with *around* ⟨he hasn't been working at all, just ~*ing* around⟩ **b :** to meddle or tamper thoughtlessly or ignorantly **:** handle recklessly — used with *with* ⟨emotions are dangerous things to ~ with⟩ or *around with* ⟨don't ~ around with that gun⟩ **c :** to act or work tentatively or unsystematically or casually — often used with *around* ⟨~*ing* around in his home laboratory⟩ ⟨~*ing* around with new wing designs⟩ ⟨he ~*ed* with farm machinery so much that he just about didn't get any farming done —Danforth Ross⟩ **d :** to deal without serious intent **:** TRIFLE, PHILANDER — often used with *around* ⟨falls into the habit of ~*ing* around with a blond instead of going dutifully home —*Time*⟩ ⟨time to stop ~*ing* around and get married and settle down⟩ **2 a :** to play or improvise a comic role **:** make comedy ⟨a master maker of comedy, he could ~ excellently —Edith Hamilton⟩ ⟨he is serious, but she likes to ~⟩ **b :** to speak in jest **:** speak or act in playful deception **:** JOKE ⟨don't be frightened, I was only ~*ing*⟩ **3 a :** to contend or fight without serious intent or with less than full strength **:** TOY — used with *with* ⟨the champion ~*ed* with him for six rounds and then knocked him out⟩ ⟨a dangerous man to ~ with⟩ **b :** to go at less than full or normal speed **:** AMBLE, LOITER — used with *along* or *about* ⟨we didn't hurry, just ~*ed* along enjoying the scenery⟩ ~ *vt* **1 a :** to make a fool of **:** DECEIVE, DUPE ⟨to ~ rustlers . . . ranchers started putting brands in two or three different places —S.E.Fletcher⟩ ⟨his disguise didn't ~ anybody⟩ ⟨~*ing* the voters with large promises⟩ **b :** to take by surprise **:** exceed or disappoint the expectations of ⟨I don't think he is ready for work, but he may ~ me⟩ **2** *obs* **:** to make foolish **:** INFATUATE ⟨for, ~*ed* with hope, men favor the deceit —John Dryden⟩ **3 :** to spend on trifles or without advantage **:** FRITTER — used with *away* ⟨~*ed* the whole afternoon away⟩ ⟨~*ed* away his week's allowance in two days⟩

³fool \"\ *adj* [partly fr. ME *fol, fool,* fr. OF *fol,* fr. LL *follus,* fr. *follis,* n.; partly fr. ¹*fool*] **:** FOOLISH, SILLY, STUPID ⟨his ~ idea of rewriting the books of authors —Bennett Cerf⟩ ⟨the dog was barking his ~ head off⟩

fool duck *n* [so called fr. its tameness that allows it to be easily caught] **:** RUDDY DUCK

fool·er \ˈfülə(r)\ *n* -s **:** one that fools **:** JOKER

fool·ery \-l(ə)rē, -ri\ *n* -ES **1 :** the habit or practice of folly or fooling **:** the behavior of a fool **:** ABSURDITY ⟨folly in fools bears not so strong a note, as ~ in the wise, when wit doth dote —Shak.⟩ **2 :** an act of folly or fooling **:** a foolish, absurd, or nonsensical performance, utterance, or belief ⟨the solemn ~ of scholarship for scholarship's sake —Aldous Huxley⟩

foolfish \ˈ=,=\ *n* **1 :** FILEFISH **2 :** the eel-back flounder or a related fish

fool-happy *adj, obs* **:** lucky without judgment or contrivance

foolhardihood \ˈ=,==,=, =ˈ==,=\ *n* **:** FOOLHARDINESS

foolhardily \ˈ=,===\ *adv* [ME *folhardily,* fr. *folhardy* + *-ly*] **:** in a foolhardy manner ⟨tried ~ to attract attention to himself⟩

foolhardiness \ˈ=,===\ *n* [ME *folhardinesse,* fr. *folhardy* + *-nesse* -ness] **:** the quality or state of being foolhardy ⟨courage . . . the mean between ~ and cowardice —G.L.Dickinson⟩

foolhardy \ˈ=,==\ *adj* -ER/-EST [ME *folhardy, foolhardy,* fr. OF *fol hardi,* fr. *fol* foolish + *hardi* bold, brave — more at FOOL, HARDY] **:** daring but lacking judgment **:** foolishly adventurous and bold **:** exhibiting or characterized by lack of regard for foreseeable or avoidable danger ⟨a ~ dive into shallow water⟩ ⟨since I had been so ~ as to come ashore with these desperadoes —R.L.Stevenson⟩ **syn** see ADVENTUROUS

fool hay *n* **1 :** ROUGH BENT **2 :** WITCHGRASS 2

foolhearted \ˈ=¦==\ *adj* **:** having the heart of a fool **:** FOOLISH

fool hen *n* [fr. its stupidity that permits it to be easily caught] **:** a grouse that exhibits little alertness or fear of man: **a :** SPRUCE GROUSE **b :** FRANKLIN GROUSE

fool·ish \ˈfülish, -lēsh\ *adj, sometimes* -ER/-EST [ME *folish, foolish,* fr. *fol, fool* + *-ish*] **1 :** marked by folly **:** lacking in judgment, fit consideration, or intelligence: as **a :** lacking in intellect **:** IDIOTIC, FEEBLEMINDED, SIMPLE **b :** lacking in discretion or consideration of effects and consequences ⟨many changes that well might seem rash, mistaken, ~ and ill-advised —J.C.Powys⟩ **c :** lacking in sense or seriousness **:** NONSENSICAL ⟨obscurely and uselessly, like a ~ suggestion —Liam O'Flaherty⟩ **d :** lacking in significance, balance, fitness, or relevance ⟨a prince who should . . . not, like a subject, ~ matters mince —John Keats⟩ **e :** lacking in prowess, cunning, or strength ⟨the line which ~ birds are caught with —William Wordsworth⟩ **f :** idly and vainly enthusiastic or enamored **:** INFATUATED ⟨when you began to feel ~ about that man, I warned you he would not make you happy —Thomas Hardy⟩ **2 a :** ABSURD, RIDICULOUS ⟨a ~ little hat⟩ **b :** NONPLUSSED, ABASHED ⟨stood looking and feeling ~ —Arnold Bennett⟩ **c** *obs* **:** DIVERTING, AMUSING **3 :** absurdly paltry, insignificant, or inadequate **:** TRIFLING, HUMBLE ⟨we have a trifling, ~ banquet toward —Shak.⟩ ⟨all our ~ little paper knives and pincushions —Compton Mackenzie⟩

syn SILLY, ABSURD, PREPOSTEROUS: FOOLISH applies to what is marked by folly and nonsense, to what is not wise, sensible, or judicious ⟨only a *foolish* optimist can deny the dark realities of the moment —F.D.Roosevelt⟩ ⟨we need courage to look into our own heart and clear it of the *foolish* desires which make us sow vain hopes and devote needless toil and anxiety to raise bitter crops of disappointment —M.R.Cohen⟩ SILLY may indicate a fatuous lack of common sense, a witless, inane, or childish lack of reason ⟨how *silly* an ardent and unsuccessful wooer can be, especially if he's getting on in years —Dashiell Hammett⟩ ⟨a circle of *silly* young officers, who talked in bellicose and boastful terms —*Times Lit. Supp.*⟩ ABSURD may apply to what is flagrantly and ridiculously inconsistent with reason and common sense ⟨it is *absurd* to suppose that the shrewd traders . . . were moved by an abstract question of hereditary right —J.R.Green⟩ PREPOSTEROUS may indicate glaring, nonsensical lack of reasonableness ⟨if a man cannot see a church, it is *preposterous* to take his opinion about its altarpiece or painted window —T.H.Huxley⟩ ⟨a *preposterous* attempt to turn back the pages of history —V.L.Parrington⟩ ⟨a *preposterous* kind of resentment which endeavors to wreak itself on the beloved object —Nathaniel Hawthorne⟩ **syn** see in addition SIMPLE

foolish guillemot *n* **:** a common murre (*Uria aalge*) of northern seas

fool·ish·ly *adv* **:** in a foolish manner

fool·ish·ment \-mənt\ *n* -s *chiefly Midland* **:** FOOLISHNESS

fool·ish·ness *n* -ES [ME *folishnes,* fr. *folish* foolish + *-nes* -ness] **1 :** the quality or state of being foolish **:** FOLLY **2 :** a foolish practice **:** ABSURDITY

foolkiller \ˈ=,==\ *n* **:** one that kills fools ⟨a sudden gale, a vicious north wind called the ~, which could blow a 40-foot boat to kingdom come —*Saturday Rev.*⟩; *esp* **:** an imaginary or legendary person whose business is destroying fools

fool·oc·ra·cy \füˈläkrəsē\ *n* -ES [¹*fool* + *-o-* + *-cracy*] **1 :** government by fools **2 :** a ruling class of fools

fool·om·e·ter \füˈlämǝd·ǝ(r)\ *n* [¹*fool* + *-o-* + *-meter*] **:** a standard for measuring folly ⟨she was also useful as a touchstone, a ~ —Rose Macaulay⟩

foolproof \ˈ=¦=\ *adj* **1 :** so simple, plain, or strong as not to be liable to be misunderstood, damaged, or misused ⟨~ tools⟩ ⟨~ automatic washer⟩ **2 :** guaranteed to operate without breakdown or failure under any conditions ⟨~ elevator⟩ ⟨~ rule of thumb⟩ ⟨the system for reducing armaments must be ~ — that is, proof against cheating by any nation —*N.Y. Herald Tribune*⟩ — **fool·proof·ness** *n* -ES

fools *pl of* FOOL, *pres 3d sing of* FOOL

fools·cap *or* **fool's cap** \ˈfülz,kap\ *n* **1 :** a cap or hood usu. with bells worn by jesters **2 :** DUNCE CAP **3** *usu* **foolscap** [so called fr. the watermark of a fool's cap formerly applied to such paper] **:** a size of paper differing somewhat in the various grades and typically about 16x13 inches for writing and drawing papers, 17x13 for printing papers and boards, and 18x14 for wrapping papers

foolscap 1

fool's-coat \ˈ=,=\ *n, pl* **fool's-coats** [so called fr. its gaudy, multicolored plumage] **:** GOLDFINCH 1

fool's cress *n* **:** FOOL'S WATERCRESS

fool's errand *n* **:** a needless or profitless errand

fool's gold *n* **1 :** PYRITE **2 :** CHALCOPYRITE

fool's huckleberry *n* **:** a straggling shrub (*Menziesia ferruginea*) of northwestern No. America with glandular hirsute petioles and pedicels

fool's paradise *n* [ME *foles paradise*] **:** a state of delusory or deceptive success or happiness **:** a state of fatuous complacency based on unreal conditions or false expectations ⟨may go on living in a *fool's paradise* until they are caught in the final crash —M.B.Foster⟩

fool's parsley *n* **:** a European weed (*Aethusa cynapium*) of the family Umbelliferae that is naturalized in America and resembles parsley but causes nausea and poisoning when eaten

fool's-stones \ˈ=,=\ *n pl but sing or pl in constr* [so called fr. the resemblance of the roots to testes] **:** any of several European orchids of the genus *Orchis*

fool's watercress *n* **:** a European perennial herb (*Apium nodiflorum*) with simple pinnate leaves and umbels of greenish white flowers

foon·er \ˈfünər\ *Scot var of* FOUNDER

¹foos·ter \ˈfüs·t(h)ər\ *n* -s [IrGael *fūstar*] *chiefly Irish* **:** FUSS, BUSTLE, TO-DO

²fooster \"\ *vi* -ED/-ING/-S *chiefly Irish* **:** to bustle around **:** FLUSTER; *esp* **:** to waste time by fussing and chattering ⟨you can't expect children to concentrate when everybody's gabbling and ~*ing* around them —Michael McLaverty⟩

¹foot \ˈfůt, *usu* -ůd·+V\ *n, pl* **feet** \ˈfēt *usu* -ēd·+V\ *also* **foot** *see numbered senses, often attrib* [ME *fot, foot,* fr. OE *fōt;* akin to OHG *fuoz* foot, ON *fōtr,* Goth *fotus,* L *ped-, pes,* Gk *pod-, pous,* Skt *pad*]

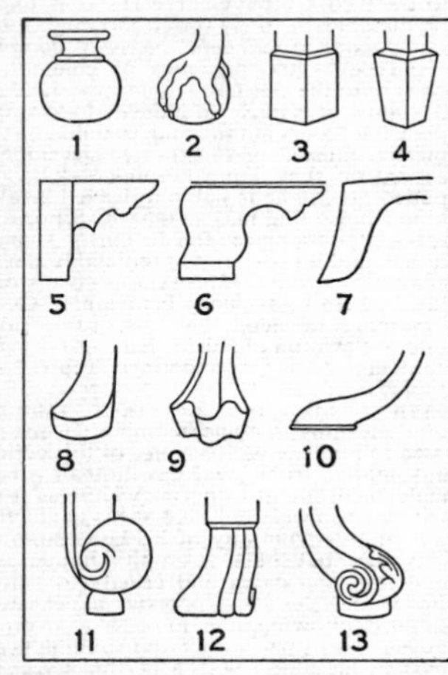

feet used in furniture: *1* ball, *2* claw and ball, *3* block, *4* spade, *5* straight bracket, *6* ogee bracket, *7* French bracket, *8* club, *9* drake, *10* snake, *11* flemish scroll, *12* Spanish scroll, *13* French scroll

1 : the terminal part of the vertebrate leg upon which an individual stands consisting in most bipeds (as man) and many quadrupeds (as the cat) of all the structures (as heel, arches, and digits) below the ankle joint or in digitigrade animals (as the horse or sheep) of the terminal parts of one or more digits often encased in a horny hoof **2 :** any of various invertebrate organs of locomotion or attachment: as **a :** a limb of an arthropod **b :** the ventral muscular surface or a ventral muscular process of a mollusk flattened for creeping in most gastropods or tapering for burrowing in many bivalves — compare PSEUDOPODIUM; see TUBE FOOT; CLAM illustration **3 :** any of various ancient and modern units of length based on the length of the human foot; *esp* **:** the unit used generally in English-speaking countries equal to ⅓ yard and comprising 12 inches ⟨a width of 16 *feet*⟩ ⟨a 5-*foot* tree⟩ ⟨six ~ tall⟩ — *pl foot* used preceded by a number and followed by a noun; *pl feet* or *foot* used preceded by a number and followed by an adverb ⟨10 *feet* tall⟩; see CAPE FOOT, GREEK FOOT, ROMAN FOOT; MEASURE table **4 :** the least bit of length, distance, or area ⟨payed out the rope to the last ~⟩ ⟨dragged along complaining every ~ of the way⟩ ⟨I'll starve ere I rob a ~ further —Shak.⟩ ⟨searched the grounds ~ by ~⟩ **5 a :** the basic unit of verse meter **:** a single instance of the recurring pattern which constitutes metrical rhythm **:** a group of syllables constituting a metrical unit **b :** the basic unit in a rhythmic series of any kind whether metrical or not — compare CADENCE, METER **6 a :** motion or power of walking or running **:** STEP, TREAD ⟨graceful and light of ~⟩ **b :** SWIFTNESS, SPEED ⟨the horse showed early ~ but tired before the end⟩ **7 :** something resembling a foot in position or use **:** the lowest supporting or structural part **:** BASE: as **a :** the lower end of the leg of a chair or table **b :** one of the areas of the base of a piece of printing type on each side of the groove; *also* **:** the corresponding area in type cast with no groove or in wood type — see TYPE illustration **c** (1) **:** the basal portion of the sporogonium in mosses embedded in the gametophyte and absorbing food from it (2) **:** a specialized outgrowth by which the embryonic sporophyte of many ferns and related plants and some seed plants absorbs nourishment from the gametophyte (3) **:** the basal portion of an epidermal hair lying within the epidermis and often differing in shape from adjacent epidermal cells **d :** the lowest part of an organ pipe **e :** a piece on a sewing machine that presses the cloth against the feed **f :** FOOTING 9 **8** *foot pl, chiefly Brit* **:** INFANTRY ⟨three regiments of ~ and two of cavalry⟩ ⟨the 41st *Foot*⟩ **9 :** the lower edge: as **a** *pl* **foots :** the bottom woven edge (as of a wicker basket) — see BASKET illustration **b :** the edge of a sail nearest the deck **c :** the bottommost part of a type page or printed page **d :** the lowermost edge of a book that is standing upright — compare BINDING EDGE, FORE EDGE, HEAD, TAIL **10 :** the lowest part **:** BOTTOM ⟨~ of a hill⟩ ⟨~ of a staircase⟩ **11 a :** the end that is lower or opposite the head ⟨~ of the bed⟩ ⟨~ of a lane⟩ ⟨~ of a line of dancers⟩ ⟨~ of the class⟩ **b :** the part that covers the foot ⟨the ~ of a stocking⟩ **12 :** something placed at the bottom: as **a** *obs* **:** the refrain of a song **b** *obs* **:** the sum of an account **13** *obs* **a :** FOOTING, BASIS, RANK **b :** customary value or price **:** standard rate of reckoning **14 :** the point of intersection of one line with another line or the point of contact with a plane **15 foots** *pl but sing or pl in constr* **:** material deposited esp. in aging or refining ⟨~*s* or soap stock precipitated in refining of fatty oils with alkali⟩ **:** SEDIMENT **:** DREGS **:** RESIDUE — compare ²BREAK 6d **16 :** FOOTWALL **17 foots** *pl* **:** FOOTLIGHTS — **at foot** *adv* **:** NEARBY **:** in the same enclosure (as for nursing) ⟨a mare with her colt *at foot*⟩ — **at one's feet :** under one's spell or influence **:** in subjection ⟨kept the audience *at her feet* for several seasons⟩ — **off its feet** *adv (or adj), of set type* **:** out of line with or inclined from the vertical (as from improper locking) — **off one's feet 1 :** in a sitting or lying position **:** not upright ⟨told by the doctor to stay *off his feet* as much as possible⟩ **2 :** beyond emotional self-control ⟨swept *off her feet* by a whirlwind courtship⟩ — **on foot** *adv* **1 :** in a walking or running state ⟨tour the campus *on foot*⟩ **2 :** under way **:** in progress ⟨plans to enlarge the campus are *on foot*⟩ — **on one's feet 1 :** in a standing position ⟨jumped and landed *on his feet*⟩ **2 :** in a position to go on ⟨the nomination put him *on his feet*⟩ **:** in an established position or state ⟨the business is finally *on its feet*⟩ **3 :** in a recovered condition (as from illness) **:** at a stage of being able to resume work or activity **4 :** without obvious deliberation or hesitation **:** EXTEMPORANEOUSLY ⟨a debater should be able to think *on his feet*⟩ — **put one's foot down :** to take a firm stand ⟨*put his foot down* on our staying out after midnight⟩ **:** give a clear or decisive order — **put one's foot into it :** to make a tactless or embarrassing blunder **:** get into trouble ⟨we can count on him to *put his foot into it* at the wrong moment⟩ — **with both feet** *adv* **:** HEAVILY, SOLIDLY, EMPHATICALLY ⟨came down *with both feet* against the proposal⟩

²foot \"\ *vb* -ED/-ING/-S [ME *foten,* fr. *fot, foot*] *vi* **1 :** to tread to music **:** DANCE, TRIP — often used with *it* ⟨~ it featly here and there —Shak.⟩ **2 :** to go on foot **:** WALK, RUN — contrasted with *ride;* often used with *it* ⟨~ it softly across the lambing fields —Roland Mathias⟩ ⟨a couple of men tearing up the path as tight as they could ~ it —Mark Twain⟩ **3** *of a falcon* **:** to seize prey with the talons **4** *of a sailboat* **:** to make speed or distance forward — contrasted with *point* ⟨under all sail . . . she ~*s* along in a light breeze —Luis Marden⟩ ~ *vt* **1 a :** to perform the movements of (a dance) ⟨~ the saraband or some other intricate forgotten dance —Dixon Wecter⟩ **b :** to walk, run, or dance on, over, or through ⟨~ the greensward⟩ ⟨the moon . . . ~*ing* the treetops —C.E.S.Wood⟩ ⟨~*ing* his way to Paris —H.O.Taylor⟩ **2** *archaic* **a :** to kick with the foot **b :** REJECT, SPURN **c :** to seize or strike with the talons **3** *archaic* **:** to set on a basis **:** ESTABLISH **4 a :** to sum up (as numbers in a column) — sometimes used with *up* ⟨~ up an account⟩ **b :** to pay or stand credit for (a bill, expenses) ⟨~ the cost of a trip to the mountains⟩ **5 :** to make or renew the foot of (as a stocking) **6 :** TRACK 1 **7** *Irish* **:** to set (turf sods) on end in small heaps to dry ⟨~*ing* turf is a job —Bryan MacMahon⟩ **8 :** to splice (an arrow) with a footing **9 :** to hold the lower edge of (a stage flat) in place with the foot to facilitate raising to vertical position

foot·age \'fu̇d·ij, -ùt|, |ēj\ *n* -S **1 :** length or quantity expressed in feet: as **a :** BOARD FEET **b :** the total number of running feet of motion-picture film used for a complete story or for one or more scenes or for any subject **2 :** payment (as of miners) by the running foot of work; *also* **:** amount so paid

foot-and-mouth disease *n* **:** an acute contagious febrile disease affecting esp. cloven-footed animals, caused by a filtrable virus, and characterized by ulcerating vesicles in the mouth, about the hoofs, and on the udder and teats — called also *aphthous fever*

footback \'ₛ,ₛ\ *adv* [¹*foot* + *back* (as in *horseback*)] *dial* **:** on foot

footbacker \'ₛ,ₛₛ\ *n* -S *dial* **:** a person traveling on foot

¹football \'ₛ,ₛ\ *n, often attrib* [ME *fotbal, football,* fr. *fot, foot* + *bal* ball — more at FOOT, BALL] **1 :** any of several games played with a football on a rectangular field having two goalposts at each end by two teams whose object is to get the ball over a goal line or between goalposts: as **a** *Brit* **:** SOCCER **b** *Brit* **:** RUGBY **c :** a game played between two teams of 11 players each in which the ball is in recognized possession of one side at a time and is advanced by running or passing, in which opposing players may stop the ballcarrier by tackling him, and in which teammates of the ballcarrier may precede him down the field to block off opponents — see AUSTRALIAN RULES FOOTBALL, CANADIAN FOOTBALL, GAELIC FOOTBALL, SIX-MAN FOOTBALL, TOUCH FOOTBALL **2 a :** an inflated oval ball made of a bladder encased usu. in leather, rubber, or plastic and used for throwing and kicking in the game of football **b** *Brit* **:** a soccer ball **3 a :** something that is tossed or kicked about **:** something or someone subjected to rough or irresponsible treatment ⟨sorry to see the GI made the ~ of politics —*N.Y. Herald Tribune*⟩ **b :** an item of merchandise priced to serve as a loss leader

diagram of intercollegiate football field: *ABBA,* field of play; *ACCA, DBBD,* end zones; *CC, DD,* end lines; *AA, BB,* goal lines; *EE, FF,* inbounds lines; *G, G,* goalposts

²football \"\ *vb* -ED/-ING/-S *vi* **:** to play football ~ *vt* **:** to sell (an item of merchandise) below cost as a loss leader

footballer \'ₛ,bȯlə(r)\ *n* **:** one that plays football or soccer

footband \'ₛ,ₛ\ *n* **1 :** a reinforcing strip of canvas on the afterpart of the foot of a sail — called also *footlining* **2 :** the bottom headband of a book — called also *tailband*

foot base *n* **:** a molding above a plinth

footbath \'ₛ,ₛ\ *n* **1 :** a bath for cleansing, warming, or disinfecting the feet (as at the entrance to an indoor swimming pool) ⟨a mustard ~ —Eric Knight⟩ **2 :** a small portable tub ⟨stepping into a ~ and washing upward —Flora Thompson⟩

footbeat \'ₛ,ₛ\ *n* **:** FOOTSTEP

foot-binding \'ₛ,ₛₛ\ *n* **:** the compressing of the feet of girls with tight bandages (as formerly in China) so as to keep the feet from being over three or four inches long

footblower \'ₛ,ₛₛ\ *n* **1 :** a bellows worked by foot **2 :** FOOTMAKER

footboard \'ₛ,ₛ\ *n* **1 :** a board or narrow platform on which one may stand or brace his feet: as **a :** the footrest of a coachman's box **b** (1) **:** FOOTPLATE (2) **:** a step slightly above track level on yard and freight locomotives for the use of train and yard personnel in yard operations **c :** a small platform at the rear of a carriage for a footman **d** (1) **:** the part of the front flooring in an automobile against which one's feet may rest (2) **:** RUNNING BOARD **2 :** a board forming the foot of a bed **3 :** TREADLE

foot bolt *n* **:** a bolt operated by foot pressure and attached to the bottom of a door to hold it in either open or closed position

footboy \'ₛ,ₛ\ *n* **:** a serving boy **:** PAGE, ATTENDANT

foot brake *n* **:** a brake operated by foot pressure

footbridge \'ₛ,ₛ\ *n* [ME *fotbrigge,* fr. *fot, foot* + *brigge,* bridge — more at BRIDGE] **:** a bridge for pedestrians

footcandle \'ₛ¦ₛₛ\ *n* **:** a unit of illuminance on a surface that is everywhere one foot from a uniform point source of light of one candle and equal to one lumen per square foot

footcandle meter *n* **:** a direct-reading illuminometer calibrated in footcandles

foot carrier *n* **:** a postal carrier who makes his mail deliveries on foot

footcloth \'ₛ,ₛ\ *n* [ME *fotcloth,* fr. *fot, foot* + *cloth*] **1 :** an ornamental cloth draped over the back of a horse to reach the ground on each side and serve to indicate the state and dignity of the rider **2** *obs* **:** CARPET, RUG

foot couple *n* **:** the couple at the end of a double line of square dancers farthest from the music — compare HEAD COUPLE

foot cut *n* **:** a cut made at the low end of a rafter for proper seating on the wall plate

foot drop *n* **1 :** an extended position of the foot caused by paralysis of the flexor muscles of the leg — called also *toedrop* **2 :** a planter with a seed-dropping mechanism to be operated by the foot

foot·ed \'fu̇d·əd, -ùtəd\ *adj* [ME *foted, footed,* fr. OE *-fōted,* fr. *fōt* foot + *-ed*] **1 :** having a foot ⟨~ creatures⟩ ⟨~ candy dish⟩ **:** having such or so many feet ⟨black-*footed*⟩ ⟨four-*footed*⟩ **:** shaped in the feet ⟨claw-*footed*⟩ **2 :** having or capable of such a gait or tread **:** having such ability with the feet ⟨fleet-*footed*⟩ ⟨nimble-*footed*⟩ ⟨soft-*footed*⟩ **3 :** composed in meter ⟨good poetry . . . without rhyme or ~ rhythms —Michael Earls⟩ **4** *of an arrow* **:** having a footing of hardwood spliced to the fore end of the shaft

foot·ed·ness *n* -ES **:** the dominance of one foot over the other ⟨ambidexterity and mixture of eyedness, handedness, and ~ —J.R.Gallagher⟩

foote·ite \'fu̇d·,īt\ *n* -S [A.E. *Foote* †1895 Am. mineral collector + E *-ite*] **:** CONNELLITE

¹foot·er \'fu̇d·ə(r), -ùtə-\ *n* -S [ME *foter, footer,* fr. *fot, foot* + *-er*] **1 :** one that goes on foot **:** PEDESTRIAN **2 :** a person or thing a (specified) number of feet in height, length, or breadth — used in combination ⟨the man is a six-*footer*⟩ ⟨the yacht was an 80-*footer*⟩ ⟨holed a 20-*footer* for par⟩ **3** *Brit* **:** RUGBY, SOCCER **4 :** the bowling mat used in lawn bowling **5 :** a hawk that seizes prey with the talons **6 a :** a machine for knitting feet on hosiery — compare LEGGER **b :** an operator of this machine **7 :** a mine worker who attaches and detaches tubs at the bottom of a haulage incline **8 :** FOOTING 7c

²foo·ter \'füd·ə(r), -ütə-\ *var of* FOUTER

³foo·ter \"\ *vi* -ED/-ING/-S [F *foutre,* lit., to copulate — more at FOUTER] **:** FOOTLE

footfall \'ₛ,ₛ\ *n* **:** the sound of a footstep ⟨walked together with hushed ~*s* —Ida A. R. Wylie⟩

foot fault *n* **1 :** a fault called against a server in tennis by reason of his failure to keep both feet behind the base line or because of walking, running, or failure to maintain contact with the ground during the delivery of a service **2 :** the stepping over the end line in volleyball while serving or over the center line while playing

footfault \'ₛ,ₛ\ *vi* [*foot fault*] **:** to commit a foot fault

footfeed \'ₛ,ₛ\ *n* **:** the pedal operating the throttle in a motor vehicle

footfolk \'ₛ,ₛ\ *n* [trans. of G *fussvolk*] *archaic* **:** INFANTRY

foot front *n* **:** FRONT FOOT

footgear \'ₛ,ₛ\ *n* **:** covering for the feet (as shoes, boots, slippers)

footglove \'ₛ,ₛ\ *n* **1 :** a heavy stocking worn over the shoe **2 :** a close-fitting sock of soft material worn to protect the foot or the stocking against harsh shoe linings

footgrip \'ₛ,ₛ\ *n* **:** a surface (as of a stair tread) roughened or grained to prevent slipping

foot guard *n* **:** a guard for the foot: as **a :** a boot or pad for a horse's foot to prevent injury to the hoof by interfering or overreaching **b :** a filler placed in the space between converging railroad rails to prevent the feet of persons from becoming wedged between the rails

foothill \'ₛ,ₛ\ *n* **1 :** a hill at the foot of higher hills **2 foothills** *pl* **:** a hilly region at the base of a mountain range

foothill death camas *n* **:** an herb (*Zigadenus paniculatus*) of the western U.S. with greenish white racemose flowers and narrow leaves that are poisonous to cattle

foothills yellow pine *n* **:** PONDEROSA PINE

foothold \'ₛ,ₛ\ *n* **1 :** a hold for the feet **:** a place where one may tread or stand **:** a stable position of the feet **:** FOOTING ⟨a layer of wooden planking . . . affording a safe ~ to the crew in wet weather⟩ ⟨pine and balsam find a precarious ~ on the shaggy cliffs —*Amer. Guide Series: Minn.*⟩ **2 :** a position providing a base for further efforts to advance (as in a military invasion) ⟨effort to win a continental ~ —*Collier's Yr. Bk.*⟩ ⟨settlers struggling to secure a ~ in the new country —*Amer. Guide Series: Oregon*⟩ **3 :** a light rubber overshoe or sandal with only a strap around the heel — called also *tip*

foothook \'ₛ,ₛ\ *n* **:** FUTTOCK

foothot \'ₛ¦ₛ\ *adv* [ME *fot hot, foot hot*] *archaic* **:** without delay **:** HASTILY

footie *var of* FOOTSIE

foot indian *n, usu cap I* **:** a South American Indian who travels by foot and not by canoe or horseback

foot·ing \'fu̇d·iŋ, -ùt|, |ēŋ\ *n* -S [ME *foting, footing,* fr. *fot, foot* + *-ing*] **1 :** a stable position of the feet **:** a surface or its condition with respect to one walking or running on it ⟨the loose stones made the ~ treacherous⟩; *specif* **:** the condition of a racetrack **2 :** the placing of the feet so as to ensure stability ⟨be careful of your ~ up here⟩ **:** ability to keep a grip with the feet on a surface so as to stay upright or move steadily forward ⟨lost her ~ and tumbled down the slope⟩ **3 :** FOOTLING **4 a :** a place or space for standing **:** basis for operations **:** FOOTHOLD ⟨a deliberate act of policy . . . in order to stake a claim for a ~ in Morocco —Wickham Steed⟩ **b :** established position **:** STATUS ⟨finally achieved a ~ at court⟩ ⟨placing the children of a former marriage on the same ~, with regard to inheritance —*Encyc. Americana*⟩ **c** *archaic* **:** payment exacted informally for entering upon a new status in a trade or profession **:** an initiation fee — used chiefly in the phrase *pay one's footing* **5 :** BASIS ⟨negotiating on a new ~ of mutual trust⟩ ⟨put the enterprise on a firm ~⟩ ⟨when the nation is on a war ~ —Zechariah Chafee⟩ **6 :** social relationship **:** terms of social intercourse ⟨tribes that are on a friendly ~ —Edward Sapir⟩ ⟨throwing our ideals overboard and meeting saints and dictators on the same ~ —*New Statesman and Nation*⟩ **7 a :** the substructure or bottom unit of a wall or column **:** BASE **b :** the part of a structure that is in contact with the soil or rock foundation **c :** an enlargement at the lower end of a foundation wall, pier, or column to distribute the load **8 a :** the straight side of an edging lace **b :** a very narrow lace or net used as an insertion, edging, or trimming **9 :** a piece of hardwood inserted into an arrow shaft and projecting into the pile **10 :** the amount or sum total of a column of figures

footing beam *n* **:** the tie beam of a roof

footing stone *n* **:** a broad flat stone for the base or lowest course of a wall

foot iron *n* **1 :** the step of a carriage **2 :** a bracket for securing scenery to the stage floor

foot jaw *n* **:** MAXILLIPED

footlambert \'ₛ¦ₛ,ₛ\ *n* **:** a unit of luminance equal to the luminance of a perfectly diffusing surface that emits or reflects one lumen per square foot

foot landraker *n, obs* **:** FOOTPAD, TRAMP

foo·tle \'füld·ᵊl, 'fu̇|, |tᵊl\ *vi* **footled; footled; footling** \|d·ᵊliŋ, |t(ᵊ)liŋ\ **footles** [alter. of ³*footer*] **1 :** to waste time **:** TRIFLE, FOOL, POTTER — used with *around* or *about* **2 :** to talk or act foolishly

foo·tler \|d·ᵊlə(r), |t(ᵊ)lə-\ *n* -S **:** one that footles **:** TRIFLER ⟨unless a writer is quite ruthless with these amiable ~*s* —*N.Y. Herald Tribune*⟩

foot·less \'fu̇tləs\ *adj* [ME *fotles footles,* fr. *fot, foot* + *-les* -less] **1 a :** lacking a foot **:** having no feet **b :** lacking foundation **:** UNSUBSTANTIAL ⟨~ halls of air —J.G.Magee⟩ **2 :** CLUMSY, STUPID, INEPT, USELESS, FUTILE ⟨~ and vacillating foreign policy —Alvin Johnson⟩ — **foot·less·ly** *adv* — **foot·less·ness** *n* -ES

footlicker \'ₛ,ₛₛ\ *n* -S **:** SYCOPHANT, BOOTLICKER

footlight \'ₛ,ₛ\ *n* **1 :** a light that casts its illumination upward from foot level; *esp* **:** one of a row of lights set across the front of a stage floor — usu. used in pl. **2 footlights** *pl* **:** the stage as a profession

footlights 1

footlike \'ₛ,ₛ\ *adj* **:** resembling a foot

foot line *n* **1 :** the weighted line of a fishing net **2 :** a line at the foot of a type page that is sometimes blank and sometimes carries the page number or signature figure or letter **3 :** FOOT SCORE

¹foot·ling \'fu̇tliŋ\ *n* -S [fr. ¹*foot* + *-ling* (n. suffix)] **:** one of the fore-and-aft strips of wood secured to the frames in the bottom of a small boat **:** FLOORBOARD — called also *footing*

²footling \"\ *adv (or adj)* [¹*foot* + *-ling* (adv. suffix)] **:** with or having the feet foremost ⟨~ presentation at delivery⟩

³foo·tling \'füld·ᵊliŋ, 'fu̇|, |t(ᵊ)liŋ\ *adj* [fr. pres. part. of *footle*] **1 :** lacking judgment, intelligence, or experience **:** FOOLISH, SILLY ⟨~ amateurs who understand nothing —E.R. Bentley⟩ **2 :** lacking importance, use, or value **:** TRIVIAL, INSIGNIFICANT ⟨a pity that such an attractive young woman should be interested in such ~ things —Nevil Shute⟩

footlining \'ₛ,ₛₛ\ *n* **:** FOOTBAND

footlock \'ₛ,ₛ\ *n* **1 :** a grip secured by the feet in climbing a rope **2 :** a level or relatively level projection temporarily fastened to a roof to provide footing for a workman

footlocker \'ₛ,ₛₛ\ *n* [¹*foot* + *locker*] **:** a small flat trunk equipped with a lock and designed to be placed at the foot of a barracks bunk

footlog \'ₛ,ₛ\ *n, chiefly Midland & West* **:** a simple footbridge consisting often of a single log hewn flat on one side ⟨crossing the ~ over Marsh Run —Conrad Richter⟩

footloose \'ₛ,ₛ\ *adj* **:** able or accustomed to act and travel about freely **:** not tied **:** WANDERING, NOMADIC ⟨Americans, from frontier times downward, have been a ~ people, always moving on —G.R.Stewart⟩ ⟨~ bachelors⟩

foot louse *n* **:** a sucking louse (*Linognathus pedalis*) on sheep congregating and feeding chiefly on the hairy skin immediately above the hooves

footmaker \'ₛ,ₛₛ\ *n* **:** a member of a chair of glassworkers who gathers and blows glass and shapes it on a marver table

foot·man \'ₛmən\ *n, pl* **footmen** [ME *fotman, footman,* fr. *fot, foot* + *man*] **1 a** *archaic* **:** a traveler on foot **:** PEDESTRIAN **b** *obs* **:** FOOTPAD **c** *obs* **:** one who runs foot races **d :** FOOT SOLDIER **2 a :** a servant in livery formerly in attendance upon a rider or required to run before his master's carriage **b :** a house servant who assists the butler in serving at table, tending the door, carrying luggage and parcels, running errands **c :** DOORMAN 1a **d :** a policeman who rides in the back of a patrol wagon and supervises the transportation of prisoners (as from a police beat to a station house or jail) — called also *wagonman* **3 :** a metal stand for holding a plate or kettle near a fire to keep it warm **4 :** BOTTOMER c

foot mange *n* **:** CHORIOPTIC MANGE

footman moth *n* [so called fr. its coloration, reminiscent of a footman's livery] **:** any of numerous moths of the family Lithosiidae

foot·man·ship \'fu̇tmən,ship\ *n, archaic* **:** speed afoot **:** prowess in running and walking

foot mantle *n* [ME *foot mantel*] **1 :** a long garment formerly worn to protect the dress in riding **2 :** FOOTCLOTH

footmark \'ₛ,ₛ\ *n* **:** FOOTPRINT

foot-mouth \'ₛ,ₛ\ *n* [by shortening] **:** FOOT-AND-MOUTH DISEASE

¹footnote \'ₛ,ₛ\ *n* [¹*foot* + *note*] **1 :** a note of reference, explanation, or comment placed below the text on a printed page or underneath a table or chart — compare REFERENCE MARK **2 :** an utterance or action that is subordinated or added to a larger statement or event **:** COMMENTARY, AFTERTHOUGHT ⟨this novel is a ~ to recent history⟩ ⟨it has been said that all philosophy is a ~ to Plato —Lionel Trilling⟩

²footnote \"\ *vt* **:** to furnish with a footnote **:** ANNOTATE

foot of the fine *n, pl* **feet of the fines** [trans. of AF *pee de la fin*] **:** the part of a tripartite indenture made in case of a fine of land made for the court's records — compare CHIROGRAPH

footpace \'ₛ,ₛ\ *n* **1 :** a walking pace ⟨the coach proceeded at a ~⟩ **2** *obs* **:** CARPET, MAT **3 a :** an elevated platform **:** DAIS **b :** a landing on a staircase **c :** PREDELLA 1a

¹footpad \'ₛ,ₛ\ *n* [¹*foot* + *pad* (highwayman)] **:** one who robs a pedestrian **:** HOLDUP MAN

²footpad \"\ *n* [¹*foot* + *pad* (thick sole)] **:** PAD 4a(1) ⟨ancient bull elephant that glides on noiseless, 28-inch ~*s* —*Time*⟩

foot page *n* [ME *fot page*] **:** an errand boy **:** ATTENDANT, FOOTBOY

foot passenger *n* **:** PEDESTRIAN, PASSERBY

footpath \'ₛ,ₛ\ *n* **:** a narrow path for pedestrians **:** FOOTWAY; *specif, Brit* **:** SIDEWALK

foot pavement *n, chiefly Brit* **:** SIDEWALK

footpick \'ₛ,ₛ\ *n* **:** a pointed pole with handgrips and foot piece for digging in hard or stony ground

footplate \'ₛ,ₛ\ *n* **1 :** a carriage step **2 a :** a platform on early locomotives for the engineer to stand on **b** *Brit* **:** the floor of a locomotive cab **3 :** a wooden sill to distribute concentrated loads in a frame construction

foot post *n* **1 :** a postal carrier who travels on foot **:** FOOT CARRIER **2 :** a mail-delivery service employing exclusively foot carriers

footpost \'ₛ,ₛ\ *n* **:** one of the posts at the foot of a bed

foot-pound \'ₛ¦ₛ\ *n, pl* **foot-pounds 1 :** a unit of work in the fps system equal to the work done by a pound-force acting through a distance of one foot in the direction of the force **2 :** a unit of torque equal to the torque produced by a pound-force acting perpendicular to and at the end of a lever arm of one foot — called also *pound-foot*

foot-poundal \'ₛ¦ₛₛ\ *n* **:** the absolute unit of work in the fps system equal to the work done by a force of one poundal acting through a distance of one foot in the direction of the force

foot-pound-second \ₛ¦ₛₛ\ *adj* **:** being or relating to a system of units based upon the foot as the unit of length, the pound as the unit of weight or mass, and the second as the unit of time — abbr. *fps*

footprint \'=,=\ *n* **1 :** an impression of the foot **2 :** TRACE

foot pump *n* **1 :** a portable hand pump held in place by the foot **:** STIRRUP PUMP **2 :** a pump operated by a treadle

footrace \'=,=\ *n* **:** a race run on foot

foot racer *n* **:** one that runs footraces

footrail \'=,=\ *n* **1 :** a crosspiece (as between the legs of a table or chair or under a car seat) serving to support the feet **2 :** the crosspiece at the foot of a bed

footrest \'=,=\ *n* **:** a support for the feet **:** FOOTRAIL **:** FOOTSTOOL

foot·rill \'fu̇·trəl, -u̇t·,ril\ *n* [perh. alter. of *foot trail*] *Brit* **:** a level or inclined road giving entrance (as by a tunnel driven in a hillside) to a mine

footrope \'=,=\ *n* **1 :** a rope rigged below a yard for men to stand on when reefing or furling — see SHIP illustration **2 :** the part of a boltrope sewed to the lower edge of a sail

foot rot *n* **1 a :** a disease (as mal di gomma of citrus) that rots the stem or trunk of an affected plant near the ground **b :** a disease of cereals (as wheat) in which the culm blackens and decays resulting in lodging — compare TAKE-ALL **2 :** a progressive inflammation of the tissues in the region of the feet (as between the digits) of sheep or cattle; *specif* **:** a necrobacillosis marked by sloughing, ulceration, suppuration, and sometimes loss of the hoof — called also *foul-foot*

foot rule *n* **:** a stick one foot long for measuring length or distance ⟨carpenter with *foot rule*, notebook, and pencil —May Sinclair⟩; *broadly* **:** a standard of measurement or judgment ⟨measured with the *foot rule* of the individual life —S.A. Coblentz⟩

foots \'fu̇ts\ *pl of* FOOT

foot scab *n* **:** CHORIOPTIC MANGE

footscald \'=,=\ *n* **:** an injury (as from a hot shoe) to the sole of a horse's foot

foot score *n* **:** a line 12 feet behind the tee and at right angles to the length of a curling rink from which a player delivers his stone — called also *foot line;* see CURLING illustration

footscraper \'=,==\ *n* **:** a sharp-edged plate or bar fixed on a doorstep for cleaning mud from the shoes before entering the house

foot screw *n* **:** an adjusting screw (as on a table leg) that serves also as a foot

footscraper

foot·sie \'fu̇tsē, -si\ *also* **foot·ie** \-u̇d·|ē, -u̇t|, |i\ *n* -s [fr. baby-talk dim. of [1]*foot*] *slang* **:** an action of flirting or becoming friendly or intimate often with covertness and sometimes with duplicity — usu. used with the verb *play* ⟨play ~ under the table⟩ ⟨if she was playing ~ with somebody else, how'd she find the opportunity for it —Bob Wicks⟩

foot·slog \'=,=\ *vi* **:** to march or tramp toilsomely through or as if through mud

foot·slog·ger \'=,==\ *n* **:** INFANTRYMAN

foot soldier *n* **:** a soldier who marches and fights on foot **:** INFANTRYMAN

footsore \'=,=\ *adj* **:** having sore or tender feet (as by reason of much walking) — **footsoreness** *n* -ES

footstalk \'=,=\ *n* **1 a :** the petiole or pedicel of a flower **b :** PEDUNCLE **2 :** the lower part of a millstone spindle

footstall \'=,=\ *n* **1 :** the stirrup of a side saddle **2 :** the plinth, base, or pedestal of a pillar

footstep \'=,=\ *n* [ME *fotstep, footstep*, fr. *fot, foot* + *step*] **1 a :** STEPPING, FOOTFALL, TREAD **b :** distance covered by a step **:** PACE **2 :** the mark of the foot **:** TRACK, TRACE, TOKEN ⟨the ~s of divine wisdom⟩ **3 :** a step on which to ascend or descend ⟨~ of a carriage⟩ **4** *or* **footstep bearing :** STEP BEARING

footstick \'=,=\ *n* **:** a wooden or iron stick that when wedged with quoins secures the foot of a locked-up type page

footstock \'=,=\ *n* **:** TAILSTOCK

footstone \'=,=\ *n* **1 :** a single stone forming a kneeler at the foot of a gable slope to resist the thrust of the coping stones above **2 :** a stone placed at the foot of a grave

footstool \'=,=\ *n* **1 :** a low stool to support the feet **:** OTTOMAN **2 :** a portable step (as for mounting a horse)

foot stove *n* **:** a box with a pan for hot coals to warm the feet

foot switch *n* **:** an electric switch operated by pressure of the foot

foot tender *n* **:** BOTTOMER c

foot-ton \'=|=\ *n, pl* **foot-tons :** a unit of energy equal to the work done in raising one ton against standard gravity through the height of one foot

foot up *vt* [[2]*foot*] **:** to make a total of (as the cost) **~** *vi* **:** to amount to when added or reckoned — usu. used with *to* ⟨his debts *foot up* to a huge sum⟩

foot-up \'=,=\ *n* -s [[1]*foot*] **:** a lifting of the foot by a scrummager in rugby before the ball is fairly in the scrummage

foot valve *n* **:** a check valve at the lower end of a suction pipe (as in a well)

foot waling *n* **:** the inside bottom planks of a ship

footwalk \'=,=\ *n* **1 :** a surface paved or constructed for walking along often with a handrail (as on a bridge or on a parapet) **2 :** SIDEWALK

footwall \'=,=\ *n* **1 :** the lower or underlying wall of a vein, ore deposit, or coal seam in a mine **:** the wall upon which a miner stands **2 :** the lower wall of an inclined fault; *also* **:** the entire mass of rock below an inclined fault — opposed to *hanging wall*

foot warmer *n* **1 :** a contrivance to keep the feet warm **2 :** a warm covering (as a lined slipper) for the foot

foot washing *n* **:** a ceremonial cleansing of the feet preparatory to worship

footway \'=,=\ *n* [ME *fotewey*, fr. *fot, foot* + *wey* — more at FOOT, WAY] **:** a footpath, sidewalk, or any way reserved for pedestrians

footwear \'=,=\ *n* **:** wearing apparel for the feet (as shoes, boots, slippers, overshoes) usu. excluding hosiery

footwell \'=,=\ *n* **:** a shallow well in the afterdeck of a sailboat

footwork \'=,=\ *n* **1 :** the management of the feet and work done with them (as in boxing, football, tennis, dancing) **2 :** the activity of moving from place to place in the fulfillment of a task or purpose; *esp* **:** the activity of a news reporter in gathering news by direct investigation ⟨the crime investigation entailed a lot of ~⟩

foo·ty \'füd·ē, 'fü-\ *adj* [F *foutu*, fr. past part. of *foutre* to copulate — more at FOUTER] **1** *chiefly dial* **:** INSIGNIFICANT, PALTRY ⟨a ~ little town⟩ **2** *chiefly dial* **:** poorly kept **:** SHODDY ⟨a pair of ~ old boots⟩

foo yong \'fü'yȯŋ, -'yəŋ\ *n* -s [Chin (Pek) *fu[2] yung[2]*, lit., hibiscus] **:** a Chinese omelette made with bean sprouts, green pepper, and onion and fried in deep fat

[1]**foo·zle** \'füzəl\ *vt* **foozled; foozled; foozling** \-z(ə)liŋ\ **foozles** [perh. fr. G dial. *fuseln* to work hurriedly or poorly] **:** to manage awkwardly **:** treat or play unskillfully **:** BUNGLE

[2]**foozle** \"\ *n* -s **:** act of foozling; *esp* **:** a bungling stroke (as in golf)

foo·zler \-z(ə)lə(r)\ *n* -s **:** one that foozles **:** BUNGLER

[1]**fop** \'fäp\ *n* -s [ME *foppe, fop;* akin to ME *fobben* to deceive, cheat, MHG (Alemannic dial.) *voppen*] **1** *obs* **:** a foolish or silly person **:** a conceited pretender to wit or accomplishments **2 :** a man who is devoted to or vain of the exquisiteness or showiness of his dress **:** COXCOMB, DANDY, DUDE

[2]**fop** *vt* **fopped; fopped; fopping; fops** *obs* **:** FOOL, DUPE, CHEAT

fop·ling \'fäpliŋ\ *n* -s [[1]*fop* + *-ling*] *archaic* **:** an insignificant or absurd man of fashion **:** PETIT MAÎTRE, LADIES' MAN

fop·pery \'fäp(ə)rē, -ri\ *n* -ES [[1]*fop* + *-ery*] **1 :** foolish character or action **:** FOLLY, ABSURDITY, VANITY ⟨let not the sound of shallow ~ enter my sober house —Shak.⟩ **2 :** the behavior, dress, or other mark of a fop **:** COXCOMBRY, AFFECTATION

fop·pish \'fäpish, -pēsh\ *adj* **1** *obs* **:** FOOLISH, SILLY, STUPID **2 :** characteristic of a fop in dress or manners ⟨a ~ embroidered nightshirt —A. Conan Doyle⟩ — **fop·pish·ly** *adv* — **fop·pish·ness** *n* -ES

fop·py \'fäpē, -pi\ *adj* -ER/-EST **:** FOPPISH

fop's alley *n* **:** a fashionable promenade (as the passage through the center of the pit) in an 18th century theater or opera house

FOQ *abbr* free on quay

[1]**for** \fə(r), (,)fȯ(ə)r, (,)fȯ(ə), *in R speech in the southern US also* (,)fär\ *prep* [ME, fr. OE; akin to OHG *fora* before, *furi* before, for, ON *fyr*, Goth *faur* before, for, L *per* through, *pro* before, for, *prae* before, Gk *pro* before, ahead, Skt *pra-* before, forward, OE *faran* to travel, go — more at FARE] **1** *obs* **:** BEFORE **2 a :** as a preparation toward ⟨dressing ~ dinner⟩ or against ⟨storing nuts ~ the winter⟩ or in view of ⟨making plans ~ retirement⟩ ⟨studying ~ examinations⟩ **:** having as goal or object ⟨volunteered ~ the air force⟩ **b :** in order to be, become, or serve as ⟨originally built ~ a church⟩ ⟨ordered eggs ~ breakfast⟩ **c :** in order to bring about or further ⟨working ~ the good of humanity⟩ **d :** to supply the need of ⟨food ~ hungry mouths⟩ **e :** with the purpose or object of ⟨an instrument ~ measuring speed⟩ **f :** adapted to ⟨suits ~ tall men⟩ ⟨a calendar ~ 1960⟩ or prerequisite to ⟨a shelf ~ books⟩ ⟨mathematics ~ engineers⟩ **g :** in order to obtain ⟨write ~ a free catalog⟩ or gain ⟨work ~ a living⟩ **h :** in order to save (something in danger) ⟨on trial ~ his life⟩ ⟨could not tell ~ the life of me whether he was serious⟩ ⟨running ~ dear life⟩ or to remedy ⟨take something ~ his cough⟩ ⟨don't like to sell the house, but there is nothing else ~ it⟩ ⟨mud is good ~ bee stings⟩ **3 a —** used as a function word to indicate the object of a feeling ⟨hungry ~ praise⟩ ⟨longing ~ home⟩ or faculty ⟨a taste ~ spicy food⟩ ⟨an eye ~ color⟩ **b :** so as to secure as a result **:** conducive to ⟨telling you ~ your own good⟩ ⟨acting ~ the best in forbidding the trip⟩ **c** (1) **:** intending to go to or toward ⟨has just left ~ the office⟩ ⟨starting out ~ a trip across the country⟩ (2) **:** on the point of **:** having the intention of ⟨was just ~ going to bed⟩ ⟨wise men will have it that he meant these islands, and I am not ~ arguing the point —Norman Douglas⟩ **d —** used as a function word to indicate the person or thing that something is to be delivered to ⟨any letters ~ me⟩ or assigned to ⟨a slot ~ out-of-town mail⟩ or used by or in connection with ⟨are these the tires ~ this car⟩ **4 :** to the amount of ⟨a check ~ $100⟩ or extent of ⟨can see ~ miles from the hilltop⟩ or duration of ⟨waited ~ several hours⟩ ⟨won't be here ~ long⟩ or value of ⟨now pull ~ all you are worth⟩ **5 a :** in place of ⟨go to the store ~ me⟩ ⟨Doe now batting ~ Roe⟩ **:** in exchange as the equivalent of ⟨all that trouble ~ nothing⟩ ⟨my kingdom ~ a horse —Shak.⟩ or in requital of ⟨he gave blow ~ blow⟩ ⟨an eye ~ an eye⟩ **b :** in behalf of ⟨his lawyer will act ~ him in this affair⟩ **:** in support of ⟨let me carry that ~ you⟩ or in defense of ⟨fighting ~ their country⟩ **:** in favor of ⟨a prayer ~ those at sea⟩ ⟨which candidate are you ~⟩ — opposed to *against* **c :** in honor of **:** AFTER ⟨named ~ his grandfather⟩ **6 a —** used with a noun or pronoun followed by an infinitive to form an equivalent to such noun clauses as *that he should, that he might* ⟨~ him to confess would be painful⟩ ⟨shouted the news ~ all to hear⟩ ⟨~ you to have to pay for this is not fair⟩ ⟨here are some books ~ you to read⟩ **b —** used chiefly South & Midland redundantly after such verbs as *like, want, choose* ⟨I'd like ~ you to go⟩ **c —** used as a function word to introduce exclamations ⟨~ her to talk to her father like that⟩ or mild oaths ⟨~ God's sake hold your tongue and let me love —John Donne⟩ **7 a :** as being ⟨know ~ a fact⟩ ⟨do you take me ~ a fool⟩ ⟨take ~ granted⟩ ⟨mere noisy shouting often passes ~ comedy⟩ ⟨left ~ dead on the field⟩ **b —** used as a function word to indicate parenthetically an actual or implied enumeration or selection from an aggregate or series ⟨~ one thing, we have no money; ~ another, we have no time⟩ ⟨people don't buy it because, ~ one thing, the price is too high⟩ ⟨I ~ one will vote for him⟩ ⟨~ the last time, will you stop that noise⟩ ⟨be sensible ~ once⟩ **8 a :** because of ⟨shouted ~ joy⟩ **:** on account of ⟨decorated ~ bravery⟩ ⟨do it ~ my sake⟩ **b** *obs* **:** in order to prevent **:** for fear of ⟨here they shall not lie, ~ catching cold —Shak.⟩ **9 —** used as a function word to indicate equality or proportion between numbers or quantities that are related, compared, or contrasted ⟨~ every good writer there are a dozen scribblers⟩ ⟨answered his argument point ~ point⟩ ⟨repeated the speech word ~ word⟩ ⟨the best fighter, weight ~ weight, in the country⟩ **10 a :** as regards **:** in respect to **:** CONCERNING ⟨a stickler ~ detail⟩ ⟨so much ~ that topic⟩ ⟨true ~ all I know⟩ ⟨safe ~ the present⟩ ⟨good country ~ deer⟩ **b :** in proportion to ⟨tall ~ his age⟩ **:** taking into account **:** CONSIDERING ⟨very cool ~ May⟩ ⟨that was a good score ~ him⟩ **c :** in spite of **:** NOTWITHSTANDING — usu. used with *all* ⟨you don't convince me ~ all your clever arguments⟩ ⟨the elephants ~ all their great size moved absolutely noiselessly —Jule Mannix⟩ ⟨a man's a man ~ a' that —Robert Burns⟩ — **for all me :** as far as I am concerned — **for all the world —** used to emphasize a likeness ⟨looked *for all the world* like a ship that had lost her foremast —Frank Yerby⟩ — **for itself 1** *of a being* **:** capable of functioning esp. in the epistemological process purely by relation to itself **:** SELF-DETERMINED **2** *of a notion* **:** related to itself or its own manifestations

[2]**for** \"\ *conj* [ME, fr. *for*, prep.] **1** *archaic* **:** by reason that **:** for the reason that **:** BECAUSE ⟨my foolish rival, that her father likes only ~ his possessions are so huge —Shak.⟩ **2 :** for this reason or on this ground **:** as indicated or shown by the following circumstance **:** in substantiation of which **:** witness the fact that — used to introduce a reason for something before advanced (as a cause, motive, explanation, justification, or proof, of an action related or a statement made) ⟨we believe that he will succeed, ~ he has talent⟩ ⟨the army should be reduced in numbers, ~ possession of large armies has led nations to war⟩ **3** *obs* **:** in order that ⟨and, ~ the time shall not seem tedious, I'll tell thee what befell me —Shak.⟩

[3]**for** \'fȯ(ə)r, 'fȯ(ə), *in R speech in the southern US also* 'fär\ *n* -s [[1]*for*] **1 :** one who takes the affirmative side **2 :** what is said or felt in favor of someone or something **:** PRO

for- *prefix* [ME, fr. OE; akin to OHG *fir-, far-, fur-* for-, OS *for-*, Goth *fra-, fair-* for-, *faur-* for-, fore-, OE *for*] **1 :** so as to involve prohibition, exclusion, omission, failure, or refusal — almost exclusively in words coined before 1600 ⟨*for*say⟩ ⟨*for*heed⟩ **2 :** destructively or detrimentally — almost exclusively in words coined before 1600 ⟨*for*hang⟩ ⟨*for*storm⟩ **3 :** completely **:** excessively **:** to exhaustion **:** to pieces — almost exclusively in words coined before 1600 ⟨*for*bruise⟩ ⟨*for*weary⟩ ⟨*for*spent⟩

for *abbr* **1** foreign **2** forel **3** forest; forestry

FOR *abbr* free on rail

fora *pl of* FORUM

for a' \fə'rȯ\ *adv, Scot* **:** NEVERTHELESS, NOTWITHSTANDING ⟨she has a bonny face for a'⟩

[1]**for·age** \'fȯrij, 'fär-, -rēj\ *n* -s *often attrib* [ME, fr. MF *fourage, forage*, fr. OF, fr. *forre, fuerre* fodder, straw, of Gmc origin; akin to OHG *fuotar* food, fodder — more at FOOD] **1 a :** vegetable food (as hay, grain) for domestic animals ⟨~ crop⟩ **b :** food that wild or domestic animals take for themselves **2** [[2]*forage*] **:** the act of foraging **:** search for provisions ⟨they skirt the land like scouts upon a ~ —Eileen Duggan⟩

[2]**for·age** \", *esp in pres part* -rəj\ *vb* -ED/-ING/-S [ME *foragen*, fr. MF *fourager*, fr. *fourage*] *vt* **1 a :** to strip of provisions **:** collect forage from **b** *archaic* **:** SPOIL, PLUNDER **2 :** to supply (as horses and cattle) with forage **3 :** to secure by foraging ⟨*foraged* a chicken for the feast⟩ **~** *vi* **1 :** to wander or rove in search of forage or food **2 :** to secure forage (as for horses and cattle) by stripping the country **3 :** RAVAGE, RAID **4 :** to make a search **:** RUMMAGE ⟨*foraging* in his pockets for a match⟩ ⟨went *foraging* for bedroom slippers, shaving mirrors, and stationery —Bill Davidson⟩

[3]**for·age** \'fȯrij\ *n* -s [by folk etymology] **:** FORE EDGE ⟨~ painting in bookbinding⟩

forage acre *n* **:** a unit of grazing value equivalent to one acre of land entirely covered with herbage that can be completely utilized by grazing animals — abbr. *F.A.*

forage cap *n* **:** a small military cap with a visor and a round flat crown to be worn with undress uniforms

forage density *n* **:** the proportion of the soil surface in a range or pasture that is covered by vegetation within the reach of animals

forage fish *n* **:** fish of value as food for other fishes more useful to man — compare FOOD FISH, GAME FISH, ROUGH FISH

forage grass *n* **:** grass used as feed for stock

forage harvester *n* **:** FIELD CHOPPER

forage poisoning *n* **:** staggers of domestic animals and birds due to toxic elements taken in with the food; *often* **:** BOTULISM

forage press *n* **:** BALER

for·ag·er \'fȯrəjə(r), 'fär-, -rēj-\ *n* -s [ME, fr. MF *fourageur*, fr. *fourager* + *-eur* -or] **1 :** one that forages **2 foragers** *pl* **a :** soldiers detailed to forage **b :** cavalrymen advancing in line with extended intervals **3 :** FORAGING ANT

forag·ing ant *n* **:** an ant (as the driver and army ant) that goes out in search of food in companies

for·a·lite \'fȯrə,līt\ *n* -s [L *forare* + E *-lite*] **:** a marking found in stratified rocks that resembles a worm's burrow

for·am \'fȯrəm\ *n* -s [NL *Foraminifera*] **:** one of the Foraminifera

fo·ra·men \fə'rāmən, fō'-\ *n, pl* **fo·ram·i·na** \-ramənə\ *or* **foramens** [L, fr. *forare* to bore, pierce — more at BORE] **1 :** a small opening, perforation, or orifice **:** FENESTRA **2** [NL, fr. L] **:** MICROPYLE 2

foramen mag·num \-'magnəm\ *n* [NL, lit., great opening] **:** the large opening in the occipital bone through which the medulla oblongata passes to become the spinal cord

foramen of ma·gen·die \-mə,zhän'dē\ *usu cap M* [after François *Magendie* †1855 Fr. physiologist] **:** a passage through the midline of the roof of the fourth ventricle of the brain which together with the foramina of Key and Retzius affords a passage for the cerebrospinal fluid from the ventricles to the subarachnoid spaces

foramen of mon·ro \-mən'rō\ *usu cap M* [after Alexander *Monro* †1817 Scot. anatomist] **:** the opening from each lateral ventricle into the third ventricle of the brain

foramen of wins·low \-'winz(,)lō\ *usu cap W* [after Jakob B. *Winslow* †1760 Dan. anatomist] **:** EPIPLOIC FORAMEN

foramen ova·le \-ō'va(,)lē, -'vā(-, -'vä(-\ *n* [NL, lit., oval opening] **1 :** an opening in the septum between the two atria of the heart that is normally open only in the fetus **2 :** an oval opening in the greater wing of the sphenoid for passage of the mandibular nerve

fo·ram·i·nal \fə'ramənᵊl\ *adj* [L *foramin-, foramen* + E *-al*] **:** of or occurring by way of a foramen ⟨~ block⟩

foramina of key and ret·zi·us \-,kān'retsēəs\ *usu cap K&R* [after Ernst A. H. *Key* †1901 and Gustaf M. *Retzius* †1919 Swed. anatomists] **:** passages at the lateral recesses of the fourth ventricle of the brain — see FORAMEN OF MAGENDIE

fo·ram·i·nate \fə'ramə,nāt\ *or* **fo·ram·i·nat·ed** \-ād·əd\ *adj* [LL *foraminatus*, fr. L *foramin-, foramen* + *-atus* -ate, -ated] **:** having foramina **:** PERFORATED

for·a·min·i·fer \,fȯrə'minəfə(r)\ *n* -s [NL *Foraminifera*] **:** one of the Foraminifera

fo·ram·i·nif·era \fə,ramə'nif(ə)rə, ,fȯrəmə'-\ *n pl* [NL, fr. L *foramin-, foramen* + NL *-i-* + *-fera* (fr. neut. pl. of L *-fer*)] **1** *cap* **:** an order of Rhizopoda comprising large chiefly marine protozoans that have one or more nuclei, that are generally enclosed in a typically calcareous shell having minute openings for slender branching pseudopodia and consisting of several successively formed communicating chambers each larger than the preceding, that have a complex life cycle in which sexual and asexual generations alternate, and that are so abundant that their shelly remains constitute a major part of various sedimentary limestones (as chalk) and serve to identify geologic horizons — compare INDEX FOSSIL; see BILOCULINA, GLOBIGERINA **2 :** organisms belonging to Foraminifera

fo·ram·i·nif·er·al \=¦==¦nif(ə)rəl, ¦===¦nif(ə)rəl\ *adj* [NL *Foraminifera* + E *-al*] **:** of, derived from, or relating to the Foraminifera or their shells

[1]**fo·ram·i·nif·er·an** \-rən\ *adj* [NL *Foraminifera* + E *-al*] **:** FORAMINIFERAL

[2]**foraminiferan** \"\ *n* -s **:** one of the Foraminifera

fo·ram·i·nif·er·ous \-rəs\ *adj* [NL *Foraminifera* + E *-ous*] **:** FORAMINIFERAL

fo·ram·i·nous \fə'ramənəs\ *adj* [L *foramin-, foramen* + E *-ous*] **:** having foramina **:** POROUS

fo·ram·i·nule \-mə,nyül\ *n* -s [L *foramin-, foramen* + E *-ule*] **:** a minute foramen

for and *conj, obs* **:** and also

for·as·much as \¦fȯrəz¦məch-, ,fərəz'm-\ *conj* [ME *for as much as*] **:** in consideration that **:** seeing that **:** SINCE ⟨*forasmuch as* the earth cannot hold aught beside them, you have dedicated the earth . . . to wisdom, liberty —E.L.Masters⟩ ⟨*forasmuch as* transatlantic firms are glad to print cheap popular translations —Caroline Ticknor⟩

for·as·te·ro \,fȯrə'ste(,)rō\ *n* -s [Sp, lit., stranger, fr. Catal *foraster, forester*, fr. OCatal, fr. OProv *forestier*, fr. *forest* hamlet, country house, fr. (assumed) VL *forestis*, fr. L *foris* outside — more at FORUM] **:** any of various very productive cacaos with thick hard shells and purple seeds — compare CRIOLLO

[1]**for·ay** \'fō,rā, =ˈ= *also* 'fä,- *or* 'fō,-\ *vb* -ED/-ING/-S [ME *forrayen*, fr. MF *forrer*, fr. *forre, fuerre* fodder, straw — more at FORAGE] *vt, archaic* **:** to ravage in search of spoils **:** PILLAGE ⟨he might ~ our lands —Sir Walter Scott⟩ **~** *vi* **:** to make a raid or brief invasion ⟨~*ed* briefly into enemy territory⟩ **:** FORAGE, PILLAGE

[2]**foray** \"\ *n* -s [ME *forray*, fr. *forrayen*, v.] **1 :** a sudden or irregular incursion for war or spoils **:** RAID ⟨abandoned its attacks against our principal ports except for attempted sneak and surprise ~s —D.D.Eisenhower⟩ **:** ATTACK ⟨these legislative ~s became tedious —*New Republic*⟩ **2** *obs* **:** spoils won in a foray **:** BOOTY

for aye *adv* [ME *for aye*] **:** ALWAYS, FOREVER, ETERNALLY

for·ay·er \-āə(r)\ *n* -s [ME *forrayer*, fr. *forrayen* + *-er*] **1 :** one that makes or joins in a foray **2** *obs* **:** one that goes before **:** HARBINGER

forb \'fȯrb\ *n* -s [Gk *phorbē* fodder, food, fr. *pherbein* to graze, pasture; akin to OE *beorgan, birgan* to taste, eat, ON *bergja* to taste] **:** an herb other than grass **:** a broadleaf herb **:** WEED

forbade *or* **forbad** *past of* FORBID

[1]**for·bear** \fȯr'be(ə)r, fər-, -'ba(a)(ə)r; fȯə'beə, fə'-, -'ba(a)ə\ *vb* **for·bore** \-'bō(ə)r, -'bȯ(ə)r; -'bōə, -'bȯ(ə)\ *or archaic* **forbare** *pronounced like* FORBEAR\ **forborne** \-'bō(ə)rn; -'bȯ(ə)n\ **forbearing; forbears** [ME *forberen*, fr. OE *forberan* (akin to OHG *firberan* to refrain from, abstain, Goth *frabairan* to endure), fr. *for-* + *beran* to bear — more at FOR-, BEAR] *vt* **1** *obs* **a :** to bear with **:** ENDURE **b :** to control (feelings) **2** *obs* **:** to leave alone **:** SHUN ⟨~ his presence —Shak.⟩ **3** *obs* **:** to do without **:** endure the privation of ⟨fruits . . . whose taste too long *forborne* —John Milton⟩ **4 :** to refrain from **:** abstain or desist from ⟨so poison-mean the marsh mosquitoes *forbore* to bite him —S.H.Adams⟩ ⟨could not ~ crying out⟩ ⟨wherever he has not the power to do or ~ any act —Frank Thilly⟩ **:** FORGO ⟨a merchant who could not ~ the fun of setting sail —*Times Lit. Supp.*⟩ **~** *vi* **1 :** to hold back **:** ABSTAIN, DECLINE ⟨~, my friends, and spare me this ovation —W.S.Gilbert⟩ ⟨I cannot ~ from expressing my surprise⟩ **2 :** to control oneself when provoked **:** be patient ⟨*forbore* with his friend's failings⟩ **syn** see FORGO, REFRAIN

[2]**forbear** *var of* FOREBEAR

for·bear·ance \-'berən(t)s, -'ba(a)r-\ *n* -s [[1]*forbear* + *-ance*] **1 :** a delay in enforcing or a suspension of or a refraining from enforcing debts, rights of action, rights, privileges, claims, or obligations — compare RENEWAL **2 :** the act of forbearing **:** the exercise of patience or restraint ⟨I believe you equal to every . . . domestic ~, so long as . . . you have an object —Jane Austen⟩ **3 :** the quality of being forbearing **:** indulgence toward offenders or enemies **:** LONG-SUFFERING, LENIENCY ⟨known . . . for her ~ with her incorrigible husband —Willa Cather⟩ ⟨grateful for the help and ~ shown to us by the police —Basil Thomson⟩ ⟨~ has broadened into unconcern —Agnes Repplier⟩ **syn** see PATIENCE

for·bear·ant \-nt\ *adj* [[1]*forbear* + *-ant*] *archaic* **:** FORBEARING ⟨equitable, nay ~ if need were —Thomas Carlyle⟩

for·bear·er \-rə(r)\ *n* -s **:** one that forbears

forbearing *adj* [ME *forbering*, fr. pres. part. of *forberen* to forbear — more at FORBEAR] **:** marked by calm patience esp. under provocation **:** slow to expression of resentment or acts of punishment or retaliation **:** PATIENT

syn TOLERANT, CLEMENT, LENIENT, MERCIFUL, INDULGENT: FORBEARING implies a calm unruffled abstention, esp. under provocation, from judging harshly or taking due action against something or somebody ⟨where life shall be seemly and noble and *forbearing* . . . yet strong enough withal to resist aggression —Learned Hand⟩ TOLERANT emphasizes the acceptance, often negative but usu. generous, of what one would be or might be expected to object to or oppose ⟨it will make us *tolerant* and forgiving, patient with stubbornness and prejudice —A.C.Benson⟩ CLEMENT emphasizes a humaneness in the exercise of a power to judge or punish ⟨he was *clement* whenever he could be *clement* with safety, and he began to pardon the proscribed —John Buchan⟩ LENIENT emphasizes the mildness of the judgment or punishment ⟨she looked on his foibles with a *lenient* eye, for she had been accustomed to such all her life —Anthony Trollope⟩ MERCIFUL emphasizes the idea of compassionate treatment, esp. with the implication of forgiveness ⟨many have had the impression that he is not very *merciful* or sympathetic to sinners or enemies of the law —M.R.Cohen⟩ INDULGENT suggests strongly a laxness, an easygoingness, as from an absence of a precise standard, and often implies a weakness in the exercise of the power to judge, restrain, or punish ⟨a main criticism is that juries are now rigorous, now *indulgent*, prone to severity in cases involving attacks on property, but to leniency in cases of assault . . .; too often swayed by local prejudices or political feeling; too susceptible to the oratory of clever criminal lawyers —F.A.Ogg & Harold Zink⟩

for·bear·ing·ly *adv* **:** in a forbearing manner ⟨under her management all beginners were treated ~⟩

for·bear·ing·ness *n* -ES **:** FORBEARANCE

forbes·ite \ˈfȯrb,zīt\ *n* -S [David *Forbes* †1876 Brit. geologist + E *-ite*] **:** a mineral $H(Ni,Co)AsO_4.3\frac{1}{2}H_2O$ consisting of a grayish white hydrous fibrocrystalline nickel cobalt arsenate

forbes scale \ˈfȯrbz-\ *n, usu cap F* [after Stephen A. *Forbes* †1930 Am. entomologist] **:** a thin grayish armored scale (*Aspidiotus forbesi*) attacking fruit trees and resembling the San Jose scale but usu. much less destructive

[1]**for·bid** \fȯr'bid, fȯ'-, fə(r)'-\ *vb* **for·bade** \-'bad\ *or* **for·bad** \-'bad, -'baa(ə)d\ **for·bid·den** \-'bidᵊn\ *or archaic* **forbid; forbidding; forbids** [ME *forbidden*, alter. (influenced by *bidden* to entreat, pray, invite, command) of *forbeden*, fr. OE *forbēodan* (akin to OFris *urbiāda* to forbid, OHG *firbiotan*, Goth *faurbiudan*), fr. *for-* + *bēodan* to offer, proclaim, command — more at BID] *vt* **1 :** to command against or contrary to **:** INTERDICT ⟨~ the banns⟩ **:** PROHIBIT ⟨order . . . *forbidding* strikes of civil-service employees —*Collier's Yr. Bk.*⟩ ⟨the law ~*s* rich and poor alike to sleep under bridges⟩ ⟨God ~ that war should come⟩ **2 a :** to exclude or warn off from by express command ⟨I ~ you the house⟩ **b :** to bar from use ⟨*forbade* . . . movie cameras at House Committee hearings —*Americana Annual*⟩ ⟨running with the ball is *forbidden* in basketball⟩ **3 :** to hinder or prevent as if by an effectual command **:** make impossible or impracticable ⟨rocky rapids *forbade* further progress up the stream⟩ ⟨space ~*s* further treatment of the subject here⟩ ⟨modesty ~*s* telling what my part in the affair was⟩ ~ *vi* **:** to utter a prohibition **:** HINDER ⟨~ who will, none shall from me withhold longer thy offered good —John Milton⟩

syn FORBID, PROHIBIT, ENJOIN, INTERDICT, INHIBIT, and BAN can mean, in common, to debar (someone) from doing, using, entering, or otherwise acting or to order (something) not to be done, used, entered, or otherwise acted upon. The more or less familiar FORBID and the more formal PROHIBIT imply the exercise of authority or the existence of imperative conditions, FORBID suggesting an expected obedience or an absolute proscription, PROHIBIT applying more particularly to official and less autocratic proscriptions ⟨*forbid* a child to go out on a rainy day⟩ ⟨a law *forbidding* the sale of liquor on Sunday⟩ ⟨limitations of space *forbid* elaborately detailed treatments of these subjects —*Amer. Guide Series: N.H.*⟩ ⟨the act was wrong in the sense that it was *prohibited* by law —B.N.Cardozo⟩ ⟨condemned for not taking active steps toward *prohibiting* an armed group from organizing on its soil —*Collier's Yr. Bk.*⟩ ⟨implements of war would be *prohibited* and prevented —Vera M. Dean⟩ ENJOIN, a legal term implying a judicial order that forbids something under penalty, suggests a strong and compelling proscription or exhortation ⟨the president, under the war powers, seized the railroads and the courts *enjoined* the strike —*Collier's Yr. Bk.*⟩ ⟨a deed of filial duty *enjoined* upon him by his father's fearful command —Karl Polanyi⟩ ⟨immediately after he had concluded his lecture, someone was certain to *enjoin* him to relax —Bryan MacMahon⟩ INTERDICT implies prohibition by authority usu. for a given time and for a salutary purpose ⟨the navy has prohibited, the church has *interdicted* the defloration ceremony, formerly an inseparable part of the marriages of girls of rank —Margaret Mead⟩ ⟨alcohol and tobacco are *interdicted* —*Yr. Bk. of Medicine*⟩ ⟨to *interdict*, or at least discourage, his visits —George Meredith⟩ INHIBIT applies to the imposition of restraints or restrictions whether by authority or by circumstances or conditions ⟨signalized the opening of a new reign by *inhibiting* stage plays —A.T.Quiller-Couch⟩ ⟨stiff royalties — payable in dollars — have *inhibited* widespread production of U. S. plays —W.H. Whyte⟩ ⟨the destructive exchange practices which *inhibited* the flow of world trade —Eugene Meyer⟩ BAN implies civil or ecclesiastical prohibition and strongly connotes condemnation or disapproval ⟨these laws . . . were specific in naming the one weapon to be *banned* —R.W.Thorp⟩ ⟨the proscribed categories of persons *banned* from Federal employment —Benjamin Ginzburg⟩ ⟨authorities *banned* the rebuilding of wooden houses in the same area —Theodore Hsi-en Chen⟩

[2]**forbid** \"\ *adj* [fr. archaic past part. of [1]*forbid*] *archaic* **:** ACCURSED ⟨she becomes a leper herself . . . and lives for years in a cave hermitage, a thing ~ —*Nation*⟩ ⟨the sensitive plant, like one ~, —P.B.Shelley⟩

for·bid·dance \fȯ(r)'bidᵊn(t)s, fə(r)-\ *n* -S **:** the act of forbidding **:** a command or edict against something **:** PROHIBITION

for·bid·den \-dᵊn\ *adj* [ME, fr. past part. of *forbidden* to forbid — more at FORBID] **1 :** not allowed **:** not permitted **:** PROHIBITED ⟨the whole attraction of such knowledge consists in the fact that it is ~ —Bertrand Russell⟩ ⟨secretly enjoying a ~ cigar⟩ **:** TABOO ⟨~ meaning of a dream⟩ **2 :** not conforming to the usual selection principles — used of quantum phenomena ⟨~ transition⟩ ⟨~ radiation⟩ ⟨the line spectrum . . . would consist of one line and be optically ~ —L.M.Branscomb⟩ — **for·bid·den·ly** *adv* — **for·bid·den·ness** *n* -ES

forbidden degree *n* **:** a degree of consanguinity or affinity within which marriage is forbidden — called also *prohibited degree;* compare LEVITICAL DEGREE

forbidden fruit *n* **1 :** an immoral pleasure (as illicit sexual intercourse) **2 a :** any of several varieties of citrus fruit; *esp* **:** a small shaddock **b :** the fruit of a Ceylonese tree (*Tabernaemontana dichotoma*) that has powerfully narcotic seeds **3** [fr. *Forbidden Fruit*, a trademark] **:** an American liqueur of orange color made from grape brandy flavored with shaddock

for·bid·der \-də(r)\ *n* -S [ME, fr. *forbidden* + *-er*] **:** one that forbids

for·bid·ding \-diŋ, -dēŋ\ *adj* [ME, fr. pres. part. of *forbidden*] **1 :** such as to make approach or passage difficult or impossible ⟨~ mountains⟩ ⟨~ walls⟩ ⟨~ terminology⟩ **2 :** DISAGREEABLE, REPELLENT ⟨desolate ~ countryside⟩ ⟨dark ~ ravines⟩ **3 :** MENACING, GRIM ⟨~ array of guns⟩ — **for·bid·ding·ly** *adv* — **for·bid·ding·ness** *n* -ES

forbids *pres 3d sing of* FORBID

for·biv·o·rous \(ˈ)fȯ(r)ˈbivərəs\ *adj* [*forb* + *-i-* + *-vorous*] **:** feeding on forbs ⟨~ grasshoppers⟩

[1]**forbode** *n* -S [ME *forbod, forbode*, fr. OE *forbod*, fr. *forbēodan* to forbid — more at FORBID] *archaic* **:** FORBIDDANCE, PROHIBITION

[2]**forbode** *var of* FOREBODE

forbore *past of* FORBEAR

forborne *past part of* FORBEAR

forbs *pl of* FORB

for·bush's sparrow \ˈfȯr,bu̇shəz-, -,bəsh-\ *n, usu cap F* [after Edward H. *Forbush* †1929 Am. ornithologist] **:** a sparrow (*Melospiza lincolnii gracilis*) of the Pacific coast closely related to the Lincoln's sparrow but browner

[1]**for·by** *or* **for·bye** \fȯrˈbī, fər-, -ˈbī\ *prep* [ME *forby*, prep. & adv., fr. *for-, fore-* fore- + *by*, prep. & adv. — more at BY] **1** *archaic* **a** *of motion* **:** PAST **b** *of position* **:** NEAR **c :** BY ⟨took her up ~ the lily hand —Edmund Spenser⟩ **2** *chiefly Scot* **:** as well as **:** BESIDES **3** *Scot* **:** EXCEPT ⟨left without a copper ~ some insurance⟩

[2]**forby** *or* **forbye** \"\ *adv* [ME *forby*] *chiefly Scot* **:** over and above **:** in addition **:** BESIDES ⟨you're a liar and a thief, lassie, and ~ ye tried to kill me too —Rose Macaulay⟩

[3]**forby** *or* **forbye** \"\ *adj, chiefly Scot* **:** UNUSUAL, UNCOMMON, REMARKABLE; *specif* **:** unusually good ⟨a ~ wife⟩

for·çat \fȯrsä\ *n* -S [F, fr. It *forzato*, fr. past part. of *forzare* to force, fr. (assumed) VL *fortiare* — more at FORCE] **:** a convict in France condemned to imprisonment with hard labor or formerly to the galleys

[1]**force** \ˈfō(ə)rs, ˈfȯ(ə)rs, ˈfōəs, ˈfȯ(ə)s\ *n* -S *often attrib* [ME, fr. MF *force*, fr. (assumed) VL *fortia*, fr. L *fortis* strong + *-ia* -y — more at FORT] **1 a :** strength or energy esp. of an exceptional degree **:** active power **:** VIGOR **b :** physical strength or vigor of a living being ⟨drained of all ~ by his mighty effort⟩ **c :** power to affect in physical relations or conditions ⟨the ~ of the blow was somewhat spent when it reached him⟩ ⟨the rising ~ of the wind⟩ **d :** moral or mental strength esp. when manifested as power of effective action (as in the overcoming of opposition) ⟨the ~ of his character had the impact of a physical pressure⟩ ⟨a man of great ~ and determination⟩ **e :** power or capacity to sway, convince, or impose obligation **:** VALIDITY, EFFECT ⟨the ~ of his arguments⟩ ⟨who could resist the ~ of such an appeal⟩; *often* **:** legal efficacy **:** operative effect ⟨that law is still in ~⟩ ⟨an agreement having the ~ of law⟩ **2 a :** might or greatness esp. of a prince or state; *often* **:** strength in or capacity for waging war ⟨the ~ of this lord was so great that no other would contest his right to rule⟩ **b** (1) **:** a group of individuals occupied with or ready for combat ⟨the entire ~ of the fortress⟩; *usu* **:** a body of troops, ships, airplanes, or combinations thereof esp. when assigned to a particular military purpose or necessity ⟨took a small ~ of infantrymen and searched the village⟩ ⟨the enemy assembled a great ~ for the spring offensive⟩ — see TASK FORCE (2) **forces** *pl* **:** the whole military strength (as of a nation) **:** ARMED FORCES **c :** a body of persons available for or serving a particular end ⟨a large available labor ~⟩; *often* **:** a more or less organized group or staff having a common responsibility or task ⟨a conscientious police ~⟩ ⟨the plantation ~ took a half holiday⟩ **3 a :** power, violence, compulsion, or constraint exerted upon or against a person or thing ⟨conciliation may succeed where ~ completely fails⟩ ⟨those who will not respond to kindness must yield to ~⟩ **b :** strength or power of any degree that is exercised without justification or contrary to law upon a person or thing **c :** violence or such threat or display of physical aggression toward a person as reasonably inspires fear of pain, bodily harm, or death **4** *dial Eng* **:** a large part, quantity, or number **5 :** an agency or influence (as a push or pull) that if applied to a free body results chiefly in an acceleration of the body and sometimes in elastic deformation and other effects (as from overcoming cohesion or adhesion or sustaining weight) **6 :** the quality of conveying impressions intensely in writing or speech (as by vividness, cogency, or passion) ⟨a stimulating essay marked by ~ and cogency⟩ **7 :** an act (as of misdirection) or course (as of play) that forces the response of another (as in a play in a game) into a predetermined pattern ⟨sometimes a ~ is useful for locating honors in the opponents' hands⟩ **8 a :** the upper hollow embossing die **:** [5]COUNTER 10b **b :** a specially formed bar or plate attached to the underside of the slide of a punch press chiefly for use in riveting and seaming **9 :** a billiards stroke made by striking a cue ball hard and just below the center so that it rebounds or stops sharply or goes off at a desired angle after striking the object ball

syn VIOLENCE, COMPULSION, COERCION, DURESS, CONSTRAINT, RESTRAINT: FORCE is a general term for exercise of strength or power, esp. physical, to overcome resistance ⟨there is the *force* used by parents when . . . they compel their children to act or refrain from acting in some particular way. There is the *force* used by attendants in an asylum when they try to prevent a maniac from hurting himself or others. There is the *force* used by the police when they control a crowd . . . there is the *force* used in war —Aldous Huxley⟩ VIOLENCE is applicable to dynamic power showing great strength, power, intensity, fury, destructiveness ⟨a wild nightmare of *violence*, noise, confusion, and pain —T.B.Costain⟩ ⟨force must not be confused with *violence* . . . the completely successful use of force implies the absence of *violence*, because those against whom force is used recognize the futility of resistance —P.M.Sweezy⟩ COMPULSION is applicable to any power or agency that compels, that makes an individual follow a will not his own ⟨*compulsion* exists where a being is inevitably determined by an external cause —Frank Thilly⟩ ⟨masterpieces I read under *compulsion* without the faintest interest —Bertrand Russell⟩ COERCION often suggests unethical, unjust compulsion, as by threat or deception ⟨a promise obtained by *coercion* is hardly binding⟩ ⟨the amiable trait in his character of an intense dislike to *coercion* —G.B.Shaw⟩ DURESS may suggest a stronger coercion in which the compelling is accomplished by confinement or violence, or dire threats of confinement or violence ⟨our *duress*, his arrogance, our awful servitude —Edna S. V. Millay⟩ ⟨a fake declaration of love by the heroine under *duress* —Dyneley Hussey⟩ CONSTRAINT may apply to the action of any agency enjoining unwilling performance or avoidance of an action ⟨the *constraint* of society had banished his former expression of easy good humor —G.B.Shaw⟩ ⟨prose is memorable speech set down without *constraint* of meter —A.T. Quiller-Couch⟩ RESTRAINT suggests an agency which checks free activity or expression or an atmosphere in which such restriction is likely or common ⟨long years of abstinence and *restraint* and an avoidance of physical contacts and emotional responses before marriage —A.C.Kinsey⟩ ⟨they rushed into freedom and enjoyment, into the unfettered use of their powers, with an energy proportional to their previous *restraint* —G.L. Dickinson⟩ **syn** see in addition POWER

— **by force of** *prep* [ME, trans. of OF *à force de*] **:** in virtue of **:** by means of **:** THROUGH ⟨*by force of* the authority vested in my present office⟩ — **in force 1 :** in great numbers **:** with many individuals ⟨the Indians invaded *in force* that winter⟩ **2 :** VALID, OPERATIVE, BINDING ⟨these antiquated laws have been *in force* since the 17th century⟩

[2]**force** \"\ *vb* -ED/-ING/-S [ME *forcen*, fr. MF *forcier, forcer* to attack, rape, compel, fr. (assumed) VL *fortiare*, fr. L *fortis* strong] *vt* **1 :** to do violence to; *esp* **:** RAPE ⟨a maiden *forced* by the intruder⟩ **2 :** to constrain or compel by physical, moral, or intellectual means or by the exigencies of circumstances ⟨*forced* by injuries to stay at home⟩ ⟨hunger *forced* him to forget his scruples⟩ ⟨such evidence ~*s* conviction on the mind⟩ ⟨financial weakness ~*s* many small businesses to the wall⟩ **3 :** to make, cause, make to be, or accomplish through natural or logical necessity ⟨~*s* the diameters to be equal —Josiah Royce⟩ **4 a :** to press, drive, attain to, or effect as indicated against resistance or inertia by some positive compelling force or action ⟨~ your way through⟩ ⟨much of the previously unobtainable oil is *forced* to the surface —*Amer. Guide Series: Pa.*⟩ ⟨basic problems *forced* on us by the age in which we live —J.B.Conant⟩ **b :** to press, impose, or thrust urgently, importunately, inexorably ⟨he *forced* his personality upon his little world by organizing an army —L.C.Powys⟩ ⟨~ his attentions on a woman⟩ **c :** to drive (as warm air) through or into a duct or channel by some impelling force (as a fan) ⟨~ the caulking compound into the crevices⟩ **5 :** to achieve or win by strength in struggle or violence: **a :** to win one's way into **:** storm successfully **:** enter in attack ⟨~ a castle⟩ **b :** to effect a passage through by overcoming defenses ⟨*forced* the mountain passes —O.L. Spaulding⟩ **c :** to break open or through ⟨~ a lock⟩ ⟨eventually the gate was *forced*⟩ **6 a :** to raise, accelerate, or heighten to the utmost ⟨*forcing* the pace⟩; *sometimes* **:** to intensify the action and pressure in (as a game) ⟨*forced* the game by a series of brilliant plays⟩ **b :** to give forth, emit, produce only with unnatural or unwilling effort, not freely, spontaneously ⟨the laughter was *forced* and unnatural —Sherwood Anderson⟩ **c :** to wrench, strain, use with marked unnaturalness and lack of ease **:** press to an unusual use, past a usual limit, or into an unusual meaning or interpretation ⟨to ~, to dislocate if necessary, language into his meaning —T.S.Eliot⟩ ⟨a *forced* interpretation of the passage⟩ **7 a :** to hasten the speed, growth, progress, developing, or maturing of (as through artificial means, maximum effort, close care, or individual attention) ⟨a *forced* march⟩ ⟨children *forced* into early maturity by heavy responsibilities⟩ **b :** to bring (plants or their wanted parts, as flowers or fruit) to maturity out of the normal season (as by the use of heat and special lighting) ⟨*forcing* lilies for the Easter trade⟩ **8 a** *archaic* **:** REINFORCE, MAN ⟨~ with soldiers⟩ **b :** to increase the intake of (as fluids) beyond the normal bodily requirement ⟨it is wise to ~ fluids when any systemic intoxication is present⟩ **9 a :** to cause (a person) to respond in a particular way in a game or trick usu. to one's own advantage (as by discarding a playing card that an opponent must take under the rules of the game) ⟨card tricks that depend on misdirection to ~ the helper to take the intended card⟩ **b :** to induce (as a particular bid or play by another player) in a card game by some conventional act, play, bid, or response ⟨doubled the opponent's bid to ~ a try for game from his partner⟩ ⟨hoped to ~ the trump ace out by leading the remaining club⟩ **10 a :** to cause (a runner in baseball) to be put out by compelling him (as by a hit) to vacate the base he has been occupying and attempt to advance to the next base **b :** to cause (a run) to be scored in baseball or (a runner) to score (as by giving a base on balls when the bases are full) **11 :** to develop (photographic material) to the limit either in time or by chemical means or both in order to obtain detail in the shadow portions of an underexposed negative or the highlights of an underexposed print ~ *vi* **1 :** to advance or progress by force ⟨our troops *forcing* ahead⟩ **2 :** to grow, advance, mature by being forced ⟨these plants ~ well⟩ **3 a :** to make a series of shots intended to put an opponent in a racket game out of position for a subsequent shot **b :** to make a bid or play in a card game that forces another player or a particular response

syn COMPEL, COERCE, CONSTRAIN, OBLIGE: FORCE is a general term indicating use of strength, power, weight, stress, duress in overcoming resistance ⟨the editors were *forced* to flee for their lives and the newspaper plant was burned —*Amer. Guide Series: Ark.*⟩ ⟨American pressure had been sufficient to *force* Germany to suspend unrestricted submarine warfare —C.E. Black & E.C.Helmreich⟩ ⟨those yield data and *force* the mind to put many queries —H.O.Taylor⟩ COMPEL may more strongly indicate irresistible overcoming of unwillingness or resistance ⟨yellow fever was raging in Charleston, and for this reason the Scots were *compelled* to remain on board —W.P. Webb⟩ ⟨the discovery of new facts *compels* the rational thinker to reexamine the adequacy of his previous generalizations —M.R.Cohen⟩ COERCE implies domineering and overriding resistance by notably unethical tactics like violence, intimidation, pressure, duress ⟨no one can claim that he was *coerced* by bribery. This is reserved for threats and direct pleas —W.D. Falk⟩ CONSTRAIN suggests forcing by something that either does or seems to constrict, press, confine, compress ⟨tied him to the wall, where he was *constrained* to stay till a kind passerby released him —John Galsworthy⟩ ⟨*constrained* through poverty to live in the houses of others —Edith Sitwell⟩ OBLIGE, although it may apply to any binding force, is common in situations involving ethical, social, or intellectual necessity, through the effect of codes or principles ⟨the Protestant missionary felt *obliged* to give the Indian a book religion —*Amer. Guide Series: Minn.*⟩ ⟨*obliged* to receive and grind grain for his fellow townsmen —*Amer. Guide Series: R.I.*⟩

— **force a safeguard :** to violate (as by overwhelming a protecting guard) protection accorded a person or property — **force one's hand :** to cause one to act precipitously ⟨his unexpected offer for the property *forced my hand*⟩**:** force one who for diplomatic or tactical reasons is passive or noncommittal to act in a way that reveals his beliefs or purposes or intentions

[3]**force** \"\ *n* -S [ME *fors, force*, fr. ON *fors, foss;* akin to Skt *pṛṣat* drop, OSlav *prachŭ* dust] *dial* **:** WATERFALL, CASCADE

[4]**force** \"\ *vt* -ED/-ING/-S [alter. (influenced by [2]*force*) of [1]*farce*] *archaic* **:** FARCE, STUFF ⟨malice *forced* with wit—Shak.⟩

force·able \-səbəl\ *adj* [by alter.] **:** FORCIBLE

force·ably \-blē, -li\ *adv* **:** FORCIBLY

force account *n* **1 :** the part of the expense account of a public body (as a municipality) resulting from the employment of a labor force (as for garbage collection and the maintenance of streets) usu. distinguished from the part resulting from contracting similar services with commercial agencies ⟨disadvantages of the *force-account* method of handling municipal maintenance⟩ **2 :** a labor force maintained under force account ⟨every public-works department requires a considerable *force account*⟩

force and arms *n* **:** VIOLENCE — used in old legal indictments and declarations in trespass

force and effect *n* **:** legal efficacy **:** the existing foundation of enforceable rights and duties ⟨the entrenched sections of the South Africa Act are still of *force and effect* —E.P.Dvorin⟩

force-break \ˈ=,=\ *vt* **:** to train (as a horse or dog) by punishing faults rather than by rewarding success

force cup *n* **:** PLUNGER 2e

forced \ˈfō(ə)rst, ˈfȯ(ə)rst, ˈfōəst, ˈfȯ(ə)st\ *adj* **1 :** compelled by force **:** INVOLUNTARY, COMPULSORY ⟨~ service⟩ ⟨a ~ landing⟩ **2 :** done or produced with or as if with notable effort, exertion, or pressure ⟨a ~ artificial style of writing⟩ ⟨a ~ laugh⟩ **3 :** produced by or subjected to forcing ⟨~ chrysanthemums⟩ ⟨*forced*-air heating⟩ ⟨furnaces of the *forced*-convection type⟩ — **for·ced·ly** \-sədlē, -stlē, -li\ *adv* — **for·ced·ness** \-sədnəs, -stnəs\ *n* -ES

forced draft *n* **:** a draft of air for use in combustion forced through a grate or other burner by or as if by a blower ⟨a *forced draft* heating unit⟩

forced heir *n* **:** an heir who cannot be disinherited except for good causes recognized by law and whose share in his ancestor's estate cannot be impaired by the will of the ancestor or even by gifts made inter vivos

forced landing *n* **:** an emergency airplane landing made under some compulsion of circumstance (as engine failure, adverse weather conditions) beyond the control of the pilot

forced march *n* **:** a march (as of a military force) greater in extent than the distance usu. covered and often carried out under difficulties (as increased pace or restricted halts)

forced oscillation *also* **forced vibration** *n* **:** an oscillation imposed upon a body or system by and with the frequency of some external vibrator of sensibly different frequency — opposed to *free oscillation*

forced saving *n* **1 :** involuntary saving by an individual resulting from restrictions imposed upon expenditures, deferred income, insurance, or other circumstances **2 :** involuntary transfer of purchasing power from consumers to investors by means of a money and credit expansion accompanied by a decrease in the value of money

forced ventilation *n* **:** mechanical ventilation

force-feed \ˈ=ˌ=\ *vt* **force-fed** *or* **forced-fed; force-fed** *or* **forced-fed; force-feeding** *or* **forced-feeding; force-feeds** [*force feed*] **1 :** to feed (as an animal) by forcible administration of food ⟨necessary to *force-feed* the young birds by pushing food well back in the throat⟩ **2 :** to cause to take in or to expand vigorously ⟨the cities never became swollen until after the Civil War, which *force-fed* urban industry —*Times Lit. Supp.*⟩ ⟨*force-fed* on propaganda, people turn from it with loathing —Eric Johnston⟩

force feed *n* **:** a lubricating system (as in an internal-combustion engine) in which the lubricant is supplied under pressure

force field *n* **:** FIELD OF FORCE

force fit *n* **:** PRESS FIT

force·ful \ˈfȯrsfəl, ˈfōrs-,ˈfōəs-, ˈfȯ(ə)s\ *adj* **:** possessing or filled with force **:** exerting or impelled by force **:** FORCIBLE, MIGHTY, EFFECTIVE ⟨a vigorous ~ personality⟩ ⟨his ~ presentation of the data⟩ ⟨won the Pulitzer prize for his ~ novel⟩ — **force·ful·ly** \-f(ə)lē, -li\ *adv* — **force·ful·ness** *n* -ES

force land *vi* [back-formation fr. *forced landing*] **:** to make a forced landing

force·less \-sləs\ *adj* **:** lacking force **:** FEEBLE, WEAK ⟨a ~ argument⟩ — **force·less·ness** *n* -ES

force main *n* **:** a principal conduit (as in a sewer system) through which water is pumped as distinguished from one through which it flows by gravity

force ma·jeure \-maˈzhər\ *n* [F, lit., superior force] **:** an event or effect that cannot reasonably be anticipated or controlled — compare ACT OF GOD, INEVITABLE ACCIDENT, VIS MAJOR

forcemeat \ˈ=,=\ *n* [[4]*force* + *meat*] **:** finely chopped and highly seasoned meat or fish that often has added eggs, cereal products, or other enrichments and is either served alone or used as a stuffing — called also *farce*

forcement *n* -s [²*force* + *-ment*] *obs* **:** an act of forcing **:** COMPULSION

for·ce·ne \ˌfȯrsəˌnā, (ˈ)fȯrˈsēn\ *adj* [F *forcené*, frantic, mad, insane, fr. OF *forsené*, past part. of *forsener* to be or become mad or furious, fr. *fors* out of, outside, except + *sen* mind, sense, of Gmc origin; akin to OHG *sin* sense, mind — more at FORECLOSE, SENSE] *of a heraldic representation of a horse* **:** depicted rearing

force of friction : the force required to initiate or to maintain relative motion against friction

force of habit : behavior made involuntary or automatic by repeated practice ⟨said no from *force of habit*⟩

force–out \ˈ=ˌ=\ *n* [fr. *force out*, v.] **:** a baseball play in which the runner is put out by a force play

force play *n* **:** a baseball play in which the runner is automatically out unless he advances to another base because the batter has become a base runner ⟨a *force play* at second base⟩

force polygon *n* **:** a closed polygon whose sides taken in order represent in magnitude and direction a system of forces in equilibrium

for·ceps \ˈfȯrsəps, ˈfō(ə)s-, -ˌseps\ *n, pl* **forceps** \ˈ"\ *also* **forcepses** \-psəz\ *or* **forci·pes** \-səˌpēz\ [L, fr. *formus* hot + *-ceps* (fr. *capere* to take) — more at WARM, HEAVE] **1 :** an instrument for grasping, holding firmly, or exerting traction upon objects that it would be inconvenient or impracticable to seize with the fingers; *esp* **:** such an instrument for delicate operations (as of jewelers, surgeons, obstetricians, dentists) **:** PINCERS, TONGS — sometimes used with *pair* ⟨a pair of ~⟩ **2** [NL, fr. L] **:** a limb resembling a forceps; *esp* **:** a pair of curved hard movable appendages at the end of the abdomen of an insect (as the earwig)

for·ceps·like \-psˌlīk\ *adj* **:** resembling a forceps esp. in having two opposable processes

force pump *n* **:** a pump with a solid piston for drawing and forcing through valves a liquid (as water) to a considerable height above the pump or under a considerable pressure

forceput \ˈ=ˌ=\ *n* [alter. of earlier *forced put*] *now chiefly dial* **:** an action that is made unavoidable or inevitable by circumstances ⟨this marry-me-quick business . . . looks too much like a *forceput* —B.A.Williams⟩

¹**forc·er** \ˈfōrsər, ˈfȯr-; ˈfōsə(r, ˈfȯ(ə)s-\ *n* -s [ME, fr. OF *forcier*, fr. *force* — more at FORCE] *archaic* **:** COFFER, CHEST

²**for·cer** \ˈ"\ *n* -s [²*force* + *-er*] **1 :** one that forces (as by driving, compelling, or pressing); *esp* **:** a person that forces crops (as for out-of-season markets) **2 a :** the solid piston of a force pump **b :** a small hand pump (as for sinking pits or draining cellars) **c :** FORCE 8 a **3 :** a plant esp. adapted to forcing

forces *pl of* FORCE, *pres 3d sing of* FORCE

forces letter *n* [(*Armed*) *Forces*] *Brit* **:** an air-letter sheet for use in writing to a member of the armed forces

forchette *var of* FOURCHETTE

forc·ibil·i·ty \ˌfō(r)səˈbilədē, ˌfȯ(r)s-\ *n* -ES **:** the quality or state of being forcible ⟨the ~ of his language⟩

forc·ible \ˈfō(r)səbəl, ˈfȯ(r)-\ *adj* [ME, fr. MF, fr. *force* + *-ible*] **1 :** effected by force used against opposition or resistance **:** obtained by compulsion or violence ⟨a ~ entry⟩ ⟨determined on ~ repatriation of the refugees⟩ **2 :** possessing force **:** characterized by force, efficiency, or energy **:** POWERFUL, EFFICACIOUS, IMPRESSIVE, CONVINCING ⟨expressed his views in very ~ words⟩ ⟨used ~ maneuvers to obtain the chairmanship⟩ — **forc·ible·ness** *n* -ES — **forc·ibly** \-blē, -li\ *adv*

forcible entry and detainer *n* **1 :** the entering upon and taking or the keeping possession of land or a tenement by actual force or by threats or display of force menacing life or limb without authority of law **2 :** the statutory proceeding to regain possession of property alienated by forcible entry and detainer

forcible-feeble \ˌ=ˌ=ˈ=ˌ=\ *adj* [fr. *Forcible Feeble*, nickname of *Francis Feeble*, character in Shakespeare's *2 Henry IV* who was a woman's tailor turned soldier] **:** seemingly vigorous but really weak or insipid

forcing *pres part of* FORCE

forcing bed *n* **:** HOTBED

forcing cone *n* **:** the portion of the boring of a shotgun in which the chamber diameter decreases to bore diameter and which in section is a truncated cone

forcing ground *n* **:** HOTBED 2

forcing house *n* **1 :** a greenhouse in which plants are forced esp. in quantities for market **2 :** HOTBED 2

forc·ing·ly *adv* [fr. *forcing* (pres. part. of ²*force*) + *-ly*] **:** so as to force or exert pressure

forcing pump *n* **:** FORCE PUMP

forcing system *n* **:** CULBERTSON SYSTEM

for·ci·pate \ˈfȯ(r)səˌpāt\ *also* **for·ci·pat·ed** \-ādəd\ *adj* [L *forcip-, forceps* + E *-ate, -ated* — more at FORCEPS] **:** shaped like a forceps **:** deeply forked

forcipes *pl of* FORCEPS

for·cip·i·form \(ˈ)fȯ(r)ˈsipəˌfȯrm\ *adj* [L *forcip-, forceps* + E *-iform*] **:** shaped like a forceps; *usu* **:** having or being forcipulate pedicellariae with two valves that cross when closed — compare FORFICIFORM

for·ci·pressure \ˈfȯ(r)sə+ˌ-\ *n* [blend of L *forcip-, forceps* and E *pressure*] **:** compression of a blood vessel with a forceps to arrest hemorrhage

for·cip·u·la·ta \fȯ(r)ˌsipyəˈlädə, -ˈlād·ə\ *n pl, cap* [NL, fr. *forcipula* (dim. of L *forcip-, forceps*) + *-ata*] **:** the most highly specialized order of starfishes, distinguished by possession of stalked forficulate pedicellariae with three ossicles

for·cip·u·late \(ˈ)fȯ(r)ˈsipyəˌlāt\ *adj* [NL *forcipula* + E *-ate*] **:** like a small forceps; *usu* **:** being or having stalked pedicellariae made up of a basal ossicle with two articulated blades — see FORCIPIFORM, FORFICIFORM; compare FORFICULATE

for·cip·u·lo·sa \fȯ(r)ˌsipyəˈlōsə\ [NL, fr. *forcipula* + *-osa* (fr. L, neut. pl. of *-osus* -ous)] *syn of* FORCIPULATA

forcive *adj* [¹*force* + *-ive*] *obs* **:** FORCIBLE

forclose *obs var of* FORECLOSE

¹**ford** \ˈfō(ə)rd, ˈfȯ(ə)rd, ˈfōəd, ˈfȯ(ə)d\ *n* -s [ME, fr. OE; akin to OFris *forda* ford, OS *ford*, OHG *furt* ford, ON *fjǫrthr* fjord, bay, W *rhyd* ford, L *portus* house door, port, *porta* gate, Av *pərətush* passage, ford, bridge, OE *faran* to travel, go — more at FARE] **1 :** a shallow and usu. narrow part of a river or other body of water that may be crossed by man or animal by wading; *broadly* **:** any shallows that may be passed through (as by a wheeled vehicle) **2** *archaic* **:** a body of water **:** STREAM

²**ford** \ˈ"\ *vb* -ED/-ING/-S *vt* **1 :** to pass or cross (as a river or other body of water) by a ford **2 :** to pass over (water) ⟨the plank that ~*ed* the creek⟩ ⟨~*ing* the river on rafts⟩ ~ *vi* **:** to cross a body of water by a ford

³**ford** \ˈ"\ *n* -s [after *Ford*, a popular low-priced automobile] *slang* **:** a highly successful fashion design; *often* **:** a low-priced copy of a successful high-priced style in women's dress

ford·able \-dəbəl\ *adj* **:** crossable by fording ⟨a ~ stream⟩

ford cup *n, usu cap F* [fr. the *Ford* Motor Company] **:** a viscometer used for testing paints, varnishes, and lacquers

fording *n* -s [fr. gerund of ²*ford*] **1 :** the act of crossing a ford **2 :** a fording place **:** FORD

ford·ism \-ˌdizəm\ *n* -s *usu cap* [Henry *Ford* †1947 Am. auto manufacturer + E *-ism*] **:** a technological system that seeks to increase production efficiency primarily through carefully engineered breakdown and interlocking of production operations and that depends for its success on mass production by assembly-line methods

ford·ize \-ˌdīz\ *vt* -ED/-ING/-S *often cap* [Henry *Ford* + E *-ize*] **1 :** to standardize in the interests of efficiency and mass production ⟨~ a plant⟩ ⟨~ the cotton industry⟩ **2 a :** to organize and control (people or their work) as if on an assembly line ⟨the medical profession cannot be *fordized* until human beings become robots —E.H.Cary⟩ ⟨an attempt to ~ high-school education —H.R.Linville⟩ **b :** to deprive of individuality ⟨can we ~ our minds as well as our motors —Glenn Frank⟩

ford·less \ˈ=ləs\ *adj* **:** lacking a ford **:** impossible to cross on foot ⟨a ~ tide⟩

for·do *or* **fore·do** \fȯrˈdü, fōr-\ *vt* **for·did** *or* **fore·did** \-ˈdid\ **for·done** *or* **foredone** \-ˈdən\ **for·do·ing** *or* **fore·do·ing** \-ˈdüiŋ\ **for·does** *or* **fore·does** \-ˈdəz\ [ME *fordon*, fr. OE *fordōn*, fr. *for-* + *dōn* to do — more at DO] **1 a** *archaic* **:** to do away with **:** KILL, ABOLISH, DESTROY **:** UNDO, RUIN **b :** to bring to an end **:** TERMINATE ⟨subject to appraisal as an affair *fordone* —H.B.Alexander⟩ **2 :** to overcome with fatigue **:** EXHAUST — used only as past participle ⟨quite *fordone* with the heat⟩

for·dyce disease \ˈfȯrˌdīs-\ *n, usu cap F* [after John A. Fordyce †1925 Am. dermatologist] **:** a common anomaly of the oral mucosa in which misplaced sebaceous glands form yellowish white nodules on the lips or the lining of the mouth

¹**fore** \ˈfō(ə)r, ˈfȯ(ə)r, ˈfōə, ˈfȯ(ə)\ *adv* [ME, adv. & prep., fr. OE; akin to OHG *fora*, adv. & prep., before, Goth *faura*, adv. & prep., OE *for*, prep., for, before — more at FOR] **1** *obs* **:** at an earlier time or period **:** FORMERLY, PREVIOUSLY **2 :** in, toward, or adjacent to the front **:** FORWARD ⟨went ~ to check his instruments⟩ ⟨the bolt struck ~ of the mast⟩ — see FORE AND AFT

²**fore** *also* **'fore** \ˈ"\ *prep* [ME *fore*] **1** *now dial* **:** BEFORE **2 :** in the presence of — used chiefly in oaths

³**fore** \ˈ"\ *adj* [*fore-*] **1 :** prior in order of occurrence **:** PREVIOUS, FORMER, EARLIER ⟨during the ~ years of the last decade⟩ **2 :** situated in front of something else **:** FORWARD ⟨the ~ body of a whale⟩ — often contrasted with *back* and *hind*

⁴**fore** \ˈ"\ *n* -s **:** something that occupies a front or anterior position: as **a** (1) **:** FOREMAST (2) **:** ⁵BOW 1 **b** (1) **:** FOREQUARTER ⟨lamb ~s are cheap now⟩ (2) **:** FORELEG ⟨a horse lame in his off ~⟩ (3) **:** FORE WING ⟨markings on the hind wing more sober than those on the ~⟩ — **at the fore** *adv* (*or adj*) **:** on the foremast usu. at the masthead — used of a flag hoisted as a signal (as for sailing) — **to the fore** *adv* (*or adj*) **1 a :** within call **b :** in a still surviving state **:** ALIVE **2 :** in available or ready condition — used of money, credit, or other resources **3 :** in a position of prominence **:** FORWARD

⁵**fore** \ˈ"\ *interj* [prob. short for *before*] — used by a golfer to warn anyone within range of the probable line of flight of his ball

fore- \ˈ"\ *comb form* [ME *for-, fore-*, fr. OE *fore-*, fr. *fore*, adv.] **1 a :** at an earlier point in time **:** beforehand ⟨*fore*see⟩ ⟨*fore*tell⟩ **b :** occurring at an earlier point in time **:** occurring beforehand ⟨*fore*payment⟩ ⟨*fore*period⟩ **c :** being an early part of (something stipulated) ⟨*fore*day⟩ ⟨*fore*summer⟩ **2 a :** situated at or toward the front **:** situated in front of something ⟨*fore*leg⟩ ⟨*fore*porch⟩ **b :** being the front part of (something stipulated) ⟨*fore*arm⟩ ⟨*fore*palate⟩

fore and aft *adv* **1 :** lengthwise of a ship **:** from stem to stern — compare ¹ATHWART 1 b **2 :** in, at, or toward both the bow and stern

fore–and–aft \ˌ=ˌ=ˈ=\ *adj* [*fore and aft*] **1 :** lying, running, or acting in the general line of the length of a ship or other construction (as a house or an airplane) **:** LONGITUDINAL ⟨a *fore-and-aft* shot⟩ — see FORE-AND-AFT SAIL **2** *of a sailing ship* **:** having no square sails — see FORE-AND-AFT RIG, SCHOONER, SLOOP **3** *of a hat or cap* **:** having peaks in front and back

fore–and–aft bridge *n* **:** a gangway that sometimes connects a ship's forward bridge and after bridge

fore–and–aft·er \ˌ=ˌ=ˈafta(r)\ *n* -s [*fore-and-aft* (*rig*) + *-er*] **1 a :** a ship with a fore-and-aft rig; *esp* **:** SCHOONER **b :** something arranged fore and aft (as a longitudinal member dividing a hatchway) **2 :** a cocked hat worn with peaks in front and back

fore–and–aft rig *n* **1 :** a sailing-ship rig in which most or all of the sails are not attached to yards but are bent to gaffs or set on the masts or on stays in the midship line of the ship — compare SQUARE RIG **2** *slang Brit* **:** the uniform of a naval rating who wears a peak cap

fore–and–aft rigged *adj* **:** equipped with a fore-and-aft rig

fore–and–aft sail *n* **:** a sail not supported by a yard and usu. carried on a gaff or stay — see SAIL illustration

¹**forearm** \(ˈ)=ˈ=\ *vt* [*fore-* + *arm* (*v*)] **:** to arm in advance for attack or resistance; *broadly* **:** PREPARE ⟨we must ~ ourselves against the coming winter⟩

²**forearm** \ˈ=ˌ=\ *n* [*fore-* + *arm* (part of the body)] **1 :** the part of the arm or forelimb between the elbow and the wrist in a primate **:** ANTEBRACHIUM; *sometimes* **:** the corresponding part in other vertebrate animals — see HORSE illustration **2 :** FORE-END 2

forebay \ˈ=ˌ=\ *n* [*fore-* + *bay*] **1 :** a reservoir or canal from which water is immediately taken to run a waterwheel, turbine, or other equipment; *broadly* **:** the discharging end of a pond or millrace **2 :** the overhanging front of the upper story of a Pennsylvania Dutch barn

fore beam *n* **:** CLOTH BEAM

fore·bear *or* **for·bear** \ˈfōrˌbe(ə)r, ˈfȯr-, -ˌba(a)(ə)r; ˈfōəˌbeə, ˈfȯ(ə)ˌ-, -ˌba(a)ə\ *n* [ME (Sc dial.) *forebear*, fr. *fore-* + *-bear* one that is (fr. *been* to be + *-ar, -er* -er) — more at BE] **:** ANCESTOR, FOREFATHER — usu. used in pl. **syn** see ANCESTOR

forebitt \ˈ=ˌ=\ *n* [*fore-* + *bitt*] **:** one of the bitts near the foremast

foreboard \ˈ=ˌ=\ *n* [*fore-* + *board*] **:** the foredeck of a ship

fore·bode *or* **for·bode** \fōrˈbōd, fȯr-, fə(r)ˈ-, fōəˈ-, fȯ(ə)ˈ-\ *vb* -ED/-ING/-S [*fore-* + *bode*] *vt* **1 :** FORETELL, PORTEND ⟨such heavy air ~s a storm⟩ **2 :** to be prescient of **:** have an inward conviction of (as of coming ill or misfortune) **:** augur despondingly ~ *vi* **:** FORETELL, PRESAGE, AUGUR, PREDICT **syn** see FORETELL

fore·bod·er \-də(r)\ *n* -s **:** one that forebodes

¹**foreboding** *n* -s [fr. gerund of *forebode*] **:** the act of one who forebodes; *also* **:** a result of foreboding **:** a presage, prediction, or presentiment esp. of coming evil **:** PORTENT ⟨I have a sort of ~ about him —Henry James †1916⟩ **syn** see APPREHENSION

²**foreboding** *adj* [fr. pres. part. of *forebode*] **:** indicative of or marked by foreboding ⟨a ~ glance⟩ ⟨troubled ~ thoughts⟩ — **fore·bod·ing·ly** *adv* — **fore·bod·ing·ness** *n* -ES

forebody \ˈ=ˌ=\ *n* [*fore-* + *body*] **1 a :** the part of a ship forward of the largest or midship cross section — compare AFTERBODY, MIDDLE BODY **b :** the part of a seaplane float or hull forward of the step; *specif* **:** the bottom surface forward of the step and below the chines **2 :** THORAX

foreboom \ˈ=ˌ=\ *n* [*fore-* + *boom*] **:** the boom of the foremast of a ship

foreboot \ˈ=ˌ=\ *n* [*fore-* + *boot*] **:** a receptacle in the front of a vehicle (as for the stowing of baggage)

forebrace \ˈ=ˌ=\ *n* [*fore-* + *brace*] **:** a brace for swinging a fore yardarm — see SHIP illustration

forebrain \ˈ=ˌ=\ *n* [*fore* + *brain*] **1 a :** the anterior of the three primary divisions of the developing vertebrate brain **b :** the part of the brain of the adult, comprising the telencephalon and diencephalon, that develops from the embryonic forebrain **c :** TELENCEPHALON **2 :** the protocerebrum of an invertebrate

forebreast \ˈ=ˌ=\ *n* [Sc *forebreist* front part, fr. ME *forebrest*, fr. *fore-* + *brest* breast — more at BREAST] **1 :** FOREFIELD 2 **2 :** the anterior part of the chest esp. of a quadruped

foreby *var of* FORBY

forecabin \ˈ=ˌ=\ *n* [*fore-* + *cabin*] **:** a cabin in the forepart of a ship

forecaddie \ˈ=ˌ=\ *n* [*fore-* + *caddie*] **:** a golf caddie who is stationed in advance of the players and who indicates the position of balls on the course

forecarriage \ˈ=ˌ=\ *n* [*fore-* + *carriage*] **1 :** the forward part of the running gear of a four-wheeled vehicle when arranged so as to permit the two front wheels to turn independently of the rear wheels **2 :** a small usu. 2-wheeled carriage attached under the front end of the beam of a heavy-duty walking plow

¹**fore·cast** \ˈfōrˌkast, ˈfȯr-, ˈfōə-, ˈfȯ(ə)ˌ-, -ˌkaa(ə)st, -ˌkaist, -ˌkȧst *also* ˈ=ˈ=\ *vb* **forecast** *or* **forecasted**; **forecast** *or* **forecasted**; **forecasting**; **forecasts** [ME *forcasten, forecasten*, fr. *for-, fore-* fore- + *casten* to cast, contrive — more at CAST] *vt* **1** *archaic* **:** to plan ahead **:** SCHEME, FOREORDAIN **2 a :** to anticipate, calculate, or predict (some future event or condition) usu. as a result of rational study and analysis of available pertinent data ⟨it should be possible to ~ accurately swings in the business cycle⟩ ⟨the guide ~ good fishing if the weather held⟩; *esp* **:** to predict (weather conditions) usu. on the basis of correlated meteorological observations **b :** to indicate or hint at as likely to occur or ensue ⟨optimists are ~*ing* an immediate upswing in business⟩ **3 :** to serve as a forecast of **:** FORETELL, PRESAGE ⟨such events ~ war⟩ ~ *vi* **1** *obs* **:** to contrive or plan beforehand **2 :** to calculate the future **:** FORESEE, FORETELL ⟨if it turns out as I ~*ed*⟩ **syn** see FORETELL

²**forecast** \ˈ=ˌ=\ *n* [ME *forcast, forecast*, fr. *for-, fore-* fore- + *cast* cast, plan — more at CAST] **1** *obs* **a :** previous contrivance or determination **b :** PLAN, DESIGN **2** *archaic* **:** foresight of consequences and provision against them **:** PREVISION, FORETHOUGHT **3 :** a prophecy, estimate, or prediction of a future happening or condition ⟨waited for the noon weather ~⟩

fore·cast·er \-tə(r) *also* ˈ=ˌ==\ *n* **:** one that forecasts; *esp* **:** one that professionally forecasts the weather

fore·cast·ing·ly \(ˈ)=ˈ===lē\ *adv* **:** so as to form or formulate a forecast **:** with foresight

fore·cas·tle *or* **fo'c'sle** \ˈfōksəl *sometimes* ˈfōrˌkasəl *or* ˈfȯr-\ *n* -s [ME *forcastel, forecastel*, fr. *for-, fore-* fore- + *castel* castle — more at CASTLE] **1 a :** an ancient warship's short upper deck forward raised like a castle in order to command an enemy's decks **b :** the part of the upper deck of a ship forward of the foremast or of the fore channels **2 :** the forward part of a merchantman where the sailors live either under the deck or in a compartment above the deck

forecastle deck *n* **:** a partial deck above the main deck at the bow of a ship over a forecastle

fore·cas·tle·head \-lˌhed\ *n* **:** the forward part of a forecastle (sense 1b)

fore–chains \ˈ=ˌ=\ *n pl* **:** the forward chains of a ship

forecheck \ˈ=ˌ=\ *vi* **:** to check an opponent in ice hockey in his own defensive zone

fore·clos·able \fōrˈklōzəbəl, fȯr-\ *adj* **:** capable of being foreclosed **:** subject to foreclosure

fore·close \(ˈ)fōrˈklōz, fȯr-, fōəˈ-, fȯ(ə)ˈ-\ *vb* [ME *forclosen*, fr. OF *forclos*, past part. of *forclore*, fr. *fors* outside, out of, except (fr. L *foris* outside) + *clore* to close — more at FORUM, CLOSE] *vt* **1 :** to shut out **:** DEBAR, PREVENT, HINDER, PRECLUDE ⟨refused to ~ the possibility of a third term⟩; *sometimes* **:** to bring to an end ⟨if he went back to his family he would ~ any chance for independent growth⟩ **2** *obs* **:** to close or block up **:** BAR **3 :** to hold exclusively **4 :** to deal with or close in advance ⟨the chairman cleverly *foreclosed* the question⟩ **5 a :** to bar or cut off (one having an equity of redemption) for a default in payment of what is due on a mortgage **:** take away the equity of redemption from **b :** to subject to foreclosure proceedings **:** take away the right of (a mortgagor or lienor) to redeem property — see EQUITY OF REDEMPTION ~ *vi* **:** to foreclose a mortgage

fore·clo·sure \-ˈlōzhə(r)\ *n* **:** an act or instance of foreclosing; *specif* **:** a legal proceeding that bars or extinguishes a mortgagor's right of redeeming a mortgaged estate

foreconceive *vt* [*fore-* + *conceive*] *obs* **:** PRECONCEIVE

foreconscious \ˈ=ˌ==\ *n* [*fore-* + *conscious*; trans. of G (*dos*) *vorbewusste*] *n* **:** PRECONSCIOUS

forecourse \ˈ=ˌ=\ *n* [*fore-* + *course*] **:** FORESAIL 1

forecourt \ˈ=ˌ=\ *n* [*fore-* + *court*] **1 :** the outer or front court of a building or group of buildings **2 :** the forward part of a court; *esp* **:** the area between the service line and the net of a lawn tennis court

foredate \ˈ=ˈ=\ *vt* [*fore-* + *date*] **:** ANTEDATE

foredawn \ˈ=ˌ=\ *n* [*fore-* + *dawn*] **:** the time immediately before dawn

foredeck \ˈ=ˌ=\ *n* [*fore-* + *deck*] **:** the forepart of the main deck of a ship

foredeem *vb* [*fore-* + *deem* (to judge)] *obs* **:** to judge in advance **:** FORECAST

foredeep \ˈ=ˌ=\ *n* [*fore-* + *deep*] **:** a deep depression in the ocean bottom fronting a mountainous land area ⟨the Tuscarora ~ lies off the coast of Japan⟩

foredestine \ˈ=ˈ==\ *vt* [ME *fordestinen, foredestinen*, fr. *for-, fore-* fore- + *destinen* to destine — more at DESTINE] **:** PREDESTINE

foredestiny *n* [*fore-* + *destiny*] **1** *obs* **:** FORECAST **2 :** PREORDINATION

foredo *var of* FORDO

foredone \(ˈ)=ˈ=\ *adj* [*fore-* + *done*] **:** previously done or made

¹**foredoom** \ˈ=ˌ=\ *n* [*fore-* + *doom* (n.)] *archaic* **:** consignment in advance to a particular fate **:** DESTINY

²**foredoom** \(ˈ)=ˈ=\ *vt* [*fore-* + *doom* (v.)] **1 :** to doom beforehand ⟨~*ed* by her unfortunate background⟩; *often* **:** to consign in advance to a particular fate ⟨efforts ~*ed* to failure⟩ **2** *archaic* **:** to predict as a doom or destiny **:** FORECAST, PRESAGE

foredoor \ˈ=ˌ=\ *n* [*fore-* + *door*] *now dial* **:** the front door of a house

foredune \ˈ=ˌ=\ *n* [*fore-* + *dune*] **:** a dune ridge (as at the landward margin of a beach) more or less completely stabilized by vegetation

fore edge \ˈ=ˌ=\ *n* [*fore-* + *edge*] **:** the edge of a book, book section, or illustration opposite the backbone

fore–edge painting *n* **:** the method or act of painting a picture on the fore edge of a book so that the picture is visible only when the pages are slightly fanned; *also* **:** a picture so painted

fore–eld·er \ˈfōrˌeldər\ *n* [ME *foreldre*, fr. *for-, fore-* fore- + *eldre* elder, ancestor — more at ELDER] *chiefly Scot* **:** ANCESTOR, FOREFATHER — usu. used in pl.

fore–end \ˈ=ˌ=\ *n* [ME *forende*, fr. *for-, fore-* fore- + *ende* end — more at END] **1 :** the anterior end or part **2 :** the part of the stock of a firearm under the barrel and forward of the trigger guard

fore–exercise \ˈ=ˈ===\ *n* [*fore-* + *exercise*] **:** a preliminary exercise; *esp* **:** one designed to acquaint students with the technique of a test about to be administered

foreface \ˈ=ˌ=\ *n* [*fore-* + *face*] **:** the part of the head of a quadruped that is in front of the eyes **:** MUZZLE

forefather \ˈ=ˌ==\ *n* [ME *forfader, forefader*, fr. *for-, fore-* fore- + *fader* father — more at FATHER] **1 :** one that precedes another in a line of descent in any degree of consanguinity but usu. in a remote degree **:** ANCESTOR **2 :** a person of an earlier period and common heritage without necessarily a traceable genealogic relationship **:** FOREBEAR — usu. used in pl. **syn** see ANCESTOR

fore·fa·ther·ly *adj, archaic* **:** of or relating to a forefather

forefather's–cup \ˈ=ˌ==ˌ=\ *n, pl* **forefather's–cups :** PITCHER PLANT a

¹**forefeel** \ˈ=ˈ=\ *vt* [*fore-* + *feel*] **:** to have a presentiment of **:** ANTICIPATE ⟨~*ing* their doom⟩

²**forefeel** \ˈ=ˌ=\ *n* **:** a presentiment or anticipatory sensation ⟨a ~ of winter in the air⟩

forefence *n* [*fore-* + *fence*] *obs* **:** a front defense

forefend *var of* FORFEND

forefield \ˈ=ˌ=\ *n* [*fore-* + *field*] **1 :** the nearest part of a field (as of view or of combat) **2** *Brit* **:** the face of a mine working — called also *forebreast*

forefinger \ˈ=ˌ==\ *n* [ME *forfinger, forefinger*, fr. *for-, fore-* fore- + *finger*] **:** the finger next to the thumb **:** INDEX FINGER

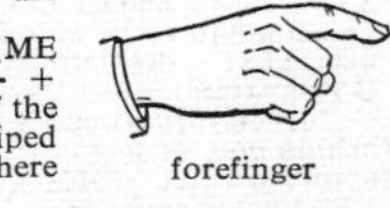

forefinger

¹**forefoot** \ˈ=ˌ=\ *n, pl* **forefeet** [ME *forfot, forefot*, fr. *for-, fore-* fore- + *fot* foot — more at FOOT] **1 :** one of the anterior feet of a quadruped or multiped **2 :** the forward part of a ship where the stem and keel meet

²**forefoot** \ˈ"\ *vt, West* **:** to rope (an animal) by the forefeet

¹**forefront** \ˈ=ˌ=\ *n* [ME *forfrount, forefrount*, fr. *for-, fore-* + *frount* front — more at FRONT] **:** the foremost part or place **:** VANGUARD ⟨had lived in the ~ of her time —Virginia Woolf⟩ ⟨in the ~ of cultural civilization —G.B.Shaw⟩

²**forefront** \ˈ"\ *vt* **:** to provide with a forefront

foregain *or* **foregainst** *prep* [ME *forgain* (fr. *for-, fore-* fore- + *again* against) & *forgaines*, fr. *for-, fore-* + *againes* against — more at AGAIN, AGAINST] *obs* **:** OPPOSITE

fore·gang·er \ˈfōrˌgaŋər, ˈfȯr-\ *n* [*fore-* + *ganger*] **1** *obs* **:** one that goes before **2 a :** a short rope grafted on a harpoon (as of a whaler) to which the longer line is attached **b :** a length of rope or chain stouter than the rest of the cable and placed next to an anchor

foregate \ˈ=ˌ=\ *n* [ME *forgate, foregate*, fr. *for-, fore-* fore- + *gate*] *archaic* **:** a main entrance or front gate

foregather *var of* FORGATHER

foregift \ˈ=ˌ=\ *n* [*fore-* + *gift*] *Brit* **:** a premium paid for a lease by a tenant; *sometimes* **:** a payment in advance (as on a lease)

foreglance \'⸗,⸗\ *n* [*fore-* + *glance*] **:** a glance forward or beforehand

foregleam \'⸗,⸗\ *n* [*fore-* + *gleam*] **:** a premonitory gleam **:** FORECAST

foreglimpse \'⸗,⸗\ *n* [*fore-* + *glimpse*] **:** a glimpse of the future **:** FOREGLEAM

[1]**fore·go** \fōr'gō, fȯr-, fōə'-, fȯ(ə)'-\ *vt* **fore·went** \-'went\ **fore·gone** \-'gȯn\ **fore·go·ing** \-'gōiŋ\ **fore·goes** \-'gōz\ [ME *forgon, forgan,* fr. OE *foregān,* fr. *fore-* + *gān* to go — more at GO] **:** to go before **:** PRECEDE ⟨the story of his mishap *forewent* him⟩

[2]**forego** *var of* FORGO

fore·go·er \-'gōə(r)\ *n* [ME *forgoer, foregoer,* fr. *forgon* + *-er*] **:** one that goes before: as **a** *obs* **:** a messenger sent ahead (as a king's purveyor) **:** FORERUNNER **b :** one that leads or goes in the van **:** EXAMPLE **c :** PREDECESSOR, ANCESTOR **d :** the foreganger of a harpoon

fore·go·ing \(')⸗¦gōiŋ, -ōeŋ\ *adj* [ME *forgoing,* fr. pres. part. of *forgon*] **:** prior in place, time, or arrangement **:** ANTECEDENT, PRECEDING ⟨the ~ paragraphs⟩

fore·gone \-¦gȯn\ *adj* [fr. past part. of [1]*forego*] **:** PREVIOUS, PAST ⟨nostalgic dreams of ~ summers⟩ — **fore·gone·ness** \-n(n)əs\ *n* -ES

foregone conclusion *n* **1 :** a conclusion that has preceded argument or examination **:** a predetermined conclusion **2 :** an inevitable result **:** CERTAINTY ⟨under the circumstances his victory was a *foregone conclusion*⟩

foregrip \'⸗,⸗\ *n* [*fore-* + *grip*] **:** the portion of a fishing rod butt lying between the forward edge of the reel seat and the forward end of the butt

foreground \'⸗,⸗\ *n* [*fore-* + *ground*] **1 :** the part of a scene or representation that is or is depicted as being nearest to and in front of the spectator — compare BACKGROUND, DISTANCE, PERSPECTIVE **2 :** a position of prominence **:** FOREFRONT ⟨in the ~ of our activities⟩

foregut \'⸗,⸗\ *n* [*fore-* + *gut*] **1 :** the anterior part of the primitive alimentary canal of a vertebrate embryo including those parts that develop into the pharynx, esophagus, stomach, and extreme anterior part of the intestine **2 :** the anterior part of the definitive alimentary canal of an invertebrate animal

forehall \'⸗,⸗\ *n* [*fore-* + *hall*] **:** a front hall esp. in a large building

forehammer \'⸗,⸗\ *n* [ME *forhamer, forehamer,* fr. *for-, fore-* fore + *hamer* hammer — more at HAMMER] **:** the hammer that strikes first when two hammers are used; *sometimes* **:** SLEDGE-HAMMER

[1]**forehand** \'⸗,⸗\ *n* [*fore-* + *hand*] **1** *archaic* **:** superior position **:** ADVANTAGE **2** *obs* **:** the chief or most important part **3 :** the part of a horse that is before the rider **4** *Brit* **:** a working foreman or supervisor; *esp* **:** one in charge of a process or apparatus in copper extracting **5 :** a forehand stroke (as in tennis or racquets) ⟨a player with an excellent ~⟩; *also* **:** the side on which such strokes are made ⟨he took the ball on his ~⟩ ⟨played to his opponent's ~⟩ — opposed to *backhand* **6** [trans. of G *vorderhand* lead] **:** the player in skat whose turn to bid comes first

forehand 5

[2]**forehand** \"\ *adv* **:** with a forehand stroke

[3]**forehand** \"\ *adj* [[2]*fore* + *hand*] **1** *obs* **:** done or given in advance **:** PRIOR, ANTICIPATIVE — see FOREHAND RENT **2** *of a stroke in racket games* **:** made on the side of the playing arm with the palm forward

forehanded \'⸗¦handəd, -aan-\ *adj* **1** *obs, of a horse* **:** having a forehand of an indicated sort **2 :** mindful of the future **:** THRIFTY, PRUDENT; *often* **:** having resources reserved for the future **3 :** FOREHAND 2

fore·hand·ed·ly *adv* **:** in a forehanded manner **:** THRIFTILY, PRUDENTLY

fore·hand·ed·ness *n* -ES **:** the quality or state of being ready and prepared (as for future need); *often* **:** THRIFT

forehand rent *n* **1** *Scots law* **:** rent made payable before the tenant's crop out of which it is to be paid has been harvested **2** *English law* **:** FOREGIFT

fore·head \'fȯrəd, 'färəd; 'fōr,hed, 'fōr,h-, 'fōə,h-, 'fȯ(ə),h-; *sometimes* 'fō,red *or* 'fä,red\ *n* [ME *forheved, forhed,* fr. OE *forhēafod,* fr. *for-, fore-* fore + *hēafod* head — more at HEAD] **1 :** the part of the face above the eyes **:** BROW **2 :** the aspect or countenance as expressing emotion or personal qualities (as of assurance or effrontery or sometimes modesty) **3 :** the front or forepart of something ⟨flames in the ~ of the morning sky —John Milton⟩ **4 :** the face of a mine working

fore·head·ed \-dəd\ *adj* **:** having or characterized by a forehead — used in combination with a qualifying adjective ⟨a low-*foreheaded* race⟩

forehearth \'⸗,⸗\ *n* [*fore-* + *hearth*] **1 :** the forward extension of the hearth of a blast furnace under the tymp; *also* **:** a similar extension of any smelting hearth **2 :** a steel furnace having an attachment in the front so as to dispense with the casting ladle **3 :** a separate receptacle taking the place of a hearth in front of a furnace for receiving molten material flowing out esp. to permit settling; *also* **:** a chamber at the end of a tank furnace from which glass is withdrawn for working

foreheater \'⸗,⸗⸗\ *n* [*fore-* + *heater*] **:** a shallow iron pan in which brine is boiled in the preparation of salt

forehold \'⸗,⸗\ *n* [*fore-* + *hold*] **:** a hold in the forward part of a ship

forehoof \'⸗,⸗\ *n, pl* **forehoofs** *also* **forehooves** [*fore-* + *hoof*] **:** the hoof of a forefoot (as of a horse)

forehook \'⸗,⸗\ *n* [*fore-* + *hook*] **:** a piece of timber placed across the stem to unite the bows and strengthen the forepart of a ship **:** BREASTHOOK

[1]**for·eign** \'fȯrən, 'fär-\ *adj* [ME *forein,* fr. OF *forain, forein,* fr. LL *foranus* situated on the outside, fr. L *foris* outside + *-anus* -an — more at FORUM] **1 :** situated outside a place or country: as **a :** situated outside one's own country ⟨~ nations⟩ ⟨~ cities⟩ **b :** situated outside a locality under consideration (as a private estate or a township) **2 :** born in, belonging to, derived from, intended for, or characteristic of some place or country (as nation) other than the one under consideration **:** not native or domestic ⟨our large ~ population⟩ ⟨~ art⟩ ⟨outgoing ~ mail⟩ ⟨incoming ~ mail⟩ **3 :** of, relating to, or proceeding from some other person, material thing, or substance than the one under consideration ⟨a man cannot save himself by ~ aid⟩ ⟨nothing is ~: parts relate to whole —Alexander Pope⟩ ⟨allergenic effects of ~ proteins⟩ ⟨the introduction of ~ genes in maize⟩ ⟨~ matter in milk⟩ **4 :** alien in character **:** not connected or pertinent **:** lacking congruity **:** INAPPROPRIATE ⟨~ to the plan⟩ ⟨this design is not ~ from some people's thoughts —Jonathan Swift⟩ **5 :** related to or dealing with other nations ⟨~ trade⟩ ⟨a ~ policy⟩ ⟨~ dividends⟩ **6 :** occurring in an abnormal situation in the living body and commonly introduced from without ⟨a sliver of wood under a fingernail or a coin in the esophagus are equally ~ bodies to the physician⟩ **7** *obs* **:** not belonging to or concerned with one's own household or family **8 a :** not being within the sphere of operation of the laws of a country under consideration — opposed to *domestic* **b :** not being within the sphere of operation of a locality (as a state or county) under consideration **9 a** *of a ship* **:** owned by a national of a foreign nation **b** *of the registry of a ship* **:** being under the flag of a nation other than that of which the owner is a national **syn** see EXTRINSIC

[2]**foreign** \"\ *n* -S [ME *forein,* fr. *forein,* adj.] **1** *obs* **:** FOREIGNER **:** a ship of foreign origin or registry **2** *obs* **:** an outlying part (as of a town or monastery) **3 :** a bond or other security originating in the jurisdiction of and usu. issued by a foreign governing body — usu. used in pl. ⟨~*s* drifted somewhat lower today⟩

foreign affairs *n pl* **:** matters relating to foreign countries **:** affairs other than domestic; *esp* **:** matters having to do with international relations and with the interests of the home country in foreign countries — see FOREIGN OFFICE

foreign aid *n* **:** economic or other assistance provided by one nation to another esp. as a tool in molding opinion in the recipient nation

foreign attachment *n* **:** a legal process by which the property of a foreign or absent debtor is attached within the jurisdiction for the satisfaction of a debt due from him to the plaintiff

foreign bill *n* **:** a bill of exchange not classified as an inland bill under the applicable law

foreign-born \'⸗⸗¦⸗\ *adj* **:** born under an alien sovereignty **:** foreign by birth whether naturalized or not

foreign car *n* **:** a freight car that is not owned by the railroad upon which it is being used — contrasted with *home car*

foreign corporation *also* **foreign company** *n* **:** a corporation or other organization having the essential attributes of a corporation that is chartered under the laws of a state or government other than that in which it is doing business

foreign correspondent *n* **:** a correspondent employed to send from a foreign country or region news or comment for publication

foreign devil *n* [trans. of Chin (Pek) *fan*[1] *kuei*[3]] **:** a foreigner in China — usu. used disparagingly

for·eign·er \'fȯrənə(r), 'fär-\ *n* -S [ME *foreiner,* fr. *forein,* adj. + *-er*] **1 :** a person belonging to or owing allegiance to a foreign country **:** ALIEN **2 :** something originating in another country; *esp* **:** a ship from abroad **3** *now dial* **:** STRANGER, OUTSIDER; *usu* **:** a nonresident or an unknown person in a community

foreign exchange *n* **1 :** a process of settling accounts or debts between persons residing in different countries **2 :** foreign coins and currency or current and short-term credit instruments payable in such currency

foreign factor *n* **:** an agent traveling on a ship and in charge of another's cargo with power to sell it for cash or exchange it for other property and to bring that property back to the port of embarkation — compare DOMESTIC FACTOR

foreign-flag \'⸗⸗¦⸗\ *adj* **:** registered under a foreign flag — used of a ship or airplane or of its owner ⟨*foreign-flag* competitors⟩ ⟨*foreign-flag* lines flying into the country⟩

for·eign·ism \'fȯrə,nizəm, 'fär-\ *n* -S **1 :** something peculiar to a foreign language or people **:** a foreign idiom or custom; *usu* **:** a feature of pronunciation or grammar or a word or word usage that is identified as foreign **2 :** imitation of foreign usage

for·eign·ize \-,nīz\ *vt* -ED/-ING/-S **:** to make foreign **:** give a foreign character or flavor to ⟨concealing fact under a *foreignized* terminology⟩

foreign jury *n* **:** a jury selected usu. because of local prejudice from a county other than that where a case is being tried

foreign legion *n* [trans. of F *légion étrangère*] **:** a volunteer corps of foreign citizens in the military service of a state

for·eign·ly *adv* **:** in a foreign manner

foreign minister *n* **:** a governmental minister for foreign affairs ⟨the *foreign minister* of the U.S. bears the title Secretary of State⟩

foreign mission *n* **:** a religious mission conducted outside the nation or national territory from which it is commissioned — compare HOME MISSION

for·eign·ness \'fȯrən(n)əs, 'fär-\ *n* -ES **1 :** the quality or state of being foreign ⟨the ~ of his background⟩ **2 :** lack of relation or appropriateness **:** IRRELEVANCY ⟨the complete ~ of such an approach weakened the force of his thesis⟩

foreign office *n* **:** a government department (as a ministry or cabinet bureau) having to do with foreign affairs and usu. headed by a minister ⟨the British *Foreign Office*⟩ ⟨caused a stir in the *foreign offices* of the democracies⟩

foreign policy *n* **:** the underlying basic direction of the activity and relationships of a sovereign state in its interaction with other sovereign states typically manifested in peace, war, neutrality, and alliance or various combinations of or approaches to these

foreign relations *n pl* **:** the relations between sovereign states **:** the manifest result of foreign policy; *broadly* **:** the field of international interaction and reaction ⟨a specialist in *foreign relations*⟩

foreigns *pl of* FOREIGN

foreign service *n* **1** [trans. of ML *servitium forinsecum*] **:** forinsec service **2 :** the field force of a foreign office comprising diplomatic personnel concerned primarily with governmental relations and consular personnel concerned largely with individual and commercial matters **3 :** service in the armed forces of a nation performed outside the national or continental boundaries but not necessarily beyond the boundaries of its sovereignty

foreign shipment *n* **:** a railroad shipment originating on or passing to another line

foreign-trade zone *n* **:** an isolated policed area adjacent to a port of entry (as a seaport or airport) where foreign goods may be unloaded for immediate transshipment or stored, repacked, sorted, mixed, or otherwise manipulated without being subject to import duties

foreign voltage *n* **:** a voltage imposed (as for the purpose of control or by accident) on an electrical circuit from some other source than the regular source

foreign word *n* **1 :** a word of a foreign language **2 :** a word taken from another language, pronounced and written as alien, and in English usu. printed in italics **3 :** a word adopted from another language **:** LOANWORD

foreintend \,⸗⸗'⸗\ *vt* [*fore-* + *intend*] **:** to plan in advance **:** intend to act or do as a result of deliberation

foreiron \'⸗,⸗⸗\ *n* [*fore-* + *iron*] **:** COLTER

[1]**fore·judge** *or* **for·judge** \fər'jəj, fōr-, fȯr-\ *vt* [ME *forjuggen,* fr. MF *forjugier, forsjugier,* fr. *fors* outside + *jugier* to judge — more at FORECLOSE, JUDGE] **1 :** to expel, oust, or put out by judgment of a court — used with *from* or *of* or with a double object **2** *obs* **:** ADJUDGE, CONDEMN

[2]**forejudge** \fōr'jəj, fȯr-\ *vt* [*fore-* + *judge*] **:** PREJUDGE

fore·judg·er *or* **for·judg·er** \fər'jəjə(r), fōr-, fȯr-\ *n* -S [ME *forjugger,* fr. MF *forjugier, forsjugier* to forejudge] **:** a judgment under English law by which one is expelled, ousted, or put out

fore·judg·ment \-'jəjmənt\ *n* [*fore-* + *judgment*] **:** FOREJUDGER

fore·know \fōr'nō, fȯr-\ *vt* [ME *foreknowen,* fr. *fore-* + *knowen* to know — more at KNOW] **:** to have previous knowledge of **:** know beforehand ⟨who would the miseries of man ~—John Dryden⟩ **syn** see FORESEE

fore·know·able \-ōəbəl\ *adj* **:** being or capable of being known in advance ⟨a ~ verdict⟩

fore·know·er \-ōə(r)\ *n* **:** one that foreknows

fore·know·ing·ly *adv* **:** with foreknowledge

foreknowledge \(')⸗¦⸗⸗\ *n* [*fore-* + *knowledge*] **:** knowledge of a thing before it happens or exists **:** PRESCIENCE, PRECOGNITION ⟨some of the tests seemed to indicate a definite ~ of what card would turn up next⟩ ⟨~ of human weakness⟩

for·el *also* **for·rel** \'färəl\ *n* -S [ME *forel* case, sheath, fr. MF *forrel, fourrel,* dim. of *fuerre* sheath — more at FUR] **1 a** *now dial Eng* **:** SHEATH, CASE **b :** a sheath or slipcase for holding a book **2 :** an inferior parchment for book covers **3 :** BURSE 2c

forelady \'⸗,⸗⸗\ *n* [*fore-* + *lady*] **:** a woman employed to supervise a group of working women (as in a factory) — called also *floorlady, floorwoman*

fore·land \'fōrlənd, 'fȯr-\ *n* [ME *forland, foreland,* fr. *for-, fore-* fore + *land*] **1 :** PROMONTORY, HEADLAND **2 :** land lying in front or forming the forward margin of something ⟨the ~ of the oil region⟩ ⟨the ~ of a national boundary⟩ **3 :** a portion of the natural shore on the outside of an embankment or sea wall that receives the shock of waves and deadens their force **4 :** a region of comparatively undisturbed rocks adjacent to an orogenic belt

forelay \'⸗'⸗\ *vb* **forelaid; forelaid; forelaying; forelays** [*fore-* + *lay*] *vt* **1** *now chiefly dial* **:** to lie in wait for **:** AMBUSH, WAYLAY **2** *archaic* **:** HINDER, OBSTRUCT **3** *dial* **:** to plan on **:** INTEND ~ *vi, dial* **:** to make arrangements beforehand

foreleech \'⸗,⸗\ *n* [*fore-* + *leech* (edge of a sail)] **:** the luff of a fore-and-aft sail

foreleg \'⸗,⸗\ *n* [ME *forlegge,* fr. *for-, fore-* fore + *legge* leg — more at LEG] **1 :** either of the anterior pair of legs of a quadruped or multiped **2 :** a front leg of a legged inanimate object (as a chair)

forelimb \'⸗,⸗\ *n* [*fore-* + *limb*] **:** an arm or a fin, wing, or leg of a vertebrate animal that is a foreleg of a quadruped or is homologous to it

[1]**forelock** \'⸗,⸗\ *n* [ME *forlok, forelok,* fr. *for-, fore-* fore + *lok* lock (fastening device) — more at LOCK] **:** COTTER PIN, SPLIT PIN, LINCHPIN

[2]**forelock** \"\ *vt* **:** to fasten with a forelock

[3]**forelock** \"\ *n* [*fore-* + *lock* (tuft of hair)] **:** a lock of hair that grows from the forepart of the head; *specif* **:** the part of a horse's mane that arises between the ears and hangs forward over the face — see HORSE illustration

forelock hook *n* **:** a hook by means of which a bunch of three yarns is twisted into a strand of rope

forelook \⸗'⸗\ *vi* [*fore-* + *look*] **:** to look ahead or toward the future

[1]**fore·man** \'fōrmən, 'fȯr-, 'fōəm-, 'fȯ(ə)m-\ *n, pl* **foremen** [ME *forman, foreman,* fr. *for- fore-* fore- + *man*] **:** a first or chief man: as **a** *obs* **:** a man who goes in advance **:** LEADER **b :** a member of a jury that acts as speaker, presides over deliberations, and conducts communication with the court **c** (1) **:** a chief and often specially trained workman who works with and commonly leads a gang or crew (2) **:** a representative of an owner or management in authority over a group of workers, a particular process or operation, a section of a plant or an entire organization ⟨the old-time ranch ~ had all the responsibilities and few of the benefits of ownership⟩ ⟨in the modern industrial plant the ~ is at once a link in the chain of management and a bridge between management and labor⟩

[2]**foreman** \"\ *vt* **foremaned** *or* **foremanned; foremaned** *or* **foremanned; foremaning** *or* **foremanning; foremans :** to supervise in the status of a foreman

fore·man·ship \-n,ship\ *n* **:** the office or occupation of a foreman ⟨took a course in ~⟩

fore·mast \'fōr,mast, 'fȯr-, 'fōə,-, 'fȯ(ə),-, -,maast, -,mȧst, -məst\ *n* [*fore-* + *mast*] **:** the mast nearest the bow of a sailing ship — see SHIP illustration

fore·mast·man \-tmən\ *also* **fore·mast·hand** \-t,hand\ *n, pl* **foremastmen** *also* **foremasthands** *n* **:** a common sailor **:** a man before the mast

forematter \'⸗,⸗⸗\ *n* [*fore-* + *matter*] **:** FRONT MATTER

foremilk \'⸗,⸗\ *n* [*fore-* + *milk*] **1 :** the first-drawn milk (as of a cow) usu. poor in fat and contaminated with bacteria from the teat canal **2 :** COLOSTRUM

[1]**fore·most** \'fōr,mōst, 'fȯr-, 'fōə,-, 'fȯ(ə),-, *also* -,məst\ *adj* [alter. (influenced by *fore-* & *most*) of ME *formest,* adj. & adv., fr. OE *formest, fyrmest,* superl. of *forma* first; akin to OS *formo* first, OS & OHG *fruma* advantage, profit, ON *frumfirst,* Goth *fruma,* OE *faran* to travel, go — more at FARE] **1 :** standing at the head, van, or front in a series or progression **:** most advanced in position **:** FIRST, HEADMOST ⟨was none who would be ~ to lead such dire attack —T.B.Macaulay⟩ **2 :** of first rank, position, influence, worth, reputation **:** leaving others behind **:** PREEMINENT ⟨great in council and great in war, ~ captain of his time —Alfred Tennyson⟩ ⟨unquestionably the ~ figure among Maine artists —*Amer. Guide Series: Maine*⟩ **syn** see CHIEF

[2]**foremost** \"\ *adv* [alter. of ME *formest,* adj. & adv.] **1 :** in the first place **:** FIRST ⟨put his best foot ~⟩ **2 :** most importantly ⟨first and ~⟩

fore·most·ly *adv* **:** before all **:** in the foremost place

foremother \'⸗,⸗⸗\ *n* [*fore-* + *mother*] **:** a woman corresponding in relationship to a forefather **:** a female ancestor or forebear

forename \'⸗,⸗\ *n* [*fore-* + *name*] **:** a name that precedes one's surname **:** a personal name by which an individual is distinguished from others with the same surname **:** a first or middle name ⟨a tendency to call men by the initials of their ~*s* —E.C.Smith⟩

fore·named \'⸗¦nāmd\ *adj* [ME *fornamed, forenamed,* fr. *for-, fore-* fore + *named,* past part. of *namen* to name — more at NAME] **:** previously mentioned **:** named before

fore·nenst *or* **fore·nent** \fə(r)-\ *var of* FORNENT

fore·night \'fōr,nīt\ *or* **fore·nicht** \-,nikt\ *n* [*fore-* + *night* or *nicht*] *Scot* **:** the part of evening between twilight and bedtime

forenoon \'⸗,⸗, ⸗'⸗\ *n* [ME *fornoon, forenoon,* fr. *for-, fore-* fore- + noon] **:** a part of day ending with noon; *usu* **:** the time between daylight or breakfast and noon

forenoon watch *n* **:** the watch on a ship from 8 a.m. to noon

forenotice \'⸗,⸗⸗\ *n* [*fore-* + *notice*] **:** notice or warning conveyed in advance

[1]**fo·ren·sic** \fə'ren(t)s|ik, (')fōr¦e-, (')fȯ¦re-, -nz|, |ēk\ *adj* [L *forensis* of a market or forum, public, forensic (fr. *forum* market, forum) + E *-ic* — more at FORUM] **1 :** belonging to courts of judicature or to public discussion and debate **2 :** used in legal proceedings or in public discussions; *broadly* **:** ARGUMENTATIVE, RHETORICAL ⟨~ eloquence⟩ **3 :** of or relating to forensics ⟨an excellent ~ program⟩ — **fo·ren·si·cal·ly** \|ək(ə)lē, |ēk-, -li\ *adv*

[2]**fo·ren·sic** \fə're-, fōr'e-, fȯ're-\ *n* -S **1 :** an argumentative exercise in the form of a speech or thesis formerly much used as an exercise in American schools and colleges **2 forensics** *pl but sing or pl in constr* **:** the art or study of argumentative discourse; *sometimes* **:** DEBATE 2

fo·ren·si·cal \|əkəl\ *adj* [L *forensis* + E *-ical*] *archaic* **:** FORENSIC

forensic ballistics *n pl but sing or pl in constr* **:** ballistics applied in the determination of legal evidence esp. as concerned with the identification of firearms, ammunition, bullets, and cartridge cases

forensic chemistry *n* **:** chemistry applied to legal questions — called also *legal chemistry*

forensic medicine *n* **:** a science that deals with the relation and application of medical facts to legal problems — called also *medical jurisprudence*

forensic psychiatry *n* **:** the application of psychiatry in courts of law (as for the determination of criminal responsibility or liability to commitment for insanity)

fore-oath \'⸗,⸗\ *n* [*fore-* + *oath*] **:** an oath required of a party bringing suit under old English law unless the cause of complaint were manifest

foreordain \,⸗,⸗'⸗\ *vt* [ME *forordeinen,* fr. *for-, fore-* fore- + *ordeinen* to ordain — more at ORDAIN] **:** to dispose or appoint in advance **:** PREDESTINATE, PREDETERMINE ⟨this ~*ed* course of events⟩ ⟨~*ed* to perish as their fathers had⟩

foreordination \,⸗,⸗⸗'⸗⸗\ *n* [*fore-* + *ordination*] **:** the quality or state of being foreordained; *esp* **:** PREDESTINATION 2

foreparent \'⸗,⸗⸗\ *n* [*fore-* + *parent*] *Midland* **:** ANCESTOR, FOREBEAR — usu. used in pl.

forepart \'⸗,⸗\ *n* [ME *forpart, forepart,* fr. *for-, fore-* fore- + *part*] **1 :** the forward or anterior part of something **:** FRONT ⟨the ~ of a ship⟩: as **a :** the forward part of a shoe or last **b :** the part of a garment (as a jacket) that covers the chest; *sometimes* **:** either of the pieces of material that when assembled form one lateral half of the forepart of a garment **2 :** the earlier part of a period of time ⟨spent the ~ of the morning on the beach⟩

forepassed *or* **forepast** \⸗'⸗\ *adj* [*fore-* + *passed, past*] **:** BYGONE

forepaw \'⸗,⸗\ *n* [*fore-* + *paw*] **:** the paw of a foreleg

forepeak \'⸗,⸗\ *n* [*fore-* + *peak*] **:** the extreme forward lower compartment or tank used for trimming or storage in a ship

forepiece \'⸗,⸗\ *n* [*fore-* + *piece*] **:** a front piece: as **a :** the flap in the forepart of a sidesaddle that guards the rider's dress **b :** CURTAIN RAISER

forepillar \'⸗,⸗⸗\ *n* [*fore-* + *pillar*] **:** PILLAR 4d

fore plane *n* [[3]*fore*] **:** a carpenter's plane usu. about 18 inches long and intermediate between the jack plane and jointer

foreplay \'⸗,⸗\ *n* [*fore-* + *play*] **:** sexual stimulation that normally tends to lead to sexual intercourse

forepleasure \'⸗,⸗⸗\ *n* [*fore-* + *pleasure*] **:** pleasurable excitement (as that induced by stimulation of erogenous zones) that tends to lead to or release a more intense emotional reaction (as in orgasm) — compare ENDPLEASURE

foreplot \⸗'⸗\ *vt* [*fore-* + *plot*] **:** to work out in advance ⟨you can ~ the course of the story easily enough⟩

forepoint *vt* [*fore-* + *point*] *obs* **:** PREDESTINE, FORECAST

[1]**forepole** *also* **forepale** \(')⸗¦⸗\ *vt* [*fore-* + *pole* or *pale* (v.)] **:** to advance (an excavation) in quicksand or caving ground by driving poles, slabs, or sheathing into the ground ahead of the excavating or simultaneously with it

[2]**forepole** \'⸗,⸗\ *n* [*fore-* + *pole* (n.)] **:** a piece of lagging, a heavy plank, or a pole, sharpened on one end and used in forepoling — called also *lath, spile, spiling*

forepost \ˈ=ˌ=\ *n* [*fore-* + *post*] **:** OUTPOST

foreprise *or* **foreprize** *vt* -ED/-ING/-S [*forprise* fr. *fore-* + *-prise* (as in *apprise*); *foreprize* alter. of *foreprise*] *obs* **:** to determine, provide for, or deal with beforehand **:** take for granted or in advance

forepump \ˈ=ˌ=\ *n* [*fore-* + *pump*] **:** a vacuum pump auxiliary to a more effective pump for which it supplies a first stage of exhaustion — called also *backing pump*

forequarter \ˈ=ˌ==\ *n* [*fore-* + *quarter*] **:** a front quarter or part; *specif* **:** the front part of the lateral half of a carcass (as of beef, veal, lamb, or mutton) usu. divided between the 12th and 13th ribs

forereach \ˈ=ˈ=\ *vb* [*fore-* + *reach*] *vi, of a ship* **:** to gain ground in going about usu. by carrying more way while in stays ~ *vt* **1 :** to gain upon (as a ship) **2 :** to overhaul and go ahead of (a ship) when close-hauled

foreribs \ˈ=ˌ=\ *n pl* [*fore-* + *ribs*] *Brit* **:** a cut of beef including the ribs immediately in front of the loin and forming one of the best roasting cuts **:** the prime ribs

fore rider *n* [ME *forerider*, fr. *fore-* + *rider*] **:** a rider in advance (as an outrider or scout)

[1]**fore·right** \ˈfōr,rīt\ *adv* [ME, fr. *fore-* + *right* (adv.)] *now dial Eng* **:** straight ahead **:** directly forward

[2]**foreright** \ˈ"\ *adj* **1** *dial Eng* **:** going straight ahead **:** STRAIGHTFORWARD, DIRECT ⟨the ~ path⟩ **2** *dial* **:** HEADSTRONG, OBSTINATE

[3]**foreright** \ˈ"\ *prep, dial Eng* **:** directly opposite **:** across from

foreroom \ˈ=ˌ=\ *n* [*fore-* + *room*] *dial* **:** LIVING ROOM, PARLOR

[1]**forerun** \=ˈ=\ *vt* [ME *forrennen, forerennen*, fr. *for-, fore-* fore- + *rennen* to run — more at RUN] **1 :** to run before **:** be in advance of (something following) **:** PRECEDE **2 :** to come before as an earnest of something to follow **:** introduce as a harbinger **:** ANNOUNCE ⟨these signs ~ the death or fall of kings —Shak.⟩ **3 :** FORESTALL, ANTICIPATE

[2]**forerun** \ˈ=ˌ=\ *or* **forerunning** \ˈ=ˌ==\ *n* **:** the first part that comes over in a distillation **:** the most volatile portion of a distilland ⟨the ~s of citronella oil⟩ — often used in pl.

forerunner \ˈ=ˌ==\ *n* [ME *forrenner, forerenner*, fr. *for-, fore-* fore- + *renner* runner; prob. trans. of L *praecursor* — more at RUNNER] **1 :** one going or sent before to give notice of the approach of others **:** HARBINGER ⟨blustery March days that are ~s of spring⟩: as **a :** a premonitory sign or symptom ⟨a stuffy feeling that is often the ~ of a cold⟩ ⟨a sudden alteration in the cost of money is a frequent ~ of economic decline⟩ **b :** one or more skiers who run the course before the start of a downhill skiing race to break trail, establish a typical time for the course, or indicate hazards **2 :** PREDECESSOR, FOREBEAR, ANCESTOR ⟨colonial administrators who . . . like their ~s . . . dedicate their lives to arduous and largely unrecognized service —*Times Lit. Supp.*⟩ ⟨a ~ of present-day cartoonists⟩ **3 a :** a piece of cloth tied on a ship's log line some fathoms from the outboard end to mark the limit of drift line **b :** FOREGANGER 2a

fores *pl of* FORE

foresaddle \ˈ=ˌ==\ *n* [*fore-* + *saddle*] **:** a wholesale cut of veal, lamb, or mutton consisting of the undivided forequarters of a carcass — compare HINDSADDLE

fore·said \ˈfōr,sed, ˈfȯr-\ *adj* [ME *forsaid, foresaid*, fr. OE *foresǣd*, fr. *fore-* + *gesǣgd, gesǣd*, past part of *secgan* to say — more at SAY] *archaic* **:** AFORESAID

fore·sail \ˈfōr,sāl, ˈfȯr-, ˈfōə,-, ˈfȯ(ə),-, -səl\ *n* [ME *foreseile*, fr. *for-, fore-* fore- + *seil, seile* sail — more at SAIL] **1 :** a sail that is carried on the foreyard of a square-rigged ship and that is the lowest sail on the foremast — called also *forecourse*; see SAIL illustration **2 :** the lower sail set abaft the foremast of a schooner — see SAIL illustration **3 :** FORESTAYSAIL

foresay \=ˈ=\ *vt* [ME *forseyen, foreseyen*, fr. OE *foresecgan*, fr. *fore-* + *secgan* to say — more at SAY] *archaic* **:** to tell in advance **:** PREDICT, FORETELL

fore·see \(ˈ)fōrˈsē, (ˈ)fȯr-, (ˈ)fōə-, (ˈ)fȯ(ə)ˈ-\ *vb* [ME *forseen, foreseen*, fr. OE *foresēon*, fr. *fore-* + *sēon* to see — more at SEE] *vt* **1 :** to see (as a future occurrence or development) as certain or unavoidable **:** look forward to with assurance ⟨should have *foreseen* the risk of economic collapse⟩ ⟨surely you can ~ what will happen next⟩ **2** *obs* **:** to provide esp. for or against **3** *obs* **:** to see, interview, or consider beforehand ~ *vi, obs* **:** to have or exercise foresight

syn FORESEE, FOREKNOW, DIVINE, APPREHEND, ANTICIPATE can mean to know or prophesy a future event or have knowledge of something prior to its manifestation. FORESEE in itself gives no hint of how the knowledge is derived or prophecy arrived at ⟨I had not *foreseen* the black depths of loneliness —Francis Stuart⟩ ⟨our failure to *foresee* all future problems —Vera M. Dean⟩ FOREKNOW, stressing the prior knowledge, usu., though not always, implies supernatural powers or the assistance of them, as divine revelation ⟨he cannot, however, *foreknow* how his opponent will behave in action —A.J.Toynbee⟩ ⟨they were willing to say that God *foreknows* the sin of those who are not elected to salvation —K.S.Latourette⟩ DIVINE, often indistinguishable from FORESEE, frequently suggests a gift, the assistance of a special power, or unusual discernment ⟨the military genius is the general who repeatedly succeeds in *divining* the unpredictable by guesswork or intuition —A.J. Toynbee⟩ ⟨impossible for him to *divine* the complexity and subtlety of these abstract mathematical ideas which were waiting for discovery —A.N.Whitehead⟩ ⟨whose talents for *divining* news and coordinating its coverage remain a matter of perpetual awe —Gladwin Hill⟩ APPREHEND often implies somewhat less certainty of what is foreseen than the previous words but a stronger emotional effect of the advance knowledge or the suspicion, often suggesting esp. a certain anxiety or dread ⟨she *apprehended*, not without good cause, that his kingdom might soon be extended to her frontiers —T.B. Macaulay⟩ ⟨his lips quivered, and she *apprehended* rather than heard what he said —Ellen Glasgow⟩ ANTICIPATE suggests an action of some kind in relation or seeming relation to the thing foreseen or prophesied, as the formulation of an historical hypothesis that makes the future event reasonable or seemingly inevitable, or an experiencing of prior joy or pain on account of the thing foreseen, or an interrelated move as one that forestalls, aggravates, or is motivated by the thing foreseen ⟨his leadership in the state has consisted of *anticipating* the thinking of the major groups of voters and following what he believes to be public opinion —Frank Tollman⟩ ⟨to *anticipate* charity by preventing poverty —Theodore Bienenstok⟩ ⟨sometimes we are able to *anticipate* a news event . . . but more often than not news breaks without any warning —S.W.Rumsam⟩ ⟨to *anticipate* the arrival of the next attack —H.G.Wells⟩

fore·see·abil·i·ty \(ˌ)=ˌsēəˈbilədē\ *n* **:** the quality or state of being foreseeable

fore·see·able \(ˈ)=ˈsēəbəl\ *adj* **1 :** being such as may reasonably be anticipated ⟨the ~ costs are well within the budget allowed⟩ ⟨~ problems⟩ **2 :** lying within the range for which forecasts are possible ⟨does not anticipate a tax cut in the ~ future⟩

fore·see·ing·ly \-ēiŋlē\ *adv* **:** with foresight

fore·se·er \(ˈ)=ˈsēə(r)\ *n* **:** one that foresees

[1]**foreset** \=ˈ=\ *vt* [*fore-* + *set*] **:** to arrange beforehand

[2]**foreset** \ˈ=ˌ=\ *adj* [*fore-* + *set* (past part. of *set*)] **:** of, relating to, or forming the steeper slope on the outer margin of a delta or the lee side of a dune or the sediments deposited on such a slope ⟨a silty ~ slope⟩

[3]**foreset** \ˈ"\ *also* **foreset bed** *n* **:** a foreset slope or layer (as of sediment or rock)

fore·sey \ˈfōrˈsī\ *n* -S [*fore-* + Sc *sey*] *Scot* **:** a cut of beef including the prime ribs and usu. some of the more anterior ribs

[1]**foreshadow** \(ˈ)=ˈ==\ *vt* [*fore-* + *shadow* (v.)] **:** to shadow or typify beforehand **:** be the archetype or prototype of **:** PREFIGURE — **foreshadower** \(ˈ)=ˈ===\ *n* -S

[2]**foreshadow** \ˈ=ˌ==\ *n* [*fore-* + *shadow* (n.)] **:** a shadow of a thing cast before; *broadly* **:** an indication of what is to come

foreshaft \ˈ=ˌ=\ *n* [*fore-* + *shaft*] **:** the forward portion of the shaft of an arrow to which the footing is joined and to which the head is attached

foreshank \ˈ=ˌ=\ *n* [*fore-* + *shank*] **:** SHIN 1b

foresheet \ˈ=ˌ=\ *n* [*fore-* + *sheet*] **1 a :** one of the sheets of a foresail **b :** the rope by which the clew of a forecourse is held down — see SHIP illustration **2 foresheets** *pl* **:** the forward portion of an open boat

foreship \ˈ=ˌ=\ *n* [ME *forship, foreship*, fr. OE *forscip*, fr. *for-, fore-* fore- + *scip* ship — more at SHIP] **:** the forward part of a ship

foreshock \ˈ=ˌ=\ *n* [*fore-* + *shock*] **:** one of the accessory or minor tremors commonly preceding the principal shock of an earthquake

foreshore \ˈ=ˌ=\ *n* [*fore-* + *shore*] **1 :** a strip of land margining a body of water (as a lake or stream) ⟨camped on the wooded ~ of the island⟩ ⟨the frozen gravel and clay thawed when exposed to the warm air, and soon innumerable small streams were running across the ~ —*Geog. Rev.*⟩ **2 :** the part of a seashore between the low-water line usu. at the seaward margin of a low-tide terrace and the upper limit of wave wash at high tide usu. marked by a beach scarp or berm ⟨under British law the ~ is ordinarily vested in the Crown⟩

foreshorten \=ˈ==\ *vt* [*fore-* + *shorten*] **1 :** to shorten (as a design) by proportionately contracting in the direction of depth so that an illusion of projection or extension in space is obtained **2 :** to make more compact **:** ABRIDGE, CONTRACT, SHORTEN ⟨distance and geography — though ~*ed* in the air age — still have strategical . . . meaning —H.W.Baldwin⟩ ⟨allows a long and scattered history to be gathered and ~*ed* —Susanne K. Langer⟩ ⟨dramatize and ~ the development of events —*Times Lit. Supp.*⟩

foreshortening *n* -S **:** the act of one that foreshortens or the state of being foreshortened; *often* **:** representation in art or literature in a foreshortened mode

foreshot \ˈ=ˌ=\ *n* [*fore-* + *shot*] **:** the forerun in the distillation of whiskey

[1]**foreshow** \=ˈ=\ *vt* [ME *forshewen, foreshewen*, fr. OE *foresceawian*, fr. *fore-* + *sceawian* to show — more at SHOW] **1 a :** FORETELL **b :** to show beforehand **2** *obs* **:** BETOKEN, SHOW ⟨your looks ~ you have a gentle heart —Shak.⟩ — **foreshow·er** \ˈ"+ə(r)\ *n*

[2]**foreshow** *n* [*fore-* + *show*] *obs* **:** FORETOKEN

foreside \ˈ=ˌ=\ *n* [ME *forside, foreside*, fr. *for-, fore-* fore + *side*] **:** the front side or part **:** FRONT

fore·sight \ˈfōr,sīt, ˈfȯr-, ˈfōə,-, ˈfȯ(ə),-, *usu* -īd.+V\ *n* [ME *forsight, foresight*, fr. *for-, fore-* fore + *sight*] **1 :** an act or the power of foreseeing **:** PRESCIENCE, FOREKNOWLEDGE **2 :** an act of looking forward; *also* **:** a view forward **3 :** action in reference to the future **:** provident care **:** PRUDENCE, FORETHOUGHT **4 :** FRONT SIGHT **5 a :** a reading taken by a surveyor in leveling to determine the elevation of the point on which the rod rests when read — called also *minus sight* **b :** a sight or bearing taken in a forward direction by a compass or transit **syn** see PRUDENCE

fore·sight·ed \ˈ=ˌsīd·əd\ *adj* **:** having foresight; *esp* **:** provident for the future — **fore·sight·ed·ly** *adv* — **fore·sight·ed·ness** *n* -ES

fore·sight·ful \ˈ=ˌsītfəl\ *adj* **:** characterized by foresight ⟨~ plans⟩ **:** FORESIGHTED

fore·sight·less \ˈ=ˌ=ləs\ *adj* **:** lacking in foresight — **foresight·less·ness** *n* -ES

foresignify \=ˈ===\ *vt* [*fore-* + *signify*] **:** to signify beforehand **:** FORESHOW, PREFIGURE

foreskin \ˈ=ˌ=\ *n* [*fore-* + *skin*] **:** a fold of skin that covers the glans of the penis — called also *prepuce*

fore·slack *var of* FORSLACK

foresleeve \ˈ=ˌ=\ *n* [ME *foresleve*, fr. *fore-* + *sleve* sleeve — more at SLEEVE] **:** an ornamental sleeve or part of a sleeve that can be slipped on or off

fore·slow *var of* FORSLOW

foresound \ˈ=ˌ=\ *n* [*fore-* + *sound*] **:** one of the audible vibrations occas. noted immediately preceding or accompanying the first disturbance of the ground during an earthquake — usu. used in pl.

[1]**forespeak** \=ˈ=\ *vt* [ME *forspeken, forespeken*, fr. *for-, fore-* fore- + *speken* to speak — more at SPEAK] **1 :** to speak of beforehand **:** FORETELL, PREDICT **2 :** to bespeak in advance ⟨all the rooms were *forespoken* weeks ago⟩

[2]**fore·speak** *var of* FORSPEAK

forespeaker \ˈ=ˌ==\ *n* [ME *forspeker*, fr. [1]*for* + *speker* speaker — more at SPEAKER] **1** *archaic* **:** one that speaks for another **2** [*fore-* + *speaker*] *obs* **:** one that speaks first

forespeaking *n* [fr. gerund of [1]*forespeak*] *obs* **:** PREDICTION

[1]**fore·spent** *var of* FORSPENT

[2]**forespent** *adj, obs* **:** already spent **:** gone by **:** PAST

forespore \ˈ=ˌ=\ *n* [*fore-* + *spore*] **:** a precursor of a spore; *specif* **:** a form preceding the endospore in some bacteria and characterized by diffuse response to chromatin stains

[1]**for·est** \ˈfȯrəst, ˈfär-\ *n* -S *often attrib* [ME, fr. OF, fr. ML *forestis*, fr. L *foris* outside — more at FORUM] **1 a :** a tract of more or less wooded land formerly set apart in England primarily for the keeping and hunting of game though often including inhabited areas, usu. belonging to the sovereign, and having its own distinctive laws, courts, and officers — compare CHASE, PARK, WARREN **b** *Scot* **:** a tract of usu. treeless upland set apart for the keeping and hunting of deer **2 a :** a dense growth of trees and underbrush covering a large tract of land; *specif* **:** an extensive plant community of shrubs and trees in all stages of growth and decay with a closed canopy having the quality of self-perpetuation or of development into an ecological climax **b :** such a growth or community together with the land on which it stands **3** *archaic* **:** an uncultivated or waste area **4** *Brit* **:** a district once wooded but now under cultivation — used chiefly in place names **5** *usu cap* **:** a usu. dense and often hilly wooded region (as in equatorial Africa) inhabited by a people whose culture has become characteristic of the region ⟨~ Pygmies⟩ — contrasted with *bush* and *jungle* **6 :** something felt to resemble a forest: as **a :** a large number of upright objects ⟨a ~ of masts⟩ **b :** a great quantity ⟨from the ~ of answers received⟩ ⟨creating whole ~s of abstract terms in striving for a narrow precision of expression⟩

[2]**forest** \ˈ"\ *vt* -ED/-ING/-S **1 :** to cover with trees or forest **:** AFFOREST, REFOREST ⟨~*ed* with pine and spruce —*Amer. Guide Series: Minn.*⟩ **2 :** to place or hide in a forest

forestaff \ˈ=ˌ=\ *n* [*fore-* + *staff*] **:** CROSS-STAFF 2

forestage \ˈ=ˌ=\ *n, often attrib* [*fore-* + *stage*] **:** a part of a theater stage nearest the audience and usu. projecting beyond the curtain **:** APRON ⟨the stage is to be forty feet deep at the center, and there will be two small ~ areas at either side and forward of the proscenium —Alice Griffin⟩

forestair \ˈ=ˌ=\ *n* [*fore-* + *stair*] *Scot* **:** an open outside staircase

for·est·al \ˈfȯrəstᵊl, ˈfär-\ *adj* **:** of, relating to, or being a forest ⟨~ resources⟩

[1]**fore·stall** \ˈfōr,stȯl, ˈfȯr-, ˈfōə,-, ˈfȯ(ə),-\ *n* -S [ME *forstall, forestall*, fr. OE *foresteall*, fr. *fore-* + *steall* position, stall — more at STALL] **1 :** an offense under old English law of feloniously waylaying on the highway; *also* **:** the feudal franchise of jurisdiction over this offense **2 a :** FRONTSTALL **b :** FRONT 2d(2)

[2]**forestall** \=ˈ=\ *vt* -ED/-ING/-S [ME *forstallen, forestallen*, to ambush, intercept, fr. *forstall, forestall*, n.] **1** *archaic* **:** to intercept, lie in wait for, or stop the passage of (a person or thing) esp. on the road or highway and for a felonious purpose **2 :** to exclude, hinder, or prevent by prior occupation or by measures taken in advance **3 a :** to get ahead of **:** act in advance of **:** take or think of beforehand **b** *obs* **:** to take possession of in advance of someone or something else esp. to the exclusion or detriment of the latter **:** deprive by prior action **4** *obs* **:** OBSTRUCT, BESET ⟨~ a road⟩ **:** prevent ingress (as of a tenant) to (rented premises) **5 :** to anticipate or prevent the normal trading in (as a market) by buying or contracting for merchandise or provisions on their way to the market with the intention of reselling at a higher price, by dissuading persons from bringing merchandise or provisions to market, or by persuading those who have brought merchandise or provisions to market to raise the price ⟨~*ing* the wheat harvest and selling it at three times its cost —G.B.Shaw⟩ **syn** see PREVENT

fore·stall·er \-lə(r)\ *n* -S [ME *forstaller, forestaller*, fr. *forstallen, forestallen* + *-er*] **1 :** one that forestalls; *broadly* **:** MIDDLEMAN 3a **2 :** the act or offense of forestalling

fore·stall·ment \-lmənt\ *n* -S [ME *forstallment, forestallment*, fr. *forstallen, forestallen* + *-ment*] **:** an act of forestalling or the result of this **:** ANTICIPATION ⟨disheartened at the ~ of his invention⟩

forestarling \ˈ=ˌ==\ *n* [*fore-* + *starling*] **:** an icebreaker in front of a bridge starling

for·est·a·tion \ˌfȯrəˈstāshən, ˌfär-\ *n* -S [[1]*forest* + *-ation*] **:** the establishment of a forest

forestay \ˈ=ˌ=\ *n* [ME *forstay, forestay*, fr. *for-, fore-* fore- + *stay*] **:** a support in front or directed to the front; *specif* **:** a stay from the foremast head usu. to the deck of a ship which supports the foremast in a fore-and-aft direction and to which the forestaysail is secured by hanks — see SHIP illustration

fore·stay·sail \=ˈ=ˌsāl, -ˌsəl\ *n* **:** the aftermost headsail of a schooner, ketch, or yawl that is triangular in shape and set on hanks on the forestay — called also *foresail*; see SAIL illustration

forest bat *n* **:** any of several brightly marked vespertilionid bats (genus *Kerivoula*) of African forests — called also *painted bat*

forest cover *n* **:** land cover consisting of forest **:** the plants of a forest together with the products of their decay

for·est·ed \ˈfȯrəstəd, ˈfär-\ *adj* **:** covered with forest **:** WOODED

forestem \ˈ=ˌ=\ *n* [ME *forstem, forestem*, fr. *for-, fore-* fore- + *stem*] *Scot* **:** STEM 2a(1)

for·est·er \ˈfȯrəstə(r), ˈfär-\ *n* -S [ME *forster, forester*, fr. OF *forestier* fr. *forest* + *-ier* -er — more at FOREST] **1 :** an officer formerly charged with the watching of a royal forest in Great Britain and with the preserving of its plants and game animals **2 a :** a person in charge of growing timber (as on an estate) **b :** a person who supervises the development, care, and management of forest land or forest parkland **3 :** an inhabitant or frequenter of the forest: as **a :** a half-wild English pony of the New Forest area **b** *also* **forester moth** (1) **:** any of various moths of the family Agaristidae — see EIGHT-SPOTTED FORESTER (2) **:** any of several brightly colored European moths of the family Zygaenidae **c** *Austral* **:** GIANT KANGAROO; *esp* **:** a male giant kangaroo **4** *usu cap* **:** a member of one of the major benevolent and fraternal orders

for·est·er·ship \-(r),ship\ *n* **:** the office of or an appointment as forester

forest fire *n* **:** an uncontrolled fire in a wooded area — see CROWN FIRE, GROUND FIRE

forest floor *n* **:** the richly organic layer of soil in a forest consisting of the more or less decayed debris (as fallen leaves and branches) that makes up the litter, duff, and leaf mold and commonly including the A-horizon, B-horizon, and C-horizon of the soil proper

forest fly *n* **:** a winged blood-sucking fly (*Hippobosca equina*) that is related to the sheep ked and that bites horses and cattle

forest green *n* **1 :** a dark green that is yellower and stronger than evergreen or average bottle green **2 :** a moderate olive green that is greener and deeper than holly green (sense 2), yellower, lighter, and stronger than cypress, and greener, stronger, and slightly darker than Lincoln green

forest hog *or* **forest pig** *n* **:** a large dark-colored wild pig (*Hylochoerus meinertzhageni*) native to the forested region of tropical Africa and closely related to the babirusa

fo·res·tial \fəˈrestēəl, -s(h)chəl\ *adj* [[1]*forest* + *-ial*] **:** FORESTAL

forestick \ˈ=ˌ=\ *n* [*fore-* + *stick*] **:** the front log of an open log fire (as in a fireplace) in which the main logs are parallel in arrangement

for·es·ti·e·ra \ˌfȯrəstēˈirə, ˌfär-, -ēˈerə, -ˈstirə\ *n* [NL, after Pierre Gaspard *Forestier* †1847 Fr. physician] **1** *cap* **:** a genus of sometimes spiny American shrubs or trees (family Oleaceae) that have simple opposite leaves and inconspicuous flowers followed by single-seeded drupes **2** -S **:** any plant of the genus *Forestiera* — see TANGLEBUSH

foresting *pres part of* FOREST

forest law *n* **:** a law (as for the protection of game or preservation of timber) that is peculiarly applicable in a forest; *esp* **:** one of several laws enacted by William I and other Norman English kings for the protection of the royal forests

for·est·less \ˈfȯrəstləs, ˈfär-\ *adj* **:** having no forests **:** lacking wooded areas ⟨the wide ~ plains⟩

forestlike \ˈ==ˌ=\ *adj* **:** like or like that of a forest

forest mahogany *n* **:** any of several Australian trees of the genus *Eucalyptus*: as **a :** TALLOWWOOD **b :** RED MAHOGANY **c :** RED GUM

forest mole *n* **:** a very large partially diurnal forest-dwelling southern African mole (*Chrysospalax trevelyani*) closely related to the golden moles

forest negro *n, often cap F, cap N* **:** an African characterized by possession of all the typical negroid traits highly developed and supposed to be most common in the forests of tropical West Africa including much of the Niger and Congo basins

forest oak *n, Austral* **:** a she-oak (esp. *Casuarina torulosa*)

forestock \ˈ=ˌ=\ *n* [*fore-* + *stock*] **:** FORE-END 2

forest of dean red *often cap F&D* [fr. *Forest of Dean*, a kind of sandstone, fr. *Forest of Dean*, Gloucestershire, Eng.] **:** ENGLISH RED 2a

forestomach \ˈ=ˌ==\ *n* [*fore-* + *stomach*] **:** the cardiac part of the stomach

forest pathology *n* **:** a branch of plant pathology that deals with diseases of trees

forest ranger *n* **:** an officer charged with the duty of patrolling and guarding a forest; *esp* **:** one in charge of the management and protection of a portion of a public forest

forest red gum *n* **:** a broad-leaved Australian eucalypt (*Eucalyptus tereticornis*) yielding a heavy durable dark red timber

forestroke \ˈ=ˌ=\ *n* [*fore-* + *stroke*] **:** a forward stroke (as in various games)

for·est·ry \ˈfȯrəstrē, ˈfär-, -ri\ *n* -ES *often attrib* [MF *foresterie*, fr. *forest* + *-erie* -ery] **1** *Scots law* **:** a right to the privileges of a royal forest; *also* **:** a tract over which such privileges are enjoyed **2 :** forest land **:** FOREST **3 :** a science of developing, caring for, or cultivating forests **:** the management of growing timber

forests *pl of* FOREST, *pres 3d sing of* FOREST

forest school *n* **:** a school of forestry

forest shrew *n* **:** any of several small shrews (genus *Sylvisorex*) found in forests at high elevations in tropical Africa

forest tea *n* **:** a Philippine plant (*Ehretia microphylla*) used as a substitute for tea in the Philippines esp. by resident Chinese

forest tent caterpillar *n* **:** a hairy orange-striped and orange-spotted bluish tent caterpillar (*Malacosoma disstria*) that is gregarious, spins a carpet rather than a tent, and is sometimes a serious defoliator of deciduous trees

forest type *n* **:** similarity of composition and development (as in two or more stands of trees) due to the impact of corresponding physical and biological factors; *sometimes* **:** a forest association

for·esty \ˈfȯrəstē, ˈfär-\ *adj* **:** covered with or abounding in forests

forest yaws *n* **:** ESPUNDIA

foreswear *var of* FORSWEAR

foretack \ˈ=ˌ=\ *n* [*fore-* + *tack*] **:** a rope by which the tack of a square foresail is hauled and held

foretackle \ˈ=ˌ==\ *n* [*fore-* + *tackle*] **:** the tackle that hooks on to the pendant on the foremast

foretake *vt* [*fore-* + *take*] *obs* **:** ANTICIPATE, PRESUPPOSE

foretalk \ˈ=ˌ=\ *also* **foretalking** \ˈ=ˈ==\ *n* **:** PREFACE

[1]**foretaste** \ˈ=ˌ=\ *n* [ME *fortaste, foretaste*, fr. *for-, fore-* fore- + *taste*] **1 :** something that serves to indicate or warn of what is to come ⟨the air held a ~ of rain⟩ **2 a :** a taste or trial in advance **:** a small anticipatory sample ⟨those brilliant February days that sometimes come as a ~ of spring⟩ ⟨a journey like this was only a ~, too rewarding not to be repeated —Van Wyck Brooks⟩

[2]**foretaste** \=ˈ=\ *vt* [ME *fortasten, foretasten*, fr. *for-, fore-* fore- + *tasten* to taste — more at TASTE] **:** to taste beforehand **:** have a foretaste of **:** ANTICIPATE ⟨*foretasting* his discharge from the army on a weekend pass⟩

fore·tast·er \ˈ"+ə(r)\ *n* **:** one that foretastes

fore·tell \(ˈ)fōrˈtel, (ˈ)fȯr, (ˈ)fōəˈ-, (ˈ)fȯ(ə)ˈ-\ *vb* [ME *fortellen, foretellen*, fr. *for-, fore-* fore- + *tellen* to tell — more at TELL] *vt* **1 :** to tell of from foreknowledge **:** PREDICT, PROPHESY **2** *obs* **:** to tell, acquaint, or command beforehand ~ *vi, obs* **:** to utter prediction **:** PROPHESY

syn PREDICT, FORECAST, PROPHESY, PROGNOSTICATE, AUGUR, PRESAGE, PORTEND, FOREBODE: FORETELL applies to procedures to telling of the coming of some future event by any procedure or source of information ⟨some sorcerer . . . had *foretold* —Alfred Tennyson⟩ ⟨the marvelous exactness with which eclipses are *foretold* —K.K.Darrow⟩ PREDICT is closely synonymous with FORETELL; it may be preferred in today's English to suggest or apply to inference from facts and laws of nature ⟨if we can trace certain changes slowly at work in the period preceding our own we may be able to *predict* with some probability that these changes will continue for some time at least to operate in the same direction —W.R.Inge⟩ ⟨astronomers, who developed mathematics to such a degree that it could *predict* the wanderings of the planets and their satellites —K.K.Darrow⟩ FORECAST may suggest concomitant anticipation, consideration of effects, and provision for one's needs ⟨he *forecast* the war, announced in his message the intention to put the state militia on a war footing —*Encyc. Americana*⟩ PROPHESY may imply mystic inspiration, real or pretended, supernatural machinery, or august or pontifical assurance ⟨ancestral voices *prophesying* war —S.T.Coleridge⟩ ⟨professional astrologists make a practice of *prophesying* the presidency for budding statesmen —S.H.Adams⟩ PROGNOSTICATE may indicate learned or skilled use of symptoms and signs; it is applicable to a physician's procedure ⟨*prognosticating* a quick recovery⟩ ⟨the slight moisture resolved itself into a monotonous smiting of earth by heaven, in torrents to which no end could be *prognosticated* —Thomas Hardy⟩ AUGUR may indicate foreknowing the future by interpreting omens; used in relation to things and conditions, it indicates presentation as an omen of good or evil ⟨the morrow brought a very sober-looking morning; the sun making only a few efforts to appear; and Catherine *augured* from it everything most favorable to her wishes —Jane Austen⟩ PRESAGE and PORTEND, the latter usu. used of evil things or adverse developments, may apply to foreshadowing or suggesting a coming event or indicating its likelihood, sometimes by occult procedures ⟨they think that the sight of a meteor *presages* some misfortune —J.G.Frazer⟩ ⟨the yellow and vapory sunset . . . had *presaged* change —Thomas Hardy⟩ ⟨all the signs, the position of the stars, and the very disposition of nature *portended* war and disaster⟩ ⟨the appearance of these spectral flames, it is claimed, is not exclusively confined to *portending* the demise of someone already ill —*Irish Digest*⟩ FOREBODE indicates a feeling, indefinable, perhaps ill-based, but insistent and worrisome, or an indication calling forth worrisome or dread feeling ⟨his heart *forebodes* a mystery —Alfred Tennyson⟩ BODE applies to indication of future probability, often indefinite and often dire ⟨an eternal nightmare which, even for the richest and safest of nations, *bodes* catastrophes —A.L.Guérard⟩ ⟨the mood of quiet, grim resolution which here prevails *bodes* ill for those who conspired and collaborated to murder world peace —F.D.Roosevelt⟩ ⟨the dynamics of social change, which is *foreboded* in the emotional tensions of individuals —Franz Alexander⟩

fore·tell·able \(ˈ)=ˌtelәbәl\ *adj* **:** being of a kind that may be anticipated and foretold ⟨a ~ disaster⟩

fore·tell·er \(ˈ)=ˈtelә(r)\ *n* **:** one that foretells **:** a predictor or prophet

forethigh \ˈ=ˌ=\ *n* [*fore-* + *thigh*] **:** the part of the forelimb of a quadruped (as a horse) lying between elbow and knee

forethink \=ˈ=\ *vb* [ME *forthinken, forethinken, forthenken, forethenken,* fr. OE *forethencan,* fr. *fore-* + *thencan* to think — more at THINK] *vt* **:** to consider (something) beforehand; *broadly* **:** to anticipate in the mind **:** PROGNOSTICATE **~** *vi, obs* **:** to think beforehand **:** PLAN

fore·think·er \"+ә(r)\ *n* **:** one that forethinks

1fore·thought \ˈfōr,thȯt, ˈfȯr-, ˈfōә,-, ˈfȯ(ә),-, *usu* -ȯd·+V\ *n* [ME *forthought, forethought,* fr. *for-, fore-* + *thought,* n.] **1 :** a thinking or planning out in advance **:** PREMEDITATION ⟨this was no spontaneous crime but a product of careful ~⟩ **2 :** prior thought **:** CONSIDERATION ⟨turned without ~ and offered his hand⟩ **3 :** prudent thought or consideration for the future **:** provident care ⟨her ~ saw that we never lacked anything we really needed⟩ **syn** see PRUDENCE

2forethought \"\ *adj* [ME *forthought, forethought,* fr. past part. of *forthinken, forethinken*] **:** thought of or planned beforehand **:** AFORETHOUGHT; *often* **:** DELIBERATE

fore·thought·ed \-ȯdәd\ *adj* **:** having or marked by forethought ⟨a ~ person who is never at a loss for the next step⟩ — **fore·thought·ed·ly** *adv*

fore·thought·ful \(ˈ)=ˌthȯtfәl\ *adj* **:** full of or having forethought **:** PROVIDENT ⟨careful ~ planning⟩ — **fore·thought·ful·ly** \-fәlē, -li\ *adv* — **fore·thought·ful·ness** *n* -ES

fore·thought·less \ˈ=,=lәs\ *adj* **:** lacking forethought

foretime \ˈ=,=\ *n* [*fore-* + *time*] **:** former or past time **:** the time before the present ⟨the heroic ~ of our remotest fathers⟩

foretimed \(ˈ)=ˌ=\ *adj* [*fore-* + *timed*] **:** existing too soon **:** ANTEDATED ⟨a man ~ by a century⟩

1foretoken \ˈ=,==\ *n* [ME *fortoken, foretoken,* fr. OE *foretācn,* fr. *fore-* + *tācn* token, sign — more at TOKEN] **:** a premonitory sign or warning

2foretoken \=ˈ==\ *vt* [ME *fortokenen, foretokenen,* fr. *fortoken, foretoken,* n.] **:** to serve as advance warning of **:** FORESHOW, PROMISE ⟨the clear air and bright sunset seemed to ~ good weather⟩

fore–tooth \ˈ=,=\ *n* [*fore-* + *tooth*] **:** one of the teeth in the forepart of the mouth **:** INCISOR

fore·top \ˈfōr,täp, ˈfȯr-, ˈfōә,-, ˈfȯ(ә),- *or in sense 3* -_tәp\ *n* [ME *fortop, foretop,* fr. *for-, fore-* fore- + *top*] **1** *archaic* **:** the front of the crown of the head; *also* **:** the crown of the head **2 :** hair on the forepart of the head: as **a** *archaic* **:** an ornamental arrangement of the front of a wig or hairdo **b :** the forelock of a horse **3 a :** the platform at the head of a ship's foremast — see SHIP illustration **b :** FORETOPMAN

fore–topgallant \ˌ=,täpˌgalәnt, -_tә(p)ˌ-\ *adj* [*fore-* + *topgallant*] **:** of, relating to, or being a part (as a mast, sail, or yard) next above the fore-topmast ⟨the *fore-topgallant* sail⟩ — see SAIL illustration

fore·top·man \=ˈtäpmәn; ˈ=,täpmәn, -_tәp-\ *n, pl* **foretopmen** [*foretop* + *man*] **:** a member of a ship's crew on duty on the foremast and above

fore–topmast \=ˈ=,mast, -,maa(ә)st, -,mȧst, -_mәst\ *n* [*fore-* + *topmast*] **:** a ship's mast next above the foremast

fore–topsail \-,sāl, -_sәl\ *n* [*fore-* + *topsail*] **:** the sail above the foresail set on the fore-topmast — see SAIL illustration

foretruck \ˈ=,=\ *n* [*fore-* + *truck*] **:** the truck at the head of a foremast

foreturn \ˈ=,=\ *n* [*fore-* + *turn*] **:** the twist of the yarns or wires composing a strand of a rope — compare AFTERTURN

1for·ev·er \fәˈrevә(r), fȯˈ- *sometimes* fәˈevә *or* fȯˈevә\ *adv* [ME *for ever*] **1 :** for a limitless time or endless ages **:** EVERLASTING, ETERNALLY **2 :** at all times **:** ALWAYS, CONTINUALLY, INCESSANTLY

2forever \"\ *n* -S **:** ETERNITY

for·ev·er·more \fә,revәrˈmō(ә)r, fȯ,-, -ˈmȯ(ә)r; fә,revәˈmōә, fȯ,-, -ˈmȯ(ә) *sometimes* fә,e- *or* fȯ,e-\ *adv* [1*for* + *evermore*] **:** FOREVER

for·ev·er·ness *n* -ES **:** ETERNITY; *often* **:** a seemingly interminable duration ⟨will never forget the ~ of that day of waiting⟩

forewarm \=ˈ=\ *vt* [*fore-* + *warm*] **:** PREHEAT — **forewarmer** \ˈ=,==\ *n*

fore·warn \fōrˈwȯ(ә)rn, fȯr-; fōәˈwȯ(ә)n, fȯ(ә)ˈ-\ *vt* [ME *forwarnen, forewarnen,* fr. *for-, fore-* fore- + *warnen* to warn — more at WARN] **:** to warn in advance: as **a :** to give previous notice or information to ⟨we were ~*ed* to expect you before dark⟩ **b :** to caution in advance esp. in the form of an admonition ⟨let me ~ you, young man, you'll be sorry if you are late for supper⟩ **syn** see WARN

fore·warn·er \-nә(r)\ *n* [ME *forwarner, forewarner,* fr. *forwarnen, forewarnen* + *-er*] **:** one that forewarns

fore·warn·ing·ly \-niŋlē\ *adv* **:** so as to forewarn

forewaters \ˈ=,==\ *n pl* [*fore-* + *waters*] **:** AMNIOTIC FLUID

forewent *past of* FOREGO

fore wing *n* [3*fore*] **:** either member of the anterior pair of wings of a 4-winged insect

forewoman \ˈ=,==\ *n, pl* **forewomen** [*fore-* + *woman*] **:** FORELADY

fore·word \ˈfōr,wәrd, ˈfȯr-, -_wәrd; ˈfōә,wәd, ˈfȯ(ә),-, -_wәd\ *n* [*fore-* + *word;* prob. trans. of G *vorwort*] **:** PREFACE; *often* **:** front matter likely to be of interest but not necessarily essential for the understanding of the text of a book and commonly written by someone other than the author of the text

foreworld \ˈ=,=\ *n* [*fore-* + *world;* prob. trans. of G *vorwelt*] **:** the primeval or ancient world

foreworn *var of* FORWORN

1foreyard \ˈ=,=\ *n* [ME *foryerd, foreyerd,* fr. *for-, fore-* fore- + *yerd* yard — more at YARD (enclosure)] **:** a yard in front

2foreyard \"\ *n* [3*fore-* + *yard* (spar)] **:** the lowest yard on a foremast — see SHIP illustration

for·fairn \fәrˈfārn\ *adj* [ME *forfaren,* past part. of *forfaren* to perish, destroy, go astray, fr. *for-* + *faran* to travel, go — more at FARE] **1** *Scot* **:** FORLORN, BEREFT **2** *Scot* **:** worn out and decrepit (as with age) **:** EXHAUSTED

for·far \ˈfȯrfәr\ *also* **for·fars** \-rz\ *n, pl* **forfars** [fr. *Forfar,* county and town in Scotland where it was first made] **:** a coarse heavy linen cloth

for·far·shire \ˈ==,shi(ә)r, -iә-, -shә(r)\ *or* **forfar** *adj, usu cap* [fr. *Forfarshire* or county of *Forfar,* Scotland] **:** ANGUS

for·fault \ˈfȯrfȯt\ *archaic Scot var of* FORFEIT

1for·feit \ˈfȯrfәt, -ȯ(ә)f-, *usu* -әd·+V\ *n* -S [ME *forfait, forfet,* fr. MF, fr. past part. of *forfaire* to commit a crime, lose possession because of a crime committed, prob. fr. *for, fors* outside, out of + *faire* to make, do, fr. L *facere* — more at FORECLOSE, DO] **1** *obs* **:** MISDEED, CRIME, HARM **2 :** something which is lost or the right to which is alienated by a crime, offense, neglect of duty, or breach of contract **:** a thing forfeit or forfeited; *often* **:** FINE, MULCT, PENALTY ⟨he who murders pays the ~ of his life⟩ **3 :** forfeiture esp. of civil rights **4 a :** something deposited (as for making some mistake in a game) and then redeemed on payment of a fine **b forfeits** *pl but sing in constr* **:** a game in which forfeits are exacted

2forfeit \"\ *vb* -ED/-ING/-S [ME *forfaiten, forfeten,* fr. *forfait, forfet,* n.] *vi* **1** *obs* **:** to be guilty of a misdeed **2 :** to yield or be subject to a forfeit ⟨if they fail or refuse to make delivery by the 15th they must ~⟩ **~** *vt* **1 :** to lose or lose the right to by some error, fault, offense, or crime **:** alienate the right to possess by some neglect or crime **:** have to pay as a forfeit ⟨~*ed* his estate by treason⟩ ⟨~*ing* respect by his actions⟩ **2 a :** to subject (as property) to confiscation as a forfeit **b** *archaic* **:** to subject to forfeiture of property **:** confiscate the estate or possessions of — used of government action **3** *obs* **:** to cause the forfeiture or loss of

3forfeit \"\ *adj* [ME *forfait, forfet,* fr. MF, fr. past part. of *forfaire*] **:** lost or alienated for an error, fault, offense, breach of condition, legal duty, or crime ⟨thy wealth being ~ to the state —Shak.⟩

for·feit·able \-fәd·әbәl\ *adj* [ME *forfaitable, forfetable,* fr. *forfaiten, forfeten* + *-able*] **:** capable of being forfeited **:** subject to forfeiture — **for·feit·able·ness** *n* -ES

for·feit·er \-fәd·ә(r)\ *n* -S [ME *forfaitour, forfetour,* fr. MF *forfaiteur, forfetour,* fr. *forfait, forfet* + *-eur* -or] **:** one that forfeits

for·feit·ure \-fә,chu̇(ә)r, -,chu̇ә, -_chә(r), -,tyu̇-, -,tu̇-\ *n* -S [ME *forfaiture, forfeture,* fr. MF, fr. *forfait, forfet* + *-ure*] **1 a :** the divesting of the ownership of particular property of a person on account of the breach of a legal duty and without any compensation to him **:** the loss of property or money on account of one's breach of the terms of an agreement, bond, or other legal obligation **b :** loss of some right, privilege, estate, honor, office, or effects in consequence of a crime, offense, breach of condition, or other act **2 :** the loss of something through one's own act ⟨repeated roughness leads to ~ of the game⟩ ⟨by his trickery he gained only complete ~ of his father's trust⟩ **3 :** something (as property or money) lost as a forfeit

forfeiture bond *n* **:** a bond providing for forfeiture of the full penalty upon breach of the condition of the bond

for·fend \(ˈ)fȯrˈfend, ˈfȯ(ә)ˈ-\ *also* **fore·fend** \(ˈ)fōrˈ-, -ȯrˈ-, -ōә-,-ȯ(ә)ˈ-\ *vt* [ME *forfenden;* fr. *for-* + *fenden* to fend — more at FEND] **1 a** *archaic* **:** FORBID, PROHIBIT **b :** to ward off **:** AVERT, PREVENT ⟨may God ~ such an unhappy fate⟩ ⟨~ the crash of civilization —*Saturday Rev.*⟩ ⟨may Heaven ~ that she should die so young⟩ **2 :** PROTECT, PRESERVE, SECURE ⟨gathered in an isolated area to ~ themselves from the epidemic⟩

for·fi·ca·tion \,fȯ(r)fәˈkāshәn\ *n* -S [L *forfic-, forfex* scissors, shears (perh. alter. of *forcip-, forceps*) + E *-ation* — more at FORCEPS] **:** a deep furcation

for·fic·i·form \fȯrˈfisә,fȯrm\ *adj* [L *forfic-, forfex* + E *-iform*] **:** shaped like a scissors; *usu* **:** having or being forcipulate pedicellariae with two valves that do not cross when closed — compare FORCIPIFORM

for·fic·u·la \-ˈfikyәlә\ *n, cap* [NL, fr. L, small scissors, dim. of *forfic-, forfex*] **:** a genus (the type of the family Forficulidae) of earwigs that are sometimes destructive to cultivated bulbs

for·fic·u·late \-lәt, -,lāt\ *adj* [L *forficula* + E *-ate*] **:** FORKED, FURCATE — used esp. of plant or animal parts (as certain pedicellariae); compare FORCIPULATE

for·fi·cu·li·dae \,fȯrfәˈkyülә,dē\ *n pl, cap* [NL, fr. *Forficula,* type genus + *-idae*] **:** a large cosmopolitan family of insects (order Dermaptera) that have the abdomen depressed and the forceps flattened or cylindrical and that comprise the typical earwigs — see FORFICULA

for·fough·en *or* **for·fouch·en** \fәrˈfōkәn, -äk-, -ȯk-\ *or* **for·fought·en** \-ktәn\ *adj* [ME *forfoughten,* fr. *for-* + *foughten,* past part. of *fighten* to fight — more at FIGHT] *chiefly Scot* **:** worn out and depressed **:** EXHAUSTED

for·gainst \fәrˈgān(t)st, -gen-\ *prep* [ME *forgaines, forgenes,* fr. *fore-* + *againes, agenes* against — more at AGAINST] *chiefly Scot* **:** AGAINST

forgat *archaic past of* FORGET

for·gath·er \(ˈ)fȯrˈgathә(r), -ȯ(ә)ˈ-\ *or* **fore·gath·er** \(ˈ)fōrˈ-, -ȯrˈ-,-ōәˈ-, -ȯ(ә)ˈ-\ *vi* [ME (Sc dial.) *forgadderen,* fr. *for-* + *gadderen* to gather — more at GATHER] **1 a :** to come together ⟨these two old buzzards have got to *foregather* in secret —P.G. Wodehouse⟩ **:** CONVENE, ASSEMBLE ⟨where young musicians could ~ for stimulus and instruction —*Atlantic*⟩ **b :** to come together in a social group **:** consort socially ⟨~*s* with a squad of his admirers for lunch —H.H.Martin⟩ **2 :** to meet someone usu. incidentally ⟨~*ed* with many a homespun philosopher in his travels⟩

forgave *past of* FORGIVE

1forge \ˈfō(ә)rj, -ȯ(ә)rj,-ōәj,-ȯ(ә)j\ *n* -S [ME, fr. OF, fr. L *fabrica* workshop of an artisan who works in hard materials, smithy, fr. *fabr-, faber* artisan, smith + *-ica* (fr. fem. of *-icus* -ic) — more at DAFT] **1 a :** a place or establishment where iron or other metal is wrought by heating and hammering; *usu* **:** a furnace or a shop with its furnace where metal is heated and wrought **:** SMITHY **b :** a workshop where wrought iron is produced directly from the ore or where iron is rendered malleable by puddling and shingling **:** SHINGLING MILL, BLOOMERY **2** *obs* **:** MANUFACTURE, FABRICATION, PRODUCTION; *sometimes* **:** the act of forging

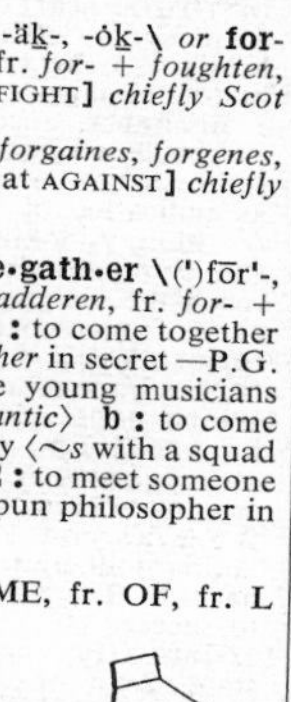

forge 1a

2forge \"\ *vb* -ED/-ING/-S [ME *forgen,* fr. MF *forgier,* fr. L *fabricare, fabricari* to fashion, construct, forge, fr. *fabrica*] *vt* **1 a :** to form by heating and hammering **:** beat (as a metal) into a particular shape ⟨Mars's armor *forged* for proof eterne —Shak.⟩ **b :** to form (metal) by a mechanical or hydraulic press with or without heat **2 :** to form or shape out in any way **:** FASHION, MAKE, PRODUCE ⟨attempting to ~ an agreement between the conflicting groups⟩ ⟨a man who has chosen to ~ himself a coherent outlook sooner than surrender to disruptive tendencies —Cecil Sprigge⟩ **3 :** to make or imitate falsely ⟨did not hesitate to ~ his own character references⟩ ⟨*forged* rare postage stamps that fooled expert philatelists⟩; *specif* **:** to alter (a writing) in respect of a material matter with intent to defraud ⟨he *forged* a check for $20⟩ **~** *vi* **1 :** to work at a forge **:** do forging **2 :** to commit forgery ⟨living by trickery and *forging*⟩ **3** *of a horse* **:** to make a clicking noise by overreaching so that a hind shoe hits a fore shoe **syn** see MAKE

3forge \"\ *vi* -ED/-ING/-S [origin unknown] **1 a :** to move forward or ahead steadily but slowly or gradually ⟨the ship continued to ~ ahead after the sails were furled⟩ **b :** to move with a sudden increase of speed and power ⟨the ship *forged* ahead as the breeze filled her sails⟩ ⟨the runner *forged* into the lead in the stretch⟩ **2 :** PROGRESS, ADVANCE ⟨companies that *forged* to prominence on a single basic invention⟩

forge·a·bil·i·ty \,=әˈbilәd·ē, -әtē, -i\ *n* **:** suitability for being forged ⟨some alloys exhibit greater ~ than others⟩

forge·able \ˈ=әbәl\ *adj* **:** capable of or suitable for being forged — used chiefly of metals

forge·man \ˈ=mәn\ *n, pl* **forgemen :** SMITH 1a

forg·er \ˈfōrjә(r), -ȯrj-, -ōәj-, -ȯ(ә)j-\ *n* -S [ME *forger, forgeour,* fr. MF *forgeur,* fr. *forgier* + *-eur* -or] **1 a** *obs* **:** an author or maker **b :** FALSIFIER; *specif* **:** a creator of false tales **c :** a person guilty of forgery (as of a document) **2 :** one that forges metals; *esp* **:** a person whose work is to forge a specified thing or material ⟨an iron ~⟩ ⟨experienced axle ~*s*⟩

for·gery \-j(ә)rē, -ri\ *n* -ES [2*forge* + *-ery*] **1** *obs* **:** the act or art of forging metal **2** *archaic* **:** the act of inventing or devising **:** INVENTION; *often* **:** FEIGNING, FICTION **3 :** an act of forging; *usu* **:** the crime of falsely and with fraudulent intent making or altering a writing or other instrument that if genuine might apparently be of legal effect on the rights of another — see FALSI CRIMEN **4 :** something produced by forging, fabricating, or counterfeiting ⟨17th century *forgeries* of medieval documents⟩ ⟨the *forgeries* of jealousy —Shak.⟩

forgery bond *n* **:** insurance against loss from forgery or alteration of negotiable instruments or evidences of debt or ownership

1for·get \fә(r)ˈget *also* fȯrˈ-, *usu* -ed·+V\ *vb* **for·got** \-gät, *usu* -äd·+V\ *or archaic* **for·gat** \-gat, *usu* -ad·+V\ **for·got·ten** \-gätᵊn\ *or* **forgot; forgetting; forgets** [ME *forgeten, foryeten,* fr. OE *forgietan, forgeotan, forgitan* (akin to OS *fargetan* to forget, OHG *firgezzan*), fr. *for-* + *-gietan, -geotan, -gitan* (akin to ON *geta* to get) — more at GET] *vt* **1 a :** to lose the remembrance of **:** let go from the memory **:** be unable to think of or recall ⟨soon *forgot* her father's warning⟩ ⟨*forgetting* past favors and old friends⟩ **b** *obs* **:** to lose the power or use of **:** cease from doing **2 :** to omit or disregard unintentionally **:** NEGLECT ⟨I *forgot* to close the door⟩ **3 :** to treat with inattention or disregard **:** SLIGHT ⟨the successful leader does not ~ his subordinates⟩ ⟨*forgot* her lessons until bedtime⟩ ⟨lend a hand and I'll not ~ you when I'm paid⟩ **4 :** to disregard intentionally **:** OVERLOOK — usu. used in the imperative ⟨~ it⟩ **~** *vi* **1 :** to cease remembering or noticing ⟨she *forgot* about the note to her mother⟩ ⟨if we forgive and ~ we may hope to be forgiven⟩ **2 :** to fail to become mindful at the intended or proper time ⟨*forgot* about paying the bill until the discount date was past⟩ ⟨if you ~ about turning down the oven you will burn the roast⟩ **syn** see NEGLECT — **forget oneself :** to do something or behave in a manner unworthy of one **:** lose one's dignity, temper, or self-control

2forget \"\ *n* -S **:** an act of forgetting

3for·get \ˈfȯrjәt, -,jet\ *n* -S [by alter.] **:** FOURCHETTE 2

for·get·ful \fә(r)ˈgetfәl *also* fȯrˈ-\ *adj* [ME *forgetful, foryetful,* fr. *forgeten, foryeten* + *-ful*] **1 :** apt to forget **:** having a poor memory ⟨he was so ~ that he constantly missed appointments⟩ **2 :** characterized by or indulging in heedless or negligent failure to remember or pay attention ⟨~ of her responsibilities⟩ **3 :** inducing oblivion **:** causing an end to awareness or consideration ⟨lulled by ~ sleep⟩

syn OBLIVIOUS, UNMINDFUL: FORGETFUL may describe a tendency not to remember through defective memory; it may imply a negligent or heedless failure to keep in mind something that should be remembered ⟨so *forgetful* as to be duped into making "deals" at the expense of our allies —F.D.Roosevelt⟩ OBLIVIOUS may suggest a failure to notice, an inability to remember due to exterior forces or conditions, or a determination to hold from one's cognition; the word is sometimes a synonym of *unconscious* and *unaware* ⟨those who hope to render themselves, through absorption in the mere habit and technique of writing poetry, *oblivious* to the harsh interruptions of reality —C.D.Lewis⟩ ⟨I was often seasick but that semicomatose condition has its advantage—it makes one *oblivious* to danger —Herbert Hoover⟩ ⟨he is *oblivious* of all distractions when he is wrapped up in his work —E.J.Kahn⟩ UNMINDFUL may be close to FORGETFUL; it may suggest inattention and heedlessness; it may indicate deliberate purposive ignoring and thrusting from the mind ⟨totally *unmindful* of their mutual dependence —*Amer. Guide Series: Minn.*⟩ ⟨we sat about *unmindful* of the winds and the snow —H.A. Chippendale⟩

for·get·ful·ly \-fәlē, -li\ *adv* **:** in a forgetful manner

for·get·ful·ness *n* -ES [ME *forgetfulnesse, foryetfulnesse,* fr. *forgetful, foryetful* + *-nesse* -ness] **:** the act or state of being forgetful

for·ge·tive \ˈfōrjә|d·iv, -ȯj-|, tiv\ *adj* [prob. fr. 2*forge* + *-tive* (as in *inventive*)] **:** INVENTIVE, PRODUCTIVE, IMAGINATIVE

forget–me–not \=ˈ=(,)=,=\ *n* -S **1 a :** any of several small herbaceous plants constituting the genus *Myosotis,* having usu. bright blue or white flowers arranged in a scorpioid raceme, and including some that are cultivated as ornamentals; *esp* **:** a perennial herb (*M. scorpioides*) with angular succulent stems, rough pubescent leaves, and sky-blue flowers with yellow centers that is prob. native to Europe but now widely distributed in temperate No. America **b :** any of various plants resembling the forget-me-nots esp. in clear blue color of flowers — usu. used with a qualifying term; see CAPE FORGET-ME-NOT, CHINESE FORGET-ME-NOT **2** *or* **forget–me–not blue a :** a variable color averaging a light blue that is greener and paler than average della Robbia blue **b :** a pale to grayish blue that is greener and less strong than Alice blue — called also *myosotis blue*

forgets *pres 3d sing of* FORGET, *pl of* FORGET

for·get·ta·ble \fә(r)ˈged·әbәl, -etәb- *also* fȯrˈ-\ *adj* [1*forget* + *-able*] **:** fit or likely to be forgotten — **for·get·ta·ble·ness** *n* -ES

for·get·ter \-ˈged·ә(r), -etә-\ *n* -S [ME *forgeter, foryeter,* fr. *forgeten, foryeten* to forget + *-er*] **:** one that forgets esp. habitually or deliberately

for·get·tery \-ed·әrē, -etә-, -ri\ *n* -ES [1*forget* + *-ery*] **:** a faculty for forgetting **:** a poor memory ⟨a remarkable ~ for those irksome little chores⟩ ⟨a well-managed ~ is often as important as a good memory⟩

forgetting *pres part of* FORGET

for·get·ting·ly *adv* **:** by forgetting **:** ABSENTMINDEDLY

forge water *n* [1*forge*] **:** a tonic formerly popular consisting of water in which heated irons have been thrust

forge welding *n* **:** the uniting of two pieces of hot metal by hammering them together on an anvil

for·gie \fәrˈgē\ *Scot var of* FORGIVE

forging *n* -S [ME, fr. gerund of *forgen* to forge — more at FORGE] **1 :** the act of one that forms by heating and hammering **2 :** a piece of forged work (as in iron) **3 :** FORGERY 3

forging machine *n* **:** a forging press that operates in a horizontal position (as for the upsetting of bolts)

forging press *n* **:** a punch press that forges metal by subjecting it to heavy pressure between dies

forging roll *n* **:** a rolling mill that forges comparatively uniform shapes by rolls of variable radii around the circumference

for·giv·able \fә(r)ˈgivәbәl *also* fȯrˈ-\ *adj* **:** being of a kind that can be forgiven ⟨a ~ error⟩ — **for·giv·able·ness** \-nәs\ *n* -ES

for·giv·ably \-әblē, -li\ *adv* **:** in a forgivable manner

for·give \fә(r)ˈgiv *also* fȯrˈ-\ *vb* **for·gave** \-ˈgāv\ **for·giv·en** \-ˈgivәn, -ibᵊm\ **forgiving; forgives** [ME *foryeven, foryiven, forgeven, forgiven,* fr. OE *forgiefan, forgifan* (akin to OS *fargeƀan* to give, forgive, promise, OHG *firgeban* to give, forgive, Goth *fragiban* to forgive), fr. *for-* + *giefan, gifan* to give — more at GIVE] *vt* **1 :** to cease to feel resentment against on account of wrong committed **:** give up claim to requital from or retribution upon (an offender) **:** ABSOLVE, PARDON ⟨Father, ~ them, for they do not know what they are doing —Lk 23:34 (NCE)⟩ **2 a :** to give up resentment of or claim to requital for (an offense or wrong) **:** remit the penalty of ⟨and their sins should be *forgiven* them —Mk 4:12 (AV)⟩ **b :** to grant relief from **:** refrain from exacting ⟨*forgave* his tenants thousands of dollars in back rent⟩ ⟨a loophole in the tax law that ~*s* all if a taxpayer is out of the U.S. —*Time*⟩ **~** *vi* **:** to grant forgiveness **syn** see EXCUSE

for·give·ness *n* -ES [ME *foryevenesse, foryivenesse, forgevenesse, forgivenesse,* fr. OE *forgifnes, forgifenes,* fr. *forgifen* (past part. of *forgiefan, forgifan*) + *-nes* -ness] **1 :** an act of forgiving or state of being forgiven; *often* **:** REMISSION ⟨the ~ of the tax liability . . . should not result in such a serious disturbance to the revenues —*Jour. of Accountancy*⟩ **2** *archaic* **:** disposition to pardon **:** willingness to forgive

for·giv·er \fə(r)ˈgivə(r) *also* fȯrˈ-\ *n* -s [ME *foryever, foryiver, forgever, forgiver,* fr. *foryeven, foryiven, forgeven, forgiven* + *-er*] **:** one that forgives

forgiving *adj* **:** willing or able to forgive **:** characterized by forgiveness ⟨a kindly ~ nature⟩ ⟨said a ~ word of welcome to his erring son⟩ — **for·giv·ing·ly** *adv* — **for·giv·ing·ness** *n* -ES

for·go \(ˈ)fȯrˈgō, ˈfȯ(ə)ˈ-\ *also* **fore·go** \(ˈ)fōr-, -ȯr-, -ōə-, -ȯ(ə)ˈ-\ *vt* **for·went** *also* **fore·went** \-ˈwent\ **for·gone** *also* **fore·gone** \-ˈgȯn\ **for·go·ing** *also* **fore·go·ing** \-ˈgōiŋ\ **forgoes** *also* **foregoes** [ME *forgon, forgan,* fr. OE *forgān* to pass by, forgo (akin to OS *fargangan* to pass away, OHG *firgangan* to pass away, Goth *faurgangan* to go by), fr. *for-* + *gān* to go — more at GO] **1** *archaic* **:** to depart from **:** QUIT, LEAVE, FORSAKE **2 :** to abstain from **:** let slip or pass **:** relinquish the enjoyment or advantage of **:** give up **:** RESIGN, RENOUNCE ⟨never *forwent* an opportunity of honest profit —R.L.Stevenson⟩ ⟨decided to ~ dessert for a few days⟩

syn ABNEGATE, ESCHEW, FORBEAR, SACRIFICE: FORGO is usu. used when one abstains from or gives up an available pleasure or advantage on the grounds of policy or expediency ⟨he agreed . . . to *forgo* all remuneration until his apprenticeship was completed —Van Wyck Brooks⟩ ⟨he has asked his people to forsake all narrow views of their own security and prosperity and . . . to *forgo* many immediate benefits —*Economist*⟩ ⟨to *forgo* wartime profits —*New Republic*⟩ ⟨this is a book no theater lover should lightly *forgo* —*Spectator*⟩ ABNEGATE is usu. used when one surrenders, relinquishes, or renounces on grounds of policy, expediency, or sometimes principle, something that one already has, the idea of self-denial often being strongly implied ⟨*abnegate* all rights to a property⟩ ⟨smile in a self-*abnegating* way⟩ ESCHEW suggests a more all-out abstinence from, often a positive avoidance of, something, usu. something inadvisable or distasteful, or something wrong but tempting ⟨the normal vegetarian only *eschews* fish, flesh, and fowl —N.C.Wright⟩ ⟨the laudable aim of *eschewing* controversial philosophical issues in a textbook —G.B.Keene⟩ ⟨it *eschews* cartoon, illustration, graph, or any device to attract attention —*Marketing*⟩ ⟨the emotions are *eschewed* as distorters of true knowledge —S.J.Beck⟩ FORBEAR is used when one exercises patient self-restraint in refraining from some action on grounds of prudence or high resolve ⟨she had forgotten several things . . . but she *forbore* to mention it —Elizabeth Goudge⟩ ⟨*forbear* to complain even though treated unjustly⟩ SACRIFICE implies and has generally implied a self-denial, a renunciation of an advantage, usu. immediate, in the interests of a future advantage or of someone or something else, as a religious or ethical value, but has come to apply more frequently to the giving up of something of value in the interests of something else, often of less value ⟨the individual will gladly *sacrifice* both time and money in the party interest —*Nation's Business*⟩ ⟨*sacrificed* their fortune in the world for theology's sake —H.O.Taylor⟩ ⟨significantly important news is often *sacrificed* for whatever can be depended on to make headlines —F.L.Mott⟩ ⟨a writer who, at times, *sacrificed* his talents to his ambition and pursuit of power —Daniel George⟩

for·go·er \-ˈgōə(r)\ *n* -s **:** one that forgoes

for good *adv* **:** PERMANENTLY ⟨I certainly hope they are gone *for good*⟩

forgot *past of* FORGET

forgotten *past part of* FORGET

forgotten man *n* **:** a person or category of persons that receives less consideration or attention than is merited ⟨one of the *forgotten men* of American literature —Jay Leyda⟩ ⟨the ultimate consumer has become a *forgotten man* to industrial designers⟩

for-hire \ˌ=ˈ=\ *adj* [fr. the phrase *for hire*] **:** available or offered for rent ⟨*for-hire* vehicles⟩

for·hoo \fərˈhü\ *or* **for·hoo·ie** \-ˈhüē\ *vt* [ME *forhowen, forhohien* to despise, reject, abandon, fr. OE *forhogian* (akin to OS *farhuggian* to despise, OHG *farhuggen*), fr. *for-* + *hogian* to care for, think about; akin to OE *hycgan* to think, consider, understand — more at HUG] *Scot* **:** to forsake or abandon

fo·rin·sec \fəˈrin(t)sək\ *adj* [ML *forinsecus,* fr. L, from outside, fr. *foris* outside + *-insecus* (as in *extrinsecus* on the outside) — more at FORUM, EXTRINSIC] *of obligations under feudal law* **:** extraordinary in nature or performed away from the holding of a mesne lord for his superior ⟨~ service included foreign military service, the supplying of labor, and certain payments⟩

fo·rint \ˈfō(ˌ)rint\ *n* -s [Hung, fr. It *fiorino* florin — more at FLORIN] **1 :** a Hungarian florin **2 a :** the basic monetary unit of Hungary as established in 1946 — see MONEY table **b :** a coin representing one forint unit

fo·ris·fa·mil·i·ate \ˌfōrəsfəˈmilēˌāt\ *vb* -ED/-ING/-S [ML *forisfamiliatus,* past part. of *forisfamiliare,* fr. L *foris* outside + *familia* family — more at FORUM, FAMILY] *vt, Scots law* **:** to portion off so as to exclude further claim of inheritance **:** emancipate from paternal authority ~ *vi* **:** to renounce a legal title to a further share of paternal inheritance — **fo·ris·fa·mil·i·a·tion** \-ˌmilēˈāshən\ *n* -s

for·jes·ket *or* **for·jes·kit** \fərˈjeskət\ *or* **for·jas·kit** \-ˈjaskət\ *adj* [alter. (influenced by *for-*) of *disjaskit*] *Scot* **:** weary or broken down **:** EXHAUSTED ⟨~ sair, with weary legs —Robert Burns⟩

forjudge *var of* FOREJUDGE

¹fork \ˈfȯ(ə)rk, ˈfō(ə)k\ *n* -s *often attrib* [ME *forke,* fr. OE & ONF; OE *force, forca,* fr. L *furca;* ONF *forque,* fr. L *furca;* perh. akin to Lith *žirklės* scissors] **1 a :** an instrument or implement consisting of a handle with a shank terminating in two or more prongs used for piercing, holding, taking up, pitching, or digging something **b :** a small instrument of this description for use in manipulating food esp. in serving and eating — see DESSERT FORK, DINNER FORK, OYSTER FORK, SALAD FORK **c :** any of various pronged grappling devices often with automatic trip arrangements that are used in conjunction with a tackle for handling loose bulky material (as hay or straw) **d :** FORKLIFT **2 :** a forked part, tool, or piece of equipment (as a tuning fork): as **a** *obs* **:** GALLOWS 1a **b :** a barbed point (as of an arrow) **c :** the lower part of the human body where the legs diverge from the trunk usu. including the legs **d :** CRUTCH 4a **e :** the end of the pallet lever of a lever-escapement watch that consists of a slot, two horns, and a guard finger and that imparts an impulse to the balance roller **f :** the front part of a saddletree **g :** FILLING FORK **h :** a long iron or steel rod with a forked end used in glass manufacturing for carrying finished articles to the lehr **i :** a forked electrical fitting for holding an insulator **j :** a 2-pronged support (as for the axle of a wheel or caster) ⟨the front ~ of a bicycle⟩ — see BICYCLE illustration **3 a :** a division into branches or the place where something divides into branches ⟨came to a ~ in the road⟩ ⟨the ~ of a fish's tail⟩ ⟨pruning should eliminate weak ~*s* at which a tree may later split⟩ **b :** a place where two or more streams flow together to form a larger waterway **:** CONFLUENCE; *often* **:** an area of land or a settlement bounded by or adjoining such a fork — often used in pl. and in place names ⟨stopped for the night at Miller's *Forks*⟩ **4 a :** one of the branches into which something forks ⟨take the left ~ at the crossroads⟩ **b :** an alternative or choice ⟨after certain basic training the student specializes in one of two ~*s*⟩ **5 a :** an attack by one chess piece (as a pawn or knight) on two pieces simultaneously **b :** TENACE **6 :** a change in elevation of artillery capable of producing a change in the range equal to four range probable errors

²fork \"\ *vb* -ED/-ING/-S [ME *forken,* fr. *forke,* n.] *vi* **1 :** to divide into two or more branches ⟨just over the hill the road ~*s*⟩ **2** *of lightning* **:** to play in zigzag or forked streaks **3 a :** to use a fork ⟨he could ~ all day against any two men in the crew⟩ **b :** to make a turn into or travel a fork ⟨the car ~*ed* to the left⟩ ~ *vt* **1 :** to give the form of a fork to **:** cause to be forked ⟨~*ing* her fingers⟩ **2 :** to raise or pitch (as hay or earth) with a fork ⟨~*ed* down a manger of hay⟩ **3 :** to attack (two chessmen) simultaneously (as with a knight or pawn) **4** *chiefly West* **:** to mount (a horse) esp. with a quick swing ⟨he jumped out of the buggy, ~*ed* his horse, and took after her —J.F.Dobie⟩ **5 :** to pay or contribute — used with *over, out,* or sometimes *up* ⟨he had to ~ over $5000 to keep the matter quiet⟩ ⟨not everybody can afford to ~ out a premium to get a new car⟩ **syn** see BRANCH

fork·able \-kəbəl\ *adj* **:** fit to handle or transport with a fork

fork ball *n* **:** a pitched ball in baseball that is gripped between the forked index and second fingers with the thumb underneath and delivered with a snap of the wrist

fork beam *n* **:** BEAM ARM 1

forked \ˈfȯ(ə)rkt, ˈfō(ə)kt, -kəd\ *adj* [ME, fr. past part. of *forken* to fork] **1 a :** resembling a fork esp. in having one end divided into two or more branches or points ⟨a bird with a ~ tail⟩ ⟨~ lightning⟩ **b :** having or distinguished by a fork or a forked part ⟨a ~ road⟩ ⟨the long-*forked* chimney swifts⟩ **2** *obs* **a :** having a double meaning **:** AMBIGUOUS, EQUIVOCAL **b :** HORNED; *often* **:** CUCKOLDED — **fork·ed·ly** \-kədlē, -li\ *adv* — **fork·ed·ness** *n* -ES

forked catchfly *or* **forking catchfly** *n* **:** a European weedy annual herb (*Silene dichotoma*) having flowers with notched petals

forked chain *n* **:** BRANCHED CHAIN

forked chickweed *n* **:** any of various plants of the genus *Paronychia; esp* **:** a slender small branching weed (*P. canadensis*)

forked leaf *also* **fork-leaf blackjack** *n* **:** TURKEY OAK b

forked worm *n* **:** GAPEWORM

for keeps *adv* **:** PERMANENTLY

fork·er \ˈfȯrkər, ˈfō(ə)kə(r\ *n* -s **1 :** one that forks; *esp* **:** a workman who lifts, transfers, or holds with a fork **2** *obs* **:** something forked

fork·ful \ˈ=ˌfu̇l\ *n, pl* **fork·fuls** \-lz\ *or* **forks·ful** \-ks,fu̇l\ **:** as much as a fork will hold

forkhead \ˈ=ˌ=\ *n* -s **1 :** an arrowhead with two or occas. three prongs pointing forward **2 :** a forked end of a rod

fork·i·ness \ˈfȯrkēnəs, -ō(ə)k-, -kin-\ *n* -ES **:** the quality or state of being forky

forking *pres part of* FORK

fork length *n* **:** the length of a fish measured from the most anterior part of the head to the deepest point of the notch in the tail fin

fork·less \ˈ=ləs\ *adj* **:** having no fork

forklift \ˈ=ˌ=\ *n* **:** a machine for hoisting heavy objects (as boxes, bales, or metal bars) by means of a row of steel fingers inserted under the load and drawn up a vertical guide to the required level usu. by hydraulic means

forklike \ˈ=ˌ=\ *adj* **:** resembling a fork or functioning like the tines of a fork

fork·man \ˈ=mən\ *n, pl* **forkmen :** FORKER 1; *usu* **:** a metalworker who with a fork or hook guides the bloom through the roughing mill or billets of nonferrous metals from furnace to extruding press

forks *pl of* FORK, *pres 3d sing of* FORK

forktail \ˈ=ˌ=\ *n* **:** any of various fork-tailed animals (as birds or fishes): as **a :** SWORDFISH **b :** KITE **c :** GRILSE **d :** any of various chiefly black and white thrushes (genus *Enicurus*) widely distributed in the Oriental region and having long deeply forked tails

forktail cat *n* **:** BLUE CATFISH

fork-tailed \ˈ=ˈ=\ *or* **forktail** \ˈ=ˌ=\ *adj* **:** having the tail or posterior end of the body deeply cleft ⟨a *fork-tailed* schistosome cercaria⟩; *usu* **:** having the outer feathers or rays of the tail much longer than the central ones — used of birds and fishes

fork-tailed flycatcher *n* **:** a tropical American flycatcher (*Muscivora tyrannus*) that is rather like a swallow in appearance, with a black head and a long deeply forked black tail

fork-tailed gull *n* **:** SABINE'S GULL

fork-tailed kite *n* **:** SWALLOW-TAILED KITE

fork-tailed petrel \ˈ=ˌ=-\ *also* **forked-tailed petrel** \ˈ=ˌ=-\ *n* **:** a bluish gray white-marked petrel (*Oceanodroma furcata*) that has a deeply forked tail and is widely distributed in the northern Pacific; *also* **:** any of several closely related birds with more or less forked tails

forktail perch *n* **:** either of two commercially important embiotocid food fishes (*Damalichthys vacca* and *Phanerodon furcatus*) of the Pacific coast of No. America

fork-tongued \ˈ=ˈ=\ *or* **forked-tongued** \ˈ=ˈ=\ *adj* **:** given to prevarication

fork truck *or* **forklift truck** \ˈ=ˌ=-\ *n* **:** a lift truck equipped with a forklift

forky \ˈfȯrkē, -ō(ə)kē, -ki\ *adj, often* -ER/-EST **:** divided into or terminating in two or more branches **:** FORKED ⟨a ~ beard⟩

for·la·na \fȯrˈlänä, -nə\ *also* **fur·la·na** \fu̇rˈ-\ *n, pl* **forla·ne** \-(ˌ)nā\ *or* **forlanas** [It, fr. fem. of *forlano, furlano,* adj., var. of *friulano* Friulian, fr. *Friuli,* former duchy in northeastern Italy] **1 :** a lively old Italian dance in 6/8 or 6/4 time **2 :** the music for a forlana

¹for·lorn \fə(r)ˈlȯ(ə)rn, -ō(ə)n\ *adj, often* -ER/-EST [ME *forloren, forlorn* (past part. of *forlesen, forleosen* to lose), fr. OE *forloren,* past part. of *forlēosan* to lose (akin to OS *farliosan* to lose, OHG *furliosan,* Goth *fraliusan*), fr. *for-* + *lēosan* to lose — more at LOSE] **1** *obs* **:** LOST, ASTRAY **:** **a :** morally abandoned **b :** RUINED, DOOMED **2 a :** FORSAKEN, DESTITUTE, BEREFT — usu. used postpositively and with *of* ⟨a person ~ of hope⟩ **b :** deserted and desolate **:** sad and lonely esp. by reason of emptiness or abandonment ⟨a ~ huddle of sagging buildings⟩ **3 a :** being in poor condition **:** MISERABLE, DISORDERED, BEDRAGGLED, WRETCHED ⟨a few ~ chickens scratched about the muddy yard⟩ ⟨never did I see such a ~ woebegone face⟩ **b :** pathetic or pitiable esp. as indicative of loneliness, distress, or sorrow ⟨a ~ cry⟩ ⟨~ hungry-looking waifs⟩ **4 :** having but the barest plausibility or promise **:** nearly hopeless ⟨one final ~ attempt to reach the sinking ship in time to rescue the crew⟩ **syn** see ALONE, DESPONDENT

²forlorn \"\ *n* -s **1** *archaic* **:** one who is forlorn **2** *obs* **a :** forlorn hope or a member of one **b :** VANGUARD

forlorn hope *n* [by folk etymology fr. D *verloren hoop,* lit., lost band] **1 a :** a body of men selected usu. from volunteers to attempt a breach, scale a wall, or perform other perilous service esp. in advance of the main force **b :** a member of such a body **2 :** a desperate or extremely difficult enterprise **:** an undertaking unlikely to be completed successfully or without great hazard **3 a :** a vain or faint hope **b :** something unlikely to succeed

for·lorn·i·ty \-nəd·ē, -ətē, -i\ *n* -ES **1 :** forlorn quality or state **2 :** a forlorn thing or person

for·lorn·ly *adv* **:** in a forlorn manner

for·lorn·ness \=ˈ=nəs\ *n* -ES [ME *forlorenesse,* fr. *forloren, forlorn* + *-nesse* -ness] **:** forlorn quality or state; *esp* **:** desolate isolated condition or location ⟨the complete ~ of the scene⟩

¹form \ˈfō(ə)rm, -ō(ə)m\ *n* -s *often attrib* [ME *forme, fourme,* fr. OF, fr. L *forma,* perh. modif. of Gk *morphē;* perh. akin to Gk *marmairein* to flash, sparkle — more at MORN] **1** *obs* **:** IMAGE, REPRESENTATION **2 a :** the shape and structure of something as distinguished from the material of which it is composed ⟨the carefully graded ~ of the curves⟩ **b :** a body esp. of a human being as distinguished (1) by external appearance or (2) from the countenance or visage **:** FIGURE ⟨the dress displayed her ~ to advantage⟩ **c** *archaic* **:** pleasing external appearance **:** BEAUTY ⟨he had no ~ or comeliness —Isa 53:2 (RSV)⟩ **3 a :** the ideal or intrinsic character of anything or something that imposes this character; *sometimes* **:** a pattern or schema **b** *in metaphysics* **:** the essential nature of a thing as distinguished from the matter in which this is embodied: as (1) *in Platonic philosophy* **:** a transcendent idea, universal essence, or subsistent entity (2) *in Aristotelian or scholastic philosophy* **:** the component of a thing that determines it in its kind or species **:** FORMAL CAUSE — often distinguished from *matter* (3) *in Baconian philosophy* **:** the basis constituting the condition for the existence of any given nature or quality (as density, heat, or color) **c** *in Kantian philosophy* **:** one of the formative modes of perception and cognition regarded as a subjective factor molding reality as given in sensation into systematic experience esp. as regards spatial and temporal order **4 a** *obs* **:** manner, method, or style (as of proceeding) **b :** established method of expression or practice **:** fixed or formal way of proceeding **:** procedure according to rule or rote **c :** a prescribed and usu. set order of words **:** FORMULA ⟨the ~ of the marriage service in the prayer book⟩ **d** *obs* **:** RECIPE, PRESCRIPTION **e** (1) **:** a printed or typed document with blank spaces for insertion of required or requested specific information ⟨a ~ for a deed⟩ ⟨be sure to fill all blanks on your tax ~⟩ (2) **:** a document of this kind which is attached to and forms an endorsement of a property insurance policy and in which is filled in a description of the property insured; *broadly* **:** such an endorsement containing alterations or modifications of the provisions of a standard policy **5 a :** conduct regulated by extraneous controls (as of custom or etiquette) **:** CEREMONY, CONVENTIONALITY, FORMALITY; *sometimes* **:** show without substance **:** empty pretentious appearance or ceremony **b :** a prescribed manner of behaving (as in society) ⟨the rigid ~ of the imperial court⟩ **:** an act of conduct or mode of procedure prescribed (as by custom or a code of etiquette) ⟨the complex ~*s* and taboos of the savage⟩ **:** FORMALITY, CEREMONY, CONVENTIONALITY ⟨knew all the ~*s* for wooing a proper young miss⟩ **c :** manner or conduct as tested by a prescribed or accepted standard — used with a qualifying adjective ⟨his behavior was often bad ~⟩ ⟨such poor ~ is to be deplored⟩ **d :** manner or style of performing or accomplishing something esp. when recognized standards of technique exist ⟨he is a strong swimmer but weak on ~⟩ **6 a :** the resting place of a hare or occas. of another animal **b :** a long seat **:** JOINT STOOL, BENCH ⟨seated on a low ~ against the wall⟩ **c :** a supporting frame model of the human figure or other device used for displaying merchandise in a store; *also* **:** a proportioned and often adjustable model for fitting clothes **d :** something that holds, supports, and gives or determines shape; *esp* **:** a mold in which concrete is placed to set **7** *obs* **a :** degree of quality, dignity, eminence, or excellence **b :** a class or rank esp. in society or official life **8 a :** the total combination of the letterpress matter imposed and locked up in a chase with the furniture, quoins, and the chase itself **b :** set-up type ⟨how to move ~*s* from the galley to the stone⟩ ⟨wind the cord clockwise around the ~⟩ **9 a :** one of the different modes of existence, action, or manifestation of a particular thing or substance **:** KIND, MODIFICATION, SPECIES, VARIETY ⟨the diamond, graphite, and soot are allotropic ~*s* of carbon⟩ ⟨the democratic ~ of government⟩ ⟨one ~ of respiratory disorder⟩ ⟨the ~ of vegetation typical of xerophytic areas⟩ **b** *also* **for·ma** \-mə\ **:** a botanical taxonomic category ranking below a variety and consisting of individuals that differ from those of related forms in one or very few characters ⟨the *discretiflorus* ~ of the rush *Juncus tenuis*⟩; *also* **:** a member of such a category **c :** a distinguishable group of organisms — commonly used by zoologists to avoid taxonomic implications ⟨the southern ~ of the hairy woodpecker⟩ **10 a :** orderly arrangement or method of arrangement (as in the presentation of ideas) **:** manner of coordinating elements (as of an artistic production or course of reasoning); *sometimes* **:** a particular kind or instance of such arrangement ⟨the sonnet is a poetical ~⟩ **b** *in logic* (1) **:** the structure, pattern, or schema possessed in common by different logical statements esp. as disclosed through the substitution of variables for different descriptive terms so that the manner in which the terms are interrelated becomes apparent (2) **:** the structure of an argument or an inference as symbolized by the use of variables (3) **:** the logical properties of a word, expression, or symbol as exhibited by its contribution to the logical form of statements in which it may properly occur **c :** the structural element, plan, or design of a work of art; *specif* **:** the combinations and relations to each other of various components (as lines, colors, and volumes in a visual work of art or themes and elaborations in an aural work of art) ⟨~ consists in a pattern of relationships that gives unity to a complex of perceptual elements —F.S.Haserot⟩ — often contrasted with *content* **d :** a relationship between or among elements of raw subject matter (as in a painting) which is sensed and made structural by the artist; *also* **:** a visible and measurable unit defined by a contour **:** a bounded surface or volume or a system of visible elements **e** (1) **:** the structural pattern of a musical composition (2) **:** a specific type (as fugue, rondo, sonata) of such pattern **11 :** a class or grade in a British secondary school or in certain American private schools — see SIXTH FORM **12 a :** the past performance of a race horse; *often* **:** a table giving details relating to a horse's past performance (as handicaps, jockeys, odds) used by bettors in making selections ⟨a ~ sheet⟩ ⟨a racing ~⟩ ⟨~ players⟩ **b :** CONDITION, FITNESS ⟨preseason workouts to get in ~ for the regular season⟩; *often* **:** known ability to perform ⟨a batter off his ~ at the plate⟩ ⟨a musician playing at the top of his ~⟩ **13 :** the combination of faces included under a general crystallographic symbol and necessary to satisfy the symmetry of the crystal ⟨a single crystal often exhibits faces of two or more crystal ~*s* which supplement one another or truncate one another's edges or corners⟩ **14 a :** LINGUISTIC FORM **b :** one of the different aspects a word may take as a result of inflection or change of spelling or pronunciation ⟨obsolete, participial, or verbal ~*s*⟩ **15** *math* **:** a rational integral homogeneous function of a set of variables **16 :** the immature flower bud of the cotton plant **17 :** BOOK 1d(1) **18 :** the profile of a screw thread

syn FORMALITY, CEREMONY, CEREMONIAL, RITE, RITUAL, LITURGY: FORM is a general word and usu. lacks any special connotation ⟨there had been no fixed order for the coronation of an English king, and the *form* which was observed at Bath was reached only after . . . two experimental drafts —F.M.Stenton⟩ ⟨his inclinations toward the *forms* of the Church of England —G.H.Genzmer⟩ ⟨made his declaration in *form* —Jane Austen⟩ Modified, as by *good* or *bad,* FORM indicates the degree of conformity to established usage or custom ⟨it was accepted poetic good *form* that the lover, writing of his lady, should inventory her charms from top to toe —J.L.Lowes⟩ ⟨nothing could be worse *form* . . . than any display of temper in a public place —Edith Wharton⟩ FORM may indicate a traditional or sanctioned procedure lacking force, significance, or real vitality ⟨if congress remains at liberty to give this court appellate jurisdiction . . . the distribution of jurisdiction made in the Constitution is *form* without substance —John Marshall⟩ FORMALITY applies either to a prescribed procedural detail, often one done perfunctorily and lacking in import, or to an attitude of punctilious, reserved stiffness ⟨the first reading of a public bill is a *formality* and is in effect little more than information given to the House that the bill is on its way —R.M.Dawson⟩ ⟨the cold *formality* of the duchess's court⟩ CEREMONY is likely to suggest dignified, impressive, elaborate, or punctilious performance of actions ranging from those of deep spiritual significance to little everyday courtesies or routine actions ⟨the *ceremonies* at the investiture of a pope⟩ ⟨*ceremonies* in honor of the martyred king⟩ ⟨the beauty of an inherited courtesy of manners, of a thousand little *ceremonies* flowing out of the most ordinary relations and observances of life —Laurence Binyon⟩ CEREMONIAL, occas. a synonym for CEREMONY, is more likely to suggest a system or code of prescribed ceremonies ⟨the gorgeous *ceremonial* of the Burgundian court —W.H.Prescott⟩ RITE indicates the prescribed speech and action of a special formal occasion, esp. a very significant or unusual one, an ordinary event treated as though of major importance, or an esoteric practice ⟨had gone through this formality as resignedly as through all the others which made of a nineteenth century New York wedding a *rite* that seemed to belong to the dawn of history —Edith Wharton⟩ ⟨the semipagan *rites* peculiar to the burial of the dead in middle-class houses —Rudyard Kipling⟩ ⟨abhorred *rites* to Hecate in their obscured haunts —John Milton⟩ RITUAL in its older sense indicates the totality of the rites of service or faith ⟨the Roman *ritual* had always a great attraction for him —Oscar Wilde⟩ More frequently today it designates any series of actions given an unusual importance and a prescribed order or manner ⟨the *ritual* of asepsis today is the same the world over —Harvey Graham⟩ ⟨it was essential to reach a cave around the next headland where she would sit down facing the sea before she thought about anything — thus making a little *ritual* against despair —Audrey Barker⟩ Where it is not an equivalent for RITUAL or RITE, LITURGY may indicate the prescribed form for an act or session of worship as written and accepted ⟨he [Henry VIII] insisted on . . . the maintenance of full ritual in the *liturgy* —Hilaire Belloc⟩

syn FIGURE, SHAPE, CONFORMATION, CONFIGURATION: FORM may suggest an appearance in which both clear outline and also structure and orderly disposition of details are presented or suggested ⟨appearing in book *form*⟩ ⟨the republican *form* of government⟩ ⟨a sense of interdependence and interrelated unity that gave *form* to intellectual stirrings that had been previously inchoate —John Dewey⟩ ⟨school architecture throughout the state is highly specialized. Rigid state laws for heating, ventilation, and lighting offer little opportunity for variation on standard *form* —*Amer. Guide Series: N.J.*⟩ FIGURE is likely to call attention to outlines, to bounding, enclosing circumference or outer lines ⟨a geometrical *figure*⟩ ⟨the *figures* of a dance⟩ ⟨the cloud *figures* in the sky —Sylvia Berkman⟩ ⟨the president rose to his great height, a somber, towering *figure* in black —Sir Winston Churchill⟩ SHAPE may sometimes suggest both outline and also content, mass, body, bulk, or detail ⟨hat *shapes* of beaver, coon, otter, and other skins —*Amer. Guide Series: Conn.*⟩ ⟨the construction of a play sets up its *shape*, and builds its skeleton —John Van Druten⟩ ⟨the *shape* of an idea emerged gradually out of the fog of words —Ellen Glasgow⟩ ⟨whole stone logs are found, some wonderfully and delicately colored, in the *shape* of the Asiatic gingko tree —*Amer. Guide Series: Wash.*⟩ CONFORMATION is usable in reference to whole complicated structure or to detailed arrangement or presentation ⟨they failed to find any relation between altitude tolerance and body stature or *conformation* —H.G.Armstrong⟩ ⟨a culture acquires its *conformation* and specificity from the uniqueness of its institutions —Abram Kardiner⟩ CONFIGURATION is applicable to a detailed outline or statement of the nature and disposition or arrangement of various parts ⟨he used to wake up and not know where he was, but the *configurations* of a dream could easily have taken on such a shape as this — the dining room of the Marlborough in the shadowy light of early morning —Hamilton Basso⟩ ⟨though the main street is wide and lined with stores, most of the others fit crookedly into the *configurations* of the valley —*Amer. Guide Series: Pa.*⟩

syn USAGE, CONVENTION, CONVENANCE: these nouns all have in common the sense of a fixed or accepted way of doing something. FORM can apply to a prescribed or approved way of behaving, method of procedure, or technique in any sphere of activity where correctness or uniformity of method or manner is thought essential ⟨the *forms* of good conduct⟩ ⟨the *forms* of worship⟩ ⟨good *form* in swimming⟩ ⟨a *form* of address⟩ USAGE implies the sanction of precedent or tradition, often designating a form preserved out of respect for a class, profession, or religion ⟨descriptions of *usages* presuppose descriptions of uses, that is, ways or techniques of doing the thing the more or less widely prevailing practice of doing which constitutes the usage —Gilbert Ryle⟩ ⟨to bury in the first furrow certain fruits of a particular structure, such as figs, pomegranates, and locust beans, is a *usage* frequently observed —J.G.Frazer⟩ CONVENTION, often interchangeable with FORM, esp. in application to social behavior, stresses general agreement and therefore applies to some set way of doing or saying something that is sanctioned or believed to be sanctioned only by general unquestioning acceptance ⟨this music followed *conventions* perfectly understood by the contemporaries —P.H.Lang⟩ ⟨certain parliamentary *conventions* which exist to supplement the rules of procedure —T.E.May⟩ ⟨this genius who was too wild and elemental ever to conform to any aesthetic *convention* —H.M.Ledig-Rowohlt⟩ CONVENANCE, a literary term still retaining some of its character as a loanword, applies only to social conventions especially regarded as essential to propriety or decorum ⟨disregarding the social *convenances*, continued to chatter on —R.H.Sampson⟩ ⟨the *convenances* of life —A.C.Benson⟩

2**form** \"\ *vb* -ED/-ING/-S [ME *formen, fourmen*, fr. OF *former, fourmer*, fr. L *formare*, fr. *forma*, n.] *vt* **1 a :** to give form or shape to **:** FRAME, CONSTRUCT, MAKE, FASHION ⟨man, ~*ed* of earth, to earth returns⟩ ⟨the skilled craftsman ~*s* and finishes the rough stone to a thing of beauty⟩ **b :** to constitute by nominating or appointing individuals to governmental positions usu. associated with membership in a cabinet or government ⟨asked to ~ a new cabinet —M.S.Stewart⟩ ⟨was called upon to ~ a government —Kenneth Lawson⟩ **2 a :** to give a particular shape to **:** shape, mold, or fashion into a certain state or condition or after a particular model **:** ARRANGE, ADJUST ⟨~ the paste into lozenges and roll them in sugar⟩ ⟨a state ~*ed* after the Roman republic⟩ **b :** to model by instruction and discipline **:** mold esp. by influence ⟨'tis education ~*s* the common mind —Alexander Pope⟩ **3 :** DEVELOP, ACQUIRE, CONTRACT ⟨~ a habit⟩ **4 :** to serve to make up or constitute **:** be a usu. essential or basic element of ⟨bonds ~*ed* the bulk of his estate⟩ ⟨her hat was ~*ed* of feathers⟩ **5 a :** to treat (plates) for use in an electrical storage battery by coating the positive plate with lead dioxide and the negative plate with spongy lead **b :** to treat (mercury arc rectifiers) to remove all moisture and gas after a period of idleness or after opening the tank **6 a :** to have (as a tense) expressed ⟨~*s* the past tense in *-ed*⟩ **b :** to combine to make (a compound word) **c :** to make up **:** CONSTITUTE ⟨~ a clause or sentence⟩ **7 :** to arrange in order **:** draw up ⟨the battalion advanced as soon as its lines were ~*ed*⟩ **8 :** to bend or stretch (metal) to conform to the shape of a die or other tool ~ *vi* **1 :** to become formed or shaped ⟨a clot ~*ed* gradually over the cut⟩ **2 :** to take form **:** come into existence **:** ARISE ⟨popular protest ~*ed* steadily⟩ ⟨thunderheads were ~*ing* over the hills⟩ **3 :** to take on a definite form, shape, or arrangement ⟨the infantry ~*ed* in columns⟩ **4** *of a hare* **:** to run to or crouch in a form **syn** see MAKE
— **form on :** to take up a formation next to ⟨ordered the group to *form on* the last platoon⟩

form- *or* **formo-** *comb form* [*formic* (*acid*)] **:** formic acid **:** formyl ⟨*form*anilide⟩ ⟨*formo*toluidide⟩

-form \ˌfȯrm\ *adj comb form* [MF and L; MF *-forme*, fr. L *-formis*, fr. *forma* form — more at FORM] **:** in the form or shape of **:** resembling **:** -MORPHOUS — preceded by *i* ⟨calci*form*⟩ ⟨ovi*form*⟩

for·ma \ˈfȯrmə, -ȯ(ə)mə\ *n, pl* **for·mae** \-ˌmē\ *also* **formas** [NL, fr. L, form] **:** FORM 9b

form·abil·i·ty \ˌ=əˈbiləd·ē, -ətē, -i\ *n* **:** capacity for being formed into new shapes ⟨the excellent ~ of modern plastics⟩

form·able \ˈ=əbəl\ *adj* [ME, fr. LL *formabilis*, fr. L *formare* to form + *-abilis* -able — more at FORM] **:** capable of being formed **:** suitable for forming ⟨~ sheet metal⟩

form·ably \-əblē, -li\ *adv* **:** so as to be formable

for·ma·gen \ˈfȯrməjən, -ˌjen\ *n* -S [L *forma* form + E *-gen*] **:** a substance having a formative effect on plants; *esp* **:** one that modifies the shape, size, or arrangement of organs — **for·ma·gen·ic** \ˌ==ˈjenik\ *adj*

for·mal \ˈfȯrməl, -ȯ(ə)m-\ *adj* [ME *formal, formel*, fr. OF & L; OF, fr. L *formalis*, fr. *forma* form + *-alis* -al] **1 a :** belonging to or being the essential constitution of a thing as distinguished from the matter composing it ⟨the ~ nature of a square is a relation of lines and angles rather than a matter of space or solidity⟩; *often* **:** having power to make a thing what it is **:** CONSTITUTIVE, ESSENTIAL ⟨divine goodwill is the ~ cause of human aspiration⟩ **b :** relating to, concerned with, or constituting the outward form, superficial qualities, or arrangement of something as distinguished from its content: as (1) **:** of, relating to, or preoccupied with the material or compositional factors in art or emphasizing these over other factors (as subject matter or content) ⟨a ~ style in painting⟩; *often* **:** having a symmetrical arrangement of elements ⟨~ balance in design⟩ ⟨a ~ composition⟩ (2) **:** consisting of, based upon, evidenced by, or considering observable similarities and differences in linguistic form as distinguished from logical, a priori, semantic, comparative, or historical similarities and differences ⟨the ~ approach to comparative linguistics⟩ ⟨a ~ classification of language⟩ (3) **:** of, relating to, or constituting logical, epistemological, or ontological forms; *also* **:** belonging to a formalized system **:** SYNTACTICAL **2 a :** following or according with established form, custom, or rule **:** not deviating from what is usual or generally acceptable **:** CONVENTIONAL ⟨still in constraint your suffering sex remains or bound in ~ or in real chains —Alexander Pope⟩ ⟨paying ~ attentions to his hostess⟩ **b :** done in due form **:** carried out with solemnity **:** CEREMONIAL ⟨no noble rite nor ~ ostentation —Shak.⟩ ⟨received a ~ rebuke before the whole congregation⟩ **c** *obs* **:** characterized by or formed in due order **:** REGULAR **3 a :** based on forms and rules, esp. such as are accepted by convention **:** of or following a prescribed form ⟨a ~ exposition⟩ ⟨~ landscape architecture⟩ ⟨a ~ reception⟩ **b :** characterized by punctilious respect for form **:** EXACT, METHODICAL, ORDERLY ⟨a man very ~ in all his dealings⟩; *often* **:** constrained by reason of excessive devotion to form **:** PRIM, RIGID, STIFF, CEREMONIOUS ⟨those stern ~ even formidable ancestors locked in their rigid armor of propriety⟩ **c** *of a legal procedure* **:** requiring special or stipulated solemnities or formalities to become effective (as in the creating of a legal relationship) **4** *obs* **a :** sound in mind **:** SANE **b :** CIRCUMSTANTIAL **5 :** having the appearance without the substance **:** being or subject to being so construed only as a matter of form ⟨~ Christians who go to church on Easter Sunday to show off their new clothes⟩ **:** NOMINAL ⟨a purely ~ requirement that can be waived without trouble⟩ ⟨a ~ party to a suit⟩ **syn** see CEREMONIAL

2**formal** \"\ *n* -S **:** something formal in character: as **a :** a social affair (as a dance) requiring formal evening dress **b** (1) **:** EVENING DRESS (2) **:** a man's formal evening costume

3**for·mal** \fȯrˈmal\ *n* -S [ISV, fr. *formaldehyde*] **1 :** METHYLAL **2 :** any acetal derived from formaldehyde and an alcohol ⟨butyl ~⟩ ⟨polyvinyl ~⟩

4**for·mal** \ˈfȯrməl\ *adj* [*form*ula + *-al*] **:** 3MOLAR 2 ⟨~ concentration of a solution⟩

formal cause *n, in Aristotelianism* **:** the structure, essence, or pattern that a fully realized thing embodies

formal contract *n* **1 :** a contract under seal or by statute having that effect **:** SPECIALTY CONTRACT **2 :** RECOGNIZANCE **3 :** a negotiable instrument

form·al·de·hyde \fȯrm+\ *n* [ISV *form-* + *aldehyde*; orig. formed as G *formaldehyd*] **:** a very reactive aldehyde $HCHO$ that has a tendency to polymerize, that is a colorless pungent irritating combustible gas when pure but is conveniently handled in the form of aqueous solutions or solid polymers (as paraformaldehyde), that is usu. made by oxidation of methanol or of gaseous hydrocarbons, and that is used chiefly as a disinfectant and preservative, as a hardening and insolubilizing agent esp. for proteins, and in the synthesis of other compounds (as pentaerythritol) and of phenolic and other synthetic resins — called also *formic aldehyde, methanal*

formaldehydesulfoxylate \=ˈ==ˌ=(ˌ)=ˈ==ˌ=\ *n* [*formaldehyde* + *sulfoxylate*] **:** a salt of formaldehydesulfoxylic acid

formaldehydesulfoxylic acid \=ˈ==ˌ=ˌ=ˌ=ˈ==-\ *n* [ISV *formaldehyde* + *sulfoxylic*] **:** an unstable acid $HOCH_2SO_2H$ known only in the form of salts (as sodium formaldehydesulfoxylate) that are strong reducing agents

formaldehyde tanning *n* **:** tanning with formaldehyde solutions esp. in the preparation of white leathers

for·mal·de·hy·do·gen·ic \=ˌ==ˌhīˌdōˈjenik\ *adj* [*formaldehyde* + *-o-* + *-genic*] **:** yielding formaldehyde ⟨~ steroids⟩

formal discipline *n* **:** disciplinary training supposedly imparted by the form of a study (as mathematics) as distinguished from its content value; *also* **:** the study itself

formal fallacy *n* **:** a violation of any rule of formal inference — called also *paralogism;* contrasted with *material fallacy* and *verbal fallacy;* compare AFFIRMATION OF THE CONSEQUENT, DENIAL OF THE ANTECEDENT, IGNORATIO ELENCHI, ILLICIT PROCESS, PETITIO PRINCIPII

formal garden *n* **:** a garden laid out with complete regularity on formal lines and in accord with the methods of classic design, the plantings being in symmetrically arranged rows or geometrical figures

For·ma·lin \ˈfȯrmələn\ *trademark* — used for a clear aqueous solution of formaldehyde that usu. contains about 37 percent formaldehyde by weight or 40 percent by volume together with a small amount of methanol for inhibiting polymerization

for·ma·lin·ize \-ləˌnīz\ *vt* -ED/-ING/-S *see -ize in Explan Notes* **:** FORMOLIZE

for·mal·ism \ˈfȯrməˌlizəm, -ȯ(ə)m-\ *n* -S [1*formal* + *-ism*] **1 a :** the practice or the doctrine of strict adherence to or dependence on prescribed or external forms ⟨the rigid ~ of the royal court⟩; *also* **:** an instance of this ⟨the petty ~*s* with which he filled his life⟩ **b :** the using or observance of external religious forms without the life and spirit of religion **c** (1) **:** any theory (as that of Kant) holding that the nature of duty is determined by purely formal principles (as the categorical imperative) rather than by a consideration of the consequences of actions (2) **:** INTUITIONISM 1 **d :** a philosophy of mathematics that seeks to establish the consistency of mathematics by metamathematical methods — compare INTUITIONISM **2 a :** emphatic or predominant attention to arrangement, style, or artistic means (as in graphic art, literature, or music) usu. with corresponding de-emphasis of content; *often* **:** strict adherence to traditional or prescribed rules and methods in the arts **b :** dramatic representation in which all the elements of production are conventionalized into simple and arbitrary terms

1**for·mal·ist** \-ləst\ *n* -S [1*formal* + *-ist*] **1 :** a person who adopts as a matter of form the current opinions and modes of action **:** TIMESERVER **2 a :** one overattentive to forms or too much confined to them **b :** one given to formalism **:** a formal person; *often* **:** an advocate or proponent of a theory of formalism **3 :** one that gives form **:** a form-giving power or element ⟨the sun and moon, the great ~*s* in the sky —R.W. Emerson⟩

2**formalist** \"\ *adj* **:** of or relating to formalists **:** FORMALISTIC

for·mal·is·tic \ˌ=məˈlistik\ *adj* **:** concerned with or characterized by formalism ⟨the ~ approach to the study of society —C.V.Woodward⟩; *often* **:** employing or advocating formalism (as in ethics) — **for·mal·is·ti·cal·ly** \-ək(ə)lē\ *adv*

for·mal·i·ter \fȯrˈmaləd·ər\ *adv* [LL, fr. L *formalis* formal — more at FORMAL] **:** FORMALLY; *esp* **:** with reference to Aristotelian form

for·mal·i·ty \fȯ(r)ˈmaləd·ē, -ətē, -i\ *n* -ES [MF *formalité*, fr. *formal* + *-ité* -ity — more at FORMAL] **1 :** the quality or state of being formal: as **a** *obs* **:** the practice or exhibition of formalism in art or music **b :** strictly ceremonious quality or state **:** precise stiff regularity or conformance **2** *archaic* **:** the distinctive quality that makes a thing what it is or defines its nature **:** ESSENCE **3 :** compliance with formal or conventional rules **:** conformity to established form or method of procedure (as in law) **:** FORM, CEREMONY, CONVENTIONALITY **4 :** the dress or insignia prescribed for academic, municipal, or sacerdotal office — usu. used in pl. ⟨the lord mayor in his *formalities* headed the procession⟩ **5 a :** an established form or formal procedure that is required or conventional esp. in religious, legal, courtly, or social matters **b :** a customary ceremony without much real significance ⟨he was installed with all the usual *formalities* —Conyers Middleton⟩ **6** *obs* **a :** ceremonious attention **b :** formal aspect **c :** invariable practice **:** ORDER, REGULARITY **d :** external appearance or form; *often* **:** form without substance **7** *in scholasticism* **a :** the manner in which a thing is conceived or constituted by an act of human thinking **b :** the result of such an act **syn** see FORM

for·mal·iz·able \ˌfȯrməˈlīzəbəl, ˈfȯ(ə)m-\ *adj* **:** capable of being formalized

for·ma·li·za·tion \ˌ=mələˈzāshən, -ˌlīˈz-\ *n* -S **:** an act of formalizing or the state of being formalized — compare AXIOMATIZATION

1**for·mal·ize** \ˈfȯrməˌlīz, ˈfȯ(ə)m-\ *vb* -ED/-ING/-S *see -ize in Explan Notes* [*formal* + *-ize*] *vt* **1** *obs* **:** to give form or formal existence to **:** ANIMATE **2 :** to give a certain or definite form to **:** SHAPE, MOLD **3 a :** to render formal; *often* **:** STYLIZE **b :** to state precise rules for the combination and transformation of (as expressions or language) usu. by replacing the original words by symbols that can be discussed without reference to their meaning — compare FORMATION RULE, TRANSFORMATION RULE **c :** to give formal status or approval to (as a decision, plan, or proposal) **4** *obs* **:** to take exception to **:** cavil at ~ *vi* **1 :** to be formal **:** affect formality **2** *obs* **:** to object without good reason **:** CAVIL, SCRUPLE — **for·mal·iz·er** \-ˌlīzə(r)\ *n* -S

2**formalize** \"\ *vt* -ED/-ING/-S [*formal*in + -ize] **:** FORMOLIZE

formal logic *n* **:** a system of logic (as Aristotelian logic or symbolic logic) that abstracts the forms of thought from its content to establish abstract criteria of consistency — contrasted with *material logic*

for·mal·ly \ˈ=məlē, -li\ *adv* [ME, fr. *formal* + *-ly*] **:** in a formal manner: as **a :** with respect to or according to form **b :** EXPRESSLY, EXPLICITLY **c :** in prescribed or customary form **d :** with formality **:** CEREMONIOUSLY ⟨inspection of the new hotel . . . which will be ~ opened for dinner this evening — D.D.Martin⟩

formal matter *n* **:** MATTER OF A PROPOSITION b

formal mode *n* **:** language that makes statements about linguistic signs without reference to their meaning or denotation — contrasted with *material mode*

for·mal·ness *n* -ES **:** the quality or state of being formal **:** FORMALITY

formal proposition *n* **:** a proposition in which no specific content is designated or a principle is stated in the manner of a formula (as "if all A is B, then no A is not B")

formals *pl of* FORMAL

formal sociology *n* **:** a branch of sociology concerned with the modes of recurrent social relationships (as competition, division of labor, supraordination, and subordination) that are conceived to exist in any type of human association

formal subject *n* **:** GRAMMATICAL SUBJECT

formal truth *n* **:** the true elaboration of concepts, meanings, or implications that is relatively independent of external existence or nonexistence ⟨the *formal truth* of a definition⟩ ⟨the truth that certain premises give a certain conclusion is a *formal truth*⟩ — called also *logical truth*

form·amide \fȯrm+\ *n* [ISV *form-* + *amide*] **:** a colorless hygroscopic liquid $HCONH_2$ made in various ways (as from ammonia and a formic ester or from ammonia and carbon monoxide under pressure) and used chiefly as a solvent and softening agent; the amide of formic acid

form·am·i·dine \fȯrˈmaməˌdēn, -ˌdən\ *n* -S [ISV *formamide* + *-ine*] **:** an unstable base $HC(=NH)NH_2$ known only in the form of its salts and other derivatives

formamido- *comb form* [*formamide*] **:** containing the univalent radical $HCONH—$ derived from formamide ⟨*para-formamido*benzoic acid⟩

for·man·ite \ˈfȯrməˌnīt\ *n* -S [Francis G. *Forman*, 20th cent. Australian geologist + E *-ite*] **:** a mineral $(U,Zr,Th,Ca)(Ta_1Nb)O_4$ consisting essentially of an oxide of uranium, zirconium, thorium, calcium, tantalum, and niobium with some rare-earth metals and isomorphous with fergusonite

for·mant \ˈfȯrmənt, -ȯ(ə)m-, -ˌmant, -aa(ə)nt\ *n* -S [G, fr. L *formant-, formans*, pres. part. of *formare* to form — more at FORM] **1 :** a characteristic component of the quality of a speech sound; *specif* **:** any of several resonance bands which are regarded as together determining the phonetic quality of a vowel **2 a :** 2DETERMINATIVE 3 **b :** a derivational affix

formas *pl of* FORMA

for·mat \ˈfȯrˌmat, -ȯ(ə)ˌm-, *usu* -ad·+V\ *n* -S [F or G; F, fr. G, fr. L *formatus*, past part. of *formare* (prob. in such contexts as NL *liber in quarto formatus* volume formed in quarto)] **1 a :** the shape and size of a publication as determined by the number of times each constituent sheet has been folded ⟨in octavo ~ each sheet is folded 3 times to produce 8 leaves⟩ — compare BOOK tables **b :** the general makeup or style of a publication ⟨a double-column ~⟩ ⟨loose-leaf ~⟩ **2 :** general plan of physical organization or arrangement (as of a television show or the design of a coin) ⟨the ~ of the new show included a careful balance of music and comedy⟩ ⟨students are given practice exercises to acquaint them with the ~ of the tests⟩ **3 :** SIZE, SHAPE, PROPORTION ⟨a rare stamp of triangular ~⟩ ⟨cameras employing ~*s* up to 24 by 36 millimeters⟩ ⟨the exceptionally tall ~ of the panels⟩

1**for·mate** \ˈfȯrˌmāt, *usu* -ād·+V\ *n* -S [*form-* + *-ate*] **:** a salt or ester of formic acid

2**formate** \"\ *vi* -ED/-ING/-S [back-formation fr. *formation*] *of aircraft* **:** to fly in or join a formation

for·ma·tion \fȯrˈmāshən, -ȯ(ə)ˈ-\ *n* -S [ME *formacioun*, fr. MF or L; MF *formation*, fr. L *formation-, formatio*, fr. *formatus* + *-ion-, -io* -ion] **1 :** an act of giving form or shape to something or of taking form **:** PRODUCTION, DEVELOPMENT ⟨planned the ~ of a social club⟩ ⟨the ~ of good habits⟩ **2 :** something that is formed ⟨new word ~*s*⟩ ⟨a greenish ~ of mold on bread⟩ **3 :** the manner in which a thing is formed **:** STRUCTURE, CONSTRUCTION, FORM ⟨the peculiar ~ of the heart⟩ **4 a :** the largest unit in ecological community organization comprising two or more associations together with the successional communities that lead to their establishment, the unit as a whole corresponding in area with a region of essentially uniform climate ⟨the grassland ~⟩ — compare BIOME **b :** a group of associations bound together by close similarity in life forms or habits and by dependence upon closely similar climates — compare CLIMAX 4 **5 a :** any particular mineral aggregate or rock — not often used technically **b :** any igneous, sedimentary, or metamorphic rock represented as a unit in geological mapping **:** a cartographic unit **c :** any sedimentary bed or consecutive series of beds sufficiently homogeneous or distinctive to be regarded as a unit ⟨the Trenton ~⟩ **6 a :** an arrangement of a body of troops in line, column, or other prescribed manner **b :** an arrangement of football players at the start of a play; *esp* **:** the deployment of the offensive backfield at the start of a play from scrimmage — usu. used in combination; see A FORMATION, DOUBLE WINGBACK FORMATION, I FORMATION, PUNT FORMATION, SINGLE WINGBACK FORMATION, SPLIT T, SPREAD FORMATION, T FORMATION **c :** an arrangement of two or more airplanes flying as a unit and for a particular purpose (as attack, protection, or review) **7 :** the arrangement of the fibers in a sheet of paper ⟨a well closed, or regular, ~⟩ ⟨a wild, or irregular, ~⟩

for·ma·tion·al \-shənᵊl, -shnəl\ *adj* **:** of or concerned with formation or a formation ⟨~ contrasts in geologic strata⟩ ⟨the ~ aspects of character building⟩ — **for·ma·tion·al·ly** \-ᵊlē, -əlē, -li\ *adv*

formation rule *n* **:** a principle in logic for establishing permissible combinations of signs (as for determining how to construct statements or formulas in a formalized language or calculus) — contrasted with *transformation rule*

1**form·a·tive** \ˈfȯ(r)məd·iv\ *adj* [MF *formatif*, fr. L *formatus* + MF *-if* -ive] **1 a :** capable of giving form **:** tending to give form **:** CONSTRUCTIVE ⟨a ~ influence⟩ ⟨farm animals . . . were brought to the colonies as a basic element of ~ equipment —E.D.Ross⟩ **b** *of an affix or other word element* **:** used in word formation or inflection **2 :** capable of or subject to alteration by growth and development; *usu* **:** producing new cells and tissues **:** MERISTEMATIC, PLASTIC ⟨a ~ zone in developing bone⟩ ⟨the ~ cambium of a woody stem⟩ **3 a :** of, relating to, or characterized by formative effects or formation **:** CREATIVE ⟨the ~ period in the life of a child⟩ ⟨~ years⟩ ⟨the ~ arts⟩ **b** *usu cap* **:** of or belonging to the period of prehistoric cultural development in Peru and Central America during which the characteristic techniques and styles were forming — compare CLASSIC, FLORESCENT — **form·a·tive·ly** \-əvlē, -li\ *adv* — **form·a·tive·ness** *n* -ES

2**formative** \"\ *n* -S **:** the element (as a prefix or termination) in a word that serves to give the word appropriate form and is no part of the base

for·ma·to·re \ˌfȯrməˈtō(ˌ)rā\ *n* -S [It, fr. L *formator* one that forms, fr. *formatus* + *-or*] **:** a molder or modeler (as of plaster or wax)

formatrix *n, pl* **formatrixes** *or* **formatrices** [LL, fem. of L *formator*] *obs* **:** a formative agent

form·a·zan \ˈfȯrməˌzan\ *n* -S [*form-* + *az-* + *-an*] **:** a hypothetical hydrazone $HN=NCH=NNH_2$ related to formic acid and known only in the form of intensely colored derivatives (as triphenyl-formazan) that are obtained either from hydrazones by coupling with diazonium compounds or from colorless tetrazolium compounds by the reducing action of living tissues, in the latter case serving as indicators of viability as a result of color production; *also* **:** any of these derivatives

form block *n* **:** a temporary die made of wood or plastic and used for forming a few experimental samples of embossed work (as of metal foil or paper)

form board *n* **:** a small board with spaces for the insertion of blocks of different shapes and sizes that is used to test an individual's speed and accuracy of insertion and his approach to the problem

form class *n* **:** a class of linguistic forms that can be used in the same position in a construction and that have one or more morphological or syntactical features in common ⟨*book, hat, going, deceased, little one*, and *rapidly flowing stream* belong to the same *form class* as shown by the fact that each can be used in the same position in the construction *the — is*⟩ ⟨*books* and *hats* belong to the *form classes* of nouns and of plurals⟩ ⟨*opened* and *walked* belong to the *form classes* of verbs and of past tenses⟩ — see MAJOR FORM CLASS

form critic *n* **:** a specialist in form criticism

form criticism *n* **:** a method of biblical criticism that seeks to classify units of scripture into literary patterns (as love poems, parables, sayings, elegies, legends) and that attempts to trace each type to its period of oral transmission in an effort to determine the original form and the relationship of the life and thought of the period to the development of the literary tradition

form cutter *n* **:** a cutting tool having its edge shaped to the profile to be imparted to the work

forme \ˈfȯ(ə)rm, -ȯ(ə)m\ *n* -S [F, lit., form — more at FORM] **1** *Brit* **:** 1FORM 8 **2 a :** a pattern of an upper of a shoe **b :** a low bench on which shoemakers formerly sat when working

formed \ˈfȯ(ə)rmd, -ȯ(ə)md\ *adj* [ME, fr. past part. of *formen* to form — more at FORM] **1 :** clearly defined **:** SETTLED, DEFINITE ⟨I have no ~ opinion about the chances of success⟩ **2 :** fully developed (as by discipline or training) **:** MATURED ⟨a ~ opposition arose over the terms of the agreement⟩ ⟨a graceful but not yet fully ~ literary style⟩ **3 :** being or having the characteristics of living matter **:** ORGANIZED ⟨~ ferments extracted from the gastric mucosa⟩ ⟨~ elements of the blood⟩ **4 :** shaped (as by pressure or carving) to fit ⟨~ plastic snugly encloses the assembly⟩ ⟨a ~ handgrip on a grease gun⟩

formed coil *n* **:** an electric coil wound by a machine upon a form and transferred afterward to an armature as distinguished from a coil wound directly on the armature

for·me·don \ˈfȯrmə,dän\ *n* -S [ME, fr. AF, fr. ML *forma doni*, lit., form of a gift] **:** a former writ of right for recovering per formam doni entailed property under English law

for·mée *also* **for·mé** \ˈfȯr,mā\ *or* **formy** \-,mē\ *adj* [ME *forme*, fr. MF *formé, fourmé*, past part. of *former, fourmer* to form — more at FORM] *of a cross* **:** having the arms narrow at the center and expanding toward the ends, the sides of the arms being either straight or concave lines and the ends of the arms cut off square or very slightly concave **:** PATTÉE — compare MALTESE CROSS 1; see CROSS illustration

forme fruste \fȯrmfrüest\ *n, pl* **formes frustes** \"\ [F, lit., worn-down form] **:** an atypical and usu. abortive manifestation of a disease

for·men·kreis \ˈfȯrmən,krīs\ *n, pl* **formenkrei·se** \-īzə\ *or* **formenkreis·es** \-īsəz\ [G, lit., cycle of forms, fr. *formen*, pl. of *form* (fr. MHG *forme*, fr. L *forma*) + *kreis* circle, cycle — more at FORM, ARTENKREIS] **:** a polytypic species (as of birds)

1**form·er** \ˈfȯrmər, ˈfȯ(ə)mə(r\ *n* -S [ME, fr. *formen* to form + *-er* — more at FORM] **1 :** one that forms **:** MAKER, CREATOR, SHAPER ⟨discipline is a ~ of character⟩ **2 :** a worker who forms materials into products or products from materials (as by cutting, pressing, bending, molding, or other hand or machine operation) — often used in combination with an attributive noun indicating the material acted on or the product produced ⟨a coil ~⟩ ⟨expert felt ~*s*⟩ **3 :** a device, tool, or machine used to form some material or product: as **a :** a shape around or by which an article is to be shaped, molded, woven, wrapped, pasted, or otherwise constructed ⟨the ~ on which paper bags are pasted⟩ **b :** a templet, pattern, gauge, guide, or block by which an article is shaped or bent **c :** FORMING DIE **d :** a device or machine for bending sheet metal into various forms (as tubes or cylinders) **e :** a machine used in ropemaking for twisting yarn into strands **4** [1*form* + *-er*] *chiefly Brit* **:** a member of a school form — usu. used in combination ⟨sixth *formers*⟩ ⟨invited the lower *formers* on a picnic⟩

2**for·mer** \"\ *adj* [ME, fr. *forme* first (fr. OE *forma*) + *-er* — more at FOREMOST] **1 a :** preceding in order of time; *usu* **:** of, relating to, or occurring in the past **:** ANTECEDENT, PREVIOUS, PRIOR, EARLIER ⟨recovered some of her ~ ease⟩ ⟨as we agreed in ~ correspondence⟩ **b** *obs* **:** being far distant in time **:** ANCIENT **2 :** near the beginning **:** PRECEDING ⟨the ~ part of a discourse or argument⟩ **3 :** first mentioned or in order of two things mentioned or understood ⟨of these two evils the ~ is the lesser⟩ **4** *obs* **:** anterior in place or situation **:** FRONT, FOREMOST **5 :** having been at some previous time **:** ONETIME, SOMETIME ⟨~ president of his fraternity⟩ ⟨~ members of the legislature⟩

former adjudication *n* **:** RES JUDICATA

for·mer·et \ˈfȯrmə,ret\ *n* -S [F, fr. MF, fr. *forme* form, large window in a church — more at FORM] **:** a wall rib in a roof vaulted with ribs

former jeopardy *n* **:** JEOPARDY 3

for·mer·ly \ˈfȯrmə(r)lē, -ȯ(ə)məlē, -li\ *adv* [2*former* + *-ly*] **1** *obs* **a :** in time immediately preceding **:** just before **b :** BEFOREHAND, FIRST **2 :** in time past **:** in the time of an earlier or previous period **:** ONCE, HERETOFORE, PREVIOUSLY ⟨~ there were giants in the world⟩ ⟨we ~ lived in the country⟩ ⟨a ~ prosperous area⟩

-for·mes \ˈfȯr,mēz\ *n pl comb form* [NL, fr. L, pl. of *-formis* -form] **:** ones having (such a) form **:** ones resembling — in names of zoological orders and certain other groups of higher rank than family ⟨Galli*formes*⟩ ⟨Passeri*formes*⟩

form factor *n* **:** the ratio between the volume of a tree and that of a geometric solid (as a cylinder) having the same diameter and height

formfitting \ˈ=ˌ==\ *adj* **:** conforming to the outline of the body **:** CLOSE-FITTING ⟨a ~ sweater⟩ ⟨a comfortably ~ armchair⟩

form·ful \ˈ=fəl\ *adj* **:** exhibiting or notable for form (as in a sport) ⟨a ~ jump —*Time*⟩

form genus *n* **:** an artificial taxonomic category established for organisms of which the true relationships are obscure due to incomplete knowledge of structure (as in some fossils) or of development or life history (as in Fungi Imperfecti and various animal parasites)

form grinder *n* **:** a grinding wheel shaped to the contour to be imparted to the work — compare FORM CUTTER

for·mic \ˈfȯrmik, -ȯəm-\ *adj* [irreg. fr. L *formica* ant — more at PISMIRE] **1 :** of or relating to ants **2 :** being or derived from formic acid

for·mi·ca \fȯrˈmīkə\ *n, cap* [NL, fr. L, ant] **:** a genus of hymenopterous insects formerly including all the ants but now restricted to various typical ants (as the mound-building ants and the sanguinary ant)

For·mi·ca \(ˈ)fȯrˌmīkə, fərˈm-\ *trademark* — used for various laminated plastic products used esp. in furniture (as for tabletops) and in building (as for wallboards)

formic acid *n* **:** a colorless pungent fuming vesicatory liquid acid HCOOH that occurs naturally in most ants and some other insects and in many plants, that is usu. made by acidification of sodium formate, and that is used chiefly in dyeing and finishing textiles as an acidifying or reducing agent — called also *methanoic acid*

formic aldehyde *n* **:** FORMALDEHYDE

for·mi·can \fȯrˈmīkən\ *adj* [L *formica* + E *-an*] **:** of or relating to ants

for·mi·ca·ri·idae \,fȯrməkəˈrīə,dē\ *n pl, cap* [NL, fr. *Formicarius*, type genus (fr. L *formica* + *-arius* -ary) + *-idae*] **:** a large family (suborder Tyranni) comprising the typical antbirds of tropical America — compare FURNARIIDAE — **for·mi·car·i·oid** \-ˈka(a)rē,ȯid\ *adj or n* — **for·mi·car·oid** \-ˈka(a),rȯid\ *adj*

for·mi·car·i·um \-ˈkerēəm, -ˈa(a)r-, -ˈär-\ *n, pl* **formicar·ia** \-rēə\ [ML] **:** FORMICARY; *specif* **:** an artificial ant nest arranged for observation or study of the activities of the insects

for·mi·cary \ˈfȯrmə,kerē, -i\ *n* -ES [ML *formicarium*, fr. L *formica* ant + *-arium* -ary] **:** the dwelling of a colony of ants **:** an ant hill or ant nest

for·mi·ca·tion \,==ˈkāshən\ *n* -S [L *formication-, formicatio*, fr. *formicatus* (past part. of *formicare* to crawl like an ant, fr. *formica* ant) + *-ion-, -io* -ion — more at PISMIRE] **:** an abnormal sensation resembling that made by insects creeping in or on the skin

for·mic·i·dae \fȯrˈmisə,dē\ *n pl, cap* [NL, fr. *Formica*, type genus + *-idae*] **:** a family of hymenopterous insects including all the ants

for·mi·cide \ˈfȯrmə,sīd\ *n* -S [L *formica* ant + E *-cide*] **:** a substance used for destroying ants

1**for·mi·cine** \-,sīn, -,sən\ *adj* [L *formicinus*, fr. *formica* ant + *-inus* -ine] **1 :** of, relating to, or resembling an ant **2** [NL *Formicinae* group of ants, fr. L, fem. pl. of *formicinus*] **:** belonging to a group of ants that resemble and are closely related to those of the genus *Formica*

2**formicine** \"\ *n* -S **:** a formicine ant

for·mi·civ·o·rous \ˌ==ˌsiv(ə)rəs\ *adj* [L *formica* ant + E *-i-* + *-vorous*] **:** feeding on ants

for·mi·coi·dea \,==ˈkȯidēə\ *n pl, cap* [NL, fr. *Formica* + *-oidea*] **:** a superfamily of aculeate hymenopterous insects consisting of the ants and being coextensive with Formicidae

for·mi·col·o·gist \-ˈkäləjəst\ *n* -S [L *formica* ant + E *-o-* + *-logist*] **:** MYRMECOLOGIST

for·mi·da·bil·i·ty \,fȯ(r)mədəˈbiləd·ē, -ətē, -i\ *n* -ES **:** formidable quality ⟨a ~, in both size and substance, which must have deterred many readers —*Times Lit. Supp.*⟩

for·mi·da·ble \ˈfȯ(r)mədəbəl, fȯ(r)ˈmid-\ *adj* [ME, fr. L *formidabilis*, fr. *formidare* to fear, dread (fr. *formido* fear, terror) + *-abilis* -able; akin to Gk *mormō* she-monster, bugbear, *mormoros* fear] **1 :** exciting fear, dread, or apprehension ⟨a grim and ~ foe⟩ ⟨a ~ prospect⟩ ⟨the first attack was dangerous, but a second must be more ~ still —William Cowper⟩ **2 :** able seriously to impede a projected interaction or course of action usu. by interposing difficulties, hardships, or obstructions ⟨the mountains were a ~ barrier to our progress⟩ ⟨these qualities . . . made the Miltonic sentence a ~ construction —R.M.Weaver⟩; *broadly* **:** DIFFICULT ⟨~ coloratura passages⟩ **3 :** tending to inspire awe or wonder usu. by reason of notable size, quantity, superiority, or excellence ⟨had a ~ array of compositions to his credit —Joseph Wechsberg⟩; *broadly* **:** LARGE, SUPERIOR, OUTSTANDING ⟨in a society based on oral tradition the memory of the elders is ~⟩ ⟨a social lioness of ~ glamour⟩ ⟨his ~ accomplishments in art⟩ — **for·mi·da·ble·ness** \-nəs\ *n* -ES — **for·mi·da·bly** \-əblē, -li\ *adv*

forming *pres part of* FORM

forming die *n* **:** a die resembling a drawing die but lacking a blank holder

forming press *n* **:** a punch press used for forming (as metal parts)

forming punch *n* **:** a punch that operates with a forming die

forming rolls *n pl* **:** a set of rolls shaped to give a predetermined contour of cross section to work run through them

forming tool *n* **1** *or* **form tool :** a tool or machine accessory so shaped that it imparts a predetermined contour or profile to the work **2 :** a pair of light tongs with broad flat ends used in manipulating and shaping softened glass

form·ism \ˈfȯ(r),mizəm\ *n* -S [1*form* + *-ism*] **:** a philosophical theory (as Platonism or Aristotelianism) assigning a preeminent place to metaphysical forms

form·ist \-,məst\ *n* -S **:** one who advocates strict adherence to forms — **form·is·tic** \(,)=ˈmistik\ *adj*

form·less \ˈ=ləs\ *adj* **:** deficient in or lacking form: as **a :** having no regular or inherent shape ⟨fluids are ~, taking the shape of their container⟩ **b :** SHAPELESS 2 ⟨a ~ old dress⟩ **c :** lacking order or arrangement **:** INCHOATE ⟨the ~ welter of his prose works —George Saintsbury⟩ **d :** having no physical existence **:** IMMATERIAL ⟨the primitive society exists in a world filled with taboos, mysteries, and ~ but often malevolent beings⟩ — **form·less·ly** *adv* — **form·less·ness** *n* -ES

form letter *n* **:** a letter on a subject of frequent recurrence (as in a business house) that can be sent to different persons without essential change other than in the address

form line *n* **:** a line drawn on a map to depict surface configuration in a generalized manner and usu. without indicating elevations — compare CONTOUR LINE

form master *n* **:** a teacher in charge of a form esp. in an English secondary school

formo- — see FORM-

form of action : one of the personal actions formerly brought at common law (as assumpsit, detinue, replevin)

form of address : a formula generally accepted as proper or suitable for addressing an individual of a particular rank or status either orally or in writing

form of discourse : one of the types into which discourses are classified according to function and which comprise exposition, argument, description, and narration

form of forms : FIRST CAUSE

form oil *n* **:** oil with which concrete forms esp. of metal are sometimes treated to prevent sticking upon removal

For·mol \ˈfȯr,mȯl, -ōl\ *trademark* — used for an aqueous solution of formaldehyde

for·mol·ize \-,līz\ *vt* -ED/-ING/-S *see -ize in Explan Notes* [*Formol* + *-ize*] **:** to treat (as a serum) with a dilute formaldehyde solution esp. for the purpose of attenuating a virus or toxin

for·mo·nitrile \fȯr,mō+\ *n* -S [ISV *form-* + *nitrile*] **:** HYDROGEN CYANIDE

for·mo·sa \fȯ(r)ˈmōsə, -zə\ *adj, usu cap* [fr. *Formosa*, island in the China Sea] **:** of or from the island of Formosa ⟨*Formosa* tea⟩ **:** of the kind or style prevalent in Formosa **:** FORMOSAN

formosa camphor *n, usu cap F* **:** dextrorotatory camphor

1**for·mo·san** \-sᵊn, -zᵊn\ *adj, usu cap* [*Formosa* + E *-an*] **1 :** of or relating to the island of Formosa or its inhabitants **2 :** of, relating to, or in the Formosan language

2**formosan** \"\ *n* -S *cap* **1 a :** a native or inhabitant of Formosa **b :** a member of one of the largely uncivilized groups of mixed Mongolian and Indonesian descent that live in the interior of the island **2 a :** the Indonesian languages of the Formosan people **b :** any of these languages

formosan pheasant *n, usu cap F* **:** a rather light-colored pheasant native to Formosa that is probably a variety of the ring-necked pheasant with which it freely interbreeds and that like the latter has been widely introduced in No. America

for·mos·i·ty \fȯrˈmäsəd·ē, -ətē, -i\ *n* -ES [ME *formosite*, fr. L *formositas*, fr. *formosus* beautiful (fr. *forma* form, beauty + *-osus* -ous) + *-itas* -ity — more at FORM] *archaic* **:** beauty or a beautiful thing

form quotient *n* **:** the ratio of the breast-high diameter of a tree to the diameter at some higher point

forms *pl of* FORM, *pres 3d sing of* FORM

form species *n* **:** a taxonomic species placed in a form genus

for·mu·la \ˈfȯrmyələ, -ȯ(ə)m-\ *n, pl* **formu·las** \-ləz\ *also* **formu·lae** \-,lē, -,lī\ *often attrib* [L, dim. of *forma* form] **1 a :** a set form of words for use in a ceremony or ritual **b :** a formal statement of religious doctrine or a written confession of faith **c :** a conventionalized statement intended to express some fundamental truth or principle esp. as a basis for negotiation, discussion, or action ⟨the two nations sought a ~ that would allow settling of the border dispute⟩ ⟨the ~ "54–40 or fight"⟩ **2 a :** a recipe or prescription giving method and proportions of ingredients for the preparation of some material (as a medicine, a blend of coffee, or a caulking compound) **b :** a milk mixture or substitute for feeding an infant typically consisting of prescribed proportions and forms of cow's milk, water, and sugar; *often* **:** a batch of this made up at one time to meet an infant's future requirements (as during a 24-hour period) **3 a :** a general fact, rule, or principle expressed in symbols ⟨certain earlier workers attempted to differentiate nematodes by a ~ of numerical ratios⟩ **b :** a symbolic expression showing the composition or constitution of a chemical substance and consisting of symbols for the elements present and subscripts to indicate the relative or total number of atoms present in a molecule ⟨the ~*s* for water, sulfuric acid, and ethyl alcohol are H_2O, H_2SO_4, and C_2H_5OH respectively⟩ — see EMPIRICAL FORMULA, GENERAL FORMULA, MOLECULAR FORMULA, STRUCTURAL FORMULA **c :** a group of symbols (as numbers, letters, or arbitrary signs) associated to express briefly a single concept; *also, in logic* **:** any combination of signs in an uninterpreted calculus **d** *in logic* **:** an expression (as a statement or matrix) stipulated to be meaningful by the rules of the calculus to which it belongs; *esp* **:** such an expression containing only variables **4 :** a prescribed or set form **:** a fixed or conventional method (as of acting, arranging, or speaking) **:** an established rule or custom — often used somewhat derogatorily ⟨many of the paintings were unimaginative ~ works⟩ ⟨the limitations of ~ fiction —Coleman Rosenberger⟩ **5 :** any of the various written forms by which the praetors of ancient Rome referred causes to judges or arbitrators for hearing and adjudication upon a summons of the defendant into court by the plaintiff

for·mu·lable \-ləbəl\ *adj* [*formul*ate + *-able*] **:** capable of being formulated

for·mu·la·ic \ˌ==ˌlā·ik\ *adj* [*formula* + *-ic*] **:** characterized by or made up of formulas **:** constituting a formula ⟨~ expression of ideas⟩ ⟨a ~ phrase⟩ — **for·mu·la·i·cal·ly** \-ək(ə)lē\ *adv*

for·mu·lar·ism \ˈfȯrmyələ,rizəm\ *n* -S [1*formulary* + *-ism*] **:** the practice of depending on or adhering strictly to set formulas — **for·mu·lar·is·tic** \ˌ===ˌristik\ *adj*

for·mu·la·ri·zable \ˌ===ˌrīzəbəl\ *adj* **:** capable of being reduced to a formula **:** FORMULABLE

for·mu·lar·iza·tion \,===rəˈzāshən, -,rīˈz-\ *n* -S **:** an act or a product of formularizing

for·mu·lar·ize \-,rīz\ *vt* -ED/-ING/-S [1*formulary* + *-ize*] **1 :** to state in or reduce to a formula **:** FORMULATE **2 :** to bind or circumscribe the action of by formulas ⟨men tricked by their own ingenuity into becoming *formularized* slaves of the machines they created⟩ — **for·mu·lar·iz·er** \-zə(r\ *n* -S

1**for·mu·lary** \ˈ==,lerē, -ri\ *n* -ES [MF *formulaire*, fr. *formule* formula (fr. L *formula*) + *-aire* -ary] **1 :** a book or other collection of stated and prescribed forms (as of oaths, declarations, or prayers) **:** a system of formulas ⟨a liturgical ~⟩ **2 :** a prescribed form or model **:** FORMULA **3 :** a book containing a list of medicinal substances and formulas for making medicines

2**formulary** \"\ *adj* [*formula* + *-ary*] **1 :** of or relating to formulas or to a formulary system **2 :** constituting a formula ⟨a ~ solution of a problem⟩ **3 :** preoccupied with or adhering to formulas ⟨a stiff ~ man⟩

formulas *pl of* FORMULA

for·mu·lat·able \ˈ==,lād·əbəl\ *adj* **:** capable of being formulated

for·mu·late \-,lāt, *usu* -ād·+V\ *vt* -ED/-ING/-S [*formula* + *-ate*] **1 a :** to reduce to or express in or as if in a formula **:** put into a systematized statement or expression **b :** to plan out in orderly fashion **:** DEVISE ⟨*formulating* expedients to meet the emergency⟩ **2 a :** to develop a formula for the preparation of (as a soap or a plastic) **:** standardize by formula **b :** to make or prepare in accord with a formula

for·mu·la·tion \,==ˈlāshən\ *n* -S **:** an act or the product of formulating ⟨his ~ of the data was clear and concise⟩ ⟨a new varnish ~⟩

for·mu·la·tive \ˈ==,lād·iv, -ātiv, -ēv\ *adj* **:** tending to effect formulation ⟨exerting ~ influences on the student's thought processes⟩

for·mu·la·tor \-,lād·ə(r), -ātə-\ *n* -S **:** one that formulates; *esp* **:** a developer of commercial and industrial formulas

for·mu·la·to·ry \-,lə,tōrē, -,ȯr-\ *adj* **:** of or relating to formulation

for·mule \ˈfȯr(,)myül\ *n* -S [F, fr. L *formula* — more at FORMULA] **:** FORMULA

for·mu·lism \-,myə,lizəm\ *n* -S [*formula* + *-ism*] **:** attachment to or reliance on formulas

for·mu·lis·tic \ˌ==ˌlistik\ *adj* **:** based on or characterized by a formula

for·mu·li·za·tion \,==ləˈzāshən, -,līˈz-\ *n* -S **:** FORMULATION

for·mu·lize \ˈ==,līz\ *vt* -ED/-ING/-S [*formula* + *-ize*] **:** FORMULATE 1

form up *vi* **:** to assume or participate in an orderly arrangement ⟨the waiting crowd *formed up* in a long line⟩ ⟨the planes *formed up* over the airfield⟩

Form·var \ˈfȯrm,vär\ *trademark* — used for various thermoplastic resins that are formals of polyvinyl alcohol and are used esp. in coatings, adhesives, and molding materials

form word *n* **:** FUNCTION WORD

formwork \ˈ=,=\ *n* **:** a set of forms in place for the reception of concrete

formy *var of* FORMÉE

for·myl \ˈfȯr,mil, -,məl\ *n* -S [ISV *form-* + *-yl*] **:** the radical HCO– of formic acid that is also characteristic of aldehydes

for·myl·ate \-,mə,lāt\ *vt* -ED/-ING/-S [*formyl* + *-ate*] **:** to introduce formyl into (a compound) — **for·myl·a·tion** \,==ˈlāshən\ *n* -S

formyl violet S4B *n, usu cap F&V* **:** an acid dye — see DYE table I (under *Acid Violet 17*)

for·nent \fə(r)ˈnent\ *or* **for·ninst** \-ˈninzt, -ˈnin(t)st\ *also* **for·nenst** \-ˈnenzt, -ˈnen(t)st\ *prep* [ME (Sc dial.) *fornent, forenent, fornentis*, fr. ME *for-, fore-* fore + *anent* or *anentes* anenst — more at ANENT, ANENST] **1** *dial* **:** in front of **:** OPPOSITE ⟨a little square ~ the church⟩ **2** *dial* **:** near to **:** alongside of **:** BESIDE, AGAINST ⟨left the shovel ~ the fence⟩

1**for·ni·cate** \ˈfȯ(r)nə,kāt, *usu* -ād·+V\ *vb* -ED/-ING/-S [LL *fornicatus*, past part. of *fornicare, fornicari*, fr. L *fornic-, fornix* arch, vault, arched basement (inhabited by people of the lower classes), brothel, prob. fr. *fornus, furnus* oven — more at FURNACE] *vi* **:** to commit fornication ~ *vt* **:** to engage in fornication with

2**for·ni·cate** \-nəkət, -nə,kāt\ *also* **for·ni·cat·ed** \-nə,kādəd\ *adj* [L *fornicatus*, fr. *fornic-, fornix* arch, vault + L *-atus* -ate, -ated] **1 :** having an arched or vaulted form ⟨a small mollusk with an abruptly ~ shell⟩ ⟨broad ~ leaves⟩ **2** *of plants* **:** having fornices

1**for·ni·ca·tion** \,fȯ(r)nəˈkāshən\ *n* -S [ME *fornicacioun*, fr. MF & LL; MF *fornication*, fr. LL *fornication-, fornicatio*, fr. *fornicatus* (past part.) + L *-ion-, -io* -ion] **1 :** human sexual intercourse other than between a man and his wife **:** sexual intercourse between a spouse and an unmarried person **:** sexual intercourse between unmarried people — used in some translations (as AV, DV) of the Bible (as in Mt 5:32) for *unchastity* (as in RSV) or *immorality* (as in NCE) to cover all sexual intercourse except between husband and wife or concubine **2 :** sexual intercourse on the part of an unmarried person accomplished with consent and not deemed adultery — compare INCEST, RAPE

2**fornication** \"\ *n* -S [L *fornication-, fornicatio*, fr. *fornicatus* vaulted + *-ion-, -io* -ion] **:** a vaulting or arching **:** vaulted construction (as of a cloister)

for·ni·ca·tor \ˈfȯ(r)nə,kād·ə(r), -ātə-\ *n* -S [ME *fornicatour*, fr. LL *fornicator*, fr. *fornicatus* (past part.) + L *-or*] **:** a person guilty of fornication — sometimes used to distinguish the male participant in such conduct; compare FORNICATRIX

for·ni·ca·to·ry \ˈfȯ(r)nəkə,tōrē, fȯ(r)ˈnik-\ *adj* [*fornicate* + *-ory*] **:** of or relating to fornication ⟨~ literature⟩

fornicatress *n* -ES [*fornicator* + *-ess*] *obs* **:** FORNICATRIX

for·ni·ca·trix \,fȯ(r)nəˈkā·triks\ *n, pl* **fornicatri·ces** \-,kəˈtrī,sēz\ [LL, fem. of *fornicator*] **:** a woman guilty of fornication — compare FORNICATOR

for·nic·i·form \(ˈ)fȯrˌnisə,fȯrm\ *adj* [L *fornic-, fornix* + E *-iform*] **:** FORNICATE

for·nix \ˈfȯrniks, -nēks\ *n, pl* **forni·ces** \-nə,sēz\ [NL, fr. L, arch, vault — more at FORNICATE] **1** *anat* **:** an arch or fold or an arched or folded structure: as **a :** the vault of the cranium **b :** the part of the conjunctiva overlying the cornea **c :** a body of nerve fibers lying beneath the corpus callosum with which they are continuous posteriorly and serving to integrate the hippocampus with other parts of the brain **d :** the vaulted upper part of the vagina surrounding the uterine cervix **e :** the fundus of the stomach **f :** the vault of the pharynx **2 :** one of the small arched scales in the throat of the corolla of some plants (as members of the genus *Myosotis*)

for·pine \fə(r)ˈpīn\ *vb* -ED/-ING/-S [ME *forpinen*, fr. *for-* + *pinen* to pine — more at PINE] *archaic* **:** to waste or pine away (as from anguish or suffering)

for·pit *or* **for·pet** \ˈfōrpət\ *n* -S [alter. of *fourth part*] *chiefly Scot* **:** ¼ peck

for·rad *or* **for·rard** \ˈfȯrə(r)d\ *dial var of* FORWARD

for·rad·er *also* **for·rard·er** \-də(r)\ *chiefly dial comparative of* FORWARD

for real *adv* **1 :** in earnest **:** SERIOUSLY ⟨this was no casual scuffling: they were fighting *for real*⟩ **2** *slang* **:** REALLY ⟨now you've messed things up *for real*⟩

forrel *var of* FOREL

for·rit \ˈfȯrət\ *chiefly Scot var of* FORWARD

for·rit·some \-tsəm\ *adj* [*forrit* + *-some*] *Scot* **:** BOLD, IMPUDENT, FORWARD

fors *pl of* FOR

for·sake \fə(r)ˈsāk, fȯrˈ-, fȯ(ə)ˈ-\ *vt* **for·sook** \-ˈsu̇k\ **for·saken** \-ˈsākən\ **forsaking; forsakes** [ME *forsaken* to reject, forsake, fr. OE *forsacan*, fr. *for-* + *sacan* to dispute, Goth *sakan* to quarrel — more at SAKE] **1 :** to renounce or surrender (as a custom or practice formerly held dear) ⟨promised to ~ his bad habits if she would marry him⟩ **2 :** to quit or leave entirely **:** depart or withdraw from **:** LEAVE, DESERT, ABANDON ⟨false friends ~ us in adversity⟩ ⟨*forsook* the theater for a career in politics⟩

forsaken *adj* [ME, fr. past part. of *forsaken*] **:** left desolate or empty **:** DESERTED ⟨the ~ slopes where children once played on their way from school); *often* : miserable and forlorn as if deserted ⟨the conviction that where one was born and lives is the best place in the world no matter how ~ a hole it may appear to an outsider —E.L.Ullman⟩ — see GODFORSAKEN — **for·sak·en·ly** *adv* — **for·sak·en·ness** \-kən(n)əs\ *n* -ES

for·sak·er \-kə(r)\ *n* -S [ME, fr. *forsaken* to forsake + *-er*] : one that forsakes

forslack *vt* [*for-* + *slack*] *obs* : to be remiss in : NEGLECT

for·slow \fə(r)'slō\ *vb* [ME *forslewen* to be slow, delay, fr. OE *forslǣwan, forslāwian*, fr. *for-* + *-slǣwan, slāwian* to be slow, fr. *slāw* slow — more at SLOW] *archaic* : to put off : DELAY

forsook *past or obs past part of* FORSAKE

for·sooth \fə(r)'süth\ *adv* [ME *for soth, for sothe*, fr. OE *forsōth*, fr. *for* + *sōth* truth — more at SOOTH] : in truth : CERTAINLY, INDEED — now often used to imply contempt or doubt ⟨a pretty story ~⟩

for·speak \fə(r)'spēk\ *vt* [ME *forspeken* to cast a bad spell over, speak evil of, fr. OE *forspecan, forsprecan* to speak in vain, deny, denounce, fr. *for-* + *specan, sprecan* to speak — more at SPEAK] **1** *now dial Brit* : to cast a bad spell over : bewitch esp. by immoderate praise ⟨don't boast about the child, lest you ~ him⟩ **2** *obs* : to speak against : ASPERSE

for·spent \fə(r)'spent\ *adj* [*for-* + *spent*] *archaic* : worn out : EXHAUSTED ⟨~ with speed —Shak.⟩

forss·man antibody \'fȯrsmən-\ *n, usu cap F* [after John *Forssman* †1947 Swedish pathologist] : an antibody (as heterophile antibody) active against a Forssman antigen

forssman antigen *n, usu cap F* [after J. *Forssman*] : an antigenic constituent occurring in animals without regard to biologic relationship (as one present in guinea pigs and sheep but absent from rabbits and cattle) : a heterophile antigen

for·ster·ite \'fō(r)stə,rīt\ *n* -S [Johann R. *Forster* †1798 Ger. traveler + E *-ite*] : a mineral consisting of magnesian olivine; *specif* : magnesium silicate Mg_2SiO_4 constituting the essential component of some refractories

forster's tern *n, usu cap F* [after Johann R. *Forster*] : a black-capped tern (*Sterna forsteri*) that is related to the common tern, breeds chiefly in marshes and on the interior lakes of No. America, and migrates southward in winter

forst·ner bit \'fōrstnər-\ *n, usu cap F* [fr. the name *Forstner*] : a spurless wood-drilling bit used esp. for drilling blind holes

for sure *adv* : CERTAINLY, INEVITABLY

for·swear *or* **fore·swear** \fȯr'swe(ə)r, -wa(a)(ə)r; fō(ə)'sweə, -wa(a)ə\ *vb* **for·swore** *or* **fore·swore** \fȯr'swō(ə)r, -wȯ(ə)r; fō(ə)'swōə, -wȯ(ə)\ **forsworn** *or* **foresworn** \fȯr'swō(ə)rn, fō(ə)'swō(ə)n\ **forswearing** *or* **foreswearing**; **forswears** *or* **foreswears** [ME *forsweren*, fr. OE *forswerian* (akin to OS *farswerian* to swear falsely, OHG *farswerren* to abjure), fr. *for-* + *swerian* to swear — more at SWEAR] *vt* **1** : to reject or renounce upon oath; *broadly* : to renounce earnestly, determinedly, or with protestations — sometimes used with an infinitive as object ⟨she had *forsworn* to wed again⟩ **2** : to deny upon oath ⟨*forswore* the debt⟩ **3 a** *archaic* : to swear to (as a matter of fact) falsely **b** : PERJURE ⟨~ himself⟩ ~ *vi* : to swear falsely : commit perjury **syn** see ABJURE

forsworn *or* **foresworn** *adj* [ME, fr. OE *forsworen*, past part. of *forswerian*] : PERJURED

for·syth·ia \fə(r)'sithēə, *chiefly Brit* fȯr'sī- *sometimes* -ithēə\ *n* [NL, fr. William *Forsyth* †1804 Brit. botanist + NL *-ia*] **1** *cap* : a small genus of ornamental Asian and European shrubs (family Oleaceae) with opposite leaves and bright yellow bell-shaped flowers which appear before the leaves in early spring **2** -S : any plant of the genus *Forsythia* **3** -S *often cap* **a** : a moderate orange yellow **b** : a brilliant yellow

¹fort \'fō(ə)r|t, -ō(ə)r|, -ōə|, -ȯ(ə)|, *usu* |d.+V\ *n* -S [ME *forte*, fr. MF *fort*, fr. *fort* strong, fortified, fr. L *fortis* strong, fr. OL *forctis*; prob. akin to OHG *berg* mountain — more at BARROW] **1** : a strong or fortified place: as **a** : a fortified place occupied only by troops and surrounded with such works as a ditch, rampart, and parapet : FORTIFICATION **b** : an enclosed work possessing bastions **c** : a permanent army post of the U.S. — often used in place names **2** : a trading post on the No. American frontier

²fort \"\ *vb* -ED/-ING/-S *vt* **1** : to protect by or station or gather in a fort **2** : to enclose by fortifications : FORTIFY ~ *vi* **1** *archaic* : to construct fortifications **2** : to gather in a strong or fortified place (as for defense)

fort *abbr* fortification; fortified

for·ta·le·za \,fō(r)də,'lāzə\ *adj, usu cap* [fr. *Fortaleza*, Brazil] : of or from the city of Fortaleza, Brazil : of the kind or style prevalent in Fortaleza

for·ta·lice \'fō(r)də̇ləs\ *n* -S [ME, fr. ML *fortalitia* — more at FORTRESS] **1** *archaic* : FORTRESS **2** *archaic* : a small fort or an outwork of a fortification

fort ancient *adj, usu cap F&A* [fr. *Fort Ancient*, Warren county, Ohio] : of or belonging to a late prehistoric aspect of the upper Mississippi culture centered in southern Ohio and Indiana and extending into Kentucky and West Virginia

¹forte \'fō(ə)r|t, -ō(ə)r|, -ōə|, -ȯ(ə)|, *usu* |d.+V *also* 'fȯr|d-(,)ā, -ō(ə)|, |(,)tā\ *n* -S [earlier *fort*, fr. MF, fr. *fort*, adj., strong — more at FORT] **1** : one's strong point : that in which one excels ⟨writing is his ~⟩ **2** : the stronger part of the blade of a sword : the part or half of a sword nearest the hilt — opposed to *foible*

²for·te \'fȯr|d·(,)ā, 'fō(ə)|, (,)tā; *also* 'fȯr|d·|ē, |t|, |i\ *adv* (*or adj*) [It, strongly, loudly, fr. *forte*, adj., strong, loud, fr. L *fortis* strong — more at FORT] : LOUDLY, POWERFULLY — used as a direction in music; opposed to *piano*; abbr. *f* or *F*

³forte \"\ *n* -S : a tone or passage played forte

for·te·men·te \,fȯrd·ə'men·(,)tā\ *adv* [It, fr. *forte*, adj.] : STRONGLY, LOUDLY — used as a direction in music

for·te·pia·no \,fȯ(r)d·ə·pyä(,)nō\ *n* [F or It; F, fr. It, fr. *forte* loud + *piano* soft] *archaic* : PIANOFORTE

forte–piano \¦=¦=(,)=\ *adj* [It, lit., loud-soft] : loud then immediately soft — used as a direction in music; abbr. *fp*

fortes *pl of* FORTIS

for·tes·cue \'fȯrd·ə,skyü\ *also* **for·tes·cure** \-yůr\ *or* **for·tes·que** \-yü\ *n* -S [alter. (influenced by the proper name *Fortescue*) of *forty-skewer*] : an Australian scorpion fish (*Centropogon australis*) having along the back venomous erectile spines capable of inflicting painful wounds — called also *forty-skewer, scorpion*

¹forth \'fō(ə)rth, 'fȯ(ə)rth, 'fōəth, 'fȯ(ə)th\ *adv* [ME, adv. & prep., fr. OE; akin to OFris & OS *forth* forward, further, MHG *vort*, and to OE *for*, prep., for, before — more at FOR] **1** : onward in time, place, or order : in advance from a given point : on to or toward the end : FORWARD ⟨from that day ~⟩ ⟨one, two, three, and so ~⟩ ⟨swaying back and ~⟩ **2** : out esp. from a state of concealment, retirement, confinement, or nondevelopment : out into notice or view ⟨the plants in spring put ~ leaves⟩ ⟨invites them ~ to labor in the sun —John Dryden⟩ ⟨a spring issuing ~ from the hill⟩ **3** *obs* : beyond a certain boundary : AWAY, ABROAD ⟨I have no mind of feasting ~ tonight —Shak.⟩

²forth \"\ *prep* [ME] **1** *obs* : forward or onward to **2** *archaic* : forth from : out of

³forth *n* -S [ME, fr. ¹*forth*] *obs* : free course : WAY — used chiefly in the phrase *have one's forth*

for that *conj, archaic* : BECAUSE

forthbringer \(')=¦==\ *n* -S [¹*forth* + *bringer*] : one that brings forth

forth·come \(')=¦kəm\ *vi* [back-formation fr. *forthcoming*] : to be forthcoming

forth·com·er \-mə(r)\ *n* -S : one that comes forth

¹forth·com·ing \(')=¦kəmiŋ, -mēŋ\ *adj* [fr. pres. part. of obs. *forthcome* to come forth, fr. ME *forthcomen*, fr. ¹*forth* + *comen* to come — more at COME] **1** : about to appear : APPROACHING ⟨the ~ holidays⟩ ⟨a new edition is reported to be ~ in the fall⟩ **2 a** : readily available ⟨new funds will be ~ after the election⟩ **b** : AFFABLE, APPROACHABLE, SOCIABLE ⟨a pleasingly ~ manner⟩

²forthcoming \"\ *n* [fr. gerund of obs. *forthcome*] **1** : a coming forth : APPROACH **2** *or* **furth·com·ing** \fərth'kəmiŋ\ : an action under Scots law by which an arrestment is perfected by sentence ordering the debt to be paid or the goods to be delivered to the creditor

forthcoming bond *n* : a bond given to a sheriff conditioned to duly produce the property levied upon

forth·com·ing·ness *n* -ES : the quality or state of being forthcoming; *usu* : APPROACHABILITY, SOCIABILITY

forthfaring \='==\ *n* -S [¹*forth* + *faring*, gerund of ¹*fare*] : an act or instance of going out : a journey forth

forthgaze \='=\ *vi* : to gaze forth

forthgoer \='==\ *n* [¹*forth* + *goer*] : one that goes forth (as from a home place or group of associates)

¹forthgoing \(')=¦gōiŋ, -ōēŋ\ *n* [ME, fr. gerund of *forthgon* to go forth, fr. ¹*forth* + *gon* to go — more at GO] : a going forth (as a departure) : something that goes forth (as an utterance)

²forthgoing \"\ *adj* : ENTHUSIASTIC, GRACIOUS

for·think \fər'thiŋk\ *vb* **for·thought** \-'thȯt\ **forthought**; **forthinking**; **forthinks** [ME *forthinken*, *forthenken* to regret, repent, displease, be displeased; partly fr. *for-* + *thinken* to seem; partly fr. OE *forthencan* to mistrust, despise, despair, fr. *for-* + *thencan* to think — more at THINK] *vt, now chiefly Scot* : to change the mind of (oneself); *often* : REGRET ~ *vi, now chiefly Scot* : to have a change of mind or a feeling of regret

forth of *prep* [¹*forth*] : out of : out from ⟨the lion came *forth of* his den⟩

forth on *adv* [ME, fr. ¹*forth* + *on* (adv.)] *obs* : ONWARD, FORTHWITH

¹forthputting \(')=¦==\ *adj* [¹*forth* + *putting*, pres. part. of *put*] : BOLD, FORWARD

²forthputting \"\ *n* [¹*forth* + *putting*, gerund of *put*] **1** : an act of putting forth ⟨his determined ~ of effort⟩ **2** : forward or aggressive conduct

¹forth·right \(')=¦=\ *adv* [ME, fr. ¹*forth* + *right* (adv.)] **1 a** : directly forth or ahead : unswervingly forward **b** : without hesitation : FRANKLY ⟨spoke ~ and to the point⟩ **2** *archaic* : STRAIGHTWAY, STRAIGHTFORWARD, IMMEDIATELY

²forthright \"\ *adj* [ME, fr. ¹*forth* + *right* (adj.)] : proceeding straight on; *usu* : lacking ambiguity : DIRECT, STRAIGHTFORWARD ⟨a ~ man⟩ ⟨a ~ approach to a problem⟩ — **forth·right·ly** *adv* — **forth·right·ness** *n* -ES

³forthright \'=,=\ *n* : a straight path or direct course (as of action)

forthsetting \='==\ *n* [¹*forth* + *setting*, gerund of *set*] *archaic* : an exhibition or setting forth

forthtell \='=\ *vt* [¹*forth* + *tell*] : to make public : PUBLISH — **forth·tell·er** \"+ə(r)\ *n*

forth·ward \'fōrthwərd, 'fȯr-\ *adv* [ME, fr. OE *forthweard* forward, continually, henceforth, fr. ¹*forth* + *-weard* -ward] *archaic* : FORWARD

forthwith \'=,=\ *adv* [ME, fr. ¹*forth* + *with*] **1** : with dispatch : without delay : within a reasonable time ⟨you are to proceed ~ to your home⟩ : IMMEDIATELY **2** : immediately after some preceding event : THEREUPON ⟨when students . . . are suspended, they must ~ leave Williamsburg —*College of William & Mary Catalog*⟩ ⟨the legislature left the capital and that city ~ became less important to the revolutionary forces⟩ ⟨immediately there fell from his eyes as it had been scales: and he received sight ~ —Acts 9:18 (AV)⟩

for thy *adv* [ME *forthy*, fr. OE *forthȳ*, fr. *for* + *thȳ*, instr. of *thæt* it, that — more at THAT] *obs* : on this account : THEREFORE ⟨have no care for *thy* —Edmund Spenser⟩

forthy \'fōrthi\ *adj* [¹*forth* + *-y*] **1** *dial Brit* : forward and enterprising : inclined to be officious **2** *dial Brit* : open and friendly in nature and disposition : AFFABLE

forties *pl of* FORTY

¹for·ti·eth \'fō(r)d·ē̇əth, -(r)t|, |iəth\ *adj* [ME *fourtithe*, adj. & n., fr. OE *fēowertigotha*, fr. *fēowertig* forty + *-otha*, *-tha* -th — more at FORTY] **1** : being number 40 in a countable series ⟨the ~ day⟩ — see NUMBER table **2** : being one of 40 equal parts into which something is divisible ⟨a ~ share of the money⟩

²fortieth \"\ *n* -S [ME *fourtithe*] **1** : number 40 in a countable series **2** : the quotient of a unit divided by 40 : one of 40 equal parts of something ⟨one ~ of the total⟩

for·ti·fi·able \'fō(r)d·ə,fīəbəl\ *adj* : capable of or suitable for being fortified

for·ti·fi·ca·tion \,fō(r)d·əfə'kāshən, -)təf-\ *n* -S [ME *fortificacioun*, fr. MF *fortification*, fr. LL *fortification-, fortificatio*, fr. *fortificatus* (past part. of *fortificare*) + L *-ion-, -io* -ion] **1** : an act or process of fortifying: as **a** : a strengthening by corroboration (as of a statement) or by reinforcement (as of a structure) **b** : the act of furnishing (as a military post) with defensive works; *also* : the art or science of fortifying places or positions **c** : increase in the content of an ingredient (as alcohol in wine or vitamins in flour) by addition : ENRICHMENT **2** : something that fortifies, defends, or strengthens; *esp* : works erected to defend a place or position

fortification agate *n* : agate having angular markings resembling the plan of a fortification

fortified wine *n* : a wine (as most dessert wines) to which alcohol usu. in the form of grape brandy has been added during or after fermentation — used descriptively but not permitted in labeling or advertising in the U.S.

for·ti·fi·er \'fȯrd·ə,fī(ə)r, -rtə,-; 'fōd·ə,fīə, -ōtə,-\ *n* -S : one that fortifies

for·ti·fy \-,fī\ *vb* -ED/-ING/-ES [ME *fortifien*, fr. MF *fortifier*, fr. LL *fortificare*, fr. L *fortis* strong + *-ficare* -fy — more at FORT] *vt* **1** : to make strong : STRENGTHEN : as **a** : to strengthen and secure (as a town) by forts or batteries or by surrounding with fortifications **b** *obs* : to equip and supply (as a garrison or fortress) **c** : to add strength by reinforcing the structure of ⟨~*ing* the dam with riprap⟩ **d** : to give physical strength, courage, or endurance to : INVIGORATE, REFRESH ⟨a balanced diet *fortifies* the system against infection⟩ ⟨*fortified* himself with a glass of wine⟩ **e** : to add mental or moral strength to : furnish with resistant power : help to endure : ENCOURAGE, CONFIRM ⟨their spirits *fortified* with prayer⟩ ⟨*fortified* by initial successes he determined to carry out his plan⟩ ⟨let thy spirit ~ me in times of trouble⟩ **2** *obs* : to make (as a way) passable **3** : to add material to for the purpose of strengthening or improving: as **a** : to add ethyl alcohol to (as wines) **b** : to enrich (as a foodstuff or diet) by increasing the content of material usu. present (as minerals or vitamins) or by adding something not normally present (as an antibiotic) **c** : to bring (as a weak or spent solution) to the proper concentration by addition of a deficient substance ⟨~*ing* spent nitric acid recovered from the nitrating of cellulose with concentrated nitric acid⟩ ~ *vi* **1** *obs* : to grow or become strong **2** : to erect fortifications : prepare military defenses **syn** see STRENGTHEN

for·ti·fy·ing·ly *adv* : so as to fortify : with or for a fortifying effect

for·tin \'fȯrd·ən\ *n* -S [F, fr. It *fortino*, dim. of *forte* fort, prob. fr. F *fort* — more at FORT] : a little fort

for·tin barometer \(')fȯr¦taⁿ-\ *also* **fortin's barometer** *n, usu cap F* [after Jean *Fortin* †1831 Fr. physicist and engineer, its inventor] : a cup barometer having an adjustable cistern

forting *pres part of* FORT

¹for·tis \'fȯr|d·əs, 'fō(ə)|, |təs\ *adj* [NL, fr. L, strong — more at FORT] *of one of two homorganic consonants* : produced with greater articulatory tenseness and stronger expiration ⟨\t\ in *toe* is ~, \d\ in *doe* is lenis⟩

²fortis \"\ *n, pl* **fortes** \|d·(,)ēz, |,tēz\ [NL, fr. *fortis*, adj.] : a fortis consonant

For·ti·san \'fō(r)d·ə,san, -,zan\ *trademark* **1** — used for a strong filament yarn made from regenerated cellulose **2** : a lightweight fabric made from Fortisan yarn and used for parachutes, clothing, curtains, bandages, and various industrial purposes

¹for·tis·si·mo \(')fō(r)¦tisə,mō\ *adv* (*or adj*) [It, fr. L *fortissimus*, superl. of *fortis* — more at FORT] : very loud — used as a direction in music; abbr. *ff*

²fortissimo \"\ *n, pl* **fortissimos** \-,mōz\ *or* **fortissi·mi** \-,mē\ [It, fr. *fortissimo*, adv.] : a very loud passage, sound, or tone

for·tis·sis·si·mo \,fō(r)d·ə¦sisə,mō\ *adv* (*or adj*) [It, fr. *fortissimo* (by reduplication of the *-iss-* of the superl. suffix)] : with greatest loudness — used as a direction in music; abbr. *fff*

for·ti·tude \'fō(r)d·ə,tüd, -)tə,-, -ə,tyüd\ *n* -S [ME, fr. L *fortitudo*, fr. *fortis* strong + *-tudo* -tude — more at FORT] **1** *obs* : STRENGTH, IMPREGNABILITY ⟨the ~ of the place is best known to you —Shak.⟩ **2** : the strength or firmness of mind that enables a person to encounter danger with coolness and courage or to bear pain or adversity without murmuring, depression, or despondency : passive courage : resolute endurance ⟨had borne her mother's death . . . with quiet ~ —Ellen Glasgow⟩ ⟨the temporary ~ they had gained from the jug —Irwin Shaw⟩

syn GRIT, BACKBONE, PLUCK, GUTS, SAND. Although these terms are often used interchangeably, the following distinctions may be made: FORTITUDE usu. indicates blended resolute courage, firm behavior, and power of prolonged endurance under duress ⟨a life of unremitting physical toil and mental anxiety combined with miserable health . . . no small test of *fortitude* —John Buchan⟩ ⟨deepest admiration of Welch's *fortitude* and indomitable spirit during these months when he was slowly dying of cancer —Eleanor M. Sickels⟩ GRIT usu. blends strength, mental firmness, and a hard or indomitable endurance of deprivation or distress ⟨the foot soldier will still have to advance against strongly entrenched and fanatical troops, through sheer *grit* and fighting skill —H.S. Truman⟩ BACKBONE may indicate resolute ability and determined independence in confronting opposition or difficulty without quailing ⟨the man's *backbone* and perseverance did not fail him once in all the years of poverty and discouragement⟩ ⟨like conscience-stricken dogs they lost *backbone*, and visibly were in a condition to submit to anything —Kenneth Roberts⟩ PLUCK usu. applies to game stoutheartedness in the face of danger or willingness to continue fighting against odds ⟨the energy, fortitude, and dogged perseverance that we technically style *pluck* —E.G.Bulwer-Lytton⟩ ⟨what indomitable courage he had, how fearless he was in the midst of danger, how keen and wary in his dealing with an enemy, and how full of resources and *pluck* when difficulties arose —H.E.Scudder⟩ GUTS, usu. forceful and sometimes considered vulgar, indicates vigorous stamina in confronting and coping with what alarms, repels, discourages, or enervates ⟨he could tell by the set of Bill's mouth that sheer *guts* was all that kept him hanging to that bull's head now —F.B.Gipson⟩ ⟨what bothered him was not the superzealot attackers so much as the lack of plain old-fashioned *guts* on the part of the people who give in to them —Elmer Davis⟩ SAND is a close synonym of GRIT, occas. somewhat weaker in its implications ⟨a fine personality, the teacher type; needs more *sand* in his blood; inclined to be apologetic —H.H.Arnold & I.C.Eaker⟩

for·ti·tu·di·nous \¦=¦tüdənəs, -¦tyü-\ *adj* [L *fortitudin-, fortitudo* + E *-ous*] : having or marked by fortitude : COURAGEOUS ⟨~ heroes —Edward Gibbon⟩

fort–lamy \,fō(r)lə¦mē\ *adj, usu cap F&L* [fr. *Fort-Lamy*, Republic of Chad] : of or relating to Fort-Lamy, the capital of the Republic of Chad : of the kind or style prevalent in Fort-Lamy

fort·let \'=lət\ *n* -S [ME *fortelet*, fr. *forte* fort + *-let* — more at FORT] : a small or rudimentary fort

fortlike \'=,=\ *adj* : resembling a fort esp. in grim solidity or in well-defended state ⟨a square ~ house⟩ ⟨secure ~ vaults⟩

fort·night \'fȯrt,nīt, 'fȯr-, 'fōət-, 'fō(ə)t-\ *n* [ME *fourtenight*, fr. earlier *fourtene night*, fr. OE *fēowertȳne niht* fourteen nights] : the space of fourteen days : two weeks

¹fort·night·ly \-lē\ *adj* [*fortnight* + *-ly* (adj. suffix)] : occurring, appearing, or being made, done, or acted upon once in two weeks or every two weeks ⟨~ meeting⟩ ⟨~ letters⟩ ⟨~ tasks⟩

²fort·night·ly *adv* [*fortnight* + *-ly* (adv. suffix)] : once in a fortnight : every fortnight

³fort·night·ly *n* -ES [¹*fortnightly*] : a publication issued fortnightly

fort·nit·er *or* **fort·night·er** \-,nīd·ə(r)\ *n* -S [fr. *Fortniter*, a trademark] : a large traveling bag with hangers in the lid for garments and compartments in the bottom for accessories (as shoes)

for to *prep* [ME, fr. ¹*for* + *to*] *now chiefly dial* : TO ⟨he did go down to the meadow *for to* mow —*Ballad Book*⟩

¹for·tress \'fōr·trəs, 'fō(ə)t-\ *n* -ES *often attrib* [ME *forteresse, fortresse*, fr. MF *fortelesce, forteresce*, fr. ML *fortalitia*, fr. L *fortis* strong — more at FORT] **1** : a fortified place : STRONGHOLD; *esp* : a large and permanent fortification sometimes including a town **2** : a center or source of assurance or protection : a refuge or support ⟨they meet in freedom and in peace, and, meeting so, are an earnest and a prayer and . . . a ~ —Bernard DeVoto⟩ **3** : a region (as central Europe) dominated by a single military power and regarded as an impregnable stronghold

²fortress \"\ *vt* -ED/-ING/-ES : to furnish or protect with or as if with a fortress : FORTIFY

fort royal *n* [¹*fort* + *royal* (adj.)] *obs* : a fort of great magnitude

forts *pres 3d sing of* FORT, *pl of* FORT

for·tu·i·tism \fō(r)'tüə,tizəm, fə(r)-, -)·'tyü-\ *n* -S [*fortuitous* + *-ism*] : the doctrine or belief that evolutionary adaptations and progress are chance results rather than determined consequences of natural law or the outcome of teleology — compare TYCHISM

for·tu·i·tist \-ləd·əst, -ləṭə̇-\ *n* -S [*fortuitous* + *-ist*] : a believer in fortuitism

for·tu·i·tous \-ləd·əs, -lətəs\ *adj* [L *fortuitus*, derivative fr. the root of *fort-, fors* chance, luck — more at FORTUNE] **1** : occurring by chance without evident causal need or relation or without deliberate intention ⟨the ~ rencounters, the strange accidents of fortune —Henry Miller⟩ ⟨by which the events of life are no longer regarded as isolated and ~ moments —P.E.More⟩ **2** : LUCKY **syn** see ACCIDENTAL

for·tu·i·tous·ly *adv* : in a fortuitous manner : by chance

for·tu·i·tous·ness *n* -ES : FORTUITY

for·tu·i·ty \-ləd·ē, -lətē, -ī\ *n* -ES [irreg. fr. *fortuitous* + *-y*] **1** : fortuitous quality or state or an appearance of this **2** : a chance event or occurrence

¹for·tu·nate \'fō(r)chənət, -chnət, *usu* -əd·+V\ *adj* [ME *fortunat*, fr. L *fortunatus*, fr. past part. of *fortunare* to make prosperous, fr. *fortuna*] **1** : coming by good luck or favorable chance : bringing some good thing not foreseen as certain : presaging happiness : AUSPICIOUS ⟨a ~ event⟩ ⟨made a ~ investment⟩ **2** : receiving some unforeseen or unexpected good or some good not dependent on one's own efforts : LUCKY ⟨how ~ we are to get such a nice room⟩ **3** *of a sign of the zodiac* : having a fortunate influence **syn** see LUCKY

²fortunate \"\ *n* -S : one that is fortunate

for·tu·nate·ly *adv* : in a fortunate manner : LUCKILY

for·tu·nate·ness *n* -ES : the quality or state of being fortunate

¹for·tune \'fȯr|chən, 'fō(ə)|, |(,)chün\ *n* -S *often attrib* [ME, fr. MF, fr. L *fortuna*, derivative fr. the root of *fort-, fors* chance, luck; akin to L *ferre* to carry — more at BEAR] **1** : a hypothetical force or power that unpredictably or capriciously determines events and issues favorably or unfavorably for persons or causes ⟨more by ~, lady, than by merit —Shak.⟩ — often personified as a mythical being and then usu. cap. ⟨turn, *Fortune*, and help thy devoted servant⟩ **2** *obs* : something that befalls one : ACCIDENT, MISHAP **3 a** : good luck : favorable issue : SUCCESS : prosperity attained partly through luck ⟨~ attended the general's campaign⟩ **b** : a turn or course of good or bad luck falling to one either by pure chance or incidentally in the course of some undertaking ⟨it was my good ~ to be present —A.N.Whitehead⟩ **c fortunes** *pl* : the turns and courses of luck accompanying the progress of an individual (as through life or toward ultimate success) ⟨following the ~s of a typical rags-to-riches hero in the comics⟩ ⟨his ~s varied but he never gave up his main objective⟩ **4** : what is to befall one : DESTINY, FATE ⟨read his ~ in his palm⟩ ⟨it may be my ~ to succeed or fail but I will not hesitate to try⟩ **5 a** : condition in life as determined by material possessions : large possessions : RICHES, WEALTH ⟨a man of ~⟩ **b** : a store of material possessions or wealth owned (as by an individual or a family) ⟨was left a ~ by his uncle⟩ — often used in pl. ⟨the family ~s had declined greatly since his grandfather's day⟩ **6** *archaic* : a woman of wealth and substance : HEIRESS **7** : one of the benevolent planets (Jupiter, Venus) in a favorable aspect **syn** see CHANCE

²fortune \"\ *vb* -ED/-ING/-S [ME *fortunen*, fr. MF *fortuner*, fr. L *fortunare*, to make prosperous] *vt* **1** *obs* : to give or ascribe either good or bad fortune to : ordain the fortune of **2** *archaic* : to provide with a fortune esp. as a dower ~ *vi*, *archaic* : to fall out : HAPPEN, CHANCE

fortune hunter *n* : a person that seeks to acquire wealth esp. by marriage

for·tune·less \-nləs\ *adj* **1** : lacking in or not conducive to good fortune : UNFORTUNATE ⟨this ~ encounter⟩ **2** : lacking wealth : POOR, IMPOVERISHED; *esp* : having no marriage portion ⟨but who would marry a ~ girl⟩

fortune line *n* : LINE OF THE SUN

for·tu·nel·la \ˌfȯ(r)chə'nelə\ *n, cap* [NL, fr. Robert *Fortune* †1880 Scot. traveler and botanist + NL *-ella*] : a genus of Asiatic evergreen citrus shrubs or small trees comprising the kumquats and being often included in the genus *Citrus* from which it is distinguished by small acid fruits with a sweet pulpy edible skin and only three to seven fruit segments

fortune-tell \'==ˌ=\ *vt* [back-formation fr. [1]*fortune-telling*] : to tell the fortune of ⟨I'll conjure you, I'll *fortune-tell* you —Shak.⟩

fortune-teller \'==ˌ==\ *n* [[1]*fortune* + *teller*] : one that tells fortunes; *esp* : a person who for payment predicts what are claimed to be future events or influences in the life of another

[1]**fortune-telling** \'==ˌ==\ *n* [[1]*fortune* + *telling*, gerund of *tell*] : the art or practice of telling fortunes

[2]**fortune-telling** \"\ *adj* [[1]*fortune* + *telling*, pres. part. of *tell*] : engaged in or practicing fortune-telling : serving to tell fortunes

fort wayne \-'wān\ *adj, usu cap F&W* [fr. *Fort Wayne*, Ind.] : of or from the city of Fort Wayne, Ind. ⟨a *Fort Wayne* hotel⟩ : of the kind or style prevalent in Fort Wayne

fort worth *adj, usu cap F&W* [fr. *Forth Worth*, Tex.] : of or from the city of Fort Worth, Texas ⟨the *Fort Worth* stockyards⟩ : of the kind or style prevalent in Fort Worth

[1]**for·ty** \'fȯr|d·|ē, 'fȯr|, 'fȯ(ə)|, 'fōə|, |t|, |i\ *adj* [ME *fourty*, fr. OE *fēowertig*, fr. *fēowertig*, n., group of 40, fr. *fēower* four + *-tig* group of 10 — more at FOUR, EIGHTY] : being one more than 39 in number ⟨~ years⟩ — see NUMBER table

[2]**forty** \"\ *pron, pl in constr* [ME *fourty*, fr. *fourty*, adj.] : 40 countable persons or things not specified but under consideration and being enumerated ⟨~ are here⟩ ⟨~ were found⟩

[3]**forty** \"\ *n* -ES **1** : four tens : twice 20 : five times eight : two twenties : eight fives : two score **2 a** : 40 units or objects ⟨a total of ~⟩ **b** : a group or set of 40 ⟨arranged by *forties*⟩ **3** : the numerable quantity symbolized by the arabic numerals 40 **4** : the 40th in a set or series; *esp* : an article of clothing of the 40th size ⟨wears a ~⟩ **5** : something having as an essential feature 40 units or members **6** : a 40-acre plot of land : one sixteenth of a section of land : a rectangular block of land with quarter-mile sides **7** : a boat of 40 tons burden **8** : three points won in a game of tennis **9 forties** *pl* **a** : the numbers 40 to 49 inclusive ⟨a score in the *forties*⟩ ⟨low grades in the *forties*⟩ **b** : the members of a series or set of successive numbers that end in 40 to 49 inclusive ⟨the *forties* of the preceding century⟩ ⟨lives in the *forties* in the next block⟩ **c** : the portion of a continuum lying between 40 and 50 on a scale of measurement or segmentation ⟨temperatures in the *forties* tomorrow⟩ ⟨a man in his *forties*⟩ ⟨dresses selling in the *forties*⟩ ⟨in the latitude of the *forties*⟩

[1]**forty-eight** \¦==¦=\ *adj* : being one more than 47 in number ⟨*forty-eight* years⟩ — see NUMBER table

[2]**forty-eight** \"\ *pron, pl in constr* : 48 countable persons or things not specified but under consideration and being enumerated ⟨*forty-eight* are here⟩ ⟨*forty-eight* were found⟩

[3]**forty-eight** \"\ *n* **1** : eight and 40 : three times 16 : four times 12 : six times eight : four dozen **2 a** : 48 units or objects ⟨a total of *forty-eight*⟩ **b** : a group or set of 48 **3** : the numerable quantity symbolized by the arabic numerals 48 **4** : the 48th in a set or series; *esp* : an article of clothing of the 48th size ⟨wears a *forty-eight*⟩ **5** : FORTY-EIGHTMO **6** : a 48-hour leave (as from military duties)

forty-eighter \ˌfȯ(r)d·ē'ād·ə(r)\ *n* -S [(*eighteen*) *forty-eight* + *-er;* trans. of G *achtundvierziger*] : a German who participated in the revolution of 1848; *specif* : one of these revolutionists who subsequently fled to the U.S.

[1]**forty-eighth** \¦==¦=\ *adj* **1** : being number 48 in a countable series ⟨the *forty-eighth* day⟩ — see NUMBER table **2** : being one of 48 equal parts into which something is divisible ⟨a *forty-eighth* share of the total⟩

[2]**forty-eighth** \"\ *n* **1** : number 48 in a countable series **2** : the quotient of a unit divided by 48 : one of 48 equal parts of something ⟨one *forty-eighth* of the total⟩

forty-eightmo \ˌfȯ(r)d·ē'āt(ˌ)mō\ *n* -S [*forty-eight* + *-mo*] : the size of a piece of paper cut 48 from a sheet; *also* : paper or a page of this size — abbr. *48mo;* symbol *48°*; see BOOK tables

[1]**forty-fifth** \¦==¦=\ *adj* **1** : being number 45 in a countable series ⟨the *forty-fifth* day⟩ — see NUMBER table **2** : being one of 45 equal parts into which something is divisible ⟨a *forty-fifth* share of the money⟩

[2]**forty-fifth** \"\ *n* **1** : number 45 in a countable series **2** : the quotient of a unit divided by 45 : one of 45 equal parts of something ⟨one *forty-fifth* of the total⟩

[1]**forty-first** \¦==¦=\ *adj* **1** : being number 41 in a countable series ⟨the *forty-first* day⟩ — see NUMBER table **2** : being one of 41 equal parts into which something is divisible ⟨a *forty-first* share of the money⟩

[2]**forty-first** \"\ *n* **1** : number 41 in a countable series **2** : the quotient of a unit divided by 41 : one of 41 equal parts of something ⟨one *forty-first* of the total⟩

[1]**forty-five** \¦==¦=\ *adj* : being one more than 44 in number ⟨*forty-five* years⟩ — see NUMBER table

[2]**forty-five** \"\ *pron, pl in constr* : 45 countable persons or things not specified but under consideration and being enumerated ⟨*forty-five* are here⟩ ⟨*forty-five* were found⟩

[3]**forty-five** \"\ *n* **1** : five and 40 : five times nine : nine fives : three fifteens **2 a** : 45 units or objects ⟨a total of *forty-five*⟩ **b** : a group or set of 45 **3** : the numerable quantity symbolized by the arabic numerals 45 **4** : the 45th in a set or series; *esp* : an article of clothing of the 45th size ⟨wears a *forty-five*⟩ **5** : a 45 caliber pistol — usu. written .45 **6** : a variation of spoil five in which points are scored on every deal and 45 points are game **7** : a microgroove phonograph record designed to be played at 45 revolutions per minute — usu. written 45

[1]**forty-four** \¦==¦=\ *adj* : being one more than 43 in number ⟨*forty-four* years⟩ — see NUMBER table

[2]**forty-four** \"\ *pron, pl in constr* : 44 countable persons or things not specified but under consideration and being enumerated ⟨*forty-four* are here⟩ ⟨*forty-four* were found⟩

[3]**forty-four** \"\ *n* **1** : four and 40 : four times 11 **2 a** : 44 units or objects ⟨a total of *forty-four*⟩ **b** : a group or set of 44 **3** : the numerable quantity symbolized by the arabic numerals 44 **4** : the 44th in a set or series; *esp* : an article of clothing of the 44th size ⟨wears a *forty-four*⟩ **5** : a 44 caliber pistol — usu. written .44

[1]**forty-fourth** \¦==¦=\ *adj* **1** : being number 44 in a countable series ⟨the *forty-fourth* day⟩ — see NUMBER table **2** : being one of 44 equal parts into which something is divisible ⟨a *forty-fourth* share of the money⟩

[2]**forty-fourth** \"\ *n* **1** : number 44 in a countable series **2** : the quotient of a unit divided by 44 : one of 44 equal parts of something ⟨one *forty-fourth* of the total⟩

for·ty·ish \'fȯ(r)d·ēish\ *adj* : approaching or being about 40 years old ⟨a pleasant ~ man⟩

forty-knot \'==ˌ=\ *n* : a prostrate tropical American herb (*Achyranthes repens*) with many-jointed stems

forty-legs \'==ˌ=\ *n pl but sing or pl in constr, Brit* : CENTIPEDE

forty-leven \¦==¦=\ *adj* [*forty* + *leven*, short for *eleven*] *dial* : extremely numerous : INNUMERABLE ⟨asked *forty-leven* questions⟩

[1]**forty-nine** \¦==¦=\ *adj* : being one more than 48 in number ⟨*forty-nine* years⟩ — see NUMBER table

[2]**forty-nine** \"\ *pron, pl in constr* : 49 countable persons or things not specified but under consideration and being enumerated ⟨*forty-nine* are here⟩ ⟨*forty-nine* were found⟩

[3]**forty-nine** \"\ *n* **1** : nine and 40 : seven sevens : the square of seven **2 a** : 49 units or objects ⟨a total of *forty-nine*⟩ **b** : a group or set of 49 **3** : the numerable quantity symbolized by the arabic numerals 49 **4** : the 49th in a set or series; *esp* : an article of clothing of the 49th size ⟨wears a *forty-nine*⟩

forty-nine dance *n* : an American Indian round dance developed under the influence of white couple dances

forty-niner \ˌfȯ(r)|d·|ē'nīnə(r), ˌfō(r)|, |t|, |i\ *n* -S [(*eighteen*) *forty-nine* + *-er*] **1** : one who went to California in the rush for gold in 1849 **2** : an enthusiastic seeker of valuable minerals; *esp* : one who participates in a rush to the site of a new strike

[1]**forty-ninth** \¦==¦=\ *adj* **1** : being number 49 in a countable series ⟨the *forty-ninth* day⟩ — see NUMBER table **2** : being one of 49 equal parts into which something is divisible ⟨a *forty-ninth* share of the money⟩

[2]**forty-ninth** \"\ *n* **1** : number 49 in a countable series **2** : the quotient of a unit divided by 49 : one of 49 equal parts of something ⟨one *forty-ninth* of the total⟩

[1]**forty-one** \¦==¦=\ *adj* : being one more than 40 in number ⟨*forty-one* years⟩ — see NUMBER table

[2]**forty-one** \"\ *pron, pl in constr* : 41 countable persons or things not specified but under consideration and being enumerated ⟨*forty-one* are here⟩ ⟨*forty-one* were found⟩

[3]**forty-one** \"\ *n* **1** : one and 40 **2 a** : 41 units or objects ⟨a total of *forty-one*⟩ **b** : a group or set of 41 **3** : the numerable quantity symbolized by the arabic numerals 41 **4** : the 41st in a set or series; *esp* : an article of clothing of the 41st size ⟨wears a *forty-one*⟩ **5** : a 41 caliber pistol — usu. written .41 **6** *or* **forty-one pool** : a pool game played with a cue ball and 15 object balls in which each player attempts to score sufficient points to total exactly 41 when added to his private number

forty-rod \'==ˌ=\ *n* [so called fr. its alleged ability to kill at forty rods] *dial* : whiskey esp. when cheap and strong

[1]**forty-second** \¦==¦==\ *adj* **1** : being number 42 in a countable series ⟨the *forty-second* day⟩ — see NUMBER table **2** : being one of 42 equal parts into which something is divisible ⟨a *forty-second* share of the money⟩

[2]**forty-second** \"\ *n* **1** : number 42 in a countable series **2** : the quotient of a unit divided by 42 : one of 42 equal parts of something ⟨one *forty-second* of the total⟩

forty-second cousin *n* : a distant relative ⟨he's some sort of a *forty-second cousin* on my father's side⟩

[1]**forty-seven** \¦==¦==\ *adj* : being one more than 46 in number ⟨*forty-seven* years⟩ — see NUMBER table

[2]**forty-seven** \"\ *pron, pl in constr* : 47 countable persons or things not specified but under consideration and being enumerated ⟨*forty-seven* are here⟩ ⟨*forty-seven* were found⟩

[3]**forty-seven** \"\ *n* **1** : seven and 40 **2 a** : 47 units or objects ⟨a total of *forty-seven*⟩ **b** : a group or set of 47 **3** : the numerable quantity symbolized by the arabic numerals 47 **4** : the 47th in a set or series; *esp* : an article of clothing of the 47th size ⟨wears a *forty-seven*⟩

[1]**forty-seventh** \¦==¦==\ *adj* **1** : being number 47 in a countable series ⟨the *forty-seventh* day⟩ — see NUMBER table **2** : being one of 47 equal parts into which something is divisible ⟨a *forty-seventh* share of the money⟩

[2]**forty-seventh** \"\ *n* **1** : number 47 in a countable series **2** : the quotient of a unit divided by 47 : one of 47 equal parts of something ⟨one *forty-seventh* of the total⟩

[1]**forty-six** \¦==¦=\ *adj* : being one more than 45 in number ⟨forty-six years⟩ — see NUMBER table

[2]**forty-six** \"\ *pron, pl in constr* : 46 countable persons or things not specified but under consideration and being enumerated ⟨*forty-six* are here⟩ ⟨*forty-six* were found⟩

[3]**forty-six** \"\ *n* **1** : six and 40 : 23 times two **2 a** : 46 units or objects ⟨a total of *forty-six*⟩ **b** : a group or set of 46 **3** : the numerable quantity symbolized by the arabic numerals 46 **4** : the 46th in a set or series; *esp* : an article of clothing of the 46th size ⟨wears a *forty-six*⟩

[1]**forty-sixth** \¦==¦=\ *adj* **1** : being number 46 in a countable series ⟨the *forty-sixth* day⟩ — see NUMBER table **2** : being one of 46 equal parts into which something is divisible ⟨a *forty-sixth* share of the money⟩

[2]**forty-sixth** \"\ *n* **1** : number 46 in a countable series **2** : the quotient of a unit divided by 46 : one of 46 equal parts of something ⟨one *forty-sixth* of the total⟩

forty-skewer \'==ˌ==\ *n* : FORTESCUE

forty-spot \'==ˌ=\ *n* : a Tasmanian diamond bird (*Pardalotus quadragintus*) having the plumage spotted with white

[1]**forty-third** \¦==¦=\ *adj* **1** : being number 43 in a countable series ⟨the *forty-third* day⟩ — see NUMBER table **2** : being one of 43 equal parts into which something is divisible ⟨a *forty-third* share of the money⟩

[2]**forty-third** \"\ *n* **1** : number 43 in a countable series **2** : the quotient of a unit divided by 43 : one of 43 equal parts of something ⟨one *forty-third* of the total⟩

[1]**forty-three** \¦==¦=\ *adj* : being one more than 42 in number ⟨*forty-three* years⟩ — see NUMBER table

[2]**forty-three** \"\ *pron, pl in constr* : 43 countable persons or things not specified but under consideration and being enumerated ⟨*forty-three* are here⟩ ⟨*forty-three* were found⟩

[3]**forty-three** \"\ *n* **1** : three and 40 **2 a** : 43 units or objects ⟨a total of *forty-three*⟩ **b** : a group or set of 43 **3** : the numerable quantity symbolized by the arabic numerals 43 **4** : the 43d in a set or series; *esp* : an article of clothing of the 43d size ⟨wears a *forty-three*⟩

[1]**forty-two** \¦==¦=\ *adj* : being one more than 41 in number ⟨*forty-two* years⟩ — see NUMBER table

[2]**forty-two** \"\ *pron, pl in constr* : 42 countable persons or things not specified but under consideration and being enumerated ⟨*forty-two* are here⟩ ⟨*forty-two* were found⟩

[3]**forty-two** \"\ *n* **1** : two and 40 : three times 14 : six times seven **2 a** : 42 units or objects ⟨a total of *forty-two*⟩ **b** : a group or set of 42 **3** : the numerable quantity symbolized by the arabic numerals 42 **4** : the 42d in a set or series; *esp* : an article of clothing of the 42d size ⟨wears a *forty-two*⟩ **5** : a game played with dominoes but resembling the card game pitch and having the sum of the counters equal 42

forty winks *n pl but sing or pl in constr* : a short sleep : NAP

fo·rum \'fōrəm, 'fȯr-\ *n, pl* **forums** \-mz\ *also* **fo·ra** \-rə\ [L; akin to L *foris, foras* outside, *foris, fores* door — more at DOOR] **1** : the marketplace or public place of an ancient Roman city consisting of an open place or square surrounded by shops or in later times by public buildings or ornamental structures (as colonnades) and forming the center of judicial and public business **2** : a judicial body or assembly : COURT, TRIBUNAL ⟨in the ~ of one's own conscience⟩; *often* : the particular court before which a case can be or is being tried **3 a** : an organization that holds public meetings for the discussion of subjects of current interest **b** : a meeting that is held by such an organization and is frequently in the form of a question period following a lecture; *broadly* : a lecture followed by audience discussion and questioning of the lecturer **c** : a program (as on radio or television) involving discussion of a problem usu. by several authorities under the supervision of a chairman or moderator and usu. providing no means of audience participation **4 a** : a public meeting place for open discussion ⟨this busy intersection had been the town's ~ for generations⟩ **b** : a medium of open discussion ⟨aims of the publication are . . . to act as a ~ in which controversial issues . . . can be discussed —*Biol. Abstracts*⟩

forum non con·ve·ni·ens \-ˌnänkən'vinēˌen(t)s\ [NL, lit., unsuitable tribunal] : a doctrine whereby a court of law having full jurisdiction over a case brought in a proper venue or district declines to determine the case on its merits because justice would be better served by the trial of the case in another jurisdiction or district

for·wan·der \fə(r)'wändə(r)\ *vi* [ME *forwandren*, fr. *for-* + *wandren* to wander — more at WANDER] *archaic* : to wander far : become weary from wandering

[1]**for·ward** \'fȯrwərd, 'fȯ(ə)wəd *also in the South* 'färwərd, 'fȧwəd *sometimes* 'fȯrəd\ *adj, sometimes* -ER/-EST [ME *forward, foreward*, fr. OE *foreweard* fore, former, toward the front, fr. *fore-* + *-weard* -ward] **1 a** : near, at, or belonging to the forepart ⟨the ~ gun in a ship⟩ **b** : situated in advance ⟨baggage is carried in the ~ cars⟩ **c** : of, being, or situated in or near the immediate vicinity of an area of actual opposition or conflict of military forces ⟨arranging ~ transport⟩ ⟨a ~ area⟩ **2 a** : strongly inclined : ANXIOUS, EAGER, READY ⟨always ~ to criticize his neighbors⟩ **b** *archaic* : ARDENT, SPIRITED, ZEALOUS **c** : tending to push oneself forward : lacking proper modesty and reserve : BRASH, BOLD, INDECOROUS ⟨badly disciplined children are often distressingly ~⟩ ⟨a flashy ~ young woman⟩ **3** : notably advanced or developed : PRECOCIOUS ⟨the child was very ~ at walking⟩: **a** (1) *of vegetation* : advanced in growth beyond what is normal for the season ⟨a location sheltered from late sun avoids too ~ blossom which might be nipped by frost⟩ (2) *of a season* : advanced beyond what is usual : EARLY ⟨spring was very ~ that year⟩ **b** *of a female animal* : far-advanced in pregnancy ⟨bring only ~ ewes into the lambing pen⟩ **c** (1) *of an animal* : large and well-grown for its age ⟨fattening ~ stocks for market⟩ (2) *of a two-year-old registered horse* : born early in the year so that when officially two years old on January first it will be nearly three years old in chronological fact ⟨the demand for ~ two-year-olds necessitates a short breeding season . . . and the months most favorable for . . . regular ovulations are lost —*Veterinary Bull.*⟩ **4 a** : moving, tending, or leading toward a position in front ⟨picked her ~ way down the cluttered aisle⟩ ⟨checked a sudden ~ movement of the dog with a word⟩ **b** : more nearly ahead of the extended line of the popping crease than usual — used of a cricket fieldsman or his position ⟨~ short leg⟩ ⟨~ point⟩ **5 a** : supporting or advocating an advanced policy or energetic action in the direction of what is considered progress ⟨~ statesmen⟩ ⟨a firm ~ policy⟩ **b** : EXTREME, RADICAL, ULTRA ⟨on the ~ fringe of liberalism⟩ **6** : of, relating to, or for the future : relating to or for future delivery ⟨~ buying of produce⟩

[2]**forward** \"\ *adv, sometimes* -ER/-EST [ME, fr. OE *forewearde*, fr. *forweard*, adj.] : to or toward what is before or in front: as **a** : toward, into, or through the future ⟨from that time ~⟩ ⟨looking ~ to the time I retire⟩ **b** : in a forward direction ⟨they went slowly ~ through the mud⟩ **c** : to or into the fore part of a ship — opposed to *aft* ⟨sent the sailors ~⟩ **d** : into prominence ⟨he first came ~ with the adoption of his control plan⟩ ⟨the brush and rocks came ~ as we approached and we saw it was no easy climb⟩ **e** : to the front of the church as a sign of conversion ⟨came ~ when the evangelist gave the invitation⟩ ⟨went ~ on the first evening of the revival⟩

[3]**forward** \"\ *n* -S **1** : the forepart of a ship **2 a** : one of the players in certain games (as soccer, hockey, basketball, or water polo) who is stationed at or relatively near the front of his side or team and whose chief duty is to carry on the offensive play — see VOLLEYBALL illustration **b** : a defensive or offensive lineman in football — compare [1]BACK 5a

[4]**forward** \"\ *vt* -ED/-ING/-S [[2]*forward*] **1** : to help onward : ADVANCE, PROMOTE, HASTEN ⟨~*ing* the growth of a plant with proper lighting⟩ ⟨his good work should ~ him in rank⟩ **2 a** : to send forward : send toward the place of destination : TRANSMIT ⟨I shall ~ the bill of lading this afternoon⟩ ⟨we will ~ the goods on receipt of your check⟩ **b** : to send or ship onward from an intermediate post or station in transit (as from one carrier to another or from the post office of address to another) ⟨left before your letter came but I ~*ed* it to her new address⟩ ⟨prepared to receive and ~ foreign shipments at minimum cost⟩ **3** : to perform on (a book) the construction operations following sewing **syn** see ADVANCE, SEND

forward air controller *n* : the person either on the ground or in the air near the front lines who in close air-support operations spots enemy troops, guns, tanks, and other targets and by radio directs fighter-bombers in attacks on these targets

for·ward·al \-dᵊl\ *n* -S : FORWARDING

forward allowance *n, Brit* : [2]LEAD 3g

forward echelon *n* : an advance element of a military headquarters or unit : an advance command post — compare REAR ECHELON

for·ward·er \-də(r)\ *n* -S [[4]*forward* + *-er*] : one that forwards: as **a** : an agent who performs services (as clearing of customs, receiving, assembling, transshipping, or delivering) designed to assure and facilitate the passage of goods of his principal to their destination — called also *freight forwarder* **b** : a bindery worker who performs any of the construction operations following sewing

forward exchange *n* : a draft or other form of foreign exchange to be delivered at a specified future date

for·ward·ing *n* -S : the act of one that forwards; *esp* : the business of a forwarder of goods

forward-looker \ˌ=='==\ *n* : one that looks to the future esp. for improvement of the world and man : VISIONARY

forward-looking \¦==¦==\ *adj* : concerned with or planning for the future ⟨*forward-looking* industrialists build up reserves in times of expansion⟩

[1]**for·ward·ly** *adv* [[1]*forward* + *-ly* (adv. suffix)] **1 a** *archaic* : with readiness, eagerness, or self-assurance **b** : in a forward manner : BOLDLY, PRESUMPTUOUSLY ⟨the pert child answered very ~⟩ **2** : at or toward the front or forward part ⟨a ~ displaced upper molar⟩

[2]**forwardly** *adj* [[1]*forward* + *-ly* (adj. suffix)] *obs* : READY, EAGER, ADVANCED, EARLY

for·ward·ness *n* -ES : the quality or state of being forward: as **a** : READINESS, EAGERNESS, ZEAL ⟨~ in propagating the gospel⟩ **b** : an advanced stage of progress or of preparation : EARLINESS, PRECOCITY ⟨the ~ of spring⟩ ⟨~ of a pupil⟩ **c** : BOLDNESS, CONFIDENCE; *often* : excessive boldness : PRESUMPTION

forward observer *n* : an observer operating with front-line troops who is trained and equipped to adjust supporting artillery fire

forward of the beam : a ship's relative bearing of less than 90 or more than 270 degrees

forward pass *n* : a pass in football made in the direction of the opponents' goal

forward play *n* : batting in cricket in which the batsman steps forward and plays the ball near or forward of the popping crease — contrasted with *back play*

for·wards *pronunc at* FORWARD + z\ *adv* [ME *forwardes, forewardes*, fr. *forward, foreward* forward + *-es* -s (adv. suffix)] : FORWARD — now used chiefly to indicate an actual direction (as of a movement)

for·warn \fər'wȯ(ə)rn\ *vt* [ME *forwernen*, fr. OE *forwiernan*, fr. *for-* + *wiernan* to forbid — more at FOR-, WARN] *archaic* : FORBID, PROHIBIT

forwaste *vt* [*for-* + *waste*] *obs* : to lay waste : make desolate

for·wea·ried \fə(r)'wirēd\ *adj* [ME *forweried*, fr. *for-* + *weried*, past part. of *werien* to weary — more at WEARY] *archaic* : EXHAUSTED

forwent *past of* FORGO

for what *conj* : for anything : for all : as far as ⟨they may all be dead, *for what* we know⟩

[1]**for·why** \fȯr'(h)wī, fȯ(ə)'-\ *adv* [ME, fr. OE *for hwī, for hwȳ*, fr. [1]*for* + *hwī, hwȳ*, instr. of *hwæt* what — more at WHAT] *chiefly dial* : WHY, WHEREFORE

[2]**forwhy** \"\ *conj* [ME, fr. *forwhy*, adv.] *archaic* : BECAUSE, FOR, SINCE

for·worn \fər'wō(ə)rn, -'wȯ(ə)-\ *also* **fore·worn** \fōr'-\ *adj* [fr. past part. of obs. *forwear, forewear* to wear out, exhaust, fr. ME *forweren, forwerien*, fr. *for-* + *weren, werien* to wear — more at WEAR] **1** *obs* : worn out by use : old and worn : TATTERED **2** : exhausted by effort or labor : greatly tired ⟨~ by the long walk under a hot sun⟩

for·zan·do \(')fȯr¦tsän(ˌ)dō\ *adj (or adv)* [It, verbal of *forzare* to force, fr. (assumed) VL *fortiare* — more at FORCE] : SFORZANDO — abbr. *fz*

for·za·to \(')fȯr¦tsäd·(ˌ)ō, -ä(ˌ)tō\ *adj (or adv)* [It, past part. of *forzare*] : SFORZANDO

FOS *abbr* free on steamer

fosh \'fōsh\ *Scot past of* FETCH

fo·sha·gite \'fōshəˌgīt\ *n* -S [William F. *Foshag* †1956 Am. geologist + E *-ite*] : a mineral $Ca_5Si_3O_{10}(OH)_2.2H_2O$ consisting of a basic hydrous calcium silicate

[1]**fos·sa** \'fäsə, 'fȯsə\ *n, pl* **fos·sae** \-ˌsē, -ˌsī\ [L, cavity, ditch, trench, fr. fem. of *fossus*, past part. of *fodere* to dig — more at BED] *anat* : PIT, CAVITY, DEPRESSION ⟨the temporal ~ of the skull⟩ ⟨the ~ of the vena cava⟩ ⟨the nasal *fossae*⟩

[2]**fossa** \"\ *n* [Malagasy] **1** *also* **fous·sa** \'füsə\ -S **a** : a slender lithe mammal (*Cryptoprocta ferox*) that is the largest carnivore of Madagascar and is intermediate in some respects between cats and civets although classed with the latter **b** : FANALOKA **2** *cap* [NL, fr. Malagasy] : a monotypic genus of Malagasy civets closely related to the Asiatic palm civets and including only the fanaloka

fos·sar·ia \=='sa(a)rēə\ *n, cap* [NL, fr. L *fossa* ditch + NL *-aria*] : a widely distributed genus of small freshwater pulmonate snails (family Lymnaeidae) including important intermediate hosts of liver flukes and possibly of other trematode worms of medical or veterinary importance

fos·sar·i·an \-ēən\ *n* -S [LL *fossarius* fossor (fr. L *fossa* + *-arius* -ary) + E *-an*] : FOSSOR

fos·sate \'=ˌsāt\ *adj* [[1]*fossa* + *-ate*] : having a pit ⟨primitive ~ tapeworms⟩

fosse *or* **foss** \'fäs, 'fȯs\ *n, pl* **fosses** [ME *fosse*, fr. OF, fr. L *fossa*] **1** : CANAL, DITCH, TRENCH: as **a** : a ditch serving as a barrier against an enemy — see CASTLE illustration **b :** a moat surrounding a castle **c :** a depression between a glacier and a moraine **2** *archaic* **:** a hole dug in the ground **:** PIT **3 :** FOSSA

fos·sette \(')fä¦set, (')fȯ¦-\ *n* -s [F, small cavity, dimple, fr. OF *fossete*, fr. *fosse* + *-ete* -ette] **:** a small fossa **:** a little hollow; *specif* **:** a depression for the resilium in bivalve shells

fosse-way \'ˌ=ˌ=\ *n, usu cap F* [so called fr. the ditch along each side] **:** any of the principal Roman roads in Britain

fos·sick \'fäsik\ *vb* -ED/-ING/-S [E dial. *fussick, fussock* to potter over one's work, bustle about, irreg. fr. E *fuss*] *vi* **1** *Austral* **:** to search for gold typically by picking over abandoned workings **2** *chiefly Austral* **:** to search about **:** RUMMAGE, PROSPECT ~ *vt, chiefly Austral* **:** to search for by or as if by rummaging **:** ferret out

fos·sick·er \-kə(r)\ *n* -s *chiefly Austral* **:** one that fossicks **:** PROSPECTOR

fos·si·form \'fäsəˌfȯrm, 'fȯs-\ *adj* [[1]fossa + *-iform*] **:** having the form of a fossa **:** DEPRESSED, GROOVED

[1]**fos·sil** \'fäsəl *also* 'fȯs- *sometimes* -(ˌ)sil\ *n* -s [L *fossilis*, adj., dug up] **1** *archaic* **:** a rock, mineral, or other substance dug out of the earth **2 :** any remains, impression, or trace of an animal or plant of past geological ages that has been preserved in the earth's crust ⟨the tangible evidences of paleobotany are ~s —W.C.Darrah⟩ **3 a :** a person whose views are outmoded **:** one whose interests are in the past ⟨one of the ~s of the old abolition party —*N. H. Patriot & State Gazette*⟩ **b :** something that has become rigidly fixed ⟨aesthetic theories are filled with ~s of antiquated psychologies —John Dewey⟩ **4 a :** a word or sense once in common use but now obsolete except in certain idioms and phrases (as *fro* in *to and fro*) **b :** a linguistic form no longer productive but preserved in certain words (as the prefix *a* in *aloft, away*)

[2]**fossil** \"\ *adj* [L *fossilis* dug up, fr. *fossus* (past part. of *fodere* to dig) + *-ilis* -ile — more at BED] **:** having the characteristics of a fossil: as **a :** extracted from the earth ⟨the main sources of concentrated energy available to man were the ~ fuels such as coal, oil, and natural gas —E.V.Murphree⟩ **b :** preserved in an identifiable and commonly more or less mineralized or petrified form through geologic ages **c :** dead to change or progress **:** rigidly fixed **:** ANTIQUATED

fossil copal *n* **:** COPALITE

fossil flour *n* **:** ground diatomite

fos·sil·if·er·ous \ˌfäsə¦lif(ə)rəs *also* ¦fȯs-\ *adj* [ISV [1]*fossil* + *-i-* + *-ferous*] **:** containing fossils

fos·sil·i·fi·ca·tion \fä̦ˌsiləfə'kāshən *also* fȯ̦ˌ-\ *n* -s [[1]*fossil* + *-i-* + *-fication*] **:** FOSSILIZATION

fos·sil·i·fy \=ˈ==ˌfī\ *vb* -ED/-ING/-ES [[1]*fossil* + *-i-* + *-fy*] **:** FOSSILIZE

fos·sil·ist \'fäsələst *also* 'fȯs-\ *n* -s **:** PALEONTOLOGIST

fossil ivory *n* **:** ivory that has been buried long enough to become yellowish, variegated, sepia, or black in color — see OLD BERING SEA

fos·sil·iza·tion \ˌ==lə'zāshən, -ˌlī'z-\ *n* -s [ISV *fossilize* + *-ation*] **:** the process of fossilizing or becoming fossilized

fos·sil·ize \'ˌ==ˌlīz\ *vb* -ED/-ING/-S *see -ize in Explan Notes* [ISV [1]*fossil* + *-ize*] *vt* **1 :** to turn into a fossil ⟨their *fossilized* remains, recovered from some limestone that they helped to build, are often wonderfully attractive —W.E.Swinton⟩ **2 :** to preserve as if in fossil form **:** make outmoded, rigid, or fixed ⟨"no" as clearly stamps one as retrogressive, *fossilized*, probably isolationist or worse —Irving Kolodin⟩ ~ *vi* **:** to become changed into a fossil ⟨not all plant materials ~ equally well —*Science News Letter*⟩

fossil man *n* **:** man known only from fossilized skeletal remains

fos·sil·o·gy \fä'siləjē *also* ˌfȯ'- *or* **fos·sil·ol·o·gy** \ˌfäsə'läləjē *also* ˌfȯs-\ *n* -ES [*fossilogy* fr. *fossil* + *-logy*; *fossilology* fr. *fossil* + *-o-* + *-logy*] *archaic* **:** PALEONTOLOGY

fossil oil *n* **:** PETROLEUM

fossil ore *n* **:** a fossiliferous ore in which the fossil fragments have turned into some compound of iron

fossil resin *n* **:** any of various hard natural resins (as amber or some copals) usu. found in the earth as exudates of trees long dead

fossil turquoise *n* **:** ODONTOLITE

fos·sor \'fäsə(r) *also* 'fȯs-\ *n* -s [LL, fr. L, digger, fr. *fossus* (past part. of *fodere* to dig) + *-or*] **:** a gravedigger in the early church

fos·so·ri·al \(')fä¦sōrēəl, -sȯr- *also* (')fȯ¦-\ *or* **fos·so·ri·ous** \-ēəs\ *adj* [ML *fossorius* adapted to digging (fr. L *fossus* + *-orius* -ory) + E *-al* or *-ous*] **:** adapted to digging ⟨a ~ foot⟩ ⟨a ~ mammal⟩ — opposed to *cursorial*

fos·su·late \'fäs(y)ələt, -ˌlāt *also* 'fȯs-\ *adj* [NL *fossula* small fossa (fr. L, small ditch, fr. *fossa* cavity, ditch, trench + *-ula*) + E *-ate* — more at FOSSA] *zool* **:** slightly hollowed or grooved

[1]**fos·ter** \'fȯstər\ *n* -s [ME, foster child, offspring, food, fr. OE *fōstor* food, feeding; akin to ON *fōstr* action of bringing up; derivative fr. the root of E *food*] *Scot* **:** a foster child

[2]**fos·ter** \'fȯstə(r), 'fäs-\ *n* -s [ME *foster, fostre*, fr. OE *-fōstre* nurse; akin to ON *fōstra* nurse; derivative fr. the root of E [1]*foster*] *archaic* **:** a foster parent

[3]**foster** \"\ *vt* **fostered; fostered; fostering** \-t(ə)riŋ\ **fosters** [ME *fostren, fostrien*; akin to ON *fōstra* to raise, bring up; derivative fr. the root of E [1]*foster*] **1** *obs* **:** to supply with food or nourishment ⟨one bred but of alms and ~*ed* with cold dishes —Shak.⟩ **2 a** *obs* **:** to bring up with parental care **b :** to bring up under fosterage ⟨the young prince was ~*ed* in the home of the duke⟩ **3 :** to keep warm **:** WARM ⟨what a viper have I been ~*ing* in my bosom —Oliver Goldsmith⟩ **4 :** to promote the growth or development of **:** promote and sustain **:** ENCOURAGE, CULTIVATE ⟨the type of civilization which ~*ed* the minstrel —C.D.Lewis⟩ ⟨~ the use of radioactive isotopes —L.V.Joseph⟩ **syn** see NURSE

[4]**foster** \"\ *adj* [ME *foster, foster-* (as first constituent in such terms as *foster moder, fostermoder* foster mother, *foster child, fosterchild* foster child), fr. OE *fōstor-*, fr. *fōstor* food, feeding] **:** affording, receiving, or sharing nourishment, upbringing, or parental care though not related by blood or legal ties: as **a :** rearing the child of another ⟨a ~ parent⟩ **b :** brought up by someone other than one's natural parent ⟨a ~ child⟩ **c :** reared in the same family but not of the same parentage ⟨~ brothers⟩

[5]**foster** *n* -s [ME, alter. of *forster* — more at FORESTER] *obs* **:** FORESTER

fos·ter·age \'fȯstərij, 'fäs-\ *n* -s [[3]*foster* + *-age*] **1 a :** the care of a foster child **b :** the state of being a foster child **2 :** the custom once widely prevalent in Ireland, Wales, and Scotland of entrusting one's child to foster parents to be nursed and brought up ⟨the ties of clanship were strengthened by ~⟩ **3 :** the act of encouraging or promoting development

foster care *n* **:** supervised care for orphaned, neglected, or delinquent children or for persons mentally ill in a substitute home or an institution on either a full-time or day-care basis

fos·ter·er \-tərə(r)\ *n* -s [ME *fostrere*, fr. *fostren* to foster + *-ere* -er] **1 :** one that fosters **2** *archaic* **:** a foster brother

foster home *n* **:** a household in which an orphaned, neglected, or delinquent child or a person mentally ill is placed for care usu. with the approval of the government or of a social-service agency

fostering *n* -s [ME *fostringe, fostring*, fr. *fostren* to foster + *-inge, -ing* -ing] **1 :** the act of one that fosters **2 :** FOSTERAGE 2

fosterland \'ˌ==ˌ=\ *n* [OE *fōstorland*, fr. *fōstor* food, feeding + *land* — more at [1]FOSTER, LAND] **:** land allotted under old English law for the maintenance esp. of monks

fos·ter·ling \'fȯstə(r)liŋ, 'fäs-\ *n* -s [ME, fr. OE *fōstorling*, fr. *fōstor* + *-ling*] **:** a foster child

[1]**foster-mother** \'ˌ==ˌ==\ *n* [*foster mother* (noun phrase) woman that feeds or brings up another's child, fr. ME *foster moder, fostermoder*, fr. OE *fōstormōdor*; akin to ON *fōstr mōthir* woman that feeds or brings up another's child; both fr. a prehistoric NGmc-WGmc compound whose first and second constituents respectively are represented by OE *fōstor* food, feeding and by OE *mōdor* mother — more at [1]FOSTER, MOTHER] *Brit* **:** a device intended to foster young animals: as **a :** a completely enclosed movable heated house and attached run for starting young chicks without a hen **b :** a many-nippled nursing bottle for feeding litters of puppies or pigs

[2]**foster-mother** \"\ *vt* [*foster mother* (noun phrase) woman that feeds or brings up another's child] **:** to serve as the mother of ⟨*foster-mother* three little children —Dorothy C. Fisher⟩

FOT *abbr* free on truck

fotch \'fäch\ *vb* **fotched** *or* **fotch; fotched** *or* **fotch; fotching; fotches** [ME *focchen*, alter. of *fecchen* to fetch — more at FETCH] *South & Midland* **:** FETCH

[1]**foth·er** \'fäthə(r)\ *or* **fod·der** \-ädə-\ *n* -s [ME, fr. OE *fōther*; akin to OHG *fuodar* cartload, OE *fæthm* embracing or outstretched arms — more at FATHOM] **1** *now dial Eng* **:** LOAD; *esp* **:** WAGONLOAD **2 :** any of various units of weight for lead; *esp* **:** a modern unit equal to 19½ hundredweights

[2]**fother** \"\ *dial var of* FODDER

[3]**fother** \"\ *vt* -ED/-ING/-S [prob. modif. of LG *fodern* to line, fr. MLG *vōderen*, fr. *vōder* lining; akin to Goth *fodr* sheath — more at FUR] **:** to cover (a sail or piece of canvas) esp. with oakum or rope yarn for use in temporarily stopping a leak in the hull of a ship

foth·er·gil·la \ˌfäthə(r)'gilə\ *n* [NL, fr. John *Fothergill* †1780 Brit. physician and botanist] **1** *cap* **:** a small genus (family Hamamelidaceae) of deciduous shrubs of the southeastern U.S. that have alternate coarsely toothed leaves with petioles and stipules and bear white apetalous flowers in terminal heads or spikes **2** -s **:** any plant of the genus *Fothergilla* — called also *witch alder*

fo·tui \'fūd·ē, fō'tüē\ *n* -s [native name in British Guiana] **:** a tropical So. American timber tree (*Jacaranda copaia*) yielding a moderately light soft whitish wood

[1]**fou** \'fü\ *adj* [ME (Sc) *fow* full, fr. ME *ful, full* — more at FULL] *Scot* **:** DRUNK

[2]**fou** \"\ *n* -s [Sc *fou*, adj., full, fr. ME (Sc) *fow*] *Scot* **:** BUSHEL

fou·cault current \(')fü¦kō-\ *n, usu cap F* [after Jean B.L.*Foucault* †1868 Fr. physicist] **:** EDDY CURRENT

foucault pendulum *n, usu cap F* [after J.B.L. *Foucault*] **:** a freely swinging pendulum that consists of a heavy mass suspended by a long line, that oscillates for long periods in the original plane of motion, and that is used to demonstrate the rotation of the earth

foud *or* **fowd** \'faud\ *n* -s [ME (Sc) *fowde*, fr. ON *fōguti* bailiff, fr. MLG *voget*, fr. ML *vocatus* legal representative, fr. L *advocatus* advocate — more at ADVOCATE] **:** a magistrate, sheriff, or bailiff in the Orkney, Shetland, and Faroe islands

fou·droy·ant \(')fü¦drȯi(y)ənt\ *adj* [F, pres. part. of *foudroyer* to strike (as lightning), blast, thunder, fr. OF *foudroier* to strike (as lightning), fr. *foudre* lightning, fr. L *fulgur*; akin to L *flagrare* to burn — more at BLACK] **1 :** THUNDERING, DAZZLING **2** *med* **:** FULMINATING, FULMINANT

fouet·té \(')fwe¦tā\ *n* -s [F, fr. past part. of *fouetter* to whip, fr. MF, fr. *fouet* whip, fr. OF, fr. *fou* beech (fr. L *fagus*) + *-et* — more at BEECH] **:** a quick whipping movement of the raised leg in ballet dancing often accompanied by continuous turning on the supporting leg

fou·gade \(')fü¦gäd\ *n* -s [F, modif. of It *fogata* chase, pursuit, light surface mine, fr. fem. of *fogato*, past part. of *fogare* to put to flight, fr. L *fugare*, fr. *fuga* flight; akin to L *fugere* to flee — more at FUGITIVE] **:** FOUGASSE

fou·gasse \-gas, -gäs\ *n* -s [F, alter. of *fougade*] **:** a land mine in which the charge is overlaid by stones or other missiles so placed as to be hurled in the desired direction

fought *past of* FIGHT

[1]**fought·en** \'fȯtᵊn\ *now dial past part of* FIGHT

[2]**fought·en** \'fȯktən\ *adj, chiefly Scot* **:** worn out **:** exhausted esp. from fighting

foughten field *n, archaic* **:** BATTLEGROUND

fough·ty \'fōti\ *adj* [origin unknown] *dial Eng* **:** MUSTY, MOLDY

foujdar *var of* FAUJDAR

[1]**foul** \'faul, *esp before pause or consonant* -auəl\ *adj, usu* -ER/-EST [ME, fr. OE *fūl*; akin to OHG *fūl* rotten, ON *fūll* foul, Goth *fūls* stinking, L *pus* pus, *putēre* to stink, Gk *pyon* pus, *pythein* to cause to rot, Skt *pūyati* it stinks] **1 a :** offensive to the senses **:** LOATHSOME ⟨in their ~ homes of dirt and rag —Bernard Gutteridge⟩ **b :** charged with offensive matter **:** ROTTEN, PUTRID ⟨the contents of the bowl are ~ and stinking —J.G.Frazer⟩ **2 :** full of dirt or mud **:** MUDDY **3 a :** morally or spiritually odious **:** WICKED ⟨how ~ are all impulses of prejudice —J.H.Holmes⟩ **b :** notably unpleasant or distressing ⟨if my day has been ~, I can turn on my . . . radio and everything's mellow —Adrian Dove⟩ **4 a :** OBSCENE, PROFANE ⟨much of this most tedious and lengthy book is ~, lewd, and revolting —Hartley Shawcross⟩ **b :** ABUSIVE ⟨it was hard for me to take all the ~ names he called me —H.A. Chippendale⟩ **c** *dial Eng* **:** bad-tempered **:** UNFRIENDLY **5 a :** wet and stormy **:** DISAGREEABLE ⟨~ weather⟩ ⟨a ~ sky⟩ **b :** obstructive to navigation **:** UNFAVORABLE, DANGEROUS ⟨we had a ~ tide —Peter Heaton⟩ ⟨always presume your course to be ~ unless you know it to be clear —H.A.Calahan⟩ **6 a** *now dial Brit* **:** not attractive **:** HOMELY, UGLY ⟨I don't look too ~ do I —A.J.Cronin⟩ **b** *of a feather or plumage* **:** of any color not accepted as standard for birds of a particular variety or breed **7 a :** grossly unfair **:** TREACHEROUS, DISHONORABLE ⟨competition was stifled by fair means or ~ —Grace L. Nute⟩ **b :** characterized by harshness, roughness, or violence ⟨war is a ~ game —R.W.Emerson⟩ **c :** constituting an infringement of rules in a game or sport ⟨a ~ hand in poker⟩ ⟨a ~ blow in boxing⟩ **8 a :** marked up **:** defaced by changes ⟨a ~ galley proof⟩ ⟨a ~ manuscript⟩ **b** *of a proof in printing* **:** pulled before the latest alterations were made in type **9 a :** encrusted, clogged, or choked with a foreign substance ⟨a ~ ship bottom⟩ ⟨a ~ chimney⟩ ⟨on ~ land weeds may get the better of clover —E.V.Wilcox⟩ **b :** littered esp. with matter that should have been put away ⟨a ~ stone in printing⟩ **10 a :** odorous and impure **:** POLLUTED ⟨~ air⟩ ⟨~ water⟩ **b** *archaic* **:** DISCOLORED ⟨we make ~ the clearness of our deservings —Shak.⟩ **11 :** hindered from freedom of motion by collision or entanglement **:** ENTANGLED ⟨a ~ fishline⟩ **12 :** eating coarse food or carrion — used esp. in the phrase *foul feeder* **13** *of a typecase* **:** containing many missorted characters **14 :** outside the foul lines in baseball — compare FOUL BALL, FOUL LINE **syn** see DIRTY

[2]**foul** \"\ *n* -s [ME, fr. OE *fūl*, fr. *fūl*, adj. — more at [1]FOUL] **1** *archaic* **:** something that is foul ⟨~ befall the man who ever lays a snare in its way —Laurence Sterne⟩ **2 :** FOOT ROT 2 **3 :** an entanglement or collision esp. in angling or sailing **4 a :** an infringement of the rules in a game or sport (as in basketball) for which a penalty is levied against the offending person or team — see PERSONAL FOUL, TECHNICAL FOUL, VIOLATION **b :** FREE THROW **5 :** FOUL BALL

[3]**foul** \"\ *adv* [ME *foule*, fr. OE *fūle*, fr. *fūl*, adj.] **:** FOULLY

[4]**foul** \"\ *vb* -ED/-ING/-S [ME *foulen*, fr. OE *fūlian*, fr. *fūl*, adj.] *vi* **1 :** to become or be foul: as **a :** to become odorous **:** DECOMPOSE, ROT ⟨it is this organic refuse which alone is ~*ing* —Emily Holt⟩ **b :** to become encrusted, clogged, or choked with a foreign substance ⟨a gun ~*s*⟩ **c :** to become entangled or come into collision ⟨this may cause . . . the suspension lines of the parachute to ~ —H.G.Armstrong⟩ **2 :** to commit a foul in a sport or game **3 :** to make an out in baseball by hitting a foul ball that is caught by a member of the opposing team ⟨the batter ~*ed* to the first baseman⟩ ~ *vt* **1 :** to make foul: as **a :** to make dirty **:** SOIL, POLLUTE ⟨air was ~*ed* and darkened by factory soot —J.D.Hart⟩ **b :** to become entangled or come into collision with ⟨a raveled rope ~*ed* a pulley —L.C.Douglas⟩ ⟨the propeller ~*ed* a treetop —T.E.McKitterick⟩ **c :** to encrust with a foreign substance ⟨when a ship's bottom is ~*ed* from sea grass and barnacles it often takes 10 percent more fuel to keep her going at normal speed —*Nat'l Geographic*⟩ **d :** OBSTRUCT, BLOCK ⟨the carrier's flight deck was ~*ed* by a crashed plane⟩ **e** *of a bird* **:** to mark with areas of plumage of a color not accepted as standard **2 :** to bring into disgrace **:** DISHONOR, DISCREDIT ⟨it is senseless to ~ our municipal personnel with unproved charges —Robert Moses⟩ **3 :** to commit a foul against (as in basketball) **4 :** to hit (a baseball) foul ⟨he ~*ed* the first pitch⟩

foul anchor *or* **fouled anchor** *n* **1 a :** an anchor whose cable has become twisted around the stock or fluke **b :** an anchor that has hooked or become entangled with another anchor **2 :** a conventionalized anchor with a section of cable entwined about its shank or hanging from its ring used on nautical insignia, seals, or pennants

foul anchor 2

fou·lard \(')fü¦lärd, fə'l-, (')fü¦l-, -läd\ *n* -s [F] **1 a :** a lightweight plainwoven or twilled silk usu. printed with a small neat evenly spaced pattern **b :** an imitation of this fabric made usu. of rayon, cotton, wool, or nylon **2 :** an article of clothing (as a tie, scarf, or handkerchief) that is made of foulard

foul ball *n* **:** a batted baseball that rolls outside an infield foul line or that lands in foul territory — compare FAIR BALL, FOUL TIP

foul berth *n* **:** a berth in which an anchored ship cannot swing without fouling another ship or in which it becomes grounded at low tide

foul bill *n* **:** FOUL BILL OF HEALTH

foul bill of health : a certificate given to a ship's master at the time of leaving port indicating that there was an epidemic at the place of departure when the ship left — compare CLEAN BILL OF HEALTH

foul bill of lading : a bill of lading with notations as to shortages or condition of goods that limits the rights of the holder — compare CLEAN BILL OF LADING

foulbrood \'ˌ=ˌ=\ *n* **:** any of three destructive bacterial diseases of the larvae of the honeybee: **a :** AMERICAN FOULBROOD **b :** EUROPEAN FOULBROOD **c :** PARAFOULBROOD

fouldcourse *var of* FOLDCOURSE

foulder *vi* -ED/-ING/-S [obs. *foulder*, n., lightning, fr. ME *fouldre, foudre*, fr. MF — more at FOUDROYANT] *obs* **:** FLASH ⟨loud thunder . . . did rend the rattling skies with flames of ~*ing* heat —Edmund Spenser⟩

fou·le \(')fü¦lā\ *n* -s [F *foulé*, past part. of *fouler* to full — more at FULL] **:** a cloth treated by fulling

fouled-up \'ˌ=ˌ=\ *adj* [*fouled* fr. past part. of [4]*foul*] **:** characterized by total confusion or disorganization **:** CONFUSED, SNAFU ⟨a fantastically *fouled-up* operation —H.H.Martin⟩ ⟨an impossibly *fouled-up* bungle —Cameron Hawley⟩

[1]**fouler** *comparative of* FOUL

[2]**foul·er** \'faulə(r)\ *n* -s [[4]*foul* + *-er*] **1 :** one that fouls **2 :** FOULING SHOT

foulest *superlative of* FOUL

foul-foot \'ˌ=ˌ=\ *n* **:** FOOT ROT 2

foul hawse *n* **:** an arrangement of starboard and port anchor cables in which the cables cross or twist with the swinging around of the ship — compare OPEN HAWSE

foul-hook \'ˌ=ˌ=\ *vt* **:** to hook (a fish) elsewhere than in the mouth

fouling *n* -s [fr. gerund of [4]*foul*] **1 :** an accumulation of deposits **:** INCRUSTATION ⟨~ in sewage pipes⟩ ⟨marine ~⟩ **2 :** a deposit left in the bore of a gun after firing that consists of the powder residue and in small arms of a thin plating of the bullet metal

fouling organism *n* **:** any of various aquatic organisms with free-swimming larvae and sedentary adult stages that cause fouling of ships and underwater structures

fouling point *n* **1 :** the point at a railroad switch or turnout beyond which cars must be placed to prevent their being struck by cars running on the line from which the switch diverges **2 :** the point at a turnout back of the frog in signaled track where insulated joints are placed

fouling shot *n* **:** one of several rounds fired before a rifle match to warm the barrel and to furnish some fouling in order that the initial rounds of record fire pass through the bore under conditions similar to those obtaining for later rounds

foul line *n* **1 :** either of two straight lines extending from the rear corner of home plate through the outer corners of first and third base respectively and prolonged to the boundary of a baseball field — see BASEBALL illustration **2 :** a line across a bowling alley 60 feet from the center of the number 1 pin spot across which a player must not step when delivering the ball

foul·ly \'faul(l)ē, -əli\ *adv* [ME, fr. OE *fūllīce, fūllīce*, fr. *fūllīc, fūllīc*, adj., foul, fr. *fūl* foul + *-līc, -lic* -ly (adj. suffix)] **:** in a foul manner: as **a :** in an obscene manner **:** LEWDLY **b :** in a shameful manner **:** WICKEDLY ⟨last June two constables were ~ murdered —Robert Sherrod⟩ **c** *archaic* **:** FETIDLY **d** *archaic* **:** GRIEVOUSLY **e :** in a coarse manner **:** INSULTINGLY ⟨an internationally honored teacher, scholar, and philosopher was ~ condemned —M.R.Cohen⟩ **f** *archaic* **:** in an ugly manner **:** HIDEOUSLY

foulmouthed \'ˌ=¦=\ *adj* **:** given to the use of obscene, profane, or abusive language ⟨so he went off cursing like the ~ blackguard that he was —A. Conan Doyle⟩ ⟨nowhere is cant at once so ~ and so tight-laced as in the penny, two-penny, threepenny, or sixpenny press —Herbert Read⟩

foul·ness *n* -ES [ME *foulnesse*, fr. OE *fūlnes*, fr. *fūl* foul + *-nes* -ness] **1 :** the quality or state of being foul: as **a** *obs* **:** physical repulsiveness ⟨the fury . . . with new methods tried the ~ of the infernal form to hide —John Dryden⟩ **b :** a deposit of foul matter **:** FILTH ⟨the floors were made of serpents encased in ~ —R.B.Anderson⟩ **c :** moral impurity, obscenity, or vulgarity ⟨the cheapness of his person and the ~ of his tongue —Hamilton Basso⟩ **d :** UNCLEANNESS, POLLUTION ⟨a medicine . . . useful in . . . ~*es* of the blood —George Berkeley⟩ **e :** an unfavorable state (as of weather) **2 :** FIREDAMP

foul out *vi* **1 :** FOUL *vi* 3 **2 :** to be put out of a basketball game for exceeding the number of fouls permitted

foul play *n* **:** unfair, dishonest, or treacherous conduct or dealing; *specif* **:** VIOLENCE ⟨met with *foul play*⟩ ⟨a victim of *foul play*⟩ — compare FAIR PLAY

fouls *pl of* FOUL, *pres 3d sing of* FOUL

foul shot *n* **:** FREE THROW

foul·some \'fü(l)səm\ *adj* [ME *foulsom*, alter. (influenced by [1]*foul*) of *fulsom* fulsome] *chiefly Scot* **:** DISGUSTING, FULSOME

foul-spoken \'ˌ=¦==\ *adj* **:** FOULMOUTHED

foul strike *n* **:** a foul that counts as a strike in baseball

foul tip *n* **:** a pitched ball in baseball that is slightly deflected by the bat; *specif* **:** a tipped pitch legally caught by the catcher and counting as a full strike with the ball remaining in play

foul up *vt* **1 :** to make dirty **:** CONTAMINATE ⟨the ranchers used water out of open creek holes that was sometimes alkali and *fouled up* by stock —Bruce Siberts⟩ **2 :** to spoil by making mistakes or using poor judgment **:** CONFUSE ⟨no army would risk *fouling up* a major landing —Linnell Jones⟩ **3 :** to have a depressing effect on **:** DARKEN **:** LOWER ⟨a sad sack like that one only *fouls up* the spirit of the ward —*Atlantic*⟩ **4 :** ENTANGLE, CHOKE, BLOCK ⟨in two or three years the ivy should have been *fouling up* the television aerial —R.M. Yoder⟩ ⟨a big car trying to get into a small parking space *fouled up* traffic —Bill Hatch⟩ ~ *vi* **:** to become confused **:** get into difficulty **:** BUNGLE ⟨he couldn't shake the feeling that it was his fault. He had *fouled up* —Pat Frank⟩

foul-up \'ˌ=ˌ=\ *n* -s [*foul up*] **1 :** a state of confusion brought on by ineptitude or mismanagement **:** MIX-UP ⟨as with all transportation there are occasional *foul-ups* which gratify nobody —Richard Thruelsen⟩ **2 :** a mechanical difficulty ⟨the added complication of a *foul-up* in the steering mechanism in her motor pilot boat —*Springfield (Mass.) Union*⟩

fou·mart *also* **foul·mart** \'fümərt, -ˌmärt\ *n* -s [ME *fulmard, fulmarde, folmarde, folmert*, prob. fr. [1]*ful* foul + (assumed) ME *marth* marten, fr. OE *mearth* — more at MARTEN] **1 :** the European polecat **2 :** a contemptible person — used as a generalized term of abuse

[1]**found** *past of* FIND

[2]**found** \'faund\ *n* -s **:** free food and lodging in addition to wages ⟨they're paid $175 a month and ~ —*New Yorker*⟩

[3]**found** \"\ *vb* -ED/-ING/-S [ME *founden*, fr. OF *fonder*, fr. L *fundare*, fr. *fundus* bottom — more at BOTTOM] *vt* **1 :** to take the first steps or measures in building **:** build for the first time ⟨~*ed* palaces and planted bowers —Matthew Prior⟩ **2 :** to lay the base or foundation of **:** set on something solid for support ⟨the winds blew and beat upon that house but it did not fall because it had been ~*ed* on the rock —Mt 7:25 (RSV)⟩ **3 :** to establish (as an institution) often with provision for future maintenance **:** ORIGINATE, INITIATE ⟨this school was ~*ed* by a bequest of . . . $1,250,000 —C.W.Dabney⟩ ⟨he had ~*ed* prizes and scholarships and endowed hospital beds and charities —Osbert Lancaster⟩ **4 a :** to establish on a firm basis **:** fix firmly ⟨the single vital principle on which the true republic must ~ itself . . . is the principle of goodwill —V.L. Parrington⟩ ⟨all his imaginative work is ~*ed* on personal reminiscences of actual incidents and people —R.W.Stallman⟩ **b :** to serve as a basis for ⟨is enough to ~ my notion of their

having . . . the relation of brothers —John Locke⟩ ~ *vi* : to have a foundation : DEPEND — used with *on* or *upon* ⟨all delineation . . . must either ~ on belief and provable fact or have no foundation at all —Thomas Carlyle⟩

syn ESTABLISH, INSTITUTE, ORGANIZE: FOUND applies to the first steps, usu. the devising of the project or providing funds for it, taken to set up a business, colony, institution, city, or the like ⟨a lottery by which $40,000 was raised to *found* the College of Medicine —*Amer. Guide Series: Md.*⟩ ⟨the Conservatory of Music, *founded* by two distinguished dancers from Latvia —*Report: (Canadian) Royal Commission on Nat'l Development*⟩ ⟨*founding* a race, a whole descent, a whole line . . . which had gone on unbroken since before the time of William the Conqueror —Louis Bromfield⟩ ⟨the baronet looked down on the generous future he thus *founded* —George Meredith⟩ ESTABLISH usu. adds to FOUND the idea of bringing into enduring existence ⟨the power which in 1644 *established* itself as the Ch'ing dynasty in Peking —C.A.Fisher⟩ ⟨follows a route to California *established* by James Beckwourth —*Amer. Guide Series: Nev.*⟩ ⟨to *establish* a business⟩ INSTITUTE stresses an origination, a taking of the first steps in establishing something, but applies more widely than FOUND or ESTABLISH, for it comprises things that do and things that do not have a long life, as, respectively, a method of teaching and a course of lectures ⟨the office of prime minister was formally *instituted* in the Gold Coast —*Americana Annual*⟩ ⟨*institute* the first large-scale reforestation project in the U. S. —*Amer. Guide Series: N.C.*⟩ ⟨the act provided that no appeal could be *instituted* at a time later than twenty-eight days after the date upon which the magistrate made his decision or order⟩ ORGANIZE can imply founding but stresses the steps taken to establish also a proper functioning of something, as by the establishing of a separation and interrelationship of necessary operations or responsibilities ⟨he determined to take upon his own shoulders the responsibility of *organizing* some amusements —Thomas Hardy⟩ ⟨a small class of 15 children was *organized* —*Amer. Guide Series: Minn.*⟩ ⟨he *organized* the Harmonia Society and presented Haydn's *The Seasons* —*Amer. Guide Series: N.Y.*⟩ ⟨the development of trade had been well begun before the town itself was *organized* —*Amer. Guide Series: La.*⟩ **syn** see in addition BASE

4found \'fün(d)\ *n* -s *Scot* : BASE, FOUNDATION

5found \'faünd\ *vt* -ED/-ING/-S [ME *founden* to mix, fr. MF *fondre* to mix, pour, melt, fr. L *fundere* to found, pour; akin to OE *gēotan* to pour, OHG *giozzan* to pour, ON *gjōta* to bring forth (young), Goth *giutan* to pour, Gk *chein* to pour, Skt *juhoti* he pours into the fire, sacrifices] **1 a** : to melt (metal) and pour into a mold **b** : to make (a metal object) in this way : CAST **2 a** : to cause (ingredients for making glass) to melt or fuse **b** : to make (glass) by this method

6found \"\ *n* -s *archaic* : an act or process of founding : CASTING

1foun·da·tion \faün'dāshən\ *n* -s [ME *foundacioun*, fr. MF *fondation*, fr. L *fundation-, fundatio*, fr. *fundatus* (past part. of *fundare* to found) + *-ion-, -io* -ion] **1** : the act of founding: as **a** : the act of taking the first steps in building or of building for the first time ⟨thy love for me before the ~ of the world —Jn 17:24 (RSV)⟩ **b** : the act of establishing on a permanent basis typically with provision for future maintenance ⟨his piety was evidenced by his ~ of several religious houses⟩ **2 a** : the basis on which something is founded : the basis upon which something stands or is supported ⟨is very little ~ for this objection either in reason or good taste —William Hazlitt⟩ **b** *archaic* : a basis of agreement : UNDERSTANDING ⟨the English might again repair to their respective houses and trade on the old ~ —Alexander Hamilton⟩ **3 a** : funds given for the permanent support of an institution or cause : ENDOWMENT ⟨we are anxious to establish scholarships and endowments; hence we solicit such ~s from our friends —*Bull. of Mt. Saint Mary's College*⟩ **b** : an organization or institution established by endowment ⟨the citizen taxpayer has succeeded the philanthropic ~ as the principal underwriter of the costs of science —*Scientific American Reader*⟩ or otherwise established with provision for future maintenance ⟨the Benedictine order is a religious ~ dating from the sixth century⟩ **4 a** : an underlying natural or prepared base or support ⟨the terrain . . . has a gracefully undulating surface over a limestone ~ —J.T.Dorris⟩ ⟨~ for the boilers and engines of a ship⟩ **b** : a means of transferring building loads to the soil below: (1) : the supporting part of a wall or structure usu. below ground level and including footings (2) : the whole masonry substructure of a building **5** : a body or ground upon which something is built up or overlaid: as **a** : a stiffening or backing piece in an article of clothing **b** : a basic stitch or pattern **c** : the form on or over which a manufactured article is constructed ⟨allow woven rush baskets to dry thoroughly before you remove them from the ~ as in this way the shape becomes properly set —F.J.Christopher⟩ **d** *or* **foundation garment** : a woman's supporting undergarment : CORSET, CORSLET, GIRDLE **e** : a cosmetic in liquid, cream, or cake form usu. used as a base for makeup **f** : a priming coat of pigment sometimes laid over canvas as a ground for oil painting **g** : a thin sheet of pressed beeswax imitating the bottoms of natural honeycomb cells that is placed in a frame or section to shorten the time for and increase uniformity in comb building by hived bees **h** : a card of a prescribed rank placed face up as the starter for a sequence in solitaire — **on the foundation** *Brit* : belonging to an endowed institution or holding an endowed scholarship or other emolument

foundation 5d

2foundation \"\ *vt* -ED/-ING/-S : 3FOUND

foun·da·tion·al \(')faün¦dāshən³l, -shnəl\ *adj* : forming or serving as a foundation : FUNDAMENTAL — **foun·da·tion·al·ly** \-³l|ē, -əl|, |ī\ *adv*

foun·da·tion·ary \faün'dāshə,nerē, -ri\ *adj* : of or relating to a foundation

foundation bed *n* : the soil immediately beneath the foundation of a building : bearing soil

foundation day *n, usu cap F&D* : AUSTRALIA DAY — used esp. in Victoria

foun·da·tion·er \faün'dāsh(ə)nə(r)\ *n* -s *Brit* : one who derives support from the funds or foundation of a college or school

foun·da·tion·less \-shənləs\ *adj* : lacking foundation : BASELESS

foundation mat *n* : FLOATING FOUNDATION

foundation member *n, Brit* : CHARTER MEMBER

foundation planting *n* : a group of plants used in landscape design to blend a building with its setting and obscure any undesirable features of the foundation

foundation seed *n* : pure seed stocks grown by or under the supervision of a public agency for use in the production of registered and certified seed

foundation stock *n* : stock directly ancestral to a herd, strain, or breed ⟨although fourteen . . . animals made up the *foundation stock* only six of these have actually made a permanent contribution to the line —David England⟩

foundation stone *n* **1** : a stone in the foundation of a building; *specif* : such a stone laid with public ceremony in celebration of the beginning of erection — compare CORNERSTONE **2** : BASIS, GROUNDWORK ⟨absolute fear of magic powers . . . was the *foundation stone* of all . . . ceremonies of oath taking —L.S.B.Leakey⟩

foundation stop *n* **1** : a stop in a pipe organ whose pipes are in unison with or one or more octaves higher or lower than the piano strings sounded by the corresponding keys — compare MUTATION STOP **2** : any one of the fundamental flue stops (as the diapasons) as contrasted with reed stops or mixture stops

founded *past of* FOUND

1found·er \'faündə(r)\ *n* -s [ME *foundere*, alter. (influenced by ME *-ere* -er) of *foundour, foundeour*, fr. OF *fondeor*, fr. L *fundator*, fr. *fundatus* (past part. of *fundare* to found) + *-or* — more at FOUND] : one that founds, establishes, or builds ⟨the ~s of the college⟩

2foun·der \"\ *vb* **foundered**; **foundered**; **foundering** \-d(ə)riŋ\ **founders** [ME *foundren* to strike down, knock to the ground, fall to the ground, fr. MF *fondrer* to send to the bottom, fall to the ground, fr. (assumed) VL *fundorare*, fr. (assumed) VL *fundor-, fundus* bottom, alter. of L *fundus* — more at BOTTOM] *vi* **1** : to become disabled: as **a** : to break down or go lame ⟨his horse ~*ed* while he was still five miles from home⟩ **b** : to become stuck ⟨the sheep ~*ed* in the deep snow⟩ **c** : to become stiff or sick from overeating ⟨the old horse ~*ed* on green corn⟩ **2 a** : to give way : COLLAPSE ⟨the palatial hotel . . . swayed and plunged then ~*ed*, turning its desk register into a death toll —*Time*⟩ **b** : to sink or slip sideways ⟨large masses of the Grenville ~*ed* and were engulfed in the granite magma —C.O.Dunbar⟩ **3** : to sink below the surface of the water ⟨a squall came up the next day and imminent was the danger that the boat would ~ —B.N. Cardozo⟩ **4 a** : to come to grief : FAIL ⟨their efforts either ~*ed* in the committees of the state legislature or were voted down at the polls —Dwight Macdonald⟩ **b** : to break down because of an immaterial obstacle ⟨the idea of the five-power conference . . . had ~*ed* up to now on the point whether it should be held before or after implementation of the . . . declaration —Arnaldo Cortesi⟩ ~ *vt* **1 a** : WRECK, DAMAGE ⟨how often have we ~*ed* progress to save some sterile principle —Richard Christopherson⟩ **b** : to cause to become disabled or lame; *esp* : to cause (an animal) to founder by overfeeding **2** : to send (a ship) to the bottom : SINK

3foun·der \"\ *n* -s **1** : laminitis esp. when of digestive origin **2** : CHEST FOUNDER

4found·er \"\ *n* -s [ME *foundour, founder*, fr. MF *fondeur*, fr. OF *fondeor*, fr. *fondre* to pour, melt + *-eor* -or — more at FOUND] **1** : one who founds metal or glass; *specif* : TYPEFOUNDER **2** : the foreman who immediately directs the operation of an iron blast furnace

foun·der·ous *or* **foun·drous** \'faünd(ə)rəs\ *adj* : likely to cause one to founder : MIRY, SWAMPY ⟨if a way becomes ~ the public may have a right to deviate —F.D.Smith & Barbara Wilcox⟩

founders' shares *n pl* [1*founder*] *chiefly Brit* : stock issued to the organizers of a public company or corporation and carrying certain special privileges — compare MANAGEMENT SHARES

founders' type *n* [4*founder*] : FOUNDRY TYPE

founding *n* -s [fr. gerund of 5*found*] : the art of melting and casting

founding father *n* [*founding* fr. pres. part. of 3*found*] : the originator of an institution or movement : FOUNDER; *specif, usu cap both Fs* : a member of the American Constitutional Convention of 1787 ⟨Benjamin Franklin, the oldest and perhaps the wisest of our *Founding Fathers* —J.F.Hopkins⟩

found·ling \'faündliŋ, -lēŋ\ *n* -s [ME *foundling, foundeling*, fr. *founde, founden* found (past part. of *finden* to find) + *-ling* — more at FIND] : an unclaimed infant : a baby deserted by unknown parents

foundling hospital *n* : an institution for foundlings

found·ress \-drəs\ *n* -ES [ME *founderesse*, fr. *foundere* founder + *-esse* -ess] : a female founder

found·ry \'faündrē, -ri\ *n* -ES *often attrib* [F *fonderie*, fr. MF, fr. *fondre* to pour, melt + *-erie* -ery] **1 a** : the act, process, or art of casting metals **b** : articles produced by founders : CASTINGS **2** : a building or establishment where metal or glass founding is carried on **3 a** : a place where stereotyping or electrotyping is done **b** : TYPEFOUNDRY **c** : a department in a printing works for the melting down of composing-machine type or slugs

foundry facing *n* : a usu. carbonaceous material applied to the surface of a sand mold to prevent the molten metal from penetrating and reacting with the sand of the mold

foundry iron *or* **foundry pig** *n* : pig iron suitable for making castings

found·ry·man \-mən\ *n, pl* **foundrymen** : a foundry worker

foundry proof *n* : a proof taken from a form that has been locked up and made ready for plating

foundry scrap *n* : IRON SCRAP 2

foundry type *n* : type cast by a typefounder esp. as distinguished from type cast by a typesetting machine

founds *pl of* FOUND, *pres 3d sing of* FOUND

1fount \'faünt\ *n* -s [ME, baptismal font, source, fr. OF *font*, fr. L *font-, fons* fountain, spring; prob. akin to Skt *dhanvati* it flows] **1 a** : a fountain or spring **b** : a reservoir for liquids: as (1) : the oil reservoir of a lamp (2) : INKWELL (3) : a drinking vessel for poultry; *esp* : one maintaining a constant water level by gravity feed **2** : something that resembles a spring or reservoir : SOURCE ⟨the people were sovereign, the sole ~ of power —John Buchan⟩

2fount \'fänt, 'faünt\ *n* -s [F *fonte*, fr. MF, act or process of casting or founding — more at FONT] *Brit* : a font of type

1foun·tain \'faünt³n, -tən\ *n* -s *often attrib* [ME *fountaine*, fr. MF *fontaine*, fr. LL *fontana*, fr. L, fem. of *fontanus* of a spring, fr. *font-, fons* spring + *-anus* -an] **1 a** (1) : a spring of water issuing from the earth ⟨the greatest objection to this country is the want of ~s and running streams —H.M.Brackenridge⟩ (2) : the point of origin or head of a stream ⟨making rivers to ascend to their ~s —John Ray⟩ **b** : something that resembles a flowing spring ⟨with purple ~s issuing from your veins —Shak.⟩ **2** : the source from which something proceeds or from which it is supplied ⟨he is the ~ of honor and all titles spring from his power of conferment —W.A.Robson⟩ **3 a** : an artificially produced jet of water **b** : the structure from which such a jet of water rises or flows **c** : DRINKING FOUNTAIN **d** : an upward jet or downward shower of something other than water ⟨spectacular ~s of lava —Howel Williams⟩ **e** : a pyrotechnic device that emits a shower of sparks in imitation of water falling from a fountain **4** *heraldry* : a roundel barry-wavy of six argent and azure **5** : a reservoir containing a liquid or other substance that can be conducted or drawn off as needed for use ⟨the ink ~ in a printing press⟩ **6** : SODA FOUNTAIN

fountain 4

2fountain \"\ *vb* -ED/-ING/-S *vi* : to flow or spout like a fountain ~ *vt* : to cause to flow like a fountain

fountain brush *n* [*fountain* (*pen*)] : a marking or painting brush with a reservoir in its handle for ink or paint

foun·tained \-³nd,-ənd\ *adj* [1*fountain* + *-ed*] : having a fountain

foun·tain·eer \¦faünt³n¦i(ə)r, -tə¦ni-\ *n* -s [F *fontenier*, fr. MF, fr. *fontaine* fountain + *-ier* -eer] **1** *obs* : one in charge of a fountain **2** [1*fountain* + *-eer*] : SODA JERK

fountain grass *n* : an ornamental grass (*Pennisetum ruppelii*) with long nodding or curving spikes of flowers that have prominent bristles extending beyond the spikelets

fountainhead \'≈≈,≈\ *n* **1** : a fountain or spring that is the head or source of a stream **2** : a place of origin or issue : principal source ⟨theory serves as a ~ of inspiration to action —John Dewey⟩

foun·tain·less \'≈≈ləs\ *adj* : being without sources of water ⟨barren desert ~ and dry —John Milton⟩

fountain moss *n* **1** : a moss of the genus *Fontinalis* (esp. *F. antipyretica*) **2** : a highly variable No. American moss (*Philonotis fontana*) that grows about springs and seeps and often forms dense thick mats

fountain of honor *or* **fountain of justice** *often cap F&H&J* : the British crown conceived as the source of all justice, honors, dignities, titles, peerages, and privileges ⟨arms and honors have always proceeded from the sovereign as the *fountain of honor* —L.G.Pine⟩

foun·tain·ous \'faünt(³)nəs, -tən-\ *adj* **1** : of, relating to, or having the characteristics of a fountain **2** : full of or containing fountains

fountain pen *n* : a pen containing a reservoir that automatically feeds the writing point with ink

fountain plant *n* **1** : a garden amaranth (*Amaranthus tricolor angustior*) **2** : a Mexican shrub or woody herb (*Odontonema cuspidatum*) of the family Acanthaceae

fountain shell *n* : a king conch (*Strombus gigas*) sometimes used for a garden ornament

fountain syringe *n* : a syringe for introducing fluid into a body space under gravity flow

fountain tree *n* [so called fr. the water obtained fr. its leaves] **1** : WATER VINE 1 **2** : DEODAR

fount·ful \'faüntfəl\ *adj, archaic* : full of springs or fountains

fou·quie·ria \fü'kirēə, ,fükē'ir-, ,fükē'er-\ *n, cap* [NL, fr. Pierre Eloi *Fouquier* †1850 Fr. physician + NL *-ia*] : a small genus of scarlet-flowered shrubs or low trees (family Fouquieriaceae) with brittle wood and spiny stems that are leafless for most of the season — see OCOTILLO

fou·quie·ri·a·ce·ae \(,)fü,kirē'āsē,ē, ,fükē,ir-, ,fükē,er-\ *n pl, cap* [NL, fr. *Fouquieria*, type genus + *-aceae*] : a small family of spiny shrubs or trees (order Parietales) of southwestern No. America

1four \'fō(ə)r, -ō(ə)r, -ōə, -ȯ(ə)\ *adj* [ME *four, foure*, fr. OE *fēower*; akin to OHG *fior* four, ON *fjōrir*, Goth *fidwor*, L *quattuor*, Gk *tettares, tessares*, Skt *catur*] : being one more than three in number ⟨~ years⟩ — see NUMBER table

2four \"\ *pron, pl in constr* [ME *four, foure*, fr. OE *fēower*, fr. *fēower*, adj.] : four countable persons or things not specified but under consideration and being enumerated ⟨~ are here⟩ ⟨~ were found⟩

3four \"\ *n* -s [ME *four, foure*, fr. *four, foure*, adj. & pron.] **1** : twice two : two times two : two twos : the square of two **2 a** : four units or objects ⟨a total of ~⟩ **b** : a group or set of four ⟨arranged by ~s⟩ **3 a** : the numerable quantity symbolized by the arabic numeral 4 **b** : the figure 4 **4** : four o'clock — compare BELL table, TIME illustration **5** : the fourth in a set or series: as **a** : a playing card marked to show that it is fourth in a suit **b** : a domino with four spots on one of its halves **c** : a die with four spots on the side uppermost **d** : an article of clothing of the fourth size ⟨wears a ~⟩ **6** : something having as an essential feature four units or members: as **a** *cricket* (1) : a hit that counts four runs (2) : a hit from which four runs are scored **b** (1) : a 4-oared racing boat (2) : the crew of such a boat (3) **fours** *pl* : races for 4-oared boats **c** : four cards of a kind (as in poker) — usu. used in pl. **d fours** *pl* : QUARTO ⟨a book printed in ~s⟩ **e** : a 4-cylinder engine or automobile **f** : a set of four players or contestants (as a table at bridge) **7 fours** *pl* : the four feet or the hands and feet or knees — see *on all fours* at ALL FOURS

four ale *n* [so called fr. its being orig. sold at fourpence a quart] *Brit* : a cheap mild ale

four back *n* : a bowling game in which only the four back pins are spotted

four-bag·ger \'≈¦bagə(r), -aag-, -aig-\ *n* [1*four* + *bag* + *-er*] : HOME RUN

four-ball \'≈,≈\ *or* **four-ball match** *n* **1** : BEST-BALL FOURSOME **2** : a golf match in which four players tee off and partners select the better drive and alternate in striking the ball

fourbe *or* **fourb** *n* -s [F *fourbe*, fem., trick & *fourbe*, masc., swindler, fr. MF, fr. *fourbir* to polish, clean, steal — more at FURBISH] **1** *obs* : TRICK **2** *obs* : IMPOSTOR

four·be·rie \¦fürbə¦rē\ *n* -s [F, fr. *fourbe* + *-erie* -ery] : TRICKERY, DECEPTION

1four·ble \'fōrbəl, 'fȯr-\ *adj* [1*four* + *-ble* (as in *double*)] *dial* : QUADRUPLE, FOURFOLD

2fourble \"\ *n* -s : a unit of pipe for drilling oil consisting of four lengths coupled together

fourble board *n* : a platform at a height of 80 feet or more above the floor of an oil derrick

four·cault process \(')fü(ə)r¦kō-, (')fō¦\ *n, usu cap F* [after Émile *Fourcault*, 20th cent. Belg. inventor] : a process of drawing molten glass vertically upward in sheet form ⟨the *Fourcault process* produces flat glass for windows —E.R.Riegel⟩

four-centered arch \'≈,≈≈-\ *n* : an arch whose intrados curve is described from four centers — compare TUDOR ARCH

four·chée *also* **four·ché** \(')fü(ə)r¦shā\ *or* **four·chy** \'fü(ə)r-shē\ *adj* [F *fourchée* (fem.) & *fourché* (masc.), fr. OF *forchiée* (fem.) & *forchié* (masc.), fr. *forchié*, past part. of *forchier* to fork, fr. *forche* fork, fr. L *furca* — more at FORK] **1** *heraldry* : having the end of each arm divided so as to terminate in a V — used of a cross; see CROSS illustration **2** *heraldry* : divided near the end into two parts ⟨a lion rampant, tail ~⟩

1four·chette \(')fü(ə)r¦shet\ *n* -s [F, lit., fork, fr. MF *forchete*, fr. *forche* + *-ete* -ette] **1 a** : a small fold of membrane connecting the labia minora in the posterior part of the vulva **b** : WISHBONE **c** : FROG 2 **2** *or* **for·chette** \(')fō(ə)r-\ : the strip or shaped piece used for the sides of the fingers of a glove — see GLOVE illustration **3** : TENACE

2four·chet·té \¦fürshə¦tā\ *adj* [modif. of F *fourcheté*, fr. *fourchette* fork] : FOURCHÉE

four-color \'≈¦≈≈\ *adj* **1** : having four colors **2** *of process printing* : using the four colors red, yellow, blue, and black — compare COLOR PHOTOGRAPHY

four-cornered \'≈¦≈≈\ *adj* [ME, fr. *four, foure* four + *cornered*] **1** : QUADRANGULAR **2** : having four participants ⟨a *four-cornered* fight⟩

four corners *n pl* **1** *sing in constr* : the intersection of two roads or the meeting of four roads : CROSSROADS ⟨a little grocery at the *four corners* —John Dos Passos⟩ **2** : the entire area comprising something ⟨in the *four corners* of the political, social, cultural, and religious horizon —A.L. Guérard⟩ **3** *sing in constr* : a skittles game with four pins

four-coupled locomotive \'≈,≈≈-\ *n* : a locomotive with two pairs of driving wheels which are connected together by coupling rods

four·croya \fůr'krȯi(y)ə, fōr-\ [NL, fr. Count Antoine F. de *Fourcroy* †1809 Fr. chemist] *syn of* FURCRAEA

four-cycle \'≈¦≈≈\ *adj* : having a four-stroke cycle ⟨a *four-cycle* internal combustion engine⟩

four-decker \'≈¦≈≈\ *n* : a ship with four decks

four-dimensional \¦≈≈¦≈(≈)≈\ *adj* : having or relating to four dimensions; *esp* : involving or relating to the fourth dimension

four-door \'≈¦≈\ *adj, of an automobile* : having two seating compartments each provided with two doors

four·drin·i·er \fůr'drinēər, -ē,ā\ *or* **fourdrinier machine** *n* -s *often cap F* [after Henry *Fourdrinier* †1854 and Sealy *Fourdrinier* †1847 Eng. papermakers and inventors] : a paper machine in which the web of paper is formed on an endless traveling wire screen that passes under a dandy roll, over suction boxes, through presses, and over dryers to the calenders and reels — compare CYLINDER MACHINE

fourdrinier wire *n, often cap F* : a continuous screen of fine wire cloth used for draining pulp in a fourdrinier machine

four-em space *n* [contr. of *four-to-em space*] : a space in printing that is ¼ of an em in thickness

four-eyed \'≈¦≈\ *adj* **1** : having or appearing to have four eyes **2** : wearing glasses ⟨getting tired of being called a *four-eyed* weakling⟩

four-eyed fish *n* : a fish of the genus *Anableps*

four-eyed opossum *n* : any of various So. American opossums that are distributed between two genera (*Metachirops* and *Metachirus*) and are distinguished by a patch of light hair above each eye

four-eyes \'≈,≈\ *n pl but sing in constr* **1** : FOUR-EYED FISH **2** : a person who wears glasses

4-f \'≈¦≈\ *n, pl* **4-f's** *usu cap F* [so called fr. the arbitrary official designation of the class of registrants consisting of those men found unfit for military service under the Selective Service System established by the U.S. during World War II] : one who is rejected for military service because of a physical, mental, or moral disability

four-five-six \¦≈,≈¦≈\ *n* : a game played with three dice in which 4-5-6 is one of the winning casts

four flush *n* [3*four* + *flush*] : four cards of the same suit in a five-card poker hand

four-flush \"\ *vi* [*four flush*] : to make a false claim : BLUFF ⟨no beating around the bush and pretending and *four-flushing* —*Amer. Mercury*⟩

four-flusher \'≈¦≈ə(r)\ *n* : one that cannot back up his pretensions : BLUFFER ⟨did you ever see a *four-flusher* that went on holding people's confidence —Sinclair Lewis⟩

1four·fold \'≈¦fōld\ *adj* [ME *fourfold, fourefold*, fr. OE *fēowerfeald*, fr. *fēower* four + *-feald* -fold] **1** : having four parts or aspects : QUADRUPLE **2** : being four times as large, as great, or as many as some understood size, degree, or amount ⟨a ~ increase⟩ **3** : TETRAD

2fourfold \"\ *adv* [ME *fourfold, fourefold*, fr. *fourfold, fourefold*, adj.] : to four times as much or as many : by four times ⟨increased ~⟩

four-foot \ˈ=,=\ *adj* [ME *fourfote, fourefote,* fr. OE *fēowerfōte,* fr. *fēower* four + *-fōte* (fr. *fōt* foot)] **1** : FOUR-FOOTED **2** : having a dimension of four feet

four-footed \ˈ=ˈ==\ *adj* [ME *fourfoted, fourefoted,* fr. OE *fēowerfōted,* fr. *fēower* four + *-fōted* footed] **1** : having four feet : QUADRUPED **2** : of, relating to, or characteristic of quadrupeds

four-footed butterfly *n* : a butterfly of the family *Nymphalidae*

four-foot octave *n* : SMALL OCTAVE

four-foot pitch *n* : the pitch of a 4-foot stop on a pipe organ

four-foot stop *n* : a pipe-organ stop sounding pitches an octave higher than the notes indicate — compare EIGHT-FOOT STOP

four-four \ˈ=ˈ=\ *or* **four-four time** *n* : the rhythmic content per measure as indicated 4/4 in a musical composition consisting of four quarter notes or tones or their equivalent

four freedoms *n pl, often cap both Fs* : the four basic human freedoms identified by F.D. Roosevelt as freedom of speech and expression, freedom of worship, freedom from want, and freedom from fear

four gents chain *or* **four ladies chain** *n* : a crossover in a square dance in which all four men or all four women join hands in the center of the set

four·gon \fürgōⁿ\ *n, pl* **fourgons** \-ōⁿ(z)\ [F, wagon for carrying baggage, poker, fr. OF *forgon* poker, fr. *forgier, furgier* to search, rummage, fr. (assumed) VL *furicare,* irreg. fr. L *fur* thief — more at FURTIVE] : a wagon for carrying baggage ⟨you look through the glassed-in windows of the promenade and see the last ~s loaded —Christopher Morley⟩

4-H \ˈ=ˈ=\ *adj, usu cap H* [so called fr. the fourfold aim of improving the head, heart, hands, and health] : of or relating to a 4-H club or the 4-H club program

four-hand \ˈ=ˈ=\ *adj* : FOUR-HANDED

four-handed \ˈ=ˈ==\ *adj* **1** : having four hands : QUADRUMANOUS **2** : designed for execution by four hands ⟨a piano duet is a *four-handed* musical composition⟩ **3** : requiring the participation of four persons ⟨a *four-handed* game⟩ ⟨*four-handed* reel⟩

4-H'er \ˈ=ˈāchə(r)\ *n -s usu cap H* : a member of a 4-H club established by the U.S. Dept. of Agriculture to instruct young people esp. in rural areas in modern farm practices and the fundamentals of good citizenship

four-hol·er \ˈ=ˈhōlə(r)\ *n* [¹*four* + *hole* + *-er*] : a privy with four openings

four-horned antelope \ˈ=,=-\ *n* : an Indian antelope (*Tetracerus quadricornis*) the male of which has two pairs of horns — called also *bekra, bhokra, doda*

four horsemen *n pl* **1** *usu cap F&H* : war, famine, pestilence, and death personified as the four major plagues of mankind ⟨the *Four Horsemen* still darken the skies —Harrison Smith⟩ — with reference to Apoc 6:2-7(NCE) **2** : four threatening forces of any kind ⟨the *four horsemen* . . . scarcities, subsidies, doles, and inflation —Raymond Moley⟩

four hundred *or* **400** *n, usu cap F&H* [so called fr. the idea that a social elite must necessarily be small in number] : the exclusive social set of a community — used with *the* ⟨a crystal-chandelier background that provided her with relatives and friends in the *400* —Marjorie B. Snyder⟩

four-hundred-day clock *n* [trans. of G *vierhunderttageuhr*] : ANNIVERSARY CLOCK

fou·ri·er analysis \ˌfu̇rēˌā-\ *n, usu cap F* [after Baron Jean Baptiste Joseph *Fourier* †1830 Fr. geometrician and physicist] : the fitting of terms of a Fourier series to periodic data

fou·ri·er·ism \ˈfu̇rēə,rizəm, ˈfōr-,ˈfyu̇r-\ *n -s usu cap* [F *fouriérisme,* fr. F. M. Charles *Fourier* †1837 Fr. social scientist and reformer + F *-isme* -ism] : a plan for the reorganization of society into cooperative communities of small groups living in common — called also *phalansterianism*

fou·ri·er·ist \-ərə̇st\ *or* **fou·ri·er·ite** \-ə,rīt\ *n -s usu cap* [*fourierist* fr. F *fouriériste,* fr. F. M. Charles *Fourier* †1837 + F *-iste* -ist; *fourierite* fr. F. M. Charles *Fourier* †1837 + E *-ite*] : an advocate of Fourierism

fou·ri·er·is·tic \ˌ===ˈristik\ *adj, usu cap* [*fourierist* + *-ic*] : of, relating to, or resembling Fourierism

fou·ri·er series \ˌfu̇rēˌā-\ *n, usu cap F* [after Baron Jean Baptiste Joseph *Fourier* †1830] *math* : an infinite series of the form $a_0/2+a_1\cos x+b_1\sin x+a_2\cos 2x+b_2\sin 2x+\cdots$ that may be used to approximate a function or to fit a given set of data (as periodic data)

fou·ri·er's theorem \-ēˌāz-\ *n, usu cap F* [after Jean Baptiste Joseph *Fourier* †1830] : a theorem in mathematics: any periodic function may be resolved into sine and cosine terms involving known constants

four-in-hand \ˈ==,=\ *n* **1 a** : a team of four horses driven by one person **b** : a vehicle drawn by such a team **2** : a necktie cut on the bias and often made with a lining and tied in a slipknot so that the long flared ends overlap vertically in front

four-in-hand 2

four-leaf clover \ˈ=,=-\ *n* **1** *also* **four-leafed clover** \ˈ=,=-\ : an atypical clover leaf with four leaflets often believed to be an omen of good luck **2** : a closed circle of four square dancers with overlapping arms

four-letter word *n* : any of a group of vulgar or obscene words typically made up of four letters ⟨books which rely for their appeal upon sensation and *four-letter words* —Louis Bromfield⟩ ⟨*four-letter words* used across the tracks —Lou Richter⟩

four-lined plant bug *also* **four-lined leaf bug** \ˈ=,=-\ *n* : a yellow or orange leaf bug (*Poecilocapsus lineatus*) that is widespread in eastern and central No. America, that has four longitudinal black stripes down the back, and that feeds on various wild and cultivated plants

four-line octave *n* [so called fr. the four accent marks of the symbol C'''' representing the third C above middle C] : the musical octave that begins on the third C above middle C — see PITCH illustration

four·ling \ˈ=liŋ\ *n -s* [³*four* + *-ling*] : a twin crystal consisting of four individuals

four·mar·i·er·ite \fu̇rˈmarēə,rīt\ *n -s* [F *fourmariérite,* fr. Paul *Fourmarier,* 20th cent. Belg. geologist + F *-ite*] : a mineral $PbU_4O_{13}.5H_2O$(?) consisting of a hydrous oxide of lead and uranium

four-masted bark \ˈ=,==-\ *n* : a 4-masted ship that is fore-and-aft rigged on the aftermost mast and square-rigged on the other three masts

four-mast·er \ˈ=ˈ=ə(r)\ *n -s* : a 4-masted ship

four-minute man *n* : one of a body of men who during World War I made short speeches esp. to promote the sale of government bonds

four noble truths *n pl, usu cap F&N&T* : the basic doctrines of Buddhism specifying that all life is subject to suffering, that the desire to live is the cause of repeated existences, that only the annihilation of desire can give release, and that the way of escape is the elimination of selfishness by means of the Eightfold Path

four-oar \ˈ=,=\ *n* : a four-oared boat

four-oared \ˈ=ˈ=\ *adj* **1** : provided with or rowed by four oars with one man to an oar **2** : participated in by four-oared boats

four-o'clock \ˈ==,=\ *n* **1** : a plant of the genus *Mirabilis:* as **a** : a common garden plant (*M. jalapa*) with fragrant yellow, red, or white flowers that open late in the afternoon — called also *marvel-of-Peru* **b** : a California plant (*M. laevis*) with red flowers **2** [so called fr. its cry] : FRIARBIRD

four-o'clock family *n* : NYCTAGINACEAE

four of a kind : four playing cards of the same rank — called also *double pair royal;* see POKER illustration

four paws *n pl but usu sing in constr* : four short chains terminating in hooks at one end and welded at the other end to a single ring for use in skidding logs — called also *four-paw grab*

four·pence *Brit* ˈ=,pən(t)s, *US* " *or* ˈ=,pen-\ *n, pl* **fourpence** *or* **fourpences** **1** : the sum of four usu. British pennies **2** : a British silver coin worth four pennies now used only as maundy money : GROAT **3** : FIPPENNY BIT

fourpence ha' penny *n* : FIPPENNY BIT

¹**four·pen·ny** \-nē,-ni, *Brit sometimes* ˈfōpni\ *adj* [ME *fourepeny-* (in *fourepenynail*), fr. *four, foure* four + *peny* penny] : amounting to, worth, or costing fourpence

²**fourpenny** \"\ *n* : FOURPENCE

fourpenny nail *n* [ME *fourepenynail* nail costing fourpence per hundred, fr. *fourepeny-* fourpenny + *nail*] : a nail 1⅜ inches long by 15½ gauge

four-pip·er \ˈ=ˈpīpə(r)\ *n* [¹*four* + *pipe,* n. + *-er*] : FOUR-STACKER

four-post·er \ˈ=ˈpōstə(r)\ *n* [¹*four* + *post,* n. + *-er*] : a bed whose tall often carved corner posts were orig. designed to support curtains or a canopy

four-poster

four·pound·er \ˈ=ˈpau̇ndə(r)\ *n* : a gun throwing a 4-pound projectile

four-quarter plan *n* : the plan of dividing the academic year into four quarters of approximately 12 weeks each

four questions *n* : the four questions concerning the meaning of Seder customs asked usu. by the youngest participant at the beginning of the Passover Seder service prompting recital of the Haggada

four·ra·gère \ˌfu̇rəˈzhe(ə)r\ *n -s* [F, fr. fem. of *fourrager,* adj., connected with or yielding forage, fr. *fourrage* forage, fr. OF *forage* — more at FORAGE] : a braided cord worn usu. around the left shoulder; *esp* : such a cord awarded as a decoration to a military unit for distinguished service or conspicuous gallantry in war — compare AIGUILLETTE

four·ri·er \ˈfu̇rēə(r)\ *n -s* [MF, forager, fr. OF *forrier,* fr. *forre, fuerre* fodder, straw — more at FORAGE] : one that goes before : FORERUNNER, PRECURSOR

four-rowed barley \ˈ=,=-\ *n* : a barley in which the overlapping of the lateral members of each cluster of three fertile spikelets makes the spike appear to have four rows — compare SIX-ROWED BARLEY, TWO-ROWED BARLEY

fours \ˈfō(ə)rz, -ó(ə)rz,-ōəz,-ó(ə)z\ *or* **four·ses** \-zə̇z\ *n pl but usu sing in constr* [*fours* fr. pl. of ³*four; fourses* fr. *fours* + *-es* (suffix forming plural of nouns)] *dial Eng* : a light meal served in the afternoon esp. to harvest workers

fourscore \ˈ=ˈ=\ *adj* [ME *fourscore, fourescore,* fr. *four, foure* four + *score*] : being 80 in number

fourscorth *adj* [*fourscore* + *-th*] *obs* : EIGHTIETH

¹**four·some** \ˈ=səm\ *n -s* [ME *foursum,* fr. (assumed) ME *foure sum* one of four, fr. OE *fēowra sum,* fr. *fēowra* (gen. of *fēower* four) + *sum* some, one — more at FOUR, SOME] **1 a** : a group of four : QUARTET **b** : two couples each of which consists of a man and a woman **2 a** : a golf match between two pairs of partners each of whom plays his own ball — compare FOUR-BALL **b** : a similar match with each side playing one ball and partners striking alternately — called also *Scotch foursome*

²**foursome** \"\ *adj* **1** *Scot* : suitable for four persons **2** *Scot* : requiring four participants

four-spined stickleback \ˈ=,=-\ *n* : a stickleback (*Apeltes quadracus*) that occurs along the New England coast

four-spot \ˈ=,=\ *n* **1** : a four in cards or dice **2** *or* **fourspot flounder** \ˈ=,=-\ *also* **four-spotted flounder** \ˈ=,==-\ : a flatfish (*Paralichthys oblongus*) of the eastern coast of the U.S.

¹**foursquare** \ˈ=ˈ=\ *adj* [ME *foursquare, foursquare,* fr. *four, foure* four + *square*] **1 a** : having four equal sides and four right angles : SQUARE ⟨a large ~ Victorian mansion —Osbert Lancaster⟩ **b** : arranged in a square ⟨a stockyard where thatched cowhouses . . . cart sheds and a great old barn . . . huddle ~ —J.W.Day⟩ **2** : characterized by boldness and conviction : sound and unswerving : FORTHRIGHT ⟨they are . . . ~ and simple and staunch —H.S.Commager⟩ **3** *usu cap* : of or relating to a fundamentalist religious cult or sectarian movement originating in southern California after World War I ⟨*Foursquare* churches⟩ ⟨the *Foursquare* technique⟩ ⟨a *Foursquare* choir⟩

²**foursquare** \ˈ=ˈ=\ *adv* **1** : in a square position : SOLIDLY ⟨their monuments stand ~ —J.E.M.White⟩ **2** : in an unequivocal manner : FORTHRIGHTLY ⟨he stood ~ for religious liberty and toleration —C.G.Bowers⟩

³**foursquare** \ˈ=,=\ *n, archaic* : a figure with four equal sides and four right angles ⟨of a shape between a circle and a ~ —William Upton⟩

four-square·ness \ˈ=ˈ=nə̇s\ *n* -ES : lack of refinement : BLUNTNESS

four-stack·er \ˈ=ˈstakə(r)\ *n* [¹*four* + *stack,* n. + *-er*] : a destroyer of World War I design with four smokestacks

four-star *or* **four-starred** \ˈ=ˈ=\ *adj* **1** : of a high degree of excellence **2** : having the military rank of general or admiral

fourstrand \ˈ=,=\ *or* **four-stranded** \ˈ=ˈ==\ *adj* [*fourstrand* fr. ¹*four* + *strand,* n.; *four-stranded* fr. ¹*four* + *strand,* n. + *-ed*] : having four strands; *specif, of a rope* : having four strands laid up right-handed with a core in the center

four-strip·er \ˈ=ˈstrīpə(r)\ *n* [so called fr. the four gold stripes worn on the sleeve of his uniform] : a captain in the U.S. Navy

four-stroke cycle *n* : a cycle in which air or an explosive mixture is drawn into the cylinder of an internal-combustion engine on a suction stroke, is compressed and ignited on a compression stroke, burns and performs useful work on an expansion stroke, and expels the products of combustion on an exhaust or scavenging stroke

¹**four·teen** \(ˈ)fō(ə)r(t)ˈtēn, -ó(ə)r|, -ōə|, -ó(ə)|\ *sometimes* |d-ˈtēn\ *adj* [ME *fourtene,* fr. OE *fēowertiene, fēowertȳne, fēowertēne* (akin to OHG *fiorzehan* fourteen, ON *fjōrtān,* Goth *fidwortaihun*), fr. *fēower* four + *-tiene, -tȳne, -tēne* (fr. *tien, tȳn, tēn* ten) — more at FOUR, TEN] : being one more than 13 ⟨~ years⟩ — see NUMBER table

²**fourteen** \"\ *pron, pl in constr* [ME *fourtene,* fr. OE *fēowertiene, fēowertȳne, fēowertēne,* fr. *fēowertiene, fēowertȳne, fēowertēne,* adj.] : 14 countable persons or things not specified but under consideration and being enumerated ⟨~ are here⟩ ⟨~ were found⟩

³**fourteen** \"\ *n -s* [ME *fourtene,* fr. OE *fēowertiene, fēowertȳne, fēowertēne,* fr. *fēowertiene, fēowertȳne, fēowertēne,* adj.] **1** : 10 and four : twice seven : seven times two **2 a** : 14 units or objects ⟨a total of ~⟩ **b** : a group or set of 14 **3** : the numerable quantity symbolized by the arabic numerals 14 **4** : the 14th in a set or series; *esp* : an article of clothing of the 14th size ⟨wears a ~⟩

four·teen·er \-nə(r)\ *n -s* **1** : a poetic line of 14 syllables; *esp* : such a line consisting of seven iambic feet **2** : a mountain peak 14,000 or more feet above sea level

fourteen-one continuous *n* : the championship game of pocket billiards in which the balklines are located fourteen inches from the cushions, a player being permitted only one shot from balk, and in which a player must call his shots and amass 150 points to win

fourteen step *n* : an ice-skating step combination of waltz and various turns

¹**four·teenth** \-n(t)th\ *adj* [ME *fourtenthe,* adj. & n., alter. (influenced by *fourtene* fourteen) of *fourtethe,* fr. OE *fēowertēotha* (akin to ON *fjōrtāndi* fourteenth), fr. *fēowertiene, fēowertȳne, fēowertēne* fourteen + *-otha, -tha* -th] **1** : being number 14 in a countable series ⟨the ~ day⟩ — see NUMBER table **2** : being one of 14 equal parts into which something is divisible ⟨a ~ share of money⟩

²**fourteenth** \"\ *n, pl* **fourteenths** \-n(t)s,-n(t)ths\ [ME *fourtenthe*] **1** : number 14 in a countable series ⟨the ~ of the month⟩ **2** : the quotient of a unit divided by 14 : one of 14 equal parts of something ⟨one ~ of the total⟩ **3** : a musical interval comprising an octave and a seventh

fourteen-two balkline *n* : a carom billiards game in which balklines are located 14 inches from the cushions and two shots are permitted from balk

¹**fourth** \ˈfō(ə)rth, -ó(ə)rth, -ōəth,-ó(ə)th\ *adj* [ME *fourthe,* adj. & n., alter. (influenced by *four, foure* four) of *ferthe,* fr. OE *fēortha, fēowertha* (akin to OHG *fiordo* fourth, ON *fjōrthi*), fr. *fēower* four + *-tha* -th — more at FOUR] **1** : being number four in a countable series ⟨the ~ day⟩ — see NUMBER table **2** : being one of four equal parts into which something is divisible ⟨a ~ share of the money⟩ **3** *in certain motor vehicles* : being the forward gear or speed next higher than third

²**fourth** \"\ *n -s* [ME *fourthe*] **1** : number four in a countable series ⟨the ~ of the month⟩ **2** : the quotient of a unit divided by four : one of four equal parts of something ⟨one ~ of the total⟩ **3 a** : the musical interval embracing four diatonic degrees **b** : the tone at this interval; *specif* : SUBDOMINANT **c** : the harmonic combination of two tones a fourth apart **4** : the fourth forward gear or speed of a motor vehicle **5 a** *usu cap* : INDEPENDENCE DAY — used with preceding *the* **b** *Brit* : the day on which bills dated the first of the month become due — used in the phrase *fourth of the month* **6** : QUARTE

³**fourth** \"\ *adv* **1** : in the fourth place **2** : with three exceptions ⟨the nation's ~ largest city⟩

fourth class *n* **1** : a class or group ranking fourth in a series **2 a** : a class of mail in the U.S. that comprises merchandise and non-second-class printed matter weighing over 8 oz. and not sealed against inspection **b** : a class of mail in Canada that comprises merchandise and printed matter exceeding certain weights

fourth cranial nerve *or* **fourth nerve** *n* : TROCHLEAR NERVE

fourth day *n, usu cap F* : WEDNESDAY — used chiefly by the Friends

fourth deck *n* : the lowest deck in a typical merchant ship of many decks; *sometimes* : ORLOP DECK — see DECK illustration

fourth dimension *n* [prob. trans. of NL *quarta dimensio*] **1** : a dimension in addition to the three dimensions length, breadth, and thickness that is assumed to exist in order to satisfy certain mathematical analogies and that in the theory of relativity constitutes the time coordinate used along with the rectangular coordinates *x, y, z* to locate a point (as for recording an event) **2** : something outside the range of ordinary experience ⟨a *fourth dimension* of meaning that transcends . . . the issue of clarity versus obscurity —Peter Viereck⟩

fourth-dimensional \ˌ=(,)=ˈ=(=)=\ *adj* : relating to the fourth dimension

fourth estate *n, often cap F&E* : a group other than the clergy, nobility, or commons that wields political power; *specif* : the public press ⟨the *Fourth Estate* . . . has genuine being in Congress and in national politics generally —W.S.White⟩ — compare ESTATE 3, FIFTH ESTATE

fourth hand *n* : the fourth player in various card games to have the right to bid or to play to any trick

fourth·ly *adv* : in the fourth place

fourth of july *usu cap F&J* : INDEPENDENCE DAY

fourth-rate \ˈ=ˈ=\ *adj* **1** : belonging or relating to a fourth rank or grade (as in order of excellence) **2** : of negligible worth — **fourth-rat·er** \ˈ=ˈrād·ə(r)\ *n*

fourth ventricle *n* : a somewhat rhomboidal ventricle of the posterior part of the brain that connects at the front with the third ventricle through the aqueduct of Sylvius and at the back with the central canal of the spinal cord

four-times accented octave *n* : FOUR-LINE OCTAVE

four-toed \ˈ=ˈ=\ *adj* : having four toes; *specif* : having four toes on each foot

four-tooth \ˈ=,=\ *n, pl* **four-tooths** : a 2-year-old sheep

four-way \ˈ=ˈ=\ *adj* **1** : allowing passage in any of four directions ⟨a *four-way* valve⟩ ⟨a *four-way* traffic light⟩ **2** : including four participants ⟨a *four-way* talk⟩

four-way cock *n, mech engin* : a cock connected with four pipes or ports and having two or more passages in the plug by which the adjacent pipes or ports may be made to communicate

four-way switch *n* : an electric switch used in house wiring so that a light may be turned on or off at three or more places

four-wheel *or* **four-wheeled** \ˈ=ˈ=\ *adj* **1** : having four wheels ⟨a *four-wheel* carriage⟩ **2** : acting on or by means of four wheels of an automotive vehicle ⟨*four-wheel* drive⟩ ⟨*four-wheel* brakes⟩

four-wheeled scraper *n* : a scraper with four wheels and a metal scoop suspended from an axle that can be raised to clear the ground after loading

four-wheel·er \ˈ=ˈ(h)wēlə(r)\ *n* : a vehicle with four wheels; *specif* : a one-horse carriage with four wheels

fous *pl of* FOU

foussa *var of* FOSSA

fout \ˈfau̇t, ˈfōt\ *dial past of* FIGHT

fou·ter \ˈfüd·ər, -ütə-\ *or* **fou·tra** \-ü·trə\ *n -s* [MF *foutre* to copulate with, copulate, fr. L *futuere;* prob. akin to L *-futare* to beat — more at BEAT] **1** *archaic* : something of little value : FIG ⟨a *foutra* for the world and worldlings base —Shak.⟩ **2 a** *chiefly Scot* (1) : an objectionable or tedious person (2) : a worthless or bungling person **b** *Scot* : CHAP, FELLOW

fouth \ˈfüth\ *n -s* [ME (Sc), fr. ME *fulth* fullness — more at FULTH] *chiefly Scot* : ABUNDANCE, PLENTY

fo·vea \ˈfōvēə\ *n, pl* **fove·ae** \-vē,ē, -vē,ī\ [L, small pit] : a small depression or pit : FOSSA: as **a** [NL, fr. L] : the hollowed leaf base in the quillwort containing a sporangium **b** *or* **fovea cen·tra·lis** \-,sen·ˈtraləs, -ral-,-ral-\ [*fovea* fr. NL, fr. L; *fovea centralis* fr. NL, central fovea] : a small rodless area of the retina affording acute vision — see EYE illustration

fo·ve·al \-vēəl\ *adj* : of or relating to a fovea (as the retinal fovea) : situated in or mediated through the fovea — **fo·ve·al·ly** \-əlē\ *adv*

fo·ve·ate \-vē,āt, -ēə̇t\ *or* **fo·ve·at·ed** \-ē,ād·ə̇d\ *adj* [*foveate* fr. NL & L *fovea* small pit + E *-ate; foveated* fr. NL & L *fovea* + E *-ate* + *-ed*] : having foveae : PITTED

fo·ve·a·tion \ˌfōvēˈāshən\ *n -s* [*foveate* + *-ion*] **1** : the act or process of forming pits **2** : the state of being pitted

fo·ve·i·form \ˈfōvēə,fȯrm, fō'v-\ *adj* [ISV *fovea* (fr. NL & L) + *-iform*] : like a fovea

fo·ve·o·la \fōˈvēələ\ *n, pl* **foveo·lae** \-,lē\ *or* **foveolas** [NL, dim. of *fovea*] : a small pit; *specif* : one of the pits in the embryonic gastric mucosa from which the gastric glands develop — **fo·ve·o·lar** \-lə(r)\ *adj*

fo·ve·o·lar·i·ous \ˌfōvēəˈla(a)rēəs\ *adj* [prob. fr. (assumed) NL *foveolarius,* fr. NL *foveola* + L *-arius* -ary] : FOVEATE

fo·ve·o·late \ˈfōvēə,lāt, fōˈvēələ̇t\ *or* **fo·ve·o·lat·ed** \-ē·ə,lād·ə̇d\ *adj* [*foveolate* prob. fr. (assumed) NL *foveolatus,* fr. NL *foveola* + L *-atus* -ate; *foveolated* prob. fr. (assumed) NL *foveolatus* + E *-ed*] : FOVEATE

fo·ve·ole \ˈfōvē,ōl\ *or* **fo·ve·o·let** \ˌfōvēəˈlet, fōˈvēələ̇t\ *n -s* [*foveole* fr. NL *foveola; foveolet* fr. *foveole* + *-et*] : FOVEOLA

¹**fow** \ˈfü\ *dial Brit var of* FULL

²**fow** \"\ *var of* FOU

³**fow** \ˈfau̇, ˈfō\ *dial Brit var of* FOUL

FOW *abbr* **1** first open water **2** free on wagon

fowd *var of* FOUD

fow·er \ˈfau̇(ə)r\ *Scot var of* FOUR

fowk \ˈfau̇k\ *chiefly Scot var of* FOLK

¹**fowl** \ˈfau̇l, *esp before pause or consonant* -au̇əl\ *n, pl* **fowl** *or* **fowls** [ME *foul,* fr. OE *fugel;* akin to OHG *fogal* bird, ON *fugl,* Goth *fugls,* and prob. to OHG *fliogan* to fly — more at FLY] **1** : a bird of any kind ⟨dominion over . . . the ~ of the air —Gen 1:28 (AV)⟩ ⟨watch the hungry ocean ~ breast its way southward —Llewelyn Powys⟩ **2 a** : a domestic cock or hen : CHICKEN; *esp* : an adult hen — see DOMESTIC FOWL **b** : any of several domesticated or wild gallinaceous birds ⟨jungle ~⟩ ⟨guinea ~⟩ **3** : the meat of fowls used as food; *esp* : the meat of domestic fowls

²**fowl** \"\ *vi* -ED/-ING/-S [ME *foulen,* fr. OE *fuglian,* fr. *fugel*] : to seek, catch, or kill wild fowl for sport or food ⟨such persons as may lawfully hunt, fish, or ~ —William Blackstone⟩

fowl cholera *n* : an acute contagious septicemic disease of birds marked by fever, weakness, diarrhea, and petechial hemorrhages in the mucous membranes, caused by a bacterium (*Pasteurella multocida syn. avicida*), and highly destructive of all types of domestic poultry and most wild birds — compare FOWL PLAGUE

fowl·er \ˈfau̇lə(r)\ *n -s* [ME *foulere,* fr. OE *fuglere,* fr. *fugel* + *-ere* -er] : one that hunts wild fowl for sport or food

fow·ler flap \"-\ *n, usu cap 1st F* [after Harlan D. *Fowler,* 20th cent. Am. aeronautical designer] : an extensible trailing-edge flap that in the deflected position exposes a slot in the airplane wing

fow·ler·ite \ˈfau̇lə,rīt\ *n -s* [Samuel *Fowler* †1844 Am. physician and mineralogist + E *-ite*] : a variety of the mineral of a zinc-bearing rhodonite

fow·ler's solution \ˈfau̇lə(r)z-\ *n, usu cap F* [after Thomas *Fowler* †1801 Eng. physician] : an alkaline aqueous solution of potassium arsenite used in medicine (as in treating some diseases of the blood or skin)

fowler's toad *n, usu cap F* [after Samuel Page *Fowler* †1888 Am. antiquarian and naturalist] : a No. American toad (*Bufo fowleri*) with long postorbital and parallel frontoparietal crests

fowling piece *n* [*fowling* fr. gerund of ²*fowl*] : a light gun for shooting birds or small quadrupeds

fowl leukemia *also* **fowl leukosis** *or* **fowl leukosis complex** *n* **:** AVIAN LEUKOSIS COMPLEX

fowl meadow grass *or* **fowl grass** *n* **:** a slender pasture grass (*Poa palustris*) of Europe and America

fowl mite *n* **1 :** CHICKEN MITE **2 :** NORTHERN FOWL MITE

fowl paralysis *n* **:** NEUROLYMPHOMATOSIS

fowl pest *n* **1 :** FOWL PLAGUE **2 :** NEWCASTLE DISEASE

fowl plague *n* **:** a highly fatal virus disease of domestic poultry excepting pigeons and of many kinds of wild birds — compare FOWL CHOLERA

fowl pox *n* **:** either of two forms of a virus disease of chickens, turkeys, and various other birds characterized by head lesions: **a :** a cutaneous form marked by pustules, warty growths, and scabs esp. on the unfeathered skin — called also *sorehead* **b :** a more serious form occurring as cheesy lesions of the mucous membranes of the mouth, throat, and eyes that sometimes coalesce into a false membrane — called also *avian diphtheria*

fowl spirochetosis *n* **:** a severe febrile disease of poultry that is marked by enteritis and diarrhea and by congestion and often localized necrosis or ecchymoses in the liver and spleen and that is caused by a spirochete (*Borrelia anserina*) which is transmitted either directly or by a biting arthropod (as the chicken tick) — compare ARGAS

fowl tick *n* **:** CHICKEN TICK

fowl typhoid *n* **:** an infectious disease of poultry characterized by diarrhea, anemia, and great prostration and caused by a bacterium (*Salmonella gallinarum*)

¹fox \ˈfäks\ *n, pl* **foxes** *or* **fox** *often attrib* [ME, fr. OE; akin to OLF *vus* fox, OHG *fuhs* fox, *foha* she-fox, ON *fōa* fox, Goth *fauho* fox, Skt *puccha* tail] **1 :** any of various alert carnivorous mammals of the family Canidae related to the wolves but smaller, with shorter legs, more pointed muzzle, large erect ears, and long bushy tail and now placed in *Vulpes* and several other genera represented by one or more species in most parts of the world — see ARCTIC FOX, FENNEC, GRAY FOX, SILVER FOX; compare COLOR PHASE **2 :** the fur of a fox **3 :** a clever crafty man **:** a sly fellow ⟨the ~*es* live by their wits and rely on fraud —J.H.Hallowell⟩ **4** *archaic*

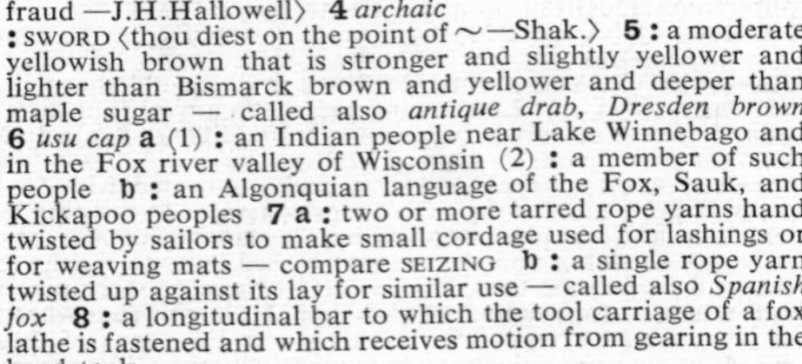
red fox

: SWORD ⟨thou diest on the point of ~ —Shak.⟩ **5 :** a moderate yellowish brown that is stronger and slightly yellower and lighter than Bismarck brown and yellower and deeper than maple sugar — called also *antique drab, Dresden brown* **6** *usu cap* **a** (1) **:** an Indian people near Lake Winnebago and in the Fox river valley of Wisconsin (2) **:** a member of such people **b :** an Algonquian language of the Fox, Sauk, and Kickapoo peoples **7 a :** two or more tarred rope yarns hand twisted by sailors to make small cordage used for lashings or for weaving mats — compare SEIZING **b :** a single rope yarn twisted up against its lay for similar use — called also *Spanish fox* **8 :** a longitudinal bar to which the tool carriage of a fox lathe is fastened and which receives motion from gearing in the headstock

²fox \"\ *vb* -ED/-ING/-ES *vt* **1 a :** to trick by ingenuity or cunning **:** FOOL, OUTWIT ⟨we would ~ him into withdrawing vitally needed strength —E.E.S.Montagu⟩ **b :** CONFUSE, BEWILDER, BAFFLE ⟨some survivors . . . were completely ~*ed* by the tragedy —Alan Villiers⟩ **2** *obs* **:** to make drunk **:** INTOXICATE ⟨I drank . . . so much wine that I was even almost ~*ed* —Samuel Pepys⟩ **3 a :** to repair (a shoe) by renewing the upper **b :** to add a strip of something to; *specif* **:** to trim (a shoe) with a strip of leather ~ *vi* **:** to act like a fox **:** DISSEMBLE ⟨you never know — he may be ~*ing* —Guthrie Wilson⟩

³fox \"\ *usu cap* — a communications code word for the letter *f*

fox and geese *n* **1 a :** a board game in which pegs or pieces representing geese can be moved only forward in their attempt to corner the fox while the piece representing the fox can move in any direction and can remove geese from the board by jumping them **b :** a similar game played on a checkerboard in which four pieces representing geese are moved forward one space at a time to try to corner the fox who can be moved one space at a time forward or back but cannot jump — called also *devil and the tailors* **2 :** a game usu. played in the snow in which one player representing the fox tries to catch one of the others representing the geese as they run around the rim and through the spokes of a wheel-shaped figure

[fox and geese figure: see caption] fox and geese 1a

foxbane \ˈ≈,≈\ *n* **:** a wolfsbane (*Aconitum lycoctonum*)

fox bat *n* **:** FRUIT BAT

fox·ber·ry \ˈfäks — *see* BERRY\ *n* **1 :** a bearberry (*Arctostaphylos uva-ursi*) **2 :** MOUNTAIN CRANBERRY

fox bolt *n* **:** an anchor bolt with a split end to receive a fox wedge for use in blind holes

fox dog *n* **1 :** FOXHOUND **2 :** Azara's dog or various related So. American wild dogs **3 :** LONG-EARED FOX

foxed \ˈfäkst\ *adj* [¹*fox* + *-ed*] **:** discolored with yellowish brown stains due to dampness, fungus activity, metallic impurities, or incipient decay ⟨~ leaves of old books⟩

fox encephalitis *n* **:** a virus disease of foxes, dogs, and related animals that is marked by virus invasion of endothelial tissues esp. of smaller blood vessels resulting in local hemorrhage which damages the tissues of the affected area and leads to inflammation of the brain or other organs

fox·er \ˈfäksə(r)\ *n* -S **:** a worker who foxes shoes or rubbers

foxfeet \ˈ≈,≈\ *n pl but sing in constr* **:** FIR CLUB MOSS

fox fire *n* [ME *foxfire*, fr. ¹*fox* + *fire*] **1 :** an eerie phosphorescent light; *esp* **:** the luminescence of decaying wood **2 :** any of various luminous fungi (as *Armillaria mellea*) that cause decaying wood to glow

foxfish \ˈ≈,≈\ *n* **:** the European dragonet

fox geranium *n* **:** HERB ROBERT

foxglove \ˈ≈,≈\ *n* [ME, alter. of *foxesglove*, fr. OE *foxes glōfa*, fr. *foxes* (gen. of ¹*fox*) + *glōfa, glōf* glove, pouch — more at GLOVE] **1 :** a plant of the genus *Digitalis*; *esp* **:** a common European biennial or perennial (*D. purpurea*) with long clusters of dotted white or purple tubular flowers — called also *fairy bell, fingerflower, fingerroot* **2 :** any of several other plants: as **a** *dial Eng* **:** MULLEIN **b :** TRUMPET CREEPER **c :** PITCHER PLANT **d :** POKEWEED

foxglove aphid *n* **:** an aphid (*Acyrthosiphon solani*) that is an economic pest of various cultivated plants (as potatoes) in temperate regions

fox grape *n* **:** any of several native grapes of eastern No. America with foxy fruit of sour or musky flavor: as **a :** MUSCADINE 2 **b :** CHICKEN GRAPE **c :** a tall-growing grape (*Vitis labrusca*) that has heavily tomentose young growth and compact thyrses of bluish black to pink or greenish white fruits which are sharp and acid until fully ripe and that is an ancestor of most hardy American cultivated grapes

foxhole \ˈ≈,≈\ *n* **:** a pit usu. dug hastily during combat for individual cover against enemy fire, sometimes large enough for two or three men, and elaborated in construction as the situation demands and materials available permit

foxhound \ˈ≈,≈\ *n* **:** any of certain large swift powerful hounds of great endurance that are used in hunting foxes, that are considered to form several breeds and many distinctive strains, and that are from 21 to 25 inches high with a dense hard glossy coat usu. of black, tan, and white, long ears, straight forelegs, heavy hind legs, and the tail carried gaily over the back — see AMERICAN FOXHOUND, ENGLISH FOXHOUND

foxier *comparative of* FOXY

foxiest *superlative of* FOXY

fox·i·ly \ˈfäksəlē, -li\ *adv* **:** in a foxy manner **:** CRAFTILY, TRICKILY

fox·i·ness \ˈfäksēnəs, -sin-\ *n* -ES **:** the quality or state of being foxy

fox·ing \ˈfäksiŋ\ *n* -S [fr. *foxed*, after such pairs as E *colored: coloring*] **1 :** DISCOLORATION; *esp* **:** brownish spots in the paper of old books **2** [fr. gerund of ²*fox*] **a :** a piece of material applied to the upper or extending around the outsole of a boot or shoe **b :** a piece of leather ornamenting the lower part of the quarter of a shoe, covering the counter, and sometimes extending to the vamp — see SHOE illustration

fox key *n* **:** a cotter secured by a fox wedge

fox lathe \ˈfäks-\ *n* [perh. after James *Fox fl*1821 Eng. toolmaker] **:** a lathe with or without a turret having a chasing bar and leaders for thread cutting and being used for turning brass

fox maggot *n* **:** a screwworm (*Wohlfahrtia opaca*) developing in the flesh of various mammals and esp. destructive to young ranch mink and foxes

fox mark *n* [*fox* (as in *foxed*) + *mark*] **:** a brownish spot; *esp* **:** a discoloration of old paper

fox moth *n* **:** a grayish brown European moth (*Macrothylacia rubi*) of the family Lasiocampidae

fox plum *n* **:** a bearberry (*Arctostaphylos uva-ursi*)

fox poison *n* **:** SPURGE LAUREL 1

fox shark *n* **:** THRESHER SHARK

fox snake *n* **:** a common rodent-eating colubrid snake (*Elaphe vulpina*) of the upper Mississippi valley

fox sparrow *n* **:** a large American sparrow (*Passerella iliaca*) typically rich chestnut above and striped below

fox squirrel *n* **:** a large stout-bodied arboreal squirrel (*Sciurus niger*) that is now rare over much of its range from the Mississippi valley and the southeastern U.S. north to New Jersey and central New York and is represented by several varieties differing chiefly in color — see BLACK SQUIRREL, CAT SQUIRREL

foxtail \ˈ≈,≈\ *n* [ME *fox tail*, fr. ¹*fox* + *tail*] **1 a :** the tail of a fox **b :** something resembling the tail of a fox ⟨there were ~*s* white and wispy all over the sky —David Walker⟩ **2 a** *or* **foxtail grass :** any of several grasses esp. of the genera *Alopecurus, Hordeum*, and *Setaria* with spikes resembling brushes — compare BRISTLE GRASS **b :** any of several ground pines; *esp* **:** a widely distributed ground pine (*Lycopodium alopecuroides*) of barren sandy or peaty moist coastal regions of eastern and southeastern U.S. that has numerous erect fertile branches thickly clothed with usu. bristly ciliate leaves **3 :** the last cinder obtained in the fining of metal

foxtail barley *n* **:** SQUIRRELTAIL

foxtail lily *n* **:** a plant of the genus *Eremurus*

foxtail millet *n* **:** a coarse drought-resistant but frost-sensitive annual grass (*Setaria italica*) with a thick heavy elongated spicate inflorescence that is probably derived from an Old World bristle grass (*S. viridis*), has differentiated into a number of varieties under cultivation, and is grown for grain, hay, and forage in the Old World and chiefly for green fodder and silage in the U. S. — called also *Hungarian grass, Italian millet;* see GERMAN MILLET, SIBERIAN MILLET

foxtail pine *n* **:** any of several American pines with a dense head of foliage: as **a :** a moderate to large pine (*Pinus balfouriana*) of upland western No. America that is initially pyramidal but becomes irregular and open with age and that has stiff crowded persistent leaves, short-stalked dark brown pendulous cones, and bark initially milk white but becoming reddish brown and deeply fissured with age **b :** BRISTLECONE PINE **c :** LOBLOLLY PINE 1

foxtail wedging *n* **:** the process of fastening by fox wedges — called also *fox wedging*

fox terrier *n* **:** either of two small-sized high-spirited terriers that were formerly used to dig out foxes, that weigh about 16 to 18 pounds, and that have a flat moderately narrow skull, very little stop, a long muzzle, small V-shaped ears which droop forward close to the cheek, straight forelegs, and muscular hindquarters without any tendency to droop or crouch: **a :** such a dog with a close smooth dense coat — called also *smooth fox terrier* **b :** such a dog with a harsh wiry coat of moderate length — called also *wirehaired fox terrier*

wirehaired fox terrier

¹fox-trot \ˈ≈,≈\ *n* **1 :** a short broken slow trotting gait in which the hind foot of the horse hits the ground a trifle before the diagonally opposite forefoot and the head nods in time to the movement **2 a :** a ballroom dance in duple time that includes slow walking steps, quick running steps, and two-steps **b :** an ice dancing step **3 :** the music to which a fox-trot is danced **:** jazz in duple rhythm fast or slow — compare BLUES, CHARLESTON

²fox-trot \"\ *vi* [¹*fox-trot*] **:** to dance the fox-trot

foxtrot \"\ *usu cap* [¹*fox-trot*] — a communications code word for the letter *f*

fox wedge *n* **:** a wedge for expanding the split end of a bolt, cotter, dowel, tenon, or other piece in order to fasten the end in a hole or mortise and prevent withdrawal

fox wolf *n* **:** any of several So. American wild dogs (as Azara's dog and the crab-eating fox)

foxy \ˈfäksē, -si\ *adj, usu* -ER/-EST [¹*fox* + *-y*] **1 a :** resembling a fox in appearance or disposition **:** SLY, WILY ⟨a strain of ~ secretiveness —Edgar Johnson⟩ **b :** alert and knowing **:** smart in appearance and behavior **:** CLEVER ⟨this ~ publicity man turned fumbling poet —Sherwood Anderson⟩ **2 a :** having the color of a fox **:** being of the color fox **b :** characterized by excessive use of reddish tints — used esp. of an oil painting ⟨such an excessive brownness in their shadows as to make them sometimes perfectly ~ —W.M.Craig⟩ **3 :** defective in color or quality esp. from age or dampness **:** FOXED ⟨this book . . . when it is old and ~ —R.L.Stevenson⟩ **4 :** having the flavor of native American grapes (as the fox grape) ⟨we say the wine tastes "grapey"; wine makers call it a ~ taste —Frank Schoonmaker & Tom Marvel⟩ **syn** see SLY

foy \ˈfȯi\ *n* -S [D dial. *fooi* feast given by a farmer to his laborers at the end of the harvest, fr. MD *foye, voye* journey, way, parting entertainment, fr. OF *voie* journey, way, fr. L *via* way — more at VIA] *chiefly Scot* **:** a farewell entertainment or feast (as at the end of a harvest or just before a marriage)

foya·ite \ˈfȯi(y)ə,īt, ˈfōyə-\ *n* -S [G *foyait*, fr. *Foya* (La Foia), mountain in Algarve province, Portugal + G *-it* -ite] **1 :** a coarse-grained hornblende-nepheline-syenite rock **2 :** a nephelite-syenite rock with trachytoid texture — **fo·ya·it·ic** \;≈≈ˈid·ik\ *adj*

foy boat \ˈfȯi-\ *n* [*foy* (origin unknown) + *boat*] **:** a pilot boat used in and about the river Tyne

foy·er \ˈfȯi(y)ə(r) *also* ˈfȯi,(y)ā *sometimes* fȯiˈ(y)ā\ *n* -S [F, lit., fireplace, fr. ML *focarius* fireplace, fr. L *focus* fireplace, hearth + *-arius* -ary — more at FOCUS] **1 a :** an anteroom or lobby esp. of a theater, library, or other public building — compare GREENROOM **b :** an entrance hallway or vestibule leading typically to stairs or to the interior of private living quarters **2 a :** a gathering place **:** CENTER ⟨a student ~ . . . where they can eat meals composed principally of soup and starches for . . . about twenty cents —Paul Bowles⟩ **b :** a focal point **:** center of concentration ⟨intended that the university . . . should become the ~ of Hellenism in a very practical sense —H.A.Gibbons⟩ **3 :** a crucible for molten metal in a furnace

fo·zi·ness \ˈfōzinəs\ *n* -ES *chiefly Scot* **:** the quality or state of being fozy: **a :** SPONGINESS **b :** OBESITY **c :** FATHEADEDNESS

fo·zy \-zi\ *adj, usu* -ER/-EST [D *voos* spongy and light-textured + E *-y*; akin to ON *fauskr* rotten log, OE *fūl* foul — more at FOUL] **1** *chiefly Scot, of a vegetable* **:** spongy and light-textured **:** OVERGROWN **2** *chiefly Scot, of a person* **a :** fat and bloated **:** OBESE **b :** dull-witted and insipid **:** FATHEADED

fp *abbr* freezing point

FP *abbr* **1** field punishment **2** fine paper **3** fireplace **4** fireplug **5** flash point **6** floating policy **7** foot-pound **8** [It *fortepiano*] loud, then soft **9** freight and passenger **10** fully paid

FPA *abbr* free of particular average

FPAAC *abbr* free of particular average, American conditions

FPAEC *abbr* free of particular average, English conditions

FPC *abbr* for private circulation

FPM *abbr* feet per minute

FPO *abbr* **1** field post office **2** fleet post office

fprf *abbr* fireproof

FPS *abbr* **1** *often not cap* feet per second **2** *usu not cap* foot-pound-second **3** *often not cap* frames per second

fqcy *abbr* frequency

fqt *abbr* frequent

fr *abbr* **1** *often cap* father **2** fragment **3** frame **4** franc **5** *often cap* [L *frater*] brother **6** frequent **7** *often cap* friar **8** from **9** front **10** fruit

FR *abbr* **1** fire resistant; fire retardant **2** freight release

Fr *symbol* francium

¹fra \ˈfrə\ *prep* [ME (northern dial.) *fra, fro*, fr. ON *frā* — more at FROM] *Scot* **:** FROM

²fra \ˈfrä\ *n* -S *usu cap* [It, short for *frate* brother, monk, fr. L *frater* brother — more at BROTHER] **:** BROTHER — often used as a title preceding the name of an Italian monk or friar ⟨*Fra* Angelo⟩ ⟨*Fra* Dominic⟩

fra·ca \frəˈkä\ *n* -S [F *fracas*] *Scot* **:** FRACAS

fra·cas \ˈfrākəs *also* ˈfrak-, *Brit usu* ˈfra(,)kä\ *n, pl* **fracases** \-səz\ *or Brit* **fracas** \-äz\ [F, din, hubbub, row, fr. MF, fr. OIt *fracasso*, fr. *fracassare* to break into pieces, shatter, destroy, fr. (assumed) VL, blend of L *frangere* to break and *quassare* to shake, break into pieces — more at BREAK, QUASH] **:** a noisy quarrel **:** BRAWL, FIGHT, ALTERCATION ⟨there was suddenly a ~, and one of them clenched his fists and hit another full in the face —E.V.Lucas⟩ ⟨the most violent ~ in . . . parliamentary history resulted in hurled benches and three injuries —*Collier's Yr. Bk.*⟩ **syn** see BRAWL

frack \ˈfrak\ *var of* FRECK

fract·ed \ˈfraktəd\ *adj* [L *fractus*, (past part.) + E *-ed*] **1** *obs* **:** BROKEN **2** *of a heraldic ordinary* **:** having a part displaced as if the charge were broken

¹frac·tion \ˈfrakshən\ *n* -S [ME *fraccioun*, fr. LL *fraction-, fractio* action of breaking, fr. L *fractus* (past part. of *frangere* to break) + *-ion-, -io* -ion — more at BREAK] **1 :** a part of a whole: as **a :** the indicated quotient of one expression divided by another — see NUMBER table **b** (1) **:** a piece broken off **:** FRAGMENT, SCRAP (2) **:** a discrete unit **:** PORTION, SECTION ⟨a minute ~ of the voters⟩ **c :** a part less than a point in a security quotation ⟨the price of U.S. steel declined a ~⟩ **2** *archaic* **a :** a rupture in relations **:** DISCORD, DISSENSION, DISHARMONY **b :** a breach of peace **:** FRACAS, RUCTION **3 a :** a breaking up **:** BREAKING; *specif, often cap* **:** the breaking of the bread by the priest before the communion in Eastern and Western Christian liturgies **b** *obs* **:** a broken place **:** FRACTURE, RUPTURE, BREACH, BREAK **4 :** LITTLE, BIT ⟨a ~ closer⟩ **5 :** one of several portions (as of a distillate or precipitate) separable by fractionation and consisting either of mixtures or of pure chemical compounds **:** CUT ⟨petroleum ~*s*⟩ ⟨gamma globulin is a ~ of blood plasma⟩ **6 :** a type character representing a mathematical fraction — see PIECE FRACTION **7 :** a group of Communists who work for reform within a non-Communist organization — compare CELL 9 **syn** see PART

²fraction \"\ *vt* -ED/-ING/-S **:** to separate or divide into portions, separable units, or discrete components; *specif* **:** FRACTIONATE 1

¹frac·tion·al \-shənᵊl, -shnəl\ *adj* **1 :** of or relating to a fraction **:** being or constituting a fraction; *esp* **:** having to do with only a small portion of a possible whole, total, or entirety ⟨showing only ~ allegiance to his country⟩ **2 :** relatively small **:** INCONSIDERABLE, INSIGNIFICANT ⟨waited only a ~ part of the time allowed⟩; *also* **:** very short ⟨spoke after a ~ pause⟩ **3 :** of, relating to, or being fractional currency ⟨a ~ coin⟩ **4 :** of or relating to any process used to separate the components of a mixture through differences in physical or chemical properties (as volatility or solubility) ⟨~ distillation of petroleum⟩ ⟨~ crystallization of the rare earths⟩

²fractional \"\ *n* -S [by shortening] **:** FRACTIONAL TIME

fractional burial *n* **:** a burial in which only part (as the head) of a body is interred

fractional currency *n* **1 :** paper money in denominations of less than one dollar issued by the U.S. 1863–76 **2 :** currency in denominations less than the basic monetary unit

fractional equation *n* **:** an equation containing the unknown in the denominator of one or more terms (as $\frac{a}{x}+\frac{b}{x+1}=c$)

frac·tion·al·ism \-shənᵊl,izəm, -shnə,li-\ *n* -S **1 :** the state of consisting of separate usu. nonhomogeneous or inharmonious units ⟨the ~ of a modern society striving toward unity⟩ **2 :** the action of forming or encouraging the formation of a fraction within the Communist party

frac·tion·al·iza·tion \,frakshənᵊləˈzāshən, -shnələ-\ *n* -S **:** the act or process of fractionalizing or the state of being fractionalized ⟨stimulates division of leadership and ~ within the electorate —V.O.Key⟩

frac·tion·al·ize \ˈfrakshənᵊl,īz, -shnə,līz\ *vt* -ED/-ING/-S [¹*fractional* + *-ize*] **:** to break up into fractions or subdivisions ⟨the *fractionalizing* of the empire into many independent nations⟩ ⟨trying to unify a *fractionalized* congress⟩

fractional lot *n* **:** ODD LOT

frac·tion·al·ly \-shənᵊlē, -shnəlē, -li\ *adv* **:** in a fractional manner **:** by a fraction **:** to the extent of a fraction ⟨the stock had declined ~⟩ **:** by fractions ⟨squirming on his belly like a lizard, moving ~ . . . one shoulder came forward, a pause, then the other —Alan Sullivan⟩ **:** to a small or insignificant extent ⟨the area had been only ~ explored⟩

fractional note *n* **1 :** a piece of postal currency **2 :** a piece of fractional paper money of government or private issue esp. in the U.S. and Canada — called also *shinplaster;* compare FRACTIONAL CURRENCY

fractional sterilization *n* **:** sterilization by repeated exposure to flowing steam at such intervals as would permit bacterial or other spores present to pass into the nonresistant negative stage between exposures

fractional substitution *n* **:** encipherment beginning with fractionating, continued by transposing the units singly, and completed by recombining the units according to the resulting juxtapositions and replacing them by letters again

fractional time *n* **:** the time made by a contestant in a race at the end of a fractional part (as a lap or a quarter mile) of the total distance covered

frac·tion·ary \-shə,nerē\ *adj* **1 :** FRACTIONAL **2 :** concerned with or done by fractions or piecemeal

frac·tion·ate \-shə,nāt, *usu* -ād.+V\ *vt* -ED/-ING/-S [¹*fraction* + *-ate*] **1 a :** to separate (a mixture) into different portions (as by distillation, precipitation, or screening) **:** subject to fractional distillation, fractional crystallization, or other fractional process **b :** to divide or break up (a whole or unit) into component parts or smaller units **:** separate into divisions, parts, sections, or fragments ⟨practically all the lands have been . . . *fractionated* through allotment —Laura Thompson⟩ ⟨suggest . . . we ~ our problem by first looking for a criterion of meaning —Gustav Bergmann⟩ **2 :** to replace (letters) by bifid or trifid substitutes

frac·tion·a·tion \,frakshəˈnāshən\ *n* -S **:** the act or process of fractionating or the state of being fractionated ⟨a mass of material (15 loose-leaf binders containing 3000 typewritten pages) which has been subjected . . . to ~ —*New Republic*⟩ ⟨land ~⟩ ⟨~ of the culture —C.P.Shaw⟩ ⟨~ of blood plasma by precipitation of proteins⟩; *specif* **:** the crystallization with falling temperature of successive minerals from a silicate magma

frac·tion·a·tor \ˈ≈≈,nād·ə(r)\ *n* -S **:** an apparatus for fractionating esp. by fractional distillation

fractioned *past of* FRACTION

fractioning *pres part of* FRACTION

frac·tion·ize \-,nīz\ *vt* -ED/-ING/-S *see -ize in Explan Notes* **:** FRACTIONATE 1b

fractions *pl of* FRACTION, *pres 3d sing of* FRACTION

frac·tious \ˈfrakshəs\ *adj* [¹*fraction* + *-ous*] **1 :** tending to cause trouble (as by disobedience or opposition to an established order) **:** hard to manage or unmanageable **:** REFRACTORY, UNRULY ⟨a ~ horse⟩ ⟨a ship with a ~ crew threatening mutiny throughout the trip⟩ **2 :** not smooth or free of trouble in operation **:** likely to function in unpredictable and troublesome ways ⟨rockets and guided missiles are much too ~ to be tested anywhere near a thickly populated area —*Time*⟩ ⟨loudspeakers remain the most ~ of all high-fidelity components —J.M.Conly⟩ **3 a :** QUARRELSOME, CONTRARY ⟨at the beginning the crowd was captious and ~, owing to delays and bad arrangements —Arnold Bennett⟩ **b :** PEEVISH, IRRITABLE ⟨a ~ child⟩ ⟨like a ~ mother hen rounding up a brood of willful chicks —H.J.Higdon⟩ **syn** see IRRITABLE

frac·tious·ly *adv* **:** in a fractious manner

frac·tious·ness *n* -ES **:** the quality or state of being fractious

fracto- *comb form* [L *fractus*] **:** broken up and ⟨*fracto*cumulus⟩ **:** fracture ⟨*fracto*graph⟩

frac·to·graph \'fraktə,graf\ *n* [*fracto-* + *-graph*] **:** a fractographic photograph

frac·to·graph·ic \¦==¦grafik\ *adj* **:** of, used in, or relating to fractography — **frac·to·graph·i·cal·ly** \-fək(ə)lē\ *adv*

frac·tog·ra·phy \frak'tägrəfē\ *n* -ES [*fracto-* + *-graphy*] **:** the microscopic study of fractured surfaces of metals at high magnification

[1]fractur *usu cap, var of* FRAKTUR

[2]frac·tur \fräk'tü(ə)r, -üə\ *or* **fractur painting** *also* **fraktur** \"\ *or* **fraktur painting** *n* -S [PaG *fraktur*, fr. G *fraktur* (formerly spelled *fractur*), a Gothic script — more at FRAKTUR] **:** illuminated writing featuring decorative motifs (as tulips, birds, and scrolls) and used by Pennsylvania Germans on documents (as wedding, birth, and baptismal certificates) often framed and hung

frac·tur·able \'frakchərəbəl, -ksh-\ *adj* **:** capable of being fractured **:** BREAKABLE

frac·tur·al \-kchərəl, -ksh(ə)rəl\ *adj* **:** of, relating to, being, or due to fracture

[1]frac·ture \'frakchə(r), -ksh-\ *n* -S [ME, fr. L *fractura*, fr. *fractus* (past part. of *frangere* to break) + *-ura* -ure — more at BREAK] **1 a :** the act or process of breaking or the state of being broken **:** rupture by a break through the entire thickness of a material **:** BREACH; *specif* **:** the breaking of hard tissue (as a bone, tooth, or cartilage) **b :** the rupture (as by tearing) of soft tissue ⟨kidney ~⟩ **2 :** the product or result of fracturing **:** BREAK, CRACK, CLEFT **3 :** the texture or general appearance of the freshly broken surface of a mineral ⟨a rock with a conchoidal ~⟩ **4 :** BREAKING 1

[2]fracture \"\ *vb* **fractured; fractured; fracturing** \-kchəriŋ, -ksh(ə)r-\ **fractures** *vt* **1 a :** to cause a fracture in **:** BREAK ⟨~ a rib⟩ ⟨the bump in the road *fractured* a spring on the car⟩ **b :** RUPTURE, TEAR, LACERATE ⟨a blow that *fractured* a kidney⟩ **2 a :** to damage or destroy as if by rupturing or tearing apart ⟨~ the newfound unity of the two parties⟩ ⟨may seriously ~ himself as he tries to patch up the rifts in the . . . party —Sidney Hyman⟩ **b :** to break into pieces **:** cause great disorder in ⟨a scream that *fractured* the peace of the night⟩ ⟨conspiracy to ~ their sensibilities —*Time*⟩ **c :** to break up **:** FRACTIONATE ⟨by *fracturing* and dispersing senatorial power —W.V.Shannon⟩ ⟨most world movements and agencies . . . have been *fractured* or assimilated by national interests in one way or another —Liston Pope⟩ **d :** to show disregard for (as a law or rule) **:** VIOLATE ⟨declared the principle of the separation of church and state *fractured* by the agreement⟩ ⟨he *fractured* many of the laws of probability —Sheldon Cheney⟩ **~** *vi* **:** to undergo fracture **:** break esp. through a total thickness ⟨under the blow the thighbone *fractured*⟩

fracture cleavage *n* **:** geologic cleavage independent of the orientation of mineral grains but due to the presence of many closely spaced fractures or incipient fractures

fracture plane *n* **:** a point in an arthropod appendage that is modified for the ready occurrence of autotomy (as by the presence of special muscles and mechanisms to prevent loss of body fluid)

frad·i·cin \'fradəsən\ *n* -S [NL *fradia* (specific epithet of *Streptomyces fradiae*) + E *-cin* (as in *actinomycin*)] **:** a crystalline antibiotic active against fungi that is produced by an actinomycete (*Streptomyces fradiae*) — compare NEOMYCIN

frae \'frā\ *prep* [ME (northern dial.) *fra, frae, fro*, fr. ON *frā* — more at FROM] *Scot* **:** FROM

fraenulum *var of* FRENULUM

fraenum *var of* FRENUM

frag \'frag\ *n* -S [by shortening] **:** FRAGMENTATION BOMB

frag *abbr* **1** fragile **2** fragment; fragmentation

fra·gar·ia \frə'ga(a)rēə\ *n, cap* [NL, fr. L *fragum* strawberry + NL *-aria*] **:** a small genus of low perennial herbs (family Rosaceae) that comprise the strawberries, have trifoliate leaves, cymose white flowers, and long slender runners, and are represented in cultivation mainly by horticultural forms derived from several wild species (as *F. vesca, F. virginiana, F. chiloensis, F. moschata*) and including many hybrids of these — see CHILEAN STRAWBERRY, STRAWBERRY, WOOD STRAWBERRY

fra·ge \'frägə, 'fräg\ *n* -S [G, lit., question, fr. OHG *frāga* — more at PRAY] **:** the lowest bid in a card game (as frog or skat)

frag·i·lar·ia \,frajə'la(a)rēə\ *n, cap* [NL, fr. L *fragilis* frail + NL *-aria*] **:** a genus (the type of the family Fragilariaceae of the order Pennales) of rectangular diatoms forming irregular colonies

frag·ile \'frajəl, *US also & Brit usu* -a,jīl\ *adj* [MF, fr. L *fragilis* — more at FRAIL] **1 a :** easily broken or destroyed **:** FRAIL ⟨the ~ stem of the tall flower⟩ ⟨a person of ~ moral convictions⟩ **b :** delicate of constitution or of health **:** barely able or unable to endure without harm the normal day-to-day physical demands of existence **:** unusually susceptible to ill health or physical harm ⟨a ~ and tottering old man⟩ ⟨too ~ to stand the Vermont winter —Sinclair Lewis⟩ **c :** giving the impression of or having qualities suggesting someone that is fragile of body or health ⟨a ~ soprano⟩ ⟨a ~ gesture⟩ ⟨~ hands⟩ **2 a :** WEAK, TENUOUS, UNSUBSTANTIAL ⟨a ~ connection with great men⟩ ⟨the ground of his faith . . . seemed to me so ~ —H.J.Laski⟩ **b :** thin and transparent ⟨a ~ skin⟩ **:** extremely light and evanescent ⟨a ~ tone⟩ **:** DIAPHANOUS ⟨a ~ taffeta⟩ **c :** extremely subtle or fine **:** calling for an extremely fine perception ⟨a ~ wine⟩ ⟨the tantalizing, ~ taste of fresh blue crab —Hugh Cave⟩ **d :** SHORT-LIVED, EVANESCENT ⟨a ~ moment⟩ **syn** see WEAK

fragile fern *n* **:** a delicate fern (*Cystopteris fragilis*) widely distributed in Europe, Asia, and No. America with 2 or 3 thin pinnatifid fronds, creeping rootstocks, and slender brittle stems — called also *brittle fern*

frag·ile·ly \-əl(l)ē, -īllē, -i\ *adv* **:** in a fragile manner

fra·gil·i·tas os·si·um \frə'jilə,tas'äsēəm\ *n* [NL, lit., fragility of bones] **:** a familial disease marked by extreme brittleness of the long bones and a bluish color of the whites of the eyes

fra·gil·i·ty \frə'jiləd·ē, -ətē, -i\ *n* -ES [ME *fragilite*, fr. MF *fragilité*, fr. L *fragilitat-, fragilitas*, fr. *fragilis* + *-itat-, -itas* -ity] **1 :** the quality or state of being fragile ⟨the extreme ~ of public order —G.W.Johnson⟩ ⟨most men's touching illusion as to the frailness of women and their spiritual ~ —Joseph Conrad⟩ ⟨worried because of the ~ of the vase⟩ **2 :** something fragile ⟨rooms . . . heavy with *fragilities* —Natacha Stewart⟩

fragility test *n* **:** a test of the relative fragility of red blood cells made by exposing them to hypotonic solutions and determining the point at which they rupture

fra·gil·o·cyte \frə'jilə,sīt\ *n* -S [L *fragil*is + E *-o-* + *-cyte*] **:** an exceptionally fragile red blood cell (as in congenital hemolytic jaundice)

fra·gil·o·cy·to·sis \frə,jilō(,)sī'tōsəs\ *n, pl* **fragilocyto·ses** \-'tō,sēz\ [NL, fr. ISV *fragilocyte* + NL *-osis*] **:** an abnormal state characterized by the presence of fragilocytes in the blood

[1]frag·ment \'fragmənt\ *n* -S [ME, fr. L *fragmentum*, fr. *frag-* (stem of *frangere* to break) + *-mentum* -ment — more at BREAK] **1 :** a part broken off **:** a small detached portion **:** an imperfect or incomplete part ⟨pieces of pottery and ~*s* that can be reconstructed —*Amer. Guide Series: N.J.*⟩ ⟨enchanting ~*s* of Irish life —John McNulty⟩ ⟨only ~*s* remain of the covered-wagon ballads —*Amer. Guide Series: Oregon*⟩ **2 :** something that is small and usu. insignificant ⟨a ~ of silence —Guy Fowler⟩ **syn** see PART

[2]frag·ment \'frag,ment, ='=\ *vb* -ED/-ING/-S *vi* **:** to break into fragments **:** FRAGMENTIZE ⟨the vase fell and ~*ed* into small pieces⟩ ⟨this pluralized and ~*ing* society —Walter Lippmann⟩ **~** *vt* **:** to break or divide into disorganized or not unified pieces ⟨a foreign policy that is ~*ed* rather than organized to a focal purpose⟩ ⟨an old woman's ~*ed* memory —Meridel Le Sueur⟩; *esp* **:** to destroy by such breaking or dividing up ⟨the remaining hopes of control of weapons have been ~*ed* by the new bomb —M.W.Straight⟩

frag·men·tal \(')frag¦mentᵊl\ *adj* **:** FRAGMENTARY **:** consisting of fragmentary or detrital material (as conglomerate, sandstone, shale, or tuff) — compare CLASTIC 2 — **frag·men·tal·ly** \-ᵊlē\ *adv*

frag·men·tal·ize \frag'mentᵊl,īz\ *vt* -ED/-ING/-S **:** FRAGMENTIZE ⟨his rapid oscillations of style and plot . . . ~ the American myth and destroy the cohesiveness of the allegory —Harvey Swados⟩

frag·men·tar·i·ly \¦fragmən·¦terəlē, -li\ *adv* **:** in a fragmentary manner ⟨the dim light penetrated only ~ into the drifting mist⟩

frag·men·tar·i·ness \-rēnəs, -rin-\ *n* -ES **:** the quality or state of being fragmentary ⟨the ~ of our approach and the unsystematic nature of our categories —Anna G. Hatcher⟩ ⟨exasperated by the ~ of the facts at my disposal —W.S.Maugham⟩

frag·men·ta·rism \'fragməntə,rizəm\ *n* -S [*fragmentary* + *-ism*] **:** FRAGMENTARINESS

frag·men·tary \'fragmən·,terē, -ri\ *adj* **1 :** consisting of or composed of fragments ⟨large leg bones, and other ~ remains of an elephant —*Amer. Guide Series: Nev.*⟩ ⟨the sampling of most authors is necessarily ~ —Uriel Weinreich⟩ ⟨historical links between certain of the more ~ letters —Robert Lawrence⟩ **:** consisting of disconnected and incomplete parts ⟨had only a ~ education⟩ **:** INCOMPLETE, PARTIAL ⟨gave only a ~ account of the incident⟩ ⟨~ and inconclusive knowledge —*Current Biog.*⟩ ⟨this viewpoint may prove to be optimistic, but ~ evidence so far has not suggested that it is —J.A.Morris b. 1904⟩ **:** DISORGANIZED ⟨our approach to the problem is still ~ —*N.Y.Times*⟩ ⟨we need wholeness, but he is ~ —E.R.Bentley⟩ **2 :** dealing in or being only a fragment of a whole ⟨every ~ science of man, such as economics —Edward Sapir⟩ **3 :** FRAGMENTAL

frag·men·tate \-,tāt\ *vb* -ED/-ING/-S [back-formation fr. *fragmentation*] **:** to break into pieces esp. explosively **:** FRACTIONATE, FRAGMENTIZE ⟨they were sure the master rods on the engines were all *fragmentating* —David Beaty⟩ ⟨permits the . . . artist to ~ a single small idea into a limitless string of daily episodes —C.W.Morton⟩

frag·men·ta·tion \,=='tāshən\ *n* -S [F, fr. *fragmenter* to divide into fragments (fr. *fragment*, n., fr. L *fragmentum*) + *-ation*] **1 :** the act or process of fragmentating or fractionating or the state of being fragmentated or fractionated ⟨the constant ~ of landholdings —J.H.Steward⟩ ⟨cried for the ~ of India —*Time*⟩ ⟨the growing ~ of the corporation into a multitude of divisions and departments —W.H.Whyte⟩ **:** the act or process of making fragmentary or the state of becoming or being fragmentary ⟨the contemporary pursuit of brevity, with its inevitable consequence of ~, in all fields of communication is alarming —F.L.Mott⟩ ⟨the ~ of the past was to be overcome by integration —*Amer. Anthropologist*⟩; *esp* **:** a shattering into numerous and widely scattered fragments (as of a fragmentation bomb) **2 :** the fragments from the fragmentation of a shell, grenade, or bomb ⟨the explosion rained ~ all about them⟩ **3 :** disorganization of mind or behavior **:** a breakdown of the usual pattern of thought or action

fragmentation bomb *or* **fragmentation shell** *n* **:** a bomb or shell whose relatively thick casing is splintered upon explosion and thrown in fragments in all directions at high speed and temperature

frag·ment·ist \'fragməntəst\ *n* -S [G, fr. *fragment* (fr. L *fragmentum*) + *-ist*] **:** a writer of a literary fragment

frag·ment·iza·tion \,fragməntə'zāshən\ *n* -S **:** the act or process of fragmentizing or the state of being fragmentized ⟨up in arms against a ~ of their native land —Sidney Wallach⟩

frag·ment·ize \'fragmən·,tīz\ *vb* -ED/-ING/-S *vt* **:** to break up or apart or into pieces, sections, or fragments **:** FRACTION, FRACTIONATE 1b ⟨the barriers of race, color, nationality, economic strife, religious belief, and political ideology which ~ our world —*Christian Science Monitor*⟩ **~** *vi* **:** to fall apart **:** break up or separate into pieces, parts, or fragments ⟨watched the bridge ~ before his eyes⟩

fra·grance \'frāgrən(t)s\ *n* -S [F or L; F, fr. L *fragrantia*, fr. *fragrant-, fragrans* + *-ia* -y] **1 :** the quality or state of having a sweet or pleasing odor **:** sweetness or pleasantness of smell ⟨the ~ of flowers⟩ ⟨the ~ of balsam⟩ **2 a :** a sweet smell or pleasing odor esp. delicate or evanescent ⟨a ~ not unpleasant to the nostrils⟩ **b :** the odor of perfume, cologne, or toilet water ⟨as close as ~ clings to a woman's robe —John Galsworthy⟩ **3 a :** a quality resembling a perfume (as in pleasantness, delicacy, or evanescence or in seeming to be an emanation) ⟨a relationship that gave something of ~ to an occupation much in need of it —L.C.Douglas⟩ ⟨she inhaled the sharp ~ of those days —Maurice Hewlett⟩ ⟨to handle a first edition of Montaigne . . . was not without its poetic ~ —H.J.Laski⟩ **b :** something having such a quality ⟨literature represents the ~ of culture —W.P.Webb⟩

syn FRAGRANCE, PERFUME, SCENT, INCENSE, REDOLENCE, and BOUQUET agree in signifying a sweet or pleasant odor. FRAGRANCE usu. suggests the odor of flowers or a like pleasing and usu. delicate emanation ⟨the soft wind from across the bayou brought in the garden *fragrance* —Stark Young⟩ ⟨their subtle *fragrance* of sandalwood, aloes, musk, cassia, and sweet calamus —Elinor Wylie⟩ ⟨none can resist the *fragrance* of pines, firs, and spruces in the forest —A.C.Morrison⟩ PERFUME differs little from FRAGRANCE except in possibly suggesting a less delicate odor and commonly implying the odor of a liquid specially manufactured to emit it ⟨the *perfume* of lilies had overcome the scent of books —John Galsworthy⟩ ⟨the strong *perfume* of orange blossoms⟩ ⟨her *perfume* was heavy and cloying⟩ SCENT in being often interchangeable with *odor* is more neutral in its connotations than FRAGRANCE or PERFUME, but in being also often interchangeable with PERFUME, esp. in British use, can apply to the fragrance as of flowers or any delicately perceived, usu. pleasant, odor ⟨the still nights in the small harbors, with a *scent* of seaweed abroad —William Black⟩ ⟨the *scent* of the apples —Robert Frost⟩ ⟨a delicate *scent* of apricots lingered in the flask at his side —Elinor Wylie⟩ INCENSE applies to the agreeably odorous smoke of burning spices or aromatic gums or to any similar penetrating odor, often, because of the association of incense with religious rites, suggesting a spiritually uplifting effect ⟨*incense*-breathing morn —Thomas Gray⟩ ⟨the *incense* of mown fields⟩ REDOLENCE now usu. suggests a mixture of fragrant, often pungent odors ⟨the *redolence* of the forest⟩ ⟨the kitchen *redolence* of Christmas cooking and baking⟩ BOUQUET in this comparison commonly applies to the distinctive and esp. delicate and agreeable odor of a good wine or liquor but can extend to any odor, as of a food, suggesting this ⟨some of the vocabulary of the winetaster has crept in, like the word *bouquet*, which means smell or scent, and yet is more descriptive of what the nose gets from a wine than either smell or scent —Mary Mabon⟩ ⟨duck that has been hung a long time, so you can smell the *bouquet* —*Time*⟩ ⟨the grateful smell of cooking pork grew every moment more perfect in *bouquet* —Ethel Anderson⟩

fra·gran·cy \-nsē, -si\ *n* -ES [L *fragrantia*] *archaic* **:** FRAGRANCE

fra·grant \-nt\ *adj* [ME *fragraunt*, fr. L *fragrant-, fragrans*, pres. part. of *fragrare* to give off an odor, be fragrant; akin to MHG *bræhen* to smell] **:** having a fragrance **:** marked by fragrance ⟨an air ~ with sweetest flowers —H.O.Taylor⟩ ⟨fresh and ~ as meadow hay —Herman Melville⟩ ⟨my sojourn in the garden of Africa has left so many ~ memories —R.S.B. Baker⟩ ⟨people talk of matters which . . . communicate a rich color, a ~ sentiment to them —A.C.Benson⟩ — **fra·grant·ly** *adv* — **fra·grant·ness** *n* -ES

fragrant balm *n* **: 1 :** OSWEGO TEA **2 :** BEE BALM 2b

fragrant bedstraw *n* **:** a bedstraw (*Galium triflorum*) that has small white flowers and is fragrant when drying

fragrant goldenrod *n* **:** BLUE MOUNTAIN TEA

fragrant shield fern *or* **fragrant cliff fern** *or* **fragrant wood fern** *n* **:** a stout pinnate-leaved fern (*Dryopteris fragrans*) of northern regions

fragrant sumac *n* **:** a sweet-scented sumac (*Rhus aromatica*) with ternate leaves, yellowish green flowers in spikes resembling catkins, and red hairy fruits

frags *pl of* FRAG

fraid \'frād\ *adj* [by shortening] *dial* **:** AFRAID

fraidy·cat \'frādē,kat, -di,-, *usu* -ad·+V\ *or* **fraid·cat** \-d,k-\ *n* [*fraidy* (fr. *fraid* + *-y*) or *fraid* + *cat*] **:** one that is timid or easily frightened — used chiefly among children or of children

[1]fraik \'frāk\ *n* -S [alter. of [1]*freak*] **1** *Scot* **:** [1]FREAK **2** *Scot* **:** FLATTERY

[2]fraik \"\ *vi, Scot* **:** to make flattering remarks **:** CAJOLE

[1]frail \'frāl, *esp before pause or consonant* -āəl\ *n* -S [ME *frayel, freyel*, fr. MF *fraiel, freel, frael*, perh. fr. *fraiel, freel, frael* piece of a vine with grapes attached, alter. of *flaiel, flael* flail, whip, piece of a vine with grapes attached — more at FLAIL] **1 :** a basket typically made of rushes and used for shipping (as of figs or raisins) **2 :** the quantity (as 32, 56, or 75 pounds) of raisins contained in a frail

[2]frail \"\ *adj* -ER/-EST [ME *frele, freel, frail*, fr. MF *fraile, frele*, fr. L *fragilis*, fr. *frag-* (stem of *frangere* to break) + *-ilis* -ile — more at BREAK] **1 a :** easily led into evil **:** morally weak ⟨a fiery sermon delivered to all of ~ humanity⟩ **b :** easily led from one's chosen course **:** lacking in general strength of character or purpose ⟨~ enough to give in if subjected to any pressure⟩ **2 a :** easily broken **:** not firm or durable ⟨a bridge with ~ construction⟩ ⟨a small and ~ ship⟩ **b :** easily destroyed **:** likely to fail or die quickly ⟨a ~ flower⟩ ⟨a ~ and very old woman⟩ **c :** unusually susceptible to disease or other infirmity ⟨a man of ~ constitution⟩ **3 a** (1) **:** lacking even normal strength or force ⟨their voices were weak and ~ —Humayun Kabir⟩ (2) **:** weak and small ⟨his steady, workman's hands looking enormous around the ~ tube of tobacco —Irwin Shaw⟩ **b** (1) **:** lacking significant substance ⟨a charming, ~, breathless book —*New Yorker*⟩ ⟨smiled a minute ~ smile —Raymond Chandler⟩ ⟨his lyrics are ~ and derivative —F.B.Millett⟩ (2) **:** tenuous and thin ⟨only ~ hope of finding more survivors existed —*N.Y. Times*⟩ ⟨how ~ the barrier between civilization and the primal jungle —Oscar Handlin⟩ ⟨the love of truth is pitifully ~ —M.R.Cohen⟩ **syn** see WEAK

[3]frail \"\ *dial var of* FLAIL

frai·le·jón \,fräēlā'hōn\ *n, pl* **frailejo·nes** \-ō,nās\ [AmerSp, aug. of Sp *fraile* friar, fr. OSp *fraire*, fr. OProv, brother, friar, fr. L *fratr-, frater* brother — more at BROTHER] **1 :** any of several xerophytic plants of the genus *Espeletia* (family Compositae) of the higher Andes (esp. *E. grandiflora*) **2 :** the tomentum of the stem and leaves of frailejón resembling wool

frail·ly \'frāl(l)ē, -i\ *adv* [ME *frelly*, fr. *frele* frail + *-ly*] **:** in a frail manner ⟨paint scenes of Venice drained of its water, with the buildings ~ poised on the oaken pilings that are their principal foundations —R.M.Coates⟩

frail·ness *n* -ES [ME *frelenesse, freelnesse, frailnesse*, fr. *frele, freel, frail* + *-nesse* -ness] **:** the quality or state of being frail ⟨the ~ of the child from birth made her susceptible to every prevailing illness⟩ ⟨a ~ of character, a tendency to give up easily⟩

frail·ty \'frā(ə)ltē, -ti\ *n* -ES [ME *frelete, freelte, frailte*, fr. MF *frailete, frelete*, fr. L *fragilitat-, fragilitas*, fr. *fragilis* + *-itat-, -itas* -ity] **1 :** the quality or state of being frail ⟨declaim against the ~ of human flesh⟩: **a :** INSUBSTANTIALITY ⟨a novel marked by ~ of subject matter⟩ **b :** TENUOUSNESS ⟨the ~ of the connection between the two sides of the family⟩ **c :** INFIRMITY ⟨always concerned for the ~ of his physical being⟩ **d :** SUSCEPTIBILITY ⟨the ~ of young lads to the charms of young ladies⟩ **2 :** an inadequacy, a fault, or a sin resulting from weakness (as of constitution or moral character) **syn** see FAULT

fraim \'frām\ *var of* FREMD

fraischeur *n* -S [MF *fraischeur, fraicheur*, fr. *fraische, fraiche*, fem. of *frais* fresh — more at FRESH] *obs* **:** FRESHNESS, COOLNESS

[1]fraise \'frāz\ *n* -S [alter. of *phrase*] **1** *or* **frase** *dial Brit* **:** a noisy confusion **:** HUBBUB **2** *Scot* **:** FLATTERY, CAJOLERY **:** empty talk

[2]fraise \"\ *vt* -ED/-ING/-S **:** FLATTER, CAJOLE

[3]fraise \"\ *n* -S [F, lit., mesentery of a calf or lamb, fr. MF, fr. *fraiser* to unwrap, shell (as a bean), fr. (assumed) VL *fresare*, fr. L *fresa* (in the term *faba fresa* ground bean), fem. of *fresus*, past part. of *frendere* to gnash, crush, grind — more at GRIND] **1 :** an obstacle used in fortification consisting of pointed stakes driven into the ramparts in a horizontal or inclined position **2 :** a style of neck ruff **3 :** a fluted reamer for enlarging holes in stone **4 :** a cutting tool for correcting the shape of the teeth of timepiece wheels

[4]fraise \"\ *vt* -ED/-ING/-S **1 :** to ream out and enlarge (as a hole in stone) **2 :** to shape or dress with a fraise

[5]fraise \"\ *n* -S [F, strawberry, fr. OF *fraise, frese*, irreg. (perh. influence of the *-s-* in *framboise* raspberry) fr. LL *fraga*, fr. L, pl. of *fragum*] **1** *also* **frase :** a heraldic representation of a strawberry blossom often not distinguished from a cinquefoil — called also *fraser* **2 :** strawberry color

frake \'frāk\ *n* -S [prob. native name in Africa] **:** LIMBA

[1]frak·tur *also* **frac·tur** \fräk'tü(ə)r, -üə\ *n* -S *usu cap* [G *fraktur* (formerly spelled *fractur*), an ornate kind of handwriting developed in the 16th cent., fraktur, fr. L *fractura* action of breaking; fr. the curlicues that broke up the continuous line of a word — more at FRACTURE] **:** a German style of black-letter text type

[2]fraktur *or* **fraktur painting** *var of* FRACTUR

fram \'fram\ *vb* **frammed; frammed; framming; frams** [origin unknown] *South & Midland* **:** POUND, BEAT

fram·able *or* **frame·able** \'frāməbəl\ *adj* **:** capable of being framed

fram·be·sia *also* **fram·boe·sia** \fram'bēzh(ē)ə, -zēə\ *n* -S [NL, fr. F *framboise* raspberry; fr. the raspberry appearance of the excrescences] **:** YAWS

fram·boise \fräⁿ'bwaz\ *n* -S [F, fr. OF, prob. modif. (perh. influenced by the *f-* in *fraise* strawberry) of a WGmc word represented by D *braambes* blackberry, MLG *brāmber*, OHG *brāmberi*, all fr. a prehistoric WGmc compound whose first constituent is represented by OHG *brāma, brāmo* bramble and whose second constituent is represented by D *bes* berry, OHG *beri* — more at BROOM, BERRY] **1 :** raspberry color **2 :** raspberry brandy usu. unsweetened

[1]frame \'frām\ *vb* -ED/-ING/-S [ME *framien, framen* to benefit, comfort, construct, fr. OE *framian, fromian* to avail, benefit, make progress; akin to OFris *framia* to carry out, further, OS gi*framōn*, ON *frama*, all fr. a prehistoric WGmc-NGmc verb derived fr. a word represented by ON *fram* forward — more at FROM] *vi* **1 a** *obs* **:** to get on **:** FARE **b** *archaic* **:** PROCEED, GO ⟨~ upstairs and make little din —Emily Brontë⟩ **2 a** *now dial Eng* **:** to show promise and adaptability **b** *archaic* **:** CONTRIVE, MANAGE **~** *vt* **1** *obs* **:** to prepare (wood) for a building (as by hewing out timbers) **2 a :** PLAN, DEVISE, CONTRIVE ⟨the committee *framed* a new method of achieving their purpose⟩ **b :** to give expression to **:** FORMULATE ⟨~ a rule that brings order into our perceptions —Virginia Woolf⟩ ⟨the specific problems . . . are still the persistent and central problems of philosophy, although perhaps not now *framed* in just his terminology —Alice Ambrose⟩ ⟨the poignancy of the hero's failure is *framed* in the plaint of that ubiquitous figure of Italian life, the sorrowing mother —C.W.White⟩ **c :** SHAPE, FASHION, FORM ⟨~ a figure out of clay⟩ **:** MAKE, CONSTRUCT ⟨a series of questions so *framed* as to involve by way of answer the plain alternative of yes or no —N.H.Snaith⟩ **d :** INVENT, FABRICATE ⟨*framed* a series of new characters for a radio drama series⟩ ⟨*framed* a device for eliminating rattles in a car⟩ **e :** CONCEIVE, IMAGINE ⟨could not ~ the man in my mind from the inadequate description⟩ **f :** to make a draft of or draw up (as a law or constitution) ⟨~ a plan for combating inflation —*Current Biog.*⟩ ⟨it was once my duty to ~ a case against a manifest thief —R.W.Chapman⟩ ⟨a subcommittee which *framed* the so-called tidelands oil bill —W.A. Clark⟩ ⟨when the Bolsheviks' five-year plan was being *framed* —G.N.S.Raghavan⟩ **3 :** to fit or adjust esp. to something or for an end **:** REGULATE, ARRANGE ⟨and ~ my face to all occasions —Shak.⟩ ⟨the professional training is *framed* to teach the student what children are like at different stages —*Choice of Careers: Local Gov't*⟩ ⟨he *framed* his model exordium to the middle-class youth in these words —Roy Lewis & Angus Maude⟩ ⟨required to pass tests which are *framed* to be within the power of a normal girl at each stage of her growth

—*Girl Guiding & The Church*⟩ **4 :** to bring about **:** CAUSE, PRODUCE ⟨fear ~*s* disorder and disorder wounds —Shak.⟩ ⟨struggling to ~ an alliance to secure southeast Asia —Benjamin Welles⟩ **5** *archaic* **:** to give direction to **:** start out on (a journey) **6 :** to put together the frame of **:** construct by fitting and uniting the parts of the skeleton of (a structure) ⟨*framed* a house at Steilacoom in 1860 and shipped it by steamer to be set up in the new settlement —*Amer. Guide Series: Wash.*⟩ ⟨*framed* a boat in the cellar and completed it outside⟩; *specif* **:** to erect the frames of (a ship) on the building ways **7 a :** UTTER, ARTICULATE ⟨*framed* a reply in words as flattering as the question⟩ **b :** to form the mouth and lips into the form for uttering but without making a vocal sound ⟨their lips ~ the words, "We're pleased to see you" —Richard Harrison⟩ ⟨tremulous lips *framed* an affirmative, but never uttered it —Zane Grey⟩ **8 a :** to provide with a frame **:** enclose in a frame ⟨~ a picture⟩; *also* **:** to enclose as if in a frame ⟨a face *framed* in a wealth of auburn hair⟩ ⟨he had had the entire lobby *framed*, at a height of about 15 feet, by slender boxes of hanging ivy and various nondescript plants —Douglas Woolf⟩ ⟨his eyes were *framed* above with unusually long eyelashes and below with the blue semicircle of ill health —Scott Fitzgerald⟩ **b :** to serve as a frame for ⟨the window *framed* a view of the lake⟩ **9 :** to run (crutched soap) into a frame to cool and solidify **10 a :** to devise falsely (as a criminal charge against an innocent man) ⟨~ a case against a neighbor to get rid of him⟩ — often used with *up* **b :** to contrive the evidence against (an innocent man) so that a verdict of guilty is assured ⟨many of the so-called anarchists . . . had been *framed* by courts and prosecutors —F.P.Adams⟩ ⟨innocent women were frequently *framed* by a ring consisting of police officers, stool pigeons, bondsmen, and lawyers —Morris Ploscowe⟩ **c :** to prearrange (as a contest or an incrimination) so that a particular outcome is assured ⟨the wrestling matches were *framed*⟩ — often used with *up* **11 :** to bring (a projected image) into register with the aperture of a motion-picture projector so that the horizontal frame line does not appear on the screen **syn** see BUILD, CONTRIVE

²frame \"\ *n* -s [ME, fr. *framien, framen*, v.] **1 a** *archaic* **:** something composed of parts fitted together and united **b** *archaic* **:** BUILDING; *esp* **:** a wooden building **c :** the form in which something is fashioned **:** SYSTEM ⟨a ~ of government⟩ ⟨how fine if we had an intimate theater . . . to produce certain works that call for a small ~ —Howard Taubman⟩; *esp* **:** the bodily structure **:** the physical construction or constitution

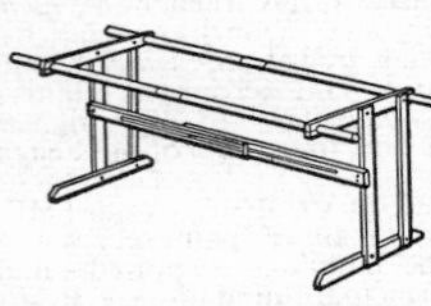
quilting frame

: BODY, FIGURE ⟨he is distinctly, almost nobly handsome, with stalwart ~ —S.H.Adams⟩ ⟨sobs swept at intervals through her ~, shaking it —Arnold Bennett⟩ **d** *archaic* **:** a proper or correct form, order, or shape ⟨before the hills in order stood, or earth received her ~ —Isaac Watts⟩ **e :** a standardized form or shape ⟨the artistry of a low comedian . . . stands out in splendid relief from the ~ of a dull musical comedy —E.R. Bentley⟩ ⟨the mock-heroic ~ is intermittent —Austin Warren⟩ **2 a :** the constructional system that gives shape or strength (as to a building) **:** an underlying structure or skeleton ⟨his enormous weight broke the ~ of the sofa⟩; *specif* **:** the arrangement of supporting girders, beams, columns, joists, or trusses forming the main support (as of a building) ⟨the ~ of the roof had begun to sag⟩ **b :** such a skeleton or outline not filled in or covered (as by the other constituents of the whole of which it is a part) ⟨the fire left only the steel ~ of the building standing⟩ **c :** a basic structural unit onto or into which other constituents of a whole are fitted, to which they attach, or with which they are integrated: as (1) **:** the basic unit of a handgun which serves as a mounting for the barrel and operating parts of the arm — compare RECEIVER (2) **:** any of the skeleton structures forming the athwart ribs of a ship — see CANT FRAME, SQUARE FRAME (3) AIRFRAME; *also* **:** a structural piece supporting the longitudinal members or skin of the fuselage, float, or hull of an airplane **d** *dial* **:** an emaciated person or animal **:** SKELETON **3 a :** an open case or structure made for admitting, enclosing, or supporting something (as one that encloses a window, door, or picture) **b :** something on, in, or across which something else is held or stretched: as (1) *archaic* **:** LOOM 3 (2) **:** a machine built upon or within a framework and used esp. in manufacture of yarn and textiles ⟨a spinning ~⟩ (3) **:** an adjustable structure of four bars forming an open square or rectangle for holding cloth (as for embroidery or quilting) — compare CURTAIN STRETCHER (4) **:** a rack used in carpet manufacturing for holding yarn packages used in the pile **c :** a foundry molding box or flask that being filled with sand around a pattern serves as a mold for castings **d :** the covered lattice structure used on the arms of a windmill **e :** the skeleton structure supporting the boiler and machinery of a locomotive upon its wheels or either of the two structures containing the axle boxes and supporting the upper part of an electric car **f :** a structural unit in an automobile chassis supported on the axles and supporting the rest of the chassis and the body **g :** the ribs and stretchers of an umbrella or similar structure with a fabric covering **h :** an openwork wooden structure usu. enclosing a sheet of foundation placed in a beehive to encourage bees to build honeycomb in an orderly fashion **i :** a board for holding coins, medals, or stamps on exhibition **j :** a stand to support printers' type cases **k** (1) **:** SAW GATE (2) **:** a piece shaped like a yoke and resembling a saw gate ⟨the ~ of a micrometer⟩ ⟨the ~ of a C-clamp⟩ **l :** a large shallow rectangular metal pan having removable sides used for the cooling and solidifying of liquid soap in soap manufacture **m** (1) **:** a part of a pair of glasses that holds one of the lenses (2) **frames** *pl* **:** the constituent of a pair of glasses other than the lenses **4 a** *obs* **:** the act of framing, constructing, or devising **b** *archaic* **:** the manner or method in which something is fashioned **5 a :** a particular state or disposition (as of the mind) ⟨left the shop in a very puzzled ~ of mind —F.W.Crofts⟩ **b** *archaic* **:** attitude of mind **:** state of feeling **:** HUMOR, MOOD ⟨we have sent him to you in the best health and in the happiest ~ —Charles Dickens⟩ **6 a :** an enclosing usu. rectangular and esp. ornamental border or a physical limitation suggesting such a border: (1) **:** a single line or an ornamental band bordering a stamp (2) **:** the lines around boxed matter in a newspaper (3) **:** the boundary of the gate of a motion-picture camera, printer, or projector (4) **:** FALSE PROSCENIUM **b :** the matter or area enclosed in such a border or as if in such a border: as (1) **:** one of the squares in which scores for each round are recorded (as in bowling); *also* **:** a round in bowling (2) **:** boxed matter in a newspaper; *esp* **:** a box of a comic strip (3) **:** one picture of the series on a length of motion-picture film or on a filmstrip or microfilm (4) **:** a complete picture or image being transmitted by television **c :** a playing unit of a game (as an inning in baseball) **d :** an abstract set of limitations (as of circumstances or considerations) within which a thing or a group of things is contained, in relation to which they are unified, or within which they acquire a usu. particular or a typical significance or expression **:** a limiting, typical, or esp. appropriate set of circumstances ⟨a joke that can be told . . . out of ~ —James Burnham⟩ ⟨within the ~ of business-as-usual —*New Republic*⟩ ⟨the ~ of experience in which the American strategic problem in the atomic age is set —H.W.Baldwin⟩ ⟨clinical studies carried on within the ~ of our own society and culture —Ralph Linton⟩ **e :** an event or set of events or circumstances that form the background for the action of a novel or dramatic work ⟨the main ~ of action of the novel is the week of a false armistice in 1918 —Carvel Collins⟩ **f :** a literary device used in a story or dramatic work to bring together into a unity the matter of the story or drama or to provide a plausible excuse for relating or presenting it; *esp* **:** such a device not essential to the story or dramatic action itself ⟨the story uses a ~ purporting to be told to the writer 20 years after the events⟩ **g :** a part of a syntactical or morphological linguistic construction that remains unchanged even though the remainder may be altered by the substitution of new items **7 :** COLD FRAME **8** *slang* **:** FRAME-UP **9 :** SLATE 3d **10 :** a listing or other scheme in statistics for identification of the elementary sampling units that constitute a population

³frame \"\ *also* **framed** \-md\ *adj* **:** having a wood frame ⟨a ~ building with brick siding⟩ ⟨inexpensive ~ houses⟩ **:** having a frame (of a specified material) ⟨a steel-*frame* office building⟩ ⟨a large building of reinforced concrete ~ construction and stone panel siding⟩

fra·mea \ˈfrāmēə\ *n, pl* **frame·ae** \-ē,ē\ [L, prob. fr. a Gmc word derived fr. a word represented by OHG *fram* forward, further — more at FROM] **:** a spear with a long shaft and iron head used by the ancient Teutons

frameable *var of* FRAMABLE

framed *past of* FRAME

frame frequency *n* **:** the number of times per second that the frame area in television is completely scanned — compare LINE FREQUENCY

frame·less \ˈfrāmləs\ *adj* **:** having no frame ⟨a ~ picture⟩

frame·man \ˈ=mən\ *n, pl* **framemen :** a telephone worker who connects the terminals of trunk and local lines on a wire-distributing frame

frame of reference 1 : an arbitrary set of usu. orthogonal axes with reference to which the position or motion of a point, body, or group of bodies is described or with reference to which physical laws are formulated **2 a :** a usu. systematic set of principles, rules, or presuppositions or a system of laws, mores, or values or an interlocking group of facts or ideas serving to orient or give particular meaning (as to a fact, statement, or point of view) or serving as a matrix for behavior or for the formation of attitudes; *broadly* **:** VIEWPOINT, THEORY ⟨give me some *frame of reference* in which to discuss his contention —*N. Y. Times*⟩ ⟨each of us views the problem from his particular and limited *frame of reference* —S.G. DiMichael⟩ ⟨the most common *frames of reference* that the term evokes — economic theories or political loyalties, specific industries or all industries, all foreign countries or particular ones —S.L.Payne⟩ **b :** the characteristics of a ground which influence or determine the perception of a figure against it

fram·er \ˈfrāmə(r)\ *n* -s **1 :** one that frames: as **a :** INVENTOR, CONTRIVER, FORMULATOR ⟨a ~ of an intricate poetic stanza⟩ ⟨a ~ of the constitution⟩ ⟨a ~ of witty turns of phrase⟩ **b :** a worker who makes frames (as of boxes) or assembles framework (as of furniture to be upholstered) **c :** a worker who puts on frames (as on pictures) **2 :** FRAME SPINNER

frames *pres 3d sing of* FRAME, *pl of* FRAME

frame spacing *n* **:** the fore-and-aft distance between the heels of two consecutive frames of a ship

frame spinner *n* **:** an operator of a frame spinning machine

frame spinning *n* **:** yarn spinning on a frame as distinguished from spinning on a mule **:** RING SPINNING

frame story *or* **frame tale** *n* [trans. of G *rahmenerzählung*] **:** a story told within a frame or a story constituting a frame for another story or a series of other stories

frame-up \ˈ=,=\ *n* -s [*frame up*] **1 :** an act or series of actions in which someone is framed ⟨points an accusing finger at overzealous prosecutors, avenging witnesses, concealment of evidence of innocence, and ruthless *frame-ups* —*Nation*⟩ **2 :** an action that is framed ⟨looked legitimate enough but at the investigation it was proved to be a *frame-up*⟩

¹framework \ˈ=,=\ *n* [²*frame* + *work*] **1 a** (1) **:** a skeletal or structural frame ⟨the ~ of the ship⟩ (2) **:** an openwork frame ⟨the vines climbed a ~⟩ (3) **:** a basic ideational or narrative structure ⟨the ~ of the political theory⟩ ⟨the ~ of the novel⟩ (4) **:** a systematic set of relationships ⟨the family was so large he had difficulty keeping the ~ of kinship clear in his mind⟩ **b :** frames or a system of frames ⟨the ~ he had constructed for a gallery of pictures⟩ **2 :** work done in or by means of a frame **3 :** a conceptual scheme, structure, or system **:** the limits or outlines esp. of a particular set of circumstances **:** FRAME OF REFERENCE **4 :** the larger branches of a tree that together determine its shape and symmetry

²framework \"\ *vt* **:** to graft scions of another variety on the framework of (as a fruit tree) after removal of all smaller laterals usu. to obtain more desirable fruit — compare TOPWORK

fram·ing \ˈfrāmiŋ, -mēŋ\ *n* -s [ME, fr. gerund of *framien, framen* to frame — more at FRAME] **:** FRAME, FRAMEWORK ⟨the ~ of the dormitories is reinforced concrete with buff-colored brick facing —*Current Biog.*⟩ ⟨the huge stone chimney and part of the ~ are probably all that is left of an original one-room house —*Amer. Guide Series: Conn.*⟩

framing chisel *n* **:** a long sturdy chisel designed for rough carpentry work

framing square *n* **:** a large carpenter's square graduated with scales typically for use in cutting off and notching (as rafters or stair joists)

frammed *past of* FRAM

framming *pres part of* FRAM

fram·mit \ˈframət\ *var of* FREMD

frampold *adj* [origin unknown] **1** *obs* **:** PEEVISH, CROSS, VEXATIOUS, QUARRELSOME **2** *obs, of a horse* **:** FIERY, SPIRITED

frams *pres 3d sing of* FRAM

franc \ˈfraŋk\ *n* -s [ME *frank*, fr. MF *franc*, fr. ML *Francus* Frenchman (in *Francorum rex* king of the French, the device on the 14th cent. francs), fr. LL, Frank — more at FRANK] **1 a :** an old French gold coin first struck in 1360 **b :** an old French silver coin issued from 1575 to 1641 **2 a** (1) **:** the basic monetary unit of modern France established during the Revolution — see MONEY table (2) **:** a coin representing this unit **b :** any of numerous monetary units (as of Belgium, Luxembourg, or Switzerland) or their corresponding coins orig. equivalent to the French franc — see MONEY table **c** [Alb *frëngë*, fr. F *franc*] **:** the former monetary unit of Albania **3 a :** any of numerous monetary units of specified French dependencies ⟨a Djibouti ~⟩ **b :** a coin representing one of these units

france \ˈfran(t)s, -aa(ə)n-, -ain-, -ȧn-\ *adj, usu cap* [fr. *France*, country in Europe] **:** of or from France **:** of the kind or style prevalent in France **:** FRENCH

france rose *n, often cap F* **:** a deep pink to purplish pink that is deeper than arbutus

fran·chis·al \ˈfran,chīzəl, -raan- *sometimes* -īsəl\ *adj* [*franchise* + *-al*] **:** of, relating to, or having the characteristics of a franchise

¹fran·chise \ˈfran,chīz, -raan- *sometimes* -īs\ *n* -s [ME, fr. OF, fr. *franchir* to free, fr. *franche* (fem. of *franc* free) + *-ise* -ice — more at FRANK] **1** *obs* **:** freedom from servitude or restraint **2 a :** freedom or immunity from some burden, exaction, restriction, or superior jurisdiction vested either in a natural or an artificial person or a particular class or order of persons **:** EXEMPTION — compare CHARTER 2b **b** *archaic* **:** the jurisdiction over which such a freedom extends **:** the limits of such an immunity **3 a :** a right or privilege conferred by grant from a sovereign or a government and vested in an individual or a group; *specif* **:** a right to do business conferred by a government — see FRANCHISE TAX **b :** a constitutional or statutory right or privilege; *esp* **:** the right to vote — usu. used with *the* **c** (1) **:** the right granted to an individual or group to market a company's goods or services in a particular territory (2) **:** the territory involved in such a right **d :** a contract for public works or public services granted by a government to an individual or company **e** (1) **:** the right of membership granted by certain professional sports leagues (2) **:** such membership itself (3) **:** a team and the professional organization operating it having such membership **f :** the right to present, broadcast, or televise the events put on by a sports league or organization **4 a :** an amount of liability (as a percentage or a sum) specified in an insurance contract below which an underwriter claims only partial liability or disclaims liability and often above which the underwriter assumes total liability **b :** group coverage insurance of fewer than the minimum number of participants required by state law for such coverage

²franchise \"\ *vt* -ED/-ING/-S [ME *fraunchisen*, fr. MF *fraunchiss-*, stem of *franchir*] **1** *archaic* **:** to set free **2 :** to grant a franchise or the franchise to **:** ENFRANCHISE ⟨an amendment *franchising* adults over 18⟩ ⟨these firms are now being *franchised* to handle this manufacturer's line —*Distribution Age*⟩

franchise bond *n* **:** a surety bond that insures a government or state against loss due to a franchise holder's failure to complete work specified in the franchise grant

fran·chise·ment \-mənt, -ˌchəzm- *sometimes* -chəsm- *or* fra(a)n'chī-\ *n* -s [MF, fr. OF *franchissement*, fr. *franchiss-* + *-ment*] **:** ENFRANCHISEMENT

fran·chiser \ˈfran,chīzə(r), -raan- *sometimes* -īsə-\ *n* -s [¹*franchise* + *-er*] **:** one that holds a franchise ⟨a four-page tabloid . . . designed to keep carbonated beverage packers and their ~*s* abreast of news in the canned soft-drink field —*Modern Packaging*⟩

franchise stamp *n* **:** a postage stamp issued by some countries for use on free mail (as that of a charitable institution)

franchise tax *n* **:** a business tax imposed upon various corporations granted a franchise

fran·cic \ˈfran(t)sik\ *adj, usu cap* [ML *Francicus*, fr. LL *Francus* Frank + L *-icus* -ic — more at FRANK] **:** FRANKISH

fran·cien \frȧⁿsyaⁿ\ *n* -s *usu cap* [F, fr. *Île-de-France* + *-ien* -ian] **:** the dialect of French used in the middle ages in Île-de-France that furnishes the basis for the literary and official form of the modern French language

¹fran·cis·can \(ˈ)fran¦siskən, -raan-\ *adj, usu cap* [*Franciscus* (St. Francis of Assisi) †1226 Ital. monk & preacher + E *-an*] **:** of or relating to St. Francis of Assisi, to the Order of St. Francis, or to the Franciscans

²franciscan \"\ *n* -s *usu cap* **:** a member of one of various religious foundations established by St. Francis of Assisi in the early 13th century including the Friars Minor, the Poor Clares, and the Franciscan tertiaries

fran·cis·can·ism \=ˈ=kə,nizəm\ *n* -s *often cap* **:** Franciscan beliefs or practices

fran·ci·um \ˈfran(t)sēəm\ *n* -s [NL, fr. *France* + NL *-ium*] **:** a radioactive element of the alkali-metal group discovered as a disintegration product of actinium and obtained artificially by the bombardment of thorium with protons — symbol *Fr;* see ACTINIUM SERIES, ELEMENT table

franck-con·don principle \ˈfraŋkˈkändən-, -räŋ-\ *n, usu cap F&C* [after James *Franck* †1964 Am. physicist born in Germany and Edward U. *Condon* b1902 Am. physicist] **:** a principle in spectroscopy: the intensities of molecular spectral bands due to electronic transitions are consistent with the assumption that the relatively large mass of the atomic nuclei in the molecule prevents appreciable change in their configuration during such transitions

franck·e·ite \ˈfräŋkə,īt\ *n* -s [G *franckeït*, fr. Carl and Ernest *Francke*, 19th cent. Ger. mining engineers + G *-it* -ite] **:** a mineral consisting of a dark gray or black massive lead antimony tin sulfide (sp. gr. 5.55)

fran·co \ˈfräŋ(,)kō\ *adj* [It (*porto*) *franco* free carriage, fr. *porto* carriage + *franco* free, fr. ML *francus* — more at FRANK] **:** free of charge **:** FRANKED: **a :** postage free **b :** delivered free

franco- *comb form, usu cap* [ML, fr. *Francus* Frenchman, fr. LL, Frank — more at FRANK] **:** French and ⟨*Franco*-Swiss⟩ **:** French ⟨*Franco*phile⟩

fran·co·ism \ˈfraŋkō,izəm, -räŋ-\ *n* -s *usu cap* [Francisco *Franco* b1892 Span. soldier and dictator of Spain + E *-ism*] **1 :** the political or social policies advocated or put into effect by the dictator Franco **2 :** the advocacy of or allegiance to Franco's policies

fran·çois pre·mier \fräⁿˈswä·prə'myā\ *n, usu cap F&P* [F, after *François premier* (Francis I) †1547 king of France] **:** a furniture style modeled on that of the Italian Renaissance and introduced into France under Francis I

fran·co·ist \ˈfraŋkōəst, -räŋ-\ *n* -s *usu cap* [Francisco *Franco* + E *-ist*] **1 :** a member of General Franco's forces in the Spanish civil war **2 :** an advocate of or adherent to Francoism

fran·co·lin \ˈfraŋkōlən, -kəl-\ *n* -s [F, fr. OF, fr. OIt *francolino*] **:** any of numerous partridges of southern Asia and Africa constituting *Francolinus* and related genera — see BLACK PARTRIDGE

¹fran·co·ni·an \(ˈ)fraŋ¦kōnēən, -an¦-, -nyən\ *adj, usu cap* [*Franconia*, former duchy of Germany + E *-an*] **1 :** of or relating to Franconia **2 :** of, relating to, or being a Franconian dialect or the Franconian dialects

²franconian \"\ *n* -s *cap* **:** the West Germanic language of the Franks esp. as represented by a group of dialects, partly Low German and partly High German, attested by written documents of which the earliest belong to the late 8th or early 9th century over an area extending from the lowest part of the Rhine as far south as the northern border of Alsace and as far east as the region around Bamberg in northern Bavaria and continuing in oral use to the present day — compare FRANKISH, LOW FRANCONIAN

fran·co·nia potatoes \-nēə-, -nyə-\ *n pl, usu cap F* **:** potatoes cooked with a roast and often basted with the drippings

¹fran·co·phile \ˈfraŋkə,fīl, -kō,-\ *or* **fran·co·phil** \-,fil\ *adj, usu cap* [*Franco-* + *-phile, -phil* (adj. comb. form)] **:** markedly friendly or attracted toward France or French culture or customs

²francophile \"\ *or* **francophil** \"\ *n* -s *usu cap* [*Franco-* + *-phile, -phil* (n. comb. form)] **:** a Francophile person

fran·co·phil·ia \,==ˈfilēə, -lyə\ *n* -s *usu cap* [NL, fr. *Franco-* + *philia*] **:** the quality or state of being Francophile

¹fran·co·phobe \ˈ==,fōb\ *adj, usu cap* [*Franco-* + *-phobe* (adj. comb. form)] **:** marked by a fear or strong dislike of France or French culture or customs

²francophobe \"\ *n* -s *usu cap* [*Franco-* + *-phobe* (n. comb. form)] **:** a Francophobe person

fran·co·pho·bia \,==ˈfōbēə\ *n* -s *usu cap* [NL, fr. *Franco-* + *-phobia*] **:** the quality or state of being Francophobe

¹franco-provençal \ˈfraŋ(,)kō+\ *adj, usu cap F&P* [*Franco-* + *Provençal;* trans. of It *franco-provenzale*] **:** of, relating to, or constituting Franco-Provençal

²franco-provençal \"\ *n, cap F&P* **:** a group of southeastern French dialects spoken in western Switzerland and the adjacent parts of France bordering on the Provençal dialect area

franc-ti·reur \ˌfräⁿtēˈrər, +V -ər·\ *n* -s [F, fr. *franc* free + *tireur* shooter, fr. MF, fr. *tirer* to pull, shoot + *-eur* -or — more at FRANK] **:** a civilian esp. French guerrilla fighter or sniper

FR and CC *abbr* free of riot and civil commotion

fran·gi·bil·i·ty \,franjəˈbilədē\ *n* -ES **:** the quality or state of being frangible

fran·gi·ble \ˈfranjəbəl\ *adj* [ME, fr. MF & ML; MF, fr. ML *frangibilis*, fr. L *frangere* to break + *-ibilis* -ible — more at BREAK] **:** capable of being broken **:** BREAKABLE, BRITTLE, FRAGILE ⟨a fire-extinguishing fluid in a ~ container⟩ ⟨these ladies' dainty and ~ shoulder blades must not be burdened by so deplorable an event —Elinor Wylie⟩ — **fran·gi·ble·ness** *n* -ES

frangible bullet *n* **:** a bullet used in firing practice that breaks into powder or fragments upon contact with the target and does not penetrate

fran·gi·pane \ˈfranjə,pān, -raan-\ *n* -s [F & It.; F, fr. It *frangipane*, a kind of perfume orig. used to perfume gloves, after the Marquis Muzio *Frangipane* or *Frangipani*, 16th cent. Ital. nobleman] **1 :** FRANGIPANI **2 a :** a dessert of almond cream flavored with frangipani or jasmine perfume **b :** a cream flavored with almonds and used as a tart filling custard cream flavored with almonds

fran·gi·pani *also* **fran·gi·pan·ni** \,==ˈpanē, -ˈpänē\ *n, pl* **frangipani** *or* **frangipanis** *also* **frangipanni** *or* **frangipannis** [modif. of F & It *frangipane*] **1 :** a perfume derived from or imitating the odor of the flower of the red jasmine **2 :** any of various tropical American shrubs or small trees of the genus *Plumeria* (as red jasmine)

fran·gu·la \ˈfraŋgyələ\ *n* -s [NL, fr. L *frangere* to break + *-ula;* fr. the frangibility of the wood] **1 :** ALDER BUCKTHORN **2 :** the bark of frangula used in medicine for its laxative properties

frangula emodin *n* **:** EMODIN

fran·gu·lin \-lən\ *n* -s [ISV *frangul-* (fr. NL *frangula*) + *-in;* orig. formed in G] **:** an orange crystalline glycoside $C_{21}H_{20}O_9$ obtained esp. from the bark of the alder buckthorn and yielding emodin and rhamnose on hydrolysis

franion *n* -s [origin unknown] *archaic* **:** an habitual pleasure seeker or merrymaker **:** IDLER, REVELER

¹frank \ˈfraŋk, -aiŋk\ *n* -s *cap* [ME *Frank, Franc*, partly fr. OE *Franca;* partly fr. OF *Franc*, fr. LL *Francus*, of Gmc origin; akin to OHG *Franko* Frank, OE *Franca*] **1 :** a member of one of the West Germanic peoples entering the Roman provinces in A.D.253, occupying the Netherlands and most of Gaul, and shortly afterward establishing themselves in two divisions along the lower and middle Rhine **2 :** a western European ⟨Europeans are still called *Franks* in the Levant —Emil Lengyel⟩

²frank \"\ *adj* -ER/-EST [ME, fr. OF *franc*, fr. ML *francus*, fr. LL *Francus*, n., Frank] **1** *obs* **a :** free from bondage or restraint **b :** free of charge or other conditions **:** UNCONDITIONAL **2** *archaic* **:** LIBERAL, GENEROUS, PROFUSE **3** *obs* **a :** superior in quality or strength **b :** LUXURIANT, RANK, VIGOROUS **4 a :** marked by free unrestrained willing expression of facts, opinions, or feelings without reticence, inhibition, or concealment ⟨forthright comments from a ~ critic⟩ ⟨a kindly but ~ warning⟩ ⟨most ~ in his confession of entire disbelief in the legends which . . . almost all thought it decent to pretend to credit —J.A.Froude⟩ **b :** marked by or suggestive of freedom and honesty in expression **:** lacking concealment, dissembling, or guile ⟨suspicion or hostility dispelled by a ~ smile⟩ **5 a :** lacking disguise or masking **:** bluntly or honestly avowed **:** downright and clearly obvious **:** sheer and utter without reservation, mitigation, or inhibition ⟨the mixture of the idea of evolution with the ~ materialism of Haeckel and the subtle agnosticism of Huxley —R.W.Murray⟩ ⟨her mouth was painted ripely with mauve as if in ~ appeal to be kissed —Edmund Wilson⟩ **b** *med* **:** UNMISTAKABLE, MANIFEST **:** clinically evident ⟨~ pus⟩ ⟨~ anemia⟩

syn CANDID, OPEN, PLAIN: FRANK may suggest a willingness to express oneself in a free and forthright way, without reservations or modifications brought about by timidity, evasiveness, or tact ⟨intelligent enough to realize just what all the theorists of his age were actually doing, and *frank* enough to announce it openly —J.H.Randall⟩ ⟨I have now told you everything without an attempt of circumlocution or concealment. Do you in your turn be as *frank* with me —A. Conan Doyle⟩ ⟨his notorious comment — which the American democrat has never forgiven him, "The people! — the people is a great beast!" — was characteristically *frank* —V.L.Parrington⟩ CANDID may suggest a sincerity and honesty marked by straightforward expression without evasion or expedient reservation ⟨I am sure that he was *candid* with me. I am certain that he had no guile —W.A.White⟩ ⟨as a leader of our party for 10 years I have never lacked *candid* critics in my own ranks —Clement Attlee⟩ OPEN may imply an inclination to ready, free, natural, honest expression lacking concealment or reserve ⟨wished her children would be more *open* with her and not have so many secrets among themselves⟩ ⟨the absurdity of her remark moved him to *open* taunts⟩ PLAIN may stress simple straightforward expression not mollified by tact or complicated by erudite language ⟨the admiral . . . made the following signal in *plain* language: "Will be compelled to return fire" —Emil Lengyel⟩ ⟨the difference between ordinary phraseology that makes its meaning *plain* and legal phraseology that makes its meaning certain —Ernest Gowers⟩

³frank \"\ *vt* -ED/-ING/-S **1 a :** to mark (a piece of mail) with an official signature indicating the right of the sender to free mailing **b :** to mark (mail) with a sign indicating the right of the sender to exemption from postage **c :** to send by mail at no expense to the sender **d :** to affix to (mail) a stamp or a marking indicating the payment of postage **:** put a postage stamp on ⟨a cover ~*ed* with two 3-cent stamps⟩ ⟨he ~*ed* his business mail with meter impressions⟩ **e :** to label (mail) as having the postage paid ⟨a commemorative stamp ~*ed* the letter⟩ **f :** to mark (mail) with a postal marking of any kind **2 :** to facilitate the passage of **:** help forward **:** enable to pass or go freely or easily **3 :** to make immune (as by a pass inscribed with an official signature) **:** EXEMPT, FREE ⟨court functionaries drew up in motorcars to my hotel, and presented me with a case all over seals and imperial devices ~*ing* me through the customs houses of the universe —W.J.Locke⟩

⁴frank \"\ *n* -S [³*frank*] **1 a :** the signature of the sender on a piece of franked mail serving in place of a postage stamp **b :** a mark or stamp on a piece of mail indicating postage paid ⟨a meter ~ on business mail⟩ **c :** a franked envelope or cover **2 :** the privilege of sending mail free of charge

⁵frank *n* -S [ME, fr. MF *franc* pigsty, fr. OLF *hranne, chramne;* akin to OS *hrama* frame, and perh. to Gk *kremannynai* to hang — more at CREMASTER] *obs* **:** a sty for boars

⁶frank *vt* -ED/-ING/-S [ME *franken*, fr. ⁵*frank*] *obs* **:** to shut up (a boar) in a frank esp. for fattening

⁷frank *n* -S [⁶*frank;* fr. its fattening properties] *obs* **:** SPURRY

⁸frank \'fraŋk, -raaŋk\ *n* -S [imit. of its cry] *dial Brit* **:** a common European heron (*Ardea cinerea*)

⁹frank \"\ *vt* -ED/-ING/-S [origin unknown] **:** to join or frame together (as molded sash bars) by mitering to the depth of the molding and cutting off the rest of each abutting piece square or finishing with a mortise-and-tenon joint

¹⁰frank \"\ *n* -S [G & Flem, fr. F *franc* — more at FRANC] **:** FRANC 2 b

¹¹frank *n* -S [by shortening] **:** FRANKFURTER

frank·al·moign *or* **frank·al·moin** *also* **frank·al·moigne** \'fraŋkal,mȯin, ˌ=ˈ=ˌ=, ˌ=ˈ=ˌ=\ *n* -S [*frank* + *almoign, almoin;* trans. of ML *eleemosyna libera*] **:** a tenure in English law by which a religious corporation holds lands given to them and their successors forever usu. on condition of praying for the soul of the donor and his heirs — compare LAY FEE

frank bank *n* [trans. of ML *francus bancus*] *obs* **:** FREE BENCH

fran·ke·nia \fran'kēnēə, -an'-\ *n, cap* [NL, after Johan *Frankenius* (Franke) †1661 Swed. professor of anatomy and botany] **:** a genus (the type of the family Frankeniaceae) of perennial herbs or undershrubs with opposite leaves and solitary pink, violet, or red flowers usu. in the forks of the branches — **fran·ke·ni·a·ceous** \ˌ=ˌ=nē'āshəs\ *adj*

fran·ke·ni·a·ce·ae \ˌ=ˌ=ˌ=ˈāsē,ē\ *n pl, cap* [NL, fr. *Frankenia*, type genus + *-aceae*] **:** a family of perennial herbs or low-growing evergreen woody plants (order Parietales) native to seacoasts in temperate and subtropical regions and sometimes used as border or ground carpet plants in light sandy soil or in rockeries — see FRANKENIA

frank·en·stein \'fraŋkən,stīn *sometimes* -tēn\ *n* -S *usu cap* [after Baron *Frankenstein*, hero of the novel *Frankenstein* (1818) by Mary W. Shelley †1851 Eng. novelist, whose life is ruined by a monster he created from parts of corpses and endowed with life; fr. his name being taken to be the name of the monster he created] **1 :** a monster in the shape of a man; *esp* **:** one resembling the man-made monster of the novel *Frankenstein* ⟨he learned the art of making theatrical masks with plastic materials . . . would appear before his mother or guests as a *Frankenstein* with a bloody hole in his forehead, from which protruded a spike —Victor Eisenstein⟩ **2 :** a work or agency that proves troublesomely uncontrollable esp. to its creator; *esp* **:** one that ultimately destroys or ruins its creator ⟨warfare has ever been the creature of man's ingenuity and has today become the *Frankenstein* that may indeed destroy the human race —A.M.Prentiss⟩ ⟨if the scientific method . . . is not to become a consuming *Frankenstein*, it must be extended to the admittedly more complex and baffling problems of human relationships —C.F.Richards⟩

fran·ken·stein·i·an \ˌ=ˌ=ˈstīnēən -tin-\ *adj, usu cap* **:** of, relating to, or resembling a Frankenstein ⟨a sort of *Frankensteinian* phobia created by factions who would have people everywhere believe there is no room in one world for more than one economic and social system —Norman Corwin⟩

frankenstein monster *also* **frankenstein's monster** *n, usu cap F* **:** FRANKENSTEIN ⟨a *Frankenstein monster* that would stand before a typecase and pluck out letters and click them into a composing stick —T.W.Duncan⟩ ⟨bureaucracy . . . become a *Frankenstein monster*, a law unto itself, interested largely in its own perpetuation and expansion —E.S.Griffith⟩ ⟨French fears that a rearmed Germany might prove to be a *Frankenstein's monster* which would turn on its creators —O.N.Bradley⟩

fran·ken·thal \'fraŋkən,thȯl, 'fräŋkən,täl *n* -S *usu cap* [fr. *Frankenthal*, city in Bavaria, Germany where it was produced] **:** faience and hard-paste porcelain produced at Frankenthal, Bavaria during the second half of the 18th century and noted for well-modeled figures

frank·er \'fraŋkə(r)\ *n* -S [³*frank* + *-er*] **:** one that franks; *esp* **:** a machine for franking mail

frank·fort \'fraŋkfə(r)t, *usu* -d.+V\ *adj, usu cap* **1** *or* **frankfurt** \", 'fräŋk,fůrt\ [fr. *Frankfurt* am Main, Germany] **:** of or from the city of Frankfurt am Main, Germany **:** of the kind or style prevalent in Frankfurt am Main **2** *or* **frankfurt** [fr. *Frankfurt* an der Oder, Germany] **:** of or from the city of Frankfurt an der Oder, Germany **:** of the kind or style prevalent in Frankfurt an der Oder **3** [fr. *Frankfort*, Ky.] **:** of or from Frankfort, the capital of Kentucky ⟨a *Frankfort* residence⟩ **:** of the kind or style prevalent in Frankfort

frankfort black *n, usu cap F* **:** a pigment made usu. by charring vegetable material (as vine twigs or the lees of wine) — called also *drop black*

frank·furt·er *or* **frank·fort·er** \R 'fraŋkfə(r)|d·ər, -k,fər|, |tər -R -kfə|d·ə(r, -k,fə|, |tə(r\ *or* **frank·furt** *or* **frank·fort** \'fraŋkfə(r)t, *usu* -d·+V\ *n* -S [*frankfurter, frankforter* fr. G *Frankfurter* of Frankfurt, fr. *Frankfurt* am Main, Germany; *frankfurt, frankfort* short for *frankfurter, frankforter*] **:** a sausage (as of beef or beef and pork or a mixture of meats and poultry) that is cured and cooked and stuffed in a casing or skinless

frankfurt horizontal *or* **frankfort horizontal** *or* **frankfurt plane** *or* **frankfort plane** *n, usu cap F* [*Frankfurt* am Main] **:** EYE-EAR PLANE

frankhearted \'=ˌ=ˌ=\ *adj* **:** having an open or honest heart

frank·in·cense \'fraŋkən,sen(t)s\ *n* -S [ME *fraunk encens*, fr. OF *fraunk, frank* free, pure + *encens* incense — more at FRANK, INCENSE] **1 :** a gum resin containing volatile oil obtained from various chiefly East African or Arabian trees of the genus *Boswellia*, valued in ancient times in worship and for embalming and fumigation, and still an important incense resin — called also *Indian frankincense* **2 :** GUM THUS 2

frankincense pine *n* **:** LOBLOLLY PINE 1

franking *n* -S [fr. gerund of ³*frank*] **1 :** the stamp or other indication relating to postage on a cover — see MIXED FRANKING **2 :** the mailing charge ⟨~ was paid by a 2-shilling stamp —L.A.Wolf⟩ **3 :** the sending of mail free of charge (as by a frank)

¹frank·ish \'fraŋkish, -raiŋ-, -kēsh\ *adj, usu cap* [¹*Frank* + *-ish*] **:** of or relating to the Franks

²frankish \"\ *n* -ES *cap* **:** the West Germanic language of the Franks esp. as represented by a large and early stratum of Germanic elements in the vocabulary of French — compare FRANCONIAN

frank·lin \'fraŋklən\ *n* -S [ME *frankeleyn, fraunkeleyn*, fr. AF *fraunclein*, fr. OF *franc, fraunc* free + *-lenc, -layn, -lein -ling* — more at FRANK, CHAMBERLAIN] **:** a substantial landowner of 14th and 15th century England who is of free but not noble birth

franklin grouse *or* **franklin's grouse** *n, usu cap F* [after Sir John *Franklin* †1847 Eng. explorer] **:** a grouse (*Canachites franklinii*) of northwestern evergreen forests closely related to or included among the spruce grouses

¹frank·lin·ia \fraŋk'linēə\ [NL, fr. Benjamin *Franklin* †1790 Am. statesman, scientist, and philosopher + NL *-ia*] *syn of* GORDONIA

²franklinia \"\ *n* -S [NL, fr. Benjamin *Franklin* + NL *-ia*] **:** a plant of the genus *Gordonia; esp* **:** FRANKLIN TREE

frank·lin·i·an \(')=ˌ=nēən\ *adj, usu cap* [Benjamin *Franklin* + E *-ian*] **:** of, relating to, or having the characteristics of Benjamin Franklin

frank·lin·i·el·la \ˌfraŋk,linē'elə\ *n, cap* [NL, prob. fr. Henry James *Franklin* †1958 Am. zoologist and entomologist + NL *-i-* + *-ella*] **:** a large genus of thrips including numerous serious pests of cultivated plants some of which are vectors of virus diseases — see FLOWER THRIPS, TOBACCO THRIPS

frank·lin·ite \'fraŋklə,nīt\ *n* -S [*Franklin*, N.J. + E *-ite*] **:** an iron-black slightly magnetic mineral $ZnFe_2O_4$ consisting of an oxide of iron and zinc occurring in octahedral crystals or massive and constituting a member of the magnetite series

franklin's gull *n, usu cap F* [after Sir John *Franklin*] **:** a small black-headed gull (*Larus pipixan*) that breeds in the western interior of No. America

franklin stove *also* **franklin** *n, usu cap F* [after Benjamin *Franklin*, its inventor] **1 :** a metal heating stove resembling an open fireplace but designed to be set out in a room so as to conserve heat and to distribute it evenly **2 :** an enclosed metal heating stove designed to be set out in a room

folding door Franklin stove

franklin tree *n, usu cap F* [after Benjamin *Franklin*] **:** a shrub or small tree (*Gordonia alatamaha*) frequently cultivated for its foliage and solitary showy white flowers

frank·ly *adv* [²*frank* + *-ly*] **1 :** in a frank manner: **a :** GENEROUSLY, UNRESERVEDLY ⟨wishing to repay the money so ~ offered to him in his need⟩ **b :** without concealment **:** OPENLY, PLAINLY, CLEARLY ⟨the ordeals he and his companions underwent are ~ harrowing —*Geoffrey Bles Annual List*⟩ ⟨the avenue now had a building that was ~ commercial as well as dignified —*Amer Guide Series: N.Y. City*⟩ ⟨the bottle was ~ enormous —Margery Allingham⟩ **c :** FORTHRIGHTLY, BLUNTLY ⟨the bold types ~ surround the table and heap up their plates with everything close at hand —*Sydney (Australia) Bull.*⟩ ⟨one needs then ~ to face oneself and to observe the particular kind of folly one is committing —H.A.Overstreet⟩ **2 :** INDEED **:** to tell the truth **:** to be sure **:** UNDOUBTEDLY ⟨~ . . . we could afford to give them the materials free —*Monsanto Mag.*⟩

frankmarriage \'=ˌ=ˌ=\ *n* [ME *franke mariage*, fr. AF *fraunk mariage*, lit., free marriage] **:** the tenure in feudal law by which a man and his wife held an estate granted by a blood relative of the wife in consideration of their marriage, whether before or after it, to be held of the donor by the issue of the marriage to not less than the fourth generation and without other service than fealty — called also *liberum maritagium*

frank·ness *n* -ES **:** the quality or state of being frank ⟨charmed by the ~ of the boy's reply⟩ ⟨told people what he thought with ~ that bordered on discourtesy⟩

frankpledge \'=ˌ=\ *n* [ME *frankplegge, fraunkplegge*, fr. AF *fraunc plege* (intended as trans. of ME *friborg*, alter. — influenced by ME *fri, fre* free — of assumed OE *frithborh*), fr. OF *fraunc, franc* free + *plege* pledge — more at FRITHBORH, FRANK, PLEDGE] **:** the system or condition in Old English law under which with certain exceptions each male member of a tithing of 12 years of age or upward was responsible for the good conduct of and for the damage done by other members of the tithing; *also* **:** the member himself or the tithing

franks *pl of* FRANK, *pres 3d sing of* FRANK

frank tenant *n* [AF *franc tenant*, fr. OF *franc* free + *tenant* tenant — more at TENANT] *Old Eng law* **:** one that holds a freehold estate

frank tenement *n* [ME, fr. AF *fraunc tenement*, fr. OF *franc, fraunc* free + *tenement* — more at TENEMENT] **:** a freehold estate

frank tenure *n* **:** a freehold tenure

fran·se·ria \fran'sirēə\ *n* [NL, fr. Antonio *Franseri*, 18th cent. Span. physician and botanist + NL *-ia*] **1** *cap* **:** a genus of annual or perennial herbs or shrubs of the family Compositae having alternate leaves and inconspicuous greenish flowers in discoid heads with pistillate heads in the axils of the upper leaves at the bases of nodding spikes or racemes of staminate heads **2** -S **:** any plant of the genus *Franseria* — called also *bur-ragweed*

fran·tic \'frantik, -raan-, -tēk\ *adj* [ME *frenetik, frentik, frantik* — more at FRENETIC] **1 a** *archaic* **:** mentally deranged **:** DELIRIOUS, INSANE, MAD ⟨sorrows, and grief of heart, makes him speak . . . like a ~ man —Shak.⟩ **b :** almost mentally deranged **:** nearly mad ⟨at the beach outside Venice they drove the caretaker ~ by demanding, one after the other, an adequately large bathing suit —Robert Berkelman⟩ **c :** emotionally out of control **:** overwhelmed with feeling to the point of wildness **:** FRENZIED ⟨~ with anger and frustration⟩ **2 a :** marked by fast and nervous, disordered, or anxiety-driven activity ⟨this almost ~ search for new writers —J.T. Farrell⟩ ⟨the most ~ dancers in the world —Wolcott Gibbs⟩ ⟨did a tumbling act, spinning across the stage in a series of ~ cartwheels as though she were made of springs —Winifred Bambrick⟩ ⟨tornadoes and ~ thunderstorms —*Springfield (Mass.) Union*⟩ ⟨there was something desperate and ~ in this gaiety —B.A.Williams⟩ **:** wild or out of control esp. with fear and anxiety ⟨after longer periods without water they sometimes become ~ —*Amer. Guide Series: Ariz.*⟩ ⟨clasping me in desperation like a person ~ with drowning —R.P.Warren⟩ ⟨destroyed the bridges . . . in spite of ~ protests from the townspeople —*Amer. Guide Series: Tenn.*⟩ **b :** noisy or active in an uncontrolled way ⟨~ applause at the end of the opera⟩ ⟨the batsman, making a ~ attempt to cover himself —Dorothy Sayers⟩ **3** *of an emotion* **:** intense to the point of hysteria ⟨~ fear and fanatical hatred —M.R.Cohen⟩ ⟨a child, playing on a damp beach, suddenly finds he can repeat, over and over, the imprint of his hand . . . will do this, then, in ~ joy —Roger Burlingame⟩ **4 :** of or befitting one that is frantic ⟨the forest seemed a vast hive of men buzzing about in ~ circles —Stephen Crane⟩ ⟨protests with ~ words and gestures that he has only desired peace —Sir Winston Churchill⟩ ⟨our ~ zeal to extend the frontiers of knowledge —E.S.McCartney⟩ ⟨the ~ beat of hoofs down the road —T.B.Costain⟩ **5 :** very great **:** EXTREME ⟨in a ~ hurry to get home⟩ — **fran·ti·cal·ly** \-tək(ə)lē, -tēk-, -li\ *adv* — **fran·tic·ly** *adv* — **fran·tic·ness** *n* -ES

²frantic *n* -S [ME *frenetik, frentik, frantik*, fr. *frenetik, frentik, frantik*, adj.] *archaic* **:** LUNATIC

fran·zy \'franzē\ *dial var of* FRENZY

frap \'frap\ *vt* **frapped; frapped; frapping; fraps** [ME *frapen, frappen*, fr. MF *fraper*, prob. of imit. origin] **1** *dial Eng* **:** STRIKE, BEAT **2 :** to draw tight **:** strengthen with bonds (as a ship by passing cables around it) **:** bind, draw together, or secure with ropes

frap·le \'frapəl\ *vi* -ED/-ING/-S [perh. freq. of *frap*] *archaic* **:** BLUSTER, WRANGLE — **frap·ler** \-plə(r)\ *n* -S

¹frap·pé *or* **frappe** \fra'pā\ *adj* [F *frappé*, fr. past part. of *frapper* to strike, chill, fr. OF *fraper* to strike, beat — more at FRAP] *of a food or beverage* **:** ICED, FROZEN ⟨wine ~⟩

²frappé \"\ *or* **frappe** \'frap\ *n* -S **1 :** an iced and flavored semiliquid mixture served in glasses **2** *usu frappé* **:** an after-dinner drink of liqueur served in a cocktail glass over shaved ice **3** *usu frappe* **:** a thick milk shake

³frap·pé \fra'pā\ *vt* **frappéed; frappéed; frappéing; frappés :** to freeze to a soft mush

⁴frappé \"\ *n* -S [F, fr. past part. of *frapper*] **:** a movement in ballet in which the free foot beats against the ankle of the supporting foot

frapping *n* -S [fr. gerund of *frap*] **:** a lashing that binds tightly or binds things together

frasch process \'fräsh-\ *or* **frasch method** *n, usu cap F* [after Herman *Frasch* †1914 Am. chemist born in Germany, its inventor] **:** a method of mining deep-lying sulfur by forcing into the deposit very hot water and pumping out the sulfur thereby melted

¹frase \'frāz\ *Scot var of* PHRASE

²frase *var of* FRAISE

fra·ser \'frāzə(r)\ *n* -S [F *fraisier* strawberry plant, fr. *fraise* strawberry, fr. OF *fraise, frese* — more at FRAISE] **:** ⁵FRAISE

fraser fir *n, usu cap 1st F* [after John *Fraser* †1811 Brit. botanist] **:** an evergreen tree (*Abies fraseri*) of the southern Alleghenies similar to the balsam fir but having leaves rarely more than ¾ inch long and rounded and notched at the apex

fras·ni·an \'frasnēən\ *adj, usu cap* [F *Frasnian*, subdivision of the Devonian, fr. *Frasne*, France + E *-ian*] **:** of or relating to a subdivision of the European Devonian — see GEOLOGIC TIME table

frass \'fras\ *n* -ES [G, lit., food, feed, fr. OHG *frāz* food, fr. OHG *frezzan* to eat voraciously, devour — more at FRET] **:** debris or excrement produced by insects

¹frat \'frat, *usu* -ad·+V\ *n* -S [by shortening] **:** FRATERNITY

²frat \"\ *vi* **fratted; fratted; fratting; frats** [short for *fraternize*] **:** to associate on friendly terms **:** FRATERNIZE

¹fratch \'frach\ *vi* -ED/-ING/-S [ME *fracchen* to creak, prob. of imit. origin] *dial Eng* **:** QUARREL, WRANGLE

²fratch \"\ *n* -ES *dial Eng* **:** DISAGREEMENT, QUARREL

fratched *adj, dial Brit* **:** IRRITATED, PEEVED

fratchy \'frachī\ *adj* -ER/-EST *dial Brit* **:** irritable and argumentative **:** PEEVISH

fra·te \'frä(,)tā\ *n, pl* **fra·ti** \-tē\ [It, lit., brother — more at FRA] **:** FRIAR — often used as a title

¹fra·ter \'frād·ə(r)\ *n* -S [ME *fraytour, frater*, fr. OF *fraitur*, short for OF *refraitur, refaitur*, fr. ML *refectorium* — more at REFECTORY] **:** a refectory of a monastery

²fra·ter \'frā|d·ə(r), -rā|, |tə-\ *n* -S [ML, fr. L, brother — more at BROTHER] **1 :** a member of certain religious orders (as the Benedictine order) who is studying for the priesthood — often used as a title or form of address esp. among members of the same or similar orders **2 a :** a fraternity brother **b :** a brother Freemason in certain Masonic orders

¹fra·ter·nal \frə'tərnᵊl, -'tən-\ *adj* [ME, fr. ML *fraternalis*, fr. L *fraternus* (fr. *frater*) + *-alis* -al] **1 a :** of, relating to, or involving brothers ⟨trying to improve the ~ relationship between the two boys even though their father did not care⟩ **b :** of, relating to, or being a fraternity or confederation ⟨a ~ order⟩ ⟨a ~ chapter house⟩ ⟨a ~ delegate to national meetings⟩ **c :** of, relating to, or being one of many men's or sometimes women's clubs or associations usu. having secret rites, restricted membership, and religious, social, charitable, or professional purposes **2** *of twins* **:** derived from two ova **:** DIZYGOTIC **3 :** FRIENDLY, BROTHERLY ⟨so we shall have ~ nations . . . instead of warring, organized interests —H.J. Mackinder⟩ — **fra·ter·nal·ly** \-ᵊlē, -ᵊli\ *adv*

²fraternal \"\ *n* -S **1 :** a member of a fraternal order **2 :** a society providing fraternal insurance

fraternal benefit society *n* **:** a fraternal order or association providing fraternal insurance

fraternal insurance *n* **:** insurance issued by a fraternal order or association to its members, formerly meeting its obligations by assessments upon members at the time obligations arose but now generally by a legal reserve

fra·ter·nal·ism \-nᵊl,izəm, -nə,li-\ *n* -S **1 a :** the state of being fraternal **b :** fraternal feeling **2 :** the theoretic justification of fraternal societies or their practices; *also* **:** the advocacy of fraternal societies

fra·ter·nal·ist \-nᵊləst, -nələ-\ *n* -S **:** a person who practices or advocates fraternalism

fraternal polyandry *n* **:** polyandry in which several brothers share one wife — contrasted with *sororal polygyny*

fraternal worker *n* **:** a person engaged professionally in the work of a church who comes from and is usu. supported by a church in another country

fra·ter·ni·ty \frə'tərnəd·ē, -'tən-, -ətē, -i\ *n* -ES [ME *fraternite*, fr. MF & L; MF *fraternite*, fr. L *fraternitat-, fraternitas*, fr. *fraternus* + *-itat-, -itas* -ity] **1 :** a group of people associated or formally organized for a common purpose, interest, or pleasure: as **a :** a religious or ecclesiastical brotherhood **b :** a usu. organized group of men of the same class, occupation, interest, or pursuit **:** COMPANY, GUILD **:** fraternal order **c :** a national or local men's student organization formed chiefly for social purposes having secret rites and a name consisting of usu. three Greek letters; *also* **:** an organization of alumni who were members of such an organization **d :** a student organization for scholastic, professional, or extracurricular activities; *esp* **:** a national honorary organization including students and alumni ⟨an honorary ~⟩ ⟨a debating ~⟩ **2 a :** the quality or state of being a brother or being brothers **:** the relationship of a brother or of brothers **b :** the quality or state of being brotherly or very friendly **:** BROTHERLINESS **c :** a brotherly commonness (as of occupation) ⟨men with a ~ of interests⟩ **3 :** men of the same class, profession, occupation, character, or tastes ⟨the legal ~⟩ ⟨the racetrack ~⟩ ⟨the despised ~ of armchair historians —T.S.Brown⟩ **4 a :** the entire progeny of a single mating **b :** a group of siblings

frat·er·ni·za·tion \ˌfrad·ə(r)nə'zāshən, -atə-, -nī'-\ *n* -S **:** the act of fraternizing

frat·er·nize \'frad·ə(r),nīz, -atə-\ *vb* -ED/-ING/-S *see -ize in Explan Notes* [F *fraterniser*, fr. ML *fraternizare*, fr. L *fraternus* brotherly (fr. *frater* brother) + ML *-izare* -ize — more at BROTHER] *vi* **1 a :** to associate or mingle as brothers or on fraternal terms **:** engage in comradely social intercourse ⟨he sent a detachment of cavalry to reconnoiter the route again and ~ with the Indians —Bernard De Voto⟩ ⟨guest of honor at a dinner . . . where he *fraternized* with seven prominent hoodlums —Polly Adler⟩ ⟨the militiamen were persuaded to lay down their arms and ~ with the strikers —*Amer. Guide Series: Md.*⟩ ⟨greater opportunities for the people of the western nations to mingle and ~ with each other —*Saturday Rev.*⟩ **b :** to associate on intimate terms with members of a hostile group (as civilians of an occupied country) esp. when contrary to military orders ⟨caught the men *fraternizing*⟩ ⟨the crime of *fraternizing* with foreigners —H.W.Carter⟩; *esp* **:** to have sexual intercourse with a woman of an occupied country ⟨by the first few weeks of occupation 70 percent of our troops had *fraternized* in husbandly fashion —John McPartland⟩ **c :** to be friendly or amiable **2** *of animals* **:** to mingle, live together, or inhabit the same area without hostility ⟨after mating, it is believed that the male lives alone and does not ~ even with others of his own sex, while the female orang retires to bear her young alone —Weston La Barre⟩ ⟨still a few antelope in the cattle country; they ~ easily with the domestic beasts —Tom Marvel⟩ **~** *vt, archaic* **:** to bring into a fraternal or friendly sympathetic relationship — **frat·er·niz·er** \-zə(r)\ *n* -s

fraters *pl of* FRATER

frati *pl of* FRATE

frat·i·cel·li \ˌfrad·əˈchelē\ *n pl, cap* [It, pl. of *fraticello,* lit., little brother, dim. of *frate* brother — more at FRA] **:** any of several small Christian sects existing chiefly in Italy from the 13th to the 15th centuries and having some connection with the Franciscans: as **a :** a band of seceders from the Franciscan order under the leadership of Angelo de Clareno (1247–1337) **b :** the Spirituals or Spiritual Franciscans who revolted against the order and defied many popes **c :** the followers of Michael of Cesena (1270–1342) who defended a theory of poverty and property for monks and ecclesiastics generally

fra·tor·i·ty \frəˈtärəd·ē, -ˈtȯr-\ *n* -ES [*frat*ernity + sor*ority*] **:** a society or club including both men and women or boys and girls

frat·ri·ci·dal \ˌfra·traˈsīdᵊl *sometimes* -rāt-\ *adj* **:** of, relating to, being, or resulting in fratricide ⟨the outbreak of one of the bloodiest, most ~ wars in Irish history —Paul Blanshard⟩

frat·ri·cide \ˈ==ˌsīd\ *n* -s [in sense 1, fr. ME, fr. MF or L; MF, fr. L *fratricida,* fr. *fratr-, frater* brother + *-cida* -cide (killer); in sense 2, fr. MF or L; MF, fr. L *fratricidium,* fr. *fratr-, frater* + *-cidium* -cide (killing) — more at BROTHER] **1 :** one that murders or kills his own brother or sister or some person (as a countryman) who stands in a relationship resembling that of a brother or sister ⟨besides being a great lady she is also a ~, a moral coward and a tosspot —*Time*⟩ **2 :** the act of a fratricide

fra·try \ˈfrā·trē\ *also* **fra·tery** \-ād·ərē\ *n* -ES [prob. fr. ¹*frater* + *-y*] **1 :** a refectory of a monastery **2 :** the residential quarters of a monastery

frats *pl of* FRAT, *pres 3d sing of* FRAT

fratted *past of* FRAT

fratting *pres part of* FRAT

frau \ˈfrau̇\ *n* [G, woman, married woman, wife, fr. OHG *frouwa* mistress, lady; akin to OE *frēa* lord, master, OS *frūa* mistress, lady, *frao* lord, master, OHG *frō* lord, master, ON *freyja* mistress, lady, Goth *frauja* lord, master, OE *faran* to travel, go — more at FARE] **1** *pl* **frauen** \-au̇ən\ *usu cap* **:** MRS. — usu. used preceding the name of a German married woman **2** -s **:** WIFE, HOUSEWIFE — sometimes used disparagingly

fraucht \ˈfrȯkt, -räkt\ *Scot var of* FRAUGHT

fraud \ˈfrȯd\ *n* -s [ME *fraude,* fr. MF, fr. L *fraud-, fraus;* akin to Skt *dhūrvati* he injures, *dhūrta* fraudulent, and prob. to OHG *triogan* to deceive, ON *draugr* ghost, Skt *droha* injury, treachery] **1 a :** an instance or an act of trickery or deceit esp. when involving misrepresentation **:** an act of deluding **:** DELUSION ⟨the presumed guarantee of standards is really a ~ —Walter Moberley⟩: as (1) *or* **fraud in fact :** an intentional misrepresentation, concealment, or nondisclosure for the purpose of inducing another in reliance upon it to part with some valuable thing belonging to him or to surrender a legal right **:** a false representation of a matter of fact by words or conduct, by false or misleading allegations, or by the concealment of what should have been disclosed that deceives or is intended to deceive another so he shall act upon it to his legal injury — called also *actual fraud* (2) *or* **fraud in equity :** an act, omission to act, or concealment by which one person obtains an advantage against conscience over another or which equity or public policy forbids as being prejudicial to another (as an act in violation of a relationship of trust and confidence) — called also *equitable fraud, legal fraud;* see CONSTRUCTIVE FRAUD **b :** a means used in trickery **:** a dishonest stratagem or a spurious thing passed off as genuine **:** TRICK, HOAX ⟨who worked the big ~ on the . . . bank —Rudyard Kipling⟩ **2 :** the quality of being deceitful **:** the disposition to deceive ⟨the dross of ~ and charlatanism —Lewis Mumford⟩ **3 :** the condition of being defrauded or beguiled **4 a :** a person who is not what he pretends to be **:** PRETENDER, HUMBUG, HYPOCRITE ⟨the pretentious ~ who assumes a love of culture that is alien to him —Richard Watts⟩ **b :** one who defrauds **:** CHEAT ⟨the ~ is simply another variety of confidence man who pretends to have influence —G.A.Graham⟩ **syn** see DECEPTION, IMPOSTURE

fraud·ful \-dfəl\ *adj* [ME, fr. *fraude* + *-ful*] *archaic* **:** marked by fraud **:** FRAUDULENT — **fraud·ful·ly** \-fəlē, -li\ *adv, archaic*

fraud in equity 1 : FRAUD 1a(2) **2 :** fraud for which a court of equity grants a remedy

fraud order *n* **:** an order issued by the U. S. postmaster general forbidding the use of the mails to a person who has used them fraudulently

fraud·u·lence \ˈfrȯjələn(t)s\ *n* -s [ME, fr. L *fraudulentia,* fr. *fraudulentus* fraudulent + *-ia* -y] **:** the quality or state of being fraudulent **:** deliberate deceit **:** DECEITFULNESS, FRAUD

fraud·u·len·cy \-nsē\ *n* -ES [L *fraudulentia*] *archaic* **:** FRAUDULENCE, FRAUD

fraud·u·lent \-nt\ *adj* [ME, fr. MF, fr. L *fraudulentus,* fr. *fraud-, fraus*] **1 :** belonging to or characterized by fraud ⟨throw off the yoke of superstition, of ~ priests and tyrannous rulers —M.R.Cohen⟩ **:** founded on fraud ⟨I should be very sorry to think that there was anything fishy or ~ about the . . . institution of Private Property —L.P.Smith⟩ **:** FALSE ⟨~ claims for unemployment compensation —*Wall Street Jour.*⟩ **:** obtained or performed by fraud ⟨~ land grants —E.G.Gudde⟩ ⟨beset with charges of ~ voting —*Amer. Guide Series: N.J.*⟩ **2** *of a legal conveyance* **:** made in fraud of others' rights; *specif* **:** made without adequate consideration in violation of the rights of creditors or made to hinder or delay them — **fraud·u·lent·ly** *adv* — **fraud·u·lent·ness** *n* -ES

fraudulent preference *n* **:** a payment to or advantage conferred on one creditor in fraud of the rights of other creditors by an insolvent debtor

fraudulent representation *n* **:** a representation that a past or present material fact is true which is made in any manner or form with the intention of inducing someone to act thereon and by one who either knows of its falsity or is ignorant of its truth or falsity or who acts recklessly without regard to its truth and which in some jurisdictions requires an actual intention to deceive for one to be held liable for damages but which is even without such intention sometimes fraudulent in law and ground for avoiding a contract — compare DECEIT, MISREPRESENTATION, WARRANTY

frauen *pl of* FRAU

1fraught \ˈfrȯkt, -räkt\ *n* -s [ME, fr. MD or MLG *vracht, vrecht,* prob. fr. an (assumed) OFris word akin to OHG *frēht* reward, earnings, fr. *fir-, fur-* for- + *ēht* property — more at AUGHT] **1** *chiefly Scot* **:** FREIGHT, PASSAGE **2** *now chiefly Scot* **a :** LOAD, CARGO **b :** the amount one person can carry at a time ⟨carry a ~ of water to the manse —J.M.Barrie⟩

2fraught \"\ *vt* **fraughted** *or* **fraught; fraughted** *or* **fraught; fraughting; fraughts** [ME *fraughten,* fr. *fraught,* n.] *now chiefly Scot* **:** LOAD, FREIGHT, FILL

3fraught \ˈfrȯt, *usu* -ȯd·+V\ *adj* [ME, fr. past part. of *fraughten*] **1** *archaic* **:** carrying as a load **:** LADEN, FREIGHTED **2 a :** burdened or menaced with ⟨the long, danger-*fraught* wait before the . . . invasion —*Manchester Guardian Weekly*⟩ ⟨an extrahazardous occupation ~ with dangers —R.M. Hutchins⟩ **:** ENDANGERED, THREATENED ⟨the changed times were ~ with other obstacles than these —Charles Dickens⟩ **b :** giving promise or prospect — used with *with* ⟨opinions that we loathe and believe to be ~ with death —O.W.Holmes †1935⟩ ⟨achievements . . . ~ with happy consequences for the future —John Buchan⟩ **c :** ACCOMPANIED, ATTENDED — used with *with* ⟨a great event which might be ~ with strange consequences —Robert Hichens⟩ ⟨the speaking of words ~ with deep emotional significance —A.T.Weaver⟩ ⟨here . . . every footstep is ~ with memories —Norman Douglas⟩

fraught·age \-ōd·ij\ *n* -s [ME, fr. ¹*fraught* + *-age*] *archaic* **:** FREIGHT

fräu·lein \ˈfrȯiˌlīn *sometimes* -rau̇,- *or* -rō,-\ *n* -s [G, fr. MHG *vrouwelīn* young lady, dim. of *vrouwe* lady, mistress, fr. OHG *frouwa* — more at FRAU] **1** *usu cap* **:** MISS — usu. used before the name of an unmarried German girl or woman **2 a :** a usu. young unmarried woman esp. of Germany ⟨an operetta about the love of an American GI for a ~ —Percy Winner⟩ ⟨a German ~ with bare and sunburned legs and plaited hair —Negley Farson⟩ **b :** a German governess ⟨the parties of children that used to be seen hurrying along the avenue at the close of the afternoon, in the care of nannies or mademoiselles or ~s —Rebecca West⟩

fraun·ho·fer lines \ˈfrau̇nˌhōfə(r)\ *n, usu cap F* [after Joseph von *Fraunhofer* †1826 Bavarian optician and physicist] **:** any of the dark lines in the spectrum of sunlight

fra·va·shi \frəˈväshē\ *n* -s [Av *fravashay-*] *Persian religion* **:** an immortal preexisting spiritual guardian or genius of each individual **:** the heavenly image and celestial archetype of each creature; *collectively* **:** the ministering angels of divine heavenly beings

frawn \ˈfrȯn\ *n* -s [IrGael *fraochān*] **:** WHORTLEBERRY 1

frax·e·tin \ˈfraksəd·ən\ *n* -s [ISV *fraxin* + *-etin*] **:** a yellow crystalline compound $C_{10}H_8O_5$ derived from coumarin and obtained by hydrolysis of fraxin

frax·in \ˈfraksən\ *n* -s [ISV *frax-* (fr. L *fraxinus*) + *-in;* orig. formed in G] **:** a bitter yellowish crystalline glucoside $C_{16}H_{18}O_{10}$ found esp. in the bark of the ash and the horse chestnut

frax·i·nel·la \ˌfraksəˈnelə\ *n* -s [NL, dim. of L *fraxinus;* fr. the similarity of its leaves to those of an ash] **:** a Eurasian perennial herb (*Dictamnus albus*) of the family Rutaceae with flowers which exhale a flammable vapor in hot weather and were formerly reputed to have the power to expel arrows from the body — called also *burning bush, gas plant*

frax·i·nus \ˈfraksənəs\ *n, cap* [NL, fr. L, ash — more at BIRCH] **:** a genus of trees or sometimes shrubs (family Oleaceae) comprising the ashes, being natives of the north temperate zone, and having thin furrowed bark, opposite pinnate leaves, and small apetalous flowers followed by fruits that are samaras

1fray \ˈfrā\ *vb* -ED/-ING/-S [ME *fraien,* short for *afraien, affraien* — more at AFFRAY] *vt* **1** *archaic* **:** FRIGHTEN, SCARE, TERRIFY **2** *archaic* **:** to frighten away **:** DISPEL **~** *vi, archaic* **:** BRAWL, QUARREL, FIGHT

2fray \"\ *n* -s [ME, short for *afray, affray* — more at AFFRAY] **1** *now chiefly Scot* **:** APPREHENSION, FRIGHT, TERROR **2 a :** COMMOTION, TUMULT **b :** QUARREL, BRAWL ⟨authority to quell all quarrels, ~s, and disorders among persons subject to this code —*U.S. Code*⟩ ⟨sometimes those cold ornery guys turned very dangerous in a ~ . . . used knucks, even knives —T.W. Duncan⟩ **c :** SKIRMISH, COMBAT, FIGHT ⟨who began this bloody ~ —Shak.⟩ ⟨picked up a club and threw himself into the ~⟩ **d :** DISPUTE, DEBATE ⟨the editor took a side opposite to the local faculty in the ~⟩ ⟨known for his scientific-political ~s as well as his chemistry —*Newsweek*⟩ **syn** see CONTEST

3fray \"\ *vb* -ED/-ING/-S [MF *frayer, froyer* to rub, fr. L *fricare* — more at BRINE] *vt* **1 a :** to rub against something ⟨a deer ~s his antlers to remove the velvet⟩ **b :** to wear (as an edge of cloth or an end of rope) or wear off by or as if by rubbing **:** FRET ⟨the friction ~*ed* the edge of the polishing cloth⟩ **c :** to separate the strands or threads at the edge or end of (as a piece of fabric or rope); *also* **:** to divide an end or edge of so that the separate divisions fan out **2 a :** to cause to lose much of an original strength, force, or essential quality ⟨the boy's gratitude became rapidly ~*ed*⟩ ⟨his boyish charm got a bit ~*ed* near the end —Crary Moore⟩ **b :** to strain and bring to an unhealthy, touchy, or inauspicious condition ⟨his temper became a bit ~*ed*⟩ ⟨relations . . . already ~*ed* as a result of disagreements —*N.Y. Times*⟩ ⟨excursions from the family circle have benefited his health and ~*ed* nerves out of recognition —Rex Ingamells⟩ **~** *vi* **1 :** to wear out or into shreds **:** come apart (as when the threads of a fabric loosen and ravel) **2 :** to thin or separate into shreds, parts, or separate units, and spread or splay — used with *out* ⟨in the dips of the road the mist ~*ed out* over the slab and blunted the headlights —R.P.Warren⟩ ⟨is our civilization widening and deepening, or is it ~*ing out* —Douglas Stewart⟩ ⟨white pelicans . . . rise, ~*ing out,* peeling off, in a slow roar of aroused wings —Marjory S. Douglas⟩ ⟨feathered lines that ~*ed out* upon the skin —Elizabeth M. Roberts⟩

4fray \"\ *n* -s **:** a raveled place or worn spot (as on fabric)

5fray \ˈfrī\ *n* [Sp, short for *fraile,* alter. of OSp *fraire,* fr. OProv, brother, monk, fr. L *fratr-, frater* brother — more at BROTHER] **:** BROTHER — a title of a clergyman of various religious orders in Spanish countries

frayed·ly *adv* **:** in the manner of one that is frayed

frayed·ness *n* -ES **:** the quality or state of being frayed

fraying *n* -s [fr. gerund of ³*fray*] **:** something rubbed or worn off by fraying: as **a :** the velvet that a deer frays from his antlers **b :** pieces of fabric worn off

frayn *or* **frayne** \ˈfrān\ *vb* -ED/-ING/-S [ME *freynen, fraynen,* fr. OE *fregnan, frignan* — more at PRAY] *vt, archaic* **:** to inquire of **:** ASK **~** *vi, obs* **:** ASK, INQUIRE

1fraze \ˈfrāz\ *n* -s [F *fraise,* fr. *fraise,* a kind of ruff; fr. the shape of some cutters — more at FRAISE] **1 a :** a small milling cutter used to cut down the ends of canes or rods to receive a ferrule **b :** the end of a cane or rod shaped as if by a fraze **2** [²*fraze*] **:** the unevenness caused by rough edges or burs

2fraze \"\ *vt* -ED/-ING/-S **:** to smooth by or as if by removing fraze; *specif* **:** to cut or shape (the end of something) to receive a ferrule — **fraz·er** \-zə(r)\ *n* -s

fra·zil \ˈfrāzəl, frəˈzil\ *or* **frazil ice** *n* -s [CanF *frasil, frazil, fraisil,* fr. F *fraisil* coal cinders, alter. of OF *faisil,* fr. (assumed) VL *facilis,* fr. L *fac-, fax* torch + *-ilis* -ile] **:** ice crystals or granules sometimes resembling slush that are formed in turbulent water

1fraz·zle \ˈfrazəl\ *vb* **frazzled; frazzled; frazzling** \-z(ə)liŋ\ **frazzles** [alter. (prob. influenced by ³*fray*) of E dial. *fazle* to tangle, fray, fr. ME *faselen* to fray, fr. *fasel,* n., fringe, frayed edge, dim. of *fas* fringe, fr. OE *fæs* — more at FASH] *vt* **1 :** ³FRAY ⟨a bedside lamp with a *frazzled* cord and torn shade —Hamilton Basso⟩ **2 a :** to reduce to a state of extreme physical or nervous fatigue ⟨as if all of these projects weren't enough to ~ him —Diane Disney Miller⟩ ⟨finally arrived . . . *frazzled* and miserable —Joseph Wechsberg⟩ **b :** to disturb greatly **:** UPSET ⟨he has probably helped to open as many curious minds as he has helped to ~ unstable ones —*Time*⟩ **~** *vi* **:** to become frazzled **:** FRAY, WEAR ⟨a thin ribbon of gray smoke . . . *frazzled* into nothingness —J.B.Clayton⟩ ⟨guaranteed not to rip in the seams or ~ at the sleeves —J.C.Harris⟩ ⟨I think he rather *frazzled* out —G.W.Johnson⟩

2frazzle \"\ *n* -s **1 :** the state of being frazzled **2 a :** a frayed or tattered end or edge **b :** a condition of fatigue or nervous exhaustion suggesting such an end or edge ⟨worn to a ~⟩

1freak \ˈfrēk\ *n* -s [perh. fr. obs. *freak* man-at-arms, human being, extraordinary or supernatural creature (in such phrases as *the freaks of Fortune,* lit., the minions of Fortune), fr. ME *freke,* fr. OE *freca* warrior, hero, fr. *frec* greedy, eager, bold, dangerous; akin to OHG *freh* untamed, greedy, ON *frekr* greedy, harsh, severe, Goth *faihufriks* covetous, greedy for money, Pol *pragnąć* to desire, Czech *prahnouti*] **1 a :** a sudden apparently causeless turn of the mind **:** WHIM, FANCY, CAPRICE ⟨the condition of the mare, and the young gentleman's strange ~ in riding her out all night —George Meredith⟩ ⟨his spurts of action are not mere ~s of a temperament that alternates between feverish exploits and slothful lethargy —Karl Polanyi⟩ ⟨you should be able to stop and go on, and follow this way or that, as the ~ takes you —R.L.Stevenson⟩; *also* **:** an odd or whimsical idea or preconception ⟨a bishop arrived who'd some strange ~s about meditation —George Bellairs⟩ **b :** an odd, unexpected, or seemingly capricious action or event ⟨by a ~ of wind the smoke had been blown high —Wallace Stegner⟩ ⟨stories about ~s of the weather, floods, and great droughts —*Amer. Guide Series: Ind.*⟩ ⟨a ~ of good fortune —*New Yorker*⟩ **2** *archaic* **:** a freakish quality or disposition **:** CAPRICIOUSNESS, WHIMSICALITY **3 a :** a product of freakish thought or action or of a freakish process **:** something markedly unusual or abnormal ⟨~s of this storm include a shingle driven through a fence post, a flock of chickens picked clean, and the walls of a house carried away bodily, leaving a cupboard full of unbroken china —*Amer. Guide Series: Minn.*⟩ ⟨the ~s of contemporary fashion —O. Elfrida Saunders⟩ ⟨no individual ~, but a confirmed habit of the species —James Stevenson-Hamilton⟩ **b :** something markedly abnormal mentally or physically esp. to the point of shocking usual expectations; *esp* **:** one with a physical oddity who appears in a circus sideshow or similar exhibition — compare MUTATION, SPORT 6 **4** *Brit* **:** a wild card in poker; *esp* **:** a wild deuce

2freak \"\ *adj* **:** having the character of a freak **:** diverging from what is natural or normal ⟨when rain comes it is often in ~ deluges —Keith Ellis⟩ ⟨the range of the four main voices, . . . is not more than four octaves . . . except in the case of Russian basses and ~ sopranos —Ralph Vaughan Williams⟩ ⟨grotesque sandstone formations, tooled by centuries of wind and weather into ~ shapes —*Amer. Guide Series: Calif.*⟩

3freak \"\ *vt* -ED/-ING/-S **:** to streak esp. with color ⟨silver and mother-of-pearl ~*ing* the intense azure —Robert Bridges †1930⟩

freaked *adj* [fr. past part. of ³*freak*] **:** marked by streaks ⟨here tall bare fells, capped and ~ with snow —John Brophy⟩; *esp* **:** colorful or vivid with contrasting streaks of color occurring capriciously ⟨the rarest moths, those ~ with azure and the deepest crimson —L.P.Smith⟩ **syn** see VARIEGATED

freak·ish \-kish, -kēsh\ *adj* **1 :** marked by freak turns of mind or actions **:** produced by such turns of mind or actions **:** WHIMSICAL, CAPRICIOUS ⟨a ~ spirit even in his kindness —Glenway Wescott⟩ ⟨a frenzied kind of person, acting on ~ impulses —Peggy Bennett⟩ ⟨a ~ structure with elaborate porches and odd-shaped windows —*Amer. Guide Series: Conn.*⟩ **2 :** being or befitting a freak **:** markedly odd or abnormal ⟨a ~ person with a great head and diminutive body⟩ ⟨a ~ gift for remembering thousands of unrelated facts⟩ ⟨how queer . . . must seem this ~ bookworm —Jean Stafford⟩ — **freak·ish·ly** *adv* — **freak·ish·ness** *n* -ES

freak of nature : FREAK 3b ⟨these *freaks of nature* include giants, dwarfs, . . . and numerous others upon whom nature has played queer tricks —A.M.Smith⟩

freakpot \ˈ==ˌ=\ *n* **1** *Brit* **:** a deal in poker with deuces wild **2 freakpots** *n pl but sing in constr, Brit* **:** a game in which deuces are always wild

freak show *n* **:** an exhibition (as a sideshow) featuring freaks of nature

freaky \ˈfrēkē\ *adj* -ER/-EST **:** FREAKISH

fream \ˈfrēm\ *vi* -ED/-ING/-S [perh. modif. of L *fremere* to roar, murmur — more at FREMITUS] *of a boar* **:** to make the roaring cry characteristic of rutting

freat \ˈfrēt\ *var of* FREIT

1freath \ˈfrēth\ *vi* -ED/-ING/-S [prob. alter. of ²*froth*] *Scot* **:** to froth and foam ⟨see the ale ~⟩

2freath \"\ *n* -s [prob. alter. of ¹*froth*] *Scot* **:** FOAM

freck \ˈfrek\ *adj* [ME *frek,* fr. OE *frec* greedy, eager, bold, dangerous — more at FREAK] **1** *dial Brit* **a :** EAGER, READY **b :** FORWARD, IMPETUOUS **2** *now chiefly Scot* **:** stout and strong **:** HEARTY

freck·en \ˈfrekən\ *n* -s [ME *freken, fraken*] *now dial* **:** FRECKLE

1freckle \ˈfrekəl\ *n* -s [ME *frekel, frakel,* alter. of *freken, fraken,* of Scand origin; akin to ON *freknōttr* freckled, Icel & Norw dial. *frekna* freckle; akin to MHG *sprinkel, sprenkel* spot, OE *spearca* spark — more at SPARK] **1 a :** a small brownish spot in the skin usu. due to precipitation of pigment on exposure to sunlight — called also *ephelis;* compare LENTIGO **b :** any spot or small bit of coloring or discoloration ⟨you felt that the sun would . . . send little ~s of light to dance upon her —Edith Sitwell⟩; *specif* **:** a superficial spot on the skin of fruits (as in peach scab) **2 :** an instance of freckling or a spotted condition produced by or resembling freckles ⟨a shadowy ~ had strewn itself throughout her ivory skin —Glenway Wescott⟩ ⟨the ~ of red villas on the coast —Virginia Woolf⟩

2freckle \"\ *vb* **freckled; freckled; freckling** \-k(ə)liŋ\ **freckles** *vt* **:** to sprinkle or mark with freckles or small spots **:** SPOT ⟨the tiny, black spots (actually, a species of mushroom) that ~ their walls —P.E.Deutschman⟩ ⟨watching the lights from outside my window ~ the ceiling with color —E.L. Wallant⟩ **~** *vi* **:** to become covered or marked with freckles ⟨a skin that ~s but does not tan in the sun⟩

freck·led \-ld\ *adj* [ME *frekled, frakled,* fr. *frekel, frakel* + *-ed*] **:** spotted with or as if with freckles **:** SPECKLED ⟨a ~ face⟩ ⟨two damp rooms with lichen-*freckled* walls —Anne S. Mehdevi⟩ — **freck·led·ness** *n* -ES

freckled duck *n* **:** an Australian and Tasmanian duck (*Stictonetta naevosa*) with speckled white-and-brown markings

freckle-faced \ˈ==ˌ=\ *adj* **:** having a noticeably freckled face ⟨a *freckle-faced* boy⟩

freckling *n* -s [fr. gerund of ²*freckle*] **1 :** a marking like a freckle ⟨a face covered with lines and ~s⟩ **2 :** a spotted condition; *also* **:** an area marked by freckles ⟨terrapins . . . with the thick ~ of golden pinhead spots —Gerald Durrell⟩

freck·ly \ˈfrek(ə)lē, -li\ *adj, often* -ER/-EST **:** marked with freckles **:** FRECKLED ⟨a ~ face⟩ ⟨a ~ skin⟩

fre·do \ˈfrā(ˌ)dō\ *adj (or adv)* [It, fr. L *frigidus* — more at FRIGID] **:** COLD, PASSIONLESS — used as a direction in music

fred·er·icks·burg \ˈfred(ə)riksˌbərg\ *adj, usu cap* [fr. *Fredericksburg,* subdivision of the Comanchean, fr. *Fredericksburg,* Texas] **:** of or relating to a subdivision of the Comanchean — see GEOLOGIC TIME table

fred·er·ic·ton \ˈfred(ə)riktən\ *adj, usu cap* [fr. *Fredericton,* New Brunswick, Canada] **:** of or from Fredericton, the capital of New Brunswick **:** of the kind or style prevalent in Fredericton

frederik *or* **fred·er·ik d'or** \ˈfred(ə)rikˈdȯ(ə)r\ *n* -s [*frederik* fr. Dan, fr. *Frederik* VI †1839 king of Denmark; *frederik d'or* fr. Dan *frederikdor,* fr. *Frederik* VI + F *d'or* of gold] **:** a gold coin of Frederick VI of Denmark

fred·er·iks·berg \ˈfred(ə)riksˌbərg\ *adj, usu cap* [fr. *Frederiksberg,* Denmark] **:** of or from the city of Frederiksberg, Denmark **:** of the kind or style prevalent in Frederiksberg

1free \ˈfrē\ *adj* **fre·er** \ˈfrēə(r), ˈfriə)r, -iə\ **fre·est** \ˈfrēəst\ [ME *fre, free,* fr. OE *frēo;* akin to OHG *frī* free, ON *frjāls* free, Goth *freis,* W *rhydd* free, Gk *prays* mild, gentle, Skt *priya* (adj.) dear, *priya* (n.) friend, husband; basic meaning: dear, hence, belonging to one's own family or clan, not being a slave] **1 a :** not being in the position of a slave or serf **:** having the freedom of action and the legal and political rights of a citizen ⟨an edict setting the slave ~⟩ **b :** not subject to a particular ruling, authority, or obligation **:** enjoying a special privilege or immunity **c** (1) **:** not being under an arbitrary, despotic, or totalitarian government **:** subject only to reasonably fixed laws that defend from encroachments upon natural or acquired rights **:** enjoying civil and political liberty ⟨~ citizens⟩ ⟨a ~ people⟩ ⟨the ~ world⟩ (2) **:** defending individual rights against encroachment **:** assuring or maintaining individual liberty **:** not arbitrary or despotic **:** maintained by a politically independent people ⟨a ~ country⟩ ⟨a ~ government⟩ **d :** enjoying political independence or freedom from outside domination ⟨a ~ city⟩ ⟨a ~ nation⟩ **e :** not subject to a parent or guardian **:** not being under guardianship, manus, or potestas **f :** SELF-RELIANT, INDEPENDENT ⟨my young friend, who seems to have as ~ and erect a mind as any I have ever met —R.W.Emerson⟩ ⟨endowed with a mind that was extraordinarily subtle, ~, and fertile in general ideas —M.R.Cohen⟩ **2 a :** not determined by anything beyond its own nature or being: as (1) **:** originating in the soul, personality, or pure ego **:** being without compulsion from the passions or habit or from the organism or environment **:** choosing or capable of choosing for itself ⟨a ~ agent⟩ (2) **:** determined by the choice of the actor or by his wishes ⟨~ actions⟩ ⟨~ choices⟩ (3) **:** determined by intrapsychic needs rather than by the objective demands of the stimulus situation **b :** made, done, or given voluntarily or spontaneously **:** SPONTANEOUS ⟨a ~ offer⟩ ⟨gave his ~ consent⟩ **3** *obs* **a :** of or marked by gentle birth and breeding **:** NOBLE **b :** magnanimous or generous in conduct or character **4 a** (1) **:** clear, exempt, relieved, or released esp. from a burdensome, noxious, oppressive, or deplorable condition or obligation ⟨~ from pain⟩ ⟨~ from disease⟩ ⟨a duty-*free* import⟩ ⟨~ from impurities⟩ ⟨the only spot where he was ~ from hay fever —S.H.Holbrook⟩ **:** RID ⟨she was glad to be ~ of old Matthew —Ellen Glasgow⟩ (2) **:** UNTOUCHED, UNTAINTED — usu. used with *from* ⟨interested in keeping local government ~ from profit —W.E.Jackson⟩ (3) **:** not bothered — usu. used with *from* ⟨at this stage the herring is ~ from invertebrate predators —W.H.Dowdeswell⟩ **b :** not bound, confined, imprisoned, or detained by or as if by force ⟨the prisoner was now ~⟩ ⟨cattle left ~ to range⟩ ⟨upon opening the skull a considerable amount of ~ blood is noted —H.G.Armstrong⟩ **c :** invested with a particular freedom or franchise **:** enjoying particular immunities or privileges — usu. used with *of* **d** (1) **:** having no trade restrictions **:** open for commercial purposes to everyone **:** exempt from liability to duty, tax, or toll (2) **:** duty free ⟨the refineries had an interest in ~ sugar —F.L.Paxson⟩ **e** (1) **:** not subject to government regulation except in legally designated areas — see FREE ECONOMY (2) **:** entailing, arising from, or being under no compulsion or coercion recognized by the courts ⟨no reasonable ground for interfering with . . . the right of ~ contract by determining the hours of labor —R.F.Peckham⟩ ⟨the employee was ~ to agree to working conditions injurious to his health⟩ (3) *of foreign exchange* **:** not subject to restriction or official control **f** (1) **:** having no obligations (as to work) or commitments (as to duty or custom) **:** not given over to one's customary employment or occupation ⟨the foreman of a trail herd allowed his cowhands a ~ evening when they camped for the night near a large town —*Amer. Guide Series: Nev.*⟩ (2) **:** untrammeled by duties or obligations ⟨she would, like most girls, like a year or two ~ before she entered upon motherhood —Ruth Park⟩ ⟨thought that the life of a bachelor would be *freer* than that of a married man⟩ **g :** LOOSE, INEXACT ⟨population in 1940 was only 18,000 and the current estimate is 58,000 with ~ talk of 100,000 by 1960 —*Newsweek*⟩ ⟨a scherzo is a ~ term for something rather humorous and sprightly that goes at a good clip —Ross Parmenter⟩ **h :** not being part of the time for which one is paid ⟨whether within or outside the plant, on ~ or on paid time —*Dun's Rev.*⟩ **5 a** (1) **:** not obstructed or impeded **:** OPEN, CLEAR ⟨raced the car along the ~ and open highway⟩ ⟨the boat had ~ passage along the channel⟩ ⟨a considerable amount of ~ floor space in addition to the space required for equipment —H.G.Armstrong⟩ ⟨the side with the *freest* access to its resources should be the ultimate victor —Michael Scully⟩ (2) **:** not being used or occupied ⟨tried to telephone five times before he got a ~ circuit⟩ ⟨lying on her bed waiting for the bathroom to be ~ —Charles Ingle⟩ ⟨a ~ position in a molecule or crystal⟩ **b :** not impeded, hampered, or restricted in its natural or normal operation **:** LOOSE, UNFETTERED ⟨the movement of the motor shaft seemed ~ enough⟩ ⟨found his hands ~ of the chains⟩ ⟨the runner fell into a ~ easy jog⟩ ⟨wheeled the cylinders to make certain they were turning ~ and fast —S.H.Holbrook⟩ ⟨flying from out of the jungle with a great ~ flapping of wings —Jack McLaren⟩ **c :** having liberty by reason of not being restrained, hindered, or compelled by an outward force ⟨~ to tell the truth as he sees it⟩ ⟨any member is ~ to raise any topic —*London Calling*⟩ ⟨she was ~ . . . to go where she liked and do what she liked . . . had no responsibilities, no cares —Arnold Bennett⟩ **d :** not interfered with by autocratic restrictions or autocratically compelling forces or agencies **:** engaged in by men who are politically and socially free ⟨~ elections⟩ **e :** executed or allowed to be executed without interference from the opposing side — used of a kick, throw, or hit in competitive sports **f** (1) **:** not fixed **:** not fastened ⟨one end of the rope was left ~ and trailed in the water behind the boat⟩ ⟨rising like a toy balloon that had slipped ~ of a child's fingers —Horace Sutton⟩ (2) **:** not supported ⟨the cantilever construction allowed the ~ end of the beam to project over 15 feet⟩ (3) **:** not confined to a particular position or place **:** free moving ⟨in twelve-tone music, no note is wholly ~ for it must hold its place in the series —J.L.Stewart⟩ (4) *of a particle or mass in physics* **:** capable of moving or turning in any direction **g** *of a foot or hand* **:** not being used in a particular operation ⟨while he was skating on one foot he held the ~ foot up in front of him⟩ ⟨held the chair tilted with one hand and pointed under it with his ~ hand⟩ **h** *of a missile* **:** not guided **:** not capable of being directed while in flight **i** *gymnastics* **:** performed without apparatus **6** *obs* **:** of, relating to, or located on a freehold **7 :** acting or prone to act in a way that is copious, ample, or profuse or that lacks constraint, restraint, or reserve: as **a :** not parsimonious with one's possessions **:** LIBERAL, OPENHANDED, LAVISH ⟨pretty ~ with his money⟩ ⟨the evidence of high living standards and ~ spending in New York —Dixon Wecter⟩ **b :** marked by freedom of expression **:** spoken or uttered without reserve or restraint **:** OUTSPOKEN **c :** availing oneself of or using without stint or reserve — now usu. used with *with* **d :** unconstrained by timidity or reserve **:** FRANK, OPEN ⟨most of these women of distinction were courtesans, ~ in spirit, manners, and finances —H.M.Parshley⟩ **e** *archaic* **:** READY, EAGER, PRONE **f :** observing or marked by few if any responsibilities or limitations ⟨the professor had made ~ use of cracks and weather marks on the stone, combining them with the hieroglyphics to make the translation come out right —Martin Gardner⟩ **g :** overly familiar or forward in action or attitude ⟨a young man who had been much too ~ with the ladies of the town —Harvey Graham⟩ **h :** going beyond decorous bounds **:** IMMODERATE, LICENTIOUS ⟨indulging in inexcusably ~ talk before the ladies⟩ ⟨resting her chin on her clasped hands, her elbows on the table, in an attitude which the older women thought shockingly ~ —Edith Wharton⟩ **i** *chiefly Brit, of a graft stock* **:** SEEDLING **8 :** individual and exclusive in nature as opposed to common — used of certain franchises **9 a :** not costing or charging anything ⟨a ~ school⟩ **b :** given or furnished without cost or payment **:** GRATUITOUS ⟨~ admission⟩ ⟨a ~ ticket to a circus⟩ **c :** admitted without payment ⟨the dance hall was largely filled with ~ customers⟩ **10 :** easily or readily worked or wrought **:** having a texture or structure that is loose, soft, malleable, or lacking in firm cohesiveness **11 a :** PERMISSIBLE ⟨it is ~ for him to think so⟩ **b :** being or feeling at liberty to use or enjoy — used with *of* ⟨made his friends ~ of his land and possessions⟩ ⟨made their children ~ of every novel in the house —*Times. Lit. Supp.*⟩ ⟨he was ~ of the house, and might be found at any moment, in the hall or patio, or sitting at ease in the study —R.P. Warren⟩ **12** *obs* **:** GUILTLESS, INNOCENT **13 a :** not united or combined with something else **:** SEPARATED, UNATTACHED ⟨a ~ ore⟩ ⟨a ~ column⟩ ⟨electrons . . . quite a number of them are ~, that is, they are not attached to any particular atom —*Magic of Communication*⟩ **b :** DISTINCT, SEPARATE ⟨having flowers with ~ whorls⟩ ⟨a vine with ~ stipules⟩ **c** (1) **:** uncombined with or not present as an element in other substances ⟨turkeys require ~ water for drinking purposes —R.E. Trippensee⟩ ⟨the slower flowing watercourses retain water, either ~ or in sand, all the year round —*Geog. Jour.*⟩ (2) **:** chemically uncombined or readily obtainable in uncombined form (as by heating) **:** AVAILABLE 6b **:** NATIVE 11a ⟨~ oxygen⟩ ⟨~ acids⟩ — opposed to *bound* **d :** not permanently attached **:** able to move about ⟨the ~ zooids of some bryozoans⟩ **e** *of a vowel* **:** not followed by a consonant in the same syllable — opposed to *checked* **f** *of accent in speech* **:** not occurring on the same syllable in all words **:** not fixed ⟨accent in English is ~⟩ **g** *of a linguistic form* **:** capable of being used alone with meaning ⟨the word *hats* is a ~ form⟩ — opposed to *bound* **14 a :** departing somewhat from faithfulness to an original form ⟨a ~ version of a Greek play⟩ ⟨a ~ rendering of a piano concerto⟩ **:** not literal or exact ⟨a ~ translation⟩ **b :** not determined or restricted by or observing or conforming to conventional or established forms ⟨a ~ use of the dance steps he had learned⟩ ⟨was considered her superior at ~ skating —*Current Biog.*⟩ ⟨his subjects were chiefly historical and marine, done in ~ and incisive lines —*Amer. Guide Series: Oreg.*⟩ ⟨~ rhythms⟩ ⟨the stone-cut inscriptions of today which employ *freer* forms —F.W.Goudy⟩ — see FREE VERSE **c :** of or relating to a free church ⟨a church that belongs to the ~ tradition⟩ ⟨whether that church is established or ~⟩ **15 :** FAVORABLE — used of a wind blowing from a direction more than six points from straight ahead **16 a :** of, relating to, or characterized by free men or freedom **:** resulting from freedom **:** produced by free men ⟨~ labor⟩ ⟨if we do not take such action, the ~ Pacific will be lost —*Time*⟩ **b :** not allowing slavery **:** making slavery illegal ⟨the territory of Iowa was shortly to be admitted to the Union as a ~ state —Marjory S. Douglas⟩ **17 a :** FREE-FOR-ALL ⟨a ~ competition⟩ ⟨that most pleasurable of Anglo-Saxon pastimes, a ~ fight —Winston Churchill⟩ **b** *of firearms* **:** being under few limitations for match firing with regard to the specifications of the arm ⟨a ~ rifle⟩ ⟨a ~ pistol⟩ **18 a :** not having or using **:** LACKING — usu. used in combination or with *from* or *of* ⟨footloose and fancy-*free*⟩ ⟨a germ-*free* atmosphere⟩ ⟨~ of imperfections⟩ ⟨a face ~ of makeup⟩ ⟨a statement ~ of any insulting implication⟩ ⟨a night ~ from terrors⟩ **b :** being outside ⟨the house was set up to be ~ of the prison confines⟩ **19** *of wool* **:** that has no defects **20 a** *of paper pulp* **:** that parts with its water readily — compare SLOW **b** *of a sheet of paper* **:** not containing groundwood pulp **21 a** *of a bid in bridge* **:** not made for the purpose of keeping the bidding open — used of a raise, response, or rebid that is just sufficient to overcall a preceding bid by the bidder's right-hand opponent **b** *of a double in bridge* **:** made when the opponent's bid is sufficient for game at its undoubted value

syn INDEPENDENT, SOVEREIGN, AUTONOMOUS, AUTARCHIC (or AUTARCHICAL, AUTARKIC, AUTARKICAL): FREE, applied to a state or people, stresses complete absence of external rule, control, or guidance with the full right to make all of one's own decisions ⟨the U.S. became a *free* country after the American Revolution⟩ ⟨for liberty is to be *free* from restraint and violence from others, which cannot be where there is no law —John Locke⟩ ⟨freedom makes a man to choose what he likes; that is, makes him *free* —A.T.Quiller-Couch⟩ INDEPENDENT may describe that which stands alone without relation or connection ⟨words have a meaning *independent* of the pattern in which they are arranged —Aldous Huxley⟩ Applied to nations, it indicates lack of connection with any state or government having power to rule or control ⟨the colony became a dominion and then, severing all ties with the motherland, became *independent*⟩ Applied to persons it indicates a disposition to stand alone and apart with self-reliance and without binding attachment or applies to one who has taken such a stand or stands as if in such a way ⟨in America it seems that almost one third of the voters classify themselves as *independent* and a large number of others do not hesitate to cross party lines to vote for candidates of the other party —E.S.Griffith⟩ SOVEREIGN implies both absence of a superior power over the thing described and unquestioned supremacy within its own sphere ⟨Puerto Rico . . . is a self-governing commonwealth under the American flag. It is *sovereign*, independent, and equal, but has of its own free choice, and for sound and practical reasons, entrusted its foreign and defense policy to the government in Washington —J.C.Harsch⟩ ⟨the alternative purpose proposed by the Scottish Nationalists — namely, the creation of a *sovereign* Scottish nation —*Scotsman*⟩ AUTONOMOUS may indicate an independence of a government in local matters but a degree of control over that government in others ⟨*autonomous* communities within the British Empire, equal in status, in no way subordinate one to another in any aspect of their domestic or external affairs, though united by a common allegiance to the Crown, and freely associated as members of the British Commonwealth of Nations —*Statute of Westminster*⟩ ⟨ANDORRA. An *autonomous* state on the south slope of the eastern Pyrenees, nominally under the joint sovereignty of France and the Spanish bishop of Urgel —*Americana Annual*⟩ AUTARCHIC and its variants now stress economic self-sufficiency more than political independence ⟨all of the countries of the Soviet bloc operate an *autarchical* type of economy. Striving for self-sufficiency, they buy only the barest minimum of goods from abroad —Clifton Daniel⟩ — **for free :** at no cost **:** for nothing **:** GRATIS, GRATUITOUS ⟨bought the entire stock and distributed them to all hands *for free* —Fletcher Pratt⟩ ⟨just across the river is an outdoor movie, with children hanging on the parapet trying to see *for free* —Claudia Cassidy⟩ ⟨where most of the best things in life are *for free* —Budd Schulberg⟩ ⟨publicity *for free* was not his motive either —Carl Jonas⟩ — **free in and out** *of cargo assigned to a chartered vessel* **:** loaded, stowed, trimmed, and discharged at the expense of the charterer or of the charterer and the consignee without cost to the shipowner — **with a free hand :** LIBERALLY, GENEROUSLY, LAVISHLY ⟨the company gave out gifts *with a free hand* at Christmas⟩

²free \ˈ"\ *vt* **freed; freed; freeing; frees** [ME *freen*, fr. OE *frēogan, frēon* to free, love; akin to MHG *vrīen* to free, woo, ON *frjā* to love, Goth *frijōn* to love, Skt *priyāyate* he makes friends with; derivative fr. the root of E ¹*free*] **1 a :** to cause to be free **:** set at liberty ⟨~ the slaves⟩ ⟨~ her husband to marry again⟩ **b :** to relieve or rid of something that confines, limits, oppresses, upsets, or embarrasses ⟨*freed* him of his chains⟩ ⟨~ a party of an obnoxious bore⟩ ⟨an Irish brogue from which she later found it difficult to ~ herself —*Current Biog.*⟩ ⟨human sensibility must be *freed* from the dust of erudition and the weight of tradition —Clive Bell⟩ ⟨~ another large portion of her import trade from quantitative restrictions —H.F.Tysser⟩ **c :** RELEASE ⟨~ a stuck door by throwing his weight against it⟩ ⟨*freed* rayon cloth distribution from control —*Times Rev. of Industry*⟩ **d :** to make immune or secure — used with *from* ⟨~ a child from danger⟩ ⟨good health can ~ the body from infection⟩ **e :** DISENTANGLE, CLEAR, DISENCUMBER ⟨~ a fishline from overhead branches⟩ ⟨~ a passage of refuse and debris⟩ ⟨the orange, peeled, carefully *freed* of every shred of white rind —Marcia Davenport⟩ **f :** to let loose **:** allow to go freely ⟨flower scents, that only nighttime ~*s* —Amy Lowell⟩ **2** *obs* **:** to get rid of **:** REMOVE, BANISH

syn RELEASE, LIBERATE, EMANCIPATE, MANUMIT, AFFRANCHISE, ENFRANCHISE, DELIVER, DISCHARGE: FREE is a general term often interchangeable with many of the following; it applies to setting at liberty from whatever binds, as dependence, restraint, obligation, oppression, or suppression ⟨*freed* from debt⟩ ⟨speculation could not *free* itself from the moving principles of Christian theology —H.O.Taylor⟩ ⟨the more progressive lawyers are trying to *free* their own writing from archaic terminology —Milton Hall⟩ ⟨*freed* from the tyranny of the classroom —Allen Johnson⟩ RELEASE may suggest more forcefully than FREE the action of unloosing from a confined or constrained situation without, however, necessarily implying the permanent liberation that FREE usu. does ⟨state institutions *released* on parole or some other form of conditional release a total of 34,032 prisoners —R.S.Banay⟩ ⟨it gave him the feeling that she had reclaimed, reappropriated him. No! That she had never for a moment *released* him —S.H.Adams⟩ ⟨only by indulging a deep impulse towards sermonizing could he *release* those other impulses which made him the great writer he was —C.H.Sykes⟩ LIBERATE may suggest the process or act of freeing or disengaging from bondage, restraint, or constriction, usu. with resulting liberty ⟨to *liberate* a certain group of individuals, those concerned in new forms of industry, commerce, and finance, from shackles inherited from feudalism —John Dewey⟩ ⟨to *liberate* Victorian women from the confining clothes of the period —Lois Long⟩ ⟨the central idea of Goethe's drama is that Orestes can be reconciled with fate and *liberated* from the furies of his conscience —W.A.Kaufmann⟩ EMANCIPATE may refer to the formal process of setting free after slavery; it may refer to a freeing or becoming free from previous restraints or shackles and attaining to independence of action ⟨the descendants of such slaves, when they shall be *emancipated*, or who are born of parents who had become free before their birth —R.B. Taney⟩ ⟨a Greek education which *emancipated* him from the superstitions of his countrymen —J.G.Frazer⟩ ⟨the vital necessity of education and its power to *emancipate* the working classes, mentally, socially, and politically —Alfred Plummer⟩ MANUMIT may refer to the formal conferring of freedman status on slave or serf, usu. by his owner ⟨it appears from the report, that Darnall was born in Maryland, and was the son of a white man by one of his slaves, and his father executed certain instruments to *manumit* him —R.B.Taney⟩ ⟨a master may *manumit* his slave in the church, or outside of it, before a judge or other person, by testament, or by letter; but he must do this in person —*Political Science Quarterly*⟩ AFFRANCHISE and the more common ENFRANCHISE imply freeing from subjection or other condition marked by lack of personal or political liberty, the latter usu. implying admission to full political rights ⟨every slave, after fifteen years, should be *affranchised* —W.S.Landor⟩ ⟨American Negroes emancipated by the proclamation of President Lincoln in 1863 but not *enfranchised* until the Fifteenth Amendment went into effect in 1870⟩ DELIVER still occasionally shows evidence that it is etymologically a cognate of LIBERATE ⟨from the fury of the Norsemen, Good Lord *deliver* us⟩ ⟨a rescue party was in time to *deliver* him with his head still on his shoulders —A.M. Young⟩ Similarly, DISCHARGE in some uses may indicate release from confinement, restraint, or constriction ⟨*discharge* a prisoner⟩ ⟨an honorably *discharged* veteran⟩ ⟨no person held to service or labor in one State, under the laws thereof, escaping into another, shall, in consequence of any law or regulation therein, be *discharged* from such service or labor —*U.S. Constitution*⟩

³free \ˈ"\ *adv* [ME *fre, free*, fr. *fre, free*, adj. — more at ¹FREE] **1 :** FREELY ⟨the high overtone of the saw penetrates every corner of the mill, singing when it runs ~ —*Amer. Guide Series: Ark.*⟩ ⟨a ~ moving joint⟩ **2 :** without charge ⟨children admitted ~⟩ ⟨people have traditionally been able to walk into museums ~ —Huntington Hartford⟩ **3 :** with the wind more than six points from dead ahead **:** not close-hauled ⟨a yacht sailing ~⟩

free air *n* **:** air not under restraint (as by pressure or flow) **:** normal atmospheric air; *specif* **:** all of the atmosphere usu. above 100 feet from the earth that is not greatly bound or restricted in its movements by surface friction of the earth and the resulting turbulence

free alms *n pl* [ME *fre almes*, trans. of ML *eleemosyna libera*] **:** FRANKALMOIGN

free alongside ship *or* **free alongside vessel** *adv (or adj)* **:** with delivery at the side of the ship free of charges, the buyer's liability then beginning

free and clear *adv (or adj)* **:** without liens or other legal claims ⟨after only a few months the property was *free and clear*⟩ ⟨they owned it and owned it *free and clear*⟩

free and common socage *n* **:** FREE SOCAGE

¹free and easy *adj* **1 :** marked by casualness, informality, and total lack of constraint ⟨a *free and easy* laugh⟩ ⟨the *free and easy*, open-air life of the plains —Allan Murray⟩ ⟨a *free and easy* relationship between the older and younger members of the family⟩ **2 :** not observant of strict demands ⟨a *free and easy* way with his literary judgments⟩ ⟨his reputation had been no worse than that of his *free and easy* young associates —S.H.Adams⟩ ⟨the incumbent had got fat by being *free and easy* with union money —Kermit Eby⟩ ⟨the fair, *free and easy* daughter of the leading publican —S.E.Morison & H.S.Commager⟩ ⟨too *free and easy* a community to put up with reformers or longhairs —W.S.Campbell⟩

²free and easy *n, pl* **free and easies 1 a :** a convivial party esp. in a public house **b :** a usu. somewhat disreputable music hall or tavern providing entertainment **2 :** a Salvation Army praise meeting at which joyousness and informality are esp. encouraged

³free and easy *adv* **:** in a free and easy manner ⟨a crew of young bloods who lived *free and easy* and were inclined to damn the consequences of most any act they took a notion to perform —F.B.Gipson⟩

free association *n* **1 a :** the verbal or written expression of all the content of consciousness without censorship or intellectual control as an aid in gaining access to unconscious processes esp. in psychoanalysis **b :** the reporting of the first thought that comes to mind in response to a given stimulus (as in the word association test) **2 :** an idea or image elicited by free association **3 :** a method using free association

free astray *n* **:** a shipment that is miscarried or unloaded at a wrong destination and then forwarded correctly free of extra charge because of being astray

free ball *n* **:** a ball other than a legal forward pass that is not dead and not in the possession of any player in a football game and that may be recovered by either side

free balloon *n* **:** a balloon which can be made to ascend by the use of ballast and to descend by the release of gas but which cannot be guided in flight

free-banking system *n* **:** a system under which all applicants are permitted to organize banking corporations or associations and under prescribed conditions issue notes (protected by deposited securities)

free baptist *n, cap F&B* **:** a freewill Baptist of the original group founded in No. Carolina in 1729

free bench *or* **free bank** *n* [trans. of ML *francus bancus*] **:** the interest formerly held in English law by a widow or sometimes a widower in the copyhold or customary lands of the deceased spouse — compare DOWER 1

free-blown \ˈ=ˌ=\ *adj, of glass* **:** blown without the assistance of a mold and with the use only of blowpipe and punty

freeboard \ˈ=ˌ=\ *n* **1 a :** the distance between the waterline and the freeboard deck of a ship **b :** the height that is above the recorded high-water mark of a structure associated with a body of water (as a dam, seawall, or culvert) and that is an allowance against overtopping by waves or other transient disturbances **2 :** the space between the surface of the ground and the undercarriage of an automobile

freeboard deck *n* **:** the deck up to which a ship's freeboard is measured and below which all bulkheads are made watertight — see DECK illustration

free·boot \ˈfrē,büt\ *vi* [back-formation fr. *freebooter*] **:** to act as a freebooter **:** PLUNDER

free·boot·er \ˈfrē,büd·ə(r), -ütə-\ *n* [part trans. of D *vrijbuiter*, fr. *vrijbuit* plunder (fr. *vrij* free — akin to OHG *frī* free — + *buit* booty, fr. *buiten* to exchange, plunder, fr. MD *būten*, fr. MLG) + *-er* (akin to OE *-ere* -er); akin to MLG *būte* exchange, distribution — more at FREE, BOOTY, -ER] **:** one that goes about plundering without the authority of national warfare **:** a member of a predatory band **:** PILLAGER, PIRATE

freebooty *n* [blend of *freebooter* and *booty*] *obs* **:** PLUNDER

free boring *n* **:** a milling of the rifling from a section of the bore of a firearm immediately forward of the chamber

freeborn \ˈ=ˈ=\ *adj* [ME *freborn, freeborn*, fr. *fre, free* free + *born*] **1 :** not born in vassalage or slavery **2 :** belonging to or befitting one that is freeborn

free capital *n* **1 :** capital that has numerous possible or actual uses as opposed to capital confined to a specialized use **2 :** capital available for investment

free cell formation *n* **:** a process of cell formation that is frequent in endosperm development and in spore formation in many fungi (esp. ascomycetes) and in which successive nuclear divisions are followed by the nuclei each appropriating a portion of cytoplasm and usu. simultaneously becoming invested with a cell wall and leaving a surplus of cytoplasm — compare CLEAVAGE 4c, EPIPLASM

free central *adj* **:** having the placentas on a central column of tissue that is not connected by partitions to the wall of the ovary

free chant *n* **:** a recitative for psalms and canticles having a 2-chord phrase for each hemistich

free chapel *n, Eng eccl law* **:** an English chapel not subject to the jurisdiction of the ordinary as a result of having been founded by the king or by a subject specially authorized

free charge *n* **:** the part of the electric charge on a conductor that escapes to earth when the conductor is grounded

¹free-choice \ˈ=ˈ=\ *adj* **:** of, relating to, or supplied according to the method of free-choice feeding ⟨fed solely on *free-choice* grains and meals —*Poultry Farming*⟩

²free-choice \ˈ"\ *adv* **:** by free-choice feeding ⟨salt may be fed *free-choice* —C.F.Rooks⟩ ⟨hogs fed *free-choice* on minerals, corn, and supplement⟩

free-choice feeding *n* **:** a method of feeding livestock in which various feeds are kept constantly available and the feeders are allowed to balance their own diet

free church *n* **1 :** a church whose sittings are for all and without charge **2** *often cap F&C* **:** a church not established or under state control: **a** *cap F&C, in Scotland* **:** the church organized by those who left the Church of Scotland in 1843 to be free from state control in spiritual matters — called also *Free Kirk* **b** *cap F&C, in England* **:** a nonconformist church

free-church \'⸗¦⸗\ *adj* [*free church*] **:** of or relating to a church that is not an established church ⟨the American *free-church* system⟩ — **free-church·ly** *adv*

free churchman *n, often cap F&C* [*free church* + *man*] **:** a member of a free church

free city *n* **:** a self-governing city or city-state usu. possessing sovereign power: as **a :** an Italian city-state of the 11th century and later **b :** certain cities of Germany since the 13th century having free institutions **c :** a territorial unit (as formerly Danzig) comprising a city and often adjacent areas that functions as a semiautonomous political entity under the authority of an international organization — compare CITY 2f

free classic *n* **:** an architectural style in England at the close of the 19th century characterized by an unconventional use of classical or baroque elements

free coinage *n* **1 a :** the conversion of bullion of any specified metal into legal-tender coins for any person who chooses to bring it to the mint **b :** such coinage when done at a certain fixed charge proportionate to the cost of the operation — compare BRASSAGE, SEIGNORAGE **2 :** legal-tender coins made by free coinage

free companion *n* **:** one of a band of medieval mercenaries available for hire by a prince or country **:** CONDOTTIERE

free company *n* **:** a band of free companions

free corps *n* [trans. of G *freikorps*] **:** a corps of usu. German volunteer soldiers

free counterpoint *n* **:** counterpoint freed from the harmonic and melodic limitations of strict counterpoint

free crushing *n* **:** a method of crushing ore in which the rate of feed is such that the crushed material passes freely through the crushing unit

free currency *n* **:** a currency not based on metal **:** inconvertible paper currency — compare NORMATIVE CURRENCY

freed *past of* FREE

free democrat *n, usu cap F&D* [trans. of G *freier demokrat*] **:** a member of a conservative and Protestant political party formed in West Germany that stresses individual freedom esp. in economics

free diver *n, Brit* **:** SKIN DIVER

free diving *n, Brit* **:** SKIN DIVING

freed·man \'frēdmən, -ˌman, -ˌmaa(ə)n\ *n, pl* **freedmen :** a man who has been a slave and has been set free; *specif* **:** an American Negro freed from slavery as a result of the Civil War

free·dom \'frēdəm\ *n* -s [ME *fredom*, fr. OE *frēodōm*, fr. *frēo* free + *-dōm* -dom] **1 :** the quality or state of being free: as **a :** the quality or state of not being coerced or constrained by fate, necessity, or circumstances in one's choices or actions ⟨the philosophical implications of the play theory are found in its opposition of ~ and necessity, of spontaneity and order —John Dewey⟩ **b** (1) **:** the status of the will as an uncaused cause of human actions **:** the absence of antecedent causal determination of human decisions (2) **:** self-realization or spiritual self-fulfillment that is not incompatible with the existence of natural causes of the will-act **:** SELF-DETERMINATION ⟨the Stoic conception of ~ is one of rational self-determination; free acts are those which are in conformity with a man's rational nature and, ultimately, with the rational nature of the universe —Frank Thilly⟩ **c** (1) **:** exemption or liberation from slavery, imprisonment, or restraint or from the undue, arbitrary, or despotic power and control of another **:** LIBERTY, INDEPENDENCE (2) **:** the ability or capacity to act without undue hindrance or restraint **d :** the quality or state of being exempt or released ⟨~ from care⟩ ⟨~ from annoyance⟩ ⟨~ from taxes⟩ **e :** GENEROSITY, LARGENESS, MAGNANIMITY ⟨betray him and announce either the ~ and nobility of his soul or its meanness and limitation —Laurence Binyon⟩ **f** (1) **:** EASE, FACILITY ⟨able to speak the foreign language with ~⟩ (2) **:** the quality or state of running or operating smoothly and without impediment ⟨the machine ran with greater ~ after greasing⟩ **g :** the quality of being frank, open, unreserved, or outspoken **h :** improper familiarity **:** undue social liberty **:** violation of the strict dictates of decorum or decency **i :** boldness or vigor of conception or execution **j :** unrestricted use ⟨give a friend the ~ of the house⟩ ⟨gave the visitor the ~ of the club⟩ **2 :** RIGHT, PRIVILEGE, FRANCHISE ⟨follow the . . . political line as a price for their limited ~ to preach and teach —T.P.Whitney⟩: as **a :** the right of participating as a member or a citizen often conferred as a mark of honorary distinction upon one who is not a member or a citizen **b :** a right or liberty guaranteed by a constitution or fundamental law ⟨formulated in their first civil contract certain ~s as essential to a happy people⟩ or granted by one in authority ⟨given the ~ to enter without showing his pass⟩ or assured by convention or popular sentiment ⟨no one cared if the beloved old man was allowed a ~ denied to law-abiding citizens⟩ **c :** the right or privilege of availing oneself of speech or of acting according to the dictates of conscience or utilizing, supporting, and acting according to one's own view of religion without undue restraints or within reasonably formulated and legally specified limits **3 :** a share of common land formerly allotted in Scotland to a freeman

free·dom·ism \'frēdəˌmizəm\ *n* -s **:** the doctrine that man has freedom of choice in his actions **:** INDETERMINISM — opposed to *determinism*

free·dom·ist \-məst\ *n* -s **:** an advocate or adherent of freedomism

free·dom·is·tic \ˌfrēdə¦mistik\ *adj* **:** of, relating to, or having the characteristics of freedomism

free·dom·ite \'frēdəˌmīt\ *n* -s *usu cap* [prob. trans. of Russ *svobodnik*] **:** a member of a Doukhobor sect emigrating from Russia to Canada at the end of the 19th century

freedom of contract : a power of freely contracting and freely determining the provisions of contracts without arbitrary or unreasonable legal restrictions guaranteed as a natural right by U.S. federal and state constitutions — called also *liberty of contract*

freedom of navigation 1 : the right recognized in international law esp. by treaties or agreements for vessels of one or all states to navigate streams passing through two or more states **2 :** FREEDOM OF THE SEAS

freedom of speech : the right to express facts and opinions subject only to reasonable limitations (as the power of the government to protect itself from a clear and present danger) guaranteed by the 1st and 14th amendments to the U.S. Constitution and similar provisions of some state constitutions

freedom of the press : the right of publishing books, pamphlets, newspapers, or periodicals without restraint or censorship subject only to the existing laws against libel, sedition, and indecency

freedom of the seas : the right of a merchant ship of any nation to travel any waters except territorial waters either in peace or war

[1]**free-drop** \'⸗¦⸗\ *n* **1 :** a dropping (as of supplies) from airplanes to the ground without parachutes **2 :** something dropped by free-drop

[2]**free-drop** \"\ *vt* **:** to drop (as supplies) by a free-drop ⟨lumber and a few other items were *free-dropped* from 100 feet —P.A.Siple⟩

freedwoman \'⸗ˌ⸗⸗\ *n, pl* **freedwomen :** a woman freed from slavery

free economy *n* **:** an economy that is based upon the principles of private enterprise and has a minimum of governmental restrictions — compare FREE ENTERPRISE; PLANNED ECONOMY

free electron *n* **1 :** an electron within a conducting substance (as a metal) but not permanently attached to any atom **2 :** an electron moving in a vacuum

free endpaper *n* **:** the inner leaf of an endpaper secured at its binding edge to the first or last page of a book and forming a flyleaf

free energy *n* **1 :** the part of the energy of a portion of matter that may be changed without change of volume **:** internal thermodynamic potential **2 :** AVAILABLE ENERGY

free enterprise *n* **1 :** an economic system in which primary reliance is placed upon private business operating in competitive markets to satisfy consumer demands and to maintain equilibrium in the national economy and in which government action in this respect is restricted to protecting the rights of individuals rather than acting as a directing economic force **2 :** a business enterprise operating under free enterprise

free fall *n* **1 a :** the fall through the air of a body free from guidance or restraint in falling (as from a parachute) **b :** the part of a parachute jump before the parachute opens **2 :** the condition of unrestrained motion in a gravitational field (as when the power that drives a rocket in flight is shut off)

free fantasia *n* **:** the development section of a piece of music composed in the sonata form

free field *n* **:** a sound-wave field devoid of obstacles causing reflection, refraction, or diffraction

free fishery *n* **:** an exclusive privilege of fishing in public waters that is derived from governmental grant and is independent of the soil

free flight *n* **:** the flight (as of a rocket) after the power is shut off

free-floating \'⸗¦⸗⸗\ *adj* **1 a :** relatively unattached or attached by a device that allows relatively free movement **:** moving or capable of moving in almost any direction ⟨a *free-floating* tone arm on a phonograph⟩ **b :** relatively uncommitted (as to a system of ideas or a particular purpose) ⟨was not sure how any of the *free-floating* intellectuals would vote⟩ **2 :** felt as an emotion without apparent cause ⟨*free-floating* anxiety⟩

[1]**free-for-all** \ˌfrēf¦(r)ȯl\ *adj* **1 :** unrestricted as to entries, participants, or users ⟨a *free-for-all* race⟩ ⟨a *free-for-all* discussion⟩ ⟨*free-for-all* use of patents during wartime⟩ **2 a :** constituting a free-for-all ⟨a *free-for-all* fight waged for several days over the passage of the law⟩ **b :** observing no rules or restrictions ⟨the game was *free-for-all* with no holds barred⟩

[2]**free-for-all** \'⸗⸗ˌ⸗\ *n* -s **1 :** a discussion, fight, or brawl unrestricted as to participants and usu. bound by no special rules ⟨the debate on the controversial bill was a *free-for-all*⟩ ⟨got into a *free-for-all* in a back alley with some thugs and had a tooth knocked out⟩ **2 :** an altercation that has got out of control ⟨the moderator at the town meeting raised the controversial issue and in five minutes the discussion became a *free-for-all*⟩

free form *n* **:** an asymmetrical biomorphic and usu. nonrectilinear shape used in works of art or of design esp. of the 20th century and found typically in the works of the 20th century painters Hans Arp and Joan Miró

free-form \'⸗¦⸗\ *adj* **:** of, relating to, or having the characteristics of a free form ⟨a *free-form* contour⟩ ⟨*free-form* art⟩ ⟨a *free-form* coffee table⟩ ⟨a *free-form* swimming pool⟩

free frank *n* **:** a postal frank indicating free postage

free gold *n* **:** gold held in excess of legal reserve requirements or gold certificates held by the U. S. Federal Reserve system over the required minimum set as backing for Federal Reserve notes and member-bank deposits

free goods *n pl* **1 :** goods admitted into a country free of duty **2 :** goods not subject to seizure in time of war **3 :** goods having utility but accessible in such abundance as to possess no economic value

free gratis *adv* (*or adj*) **:** without cost **:** FREE, GRATIS — not often in formal use ⟨the car was given *free gratis* to anyone guessing the right number⟩ ⟨souvenirs were *free gratis*⟩

free gunnery *n* **:** FLEXIBLE GUNNERY

[1]**freehand** \'⸗ˌ⸗\ *adj* [[1]*free* + *hand*] **1 :** executed without mechanical aids or devices ⟨a ~ sketch of a child⟩ ⟨took a course in ~ drawing⟩ ⟨~ grinding⟩ ⟨~ lettering⟩ **2 a :** not conforming strictly to an established or conventional form or pattern **:** FREE ⟨matching ribbon four inches wide makes a vast ~ X under one side of the bosom —Lois Long⟩ ⟨the procedure he used was a ~ adaptation of the one he had developed in his most recent experiments with dogs —Berton Roueché⟩ **b :** UNRESTRAINED ⟨the wealth of inspiration in the ~ imagination and fantasy of these mountaineers —Sacheverell Sitwell⟩ ⟨settled down to ~ drinking —Martin Quigley⟩

[2]**freehand** \"\ *adv* [[1]*freehand*] **:** in a freehand manner ⟨drew a sketch ~⟩

free hand \'⸗'⸗\ *n* [[1]*free* + *hand*] **:** freedom of action or decision ⟨gave him a *free hand* in running the business⟩

freehanded \'⸗¦⸗⸗\ *adj* **1 :** OPENHANDED, LIBERAL, GENEROUS ⟨for he was as ~ a young fellow as any in the army —W.M. Thackeray⟩ **2 :** FREEHAND ⟨a ~ drawing of a child⟩ ⟨dealing in pretty ~ overstatement⟩ — **free·hand·ed·ly** *adv*

free handicap *n* **:** a handicap in horse racing in which no liability for entrance money, stake, or forfeit is incurred until the weight assigned has been accepted explicitly or by default

freehearted \'⸗¦⸗⸗\ *adj* [ME *fre herted*, fr. *fre* free + *herted* hearted] **1 :** FRANK, OPEN, UNRESERVED **2 :** GENEROUS, LIBERAL — **free·heart·ed·ly** *adv*

[1]**freehold** \'⸗ˌ⸗\ *n* [ME *frehold* (trans. of AF *fraunc tenement* frank tenement), fr. *fre* free + *hold* (n.)] **1 a :** a tenure of real property by which an estate of inheritance in fee simple or fee tail or for life is held **b :** an estate held by such tenure — compare [2]FEE 1 **2 :** a tenure of an office or dignity similar to a freehold

[2]**freehold** \"\ *adv* **:** by freehold ⟨he owns, ~, an estate which is rich, though unimproved —Ian Watt⟩

free·hold·er \'⸗ˌ⸗ə(r)\ *n* [ME *freholder* (trans. of AF *fraunc tenaunt* frank tenant), fr. *fre* free + *holder*] **1 :** the owner of a freehold **2 :** a public officer in New Jersey serving on a board that has charge of the property, finances, and affairs of a county and being similar to a county commissioner or supervisor

free house *n* **:** a British inn or public house not committed to the purchase of supplies from a particular brewery

free-in-county \¦⸗⸗¦⸗⸗\ *adj* **:** mailable free of postage when sent to an address within the county where printed — used of second-class mail matter and specif. newspapers

freeing *pres part of* FREE

freeing port *n* [fr. gerund of *free*] **:** an opening covered by a hinged plate in the lower part of the bulwarks of a ship to allow deck water to run overboard

free kick *n* **:** a kick in football (as after a safety) that the opponents may not block but may run back after receiving

free kirk *n, cap F&K, Scot* **:** FREE CHURCH 2a

free kirker *n, usu cap F&K* **:** a member or adherent of the Free Church of Scotland

free·lage \'frēlij\ *n* -s [ME (Sc) *frelage*, fr. ME *fre* free + ME (northern dial.) *-lage* (as in *knawlage*, n., knowledge)] *dial Brit* **:** FREEDOM, FRANCHISE

free lance *n* [[1]*free* + *lance*] **1 a :** a knight or roving soldier available for hire by a state or commander **:** FREE COMPANION, CONDOTTIERE **b :** one who acts on his own responsibility without regard to party lines or deference to authority **2 :** one who pursues a profession or occupation usu. in the arts under no long-term contractual commitments to any one employer or company ⟨the *free lance* works from his own studio, contacting his clients when necessary . . . is paid by the job, and the number and importance of his jobs depends largely on the reputation he has built —*Design*⟩; *esp* **:** a writer who writes stories or articles for the open market with long-term commitments to no one publisher or periodical

[1]**free-lance** \'⸗¦⸗\ *adj* [*free lance*] **:** of, relating to, or befitting a free lance ⟨*free-lance* factual articles —*Americana Annual*⟩ ⟨sold . . . *free-lance* material to newsreel companies —*Current Biog.*⟩ ⟨*free-lance* illustrating —*Print*⟩; *esp* **:** independent or being under no long-term esp. contractual commitment to any person, company, group, or ideology ⟨a *free-lance* writer⟩ ⟨a *free-lance* designer of window displays —*Current Biog.*⟩ ⟨the alliance in this country between *free-lance* intellect and formal political power —*Times Lit. Supp.*⟩ ⟨left shortly for a period of *free-lance* missionary work in Chicago —Carey McWilliams⟩ ⟨a *free-lance* wearing-apparel salesman —*N.Y. Times*⟩ ⟨the *free-lance* or lone-wolf gambler is a survival of the old frontier days —D.W.Maurer⟩

[2]**free-lance** \"\ *vb* [*free lance*] *vi* **:** to act as a free lance ⟨spent ten years on the *Times*, until 1924, when he left to *free-lance*; has written novels; has contributed to magazines —Bernard Kalb⟩ **~** *vt* **:** to offer or contract for the purchase of in the manner of a free lance ⟨tried *free-lancing* his sketches in New York and London⟩ ⟨the others still *free-lance* their instrumental talents or sing at churches and with choral groups —Martin Mayer⟩; *esp* **:** to write and submit for publication in the manner of a free-lance writer ⟨he *free-lanced* pieces for British publications⟩

free-lanc·er \"+ə(r)\ *n* [[2]*free-lance* + *-er*] **:** FREE LANCE; *esp* **:** a free-lance writer

free list *n* **:** a list of persons or things for which no charge is made in circumstances when a charge is usual; *specif* **:** a schedule of commodities admitted to a country free of duty

free-liv·er \'frē'livə(r)\ *n* **:** one who lives with more than usual freedom in the gratification of physical appetites

free-living \'⸗¦⸗⸗\ *adj* **1 :** marked by more than usual freedom in the gratification of physical appetites **2** *biol* **a :** not fixed to a substrate **:** capable of motility **b :** metabolically independent — compare PARASITIC, SYMBIOTIC

freeload \'⸗¦⸗\ *vi* **1 :** to impose upon another's generosity or hospitality (as in entertaining) without sharing in the cost or responsibility involved or without making an effort to return the favor or remove the obligation ⟨big parties attended by ~*ing* pseudo opera stars —John Brooks⟩ **2 :** to take advantage of an opportunity to use without obligation property or facilities belonging to another (as a club) ⟨~*ing* public servants who dote on hauling their relatives all over the lot at public expense —*Time*⟩ — **free·load·er** \"+ə(r)\ *n* -s

freeloading *n* [fr. gerund of *freeload*] **:** the activity or practice of one that freeloads ⟨undertakes to instruct the narrator in the arts of ~ and benign swindling —*New Yorker*⟩

free love *n* **1 :** sexual intercourse or cohabitation without a legal wedding — compare COMMON-LAW MARRIAGE **2 :** the doctrine that advocates the legalization of free love

free lunch *n* **:** a buffet lunch formerly available in certain bars or saloons to those buying drinks

free·ly *adv* [ME *frely*, fr. OE *frēolīce*, fr. *frēolīc*, adj., free, freeborn, noble, fr. *frēo* free + *-līc* -ly] **:** in a free manner: as **a :** of one's own accord **:** WILLINGLY ⟨he ~ shared his supply with the needy settlers about him —*Amer. Guide Series: N.H.*⟩ ⟨asserts its intention to become a member of the international organizations of the free world and ~ undertakes to participate in the European Defense Community —*Current History*⟩ **b** (1) **:** not in bondage **:** in freedom (2) **:** by free men ⟨~ elected governments —C. E. Black & E. C. Helmreich⟩ **c** (1) **:** without restraint or reserve **:** PLENTIFULLY, ABUNDANTLY ⟨a ~ growing plant⟩ ⟨gave out largesse ~⟩ (2) **:** OPENLY, FRANKLY ⟨sometimes spoken my opinion of him, and to him, too ~ —Jane Austen⟩ ⟨he came to admit ~ that the future belonged to the man of statistics and economics —M.R.Cohen⟩ **d :** without hindrance **:** UNCONSTRAINEDLY ⟨its doors swing ~ open to all who come —*Amer. Guide Series: N.H.*⟩ ⟨within a few years the world's major currencies would be ~ convertible, freed from exchange restrictions —Fritz Machlup⟩ ⟨the wood burns fiercely and ~ in a pile —*Sydney* (*Australia*) *Bull.*⟩ **e :** with freedom from strict observance of any model, pattern, convention, or rule ⟨the detail is ~ executed —*Amer. Guide Series: Minn.*⟩ ⟨a ~ flowing line⟩

free·man \'frēmən, -ˌman, -ˌmaa(ə)n\ *n, pl* **freemen** [ME *freman*, fr. OE *frēoman*, fr. *frēo* free + *man*, *mann* man] **1 a :** one not subject to the will of another; *specif* **:** one not a slave or vassal **b :** one enjoying civil or political liberty **2 :** one having the freedom of a company or municipality **:** a member of a corporation or company or one with the full rights of a citizen

free market *n* **:** an economic market operating by free competition **:** an economic condition of unrestricted buying and selling

free-mar·tin \'frēˌmär|tᵊn, -mȧ|, |d-ən, |tən\ *n* [prob. fr. [1]*free* + *-martin* (perh. alter. of *mart* beef animal fattened for slaughter) — more at MART] **:** a sexually imperfect usu. sterile female calf twinborn with a male; *also* **:** a similar female of another species

free·ma·son \'frē¦māsᵊn\ *n* [ME *fremason*, fr. *fre* free + *mason*] **1** *obs* **:** one of a class of itinerant skilled masons of medieval and early modern times who formed associations and had secret signs as means of recognition **2** *usu cap* **:** a member of a widespread secret society called Free and Accepted Masons made up of persons who are united for fraternal purposes — called also *Mason*

free·ma·son·ry \-nrē, -ri\ *n* [ME *fremasonry*, fr. *fremason* + *-ry*] **1** *obs* **:** the craft or labor of a freemason **2** *usu cap* **:** the principles, institutions, or practices of Freemasons — called also *Masonry* **3 :** natural or instinctive fellowship or sympathy ⟨that feeling of participation in the ~ of the sea that sets the seaman apart from the ordinary chap —Peter Heaton⟩ ⟨there is no ~ like the passion for books, unless it be that of love —J.C.Snaith⟩

free methodist *n, usu cap F&M* **:** a member of a fundamentalist Methodist group organized in 1860 and dedicated to Wesleyan simplicity and an experience by each member of complete renewal in holiness

[1]**free milling** *n* **:** the treatment of gold or silver ore by crushing and amalgamation

[2]**free milling** *adj, of gold or silver ore* **:** lending itself to free milling **:** in native form and easily amalgamated or cyanided

free-minded \'⸗¦⸗⸗\ *adj* **:** having a mind free from care

free miner *n* **:** a person or association holding a purchased, limited, revocable, and renewable mining license under Canadian Dominion laws and British Columbia provincial laws and thereby authorized to prospect on unoccupied lands and to carry on mining operations subject to other conditions imposed by the law

freend \'frēnd\ *Scot var of* FRIEND

free·ness *n* -ES [ME *frenesse*, fr. *fre* free + *-nesse* -ness] **:** FREEDOM

free nuclear stage *n* **:** an early stage in the development of a female gametophyte or an embryo of most gymnosperms in which repeated nuclear divisions occur without cell-wall formation

free on board *adv* (*or adj*) **:** without charge for delivery to and placing on board a carrier at a specified point — abbr. *f.o.b.*

free oscillation *n* **1 :** the oscillation of a body or system with its own natural frequency and under no external influence other than the impulse that initiated the motion — called also *free vibration;* opposed to *forced oscillation* **2 :** damped alternating current produced by an electric impulse in a circuit but flowing while no external electromotive force is being applied

free overside *or* **free overboard** *adv* (*or adj*) **:** EX SHIP

free paper *n* **:** a certificate of manumission issued to freed slaves — usu. used in pl.

free part *n* **:** an independent part of a canon or fugue added to fill out the harmony

free pass *n* **:** [3]PASS 4d

free path *n* **:** MEAN FREE PATH

free perspective *n* **:** intentional falsification of perspective (as in painting or stage designing) for a particular effect such as the illusion of great depth or distance

free piston *n* **:** a combination of two pistons that are usu. of different diameters, are rigidly attached to the same piston rod, work in different cylinders without external connection, and are used in some pumps and pressure gauges

free place *n* **:** a scholarship granting free tuition in a British secondary school

free plac·er \'frē¦plāsə(r)\ *n* [*free place* + *-er*] **:** a secondary-school student holding a free place

free play *n* **:** unrestricted movement, activity, or interplay ⟨*free play* was being given to private enterprise and individual initiative —*Americana Annual*⟩

free port *n* **:** FOREIGN-TRADE ZONE

[1]**freer** *comparative of* FREE

[2]**freer** \'frē(ə)r\ *archaic Scot var of* FRIAR

[3]**fre·er** \'frēə(r), 'fri(ə)r, -iə\ *n* -s [[2]*free* + *-er*] **:** one that frees ⟨the ~ of the slaves⟩

free radical *n* **:** an atom or a group of atoms [as triphenylmethyl $(C_6H_5)_3C\cdot$ or hydroxyl $OH\cdot$] characterized by the presence of at least one unpaired electron and held to participate in many reactions (as polymerization and reactions in biological systems)

free rate *n* **:** the quotation established for a currency in the free foreign-exchange market as distinguished from the restricted or official rate

free reach *n* **:** a sailing reach with the wind abaft the beam

free reed *n* **:** a reed in a musical wind instrument whose edges do not overlap the edges of the opening over which it is fixed and that is used typically in the harmonium or concertina — compare BEATING REED

free rein *n* **:** unrestricted liberty of action or decision ⟨the dictator had *free rein* to do as he pleased⟩

free ride *n* **1 :** a benefit (as food, entertainment, or acclaim) gained or accepted at another's expense or without cost to or effort by the one benefiting **2 a :** a subscription to a new security offering with the hope that the bonds or shares allotted can be sold out at a profit before actual payment is made **b :** a speculation on a very thin margin or where a quick profit seems assured by government or other action **3 :** the right to receive another card in stud poker without putting any chips in the pot

free rider *n* **:** one who gets or tries to benefit by a free ride ⟨tried to run a restaurant but failed because of too many friends who were *free riders*⟩; *specif* **:** a worker who enjoys the benefits derived from a union contract and activities without becoming a member of the union

free run *also* **free run wine** *n* **:** wine consisting of juice that ran freely from the pomace after fermentation without being pressed out

frees *pres 3d sing of* FREE

free sample *n* **:** a usu. small and packaged portion of merchandise distributed free esp. as an introduction to potential customers

free service *n* [ME *fre service* (trans. of ML *liberum servitium*), fr. *fre* free + *service, servise* service] *old English law* **:** one of such feudal services as were not unbecoming the character of a soldier or a freeman to perform (as to serve under his lord in war) — usu. used in pl.

free ship *n* **:** a ship of a neutral nation free from capture in time of war even though carrying an enemy's goods — compare CONTRABAND OF WAR

free·sia \ˈfrēzh(ē)ə, -zēə\ *n* [NL, fr. F.H.T.*Freese* †1876 Ger. physician + NL *-ia*] **1** *cap* **:** a genus of sweet-scented African herbs (family Iridaceae) with bulbous tunicate corms and narrow funnelform or tubular red, white, or yellow flowers **2** -s **:** any plant of the genus *Freesia*

free silver *n* **1 :** the free coinage of silver often at a fixed ratio with gold **2 :** the advocacy of or political philosophy favoring free silver

free skating *n* **:** figure skating esp. in competition in which the skater executes skating figures or steps in an arrangement of his own devising to music of his own choice

free socage *n* [ME *fre socage* (trans. of ML *socagium liberum*), fr. *fre* free + *socage*] **:** a free tenure of land held by services of an honorable but not spiritual, military, or serviential nature — called also *free and common socage*

free soil *n* [¹*free* + *soil*] **1 :** an area in which slavery is prohibited; *esp* **:** U.S. territory where prior to the Civil War slavery was prohibited — compare SLAVE STATE **2 :** free-soil principles or beliefs

free-soil \ˈ⸗ˌ⸗\ *adj* [*free soil*] **1 :** of, relating to, or advocating the prohibiting of the extension of slavery to the territories of the U.S. prior to the Civil War **2** *usu cap F&S* **:** of or belonging to the Free-Soil party which was active during the period 1848–54 in opposing the extension of slavery to the territories of the U.S. and the admission of slave states into the Union

free-soil·er \ˈ⸗ˌsȯilə(r)\ *n, usu cap F&S* [*free soil* + *-er*] **:** one that is in favor of free soil or a member of the Free-Soil party

free-soil·ism \-ˌlizəm\ *n* -s *usu cap F&S* [*free soil* + *-ism*] **:** the advocacy of free soil

free speech *n* **:** FREEDOM OF SPEECH ⟨the first amendment to the Constitution guarantees *free speech*⟩

free-spoken \ˈ⸗ˈ⸗⸗\ *adj* **:** speaking freely **:** OUTSPOKEN

free spool *n* **:** the spool of a fishing reel equipped with a device that allows the spool to revolve without any tension on the line (as in the process of casting or trolling)

free-spool \ˈ⸗ˈ⸗\ *vt* **:** to set a device controlling the free spool of (a fishing reel) to permit the line to unreel without tension

freest *superlative of* FREE

freestanding \ˈ⸗ˈ⸗⸗\ *adj* **:** standing alone and on its own foundation free of architectural or supporting frame or attachment ⟨a ~ wall⟩ ⟨a ~ stairway⟩ ⟨a piece of ~ sculpture⟩

free state *n, usu cap F&S* **:** a state of the U.S. in which slavery was prohibited before the Civil War

free-state man *n* **:** a resident of Kansas who was opposed to slavery in the territory before its admission to the union

free stater \ˈ⸗ˌstād·ə(r), -ātə-\ *n, cap F&S* **1 :** a native or resident white of the former Orange Free State **2 a :** a native or inhabitant of the Irish Free State **b :** one professing allegiance to the Irish Free State rather than to an Irish republic **3 :** MARYLANDER

¹freestone \ˈ⸗ˌ⸗\ *n* [ME *freston*, fr. *fre* free + *stoon, ston* stone] **1 :** a stone (as sandstone or limestone) that may be cut freely in any direction without splitting **2** [¹*free* + *stone*] **a :** a fruit stone to which (as in certain varieties of peach, plum, or cherry) the flesh does not cling **b :** a fruit having such a stone — compare CLINGSTONE **3 :** a pale orange yellow that is yellower, less strong, and slightly lighter than sunset and yellower and less strong than peachblow — called also *Bath stone, Caen stone*

²freestone \"\ *or* **freestone water** *n* **:** water containing little or no dissolved substances (as calcium)

freestyle \ˈ⸗ˌ⸗\ *n, often attrib* **:** a race in which a contestant uses a style (as of swimming) of his choice instead of a specified style (as a breaststroke) to be used by all entrants ⟨the one-mile ~⟩ ⟨the prestige of winning the ~ —Shelley Mann⟩ ⟨~ skating⟩

free·styl·er \ˈ⸗ˌstīlə(r)\ *n* **:** a competitive swimmer noted for his ability in freestyle events

free-swimming \ˈ⸗ˈ⸗⸗\ *adj* **:** able to swim about **:** not attached

free-swinging \ˈ⸗ˈ⸗⸗\ *adj* **:** bold, forthright, and heedless of personal consequences or feelings ⟨a *free-swinging* soldier of fortune —Will Herberg⟩ ⟨an energetic, *free-swinging* examination of every facet of the present American educational system —*Saturday Rev.*⟩ ⟨a wrathful, indignant, and *free-swinging* account of the town's crime —Herman Kogan⟩

¹freet \ˈfrāt, ˈfrēt\ *var of* FREIT

²freet \ˈfrēt\ *dial Brit var of* ¹FRET 1

free-tailed bat \ˈ⸗ˌ⸗-\ *n* **:** a bat of the families Emballonuridae or Molossidae in which the tail is more or less independent of the posterior portion of the flight membrane

free tenement *n* [ME *fre tenement* (trans. of AF *fraunc tenement* frank tenement), fr. *fre* free + *tenement*] *English law* **:** a freehold tenement

freethinker \ˈ⸗ˈ⸗⸗\ *n* **1 :** one that forms opinions (as about religious matters) on the basis of reason independently of authority; *esp* **:** one whose beliefs differ markedly from those of an established religion usu. in the direction of skepticism or denial of established belief ⟨was far from being a religious skeptic (he scorned ~s, and was passionately devoted to the example of Christ —*Time*⟩ **2 :** AGNOSTIC **syn** see AGNOSTIC

¹freethinking \ˈ⸗ˈ⸗⸗\ *n* [¹*free* + *thinking*, n.] **:** the beliefs of a freethinker ⟨seduced by the intellectual charms of utopian socialism and atheistic ~ —G.L.Kline⟩

²freethinking \"\ *adj* [²*free* + *thinking*, adj.] **:** holding the beliefs or engaging in the reasoning of a freethinker ⟨discoveries made and offered to a ~ democracy are the basis of tomorrow's decisions —A.A.Berle⟩ ⟨reared in liberal and ~ circles —*Amer. Guide Series: Tenn.*⟩ ⟨under both church and ~ auspices —Oscar Handlin⟩

free thought *n* **:** free thinking or unorthodox thought; *specif* **:** 18th century deism ⟨the line between tutelage and *free thought* varies from individual to individual —G.B.Shaw⟩ ⟨heresies naturally grew also; orthodox thought was followed by *free thought* —G.G.Coulton⟩

free throw *n* **:** an unhindered shot in basketball that is made from behind a line established for the purpose and usu. because of a foul by an opponent and that if successful counts one point — compare BASKET; see BASKETBALL illustration

free time *n* **:** a period allowed shippers or consignees to load or unload cargo before demurrage or storage charges accrue

free trade *n* **1 a :** trade based upon the unrestricted international exchange of goods with tariffs used only as a source of revenue not as instruments to influence the quantity, direction, or price of goods traded **b :** the principles or policy advocating such unrestricted trade — compare PROTECTION 4b **2** *chiefly Scot* **:** SMUGGLING

free trader \ˈ⸗ˈtrādə(r)\ *n* [¹*free* + *trader*] **1 :** a trader among the American Indians who was not in the service of a trading company **2** [*free trade* + *-er*] **:** one that practices, supports, or advocates free trade

free-trade zone *n* **:** FOREIGN-TRADE ZONE

free union *n* [trans. of F *union libre*] **:** cohabitation without marriage

free variable *n* **:** a variable whose range is not restricted by quantification

free variation *n* **:** use or usability in the same environment by different speakers or in different utterances of linguistic items that are perceptually different but semantically the same and idiomatically normal (as using either an unreleased or a released \t\ in *cat* or using either \with\ or \with\ for *with*)

free verse *n* [trans. of F *vers libre*] **:** verse whose meter is irregular in some respect or whose rhythm is not metrical

free vibration *n* **:** FREE OSCILLATION

free water *n* **:** water that is free: **a :** water that will settle from oil rapidly **b :** water in ore analysis that is not in chemical combination with mineral matter **c :** ground water free to move in response to gravity — called also *gravitational water*

freeway \ˈ⸗ˌ⸗\ *n* **1 :** an expressway with fully controlled access **2 :** a toll-free highway — compare PARKWAY, TURNPIKE

¹freewheel \ˈ⸗ˈ⸗\ *n* **1 :** a power-transmission system in a motor vehicle comprising an overrunning clutch that is interposed between the gearbox mechanism and the final drive and that makes the connection for a positive drive between the engine shaft and propeller shaft but permits the propeller shaft to run freely when its speed is greater than that of the engine shaft **2 :** a clutch that is fitted in the rear hub of a bicycle and that engages the rear sprocket with the rear wheel when the pedals are rotated forward and permits the rear wheel to run on free from the rear sprocket when the pedals are stopped or rotated backward — compare COASTER BRAKE

²freewheel \"\ *vi* **1 a :** to run freely independently of a gear by the use of a freewheel — used of a bicycle, bicyclist, or motor vehicle ⟨he ~ed down the long hill —Bruce Marshall⟩ **b** *of a clutch* **:** to operate like a freewheel **2 :** to move, act, live, or drift along freely, independently, or irresponsibly or heedless of rules, responsibilities, or consequences

free-wheel·er \"+ə(r)\ *n* **:** one that freewheels; *esp* **:** a freewheeling bicycle or motor vehicle

¹freewheeling *n* [fr. gerund of ²*freewheel*] **:** the action of one (as a bicycle) that freewheels

²freewheeling *adj* [fr. pres. part. of ²*freewheel*] **:** befitting one that freewheels **:** relatively heedless of forms, rules, responsibilities, or consequences ⟨a ~ logic —Stanley Newman⟩ ⟨reverting to . . . ~ foolishness —*Time*⟩ ⟨roams about the West in ~ style —John McCarten⟩ ⟨~ generalities —*New Yorker*⟩ ⟨a God-sent warning of his ~ grammar and spelling —Bice Clemow⟩ — **freewheelingness** *n* -ES

free will *n* [ME *fre wil*, fr. *fre* free + *wil, will* will, n.] **1 :** the power asserted of moral beings of willing or choosing within certain limitations or with respect to certain matters without the restraints of physical or divinely imposed necessity or outside causal law **:** spontaneous will or partially causeless volition **2 :** the ability to choose between alternative possibilities in such a way that the choice and action are to some extent creatively determined by the conscious subject at the time

freewill \ˈ⸗ˈ⸗\ *adj* [*free will*] **1 :** of or belonging to free will **:** VOLUNTARY, SPONTANEOUS ⟨a ~ offering⟩ **2** *cap* **:** of or relating to Freewill Baptists ⟨*Freewill* churches⟩

freewill baptist *n, usu cap F&B* **:** a member of one of three Baptist groups including an original group and dissenting Bullockites and United American Freewill Baptists that hold Arminian doctrines and observe open communion and except among the Bullockites usu. foot washing and anointing

free-will·er \ˈ⸗ˌwilə(r)\ *n* **1 :** a believer in or advocate of a doctrine of free will **:** LIBERTARIAN **2 :** FREEWILL BAPTIST

free-will·ist \-ləst\ *n* -S **:** FREE-WILLER 1

freewill offering *n* **:** a voluntary religious offering made in addition to what is required by a vow, tithe, or pledge ⟨she preached on shipboard and a *freewill offering* from the passengers enabled her to get back east —M.L.Bach⟩

freez·able \ˈfrēzəbəl\ *adj* **:** capable of or susceptible to being frozen

¹freeze \ˈfrēz\ *vb* **froze** \ˈfrōz\ *or dial* **friz** \ˈfriz\ **fro·zen** \ˈfrōzᵊn\ *or chiefly dial* **froze** *or dial* **friz**; **freezing**; **freezes** [ME *fresen*, fr. OE *frēosan*; akin to OHG *friosan* to freeze, ON *frjōsa* to freeze, Goth *frius* coldness, L *pruina* hoarfrost, Skt *pruṣvā* drop of water, ice] *vi* **1 a :** to become congealed into ice by cold ⟨fresh water ~s at 32° Fahrenheit⟩ **b :** to become hardened into a solid body by the abstraction of heat ⟨the melting was done in an Arsem vacuum furnace and the molten metal allowed to ~ slowly —*Jour. of Research*⟩ **2 a :** to become chilled with cold **:** be very cold ⟨the furnace went out and we *froze* trying to get it going again⟩; *also* **:** to suffer loss of animation or life by lack of heat ⟨the lost climber became exhausted and almost *froze* to death⟩ **b :** to become coldly formal in manner **:** act coldly ⟨the hostess *froze* and avoided us during the party⟩ **c :** to cause loss of sensitivity in or to anesthetize a part esp. by cold ⟨some dentists prefer *freezing* to the administering of gas before tooth extraction⟩ **3 a :** to remain solidly in contact or affixed by reason of freezing — used with *to* ⟨the damp clothes *froze* to the clothes-line⟩ **b :** to adhere solidly or stay immovably fixed — used with *to* ⟨the brake shoe *froze* to the brake drum⟩ ⟨a large nut to be removed had *frozen* to its bolt —G.F.Burnley⟩ ⟨under pressure and movement, two clean metal surfaces . . . will weld or ~ together, often with severe consequences —C.H. Hack⟩ **c :** to grip very tightly (as from fear) — used with *to* ⟨the terrified driver *froze* to the wheel⟩ **d** (1) *of a billiard or pool ball* **:** to come to rest in contact with another ball or with a cushion (2) *of a curling stone* **:** to come to rest against another stone **4 a :** to have its liquid content freeze **:** become clogged with ice ⟨in the winter the water pipes *froze*⟩ ⟨so cold the car radiator *froze*⟩ **b** *of a car* **:** to have the radiator liquid freeze ⟨we left the car out all night and it *froze*⟩ **5 :** to become motionless as if suddenly frozen: **a :** to stand or remain without movement or activity of any kind ⟨at the least sign of alarm, ~ in your tracks and don't move a muscle —*Boy Scout Handbook*⟩; *esp* **:** to become incapable of acting or speaking (as from fright) ⟨when I put a mike in front of her she'd ~ —Pete Martin⟩ — often used with *up* **b :** to become fixed and unalterable ⟨a perceptible tendency for the techniques of microprinting to ~ at present levels —H.M.Silver⟩ **c** *of a mechanism or moving part* **:** to cease to function or to resist movement by reason of jamming, locking, or damage **:** stick in operation ⟨the intense heat caused too great an expansion and the piston *froze* in the cylinder⟩ ⟨the speedometer *froze* at 90 miles an hour when the car overturned⟩ **6 :** to become fixed and motionless or unalterable as if by freezing ⟨the whole crowd had *frozen* into fascinated attention —Dorothy Sayers⟩ ⟨his anger *froze* into fear⟩ ⟨smiles which readers prepare for his latest effort may ~ on their faces —Laurent LeSage⟩ ~ *vt* **1 a :** to harden into ice **:** convert from a liquid to a solid by cold ⟨the low temperature *froze* the water in the birdbath⟩ **b :** to clog with ice ⟨the intense cold *froze* the water pipes⟩ **c** (1) **:** to subject in storage to a temperature below freezing ⟨~ meat to preserve it during the summer⟩ (2) **:** to subject (food packages) to intense cold and solidification into a block like ice for preservation ⟨patrons prepared and wrapped meats at home and *froze* them in their lockers —*Pa. State Bull. 433*⟩ **2 a :** to make extremely cold **:** give a sensation of extreme cold or an all-embracing sense of coldness to **:** CHILL ⟨the spectators at the game were *frozen* by the unseasonably low temperature⟩ **b :** to act toward in a stiff and formal unfriendly way **:** discourage or dampen the enthusiasm of by coldness of demeanor ⟨conducted herself with hauteur and *froze* her neighbors⟩ ⟨the director tended to ~ newcomers who stepped out of line⟩ **c :** to cause to act adversely **:** ALIENATE ⟨the object of this book being largely to persuade the prospective reader, and not to ~ him with assumptions of his mental inadequacy —C.D.Lewis⟩ **3 a :** to harden, damage, kill, or have other effect upon by the action of frost ⟨one night of frost *froze* the ground surface solid⟩ ⟨found her annuals in the garden *frozen* and blackened in the morning after the cold night⟩ **b :** to cause loss of animation or life in from lack of heat ⟨the winter struck early and *froze* several tramps sleeping in alleyways⟩ **c :** to anesthetize (a part) by or as if by cold ⟨had the inflamed appendix *frozen* —*Current Biog.*⟩ ⟨a face nicely *frozen* from injections —Monica Stirling⟩ **4 a :** to cause to adhere by or as if by the effect of intense cold ⟨the low temperature *froze* the damp clothes to the line⟩ ⟨the heat of friction *froze* the two metal surfaces together⟩ **b :** to cause (a billiard or pool ball) to come to rest in contact with another ball or with a cushion **c :** to cause to grip tightly or remain in immovable contact as if paralyzed ⟨fear *froze* the pilot to the controls⟩ **5 :** to make or cause to become fixed, immovable, inflexible, or unalterable: as **a :** to cause to stand or remain rigidly motionless ⟨the sudden noise *froze* the animal in an attitude of fright⟩ ⟨the sound of her name . . . *froze* her on the bottom step —Berton Roueché⟩ ⟨it isn't fear-paralysis that keeps a rabbit *frozen* in its squat at the sound of a shot —*Sydney (Australia) Bull.*⟩ **b :** to fix securely, permanently, or irremovably ⟨premature choices tend to lead you into, and ~ you in, occupations which will be inadequately rewarding spiritually —H.M.Wriston⟩ ⟨he had concluded that the city-manager plan would tend to ~ in office whoever won the first election —Darrell Garwood⟩ **c :** to harden into inflexibility or convert as if by hardening into a rigid unchanging form ⟨his mind shut hard . . . upon his first impressions and *froze* them to unalterable convictions —Virginia Woolf⟩ ⟨most social planning to date aims essentially to ~ most of the existing cultural values —A.L.Kroeber⟩ ⟨a scholastic tendency to ~ our concepts of a writer's life —Jay Leyda⟩ ⟨tend to ~ his message into an orthodoxy —André Martinet⟩ **d :** to fix so as to maintain unaltered in form, condition, or relationship: (1) **:** to stop any further alteration in ⟨a system of rules which ~s a social position and keeps one class or race on top of another —Philip Mason⟩ ⟨~ designs and go into production on current aircraft models —*Newsweek*⟩ ⟨that all unresolved problems . . . be *frozen* for ten years during which concerted efforts would be made to seek permanent peaceful solutions —*N.Y. Times*⟩ ⟨*freezing* the status quo —A.H.Vandenberg †1951⟩ (2) **:** to fix inflexibly (as by executive order) at a point or in a status governing or prevailing on a particular day ⟨~ the price on essential commodities⟩ ⟨~ wages as of the last pay period⟩ (3) **:** to forbid further manufacture, use, or sale of (a raw material) (4) **:** to immobilize by governmental regulation or legislation the expenditure, withdrawal, or exchange of (foreign-owned bank balances) — compare BLOCK *vt* 1h (5) **:** to forbid (a worker) to leave or change a job (6) **:** to counteract the growth, expansion, or development of ⟨the older generation was trying to ~ the country and make it static —Hugh MacLennan⟩ (7) **:** to prevent the use of (money) by tying up (as in capital stock or inventory) ⟨the amount of additional capital *frozen* into the inventory of every tire or oil outlet by the new taxes —T.H.White b. 1915⟩ ⟨another step to free *frozen* money —P.J.O'Brien⟩ **6 a :** to make (as the face) expressionless ⟨with instructions to recognize no one; and in fact he did ~ his face up when an old acquaintance hailed him —Fletcher Pratt⟩ ⟨a look of incredulity *froze* his face . . . and his eyes went blank with surprise —Hamilton Basso⟩ **b :** to preserve rigidly a particular expression on ⟨he still sat, his face *frozen* in shame and misery —Agnes S. Turnbull⟩ **7 :** to make inaccessible **:** prevent access to or use of ⟨police chiefs here and there are constantly *freezing* their records to protect someone —*Quill*⟩ **8 a :** to photograph as static a single point in (fast action) or in the action of (something in fast motion) ⟨pictures made with speedlights . . . ~ action completely —Bruce Downes⟩ ⟨the camera . . . is capable of *freezing* the whirring of a moving fan blade —*Science News Letter*⟩ ⟨high speed photography that *freezes* bullets in flight —*Time*⟩ **b :** to preserve in a relatively permanent and unalterable form ⟨the tape could ~ the speech of a native and repeat it as often as desired —N.A.McQuown⟩ **9 :** to attempt to keep possession of (a ball or puck) in the closing minutes of play (as in a basketball or hockey game) without an attempt to score in order to protect a small lead ⟨they decided to play a defensive game and ~ the ball —A.J.Liebling⟩ **10 :** to play a wild card on (the discard pile) in canasta and related games — compare FROZEN 2e

²freeze \"\ *n* -s [ME *frese*, fr. *fresen*, v. — more at ¹FREEZE] **1 :** a state of weather marked by unusually low temperature esp. when below the freezing point ⟨the ~ . . . destroyed the citrus groves —*Amer. Guide Series: Fla.*⟩ **2 :** an act or instance of freezing **:** the state of being frozen **3 a :** a legislative or administrative and usu. emergency action intended to restrict or forbid something (as the use or manufacture of goods needed in a war effort) or prevent alteration (as in wages, prices, job positions, or manufacturing quotas) ⟨clamped a ~ on certain steel stocks, ordered warehouses to ship them only to defense contractors —*Time*⟩ ⟨the military ~ on all multi-engine helicopter production —F.B.Lee⟩ ⟨a three-and-a-half-year Federal ~ on station building —*Newsweek*⟩ ⟨a ~ is the logical first technique in price control —T.B.Worsley⟩ ⟨the 60-day temporary ~ of food prices —*Business Week*⟩ **b** *slang* **:** cold and unfriendly treatment **c :** a keeping possession of the ball or puck (as in basketball or hockey) with no effort at scoring often in the last minutes of play in order to prevent scoring by one's opponent ⟨one never knows when the ~ will be needed to stave off the last-minute rally of an opponent —*Athletic Jour.*⟩

freeze-dry \ˈ⸗ˈ⸗\ *vt* **:** to dry in a frozen state under high vacuum so that ice or other frozen solvent sublimes rapidly and a porous solid remains **:** LYOPHILIZE

freeze dryer *n* **:** an apparatus used for freeze-drying

freeze-drying *n* -s [fr. gerund of *freeze-dry*] **:** the process by which matter is freeze-dried **:** LYOPHILIZATION

freeze·me·ter \ˈfrēzˌmēd·ə(r)\ *n* [*freeze* + *-meter*] **:** a hydrometer designed to test the strength of antifreeze solutions in automobile radiators

freeze out *vt* [¹*freeze* + *out*] **1 a :** to drive out or exclude by cold ⟨the drop in temperature when the furnace went out *froze out* the club meeting⟩ **b :** to drive out or eliminate from competition or eliminate or exclude from a position of intimacy, significance, influence, or authority esp. by stratagem, by coldly formal rejection, or by force ⟨the depression *froze out* most of his competitors⟩ ⟨the majority stockholders *froze out* the minority and took over the business⟩ ⟨tended to *freeze* out newcomers until their family and educational backgrounds had been ascertained⟩ **2 :** to eliminate from a game of freeze-out

freeze-out \ˈ⸗ˌ⸗\ *n* -s [*freeze out*] **1 :** elimination or exclusion by freezing out **2 :** a method of playing poker by which the players start with agreed-upon capital to which they cannot add or from which they can withdraw nothing, each player being forced to drop out of the game as soon as his capital is lost and all stakes thus going to the last remaining player; *also* **:** a poker game played by this method

freeze over *vb* [¹*freeze* + *over*] *vi* **:** to become covered with a layer of ice ⟨the pond *froze over* as early as October⟩ ~ *vt* **:** to cause to become covered with a layer of ice ⟨a single night's cold was enough to *freeze over* the pond⟩

freeze-over \ˈ⸗ˌ⸗⸗\ *n* -s [*freeze over*] **:** an instance of freezing over ⟨going skating at the first *freeze-over* on the pond⟩

freeze-proof \ˈ⸗ˈ⸗\ *vt* [²*freeze* + *-proof* (as in *waterproof*, v.)] **:** to protect (as shipments of coal) from forming a hard solid mass in cold weather

freez·er \ˈfrēzə(r)\ *n* -s **1 :** one that freezes or keeps very cold: **a :** a hand-operated machine that freezes ice cream **b :** an operator of an ice-cream freezing machine **c :** a railroad refrigerator car **d** (1) **:** an insulated compartment or room equipped to freeze perishable foods rapidly at a temperature of −10° to −30° F to prepare them for storage in a locker at subfreezing temperature (2) **:** a cabinet equipped with both a quick-freezing unit and a storage locker or a single compartment for both quick-freezing and storage esp. for the use of one family — called also *home freezer* (3) **:** a refrigerated room **e :** a food processor who operates a food-freezing plant **2** *Austral* **:** a sheep bred and raised for export as frozen meat **3 :** a tool used in metalcraft for retouching castings **4** *slang* **:** PRISON, JAIL

freezer 1a

freezer burn *n* **:** light-colored spots developed in frozen foods (as poultry and meat) as a result of surface evaporation and

drying when improperly or inadequately wrapped or packaged
freezer locker *n* **:** a storage unit in a commercial food-freezing plant
freez·er·ship \'==,ship\ *n* **:** a ship designed for the transporting of frozen fish
freezes *pres 3d sing of* FREEZE, *pl of* FREEZE
freeze–up \'=,=\ *n* -s [*freeze up* (verb phrase), fr. 1*freeze* + *up*] **1 :** a freezing over of a body of water esp. when marking the onset of winter ⟨goes on duty in April, just before the swans arrive, and stays with them until they leave at *freeze-up* —Lyn Harrington⟩ **2 :** a period during which the bodies of water in an area are frozen over ⟨the *freeze-up* lasted six weeks last year⟩ ⟨before the *freeze-up* sets in —V.E.Fuchs⟩ ⟨all their food for seven months had to be taken to camp before the winter *freeze-up* —Bill Wolf⟩
1**freezing** *adj* [fr. pres. part. of 1*freeze*] **1 :** being at or below freezing point ⟨the temperature is ~⟩ **2 :** very cold ⟨hurry up and let's get indoors because I'm ~⟩ **3** *of precipitation* **:** falling to earth in a liquid state and then usu. partially freezing on exposed surfaces ⟨a ~ drizzle⟩ ⟨a ~ rain⟩ — **freez·ing·ly** *adv*
2**freezing** *adv* **:** to a freezing degree ⟨~ cold weather⟩
3**freezing** *n* -s [fr. gerund of 1*freeze*] **:** the method by which foods are frozen to preserve them
freezing mixture *n* [*freezing* fr. gerund of 1*freeze*] **:** a mixture (as of salt and ice or of dry ice and acetone) for producing intense cold
freezing point *n* [*freezing* fr. gerund of 1*freeze*] **:** the temperature at which a liquid solidifies; *specif* **:** the temperature at which the liquid and solid states of the substance are in equilibrium at atmospheric pressure **:** MELTING POINT ⟨the *freezing point* of water is 0°C or 32°F⟩
freezing–point law *n* **:** a law of physical chemistry: the freezing point of a dilute binary solution is lower than that of the pure solvent by an amount proportional to the concentration of the solute
freezing process *n* [*freezing* fr. gerund of 1*freeze*] **1 :** a process of excavating shafts or tunnels in unstable material (as quicksand) by freezing an area larger than the intended work and excavating in the frozen earth **2 :** a method of sinking a shaft through watery strata during the winter by thawing part way through the frozen surface with fire, digging out the softened earth, and then allowing another frozen crust to form and repeating the operations as needed
free zone *n* **:** FOREIGN-TRADE ZONE
freezy \'frēzē\ *adj* -ER/-EST [1*freeze* + *-y*] *slang* **:** FREEZING
fre·ga·tae \frə'gā,tē\ *n pl, cap* [NL, fr. pl. of *Fregata*] **:** a suborder of the order Pelecaniformes that is coextensive with the family Fregatidae
fre·gat·i·dae \frə'gad·ə,dē\ *n pl, cap* [NL, fr. *Fregata*, type genus (fr. F *frégate* frigate bird, frigate) + *-idae*] **:** a family of web-footed sea birds comprising the frigate birds — see FREGATAE
fre·ge·an \'frāgēən\ *adj, usu cap* [Friedrich Ludwig Gottlob *Frege* †1925 Ger. mathematician + E *-an*] **:** of or relating to F. L. Gottlob Frege or his contributions to the development of symbolic logic and the foundations of arithmetic
f region *n, cap F* [1*f* + *region*] **:** the highest region of the ionosphere occurring from 90 to more than 250 miles above the earth's surface and often splitting in the daytime into two layers whose heights vary — see F_1 LAYER, F_2 LAYER
frei·berg·ite \'frī,bər,gīt\ *n* -s [G *freibergit*, fr. *Freiberg*, Saxony, Germany, its locality + G *-it* -ite] **:** argentian tetrahedrite
frei·burg \'frī,bərg, -ēg, *Ger* -bu̇rk\ *adj, usu cap* [*Freiburg* im Breisgau, Germany] **:** of or from the city of Freiburg im Breisgau, Germany **:** of the kind or style prevalent in Freiburg
frei·es·le·ben·ite \,frīəs'lābə,nīt\ *n* -s [G *freieslebenit*, fr. Johann K. *Freiesleben* †1846 Ger. mineralogist + G *-it* -ite] **:** a mineral $Pb_3Ag_5Sb_5S_{12}$ consisting of a gray metallic-looking sulfide of antimony, lead, and silver
1**freight** \'frāt, *usu* -ād·+V\ *n* -s *often attrib* [ME, fr. MD or MLG *vracht, vrecht* — more at FRAUGHT] **1 :** the compensation paid for the transportation of goods or for the use of all or part of a ship, train, plane, or other means of such transportation — called also *freightage* **2 a :** something that is loaded for transportation **:** CARGO ⟨an airplane carrying a very heavy ~⟩ — see AIRFREIGHT **b :** LOAD, BURDEN ⟨a man staggering under a ~ of small logs in a basket⟩ ⟨burdened by a ~ of woes⟩ ⟨the silvery blue larkspur bending under a ~ of bees —D.C.Peattie⟩ **3 a :** freight transportation; *specif* **:** the ordinary transportation of goods afforded by a common carrier and distinguished from express usu. by lower rates, deferred dispatch, extra charge for pickup and delivery, or larger volume minimum ⟨~ is less expensive than express⟩ ⟨a ~ charge⟩ ⟨~ service⟩ **b :** a train designed or used for such transportation ⟨a 100-car ~ pounding the rails beside us —Richard Bissell⟩
2**freight** \"\ *vt* -ED/-ING/-S [ME *freighten*, fr. *freight*, n.] **1 a :** to load (as a ship or plane) with goods for transportation **:** furnish with freight ⟨a ship being ~*ed* at the dockside⟩ **b :** to weigh down **:** LOAD, BURDEN ⟨a time . . . so ~*ed* with conflicting and violent emotion —Marya Mannes⟩ ⟨~*ed* with the . . . fears of millions of mankind —A.E.Stevenson b.1900⟩ **:** CHARGE ⟨persistent delinquency . . . heavily ~*ed* with neurotic complications —Edwin Powers & Helen Witmer⟩ ⟨every word he spoke was ~*ed* with meaning for the American way of self-government —C.A.Beard⟩ ⟨~*ed* with dark torment and intimate self-revelation —A.M.Schlesinger b.1917⟩; *esp* **:** to charge or burden (as a piece of writing) with significance or meanings esp. too heavily ⟨his gaiety was serious . . . his comedy was ~*ed* —Francis Hackett⟩ ⟨there is a minimum of ~*ed* sermonizing, which usually bores the reader and consequently wastes the message —Siegfried Mandel⟩ ⟨those oddly associated adjectives were ~*ed* for him beyond their usual connotations —F.O.Matthiessen⟩ ⟨his means of expression are so elaborate and so heavily ~*ed* —Winthrop Sargeant⟩ **c :** to make rich (as in hope or joy) ⟨their counsel is ~*ed* with the rich experience of many years of successful work —J.A.O'Brien⟩ ⟨he is ~*ed* with honors which he wears invisibly —Lucien Price⟩ **2 :** to hire or let for transportation of goods or passengers **3 :** to transport, carry, or ship by freight ⟨boats ~*ed* hogsheads of tar to the canal communities —S.H.Adams⟩ ⟨beef, pork, mutton, butter, cheese, and grain were ~*ed* out in winter on sleds —*Amer. Guide Series: Vt.*⟩
3**freight** *adj* [ME, past part. of *freighten* to freight] *obs* **:** LADEN, FRAUGHT
freight·age \'frād·ij, -āt|, |ēj\ *n* -s **:** FREIGHT
freight agent *n* **:** a carrier employee who receives, forwards, or delivers goods or who represents or directs locally the freight functions of a carrier
freight bill *n* **:** a bill rendered by a carrier to a consignee of freight and containing an identifying description of the freight, the name of the shipper, the point of origin of the shipment, its weight, and the amount of charges
freight bureau *or* **freight conference** *n* **:** a regional organization of carriers that represents all of the participating members in rate and tariff matters and in the publication of tariffs
freight car *n* **:** a railroad car for the transportation of freight
freight claim *n* **:** a demand by a shipper or consignee upon a carrier (as for reimbursement of an overcharge or for loss or damage to goods accepted for transportation)
freight·er \'frād·ə(r), -ātə-\ *n* -s **1 :** one that loads or charters and loads a ship **2 :** one whose business is freighting; *esp* **:** one engaged in the former business of shipping goods by wagon across the western plains of the U.S. ⟨the city's history is rife with stories of the wild behavior of cowboys, soldiers, trail drivers, and ~*s* —*Amer. Guide Series: Texas*⟩ ⟨as a ~ . . . his eight-mule wagon was held up by a band of one hundred raiding Sioux —S.H.Adams⟩ **3 :** SHIPPER **4 :** a ship or airplane used chiefly to carry freight ⟨makes air ~*s* out of conventional commercial aircraft —*N.Y. Times*⟩
freight house *n* **:** a facility owned and operated by a railroad for receiving, delivering, or dispatching freight
freighting *n* -s [ME, fr. *freighten* to freight + *-ing*] **:** the transporting of freight as a business or occupation
freight insurance *n* **:** insurance for indemnifying the policyholder against loss of the freight money if the shipowner cannot complete his contract of carriage because of unavoidable peril
freight rate *n* **:** the charge per unit (as per hundred pounds or per ton) by a carrier for the transportation of cargo generally published in a freight tariff
frei·jo \'frā,jō, (')frā'zhō\ *n* -s [modif. of Pg *Frei-Jorge*, lit., friar George, fr. *frei* brother, friar (short for *freire*, fr. OProv *fraire*, fr. L *frater* brother) + *Jorge* George — more at BROTHER] **1 :** the hard strong wood of a timber tree (*Cordia golldiana*) of the lower Amazon used in making pails and casks — called also *Jenny wood* **2 :** the tree that yields freijo
frei·ri·nite \frā'rē,nīt\ *n* -s *often cap* [*Freirina*, north central Chile, its locality + E *-ite*] **:** a mineral $Na_3Cu_3(AsO_4)_2(OH)_3.H_2O$ consisting of a basic hydrous arsenate of sodium and copper
freit \'frāt, 'frēt\ *n* -s [ME *frete* divination, fr. ON *frētt* news, inquiry; akin to ON *fregna* to inquire, find out — more at PRAY] **1** *chiefly Scot* **:** a superstitious observance or idea ⟨an idle ~⟩ **2** *chiefly Scot* **:** a saying or saw conveying a superstition ⟨an old ~ about the weather⟩ **3** *chiefly Scot* **:** an omen esp. of misfortune
frei test \'frī-\ *n, usu cap F* [after Wilhelm Siegmund *Frei* †1943 Ger. dermatologist] **:** a serologic test for the identification of lymphogranuloma venereum
freity \'frād·i, -ēd·i\ *adj* -ER/-EST [*freit* + *-y*] *chiefly Scot* **:** SUPERSTITIOUS
fremd \'fremd\ *adj* [ME *fremd, fremde*, fr. OE *fremde*; akin to OHG *fremidi, framadi* strange, Goth *framatheis* strange, belonging to someone else, alienated; all fr. a prehistoric EGmc-WGmc adjective derived from a word represented by OE *fram* from, away — more at FROM] **1** *now chiefly Scot* **:** FOREIGN, UNFAMILIAR **2** *now chiefly Scot* **:** not belonging to one's own family or household **:** UNRELATED — **fremd·ly** *adv* — **fremd·ness** *n* -ES
frem·i·tus \'fremәd·əs\ *n* -ES [L, murmur, roar, fr. *fremitus*, past part. of *fremere* to murmur, roar; akin to OE *bremman* to roar, OHG *breman* to murmur, Skt *bhramara* bee] **:** a sensation felt by the hand when it is placed on a part of the body (as the chest) that vibrates during speech
fre·mont cottonwood \'frē,mänt-\ *n, usu cap F* [after John *Frémont* †1890 Am. explorer] **:** a poplar (*Populus fremontii*) of the southwestern U.S. and esp. California and Arizona with whitish bark and deltoid orbicular yellowish green leaves
fre·mon·tia \frə'mäntēə, frē'-, -änch(ē)ə\ *n* [NL, fr. John C. *Frémont* †1890 + NL *-ia*] **1** *cap* **:** a genus of Californian and Mexican shrubs (family Sterculiaceae) with alternate leaves and showy yellow flowers **2** -s **:** any plant of the genus *Fremontia* — see FLANNELBUSH
fre·mon·to·den·dron \frə,män·,tō'dendrən, frē,-\ [NL, fr. John C. *Frémont* †1890 + NL *-o-* + *-dendron*] *syn of* FREMONTIA
fremont's pine *or* **fremont's nut pine** *n, usu cap F* **:** a pine (*Pinus monophylla*) of the western U.S. with leaves usu. solitary or in pairs
fremont's squirrel *n, usu cap F* **:** a Rocky mountain squirrel (*Sciurus fremonti*) with a conspicuously white-fringed tail
frena *pl of* FRENUM
fre·nal \'frēn°l\ *adj* [ISV *fren*um + *-al*] **1 :** of or relating to a frenum **2 :** LORAL
fre·na·tae \'frēnə,tē\ *n pl, cap* [NL, fem. pl. of *frenatus* having a frenum or frenulum] *in some classifications* **:** a group of Lepidoptera comprising most that have a frenulum and including the butterflies and the majority of the moths
1**fre·nate** \'frē,nāt\ *adj* [NL *frenatus*, fr. L, bridled, past part. of *frenare* to bridle, fr. *frenum* bridle — more at FRENUM] **:** having a frenum or frenulum
2**frenate** \"\ *adj* [NL *Frenatae*] **:** of or relating to the Frenatae
3**frenate** \"\ *n* -s [NL *Frenatae*] **:** a butterfly or moth of the group Frenatae
1**french** \'french\ *adj, usu cap* [ME *french, frensh*, fr. OE *frencisc*, fr. *Franca* Frank + *-isc* -ish] **1 a :** of or belonging to the people, the culture, or the civilization of France ⟨the *French* nation⟩ ⟨the *French* army⟩ ⟨the *French* countryside⟩ **b :** befitting, derived from, or suggesting the people or the culture of France ⟨*French* cooking⟩ ⟨*French* attitudes⟩ **:** made in France or copied from articles designed in or associated with France ⟨a *French* hat⟩ ⟨a *French* fabric⟩ **:** settled by the French ⟨a *French* section of the territory⟩ or made up of French people ⟨a *French* group⟩ **2 :** of, belonging to, or in French ⟨a *French* lesson⟩ ⟨a *French* book⟩ **3 :** of or belonging to the overseas descendants of the French people (as the French Canadians) — **french·ly** *adv, usu cap*
2**french** \"\ *n, cap* [ME *french, frensh*, fr. OE *frencisc*, fr. *frencisc*, adj.] **1** -ES **:** a Romance language that developed out of the Vulgar Latin of all of Transalpine Gaul except the southern part and that is the vehicle of an important literature at first in a wide variety of dialects with the earliest texts dating from the 9th century and that became in a form based on the Francien dialect the literary and official language of France — see ANGLO-FRENCH, MIDDLE FRENCH, OLD FRENCH, OLD NORTH FRENCH; compare PROVENÇAL **2** *pl in constr* **:** the French people
3**french** \"\ *vb* -ED/-ING/-ES *often cap* [1*french*] *vt* **1 :** to make French in form **2 :** to prepare in a French manner: as **a :** to cut (snap beans) in strips lengthwise before cooking **b :** to cut off the strip of meat along the bone of (a rib chop) **c :** to cut (a tenderloin) into slices and pound the slices flat before cooking **3** *slang* **:** to engage (someone) in cunnilingus or fellatio ~ *vi* **:** to undergo frenching
french anemone *n, usu cap F* **:** one of several horticultural varieties of the poppy anemone
french arch *n, usu cap F* **:** a masonry construction that consists of bricks laid sloping on each side so as to meet in the center at an angle and that is used instead of a true flat arch
french bean *n, usu cap F* **1** *chiefly Brit* **:** a bean of which the whole young pod is eaten (as a green bean, wax bean) **:** SNAP BEAN **2** *chiefly Brit* **:** KIDNEY BEAN
french beaver *n, usu cap F* **:** European rabbit fur processed to simulate nutria or beaver
french bed *n, usu cap F* **1 :** a bedstead with head and foot rolled outward in scroll form **2 :** a short-sheeted bed
french beige *n, often cap F* **:** a light brown that is darker and slightly yellower than blush, deeper and slightly yellower than alesan, and redder and slightly darker than cork — called also *hopi, sunburn*
french berry *n, usu cap F* **:** AVIGNON BERRY
french blue *n, often cap F* **1 :** a strong purplish blue that is the color of ultramarine prepared artificially — called also *artificial ultramarine, French ultramarine, Gmelin's blue, Guimet's blue, lime blue, new blue, permanent blue* **2 :** ULTRAMARINE 1b
french boston *n, usu cap F* **:** a card game consisting of a variety of boston in which the bidder can either have a partner or play alone
french bowline *n, usu cap F* **:** PORTUGUESE BOWLINE
french bracken *n, usu cap F* **:** ROYAL FERN
french bracket foot *n, usu cap 1st F* **:** a bracket foot marked by simple long S-curve inner lines and slightly concave vertical outer line — see FOOT illustration
french bread *n, usu cap F* [ME *frensh breed*] **1 :** a bread with a crisp crust and little crumbling made with flour, water, salt, and leaven and baked in a stick about 18 inches long **2 :** any of various fancy-shaped breads (as French rolls and crescents)
french brier *n, usu cap F* **:** the root of brier used in pipe manufacturing
french bulldog *n* **1** *usu cap F* **:** a breed of small bat-eared dog that was developed in France supposedly from a crossing of small English bulldogs with native dogs, that is active, muscular, heavy-boned, compactly built, and weighs up to 28 pounds, and that has a large square head with well-defined stop, short nose, and a less prominent under jaw than the English bulldog **2** *often cap F* **:** a dog of the French bulldog breed
french canadian *n, usu cap F&C* [1*french* + *canadian*, n.] **1 a :** a French settler in Canada — compare ACADIAN, HABITANT **b :** one of the descendants of French settlers in lower Canada now predominating in the population of the province of Quebec but found throughout Canada as well as in New England and along the northern border of the U. S. **2 :** French as spoken in Canada **:** CANADIAN FRENCH
french–canadian *adj, usu cap F&C* [*french canadian*] **1 :** of, relating to, or characteristic of the French Canadians **2 :** of, relating to, or characteristic of the Canadian-French language
french canadianism *n, usu cap F&C* [*french canadian* + *-ism*] **:** the movement advocating the political independence of French Canada and its culture
french canna *n, usu cap F* **:** any of various large-flowered dwarf cannas that are used extensively as ornamental bedding plants
french chalk *n, usu cap F* **:** a soft white granular variety of steatite used as a grease remover in dry cleaning or for drawing lines on cloth or other special uses
french chestnut *n, usu cap F* **:** SPANISH CHESTNUT
french chippendale *n, usu cap F&C* **:** a Chippendale furniture with elaborate detail like Louis Quatorze and Louis Quinze furniture
french chop *n, usu cap F* **:** a rib chop with the meat trimmed from the end of the rib
french cleaner *n, usu cap F* **:** DRY CLEANER
french cleaning *n, usu cap F* **:** DRY CLEANING
french clover *n, usu cap F* **:** CRIMSON CLOVER
french cocklebur *n, usu cap F* **:** CAESAR WEED
french column *n, usu cap F* **:** an apparatus that is used for effecting fractional condensation and that consists of a chambered column or dephlegmator with which is connected a series of U-tubes
french combing wool *n, usu cap F* **:** wool having a staple length intermediate between that of clothing wool and combing wool
french crown *n, usu cap F, obs* **:** ECU 1
french cuff *n, usu cap F* **:** a soft double cuff that is made by turning back part of a wide cuff band and that fastens by cuff buttons or cuff links — distinguished from *barrel cuff*
french curve *n, often cap F* **:** a curved piece of flat material (as wood, ebonite, celluloid) often in the form of a scroll and used as an aid in drawing noncircular curves
french disease *n, usu cap F, archaic* **:** SYPHILIS
french door *n, usu cap F* **:** a light door in which the area included between the outer stiles and rails is divided by muntins into rectangular units provided with panes of glass; *also* **:** one of a pair of such doors mounted in a single frame

French cuff

french doughnut *n, usu cap F* **:** a doughnut shaped of cream-puff dough and fried in deep fat
french drain *n, usu cap F* **:** a drain consisting of an underground passage made by filling a trench with loose stones and covering with earth — called also *rubble drain*
french dressing *n, usu cap F* **:** a salad dressing of oil and vinegar or lemon juice seasoned with salt, pepper, mustard, or other condiments
french drip *n, often cap F* **:** DRIP COFFEE
frenched *adj* [fr. past part. of 3*french*] *of a plant* **:** affected by frenching
french endive *n, usu cap F* **:** ENDIVE 2
french·er \'frenchə(r)\ *n* -s *cap* [1*french* + *-er*] *archaic* **:** FRENCHMAN — usu. used disparagingly
frenches *pl of* FRENCH, *pres 3d sing of* FRENCH
french fake *n, usu cap 1st F* **:** a mode of coiling a rope by running it backward and forward in parallel bends; *also* **:** a modification of a Flemish coil
french flat *n, usu cap 1st F, archaic* **:** APARTMENT 1
french fold *n, often cap 1st F* **:** a folding of a sheet printed on one side into four or more leaves so that the outside pages read consecutively; *also* **:** a sheet folded in this manner
french folio *n, usu cap 1st F* **:** a lightweight writing paper often used in manifolding and for printers' proofs
french foot *n, usu cap 1st F* **1 :** a hosiery foot used in full-fashioned stockings in which the back seam of the leg is continued through the middle of the sole — compare ENGLISH FOOT **2 :** FRENCH BRACKET FOOT
french fried potato *n, often cap 1st F* [1*french* + *fried potato* (noun phrase)] **:** FRENCH FRY — usu. used in pl.
1**french fry** *vt, often cap 1st F* [back-formation fr. *french fried* (in *french fried potato*)] **1 :** to fry strips of (potato) in deep fat until brown **2 :** to cook by frying in deep fat until brown ⟨*french fried* onions⟩ ⟨*french fried* shrimp⟩
2**french fry** *also* **french fried**, *n, pl* **french fries** *also* **french frieds** *often cap 1st F* [short for *french fried potato*] **:** one of the strips of a potato that has been cut into long strips of triangular or rectangular cross section and fried in deep fat until brown — usu. used in pl.
french fryer *n, often cap 1st F* [1*french fry* + *-er*] **:** a deep open pan or kettle fitted with a wire basket in which food is placed for deep-fat frying
french gray *n, often cap F* **:** a light greenish gray that is bluer and duller than ash gray or lichen green
french green *n, often cap F* **:** a moderate yellowish green that is greener and darker than tarragon, greener and duller than malachite green, and duller and slightly greener than verdigris

french fryer

french grunt *n, usu cap F* **:** a grunt (*Haemulon flaveolineatum*) of Florida and the West Indies — called also *openmouthed grunt*
1**french guianese** *also* **french guianan** *adj, usu cap F&G* [*French Guiana*, French overseas department on northeast coast of So. America + E *-ese* or *-an*] **1 :** of, relating to, or characteristic of French Guiana **2 :** of, relating to, or characteristic of the people of French Guiana
2**french guianese** *also* **french guianan** *n, cap F&G* **:** a native or inhabitant of French Guiana
french hand work *n, usu cap F* **:** a laundry service in which fancy articles are washed and ironed by hand
french harp *n, usu cap F, chiefly Midland* **:** HARMONICA 3
french–headed \'=¦=\ *adj, usu cap F* **:** provided with pinch pleats ⟨full *French-headed* flounces⟩ ⟨*French-headed* curtains⟩
french heading *n, usu cap F* **:** PINCH PLEAT
french heath *n, usu cap F* **:** FRENCH BRIER
french heel *n, usu cap F* **1 :** a woman's shoe heel that is usu. high and pitched well forward and has a back line and breast line with a pronounced curve — see LOUIS HEEL **2 :** a narrow heel reinforcement for hosiery
french hem *n, usu cap F* **:** a small hem similar to a French seam
french honeysuckle *n, usu cap F* **1 :** SULLA **2 :** RED VALERIAN
french hood *n, usu cap F* **:** a 16th century woman's headdress covering the hair except in front and having a jeweled crescent-shaped framework sometimes with a fall of cloth and set back on the head
french horn *n, usu cap F* **1 :** a brass wind musical instrument derived from the hunting horn and consisting of a long conical tube with a narrow funnel-shaped mouthpiece at one end, a flaring bell at the other, and keys or valves and having a range in pitch of more than three octaves upward from two octaves below middle C **2 :** an 8-foot pipe-organ reed stop having a quality similar to that of a French horn
french ice cream *n, usu cap F* **:** a frozen yellow custard made with cream and egg yolks

French horn

frenchier *comparative of* FRENCHY
frenchies *pl of* FRENCHY
frenchiest *superlative of* FRENCHY
french·i·fi·ca·tion \,frenchəfə'kāshən\ *n* -s *often cap* [fr. *frenchify*, after such pairs as E *amplify: amplification*] **:** the act of frenchifying or the state of being frenchified
french·ify \'frenchə,fī\ *vb* -ED/-ING/-ES *often cap* [1*french* + *-i-* + *-fy*] *vt* **1 a :** to make French in qualities, traits, or typical ideas or practices ⟨his residence in Paris *frenchified* him in many ways⟩ ⟨the foreign intelligence agent *frenchified* his behavior and accent⟩ **b :** to make over to accord with French policies or organizational plan ⟨~ the schools of the

colony⟩ : subject to French civil or cultural control ⟨~ the islands⟩ **2 a** : to make superficially or spuriously French in qualities or actions ⟨*frenchified* bistro entertainers⟩ **b** : to make affected or somewhat effeminate : DANDIFY ⟨a mincing *frenchified* walk⟩ **3** : to make (a linguistic form) accord with typical French linguistic forms ⟨*frenchified* his name from Thomas Becket to Thomas à Becket⟩ : change (a linguistic form) to a French equivalent ⟨*frenchified* his name from Jacob to Jaques⟩ ~ *vi* : to acquire French qualities, traits, or ideas

french·i·ly \-ələ̄\ *adv, usu cap F* [*frenchy* + *-ly*] : in a Frenchy manner ⟨a *Frenchily* farcical situation —S.H.Adams⟩

french indian *n, cap F&I* : an Indian who was friendly to or strongly influenced by the French in prerevolutionary America

french·i·ness \'frenchēnəs, -chin-\ *n* -ES *usu cap* [*frenchy* + *-ness*] : the quality or state of being French or Frenchy

frenching *n* -S [fr. gerund of ³*french*] **1** : a narrowing, thickening, and crinkling of leaves characteristic of various plant diseases of which virus, nutritional deficiency, or physiological factors may be the cause **2** *in Florida* : MOTTLE-LEAF

french·ism \'fren‚chizəm\ *n* -S *usu cap F* : GALLICISM 1

french·ize \-‚chīz\ *vt* -ED/-ING/-S *often cap* : FRENCHIFY; *esp* : to alter in linguistic or literary form to approximate that of the French language ⟨"riding coat" *frenchized* to "redingote"⟩

french kid *n, usu cap F* : fine kidskin leather that is alum tanned or vegetable tanned and finished to resemble leather orig. made in France

french kiss *n, sometimes cap F* : DEEP KISS

french knot *n, usu cap F* : a decorative stitch made by winding the thread one or more times around the needle and drawing the needle back through the material at the point where it came out

french lavender *n, usu cap F* **1** : a shrubby grayish lavender (*Lavandula stoechas*) native to southwestern Europe **2** : SPIKE LAVENDER

french leave *n, usu cap F* [so called fr. an 18th century French custom of leaving a reception without taking leave of the host or hostess] : an informal, hasty, or secret departure; *esp* : the leaving of a place without paying one's debts

french leg *n, usu cap F* : a cabriole leg that is light in construction and terminates without enlargement or with a slight bulk above the foot

french letter *n, usu cap F, slang Brit* : CONDOM

french lug *n, usu cap F* : BALANCE LUGSAIL

french·man \'=mən\ *n, pl* **frenchmen** [ME *Frenshman, frensh man*, fr. OE *frencisc man*, fr. *frencisc* French + *man, mann* man] **1** *cap* **a** : a native or inhabitant of France **b** : one that is of French descent **2** *usu cap* : a French ship **3** *usu cap* : a frenched plant (as of tobacco) **4** *usu cap, Brit* : RED-LEGGED PARTRIDGE

french marigold *n, usu cap F* : a strong-scented bushy annual herb (*Tagetes patula*) having flower heads usu. about 1½ inches across and marked with red

french molt *n, usu cap F* : an irregular and atypical molt of young cage birds by some attributed to dietary deficiency and by others to the attack of an unidentified mite

french morocco *n, usu cap F* : a morocco made from sheepskin

french mulberry *n, usu cap F* **1** : a shrub (*Callicarpa americana*) of the southern U.S. with clusters of small pink flowers and purple berries that is often used as an ornamental **2** : WHITE MULBERRY

french nude *n, often cap F* : ALESAN

french ocher *n, often cap F* : YELLOW OCHER

french order *n, usu cap F* : a style of architecture characterized esp. by the use of rusticated columns and introduced by the French architect Delorme (1515–70)

french partridge *n, usu cap F* : RED-LEGGED PARTRIDGE

french pastry *n, usu cap F* : fancy pastry made usu. of puff paste baked in individual portions varying in shape and filled (as with custard or preserved fruit)

french pea *n, usu cap F* : PETITS POIS

french pink *n, usu cap F* **1** : CORNFLOWER 1b **2** : THRIFT 6

french pitch *n, usu cap F* : DIAPASON NORMAL

french plague *or* **french pox** *n, usu cap F, obs* : SYPHILIS

french polish *n, usu cap F* **1** : a rubbed and polished finish for furniture using oil and shellac; *also* : the glossy surface of such a finish **2** : a preparation usu. of shellac and oil used as a furniture polish

french provincial *n, usu cap F & often cap P* : a style of furniture, architecture, or fabric design originating in the 17th and 18th century French provinces or a style derived from or associated with this

french pusley *n, usu cap F* : a portulaca (*Portulaca grandiflora*)

french reef *n, usu cap F* : a reef in a square sail made with a jackstay on the reef band and a becket on the yard

french roast *n, usu cap F* : coffee of a darker roast than is usual in the U.S. but not as dark as Italian roast

french roll *n, usu cap F* : a roll resembling French bread in texture and oval in shape

french roof *n, usu cap F* : a curb roof much like the mansard

french rose *n, usu cap F* : a common red rose (*Rosa gallica*) the petals of which are the source of an oil used chiefly in perfumery

french sage *n, usu cap F* : JERUSALEM SAGE

french sash *n, usu cap F* : a casement swinging on hinges — compare FRENCH WINDOW

french scarlet *n, often cap F* : SCARLET 2b

french scroll *n, usu cap F* : a ball-shaped furniture scroll with spirals nearly horizontal in position — see FOOT illustration

french seal *n, usu cap F* : rabbit fur processed to simulate seal

french seam *n, usu cap F* : a standing seam made by stitching on the right side, trimming closely, turning, and stitching on the wrong side so as to enclose all raw edges

French seam

french sennit *n, usu cap F* : a sennit more open than flat and braided of an odd number (as five or seven) of rope yarns

french 75 *n, pl* **french 75's** *usu cap F* : a cocktail consisting of lemon juice, gin, angostura bitters, and sugar added to a base of chilled champagne

french silver *n, usu cap F & often cap S* : a breed of large domestic rabbits of French origin having the undercoat blue with a mingling of black and white hairs and a silvery outer coat

french sixth *n, usu cap F* : an augmented sixth chord consisting of a major third, an augmented fourth, and an augmented sixth above the lowest tone (as A♭, C, D, F♯)

french sole *n, usu cap F* : a European sole (*Solea pegusa*)

french sorrel *n, usu cap F* **1** : a wood sorrel (*Oxalis montana*) **2** : a European garden sorrel (*Rumex scutatus*)

french spinach *n, usu cap F* : RED GOOSEFOOT

french spun *n, pl* **french spuns** *usu cap F* : soft worsted yarn made by the French system

french square *n, usu cap F* : a square bottle with flattened corners used in the dispensing of liquid medicines

french system *n, usu cap F* : a method of spinning worsted yarn esp. for wools shorter than three inches — called also *continental system;* compare BRADFORD SYSTEM

french tack *n, usu cap F* : a loose invisible joining between two parts of a garment that consists of blanket stitches worked across several threads to form a bar

french tamarisk *n, usu cap F* : a Eurasian shrub or small tree (*Tamarix gallica*) with white or pink flowers that is often found as an escape in the southern U.S.

french tea *n, usu cap F* **1** : an aromatic herb (*Micheliella anisata*) of the mint family of the southeastern U.S. **2** : a tea made from a sage (*Salvia officinalis*) of southern France — called also *green tea*

french telephone *n, usu cap F* : HANDSET

french tip *n, usu cap F* : a guard formed in bookbinding by folding a narrow strip of the binding edge of an insert and tipped in by wrapping but not pasting around a fold of a signature

french toast *n, usu cap F* : bread dipped in a mixture of egg and milk and then sautéed

french toe *n, usu cap F* : a toe of a shoe having a square tip

french trumpet *n, usu cap F* : an 8-foot reed pipe-organ stop of brilliant tone

french ultramarine *n, often cap F* : FRENCH BLUE

french varnish *n, usu cap F* : FRENCH POLISH

french vermilion *n, often cap F* : a strong to vivid reddish orange that is redder and darker than mikado — called also *cadmium red*

french vermouth *n, usu cap F* : dry vermouth

french veronese green *n, often cap F&V* : VIRIDIAN 2

french walnut *n, usu cap F* : ENGLISH WALNUT

frenchweed \'=,=\ *n, usu cap* **1** : PENNYCRESS **2** : a tropical American plant (*Galinsoga parviflora*) naturalized and troublesome as a weed in Europe and No. America

french willow *n, usu cap F* **1** : ALMOND WILLOW 1 **2** : FIREWEED b

french window *n, usu cap F* **1** : a French door placed in an exterior wall and opening usu. onto a porch or terrace **2** : CASEMENT 2b

French window 1

frenchwoman \'=,=\ *n, pl* **frenchwomen** *cap* : a woman who is French

¹**frenchy** \'frenchē, -chi\ *adj, often* -ER/-EST *usu cap* [¹*french* + *-y*] : French in quality ⟨the little daughter of a very *Frenchy* lady —William Soskin⟩ ⟨a score that briskly sets about creating a *Frenchy* atmosphere —Douglas Watt⟩; *esp* : markedly, affectedly, or spuriously French in quality or French in a superficial usu. frivolous sense

²**frenchy** \"\ *n* -ES *cap* : a Frenchman or French woman

french yellow *n, often cap F* : a brownish orange to strong yellowish brown — called also *Cathay, Mexican, Yucatan*

fre·net·ic \frə'ned·ik, -etik\ *adj* [ME *frenetik* insane, fr. MF *frenetique*, fr. L *phreneticus*, modif. of Gk *phrenitikos*, fr. *phrenitis* inflammation of the brain (fr. *phren-, phrēn* mind + *-itis*) + *-ikos* -ic; akin to ON *grunr* suspicion] **1 a** : FRENZIED, FRANTIC, HECTIC ⟨a ~ but unsuccessful attempt to beat a deadline⟩ ⟨a woman who let out ~ screams after a car accident⟩ ⟨the ~ bustle on the stock-market floor following a sharp decline in stocks⟩ **b** : wild and excited ⟨a noisy ~ celebration⟩ ⟨~ cheering⟩ **2** : tense and marked by a tendency to overexcitement ⟨a thin ~ woman —C.O.Gorham⟩ — **fre·net·i·cal·ly** \-ək(ə)lē, -ēk-, -li\ *adv*

fre·net·i·cal \-əkəl\ *adj* [*frenetic* + *-al*] *archaic* : FRENETIC

fren·tón \'fren,tän, =ˈ=\ *n, pl* **fren·to·nes** \fren'tōnēz\ *usu cap* [AmerSp, fr. Sp *frentón*, adj., having a large forehead, aug. of *frente* forehead, fr. L *front-, frons* — more at BRINK] : a member of an Indian people constituting a division of the Guaicuru and comprising the Mocoví and Toba and formerly the Abipón

fren·u·lar \'frenyələ(r)\ *adj* [*frenulum* + *-ar*] : of or relating to a frenulum

fren·u·lum \'frenyələm\ *also* **frae·nu·lum** \'frēnyə-, 'frenyə-\ *n, pl* **frenu·la** *also* **fraenu·la** \-lə\ [NL, dim. of L *frenum, fraenum*] **1** : a frenum esp. when small; *specif* : a narrow band of white matter in the brain running between the upper surface of the anterior medullary velum and the corpora quadrigemina **2** : a bristle or group of bristles on the front edge of the posterior wings of many lepidopterous insects that interlocks with a process on the front wings and thus unites the wings

fre·num *also* **frae·num** \'frēnəm\ *n, pl* **fre·nums** \-nəmz\ *or* **fre·na** \-nə\ [L, lit., bridle; akin to L *fretus* relying, *firmus* firm — more at FIRM] **1** : a connecting fold of membrane serving to support or restrain (as the underside of the tongue) **2** : a fold or ridge extending from the scutellum of an insect to the base of each anterior wing **3** : a stripe of color on the cheek

frenzical *adj* [obs. E *frenzic* insane, delirious (fr. E ¹*frenzy* + *-ic*) + E *-al*] *obs* : INSANE, DELIRIOUS ⟨a certain ~ malady they call love —Philip Sidney⟩

fren·zied \'frenzēd, -zid\ *adj* [¹*frenzy* + *-ed*] : marked by frenzy : giving evidence of abnormal excitement or emotional disturbance : extremely stirred up : HECTIC ⟨could hear the prosecutor's ~ denunciations of the accused —H.W.Carter⟩ ⟨a ~ look in the eye⟩: *as* **a** : marked by extreme tense persistent and often disorderly activity ⟨a ~ buying on the stock exchange⟩ ⟨the last few ~ moments of rehearsals —*Amer. Guide Series: Calif.*⟩ ⟨wrote with a ~ facility —V.S. Pritchett⟩ **b** : loud and insistent ⟨a ~ clamor⟩ ⟨~ applause⟩ — **fren·zied·ly** *adv*

¹**fren·zy** *or* **phren·sy** \-zē, -zi\ *n* -ES [ME *frenesie*, fr. MF, fr. ML *phrenesia*, alter. of L *phrenesis*, fr. *phreneticus*, after such pairs as L *poeticus* poetic: *poesis* poetry, poesy] **1 a** : a temporary madness or insane derangement : a paroxysm from a mania ⟨was generally docile but became uncontrollable in his *frenzies*⟩ ⟨in a rage amounting to a ~⟩ **b** : a strong mental disturbance resembling such a derangement and usu. resulting in a violent passion ⟨the old man's drunken *frenzies* and the way his mulatto brood ran shrieking . . . when he turned on them with a horsewhip —Ellen Glasgow⟩ **c** : a violent mental or emotional agitation : abnormal or unusual excitement ⟨a disturbing air of ~ about his writing⟩ ⟨a ~ of delight⟩ ⟨the sexual ~ —E.A.Armstrong⟩ ⟨a ~ of resentment —*Amer. Guide Series: Oregon*⟩ ⟨a ~ of mystical exaltation —C.S. Kilby⟩ **2 a** : the activity of one that is frenzied ⟨a ~ of skiing⟩ ⟨small watercourses race in a white-capped ~ down mountain and forest slope —*Amer. Guide Series: Oregon*⟩; *esp* : intense persistent usu. wild and often disorderly compulsive or agitated activity ⟨the wild ~ of religious camp meetings —J.T.Adams⟩ ⟨the ~ of the geysers —Margaret Clarke⟩ **b** : an activity of this kind ⟨until the imagination is tortured into a ~ of baffled guessing —J.W.Beach⟩ ⟨a ~ of high living —Arnold Bennett⟩ ⟨the ~ of wartime production —*Amer. Guide Series: Mich.*⟩ ⟨a ~ of abuse⟩ **c** : intensity of effort ⟨in order to wrest a living from the soil . . . had to toil with a ~ approaching desperation —D.L.Cohn⟩ **syn** see MANIA

²**frenzy** \"\ *adj* -ER/-EST *dial Eng* : ANGRY

³**frenzy** \"\ *vt* -ED/-ING/-ES : to affect with frenzy : drive to madness ⟨the sport which *frenzies* our colleges each autumn —Frederic Morton⟩

Fre·on \'frē,än\ *trademark* — used for any of a series of nonflammable gaseous and liquid paraffin hydrocarbons that contain one or more fluorine atoms in the molecule and are used chiefly as refrigerants and as propellants for aerosols

freq *abbr* frequency; frequent; frequentative

fre·quence \'frēkwən(t)s\ *n* -S [ME, crowd, fr. L *frequentia*] **1** *archaic* : crowded state : CONCOURSE, CROWD **2 a** *obs* : frequent use or practice : FAMILIARITY **b** : FREQUENCY 1b

fre·quen·cy \'nsē, -si\ *n* -ES [L *frequentia* crowd, fr. *frequent-, frequens* crowded, frequent + *-ia* -y] **1** : the quality or state of being frequent: as **a** *obs* : frequent use or practice : FAMILIARITY **b** : the fact or condition of occurring frequently : occurrence often repeated : common occurrence ⟨the ~ of crimes has aroused the public⟩ **2 a** : the number of times that a periodic function takes on the same sequence of values as the independent variable (as one that represents time) varies through one unit : the reciprocal of the period **b** : the number of individuals falling within a single class when objects are classified according to variations in a set of one or more specified attributes **3** : the number of repetitions of a periodic process in a unit of time: as **a** : the number of complete alternations per second of an alternating electric current **b** : the number of sound waves per second produced by a sounding body (as a tuning fork) **c** : the number of complete oscillations per second of the electric or magnetic component of an electromagnetic wave

frequency band *n* : one of a succession of acoustic, radio, or spectral frequency ranges each beginning where the preceding one leaves off — compare RADIO FREQUENCY

frequency changer *or* **frequency converter** *n* : a motor generator used to change the frequency of an alternating-current circuit with or without a phase or voltage change

frequency curve *n* : a curve that graphically represents a frequency distribution

frequency distribution *n* : a systematic arrangement of statistical data that exhibits the division of the values of the variable into classes and that indicates the frequencies or relative frequencies that correspond to each of the classes

frequency indicator *n* : a one-point frequency meter that measures one frequency only and that is used in transmitting stations to maintain constant frequency

frequency meter *n* : an instrument for measuring the frequency in cycles per second of an alternating current or of a radio wave

frequency-modulated \'=‚=‚=‚=\ *adj* : modulated by frequency modulation : of, using, or relating to waves so modulated

frequency modulation *n* : modulation of the frequency of the carrier wave in accordance with speech or a signal; *specif* : the system of broadcasting using this method of modulation — abbr. *FM;* compare AMPLITUDE MODULATION

frequency multiplier *n* : a device (as a frequency changer) for multiplying by an integer the frequency of a circuit

frequency polygon *n* : a frequency curve made up of straight lines

frequency rate *n* : the number of disabling injuries of given types resulting from industrial accident per million man-hours worked

frequency response *n* : a response depicting the output-to-input ratio of a transducer as a function of frequency

frequency shift *n* : a method of communication in radiotelegraphy based on slight shifts in the carrier frequency in accordance with the code signals

¹**fre·quent** \'frēkwənt\ *adj, sometimes* -ER/-EST [ME, ample, abundant, fr. MF or L; MF, crowded, fr. L *frequent-, frequens* crowded; frequent; prob. akin to L *farcire* to stuff — more at FARCE] **1** *obs* **a** : FILLED, THRONGED — used of a place **b** : FULL, NUMEROUS — used of an attendance or assembly **2 a** : COMMON, FAMILIAR, CURRENT, USUAL ⟨cannibalism is not a ~ practice among these Indians⟩ ⟨degenerative changes are somewhat *frequenter* in patients with backache —*Jour. Amer. Med. Assoc.*⟩ **b** : happening or found at short intervals : often repeated or occurring ⟨~ visits⟩ ⟨the inns are very ~ on this road⟩ ⟨bootleg coal workings are ~ —*Amer. Guide Series: Pa.*⟩ **3** : given to some practice : HABITUAL, PERSISTENT ⟨were not ~ at visiting —Pearl Buck⟩ ⟨a ~ guest at my house⟩ **4** *archaic* : familiarly associated (as in friendship or understanding) : INTIMATE, VERSED

²**fre·quent** \(')frē¦kwent, 'frēkwənt\ *vb* -ED/-ING/-S [ME *frequenten*, fr. MF or L; MF *frequenter*, fr. L *frequentare*, fr. *frequent-, frequens*] *vt* **1 a** : to associate with, be in, or resort to often or habitually : visit often ⟨gray and white herons ~ the marshes —*Amer. Guide Series: Fla.*⟩ ⟨many ships ~ the port⟩ ⟨when I first began to ~ her house —W.B.Yeats⟩ **b** : to read systematically or habitually : familiarize oneself with the thought or writings of ⟨the lessons he proposes as the profit of ~*ing* Milton would . . . be more reasonably sought elsewhere —F.R.Leavis⟩ **2** *obs* : to use, practice, celebrate, or partake of frequently **3** *obs* : to crowd or fill **4** *obs* **a** : FAMILIARIZE **b** : to furnish abundantly ~ *vi, archaic* : to visit regularly or frequently ⟨every track nor pathway might declare that human foot ~*ed* there —Sir Walter Scott⟩

fre·quen·ta·tion \‚frēk‚wen'tāshən, -‚wən-\ *n* -S [ME *frequentacioun* frequent gathering, fr. LL *frequentation-, frequentatio*, fr. L, action of crowding or packing together, fr. *frequentatus* (past part. of *frequentare* to frequent, crowd) + *-ion-, -io* -ion] **1 a** : the act, habit, or an instance of frequenting or visiting often ⟨my ~ of the late major all the time he has been living here —Glenway Wescott⟩ ⟨his ~*s* among the scum . . . were . . . distinctly insalubrious —Augustus John⟩ **b** : systematic or habitual reading ⟨only the ~ of the old masters enables us to judge the new —Meyer Schapiro⟩ ⟨one whose mind is trained by the ~ of newspaper columns —Pier-Maria Pasinetti⟩ **2** *archaic* : frequent use, practice, or celebration

¹**fre·quen·ta·tive** \frē'kwentəd·iv, -ətiv\ *adj* [L *frequentativus*, fr. *frequentatus* (past part. of *frequentare* to frequent, crowd, do repeatedly) + *-ivus* -ive] : denoting repeated or recurrent action or state — used of a verb aspect, verb form, or meaning; compare ITERATIVE

²**frequentative** \"\ *n* -S : a frequentative verb or verb form

fre·quent·er \frē'kwentə(r), 'frēkwən-\ *n* -S : one that frequents

fre·quent·ly *adv* : at frequent or short intervals

fre·quent·ness *n* -ES : the quality or state of being frequent : FREQUENCY

fres·cade \fres'kād, -äd\ *n* -S [obs. F, fr. MF, prob. fr. (assumed) OProv *frescada* cool of the evening, cool drink (whence Prov *frescado*), fr. OProv *fresc* fresh, of Gmc origin; akin to OHG *frisc* fresh] : a cool walk : shady place ⟨where each ~ rings with melodious booing —W.H.Auden⟩

¹**fres·co** \'fres,kō\ *n, pl* **frescoes** *or* **frescos** [It, fresh plaster on which one may paint, coolness, fr. *fresco*, adj., cool, fresh, of Gmc origin; akin to OHG *frisc* fresh] **1 a** (1) : the art of painting on freshly spread moist lime plaster with pigments suspended in a water vehicle — called also *buon fresco* (2) : a painting so executed **b** : SECCO **c** : mural painting; *also* : MURAL **2** *obs* : cool refreshing air : SHADE

²**fresco** \"\ *vt* -ED/-ING/-ES **1** : to paint in fresco ⟨a ceiling decoration for the . . . Louvre has just been ~*ed* —Janet Flanner⟩ **2** : to cover (a vertical surface) : decorate heavily ⟨walls ~*ed* with little drawings in heavy frames⟩

fresco secco *n* [It, dry fresco] : SECCO

¹**fresh** \'fresh\ *adj* -ER/-EST [ME *fresh, fersh*, fr. OE & OF; OE *fersc* fresh, not salt, unsalted; akin to OFris *fersk* fresh, MD *versch*, OHG *frisc* fresh, and perh. to Russ *presnyi* fresh, sweet, unleavened; OF *freis* fresh (fem. *fresche*), of Gmc origin; akin to OHG *frisc* fresh] **1 a** : not containing or composed of salt water : not salt ⟨sediment . . . is carried out to sea much farther than if the ocean were ~ —G.E. & Nettie MacGinitie⟩ ⟨~ water⟩ **b** (1) : having or conveying no taint : PURE, INVIGORATING, LIVELY, BRISK ⟨how sweet it was to breathe the ~ air —Bram Stoker⟩ ⟨a ~ dewy morning⟩ (2) *of wind* : STRONG — see FRESH BREEZE, FRESH GALE (3) *chiefly Scot* : free from frost : OPEN ⟨our winters have been ~ of late⟩ **2 a** : newly produced, gathered, or made : not stored, cured, or preserved (as by pickling in salt or vinegar or by refrigeration) ⟨~ vegetables⟩ ⟨~ fruit⟩ **b** : having its original qualities unimpaired: as (1) : not exhausted or fatigued : full of or renewed in vigor or readiness for action : FRESHENED, REFRESHED, ACTIVE ⟨next morning he was ~ and gay, all his weariness gone⟩ ⟨had I been as ~ as when I arose —R.L.Stevenson⟩; *specif, of land* : not depleted of its fertility : recently put into cultivation ⟨New England had its troubles . . . when . . . the greater product of *fresher* lands came flooding eastward —Russell Lord⟩ (2) : not stale, sour, decayed, or deteriorated in any way ⟨meat kept ~ by refrigeration⟩ ⟨~ bread⟩ (3) : not faded or tarnished : not dim : BRIGHT, ALIVE ⟨the beams and paint are as ~ as spring —Sacheverell Sitwell⟩ ⟨the big trucks are painted a ~ white —J.K.Howard⟩ ⟨his memory is still ~ in the hearts of his people⟩ : not worn or rumpled : SPRUCE ⟨he always keeps his clothes ~ and tidy⟩ ⟨made herself ~ and recombed her hair —Agnes S. Turnbull⟩ (4) *of rock* : unaltered by surface agencies (as rain, wind, or frost) (5) *chiefly Scot* : not under the influence of drink : SOBER — used esp of someone who has just sobered up **3 a** (1) : experienced newly or anew : not known or experienced before : NEW ⟨a considerable number of ~ Lincoln letters were turned up —Bernard Kalb⟩ ⟨I got a ~ cold in my head —Tobias Smollett⟩ : ADDITIONAL, ANOTHER, DIFFERENT ⟨we must make a ~ start⟩ ⟨begin a ~ paragraph⟩ (2) : not trite or hackneyed : ORIGINAL, STRIKING, VIVID, NOVEL, VITAL ⟨can anyone hope to say anything not new, but even ~, on a topic so well worn? —H.S.Bennett⟩ ⟨language and metaphor that are . . . ~ and . . . singular today —H.V. Gregory⟩ ⟨his material is familiar; his handling of it, however, is notably ~ —M.A.Hamilton⟩ **b** : newly or recently made or received : RECENT ⟨the news he brought was not very ~⟩ ⟨those scratches are all ~ —Erle Stanley Gardner⟩ ⟨a ~ wound⟩ ⟨on striking ~ lion spoor the trackers follow on it —James Stevenson-Hamilton⟩ **c** : having little or no experience : INEXPERIENCED, RAW, GREEN ⟨coming ~ to the job —Helen Howe⟩ **d** : newly or just come or arrived ⟨the engineer, ~ out of college —Richard Joseph⟩ ⟨a new car ~ from the assembly line —F.L.Allen⟩ ⟨weekly newspaper ~ off the press —Lewis Nordyke⟩ **e** *of a cow or other female mammal* (1) : having the milk flow recently established (2) : having recently calved (3) : giving milk **f** *of a bird* : newly molted : having the feathers unworn and unmarred **4** [prob. by folk etymology fr. G *frech*, fr. OHG *freh* untamed, greedy — more at FREAK] : disposed to take liberties : SAUCY, IMPUDENT,

IMPERTINENT, RUDE ⟨he was ~ with the nurses while on duty —Greer Williams⟩ ⟨his teacher reprimanded him for being ~ —Priscilla Noddin⟩ ⟨don't get ~ with mother⟩ **syn** see NEW

2fresh \"\ *vb* -ED/-ING/-ES [ME *freshen*, fr. *fresh, fersh*, adj.] *vt* **:** to make fresh or spruce **:** FRESHEN, REFRESH, RENEW — often used with *up* ⟨back to the hotel to ~ himself up⟩ **~** *vi* **1 :** to become fresh — often used with *up* ⟨the sea was beginning to ~ up⟩ **2 :** to make oneself fresh — often used with *up* ⟨going to ~ up⟩

3fresh \"\ *adv* [ME *freshe*, fr. *fresh, fersh*, adj.] **:** just recently **:** just now **:** FRESHLY ⟨stocking his cigar case from a bundle ~ in —John Galsworthy⟩ ⟨we're ~ out of tomatoes⟩ ⟨the circus was ~ out of funds —Henry LaCossitt⟩ ⟨a ~ laid egg⟩ ⟨a ~ caught fish⟩ ⟨the sheepskin was ~ dried —Ernest Hemingway⟩

4fresh \"\ *n* -ES [1*fresh*] **1 a :** an increased flow or rush of water **:** FRESHET, FLUSH **b :** a stream, spring, or pool of fresh water **c** (1) **:** a stream of fresh water running into salt water **:** the mingling of fresh and salt waters (2) **:** the part of a river or its shores above the flow of tidal seawater **2** *chiefly Scot* **:** a period of open weather ending a frost **:** THAW **3 :** the early or beginning part of a duration (as a day, a year, or a lifetime)

fresh air *adj* [fr. *fresh air* (noun phrase)] **:** relating to a movement, place, or activity providing rural or outdoor facilities (as for health or recreation) esp. for underprivileged children ⟨a *fresh air* farm for convalescent children —M.V. Merrick⟩ ⟨*fresh air* work —J.T.McDonnell⟩

fresh breeze *n* **:** wind having a speed of 19 to 24 miles per hour — see BEAUFORT SCALE table

fresh·en \'freshən\ *vb* **freshened; freshened; freshening** \-sh(ə)niŋ\ **freshens** *vi* **1 :** to grow or become fresh: as **a** *of wind* **:** to increase in strength **:** grow more brisk ⟨the wind ~*ed* from the north quarter⟩ **b :** to become fresh in appearance **:** become brighter, more vivid, or stronger in color or vitality ⟨the flowers ~*ed* after a good watering and some warm weather⟩ ⟨at the compliment, the young girl's face ~*ed*⟩ **c** *of water* **:** to lose saltiness ⟨the water ~*s* quickly as one moves upstream from the sea⟩ **2 a** *of a cow or other milch animal* **:** to come into milk **b :** to give birth to young **3 :** to wash the hands and face, take a shower, put on clean clothes, or perform other operations designed to improve one's appearance or encourage a sense of well-being — usu. used with *up* ⟨went back to the hotel to ~ up before going out to dinner⟩ ⟨went to her room to ~ after the long night and day journey —James Reynolds⟩ **~** *vt* **1 :** to make fresh: as **a :** to separate (as water) from saline ingredients **:** make less salty ⟨~ salt fish⟩ **b :** to make fresher, newer, or more interesting in appearance or constitution **:** make brighter, more vivid, or stronger in color or vitality — sometimes used with *up; also* **:** REFRESH, REVIVE ⟨like a wind of morning rising from the sea, it stirred his hair and ~*ed* him —R.O.Bowen⟩ ⟨in season pink and white dogwood ~ the scene —*Amer. Guide Series: Pa.*⟩ ⟨the sun departed, leaving the soothing fingers of the darkness to ~ up the herbage and cool down the hot sands —Myrtle R. White⟩ ⟨crews of painters are now ~*ing* up several of the buildings —*Springfield (Mass.) Daily News*⟩ ⟨the gown that she wore . . . was very old, though some attempt had been made to ~ it —Edith Sitwell⟩ **c :** to give (tissues) a fresh raw surface (as by scraping fibrous tissue from a fracture site) esp. to promote union and healing **d :** to improve (a stale drink) by adding fresh matter ⟨poured some more coffee in the cup to ~ it⟩ ⟨~ the highball with more ice⟩ **2 :** to put (as oysters or clams) in fresher water **3 a :** to relieve (as a rope) by change of place or position where friction causes wear **b :** SHIFT, REDISTRIBUTE ⟨~ a ship's ballast⟩ **4 :** to improve the appearance or restore or increase the sense of well-being of (oneself) by freshening — usu. used with *up*

fresh·en·er \-sh(ə)nə(r)\ *n* -S **:** one that freshens: as **a :** a drink that revives or cheers **b :** an astringent lotion for cleansing the skin

1fresher *comparative of* FRESH

2fresh·er \-shə(r\ *n* -S [1*fresh* + *-er*] *Brit* **:** FRESHMAN

freshest *superlative of* FRESH

fresh·et \'freshət, *usu* -əd·+V\ *n* -S [4*fresh* + *-et*] **1 a** *archaic* **:** a stream of fresh water **b :** a stream or current of fresh water that flows into the sea **2 a :** a great rise or a flood or overflowing of a stream caused by heavy rains or melted snow **:** a sudden inundation **b :** something resembling or suggesting a freshet esp. in being in sudden large supply ⟨rewarded handsomely by ~*s* of applause —Douglas Watt⟩ ⟨this quickened interest is shown in a ~ of publications —*Amer. Polit. Sci. Rev.*⟩ ⟨the almost endless and endlessly varied ~ of letters —*New Yorker*⟩ ⟨the ~*s* of welcome —Clemence Dane⟩

fresh gale *n* **:** wind having a speed of 39 to 46 miles per hour — see BEAUFORT SCALE table

freshing *n* -S [fr. gerund of 2*fresh*] **:** the recutting of worn rifling in the barrel of a firearm — often used with *out* ⟨the barrel needs ~ out⟩

fresh·ly *adv* [ME, fr. *fresh, fersh* fresh + *-ly*] **:** in a fresh manner: as **a :** NEWLY, RECENTLY ⟨a ~ cleaned floor⟩ ⟨a ~ acquired egg⟩ **b :** STRONGLY, VIGOROUSLY ⟨a ~ blowing breeze⟩ **c :** BRIGHTLY, VIVIDLY ⟨a ~ green leaf⟩ **d :** STRIKINGLY ⟨a ~ original poem⟩ **e :** IMPUDENTLY ⟨a ~ forward remark⟩

fresh·man \'⸗mən\ *n, pl* **freshmen** *often attrib* **1 :** one having as yet only the rudiments of knowledge esp. in a particular field or occupation **2 a :** a student in his first year or having chiefly first-year standing at a college or university **b :** a student in his first year in a secondary school **3 :** a newcomer in an occupation or activity requiring expert skill ⟨the tradition that Senate *freshmen* should be seen and not heard —*Time*⟩ ⟨a busy Congress, with a large contingent of *freshmen* —*Congressional Highlights*⟩ ⟨his ~ year in the major leagues⟩ ⟨made her ~ appearances in silent films⟩

freshman composition *n* **1 :** an elementary composition course usu. required in most colleges **2 :** a composition written as an assignment in a freshman course

fresh·man·ic \(')fresh'manik\ *adj* **:** of, belonging to, or befitting a freshman (as in college) ⟨a ~ innocence of outlook⟩

fresh·man·ship \'freshmən,ship\ *n* **:** the quality or state of being a freshman

freshman week *n* **:** a week usu. just before the beginning of the college year given over to activities intended to orient entering students

fresh meadow *n* **:** a low-lying meadow made marshy or subject to inundation by fresh water

fresh·ness *n* -ES [ME *freshnesse*, fr. *fresh, fersh* fresh + *-nesse* -ness] **:** the quality or state of being fresh

fresh pursuit *or* **fresh suit** *n* [*fresh pursuit* prob. trans. of AF *fresche sute; fresh suit* fr. ME *vers siute* (trans. of AF *fresche sute*), fr. *fresh, fersh, vers* fresh + *sute* pursuit — more at SUIT] **:** a pursuit undertaken immediately or while the circumstances still indicate a reasonable chance for success to recapture property illegally taken or being moved in violation of law, to claim property in something not yet reduced to ownership, or to capture someone detected in a violation of law

fresh-run *adj, of an anadromous salmon* **:** recently returned to fresh water

1freshwater \'⸗¦⸗⸗\ *n* [ME *fresh water* (noun phrase), fr. *fresh, fersh* fresh + *water*] **:** a freshwater pond, lake, stream, or river

2freshwater \"\ *adj* [ME *fresh water* (noun phrase used attributively), fr. *fresh water* (noun phrase)] **1 :** of or belonging to water that is not salt **:** living in or taken from fresh water or a body of fresh water ⟨~ fish⟩ ⟨~ mussels⟩ **:** consisting of fresh as opposed to salt water ⟨a ~ stream⟩ **:** marked by bodies of fresh as opposed to salt water ⟨~ areas⟩ **:** taking place in a body of fresh water ⟨~ battles —Martin Levin⟩ **2 a :** accustomed to navigating only in freshwaters ⟨a ~ sailor⟩ **b** *obs* **:** UNTRAINED, UNSKILLED **3 :** inland and usu. provincial ⟨a small ~ town —G.Patton⟩ ⟨a ~ college⟩

freshwater catfish *n* **:** an Australian catfish (*Tandanus tandanus*) that is sometimes smoked and is also an excellent hardy aquarium fish — see NEW ZEALAND BLUE COD

freshwater clam *n* **:** MUSSEL 2

freshwater cod *or* **freshwater cusk** *n* **:** BURBOT

freshwater crab *n* **:** a small crab (*Sesarma bidentatum*) from upland streams of Jamaica

freshwater drum *n* **:** a croaker (*Aplodinotus grunniens*) of the Great Lakes and Mississippi valley that sometimes attains a weight of 50 pounds or more — called also *bubbler*

freshwater flying fish *n* **:** FLYING FISH 2

freshwater herring *n* **:** any of various fishes (as the Australian grayling or the Columbia chub) not closely related to herrings but likened to the herring in size or appearance or food qualities

freshwater limpet *n* **:** any minute conical gastropod (family Ancylidae) superficially resembling a limpet but living and feeding on freshwater plants — called also *river limpet*

freshwater medusa *n* **:** a jellyfish of the genus *Craspedacusta*

freshwater mussel *n* **:** MUSSEL 2

freshwater polyp *n* **:** HYDRA

freshwater shipworm *n, Austral* **:** a voracious and destructive shipworm (*Nausitora meselli*) inhabiting fresh and brackish waters

freshwater shrimp *n* **1 :** a member of the malacostracan order Amphipoda; *esp* **:** a member of a common genus (*Talitrus*) of relatively large amphipods **2** *Austral* **:** a small translucent decapod (*Paratypa australiense*) common in backwaters of the Murray river

freshy \'freshē, -shi\ *n* -ES [*freshman* + *-y*] *slang* **:** a freshman in a college, university, or secondary school

fres·nel \frā'nel\ *n* -S [after Augustin J. *Fresnel* †1827 Fr. physicist] **:** a unit of frequency equal to one trillion cycles per second

fresnel biprism *n, usu cap F* **:** BIPRISM

fresnel lens *n, usu cap F* **:** a lens that has a surface consisting of a concentric series of simple lens sections so that a thin lens with a short focal length and large diameter is possible and that is used esp. in searchlights and viewing devices

fresnel mirrors *n, usu cap F* **:** two plane mirrors hinged so that there is no gap between the edges and so that the two planes make an angle with each other of nearly 180 degrees and used in demonstrating interference phenomena

fresnel rhomb *n, usu cap F* **:** a rhombic prism of glass used to transform plane polarized light into circularly polarized or elliptically polarized light

fres·no scraper \'frez,nō-\ *or* **fresno** *n* -S *sometimes cap F* [*Fresno* Agricultural Works, Fresno, California, where it is made] **:** BUCK SCRAPER

fres·son process \fre'sōⁿ-\ *n, usu cap F* [after Henri T. *Fresson* †1951 Fr. agricultural engineer] **:** a printing process in photography which is similar to the carbon process but with no transferring and in which development of the image occurs when pigment is removed from the unexposed portions of the image by washing the print surface with finely divided wet sawdust

1fret \'fret, *usu* -ed·+V\ *vb* **fretted; fretted; fretting; frets** [ME *freten*, fr. OE *fretan*; akin to OHG *frezzan* to devour, Goth *fraitan*; all fr. a prehistoric EGmc-WGmc compound whose first and second constituents respectively are represented by Goth *fra-* for- and by Goth *itan* to eat — more at FOR-, EAT] *vt* **1 a** *obs* **:** EAT, DEVOUR **b** *archaic* **:** CONSUME ⟨our thin wardrobe eaten and *fretted* . . . by moths —Charles Lamb⟩ **2 a :** to cause to suffer emotional wear and tear **:** trouble persistently **:** VEX, TORMENT, WORRY ⟨misgiving *fretted* him —Carson McCullers⟩ ⟨don't you ~ yourself about me —J.C. Powys⟩ **b :** to bring by bothering or tormenting ⟨*fretted* to irritation by the remarks⟩ ⟨*fretted* out of her coma by a violent thirstiness —Florence Gould⟩ **3 a :** to eat into or wear away **:** CORRODE ⟨the acid *fretted* the metal⟩ ⟨the river *fretted* the soft banks⟩ ⟨rainwater ~*s* the rocks⟩; *also* **:** to make irregular esp. along an edge as if by eating **:** FRAY, RAVEL ⟨the horizon was *fretted* by long thin lines of spruce and fir —O.S.J.Gogarty⟩ ⟨honeycombed and *fretted* and pocked —M.S.Douglas⟩ **b :** RUB, CHAFE, GALL ⟨a harness strap was *fretting* the horse so that he became almost unmanageable⟩ **c :** to diminish or lessen by slow consumption or using up ⟨his *fretted* fortunes gave him hope and fear —Shak.⟩ **d :** to make by wearing away a substance ⟨the stream *fretted* a channel for itself through the soft earth⟩ **4 :** to pass, occupy, or waste (as time or life) in fretting ⟨a poor player that struts and ~*s* his hour upon the stage —Shak.⟩ — often used with *away* or *out* **5 :** ROUGHEN, AGITATE, DISTURB **:** cause to ripple ⟨~ the surface of the lake⟩ **~** *vi* **1 a :** to eat into something **:** make a way by wearing away or off or by corrosion **b :** RANKLE ⟨the insult *fretted* in his breast for some time⟩ **c :** to affect something as if by gnawing or biting **:** GRATE ⟨the . . . urgent voice *fretted* at his nerves —Graham Greene⟩ ⟨the familiar objects *fretted* on his mood —S.E.White⟩ **2 :** WEAR, CORRODE ⟨marble one expects to ~ away, for it is merely fused limestone, very subject to the solvent action of rain —*Sydney (Australia) Bulletin*⟩ **:** CHAFE ⟨his back where the harness rubbed began to ~⟩ **:** FRAY, RAVEL **3 a :** to become vexed, worried, impatient, or irritated ⟨*fretting* over the high cost of feeding their families —Vance Packard⟩ ⟨when I *fretted* with impatience —Isaac Rosenfeld⟩ **b** *of running water* **:** to become agitated ⟨a brook *fretting* over rocks⟩ **c :** to occupy oneself fretfully or impatiently **:** FUSS ⟨the cook had dinner simmering on the stove . . . and *fretted* with brooms, linens, mops —Frederick Way⟩ **d :** to feel impatient or irritated and usu. passive opposition ⟨tribes of hostile Indians who *fretted* against forward thrust of settlement —V.L.Parrington⟩ ⟨the younger son, *fretting* against parental opposition —C.D.Lewis⟩ **4** *now dial Eng* **:** FERMENT, WORK ⟨sweet wine is liable to ~⟩ **syn** see WORRY

2fret \"\ *n* -S [ME, action of gnawing, fr. *freten* to eat, devour, gnaw — more at 1FRET] **1 a :** the action of eroding **:** a wasting away or being wasted away as if by being gnawed or eaten **b :** a worn or eroded spot (as in an asphalt highway or the insulation of an electric wire) **c** *obs* **:** a spot of decay **:** ULCER **2 a :** an agitation of mind marked by complaint and impatience **:** IRRITATION, FRETTING ⟨the cook was in a marked ~ because the potatoes had burned⟩ ⟨trying to curb his constant worry and ~⟩ **b :** something that frets the mind or temper ⟨one of those still moments when the small ~*s* vanish —D.H.Lawrence⟩ ⟨the great peace beyond all this turmoil and ~ —L.P. Smith⟩ ⟨relief from domestic ~*s* —S.H.Adams⟩ **3** *obs* **:** FLURRY, SQUALL **4 :** fermentation effervescence (as of liquor) **5 :** CHRYSAL

3fret \"\ *vt* **fretted; fretted; fretting; frets** [ME *fretten*, fr. MF *freter* to decorate with interlaced designs, bind with a ferrule, fr. OF, fr. *frete* ferrule] **1 a :** to decorate with interlaced designs **:** embroider with gold or silver **b :** to mark decoratively esp. with a network of things **:** form a pattern or design upon ⟨the air was *fretted* with a kaleidoscopic network of swifts —William Beebe⟩ **2 :** to enrich (as a ceiling) with embossed or pierced carved patterns

4fret \"\ *n* -S [ME, fr. MF *frete* interlaced design on a shield, fr. *freter* to decorate with interlaced designs] **1 :** an ornamental network; *esp* **:** a medieval net of gold, silver, or jewels for a woman's headdress **2 :** an ornament or ornamental work often in relief consisting of small straight bars intersecting one another in right or oblique angles or often of solid slats intersecting each other **3 a :** a heraldic device consisting of narrow bends crossed saltirewise and interlaced **b :** a heraldic device consisting of two narrow bends in saltire interlaced with a voided lozenge

1 2 3 4 5

fret 2: *1, 2, 3, 4,* Greek frets; *5* Japanese fret

5fret \"\ *n* -S [prob. fr. MF *frete* ferrule, fr. OF, prob. of Gmc origin; akin to OE *fetor* fetter — more at FETTER] **:** one of a series of ridges of metal, ivory, or other material fixed across the fingerboard of a guitar or similar instrument

6fret \"\ *vt* **fretted; fretted; fretting; frets :** to furnish with frets (as a stringed instrument)

7fret \"\ *n* -S [L *fretum* — more at FRETUM] *archaic* **:** STRAIT

fret·ful \'fretfəl\ *adj* [1*fret* + *-ful*] **1** *obs* **:** GNAWING, CORROSIVE, IRRITATING **2 a :** disposed to fret ⟨a ~ baby⟩ **:** PEEVISH ⟨a ~ and cantankerous old man⟩ **:** IMPATIENT, RESTLESS ⟨turned a ~ hungry eye upon the calendar, counting the days that intervened —A.J.Cronin⟩ ⟨a constant ~ stamping of hoofs upon splintery planks —Kenneth Roberts⟩ **b :** ILL-HUMORED, ANGRY ⟨weary days of ~ argument —C.A. & Mary Beard⟩ **3 a** *of water* **:** showing agitation **:** TROUBLED ⟨the ~ waters of the Rogue river —*Amer. Guide Series: Oregon*⟩ **b** *of wind* **:** coming brokenly **:** GUSTY **syn** see IRRITABLE

fret·ful·ly \-fəlē, -li\ *adv* **:** in a fretful manner

fret·ful·ness *n* -ES **:** the quality or state of being fretful

fretize *vt* -ED/-ING/-S [perh. fr. 4*fret* + *-ize*] *obs* **:** to ornament with fretwork

fret·less \'fretləs\ *adj* **:** having no frets

frets *pres 3d sing of* FRET, *pl of* FRET

fretsaw \'⸗,⸗\ *n* [4*fret*] **:** a narrow-bladed fine-toothed saw held under tension in a frame and used for cutting frets, scrolls, and other curved outlines; *also* **:** COMPASS SAW, COPING SAW

fret·some \'fretsəm\ *adj* [1*fret* + *-some*] **:** ANNOYING, IRRITATING, BOTHERSOME

fretted *adj* [fr. past part. of 3*fret*] *of heraldic charges or ordinaries* **:** interlaced with one another — see PARTED AND FRETTED

fret·ter \'fred·ə(r), -etə-\ *n* -S [1*fret* + *-er*] **:** one that frets

1fretting *n* -S [ME *freting*, fr. *freten* to eat, devour, gnaw + *-inge, -ing* -ing — more at FRET] **:** damage caused by rubbing, chafing, or wearing away

2fretting *n* -S [ME *freting*, fr. *freten, fretten* to decorate with interlaced designs + *-inge, -ing* -ing — more at FRET] **:** FRETWORK

fret·ting·ly *adv* [ME *fretingly*, fr. *freting* (fr. *freten* to fret, devour + *-ing*, adj. suffix used to form the present participle) + *-ly* — more at FRET] **:** in the manner of one that frets ⟨hung around the house ~ occupying himself with trivialities⟩

1fret·ty \'fred·ē, -etē, -i\ *adj* [ME *frette*, fr. MF *fretté*, fr. OF, past part. of *freter* to decorate with interlaced designs — more at FRET] **1** *heraldry* **:** covered with narrow bands interlacing saltirewise **2** *heraldry* **:** FRETTED

2fretty \"\ *adj* -ER/-EST [1*fret* + *-y*] **:** FRETFUL ⟨baby made ~ resentful sounds —Ethel Wilson⟩

fre·tum \'frēd·əm, -ētəm\ *n, pl* **fre·ta** \-ēd·ə, -ētə\ [L; prob. akin to L *fervēre* to boil — more at BURN] **:** an arm of the sea **:** STRAIT

fretwork \'⸗,⸗\ *n* [4*fret* + *work*] **1 a :** decoration consisting of work carved, pierced, or otherwise adorned with frets **b :** ornamental openwork or work in relief esp. when elaborate or intricate **2 :** something suggesting intricate fretwork ⟨the ~ of shade and sunshine —T.B.Macaulay⟩ ⟨the ~ of trees —Ellen Glasgow⟩

fretworked \'⸗,⸗\ *adj* **:** decorated with fretwork ⟨a ~ handle on the box⟩ **:** done in fretwork ⟨a ~ motto on the postcard⟩

1freud·i·an \'frȯidēən\ *adj, often cap* [Sigmund *Freud* †1939 Austrian neurologist, founder of psychoanalysis + E *-ian*] **1 :** of, relating to, or according with the theories or practices of Sigmund Freud and his system of psychoanalysis ⟨~ theories⟩ ⟨~ repressions⟩ **2 a :** readily interpretable in psychoanalytic terms **:** characterized by thinly veiled psychodynamics ⟨a clear ~ reason for his action⟩ ⟨a ~ slip of the tongue⟩ **b :** arising from or belonging to repressed libidinal impulses ⟨a ~ compulsion⟩ **c :** SEXY, SMUTTY ⟨a bit too ~ in his remarks for polite society⟩ — **freud·i·an·ism** \-ə,nizəm\ *n* -S *usu cap*

2freudian \"\ *n* -S *usu cap* **:** an adherent of the Freudian school of psychoanalysis **:** an orthodox psychoanalyst

freud·ism \-,dizəm\ *n* -S *usu cap* **:** FREUDIANISM

freund's adjuvant \'frȯin(d)z-\ *n, usu cap F* [after Jules T. *Freund* b1890 Am. immunologist] **:** any of various substances (as lanolin, paraffin oil, or killed tubercle bacilli) added to an antigen to enhance its antigenicity

frey·ci·ne·tia \,frāsə'nēsh(ē)ə\ *n* [NL, fr. Louis C. de Saulces de *Freycinet* †1842 Fr. naval officer + NL *-ia*] **1** *cap* **:** a genus of Asiatic evergreen woody climbers (family Pandanaceae) with fleshy often brightly colored bracts and red berries **2** -S **:** any plant of the genus *Freycinetia*

fri·a·bil·i·ty \,frīə'biləd·ē, -ətē, -i\ *n* -ES **:** the condition of being friable

fri·a·ble \'frīəbəl\ *adj* [MF or L; MF, fr. L *friabilis*, fr. *friare* to rub, crumble + *-abilis* -able — more at FRICTION] **:** easily crumbled, pulverized, or reduced to powder ⟨~ sandstone⟩ ⟨~ carcinomatous tissue⟩ ⟨~ curds formed in the stomach⟩ — **fri·a·ble·ness** *n* -ES

fri·and \'frē,änd, *F* frēäⁿ\ *adj* [F, fr. OF *friant*, fr. pres. part. of *frire* to fry, roast — more at FRY] *archaic* **:** dainty or fond of dainties

fri·ar \'frī(ə)r, -īə\ *n* -S [ME *frere, fryer*, fr. OF *frere*, lit., brother, fr. L *fratr-, frater* — more at BROTHER] **1 a :** a member of a mendicant order **b :** MONK **2 :** SILVERSIDES **3** *archaic* **:** a white or pale patch on a printed sheet caused by insufficient deposition of ink — compare MONK **4 :** PILGRIM BROWN

friarbird \'⸗,⸗\ *n* [so called fr. its bare head and neck] **1 :** an Australian honey eater (*Philemon corniculatus*) having the head black and destitute of feathers — called also *four-o'clock* **2 :** any of various birds of Australia, New Guinea, and the southwest Pacific islands that are related to the friarbird

fri·ar·ly \-ī(ə)rlē, -īəl-, -li\ *adj* **:** like a friar **:** relating to friars

friar minor *n, pl* **friars minor** *usu cap F&M* [ME *frere menour*, fr. OF *frere meneur*] **:** a friar belonging to a division of the Franciscan order that follows the unmodified rule of St. Francis

friar minor conventual *n, pl* **friars minor conventual** *usu cap F&M&C* **:** a friar belonging to a division of the Franciscan order that follows a modified rule of St. Francis

friar preacher *n, pl* **friars preachers** *or* **friar preachers** *usu cap F&P* [ME *frere prechour*, fr. OF *frere preecheur*] **:** DOMINICAN

friar's balsam *n* **:** an alcoholic solution containing essentially benzoin, storax, balsam of Tolu, and aloes used chiefly as a local application (as for small fissures) and after addition to hot water as an inhalant in bronchitis — called also *compound benzoin tincture*

friar's chicken *n, Scot* **:** chicken broth with eggs in it

friar's cloth *n* **:** MONK'S CLOTH

friar's-cowl \'⸗⸗,⸗\ *n, pl* **friar's-cowls :** any of several plants having a cowled flower or inflorescence: as **a :** a European arum (*Arisarum vulgare*) with a cowl-shaped spathe **b :** CUCKOOPINT **c :** a common Old World monkshood (*Aconitum napellus*) having flowers with the helmet convex to hemispherical or arched

friar skate *n* **:** a European skate (*Raja alba*) or related fish

fri·ary \'frī(ə)rē, -ri\ *n* -ES [alter. (influenced by *friar*) of earlier *frary* friary, brotherhood, fr. ME *frarie, frerie*, fr. MF *frarie, frairie, frerie*, fr. ML *fratria*, fr. *fratr-, frater* friar, monk (fr. L, brother) + L *-ia* -y — more at BROTHER] **:** a convent or brotherhood of friars **:** MONASTERY

frib \'frib\ *n* -S [origin unknown] **:** a short small dirty lock of wool

1frib·ble \'fribəl\ *vb* **fribbled; fribbled; fribbling** \-b(ə)liŋ\ **fribbles** [origin unknown] *vi* **1 :** to act in a trifling or foolish manner **:** act frivolously **2** *obs* **:** TOTTER, STAMMER, FALTER **~** *vt* **:** to trifle or fool away

2fribble \"\ *n* -S **:** a frivolous person, thing, or idea **:** TRIFLER ⟨a man whom he pilloried as a ~ and a dilettante —Leonard Bacon⟩

3fribble \"\ *adj* **:** FRIVOLOUS, TRIFLING ⟨a ~ fellow who orders his dressing gown to match his sheets —*Time*⟩

fribbling *adj* **:** FRIVOLOUS, TRIFLING, CAPTIOUS ⟨~ banalities —P.A.Samuelson⟩

frib·by \'fribē\ *adj* -ER/-EST [*frib* + *-y*] *chiefly Brit* **:** SMALL, SHORT — used of locks of wool

fri·bourg \'frē,bu̇(ə)r\ *n, usu cap* [fr. *Fribourg*, canton of Switzerland] **:** a Swiss breed of black and white cattle used for dairy, meat, and draft

fric·an·deau *also* **fric·an·do** \'frikən,dō, ⸗⸗'⸗\ *n, pl* **fricandeaus** \-ōz\ *or* **fricandeaux** \-ōz\ *also* **fricandoes** [F *fricandeau*, fr. MF, irreg. fr. *fricasser*] **:** larded veal roasted and glazed in its own juices

1fric·as·see \'frikə,sē, ⸗⸗'⸗ *sometimes* ¦zē\ *n* -S [MF, fr. fem. of *fricassé*, past part. of *fricasser* to fricassee, perh. fr. *frire* to fry + *casse* ladle, dripping pan, kettle — more at FRY, CASSEROLE] **1 :** a stew formerly of light-colored meat (as veal or chicken) in a light gravy **2 :** a stew of meat or other foods in light or brown gravy

2fricassee \"\ *vt* **fricasseed; fricasseed; fricasseeing; fricassees :** to cook as a fricassee

fri·ca·tion \fri'kāshən\ *n* -S [ME *fricacioun*, fr. L *frication-*, *fricatio,* fr. *fricatus* (past part. of *fricare* to rub) + *-ion-, -io* -ion — more at FRICTION] **1** *obs* **:** FRICTION; *specif* **:** a rubbing of the body with the hands **2 a :** a fricative sound **b :** the frictional rustling of a fricative sound

¹fric·a·tive \ˈfrikəd·iv, -ətiv\ *adj* [L *fricatus* + E *-ive*] **:** characterized by frictional passage of the expired voiced or voiceless breath against a narrowing at some point in the vocal tract ⟨\f v th t͟h s z sh zh h\ are ~⟩ — compare SPIRANT

²fricative \"\ *n* -s **:** a fricative consonant

fric·a·trice \ˈfrikə·trə̇s\ *n* -s [MF, female homosexual, fr. L *fricare* to rub + MF *-trice* -trix (fr. L *tric-, -trix*); trans. of L & Gk *tribas* — more at TRIBADE] *archaic* **:** a lewd woman **:** HARLOT; *specif* **:** a female homosexual

fricht \ˈfrikt\ *Scot var of* FRIGHT

fricht·some \-səm\ *adj* [*fricht* + *-some*] *Scot* **:** FRIGHTFUL, TERRIBLE ⟨a ~ rain storm⟩

¹fric·tion \ˈfrikshən\ *n* -s [MF or L; MF, fr. L *friction-, frictio,* fr. *frictus* (past part. of *fricare* to rub) + *-ion-, -io* -ion; akin to L *friare* to rub, crumble, OIr *brissim* I break, Skt *bhrīṇanti* they injure, hurt] **1 a :** the act of rubbing one body against another **:** ATTRITION; *specif* **:** the act of rubbing the body esp. to stimulate the skin ⟨after the haircut, I had a shampoo, some ~, a little brilliantine —O.F.Karaka⟩ **b :** resistance to the relative motion of one body sliding, rolling, or flowing over another with which it is in contact **c :** the clashing between two persons or parties of opposed views **:** disagreement tending to prevent or retard progress **2 :** rubber forced into textile fabric by calendering **3 :** nonvibratory sound produced by impingement of air against some part of the respiratory tract

²friction \"\ *vt* -ED/-ING/-S **:** to impregnate (textile fabric) with rubber by calendering **:** RUBBERIZE

fric·tion·al \-shənᵊl,-shnəl\ *adj* **:** relating to friction **:** moved by friction **:** produced by friction ⟨~ electricity⟩ — **fric·tion·al·ly** \-ᵊlē,-əl|, |ī\ *adv*

frictional gearing *n* **:** FRICTION GEARING

frictional unemployment *n* **:** the temporary unemployment of resources (as labor) resulting from job changes, imbalance of factors of production, or short term lack of mobility preventing continuous employment

friction bearing *n* **:** a solid bearing on a railroad freight car usu. of brass construction with babbitt lining whose interior surface is in direct contact with the surface of the axle end which it supports

friction board *n* **:** a heavy compressed impregnated solid paperboard used for making pulleys usu. by cutting into disks that are then compacted together coaxially

friction brake *n* **1 :** a brake operating by friction **2 :** an absorption dynamometer that absorbs energy by friction

friction breccia *n* **:** a breccia composed of rocks shattered and crushed under friction

friction calender *n* **:** a calender used for friction glazing — compare SUPERCALENDER

friction clamp *n* **:** a clamp that holds or supports by friction alone without indentation or deformation of the bodies concerned

friction clutch *n* **:** a clutch in which connection is made through sliding friction

friction composition *n* **:** a composition that readily ignites by friction — compare ³MATCH 3

friction crack *n* **:** a short crack in glaciated rock that is transverse to the direction of ice movement and that presumably results from local increase in friction between ice and rock

friction drive *n* **:** an automobile power-transmission system in which the gearbox is replaced by a friction gearing the driver and follower of which are arranged so that by varying their position relative to one another a full range of variation in desired speed ratios may be obtained

friction gearing *also* **friction gear** *n* **:** a gearing for transmitting motion by surface friction instead of by teeth

friction-glazed \ˈ≈≈,≈\ *adj, of paper* **:** glazed by being passed in a continuous sheet between two calender rolls one of which by revolving faster than the other burnishes the surface — compare FLINT-GLAZED — **friction glazing** *n*

friction head *n* **:** the head (sense 14a) lost by flowing water as a result of friction between the moving water and the walls of its conduit plus intermolecular disturbances

friction horsepower *n* **:** power lost esp. in an internal-combustion engine through friction between parts of the machine itself

fric·tion·ize \ˈfrikshə,nīz\ *vt* -ED/-ING/-S **:** to act upon by friction or rubbing

friction jewel *n* **:** a bearing jewel that is press-fit into place in a watch plate

fric·tion·less \ˈfrikshənlə̇s\ *adj* **1 :** devoid of friction ⟨a ~ connection between the two moving parts⟩ **:** operating without significant friction ⟨a ~ bearing⟩ **2 :** AMICABLE ⟨a totally ~ relationship existed between the two people⟩ — **fric·tion·less·ly** *adv*

friction match *n* **:** a match that is ignited by friction and has a tip usu. containing phosphorus sulfide mixed with other combustibles and with oxidizing material (as potassium chlorate, saltpeter, or red lead)

friction primer *n* **:** a device operating by friction used for igniting the charge in a cannon

friction ridge *n* **:** one of the corrugated ridges characteristic of the skin of the palmar and plantar surfaces of primates

frictions *pl of* FRICTION, *pres 3d sing of* FRICTION

friction saw *n* **:** a toothless circular saw used for cutting metals or other materials by fusion in the cut due to frictional heat — **friction sawing** *n*

friction slip *n* **:** a slipping friction clutch or coupling

friction socket *n* **:** a tool used for recovering tools of small diameter from a well

friction sound *n* **:** an auscultatory sound caused by the rubbing together of two inflamed serous surfaces (as of the pleural membranes in pleurisy)

friction tape *n* **:** cotton tape impregnated with water-resistant insulating material and an adhesive and used esp. to protect, insulate, and support electrical conductors — called also *electric tape*

friction-tight \ˈ≈≈ˈ≈\ *adj* **:** tight enough to operate by means of friction

friction top *n* **:** a top for a container held in place by friction between the mating parts

friction wheel *or* **friction pulley** *n* **:** a wheel operating by friction (as in a friction gearing)

fri·day \ˈfrīdē, -di *also* -(,)dā\ *n* -s *usu cap* [ME, fr. OE *frīgedæg;* akin to OFris *frīadei, frīgendei* Friday, OHG *frīatag;* all fr. a prehistoric WGmc compound formed from components represented by OHG *Frīa,* the Germanic goddess of love, and *tag* day; trans. of L *Veneris dies,* lit., day of Venus (the Roman goddess of love and the planet Venus) — more at DAY] **:** the sixth day of the week **:** the day following Thursday

fri·days \"+z\ *adv, usu cap* **:** on Friday repeatedly **:** on any Friday

¹fridge \ˈfrij\ *vb* -ED/-ING/-S [prob. alter. of ¹*frig*] *vt, dial Eng* **:** RUB, FRAY, IRRITATE ~ *vi, dial Eng* **:** FIDGET, CHAFE

²fridge \"\ *n* -s [by shortening and alter.] *chiefly Brit* **:** REFRIGERATOR

fridstool *var of* FRITHSTOOL

fried \ˈfrīd\ *adj* [ME, fr. past part. of *frien* to fry — more at FRY] **1** *of food* **:** cooked by frying **2 :** INTOXICATED ⟨he was plenty ~ when he left here —William Ward⟩

friedcake \ˈ≈,≈\ *n* **:** a cake in the form of a ring, twist, ball, or strip fried in deep fat **:** DOUGHNUT, CRULLER

frie·del-crafts reaction \frē,del|el'kraf(t)s-, ¦fre,dᵊl\ *n, usu cap F&C* [after Charles *Friedel* †1899 Fr. chemist & James M. *Crafts* †1917 Am. chemist] **:** a synthetic reaction in organic chemistry in which anhydrous aluminum chloride acts as the typical catalyst: as **a :** the synthesis of a hydrocarbon (as ethylbenzene) by alkylation of an aromatic hydrocarbon with an alkyl halide **b :** the synthesis of a ketone (as benzophenone) by acylation of an aromatic hydrocarbon with an acyl chloride or acid anhydride

frie·del·in \frēˈdelə̇n\ *n* -s [Charles *Friedel* + E *-in*] **:** a crystalline triterpenoid ketone $C_{30}H_{50}O$ extracted esp. from cork

frie·del·ite \-,līt\ *n* -s [F, fr. Charles *Friedel* + F *-ite*] **:** a mineral $Mn_8Si_6O_{18}(OH, Cl)_4.3H_2O$ consisting of a rose-red manganese silicate containing chlorine (hardness 4–5, sp. gr. 3.07)

fried·länd·er's bacillus \ˈfrēt|,lendə(r)z-, -ēd|\ *also* **friedländer bacillus** *or* **friedländer's pneumobacillus** *n, usu cap F* [after Carl *Friedländer* †1887 Ger. pathologist] **:** PNEUMOBACILLUS

fried·man test \ˈfrēdmən-\ *also* **friedman's test** *n, usu cap F* [after Maurice H. *Friedman b*1903 Am. physiologist] **:** a modification of the Aschheim-Zondek test for pregnancy using rabbits as test animals

fried pie *n* **:** a turnover fried in deep fat

fried·reich's ataxia \ˈfrē,drīks-, -īks\ *also* **friedreich's disease** *n, usu cap F* [after Nikolaus *Friedreich* †1882 Ger. physician] **:** a recessive hereditary anomaly marked by muscular incoordination and twitching and usu. becoming manifest in the adult

fried·richs·dor \ˈfrēdriks¦dȯ(ə)r, -iks-\ *n* -s [G, fr. *Friedrich* Frederick II †1786 king of Prussia + F *d'or* of gold] **1 :** a former gold coin of Prussia equal to five silver talers first struck by Frederick II **2 :** FREDERIK

¹friend \ˈfrend\ *n* -s [ME *frend,* fr. OE *frēond;* akin to OHG *friunt* friend, relative, ON *frǣndi* blood relative, friend, Goth *frijonds* friend; all fr. the pres. part. of a Gmc verb represented by OE *frēogan, frēon* to love, OS *friohan, friehan,* ON *frjā,* Goth *frijon;* akin to OE *frēo* free — more at FREE] **1 a :** one that seeks the society or welfare of another whom he holds in affection, respect, or esteem or whose companionship and personality are pleasurable **:** an intimate associate esp. when other than a lover or relative — often used as a form of address **b :** ACQUAINTANCE **2 a :** one not hostile or not an enemy **b :** one that is of the same nation, party, or other group and whose friendly feelings are assumed or from whom sympathy or cooperation is expected **3 :** one that gives assistance or that favors or promotes something (as a cause, institution, or project) ⟨~s of divorce and birth control, or critics of denominational education —Paul Blanshard⟩ ⟨the inexhaustible ~ of all good causes —Van Wyck Brooks⟩ ⟨this trend has alarmed ~s of the liberal arts —Raymond Walters b. 1885⟩ ⟨nature is still the painter's nearest ~ —F.J.Mather⟩ **4** *now chiefly Scot* **:** KINSMAN **5 a** *obs* **:** PARAMOUR **b :** a favored date **:** a boyfriend or girlfriend **:** SWEETHEART **6** *cap* **:** one of a religious group of Christians that lay special stress on the guidance of the Holy Spirit, that reject outward rites and an ordained ministry, that practice simplicity of dress and speech, and that have a long tradition of actively working for peace and opposing war — called also *Quaker* **7 :** a troublesome acquaintance **:** one causing or likely to cause annoyance ⟨has your ~ been up bothering you lately⟩

syn ACQUAINTANCE, INTIMATE, CONFIDANT: FRIEND applies to a person one has regarded with liking and a degree of respect and has known for a time in a pleasurable relationship neither notably intimate nor dependent wholly on business or professional ties ⟨a *friend* is one who knows all about us, but is loyal to us just the same —C.A.Dial⟩ ⟨a companion loves some agreeable qualities which a man may possess, but a *friend* loves the man himself —James Boswell⟩ ACQUAINTANCE is likely to indicate one known, usu. not unfavorably, with less familiarity, closeness, fellowship, and well-wishing than FRIEND ⟨you understand that I am not their friend. I am only a holiday *acquaintance* —Joseph Conrad⟩ INTIMATE implies a closeness precluding reserve or reservation ⟨a few *intimates* in whose critical judgment he had confidence —Allen Johnson⟩ CONFIDANT (applicable to persons of either sex, although the feminine form *confidante* is still used) indicates a person in whom one confides secrets, usu. but not necessarily an intimate ⟨the same detective and his friend and *confidant,* Dr. Watson —A.C.Ward⟩ ⟨could she make a *confidant* of such a man? Something in her yearned to unburden itself in a torrent of pitiful words —J.C.Powys⟩

— **be friends with :** to have friendly relations with ⟨making an effort to *be friends with* people they essentially disliked⟩ — **make friends with :** to become friendly with **:** establish friendly relations with ⟨advised the child to *make friends with* as many of his classmates as possible⟩ — compare MAKE *vt* 24a

²friend \"\ *vt* -ED/-ING/-S [ME *frenden,* fr. *frend,* n.] **1** *obs* **:** to make friends of **:** join as friends **2 :** to act as the friend of **:** BEFRIEND, AID, SERVE ⟨and I will ~ you, if I may, in the dark and cloudy day —A.E.Housman⟩

friend at court *or* **friend in court** [ME *frend in court*] **:** one in a position of importance or influence who is disposed to act in one's behalf

friend·ed \-dəd\ *adj* [ME *frended,* fr. past part. of *frenden*] *archaic* **:** provided with friends

friending *n* -s [fr. gerund of ²*friend*] *obs* **:** FRIENDLINESS

friend·less \ˈfrendlə̇s, *rapid* -nl-\ *adj* [ME *frendles,* fr. OE *frēondlēas,* fr. *frēond* friend + *-lēas* -less] **:** having no friends — **friend·less·ness** *n* -ES

friend·li·ly \-lə̇lē,-lə̇li\ *adv* [¹*friendly* + *-ly*] **:** in a friendly manner

friend·li·ness \ˈfrendlēnə̇s, -lin-, *rapid* -enl-\ *n* -ES [ME *frendlinesse,* fr. *frendly* + *-nesse* -ness] **:** the quality or state of being friendly ⟨a certain indescribable kindliness or ~ of spirit —P.E.More⟩

¹friend·ly \-lē,-li\ *adj* -ER/-EST [ME *frendly,* fr. OE *frēondlic,* fr. *frēond* friend + *-lic* -ly — more at FRIEND] **1 :** of, relating to, befitting, or typical of a friend, of friends, or of friendship: as **a :** showing or marked by the disposition or attitude of one that is or wishes to be a friend **:** manifesting or disposed to goodwill, kindly interest, pleasant warmth, or familiar sociability ⟨~ neighbors⟩ ⟨a ~, approachable person —C.H. Voss⟩ ⟨wished to be ~ to even the worst members of the club⟩ **:** prone to favor, support, or aid ⟨a teacher not too ~ toward independent students⟩ ⟨an administration ~ to experimentation⟩ ⟨a ~ correspondence with a former rival⟩ **b :** not hostile or antagonistic ⟨a ~ state⟩ ⟨~ Indians⟩; *specif* **:** belonging to one's own country's forces or those of an ally ⟨~ planes⟩ ⟨in ~ territory⟩ ⟨an unduly heavy price in ~ casualties —*N.Y. Times*⟩ ⟨fell victim to a ~ destroyer which . . . would not listen to her frantic signals —E.L.Beach⟩ **c** (1) **:** warm and comforting or cheerful ⟨sitting in the ~ glow of the fire⟩ ⟨came out of a drab side street into the ~ lights of the theater district⟩ (2) **:** having qualities that attract and none that are forbidding in any way ⟨~ and charming hills —Mark Saxton⟩ (3) **:** conducing to amicable feeling and goodwill ⟨the ~ rooms of the club⟩ **2 :** serving a beneficial or helpful purpose **:** FAVORABLE, PROPITIOUS ⟨a ~ breeze finally drove the boat into harbor⟩ ⟨official attitudes that are ~ to private investors —*U.S.News & World Report*⟩ **3 :** marked by a lack of fierce zeal for victory **:** engaged in for sport or recreation rather than for stakes or prizes **:** not bitterly, savagely, or hotly contested ⟨a ~ game of tennis⟩ ⟨a ~ game of poker with a maximum raise of two cents⟩ **4** *usu cap* **:** of or relating to the Friends **syn** see AMICABLE

²friendly \"\ *adv, usu* -ER/-EST [ME *frendly,* fr. OE *frēondlice,* fr. *frēondlic,* adj.] **:** in a friendly manner **:** AMICABLY, FRIENDLILY ⟨he was . . . ~ disposed toward the British —W.G. Harmon⟩

³friendly \"\ *n* -ES [¹*friendly*] **:** one that is friendly; *esp* **:** a native who is friendly to settlers or invaders ⟨but bands began to form and the cry rose, "Kill the whites! Kill the *friendlies!*" —Meridel Le Sueur⟩

friendly crab *n* **:** ²VOOD CRAB

friendly fire *n* **:** a fire contained within the receptacle provided for it (as a boiler or heater), no liability being assumed in a fire insurance contract by the underwriter for property destroyed by the fire while thus contained — compare HOSTILE FIRE

friendly society *n, Brit* **:** BENEFIT SOCIETY

friend of god *usu cap F&G* [trans. of G *gottes freund*] **:** a clerical or lay mystic of a 14th century Rhenish and Swiss movement that sought holiness not in ceremonies and creeds but in a direct personal relationship with God

friend of the court 1 : AMICUS CURIAE **2 :** a public officer in Michigan who assists the court, aids in carrying out its orders and decrees, and advises the public in many matters (as those involving domestic relations)

friends *pl of* FRIEND, *pres 3d sing of* FRIEND

friend·ship \ˈfren(d),ship, -n,chip\ *n* [ME *frendship,* fr. OE *frēondscipe,* fr. *frēond* friend + *-scipe* -ship] **1 a :** the state of being friends ⟨the two men valued their long-standing ~⟩ **:** the state of being in a friendly relationship ⟨the two countries made enough concessions to each other so that their ~ was not endangered by the crisis⟩ **b :** the state of being a friend ⟨the man valued his neighbor's ~⟩ **2 :** friendly feeling **:** FRIENDLINESS ⟨felt encouraged by the ~ his fellow employees showed him⟩ **3** *obs* **:** AID, HELP, ASSISTANCE

friendship sloop \"-\ *n, usu cap F* [fr. *Friendship,* Maine] **:** a sloop-rigged centerboard fishing boat typically about 30 feet overall that has a clipper bow and strong sheer and that is popular along the Maine coast

frier *var of* FRYER

fries *pl of* FRY, *pres 3d sing of* FRY

¹frie·sian \ˈfrēzhən *also* -zhēən\ *usu cap, var of* FRISIAN

²friesian \"\ *n* -s *usu cap, chiefly Brit* **:** HOLSTEIN-FRIESIAN

fries·land \ˈfrēz|lənd, -ēsl-, -,land\ *n, often cap* [fr. *Friesland,* province in the Netherlands] *southern Africa* **:** HOLSTEIN-FRIESIAN

fries reaction \ˈfrēs-, -ēz-\ *n, usu cap F* [after Karl *Fries b*1875 Ger. chemist] **:** the isomerization of an aryl ester of a carboxylic acid into a phenolic ketone by means of anhydrous aluminum chloride

¹frieze \ˈfrēz, frēˈzā, frə̇ˈzā\ *n* -s [ME *frise,* fr. MF *frise,* fr. MD *friese, vriese* — more at FRIZZLE] **1 a :** a heavy durable fabric with a rough surface that is woven of coarse wool and shoddy in gray or mixed colors and is made esp. in Ireland for overcoats **b :** a wiry upholstery fabric with patterns in cut and uncut loops that is made with a cotton backing and a wool, mohair, or rayon pile **2 a :** a pile surface of uncut loops or of patterned cut and uncut loops; *also* **:** the yarn used for such a surface **b :** a carpet having a pile of tightly twisted yarn

²frieze \ˈfrēz\ *vt* -ED/-ING/-S [ME *frisen,* fr. *frise,* n.] **:** to make a nap on (cloth)

³frieze \ˈfrēz\ *n* -s [MF *frise,* perh. fr. ML *phrygium, frigium, frisium* embroidery, embroidered cloth, fr. L *Phrygium,* neut. of *Phrygius* Phrygian, fr. *Phrygia,* noted for its fine embroidery; fr. the fancy decorations reminiscent of embroidery on some friezes] **1 a :** the part of an entablature that is between the architrave and the cornice **b :** a sculptured or richly ornamented band (as on a building or a piece of furniture) — see ENTABLATURE illustration **2 :** a band, line, or series suggesting a frieze ⟨a ~ of willows —C.B.Firestone⟩ ⟨a constant ~ of visitors wound its way around the . . . ruins —Mollie Panter-Downes⟩ ⟨an interminable ~ of sobbing boys, dying dogs and disabled children —*Time*⟩

⁴frieze \"\ *vt* -ED/-ING/-S **:** to adorn with a frieze

frieze rail *n* [³*frieze*] **:** the rail below a frieze panel

friez·ing \ˈfrēziŋ\ *n* -s [³*frieze* + *-ing*] **:** a frieze esp. along a ship's quarter

friezy \-zē\ *adj* -ER/-EST [¹*frieze* + *-y*] **:** made of frieze or of a rough cloth resembling frieze ⟨a ~ coat⟩ **:** resembling frieze ⟨a ~ cloth⟩

¹frig \ˈfrig\ *vb* **frigged; frigged; frigging; frigs** [ME *friggen*] *vi, now dial Eng* **:** WRIGGLE ~ *vt, dial chiefly Eng* **:** RUB, CHAFE

²frig \"\ *vb* **frigged; frigged; frigging; frigs** [prob. fr. ¹*frig*] *vt* **:** to copulate with — usu. considered vulgar ~ *vi* **1 :** COPULATE — usu. considered vulgar; in its *-ing* form often in speech a meaningless intensive **2 :** to waste time in a futile or fooling manner — often used with *around*

³frig \ˈfrij\ *n* -s [by shortening] *Brit* **:** REFRIGERATOR

frig·ate \ˈfrigə̇t, *usu* -əd.+V\ *n* -s [MF *frigate,* fr. It *fregata*] **1 :** a light boat propelled orig. by oars but later by sails **2 :** a ship of a former class of ship-rigged war vessels intermediate between corvettes and ships of the line usu. with a full battery on the gun deck and a light battery on the spar deck **3 :** a British or Canadian escort ship between a corvette and a destroyer in size and corresponding to a U. S. destroyer escort **4 :** a ship of a class of U. S. warships of 5000 to 7000 tons that is smaller than a cruiser and larger than a destroyer

frigate 2

frigate bird *n* **:** any of several long-winged strong-flying sea birds chiefly of tropical seas (family Fregatidae) that are noted for their rapacious habits and obtain much of their diet of chiefly fish by robbing other birds — called also *man-o'-war bird*

frigate-built \ˈ≈≈ˌ≈\ *adj, of a ship* **:** built with a raised quarter-deck and forecastle

frigate mackerel *n* **:** a small scombroid fish (*Auxis thazard*) that is bluish green above and silvery beneath and often marked with black spots or wavy bars and that is very oily and little sought for food or game though widely available in warm seas

frigefact *vt* -ED/-ING/-S [L *frigefactare,* fr. *frigēre* to be cold, freeze + *factare* to make, do, freq. of *facere* to make, do — more at FRIGID, DO] *obs* **:** CHILL — **frigefaction** *n* -s *obs* — **frigefactive** *adj, obs*

frig·gle \ˈfrigəl\ *vi* -ED/-ING/-S [freq. of ¹*frig*] *dial Brit* **:** to fuss over trifles **:** PUTTER

¹fright \ˈfrīt, *usu* -īd.+V\ *n* -s [ME, fr. OE *fyrhto, fryhto* fear, fright; akin to OE *forht* afraid, fearful, OFris *fruchte* fear, OS & OHG *forht, foraht* afraid, *forhta* fear, Goth *faurhts* afraid, *fauhrtei* fear, and perh. to Toch A *pärsk-, prask-* to fear, *praski* fear, Toch B *pärsk-, prāsk-* to fear, *prosko, proskye* fear] **1 a :** terror excited by sudden danger **:** sudden and violent fear usu. of short duration **:** ALARM ⟨familiarity rubbed away the ~ at the strangeness and dissipated the prejudice born of ignorance —Oscar Handlin⟩ **b :** an instance of such terror, fear, or alarm ⟨the sudden apparition gave him a ~⟩ **c :** FEAR ⟨incessant ~ of the future —Oscar Handlin⟩ **2 :** something strange, ugly, unsightly, or shocking ⟨he was a bundle of rags, his hair had grown prodigiously, his beard was a ~ —I.L.Idriess⟩ **syn** see FEAR

²fright \"\ *vt* -ED/-ING/-S [ME *frighten,* fr. OE *fyrhtan, fryhtan;* akin to OE *forhtian* to fear, OFris *fruchtia,* OS *forhtian,* OHG *furhten, forhten,* Goth *faurhtjan* to fear, OE *fyrhto, fryhto,* n.] **:** to alarm suddenly **:** SCARE, FRIGHTEN ⟨are not easily ~*ed* by politics —*Kiplinger Washington Letter*⟩ **syn** see FRIGHTEN

fright disease *n* **:** CANINE HYSTERIA

fright·en \ˈfrītᵊn\ *vb* **frightened; frightened; frightening** \-t(ᵊ)niŋ\ **frightens** [¹*fright* + *-en*] *vt* **1 :** to markedly disturb with fear **:** throw into a state of alarm **:** make afraid **:** TERRIFY ⟨the mask ~*ed* the child⟩ **2 a :** to impel or drive by frightening ⟨~*ed* the boy into confessing his crime⟩ ⟨~*ed* the prowler away⟩ **b :** to evoke by the use of frightening methods ⟨~ the secret out of the man⟩ **3** *dial Eng* **:** to take by surprise **:** AMAZE ⟨I shouldn't be ~*ed* if it rained today⟩ ~ *vi* **1 :** to produce fright **:** SCARE, TERRIFY ⟨a costume designed to ~⟩ **2 :** to become frightened ⟨not a man who ~s easily⟩

syn FRIGHT, SCARE, ALARM, TERRIFY, TERRORIZE, STARTLE, AFFRAY, AFFRIGHT: these verbs have in common the meaning of to fill with fear or dread. FRIGHTEN, perhaps the most general, may apply to a momentary reaction of mild or acute apprehension or to a long-standing state of mind in which fear or dread prevails, although more frequently implying a shortish reaction of acute apprehension and generally suggesting a paralyzing effect upon the body or the will ⟨children *frightened* by thunder⟩ ⟨the silence of the house for a long time *frightened* Clara —Sherwood Anderson⟩ ⟨when I started down that precipice I was *frightened,* literally scared numb and stiff —W.A.White⟩ FRIGHT is an older and now almost solely literary or dialect form of FRIGHTEN ⟨you have Death perpetually before your eyes, only so far removed as to compose the mind without *frighting* it —Thomas Gray⟩ Often equivalent to FRIGHTEN in conversational use, SCARE usu. implies a quick fear that causes one to run, shy, or tremble ⟨the near approach of death *scared* him into sincerity —T.B. Macaulay⟩ ⟨sensational books commonly try to *scare* the reader —C.E.Kellogg⟩ ALARM, in modern use, stresses apprehension or anxiety ⟨they had been *alarmed* during the night by loud noises that must have been demolitions of some kind —Eric Linklater⟩ ⟨my mother, *alarmed* by the cries and fighting, came running downstairs to help me —R.L.Stevenson⟩ TERRIFY puts stress upon acute fear and agitation, usu. suggesting a state of mind in which self-control or self-direction are impossible ⟨something in his face and in his voice *terrified* her heart —Robert Hichins⟩ ⟨these things *terrified* the people to the last degree —Daniel Defoe⟩ TERRORIZE, as distinct from TERRIFY, often implies an intentional affecting with terror ⟨a band of cutthroats and thieves that *terrorized* the lower Mississippi valley —*Amer. Guide Series: Tenn.*⟩ ⟨he delighted in *terrorizing* the guests by his bullying and swaggering ways —E.V.Buckholder⟩ STARTLE always implies surprise or a sudden usu. light shock that causes one to jump or shrink ⟨an infant is *startled* by a loud noise —Morris Fishbein⟩ ⟨suddenly she was *startled* into an upright position, with her eyes staring and her mouth wide open —Liam O'Flaherty⟩ AFFRAY and AFFRIGHT are now archaic and found usu. in poetic works; AFFRAY is very close to TERRIFY, AFFRIGHT close to FRIGHTEN ⟨blastings and blightings of hope and love, and rude shocks that *affray* —Robert Bridges †1930⟩ ⟨I was *affrighted* by that impossible novel —W.B.Yeats⟩ ⟨a picture of Purgatory which made the hair of those who gazed on it stand on end in terror, and so *affrighted* the butchers and the fishmongers that they abandoned their trade of taking life —Laurence Binyon⟩

fright·en·able \-t(ᵊ)nəbəl\ *adj* : capable of being frightened ⟨a child too easily ~⟩

frightened *adj* : affected with fright : made afraid : SCARED ⟨a ~ child⟩ ⟨~ of doing wrong⟩ **syn** see AFRAID

fright·ened·ly \-t(ᵊ)n(ə)dlē, -li\ *adv* : in a frightened manner

frightening *adj* : tending to frighten : exciting alarm ⟨a ~ display of air power⟩ ⟨a ~ apparition⟩ — **fright·en·ing·ly** *adv*

fright·ful \ˈfrītfəl\ *adj, sometimes* **frightfuller; frightfullest** [ME, fr. ¹*fright* + *-ful*] **1 a** *archaic* : tending to frighten easily : TIMID **b** *dial chiefly Eng* : ALARMED, FRIGHTENED **2** : conducive to fright : likely to arouse the emotions of fright, fear, or alarm ⟨the gods, as they appear to men, are radiant . . . the demons are ~, producing perturbation and terror —H.O. Taylor⟩ ⟨seeing some ~ specter —Charles Lamb⟩ **3** : egregious, startling, objectionable, or terrible (as because of enormity, outrageousness, or grotesqueness) and likely to shock, alarm, revolt, or stun ⟨its cost in money, property loss, and lives was ~ —Allan Nevins & H.S.Commager⟩ ⟨they talked most ~ scandal —George Meredith⟩ ⟨regard the most ~ things as normal —H.M.Parshley⟩ **4** : EXTREME, AWFUL ⟨a ~ thirst⟩ ⟨a ~ snob⟩ **syn** see FEARFUL

fright·ful·ly \-f(ə)lē, -li\ *adv* : in a frightful manner: as **a** : ALARMINGLY ⟨worried by the ~ fast movement of the car over the dark road⟩ **b** : EGREGIOUSLY, SHOCKINGLY ⟨the ~ cruel treatment of the animal⟩ **c** : VERY, EXTREMELY ⟨I'm ~ sorry I inconvenienced you⟩

fright·ful·ness \-fəlnəs\ *n* -ES **1** : the quality or state of being frightful **2** [trans. of G *schrecklichkeit*] : action or policy intended to terrorize esp. in warfare

frighting *pres part of* FRIGHT

frights *pl of* FRIGHT, *pres 3d sing of* FRIGHT

fright wig *n* : a costume wig with hair that stands out from the head or that may be made to stand out when the wearer wants it to

frig·id \ˈfrijəd\ *adj* [L *frigidus*, fr. *frigēre* to be cold; akin to L *frigus* frost, cold, Gk *rhigos*] **1 a** : very cold : markedly lacking heat or warmth ⟨a ~ climate⟩ ⟨a ~ day⟩ ⟨natural caves where the ~ water coats the surroundings with ice —*Amer. Guide Series: N.H.*⟩ **b** : lacking warmth, ardor, or vivacity of feeling : forbidding in manner : stiff and formal **c** : indifferent or hostile ⟨felt ~ toward the plan⟩ **2** : lacking imaginative qualities : INSIPID, PLODDING, DULL ⟨an artist's ~ conception⟩ ⟨writing a precise and ~ poetry⟩; *also* : POINTLESS, SENSELESS **3 a** : abnormally averse to sexual intercourse — used esp. of women **b** *obs* : lacking sexual vigor : IMPOTENT **c** *of a female* : unable to achieve orgasm during sexual intercourse — **frig·id·ly** *adv* — **frig·id·ness** *n* -ES

Frig·i·daire \ˌfrijəˈda(a)(ə)r, -de|, |ə\ *trademark* — used for a mechanical refrigerator

frig·i·dar·i·um \ˌfrijəˈda(a)rēəm\ *n, pl* **frigidar·ia** \-ēə\ [L, fr. *frigidus* + *-arium*] : a room of the ancient Roman thermae furnished with a cold bath and used for cooling off

fri·gid·i·ty \frəˈjidəd·ē, -ətē, -i\ *n* -ES [ME *frigidite*, fr. LL *frigiditas*, fr. L *frigidus* + *-itas* -ity] : the quality or state of being frigid; *specif* : marked or abnormal sexual indifference esp. in a woman

frigid zone *n* : the area or region between the arctic circle and the north pole or between the antarctic circle and the south pole — see ZONE illustration

frigo- *comb form* [ISV, fr. L *frigus* frost, cold] : cold ⟨*frigo*stable⟩ ⟨*frigo*therapy⟩

frig·o·rif·ic \ˌfrigəˈrifik\ *adj* [L *frigorificus*, fr. *frigor-*, *frigus* frost, cold + *-i-* + *-ficus* -fic — more at FRIGID] : causing cold : COOLING, CHILLING

fri·go·ri·fi·co \ˌfrigəˈrifəˌkō\ *n* -S [AmerSp *frigorífico*, fr. Sp, adj., chilling, fr. L *frigorificus*] **1** : a So. American meat-packing plant primarily for the exportation of frozen meat **2** *or* **frigorifico hide** : a So. American cattle hide from a frigorifico

frig·o·rim·e·ter \ˌfrigəˈriməd·ə(r)\ *n* [L *frigor-*, *frigus* coldness + E *-i-* + *-meter*] : a low-temperature thermometer

frigs *pres 3d sing of* FRIG, *pl of* FRIG

fri·jol \(ˈ)frēˈhōl, -hōl\ *also* **fri·jole** \", frēˈhōlē\ *n, pl* **fri·jo·les** \frēˈhōlēz, -ˈhō,lās, -ˈhō,lās\ [Sp *frijol*, fr. earlier *fesol*, *fresol*, fr. Pg *feijão* or Pg dial. (Galicia) *freixó*, *feixoo*, fr. L *phaseolus* kidney bean, dim. of *phaselus*, fr. Gk *phasēlos*] *chiefly Southwest* : BEAN 1b: as **a** : KIDNEY BEAN **b** : COWPEA 1b

fri·jo·li·llo \ˌfrē(h)əˈlē(ˌ)(y)ō\ *n* -S [AmerSp, dim. of Sp *frijol*] : any of several leguminous herbs or trees: as **a** : CORAL BEAN **2 b** : LOCOWEED

¹frill \ˈfril\ *vb* -ED/-ING/-S [perh. fr. Flem *frullen*, fr. *frul*, n.] *vt* **1 a** : to provide or decorate with a frill ⟨~ a cap⟩ : crimp or pleat an edge of **b** : to serve as a frill for ⟨if you look up . . . you see that clouds ~ the sky —Leo Sinden⟩ **2** *Austral* : to ring (a tree) with a frill : FRILL-BARK ~ *vi, of a photographic emulsion* : to wrinkle and loosen from the film or plate support

²frill \"\ *n* -S [perh. fr. Flem *frul*] **1** : an ornamental flared or ruffled edge: as **a** : a gathered, pleated, or bias-cut fabric edging used on clothing **b** : a strip of paper curled at one end and rolled to be slipped over the bone end (as of a chop) in serving **2** : something resembling a frill ⟨a ~ of white beard edging his face —Victoria Sackville-West⟩ as: **a** : a fold of hair or feathers about the neck of an animal **b** : an architectural ornamental trimming ⟨gables decorated with jigsaw ~s —*Amer. Guide Series: Tenn.*⟩ ⟨varicolored houses often ornamented with little baroque ~s in white —Christopher Rand⟩ **c** : AFFECTATION, AIR — usu. used in pl. ⟨an honest, just, ever generous man who had no ~s, no side, no nonsense about him —W.A.White⟩ **d** : something that has only decorative significance and can be dispensed with : something refined, tasty, or elegant but unsubstantial : something not essential : SUPERFLUITY, EXTRAVAGANCE, DAINTY, DELICACY, LUXURY ⟨the elimination of typographic ~s and unnecessary elaboration —*Linotype News*⟩ ⟨one man's fundamentals may be another man's ~s —Bice Clemow⟩ ⟨detestation of anything resembling ~s and fancies in food and drink and clothing⟩ **3** *Austral* : a border made by forcing back a narrow strip of bark below a groove cut around the trunk of a tree **4** *often cap* : a canary of a domestic variety marked by frilled and curled feathers

frill 1b

frill-bark \ˈ=,=\ *vt, Austral* : to ring (a tree) with a frill

frilled lizard *n* : a large Australian agamoid lizard (*Chlamydosaurus kingii*) having a broad frill on each side of the neck

frilled shark *or* **frill shark** *n* : an eel-shaped shark (*Chlamydoselachus anguineus*) found in deep water off the coast of Japan and in parts of the Atlantic that has six pairs of gill slits with broad frilled margins and a terminal mouth

frill·ery \ˈfrilərē\ *n* -ES [²*frill* + *-ery*] : an arrangement of frills (as on a dress) : FRILL

frill·ies \ˈfrilēz\ *n pl* [*frilly* + *-es* (pl. suffix)] : women's clothing with ruffles : TRIMMINGS; *esp* : frilled lingerie

frill·i·ness \ˈfrilēnəs, -lin-\ *n* -ES : the quality of being frilly

frill·ing \ˈfriliŋ\ *n* -S : a frill or arrangement of frills : an edging gathered into a frill

frilly \ˈfrilē, -li\ *adj* -ER/-EST : having or resembling a frill : NONESSENTIAL, ORNAMENTAL, FRIVOLOUS, TRIFLING ⟨get out of my field clothes and sun helmet into something ~ —Eve Langley⟩ ⟨like her earlier writing, it is . . . rather ~ here and there —E.A.Speiser⟩ ⟨~ cakes coated with icing —*New Yorker*⟩

frim \ˈfrim\ *adj* [ME, abundant, flourishing, prob. fr. OE *freme* good, excellent; akin to OE *fram* bold, strong, ON *framr* foremost, *fram* forward — more at FROM] **1** *dial Eng* : marked by good physical condition : FLOURISHING ⟨a ~ calf⟩ **2** *dial Eng* : tender and succulent ⟨in the spring when the grass is young and ~⟩

¹fringe \ˈfrinj\ *n* -S *often attrib* [ME *frenge*, fr. MF *frenge*, *frange*, *fringe*, fr. (assumed) VL *frimbia*, fr. L *fimbria*] **1** : an ornamental border (as for clothing, upholstery, curtains) consisting of short lengths of straight or twisted thread, cord, or leather hanging from cut or raveled edges of garments or from a separate band and often grouped or knotted in various designs **2** : something resembling a fringe : BORDER, EDGING, MARGIN, PERIPHERY ⟨the . . . people who lived just outside the ~ of the drought area —R.W.Murray⟩ ⟨a narrow ~ of continental coast —*Encyc. Americana*⟩: as **a** : a growth like a fringe (as of hair or bristles) ⟨hair forming a ~ around his bald head —Frances H. Eliot⟩ **b** : ⁵BANG **c** : a fimbriate border (as that of certain petals); *specif* : the peristome of a moss **d** : the confused double outline produced by lack of registration between two or more component pictures of a color photograph **e** : one of various light or dark bands produced by the interference or diffraction of light **f** : vague images and feelings attending a definite idea or sometimes present when the idea cannot be recalled **3 a** : something that is marginal, borderline, or introductory in relation to some activity, process, or subject matter : something that is secondary or supplementary to what is basic or central in importance or value ⟨this is an enormous field of which I can here touch only the ~ —G.G.Coulton⟩ ⟨education for an age in which leisure is the center rather than the ~ —John Diebold⟩ **b** : a group of persons occupying a marginal, extremist, or markedly deviant position (as economically, socially, politically, or culturally) ⟨an unwashed child from the criminal ~ of town —Frances G. Patton⟩ ⟨the ~s of Salem society were superstitious —Van Wyck Brooks⟩ ⟨this attack has been well organized by ~ groups —*New Republic*⟩ ⟨that is what they talk about in the ~ sects, not in proper congregations —*Time*⟩ ⟨the ~ types — the pathological and near pathological —John McPartland⟩ — see LUNATIC FRINGE **c** : FRINGE BENEFIT ⟨most unions want higher pensions, health and welfare, other ~s —*Kiplinger Washington Letter*⟩

²fringe \"\ *vb* -ED/-ING/-S *vt* **1** : to furnish or adorn with or as if with a fringe ⟨the cloth over the tea table is *fringed* with blue elephants —*New Yorker*⟩ ⟨~ a rug⟩ **2** : to serve as a fringe for ⟨grass *fringed* the stream⟩ ~ *vi* : to spread out like a fringe ⟨in that medieval time the cathedral *fringed* out into the university —Francis Hackett⟩

fringe area *n* : a region in which reception from a given broadcasting station is weak or subject to serious distortion due to distance, obstructions, or other causes

fringe benefit *n* : an employment benefit (as a pension, a paid holiday, or health insurance) granted by an employer that involves a money cost without affecting basic wage rates

fringe bush *n* : FRINGE TREE

fringe cup *n* **1** : MITERWORT 1 **2** *also* **fringe cups** *pl but sing or pl in constr* : FALSE ALUMROOT

fringed \ˈfrinjd\ *adj* [ME *frenged*, fr. *frenge* + *-ed*] : furnished with a fringe

fringed fern *n* : CLIMBING FERN

fringed gecko *n* : FLYING GECKO

fringed gentian *n* : any of several No. American herbs of the genus *Gentiana* having the margin of the corolla lobes fringed: as **a** : a widely but irregularly distributed annual or biennial herb (*G. crinita*) of eastern and central No. America that has violet-blue or white fringed flowers **b** : a similar but somewhat smaller blue-flowered plant (*G. procera*) of central and western No. America

fringed heath *n* : a prostrate European shrub (*Erica ciliaris*) with small rosy purple flowers and glandular-ciliate leaves

fringed loosestrife *n* : a perennial leafy herb (*Lysimachia ciliatum*) of eastern No. America having ciliate leaves and yellow flowers

fringed gentian a

fringed orchis *also* **fringed orchid** *n* : any of several summer-flowering American orchids of the genus *Habenaria* distinguished by a fringed or lacerated lip

fringed pink *n* **1** : any of several pinks with laciniate petals; *esp* : a Eurasian perennial herb (*Dianthus superbus*) sometimes cultivated for its showy fragrant lilac or rose flowers with deeply fringed margins **2** : a low wiry-stemmed branching herb (*Linanthus dianthiflorus*) of southern California with fringed pink flowers

fringed polygala *n* : GAYWINGS

fringed poppy mallow *n* : a poppy mallow (*Callirhoë digitata*) of the Great Plains

fringed tapeworm *n* : a cyclophyllidean tapeworm (*Thysanosoma actinioides*) found in the intestine and bile ducts of sheep and goats esp. in the western U.S. and having the hinder margin of each segment fringed

fringe-flower \ˈ=,=\ *n* : BUTTERFLY FLOWER

fringefoot \ˈ=,=\ *n, pl* **fringefoots** : any of numerous iguanid lizards (genus *Uma*) living in desert areas of the southwestern U.S. and adjacent Mexico and having the feet modified for movement over loose sand by elongated pointed scales fringing the digits

fringepod \ˈ=,=\ *n* : a plant of the genus *Thysanocarpus*

fring·er \ˈfrinjə(r)\ *n* -S **1** : one that fringes or makes a fringe **2** : one who is a member of a fringe ⟨made himself just as unpopular with ~s on the right as with those on the left —*Time*⟩

fringes *pl of* FRINGE, *pres 3d sing of* FRINGE

fringetail \ˈ=,=\ *n* : a goldfish with some of the fins long and fringed

fringe tree *n* : a small tree or shrub of the genus *Chionanthus*; *esp* : a small tree (*C. virginica*) occurring in the southern U.S. but used as an ornamental further north esp. in sheltered locations and having clusters of white flowers — called also *fringe bush*

fringe-tree bark *n* : the dried root bark of the fringe tree (*Chionanthus virginica*) formerly used as a diuretic

frin·gil·la \frinˈjilə\ *n, cap* [NL, fr. L *fringilla*, *fringuilla* chaffinch] : a genus (the type of the family Fringillidae) of singing birds including the chaffinch, brambling, and related forms

¹frin·gil·lid \(ˈ)frinˈjiləd\ *adj* [NL *Fringillidae*] : of or relating to the Fringillidae or a finch

²fringillid \"\ *n* -S : one of the Fringillidae : FINCH

frin·gil·li·dae \frinˈjiləˌdē\ *n pl, cap* [NL, fr. *Fringilla*, type genus + *-idae*] : a family of small seed-eating passerine birds that comprise the finches, that have strong bills which are short and usu. thick at the base, and that often exhibit well-marked sexual dimorphism with the juveniles resembling the females

fringing *adj* : forming a fringe ⟨that same rugged west coast with its deep fiords and its innumerable ~ islands —L.D. Stamp⟩

fringing forest *n* : a forest growing along a watercourse in a region otherwise devoid of trees

fringing reef *n* : a coral reef that borders the land

fringy \ˈfrinjē, -ji\ *adj* -ER/-EST : adorned with fringes : resembling fringe ⟨the gracefullest little ~ films of lace —Mark Twain⟩

frip·per \ˈfripə(r)\ *also* **frip·per·er** \-pərə(r)\ *n* -S [*fripper* fr. MF *fripier*, fr. OF *frepier*, fr. *frepe* + *-ier* -er; *fripperer* fr. MF *fripier* + E *-er*] *archaic* : one who deals in frippery or in old clothes

¹frip·pery \ˈfrip(ə)rē, -ri\ *n* -ES [MF *friperie* rags, old clothes, fr. OF *freperie*, fr. *frepe*, *ferpe*, *feupe* rag, old garment (fr. ML *faluppa* piece of straw, splinter) + *-erie* -ery] **1** *obs* **a** : castoff clothes **b** : a place where old clothes are sold **2 a** : a piece of finery : FINERY; *esp* : a showy nonessential article of dress that may be cheap and tawdry, excessively detailed and ornamented, or elegant and rich ⟨the *fripperies* of her elegant bonnet trembling —Arnold Bennett⟩ **b** : affected elegance : OSTENTATION

²frippery \"\ *adj* : TRIFLING, CONTEMPTIBLE

friscal *n* -S [prob. alter. of ¹*frisk* + *-al*] *obs* : FRISK, CAPER

¹frisco *n* -ES [prob. alter. of ¹*frisk* + *-o* (common Sp & It n. ending)] *obs* : FRISCAL

²fris·co \ˈfri(ˌ)skō\ *adj, usu cap* [fr. *Frisco*, short for *San Francisco*, Calif.] *slang* : of or relating to the city of San Francisco, Calif. ⟨the *Frisco* convention⟩

fri·sé \frēˈzā, frəˈ-\ *n* -S [F, fr. past part. of *friser* to curl, frieze — more at FRIZZ] : FRIEZE 1b, 2a

frise aileron \ˈfrēz-\ *n, usu cap F* [after Leslie G. *Frise* b 1897 Eng. engineer] : an aileron having a nose portion projecting ahead of the hinge axis and a lower surface in line with the lower surface of the wing so that when the trailing edge of the aileron is raised the nose portion protrudes below the lower surface of the wing thus increasing the drag

fri·sette \frēˈzet, frəˈ-\ *n* -S [F, fr. *friser* to curl + *-ette* — more at FRIZZ] *archaic* : a fringe of hair or curls worn on the forehead by women

fri·seur \frēˈzər\ *n* -S [F, fr. *friser* + *-eur* -or] : HAIRDRESSER

¹fri·sian \ˈfrizhən, ˈfrē| *also* |zhēən\ *adj, usu cap* [L *Frisii* + E *-an*] **1 a** : of, relating to, or characteristic of Friesland **b** : of, relating to, or characteristic of the Frisians. **2** : of, relating to, or characteristic of the Frisian language

²frisian \"\ *n* -S *cap* **1 a** : a member of the Frisii **b** : one of the modern descendants of the Frisii that inhabit principally the Netherlands province of Friesland and the Frisian islands in the North sea **2** : the West Germanic language of the Frisian people — see INDO-EUROPEAN LANGUAGES table

fri·sii \ˈfriz(h)ēˌī, -zēˌē\ *n pl, cap* [L] : a Germanic people that settled along the coast of the North sea in prehistoric times

¹frisk \ˈfrisk\ *vb* -ED/-ING/-S [obs. *frisk*, adj., lively, brisk, fr. ME, fr. MF *frisque*, *frique*, of Gmc origin; akin to OHG *frisc* fresh, lively — more at FRESH] *vi* : to leap, skip, dance, or gambol esp. in frolic : move briskly and sportively or playfully ⟨the innocent voices laughing in the evening, the dogs ~*ing* —T.H.White b.1915⟩ ⟨filling in the time . . . by ~*ing* about —T. B.Costain⟩ ~ *vt* **1** : to move in a frisking manner ⟨a milk-cart pony rattles down the street, ~*ing* his mane —*Times Lit. Supp.*⟩ ⟨~*ing* about the hem of her skirt —T.B.Costain⟩ **2 a** : to search or go through esp. for concealed weapons or stolen articles ⟨they'd used this fake bell boy to ~ my coat while I was washing —Erle Stanley Gardner⟩ ⟨~*ing* the ladies' cabins in their absence —*New Yorker*⟩; *esp* : to search (a person) for such purpose usu. by running the hand rapidly over the clothing and through the pockets ⟨I went behind him and ~*ed* him carefully —Hartley Howard⟩ **b** : to take or steal from esp. by such frisking ⟨a certain soldier was ~*ed* of $800 when boarding the train for home —Dixon Wecter⟩

²frisk \"\ *n* -S **1 a** *archaic* : CARACOLE, CAPER, JIG **b** : a frolicking movement : GAMBOL, ROMP ⟨in a few minutes . . . she was exploring the yard with ~s of pleasure —Mary Mian⟩ **c** : a gay time : FROLIC, DIVERSION ⟨so come . . . it will be a ~ that will do you good —Mary W. Shelley⟩ **2** : a frisking esp. for concealed weapons or stolen articles ⟨a quick ~ of the coats in the coatroom of the hall —W.L.Gresham⟩

frisk·er \-kə(r)\ *n* -S [*frisk* + *-er*] : one that frisks

fris·ket \ˈfriskət\ *n* -S [F *frisquette*, fr. MF, fr. fem. of *frisquet* vivacious, flirtatious, fr. *frisque*, *frique* lively — more at FRISK] **1** : a light frame to hold the sheet of paper to the tympan in printing on a hand press; *also* : a sheet stretched in a frame with parts cut out to lay over an inked form so that only certain parts shall be printed **2** : a masking device comparable to a frisket used in photography and photoengraving

frisk·i·ly \ˈfriskəlē, -li\ *adv* : in a frisky manner ⟨moves about ~ despite his age⟩

friskin *n* -S [prob. alter. of *frisking*, gerund of ¹*frisk*] *obs* : a frisky action or person

frisk·i·ness \ˈfriskēnəs, -kin-\ *n* -ES : the quality or state of being frisky ⟨the ~ of young colts just put out to pasture⟩

frisk·ing·ly *adv* : in a frisking manner

frisky \ˈfriskē, -ki\ *adj* -ER/-EST [obs. *frisk* lively, frisk + *-y* — more at FRISK] : inclined to frisk : FROLICSOME, GAY, PLAYFUL ⟨still dancing with ~ step —Nathaniel Hawthorne⟩ ⟨the mood of the picture is ~ —Bosley Crowther⟩ ⟨too ~ for an old man —Francis Jeffrey⟩

fri·so·lée \ˌfrēzəˈlā\ *n* -S [F *frisolée*, *friselée*, fr. fem. of *friselé*, past part. of *friseler* to curl, fr. *friser* — more at FRIZZ] : MOSAIC

fri·son \frēˈzōⁿ\ *n* -S [F, fr. *friser* to curl] : waste silk usu. taken from the outside of the cocoon

friss \ˈfrish\ *also* **frisz·ka** \ˈfrishkə\ *n, pl* **frisses** *also* **friszkas** [*friss* fr. Hung; *friszka* fr. Pol, fr. Hung *friss*] : the fast section of a czardas — contrasted with *lassú*

fris·son \frēˈsōⁿ\ *n, pl* **frissons** \-ōⁿ(z)\ [F, fr. LL *friction-*, *frictio*, irreg. (influence of L *friction-*, *frictio* friction), fr. L *frigēre* to be cold + *-ion-*, *-io* -ion — more at FRIGID] : SHUDDER, QUIVER, CHILL, TINGLE ⟨and again a ~ of surprise shot through him —Kathleen Freeman⟩ ⟨a little ~ of fear — Kathryn Hulme⟩; *esp* : a pleasurable sensation of fright or gloom : THRILL ⟨made a lucrative living from thrillers with a certain psychological ~ —Vernon Young⟩

fri·sure \ˈfrizhər, frəˈzhü(ə)r\ *n* -S [F, fr. *friser* to curl + *-ure* — more at FRIZZ] : a style of curling or dressing the hair : HAIRDRESSING, HAIRDO

¹frit \ˈfrit\ *n* -S [It *fritta*, fr. fem. of *fritto*, past part. of *friggere* to fry, fr. L *frigere* — more at FRY] **1** : the materials of which glass is made after having been calcined or partly fused in a furnace but before vitrification **2** : glass variously compounded that is quenched and ground as a basis for glazes or enamels

²frit \"\ *vt* **fritted; fritted; fritting; frits** : to prepare (materials for glass) by heat : FUSE

³frit \"\ *adj* [fr. E dial. past part. of ²*fright*] *dial Eng* : FRIGHTENED

frit fly \"-\ *n* [origin unknown] : a fly of the family Chloropidae (esp. *Oscinella frit*) injurious to grain in Europe

¹frith \ˈfrith\ *n* -S [ME, fr. OE *fyrhthe* wooded country] **1** *dial Eng* **a** : a tract of land grown with copsewood : COPPICE **b** : a clearing within a wooded area **2** *dial Eng* **a** : BRUSHWOOD, UNDERWOOD; *esp* : brushwood suitable for wattling **b** : HURDLE, HEDGE; *esp* : one made or mended with wattled brushwood

²frith \"\ *n* -S [alter. of *firth*] : a narrow arm of the sea : the opening of a river into the sea : FIRTH

frithborh *also* **frithborgh** *n* [ME *frithborg*, fr. (assumed) OE *frithborh*, fr. *frith* peace + *borh* pledge; akin to OE *frithu* peace, OHG *fridu*, ON *frithr* peace, Goth *gafrithon* to reconcile, OE *frēo* free — more at FREE, BORROW] *obs* : FRANKPLEDGE

frith·stool \ˈfrith,stül\ *also* **frid·stool** \ˈ-, -id,s-\ *n* [OE *frithstōl* place of safety or refuge, fr. *frith* peace + *stōl* chair, seat — more at STOOL] : a seat of sanctuary or refuge placed in ancient times in some English churches

frit·il·lar·ia \ˌfrid·ᵊlˈa(a)rēə\ *n* [NL, fr. L *fritillus* dice-cup + NL *-aria*; fr. the checkered markings of the petals] **1** *cap* : a genus of bulbous herbs (family Liliaceae) of north temperate regions having checkered or checkered nodding flowers — see CHECKERED LILY, CROWN IMPERIAL **2** -S : any plant, bulb, or flower of the genus *Fritillaria*

frit·il·lary \ˈfrid·ᵊlˌerē, *chiefly Brit* frəˈtiləri\ *n* -ES [NL *Fritillaria*] **1** : a plant of the genus *Fritillaria* **2** : any of numerous butterflies of *Speyeria*, *Argynnis*, and related genera — compare SILVERSPOT

Fri·tos \ˈfrē(ˌ)tōz, -ōs\ *trademark* — used for corn chips

¹frit·ter \ˈfrid·ə(r), -itə-\ *n* -S [ME *fritour*, *fritur*, *frutour*, *frutur*, fr. MF *friture*, fr. (assumed) VL *frictura*, fr. L *frictus* (past part. of *frigere* to roast, fry) + *-ura* -ure] **1** : a small quantity of batter often containing fruit or meat and fried in deep fat or sautéed ⟨apple ~s⟩ ⟨corn ~s⟩ ⟨clam ~s⟩ **2** *New Eng* : GRIDDLE CAKE

[2]**fritter** \"\ *n* -s [alter. of *fitter*] : FRAGMENT, SHRED ⟨each . . . morsel, crumb, scrag and ~ from the bins —Edith Sitwell⟩
[3]**fritter** \"\ *vb* -ED/-ING/-s *vt* **1** : to reduce or waste piecemeal : DIMINISH, CONSUME, DISSIPATE — used chiefly with *away* ⟨foolishly ~*ing* away time and energy⟩ ⟨~*ing* our time and thoughts away on trivial things —Dorothy C. Fisher⟩ **2** : to cut or break into small pieces or fragments : DISPERSE ⟨the responsibility for measures is ~*ed* and divided among a triad of authorities —Ernest Barker⟩ ~ *vi* **1** : to break up : divide into fragments ⟨there is formed . . . a slag which ~*s* on cooling —*Chem. Abstracts*⟩ **2** : to dissipate itself : DWINDLE ⟨the threat of economic sanctions ~*ed* into impotent "moral" protest —*Fortune*⟩ ⟨the conspiracy ~*ed* away to an ignominious conclusion —*Amer. Guide Series: Ind.*⟩ **syn** see WASTE
frit·ter·er \-id·ə·rə(r), -itə-\ *n* -s : one that fritters
fritting *n* -s [fr. gerund of [2]*frit*] **1** : the act or process of quenching from a molten condition in preparation of a frit for glaze or enamel **2** : the act or process of fusing into a glass the otherwise soluble components of a glaze or enamel
frit·to mi·sto \ˌfrē(ˌ)tō'mē(ˌ)stō\ *n* [It, mixed fried food] : MIXED GRILL
fritz \'frits\ *n* -ES *usu cap* [G, nickname for *Friedrich* (Frederick), a common German given name] : GERMAN ⟨it was the first I'd seen since the *Fritzes* cleared out —Kay Boyle⟩ — usu. used disparagingly — **on the fritz** *adv (or adj)* [origin unknown] : in a state of disrepair — usu. used with *go* ⟨his supercharger had gone *on the fritz* —G.P.Elliott⟩
fri·u·li·an \(')frē¦ülēən\ *n* -s *cap* [*Friuli*, district in Italy + E *-an*] **1** : a member of a people in northeastern Italy of the district of Friuli — called also *Furlan* **2** : the Rhaeto-Romanic dialect of the Friulians
[1]**friv·ol** \'frivəl\ *vi* **frivoled** *or* **frivolled**; **frivoled** *or* **frivolled**; **frivoling** *or* **frivolling** \-v(ə)liŋ\ **frivols** [back-formation fr. *frivolous*] : to act frivolously : TRIFLE ⟨a man of weight . . . does not come and ~ in the typists' room —Dorothy Sayers⟩ — **friv·ol·er** *or* **friv·ol·ler** \-v(ə)lə(r)\ *n* -s
[2]**frivol** \"\ *n* -s [back-formation fr. *frivolous*] : something that is frivolous : TRIFLE ⟨a restful holiday may be spent away from fashions and ~*s* —Napier Devitt⟩
frivol away *vt* : to spend frivolously : fritter away ⟨you who would *frivol* life *away* in charming play —Ethna MacCarthy⟩
fri·vol·i·ty \frə'välǝd·ē, -ətē, -i\ *n* -ES [F *frivolité*, fr. *frivole* frivolous (fr. L *frivolus*) + *-ité* -ity] **1** : the quality or state of being frivolous : the fact or habit of trifling : lack of seriousness : unbecoming levity ⟨greatness can never be founded upon ~ and corruption —Matthew Arnold⟩ **2** : an act or thing that is frivolous ⟨free from the vices and *frivolities* of the Court —Max Peacock⟩ ⟨nosegays and other *frivolities* for Easter —*New Yorker*⟩
friv·o·lous \'friv(ə)ləs\ *adj* [ME, fr. L *frivolus*, prob. fr. *friare* to rub, crumble — more at FRICTION] **1** : of little weight or importance : having no basis in law or fact : LIGHT, SLIGHT, SHAM, IRRELEVANT, SUPERFICIAL ⟨the procedure encourages ~ cases —David Fellman⟩ ⟨is it not possible to screen out ~ charges —A.F.Westin⟩ ⟨a ~ argument⟩ **2** : given to trifling or unbecoming levity : not grave or serious in demeanor, purpose, or acts : LIGHT-MINDED ⟨as ~ as his eldest son —C.H. Sykes⟩ ⟨she spends . . . too much time at soda fountains . . . it makes her appear ~ —Ellen Glasgow⟩ ⟨the . . . ~ existence of a public official mingling in corrupt social circles —*Encyc. Americana*⟩ : not serious or practical (as in content or form) : LIGHT, GAY, PLAYFUL ⟨this letter is, on the whole, ~ in its temper —Irving Kristol⟩ ⟨some ~ lapel pins . . . in the form of heads of young girls —*New Yorker*⟩ — **friv·o·lous·ly** *adv*
friv·o·lous·ness *n* -ES : the quality or state of being frivolous : FRIVOLITY
friz *dial past of* FREEZE
frize \'frēz\ *archaic var of* FRIZZ
friz·er *also* **frizz·er** \'frizə(r)\ *n* -s : one that frizzes
[1]**frizz** *also* **friz** \'friz\ *vb* **frizzed**; **frizzed**; **frizzing**; **frizzes** [alter. (influenced by *frizzle*) of F *friser* to shrivel up (as meat when fried), curl, crimp, prob. fr. *fris-*, stem of *frire* to fry — more at FRY] *vt* **1** : to form into small tight curls : CURL ⟨plays a ~*ed* girl of the 20s —*Time*⟩ — often used with *up* ⟨a young girl ~*ing* up her hair in preparation for a date⟩ **2** : to remove a thin layer of the grain side of (a skin) in leather manufacture (as by rubbing with pumice stone or a blunt instrument after prolonged liming); *also* : to pare off with a sharp knife (as in the making of glove leather) ~ *vi, of hair* : to form or be in or form into a mass of tight curls
[2]**frizz** *also* **friz** \"\ *n* -ES **1** : a tight curl or curls ⟨she took a pencil from the *frizz* behind her ear —Elizabeth Taylor⟩ **2** : hair that is tightly curled
[3]**frizz** \"\ *vb* -ED/-ING/-ES [alter. (influenced by *sizzle*) of [1]*fry*] : to fry, cook, or sear with a sizzling noise : SIZZLE
friz·zen \'friz°n\ *n* -s [alter. of earlier *frizzle*, of unknown origin] : the pivoted metal upright of the action of a flintlock against which the flint strikes upon firing
frizz·i·ly \-zəlē, -li\ *adv* : in a frizzy manner ⟨a head of hair curled a little too ~⟩
frizz·i·ness \-zēnə̇s, -zin-\ *n* -ES : the quality or state of being frizzy ⟨had trouble combing out the ~ of the dog's coat⟩
[1]**friz·zle** \'frizəl\ *vb* **frizzled**; **frizzled**; **frizzling** \-z(ə)liŋ\ **frizzles** [prob. akin to OE *fris* curly, OFris *frisle*, *fresle* curl, lock of hair] *vt* : to curl or crisp (as the hair) usu. with heat : FRIZZ — often used with *up* ⟨*frizzled* up her locks for the occasion⟩ ~ *vi* : CURL, CRISP — used esp. of hair; often used with *up*
[2]**frizzle** \"\ *n* -s **1 a** : a crisp curl or curls **b** : the state of being frizzed **2** *often cap* : a domestic fowl having the feathers curled backward that is in some areas regarded as constituting a separate breed but prob. represents a simple genetic variation
[3]**frizzle** \"\ *vb* -ED/-ING/-S [blend of [1]*fry* and *sizzle*] *vt* **1** : to fry until crisp and curled ⟨*frizzled* beef⟩ **2** : to burn, scorch, or sear by the application of heat ⟨if you touch a turbine in the wrong place, you get *frizzled* —Ann Bridge⟩ ⟨sometimes the brown grass was dark and *frizzled* with heat —Eve Langley⟩ ~ *vi* : to cook with a sizzling noise ⟨I could smell the bacon *frizzling* downstairs —E.L.Thomas⟩
[4]**frizzle** \"\ *n* -s : the act or noise of frizzling ⟨letting escape the sudden ~ and fragrance of the roast —Adrian Bell⟩
friz·zly \'friz(ə)lē\ *adj, sometimes* -ER/-EST : FRIZZY ⟨~ hair⟩
frizzy \'frizē -zi\ *adj* -ER/-EST **1** *of hair* : tightly curled ⟨the aborigine's mass of short ~ hair⟩ **2** : FRILLED
frl *abbr* fractional
frm *abbr* **1** frame; framing **2** from
[1]**fro** \frə, (ˌ)frō\ *prep* [ME *fra*, *fro*, fr. ON *frā* — more at FROM] *dial Brit* : FROM
[2]**fro** \'frō\ *adv* [ME *fra*, *fro*, fr. *fra*, *fro*, prep.] : BACK, BACKWARD, FROM, AWAY — used correlatively with *to* in the phrase *to and fro*
[1]**frock** \'fräk\ *n* -s [ME *frok*, *frokke*, fr. MF *froc*, of Gmc origin; akin to OS *hroc* mantle, coat, OFris *hrock*, OHG *hroch*, and prob. to OE *rocc*, OS *rok*, OHG *roc*, *roch*, OIr *rucht*, MW *rhuch*] **1** : an outer garment worn by monks and friars : HABIT **2** : an outer garment worn chiefly by men: **a** : a long loose mantle **b** : COAT OF MAIL **c** : a workman's outer shirt; *esp* : SMOCK FROCK **d** : a woolen jersey worn esp. by sailors **e** : FROCK COAT; *also* : a military coat of similar cut **3 a** : a woman's dress **b** : a dress worn by a girl and formerly by both boys and girls
[2]**frock** \"\ *vt* -ED/-ING/-S **1** : to clothe in a frock ⟨~*ed* in dusty pink with a musquash coat —*Perth (Australia) Sunday Times Mag.*⟩ **2** : to make a cleric of — compare UNFROCK
frock coat *n* : a man's usu. double-breasted coat having knee-length skirts front and back
frock·ing \-kiŋ\ *n* -s [[1]*frock* + *-ing*] : cloth suitable for a frock
froe *or* **frow** \'frō\ *n* -s [alter. of *frower*] **1** : a cleaving tool with handle at right angles to the blade for splitting cask staves and shingles from the block **2** : a steel wedge for splitting logs
[1]**froe·be·lian** \(')frā¦bēlēən, (')frē¦-, (')frœ¦-, -bel-, -lyən\ *adj, usu cap* [Friedrich *Froebel* †1852 Ger. educator who founded the kindergarten system + E *-ian*] : relating to or derived from Friedrich Froebel or his kindergarten system of education
[2]**froebelian** \"\ *n* -s *usu cap* : a person who teaches by or favors the Froebelian system
froehlich's syndrome *usu cap F, var of* FRÖHLICH'S SYNDROME
froe·man \'frōmən\ *n, pl* **froemen** [*froe* + *man*] : [2]RIVER
FROF *abbr* fire risk on freight

[1]**frog** \'frȯg, 'fräg\ *n* -s [ME *frogge*, fr. OE *frogga*; akin to OE *frosc*, *frox*, *forsc* frog, OHG *frosk*, ON *frauki* & *froskr* frog, Skt *pravate* he jumps up, *plava* frog; basic meaning: jumping, hopping] **1 a** : any of various smooth-skinned web-footed tailless agile leaping amphibians (as of the suborder Diplasiocoela) being largely aquatic, feeding chiefly on insect larvae, small fishes, and other water dwellers, and laying eggs in clusters enclosed in a gelatinous matrix from which hatch the tailed gilled limbless larvae that later metamorphose into 4-limbed adults without tails or gills : one of the more aquatic members of the order Salientia as distinguished from the more terrestrial toads — compare BUFO, RANA, TADPOLE **b** : an amphibian of the order Salientia **c** [so called fr. their reputation for eating frogs] : FRENCHMAN — usu. taken to be offensive **d** : a throat condition that produces hoarseness — often used in the phrase *frog in the throat* **2** : the triangular elastic horny pad in the middle of the sole of the foot of the horse and related animals — see FRUSH **3 a** (1) : a looped device attached to a belt for holding a weapon or tool (2) : a front fastening for a garment (as a coat, jacket, dress) that is made usu. of braid in an ornamental looped design with a bar-shaped button or thick knot on one edge of the opening to fit into a loop on the other **b** : a device made of rail sections constructed and assembled to permit the wheels on one rail of a track to cross another rail of an intersecting track **c** : a shallow place for mortar in the upper face of a brick **d** : the frame or block to which the share, moldboard, landside, or beam of a plow are secured **e** : the nut of a violin bow : HEEL — see BOW illustration **f** (1) : the junction of two branches of a flume (2) : a guiding timber at the mouth of a slide **g** : a device for supporting and mutually insulating trolley wires that cross each other **h** : the seat for the plane iron in the stock of a carpenter's plane **i** : a loom device that actuates a stop motion when the shuttle is out of position **4** : an imperfectly ripened prune of inferior quality **5** [by folk etymology fr. *frage*] **a** : a card game developed from tarok and popular esp. in Mexico **b** : the lowest bid in this and similar games — compare CHICO, FRAGE

frog 3a(2)

[2]**frog** \"\ *vi* **frogged**; **frogged**; **frogging**; **frogs** : to catch or look for frogs
frogbit *or* **frog's-bit** \'=,=\ *n, pl* **frogbits** *or* **frog's-bits** **1** : a European aquatic floating herb (*Hydrocharis morsus-ranae*) with roundish heart-shaped leaves and small white flowers **2** : an American aquatic plant (*Limnobium spongia*) with round-cordate or reniform leaves and sessile or short-stalked spathes
frogbit family *or* **frog's-bit family** *n* : HYDROCHARITACEAE
frog boot *n* : a cushion (as of rubber or leather) fitted around the frog of a horse's foot to prevent shock — called also *frog pad*
frog breathing *n* : a technique using mouth and tongue to force air into the lungs that was developed by some patients suffering from poliomyelitic paralysis of respiratory muscles
frog cheese *n* : a young puffball
frog crab *n* : any of numerous crabs constituting the family Raninidae, having an elongated carapace, flattened legs, and a stance like that of a frog, and being widely distributed in shallow or moderately deep tropical seas
frog duck *n* : HOODED MERGANSER
frogeater \'=,==\ *n* **1** : one that eats frogs **2** *usu cap* : FRENCHMAN — usu. taken to be offensive
frogeye \'=,=\ *n* : any of numerous leaf diseases characterized by the concentric rings about the diseased spots: as **a** (1) : a disease of growing tobacco caused by a parasitic fungus (*Cercospora nicotianae*) (2) : a similar and often severely defoliating disease of soybeans caused by a related fungus (*Cercospora diazu*) **b** : a phase of black rot of apples in which the leaves are so spotted — **frog-eyed** \'=,=\ *adj*
frogface \'=,=\ *n* : a face resembling a frog's; *specif* : one with the nose broadened by polyps
frogfish \'=,=\ *n* **1** : a fish (as the angler) of the family Antennariidae; *broadly* : one of the order Pediculati **2** : TOADFISH 1
frogged \'frȯgd, 'frägd\ *adj* [[1]*frog* + *-ed*] : decorated or fastened with frogs
frog·ger \-gə(r)\ *n* -s [[1]*frog* + *-er*] **1** : a logger who helps to load logs and timber on sleds or drays for removal from the forest — called also *trailer, zoogler* **2** : CHASER 3a
frog·gery \-gərē\ *n* -ES [[1]*frog* + *-ery*] : a gathering of frogs; *also* : a place where frogs abound
frog·ging \-giŋ\ *n* -s [[1]*frog* + *-ing*] : FROG 3a(2) : an ornamentation with frogs
frog·gish \-gish\ *adj* : characteristic of a frog
frog·gy \-gē, -gi\ *adj* -ER/-EST : abounding in frogs : of, relating to, or resembling frogs ⟨his gruff, ~ voice —E.J.Kahn⟩
froghopper \'=,==\ *n* : a member of the Cercopidae : SPITTLE INSECT
frog kick *n* : the breaststroke kick when it is executed with the hip joints in a position with the knees apart
frog·let \-glə̇t\ *n* -s [[1]*frog* + *-let*] **1** : a small or young frog **2** : a small tree toad (as *Crinia laevis* of Tasmania)
frog lily *n* **1** : SPATTERDOCK **2** : a plant of the genus *Potamogeton*
frog·ling \-gliŋ\ *n* -s [[1]*frog* + *-ling*] : a small or young frog : FROGLET
frog·man \-,man, -,mən, -,maa(ə)n\ *n, pl* **frogmen** : a person equipped with a face mask, flippers, a rubber suit, or other devices for swimming under water for extended periods; *esp* : a person so equipped for military reconnaissance and demolition of underwater obstacles
frog-march \'=,=\ *vt* : to carry (as a resisting prisoner) face downward by the arms and legs
frogmouth \'=,=\ *n* : any of various birds of Oriental and Australian regions related to the goatsuckers and constituting the family Podargidae
frog orchis *or* **frog orchid** *n* : any of several green-flowered orchids of the genus *Habenaria*
frog pad *n* : FROG BOOT
frog plant *n* : ORPINE
frogs *pres 3d sing of* FROG, *pl of* FROG
frog's-bit *var of* FROGBIT
frog's-bladder \'=,==\ *n, pl* **frog's-bladders** : ORPINE
frog shell *n* : any of numerous chiefly tropical gastropod mollusks (family Cymatiidae) that resemble the related tritons but have notably thick heavy rugose or tuberculated shells; *also* : a shell of one of these mollusks
frogskin \'=,=\ *n* [so called fr. the green back] *slang* : a piece of paper money; *esp* : a dollar bill
frog spawn *n* **1** : a red alga of the genus *Batrachospermum* **2** : FROG SPIT 2
frog spit *or* **frog spittle** *n* **1** : CUCKOO SPIT 1a **2** : an alga (as of the family Chlorophyceae) that forms slimy masses on ponds or other quiet water
frogsticker \'=,==\ *n, Midland* : POCKETKNIFE
frogstool \'=,=\ *n* : TOADSTOOL
froh·berg·ite \'frō,bər,gīt\ *n* -s [Max H. *Frohberg* b1901 Canadian geologist born in Germany + E *-ite*] : a mineral $FeTe_2$ consisting of a telluride of iron and belonging to the marcasite group
fröh·lich \'frœlik\ *adj* [G, fr. OHG *frōlih*, fr. *frō* happy, cheerful + *-lih* -ly — more at FROLIC] *adj* : JOYOUS, HAPPY — used as a direction in music
fröh·lich's syndrome *or* **froeh·lich's syndrome** \'frā¦lik(s)-, 'frō¦, 'frœ¦, -ik(s)-\ *n, usu cap F* [after Alfred *Fröhlich* †1953 Austrian neurologist] : ADIPOSOGENITAL DYSTROPHY
froise \'frȯiz\ *n* -s [ME] *dial Eng* : a large thick pancake often served with bacon
[1]**frol·ic** \'frälik, -lēk\ *adj* [D *vroolijk*, fr. MD *vrolijc*, fr. *vro* happy, joyful + *-lijc* -ly (akin to OHG *-līh*); akin to OFris *frō* happy, OS *frā*, *frō*, *fraho*, OHG *frō* happy, ON *frār* swift, OE *frogga* frog — more at FROG] : full of fun or mirth : dancing, playing, or frisking about : GAY, MERRY ⟨contrasting the stern anxiety of his present mood with the ~ spirit of the preceding year —Nathaniel Hawthorne⟩ — **frol·ic·ly** \-ləklē, -li\ *adv*
[2]**frolic** \", *chiefly in pres part* -lək\ *vi* **frolicked**; **frolicked**; **frolicking**; **frolics** **1** : to amuse oneself : make merry : make fun : DISPORT, REVEL ⟨who has *frolicked* with him the night before and little dreams that he is to leave her —*Encyc. Americana*⟩ **2** : to move gaily or sportively : play about happily : ROMP, CAPER, GAMBOL ⟨two white pigeons *frolicking* on the green lawn —*N.Y. Times*⟩ ⟨a young daughter who . . . *frolicked* around the bar, the storerooms, and the wine cellars —*New Yorker*⟩ **syn** see PLAY
[3]**frolic** \"\ *n* -s [[2]*frolic*] **1** : a playful, sportive, or gaily mischievous action : a good time : PRANK, LARK ⟨would ask a visitor if she wanted onions in her cocoa . . . had always been up to some ~ like that —Jean Stafford⟩ ⟨boys bent on a ~ —Margaret Mead⟩ ⟨for the first ten months the klan existed mainly as a ~ —Dixon Wecter⟩ **2 a** : FUN, MERRIMENT, GAIETY ⟨their sedateness is as comical as their ~ —George Meredith⟩ ⟨can read and enjoy him for his lively sense of adventure and ~ —Richard McLaughlin⟩ ⟨expecting to indulge in an evening of lightsome ~ —Theodore Dreiser⟩ **b** : an occasion or scene of gaiety and mirth : DANCE, PARTY, PICNIC ⟨working in behalf of the seventh annual spring ~, a tea dance —*N.Y. Times*⟩ ⟨~*s* at the officers' club —H.H. Martin⟩: as (1) *dial* : BEE 3 ⟨quilting ~⟩ (2) *dial* : a lively country party usu. with dancing and games **syn** see [2]PLAY
frol·ic·some \-səm\ *adj* : full of gaiety and mirth : given to pranks : SPORTIVE, PLAYFUL ⟨treated the whole affair as a ~ adventure —Herman Melville⟩ ⟨a ~ young thing⟩ — **frol·ic·some·ly** *adv* — **frol·ic·some·ness** *n* -ES
from _f(r)əm, f°m, ¦främ, ¦frəm, _främ\ *prep* [ME *fram*, *from*, fr. OE; akin to OE & OHG *fram*, adv., forth, away, forward, ON *frā*, prep., from, *fram*, adv., forward, Goth, prep., from, OE *faran* to travel, go — more at FARE] **1** — used as a function word to indicate a starting point: as (1) a point or place where an actual physical movement (as of departure, withdrawal, or dropping) has its beginning ⟨he set out ~ town this morning⟩ ⟨held the funeral ~ the funeral parlor —R.O.Bowen⟩ ⟨shrinking ~ his touch⟩ ⟨a fall ~ a horse⟩ ⟨the first pigeon race . . . ever held ~ this city —*Springfield (Mass.) Daily News*⟩ ⟨he comes ~ beyond the sea⟩ ⟨came out ~ under the table⟩ ⟨five tanks were shot ~ under him —*Current Biog.*⟩; (2) something that is taken as a starting point in measuring or reckoning or in a statement of limits ⟨it is 20 miles ~ here to the nearest town⟩ ⟨three years ~ that day⟩ ⟨ready to go home within a fortnight ~ the operation —*Lancet*⟩ ⟨~ five to ten years are needed for the project⟩ ⟨~ childhood he displayed great ability⟩ ⟨frames and trays range ~ $1 —*N.Y. Herald Tribune*⟩; (3) the starting or focal point of any activity or movement ⟨will fight you ~ our beaches and ~ our ruined homes⟩ ⟨looked at me ~ under her glasses⟩ ⟨~ one point of view you are right⟩ ⟨I speak ~ the heart⟩ ⟨shot straight ~ the hip⟩; often used with words that express the condition of being suspended or pendent ⟨ornaments hanging ~ a Christmas tree⟩ **2** — used as a function word to indicate (1) the fact or condition of spatial or physical absence, separation, remoteness, or disjunction ⟨an ocean separates America ~ Europe⟩ ⟨the wind was ~ them⟩ ⟨a dunlin, disturbed ~ its young, creeps along the ground —E.A.Armstrong⟩; often used, chiefly Brit., in the phrase *from home* ⟨seemed to discover a home ~ home in our house —Adrian Bell⟩ ⟨he had been ~ home . . . during most of the period mentioned —F.W. Crofts⟩; also in obs. usage to indicate qualitative remoteness or unlikeness; (2) the act, fact, or condition of removal, withdrawal, abstention, separation, dissent, discrimination, qualification, or differentiation of any kind ⟨the most extensive file . . . lacks only five numbers ~ being complete —B.A.Botkin & A.F.Harlow⟩ ⟨asked him to refrain ~ interrupting⟩ ⟨exclude a man ~ membership⟩ ⟨he differs ~ his brother in every particular⟩ ⟨purging its abuses ~ the faith⟩ ⟨put his wife ~ him⟩ ⟨set men free ~ superstition⟩; (3) change or transition from one state or condition to another or replacement of one thing by another ⟨~ the defense they sprang to the attack⟩ ⟨things go ~ bad to worse⟩ ⟨transformed wretched serfs into proud freemen⟩ ⟨turned ~ their books to the grim business of war⟩ **3** — used as a function word to indicate the source or original or moving force of something: as (1) the source, cause, means, or ultimate agent of an action or condition ⟨all his misfortunes spring ~ that piece of folly⟩ ⟨you will hear ~ my lawyer⟩ ⟨he holds his appointment ~ the trustees⟩ ⟨smoking a cigarette ~ one hand and sipping chocolate ice-cream soda . . . ~ the other —Frances Perkins⟩ ⟨emissaries ~ a barbarian king⟩ ⟨these lakes . . . are, ~ their low temperature, entirely destitute of fish —*Encyc. Americana*⟩ ⟨tea time when visits ~ her family usually occurred —Osbert Lancaster⟩; (2) the ground, reason, or basis (as of a judgment, belief, finding, or action) ⟨its composition appears to be uncertain ~ the physical facts —W.E.Swinton⟩ ⟨cannot generalize ~ the state of the weather in Great Britain and Ireland —Geoffrey Jefferson⟩ ⟨negotiations ~ strength⟩; (3) descent, ancestry, or birth ⟨descended ~ a long line of kings⟩ ⟨two colts ~ the same dam⟩; (4) the place of origin, source, or derivation of a material or immaterial thing ⟨all creation is ~ conflict —W.B.Yeats⟩ ⟨assigned two chapters ~ the text⟩ ⟨took a dime ~ his pocket⟩; (5) the model or original (as of a work of art) ⟨painting done directly ~ nature⟩ ⟨the church was built ~ his plans⟩; also used to indicate a person or thing that another is named for ⟨the name was soon changed to Jamaica, ~ the Jameco Indians, the aboriginal settlers —*Amer. Guide Series: N.Y. City*⟩; (6) the fact or condition of being suspended or pendent ⟨wear it ~ the principal masthead when the yacht is in commission —Peter Heaton⟩; (7) selection out of a number of individuals ⟨chosen ~ a large number of competitors⟩; (8) the fact or condition of being native to or a resident of ⟨people ~ Ohio are often called Buckeyes⟩ — **from . . . to . . .** — used (1) with a repeated noun to indicate recurrence or continued succession ⟨beg *from* door *to* door⟩ ⟨a ration issued *from* day *to* day⟩ and (2) with extremes or extremely unlike objects to indicate a wide range ⟨known *from* Maine *to* California⟩ ⟨a noncommittal word that might be used of anything *from* babies *to* furnaces —J.C.Swaim⟩
[1]**from·ward** \'främwə(r)d, 'frəm-\ *also* **from·wards** \-dz\ *adv* [ME *fromward*, *framward*, fr. OE *framweard*, *framweardes*, fr. *fram* from + *-weard*, *-weardes* -ward, -wards] *now dial Eng* : away from : AWAY
[2]**fromward** \"\ *also* **fromwards** \"\ *prep* [ME *fromward*, *framward*, fr. *fromward*, *framward*, adv.] *now dial Eng* : FROM
frond \'fränd\ *n* -s [L *frond-*, *frons* leafy branch, foliage — more at BRIM] **1** : LEAF; *esp* : the leaf of a palm ⟨beyond the dim, stirring ~*s* of the palm trees —*Omnibook*⟩ **2 a** : a foliaceous thallus or thalloid shoot ⟨the ~ of a lichen⟩ ⟨the ~*s* of duckweed⟩ **b** : the leaf of a fern whether a foliage leaf or a sporophyll — see CIRCINATE, CROSIER 3 **3** : something resembling a frond ⟨the sensitive ~*s* of some complex insect antennae⟩ ⟨the ~*s* of his hair were all dabbled and stiff —Edith Sitwell⟩
frond·age \-dij\ *n* -s [*frond* + *-age*] : a collection of fronds : leafy foliage
frond·ed \-dəd\ *adj* : furnished with fronds ⟨~ palms⟩
fron·del·ite \frän'de,līt\ *n* -s [Clifford *Frondel* b1907 Am. mineralogist + E *-ite*] : a mineral $MnFe_4(PO_4)_3(OH)_5$ consisting of a basic phosphate of manganese and iron and isomorphous with rockbridgeite

frond of a fern

fron·dent \'fränd°nt\ *adj* [L *frondent-*, *frondens*, pres. part. of *frondēre* to be in leaf, put forth leaves, fr. *frond-*, *frons*] : having fronds
fron·des·cence \frän'des°n(t)s\ *n* -s [NL *frondescentia*, fr. L *frondescent-*, *frondescens* (pres. part. of *frondescere* to become leafy, incho. of *frondēre*) + *-ia* -y — more at FROND] **1** : the condition or period of unfolding of leaves **2** : FOLIAGE — **fron·des·cent** \(')frän¦des°nt\ *adj*
fron·deur \frō'dœr\ *n, pl* **frondeurs** \-r(z)\ [F, slinger, participant in a 17th cent. French revolt in which parliamentarians were compared to schoolboys who use their slings only when the teacher is not looking, rebel, malcontent, fr. *fronde* sling (fr. OF *fonde*, *fronde*, fr. — assumed — VL *fundula*, dim. of L *funda*) + *-eur* -or] : REBEL, MALCONTENT, DISSIDENT ⟨he did exhibit the spirit of a ~ —H.A.Gibbons⟩

fron·dif·er·ous \(ˈ)frän¦dif(ə)rəs\ *adj* [L *frondifer*, fr. *frond-, frons* leaf + *-i-* + *-fer* -ferous] **:** bearing fronds or leaves
frond·let \ˈfrändlət\ *n* -s **:** a small frond
fron·dose \ˈfrän,dōs\ *adj* [L *frondosus*, fr. *frond-* *frons* + *-osus* -ose] **:** bearing fronds **:** resembling a frond **:** THALLOID — **fron·dose·ly** *adv*
frons \ˈfränz\ *n, pl* **fron·tes** \-n·,tēz\ [L] **1 :** FOREHEAD **2** [NL, fr. L] **:** the upper anterior part of the head capsule of an insect usu. consisting of a separate sclerite between the epicranium and clypeus
¹front \ˈfrənt\ *n* -s [ME *frount, front*, fr. OF *front*, fr. L *front-, frons* — more at BRINK] **1 a :** FOREHEAD, BROW ⟨slavery will be branded on our ~ —W.E.Channing⟩; *also* **:** the whole face ⟨tears ran down that noble ~⟩ **b** (1) **:** countenance, demeanor, bearing, or posture esp. in the face of danger or other trial ⟨let us . . . take with unshaken ~ what comes —Theodore Roosevelt⟩ ⟨appeared with dauntless ~, accompanied by his paramour —T.B.Macaulay⟩ (2) **:** the outward, visible, or feigned bearing or behavior of a person as contrasted with his true or essential character, feelings, or condition ⟨the brave ~ she had maintained so long —T.B.Costain⟩ ⟨has good within him, behind a perfectly abominable ~ —Irving Stone⟩ ⟨a perpetually phony ~ of good fellowship is maintained —V.A. Young⟩ ⟨was putting up a ~ . . . in order not to distress this girl —Mary R. Rinehart⟩; *also* **:** external and often feigned appearance (as of material prosperity or high social position) ⟨very good clothes at bargain prices — important to a man who must maintain a ~ —R.M.Yoder⟩ (3) **:** an artificial, affected, or self-important manner **:** show of vanity or haughtiness **:** AIRS ⟨he was very humble and had no ~ for a prince —*Time*⟩ (4) **:** stand or posture in reference to some issue or problem **:** POINT OF VIEW, OUTLOOK, POLICY, POSITION — chiefly used with *change* ⟨a change of ~ was signaled by his offer to come to terms⟩ ⟨suddenly changed ~ and threw in with the opposition⟩ **c** (1) **:** the foremost rank (as of an army) **:** VAN (2) **:** a line of battle (3) *often cap* **:** a zone of conflict esp. between armies ⟨a division going up to the ~⟩ (4) **:** lateral space occupied by a military unit (5) — used as a military command of execution for individuals to turn their heads straight forward (as after dressing to the right) ⟨ready, ~!⟩ (6) — used as a call by a hotel desk clerk in summoning a bellboy (7) **:** a sphere or area of conflict or activity ⟨while men are always on fire over their opinions, they are rarely so on more than one ~ at a time —Curtis Bok⟩ ⟨the four ~s are military, economic, political, and psychological —*Congressional Record*⟩ ⟨progress on the educational ~⟩ ⟨a fairly quiet month on the athletic ~ —*Dartmouth Alumni Mag.*⟩ **d** (1) **:** a coalition or movement linking persons, elements, or groups often of diverse political, ideological, or other tendency in an effort to achieve certain common objectives ⟨common unity and a common ~ are surely a pressing political need —Christopher Fremantle⟩ ⟨announced his purpose to be the erection of a solid ~ . . . a hemisphere wholly prepared to consult together for our mutual safety —R.W. Van Alstyne⟩ ⟨a united psychiatric ~ to frustrate the drive of courts and lawyers to make psychiatric testimony conform to antiquated concepts —Edward de Grazia⟩; *specif* **:** a coalition of political parties of diverse ideological or other tendency for the achievement of certain common objectives — usu. used with a qualifier ⟨and to create a popular democratic ~ —*Collier's Yr. Bk.*⟩ ⟨the people's ~s represented an intermediate stage between Western and Soviet forms of democracy —Taylor Cole⟩ (2) **:** a person, group, or thing that is used to cover up or mislead concerning the identity or the usu. illegal, harmful, or self-serving true character, purpose, or activity of the actual controlling or directing agent **:** FACADE ⟨uses her as a ~ for his sinister machinations —*N.Y.Times Bk. Rev.*⟩ ⟨operated a florist shop as a ~ —Robert Shaplen⟩ ⟨assailed the . . . nominees as ~s for a party of privilege —*Collier's Yr. Bk.*⟩ ⟨all political groups and mass organizations are useful ~s to strengthen the party's influence —N.D.Palmer & S.C.Leng⟩ (3) **:** a person who serves as the official though often only nominal head or spokesman of an enterprise or group to lend it prestige **:** FIGUREHEAD ⟨a retired general with an impressive war record made an excellent ~ for the company⟩ **2 :** something that confronts or faces forward: as **a** (1) **:** a face of a building; *esp* **:** the face that contains the principal entrance (2) **:** the part of a theater in front of the curtain; *also* **:** the personnel engaged to work there (3) **:** the faceplate of a mortise lock through which the ends of the bolt are projected (4) **:** the part of a crab's carapace between the eyes (5) **:** FRONS 2 (6) **:** the forepart of the chest and forelegs in a quadruped (7) **:** the forepart of a garment ⟨a book . . . propped against his meager ~ of tweed —James Stern⟩ (8) **:** SHIRTFRONT (9) **:** DICKEY (10) **:** the part of the human figure opposite to the back ⟨lying on his ~⟩ **b** (1) **:** the part or surface of something that seems to look out or be directed forward **:** the fore or forward part ⟨a grasshopper's back is really his ~ —J.B.S.Haldane⟩ (2) **:** land that faces or abuts (as on a body of water, a river, a road) **:** FRONTAGE ⟨a lake ~⟩; *also* **:** a promenade along the beach at a seaside resort ⟨they walked on the ~ together —W.S.Maugham⟩ (3) **:** a relatively narrow zone of rock characterized by concentration of some elements or scarcity of others relative to adjacent zones (4) **:** the end of a dynamo or motor shaft opposite to the end that carries the pulley or other coupling member (5) **:** the side of a paper machine from which it is operated (6) **:** the boundary between two dissimilar air masses — see COLD FRONT, WARM FRONT (7) **:** the part of the upper surface of the tongue behind the blade that lies opposite the hard palate when the tongue is at rest (8) **:** BELLY 5d **c :** the first part of something: as (1) *archaic* **:** the first part of a season or other unit of time **:** BEGINNING (2) **fronts** *pl* **:** the first portion of a distillate ⟨benzene ~s⟩ **d :** something attached to the forepart: as (1) **:** false hair worn over the forehead by a woman (2) **:** the part of a bridle that crosses the forehead — see BRIDLE illustration **3 a :** a position directly before or ahead of a person or before the foremost part of a thing ⟨with six seconds to go he forged out in the ~ of his rivals⟩ ⟨a tree stood in the ~ of the yard⟩ **b :** a position of leadership, advantage, or superiority in any field ⟨an indefatigable worker, he rapidly made his way to the ~ of his profession⟩ — **front and center 1** — used as a preparatory military command before "march" for certain designated individuals to march to the front of the center of a formation **2** — used as a call for someone not in sight to come forward — **in front of** *prep* **:** directly before **:** before the foremost part of **:** ahead of ⟨watching the road *in front of* him⟩ ⟨a tree stood *in front of* the house⟩ ⟨frightened of what lies *in front of* them —*Isis*⟩ ⟨*in front of* him were two Union lines —G.J.Fiebeger⟩ — **out front** *adv* **:** in the audience

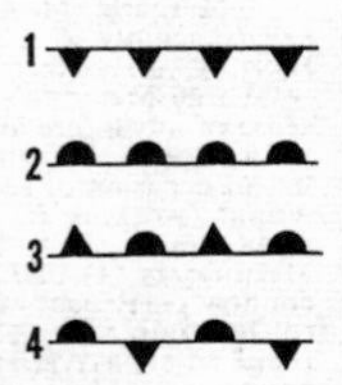

front 2b(6): symbols used on weather maps to indicate *1* cold front, *2* warm front, *3* occluded front, *4* stationary front

²front \"\ *vb* -ED/-ING/-S [partly fr. MF *fronter*, fr. *front*, n.; partly fr. ¹*front*] *vi* **1 :** to have or turn the face or front in a specified direction **:** FACE ⟨the house ~s toward the east⟩ **2 a :** to act as a sponsor, advocate, or spokesman ⟨the persons who had gotten them jobs ~ed for them in time of stress —C.R.Cooper⟩ ⟨his ability to . . . ~ for the U.S. in world affairs —*Time*⟩ **b :** to serve as a front ⟨~*ing* for oil interests —*Current Biog.*⟩ ⟨the top men in the community have little time for committee meetings; they send a lesser man to ~ for them —O.S.Strong⟩ ~ *vt* **1 a :** to face up to **:** CONFRONT ⟨went to the woods because I wished . . . to ~ only the essential facts of life —H.D.Thoreau⟩ ⟨loses his job . . . and with it his ability to ~ life benignly —J.P.Bishop⟩ **b :** to appear before **:** meet face-to-face ⟨daily ~*ed* him in some fresh splendor —Alfred Tennyson⟩ **2 a :** to stand in front of **:** serve as a front to ⟨a lawn ~*ing* a house⟩ **b :** to be the leader of (a dance orchestra) ⟨appeared as soloist in reviews, in addition to ~*ing* bands —*Esquire's Jazz Bk.*⟩ **3** *obs* **:** BEGIN, INTRODUCE, PREFACE **4 :** to supply a front to **:** put a facing upon ⟨~*ed* the building with brick⟩ **5 :** to face or look toward **:** have the front toward, opposite, or over against ⟨the house ~s the street⟩ **6 :** to articulate (a sound) with the tongue further forward
³front \"\ *adj* [¹*front*] **1 :** of or relating to the front or forward part **:** situated in front ⟨a ~ view⟩ ⟨~ seats at the opera⟩ **2** *comparative sometimes* **fronter :** articulated at or toward the front of the oral passage ⟨\ē\, \a\, \s\, and \p\ are ~ sounds⟩
⁴front \"\ *adv* [¹*front*] **:** toward, in, or at the front or forward position ⟨a pale boy rose and came ~ of the class —Willa Cather⟩ ⟨those who are older and sit farther ~ than I do —Henry Hewes⟩ — often used in the phrases *up front* and *out front* ⟨a few riflemen might be needed up ~ later —*Combat Forces Jour.*⟩ ⟨way out ~ in the race —T.M.Pryor⟩
front *abbr* frontispiece
front·ad \ˈfrənt·,ad, -n·,tad\ *adv* [¹*front* + *-ad*] **:** toward the front ⟨outside the eye the infraorbital line runs ~ —Nils Holmgren⟩
front·age \ˈfrəntij, -tēj\ *n* -s [¹*front* + *-age*] **1 a :** a portion of land that fronts (as on a stream, body of water, or road) ⟨the Romans won . . . a ~ on the Atlantic ocean —A.J. Toynbee⟩ ⟨states of the Union . . . which have a salt-water ~ —*Congressional Record*⟩; *also* **:** the extent of front ⟨has a lake ~ of approximately two miles —*Amer. Guide Series: La.*⟩ **b :** the land between the front of a building and the street **2 :** the front part or face of a building ⟨dirty plaster ~s embossed with scrollwork and heraldic devices —Christopher Isherwood⟩ ⟨the pillars of its colonnaded ~ —Claud Cockburn⟩ **3 :** the act or fact of facing a given way **:** EXPOSURE **4 :** something that belongs to, is part of, or appears in or on a front ⟨a dazzling ~ of flowers and faces —Leonard Merrick⟩ **5 :** the lateral extent of responsibility of a military unit **:** the width of a zone of military action in an attack **:** the width of a military sector in defense
front·ag·er \-jə(r)\ *n* -s **:** one that holds the frontage (as on a road or on water)
frontage road *n* **:** a local street or road generally paralleling an expressway or through street on one or both of its sides to collect local traffic and provide access to property isolated from the expressway through access controls — called also *service road*
¹fron·tal \ˈfrəntᵊl *sometimes* -rän-\ *n* -s [in sense 1, fr. ME *frountel, frontel*, fr. MF *frontel*, fr. L *frontale*, fr. *front-, frons* + *-ale* (neut. of *-alis* -al); in sense 2, fr. ME *frountel, frontel*, fr. ML *frontellum*, dim. of L *front-, frons*; in other senses, fr. ²*frontal*] **1 :** something worn across the forehead; *specif* **:** an ornamental band often of jewels **2 :** a movable decorative piece (as of rich stuff or embroidery) covering the front of an altar in a church **3 :** FACADE **4 a :** FRONTAL BONE **b :** a frontal scale or plate
²frontal \"\ *adj* [NL *frontalis*, fr. L *front-, frons* forehead + *-alis* -al — more at BRINK] **1 a :** of or relating to the forehead or the frontal bone **b :** of or being a scale or plate lying between the eyes and over the frontal bone in a reptile **2 a :** belonging to the front part ⟨a ~ appendage⟩ **b :** of or relating to the front **:** taking place from or at the front ⟨to cease all ~ resistance and to limit its activity to guerrilla warfare —D.J. Dallin⟩ **c :** directed against the front **:** delivered upon the main or essential point or issue **:** DIRECT ⟨a ~ assault on the enemy⟩ ⟨~ attack . . . on broad problems of human nature —F.A.Geldard⟩ **3 a :** parallel to the main axis of the body and at right angles to the sagittal plane **b :** having or showing frontality **4 :** of or relating to a meteorological front **5 :** FRONT 2 — **fron·tal·ly** \-ᵊlē, -ᵊli\ *adv*
frontal angle *n* **:** the angle formed by the intersection of lines from the bregma and glabella to the auricular point
frontal apron *n* **:** APRON 5
frontal artery *n* **:** one of the terminal branches of the ophthalmic artery
frontal bone *n* **:** one of a pair of membrane bones of the upper front part of the cranium next anterior to the parietals, in man becoming united into a single bone that forms the forehead and upper part of the orbits
frontal convolution *or* **frontal gyrus** *n* **:** any of the convolutions of the outer surface of the frontal lobe of the brain
frontal crest *n* **:** a median ridge on the internal surface of the vertical part of the human frontal bone
frontal eminence *n* **:** the prominence of the human frontal bone above each superciliary ridge
frontal gibbosity *n* **:** a protuberance on the head of certain male fishes prominent as sexual maturity is reached
frontal index *n* **:** the ratio of the least breadth of the forehead to its greatest breadth multiplied by 100
fron·ta·lis \,frən·ˈtaləs, frän-, -tāl-,-tāl-\ *n* -ES [NL, fr. *frontalis* frontal] **:** the muscle of the forehead that forms part of the occipitofrontalis
fron·tal·i·ty \,frən·ˈtaləd·ē, frän-\ *n* -ES **1** *in sculpture* **:** a schematic composition of the front view that is complete without lateral movement **2** *in the pictorial arts* **:** an arrangement of one or more planes parallel to the picture plane
frontal lobe *n* **:** the anterior division of each cerebral hemisphere having its lower part in the anterior fossa of the skull and being bordered behind by the central sulcus
frontal nasal spine *n* **:** a median process projecting down from the frontal bone and articulating with the two nasal bones — called also *superior nasal spine*
frontal nerve *n* **:** a branch of the ophthalmic nerve supplying the forehead, scalp, and adjoining parts
frontal shield *also* **frontal plate** *n* **:** a platelike prolongation of the base of the upper mandible over the forehead that is a characteristic feature of the coots and gallinules
frontal sinus *n* **:** either of two air spaces lined with mucous membrane that lie within the frontal bone above the orbit on each side
frontal vein *n* **:** a vein of the middle of the forehead that unites with the supraorbital to form the angular vein near the inner angle of the orbit
front bench *n* **:** either of the two benches nearest the chair in the British House of Commons for occupation by the ministers and by the leaders of the opposition — compare BACK BENCH
front bencher *n* **:** a minister or a leader of the opposition in the British House of Commons
front-connected switch \ˈ=¦==-\ *n* **:** a switch in which the conductors are fastened to terminals in front of the mounting
front court *n* **:** a basketball team's offensive half of the court
front dive *n* **1 :** a dive in which for the takeoff the diver faces the water **2 :** one of several competitive dives including those in which the body rotates forward from a front takeoff — compare BACK DIVE, INWARD DIVE, REVERSE DIVE, TWIST DIVE
front door *n* **1 :** the main entrance to a dwelling or apartment having more than one entrance **:** a doorway fronting on or giving direct access to a street or road **2 a :** a place or area affording the main or best approach or access (as to a country) ⟨the war would then be brought directly to the *front door* of the Americas —Emil Lengyel⟩ **b :** an open direct forthright approach or a legal approach toward gaining some object ⟨should do it directly and openly, through the *front door* —*Yale Rev.*⟩
front drop *n* **:** a fundamental trampoline stunt consisting of dropping to a prone position on the bed with the head up and then rebounding to a standing position
front·ed \ˈfrəntəd\ *adj* **:** having or furnished with a front of a specified kind or quality ⟨plaster-*fronted* houses . . . painted in garish colors —James Reach⟩ ⟨a tuck-*fronted* shirt —*New Yorker*⟩ ⟨smartly ~ little restaurants —*Amer. Guide Series: Ind.*⟩
¹fronter *comparative of* FRONT
²fronter *n* -s [¹*front* + *-er*] **:** one who is a member of an organization which is or is alleged to be a front ⟨a Communist ~ —Hillel Silver⟩
frontes *pl of* FRONS
front-fanged \ˈ=¦=\ *adj* **:** having grooved or perforated venom-conducting teeth in the front of the mouth — used chiefly of members of the Proteroglypha; compare BACK-FANGED, PIT VIPER
front flap *n* **:** the part of a book jacket that folds over and onto the inside of the front board
front foot *n* **:** a foot measured along the front of a piece of property — called also *foot front*
front-foot rule *n* **:** a method of property assessment based upon the length of frontage of the property
¹fron·tier \,frən·ˈti(ə)r, -ˈtiə, ˈ=,= *also* frän·ˈ- *or* ˈfrän·,- *sometimes* ,frən·ˈ-, *chiefly Brit* ˈ=·,tiə(r *or* ˈ=·,tyə(r\ *n* -s [ME *frounter, fronter*, fr. MF *frontiere*, fr. *front* — more at FRONT] **1 a** (1) **:** a part of a country that fronts or faces another country ⟨the inhabitants of the ~ between Canada and the U.S.⟩; *specif* **:** a demarcated boundary between countries ⟨crossed the ~ into Mexico⟩ (2) **:** a boundary between territorial units ⟨lived on the edge of the river that defined the ~ between the two counties⟩ **b** *obs* **:** BARRIER, DEFENSE; *specif* **:** a stronghold upon a border province or frontier **2 a :** a typically shifting or advancing zone or region esp. in No. America that marks the successive limits of settlement and civilization **:** a zone or region that forms the margin of settled or developed territory ⟨the ~, where people . . . lead rough lives and seldom meet together for pleasure —Willa Cather⟩ **b :** an area (as of thought or investigation) that constitutes the most advanced, obscure, or unexploited field or line of inquiry with respect to a particular subject **:** the farthermost limits of knowledge or achievement ⟨the latest ~s of linguistic research⟩ ⟨the study advances appreciably the ~ of political analysis —R.M.Goldman⟩ ⟨progress on the atomic ~ last week —*Time*⟩ ⟨work on one of the ~s of modern science—the geology of the deeper parts of the earth's crust —W.H.Bucher⟩ **c :** a line of division between different or opposed things ⟨the ~ of melodrama and melodrama is vague —T.S.Eliot⟩ **d :** a new or relatively unexploited field that offers scope for large exploitative or developmental activity ⟨a large economic ~ right at home —T.J.Kreps⟩ ⟨is television destined to become a great new educational ~ —*Mich. Alumnus*⟩ ⟨the ~s of the future are marketing ~s —Bud Wilson⟩
²frontier \"\ *adj* **1 :** situated on a frontier between countries **:** BORDERING, CONTERMINOUS ⟨all ~ garrisons were ordered withdrawn⟩ **2 :** of or relating to a frontier esp. in No. America **:** characteristic of people living on such a frontier ⟨turning to the task with typical ~ ingenuity —R.A.Billington⟩ ⟨the hardships of ~ life⟩ ⟨one of the last real ~ towns⟩ **3 :** advancing or pushing back the frontiers of knowledge or achievement **:** EXPLORATORY, PIONEERING ⟨~ research in the humanities —C.E.Odegaard⟩ ⟨a ~ report in the field⟩
³frontier \"\ *vt* -ED/-ING/-S *archaic* **:** BORDER, FACE
fron·tiers·man \-rzmən, -əz-\ *n, pl* **frontiersmen :** a man living on the frontier
fronting *pres part of* FRONT
fron·tis \ˈfrəntəs *sometimes* -rän-\ *n* -ES [by shortening] **:** FRONTISPIECE
¹fron·tis·piece \ˈfrəntə,spēs *sometimes* -rän-\ *n* -s [alter. (influenced by *piece*) of earlier *frontispice*, fr. MF, fr. LL *frontispicium* front of a building, lit., looking at the forehead, fr. L *front-, frons* forehead, brow, front + *-i-* + *-spicium* (fr. *specere* to look, look at) — more at FRONT, SPY] **1 a :** the principal front of a building; *esp* **:** the entryway of a building when decoratively treated **b :** an ornamental or decorated pediment (as over a portico or window); *also* **:** a sculptured panel (as of a door) **2 a** *obs* **:** TITLE PAGE **b** *archaic* **:** an ornamental figure or illustration on the first page of a book or pamphlet; *also* **:** the page itself **c :** an illustration preceding and usu. facing the title page of a book or magazine or of a major section of a book; *also* **:** the page itself **3 :** an architectural drawing in which details are assembled and presented in an attractive way
²frontispiece \"\ *vt* -ED/-ING/-S **:** to supply with, show on, or act as a frontispiece
front·less \ˈfrəntləs\ *adj* **1 :** being without face or front **2** *archaic* **:** SHAMELESS
front·let \-lət, *usu* -ləd·+V\ *n* -s [in sense 1, fr. ME *frontlette*, fr. MF *frontelet*, dim. of *frontel*; in other senses, fr. ¹*front* + *-let* — more at FRONTAL] **1 a :** FRONTAL, BROWBAND ⟨a black velvet ~ just visible as a loop on the forehead —Doreen Yarwood⟩ **b :** PHYLACTERY ⟨~s between thine eyes —Deut 6:8(AV)⟩ **2 :** a fronting piece: as **a :** an architectural facade **b :** SUPERFRONTAL; *also* **:** a short valance over an altar frontal **3 a :** the forehead esp. of a quadruped mammal **b :** the forehead of a bird when distinguished by a different color or texture of plumage
frontlighting \ˈ=¦=\ *n* **:** the broad basic lighting of a photographic subject from the front or the side toward the camera
front line *n* **1 :** a military line formed by the most advanced tactical units in a combat situation; *also* **:** the line or zone of contact with an enemy **:** FRONT **2 :** the most advanced, responsible, or vanguard position in any field of activity or struggle ⟨constantly in the *front line* of antislavery agitation —F.S.Philbrick⟩
frontline \ˈ=¦=\ *adj* [*front line*] **:** situated or suitable for use at the front ⟨a new ~ ambulance —*Army Reserve Training Bull.*⟩ **:** relating to advance activity or procedure ⟨~ agricultural news —*Atlantic*⟩ ⟨in the cultural struggle . . . the schools are the ~ trenches —Paul Blanshard⟩
front man \ˈ=,=\ *n, pl* **front men** [¹*front*] **1 :** FRONT ⟨would almost certainly be used as a *front man* by whatever group succeeded in capturing him —R.C.Doty⟩ ⟨the *front men* of the leading law firms . . . are usually chosen . . . for their glamour or histrionic abilities —*Harper's*⟩ ⟨does business anonymously through *front men*⟩ ⟨has had a long career as a professional *front man* with no power —E.D.Canham⟩ **2 a :** a barker esp. for a show or circus ⟨also acted for a short time as *front man* for a magician —*Current Biog.*⟩ **b :** one who leads a dance orchestra ⟨big bands used to take their personality from the improvisations of the *front men* —*Time*⟩
front matter *n* **:** matter preceding the main text of a book — called also *preliminaries*; compare BACK MATTER
fronto- *comb form* [ISV, fr. L *front-, frons* forehead, brow, front — more at BRINK] **1 :** frontal bone and ⟨*fronto*parietal⟩ **:** frontal lobe and ⟨*fronto*pontine⟩ **2** [¹*front* + *-o-*] **:** boundary of an air mass ⟨*fronto*genesis⟩
front office *n* **:** the head or executive office; *specif* **:** the policy-making staff ⟨play the genial host while . . . worrying about what the *front office* will say when they turn in the liquor bill —R.D.Altick⟩
fron·to·genesis \¦frəntō, -rän-+\ *n* [NL, fr. *fronto-* + L *genesis*] **:** the coming together of two dissimilar masses or currents of air in such a way that a distinct front is formed or sharpened between them and that they commonly react upon each other to induce cloud and precipitation
front·o·ly·sis \,frənt·ˈäləsəs, ,frən·ˈtä-, frän·ˈtä-\ *n, pl* **frontoly·ses** \-ə,sēz\ [NL, fr. *fronto-* + *-lysis*] **:** a process tending to destroy a meteorological front (as by horizontal mixing and divergence of the air)
¹fron·ton \,frən·ˈtōn, frän-\ *n, pl* **frontons** \-tōⁿ(z)\ [F, fr. It *frontone*, aug. of *fronte* forehead, front, fr. L *front-, frons* — more at BRINK] **:** a pediment esp. over a door or window **:** FRONTAL
²fron·ton \ˈfrän·,tän, =·ˈ=\ *n* -s [Sp *frontón*, irreg. aug. (influence of L *front-, frons*) of *frente* forehead, front, fr. L *front-, frons* — more at BRINK] **:** a court or building for the game of jai alai
fron·to-occipital \¦frəntō, -rän-+\ *adj* [*fronto-* + *occipital*] **:** of or pertaining to the forehead and occiput
fron·to·parietal \"+\ *adj* [*fronto-* + *parietal*] **:** of, relating to, or involving both the frontal and parietal bones of the skull
frontoparietal suture *n* **:** CORONAL SUTURE
fron·to·pontine \"+\ *adj* [*fronto-* + L *pont-, pons* bridge + E *-ine*] **:** of or relating to both the frontal lobe and the pons
frontopontine tract *n* **:** a neural tract beginning in the frontal cortex and ending in the pons
¹front-page \ˈ=¦=\ *adj* [*front page*] **:** of, relating to, or appearing on the front page of a newspaper **:** very newsworthy ⟨*front-page* news⟩ — opposed to *back-page*
²front-page \"\ *vt* [*front page*] **:** to print (news) or report (an event) on the front page of a newspaper or periodical ⟨every newspaper . . . *front-paged* the story —Walter White⟩
frontpiece \ˈ=¦=\ *n* **:** the piece or part in or at the front of something
front-porch campaign *n* **:** a presidential campaign in which the candidate instead of stumping the country stays at home issuing written statements and making most of his speeches in his home community (as from his front porch)
front-rank \ˈ=¦=\ *adj* [*front rank*] **:** being in the front rank **:** ranking among the best **:** of the first quality or importance **:** FIRST-RATE ⟨emerges as a figure of *front-rank* importance in

the American social sciences —Eric Goldman⟩ ⟨a *front-rank* university⟩
front room *n* **:** LIVING ROOM, PARLOR
front–runner \ˈ=ˌ==\ *n* **1 :** a contestant who runs best when in the lead; *also* **:** one who can set his own fast pace **2 :** the leading contestant or one of the leading contestants in any rivalry or competition ⟨the *front-runner* . . . on two ballots —T.L.Stokes⟩ ⟨one of the *front-runners* in the postwar frozen-orange-juice derby —E.J.Kahn⟩
fronts *pres 3d sing of* FRONT, *pl of* FRONT
front sight *n* **:** the sight of a weapon nearest the muzzle
frontstall \ˈ=ˌ=\ *n* **:** a plate of armor attached to a horse's bridle with holes for the eyes and nostrils
front string *n* **:** an exposed stair stringer
front vault *n* **:** a vault in gymnastics executed to the right or left in which the body is raised sideward and then rotated a quarter turn inward so that the front of the body passes over the apparatus
front wall *n* **:** the wall against which the ball is served in a rackets game and from which every fair hit must rebound
front·ward \ˈfrəntwə(r)d\ *also* **front·wards** \-dz\ *adv* **:** toward the front **:** in a frontal direction ⟨a strip reading . . . *frontwards* over a distance of hundreds of miles —Bruce Bliven b.1889⟩ ⟨practice sewing backward as well as ~ —Clarence Poulin⟩
front·ways \-ˌwāz\ *adv* **:** from the front ⟨looked at the statue first sideways and then ~⟩
front–wheel \ˈ=ˌ=\ *adj* [*front wheel*] **:** operative on the front wheels of a vehicle ⟨*front-wheel* drive⟩ ⟨*front-wheel* brake⟩
frop·pish \ˈfräpish\ *adj* [alter. of earlier *frappish*, fr. *frap* + *-ish*] *archaic* **:** PEEVISH, FRETFUL
frore \ˈfrō(ə)r, -ō(ə)r,-ōə,-ó(ə)\ *adj* [ME *froren*, fr. OE, past part. of *frēosan* to freeze — more at FREEZE] **:** FROSTY, COLD, FROZEN ⟨the evenings, whatever they be — frosty and ~, warm and wet —C.G.Glover⟩ ⟨stood in a ~ and fearful silence —Eric Linklater⟩
frory \-ōrē,-órē, -ri\ *adj* [*frore* + *-y*] *archaic* **:** FROZEN, FROSTY
[1]**frosh** \ˈfräsh\ *also* **frosk** \-sk\ *n* [ME *frosk, frosh, frush, frosse*, fr. OE *frosc, frox, forsc* & ON *froskr* — more at FROG] *now dial Eng* **:** FROG
[2]**frosh** \ˈfräsh\ *n, pl* **frosh** [by shortening & alter.] **:** FRESHMAN
[1]**frost** \ˈfrȯst *also* -ä-\ *n* -s [ME *frost, forst*, fr. OE; *akin to* OS, OHG, & ON *frost;* derivatives fr. the root of E *freeze*] **1 a :** the process of freezing **:** congelation of fluids, esp. water **b (1) :** the condition or temperature of the air that causes the freezing of water **:** freezing weather **(2) :** a frozen condition **c (1) :** a covering of minute ice crystals on a cold surface that is formed by the condensation of atmospheric vapor at temperatures below freezing — called also *hoarfrost, white frost;* compare BLACK FROST **(2) :** the cause of such crystallization and freezing regarded as a special agency — compare JACK FROST **2 a :** coldness of deportment or temperament **:** an indifferent, reserved, or unfriendly manner ⟨our friends have . . . a slight ~ or tartness in their speech —F.A.Swinnerton⟩ **b :** something that meets with a cold reception **:** FIASCO, FAILURE ⟨one small meeting can be a ~ and another a crashing success —R.H.Rovere⟩ ⟨the trip proved to be a ~ —R.L. Taylor⟩ ⟨the play was . . . a most dreadful ~ —Arnold Bennett⟩
[2]**frost** \ˈ"\ *vb* -ED/-ING/-S *vt* **1 :** to roughen or sharpen (as the nailheads or calks of horseshoes) so as to prevent slipping on ice **2 a :** to cover with or as if with frost or a surface resembling frost ⟨white pleated panels ~ a pastel dress —*McCall's Needlework*⟩ ⟨a face mask . . . tends to produce fogging of the goggles . . . and to ~ them over below −10°F —H.G. Armstrong⟩ **b :** to produce on (as metal or glass) a fine-grained sparkling slightly roughened surface with a distinctive pattern **c :** to pit or etch (a rock) by wind action **3 a :** to injure by frost **:** FREEZE ⟨froze to death 2000 of their birds and ~*ed* the remaining 1000 . . . badly —John Bird⟩ **b :** to freeze so as to kill (as plants) or cause to drop (as buds) ~ *vi* **1 :** to become frosted **:** FREEZE ⟨I've had tumblers ~*ing* all day —Eugene Walter⟩ ⟨the fur parka . . . began to ~ up —Robert Murphy⟩ ⟨I have on various evenings hugged the open fire . . . to keep my bones from ~*ing* —W.A.Krauss⟩ — often used with *over* ⟨all of the cabin windows will ~ over —H.G.Armstrong⟩ **2 :** to dry with the appearance of a frosty window — used esp. of varnish and oil films
frostbird \ˈ=ˌ=\ *n* **:** any of various migratory birds that appear at about the time of the first frost; *esp* **:** GOLDEN PLOVER
[1]**frostbite** \ˈ=ˌ=\ *vt* **frostbit; frostbitten** *also* **frostbit; frostbiting; frostbites :** to blight or nip with frost **:** damage by freezing
[2]**frostbite** \ˈ"\ *n* **:** the freezing or the local effect of a partial freezing of some part of the body (as the ears or nose)
frostbitten \ˈ=ˌ==\ *adj* **:** injured, nipped, or withered by frost or freezing ⟨~ grapes unsalable as fresh fruit —*Time*⟩
frost–blite \ˈ=ˌ=\ *n* **1 :** LAMB'S-QUARTERS **2 :** a plant of the genus *Atriplex*
frost boil *n* **:** a defective spot in the surface of a pavement due to the pulverizing and swelling action of frost
frostbow \ˈ=ˌ=\ *n* **:** a white arc in the sky that occurs in frosty weather and is formed by reflection of sunlight from floating ice crystals **:** the parhelic circle that has its center at the zenith and is not to be confused with the white rainbow
frost crack *n* **:** a split in a tree trunk due to uneven shrinkage during severe frost
[1]**frost·ed** \-təd\ *adj* [fr. past part. of [2]*frost*] **1 a :** covered with hoarfrost or something like hoarfrost ⟨a ~ windowpane⟩ **b :** ornamented with frosting ⟨a ~ cake⟩ **c :** FROSTBITTEN **2 :** etched with or as if with sand ⟨a ~ electric light bulb⟩ **3 :** made white or dim by age ⟨a wild red mustache, ~ now —Judson Philips⟩ ⟨his eyes were at moments ~ by age —John Mason Brown⟩ **4 :** cold or distant in manner or temperament **:** ARROGANT, STUCK-UP ⟨they . . . come back as ~ little snobs —*Time*⟩ **5 :** quick-frozen for preservation and commercial distribution ⟨~ vegetables⟩
[2]**frosted** \ˈ"\ *n* -s **:** ice cream added to a liquid (as milk and chocolate syrup) and shaken or stirred until almost melted ⟨chocolate ~⟩ — compare FLOAT 14
frosted bat *n* **:** any of various bats having the basic fur color obscured by intermingled white or white-tipped hairs; *esp* **:** a common Eurasian bat (*Vespertilio murinus*)
frosted rustic *adj* **:** having the margins of the stones cut to a plane parallel to the plane of the wall with the intermediate part having an irregular surface — used esp. in the phrase *frosted rustic work*
frosted scale *n* **:** an unarmored scale (*Lecanium pruinosum*) that has a body covered with a frosting of wax and is a pest on peach and apricot trees
frost·er \-tə(r)\ *n* -s **1 :** one that frosts: as **a :** a sand blaster who produces a frosted appearance on glass **b :** one who frosts baked goods by hand or by machine **2 :** one who roughs out the ground for a wood carving with a punch
frostfish \ˈ=ˌ=\ *n* **1 :** TOMCOD 1a **2 :** SMELT 1a(1) **3** *New Zeal* **:** a scabbard fish (*Lepidopus caudatus*)
frost flower *n* **1 a :** a small bulbous herb (*Milla biflora*) of Mexico and the southwestern U.S.; *also* **:** its star-shaped flower — called also *floating star* **b :** a plant of the genus *Aster* **c :** FROSTWEED **2 :** an ice crystal resembling a flower; *esp* **:** one formed on the ground or in the subsoil
frost grape *n* **1 :** CHICKEN GRAPE **2 :** RIVERBANK GRAPE
frost gray *n* **:** a nearly neutral slightly purplish medium gray that is very slightly bluer than Quaker drab — called also *chateau gray*
frost gull *n* **:** BONAPARTE'S GULL
frost heave *or* **frost heaving** *n* **:** an upthrust of ground caused by freezing of moist soil (as under a footing or pavement)
frost·i·ly \-təlē, -li\ *adv* **:** to a frosty or chilling degree **:** in a chilly, reserved, or distant manner ⟨he smiled ~⟩
frost·i·ness \-tēnəs, -tin-\ *n* -ES **:** the quality or state of being frosty or frigid ⟨often criticized for his excessive ~ toward modern art —*Newsweek*⟩
frost·ing \-tiŋ,-tēŋ\ *n* -s **1 a :** ICING **b :** a trimming on a garment ⟨white angora ~ on cuffs and collar of a box jacket —*McCall's Needlework*⟩ **2 :** lusterless finish of metal or glass **:** MAT **3 :** a finely pulverized glass used with a mixture of varnish and glue esp. to frost paper shades **4 :** a light tracery of lines or scratches machined on polished machine parts for ornamental effect and sometimes also for better retention of lubricant
frost·less \-tləs\ *adj* **:** not marked or hardened by frost ⟨a ~ night⟩ ⟨the water was soaking into the ~ ground —J.P. Marquand⟩
frost line *n* **:** the depth to which frost penetrates the soil
frost necrosis *n* **:** death of plant tissue due to low temperature
frost plant *n* **:** FROSTWEED
frost pocket *n* **:** a small low area that has poor aerial drainage and is subject to frequent frosts
frost rib *or* **frost ridge** *n* **:** a ridge on a tree trunk caused by the healing and recurrence of frost cracks
frost ring *n* **:** a false annual ring in the trunk of a tree that is often evident only as a brownish line of collapsed or abnormal cells and is caused by defoliation due to frost and subsequent leafing out again
frostroot \ˈ=ˌ=\ *n* **:** SKEVISH
frosts *pres 3d sing of* FROST, *pl of* FROST
frost smoke *n* **:** frozen fog over water esp. in polar regions
frost snipe *n* **1 :** STILT SANDPIPER **2 :** RED-BACKED SANDPIPER
frost thrusting *n* **:** the movement of rock fragments by frost action; *also* **:** the result of such movement
frost valve *n* **:** a valve to drain the part of a pipe, hydrant, or pump where water would be liable to freeze
frostweed \ˈ=ˌ=\ *n* **:** any of several plants upon which ice crystals form during the first frosts: as **a :** an American plant of the genus *Helianthemum* — see FROSTWORT **b :** a salt-marsh fleabane (*Pluchea camphorata*)
frostweed aster *n* **:** HEATH ASTER
frostwork \ˈ=ˌ=\ *n* **1 :** the figures that moisture sometimes forms in freezing (as on a windowpane) **2 :** ornamentation (as on silver, glass, paper) imitative of frost figures
frostwort \ˈ=ˌ=\ *n* **:** a shrubby frostweed (*Helianthemum canadense*) of northeastern No. America with solitary terminal petalous flowers and few apetalous cleistogamous flowers
frosty \ˈfrȯstē, -ti *also* -rä-\ *adj* -ER/-EST [ME, fr. *frost* + *-y*] **1 :** attended with or producing frost **:** having power to congeal water **:** COLD, FREEZING ⟨a ~ night⟩ **2 a :** covered with or as if with hoarfrost **:** HOARY; *esp* **:** GRAY ⟨ran his thin brown fingers through his ~ hair —Elinor Wylie⟩ **b :** of a pure or glistening white **:** producing an effect of crispness or coolness ⟨the bride . . . was the traditional vision in white satin and . . . ~ lace veil —James Reynolds⟩ **3 :** marked by coolness or extreme reserve in manner **:** SEVERE, FRIGID, CHILL, UNFRIENDLY ⟨he got a ~ reception from the Senate group —*N.Y. Times*⟩ ⟨his smile was distinctly ~ —Erle Stanley Gardner⟩ ⟨the night superintendent was a man ~ and suspicious —Sinclair Lewis⟩
frosty–beak \ˈ==ˌ=\ *n* **:** MALLARD 1
frosty green *n* **:** NICKEL GREEN
frosty mildew *n* **:** a leaf spot of various plants caused by fungi of the genus *Cercosporella* and characterized by pale to white usu. circumscribed lesions on affected foliage
[1]**froth** \ˈfrȯth *also* -ä-\ *n, pl* **froths** \-ths,-thz\ [ME *froth, frooth*, fr. ON *frotha*; akin to ON *frauth* froth, *frȳsa* to snort, OE *āfrēothan* to froth, Gk *prēthein* to blow up, Skt *prothati* he snorts] **1 a :** an aggregation of bubbles formed in or on a liquid (as by fermentation or agitation) **:** FOAM, SPUME, SCUM **b :** a foamy slaver sometimes accompanying disease (as rabies) or exhaustion **2 :** something light, unsubstantial, or of little value ⟨it is common belief that ~ must be offered to viewers in the summer —*N.Y. Times*⟩ ⟨the writing of some folk is nothing but a ~ of words —G.D.Brown⟩
[2]**froth** \-th,-th\ *vb* -ED/-ING/-S [ME *frothen*, fr. *froth*, n.] *vt* **1 :** to cause to foam **:** cause froth on the surface of ⟨with which to ~ chocolate, a favorite drink —*Amer. Guide Series: Texas*⟩ **2 :** VENT, VOICE ⟨belligerently ~*ing* a rush of hasty and intemperate words⟩ ⟨came out of classes ~*ing* ideas —*Time*⟩ **3 :** to cover with froth ⟨a horse ~*s* his chain⟩ ~ *vi* **1 :** to foam at the mouth ⟨it hit him square and he died ~*ing* —Richard Bissell⟩ **2 :** to throw froth out or up **:** FOAM ⟨liquids which ~ to a troublesome extent during distillation —*Pharmacopoeia of the U.S.A.*⟩ ⟨surging, ~*ing*, heaving water —Gavin Casey⟩
froth·er \-thə(r), -th-\ *n* -s [[2]*froth* + *-er*] **:** an agent (as pine oil or cresol) that is active in froth flotation through its ability to change the surface tension of a liquid and consequently decrease the wettability of the particles to be recovered
froth flotation *n* **:** flotation in which air bubbles are introduced into a mixture of finely divided ore or other material with water and a chemical that aids attachment of the bubbles to the particles of the desired material and its recovery as a froth
froth·i·ly \-thəlē, -th-, -li\ *adv* **:** in a frothy manner
froth·i·ness \-thēnəs, -th, |in-\ *n* -ES **:** the quality or state of being frothy
froth insect *also* **froth hopper** *or* **froth worm** *n* **:** SPITTLE INSECT
froth pit *n* **:** a minute depression in the surface of a coated paper caused by froth in the coating mixture used
frothy \-thē, -th, |i\ *adj* -ER/-EST **1 :** full of or consisting of foam, froth, or light bubbles **:** SPUMOUS, FOAMY ⟨~ waves⟩ **2 a :** gaily frivolous, superficial, or light in content or treatment **:** INSUBSTANTIAL, SHALLOW ⟨a ~ comedy⟩ ⟨the symphony . . . is ~, brilliant, without much thematic development —E.T. Canby⟩ ⟨a ~ and rhetorical exposition of meager doctrine without pretense of scholarship —H.J.Laski⟩ **b :** made of light thin material **:** having frilly trimmings ⟨~ garments lying all about on chairs and in the box —Arnold Bennett⟩ ⟨a ~ creation of white nylon tulle —*New Yorker*⟩
frot·tage \frōˈtäzh, frə-\ *n* -s [F, fr. *frotter* to rub + *-age*] **1 :** RUBBING, POLISHING ⟨gasoline . . . is applied with gauze . . . by ~ to each local itching area —*Jour. Amer. Med. Assoc.*⟩ **2 a :** the artistic process of composing directly on paper a variety of shapes and motifs produced from rubbings **b :** a composition made by this process **c :** a drawing or painting modeled on images produced from rubbings **3 :** masturbation by rubbing against another person
frot·to·la \ˈfrōdᵊlə, ˈfräd-, *It* ˈfrōttōlä\ *n, pl* **frotto·le** \-ᵊlˌā, -ōlā\ [It, fr. OIt, fr. *frotta* crowd, multitude, fr. MF *flote*, fr. OF, fr. (assumed) OIt *flotta*, alter. of (assumed) *flotto*, fr. L *fluctus* action of flowing, flood, wave — more at FLUCTUATE] **:** a secular part-song of Italy of the 15th and 16th centuries that is largely homophonic and has the music repeated with each verse
frot·ton \(ˈ)frō¦tōⁿ\ *n, pl* **frottons** \-ōⁿ(z)\ [F, fr. *frotter* to rub] **:** a burnisher for rubbing the back of paper in block printing
frou·frou \ˈfrüˌfrü\ *n* -s [F, of imit. origin] **1 :** a rustling esp. of a woman's skirts **2 :** frilly trimming; *esp* **:** abundant or excessive ornamentation (as ruffles, beading, flowers, veiling) in women's clothing **3 :** fussy details or showy accessories and amenities esp. in a social setting ⟨the ~ of Victorian decor⟩
frough *also* **frow** *adj* [ME] *obs* **:** BRITTLE, FRAGILE
frounce \ˈfraün(t)s\ *vt* -ED/-ING/-S [ME *frouncen*, fr. MF *froncir*, of Gmc origin; akin to OHG *runzala* wrinkle, ON *hrukka*] *archaic* **:** CURL, FRIZZLE ⟨not tricked and *frounced* —John Milton⟩
frouzy *var of* FROWZY
[1]**frow** \ˈfraü, ˈfrō\ *n* -s [ME *frowe*, fr. MD *vrouwe* lady, woman; akin to OHG *frouwa* mistress, lady — more at FRAU] **1 a :** a Dutch or German woman **b :** WOMAN, WIFE, HOUSEWIFE ⟨I'm not going to settle down into a ~ until I've had some fun —Joyce Cary⟩ ⟨a crocodile-hided . . . old ~ —A.M. Mizener⟩ **2 a** *obs* **:** MAENAD, BACCHANTE **b** *dial Brit* **:** an untidy messy woman; *specif* **:** one of loose morals
[2]**frow** \ˈfrō\ *var of* FROE
fro·ward \ˈfrō(w)ə(r)d, -ōrd\ *adj* [ME *froward, fraward*, fr. *fra, fro* from + *-ward* — more at FRO] **1 :** habitually disposed to disobedience and opposition **:** PERVERSE ⟨of a vehement and untamable mind, ~ beyond control —John Bennett⟩ **2** *archaic* **:** ADVERSE, UNFAVORABLE **syn** see CONTRARY
fro·ward·ly *adv* **:** in a froward manner
fro·ward·ness *n* -ES **:** the quality or state of being froward
frow·er \ˈfrō(ə)r, -ōə\ *n* -s [perh. alter. of obs. *froward* turned away, fr. *fro* + *-ward*; fr. the position of the handle] **:** FROE
[1]**frown** \ˈfraün\ *vb* -ED/-ING/-S [ME *frounen*, fr. MF *froigner, frogner* to snort, turn up one's nose, frown, of Celt origin; akin to MBret *froan* nostril, W *ffroen* nostril, OIr *srōn* nose] *vi* **1 a :** to contract the brow (as in displeasure, sternness, or concentration) **:** put on a stern, grim, or surly look **:** SCOWL ⟨she looked away, ~*ing* —Richard Llewellyn⟩ ⟨he ~*ed* in astonishment —Louis Auchincloss⟩ **b :** to present a somber or menacing appearance — used of inanimate objects ⟨grim gray towers . . . ~ down upon this dignified old town —*Amer. Guide Series: Texas*⟩ **2 a :** to give evidence of displeasure or disapproval by facial expression — used chiefly with *at* ⟨his neighbors ~*ed* at him with impatience —Margaret Deland⟩ **b :** to give evidence of displeasure or disapproval by other means — used chiefly with *on* or *upon* ⟨his religion ~*s* upon smoking, drinking, and modern faddism —*Current Biog.*⟩ ⟨society ~*s* on such deviations from good taste⟩ ~ *vt* **:** to show displeasure with or disapproval of by facial expression or other means ⟨I will be neither ~*ed* nor ridiculed into error —Noah Webster⟩
[2]**frown** \ˈ"\ *n* -s **1 :** a wrinkling of the brow (as in displeasure or concentration) **:** a severe, reproving, or stern look **:** SCOWL ⟨looked about him with a ~⟩ **2 :** an expression of displeasure ⟨the book received critical ~*s*⟩
frown·er \-nə(r)\ *n* -s [ME *frouner*, fr. *frounen* + *-er*] **:** one that frowns
frown·ing·ly *adv* **:** in a frowning manner ⟨meditated ~ over a cup of tea⟩
[1]**frowst** \ˈfraüst\ *n* -s [back-formation fr. *frowsty*] *chiefly Brit* **:** stale stuffy atmosphere **:** offensive or musty odor ⟨the ~ that rose . . . from my bedding —Monica Baldwin⟩ ⟨the ~ of a third-class carriage full of sleepy travelers —John Buchan⟩
[2]**frowst** \ˈ"\ *or* **froust** \ˈ"\ *vi* -ED/-ING/-S *Brit* **:** to loll or lounge esp. indoors ⟨why should one ~ within four walls on such a night —J.C.Snaith⟩
frows·ty *or* **frous·ty** \-ti\ *adj* -ER/-EST [alter. of *frowzy*] *chiefly Brit* **:** musty and stuffy **:** having an unpleasant smell ⟨cool night air rushed into the ~ little room —Carol Bache⟩
frowy \ˈfraüē\ *adj* [*frough, frow* + *-y*] *chiefly New Eng* **:** STALE, RANCID
frowze *n* -s [origin unknown] *obs* **:** frizzed hair; *specif* **:** a frizzed wig
frow·zled \ˈfraüzəld\ *also* **frow·zly** \-z(ə)lē\ *adj* [blend of *frowzy* and *tousled*] **:** FROWZY, DISHEVELED, UNKEMPT ⟨powder-smeared and ~ —Stephen Crane⟩
frow·zy *or* **frow·sy** *or* **frou·zy** \ˈfraüzē, -zi\ *adj* -ER/-EST [origin unknown] **1 :** having a slatternly, slovenly, unkempt, or uncared-for appearance **:** SHABBY, MEAN, SQUALID, DISHEVELED ⟨filled the entrance with her ~ bulk —Arthur Morrison⟩ ⟨~ white hair⟩ ⟨a ~ old office⟩ ⟨reduced to a daily diet of ~ economy —F.A.Swinnerton⟩ **2 :** MUSTY, STALE ⟨a ~ smell of stale beer and stale smoke —W.S.Maugham⟩ ⟨this must render the air moist, ~, and even putrid —Tobias Smollett⟩ **syn** see SLATTERNLY
froze *past or chiefly dial past part of* FREEZE
fro·zen \ˈfrōzᵊn\ *adj* [ME *frosen*, alter. (influenced by *fresen* to freeze) of *froren*, fr. past part. of *fresen* to freeze — more at FREEZE] **1 a :** congealed by cold **:** affected or crusted over by freezing ⟨a ~ brook⟩ **b :** subject to frost or to long and severe cold **:** CHILLY ⟨the ~ north⟩ **c (1) :** clogged with ice ⟨~ water pipes⟩ **(2) :** injured or killed by cold ⟨~ plants⟩ **d :** CHILLED, REFRIGERATED — used of foods prepared for the table ⟨~ custard⟩ ⟨~ fruit salad⟩ **2 a (1) :** not susceptible or responsive to feeling **:** drained or incapable of emotion **:** BENUMBED ⟨~ and bitter and visibly tortured by loneliness —Marcia Davenport⟩ **(2) :** expressing coldness or unfriendliness **:** not heartfelt or sincere **:** IMPASSIVE, FRIGID, MECHANICAL, STIFF ⟨friends give you that ~ look —Clyde Martin⟩ **b :** incapable of being changed, moved, or undone **:** not subject to change or movement **:** not flexible, dynamic, or plastic **:** IMMOBILE, RIGID, PETRIFIED, FIXED ⟨in the United States today institutions are not ~ —Zechariah Chafee⟩ ⟨a ~ social system⟩ ⟨stood ~ with terror⟩ ⟨thinks there should be no ~ agenda for any meeting —*Kiplinger Washington Letter*⟩; *specif* **:** debarred from change in status or from movement by law or other official action ⟨workers are ~ in their jobs for the duration of the war⟩ ⟨prices and wages are ~ for the emergency⟩ **c :** not available for present use **:** not liquid ⟨~ inventories⟩ ⟨~ capital⟩ **d** *of a billiard ball* **:** resting against another ball or a cushion **e :** not subject to being taken unless a player holds a pair to match the top card in rank — used of the discard pile in canasta and related games — **fro·zen·ly** \-ᵊnlē, -li\ *adv* — **fro·zen·ness** \-ᵊn(n)əs\ *n* -ES
frozen account *n* **:** a bank, trust-company, or brokerage account from which withdrawals are barred by court or government order
frozen asset *n* **:** an asset that cannot readily be turned into cash without heavy loss
frozen credit *n* **:** extended credit on a loan that cannot be paid off when due or in the foreseeable future
frozen daiquiri *n* **:** a daiquiri beaten into shaved ice to a consistency resembling that of a sherbet and drunk through straws
frozen food *n* **:** food that has been subjected to rapid freezing and is kept frozen until used
frozen–pack \ˈ==ˌ=\ *n* **:** the preserving of food (as fruits and vegetables) by packaging and quick-freezing
frozen pudding *n* **:** a rich frozen custard containing nuts and candied fruit and sometimes flavored with rum or sherry
frozen shoulder *n* **:** a shoulder afflicted with severe pain and stiffening
frozen sleep *n* **:** local or systemic reduction of temperature in an unconscious patient (as for the relief of pain in inoperable cancer)
frt *abbr* freight
fruct·ed \ˈfrəktəd, -rük-,-rük-\ *adj* [L *fructus* fruit + E *-ed* — more at FRUIT] **:** bearing fruit — used of a heraldic tree or plant
fruc·tes·cence \ˌfrəkˈtesᵊn(t)s, frük-,frük-\ *n* -s [NL *fructescentia*, fr. L *fructescent-, fructescens*, pres. part. of *fructescere* to produce fruit, fr. *fructus* fruit] **:** the period of maturing of fruit — **fruc·tes·cent** \¦frək¦tesᵊnt, (ˈ)frük-, (ˈ)frük-\ *adj*
fructi– *comb form* [L, fr. *fructus* — more at FRUIT] **:** fruit ⟨*fructiculture*⟩ ⟨*fructicolous*⟩
fruc·tif·er·ous \¦frək¦tif(ə)rəs, (ˈ)frük-, (ˈ)frük-\ *adj* [L *fructifer*, fr. *fructi-* + *-fer* -ferous] **:** bearing or producing fruit — **fruc·tif·er·ous·ly** *adv*
fruc·ti·fi·ca·tion \ˌfrəktəfəˈkāshən, ˌfrük-, ˌfrük-\ *n* -s [LL *fructification-, fructificatio*, fr. L *fructificatus* (past part. of *fructificare* to bear fruit) + *-ion-, -io* -ion — more at FRUCTIFY] **1 :** the action of forming or producing fruit **:** FRUITING **2 a :** the ripened plant ovary and its appendages **:** FRUIT **b :** a sporophore or sporogenous structure ⟨the ~ of a fungus⟩
fruc·ti·fi·ca·tive \ˈ===ˌkād·iv, ¦frəktifəkəd-, (ˈ)frük¦-, (ˈ)frük¦-\ *adj* [*fructification* + *-ive*] **:** having the capacity for fructification
fruc·ti·fi·er \ˈ=ˌtəˌfī(ə)r\ *n* -s **:** something that fructifies ⟨the local deities . . . ~*s* of the soil —A.P.Davies⟩
fruc·ti·form \-ˌfórm\ *adj* [*fructi-* + *-form*] **:** having the form of a fruit
fruc·ti·fy \ˈfrəktəˌfī, -rük-,-rük-\ *vb* -ED/-ING/-ES [ME *fructifien*, fr. MF *fructifier*, fr. L *fructificare*, fr. *fructi-* + *-ficare* -fy] *vi* **:** to bear fruit ⟨its seeds shall ~ —Amy Lowell⟩ ~ *vt* **:** to make fruitful **:** make productive ⟨then he kisses the earth she *fructifies* —Francis Yeats-Brown⟩
fruc·tiv·o·rae \ˌfrəkˈtivəˌrē, frük-,frük-\ [NL, fr. *fructi-* + L *-vorae* (fem. pl. of *-vorus* -vorous)] *syn of* MEGACHIROPTERA
fruc·tiv·o·rous \¦frək¦tivərəs, (ˈ)frük-, (ˈ)frük-\ *adj* [*fructi-* + *-vorous*] **:** FRUGIVOROUS
fruc·tol·y·sis \ˌfrəkˈtäləsəs, frük-,frük-\ *n, pl* **fructoly·ses** \-ləˌsēz\ [NL, fr. L *fructus* fruit + NL *-o-* + *-lysis* — more at FRUIT] **:** the breakdown of fructose esp. in the metabolism of stored sperm
fruc·to·san \ˈfrəktəˌsan, -rük-,-rük-\ *n* -s [*fructose* + *-an*] **:** a polysaccharide (as inulin) yielding primarily fructose on hydrolysis
fruc·tose \-ˌtōs *also* -ōz\ *n* -s [ISV *fruct-* (fr. L *fructus* fruit) + *-ose*] **:** a ketose sugar $HOCH_2(CHOH)_3COCH_2OH$ known in levorotatory, dextrorotatory, and racemic forms; *esp* **:** the very sweet soluble levorotatory D-form that occurs esp. in fruit juices and honey and combined in many disaccharides and polysaccharides — see INVERT SUGAR, LEVULOSE, SUCROSE
fruc·to·side \-təˌsīd\ *n* -s [*fructose* + *-ide*] **:** a glycoside that yields fructose on hydrolysis — **fruc·to·sid·ic** \¦==¦sidik\ *adj*
[1]**fruc·tu·ary** \ˈfrəkchəˌwerē, -ksh-\ *n* -ES [LL *fructuarius*, fr. *fructuarius*, adj.] **:** USUFRUCTUARY

[2]**fructuary** \"\ *adj* [LL *fructuarius*, fr. L, of fruit, fruit-bearing, fr. *fructus* + *-arius* -ary] **:** of or relating to a usufruct — used of a stipulation in Roman and civil law

fruc·tu·ous \-chəwəs, -sh-\ *adj* [ME, fr. MF & L; MF *fructueux*, fr. L *fructuosus*, fr. *fructus* fruit + *-osus* -ous] **:** FRUITFUL, PRODUCTIVE, PROFITABLE ⟨a ~ land⟩ — **fruc·tu·ous·ly** *adv* — **fruc·tu·ous·ness** *n* -ES

fruc·tus in·dus·tri·a·les \'frûktə,sin,dûstrē'ä,lās\ *n pl* [NL] **:** crops (as wheat, corn) produced by labor on the part of man — distinguished from *fructus naturales*

fruc·tus nat·ur·a·les \-,näd·ə'rä,lās\ *n pl* [NL, lit., natural fruits] **:** crops produced without any substantial assistance from man — distinguished from *fructus industriales*

fru·gal \'frügəl\ *adj* [MF or L; MF, fr. L *frugalis*, back-formation fr. *frugaliter*, adv., economically, frugally, fr. *frugi* fit, economical, frugal, fr. dat. of *frux* fruit, produce, value (in such phrases as *esse frugi bonae* to be capable of a good harvest or revenue); akin to L *frui* to enjoy, have the use and enjoyment of — more at BROOK] **1 :** economical in the use or expenditure of resources **:** not wasteful or lavish **:** SAVING, THRIFTY ⟨the cost of the war was appalling to his ~ mind —C.S.Forester⟩ ⟨a ~ farm family⟩ **2 :** reflecting or displaying economy in the use or expenditure of resources **:** SCANTY, MEAN ⟨a small and ~ apartment —T.B.Costain⟩ ⟨insistence on a ~ diet —Lillian Smith⟩ **syn** see SPARING

fru·gal·i·ty \frü'galəd·ē, -ətē, -i\ *n* -ES [L *frugalitas*, fr. *frugalis* + *-itas* -ity] **:** the quality or state of being frugal **:** careful management of resources **:** THRIFT ⟨lived with great ~⟩

fru·gal·ly \'frügəlē, -li\ *adv* **:** in a frugal manner

fru·gal·ness \-əlnəs\ *n* -ES **:** the quality or state of being frugal

fru·giv·o·ra \frü'jivərə\ [NL, fr. L *frugi-* (fr. *frug-*, *frux*) + NL *-vora*] *syn of* MEGACHIROPTERA

fru·giv·o·rous \(')⸗¦⸗⸗rəs\ *adj* [L *frugi-* + E *-vorous*] **1 :** feeding on fruit **2 :** of or relating to the Megachiroptera

[1]**fruit** \'früt, *usu* -üd·+V\ *n* -S *often attrib* [ME, fr. OF, fr. L *fructus* use, enjoyment, product, fruit, fr. *fructus*, past part. of *frui* to enjoy, have the use and enjoyment of — more at BROOK] **1 a :** a product of plant growth useful to man or animals (as grain, vegetables, cotton, flax) — usu. used in pl. ⟨the ~*s* of the field⟩ **b** (1) **:** the reproductive body of a seed plant consisting of one or more seeds and usu. various protective and supporting structures — used esp. of edible bodies ⟨squash vines full of green ~*s* that will be killed by frost⟩ (2) **:** such a fruit having an edible more or less sweet pulp associated with the seed and usu. being used as or in a dessert or sweet course ⟨apples, peaches, plums, and berries are among our best native ~*s*⟩ — contrasted with *vegetable* ⟨pears and cherries are ~*s* while squashes and beans are vegetables⟩ (3) **:** a succulent plant part used chiefly in a dessert or sweet course ⟨rhubarb though actually the petiole of a leaf is considered a ~⟩ **c :** a dish, selection, or diet of fruits ⟨pass the ~⟩ ⟨live on ~⟩ **d :** a product of fertilization in a plant with its modified envelopes or appendages (as the cystocarp in various algae or the sporogonium of a moss); *specif* **:** the ripened ovary of a seed plant and its contents including such adjacent tissues as may be inseparably connected with it (as the pod of a pea or the capsule of many annuals) — compare SEED **2 :** OFFSPRING, YOUNG, PROGENY ⟨the ~ of the womb⟩ **3 :** the effect or consequence of an action or operation **:** ISSUE, RESULT ⟨that policy bore ~⟩ ⟨the ~*s* of crime⟩ ⟨the ~*s* of sound instruction⟩ **4** *slang* **:** HOMOSEXUAL

[2]**fruit** \"\ *vb* -ED/-ING/-S [ME *fruiten*, fr. *fruit*, n.] *vi* **:** to bear or produce fruit **:** come to fruition ⟨a tree that ~*s* annually⟩ ⟨some of the tomatoes blossomed but didn't ~⟩ ⟨the culture he served . . . never ~*ed* in wisdom —V.L.Parrington⟩ ~ *vt* **:** to cause to bear fruit **:** develop fruit upon ⟨~*ed* the seedlings⟩

fruit·age \'früd·|ij, -üt|, |ēj\ *n* -S [MF, fr. *fruiter* to bear fruit (fr. *fruit*, n.) + *-age*] **1 a :** the condition or process of bearing fruit **b :** a quantity of fruit ⟨a tree bending with ~⟩ **:** yield of fruit ⟨the bark of this tree is so beautiful itself that it would be worth planting if there were not the rich ~ —*Horticulture*⟩ **c :** OFFSPRING, PROGENY ⟨their marriage had five children as its ~⟩ **2 :** the product or result of an action **:** good or bad effect ⟨seldom is it given to any man to see . . . the ~ of his life —*Christian Century*⟩

fruit·ar·i·an \früd·'|erēən, -ü't|, |a(a)r-, |ār-\ *n* -S [[1]*fruit* + *-arian* (as in *vegetarian*)] **:** one who lives chiefly on fruit

fruit bark beetle *n* **:** SHOT-HOLE BORER

fruit bat *n* **:** any of numerous large bats that constitute the suborder Megachiroptera, are confined to the warm parts of the Old World, and feed on fruit — called also *flying fox*

fruit body *n* **:** FRUITING BODY

fruit bud *n* **1 :** a bud that produces flowers and, if fertilized, fruit **2 :** a bud that produces both leaves and flowers (as in the apple, pear, and blackberry) — compare MIXED BUD

fruitcake \'⸗,⸗\ *n* **:** a rich light or dark cake that usu. contains a variety of nuts and dried or candied fruits and is often highly spiced

fruit cocktail *n* **:** a mixture of usu. tart and sweet fruits sometimes flavored with a liquor (as sherry) and served in a small stemmed glass as a first course — compare FRUIT CUP

fruit cup *n* **:** a mixture of fruits sometimes topped with a small ball of fruit ice and served in a medium-sized stemmed glass as a dessert course — compare FRUIT COCKTAIL

fruit dot *n* **:** SORUS

fruit dove *n* **:** any of numerous small brightly colored fruit-eating pigeons that have bright red or yellow feet and legs, that are usu. made a subfamily of Columbidae but sometimes a separate family, and that are found mainly in an area extending from India to Polynesia and south to Australia — called also *fruit pigeon*

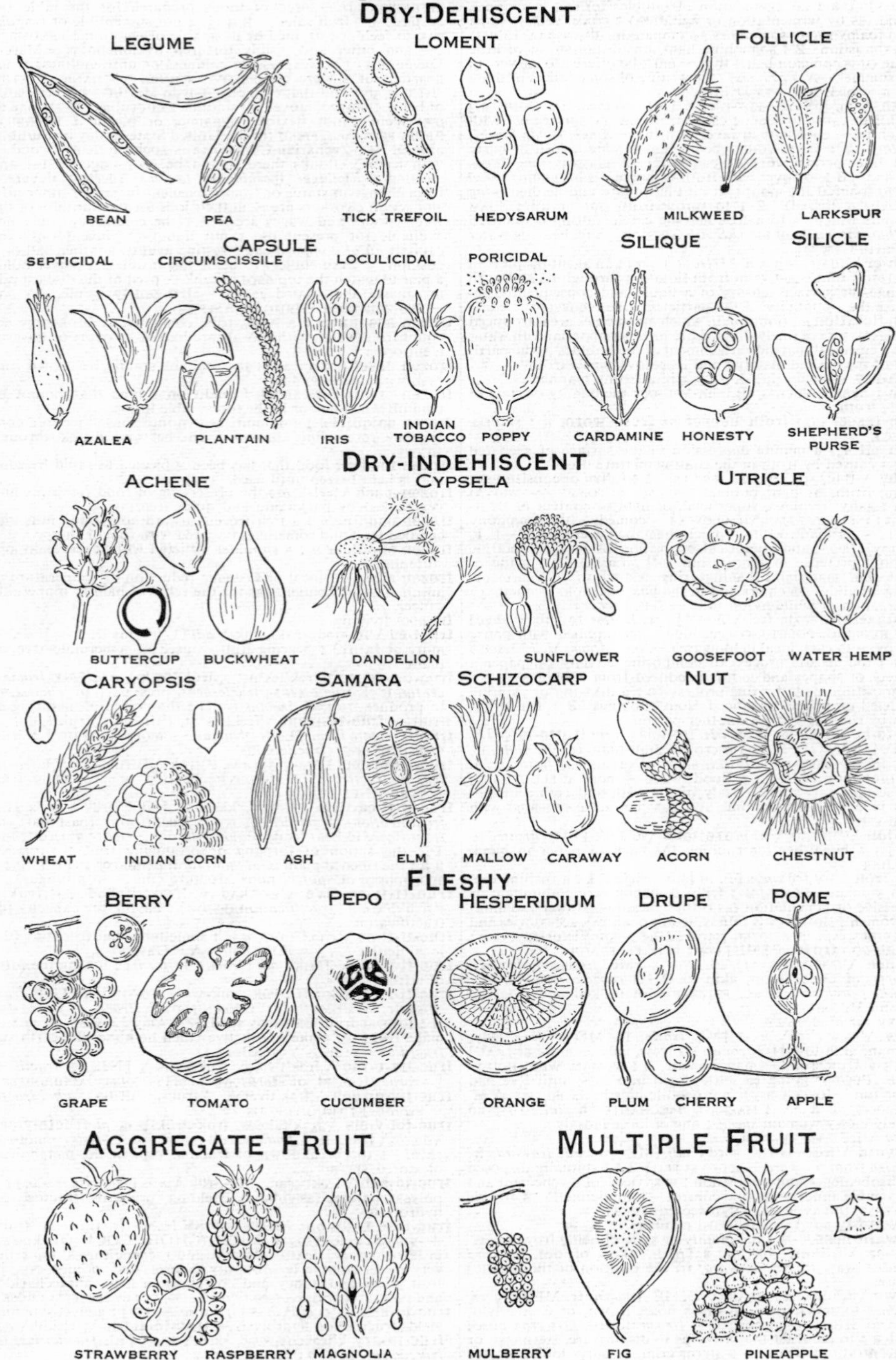

fruit·ed \¦früd·əd, -ütəd\ *adj* **1 :** bearing fruit ⟨a heavily ~ plant⟩ **2 :** having fruit added ⟨~ cereal⟩ ⟨~ jello⟩

fruit·er \-üd·ə(r), -ütə-\ *n* -S [[1]*fruit* + *-er*] **1 :** a ship for carrying fruit **2 :** a tree or plant that bears fruit

fruit·er·er \-üd·ərə(r), -ütə-\ *n* -S [ME, fr. *fruiter* fruiterer (fr. MF *fruitier*, fr. *fruit* + *-ier* -er) + *-er*] **:** one who deals in fruit **:** a seller of fruits

fruit·er·ess \-üd·ərəs, -ütə-\ *n* -ES **:** a female seller of fruit

fruit·ery \-üd·ərē, -ütə-\ *n* -ES [[1]*fruit* + *-ery*] *archaic* **:** FRUIT

fruit fly *n* **:** any of various small acalyptrate flies whose larvae feed on fruit or decaying vegetable matter: as **a :** a member of the genus *Drosophila* **b :** any of various members of the family Trypetidae (as the Mediterranean fruit fly)

fruit·ful \'frütfəl\ *adj, sometimes* **fruitfuller**; *sometimes* **fruitfullest** [ME, fr. [1]*fruit* + *-ful*] **1 a** (1) **:** yielding or producing fruit ⟨a ~ soil⟩ ⟨a ~ womb⟩ (2) **:** conducive to an abundant yield ⟨a ~ rain⟩ **b** *obs* **:** COPIOUS, ABUNDANT **2 :** abundantly productive ⟨regarded as the great waster, the ~ mother of social misery —V.L.Parrington⟩ ⟨a ~ writer⟩; *esp* **:** abundantly productive of desirable results ⟨a brilliant culmination of a rich and ~ career —F.E.Egler⟩ ⟨a ~ discussion⟩ ⟨made a number of ~ suggestions⟩ **syn** see FERTILE

fruit·ful·ly \-fəlē, -li\ *adv* [ME, fr. *fruitful* + *-ly*] **:** in a fruitful manner

fruit·ful·ness *n* -ES [ME *fruitfulnes*, fr. *fruitful* + *-nes* -ness] **:** the quality or state of being fruitful ⟨the ~ of this type of research —Edward Sapir⟩

fruit head *n* **:** a capitate inflorescence (as of the hop) in the fruiting stage

fruitier *comparative of* FRUITY

fruitiest *superlative of* FRUITY

fruit·i·ness \'früd·|ēnəs, -üt|, |in-\ *n* -ES **:** the quality or state of being fruity

fruiting *pres part of* FRUIT

fruiting body *n* **:** an organ (as an apothecium or the sporophore of mushrooms, mosses, liverworts) specialized for producing spores — called also *spore fruit*

fruiting calyx *n* **:** a calyx subtending a mature ovary; *esp* **:** one modified to form part of the fruit

fru·i·tion \frü'ishən\ *n* -S [ME *fruicioun*, fr. MF or LL; MF *fruition*, fr. LL *fruition-*, *fruitio*, fr. L *fruitus* (alter. of *fructus*, past part. of *frui* to enjoy, have the use and enjoyment of) + *-ion-*, *-io* -ion — more at BROOK] **1 :** the pleasurable use or possession of something **:** ENJOYMENT ⟨the sweet ~ of an earthly crown —Christopher Marlowe⟩ **2** [influenced in meaning by [1]*fruit*] **a :** the state of bearing fruit ⟨the fields needed rain for ~ —Pearl Buck⟩ **b :** REALIZATION, ACCOMPLISHMENT, CONCLUSION ⟨the ~ of a farsighted policy —Marquis James⟩ ⟨carry that mission to a successful ~ —J.C. Lincoln⟩ **syn** see PLEASURE

fru·i·tive \'früəd·iv\ *adj* [ML *fruitivus*, fr. L *fruitus* + *-ivus* -ive] **1 :** ENJOYING, POSSESSING **2** [*fruition* + *-ive*] **:** capable of producing fruit **:** FRUITFUL ⟨the big garden lying warm and brown and ~ in the sun —Nancy Hale⟩

fruit knife *n* **:** a small knife usu. with a fancy handle and a blade sharp enough to pare and cut fruit at table

fruit·less \'frütləs\ *adj* [ME, fr. [1]*fruit* + *-less*] **1 :** lacking or not bearing fruit **:** BARREN ⟨a ~ tree⟩ **2 :** productive of no advantage or good effect **:** VAIN, UNSUCCESSFUL, UNPROFITABLE ⟨a ~ effort⟩ ⟨~ negotiations⟩ — **fruit·less·ly** *adv* — **fruit·less·ness** *n* -ES

fruit·let \-lət\ *n* -S [[1]*fruit* + *-let*] **1 :** a fruit of small size **2 :** a unit or member of a collective fruit

fruit liqueur *n* **:** a liqueur made chiefly by a maceration process from fruit and neutral spirits or brandy — compare PLANT LIQUEUR

fruit pigeon *n* **1 :** FRUIT DOVE **2 :** GREEN PIGEON

fruit pit *n* **:** BITTER PIT

fruit pox *n* **:** a nonparasitic disease of unknown origin characterized by dark green dots that later become sunken and sometimes coalesce to form streaks esp. on greenwrap tomato fruits

fruits *pl of* FRUIT, *pres 3d sing of* FRUIT

fruit salad *n, slang* **:** military service ribbons and decorations ⟨peeking up at three rows of *fruit salad* on his chest —K.M. Dodson⟩ ⟨twenty thousand medals for . . . one year of combat is a lot of *fruit salad* —John Ciardi⟩

fruit-set \'⸗,⸗\ *n* **:** SET 17d

fruit spot *n* **:** any of various diseases of plants characterized by the occurrence of sunken, pithy, or discolored local lesions on the fruits and commonly caused by parasitic fungi — see CYLINDROSPORIUM

fruit spur *n* **:** a short stout twig that bears the fruit buds in a fruit tree (as the apple or pear)

fruitstalk \'⸗,⸗\ *n* **:** PEDUNCLE

fruitsucker \'⸗,⸗⸗\ *n* **:** GREEN BULBUL

fruit-tree bark beetle *n* **:** SHOT-HOLE BORER

fruit-tree leaf roller *n* **:** a small tortricid moth (*Archips argyrospila*) having larvae that are leaf rollers feeding on apple and other fruit trees

fruit wine *n* **:** a wine fermented from fruit other than grapes

fruitwood \'⸗,⸗\ *n* **1 :** the wood of a fruit tree; *esp* **:** the wood of such a tree used for furniture **2 :** the twigs or shoots of a plant that produce flower buds as distinguished from those that bear only leaf buds

fruitworm \'⸗,⸗\ *n* **:** any of numerous insect larvae mainly of the orders Diptera and Lepidoptera that feed on or in fruits

fruit wrap *or* **fruit wrapper** *n* **:** a strong thin paper sometimes treated for use as a protective covering for fruit

fruity \'früd·|ē, -üt|, |i\ *adj* -ER/-EST **1 a :** relating to a fruit **:** resembling or suggesting a fruit (as in taste or odor) **:** rich with or as if with fruits or fruit flavor ⟨the ~ fragrance always surprised them —Jean Stafford⟩ ⟨a ~ cake⟩ ⟨a ~ scent, possibly orange —*New Yorker*⟩ **b :** retaining the flavor and fragrance of the grape **:** rich in flavor — used of wines **2 a :** having a rich, strong, or spicy quality **:** extremely effective, interesting, or enjoyable **:** JUICY, ATTRACTIVE ⟨described postmortems, good rich ~ ones —Thomas Wood †1950⟩ ⟨dialogue . . . highly characterized in a finely ~ southern vein —E.R.Bentley⟩ ⟨his comparisons are not only humorous but ~ and unfaded —R.F.Adams⟩ **b :** sweet or sentimental esp. to excess **:** SYRUPY ⟨his voice was rich and arrogant, with a mellow ~ note —George Bellairs⟩ ⟨an educational bureaucrat . . . from his cameo ring to his ~ smile —*Time*⟩ ⟨~ bits of poetry —David Swift⟩ **c** *slang* **:** mentally unbalanced **:** CRAZY, NUTTY, SILLY, WACKY ⟨knocked me *fruitier* than a nutcake —E.J.Kahn⟩ ⟨I tell you he's ~ —J.T.Farrell⟩ ⟨the drugstore man thought I was ~ —C.C.Dewey⟩ **d** *slang* **:** HOMOSEXUAL

frum \'frûm, 'frəm\ *var of* FRIM

fru·men·ta·ceous \¦frümən·¦tāshəs\ *adj* [LL *frumentaceus*, fr. L *frumentum* grain (fr. *frui* to enjoy) + *-aceus* -aceous — more at BROOK] **:** made or or resembling wheat or other grain

fru·men·ty \'früməntē, 'frûm-\ *or* **fur·men·ty** \'fərm-\ *or* **fur·me·ty** *or* **fur·mi·ty** \-məd·ē\ *n* -ES [ME *furmente*, *frumente*, *frumenty*, fr. MF *furmentee*, *formentee*, *frumentee*, *fromentee*, fr. *furment*, *forment*, *frument*, *froment* grain, wheat, fr. L *frumentum*] **1 :** a dish of wheat boiled in milk and usu. flavored with sugar, spice, and raisins **2 :** a cereal dessert set in a mold

frum·er·ty *or* **frum·e·ty** \'frûmə(r)d·i, 'frəm-\ *dial Eng var of* FRUMENTY

[1]**frump** \'frəmp\ *vb* -ED/-ING/-S [perh. short for *frumple;* fr. the distortion of the face in a sneer] *vt* **1** *archaic* **:** INSULT, FLOUT, MOCK, SNUB **2** *archaic* **:** PROVOKE, IRRITATE, VEX ~ *vi, archaic* **:** SULK

[2]**frump** \", *dial Brit* " *or* 'frûmp\ *n* -S **1 frumps** *pl, dial Brit* **:** a cross mood **:** SULKS **2** [short for *frumple*] **a :** a dowdy, unattractive, or generally uninteresting girl or woman ⟨a terribly plain little ~ —Jessamyn West⟩ ⟨weighs about two hundred pounds, doesn't know how to dress, and, briefly, is an awful ~ —Olive H. Prouty⟩ **b :** a staid, drab, old-fashioned person ⟨representing the New England founding fathers as the usual reputable ~*s* —John McCarten⟩

frump·i·ly \-pəlē, -li\ *adv* **:** in a frumpy manner

frump·i·ness \-pēnəs, -pin-\ *n* -ES **:** the quality or state of being frumpy

frump·ish \'frəmpish, -pēsh\ *adj* **1** *archaic* **:** CROSS, SCORNFUL **2 :** generally uninteresting or unattractive **:** DOWDY, DULL, OLD-FASHIONED ⟨nothing is so ~ as last year's gambling game —Nancy Mitford⟩ — used esp. of a woman ⟨a ~ middle-aged spinster —Carol Field⟩ ⟨~ in a lacy old-fashioned way —Edmund Wilson⟩ ⟨a ~ old maid —Louis Bromfield⟩ — **frump·ish·ly** *adv* — **frump·ish·ness** *n* -ES

frum·ple \'frəmpəl, 'frəm-\ *vt* -ED/-ING/-S [ME *fromplen*, fr. MD *verrompelen*, fr. *ver-* for- (akin to OHG *fir-*) + *rompelen* to wrinkle — more at RUMPLE] *dial Brit* **:** WRINKLE, CRUMPLE

frumpy \'frəmpē, -pi\ *adj* -ER/-EST **:** DULL, FRUMPISH, DOWDY, DRAB ⟨a dull ~ Victorian society —Anita Leslie⟩ ⟨enraged all the ~ bluestockings by the smartness of her toilet —V.L. Parrington⟩

¹frush \'frəsh\ *n* -ES [perh. alter. of ¹*frosh*] **1 :** the frog of a horse's foot **2 :** a discharge from the frog of a horse's foot; *also* **:** THRUSH

²frush \'frùsh, 'frəsh\ *adj* [perh. alter of *frough*] **1** *dial Brit, of timber or cloth* **:** decayed to the point of brittleness **:** lacking tensile strength **2** *dial Brit, of soil* **:** friable and mellow

frusta *pl of* FRUSTUM

frus·to·conical \¦frə(,)stō+\ *adj* [*frustum* + *-o-* + *conical*] **:** of the shape of a frustum of a cone

frustra *pl of* FRUSTRUM

frus·tra·ne·ous \¦frə¦strānēəs, ¸frə's-\ *adj* [L *frustra* + E *-aneous* (as in *extraneous*)] **:** leading to frustration **:** VAIN, UNPROFITABLE

¹frus·trate \'frə,strāt, *chiefly Brit* (,)=¦= ; *usu* -ād·+V\ *vt* -ED/-ING/-S [ME *frustraten*, fr. L *frustratus*, past part. of *frustrare, frustrari* to deceive, disappoint, frustrate, fr. *frustra* in error, in vain; akin to L *fraud-, fraus* deception, fraud — more at FRAUD] **1 a :** to check, balk, or defeat in an endeavor or purpose **:** prevent from attaining ⟨*frustrated* by army routine —Darrell Berrigan⟩ ⟨*frustrated* by a blank wall of suspicion . . . and bureaucratic inertia —H.W.Carter⟩ **b :** to induce feelings of frustration or discouragement in ⟨brought the short story to a harsh perfection that ~*s* contemporary short-story writers —Alfred Kazin⟩ ⟨the story of a personality *frustrated* by the practical temper of America —J.D.Hart⟩ **2 a :** to make ineffectual **:** bring to nothing **:** DEFEAT, BAFFLE, FOIL ⟨nature . . . supports as well as ~*s* our lofty aspirations —H.J. Muller⟩ ⟨illness *frustrated* his plans for college⟩ ⟨did all they could to ~ . . . the inquiry —William McFee⟩ **b :** to make null or ineffectual **:** make invalid or of no effect **:** NULLIFY

syn THWART, BALK, FOIL, BAFFLE, OUTWIT, CIRCUMVENT: FRUSTRATE indicates a check, repelling, defeating of a sort that makes efforts vain, ineffectual, often with ego depreciation ⟨if waves of black pessimism swept over him in those unhappy later years when his ambitions were hopelessly *frustrated*, there was provocation enough —V.L.Parrington⟩ THWART may suggest a defeating, checking, or frustrating by obstructing one's course with some block or barrier ⟨his hatred of pioneer life and all its conditions, those conditions that were *thwarting* his creative life —Van Wyck Brooks⟩ ⟨I was anxious about her but I did not like to *thwart* her in her present mood —Rose Macaulay⟩ BALK likewise indicates frustrating by obstacles and obstructions, esp. those that hamper or hobble ⟨these regulations frequently *balked* the efforts of our Intelligence Corps to pry vital information from prisoners —*Saturday Rev.*⟩ ⟨I've always been *balked* or bullied out of having what I wanted —Ellen Glasgow⟩ FOIL indicates checking or defeating with galling or disheartening discomfiture ⟨*foiled*, he sank down again —Robert Browning⟩ BAFFLE indicates frustrating defeat by something confusing, perplexing, and vexing ⟨such knotty problems of alleys . . . such sphinx's riddles of streets . . . as must, I conceive, *baffle* the audacity of porters —Thomas De Quincey⟩ ⟨all these complexities and bonds that *baffled* him —James Boyd⟩ OUTWIT and CIRCUMVENT are more likely to stress the fact of defeat or escape by greater wit, craft, ingenuity, perception, or stratagem and less likely to suggest resulting disposition or attitude ⟨the skill with which she had hoodwinked and *outwitted* every statesman in Europe during fifty years —J.R.Green⟩ ⟨the *Defiance* was an opposition boat and had been refused a license to carry passengers on San Francisco Bay. But her captain had a plan to *circumvent* the dastardly port officials —Julian Dana⟩

²frustrate \"\ *adj* [ME *frustrat*, fr. L *frustratus*, past part.] **1 a :** balked in some endeavor, purpose, or action **:** FRUSTRATED, BAFFLED ⟨tore at the lock, ~ in fear —G.D.Brown⟩ ⟨~ and unhappy lovers —Elinor Wylie⟩ **b :** reflecting or indicating frustration ⟨turned a ~ eye upon me⟩ ⟨gave him a ~ look⟩ **2 :** of no effect **:** VAIN, UNPROFITABLE, NULL ⟨makes love itself seem ~, vulgar, or disgusting —W.Y.Tindall⟩ ⟨his ~ and unhopeful quest —M.G.Bishop⟩

³frustrate \'=,=\ *n* -S **:** a person who is frustrated

frustrated *adj* **1 a :** balked in some endeavor or purpose **:** THWARTED, DISAPPOINTED ⟨the Irish writer is a ~ talker —H.M.Reynolds⟩ ⟨a ~ jail break⟩ **b :** reflecting or indicating frustration ⟨gave a ~ shrug —Winifred Bambrick⟩ ⟨the venom with which he was attacked . . . may be attributed to their ~ rage —J.H.Plumb⟩ **c :** filled with a sense of frustration **:** filled with a deep chronic sense of insecurity, discouragement, and dissatisfaction as a result of thwarted desires, inner conflicts, or other unresolved problems ⟨a ~ man, divided against himself —P.M.Clyde⟩ ⟨a morbid, ~, sensitive . . . man —William Phillips b. 1907⟩ ⟨~ because . . . constantly worried about being fired —*Time*⟩ ⟨the world is full of anxious, frightened, ~, hurt people —*Episcopal Churchnews*⟩ **2 :** delayed in or prevented from being shipped for any reason — used of cargo, goods, or supplies ⟨bogus documents describing the goods as rejected or ~ exports —*Criminal Law Rev.*⟩ ⟨permission recently given to manufacturers to sell ~ export garments . . . on the home market —*Times Rev. of Industry*⟩

frus·trat·er \'=,strād·ə(r), -ātə-, *chiefly Brit* (,)=¦==\ *n* -S **:** one that frustrates ⟨a city need not be a ~ of life —Julian Huxley⟩

frus·trat·ing·ly *adv* **:** in a frustrating manner ⟨~ unresolved and inconclusive —W.V.Taylor⟩

frus·tra·tion \(,)frə'strāshən\ *n* -S [ME *frustracioun*, fr. L *frustration-, frustratio* deception, disappointment, frustration, fr. *frustratus* + *-ion-, -io* -ion] **1 a :** the act of frustrating ⟨will make parliamentary alliances . . . with a view to obstruction and ~ —A.E.Stevenson b. 1900⟩ ⟨the ~ of creative instinct is a notorious evil of the machine age —*Times Lit. Supp.*⟩ **b** (1) **:** the condition or an instance of being frustrated in some purpose **:** DISAPPOINTMENT, DEFEAT ⟨cruel ~*s* had eaten away that confidence —Oscar Handlin⟩ ⟨you've never experienced ~ until you watch a one-channel television set —Goodman Ace⟩ ⟨life became for him a series of great ~*s*⟩ ⟨the life of the admiral closed on a note of ~ —S.E.Morison⟩ (2) **:** a deep chronic sense or condition of insecurity, discouragement, and dissatisfaction arising from thwarted desires, inner conflicts, or other unresolved problems ⟨~ brought about by the constant inner conflict between the desire to possess and the yearning to renounce —*Orient Bk. World*⟩ ⟨the child seeks to retaliate for ~ by biting —G.S.Blum⟩ ⟨loneliness and ~: those are two constant themes in American literature —Malcolm Cowley⟩ ⟨the gusto and excitement concealed a certain ominous shallowness and ~ —Richard Watts⟩ ⟨a lifelong ~ —H.S.Canby⟩ **c :** something that frustrates ⟨as a work of serious reference the volume is full of ~*s* —*Saturday Rev.*⟩ ⟨escape lodges, women's clubs, bridge clubs, and other modern ~*s* —*Current Biog.*⟩ ⟨postwar Britain was a ~ . . . to the advertising man —E.S.Turner⟩ **2 :** a doctrine in the law of contracts whereby courts depart from the general rule that impossibility does not excuse performance and does not terminate contracts and instead adjust equitably conflicting rights as if the original state of affairs had continued although the value of an expected performance has been destroyed by fortuitous circumstances which the parties were not negligent in failing to guard against or by a radical change in the state of affairs (as war, government orders, cancellation of unique events) which the parties were not bound to have foreseen

frus·tra·tive \'frə,strā|d·|iv, 'frəstrə|, (,)frə'strā|, |t|, |ēv\ *adj* **:** tending to frustrate

frus·tu·la·tion \,frəschə'lāshən\ *n* -S [NL *frustulum* bud from a hydroid (fr. L, small piece) + E *-ation*] **:** constriction of small buds that settle down and grow into new hydranths from a hydroid

frus·tule \'frəs,chül\ *n* -S [F, fr. L *frustulum* small piece] **:** the siliceous shell of a diatom composed of two valves that overlap; *often* **:** the siliceous shell of a diatom together with the protoplast — see EPITHECA

frus·tu·lum \'frəschələm\ *n, pl* **frustu·la** \-lə\ [NL, fr. L, small piece] **:** a light breakfast allowed on fast days in the Roman Catholic Church

frus·tum \'frəstəm\ *also* **frus·trum** \-trəm\ *n, pl* **frustums** \-təmz\ *or* **frus·ta** \-tə\ *also* **frustrums** \-trəmz\ *or* **frus·tra** \-trə\ [NL, fr. ML & L; ML *frustrum* piece, bit, alter. of L *frustum* — more at BRUISE] **1 :** the part of a cone-shaped solid next to the base and formed by cutting off the top by a plane parallel to the base; *also* **:** the part of a solid (as a cone or pyramid) intersected between two planes that are either parallel or sometimes inclined to each other **2 :** one of the drums of the shaft of a column

frustums 1

fru·tes·cence \frü'tesᵊn(t)s\ *n* -S **:** the quality or state of being frutescent

fru·tes·cent \(')frü¦tesᵊnt\ *adj* [L *frutex* shrub, bush + E *-escent*] **:** having or approaching the appearance or habit of a shrub **:** SHRUBBY

fruti- *comb form* [L *frutic-, frutex*] **:** shrub ⟨*fruticolous*⟩

fru·ti·ce·tum \,früd·ə'sēd·əm\ *n, pl* **frutice·ta** \-ēd·ə\ [NL, fr. L, place full of shrubs, fr. *frutic-, frutex* + *-etum*] **:** a collection of shrubs grown for ornament or study (as in a botanical garden) — compare ARBORETUM

fru·ti·cose \'früd·ə,kōs\ *adj* [L *fruticosus*, fr. *frutic-, frutex* shrub + *-osus* -ose; akin to MHG *briezen* to bud, swell, OHG *broz* bud, sprout, OIr *broth* whisker, hair] **:** occurring in the form of or resembling a shrub **:** SHRUBBY ⟨a ~ chrysanthemum⟩ ⟨herbaceous or sometimes ~ perennials⟩; *esp, of a lichen* **:** having a shrubby bushy thallus with flattened or cylindrical branches

fru·tic·u·lose \frü'tikyə,lōs\ *adj* [L *frutic-, frutex* + *-ulus* (dim. suffix) + E *-ose*] **:** resembling a small shrub

fru·ti·lla \frü'tē(y)ə\ *n* -S [Sp, dim. of *fruta* edible fruit, fr. ML *fructa*, pl. of *fructum*, alter. of L *fructus* — more at FRUIT] **:** CHILEAN STRAWBERRY

frwy *abbr* freeway

¹fry \'frī\ *vb* **fried; fried; frying; fries** [ME *frien*, fr. OF *frire*, fr. L *frigere* to roast, fry; akin to Gk *phrygein* to roast, fry, Skt *bhṛjjati* he roasts] *vt* **:** to cook in a pan or on a griddle by heating over a fire esp. with the use of fat **:** cook in hot fat ⟨~ fish⟩ — compare BROIL **~** *vi* **1 :** to undergo the process of frying **:** become subject to the action of heat in a frying pan or on a griddle **2** *slang* **:** to suffer execution in the electric chair ⟨if I burn, you'll ~ along with me —Barton Black⟩

²fry \"\ *n* -ES **1 a** (1) **:** a dish of something fried ⟨a mixed ~ of . . . tiny crayfish and squid —P.E.Deutschman⟩ (2) **:** FRENCH FRY **b :** a social gathering or picnic at which food is fried and eaten ⟨a fish ~⟩ ⟨a steak ~⟩ ⟨organized a ~⟩ **c** *or* **fry meat** *chiefly Midland* (1) **:** a portion of fried meat (2) **:** meat suitable for frying **2 :** an internal part or organ of an animal (as pig's liver, calf's pluck) that is usu. eaten fried — usu. used in pl. **3 :** a state of excitement ⟨he was in an awful ~⟩

³fry \"\ *n, pl* **fry** [ME *frie, fry*, prob. fr. ONF *fri*, fr. OF *froyer, frayer, frier* to rub, spawn — more at FRAY] **1 a :** young or recently hatched fishes — compare FINGERLING **b :** the young or brood of other animals (as oysters or birds) **c** *obs* **:** human offspring **2 :** very small adult fishes; *esp* **:** those (as various anchovies) that swim in schools **3 :** members of a group or class **:** PERSONS, INDIVIDUALS — often used disparagingly ⟨a great part of the earth is peopled with these ~ —Katherine Mansfield⟩ or with a qualifier indicating smallness, youth, or insignificance ⟨the lesser ~ of the expedition march side by side with natives —Gordon Nares⟩ ⟨small ~ such as voles and field mice —Douglas Carruthers⟩ ⟨sturdy school shoe for the young ~ —*Footwear News*⟩ ⟨so beautifully illustrated that you and the young ~ will read it like a book —*Parents' Mag.*⟩

fry cook *n* **:** a cook who specializes in fried foods

fry·er *also* **fri·er** \'frī(ə)r, -īə\ *n* -S **1 :** one that fries **2 :** something intended for or used in frying: as **a :** a young chicken; *esp* **:** one weighing between 2½ and 4 pounds — compare BROILER **b :** a rabbit of 2½ to 3 months of age **c :** a deep utensil for frying foods sometimes with a cover and fitted with a basket

frying pan *n* [ME, fr. *frying* (gerund of *frien* to fry) + *pan*] **:** a metal pan with a handle used for frying foods **:** SPIDER — **out of the frying pan into the fire :** clear of one difficulty only to fall into a greater one

frypan \'=,=\ *n* **:** FRYING PAN

fs *abbr* facsimile

FS *abbr* **1** factor of safety **2** [F *faire suivre*] please forward **3** field service **4** filmstrip **5** final statement **6** financial secretary

f's *or* **fs** *pl of* F

FSH *abbr* follicle-stimulating hormone

f sharp \'=¦=\ *n, usu cap F* **1 :** the keynote of F-sharp major or F-sharp minor **2 :** the tone a half step above F

f-sharp major \'=,=¦==\ *n, usu cap F* **:** the major musical key having a signature of six sharps

frying pans: *1* used over source of heat; *2* heated electrically

f-sharp minor \'=,=¦==\ *n, usu cap F* **:** the minor musical key having a signature of three sharps

fspc *abbr* frontispiece

fst *abbr* fast

f star *n, usu cap F* **:** a star of spectral type F — see SPECTRAL TYPE table

f-stop \'=,=\ *n* [*f* (symbol for *focal length*)] **:** a camera lens aperture setting indicated by an f-number

f-system \'=,==\ *n* [*f* (symbol for *focal length*)] **:** a system of camera lens aperture markings that uses f-numbers

ft *abbr* **1** [L *fiat*] let it be done; let it be made **2** foot; feet **3** forint **4** fort; fortification; fortified

FT *abbr* **1** full terms **2** fume tight

ftd *abbr* fortified

fth *or* **fthm** *abbr* fathom

FTI *abbr* federal tax included

ftr *abbr* **1** fighter **2** fitter

f_2 layer \'ef¦tü-\ *n, cap F* **:** the upper and usu. more densely ionized of the two layers into which the F region of the ionosphere splits in the daytime, occurring at varying heights from about 150 to 250 miles or more above the earth's surface

fu' \'fü\ *chiefly Scot var of* FULL

Fu·a·din \'fyüədᵊn\ *trademark* — used for stibophen

fub \'fəb\ *archaic var of* FOB

fub·sy \'fəbsi, 'fəb-\ *adj* [obs. E *fubs* chubby person + E *-y*] *dial chiefly Eng* **:** chubby and somewhat squat

fuc- *or* **fuco-** *or* **fuci-** *comb form* [NL, fr. *Fucus*] **1 :** derived from or related to the alga fucus ⟨*fucic* acid⟩ ⟨*fuci*phagous⟩ **2 :** fucose ⟨*fucoside*⟩ ⟨*fuco*pyranoside⟩

fu·ca·ce·ae \fyü'kāsē,ē\ *n pl, cap* [NL, fr. *Fucus*, type genus + *-aceae* — more at FUCUS] **:** a small family of brown algae (order Fucales) including the gulfweeds and rockweeds

fu·ca·ceous \(')=¦=shəs\ *adj* [NL *Fucaceae* + E *-ous*] **:** of or relating to the Fucaceae

fu·ca·le·an \(')fyü¦kālēən\ *adj* [NL *Fucales* + E *-an*] **:** of or relating to the Fucales

fu·ca·les \fyü'kā(,)lēz\ *n pl, cap* [NL, fr. *Fucus* + *-ales*] **:** an order of brown algae coextensive with the family Fucaceae and including exclusively diploid plants — compare LAMINARIALES

fuch·sia \'fyüshə *sometimes* -üshēə *or* -üksēə\ *n* [NL, fr. L. Leonhard *Fuchs* †1566 Ger. botanist + NL *-ia*] **1** *cap* **:** a genus of decorative shrubs (family Onagraceae) with pendulous tetramerous flowers found chiefly in tropical America but often cultivated as pot plants **2** -S **:** any plant of the genus *Fuchsia* **3** -S **:** a vivid reddish purple — compare FUCHSIA PURPLE

fuchsia pink *n* **:** a moderate purplish pink that is bluer and deeper than Vassar rose (sense 2)

fuchsia purple *n* **:** a variable color averaging a strong reddish purple that is redder and less strong than purple orchid and redder and duller than phlox purple — compare FUCHSIA

fuchsia red *n* **:** a moderate to deep purplish red — called also *magenta*

fuchsia rose *n* **:** a variable color averaging a moderate purplish red that is bluer and deeper than average rose, redder and deeper than violine pink, redder, lighter, and stronger than magenta rose, and bluer and stronger than solferino

fuch·sine *or* **fuch·sin** \'fyüksən, -k,sēn *also* 'fyü(,)sh| *or* 'fük(,)s|\ *n* -S [F *fuchsine*, prob. fr. *fuchsia* (fr. NL *Fuchsia*) + *-ine*; fr. its color] **1** *often cap* **:** a triphenylmethane dye that is made usu. in the form of the chloride by oxidation of a mixture of aniline and toluidines, that gives a brilliant bluish red solution and dyes wool or silk directly or mordanted cotton, but is used chiefly in coloring paper and as a biological stain — called also *magenta, rosaniline*; see DYE table I (under *Basic Violet 14* and *Solvent Red 41*); compare ACID FUCHSINE, NEW FUCHSINE, PARA FUCHSINE **2 :** FUCHSIA 3

fuch·sin·o·phil \f(y)ük'sinə,fil\ *also* **fuch·sin·o·phile** \-fīl\ *or* **fuch·si·no·phil·ic** \(¦)f(y)ük¦sinə¦filik\ *adj* [*fuchsinophil, fuchsinophile* fr. ISV *fuchsine* + *-o-* + *-phil, -phile*; *fuchsinophilic* fr. *fuchsinophil, fuchsinophile* + *-ic*] **:** having an affinity for the acid dye fuchsine ⟨~ cytoplasmic granules⟩ or depending on such affinity ⟨the ~ mitochondrial reaction⟩

fuchs·ite \'f(y)ük,sīt\ *n* -S [G *fuchsit*, fr. Johann N. von *Fuchs* †1856 Ger. mineralogist + G *-it* -ite] **:** a mineral consisting of a common mica containing chromium

¹fu·coid \'fyü,kȯid\ *or* **fu·coi·dal** \(')fyü¦kȯidᵊl\ *adj* [*fucoid* prob. fr. (assumed) NL *fucoides*, fr. NL *Fucus* + L *-oides* -oid; *fucoidal* fr. *fucoid* + *-al*] **1 a :** of, relating to, or resembling algae of the order Fucales **b :** resembling or having the nature of seaweeds **2 :** of, relating to, or containing impressions of fossil fucoids or markings that resemble such impressions

²fucoid \"\ *n* -S [prob. fr. NL *fucoides*, fr. (assumed) NL *fucoides*, adj.] **1 :** a seaweed of the order Fucales **2 :** a fossil of an alga or a plant resembling an alga

fu·coi·din \fyü'kȯidᵊn\ *n* -S [ISV ²*fucoid* + *-in*] **:** a sulfuric ester of fucosan obtained from various brown algae (as those of the genus *Fucus*)

fu·co·san \'fyükə,san\ *n* -S [prob. ISV *fucose* + *-an*] **:** a polysaccharide occurring in various brown algae (as those of the genus *Fucus*) and yielding fucose on hydrolysis

fu·cose \'fyü,kōs\ *n* -S [ISV *fuc-* + *-ose*] **:** an aldose sugar $CH_3(CHOH)_4CHO$ occurring combined in the dextrorotatory D-form in various glycosides (as jalapin) and in the levorotatory L-form in fucosan, fucoidin, and polysaccharides typical of some blood groups; 6-deoxy-galactose — compare GLUCOSE

fu·cos·ter·ol \fyü'kästə,rōl, -rōl\ *n* [*fuc-* + *sterol*] **:** a crystalline sterol $C_{29}H_{47}OH$ occurring in various algae (as *Fucus vesiculosus*)

fu·co·xanthin \¦fyükō+\ *n* [ISV *fuc-* + *xanthin*] **:** a brown crystalline carotenoid pigment $C_{40}H_{60}O_6$ occurring esp. in the ova of brown algae

fu·cus \'fyükəs\ *n* [L, archil, red dye, rouge, deceit, fr. Gk *phykos* seaweed, rouge, of Sem origin; akin to Heb *pūk* antimony used as a cosmetic] **1** -ES *obs* **a :** a face paint or complexion aid **:** COSMETIC **b :** outward show **:** FACADE ⟨God . . . sees through all the daubings and ~*es* of hypocrisy —John Scott⟩ **2** [NL, fr. L] *cap* **:** a genus (the type of the family Fucaceae) of cartilaginous dichotomously branched brown algae that are blackish brown to olive green in color, have the reproductive cavities restricted to the bladder-shaped branch buds, and are used in the kelp industry and as a source of algin — compare ASCOPHYLLUM **3** -ES **:** any of various brown algae; *esp* **:** any plant of the genus *Fucus*

fu·cused \-st\ *adj, archaic* **:** artificially embellished

fud \'fəd\ *n* -S [perh. of Scand origin; akin to ON *futh* vulva, Norw dial. *fud* buttocks; akin to MHG *vut* vulva, Skt *puta* buttock, OE *fūl* foul — more at FOUL] **1** *chiefly Scot* **a :** BUTTOCKS, RUMP **b :** the tail of an animal (as a rabbit or hare) **2** [perh. alter. of *food*] *chiefly Brit* **:** waste from wool carding **3** [by shortening] **:** FUDDY-DUDDY ⟨old ~*s* like that never . . . retire —R.L.Scott⟩

¹fud·dle \'fədᵊl\ *vb* **fuddled; fuddled; fuddling** \-d(ᵊ)liŋ\ **fuddles** [origin unknown] *vi* **:** to take part in a drinking bout **:** TIPPLE ⟨then there's *fuddling* about in the public houses, and drinking bad spirits —Thomas Hughes⟩ **~** *vt* **1 :** to make drunk **:** INTOXICATE ⟨she would ~ herself every night with ale and whiskey —Richard Free⟩ **2 :** to make confused **:** MUDDLE ⟨corridors, archways, recesses . . . combined to ~ any sense of direction —Elizabeth Bowen⟩ **3 :** to make (a fish) torpid **:** STUPEFY ⟨catch a trout by *fuddling* him —A.A.Horn⟩

²fuddle \"\ *n* -S **1** *obs* **:** LIQUOR ⟨we sipped our ~ —Ned Ward⟩ **2 :** INTOXICATION ⟨a venerable toper . . . whom the oldest inhabitant had never seen otherwise than in a state of benevolent ~ —Norman Douglas⟩ **3** *chiefly Brit* **:** a prolonged drinking spell — used esp. in the phrase *on the fuddle* **4 :** a confused mixture **:** JUMBLE ⟨in front of a side altar a ~ of candles burned —Bruce Marshall⟩

fud·dler \'fəd(ᵊ)lə(r)\ *n* -S **:** DRUNKARD

¹fuddy-duddy \'fədē,dədē, 'fədi,dədi, ,==¦==\ *n* -ES [perh. redupl. of Sc *fuddy, fuddie* tail of an animal, short-tailed animal, fr. *fud* buttocks, tail of an animal + E *-y*] **1 :** one who is old-fashioned or ultraconservative **:** FOGY ⟨anybody over thirty has to . . . ask himself just how much of a *fuddy-duddy* he really is —Alistair Cooke⟩ **2 :** one who is pompous and unimaginative **:** STUFFED SHIRT ⟨the general impression . . . that anyone from a colonel up is a frozen-faced *fuddy-duddy* —Fletcher Pratt⟩ **3 :** one who is concerned about trifles **:** FUSSBUDGET ⟨an academic *fuddy-duddy* counting the semicolons —S.E.Hyman⟩

²fuddy-duddy \"\ *adj* **1 :** prim and conservative **:** FUSSY ⟨a *fuddy-duddy* professor in a classroom of rowdy boys —*Time*⟩ **2 :** OLD-FASHIONED, OUTDATED ⟨the atom bomb is already *fuddy-duddy* —Ellery Queen⟩

¹fudge \'fəj\ *vb* -ED/-ING/-S [prob. alter. of ²*fadge*] *vi* **1** *archaic* **:** to work out **:** RESULT ⟨we will see how this will ~ —Sir Walter Scott⟩ **2 a :** to act dishonestly **:** CHEAT; *specif* **:** to move a taw forward beyond the proper limits when starting to shoot in a game of marbles ⟨you *fudged* a mile —W.D.Steele⟩ **b :** to fail to live up to something **:** WELSH ⟨a man who would ~ on his oath of office —Harold Benjamin⟩ **3 :** to insert a last-minute newspaper item **4 :** to move slowly or cautiously ⟨you keep *fudging* along —K.M.Dodson⟩ **5 :** to avoid commitment **:** HEDGE ⟨we object to that kind of *fudging* off and whitewashing —R.E.Danielson⟩ **~** *vt* **1 a :** to devise as a substitute **:** contrive without adequate basis **:** FAKE ⟨it is not necessary to ~ anecdotes when there are so many of them —A.J.Liebling⟩ **b :** EMBELLISH, DISTORT ⟨used to ~ the accounts to the credit of the latter —J.V.DeMorgan⟩ **c :** to spoil the line of **:** BLUR ⟨the outlines of lips and nostrils had been *fudged* in the drawing —Oliver La Farge⟩ **2 :** to squeeze in belatedly **:** INTERPOLATE; *specif* **:** to insert (a news item) at the last minute **3 :** to fail to come to grips with **:** DODGE ⟨has too often blessed war, condoned injustice, *fudged* the racial issue, and shared the profits of acquiescence —M.A. Kapp⟩

²fudge \"\ *n* -S **1 :** a piece of foolish nonsense **:** BUNKUM, TWADDLE — often used interjectionally to express annoyance, disappointment, or disbelief ⟨oh, ~, she says they can't come⟩ **2 :** an item (as a news flash received too late for plating) typeset and inserted directly on the printing press — compare STOP PRESS **3 :** a soft candy made typically of sugar, milk, butter, and chocolate cooked together and beaten to a creamy consistency **4 :** RUSSIAN CALF

fudge box *n* **:** the metal container in a newspaper printing press for holding fudge matter **2 :** newspaper space left blank for the insertion of last-minute items

fudge edge *n* **:** a shoe sole or sole edge stitched and trimmed very close to the upper

fudg·er \'fəjə(r)\ *n* -S **:** a worker in a shoe factory who finishes the edge of a sole

fudge wheel *n* **:** a tool used in shoe manufacturing to ornament the edge of a sole or welt in imitation of welt stitching

fu dog *or* **foo dog** \'fü-\ *n, usu cap F* [Chin *fu²* happiness] **:** a mythical lion-dog used as a decorative motif in Far Eastern art — called also *Fu lion*

fue·gi·an \f(y)ü'āgēən, 'fwāg-\ *n* -S *usu cap* [Tierra del *Fuego*, archipelago at southern end of So. America + E *-ian*] **1 :** an Indian people of Tierra del Fuego — compare ALACALUF, ONA, YAHGAN **2 :** a member of the Fuegian people

fuehrer *sometimes cap, var of* FÜHRER

1**fu·el** \'fyüəl, -üəl *also* -ül, *chiefly Brit* |(,)il\ *n* -s *often attrib* [ME *fewel*, fr. OF *fouaille, fuaille*, fr. *feu* fire, fr. LL *focus*, fr. L, hearth — more at FOCUS] **1 a :** a material (as coal, coke, gas, oil, peat, wood) used to produce heat or power by burning : something that feeds fire **b :** nutritive material : FOOD : ALIMENT ⟨animals take food to obtain ~ or energy to carry on all their life activities —G.E. & Nettie MacGinitie⟩ **c :** any material from which atomic energy can be liberated; *esp* : fissionable material used in a nuclear reactor — called also *nuclear fuel* **2 :** a source of sustenance or additional incentive : REINFORCEMENT ⟨public opinion . . . ought to provide the ~ to carry American foreign policy forward —H.J. Morgenthau⟩

2**fuel** \"\ *vb* **fueled** *or* **fuelled; fueled** *or* **fuelled; fueling** *or* **fuelling; fuels** *vt* **1 :** to provide with material for burning ⟨the virgin stand of big trees . . . went long ago . . . to ~ the furnaces —J.W.Schaefer⟩ **2 :** SUPPORT, STIMULATE ⟨the country might be on its way to self-sufficiency in petroleum instead of . . . scrabbling for supplies to ~ its industrial development —S.G.Hanson⟩ ~ *vi* **:** to take in fuel : become provided with fuel — often used with *up* ⟨the plane's ~*ing* up —Kay Boyle⟩

fuel dope *n* : DOPE 2d

fu·el·er *or* **fu·el·ler** \-lə(r)\ *n* -s [ME *fewelere*, fr. *fewel* fuel + *-ere* -er] : one that supplies fuel or feeds fires

fuel filter *n* : an attachment to the fuel line of an automotive internal-combustion engine that filters the liquid before it enters the carburetor

fuel injector *n* : a pump and valve mechanism that sprays liquid fuel intermittently into the cylinder of a diesel engine

fuel-mixture indicator *n* : EXHAUST-GAS ANALYZER

fuel oil *n* : an oil used for fuel esp. in a furnace or heater and usu. having a flash point higher than that of kerosine

fuel pump *n* : a pump in a motor vehicle that propels liquid fuel from the tank to the carburetor

fuerth *usu cap, var of* FÜRTH

1**fuff** \'fəf\ *vb* -ED/-ING/-S [imit.] *vi* **1** *chiefly Scot* **a :** to puff and blow : PANT **b :** to give off puffs of vapor **2** *chiefly Scot* **:** to spit and hiss **3** *chiefly Scot* **:** to fly into a rage : have a fit of temper ~ *vt, chiefly Scot* **:** to cause to give off puffs; *specif* : SMOKE

2**fuff** \"\ *n* -s **1** *chiefly Scot* **:** a gust or puff esp. of wind **2** *chiefly Scot* **:** an outburst of temper : RAGE

fuf·fle \'fəfəl\ *vb* -ED/-ING/-S [perh. freq. of 1*fuff*] *vi, Scot* : to become disheveled or mussed up ~ *vt, Scot* : DISARRAY, MUSS

1**fug** \'fəg\ *n* -s [by alter.] *Scot* : 1FOG

2**fug** \"\ *n* -s [prob. alter. of 3*fog*] : an odorous emanation; *esp* : the stuffy atmosphere of a hot crowded poorly ventilated space ⟨cooking and breathing soon produced a pleasant ~ in the tents —J.R.Ullman⟩

3**fug** \"\ *vb* **fugged; fugged; fugging; fugs** *vi* : to loll indoors in a stuffy atmosphere ⟨we retired . . . to steam and ~ for fourteen long hours —Frank Hurley⟩ ~ *vt* : to make stuffy and odorous ⟨the small tent was *fugged* —Walter Macken⟩

fu·ga \'fügə\ *n* -s [It — more at FUGUE] **1 :** FUGUE **2 :** a canon in medieval music

fu·ga·cious \(')fyü'gāshəs\ *adj* [L *fugac-, fugax* swift, fleeting (fr. *fugere* to run away) + E *-ious* — more at FUGITIVE] **1 a :** of an unsubstantial nature : lasting a short time : EVANESCENT ⟨the painter's fame is based on the most ~ of substances — public favor —Frederic Taubes⟩ **b** *also* **fugaceous :** falling off or disappearing before the usual time — used chiefly of plant parts other than floral organs (as stipules or moss calyptras); opposed to *persistent;* compare CADUCOUS, DECIDUOUS **2 :** not fixed in a certain place : WANDERING ⟨unlike other minerals . . . oil and gas are . . . ~ —Robert Kratovil⟩

fu·ga·cious·ness *n* -ES : the quality or state of being fugacious

fu·gac·i·ty \fyü'gasəd·ē\ *n* -ES [fr. *fugacious*, after such pairs as E *capacious: capacity*] **1 :** lack of enduring qualities : TRANSIENCE ⟨that the fresh bloom of the carol was evanescent . . . I always knew; but never realized its extreme ~ until five years ago —A.T.Quiller-Couch⟩ **2 a :** the vapor pressure of a vapor assumed to be an ideal gas obtained by correcting the determined vapor pressure and useful as a measure of the escaping tendency of a substance from a heterogeneous system **b :** a correction for the deviation in the behavior of an actual solution from that of an ideal solution — compare ACTIVITY 6b

fu·gae warrant *also* **fu·gie warrant** \'f(y)ü(,)jē-\ *n* [*fugae* prob. alter. (influenced by L *fugae* of running away — in the Scots law phrase used in reference to an absconding debtor NL *in meditatione fugae* in contemplation of running away — gen. of *fuga* flight, running away) of *fugie*, prob. by shortening & alter. fr. 2*fugitive*] *Scots law* : a warrant to attach an absconding debtor

fu·gal \'fyügəl\ *adj* [1*fugue* + *-al*] : of, relating to, or in the style of a musical fugue — **fu·gal·ly** \-əlē,-əli\ *adv*

-fu·gal \,fyəgəl, ,fəgə-, ,fēg-, |k-, *chiefly Brit* 'fyügəl\ *adj comb form* [prob. fr. (assumed) NL *-fuga* -fuge + E *-al*] : fleeing : passing from ⟨centri*fugal*⟩ — **-fu·gal·ly** \gəlē, -li\ *adv comb form*

fu·ga·ra \fü'gärə\ *n* -s [It, fr. Pol *fujara* shepherd's flute] : a labial pipe-organ stop of 8-foot or 4-foot pitch and of string quality

1**fu·ga·to** \fü'gäd·(,)ō\ *adv (or adj)* [It, fr. past part. of *fugare* to compose as a fugue, fr. *fuga* fugue — more at FUGUE] : in the style of but not strictly in the form of a musical fugue

2**fugato** \"\ *n* -s [It, fr. past part. of *fugare* to compose as a fugue] : a musical passage in fugato style

fuge \'fyüg\ *n* -s [earlier spelling of 1*fugue*] : FUGUING TUNE

-fuge \,fyüj\ *n comb form* -s [F, prob. fr. (assumed) NL *-fuga*, fr. LL *-fuga, -fugia* (in *febrifuga, febrifugia* centaury), fr. L *fugare* to put to flight, fr. *fuga* flight — more at FUGUE] : one that drives away ⟨dolori*fuge*⟩ ⟨vermi*fuge*⟩

fug·gy \'fəgē\ *adj, usu* -ER/-EST [2*fug* + *-y*] : stuffy and smelly ⟨the air was ~; the light dim —Virginia Woolf⟩

fu·ghet·ta \f(y)ü'ged·ə\ *n* -s [It, dim. of *fuga* fugue] : a short or condensed fugue

fugi *var of* FUJI

fu·gie \'fyüjē\ *n* -s [prob. by shortening & alter.] **1** *Scot* : FUGITIVE **2** *Scot* **a :** a fighting cock that will not fight **b :** a cowardly person

fu·gi·tate \'fyüjə,tāt\ *vb* -ED/-ING/-S [1*fugitive* + *-ate* (v. suffix)] *vt, Scots law* : to declare judicially to be a fugitive from justice and thereby cause the escheat of the fugitive's movable property to the crown : OUTLAW ~ *vi* : to run away

fu·gi·ta·tion \,==' tāshən\ *n* -s [*fugitate* + *-ion*] **1** *Scots law* : a judicial declaration of outlawry **2 :** the act of fleeing

1**fu·gi·tive** \'fyüjəd·iv, -ətiv\ *adj* [ME *fugitif, fugitive*, fr. MF & L; MF *fugitif*, fr. L *fugitivus*, fr. *fugere* to run away, flee; akin to Gk *pheugein* to run away, flee, Lith *baugus* timorous, and prob. to OHG *biogan* to bend — more at BOW] **1 :** running away or intending flight (as from an enemy, a master, duty, or justice) : FLEEING ⟨a ~ slave⟩ ⟨a ~ debtor⟩ ⟨the new note served notice that neither the ~ . . . diplomat nor his wife would be handed over —*Wall Street Jour.*⟩ **2 :** moving from place to place : WANDERING ⟨a ~ theatrical company⟩ ⟨the ~ clouds of the sky —K.K.Darrow⟩ **3 a :** being of short duration : FLEETING ⟨the journalist . . . is concerned only with the ~ moment —A.L.Guérard⟩ **b :** difficult to grasp or retain : ELUSIVE ⟨thought is clear or muddy, graspable or ~, according to the purity of the medium —J.M.Barzun⟩ **c :** likely to evaporate : VOLATILE ⟨~ elements escape from the magma in rock crystallization⟩ **d :** likely to deteriorate : PERISHABLE ⟨a great deal of valuable material is mounted on ~ cardboard —*All The King's Horses*⟩ **e :** subject to change : not fixed ⟨its membership is ~ but the institution . . . requires continuity —O.W.Phelps⟩; *specif* : fading when exposed to light ⟨many of these dyes . . . are so ~ to light that dyed material if left uncovered in a mill room during a weekend . . . may be found to have faded —C.M.Whittaker & C.C.Wilcock⟩ **f :** likely to disappear or fall away; *specif* : not permanently established — used esp. of a botanical species **4 a :** SCATTERED, INFREQUENT, OCCASIONAL ⟨he has only to collect his ~ pieces to have . . . a book of deep significance —T.V.Smith⟩ **b :** being of transient interest : EPHEMERAL ⟨the press ranges from the superficiality of fragmentary items in the most ~ tabloid to the rich fare of the *New York Times* —William Albig⟩ **syn** see TRANSIENT

2**fugitive** \"\ *n* -s [ME *fugitif, fugitive*, fr. MF & L; MF *fugitif*, fr. L *fugitivus*, fr. *fugitivus*, adj.] **1 :** one who flees or tries to escape: as **a :** one who runs away from a master or employer or from uncongenial surroundings ⟨a ~ from a sweatshop —A.E.Stevenson b.1900⟩ **b :** one who tries to elude justice ⟨surrender of the ~ for trial —R.G.Neumann⟩ **c :** one who flees or is forced to leave his country : EXILE, REFUGEE ⟨for the doubtful benefit of the political ~ —Alona Evans⟩ **2 :** one who goes from place to place usu. without a fixed purpose or direction : WANDERER **3 :** something elusive or hard to find ⟨what muse but his can nature's beauties hit, or catch that airy ~ called wit —Walter Harte⟩ **4 a :** a dye that is not fast **b :** an article colored with such a dye ⟨cotton ~*s* are simply dyed with alkali and common salt —G.H.Johnson⟩

fugitive from justice : one who having committed or being accused of a crime in one jurisdiction is absent for any reason from that jurisdiction; *specif* : one who flees to avoid punishment

fu·gi·tive·ly \-d·ə̇vlē, -tə̇-, -li\ *adv* : in a fugitive manner : in the manner of a fugitive

fu·gi·tive·ness \-d·ivnəs, -ti-\ *n* -ES : the quality or state of being fugitive

fugitive warrant *n* : a warrant providing for the arrest and detention of an alleged fugitive from justice pending the extradition proceeding

fu·gi·tiv·i·ty \,fyüjə'tivəd·ē\ *n* -ES : FUGITIVENESS

fu·gle \'fyügəl\ *vi* -ED/-ING/-S [back-formation fr. *fugleman*] *archaic* : to act as fugleman

fu·gle·man \-mən, -,man\ *n, pl* also **flu·gel·man** \'flü-\ *n, pl* **fuglemen** *also* **flugelmen** [modif. of G *flügelmann*, fr. *flügel* wing (fr. MHG *vlügel*) + *mann* man, fr. OHG *man;* akin to OHG *fliogan* to fly — more at FLY, MAN] **1 :** a trained soldier formerly posted in front of a line of men at drill to serve as a model in their exercises **2 :** one who heads a group : LEADER ⟨their ~ was an accomplished man of letters but in his followers his . . . virtues disappeared —John Buchan⟩; *specif* : a political manager ⟨the politician in the frock coat who was the . . . chief ~ —Robert Grant †1940⟩

fugs *pl of* FUG, *pres 3d sing of* FUG

fu·gu \'fü(,)gü\ *n* -s [Jap] : any of various globefishes that contain a heat-stable toxic principle resembling curare and are sometimes eaten in Japan with suicidal intent

1**fugue** \'fyüg\ *n* -s [alter. (influenced by F *fugue*, fr. It *fuga*) of earlier *fuge*, prob. fr. It *fuga* fugue, act of running away, flight, fr. L, act of running away, flight; akin to L *fugere* to run away, flee — more at FUGITIVE] **1 :** a contrapuntal musical composition in which one or two melodic themes are repeated or imitated by the successively entering voices and developed in a continuous interweaving of the voice parts into a well-defined single structure — compare CANON **2 :** something having a thematic structure that is suggestive of a musical fugue ⟨it was an immense, dissonant ~ in black with incidental color —Alfred Frankenstein⟩ **3 :** a pathological disturbance of consciousness during which the patient performs acts of which he appears to be conscious but of which on recovery he has no recollection

2**fugue** \"\ *vb* -ED/-ING/-S *vi* : to compose or perform a musical fugue ~ *vt* : to make a fugue of

fuguing tune *or* **fuguing piece** *n* [*fuguing* fr. gerund of 2*fugue*] : an early 19th century hymn characterized by polyphony and imitation — called also *fuge*

fugu·ist \'fyügəst\ *n* -s : one who composes or performs fugues

füh·rer *or* **fueh·rer** *also* **fuh·rer** \'fyürə(r), 'fir-, *G* 'fü̅rər\ *n* -s *sometimes cap* [G *führer* leader, guide, fr. MHG *vüerer* wagoner, bearer, fr. *vüeren* to lead, drive, bear (fr. OHG *fuoren* to lead, set in motion) + *-er* -er, fr. OHG *-āri*; akin to OE *fēran* to go, ON *fœra* to bring; derivative fr. the root of OE *faran* to go — more at FARE] : one in a position of authority : LEADER; *esp* : TYRANT ⟨an epoch of ~*s* and generalissimos backed by . . . unprecedented instruments of coercion —Leland Stowe⟩

fui·dhir \'fwi,thi(ə)r\ *n* -s [MIr *fuidir*] : a stranger or refugee in ancient Ireland placing himself under the protection of a chief and becoming his tenant

fuil \'fœl, 'fœl\ *Scot var of* FOOL

fu·i·re·na \,fyüə'rēnə\ *n, cap* [NL, fr. Georg *Fuiren* †1628 Dan. physician] : a genus of sedges (family Cyperaceae) with leafy culms and many-flowered terete spikelets in terminal or axillary clusters — see UMBRELLA GRASS c

fu·ji \'f(y)ü(,)jē\ *n* -s [in sense 1, fr. Jap; in other senses, fr. *Fuji*, sacred mountain in south central Honshu, Japan] **1 :** a wisteria (*Wistaria sinensis*) **2** *also* **fuji cherry :** a shrubby Japanese flowering cherry with pale pink petals and red filaments that persist after the petals fall **3** *also* **fu·gi** \-(,)jē\ **a :** a spun silk clothing fabric in plain weave orig. made in Japan **b :** a rayon imitation of this fabric

fu·ku·o·ka \,fü(,)kü'ōkə\ *adj, usu cap* [fr. *Fukuoka*, city in northern Kyushu, Japan] : of or from the city of Fukuoka, Japan : of the kind or style prevalent in Fukuoka

1**-ful** \fəl *sometimes* (,)fül *esp when an unstressed vowel precedes*\ *adj suffix* [ME, fr. OE, fr. *full*, adj.] **1 :** full of ⟨event*ful*⟩ **2 :** characterized by : -OUS ⟨peace*ful*⟩ ⟨boast*ful*⟩ **3 :** having the qualities of : resembling ⟨master*ful*⟩ **4 :** -ABLE ⟨bash*ful*⟩ ⟨mourn*ful*⟩

2**-ful** *also* **-full** \,fül\ *n suffix* -s [ME *-ful*, fr. OE *-ful, -full*, fr. *full*, adj.] : number or quantity that fills or would fill ⟨cup*ful*⟩ ⟨room*ful*⟩ ⟨belly*ful*⟩ — sometimes after pl. nouns ⟨bags*ful*⟩

fu·la *or* **fu·lah** \'fülə, 'fulə\ *also* **ful** \'fül, 'ful\ *n, pl* **fula** *or* **fulas** *or* **fulah** *or* **fulahs** *also* **ful** *or* **fuls** *usu cap* **1 a :** a Sudanese people of African Negroid stock and Mediterranean Caucasoid admixture with highly variable skin color that is often reddish brown, hair wavy to crisp, and slender figure — called also *Fellata, Fulani, Fulbe* **b :** a member of such people **2 :** FULANI 2a

fu·la·ni \'fü,läne, fü'l-\ *n, usu cap* **1** *pl* **fulani** *or* **fulanis** **a :** FULA 1a; *esp* : the Fula of northern Nigeria and adjacent areas **b :** a member of such people **2** *pl* **fulani** *or* **fulanis** **a :** the language of the Fula people now classified as West-Atlantic and most closely related to Serer — called also *Fula, Fulfulde, Peul* **b :** a trade language used by other tribes in many areas of West Africa **3 a :** a West African breed of large white-coated black-skinned humped cattle with horns rising in a lyre-shaped curve **b** *pl* **fulani** *or* **fulanis :** an animal of this breed

ful·be \'fül(,)bā\ *n, pl* **fulbe** *or* **fulbes** *usu cap* : FULA 1

ful·bright \'ful,brīt, *usu* -īd·+V\ *n* -s *usu cap* [after James William *Fulbright* b1905 U. S. senator] : a grant awarded under the Fulbright Act that makes U. S. surplus property in foreign countries available to finance lectures or research abroad by American students and professors

ful·chronograph \(')fül, |fəl+\ *n* [L *fulgur* lightning (fr. *fulgēre* to shine, flash) + E *chronograph*] : a lightning-recording device that consists of a revolving aluminum disk having on its rim several hundred steel fins which, as they pass successively every forty-millionth of a second between two coils carrying the surge current of a lightning stroke, become proportionately magnetized and register the duration and intensity of the strokes

ful·ci·ment \'fulsəmənt, 'fəl-\ *n* -s [L *fulcimentum*, fr. *fulcire* to prop + *-mentum* -ment] *archaic* : PROP

ful·cral \'fulkrəl, 'fəl-\ *adj* [*fulcrum* + *-al*] : of or relating to a fulcrum

ful·crate \-,krāt\ *adj* [prob. fr. (assumed) NL *fulcratus*, fr. NL *fulcrum* + L *-atus* -ate] *biol* : having a fulcrum

1**ful·crum** \'fulkrəm, 'fəl-\ *n, pl* **fulcrums** \-mz\ *or* **ful·cra** \-rə\ [LL, fr. L, bedpost, fr. *fulcire* to prop — more at BALK] **1 a :** PROP, SUPPORT; *specif* : the support about which a lever turns ⟨an oar rests against some kind of ~ on the boat —*Notes & Queries on Anthropology*⟩ — see LEVER illustration **b :** one that supplies leverage for action ⟨he is . . . the reader's eyes and ears and the ~ of his judgment —Bernard De Voto⟩ **2** [NL, fr. LL] **:** a part of an animal that serves as a hinge or support: **a :** one of the small modified scales or spines on the anterior edge of the fins of many ganoid and a few teleost fishes **b :** the horny inferior surface of the ligula of various insects; *specif* : a chitinous framework at the base of the proboscis of insects of the order Diptera **c :** the stem or median part of the incus of the mastax of certain rotifers

2**fulcrum** \"\ *vt* -ED/-ING/-S : to furnish with a fulcrum : apply a fulcrum to : make a fulcrum of

fule \'fæl\ *Scot var of* FOOL

ful·fill *or* **ful·fil** \(')fül'fil *sometimes* fəl'f-, *rapid sometimes* fə'f- *or* fə'f- *by* l-*dissimilation*\ *vt* **fulfilled; fulfilled; fulfilling; fulfills** *or* **fulfils** [ME *fulfillen*, fr. OE *fullfyllan*, fr. 1*full* + *fyllan* to fill — more at FULL, FILL] **1** *archaic* : to make full : FILL ⟨the world has received animals . . . and is ~*ed* with them —Benjamin Jowett⟩ ⟨her subtle, warm, and golden breath . . . ~*s* him with beatitude —Alfred Tennyson⟩ **2 :** to supply the missing parts of : make whole : INTEGRATE ⟨admirable though the illustrations are, their virtue is . . . that they ~ the text —*Times Lit. Supp.*⟩ **3 a :** to carry out : ACCOMPLISH, EXECUTE ⟨he had struck out into the wilderness . . . partly for reasons of his own, partly to ~ an order of his superior —Vicki Baum⟩ **b :** to finish out : bring to an end ⟨she came to install herself and ~ her time at the house —Willa Cather⟩ **c :** to come up to (as a requirement) : MEET, ANSWER, SATISFY ⟨this work ~*s* a need that lawyers have felt for many years —*Columbia Univ. Press Books*⟩ **4 a :** to measure up to : convert into reality ⟨pioneering courage balanced by a sense of the failure of life to ~ its ultimate expectations —Leslie Rees⟩ **b :** to realize the full potentialities of : develop completely : CONSUMMATE ⟨the inalienable right of a man to realize his potentialities, to ~ himself, to enter upon his destiny —August Heckscher b. 1913⟩ **syn** see PERFORM, SATISFY

ful·fill·er \-lə(r)\ *n* [ME, fr. *fulfillen* + *-er*] : one that fulfills

ful·fill·ment *or* **ful·fil·ment** \='=mənt\ *n* -s **1 :** the act or process of fulfilling : EXECUTION ⟨participation in the ~ of mother's dreams —C.S.Hill⟩ **2 :** the quality or state of being fulfilled : COMPLETION ⟨a patchwork quilt which I was well aware would never reach ~ —Agnes Repplier⟩

ful·ful·de \ful'fuldē\ *n, pl* **fulfulde** *or* **fulfuldes** *usu cap* : FULANI 2a

ful·gence \'fulјən(t)s, 'fəl-\ *or* **ful·gen·cy** \-nsē\ *n, pl* **fulgences** *or* **fulgencies** [*fulgence* fr. ME, fr. *fulgent*, after such pairs as ME *excellent: excellence; fulgency* fr. *fulgent* + *-cy*] : brilliant luster : RESPLENDENCE

ful·gen·ic acid \(')fu|l'jenik-, |fəl\ *n* [*fulgenic* fr. G *fulgen-* (fr. L *fulgens* fulgent) + E *-ic*] : a dicarboxylic acid $[CH_2{=}C(COOH){-}]_2$ known in the form of derivatives

ful·gent \'fuljənt, 'fəl-\ *adj* [ME, fr. L *fulgent-, fulgens*, pres. part. of *fulgēre* to shine, flash; akin to L *flagrare* to burn — more at BLACK] : dazzlingly bright : RADIANT ⟨the sun was ~ —Dan Levin⟩ ⟨lilac and wistaria . . . ~, with a burning scent —William Faulkner⟩ — **ful·gent·ly** *adv*

ful·gid \-jəd\ *adj* [L *fulgidus*, fr. *fulgēre*] **1** *archaic* : shining brightly : GLITTERING ⟨the ~ sunbeams spread abroad their animating light —William Bartram⟩ **2** *zool* : fiery red with metallic reflections

ful·gide \-,jīd, -jəd\ *n* -s [G *fulgid*, fr. *fulg-* (fr. L *fulgēre*) + *-id* -ide] **1 :** the anhydride $C_6H_4O_3$ of fulgenic acid **2 :** a derivative of fulgenic acid (as some aryl derivatives used in photography to produce removable light images in blue and black tones)

ful·gor \'fulgər, 'fəl-, -,gȯ(ə)r\ *or* **ful·gour** \-,gər\ *n* -s [L *fulgor*, fr. *fulgēre*] *archaic* : dazzling brightness : SPLENDOR — **ful·gor·ous** \-gərəs\ *adj*

ful·go·ra \'fulgərə, 'fəl-\ *n, cap* [NL, fr. L *Fulgora*, goddess of lightning] : the type genus of the family Fulgoridae

1**ful·go·rid** \-rəd, -,rid\ *adj* [NL *Fulgoridae*] : of or relating to the Fulgoridae

2**fulgorid** \"\ *n* -s [NL *Fulgoridae*] : an insect of the family Fulgoridae

ful·gor·i·dae \ful'gȯrə,dē, ,fəl-\ *n pl, cap* [NL, fr. *Fulgora*, type genus + *-idae*] : a family of chiefly tropical often grotesquely formed plant-feeding insects (superfamily Fulguroidea) that have the beak obviously arising from the base of the head and the ocelli near or below the eyes — see LANTERN FLY

ful·go·roi·dea \,fulgə'rȯidēə, ,fəl-\ *n pl, cap* [NL, fr. *Fulgora* + *-oidea*] : a superfamily of insects (suborder Homoptera) that usu. have ocelli in cavities of the cheeks and the anal veins of the fore wings fused apically to form a Y — see LANTERN FLY

ful·gu·ral \'fulg(y)ərəl, 'fəl-\ *adj* [L *fulguralis*, fr. *fulgur* lightning + *-alis* -al] *archaic* : of or relating to lightning

ful·gu·rant \-rənt\ *adj* [L *fulgurant-, fulgurans*, pres. part. of *fulgurare*] : flashing like lightning : DAZZLING ⟨these great best canvases still look as astonishing and as invitingly new as they did . . . when . . . his ~ popularity was in full growth —Janet Flanner⟩

ful·gu·rate \-,rāt\ *vb* -ED/-ING/-S [L *fulguratus*, past part. of *fulgurare* to lightning, flash like lightning, fr. *fulgur* lightning, fr. *fulgēre* to shine, flash] *vi, obs* : to flash like lightning ~ *vt* **1 :** to emit flashes of ⟨he is said to have been conspicuously handsome: well built, of soldierly bearing, with . . . blue eyes that *fulgurated* . . . terror, love, or hate —*New Yorker*⟩ **2 :** to perform electrodesiccation on : remove or destroy by means of electrodesiccation ⟨relieved the patient's discomfort by *fulgurating* the uterine mass⟩

ful·gu·ra·tion \,=='rāshən\ *n* -s [L *fulguration, fulguratio* sheet lightning, fr. *fulguratus* + *-ion-, -io* -ion] **1 a :** the act or process of flashing like lightning : a lightning flash ⟨it was pleasant to be sitting there while the sultriest ~*s*, flickering, cast corners in the glass —Wallace Stevens⟩ **b :** a spiritual radiation or divine manifestation **c :** *Leibnizianism* : the monads that are coeternal with God **2 :** the sudden brightening of a fused globule of gold or silver when the last film of oxide of lead or copper leaves its surface in assaying **3 :** ELECTRODESICCATION

ful·gu·rite \'==,rīt\ *n* -s [ISV *fulgur-* (fr. L *fulgur*) + *-ite*] : an often tubular vitrified crust produced by the fusion of sand or rock by lightning

ful·gu·rous \-rəs\ *adj* [L *fulgur* + E *-ous*] : charged with or emitting flashes of or like lightning ⟨adventures related often with raffish gusto, in style both vivid and ~ —Idwal Jones⟩

ful·ham \'fuləm\ *n* -s [perh. by folk etymology (influence of *Fulham*, London borough formerly much frequented by professional gamblers) fr. earlier *fullan*, perh. fr. 1*full* + *one*, n.] *archaic* : a loaded die ⟨there is no loading of the dice or throwing of ~*s* —A. Conan Doyle⟩

fu·li·ca \'fyüləkə\ *n, cap* [NL, fr. L, coot — more at BALD] : a genus of aquatic birds (family Rallidae) comprising the coots and being distinguished from the typical rails by the presence of a frontal shield and lobed toes — compare GALLINULE

fu·li·cine \-lə,sīn, -,sən\ *adj* [NL *Fulicinae* subfamily comprising the coots, fr. *Fulica* + *-inae*] : of or relating to the genus *Fulica*

fu·lig·i·nos·i·ty \(,)fyü,lijə'näsəd·ē\ *n* -ES [F *fuliginosité*, fr. MF, fr. LL *fuliginosus* sooty + MF *-ité* -ity] : the quality or state of being fuliginous

fu·lig·i·nous \(')fyü'lijənəs\ *adj* [LL *fuliginosus* sooty, fr. L *fuligin-, fuligo* soot + *-osus* -ose; akin to MIr *dúil* wish, Lith *dulsvas* smoke-colored, L *fumus* smoke — more at FUME] **1** *obs* : of or relating to certain noxious bodily vapors formerly held to be produced by organic processes ⟨it is not amiss to bore the skull with an instrument to let out the ~ vapors —Robert Burton⟩ **2 a :** of, relating to, or containing soot : SOOTY ⟨plenty of Londoners who are fed up with the current spell of ~, choking weather —Mollie Panter-Downes⟩ **b :** CLOUDED, OBSCURE, MURKY ⟨a ~ sense of ironical humor —W.J.Locke⟩ **3 :** having the color of soot : DARK, DUSKY — **fu·lig·i·nous·ly** *adv*

fu·li·go \fyü'lī(,)gō, fyü'lē(-\ *n, cap* [NL, fr. L, soot] : a widely distributed genus of large slime molds with the sporangia gathered in an aethalium and the plasmodium commonly bright yellow

fu lion *n, usu cap F* [Chin *fu*[2] happiness] : FU DOG

fulk \'fəlk, 'fulk\ *vi* -ED/-ING/-S [origin unknown] : to move the hand unfairly in shooting marbles

1**full** \'ful\ *adj* -ER/-EST [ME *ful, full*, fr. OE *full;* akin to OHG *fol* full, ON *fullr*, Goth *fulls*, L *plenus* full, *plēre* to fill, Gk *plērēs* full, *plēthein* to be full, Skt *pūrṇa* full] **1 a :** containing all that possibly can be placed or put within ⟨a ~ hamper⟩ ⟨a ~ magazine⟩ — often used with *of* ⟨a bin ~ of corn⟩ **b :** having the normal or intended capacity supplied or accommodated : entirely occupied ⟨a ~ bus⟩ ⟨a ~ house⟩ **c** : occupying completely the requisite space ⟨a ~ cargo⟩ ⟨a ~ audience⟩ **d** : possessed of the appropriate or normal complement ⟨a ~ dramatic company⟩ ⟨a ~ jury⟩ **e** : regularly allotted : normally apportioned ⟨more than its ~ share of lovely old American houses —Jerome Weidman⟩ **f** *of an ablaut grade* : NORMAL **2 a** (1) : lacking restraint or check : PRECIPITOUS, HEADLONG ⟨~ retreat⟩ (2) : being without reservation : UNQUALIFIED ⟨~ supporters of a policy⟩ **b** : possessing the maximum strength or force ⟨a ~ gale⟩ **c** (1) : followed to the greatest extent feasible : all possible ⟨making ~ use of a library's resources⟩ (2) : greatest or highest potential ⟨a ship going at ~ speed⟩ ⟨a machine operating at ~ capacity⟩ (3) : being at or of the greatest or highest degree : MAXIMUM ⟨~ strength⟩ ⟨~ potency⟩ **3 a** : rounded in outline ⟨a ~ face⟩ : well filled out : PLUMP ⟨a ~ figure⟩ : generously formed : SWELLING ⟨~ lips⟩ **b** (1) : filled or distended by wind ⟨~ sails⟩ (2) *of a ship* : having the sails filled with wind **c** : big with young or eggs **d** : having an abundance of material esp. in the form of gathered, pleated, or flared parts ⟨a ~ skirt⟩ **e** (1) : slightly oversize, projecting, or standing out usu. so as to require more tooling (2) : risen above the normal level : SWOLLEN ⟨in spring when the rivers and streams are ~⟩ **4 a** : possessing, containing, or furnished with an abundance or great number — used with *of* ⟨a face ~ of wrinkles⟩ ⟨a city ~ of soldiers⟩ ⟨a room ~ of pictures⟩ **b** : possessing all particulars : completely familiar or expert — used with *of* ⟨he is ~ of his subject and our foremost authority —W.O.Douglas⟩ **c** : packed with variety of experience ⟨a ~ life⟩; *also* : possessing much knowledge ⟨education having made him a ~ man⟩ **5 a** : satisfied esp. with food or drink : REPLETE **b** : large enough so as to satisfy ⟨a ~ meal⟩ **6 a** (1) : enjoying or possessed of all recognized or authorized prerogatives, rights, and privileges : not temporary, substitute, or provisional ⟨a ~ member⟩ (2) : being without reduction or subtraction : REGULAR ⟨working only half time but drawing ~ salary⟩ ⟨maintaining ~ diplomatic relations with a foreign country⟩ ⟨a ~ term of office⟩ (3) : being without truncation : UNABBREVIATED ⟨~ words⟩ **b** (1) : containing all details : COMPLETE ⟨a ~ statement⟩ ⟨a ~ report⟩ (2) : not lacking in any feature, quality, or accomplishment : PERFECT ⟨quite old but in ~ possession of his faculties⟩ **7** *archaic* : completely weary : utterly sick — used with *of* **8** : filled with emotion ⟨a ~ heart⟩ **9 a** : having the limit or near limit — used with *of* ⟨a man weary and ~ of years⟩ **b** (1) : being at the height of development ⟨a flower in ~ bloom⟩ ⟨the tide at ~ flood⟩ ⟨a moon nearly ~⟩ (2) : MATURE, ADULT ⟨men and women of ~ age⟩ **10** : having the same parents ⟨~ sisters⟩ **11** *of a color* : PURE **12 a** : carried to the greatest practical extent ⟨a shotgun with a ~ choke⟩ **b** : extended to or occupying the largest possible space, area, or dimensions ⟨a ~ basement⟩ **c** : completely covering the boards and backbone ⟨a book bound in ~ crushed blue morocco with gilt edges and blind tooling⟩ — compare HALF **13 a** : having marked volume or depth ⟨a ~ voice⟩ ⟨a ~ tone⟩ **b** *of a vowel* : BACK 1c **14 a** : squarely facing ahead ⟨a *full*-face portrait⟩ **b** : being in dead center : DIRECT ⟨a cue ball making a ~ hit on the object ball⟩ **15** : completely occupied : ENGROSSED — used with *of* ⟨I have been ~ of work since I wrote last —H.J.Laski⟩ **16** : being the rank of the three of a kind in a full house in poker — used postpositively ⟨jacks ~⟩ **17** : possessing a rich or pronounced quality ⟨a wine of ~ body⟩ ⟨a food of ~ flavor⟩

²full \"\ *adv* [ME *ful, full,* fr. OE *full,* fr. *full,* adj.] **1 a** : VERY, EXTREMELY ⟨I knew ~ well he had lied to me⟩ **b** : ENTIRELY, COMPLETELY, QUITE ⟨it was ~ dark by then —A.J.Liebling⟩ ⟨swung ~ around —Morley Callaghan⟩ **2** : to the full : to the utmost extent : to the highest degree, state, or condition ⟨the sun was ~ on the suburb —Herbert Gold⟩ **3 a** *of a position* : EXACTLY ⟨~ in the center of the sacred wood —Joseph Addison⟩ **b** *of a direction* : STRAIGHT, SQUARELY ⟨the blow hit him ~ in the face⟩ ⟨he turned and looked ~ at me —Nigel Balchin⟩

³full \"\ *n* -s [ME *fulle,* fr. OE *fulla,* fr. *full,* adj.] **1 a** : the utmost extent ⟨enjoy a book to the ~⟩ **b** : the highest or fullest state, condition, or degree ⟨the ~ of the moon⟩ ⟨the ~ of the tide⟩ ⟨when the moon is at ~⟩ **2** : a satiating or glutting share or portion — often used with the possessive adjective ⟨had his ~ of that job⟩ **3** : the requisite or complete amount — often used with *in* ⟨paid in ~⟩ **4** *Brit* : BEACH RIDGE **5** : FULL HOUSE

⁴full \"\ *vb* -ED/-ING/-S [ME *fullen* to become full, fill, fr. *ful, full,* adj. — more at ¹FULL] *vi, of the moon* : to become full ~ *vt* **1** : to make full in sewing esp. by gathering or pleating **2** : to distribute (fullness) by fitting a longer edge to a shorter edge smoothly in sewing — often used with *on*

⁵full \"\ *vt* -ED/-ING/-S [ME *fullen,* fr. MF *fouler,* fr. (assumed) VL *fullare,* fr. L *fullo* fuller; perh. akin to Skt *bhāla* luster — more at BALD] : to shrink and thicken (woolen cloth) by fulling

-full — see -FUL

full age *n* [ME *ful age, full age*] : mature age or legal majority; *specif* : the time of life at which one attains full personal rights and capacities, which under common law is attained upon the last day of completing 21 years or specif. on the first instant of the day preceding the 21st birthday and under civil law is attained upon completing 25 years, and which in some states is attained by women upon completing 18 years

fullam *var of* FULHAM

full and by *also* **full and bye** *adj* [ME *full and by*] : sailing with all sails full and lying as near the wind as possible : CLOSE-HAULED

full and down *adj, of a ship* : having all cargo space filled and being so weighted as to have the hull down exactly to the Plimsoll mark

full anthem *n* : an anthem entirely of chorus parts — compare VERSE ANTHEM

full automatic *adj* : AUTOMATIC 5

fullback \'=,=\ *n* [¹*full* + *back,* n.] **1** : a football back who is used primarily for line plunges and blocking on offense and who usu. backs up the line on defense **2** : a primarily defensive member of a team usu. stationed near the defended goal (as in soccer, speedball, field hockey, rugby)

full binding *n* : a book binding wholly of leather — called also *whole binding;* compare HALF BINDING, QUARTER BINDING, THREE-QUARTER BINDING

full blast *adv* : at full capacity : with great intensity

full blood *n* **1** : descent from parents both of one pure breed — called also *whole blood;* compare BLOOD 2g, PUREBRED **2 a** : person or animal of full blood

full-blooded \'=¦==\ *adj* **1** : of unmixed ancestry : PUREBRED ⟨*full-blooded* Indians⟩ **2** : FLORID, RUDDY ⟨a *full-blooded* face⟩ **3 a** : SANGUINE, ARDENT ⟨a *full-blooded* personality⟩ ⟨*full-blooded* generosity⟩ **b** : IMPELLING, FORCEFUL ⟨a *full-blooded* argument⟩ ⟨a *full-blooded* prose style⟩ **4 a** : lacking no particulars : GENUINE ⟨a *full-blooded* war⟩ ⟨a *full-blooded* socialist⟩ **b** : extremely thorough or complete ⟨a *full-blooded* analysis⟩ **c** : containing fullness of substance : RICH ⟨a *full-blooded* narrative⟩ — **full-blood·ed·ness** *n* -ES

full-blown \'=¦=\ *adj* **1 a** : being at the height of bloom ⟨a *full-blown* rose⟩ **b** : fully ripe, mature, or mellow : LUSH ⟨a woman of *full-blown* charms⟩ **2** : possessing all the usual or necessary features, attributes, or qualities ⟨a *full-blown* scandal⟩ ⟨a *full-blown* atomic power plant⟩ ⟨ideas that did not emerge *full-blown* but took years to develop⟩

full-bod·ied \'=¦bädēd, -did\ *adj* **1** : having a large body : STOUT, CORPULENT ⟨his mother, *full-bodied,* with a mop of thick dark hair —Crichton Porteous⟩ ⟨dangerously *full-bodied*⟩ **2 a** : marked by richness and fullness of flavor ⟨a *full-bodied* red wine⟩ **b** : marked by fullness of body ⟨*full-bodied* ink⟩ ⟨*full-bodied* varnish⟩ **3** : marked by breadth of scope, excellence of texture, or richness of tone : SUBSTANTIAL ⟨this *full-bodied* novel, fresh, dramatic, violent —R.L.Blakesley⟩ ⟨the brilliant *full-bodied* numbers that our modern composers turn out —Deems Taylor⟩ **4** : having importance, significance, or meaningfulness ⟨the U.S. played a *full-bodied* role in the world and did not attempt to secede from it —Roscoe Drummond⟩

full-bodied money *n* : money which has a face value not in excess of its intrinsic value as a commodity

full-boled \'=¦=\ *adj, of a tree trunk or log* : having the same or nearly the same diameter from one end to the other

full bond *n* : a bond in masonry where all bricks are laid as headers

full-bosomed \'=¦==\ *adj* : having an amply developed bosom ⟨a pretty, *full-bosomed,* physically and emotionally precocious schoolgirl —S.H.Adams⟩

full bottom *n* : a full-bottomed wig worn esp. by some barristers

full-bot·tomed \'=¦bädəmd, -ätə-\ *adj* [¹*full* + *bottom,* n. + *-ed*] **1** *of a wig* : large and having curled sections falling below the shoulders **2** : of great capacity below the waterline (as a ship having a small rise of floor)

full-bound \'=¦=\ *adj* **1** *of a book* : having full binding **2** *carpentry* : having an equal amount of wood in all rails — used of sashes

full cadence *n* : PERFECT CADENCE

full capping *n* [*capping* fr. gerund of ²*cap*] : the application of camelback to the entire area of a worn tire tread including the shoulders — compare TOP CAPPING

full-cell process *or* **full-cell treatment** *n* : a method of treating wood so that a preservative chemical partially or completely fills the cells in the treated portion (as in the Bethell process) — compare EMPTY-CELL PROCESS

full cock *n* : the position of the hammer of a firearm when fully retracted and ready to be released by the sear — compare HALF COCK

full-court press *n* : a press employed in basketball on both halves of the court — called also *all-court press*

full cousin *n* : COUSIN 1b

full coverage *n* : insurance that provides payment for all losses up to the limit of the policy without any deductions

full-cream cheese *n* : cheese made from unskimmed milk

full-crew law *n* : a law establishing standards about the number of employees to be used on trains

full-crown fender *n* : an automobile fender arched across its entire width

full cry *n* : eager chase — used of hounds that have caught the scent and give tongue together

full dress *n* : the style of dress prescribed by fashion or governmental regulation for ceremonial or formal social occasions — compare EVENING DRESS, FULL-DRESS UNIFORM

full-dress \'=¦=\ *adj* [*full dress*] **1** : complete down to the last formal detail ⟨a *full-dress* welcome⟩ ⟨a *full-dress* biography⟩ **2** : carried out by all possible means or from all possible approaches ⟨a *full-dress* investigation⟩

full-dressed \'=¦=\ *adj* **1** *of poultry* : dressed completely with feathers, viscera, and usu. head and feet removed — compare NEW YORK DRESSED **2** *of a ship* : dressed with ensigns and a line of pennants — compare *dress ship* 1 at ¹DRESS

full dress ship *n* : a ship dressed with ensigns and a line of pennants — compare *dress ship* 1 at ¹DRESS

full-dress uniform *n* : the military or naval uniform established by regulations for wear on a ceremonial occasion — compare DRESS UNIFORM

fulled *past of* FULL

¹full·er \'fu̇lə(r)\ *n* -s [ME *fullere,* fr. OE, fr. L *fullo* fuller + OE *-ere* -er — more at ⁵FULL] **1** : one that fulls cloth **2** : WEIGHTER

²ful·ler \"\ *vt* -ED/-ING/-S [prob. fr. the name *Fuller*] : to form a groove or channel in ⟨~ a bayonet⟩

³ful·ler \"\ *n* -s **1** : a blacksmithing set hammer with a longitudinally half-round peen or a form of bottom tool with a similar working end sometimes used in conjunction with the first for grooving and spreading iron; *also* : a groove made by such a tool or any groove or fluting **2** : the portion of a forging die that reduces the cross-sectional area between the ends of the stock and permits the metal to move outward during preliminary forging

fuller 1

ful·ler·board \'==,=\ *n* [prob. fr. the name *Fuller*] : a paperboard which may be pressed into various forms and used as an electrical insulator in low-voltage work — called also *pressboard*

fuller faucet *also* **fuller bibcock** *or* **fuller cock** *n* [fr. *Fuller,* a trademark] : a faucet opened and closed by means of a lever and eccentric

ful·ler·ing tool *n* [*fullering* fr. gerund of ²*fuller*] : a blacksmith's fuller; *also* : a tool for caulking metal plates

ful·ler rose beetle *or* **fuller's rose weevil** *n, usu cap F* [perh. after Andrew S. *Fuller* †1896 Am. horticulturist] : a small broad-snouted grayish weevil (*Pantomorus godmani*) feeding on the leaves of numerous cultivated plants and being esp. destructive to citrus and certain ornamentals

full·er's card *n* [*fuller's* (poss. of ¹*fuller*) + *card*] : WILD TEASEL

full·er's earth *n* [ME *fulleres erthe*] : a white to brown naturally occurring earthy substance resembling potter's clay but lacking in plasticity, consisting chiefly of the clay minerals montmorillonite and attapulgite, and used in fulling cloth and now esp. as an adsorbent (as in refining and decolorizing oils and fats) and as a catalyst

full·er's herb *n* [so called fr. its former use in removing stains from cloth] : SOAPWORT

full·er's teasel *n* [ME *fulleres tesel*] : a teasel (*Dipsacus fullonum*) having heads with curved barbed bracts that are used in the woolen industry for gigging and napping

full·er's thistle *n* : TEASEL 1

fullface \'=,=\ *n* : BOLDFACE 2

full faith and credit *n* : an obligation under the U.S. Constitution of one state to recognize and give effect to the public acts, records, and judicial proceedings of her sister states

full-fashioned \'=¦==\ *also* **fully fashioned** *adj* : employing or produced by a flat-knit process for shaping to conform to body lines ⟨*full-fashioned* knitting⟩ ⟨*full-fashioned* hosiery⟩

full-feathering \'=¦=(=)=\ *adj, of an airplane propeller* : capable of being feathered in flight to a pitch angle of approximately 90 degrees so that the drag is a minimum and there is no tendency to rotate

full-feed \'=¦=\ *vt* : to feed (an animal) to the full extent of its needs

full-fledged \'=¦=\ *adj* **1** : fully developed : MATURE **2** *of a bird* : fully fledged **3** : having attained complete status : GENUINE ⟨a *full-fledged* lawyer⟩

full force and effect *n* : FORCE AND EFFECT

full-form insurance *n* : marine insurance covering partial as well as total loss

full frame *n* : BRACED FRAME

full framing *n* : BRACED FRAMING

full gainer *n* : GAINER

full gate *n* : the adjustment of a water turbine to utilize its full capacity ⟨working at *full gate*⟩

full gear *n* : the condition of a steam engine with valves worked by a link motion where the link motion operates the valve to the fullest extent

full gilt *n* : a book having gilt on all three edges

full gospel *n, usu cap F&G* : an American fundamentalistic sect originating in the South about 1935

full grain *or* **full grain leather** *n* : leather retaining original grain surface with only hair and associated epidermis removed

full-grooved ax \'=¦=-\ *n* : a prehistoric grooved ax having the groove completely encircling the area where the ax handle was attached

full-grown \'=¦=\ *adj* : having reached full growth or development : MATURE

full gum *n* : ORIGINAL GUM

full habit *n* : a condition of the body characterized by congestion of the visible blood vessels and tendency to stoutness — compare ENDOMORPHIC, HABIT

fullhearted \'=¦==\ *adj* : having a heart full of courage or confidence or understanding ⟨~ support⟩ ⟨~ recognition of the 19th century and its greatness —*Times Lit. Supp.*⟩ — **full·heart·ed·ly** *adv* — **full·heart·ed·ness** *n* -ES

full house *or* **full hand** *n* : a poker hand containing three of a kind and a pair (as three aces and two tens) and ranking above a flush and below four of a kind — see POKER illustration

full·ing \'fu̇liŋ, -lēŋ\ *n* -s [ME *fullinge,* fr. *fullen* to full + *-inge* -ing — more at ⁵FULL] : the process of shrinking and thickening woolen fabric by application of moisture, heat, friction, and pressure that causes the fibers to felt

fulling mill *n* [ME *fullinge mille*] **1** : a machine for fulling cloth **2** : a factory where cloth is fulled

fulling stock *n* **1** : a wooden beater for fulling cloth **2 a** : a mallet for beating oil into hides **b** : a machine in which such mallets form the essential feature — usu. used in pl.

full-jacket \'=¦==\ *or* **full-jacketed** \'=¦===\ *adj, of a bullet* : having the core covered with a jacket

full-length \'=¦=\ *adj* **1** : having the full or usual length of its kind : not curtailed or skimpy ⟨a *full-length* play⟩ ⟨a *full-length* book⟩ **2** : having, accommodating, or representing the full height of the human figure ⟨a *full-length* mirror⟩

full lot *n* : BOARD LOT

full marks *n pl* : complete credit : due commendation ⟨*full marks* must be given the victor⟩

full moon *n* [ME *ful mone, ful moone,* fr. OE *full mōna*] **1 a** : the moon with its whole apparent disk illuminated appearing when the moon is in opposition to the sun — see MOON illustration **b** : the time when the moon is full **2** : the 14th day of the moon occurring regularly according to a set of calendar rules without regard to the real moon of the sky

full-moon maple *n* : JAPANESE MAPLE

fullmouth \'=,=\ *n* : a fullmouthed animal (as a sheep or cow); *also* : the mouth of such an animal

fullmouthed \'=¦=\ *adj* **1** : having a full mouth; *esp* : having a full complement of teeth — used esp. of sheep and cattle **2** : uttered as with full power or sound : LOUD, NOISY ⟨a ~ welcome⟩

full nelson *n* : a hold gained by a wrestler who from a position behind his opponent places both arms under his opponent's arms and clasps his hands or wrists behind the opponent's neck — compare HALF NELSON, QUARTER NELSON, THREE-QUARTER NELSON

full·ness *also* **ful·ness** \'fu̇lnəs\ *n* -ES [ME *fulnesse,* fr. *ful, full* full + *-nesse* -ness] : the quality or state of being full

full of the moon [ME *fulle of the mone*] : the time or condition of complete illumination of the lunar disk

full-orbed \'=¦ȯ(ə)rbd\ *adj* : having or forming a full orb ⟨the *full-orbed* moon⟩ ⟨the *full-orbed* pumpkins —Van Wyck Brooks⟩

full organ *adv (or adj)* : with all or most of the stops drawn so that the full power of the instrument is heard — often used as a direction in music

full-out \'=¦=\ *adj* **1** : flush left — used of a typeset or typewritten line **2** : COMPLETE, TOTAL ⟨a *full-out* war effort⟩

full-paid \'=¦=\ *adj* : FULLY PAID

full-patch \'=¦=\ *adj* : FULL-JACKET

full-pitch winding *n* : the winding of an armature in which the two sides of the armature coil span a distance equal to the pole pitch

full plate *n* : a watch having all its train wheels and escapement under one plate with only the balance exposed

full position *n* : the position of an advertisement that has reading matter on two sides or that is at the top of a column and has reading matter on at least one side

full reporting clause *n* : a clause in an insurance policy that provides that the indemnity will not exceed that proportion of loss which the last reported value of the property bears to the actual value

full-rigged \'=¦=\ *adj* **1** : having all the sails and rigging necessary; *esp* : having three or more masts each with its full complement of square sails ⟨a *full-rigged* ship⟩ — see SAIL illustration **2** : completely equipped

full-rig·ger \'=¦rigə(r)\ *n* [*full rig* (noun phrase) + *-er*] : a ship having a full rig

full rudder *n* : the maximum angle with the keel to which the rudder of a boat may be moved

full run *n* : a contract purchased from an advertising agency whereby a card of a type suitable for bus, subway, or train advertising is required to be placed in every car in a specified district

fulls *pl of* FULL, *pres 3d sing of* FULL

-fulls *pl of* -FULL

full-scale \'=¦=\ *adj* **1** : identical to an original in proportion and size ⟨a *full-scale* drawing⟩ **2 a** : ABSOLUTE, COMPLETE ⟨help them . . . towards *full-scale* success in the larger theatre —Leslie Rees⟩ **b** : involving full use of available resources ⟨a *full-scale* civil war⟩ ⟨started *full-scale* production⟩

full score *n* : a musical score in which all the parts of a composition are given; *esp* : one in which each vocal or instrumental part is on a separate staff

full sea *n, archaic* : FLOOD TIDE

full seamark *n* : the limit of flood tide

full service *n* : a musical setting of all the canticles used in the liturgy of the Anglican church esp. for chorus only with no solo parts — compare FULL ANTHEM

full-shroud \'=¦=\ *vt* : to provide (a gear wheel) with shrouds extending to the tops of the teeth

full sight *n* : a sight or aim in which all the front sight of a gun is seen in the notch of the rear sight

full snipe *n* : a common European snipe (*Capella gallinago*)

full speed *n* : top or utmost speed; *specif* : a speed one eighth more than standard speed

full stop *or* **full point** *n* : PERIOD 5a

full-summed \'=¦=\ *adj* : FULL-FLEDGED 2

full swell *adv (or adj)* : with all stops on the swell manual drawn — often used as a direction in music

full-term \'=¦=\ *adj, of an infant* : retained in the uterus for the entire normal gestation period

full tilt *adv* [¹*full* + *tilt* (single combat between mounted men)] : at high speed : with a rush

full time *n* : the amount of time considered the normal or standard amount for working during a given period (as a day, week, or month)

full-time \'=¦=\ *adj* [*full time*] **1** : employed for or working the amount of time considered customary or standard ⟨*full-time* clerks⟩ **2** : involving or operating the amount of time considered customary or standard ⟨*full-time* teaching⟩

full to fifteenth : full organ excepting reeds and mixtures — used as a direction in organ music

full toss *or* **full pitch** *or* **full volley** *n* : a bowled ball in cricket so pitched that it will if left alone hit or land close to the stumps before touching the ground

full-track vehicle *n* : a vehicle (as a tank) that is entirely supported, driven, and steered by a caterpillar tread

full trailer *n* : a trailer whose weight is carried entirely on its own wheels — compare SEMITRAILER

full twist *n* : a front or back dive in which the diver executes a complete turn of the body on a vertical axis without bending the body — compare HALF TWIST

full vamp *n* : a one-piece upper seamed at the center of the heel

full verb *n* : a verb with full meaning — compare LINK VERB

full-wave rectifier *n* : a rectifier that converts alternating current into continuous current and that utilizes both halves of each cycle of the alternating current

full word *n* : a word conveying an idea or image : SEMANTEME — compare FUNCTION WORD

ful·ly \'fu̇l(l)ē, |i, *when emphatic also* 'fu̇l|l\ *adv* [ME, fr. OE *fullīce,* fr. OE *full* + *-līce* -ly — more at FULL] **1** : in a full manner : to a full degree : COMPLETELY, ENTIRELY, THOROUGHLY **2** : at least ⟨~ half the class⟩

fully fashioned *var of* FULL-FASHIONED

fully fledged *adj, chiefly Brit* : FULL-FLEDGED

fully found *adj, of a boat* : completely equipped for service

fully insured *adj, under old age and survivors insurance* : having at age 65 or at death at least one quarter of coverage for each two calendar quarters since December 31, 1950, or since reaching age 21, whichever is later, at least six quarters of coverage being required

fully insured for life *under old age and survivors insurance* : having 40 quarters of coverage

fully paid *adj, of corporate shares* : paid for at full face value with no further money due from the stockholder

ful·mar \'fu̇lmər, -,mär\ *also* **fulmar petrel** *n* -s [of Scand origin; akin to ON *fūlmār,* fr. *fūll* foul + *mār* gull — more at FOUL, MEW] **1** : an Arctic sea bird (*Fulmarus glacialis*) that is closely related to the petrels, resembles the herring gull in size and color, is very abundant on the northern No. Atlantic, breeds on cliffs, feeds chiefly on fish and floating offal and is esp. fond of whale blubber, and is valued for its eggs, oil, and feathers and for the strong-scented flesh of young birds which is sometimes used as food **2 :** any of several birds of southern seas that are related to the fulmar

ful·mi·nant \'fəlmənənt *also* 'fəl-\ *adj* [L *fulminant-, fulminans,* pres. part. of *fulminare* to lightning] **:** FULMINATING 3

¹ful·mi·nate \-,nāt, *usu* -ād.+V\ *vb* -ED/-ING/-S [ME *fulminaten,* fr. ML *fulminatus,* past part. of *fulminare,* fr. L, to lightning, strike with lightning, fr. *fulmin-, fulmen* lightning, stroke of lightning; akin to L *fulgēre* to shine, flash, *flagrare* to burn — more at BLACK] *vt* **1 :** to utter or send out with denunciation or censures ⟨~ a decree⟩ **2 :** to cause to explode ~ *vi* **1 :** to issue or send forth censures or invectives menacingly or authoritatively **2 :** to make a sudden loud noise **:** DETONATE, EXPLODE **3** *of a disease* **:** to come on suddenly and intensely

²fulminate \"\ *n* -S [ISV *fulmin-* (fr. L *fulmin-, fulmen* lightning) + *-ate*] **:** a salt of fulminic acid; *esp* **:** MERCURY FULMINATE

fulminate of mercury : MERCURY FULMINATE

fulminating *adj* [fr. pres. part. of ¹*fulminate*] **1 :** exploding with a vivid flash **:** THUNDERING **2 :** hurling denunciations, menaces, or censures ⟨a ~ bishop⟩ **3 :** coming on suddenly with great severity **:** characterized by a rapid and severe course ⟨a ~ disease⟩

fulminating gold *n* **:** any of several explosive substances containing gold and nitrogen (as a powder obtained by the action of ammonia on gold oxide)

fulminating material *n* **:** a detonating substance that appears during thunderstorms as luminous balls

fulminating mercury *n* **:** MERCURY FULMINATE

fulminating silver *n* **1 :** a black crystalline explosive substance obtained by the action of ammonia on silver oxide **2 :** SILVER FULMINATE

ful·mi·na·tion \,fu̇lmə'nāshən *also* ,fəl-\ *n* -S [MF, pronouncement of an ecclesiastical sentence or censure, fr. L *fulmination-, fulminatio* lightning, fr. *fulminatus* (past part. of *fulminare* to lightning) + *-ion-, -io* -ion] **1 :** vehement menace or censure ⟨uncowed by police ~⟩ **2 :** something that is thundered forth ⟨ecclesiastical ~s⟩ **3 :** the act or action of exploding

ful·mi·na·tor \'==,nād·ə(r), -ātə-\ *n* -S [L, hurler of lightning, fr. *fulminatus* (past part. of *fulminare* to lightning, strike with lightning) + *-or*] **:** one that fulminates

ful·mine \'fu̇lmən, 'fəl-\ *vb* -ED/-ING/-S [MF *fulminer,* fr. L *fulminare*] *archaic* **:** FULMINATE

ful·min·e·ous \(')fu̇l¦minēəs, ¦fəl¦-\ *adj* [L *fulmineus,* fr. *fulmin-, fulmen* lightning + *-eus* -eous] **:** FULMINIC

ful·min·ic acid \(')fu̇l¦minik-, ¦fəl¦-\ *n* [*fulminic* ISV *fulmin-* (fr. L *fulmin-, fulmen* lightning) + *-ic*] **:** an unstable acid CNOH isomeric with cyanic acid and known only in solution (as ether, in which it polymerizes rapidly) and in the form of highly explosive salts

ful·mi·nous \'fu̇lmənəs, 'fəl-\ *adj* [L *fulmin-, fulmen* + E *-ous*] **:** of, relating to, or resembling thunder and lightning

ful·min·uric acid \,fu̇l¦mə¦n(y)u̇rik-, ¦fəl¦-\ *n* [*fulminuric* ISV *fulmin-* (as in *fulminic*) + *uric*] **:** a white crystalline explosive acid $NCCH(NO_2)CONH_2$ structurally related to nitromethane and obtainable in the form of salts by boiling mercury fulminate with potassium chloride solution

fulness *var of* FULLNESS

ful·nio \'fu̇lnē,ō\ *n, pl* **fulnio** *or* **fulnios** *usu cap* **1 a :** a people of the state of Pernambuco, Brazil **b :** a member of such people **2 :** the language of the Fulnio people

fü·löpp·ite *also* **ful·lopp·ite** *or* **ful·opp·ite** \'fu̇lə,pīt, 'fil-\ *n* -S [Bela *Fülöpp,* 20th cent. Hung. mineral collector + E *-ite*] **:** a lead-gray mineral $Pb_3Sb_8S_{15}$ consisting of lead, antimony, and sulfur

fuls *pl of* FUL

-fuls *pl of* -FUL

ful·some \'fu̇lsəm *also* -lts-\ *adj* [ME *fulsom,* fr. *ful, full* full + *-som* -some — more at FULL (adj.)] **1 a :** COPIOUS, ABUNDANT **b** *obs* **:** PLUMP, FAT **2** *obs* **:** LUSTFUL, WANTON **3 a :** offensive to sense or appetite **:** NAUSEATING, SICKENING ⟨~ richness of the food⟩ **b :** offensive to moral or aesthetic sensibility **:** REPULSIVE, DISGUSTING ⟨~ prejudices⟩ ⟨~ language⟩ **c :** offensive from insincerity or baseness of motive ⟨~ politeness⟩ ⟨~ praise⟩ ⟨~ compliments⟩ ⟨trying not to be ~ to make up for his coldness at the governor's party —C.S.Forester⟩ **4 :** counter to the norms of propriety or social usage **:** displaying bad taste ⟨the ~ chromium glitter of the escalators —Lewis Mumford⟩ ⟨a ~ prose style⟩ — **ful·some·ly** *adv* — **ful·some·ness** *n* -ES

fulth \'fu̇l(t)th\ *n* -S [ME *fulthe, fulth,* fr. *ful, full* full + *-the, -th* -th] *now dial Eng* **:** FULLNESS, REPLETION

ful·ton cat \'fu̇ltᵊn-\ *n, usu cap F* [prob. fr. the name *Fulton*] **:** WILLOW CAT

fulup *usu cap, var of* FELUP

ful·vene \'fu̇l,vēn, 'fəl-\ *n* -S [G *fulven,* fr. L *fulvus* tawny + G *-en* -ene] **:** an unstable yellow hydrocarbon C_6H_6 that is a methylene derivative of cyclopentadiene; *also* **:** any of a series of its derivatives

ful·ves·cent \(')fu̇l'vesᵊnt, ¦fəl¦-\ *adj* [L *fulvus* + E *-escent*] **:** somewhat fulvous

ful·vid \'fu̇lvəd, 'fəl-\ *adj* [LL *fulvidus,* fr. L *fulvus*] **:** FULVOUS

ful·vous \-vəs\ *adj* [L *fulvus;* perh. akin to L *flavus* yellow — more at BLUE] **:** dull brownish yellow **:** TAWNY ⟨my neighbor's field turned to a stretch of ~ stubble —Lori Petri⟩ ⟨staining the clearness with its ~ storm water —Victor Canning⟩

fulvous tree duck *n* **:** a long-legged long-necked brownish duck (*Dendrocygna bicolor*) known from several widely separated populations in the Americas, India, and eastern Africa

ful·yie *or* **ful·zie** \'fül(y)ē\ *n* -S [ME (Sc) *fulȝe* dung] *Scot* **:** DIRT, FILTH; *specif* **:** street sweepings

fum \'fəm\ *n* -S **:** FÊNG HUANG

fumadiddle *var of* FLUMMADIDDLE

fu·ma·gil·lin \,fyümə'jilən\ *n* -S [*fumagill-* (rearrangement of some of the letters of the species name NL *Aspergillus fumigatus,* fr. *Aspergillus,* genus name + *fumigatus,* specific epithet, fr. L, past part. of *fumigare* to fumigate) + *-in* — more at ASPERGILLUS, FUMIGATE] **:** a crystalline orally effective antibiotic ester of an unsaturated acid produced by a soil fungus (*Aspergillus fumigatus*) and used in the treatment of amebiasis

fu·ma·gine \'fyümə,jēn\ *n* -S [F, fr. NL *Fumagin-, Fumago,* former genus name, fr. L *fumus* smoke] **:** a dark-colored sooty mold found chiefly on greenhouse plants or in southern latitudes and caused by various fungi of the order Erysiphales

fumar- *or* **fumaro-** *comb form* [ISV, fr. NL *Fumaria*] **:** fumaric acid ⟨*fumaramide*⟩ ⟨*fumaronitrile*⟩

fu·ma·rase \'fyümə,rās, -āz\ *n* -S [ISV *fumar-* + *-ase*] **:** a crystalline enzyme occurring in many animal and plant tissues that accelerates the interconversion of fumaric acid and L-malic acid by hydration and dehydration (as in the Krebs cycle)

fu·ma·rate \-,rāt, -rət\ *n* -S [ISV *fumar-* + *-ate*] **:** a salt or ester of fumaric acid

fu·mar·ia \fyü'ma(a)rēə\ *n* [NL, fr. LL, fumitory, fr. L *fumus* smoke + *-aria*] **1** *cap* **:** a genus of annual herbs (family Fumariaceae) with only one petal spurred at the base and a one-seeded globose capsule **2** *pl* **fumari·ae** \-ē,ē\ **:** an extract or dried leaves of the common fumitory formerly used as a tonic and alterative

fu·mar·i·a·ce·ae \fyü,ma(a)rē'āsē,ē\ *n pl, cap* [NL, fr. *Fumaria,* type genus + *-aceae*] **:** a family of erect or climbing herbs (order Papaverales) of the northern hemisphere and southern Africa with basal or alternate dissected leaves, irregular spurred flowers, and capsular fruit — **fu·mar·i·a·ceous** \=¦==¦āshəs\ *adj*

fu·mar·ic acid \(')fyü¦marik-\ *n* [*fumaric* ISV *fumar-* + *-ic*] **:** a crystalline unsaturated dicarboxylic acid HOOCCH= CHCOOH that is found in fumitory and many other plants and is formed from succinic acid as an intermediate in the Krebs cycle, that is made synthetically (as by heating maleic acid), and that is used chiefly in making polyester resins; *trans-*butene-dioic acid — see CIS-TRANS ISOMERISM a

fu·ma·rine \'fyümə,rēn, -,rən\ *n* -S [prob. fr. F, fr. NL *Fumaria* + F *-ine*] **:** PROTOPINE

fu·ma·role *also* **fu·me·role** \'fyümə,rōl\ *n* -S [It *fumarola,* modif. of LL *fumariolum* vent, smoke hole, dim. of *fumarium* vent, smoke hole, fr. L, smoke chamber for aging wine, fr. *fumus* smoke + *-arium* -ary] **:** a hole in a volcanic region and usu. in lava from which issue gases and vapors at high temperature — **fu·ma·rol·ic** \¦==¦rōlik, -¦räl-\ *adj*

fu·mar·o·yl \fyü'marə,wil\ *or* **fu·ma·ryl** \'fyümə,ril\ *n* -S [ISV *fumar-* + *-oyl* or *-yl*] **:** the radical —COCH=CHCO— of fumaric acid

fu·ma·to·ri·um \,fyümə'tōrēəm\ *n* -S [NL, fr. L *fumatus* (past part. of *fumare* to smoke, fr. *fumus* smoke) + *-orium* -ory] **:** an airtight compartment in which vapor may be generated to destroy fungous or insect pests (as on growing plants) **:** a fumigation chamber

¹fum·ble \'fəmbəl\ *vb* **fumbled; fumbled; fumbling** \-b(ə)liŋ\ **fumbles** [prob. of Scand origin; akin to Sw *fumla* to fumble, bungle, Norw dial. *fumla*] *vi* **1 a :** to grope for or handle something clumsily, perplexedly, or aimlessly ⟨*fumbled* nervously with her necklace before she answered⟩ **b :** make awkward attempts to do or find something ⟨his numb hands ~ with the shoestring⟩ ⟨*fumbled* in his pocket for a coin⟩ **c :** search by trial and error ⟨a generation that ~s after a fresh outlook on life⟩ **d :** BLUNDER ⟨just when the whole scheme hung in balance he *fumbled*⟩ **2** *archaic* **:** to be impotent in sexual relations **3 :** to speak gropingly or indistinctly ⟨he *fumbled* in answering and made them suspicious⟩ **:** MUMBLE ⟨shyness made his tongue ~⟩ **4 :** to feel one's way or move awkwardly ⟨they *fumbled* along the dark path⟩ ⟨*jumbled* about until the admiral indicated where he was to sit —J.A.Michener⟩ **5 a :** to drop or juggle or fail to play cleanly a ground ball — compare MUFF **b :** to lose hold of a football while handling or running with it ~ *vt* **1 :** to accomplish or bring about by clumsy or groping manipulation ⟨*fumbled* the door open⟩ **2 a :** to feel or handle gropingly or clumsily ⟨his toes *fumbling* the rough edge of a big rip in the carpet —Raymond Chandler⟩ ⟨he *fumbled* the pages looking for the place⟩ **b :** to deal with in an awkward or blundering way **:** BUNGLE ⟨where adept decisive action is needed he ~s the problem⟩ ⟨he *fumbled* a chance to take the fort by surprise⟩ **3 :** to utter in a groping, indistinct, or blundering way ⟨startled into confusion, he ~s out a few broken sentences⟩ ⟨made to feel inferior if we ~ an unusual word —G.A.Miller⟩ **4** *archaic* **:** to bundle cumbrously or confusedly ⟨send them forth so covered, veiled, and *fumbled* up —John Molle⟩ ⟨~ this, next, and last week's devotion all in a prayer —Thomas Fuller⟩ **5 :** to make (one's way) in a clumsy or groping manner ⟨the baby turtles will ~ their way down to the water's edge —Alan Moorehead⟩ ⟨watch a growing community ~ its way to maturity —T.H. White b.1915⟩ **6 a :** MISPLAY ⟨~ a ground ball⟩ **b :** to lose hold of (a football) while handling or running

²fumble \"\ *n* -S **1 :** an act or instance of fumbling ⟨a long evolution that begins with the ~s, trials and errors of practical men —Charles Frankel⟩ ⟨safe on the shortstop's ~⟩ **2 :** a fumbled ball ⟨fell on the quarterback's ~⟩

fum·bler \'fəmb(ə)lə(r)\ *n* -S **:** one that fumbles

fumbling *adj* [fr. pres. part. of *fumble*] **:** marked by groping or clumsiness ⟨a writer . . . so preoccupied with his matter as to be careless and ~ in his manner —Brand Blanshard⟩ — **fum·bling·ly** *adv*

fum·bling·ness *n* -ES **:** the quality or state of being fumbling ⟨was entirely self-taught, and his earliest paintings reveal a certain ~ —R.M.Coates⟩

¹fume \'fyüm\ *n* -S [ME, fr. MF *fum,* fr. L *fumus;* akin to OHG *toumen* to be fragrant, Gk *thymos* spirit, mind, courage, Skt *dhūma* smoke] **1 a :** a gaseous emission (as from a burning or evaporating substance) that is usu. odorous and sometimes noxious **:** SMOKE ⟨a thin ~ rising from his pipe and scenting the library⟩ **:** VAPOR ⟨the rain . . . sprang back on itself and the ground was hidden by a white ~ —Audrey Barker⟩ **:** ODOR ⟨noticed the ~s of whiskey when he talked⟩ **b :** an often noxious suspension of particles in air or gas that may be formed in various ways (as by condensation of vapors or by chemical reaction) ⟨the air pollution aspects of smoke and ~s⟩ — usu. used in pl. and sometimes only of suspensions of solid particles in distinction from *mist* **c :** solid material deposited by condensation of fumes ⟨the baghouse ~ in lead smelting⟩ **2 a :** a noxious vapor formerly supposed to rise to the brain from the stomach (as from alcoholic drinks) ⟨a day's idleness to let the ~s of rum-punch . . . get out of his head —David Garnett⟩ **b :** something (as an emotion) that impairs one's reasoning ⟨until the ~s of passion cleared away⟩ **3 :** a state of excited irritation or anger — usu. used in the phrase *in a fume* ⟨might go away in a ~ muttering —Thomas Wood †1950⟩ **4 :** something like a fume in being transient or unsubstantial and noxious or offensive ⟨the all-pervading ~s of sanctimoniousness —Max Ascoli⟩

²fume \"\ *vb* -ED/-ING/-S [ME *fumen,* fr. MF *fumer* to smoke, fr. L *fumare* to smoke, fr. *fumus*] *vt* **1 a :** to expose to fumes; *esp* **:** to treat with acid vapors to develop color ⟨~ a fabric with acid vapors⟩ **b :** to fill or permeate with fumes (as of incense) ⟨sheets *fumed* with violets —John Marston⟩ **c** *obs* **:** PERFUME **2 :** to give off in or as if in fumes ⟨the freighter was *fuming* thick black smoke⟩ ⟨an itinerant agitator who *fumed* race hatred⟩ **3 a :** to cause (a substance) to emit fumes (as by heating) ⟨~ the slag in a furnace to recover the lead contained⟩ **b :** to produce by fuming; *esp* **:** SUBLIME 1a — usu. used as a past participle ⟨*fumed* litharge⟩ ~ *vi* **1 a :** to emit fumes (as in combustion or chemical action) ⟨hydrogen chloride ~s in moist air⟩ **:** SMOKE, REEK ⟨a cigarette ~s forgotten in the ash tray⟩ ⟨the refinery area ~s with oil⟩ **b :** to act as if generating fumes: as (1) **:** to be in a state of excited irritation or anger ⟨he fretted and *fumed* over the delay⟩ (2) **:** to speak in a fuming manner ⟨he *fumed* at his opponent in an arm-waving, name-calling harangue⟩ **2 :** to rise and pass away in or as if in fumes ⟨a cloud of incense ~s from the censer⟩ ⟨their happiness had suddenly *fumed* away⟩ — **fum·er** \-mə(r)\ *n* -S

fume chamber *or* **fume cupboard** *n, chiefly Brit* **:** a chamber with forced draft used for eliminating undesirable fumes — compare HOOD 3d (2)

fumed oak *n* [*fumed* fr. past part. of ²*fume*] **:** oak given a weathered appearance by exposure to fumes of ammonia

fume·less \'fyümləs\ *adj* **:** free from fumes

fumerole *var of* FUMAROLE

¹fu·met \'fyümət\ *n* -S [prob. alter. of ME *fume,* fr. MF *fumee,* fr. OF, excrement, fr. fem. of *fumé, femé,* past part. of *fumer, femer* to fertilize with dung, discharge excrement, fr. ML *fimare* to fertilize with dung, fr. L *fimus* dung; prob. akin to L *fumus* smoke] *archaic* **:** the dung of deer

²fumet \"\ *also* **fu·mette** \(')fyü¦met\ *n* -S [F *fumet* odor, fume of wine or meat, fr. MF, fr. *fumer* to smoke, expose to fumes] **:** a concentrated essence of game or fish, herbs, and spices used in flavoring a sauce

fumewort *or* **fumeroot** \'=,=\ *n* **:** FUMITORY; *broadly* **:** any of several plants closely related to the fumitories (as some members of the genus *Corydalis*) — often used in combination ⟨the yellow and slender ~s⟩

fumid *adj* [L *fumidus* smoky, fr. *fumus* smoke] *obs* **:** SMOKY, VAPOROUS

fu·mig·a·cin \fyü'migəsən\ *n* -S [*fumiga-* (fr. NL *fumigatus,* specific epithet of *Aspergillus fumigatus*) + *-cin* (as in *actinomycin, streptothricin*) — more at FUMAGILLIN] **:** a crystalline antibiotic acid $C_{32}H_{44}O_8$ obtained from a soil fungus (*Aspergillus fumigatus*) — called also *helvolic acid*

fu·mi·gant \'fyüməgənt, -mēg-\ *n* -S [*fumigate* + *-ant*] **:** a gaseous or readily volatilizable chemical (as hydrogen cyanide or paradichlorobenzene) used as a disinfectant or pesticide — compare AEROSOL 2

fu·mi·gate \'fyümə,gāt, *usu* -ād.+V\ *vt* -ED/-ING/-S [L *fumigatus,* past part. of *fumigare,* fr. *fumus* smoke + *-igare* (akin to L *agere* to drive) — more at AGENT] **1 :** to apply smoke, vapor, or gas to ⟨tribes that ~ bodies to dry and preserve them⟩: as **a** *archaic* **:** to scent with incense or perfume ⟨with fragrant thyme the city ~ —John Dryden⟩ **b :** to treat (as a house or room) with a gas for the purpose of disinfecting or of destroying pests **c :** to make an odor imperceptible in (as a room) esp. by permeation with aromatic fumes **2 :** to remove or conceal what is offensive in ⟨the descriptions of . . . illnesses might very well have been *fumigated* —Clifton Fadiman⟩

fu·mi·ga·tion \,fyümə'gāshən\ *n* -S [ME *fumigacioun,* fr. MF *fumigation,* fr. LL *fumigation-, fumigatio,* fr. L *fumigatus* + *-ion-, -io* -ion] **:** the act or process of fumigating ⟨~ of infested but irreplaceable trees⟩ ⟨jeered at the preliminary charity bout as crass ~⟩

fu·mi·ga·tor \'fyümə,gād·ə(r), -ātə-\ *n* -S [ISV *fumigate* + *-or*] **:** one that fumigates: as **a :** a device or apparatus that generates a gas or vapor for use as a fumigant **b :** FUMIGANT **c** (1) **:** EXTERMINATOR a (2) **:** one who kills insect pests on trees or shrubs by treatment with poisonous gas (3) **:** one who cleans and moth-proofs rugs and upholstered furniture and fumigates them by placing them in an airtight chamber with disks impregnated with hydrocyanic acid

fu·mi·ga·to·ri·um \,fyüməgə'tōrēəm\ *n* -S [NL, fr. L *fumigatus* + *-orium* -ory] **:** FUMATORIUM

fu·mi·ga·to·ry \'fyüməgə,tōrē, -mēg-, -tōr-, -ri\ *adj* [*fumigate* + *-ory*] **:** having the quality of fumigating

fum·i·ly \'fyüməlē\ *adv* **:** in a fumy manner

fum·ing·ly *adv* [*fuming* (pres. part. of ²*fume*) + *-ly*] **:** in a fuming manner **:** ANGRILY ⟨exclaimed ~ that he was not accustomed to such treatment⟩

fuming nitric acid *n* **:** concentrated nitric acid containing dissolved nitrogen oxides prepared as either a colorless to pale yellow or a red to brown corrosive poisonous liquid and used esp. as a nitrating agent and as a powerful oxidizing agent (as in rocket propellants)

fuming sulfuric acid *n* **:** OLEUM 2

fum·ish \'fyümish\ *adj, obs* **1 :** emitting or having the character of fumes **:** SMOKY **2 :** tending to fume **:** CHOLERIC

fu·mi·to·ry \'fyümə,tōrē\ *n* -ES [alter. (influenced by E *-ory*) of earlier *fumeterre,* fr. ME *fumetere,* fr. MF, fr. ML *fumus terrae,* fr. L *fumus* smoke + *terrae,* gen. of *terra* earth — more at TERRACE] **:** a plant of the genus *Fumaria; esp* **:** a common European herb (*F. officinalis*)

fumitory family *n* **:** FUMARIACEAE

fumosity *n* -ES [ME *fumosite,* fr. MF & ML; MF *fumosité,* fr. ML *fumositat-, fumositas,* fr. L *fumosus* + *-itat-, -itas* -ity] **1** *obs* **:** the quality or state of having or emitting fumes **2** *obs* **:** a fumy exhalation

fumous *also* **fumose** *adj* [ME, fr. L *fumosus,* fr. *fumus* smoke + *-osus* -ose] *obs* **:** producing, full of, or consisting of fumes **:** SMOKY

fums *pl of* FUM

fu·mu·lus \'fyümyələs\ *n* -ES [NL, fr. L *fumus* smoke + NL *-ulus*] **:** a thin cloud resembling a veil and forming at any level

fumy \'fyümē\ *adj* **fumier; fumiest** [¹*fume* + *-y*] **:** producing or full of fumes ⟨a bottle of ~ household bleach⟩ ⟨a ~ café⟩

¹fun \'fən\ *vb* **funned; funned; funning; funs** [perh. alter. of ME *fonnen* to fool, make a fool of, fr. *fonne* fool, dupe] *vt, now dial* **:** HOAX, TEASE, TRICK, KID ~ *vi* [fr. ²*fun*] **:** to indulge in banter or play **:** speak or act in fun **:** JOKE, FOOL ⟨*funning* about the marriage⟩ ⟨passed the time *funning* till others tired of his horseplay⟩

²fun \"\ *n* -S **1** *obs* **:** a practical joke **:** TRICK, HOAX **2 :** what provides amusement or enjoyment ⟨a book that is ~ to read⟩ ⟨a fellow who is ~ to have around⟩ **:** enjoyable activity ⟨the game was no ~⟩ ⟨picnics are great ~⟩ ⟨didn't know hard study could be so much ~⟩ ⟨sitting on the ground was part of the ~⟩; *specif* **:** playful often boisterous action or speech **:** JOCULARITY **:** RIDICULE ⟨made myself a fine figure of ~ for someone outside —Arthur Grimble⟩ **3 :** the disposition or mood to find or make a cause for amusement **:** PLAYFULNESS ⟨a carefree man who was always full of ~⟩ ⟨has a lot of ~ in him⟩ ⟨don't say that even in ~⟩ **4 :** AMUSEMENT, ENJOYMENT ⟨have ~ at the party⟩ ⟨the baby had a lot of ~ with the blocks⟩ ⟨robbed him just for the ~ of it⟩ ⟨play cards for ~⟩ ⟨never got any ~ out of listening to serious music⟩ **5 :** violent or excited activity or argument **:** FIREWORKS ⟨a rabbit stampeded the herd and then the ~ began⟩ ⟨just toss in the South as a conversation piece and watch the ~ —James Street⟩

syn FUN, JEST, SPORT, GAME, and PLAY agree in designating what provides diversion or amusement or is intended to arouse laughter. FUN implies amusement or applies to what provides what interests as an end in itself or applies to what provides this amusement or interest, often also implying a propensity for laughing or for finding a usu. genial cause for laughter or amusement ⟨had such a zest for everything and thought it all such *fun* —O.E.Rölvaag⟩ ⟨make living more *fun,* life more complete —*Printers' Ink*⟩ ⟨a man full of *fun*⟩ JEST occurs in phrases (as *in jest*) or applies to activity or utterance not to be taken seriously, sometimes carrying an implication of ridicule or hoaxing ⟨a man given to making his most significant remarks in *jest*⟩ ⟨make *jest* of very serious problems⟩ SPORT, often interchangeable with FUN ⟨there is a good deal of *sport* in many serious activities⟩ or JEST ⟨play a trick on a friend for the *sport* of it⟩ or GAME, although here usu. generic or applying to activity calling for a certain skill ⟨go at *sport* as if it were a way of life⟩ ⟨the *sport* of fly casting⟩ ⟨the *sport* of tennis⟩ can also imply amusement or provoking of laughter by putting someone or something up to gentle or malicious ridicule ⟨make *sport* of a suggestion⟩ ⟨make a good deal of *sport* out of someone else's misfortune⟩ GAME in a now rare earlier sense of FUN implies a certain ridicule ⟨make *game* of an unfortunate rival⟩ More commonly today it applies to any activity engaged in for fun ⟨a *game* of tennis⟩ ⟨*games* to keep children amused⟩ PLAY, a generic term for all games or amusements, stresses in all senses an opposition to *earnest,* carrying no suggestion of anything but an intent to divert or be diverted ⟨*play* time in a nursery⟩ ⟨made his work *play* by enjoying it thoroughly⟩ ⟨pretend to spank a child in *play*⟩

³fun \"\ *adj* [²*fun*] **1 :** providing fun, entertainment, or amusement ⟨a ~ party⟩ ⟨~ hat⟩ **2 :** full of fun **:** PLEASANT ⟨a ~ night⟩ ⟨have a ~ time⟩

⁴fun \"\ *n* -S [alter. of *whin*] *Scot* **:** FURZE

⁵fun \'fün, -üŋ\ *n, pl* **fun** [Jap] **:** a Japanese unit of weight equal to 1/10 momme, .375 grams, or 5.79 grains

fu·nam·bu·la·tion \(,)fyü,nambyə'lāshən\ *n* -S [prob. fr. *funambulator,* after such pairs as E *perambulator: perambulation*] **:** ROPEDANCING

fu·nam·bu·la·tor \=¦==,lād·ə(r)\ *n* -S [perh. fr. obs. E *funambule,* v., to walk or dance on a rope (prob. fr. L *funambulus,* n., funambulist) + E *-ator*] **:** FUNAMBULIST

fu·nam·bu·la·to·ry \-lə,tōrē\ *adj* [prob. fr. *funambulator,* after such pairs as E *auditor: auditory*] **1 :** relating to or resembling ropedancing **2 :** performing or as if a ropedancer

fu·nam·bu·list \-ləst\ *n* -S [prob. fr. L *funambulus* funambulist (fr. *funis* rope + *-ambulus* — fr. *ambulare* to walk) + E *-ist* — more at FUNICULUS, AMBLE] **:** ROPEWALKER, ROPEDANCER

fu·nam·bu·lo \-,lō\ *n* -ES [It *funambolo, funambulo,* fr. L *funambulus*] **:** FUNAMBULIST

funambulus *n, pl* **funambuli** [L] *obs* **:** FUNAMBULIST

fu·nar·ia \fyü'na(a)rēə\ *n, cap* [NL, fr. L *funis* rope + NL *-aria*] **:** the type genus of Funariaceae comprising the cord mosses and being characterized by filamentous setae, a gibbous obtusely pyriform capsule, and usu. a double peristome of 16 teeth

fu·nar·i·a·ce·ae \fyü,na(a)rē'āsē,ē\ *n pl, cap* [NL, fr. *Funaria* + *-aceae*] **:** a family of acrocarpous true mosses (order Funariales) with annual or biennial erect gametophores — see FUNARIA — **fu·nar·i·a·ceous** \=¦=¦=¦āshəs\ *adj*

fu·nar·i·a·les \-ā(,)lēz\ *n pl, cap* [NL, fr. *Funaria* + *-ales*] **:** an order of usu. acrocarpous mosses having erect gametophores with an apical rosette of leaves

¹func·tion \'fəŋ(k)shən\ *n* -S [L *function-, functio* performance, fr. *functus* (past part. of *fungi* to perform) + *-ion-, -io* -ion; prob. akin to Skt *bhuṅkte* he enjoys] **1 a :** professional or official position **:** OCCUPATION ⟨big business has elevated the ~ of management to the status of the learned professions —*Nation's Business*⟩ ⟨a man combining the dual ~s of chief and sorcerer —J.G.Frazer⟩ **b** *obs* **:** those engaged in an occupation ⟨the scribes are not a sect but a ~ —Samuel Purchas⟩ **2 :** the action for which a person or thing is specially fitted, used, or responsible or for which a thing exists **:** the activity appropriate to the nature or position of a person or thing **:** ROLE, DUTY, WORK ⟨the ~ that older people can perform in city life today⟩ ⟨it is the ~ of stockholders to assume the risk⟩ ⟨outlined the required and permitted ~s vested in the committee⟩ ⟨discharged the ~s of his office with distinction⟩ **:** USE ⟨form follows ~⟩ ⟨glass has an important ~ in modern architecture⟩ **:** PURPOSE ⟨literary criticism serves complex psychological and sociological ~s⟩ ⟨poetry fulfills its ~ when it introduces us to life⟩ **3** *obs* **:** bodily or mental action **:** BEHAVIOR, PERFORMANCE ⟨~ is smothered in surmise —Shak.⟩ **4 a :** an impressive and elaborate religious ceremony **b :** an often formal public or social ceremony or gathering (as a dinner or reception) ⟨seating notables at official diplomatic ~s⟩ **5 :** one of a group of related actions contributing to a larger action **:** OPERATION ⟨marketing involves the propaganda ~⟩ ⟨the higher human ~s of interpretation and decision⟩: as **a :** the normal and specific contribution of any bodily part (as a tissue, organ, or system) to the economy of a living organism ⟨the primary ~ of any gland is secretion⟩ **b :** syntactic relation (as subject, predicate, qualifier) ⟨*round* has a qualifying ~ in "round eyes"⟩ **c :** a feature of meaning distinguished as characteristic of a type of word ⟨number is a ~ of nouns; tense, of verbs⟩ **d :** the contribution (as of an element, trait, activity) to the consistency or equilibrium of a culture **6 :** either of two magnitudes so related to each other that to values of one there correspond values of the other **:** a correspondence that associates a unique number represented symbolically by $f(x, y, z \ldots)$ with every ordered set of numbers $(x, y, z \ldots)$ each over its domain ⟨the area of a circle is a ~ of its radius because to every value of the radius *r* there corresponds a unique value of the area *A*⟩ **7 :** any quality, trait, or fact so related to another that it is dependent upon and varies with it ⟨sand height is not a ~ of sea-level height —*Science*⟩ **8 a :** an expression which contains a variable term and whose meaning or truth is determined when concrete values of the variable are specified **b :** a propositional or sentential function — compare PREDICATE 1b **c :** the rule, law, relation, or operation denoted by such an expression **9 :** characteristic behavior of a compound due to the presence of a particular atom, group of atoms (as an amino group), or mode of union of atoms (as a double bond); *also* **:** the atom, group, or arrangement causing such behavior ⟨a compound of simple ~ is one containing only one kind of ~ —*Chem. Abstracts*⟩ **10 :** the performance or fulfillment of a function **:** FUNCTIONING ⟨the bubbles in the tissues . . . causing altered sensory or motor ~s —H.G.Armstrong⟩ **11 :** an organizational unit performing a group of related acts and processes **:** ACTIVITY ⟨directed all ~s of the department to effect a reduction in force⟩

syn FUNCTION, OFFICE, DUTY, and PROVINCE can signify in common the acts, activity, or operations expected of a person or thing by virtue of his or its nature, structure, status, or position. FUNCTION can apply very comprehensively to person or thing ⟨to fulfill one's *function* as a human being⟩ ⟨one of the *functions* of a chairman is to preside over meetings⟩ ⟨the *function* of the appendix is unknown⟩ ⟨the main *function* of a language is to communicate ideas or feelings⟩ OFFICE, often close to FUNCTION in application to things, usu. applies to the function or work expected of a person by virtue of his trade, profession, or position in relation to others ⟨the *office* of books is not to create bookworms, but independent souls —Howard M. Jones⟩ ⟨the view here taken of the work and *office* of philosophy —John Dewey⟩ ⟨for all these the good *offices* of an editor are needed —*Times Lit. Supp.*⟩ ⟨the hangman addressed himself to his *office* —T.B.Macaulay⟩ ⟨performing the *office* of president in his absence⟩ ⟨it is not the *office* of a friend to meddle too much⟩ DUTY, in this connection, applies to a task one is expected to perform by reason of the obligation inherent in one's position, relationship, or calling ⟨one's *duty* as a citizen is to vote intelligently⟩ ⟨the *duties* of a school principal⟩ ⟨the *duty* of the vicar as a husband and father should not clash with his *duties* as a clergyman⟩ ⟨the *duties* of a clerk⟩ PROVINCE may apply to any duty or function falling under one's jurisdiction, power, competence, and so on ⟨the historian takes for his *province* those human activities which flow from thought —E.J.Tapp⟩ ⟨a question of universal interest which lies in the *province* of the biologist, How did life make its appearance on our planet? —W.J.V.Osterhout⟩ ⟨such issues are deemed beyond the *province* of a court —Felix Frankfurter⟩

[2]function \"\ *vi* **functioned; functioned; functioning** \-sh(ə)niŋ\ **functions 1 :** to have a function **:** SERVE ⟨shivering ~s to maintain the heat of the body⟩ ⟨an attributive noun ~s as an adjective⟩ **2 :** to carry on a function or be in action **:** OPERATE, WORK ⟨a government ~s through numerous divisions⟩ ⟨war was, when seen ~*ing*, senseless and horrible —Rose Macaulay⟩ ⟨a conductor who ~*ed* also for a time as a music critic —Harriett Johnson⟩ **syn** see ACT

functionaire *var of* [1]FUNCTIONARY

func·tion·al \'fəŋ(k)shənᵊl, -shnəl\ *adj* **1 a :** of, connected with, or being a function ⟨replace the foreman who supervised all aspects of work with several ~ foremen⟩ ⟨a manager who has ~ authority over a specified process through the several departments⟩ **:** dependently related ⟨many similarities, some ~ to the pastoral nomadic way of life, some due to historical relationship —Elizabeth Bacon⟩ **b :** of, relating to, or based on function or functioning ⟨the problem now is not a constitutional one, it is a ~ one . . . to make the machinery established at San Francisco work —C.M.Eichelberger⟩ ⟨a ~ expert, available to keep the administrative organization . . . in good running order —F.R.M.de Paula⟩ ⟨a ~ presentation of government activities that groups related items regardless of agency or location⟩: as (1) **:** affecting functions but not structure — compare ANATOMIC, ORGANIC, PSYCHOGENIC (2) **:** of or selected by functional representation ⟨delegates elected on a ~ rather than geographical basis⟩ **:** OCCUPATIONAL (3) **:** of or affecting the adaptation of a property (as equipment or a building) to prevailing standards or use ⟨the air-conditioned coach resulted in the ~ obsolescence of the old day coach⟩ **2 :** existing or used to contribute to the development or maintenance of a larger whole **:** having a useful function ⟨a style of writing in which every word is ~⟩ ⟨its trunk and branches were a ~ part of the tree house⟩: as **a :** designed or developed chiefly from the point of view of use **:** UTILITARIAN ⟨~ architecture⟩ ⟨~ fabrics⟩ ⟨the play's dialogue was strictly ~⟩ **b :** relating directly to everyday needs and interests **:** concerned with application in activity **:** PRACTICAL ⟨~ education selects knowledge that is concrete and usable, not abstract and theoretical⟩ **c :** carrying out or consisting of a group of related activities **:** performing a specialized service ⟨the European Defense Community and other ~ arms of the emerging political structure —*New Republic*⟩ ⟨whether ~ cooperation would lead to structural union⟩ **3 :** performing or able to perform its regular function **:** in a functioning condition ⟨vision that is ~ only in bright light⟩ **:** WORKING ⟨the flashlight was still ~ after being dropped⟩ **4 :** placing related functions in an industry or business under the direction of a specialist **:** having specialized administration ⟨~ organization⟩ ⟨~ management⟩ **5 :** FUNCTIONALIST **6 :** relating or attempting to demonstrate the relatedness of any single aspect of culture to the maintenance of an integrated sociocultural whole ⟨in our western civilization the personal life and the ~ life have fallen apart —P.C.W.Gutkind⟩ ⟨~ sociology⟩ **7 :** having no neurological or organic pathology ⟨a ~ psychosis caused by maladjustment⟩ ⟨in the ~ . . . disorders the amount of organ pathology which is discovered, even with careful and thorough examination, is neither sufficient nor impressive enough to account for the symptoms —E.A.Strecker⟩

functional calculus *n* **:** a branch of symbolic logic that utilizes quantifiers in order to deal with propositional functions in addition to the unanalyzed propositions of propositional calculus — called also *predicate calculus;* see HIGHER FUNCTIONAL CALCULUS, LOWER FUNCTIONAL CALCULUS

functional determinant *n* **:** a determinant whose constituents are partial derivatives of one set of variables as to another set, each row containing derivatives of only one variable and each column derivatives as to only one variable

functional finance *n* **:** management of the public debt of a country designed to balance its economy

functional group *n* **:** [1]FUNCTION 9

functional illiterate *n* **:** a person unable to read and understand directions ⟨Selective Service ruled that all examinees with less than five years of schooling were *functional illiterates*⟩

func·tion·al·ism \-shənᵊl,izəm, -shnə,li-\ *n* -s **1 :** a psychology in which mental or behavioral processes are viewed as adaptive responses of the whole organism **:** instrumental psychology **2 a :** a philosophy of design (as in architecture) holding that form should be adapted to use, material, and structure **b :** design in which the functionalist principle dominates **3 :** a theory of culture which analyzes the interrelatedness and interdependence of patterns and institutions within a cultural complex or social system and which emphasizes the interaction of these forms in the maintenance of sociocultural unity or in meeting biosocial requirements **4 :** any doctrine or practice that emphasizes practical utility or functional relations ⟨the prevailing outlook of ~ in which a man asks of a thing only "What's it good for?"⟩ **5 :** a system of functional organization or representation **6 :** the theory or practice of achieving cooperation or union between governmental units by gradual integration of economic and other functions rather than immediate political federation ⟨~ in contrast to federalism as a road to European unity —D.C.Stone⟩

[1]func·tion·al·ist \-shənᵊləst, -shnəl-\ *n* -s **:** one who advocates or employs functionalism

[2]functionalist \"\ *or* **func·tion·al·is·tic** \ˌfəŋ(k)shənᵊlˈistik, -shnəˈli-\ *adj* [*functionalist* fr. [1]*functionalist; functionalistic* fr. [1]*functionalist* + *-ic*] **:** of or relating to functionalism (as in architecture or sociology) ⟨the ~ theory of mind⟩

func·tion·al·i·ty \ˌfəŋ(k)shəˈnaləd·ē\ *n* -ES **:** the quality, state, or relation of being functional **:** UTILITY **:** INTERRELATION

func·tion·al·iza·tion \ˌfəŋ(k)shənᵊləˈzāshən, -shnəl-, -ᵊlˌīˈz-, -əˌlīˈz-\ *n* -s **1 :** the act or process of functionalizing **2 :** the quality or state of being functionalized

func·tion·al·ize \ˈfəŋ(k)shənᵊlˌīz, -shnəˌlīz\ *vt* -ED/-ING/-S **1 :** to cause to be functional **2 :** to organize (as work or management) into units performing specialized tasks

functional load *also* **functional burden** *or* **functional burdening** *n* [prob. trans. of G *funktionelle belastung*] **:** the measure of the actual functioning of a usu. phonemic difference as the sole distinction between two otherwise identical elements (as morphemes or words) of a language

func·tion·al·ly \ˈfəŋ(k)shənᵊl|ē, -shnəl|, |i\ *adv* **1 :** as regards function ⟨ornamental columns that were ~ unnecessary⟩ **2 :** in a functional manner ⟨a ~ designed auditorium⟩

functional middleman *n* **:** AGENT MIDDLEMAN

functional psychology *n* **:** FUNCTIONALISM 1

functional representation *n* **:** representation in legislative or other political bodies based on the economic and social groups of a community

functional shift *or* **functional change** *n* **:** the process by which a word or form comes to be used in a second or third grammatical function (as a noun used in a verb function) — compare CLASS CLEAVAGE

functional yield *n* [prob. trans. of F *rendement fonctionnel*] **:** FUNCTIONAL LOAD

func·tion·a·rism \ˈfəŋ(k)sh(ə)nəˌrizəm\ *n* -s [*functionary* + *-ism*] **:** administration by functionaries **:** OFFICIALISM

[1]func·tion·ary \ˈfəŋ(k)shəˌnerē, -ri\ *also* **func·tion·aire** *or* **func·tion·naire** \ˌ==ˈna(a)|(ə)r, -ˈne|, |ə\ *n, pl* **functionaries** *also* **functionaires** *or* **functionnaires** [*functionary* (trans. of F *fonctionnaire*) fr. [1]*function* + *-ary* (n. suffix); *functionaire, functionnaire* modif. (influenced by E [1]*function*) of F *fonctionnaire*, fr. *fonction* function (fr. L *function-, functio* performance) + *-aire* -ary — more at FUNCTION] **:** one who serves in a certain function ⟨characters in melodrama . . . are rather *functionaries* in a preconceived plot —Roger Manvell⟩ ⟨the *functionaries* who summon motorcars for the clubhouse patrons —Frank Sullivan⟩; *esp* **:** one holding a paid position or office in a government or party **:** CIVIL SERVANT ⟨the bureaucracy . . . includes a number of functionaries . . . 1 court clerk . . . 1 forest guard . . . 1 market sweeper —Mary Tew⟩ **:** OFFICIAL ⟨the distinction between members of the Communist party and *functionaries* —Sidney Hook⟩

[2]functionary \"\ *adj* [[1]*function* + *-ary* (adj. suffix)] **:** FUNCTIONAL 1b

func·tion·ate \ˈ==ˌnāt\ *vi* -ED/-ING/-S **:** to carry on a natural esp. organic function ⟨interferes with the normal action of the auricle, rendering it . . . powerless to ~ properly —F.A. Faught⟩ — **func·tion·a·tion** \ˌ==ˈnāshən\ *n* -s

functioned *past of* FUNCTION

functioning *pres part of* FUNCTION

func·tion·less \ˈfəŋ(k)shənləs\ *adj* **:** having no useful unction

functions *pl of* FUNCTION, *pres 3d sing of* FUNCTION

function word *n* **:** a word expressing primarily grammatical relationship (as a preposition, auxiliary verb, conjunction, conjunctive adverb, or relative) — called also *empty word, form word;* compare FULL WORD

func·tor \ˈfəŋ(k)tə(r)\ *n* -s [NL, fr. L *functus* (past part. of *fungi* to perform) + NL *-or* — more at FUNCTION] **1 :** something that performs a function or operation **2 :** a sign for a nonpropositional function; *esp* **:** a syncategorematic sign used to indicate operations in symbolic logic — **func·to·ri·al** \ˌfəŋ(k)ˈtōrēəl\ *adj*

func·tus of·fi·cio \ˌfəŋ(k)təsəˈfishēˌō\ *adj* [L, having performed his duty, having served its purpose] **:** of no further official authority or legal efficacy — used of an officer no longer in office or of an instrument, power, or agency that has fulfilled the purpose of its creation ⟨once exercised, their power of approval or disapproval is *functus officio* —*U.S. Fed. Supp.*⟩

[1]fund \ˈfənd\ *n* -s [F & L; F *fond* bottom, innermost part, basis & F *fonds* stock or capital, piece of landed property, fr. L *fundus* bottom, piece of landed property — more at BOTTOM] **1** *obs* **a :** the lowest or innermost part **:** BOTTOM **b :** BASIS 3 ⟨what may afford ~ enough for ridicule —Joseph Butler⟩ **2** *obs* **:** FONT **3 a :** a quantity of material resources maintained or available as a source of supply ⟨of a large ~ of land and of a considerable reserve of labor seeking employment in agriculture —Peter Struve⟩ **b :** a supply of intangible resources (as of information, stories, wisdom, goodwill) **4 :** an appropriation (as of permanent revenue) or a deposit or collection of money or its equivalent used as a resource or security: **a :** a sum of money or other resources the principal or interest of which is set apart for a specific objective or activity ⟨a ~ for retirement of bonds⟩ ⟨a campaign ~⟩; *specif* **:** a reserve or accumulation set up by a self-insurer or some public body (as the federal or a state government) for the assumption of certain risks **b :** money on deposit which is held at a specified place and on which checks or drafts can be drawn — usu. used in pl. ⟨prefers payment from foreign concerns in New York ~s⟩ **c :** STOCK, CAPITAL ⟨the ~ of a bank⟩ **d funds** *pl* **:** the stock of the British national debt — called also *public funds;* usu. used with *the* ⟨the holdings of these men in the ~s —W.O. Aydelotte⟩ **5 funds** *pl* **:** available pecuniary resources ordinarily including cash and negotiable paper that can be converted to cash at any time without loss ⟨will be in ~s again after payday⟩ **6 :** an organization administering a special fund ⟨the International Monetary *Fund* . . . conferred with its members —*Britannica Bk. of the Yr.*⟩

[2]fund \"\ *vt* -ED/-ING/-S **1 a :** to provide and appropriate a fund or permanent revenue to pay the interest of **:** make permanent provision of resources for discharging the interest or principal of ⟨a pledge of customs revenue to ~ government notes⟩ ⟨~ employees' pensions⟩ **b :** to make provision for meeting (a recurrent future liability) by systematic accumulation of a fund ⟨~ a pension plan⟩ **2 :** to place in a fund **:** store up **:** ACCUMULATE ⟨a background of . . . ~*ed* notions of the beautiful —F.J.Mather⟩ **3 :** to convert (a floating or short-time debt or a number of different debts) into a debt that is payable either at a distant date usu. with an option to the debtor to redeem after a certain time or at no definite date and that bears a fixed interest **4 :** to invest (money) in the British public funds

fun·dal \ˈfəndᵊl\ *adj* [*fundus* + *-al*] **:** FUNDIC

fun·da·ment \ˈfəndəmənt\ *n* -s [ME, foundation, alter. (influenced by L *fundamentum*) of *foundement, fundement*, fr. OF *fondement*, fr. L *fundamentum*, fr. *fundare* to found (fr. *fundus* bottom) + *-mentum* -ment] **1 a** *obs* **:** the base on which a structure (as a building or wall) is erected **b :** an underlying ground or theory **:** basic principle ⟨relations between countries based on the ~s of mutual respect and neighborliness⟩ **:** FOUNDATION ⟨archaeology and history are giving us a firm ~ of facts —W.W.Hill⟩ **2 a :** the part of the body on which one sits **:** BUTTOCKS **b :** ANUS **3** *biol* **:** ANLAGE **4 :** the part of a land surface that has not been altered by human activities

[1]fun·da·men·tal \ˌfəndəˈmentᵊl\ *adj* [ME, fr. LL *fundamentalis* of a foundation, fr. L *fundamentum* + *-alis* -al] **1 :** producing, supporting, regulating, or conditioning something (as a development or system) **:** BASIC, UNDERLYING — often used with *to* ⟨responsibility is ~ to democracy⟩: **a :** serving as an original or generating source **:** being the one from which others are derived **:** PRIMARY ⟨the chronicle is the ~ account of the era from which all later historians drew⟩ **:** FORMATIVE ⟨the various theories developed from that ~ idea⟩ **b :** serving as a basis supporting existence or determining essential structure or function **:** forming the foundation on which something immaterial is built ⟨the productivity ~ to a sound economy⟩ ⟨the ~ rules governing all scientific experiments⟩ **c :** constituting a necessary or elemental quality, part, or condition **:** INDISPENSABLE ⟨American business sagacity had been ~ in that triumph —Bernard DeVoto⟩ **:** IRREDUCIBLE ⟨considered the atom the ~ unit of matter⟩ **2 a :** of or extending or relating to essential structure, function, or facts **:** going to the root of the matter ⟨naïve as the child's questions may sound, they are ~ —W.K.Livingstone⟩ **:** RADICAL ⟨distinguish ~ from superficial differences⟩ ⟨monarchy had undergone ~ changes beneath its continuing forms⟩ **:** ELEMENTARY ⟨less ~ and general instruction and more advanced and specialized study⟩; *specif* **:** of or dealing with general principles (as of a chemical or electrical process) rather than practical application **:** PURE ⟨~ science⟩ **b :** concerned with fundamentals (as of life or religion); *specif* **:** FUNDAMENTALIST ⟨replace modernist with ~ Bible lessons⟩ ⟨a preacher who is evangelical, Bible-teaching, and ~⟩ **3 :** serving as or employing an arbitrarily established standard, reference point, or basis of reckoning ⟨~ units of measurement⟩ ⟨taking the equator as the ~ circle⟩ **4 a** *of a musical chord or its position* **:** having the root in the bass **b :** of, relating to, or produced by the lowest component of a complex vibration **5 :** being or constituting the lowest geological formation **:** BASAL ⟨the ~ gneiss of the British isles⟩ **6 :** of central importance **:** PRINCIPAL ⟨lost sight of his ~ purpose in the pursuit of secondary aims⟩ **:** VITAL ⟨such ~ events as birth, marriage, and death⟩ **7 :** forming a sustained or recurring element **:** serving as a background or starting point ⟨used black jute as the ~ material with patterns in colored thread⟩ ⟨in the ~ position the boxer's right arm is leading, his left guarding⟩; *specif* **:** forming the underlying pattern or image in a work of art ⟨the conductor feels . . . doubt as to whether he should beat auxiliary beats or ~ beats —Warwick Braithwaite⟩ ⟨obscures the ~ image of his poem with ornate metaphor⟩ **8 :** belonging to one's innate or ingrained characteristics **:** DEEP-ROOTED ⟨fatigue nor worry nor professordom could extinguish his ~ gaiety —John Mason Brown⟩ **syn** see ESSENTIAL

[2]fundamental \"\ *n* -s **1 :** something fundamental; *esp* **:** one of the minimum constituents without which a thing would not be what it is or on which all further development is founded — often used in pl. ⟨reading, writing, spelling, and arithmetic are ~s of education⟩ **2 a :** the prime tone of any given harmonic series that gives the heard pitch of the tone sounded — compare OVERTONE **b :** the root of a chord **3 :** the harmonic component of a complex vibration or wave train (as a sound wave) that has the lowest frequency and commonly the greatest amplitude **syn** see PRINCIPLE

fundamental bass *n* **1 :** the root note of a musical chord **2 :** the generating tone of a series of harmonics **3 :** a bass formed of the roots of a succession of harmonics

fundamental complex *n* **1 :** a widespread complex assemblage of highly metamorphic rocks that is the foundation of the geological column **:** the Archean rocks **2 :** an assemblage of metamorphic rocks in any region and of any age that unconformably underlies the sedimentary or unmetamorphosed rocks of the region

fundamental education *n* **:** preparation of children or adults without opportunity for traditional formal schooling (as in underdeveloped areas) for effective participation in community life through instruction in basic facts and skills (as of literacy, agriculture, homemaking, hygiene, citizenship)

fun·da·men·tal·ism \ˌ==ˈmentᵊlˌizəm\ *n* -s [[1]*fundamental* + *-ism*] **1 a** *often cap* **:** a militantly conservative movement in American Protestantism originating around the beginning of the 20th century in opposition to modernist tendencies and emphasizing as fundamental to Christianity the literal interpretation and absolute inerrancy of the Scriptures, the imminent and physical second coming of Jesus Christ, the virgin birth, physical resurrection, and substitutionary atonement **b :** the beliefs on which this movement was founded **c :** adherence to the attitude opposing modernism and to the literalist doctrines of fundamentalism ⟨a minister noted for his strict ~⟩ **2 :** a movement or attitude similar in a significant respect (as literalism or strict adherence to traditional beliefs) to the American religious fundamentalism ⟨Muslim ~⟩ ⟨~ in education stresses the three R's⟩

[1]fun·da·men·tal·ist \-ᵊləst\ *n* -s [[1]*fundamental* + *-ist*] **1** *sometimes cap* **:** an adherent or proponent of Protestant fundamentalism **2 :** an extreme conservative; *esp* **:** one who attacks any deviation from certain doctrines and practices he considers essential (as to a religious, political, or educational system) ⟨a political ~ . . . could reduce the shadings of any political controversy into a black-and-white conflict between free enterprise and socialism —*Time*⟩ **3** *often cap* **:** a member of a small dissident Mormon sect continuing to practice polygamy after its outlawry in 1890

[2]fundamentalist \ˈ==ˈ===\ *or* **fun·da·men·tal·is·tic** \ˈ==ˌ==ˈistik, -tēk\ *adj* [[2]*fundamentalist* fr. [1]*fundamentalist; fundamentalistic* fr. [1]*fundamentalist* + *-ic*] **:** of, adhering to, or marked by fundamentalism ⟨comparing the neoorthodox with the ~ position⟩ ⟨a ~ revival preacher⟩ ⟨an economic outlook strongly ~ in tone⟩

fun·da·men·tal·i·ty \ˌfəndəˌmen·ˈtaləd·ē, -ˌmən·-\ *n* -ES **:** the quality or state of being fundamental

fundamental law *n* **:** the organic or basic law of a state or political subdivision with which all departments of government including the lawmaking body must conform **:** CONSTITUTION ⟨judged the statute passed by the legislature to be contrary to the *fundamental law* of the land⟩

fun·da·men·tal·ly \ˈfəndəˈmentᵊlē, -ᵊli *sometimes* ÷-tlē *or* ÷-tli\ *adv* [ME *fundamentali*, fr. *fundamental* + *-li* -ly] **:** in a fundamental manner **:** in the manner of a primary source ⟨animals are ~ dependent on plant life⟩ **:** in essential structure or function ⟨systems ~ different⟩ ⟨~ all forms of mathematics are short cuts for the operations of grade-school arithmetic —Robert Bendiner⟩ **:** in fundamental disposition ⟨a ~ honest person⟩ **:** BASICALLY

fun·da·men·tal·ness \ˌ==ˈmentᵊlnəs\ *n* -ES **:** the quality or state of being fundamental

fundamental particle *n* **:** ELEMENTARY PARTICLE

fundamental tissue *n* **:** plant tissue other than dermal and vascular tissues that consists typically of relatively undifferentiated parenchymatous and supportive cells

fundamental tone *n* **:** FUNDAMENTAL 2

fundaments *pl of* FUNDAMENT

fun·da·men·tum \ˌfəndəˈmentəm\ *n* -s [L, lit., foundation — more at FUNDAMENT] **:** a logical basis or ruling principle **:** GROUND

fun·da·tri·ge·nia \ˌfənˌdā·trəˈjēnyə, -nēə\ *n, pl* **fundatri·geni·ae** \-nēˌē\ [NL, fr. *fundatri-* (fr. *fundatrix*) + *-genia* (irreg. fr. Gk *-genēs* born) — more at -GEN] **:** a viviparous parthenogenetic wingless female aphid produced by a fundatrix and giving rise to further wingless forms or to migrantes — **fun·da·tri·gen·ic** \ˈ=ˌ==ˈjenik\ *adj*

fun·da·trix \ˌfənˈdā·triks\ *n, pl* **fundatri·ces** \ˌfənˈdā·trəˌsēz, ˌfəndə·ˈtrī(ˌ)sēz\ [NL, fr. LL, foundress, fem. of L *fundator* founder, fr. *fundatus* (past part. of *fundare* to found, fr. *fundus* bottom) + *-or* — more at BOTTOM, -TRIX] **:** a viviparous parthenogenetic winged or wingless female aphid produced on the primary host plant from an overwintering fertilized egg

funded *past of* FUND

funded debt *also* **funded liability** *n* [*funded* fr. past part. of [2]*fund*] **:** FIXED LIABILITY; *specif* **:** BONDED DEBT

fundholder \ˈ=ˌ==\ *n* **1 :** one that has money invested in the British public funds **2 :** one that holds stocks, bonds, or other funds as a mere investment

[1]fundi *pl of* FUNDUS

[2]fun·di \ˈfəndē\ *n* -s [perh. fr. Limba *fandi ha* grass] **:** a tropical African grass (*Digitaria exilis*) cultivated for its seed that resembles millet

fun·dic \ˈfəndik\ *adj* [*fundus* + *-ic*] **:** of or relating to a fundus

fundic gland *n* **:** one of the tubular glands of the fundus of the stomach secreting pepsin and mucus — compare CHIEF CELL 1, PARIETAL CELL

funding *pres part of* FUND

fund·less \'fəndləs\ *adj* **:** being without funds

fun·do \'fün(,)dō\ *n* -s [Sp, country estate, fr. L *fundus* bottom, piece of landed property] **:** a large agricultural estate in Chile

funds *pl of* FUND, *pres 3d sing of* FUND

funduck *var of* FONDUK

fun·du·line \'fəndə,līn, 'fənjə-\ *adj* [NL *Fundulinae* subfamily of fishes including the common killifishes, fr. *Fundulus*, type genus + *-inae*] **:** of or relating to the genus *Fundulus*

fun·du·lus \-ləs\ *n* [NL, fr. L *fundus* bottom + NL *-ulus*] **1** *cap* **:** a genus of carnivorous cyprinodont fishes including the common killifishes **2** *pl* **fundulus :** any fish of the genus *Fundulus*

fun·dus \'fəndəs\ *n, pl* **fun·di** \-,dī\ [NL, fr. L, bottom, piece of landed property — more at BOTTOM] **1 :** the bottom of or part opposite the aperture of the internal surface of a hollow organ of the body: as **a :** the greater curvature of the stomach **b :** the lower back part of the bladder **c :** the large upper end of the uterus **d :** the part of the eye opposite the pupil **2** [L] *Roman & civil law* **:** LAND, BUILDINGS **:** land with buildings affixed thereto **:** REAL ESTATE

fun·du·scop·ic *also* **fun·do·scop·ic** \¦fəndə¦skäpik\ *adj* [*funduscopic* fr. *fundus* + *-scopic* (as in *microscopic*); *fundoscopic* fr. *fundo-* (fr. *fundus*) + *-scopic* (as in *microscopic*)] **:** of, relating to, or by means of funduscopy

fun·dus·co·py \,fən'dəskəpē\ *also* **fun·dos·co·py** \-däs-\ *n* -ES [*funduscopy* fr. *fundus* + *-scopy; fundoscopy* fr. *fundo-* (fr. *fundus*) + *-scopy*] **:** ophthalmoscopic examination of the fundus of the eye

fu·ne·bri·al \(')fyü¦nēbrēəl, -neb-\ *adj* [L *funebris* funereal (fr. *funus* funeral) + E *-al*] **:** FUNEREAL

funebrious *or* **funebrous** *adj* [*funebrious* fr. L *funebris* + E *-ous; funebrous* fr. L *funebris* + E *-ous*] *obs* **:** FUNEREAL

[1]**fu·ner·al** \'fyün(ə)rəl\ *adj* [ME, fr. LL *funeralis*, fr. L *funer-, funus* funeral (n.) + *-alis* -al; perh. akin to ON *deyja* to die — more at DIE] **1 :** of, relating to, or constituting a funeral ⟨~ notices in the newspaper⟩ ⟨made the ~ arrangements⟩ ⟨attended his ~ service⟩ **2 :** forming part of, connected with, or used in connection with a funeral or related observances ⟨preached the ~ sermon⟩ ⟨marched in the ~ procession⟩ ⟨a grave covered with ~ flowers⟩ ⟨insurance covered all the ~ expenses⟩ **3 :** FUNEREAL 2 ⟨a sky that was dull and ~⟩

[2]**funeral** \"\ *n* -s [ME *funerelles* (pl.), fr. MF *funerailles* (pl.), fr. ML *funeralia* (pl.), fr. LL *funeralia*, neut. pl. of *funeralis*, adj.] **1 a :** the observances held in honor or on behalf of one who has died ⟨dances held on the occasion of a chieftain's ~⟩ ⟨Egyptian animals had their ranks . . . and their ~*s* sometimes rivaled in magnificence those of the pharaohs —Elizabeth Lee⟩; *esp* **:** a rite or service for a dead person held ordinarily in the presence of the body before burial or cremation ⟨a church ~ with a Scripture reading and a eulogy⟩ ⟨a ~ conducted by his fellow Masons⟩ ⟨given a military ~ in the fort⟩ — compare COMMITTAL, MEMORIAL SERVICE, REQUIEM **b funerals** *pl, obs* **:** a funeral ceremony or sermon **:** OBSEQUIES ⟨his ~*s* were performed very solemnly in the collegiate church at Westminster —Thomas Fuller⟩ **2** *now dial* **:** a funeral sermon ⟨after preaching a man's ~ he walked down to pay his respects to the departed —A.W.Long⟩ **3 :** a funeral party on its way to the funeral or committal **:** a funeral procession ⟨the ~ is expected to reach the cemetery at 1:30⟩ **4 a :** the end of the existence of something ⟨planning the ~ of the opposition party⟩ **b** *obs* **:** DEATH **5 :** a matter of concern to one **:** a problem that one must solve **:** LOOKOUT ⟨I didn't see how the prom committee could handle it, but it wasn't my ~ —Albert Halper⟩

funeral car *or* **funeral coach** *n* **:** HEARSE 4

funeral certificate *n* **:** a certificate filed in 16th and 17th century England and Ireland by an officer of arms attesting the use of only authorized arms at the funeral of an armigerous person and now valued as a source of detailed genealogical and armorial information

funeral chapel *n* **1 :** a room in a funeral home used for funerals and often for the viewing of the deceased by mourners **2 :** a building containing a funeral chapel **:** FUNERAL HOME

funeral director *n* **:** one whose profession is the management of funeral and burial preparations and observances and who is usu. an embalmer — called also *mortician, undertaker*

funeral home *or* **funeral parlor** *n* **:** an establishment with facilities for the preparation of the dead for burial or cremation, for the viewing of the body, and for funerals

fu·ner·al·ize \'fyün(ə)rə,līz\ *vt* -ED/-ING/-S *dial* **:** to hold a funeral or memorial service for ⟨put off *funeralizing* him⟩

funeral pie *n* [prob. so called fr. a Pennsylvania Dutch custom of serving it at funerals] **:** pie made of raisins

fu·ner·ary \'fyünə,rerē, -eri\ *adj* [L *funerarius*, fr. *funer-, funus* + *-arius* -ary] **:** of, used for, or associated with burial **:** FUNERAL ⟨the ~ rites of the deceased ruler⟩ **:** MORTUARY ⟨a ~ monument⟩ **:** BURIAL ⟨a pharaoh's ~ chamber⟩

fu·ne·re·al \(')fyü¦nirēəl, -nēr-\ *adj* [L *funereus* funereal (fr. *funer-, funus* + *-eus* -eous) + E *-al*] **1 :** of or belonging to a funeral ⟨organ works . . . suited to both marital and ~ occasions —Virgil Thomson⟩ **2 :** befitting or suggesting a funeral (as in appearance or mood) ⟨an almost ~ gloom seemed to have descended —Jack London⟩ ⟨the ~ pace of the bullock carts —E.E.Shipton⟩ **:** oppressively solemn ⟨the butler . . . admitted us with silent ~ dignity —W.H.Wright⟩ **:** GLOOMY ⟨a large dark room furnished in a ~ manner with black horsehair —Charles Dickens⟩ — **fu·ne·re·al·ly** \-əlē, -li\ *adv*

fu·nest \(')fyü¦nest\ *adj* [F *funeste*, fr. L *funestus*, fr. *funer-, funus*] **:** portending death or evil **:** FATAL, DIRE, DOLEFUL

fun fair *n, chiefly Brit* **:** AMUSEMENT PARK

funfest \'=,=\ *n* **:** a gathering for amusements ⟨turned the monthly meeting of their dance group into a public ~⟩ ⟨the town's annual ~ attracts crowds of tourists⟩

[1]**fung** \'fəŋ\ *Scot var of* FUNK

[2]**fung** \'fu̇|ŋ\ *also* **funj** \|nj\ *or* **fun·ji** \|n(,)jē\ *n, pl* **fung** *or* **fungs** *also* **funj** *or* **funjes** *or* **funji** *or* **funjis** *usu cap* **1 :** a Negroid people dominant in Sennar **2 :** a member of such people **3 :** the language of the Fung people

[1]**fun·gal** \'fəŋgəl\ *adj* [NL *Fungales*] **1 :** FUNGOUS **2 :** consisting of fungi

[2]**fungal** \"\ *n* -s [NL *Fungales*] **:** FUNGUS

fun·ga·les \,fəŋ'gā(,)lēz\ *n pl, cap* [NL, fr. L *fungus* + NL *-ales*] *in some esp former classifications* **:** a group coextensive with Fungi

fun·gate \'fəŋ,gāt\ *vi* -ED/-ING/-S [*fungus* + *-ate*] **:** to assume a fungous form or grow rapidly like a fungus — **fun·ga·tion** \,fəŋ'gāshən\ *n* -s

fung–hwang *var of* FÊNG HUANG

[1]**fungi** *pl of* FUNGUS

[2]**fun·gi** \'fən,jī, 'fəŋ,gī\ *n pl, cap* [NL, fr. L, pl. of *fungus* — more at FUNGUS] **:** a division or other major group of lower plants that is often included in Thallophyta coordinate to Algae, that includes a varied assemblage of saprophytic and parasitic plants which lack chlorophyll, and that comprises the classes Phycomycetes, Ascomycetes, Basidiomycetes, and Fungi Imperfecti, and usu. also the Myxomycetes and Schizomycetes

fungi- *comb form* [perh. fr. NL, fr. L *fungus*] **:** fungus ⟨*fungi*colous⟩ ⟨*fungi*form⟩

fun·gia \'fənjēə, 'fəŋgēə\ *n, cap* [NL, fr. L *fungus* + NL *-ia*] **:** a genus (the type of the family Fungiidae) of madrepores comprising the typical mushroom corals — **fun·gi·an** \-ēən\ *adj or n*

fun·gi·bil·i·ty \,fənjə'biləd·ē\ *n* -ES **:** the quality or state of being fungible

[1]**fun·gi·ble** \'fənjəbəl\ *n* -s [NL *fungibilis*, adj., fungible] **:** goods that are fungible — usu. used in pl. ⟨~*s* loaned under a contract of mutuum⟩

[2]**fungible** \"\ *adj* [NL *fungibilis*, fr. L *fungi* to perform + *-ibilis* -ible — more at FUNCTION] **1 :** of such a kind or nature that one specimen or part may be used in place of another specimen or equal part in the satisfaction of an obligation — used of things that can be counted, weighed, or measured and are consumed or alienated by use (as food, coal, oil, lumber) ⟨~ goods enjoyed under the usufruct of property⟩ **2 :** capable of mutual substitution **:** INTERCHANGEABLE

fun·gic \'fənjik, 'fəŋgik\ *adj* [ISV *fung-* (fr. L *fungus*) + *-ic*; orig. formed as F *fongique*] **:** of or relating to fungi

fun·gi·ci·dal \¦fənjə¦sīdᵊl, ¦fəŋgə-\ *adj* [*fungicide* + *-al*] **1 :** destroying fungi ⟨a ~ compound for use in skin infections⟩; *broadly* **:** preventing further ravage (as of plants, cloth, or wood) by a fungus by killing or inactivating it ⟨the ~ action of the solution in the timber⟩ **2 :** of or relating to a fungicide — compare FUNGISTATIC — **fun·gi·cid·al·ly** \-ᵊlē,-ᵊli\ *adv*

fun·gi·cide \'==,sīd\ *n* -s [ISV *fungi-* + *-cide*] **:** an agent that destroys fungi; *broadly* **:** an agent hostile to fungi (as a fungistat or seed disinfectant)

fun·gi·ci·din \¦==¦sīdᵊn\ *n* -s [*fungicide* + *-in*] **:** NYSTATIN

[1]**fun·gid** \'fənjəd, 'fəŋgəd\ *adj* [prob. irreg. fr. NL *Fungiidae*, fr. *Fungia* + *-idae*] **:** of or relating to the genus *Fungia* or the family Fungiidae

[2]**fungid** \"\ *n* -s [prob. irreg. fr. NL *Fungiidae*] **:** a madrepore of the genus *Fungia* or the family Fungiidae

fun·gi·form \'fənjə,fȯrm 'fəŋgə-\ *adj* [prob. fr. NL *fungiformis*, fr. *fungi-* + *-formis* -form] **:** shaped like a mushroom

fungiform papilla *n* [prob. trans. of NL *papilla fungiformis*] **:** any of numerous papillae on the upper surface of the tongue that are flat-topped and noticeably red from the richly vascular stroma and that usu. contain taste buds

fungi im·per·fec·ti \-,impə(r)'fek,tī\ *n pl, cap F&I* [NL, lit., imperfect fungi] **:** a large and heterogeneous group of fungi comprising forms whose life cycle is imperfectly known or lacks the sexual stage, including many that are undoubtedly ascomycetes or more rarely basidiomycetes for which the perfect stage exists but has not been identified, and being usu. divided among the orders Sphaeropsidales, Melanconiales, Moniliales, and Mycelia sterilia

fung·inert \'fənjə,nərt, 'fəŋgə-, ,=='=\ *adj* [*fungus* + *inert*] **:** not supporting fungous growth

fun·gi·sta·sis \,fənjə'stāsəs, ,fəŋgə-, -'stasəs; ,fən'jistəsəs, ,fəŋ'gi-\ *n* [*fungi-* + *-stasis*] **:** fungistatic action

fun·gi·stat \'fənjə,stat, 'fəŋgə-\ *n* -s [*fungi-* + *-stat*] **:** a fungistatic agent

fun·gi·stat·ic \¦==¦stad·ik\ *adj* [*fungi-* + *static*] **:** capable of inhibiting the growth of fungi without destroying them — compare FUNGICIDAL — **fun·gi·stat·i·cal·ly** \-d·ək(ə)lē\ *adv*

fun·gi·tox·ic \-¦täksik\ *adj* [*fungi-* + *toxic*] **:** toxic to fungi — **fun·gi·tox·ic·i·ty** \,==,täk'sisəd·ē\ *n*

fun·giv·o·rous \¦fən¦jivərəs, ¦fəŋ¦gi-\ *adj* [prob. fr. (assumed) NL *fungivorus*, fr. NL *fungi-* + L *-vorus* -vorous] **:** feeding customarily on or in fungi **:** MYCETOPHAGOUS

fun·go \'fəŋ(,)gō\ *n, pl* **fungoes** [origin unknown] **1 :** a fly ball hit for practice purposes by a player who tosses the ball into the air and bats it as it comes down **2** *or* **fungo bat :** a lightweight bat that is longer and thinner than the ordinary bat and is used for fungo hitting

[1]**fun·goid** \'fəŋ,gȯid\ *adj* [prob. fr. (assumed) NL *fungoides*, fr. L *fungus* + NL *-oides* -oid] **1 :** resembling a fungus: as **a :** having a mushroom shape or spongy or fleshy texture ⟨a ~ ulcer⟩ **b :** growing rapidly ⟨the ~ growth of bureaucracy —Eric Partridge⟩ **2** *chiefly Brit* **:** FUNGOUS 1a, 1b ⟨dampness promotes ~ growth⟩

[2]**fungoid** \"\ *n* -s **:** a fungoid growth

fun·gol·o·gist \,fəŋ'gäləjəst\ *n* -s [*fungology* + *-ist*] **:** MYCOLOGIST

fun·gol·o·gy \-jē\ *n* -ES [*fungus* + *-o-* + *-logy*] **:** MYCOLOGY

fun·gose \'fəŋ,gōs\ *adj* [L *fungosus*] **:** FUNGOUS

fun·gos·i·ty \,fəŋ'gäsəd·ē\ *n* -ES [prob. fr. (assumed) NL *fungositat-, fungositas*, fr. L *fungosus* fungous + *-itat-, -itas* -ity] **1 :** the quality or state of being fungous **2 :** a fungous excrescence

fun·gous *also* **fun·gus** \'fəŋgəs\ *adj* [*fungous* fr. ME, fr. L *fungosus*, fr. *fungus* + *-osus* -ose; *fungus* alter. (influenced by *fungus*, n.) of *fungous*] **1 a :** of, relating to, or having the characteristics of a fungus or the Fungi ⟨an old stump with a flourishing ~ growth⟩ **b :** caused by a fungus ⟨a ~ disease⟩ **c :** infected by a fungus ⟨a dangerous shower stall with . . . *fungus* walls —Jean Stafford⟩ **2 :** FUNGOID 1

[1]**fun·gus** \'fəŋgəs\ *n, pl* **fun·gi** \'fən,jī, 'fəŋ,gī\ *also* **funguses** [L, prob. modif. of Gk *spongos* sponge, prob. of non-IE origin; akin to the source of Arm *sung* sponge] **1 :** any of numerous chiefly saprophytic or parasitic plants that constitute the division Fungi; lack true chlorophyll; have a body made up of single cells or of filamentous coenocytic or septate hyphae arranged in a soft mycelium or in some cases partially disposed in complex highly specialized and characteristic fruiting bodies; often exhibit complex alternation of generations with very distinct sexual and asexual phases; include the molds, mildews, rusts, smuts, mushrooms, toadstools, and puffballs, and usu. the yeasts, bacteria, and slime molds; and are often destructive pathogens of plants, man, and lower animals but have representatives that are used for food or are greatly valued for the organic fermentations that they produce ⟨a cellar wall covered with ~⟩ ⟨a *fungus*-proof coating for leather⟩ ⟨edible ground *fungi*⟩ **2** [LL or obs. F; obs. F, fr. MF, fr. LL, fr. L, fungus (plant)] **:** an abnormal spongy growth; *esp* **:** a mass of spongy granulations **3 :** infection with a fungus or disease caused by it; *specif* **:** a serious highly contagious skin disease of freshwater fishes esp. in hatcheries and aquaria caused by a mold (*Saprolegnia ferax*) **4 :** something resembling a fungus ⟨the blighting of everything fair . . . with the garish ~ of greed —Herman Wouk⟩

[2]**fungus** \"\ *vi* -ED/-ING/-ES **:** to become infected with a fungus ⟨a few impounded Chinook, however, ~*ed* rapidly and . . . usually died —*Scientific American*⟩

fungused *adj* [fr. past part. of [2]*fungus*] **:** infected with or affected by fungus **:** having a fungous growth

fungus gall *n* **:** a malformation of a plant resulting from an attack of a parasitic fungus

fungus garden *n* **:** a growth of fungus in the nests of various ants and beetles that is tended and used by them for food — compare AMBROSIA BEETLE, BROMATIUM

fungus gnat *n* **:** any of numerous small two-winged flies constituting the families Mycetophilidae and Sciaridae and having larvae that feed on fungi

fungus root *n* **:** MYCORRHIZA

fun house *n* **:** a building in an amusement park containing various devices designed to startle or amuse (as distorting mirrors, unexpected air blasts, fantastic lighted scenes) and arranged along a passage through which patrons walk

fu·nic \'fyünik\ *adj* [*funis* + *-ic*] **:** of, relating to, or originating in the umbilical cord

fu·ni·cle \'fyünəkəl\ *n* -s [NL *funiculus*] **:** FUNICULUS

[1]**fu·nic·u·lar** \(')fyü¦nikyələ(r), f(y)ə'n-\ *adj* [L *funiculus* + E *-ar*] **1 :** dependent on the tension of a cord or cable **2 :** having the form of or associated with a cord **3** [NL *funiculus* + E *-ar*] **:** of or consisting of a funiculus

[2]**funicular** \"\ *or* **funicular railway** *also* **fu·nic·u·laire** \=¦==¦la(a)|(ə)r, -¦le|, |ə\ *n* -s [[2]*funicular* (trans. of F *funiculaire*, n.) fr. [1]*funicular*; *funicular railway* (prob. trans. of F *chemin de fer funiculaire*) fr. [1]*funicular* + *railway*; *funiculaire* fr. F *funiculaire*, n., fr. *funiculaire*, adj., funicular, fr. L *funiculus* + F *-aire* -ary (fr. L *-arius*)] **:** a cable railway ascending a mountain; *esp* **:** one having the weight of an ascending car partly or wholly counterbalanced by the weight of a descending car

funicular polygon *n* **1 :** an open or closed figure that is not necessarily plane and that is formed by a rope or cord acted upon at a number of points by forces acting in various directions **2 :** a figure representing lines of resultant stress in a rigid body acted upon at various points by forces that may or may not be concurrent and may or may not be coplanar

fu·nic·u·li·tis \=,=='līd·əs\ *n* -ES [NL, fr. *funiculus* + *-itis*] **:** inflammation of the spermatic cord

fu·nic·u·lus \fyü'nikyələs, f(y)ə'n-\ *n, pl* **funicu·li** \-,lī, -,lē\ [NL, fr. L, small rope, dim. of *funis* rope; perh. akin to Gk *thōminx* cord] **1 :** any of various bodily structures more or less like a cord in form: **a :** UMBILICAL CORD **b :** one of the small bundles of fibers of which large nerves are made up **c :** any of certain bands of white matter in the brain and spinal cord; *specif* **:** COLUMN 6 c(1) **d :** SPERMATIC CORD **2 a :** the stalk of an ovule **b :** the hyphal cord attaching the peridiole to the peridium in certain fungi of the family Nidulariaceae **3 a :** a band of mesoblastic tissue extending from the stomach to the body wall in bryozoans **b :** the part of the antenna of an insect situated between the pedicel and the club **c :** a dorsal ligament connecting the petiole and propodeum of certain hymenoptera

fu·ni·pendulous \¦fyünə+\ *adj* [L *funis* rope + E *pendulous*] **:** suspended by a rope or cord

fu·nis \'fyünəs\ *n* -ES [NL, fr. L, rope] **:** UMBILICAL CORD

funj *or* **funji** *var of* FUNG

[1]**funk** \'fəŋk\ *n* -s [prob. of F dial. origin; akin to F dial. (French Flanders) *funquer* to give off smoke, F dial. (Picardy) *funquer, finquer*; these fr. ONF *funkier* to give off smoke, fr. (assumed) VL *fumicare*, alter. (influenced by such words as L *communicare* to share, impart, communicate) of L *fumigare* to give off smoke, fumigate — more at FUMIGATE] **:** a strong offensive smell

[2]**funk** \"\ *vb* -ED/-ING/-S [prob. of F dial. origin; akin to F dial. (French Flanders) *funquer* to give off smoke, F dial. (Picardy) *funquer, finquer*] *vt* **1 :** to subject to offensive smell or smoke **2 :** to use (as a pipe) in smoking ~ *vi* **:** to emit an offensive smell or smoke

[3]**funk** \'fu̇ŋk, 'fəŋk\ *n* -s [perh. fr. (assumed) obs. E *funk* spark, fr. ME *funke*, prob. fr. MD *vonke, vunke*; akin to OHG *funcho* spark, ON *funi* fire, Goth *fon*, OPruss *panno*, OHG *fiur* — more at FIRE] *dial Brit* **:** [3]PUNK 2

[4]**funk** \'fəŋk\ *vi* -ED/-ING/-S [prob. imit.] **1** *chiefly Scot* **:** [1]KICK 1 **2** *chiefly Scot* **:** to give vent to a rage or temper

[5]**funk** \", *dial Brit* " *or* 'fu̇ŋk\ *n* -s **1** *dial Brit* **:** BLOW; *specif* **:** [2]KICK 1 **2 :** a fit of ill humor **:** RAGE

[6]**funk** \'fəŋk\ *n* -s [prob. fr. obs. Flem *fonck* perturbation] **1 a :** a state of paralyzing fear or timidity ⟨the man was in such a ~ that he would not use his legs —Sinclair Lewis⟩ ⟨pure nerve and bluff on his part and pure ~ on the part of his opponents then saved him —*Nation*⟩ **b :** a depressed state of mind ⟨in a deep, blue ~ about life in the city . . ., she wanted to flee —Bill Hosokawa⟩ **2** [[7]*funk*] **:** one that funks **:** SHIRKER, COWARD ⟨he must be a bit of a ~ . . . to be afraid of a poor old lady —L.P.Hartley⟩

[7]**funk** \"\ *vb* -ED/-ING/-S [prob. fr. [6]*funk*] *vi* **:** to become frightened and shrink back **:** FLINCH, PANIC ⟨often . . . I have ~*ed* completely, such as the time I went up to the top of the 30-foot Olympic diving tower —Paul Gallico⟩ ~ *vt* **:** to funk at: **a :** to be afraid of **:** DREAD ⟨the seventeen-year-old . . . ~*s* riding the black horse but takes it on to please his dad —Leslie Rees⟩ ⟨it isn't a natural thing for a boy to ~ water —*Strand Mag.*⟩ **b :** to shrink from undertaking or facing ⟨every officer had either bungled or had ~*ed* the fight —R.H. Davis⟩ ⟨if the colleges ~ their job of turning out fully educated men —*New Yorker*⟩

[8]**funk** \"\ *n* -s *usu cap* [*Funk* (surname of *Peter Funk*) — more at PETER FUNK] **:** PETER FUNK

funk·er \'fəŋkə(r)\ *n* -s [[7]*funk* + *-er*] **:** [6]FUNK 2

funk hole *n* [[6]*funk*] **1 :** DUGOUT 2 **2 :** a place of safe retreat ⟨*funk holes* on the bridge and below decks plated with armor —Hanson W. Baldwin⟩ ⟨joined a volunteer corps as a *funk hole* to evade real military service —*Times Hist. of the War*⟩

[1]**fun·kia** \'fəŋkēə, 'fu̇ŋ-\ [NL, irreg. fr. C. H. *Funck* †1839 Ger. druggist and botanist + NL *-ia*] *syn of* HOSTA

[2]**funkia** \"\ *n* -s [NL *Funkia*] **:** PLANTAIN LILY

funk·i·ness \'fəŋkēnəs\ *n* -ES **:** the quality or state of being funky

funk money *n* [[6]*funk*] *Brit* **:** HOT MONEY

[1]**funky** \'fəŋkē\ *adj* -ER/-EST [[6]*funk* + *-y*] **:** being in a state of funk **:** PANICKY ⟨if he did not give up to you like a ~ traveler to a highwayman —George Meredith⟩

[2]**funky** \"\ *adj* -ER/-EST [[1]*funk* + *-y*] **1 :** MUSTY 2 **2 :** having an offensive odor **:** FOUL ⟨the ~ smell of stale bedclothes —James Jones⟩

funmaker \'=,==\ *n* **1 :** one that is given to playing jokes or setting up humorous situations ⟨evinced some disdain for the ~*s* —Walter Goodman⟩ **2 :** HUMORIST, COMEDIAN

funned *past of* FUN

[1]**fun·nel** \'fənᵊl\ *n* -s *often attrib* [ME *fonel, funel*, fr. OProv *fonilh*, fr. ML *fundibulum*, short for L *infundibulum*, fr. *infundere* to pour in, fr. *in* + *fundere* to pour — more at IN, FOUND] **1 a :** a utensil that has typically the shape of a hollow cone with a tube extending from the point, is designed to catch and direct a downward flow of liquid or some other substance, and is sometimes fitted or combined with a strainer or filter — see SEPARATORY FUNNEL **b :** something shaped like a funnel (as a conical part, passage, or hole); *specif* **:** the swimming funnel of a cephalopod **c :** one that serves as a constricted channel or central agent or organization through which something passes or is transmitted **2 :** a stack or flue for the escape of smoke or for ventilation; *specif* **:** the stack of a ship **3 :** a cylindrical band of metal; *esp* **:** one around the top of an upper mast around which the rigging fits **4 :** RUNNING GATE **5 :** FUNNEL CLOUD **6 :** a black usu. cylindrical metal hood attached to a spotlight to prevent the spill of light outside the illuminated area of a stage

funnel 1a

[2]**funnel** \"\ *vb* **funneled** *also* **funnelled**; **funneled** *also* **funnelled**; **funneling** *also* **funnelling**; **funnels** *vi* **1 :** to have or take the shape of a funnel **:** NARROW, WIDEN ⟨a shallow, rounded valley bottom ~*s* into a miniature gorge with steep bluffs —*Jour. of Geol.*⟩ **2 :** to move to or from a focal point or into a central channel ⟨the gang . . . ~*ed* onto the end of the jetty off the slope —R.O.Bowen⟩ ⟨orders were ~*ing* out to the ships from the flagship —Alexander Griffin⟩ **3 :** to pass through or as if through a funnel; *specif* **:** to move through a constricted passage or central medium ⟨the fierce winds which ~*ed* up the valley center —John Steinbeck⟩ ⟨through the great port ~*s* much of the overseas commerce —*Newsweek*⟩ ⟨thousands of pictures . . . ~*ed* back to the press and public through the public-relations division —Robert Moora⟩ ~ *vt* **1 :** to cause to funnel: **a :** to form into the shape of a funnel ⟨~*s* his hands and shouts through them⟩ **b :** to cause to move to or from a focal point or into a central channel ⟨traffic is ~*ed* into consolidation stations . . . and fanned out to destinations —*Distribution Age*⟩ ⟨airlift's traffic pattern ~*s* planes from widely separated . . . bases into two 20-mile-wide corridors —*Nat'l Geographic*⟩ **c :** to direct to a single recipient or distribute from a single source ⟨impurities ~*ed* into the air by automobiles, backyard bonfires, and factory chimneys —*N.Y. Times*⟩ ⟨~ the kerosine into the tank⟩ **d :** to send or direct through a narrow passage or central medium ⟨pass . . . through which were ~*ed* troops and supplies —F.T.Chapman⟩ ⟨cupped her hands over the lens of the flashlight, ~*ing* the light through a small opening —E.S. Gardner⟩ ⟨if a bank ~*s* its news through a public-relations firm —*Banking*⟩ **2 :** to serve as a means for the transmission or direction of ⟨accused the press of ~*ing* secret military information to Soviet Russia —*Newsweek*⟩ ⟨~ . . . high-caliber young people to the agency business —*Printers' Ink*⟩

[3]**fun·nel** \'fu̇nᵊl, 'fən-\ *n* -s [origin unknown] *dial Eng* **:** HINNY

funnel chest *also* **funnel breast** *n* **:** a depression of the anterior wall of the chest produced by a sinking in of the sternum

funnel cloud *n* **:** a funnel-shaped cloud that hangs below the greater thundercloud mass of a tornado

fun·nel·form \'fənᵊl,fȯrm\ *adj, of a corolla of a flower* **:** INFUNDIBULIFORM

funnel tube *n* **:** a long usu. glass tube that has a conical or bulging thistle-shaped top and sometimes a loop with or without bulbs serving as a safety trap and that is used esp. in the chemical laboratory for pouring liquid into an apparatus

fun·ni·ly \'fənᵊl|ē, -nəl|, |i\ *adv* **:** in a funny manner **:** ODDLY, LAUGHABLY ⟨~ enough I've wanted to talk to you for a month —Eden Phillpotts⟩

fun·ni·ment \-nēmənt, -nim-\ *n* -s **:** a funny saying or action

fun·ni·ness \-nēnəs, -nin-\ *n* -ES **:** the quality or state of being funny

funning *pres part of* FUN

[1]**fun·ny** \'fənē, -ni\ *adj* -ER/-EST [[2]*fun* + *-y*] **1 a :** affording light mirth and laughter typically by means of absurdity or oddness without much subtlety **:** AMUSING ⟨when they laughed it was not because they thought it was ~ but out of embarrassment —Barnaby Conrad⟩ ⟨he is the *funniest* writer in the world, with more kinds of fun than any other,

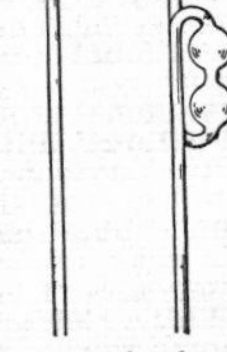

funnel tubes

from the broadest burlesque . . . to the final subtlety of the tear-stained smile —Robert Morse⟩ **b :** seeking or intended to amuse **:** FACETIOUS, TRIFLING ⟨don't take him so seriously; he was just being ~⟩ ⟨cut out the ~ business and get to work⟩ ⟨a tactical mistake — to . . . get ~ with an official —*Irish Digest*⟩ **2 a :** differing from the ordinary in a suspicious, perplexing, quaint, or eccentric way **:** QUEER, ODD, FISHY ⟨they'd surely think it ~ if we shot up the price now —C.G. Benjamin⟩ **b :** ILL ⟨came to the doctor with the vague complaint that he felt ~ all over⟩ ⟨he had been a bit ~ in the top story —Norman Lewis⟩ **c :** INTOXICATED **3 :** involving trickery or deception **:** SPURIOUS, UNDERHANDED ⟨warned them he would shoot if they tried any ~ stuff⟩ ⟨fake bidding and other ~ business at the auction⟩ **4 :** COMIC 3 ⟨reading the ~ page in a daily paper⟩ **syn** see LAUGHABLE

[2]funny \"\ *n* -ES [perh. fr. [1]*funny*] **:** a narrow clinker-built British scull with one pair of outriggers for the oarlocks

[3]funny \"\ *n* -ES [[1]*funny*] **1 :** one that is funny ⟨cast him as one of the *funnies* —Robertson Davies⟩ **2 :** a comic strip or comic section of a newspaper or periodical — usu. used in pl. ⟨follow their adventures in the *funnies*⟩ ⟨look at the *funnies*⟩

[4]funny *adv* **:** in an odd or amusing way ⟨made them suspicious when he began acting ~⟩

funny bone *n* [so called fr. the tingling felt when it is struck] **1 :** the place at the back of the elbow where the ulnar nerve rests against the medial condyle of the humerus **:** OLECRANON — called also *crazy bone* **2 :** SENSE OF HUMOR ⟨a joke that tickled his *funny bone*⟩

funny book *n* **:** COMIC BOOK

fun·ny·man \'==,man, -,maa(ə)n\ *n, pl* **funnymen :** a man with a reputation for humor **:** JOKER; *esp* **:** a professional humorist or comedian

funny-money \'==,==\ *n* **:** inflated currency; *esp* **:** currency inflated or otherwise manipulated for political or social purposes ⟨his opposition to the *funny-money* manipulations . . . brought him into disfavor —*Newsweek*⟩

funny paper *n* **:** FUNNY 2

fu·no·ri \fü'nōrē\ *n* -S [Jap] **1 :** any of several succulent marine algae esp. of the genus *Gloiopeltis* that furnish a tough glue **2** *or* **fu·no·rin** \-rən\ **:** a glue made from funori and used in the Orient as a size for textiles and paper

funs *pres 3d sing of* FUN, *pl of* FUN

fun·ster \'fənztə(r), -n(t)st-\ *n* -S **:** a person who seeks to amuse others **:** COMEDIAN, HUMORIST

fun·tu·mia \,fən·'t(y)ümēə\ *n* [NL, prob. fr. Ewe dial. *funtum* funtumia + NL *-ia*] **1** *cap* **:** a small genus of tropical African trees (family Apocynaceae) with opposite leaves and small axillary cymes of yellowish white flowers — see LAGOS RUBBER **2** -S **:** any tree of the genus *Funtumia*

[1]fur \R 'fər, + *vowel* 'fər·; –R 'fə̄, + *suffixal vowel* 'fər· *also* 'fə̄r, + *vowel in a following word* 'fər· *or* 'fə̄ *also* 'fə̄r\ *dial var of* FAR

[2]fur \"\ *vb* **furred; furred; furring; furs** [ME *furren*, fr. MF *fourrer* to line a garment, fr. OF *forrer*, fr. *fuerre* sheath, of Gmc origin; akin to OE *fōdder* case, sheath, OFris *fōder* lining of a coat, OHG *fuotar* case, sheath, Goth *fodr* sheath; akin to Gk *pōy* herd, flock, Skt *pāti* he watches over, protects; basic meaning: guarding cattle] *vt* **1 :** to cover, line, or trim with fur or a fabric resembling fur ⟨russet velvet *furred* with sables —Francis Hackett⟩ **2 a :** to clothe with fur — usu. used in passive ⟨it was the 29th May . . . and still the fair were *furred* —*Tinsley's Mag.*⟩ **b :** to facilitate the growth of fur on (an animal) ⟨the same house will be used in September through November for *furring* about 600 mink —*Nat'l Fur News*⟩ **3 :** to coat or clog as if with fur ⟨dust had *furred* the beams and lodged on ridges in the plaster —Clemence Dane⟩ **4** *carpentry* **:** to apply furring to **:** support on furring — often used with *down, out, up* ⟨~ down a ceiling⟩ **~** *vi* **1 a :** to become coated or clogged as if with fur ⟨the pipes . . . *furred* up with lime —*English Digest*⟩ **b :** to become fluffy ⟨her tail *furred* out, her hair rose, and she assumed the typical attitude of a cat close-cornered by a dog —Archibald Rutledge⟩ **2 :** to grow fur ⟨mink ~ better in cool regions⟩

[3]fur \"\ *n* -S *see sense 4b* [ME *furre*, prob. fr. *furren*, v.] **1 :** a piece of the dressed pelt of an animal (as ermine, rabbit, seal) used as a material to make, trim, or line wearing apparel or other articles ⟨advertisers should invariably indicate by suitable descriptive matter . . . just what the ~ is —*Chamber of Commerce Bull.*⟩ **2 a :** an article of clothing made of fur ⟨her new ~ was a full-length muskrat coat⟩ **b :** one or more dressed pelts fashioned into a woman's neckpiece — usu. used in pl. ⟨a set of ~s⟩ **c :** a trimming or lining of fur on a garment worn as a mark of office or state or as a badge of a university degree ⟨add . . . wisdom to the ~s of power —William Shenstone⟩ **3 :** the fine soft thick hairy covering or coat of a mammal usu. consisting of a double coating of hair that includes a layer of comparatively short soft curly barbed hairs next to the skin protected by longer smoother stiffer hairs that grow up through these — compare HAIR 2, PELAGE, WOOL 1 **4 a furs** *pl* **:** the skins of animals with the fur attached **:** PELTRY ⟨a cargo of ~s⟩ **b** *pl usu* **fur :** fur-bearing animals ⟨many trainers break their retrievers of ~ altogether, not allowing them to see or carry rabbits for at least the first two seasons —P.R.A.Moxon⟩ **5 :** any of several patterns used in heraldry that are conventionally classified as tinctures **6 :** a coating resembling or suggesting fur: as **a :** a coat of epithelial debris on the tongue **b :** a deposit formed on the interior of boilers and other vessels by hard water and composed chiefly of carbonates **c :** the thick pile of a fabric (as chenille) **d :** the rough surface of lumber after sawing **7 :** a piece of wood nailed on a wall or ceiling to serve as base for a finished surface — compare FURRING 3b(1)

[4]fur \"\ *adj* **:** of or relating to fur

[5]fur \"\ *n* -S [ME, var. of *furgh, forwe, forow* — more at FURROW] *dial Brit* **:** FURROW

fur- *or* **furo-** *comb form* [ISV, fr. *furfural*] **1 :** related to furan ⟨*fur*odiazole⟩, furfural ⟨*fur*oin⟩, or furoic acid ⟨2-*fur*amide⟩ **2 :** containing a furan ring fused on one side to one side of another ring ⟨*furo*quinoline⟩

fur *abbr* **1** furlong **2** furlough **3** further

Fu·ra·cin \'fyùrəsən\ *trademark* — used for nitrofurazone

fu·ra·cious \fyə'rāshəs\ *adj* [L *furac-, furax* thievish (fr. *fur* thief) + E *-ious* — more at FURTIVE] *archaic* **:** given to theft **:** THIEVISH

fu·ral \'fyù,ral\ *n* -S [ISV *fur-* + *-al*] **:** FURFURYLIDENE

fur·aldehyde \fyə'r, (')fyù¦r+,\ *n* [alter. of *furfuraldehyde* — more at FURFURAL] **:** FURFURAL 1

fu·ran \'fyù,ran, fyə'r-\ *also* **fu·rane** \-rān\ *n* -S [*furan*, *furane*, ISV *fur-* + *-an* or *-ane*] **1 :** a flammable liquid compound C_4H_4O that contains four carbon atoms and one oxygen atom in a ring, that is obtained from wood oils of certain pines but is usu. made synthetically from furfural by catalytic removal of the aldehyde group, and that is used chiefly in making tetrahydrofuran and other intermediates for the manufacture of nylon — compare STRUCTURAL FORMULA **2 :** a derivative of furan containing the furan ring

O; α·HC 5 1 2 CH α; β·HC 4 3 CH β

furan

fu·ra·noid \'fyùrə,nȯid\ *also* **fu·roid** \-ü,rȯid\ *adj* [*furan* or *fur-* + *-oid*] **:** resembling furan in chemical structure **:** characterized by the presence of the furan ring

fu·ra·nose \'fyùrə,nōs *also* -ōz\ *n* -S [*furan* + *-ose*] **:** a glycose sugar in the form of a cyclic hemiacetal containing a 5-member ring

fu·ran·o·side \fyə'ranə,sīd, -,səd\ *n* -S [*furanose* + *-ide*] **:** a glycoside containing the ring characteristic of a furanose

furan resin *n* **:** any of numerous resins made from derivatives of furan (as furfuryl alcohol or furfural) and used chiefly in adhesives and in impregnating and coating compositions

furbearer \'=,==\ *n* **:** an animal that bears fur esp. of a commercially desired quality

[1]fur·be·low \'fərbə,lō, 'fə̄b-,'fəib-\ *n* -S [by folk etymology fr. F dial. *farbella, ferbela*] **1 a :** a pleated or gathered piece of material **:** RUFFLE; *specif* **:** a flounce on women's clothing ⟨your slip . . . uncluttered by the conventional ~s of women's dresses —Lois Long⟩ **b :** something that resembles or suggests a furbelow esp. in being showy or superfluous ⟨its plate glass and the intricate ~s of its facade testified to suddenly acquired money —Jean Stafford⟩ ⟨dealt with . . . all phases and facets and ~s of our literary effort —Harvey Breit⟩ **2** *dial Eng* **:** a sea tangle (*Laminaria bulbosa*)

[2]furbelow \"\ *vt* -ED/-ING/-S **:** to trim with or as if with a furbelow ⟨it is the same old capitalist dog ~*ed* in bright nationalist ribbons —John Gunther⟩

fur·bish \'fərbish, 'fə̄b-, 'fəib-, -bēsh, *chiefly in pres part* -bəsh\ *vt* -ED/-ING/-ES [ME *furbisshen*, fr. MF *fourbiss-*, stem of *fourbir* to polish, of Gmc origin; akin to OHG *furben* to clean, sweep, polish] **1 :** to make lustrous **:** BURNISH, POLISH ⟨his coat of mail, ~*ed* so recently and so zealously that it shone like glass —T.B.Costain⟩ ⟨where the Bible is being revised . . . the church has reached maturity and seeks to improve and ~ its own weapons —Eric Fenn⟩ **2 :** to give a new look to **:** RENOVATE, REVIVE — often used with *up* ⟨aim of the restoration has been . . . to ~ up an old town —J.P.Bishop⟩ ⟨I am convinced we should take out the copybooks and ~ up their maxims —E.F.Mohler⟩

fur·bish·er \-shə(r)\ *n* -S [ME *furbissher*, fr. *furbisshen* + *-er*] *archaic* **:** one that furbishes; *esp* **:** one that furbishes arms and armor

fur breeder *n* **:** one that breeds fur-bearing animals esp. for commercial purposes

fur·ca \'fərkə\ *n, pl* **fur·cae** \-r,kī, -r,sē\ [NL, fr. L, fork — more at FORK] **:** a forked process: **a :** an internal skeletal projection from the ventral thoracic wall in certain insects **b :** a chitinous structure in the proboscis of certain flies **c :** the two-forked last abdominal segment of certain crustaceans **d :** FORCEPS 2

fur·cal \-rkəl\ *adj* [L *furca* + E *-al*] **:** FORKED, FURCATE — used chiefly of anatomical structures

fur·ca·sternum \¦fərkə+\ *n, pl* **furcasterna** *or* **furcasternums** [NL, fr. *furca* + *sternum*] **1 :** a part of the insect sternum bearing the furca **2 :** the posterior plate of an insect sternum **:** STERNELLUM

[1]fur·cate \'fər,kāt, -,kət\ *adj* [LL *furcatus*, fr. L *furca* + *-atus* -ate] **:** branching like a fork **:** FORKED — **fur·cate·ly** *adv*

[2]fur·cate \-,kāt\ *vi* -ED/-ING/-S [ML *furcatus*, past part. of *furcare*, fr. L *furca*] **:** to branch like a fork **syn** see BRANCH

fur·ca·tion \,fər'kāshən\ *n* -S [ML *furcation-, furcatio*, fr. *furcatus* + L *-ion-, -io* -ion] **1 :** something that is branched **:** FORK **2 :** the act or process of branching

fur·cel·lar·ia \,fərsə'la(a)rēə\ *n, cap* [irreg. fr. L *furcilla* small fork (dim. of *furca*) + NL *-aria*] **:** a genus of red algae of the family Nemastomaceae whose only known species (*F. fastigiata*) is common in the No. Atlantic

fur·cel·late \'fərsə,lāt, ,fər'selət\ *adj* [irreg. fr. L *furcilla* + E *-ate*] **:** minutely or slightly furcate

fur·cif·er·ous \¦fər¦sif(ə)rəs\ *adj* [L *furci-* (fr. *furca* fork) + E *-ferous* — more at FORK] **:** having a forked appendage — used esp. of certain lepidopterous larvae

fur·ci·form \'fərsə,fȯrm\ *adj* [L *furci-* + E *-form*] **:** FORKED

fur·cil·ia \,fər'silēə\ *n* -S [NL, fr. L *furca*] **:** an intermediate larva of a euphausid in which eye development is nearly adult but biramous swimming appendages are retained

fur·co·cer·cous \¦fərkō¦sərkəs\ *adj* [*furco-* (fr. L *furca*) + *-cercous* (fr. Gk *kerkos* tail)] *of a cercaria* **:** having the tail forked

fur·craea \,fər'krēə, '==\ *n, cap* [NL, after Count Antoine F. de *Fourcroy* †1809 Fr. chemist] **:** a small genus of tropical American plants (family Amaryllidaceae) closely related to and resembling *Agave* but distinguished by rotate white flowers — see CAJUN

fur·cu·la \'fərkyələ\ *n, pl* **furcu·lae** \-,lē\ [NL, fr. L, forked prop, dim. of *furca* fork — more at FORK] **1 :** a forked process or structure; *specif* **:** WISHBONE **2 :** an elevation on the embryonic floor of the pharynx from which the epiglottis develops **3 :** any of various appendages of insects; *specif* **:** the forked leaping appendage arising from the fourth abdominal segment of a collembolan — **fur·cu·lar** \-lə(r)\ *adj*

fur·cu·lum \-ləm\ *n, pl* **furcu·la** \-lə\ [NL, fr. L *furca* + *-ulum* (neut. dim. suffix)] **:** FURCULA; *esp* **:** WISHBONE

fur·dle \'fərdᵊl\ *vt* -ED/-ING/-S [modif. of MF *fardeler* to pack up — more at FARDEL] *now dial Eng* **:** to fold up **:** FURL

fur fabric *n* **:** a fabric usu. woven or knitted from rayon, wool, or cotton and made with a pile that is dyed and finished to resemble an animal's fur

fur farm *n* **:** a farm devoted to the raising of fur-bearing animals in a state of semidomestication typically in pens or on protected islands

fur farming *n* **:** the act or process of raising fur-bearing animals commercially for their pelts

fur·fur \'fərfər\ *n* -ES [L (also, bran); akin to L *frendere* to crush, bruise, grind — more at GRIND] **1 :** an exfoliation of a surface esp. of the epidermis **:** DANDRUFF, SCURF **2 fur·fu·res** \-rf(y)ə,rēz\ *pl* **:** flaky particles (as of scurf)

fur·fu·ra·ceous \¦fərf(y)ə¦rāshəs\ *adj* [LL *furfuraceus*, fr. L *furfur* + *-aceus* -aceous] **:** consisting of or covered with flaky particles **:** SCALY, SCURFY

fur·fu·ral \'fərf(y)ə,ral\ *n* [*furfural*, ISV, short for *furfuraldehyde*, fr. L *furfur* bran + ISV *aldehyde*] **1** *also* **fur·fur·aldehyde** \¦fərf(y)ə¦r+-\ **:** a liquid aldehyde C_4H_3OCHO that turns yellow to brown in air and has a penetrating odor, that is usu. made from corncobs, oat hulls, cottonseed hulls, or other materials containing pentosans by digestion with acid, and that is used chiefly in making furan and its derivatives (as intermediates for the manufacture of nylon), in making phenolic resins, and as a solvent (as for refining oils from petroleum) — called also *furaldehyde, 2-furaldehyde* **2 :** FURFURYLIDENE

fur·fu·ran \'fərf(y)ə,ran\ *n* [ISV *furfural* + *-an*] **:** FURAN

fur·fu·ra·tion \,fərf(y)ə'rāshən\ *n* -S [L *furfur* scurf + E *-ation*] **:** a scaling off (as of dandruff) **:** DESQUAMATION

fur·fu·rous \'fərf(y)ərəs\ *adj* [L *furfurosus* resembling bran, fr. *furfur* + *-osus* -ous] *archaic* **:** FURFURACEOUS

fur·fu·ryl \'fərf(y)ərəl, -)ə(,)ril\ *n* [ISV *furfural* + *-yl*] **:** the univalent radical $C_4H_3OCH_2$ derived from furfuryl alcohol by removal of the hydroxyl group; 2-furyl-methyl

furfuryl alcohol *n* **:** a liquid $C_4H_3OCH_2OH$ that turns amber to black in air, that occurs in the oil of roasted coffee and in cloves and is made by catalytic hydrogenation of furfural, and that is used chiefly in making dark corrosion-resistant resins and as a solvent; 2-furan-methanol

fur·fu·ryl·i·dene \,fərf(y)ə'rilə,dēn\ *n* -S [ISV *furfuryl* + *-idene*] **:** the bivalent radical C_4H_3OCH< derived from furfural by removal of the aldehydic oxygen atom

fu·ri·ant \'f(y)ùrē,änt, ,==\ *n* -S [G & Czech, fr. L *furiant-*, *furians* pres. part. of *furiare* to enrage, fr. *furia* madness, fury — more at FURY] **:** a spirited Bohemian dance tune in ¾ time with shifting accents

fu·ri·bund \'fyùrə(,)bənd\ *adj* [L *furibundus*, fr. *furere* to be mad, rage — more at DUST] **:** full of fury **:** FRENZIED, RAGING

furies *pl of* FURY

fu·rio·sa·men·te \,fyùrē,ōsə'men·(,)tā, (,)fyùr,yō\ *adv* [It, fr. *furioso*] **:** FURIOUSLY — used as a direction in music

fu·ri·os·i·ty \,fyùrē'äsəd·ē\ *n* -ES [ME *furiosite*, fr. MF or LL; MF *furiosité*, fr. LL *furiositat-, furiositas*, fr. L *furiosus* + *-itat-, -itas* -ity] **1** *Scots law* **:** INSANITY **2 :** the quality or state of being furious **:** FURY

[1]fu·ri·o·so \,fyùrē'ō(,)sō, fyùr'yō-\ *n* -S [It, fr. *furioso*, adj.] **:** a furious or insane man **:** FANATIC

[2]furioso \"\ *adj* (*or adv*) [It, fr. L *furiosus*] **:** with great force or vigor — used chiefly as a direction in music

fu·ri·ous \'fyùrēəs, -ür-\ *adj* [ME, fr. MF *furieus*, fr. L *furiosus*, fr. *furia* madness, rage, fury + *-osus* -ous — more at FURY] **1 a :** exhibiting or goaded by anger or passion **:** FIERCE, VIOLENT ⟨fully expects a ~ renewal of the attacks against him —Howard Rushmore⟩ ⟨makes me ~ to think what slaves we were —Corra Harris⟩ **b :** appearing or moving as if angry **:** STORMY, TURBULENT ⟨the ~ outbursts of swirling flame from the palaces which have been set on fire —Laurence Binyon⟩ **c :** full of noise and excitement **:** BOISTEROUS ⟨ducking one another, dashing water with cupped hands, the fun was fast and ~ —C.P.Conigrave⟩ **d :** full of activity **:** ENERGETIC, VIGOROUS ⟨this loading job normally consumed for the . . . crew a leisurely day — or a ~ half of one —Wirt Williams⟩ **2 a :** existing in the height of its distinctive character **:** INTENSE ⟨everywhere the ecstatic green of California's brief and ~ spring —Wallace Stegner⟩ **b :** characterized by excess **:** EXTRAVAGANT ⟨lost such ~ sums —Mary W. Montagu⟩ **3 a** *Scots law* **:** mentally deranged **:** INSANE **b :** characterized by unreasoned enthusiasm **:** FANATICAL ⟨gradually formulated a theory to support his ~ conviction —*Time*⟩

furious fits *n pl but sing in constr* **:** CANINE HYSTERIA

fu·ri·ous·ly *adv* [ME, fr. *furious* + *-ly*] **1 a :** in an impassioned manner **:** ANGRILY, HOTLY ⟨an alarm is raised and a number of Moors on horseback ~ pursue them —Bernard De Voto⟩ **b :** in a turbulent manner **:** WILDLY ⟨the wind ran ~, tearing leaves off trees, carrying great volumes of dust before it —Sherwood Anderson⟩ **2 :** in a lively manner **:** ENERGETICALLY ⟨she would heave her huge body onto the saddle and go pedaling ~ up the narrow street —Arnold Hill⟩ **3 :** in an intensive manner or degree **:** EXTREMELY ⟨decorated with ~ modern murals —Frederic Morton⟩ ⟨a ~ colorful futurist study —S.E.Hyman⟩

fu·ri·ous·ness *n* -ES *archaic* **:** the quality or state of being furious

furious rabies *n* **:** rabies characterized by spasm of the muscles of throat and diaphragm, choking, salivation, extreme excitement, and evidence of fear often manifested by indiscriminate snapping at objects — compare DUMB RABIES

fu·ri·son \'fyùrəsən, -rəzən\ *n* -S [LG *vūrisern*, fr. MLG, fr. *vūr* fire (akin to OHG *fiur*) + *īsern* iron; akin to OHG *īsan*, *īsarn* — more at FIRE, IRON] **:** an iron used to strike fire from a flint — used esp. in heraldry

[1]furl \'fərl, *esp before pause or consonant* 'fər·əl; 'fə̄l, 'fəil\ *vb* -ED/-ING/-S [MF *ferler*, fr. ONF *ferlier* to tie tightly, fr. OF *fer, ferm* tight, fast (fr. L *firmus* firm) + *lier* to tie (fr. L *ligare*) — more at FIRM, LIGATURE] *vt* **1 a :** to roll up or gather in (a sail) and fasten close to a yard or mast **b :** to draw in (a flag) and secure to a staff **c :** to roll up as if furling a sail or a flag ⟨he was supposed to ~ the side flaps in the morning and let them down at night —Norman Mailer⟩ **2 :** to draw into ripples or folds **:** CURL, WRINKLE ⟨it shrivels behind ~*ed* leaves —Clive Arden⟩ **3 :** COVER, WRAP, ENFOLD ⟨the peacock . . . was itself ~*ed* into the night and the blackness closed in on them again —Rebecca West⟩ **~** *vi* **1 :** to curl or fold spirally ⟨she looked at the trees and at the ~*ing* blooms of the iris —Millen Brand⟩ **2 :** to roll away ⟨years of misery and sin ~ off and leave her heaven blue —J.R.Lowell⟩

[2]furl \"\ *n* -S **:** the act of furling or state of being furled **:** something that is furled

fur·lan \'fù(ə)rlən, fùr'län\ *n* -S *cap* [It *furlano, forlano, friulano*, fr. *Friuli*, district in Italy + It *-ano* -an] **:** FRIULIAN

furlana *var of* FORLANA

furl·er \'fərlər; 'fə̄lə(r, 'fəil-\ *n* -S **:** one that furls

fur·less \'fərləs, 'fə̄l-\ *adj* **:** lacking fur ⟨a ~ animal⟩

fur·long \'fər,lȯŋ, 'fə̄,l-, 'fəi,l- *also* -läŋ\ *n* -S [ME, fr. OE *furlang*, fr. *furh* furrow + *lang* long — more at FURROW, LONG] **1 a :** a unit of distance equal to ⅛ statute mile, 40 rods, 220 yards, or 201.17 meters **b :** SQUARE FURLONG **2** *now dial Eng* **a :** a division of an unenclosed field **b :** a strip of newly plowed land between main furrows

[1]fur·lough \'fər(,)lō, 'fə̄(-, 'fəi(-\ *n* -S [D *verlof*, lit., permission, fr. MD *verlof*, fr. *ver-* for- (akin to OHG *fir-*) + *lof* permission; akin to MHG *loube* permission — more at LEAVE] **1 a :** a leave of absence granted to a governmental or institutional employee (as a soldier, civil servant, or missionary) **b :** a document authorizing such a leave of absence **2 a :** a leave of absence granted by an employer to an employee; *esp* **:** a leave of absence granted at the employee's request **b :** a temporary lack of employment due to economic conditions **:** LAYOFF

[2]furlough \"\ *vb* -ED/-ING/-S *vt* **1 :** to grant a leave of absence to ⟨it is doubtful that the army will cooperate in extending deferments or in ~*ing* skilled workers —*Atlantic*⟩ **2 :** to subject to an enforced leave of absence **:** lay off ⟨the railroad recently announced it would ~ more than 2250 employees for five days . . . because of a continued decline in business —*Wall Street Jour.*⟩ **~** *vi* **:** to spend a furlough ⟨throngs of ~*ing* service people and chippies on . . . Broadway and Times Square —R.A.Gunnison⟩

furm \'fürm\ *Scot var of* [1]FORM 6b

furmenty *or* **furmety** *or* **furmity** *var of* FRUMENTY

furn *abbr* **1** furnished **2** furniture

[1]fur·nace \'fərnəs, 'fə̄n-,'fəin-\ *n* -S *often attrib* [ME *furneis, furnas*, fr. OF *fornaise, fournaise*, fr. L *fornac-, fornax*; akin to L *formus* warm — more at WARM] **1 :** an apparatus for the production or application of heat: as **a :** an enclosed structure for reducing ore or melting or heat-treating metal by the application of intense heat produced typically by full combustion — compare HEARTH **b :** an oven for firing pottery **:** KILN **c :** an apparatus usu. consisting of a firepot and a system of pipes to carry heat to all parts of a building **d :** an atomic reactor **2** *archaic* **:** a boiler or crucible **3 :** something that resembles or has the effect of a furnace ⟨the immense ~s of the stars —J.A.Thomson & Patrick Geddes⟩ ⟨as gold is refined in the crucible so do the great Christian virtues . . . flow in all their purity from the ~ of man's affliction —W.F.Hambly⟩

[2]furnace \"\ *vt* -ED/-ING/-S **1** *obs* **:** to give forth like a furnace ⟨he ~s the thick sighs from him —Shak.⟩ **2 a :** to subject to heat ⟨a mixture of extremely fine silica and . . . lead oxide is *furnaced* for two hours at 625°C —E.R.Riegel⟩ **b :** to appear to heat **:** make glow ⟨the Indian House stood *furnaced* in melancholy red by a September sunset —William Sansom⟩

furnace black *or* **furnace combustion black** *n* **:** a carbon black made by the partial combustion of liquid and gaseous hydrocarbons (as petroleum distillates or refinery residues, natural gas, or a mixture of gas and oil) in a closed furnace or retort

fur·nace·man \-,man, -,mən\ *n, pl* **furnacemen 1 :** one who installs and repairs hot-air furnaces **2 :** a man who tends a furnace esp. a metallurgical furnace

furnace oil *n* **:** a fuel oil that can be burned in an atomizing burner and that is usu. a distilled product having a gravity of from 36° to 40° Bé

Fur·nace·stat \-nə(s)s,tat\ *trademark* — used for a thermostatic control for a hot-air-furnace fan to ensure delivery of properly heated air

furnace thermal black *n* **:** THERMAL BLACK

fur·nage \'fərnij\ *n* -S [ME, fr. MF *fornage*, fr. *forn, for, four* oven (fr. L *furnus*) + *-age*; akin to L *formus* warm — more at WARM] **:** a price paid for the use of an oven; *specif* **:** the fee paid a feudal lord by his tenants for the right to bake in his oven

fur·na·ri·idae \,fərnə'rīə,dē\ *n pl, cap* [NL, fr. *Furnarius*, type genus (fr. L *furnarius* baker, fr. *furnus* + *-arius* -ary) + *-idae*] **:** a family of tropical American birds comprising the ovenbirds and related forms and with the woodhewers, the antbirds, and several other tropical American birds forming a superfamily of the Tyranni

[1]fur·nish \'fərnish, 'fə̄n-,'fəin-, -nēsh, *chiefly in pres part* -nəsh\ *vb* -ED/-ING/-ES [ME *furnisshen*, fr. MF *furniss-, fourniss-, forniss-*, stem of *furnir, fournir, fornir* to complete, carry out, equip, of Gmc origin; akin to OHG *frummen* to carry out, complete, OS *frummian*; causative-denominatives fr. the n. represented by OHG *fruma* advantage, profit — more at FOREMOST] *vt* **1 a :** to provide or supply with what is needed, useful, or desirable **:** EQUIP ⟨'tis now but four o'clock. We have two hours to ~ us —Shak.⟩ — usu. used with following *with* ⟨the wary collector sends for someone who can ~ him with . . . evidence of the authenticity of his picture —Clive Bell⟩ ⟨fins . . . ~*ed* with strong pointed spines — Richard Semon⟩ **b :** to supply (as a room or building) with furniture or appliances **:** equip for use ⟨a luxuriously ~*ed* reception room —John Pudney⟩ **2** *obs* **:** to fit out for work or active service ⟨Bucephalus . . . being saddled and ~*ed* . . . could endure none but Alexander —Edward Topsell⟩ **3** *obs* **:** ORNAMENT, DECORATE ⟨I'll show thee some attires and have thy counsel which is the best to ~ me tomorrow —Shak.⟩ **4 :** to make a gift of (something needed or desirable) **:** CONTRIBUTE, AFFORD, YIELD ⟨the southeast trade winds and the tropical foliage ~ alleviating coolness —H.A.Chippendale⟩ **~** *vi* **1 :** to equip living quarters with furniture and appliances ⟨the modern young couple about to ~ —R.D.Benn⟩ **2** *chiefly dial Brit* **:** to gain strength and weight **:** become fully developed **:** MATURE: as **a** *of a horse* **:** to gain strength and stamina

b : to have a fully developed comb, hackle, saddle, and tail ⟨in White Leghorns . . . there is the type which ~*es* slowly, the comb being slow in the growing and the feathering long —*Australasian*⟩

syn EQUIP, OUTFIT, APPOINT, ARM, ACCOUTER: FURNISH is a general term indicating supplying and providing; it may apply to anything supplied ⟨music was *furnished* by the United States Army Band —*Amer. Guide Series: Oreg.*⟩ ⟨such education as the local schools could *furnish* —G.F.Smythe⟩ but is used typically with tangible more or less permanent articles for use ⟨to *furnish* a room⟩ EQUIP, likewise wide in application ⟨*equip* oneself to practice law⟩, applies often to the provision of specific things making for greater convenience or utility ⟨the house is three stories high, and is *equipped* with a conservatory —*Amer. Guide Series: N. J.*⟩ ⟨delightful picnic spots along the way, *equipped* with outdoor fireplaces, lunch tables, and springwater —*Amer. Guide Series: Vt.*⟩ OUTFIT suggests provision of various things needed for a journey, expedition, or occasion ⟨it took several days to *outfit* me for my journey to Washington —Willa Cather⟩ ⟨an English ship *outfitted* by Raleigh arrived with supplies and reinforcements —*Amer. Guide Series: N. C.*⟩ APPOINT may suggest elegant equipment; the word is less used today in this sense than previously ⟨the interior has been *appointed* with pieces associated with the Colonial period —*Amer. Guide Series: N. Y. City*⟩ ⟨it has beautifully *appointed* lounges, cafeteria, dining room, meeting rooms —*Amer. Guide Series: Mich.*⟩ ARM often applies to supplying or furnishing that which adds to strength or security, to means of defense or offense ⟨ever youthful in ardor, and *armed* with the shining sword of truth, he fought and killed many ogres who oppressed the children of the light —M.R.Cohen⟩ ⟨*armed* with wide powers and unlimited resources —T.D.McCormick⟩ ACCOUTER indicates the providing of dress, personal equipment, and weapons for combat or as if for combat ⟨lying hidden in her bosom was a loaded pistol. Lying hidden at her waist was a sharpened dagger. Thus *accoutered* . . . Madame Defarge took her way —Charles Dickens⟩ ⟨the fully *accoutered* members of a Wild West show —*Saturday Rev.*⟩ **syn** see in addition PROVIDE

²furnish \"\ *n* -ES **1 :** an act or instance of furnishing **2 :** something furnished: as **a :** the raw materials placed in a beater for making paper pulp **b** *South* **:** groceries and supplies provided on credit to a plantation tenant by the owner

furnished *adj* [ME *furnisshed*, fr. past part. of *furnisshen*] **1 :** provided with essentials **:** EQUIPPED ⟨a completely ~ toolbox⟩ **2** *obs* **:** possessing a quantity **:** STOCKED ⟨these rivers are very well ~ with fish —Daniel Denton⟩ **3 :** containing furniture ⟨the tenant of a ~ house —F.M.Ford⟩ **4** *heraldry* **:** provided with equipment ⟨a horse passant ~⟩

fur·nish·er \-shə(r)\ *n* -S **1 :** one that furnishes; *specif* **:** a dealer in men's furnishings **2 :** a revolving brush or roller that supplies the color used in printing textiles

furnishing *n* -S [ME *furnisshing*, fr. gerund of *furnisshen*] **1** *archaic* **:** the act or process of supplying furniture or equipment ⟨rudder irons . . . of this company's ~ —Thomas Hale⟩ **2 a :** an article or accessory of dress; *specif* **:** HABERDASHERY — usu. used in pl. ⟨a sale on shirts and other ~*s* for men⟩ **b :** an ornamental appendage of an animal ⟨the unusual butterfly comb, the crest and muffled face, look quite attractive . . . but such ~*s* do not appeal to the usual run of commercial poultry keepers —*Farmer's Weekly (So. Africa)*⟩ **3 :** an object or fixture that tends to increase comfort or utility ⟨dead bodies . . . surrounded by all the ~*s* they had made use of in life —Edith Hamilton⟩ ⟨a remarkable ability to . . . depict the ~*s* of a small town —J.D.Hart⟩; *specif* **:** an article of furniture for the interior of a building — usu. used in pl. ⟨a variety of ~*s*, among them such important upholstered pieces as an elegant long couch with loose down cushions —*New Yorker*⟩

fur·nish·ment \-shmənt\ *n* -S **1 a :** the act or process of furnishing **b :** the quality or state of being furnished **2 furnishments** *pl, archaic* **:** necessary equipment and supplies; *specif* **:** MUNITIONS ⟨purveyor for the army . . . vastly rich; grown so as contractor of ~*s* which he never furnishes —Lew Wallace⟩

furnish out *vt* **1 :** to provide a supply of (what is needed) **:** COMPLETE ⟨from among the impoverished citizens he *furnished out* masses of colonists to repair the decay of ancient cities —J.A.Froude⟩ **2 :** to provide material for **:** SUPPLY ⟨the assorted sins and failings which *furnish out* so many of the pages in . . . biographies —F.L.Mott⟩ **3** *obs* **:** to outfit esp. for military action **:** EQUIP

fur·ni·ture \ˈfərnəchər, ˈfə̄nəchə(r), ˈfəinəchə(r, -nēch- *sometimes* -ˌchu̇(ə)r *or* -u̇ə\ *n* -S *often attrib* [MF *fourniture*, fr. *fournir, furnir, fornir* to complete, carry out, equip — more at FURNISH] **1** *obs* **a** (1) **:** the act of furnishing or decorating (2) **:** an article of decoration **:** ORNAMENT ⟨see the barge be ready and fit it with such ~ as suits the greatness of his person —Shak.⟩ **b :** the execution of a plan ⟨toward the ~ of his hostile designs he had extraordinary subsidy —John Speed⟩ **2 a** *obs* **:** STOCK, STORE, SUPPLY ⟨we were particularly searched to the effect we carried in no ~ of arms nor powder —William Lithgow⟩ **b :** that by which something is filled **:** CONTENTS ⟨the Constitution has the normal ~ of all constitutions—provisions for amendment, for admitting member states —T.H.White *b*1915⟩ **3 :** something that is necessary, useful, or desirable: as **a** *archaic* **:** the harness and trappings esp. of a horse ⟨the saddles and rich ~ of the cavalry —Edward Gibbon⟩ **b :** a fund of ideas or information **:** mental equipment ⟨my intellectual ~ consists of an assortment of general propositions —O.W.Holmes †1935⟩ **c** *obs* **:** personal belongings **:** CLOTHING, ARMOR ⟨the king would find himself incommoded with all that ~ upon his back —Andrew Marvell⟩ **d :** articles of convenience or decoration used to furnish living quarters, offices, public and private buildings — usu. used of movable articles (as tables and chairs) as distinguished from such permanent installations as bathroom fixtures **e :** equipment needed for work or active service; *specif* **:** the tackle of a ship **f :** a mixture stop in a pipe organ **4** *archaic* **:** the state of being equipped **:** readiness for action ⟨you will inform yourself of the ~ of the French on the Mediterranean seas —John Evelyn⟩ **5 :** useful or decorative appendages **:** ACCESSORIES: as **a :** the mountings of a gun **b :** pieces of wood or metal less than type high that are placed in printing forms to fill in blank spaces or used with quoins to fasten matter in a chase **c :** HARDWARE; *specif* **:** the metal trimmings on a coffin **d :** background details ⟨mere ~ counts for a good deal in the best romances, and they are full of descriptions of riches and splendors —W.P.Ker⟩

furniture beetle *also* **furniture borer** *n* **:** a small borer beetle (*Anobium punctatum*) resembling a powder-post beetle but having the head bent under the thorax and feeding on both sapwood and heartwood of seasoned timber; *broadly* **:** a beetle of the family Anobiidae

furniture worker *n* **:** a worker who constructs wooden furniture and accessories to be installed in airplanes

furo- — see FUR-

fu·ro·ate \ˈfyu̇rəˌwāt\ *n* -S [*fur-* + *-ate*] **:** a salt or ester of furoic acid

fu·ro·ic acid \(ˈ)fyu̇ˈrōik-\ *n* [*fur-* + *-ic*] **:** either of two crystalline monocarboxylic acids C_4H_3OCOOH derived from furan; *esp* **:** the alpha or 2-derivative obtained by oxidation of furfural and used chiefly as a preservative

furoid *var of* FURANOID

fu·role \ˈfyu̇ˌrōl, =ˈ=\ *n* -S [F, fr. MF *fuirole*, prob. of Gmc origin; akin to OE *fȳr* fire — more at FIRE] *archaic* **:** SAINT ELMO'S FIRE

fu·ror \ˈfyu̇ˌrȯ(ə)r, ˈfyü,-, -ˌrō(ə)r, -ˌrȯ(ə), -ˌrōə *sometimes* f(y)ə'- *or* fyu̇'- *or* ˈfyu̇rə(r) *or* ˈfyürə(r)\ *n* -S [MF & L; MF *fureur, furor*, fr. L *furor*, fr. *furere* to be mad, rage + *-or* — more at DUST] **1 a :** an angry or maniacal fit **:** RAGE ⟨in mixed terror and ~ —Thomas Carlyle⟩ **b :** something that resembles such a fit ⟨strong dikes defend the land against the ~ of winter storms —Samuel Van Valkenburg & Ellsworth Huntington⟩ **c :** enraged behavior as a manifestation of epilepsy **d** *archaic* **:** a state of fervent inspiration **:** FRENZY ⟨poetic ~ may have betrayed me into some indecency —Samuel Foote⟩ **2 :** FURORE

fu·rore \", *chiefly Brit* fyu̇ˈrȯri\ *n* -S [It, fr. L *furor*] **1 :** a contagious excitement **:** general commotion **:** STIR ⟨had not let the ~ of the catch distract him from the other whales —R.B.Robertson⟩; *specif* **:** a fashionable craze ⟨a man struck the match that started the women's pipe ~ —Marybeth Weinstein⟩ **2 :** a public disturbance **:** CONTROVERSY, UPROAR ⟨the ~ over corruption in the executive departments has just about disappeared —R.H.Rovere⟩

fur·phy \ˈfərfē\ *n* -ES [fr. *Furphy (carts)*, water and sanitation carts used during World War I in Australia, fr. the *Furphy* manufacturing company, Shepparton, Victoria, Australia] *slang Austral* **:** a false report **:** RUMOR

furr \ˈfər, ˈfə̄(r\ *n* -S [ME *fur* — more at FUR (furrow)] *dial Brit* **:** FURROW

furr-ahin \ˌfə̄rəˈhin\ *n* -S [*furr* + Sc *ahin* behind, alter. of *ahind*] *Scot* **:** the right-hand hindmost horse that walks in the furrow in plowing

furred \ˈfərd, ˈfə̄d\ *adj* [ME, fr. past part. of *furren* to line with fur — more at FUR] **1 :** lined, trimmed, or faced with fur ⟨the original painted by himself with a black cap and ~ gown —Horace Walpole⟩ **2 :** coated as if with fur; *specif* **:** having a coating consisting chiefly of mucus and dead epithelial cells ⟨a ~ tongue⟩ **3 a :** covered with or bearing fur ⟨~ animals thrive in cold climates⟩ **b :** wearing fur ⟨~ ladies in ermine and sable⟩ **4** *archit* **:** provided with furring

¹fur·ri·er \ˈfərēə(r *also* ˈfə·rē-\ *n* -S [alter. of ME *furrer*, fr. AF *furrere*, fr. OF *forrer, fourrer* to fur + *-ere* -er — more at FUR] **1 :** one that buys and sells furs or fur products **:** fur dealer **2 a :** one that dresses furs **b :** one that makes, repairs, alters, or cleans fur garments

²furrier *comparative of* FURRY

fur·ri·ery \-ēərē, -ri\ *n* -ES **1 furrieries** *pl, archaic* **:** FURS **2 a :** the fur business **:** trade in furs **b :** the furrier's art **:** fur craftsmanship

furriest *superlative of* FURRY

fur·ri·ner \ˈfərənə(r)\, ˈfə·rə-\ *n* -S [by alter.] *dial* **:** FOREIGNER; *specif* **:** a person not a native of a given locality ⟨a mountain neighbor in a community that didn't take kindly to ~*s* —Frances Witherspoon⟩

fur·ri·ness \ˈfər·ēnəs, -r·in-\ *n* -ES **:** the quality or state of being furry

fur·ring \ˈfər·|iŋ, |ēŋ *also* ˈfə̄r|\ *n* -S [ME, fr. gerund of *furren* to line with fur — more at FUR] **1** *archaic* **:** a fur trimming or lining ⟨among the clergy of the lower grade in a cathedral there was a distinction marked by the ~ of the amice —Daniel Rock⟩ **2 a :** the process of incrustation or of clogging as if with fur ⟨the ~ of the mouth and the throat in fevers —John Woodall⟩ **b :** a coating of or as if of fur; *specif* **:** a deposit from water that collects on the inside of a boiler **3 a** (1) **:** the process of double-planking a ship's sides (2) **:** the material used in this process (3) **:** strips of wood fastened to the frames or joists of a ship to shape or level them for the attachment of a finished surface (as sheathing) **b** (1) **:** the application of thin wood, brick, or metal pieces to the joists, studs, or walls of a building to form a level surface (as for lathing, plastering, or attaching wallboard), to form an air space, or to make the wall look thicker and the window jambs deeper — called also *firring* (2) **:** the material used in this process

furring brick *n* **:** a hollow brick large enough to bond and grooved to afford a key for plastering

furring insert *n* **:** a wire device inserted into concrete or masonry that serves as an anchor for the attachment of furring

furring strip *n* **:** a strip of wood or very light steel channel to support lath esp. in furring masonry walls

furring tile *n* **:** a structural clay tile that is used for lining the inside of a wall and carries no superimposed load

¹fur·row \ˈfər·(ˌ)ō, ˈfə·(ˌ)rō, -ərə,-ə·rə, *often* -ər·əw *or* -ə·rəw +V\ *n* -S *often attrib* [ME *furgh, forwe, forow*, fr. OE *furh*; akin to OHG *furuh* furrow, ON *for* furrow, drainage ditch, L *porca*, and perh. to Skt *parśāna* precipice, chasm] **1 a :** a trench in the earth made by a plow ⟨twites nest under ~*s* and ringed plovers amid rows of potato plants —*Brit. Birds in Colour*⟩ **b :** a plowed field or farm ⟨artists frequently spring from sidewalks and ~*s* —A.W.Long⟩ **c :** something that resembles the track of a plow ⟨plowing a ~ across the Atlantic ocean —*N.Y. Times*⟩ **d** *Scot* **:** the earth turned over in plowing ⟨till crushed beneath the ~'*s* weight shall be thy doom —Robert Burns⟩ **2** *now chiefly Africa* **:** a natural or artificial watercourse for drainage or irrigation ⟨when leading water in concrete ~*s* it will run twice as quickly for the same fall as in an earth ~ —*Farmer's Weekly (So. Africa)*⟩ **3 :** a long and narrow indentation: as **a :** natural depression **:** GROOVE, CHANNEL ⟨tracing a fingernail along a ~ in the corduroy of her housecoat —Douglass Wallop⟩ ⟨major tectonic ~*s* or fault angles —C.A.Cotton⟩; *specif* **:** a groove in the face of a millstone **b :** a deep wrinkle on the face ⟨leathery folds and humorous wrinkles about his eyes deepening into a hundred crevices and ~*s* —J.C.Powys⟩ **c :** a crease in a plant or one of its parts ⟨seed single . . . marked with a ~ lengthwise —William Withering⟩ **d :** an indentation from the top of a dog's skull to the stop dividing the forehead into two lateral halves

²furrow \"\ *vb* -ED/-ING/-S *vt* **1 a :** to make a furrow in (earth) **:** PLOW **b :** to till as if with a plow **:** CULTIVATE ⟨plows literary ground that has been ~*ed* on innumerable occasions in the past —R.L.Neuberger⟩ **c :** to cut through **:** CLEAVE ⟨a road ~*ed* through the woods⟩ **2 a** (1) **:** to make a channel in **:** SCORE ⟨the rocket ~*s* the dark and falls —C.P.Aiken⟩ (2) **:** to make streaks in ⟨fair cheeks were ~*ed* with hot tears —Lord Byron⟩ **b :** to shape into alternate ridges and grooves ⟨one of the thousands of canyons that ~ the wide coast range —Frank Cameron⟩; *specif* **:** to make wrinkles in (the brow) ⟨he may sweat and ~ his brow —J.N. Leonard⟩ ~ *vi* **1** *archaic* **:** to make a furrow **:** PLOW **2 :** to make a channel **:** COURSE ⟨without warning the tears began to ~ down his cheeks —Margaret O. R. Cole⟩ **3 :** to make an indentation or groove **:** WRINKLE ⟨any educator's brow will automatically ~, contemplating the sober prediction —*Newsweek*⟩

furrow drill *n* **:** a grain drill that opens furrows at intervals of 10 to 18 inches and deposits seed in them

furrowed *adj* **:** having furrows **:** WRINKLED, CORRUGATED ⟨his ~ face is occasionally lit by a warming smile —Colm Brogan⟩

furrowed prawn *n* **:** an Australian prawn (*Peneus latisulcatus*) that attains a length of nine inches and sometimes appears on the market as shrimp

fur·row·er \ˈfərəwə(r), ˈfə·rəw-; ˈfər·ōə(r), ˈfə·rō\ *n* -S **:** one that furrows

furrowing *n* -S **:** a process of cell division in certain plants in which cleavage furrows begin at the existing cell wall and progress inwardly until they meet (as in spore formation in certain algae and fungi and development of the endosperm in certain seed plants)

furrow irrigation *n* **:** irrigation of farmland by water run in furrows between the crop rows

furrow pan *n* **:** PLOW SOLE

furrow press *n* **:** a heavy wheel or bar attached to the rear of a plow to travel in the furrow and firm the seedbed

furrow slice *n* **:** the ridge of earth turned by a plow ⟨this plow may be adjusted to set the *furrow slice* on edge —A.F.Gustafson⟩

fur·rowy \ˈfər·əw|ē, ˈfə·rəw|, ˈfər·ō|, ˈfə·rō|, |i\ *adj* **:** FURROWED

furs *pl of* FUR

fur·ry \ˈfər·|ē, |i *also* ˈfə̄r|\ *adj* -ER/-EST [²*fur* + *-y*] **1 :** consisting of or resembling fur ⟨one of those beautiful storms that wrap Denver in dry ~ snow —Willa Cather⟩ **2 :** covered with or as if with fur ⟨the ~ bulk of the bear —C.G.D. Roberts⟩ ⟨a lush ~ growth made up of algae, sea moss, tube worms, barnacles —Joseph Mitchell⟩ **3 :** clogged as if with fur ⟨his voice was tender and ~ —Frederic Prokosch⟩

furry dance \"-\ *n* [perh. by folk etymology fr. Corn *fēr* fair, market, fr. ML *feria* — more at FAIR] **:** a springtime serpentine dance through the streets of Helston, Cornwall

furs *pres 3d sing of* FUR, *pl of* FUR

fur seal *n* **:** any of various eared seals that have a double coat with a dense soft underfur highly valued for clothing and trimmings and that are now nearly extinct except at a few protected breeding places: **a :** a seal of the genus *Arctocephalus* **b :** a seal of the genus *Callorhinus*; *specif* **:** a seal (*C. alascanus*) that breeds on the Pribilof islands

furta *pl of* FURTUM

furta usus *pl of* FURTUM USUS

¹furth \ˈfərth\ *Scot var of* FORTH

²fürth *or* **fuerth** *or* **furth** \ˈfi(ə)rt, *Ger* ˈfɛrt\ *adj, usu cap* [fr. *Fürth*, Germany] **:** of or from the city of Fürth, Germany **:** of the kind or style prevalent in Fürth

furthcoming *var of* FORTHCOMING

¹fur·ther \ˈfərthər, ˈfə̄thə(r, ˈfəithə(r, *in Southern US often* ˈfəthə(r *or* ˈfəthər\ *adv* [ME, fr. OE *furthor*; akin to OHG *furthar, furdir* further, OS *furthor*; comparative fr. the root of E *forth*] **1 :** ¹FARTHER 1 **2 :** ¹FARTHER 2 **3 :** in addition **:** MOREOVER ⟨if we ~ suppose —C.H.Sykes⟩ ⟨~, when writing was finally popularized —A.N.Whitehead⟩ ⟨he felt ~ that it was his place to be there —Ira Wolfert⟩ ⟨the soil is ~ enriched by abundant applications of sheep manure —Tom Marvel⟩ **4 :** ¹FARTHER 4

²further \"\ *adj* [ME, fr. OE *furthra*, fr. *furthor*, adv.] **1 :** ²FARTHER 1 **2 :** going or extending beyond what exists **:** ADDITIONAL ⟨a ~ volume —Carl Van Doren⟩ ⟨she may obtain ~ education on the side —J.B.Conant⟩ ⟨people can have no ~ illusions about it —F.D.Roosevelt⟩ ⟨I know nothing ~ of them —Pearl Buck⟩ **3 :** ²FARTHER 3

³further \"\ *vb* **furthered; furthered; furthering** \-th(ə)riŋ\ **furthers** [ME *furtheren*, alter. (influenced by ¹*further* and ²*further*) of OE *fyrthrian*, fr. *furthor*] *vt* **:** to help forward **:** PROMOTE, ADVANCE ⟨does the music ~ the dramatic purpose —Irving Kolodin⟩ ~ *vi, now chiefly Scot* **:** to go on **:** make progress **syn** see ADVANCE

⁴further \"\ *n* -S *dial Brit* **:** good fortune **:** SUCCESS

fur·ther·ance \-th(ə)rən(t)s\ *n* -S [ME *furtheraunce*, fr. *furtheren* + *-aunce* -ance] **:** the act of preferment **:** ADVANCEMENT, PROMOTION ⟨the elimination of poverty and the ~ of social justice —Oscar Handlin⟩

further education *n, Brit* **:** ADULT EDUCATION

fur·ther·er \-thərə(r)\ *n* -S [ME, fr. *furtheren* + *-er*] **:** one that furthers

fur·ther·ly \-th(ə)(r)lē\ *adj, now dial Eng, of crops* **:** EARLY, FORWARD

fur·ther·more \ˈ==,=, ,==ˈ=\ *adv* [ME, fr. *further* + *more*] **:** in addition to what precedes **:** BESIDES, MOREOVER

fur·ther·most \ˈ==ˌmōst\ *adj* **:** most distant **:** FARTHEST

fur·ther·some \-ˌsəm\ *adj* [³*further* + *-some*] **1** *archaic* **:** encouraging advance **:** BENEFICIAL, USEFUL **2** *Scot* **:** VENTURESOME, RASH

fur·thest \-thəst\ *adv (or adj)* [ME, fr. *further* + *-est*] **:** FARTHEST

furthy \ˈfərthi\ *Scot var of* FORTHY

fur·tive \ˈfər|d·|iv, ˈfə̄|, ˈfəi|, |t|, |ēv\ *adj* [F or L; F *furtif*, fr. L *furtivus*, fr. *furtum* theft (fr. *fur* thief) + *-ivus* -ive; akin to Gk *phōr* thief, L *ferre* to carry — more at BEAR] **1 a :** done by stealth **:** SECRET, SURREPTITIOUS ⟨a ~ glance told her worlds —Mark Twain⟩ **b :** expressive of stealth **:** SNEAKY, SLY ⟨the ~ look of those who know they ought to be doing something else —Alan Ross⟩ **2 a :** obtained underhandedly **:** STOLEN **b** *archaic* **:** given to stealing **:** THIEVISH ⟨the farmers were so much plagued by the ~ bird —J.H.Burton⟩ **syn** see SECRET

fur·tive·ly \|əvlē, -li\ *adv* **:** in a furtive manner

fur·tive·ness \|ivnəs, |ēv-\ *n* -ES **:** the quality or state of being furtive

fur·tum \ˈfərd·əm\ *n, pl* **fur·ta** \-d·ə\ [L] *Roman & civil law* **:** the unauthorized making of a profit from or appropriation to one's use of another's property **:** a trespass on movable property **:** THEFT

furtum usus \-ˈyüsəs\ *n, pl* **furta usus** [L, theft of use] *Scots law* **:** a trespass by temporarily depriving an owner of his movable property

fu·run·cle \ˈfyu̇ˌrəŋkəl\ *n* -S [L *furunculus* petty thief, secondary branch of a vine (that robs the main branches of sap), knob on a vine, furuncle, dim. of *furon-, furo* ferret, thief, fr. *fur* thief — more at FURTIVE] **:** a localized inflammatory swelling of the skin and underlying tissues that is caused by infection by a bacterium (esp. *Staphylococcus aureus*) in a hair follicle or skin gland and that discharges pus and a central core of dead tissue — called also *boil*; compare CARBUNCLE

fu·run·cu·lar \fyəˈrəŋkyələ(r), (ˈ)fyu̇ˌr-\ *or* **fu·run·cu·lous** \-ləs\ *adj* [L *furunculus* + E *-ar* or *-ous*] **1 :** having or tending to produce furuncles **2 :** resembling a furuncle

fu·run·cu·loid \-ˌlȯid\ *adj* [L *furunculus* + E *-oid*] **:** resembling a furuncle

fu·run·cu·lo·sis \fyəˌrəŋkyəˈlōsəs, (ˌ)fyu̇ˌr-\ *n, pl* **furunculoses** \-ōˌsēz\ [NL, fr. L *furunculus* + NL *-osis*] **1 :** the condition of having or tending to develop multiple furuncles **2 :** a highly infectious disease of the salmons and related fishes that is caused by a bacterium (*Bacterium salmonicida*), is characterized by purplish blotches followed by deep erosive ulcers of the skin and subcutaneous tissues, and is esp. virulent in hatcheries or other areas of heavy fish population

fu·run·cu·lus \fyəˈrəŋkyələs, fyu̇ˈr-\ *n, pl* **furuncu·li** \-ˌlī\ [L] **:** FURUNCLE

fu·ry \ˈfyu̇rē, ˈfyür-, -ri\ *n* -ES [ME *furie*, fr. MF & L; MF, fr. L *furia*, fr. *furere* to be mad, rage + *-ia* -y — more at DUST] **1 a :** violent anger **:** extreme wrath **:** RAGE ⟨heaven has no rage like love to hatred turned, nor hell a ~ like a woman scorned —William Congreve⟩ **b :** a passionate fit **:** FRENZY ⟨roused his listeners to a ~ of compassionate indignation —*Amer. Guide Series: N.Y. City*⟩ **c :** something that appears to be driven by rage **:** violent turbulence ⟨the first ~ of the storm had spent itself —E.A.Poe⟩ **d :** the savagery of an animal ⟨taught them how to match their skill against the cunning and fierce ~ of the fastest of the ocean denizens —T. C.Roughley⟩ **2** [ME *furie*, fr. MF or L; MF, fr. L *Furiae*, fr. pl. of *furia*] **a** *usu cap* **:** an avenging deity of ancient Greece and Rome **b :** an avenging or infernal spirit ⟨liberated from the *furies* of his conscience —W.A.Kaufmann⟩ **c :** one who resembles an avenging or infernal spirit; *esp* **:** a malicious or spiteful woman ⟨sometimes she behaves like . . . a vindictive ~ —Rosemary Benet⟩ **3 :** extreme impetuosity or violence **:** unrestrained force ⟨attacked with ~ and precision —T.R. Hay⟩ **4 :** a state of inspired exaltation **:** AFFLATUS ⟨in an age of formalism, poetic ~ itself became a formal requirement —Irving Babbitt⟩ **syn** see ANGER — **like fury :** to an intense or extreme degree or extent ⟨kicked and plunged *like fury* —Henry Wynmalen⟩

fu·ryl \ˈfyu̇rəl, -(ˌ)ril\ *n* -S [ISV *fur-* + *-yl*] **:** either of two univalent radicals C_4H_3O derived from furan by removal of one hydrogen atom; *esp* **:** the alpha or 2-radical

furze \ˈfərz\ *n* -S [ME *firse, furse*, fr. OE *fyrs*; akin to Gk *pyros* wheat, *pyrēn* pit (of fruit), Lith *pūrai* winter wheat, OSlav *pyro* spelt] **:** any of several plants of the genera *Ulex* and *Genista*; *esp* **:** a spiny evergreen shrub (*U. europaeus*) with yellow flowers that is very common throughout Europe and is often used for fuel and fodder — called also *gorse, whin*

furzechat \ˈ=ˌ=\ *n* [*furze* + *chat* (bird)] **1 :** WHINCHAT **2 :** STONECHAT

furze lark *n* **:** MEADOW PIPIT

furze·ling \-ˌliŋ\ *n* -S [*furze* + *-ling*] **:** DARTFORD WARBLER

furze wren *n* **:** DARTFORD WARBLER

furzy \ˈfərzē\ *adj* -ER/-EST **:** abounding in or overgrown with or as if with furze ⟨his ~ brown chest half bare —J.R.Lowell⟩

fus *abbr* **1** fuselage **2** fusilier

fu·sain \ˈfyüˌzān, =ˈ=\ *n* -S [F, spindle tree, charcoal made from spindle-tree wood, fusain, fr. (assumed) VL *fusagin-, fusago*, fr. L *fusus* spindle; fr. the fact that the wood of the tree was used for spindles] **:** a dull constituent closely resembling charcoal that is present in banded bituminous coals and causes much of the dust in coal mines — compare CLARAIN, DURAIN, VITRAIN

fu·sar·i·al \(ˈ)fyüˈza(a)rēəl\ *adj* [NL *Fusarium* + E *-al*] **:** of or relating to a fungus of the genus *Fusarium*

fu·sar·i·um \=ˈ==əm\ *n* [NL, fr. L *fusus* spindle + NL *-arium*] **1** *cap* **:** a form genus of fungi (family Tuberculariaceae) having a microconidium and a crescent-shaped or fusiform macroconidium — see DRY ROT 2 b **2** *pl* **fusar·ia** \-ēə\ **:** any fungus of the genus *Fusarium*

fusarium wilt *n* **:** any of various plant wilt diseases caused by fungi of the genus Fusarium — compare DRY ROT

fu·sa·role \ˈfyüzəˌrōl\ *n* -S [F *fusarolle, fusarole*, fr. obs It. *fusarola* (now *fusaiuola*), fr. *fuso* spindle, shaft of a column, fr. L *fusus* spindle] **:** a rounded usu. beaded convex molding placed under the echinus of capitals in the Doric, Ionic, and Corinthian orders

fu·sate \'fyü,zāt\ *adj* [L *fus*us + E *-ate*] : FUSIFORM

fusco- *comb form* [ISV, fr. L *fuscus*] : having a dark color : tawny ⟨*fusco*chlorin⟩ ⟨*fusco*ferruginous⟩

fus·cous \'fəskəs\ *adj* [L *fuscus* — more at DUSK] : of any of several colors averaging a brownish gray which is lighter than taupe (sense 1), lighter and less strong than average chocolate, and less strong and slightly redder than mouse gray

[1]**fuse** \'fyüz\ *n* -s *often attrib* [It *fuso* spindle, fr. L *fusus*] **1** : a continuous train of explosive enclosed in a flexible waterproof cord or cable for setting off a charge (as dynamite) by communication of either fire or detonation ⟨detonating ~*s*⟩ — see SAFETY FUSE 1 **2** *usu* **fuze** \"\ : a detonating device for setting off (as by percussion) the bursting charge of a projectile, bomb, or torpedo ⟨our new proximity ~ which enabled artillery shells to burst automatically —F.E.Fox⟩

[2]**fuse** *or* **fuze** \"\ *vt* -ED/-ING/-S [[1]*fuse* & [4]*fuse*] : to equip with a fuse

[3]**fuse** \"\ *vb* -ED/-ING/-S [L *fusus*, past part. of *fundere* to pour, to melt — more at FOUND] *vt* **1 a** : to reduce to a liquid or plastic state by heat : DISSOLVE, MELT ⟨the thunderstorm had *fused* the electric mains —C.K.Finlay⟩ **b** : to blend by melting together : unite by heating ⟨foundries which ~ zinc and copper into hard, bright brass —*Newsweek*⟩ **c** *archaic* : to thin or dilute (the blood) ⟨purgatives are . . . to ~ and thin the blood —George Cheyne⟩ **2** : to unite as if by melting together : BLEND, INTEGRATE ⟨~*s* the clutter of detail into a rich and fascinating narrative —A.M.Schlesinger b.1917⟩; *specif* : to join (two adjacent bony surfaces) by surgery ~ *vi* **1** : to become fluid with heat : LIQUEFY, MELT ⟨acetate rayon tends to ~ if pressed at too high a temperature —W.L.Carmichael⟩; *specif* : to fail because of the melting of a link in an electrical circuit ⟨all the lights in the house have *fused* —*Christian Science Monitor*⟩ **2** : to become integrated : UNITE, MERGE ⟨the passion for service must ~ with the passion for knowledge —C.W.Eliot⟩ **syn** see MIX

[4]**fuse** \"\ *n* -S : a wire, bar, or strip of metal with a very low melting point that melts and breaks the circuit when an electric current exceeds a specified amperage ⟨plug ~*s* . . . have transparent windows at the top which enable the homeowner to see when they are blown —Bernard Gladstone⟩

fu·seau \(')fyü¦zō\ *n, pl* **fu·seaux** \-ōz\ [F, lit., spindle, fr. OF *fusel*, dim. of *fus*, fr. L *fusus*] : a fusiform multicellular body that resembles a spore and that is characteristic of various fungi of the genus *Trichophyton*

fuse block *n* **1** : FUSE GAUGE **2** *also* **fuse cutout** : a block of porcelain, slate, or other refractory material supporting a mounting for an electrical fuse

fuseboard \'=,=\ *n* : a slab of incombustible insulating material on which electrical safety fuses are mounted

fuse box *or* **fuse cabinet** *n* : CUTOUT BOX

fuse clip *n* : a spring clip supporting one end of a cartridge fuse and providing electrical connection with it

fused \'fyüzd\ *adj* **1 a** : melted together : united by heating; *specif, of a shirt collar* : stiffened by bonding an acetate interlining to the outside layers ⟨cotton broadcloth with ~ collar that does not need starching —*Eaton's Catalogue*⟩ **b** : reduced to liquid by heat : MOLTEN ⟨plating . . . consists in enveloping the metal with the higher melting point by the ~ bath of the metal with the lower melting point —*Scientific American*⟩ **c** : having atoms in common — used of ring systems in chemical compounds (as benzanthracene) **2** : MINGLED, BLENDED, INTEGRATED ⟨two sentences ~ into one⟩ ⟨a meandering fancy rather than a ~ vision —*Time*⟩

fused quartz *or* **fused silica** *n* : VITREOUS SILICA

[1]**fu·see** *or* **fu·zee** \(')fyü¦zē\ *n* -S [F *fusée*, lit., spindleful of yarn, fr. OF *fusee*, fr. *fus* spindle, fr. L *fusus*] **1** : a conical spirally grooved pulley in a timepiece from which a cord or chain unwinds onto a barrel containing the spring, the increasing diameter of the pulley compensating for the lessening power of the spring **2** : [1]FUSE 1 **3** *obs* : a bony growth on the leg of a horse **4 a** : a wooden match with a bulbous head not easily blown out when ignited **b** : a paper match impregnated with niter and tipped with sulfur **5** : a red signal flare used esp. for protecting stalled trains and trucks

[2]**fusee** *or* **fuzee** \"\ *n* -S [modif. of F *fusil* — more at FUSIL] **1** : a flintlock gun : FIRELOCK **2** : FUSILIER

fuse gauge *also* **fuse cutter** *n* : an instrument for cutting fuses that consists of a block with a brass scale on one side and a hinged knife — called also *fuse block*

fu·se·lage \'fyüsə,läzh, -làzh *also* -üzə- *or* -läj *or* -làj *or* ,==' = *sometimes* '==‚lij *or* 'fyü(,)sl- *or* -fyüz(,)l-\ *n* -S [F, fr. *fuselé* spindle-shaped (fr. MF, fr. *fusel* spindle + *-é* -ate, fr. L *-atus*) + *-age* — more at FUSEAU] : the central body portion of an airplane designed to accommodate the crew and the passengers or cargo

fu·sel oil \'fyüzəl-\ *n* [G *fusel* bad liquor] **1** : an acrid oily liquid that has an unpleasant odor, that is obtained in small amounts as a by-product in alcoholic fermentation (as of potatoes, grain, or molasses), that consists of a mixture chiefly of alcohols (as isopentyl, active amyl, isobutyl, and normal propyl alcohols), and that is used esp. as a source of alcohols and as a solvent **2** : AMYL ALCOHOL 2a

fuseplug \'=,=\ *n* **1** : a plug fitted to the fuse hole of a military projectile to hold the fuse **2** : PLUG FUSE

fuses *pl of* FUSE, *pres 3d sing of* FUSE

fu·shion \'füzhən\ *var of* FOISON

fu·shion·less \-ləs\ *adj* **1** *Scot, of food or drink* : lacking in flavor or nourishment : INSIPID **2** *Scot, of a person* **a** : physically weak : lacking energy **b** : mentally or spiritually dull

fu·shun \'fü¦shu̇n\ *adj, usu cap* [fr. *Fushun*, Manchuria] : of or from the city of Fushun, Manchuria : of the kind or style prevalent in Fushun

fusi- *comb form* [L *fusus* spindle] : spindle ⟨*fusi*form⟩ : spindle-shaped ⟨*Fusi*coccum⟩

fu·si·bil·i·ty \,fyüzə'biləd·ē, -ətē, -i\ *n* -ES [F *fusibilité*, fr. MF, fr. *fusible* + *-ité* -ity] : the quality, state, or degree of being fusible

fu·si·ble \'fyüzəbəl\ *adj* [F or ML; F, fr. MF, fr. ML *fusibilis*, fr. L *fusus* (past part. of *fundere* to pour, melt) + *-ibilis* -ible — more at FOUND] : capable of being fused; *esp* : capable of being liquefied by heat

fusible metal *or* **fusible alloy** *n* : a metal or alloy (as of bismuth, lead, and tin or of these three metals and cadmium or indium) having a low melting point usu. below 300°F and used typically for dies, fixtures, molds, patterns, boiler safety plugs, and automatic-sprinkler fuses

fu·si·cla·di·um \,fyüzə'klādēəm\ *n, cap* [NL, fr. *fusi-* + Gk *kladion* twig, shoot, dim. of *klados* branch, shoot — more at GLADIATOR] : a form genus of imperfect fungi (family Dematiaceae) that produces one-celled or once-septate spores on short conidiophores usu. in extensive groups

fu·si·coc·cum \-'käkəm\ *n, cap* [NL, fr. *fusi-* + *-coccum* (fr. Gk *kokkos* grain, seed, kermes berry)] : a form genus of imperfect fungi (family Sphaeropsidaceae) that have hyaline unicellular fusiform spores in several-chambered pycnidia

fu·si·form \'fyüzə,fȯrm\ *adj* [*fusi-* + *-form*] : shaped like a spindle : tapering toward each end — see ROOT illustration

fusiform bacillus *n* : a rod-shaped bacterium (*Fusobacterium fusiforme* or *Fusiformis plauti-vincenti*) having one blunt and one pointed end and being typically associated in pairs with the blunt ends apposed forming a fusiform figure — see VINCENT'S INFECTION

fusiform initial *n* : an elongated tapering cell in the cambium that through repeated division gives rise to vertically arranged cells — compare RAY INITIAL

fu·si·for·mis \,=='fȯrməs\ *n, cap* [NL, fr. ISV *fusiform*] *in some classifications* : a genus of parasitic anaerobic or microaerophilic nonmotile bacteria (family Bacteroidaceae) that stain unevenly, form no spores, and are often associated with purulent lesions

fusiform rust *n* : a rust esp. of loblolly and Caribbean pine seedlings caused by a fungus (*Cronartium fusiforme*) that produces distinctive spindle-shaped cankers on the stems

[1]**fu·sil** \'fyüzəl\ *or* **fu·sile** \", -ü,zīl, -,sīl\ *adj* [ME *fusil*, fr. L *fusilis*, fr. *fusus* (past part. of *fundere* to pour, melt) + *-ilis* -ile — more at FOUND] **1** *archaic* **a** : made by melting and pouring into forms : CAST ⟨wrought ~ or graven in metal —John Milton⟩ **b** : liquefied by heat : melted and flowing ⟨o'er the silver pours the ~ gold —Alexander Pope⟩ **2** *archaic* : susceptible to melting : FUSIBLE

[2]**fu·sil** \'fyüzəl\ *n* -S [ME, fr. MF *fusel, fusil* spindle — more at FUSEAU] **1** : a rhomboidal heraldic bearing longer in proportion to its width than a lozenge **2** : a spindle-shaped siliceous concretion

fusil 1

[3]**fusil** \"\ *also* **fu·zil** \"\ *n* -S [F *fusil* steel for striking fire, musket, fr. OF *foisil, fuisil* steel for striking fire, fr. (assumed) VL *focilis*, fr. LL *focus* fire (fr. L, fireplace, hearth) + L *-ilis* -ile — more at FOCUS] : a light flintlock musket

fu·si·lier *or* **fu·si·leer** \¦fyüzə¦li(ə)r, -iə\ *n* -S [F *fusilier*, fr. *fusil* + *-ier* -er] **1** : a soldier armed with a fusil **2** : a member of one of the British regiments that were formerly armed with fusils

[1]**fu·sil·lade** \'fyüsə,lād, -üzə-, -äd, -ȧd, ,=='=\ *n* -S [F, fr. *fusiller* to shoot (fr. *fusil*) + *-ade*] **1 a** : a number of shots fired simultaneously or in rapid succession esp. with small arms : VOLLEY ⟨a ~ of buckshot —Horace Sutton⟩ **b** : FIRING SQUAD ⟨he was condemned to death . . . and died by the ~ —W. O.Scroggs⟩ **2** : a spirited outburst of any sort ⟨a ~ of marimba music —Maud Oakes⟩; *specif* : a barrage of criticism ⟨never . . . has a new head of government come under such a ~ from his own party —*Atlantic*⟩

[2]**fusillade** \"\ *vt* -ED/-ING/-S : to attack or shoot down by simultaneous or rapidly successive gunfire

fu·sil·ly \'fyüzəlē\ *adj* [ME *fusile*, fr. *fusil*] **1** : divided into fusil-shaped compartments — used of a heraldic field or bearing **2** : made of a row of fusils — used of a heraldic bearing

fusing *pres part of* FUSE

fusing disk *n* : a steel disk that causes fusion by the heat from its rapid rotation and is used to cut metal

fu·si·nite \'fyüzᵊn,īt\ *n* -S [alter. of *fusain* + *-ite*] : the opaque carbonized cell structure found in fusain and sometimes considered a mineral

fu·si·ni·za·tion \,fyüzᵊnə'zāshən, -,nī'z-\ *n* -S [alter. of *fusain* + *-ization*] : the transformation of plant material to fusain

fu·sion \'fyüzhən\ *n* -S *often attrib* [L *fusion-, fusio*, fr. *fusus* (past part. of *fundere* to pour, melt) + *-ion-* *-io* -ion — more at FOUND] **1 a** : the act or process of liquefying or rendering plastic by heat : transition of a substance from a solid to a liquid : MELTING ⟨welds accompanied by ~ are by far the most common —*Welding Handbook*⟩ **b** : the quality or state of flowing induced by this process ⟨that degree of heat must be employed which will give perfect ~ to the glaze —G.R. Porter⟩ **2** : a union by or as if by melting: as **a** : a merging of diverse elements into a unified whole : SYNTHESIS ⟨opera is the ~ of five arts into a composite whole —Warwick Braithwaite⟩; *specif* : the blending of retinal images in binocular vision **b** : a combination of ingredients achieved by heating and mixing together ⟨cement is a ~ formed from exact proportions of shale and limestone —E.S.Perry⟩ **c** : a political partnership : COALITION ⟨a ~ of Democrats and independent Republicans —*N.Y. Times*⟩ ⟨elected on a ~ ticket —F. H. LaGuardia⟩ **d** (1) : a blend of sensations, perceptions, ideas, or attitudes such that the component elements can seldom be identified by introspective analysis (2) : the perception of light from a source that is intermittent above a critical frequency as if the source were continuous — contrasted with *flicker;* see CRITICAL FLICKER FREQUENCY **e** : a coalescence into a solid unit : WELDING; *specif* : the surgical immobilization of a joint ⟨spinal ~⟩ **f** : coalescence between root and affix in a language (as in Latin *pēs* "foot" from assumed earlier *peds* with the root *ped-* and the nominative singular ending *-s*) — compare INFLECTIONAL **g** : the union of atomic nuclei to form heavier nuclei resulting in the release of enormous quantities of energy when certain light elements unite (as in the combination of heavy-hydrogen nuclei to form helium nuclei that takes place in the sun or in a hydrogen bomb) — called also *nuclear fusion;* contrasted with *fission*

fu·sion·al \-zhənᵊl,-zhnəl\ *adj* : relating to or characterized by fusion; *specif* : being or relating to a process, language, or type of linguistic structure in which fusion occurs

fusion bomb *n* : a bomb in which nuclei of a light chemical element unite to form nuclei of heavier elements with a release of energy; *esp* : HYDROGEN BOMB — compare ATOM BOMB

fusion frequency *n* : CRITICAL FLICKER FREQUENCY

fu·sion·ist \-zh(ə)nəst\ *n* -S [F *fusionniste*, fr. *fusion* (fr. L *fusion-, fusio*) + *-iste* -ist] : one who promotes or takes part in a coalition esp. of political parties

fu·sion·less \'füzhənləs\ *var of* FUSHIONLESS

fusion nucleus *n* **1 a** : PRIMARY ENDOSPERM NUCLEUS **b** : the triploid nucleus resulting from double fertilization that produces the endosperm nuclei in seed plants **2 a** : SYNKARYON **b** : ZYGOTE

fusion point *n* : MELTING POINT

fusion welding *n* : the welding of metals in a molten state without mechanical pressure or pounding

fu·site \'fyü,zīt\ *n* -S [*fus*ain + *-ite*] : FUSINITE

fuso- *comb form* [L *fusus* spindle] **1** : shaped like a spindle ⟨*fuso*cellular⟩ **2** : fusiform bacillus and ⟨*fuso*spirillar⟩ ⟨*fuso*spirochetal⟩

fu·so·bacterium \¦fyü(,)zō+\ *n* [NL, fr. *fuso-* + *bacterium*] **1** *cap* : a genus of gram-negative anaerobic strictly parasitic rod-shaped bacteria usu. placed among the Bacteroidaceae and sometimes included in *Fusiformis* — see FUSIFORM BACILLUS **2** *pl* **fusobacteria** : any organism of the genus *Fusobacterium*

fu·so·cellular \"+\ *adj* [ISV *fuso-* + *cellular*] : composed of fusiform cells

fu·soid \'fyü,zȯid\ *adj* [L *fus*us spindle + E *-oid*] : FUSIFORM

fu·so·spirochetal \¦fyü(,)zō+\ *adj* [*fuso-* + *spirochetal*] : of, relating to, or caused by the fusiform bacillus and spirochetes — compare VINCENT'S INFECTION

fu·so·spirochete \"+\ *n* -S [ISV *fuso-* + *spirochete*] : the associated bacterium and spirochete that are typically present together in Vincent's infection

fu·so·spirochetosis \"+\ *n, pl* **fusospirochetoses** [NL, fr. ISV *fusospirochete* + NL *-osis*] : VINCENT'S INFECTION

[1]**fuss** *n* -ES [origin unknown] *obs* : FUSSOCK

[2]**fuss** \'fəs\ *n* -ES [perh. of imit. origin] **1 a** : needless bustle or excitement : COMMOTION ⟨he found a point of vantage and settled himself with all the ~ of an audience in a theater —Audrey Barker⟩ **b** : effusive praise : TO-DO ⟨stand by this old man and make a big ~ over his ability to cook beans —L.C.Douglas⟩ **2 a** : a state of agitation esp. over a trivial matter ⟨in a ~ and a stew all afternoon —Molly L. Bar-David⟩ **b** : COMPLAINT, OBJECTION, PROTEST ⟨no ~ was made in his day if a new writer took from an old one whatever material he found congenial —C.E.Montague⟩ **c** : an angry dispute : QUARREL ⟨as a dying phase of the ~ they are raising a controversy over certain words and phrases —B.J.Hendrick⟩ **3** : an ornamental flourish : DECORATION ⟨printed in Caslon without ~ —*Times Lit. Supp.*⟩ **syn** see STIR

[3]**fuss** \"\ *vb* -ED/-ING/-ES *vi* **1 a** : to create or be in a state of restless activity : BUSTLE ⟨a fleet of small tugs . . . ~*ed* up and down continually —Leslie Richardson⟩; *specif* : to shower flattering attentions — usu. used with *over* ⟨the children kissed me and patted me and ~*ed* over me —Polly Adler⟩ **b** : to pay undue attention to small details : PUTTER ⟨~ with his clothes —J.B.Benefield⟩ **2** *slang* : to court a girl : DATE ⟨have the best time in college: dramatics and basketball and ~*ing* and dancing —Sinclair Lewis⟩ **3 a** : to become upset : FRET, WORRY ⟨I know I'm an idiot to ~ but they're two hours late —David Walker⟩ **b** (1) : NAG, COMPLAIN : ARGUE, PROTEST ⟨tears and ~*ing* are hard for a parent to take but some release is better for a child than attempts at Spartan bravery —Dorothy Barclay⟩ (2) *dial* : SCOLD, CHIDE — usu. used with *at* ⟨I don't like to be ~*ed* at in public —Eudora Welty⟩ ~ *vt* **1** : to stir up : ANNOY, AGITATE, UPSET ⟨she ~*ed* one; she was always in a state of emotion —Virginia Woolf⟩ **2** *slang* : COURT, DATE

fuss and feathers *n pl but usu sing in constr* : fanfare and ostentation ⟨official holidays . . . were celebrated with a maximum of *fuss and feathers* —A.T.Bouscaren⟩

fuss·budg·et \'fəs,bəjət, *usu* -əd·+V\ *n* -S : one who fusses or frets about trifles ⟨funny old ~*s* without much practical sense —M.M.Mathews⟩ — **fuss·budg·ety** \-əd·ē\ *adj*

fuss·er \'fəsə(r)\ *n* -S : one that fusses

fuss·i·ly \'fəsəlē, -li\ *adv* : in a fussy manner

fuss·i·ness \-sēnəs, -sin-\ *n* -ES : the quality or state of being fussy

fus·sle \'fəsəl\ *Scot var of* WHISTLE

fuss mill *n* : ATTRITION MILL

fus·sock \'fu̇sək, 'fəs-\ *n* -S [origin unknown] *dial Eng* **1** : DONKEY **2** : a pudgy or stupid person

fuss·pot \'fə,spät\ *n* -S : FUSSBUDGET

fuss up *vt, dial* : to make pretty : EMBELLISH ⟨*fuss up* the stage with superfluous people and superfluous action —*N.Y. Times*⟩

fussy \'fəsē, -si\ *adj* -ER/-EST **1 a** : nervous or easily upset : IRRITABLE ⟨a ~ manner that covered a nervousness he had never been able to conquer —J.D.Beresford⟩ **b** : full of commotion : BUSTLING ⟨~ . . . locomotives snort and wheeze as they drag heavily laden cane trucks to sugar factories —J.W.Coulter⟩ **2** : provided with an abundance of decorative detail : ORNATE ⟨the white curtains starched and all the ~ gilt handles rubbed up —Helen Shaw⟩ **3 a** : requiring or giving close attention to petty details : METICULOUS ⟨looked like a natural for the ~ bookkeeping routine of an orderly room —Earle Birney⟩ **b** : revealing a finicky concern for niceties : FASTIDIOUS, CHOOSY ⟨a man who was ~ about his food⟩ **syn** see NICE

[1]**fust** \'fu̇st, 'fəst\ *n* -S [back-formation fr. *fusty*] *dial Brit* : a strong musty smell : MUSTINESS

[2]**fust** \"\ *vi* -ED/-ING/-S **1** *archaic* : to become moldy through disuse ⟨sure he that made us . . . gave us not that capability and godlike reason to ~ in us unused —Shak.⟩ **2** *archaic, of food or drink* : to taste or smell moldy or stale

[3]**fust** \'fəst\ *n* -S [It *fusto*, lit., trunk (of a tree), fr. L *fustis* club, staff — more at BEAT] : the shaft of a column or pilaster

[4]**fust** \"\ *dial var of* FIRST

fus·ta·nel·la \,fəstə'nelə, ,füs-\ *n* -S [It, fr. NGk *phoustanella*, dim. of *phoustani* woman's dress, fr. It *fustagno* fustian, fr. ML *fustaneum* — more at FUSTIAN] : a short full skirt of stiff white linen or cotton worn by men (as the evzones) in some Balkan countries

fus·tet \¦fə¦stet\ *n* -S [F, fr. MF *fustet, fustel*, fr. OProv, prob. fr. OCatal *fustet*, fr. Ar *fustaq, fustuq* — more at FUSTIC] **1** : SMOKE TREE 1a **2** : the yellow dyewood of the European smoke tree — called also *young fustic*

[1]**fus·tian** \'fəschən, *chiefly Brit* -stiən *or* -styən\ *n* -S [ME *fustane, fustian*, fr. OF *fustane, fustaine*, fr. ML *fustaneum*, prob. fr. ML *fustis* tree trunk, fr. L, club, staff; trans. of Gk *xylinon* cotton, fr. neut. of *xylinos* wooden, fr. *xylon* wood, club] **1 a** : a strong cotton and linen fabric used for clothing and bedding **b** : a class of cotton fabrics usu. having a pile face and twill weave ⟨corduroys and velveteens belong to a group of filling-faced fabrics known by the old term ~ —John Hoye⟩ **2** : pretentious writing or speech : an inflated style : BOMBAST ⟨pure ~ — an appropriate accompaniment for some melodramatic stage spectacle —Winthrop Sargeant⟩ — often used interjectionally to express disbelief or disdain ⟨nonsense! ~! Good day to you! —S.H.Adams⟩ **syn** see BOMBAST

[2]**fustian** \"\ *adj* **1** : made of fustian ⟨a ~ coat⟩ **2** : pompous and overdone : EXAGGERATED ⟨~ antique heroes —H.O. Taylor⟩ **3** : GOOD-FOR-NOTHING, WORTHLESS ⟨a ~ rascal —Leslie Hotson⟩

fus·tic \'fəstik\ *n* -S [ME *fustik*, fr. MF *fustoc*, fr. Ar *fustuq, fustaq*, fr. Gk *pistakē* pistachio tree — more at PISTACHIO] **1** : any of several dyewoods: as **a** : the yellow wood of a common tropical American tree (*Chlorophora tinctoria*) — called also *dyer's mulberry, old fustic* **b** : FUSTET 2 **2** : the tree that yields old fustic — called also *dyer's mulberry* **3** : the yellow coloring matter extracted from old fustic and used esp. in dyeing wool — see DYE table I (under *Natural Yellow 11*) **4** : [6]LIME 3

fus·ti·gate \'fəstə,gāt\ *vt* -ED/-ING/-S [LL *fustigatus*, past part. of *fustigare*, fr. L *fustis* club, staff + *-igare* (akin to *agere* to drive, act, do) — more at BEAT, AGENT] **1** : to beat with a stick : CUDGEL **2** : to criticize severely : CASTIGATE — **fus·ti·ga·tion** \,=='gāshən\ *n* -S

fus·ti·ga·tor \'==,gād·ə(r)\ *n* -S : one that fustigates

fus·ti·lugs \'fəstē,ləgz\ *n, pl* **fustilugs** [*fusty* + *lugs*, pl. of *lug*] *archaic* : a ponderous clumsy person; *esp* : a fat and slovenly woman

fus·ti·ly \'fəstəlē, -li\ *adv* : in a fusty manner

fus·tin \'fəstən\ *n* -S [G, fr. F *fustet* + G *-in*] : a crystalline compound $C_{15}H_{12}O_6$ obtained from the wood of various plants (as the smoke tree); dihydro-fisetin

fus·ti·ness \'fəstēnəs, -tin-\ *n* -ES : the quality or state of being fusty

fus·tle \'fu̇səl, 'fəs-\ *vi* -ED/-ING/-S [blend of *fuss* and *bustle*] *dial Brit* : to fuss and bustle

fus·ty \'fəstē, -ti\ *adj* -ER/-EST [ME, fr. *fust* wine cask (fr. MF, club, stick, tree, cask, fr. L *fustis* club, staff) + *-y* — more at BEAT] **1** *Brit* : impaired by age or dampness : MOLDY ⟨~ hay⟩ **2** : saturated with dust and stale odors : MUSTY ⟨rummage into ~ rooms —Howard Griffin⟩ **3** : old-fashioned or rigidly conservative : ANTIQUATED ⟨a ~ elderly gentleman in a threadbare morning coat —George Bellairs⟩

fu·su·la \'fyüzələ\ *n, pl* **fusu·lae** \-,lē, -,lī\ *or* **fusulas** [NL, fr. L *fusus* spindle + *-ula* (fem. dim. suffix)] : a terminal projection of the spinneret of a spider through which the silk gland opens

fu·su·li·na \,fyüzə'līnə, -lēnə\ *n* [NL, fr. L *fusus* spindle + *-ulus* (dim. suffix) + NL *-ina*] **1** *cap* : a genus (the type of the family Fusulinidae) of large fossil spindle-shaped foraminiferans having a test with 4-layered walls and deeply folded septa and serving as an index fossil in various Lower and Middle Pennsylvanian rocks **2** -S : an animal or fossil of *Fusulina* or a related genus

[1]**fu·su·lin·id** \¦==¦=nəd, -¦linəd\ *adj* [NL *Fusulinidae*] : of or relating to the family Fusulinidae

[2]**fusulinid** \"\ *or* **fu·su·line** \'fyüzə,līn\ *n* -S : an animal or fossil of the family Fusulinidae

fu·su·lin·i·dae \,fyüzə'linə,dē\ *n pl, cap* [NL, fr. *Fusulina*, type genus + *-idae*] : a large family of Paleozoic foraminiferans known from their tests which form a major component of one widely distributed kind of Carboniferous limestone

fu·su·ma \'füsə,mä\ *n* -S [Jap] : a framed and papered sliding door used to partition off rooms in a Japanese house

fut *abbr* future; futures

futch·el *or* **futch·ell** \'fəchəl\ *n* -S [origin unknown] : one of the pieces of wood or metal forming a socket for the pole of a carriage and uniting the splinter bar and the fore axletree

fu·thark \'fü,thärk\ *also* **fu·thorc** *or* **fu·thork** \-thȯrk\ *n* -S [*futhark* fr. the first 6 letters (including *thorn* for *th*) of the Scandinavian and continental runic alphabets; *futhorc, futhork* fr. the first 6 letters of the Anglo-Saxon runic alphabet] : RUNIC ALPHABET

fu·tile \'fyüd·ᵊl, -ütᵊl, *also* -ü,tīl *sometimes* -ü(,)til\ *adj* [MF or L; MF *futile*, fr. L *futtilis, futilis* that easily pours out, vain, worthless, fr. *futt-, fut-* (fr. *fundere* to pour, melt) + *-ilis* -ile — more at FOUND] **1** : serving no useful purpose : INEFFECTIVE, FRUITLESS ⟨opposition . . . had been so ~ that surrender seemed the only course open —C.L.Jones⟩ **2** : occupied with trifles : FRIVOLOUS ⟨a ~ vain man —John Buchan⟩ — **fu·tile·ly** \-ᵊl(l)|ē, -īl|, -il(l)|, |i\ *adv* — **fu·tile·ness** \-ᵊlnəs, -īln-,-iln-\ *n* -ES

[1]**fu·til·i·tar·i·an** \(,)fyü,tilə'terēən, -'ta(a)r-,-'tār-\ *n* -S [blend of *futile* and *utilitarian*] **1** : one who engages in futile pursuits **2** : one who believes in the futility of human striving and aspiration — **fu·til·i·tar·i·an·ism** \-ēə,nizəm\ *n* -S

[2]**futilitarian** \(¦)=¦==¦===\ *adj* : exhibiting or based on an attitude of futility ⟨~ defeatism of the . . . recent posthumous volume —Fred Rodell⟩

fu·til·i·ty \fyü'tiləd·ē, -ətē, -i\ *n* -ES [L *futilitas*, fr. *futilis* + *-itas* -ity] **1** : the quality or state of being futile : USELESSNESS ⟨the economic ~ of military power —Norman Angell⟩ **2** : an abortive attempt or useless gesture ⟨as startling as the aptness of flower and insect symbiosis are their unsuccesses and *futilities* —D.C.Peattie⟩ ⟨the *futilities* of debate for its own sake —W.A.White⟩ **3** : a lack of serious purpose : FRIVOLITY ⟨the pure *futilities* and unmitigated flirtations of an aristocracy —Walter Bagehot⟩

futilous *adj* [L *futil*is + E *-ous*] *obs* : FUTILE

fut·tock \'fəd·ək, -ətək\ *n* -s [prob. alter. of *foothook*] **:** one of the curved timbers scarfed together to form the lower part of the compound rib of a ship; *esp* **:** one of the transverse framing timbers passing across the keel — see SHIP illustration

futtock hoop *or* **futtock band** *n* **:** an iron band located near the top of a lower mast and to which the futtock shrouds are secured

futtock plate *n* **:** an iron plate fastened to the top of a lower mast and equipped with deadeyes to which the topmast rigging and the upper ends of the futtock shrouds are secured

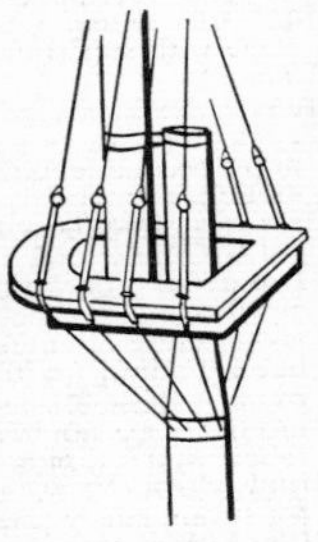

futtock plate

futtock shroud *n* **:** a short iron rod leading from the futtock hoop to the futtock plate and connecting the topmast rigging with the lower mast — see SHIP illustration

futtock staff *n* **:** a short wooden or iron bar covered with leather or canvas and seized across the topmast rigging above the top

futtock stave *n, obs* **:** a short rope used to confine shrouds near a masthead

fu·tu·nan \fə'tünən, fü'-\ *n* -s *usu cap* [*Futuna* islands, southwestern Pacific + E *-an*] **1 a :** a Polynesian people of the Futuna islands **b :** a member of such people **2** *also* **futuna :** the Polynesian language of the Futunan people — compare AUSTRONESIAN

fu·tu·rama \ˌfyüchə'ramə, -rämə\ *n* -s [fr. *Futurama*, an exhibit at the New York World's Fair (1939-40)] **:** a preview of something that is not yet a reality **:** indication of potential ⟨a model, a full-scale ~ of what a democratic city should be —Alden Stevens⟩

fu·tu·ram·ic \¦==¦ramik\ *adj* **:** of advanced design ⟨a ~ car⟩

[1]**fu·ture** \'fyüchə(r)\ *adj* [ME, fr. OF & L; OF *futur*, fr. L *futurus* about to be (suppletive fut. part. of *esse* to be) — more at BE] **1 :** that is to be **:** still to come ⟨some ~ day⟩; *specif* **:** existing after death ⟨doctrine of a ~ life —John Kenrick⟩ **2 :** of, relating to, or constituting the future tense ⟨a ~ auxiliary⟩ **3 :** existing or occurring at a later time **:** SUBSEQUENT ⟨at 18 the ~ chairman of the board joined the company as a shipping clerk⟩

[2]**future** \"\ *n* -s [ME, fr. *future*, adj.] **1 a :** time that is to come ⟨car of the ~⟩ ⟨do better in ~⟩ ⟨be more tidy in ~ —*Blackwood's*⟩ **b :** what is going to happen ⟨the past determines the ~⟩ ⟨never tell the ~ —Graham Greene⟩ **2 a :** a prospective usu. improved condition ⟨expectation of a ~ worthy of the past⟩; *specif* **:** one held to follow mortal life **b :** an expectation of advancement **:** prospect for progressive development ⟨man with a ~⟩ ⟨discussed the ~ of electronics⟩ **3 a :** a stock or commodity bought and sold for delivery at a future time — usu. used in pl. ⟨speculated heavily in soybean ~*s* —Douglass Cater⟩ **b :** a contract for the purchase or sale of something to be delivered at a definite future time and at a specified price **4** [ML *futurum*, fr. neut. of L *futurus*] **:** the future tense of a language **:** a verb form in the future tense

[3]**future** *vb* -ED/-ING/-S *obs* **:** POSTPONE, DELAY

future farmer *n, usu cap both Fs* **:** a member of the national organization of boys enrolled in vocational agriculture courses in high schools in the U.S. called Future Farmers of America

future interest *or* **future estate** *n* **:** an interest or estate in property limited or created so that its owner will come into the use, possession, or enjoyment of it at some future time **:** ESTATE IN EXPECTANCY

fu·ture·less \'fyüchə(r)ləs\ *adj* **:** lacking the prospect of a future

futurely *adv, obs* **:** in future

fu·ture·ness *n* -ES **:** the quality or state of existing in the future

[1]**future perfect** *adj* **:** of, relating to, or constituting a verb tense that is traditionally formed in English with *will have* and *shall have* and that expresses completion of an action by a specified time that is yet to come ⟨*will have left* in "they will have left before we arrive" is a *future perfect* tense⟩

[2]**future perfect** *n* **:** the future perfect tense of a language **:** a verb form in the future perfect tense

future price *n* **:** the price of a stock or commodity on a futures contract — contrasted with *spot price*

future service benefit *n* **:** a pension benefit based on length of prospective service between employment date and retirement age and payable out of funds contributed by the employer, the employee, or both

future tense *n* **:** a verb tense traditionally formed in English with *will* and *shall* and expressive of time yet to come

fu·tur·ism \'fyüchəˌrizəm\ *n* -s [It *futurismo*, fr. *futuro* future (fr. L *futurus*) + *-ismo* -ism] **1 :** a point of view that seeks life's meaning or fulfillment in the future rather than in the past or present **:** UTOPIANISM — compare ARCHAISM 3c **2 :** a movement in art, music, and literature begun in Italy about 1910 and marked esp. by violent rejection of tradition and an effort to give formal expression to the dynamic energy and movement of mechanical processes

fu·tur·ist \-rəst\ *n* -s [It *futurista*, fr. *futuro* + *-ista* -ist] **1 :** one who holds that the prophecies of the Bible are still to be realized — compare PRESENTIST, PRETERIST **2 :** one who practices or advocates futurism

fu·tur·is·tic \¦fyüchə¦ristik, -tēk\ *adj* **:** of or relating to the future or to futurism ⟨the scene of the most ~ battle of the last war —Alan Moorehead⟩ — **fu·tur·is·ti·cal·ly** \-tək(ə)lē, -tēk-, -li\ *adv*

futuristic garden *n* **:** a garden design based on the volume of foliage and architectural masses and the air masses between them and uniting all three into a single pattern

fu·tu·ri·tion \ˌfyüchə'rishən\ *n* -s [ML *futurition-*, *futuritio*, fr. L *futurus* about to be + *-ition-*, *-itio* -ition — more at BE] **1** *archaic* **:** future existence **:** FUTURITY ⟨the ~ of salvation —John Pearson⟩ **2** *archaic* **:** assurance of a future ⟨had a fixed ~ from eternity —Jonathan Edwards⟩

fu·tu·ri·ty \fyü't|ürəd·ē, fyü·'ty|, fyü'ch|, |ür-, -ətē, -i\ *n* -ES [[1]*future* + *-ity*] **1 :** time to come **:** FUTURE ⟨neither service past, nor present sorrows, nor purposed merit in ~ can ransom me into his love again —Shak.⟩ **2 :** the quality or state of being future ⟨~ of current architecture⟩ **3 a futurities** *pl* **:** future events or prospects ⟨the reader whose scholarship is still among his *futurities* —Thomas De Quincey⟩ **b :** what will exist or happen in the future ⟨gazing . . . into ~ across the groom's shoulder —Marguerite Steen⟩; *specif* **:** POSTERITY **c :** a prospective future state; *specif* **:** life after death ⟨from this earth set free in some remote ~ —Walter de la Mare⟩ **4 :** FUTURITY RACE

futurity cocktail *n* **:** a cocktail made of sloe gin, vermouth, and sometimes rum and flavored with lemon juice, grenadine, and bitters

futurity race *n* **1 :** a horse race usu. for two-year-olds in which the competitors are nominated at birth or before — compare PRODUCE RACE **2 :** a race or competition (as a field trial) for which entries are made well in advance of the event

fuze *var of* FUSE

fuzee *var of* FUSEE

fuzil *var of* FUSIL

[1]**fuzz** \'fəz\ *n* -ES [prob. back-formation fr. *fuzzy*] **1** *obs* **:** PUFFBALL 1 **2 :** a mass of fluffy particles or fibers: as **a :** the short hairs remaining on the seed of most cotton varieties after removal of the longer lint fibers **b :** fibers that project from the surface of a sheet of paper or are not firmly incorporated into it **c :** the beard of an adolescent boy ⟨although a little ~ had recently begun to appear, had no real excuse for shaving —J.R.Gallagher⟩ **3 :** a blurred effect ⟨the rainbow-colored ~ of streetlight nebula —MacKinlay Kantor⟩ **4** *slang* **:** an officer of the law **:** POLICEMAN

[2]**fuzz** \"\ *vb* -ED/-ING/-ES *vi* **:** to fly off in or become covered with fluffy particles **:** become fuzzy ⟨angora tends to ~⟩ — often used with *out* ⟨watch the cat's tail ~ out when she's angry⟩ ⟨~*ing* out of the legal concept . . . to comprise another new crime —Gerard Piel⟩ ~ *vt* **1 :** to cover with fluff **:** make fuzzy ⟨the land was ~*ed* with buffalo grass —W.A.White⟩ **2 :** to envelop in a haze **:** BLUR ⟨my head was still badly ~*ed* from the drink —Ralph Ellison⟩ — usu. used with *up* ⟨~ up the argument⟩ ⟨if a little haze ~*es* up the lamps they say it's all closed in —C.A.Lindbergh b.1902⟩

fuzzball \'=,=\ *n, dial chiefly Eng* **:** PUFFBALL 1

fuzz·i·ly \'fəzəlē, -li\ *adv* **:** in a fuzzy manner

fuzz·i·ness \-zēnəs, -zin-\ *n* -ES **:** the quality or state of being fuzzy

fuzz stick *n* **:** a short stick of dead wood with the wet outer layer cut away and the dry center trimmed down into feathers that is used by campers to start a fire when the fuel is damp

fuzztail \'=,=\ *n* -s *West* **:** a wild horse — compare BROOMTAIL

[1]**fuzzy** \'fəzē, -zi\ *adj* -ER/-EST [perh. fr. LG *fussig* loose, light, spongy; akin to D *voos* spongy, ON *fauskr* rotten wood, OHG *fūl* rotten — more at FOUL] **1** *now dial Eng* **:** not firm **:** SPONGY **2 :** having a furry or downy appearance **:** covered with fuzz ⟨deep-piled ~ felts —Lois Long⟩ ⟨an inviting carpet of ~ green moss —Tom Marvel⟩ **3 :** lacking in clarity or definition: as **a :** indistinct in outline **:** not in focus **:** BLURRED ⟨camera movement is a very likely cause of ~ photos —*Kodak Photo Notes*⟩; *specif* **:** lacking in musical clarity ⟨the loud fugue gets ~ towards end —*Saturday Rev.*⟩ **b :** VAGUE, INCONCLUSIVE, INDEFINITE ⟨like many crusaders . . . vehement in assault but ~ as to the nature of his reforms —Charles Lee⟩ **c :** CONFUSED, INCOHERENT, MUDDLED ⟨when a man's thinking is ~ or involved, so will his writing be —W.R.Parker⟩; *specif* **:** muddled by drink ⟨drank faster than anybody else without becoming ~ —Herman Wouk⟩ **4 :** CURLED, CRISPED, FRIZZY ⟨~'red wigs stuck with jewels —G.W.Thornbury⟩

[2]**fuzzy** \"\ *n* -ES **1 :** FUZZY-WUZZY **2 :** FUZZTAIL

fuzzy-guzzy \¦==¦gəzē\ *n* -s [redupl. & alter. of [1]*fuzzy*] **:** a balsamweed (*Gnaphalium obtusifolium*) with glandular villous stem

fuzzy-headed \¦==¦==\ *adj* **1 :** having a head with a woolly or downy surface ⟨*fuzzy-headed* dandelion⟩ **2 :** FUZZY 3c

fuzzy-wuzzy \¦==¦wəzē\ *n* -ES *usu cap F&W* [redupl. & alter. of [1]*fuzzy*] **1 :** a Negro of the Republic of the Sudan **2 :** a native of New Guinea or the Solomon islands

FV *abbr* [L *folio verso*] on the back of the page

f-value \'=,==\ *n* **:** F-NUMBER

FW *abbr* fresh water

FWB *abbr* four-wheel brake

FWD *abbr* **1** four-wheel drive **2** freshwater damage

fwd *abbr* forward

fwdd *abbr* forwarded

FWE *abbr* finished with engines

fx *abbr* foxed

FX *abbr* foreign exchange

fx station *n, usu cap F&X* **:** FIXED STATION

-fy \-ˌfī\ *vb suffix* -ED/-ING/-ES [ME *-fien*, fr. OF *-fier*, fr. L *-ficare*, fr. *-ficus* -fic] **1 :** make **:** form into ⟨dandi*fy*⟩ ⟨gaudi*fy*⟩ **2 :** invest with the attributes of **:** make similar to ⟨citi*fy*⟩

fy *abbr* ferry

FY *abbr* fiscal year

fyce \'fīs\ *var of* FEIST

FYI *abbr* for your information

[1]**fyke** \'fīk\ *var of* FIKE

[2]**fyke** \"\ *or* **fike** \"\ *n* -s [D *fuik* bow net, fr. MD *fūke*, *fuycke*] **:** a long bag net kept open by a series of hoops

fyke net *n* **:** FYKE; *esp* **:** a fyke equipped with one or more cork-floated wing nets designed to direct the fish toward the mouth of the fyke proper

fykie *var of* FIKIE

fyle *Scot var of* [3]FILE

fyl·fot \'filˌfät\ *n* -s [ME, painted device to fill the lower part of a painted window, fr. *fillen* to fill + *foot*] **:** SWASTIKA 1

fyrd \'fərd, 'fi(ə)rd\ *n* -s [OE *fierd*, *fyrd* (also, campaign, camp); akin to OHG *fart* journey, ON *ferth*, Goth us*fartho* departure; derivatives fr. the root of E *fare*] **1 :** the national militia in England prior to the Norman Conquest ⟨men of the ~ were mustered and their weapons counted —Hope Muntz⟩ **2 :** the duty to serve in the fyrd

fytte \'fit\ *archaic var of* [1]FIT

fz *abbr* [It *forzando; forzato*] accented

¹g \'jē\ *n, pl* **g's** *or* **gs** \'jēz\ *often cap, often attrib* **1 a :** the seventh letter of the English alphabet **b :** an instance of this letter printed, written, or otherwise represented **c :** a speech counterpart of orthographic *g* (as hard *g* in *go, sagged,* or soft *g* in *gem*) **2 a :** the keynote of G major or G minor **b :** the tone G **3 :** a printer's type, a stamp, or some other instrument for reproducing the letter *g* **4 :** someone or something arbitrarily or conveniently designated *g* esp. as the seventh in order or class **5 :** a unit of force applied to a body at rest equal to the force exerted on it by gravity **:** one of several such units applied to a body when accelerated (as when an airplane pulls out of a dive or makes a sharp turn) **6 a :** a general factor in intelligence **b** [symbol for *general ability*] **:** ABILITY 2 **7** *slang* **:** a sum of 1000 dollars

²g *abbr, often cap* **1** game **2** garage **3** [F *gauche*] left **4** gauge **5** gauss **6** gelding **7** gender **8** general **9** genitive **10** German **11** gilbert **12** gilt **13** glider **14** gloom **15** goal; goalie **16** gold **17** good **18** gourde **19** government **20** grain **21** gram **22** grand **23** gravity; acceleration of gravity **24** great **25** green **26** Greenwich time **27** grid **28** groschen **29** gross **30** group **31** guard **32** guardian **33** guide **34** guilder **35** guinea **36** gulden **37** gulf

³g *symbol, often cap* conductance

-g *abbr* -ing — used esp. in standard abbreviations of the present participle forms of verbs (as *actg* for *acting*)

ga \'gä\ *n, pl* **ga** \"\ *or* **gas** \'gäz\ *usu cap* **1 a :** a people of Ghana linguistically and culturally related to the Ashanti and others of the region — called also *Akra, Incra* **b :** a member of such people **2 :** a Kwa language of the Ga people

ga' \'gä\ *Scot var of* GALL

ga *abbr* gauge

GA *abbr* **1** general agent **2** general assembly **3** general assistance **4** general average

Ga *symbol* gallium

¹gab \'gab\ *n* -s [prob. alter. of ²*gob*] **1** *chiefly Scot* **a :** MOUTH **b :** TONGUE **2** *chiefly Scot* **:** TASTE

²gab \'gab, 'gaa(ə)b\ *vi* **gabbed; gabbed; gabbing; gabs** [prob. short for *gabble*] **:** to talk in an idle, rapid, or thoughtless manner **:** CHATTER ⟨*gabbed* . . . about his six kids —*Time*⟩ ⟨she'll probably ~ about it tomorrow at the office until I have to shut her up —Edna Ferber⟩

³gab \"\ *n* -s **:** TALK; *esp* **:** idle talk ⟨luncheon ~ among women —John Portz⟩

⁴gab \"\ *n* -s [prob. fr. Flem *gabbe* notch, gash] **:** a hook or notch (as in an eccentric rod for a valve motion) designed to drop over a rod or lever to make a temporary connection

⁵gab \"\ *vi* **gabbed; gabbed; gabbing; gabs** [F *gaber,* fr. ON *gabba;* akin to ME *gabben* to scoff, lie, D *gabberen* to joke, and perh. to OE *geonian, ginian* to yawn — more at YAWN] *archaic* **:** BOAST

⁶gab \"\ *n* -s [by shortening] **:** GABARDINE

ga·bar \'gäbər\ *n* -s *usu cap* [Per, fr. Ar *kāfir* unbeliever] **:** a Zoroastrian of Iran — compare PARSI

gab·ar·dine \'gabə(r),dēn, ˌ≈≈'≈\ *n* -s [MF *gaverdine, galvardine*] **1 :** GABERDINE **2 :** a garment of gabardine; *esp* **:** a gabardine coat or suit **3 :** a firm durable fabric with a steep twill weave forming fine distinct diagonal ribs on the right side that is given a smooth hard finish with or without sheen and is made of various fibers and in many weights for clothing

ga·ba·rit \ˌgabə¦rē\ *n* -s [F, fr. Prov *gabarrit* ship's model, blend of *gabarro* ship (fr. OProv *gabarra,* prob. modif. of LL *carabus* boat resembling a coracle) and *garbi* ship's model, form, of Gmc origin; perh. akin to OHG *garawen* to prepare — more at CARAVEL, YARE] **1 :** an outline on a drawing of an object (as a machine part) intended to move showing the space necessary to permit its motion **2 :** an outline on a drawing of a stationary object showing the space that must be kept clear for necessary access to it

gab·bai \gä'bī, '≈,≈\ *n, pl* **gab·ba·im** \-īəm,-ī(,)ēm\ *also* **gabbais** [Heb *gabbay* collector, treasurer] **1 :** a collector of charitable gifts of taxes among the Jews in talmudic times **2 :** a synagogue official; *esp* **:** a treasurer or administrator of synagogue funds

gab·bard \'gabərd\ *or* **gab·bart** \-rt\ *n* -s [modif. (influenced by *-ard, -art*) of MF *gabarre, gabbarre* ship, fr. OProv *gabarra*] **:** a small ship (as a lighter or barge) formerly much used in inland navigation in Scotland

¹gab·ber \'gabə(r)\ *vb* [prob. of imit. origin] *archaic* **:** JABBER

²gabber \"\ *n* -s [¹*gabber*] *archaic* **:** fast and incoherent or unintelligible talk

³gabber \", 'gaab-\ *n* -s [²*gab* + *-er*] **:** one that talks much, habitually, and usu. idly **:** CHATTERER

¹gab·ble \'gabəl\ *vb* **gabbled; gabbled; gabbling** \-b(ə)liŋ\ **gabbles** [prob. of imit. origin] *vi* **1 :** to talk fast, idly, foolishly, or without meaning **:** JABBER, CHATTER ⟨with a mighty throat clearing, he would ~ through his prayer —Ernest Beaglehole⟩ ⟨he loves to ~ with housewives at church suppers —Andrew Hamilton⟩ ⟨spent his time *gabbling* in bars⟩ ⟨the clerk had *gabbled* about a fee due⟩ ⟨saying nothing comprehensible, just babbling and *gabbling,* half unconsciously —Arnold Bennett⟩ **2 :** to utter inarticulate sounds (as of a chicken) rapidly ⟨a skein of duck came across, *gabbling* softly to themselves in the high air —Naomi Mitchison⟩ ~ *vt* **:** to say with incoherent rapidity **:** BABBLE ⟨our excitement exploded and we *gabbled* the story over and over —Santha Rama Rau⟩

²gabble \"\ *n* -s **1 :** loud or rapid talk with little or no meaning **:** nonsense talk ⟨subjected to ~ about fifteenth-century politics —John McCarten⟩ **2 :** meaningless sounds rapidly uttered (as by chickens) or given out (as by a stream running over rocks) ⟨discriminating between music and ~ —R.L.Ives⟩ ⟨listening to the avid ~ of water running from a gargoyle at the corner of the schoolhouse —Eve Langley⟩

gab·ble·ment \-bəlmənt\ *n* -s *archaic* **:** GABBLE

gab·bler \'gab(ə)lə(r)\ *n* -s **:** one that gabbles

gab·ble rat·chet \'gabəl,rachət\ *or* **gabble rack·et** \-,rakət\ *var of* GABRIEL RATCHET

gab·bro \'ga(,)brō\ *n* -s [It, prob. modif. of L *glaber* bare, smooth — more at GLAD] **:** a rock of a family of granular igneous rocks composed essentially of calcic plagioclase (as labradorite), a ferromagnesian mineral (as augite, hypersthene, olivine, or hornblende), and accessory minerals (as apatite, magnetite, ilmenite) — **gab·bro·ic** \(')ga¦brōik\ *adj* — **gab·bro·it·ic** \¦≈(,)≈¦id·ik\ *adj*

gab·broid \'ga,brȯid\ *adj* [*gabbro* + *-oid*] **:** resembling gabbro

gab·by \'gabē, 'gaab-, -bi\ *adj* -ER/-EST **:** fond of talking **:** TALKATIVE, GARRULOUS ⟨kept from his duties by ~ colleagues⟩ ⟨always liked a ~ team in practice, a team that shouted as it ran signals —Harry Sylvester⟩

ga·belle \gə'bel\ *n* -s [ME, fr. MF, fr. OIt *gabella,* fr. Ar *qabālah*] **:** TAX; *specif* **:** an impost on salt (as in France for several centuries prior to 1790)

gab·er·dine \'gabə(r),dēn, ˌ≈≈'≈\ *n* -s [MF *gaverdine*] **1 a :** a coarse long coat or smock worn chiefly by Jews in medieval times **b :** a loose garment like a smock worn by English laborers **c :** something that covers and protects **2** *dial Eng* **:** PINAFORE **3 :** GABARDINE

gab·er·lun·zie \ˌgabər'lənzi, -lin-, *archaic* -lün(y)i\ *n* -s [earlier *gaberlungy*] **1** *Scot* **:** BEGGAR, MENDICANT; *esp* **:** a former licensed professional beggar **2** *Scot* **:** a wandering ne'er-do-well

gab·fest \'≈,fest\ *n* -s [³*gab* + G *fest* festival — more at -FEST] **:** an occasion marked chiefly by conversation (as gab) ⟨the inevitable and excited curbstone political ~*s* —*World Report*⟩ ⟨dinners and evening ~*s* with national union chiefs —*Newsweek*⟩ ⟨his own drugstore — where the teenagers gather for a soda and a ~ —W.F.McDermott⟩

gab·gab \'gäb,gäb, 'gab,gab\ *n* [Chamorro] **1 :** CORAL TREE a **2 :** PIA

ga·bi *or* **ga·be** \'gäbē\ *n* -s [Tag *gabi*] *Philippines* **:** TARO

gabies *pl of* GABY

ga·bi·on \'gābēən\ *n* -s [MF, fr. OIt *gabbione,* lit., large cage, aug. of *gabbia* cage, fr. L *cavea* — more at CAGE] **1 :** a hollow cylinder of wickerwork or strap iron like a basket without a bottom that is filled with earth and used in building fieldworks or in mining as revetments or as shelter from an enemy's fire **2 :** a contrivance like a gabion filled with stones and sunk to assist in forming a bar, dike, or similar structure (as in harbor works)

ga·bi·o·nade \ˌgābēə¦nād, -näd\ *n* -s [F *gabionnade,* fr. MF, fr. OIt *gabbionata,* fr. *gabbione* gabion + *-ata* -ade] **1 :** a work of fortification thrown up with gabions **2 :** a structure of gabions sunk in lines as a core for a sandbar in harbor improvements

ga·bi·oned \'gābēənd\ *adj* **:** furnished with gabions

ga·ble \'gābəl\ *n* -s [ME, fr. MF, fr. ONF, of Gmc origin; akin to ON *gafl* gable — more at CEPHALIC] **1 a :** the vertical triangular portion of the end of a building from the level of the cornice or eaves to the ridge of the roof **b :** a similar end when not triangular in shape (as of a gambrel roof) **c :** the end wall of a building as distinguished from the front or rear side **2 :** something resembling or suggesting a gable esp. in shape ⟨an immense mountain mass with three ~*s* fronting the valley —John Muir †1914⟩: as **a :** a decorative usu. triangular member (as on a piece of furniture or above a Gothic doorway arch) — see BELL GABLE **b** *or* **gable hood :** a heavy hooded headdress made with a peaked band similar to a gable framing the face and worn by women during Henry VIII's reign

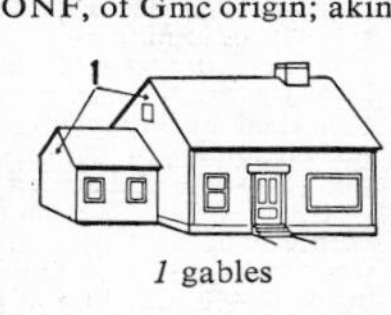

1 gables

gableboard \'≈≈,≈\ *n* **:** BARGEBOARD

ga·bled \-bəld\ *adj* **:** furnished or constructed with a gable ⟨a ~ house⟩ ⟨a ~ roof⟩ ⟨a ~ lintel⟩

gable end *n* [ME *gable ende,* fr. *gable* + *ende* end — more at END] **:** a gabled end wall (as of a wing of a building)

gable roof *n* **:** a double-sloping roof that forms a gable at each end — see ROOF illustration

ga·blet \'gāblət\ *n* -s [ME, fr. AF, dim. of ONF *gable*] **:** a small gable or canopy shaped like a gable (as over a tabernacle, niche, buttress)

gable wall *n* **:** a wall surmounted by a gable

gable window *n* **1 :** a window in a gable **2 :** a window with a gable

gab·lock \'gablək\ *var of* GAVELOCK

ga·bon \gə'bōn, -bän\ *adj, usu cap* [fr. *Gabon* Republic in Africa] **:** of or relating to Gabon **:** of the kind or style prevalent in Gabon

gabo·nese \ˌgabə¦nēz, ¦gäb-, -ēs\ *n, pl* **gabonese** *cap* [*Gabon* + *-ese*] **:** a native or inhabitant of Gabon

¹ga·boon *or* **ga·bun** \gə'bün, (')ga¦b-, (')gä¦b-\ *n* -s **1** *cap, in former classifications* **:** any of the Negro people of the Gabon Republic **2 a** *or* **gaboon mahogany** (1) **:** a light soft attractively grained pink to pinkish brown African wood (2) **:** a tree yielding gaboon (esp. *Aucoumea klaineana* and *Canarium schweinfurthii*) **b :** a high-grade black ebony obtained chiefly from the Gabon region of Africa

²ga·boon \(')gä¦bün, gə'b-\ *n* -s [alter. of ¹*gob* (lump of tobacco) + *-oon* (as in *spittoon*)] *dial* **:** CUSPIDOR, SPITTOON

gaboon chocolate *n, usu cap G* **:** DIKA BREAD

gaboon viper *n, usu cap G* **:** a large heavy-bodied brilliantly marked extremely venomous West African viper (*Bitis gabonica*) of sluggish and unaggressive disposition

ga·bri·e·li·no *or* **ga·bri·e·le·no** \ˌgäbrēə'lē(,)nō\ *n, pl* **gabrielino** *or* **gabrielinos** *or* **gabrieleno** *or* **gabrielenos** *usu cap* [Sp *gabrieleño,* fr. San *Gabriel,* a mission in Los Angeles county, Calif. + Sp *-eño* (suffix added to place names to form names of inhabitants)] **1 a :** a Shoshonean people of Los Angeles and Orange counties, California **b :** a member of such people **2 :** the language of the Gabrielino people

ga·bri·el rat·chet \'gābrēəl,rachət\ *n* [ME *Gabrielle rache,* fr. *Gabriel,* one of the seven archangels, the herald of good tidings (Lk 1), thought of as blowing a trumpet on Judgment Day + *rache* hound — more at RACH] *dial* **:** the cries of migrating wild geese flying by night which are often popularly explained as the baying of a supernatural pack of hounds and to which various superstitious significances (as forebodings of evil) are attributed

gabs *pl of* GAB, *pres 3d sing of* GAB

gab session *n, slang* **:** GABFEST

ga·by \'gābi, 'gōbi\ *n* -ES [perh. of Scand origin; akin to Icel *gapi* reckless or frivolous person, fr. *gapa* to gape — more at GAPE] *now dial Eng* **:** SIMPLETON ⟨still whimpering after that ~ of a husband —W.M.Thackeray⟩

ga·chu·pin \ˌgächə¦pēn\ *n* -s [AmerSp *gachupin, cachupin,* fr. obs. Sp *cachopin* block, trunk, blockhead, fr. *cachopo* hollow or dry trunk of a tree, fr. *cacho* pot, shard — more at CACHUCHA] *chiefly Southwest* **:** a Spanish settler in America who immigrated from Spain — sometimes used disparagingly

g acid *n, usu cap G* **:** an acid $HOC_{10}H_5(SO_3H)_2$ made by sulfonating beta-naphthol and used as an intermediate for azo dyes; 2-naphthol-6,8-disulfonic acid

¹gad \'gad, 'gaa(ə)d\ *n* -s [ME *gad, gadd,* fr. ON *gaddr* spike, sting — more at YARD (measure)] **1 a** *obs* **:** a sharp-pointed metal rod or stylus **b** *archaic* **:** SPEAR **c :** a chisel or pointed or wedge-shaped bar of iron or steel for breaking or loosening ore or rock **d** *West* **:** SPUR **2 a** *archaic* **:** a bar or ingot of metal **b :** a heraldic bearing supposed to represent such a gad sometimes depicted as a plain rectangle with the vertical dimension greater than the horizontal one and sometimes with a third dimension showing along the edge **3** *dial* **:** ROD, STICK: as **a :** a stiff whip or switch **b** *chiefly Scot* **:** FISHING ROD

²gad \"\ *vb* **gadded; gadded; gadding; gads** *vi* **:** to use a gad ~ *vt* **:** to break or loosen (as rock) with a gad in mining

³gad \"\ *vi* **gadded; gadded; gadding; gads** [ME *gadden*] **1 a :** to go or wander about esp. idly or on trivial purposes (as to gossip) — often used with *about* ⟨the women were *gadding* about gossiping instead of spending the day industriously —Ernest Beaglehole⟩ ⟨*gadding* about at political meetings —H.M.Parshley⟩ **b** *obs* **:** to run wild **:** dash about in an uncontrolled manner **2** *of an arrow* **:** to fly erratically

⁴gad \"\ *n* -s **:** the act of gadding **:** a wandering about usu. on rather trivial errands — now used chiefly in the phrases *on the gad* and *upon the gad*

⁵gad \"\ *interj* [euphemism for *God*] — a mild oath

⁶gad \"\ *n* -s [IrGael, fr. MIr *gat* willow twig — more at YARD (measure)] **:** a band or rope made of twisted straw or osiers

gad·a·ba \'gadəbə\ *n* -s *usu cap* **1 :** one of a people of primitive hoe cultivators in eastern India **2 :** the Munda language of the Gadabas

¹gadabout \'≈≈,≈\ *adj* [fr. *gad about,* v., fr. ³*gad*] **:** being a gadabout ⟨a ~ brother who refused to settle down⟩

²gadabout \"\ *n* -s [fr. *gad about,* v.] **:** one that moves or wanders from place to place often with somewhat trivial purposes **:** GADDER ⟨social whirlers are of two kinds, the ones who concentrate on doing a lot of entertaining at home, and the ones who are ~*s* —A.C.Spectorsky⟩

gad·a·rene \'gadə,rēn, ˌ≈≈'≈\ *adj* [LL *Gadarenus,* fr. Gk *Gadarēnos* inhabitant of Gadara, fr. *Gadara,* ancient town near the Sea of Galilee in northern Palestine] **1** *usu cap* **:** of or relating to Gadara or its inhabitants **2** *often cap* [fr. the *Gadarene* swine (Mt 8: 28) that rushed into the sea and drowned when Jesus sent into them demons exorcised from a demoniac person] **:** rushing precipitously forward **:** engaged in headlong flight ⟨watching the *Gadarene* swarms surging along the pavements of cities —Bruce Marshall⟩ ⟨perceiving this pitfall and attempting to prevent his ardent followers from making a ~ plunge into it —Bergen Evans⟩

ga·da·ria \gə'dərēə\ *n* -s *usu cap* [Hindi *gaḍariyā,* fr. *gāḍar* sheep] **:** one of a caste of shepherds of central and northeastern India

gad·dang \'gä,däŋ, ≈'≈\ *n, pl* **gaddang** *or* **gaddangs** *usu cap* [native name in the Philippines] **1 a :** a people inhabiting northern Luzon in the Philippines **b :** a member of such people **2 :** the Austronesian language of the Gaddang people

¹gad·der \'gadə(r), -aad-\ *n* -s [³*gad* + *-er*] **:** one that travels about habitually, restlessly, or with chiefly social purposes

²gadder \"\ *n* -s [²*gad* + *-er*] **:** a traveling drilling machine used in quarrying to make a line of holes into which gads are driven to break out the stone

¹gad·di *or* **ga·di** \gə'dē, '≈≈\ *n* -s [Hindi *gaddī*] **1** *India* **a :** a cushion esp. for a throne **b :** THRONE ⟨the succession to the ~ was not in all cases hereditary —*White Paper on Indian States*⟩ ⟨succeeded to the ~ in 1899 —*Statesman's Yr. Bk.*⟩ **2** *India* **:** a high ruling position ⟨helping the smaller ones of his tribe into ministerial ~*s* —*Weekly Observer*⟩

²gaddi \"\ *n, pl* **gaddi** *or* **gaddis** *usu cap* **1 :** a low-caste chiefly shepherd people in Kashmir **2 :** a member of the Gaddi people

gade \'gād\ *n* -s [NL *Gadus,* genus name] **:** a gadoid fish; *esp* **:** ROCKLING

gadfly \'≈,≈\ *n* [¹*gad* + *fly*] **1 :** any of various flies (as a tabanid, botfly, or warble fly) that bite or annoy livestock **2 :** a usu. purposely annoying or provoking person; *esp* **:** one that stimulates or provokes to activity and esp. to the analysis and defense of ideas by persistent criticism esp. of an irritating pointed kind ⟨an immensely busy writer on various subjects, a ~ to the respectable —Carl Van Doren⟩ ⟨a ~, buzzing with ideas both for political strategy and the improvement of things in Oregon —*U. S. News & World Report*⟩

gadge \'gaj, -äj\ *dial Brit var of* GAUGE

¹gad·get \'gajət, *usu* -əd·+V\ *n* -s [origin unknown] **1 :** a usu. small and often novel mechanical or electronic device or contrivance esp. on a piece of machinery ⟨the garden tools and ~*s* which make gardening so much more fun —Una Van der Spuy⟩ ⟨radio was one of our greatest ~*s* —M.C.Faught⟩ ⟨relatively complicated ~*s,* like hay-loaders and elevators —G.E.Fussell⟩ ⟨swings, pushcarts, car seats, or any kind of ~ in which a baby may be left sitting —*Infant Care*⟩ ⟨interesting social ~*s,* the crèche, where the women workers' babies were cared for, the hospitals, the showers and the gymnasium —W.A.White⟩ ⟨promised to bring the fire truck to school to explain the purpose and use of various ~*s* and devices on the truck —*Deerfield* (*Wisc.*) *Independent*⟩ **2 :** a spring clip attached to the end of a punty in glass manufacturing

²gadget \"\ *vt* -ED/-ING/-S **:** to equip with or as if with gadgets ⟨our homes, ~*ed* to the last push button —James Street⟩

gad·ge·teer \ˌgajə¦ti(ə)r, -iə\ *n* -s **:** one markedly fond of devising or employing gadgets ⟨an incorrigible ~, a manipulator and inventor of small marvels —G.W.Brace⟩ ⟨a short, stocky, energetic ~ . . . had an early flair for electrical devices —*Newsweek*⟩ ⟨the ~*s* who ride on our trains fascinate me, especially the compass carriers, who have to check every so often which way the train is going —F.J.Taylor⟩

gad·ge·teer·ing \-iriŋ\ *n* -s **:** the devising of gadgets ⟨spent his life at ~⟩ ⟨first step in tin can ~ is finding the right size cans —*Boy Scout Handbook*⟩

gad·get·ry \'gajətrē, -ri\ *n* -ES **1 :** GADGETEERING ⟨the ~ of science costs huge sums —W.A.Noyes b. 1898⟩ **2 :** GADGETS ⟨a world of mechanical ~ —A.C.Fisher⟩ ⟨the marvels of modern ~ that could reduce hard work to a minimum of effort —James Aldredge⟩ ⟨labor-saving ~ —J.I.Rodale⟩

gad·gety \-jəd·ē, -ət\, \i\ *adj* **1 :** of or relating to a gadget ⟨the ~ handiness of a folding stool⟩ **:** consisting of or being a gadget ⟨~ merchandise —*Amer. Perfumer*⟩ **:** having the qualities of a gadget ⟨recommended . . . as the most compact, the simplest, the least ~ —E.T.Canby⟩ ⟨a very ~ gold pen —Cyril Ray⟩ **2 :** fond of gadgets or gadgeteering ⟨so ~ have we become, a new magazine is started to keep us informed on latest gadgets —*N.Y.Daily News*⟩ ⟨a ~ old gentleman who fiddled with rotary steam engines —W.S.Lynch⟩

¹ga·dhel·ic \gə'delik, (')ga¦d-\ *adj, usu cap* [ScGael *Gāidheal* & IrGael *Gaedheal* Gael + E *-ic* — more at GAEL] **:** GOIDELIC

²gadhelic \"\ *n* -s *cap* **:** GOIDELIC

¹gadid \'gädəd, 'gad-\ *adj* [NL *Gadidae*] **:** of or relating to the Gadidae

²gadid \"\ *n* -s **:** a fish of the family Gadidae

gad·i·dae \'gadə,dē\ *n pl, cap* [NL, fr. *Gadus,* type genus + *-idae*] **:** a large family of soft-finned fishes of the order Anacanthini including many important food fishes (as the cod, haddock, tomcods, pollacks) that are chiefly marine although one genus (*Lota*) is confined to fresh water and that have a rather elongated body, small cycloid scales, a large mouth, wide gill openings, and usu. a barbel on the chin

gad·i·for·mes \ˌgadə'fȯr,mēz\ *n pl, cap* [NL, fr. *Gadus* + *-iformes*] *in some classifications* **:** an order or other division of teleost fishes including the cods and closely related forms but usu. more restricted than the order Anacanthini to which it is partially equivalent

gad·i·tan \'gadətən, -ət°n, -ə,tan\ *also* **gad·i·tane** \-ə,tān\ *adj, usu cap* [L *Gaditanus,* fr. *Gades* Cádiz, Spain, after such pairs as L *Neapolis* Naples: *Neapolitanus* Neapolitan] **:** of or relating to Cádiz (anciently Gadir), in Spain

gad·ite \'ga,dīt\ *n* -s *usu cap* [*Gad,* 7th son of Jacob (Gen 30:11), the eponymous ancestor of the Gadites (Josh 1:12) + E *-ite*] **:** a member of the Hebrew tribe of Gad **:** a descendant of Gad

gad·man \'gadmən\ *n, pl* **gadmen** [ME, fr. ¹*gad* + *man*] *dial Brit* **:** GOADMAN

¹gadoid \'gā,dȯid, 'ga,-\ *adj* [NL *Gadus,* genus name + E *-oid*] **:** resembling or relating to the Gadidae

²gadoid \"\ *n* -s **:** a gadoid fish

gad·ole·ic acid \ˌgadə¦lēik-\ *n* [NL *Gadus* + E *oleic*] **:** an unsaturated fatty acid $C_{19}H_{37}COOH$ occurring in the form of glycerides in whale oil and many fish oils

gad·o·lin·ite \'gad°lə,nīt\ *n* -s [G *gadolinit,* fr. Johann *Gadolin* †1852 Finn. chemist + G *-it* -ite] **:** a mineral mainly $Be_2FeY_2Si_2O_{10}$ that is a source of rare earths and consists of a black or brown vitreous silicate of iron, beryllium, yttrium, cerium, and erbium (hardness 6.5–7, sp. gr. 4–4.5)

gad·o·lin·i·um \ˌgad°l'inēəm\ *n* -s [NL, fr. *J.Gadolin* + NL *-ium*] **:** a trivalent magnetic metallic element of the rare-earth group occurring in combination in gadolinite, samarskite, and certain other minerals — symbol *Gd;* see ELEMENT table

ga·dop·sis \gə'däpsəs\ *n, cap* [NL, fr. *Gadus* + *-opsis*] **:** a genus of Australian and Tasmanian percoid freshwater fishes that resemble the cods

¹ga·droon \gə'drün\ *n* -s [F *godron* round plait, gadroon, fr. MF *goderon,* perh. dim. of OF *godet* drinking cup] **1 :** an ornament produced by notching or carving a rounded molding **2 :** a fluting or reeding that is usu. short in proportion to its width and often approaches an oval form and that is used decoratively (as in silverware, furniture, glassware, porcelain) — **ga·droon·ing** \-niŋ\ *n* -s

²gadroon \"\ *vt* -ED/-ING/-S **:** to decorate with gadroons

gads *pl of* GAD, *pres 3d sing of* GAD

gads·bod·i·kins \(')gadz'bädəkənz, -dēk-\ *interj, often cap* [euphemism for *God's bodykins*] — a mild oath

ga·dus \'gādəs\ *n, cap* [NL, fr. Gk *gados,* a fish] **:** the type genus of the family Gadidae consisting of the typical codfishes

gad·wall \'ga,dwȯl\ *also* **gad·wale** \-wāl\ *or* **gad·well** \-wel\ *n, pl* **gadwalls** *or* **gadwall** [origin unknown] **:** a grayish brown dabbling duck (*Anas strepera* or *Chaulelasmus streperus*) of approximately the size of the mallard

gad·zooks \gad'züks, -üks\ *interj, often cap* [*gads* (euphemism for *God's*) + *zooks,* origin unknown] *archaic* — a mild oath

gae \'gā, _gə\ *vi* **gaed** \'gād\ **gane** \'gān\ **gaun** \'gȯn\ **gaes** [ME (northern dial.) *gan* — more at GO] *Scot* **:** GO

-gaea *or* **-gea** \'jēə\ *n comb form* -s [NL, fr. Gk *gaia* land, earth] **:** a (specified) geographical area ⟨Afrogaea⟩ ⟨Neogaea⟩

gae·down \'gā,dün, '≈,≈\ *n* -s [*gae* + *down*] *archaic Scot* **:** a drinking bout

gael \'gāl, *esp before pause or consonant* -āəl\ *n* -s *cap* [ScGael *Gàidheal* & IrGael *Gaedheal,* fr. or akin to MIr *Gōidel*] **1 :** a Scottish Highlander **2 a :** a Celtic esp. Gaelic-speaking inhabitant of Ireland, Scotland, or the Isle of Man **:** a member of the Gaelic-speaking division of the Celts **b :** a member of the Gaelic or Gallic Celts of Great Britain esp. as opposed to the Cymric or Gallic Celts of Great Britain and the European continent **b :** IRISHMAN **c :** SCOTCHMAN I

gael·dom \-dəm\ *n* -s *usu cap* **:** the realm or social order of the Gael or Gaelic civilization

¹gael·ic \'gālik, -lēk\ *adj, usu cap* [ScGael *Gàidhealach* (fr. *Gàidheal*) & IrGael *Gaedhealach,* fr. *Gaedheal*] **1 :** of, relating to, or characteristic of the Gaels or esp. the Celtic Highlanders of Scotland — compare GOIDELIC **2 :** of, relating to, or characteristic of the language of the Gaels or of the Celtic Highlanders of Scotland

²gaelic \"\ *n* -s [ScGael *Gàidhlig* (fr. *Gàidheal*) & IrGael *Gaedhealg, Gaedhilge,* fr. *Gaedheal*] **:** the Goidelic speech of the Celts in Ireland, the Isle of Man, and esp. in the Highlands of Scotland, the Hebrides, and other Scottish islands — compare IRISH, IRISH GAELIC, MANX, SCOTTISH GAELIC

gaelic football *n, usu cap G* : football played chiefly in Ireland between teams of 15 players who are permitted to dribble, kick, punt, or punch the ball with the fists but may not throw it or run with it

gael·i·cist \'gāləsəst\ *n* -s *usu cap* **1 :** an expert in Gaelic study **2 :** an advocate of Gaelic as a living tongue

gael·i·cize \-,sīz\ *vt* -ED/-ING/-S *sometimes cap* : to make Gaelic in form, quality, or customs

gael·tacht \'gā(ə)ltəkt\ *n* -s *cap* [IrGael *Gaedhealtacht*, fr. *Gaedheal* Gael] **1 :** the state of being Gaelic **2 a :** the Gaelic-speaking or Irish-speaking districts **b :** the population of such districts **3 :** the native race of Ireland

gaert·ner bacillus \'gertnər-\ *n, usu cap G* [after August *Gärtner* †1934 Ger. bacteriologist] : a motile salmonella (*Salmonella enteritidis*) that causes enteritidis and is widely distributed in the intestinal tract of man and various other mammals

gaertner's canal *or* **gaertner's duct** *n, usu cap G* : DUCT OF GAERTNER

gae·tu·li \jē'tü,lī, jē-'tyü-, gī'tü(,)lē\ *n pl, cap* [L] : a Berber people living in ancient times to the south of Mauretania and Numidia

¹**gae·tu·li·an** \(')=¦=lēən\ *adj, usu cap* [*Gaetuli* + *-an*] **1 :** of, relating to, characteristic of, or being a member of the Gaetuli **2 :** of, relating to, characteristic of, or derived from Gaetulia, the region inhabited by the Gaetuli

²**gaetulian** \"\ *n* -s *usu cap* : a member of the Gaetuli

ga·fat \gə'fät\ *n* -s *usu cap* : a Semitic language formerly spoken in western Ethiopia but now replaced by Amharic

¹**gaff** \'gaf, -áf\ *n* -s [prob. of imit. origin] *chiefly Scot* : a loud laugh : GUFFAW

²**gaff** \"\ *vi* -ED/-ING/-S [¹*gaff*] *chiefly Scot* : to laugh loudly

³**gaff** \'gaf, -aa(ə)f,-aif\ *n* -s [F *gaffe*, fr. Prov *gaf*] **1 a :** a barbed spear or spearhead for taking fish or turtle **b :** an iron hook with a handle for holding or lifting heavy fish (as into a boat) **c :** the steel point of a pole used in logging **d :** a metal spur for a gamecock **e :** a butcher's hook **f** (1) **:** a climbing iron used by a telephone lineman (2) the steel point or the shank and steel point of such a climbing iron **2 a :** the spar upon which the head of a fore-and-aft sail is extended **b :** a similar spar on a ship without sails sometimes used when under way for hoisting colors **3 a :** HOAX, FRAUD **b :** GIMMICK, TRICK ⟨professional gamblers can be trusted to work out some sort of ~ to loosen up the percentage on any game of chance —C.B.Davis⟩ **4 a :** something painful or difficult to bear : ORDEAL ⟨was forced to drop out of competition because he couldn't stand the ~⟩; *esp* : persistent raillery or criticism **b :** wear and tear : roughness of treatment : ABUSE ⟨fabric that could take a great deal of ~⟩ **5 :** GAFFE

gaff 1b

⁴**gaff** \"\ *vt* -ED/-ING/-S [³*gaff*] **1 a :** to strike or secure with a gaff ⟨~ a salmon⟩ **b :** to fit or provide (as a gamecock) with a gaff **2 :** DECEIVE, TRICK; *also* : FLEECE **3 :** to tamper with for the purpose of cheating : FIX, GIMMICK ⟨gaming wheels and dice are often ~*ed* so that the player cannot win⟩

⁵**gaff** \"\ *n* -s [origin unknown] *Brit* : a cheap place of amusement; *esp* : a low-class theater or music hall — called also *penny gaff*

⁶**gaff** \"\ *vi* -ED/-ING/-S [origin unknown] *slang Brit* : to gamble esp. by tossing coins

⁷**gaff** \"\ *n* -s [origin unknown] **1 :** talk esp. when idle or foolish **2 :** OUTCRY, CLAMOR — **blow the gaff** *slang* : to give away a secret : BLAB

gaffe \'gaf, -aa(ə)f,-aif\ *n* -s [F, gaff, gaffe — more at ³GAFF] : a marked esp. social or diplomatic blunder or clumsy mistake : FAUX PAS ⟨mere social ~s and unfortunate encounters of the sort which used to provide copy for . . . society jokes —*Times Lit. Supp.*⟩ ⟨his attention to detail is really remarkable and seldom permits a major ~ —W.F.Albright⟩ ⟨like all newspapers it sometimes commits a ~ —Stuart Keate⟩

gaf·fer \'gafə(r)\ *n* -s [prob. contr. of *godfather*] **1 :** old man : old fellow — often used formerly as a form of friendly address **2** *Brit* **a :** EMPLOYER **b :** FOREMAN, OVERSEER **3 :** the master glass blower in charge of a shop in glassworking **4 :** an electrician in charge of the lighting of motion-picture or television sets

gaff-headed \'=¦==\ *adj* [³*gaff*] *of a sail* : having four sides with the head laced along a gaff — compare JIB-HEADED

gaff·kya \'gafkēə\ *n, cap* [NL, after Georg *Gaffky* †1918 Ger. bacteriologist] *in some classifications* : a genus of parasitic gram-positive bacteria (family Micrococcaceae) that are now usu. placed in *Micrococcus*

gaffle *n* -s [ME *gaffole*, fr. MD *gaffel, gafel* fork; akin to OE *gafol, geafel* fork, OHG *gabala*, OS *gafala* fork, OIr *gabul* forked branch, fork, vulva] *obs* : a steel lever used to bend a crossbow

gaff-rigged \'=¦rigd\ *adj, of a boat* : having a gaff-headed mainsail and sometimes other gaff-headed sails

gaff·sail \'=,sāl, -,səl\ *n* [³*gaff* + *sail*] : a fore-and-aft sail suspended from a gaff

gaff-topsail \=¦=(,)=, '=,==\ *n* **1 :** a usu. triangular topsail with its foot extended upon the gaff and its luff upon the topmast — see SAIL illustration **2 :** GAFF-TOPSAIL CATFISH **3** *or* **gaff-topsail pompano** : LONGFIN POMPANO

gaff-topsail catfish *n* : a sea catfish (*Bagre marina* syn. *Felichthys felis*) of the Atlantic and Gulf coasts of the U.S.

¹**gag** \'gag, -aa(ə)g, -aig\ *vb* **gagged; gagged; gagging; gags** [ME *gaggen* to strangle, of imit. origin] *vt* **1 :** to apply a gag to: **a :** to stop the mouth of by thrusting something in it in order to hinder or prevent speaking or outcry **b :** to pry or hold open by means of a gag **c :** to silence by the force of authority or violence : prevent from exercising freedom of speech or expression ⟨the dictator's first act was to ~ all newspapers⟩ ⟨the opposition refused to be *gagged* and found new means of putting their ideas across to the public⟩ **2 :** to cause to heave (as with nausea) : cause to retch **3 :** OBSTRUCT, CHOKE ⟨~ a valve⟩ ⟨was struck by a sudden terror which transfixed him on the spot and *gagged* his throat —S.B. Kaiser⟩ **4 :** to straighten (rails) with a gag **5 :** to introduce gags into : provide gags for : fill with remarks or situations intended to arouse laughter ⟨an amply *gagged* musical comedy⟩ ⟨asked to ~ a new movie by a famous producer⟩ — often used with *up* ~ *vi* **1 :** HEAVE, RETCH **2 :** to be unable to endure something : BALK ⟨*gagged* at the sort of painting she was being taught, went off to earn her living in various advertising agencies —*Time*⟩ ⟨the defense was cunning beyond belief, and unscrupulous in its use of propaganda — they *gagged* at nothing —Maxwell Anderson⟩ **3 :** to make gags : engage in an interchange intended to arouse laughter ⟨no false notes in his testimony, no mugging and *gagging* —*New Republic*⟩ ⟨*gagging* with his mates —*Life*⟩

²**gag** \"\ *n* -s [¹*gag*] **1 :** something thrust into the mouth to keep it open; *specif* : a medical device for keeping the mouth open **2 a :** something thrust into the mouth or throat to prevent or hinder speaking or outcry **b :** CLOTURE **c :** a device or action that hinders or prevents free expression of ideas **3 :** a laugh-provoking remark, story, device, or action or one intended to amuse or arouse laughter: **a :** an interpolation orig. of an amusing local or topical allusion or bit of byplay by an actor in his lines **b :** a clever, witty, or comic remark, stunt, trick, or piece of action or construction (as in a stage, motion-picture, radio, or television presentation or in a work of literature or art) esp. designed to arouse quick and broad laughter ⟨two comedians with dialogue full of fast ~s⟩ ⟨a partygoer who insists on wearing a lampshade for a hat as a ~⟩ ⟨improvise dialogue, ~s, and situations as they go along —*Current Biog.*⟩ ⟨his standard of humor was set by the ~s of the variety shows —S.H.Adams⟩ ⟨many a glamour girl got in a WAC recruiting line just for the ~ —*Time*⟩ **4 a :** a made-up story told plausibly or a contrived action to hoax or impose upon someone or to provide a pretext (as for evading something) ⟨when he picked up the telephone and demanded the general manager I thought it was just a ~ —Henry Miller⟩ **b :** a story of this kind used so frequently as to have become hackneyed ⟨the office boy's ~ about a death in the family so he can get a day off⟩ **c :** a trick of imposture or deception (as for making someone ridiculous or for gaining publicity) ⟨got himself arrested falsely as a ~ to get his name in the papers⟩ **5 :** a bit with rings at each end through which the cheekpiece of the bridle is continuous with the reins used to keep the horse's head properly up; *esp* : a light snaffle of this kind **6 :** a fuller used to straighten railway rails **7 :** a hand-controlled attachment used to prevent the operation of a punch when a hole is to be omitted **syn** see JOKE

³**gag** \"\ *n* -s [origin unknown] : a small grouper (*Mycteroperca microlepis*) of the coasts of the southern U.S. highly esteemed for food; *also* : any of several related fishes (as the yellowfin grouper)

ga·ga \'gä¦gä, 'gá¦gá, |gə\ *adj* [F, fr. *gaga*, n., fool, dodderer, of imit. origin] **1 a :** mentally foolish : CRAZY, DOTING ⟨slowly becoming ~ . . . becoming a senile imbecile —Aldous Huxley⟩ **b :** characterized by a marked and interesting or foolish variation from a conventional or expected pattern : marked by interesting or foolish incongruities or surprises (as in quality or action) ⟨a ~ comedian⟩ ⟨~ misadventures that, on stage and screen, forever befall high-school or college youths —*Life*⟩ **2 :** markedly or wildly and often foolishly enthusiastic (as from love or infatuation) ⟨a hatcheck girl went simply ~ over the clothes —*Star Detective Cases*⟩ ⟨had been so ~ about him at first —Dawn Powell⟩

¹**gage** \'gāj\ *n* -s [ME, fr. MF, of Gmc origin; akin to Goth *wadi* pledge — more at WED] **1 :** a personal pledge that one will appear to support by combat his assertions or claims; *esp* : a glove, cap, or other personal belonging cast on the ground to be taken up by an opponent as a pledge of combat **2 :** something deposited or given to or taken by another as a security for the performance of some act by the person depositing it or giving it up and forfeited by nonperformance : SECURITY; *also* : the transaction by which the security is given or taken — compare MORTGAGE, PLEDGE — **throw down the gage** : CHALLENGE, DEFY

²**gage** \"\ *vt* -ED/-ING/-S [MF *gager*, fr. OF *gagier*, fr. *gage*, n.] **1** *archaic* : to give or deposit as a gage : give as security for some act : offer as a forfeit : PLEDGE **2** *archaic* : STAKE, RISK

³**gage** *var of* GAUGE

⁴**gage** \'gāj\ *n* -s [by shortening] : GREENGAGE

gage block *n* : a hardened steel block that is used by machinists for extremely accurate measurement and has two opposite surfaces ground and lapped plane and parallel to a thickness within a few millionths of an inch of its designated size and usu. forms one of a graduated set of which two or more are often used in combination — called also *precision block, size block*

gage green *n* [⁴*gage*] : a grayish to moderate yellow green that is yellower and darker than mytho green and greener and very slightly darker than pois green

gage·ite \'gā,jīt\ *n* -s [R. B. *Gage*, 20th cent. Am. collector of specimens in N.J. + E *-ite*] : a mineral $(Mn,Mg,Zn)_8Si_3O_{14}.2$ (or 3?)H_2O consisting of a hydrous silicate of manganese, magnesium, and zinc

gage plate *n* : a metal plate placed between parallel running rails to maintain the gage on a railroad track

¹**gag·er** \'gājə(r)\ *n* -s [prob. fr. MF, lit., to gage, fr. OF *gagier*] the transaction of giving a gage : the action of providing security for a pledge

²**gager** *var of* GAUGER

gagged *past of* GAG

gag·ger \'gagə(r), -aag-,-aig-\ *n* -s **1 :** one that gags; *specif* : a workman who takes the bends out of rails at a straightening press with a steel gag **2 a :** a foundry lifter **b :** a piece of iron used in a foundry mold to keep the sand or a core in place **3 :** one that thinks up gags : JOKER, GAGMAN

gagging *pres part of* GAG

¹**gag·gle** \'gagəl, 'gaig-\ *vi* **gaggled; gaggled; gaggling** \-g(ə)liŋ\ **gaggles** [ME *gagelen*; prob. of imit. origin like MHG *gāgen* to gaggle, ON *gaga* to mock, *gagl* wild goose] : to make a noise like that of a goose : CACKLE, GABBLE

²**gaggle** \"\ *n* -s [ME *gagyll*, fr. *gagelen*, v.] **1 :** a flock of geese esp. when on the water — compare SKEIN **2 :** a group of people bonded because of some common element : BUNCH, GANG ⟨a whole ~ of photographers and reporters⟩ ⟨a ~ of gossiping women⟩ **3 :** a number of disorganized but related things ⟨a ~ of eponyms, synonyms, and terms that confront the medical student⟩ ⟨a ~ of little railroads between cities⟩

gag law *n* : a law or ruling prohibiting free debate or expression of opinion (as in a deliberative body) : CLOTURE; *also* : legislation restricting freedom of the press

gag line *n* : a remark or line (as in a comic cartoon) that constitutes a gag or is the climax of one

gag·man \'=,man, -,maa(ə)n\ *n, pl* **gagmen 1 :** one who contrives gags for comedians or other entertainers **2 :** a comedian often good at ad-libbing whose act consists chiefly of laugh-provoking remarks

gag rein *n* : a rein for use with a gag — **gag-reined** \'=¦=\ *adj*

gag resolution *n* : one of several resolutions passed in Congress between 1836 and 1844 providing in effect that no petition against slavery should be received or heard by the House

gagroot \'=,=\ *n* [so called fr. its use as an emetic] : INDIAN TOBACCO

gag rule *n* : GAG LAW, GAG RESOLUTION; *also* : ruling by gag law

gags *pres 3d sing of* GAG, *pl of* GAG

gag·ster \'gagztə(r), 'gaa|, 'gai|, |gst-\ *n* -s : GAGMAN; *also* : PRACTICAL JOKER

gagtooth \'=,=\ *n, pl* **gagteeth** [E dial. *gag* to project, stick out (of Scand origin; akin to ON *gaghals* having the head thrown back, Icel *gagur* bent backward, turned askew, Norw *gag* bent back, *gaga* to bend back) + *tooth*; akin to OE *gēagl* throat, jaws, MHG *gagen* to fidget and perh. to OE *geonian, ginian* to yawn — more at YAWN] : a projecting tooth — **gagtoothed** \'=¦=\ *adj*

ga·he \'gä(,)hā\ *n pl* [Apache] : grotesque masked dancers with yucca crowns representing mountain spirits in Apache Indian ceremonies — called also *crown dancers*; see APACHE DEVIL DANCE

gahn·ite \'gä,nīt\ *n* -s [G *gahnit*, fr. Johan G. *Gahn* †1818 Sw. chemist + G *-it* -ite] : a usu. dark green mineral $ZnAl_2O_4$ consisting of an oxide of zinc and aluminum and constituting a member of the spinel series

gaiac *var of* GUAIAC

gai·as·sa \gī'asə\ *n* -s [Ar *qayyāsah*, a kind of barge] : a Nile cargo boat with high stem and lateen rig

gai·ety *or* **gay·ety** \'gāəd-ē, -ətē, -i\ *n* -ES [F *gaieté*, fr. OF, fr. *gai* gay + *-té* -ty — more at GAY] **1 a :** MERRYMAKING, ENTERTAINMENT, FESTIVITY ⟨did not feel like joining in the ~ of the season⟩ ⟨paper bags filled with water dropped from windows, and other freshman *gaieties* marked the convention's sideshow —C.W.Ferguson⟩ **b :** the quality or state of being gay ⟨the face was in profile but the visible eye seemed to have ~ in it —Raymond Chandler⟩ : high spirits : MERRIMENT ⟨the high ~ of cocktail parties —R.L.Taylor⟩ : marked liveliness or cheerfulness ⟨a jumble of unmatched colors, which are said to lend ~ to the table —*New Yorker*⟩ **2 a :** FINERY, ELEGANCE ⟨a ~ of dress and manner⟩ **b :** an instance of such finery (as in dress) ⟨youthful *gaieties*, such as a raspberry fleece greatcoat with low patch pockets and a deep oblong collar in back —Lois Long⟩ **3 :** BEGONIA 3

gail *var of* GYLE

gaillard *var of* GALLIARD

gail·lar·dia \gə'lärdēə, ÷ -dəə\ *n* [NL, fr. *Gaillard* de Marentonneau, 18th cent. Fr. botanist + NL *-ia*] **1** *cap* : a genus of chiefly western American herbs (family Compositae) having hairy foliage and long stalked flower heads with showy yellow, purple, or variegated rays **2** -s : any plant or flower of the genus *Gaillardia*

gai·ly *or* **gay·ly** \'gālē, -li\ *adv* [ME *gayly*, fr. *gay* + *-ly*] **1 :** in a gay manner: **a :** with marked liveliness, cheerfulness, or high spirits ⟨she then ran ~ off, rejoicing —Jane Austen⟩ : MERRILY **b :** with finery, elegance, or showiness (as of dress) ⟨ladies ~ dressed⟩ **c :** in a manner that is colorful and tends to arouse gaiety ⟨~ decorated floats⟩ **2** *chiefly Scot* : pretty much : to a considerable extent or degree

¹**gain** \'gān\ *adj* -ER/-EST [ME *gayn, geyn*, fr. OE *gēn*, fr. ON *gegn* — more at AGAIN] **1** *dial Brit, of a route* : direct and straight ⟨the ~*est* way to the glen⟩ **2** *dial Brit* : useful and convenient : HANDY ⟨a ~ tool⟩

²**gain** \"\ *adv* -ER/-EST [ME *gayn*, fr. *gayn*, adj.] *dial Brit* : NEARLY, APPROXIMATELY

³**gain** *vi* -ED/-ING/-S [ME *gaynen, geinen*, fr. ON *gegna*, fr. *gegn*, adj.] : to be of advantage or help : be suitable or sufficient

⁴**gain** \'gān\ *n* -s [ME *gayne*, fr. MF *gain* (fr. OF *gaaing*, fr. *gaaignier* to gain) & *gaigne*, fr. OF *gaaigne*, fr. *gaaignier*] **1 :** an increase in or addition to what is of profit, advantage, or benefit : resources or advantage acquired or increased : PROFIT ⟨the moral and cultural ~s of the last 1000 years⟩ ⟨a lottery for private ~⟩ ⟨the practice resulted in quite a ~ in confidence in the driver⟩ ⟨the difficulties encountered, the compromises reached, the ~s achieved —Vera M. Dean⟩: as **a :** an increase of value (as from business transactions or increase in capital) ⟨the loss or ~ in a company's assets⟩ **b :** an increase in resources or business advantages resulting from business transactions or dealings **c :** a profit in the form of a sum of money, an acquired asset, or a reduction in liability arising from business transactions but not including mere advances in value — usu. used in pl. ⟨capital ~s to be entered separately on the income-tax form⟩ **2 :** the act of gaining something; *esp* : the act of obtaining or accumulating profit or valuable possessions **3 :** an increase in amount, magnitude, or degree ⟨the ~ in weight of the cattle over a period of weeks was recorded⟩ ⟨the ~ in efficiency is more than worth the heat loss —*Modern Industry*⟩ ⟨sales aggregated 84,293,729 barrels, a ~ of 1.3 percent over 1951 —*Americana Annual*⟩ ⟨its absence would mean . . . more loss than ~ in social relations —W.C.Brownell⟩; *specif* : the ratio of increase of output current, power, or voltage over input (as in an amplifier)

⁵**gain** \"\ *vb* -ED/-ING/-S [MF *gaigner*, fr. OF *gaaignier* to till, earn, win, gain, of Gmc origin; akin to OHG *weidanōn* to hunt, search for food; akin to OE *wāth* hunt, wandering, OHG *weida* pasture, fodder, food, ON *veithr* hunt, hunting, fishing, L *vis* power, force — more at VIM] *vt* **1 a :** to get or attain to possession, control, use, or benefit of (as an advantage) by industry, initiative, merit, or craft : OBTAIN, PROCURE, SECURE ⟨~ a sum of money⟩ ⟨~ a good reputation⟩ ⟨~ recognition⟩ ⟨~ admittance⟩ ⟨~ popularity⟩ ⟨~ a livelihood⟩ ⟨~ insight⟩ ⟨after climbing all the morning he had failed to ~ another glimpse of the great brown ram —C.G.D.Roberts⟩ ⟨~ the goodwill of the people —H.C.Atyeo⟩ ⟨a great aid to us in ~*ing* an inspection of the grounds —A.W.O'Neil⟩ **b** (1) **:** to get in competition ⟨~ a prize in a tennis match⟩ (2) **:** to come off winner or victor in ⟨~ a battle⟩ ⟨~ a suit at law⟩ **c :** to get or incur by a natural development, advance, or increment or by the normal exercise of one's function : come to have : RECEIVE ⟨the invalid ~*ed* strength under the doctor's care⟩ ⟨the writing was such that the reader actually ~*ed* the illusion of a cruise⟩ ⟨the false story ~*ed* credence⟩ ⟨the impression was ~*ed* that the divisional heads would hold key positions —*Farmer's Weekly (So. Africa)*⟩ ⟨a child is ~*ing* a sense of rhythm and balance —*Handwriting Today*⟩ **d :** to obtain by reclamation ⟨land ~*ed* from the sea⟩ **e :** to make or acquire (as a friend) ⟨~ an acquaintance⟩ **f :** to advance to the distance of by striving against odds or an opposing force ⟨the football team ~*ed* forty yards in the first three plays⟩ **g :** SUFFER ⟨~*ed* a black eye for his trouble⟩ ⟨the participants ~*ed* only ignominy and unhappiness⟩ **2 :** to draw to one's particular interest or party : win to one's side : PERSUADE ⟨~ adherents for his religious doctrines⟩ — often used with *over* ⟨had been ~*ed* over to urge this fatal course by a gift —*Encyc. Americana*⟩ **3 :** to arrive at ⟨the first ones to ~ the top of the mountain held it against attack⟩ ⟨~ a goal⟩ : REACH, ATTAIN ⟨he ~*ed* his car and he was safe —Jean Stafford⟩ **4 :** to cause to be obtained or given : AROUSE ⟨misfortune ~*s* the sympathy of friends⟩ ⟨~ the audience's attention⟩ **5 :** to increase in ⟨~ momentum⟩ ⟨~ impetus⟩ ⟨does not mean that the actual aesthetic experience ~*s* nothing when it is studied in the context of our total experience —Hunter Mead⟩ **6 :** to establish or reestablish a usual or normal use or position of ⟨~*ed* his feet after a fall⟩ ⟨~ my equilibrium⟩ **7** *of a timepiece* : to run fast by the amount of ⟨~*s* a minute a day⟩ ~ *vi* **1 :** to secure advantage or profit : acquire gain ⟨the man supplying the capital expected to ~ considerably by the enterprise⟩ **2 a :** INCREASE ⟨the child ~*ed* in weight⟩ ⟨~ in influence⟩ ⟨~ in reputation⟩ ⟨the day was ~*ing* in warmth⟩ **b :** to increase in weight ⟨despite her diet the woman continued to ~⟩ **c :** to improve in health ⟨the patient ~*ed* daily⟩ **d :** to become greater ⟨the water ~*ed* so frightfully in the ship that it seemed certain she would sink —Fletcher Pratt⟩ **3** *of a timepiece* : to run so that it is fast : register a time ahead of the correct time ⟨~*s* by an hour a day⟩ **syn** see GET, REACH — **gain a point** : to make a point — **gain face** : to establish or increase one's authority, influence, or reputation ⟨a petty official trying to *gain face* by treating his subordinates arrogantly⟩ ⟨she had *gained face*, for the time being, from the length of her conversation with Colonel Pole; three or four more of the family, after that, had bowed or briefly spoken to her —Elizabeth Bowen⟩ — **gain ground** : to make progress : improve esp. by getting larger, more valuable, or healthier ⟨stocks *gained ground* during the morning's trading⟩ ⟨the patient *gained ground* daily⟩ — **gain on** *or* **gain upon 1** *archaic* : to obtain influence or favor with **2 :** to encroach upon ⟨where the sea *gains on* the land⟩ **3 a :** to come nearer to by running faster than (one ahead in a race) **b :** to increase the distance from by running faster than (one behind in a race) ⟨his quarry was *gaining on* him every minute —Dale Van Every⟩ — **gain the wind** : to reach the windward side (as of another boat) when beating — **gain time** : to obtain or effect a delay in an action (as by pretexts)

⁶**gain** \"\ *n* -s [origin unknown] **1 :** a beveled shoulder above a tenon in carpentry **2 :** a notch, mortise, or groove (as in a timber or wall) for a girder or joist

gaincope *vt* -ED/-ING/-S [ME *geynecowpen*, fr. *geyne-* against (fr. OE *gēan-, gēn-* against, again) + *cowpen, copen* to strike — more at AGAIN, COPE (strike)] *obs* : to meet or intercept by a short cut

gaine \'gān\ *n* -s [F, lit., sheath, fr. OF, fr. L *vagina* — more at VAGINA] **1 :** the part of a term or similar support below a sculptured bust or head commonly in the form of a quadrangular pillar diminishing toward the base **2 :** the term-shaped lower part or body of a caryatid

gained *past of* GAIN

¹**gain·er** *comparative of* GAIN

²**gai·ner** \'gānə(r)\ *n* -s **1 :** a fancy dive in which the diver from a forward approach rotates backward in tuck, pike, or layout position and enters the water feet first and facing away from the board — called also *full gainer* **2 :** one of a former group of competitive dives including reverse dives

gainest *superlative of* GAIN

gain·ful \'gānfəl\ *adj* **1 :** productive of gain : PROFITABLE, REMUNERATIVE; *esp* : providing an income ⟨a ~ occupation⟩ **2 :** customarily employed at a gainful occupation ⟨a ~ worker⟩ — **gain·ful·ly** \-fəlē, -li\ *adv* — **gain·ful·ness** *n* -ES

gain·giv·ing \'gān,==\ *n* [*gain-* (fr. ME *gayn-, geyne-* against) + *giving* (fr. gerund of *give*)] *archaic* : MISGIVING

gaining *pres part of* GAIN

gaining machine *n* [⁶*gain* + *-ing*] : a machine for cutting a gain

gain·less \'gānləs\ *adj* [⁴*gain* + *-less*] **1 :** not producing gain : UNPROFITABLE, UNAVAILING **2 :** making no advances : achieving no gains ⟨a saving and ~ life —John Cheever⟩ — **gain·less·ness** *n* -ES

¹**gain·ly** \'gānlē, -li\ *adv* -ER/-EST [¹*gain* + *-ly*] **1** *chiefly dial* : VERY, COMPLETELY **2** *chiefly dial* : NEARBY, HANDILY ⟨the birds singing ~ that came at my call —J.H.Payne⟩

²**gainly** \"\ *adj* [¹*gain* + *-ly*] **1** *chiefly dial* : SUITABLE, BECOMING ⟨a ~ word⟩ **2 :** graceful and generally pleasing ⟨~ conduct⟩ ⟨a ~ youth with dark hair and eyes⟩

gai·nor \'gānə(r)\ *n* -s [AF *gainour*, fr. OF *gaaigneure*, fr. *gaaignier* to till, gain + *-eure* -ure — more at GAIN (obtain)] *Old Eng law* : TILLAGE, HUSBANDRY ⟨land in ~⟩

gains *pres 3d sing of* GAIN, *pl of* GAIN

gain·say \(')gān¦sā\ *vt* **gain·said** \-sād,-sed\ **gainsaid** \"\ **gainsaying** \-sāiŋ\ **gain·says** \-sāz,-sez\ [ME *gaynsayen*, fr. *gayn-* against + *sayen* to say — more at SAY] **1 :** DENY ⟨that capitalism had long existed in rudimentary form cannot be *gainsaid* —W.P.Webb⟩ ⟨a churlish critic who would ~ people the solace of fairy tales —W.H.Whyte⟩ **2 :** to speak against : CONTRADICT, CONTROVERT ⟨though I disagree with him, I will not ~ him⟩ **3 :** OPPOSE, RESIST ⟨standing armies that will permit us to grasp whatever we may desire, because no other nation or combination of nations is strong enough to ~ us —F.D.Roosevelt⟩ ⟨the development of a manner . . . that ~s the very purpose of criticism —F.R.Leavis⟩; *also* **:** SUBVERT ⟨his mother, whom he could not ~, was unconsciously but inflexibly set against his genius —Van Wyck Brooks⟩ **syn** see DENY

gainst *prep* [by shortening] *obs* **:** AGAINST

gain·stand \(ˈ)gān¦stand, -taa(ə)nd\ *vt* [ME *gaynstanden*, fr. *gayn-* against + *standen* to stand — more at STAND] *chiefly Scot* **:** WITHSTAND, RESIST

gain twist *n* [⁵*gain*] **:** a twist that is more rapid at the muzzle of a firearm than at the breech in order to increase gradually the rapidity of rotation of a projectile

¹gair \ˈgār\ *n* -s [ME (northern dial.) *gare*, fr. OE *gāra* — more at GORE] *Scot* **:** ²GORE 1a

²gair \"\ *adj* -ER/-EST [of Scand origin; akin to ON *gerr* greedy; prob. akin to ON *gjarn* eager, greedy — more at YEARN] **1** *Scot* **:** GREEDY, COVETOUS **2** *Scot* **:** PARSIMONIOUS, STINGY

gaird \ˈgārd\ *Scot var of* GUARD

gair·den \ˈgārdᵊn, ˈger-\ *Scot var of* GARDEN

gair·ten \ˈgārtᵊn, ˈger-\ *var of* GARTEN

gais·ling \ˈgāzlən, -liŋ\ *n* -s [ME *geslyng*, prob. fr. ON *gæslingr*, fr. *gās* goose + *-lingr* -ling — more at GOOSE] *Scot* **:** GOSLING

gaist \ˈgāst\ *Scot var of* GHOST

¹gait \ˈgāt, *usu* -ād·+V\ *n* -s [ME *gait, gate* — more at GATE (way)] **1** *archaic* **:** ³GATE 1 **2** *now dial* **:** ³GATE 2 **3** *Scot* **:** ³GATE 3 **4 a :** the manner of walking, running, or moving on foot ⟨a fast ~⟩ ⟨an awkward ~⟩ ⟨the ~ of a cowboy —*Current Biog.*⟩ **b :** any of the sequences of foot movement (as the walk, trot, pace, or canter) by which a horse moves forward **c :** the manner of moving forward in a vehicle ⟨everything swayed and veered in obedience to the ~ of the train —Nadine Gordimer⟩ ⟨step up our ~ to near the posted speed limit of 55 —*Sat. Eve. Post*⟩ **5 a :** the general speed or rate at which life proceeds or at which activities are pursued ⟨life in the summer slowed down to a leisurely ~⟩ **b :** the speed or rate of performance or accomplishment (as of production) ⟨after the speedup, the ~ was 300 airplanes a month⟩

²gait \"\ *vt* -ED/-ING/-S **1 :** to train (a horse) to use a particular gait or set of gaits **2 :** to lead (a show dog) before a judge to display carriage and movement

³gait \"\ *n* -s [prob. alter. of ¹*gate*] **1 :** the distance between two adjoining carriages of a lace frame in textile manufacturing **2** *Brit* **:** a full repeat of a pattern in harness weaving — used in the woolen trade

⁴gait \"\ *vt* -ED/-ING/-S [by alter.] **:** ²GATE 3

gait·ed \ˈgād·əd, -ātəd\ *adj* **1 a :** having a particular kind of gait — used in combination ⟨a stiff-*gaited* man⟩ ⟨a slow-*gaited* life⟩ **b** *of a horse* **:** trained to use particular gaits — often used in combination ⟨a 3-*gaited* bay gelding⟩ **2 :** specially fitted, trained, adjusted, or conditioned ⟨the sort of story that television is ~ to handle well —Douglas Mackenzie⟩ ⟨better ~ for the slower, more intimate aspects of Schumann than she is for such movement as the sonata opening —Irving Kolodin⟩ ⟨men who aren't ~ to decorating a house —Debs Myers⟩ ⟨the subject matter is ~ to the boy's expanding interests —O.W.Bennett⟩

gai·ter \ˈgād·ə(r), -ātə-\ *n* -s [F *guêtre*, fr. MF *guestre, guiestre*, prob. of Gmc origin; akin to OE *wrist* — more at WRIST] **1 :** a cloth or leather leg covering reaching from the instep to ankle, mid-calf, or knee, usu. fastened by buttons or buckles, and held by a strap under the shank of the shoe ⟨bishops and archdeacons, as well as deans, wear aprons and ~s —F.C. Happold⟩ **2 a :** an ankle-high shoe with elastic gores in the sides — compare CONGRESS GAITER, ROMEO **b :** an overshoe reaching to the ankle or above and having a fabric upper — compare ARCTIC **3 :** a protective covering (as for a leaf spring or over a weak spot in a fire hose)

gaiter 2a

gai·ter·less \-ləs\ *adj* **:** not wearing or not having gaiters ⟨a ~ farmer⟩ ⟨a ~ leg⟩

gai·ther \ˈgāthər\ *Scot var of* GATHER

¹gal \ˈgal\ *n* -s [by alter.] **:** GIRL

²gal \"\ *n* -s [after *Galileo* †1642 Ital. astronomer and physicist] **:** a unit of acceleration equivalent to one centimeter per second per second — used esp. for values of gravity

gal *abbr* **1** gallery **2** galley **3** gallon

¹gala \ˈgālə *also* ˈgalə *sometimes* ˈgälə *or* ˈgȧlə\ *n* -s [It, fr. MF *gale* merrymaking, festivity, pleasure — more at GALLANT] **1** *archaic* **a :** festive dress or decoration **b :** FESTIVITY, GAIETY **2 a :** a gay and lively celebration **:** a gala entertainment **:** FESTIVAL, FAIR; *specif* **:** an entertainment or entertaining presentation constituting a special occasion **b** *Brit* **:** an athletic meet esp. marking a special occasion **3 :** a gay and lively group ⟨a ~ of actresses and society women with a flair for dress —*Brit. Bk. News*⟩

²gala \"\ *adj* **:** belonging to, deserving, or attended by festivities **:** suitable for festivity ⟨a ~ dress⟩ ⟨a ~ day⟩ ⟨a ~ occasion⟩

³gala *usu cap, var of* GALLA

gala- *or* **galacto-** *comb form, usu ital* [ISV, fr. *galactose*] **:** having the stereochemical arrangement of atoms or groups found in galactose ⟨L-*gala*-heptulose⟩

gal·a·bia *or* **gal·a·bi·eh** *or* **gal·a·be·ah** *or* **gal·la·bi·ya** \ˌgaləˈbē(y)ə\ *n* -s [Ar *jallabīyah*] **:** a loose cloak or robe usu. of homespun worn by the poorer people of Arabic-speaking countries of the Mediterranean

galact- *or* **galacto-** *comb form* [*galact-* fr. MF or L; MF *galact-*, fr. L, fr. Gk *galakt-*, fr. *galakt-*, *gala*; *galacto-* fr. Gk *galakto-*, fr. *galakt-*, *gala* — more at GALAXY] **1 :** milk, milky fluid ⟨*galact*idrosis⟩ ⟨*galact*emia⟩ ⟨*galacto*rrhea⟩ **2** [ISV, fr. *galactose*] **:** related to galactose ⟨*galacto*pyranose⟩ — compare GALA- **3** [*galactic*] **:** galaxy; *specif* **:** the Milky Way galaxy ⟨*galacto*centric⟩

¹ga·lac·ta·gogue *or* **ga·lac·to·gogue** \gəˈlaktəˌgäg *sometimes* -gȯg\ *adj* [prob. fr. NL *galactagogus*, fr. *galact-* + *-agogus* -agogue] **:** promoting secretion of milk

²galactagogue *or* **galactogogue** \"\ *n* -s **:** a galactagogue agent

ga·lac·tan \gəˈlaktən, -ˌtan\ *n* -s [ISV *galact-* + *-an*] **:** any of several polysaccharides of plant or animal origin (as agar, arabogalactans, and the galactan occurring in the albumin glands of the snail *Helix pomatia*) that yield galactose on hydrolysis

ga·lac·tia \gəˈlakshēə, -ktēə\ *n, cap* [NL, fr. *galact-* + *-ia*] **:** a large genus of twining herbs or erect shrubs (family Leguminosae) that are found chiefly in warm regions and have pinnately trifoliate leaves and purple racemose flowers — see MILK PEA

ga·lac·tic \gəˈlaktik, -tēk\ *adj* [LL *galacticus* milky, fr. LGk *galaktikos*, fr. Gk *galakt-*, *gala* milk + *-ikos* -ic] **1 :** of or relating to a galaxy (as the Milky Way) **2 :** extremely great **:** HUGE ⟨a ~ profusion of merchandise —*Steelways*⟩ ⟨the ~ figure of one trillion, 370 billion francs —*Time*⟩

galactic coordinate *n* **:** a member of a system of celestial coordinates based on the equatorial plane of the Milky Way galaxy

galactic equator *n* **:** the great circle of the celestial sphere halfway between the galactic poles parallel to and about 1 degree north of the center line of the Milky Way and inclined about 62 degrees to the celestial equator

galactic latitude *n* **:** latitude in the system of galactic coordinates measured as distance north or south of the galactic equator

galactic longitude *n* **:** longitude in the system of galactic coordinates measured in degrees eastward from the point where the galactic equator crosses the celestial equator in the constellation Aquila

galactic noise *n* **:** radio-frequency radiation coming from the Milky Way that may be detected by radio receivers — called also *cosmic noise*; compare RADIO STAR

galactic pole *n* **:** either of the two opposite points of the celestial sphere that are at the greatest average distance from the Milky Way and are located one in the constellation of Coma Berenices and the other in the constellation of Sculptor — called also respectively *north galactic pole, south galactic pole*

ga·lac·tin \gəˈlaktən, -(ˌ)tin\ *n* -s [*galact-* (fr. Gk *galakt-*, *gala* milk) + *-in*] **:** LACTOGENIC HORMONE

ga·lac·tite \gəˈlakˌtīt\ *n* -s [MF or L; MF *galactite*, fr. L *galactites*, fr. Gk *galaktitēs* (*lithos*) stone that makes water milky, fr. *galakt-*, *gala* milk] **:** an unidentified soluble stone possibly of calcium nitrate whose milky solution gave rise to many legends and superstitions in medieval times

galacto- — see GALA-, GALACT-

ga·lac·to·cele \gəˈlaktəˌsēl\ *n* -s [prob. fr. NL *galactocele*, fr. *galact-* + *-cele*] **:** a cystic tumor containing milk or a milky fluid; *esp* **:** a tumor of this character in a mammary gland

ga·lac·to·cen·tric \gəˌlaktəˈsen·trik\ *adj* [*galact-* + *-centric*] **:** having or relating to the Milky Way as the center ⟨a ~ universe⟩

ga·lac·to·lipide *or* **ga·lac·to·lipid** *or* **ga·lac·to·lipin** \gəˌlaktə+\ *n* [*galact-* + *lipide* or *lipid* or *lipin*] **:** a glycolipide that yields galactose on hydrolysis — compare CEREBROSIDE

ga·lac·to·mannan \"+\ *n* [*galact-* + *mannan*] **:** any of several polysaccharides that occur esp. in seeds (as locust beans) and yield galactose and mannose on hydrolysis

gal·ac·ton·ic acid \ˌgaˌlak¦tänik-\ *n* [ISV *galact-* + *-onic*] **:** a crystalline acid $HOCH_2(CHOH)_4COOH$ obtained by oxidation of galactose

ga·lac·to·phore \gəˈlaktəˌfō(ə)r\ *n* -s [*galact-* + *-phore*] **:** a duct carrying milk

gal·ac·toph·o·rous \ˌgaˌlak¦täf(ə)rəs\ *adj* [Gk *galaktophoros*, fr. *galakt-* galact- + *-phoros* -phorous] **:** conveying milk ⟨a ~ duct⟩

ga·lac·to·poi·e·sis \gəˌlaktəˌpȯiˈēsəs\ *n, pl* **galactopoieses** \-ēˌsēz\ [NL, fr. *galact-* + *-poiesis*] **:** formation and secretion of milk

¹ga·lac·to·poi·et·ic \-¦==¦ed·ik\ *adj* [*galact-* + *-poietic*] **:** inducing galactopoiesis

²galactopoietic \"\ *n* -s **:** a galactopoietic agent

ga·lac·tor·rhea *or* **ga·lac·tor·rhoea** \gəˌlaktəˈrēə\ *n* -s [NL, fr. *galact-* + *-rrhea* or *-rrhoea*] **:** a spontaneous flow of milk from the nipple

ga·lac·tos·amine \gəˌlakˈtōsəˌmēn, ˌgaˌl-, (ˌ)=¦==¦=; gəˌlak(ˌ)tōˈsamən\ *n* [*galactose* + *amine*] **:** a crystalline amino derivative $HOCH_2(CHOH)_3CH(NH_2)CHO$ of galactose occurring in the D-form as chondrosamine; 2-deoxy-2-amino-galactose

ga·lac·tose \gəˈlakˌtōs *also* -ōz\ *n* -s [F, fr. *galact-* + *-ose*] **:** an aldose sugar $HOCH_2(CHOH)_4CHO$ that is less soluble and less sweet than glucose and that is known in dextrorotatory, levorotatory, and racemic forms of which the dextrorotatory D-form is obtained by hydrolysis of lactose melibiose, raffinose, or certain polysaccharides (as agar and pectin) and the levorotatory L-form by hydrolysis of flaxseed mucilage — compare GLUCOSE illustration

ga·lac·tos·emia \gəˌlak(ˌ)tōˈsēmēə\ *n* -s [NL, fr. ISV *galactose* + NL *-emia*] **:** galactose in the blood of infants due to an inability to utilize galactose because of a congenital absence of an enzyme that normally changes the galactose of galactose-containing foods into glucose

ga·lac·to·sid·ase \gəˌlaktəˈsīˌdās, -āz\ *n* -s [*galactoside* + *-ase*] **:** an enzyme (as lactase) that hydrolyzes a galactoside

ga·lac·to·side \gəˈlaktəˌsīd, -sᵊd\ *n* -s [*galactose* + *-ide*] **:** a glycoside that yields galactose on hydrolysis ⟨methol ~⟩

gal·ac·to·sis \ˌgaˌlakˈtōsəs\ *n, pl* **galacto·ses** \-ōˌsēz\ [NL, fr. Gk *galaktōsis* act of changing into milk, fr. *galaktousthai* to become milk (fr. *galakt-*, *gala* milk) + *-ōsis* -osis — more at GALAXY] **:** a secretion of milk

ga·lac·tos·uria \gəˌlak(ˌ)tōˈs(h)u̇rēə, -ōsˈyu̇-\ *n* -s [NL, fr. ISV *galactose* + NL *-uria*] **:** an excretion of urine containing galactose

ga·lac·to·syl \gəˈlaktəˌsil\ *n* -s [*galactose* + *-yl*] **:** a glycosyl radical $C_6H_{11}O_5$ that is derived from galactose — compare LACTOSE

ga·lac·tu·ron·ic acid \gəˌlaktyəˈränik-\ *n* [ISV *galact-* + *-uronic*] **:** a crystalline aldehyde-acid $HOOC(CHOH)_4CHO$ that is obtainable from pectic substances by hydrolysis or from methyl galactoside by oxidation and that is oxidizable to mucic acid

ga·la·fa·te \ˌgaləˈfä(ˌ)tā\ *n* -s [AmerSp (Cuba)] **:** a black oldwife (*Melichthys piceus*) of the western Atlantic from the West Indies to Brazil

gala·go \gəˈlā(ˌ)gō, -ˈlä(-; ˈgaləˌgō, ˈgälə-\ *n* [NL, perh. fr. Wolof *golokh* monkey] **1** *cap* **:** a genus of small actively nocturnal African primates (family Lorisidae) with elongated hind limbs that enable them to leap with great agility **2** -s **:** any primate of *Galago* or a closely related genus which genera together often form a subfamily of the family Lorisidae

ga·lah \gəˈlä\ *n* -s [native name in Australia] **1 :** an Australian cockatoo (*Kakatoë roseicapilla*) that has the back, wings, and tail gray and the head and underparts various shades of rosy pink, that feeds on seeds and bulbous roots, that often is a destructive pest in wheat-growing areas, and that is often kept as a cage bird **2** *slang Austral* **:** FOOL, SIMPLETON

gal·a·had \ˈgaləˌhad, -haa(ə)d\ *n* -s *usu cap* [after *Sir Galahad*, a knight in Arthurian legend who achieved the quest of the Holy Grail] **:** a man marked by unusual purity and self-sacrificing devotion to a noble cause

Gal·a·lith \ˈgaləˌlith\ *trademark* — used for a hornlike plastic made from casein and formaldehyde and used esp. in making small molded objects (as buttons, beads, or combs)

ga·la·nas \gäˈlänəs\ *n* -ES [W, murder] **:** a fine for murder in early Welsh law assessed upon the slayer and his kinsfolk and measured in cattle or money — compare ERIC

ga·lan·ga \gəˈlaŋgə\ *n* -s [ME *galonga, galinga*, fr. ML *galanga, galinga*, fr. Ar *khalanjān*] **:** GALINGALE 1

galangal *or* **galangale** *var of* GALINGALE

galan·gin \gəˈlanjən, gəˈlaŋgən, ˈgalənjən\ *n* -s [*galanga* + *-in*] **:** a yellowish crystalline flavone pigment $C_{15}H_{10}O_5$ found in galingale

ga·lant \gəˈlant, -lȧnt\ *adj* [F, galant, gallant — more at GALLANT] **:** of, relating to, or composed in the galant style of musical composition

ga·lante *like* ²GALLANT 4\ *adj* [F, fem. of *galant*] **:** GALLANT 4

ga·lan·te·rie \gə¦läntə(ˌ)rē, -län-\ *n, pl* **galanteri·en** \=ˌ==ˈrēən\ *or* **galanteries** [G & F; G, lit., gallantry, courtesy, fr. F — more at GALLANTRY] **:** a nonessential movement added to or inserted in the classical musical suite (as minuet, loure, air)

ga·lan·thus \gəˈlan(t)thəs\ *n, cap* [NL, fr. Gk *gala* milk + NL *-anthus*; fr. its white flowers — more at GALAXY] **:** a small genus of European bulbous herbs (family Amaryllidaceae) comprising the snowdrops and having solid scapes and nodding flowers with three larger outer perianth segments and three smaller inner ones with 2-lobed tips

gal·an·tine *or* **gal·a·tine** \ˈgalə(n·)ˌtēn, ==ˈ=\ *n* -s [F *galantine*, fr. OF *galentine, galatine* fish sauce, fr. ML *galatina*, prob. fr. L *gelatus*, past part. of *gelare* to freeze, congeal — more at COLD] **:** a dish of poultry, fish, game, or other meat boned, stuffed with forcemeat, cooked, pressed, covered with aspic, and served cold

galant style *n* [trans. of F *style galant*] **:** a light and elegant free homophonic style of musical composition in the 18th century with rococo ornamentation as contrasted with the serious fugal style of the baroque era

ga·lan·ty show \gəˈlantē-\ *n* [perh. fr. It *galante* gallant, fr. MF *galant* — more at GALLANT] **:** an entertainment consisting of the telling of a story by means of the shadows of miniature figures thrown on a wall or screen

ga·la·pa·go \gəˈläpəˌgō, -lap-\ *n, pl* **galapagos** \-ˌgəs, -ˌgōz\ [Sp *galápago*] **:** TORTOISE; *specif* **:** one of the very large land tortoises of the Galápagos islands

galas *pl of* GALA

gal·a·tea \ˌgaləˈtēə\ *n* -s [after the *Galatea*, a 19th cent. British man-of-war; fr. its being originally used for children's sailor suits] **:** a striped cotton cloth in twill weave similar to a lightweight denim and formerly popular for uniforms and playclothes

ga·la·ti \gəˈläts(ē)\ *adj, usu cap* [fr. *Galati*, Romania] **:** of or from the city of Galati, Romania **:** of the kind or style prevalent in Galati

¹ga·la·tian \gəˈlāsh(ē)ən\ *n* -s *cap* [*Galatia*, ancient country in Asia Minor (fr. L) + E *-an*] **:** a native or inhabitant of Galatia in Asia Minor; *esp* **:** a member of a people believed to have been Gauls who conquered and settled Galatia in the 3d century B.C. or of the descendants of such people

²galatian \"\ *adj, usu cap* **:** of or relating to the Galatians or to Galatia

ga·la·tic \gəˈlad·ik\ *adj, usu cap* [L *Galaticus*, fr. Gk *Galatikos*, fr. *Galatai* Galatians + *-ikos* -ic] **:** GALATIAN

galavant *var of* GALLIVANT

ga·lax \ˈgāˌlaks\ *n* [NL, prob. fr. Gk *galaxias* Milky Way galaxy] **1** *cap* **:** a monotypic genus of evergreen herbs (family Diapensiaceae) of the southeastern U.S. with round to heart-shaped leaves that turn maroon, coppery, or purplish in the fall and are much used for funeral and other decorations **2** -ES **:** any plant of the genus *Galax*

ga·lax·i·al \gəˈlaksēəl\ *or* **ga·lax·i·an** \-ēən\ *adj* [*galaxy* + *-al* or *-an*] **:** GALACTIC

ga·lax·i·as \gəˈlaksēəs\ *n, cap* [NL, fr. Gk, a kind of fish (also, Milky Way galaxy)] **:** the type genus of the Galaxiidae

gal·ax·i·idae \ˌgaləkˈsīəˌdē, ˌgaˌlak-\ *n pl, cap* [NL, fr. *Galaxias*, type genus + *-idae*] **:** a family of scaleless freshwater and marine salmonoid fishes of the southern hemisphere

ga·lax·ite \ˈgāˌlakˌsīt, -lək-\ *n* -s [*Galax*, Va., its locality + E *-ite*] **:** a black mineral $MnAl_2O_4$ consisting of an oxide of manganese and aluminum and constituting a member of the spinel series

gal·axy \ˈgaləksē, -si *sometimes* ˈgäl-\ *n* -ES [ME *galaxie, galaxias*, fr. ML & L; ML *galaxia*, fr. L *galaxias*, fr. Gk, fr. *galakt-*, *gala* milk; akin to L *lac* milk] **1 a** *often cap* **:** MILKY WAY GALAXY **b :** one of billions of large systems of stars including not only stars but nebulae, star clusters, globular clusters, and interstellar matter that make up the universe — called also *extragalactic nebula* **2 :** an assemblage of brilliant, noted, or notable persons or things ⟨a ~ of foreign diplomats⟩ ⟨a ~ of fireworks went up —J.M.Flagler⟩ **3 :** GALAX 2

¹gal·ba \ˈgalbə, ˈgȯl-\ *n, cap* [NL, fr. L, a small worm, ash borer, fat man, fr. Gaulish, fat man — more at CALF] **:** a widely distributed genus of freshwater snails (family Lymnaeidae) that include important Old World hosts of the liver fluke (*Fasciola hepatica*) and that are sometimes considered indistinguishable from the genus *Lymnaea*

²galba \"\ *n* -s [alter. of *calaba*] **:** SANTA MARIA TREE

gal·ba·num \ˈgalbənəm, ˈgȯl-\ *n* -s [ME, fr. L, fr. Gk *chalbanē*, fr. Heb *ḥelbĕnāh*] **:** a yellowish to green or brown aromatic bitter gum resin that contains also some essential oil, that is derived from several Asiatic plants (as *Ferula galbaniflua*), and that resembles asafetida and has been used for similar medicinal purposes and also in incense

gal·bu·la \-byələ\ *n, cap* [NL, fr. L, a small bird, prob. of Celt origin; akin to OIr *gel* white — more at YELLOW] **:** the type genus of Galbulidae including certain typical jacamars

gal·bu·lae \-ˌlē\ *n pl, cap* [NL, fr. L, pl. of *galbula*] **:** a suborder of Piciformes consisting of the jacamars, puffbirds, toucans, barbets, and honey guides

gal·bu·li·dae \=ˈbyüləˌdē\ *n pl, cap* [NL, fr. *Galbula*, type genus + *-idae*] **:** a family of brightly colored, long-billed, tropical American birds (order Piciformes) containing the jacamars, and in some classifications the puffbirds — compare BUCCONIDAE

gal·bu·lus \ˈgalbyələs, ˈgȯl-\ *n, pl* **galbu·li** \-ˌlī\ [L; perh. akin to L *galba* fat man, ash borer] **:** a spherical closed fleshy cone of thickened or fleshy peltate scales (as in the cypress)

gal·cha \ˈgalchə, ˈgȯl-\ *n, pl* **galcha** *or* **galchas** *usu cap* **1 a :** an Iranian people constituting a division of the Tajik and living in the Pamirs and on the slopes of the Hindu Kush **b :** a member of such people **2 :** the language of the Galcha — **gal·chic** \-chik\ *adj, usu cap*

¹gale \ˈgāl, *esp before pause or consonant* -āəl\ *n* -s [origin unknown] **1 a :** a strong current of air; *specif* **:** a wind having a speed from 32 to 63 miles per hour — see FRESH GALE, MODERATE GALE, STRONG GALE, WHOLE GALE; BEAUFORT SCALE table **b** *archaic* **:** a mild wind or current of air **:** BREEZE **2 a :** an emotional outburst (as of laughter) ⟨a ~ of merriment⟩ ⟨~s of hysterical patriotism —W.L.Sperry⟩ ⟨a ~ of excited conjecture —Carol Bache⟩ **b :** a strong continuous outpouring suggesting a gale ⟨earnestly shouted . . . into the teeth of the ~ of prevailing public opinion —Wendell Johnson⟩ ⟨~s of talk⟩ **syn** see WIND

²gale \"\ *n* -s [prob. alter. of ¹*gavel*] **1 a** *Brit* **:** an amount paid periodically as rent **b :** the royalty paid in English law for the right to work a mine; *also* **:** the right itself **2 :** a grant of land in English law; *also* **:** the land granted

ga·lea \ˈgālēə\ *n* -s [NL, fr. L, leather helmet, helmet, fr. Gk *galē, galeē* weasel, ferret; perh. akin to L *glis* dormouse] **1 a :** CASQUE 3 **b :** ¹CAUL 2 b **c** *or* **galea apo·neu·ro·ti·ca** \-ˌapōn(y)əˈrädəkə\ **:** a cap or a membrane fitting like a helmet; *esp* **:** the aponeurosis underlying the scalp and linking the frontal and occipital muscles **2 :** a helmet-shaped part of a calyx or corolla; *esp* **:** the upper lip of a ringent or labiate corolla — compare LABIUM **3 a :** the outer or lateral lobe of the maxilla in mandibulate insects **b :** the spinneret on the movable finger of the chelicera of a pseudoscorpion

gale·age \ˈgālij\ *n* -s [²*gale* + *-age*] **:** ²GALE 2

ga·le·ate \ˈgālēˌāt, -ēət\ *also* **ga·le·at·ed** \-ēˌād·əd\ *adj* [L *galeatus* helmeted, fr. *galea* helmet + *-atus* -ate (adj. suffix)] **:** helmet-shaped **:** having a galea **:** HOODED

gale day *n, Brit* **:** the day on which rent or interest is due

ga·lee·ny \gəˈlēnē\ *n* -ES [Sp *gallina* (*morisca*), lit., Moorish hen, fr. L *gallina* hen, fr. *gallus* cock — more at GALLUS] *dial Eng* **:** GUINEA FOWL

ga·le·ga \gəˈlēgə\ *n, cap* [NL, prob. fr. It, fr. ML (*herba*) *Gallica*, lit., Gallic herb, fr. fem. of L *Gallicus* Gallic — more at GALLIC] **:** a small genus of tall perennial Eurasian herbs (family Leguminosae) with compound leaves and racemose blue or white flowers — see GOAT'S RUE 1

ga·le·gine \gəˈlējən, -ˌjēn\ *n* -s [ISV *galeg-* (fr. NL *Galega*) + *-ine*] **:** a bitter crystalline base $C_5H_9NHC(=NH)NH_2$ that is derived from guanidine and is obtained esp. from European goat's rue

ga·lei \ˈgālēˌī\ [NL, pl., fr. Gk *galeos* dogfish, shark] *syn of* PLEUROTREMATA

¹ga·le·id \-ēəd\ *adj* [NL *Galeidae*] **:** of or relating to the Carcharhinidae

²galeid \"\ *n* -s **:** a shark of the family Carcharhinidae

ga·le·idae \gəˈlēəˌdē, gäˈlē-\ [NL, fr. *Galeus* + *-idae*] *syn of* CARCHARHINIDAE

ga·le·iform \gəˈlēəˌfȯrm, gäˈlē-ˌˈgālē-\ *adj* [prob. fr. F *galéiforme*, fr. L *galea* helmet + F *-iforme* -iform] **1 :** shaped like a helmet **2** [NL *Galeus* + E *-iform*] **:** resembling one of the Carcharhinidae **:** like a typical shark

ga·le·na \gəˈlēnə\ *n* -s [L, lead ore, dross that remains after melting lead] **:** a mineral PbS consisting of native lead sulfide occurring in cubic or octahedral crystals or massive, bluish gray in color with metallic luster, showing highly perfect cubic cleavage, and constituting the principal ore of lead

ga·le·ni·an \(ˈ)gāˈlēnēən, gəˈl-\ *adj, usu cap* [*Galen*, Greek physician + E *-ian*] **:** GALENIC

galenian figure *n, usu cap G* [so called fr. the fact that it was reputedly added by Galen to the three figures formulated by Aristotle †322 B.C. Greek philosopher] **:** the fourth syllogistic figure in logic

¹ga·len·ic \(ˈ)gā¦lenik, gəˈl-, -nēk\ *also* **ga·len·i·cal** \-nəkəl, -nēk-\ *adj* [*Galen fl* 2d cent. A.D. Greek physician and medical writer + E *-ic, -ical*] **1** *usu cap* **:** of or relating to Galen or his medical principles or method **2 :** constituting a galenical

²ga·le·nic \gəˈlēnik, -len-, -nēk\ *or* **ga·le·ni·cal** \-nəkəl, -nēk-\ *adj* [*galena* + *-ic, -ical*] **:** belonging to or containing galena

ga·len·i·cal \gäˈlenəkəl, gəˈ-, -nēk-\ *n* -s [¹*galenical* (adj.)] **:** a standard medicinal preparation (as extract, tincture) containing usu. one or more active constituents of a plant and made by a process that leaves the inert and other undesirable constituents of the plant undissolved

galenic pharmacy *n, usu cap G* **:** the preparation of galenicals

ga·len·ism \ˈgāləˌnizəm\ *n, usu cap* **:** the Galenic system of medical practice

ga·len·ist \-nəst\ *n* -s *usu cap* **:** a follower or disciple of the ancient physician Galen

ga·le·nite \gəˈlēˌnīt\ *n* -s [G *galenit*, fr. L *galena* lead ore + G *-it* -ite] **:** GALENA

ga·le·no·bismutite \gə¦lēnō+\ *n* [ISV *galena* + *-o-* + *bismutite;* orig. formed as Sw *galenobismutit*] : a mineral $PbBi_2S_4$ consisting of a lead-gray or tin-white lead bismuth sulfide (sp. gr. 6.9)

ga·le·noid \gə'lē,nȯid\ *adj* [*galena* + *-oid*] : resembling galena

gal·en·so·ga *n, pl* **galensoga** [by alter.] : GALINSOGA 2

ga·len's vein \'gālənz-\ *n, usu cap G* [after *Galen,* Greek physician] **1** : either of a pair of veins in the roof of the third ventricle that drain the interior of the brain **2** : GREAT CEREBRAL VEIN

ga·le·o·cer·do \,gālēō'sər(,)dō\ *n, cap* [NL, fr. Gk *galeos* dogfish, shark + *kerdō* wily one, fox; akin to Gk *kerdos* profit — more at CAIRD (tinker)] : a genus of sharks (family Carcharhinidae) comprising the tiger shark

[1]**ga·le·oid** \'gālē,ȯid\ *adj* [NL *Galeoidea*] : of or relating to the Galeoidea

[2]**galeoid** \"\ *n* -s : a shark of the suborder Galeoidea

ga·le·oi·dea \,gālē'ȯidēə\ *n pl, cap* [NL, fr. *Galeus* + NL *-oidea*] : a suborder of Pleurotremata comprising typical active predaceous fusiform sharks with the spiracle small or absent and an anal fin always present

ga·leo·pi·the·cus \,gālē(,)ōpə'thēkəs, -'pithəkəs\ [NL, fr. *galeo-* (fr. Gk *galeē* weasel) + *-pithecus* — more at GALEA] *syn of* CYNOCEPHALUS 2

ga·le·op·sis \,gālē'äpsəs\ *n, cap* [NL, fr. L, a nettle, fr. Gk *galeōpsis,* fr. *galē, galeē* weasel + *-opsis*] : a small genus of coarse annual Old World herbs (family Labiatae) distinguished by the calyx that has 5 to 10 nerves and the transversely 2-valved anther sacs — see HEMP NETTLE

ga·le·o·rhin·i·dae \,gālēō'rinə,dē\ *n pl, cap* [NL, fr. *Galeorhinus,* type genus + *-idae*] **1** *in some classifications* : a family of sharks equivalent to or more inclusive than Carchariidae **2** *in some classifications* : a family of sharks comprising the smooth dogfishes and related forms

ga·le·o·rhi·nus \-'rīnəs\ *n, cap* [NL, fr. Gk *galeos* dogfish, shark + NL *-rhinus* (fr. Gk *rhinē,* a shark)] **1** : a genus of sharks including the topes and soupfin sharks **2** *in some classifications* : a genus of sharks comprising the smooth dogfishes

ga·le·ra \gə'lirə\ *n* [NL, fr. L, helmet, helmetlike cap of undressed skin, fr. *galea* helmet — more at GALEA] **1** *cap* : a genus of the family Viverridae comprising the tayra **2** -s : TAYRA

ga·lère \gə'le(ə)r\ *n* -s [F, lit., galley, slave ship, fr. MF, fr. OCatal *galera* galley, alter. of *galea* — more at GALLEY] : a group of people having a marked common quality or relationship

ga·le·rie \gal'rē\ *n* -s [AmerFr (Miss. Valley), fr. F, gallery — more at GALLERY] : GALLERY, VERANDA, PORCH — often used in areas of the South where French or creole dialect is spoken

gal·e·ru·ci·dae \,galə'rüsə,dē\ *n pl, cap* [NL, fr. *Galeruca,* type genus + *-idae*] : a small but widely distributed family of leaf-eating beetles formerly usu. included in Chrysomelidae

gales *pl of* GALE

gal·e·saur \'galə,sȯ(ə)r\ *n* -s [NL *Galesaurus*] : a reptile of the genus *Galesaurus* or the family Galesauridae

[1]**gal·e·sau·rid** \¦==¦sȯrəd\ *adj* [NL *Galesauridae,* a family of reptiles, fr. *Galesaurus,* type genus + *-idae*] : of or relating to the genus *Galesaurus* or the family Galesauridae

[2]**galesaurid** \"\ *n* -s : GALESAUR

gal·e·sau·rus \,==¦sȯrəs\ *n, cap* [NL, fr. Gk *galeos* dogfish, shark + NL *-saurus*] : a genus (the type of the family Galesauridae) of advanced cynodont reptiles of the Karroo formation that have teeth suggesting those of a carnivorous mammal

[1]**ga·let** \'galət\ *n* -s [modif. of Gk *galeē, galē* weasel, ferret] : [2]FOSSA

[2]**gal·et** \'galət\ *var of* GALLET

ga·lette \gə'let\ *n* -s [F, fr. MF, fr. OF *galete,* fr. *galet* pebble — more at GALLET] : a flat round cake of pastry usu. sprinkled with sugar before baking

ga·le·us \'gālēəs\ *n, cap* [NL, fr. Gk *galeos* dogfish, shark] **1** *in some classifications* : a genus of sharks including the topes and related forms and being nearly coextensive with *Galeorhinus* **2** *in some classifications* : a genus of sharks including dogfishes that are usu. placed in *Mustelus*

ga·li·bi \gə'lēbē\ *n, pl* **galibi** *or* **galibis** *usu cap* [Carib *galibi* Caribs — more at CANNIBAL] **1 a** : a Carib people of French Guiana **b** : a member of such people **2** : the language of the Galibi people

[1]**ga·li·cian** \gə'lishən\ *n* -s *cap* [*Galicia,* region and ancient kingdom in northwest Spain + E *-an*] **1** : a native or inhabitant of Spanish Galicia **2** : the language of the Galicians

[2]**galician** \"\ *adj, usu cap* **1** : of or relating to Galicia, a division of Spain north of Portugal, or to the Galicians **2** : of, relating to, or being the Galician language

[3]**galician** \", gə'lētsēən\ *adj, usu cap* [*Galicia,* former Austrian crownland in east central Europe + E *-an*] : of or relating to Galicia, a former province of the Austro-Hungarian empire now a region of southwestern Poland and western U.S.S.R.

[4]**galician** *like* [3]GALICIAN\ *n* -s *cap* **1** : a native or inhabitant of the former Austrian crownland Galicia **2** : a Galician Jew of Poland : a speaker of one of the several Yiddish dialects among eastern European Jews

ga·lic·tis \gə'liktəs\ *n, cap* [NL, fr. Gk *galē* weasel + *iktis* yellow-breasted marten — more at GALEA] *in some classifications* : a genus of Mustelidae comprising the grison and the tayra of So. America

ga·lid·ia \gə'lidēə\ *n, cap* [NL, fr. Gk *galideus* young weasel (dim. of *galeē* weasel) + NL *-ia*] : a genus of Malagasy mongooses comprising a single species (*G. elegans*) distinguished by a black-ringed tail

gal·i·dic·tis \,galə'diktəs\ *n, cap* [NL, fr. Gk *galideus* young weasel + *iktis* yellow-breasted marten] : a genus of Malagasy mongooses marked with dark longitudinal stripes

[1]**gal·i·le·an** *also* **gal·i·lae·an** \,galə'lēən\ *n* -s *cap* [L *Galilaea* Galilee, Roman province in northern Palestine (fr. Gk *Galilaia,* hilly region of northern Palestine) + E *-an*] : a native or inhabitant of Galilee

[2]**galilean** *also* **galilaean** \¦==¦==\ *adj, usu cap* : of or relating to Galilee, the northern province of Palestine under the Romans

[3]**gal·i·le·an** \", -lāən\ *adj, usu cap* [*Galileo* †1642 Ital. astronomer and physicist + E *-an*] : of or relating to Galileo Galilei, founder of experimental physics and astronomy

galilean glass *n, usu cap 1st G* : a Galilean telescope usu. binocular in form

galilean telescope *n, usu cap G* [[3]*galilean*] : the first form of refracting telescope including a positive objective lens and a negative eye lens and giving an erect image and a restricted field of view

gal·i·lee \'galə,lē\ *n* -s [AF, fr. ML *galilaea* porch of a church, prob. fr. L *Galilaea* Galilee] : a chapel or porch at the entrance of an English church (as at Durham, Ely, and Lincoln) used in various ways as an accessory room

gal·i·ma·ti·as \,galə'māshēəs, -'mad·ē-, ¦==‚ma·¦tyä\ *n* -ES [F, fr. MF] : confused and meaningless talk : NONSENSE, GIBBERISH

gal·in·gale \'galən,gāl, -liŋ,-\ *also* **gal·an·gal** \-lən,gal, -liŋ,-\ *or* **gal·an·gale** \-,gāl\ *or* **cal·an·gall** \'kalən,gȯl, -liŋ,-\ *n* -s [ME *galyngale,* fr. MF *galingal, garingal,* fr. OF, fr. Ar *khalanjān*] **1 a** : a pungent aromatic rhizome produced in eastern Asia by plants related to the true ginger and formerly used in medicine and cookery **b** : either of two plants of the family Zingiberaceae that yield galingale: (1) : a Chinese perennial herb (*Alpinia officinalis*) with pyramidal racemes of rose-veined white flowers (2) : a stemless perennial herb (*Kaempferia galanga*) of southeastern Asia with fragrant short-lived largely white flowers **2** : an Old World sedge (*Cyperus longus*) with a root having properties like and sometimes used in place of galingale; *broadly* : a plant of the genus *Cyperus*

gal·in·so·ga \,galən'sōgə\ *n* [NL, after Mariano M. de *Galinsoga* †1797 Span. botanist] **1** *cap* : a small genus of weedy tropical American herbs (family Compositae) with opposite leaves and small heads of yellowish flowers some of which have become naturalized in Europe and No. America — see FRENCHWEED **2** *pl* **galinsoga** : any plant of the genus *Galinsoga*

gal·ion·gee \'galyən,jē, -lēə-, ,==(=)'=\ *n* -s [Turk *kalyoncı* man-of-war's man, fr. *kalyon* man-of-war, galleon, fr. It *galeone,* fr. OSp *galeón* — more at GALLEON] : a Turkish sailor

galiot *var of* GALLIOT

gal·i·pine \'galə,pēn, -,pən\ *n* -s [ISV *galip-* (fr. NL *Galipea,* genus of So. American evergreen plants + *-ine*] : a crystalline alkaloid $C_{20}H_{21}NO_3$ derived from quinoline and found in angostura bark

gal·i·pot \'galə,pät, -,pō\ *n* -s [F] : the crude turpentine oleoresin formed as an exudation upon the bark of the cluster pine in southern Europe (as in France) — called also *Bordeaux turpentine*

ga·lise creek indian *or* **ga·lice creek indian** \gə'lēs-\ *n, usu cap G&C&I* [after *Galise Creek* or *Galice Creek,* Oregon] : TALTUSHTUNTUDE

ga·li·um \'gālēəm\ *n, cap* [NL, fr. Gk *galion* bedstraw, prob. fr. *gala* milk; fr. its use to curdle milk] : a large genus of cosmopolitan usu. trailing herbs (family Rubiaceae) with angled stems, opposite or whorled leaves, and small flowers — see CLEAVERS, WILD LICORICE

gal·joen \gal'yün\ *n* -s [Afrik, galleon, galjoen, fr. D, galleon, fr. MD *galioen,* prob. fr. MF *galion* — more at GALLEON] : a compressed deep-bodied percoid food and sport fish (*Dichistius capensis*) common in shallow water and surf along the coasts of southern Africa; *also* : any of several related fishes — often used with a qualifying term

[1]**gall** \'gȯl\ *n* -s [ME, fr. OE *gealla;* akin to OHG *galla* gall, bile, ON *gall,* L *fel,* Gk *cholē, cholos* gall, bile, OE *geolu* yellow — more at YELLOW] **1 a** : BILE; *esp* : bile obtained from the gallbladder of an animal (as the ox) for use in the arts and in medicine **b** : something bitter to endure ⟨the ~ of repentance⟩ **c** : bitterness of spirit : RANCOR **2** : GALLBLADDER **3** : brazen boldness with impudent assurance and rankling insolence ⟨the small stockholder who . . . has the ~ to ask questions about the management —D.L.Cohn⟩ **4** : GLASS GALL **syn** see TEMERITY

[2]**gall** \"\ *n* -s [ME *galle,* fr. OE *gealla,* fr. L *galla* gallnut] **1 a** : a sore or a granulating wound of the skin caused by chronic irritation (as on the back or withers of a horse due to rubbing or chafing of saddle or harness) — see SADDLE SORE **b** (1) : something that irritates or causes carking exasperation (2) : a state of irritation or exasperation (3) : the inner source or spring of such irritation or exasperation **2 a** *archaic* : a bare or weak spot (as on a string) : FLAW, BLEMISH; *also* : a lesion in wood (as around a knot) used in or intended for use in archery **b** *dial* : an unfertile or barren spot where the topsoil has been removed by erosion

[3]**gall** \"\ *vb* -ED/-ING/-S [ME *gallen,* fr. *galle* gall, sore] *vt* **1 a** : to fret and wear away by friction : hurt or break the skin of by rubbing : CHAFE ⟨a saddle often ~s the back of a horse⟩ ⟨constant friction against the ship's side soon ~*ed* the cable⟩ **b** : FRET, ANNOY, IRRITATE ⟨be ~*ed* by sarcasm⟩ **2** : to harass by shooting at ⟨~*ed* by enemy fire⟩ ~ *vi* **1** : to become sore or worn by rubbing **2** : SEIZE *vi* 2

[4]**gall** \"\ *n* -s [ME *galle,* fr. MF, fr. L *galla* gallnut, gall on a plant; perh. akin to Gk *ganglion* cystic tumor, mass of nerve tissue, Skt *glau* round lump; basic meaning: ball, rounded object] **1** : a swelling or excrescence of the tissues of a plant that results usu. from the attacks of parasites (as fungi, bacteria, insects), is often distinguished by characteristic shape or color, and in some instances forms an important source of tannin — see ALEPPO GALL, BLUE GALL, GREEN GALL; NUTGALL, OAK APPLE; GALL MIDGE **2** : a small generally flattened pellet of clay found in some sandstones and sandy shales — called also *clay gall*

[5]**gall** \"\ *vb* -ED/-ING/-S *vt* : to cause galls to form on (as a tree) ~ *vi* : to form galls

gall- *or* **gallo-** *comb form* [*gallic acid*] : gallic acid ⟨*gall*aldehyde⟩

[1]**gal·la** \'galə, 'gȯlə\ *n* -s [L] : any of certain nutgalls from oaks that are used in pharmacy for their astringent properties

[2]**gal·la** *or* **ga·la** \'galə, 'gälə\ *n, pl* **galla** *or* **gallas** *or* **gala** *or* **galas** *usu cap* [perh. fr. Ar *ghaliẓ* rough, wild] **1 a** : any of several groups of Cushitic-speaking peoples occupying British East Africa and southern Ethiopia **b** : a member of any of these groups **2** : the Cushitic language of the Galla

gallabiya *var of* GALABIA

gall·acetophenone \(¦)gal, (¦)gȯl+\ *n* [ISV *gall-* + *acet-* + *phenyl* + *-one;* prob. orig. formed as G *gallazetophenon*] : a yellow crystalline compound $C_6H_3(OH)_3COCH_3$ formerly used as a mordant dye and also locally as an antiseptic; 2,3,4-trihydroxy-acetophenone — called also *Alizarine Yellow C*

gal·lah *also* **gal·lach** \'gäləḵ, gä'läḵ\ *n, pl* **gallahim** *also* **galla·chim** \gä'lōḵəm, -ḵēm, ,gälō'ḵēm\ [Heb *gallāḥ,* lit., one who shaves] *among the Jews* : a Christian minister or cleric; *esp* : a Roman Catholic priest or monk

gal·la·mine triethiodide \'galə,mēn-\ *n* [*gallamine* fr. pyrogallol + *amine*] : a substituted ammonium salt $C_6H_3[OCH_2CH_2N(C_2H_5)_3]_3I_3$ derived from pyrogallol and used to produce muscle relaxation esp. during anesthesia

gall·anilide *also* **gall·anilid** \(')gal, (')gȯl+\ *n* [ISV *gall-* + *anilide;* orig. formed as G *gallanilid*] : the anilide $C_{13}H_{11}NO_4$ of gallic acid used locally for skin diseases

[1]**gal·lant** *in current senses usu* ='= — *see* [2]GALLANT\ *n* -s [ME *galaunt,* fr. MF *galant,* fr. *galant,* adj.] **1 a** (1) : a man of fashion : a young blood (2) *archaic* : GENTLEMAN — usu. used in pl. as a noun of address ⟨good morrow ~*s!* Want ye corn for bread? —Shak.⟩ **b** *obs* : a fashionably dressed woman **2** : one who is gallant to ladies: **a** : ESCORT, DATE ⟨her ~ was now more than an hour overdue —Dorothy Barclay⟩ **b** : SUITOR **c** : LOVER

[2]**gal·lant** \'galənt *in sense 4 usu* gə'lant *or* ga'- *or* -'länt *or* -'laa(ə)nt *or* -'lȧnt\ *adj* [ME *galaunt,* fr. MF *galant,* fr. OF *galant,* pres. part. of *galer* to rejoice, have a good time, fr. *gale* pleasure, merrymaking, of Gmc origin; akin to OE *wela* weal — more at WEAL] **1 a** : marked by show, color, smartness, or splendor esp. in dress ⟨a ~ figure, with his sword, his rich-laced uniform, his cocked hat and powdered queue —C.B.Nordhoff & J.N.Hall⟩ ⟨the loveliest, the most ~ and dashing of the beauties of the end of Queen Victoria's reign —W.S.Maugham⟩ **b** *obs, of a woman* : HANDSOME **2** *archaic* : FINE, WONDERFUL, EXCELLENT — a generalized expression of admiration **3 a** : marked by dash and valor or by the promise or show of lively, valiant, or resolute performance; *broadly* : SPLENDID, STATELY ⟨command of a tall and ~ ship speeding over blue water —S.E.Morison⟩ **b** : marked by a blend of the high-spirited, brave, dashing, and chivalrous : inspiring admiration : showing courageous fortitude and ready resolution esp. in the face of defeat ⟨Pickett's desperate charge . . . facing a terrific fire, was one of the most ~ efforts —Allan Nevins & H.S.Commager⟩ ⟨losing a ~ fight for life⟩ **c** : noble, chivalrous, and often self-sacrificing ⟨a ~ white lie . . . that brings a measure of understanding to the estranged husband and wife —*Newsweek*⟩ **d** *in British parliamentary and formal use* : distinguished by being in the armed services ⟨the honorable and ~ member from Kent⟩ **4** [F *galant,* fr. It *galante* courteous, attentive to women, fr. MF *galant* dashing, lively, bold] **a** : notably marked by courtesy and attentiveness to women esp. in a spirited and dashing or elaborate way ⟨a ~ escort⟩ **b** : given to amorous quest and intrigue : concerned with amatory ventures ⟨~ enough to have made a distinguished marriage by an elopement —G.B.Shaw⟩ **syn** see CIVIL

[3]**gallant** *usu* ='=\ *vb* -ED/-ING/-S *vt* **1** : to bestow gallant attentions on (a lady) : pay court to : act as a suitor or lover toward **2 a** : to act as an escort to or attend upon (a lady) **b** : ESCORT, CONDUCT **3** *obs* : to handle or manipulate (a fan) in a modish manner ~ *vi* **1** : to act in the manner of a gallant : pay court : FLIRT : make love ⟨spent his evenings ~*ing* with the ladies of the town⟩ **2** : to gad about or gallivant esp. with the opposite sex

gal·lant·ize \-n,tīz, -nt·,īz; *stressed* ='=,= *or* '==,=\ *vt* -ED/-ING/-S : to act as a gallant toward : pay special courtesy or amorous attention to

gal·lant·ly *adv* : in a gallant manner ⟨~ offering his seat to a lady⟩ ⟨~ fighting a losing battle⟩ ⟨sailing ~ into battle⟩

gal·lant·ness *n* -ES [ME *galantnesse,* fr. *galant, galaunt* gallant, adj. + *-nesse* -ness] : the quality or state of being gallant ⟨the ~ of the futile charge against the enemy⟩ ⟨said he had no use for ~ or other useless courtesy⟩

gal·lant·ry \'galəntrē, -ri\ *n* -ES [partly fr. *gallant,* adj. & n. + *-ry* and partly fr. F *galanterie,* fr. MF, fr. *galant,* adj. & n., gallant + *-erie* -ery] **1** *obs* : GALLANTS ⟨all the ~ of Troy —Shak.⟩ **2** *archaic* : gallant appearance : fine or ostentatious display : SPLENDOR **3** : a markedly civil or courteous act or statement **4** : the conduct of a gallant: as **a** : marked civility or markedly courteous attention to a lady ⟨his vivacious ~ stole away the hearts of all the women —T.B.Macaulay⟩ **b** : markedly amorous attention to a female; *esp* : such attention designed to win sexual favors **5 a** : bravery, intrepidity, or fortitude (as against great odds) esp. marked by dashing or heroic acts ⟨the desperate ~ of our naval task forces —G.C.Marshall⟩ ⟨~ in action⟩ **b** : an instance of this ⟨eyewitness's accounts of the rearguard *gallantries* and counterattacks . . . in the great retreat to the coast —*Times Lit. Supp.*⟩

gallant soldier *n* [by folk etymology fr. NL *Galinsoga*] : an annual So. American composite herb (*Galinsoga parviflora*) now a cosmopolitan weed with an erect much-branched stem, opposite leaves, and flower heads in clusters with their branches nearly opposite and equal

gall aphid *n* : an aphid that causes the formation of a gall on the plant on which it lives; *esp* : a member of the family Psyllidae

gallas *pl of* GALLA

gal·late \'ga,lāt, 'gȯ,-\ *n* -s [*gall-* + *-ate*] : a salt or ester of gallic acid

gallavant *var of* GALLIVANT

gall·ber·ry \'gȯl- — *see* BERRY\ *n* [[4]*gall* + *berry*] : INKBERRY 1

gallbladder \'=,==\ *n* [[1]*gall* + *bladder*] : a membranous muscular sac present in most vertebrates in which the bile from the liver is stored until required, in man being pear-shaped and lodged in a fossa on the undersurface of the right lobe of the liver and opening by the cystic duct which joins the hepatic duct to form the common bile duct — see DIGESTION illustration

gal·le·ass *also* **gal·li·ass** \'galēəs, -ē,as\ *n* -ES [MF *galeasse, galiace,* fr. OIt *galeazza,* lit., large galley, aug. of *galea* galley, fr. ML, fr. MGk — more at GALLEY] : a large fast galley propelled by both sails and oars and mounting guns; *esp* : such a ship used by nations of southern Europe in the 16th and 17th centuries

galled \'gȯld\ *adj* [ME, fr. OE *geallede,* fr. *gealla* gall, sore + *-ede* -ed — more at GALL (sore)] **1** : subjected to galling : having galls **2** : sterile from exhaustion or removal of soil; *also* : rendered infertile by erosion

galle·gan \gə(l)'yāgən, gə'lēg-\ *adj, usu cap* [*gallego* + *-an*] : [2]GALICIAN

galle·go \gə(l)'yā(,)gō\ *n* -s *cap* [Sp, n. & adj., Galician, fr. L *Gallaicus* of the Gallaeci, fr. *Gallaeci,* an ancient people in western Spain] : [1]GALICIAN

gal·le·in \'galēən, 'gȯl-\ *n* -s [ISV *gall-* + phthalein; orig. formed in G] : a metallic-green crystalline phthalein dye $C_{20}H_{12}O_7$ made from phthalic anhydride and gallic acid or pyrogallol and used esp. in dyeing violet and as an indicator

gal·leon \'galēən, 'lyən\ *n* -s [OSp *galeón,* fr. MF *galion* large war galley, fr. OF *galie* galley — more at GALLEY] **1** : a heavily built chiefly square-rigged sailing ship of the 15th to early 18th centuries usu. having a high, fortified, and sometimes elaborately decorated forecastle and poop and often three or four decks and being used for war or commerce esp. by the Spanish as treasure ships in their American trade **2** : a large esp. stately sailing ship suggesting a galleon

gal·le·ri·an \gə'lirēən ga'-\ *n* -s [F *galérien,* fr. *galère* galley + *-ien* -an] *archaic* : GALLEY SLAVE

gal·ler·ied \'gal(ə)rēd, -rid\ *adj* : provided or decorated with a gallery ⟨~ country houses⟩ ⟨the fortified, ~ and intimidating great rock —Rose Macaulay⟩

gal·lery \'gal(ə)rē, -ri\ *n* -ES [MF *galerie,* fr. ML *galeria,* prob. alter. of *galilea, galilaea* galilee — more at GALILEE] **1 a** : a covered space more or less open at the sides for walking : a roofed promenade : AMBULATORY, PORTICO, COLONNADE **b** : a main corridor with windows running continuously on one side in an English country house **2 a** : a platform or passageway above ground level resembling a corridor, projecting from an outside wall, and open at the outer edge or having there only a rail or balustrade : BALCONY; *also, South & Midland* : PORCH, VERANDA **b** : a similar raised platform or passageway on the roof of a building **c** (1) : a platform at the quarter or around the stern of a ship — see QUARTER GALLERY, STERN GALLERY (2) : a gun platform or gun emplacement on a ship or aircraft carrier **d** : a raised usu. railed walk (as around the upper part of a large engine) to facilitate oiling or inspection **3 a** : a long and narrow passage, apartment, or corridor **b** : a horizontal or nearly horizontal subterranean passageway (as in a cave or excavated part of a military mining system); *also* : a working drift or level in mining **c** : a sunk or cut passageway in a fortification that is covered overhead as well as at the sides **d** : a passageway either within the thickness of a wall or projecting on corbels or between a main wall and an arcade (as in the front or flank of a Gothic church) **e** : a passage made underground by an animal (as a mole or ant) or in wood by an insect (as a beetle larva) **f** : BURROW 2 **g** : an artificial chamber provided for the collection of groundwater **4 a** : a room, series of rooms, wide corridor, or building devoted to the exhibition of works of art ⟨sculpture displayed in the north ~⟩; *also* : a long room or unusually wide corridor used for exhibitions or special ceremonials **b** : an institution devoted to the collection and exhibition of works of art ⟨the National *Gallery*⟩ **c** : a business establishment devoted to the exhibition and sale of works of art ⟨a new ~ showing modern prints⟩ **d** : ROGUES' GALLERY **e** : a collection or aggregation (as of varied specimens of one kind of thing) worthy of being put on display as if in a gallery ⟨what a ~ of men these are who line Ireland's Hall of Fame —*Saturday Rev.*⟩ ⟨the rich ~ of characters in this novel —H.S.Canby⟩ ⟨the world's ~ of attractive animals —W.E.Swinton⟩ ⟨in portraying his ~ of grotesques —Bergen Evans⟩ ⟨cameramen pick up a ~ of faces of every age, shade, and nationality —*Newsweek*⟩ ⟨his ~ of humors varies —*Encyc. Americana*⟩ **5 a** : a platform projecting from one or more interior walls (as of a church or theater) for additional accommodation (as of part of a congregation or audience) or for special use; *esp* : the highest of such platforms in a theatre commonly having the cheapest seats **b** : the occupants of a gallery; *esp* : the part of a theater audience that is seated in the top gallery or in the cheapest seats **c** : a part of the general public lacking the discriminating taste of the connoisseur **d** : a body of spectators (as at a tennis match) or listeners (as at a debate) **6** : any of several netted openings in court tennis below the side penthouse — see WINNING GALLERY **7 a** : a small ornamental barrier or railing (as along the edge of a table or shelf) **b** : an often ornamental ring to support a lampshade or globe **c** : a bandlike jewelry setting usu. with a pierced or raised design **8** : SHOOTING GALLERY; *esp* : an indoor shooting range **9** : a photographer's studio **10** : an upper-floor area open to and projecting over a lower-floor area of a house **syn** see BALCONY

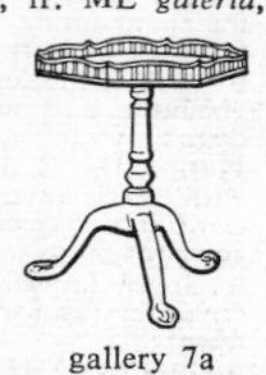

gallery 7a

gallery car *n* : a double-decked railroad car used in suburban service

gallery deck *n* : a gallery or bay for gun emplacements on a ship or aircraft carrier

gallery forest *n* : FRINGING FOREST

gallery god *n* : an occupant of the gallery of a theater

gal·lery·ite \'gal(ə)rē,īt\ *n* -s : an occupant of a gallery esp. of a theater

gallerylike \'=(=)=,=\ *adj* : resembling a gallery

gallery load *n* : a cartridge designed for firing in a gallery

gallery organ *n* : a division of a pipe organ placed at the end of the nave in a gallery

[1]**gal·let** *also* **gal·et** \'galət\ *n* -s [F *galet* pebble, fr. MF, fr. OF, dim. of *gal,* prob. of Celt origin; akin to OIr *gall* stone pillar] : a chip of stone : SPALL

[2]**gallet** *also* **galet** \"\ *vt* -ED/-ING/-S : to fill in the fresh mortar joints of (rubble masonry) with gallets

galle·ta grass *also* **galleta** \gə(l)'yed·ə, gī'|, |äd·ə\ *n* -s [Sp *galleta* hardtack, fr. F *galette* flat round cake of pastry, hardtack — more at GALETTE] : either of two perennial forage grasses (*Hilaria rigida* and *H. jamesii*) used for hay in southwestern U.S. and Mexico

gal·ley \'galē, -li\ *n* -s *often attrib* [ME *galeie*, fr. OF *galee*, *galie*, prob. fr. OCatal or fr. OProv *galea*, fr. MGk, prob. fr. Gk *galeē*, *galē* weasel, marten, a small fish — more at GALEA] **1 a :** a large low usu. one-decked ship propelled by both sails and oars, typically being 100 to 200 feet long, often having 20 oars on each side with many rowers to each oar, 2 or 3 masts rigged with lateen sails, guns at prow and stern, and a complement of 1000 to 1200 men, and used throughout medieval times esp. in the Mediterranean for war, trading, ceremonial, and pleasure purposes — see GALLEASS, GALLIOT, QUARTER GALLEY; compare GALLEON **b :** LYMPHAD 2 **2 :** a short crescent-shaped seagoing ship of classical antiquity propelled chiefly by oars though generally having a mast carrying an oblong sail — compare BIREME, PENTECONTER, QUADRIREME, QUINQUEREME, TESSARACONTER, TRIACONTER, TRIREME **3 :** a large open rowing boat formerly used in England by customs officers or press-gangs, by captains of warships, and as a river pleasure boat **4 a :** the kitchen and cooking apparatus of a ship, airplane, or trailer — see ¹CABOOSE 1a **b :** COOKHOUSE, KITCHEN **5 a :** an oblong tray commonly of pressed steel with upright sides to hold set type **b :** GALLEY PROOF **6 :** an inward circle made with the free foot during a hop in Cotswold morris dancing — **in this galley** *adv* **:** in this markedly incongruous place or group

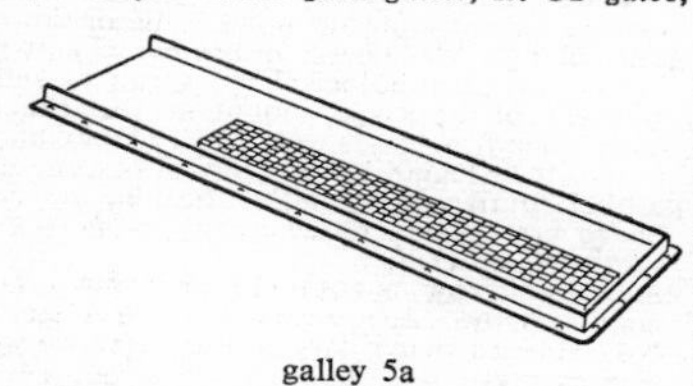

galley 5a

galley halfpenny *n* [ME *galey halfpeni*, fr. *galey*, *galeie* galley + *halfpeni* halfpenny; fr. its alleged introduction to London by Genoese traders — more at HALFPENNY] **:** a small base silver denier from the Continent that circulated in England in the 13th and 14th centuries

galley line *n* **:** an identifying line at the top of a galley of typeset matter

gal·ley·man \'==mən\ *n*, *pl* **galleymen** [ME *galay man*, fr. *galay*, *galeie* galley + *man*] **1 :** one who rows, works, or carries on trade in a galley **2 :** a utility man on a ship

galley method *n* [prob. fr. It *galea* galley, fr. ML, fr. MGk; fr. the supposed resemblance of the outline of the figures to a galley] **:** SCRATCH DIVISION

galley operator *n* **:** a regional wholesaler engaged in distributing or reshipping books and periodicals to individual dealers in rural or suburban areas

galley proof *n* **:** a proof from type on a galley before it is made up in pages

galley punt *n* **:** a clinker-built open boat with dipping lugsail and oars used esp. by English pilots

galley slave *n* **1 a :** a slave acting as a rower on a galley **b :** a criminal condemned to row on a galley **2 :** DRUDGE 1

galley slug *n* **:** SLUG 2b

galley-tile *n* [so called fr. its being originally transported by galley] *obs* **:** a tile of glazed earthenware

gal·ley-west \,galē'west\ *adv* [prob. alter. of E dial. *collywest*, *collyweston* in an opposite direction, badly askew, awry, perh. fr. a personal name] **:** into a condition of total disorder, destruction, confusion, or uselessness — used in the phrase *to knock galley-west* ⟨the trade was knocked *galley-west* when the government struck at its roots, jailed 30 of the biggest smugglers —*Today*⟩ ⟨hit him as hard as he could and knocked him *galley-west*⟩

gall fig *n* [⁴*gall*; fr. the fact that the fig wasp develops in galls produced in these figs] **:** CAPRIFIG

gallflower \'=,=\ *n* **:** a degenerate pistillate flower that occurs in some cultivated figs and is characterized by an aborted ovary incapable of developing seeds

gallfly \'=,=\ *n* **:** an insect that deposits its eggs in plants and causes galls in which the larvae feed

gall gnat *n* [⁴*gall*] **:** GALL MIDGE

gal·li \'ga,lī\ *n pl*, *cap* [NL, fr. L, pl. of *gallus* cock — more at GALLUS] **:** a suborder of Galliformes consisting of the megapodes, curassows, and pheasants and related birds (as the turkey)

¹**gal·li·am·bic** \,galē'ambik\ *n* -s [L *galliambus*, a song of the priests of Cybele, ancient nature goddess of Anatolia (fr. *Gallus*, eunuch priest of Cybele — fr. Gk *Gallos* — + L *iambus*) + E *-ic*] **:** a galliambic verse or meter

²**galliambic** \;==;==\ *adj*, *in classical prosody* **:** consisting of two iambic dimeters catalectic of which the last lacks the final syllable **:** consisting of four Ionic a minore feet varied by resolution or contraction

gallian *adj*, *cap* [L *Gallia* Gaul + E *-an*] *obs* **:** GALLIC, FRENCH

¹**gal·liard** *also* **gail·lard** \'galyə(r)d\ *adj* [ME *gaillard*, *galiard*, fr. MF *gaillard*, fr. OF, prob. of Celt origin; akin to OIr *gal* bravery, Corn *gallos* power, W *gallu* to be able; akin to Lith *galėti* to be able] **1** *archaic* **:** gay in spirits or appearance **:** LIVELY **2** *archaic* **:** HARDY, VALIANT

²**galliard** *also* **gaillard** \"\ *n* -s **1** *archaic* **:** a galliard man **2 a** [MF *gaillarde*, fem. of *gaillard*, adj.] **:** a gay dance with five steps to a phrase popular in the 16th century as a sequel to the stately pavane **b :** a 16th century dance tune in moderately quick triple time with or without an upbeat

gal·liar·dise \'galyə(r),dīz, -dēz\ *n* -s [MF *gaillardise*, fr. *gaillard* (adj.) + *-ise* -ice] *archaic* **:** extreme gaiety **:** MERRIMENT

galliass *var of* GALLEASS

gal·lic \'galik, -lēk\ *adj*, *usu cap* [ML *Gallicus*, fr. L, of the Gauls] **1 :** French esp. in quality ⟨*Gallic* wit and sophistication⟩ **2** [L *Gallicus*, fr. *Galli* Gauls, inhabitants of Gaul, *Gallia* Gaul, ancient country of Europe + *-icus* -ic] **a :** of or relating to Gaul ⟨Caesar . . . received the *Gallic* military post as a reward for party services —*Current History*⟩ **b :** of or relating to the Gauls — **gal·li·cal·ly** \-lək(ə)lē, -lēk-, -li\ *adv*, *usu cap*

gal·lic acid \'ga|lik-, 'gȯ|, \|lēk-\ *n* [part trans. of F *acide gallique*, fr. *acide* acid + *gallique* of gall, derived from gall, fr. *galle* gall + *-ique* -ic — more at GALL (excrescence)] **:** a white crystalline acid $C_6H_2(OH)_3COOH.H_2O$ that occurs widely in plants both in the free form (as in galls and in tea leaves) and combined in tannins from which it can be obtained by the action of molds or alkali and that is used chiefly in making pyrogallol, dyes, and writing ink and as a photographic developer; 3,4,5-trihydroxy-benzoic acid

¹**gal·li·can** \'galəkən, -lēk-\ *adj* [in sense 1, fr. L *Gallicanus* of the Roman province of Gaul, fr. *Gallicus* Gallic + *-anus* -an; in sense 2, fr. ML *Gallicanus* French, fr. L] **1** *usu cap* **:** GALLIC **2** *often cap* **:** of or relating to Gallicanism **:** marked by Gallicanism **:** advocating Gallicanism

²**gallican** \"\ *n* -s *usu cap* **:** one that advocates Gallicanism

gal·li·can·ism \-,nizəm\ *n* -s *usu cap* [F *gallicanisme* theory advocating administrative independence from papal control for the Roman Catholic Church in France, fr. MF *gallican* of the Roman Catholic Church in France, French (fr. ML *Gallicanus* French) + *-isme* -ism] **1 :** a theory orig. formulated in France advocating administrative independence from papal control for the Roman Catholic Church in each nation — compare ULTRAMONTANISM **2 :** advocacy of or devotion to Gallicanism or the independence it is designed to achieve

gal·li·cism \'galə,sizəm\ *n* -s *often cap* [F *gallicisme*, fr. MF, fr. ML *Gallicus* Gallic + MF *-isme* -ism] **1 a :** a word, expression, or grammatical construction distinctive of French appearing esp. in a context in another language ⟨an English novel full of ~*s*⟩ **b :** a word or expression that is adapted to another language from French by translation and that retains a distinctively French construction or word sense (as in *attorney general* or *it is to laugh* [from *c'est à rire*]) **2 a :** a mode of thought or an outlook that is distinctive of the French ⟨the ~ in French-Canadian novels⟩ **b :** a distinctively French action ⟨cheek kissing is a ~⟩

gal·li·ci·za·tion \,galəsə'zāshən, -,sī'z-\ *n* -s *usu cap* **:** the process or result of gallicizing or being gallicized

gal·li·cize \'galə,sīz\ *vb* -ED/-ING/-S *sometimes cap* [*gallic* + *-ize*] *vt* **1 :** to cause to acquire French quality or qualities or traits ⟨~ American architecture⟩ ⟨~ an English writer⟩; *also* **:** to cause to adopt French customs or modes of thought or conduct ⟨*gallicized* by an education in France⟩ **2 :** to make (a foreign word or phrase) French by adapting to French spelling or pronunciation ⟨Napoleon *gallicized* his Corsican name⟩ or by substituting a closely equivalent French word or phrase ⟨Walker *gallicized* his name to Marcheur⟩ ~ *vi* **:** to become French or adapt to French ways in speech, thought, or outlook

gal·lic·o·la \gȯ'likələ, ga'-,gə'-\ *n* -s [NL, fr. *galli-* (fr. L *galla* gall) + *-cola* — more at GALL (excrescence)] **:** the stage or an individual of some gall aphids and phylloxerans that produces leaf galls

gal·lic·o·lous \(')gȯ¦likələs, (')ga¦l-, gə'l-\ *adj* [L *galla* gall + E *-i-* + *-colous*] **:** producing and inhabiting galls

gal·li·crow \'galə,krō\ *n* [²*gally* + *crow* (bird)] *dial Eng* **:** SCARECROW

gallied *past of* GALLY

gallies *pres 3d sing of* GALLY

gal·li·form \'galə,fȯrm\ *adj* [NL *Galliformes*] **:** of or relating to the Galliformes

gal·li·for·mes \,==fȯr,mēz\ *n pl*, *cap* [NL, fr. *galli-* (fr. *Gallus*) + *-formes*] **:** an order of birds of largely terrestrial habits that are mostly rather large and heavy-bodied with short wings, legs adapted for running and scratching the ground where most of their food (as seeds or worms) is found, a large crop, and a muscular gizzard, that nest usu. on the ground, that produce numerous eggs and young which are precocial, and that include the pheasants, turkeys, grouse, partridges, quails, and related birds (as the common domestic fowl, the megapodes and curassows, and the hoatzins) — see GALLI, OPISTHOCOMI

gal·li·gas·kins \,galə'gaskənz, -lē'g-\ *n pl* [prob. modif. of MF *garguesques*, *greguesques*, fr. OSp *gregüescos*, fr. *griego* Greek, fr. L *Graecus* — more at GREEK] **1 a :** loose wide hose or breeches worn in the 16th and 17th centuries **b :** very loose trousers **2** *chiefly Scot* **:** LEGGINGS

gal·li·mau·fry \,galə'mȯfrē\ *n* -ES [MF *galimafree*, *calimafree* ragout, hash] **:** MEDLEY, MIXTURE, HODGEPODGE, JUMBLE ⟨written in a remarkable ~ of languages —*Times Lit. Supp.*⟩ ⟨a unique ~ of contestants —H.W.Wind⟩ ⟨a ~ of didactic speeches, romantic flourishes and characters for several unrelated kinds of plays —*Time*⟩

gal·li·na \gə'lēnə, gī'ēnə\ *adj*, *usu cap* [fr. *Gallina*, N.M.] **:** of or relating to an ancient culture in New Mexico contemporaneous with Anasazi and characterized by unpainted pottery resembling the Shoshoni utility types, painted pottery similar to Anasazi types, and leaf-shaped stone blades having a notch on each side halfway between the point and the base

gal·li·na·cean \,galə'nāshən\ *n* -s [NL *Gallinaceae*, a group of birds (fr. L *gallinaceae*, fem. pl. of *gallinaceus*) + E *-an*] **:** a gallinaceous bird

gal·li·na·ceous \;==;=shəs\ *adj* [L *gallinaceus* of domestic fowl, fr. *gallina* hen (fr. *gallus* cock) + *-aceus* -aceous — more at GALLUS] **1 :** resembling a bird (as a domestic fowl) of the order Galliformes ⟨a ~ pigeon⟩ **2 :** of or relating to the Galliformes ⟨~ birds⟩

gal·li·nae \gə'lī,nē\ *n pl* [NL, fr. L *gallinae*, pl. of *gallina* hen] **1** *usu cap* **:** a group of birds usu. nearly equivalent to Galliformes **2** *often cap* **:** wild birds (as wild turkey, grouse, pheasant, partridge, and quail) of the order Galliformes that are fit or lawful for hunting

galli·na·zo \¦gä(y)ē¦nä(,)sō\ *adj*, *usu cap* [Sp, turkey buzzard, fr. *gallina* hen, fr. L] **:** of or relating to an ancient culture of the Viru valley in northern Peru characterized esp. by negative-painted pottery, artificial irrigation, textiles, and limited metallurgy

gal·line \'ga,līn\ *adj* [L *gallus* cock + E *-ine*] **:** GALLINACEOUS

gal·li·ney \gə'lēnē\ *var of* GALEENY

¹**galling** *n* -s [fr. the gerund of ³*gall*] **:** the action or the results of galling ⟨resistance of stainless steel . . . to erosion, ~, and scoring —*Crane Co. Catalogue*⟩

²**galling** *adj* [fr. the pres. part. of ³*gall*] **:** of such a character as to gall **:** markedly irritating **:** CHAFING ⟨he has borne these assaults with a dignity ~ to his enemies —*New Republic*⟩ ⟨the attempts . . . to exchange the ~ status of wards for the honorable role of trading partners —D.L.Hurwood⟩ — **gall·ing·ly** *adv* — **gall·ing·ness** *n* -ES

gal·li·nip·per *also* **gal·ly·nip·per** \'galə,nipə(r), -lē,-\ *n* -s [origin unknown] **:** a biting insect: as **a :** a very large American mosquito (*Psorophora ciliata*) **b :** BEDBUG

gal·li·nule \'galə,n(y)ül\ *n* -s [NL *Gallinula*, genus of birds, fr. L *gallinula* pullet, chicken, dim. of *gallina* hen] **:** any of several aquatic birds that constitute a subfamily of the family Rallidae, are distinguished from the coots by the unlobed feet and from the rails by the presence of a frontal shield, and resemble a small domestic hen in general proportions and carriage — called also *marsh hen, swamphen, water hen*

gal·lio \'galē,ō\ *n* -s *usu cap* [after Junius Annaeus *Gallio* †*ab* A.D. 65 Roman proconsul of Achaia who dismissed the Jews' accusation against Paul (Acts 18:12-17), fr. L] **:** one that is Gallionic

gal·li·on·ic \;==;änik\ *adj*, *usu cap* [L *Gallion-*, *Gallio* + E *-ic*] **:** marked by indifference or easygoing carelessness or irresponsibility

gal·li·ot *or* **gal·i·ot** \'galēət, -ē,ät\ *n* -s [in sense 1, fr. ME *galiote*, fr. MF, fr. ML *galeota*, dim. of *galea* galley, fr. MGk; in sense 2, fr. D *galjoot*, fr. MD *galiōte*, fr. MF *galiote* — more at GALLEY] **1 :** a small swift galley formerly used in the Mediterranean and moved both by sails and oars **2 :** a long narrow light-draft Dutch merchant ship carrying a mainmast and a jigger with a mainsail having a long foot and short gaff

gal·liph·a·gous \(')gȯ¦lifəgəs, (')ga¦-\ *adj* [L *galla* gall + E *-i-* + *-phagous* — more at GALL (excrescence)] **:** GALLIVOROUS

gal·li·pot \'galə,pät\ *n* [ME *galy pott*, prob. fr. *galy*, *galeie* galley + *pott* pot; fr. its being originally transported by galley — more at GALLEY, POT (earthen vessel)] **1 :** a small usu. ceramic vessel with a small mouth; *esp* **:** one used by apothecaries to hold medicines **2 :** DRUGGIST

gal·li·um \'galēəm\ *n* -s [NL, fr. L *gallus* cock (intended as trans. of Paul É. *Lecoq* de Boisbaudran †*ab* 1912 Fr. chemist, its discoverer) + NL *-ium*] **:** a rare bluish white usu. trivalent metallic element that is hard and brittle at low temperatures but melts just above room temperature and expands on freezing and that is obtained usu. as a by-product in the extraction of aluminum from bauxite or of zinc from zinc ores — symbol *Ga*; see ELEMENT table

gal·li·vant *also* **gal·a·vant** *or* **gal·la·vant** \'galə,vant, -vaə(ə)nt *sometimes* ,==¦=\ *vi* -ED/-ING/-S [perh. alter. of ³*gallant*] **1 :** to act as a gallant **:** attend gallantly or amorously upon a member of the opposite sex **:** go about usu. ostentatiously or indiscreetly with members of the opposite sex ⟨left his wife to go ~*ing* with other women⟩ **2 a :** to travel or roam for mere pleasure ⟨~*ed* around Europe —Louis Auchincloss⟩ **b :** MOVE, GO, TRAVEL ⟨the porters . . . ~*ed* along like a cheerful bunch of boys —Edmund Hillary⟩ ⟨the flames ~*ing* up the chimney —Helen Shaw⟩

gal·li·vat \'galə,vat\ *n* -s [prob. modif. of Pg *galeota* galliot, fr. Sp, fr. ML] **:** an East Indian ship propelled by sails and oars and often armed and used by pirates

gal·liv·o·rous \(,)gȯ¦liv(ə)rəs, (')ga¦-\ *adj* [L *galla* gall + E *-i-* + *-vorous*] **:** feeding on galls or gall tissue (as the larvae of gall insects)

gal·li·wasp \'galə,wäsp, -wȯsp\ *n* [origin unknown] **:** a harmless lizard (*Diploglossus monotropis*) of eastern Central America; *also* **:** either of two similar related lizards of Jamaica

gall midge *n* **:** any of numerous minute two-winged flies of the family Cecidomyiidae most of which cause gall formation on various plants — called also *gall gnat*

gall mite *n* **:** any of various minute 4-legged mites that form galls on plants and are members of the family Eriophyidae — compare BLISTER MITE

gallnut \'=,=\ *n* [⁴*gall*] **:** a gall resembling a nut

¹**gallo-** *comb form* [L *Gallo-*, fr. *Gallus* Gaul, inhabitant of ancient Gaul] **1** *cap* **:** Gaulish and ⟨*Gallo*-Roman⟩ **2** *cap* **:** French and ⟨*Gallo*-Briton⟩ **3** *often cap* **:** France ⟨*gallo*centric⟩

²**gallo-** — see GALL-

gall oak *n* **:** an oak producing gallnuts; *esp* **:** a Spanish and Portuguese oak (*Quercus lusitanica*) that produces gallnuts

gal·lo·cy·a·nine \,ga(,)lō'sīə,nēn, ,gȯ(-, -,nən\ *n* [ISV *gall-* + *cyan-* + *-ine*] **:** an oxazine dye $C_{15}H_{12}N_2O_5$ made from gallic acid and a nitroso derivative of aniline and used in dyeing mordanted wool and cotton bluish violet — see DYE table I (under *Mordant Blue 10*)

gall of the earth [earlier *gall of the earth* lesser centaury (trans. of MF *fiel de terre*, trans. of L *fel terrae*), fr. ¹*gall*] **1 :** a lion's foot of the genus *Prenanthes*; *esp* **:** a common perennial herb (*P. serpentaria*) that is widely distributed in the southern and eastern U.S. and has thick variable basal leaves and clusters of pink to white flower heads **2 :** a wild plant of the genus *Lactuca* **3 :** PINEDROPS 1

galloglass *archaic var of* GALLOWGLASS

gal·lo·man \'galō,man\ *n*, *pl* **gallo·men** \-,men\ *usu cap* [¹*Gallo-* + *-man* maniac (fr. F *-mane*, back-formation fr. *manie* mania) — more at BIBLIOMANIA] **:** FRANCOPHILE

gal·lo·ma·nia \,galō'mānēə, -nyə\ *n*, *usu cap* [F *gallomanie*, fr. ¹*Gallo-* + *manie* mania] **:** a strong prejudice in favor of what is French — **gal·lo·ma·ni·ac** \-nē,ak\ *n*, *usu cap*

gal·lon \'galən\ *n* -s *often attrib* [ME *galon*, *galun*, a liquid measure, fr. ONF *galon*; akin to OF *jalaie*, a measure of capacity; both directly or indirectly fr. ML *galeta* jug, pail, a liquid measure] **1 :** any of various units of capacity: as **a :** a unit of liquid capacity equal to 231 cubic inches ⟨a ~ jug⟩ **b :** a British unit of liquid and dry capacity equal to 277.42 cubic inches — called also *imperial gallon*; see ALE GALLON, WINE GALLON; MEASURE table **2 :** an extremely large quantity or number — usu. used in pl. ⟨~*s* of tea, which seems to have no effect on the nerves here —Fanny K. Wister⟩ ⟨in North America there are ~*s* of language families, each with one or two ~*s* of languages —C.F.Voegelin & T.A.Sebeok⟩

gal·lon·age \-nij\ *n* -s **:** amount in gallons

gal·loon \gə'lün\ *n* -s [F *galon*, fr. MF, fr. OF *galonner* to adorn with galloons] **:** a narrow ornamental fabric for trimming or finishing clothes or upholstery; *esp* **:** a braid with gold or silver threads or a strip of lace or embroidery with both edges scalloped or indented

gal·looned \-nd\ *adj* **:** trimmed or ornamented with galloon ⟨~ watchcases⟩

¹**gal·lop** \'galəp\ *n* -s [MF *galop*, fr. OF, prob. fr. *galoper*, v.] **1 a :** a springing gait of various quadrupeds; *specif* **:** a fast natural 3-beat gait of the horse in which one or two feet touch the ground in the order of one hind foot, diagonal biped including opposite hind foot, remaining forefoot — compare CANTER, RUN **b :** a ride or run at a gallop **c :** a stretch of land used for galloping horses ⟨horses, trained in seclusion on private ~*s* —A.J.Liebling⟩ **2 :** a rapid rate or pace ⟨the child went at a ~ to get his ice-cream cone⟩ ⟨this is not a book to be read at a ~ —Hal Lehrman⟩

²**gallop** \"\ *vb* -ED/-ING/-S [MF *galoper*, fr. OF] *vi* **1 a :** to move or run in a gallop (as of a horse) **b :** to ride at a gallop **:** ride at full speed ⟨~*ing* over the moors on a stallion⟩ **2 :** to go at great speed or as fast as possible ⟨dawdle to school but ~ home⟩ ⟨he ~*ed* over the dunes barefoot —Mary H. Vorse⟩ ~ *vt* **1 :** to cause to gallop ⟨~ a horse for miles⟩ **2 :** to transport at a gallop ⟨~*ed* the general over to headquarters⟩ ⟨we are ~*ed* to them over every obstacle on the pounding hoofs of rhapsodical prose —Virginia Woolf⟩ **3 :** to ride over at a gallop ⟨each knight must ~ the course three times —*Amer. Guide Series: Md.*⟩

¹**gal·lo·pade** *also* **gal·o·pade** \¦galə¦pād, -päd\ *n* -s [F *galopade*, lit., act of galloping, fr. *galoper* to gallop + *-ade*] **:** GALOP

²**gallopade** *also* **galopade** \"\ *vi* -ED/-ING/-S **:** to dance a gallopade

gal·lop·er \'galəpə(r)\ *n* -s **1 :** a horseman that gallops **2 :** a horse that gallops fast **3 a :** a light fieldpiece on a carriage drawn without a limber that was formerly used by English regiments **b :** the carriage of such a gun **4** *Brit* **:** a military aide

¹**gal·lo·phile** \'galə,fīl\ *n* -s *usu cap* [¹*gallo-* + *-phile*] **:** ²FRANCOPHILE

²**gallophile** \"\ *adj*, *usu cap* **:** ¹FRANCOPHILE

gal·lo·phobe \-,fōb\ *n* -s *usu cap* [¹*gallo-* + *-phobe*] **:** FRANCOPHOBE

gal·lo·pho·bia \,==¦fōbēə\ *n*, *usu cap* [NL, fr. ¹*Gallo-* + *-phobia*] **:** FRANCOPHOBIA

galloping *adj* **1 :** marked by a motion like that of one galloping **:** fast moving **:** rapidly developing or increasing ⟨the ~ trend toward federal monopoly of power and other industries —Ray Tucker⟩ ⟨a ~ case of nerves —*Newsweek*⟩ ⟨~ inflation⟩ **2** *of a disease* **:** progressing rapidly toward a fatal conclusion ⟨~ consumption⟩ — **gal·lop·ing·ly** *adv*

galloping dominoes *or* **galloping ivories** *n pl*, *slang* **:** DICE

gallop rhythm *also* **gallop** *n* -s **:** an abnormal heart rhythm marked by the occurrence of three distinct sounds in each heartbeat like the sound of a galloping horse

gallo-roman \¦ga(,)lō+\ *adj*, *usu cap G&R* [¹*Gallo-* + *Roman*] **:** of or relating to Gaul under Roman rule

gallo-romance \"+\ *n*, *cap G&R* [¹*Gallo-* + *Romance*] **:** the Romance speech that developed out of Vulgar Latin in Transalpine Gaul — compare FRENCH, PROVENÇAL

gal·lo·tannic acid \¦galō, ¦gȯlō+ . . . -\ *n* [*gallo-* (fr. L *galla* gall) + *tannic* — more at GALL (excrescence)] **:** GALLOTANNIN

gal·lo·tannin \"+\ *n* [*gallo-* (fr. L *galla* gall) + *tannin*] **:** a tannin occurring esp. in extracts from gall and yielding gallic acid on hydrolysis

gallous *var of* GALLOWS

¹**gal·lo·vid·i·an** \¦galə¦vidēən\ *adj*, *usu cap* [ML *Gallovidia* Galloway (district in southwestern Scotland) + E *-an*] **:** GALWEGIAN

²**gallovidian** \"\ *n* -s *cap* **:** GALWEGIAN

gal·low \'galō\ *var of* ²GALLY

gal·lo·way \'galə,wā\ *n* [fr. *Galloway*, a district in Scotland] **1** *often cap* **a :** a breed of small hardy horses of former times originating in Galloway, Scotland **b** -s **:** a large pony or small horse **2** *usu cap* **:** a breed of hardy medium-sized hornless chiefly black beef cattle native to southwestern Scotland and distinguished from the Aberdeen Angus chiefly by the very heavy curly coat

gal·low·glass \'galō,glas\ *n* -ES [IrGael *gallōglach*, fr. *gall* foreigner + *ōglach* servant, soldier, youth, fr. OIr *ōclach* youth, fr. *ōac* young; akin to W *ieuanc* young, OE *geong* — more at YOUNG] **1 :** one of a class of soldiers (as mercenaries or retainers) formerly maintained by an Irish chief **2 :** a heavily armed Irish foot soldier — compare KERN

gal·low-grass \'galō+,-\ *n* [obs. *gallow* gallows (fr. ME *galwe*) + *grass*; fr. its use for making ropes] **:** HEMP

¹**gal·lows** \'ga(,)lōz, -ləz, *in sense 3 & archaic or dial in other senses* -ləs\ *n*, *pl* **gallows** *or* **gallowses** [ME *galwes*, pl. of *galwe*, fr. OE *galga*, *gealga*; akin to OHG *galgo* gallows, ON *galgi* gallows, Goth *galga* cross, Arm *jatk* twig] **1 a :** a frame usu. of two upright posts and a crossbeam from which is suspended the rope with which criminals are executed by hanging — compare GIBBET **b :** the punishment of hanging ⟨a crime worthy of the ~⟩ **c :** GALLOWS BIRD **2 :** a structure consisting of an upright frame with a crosspiece: as **a :** a rest for the tympan of a hand printing press when raised **b :** GALLOWS BITT **c** *or* **gallows frame :** the headframe of a mine **d :** a timber structure for butchering cattle **3 :** ³GALLUS

²**gallows** \"\ *or* **gal·lous** *or* **gal·lus** \-ləs\ *adj* [ME *galwous*, fr. *galwes*, n.] **1 :** deserving the gallows **2** *now dial chiefly Brit* **a :** wild and villainous **b :** MISCHIEVOUS, RASCALLY

gallows bird *n* **:** one who deserves hanging

gallows bitt *also* **gallows frame** *n* **:** one of two or more frames amidships to support spare spars

gallows tree *or* **gallow tree** *n* [*gallows tree* fr. earlier *gallow tree*, fr. ME *galwe tree*, fr. OE *galgatrē*, *galgtrēow*, fr. *galga* gallows + *trē*, *trēow* tree — more at TREE] **:** GALLOWS

galls *pres 3d sing of* GALL, *pl of* GALL

gallsick \'=,=\ *adj* [¹*gall* + *sick*; trans. of Afrik *galsiek*] **1 :** suffering from gall sickness ⟨a herd of ~ cattle⟩ **2 :** producing or having the conditions to produce gall sickness ⟨~ pastureland⟩

gall sickness *n* [¹*gall*; trans. of Afrik *galsiekte*] **:** ANAPLASMOSIS

gallstone \'=,=\ *n* [¹*gall* + *stone*] **1 :** calculus formed in the gallbladder or biliary passages — called also *biliary calculus* **2 :** LIGHT CHROME YELLOW

gallumph *var of* GALUMPH

gal·lup poll \'galə(p)¦pōl\ *n*, *usu cap G* [after George H.

*Gallup b*1901 Am. statistician] **:** a sampling of public opinion on a particular issue or of the degree of information among the public about a particular thing or of opinion or information in a particular group taken by questioning a representative cross section ⟨belongs certainly among the most remarkable stars visible with the naked eye; a *Gallup poll* among amateurs and professional astronomers alike would undoubtedly confirm this —*Sky & Telescope*⟩ ⟨contests of all kinds, questionnaires, and *Gallup polls* have become enormously popular —*Westralian Farmers Co-op. Gazette*⟩ ⟨we can . . . find out who are the supporters only by organized inquiries and *Gallup polls* —Barbara & Robert North⟩ ⟨an amateur *Gallup poll* to discover what modern American short-story writers are well known to the intelligent reading public in England —*Times Lit. Supp.*⟩

gal·lup·tious \gə'ləpshəs\ *adj* [fr. earlier *galoptious*, perh. alter. of *voluptuous*] *slang* **:** WONDERFUL, DELIGHTFUL, DELICIOUS

¹gal·lus \'galəs\ *n, cap* [NL, fr. L, cock; perh. akin to ON *kalla* to call — more at CALL] **:** a genus of birds (family Phasianidae) that consists of the common domestic fowl and related wild birds — see JUNGLE FOWL

²gallus *var of* GALLOWS

³gal·lus \'galəs\ *n* -ES *often attrib* [alter. of ¹*gallows*] *chiefly dial* **:** SUSPENDER 2a ⟨worn close to the left-hand ~ —J.C. Furnas⟩ — usu. used in pl.

gal·lused \-st\ *adj, chiefly dial* **:** wearing galluses ⟨a coatless, ~ man —*Nation*⟩ ⟨~, austere farmers —David Roman⟩

gall wasp *n* [⁴*gall*; fr. the fact that it lives in galls] **:** one of the Cynipidae **:** a hymenopterous gallfly

¹gally \'gȯlē\ *adj* [²*gall* + -*y*] **:** marked by bare spots or areas lacking vegetation (as from excessive wetness or erosion)

²gal·ly \'galē\ *vt* -ED/-ING/-ES [origin unknown] **1** *now chiefly dial* **:** FRIGHTEN, TERRIFY ⟨we've been *gallied* at a terrible affliction —Thomas Hardy⟩ **2 :** to put to flight (a whale) by frightening ⟨don't want to ~ those critters till we're fast to them —A.B.C.Whipple⟩

gallynipper *var of* GALLINIPPER

gal·ly·ware \'galē+,-\ *n* [perh. fr. *galley* + *ware*] **:** earthenware. usu. tin-glazed

ga·lois theory \'gal,wä-\ *n, usu cap G* **:** a part of the theory of mathematical groups that is applied esp. to showing which algebraic equations can be solved by sequences of rational operations and by the extraction of integral roots of already known quantities and to proving that a quintic equation exists that cannot be solved by such procedures

¹ga·loot \gə'lüt, *usu* -üd·+V\ *n* -S [origin unknown] **:** ROSS'S GOOSE

²galoot \"\ *n* -S [origin unknown] *slang* **:** FELLOW, PERSON; *esp* **:** a man who is strange, odd, or foolish ⟨such a simple-minded, honest kind of ~ —Robert Lowry⟩ ⟨till that crazy ~ . . . caught up with me —Earle Birney⟩ ⟨a man of any size feels like a ~ in that tomfool outfit —Jean Stafford⟩ ⟨tell me to my face that I'm a ~ . . . and a hick —Sinclair Lewis⟩

¹gal·op \'galəp, (')ga¦lō\ *n* -S [F — more at GALLOP] **:** a lively dance in duple measure performed with sliding steps from side to side and popular in the 19th century; *also* **:** music for this dance

²galop \"\ *vi* -ED/-ING/-S **:** to dance a galop

galopade *var of* GALLOPADE

gal·o·pin \'galə,pan\ *n* -S [MF, fr. OF, one that gallops, fr. *galoper* to gallop] *archaic* **:** a kitchen helper **:** SCULLION

gal·lop·tious \gə'läpshəs\ *or* **ga·lup·tious** \-'ləp-\ *var of* GALLUPTIOUS

ga·lore \gə'lō(ə)r, -ō(ə)r, -ōə, -ō(ə)\ *adj* [IrGael *go leor* enough, fr. *go* to (fr. OIr *co, cu*) + *leor* enough (fr. OIr *lour, loor*); akin to W *llawer* much, many, OIr *lōg* reward, price — more at LUCRE] **:** ABUNDANT, PLENTIFUL, PROFUSE — used postpositively ⟨bargains ~ for sharp-eyed buyers —H.T. Simmons⟩ ⟨women's clubs and lodges, and other organizations ~ —F.L.Mott⟩ ⟨Philadelphia, which boasts history ~ —Lewis Mumford⟩

¹ga·losh \gə'läsh\ *n* -ES [ME *galoche*, fr. MF, perh. alter. of *galette* flat round cake — more at GALETTE] **1** *obs* **:** a clog, patten, or shoe with a heavy sole **2 :** an overshoe designed to protect the shoe in wet weather or in wet areas and usu. made with a rubber or water-repellent fabric upper reaching to the ankle or somewhat higher **:** ²ARCTIC **3 :** a strip of material (as leather) running around a shoe at and above the sole for protection or ornament

²galosh \"\ *vt* -ED/-ING/-ES **:** to put a galosh on ⟨~ a shoe⟩; *also* **:** provide with a galosh

ga·lou·bet \¦ga(,)lü¦bā\ *n* -S [F, fr. Prov] **:** PIPE 1a(1)

galravage *var of* GILRAVAGE

gals *pl of* GAL

gal·siek·te \'gäl,sēktə\ *n* -S [Afrik, fr. *gal* gall, bile (fr. MD *galle*) + *siekte* sickness (fr. MD *siecte*, fr. *siec* sick); akin to OHG *galla* gall, bile — more at GALL (bile), SICK] *Africa* **:** ANAPLASMOSIS

¹galt \'gält, 'gȯ(l)t\ *n* -S [ME, fr. ON *göltr, galti*; akin to ON *gyltr* young sow — more at GILT] *dial Eng* **:** ¹HOG 1; *usu* **:** a gelded male swine **:** BARROW

²galt *var of* GAULT

gal·ton bar \'gȯltᵊn-\ *n, usu cap G* [after Sir Francis *Galton* †1911 Eng. scientist, its inventor] **:** an instrument used in tests of the accuracy of estimate of visible lengths that consists of a horizontal bar to be bisected by an adjustable vertical line

gal·to·nia \gȯl'tōnēə\ *n* [NL, fr. Sir Francis *Galton* + NL -*ia*] **1** *cap* **:** a small genus of southern African bulbous plants (family Liliaceae) that was formerly included in *Hyacinthus* but is distinguished by the large two to three foot long somewhat fleshy leaves and larger flowers in long loose racemes — see SUMMER HYACINTH **2** -S **:** any plant of the genus *Galtonia*

gal·to·ni·an \(')ˈ=¦==ən\ *adj, usu cap* [Sir Francis *Galton* + E -*ian*] **:** of or relating to the English scientist Francis Galton or his work

galton's law of inheritance *or* **galton's theory of inheritance** *usu cap G* [after Sir Francis *Galton*, its formulator] **:** a theory in genetics: the parents of an individual together contribute on an average 50 percent of the total inherited characters, the 4 grandparents together 25 percent, the 3d generation of ancestors together 12.5 percent, etc. — compare MENDEL'S LAW

galton whistle *n, usu cap G* [after Sir Francis *Galton*, its inventor] **:** a whistle of variable high pitch used to test the upper limit of audibility

gal·trap \'galtrəp, 'gȯl-\ *var of* CALTRAP

ga·lu·chat \¦ga(,)lü¦shä\ *n* -S [F, fr. Jean-Claude *Galluchat* †1774 Fr. leather craftsman] **:** an ornamented shagreen

ga·lumph *or* **gal·lumph** \gə'ləm(p)f\ *vi* -ED/-ING/-S [prob. alter. of ²*gallop*] **:** to move or progress with a clumsy bumping thudding heavy tread ⟨the elephant paid no heed to her calls and ~*ed* off again —*Newsweek*⟩ ⟨~*ing* along the bridle path on their mounts —Mollie Panter-Downes⟩ ⟨several pairs of feet ~*ed* down the passage —Monica Stirling⟩; *also* **:** to act in a way suggesting such a manner of moving ⟨my heart ~*ing* as I stood up —Vincent McHugh⟩

ga·luth *or* **ga·lut** \gä'lüt(h), 'gōləs\ *n, often cap* [Heb *gālūth* exile] **:** exile of the Jews from Palestine **:** DIASPORA

galv *abbr* galvanic; galvanism; galvanized

gal·van·ic \(')gal¦vanik, -nēk\ *adj* [F or It; F *galvanique*, fr. It *galvanico*, fr. Luigi *Galvani* + It -*ico* -ic] **1 a :** of, relating to, or producing galvanism **:** VOLTAIC — distinguished from *faradic* ⟨~ electricity⟩ ⟨~ battery⟩ ⟨~ current⟩ ⟨~ cell⟩ **b :** caused by galvanism — used esp. of the corrosion of metallic objects in damp earth as a result of electrolytic action **2 a :** having a sharp, marked, or jolting effect suggesting that of an electric shock **:** markedly engaging the interest, arousing to activity, or stimulating vitality ⟨a ~ speech⟩ ⟨a ~ personality⟩ ⟨made no secret in private of the ~ effect Napoleon's coronation worked in him —Lee Ellerich⟩ ⟨the most ~ religious music ever recorded —*Saturday Rev.*⟩ ⟨the product of mental energy and a ~ temperament —R.L.Cook⟩ **b :** produced as if by an electric shock ⟨a ~ reaction⟩ — **gal·van·i·cal·ly** \-nək(ə)lē, -nēk-, -li\ *adv*

galvanic couple *n* **:** a pair of dissimilar substances (as metals) capable of acting together as an electric source when brought in contact with an electrolyte

gal·va·nism \'galvə,nizəm\ *n* -S [F or It; F *galvanisme*, fr. It *galvanismo*, fr. Luigi *Galvani* †1798 Ital. physician and physicist who first described it + It -*ismo* -ism] **1 :** a direct current of electricity; *esp* **:** such a current produced by chemical action (as in a storage battery) **2 :** the therapeutic use of direct electric current **3 :** vital or forceful activity suggesting activation by a strong and continuous electric current

gal·va·ni·za·tion \,galvənə'zāshən, -,nī'z-\ *n* -S **:** the act or process of galvanizing; *specif* **:** the application of an electric current to the human body for medical purposes

gal·va·nize \'galvə,nīz\ *vt* -ED/-ING/-S [F *galvaniser*, fr. Luigi *Galvani* + F -*iser* -ize] **1 a :** to subject to the action of an electric current **b :** to arouse, stimulate, or excite as if by the application of an electric current ⟨the news *galvanized* the campers into a fury of activity⟩ ⟨~ the alliance, restore its confidence, and lead it to move and act in unison —*Newsweek*⟩ ⟨~ the government into vehement and extraordinary preparation —Sir Winston Churchill⟩ **2 :** to coat (iron or steel) with zinc — compare ELECTROGALVANIZE

galvanized iron *n* **:** iron or steel coated with zinc to protect it from rust

gal·va·niz·er \-zə(r)\ *n* -S **:** one that galvanizes ⟨serve as the chief ~ and spokesman —F.L.Allen⟩; *specif* **:** a worker who coats iron or steel with zinc

galv·an·neal \¦galv+\ *vt* [blend of *galvanize* and *anneal*] **:** to coat with an alloy of iron or steel and zinc produced by heating a surface already galvanized with zinc ⟨~*ed* wire⟩

galvano- *comb form* [*galvanic* + -*o*-] **:** galvanic current ⟨*galvanometer*⟩ **:** using or produced by galvanic current ⟨*galvanocautery*⟩ ⟨*galvanoplastics*⟩

gal·va·no·graph \gal'vanə,graf, 'galvənē,-, -räf\ *n* [*galvano-* + -*graph*] **:** a copperplate engraving produced by galvanography; *also* **:** a picture printed from such a plate — **gal·vano·graph·ic** \(¦)gal¦vanə¦grafik, ¦galvənō¦-\ *adj*

gal·va·nog·ra·phy \,galvə'nägrəfē\ *n* -ES [ISV *galvano-* + -*graphy*] **:** a method similar to electrotyping of producing an intaglio-printing plate on copper

gal·vano·luminescence \¦galvə(,)nō, gal¦va-+\ *n* [*galvano-* + *luminescence*] **:** luminescence arising at the anode in an electrolytic cell (as with aluminum electrodes in sodium bicarbonate solution)

gal·vano·magnetic \"+\ *adj* [ISV *galvano-* + *magnetic*] **:** ELECTROMAGNETIC

gal·va·nom·e·ter \,galvə'nämədə(r)\ *n* [*galvano-* + -*meter*] **:** an instrument for measuring a small electric current or for detecting its presence or direction by means of the movements of a magnetic needle or of a coil in a magnetic field that registers usu. on a scale or by a moving beam of light reflected from a mirror attached to the needle or the coil

gal·vano·met·ric \¦galvənō¦me·trik, (¦)gal¦van-\ *adj* [*galvano-* + -*metric*] **:** measured by a galvanometer

gal·vano·plastics \¦galvə(,)nō, gal¦va(+\ *n pl but sing in constr* [*galvano-* + *plastics*] **:** a science of electroforming

gal·vano·plas·ty \gal'vanə,plastē, 'galvənō,-\ *n* -ES [*galvano-* + -*plasty*] **:** GALVANOPLASTICS

gal·vano·scope \-,skōp\ *n* [*galvano-* + -*scope*] **:** an instrument for detecting the presence and direction of an electric current (as of feeble intensity) by the deflection of a magnetic needle — compare GALVANOMETER

gal·vano·tac·tic \¦galvənō¦taktik, gal¦van-\ *adj* [*galvano-* + -*tactic*] **:** of, relating to, or being galvanotaxis

gal·vano·tax·is \-¦taksəs\ *n* [NL, fr. *galvano-* + -*taxis*] **:** a taxis in which a direct electric current is the directive factor

gal·vano·trop·ic \-¦träpik\ *adj* [ISV *galvano-* + -*tropic*] **:** characterized by galvanotropism

gal·va·not·ro·pism \,galvə'nä·trə,pizəm\ *n* [ISV *galvano-* + -*tropism*] **:** a tropism in which electricity is the stimulus

gal·ves·to·nian \,galvə'stōnēən, -nyən\ *n* -S *cap* [*Galveston*, Texas + E -*ian*] **:** a native or resident of Galveston, Texas

gal·way \'gȯl,wā\ *adj, usu cap* [fr. *Galway*, urban district and county in Ireland] **1 :** of or from the urban district of Galway, Ireland **:** of the kind or style prevalent in Galway **2 :** of or from County Galway, Ireland **:** of the kind or style prevalent in County Galway

galway hooker *n, usu cap G* [fr. *Galway*, seaport in Ireland] **:** a small Irish coasting cutter-rigged boat

gal·ways \-āz\ *n pl, often cap* [prob. fr. County *Galway*, Ireland] **:** whiskers following the line of the chin

¹gal·we·gian \(')gal¦wēj(ē)ən\ *adj, usu cap* [irreg. (influence of *Norwegian*) fr. ML *Galwedia* Galloway (district in southwestern Scotland) + E -*an*] **:** of or relating to the district of Galloway, Scotland

²galwegian \"\ *n* -S *cap* **:** a native or resident of Galloway, Scotland

gal·yak *also* **gal·yac** \'gal,yak, 'gȯl,-, gəl'yak\ *n* -S [native name in Uzbekistan, U.S.S.R.] **:** a short-haired flat or slightly moiré fur derived from the pelt of a stillborn lamb, kid, or sometimes other hoofed mammal

gal·ziek·te \'gäl,zēktə, -,sē-\ *n* -S [obs. Afrik (now *galsiekte*) — more at GALSIEKTE] **:** ANAPLASMOSIS

¹gam \'gam\ *n* -S [origin unknown] **1** *Scot* **:** TOOTH; *esp* **:** a large or crooked tooth **2** *Scot* **:** MOUTH

²gam \'gam, 'gaa(ə)m\ *n* -S [prob. fr. F dial. (northern) *gambe*] *slang* **:** LEG ⟨those trim ~*s* of yours —J.H.Burns⟩ ⟨most people . . . think I have nice ~*s* —Ethel Merman⟩

³gam \"\ *n* -S [perh. short for obs. *gammon* talk, chatter — more at GAMMON] **1 :** a visit or friendly conversation esp. between whalers or other seamen at sea or ashore ⟨the story . . . had been told, in ~ after ~, wherever whaleships met —A.B.C.Whipple⟩ ⟨there'd be a famous ~ up and down the sandy beach —Alan Villiers⟩ **2 :** a school of whales **:** POD

⁴gam \"\ *vb* **gammed; gammed; gamming; gams** *vi* **:** to engage in a gam ⟨whalers *gammed* in midocean on a hot tropical day —A.B.C.Whipple⟩ ~ *vt* **1 :** to have a gam with **:** visit with ⟨I decided to ~ some friends of mine —H.A. Chippendale⟩ **2 :** to pass in conversation **:** WHILE ⟨congregate . . . to ~ the hours away —H.A.Chippendale⟩

gam- *or* **gamo-** *comb form* [NL, fr. Gk, marriage, fr. *gamos* — more at BIGAMY] **1 :** united **:** joined ⟨*gamophyllous*⟩ ⟨*gamosepalous*⟩ **2 :** sexual **:** sexuality ⟨*gamic*⟩ ⟨*gamobium*⟩ ⟨*gamogenesis*⟩

-gam \,gam, ,gaa(ə)m\ *n comb form* -S [NL -*gamia* class of plants having a (specified) means of reproduction, fr. Gk -*gamia* -gamy] **:** plant belonging to a group having a (specified) means of reproduction ⟨*cryptogam*⟩

gam *abbr* gamut

gama \'gamə\ *or* **gama grass** *n* -S [prob. alter. of *grama, grama grass*] **:** a tall coarse American grass (*Tripsacum dactyloides*) valuable for forage

-gamae \gə,mē\ *n pl comb form* [NL, fem. pl. of -*gamus* -gamous] **:** plants having (such) sexual organs or (such) a means of reproduction — in taxonomic names in botany ⟨*Agamae*⟩

ga·ma·ri \gə'märē\ *n* -S [Beng *gāmāri*, fr. Skt *gambhārī*] **:** GUMHAR

ga·mash·es \gə'mashəz\ *n pl* [MF *gamaches*, pl. of *gamache*, modif. of OProv *garamacha, galamacha*, modif. of OSp *guadameci* colored or embossed leather, fr. *guadameci*, adj., colored or embossed (said of leather), modif. of Ar *ghadāmasīy* of Gadāmes, town in Tripoli where ornate leather was made] *archaic Scot* **:** leggings or gaiters worn by horseback riders

gamb *or* **gambe** \'gam(b), -aa(ə)m-\ *n* -S [F dial. (northern) *gambe* leg, fr. ONF, fr. LL *gamba, camba* hock (of a horse), leg — more at GAMBOL] **:** LEG, SHANK — used chiefly in heraldry

gam·ba \'gämbə, 'gam-,'gaam-,'gȧm-\ *n* -S [It *gamba* leg (in *viola da gamba*), fr. LL *gamba, camba*] **:** VIOLA DA GAMBA

gamba bass *n* **:** a labial pipe-organ stop of 16-foot pitch and string quality

gam·bade \(')gam¦bād, -bäd\ *n* -S [F — more at GAMBOL] **:** ²GAMBADO ⟨a particularly explosive ~ that assaulted the rider after he had completely left the saddle —P.A.Rollins⟩ ⟨in his early youth . . . had himself tried musical and poetic ~*s* —Francis Hackett⟩

¹gam·ba·do \gam'bā(,)dō, -bä(-\ *n, pl* **gambadoes** *also* **gambados** [perh. modif. (influenced by E -*ado* in such words as *bastinado, palisado*) of It *gambale* boot top, legging, greave, fr. *gamba* leg] **1 :** a long boot or legging attached to each side of a saddle to protect the rider's feet and legs from the wet or cold **2 :** a long gaiter or legging

²gambado \"\ *n, pl* **gambadoes** *also* **gambados** [modif. (influenced by E ¹*gambado*) of F *gambade*] **1 :** a spring of a horse **2 a :** a droll or fantastic movement **:** CAPER, GAMBOL ⟨pirouetted into a reckless ~ —L.C.Douglas⟩ **b :** a sudden, unexpected, or fantastic move, sally, or flourish **:** ANTIC

gam·bel oak \'gambəl-\ *n, usu cap G* [after William *Gambel* †1849 Am. ornithologist] **:** a shrub or small tree (*Quercus gambelii*) of the Rocky mountains with thin scaly gray-brown bark, thick firm leaves with 7 to 11 lobes, and acorns enclosed to half their length by the scaly pubescent cup

gambel quail *or* **gambel's quail** *n, usu cap G* **:** a largely bluish gray black-crested quail (*Lophortyx gambelii*) of the southwestern U.S.

gambel sparrow *or* **gambel's sparrow** *n, usu cap G* **:** a common sparrow (*Zonotrichia leucophrys gambelii*) of western No. America that is largely brown above with a white stripe over each eye

gam·ben bass \'gäm|bən-, 'gam|, 'gaam|, 'gȧm|\ *n* [*gamben* prob. fr. G, pl. of *gambe* viola da gamba, fr. It *gamba* leg (in *viola da gamba*)] **:** GAMBA BASS

gam·be·son \'gambəsən, -bəzən\ *n* -S [ME *gambesoun*, fr. MF *gambeson, gambeison*, fr. OF, aug. of *gambais*, of Gmc origin; akin to OHG *wamba* belly — more at WOMB] **:** a medieval garment of stuffed and quilted cloth or leather orig. worn under the hauberk as a pad but later used alone as a defensive garment

gam·bet \'gambət\ *n* -S [earlier *gambetta*, fr. NL, fr. It, dim. of *gamba* leg] **:** REDSHANK 1

gam·bette \(')gam¦bet\ *n* -S [prob. fr. *gamba* + -*ette*] **:** a 4-foot pipe-organ stop of the viola da gamba family

gam·bia \'gambēə\ *adj, usu cap* [fr. *Gambia*, country in western Africa] **:** of or from the country of Gambia **:** of the kind or style prevalent in Gambia

gam·bi·ae \'gambē,ē\ *n* -S [NL *gambiae* (specific epithet of *Anopheles gambiae*), fr. *Gambiae*, gen. of *Gambia*, country in West Africa] **:** an African mosquito (*Anopheles gambiae*) introduced into Brazil that is a very efficient vector of malaria

gambia fever *n, usu cap G* **:** a trypanosomiasis of cattle and sometimes other domestic animals in central Africa that resembles nagana but appears to be caused by a different trypanosome — called also *paranagana*

gam·bi·an \-ēən\ *n* -S *cap* [*Gambia*, Africa + E -*an*] **:** a native or inhabitant of Gambia — **gambian** *adj, usu cap*

gambia pod *n, usu cap G* **:** the pod of babul

gam·bier *also* **gam·bir** \'gam,bi(ə)r, -iə\ *n* -S [Malay *gambir*] **:** a yellowish catechu obtained from a Malayan woody vine (*Uncaria gambir*) of the family Rubiaceae, used for chewing with the betel nut, and exported for tanning and dyeing — called also *pale catechu, terra japonica, white cutch*; see DYE table I (under *Natural Brown 3*)

gam·bist \'gambəst, 'gäm-,'gaam-,'gȧm-\ *n* -S [*gamba* + -*ist*] **:** a performer on the viola da gamba

¹gam·bit \'gambət, 'gaam-, *usu* -əd·+V\ *n* -S [alter. (prob. influenced by F *gambit*, fr. Sp *gambito*, modif. of It *gambetto*) of earlier *gambet, gambett*, fr. It *gambetto* gambit, act of tripping someone, fr. *gamba* leg] **1 :** a chess opening in which a player voluntarily risks one or more pawns or a minor piece to gain an advantage in position **2 a** (1) **:** a remark or comment designed to launch a conversation or to make a telling point **:** SALLY ⟨"I decided to see you myself," was his opening ~ —*Newsweek*⟩ ⟨opened . . . with the ~ of inquiring whether present conditions were satisfactory —Jeremy Potter⟩ ⟨this was her usual opening ~ with the young —Elizabeth Goudge⟩ ⟨he could not, if he had pondered conversational ~*s* for an hour, have hit on a more successful one —C.D.Lewis⟩ (2) **:** TOPIC ⟨to smoke or not to smoke still flourishes as a useful conversational ~ —*Saturday Rev.*⟩ ⟨three other popular conversational ~*s* —Harold Strauss⟩ **b** (1) **:** a calculated move, maneuver, or device ⟨employs the classic melodramatic ~ of the innocent who walks straight into somebody else's intrigue —*Time*⟩ ⟨worked up a neat legislative ~ to further their interests —*New Republic*⟩ ⟨threw up its hands and retired to think up a new ~ —Richard Thruelsen⟩ (2) **:** a tactical maneuver in which an airplane awaiting favorable opportunity to attack keeps out of sight of a submarine periscope

²gambit \"\ *vi* -ED/-ING/-S **:** to make a gambit

¹gam·ble \'gambəl\ *Midland var of* GAMBREL 2

²gam·ble \'gambəl, 'gaam-\ *vb* **gambled; gambled; gambling** \-b(ə)liŋ\ **gambles** [prob. back-formation fr. *gambler*] *vi* **1 a :** to play a game of chance for money or other stakes **b :** to wager money or other stakes on an uncertain outcome (as of a horse race or an athletic game) **2 :** to stake something of value on an uncertain event or contingency **:** take a chance **:** speculate esp. recklessly ⟨*gambled* on beating the Americans in air transport with jet airliners —Howard Marshall⟩ ⟨we cannot ~ on offending anyone —*Reporter*⟩ ⟨~ in the stock market⟩ ~ *vt* **1 :** to risk or lose by gambling **:** WAGER, BET ⟨they've all been *gambled* and lost by her husband that morning —Henri Michaux⟩ — often used with *away* ⟨*gambled* away his inheritance⟩ **2 :** to expose (something of value) to risk or hazard in the hope of advantage or gain ⟨decided to ~ my ship and our lives by going left —H.A.Chippendale⟩ ⟨*gambled* hundreds of thousands of dollars in research funds to work on the project —*Phoenix Flame*⟩

³gamble \"\ *n* -S **1 :** an act of playing a game of chance for money or other stakes ⟨the bishop . . . has not the slightest objection to a gentlemanly ~ —Norman Douglas⟩ **2 a :** an act or transaction having an element of risk or uncertainty **:** CHANCE, RISK ⟨a joint tenancy involves a ~ as to who dies first —*Deerfield (Wisc.) Independent*⟩ ⟨spent two billion dollars on the greatest scientific ~ in history —H.S.Truman⟩ ⟨companies . . . were unwilling to take the ~ and declined to go along —Freeman Lincoln⟩ **b :** something that is the object of a gamble ⟨every crop was a ~ —F.L.Paxson⟩

gam·bler \-blə(r)\ *n* -S [prob. alter. of obs. E *gamner, gamener*, fr. obs. E *gamen*, v., to play (fr. ME *gamenen*, fr. OE *gamenian*) + E -*er*; akin to ON *gamna* to amuse; denominative fr. the root of OE *gamen* game — more at GAME] **:** one that gambles: as **a :** one that habitually plays games of chance for money **:** GAMESTER **b :** one that for pay or other financial advantage provides the space and equipment needed to permit others to gamble **c :** one that takes risks (if a publisher doesn't want to be a ~, he shouldn't be a publisher —*Publishers' Weekly*); *specif* **:** SPECULATOR ⟨the . . . financial ~*s* who now have all our livelihoods at their mercy —G.B.Shaw⟩

gambling *n* -S [fr. gerund of ²*gamble*] **1 :** the act or practice of betting **:** the act of playing a game and consciously risking money or other stakes on its outcome **2 :** the act of risking something on an uncertain event **:** WAGERING; *specif* **:** speculation in securities by uninformed persons or on thin margins

gambling device *n* **:** an instrumentality, contrivance, or apparatus reasonably designed and intended for the playing of a game for a reward of money or something of value for the player in which chance is a substantial factor

gambling house *or* **gambling hell** *n* **:** a place where gambling is carried on or allowed as a business **:** a place kept as a gambling resort

gam·bo \'gam(,)bō\ *n* -S [W] **:** a farm cart used esp. in Wales

gam·boge \(')gam¦bō|j, -aam-, -bü|, |zh\ *n* -S [NL *gambogium*, alter. of *cambugium*, irreg. fr. *Cambodia*, region (now country) in southeast Indochina] **1** *or* **cam·boge** \(')kam-, (')kaam-\ **:** an orange to brown gum resin that becomes bright yellow when powdered, is obtained from various southeast Asian trees of the genus *Garcinia* (as *G. hanburyi*), and is used by artists as a yellow pigment and in medicine as a cathartic **2** *or* **gamboge yellow :** a strong yellow that is redder and less strong than yolk yellow or light chrome yellow

gam·bo hemp \'gam(,)bō-\ *n* [*gambo* fr. Bare'e (Austronesian language spoken in central Celebes) *gambu* fiber] **:** AMBARI HEMP

¹gam·bol \'gambəl, 'gaam-\ *n* -S [earlier *gambolde, gambalde*, modif. of MF *gambade* spring of a horse, gambol, prob. fr. (assumed) OProv *gambada, cambada* (whence Prov *gambado, cambado*), fr. OProv *camba* leg, fr. LL *gamba, camba* hock (of a horse), leg, modif. of Gk *kampē* bend — more at CAMP] **:** a skipping or leaping about in play **:** a frolicking movement **syn** see ²PLAY

²gambol \"\ *vi* **gamboled** *or* **gambolled; gamboled** *or* **gambolled; gamboling** *or* **gambolling** \-b(ə)liŋ\ **gambols :** to bound or spring as in dancing or play **:** skip about **:** FRISK, CAVORT **syn** see PLAY

gam·brel \'gambrəl, 'gaam-\ *n* -S [ONF *gamberel* crooked stick used by butchers in suspending slaughtered animals, dim. of (assumed) ONF *gambier* crooked stick used by butchers in suspending slaughtered animals (var. of ONF *jambier*), fr. ONF *gambe* leg, fr. LL *gamba, camba*] **1 :** the hock of an animal (as a horse) **2** *or* **gambrel stick :** a stick or iron crooked like a horse's hind leg and used by butchers in suspending slaughtered animals **3 :** GAMBREL ROOF

gambrel roof *n* **:** a curb roof of the same section in all parts with a lower steeper slope and an upper flatter one — compare MANSARD

gambrel roof

gambs *pl of* GAMB

gam·bu·sia \gam'byüzh(ē)ə\ *n* [NL, modif. of AmerSp (Cuban) *gambusino* gambusia] **1** *cap* **:** a genus of topminnows (family Poeciliidae) of the warmer parts of No. America and the West Indies that feed largely on aquatic larvae and have been introduced as valuable exterminators of mosquito larvae **2** *pl* **gambusia** *or* **gambusias :** any fish of the genus *Gambusia*

¹game \'gām\ *n* -s [ME, fr. *gamen*, fr. OE; akin to OHG & ON *gaman* pleasure, amusement] **1 a** (1) **:** an amusement or pastime **:** DIVERSION, PLAY ⟨children at their ∼*s*⟩ ⟨regarded his poetic activity as a ∼ to while away tedious hours⟩ (2) **:** the equipment used to play a game ⟨what ∼*s* will you buy the children for Christmas⟩ **b :** a practical joke **:** FOOLERY, FUN, PRANK, SPORT, LARK ⟨don't get mad, it was all a ∼⟩ ⟨I'm tired of your ∼*s*⟩ — often used in the phrase *to make game* ⟨the women were always making ∼ of her —W.D.Steele⟩ ⟨the queer wicked grin . . . you do have the time you're making ∼ with a man —J.M.Synge⟩ **2 a :** a scheme or strategy employed in the pursuit of an object or purpose **:** method of procedure **:** COURSE, PLAN, TACTIC ⟨the authorities decided to play a waiting ∼ —Philip Rooney⟩ ⟨the ∼ was to look frightened and then relieved —Alan Harrington⟩ ⟨the president tried another ∼ —S.E.Morison & H.S.Commager⟩ ⟨the ∼ is up⟩ **b** (1) **:** an illegal, fraudulent, or shady scheme or maneuver **:** RACKET, DODGE, TRICK ⟨a bad plan for that kind of ∼ — our police are too good —John Buchan⟩ ⟨picked up after bilking a filling-station attendant in a short-change ∼ —*Springfield (Mass.) Union*⟩ (2) **:** a particular occupation, profession, or other field of gainful activity **:** LINE ⟨the fight ∼⟩ ⟨the newspaper ∼⟩ ⟨a commercial traveler in the hardware ∼ —Richard Bissell⟩ (3) **:** a specified type of activity or mode of behavior ⟨the ∼ of sin is never worth while —F.A.Swinnerton⟩ ⟨the ∼ of love⟩ ⟨the ∼ of politics⟩ **3 a** (1) **:** a physical or mental competition conducted according to rules in which the participants play in direct opposition to each other, each side striving to win and to keep the other side from doing so — see GAME OF CHANCE (2) **:** a division or subdivision of a larger contest ⟨two ∼*s* in a row gave them a 700-point rubber⟩ ⟨he won the first set by a score of six ∼*s* to two but lost the match⟩ (3) **:** a single contest lasting until a designated limit (as a set time or a certain number of innings or points) is reached (4) **:** the number of points necessary to be scored in order to win ⟨in casino 21 points is ∼⟩ ⟨in shuffleboard 50 points is ∼⟩ (5) **:** points credited on the score in some card games (as seven-up) to the player whose cards count up the highest (6) **:** the ten-spot of trumps counting a point to the one securing it in play in pedro, cinch, and certain other card games (7) **:** any of the available bids or declarations that impose specific obligations on the bidder in skat and related games (8) **:** SCORE ⟨the bowler's ∼*s* were 197, 189, and 200⟩ (9) **:** a statistical unit for measuring the relative competitive standing of the teams in a league ⟨three ∼*s* behind⟩ (10) **:** the manner, quality, or style of playing in a contest ⟨they play a very rough ∼⟩ ⟨occasionally . . . put aside domestic cares to keep up her ∼ at the local country club —M.F. & Katharine Pringle⟩ ⟨he is off his ∼⟩ ⟨shoots in the low 80s when he is on his ∼ —*Time*⟩ (11) **:** the set of rules according to which a game is played ⟨will you teach me the ∼⟩ **b games** *pl* **:** organized athletics ⟨∼*s* and circuses are not as good as art, music, and literature —Walter Moberly⟩ **c :** CHARADES — used with *the* **d :** a contest, rivalry, or struggle of any kind ⟨delegates who are anxious to back a winner . . . early in the ∼ —*Newsweek*⟩ **4 a** *obs* **:** sport in the hunting field **b** (1) **:** animals under pursuit or taken in hunting **:** QUARRY (2) **:** animals considered worthy of pursuit by sportsmen; *esp* **:** wild animals hunted for sport or food (3) **:** the flesh of a game animal considered as food **c** (1) **:** a kept herd or flock — now used of swans (2) **:** GAME FOWL (3) *archaic* **:** the characteristics of game fowl **:** combative spirit **:** PLUCK, INTREPIDITY, ENDURANCE **d :** a butt, target, or object esp. of ridicule, exploitation, pursuit, or attack ⟨they are also bores — always the richest ∼ for the comic instinct —V.S.Pritchett⟩ ⟨petty bourgeois . . . were easy ∼ for fascism —Max Ascoli⟩ — often used in the phrase *fair game* ⟨all the customers in the speakeasies were fair ∼ —George Raft⟩ **syn** see FUN

²game \"\ *vb* -ED/-ING/-S [ME *gamen* to play, fr. *game*, n. — more at ¹GAME] *vi* **:** to play for a stake (as with cards, dice, or billiards) ⟨the men became sufficiently acquainted to ∼ together —Frances Trollope⟩ ∼ *vt, archaic* **:** to lose or squander by gambling — used chiefly with *away*

³game \"\ *adj* -ER/-EST [¹*game*] **1 :** having a resolute unyielding spirit ⟨he was ∼ to the end⟩ **2 :** of or relating to game ⟨∼ laws⟩ ⟨∼ warden⟩

⁴game \"\ *adj, sometimes* -ER/-EST [perh. fr. ³*game*] **:** LAME ⟨a ∼ leg⟩

game animal *n* [¹*game*] **:** an animal made legitimate quarry by state or other law

game bag *n* **:** a pouch usu. equipped with straps for wearing on the back and used esp. by bird hunters for carrying their take

game ball *n* **:** the service that wins a racket game for the server if it results in his scoring a point

game bird *n* **1 :** a bird made legitimate quarry for hunters by state or other law **2** *badminton* **:** GAME BALL

game cart *n* **:** a four-wheeled dogcart

gamecock \'ₛ,ₛ\ *n* [¹*game*] **1 :** a male game fowl **2 :** a combative indomitable plucky person ⟨fierce little ∼ of a commander —Dixon Wecter⟩ ⟨the slim and defiant little ∼ of a man —Edgar Johnson⟩

game fish *n* **1 :** a fish of the family Salmonidae **2 :** SPORT FISH; *esp* **:** any of various fishes made a legal catch by specific legislation

game fowl *n* [¹*game*] **:** a bird of any of various strains of domestic fowls developed orig. chiefly for the production of fighting cocks — see MODERN GAME, OLD ENGLISH GAME

gamekeeper \'ₛ,ₛₛ\ *n* **:** one who has charge of the breeding and protection of game animals or birds on private preserves

gam·e·lan \'gamə,lan, -lən\ *also* **gam·e·lang** \-,laŋ\ *or* **gam·e·lin** \-,lən\ *n* -s [Jav *gamelan*] percussion instrument related to the xylophone] **1 a :** an orchestra of varying size originating in the islands of southeastern Asia and consisting chiefly of percussion instruments of both definite and indefinite pitch, flutes, and bowed instruments **b :** the music of such an orchestra **2 :** an East Asian percussion instrument that is akin to the xylophone and is used in gamelan orchestras

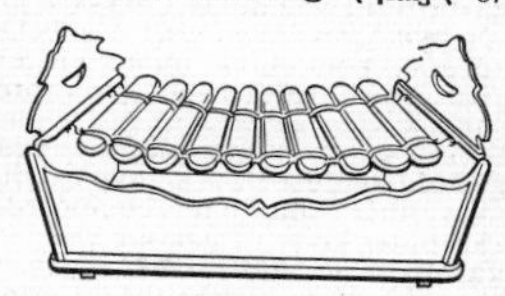
gamelan 2

ga·me·lo·te \,gamə'lōd·ē\ *n* -s [AmerSp, alter. of *gramalote*, fr. Sp *gramal* field of coarse grass, fr. *grama* coarse grass — more at GRAMA] **:** any of several grasses: as **a :** GUINEA GRASS **1 b :** either of two foxtails of the West Indies (*Setaria porretiana* and *S. paniculifera*)

game·ly *adv* [³*game* + *-ly*] **:** in a plucky manner **:** SPIRITEDLY ⟨fought a losing battle ∼ —H.L.Merillat⟩

game·ness *n* -ES [³*game* + *-ness*] **:** ENDURANCE, PLUCK

game of chance : a game (as a dice game) in which chance rather than skill determines the outcome

game of skill : a game (as chess) in which skill rather than chance determines the outcome

game point *n* **:** the point that wins a game for one side or the other

game room *n* **:** a recreation room; *esp* **:** one fitted out for the playing of table games

games *pl of* GAME, *pres 3d sing of* GAME

games-all \(')ₛₛ'ₛ\ *n* -s [*games* pl. of ¹*game*] **:** a tie score in tennis at five games or more each

games·man \'gāmzmən\ *n, pl* **gamesmen** [¹*game* + *-s-* (as in *craftsman*) + *man*] **:** one who practices gamesmanship

games·man·ship \-,ship\ *n* -s **1 :** the art or practice of winning a sports contest by expedients of doubtful propriety (as by distracting an opponent) without actual violation of the rules of the game ⟨∼ is practiced in golf more freely than in any other sport —*Time*⟩ **2 :** the use of ethically or intellectually dubious methods to achieve an objective ⟨the proposed analysis . . . is pure ∼, supported neither by phonetic nor by phonemic data —H.G.Lunt⟩

games master *n, Brit* **:** a schoolteacher who organizes, directs, and leads games and play

games mistress *n, Brit* **:** a female games master

game·some \'gāmsəm\ *adj* [ME *gamsum*, fr. *game, gam* game + *-some, -som, -sum* -some] **:** GAY, SPORTIVE, PLAYFUL, FROLICSOME, MERRY ⟨a woman that's joyous and ∼ and witty —Donagh MacDonagh⟩ — **game·some·ly** *adv* — **game·some·ness** *n* -ES

gamest superlative of GAME

game·ster \-mztə(r), -mst-\ *n* -s **1 :** one who plays games (as games of chance) **2 a** *obs* **:** a competitor in a game or contest **:** ATHLETE **b** *dial Eng* **:** a player at cudgels or singlestick

gamet- *or* **gameto-** *comb form* [NL, fr. *gameta*] **:** gamete ⟨*gametal*⟩ ⟨*gametocide*⟩

ga·me·tal \gə'mēd·ᵊl, 'ga,m-\ *adj* [*gamet-* + *-al*] **:** GAMETIC

gam·e·tan·gial \,gamə'tanj(ē)əl\ *adj* [*gametangium* + *-al*] **:** of or relating to a gametangium

gam·e·tan·gi·um \,ₛₛ'ₛjēəm\ *n, pl* **gametan·gia** \-jēə\ [NL, fr. *gamet-* + *-angium*] **:** the cell or organ in which gametes are developed — compare SPORANGIUM

ga·mete \gə'mēt, 'ga,mēt\ *n* -s [NL *gameta*, fr. Gk *gametēs* husband & *gametē* wife, fr. *gamein* to marry, fr. *gamos* marriage — more at BIGAMY] **:** a mature germ cell (as a sperm or egg) possessing a haploid chromosome set and capable of initiating formation of a new individual by fusion with another gamete — compare FERTILIZATION, MATURATION, ZYGOTE

game theory *n* **:** THEORY OF GAMES

ga·met·ic \gə'med·ik, 'ga,m-\ *adj* [*gamet-* + *-ic*] **:** of, relating to, being, or derived from a gamete — **ga·met·i·cal·ly** \-d·ək(ə)lē, -li\ *adv*

gametic number *n* **:** the haploid number of chromosomes typical of gametes

ga·me·to·cide \gə'mēd·ə,sīd\ *n* -s [*gamet-* + *-cide*] **:** an agent that destroys the gametocytes of a malaria parasite

ga·me·to·cyte \-,sīt\ *n* -s [ISV *gamet-* + *-cyte*] **:** a cell that divides to produce gametes **:** SPERMATOCYTE **:** OOCYTE

game·to·gen·e·sis \gə,mēd·ə'jenəsəs, ,gamə(,)tō'j-\ *n* [NL, fr. *gamet-* + L *genesis*] **:** the production of gametes — compare MATURATION — **ga·me·to·gen·ic** \gə¦mēd·ə¦jenik, ¦gamə(,)tō¦j-\ *or* **gam·e·tog·e·nous** \¦gamə¦täjənəs\ *adj* — **gam·e·tog·e·ny** \,gamə'täjənē\ *n* -ES

game·to·go·ni·um \gə,mēd·ə'gōnēəm, ,gamətō'g-\ *n, pl* **gametogo·nia** \-nēə\ [NL, fr. *gamet-* + *-gonium*] **:** GAMETOCYTE

gam·e·tog·o·ny \,gamə'tägənē\ *n* -ES [ISV *gamet-* + *-gony*] **:** GAMOGAMY

gam·e·toid \'gamə,tȯid\ *n* -s [*gamet-* + *-oid*] **:** a multinucleate gamete

game·to·kinetic hormone \gə'mēd·ō, ¦gamə(,)tō+ . . . -\ *n* [*gametokinetic* fr. *gamet-* + *kinetic*] **:** FOLLICLE-STIMULATING HORMONE

ga·me·to·phore \gə'mēd·ə,fō(ə)r\ *n* -s [*gamet-* + *-phore*] **:** a modified branch bearing gametangia (as in the thalloid liverworts) — **ga·me·to·phor·ic** \gə¦mēd·ə¦fórik\ *adj*

ga·me·to·phyte \gə'mēd·ə,fīt\ *n* -s [ISV *gamet-* + *-phyte*] **:** the individual or generation of a plant exhibiting alternation of generations that bears sex organs, constitutes the major part of the plant body in most algae, fungi, and mosses, exists as an independent transitory thalloid body in ferns and related plants, and is reduced to a microscopic or rudimentary structure in seed plants — distinguished from *sporophyte* — **ga·me·to·phyt·ic** \ₛ¦ₛₛ¦fid·ik\ *adj*

gamey *var of* GAMY

gam·ic \'gamik\ *adj* [*gam-* + *-ic*] **:** requiring fertilization **:** SEXUAL ⟨a ∼ egg⟩ ⟨∼ reproduction⟩

-gam·ic \¦gamik, -mēk\ *adj comb form* [ISV *-gam-* (fr. NL *-gamia* — as in *Cryptogamia* —, fr. Gk *-gamia* -gamy) + *-ic*] **1 :** having (such) reproductive organs ⟨*cleistogamic*⟩ ⟨*dichogamic*⟩ **2 :** having (such) a mode of fertilization ⟨*porogamic*⟩

gam·ie \'gāmē\ *n* -s [*game* (in *gamekeeper*) + *-ie*] *Scot* **:** GAMEKEEPER

gamier *comparative of* GAMY

-gamies *pl of* -GAMY

gamiest *superlative of* GAMY

gam·i·ly \'gāmәlē, -li\ *adv* **:** in a gamy manner **:** PLUCKILY ⟨expressing himself quite ∼ about the grosser aspects of love —Winthrop Sargeant⟩

¹gam·in \'gamən\ *n* -s [F] **1 :** a boy who runs the streets **:** a roguish impudent boy **:** URCHIN ⟨won the confidence of the street ∼*s* —E.S.Bates⟩ ⟨the jeers and stones of . . . ∼*s* flung at outraged farmers —Harriot B. Barbour⟩ **2 :** GAMINE 2

²gamin \"\ *adj* **:** of, relating to, or having the characteristics of a gamin ⟨a snub nose and a ∼ smile —*Danceland*⟩ ⟨as debonair, as ∼ . . . as ever —*Time*⟩ ⟨tough fifty-year-old ∼ face —Eleanor Clark⟩

¹gam·ine \(')ga¦mēn, 'gamən\ *n* -s [F, fem. of *gamin*] **1 :** a girl who runs the streets **:** TOMBOY ⟨a tough little ∼ —Geoffrey Household⟩ ⟨as ignorant as a ∼ —T.B.Costain⟩ **2 :** a girl of ingratiating qualities, typically slight build, and a pert and saucy air or a wistful and elfish charm ⟨a trio of glamorous ∼*s* —Lois Long⟩ ⟨a droll, touching ∼ —Constance Tomkinson⟩ ⟨one of the most coquettish ∼*s* I have ever watched —*New Yorker*⟩

²gamine \"\ *adj* **:** of or relating to a gamine ⟨her oddly ∼ . . . face —C.A.Lejeune⟩ ⟨the girls are built along shapely . . . ∼ lines —Winthrop Sargeant⟩

gam·ine·rie \'gamənrē, ga,mēn(ə)'rē\ *n* -s [F, fr. *gamin* + *-erie* -ery] **:** impudent, roguish, or wisecracking spirit ⟨there is just the same ∼ and contempt of the conventional —*Times Lit. Supp.*⟩

gam·i·ness \'gāmēnəs, -min-\ *n* -ES **:** the quality or state of being gamy

gaming *n* -s [fr. gerund of ²*game*] **:** the act or practice of playing games for stakes ⟨a passion for ∼⟩

gaming house *n* **:** GAMBLING HOUSE

gaming room *n* **:** a room habitually used for gambling

gaming table *n* **1 :** a table that is designed esp. for gambling and that often has depressions for counters and designs painted, inlaid, or in needlework appropriate to gaming **2 :** a table where gambling games are played

¹gam·ma \'gamə\ *n* -s [ME, fr. LL, fr. Gk, of Sem origin; akin to Heb *gimel* gimel] **1 :** the third letter of the Greek alphabet — symbol Γ or γ; see ALPHABET table **2 a :** the degree of contrast of a developed photographic image **b :** the slope of the straight-line portion of the characteristic curve of a photographic material or process **c :** a measure of the faithfulness with which the brightness variation in a television scene is reproduced in the displayed picture **3 a :** a unit of magnetic intensity equal to 0.00001 oersted **b :** a gamma-ray quantum **c :** one millionth of a gram **:** MICROGRAM

²gamma \"\ *or* γ- \"\ *adj* **1 :** of or relating to one of three or more closely related chemical substances ⟨γ-yohimbine⟩ — used somewhat arbitrarily to specify ordinal relationship or to specify a particular physical form, esp. an allotropic modification (as in γ-iron), or an isomeric or stereoisomeric form (as in γ-benzene hexachloride) **2 :** third in position in the structure of an organic molecule from a particular group or atom or having a structure characterized by such a position ⟨γ-hydroxy acids⟩ ⟨γ-lactones⟩ **3 :** third in order of brightness — used of a star in a constellation **4** *of streptococci* **:** producing no hemolysis on blood agar plates

gamma acid *n* [¹*gamma*] **:** a crystalline acid $HOC_{10}H_5(NH_2)SO_3H$ made from G acid and used as an intermediate for azo dyes; 7-amino-1-naphthol-3-sulfonic acid

gamma-benzene hexachloride *n* [²*gamma*] **:** LINDANE

gamma cellulose *n* [²*gamma*] **:** CELLULOSE d

gam·ma·cism \'gamə,sizəm\ *also* **gam·ma·cis·mus** \,ₛₛ'sizməs\ *n, pl* **gammacisms** *also* **gammacismuses** [*gammacism* fr. NL *gammacismus*, fr. LL *gamma* + *-cismus* (as in *iotacismus* iotacism); *gammacismus* NL] **:** difficulty in pronouncing velar consonants (as \g\ and \k\)

gamma cross *n* [¹*gamma*] **:** GAMMADION

gam·ma·di·on \gə'mādē,än, ga'-, -madē-, -ēən\ *also* **gam·mat·i·on** \-mad·ē-\ *n, pl* **gam·ma·dia** *also* **gammat·ia** \-ēə\ [modif. of ML *gammadium*, irreg. fr. LL *gamma*] **:** a cross formed of four capital gammas esp. in the figure of a swastika or in that of a voided Greek cross — called also *crux gammata, gammate cross*

gammadion: *1* swastika; *2* voided Greek cross

gamma function *n* [¹*gamma*] **:** a function of a variable γ defined by the definite integral $\Gamma(\gamma)=\int_0^\infty x^{\gamma-1}e^{-x}dx$

gamma globulin *n* [ISV ²*gamma* + *globulin*] **:** any of several globulins of plasma or serum that have less electrophoretic mobility at alkaline pH than serum albumins, alpha globulins, or beta globulins and that include most antibodies

gam·ma·graph \'gamə,graf, -rȧf\ *n* [¹*gamma* + *-graph*] **:** a radiograph produced by gamma rays — **gam·ma·graph·ic** \¦ₛₛ¦grafik\ *adj*

gamma infinity *n* [¹*gamma*] **:** the maximum degree of contrast to which a sensitive photographic material can be developed

gamma iron *n* [²*gamma*] **:** an iron that is stable between 910°C and 1400° C and that is characterized by a face-centered cubic crystal structure — compare ALPHA IRON, DELTA IRON

gamma moth *n* [NL *gamma* (specific epithet of *Plusia gamma*), fr. LL, third letter of the Greek alphabet; fr. the likeness in shape of the marks on the forewings to small gammas] **:** a migratory European noctuid moth (*Plusia gamma*) having a bright silvery Y-shaped mark on each of the fore wings and a larva that feeds on the cabbage and other vegetables — called also *silver Y moth*

gamma nasal *n* [¹*gamma* + *nasal*, adj.] *in ancient and modern Greek* **:** gamma pronounced \ŋ\, its value before κ, χ, ξ, or another gamma

gamma ray *n* [¹*gamma*] **1 :** a photon or radiation quantum emitted spontaneously by a radioactive substance **2** *or* **gamma radiation :** a continuous stream of gamma rays

¹gammarid \"\ *adj* [NL *Gammaridae*] **:** of or relating to the family Gammaridae

²gam·ma·rid \'gamərəd, -,rid\ *n* -s [NL *Gammaridae*] **:** an amphipod crustacean of the family Gammaridae

gam·mar·i·dae \gə'marə,dē, ga'-\ *n pl, cap* [NL, fr. *Gammarus*, type genus + *-idae*] **:** a large family of swimming amphipod crustaceans of both marine and freshwater forms

gam·ma·rus \'gamərəs\ *n, cap* [NL, alter. (influenced by LL *gambarus*, alter. of L *cammarus*) of L *cammarus* sea crab, lobster — more at CAMBARUS] **:** a genus (the type of the family Gammaridae) of swimming amphipod crustaceans

gam·mate cross \'ga,māt-\ *n* [part trans. of NL *crux gammata*, fr. L *crux* cross + NL *gammata*, fem. of *gammatus* composed of gammas, fr. ML, shaped like a gamma, fr. LL *gamma* + L *-atus* -ate] **:** GAMMADION

gamme \'gam\ *n* -s [F, fr. OF *game*, fr. ML *gamma*, fr. LL, third letter of the Greek alphabet; fr. the use of the letter gamma by Guido d'Arezzo †1050? Benedictine monk and musical reformer to represent the lowest note of the gamut] **:** GAMUT ⟨produces a ∼ of sounds that are beautiful —Janet Flanner⟩ ⟨a recurrent ∼ of color —Helen Gardner⟩

gammed *past of* GAM

gam·mel·ost \'gamə,lōst\ *also* **gammelost cheese** *n* -s [Norw, fr. *gammel* old (fr. ON *gamall*) + *ost* cheese, fr. ON *ostr*; akin to OE *gamol* old and perh. to L *hiems* winter — more at HIBERNATE, JUICE] **:** a Norwegian blue-mold cheese made from soured skim milk

gam·mer \'gamə(r)\ *n* -s [prob. contr. of *godmother*] **:** an old woman — compare GAFFER

Gam·mex·ane \ga'mek,sān, gə'-; 'gamik-\ *trademark* — used for lindane

gamming *pres part of* GAM

¹gam·mon \'gamən\ *n* -s [ONF *gambon* ham (of a hog), aug. of *gambe* leg — more at GAMB] **1** *dial* **a :** LEG **b :** THIGH **2 a :** a ham or flitch of cured bacon ⟨the ∼ was given as a reward and encouragement to handfasting couples —Dorothy G. Spicer⟩ **b :** the lower end of a side of bacon

²gammon \"\ *n* -s [origin unknown] **:** GAMMONING

³gammon \"\ *vt* -ED/-ING/-S **:** to fasten (a bowsprit) to the stem of a ship by lashings of rope or chain or by a band of iron

⁴gammon \"\ *n* -s [perh. alter. of ME *gamen* game, sport — more at GAME] **1** *archaic* **:** BACKGAMMON **2 :** the winning of a backgammon game before the loser has borne off any men

⁵gammon \"\ *vt* -ED/-ING/-S **:** to beat by scoring a gammon

⁶gammon \"\ *n* -s [perh. fr. obs. E *gammon* talk, chatter, perh. fr. obs. E slang *gammon* (in the expressions *give someone gammon* to stand close to someone while another person is picking his pocket, *keep someone in gammon* to divert someone's attention while another person is robbing him), perh. fr. E *gammon* leg, thigh, flitch of cured bacon — more at ¹GAMMON] **:** talk intended to deceive **:** HUMBUG ⟨it's all ∼ —G.B.Shaw⟩

⁷gammon \"\ *vb* -ED/-ING/-S *vi* **1 :** to talk gammon **2 :** PRETEND, FEIGN ∼ *vt* **:** to influence with gammon **:** put upon **:** DECEIVE, FOOL ⟨critics were not ∼*ed* by this latest prodigy —Roland Gelatt⟩

gammoning *n* -s [fr. gerund of ³*gammon*] **:** the lashing or iron band by which the bowsprit of a ship is fixed to the stem

gammon iron *n* [²*gammon*] **:** a metal hoop or band attached to the stemhead of a yacht through which the bowsprit runs

gam·my \'gamē\, *adj* -ER/-EST [prob. irreg. fr. ⁴*game* + *-y*] *dial Brit* **:** LAME, SORE ⟨a ∼ foot⟩

gamo- — see GAM-

ga·mo·bi·um \gə'mōbēəm, ga'-\ *n, pl* **gamo·bia** \-ēə\ [NL, fr. *gam-* + *-bium*] **:** the sexually reproducing generation when sexual and asexual generations alternate

gam·o·deme \'gamə,dēm\ *n* [*gam-* + *deme*] **:** a more or less isolated breeding community of organisms

ga·mog·a·my \gə'mägəmē, ga'-\ *n* -ES [*gam-* + *-gamy*] **:** gamogenesis esp. of protozoans

gam·o·gen·e·sis \,gamə'jenəsəs\ *n* [*gam-* + *genesis*] **:** reproduction by means of gametes **:** sexual reproduction — **gam·o·ge·net·ic** \¦gaməjə¦ned·ik\ *adj* — **gam·o·ge·net·i·cal·ly** \-d·ək(ə)lē\ *adv*

gam·o·gen·ic \¦gamə¦jenik\ *adj* [*gam-* + *-genic*] **:** produced by sexual reproduction

ga·mog·e·ny \gə'mäjənē, ga'-\ *n* -ES [*gam-* + *-geny*] **:** GAMOGENESIS

ga·mog·o·ny \gə'mägənē, ga'-\ *n* -ES [ISV *gam-* + *-gony*] **1 a :** GAMOGENESIS **b :** multiple fission producing sporozoan gametes **2 :** SPOROGONY

ga·mol·e·pis \gə'mäləpəs\ *n, cap* [NL, fr. *gam-* + *-lepis*] **:** a small genus of southern African herbs or shrubs (family Compositae) with alternate pinnatisect leaves and flowers resembling marigolds and having the bracts of the involucre united for one third or one half their length

gam·one \'ga,mōn\ *n* -s [ISV *gam-* + *-one* (as in *hormone*); prob. orig. formed as G *gamon*] **:** any of various substances believed to be liberated by eggs or sperms and to affect germ cells of the opposite sex

gam·ont \'ga,mänt\ *n* -s [ISV *gam-* + *-ont*] **:** a protozoan gametocyte

gamoos *or* **gamouse** *var of* ZAMOUSE

gam·o·pet·a·lae \,gamə'ped·ᵊl,ē\ [NL, fr. *gam-* + *-petalae*] *syn of* METACHLAMYDEAE

gam·o·pet·a·lous \¦ₛₛ¦ₛᵊləs\ *adj* [NL *gamopetalus*, fr. *gam-* + *-petalus* -petalous] **1 :** having the corolla composed of united petals ⟨the morning glory is ∼⟩ **2 :** of or relating to the Metachlamydeae

gam·o·phyl·lous \¦gamə¦filəs\ *adj* [prob. fr. (assumed) NL *gamophyllus*, fr. NL *gam-* + *-phyllus* -phyllous] **:** having united leaves or parts resembling leaves — used esp. of a floral envelope not differentiated into calyx and corolla

gam·o·sep·a·lous \¦gamō¦sepələs\ *adj* [prob. fr. (assumed) NL *gamosepalus*, fr. NL *gam-* + *-sepalus* -sepalous] **:** having the sepals united

-gamous \-gəməs\ *adj comb form* [Gk *-gamos*, fr. *gamos*

marriage — more at BIGAMY] **1 :** characterized by having or practicing (such) a marriage or (such or so many) marriages ⟨endo*gamous*⟩ ⟨exo*gamous*⟩ **2** [prob. fr. NL *-gamus,* prob. fr. LL, characterized by having (such) a marriage or (such or so many) marriages, fr. Gk *-gamos*] **:** -GAMIC 1

ga·mow barrier \ˈgä,mȯv-\ *n, usu cap G* [after George *Gamow* b1904 Am. physicist] **:** the potential barrier that in wave-mechanical theory is assumed to oppose the escape of alpha particles from an atomic nucleus in radioactive disintegration

gamp \ˈgamp\ *n* -S [after Sarah *Gamp,* nurse with a large cotton umbrella in Charles Dickens's *Martin Chuzzlewit* (1843-44)] *Brit* **:** a large umbrella ⟨halfway to the station my ~ blew inside out —*Sydney (Australia) Bulletin*⟩; *often* **:** one that is untidily or loosely tied up ⟨if you carry an umbrella use it tightly rolled and never as a ~ —S.D.Barney⟩

gam·phrel \ˈgamfrəl\ *n* -S [origin unknown] *Scot* **:** a stupid person **:** BLOCKHEAD

gams *pl of* GAM, *pres 3d sing of* GAM

-gams *pl of* -GAM

gam·ut \ˈgamət, -əd·+V\ *n* -S [prob. modif. of (assumed) ML *gamma ut,* fr. ML *gamma* lowest note of each hexachord in Guido's scale (fr. LL, third letter of the Greek alphabet) + *ut* lowest note of Guido's scale — more at GAMMA, UT] **1 a :** the first or lowest note of Guido's great scale **b :** GREAT SCALE **c :** the whole series of recognized musical notes; *sometimes* **:** a recognized scale **d :** the compass of a voice or instrument **2 :** an entire range from one extreme to another **:** a graded series including all kinds ⟨an Italian running through his whole possible ~ of tone —Edward Sapir⟩ ⟨the pets . . . ranged the ~ of animal life about us —Agnes M. Cleaveland⟩ ⟨deliberate murder (with a whole ~ of possible motives) —A.L.Guérard⟩ ⟨the complete ~ of the spectrum —C.T.Elvey⟩ **syn** see RANGE

gamy *also* **gam·ey** \ˈgāmē, -mi\ *adj* **gamier; gamiest** [*¹game* + *-y*] **1 :** showing an unyielding spirit to the last **:** PLUCKY, GAME — used esp. of animals ⟨the ~ fish does most of its fighting below the surface —*Nat'l Geographic*⟩ ⟨a ~ cow pony⟩ **2 a :** having or suggesting the flavor of game ⟨begins to lose its rich ~ flavor when it has been out of the water less than an hour —*Ford Times*⟩; *esp* **:** having the flavor of game kept uncooked till near the condition of tainting **b :** MALODOROUS ⟨she had a huge brown billy goat . . . so she was usually pretty ~ herself —Crary Moore⟩ **3 a :** treating of scandalous or sensational themes or happenings **:** SPICY, RACY, SORDID, TITILLATING ⟨three other episodes are rather broad and ~ —John McCarten⟩ ⟨skips the asterisks and gives you the ~ details —V.P.Hass⟩ ⟨a ~ rape story —*Time*⟩ **b :** morally tainted **:** DISREPUTABLE ⟨as ~ an assemblage of solons as the nation then offered —Dwight Macdonald⟩ ⟨a ~ character⟩

-gamy \gəmē, -mi\ *n comb form* -ES [ME *-gamie,* fr. LL *-gamia,* fr. Gk — more at BIGAMY] **1 a :** marriage ⟨exo*gamy*⟩ **b :** union for propagation or reproduction ⟨allo*gamy*⟩ **2** [NL *-gamia* (as in *Cryptogamia*), fr. Gk *-gamia* -gamy (marriage)] **a :** possession of (such) reproductive organs ⟨cleisto*gamy*⟩ **b :** possession of (such) a mode of fertilization ⟨poro*gamy*⟩

gan *past of* GIN

ga·nan·cial \gəˈnanchəl, *Sp* gänänˈthyäl *or* -ˈsyäl\ *adj* [Sp, relating to profit, held jointly by husband and wife, fr. *ganancia* profit, fr. *ganar* to gain, earn, perh. of Gmc origin; akin to ON *gana* to gape, stare; akin to Gk *chaskein* to gape, yawn] **:** being, relating to, or held under the Spanish system of law that controls the title and disposition of the property acquired during marriage by a spouse

ganch *also* **gansh** \ˈganch, -ä-\ *vt* -ED/-ING/-ES [modif. of Turk *kancalamak* to put on a hook, fr. *kanca* large hook, modif. of Gk *gampsos* curved] **:** to execute or kill by impaling on stakes or hooks ⟨field mice . . . ~*ed* upon the hooks —D.C. Peattie⟩

gan·da \ˈgandə, ˈgän-\ *n, pl* **ganda** *or* **gandas** *usu cap* **1 a :** a Bantu-speaking people of Uganda **b :** a member of such people **2 :** the Bantu language of the Ganda people spoken also with slight differences by several neighboring peoples and used as the official language of Uganda

¹gan·der \ˈgandə(r), ˈgaan-\ *n* -S [ME, fr. OE *gandra;* akin to D *gander,* MLG *ganre* gander, OE *gōs* goose — more at GOOSE] **1 :** the adult male goose **2 :** a stupid or foolish fellow **:** SIMPLETON ⟨a silly, immature little ~ —Elizabeth Bowen⟩

²gander \"\ *vi* -ED/-ING/-S *dial* **:** WANDER, STROLL ⟨~*ed* down to . . . the great whaling port —H.A.Chippendale⟩ ⟨a man could ~ around and have his pleasure —Conrad Richter⟩

³gander \"\ *n* -S [prob. fr. *¹gander;* fr. the outstretched neck of a person craning to look at something] *slang* **:** LOOK, GLANCE ⟨take a ~ at that picture⟩

gander pull *or* **gander pulling** *n* **:** a pastime esp. formerly in the South and Southwest in which a person on horseback rides rapidly past a goose hanging with its neck down and greased and tries to pull off its head

gan·dha·ra \ˌgənˈdärə, -gən'd-\ *or* **gan·dha·ran** \-rən\ *adj, usu cap* [*Gandhara,* ancient region in northwest Punjab and part of eastern Afghanistan] **:** of or relating to ancient Gandhara, its people, or its hybrid Greco-Buddhist art

gan·dhi·an \ˈgändēən, ˈgan-,ˈgaan-,ˈgän-, -diən\ *adj, usu cap* [Mohandas K. *Gandhi* †1948 Indian nationalist leader + E *-an*] **:** of or relating to the Indian political and spiritual leader Mohandas K. Gandhi or his principle of nonviolence ⟨resigned myself with a *Gandhian* shrug —Herbert Passin⟩ ⟨*Gandhian* prejudice against violent pressures —Edmond Taylor⟩

gan·dhi cap \-dē-, -di-\ *n, usu cap G* **:** a white cap worn in India that has a wide band and narrow crown and is similar in outline to an overseas cap

gan·dhism \-,dizəm\ *or* **gan·dhi·ism** \-dē,izəm, -di,iz-\ *n* -S *usu cap* **:** SATYAGRAHA

gan·dou·ra *or* **gan·dou·rah** \ganˈdúrə, gän-\ *n* -S [Ar *qandūrah*] **:** a long loose gown with or without sleeves that is worn chiefly in northern Africa

gan·dy dancer \ˈgandē-\ *n* [perh. fr. the now defunct *Gandy* Manufacturing Company, Chicago, Illinois, which made tools used by railroad laborers] **1 :** a laborer in a railroad section gang **2 :** an itinerant or seasonal laborer

gane *past part of* GAE

ga·nef \ˈgänəf\ *n* -S [Yiddish *ganef, gannef,* fr. Heb *gannābh* thief] *slang* **:** THIEF, RASCAL

¹gang \ˈgaŋ, ˈgaiŋ\ *n* -S *often attrib* [ME, fr. OE; akin to OHG *gang* act of going, ON *gangr* act of going, Goth *gagg* street, Gk *kochōnē* perineum, Skt *jaṅgha* shank] **1 :** the act, manner, or means of going **:** PASSAGE, COURSE, JOURNEY; *also* **:** GAIT **2 a** *dial chiefly Brit* (1) **:** PASSAGE, WAY, ROAD, LANE (2) **:** a pasturage for cattle **b** *chiefly Scot* **:** JOURNEY; *esp* **:** one undertaken to perform an errand **c** *chiefly Scot* **:** the amount (as of wood, water, or peat) that can be carried at one time or in one trip **3 a** (1) **:** a set or full complement of articles **:** OUTFIT ⟨a ~ of oars⟩ (2) **:** a combination of similar implements or other items arranged so as to act together to save time or labor ⟨a ~ of saws⟩ or to produce in one operation or as one unit ⟨a ~ of printing plates printing several jobs on a single sheet⟩ **b :** a number of individuals making up a group: as (1) **:** a group of persons working under the same direction or at the same task ⟨migrants . . . laboring in ~*s* in the woods, mines, and fields —*Amer. Guide Series: Wash.*⟩ ⟨~*s* of expert bottomers —B.H.Sprague⟩ (2) **:** a company of criminals ⟨a ~ of desperate banditti —Tobias Smollett⟩ ⟨squealed on the other members of the ~⟩ (3) **:** an elementary and close-knit social group of spontaneous origin; *esp* **:** such a unit composed of antisocial adolescents ⟨teen-age ~*s*⟩ (4) **:** a group of persons acting in accord who are believed to engage in improper acts or to be influenced by self-seeking, corrupt, or unworthy motives ⟨made captive by the ~ which seized power —A.H. Sulzberger⟩ ⟨denounced the musical ~ then in power —Virgil Thomson⟩ ⟨a political ~ . . . dragged out the racial issue to divert attention from itself —Oscar Handlin⟩ (5) **:** a group of congenial persons having close and informal social relations **:** a group of persons drawn together by a community of tastes, interests, or activity ⟨one of a ~ that call one another great —O.W.Holmes †1935⟩ ⟨invite the ~ plus some pretty girls —D.E.Bradbury⟩ ⟨where's the ~ going tonight⟩ ⟨the ~ in the office⟩ (6) **:** a flock or herd of animals ⟨a ~ of little chickens —J.H.Stuart⟩ ⟨a ~ of elk⟩

²gang \"\ *vb* -ED/-ING/-S *vt* **1 :** to attack (a person) as a gang ⟨young hoodlums . . . always ~ you —W.R.Burnett⟩ ⟨try to ~ him and take it away from him —*Springfield (Mass.) Union*⟩ **2 a :** to assemble or operate (mechanical or electronic parts) simultaneously as a group ⟨circuits ~*ed* together by gears⟩ **b :** to arrange in or produce as a gang (as type pages or printed sheets) — often used with *up* **~** *vi* **:** to form a group or gang **:** keep company **:** GO, TRAVEL ⟨empty-headed, idle-handed widows who ~ together —Henry Miller⟩ ⟨~*s* with those kids on the next block⟩ — often used with *up* ⟨the boys would ~ up around the corner drugstore⟩

³gang \"\ *vi* [ME *gangen* to go, walk, fr. OE *gangan;* akin to OHG *gangan* to go, ON *ganga,* Goth *gaggan* to go, OE *gang* act of going] *Scot* **:** GO

⁴gang *var of* GANGUE

gan·ga·mop·ter·is \ˌgaŋgəˈmäptərəs\ *n, cap* [NL, fr. Gk *gangamon* small round oyster net + NL *-pteris*] **:** a genus of fossil plants of Permian and Lower Triassic resembling ferns

gan·gava \ganˈgavə, gaŋ'-, -ˈgävə\ *n* -S [NGk *gangaba,* irreg. fr. Gk *gangamon*] **:** a widemouthed dredge for taking sponges from the sea bottom

gangboard \ˈ=,=\ *n* [*¹gang* + *board*] **1 :** a narrow platform extending from the quarterdeck to the forecastle of a deep-waisted ship for use esp. as a passageway **2 :** GANGPLANK

gang days *n pl* [ME *gang dayes,* fr. OE *gangdagas,* fr. *gang* act of going + *dagas,* pl. of *dæg* day] **:** ROGATION DAYS

gange \ˈganj\ *vt* -ED/-ING/-S [origin unknown] **:** to protect (the part of a line next a fishhook or the hook itself) by winding with wire

¹gang·er \ˈgaŋə(r)\ *n* -S [ME, fr. *gangen* to go, walk + *-er*] **1** *Scot* **:** a foot traveler **:** WALKER **2** *dial Brit* **:** a fast horse

²ganger \"\ *n* -S [*¹gang* + *-er*] *Brit* **:** a work gang foreman

gang·er·el \ˈgaŋ(ə)rəl\ *var of* GANGREL

gan·ges dolphin \ˈgan|(,)jēz-, ˈgaan|\ *n, usu cap G* [*Ganges,* river of north and northeast India and East Pakistan] **:** SUSU

ganges shark *n, usu cap G* **:** a shark (*Carcharhinus gangeticus*) of southeastern Asia and the East Indies that commonly enters fresh water

gan·get·ic \(ˈ)=ˈjed·ik\ *adj, usu cap* [L *gangeticus,* fr. Gk *gangētikos,* irreg. fr. *Gangēs* Ganges] **:** of or relating to the Ganges

gang·gang \ˈgaŋ,gaŋ\ *also* **gan·ga** \ˈgaŋgə\ *or* **gan·gan** \ˈgaŋ,gaŋ\ *n* -S [native name in Australia] **:** a small cockatoo (*Callocephalon fimbriatum*) of Australia and Tasmania that is largely gray with the male distinguished by a scarlet crest

gang hook *n* [*¹gang* + *hook*] **:** two or three fishhooks with their shanks joined together

¹ganging *pres part of* GANG

²gang·ing \ˈgaŋiŋ, -jəŋ\ *n* -S [fr. gerund of *gange*] **1 :** the special or protected part of a fishline to which the hook is ganged or fastened **:** SNELL **2 :** GANGION

gan·gion \ˈganjēən, -jən\ *or* **gang·in** *also* **gang·en** \-jən\ *n* -S [alter. of *ganging*] **:** one of the short lengths of moderate-weight line that bear hooks and are attached at regular intervals to the groundline of a setline by beckets of heavy twine

gang·land \ˈgaŋ,land, ˈgaiŋ-, -lənd, -,laa(ə)nd\ *n, often attrib* [*¹gang* + *land*] **:** organized crime **:** the criminal element **:** UNDERWORLD ⟨~ . . . demands that he permit the opening of a gambling joint —Frederic Morton⟩

gangli- *or* **ganglio-** *comb form* [NL, fr. Gk *ganglion*] **:** ganglion ⟨*gangli*ectomy⟩ ⟨*ganglio*plexus⟩

gan·gli·al \ˈgaŋglēəl, -aiŋ-\ *adj* [*gangli-* + *-al*] **:** of, relating to, or like a ganglion

gan·gli·ar \-ēə(r), -ē,är\ *adj* [*gangli-* + *-ar*] **:** GANGLIAL **:** GANGLIONIC

gan·gli·at·ed \-ē,ād·əd\ *also* **gan·gli·ate** \-,āt, -,ət\ *adj* [*gangliated* fr. *gangli-* + *-ate* + *-ed; gangliate* fr. *gangli-* + *-ate*] **:** GANGLIONATED

gangliated cord *n* **:** either of the two main trunks of the sympathetic nervous system, one on each side of the spinal column

gan·gli·form \-lə,fȯrm\ *adj* [ISV *gangli-* + *-form*] **:** having the form of a ganglion

gan·gling \ˈgaŋgliŋ, -aiŋ-, -lēŋ\ *adj* [perh. irreg. fr. *gangrel*] **:** having a spindling or awkwardly long growth **:** loosely built **:** LANKY ⟨a ~ gawky child . . . whose legs were too long for her skirts —Edna Ferber⟩

gan·gli·o·blast \ˈgaŋglēō,blast\ *n* [*gangli-* + *-blast*] **:** an embryonic cell that produces gangliocytes

gan·gli·o·cyte \-,sīt\ *n* -S [*gangli-* + *-cyte*] **:** a nerve cell having its body outside the central nervous system — called also *ganglion cell*

gan·gli·o·ma \,gaŋglēˈōmə\ *n, pl* **gangliomas** *or* **ganglio·ma·ta** \-məd·ə\ [NL, fr. *gangli-* + *-oma*] **:** a tumor of a ganglion

gan·gli·on \ˈgaŋglēən, -aiŋ-\ *n, pl* **gan·glia** \-ēə\ *also* **gan·glions** [LL & Gk; LL, cystic tumor, fr. Gk, cystic tumor, mass of nerve tissue — more at GALL (excrescence)] **1 a :** a small cystic tumor containing viscid fluid and connected either with a joint membrane or tendon sheath esp. about the wrist or ankle **b :** a mass of nerve tissue containing nerve cells: (1) **:** an aggregation of such cells forming an enlargement upon a nerve or upon two or more nerves at their point of junction or separation (2) **:** a mass of gray matter within the brain or spinal cord **:** NUCLEUS — see BASAL GANGLION **2 :** a center or focus esp. of strength or energy ⟨the central ~ of the world's largest . . . chemical empire —J.W.Bellah⟩

gan·gli·on·ary \-ēə,nerē\ *adj* [ISV *ganglion* + *-ary*] **:** GANGLIONIC

gan·gli·on·at·ed \-,nād·əd\ *also* **gan·gli·on·ate** \-,nāt\ *adj* [*ganglionated* fr. (assumed) NL *ganglionatus* (fr. NL *ganglion* — fr. LL & Gk — + L *-atus* -ate) + E *-ed; ganglionate* fr. (assumed) NL *ganglionatus*] **:** furnished with ganglia

ganglion cell *n* **:** GANGLIOCYTE

gan·gli·on·ec·to·my \,=ˈ=ˈnektəmē\ *n* -ES [ISV *ganglion* + *-ectomy*] **:** surgical removal of a ganglion

gan·glio·neuroma \ˌgaŋglē(,)ō+\ *n* [NL, fr. *gangli-* + *neuroma*] **:** a neuroma derived from ganglion cells

gan·gli·on·ic \,gaŋglēˈänik, ,gaiŋ-, -nēk\ *adj* [ISV *ganglion* + *-ic*] **:** of, containing, or affecting ganglia or gangliocytes

gan·gli·on·it·is \,gaŋglēəˈnīd·əs\ *n* -ES [NL, fr. *ganglion* + *-itis*] **:** inflammation of a ganglion

gan·gli·o·side \ˈgaŋglēə,sīd\ *n* -S [ISV *gangli-* + *-oside*] **:** any of a group of glycolipides closely related to the cerebrosides and found mainly in the ganglion cells of the nervous system and in increased amounts in certain lipoidoses

gan·gly \ˈgaŋglē, -aiŋ-, -li\ *adj, often* -ER/-EST [alter. (influenced by *-y*) of *gangling*] **:** GANGLING, LANKY ⟨a hawk-beaked ~ man —Flora Lewis⟩

gang mill *n* [*¹gang* + *mill*] **1 :** a sawing machine used in lumbering that has a heavy frame supporting numerous saw blades **2 :** a composite milling cutter made up of several cutters set in the same arbor in such relation as to give a cut having some desired profile — **gang milling** *n*

gang net *n* [*¹gang* + *net*] **:** a series of gill nets fastened together and fished as a unit

gan·go·sa \ganˈgōsə\ *n* -S [Sp, fem. of *gangoso* that talks through the nose, characterized by nasal resonance, of imit. origin] **:** a destructive ulcerative condition believed to be a manifestation of yaws that usu. originates about the soft palate and spreads into the hard palate, nasal structures, and outward to the face, eroding intervening bone, cartilage, and soft tissues

gangplank \ˈ=,=\ *n* [*¹gang* + *plank*] **:** a long narrow movable platform or bridge used in entering or leaving a ship (as from a wharf) — called also *gangboard*

gangplank

gangplow \ˈ=,=\ *n* [*¹gang* + *plow*] **:** a plow with two or more moldboard or disc bottoms operating together to turn parallel furrows

gang press *n* [*¹gang* + *press*] **:** MULTIPLE-DIE PRESS

¹gang punch *n* [*¹gang* + *punch* (n.)] **:** a device used for gang punching

²gang punch *vt* [*¹gang punch*] **:** to punch (common information) into a number of cards

gang·rel \ˈgaŋ(ə)rəl\ *n* -S [ME, irreg. fr. *gangen* to go — more at GANG] **1** *chiefly Scot* **a :** VAGABOND, ROVER **b :** TRAMP, VAGRANT **2** *chiefly Scot* **a :** a child just beginning to walk **:** TODDLER **b :** a gangling lanky person

¹gan·grene \ˈgaŋ,grēn, ˈgan,-, ˈgaiŋ-, ˈgaan,-, =ˈ=\ *n* -S [L *gangraena,* fr. Gk *gangraina;* akin to Gk *gran* to gnaw — more at CRESS] **1 :** local death of soft tissues (as from disease, injury, or infection) resulting from loss of blood supply — see DRY GANGRENE, GAS GANGRENE, MOIST GANGRENE, SENILE GANGRENE **2 :** a pervasive, deeply rooted moral, social, or other nonphysical evil that endangers (as moral or social health) ⟨the germs of a moral ~ which will soon . . . bear its fruit —Bela Menczer⟩

²gangrene \"\ *vb* -ED/-ING/-S *vt* **:** to produce gangrene in **:** make gangrenous **~** *vi* **:** to become affected with gangrene **:** become gangrenous ⟨a bullet wound that *gangrened*⟩

gan·gre·nous \ˈgaŋgrənəs, ˈgaiŋ-\ *adj* [prob. fr. F *gangréneux,* fr. MF *gangreneux,* fr. *gangrene* (fr. L *gangraena*) + *-eux* -ous] **:** affected by, characterized by, or likened to gangrene ⟨a ~ foot⟩ ⟨~ stomatitis⟩ ⟨~ septicemia⟩ ⟨a ~ racial problem —G.W.Johnson⟩

gangs *pl of* GANG, *pres 3d sing of* GANG

gang saw *n* **1 :** one of the thin toothed saw blades 6 to 10 inches wide used in a gang mill **2 :** GANG MILL

gang sawyer *n* **:** an operator of a gang saw

gang·ster \ˈgaŋ(k)stə(r), ˈgaiŋ-, -ŋ(k)st-\ *n* -S [*¹gang* + *-ster*] **:** a member of a gang of criminals **:** GUNMAN, THUG; *also* **:** a person who uses violence, intimidation, or other extralegal means of coercion for business ends **:** RACKETEER ⟨a ~ . . . in some kind of syndicate that controls stores and nightclubs —Chandler Brossard⟩ ⟨named one ~ as the real boss of the city —*Current Biog.*⟩

gang·ster·ism \-tə,rizəm\ *n* -S **:** the organized use of violence, intimidation, or other extralegal means of coercion for personal or group ends **:** underworld activity ⟨criminal activities suggest ties between politics and ~ —*Americana Annual*⟩

gang switch *n* [*¹gang* + *switch*] **1 :** a set of two or more switches in as many circuits operated simultaneously by a single control **2 :** a number of independent switches side by side and having a common switch plate

gang-there-out \ˈ=(,)=ˈ=\ *adj* [*³gang* + *there* + *out*] *archaic Scot* **:** VAGRANT

gangue *also* **gang** \ˈgaŋ, -anj\ *n* -S [F & G; F *gangue,* fr. G *gang* vein of metal, course, act of going, fr. OHG, act of going — more at GANG] **:** the worthless rock or vein matter in which valuable metals or minerals occur

gang up *vi* [*²gang* + *up*] **1 :** to combine for a specific purpose ⟨sellers *gang up* to raise prices —*Picture Post*⟩ ⟨*ganged up* to kill the bill⟩ **:** attack or oppose someone or something as a group — often used with *on* or *against* ⟨planning to *gang up* on us and push us around —Dorothy C. Fisher⟩ ⟨*ganged up* on him one night and beat him up⟩ ⟨all *ganged up* against each power that in succession became strongest —Elmer Davis⟩ ⟨the whole world *ganged up* against Britain —H.L.Matthews⟩ **2 :** to take sides ⟨gave . . . an impression of *ganging up* with her against me —Nigel Balchin⟩

gan·gwa \ˈgaŋ(g)wə\ *n* -S [origin unknown] **:** BLIND-YOUR-EYES

gang war *or* **gang warfare** *n* **:** feuding between gangs; *esp* **:** feuding between groups of gangsters

gangway \ˈ=,=\ *n* [*¹gang* + *way*] **1 :** a passage or way into, through, or out of any place **2 a** *archaic* **:** GANGBOARD 1 **b :** either of the sides of the upper deck of a ship between the deckhouse and the rail and the quarterdeck and forecastle **c :** the opening through the bulwarks of a ship by which persons enter or leave it **d :** GANGPLANK **3** *Brit* **:** a passage between rows of seats **:** AISLE ⟨we hear a disturbance at the back of the auditorium and three men in uniform dash down the ~ and leap on to the stage —R.W.Speaight⟩ **4 :** a main level or haulageway in a mine **5 :** JACK LADDER 2a **6 a :** a narrow aisle running crosswise dividing the front benches from the back benches in the British House of Commons **b :** a broad aisle in the British House of Commons and other British Parliamentary buildings that divides the chamber lengthwise with the benches on each side facing each other, those to the right of the speaker for members of the government party and those to the left for the opposition party **7 :** a temporary way of planks **8 :** a clear passage (as through a crowd) ⟨shouted out: "A ~, lads," and they made . . . room for me to go into the center —Arnold Bennett⟩

gang week *n* [*¹gang* + *week*] **:** ROGATION WEEK

gan·is·ter *also* **gan·nis·ter** \ˈganəstə(r)\ *n* -S [origin unknown] **1 :** a fine-grained quartzite used in the manufacture of silica brick **2 :** a mixture of ground quartz and fireclay used for lining certain metallurgical furnaces

gan·ja *also* **gan·jah** \ˈgänjə, ˈgan-, -(,)jä\ *or* **gun·ja** *or* **gun·jah** \ˈgənjə, -(,)jä, (,)gənˈjä\ *n* -S [Hindi *gā̃jā,* fr. Skt *gr̥ñja, gañjā*] **:** cannabis used esp. in India for smoking — compare BHANG, HASHISH, MARIHUANA

gan·ner \ˈganə(r)\ *dial Brit var of* GANDER

gan·net \ˈganət, *usu* -əd·+V\ *n, pl* **gannets** *also* **gannet** [ME *ganet,* fr. OE *ganot;* akin to OHG *ganazzo* gander, OE *gōs* goose — more at GOOSE] **1 :** any of several large web-footed fish-eating sea birds constituting a family (Sulidae), flying great distances and remaining at sea for long periods, and breeding in large colonies chiefly on offshore islands **2 :** WOOD IBIS

gan·net·ry \-ətrē\ *n* -ES **:** a breeding colony of gannets; *also* **:** the place of such colony whether birds are in residence or not

gan·o·ceph·a·la \,ganōˈsefələ\ *n pl, cap* [NL, fr. *gano-* (fr. Gk *ganos* brightness, joy) + *-cephala;* fr. the brightness of the bony plates; akin to Gk *gēthein* to rejoice — more at JOY] *in some classifications* **:** a group of labyrinthodonts including *Archegosaurus* and related genera having the head armored with bony plates — **gan·o·ceph·a·lan** \ˈ=ˈ=ˈ=lən\ *adj or n* — **gan·o·ceph·a·lous** \-ləs\ *adj*

gan·o·der·ma \,ganōˈdərmə\ *n, cap* [NL, fr. *gano-* + *-derma*] *in some classifications* **:** a genus of bracket fungi (family Polyporaceae) that are often included in the genus *Fomes* but when separated are distinguished on the basis of having double-walled spores with one end truncated and with a spiny brownish endospore

¹gan·o·dont \ˈganə,dänt\ *adj* [NL *Ganodonta*] **:** of or relating to the Taeniodonta

²ganodont \"\ *n* -S [NL *Ganodonta*] **:** TAENIODONT

gan·o·don·ta \,ganəˈdäntə\ [NL, fr. *gan-* (fr. Gk *ganos*) + *-odonta*] *syn of* TAENIODONTA

gan·o·dus \ˈganədəs\ *n, cap* [NL, fr. *gan-* + *-odus*] **:** a genus of Jurassic chimaeroid fishes

¹gan·oid \ˈga,nȯid\ *adj* [NL *Ganoidei*] **:** of or relating to the Ganoidei **:** having ganoid scales

²ganoid \"\ *n* -S [NL *Ganoidei*] **:** a ganoid fish; *broadly* **:** a primitive-looking fish having thick, shiny, though not necessarily ganoid scales — **ga·noi·dal** \(ˈ)gaˈnȯidᵊl, gəˈn-\ *adj* — **ga·noi·de·an** *adj or n* — **ga·noi·di·an** \-dēən\ *adj or n*

ga·noi·dei \gaˈnȯidē,ī, gəˈ-\ *n pl, cap* [NL, fr. *gan-* + *-oidei*] *in some classifications* **:** a subclass or other division of Teleostomi containing numerous extinct fishes and the living sturgeons, paddlefishes, gars (order Ginglymodi), and bowfin and having at least in the living forms a conus arteriosus, a spiral valve in the intestine, and an optic chiasma

ganoid scale *n* **:** a scale typical of the Ganoidei and found in a few other fishes that is composed of an inner layer of bone and an outer layer of ganoin

gan·o·in *or* **gan·o·ine** \ˈganəwən\ *n* -S [ISV *gano-* (fr. *ganoid*) + *-in, -ine*] **:** the covering of a ganoid scale composed of a shining material that resembles enamel

ga·nom·a·lite \gəˈnäməˌlīt\ *n* -S [Sw *ganomalit,* fr. Gk *ganōma* brightness (fr. *ganos*) + Sw *-lit* -lite] **:** a mineral $Ca_2Pb_3Si_3O_{11}$ consisting of a colorless to gray silicate of lead and calcium in tetragonal crystals or massive

gan·o·phyl·lite \,ganəˈfi,līt\ *n* -S [Sw *ganophyllit,* fr. *gano-* (fr. Gk *ganos*) + *phyll-* + *-it* -ite] **:** a mineral consisting of a brown hydrous silicate of manganese and aluminum in prismatic crystals or foliated

ga·no·sis \gəˈnōsəs\ *n, pl* **gano·ses** \-ō,sēz\ [Gk *ganōsis* action of polishing, fr. *ganoun* to polish, fr. *ganos* brightness] **:** a process of toning down the glare of marble esp. on nude parts as practiced by sculptors in classical antiquity

gan·sel \ˈgan(t)səl\ *n* -S [ME (Sc) *gansell,* fr. ME, garlic sauce, fr. MF *ganse aillie*] *Scot* **:** a sharp remark or rebuke

gan·ser syndrome \ˈgänz|ə(r)-, ˈganz|, ˈgan(t)s|\ *n, usu cap G* [after Sigbert *Ganser* †1931 Ger. psychiatrist] **:** a pattern of psychopathological behavior (as verbal) characterized by the giving of approximate answers (as 2x2 = about 5) and found in prisoners and in others who consciously or unconsciously seek to give misleading information regarding their mental state

gan·sey \'ganzi\ *n* -s [irreg. fr. *Guernsey*, one of the Channel islands] *dial Brit* : a knitted jacket or sweater : JERSEY

gansh *var of* GANCH

¹gant \'gant, -á-,-ō-\ *vi* -ED/-ING/-S [ME (Sc) *ganten*; perh. akin to OE *gānian* to gape, yawn, L *hiare* — more at YAWN] *chiefly Scot* : YAWN

²gant \"\ *n* -s [ME (Sc) *gant*, fr. *ganten*] *chiefly Scot* : YAWN

³gant \'gant\ *dial var of* GAUNT

⁴gant \"\ *vt* -ED/-ING/-S *dial* : to make thin or lean by insufficient feeding ⟨I rode two nights and ~*ed* a mule looking for a place to sleep —Alan LeMay⟩ — often used with *up*

gan·te·lope \'gant°l,ōp\ *or* **gant·lope** \-t,lōp\ *n* -s [modif. of Sw *gatlopp*, fr. OSw *gatulop*, fr. *gata* road, lane + *lop* course, run, fr. MLG *lōp*; akin to ON *gata* road, lane and to ON *hlaup* leap — more at GATE, LOPE] *archaic* : GAUNTLET

¹gantlet *var of* GAUNTLET

²gant·let \'gōntlət, 'gän-,'gan-, *usu* -əd.+V\ *n* -s [²*gauntlet*] : a stretch of railroad track (as over a bridge or in a narrow pass) where two lines of track overlap so that one rail of each track is within the rails of the other in order to obviate switching

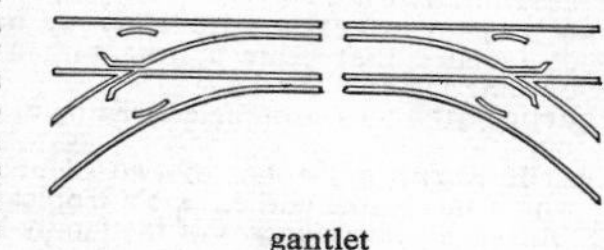
gantlet

³gantlet \"\ *vt* -ED/-ING/-S : to run together (railroad tracks) so as to make a gantlet

gant·line \'gant,līn\ *n* [perh. alter. of *girtline*] : a line rove through a block (as at the end of a bowsprit) for hoisting rigging or hanging clothing — called also *girtline*

Gan·tri·sin \'gan·trəsən\ *trademark* — used for sulfisoxazole

gan·try *also* **gan·tree** \'gan·trē, -ri\ *n*, *pl* **gantries** *also* **gantrees** *sometimes sing in constr* [perh. modif. of ONF *gantier*, fr. L *cantherius* trellis, rafter, gelding, prob. of non-IE origin; akin to the source of Gk *kanthēlios* pack ass] **1** : a frame used for supporting barrels (as in a cellar) or for rolling barrels to a higher level **2** : a frame structure raised on side supports so as to span over or around something and usu. of large dimensions: as **a** : a bridge or platform carrying a traveling crane or winch and supported by a pair of towers or by trestles or side frames running on parallel tracks **b** : a structure supporting a number of railroad signals for several tracks

gantry crane *n* : a bridge crane in which the beam or bridge is carried at each end by a trestle that travels on tracks on the ground

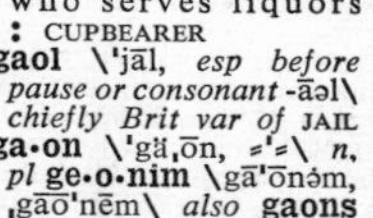
gantry crane

gan·y·mede \'ganə-,mēd\ *n* -s *usu cap* [L *Ganymedes*, cupbearer of the gods, fr. Gk *Ganymēdēs*] : a youth who serves liquors : CUPBEARER

gaol \'jāl, *esp before pause or consonant* -āəl\ *chiefly Brit var of* JAIL

ga·on \'gä,ōn, ==\ *n*, *pl* **ge·o·nim** \gā'ōnəm, ,gāō'nēm\ *also* **gaons** *often cap* [Heb *gā'ōn* majesty, excellence (pl. *gĕ'ōnīm*)] **1** : a Jewish head of one of the Babylonian academies at Sura and Pumbedita from about A.D. 589–1038 and usu. an eminent religious scholar and judicial authority — used as a title of honor; compare EXILARCH **2** : an outstanding intellectual and Talmudic scholar ⟨the celebrated 18th century ~ of Vilna⟩

ga·on·ate \-ō,nāt\ *n* -s *often cap* : the office of gaon

gaonic *often cap, var of* GEONIC

¹gap \'gap\ *n* -s [ME *gap*, *gappe*, fr. ON *gap* chasm, hole; akin to ON *gapa* to gape — more at GAPE] **1 a** : a break in a barrier (as a wall or hedge); *specif* : a breach in a line of military defense ⟨a ~ appeared in the front ranks of the Macedonian army —Tom Wintringham⟩ **b** : an assailable position : VULNERABILITY ⟨a fatal ~ in our security structure —H.S.Truman⟩ **2** : a small cleft or notch ⟨a pipe wedged between a ~ in his teeth —Judson Philips⟩ **3 a** : a notch in the crest of a ridge : mountain pass : COL ⟨US 64 enters a ~ in Crowley's Ridge and passes between the rolling slopes —*Amer. Guide Series: Ark.*⟩ **b** : a gorge cutting through a ridge : RAVINE — compare WATER GAP, WIND GAP **c** *archaic* : a hole in the ground : CHASM ⟨great holes and ~*s* had worn into the soil —Charles Dickens⟩ **d** : a break in a levee through which a distributary stream may flow : tidal inlet ⟨the tide . . . flows in and out through ~*s* —V.C.Finch & G.T.Trewartha⟩ **e** : a steep-sided furrow that cuts transversely across a ridge in the ocean bottom **4 a** : a separation in space : an intervening distance: as (1) : the shortest distance between the planes of the chords of the upper and lower wings of a biplane (2) : SPARK GAP **b** : a place from which something is missing ⟨into the ~ left by mobilized men have come women —A.R. Williams⟩ **5** : a break in continuity : INTERVAL, HIATUS ⟨intervening ~ of over thirty years —Osbert Sitwell⟩ **6** : a break in the vascular cylinder of a plant where a vascular trace departs from the central cylinder — see BRANCH GAP, LEAF GAP **7 a** : a wide difference in character or attitude ⟨~ between generations⟩ **b** : a wide difference in condition or quality ⟨~ between rich and poor⟩ **8** : a lack of balance between exports and imports : DOLLAR GAP ⟨half the ~ in the trade balance represented machinery —Harry Gilroy⟩ **syn** see BREAK

²gap \"\ *vb* **gapped; gapped; gapping; gaps** *vt* **1** : to make jagged : NOTCH **2** : to make an opening in : BREACH — usu. used in past tense ⟨the magnificent row of houses was *gapped* in two places where bombs had fallen —C.D.Lewis⟩ **3** : to adjust the space between the electrodes of (a spark plug) ~ *vi* **1** : to become notched or jagged ⟨steel *gapped* and lost its edge —*Reader*⟩ **2** : to become separated ⟨do not let the collar . . . ~ away from the neck —*N.Y. Herald Tribune*⟩ ⟨causing his . . . shirt to ~ open —Calvin Kentfield⟩

³gap \"\ *dial var of* GAPE

¹gape \'gāp *sometimes* 'gap *or* 'gaa(ə)p\ *vb* -ED/-ING/-S [ME *gapen*, fr. ON *gapa*; akin to OE *ofergapian* to neglect, MD *gapen* to gape, MHG *gaffen* to stare with open mouth, OHG *geffida* observation, L *hiare* to gape, yawn — more at YAWN] *vi* **1 a** : to open the mouth wide esp. with intent to bite or swallow ⟨baby birds ~ until they are fed⟩ **b** : to open like a mouth : spread apart along an edge or make a cavity ⟨the shell of a clam ~*s*⟩ ⟨holes ~ in pavements after floods⟩ **2 a** : to stare openmouthed in surprise or admiration — usu. used with *at* ⟨the men *gaped* at me in utter amazement —R.H. Davis⟩ ⟨~*s* round-eyed at the astonishing world —Rose Macaulay⟩ **b** : to stare with the mouth open vacantly as if not comprehending ⟨*gaped* vaguely at the skylight —Dorothy Sayers⟩ ⟨depicts man lost and blindly *gaping* amidst the chaos —Rhys Gwyn⟩ **3** *archaic* **a** : to yearn esp. for something of questionable value — usu. used with *after* or *for* ⟨~ after new spiritual incarnations —J.C.Hare⟩ **b** : to want earnestly to do something : CRAVE — used with infinitive ⟨*gaping* with mouths wide open to have their curiosity satisfied —*Sporting Mag.*⟩ **4** : to draw a deep involuntary breath with the mouth open esp. as a result of fatigue or boredom : YAWN ⟨a dull lecture makes the students ~⟩ **5** *archaic* : SHOUT, BELLOW ⟨you'll leave your noise anon . . . ye rude slaves leave your *gaping* —Shak.⟩ ~ *vt* : to make an opening in ⟨a fearful battlefield, the earth of it *gaped* open by shells and bombs —Ira Wolfert⟩ **syn** see GAZE

²gape \"\ *n* -s **1** : an act of gaping: **a** : YAWN **b** : an openmouthed stare **c** *archaic* : an eager search after : QUEST ⟨a perpetual ~ after knowledge —Joseph Addison⟩ **2** : an unfilled space or extent : VACUUM ⟨the huge attentive ~ of emptiness —Thomas Wolfe⟩ **3 a** : the median margin-to-margin length of the open mouth **b** : the line along which the mandibles of a bird close **c** : an opening at the edge of a mollusk shell when the valves are shut **d** : the width of an opening that resembles a mouth ⟨gyratory crushers having a ~ suitable for the coarsest crushing —A.M.Gaudin⟩ **e** : the distance between the barb and shank on a fishhook **4 gapes** *pl but sing in constr* **a** : a disease of young chickens, turkeys, and other birds in which nematode worms (*Syngamus trachea*) invade and irritate the trachea causing coughing and labored breathing often with the neck extended and the beak open ⟨~*s* is a common disease of chicks aged three to eight weeks —W.P.Blount⟩ — see GAPEWORM **b** : a fit of yawning — used with *the* ⟨as the lecture dragged on, he got the ~*s*⟩

gap·er \-pə(r)\ *n* -s **1** : one that gapes ⟨made herself the center of a crowd of ~*s* —Arnold Bennett⟩ **2** : any of several comparatively large sluggish burrowing clams (family Myacidae) having a shell that flares out at each end including several excellent food clams

gapeseed \'=,=\ *n* **1** *dial Brit* : something that causes gaping looks **2** *dial Brit* : a person who looks or stares gapingly

gapeworm \'=,=\ *n* : a strongyloid nematode worm (*Syngamus trachea* or *S. trachealis*) that infests the trachea and bronchi of birds and causes gapes

gap-framepress *n* : a punch press with an opening in the front of the frame at a level with the bed to permit the insertion of wide work or the feeding of strip stock across the bed from one side to the other

gaping *adj* [fr. pres. part. of ¹*gape*] **1** : wide open ⟨~ wounds⟩ ⟨a ~ gravel pit⟩ **2** : exhibiting desire, wonder, or vacuity : AGAPE ⟨with their ~ eyes and their sweet words —J.M. Synge⟩ **3** : of broad extent : GREAT, IMPORTANT ⟨~ omissions⟩ — **gap·ing·ly** *adv*

gapped *past of* GAP

gapped scale *n* [*gapped* past part. of ²*gap*] : an incomplete musical scale; *specif* : a scale established or patterned on the omission of certain notes or tones from a complete tonal series

gap·per \'gapə(r\ *n* -s *Brit* : a machine for thinning sugar beets or other crops by cutting gaps in the row

gapping *pres part of* GAP

gap·py \'gapē, -pi\ *adj, often* -ER/-EST [¹*gap* + -*y*] : having gaps : BROKEN, UNCONNECTED ⟨a ~ hedge⟩ ⟨a ~ history⟩

gaps *pl of* GAP, *pres 3d sing of* GAP

gap-toothed \'=;=\ *adj* : having gaps between the teeth

¹gar \'gär\ *vt* **garred; garred; garring; gars** [ME *geren*, *garen*, fr. ON *gera*, *göra*, *gørva* to prepare, make, do; akin to OE *gierwan* to prepare, OHG *garawen*; causative-denominative fr. the root of OE *gearu*, *gearo* ready — more at YARE] *now chiefly Scot* : to make (a person) do something : COMPEL, FORCE ⟨good manners ~ us keep the Sabbath inviolate — William Black⟩

²gar \'gär, 'gá(r\ *interj* [euphemistic alter. of *God*] — a mild oath

³gar \"\ *n* -s [short for *garfish*] : any of various fishes that have an elongate body resembling that of a pike and long and narrow jaws: as **a** : NEEDLEFISH **b** : any of various halfbeaks of Australia and New Zealand **c** : any of several freshwater ganoid fishes forming an order Ginglymodi and family Lepisosteidae, having hard shining rhombic scales and flesh that is rank and tough, and being destructive of other fishes — see ALLIGATOR GAR, LONGNOSE GAR, SHORTNOSE GAR

gar *abbr* garage

gar·ad pod \'garəd-\ *n* [Ar *qaraḍ*] : the pod of babul

¹ga·rage \gə'rä|zh, -rá|, |j, *chiefly Brit* 'ga,räzh *sometimes* 'garij\ *n* -s [F, garage, act of docking (a ship), act of sidetracking, fr. *garer* to dock, sidetrack, move out of the way (fr. MF, to dock) + -*age*; MF *garer* of Gmc origin; akin to OHG *biwarōn* to keep, protect — more at WARE] **1** : a building or compartment of a building used for housing an automotive vehicle **2** : a repair shop for automotive vehicles **3** : a siding in a canal

²garage \"\ *vt* -ED/-ING/-S : to keep or put in a garage ⟨automobile owners are advised to ~ their cars at night to preserve the finish —*Science News Letter*⟩

ga·rage·man \-,man, -,maa(ə)n\ *n*, *pl* **garagemen** : a worker in a garage

garage-porch \=';=,=\ *n* : CARPORT

gar·a·man·tes \,garə'man(,)tēz\ *n pl*, *usu cap* [L, fr. Gk] : an ancient Hamitic people of the eastern Sahara region from the time of Herodotus into the Roman period

ga·ram·bul·la \,gäräm'bü(y)ə\ *or* **ga·ram·bu·llo** \-ü(,)(y)ō\ *n* -s [MexSp *garambullo*, perh. alter. of Sp *carambolo* carambola (tree), fr. *carambola* carambola (fruit), fr. Marathi *karambal*] **1** : an arborescent cactus (*Myrtillocactus geometrizans*) of western Mexico that bears a small oblong edible berry **2** : the fruit of the garambulla

gar·an·cine \,garən'sēn\ *n* -s [F, fr. *garance* madder (fr. OF) + -*ine*; OF *garance*, of Gmc origin; akin to OHG *rezza* madder] : a dye or pigment made by treating ground madder with sulfuric acid

garand *or* **garand rifle** \gə'rand-, -'raa(ə)nd-, 'garənd-\ *n* -s *usu cap G* [after John C. *Garand* b1888 Am. inventor who designed it] : M-1 — see RIFLE illustration

ga·ra·pa·ta \,garə'päd·ə\ *also* **ga·ra·pa·to** \-d·(,)ō\ *n* -s [Sp *garrapata*] : TICK; *esp* : the spiny ear tick — compare CARRAPATO

gar·a·vance \'garə,van(t)s\ *also* **car·a·vance** \'ka-\ *or* **cal·a·vance** \'kalə-\ *n* -s [modif. of Sp *garbanzo*] : CHICK-PEA

gar·a·wi \'garə(,)wē\ *n*, *pl* **garawi** [EgyptAr *garwi* white poppy, small colocynth] : SUDAN GRASS

¹garb \'gärb, 'gáb\ *n* -s [ONF *garbe*, of Gmc origin; akin to OHG *garba* sheaf; akin to Skt *gṛbhṇāti*, *gṛhṇāti* he seizes — more at GRAB] *heraldry* : a sheaf of grain (as wheat)

²garb \"\ *n* -s [MF or OIt; MF *garbe* graceful outline, contour, grace, fr. OIt *garbo* grace, perh. modif. of Ar *qālab* mold, model] **1** *obs* : stylishness in looks or bearing : ELEGANCE ⟨ladies and gentlemen that are of any ~ —Richard Lassels⟩ **2** : prevailing mode : STYLE ⟨could not speak English in the native ~ —Shak.⟩ **3** *obs* : manner of behavior : CONDUCT ⟨this sullen ~, this moody discontent —Nicholas Rowe⟩ **4 a** : style of apparel : COSTUME ⟨in formal ~, a tail coat with silk binding . . . gray spats and shiny patent leather shoes — W.A.White⟩ **b** : style of expression : outward form ⟨give their lie the further appearance of truth and their madness the outward ~ of sanity —Lewis Mumford⟩

³garb \"\ *vt* -ED/-ING/-S **1** : to cover with clothing : DRESS ⟨~*ed* themselves in cowboy outfits —*Savings Banker*⟩ **2** : to cover as if with clothing : INVEST ⟨~*ed* each one of them with . . . individual dignity —R.G.Swing⟩

¹gar·bage \'gärbij, 'gáb-, -bēj\ *n* -s *often attrib* [ME] **1** *archaic* : the internal parts of an animal : VISCERA ⟨in Newfoundland they improve their ground with the ~ of fish —John Mortimer⟩ **2** *archaic* : a sheaf esp. of grain : FAGOT, BUNDLE ⟨all such horses . . . to be substantially served . . . in hay, ~, and litter — *Household Ordinances*⟩ **3 a** : refuse of any kind : WASTE ⟨an infinite variety of industrial ~ and poisons —K.S.Dixon⟩ **b** : refuse resulting from the preparation, cooking, and dispensing of food : SCRAPS ⟨scrape the plates and take out the ~⟩ **4** : worthless or objectionable matter put into writing or speech : TRASH ⟨one publisher's idea of a fine book may be a competitor's idea of ~ —Bennett Cerf⟩ **5** : a card game in which each player is dealt five cards which he plays in a series of different games **syn** see REFUSE

²garbage \"\ *vb* -ED/-ING/-S *vt*, *obs* : to remove the entrails from : EVISCERATE ⟨a turkey cock that when he was pulled and *garbaged* weighed thirty pounds —John Josselyn⟩ ~ *vi* : to feed on or as if on garbage : SCAVENGE ⟨the finest diet won't stop a dog from *garbaging* —B.J.Rowles⟩

garbage tankage *n* : a fertilizer material made by rendering, drying, and grinding garbage

garbage worm *n* : TRICHINA

gar·ban·zo \gär'ban(,)zō\ *also* **gar·ban·za** \-nzə\ *or* **gar·van·zo** \-'van(,)zō\ *n* -s [Sp *garbanzo*, alter. (prob. influenced by OSp *garroba* carob, fr. Ar *kharrūbah*) of OSp *arvanço*, perh. of Gmc origin; akin to OHG *araweiz* pea — more at ERS] : CHICK-PEA

garbill \'=,=\ *n* [³*gar* + *bill*] : RED-BREASTED MERGANSER

¹gar·ble \'gärbəl, 'gáb-\ *vt* **garbled; garbled; garbling** \-b(ə)liŋ\ **garbles** [ME *garbelen*, fr. OIt *garbellare* to sift, fr. Ar *gharbala* to sift, *ghirbāl* sieve, fr. LL *cribellum* small sieve — more at CRIBELLUM] **1** *archaic* **a** : to sort or pick out : select the best parts of : CULL **2** : to remove dross or dirt from : REFINE; *specif* : to sift impurities from (as spices) ⟨*garbled* Tellicherry pepper . . . sells for ¼¢ a pound above the ungarbled —F.P.Tucker⟩ **3 a** : to make misleading selections from : deliberately pervert : DISTORT ⟨their disputes on the merits of these arguments have not been edifying, since both sides have been apt to ~ the question —Gilbert Ryle⟩ **b** : to mix up through accident or ignorance : MUTILATE, DISARRANGE, JUMBLE ⟨statements . . . *garbled* into absurdity when copied into the newspapers —Havelock Ellis⟩; *specif* : to introduce textual error into (a message) by inaccurate enciphering, transmitting, or receiving

²garble \"\ *n* -s **1** : worthless material : WASTE; *specif* : the impurities removed from spices **2** *archaic* : ALLOY **3** : an act or instance of garbling; *specif* : an error in the encipherment, transmission, or reception of a message ⟨there is a ~ in "8" and the following telegram corrects the ~ —*N.Y.Times*⟩

gar·ble·able \-bələbəl\ *adj*, *archaic* : that can be or is likely to be garbled ⟨all sorts of wares or merchandise ~, as sugar, pepper, cloves —William Leybourn⟩

gar·bler \-b(ə)lə(r)\ *n* -s : one that garbles; *specif* : one that sifts spices

garb·less \-bləs\ *adj* : being without garb

garble table *n* : PERMUTATION TABLE

gar·bling \-b(ə)liŋ, -lēŋ\ *n* -s [ME *garbeling*, fr. *garbelen* + -*ing*] **1** *archaic* **a** : the act or process of sorting out the best part : CULLING; *specif* : the sifting of spices **b** : the refuse produced by culling — usu. used in pl. **2** : an act or instance of distortion : GARBLE ⟨a wholesale ~ of titles and proper names —J.H.Buckley⟩

gar·board \'gär,bō(ə)rd\ *or* **garboard strake** *n* [obs. D *gaarboord*, fr. obs. D *gaar*- (perh. fr. D *garen* to gather, fr. MD, contr. of *gaderen*) + D *boord* board, ship's side; akin to OE *gaderian* to gather and to OE *bord* board, ship's side — more at GATHER, BOARD] : the plank or planking in a wooden ship and the plate or plating in a steel ship lying next to the keel — see SHIP illustration

gar·boil \'gär,bȯil\ *n* -s [MF *garbouil*, fr. OIt *garbuglio*] *archaic* : a state of disturbance : TURMOIL

gar·bure \(')gär¦byü(ə)r\ *n* -s [F, fr. Prov *garburo*] : a thick soup of bacon and cabbage or other vegetables usu. with cheese and stale bread added

gar·butt rod *also* **gar·bet rod** \'gärbət-\ *n* [perh. fr. the name *Garbet*] : a rod attached to the cage of a standing valve of an oil-well pump in such a way that the standing valve is lifted out of the well when the plunger is withdrawn

garb willow *n* : WEEPING WILLOW

gar·cin·ia \gär'sinēə\ *n* [NL, fr. Laurent *Garcin* †1751 Fr. botanist + NL -*ia*] **1** *cap* : a large genus of tropical Asiatic trees (family Guttiferae) having thick coriaceous leaves and baccate fruit with arilled seed — see GAMBOGE, KOKUM BUTTER, MANGOSTEEN **2** -s : any tree of the genus *Garcinia*

gar·çon \(')gär¦sōⁿ, *F* gársōⁿ\ *n*, *pl* **garçons** \-ōⁿ(z)\ [F, boy, servant, fr. OF, boy, menial, knave, prob. of Gmc origin; akin to OHG *reccho*, *reckio* banished man — more at WRETCH] : a serving man; *esp* : a waiter in a French restaurant

gardant *var of* GUARDANT

garde·bras \,gärdə¦brä\ *n*, *pl* **gardebras** \-rä(z)\ [alter. (influenced by MF *garde-bras*) of ME *garbrasse*, modif. of MF *garde-bras*, fr. *garder* to guard + *bras* arm, fr. L *brachium* — more at GUARD, BRACE] : a piece of armor to protect the arm

garde-collet \¦gärdə(,)kō¦lā\ *n* [F, fr. *garder* to guard + *collet* collar — more at COLLET] : a raised plate or ridge on the shoulder piece of armor to protect the neck

gar·deen \(')gär¦dēn\ *dial var of* GUARDIAN

garde-manger \¦gärd(ə),mäⁿ¦zhā\ *n* -s [F, fr. OF *garde-mangier* official in charge of the kitchen in a royal household, fr. *garder* to guard + *mangier* food — more at BLANCMANGE] **1** : a cook who specializes in the preparation of cold meat dishes **2** : a refrigerated pantry unit where cold dishes are prepared

¹gar·den \'gärdᵊn, 'gád-\ *n* -s [ME *gardin*, fr. ONF, fr. *gart* garden, of Gmc origin; akin to OHG *gart* enclosure — more at YARD] **1 a** : a plot of cultivated ground adjacent to a dwelling and usu. devoted in whole or in part to the growing of herbs, fruits, flowers, or vegetables for household use — compare KITCHEN GARDEN, YARD **b** (1) : a tract of land devoted to the raising of crops ⟨the date ~*s* extend for over 150 miles —*Statesman's Yr. Bk.*⟩ (2) *dial Brit* : a usu. small field in which a crop is grown ⟨potato ~⟩ (3) : a natural grove ⟨vast ~*s* of wild oranges⟩ (4) : an area devoted to the raising of animals ⟨underseas ~*s* in which the oysters are planted —*Amer. Guide Series: Conn.*⟩ **c** : something that resembles a garden ⟨coral ~*s* that delight the imagination —J.A.Michener⟩ ⟨~ of memories —Van Wyck Brooks⟩ **d** : a rich well-cultivated region ⟨a semitropical ~ of sugarcane, pineapples, and sunshine —*N.Y.Herald Tribune*⟩ **2 a** : a public recreation area or park ⟨[the] usually staid Public *Garden* assumes an air of gaiety as the annual Festival of Arts takes up its stand —C.M.Barss⟩; *specif* : an open-air establishment furnished with tables and chairs and serving refreshments — see BEER GARDEN, TEA GARDEN **b** : a large hall for an indoor athletic contest (as basketball, hockey, racing, boxing), a spectacular show (as of horses, motorboats, flowers), or a circus ⟨coliseums, ~*s*, and convention halls are springing up everywhere —E.M.Smith⟩ **3** *slang* : the outfield of a baseball diamond

²garden \"\ *vb* **gardened; gardened; gardening** \-d(ᵊ)niŋ\ **gardens** *vi* **1** : to lay out or work in a garden : practice horticulture ⟨bought a house in the country so he could ~⟩ **2** : to attempt to level an uneven spot on a cricket wicket by patting it with one's bat ~ *vt* **1** : to make into a garden : bring under cultivation ⟨the long landscape . . . ~*ed* into more perfect beauty —Bayard Taylor⟩ **2** : to ornament with gardens ⟨a ~*ed* esplanade —*Amer. Guide Series: N.C.*⟩

³garden \"\ *adj* **1 a** : of or relating to a garden ⟨~ gate⟩ **b** : used in or frequenting the garden ⟨~ hose⟩ ⟨~ toad⟩ **2 a** : of a kind that is grown in the garden esp. as distinguished from a more delicate hothouse variety ⟨~ chrysanthemum⟩ **b** : of a familiar kind : COMMONPLACE ⟨domestic shorthairs as the ~ variety of cat is technically known to fanciers —*Nat'l Geographic*⟩ **3** : having a garden ⟨~ community⟩

gar·den·age \-ᵊnij\ *n* -s **1** *archaic* : HORTICULTURE **2** *archaic* : garden produce

garden apartment *n* **1** : a ground floor apartment whose rental includes the use of a garden **2** : an apartment building enclosing a gardened court for the use of the tenants

garden bagworm *n* : a European bagworm (*Apterona crenulella*) with a case resembling a snail shell that is now established in the western U. S. and is apparently parthenogenetic as no males are known

garden balm *n* : LEMON BALM

garden balsam *n* : a plant (*Impatiens balsamina*) having a more or less pubescent stem, lanceolate sharply serrate leaves tapering to a short petiole, and flowers borne in the axils of the leaves and varying in color from white to purple and rose — called also *balsam*, *balsamine*

garden bond *n* : a pattern of bricklaying in which each course usu. consists of three stretchers followed by a header

garden burnet *n* : SALAD BURNET

garden buttercup *n* : a commonly cultivated European crowfoot (*Ranunculus aconitifolius*) with white or yellow often double flowers

garden catchfly *n* : LOBEL'S CATCHFLY

garden celandine *n* : CELANDINE 1

garden centipede *n* : a minute symphilid (*Scutigerella immaculata*) that often infests the underground parts of truck and greenhouse crops — called also *garden symphilid*

garden chafer *n* : a European beetle (*Phyllopertha horticola*) that resembles a scarab and feeds on the blossoms and leaves of fruit trees and rosebushes

garden city *n*, *sometimes cap G&C* : a real-estate movement originating in England about 1875 and advocating the development of planned residential communities with park and planted areas

garden columbine *n* : a commonly cultivated Eurasian herb (*Aquilegia vulgaris*) with spurred blue and purple flowers

garden cress *also* **garden pepper cress** *n* : an Asiatic annual herb (*Lepidium sativum*) that is sometimes cultivated for its pungent basal leaves and that has small whitish flowers followed by round flattened pods

garden currant *n* **:** a European red currant (*Ribes sativum*) with greenish yellow flowers in drooping racemes
garden egg *n* **:** EGGPLANT
gar·den·er \'gärd(ᵊ)nər, 'gȧd(ᵊ)nə(r\ *n* -s [ME *gardiner*, prob. fr. ONF *gardinier*, fr. *gardin* garden + *-ier* (fr. L *-arius* -ary)] **1 :** one that gardens; *specif* **:** one employed to care for the gardens or grounds about a home, business concern, or other property **2** *slang* **:** a baseball outfielder
gardener bird *n* **:** any of several small plainly colored bowerbirds (genus *Amblyornis*) of New Guinea that make a garden of moss ornamented with flowers in front of the bower
gardener's-delight \'≈(≈)≈ₛ≈\ *n, pl* **gardener's-delights :** MULLEIN PINK
gardener's-garters \'≈(≈)≈ₛ≈\ *n pl but sing or pl in constr* **:** RIBBON GRASS
gar·den·esque \ˌgärdᵊnˈesk\ *adj* **:** of, relating to, or resembling a garden ⟨~ lily⟩ ⟨~ factory grounds⟩
garden flea *n* **:** FLEA BEETLE
garden fleahopper *n* **:** a widely distributed black fleahopper (*Halticus bracteatus*) that sometimes feeds destructively on the foliage of various cultivated plants causing white spots and when abundant the death of infested foliage
garden-fresh \'≈≈ˈ≈\ *adj* **1 :** being picked or dug extremely recently ⟨*garden-fresh* fruit⟩ ⟨*garden-fresh* vegetables⟩ **2 :** consisting of garden-fresh produce ⟨a *garden-fresh* salad⟩ **3 :** having the desirable taste or quality of garden-fresh produce ⟨*garden-fresh* cottage cheese⟩
gar·den·ful \'gärdᵊnˌfu̇l\ *n* -s **:** a quantity sufficient to fill a garden ⟨~ of roses⟩
garden-gate \'≈≈ˈ≈\ *n* **1** *dial Eng* **:** HEARTSEASE 2a(1) **2** *dial Eng* **:** HERB ROBERT
garden heliotrope *n* **1 :** a tall perennial rhizomatous herb (*Valeriana officinalis*) that is native to Europe and northern Asia but widely naturalized as an escape and has very fragrant tiny white, pinkish, lavender, or sometimes red flowers in large paniculate corymbs and roots and rhizomes which yield the drug valerian — called also *valerian* **2 :** a shrubby Peruvian heliotrope (*Heliotropium arborescens*) widely cultivated in mild regions for its very fragrant usu. lilac or violet flowers — called also *common heliotrope*
garden house *n* **1 :** a small usu. open structure providing shelter in a garden **2** *chiefly South & Midland* **:** PRIVY
garden huckleberry *n* **1 :** BLACK NIGHTSHADE **2 :** the fruit of black nightshade
gar·de·nia \gärˈdēnyə, gȧg-, -nēə\ *n* [NL, fr. Alexander *Garden* †1791 Scot. naturalist + NL *-ia*] **1** *cap* **:** a large genus of Old World tropical trees and shrubs (family Rubiaceae) having showy fragrant white or yellow flowers **2** -s **:** any plant or flower of the genus *Gardenia; esp* **:** CAPE JASMINE
gardening *n* -s [fr. gerund of ²*garden*] **:** the laying out or care of gardens
gar·den·ize \'gärdᵊnˌīz\ *vb* -ED/-ING/-S *vi* **:** GARDEN ~ *vt* **1 :** to transform into or supply with a garden ⟨this world shall be *gardenized* —*Voice*⟩ **2 :** to cultivate (a native or wild plant) in a garden ⟨~ arbutus⟩
gar·den·less \-ᵊnləs\ *adj* **:** lacking a garden
gar·den·ly \-ᵊnlē\ *adj* **:** resembling a garden
garden mint *n* **:** SPEARMINT
garden nasturtium *n* **:** a cultivated plant of the genus *Tropaeolum* (esp. *T. majus*)
garden nightshade *n* **:** BLACK NIGHTSHADE
garden of eden \ˌgärd(ᵊ)nəˈvēdᵊn, ˌgȧd-\ *usu cap G&E* [*Eden*, the garden where Adam and Eve resided before the fall (Gen 3) — more at EDEN] **:** PARADISE 2
garden orache *n* **:** an Asiatic herb (*Atriplex hortensis*) resembling spinach and often used as a potherb
garden orpine *n* **:** a cultivated orpine or one common in cultivation (as *Sedum triphyllum*)
garden party *n* **:** a social affair held in an outdoor setting
garden peppergrass *n* **:** GARDEN CRESS
garden pink *n* **:** any of several plants of the genus *Dianthus; esp* **:** COTTAGE PINK
garden plague *n* **:** GOUTWEED
garden plow *n* **:** HAND PLOW
garden poppy *n* **:** a cultivated plant of the genus *Papaver; esp* **:** OPIUM POPPY
garden portulaca *n* **:** a portulaca (*Portulaca grandiflora*)
garden rocket *n* **1 :** an erect much-branched European annual herb (*Eruca sativa*) sometimes grown for salad and having pinnately lobed leaves and whitish yellow flowers **2 :** DAME'S VIOLET
gardens *pl of* GARDEN, *pres 3d sing of* GARDEN
garden sage *n* **:** SAGE 1a
garden sass *n, chiefly Midland* **:** ¹SASS
garden slug *n* **:** a slug infesting cultivated areas; *esp* **:** the gray garden slug (*Deroceras agrestis* or *D. reticulatum*)
garden snail *n* **:** any of several snails (esp. *Helix aspersa* and *H. hortensis*) often destructive in gardens — compare BROWN SNAIL
garden sorrel *n* **:** a European sorrel (*Rumex acetosa*) with hastate leaves usu. much longer than broad that is grown for salad and spring greens
garden speedwell *n* **:** FIELD SPEEDWELL
garden spider *n* **:** a garden-frequenting spider esp. of the family Argiopidae: as **a :** a common European spider (*Aranea diademata*) **b :** a widely distributed No. American spider (*Argiope aurantia*) with bright yellow markings on a dark gray or black background
garden spot *n* **1 :** a space set aside for gardening ⟨window overlooking the *garden spot*⟩ **2 :** an esp. fertile region ⟨owning twenty-six thousand acres of land in one of the *garden spots* of Iowa —Bertha M. H. Shambaugh⟩
garden springtail *n* **:** a common springtail (*Bourletiella hortensis*) that is destructive to seedlings in parts of northern No. America
garden stuff *n* **:** vegetables grown in a garden
garden symphylan *n* **:** GARDEN CENTIPEDE
garden truck *n* **:** GARDEN STUFF; *specif* **:** vegetables raised for market
garden valerian *n* **:** GARDEN HELIOTROPE 1
garden-variety \'≈≈ˈ≈≈≈\ *adj* **:** ³GARDEN 2b
garden verbena *n* **:** VERBENA 2
garden violet *n* **:** SWEET VIOLET
garden wall bond *n* **:** GARDEN BOND — see ENGLISH GARDEN WALL BOND, FLEMISH GARDEN WALL BOND, GARDEN WALL CROSS BOND
garden wall cross bond *n* **:** a pattern in bricklaying in which a course of stretchers alternates with a course consisting of one header followed by three stretchers
garden warbler *n* **:** a brownish gray European warbler (*Sylvia borin*) — compare BECCAFICO
garden webworm *n* **:** the web-making larva of a pyralidid moth (*Loxostege similalis*) injurious to vegetables esp. in No. and So. America
garden white *n* **:** any of several small white butterflies (as the cabbage butterfly) constituting the genus *Pieris*
gar·deny \'gärd(ᵊ)nē\ *adj* [¹*garden* + *-y*] **:** suggestive of a garden ⟨a real ~ place to shut out the gales —Sinclair Lewis⟩
garde·robe \'gärˌdrōb\ *n* [ME, fr. MF; akin to ONF *warderobe* wardrobe — more at WARDROBE] **1 :** a wardrobe or its contents **2 :** a private room **:** BEDROOM **3 :** PRIVY
gar·de·vin \'gärdəˌvin\ *or* **gar·de·vine** \-ˌvēn, -ˌvīn\ *n* -s [F *garder* to keep, guard + *vin* wine, fr. L *vinum* — more at GUARD, WINE] **1** *Scot* **:** a large bottle or decanter for wine ⟨a tumbler and the ~ for the dominie —D.S.Meldrum⟩ **2** *Scot* **:** a wine closet
gar·dez \(ˈ)gärˈdā\ *v imper* [short for earlier *gardez la reine*, fr. F, guard the queen] — used to warn a chess opponent that his queen is in danger of immediate capture
gar·di·nol \'gärdᵊnˌȯl, -ˌōl\ *n* -s [fr. *Gardinol*, a trademark] **:** any of various commercially produced detergents consisting essentially of salts of sulfated fatty alcohols (as sodium lauryl sulfate)
gar·dy \'gärdē\ *n* -ES [origin unknown] *Scot* **:** ARM
gar·dy·loo \ˌgärdiˈlü\ *v imper* [perh. fr. F *garde à l'eau!* attention to the water!] — used as a warning shout in Scotland when it was customary to throw household slops from upstairs windows
¹**gare** \'gär\ *Scot var of* ²GORE
²**gare** \"\ *var of* GAIR
gare·fowl \'ga(a)(ə)rˌfau̇l\ *n, pl* **garefowl** *or* **garefowls** [of Scand origin; akin to ON *geirfugl* great auk, fr. *geirr* spear + *fugl* bird — more at GORE, FOWL] **:** GREAT AUK
garfish \'≈ˌ≈\ *n* [ME *garfysshe*, prob. fr. ME (northern) *gar*, *gare* spear (fr. OE *gār*) + ME *fysshe, fish* fish — more at GORE, FISH] **:** GAR
gar·ga·ney \'gärgənē\ *n* -s [It dial. (16th cent., region of Bellinzona, Ticino canton, southern Switzerland) *garganei*, of imit. origin] **:** a European teal (*Anas querquedula*) having the male distinguished by a broad white stripe from eye to nape
gar·gan·tuan \(ˈ)gärˈganch(əw)ən, (ˈ)gȧˈ-, -ˈgaan-\ *adj, often cap* [*Gargantua*, gigantic king who is the hero of the novel *Gargantua* (1535) by François Rabelais †1553 Fr. humorist and satirist + E *-an*] **:** of tremendous size or volume **:** GIGANTIC, COLOSSAL ⟨a ~ land of rolling prairies, grass-blanketed plains, towering mountains —R.A.Billington⟩ ⟨~ laughter like the bellow of a joyful bull —Leslie Charteris⟩ **syn** see HUGE
gar·get \'gärgət\ *n* -s [prob. fr. (assumed) obs. E *garget* throat, fr. ME *garget, gargat*, fr. MF *gargate*, fr. OF, of imit. origin] **1** *archaic* **:** a disease in swine and cattle marked by inflammation of the head or throat **2 :** mastitis of domestic animals; *esp* **:** chronic bovine mastitis with gross changes in the form and texture of the udder **3** *or* **garget plant** *or* **garget root :** POKEWEED
gar·gety \-ədˌē\ *adj* [*garget* + *-y*] **:** of, relating to, or affected with garget; *specif* **:** STRINGY, CLOTTED — used esp. of milk drawn from cows afflicted with mastitis
¹**gar·gle** \'gärgəl, 'gȧg-\ *vb* **gargled; gargled; gargling** \-g(ə)liŋ\ **gargles** [modif. of MF *gargouiller* to gurgle, bubble, of imit. origin] *vt* **1 a :** to hold (a liquid) in the mouth or throat and keep in motion by a stream of air from the lungs ⟨~ salt water⟩ **b :** to cleanse or disinfect (the inside of the mouth) in this manner ⟨~ a sore throat⟩ **2 :** to utter with a gargling sound ⟨~s his words⟩ ~ *vi* **1 :** to use a gargle ⟨~ every morning⟩ **2 :** to utter as if gargling ⟨soprano with a tendency to ~ on the high notes⟩ **3 :** to make a sound that resembles a gargle ⟨a camel . . . ~*ing* as it were with rage —Nathan Davis⟩
²**gargle** \"\ *n* -s **1 a :** a liquid (as a mouthwash) intended for use in the mouth and throat **b :** an act of gargling ⟨a ~ with a small amount of baking soda will help to clear the throat —Morris Fishbein⟩ **2 :** a sound that resembles that of a liquid being gargled ⟨heard his breath go out in a ~ —Marcia Davenport⟩
gar·gler \-g(ə)lə(r)\ *n* -s **:** one that gargles
gargling *n* -s [fr. gerund of ¹*gargle*] **:** liquid gargled by a patient and then subjected to laboratory analysis — usu. used in pl.
gar·gouil·lade \ˌgär(ˌ)güˈyäd\ *n* -s [F, fr. *gargouiller* to gurgle, bubble + *-ade*] *ballet* **:** a pas de chat with a double rond de jambe
gar·goyle \'gärˌgȯil, 'gȧ-, 'gä-\ *also* **gur·goyle** \'gər-, 'gə̄-, 'gəi-\ *n* -s [ME *gargoyl*, fr. MF *gargouille, gargoule*, fr. OF *gargoule*, of imit. origin] **1 a :** a spout often having the form of a grotesque figure or animal and projecting from a roof gutter to throw rainwater clear of a building ⟨listening to the avid gabble of water running from a ~ at the corner of the schoolhouse —Eve Langley⟩ **b :** any grotesquely carved figure ⟨strange Ethiopian ~s carved upon the ebony footposts of his bed —Hervey Allen⟩ **2 :** a person with a face resembling that of a gargoyle ⟨what you need is a woman — older, of course . . . but not a gorgon or a ~ —Mary Fitt⟩

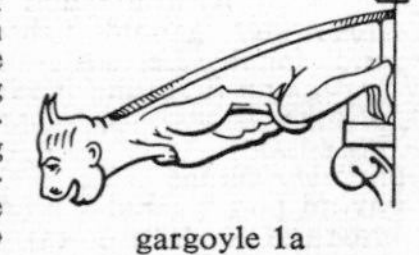
gargoyle 1a

gar·goyled \-ld\ *adj* [¹*gargoyle* + *-ed*] **:** decorated with gargoyles ⟨the ~ tops of cathedrals —*Times Lit. Supp.*⟩ ⟨the ~ and crenelated skyline —Frederic Marton⟩
gar·goyl·ism \-ȯiˌlizəm\ *n* -s **:** a genetic variation in man involving extensive structural defects of the skeleton and gross mental deficiency
garh·wa·li \gərˈwälē\ *n* -s *usu cap* **:** a Pahari dialect spoken in Garhwal, India
gar·i·bal·di \ˌgarəˈbȯldē, -di *also* ˌger-\ *n* -ES [after Giuseppe *Garibaldi* †1882 Ital. patriot] **1 :** a woman's blouse copied from the red shirt worn by the Italian patriot Garibaldi **2 :** a brilliant orange-red California market fish (*Hypsypops rubicundus*) of the family Pomacentridae
¹**gar·i·bal·di·an** \ˌ≈≈ˈ≈dēən, -diən\ *adj, usu cap* [Giuseppe *Garibaldi* †1882 + E *-an*] **:** of, relating to, or supporting Garibaldi
²**garibaldian** \"\ *or* **gar·i·bal·dist** \ˌ≈≈ˈ≈dəst\ *n* -s *usu cap* [Giuseppe *Garibaldi* †1882 + E *-an* or *-ist*] **:** a supporter of Garibaldi
ga·rigue *also* **gar·rigue** \gəˈrēg\ *n* -s [F *garrigue*, fr. MF, fr. OProv *garriga*, fr. *garric* kermes oak, prob. of non-IE origin; akin to the source of Sp *carrasca* kermes oak] **:** a low open scrubland characterized by many evergreen shrubs, low trees, and bunchgrasses and found in poor land in the Mediterranean region
gar·ish \'ga(a)rish, 'ger-, -rēsh\ *adj* [origin unknown] **1 :** clothed in vivid colors ⟨as ~ as a gypsy —Victoria Sackville-West⟩ **2 a :** excessively vivid **:** FLASHY ⟨~ colors⟩ ⟨~ oratory⟩ **b :** offensively bright **:** GLARING ⟨~ klieg lights⟩ **c :** vulgarly obtrusive **:** BLATANT ⟨~ perfume⟩ **3 a :** tastelessly showy or overdecorated **:** FLAMBOYANT ⟨this front room is furnished with ~ theatrical magnificence —Arnold Bennett⟩ **b :** offensive to the sensibilities **:** REVOLTING ⟨its cynical and corrupt elements, its ~ violence —Orville Prescott⟩ **syn** see GAUDY
gar·ish·ly *adv* **:** in a garish manner
gar·ish·ness *n* -ES **:** the quality or state of being garish
¹**gar·land** \'gärlənd, 'gȧl-\ *n* -s [ME *gerland, garland*, fr. MF *garlande*, fr. OF, perh. of Gmc origin; akin to MHG *wieren* to adorn, OHG *wiara* fine gold — more at WIRE] **1 a :** a wreath, chaplet, or coronet worn as a mark of distinction: as (1) *obs* **:** a royal crown ⟨till Richard wear the ~ of the realm —Shak.⟩ (2) **:** a wreath awarded to a hero or to the victor in ancient games ⟨where one gaineth a ~ of bays, hundreds have had a wreath of hemp —Thomas Fuller⟩ **b :** a mark of esteem or affection **:** ACCOLADE ⟨so beloved a . . . minister that he held one charge for 40 years and was retired with ~s —A.W.Long⟩ **c** *obs* **:** a person who is highly prized **:** JEWEL ⟨call him noble that was now your hate, him vile that was your ~ —Shak.⟩ **2 :** a headband of gold, silver, precious stones, or other costly material ⟨a dazzling ~ of diamonds for the hair —A.P.Herbert⟩ **3 :** a wreath or festoon of leaves or flowers to be worn on the head or used to decorate an object ⟨crowned the May queen with a ~⟩ ⟨laid a ~ of oak leaves at the foot of the statue⟩ **4 :** something that resembles a garland: as **a :** an object that reminds one of a wreath or festoon ⟨~s of lights on the ferries —Brooks Atkinson⟩ **b** (1) **:** a grommet or ring of rope used for various purposes aboard ship (2) *archaic* **:** a band of rope, iron, or wood used on ships or in shore batteries to hold shot in place **c :** a carved wreath serving as a decorative motif ⟨an ornate fireplace carved in oak with . . . high-relief ~s and swags —H.S.Morrison⟩ **d :** a heraldic wreath of laurel or of oak leaves and acorns **e :** a strip of cotton cloth or burlap used in military camouflaging to thicken overhead cover or to conceal edges of a net ⟨tie ~s of colored cloth onto a fishnet to make it resemble foliage —Carl Mann⟩ **5 :** a collection of extracts **:** ANTHOLOGY ⟨several of these essays make up a kind of friendship's ~ —Willard Thorp⟩; *esp* **:** a chapbook containing ballads or songs
²**garland** \"\ *vt* -ED/-ING/-S [ME *garlanden*, fr. *garland*, n.] **1 :** to form into a garland ⟨thine are these early wilding flowers though ~*ed* by me —P.B.Shelley⟩ **2 a :** to crown with or as if with a garland ⟨~*ed* his shaggy head with roses —P.B.Kyne⟩ ⟨goose stealers sat in the stocks ~*ed* with goose wings —S.P.B.Mais⟩ **b :** to confer an accolade upon ⟨~*ed* as a brilliant leader after the first Battle of Bull Run —A.W.Long⟩ **3 :** to surround or deck with or as if with a garland **:** ENGARLAND ⟨~ the crowns of profile hats —Lois Long⟩ ⟨one of the devices of the modern camoufleur is the use of nets ~*ed* with strips of burlap —*Newsweek*⟩
garland chrysanthemum *n* **:** a European herb (*Chrysanthemum coronarium*) with white or yellowish flowers
garland crab *n* **:** AMERICAN CRAB APPLE
garland dance *n* **:** a folk dance in which the dancers carry garlands
garland flower *n* **1 :** BUTTERFLY LILY **2 :** a widely cultivated low evergreen shrub (*Daphne cneorum*) with fragrant pink to rose-red flowers in dense terminal clusters **3 :** a heath (*Erica persoluta*) of southern Africa
gar·land·less \-n(d)ləs\ *adj* **:** lacking a garland
gar·lic \'gärlik, 'gȧl-, -lēk\ *n* -s *often attrib* [ME *garlek*, fr. OE *gārlēac*, fr. *gār* spear + *lēac* leek — more at GORE, LEEK] **1 :** any of several plants of the genus *Allium; esp* **:** a European bulbous herb (*A. sativum*) now widely naturalized elsewhere **2 :** the bulb of the garlic plant which has a strong and persistent odor and taste, is composed of a number of smaller bulbs, and is used as a condiment — see ¹CLOVE
garlic bread *n* **:** slices of French or Italian bread spread with garlic-seasoned butter and heated in the oven until crisp
garlic germander *n* **:** WATER GERMANDER
gar·licky \-ləkē, -ki\ *adj* [*garlic* + *-y*] **1 :** resembling or containing garlic ⟨~ wheat⟩ **2 :** smelling or tasting of garlic ⟨~ breath⟩ ⟨~ stew⟩
garlic mustard *n* **:** a European herb (*Alliaria officinalis*) that smells like garlic — called also *hedge garlic*
garlic oil *n* **:** a yellowish essential oil that has a strong odor of garlic and that is obtained by steam distillation of garlic and used in flavoring
garlic pear *or* **garlic pear tree** *n* **:** a tree (*Crataeva gynandra*) of Jamaica that bears a fruit with a scent of garlic and a burning taste
garlic salt *n* **:** a seasoning consisting of ground dried garlic and salt
garlic shrub *n* **:** either of two plants the bruised foliage of which smells like garlic: **a :** a tropical American woody vine (*Adenocalymna alliaceа*) of the family Bignoniaceae **b :** GUINEA-HEN WEED
gar·lion \'gärlyən\ *n* -s [*garlic* + *onion*] **:** a hybrid vegetable resulting from a cross between garlic and onion
¹**gar·ment** \'gärmənt, 'gȧm-\ *n* -s *often attrib* [ME *garment, garnement*, fr. MF *garnement, garniment* article of clothing or armor, fr. OF, fr. *garnir* to equip, prepare + *-ment* — more at GARNISH] **1 a :** an article of outer clothing (as a coat or dress) usu. exclusive of accessories **b :** an article of underclothing; *specif* **:** FOUNDATION GARMENT ⟨a ~ that gives you the bust and waistline contours the new fashions demand —*McCall's*⟩ **2 :** the outward dress in which something is seen ⟨clothe his ideas in a ~ of reality —Bertrand Russell⟩ ⟨our birch in its spring ~ —Richard Semon⟩
²**garment** \"\ *vt* -ED/-ING/-S **:** to clothe with or as if with a garment — used chiefly in past participle ⟨went about oddly ~*ed* —W.J.Ghent⟩ ⟨~*ed* in high poetry —G.C.Sellery⟩
gar·ment·less \-ləs\ *adj* **:** lacking a garment
¹**garn** \'gärn\ *n* -s [ME, fr. ON — more at YARN] *dial Eng* **:** YARN
²**garn** \"\ *v imper* [alter. of *go on*] *Brit.* — used interjectionally to express disbelief or ridicule
¹**gar·ner** \'gärnər, 'gȧnə(r\ *n* -s [ME *garner, gerner*, fr. OF *gernier, grenier*, fr. L *granarium*, fr. *granum* grain + *-arium* -ary — more at CORN] **1 a :** a building in which grain is stored **:** GRANARY **b :** a bin for the storage of grain; *specif* **:** a bin in a grain elevator in which grain is collected for weighing **c :** something that resembles a garner ⟨you may be gathered into the ~ of mortality before me —Sir Walter Scott⟩ **2 :** something that is collected **:** ACCUMULATION ⟨makes an entirely fresh ~ each year —Donald Davidson⟩
²**garner** \"\ *vb* -ED/-ING/-S [ME *garneren*, fr. *garner*, n.] *vt* **1 a :** to gather into a granary **:** STORE ⟨the new crop was not yet ~*ed* and the last year's grain was getting low —Willa Cather⟩ **b :** to deposit as if in a granary ⟨volumes in which he has ~*ed* the fruits of his lifetime labors —Reinhold Niebuhr⟩ **2 a :** to acquire as the result of effort **:** EARN, REAP ⟨~ financial support from business circles —W.J.Jorden⟩ ⟨~s publicity by floating through the air from a flying trapeze beneath a helicopter —*Newsweek*⟩ **b :** to pick up **:** ACCUMULATE, COLLECT ⟨~*ed* the spoils with an all-encompassing rake —Sidney Warren⟩ ⟨~*ed* a fine array of folk songs —Julian Dana⟩ ~ *vi* **:** to become stored **:** ACCUMULATE ⟨wrath that ~s in my heart —Alfred Tennyson⟩ **syn** see REAP
garnering *n* -s [fr. gerund of ²*garner*] **:** something that has been garnered ⟨did add their ~s to their nests —E.A.Armstrong⟩
¹**gar·net** \'gärnət, 'gȧn-, usu -əd·+V\ *n* -s [ME *gernet, grenat*, fr. MF *grenat*, fr. OF, fr. *grenat*, adj., red like a pomegranate, fr. *grenate* (in *pome grenate* pomegranate) — more at POMEGRANATE] **1 :** a brittle and transparent to subtransparent silicate mineral of the general formula $R_3''R_2'''(SiO_4)_3$ in which R″ may be calcium, magnesium, ferrous iron, or manganese and R‴ aluminum or some other trivalent element having a vitreous luster and usu. red color, occurring mainly in crystals but also massive and in grains, found commonly in gneiss and mica schist, and used as a semiprecious stone and as an abrasive (hardness 6.5–7.5, sp. gr. 3.15–4.3) **2 :** a variable color averaging a dark red that is yellower and duller than cranberry, bluer and duller than pomegranate, and bluer, stronger, and very slightly darker than average wine
²**garnet** \"\ *n* -s [ME *garnett*] **:** GARNET HINGE
³**garnet** \"\ *n* -s [ME *garnett*] **1 :** a tackle usu. rigged on the mainstay of a sailing ship for hoisting cargo in or out **2 :** CLEW GARNET
garnetberry \'≈≈- — *see* BERRY\ *n* **:** a common red currant (*Ribes rubrum*) grown in gardens
garnet brown *n* **:** a dark red to moderate reddish brown that is redder than wallflower
garnet cloth *n* **:** a cloth similar to garnet paper in preparation and uses
garnet hinge *n* [²*garnet*] **:** a hinge with an upright bar and a horizontal strap
gar·net·if·er·ous \ˌ≈nədˈif(ə)rəs\ *adj* **:** containing garnets ⟨~ schist⟩
garnet lac *n* **:** lac refined by treating with a solvent and marketed in irregularly shaped pieces having a garnet color
garnet paper *n* **:** paper covered with crushed garnet on one side and used as an abrasive and polisher
garnet red *n* **:** a dark to deep red that is bluer and slightly darker than chrysanthemum
¹**gar·nett** \(ˈ)gärˈnet\ *n* -s [prob. fr. the name *Garnett*] **1 a :** a machine of the breaker type used to remove foreign matter from fiber (as wool) before carding **b :** a similar machine used to reduce textile waste to fibrous form **2 :** the waste produced by the operation of a garnett machine
²**garnett** \"\ *vt* -ED/-ING/-S **:** to remove foreign substances from (fiber) or to reduce (textile waste) to fiber by passing through a machine provided with garnett wire
garnett wire *n* **:** a steel ribbon with teeth for use in the spiral groove of a cylinder on a garnett
gar·ni \gärˈnē\ *adj* [F, past part. of *garnir* to garnish, equip, prepare] **:** GARNISHED
gar·ni·er·ite \'gärnēəˌrīt, gärˈniˌr-\ *n* -s [Jules *Garnier* †1904 Fr. geologist + E *-ite*] **:** a soft mineral prob. $(Mg,Ni)_3Si_2O_5(OH)_4$ consisting of hydrous nickel magnesium silicate having an earthy luster and an apple-green or pale green color, having no crystal structure, and constituting an important ore of nickel (sp. gr. 2.3–2.8)
¹**gar·nish** \'gärnish, 'gȧn-, -nēsh, *esp in pres part* -nəsh\ *vt* -ED/-ING/-ES [ME *garnishen* to embellish, equip., fr. MF *garniss-*, stem of *garnir* to garnish, equip, prepare, arn, of Gmc origin; akin to OHG *wernen* to refuse, *warnōn* to take heed — more at WARN] **1 a :** to make fancy or striking **:** EMBELLISH ⟨a very handsome demi-peaked saddle . . . ~*ed* with a double row of silver-headed studs —Laurence Sterne⟩ ⟨the heroism of the men of the Alamo needs no ~*ing* —*Amer. Guide Series: Texas*⟩; *specif* **:** to add garlands to (a camouflage net) **b :** to add decorative or savory touches to (food) ⟨the chef had ~*ed* her entree with Chinese vegetable leaves —Thomas Gallagher⟩ **2 a** *obs* **:** to equip or arm (oneself) ⟨~*ed* for the chase —William Shenstone⟩ **b :** to equip for use **:** FURNISH ⟨huge stone fireplaces ~*ed* with shining copper warming pans and cooking utensils —Richard Joseph⟩ **3 :** GARNISHEE **syn** see ADORN
²**garnish** \"\ *n* -ES [ME, fr. *garnishen*, v.] **1 :** a set of flatware (as of pewter) **2 a :** something added for decoration **:** EMBELLISHMENT ⟨coat with a ~ of fur⟩ ⟨after-dinner speeches that have a ~ of humor⟩ **b :** a decorative or flavorful adjunct to a dish prepared for the table ⟨~ of parsley⟩ **3 a :** an unauthorized fee (as drink money for the other prisoners)

GEMS

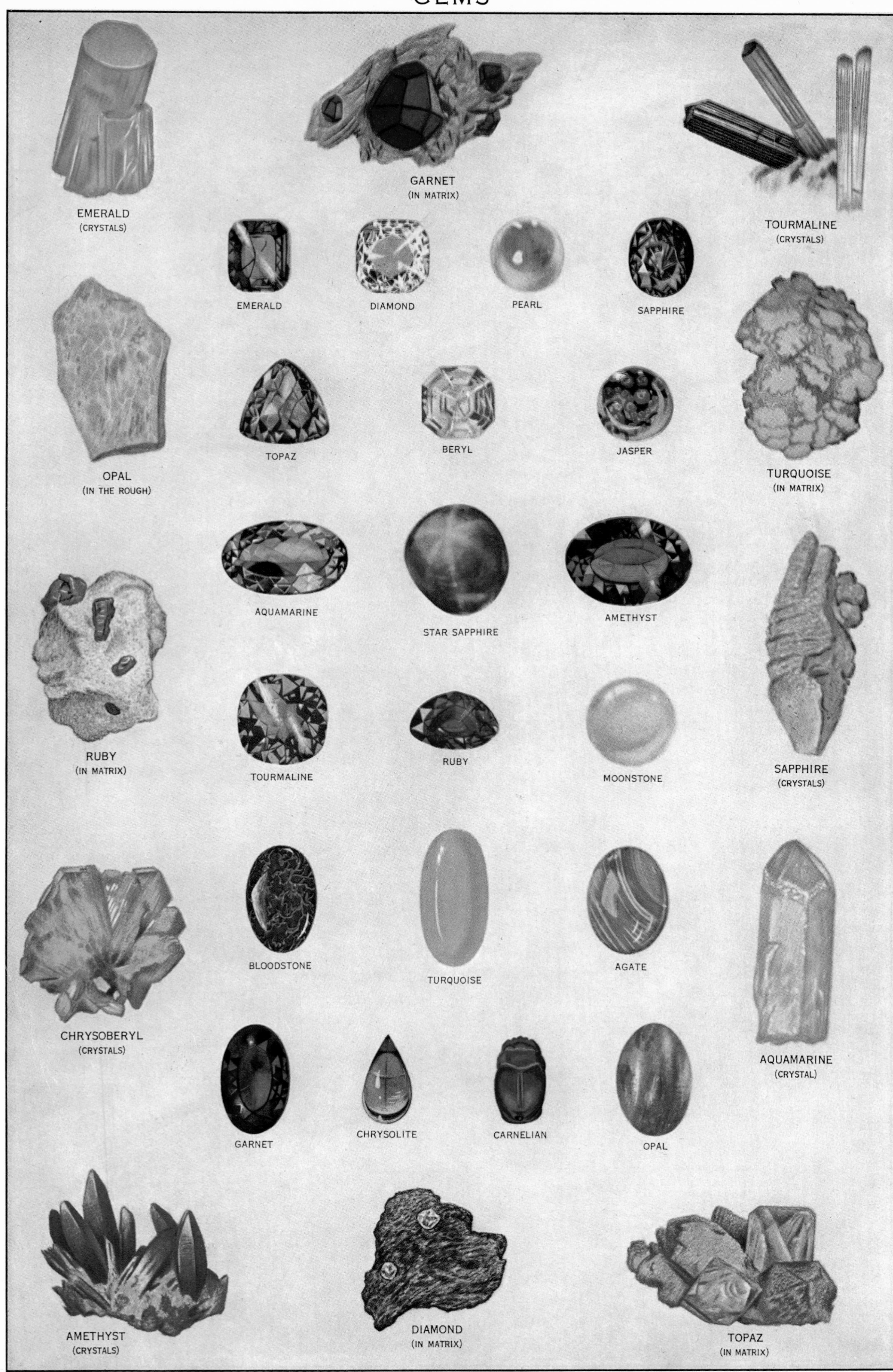
EMERALD
(CRYSTALS)
GARNET
(IN MATRIX)
TOURMALINE
(CRYSTALS)
EMERALD
DIAMOND
PEARL
SAPPHIRE
OPAL
(IN THE ROUGH)
TOPAZ
BERYL
JASPER
TURQUOISE
(IN MATRIX)
AQUAMARINE
STAR SAPPHIRE
AMETHYST
RUBY
(IN MATRIX)
TOURMALINE
RUBY
MOONSTONE
SAPPHIRE
(CRYSTALS)
BLOODSTONE
TURQUOISE
AGATE
CHRYSOBERYL
(CRYSTALS)
GARNET
CHRYSOLITE
CARNELIAN
OPAL
AQUAMARINE
(CRYSTAL)
AMETHYST
(CRYSTALS)
DIAMOND
(IN MATRIX)
TOPAZ
(IN MATRIX)

gas grenade *n* : a grenade containing gas in liquid form which is released by the bursting of the grenade

¹**gash** \ˈgash, -aa(ə)sh,-aish\ *vb* -ED/-ING/-ES [alter. of ME *garsen*, fr. ONF *garser* to scarify, wound, fr. (assumed) VL *charissare*, fr. Gk *charassein* to sharpen, cut into furrows, engrave, carve — more at CHARACTER] *vt* **1** : to make a gash in : cut or disrupt the surface of ⟨turpentiners who ~ the southern pines⟩ ⟨the knife slipped and ~*ed* his finger⟩ ⟨moldboard plows ~*ing* the prairie⟩ **2** : to rough-mill or rough-hob (the teeth of a gear wheel) preparatory to finish-machining ~ *vi* : to make a gash : CUT, SLASH ⟨blades that ~ and tear⟩

²**gash** \"\ *n* -ES [alter. of ME *garse*, fr. *garsen*, v.] **1 a** : a deep long cut esp. in flesh ⟨came out of the wreck bruised and shaken and with a long ~ over one eye⟩ **b** : a deep narrow depression in land whether natural (as a gorge or cleft between rocks) or made by man (as in road building) **c** : the female pudenda : an object of male sexual desire; *also* : SEXUAL INTERCOURSE — usu. considered vulgar **2** : an act or instance of gashing ⟨gave the sack a ~ with his knife so that flour ran over the ground⟩

³**gash** \"\ *adj* [origin unknown] *archaic Scot* : dismal or grim in appearance

⁴**gash** \"\ *adj* -ER/-EST [origin unknown] **1** *chiefly Scot* : KNOWING, SHREWD, WITTY, SHARP **2** *chiefly Scot* : having a fine appearance or air : well dressed : TRIM **3** *Scot* : TALKATIVE

⁵**gash** \"\ *vi*, *Scot* : to chatter idly : PALAVER

⁶**gash** \"\ *n* -ES *Scot* : empty talk : CHITCHAT

⁷**gash** \"\ *n* -ES [origin unknown] *slang* : extra food (as a second helping or leftovers); *often* : the garbage remaining after a meal ⟨all ~ should be burned or buried⟩

gas helmet *n* : GAS MASK

gash fracture *n* : a rock fracture due to tension and therefore tending to remain open — opposed to *shear fracture*

gash·ful \ˈgashfəl\ *adj* [alter. (influenced by ²*gash*) of *ghastful*] *now dial Brit* : GHASTLY, FRIGHTFUL

gasholder \ˈ≈,≈\ *n* : a container for gas; *esp* : a large gastight cylindrical or spherical tank for storing combustible gases for use as fuel

gashouse \ˈ≈,≈\ *n* : GASWORKS; *sometimes* : a building in which gas is made (as for heating or illumination)

gash vein *n* : a vein resulting from the filling and sometimes enlargement of a joint or crack that does not extend beyond the stratum in which it occurs

gashy \ˈgashē\ *adj* -ER/-EST : resembling or having a gash

gasholder (simple type): *a,a*, steel structure to guide cylindrical gas tank, *b*, in rising or falling through contact with wheels, *c,c,c,c*; *d,d*, masonry or steel tank containing water, *e*; *f* inlet, *g* outlet, gas pipes

gas·i·fi·ca·tion \,gasəfəˈkāshən\ *n* -S : an act or a process of gasifying (as of a fuel) ⟨~ of coal by burning or by reaction with oxygen and superheated steam⟩

gas·i·fi·er \ˈgasə,fī(ə)r\ *n* -S : an apparatus for manufacturing gas (as synthesis gas from coal)

gas·i·form \-,fȯrm\ *adj* [¹*gas* + *-iform*] : in the form of gas : GASEOUS

gas·i·fy \-,fī\ *vb* -ED/-ING/-ES [¹*gas* + *-ify*] *vt* : to convert (a solid or liquid) into gas (as by heat or a chemical process) ~ *vi* : to become gaseous ⟨liquid ammonia *gasifies* readily⟩

gas jet *n* : a flame of illuminating gas; *also* : GAS BURNER ⟨ill-kept glass box lit by a small *gas jet* —W.J.Locke⟩

¹**gas·ket** \ˈgaskət, -aas-,-ais-, *usu* -əd·+V\ *n* -S [prob. alter. of F *garcette*, fr. OF, girl, dim. of *garce* girl, prostitute, fr. *gars, garz, garçon* boy, servant, wretch, scoundrel — more at GARÇON] **1** : a line or band used to lash a furled sail securely — see HARBOR GASKET, SEA GASKET **2 a** : plaited hemp or tallowed rope for packing pistons or for making pipe joints or other joints fluid-tight **b** : packing for the same purpose made of rubber, asbestos, metal, or other elastic material usu. in the form of sheets or rings — see SPARK PLUG illustration **c** : a separate or attached sealer used in making and closing hermetic or liquid containers to ensure tightness

²**gasket** \"\ *vt* -ED/-ING/-S **1** : to fasten (a sail) with a gasket **2** : to seal (as mechanical parts) fluid-tight by means of a gasket

¹**gas·kin** \ˈgaskən\ *n* -S [prob. short for *galligaskin*] **1** *obs* : HOSE, BREECHES **2** : a part of the hind leg of a horse or other quadruped between the stifle and the hock — see HORSE illustration

²**gaskin** \"\ *also* **gas·king** \-kiŋ\ *n* -S [by alter.] : GASKET

gas lamp *n* : a lamp burning illuminating gas; *esp* : one on a public way

gas law *n* : any of several statements of physics and chemistry relating to the behavior of gases: as **a** : BOYLE'S LAW **b** : CHARLES'S LAW **c** : a statement that the product of the pressure and volume of one mole of a gas equals the product of the gas constant by the absolute temperature (as expressed by the equation $pv=RT$) — called also *ideal-gas law*; compare VAN DER WAALS'S EQUATION

gas·less \ˈ≈ləs\ *adj* : having no gas : using or producing no gas

gas lift *n* : the flowing of oil from a well due to natural-gas pressure or to pressure of gas forced into the well by pumping

gaslight \ˈ≈,≈\ *n, often attrib* **1** : light yielded by the combustion of illuminating gas ⟨the mellow radiance of ~⟩ **2** : a gas jet or gas burner; *also* : GAS LAMP — **gaslighted** \ˈ≈,≈≈\ *adj*

gas–lighting \ˈ≈,≈≈\ *n* : lighting by means of gaslight

gaslight paper *n* : a slow developing-out photographic paper

gas lime *n* : hydrated lime that has been used in purifying gas, contains other compounds (as calcium carbonate, calcium sulfide), and is used as a land dressing

gas liquor *n* : ammonia liquor obtained in the manufacture of coal gas or coke-oven gas

gaslit \ˈ≈,≈\ *adj* : illuminated by gaslight

gas log *n* : a hollow perforated imitation of a log used as a gas burner in a fireplace

gas·man \ˈ≈,man, -aa(ə)n\ *n, pl* **gasmen** **1** : one connected with the distribution, installation, or sale of gas: as **a** : a producer or manufacturer of gas for heating or illumination **b** : a supervisor of the gas lamps formerly used for theatrical illumination **c** : GAS FITTER **d** : a person who tests or reads gas meters **e** : a worker who operates units that produce fuel gas **2** : FIRE BOSS

gas mask *n* : a close-fitting facepiece connected to a canister through which all air breathed is drawn to protect the respiratory tract and face against irritating and poisonous gases : RESPIRATOR

gas meter *n* : an instrument for recording the quantity of gas passing through a particular outlet

gas·o·gene \ˈgasə,jēn\ *or* **gaz·o·gene** \-azə-\ *also* **gas·o·gen** \-asəjən, -jen\ *n* -S [F *gazogène*, fr. *gaz* gas (fr. NL *gas*) + *-o-* + *-gène* -gen — more at GAS] **1 a** : an apparatus for attachment to a vehicle (as an automobile) that produces a combustible gas for a motor fuel by partial burning esp. of charcoal or wood **b** : the motor fuel produced by a gasogene **2** : a portable apparatus for carbonating liquids

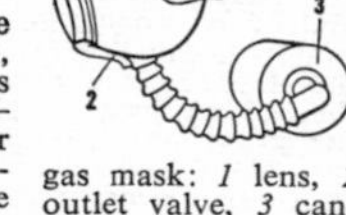

gas mask: *1* lens, *2* outlet valve, *3* canister

gas oil *n* : any of various hydrocarbon oils used esp. formerly for making oil gas or carbureted water gas and now used chiefly as diesel oils, fuel oils, or feedstock for cracking operations; *specif* : a petroleum distillate intermediate in boiling range and viscosity between kerosine and lubricating oil

gas·o·lier *also* **gas·e·lier** \,gasəˈli(ə)r, -iə\ *n* -S [*gasolier* alter. of *gaselier*; *gaselier* fr. ¹*gas* + *-elier* (as in *chandelier*)] : a chandelier equipped with gaslights

gas·o·line *also* **gas·o·lene** \,ga|səˈlēn, ,gaa|, ,gai|, ˈ≈≈,≈ *sometimes* |zə-\ *n* -S [¹*gas* + *-ol* + *-ine* or *-ene*] : a volatile flammable liquid hydrocarbon mixture suitable for use as a fuel esp. for internal-combustion engines and now consisting usu. of a blend of several products from natural gas and petroleum (as natural gasoline, straight-run gasoline, cracked gasoline, alkylates) or of products from other sources (as from the hydrogenation of coal gas or water gas) together with antiknock agents, antioxidants, or other additives — called also *petrol*; compare NAPHTHA — **gasolinic** *adj*

gasoline–electric \ˈ≈≈,≈≈ˈ≈≈\ *adj* : propelled by electricity furnished from an engine generator driven by gasoline or oil

gasoline engine *n* : an internal-combustion engine having its piston driven by explosions of a mixture of air and vapor of gasoline or other volatile fuel ignited by an electric spark

gas·o·line·less \,≈≈ˈ≈ləs, ˈ≈≈,≈-\ *adj* : having no gasoline; *often* : characterized by restriction or prohibition of the sale or use of gasoline ⟨~ Sundays during the war⟩

gasoline pump *n* : a filling-station unit that meters and supplies gasoline to motor vehicles

gas·o·lin·er \,≈≈ˈlēnə(r), ˈ≈≈,l-\ *n* -S : a powerboat with a gasoline engine

gas·om·e·ter \gaˈsämədˑə(r) *sometimes* -ˈzä-\ *n* [F *gazomètre*, fr. *gaz* gas + *-o-* + *-mètre* -meter] **1** : a laboratory apparatus (as a graduated glass tube or bottle with inlet and outlet tubes fitted with stopcocks) for holding and measuring gases **2** : GASHOLDER

gas·o·met·ric \ˌgasəˈme·trik *sometimes* ˌgazə-\ *adj* [¹*gas* + *-o-* + *-metric*] : of or relating to the measurement of gases (as in chemical analysis) — **gas·o·met·ri·cal·ly** \-rək(ə)lē\ *adv*

gas–operated \ˈ≈ˈ≈≈,≈≈\ *adj, of an automatic or autoloading weapon* : utilizing part of the powder gases to operate the action

¹**gasp** \ˈgasp, -aa(ə)sp, -aisp, -ȧsp\ *vb* -ED/-ING/-S [ME *gaspen*; akin to ON *geispa* to yawn & perh. to OE *geonian* — more at YAWN] *vi* **1** : to catch the breath convulsively and audibly often as an expression of shock, concern, or emotion ⟨he ~*ed* as he stepped into the icy water⟩ ⟨~*ing* with surprise as he saw the new house⟩ **2** : to breathe laboriously with open mouth : pant strongly and audibly ⟨the exhausted runner threw himself down and ~*ed*⟩ ⟨a dying man ~*ing* for breath⟩; *broadly* : to become completely exhausted ⟨a handful of hypertrophied capitalists ~*ing* under the load of their growing millions —G.B.Shaw⟩ **3** : to make a sound like that of a gasped breath ⟨cans ~*ed* under the knives —W.W.Haines⟩ ⟨the engine ~*ed*, caught, and settled into a smooth purr⟩ ~ *vt* : to emit or utter with gasps ⟨she ~*ed* a shocked denial⟩ — often used with *forth, out, away* ⟨he ~*ed* out a plea for mercy⟩

²**gasp** \"\ *n* -S : an act of gasping or a gasping utterance

gas packing *n* : packing (as of a food) in an airtight container in which the air has been replaced by an oxygen-free gas to prevent oxidative deterioration of the stored product

gasp·er \-pə(r)\ *n* -S **1** : one that gasps **2** *slang Brit* : CIGARETTE

gas·per·eau \ˈgaspə,rō\ *n* -S [CanF *gaspareau, gasparot*, fr. F *gasparot*, a kind of herring] *Canad* : ALEWIFE 1 a

gas·per·gou \ˈgaspə(r)ˌgü\ *n* -S [LaF *casburgot, casseburgau*, fr. F dial *casse-burgot*, a kind of fish, fr. *casser* to break + *burgau*, a kind of shellfish — more at QUASH] : FRESHWATER DRUM — used chiefly in Louisiana

gasp·i·ness \ˈgaspēnəs\ *n* -ES : the quality or state of being gaspy ⟨reduced to breathless ~ by the climb⟩

gasping disease *n* : INFECTIOUS BRONCHITIS 1

gasp·ing·ly *adv* **1** : in a gasping manner ⟨read her lines ~⟩ **2** : with great or excessive responsiveness ⟨~ ardent attention⟩ ⟨~ enthusiastic⟩

gas pipe *n* **1** : a pipe for conveying gas **2** : something resembling a gas pipe (as a single-barreled shotgun)

gas plant *n* : FRAXINELLA

gas plate *n* **1** : a hot plate using gas **2** : a steel plate in a gun breech mechanism resting in a recess in the face of the breechblock and supporting the obturator ring

gas pliers *n pl* : stout pliers designed for gripping small pipe, rods, or other round objects

gas pool *n* : a continuous area of sedimentary rocks that when drilled yields natural gas in commercial quantities

gas port *n* : a small hole in the barrel of a gas-operated rifle for allowing sufficient controlled escape of gas to insure proper functioning

gas producer *n* : PRODUCER 3

gasproof \ˈ≈ˈ≈\ *adj* : proof against the entry or damaging action of gases ⟨a ~ compartment⟩ ⟨~ varnishes⟩

gaspy \ˈgaspē\ *adj* -ER/-EST : marked by or given to gasping ⟨a tense ~ voice⟩

gas refrigeration *n* : refrigeration that involves the use of machinery in which the refrigerant is heated by a gas flame

gas retort *n* : ³RETORT 1b

gas ring *n* **1** : an obturator ring **2** : a ring-shaped portable gas burner with stand and sometimes a handle

gas sand *n* : a sandstone or other rock containing natural gas

gassed *past of* GAS

gas·ser \ˈgasə(r), ˈgaas-,ˈgais-\ *n* -S **1** : one that gasses: as **a** : a well (as an oil well) that yields gas **b** *slang* : a talkative or bragging person **c** : a worker who singes cloth, yarn, or thread **2** *slang* : something outstanding of its kind ⟨the new show is a real ~⟩

gas·se·ri·an ganglion \(ˈ)gaˈsirēən-\ *n, sometimes cap 1st G* [Johann L. Gasser †1765 Austrian anatomist + E *-ian*] : the large flattened sensory root ganglion of the trigeminal nerve lying within the skull and behind the orbit — called also *semilunar ganglion*

gasses *pl of* GAS, *pres 3d sing of* GAS

gas shell *n* : GAS BOMB

gas·si·ness \ˈgasēnəs, ˈgaas-,ˈgais-, -sin-\ *n* -ES : the quality or state of being gassy

gassing *n* -S [fr. gerund of ²*gas*] **1** : an act or process of causing something to interact with gas **2 a** : the deliberate or inadvertent poisoning of persons exposed to noxious gases or fumes **b** : the destruction of pests (as insects) by the use of poisonous gases (as hydrogen cyanide or methyl bromide) : FUMIGATION **3** : the evolution of gas bubbles from the acid in a lead storage battery while charging

gas spurt *n* : one of the little heaps that occur on the surface of certain geological strata containing organic matter and that are believed to be due to the escape of gas during early formative stages of the strata

gas station *n* : FILLING STATION

gas storage *n* : storage of fruits or vegetables in an atmosphere high in carbon dioxide and low in oxygen to delay ripening

gas·sy \ˈgasē, ˈgaas-,ˈgais-, -si\ *adj* -ER/-EST [¹*gas* + *-y*] **1 a** : full of or containing gas **b** *of a vacuum tube* : defective by reason of accumulated gas developed in service from structural components **2** : having the characteristics of gas ⟨a ~ odor⟩ **3** : full of boastful or insincere talk : INFLATED, WINDY ⟨a ~ speaker⟩ ⟨~ oratory⟩

¹**gast** *vt* -ED/-ING/-S [ME *gasten*, fr. *gast, gost* soul, spirit, ghost — more at GHOST] *obs* : SCARE ⟨~*ed* by the noise I made, full suddenly he fled —Shak.⟩

²**gast** \ˈgäst\ *n* -S *Scot* : a state of fright or alarm

³**gast** \"\ *adj* [akin to OFris *gēst, gâst* high, dry, barren, MLG *gēst* high dry land near the sea, OSw *gistiun* cracked open from dryness, and perh. to OE *geonian* to yawn — more at YAWN] *dial Eng* : BARREN — used of a domestic animal

gas·tal·do \gəˈstäl(,)dō\ *n, pl* **gastal·di** \-(,)dē\ [It *castaldo, gastaldo*, fr. ML *castaldus, gastaldus*, fr. a Lombard word akin to OE *gesteald* abode, fr. *ge-* (perfective & collective prefix) + *-steald* (akin to OE *stealdan* to possess); akin to OHG *hagustalt* day laborer, bachelor, Goth *gastaldan* to acquire, possess, OE *steall* place, position, stall — more at STALL] **1** : the representative of a king on his domains in medieval Italy esp. among the Lombards **2** : a steward in a nobleman's household

gas tank *n* **1** : a tank for the storage of natural or manufactured gas **2** : the fuel tank supplying a gasoline engine

gas·ter \ˈgastə(r)\ *n* -S [NL, fr. Gk *gastēr* belly — more at GASTRIC] : the enlarged part of the abdomen behind the pedicel in ants and other hymenopterous insects

gaster- *or* **gastero-** *comb form* [NL, fr. Gk *gastero-* belly, fr. *gaster-, gastēr*] **1** : ventral area ⟨*Gastero*poda⟩ ⟨*gastero*stome⟩ **2** : stomach ⟨*gaster*algia⟩ ⟨*Gastero*philus⟩

-gaster \ˈgastə(r), ˌgaas-, ˌgais-\ *n comb form* -S [NL, fr. Gk *gastēr*] **1** : part having a (specified) relation to the stomach ⟨meso*gaster*⟩ ⟨meta*gaster*⟩ **2** : organism having a (specified) type of digestive tract — esp. in generic names ⟨Micro*gaster*⟩ ⟨myxo*gaster*⟩

gas·te·ria \gaˈstirēə\ *n* [NL, fr. *gaster-* + *-ia*] **1** *cap* : a genus of usu. stemless southern African plants (family Liliaceae) having thick succulent leaves arranged in two ranks or a rosette and long racemes of scattered largely greenish flowers, being closely related to the aloes, growing in desert regions, and including several plants that are cultivated as ornamentals in warm dry regions or in the greenhouse **2** -S : any plant of the genus *Gasteria*

gas·tero·lichenes \ˌgastə(,)rō+\ *n pl, cap* [NL, fr. *gaster-* + *Lichenes*] *in some classifications* : a group of angiocarpous lichens in which the fungus is a gasteromycete

gas·tero·my·cete \"+ˌmīˈsēt *or* ˌmī,s-\ *n* -S [NL *Gasteromycetes*] : a fungus of the class Gasteromycetes : a basidiomycete with basidia and spores enclosed in a peridium — **gas·tero·my·ce·tous** \-ˈēd·əs\ *adj*

gas·tero·my·ce·te·ae \"+ˌmīˈsēd·ē,ē\ [NL, fr. *gaster-* + *-mycetes* + *-eae*] *syn of* GASTEROMYCETES

gas·tero·my·ce·tes \ˌgastə(,)rō,mīˈsēd·(,)ēz\ *n pl, cap* [NL, fr. *gaster-* + *-mycetes*] *in some classifications* : a class or subclass of fungi including all basidiomycetes with the basidia and spores enclosed in a peridium (as the puffballs and stinkhorns)

gas·tero·phil·i·dae \ˌgastə(,)rōˈfiləˌdē\ *n pl, cap* [NL, fr. *Gasterophilus*, type genus + *-idae*] : a family of two-winged flies comprising the horse botflies, resembling honeybees in size and proportions, and having the adult mouthparts vestigial and the antennae sunken in facial grooves

gas·ter·oph·i·lo·sis \ˌgastə,räfəˈlōsəs\ *n, pl* **gasterophiloses** \-ō,sēz\ [NL, fr. *Gasterophilus* + *-osis*] : infestation with horse botflies

gas·ter·oph·i·lus \-ˈräfələs\ *n, cap* [NL, fr. *gaster-* + *-philus*] : a genus of botflies containing one form (*G. intestinalis*) that commonly infests the horse

gas·ter·o·pod \ˈgast(ə)rə,päd\ *adj or n* [NL *Gasteropoda*, syn. of *Gastropoda*, fr. *gaster-* + *-poda*] : GASTROPOD

¹**gas·ter·os·te·id** \ˌgastəˈrästēəd\ *adj* [NL *Gasterosteidae*] : of or relating to the Gasterosteidae

²**gasterosteid** \"\ *n* -S : a fish of the family Gasterosteidae : STICKLEBACK

gas·ter·o·ste·idae \ˌgastərōˈstēəˌdē\ *n pl, cap* [NL, fr. *Gasterosteus*, type genus (fr. *gaster-* + *osteus*) + *-idae*] : a family of small spiny-finned freshwater or salt-water fishes that consists of the sticklebacks and constitutes with related forms a suborder of Scleroparei or is placed with the cornetfishes and pipefishes in the order Solenichthyes — **gas·ter·os·te·i·form** \ˌgastəˈrästēə,fȯrm\ *adj* — **gas·ter·os·te·oid** \-stē,ȯid\ *adj*

gas·ter·o·sto·ma·ta \ˌgastərōˈstōməd·ə\ *n pl, cap* [NL, fr. *Gasterostomum* genus of trematode worms (fr. *gaster-* + *-stomum*) + *-ata*] *in some classifications* : an order of Digenea coextensive with the family Bucephalidae — compare PROSOSTOMATA

gas·ter·o·stome \ˈgastərō,stōm\ *n* -S [NL *Gasterostomata*] : a trematode of the family Bucephalidae

gast·haus \ˈgäst,haůs\ *n, pl* **gasthauses** \-haůzəz\ *or* **gast·häus·er** \-hȯizə(r)\ [G, fr. OHG *gasthūs*, fr. *gast* guest + *hūs* house — more at GUEST, HOUSE] : a German inn or tavern

gas thermometer *n* : a thermometer containing gas (as hydrogen) as the enclosed thermometric substance, variations in temperature being indicated by the change in pressure of a fixed quantity of gas required to maintain the gas at a constant volume or the change in volume of a fixed quantity of gas maintained at a constant pressure

gastight \ˈ≈ˈ≈\ *adj* **1** : impervious to gas **2** : constructed or arranged so that gas (as a noxious or flammable gas) will not enter an enclosed space under specified conditions (as of pressure) — **gas·tight·ness** *n*

gastness *n* -ES [ME *gastnesse*, fr. *gast* afraid (fr. past part. of *gasten* to frighten) + *-nesse* -ness — more at GAST] *obs* : FRIGHT, DREAD

gas·tor·nis \gaˈstȯrnəs\ *n, cap* [NL, fr. Gaston Planté †1889 Fr. physician + Gk *ornis* bird — more at ERNE] : a genus of large extinct birds (order Diatrymiformes) from the Eocene formations of the Paris basin that are similar and related to those of the genus *Diatryma*

gastr- *or* **gastro-** *also* **gastri-** *comb form* [Gk, belly, fr. *gastr-, gastēr* — more at GASTRIC] **1** : ventral area ⟨*gastro*pod⟩ **2** : stomach ⟨*gastr*ectomy⟩ ⟨*gastro*logy⟩ **3** : gastric and ⟨*gastro*duodenal⟩ ⟨*gastro*hepatic⟩

gas·traea *also* **gas·trea** \gaˈstrēə\ *n* -S [NL, fr. Gk *gastr-, gastēr* belly] : a hypothetical metazoan ancestral form corresponding in organization to a simple invaginated gastrula — **gas·trae·al** \(ˈ)gaˈstrēəl\ *adj*

gas·trae·adae \gaˈstrēə,dē\ *n pl, cap* [NL, irreg. fr. *Gastraea* + *-idae*] : a hypothetical group of ancestral metazoan animals structurally comparable to the gastrula

gas·tral \ˈgastrəl\ *adj* [*gastr-* + *-al*] : of or relating to the stomach or digestive tract ⟨the ~ cavity of a sea anemone —C.L.Prosser⟩

gas·tral·gia \gaˈstralj(ē)ə\ *n* -S [NL, fr. *gastr-* + *-algia*] : pain in the stomach or epigastrium esp. of a neuralgic type — **gas·tral·gic** \(ˈ)gaˈstraljik\ *adj*

gas·tra·li·um \gaˈstrālēəm\ *n, pl* **gastra·lia** \-ēə\ [NL, fr. *gastr-* + L *-alis* -al + NL *-ium*] **1** : ABDOMINAL RIB **2** : a spicule located immediately beneath the inner cellular wall of a sponge

gas trap *n* **1** : a drain trap : sewer trap **2** : an apparatus for separating natural gas from the petroleum in which it is dissolved

gas·trec·to·my \gaˈstrektəmē\ *n* -ES [ISV *gastr-* + *-ectomy*] : surgical removal of all or part of the stomach

-gastria \ˈgastrēə\ *n comb form* -S [NL, fr. *gastr-* + *-ia*] : condition of having (such) a stomach or (such or so many) stomachs ⟨micro*gastria*⟩ ⟨poly*gastria*⟩

gas·tric \ˈgastrik, -aas-,-ais-, -rēk\ *adj* [Gk *gastr-, gastēr* belly, paunch, womb (alter. of — assumed — Gk *grastēr*, fr. Gk *gran* to gnaw, eat) + E *-ic* — more at CRESS] **1** : of, relating to situated near, or originating in the stomach ⟨~ disorders⟩ **2** : resembling a stomach in form or function ⟨a ~ polyp⟩ ⟨a ~ vacuole⟩

gastric artery *n* **1** : a branch of the coeliac artery that passes to the cardiac end of the stomach and along the lesser curvature **2** : any of several branches of the splenic artery distributed to the greater curvature of the stomach

gastric cecum *n* : one of the elongated pouches projecting from the upper end of the insect stomach

gastric gland *n* : any of various glands in the walls of the stomach that secrete the gastric juice

gastric juice *n* : the digestive fluid secreted by the glands in the mucous membrane of the stomach consisting of a thin watery fluid with an acid reaction because of the presence of 0.2 to 0.4 percent of free hydrochloric acid and containing several enzymes (as pepsin and rennin)

gastric mill *n* : a grinding apparatus consisting of several movable calcareous or chitinous pieces in the pharynx or stomach of certain invertebrates

gastric ostium *n* : the opening leading into a gastric pouch in scyphozoans

gastric pouch *n* : any of the pouched radial divisions of the stomach in scyphozoans

gastric ulcer *n* : a peptic ulcer situated in the stomach

gas·tril·e·gous \(ˈ)gaˈstriləgəs\ *adj* [*gastr-* + L *legere* to gather + E *-ous* — more at LEGEND] : gathering pollen by means of a pollen brush on the abdomen ⟨~ bees⟩ — compare PODILEGOUS

gas·tril·o·quist \gaˈstriləkwəst\ *n* -S [*gastr-* + *-loquist* (as in *ventriloquist*)] : VENTRILOQUIST

gas·trin \ˈgastrən\ *n* -S [ISV *gastr-* + *-in*] : a hormone that is produced chiefly in the antrum of the stomach, induces secretion of gastric juice, and may be identical with histamine

formerly extorted from a new inmate by the keeper of an English jail **b :** a similar payment required of a workman in celebration of his first job
gar·nish·able \-shəbəl\ *adj* **:** suitable for being garnished
garnished *adj* [ME, fr. past part. of *garnishen* to garnish] **1 :** EQUIPPED, EMBELLISHED **2** *heraldry* **:** TRIMMED, ADORNED, DECORATED — used with either specification of a tincture or name of an adornment ⟨four batons argent ~ azure⟩ ⟨a ring ~ with a sapphire⟩
¹gar·nish·ee \ˌ≈nəˈshē\ *n* -s [¹*garnish* + *-ee*] **:** one who is served with a garnishment
²garnishee \"\ *vt* **garnisheed; garnisheed; garnisheeing; garnishees 1 :** to serve with a garnishment **2 :** to attach (the wages or other property belonging to a debtor)
garnishee order *n* **:** an order served upon a person by way of garnishment
gar·nish·er \ˈ≈nishə(r), -nēsh-\ *n* -s **:** one that garnishes
gar·nish·ment \ˈ≈nishmənt, -nēsh-\ *n* -s [MF *garnissement* equipment & AF *garnissement* legal garnishment, fr. OF *garnissement* equipment, fr. *garniss-, garnisse-* (stem of *garnir*) + *-ment*] **1 :** GARNISH **2 :** a legal notice concerning the attachment of property to satisfy a debt: as **a :** a summons to a third party to appear in court and answer to the suit of the plaintiff to the extent of his liability to the defendant **b :** a warning to a person holding property belonging to a debtor not to deliver it to him pending the outcome of litigation **3 :** a legal proceeding begun by the service of a garnishment **4 :** a stoppage of a specified sum from wages to satisfy a creditor
gar·nish·ry \-nəshrē\ *n* -ES [*garnish* + *-ry*] **:** DECORATION ⟨saw in the stars mere ~ of heaven —Robert Browning⟩
gar·ni·ture \-nəchə(r), -nēch-, -ˌchu(ə)r, -ˌtu̇ə\ *n* -s [MF *garniture* equipment, alter. of OF *garneture, garnesture,* fr. *garnir*] **1 :** something that equips or furnishes ⟨mantelpiece ~⟩; *specif* **:** the material in fireworks that produces stars, fiery rain, or other display after explosion **2 a :** an accessory of dress **:** TRIMMING **b :** a decorative accessory **:** ORNAMENT; *specif* **:** a usu. ceramic set of objects designed for use on a mantel or cabinet top ⟨dessert services and mantel ~*s* —*N.Y.Times*⟩ **3 :** GARNISH 2
garns *pl of* GARN
ga·ro \ˈgä(ˌ)rō\ *n, pl* **garo** *or* **garos** *usu cap* **1 a :** a Mongoloid people of the Garo hills, Assam **b :** a member of such people **2 :** the Sino-Tibetan language of the Garo people
ga·roo \ˈgä(ˌ)rü, gəˈrü\ *n* -s [Malay *gaharu*] **:** AGALLOCH
ga·roo·kuh \gəˈrükə\ *n* -s [origin unknown] **:** a short-keeled fishing boat used in the Persian gulf
garotte *var of* GARROTE
garpike \ˈ≈ˌ≈\ *n* **:** ³GAR c
garran *var of* GARRON
gar·ra·pa·ta \ˌgarəˈpäd·ə\ *n* -s [Sp] **:** TICK; *esp* **:** CATTLE TICK
garred *past of* GAR
¹gar·ret \ˈgarət *also* ˈger-, *usu* -əd·+V\ *n* -s [ME *garette, garite* watchtower, fr. MF *garite* watchtower, place of refuge, perh. modif. of OProv *garida,* fr. *garir* to protect, of Gmc origin; akin to OHG *werien* to defend — more at WEIR] **1 a :** an unfinished part of a house immediately under or within the roof **:** LOFT — compare ATTIC 1c ⟨new college edifice . . . three stories and ~ in height —H.S.Morrison⟩ **b :** a room on the top floor of a house ⟨lives a recluse in a ~ —R.L.Stevenson⟩ **2** *slang* **:** a person's head **:** UPPER STORY
²garret \"\ *vt* -ED/-ING/-s [prob. by alter.] **:** GALLET
gar·re·teer \ˌgarəˈti(ə)r, -rəd·ˈi-\ *n* -s *archaic* **:** one that lives in a garret; *esp* **:** a literary hack
gar·rick \ˈgarik\ *n* -s [origin unknown] **:** LEERFISH
garrigue *var of* GARIGUE
garring *pres part of* GAR
¹gar·ri·son \ˈgarəsən *also* ˈger-\ *n* -s *often attrib* [ME *garisoun* protection, treasure, stronghold, fr. OF *garison* protection, provisions, fr. *garir* to protect, of Gmc origin; akin to OHG *werien* to defend] **1 :** a place of security **:** STRONGHOLD; *specif* **:** GARRISON HOUSE **2 a :** a place in which troops are quartered **:** MILITARY POST; *esp* **:** a permanent military installation **b :** a group of people associated with a military installation ⟨the ~ is small, consisting largely of expert workmen employed in the machine shops —*Amer. Guide Series: Texas*⟩; *specif* **:** a body of troops stationed at a military post ⟨a colony of Moors left as ~ by the old-time Turkish government —G.W.Murray⟩ **c :** something that resembles a defensive stronghold ⟨storming Conservative ~*s* with his Liberal dervishes —V.L.Albjerg⟩ **d :** a place that is used as a military stronghold ⟨Berlin . . . has become a ~ of the Allies —Eric Linklater⟩ — **in garrison** *usu.* manning a usu. permanent military post
²garrison \"\ *vt* -ED/-ING/-s **1 :** to furnish with soldiers **:** supply (a military post) with troops for defense ⟨a small stockaded Fort Sackville was built but not permanently ~*ed* —T.R.Hay⟩ **2 a :** to assign as a garrison **:** STATION ⟨did not ~ any troops in Manchuria —H.E.Abend⟩ **b :** to secure or defend by manning with troops **:** OCCUPY ⟨these three areas are the strategic heart of Europe and there can be no real peace or relaxation of tension as long as . . . troops ~ them —H.W. Baldwin⟩ **3 a :** to cause to serve in a garrison ⟨petty duties that become tragedies to ~*ed* soldiers —*Combat Forces Jour.*⟩ **b :** to furnish living quarters for (a garrison) **:** ACCOMMODATE ⟨temporary sheet-iron buildings . . . capable of ~*ing* about 1500 soldiers —*Amer. Guide Series: La.*⟩
garrison backstay *n* **:** a broad piece of leather covering the back seam of a shoe and extending forward on each side to the breast of the heel
garrison cap *n* **:** a visorless folding textile cap worn as part of a military uniform ⟨all officers wear grade insignia on the left side of *garrison caps* —*Nat'l Geographic*⟩ — compare SERVICE CAP
garrison court-martial *n* **:** a military court for the trial of other than capital offenses now superseded by the special court-martial — compare COURT-MARTIAL

garrison cap

gar·ri·son finish \ˈga|rəsən- *also* ˈge|\ *n, usu cap G* [prob. after Snapper *Garrison,* 19th cent. Am. jockey who came from behind to win the Suburban Handicap in 1892] **:** an unexpected last-minute victory in a contest ⟨another *Garrison finish:* . . . drop-kicked a field goal in the last 40 seconds —*Time*⟩ ⟨hard put to pay for his "whistle stop" campaign . . . but money flowed in from somewhere for his last week's *Garrison finish* —Ray Tucker⟩
garrison flag *n* [¹*garrison*] **:** the largest size of national flag used by the U.S. army and flown on national holidays and special occasions — compare HOLIDAY FLAG
garrison house *n* **1 :** a fortified house with thick protective walls used by American settlers as a protection against Indian attack **2 :** BLOCKHOUSE **3 :** a house (as of colonial times) having the second story overhanging the first in the front elevation
gar·ri·so·nian \ˌgarəˈsōnēən, -ōnyən *also* ˌger-\ *or* **gar·ri·son·ite** \ˈ≈≈səˌnīt\ *n* -s *usu cap* [William Lloyd *Garrison* †1879 Am. abolitionist + E *-ian* or *-ite*] **:** an advocate of direct emancipation of slaves in America without compensation to their owners
gar·ri·son·ism \ˈ≈≈səˌnizəm\ *n* -s *usu cap* [William L. *Garrison* †1879 + E *-ism*] **:** the principles or doctrines of the Garrisonians
garrison prisoner *n* **:** a prisoner at a military post or garrison charged with an offense not entailing dismissal or dishonorable discharge — compare GENERAL PRISONER
garrison ration *n* **:** the food allowance for one soldier for one day used as the basis for calculating the money credit to be allotted a company commander to purchase food for his men
garrison state *n* **:** a centralized state dominated by military rather than by civilian personnel and policies; *esp* **:** one whose military preparations threaten to convert it into a totalitarian state — compare POLICE STATE
gar·ron *or* **gar·ran** \ˈgarən, ˈger-\ *n* -s [IrGael *gearrān* gelding, horse & ScGael *gearran* gelding, fr. MIr *gerrān* gelding, fr. *gerraim* I cut; akin to Skt *hrasva* short — more at CHRESTOMATHY] **1** *Scot & Irish* **:** a small sturdy work horse **2** *Scot & Irish* **:** an old broken-down worn-out horse
ˈr·rot \gäˈrō\ *n, pl* **garrots** \-ō(z)\ [F] **:** GOLDENEYE 1
·rote *or* **gar·rotte** *also* **garotte** \gəˈrä|t, gaˈr-, -ˈrō|, \| *also* ˈgerə|, *usu* |d·+V\ *n* -s [Sp *garrote* club, garrote, prob. fr. MF *garrot* heavy wooden projectile] **1 a :** a Spanish method of execution by means of an iron collar affixed to a post and tightened by a screw until the victim is strangled **b :** the instrument with which the execution is effected ⟨before each turn of the *garrotte* the Greek was ordered to tell the truth —W.S.Maugham⟩ **2 a :** strangulation as if with the garrote esp. with robbery as the motive **b :** an implement (as a length of piano wire with wooden handles) used for this purpose
²garrote *or* **garrotte** *also* **garotte** \"\ *vt* **garroted** *or* **garrotted** *also* **garotted; garroted** *or* **garrotted** *also* **garotted; garroting** *or* **garrotting** *also* **garotting; garrotes** *or* **garrottes** *also* **garottes 1 :** to execute with or as if with a garrote ⟨the rule now is to ~ culprits within the walls of the prison —*Westminster Gazette*⟩ **2 :** to seize by the throat from behind in order to strangle and rob ⟨men . . . who would rather ~ a traveler than anything else in the world —Nicholas Monsarrat⟩
gar·rot·er *or* **gar·rot·ter** \-d·ə(r), -tə-\ *n* -s **:** one that garrotes
gar·ru·li·ty \gəˈrüləd·ē, gaˈ-,ge'-, -ətē, -i *sometimes* gərˈyü- *or* garˈyü- *or* gerˈyü-\ *n* -ES [MF or L; MF *garrulité,* fr. L *garrulitat-, garrulitas,* fr. *garrulus* + *-itat-, -itas* -ity] **:** the quality or state of being garrulous **:** LOQUACITY, TALKATIVENESS, GARRULOUSNESS
gar·ru·lous \ˈgarələs *also* ˈger- *or* -ryə-\ *adj* [L *garrulus,* fr. *garrire* to babble, chatter — more at CARE] **1 a :** given to conversation **:** LOQUACIOUS, TALKATIVE ⟨~ . . . when talking of war or of his own experiences —C.S.Forester⟩ **b :** characterized by long-winded or diffuse statements **:** WORDY ⟨all day ~ speeches had echoed from the tribune —*Newsweek*⟩ **c :** full of rambling detail **:** CHATTY ⟨this delightfully ~ volume of memoirs —*Book-of-the-Month Club News*⟩ **2 :** suggestive of or having the effect of loquacity ⟨~ chattering of birds⟩ ⟨ruins . . . ~ of better days —John Ruskin⟩ **syn** see TALKATIVE
gar·ru·lous·ly *adv* **:** in a garrulous manner
gar·ru·lous·ness *n* -ES **:** the quality or state of being garrulous **:** GARRULITY
gar·ru·lus \-ləs\ *n, cap* [NL, fr. L, garrulous] **:** a large genus of Old World jays including the common jay of Britain and Europe
gar·ru·pa \gəˈrüpə\ *n* [Pg *garoupa* — more at GROUPER (fish)] **1** -s **:** a grouper esp. in Spanish America **2** -s **:** a Californian rockfish **3** *cap* [NL, fr. Pg *garoupa*] **:** a genus of Serranidae comprising the black jewfish
gar·rya \ˈgarēə\ *n, cap* [NL, fr. Nicholas *Garry,* 19th cent. official of Hudson's Bay Co.] **:** a genus of evergreen shrubs and small trees (family Cornaceae) with coriaceous opposite leaves and small dioecious flowers that are borne in silky racemes which resemble catkins and are pistillate with two stipes — see BEAR BRUSH, GARRYACEAE
gar·ry·a·ce·ae \ˌgarēˈāsēˌē\ *n pl, cap* [NL, fr. *Garrya,* type genus + *-aceae*] *in some classifications* **:** a family of dicotyledonous plants coextensive with the genus *Garrya*
gar·ry oak \ˈgarē-\ *n, usu cap G* [after Nicholas *Garry*] **:** OREGON OAK
gars *pres 3d sing of* GAR, *pl of* GAR
garse \ˈgärs\ *archaic var of* GRASS
garshuni *usu cap, var of* KARSHUNI
gar·sil \ˈgärsəl\ *n* -s [ME *garsell,* of Scand origin; akin to OSw *gærthsl* fencing material, Norw dial. *gjerdsl;* suffixal derivative fr. the verb represented by OSw *gærtha* to fence in, denominative fr. the noun represented by ON *garthr* yard — more at YARD] *dial Eng* **:** UNDERBRUSH
gar·ten \ˈgärtᵊn\ *n* -s [by alter.] *Scot* **:** GARTER ⟨wear yellow ~*s* —P.M.Preston⟩
¹gar·ter \ˈgär|d·ər, ˈgȧ|d·ə(r, |tə-\ *n* -s [ME, fr. ONF *gartier,* fr. *garet, garret* bend of the knee, hock, of Celt origin; akin to W *gar* shank, OIr *gairri* calves (of the legs)] **1 a :** a circular band of elastic with or without a fastener worn to hold up a stocking or sock — called also *suspender* **b :** a strap of elastic hanging from a girdle, corset, or belt and having a fastener to support a stocking **c :** a circular band of elastic worn over a shirt sleeve to regulate its length — called also *arm garter, sleeve garter* **2** *usu cap* **a :** the distinguishing badge of Great Britain's Order of the Garter consisting of a strip of dark blue velvet edged with gold, having a buckle and pendant of gold, and worn below the left knee by men and on the left arm by women **b :** membership in the Order of the Garter ⟨he declined the offer of the *Garter*⟩ **c :** GARTER KING OF ARMS **d :** a circular band borne on the collar, badge, and star and about the armorial escutcheon of a member of the Order of the Garter that is inscribed with the motto of the Order and merges at its bottom into a representation of the buckle and free end as they appear when the garter is worn buckled in the prescribed manner — compare CIRCLET 1c **3 :** a wavy band that resembles a heraldic garter and is incorporated into an emblem or seal usu. to carry a motto ⟨the U.S. shield, encircled with a ~ bearing the words *E Pluribus Unum* —Elizabeth W. King⟩ **4 :** a tape or streamer held for a circus performer to leap over **5 :** GARTER SNAKE

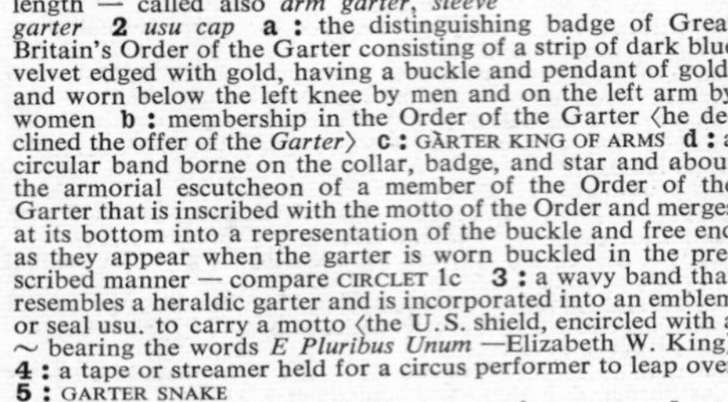

garters 1

²garter \"\ *vt* -ED/-ING/-s [ME *garteren,* fr. *garter,* n.] **:** to fasten with or as if with a garter ⟨see to ~ his hose —Shak.⟩
garter belt *n* **:** a woman's undergarment consisting of a relatively narrow band of fabric to which long garters are attached for the support of stockings — called also *suspender belt*
garter-blue \ˈ≈≈ˈ≈\ *adj* **:** of a dark blue resembling the ribbon of the Knights of the Garter
gartered *adj* [fr. past part. of ²*garter*] **1 :** having garters **2 :** invested with the badge of the Order of the Garter **3 :** surrounded or supplied with a heraldic garter
garter king of arms *usu cap G&K&A* **:** the highest-ranking king of arms in the English College of Arms who has concurrent jurisdiction with the provincial kings of arms in their respective provinces and who also is king of arms of the Order of the Garter — compare CLARENCEUX KING OF ARMS, NORROY AND ULSTER KING OF ARMS, NORROY KING OF ARMS
gar·ter·less \-ə(r)ləs\ *adj* **:** lacking a garter
garter mission *n, usu cap G&M* **:** a mission by a delegation headed by the Garter King of Arms to confer the Order of the Garter on a foreigner
garter snake *n* **1 :** any of numerous widely distributed active viviparous harmless American colubrid snakes constituting the genus *Thamnophis* and having more or less distinct longitudinal stripes on the back **2 :** any of several venomous African ringed elapid snakes of the genera *Elapsoidea* and *Elaps* related to the New World coral snakes
garter spring *n* **:** a spiral steel spring formed into a closed elastic ring
garter stitch *n* **:** a pattern of horizontal ridges formed by knitting both sides of a fabric instead of knitting one side and purling the other

garter stitch

¹garth \ˈgärth\ *n* -s [ME, fr. ON *garthr* yard — more at YARD] **1 a** *archaic* **:** a small yard or enclosure **:** CLOSE **b :** CLOISTER GARTH **2 :** a dam or weir for catching fish
²garth \"\ *dial Eng var of* GIRTH
gärtner's duct *n, usu cap G* [after Hermann T. *Gärtner* †1827 Dan. anatomist] **:** DUCT OF GAERTNER
garvanzo *var of* GARBANZO
gar·vey \ˈgärvē\ *n* -s [prob. fr. the name *Garvey*] **:** a small scow of the New Jersey coast
gar·vie \ˈgärvi\ *n* -s [origin unknown] *Scot* **:** SPRAT
gary \ˈga(a)rē, ˈger-,ˈgär-, -ri\ *adj, usu cap* [fr. *Gary,* Indiana] **:** of or from the city of Gary, Indiana ⟨*Gary* steel mills⟩ **:** of the kind or style prevalent in Gary
¹gas \ˈgas, -aa(ə)s, -ais\ *n, pl* **gases** *also* **gasses** *often attrib* [NL, alter. of *chaos* air, fr. L, chaos — more at CHAOS] **1 :** a fluid (as air) that has neither independent shape nor volume but tends to expand indefinitely **:** a substance at a temperature above its critical temperature and therefore not liquefiable by pressure alone — compare KINETIC THEORY, PERMANENT GAS, STATE OF AGGREGATION; LIQUID 1, VAPOR 2 **2 a :** a gas or gaseous mixture with the exception of atmospheric air — not used scientifically **b :** a gas or gaseous mixture (as laughing gas or ethylene) used to produce anesthesia **c :** a combustible gaseous mixture (as for fuel or illumination) ⟨heated his house with ~⟩ — see LIQUEFIED PETROLEUM GAS, MANUFACTURED GAS, NATURAL GAS **3 :** a substance (as a war gas or tear gas) whether gaseous, liquid, or solid under ordinary conditions that can be used to produce a poisonous, asphyxiating, or irritant atmosphere — compare SMOKE 1b **4** *slang* **:** empty boasting talk **:** BOMBAST, HUMBUG, NONSENSE **5 a :** GASOLINE **b :** the accelerator of a gasoline-powered vehicle ⟨had the ~ to the floor most of the way⟩
²gas \"\ *vb* **gassed; gassed; gassing; gasses** *vt* **1 :** to affect or treat with gas: as **a :** SINGE 1b **b :** to subject to the action of gas ⟨fruit *gassed* with ethylene⟩; *sometimes* **:** to injure or cause to deteriorate by the action of gas **c :** to poison or asphyxiate with a gas esp. in warfare **d :** to cause (as a metal) to absorb gas **2** *slang* **:** to address gas to **:** deceive or befuddle with idle boasting talk **3 :** to supply with gas or esp. gasoline — often used with *up* ⟨decided to ~ up the car the night before they were to start⟩ ~ *vi* **1 :** to give off gas (as of a storage battery during charging or a molten metal during cooling) ⟨the new well *gassed* for several days before oil appeared⟩ **2** *slang* **:** to indulge in idle, garrulous, or boastful talk **:** chat idly or casually ⟨stopped in to ~ with the boys⟩ **3 :** to fill the tank (as of a car, airplane, or motor) with gasoline — often used with *up* ⟨stop and ~ up on the way back⟩
³gas *pl of* GA
gasal *var of* GHAZEL
gas attack *n* **:** a military attack in which gas is used as a weapon
gas bacillus *n* **:** any of several bacteria that form gas in wounds infected with them (esp. *Clostridium perfringens* syn. *C. welchii*)
gasbag \ˈ≈ˌ≈\ *n* **1 :** a bag for holding gas: as **a :** a bag inserted empty into a gas or other line and inflated to serve as a temporary plug (as during repair or alteration) **b :** one of the gas-filled bags or a single such bag making up the inflated buoyant envelope of an airship or balloon; *broadly* **:** AIRSHIP, BALLOON **2** *slang* **:** a person given to idle boastful talk **:** one that gasses
gas black *n* **:** CHANNEL BLACK
gasboat \ˈ≈ˌ≈\ *n* **:** a boat powered by a gasoline motor; *esp* **:** one using a converted automobile engine
gas bomb *n* **:** a military explosive projectile filled with noxious gas that is usu. liquefied under pressure and released when the projectile explodes — called also *gas shell*
gas buoy *n* **:** a metal buoy filled with a compressed illuminating gas and surmounted by a lantern where a light fed by the gas burns night and day
gas burner *n* **:** a nozzle or a set of openings through which combustible gas escapes and burns
gas carbon *n* **:** carbon in a dense form deposited on the interior of a gas retort
gas cell *n* **:** a cell containing a gas electrode
gas chamber *n* **:** a chamber in which prisoners are executed by poisonous gas
gascheck \ˈ≈ˌ≈\ *n* **1 :** a device in a gun or chemical projector that prevents escape of gas **2 :** a small copper cup fitted to the base of a lead bullet for small arms to prevent the melting of the base at the temperatures and pressures created by high-velocity smokeless powder
gas checking *n* **:** a frosty wrinkled appearance of some coatings (as various tung-oil varnishes) caused by exposure to gas fumes
gas coal *n* **:** a coal used for making gas by distillation ordinarily being a caking bituminous coal
gas coke *n* **:** coke made in a gas retort as distinguished from that made in a coke oven
gas company *n* **:** a utilities company supplying gas
¹gas·con \ˈgaskən, -aas-, -ais-\ *n* -s *usu cap* [ME *Gascoun,* fr. MF *gascon*] **1 a :** a native or inhabitant of Gascony **b :** a boastful swaggering person **2 :** a Romance speech of the area between the Garonne river and the Pyrenees that is sometimes classified as a dialect of Provençal but that is in some respects more closely allied to Aragonese and Catalan **3 :** a common widely distributed saurel (*Trachurus trachurus*)
²gascon \"\ *adj* **1** *usu cap* **a :** of, relating to, or characteristic of Gascony in southwestern France **b :** of, relating to, or characteristic of the people of Gascony **2** *usu cap* **:** of, relating to, or characteristic of the Gascon language **3 :** BRAGGART, SWAGGERING
¹gas·con·ade \ˌ≈skəˈnād\ *n* -s [F *gasconnade,* fr. *gasconner* to boast (fr. *gascon* boaster, Gascon) + *-ade*] **:** BOAST, BOASTING, BRAVADO
²gasconade \"\ *vi* -ED/-ING/-s **:** to boast or bluster esp. to excess **:** show off by lauding oneself or one's accomplishments **:** BRAG **syn** see BOAST
gas·con·ad·er \-də(r)\ *n* -s **:** one that gasconades **:** BRAGGART, SHOW-OFF
gas·con·ism \ˈgaskəˌnizəm\ *n* -s *often cap* [¹*Gascon* + *-ism*] **:** a bombastic boastful way or spirit **:** BRAVADO
gas constant *n* **:** a general constant in the equation of state of gases that is equal in the case of an ideal gas to the product of the pressure and volume of one mole divided by the absolute temperature — see GAS LAW c
gas cutting *n* **:** the cutting of a preheated metal by a jet of oxygen
gas disease *n* **:** a disorder of fishes marked by formation of gas bubbles in the tissues and body fluids and occurring when the tension of gases becomes higher in the body fluids than in the surrounding water
gas edema *n* **:** any of several diseases (as blackleg or malignant edema) found in mammals and marked by crepitating gassy swelling of the tissues
gas·e·i·ty \gaˈsēəd·ē\ *n* -ES [*gaseous* + *-ity*] **:** GASEOUSNESS
gas-electric \ˈ≈ˌ≈ˈ≈\ *adj* **:** GASOLINE-ELECTRIC
gas electrode *n* **:** an electrode consisting of a conductor covered with a gas
gaselier *var of* GASOLIER
gas engine *n* **:** an internal-combustion engine similar to a gasoline engine but using natural or manufactured gas instead of gasoline vapor; *broadly* **:** INTERNAL-COMBUSTION ENGINE
gas·e·ous \ˈga|sēəs, ˈgaa|, |sh(y)əs, *Brit often* ˈgāziəs *or* ˈgāsi-\ *adj* [¹*gas* + *-eous*] **1 a :** having the form of or being gas ⟨~ matter⟩ **:** of or relating to gases ⟨~ laws⟩ ⟨~ content⟩ **b :** SUPERHEATED ⟨use of ~ steam in industrial boilers⟩ **2 :** lacking substance or solidity **:** TENUOUS ⟨unconnected, ~ information —James Stephen⟩
gaseous diffusion *n* **:** diffusion of gases through a porous barrier at a rate of speed in direct proportion to the weight of the molecules, being used as the basis of a method of separating isotopes (as fissionable uranium 235 from the nonfissionable uranium 238)
gas·e·ous·ness *n* -ES **:** the quality or state of being gaseous; *often* **:** EFFERVESCENCE
gases *pl of* GAS
gas field *n* **:** a district where natural gas is produced in commercial quantities
gas-filled tube \ˈ≈ˌ≈-\ *n* **:** GAS TUBE
gas-fired \ˈ≈ˈ≈\ *adj* **:** heated by the combustion of gaseous fuel ⟨*gas-fired* furnace⟩
gas fitter *n* **:** a workman who installs or repairs gas pipes and appliances
gas fitting *n* **1 :** the trade or occupation of a gas fitter **2 a gas fittings** *pl, archaic* **:** the equipment (as piping, valves, and meters) conveying gas from the main to the fixtures of an individual installation **b :** one of the pipe fittings of a gas-supply installation
gas fixture *n* **:** a device for conveying illuminating or combustible gas from the pipe to the gas burner
gas gangrene *n* **:** progressive gangrene marked by impregnation of the dead and dying tissue with gas and caused by one or more toxin-producing clostridia that enter the body through wounds and proliferate in necrotic tissue
gas generator *n* **:** an apparatus for generating gas: as **a :** a laboratory apparatus (as a Kipp generator) for the production of carbon dioxide, hydrogen, chlorine, or other gases **b :** GENERATOR 2b
gas gland *n* **:** a glandular structure that secretes a gas (as the oxygen-releasing mechanism of a fish's air bladder)

gas·tri·tis \ga'strīd·əs\ *n, pl* **gastrit·i·des** \-rid·ə,dēz\ [NL, fr. *gastr-* + *-itis*] **:** inflammation of the stomach esp. of its mucous membrane
gastro- — see GASTR-
gas·tro·anastomosis \¦ga(,)strō+\ *n* [NL, fr. *gastr-* + *anastomosis*] **:** the formation by surgical means of a communication between the pyloric and cardiac ends of the stomach when the normal channel is obstructed or contracted
gas·tro·blast \'gastrə,blast\ *n* [*gastr-* + *-blast*] **:** a nutritive zooid of a tunicate colony
gas·tro·cen·tral \¦gastrō¦sen·trəl\ *or* **gas·tro·cen·trous** \-rəs\ *adj* [*gastr-* + *central* or *-centrous* (fr. NL *centrum* + E *-ous*)] **1 :** having the centrum formed of the interventral elements **2 :** having gastrocentral vertebrae ⟨~ reptiles⟩
gas·tro·chae·na \,==¦kēnə\ *n, cap* [NL, fr. *gastr-* + *-chaena* (fr. Gk *chainein* to yawn, gape) — more at YAWN] **:** a genus of bivalve mollusks (order Eulamellibranchia) that bore in coral, soft rock, or hardened mud and have long siphons and a widely gaping shell
gas·trocne·mi·al \¦gastrō¦nēmēəl, -,sträk¦n-\ *adj* [NL *gastrocnemius* + E *-al*] **:** of or relating to the gastrocnemius
gas·trocne·mi·us \,==¦mēəs\ *n, pl* **gastrocne·mii** \-mē,ī\ [NL, fr. Gk *gastroknēmē* calf of the leg, fr. *gastro-* belly + *knēmē* shin, leg — more at GASTR-] **:** the largest and most superficial muscle of the calf of the leg arising by two heads from the condyles of the femur and having its tendon of insertion united with that of the soleus to form the Achilles' tendon
gas·tro·coel *also* **gas·tro·coele** \'gastrō,sēl\ *n* -S [F *gastrocèle*, fr. *gastr-* + *-cèle* -coele] **:** ARCHENTERON
gas·tro·colic \¦gastrō+\ *adj* [ISV *gastr-* + *colic*] **:** of, relating to, or uniting the stomach and colon ⟨~ ligament⟩
gastrocolic omentum *n* **:** GREATER OMENTUM
gas·tro·dermal \"+\ *adj* [NL *gastrodermis* + E *-al*] **:** of, relating to, or consisting of gastrodermis
gas·tro·dermis \"+\ *n* [NL, fr. *gastr-* + *-dermis*] **:** the lining membrane of the alimentary tract of an invertebrate — used esp. when the germ-layer origin is obscure
gas·tro·dis·coi·des \,==də'skȯi(,)dēz\ *n, cap* [NL, fr. *gastr-* + LL *discoides* quoit-shaped — more at DISCOID] **:** a genus of amphistome trematode worms including a common intestinal parasite (*G. hominis*) of man and swine in southeastern Asia
gas·tro·duodenal \¦ga(,)strō+\ *adj* [ISV *gastr-* + *duodenal*] **:** of, relating to, or involving both the stomach and duodenum ⟨a ~ ulcer⟩
gas·tro·duodenitis \"+\ *n* [NL, fr. *gastr-* + *duodenitis*] **:** inflammation of the stomach and duodenum
gas·tro·enteric \"+\ *adj* [*gastr-* + *enteric*] **:** GASTROINTESTINAL
gas·tro·enteritis \"+\ *n* [NL, fr. *gastr-* + *enteritis*] **:** inflammation of the lining membrane of the stomach and the intestines
gas·tro·en·ter·ol·o·gist \,ga(,)strō,ent·ə'räləjəst\ *n* -S **:** a specialist in gastroenterology; *specif* **:** a physician specializing in the diagnosis and treatment of gastrointestinal disorders
gas·tro·en·ter·ol·o·gy \-jē\ *n* -ES [ISV *gastr-* + *enter-* + *-logy*] **:** the study of the stomach and the intestines esp. in respect to their diseases and pathology
gas·tro·en·ter·os·to·my \-ästəmē\ *n* [ISV *gastr-* + *enterostomy*] **:** the surgical formation of a passage between the stomach and small intestine
gas·tro·epiploic artery \¦ga(,)strō+ . . . -\ *n* [*gastr-* + *epiploic*] **:** either of two arteries forming an anastomosis along the greater curvature of the stomach, the right being derived from the gastroduodenal artery and the left from the splenic artery
gas·tro·esophageal \"+\ *adj* [*gastr-* + *esophageal*] **:** of, relating to, or involving the stomach and esophagus
gas·tro·gen·ic \¦gastrə¦jenik\ *or* **gas·trog·e·nous** \(')ga¦sträjənəs\ *adj* [*gastr-* + *-genic*, *-genous*] **:** of gastric origin **:** being due to causes originating in the stomach ⟨~ anemia⟩
gas·tro·intestinal \¦ga(,)strō+\ *adj* [*gastr-* + *intestinal*] **1 :** of, relating to, consisting of, or involving both stomach and intestine ⟨~ inflammation⟩ **2 :** of or from the gastrointestinal tract ⟨the ~ wall⟩ ⟨~ absorption⟩
gastrointestinal tract *n* **:** the stomach and intestine as a functional unit
gas·tro·jejunal \"+\ *adj* [*gastr-* + *jejunal*] **:** of, relating to, or involving both stomach and jejunum ⟨~ lesions⟩
gas·tro·jejunostomy \"+\ *n* [ISV *gastr-* + *jejunostomy*] **:** the surgical formation of a passage between the stomach and jejunum **:** GASTROENTEROSTOMY
gas·tro·lith \'gastrə,lith\ *n* -S [ISV *gastr-* + *-lith*] **1 a :** CRAB'S-EYE 1 **b :** a stone or pebble found in the stomach of some fishes and reptiles and presumably used for grinding up their food **2 :** a gastric calculus
gas·tro·lo·bi·um \,gastrə'lōbēəm\ *n* [NL, fr. *gastr-* + *-lobium* (fr. Gk *lobion*, dim. of *lobos* lobe) — more at LOBE] **1** *cap* **:** a genus of Australian evergreen leguminous shrubs that have opposite or whorled compound leaves which are poisonous to livestock, showy yellow to deep orange flowers with a reddish purple keel, and 2-seeded pods **2** -S **:** any plant of the genus *Gastrolobium* **:** POISON BUSH
gas·trol·o·ger \ga'străləjə(r)\ *n* -S **:** GOURMET
gas·tro·log·i·cal \¦gastrə¦läjəkəl\ *adj* **:** of, relating to, or concerned with the needs and demands of the stomach
gas·trol·o·gist \ga'străləjəst\ *n* -S **:** a specialist in gastrology
gas·trol·o·gy \-jē\ *n* -ES [Gk *gastrologia*, title given to a poem describing a gastronomical tour of the known world, by Archestratos, 4th cent. B.C. Greek poet, fr. *gastro-* belly + *-logia* -logy — more at GASTR-] **:** the art or science of caring for the stomach either medically or gastronomically
gas·trol·y·sis \ga'străləsəs\ *n* [NL, fr. *gastr-* + *-lysis*] **:** the surgical operation of freeing the stomach from adhesions
gas·tro·my·ce·tes \,gastrō,mī'sēd·(,)ēz\ [NL, fr. *gastr-* + *Mycetes*] *syn of* GASTEROMYCETES
gas·tro·nome \'gastrə,nōm\ *n* -S [F, back-formation fr. *gastronomie* gastronomy] **1 :** one fond of good living **:** EPICURE; *esp* **:** an enthusiast over and expert judge of excellence in food and drink **2** *or* **gas·tro·nom** \¦gastrə¦näm\ [Russ *gastronom*, lit., gastronome (sense 1), fr. F *gastronome*] **:** a delicatessen in the U.S.S.R. **syn** see EPICURE
gas·tron·o·mer \ga'stränəmə(r)\ *n* -S [fr. *gastronomy*, after such pairs as *astronomy*: *astronomer*] **:** GASTRONOME 1 **syn** see EPICURE
gas·tro·nom·ic \¦gastrə¦nämik, -mēk\ *also* **gas·tro·nom·i·cal** \-məkəl, -mēk-\ *adj* [F *gastronomique*, fr. *gastronomie* + *-ique* -ic, -ical] **:** of or relating to gastronomy — **gas·tro·nom·i·cal·ly** \-mək(ə)lē, -mēk-, -li\ *adv*
gas·tron·o·mist \ga'stränəməst\ *n* -S **:** a specialist in gastronomy **:** GASTRONOME
gas·tron·o·my \-mē,-mi\ *n* -ES [F *gastronomie*, fr. Gk *gastronomia*, title given to a 4th cent B.C. poem also called *Gastrologia*, fr. *gastro-* belly + *-nomia* -nomy — more at GASTROLOGY, GASTR-] **1 :** the art or science of good eating **:** EPICURISM **2 :** culinary customs or style (as of a particular region) ⟨why not introduce oriental ~ to the Western menu —Norbert Mühlen⟩
gas·tro·pancreatic fold \¦ga(,)strō+ . . . -\ *or* **gastropancreatic ligament** *n* [*gastr-* + *pancreatic*] **:** a peritoneal fold extending from the pylorus to the pancreas
gas·tro·parietal \"+\ *adj* [*gastr-* + *parietal*] **:** connecting the stomach and body wall
gas·tro·pexy \'gastrə,peksē\ *n* -ES [ISV *gastr-* + *-pexy*] **:** a surgical operation in which the stomach is sutured to the abdominal wall
gas·troph·i·lus \ga'sträfələs\ [NL, fr. *gastr-* + *-philus*] *syn of* GASTEROPHILUS
gas·tro·phren·ic \¦gastrə¦frenik\ *adj* [ISV *gastr-* + *phrenic*] **:** of, relating to, or connecting the stomach and diaphragm
gas·tro·plication \¦ga(,)strō+\ *n* -S [ISV *gastr-* + *plication*] **:** a surgical operation for reducing chronic stomach dilatation by plication
¹gas·tro·pod \'gastrə,päd\ *also* **gas·trop·o·dan** \(')ga¦sträpəd³n\ *adj* [*gastropod* fr. NL *Gastropoda*; *gastropodan* fr. NL *Gastropoda* + E *-an*] **:** of, relating to, or characteristic of the class Gastropoda ⟨~ anatomy⟩
²gastropod \"\ *also* **gastropodan** \"\ *n* -S **:** a mollusk of the class Gastropoda **:** a snail, slug, or related mollusk
gas·trop·o·da \ga'sträpədə\ *n pl, cap* [NL, fr. *gastr-* + *-poda*] **:** a large and varied class of Mollusca known from the Cambrian on that includes mollusks with a univalve shell (as a periwinkle or whelk) which is not divided into chambers and is usu. spirally coiled and some (as the slugs and heteropods) with the shell greatly reduced or lacking, usu. with a definite head bearing one or two pairs of sensory tentacles, a pair of eyes sometimes at the end of the tentacles, and a mouth often at the end of a proboscis and in some instances fitted with a toothed radula, with the ventral surface modified into a flattened foot used in creeping or lobed (as in pteropods) for swimming, and with oviparous or sometimes ovoviviparous reproduction, and usu. with distinct larval trochophore and veliger stages — see EUTHYNEURA, STREPTONEURA; compare SCAPHOPODA — **gastropodous** *adj*
gas·tro·pore \'gastrə,pō(ə)r\ *n* [*gastr-* + *pore*] **:** a pore occupied by a gastrozooid in a hydrozoan coral
gas·tro·pri·val \¦gastrō¦prīvəl\ *adj* [*gastr-* + L *privare* to deprive + E *-al* — more at PRIVATE] **:** caused by or associated with lack of essential gastric factors or substances ⟨~ pellagra⟩
gas·trop·to·sis \,ga,sträp'tōsəs\ *n* [NL, fr. *gastr-* + *ptosis*] **:** abnormal sagging of the stomach into the lower abdomen
gas·tros·chi·sis \ga'sträskəsəs\ *n* -ES [NL, fr. *gastr-* + *-schisis*] **:** congenital fissure of the ventral abdominal wall
gas·tro·scope \'gastrə,skōp\ *n* [ISV *gastr-* + *-scope*] **:** a hollow tubular instrument designed to pass into the stomach by way of the mouth and esophagus and fitted with optical and lighting equipment that permits visual inspection of the stomach — **gas·tro·scop·ic** \¦gastrə¦skäpik\ *adj* — **gas·tros·co·pist** \ga'sträskəpəst\ *n* -S — **gas·tros·co·py** \-pē\ *n* -ES
gas·tro·splenic ligament \¦gastrō+. . .-\ *n* [*gastrosplenic*, fr. *gastr-* + *splenic*] **:** a mesenteric fold passing from the greater curvature of the stomach to the spleen
gas·tros·te·gal \(')ga¦strästəgəl\ *adj* **:** of, relating to, or being a gastrostege
gas·tro·stege \'gastrə,stēj\ *n* -S [*gastr-* + *-stege*] **:** one of the large linearly ordered scales on the ventral surface of most snakes
gas·tro·ste·idae \,gastrə'stēə,dē\ [NL, alter. of *Gasterosteidae*] *syn of* GASTEROSTEIDAE
gas·tro·stome \'gastrə,stōm\ *n* -S [*gastr-* + *-stome*] **:** the orifice of a gastropore
gas·tros·to·my \ga'strästəmē\ *n* -ES [ISV *gastr-* + *-stomy*; prob. orig. formed as F *gastrostomie*] **1 :** the surgical formation of an opening through the abdominal wall into the stomach to serve for the introduction of food **2 :** the opening made by gastrostomy
gas·tro·style \'gastrə,stīl\ *n* [*gastr-* + *style*] **:** a spiculated projection at the base of a gastropore extending into the gastrozooid
gas·tro·trich \'gastrə·,trik\ *n* -S [NL *Gastrotricha*] **:** an animal of the group Gastrotricha

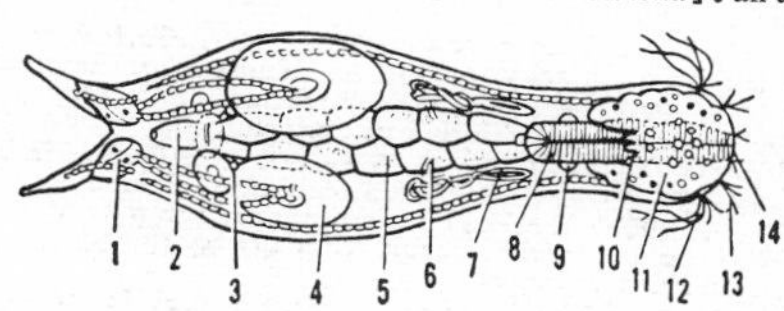

gastrotrich: dorsal view of adult female: *1* cement gland, *2* rectum, *3* ovary, *4* egg, *5* intestine, *6* excretory pore, *7* excretory canal, *8* pharynx, *9* posterior salivary gland, *10* anterior salivary gland, *11* brain, *12* posterolateral bristles, *13* anterolateral bristles, *14* mouth

gas·trot·ri·cha \ga'strä·trəkə\ *n pl, cap* [NL, fr. *gastr-* + *-tricha*] **:** a small class or other group of minute freshwater multicellular animals superficially resembling infusorians, having cilia on the ventral side, and being related to the rotifers and with these included in the phylum Aschelminthes —**gas·trot·ri·chan** \(')ga¦strä·trəkən\ *adj*
gas·tro·vascular \¦ga(,)strō+\ *adj* [ISV *gastr-* + *vascular*] **:** functioning in both digestion and circulation ⟨the coelenteron of a medusa serves as a ~ system⟩
gas·tro·zooid \¦gastrə+\ *n* [ISV *gastr-* + *zooid*] **:** a zooid provided with a mouth and digestive organs **:** TROPHOZOOID
gas·tru·la \'gastrələ\ *n, pl* **gastrulas** \-ləz\ *or* **gastru·lae** \-,lē, -,lī\ [NL, fr. *gastr* + L *-ula* (fem. dim. suffix)] **:** an early metazoan embryo consisting of a hollow 2-layered cellular cup made up of an outer epiblast and an inner hypoblast that meet along the marginal line of a blastopore and jointly enclose the archenteron, forming typically by invagination of part of the blastula wall or in many yolk-filled eggs by overgrowth of cells formed about the animal pole and epiboly, and in eggs producing discoblastulas and in mammalian eggs being greatly modified in both organization and course of formation — see DELAMINATION, INVOLUTION; compare BLASTULA, MORULA — **gas·tru·lar** \-lə(r)\ *adj*
gas·tru·late \-,lāt\ *vi* -ED/-ING/-S [NL *gastrula* + E *-ate*] **:** to become or form a gastrula ⟨*gastrulating* embryos of the frog⟩ — **gas·tru·la·tion** \,==¦lāshən\ *n* -S
gasts *pres 3d sing of* GAST, *pl of* GAST
gas tube *n* **:** an electron tube containing gas at a low pressure sufficient to influence the electrical performance of the tube
gas turbine *n* **:** an internal-combustion engine in which air compressed in a compressor goes into a combustion chamber and is compressed further by the combustion of sprayed liquid or powdered fuel, the hot compressed gases of combustion then expanding and driving a turbine having blades similar to those of a steam turbine
gas turbine locomotive *n* **:** a locomotive powered by a gas-turbine engine
gas vent *n* **1 :** a passage or slot built into a sedimentation chamber to allow the escape of gas and prevent its passage through the settling chamber **2 :** a vent pipe leading to the outer air from a gas furnace, oven, or other gas-fired equipment for removal of products of combustion
gas warfare *n* **:** warfare in which poisonous, asphyxiating, and corrosive gases are used as weapons
gas welding *n* **:** fusion welding in which the required heat is obtained from a gas flame
gas well *n* **:** a well that produces chiefly natural gas
gasworker \'=,==\ *n* **:** a gasworks laborer
gasworks \'=,=\ *n pl but sing in constr* **:** a plant for manufacturing gas
gas zone *n* **:** a rock formation holding gas at a pressure great enough to discharge it at the surface through a well
¹gat *archaic past of* GET
²gat \'gat, *usu* -ad·+V\ *n* -S [prob. fr. D, lit., hole, opening, fr. MD; akin to OE *geat* door, opening — more at GATE] **:** a channel or passage from a shore inland (as between sandbanks or cliffs) or from one body of water to another
³gat \"\ *n* -S [short for *gatling*, fr. *Gatling* (*gun*)] *slang* **:** PISTOL
GAT *abbr* Greenwich apparent time
ga·ta \'gäd·ə\ *n* -S [AmerSp, fr. Sp, female cat, fr. LL *catta* cat — more at CAT] **:** a shark (*Ginglymostoma cirratum*) of the warmer parts of the Atlantic ocean — called also *nurse shark*
gatch \'gach, 'gäch\ *n* -ES [Per *gach*, fr. MPer] **:** a plaster used esp. in Persian architectural ornamentation
gatch bed \'gach-\ *n, usu cap G* [after Willis D. *Gatch* b1878 Am. surgeon] **:** HOSPITAL BED
gatchwork \'=,=\ *n* **:** work in which gatch is used; *also* **:** ornamentation with gatch
¹gate \'gāt, *usu* -ād·+V\ *n* -S *often attrib* [ME *gat, gate, yate*, fr. OE *geat, gæt* door, gate, opening; akin to OFris *jet* hole, opening, OS & ON *gat*, Gk *chezein* to defecate, Skt *hadati* he defecates] **1 :** an opening for passage in an enclosing wall, fence, or barrier; *esp* **:** such an opening with a movable frame or door for closing it ⟨rushed down the path and through the ~⟩ **2 :** a structure or part of a structure comprising a passageway with its collateral structures (as towers, approaches) esp. when designed for defense ⟨the ~ of a walled city⟩ ⟨a temple ~⟩ **3 a :** the frame or door that closes a gate and is legally a part of the wall, fence, or other enclosure which it interrupts **:** a swinging or sliding barrier used to fill or close a gateway esp. when made of a grating or open frame or forming a heavy or rough structure **b :** a movable barrier that can be placed (as by swinging or lowering) so as to block passage along a way (as at a railroad crossing) **4 a :** a means of entrance or sometimes egress ⟨I'll lock up all the ~s of love —Shak.⟩ ⟨determination is a ~ to success⟩ ⟨a small untended wound may become a ~ for infection⟩ **b :** a pass or defile in mountains serving as a way of entrance into a country **c** (1) **:** a usu. numbered gate from a passenger terminal or pier to an embarkation area (2) **:** such a gate together with the embarkation area (as a railroad loading platform) to which it gives access **d :** STARTING GATE **e :** an opening between two flags through which a skier must pass in a slalom race **5 :** something shaped or functioning like a gate: as **a :** a door, valve, or other device for controlling the passage of fluid or other material (as through a sluice, channel, or pipe) ⟨a penstock ~ for a waterwheel⟩ ⟨a blast ~ for a forge⟩ ⟨an oil ~⟩ **b :** GATING 1 **c :** ²SASH 2 **d** *slang* **:** a railroad track switch **e :** a signal (as a square-wave signal) that makes an electronic circuit operative for a chosen short period **f :** a device used in gating (sense 2) **g** *or* **gateleg** \'=,=\ **:** a movable supporting bracket for a drop leaf consisting of a pair of legs separated and stabilized by horizontal spreaders and arranged to fold against the frame of the piece of furniture when the leaf is dropped **6 :** a hinged iron band secured to the topmast trestletrees to hold in place the heel of the topgallant mast **7 a :** a metal part behind the cylinder in old-pattern revolvers that in loading is turned outward to expose the chambers **b :** the cover for the magazine opening in a breech-loading rifle **8 a** (1) **:** a channel in a foundry mold through which the molten metal flows into the cavity made by the pattern **:** INGATE (2) **:** the waste piece of metal cast in the opening of a gate **b :** the channel in each impression of a set of drop-forging dies that connects the flash with the sprue **9 a** *also* **gate money :** the total admission receipts esp. of a sports event **b :** the number of spectators admitted **10** *slang* **:** a state of rejection or separation (as from employment or intimate association) — used esp. in the phrase *give (one) the gate* ⟨after the quarrel she gave her boyfriend the ~⟩ ⟨got the ~ for being late too often⟩ **11 :** the part of a camera, printer, or projector that includes the picture mask or aperture and the guiding tracks and surfaces which assist in positioning the film **12 :** the slotted guide for the gearshift lever of a multiple-speed automobile transmission **13 :** an electronic circuit having an output and two or more inputs so arranged that the output is energized only under certain conditions (as when both of two input wires receive pulses) **14 :** ³GAIT

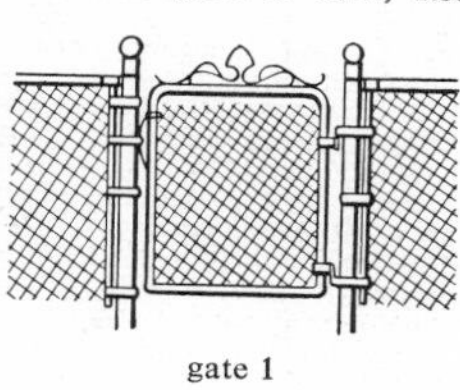
gate 1

²gate \"\ *vt* -ED/-ING/-S **1 :** to supply with a gate **2** *Brit* **:** CAMPUS **3 :** to adjust (a loom) esp. for actual weaving **4 a :** to control by means of a gate (sense 5a) **b :** to make (an electronic device) operate in accordance with a gate **5 a :** to supply (a foundry pattern) with extra parts to bring about the molding of the necessary gates **b :** to supply (a foundry mold) with gates
³gate \"\ *n* -S [ME, fr. ON *gata* road, path; akin to OHG *gazza* road, street, Goth *gatwo* street, and perh. to OE *geat* door, opening] **1** *archaic* **:** a way for travel **:** STREET, PATH ⟨gang down the ~ to Luckie Gregson's —Sir Walter Scott⟩ **2** *now dial* **a :** METHOD, WAY, TECHNIQUE **b :** customary or habitual style **3** *Scot* **:** JOURNEY, TRIP **4** *chiefly Scot* **:** route of travel **:** DIRECTION ⟨he's gone some other ~⟩ **5** *chiefly Scot* **:** DISTANCE ⟨a long ~ from Heddon Rig⟩ **6** *dial Eng* **:** pasturage on common lands
ga·te·a·do \,gäd·ē'ä(,)dō, ¦gäd·ē¦aů\ *n* -S [AmerSp, fr. Sp, adj., catlike, striped like a civet cat, fr. *gato* cat, fr. LL *cattus*; fr. the streaks in the wood — more at CAT] **:** a tropical American timber tree (*Astronium graveolens*) of the family Anacardiaceae that yields a hard dense heavy black-streaked brown timber used as a cabinet wood and that has bark rich in tannin
gate·age \'gād·ij\ *n* -S [¹*gate* + *-age*] **1 a :** the use of gates (as in controlling flow of water) **b :** the gates so used **2 :** the area of gate opening (as of a turbine gate)
ga·teau \(')ga¦tō\ *n, pl* **ga·teaux** \-ō(z)\ [F *gâteau*, fr. OF *gastel*, prob. of Gmc origin; akin to OS *wist* food, OHG, sojourn, dwelling place, food, ON *vist*, Goth *wists* being, nature, OE *wesan* to be — more at WAS] **:** CAKE; *esp* **:** a fancy cake filled with custard and glacéed fruits and nuts
gate-crash \'=,=\ *vb* [back-formation fr. *gate-crasher*] *vt* **:** to enter, attend, or participate in without invitation or ticket and often by misrepresenting oneself **~** *vi* **:** to engage in gate-crashing
gate-crasher \'=,==\ *n* [fr. the phrase *crash the gate*] **:** one that engages in gate-crashing
gat·ed \¦gād·əd, -ātəd\ *adj* [¹*gate* + *-ed*] **:** having or controlled by a gate ⟨~ sluiceways⟩ ⟨a ~ microphone⟩
gatefold \'=,=\ *n* [¹*gate* + *fold*] **:** a folded insert (as a map) in a book or other publication larger in some dimension than the page
gatehouse \'=,=\ *n* [ME *gatehous*, fr. *gate* + *hous* house] **:** a house or other building connected or associated with a gate: as **a :** a part of a gate (as of a city wall or palace) with rooms often formerly used for prisoners or guards **b :** an erection (as a power station) over a dam from which the gates are controlled
gatekeeper \'=,==\ *n* **1 :** a person who tends or guards a gate **2 :** a mottled brown Old World butterfly (*Pararge megaera*)
gateleg table \'=,=-\ *also* **gate-legged table** \'gāt,leg(d)-, -gəd-\ *n* **:** a drop-leaf table with leaves supported by movable brackets consisting of paired legs linked by horizontal stretchers which fold against the frame when the leaves are dropped

gateleg table

gate·less \'gātləs\ *adj* **:** lacking a gate ⟨a ~ valve⟩ — **gate·less·ly** *adv*
gatelike \'=,=\ *adj* **:** resembling a gate
gate·man \'=mən, -,man\ *n, pl* **gatemen 1 :** a man who tends a gate; *esp* **:** one who checks and supervises the traffic that flows through a gate **2 :** an attendant at a railroad grade crossing who bars traffic from the crossing when a train approaches
gate money *n* **:** GATE 9a
gate net *n* **:** a net used chiefly by poachers to catch hares seeking escape by a gate
gate pin *n* **:** a vertical runner used in founding to connect the pouring basin with the gates below
gatepost \'=,=\ *n* **:** either of two posts that bound and support a gate: **a :** the post to which a gate is hung — called also *hinging post, swinging post* **b :** the post against which a gate closes — called also *shutting post*
gat·er \'gād·ə(r)\ *n* -S [¹*gate* + *-er*] **:** SPRUER
gates *pl of* GATE, *pres 3d sing of* GATE
gates-ajar collar \'gātsə,jär-\ *n, slang* **:** WING COLLAR
gates·head \'gāts,hed\ *adj, usu cap* [fr. *Gateshead*, England] **:** of or from the county borough of Gateshead, England **:** of the kind or style prevalent in Gateshead
gate valve *n* **:** a valve in a pipeline consisting essentially of a flat or wedge-shaped gate that can be lowered into a seat to seal off the line or raised into an external recess so that the full area of the line is open — compare GLOBE VALVE
gate·ward \'gāt,wȯ(ə)rd\ *n* -S [ME, fr. OE *geatweard*, fr. *geat* door, gate, opening + *weard* guard — more at GATE, WARD] *archaic* **:** GATEKEEPER
gate·wards \'gātərdz, -t·wə-\ *adv* [³*gate* + *-wards*] *archaic Scot* **:** directly toward **:** along the road to
gateway \'=,=\ *n* **1 a :** ¹GATE 1,2 **b :** a supporting frame or arch in which a gate is hung **2 a :** GATE 4a **b :** a passage for navigation or travel: as (1) **:** any one of a limited number of points by which the traffic of a defined region can enter (2) **:** a point at which freight moving from one such region to

another is interchanged **c :** a basing point on or near the boundary of a rate or classification territory on which freight rates are constructed

ga·tha \'gätə, -(,)tä\ *n* -s *often cap* [Av *gāthā-;* akin to Skt *gāthā* song, verse, *gāyati* he sings — more at CHOUGH] **:** one of 17 hymns or psalms traditionally attributed to Zoroaster that form an important part of the Avesta

¹**gath·er** \'gath̲ə(r), 'geth̲- *sometimes* 'gäth̲-\ *vb* **gathered; gathered; gathering** \-th̲(ə)riŋ\ **gathers** [ME *gaderen,* fr. OE *gadrian, gaderian;* akin to OFris *gaderia* to gather, MLG *gadderen* to gather, MHG *gatern* to unite, OFris *gadia* — more at GOOD] *vt* **1 a :** to bring together into a crowd, group, body, or mass **:** CONCENTRATE, COLLECT ⟨the balloon start had ~*ed* a little crowd of people —H.G.Wells⟩ ⟨reformers ~*ing* their forces against corrupt city administrations —*Amer. Guide Series: N. Y. City*⟩ ⟨~ a supply of firewood⟩ ⟨~*ing* the frightened children about her⟩ **b** (1) **:** to draw up or together **:** ACCUMULATE (2) **:** to gain gradually with steady increase or acceleration ⟨art will ~ social purpose —J.T.Farrell⟩ ⟨a movement ~*ing* force⟩ ⟨the car ~*ed* speed⟩ **c :** to collect (melted glass) on the end of a tube for samples or for blowing **2 a :** PICK, PLUCK, HARVEST ⟨~*ed* a bunch of flowers⟩ ⟨~*ing* walnuts⟩ **b :** to cull, take, pick up, receive, or appropriate by or as if by picking or harvesting ⟨many souvenirs . . . ~*ed* from all parts of the world —*Amer. Guide Series: Maine*⟩ ⟨the vigilantes ~*ed* up Plummer and his gang and hanged them —Seth Agnew⟩ ⟨~ meaning not from reading the Constitution but from reading life —Felix Frankfurter⟩ **c :** to accumulate and place in order or readiness for being used or carried — often used with *up* ⟨he ~*ed* up his tools⟩ **d :** to assemble in sequence (the signatures and inserts of a volume) for binding **e** (1) *chiefly Brit* **:** to scoop up (as a rolling ball) neatly off the ground (2) **:** to catch (a baseball) on the fly — usu. used with *in* ⟨the shortstop easily ~*ed* in the soft liner⟩ **3 :** to attract or serve as a center of attraction for **:** cause or facilitate a bringing together or accumulating of ⟨the past . . . ~*s* round it all the inscrutable mystery of life and death —G.M.Trevelyan⟩ ⟨Puritanism . . . ~*ed* about it . . . all the forces of unrest —V.L.Parrington⟩ ⟨an age devoted to ornate decor that ~*ed* dust and moths⟩ **4 :** to effect the collection of (as tax, tribute, dues, contributions) ⟨~ tax moneys for the king⟩ **5 a :** to summon up **:** muster together **:** ACCUMULATE **:** bring together and coordinate ⟨his poor, shattered soul had ~*ed* to itself just then a great courage —Liam O'Flaherty⟩ ⟨we must . . . get out of the tumult of the market place to ~ our thoughts —M.R.Cohen⟩ ⟨reporters ~*ing* the news of the campaign⟩ **b :** to prepare (as oneself) by mustering strength and force ⟨the victim had been ~*ing* himself to run across the court —T.B.Costain⟩ **6 a :** to bring or draw together the parts of **:** collect and compress by or as if by grasping and holding ⟨~*ed* her long full skirt in each hand and sprang across the little stream⟩ **b :** to draw (as a covering) over, about, or close to something ⟨seizing his hat and ~*ing* his cloak about him⟩ ⟨~*ed* the bedclothes up to his neck⟩ **c :** to pull (fabric) along one or two lines of stitching so as to draw into puckers **:** PLAIT ⟨~ the neckline and stitch on the binding⟩ **d** (1) **:** to haul in or take up (as slack of a rope) (2) **:** to begin or increase movement in (a way or direction specified) ⟨the ship ~*ed* headway⟩ **e :** to cause (opposite walls of masonry) to approach or come together (as in the abrupt narrowing of the upper part of a fireplace to meet the flue) **7 :** to conclude on reflection **:** draw as an inference **:** DEDUCE, INFER **:** presume to be the case ⟨I ~ that the meeting was not a success⟩ **8 :** COLLECT 5a ~ *vi* **1 a :** to come together in a body, group, crowd, cluster, heap, or mass ⟨a crowd quickly ~*ed* and shouted for a speech —*Amer. Guide Series: Md.*⟩ ⟨the swallows . . . are ~*ing* to fly farther away —Padraic Colum⟩ ⟨the way the wrinkles ~*ed* about his merry gray eyes —Ellen Glasgow⟩ **b :** to accumulate, cluster, or form around a focus of attraction ⟨a romance . . . ~*s* round the wedge-shaped or cuneiform characters —Edward Clodd⟩ ⟨the unpopularity that ~*ed* about the name of Mather —V.L.Parrington⟩ **2 a :** to enlarge in coming to a head **:** swell and fill with pus **:** HEAD ⟨the boil is ~*ing*⟩ **b :** to become concentrated or intense **:** GROW, INCREASE ⟨where the cold ~*ed* more thickly —E.H.Collis⟩ ⟨a time when the ~*ing* dangers were only too apparent —Sir Winston Churchill⟩ **3 :** to become drawn or compressed together often in folds or creases ⟨a coat that ~*s* over the shoulders⟩ **4** *of a ship* **:** to make progress **:** APPROACH ⟨the boat continued to ~ toward the southeast⟩ ⟨swiftly ~*ing* on the ship ahead⟩

syn COLLECT, ASSEMBLE, CONGREGATE: GATHER, a general term, indicates the fact of bringing or coming together and lacks much especial connotation ⟨it was customary for merchants to *gather* outside to discuss business affairs —*Amer. Guide Series: R. I.*⟩ It may suggest a picking, culling, or harvesting ⟨a trading post to collect goods already *gathered* by the native population —R.A.Billington⟩ COLLECT is often interchangeable with GATHER but may imply greater purposiveness and more careful selectivity ⟨Columbus was forced to *collect* the natives one night and threaten to darken the moon —Stringfellow Barr⟩ ⟨the mass of movable wealth *collected* in the shops and warehouses of London alone —T.B.Macaulay⟩ Used in reference to persons coming together, ASSEMBLE may stress a definite aim or purpose and may suggest greater unity or organization in the group formed; used in reference to things brought together, it suggests a logical ordering or uniting ⟨Flandrau . . . *assembled* a force of volunteers at St. Peter and hastened to the relief of the village —*Amer. Guide Series: Minn.*⟩ ⟨immediately after they shall be *assembled* in consequence of the first election —*U.S.Constitution*⟩ ⟨*assembling* and interpreting statistics on the nation's war programs —*Current Biog.*⟩ CONGREGATE may apply to a gregarious flocking together of similar types ⟨the drivers *congregated* in saloons around the square —Green Peyton⟩ ⟨the older people sat rather stiffly in the corners, the young men *congregated* uneasily in impermanent groups —Irwin Shaw⟩ **syn** see in addition INFER, REAP

²**gather** \"\ *n* -s **1 :** something that is gathered ⟨the final ~ of the harvest⟩ ⟨smoothing out the ~*s* of thought between her brows⟩: as **a :** a puckering in cloth made by gathering — usu. used in pl. ⟨adjust the ~*s* evenly and sew on the waistband⟩ **b :** a mass of molten glass collected on a gathering iron for use in glassblowing **c :** a lightly collected stance of a horse **2 :** an act or instance of gathering ⟨made a final ~ of the trash before they left the picnic grounds⟩; *esp, West* **:** a roundup of cattle **3 :** the soffit of masonry formed by gathering

gath·er·able \-th̲(ə)rəbəl\ *adj* **:** capable of being gathered; *esp* **:** INFERABLE

gathered *past of* GATHER

gath·er·er \-th̲ərə(r)\ *n* -s [ME *gaderer,* fr. *gaderen* to gather + *-er* — more at GATHER] **1 :** one that collects and brings together **:** COLLECTOR, COMPILER ⟨a ~ of moral anecdotes⟩ ⟨these ~*s* of dead statistics⟩ **2 a :** a collector of money (as for fees, taxes, or other fixed charges) — often used in combination ⟨a tax *gatherer*⟩ ⟨rent *gatherers*⟩ **b** *obs* **:** MISER **3 :** a worker or device that gathers something: as **a :** one that gathers molten glass on the end of a blowpipe **b :** a person or machine that gathers sheets, leaves, or signatures for binding **c :** a sewing-machine operator or attachment that gathers fabric **4 :** an incisor of a horse

gath·er·ing \-th̲(ə)riŋ, -rēŋ\ *n* -s [ME *gadering, gaderung,* fr. OE *gaderung,* fr. *gadrian, gaderian* to gather + *-ung, -ing* -ing — more at GATHER] **1 a :** the action or an instance of coming together or accumulating ⟨a ~ of dust on the shelves⟩ ⟨that black ~ of clouds foretold a shower⟩ ⟨the ~ of melted snow into little streams⟩ **b :** a coming together of people in a group (as for social, religious, or political purposes) **:** ASSEMBLY, MEETING ⟨cultural and civic ~*s*⟩ ⟨the outstanding social ~ of the year⟩ **c :** a suppurating swelling **:** ABSCESS **2 a :** the act or work of a gatherer (as in contracting, accumulating, or assembling something) **b :** the collecting or gleaning of food and other raw materials from the wild ⟨peoples whose economy is based on ~ are ill-situated to attain the stability essential to any high level of civilization⟩ **3 :** something that is gathered: as **a :** a collection (as of money for charity) or compilation (as of literary fragments) **b :** PARISON **c :** a gather in cloth **d :** the leaves of a book that are folded and stitched into one signature **e :** sap collected at one time in a sugar-maple orchard ⟨the evening ~ is usually much larger than the morning one is⟩

gathering coal *n* **:** a large lump of coal left smothered in embers to hold a fire (as during the night)

gathering hoop *n* **:** a hoop used by coopers to draw together the ends of barrel staves so that the hoops can be put on

gathering iron *or* **gathering rod** *n* **:** an iron rod used for gathering molten glass for glassblowing

gathering machine *n* **:** a machine consisting of pockets or bins with devices for removing book signatures placed in each bin, dropping them on a movable chain belt, and delivering the assembled books complete

gathering pallet *n* **:** a revolving finger in striking clocks and repeating watches that moves the rack for each blow struck — compare TUMBLER 3c(1)

gathering peat *n* **1 :** a peat used as a gathering coal **2 :** a fiery peat formerly sent round by the Scottish borderers as an alarm signal — compare FIERY CROSS

gathering ring *n* **:** one of the clay rings placed on molten glass to keep surface impurities from the center area and provide space where highest quality glass can be gathered

gathering table *n* **1 :** a table or board on which book signatures are laid out to be gathered **2 :** a circular revolving table used for gathering book signatures

gathers *pres 3d sing of* GATHER, *pl of* GATHER

gather shot *n* **:** a billiards shot that brings the object balls back into favorable position for the succeeding shot

gath·er·um \-th̲ərəm\ *n* -s [¹*gather* + L *-um* (neut. n. ending)] **:** a collection esp. of miscellaneous items

ga·thic \'gätik\ *n* -s *usu cap* [*Gatha* + *-ic*] **:** a language of ancient Persia in which the Gathas were composed

gat·ing \'gād·iŋ\ *n* -s [¹*gate* + *-ing*] **1 :** an opening in a lock tumbler into or through which the fence passes upon the operation of the bolt **2 :** the process of selecting those parts of an electromagnetic wave that exist during a selected time interval or that have magnitudes between selected limits

gat·ling gun \'gatliŋ-, -lēŋ-\ *also* **gatling** *n* -s *usu cap Gatling* [after Richard J. *Gatling* †1903 Am. inventor] **:** a machine gun consisting of a cluster of barrels that when revolved by a crank are loaded and fired once each during a revolution of the group

ga·to \'gä(,)tō\ *n* -s [AmerSp, lit., cat, fr. LL *cattus* — more at CAT] **:** an Argentine composition in lively ¾ time for singing and dancing

ga·tor \'gād·ə(r), -ātə-\ *n* -s [by shortening] **:** ALLIGATOR

gats *pl of* GAT

gat·ter·mann-koch reaction \'gäl|d·ə(r)mən'kōk-, 'gäl|, -kōk-,-kōk-,-käk-\ *n, usu cap G&K* [after Ludwig *Gattermann* †1920 and J.A. *Koch fl*1897 Ger. chemists] **:** a synthesis of an aldehyde from an aromatic hydrocarbon, carbon monoxide, hydrogen chloride, and a catalyst containing aluminum chloride

gattermann reaction *n, usu cap G* [after L.*Gattermann*] **:** a synthesis of an aldehyde from an aromatic or heterocyclic compound, hydrogen cyanide, hydrogen chloride, and a catalyst of aluminum chloride or zinc chloride

gat·ti·na·ra \,gäd·ē'närə\ *n* -s [It, fr. *Gattinara,* town in northwestern Italy] **:** a dark red Italian table wine

gat·tine \(')ga¦tēn\ *n* -s [F] **:** an epidemic and fatal disease of silkworms believed to result from the combined action of a virus and a streptococcus

gau \'gaů\ *n, pl* **gaus** \-aůz\ *or* **gaue** \-aůə\ [G, fr. OHG *gouw-, gewi* district, region; akin to OE *-gē* district, region (in place names), OFris *gā,* OS *-gō* (in place names), Goth *gawi;* all prob. fr. a prehistoric WGmc-EGmc compound whose components are represented respectively by OHG *gi-* (perfective and collective prefix) and *ouwa* land by water, meadow — more at YCLEPT, ISLAND] **1 :** a region or district in German tribal organization including two or more marks and inhabited by kindred tribes **2 :** one of the 20 party districts into which Germany including Austria was divided by the National Socialists

gau·by \'gōbi\ *var of* GABY

gauche \'gōsh\ *adj, sometimes* -ER/-EST [F, lit., left, on the left, fr. MF, fr. *gauchir* to turn aside, swerve, alter. of *guenchir,* of Gmc origin; akin to OHG *wankōn* to stagger, sway — more at WINK] **1 a :** lacking in social graces or ease, tact, and familiarity with polite usage **:** likely or inclined to commit social blunders esp. from lack of experience or training **b :** lacking finish or exhibiting crudity (as of style, form, or technique) ⟨an excellent script and cast wasted by ~ direction⟩ ⟨a ~ turn of phrase⟩ **2 :** not plane **:** TWISTED, SKEW ⟨a ~ curve⟩ **3 :** being or designed for use with the left hand **:** LEFT-HAND ⟨a ~ or left-hand weapon, used mainly for guarding and reserve —Foster Harris⟩ **syn** see AWKWARD

gauche·ly *adv* **:** in a gauche manner **:** AWKWARDLY, CLUMSILY, CRUDELY

gauche·ness *n* -ES **:** the quality or state of being gauche ⟨the ~ of such a remark⟩

gau·che·rie \,gōshə¦rē, (')gō¦shrē; 'gōsh(ə)rē, -)ri\ *n* -s [F, fr. *gauche* + *-erie* -ery] **1 :** a tactless or awkward action; *often* **:** a bit of social or literary crudity ⟨the claptrap and ~*s* that too often fill the daily papers⟩

gau·cher's disease \(')gō¦shāz-\ *n, usu cap G* [after Philippe C.E.*Gaucher* †1918 Fr. physician] **:** a rare chronic disorder prob. of genetic origin that is characterized by enormous enlargement of the spleen, pigmentation of the skin, and bone lesions and is marked by the presence of large amounts of kerasin in the cells of the reticuloendothelial system

gau·cho \'gaů(,)chō\ *also* **gua·cho** \'gwä(-\ *n* -s *often attrib* [AmerSp *gaucho,* prob. fr. Quechua *wáhcha* poor person, orphan] **:** a cowboy or herdsman of the pampas usu. of mixed Spanish and Indian descent ⟨~*s* . . . wearing loose trousers with tight cuffs at the ankles, soft hats, and long wool ponchos —Natalie Raymond⟩ ⟨bright ~ shirts⟩

gau·cie *or* **gau·cy** *var of* GAWSIE

¹**gaud** \'gȯd, 'gäd\ *n* -s [ME *gaude,* prob. fr. OF *gaudir* to enjoy, rejoice, have a good time, fr. L *gaudēre* to rejoice — more at JOY] **1** *archaic* **:** a gay trick or jape; *sometimes* **:** a deceitful trick or artifice **:** FRAUD **2 :** ORNAMENT; *esp* **:** a showy or flashy bit of jewelry or finery **3 :** showy and often empty display or ceremony — usu. used in pl. ⟨surrounded by the pointless ~*s* of a royal household⟩

²**gaud** \"\ *vt* -ED/-ING/-S *archaic* **:** to decorate with gauds **:** ADORN, PAINT

³**gaud** \"\ *n* -s [ME *gaude*] **:** a distinctive bead used to mark a division in a rosary

⁴**gaud** \'gōd, 'gäd\ *Scot var of* GOAD

⁵**gaud** \"\ *Scot var of* GAD

gaude lake \'gōd-\ *n* [F *gaude* weld (dyestuff), of Gmc origin; akin to MLG *wolde* weld — more at WELD] **:** MIMOSA 3

gaud·ery \'gȯdərē, 'gäd-, -ri\ *n* -ES [¹*gaud* + *-ery*] **:** ostentatious display esp. in dress or belongings; *also* **:** an instance or product contributing to such display **:** FRIPPERIES, FINERY

gau·di·an \gaů'dēən\ *adj, usu cap* [Antonio *Gaudí* y Cornet †1926 Catalan architect + E *-an*] **:** of, relating to, or resembling the architect Gaudí or his style marked esp. by fantastic and elaborate detail

gaud·i·fy \-də,fī\ *vt* -ED/-ING/-ES [*gaudy* + *-fy*] **:** to make showy

gaud·i·ly \-dᵊl|ē, -dəl|, |i\ *adv* **:** in a gaudy manner **:** SHOWILY, GARISHLY

gaud·i·ness \-dēnəs, -din-\ *n* -ES **:** the quality or state of being gaudy **:** SHOWINESS

gauds·man \'gȯdzmən, 'gädz-\ *n, pl* **gaudsmen** [by alter.] *Scot* **:** GOADMAN

¹**gaudy** \'gȯdē, 'gäd-, -di\ *adj* -ER/-EST [¹*gaud* + *-y*] **:** ostentatiously fine **:** making a pretentious but often hollow show of excellence, elegance, beauty, richness, or worth **:** having show without substance

syn TAWDRY, GARISH, FLASHY, METERICIOUS: GAUDY may suggest cheap showiness of taste, over-bright coloration, or vulgarly excessive and conspicuous ornamentation ⟨he was dressed in a *gaudy* costume, resembling on the whole that of a Highland chieftain. His knees, wrists, and throat were tattooed in bright blue patterns; and he carried sword and dagger, a gold ring round his neck, and gold rings on his wrists —Charles Kingsley⟩ ⟨swarthy Mojaves, garbed in *gaudy* scarlets, blues, and yellows —*Amer. Guide Series: Calif.*⟩ TAWDRY always adds connotations of cheap pretension to those of GAUDY ⟨decorated in *tawdry* baroque, it might have been built about thirty years ago and not repainted since. On the ceiling, an immense pink, blue and gold design of cherubim, roses, and clouds was peeled and patched with damp —Christopher Isherwood⟩ GARISH may suggest offensive or harsh unrestrained brightness ⟨the *garish* splendor of the orchis —D.G.Hoffman⟩ ⟨"a red scarf?" said John pensively. "I have noted his taste for colors more *garish* than perhaps beseems a servant. Usually it was violet, whether scarf or cloak" —J.H.Wheelwright⟩ FLASHY may apply to the facilely gay or momentarily dazzling that is speedily revealed as shallow and vulgar ⟨I liked the flaring yellow scarf bound loose about her throat, I liked her showy purple gown and *flashy* velvet coat —Ralph Hodgson⟩ MERETRICIOUS may suggest the tawdry allure of false show or promise ⟨his smile was wide and rather *meretricious,* that exaggerated photograph-smile so often seen (as if only happiness should be recorded). She could imagine how it had faded the moment the camera clicked —Elizabeth Taylor⟩ ⟨girls who deck themselves with gems, false hair, and *meretricious* ornament, to chain the fleeting fancy of a man —W.S.Gilbert⟩

²**gau·dy** \"\ *n* -ES [prob. fr. L *gaudium* joy — more at JOY] **:** a feast, festival, or entertainment esp. in the form of an annual college dinner in a British university

gaudy dutch *or* **gaudy welsh** *n, usu cap G&D&W* **:** earthenware with colorful bold designs made in Staffordshire, England in the first quarter of the 19th century

gaudy green \"*gaudy*" *like* ¹GAUDY\ *n* [ME *gaude grene, gaudy grene,* fr. MF *gaude* weld + ME *grene* green — more at GAUDE LAKE, GREEN] **:** SPINACH GREEN

gaudy night *n* **:** a festal night

gaudy·ware \'==,=\ *n* **:** GAUDY DUTCH

gaue *pl of* GAU

gauffer *var of* GOFFER

gauffered *or* **gauffred** *var of* GOFFERED

gauf·frage \'gōfrij, 'gōf-; (')gō¦fräzh, (')gō¦-\ *n* -s [F *gaufrage,* fr. *gaufrer* to emboss, goffer + *-age* — more at GOFFER] **:** ornamentation with goffering

gauf·fre *also* **gau·fre** \(')gō¦frā, (')gō¦-\ *adj* [F *gaufré,* fr. past part. of *gaufrer*] **:** GOFFERED; *often* **:** ornamented with embossing ⟨~ velvet⟩

gau·fre \'gōfr(ᵊ), -f(rə); 'gōfə(r), 'gōf-\ *n, pl* **gaufres** \-fr(ᵊ), -f(rə), -fə(r)z\ [F, fr. OF — more at GOFFER] **:** a very thin crisp wafer baked with a wafer iron

gau·frette \(')gō¦fret, (')gō¦-\ *n* -s [F, dim. of *gaufre*] **:** a wafer of crisply fried potato cut to resemble a small waffle

¹**gauge** *or* **gage** \'gāj\ *n* -s [ME *gauge,* fr. ONF, prob. of Gmc origin; akin to OHG *galgo* cross, gallows — more at GALLOWS] **1 a :** measurement esp. according to some standard or system ⟨make a note of the ~ of each barrel⟩ **b :** the dimensions or extent of something ⟨cannot mark the ~ of her sufferings⟩ ⟨glanced about to take the ~ of the situation⟩ **2 a :** an instrument for or means of testing ⟨used a notched rod for a ~ to estimate the content of the barrels⟩ **b** *usu gage* **:** an instrument for checking or measuring a particular dimension of an object (as thickness, depth, or diameter) **c :** a carpenter's tool for scribing a line parallel to the edge of a piece of work — called also *marking gauge;* compare MORTISE GAUGE **d** *usu gage* **:** any of various instruments usu. provided with a graduated scale or dial for measuring or indicating quantity ⟨gasoline *gage*⟩ **e :** a bookbinders tool used to secure uniform size, spacing, or position of materials **f :** PERFORATION GAUGE; *sometimes* **:** PERFORATION NUMBER **g** *printing* (1) **:** GUIDE (2) **:** HEIGHT GAUGE 2 (3) **:** LINE GAUGE (4) **:** PAGE GAUGE **3 a :** relative position of a ship with reference to another ship and the wind — see LEE GAUGE, WEATHER GAUGE **b :** the depth to which a ship sinks in the water when fully loaded **4 a** *usu gage* **:** the distance between the heads of the rails of a railroad measured at right angles thereto at a point ⅝ inch below the top of the rail, standard gage in most countries being now 4 feet 8½ inches **b :** the distance between a pair of wheels on an axle — compare WHEELBASE **5 :** the quantity of plaster of paris used with mortar to accelerate its setting for special purposes — see GAUGE STUFF **6 :** the size of a shotgun expressed as the number in a pound of round lead balls of a size to just fit into the barrel ⟨a 12-*gauge* shotgun⟩ ⟨shotguns of different ~*s*⟩ — compare BORE, CALIBER **7 :** the thickness esp. of sheet metal or the diameter esp. of wire, a hypodermic needle, or a screw — see WIRE GAUGE 2 **8 a :** the number of needles in 1½ inches of the needlebar of a knitting machine **b :** the fineness of a knitted fabric determined by the number of loops per 1½ inch based in turn on the number of needles per 1½ inch ⟨51-*gauge* hosiery is sheerer than 45-*gauge*⟩ **c :** the number of stitches per inch in hand knitting and crocheting — used esp. in describing patterns **syn** see STANDARD

²**gauge** *or* **gage** \"\ *vt* -ED/-ING/-S [ME *gaugen,* fr. ONF *gaugier,* fr. *gauge,* n.] **1 a :** to measure exactly **:** determine precisely the size of (as a standardized part), amount of (as rainfall), dimensions, or other measurable value of (as intensity

PRINCIPAL RAILROAD GAGES OF THE WORLD

WIDTH English units	WIDTH metric units	PLACE
5′6″	1.676 m	Argentina, Ceylon, Chile, India, Pakistan, Portugal, Spain
5′3″	1.600 m	Brazil, Ireland, Australia
5′	1.524 m	Finland, Panama, U.S.S.R.
4′9¼″	1.45 m	Algeria
4′8⅝″	1.44 m	France, Tunisia
4′8½″	1.435 m	Algeria, Argentina, Australia, Canada (except Newfoundland), Chile, China, Cuba, European continent (except Spain), Finland, Great Britain, Iran, Iraq, Jamaica, Japan, Korea, Lebanon, Mauritius, Mexico, Morocco, Paraguay, Peru, Portugal, Saudi Arabia, Syria, Trinidad, Turkey, U.A.R., U.S.S.R., U.S., Uruguay
3′6″	1.067 m	Angola, Australia, Chile, Congo (Kinshasa), Costa Rica, Ecuador, China (Taiwan), Ghana, Haiti, Honduras, Indonesia, Japan, Malawi, Mozambique, Newfoundland, New Zealand, Nicaragua, Nigeria, Philippines, Republic of So. Africa, Rhodesia, Sudan, Sweden, West Africa, Western Australia, Zambia
3′5¼″	1.05 m	Algeria, Jordan, Syria
3′3⅜″	1.00 m	Algeria, Argentina, Bolivia, Brazil, Burma, Cambodia, Chile, China, Colombia, East Africa, Ecuador, Ethiopia, Greece, India, Iraq, Malaysia, Pakistan, Paraguay, Portugal, Spain, Surinam, Switzerland, Thailand, Tunisia, U.A.R., Vietnam, West Africa, Yugoslavia
3′1⅜″	0.95 m	Ethiopia, Italy
3′	0.914 m	Colombia, El Salvador, Guatemala, Ireland, Mexico, Panama, Peru, Spain
2′11″	0.891 m	Sweden
2′6″	0.762 m	Bulgaria, Ceylon, Chile, China (Taiwan), India, Nigeria, Pakistan, Sierra Leone, Yugoslavia
2′5½″	0.750 m	Argentina, Ecuador, Turkey, U.A.R.
2′	0.610 m	India, Republic of So. Africa, Venezuela
1′11⅝″	0.60 m	Algeria, Bulgaria, Chile, Indonesia

COMMON SHOTGUN GAUGES

GAUGE	INTERIOR DIAMETER OF BARREL	GAUGE	INTERIOR DIAMETER OF BARREL
10	.775 inches	20	.615 inches
12	.729 inches	28	.550 inches
16	.662 inches	.410[1]	.410 inches

[1]actually a caliber but called a gauge

or velocity); *broadly* **:** to estimate (some quantity) by practical or logical means ⟨*gauging* his progress by the milestones he passed⟩ **b :** to determine the capacity or amount of contents of (as a cask or comparable vessel) **c :** to measure the capacity, character, or ability of **:** APPRAISE, JUDGE ⟨*gauging* the probable response of the electorate by sampling techniques⟩ ⟨I would not ~ the future on what I know of the past⟩ ⟨how would you ~ his conduct?⟩ **d** *usu gage* **:** to determine the flow of (a stream) by measurement of the cross section and the velocity **2 a :** to check or limit with or as if with a gauge ⟨he *gauged* each part of the model with calipers⟩; *broadly* **:** to cause to conform to a standard (as of measurement or performance) **b :** to measure off or set out ⟨~ the line for the foundation⟩; *sometimes* **:** to set bounds to **c** (1) **:** to determine the perforation number of (a stamp) (2) **:** to have (an indicated perforation number) by measurement ⟨a stamp *gauging* 10⟩ **3 :** to mix (plaster) in certain definite proportions (as for quick drying) **:** mix plaster of paris with (mortar) for quick setting **4 :** to dress (bricks or stones) to size by rubbing or chipping **5 :** to set (an insert) in the right position in bookbinding **6 a :** to gather (sewing) with alternating short and long stitches **b :** to hold evenly distributed gathers with (as smocking)

gauge·able \-jəbəl\ *adj* **:** capable of being gauged **:** measurable or determinable by gauging — **gauge·ably** \-blē\ *adv*

gauge cock *n* **:** a vent cock used to ascertain the level of liquid in a container

gauged arch *n* **:** a masonry arch that has bricks or stones gauged in such a manner that the joints radiate from a common center

gauge glass *n* **:** the glass tube of a water gauge by which the water level in a boiler or tank is observed

gauge knife *n* **:** a knife with a gauge to limit the cut

gauge line *n* **:** a line ⅝ inch below the center of the running surface of a railroad rail along the side of the head nearer the center of track

gauge pin *n* **:** a pin attached to the tympan of a platen press to hold the sheet and act as a feed guide

gauge point *n* **:** a reference point to which a gauge is applied or from which measurements are taken in gauging

gauge pressure *n* **:** the pressure at a point in a fluid above that of the atmosphere — compare ABSOLUTE PRESSURE

gaug·er *or* **gag·er** \ˈgājə(r)\ *n* -S [ME, fr. AF *gaugeour*, fr. ONF *gaugier* + AF *-our* -or] **:** one that gauges: as **a** *chiefly Brit* **:** an exciseman or customs officer who checks, measures, and sometimes assesses the levy on dutiable bulk goods (as liquors) **b :** a worker who inspects and checks the dimensions of small parts in a machine shop **c :** one that gauges the quantity and temperature of oil in storage tanks and controls the flow of oil into pipelines

gaug·er·ship \-ˌship\ *n* **:** the office of a gauger

gauge stuff *n* **:** gauged mortar used for making specialized structures (as cornices or moldings) in which speedy setting is important

gauge wheel *n* **:** an adjustable wheel attached to a plow or planter that regulates the depth of penetration into the soil

gauging plaster *n* **:** a special gypsum plaster mixed with lime putty for use in finishing plastered surfaces

gaul \ˈgȯl\ *n* -S *cap* [fr. *Gaul*, ancient region of Europe including most of what is now France and in earliest times also including northern Italy, fr. F *Gaule*, fr. L *Gallia*] **1 :** a member of the Celtic people that inhabited ancient Gaul as well as areas in the Balkans and Asia Minor — compare GALATIAN **2 :** FRENCHMAN

gaul·ding \ˈgȯl(d)ən, -ldiŋ\ *also* **gaul·lin** \-lən\ *n* -S [origin unknown] *West Indies* **:** HERON

gau·lei·ter \ˈgau̇ˌlīd·ə(r)\ *n* -S [G, fr. *gau* + *leiter* leader, fr. OHG *leitāri*, fr. *leiten* to lead + *-āri* -er — more at LEAD] **1 a :** a district leader of the German National Socialist party formerly serving in his territory as provincial governor **b :** a political functionary occupying a similar subordinate but important position in a totalitarian regime or hierarchy **2 :** a person that in outlook and social responses may be likened to a gauleiter; *often* **:** an arrogant overbearing subordinate or henchman ⟨how these conductors feel their oats. They are ~s of music in their respective cities —D.S.Moore⟩ ⟨recognized ~s in penology —*Prison World*⟩

gaul·ic \ˈgȯlik\ *adj, usu cap* [*Gaul* (country) + E *-ic*] **:** GALLIC

¹gaul·ish \ˈgȯlish\ *adj, usu cap* [*Gaul* (country) + E *-ish*] **:** of or relating to the Gauls, their language, or land

²gaulish \"\ *n* -ES *cap* **:** the Celtic language of the ancient Gauls esp. as represented by Celtic loanwords in Latin and Old French — called also *Continental Celtic*; see INDO-EUROPEAN LANGUAGES table

gaull·ism \ˈgōˌlizəm, ˈgȯ-,\ *n* -S *usu cap* [F *Gaullisme*, fr. Gen. Charles de *Gaulle* b1890 Fr. soldier and political leader + F *-isme* -ism] **1 :** a political movement among Frenchmen during World War II characterized by allegiance to policies of Charles de Gaulle and by opposition to the Vichy regime **2 a :** a political movement emerging in France after World War II under the leadership of Charles de Gaulle and usu. associated with rightist policies **b :** the principles and beliefs associated with this movement

gaull·ist \-ˌləst\ *n* -S *usu cap* [F *gaulliste*, fr. Gen. de *Gaulle* + F *-iste* -ist] **:** a follower of the French military and political leader Charles de Gaulle either during World War II or in postwar French rightist politics

gault *also* **galt** \ˈgȯlt\ *n* -S [prob. of Scand origin; akin to ON *galdr*, *gald* hard-packed snow, Norw dial. *gald* hard ground, mountain path, and prob. to ON *gadd* hard-packed snow, Norw dial., trampled spot of ground, Sw dial, narrow path, rabbit track] **:** a heavy thick clay soil

gaul·the·ria \gȯlˈthirēə\ *n* [NL, irreg. fr. Jean-François *Gaultier* †1756 Fr. botanist in Canada + NL *-ia*] **1** *cap* **:** a widely distributed genus of evergreen shrubs (family Ericaceae) that are upright or creeping in growth, have opposite leaves and axillary white flowers, and produce small often aromatic fruits resembling berries — see CREEPING SNOWBERRY, SALAL, WINTERGREEN **2** -S **:** any plant of the genus *Gaultheria* (as the checkerberry)

gaultheria oil *n* **:** WINTERGREEN OIL

gaul·therin \ˈgȯlthərən, gȯlˈthir-\ *n* -S [ISV *gaulther-* (fr. NL *Gaultheria*) + *-in*] **:** a crystalline glycoside $C_{19}H_{26}O_{12}$ of methyl salicylate found esp. in sweet birch and various gaultherias

¹gaum \ˈgȯm, ˈgäm\ *n* -S [ME *gome*, fr. ON *gaum*, *gaumr*; akin to OE *gīeme* care, OHG *gouma* attention, ON *geyma* to keep, watch, heed, mind — more at FAVOR] **1** *dial Eng* **:** HEED, ATTENTION **2** *dial Eng* **:** UNDERSTANDING, PERCEPTION

²gaum \"\ *vt* -ED/-ING/-S **1** *dial Eng* **:** to pay attention to **:** HEED **2** *dial Eng* **:** to perceive the significance of **:** UNDERSTAND

³gaum \"\ *n* -S [perh. alter. of *³gum*] *dial* **:** a greasy or sticky mess

⁴gaum \"\ *vt* -ED/-ING/-S [perh. alter. of *⁴gum*] *dial* **:** to smudge or smear esp. with something sticky or greasy — often used with *up* ⟨the kitchen floor was all ~*ed* up with spilled molasses⟩

⁵gaum \"\ *vi* -ED/-ING/-S [origin unknown] *dial* **:** to behave in a stupid or awkward manner (as by staring or gaping)

⁶gaum \"\ *n* -S *dial* **:** an awkward lout **:** a stupid doltish person **:** CLOWN

gaum·less \-ləs\ *adj* [*¹gaum* + *-less*] *dial* **:** lacking comprehension or awareness **:** dull and stupid

gaumy \-mē\ *adj* [*³gaum* + *-y*] **1** *dial* **:** SMEARED, STICKY **2** *dial* **:** UNTIDY, SLOVENLY, DISORDERED; *broadly* **:** awkward and clumsy

gaun \ˈgȯn, ˈgän\ *dial Brit pres part of* GO *or pres part of* GAE

gaung·baung \ˈgau̇ŋˌbau̇ŋ\ *n* -S [native name in Burma] **:** a Burmese headcloth usu. of bright colored silk

¹gaunt \ˈgȯnt, ˈgänt, ˈgȧnt\ *adj* -ER/-EST [ME, perh. of Scand origin; akin to Icel *gandur* stick, Norw dial. *gand* thin stick] **1** *of a person* **a** *archaic* **:** desirably or pleasingly slim **:** of slender form or build **b :** thin and angular **:** attenuated esp. by fasting or suffering **:** LANK, HAGGARD **2 :** grim and forbidding **:** BARREN, DESOLATE ⟨the ~ leafless trees⟩ ⟨a ~ heath⟩ **syn** see LEAN

²gaunt \"\ *vt* -ED/-ING/-S **:** to make (an individual) gaunt ⟨~*ed* and hollow-eyed —Alan LeMay⟩; *usu* **:** to train fine (as for a race)

³gaunt \"\ *n* -S [prob. alter. of *gant*, obs. var. of *gannet*] **:** GREAT CRESTED GREBE

⁴gaunt \"\ *chiefly Scot var of* ¹GANT, ²GANT

¹gaunt·let \ˈgȯntlət, ˈgän-,ˈgȧn-, *usu* -ȯd·+V\ *n* -S [ME *gauntelette*, fr. MF *gantelet*, dim. of *gant* glove, of Scand origin; akin to MLG & MD *want*, *wante* mitten, ON *vöttr* gloves and perh. to ON *vöndr* wand — more at WAND] **1 :** a glove designed to protect the hand from injury: as **a :** a reinforced glove used with armor during the middle ages and evolving with such armor to become in the 14th century a covering of small minutely articulated steel plates for the whole back of the hand, fingers, and thumb — see ARMOR illustration **b :** ²CESTUS **c :** any of various gloves used primarily for protection of the hands (as in industry), extending usu. well above the wrist, and being of strong and often impervious material (as rubber or asbestos) **2 :** a challenge to combat — usu. used as the object of *throw down* or *take up* ⟨threw down the ~, defying the whole world⟩ ⟨a tense situation and apparently no one dared to take up the ~⟩ **3 a** *also* **gauntlet glove :** a dress glove extending above the wrist and having a deep flared, circular, or otherwise expanded cuff **b :** the cuff of any gauntlet

gauntlet 1c

²gauntlet \"\ *or* **gant·let** \"\ *n* -S [by folk etymology (influence of ¹*gauntlet*) fr. *gantelope*] **1 :** two rows of men facing each other and armed with clubs or other weapons with which they strike at an individual who is made to run between them ⟨forced to run a ~ of clubs, revolver butts, and blackjacks —*Harper's*⟩ ⟨some had been beaten with gun butts, some made to run a ~ barefoot —*Newsweek*⟩ **2 :** a cross fire of any kind ⟨run the ~ of cannon and machine-gun blasts from each level —Byron Kennerly⟩ ⟨walked a ~ of spitting demonstrators at the airport —*United Press*⟩ ⟨ran the candidate through a savage ~ of technical questions —Alva Johnston⟩ ⟨ran the ~ of interested glances —Hortense Calisher⟩; *broadly* **:** an ordeal or test ⟨American graduates must run the ~ of American life —Perry Miller⟩ ⟨the treaty has to run a formidable ~ —*New Republic*⟩

gauntlet cuff *n* **:** a cuff (as on women's wear) narrow at the wrist and flaring above in resemblance to the cuff of a gauntlet

gaunt·let·ed *or* **gaunt·let·ted** \-lət·əd\ *adj* **:** having, wearing, or protected by a gauntlet ⟨a ~ glove⟩

gaunt·ly *adv, sometimes* -ER/-EST **:** in a gaunt manner **:** with a gaunt appearance

gaunt·ness *n* -ES **:** the quality or state of being gaunt

gaunty \ˈgȯntē, ˈgän-,ˈgȧn-, -ti\ *adj, often* -ER/-EST [¹*gaunt* + *-y*] **:** somewhat gaunt **:** rather lean

gaup \ˈgȯp\ *vb* -ED/-ING/-S [alter. of ME *galpen* to yawn, gape; akin to OE *gielpan* to boast, praise — more at YELP] *vi, dial* **:** STARE, GAPE ~ *vt, dial* **:** to gulp or swallow greedily

gaur \ˈgau̇(ə)r\ *n, pl* **gaur** *also* **gaurs** [Hindi, fr. Skt *gaura*; akin to Skt *go* bull, cow — more at COW] **:** a large East Indian wild ox (*Bibos gaurus*) with a broad forehead and short thick conical horns — compare GAYAL

gau·ra \ˈgȯrə\ *n* [NL, fr. Gk *gaurē*, fem. of *gauros* majestic, splendid; fr. the beautiful flowers of some of the species] **1** *cap* **:** a genus of American herbs (family Onagraceae) having flowers in terminal spikes or racemes **2** -S **:** any plant of the genus *Gaura*

gaus *pl of* GAU

gau·se's principle *also* **gause's rule** \ˈgau̇zəz-\ *n, usu cap G* [after G. F. *Gause*, b1910 Am. ecologist] **:** a statement in ecology: two species that have identical ecological requirements cannot exist in the same area at the same time

gau·sha·la \ˈgau̇shələ\ *n* -S [Skt *gośālā* cowshed, fr. *go* cow + *śālā* shed, hall — more at COW, HALL] **:** an Indian shelter for homeless or unwanted cattle that often also serves as a center for breed improvement and for study of bovine nutrition and welfare

gausie *var of* GAWSIE

gauss \ˈgau̇s\ *n, pl* **gauss** *also* **gausses** [after Karl Friedrich *Gauss* †1855 Ger. mathematician] **1 :** OERSTED — used before official adoption of *oersted* in 1932 **2 :** the cgs electromagnetic unit of magnetic induction equal to the magnetic flux density that will induce an electromotive force of one abvolt in each linear centimeter of a wire moving laterally with a speed of one centimeter per second at right angles to a magnetic flux

gauss·i·an curvature \-sēən-\ *or* **gauss curvature** *n, usu cap G* [K. F. *Gauss* †1855 + E *-ian*] **:** the reciprocal of the product of the two principal radii of curvature of a surface at any of its points

gaussian curve *n, usu cap G* **:** PROBABILITY CURVE

gaussian distribution *n, usu cap G* **:** a theoretical frequency distribution used in statistics that is bell-shaped, symmetrical, and of infinite extent

gauss meter *n* [after K. F. *Gauss*] **:** an instrument that indicates the strength of a magnetic field at any point directly in gauss

gauss point *n, usu cap G* [after K. F. *Gauss*] **:** CARDINAL POINT 2

gauss' theorem *or* **gauss's theorem** \ˈgau̇s(əz)-\ *n, usu cap G* [after K. F. *Gauss*] **:** a statement in physics: the total electric flux across any closed surface in an electric field equals 4π times the electric charge enclosed by it

gaus·ter \ˈgȯstə(r), ˈgäs-\ *vi* -ED/-ING/-S [ME *galstern*] **1** *dial Brit* **:** to behave boldly or boisterously **:** SWAGGER, BULLY **2** *dial Brit* **:** to waste time conspicuously esp. by talking and gossiping

¹gauze \ˈgȯz\ *n* -S *often attrib* [MF *gaze*, prob. fr. *Gaza*, city in Palestine] **1 a :** a thin open often transparent woven fabric: as (1) **:** any of various sheer textile fabrics used chiefly for clothing or draperies (2) **:** a loosely woven cotton fabric similar to cheesecloth that is extensively used for surgical dressings (3) **:** a firm woven fabric of metal or plastic filaments — usu. used with a qualifying term ⟨plastic ~*s* for screening windows⟩ **b :** LENO 1 **2 :** HAZE, MIST

²gauze \"\ *vt* -ED/-ING/-S *chiefly Brit* **:** to cover with gauze or give a gauzy appearance to ⟨midges *gauzed* the air —Elizabeth Bowen⟩; *esp* **:** to screen (as a window) with wire gauze

gauzelike \ˈ≈,≈\ *adj* **:** resembling gauze esp. in sheer transparent texture **:** GAUZY

gauz·i·ly \ˈgȯzəlē, -li\ *adv* **:** in a gauzy manner **:** so as to resemble gauze ⟨cobwebs floating ~ in the light air⟩

gauz·i·ness \-zēnəs, -zin-\ *n* -ES **:** the quality or state of being gauzy **:** resemblance to gauze ⟨a ~ in the air that dimmed the further hills⟩

gauzy \ˈgȯzē, -zi\ *adj* -ER/-EST **:** of, relating to, or resembling gauze **:** thin and slight as gauze

ga·vage \gəˈväzh\ *n* -S [F, fr. *gaver* to stuff, feed forcibly (fr. F dial. — Picardy —, fr. *gave* gullet, gizzard, fr. OF) + *-age*] **:** introduction of material (as nutrients) into the stomach by means of a stomach tube

gave *past of* GIVE

¹gav·el \ˈgavəl\ *n* -S *often attrib* [ME, fr. OE *gafol*, fr. the stem of *giefan* to give — more at GIVE] **1 :** periodic payment (as of rent or tribute) to a superior in ancient and medieval England whether in service or produce **2** *obs* **:** interest on money **:** USURY

²ga·vel \ˈgāvəl\ *chiefly Scot var of* GABLE

³gav·el \ˈgavəl\ *n* -S [ME, fr. ONF *gavelle* sheaf, bundle of fagots, perh. fr. (assumed) VL *cavella*, dim. of LL *cavus*, fr. L, hollow — more at CAVE] **1 :** a quantity of mowed grain sufficient to make a sheaf; *esp* **:** grain dropped in a straight pile from a cradle or reaper after cutting **2 a :** a bundle (as a sheaf or shock) of grain, hay, or straw **b** *Brit* **:** a bundle of straw or reeds ready for use in thatching

⁴gavel \"\ *vt* **gaveled** *or* **gavelled; gaveled** *or* **gavelled; gaveling** *or* **gavelling** \-v(ə)liŋ\ **gavels** [ME *gavelen*, fr. *gavel*, n.] **:** to rake or collect (grain or hay) in gavels

⁵gavel \"\ *n* -S [short for *gavelkind*] **1 :** GAVELKIND 2 **2 :** a body of joint tenants (as under gavelkind) that are usu. blood relatives

⁶gavel \"\ *vt* **gaveled** *or* **gavelled; gaveled** *or* **gavelled; gaveling** *or* **gavelling** \-v(ə)liŋ\ **gavels :** to subject to or distribute according to the custom of gavelkind

⁷gavel \"\ *n* -S [origin unknown] **1 :** a mason's setting maul **2 a :** the mallet of a presiding officer (as in a legislative body, public assembly, court) **b :** a mallet used (as by an auctioneer) to attract or command attention or to confirm an act (as of selling)

gavel 2

⁸gavel \"\ *vt* **gaveled** *or* **gavelled; gaveled** *or* **gavelled; gaveling** *or* **gavelling** \-v(ə)liŋ\ **gavels 1 :** to demand, require, or force by use of the gavel usu. with disregard of parliamentary courtesies ⟨a sound that the presiding officer . . . ~*ed* into silence —F.G.Slaughter⟩ **2 :** to declare arbitrarily without regard to parliamentary practice — compare STEAMROLLER

gav·el·age \ˈgav(ə)lij\ *n* -S [ME *gaffelage*, fr. *gavel*, *gaffel* (tribute) + *-age*] *archaic* **:** ¹GAVEL 1

gav·el·kind \ˈgavəlˌkīnd\ *n* [ME *gavelkynde*, fr. ¹*gavel* + *kynde*, *kinde* kind — more at KIND] **1 :** a common-law tenure of land abolished by 1926 but existing chiefly in Kent from Anglo-Saxon times and marked by various peculiar features among which are that (1) upon the death of the tenant in fee intestate the land is divided equally among all the sons or among brothers or other collateral heirs on failure of direct or nearer heirs, (2) a tenant in fee can make disposal of his land by feoffment at the age of 15, (3) there is no escheat upon judgment of death for felony, and (4) the right of dower or curtesy vests in the surviving spouse **2 :** the custom of dividing an intestate's estate equally among the sons or other heirs

gav·el·kind·er \-də(r)\ *n* -S **:** a tenant by gavelkind

gav·el·ler *also* **gav·el·er** \ˈgav(ə)lə(r)\ *n* -S [¹*gavel* + *-er*] **1 :** an officer of the British crown granting plots in the Forest of Dean to miners for mining on a royalty basis **2 :** a tenant paying gavel for land in Britain

gav·el·man \-vəlmən\ *n, pl* **gavelmen** [¹*gavel* + *man*] *archaic* **:** a person paying gavel

gav·elock \ˈgavlək\ *n* -S [ME *gavelok*, fr. OE *gafeluc*, of Celt origin; akin to W *gaflach* javelin, *gafl* forked branch, fork — more at GAFFLE] **1** *archaic* **:** a spear or dart **:** JAVELIN **2** *dial Brit* **:** an iron crowbar or lever

ga·via \ˈgāvēə\ *n, cap* [NL, fr. L, a bird (prob. sea mew)] **:** a genus of somewhat primitive aquatic birds comprising the loons and having the legs placed far back under the body which results in a clumsy floundering gait on land — see GAVIIFORMES

ga·vi·al \ˈgāvēəl\ *also* **gha·ri·al** \ˈgərēəl\ *n* -S [F, modif. of Hindi *ghariyāl*] **1 :** a large crocodilian (*Gavialis gangeticus*) of India inhabiting chiefly the basins of the Ganges, Brahmaputra, and Indus rivers and distinguished from the typical crocodiles by long slender jaws with teeth of nearly uniform size and soft, swollen, and inflatable nose tip and by completely webbed feet **2 :** any of several living or extinct reptiles related to and resembling the gavial including one extinct Asiatic form (*Ramphosuchus crassidens*) of more than 50 feet in length — **ga·vi·al·oid** \-əˌlȯid\ *adj*

ga·vi·al·i·dae \ˌgāvēˈaləˌdē\ *n pl, cap* [NL, fr. *Gavialis*, type genus (fr. F *gavial*) + *-idae*] *in some classifications* **:** a family of crocodilians comprising the gavials and a few related extinct forms

ga·vi·ifor·mes \ˌgāvēəˈfȯrˌmēz\ *n pl, cap* [NL, fr. *Gavia* + *-i-* + *-formes*] **:** an order of large aquatic birds including those of the genus *Gavia* and a few related extinct birds — compare LOON

¹ga·votte *also* **ga·vot** \gəˈvät, *usu* -äd·+V\ *n* -S [F *gavotte*, fr. MF, fr. OProv *gavoto*, fr. *gavot* Alpine dweller, fr. *gava* crop, goiter] **1 :** a dance of French peasant origin characterized by the raising rather than sliding of the feet **2 :** a French dance tune in moderately quick ¼ time comprised of two sections each of which is repeated and always beginning on the third beat

²gavotte \"\ *vi* -ED/-ING/-S **:** to dance a gavotte

¹gaw \ˈgȯ, ˈgä\ *n* -S [alter. of ²*gall*] *chiefly Scot* **1 :** ²GALL 1a, 2a **2 :** a small channel cut for drainage purposes **:** FURROW, TRENCH

²gaw \ˈgȯ\ *dial Brit var of* GOD

GAW *abbr* guaranteed annual wage

gaw·bli·my \gȯˈblīmi\ *var of* GORBLIMY

gawd *archaic var of* ¹GAUD

gawdy *archaic var of* ¹GAUDY

¹gawk \ˈgȯk, ˈgäk\ *vi* -ED/-ING/-S [perh. alter. (influenced by E dial. *gawk* left-handed) of obs. E *gaw* to stare, fr. ME *gawen*, fr. ON *gā* to heed, mark — more at FAVOR] **:** to look without intelligent awareness **:** gape or stare stupidly — often used with *at* ⟨passers-by ~*ed* at the wreck⟩ — **gawker** *n* -S

²gawk \"\ *n* -S [prob. fr. E dial. *gawk* left-handed] **:** an ungainly clumsy stupid person **:** LOUT

gawk·ham·mer \ˈgau̇kˌhamə(r), ˈgȯk-,ˈgäk-\ *adj* [²*gawk* + E dial. *hammer* clumsy person] *dial Eng* **:** AWKWARD, CLUMSY

gawk·i·ly \ˈgȯkəlē, ˈgäk-, -li\ *adv* **:** in a gawky manner **:** with gawkiness ⟨held herself ~ as though she didn't know how to cope with the length of her limbs —W.S.Maugham⟩

gawk·i·ness \-kēnəs, -kin-\ *n* -ES **:** the quality or state of being gawky

gawk·ish \ˈgȯkish, ˈgäk-, -kēsh\ *adj* [²*gawk* + *-ish*] **:** being like a gawk **:** awkward, shy, and stupid — **gawk·ish·ly** *adv* — **gawk·ish·ness** *n* -ES

¹gawky \ˈgȯkē, ˈgäk-, -ki\ *adj* -ER/-EST [²*gawk* + *-y*] **:** lacking grace or elegance often from being too large or awkwardly put together ⟨a tall ~ house⟩; *often* **:** overgrown and gangling and consequently self-conscious and awkward ⟨a ~ lad, at that uncomfortable age when . . . the great hands and ankles protrude a long way from garments which have grown too tight for them —W.M.Thackeray⟩ **syn** see AWKWARD

²gawky \"\ *n* -ES **:** a gawky person

gawm *var of* ⁴GAUM

gaw·ney \ˈgȯni\ *n* -S [origin unknown] *chiefly dial Eng* **:** SIMPLETON, GAWK

¹gawp *var of* GAUP

²gawp \ˈgȯp\ *n* -S [¹*gawp*] *dial* **:** a stupid awkward person **:** SIMPLETON

gaw·sie *or* **gaw·cie** *or* **gaw·cey** \ˈgȯsē\ *adj* [origin unknown] **1** *Scot, of a person* **:** well-fed and hearty looking **:** plump and cheerful **2** *Scot, of a domestic animal* **:** well filled out **:** in good condition **3** *Scot* **:** good-sized **:** presenting an imposing and ample appearance ⟨the house . . . *gawcey* and substantial —G.D.Brown⟩

¹gay \ˈgā\ *adj* -ER/-EST [ME, fr. MF *gai*, prob. fr. OProv, of Gmc origin; akin to OHG *gāhi* rapid, hurried, impetuous] **1 :** excited and merry **:** manifesting or inclined to joyous exhibition of content or pleasure ⟨~ carefree children⟩ ⟨a ~ word of greeting⟩ **2 a :** bright and lively in appearance ⟨~ sunny meadows⟩ **b :** brilliant in color ⟨the dress a bit too ~ for her years⟩ **c** *chiefly Brit, of poultry* **:** marked with white ⟨Anconas often become *gayer* with age⟩ **3** *obs* **a :** FIRST-CLASS, FINE, EXCELLENT **b :** speciously or artfully brilliant — used of things immaterial (as reasoning or rhetoric) **4 a :** given to social pleasures **b :** inclined to the dissipations of society **:** LICENTIOUS, LOOSE **c** *of a woman* **:** leading an immoral life; *esp* **:** engaging in prostitution **5** *dial Eng, of health or physical condition* **:** good ⟨not feeling so ~ today⟩ ⟨looked quite ~ after his spell⟩ **6 a** *of an animal* **:** ALERT, KEEN, LIVELY **b** *of a tail* **:** carried high, erect, or curled over the back ⟨the tail of a Persian cat should never be ~⟩ **7 :** impertinent and forward **:** BRASH, FRESH — usu. used with *get* ⟨don't get ~ with me if you want to keep out of trouble⟩ **8 a :** HOMOSEXUAL **b :** of, relating to, or being a socially integrated group oriented toward and concerned with the welfare of the homosexual ⟨a ~ newspaper⟩ **syn** see LIVELY

²gay \"\ *n* -S [ME, fr. *gay*, adj.] **1** *obs* **:** a gay person or pastime **2** *dial Eng* **a :** a toy or ornament esp. for a child **b :** an illustration in a book or paper ⟨haven't got my glasses but I can still read the *gays*⟩

³gay \"\ *adv* [ME, fr. *gay*, adj.] **:** GAILY, BRIGHTLY, JOYOUSLY — used in combination ⟨the *gay*-colored flowers⟩

⁴gay \"\ *vb* -ED/-ING/-S [¹*gay*] *vi* **:** to behave gaily **:** become gay ⟨a bird ~*ing* on a branch before the window⟩ ~ *vt* **:** to make gay, bright, or cheerful — usu. used with *up* ⟨fresh paint and new curtains will ~ up a dingy kitchen⟩

⁵gay *var of* GEY

ga·ya \gə'yä\ *adj, usu cap* [fr. *Gaya*, India] **:** of or from the city of Gaya, India **:** of the kind or style prevalent in Gaya

ga·yal \gə'yäl\ *n, pl* **gayals** *also* **gayal** [Beng *gayāl*; akin to Skt *go* bull, cow — more at COW] **:** an ox (*Bibos frontalis*) domesticated in India that differs from the gaur of which it may be a domesticated variety in its longer slenderer horns and white legs

ga·ya·tri \'gäyə,trē\ *n* -s [Skt *gāyatrī*, fr. *gāyatra* song, hymn, fr. *gāyati* he sings — more at CHOUGH] **1 :** an ancient Vedic meter of 24 syllables generally arranged in a triplet **2 :** a composition in this meter (as a noted Hindu mantra used daily by the devout)

gaycat \'ˌ=ˌ=\ *n* **1** *slang* **:** a tramp who will work if the inducement is sufficient **2** *slang* **:** a young and inexperienced tramp

gay·di·ang \'gīdē,aŋ\ *n* -s [Annamese] **:** an Annamese ship with two or three masts and lofty triangular sails

gay dog *n* **:** a man given to gay or licentious self-indulgence

gayety *var of* GAIETY

gayfeather \'ˌ=ˌ==\ *n* **:** BUTTON SNAKEROOT 1; *esp* **:** a widely distributed purple-flowered perennial herb (*Liatris pycnostachya*) of central No. America that is sometimes cultivated as an ornamental and for cut flowers

gay lady's-slipper *n* **:** SHOWY LADY'S-SLIPPER

gaylies *var of* GEYLIES

gay-lus·sac \ˌgālə'sak\ *adj, usu cap G&L* [after Joseph L. *Gay-Lussac* †1850 Fr. chemist and physicist] **:** of, relating to, or developed by the French chemist Joseph L. Gay-Lussac

gay·lus·sacia \ˌgālə'sash(ē)ə, -'sakēə\ *n, cap* [NL, fr. J. L. *Gay-Lussac* + NL *-ia*] **:** a large genus of American shrubs (family Ericaceae) comprising the true huckleberries and being distinguished by a 10-locular 10-ovuled ovary and anthers without awns

gay-lussac's law *n, usu cap G&1stL* [after J. L. *Gay-Lussac*] **:** a statement in chemistry and physics: when two or more gaseous substances combine to form a gaseous compound the volume of the product is either equal to the sum of the volumes of the factors or is less than and bears a simple ratio to this sum — called also *law of combining volumes;* compare AVOGADRO'S LAW **2 :** CHARLES'S LAW

gay-lussac tower *n, usu cap G&L* [after J. L. *Gay-Lussac*] **:** a large packed tower that is situated after the chambers in the chamber process of making sulfuric acid and that contains strong sulfuric acid for absorbing nitrogen oxides from the spent gases with the formation of nitrous vitriol — see GLOVER TOWER

gay·lus·site \'gālə,sīt\ *n* -s [F, fr. J. L. *Gay-Lussac* + F *-ite*] **:** a mineral $Na_2Ca(CO_3)_2.5H_2O$ consisting of a yellowish white translucent hydrous carbonate of calcium and sodium

gayly *var of* GAILY

gay·ness *n* -ES [ME *gaynesse*, fr. ¹*gay* + *-nesse* -ness] **:** the quality or state of being gay **:** GAIETY

ga·yo \'gī(,)ō, 'gä(,)yō\ *n, pl* **gayo** *or* **gayos** *usu cap* [native name in northern Sumatra] **1 :** an Indonesian people of northern Sumatra **2 :** a member of the Gayo people

gay science *n* **:** POETRY; *esp* **:** amatory poetry

gay·some \'gāsəm\ *adj* [¹*gay* + *-some*] **:** full of gaiety **:** BLITHE, CHEERY

gayway \'ˌ=ˌ=\ *n* **:** MIDWAY 3a

gaywings \'ˌ=ˌ=\ *n pl but sing or pl in constr* **:** a common trailing perennial milkwort (*Polygala paucifolia*) of eastern No. America having leaves suggesting those of the wintergreen and rosy purple or occasionally white flowers with winged sepals and fringed crest on the corolla — called also *flowering wintergreen, fringed polygala*

gay·you \'gä|(,)(y)ü, 'gī|\ *n* -s [Annamese *ghe hâu* fine boat] **:** an Annamese narrow flat-bottomed boat with an outrigger and two or three masts with square sails or lugsails

gaz *abbr* gazette; gazetted; gazetteer

¹**gazabo** *var of* GAZEBO

²**ga·za·bo** \gə'zā(,)bō\ *n* -s [origin unknown] *slang* **:** FELLOW, PERSON, GUY

ga·za·nia \gə'zānēə\ *n* [NL, irreg. fr. Teodoro *Gaza*, 15th cent. Greek scholar + NL *-ia*] **1** *cap* **:** a genus of southern African tomentose herbs (family Compositae) that are often cultivated for their brilliant flower heads which usu. have conspicuous ray florets variously colored in red and yellow **2** -s **:** any plant of the genus *Gazania*

¹**gaze** \'gāz\ *vb* -ED/-ING/-S [ME *gasen, gazen*, prob. of Scand origin; akin to Sw dial. *gasa* to stare, Norw dial. *gase* fool, *gasa* to rush forward, and perh. to ON *gassi* reckless person, Icel, gander, Dan dial. *gåse* gander, ON *gās* goose — more at GOOSE] *vi* **:** to fix the eyes in a steady and intent look **:** look with eagerness (as in admiration, wonder) or with studious attention ⟨*gazed* delighted at the scurrying throng⟩ ⟨*gazing* after the slowly vanishing boat⟩ ~ *vt, archaic* **:** to view with attention **:** gaze on

syn GAZE, GAPE, STARE, GLARE, PEER, and GLOAT can mean in common, but with marked differences, to look at long and attentively. GAZE usu. implies fixed and prolonged attention ⟨*gaze* absently into the distance⟩ ⟨could only sigh, and *gaze* at her wonderingly —George Meredith⟩ ⟨she *gazed* into his faded blue eyes as if yearning to be understood —Joseph Conrad⟩ GAPE usu. implies an open-mouthed, often stupid, wonder ⟨*gape* at an apparition in astonishment⟩ ⟨sit *gaping* at the spring sunshine⟩ STARE implies a fixed and direct, unwavering gaze ⟨*stare* at a stranger impolitely⟩ ⟨*stare* at a TV screen⟩ GLARE adds to STARE the idea of intenseness, usu. of fierceness or anger ⟨he *stared* at her from doorways, and *glared* at her from passages as she went about with her partners; and the more he *stared*, the more taken was he —Rudyard Kipling⟩ ⟨*glare* at a disobedient child⟩ ⟨he put his paw on the prize, and *glared* across the water with a defiant growl —C.G.D. Roberts⟩ PEER suggests a looking closely or curiously, esp. with partly closed eyes or from behind something ⟨the haggard face . . . that *peered* at him out of the angle of the wall —Liam O'Flaherty⟩ ⟨we *peered* at the muddy waters through an intricate pattern of bridgework —David Fairchild⟩ ⟨she had *peered* at it keenly through her spectacles —Agnes S. Turnbull⟩ GLOAT implies prolonged or frequent gazing upon something, usu. with profound, often unholy satisfaction ⟨there were residents of Boston who couldn't take their eyes from the passing carts, but stood and *gloated* —Kenneth Roberts⟩ ⟨as a boy he used to *gloat* in the Museum of Düsseldorf over the wood-carvings —G.G.Coulton⟩ ⟨spent hours *gloating* over his money⟩

²**gaze** \"\ *n* -s **1** *archaic* **:** an object gazed on **2 a :** act of looking fixedly ⟨made a long slow ~ the length of the ridge⟩ **b :** a fixed intent look **:** a continued look of attention ⟨his ~ was steady, his mien reproachful⟩ — **at gaze 1 :** depicted with the face turned directly to the front — used of heraldic representations of beasts of chase **2 a** *of a stag or other deer* **:** assuming a position expressing sudden fear or surprise (as when first hearing hounds) **b :** standing staring (as in wonder, alarm, dismay) **:** GAZING

¹**ga·ze·bo** *also* **ga·zee·bo** \gə'zē(,)bō, -zē(-\ *or* **ga·za·bo** \-zā(-\ *n, pl* **gazebos** *or* **gazeboes** [perh. fr. ¹*gaze* + L *-ebo* (as in *videbo* I shall see)] **:** BELVEDERE

²**ga·ze·bo** \gə'zā(,)bō, -zē(-\ *var of* ²GAZABO

gazehound \'ˌ=ˌ=\ *n* **:** a dog that hunts by sight rather than by scent; *sometimes* **:** GREYHOUND

gazel *var of* GHAZEL

gaze·less \'gāzləs\ *adj* **:** UNSEEING **:** lacking power of sight ⟨turned blind and ~ eyes⟩

ga·zel·la \gə'zelə\ *n, cap* [NL, fr. F *gazelle*] **:** a genus of antelopes comprising the typical gazelles — **ga·zel·line** \-e,līn, -elən\ *adj*

¹**ga·zelle** \gə'zel\ *n, pl* **gazelles** *also* **gazelle** [F, fr. MF, fr. Ar *ghazāl*] **1 :** any of numerous small graceful and swift African and Asiatic antelopes constituting *Gazella* and related genera and noted for the luster and soft expression of their eyes **2** *or* **gazelle brown :** a grayish brown to grayish yellowish brown that is paler than soot brown or gold bronze and slightly greener and lighter than mummy brown (sense 2b) — called also *grouse, racquet*

²**gazelle** \"\ *vi* -ED/-ING/-S **:** to move in easy leaps suggesting those of a gazelle ⟨*gazelling* over the hurdles —*Newsweek*⟩

gazelle-eyed \=ˈ=ˌ=\ *adj* **:** having soft lustrous expressive eyes

gazelle-faced wallaby \=ˈ=ˌ=-\ *n* **:** any of various naked-eared wallabies of New Guinea that constitute the genus *Dorcopsis* and resemble the pademelons

gazelle hound *n* **:** a dog (as the saluki) used for coursing gazelles

gaze·ment \'gāzmənt\ *n* -s [¹*gaze* + *-ment*] *archaic* **:** prolonged observation or a stare

gaz·er \'gāzə(r)\ *n* -s **1 :** one that gazes **2** *slang* **:** a policeman or government narcotic agent

gazes *pres 3d sing of* GAZE, *pl of* GAZE

ga·zet *or* **ga·zett** \gə(d)'zet\ *n* -s [It *gazzetta*, fr. Venetian dial. *gazeta*, perh. dim. of *gaza* magpie, fr. L *Gaja*, a name for women] **:** a small Venetian copper coin of the 16th and 17th centuries

ga·zet·tal \gə'zed·ᵊl, -etᵊl\ *n* -s *Brit* **:** an act of gazetting ⟨~ of new appointments⟩

¹**ga·zette** \gə'zet, *usu* -ed·+V\ *n* -s [F, fr. It *gazzetta*, fr. Venetian dial. *gazeta* gazet, periodical that sold for a gazet] **1 :** a news sheet published periodically **:** NEWSPAPER — used chiefly in the names of newspapers **2 :** an official journal published at regular intervals (as twice a week in London and Edinburgh) containing records of various official acts, lists of promotions and honors, names of bankrupts, and public notices **3** *Brit* **:** an announcement in an official gazette ⟨just saw the ~ of his appointment⟩

²**gazette** \"\ *vt* -ED/-ING/-S **1** *chiefly Brit* **:** to announce or publish in a gazette **:** announce (as an appointment or a case of bankruptcy) publicly ⟨an Order in Council *gazetted* in Jerusalem —*Manchester Guardian Weekly*⟩ **2** *Brit* **:** to announce the appointment or status of in an official gazette ⟨he was *gazetted* to the regiment in 1932⟩ ⟨white troops *gazetted* for permanent duty in Africa —*N.Y. Times*⟩

¹**gaz·et·teer** \ˌgazə'ti(ə)r, -iə\ *n* -s [prob. fr. F *gazetier* (formerly spelled *gazettier*), fr. *gazette* + *-ier* -er] **1 a** *archaic* **:** a writer for a newspaper **b** *Brit* **:** a journalist in government employment serving usu. as a public-relations officer or publicist **2** *obs* **:** NEWSPAPER, GAZETTE **3** [fr. the *Gazetteer*, shortened form of *The Gazetteer's: or, Newsman's Interpreter: Being a Geographical Index* (1693), edited by Laurence Echard †1730 Eng. historian] **:** a geographical dictionary in which names and descriptions of places are usu. given in alphabetical order; *often* **:** a book in which something (as wines or restaurants) is treated esp. in regard to geographical distribution and regional specialization

²**gazetteer** \"\ *vt* -ED/-ING/-S **:** to describe in a gazetteer

gazi *often cap, var of* GHAZI

gazing *pres part. of* GAZE

gazing ball *n* **1 :** a glass ball used in crystal gazing **2 :** GAZING GLOBE

gazing globe *n* **:** a mirrored metallic often colored globe usu. mounted on a pedestal and used as a garden ornament

gaz·ing·ly *adv* **:** in a gazing manner **:** with an intent look

gazingstock \'ˌ=ˌ=\ *n* -s **:** a person or thing gazed at by many esp. with curiosity or contempt

gazogene *var of* GASOGENE

gazoo *var of* KAZOO

ga·zook \gə'zük, -zu̇k\ *n* -s [origin unknown] *slang* **:** GUY

ga·zoz \gə'zōz\ *n* -ES [Ar *gāzūzah* (dial. *gāzōza*), fr. It *gazzosa, gassosa*, fr. fem. of *gazzoso, gassoso* gassy, fr. *gas* (fr. NL) + *-oso* -ous (fr. L *-osus*) — more at GAS] **:** a carbonated nonalcoholic drink

gaz·pa·cho \gäth'pä(,)chō, gä'sp-\ *n, pl* **gazpachos** \-ōz, -ōs\ [Sp] **:** a soup made of uncooked chopped tomatoes, cucumbers, peppers, onion, garlic with vinegar, oil, and condiments, often thickened with bread crumbs, and served cold

GB *abbr* **1** games behind **2** gold bond **3** guidebook **4** gunboat

gba·ri \gə'bärē\ *or* **gwa·ri** \'gwärē, gə'w-\ *n, pl* **gbari** *or* **gbaris** *or* **gwari** *or* **gwaris** *usu cap* **:** a widespread peasant people of west central Nigeria to the north of the Niger-Benue confluence who are linguistically related to the Yoruba

gbo \gə'bō\ *n, pl* **gbo** [native name in Dahomey, Africa] **:** a charm that protects its owner from evil and has the power to hurt its owner's enemies

GC *abbr* **1** general circular **2** golf club **3** grand commander **4** grand cross **5** great circle **6** group captain **7** gun control

GCA *abbr* **1** general claim agent **2** ground-controlled approach

GCD *abbr* greatest common divisor

GCF *abbr* greatest common factor

GCI *abbr* ground-controlled interception

GCL *abbr* ground-controlled landing

g clef *n, usu cap G* **:** a clef that places G above middle C, on the second line of the staff — called also *treble clef;* see CLEF illustration

GCM *abbr* general court-martial

GCT *abbr* Greenwich civil time

gd *abbr* **1** good **2** ground **3** guard

GD *abbr* **1** general delivery **2** general duty **3** good delivery **4** granddaughter **5** grand duchess; grand duchy; grand duke

Gd *symbol* gadolinium

gdansk \gə'dänzk, -dan-, -n(t)sk\ *adj, usu cap* [Pol *Gdańsk* Danzig] **:** DANZIG

gde *abbr* gourde

gdn *abbr* **1** garden **2** guardian

gds *abbr* goods

gdsm *abbr* guardsman

gdyn·ia \gə'dinēə\ *adj, usu cap* [fr. *Gdynia*, Poland] **:** of or from the city of Gdynia, Poland **:** of the kind or style prevalent in Gdynia

¹**ge** *var of* GEE

²**ge** \'zhā\ *n, pl* **ge** *or* **ges** *usu cap* [Pg *gê*, of AmerInd origin] **1 a :** a group of Indian peoples of eastern Brazil **b :** a member of any of such peoples **2 :** the language of the Ge peoples

ge- *or* **geo-** *comb form* [ME *geo-*, fr. MF & L; MF, fr. L, fr. Gk *gē-, ge-, geō-*, fr. *gē* earth, land] **1 :** earth, ground, soil ⟨*geo*biology⟩ ⟨*geo*genic⟩ ⟨*geo*phyte⟩ ⟨*geo*tropic⟩ **2** geographical **:** geography and ⟨*geo*history⟩ ⟨*geo*politics⟩

GE *abbr* gilt edges

Ge *symbol* germanium

-gea — see -GAEA

¹**geal** \'jē(ə)l\ *vi* -ED/-ING/-S [ME *gellen*, fr. MF *geler* to freeze, fr. L *gelare* to freeze, congeal — more at COLD] *now dial* **:** CONGEAL

²**geal** \"\ *n* -s *dial* **:** JELLY

³**ge·al** \'jēəl\ *adj* [*ge-* + *-al*] **:** of, relating to, or caused by the earth

gean \'gēn\ *n* -s [MF *guisne, guine*] **1 a** *chiefly Brit* **:** SWEET CHERRY 1; *esp* **:** a wild sweet cherry **b :** HEART CHERRY **2 :** the fruit of a gean

ge·anticlinal \(ˌ)jē+\ *adj* [*ge-* + *anticlinal*] **:** of, relating to, or having geanticlines

ge·anticline \(')jē+\ *also* **geo·anticline** \ˌjē(,)ō+\ *or* **ge·anticlinal** \(ˌ)jē+\ *n* [*geanticline, geoanticline* fr. *ge-* + *anticline; geanticlinal* fr. *ge-* + *anticlinal*] **:** a great upward flexure of the earth's crust — opposed to *geosyncline*

¹**gear** \'gi(ə)r, -iə\ *n* -s [ME *gere*, fr. OE *gearwe;* akin to OS & OHG *garuwi* equipment, clothing, ON *gervi, görvi;* derivatives fr. the root of E *yare*] **1 a :** CLOTHING, GARMENTS **b :** personal belongings or equipment ⟨the sheds where the cowboys kept their ~⟩ **c :** movable property **:** household stuff **:** GOODS ⟨all the ~ that goes with a summer cottage⟩ **d** *dial chiefly Brit* **:** food and liquor **:** SUSTENANCE **2 :** EQUIPMENT, PARAPHERNALIA ⟨photographic ~⟩ ⟨fishing ~⟩ ⟨military ~⟩ **3 a** (1) **:** RIGGING; *specif* **:** the equipment required for any particular sail, spar, or function (2) **:** the harness of horses or cattle **:** TRAPPINGS **b** *archaic* **:** the organs of generation **4 a** *obs* **:** a leaf of heddles **b :** a single complete setline **5** *dial chiefly Brit* **:** RUBBISH, TRASH, JUNK **6** *dial chiefly Brit* **:** CONCERN, DOINGS **7 a** (1) **:** a mechanism that performs a specific function in a complete machine ⟨a valve ~⟩ ⟨a steering ~⟩ (2) **:** a toothed wheel ⟨a bevel ~⟩ ⟨a spur ~⟩ ⟨a train of ~s⟩ (3) **:** working relation or adjustment ⟨in ~⟩ ⟨out of ~⟩ **b :** one of two to several adjustments of a motor-vehicle transmission that determine mechanical advantage, relative speed, and direction of travel — compare ¹HIGH 1c(6), ⁴LOW 3f **syn** see EQUIPMENT

²**gear** \"\ *vb* -ED/-ING/-S [ME *geren*, fr. *gere*, n.] *vt* **1 :** DRESS, EQUIP ⟨now women ~*ed* out in the height of fashion⟩ **2 a :** to provide (as machinery) with gearing **:** connect by gearing **:** put into gear **b :** to harness (as a work animal) — often used with *up* **3 a :** to put into a desired state of thorough internal coordination for effective and usu. immediate operation ⟨soldiers ~*ed* to strike in instantaneous retaliation⟩ **b :** to bring into precise adjustment so as to satisfy, conform, or harmonize or into close working relation so as to keep pace or qualify for integration ⟨an institution ~*ed* to the needs of the blind⟩ ⟨is the program ~*ed* to a fixed salary increase schedule? —W.H. Whyte⟩ ~ *vi* **1** *of machinery* **:** to be in or come into gear **2 :** to adjust or become adjusted so as to match, blend, or harmonize ⟨industry ~*ing* with consumer needs⟩

gearbox \'ˌ=ˌ=\ *n* **:** TRANSMISSION 2

gear change *n, Brit* **:** GEAR SHIFT

gear cluster *n* **:** CLUSTER GEAR

gear cutter *n* **1 :** a machine for milling, hobbing, planing, or shaping gear teeth — compare GEAR HOBBER, GEAR SHAPER **2 :** a milling cutter esp. contoured to cut gear teeth — see MILLING CUTTER illustration

gear down *vt* **:** to gear so that the driven part goes slower than the driving part

geared *adj* **1 :** having gears **2 :** being in gear

geared turbine *n* **:** a turbine having its drive shaft attached to a set of reduction gears

gear hobber *n* **:** a machine for milling gear teeth by means of a hob rotated at an angular velocity having a definite ratio to that of the work

gearing *n* -s **1 :** the act or process of providing or fitting with gears **2 a** *chiefly dial* **:** HARNESS **b :** the parts by which motion is transmitted from one portion of machinery to another **:** GEAR; *specif* **:** a train of gear wheels

gearing chain *n* **:** an endless chain to transmit motion from one sprocket wheel to another

ge·ark·sut·ite \jē'ärksə,tīt\ *n* -s [*ge-* + *arksutite* $Na_5Al_3F_{14}$ fr. *Arksut* (*Arsuk*) fjord, Greenland + E *-ite*] **:** a mineral $CaAl(OH)F_4.H_2O$ consisting of an earthy clayey hydrous calcium aluminum fluoride occurring with cryolite

gear·less \'gi(ə)rləs, -iəl-\ *adj* **:** having no gear **:** operating without a gear

gearless traction *n* **:** traction without reduction gears (as in a high-speed electric elevator drive in which the driving sheave is mounted directly on the armature shaft)

gear level *vt* **:** to gear so that the driven part goes at the same rate as the driving part — compare GEAR DOWN, GEAR UP

gear·man \'=mən\ *n, pl* **gearmen 1 :** one that looks after gears **2 :** a keeper of engine-room stores aboard a ship

gearmotor \'ˌ=ˌ==\ *n* **:** an electric motor with various output speeds secured by attached combinations of gears

gear pump *n* **:** a rotary pump consisting of two meshing gear wheels in a suitable casing whose contrarotation entrains the fluid on one side and discharges it on the other

gear ratio *n* **:** the ratio of the angular speed of the initial or driving member of a gear train or equivalent mechanism to that of the final or driven member; *specif* **:** the number of engine revolutions per revolution of the rear wheels of an automobile

gears \'gi(ə)rz\ *n pl* [ME *geres*, pl. of *gere* gear — more at GEAR] *Midland* **:** HARNESS

gearset \'ˌ=ˌ=\ *n* **:** a set of gears forming a unit group

gear shaper *n* **:** a machine in which gear teeth are shaped by a cutter in the form of a pinion; *also* **:** one that shapes gears

gearshift \'ˌ=ˌ=\ *n* **:** a mechanism by which the transmission gears in a power-transmission system are engaged and disengaged; *also* **:** the functioning of such a mechanism

gear up *vt* **1 :** to gear so that the driven part goes faster than the driving part **2 :** to speed up ⟨*gear up* production to meet military needs⟩ **:** ACCELERATE

gear wheel *n* **:** a wheel that gears with another piece; *specif* **:** COGWHEEL

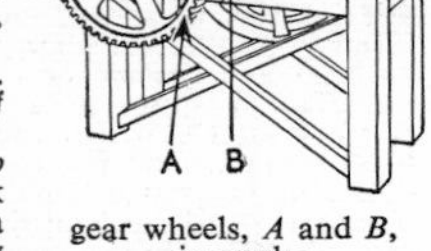

gear wheels, *A* and *B*, in mesh

geason *adj* [ME *geson*, fr. OE *gǣsne;* akin to OHG *geisinī* barrenness, and perh. to OE *gād* lack, need, desire, Goth *gaidw* lack, OE *gān* to go — more at GO] *obs* **:** UNPRODUCTIVE, SCANT, SCARCE

ge·aster \(')jē'astə(r)\ *n* [NL, fr. *ge-* + *-aster* (star)] *syn of* GEASTRUM

ge·as·trum \jē'astrəm\ *n, cap* [NL, fr. *ge-* + *-astrum* (fr. Gk *astēr* star) — more at STAR] **:** a genus (the type of the family Geastraceae) of basidiomycetous fungi having the outer peridium when dry splitting into starlike segments — compare EARTHSTAR

geat \'ya(ə)t, 'yēət\ *n, pl* **geats** \-əts\ *also* **gea·tas** \-ə,täs\ *usu cap* [OE *Gēat*] **:** a Scandinavian people of southern Sweden subjugated by the Swedes in the 6th century and believed to be ancestors of the Gotlanders — **geat·ish** *adj, usu cap*

ge·bang \gə'baŋ, -bäŋ\ *or* **gebang palm** *n* -s [Malay *gĕbang*] **:** a Malayan fan palm (*Corypha gebanga*) having large leaves that are split and used for thatching or plaiting into containers

ge·ban·ga \-ŋgə\ *n* -s [NL (specific epithet of *Corypha gebanga*), fr. Malay *gĕbang*] **:** the leaf fiber of the gebang palm

ge·brauchs·mu·sik \gə'brau̇ks(,)mü,zēk\ *n, usu cap* [G, fr. *gebrauch* use + *musik* music] **:** music composed for use outside the concert field (as for amateur groups, celebrations, films)

ge·car·cin·i·dae \ˌjē,kär'sinə,dē\ *n pl, cap* [NL, fr. *Gecarcinus*, type genus + *-idae*] **:** a family of brachyuran crabs comprising the common land crabs — see GECARCINUS

ge·car·ci·nus \jē'kärs'nəs\ *n, cap* [NL, fr. *ge-* + Gk *karkinos* crab] **:** the type genus of the family Gecarcinidae comprising the black crab and other land crabs of the West Indies and tropical western Africa

gecconid *var of* GEKKONID

gec·con·i·dae \ge'känə,dē\ *syn of* GEKKONIDAE

geck \'gek\ *vi* -ED/-ING/-S [LG *gecken* to make a fool of, fr. MLG, fr. *geck* fool] **1** *chiefly Scot* **:** to be scornful or derisive **:** MOCK — usu. used with *at* ⟨~ at me because I'm poor —Robert Burns⟩ **2** *chiefly Scot* **:** to show scorn or derision by tossing the head or casting sidelong glances

¹**gecko** *also* **gec·co** \'ge(,)kō\ *n, pl* **geckos** *or* **geckoes** *also* **geccos** *or* **geccoes** [Malay *ge'kok*, of imit. origin] **:** any of numerous small chiefly tropical usu. nocturnal lizards (family Gekkonidae) that have large eyes and vertical elliptical pupils, amphicoelous vertebrae, and toes generally expanded and furnished with adhesive disks and that are completely harmless and valuable destroyers of insects though often locally reputed to be venomous

²**gecko** \"\ [NL, fr. Malay *ge'kok*] *syn of* GEKKO

geck·oid \'ge,kȯid\ *n or adj* [NL *gecko* + E *-oid*] **:** GEKKONOID

geck·o·nes \'gekə,nēz, ge'kō(,)n-\ *syn of* GEKKONES

geck·on·i·dae \ge'känə,dē\ *syn of* GEKKONIDAE

ged *or* **gedd** \'ged\ *n* -s [ME *gedd, gedde*, fr. ON *gedda* — more at GOAD] *chiefly Scot* **:** ⁴PIKE 1a

ged·a·nite \'gedᵊn,īt, 'je-\ *n* -s [G *gedanit*, fr. *Gedanum* Danzig, city in northern Poland + G *-it* -ite] **:** a fossil resin similar to amber

ge·dank·en·experiment \gə'däŋkən+ˌ=ˌ==\ *n* [G, fr. *gedanke* thought + *experiment*] **:** an experiment carried out by proposing a hypothesis in thought only

ge·deckt \gə'dekt\ *or* **ge·dackt** *also* **ge·dact** \-däkt, -dakt\ *n* -s [*gedeckt* fr. G, fr. past part. of *decken* to cover, fr. OHG *deckan; gedackt, gedact* fr. G *gedackt*, fr. archaic past part. of *decken* — more at THATCH] **:** a labial pipe-organ stop of 2-foot, 4-foot, 8-foot, 16-foot, or 32-foot pitch and of flute quality

gedeckt pom·mer \-,pämə(r), -,pȯm-\ *n* [G *gedacktpommer, gedecktpommer*, fr. *gedackt, gedeckt* + *pommer*] **:** a gedeckt pipe-organ mixture stop that is used to produce a strong harmonic at the twelfth as well as the fundamental tone

ge·deckt·work \-k,twərk\ *n* **:** the flue stops in a pipe organ with covered pipes

ge·din·ni·an \jə'dinēən, zhə'-\ *adj, usu cap* [fr. *Gedinnian*, subdivision of the European Devonian, fr. F *Gédinnien*, fr. *Gédinne*, village in Belgium + F *-ien* -ian] **:** of, relating to, or constituting a subdivision of the European Devonian — see GEOLOGIC TIME table

ged·rite \'je,drīt\ *n* -s [F *gédrite*, fr. *Gèdre*, village in southern France + F *-ite*] **:** a mineral consisting of an aluminous variety of anthophyllite

ge·dunk \'gē,dəŋk\ *n* -s [origin unknown] *slang* **:** something (as a sundae) sold at a soda fountain or snack bar

¹**gee** \'jē\ *v imper* [origin unknown] — used (1) as a command to a team or draft animal to turn to the right or move ahead or (2) as a call in square dancing to progress to the right; compare

⁵haw ~ *vi* **geed; geed; geeing; gees 1 :** to cry out the command *gee* to a draft animal ⟨we *geed* and hawed until we were hoarse —A.M.Bailey⟩ **2 :** to turn to the off or right side ⟨the mare *geed* when she should have hawed⟩ **3 :** to obey the command *gee* ⟨teaching a pair of young steers to ~⟩

²**gee** \"\ *n* -s *slang Brit* **:** HORSE

³**gee** *also* **ge** \"\ *n* -s **1 :** the letter *g* **2** [fr. the initial letter of *grand*] *slang* **:** a thousand dollars **3** [fr. the initial letter of *guy*] *slang* **:** MAN, INDIVIDUAL ⟨nobody is gettin' away with anything on this ~ —J.T.Farrell⟩

⁴**gee** \"\ *vi* **geed; geed; geeing; gees** [origin unknown] *chiefly dial* **:** to get along **:** AGREE, JIBE ⟨these various powerful themes do not always quite ~ —*Time*⟩

⁵**gee** \ˈgē\ *n* -s [origin unknown] *chiefly Scot* **:** a capricious notion **:** WHIM; *esp* **:** a perverse inclination

⁶**gee** *or* **jee** \ˈjē\ *interj* [euphemism for *Jesus*] — often used as an introductory expletive for emphasis and sometimes to express surprise or enthusiasm

⁷**gee** \"\ *n* -s *usu cap* [origin unknown] **:** an aeronautical navigation system similar to loran and developed in England during World War II as a bombing aid

gee·bung \ˈjē,bəŋ\ *n* -s [native name in Australia] **:** any of numerous chiefly Australian shrubs and small trees that constitute a genus (*Persoonia*) of the family Proteaceae, have hard narrow leaves and long-lasting yellow or white flowers, and produce small edible but insipid 1-celled or 2-celled drupes

gee·chee \ˈgēchē\ *n* -s *usu cap* [fr. the *Ogeechee* river, Ga.] **1 :** a dialect containing English words and words of native African origin spoken chiefly by the descendants of Negro slaves settled on the Ogeechee river in Georgia — compare GULLAH **2 :** a Geechee-speaking Negro

geegaw *var of* GEWGAW

gee–gee \ˈjē(,)jē\ *n* -s [redupl. of ¹*gee*] *slang* **:** HORSE; *esp* **:** RACEHORSE

gee ho \(ˈ)jē¦hō\ *v imper* **:** ¹GEE

geek \ˈgēk\ *n* -s [prob. fr. E dial. *geek, geck* fool, fr. LG *geck*, fr. MLG] **:** a carnival performer often billed as a wild man whose act usu. includes biting the head off a live chicken or snake

geel·bec *or* **geel·bek** *or* **geel·beck** \ˈgēl,bek\ *n* -s [Afrik *geelbek*, fr. *geel* yellow (fr. MD *ghele*) + *bek* beak, fr. MD *bec*, fr. OF; akin to OHG *gelo* yellow — more at YELLOW, BEAK] **1 :** a wild yellow-billed duck (*Anas undulata*) of Africa **2 :** a large sciaenid fish (*Atractoscion aequidens*) shaped like a mackerel and favored as a leading food and game fish in southern Africa and Australia

geel·dik·kop \ˈgēl'di,käp\ *n* -s [Afrik, fr. *geel* yellow + *dikkop*, a disease of sheep, fr. *dik* thick + *kop* head — more at DIKKOP] **:** a serious photodynamic disease of southern African sheep due to sensitization to light following the ingestion of certain plants and characterized by intense jaundice and a severe facial edema

geel·hout \ˈgēl,hau̇t\ *n* -s [Afrik, fr. *geel* yellow + *hout* wood; akin to OHG *holz* wood — more at HOLT] **:** any of several southern African trees of the genera *Podocarpus* and *Elaeodendron* whose wood is sometimes used for interior work

gee pole *n* [¹*gee*] **:** a steering pole at the front of a dog sled

geepound \ˈ=,=\ *n* [³*gee* (the initial letter of *gravity*) + *pound*] **:** ³SLUG 10

geese *pl of* GOOSE

geest \ˈgāst, ˈgēst\ *n* -s [G, fr. LG, high dry land near the sea, fr. MLG *gēst* — more at GAST] **1 :** alluvial matter not of recent origin on the surface of land **2 :** loose material (as earth or soil) formed by decay of rocks in a place — compare LATERITE, SAPROLITE

gee string *var of* G-STRING

geet \(ˈ)gēt\ *Scot var of* GET

gee–throw \ˈ=,=\ *n* [¹*gee*] **:** a strong wooden lever with a curved metal point used to break out logging sleds

gee–up *also* **gee–hup** \(ˈ)jē¦(h)əp\ *v imper* **:** ¹GEE

gee whiz *also* **gee whizz** \(ˈ)jē¦(h)wiz\ *or* **gee whil·i·kers** \-(h)wiləkə(r)z, -lēk-\ *or* **gee whil·li·kins** \-kənz\ *interj* [⁶*gee* + *whiz* or *whizz* or *whillikers* or *whillikins*, of unknown origin] **:** ⁶GEE

¹**geez** *var of* JEEZ

²**ge·ez** \gēˈez, gäˈ-\ *n, cap* **:** ETHIOPIC 1

gee·zer \ˈgēzə(r)\ *n* -s [prob. alter. of *guiser*] *slang* **:** a queer, odd, or eccentric man

ge·fil·te fish *also* **ge·fül·te fish** *or* **ge·fill·te fish** \gəˈfiltə-\ *n* [Yiddish *gefilte fish*, lit., filled fish] **:** a Jewish dish of stewed or baked fish stuffed with a mixture of the fish flesh, bread crumbs, eggs, and seasoning or prepared as balls or oval cakes boiled in a fish stock

geg *usu cap, var of* GHEG

ge·gen·ion \ˈgāgən+,-\ *n* -s [G, fr. *gegen* against, counter- + *ion*] **:** COUNTERION

ge·gen·schein \ˈgāgən,shīn\ *n* -s *often cap* [G, fr. *gegen* against, counter- + *schein* shine] **:** a faint elliptical nebulous light about 20° across on the ecliptic and opposite the sun best seen during September and October when in the constellations Aquarius and Pisces and probably associated in origin with the zodiacal light — called also *counterglow*

ge·gen·stands·the·o·rie \ˈ=,=shtän(t)s,tāō,rē\ *n* -s *usu cap* [G, fr. *gegenstand* object + *theorie* theory] **:** a theory of objects; *esp* **:** a theory of intentional objects

ge·heim·rat \gəˈhīm,rät, G -räät\ *n* -s *usu cap* [G, fr. older *geheimerat*, fr. *geheime, geheimde* secrecy (fr. *geheim*, adj. secret, fr. MHG, secret, familiar, pertaining to the household, fr. *ge-*, collective prefix — fr. OHG *gi-* — + *heim* house, dwelling, fr. OHG) + *rat* counselor, counsel, fr. OHG *rāt* advice, provisions — more at CO-, HOME, READ] **:** PRIVY COUNCILOR

ge·hen·na \gəˈhenə\ *n* -s *usu cap* [LL *Gehenna, Geenna*, fr. Gk *Geenna*, fr. Heb *Gē' Hinnōm* lit., valley of Hinnom] **1 :** HELL 1a(2) **2 :** a place or state of misery ⟨all around you a ~ of mad industrial life —Norman Douglas⟩

geh·len·ite \ˈgālə,nīt\ *n* -s [G *gehlenit*, fr. A. F. *Gehlen*, 19th cent. Ger. chemist + G *-it* -ite] **:** a mineral $Ca_2Al_2SiO_7$ consisting of calcium aluminum silicate occurring in prismatic crystals isomorphous with akermanite

gei·ge \ˈgīgə\ *n, pl* **gei·gen** \-gən\ [G, fr. OHG *gīga* — more at JIG] **:** FIDDLE, VIOLIN

gei·gen principal \ˈgīgən-\ *n* [G *geigenprinzipal*, fr. *geige* + *prinzipal* open diapason] **:** VIOLIN DIAPASON

gei·ger \ˈgīgə(r)\ *n* -s *usu cap* [by shortening] **1 :** GEIGER COUNTER **2 :** a particle capable of detection by a Geiger counter

geiger counter \ˈ=¦=¦=\ *or* **geiger–mül·ler counter** \ˈ=-¦=¦=— -ˈmyü(ˌ)lə(r)-, -ˈmil, -ˈmül, -ˈmə|\ *n, usu cap G&M* [after Hans *Geiger* †1945 Ger. physicist and W. *Müller*, 20th cent. Ger. physicist, its inventors] **1 :** GEIGER-MÜLLER TUBE **2 :** an instrument consisting of a Geiger-Müller tube and the electronic equipment used in conjunction with it to record (as by a series of clicks) the momentary current pulsations in the tube gas

geiger–müller tube *or* **geiger tube** *n, usu cap G&M* [after H. *Geiger* and W. *Müller*] **:** a gas-filled counting tube with a cylindrical cathode and axial wire electrode for detecting the presence of cosmic rays or radioactive substances by means of the ionizing particles that penetrate its envelope and set up momentary current pulsations in the gas

geiger–nut·tall law *also* **geiger–nuttall relation** \ˈ=¦=ˈnəd-, -ȯl-\ *n, usu cap G&N* [after H. *Geiger* and John M. *Nuttall* †1958 Brit. physicist] **:** a statement in nuclear physics: for an alpha-emitting radioactive substance the logarithm of the decay constant and the logarithm of the range in air of the emitted alpha rays are in linear relation to each other

geiger tree *n* [after John *Geiger fl ab* 1832 Am. friend of Audubon] **:** a small often shrubby tropical American evergreen tree (*Cordia sebestena*) with thick rough deep-green leaves, orange or scarlet flowers borne in large open terminal clusters, and fruit that is a small white 4-celled edible drupe

gei·kia \ˈgēkēə\ *n, cap* [NL, fr. Sir Archibald *Geikie* †1924 Scot. geologist + NL *-ia*] **:** a genus of rather small toothless dicynodont reptiles from the Upper Permian of Scotland

gei·kie·lite \ˈgēkē,līt\ *n* -s [Sir Archibald *Geikie* †1924 + E *-lite*] **:** a mineral $MgTiO_3$ consisting of magnesium titanate, being isomorphous with pyrophanite, and occurring as bluish black or brownish black rolled pebbles

geil·siek·te \ˈgāl,sēktə\ *n* -s [Afrik, fr. *geil* fertile, rich, rank + *siekte* disease] **:** a hydrocyanic-acid poisoning in southern African sheep and goats due to forage high in cyanogenetic glucosides

gei·sha \ˈgāshə, ˈgē|\ *n, pl* **geisha** *or* **geishas** [Jap, fr. *gei* art, performance + *-sha* person] **1 :** a Japanese girl who is trained to provide (as by playing on the samisen, dancing, serving food or drinks or by sympathetic, witty, or amusing talk) entertaining and lighthearted company (as for a man or a group of men) **2 :** COURTESAN

gei·son \ˈgā,sän, ˈgī,-\ *n, pl* **gei·sa** \-(,)sä\ [Gk *geison, geisson*, prob. of non-IE origin] **:** CORNICE

ge·isotherm \(ˈ)jē+\ *n* -s [*ge-* + *isotherm*] **:** ISOGEOTHERM — **ge·isothermal** \(¦)jē+\ *adj*

geiss·ler bulb \ˈgīslə(r)-\ *n, usu cap G* [after Heinrich *Geissler* †1879 Ger. mechanic] **:** a potash bulb consisting usu. of two upper bulbs connected by three lower smaller bulbs — often used in pl.

geissler pump *n, usu cap G* [after H. *Geissler*] **:** an air pump based on the principle of the Torricellian vacuum and having its vacuum produced by the flow of mercury back and forth between a fixed and a vertically adjustable reservoir

geissler tube *n, usu cap G* [after Heinrich *Geissler*] **:** a gas-filled discharge tube having various shapes and usu. a narrowly constricted portion in which the luminosity is intensified

Geissler tubes

geisso- *comb form* [NL, fr. Gk *geisson, geison* cornice] **:** like a cornice ⟨*Geissorhiza*⟩

geist·lich \ˈgīstlik\ *adv* (*or adj*) [G, fr. OHG *geistlīch* (trans. of L *spiritualis*), fr. *geist* spirit + *-līch* -ly — more at GHOST] **:** with deep feeling **:** SOULFULLY — used as a direction in music

gei·to·nog·a·mous \ˌgītᵊnˈägəməs\ *adj* **:** of or relating to geitonogamy

gei·to·nog·a·my \ˌ=ˈ==mē\ *n* -ES [ISV *geitono-* (fr. Gk *geitōn* neighbor) + *-gamy*] **:** pollination of one flower by another growing on the same plant

gek·ko \ˈge(,)kō\ *n, cap* [NL, fr. Malay *ge'kok*, of imit. origin] **:** the type genus of Gekkonidae comprising a number of typical geckos

gek·ko·nes \ˈgekə,nēz, geˈkō(,)n-\ *n pl, cap* [NL, fr. *Gekko*] *in some classifications* **:** a major division of Lacertilia comprising the family Gekkonidae and a few related extinct lizards

¹**gek·ko·nid** *also* **gec·co·nid** \ˈgekə,nid, -ˌnəd\ *adj* [NL *Gekkonidae*] **:** of or relating to the family Gekkonidae

²**gekkonid** *also* **gecconid** \"\ *n* -s **:** a lizard of the family Gekkonidae **:** GECKO

gek·kon·i·dae \geˈkänə,dē\ *n pl, cap* [NL, fr. *Gekkon-, Gekko*, type genus + *-idae*] **:** a large family of Old World and New World lizards with amphicoelous vertebrae and other apparently primitive characters — see GEKKO

¹**gek·ko·noid** \ˈgekə,nȯid\ *adj* [NL *Gekkones* + E *-oid*] **:** of or relating to the group Gekkones or to the geckos

²**gekkonoid** \"\ *n* -s **:** a lizard of the group Gekkones

gek·ko·ta \geˈkōd·ə\ [NL, fr. NL *Gekko*] *syn of* GEKKONES

¹**gel** \ˈjel\ *n* -s [*-gel* (as in *hydrogel, alcogel*), fr. *gelatin*] **:** a colloid in a more solid form than a sol: as **a :** a semisolid apparently homogeneous substance that may be elastic and jellylike (as gelatin) or more or less rigid (as silica gel) and that is formed by coagulation of a sol in various ways (as by cooling, by evaporation, or by precipitation with an electrolyte) **:** a disperse system consisting typically of a high-molecular-weight compound or an aggregate of small particles in very close association with a liquid — see AEROGEL, JELLY 2a, XEROGEL **b :** a nonhomogeneous gelatinous precipitate **:** COAGEL

²**gel** \"\ *vi* **gelled; gelled; gelling; gels :** to change into or take on the form of a gel **:** become more solid **:** SET — compare SOLATE — **gel·able** \-ləbəl\ *adj*

gel *abbr* gelatinous

gela·da \ˈjelədə, ˈge-; jəˈlädə, gəˈ-\ *n* -s [prob. fr. Ar *qilādah* collar, mane] **:** an ape (*Theropithecus gelada*) of Ethiopia remarkable for the long mane of hair on the neck and shoulders of the adult male

ge·län·de·läu·fer \gəˈlendə,lȯifə(r)\ *n* -s [G, fr. *gelände* open field + *läufer* runner] **:** a skier making a cross-country run **:** LANGLÄUFER

ge·län·de·sprung \-,s(h)pru̇ŋ\ *also* **gelände jump** *n* -s [G, fr. *gelände* open field + *sprung* jump] **:** a jump in skiing made from a low crouching position with the aid of both ski poles and usu. over an obstacle

ge·la·sian \jəˈlāzh(ē)ən\ *adj, usu cap* [*Gelasius* I †496 + E *-an*] **:** of or relating to Pope Gelasius

ge·las·i·mus \jəˈlasəməs\ [NL, fr. Gk *gelasimos* laughable, fr. *gelan* to laugh] *syn of* UCA

ge·las·tic \jəˈlastik\ *adj* [Gk *gelastikos* able to laugh, fr. *gelastos* laughable (fr. *gelan* to laugh) + *-ikos* -ic; akin to Arm *całr* laughter — more at CLEAN] **:** RISIBLE

ge·las·to·cor·i·dae \jə,lastōˈkȯrə,dē\ *n pl, cap* [NL, fr. *Gelastocoris*, type genus (fr. Gk *gelastos* laughable + *koris* bug) + *-idae*] **:** a family of bugs (order Hemiptera) consisting of the toad bugs

gel·ate \ˈje,lāt\ *vi* -ED/-ING/-S [¹*gel* + *-ate*] **:** ²GEL

ge·lat·i·fi·ca·tion \jə,lad·əfəˈkāshən\ *n* -s [*gelatin* + *-fication*] **:** GELATINIZATION

gel·a·tig·e·nous \ˌjeləˈtijənəs\ *adj* [*gelatin* + *-genous*] **:** producing or yielding gelatin

gel·a·tin *also* **gel·a·tine** \ˈjelətᵊn, -ət·ən, -əd·ən, *chiefly Brit* -ə,tēn *or* ˌ=ˈtēn\ *n* -s [F *gélatine* (originally, a kind of thick broth), fr. It *gelatina*, fr. *gelato* (past part. of *gelare* to freeze, congeal, fr. L) + *-ina* (fr. L, fem. of *-inus* ¹ine) — more at COLD] **1 :** animal jelly **:** glutinous material obtained from animal tissues by prolonged boiling; *esp* **:** a colorless to yellowish transparent colloidal protein that is hard and brittle when dry but swells in water, dissolving in hot water and forming a jelly on cooling, that is obtained usu. in sheets, flakes, or powder by the partial hydrolysis of collagen from animal skins, tendons, ligaments, and bones by cooking in water, and that is used chiefly as a food, in photography, and in medicine — compare GLUE 1, ISINGLASS **2 a :** any of various substances (as agar) resembling gelatin in physical properties ⟨vegetable ~*s*⟩ **b :** an edible jelly formed with gelatin **c :** any of several jellylike blasting explosives (as blasting gelatin or gelatin dynamite) **d :** a thin colored transparent sheet used over a stage light in order to color it

gel·a·tin·ase \ˈjelətə,nās, -āz, jəˈlatᵊn,ā-\ *n* -s [*gelatin* + *-ase*] **:** an enzyme causing liquefaction or hydrolysis of gelatin and occurring esp. in bacteria

ge·lat·i·nate \jəˈlatᵊn,āt\ *vb* -ED/-ING/-S [*gelatin* + *-ate*] **:** GELATINIZE — **ge·lat·i·na·tion** \ˌ=,==ˈāshən\ *n* -s

gelatin boot *n* **:** a dressing for varicose veins or ulcers consisting of a paste made of zinc oxide, gelatin, glycerin, and water that is applied first directly to the lower leg before it is wrapped in a spiral bandage and then again to the outside of the bandage — called also *Unna's boot*

gelatin dynamite *n* **:** a powerful water-resistant blasting explosive consisting of a jellylike mass of nitroglycerin and lower-nitrated cellulose nitrate incorporated with a base (as wood pulp mixed with sodium nitrate) — compare AMMONIA GELATIN, BLASTING GELATIN

gel·a·tined *pronunc at* GELATIN + d\ *adj* **:** coated with gelatin

gelatin film *n* **:** a pliable translucent absorbable film used in the surgical repair of defects

gel·a·tin·ig·er·ous \ˌjelətᵊˈnijərəs\ *adj* [*gelatin* + *-i-* + *-gerous*] **:** secreting a gelatinous covering — used of certain choanoflagellates

ge·lat·i·ni·za·tion \jə,latᵊnəˈzāshən, ˌjelətᵊnə-, -ᵊn,ī'z-, -ə,nīˈz-\ *n* -s **:** the process of gelatinizing

ge·lat·i·nize \jəˈlatᵊn,īz, ˈjelətᵊ,nīz\ *vb* -ED/-ING/-S [*gelatin* + *-ize*] *vt* **1 :** to convert into a gelatinous form or into a jelly ⟨strong heating with water ~*s* starch⟩ — compare JELLY **2 :** to coat or treat with gelatin ~ *vi* **:** to become gelatinous or change into a jelly

ge·lat·i·niz·er \-zə(r)\ *n* -s **:** one that gelatinizes

ge·lat·i·no·bromide \jə¦latᵊn(,)ō, ˌjelə¦tinə +\ *n* [*gelatin* + *-o-* + *bromide*] **:** a light-sensitive preparation of gelatin and silver bromide used in photography

ge·lat·i·no·chloride \"+\ *n* [*gelatin* + *-o-* + *chloride*] **:** a light-sensitive preparation of gelatin and silver chloride used in photography

ge·lat·i·nous \jəˈlatᵊnəs\ *adj* **1 :** resembling gelatin or jelly esp. in appearance and consistency **:** VISCOUS, FLOCCULENT ⟨~ ferric hydroxide⟩ **2 :** of, relating to, or containing gelatin — **ge·lat·i·nous·ly** *adv* — **ge·lat·i·nous·ness** *n* -ES

gelatinous fiber *n* **:** a plant fiber having a jellylike inner wall

gelatin process *n* **:** any of various processes involving the use of gelatin: as **a :** a photographic process in which gelatin is used as the dispersing vehicle for the sensitive silver salts **b :** a printing process for reproducing pictures or drawings based upon the action of light on a bichromated gelatin film — compare AQUATONE, CARBON PROCESS **c :** a method of producing facsimile copies of a written or drawn original with a pad of gelatin (as in a hectograph)

gelatin sponge *also* **gelatin foam** *n* **:** a sterile absorbable porous gelatin product that is used for the control of bleeding in surgery

¹**ge·la·tion** \jəˈlāshən, jēˈ-\ *n* -s [L *gelation-, gelatio*, fr. *gelatus* (past part. of *gelare* to freeze, congeal) + *-ion-, -io* -ion — more at COLD] **:** the action or process of freezing

²**ge·la·tion** \jeˈlāshən, jəˈ-\ *n* [¹*gel* + *-ation*] **:** the formation of a gel from a sol

¹**geld** \ˈgel(d)\ *adj* [ME, fr. ON *geldr*; akin to OE *gelde* barren, sterile, OHG *galt*, ON *gelda* to castrate — more at ²GELD] *dial chiefly Eng, of an animal* **:** not producing young **:** BARREN, STERILE

²**geld** \ˈgeld\ *vt* **gelded** \-ldəd\ *also* **gelt** \-lt\ **gelded** *also* **gelt; gelding; gelds** [ME *gelden*, fr. ON *gelda*; akin to OE *gelte* young sow, OHG *galza, gelza* castrated swine, ON *göltr, galti* boar, MW *geleu, gelyf* knife, Gk *gallos* priest of Cybele, eunuch, Skt *hala* plow; basic meaning: cutting] **1 :** CASTRATE, EMASCULATE; *also* **:** SPAY **2 :** to remove the husks and chaff from **:** PRUNE **3 a :** DEPRIVE, EXCISE ⟨a man ~*ed* of his wages⟩ **b :** to lessen the force of ⟨~ an argument⟩ **c :** EXPURGATE ⟨~ a book⟩

³**geld** \"\ *also* **gelt** \-lt\ *n* -s [OE *gield, geld, gild* service, sacrifice, tax, tribute; akin to OHG *gelt* retribution, compensation, income, value, ON *gjald* tribute, payment, retribution, Goth *gild* tax, OE *gieldan* to pay, pay for — more at YIELD] **:** the crown tax paid under Anglo-Saxon and Norman kings; *also* **:** a division of people or territory paying it

⁴**geld** \ˈgeld\ *vb* -ED/-ING/-S *vt* **:** to levy a geld on ~ *vi* **:** to pay geld

geld·ing \ˈgeldiŋ, -dēŋ\ *n* -s [ME, fr. ON *geldingr*, fr. *gelda* to castrate + *-ingr* -ing] **1 :** a castrated animal; *specif* **:** a castrated male horse **2 :** EUNUCH

¹**ge·lech·i·id** \jəˈlekēəd\ *adj* [NL *Gelechiidae*] **:** of or relating to the Gelechiidae

²**gelechiid** \"\ *n* -s **:** any moth of the family Gelechiidae

gel·e·chi·idae \ˌjeləˈkīə,dē\ *n pl, cap* [NL, fr. *Gelechia*, type genus (fr. Gk *gelechēs* sleeping on the earth + NL *-ia*) + *-idae*] **:** a large family of small moths having slender wings with the outer margin of the hind wing usu. concave and including important economic insects (as the pink bollworm, the Angoumois grain moth, and various leaf rollers)

Gel·foam \ˈjel,fōm\ *trademark* — used for a gelatin sponge

gel·id \ˈjeləd\ *adj* [L *gelidus*, fr. *gelu* cold, frost — more at COLD] **:** extremely cold **:** ICY ⟨the ~ waters of the Atlantic⟩ ⟨a man of ~ reserve —*New Yorker*⟩ — **ge·lid·i·ty** \jəˈlidəd·ē, jeˈ-\ *n* -ES — **gel·id·ly** \ˈjelədlē\ *adv*

ge·lid·i·a·ce·ae \jə,lidēˈāsē,ē\ *n pl, cap* [NL, fr. *Gelidium*, type genus + *-aceae*] **:** a family of red algae coextensive with the order Gelidiales

ge·lid·i·a·les \jə,lidēˈā(,)lēz\ *n pl, cap* [NL, fr. *Gelidium* + *-ales*] **:** a small order of red algae (subclass Florideae) containing a single family and including *Gelidium* and a few related genera that are sometimes placed in Nemalionales

ge·lid·i·um \jəˈlidēəm\ *n* [NL, fr. L *gelidus* (influenced in meaning by L *gelare* to freeze, congeal) + NL *-ium*; fr. the fact that the plants are boiled down to make a jelly] **1** *cap* **:** a genus of red algae (family Gelidiaceae) having cartilaginous terete or compressed much-branched fronds and cystocarps immersed in swollen branchlets and being important sources of agar — see GELIDIALES **2** -s **:** any alga of the genus *Gelidium*

gel·ig·nite \ˈjelig,nīt\ *n* -s [*gelatin* + L *ignis* fire + E *-ite* — more at IGNITE] **:** a gelatin dynamite in which the adsorbent base is largely potassium nitrate or a similar nitrate usu. with some wood pulp

ge·li·lah \gəˈlēlə\ *n* -s [Heb *gĕlīlāh*, lit., rolling, wrapping] **:** the rolling up of the scroll of the law preparatory to wrapping it in its vestments after reading from it in the synagogue

ge·li·notte \zhəlēnōt\ *n, pl* **gelinottes** \-t(s)\ [F, fr. MF, dim. of *geline* hen, fr. L *gallina* — more at GALLINACEOUS] **:** HAZEL HEN

gell \ˈgel\ *n* -s [alter. of *gale*] **1** *Scot* **:** GALE **2** *Scot* **:** SPREE

gelled *past of* GEL

gelling *pres part of* GEL

gel mineral *n* **:** a noncrystalline mineral that originated as a gel — compare MINERALOID

gel·om·e·ter \jeˈläməd·ə(r)\ *n* [¹*gel* + *-o-* + *-meter*] **:** an instrument for measuring jelly strength

ge·long \ˈgā,lȯŋ\ *n* -s [Tibetan *geloṅ* (*dgesloṅ*), fr. *dgeba* (*gewa*) virtue + *sloṅ* (*loṅ*) to beg] **:** a Lamaist mendicant friar, bhikshu, or ordained priest

gel·ose \ˈje,lōs *also* -ōz\ *n* -s [ISV ¹*gel* + *-ose*] **:** an amorphous polysaccharide obtained from agar and like gelatin in its ability to form a jelly; *broadly* **:** a polysaccharide (as agar) occurring in red algae and capable of forming a jelly

gels *pl of* GEL, *pres 3d sing of* GEL

gel·se·mic acid \(ˈ)jel¦semik-, -semik-\ *or* **gel·se·min·ic acid** \ˌjelsə¦minik-\ *n* [*gelsemic*, ISV, fr. *gelsem-* (fr. NL *Gelsemium*) + *-ic*; *gelseminic*, ISV, fr. *gelsemin-* (fr. NL *Gelseminium*, alter. of *Gelsemium*) + *-ic*] **:** SCOPOLETIN

gel·se·mine \ˈjelsə,mēn, -mən\ *n* -s [ISV *gelsem-* (fr. NL *Gelsemium*, genus name of *Gelsemium sempervirens*) + *-ine*] **:** a crystalline alkaloid $C_{20}H_{22}N_2O_2$ from gelsemium

gel·se·mi·um \jelˈsēmēəm\ *n* [NL, modif. of It *gelsomino* jasmine, fr. Ar *yāsamīn* jasmine — more at JASMINE] **1** *cap* **:** a small genus of woody vines (family Loganiaceae) of Asia and the southern U. S. — see YELLOW JESSAMINE **2** *pl* **gelsemiums** \-mēəmz\ *or* **gelsemia** \-mēə\ **:** the root of the yellow jessamine formerly used in medicine

gel·sen·kir·chen \ˌgelzən¦kirkən\ *adj, usu cap* [fr. *Gelsenkirchen*, Germany] **:** of or from the city of Gelsenkirchen, Germany **:** of the kind or style prevalent in Gelsenkirchen

gel strength *n* **:** JELLY STRENGTH

¹**gelt** \ˈgelt\ *var of* GELD

²**gelt** \"\ *past of* GELD

³**gelt** \"\ *n* -s [D *geld* (fr. MD *ghelt* payment, money) & G *geld* & Yiddish *gelt*, both fr. OHG *gelt* retribution, compensation, income, value — more at GELD] *slang* **:** MONEY

¹**gem** \ˈjem\ *n* -s [ME *gemme*, fr. MF, fr. L *gemma* bud, gem; prob. akin to OE *camb* comb — more at COMB] **1 a :** a jewel (as a stone or pearl) having value and beauty that are intrinsic and not derived from its setting **:** a precious or sometimes semiprecious stone cut and polished for ornament **b :** a semiprecious stone (as a cameo or intaglio) of value because carved or engraved **2 a :** something (as a work of art or poem) prized esp. for great beauty or perfection **b :** a highly prized or well-beloved person **3 :** an old size of type between brilliant and diamond **4 :** MUFFIN 1a ⟨graham ~*s*⟩

²**gem** \"\ *vt* **gemmed; gemmed; gemming; gems 1** *archaic* **:** to put forth (as blossoms or fruit) **2 :** BEGEM ⟨millionaires ~ the hills with villas —Lucien Price⟩

gem- *comb form, usu ital* [¹*geminate*] **:** having two like groups attached to the same atom ⟨*gem*-dimethyl-piperidine⟩ — esp. in names of organic compounds

ge·ma·ra \gəˈmärə, -ˈmȯrə\ *n* -s *usu cap* [Aram *gĕmārā* completion] **:** a rabbinic commentary on and interpretation of the Mishnah; *broadly* **:** TALMUD

ge·ma·ric \-rik\ *adj, usu cap* **:** of or relating to the Gemara

ge·ma·rist \-rəst\ *n* -s *usu cap* **:** a specialist in the study of the Gemara

ge·ma·tria \gəˈmā·trēə, ˌgemə'trēə\ *n, pl* **gematri·ot** \-ē,ōt\ [LHeb *gīmaṭriyā*, fr. Gk *geōmetria* — more at GEOMETRY] **1 :** a cryptograph in the form of a word whose letters have the numerical values of a word taken as the hidden meaning **2 :** the cabalistic method of explaining the Hebrew Scriptures by means of the cryptographic significance of the words

ge·ma·tri·al \-ēəl\ *or* **ge·ma·tri·cal** \gə'mā·trəkəl\ *adj* **:** of or relating to gematria

ge·mauve \gə'mōv\ *n* -s [modif. of F *guimauve*, fr. OF *widmalve*, *vimauve*, modif. (influenced by *vist* mistletoe and *malve*, *mauve* mallow) of L *hibiscus* marsh mallow] **:** a tropical mallow (*Malachra capitata*) with yellow flowers in loose axillary heads that is important in harboring the cotton stainer bug

ge·mein·de \gə'mīndə\ *n*, *pl* **gemein·den** \-dən\ [G, community, congregation, fr. OHG *gimeinida* community, congregation, fr. *gimeini* common, general — more at MEAN] **:** a unit of local government in Germany corresponding to a municipality

ge·mein·schaft \gə'mīn,shäft\ *n*, *pl* **gemeinschaf·ten** \-tən\ [G, community, fr. *gemein* common, general (fr. OHG *gimeini*) + *-schaft* -ship (fr. OHG *-scaf*)] **:** a spontaneously arising organismic social relationship characterized by strong reciprocal bonds of sentiment and kinship within a common tradition; *also* **:** a community or society characterized by such a relationship — contrasted with *gesellschaft*

¹gem·el *also* **gem·mel** \'jeməl\ *n* -s [ME, twin, fr. MF *gemel*, fr. L *gemellus*, dim. of *geminus* — more at GEMINATE] **1** *obs* **:** HINGE **2 :** a ring of two separable hoops — compare GIMBAL **3** *or* **gemel bar** *also* **ge·melle** *or* **ge·mell** \jə'mel, 'jeməl\ **:** BAR GEMEL **4 :** a pair of glass bottles blown separately and then fused usu. with the two necks pointing in different directions

gemel 4

²gemel \"\ *adj* [ME, twin] **:** PAIRED **:** TWIN ⟨a ~ arch⟩

gem·eled \'jeməld\ *or* **gemelled** \", jə'meld\ *adj* **:** PAIRED

gemel hinge *n* **:** a hinge consisting of an eye or loop and a hook

ge·mel·lion \jə'melyən\ *n* -s [ML *gemellion-*, *gemellio*, fr. L *gemellus* twin + *-ion-*, *-io* -ion] **:** one of a pair of basins formerly used to wash the hands at meals

ge·mel·lus \jə'meləs\ *n*, *pl* **gemel·li** \-,lī\ *also* **gemelluses** [NL, fr. L, twin] **:** either of two small muscles of the hip that insert into the tendon of the internal obturator, a superior originating chiefly from the outer surface of the ischial spine and an inferior originating chiefly from the ischial tuberosity

gemel window *n* **:** a window filling a pair of openings

gem-fruit \'ˌ=ˌ=\ *n* **:** FALSE MITERWORT

¹gem·i·nate \'jemənə̇t, -,nāt, *usu* \|d·+V\ *adj* [L *geminatus*, past part. of *geminare* to double, fr. *geminus* twin; akin to MIr *emon*, *emuin* pair of twins, Skt *yama* twin] **1 :** BINATE ⟨~ flowers⟩ **2 :** GEMINATED — **gem·i·nate·ly** *adv*

²gem·i·nate \-,nāt, *usu* -ād·+V\ *vb* -ED/-ING/-S [L *geminatus*, past part.] *vt* **:** to cause to become geminated **:** DOUBLE ~ *vi* **:** to become double or paired

³gem·i·nate \-nə̇t, -,nāt, *usu* \|d·+V\ *n* -s [¹*geminate*] **:** a geminated consonant or vowel

geminated *adj* **1** *of a consonant or vowel letter or phonetic symbol* **:** occurring twice in succession in a transcription ⟨the ~ *-dd-* in *ladder*⟩ **2** *of a consonant or vowel sound* **a :** occurring twice in succession and receiving individual pronunciation ⟨the *-tt-* in *cattail* is ~⟩ **b :** LONG 5

gem·i·na·tion \,jemə'nāshən\ *n* -s [L *gemination-*, *geminatio*, fr. *geminatus* (past part. of *geminare*) + *-ion-*, *-io* -ion] **:** a doubling, duplication, or repetition: as **a :** a formation of two teeth from a single tooth germ **b** (1) **:** a writing of a letter twice in succession in the spelling of a word (2) **:** a making, becoming, or being geminated

¹gem·i·na·tive \'jemə,nād·iv\ *adj* [L *geminatus* + E *-ive*] **:** relating to, produced by, or showing gemination

²geminative \"\ *n* -s **:** a geminated letter or sound

gem·i·ni \'jemə(,)nē, 'jemə,nī, 'gemə,nē\ *n pl* [ME, fr. L, twins, pl. of *geminus* — more at GEMINATE] **1** *usu sing in constr, usu cap* **:** the 3d sign of the zodiac — see SIGN table; ZODIAC illustration **2** *often sing in constr, obs* **:** PAIR, COUPLE ⟨a ~ of asses . . . would make just four of you —William Congreve⟩ **3** [prob. euphemism for LL *Jesu domine* Jesus lord!] *archaic* — used as an interjection **4 :** bivalent chromosomes

gem·i·ni·flo·rous \ˌjemənē'flōrəs\ *adj* [L *geminus* + E *-i-* + *-florous*] **:** having flowers in pairs

gem·i·nous \'jemənəs\ *adj* [L *geminus*, fr. *geminus*, n., twin — more at GEMINATE] **:** DOUBLED, PAIRED

gemlike \'ˌ=ˌ=\ *adj* **1 :** resembling a gem **2 :** PERFECT, EXQUISITE ⟨~ beauty⟩ ⟨~ stories⟩

gem·ma \'jemə\ *n* [L, bud, gem — more at GEM] **1** *pl* **gem·mae** \-(,)mē\ **:** BUD; *broadly* **:** an asexual reproductive body that becomes detached from a parent plant and is unicellular in algae and fungi and some hepatics but multicellular in many mosses, hepatics, and some ferns — compare CHLAMYDOSPORE, GEMMATION **2** [NL, fr. L] *cap* **:** a monotypic genus of small round clams (family Veneridae) having a shining white, yellow, or pink shell marked with amethyst and being widely distributed on both coasts of No. America

gem·ma·ceous \(')je¦māshəs\ *adj* **:** of or relating to gemmae

gemma cup *n* **:** the cupule of a liverwort

gem·ma·ry \'jemərē\ *n* -ES [¹*gem* + *-ary*] **:** the science of gems

¹gem·mate \'je,māt\ *adj* [L *gemmatus*, past part.] **1 :** having gemmae **2 :** reproducing by a bud

²gemmate \"\ *vi* -ED/-ING/-S [L *gemmatus*, fr. *gemmatus* past part. of *gemmare* to put forth buds, fr. *gemma* bud — more at GEM] *of coral* **:** to produce or propagate by a bud

gem·ma·tion \je'māshən\ *n* -s [L *gemmatus* + E *-ion*] **:** asexual reproduction in which a new organism originates as a localized area of growth on the surface or within the body of the parent subsequently differentiating into a new individual

gem·ma·tive \'je,mād·iv, -,məd-\ *adj* [*gemmation* + *-ive*] **:** of or relating to gemmation

gemmed *past of* GEM

gemmel *var of* GEMEL

gem·mer \'jemə(r)\ *n* -s [¹*gem* + *-er*] **:** one that seeks or mines for gems

gem·mif·er·ous \(')je¦mif(ə)rəs\ *adj* [L *gemma* + E *-i-* + *-ferous*] **1 :** producing or containing gems **2** [NL *gemma* + E *-i-* + *-ferous*] **:** bearing or reproducing by a gemma

gem·mi·fi·ca·tion \,jeməfə'kāshən\ *n* -s [NL *gemma* + E *-i-* + *-fication*] **:** production of a gemma

gem·mi·form \'jemə,fȯrm\ *adj* [ISV *gemma* + *-i-* + *-form*] **:** resembling a gemma

gem·mi·ly \'jemə̇lē\ *adv* **:** in such a manner as to resemble or suggest a gem

gemming *pres part of* GEM

gem·mip·a·ra \je'mipərə\ *or* **gem·mip·a·res** \-,rēz\ *n pl* [NL, fr. L *gemma* bud + NL *-para* or *-pares* (fr. L *parere* to bear) — more at PARE] **:** animals that reproduce by budding

gem·mip·a·rous \(')je¦mipərəs\ *adj* [NL *gemmiparus*, fr. L *gemma* bud + *-parus* -parous] **:** producing, bearing, or reproducing by a bud — **gem·mip·a·rous·ly** *adv*

gem·moid \'je,mȯid\ *adj* [NL *gemma* + E *-oid*] **:** resembling a gemma

gem·mo·log·i·cal *or* **gem·o·log·i·cal** \¦jemə¦läjəkəl\ *adj* **:** of or relating to a gem or gemmology

gem·mol·o·gist *or* **gem·ol·o·gist** \je'mäləjə̇st\ *n* -s **:** a specialist in gems; *specif* **:** one who appraises gems

gem·mol·o·gy *or* **gem·ol·o·gy** \je'mäləjē\ *n* -ES [*gemmology* fr. L *gemma* bud, gem + E *-o-* + *-logy*; *gemology* alter. (influenced by ¹*gem*) of *gemmology*] **:** the science of gems

gem·mu·la \'jemyələ\ *n*, *pl* **gemmu·lae** \-,lē\ [NL, fr. L, little bud] **:** GEMMULE

gem·mu·la·tion \,jemyə'lāshən\ *n* -s [ISV *gemmule* + *-ation*] **:** GEMMATION

gem·mule \'je(,)myül\ *n* -s [F, fr. L *gemmula* little bud, dim. of *gemma* bud, gem — more at GEM] **1 :** a small plant bud **2 :** any of various minute self-multiplying particles considered in the theory of pangenesis to be transmitted from somatic to germ cells and to mediate the production in a new individual of cells like those in which they originated — compare BIOPHORE **3 :** a bud produced in gemmation; *esp* **:** an internal resistant asexual reproductive body of sponges (as of the genus *Spongilla*)

gem·mu·lif·er·ous \¦jemyə¦lif(ə)rəs\ *adj* [*gemmule* + *-i-* + *-ferous*] **:** bearing or producing a gemmule

gem·my \'jemē\ *adj* -ER/-EST [¹*gem* + *-y*] **1 :** having the characteristics (as hardness, brilliance, color) desired in a gemstone ⟨~ rock crystal⟩ **2 :** GLITTERING, BRIGHT ⟨a ~ spring day⟩

ge·mot *or* **ge·mote** \gə'mōt\ *n* -s [OE *gemōt*, fr. *ge-* (perfective and collective prefix) + *mōt* assembly, council — more at YCLEPT, MOOT] **:** a judicial or legislative assembly in England before the Norman conquest — compare FOLKMOOT, MOOT; see WITENAGEMOT

gem peg *var of* GIM PEG

gem·pyl·i·dae \jem'pilə,dē\ *n pl*, *cap* [NL, fr. *Gempylus*, type genus (fr. Gk *gempylos* young tunny) + *-idae*] **:** a family of elongated oily-fleshed percomorph fishes of open seas that resemble mackerels and comprise the escolars

¹gems *pl of* GEM, *pres 3d sing of* GEM

²gems \'gem(p)s\ *or* **gem·se** \-mzə\ *n*, *pl* **gems·es** \-m(p)sə̇z, -mzəz\ [G, fr. OHG *gamiza*, fr. LL *camoc-*, *camox*] **:** CHAMOIS

gems·bok \'gemz,bäk\ *n*, *pl* **gemsbok** *also* **gemsboks** [Afrik, lit., male chamois, fr. G *gemsbock*, fr. *gems*, *gemse* chamois + *bock* male goat or antelope, fr. OHG *boc* male goat — more at BUCK] **:** a large strikingly marked oryx (*Oryx gazella*) formerly abundant in parts of southern Africa; *also* **:** any of several related oryxes

gems·buck \-,bək\ *n*, *pl* **gemsbuck** *also* **gemsbucks** [part trans. of Afrik *gemsbok*] **:** GEMSBOK

gem shell *n* **:** a clam of the genus *Gemma*

gems·horn \'gem(p)s, 'gemz +\ *n* [G, fr. *gems*, *gemse* chamois + *horn*, fr. OHG — more at HORN] **:** a labial pipe-organ stop intermediate in quality between a string tone and a reed tone

gem stick *n* **:** a stick on which gems are cemented preparatory to cutting

gemstone \'ˌ=ˌ=\ *n* [¹*gem* + *stone*] **:** a mineral or petrified material that when cut and polished can be used in jewelry

gemul *var of* GUEMAL

gen \'jen\ *n* -s [short for *general*] *slang Brit* **:** general information

¹gen- *or* **geno-** *comb form* [Gk *genos* race, descent, kin, sex, kind, fr. the stem of *gignesthai* to be born — more at KIN] **1 :** generating **:** offspring ⟨*geno*blast⟩ **2 :** race ⟨*geno*cide⟩ **3 :** sex ⟨*geno*phobia⟩ **4** [influenced in meaning by NL *genus*] **:** genus **:** kind ⟨*geno*type⟩ **5** [*generate*] **:** a substance that produces or generates — specif. in names of oxides of alkaloids in which the oxygen is attached to nitrogen ⟨*gen*alkaloids⟩ ⟨*geno*morphine⟩

²gen- *or* **geno-** *comb form* [²*gene*] **:** gene ⟨*gen*oid⟩ ⟨*geno*cline⟩

-gen \jən, ,jen\ *also* **-gene** \,jēn\ *n comb form* -s [F *-gène*, fr. Gk *-genēs* born, fr. root of *gignesthai* to be born — more at KIN] **1 :** one that generates ⟨halo*gen*⟩ ⟨melano*gen*⟩ ⟨andro*gen*⟩ **2 :** one that is produced or generated ⟨exo*gen*⟩ ⟨culti*gen*⟩ ⟨phos*gene*⟩

gen *abbr* **1** gender **2** general **3** generation **4** generator **5** generic **6** genetics **7** genitive **8** genus

ge·na \'jēnə, 'genə\ *n*, *pl* **ge·nae** \'jē,nē, 'ge,nī\ [L, cheek — more at CHIN] **:** the cheek or lateral part of the head: as **a :** the feathered side of the under mandible of a bird **b :** the lateral part of the cephalic shield of a trilobite **c :** the lateral part of the head capsule of an insect bounded above by the margin of the eye

¹ge·nal \'jēnᵊl, 'gen-\ *adj* [*gena* + *-al*] **:** of, relating to, or constituting the cheek or broadly the lateral part of the head ⟨the ~ combs of a flea⟩

²gen·al \'jenᵊl\ *adj* [¹*gene* + *-al*] **:** of, relating to, or caused by a gene

¹ge·nappe \jə'nap, zhə-\ *n* -s [fr. *Genappe*, Belgium] **:** a smooth worsted yarn that has been genapped

²genappe \"\ *vt* -ED/-ING/-S **:** to subject (worsted yarns) to singeing

gen·darme \'zhän,därm, -dam *also* 'jän- *or* 'jen-\ *n* -s [F, fr. MF, back-formation fr. *gensdarmes*, pl. of *gent d'armes*, lit., armed people] **1 :** a cavalryman in the old French army **2 a** (1) **:** a rural policeman esp. in France (2) **:** a continental European policeman or a policeman elsewhere resembling a continental European policeman; *esp* **:** a French policeman **b** *slang* **:** POLICEMAN **3 :** a pinnacle of rock on a ridge **4 :** a flaw in a diamond or other precious stone **5** *or* **gendarme blue :** a moderate bluish green to greenish blue that is deeper than cyan blue and duller than parrot blue

gen·dar·mer·ie *or* **gen·dar·mery** \-ˌ=ərē, -əri, 'ˌ=ˌ=ˌ=ˌ=\ *n*, *pl* **gendarmeries** [MF *gendarmerie*, fr. *gendarme* + *-erie* -ery] **:** a body of gendarmes

¹gen·der \'jendə(r)\ *n* -s [ME *gendre*, fr. MF *gendre*, *genre*, fr. L *gener-*, *genus* birth, race, kind, class — more at KIN] **1 a** *archaic* **:** KIND, SORT **b :** SEX ⟨black divinities of the feminine ~ —Charles Dickens⟩ **2** *linguistics* **a :** any of two or more subclasses within a grammatical class of a language (such as noun, pronoun, adjective, verb) that are partly arbitrary but also partly based on distinguishable characteristics such as shape, social rank, manner of existence (as animate or inanimate), or sex (as masculine, feminine, or neuter) and that determine agreement with and selection of other words or grammatical forms ⟨Latin has three ~*s*, masculine, feminine, and neuter⟩ ⟨French has two ~*s*, masculine and feminine⟩ **b :** membership of a word or a grammatical form in such a subclass ⟨a Latin noun has ~, number, and case⟩ ⟨an English noun has, strictly speaking, no ~⟩ **c :** an inflectional form showing membership in such a subclass ⟨a Latin adjective agrees in ~ with the noun it modifies⟩

²gender \"\ *vb* **gendered; gendered; gendering** \-d(ə)riŋ\ **genders** [ME *gendren*, *genderen*, fr. MF *gendrer*, fr. L *generare*, fr. L *gener-* *genus*] *vt* **:** BREED ~ *vi* **:** COPULATE

³gen·der \'gen,de(ə)r, ='ˌ=, gən'd-\ *n* -s [Jav *gendèr*] **:** a Javanese percussion instrument like a xylophone

¹gene \'zhen, 'zhān, *F* zheen\ *n* -s [F *gêne*, fr. OF *gehine* torture (to make one confess), fr. *gehir*, *jehir* to confess, of Gmc origin; akin to OHG *jehan* to speak, say — more at JOKE] **:** EMBARRASSMENT, UNEASINESS ⟨a certain amount of ~ with relatives —Evelyn Waugh⟩

²gene \'jēn\ *n* -s [G *gen*, short for *pangen*] **:** one of the elements of the germ plasm serving as specific transmitters of hereditary characters and usu. regarded as portions of deoxyribonucleic acids linearly arranged in fixed positions and as functioning through control of the synthesis of specific polypeptide chains

-gene — see -GEN

gene·a·log·i·cal \¦jēnēə¦läjəkəl, -äjēk- *also* ¦jen-\ *also* **gene·a·log·ic** \-äjik,-äjēk\ *adj* [MF *genealogique*, fr. *genealogie* + *-ique* -ical, -ic] **1 :** of or relating to genealogy — **gene·a·log·i·cal·ly** \-jək(ə)lē, -jēk-, -li\ *adv*

gene·al·o·gist \ˌ÷ˌ=ˌ='äləjə̇st, \|al- *sometimes* jēn'y\| *or* jen'y\| *n* -s **1 :** a specialist or expert in genealogy **2 :** a person who traces, makes studies of, or records genealogies

gene·al·o·gize \-,jīz\ *vb* -ED/-ING/-S *vi* **:** to investigate or relate the history of descents ⟨the grotesque *genealogizing* that decaying aristocracies affect —H.L.Mencken⟩ ~ *vt* **:** to trace or chart the genealogy of

gene·al·o·giz·er \-zə(r)\ *n* -s **:** one that genealogizes

gene·al·o·gy \-jē, -ji\ *n* -ES [ME *genealogie*, fr. MF, fr. LL *genealogia*, fr. Gk, fr. *genea* race, family + *-logia* -logy — more at KIN] **1 :** an account or history of the descent of a person, family, or group from an ancestor or ancestors or from older forms **:** an enumeration of ancestors and their descendants in the natural order of succession **2 :** regular descent of a person, family, or group of organisms from a progenitor or older form **:** PEDIGREE, LINEAGE **3 :** a study of family pedigrees and the methods of investigation of them **4 :** an account of the descent of property with respect to its previous owners

gen·ecologic *or* **gen·ecological** \(¦)jēn, (¦)jen+\ *adj* **:** of or relating to genecology—**gen·ecologically** *adv*

gen·ecologist \¦jēn, ¦jen +\ *n* **:** a specialist in genecology

gen·ecology \'jēn, ¦jen+\ *n* -ES [Gk *genos* race (fr. *gignesthai* to be born) + E *ecology* — more at KIN] **:** a branch of ecology concerned primarily with the species and its genetically variant subdivisions, with their position in nature and, with the controlling genetic and ecological factors

gene complex *n* [²*gene*] **:** all the genes of an individual or of a potentially interbreeding group that constitute an interacting functional unit

gene flow *n* **:** the passage and establishment of genes typical of one breeding population into the gene complex of another through hybridization and backcrossing

gene frequency *n* **:** the percentage of occurrence of a specified gene in the chromosomes of a population

gen·emo·tor \'jenə+,-\ *n* -s [*generator* + *motor*] **:** DYNAMOTOR

gene mutation *n* **:** mutation due to fundamental intramolecular reorganization of a gene

ge·ner \'ge,ne(ə)r\ *n* -s [L; akin to Gk *gambros* son-in-law, Skt *jāmātā*, Lith *žéntas*, & prob. to L *gignere* to beget — more at KIN] *Roman & civil law* **:** SON-IN-LAW

genera *pl of* GENUS

gen·er·a·ble \'jen(ə)rəbəl\ *adj* [ME, fr. L *generabilis*, fr. *generare* to beget, create + *-abilis* -able — more at GENERATE] **:** capable of being created or produced (as by human intellect or imagination)

¹gen·er·al \'jen(ə)rəl\ *adj* [ME, fr. MF, fr. L *generalis*, fr. *gener-*, *genus* birth, race, class, kind + *-alis* -al — more at KIN] **1 :** involving or belonging to the whole of a body, group, class, or type **:** applicable or relevant to the whole rather than to a limited part, group, or section ⟨appearance of ~ decay⟩ ⟨a ~ change in temperature⟩ **2 :** involving or belonging to every member of a class, kind, or group **:** applicable to every one in the unit referred to **:** not exclusive or excluding ⟨ladies, a ~ welcome from his grace salutes ye all —Shak.⟩ ⟨those first assemblies were ~, with all freemen bound to attend —*Amer. Guide Series: Md.*⟩ **3 a :** applicable or pertinent to the majority of individuals involved **:** characteristic of the majority **:** PREVALENT, USUAL, WIDESPREAD ⟨the ~ opinion⟩ ⟨a custom ~ in these areas⟩ ⟨the conflict became ~⟩ ⟨we, the people of the United States, in order to . . . promote the ~ welfare —*U.S.Constitution*⟩ **b :** concerned or dealing with universal rather than particular aspects ⟨~ history⟩ **4 :** marked by broad overall character without being limited, modified, or checked by narrow precise considerations **:** concerned with main elements, major matters rather than limited details, or universals rather than particulars **:** approximate rather than strictly accurate ⟨a ~ outline⟩ ⟨bearing a ~ resemblance to the original⟩ ⟨the rock formations of the state have a ~ northeast-southwest trend —*Amer. Guide Series: N.H.*⟩ **5 :** not confined by specialization or careful limitation **:** not limited to a particular class, type, or field **:** inclusive and manifesting or characterized by scope, diversity, or variety **:** BROAD, CATHOLIC, COMPREHENSIVE ⟨a ~ drugstore⟩ ⟨a ~ surgeon⟩ **6 :** belonging to the common nature (as of a group of like individuals) **:** GENERIC ⟨the ~ characteristics of a species⟩ ⟨long shaggy hair is ~ among bears⟩ **7 :** holding superior rank **:** taking precedence (as over others similarly titled) ⟨~ manager⟩ **:** having wide authority or responsibility ⟨a ~ captain⟩ ⟨the ~ board⟩ — sometimes used postpositively ⟨the master ~⟩ **8 :** designed for students without special ability or vocational plans ⟨a ~ course in science⟩ — compare COLLEGE-PREPARATORY, COMMERCIAL **9 :** of or relating to a universal term or proposition or a quantified statement in logic — opposed to *singular* **10 :** involving or affecting practically the entire organism **:** not local ⟨~ nervousness⟩ **syn** see UNIVERSAL

²general \"\ *n* -s **1** *archaic* **:** WHOLE, TOTAL **2 a :** something (as a concept, fact, idea, principle, proposition, or statement) that comprehends the whole or total ⟨a description that spends too much time on the ~ and too little on the particular⟩; *specif* **:** GENERALITY **b :** GENUS, UNIVERSAL **3 a** *archaic* **:** the general public **:** PEOPLE **b** *Brit* **:** a servant for general work **4** [ML *generalis*, fr. L *generalis*, adj. (in such phrases as *abbas generalis*, lit., general abbot)] **:** the chief of a religious order of all houses or congregations under one religious rule; *specif* **:** SUPERIOR GENERAL **5** [MF, fr. OIt *generale* (also, chief of a religious order), fr. ML *generalis*] *archaic* **:** the commander in chief of an army **6 a :** a military officer of high rank — see BRIGADIER GENERAL, GENERAL OF THE AIR FORCE, GENERAL OF THE ARMY, LIEUTENANT GENERAL, MAJOR GENERAL **b :** a military officer who is junior only to a general of the army, to a general of the air force, or to a field marshal, wears 4 stars, and ranks with a four-star admiral of the navy **7 :** the supreme commander of the Salvation Army — compare SALVATIONIST — **in general** *adv* **1** *obs* **a :** without exception **:** INCLUSIVELY **b :** in all things **:** in all respects **2 :** for the most part **:** GENERALLY

general ability *n* **:** ABILITY 2

general acceptance *n* **:** an unqualified acceptance bill

general act *n* **:** GENERAL LAW

general administrator *n* **:** a legal administrator appointed at the domicile of a deceased person to settle and distribute the entire estate of the decedent or in case a will is annexed to his appointment to execute the will in accordance with law — compare PUBLIC ADMINISTRATOR

general agent *n* **1 :** one employed to transact generally all legal business of his principal entrusted to him or to do all acts connected with a particular trade, business, or employment esp. at a particular place **:** one whose authority is to conduct a series of transactions in the continuous service of his principal **2 :** a representative of an insurance company or often of several companies (as in fire insurance) who appoints and supervises selling agents and administers the company's business within a specified territory

general american *n*, *sometimes cap G & cap A* **:** the native speech of natives of the U. S. whose speech is not that of the South or of the *r*-dropping Northeast; *specif* **:** such speech excluding that of the Middle Atlantic states and western Pennsylvania

general anesthesia *n* **:** anesthesia affecting the entire body and accompanied by loss of consciousness

general appearance *n* **:** an appearance made in general terms giving a court full and absolute jurisdiction in the matter in issue (as by asking for any relief other than a ruling that the court has no jurisdiction over the person of the party)

general assembly *n* **1 :** the highest ecclesiastical judiciary or governing board of certain national churches (as of the Presbyterian Church) **2 :** a legislative body; *specif* **:** the legislature of some states of the U.S. (as So. Carolina) **3 :** a supreme deliberative body (as of the United Nations)

general assignment *n* **:** an assignment of all one's property not exempt by law for the benefit of all one's creditors with only such preferences as may be allowed

general assumpsit *n* **:** COMMON ASSUMPSIT

general atonement *n* **:** a theological doctrine that the reconciliation effected between God and man by the sufferings of Jesus Christ was efficacious for all men — compare LIMITED ATONEMENT

general average *n* **:** a loss that arises from the voluntary sacrifice of part of a ship or cargo to save the residue of the ship or cargo or from extraordinary expenses incurred in protecting the interests involved under pressure of a common risk and that is shared proportionally by all parties concerned — compare PARTICULAR AVERAGE

general baptist *n*, *usu cap G&B* **:** a member of a British Baptist body of the 17th to 19th centuries that held Arminian doctrines or a member of a similar Baptist sect in the U. S. — called also *Arminian Baptist*; compare PARTICULAR BAPTIST

general bass *n* **:** CONTINUO

general canon *n* **:** a canon enacted at a general convention of the Protestant Episcopal Church and effective within all dioceses

general cargo *n* **:** a mixed cargo (as carried by ships that take merchandise for all persons indifferently)

general certificate of education : a certificate awarded on the successful completion of an examination taken by British secondary-school students

general conference *n*, *usu cap G&C* **:** the highest legislative and judicial body in various religious denominations ⟨the *General Conference* of the Methodist Church⟩

general confession *n* **1 :** confession of sins made by a number of persons in common (as in public prayer) **2 :** a confession in which the penitent gives a summary of his sins

general convention *n* **:** a legislative body of a church (as of the Protestant Episcopal Church)

general counsel *n* **:** a lawyer at the head of the legal department (as of a corporation or governmental subdivision)

general course *n* **:** the pass course at British universities

general court *n*, *usu cap G&C* **:** the legislature of the states of Massachusetts and New Hampshire

general court-martial *n* **:** a court-martial consisting of at least five officers one of whom is a law member and having authority to impose a sentence of dishonorable discharge or death — compare SPECIAL COURT-MARTIAL, SUMMARY COURT-MARTIAL

general cover *n* **:** insurance covering fluctuating quantities of goods at locations specified and subject to limitations as imposed by contract

general creditor *n* **:** a creditor not secured by a lien or other security **:** a creditor not having a preference

general custom *n* **:** a custom or usage throughout the jurisdiction that is general, uniform, and certain and of such long standing that the courts will take judicial notice of its existence as part of the common law of the jurisdiction — compare PARTICULAR CUSTOM

gen·er·al·cy \ˈjen(ə)rəlsē, -si\ *n* -ES **:** the office or term of a general

general damages *n pl* **:** damages awarded for injury (as from defamation) in the absence of any specific pecuniary loss

general degree *n* **:** PASS DEGREE

general delivery *n* **:** a mail-delivery service or a department of a post office that handles the delivery of mail at a post office window to persons who do not have any permanent street address or for other reasons call for it or to persons who call for their mail without waiting for or in the absence of carrier service — often used as an address

general deposit *n* **:** a deposit of money under common law made by a depositor in a banking institution that creates a debt of the bank to the depositor to be paid by an equivalent sum but not by return of the identical money and that resembles the irregular deposit of the civil law

general deputy *n* **:** a deputy authorized to exercise the whole of the powers of another official

general discharge *n* **:** a formal release from military service given under honorable conditions and for satisfactory service to a member of the armed forces not qualifying for an honorable discharge — compare DISCHARGE

general editor *n* **:** one who supervises other editors or publications issued in a series — compare EDITOR IN CHIEF, MANAGING EDITOR

general education *n* **:** a program of education (as in some liberal-arts colleges and secondary schools) intended to develop students as personalities rather than trained specialists and to transmit a common cultural heritage — compare LIBERAL EDUCATION

general election *n* **:** an election usu. held at regular intervals prescribed by law or custom in which candidates are chosen in all or most constituencies of a nation or state ⟨the promptness with which Parliament meets . . . after a *general election* —F.A.Ogg & Harold Zink⟩ ⟨as well qualified to vote at a primary as at a *general election* —E.C.Meyer⟩ — compare BY-ELECTION, PRIMARY 6b

general endorsement *n* **:** an endorsement (as on a check) that does not specify a payee

general equilibrium *n* **:** simultaneous equilibrium for all economic variables

general expense *or* **general charge** *n* **:** an overhead expense not directly identifiable with a particular activity or department; *specif* **:** a charge in railroads incurred for the benefit of the road as a whole

general failure of issue : INDEFINITE FAILURE OF ISSUE

general farmer *n* **:** a farmer producing several commodities none of which represents as much as 40 percent of the total value of the products of the farm

general formula *n* **:** a chemical formula applicable to a series of compounds (as MNO_2 for metallic nitrites, ROH for alcohols, C_nH_{2n+2} for alkanes where *n* is an integer)

general grammar *n* **:** the study of general principles believed to underlie the grammatical phenomena of all languages — called also *philosophical grammar, universal grammar*

general headquarters *n* **:** the headquarters of an officer in command of all armed forces of a unit

general hospital *n* **1 :** a hospital in which patients with many different types of ailments are given care **2 :** a military hospital usu. located in a communications zone that gives treatment to all kinds of cases

gen·er·a·lia \ˌjenəˈrālēə, -lyə\ *n pl* [L, pl. of *generale* generality, fr. neut. of *generalis*] **:** general principles **:** GENERALITIES

general–in–chief \ˌ=(=)==ˈ=\ *n, pl* **generals–in–chief :** a military officer in chief command (as of the entire armed forces operating at a front or in some services of an army division)

general integral *n* **:** GENERAL SOLUTION

gen·er·a·lis·si·mo \ˌjen(ə)rəˈlisəˌmō, *rapid* -nərˈl-\ *n* -S [It, fr. *generale* general + *-issimo* superlative suffix (fr. L *-issimus*] **1 :** the chief commander of an army **:** COMMANDER IN CHIEF **2 :** one of the officers of a commandery of Knights Templar

general issue *n* **:** a legal plea that traverses and denies an indictment, declaration, petition, or complaint in its entirety without admitting the truth of any allegations and without offering special matters to avoid the legal effect of the allegations set forth — compare SPECIAL ISSUE

gen·er·al·ist \ˈjen(ə)rələst, *rapid* -nərl-\ *n* -S [[1]*general* + *-ist*] **:** one who devotes himself to, is conversant with, or can handle several different skills, fields, or aptitudes — opposed to *specialist*

gen·er·al·i·ty \ˌjenəˈralədˌē, -lətē, -i\ *n* -ES [ME *generalite*, fr. MF *generauté, generalité*, fr. LL *generalitat-, generalitas*, fr. *generalis* general + *-itat-, -itas* -ity — more at GENERAL] **1 :** the quality or state of being general **:** total applicability **2 a :** a general statement, law, principle, or proposition **b :** a vague, insufficient, or inadequate statement **3 :** the main body **:** the greatest part **:** BULK ⟨the complaint of the ~ of the nation's taxpayers —Raymond Moley⟩ **4 :** a fiscal and civil administrative district of France under the kingdom — **for the generality** *or* **in the generality** *adv, obs* **:** in general

gen·er·al·iz·able \ˈjen(ə)rəˌlīzəbəl, *rapid* ˈjenərˌl-; ˌ=(=)=ˈ===\ *adj* **:** that may be generalized

gen·er·al·iza·tion \ˌjen(ə)rələˈzāshən, -ˌlīˈz-, *rapid* ˌjenər(ˌ)l-\ *n* -S **1 :** the act or action of generalizing **2 :** the result of the process of generalizing: as **a :** a general concept, idea, or notion **b :** a general inference or proposition **:** a quantified statement **3 :** the act or process whereby response is made to a stimulus similar to but not identical with a reference stimulus

gen·er·al·ize \ˈjen(ə)rəˌlīz, *rapid* -nərˌl-\ *vb* -ED/-ING/-S *see -ize in Explan Notes* [F *généraliser*, fr. *général* general + *-iser* -ize] *vt* **1 :** to make general **:** reduce to general laws **:** give a general form to **2 a :** to derive or induce (a general conception or principle) from particulars **b :** to derive or induce a general conception, principle, or inference from **3 :** to make general (as by existential or universal qualification) **:** render applicable to a wider class **4 :** to give general applicability to ⟨~ a law⟩; *also* **:** to make indefinite (as by blurring particular features) **5 a :** to modify or eliminate (nonessential details on a map) for improving the legibility or for emphasizing some particular feature (as the location of mountains or the essential character of a coastline) **b :** to portray or emphasize in painting general rather than particular features and characteristics of ~ *vi* **1 :** to form generalizations **:** make inductions or general inferences; *also* **:** to be prone to make vague or indefinite statements **2 :** to become extended throughout the human body **3 :** to generalize the details on a map

generalized *adj* **:** made general **:** extended into a generalization; *esp* **:** not highly differentiated biologically nor strictly adapted to a particular environment ⟨the modern hedgehog, a persistently primitive and ~ mammal —C.O.Dunbar⟩

generalized coordinate *n* **:** [3]COORDINATE 2b

generalized edema *n* **:** ANASARCA

gen·er·al·iz·er \-zə(r)\ *n* -S **:** one that generalizes

general journal *n* **:** JOURNAL 1 b(2)

general law *n* **:** a law unrestricted as to time and applicable throughout the entire territory subject to the power of the legislature that enacted it and applying to all persons in the same class in the same situation — called also *general act, general statute;* distinguished from *local law* and *special law;* compare PUBLIC LAW

general ledger *n* **:** the principal and controlling ledger of a business enterprise containing individual or controlling accounts for all assets, liabilities, net worth items, revenue, and expenses

general legacy *n* **:** a testamentary gift of tangible or intangible personal property not amounting to a bequest of specific money or of a particular thing and not identified by a description that sets it apart from all other assets of the same kind in the testator's estate — compare SPECIFIC LEGACY

general license *n* **:** a license permitting exportations within certain limitations without a specific license document

general lien *n* **:** a lien for the satisfaction of a balance due from an owner of personal property not confined to the amount due in respect of the property itself — compare PARTICULAR LIEN

general linguistics *n* **:** a study of the phenomena, historical changes, and functions of language without restriction to a particular language or to a particular aspect (as phonetics, grammar, stylistics) of language

general listing *n* **:** MULTIPLE LISTING

gen·er·al·ly \ˈjen(ə)rəlē, -nərlē, -li, *-R rapid* -nᵊl-\ *adv* [ME, fr. [1]*general* + *-ly*] **:** in a general manner: as **a** *obs* **:** as a whole **:** COLLECTIVELY **b** *obs* **:** with respect to all **:** UNIVERSALLY **c :** in a reasonably inclusive manner **:** in disregard of specific instances and with regard to an overall picture ⟨~ speaking⟩ ⟨inflation ~ assumed to have been caused by war⟩ **d :** on the whole **:** as a rule ⟨elections are held ~ every other year⟩

general mortgage *n* **:** BLANKET MORTGAGE

gen·er·al·ness *n* -ES **:** the quality or state of being general

general officer *n* **:** [2]GENERAL 6a — compare FLAG OFFICER

general of the air force : an air force officer of the highest rank whose insignia is five stars

general of the armies : the highest U. S. Army rank of World War I (as conferred upon General John J. Pershing upon his retirement)

general of the army : an army officer of the highest rank whose insignia is five stars

general order *n* **1 :** any one of the orders issued by an authorized military headquarters that include important permanent directive matter of general interest — usu. used in pl.; compare SPECIAL ORDER **2 :** any one of the permanent guard orders that govern the duties of all sentries — usu. used in pl.

general paresis *also* **general paralysis** *n* **:** syphilis of the cerebral cortex and overlying membranes usu. of insidious onset with personality changes and protean manifestations that change from month to month progressing to dementia and paralysis

general partner *n* **:** a partner whose liability for partnership debts and obligations is unlimited — distinguished from *special partner*

general partnership *n* **:** a common-law partnership in which each partner has a general liability for all partnership debts and obligations in full — compare LIMITED PARTNERSHIP

general pause *n* **:** a nonrhythmic rest in all parts in ensemble music — abbr *G. P.;* called also *cutoff*

general physiology *n* **:** a branch of physiology concerned with the basic functional activities of living matter **:** protoplasmic physiology

general post *n* **1 :** blindman's buff in which players are designated by place names and are called upon to change seats two at a time until the call "general post" when all exchange **2** *chiefly Brit* **:** a general exchange of positions or locations

general post office *n, usu cap G&P&O* **:** a main post office in a capital or a large city (as London); *also* **:** a postal system

general power of appointment : a power to appoint property that can be exercised entirely in favor of the donee, his nominee, or his estate — compare SPECIAL POWER

general practitioner *n* **:** a physician or veterinarian who does not limit his practice to a specialty

general prisoner *n* **:** a military prisoner who has been sentenced to confinement and to dismissal or discharge — compare GARRISON PRISONER

general property *n* **:** the absolute ownership usu. of personal property with the right of complete dominion over it including the incidental rights of possession, of use and enjoyment, and of disposition or alienation — distinguished from *special property*

general property tax *n* **:** a tax levied on the assessed value of all nonexempt property

general proposition *n* **:** a universal proposition; *also* **:** a law or principle

general–purpose \ˈ=(=)=ˈ==\ *adj* **:** utilized or designed to be used for two or more basic purposes, products, or functions

general–purpose bomb *n* **:** a bomb designed to be effective against both troops and materiel

general–purpose flour *n* **:** ALL-PURPOSE FLOUR

general quarters *n pl* **:** a condition of maximum readiness of a warship for action with all hands at battle stations

general retainer *n* **:** a retainer of an attorney by a client to advise and represent the client for compensation and for a fixed time in all legal matters in which he may seek legal assistance; *also* **:** the retaining fee itself

general revelation *n* **:** revelation available to all men — compare SPECIAL REVELATION

general rule *n* **:** a standing order governing practice and general procedure in a court — compare SPECIAL RULE

generals *pl of* GENERAL

general science *n* **:** a subject or course of study in school or college in which the elements of several sciences are studied

general semantics *n pl but usu sing in constr* **:** a doctrine and educational discipline due to Alfred Korzybski (1879–1950) intended to improve habits of response of human beings to their environment and one another esp. by training in the better and more critical uses of words and other symbols

general service car *n* **:** a railroad car suitable for carrying a variety of classes of freight; *esp* **:** a gondola car having practically the entire bottom composed of drop doors hinged at the center to dump outside of the rails

general service school *n* **:** a unit in the system of military education at which officers and enlisted men of all arms and services are given advanced training — compare SPECIAL SERVICE SCHOOL

general sessions *n pl* **:** a court of general criminal jurisdiction

gen·er·al·ship \ˈ=(=)=ˌship\ *n* -S **1 :** office or tenure of office of a general **:** exercise of the functions of a general **2 :** military skill in a general officer or high commander **3 :** LEADERSHIP, MANAGEMENT

general ship *n* **:** a ship not chartered or let to particular parties but advertised for the general receipt of goods from the public indiscriminately to be carried on a voyage

general six–principle baptist *n, usu cap G&S&P&B* **:** a member of an Arminian Baptist sect founded in Providence, R. I., in 1653 on the six principles of repentance, faith, baptism, laying on of hands, resurrection of the dead, and eternal judgment

general solution *n* **1 :** a solution of an ordinary differential equation of order *n* that involves exactly *n* essential arbitrary constants — called also *complete solution, general integral* **2 :** a solution of a partial differential equation that involves arbitrary functions — called also *general integral*

general staff *n* **:** a group of officers in an army division or similar or larger unit who assist their commander in planning, coordinating, and supervising operations; *also* **:** a similar group assisting a chief of staff — compare SPECIAL STAFF

general statement *n* **:** a statement in logic that contains one or more bound variables — contrasted with *singular statement*

general statute *n* **:** GENERAL LAW

general store *n* **:** a retail store located usu. in a small or rural community which carries a wide variety of consumer convenience goods including groceries but is not departmentized

general strike *n* **:** a simultaneous striking by all unionized workers of all trades and industries

general synod *n, often cap G&S* **:** the highest governing body of a church ⟨the *General Synod* of the United Church of Christ⟩

general tail *n* **:** a fee-tail estate not restricted to particular descendants of the first owner thereof but designed to pass to all of said owner's descendants so long as such issue is alive

gen·er·al·ty \ˈjen(ə)rəltē\ *n* -ES [ME *generalte*, fr. MF *generauté, generalité* — more at GENERALITY] *archaic* **:** GENERALITY

general will *n* **:** the will of a community which is the embodiment or expression of its common interest; *specif* **:** the social or collective will of a community resulting from the interrelations (as the exchange of opinion) between its members

[1]**gen·er·ate** \ˈjenəˌrāt, *usu* -ād.+V\ *vb* -ED/-ING/-S [L *generatus*, past part. of *generare* to beget, create, fr. *gener-, genus* birth, race, class, kind — more at KIN] *vt* **1 :** to cause to be **:** bring into existence; *esp* **:** PROCREATE ⟨~ innumerable offspring⟩ **2 :** to originate (something material) by a physical or chemical process **:** PRODUCE ⟨would ~ a tremendous amount of electricity —*Collier's Yr. Bk.*⟩ ⟨mountain ranges . . . should ~ more heat than low-lying plains —A.E.Benfield⟩ **3 :** to define (as a mathematical or linguistic set or structure) by the application of one or more rules or operations to given quantities ⟨a mathematical group consisting of the powers of one element A is said to be *generated* by A⟩ ⟨a set of phrase structure rewriting rules that ~ underlying sentence structures —P.S.Rosenbaum⟩; *esp* **:** to trace out (as a curve) by a moving point or (as a surface) by a moving curve — see CYCLOID illustration **4 :** to form (gear teeth or screw threads) with theoretical accuracy **5 :** to be the cause of (a state of mind, an action, or something immaterial or intangible) ⟨forces *generating* interracial conflict⟩ ⟨these stories . . . ~ a good deal of psychological suspense —*Atlantic*⟩ ⟨~s mistaken opinions, wrong attitudes —H.A.Overstreet⟩ ~ *vi* **1 :** to produce offspring **:** PROPAGATE **2 :** to come into existence **:** ORIGINATE, ARISE

[2]**gen·er·ate** \ˈjen(ə)rət\ *adj* [L *generatus*] **:** GENERATED

generating station *n* **:** a plant for generating electric power

gen·er·a·tion \ˌjenəˈrāshən\ *n* -S [ME *generacioun*, fr. MF *generation*, fr. L *generation-, generatio*, fr. *generatus* + *-ion-, -io* -ion] **1 a :** a body of men, animals, or plants having a common parent or parents and constituting a single degree or step in the line of descent from an ancestor ⟨five ~s are shown in this family portrait⟩ ⟨its surface enriched with the . . . carcasses of hundreds of ~s of buffalo —B.K.Sandwell⟩ ⟨studied a bacterial culture through 60 ~s⟩ **b** (1) **:** the whole number of human beings born and living contemporaneously ⟨our ~ has seen immense changes⟩ ⟨his work affected the life and thought of later ~s⟩ (2) **:** a particular category of individuals born and living contemporaneously ⟨inspired . . . a whole ~ of theoreticians —*Newsweek*⟩ ⟨long after that ~ of scholars had passed away —G.B.Shaw⟩ ⟨uses the vocabulary of his philosophic ~ —John Dewey⟩ ⟨the present ~ of insects appears to have developed immunity to the spray⟩ (3) **:** the average span of time variously computed and varying according to cultural and other conditions between the birth of parents and that of their children ⟨among primitive peoples twenty years may make a ~⟩ ⟨a ~ . . . is roughly equal to the mean age of mothers at the birth of their daughters —*Demographic Yearbook*⟩ ⟨fifty years constitutes roughly a working lifetime, a period covering two ~s —Arthur Geddes⟩ ⟨the cornerstone of the moral system . . . for ~s —Joe Alvin⟩ (4) **:** a group of individuals having contemporaneously a status (as that of students in a school) which each one holds only for a limited period ⟨repeated by ~ after ~ of pupils —H.G.G. Herklots⟩ (5) **:** a type or class of objects derived or developed from an earlier type ⟨the Air Force's new ~ of powerful supersonic fighters —Kenneth Koyen⟩ **2 a :** the act or process of producing offspring **:** PROCREATION ⟨the organs of ~⟩ **b :** origination by some mathematical, chemical, or other process **:** PRODUCTION, FORMATION ⟨the ~ of heat⟩ ⟨the ~ of sounds⟩; *specif* **:** the formation of a geometrical figure by the motion of some other figure ⟨the ~ of a line by a point⟩ **c :** the process of coming into being **:** GENESIS, DEVELOPMENT, RISE ⟨the spontaneous ~ of these churches —Oscar Handlin⟩ ⟨factors in the ~ of income —G.V.Cox⟩ **3** *obs* **:** RACE, KIND, BREED, STOCK, FAMILY

gen·er·a·tion·al \ˌjenəˈrāshənᵊl, -shnəl\ *adj* **1 :** of or relating to generation ⟨~ sterility⟩ **2 :** of or relating to a generation or to the relations between generations ⟨an example of a ~ . . . difference in language —Paul Schach⟩

gen·er·a·tion·ism \ˌjenəˈrāshəˌnizəm\ *n* -S **:** TRADUCIANISM; *also* **:** CREATIONISM

gen·er·a·tive \ˈjenəˌrā|d·|iv, ˈjen(ə)rə|, |t|, |ēv *also* |əv\ *adj* [ME, fr. MF *generatif*, fr. LL *generativus*, fr. L *generatus* (past part. of *generare* to beget, create) + *-ivus* -ive — more at GENERATE] **1 :** having the power or function of generating, propagating, originating, producing, or reproducing ⟨~ organs⟩ **2 :** of, relating to, or acting in generation ⟨grew out of a long ~ process —Owen & Eleanor Lattimore⟩ — **gen·er·a·tive·ly** \|əvlē, -li\ *adv*

generative cell *n* **:** a sexual reproductive cell **:** GAMETE; *esp* **:** a generative nucleus together with its associated cytoplasm — see BODY CELL 2

generative nucleus *n* **:** the one of the two nuclei resulting from the first division in the pollen grain of a seed plant that gives rise to sperm nuclei — see GENERATIVE CELL; compare TUBE NUCLEUS

gen·er·a·tor \ˈjenəˌrād·ə(r), -ātə-\ *n* -S [L, fr. *generatus* + *-or*] **1 :** one that generates, causes, or produces **:** ORIGINATOR ⟨the most important ~ of industrial expansion —Andrew Shonfield⟩ ⟨rival ~s or experts in foreign policy —E.S.Griffith⟩ **2 a :** an apparatus (as a steam boiler) in which vapor or gas is formed from a liquid or solid by heat or a chemical process **b :** an apparatus for the manufacture of gas (as water gas) involving the combustion of fuel; *esp* **:** the chamber for holding the fuel — compare PRODUCER 3 **c :** GAS GENERATOR **a 3 :** a machine by which mechanical energy is changed into electrical energy usu. by electromagnetic induction **:** DYNAMO — compare ELECTROSTATIC GENERATOR

gen·er·a·trix \ˌjenəˈrā·triks\ *n, pl* **generatri·ces** \ˌjenəˈrā·trəˌsēz, -rəˈtrī(ˌ)sēz\ [NL, fr. L, fem. of *generator*] **1 :** a point, line, or surface whose motion generates a line, surface, or solid **2 :** a set of elements in a cryptological tabulation which form a line in any direction and have significance as a set

[1]**ge·ner·ic** \jəˈnerik, -rēk\ *adj* [F *générique*, fr. L *gener-, genus* birth, race, class, kind + F *-ique* -ic — more at KIN] **1 a :** relating or applied to or descriptive of all members of a genus, species, class, or group **:** common to or characteristic of a whole group or class **:** typifying or subsuming **:** not specific or individual **:** GENERAL ⟨the diseases grouped under the ~ heading of regional enteritis —W.H.Hale⟩ ⟨there is no such thing as a ~ "Asian" mind —R.A.Smith⟩ ⟨the same ~ similarity that one finds in the professional officers of any armed service —Joseph Alsop⟩ ⟨the novel has always had a ~ habit of reaching out to the extremes of literary expression —Mark Schorer⟩ **b :** available for common use **:** not protected by trademark registration **:** NONPROPRIETARY ⟨nylon and aspirin are ~ names⟩ — used esp. in trademark law **2 :** relating to or having the rank of a biological genus **syn** see UNIVERSAL

[2]**generic** \"\ *n* -S **:** an element of a compound proper name that is general and often lowercased (as *river* in "Mississippi River" and *store* in "XYZ Store")

ge·ner·i·cal \-rəkəl, -rēk-\ *adj* [F *générique* + E *-al*] *archaic* **:** GENERIC

ge·ner·i·cal·ly \-k(ə)lē, -li\ *adv* **:** in a generic manner ⟨those pioneering tales now ~ called "Westerns" —Saxe Commins⟩ ⟨the dowdy . . . people whom you call, ~, suffragettes —G.B. Shaw⟩

generic judgment *n* **:** a judgment in logic in which the predicate gives generic characteristics of the subject **:** a universal judgment

ge·ner·ic·ness *n* -ES **:** the quality or state of being generic

generic wine *n* **:** a wine (as California burgundy or New York State sherry) named from the geographical location where the wine type to which it belongs originated — compare VARIETAL WINE

ge·ner·i·type *also* **ge·ner·o·type** \jəˈnerəˌtīp\ *n* [NL *gener-, genus* + E *-i-* or *-o-* + *type*] **:** GENOTYPE

gen·er·os·i·ty \ˌjenəˈräsəd·ē, -s(ə)tē, -i\ *n* -ES [ME *generosite*, fr. L *generositat-, generositas*, fr. *generosus* + *-itat-, -itas* -ity] **1** *archaic* **:** nobility of birth or breeding **:** high quality **2 a :** liberality in spirit or act **:** MAGNANIMITY, BENEVOLENCE ⟨pleads for greater ~ in regard to immigration —S.K.Padover⟩ ⟨will make gestures of the greatest ~ to his opposition —W.S. White⟩; *esp* **:** liberality in giving **b :** an act or instance of magnanimity or munificence ⟨his countless *generosities*⟩ **3 :** ABUNDANCE, COPIOUSNESS ⟨the extreme ~ of technical illustration —*Science*⟩ **:** LARGENESS, AMPLITUDE ⟨a . . . ~ of hips not sanctioned by the styles —Mary Deasy⟩

gen·er·ous \ˈjen(ə)rəs\ *adj* [MF or L; MF *genereus*, fr. L *generosus*, fr. *gener-, genus* birth, race, class, kind + *-osus* -ous — more at KIN] **1** *archaic* **:** of honorable birth or origin **:** of good stock **:** HIGHBORN **2 a :** characterized by a noble or forbearing spirit **:** animated by or exhibiting high ideals **:** MAGNANIMOUS, LOFTY, BENEVOLENT, KINDLY ⟨unusually ~ in his judgments of people —Osbert Sitwell⟩ ⟨projecting a more ~ basis for the reorganization of society —V.L.Parrington⟩ ⟨a ~ national credo which actuality often fails to live up to

—C.J.Rolo⟩ ⟨capable of ~ enthusiasms —Alfred Buchanan⟩ ⟨the dreams of all the ~ visionaries of the past —Carl Van Doren⟩ **b :** liberal or reflecting liberality in giving **:** not stingy or niggardly **:** OPENHANDED ⟨a ~ hospitality⟩ ⟨~ with the loot he has accumulated from his victims —Frederic Morton⟩ ⟨advocating a ~ system of old age pensions⟩ ⟨of a ~ disposition, he freely shared his supply —*Amer. Guide Series: N. H.*⟩ **c** (1) **:** marked by abundance or ample proportions **:** furnished without stint **:** COPIOUS, EXPANSIVE, LAVISH ⟨set himself up in ~ style —*Amer. Guide Series: Maine*⟩ ⟨the harvests . . . were ~ —Theodore Saloutos⟩ ⟨wide overhangs and ~ verandas —Lewis Mumford⟩ ⟨~ portions of food⟩ ⟨sets a ~ table⟩ ⟨a shirt with ~ cuffs⟩ (2) *of a wine* **:** full of spirit or strength **:** STIMULATING, RICH ⟨like a draught of some ~ southern wine —Norman Douglas⟩ **syn** see LIBERAL

gen·er·ous·ly *adv* **:** in a generous manner

gen·er·ous·ness *n* -ES **:** the quality or state of being generous ⟨an unusual ~ of spirit —T.O.Heggen⟩

genes *pl of* GENE

-genes *pl of* -GENE

gen·eserine \jən+\ *n* [ISV ²*gen-* (fr. L *generare* to beget, create) + *eserine* — more at GENERATE] **:** a crystalline alkaloid $C_{15}H_{21}N_3O_3$ found in the Calabar bean **:** an *N*-oxide of physostigmine

-ge·ne·sia \jə'nēzh(ē)ə\ *n comb form, pl* **-genesi·ae** \-z(h)ē,ē\ [NL, fr. Gk, fr. *genesis* + *-ia* -y] **:** genesis **:** formation ⟨para*genesia*⟩

ge·nesic \jə'nesik, -nēsik,-nēzik\ *adj* [*genesis* + *-ic*] **:** GENERATIVE

gen·e·sis \'jenəsəs\ *n, pl* **gene·ses** \-ə,sēz\ [L, fr. Gk, fr. the stem of *gignesthai* to be born — more at KIN] **:** the origin or coming into being of anything **:** development into being esp. by growth or evolution **:** the process or mode of origin ⟨the ~ of a book⟩ ⟨the ~ of a culture pattern⟩ ⟨the ~ of a disease⟩

gene–spread \'=,=\ *n* **:** GENE FLOW

gene–string \'=,=\ *n* **:** the linear functional gene group of a chromosome **:** a chromonema with the genes it carries

ge·nes·trole \jə'ne,strōl\ *n* -s [F, fr. Prov *genestrolo*, fr. *genesto* broom, fr. OProv *genesta*, fr. L *genista*] **:** DYER'S BROOM

¹**gen·et** \'jenət\ *also* **ge·nette** \jə'net\ *n* -s [ME *jonet, genete*, fr. MF *genete*, fr. Ar *jarnayṭ*] **:** any of several small Old World carnivorous mammals comprising the genus *Genetta* and related to the civets but having the scent glands less developed and the claws perfectly retractile

²**gen·et** \'jenət\ *var of* JENNET

³**ge·net** \zhə'nā\ *n, pl* **genets** \-āz\ [F *genêt* (also, broom), fr. L *genista, genesta* broom] **1 :** WOODWAXEN **2 :** DYER'S BROOM

¹**ge·neth·li·ac** \jə'nethlē,ak\ *n* -s [in sense 1, fr. LL *genethliacus*, fr. Gk *genethliakos*, fr. *genethliakos*, adj.; in sense 2, fr. LL *genethliace*, fr. (assumed) Gk *genethliakē*, fr. fem. of *genethliakos*, adj.] **1** *archaic* **:** a calculator of nativities **2** *archaic* **:** NATIVITY

²**genethliac** \"\ *or* **gen·eth·li·a·cal** \,je,neth'līəkəl, -,nəth-\ *adj* [*genethliac* fr. LL *genethliacus*, fr. Gk *genethliakos*, fr. *genethlē* race, stock, family, offspring, fr. the stem of *gignesthai* to be born; *genethliacal* fr. LL *genethliacus* + E *-al*] **:** relating to nativities or birthdays **:** showing position and influence of stars at one's birth — **gen·eth·li·a·cal·ly** \'=(,)='līək(ə)lē\ *adv*

ge·net·ic \jə'ned·|ik, -et|, |ēk\ *also* **ge·net·i·cal** \|əkəl, |ēk-\ *adj* [fr. *genesis*, after such pairs as *antithesis: antithetic, antithetical*] **1 a :** relating to or determined by the origin, development, prior history, or causal antecedents of some phenomenon **:** CAUSAL, HISTORICAL, EVOLUTIONARY ⟨the ~ factors in juvenile delinquency⟩ ⟨the ~ features of rocks —L.V.Pirsson⟩ ⟨the ~ development of a legal doctrine⟩ ⟨traces the ~ development . . . of his neurotic conflict —Lionel Ovesey⟩ **b :** based on or determined by evolution from a common source ⟨the relationship . . . is not causal but ~ . . . both are derived from a common source, a literary convention —F.H.Ellis⟩ — used esp. of relations among languages or among words and grammatical forms of languages ⟨classes of words . . . relied upon in establishing ~ connections between languages —M.J.Andrade⟩ **c :** concerned with or seeking to explain, interpret, or understand (as a literary or psychological phenomenon) in terms of its origin and development or of its causal antecedents ⟨the general reaction against . . . historical or ~ criticism of any type —Malcolm Cowley⟩ ⟨what we call the evolutionary approach or the historical attitude is technically labeled the ~ method —John Dewey⟩ ⟨~ psychology⟩ **2 :** of or relating to genetics **:** characterized or produced by the agencies and operations of genetics **:** employed in the processes of genetics ⟨~ studies⟩ **3 :** of, relating to, produced by, or being a gene **:** GENIC ⟨~ combinations⟩ — **ge·net·i·cal·ly** \|ək(ə)lē, |ēk-, -li\ *adv*

-genetic \=|==\ *adj comb form* **1 :** relating to generation or genesis ⟨spermato*genetic*⟩ ⟨pan*genetic*⟩ **2 :** generating **:** producing **:** yielding ⟨cyto*genetic*⟩ **3 :** generated **:** produced **:** yielded ⟨psycho*genetic*⟩

genetic aggregation *n* **:** a group of blood kindred **:** a population descended through common lines undisturbed by immigration

genetic definition *n* **:** a definition that indicates how that to which a word or expression refers comes into existence (as "a circle is a closed plane curve generated by the motion of a point at a constant distance from a fixed point")

genetic drift *n* **:** random changes in the gene complex of a population due to chance preservation or extinction of particular genes

genetic fallacy *n* **:** the fallacy of employing the genetic method under inapplicable circumstances or in inappropriate ways; *esp* **:** an invalid resolution of phenomena into their antecedents

genetic individual *n* **:** INDIVIDUAL 1c, 1d

ge·net·i·cism \jə'ned·|ə,sizəm, -et|\ *n* -s **:** a theory explaining the perceptions, attitudes, and behavior of an individual primarily in terms of his heredity and development — compare NATIVISM

ge·net·i·cist \-.səst\ *n* -s **:** a specialist in genetics

ge·net·ics \|iks, |ēks\ *n pl but sing in constr* **1 a :** a branch of biology that deals with the heredity and variation of organisms and with the mechanisms by which these are effected **b :** a treatise or textbook on this subject **2 :** the genetic makeup and phenomena of an organism, type, group, or condition ⟨the ~ of drosophila⟩ **3 :** GENESIS ⟨the psychological analysis of religious experience; its ~ and causal conditions —F.P. Clarke⟩ ⟨a classification of clouds based on . . . their physical and meteorological ~ and structure —D.W.Perrie⟩

genetic spiral *n* **:** a spiral formed by passing a line through the point of insertion of each leaf on a stem from the lowest to the highest

ge·neto·troph·ic \jə¦ned·ə¦träfik, -rōf-\ *adj* [*genetic* + *-o-* + *-trophic*] **:** relating to or involving genetic predisposing and nutritional precipitating factors — used esp. of certain deficiency diseases

gen·e·trix \'jenə·(,)triks\ *n, pl* **genetri·ces** \,jenə·'trī(,)sēz\ [L, fr. the stem of *gignere* to beget — more at KIN] **:** MOTHER ⟨a ~ of aldermen and beadles —Francis Berry⟩

genets *pl of* GENET

ge·net·ta \jə'ned·ə\ *n, cap* [NL, fr. F *genette* genet, fr. MF *genete* — more at GENET] **:** a genus of Old World mammals (family Viverridae) comprising the genets

genette *var of* GENET

¹**ge·ne·va** \jə'nēvə\ *adj, usu cap* [fr. *Geneva*, Switzerland] **:** of or from the city of Geneva, Switzerland **:** of the kind or style prevalent in Geneva **:** GENEVAN, GENEVESE

²**geneva** \"\ *n* -s [modif. (influenced by *Geneva*, city in Switzerland) of obs. D *genever* (now *jenever*), lit., juniper, fr. MD *geniver, genēver*, fr. OF *geneivre, genevre*, fr. (assumed) VL *jeniperus*, fr. L *juniperus* — more at JUNIPER] **:** a strongly alcoholic liquor flavored with juniper berries and made in the Netherlands **:** HOLLANDS

Geneva bands

geneva bands *n pl, usu cap G* **:** clerical bands consisting of two narrow strips of white cloth hanging down from the front collar of the ecclesiastical dress of some Protestant clergymen and modeled after the bands worn by the Calvinist clergy of Switzerland

geneva convention *n, usu cap G* **:** one of a series of agreements concerning both the treatment of prisoners of war, the sick, wounded, and dead in battle and the status of those responsible for them first made and signed at Geneva, Switzerland, in 1864 and subsequently accepted in later revisions by the majority of nations

geneva cross *n, usu cap G* **:** RED CROSS

geneva crystal *n, usu cap G* **:** a very thin round watch glass used in closed-top pocket watches

geneva gown *n, usu cap 1st G* **:** a loose large-sleeved black academic gown adopted as a vestment for preaching by the Calvinistic clergy of Geneva and widely used by Protestants

geneva movement *n, often cap G* **1** *or* **geneva motion :** a device for obtaining intermittent motion in which a cam on a driving wheel engages slots in a driven wheel **2 :** BAR MOVEMENT

¹**ge·ne·van** \jə'nēvən\ *n* -s *cap* [*Geneva*, Switzerland + E *-an*] **1 :** a native or resident of Geneva, Switzerland **2 :** a supporter of Genevan doctrines **:** CALVINIST

²**genevan** \"\ *adj, usu cap* **1 :** of or relating to Geneva, Switzerland **2 :** of or relating to Geneva about the time of John Calvin and the beginning of the Reformation **:** PROTESTANT, CALVINISTIC ⟨*Genevan* theology⟩

geneva stop *n, usu cap G* **1 :** a device used in watches with going barrels that limits the power of the mainspring to its middle portion so that the action starts with the same even force as when it abruptly stops rather than gradually running down **2 :** MALTESE CROSS

geneva system *or* **geneva nomenclature** *n, usu cap G* **:** a system of nomenclature adopted by an international congress of organic chemists in Geneva in 1892 and later modified and added to by the International Union of *Pure and Applied* Chemistry resulting in a systematic nomenclature in which names of compounds are formed from those of parent hydrocarbons with use of prefixes and suffixes (as 2-methylbutane for isopentane, butanone for methyl ethyl ketone, hexanoic acid for caproic acid)

gen·e·vese \,jenə¦vēz, -ēs\ *n or adj, usu cap* [*Geneva*, Switzerland + E *-ese*] **:** GENEVAN

¹**ge·nial** \'jēnyəl, -nēəl\ *adj* [L *genialis*, fr. *genius* + *-alis* -al — more at GENIUS] **1** *archaic* **:** of or relating to marriage or generation **:** NUPTIAL, GENERATIVE ⟨the ~ bed —John Milton⟩ **2 a :** favorable to growth or human comfort **:** not harsh or severe **:** pleasantly warm **:** MILD ⟨in these ~ regions . . . one's wants are naturally diminished —Herman Melville⟩ ⟨a sun as bright and ~ as we would desire —Tyrone Power †1841⟩ ⟨the climate should be ~ . . . with ample rainfall —W.C. Bennett⟩ **b :** marked by or diffusing good cheer, warmth, sympathy, or friendliness **:** KINDLY, AFFABLE, AMIABLE ⟨the handsome, ~ face with its kindliness of glance, its smiling mouth —S.H.Adams⟩ ⟨the pleasure-loving, ~, imperturbable traveler —Saxe Commins⟩ ⟨the extremely comfortable and ~ atmosphere of the upper middle class —*Amer. Guide Series: Ind.*⟩ **3** *obs* **:** belonging to one's genius or nature **:** NATIVE, INBORN **4 :** displaying or marked by genius ⟨new, ~ insights —Susanne K. Langer⟩ ⟨however ~ his intuitions may be —George Santayana⟩ ⟨we rarely read . . . to share some ~ vision —Herbert Read⟩ **syn** see GRACIOUS

²**ge·ni·al** \jə'nī(ə)l\ *adj* [Gk *geneion* chin, beard (fr. *genys* jaw) + E *-al* — more at CHIN] **:** of or relating to the chin

ge·nial·i·ty \,jēnē'aləd·ē, jēn'ya-, -ətē, -i\ *n* -ES [LL *genialitas*, fr. L *genialis* + *-itas* -ity] **:** the quality of being genial; *esp* **:** sympathetic cheerfulness **:** warmth of disposition and manners ⟨overflowing with joy and a noisy, hearty ~ —Vicki Baum⟩

ge·nial·ize \'jēnyə,līz, 'jēnēə,-\ *vt* -ED/-ING/-S **:** to make genial ⟨scheme for *genializing* the world —D.G.Hoffman⟩

ge·nial·ly \-əlē,-əli\ *adv* **1** *obs* **:** by genius or nature **:** NATURALLY **2 :** in a genial manner **:** CHEERFULLY, PLEASANTLY

ge·nial·ness \-əlnəs\ *n* -ES **:** the quality or state of being genial

gen·ic \'jēnik, 'jen-, -nēk\ *adj* [²*gene* + *-ic*] **:** of, relating to, produced by, or being a gene **:** GENETIC — compare ACQUIRED — **gen·i·cal·ly** \-nək(ə)lē, -nēk-, -li\ *adv*

-gen·ic \¦jenik, -nēk, *in sense 3* \¦jēn- *or* ¦jen-\ *adj comb form* [ISV *-gen* & *-geny* + *-ic*] **1 :** producing **:** forming ⟨carcino*genic*⟩ ⟨acro*genic*⟩ **2 :** produced by **:** formed from ⟨nephro*genic*⟩ **3** [*genic*] **:** of or relating to a gene ⟨intra*genic*⟩: having (a stipulated kind or number of) genes ⟨poly*genic*⟩ **4** [photo*genic*] **:** suitable for production or reproduction by a (given) medium ⟨tele*genic*⟩

genic balance *n* **:** the relation whereby a specific gene acts as a part of the entire gene complex in the production of a particular phenotypic character

ge·nic·u·late \jə'nikyələt, -,lāt\ *or* **ge·nic·u·lat·ed** \-,lād·əd\ *adj* [L *geniculatus*, fr. *geniculum* small knee, knot (dim. of *genu* knee, knot) + *-atus* -ate, -ated — more at KNEE] **1 :** bent abruptly at an angle like a bent knee ⟨a ~ twin crystal⟩ **2 :** relating to the geniculate ganglion ⟨~ neuralgia⟩ — **ge·nic·u·late·ly** \-,lətlē, -,lāt-\ *adv*

geniculate body *n* **:** any of four oval prominences of the diencephalon functioning as centers of synapse in paths to the cerebral cortex

geniculate ganglion *n* **:** a small reddish ganglion consisting of sensory and sympathetic nerve cells located at the sharp backward bend of the facial nerve

ge·nic·u·lum \-,ləm\ *n, pl* **genicu·la** \-lə\ [NL, fr. L, knee, knot] **:** a small knee-shaped anatomical structure or abrupt bend

ge·nie \'jēnē, 'jenē, -ni\ *n, pl* **genies** *also* **ge·nii** \'jēnē,ī *also* -n,yī\ [F *génie*, modif. (influenced by *génie* genius, fr. L *genius*) of Ar *jinnīy* demon, spirit] **:** JINN ⟨the invisible ~*s*, water and heat —T.M.Longstreth⟩ ⟨all the good *genii* of the universe —Joseph Tetlie⟩

-genies *pl of* -GENY

genii *pl of* GENIUS *or of* GENIE

gen·in \'jenən, jə'nēn\ *n* -s [*-genin*] **:** any of numerous aglycons or similar compounds obtained by hydrolysis of compounds that are not glycosides — compare BUFAGIN, SAPOGENIN

-genin \'jenən; jənən, -,nēn\ *n comb form* -s [ISV ²*gen* + *-in*] **:** compound formed from another compound — in names of aglycons or similar compounds derived from the names of the parent compounds ⟨sali*genin* from salicin⟩ ⟨digito*genin* from digitonin⟩

genio- *comb form* [ISV, fr. Gk *geneio-*, fr. *geneion* chin, beard — more at GENIAL] **1 :** chin ⟨*genio*plasty⟩ **2 :** chin and ⟨*genio*glossal⟩

ge·nio·glossal \jə¦nīō+\ *adj* [*genio-* + *glossal*] **:** of or relating to the chin and tongue

ge·nio·glos·sus \=,==glä|səs, -lȯ|-\ *n, pl* **genioglos·si** \|,sī\ [NL, fr. *genio-* + *-glossus* (fr. Gk *glōssa* tongue) — more at GLOSS] **:** either of a pair of fan-shaped muscles arising from the superior mental spine and inserting on the hyoid bone and into the tongue that serve to advance and retract and also to depress the tongue

ge·nio·hyoglossus \jə¦nīō+\ *n, pl* **geniohyoglossi** [NL, fr. *genio-* + *hyoglossus*] **:** GENIOGLOSSUS

ge·nio·hyoid \"+\ *adj* [*genio-* + *hyoid*] **:** of or relating to the chin and hyoid bone — used chiefly of a pair of slender muscles arising from the inner side of the symphysis of the lower jaw and inserted on the hyoid bone

ge·nip *or* **gi·nep** \k|ə'nep, g|, |a'-, -'nip\ *n* -s [Sp *genipa*, fr. F *genipa, genipat*, fr. Guarani] **1 :** a plant or fruit of the genus *Genipa; esp* **:** GENIPAP **2 a :** a West Indian tree (*Melicocca bijuga*) **b :** the fruit of this tree

ge·ni·pa \jə'nēpə, -nīpə\ *n* [NL, fr. Sp *genipa* genip] **1** *cap* **:** a genus of tropical American trees (family Rubiaceae) bearing yellow flowers and succulent edible fruit with a thick rind — see GENIPAP **2** -s **:** any tree or fruit of the genus *Genipa*

gen·i·pap \'jenə,pap\ *also* **gen·i·pa·po** \,jenə'pa(,)pō, ,zhenə'pa(,)pü\ *n* -s [Pg *genipapo*, fr. Tupi] **1 :** a tree (*Genipa americana*) of the West Indies and northern So. America **2 :** the edible orange-sized fruit of genipap

ge·ni·sa·ro *or* **ge·ni·ze·ro** *or* **ge·ni·za·ro** \he'nēsə,rō, ge-,je-\ *n* -s [AmerSp (Nicaragua) *jenísero, jenízaro*] **:** RAIN TREE

ge·nis·ta \jə'nistə\ *n* [NL, fr. L, broom] **1** *cap* **:** a large genus of Old World often spiny shrubs (family Leguminosae) with simple leaves and yellow flowers **2** -s **:** CANARY BROOM

ge·nis·te·in \jə'nistēən, -'ni,stēn\ *n* -s [ISV *Genista, genist-* (fr. NL genus name of *Genista tinctoria*) + *-ein*] **:** a colorless crystalline compound $C_{15}H_{10}O_5$ derived from isoflavone, occurring usu. combined as genistin, and dyeing pale yellow

ge·nis·tin \jə'nistən\ *n* -s [NL *Genista* + E *-in*] **:** a pale yellow glucoside $C_{21}H_{20}O_9$ obtained from woodwaxen or soybean meal and yielding genistein and glucose on hydrolysis

gen·i·tal \'jenəd·ᵊl, -nətᵊl\ *adj* [ME, fr. L *genitalis*, fr. *genitus* (past part. of *gignere* to beget) + *-alis* -al — more at KIN] **1 :** GENERATIVE **2 :** of, relating to, or being a sexual organ **3 :** of, relating to, or characterized by the stage of mature psychosexual development in which oral and anal impulses are subordinated to adaptive interpersonal mechanisms

genital bulb *n* **:** BULB 5e

genital cord *n* **:** a mesenchymal shelf in the female mammalian fetus enclosing the developing uterus and the posterior part of the wolffian ducts and giving rise to the broad ligaments of the uterus

genital crisis *n* **:** an adult sexual phenomenon (as transitory uterine bleeding) occurring in the newborn presumably as a result of transplacental passage of maternal hormones

genital gland *n* **:** a gland producing or capable of producing germ cells **:** OVOTESTIS, OVARY, TESTIS

genital glanders *n pl but sing or pl in constr* **:** DOURINE

genital horsepox *n* **:** coital exanthema of the horse

gen·i·ta·lia \,jenə'tālēə, -lyə\ *n pl* [L, fr. neut. pl. of *genitalis*] **:** the organs of the reproductive system; *esp* **:** the external genital organs

gen·i·ta·lic \,jenə¦talik\ *also* **gen·i·ta·li·al** \-tālēəl\ *adj* [*genitalia* + *-ic* or *-al*] **:** of or relating to the genitalia

gen·i·tal·i·ty \,jenə'taləd·ē\ *n* -ES [prob. fr. F *génitalité*, fr. *génital* (fr. L *genitalis*) + *-ité* -ity] **:** possession of full genital sensitivity and capacity to develop orgasmic potency in relation to a sexual partner of the opposite sex

genital ridge *n* **:** a ridge of embryonic mesoblast developing from the wolffian body and giving rise to the gonad on either side of the body

gen·i·tals \'jenəd·ᵊlz, -nətᵊlz\ *n pl* [ME, fr. *genital*, adj. + *-s*] **:** GENITALIA

genital wart *n* **:** CONDYLOMA

gen·i·ti·val \,jenə¦tīvəl\ *adj* [*genitive* + *-al*] **:** possessing genitive form **:** relating to or derived from the genitive case ⟨*anyways, needs, backwards* are ~ adverbs⟩ — **gen·i·ti·val·ly** \-vəlē\ *adv*

¹**gen·i·tive** \'jenəd·iv, -ətiv\ *adj* [ME, fr. L *genetivus, genitivus*, lit., of generation (trans. of Gk *genikos* in *genikē ptōsis* genitive case), irreg. fr. *gener-, genus* birth, race, class, kind + *-ivus* -ive — more at KIN] **1** *of a grammatical case* **:** marking typically a relatively close, unchanging, and exclusive relationship such as that of possessor or source ⟨the words ending in *'s* in the phrases *the boy's shoes, the sun's light, the speaker's arrival*, and *a member's expulsion from the club* are in the ~ case⟩ — compare POSSESSIVE **2** *of a word or word group* **:** not characterized by case inflection but nevertheless expressing a relationship that in some inflected languages is often marked by a genitive case — used esp. of English prepositional phrases introduced by *of* ⟨the phrases *of the sun* in "the light of the sun" and *of the speaker* in "the arrival of the speaker" are ~ phrases⟩ **3 :** of or relating to the genitive case ⟨a ~ ending⟩

²**genitive** \"\ *n* -s [L *genitivus, genetivus* (trans. of Gk *genikē*), fr. *genitivus, genetivus*, adj.] **1 :** a genitive case **2 :** a genitive word or word group

genitive absolute *n* **:** a construction in Greek in which a noun or pronoun and its adjunct both in the genitive case form together an adverbial phrase expressing generally the time, cause, or an attendant circumstance of an action (as *Konōnos stratēgountos* in *taut' epracthē Konōnos stratēgountos* "this was done when Conon was general")

genito- *comb form* [*genital*] **:** genital and ⟨*genito*urinary⟩

gen·i·to·crural \¦jenə(,)tō+\ *adj* [*genito-* + *crural*] **:** GENITOFEMORAL

gen·i·to·femoral \"+\ *adj* [*genito-* + *femoral*] **:** of or relating to the genital organs and the thigh ⟨the ~ nerve⟩

gen·i·tor \'jenəd·ər, -nə,tȯ(ə)r\ *n* -s [ME *genytur*, fr. L *genitor*, fr. *genitus* (past part. of *gignere* to beget) + *-or* — more at KIN] **:** one who begets **:** FATHER, PARENT ⟨the ~ of that political hybrid, the corporate state —Avro Manhattan⟩; *specif* **:** the biological as distinguished from the legal father among certain primitive peoples — compare PATER

gen·i·to·urinary \¦jenə(,)tō+\ *adj* [ISV *genito-* + *urinary*] **1 :** of or relating to the genital and urinary organs or functions **2 :** specializing in care of genitourinary diseases ⟨a ~ surgeon⟩ ⟨~ dispensaries⟩

gen·i·ture \'jenə,chü(ə)r, -nəchər\ *n* -s [L *genitura*, fr. *genitus* + *-ura* -ure] **:** NATIVITY, BIRTH ⟨a man's lineage and ~ —A.T. Quiller-Couch⟩ ⟨the ~ of a prince may involve the slaughter of vast multitudes —Lynn Thorndike⟩

ge·nius \'jēnyəs *also* -nēəs\ *n, pl* **geniuses** \-əsəz\ *or* **ge·nii** \-nē,ī *also* -n,yī\ *see numbered senses* [L, fr. *gignere* to beget — more at KIN] **1** *pl* **genii :** an attendant spirit of a person or place **:** tutelary deity ⟨every human being has a ~ . . . associated with him from the moment of conception —C.D. Forde & G.I. Jones⟩ **2 a :** a strong leaning or inclination **:** decided taste **:** BENT, PENCHANT ⟨fate did not allow him to indulge his ~ till those last few years —Norman Douglas⟩ **b** (1) **:** peculiar, distinctive, or identifying character **:** essential nature or spirit **:** prevailing taste or sentiment ⟨at odds with the ~ of the theater —*Time*⟩ ⟨a spirit hostile to the ~ of our government —John Marshall⟩ ⟨suited to the ~ of a free people —Robert Cutler⟩ ⟨the ~ of the age we have under discussion —Benjamin Farrington⟩ ⟨the ~ of Elizabethan literature⟩ (2) **:** a personification or embodiment esp. of a quality or condition **:** INCARNATION ⟨essentially the ~ of the mediocre —H.J.Laski⟩ **c :** the distinctive character or quality of a place or the body of traditions and influences associated with it ⟨under the spell of the ~ of the ancient university town⟩ ⟨the ~ of this land was in its great irregularity and variety —Donald Davidson⟩ **3** *pl usu* **genii a :** a nature spirit or an elemental spirit **:** GENIE, DEMON ⟨these malevolent *genii* of the deep —Norman Douglas⟩ **b :** a person who influences another (as in character or behavior) for good or bad ⟨he was the evil ~ of that unhappy prince⟩ **4** *pl usu* **geniuses a** (1) **:** a singular strongly marked capacity or aptitude **:** notable talent ⟨had a ~ for getting along with boys —Mary Ross⟩ ⟨a ~ at . . . carpentry —Tom Corkery⟩ ⟨has a ~ for cooking —H.E.Scudder⟩ (2) **:** a strongly marked tendency, disposition, or flair of any kind ⟨developing a ~ for making people furious —W.J.Reilly⟩ ⟨has a ~ for understatement —John Buchan⟩ ⟨has a positive ~ for saying the wrong thing⟩ **b :** extraordinary native intellectual power esp. as manifested in unusual capacity for creative activity of any kind ⟨in the contemporary novel ~ is hard to find, talent is abundant —*Brit. Book News*⟩ **c :** a person endowed with transcendent mental superiority, inventiveness, and ability ⟨the rare, fortunate ~*es* like the Curies, Darwin, or Newton —Oliver La Farge⟩; *specif* **:** a person with a very high intelligence quotient usu. in the range of 140 or above **syn** see GIFT

genius lo·ci \-'lō,sī, -,sē, -,kē\ *n* [L] **1 :** a tutelary deity or spirit of a place ⟨a priest or prophet who serves . . . the *genius loci* —*Hibbert Jour.*⟩ **2 :** the cluster of associations identified with a place **:** pervading spirit ⟨whoso hurries unduly will never catch the *genius loci* of these regions —Norman Douglas⟩ ⟨its *genius loci* . . . eluded the researchers altogether —*Times Lit. Supp.*⟩

ge·ni·zah \gə,nē'zä, -'nēzə\ *n, pl* **geni·zoth** *or* **geni·zot** \-,nē-'zōt(h), -'nē,zōs\ *or* **genizahs** [Heb *gĕnīzāh*] **1 :** a storeroom or repository in a synagogue used for discarded, damaged, or defective books and papers and sacred objects ⟨valuable old manuscripts found in the ~ at Cairo⟩ **2 :** the contents of a genizah

genizero *or* **genizaro** *var of* GENISARO

genl *abbr* general

gennet *var of* JENNET

geno- — see GEN-

gen·oa \'jenəwə, *chiefly in substand speech* jə'nōə\ *adj, usu cap* [fr. *Genoa*, Italy] **:** of or from the city of Genoa, Italy **:** of the kind or style prevalent in Genoa **:** GENOESE

genoa jib *n, often cap* **:** an oversize jib which overlaps the mainsail and is controlled outside the rigging and is used chiefly in races to give a boat more speed

gen·o·blast \'jenə,blast\ *n* [¹*gen-* + *-blast*] **:** a matured germ cell — **gen·o·blas·tic** \¦==¦blastik\ *adj*

gen·o·ci·dal \¦jenə¦sīdᵊl\ *adj* [*genocide* + *-al*] **:** tending toward or producing genocide ⟨~ acts⟩ ⟨the degradation of anthropology to a ~ weapon by the Nazis —*Scientific Monthly*⟩

gen·o·cide \'jenə,sīd\ *n* -s [¹*gen-* + *-cide*] **1 :** the use of deliberate systematic measures (as killing, bodily or mental injury, unlivable conditions, prevention of births) calculated to bring about the extermination of a racial, political, or cultural group or to destroy the language, religion, or culture of a group **2 :** one who advocates or practices genocide

gen·o·cline \'jenə,klīn\ *n* [²*gen-* + *cline*] **:** a sequence of intergrading forms produced by hybridization between adjacent genetically distinct populations — compare ECOCLINE, GENE FLOW

¹**gen·o·ese** \¦jenə¦wēz, -ēs\ *adj, usu cap* [*Genoa*, Italy + E *-ese*] **1 :** of, relating to, or characteristic of Genoa, Italy **2 :** of, relating to, or characteristic of the Genoese

²**genoese** \"\ *n, pl* **genoese** *cap* **:** a native or resident of Genoa, Italy

genoese jib *n, often cap* **:** GENOA JIB

ge·noid \'jē,nȯid\ *n* -s [ISV ²*gen-* + *-oid*] **:** a cytoplasmic body resembling a virus and functioning in the manner of a gene **:** PLASMAGENE

ge·nome \'jē,nōm\ *or* **ge·nom** \-näm\ *n* -s [G *genom*, fr. ²*gen-* + *chromosom* chromosome] **:** one haploid set of chromosomes with the genes they contain — **ge·nomic** \(')jē¦nōmik, -näm-\ *adj*

ge·no·mere \'jēnə,mi(ə)r\ *n* -s [²*gen-* + *-mere*] **:** a hypothetical subsection of a gene

ge·no·ne·ma \,jēnə'nēmə\ *n* -s [NL, fr. ²*gen-* + *-nema*] **:** CHROMONEMA

ge·no·some \'jēnə,sōm\ *n* -s [²*gen-* + chromo*some*] **:** a portion of a chromosome that is coextensive with a given gene

ge·no·species \¦jēnō+\ *n* [¹*gen-* + *species*] **1 :** PURE LINE **2 :** the sum of the genotypes of a taxonomic species

geno·type \'jēnə,tīp, 'jen-\ *n* [in sense 1, fr. ¹*gen-* + *type*; in sense 2, fr. ²*gen-* + *type*] **1 :** the type species of a genus **2 a :** the genetic constitution of an individual or group **:** the totality of genes possessed by an individual or group **b :** a class or group of individuals sharing a specified genetic makeup — compare PHENOTYPE — **geno·typ·ic** \¦==¦tipik\ *also* **geno·typ·i·cal** \-pə̇kəl\ *adj* — **geno·typ·i·cal·ly** \-k(ə)lē\ *adv* — **geno·ty·pic·i·ty** \,==,tī'pisəd·ē\ *n* -ES

-ge·nous \jənəs\ *adj comb form* [*-gen* + *-ous*] **1 :** producing **:** yielding ⟨alkali*genous*⟩ **2 :** produced by **:** arising or originating in ⟨neuro*genous*⟩ ⟨endo*genous*⟩

gen·o·vese \¦jenə¦vēz, -ēs\ *adj or n, usu cap* [It, fr. *Genova* Genoa, Italy + *-ese*] **:** GENOESE

genre \'zhäⁿrə, ¦(ə)r, ¦nrə, ¦nə(r), ¦nə(r), ¦n, ¦nᵊ\ *n* -s *often attrib* [F, fr. OF *genre*, *gendre* — more at GENDER] **1 :** KIND, SORT, STYLE, SPECIES, CATEGORY ⟨a singer of quite a different ~ —Thomas Heinitz⟩ ⟨infantrymen without bluster, tall and imperturbable, they share one military ~ —A.J.Liebling⟩ ⟨large flappy rag dolls, a ~ favored by two-year-olds —*New Yorker*⟩ **2 :** a category of artistic composition characterized by a particular style, form, or content ⟨a fine introduction to twelve-tone music for those who have had little experience with the ~ —Arthur Berger⟩: as **a :** paintings that depict scenes or events from everyday life usu. realistically ⟨painters of ~ who . . . paint informal subjects, typical situations in the everyday world —Dorothy Adlow⟩; *also* **:** the school or style of painting featured by the use of such subject matter ⟨examples in which romanticism begins to blend with pure ~ —R.M.Coates⟩ **b :** a distinctive type or category of literary composition ⟨such unpromising ~*s* as Indian treaties, Colonial promotional tracts, and theological works —*New Yorker*⟩ ⟨an essay in that difficult ~, contemporary history —F.C. Barghoorn⟩ ⟨the noblest of ~*s*, the epic —George Sherburn⟩ **syn** see CLASS

gen·ro \'gen¦rō, =¦=\ *n pl, often cap* [Jap *genrō*, lit., principal elders] **:** the elder statesmen of Japan

¹**gens** \'jenz, 'genz, 'gen(t)s\ *n, pl* **gen·tes** \'jen·,tēz, 'gen·,tās\ [L — more at GENTLE] **1 :** a Roman clan embracing the families of the same stock in the male line with the members having a common name and being united in worship of their common ancestor — compare CURIA 1a **2 :** CLAN; *esp* **:** the patrilineal clan **3** [NL, fr. L] **:** a distinguishable group of related organisms: **a :** a subspecific biological group isolated by its habits **b :** a temporal sequence of extinct biological forms of which the divergence between extremes approaches the generic level

²**gens** *pl of* GEN

-gens *pl of* -GEN

genseng *var of* GINSENG

¹**gent** \'jent\ *adj* [ME, fr. OF, fr. L *genitus*, past. part. of *gignere* to beget — more at KIN] **1** *archaic* **:** GRACEFUL, PRETTY, ELEGANT **2** *obs* **:** of gentle birth **:** NOBLE

²**gent** \"\ *n* -s [short for *gentleman*] **:** MAN, FELLOW, GUY ⟨a big shaggy ~ with broad shoulders and a lot of rampant black hair —E.C.Marston⟩ ⟨was easier to be a vagabond than a landed ~ with no land —Claud Cockburn⟩

¹**gen·teel** \(')jen¦tēl, *esp before pause or consonant* -ēəl\ *adj, sometimes* **genteeler**; *sometimes* **genteelest** [MF *gentil* — more at GENTLE] **1 a :** appropriate to the status or manners of the gentry or upper class **:** having an aristocratic quality or flavor **:** STYLISH, FASHIONABLE ⟨Latin is ~, and I have sent my eldest boy to learn it —George Borrow⟩ ⟨like ~ tailors, they rated their services very high —Herman Melville⟩ ⟨call it very ~ . . . real stylish —John Buchan⟩ ⟨say a bouquet . . . 'tis more ~ —W.M.Thackeray⟩ ⟨preferred the ~ sword cane and the pistol —Green Peyton⟩ **b :** characteristic of or relating to the gentry or upper class **:** of or relating to a class ranking above the commonalty ⟨not a ~ face to be seen —Jane Austen⟩ ⟨a patrician with a ~ background —A.S. Link⟩ ⟨by their education . . . the boys came to occupy a ~ position —G.F.Whicher⟩ **c :** elegant or graceful in manner, appearance, or shape ⟨looking at the misty autumn landscape of a ~ park —Anthony West⟩ ⟨a graceful speaker with ~ motions —Earl of Chesterfield⟩ **d :** free from vulgarity or rudeness **:** marked by delicacy of manner **:** POLITE, COURTEOUS, POLISHED ⟨impeccably ~, she said "Yes, that's exactly what I wanted" —Helen Howe⟩ ⟨her letter, couched in majestic but most ~ phrase —Margaret Deland⟩ ⟨the symbol of the privileged classes . . . ~ on the surface, hard as nails underneath —Martin Turnell⟩ **2 a :** maintaining or striving to maintain the air, forms, or pretense of superior or middle-class social status or respectability ⟨a shabby ~ residential district —W.L.Sperry⟩ ⟨a . . . mansion of faded charm and ~ shabbiness —*Amer. Guide Series: Del.*⟩ ⟨spent most of her declining years in ~ poverty —F.H.Cramer⟩ ⟨people seem to think that an antique dealer is a ~ crook —Sam Boal⟩ **b** (1) **:** characterized by extreme or excessive regard for conventional morality or ideals **:** marked by false delicacy, prudery, or affectation **:** excessively nice or refined **:** PURITANICAL, VICTORIAN ⟨readers are tired of delicate ~ novels —David Daiches⟩ ⟨her ideas were ~ and middle-class —Charles Partridge⟩ ⟨escaping from the ~ censorship that had been a nuisance to literature —Edmund Wilson⟩ ⟨the ~ expression is "bovine attendant" —F.D.Smith & Barbara Wilcox⟩ (2) **:** conventionally or insipidly pretty **:** conforming to traditional canons **:** not bold or vigorous ⟨a timid and ~ artistic style⟩

²**genteel** \"\ *n* -s **:** a genteel person

gen·teel·ism \jen·'tē,lizəm\ *n* -s **:** a word (as *paying guest* or *perspiration*) believed by its user to be socially preferable to a common synonym (as *boarder* or *sweat*) ⟨threatened and debased on all sides by jargon, wrong constructions, solecisms, ~*s* —*Atlantic*⟩

gen·teel·ly \-ē(ə)l(l)ē, -)i\ *adv* **:** in a genteel manner ⟨frowned on Asian guests and members —Peggy Durdin⟩

gen·teel·ness \-ē(ə)lnə̇s\ *n* -ES **:** the quality or state of being genteel

gentes *pl of* GENS

genthel·vite \'gen(t)thəl,vīt, (')gent¦hel,-, gen'thel,-\ *n* -s [Frederick A. *Genth* †1893 Am. mineralogist born in Germany + E *helvite*] **:** a mineral $(Zn,Fe,Mn)_8Be_6Si_6O_{24}S_2$ consisting of a silicate and sulfide of zinc and beryllium and usu. containing also iron and manganese isomorphous with danalite and helvite

genth·ite \'gen,thīt\ *n* -s [F.A.*Genth* + E *-ite*] **:** a mineral approximately $(Ni,Mg)_4Si_3O_{10}.6H_2O$, consisting of a soft amorphous pale green or yellowish nickel magnesium silicate

gen·tian \'jenchən\ *n* -s [ME *gencian*, fr. MF *genciane*, *gentiane*, fr. L *gentiana*, perh. after *Gentius*, 2d cent. B.C. Illyrian king said to have discovered its virtues] **1 :** a plant of the genus *Gentiana* — see CLOSED GENTIAN, FRINGED GENTIAN **2** *also* **gentian root :** the rhizome and roots of the yellow gentian (*Gentiana lutea*) used as a tonic and stomachic

gentian of the Old World

gen·ti·ana \,jenchē'anə, -'änə,-'ānə\ *n, cap* [NL, fr. L, gentian] **:** the type genus of Gentianaceae comprising numerous annual, biennial, or perennial herbs which have smooth opposite leaves and showy solitary or cymose flowers with 4-lobed or 5-lobed corolla and some of which contain a bitter glycoside often used as a tonic — see GENTIAN

gen·tia·na·ce·ae \,jench(ē)ə'nāsē,ē\ *n pl, cap* [NL, fr. *Gentiana*, type genus + *-aceae*] **:** a large nearly cosmopolitan family of chiefly herbaceous plants (order Gentianales) that usu. have showy flowers with tubular or segmented calyx and lobed corolla — see GENTIANA — **gen·tia·na·ceous** \¦=(=)=¦nāshəs\ *adj*

gen·tia·na·les \-ā(,)lēz\ *n pl, cap* [NL, fr. *Gentiana* + *-ales*] **:** an order of dicotyledonous plants having gamopetalous and usu. actinomorphic flowers with two carpels and mostly opposite leaves — compare APOCYNACEAE, ASCLEPIADACEAE, GENTIANACEAE, LOGANIACEAE, OLEACEAE, SALVADORACEAE

gentian blue *n* **:** a moderate purplish blue that is redder, lighter, and stronger than marine blue, bluer and duller than average cornflower, and bluer and lighter than old glory blue

gen·tia·nel·la \,jench(ē)ə'nelə\ *n* -s [NL, dim. of L *gentiana*] **:** any of several gentians; *esp* **:** a low-growing perennial alpine gentian (*Gentiana acaulis*) that is often cultivated for its large showy typically blue flowers

gentian family *n* **:** GENTIANACEAE

gen·tian·in \'jenchənə̇n\ *n* -s [ISV *gentian-* (fr. NL *Gentiana*) + *-in*] **1 :** GENTISIN **2 :** a bluish red anthocyanin pigment obtained in the form of the chloride $C_{30}H_{27}ClO_{14}$ from the petals of a blue gentian (*Gentiana acaulis*)

gen·tian·ose \-chə,nōs *also* -ōz\ *n* -s [ISV *gentian-* (fr. NL *Gentiana*) + *-ose*] **:** a crystalline nonreducing trisaccharide $C_{18}H_{32}O_{16}$ obtained from fresh gentian root

gentian violet *n, often cap G&V* **:** a dye consisting of one or more methyl derivatives of pararosaniline used as a biological stain, as a bactericide, fungicide, and anthelmintic, and in the treatment of burns: as **a :** CRYSTAL VIOLET **b :** METHYL VIOLET a **c :** a mixture of crystal violet and methyl violet

gentian violet lake *n, usu cap G&V&L* **:** an organic pigment — see DYE table I (under *Pigment Violet 3*)

¹**gen·tile** \'jen·,tīl\ *n* -s [ME *gentil*, *gentile*, fr. LL *gentilis* foreigner, heathen, fr. L, member of the same family or gens, fellow countryman, fr. *gentilis*, adj.] **1 a** *often cap* **:** a person of a non-Jewish nation or of non-Jewish faith; *esp* **:** a Christian as distinguished from a Jew — used esp. by Jews **b :** HEATHEN, PAGAN ⟨earnest exhortations to the ~*s* —David Daiches⟩ **c** *among the Mormons, often cap* **:** a non-Mormon **2 :** a word denoting country, race, or nationality **3** [L *gentilis*] *in Roman law* **:** a member of the same Roman gens

²**gentile** \"\ *adj* [ME *gentil*, *gentile*, fr. LL *gentilis* foreign, heathen, fr. L, of the same clan or family, of the same nation — more at GENTLE] **1** *often cap* **a :** belonging to the nations at large as distinguished from the Jews; *also* **:** belonging or relating to Christians as distinguished from the Jews **b :** belonging or relating to non-Mormons **2 :** PAGAN, HEATHEN **3** [L *gentilis*] **:** relating to a tribe or clan ⟨the science of ~ or tribal society —Benjamin Farrington⟩ **4 :** denoting a people or country **:** GENTILIC ⟨*Canadian* and *Irish* are ~ nouns⟩

gen·ti·lesse \¦jentə¦les\ *n* -s [ME, fr. MF *gentilesce*, fr. *gentil* noble, pleasant, friendly + *-esce*, *-esse* -ess — more at GENTLE] *archaic* **:** the quality of being genteel **:** good breeding

¹**gen·til·ic** \(')jen·¦tilik\ *adj* [L *gentilis* + E *-ic*] **1 :** TRIBAL, RACIAL, NATIONAL **2 :** of or relating to a noun or adjective that denotes ethnic or national affiliation

²**gentilic** \"\ *n* -s **:** a name with gentilic value

gentilish *adj* [²*gentile* + *-ish*] *obs* **:** HEATHENISH, GENTILE

gentilism *n* -s [¹*gentile* + *-ism*] *obs* **:** HEATHENISM, PAGANISM

gen·ti·li·tial \¦jentə¦lishəl\ *adj* [L *gentilicius*, *gentilitius* (fr. *gent-*, *gens* clan, family, race, people) + E *-al* — more at GENTLE] **1 :** relating or peculiar to a people or family **2 :** of gentle birth **:** GENTLE

gen·ti·li·tious \-shəs\ *adj* [L *gentilicius*, *gentilitius*] **:** GENTILITIAL

gen·til·i·ty \jen·'tiləd·ē, -ətē, -i\ *n* -ES [ME *gentilete*, fr. MF *gentileté*, fr. L *gentilitat-*, *gentilitas* state or condition of belonging to the same clan or family, fr. *gentilis* of the same clan or family + *-itat-*, *-itas* -ity — more at GENTLE] **1 a :** the condition of belonging to the gentry or to a class ranking above the commonalty **:** gentle birth or status ⟨when her family lost its money . . . she lost her ~ and was allowed to work —Virginia Woolf⟩ **b :** the members of the upper class **:** GENTLEFOLK, GENTRY ⟨a ball given by the governor for the ~ —Esther Forbes⟩ ⟨the social strata midway between the lower ~ and the upper class of poor white —Ellen Glasgow⟩ ⟨recruit its nobility and ~ from loyal servants of . . . middle-class origin —J.W.Saunders⟩ **c :** the rank or heraldic status of a gentleman ⟨the purchase of ~ from the heralds was resented by the county gentry —F.P.Bornard⟩ **2 a** (1) **:** niceness, refinement, or decorum of conduct or manner **:** CIVILITY, POLISH, ELEGANCE, POLITENESS ⟨the ~ and sweet tolerance of liberal methods of government —S.L.A.Marshall⟩ ⟨combined . . . natural ~ and refinement of manner —G.R.Stewart⟩ ⟨a French trading post . . . with morals and manners that did not err on the side of ~ —*Amer. Guide Series: Mich.*⟩ (2) **:** extreme or excessive regard for conventional morality or ideals **:** the display of false delicacy, prudery, affectation, or excessive refinement esp. in cultural attitudes or activity ⟨instrumental in . . . the freeing of American letters from the bonds of ~ —Alexander Klein⟩ ⟨an impassioned diatribe against ~ in American literature —Mark Schorer⟩ ⟨the pervading malady of educated folk in late-nineteenth-century America — ~ —F.L.Allen⟩ **b** (1) **:** superior social status or prestige evidenced by manners, possessions, mode of life, or associations ⟨an academy . . . famous for its ~ —Nathaniel Burt⟩ ⟨the hat, like the sandals . . . were marks of ~ —Elizabeth Janeway⟩ ⟨the characteristic American attempt to maintain ~ by means of a detached house —G.R.Stewart⟩ (2) **:** the maintenance of the air, forms, or pretense of superior or middle-class social status esp. in the face of decayed elegance or prosperity ⟨a shabby ~ displayed against a . . . dreary background —David Daiches⟩ ⟨look of respectable but threadbare ~ —*N.Y.Times*⟩

gen·ti·o·bi·ose \,jenchēō'bī,ōs *also* -ōz\ *n* -s [ISV, blend of *gentianose* and *bi-*] **:** a crystalline dextrorotatory disaccharide $C_{12}H_{22}O_{11}$ that is not fermented by top yeasts and that is obtained from gentianose by hydrolysis or from glucose by the action of acids; 6-β-D-glucosyl-D-glucose

gen·ti·o·pic·rin \-'pikrə̇n\ *n* -s [ISV *gentio-* (fr. NL *Gentiana*) + *-picrin*] **:** a bitter crystalline glucoside $C_{16}H_{20}O_9$ obtained esp. from gentian root

gen·ti·sate \'jentə,sāt\ *n* -s [*gentis*ic + *-ate*] **:** a salt or ester of gentisic acid

gen·tis·ic acid \(')jen·¦tis¦ik-, ¦zik-\ *n* [ISV *gentis*in + *-ic*] **:** a crystalline acid $C_6H_3(OH)_2COOH$ formed by fusion of gentisin with caustic and by biological oxidation of salicylic acid and used in medicine in the form of its sodium salt similarly to sodium salicylate; 2,5-dihydroxy-benzoic acid

gen·ti·sin \'jentəsə̇n\ *n* -s [ISV *genti-* (fr. NL *Gentiana*, genus name of *Gentiana lutea*) + *-sin* (as in *pepsin*, *trypsin*)] **:** a yellow crystalline anthoxanthin pigment $C_{14}H_{10}O_5$ obtained from gentian root

¹**gen·tle** \'jentᵊl\ *adj* **gentler** \-t(ᵊ)lə(r)\ **gentlest** \-t(ᵊ)l-\ [ME *gentil*, fr. OF, fr. L *gentilis* of the same clan or family or race, fr. *gent-*, *gens* clan, family, race (fr. the stem of *gignere* to beget) + *-ilis* -ile — more at KIN] **1 a :** belonging to a family of high social station **:** of noble or aristocratic birth ⟨two distinct classes; the ~ . . . and the ungentle —E.E.Reynolds⟩; *specif* **:** having the rank or status of a gentleman (sense 1b) **b** *archaic* **:** having the qualities ascribed to a person of noble birth **:** CHIVALROUS, COURTEOUS **c :** HONORABLE, NOBLE, DISTINGUISHED ⟨we were both of ~ blood —T.B.Costain⟩; *specif* **:** of or relating to a gentleman ⟨a man of ~ birth, as "Mr." prefixed to his name . . . indicates —Eleanor Dobson⟩ **d :** KIND, AMIABLE — used esp. in address as a complimentary epithet ⟨what ought we to do, ~ sisters —W.S.Gilbert⟩ ⟨let not the ~ reader rush in blithely —D.F.Fleming⟩ **e :** suited to a person of noble birth or high social station **:** WORTHY, ESTIMABLE ⟨the ~ art of angling⟩ **2 a :** TAMED, DOMESTICATED **:** quiet, tractable, and docile ⟨a ~ horse⟩ **b** (1) **:** benignly gracious or kind in manner **:** not harsh or stern **:** MILD, CONSIDERATE, TENDER ⟨a vein of ~ irony that makes us smile —R.A.Hall b.1911⟩ ⟨the ~ eyes of my professor —*Years of the Modern*⟩ ⟨his speech was soft, his manners ~⟩ (2) **:** not violent **:** PEACEFUL ⟨convert the natives by ~ means⟩ ⟨bring about peaceful social revolution by ~ persuasion —*Current Biog.*⟩ ⟨bring about the ~ coexistence of Communists and non-Communists —Max Ascoli⟩ (3) **:** not boisterously energetic ⟨his mother came of a *gentler* and less adventurous stock —W.B.Parker⟩ **3 a** (1) **:** not rough **:** SOFT ⟨the ~ touch of her hand⟩ ⟨a ~ mind⟩ ⟨his ~ tongue —Jean Stafford⟩ (2) **:** not flowing roughly or rapidly ⟨a ~ stream⟩ **b** (1) **:** not loud or noisy **:** SOOTHING, SOFT, LOW, HUSHED ⟨a ~ voice⟩ ⟨heard a ~ knock on the door⟩ (2) **:** delicate in mood, texture, or taste **:** not harsh or blatant ⟨a ~ nocturne⟩ ⟨the most delicate and ~ pink —Geoffrey Grigson⟩ ⟨a ~ wine⟩ **4 a :** moderate in operation or degree ⟨a ~ sun shone down⟩ ⟨a ~ heat⟩ ⟨give ~ exercise every day —Emily Holt⟩ **b :** not steep ⟨a ~ hill⟩ ⟨a ~ slope⟩ **5** *dial Brit* **:** of, relating to, or frequented by fairies ⟨a ~ place⟩ ⟨~ bushes⟩ **syn** see SOFT

²**gentle** \"\ *n* -s [ME *gentil*, fr. MF, fr. *gentil*, adj.] **1 :** a person of gentle birth or status **:** GENTLEMAN ⟨a custom . . . merging the ~*s* with the burghers —G.M.Trevelyan⟩ ⟨the whole lot of them, ~*s* and simples —Virginia Woolf⟩ **2 :** MAGGOT; *esp* **:** one used as bait or as food for birds or small animals

³**gentle** \"\ *vb* -ED/-ING/-S [¹*gentle*] *vt* **1 :** to raise from the commonalty **:** ENNOBLE ⟨trading class, which having enriched itself, sought desperately to ~ itself —Sam Pollock⟩ **2 a :** to make gentle or mild in character or manner ⟨honored for *gentling* the barbarian —*New Yorker*⟩ ⟨the tough admiral *gentled* by memories of personal loss —Lee Rogow⟩ **b :** to make (an animal) tame and docile ⟨a wild pony that nobody could ~⟩ ⟨as a lion man ~*s* a cageful of cats —R.L.Taylor⟩ **c :** MOLLIFY, APPEASE, SOFTEN, PLACATE ⟨the old man is in a rage of excitement and has to be *gentled* incessantly —Clemence Dane⟩ **d** (1) **:** to make soft or smooth (as in texture, tone, or appearance) ⟨time may have *gentled* her face and hair —Kathryn Grondahl⟩ ⟨a liquid blend of herbs which ~*s* the taste of liquor —*Time*⟩ (2) **:** to make moderate (as in degree or intensity) **:** CALM ⟨play the music a little too fast . . . while others ~ it down —*New Yorker*⟩ ⟨*gentled* her nerves by reading the glad tidings again —Jean Stafford⟩ (3) **:** to stroke gently or soothingly **:** PET, FONDLE ⟨*gentled* the panther for a few minutes —Rudyard Kipling⟩ ⟨listened quietly, *gentling* a dog's ear meanwhile —James Reynolds⟩ **3 :** to make (one's way) gently ⟨a light that *gentled* its way into my parents' bedroom —Richard Church⟩ ⟨the broad-shouldered train ~*s* its way —Karl Shapiro⟩ ~ *vi* **:** to become gentle ⟨some cows never ~ —Agnes M. Cleaveland⟩ ⟨the wind *gentled* to a murmur —Kris Neville⟩ ⟨wine which . . . ~*s* with age —*Sunset*⟩

gentleboy \'==,=\ *n* **:** a young gentleman ⟨accused me . . . of masquerading in the discarded cap of a ~ —F.A.Swinnerton⟩

gentle breeze *n* **:** wind having a speed of 8 to 12 miles per hour — see BEAUFORT SCALE table

gentlefolk *also* **gentlefolks** \'==,=\ *n pl* **:** persons of gentle or good family and breeding ⟨~ too sure of themselves to alter their ways —S.H.Adams⟩

gentlehearted \¦==¦==\ *adj* **:** having a gentle heart

gen·tle·hood \'==,hu̇d\ *n* **:** the state or position of one who is of gentle birth or nature

gentle lemur *n* **:** any of several small nocturnal lemurs (genus *Cheirogaleus* or *Mioxicebus*) living in bamboo jungles of northeastern Madagascar and feeding on shoots and roots of the bamboo

gen·tle·man \'jentᵊlmən, ÷-nᵊl-\ *n, pl* **gentlemen** *often attrib* [ME *gentilman*, fr. *gentil* noble, gentle + *man* — more at GENTLE] **1 a :** a man of noble or gentle birth **:** one belonging to the nobility or aristocracy **:** a man of quality ⟨the count . . . though a rogue was a ~ by birth —W.S.Maugham⟩ **b :** a man entitled to bear a coat of arms though not of noble rank **:** a member of the gentry ⟨those whose right to bear arms was not established had to sign a form of disclaimer . . . to the title of ~ —A.R.Wagner⟩ ⟨this great revolution had been brought about by the *gentlemen* of England —L.G.Pine⟩ **c** (1) **:** a man who combines gentle birth or rank with chivalrous qualities (2) **:** a man irrespective of social status having chivalrous qualities **:** a man whose conduct conforms to a certain standard of propriety or correct behavior ⟨being a ~, he rose and gave the lady his seat⟩ ⟨no girl should go out with that man; he's no ~⟩ ⟨a ~ will never let you down —Katharine F. Gerould⟩ ⟨the law of the land requires an officer of the U.S. armed forces to be a ~ —*Time*⟩ **d** (1) **:** a man of independent means who does not engage in any occupation or profession for gain **:** a man of wealth and leisure ⟨anyone in Suffolk who is not engaged in farming and appears to exist on private means is designated a ~ —Adrian Bell⟩ ⟨the curriculum was constructed for *gentlemen;* technical or vocational subjects were unknown —Benjamin Fine⟩ (2) **:** a man who does not engage in any menial occupation or in manual labor for gain ⟨ruled that he could not compete because he had once worked with his hands and was therefore not a ~ —*Time*⟩ **2 a :** VALET — often used in the phrase *gentleman's gentleman* ⟨the unctuous conversation of gentlemen's *gentlemen* —F.A.Swinnerton⟩ **b :** an attendant upon a sovereign or other person of high station who is himself of noble or gentle birth or rank **3 a :** a man whose dress, refined speech, manners, or regard for punctilio marks him as a member of the educated or upper class ⟨a ~ . . . was a man who used a butter knife even when alone —Robertson Davies⟩ ⟨a ~ don't fling stones —George Meredith⟩ **b :** a man of a lower, uneducated, or undeterminate social class or condition who is called a gentleman ⟨drayate social class⟩ ⟨draymen . . . and the laborers on the canal were . . . denominated "them *gentlemen*" —Frances Trollope⟩ ⟨retired private chauffeur with 1953 car seeks another retired ~ —*N. Y. Herald Tribune*⟩ — often used in the pl. in addressing the men in an audience or group ⟨ladies and *gentlemen*⟩ ⟨these rambling talks have come to an end, *gentlemen* —Bliss Perry⟩ **c :** a man who is a member of a representative legislative body (as the U.S. House of Representatives) — used with *the* ⟨the time of the ~ from Kansas has expired —*Congressional Record*⟩ **d :** an amateur cricketer — contrasted with *player* **4 :** a formidable or dangerous opponent not to be trifled with or underrated ⟨must confess I do not like the ~, and would rather fight two Indians than one of these bears —Edmund Christopherson⟩

gentleman-at-arms \¦====¦=\ *n, pl* **gentlemen-at-arms :** one of a military corps of forty gentlemen who attend the British sovereign on state occasions — called also *gentleman pensioner*

gentleman-commoner \¦===¦===\ *n, pl* **gentlemen-commoners :** one of a privileged class of commoners formerly required to pay higher fees than ordinary commoners at the universities of Oxford and Cambridge

gentleman cow *n, pl* **gentlemen cows** *dial* **:** BULL

gentleman farmer *n, pl* **gentlemen farmers :** a man who farms for pleasure rather than for profit

gentleman friend *n, pl* **gentlemen friends :** a woman's male friend **:** BOYFRIEND ⟨a charming girl whose *gentleman friend* was said to be . . . high up in the fur business —Sinclair Lewis⟩

gentlemanlike \'===,=\ *adj* **:** resembling or appropriate to a gentleman ⟨a very kind and ~ individual —W.M.Thackeray⟩ — **gen·tle·man·like·ness** *n* -ES

gen·tle·man·li·ness \'===lēnə̇s, -lin-\ *n* -ES **:** the quality or state of being gentlemanly

¹**gen·tle·man·ly** \-lē, -li\ *adv* [ME *gentilmanly*, fr. *gentilman* + *-ly* (adv. suffix)] **:** in the manner of a gentleman ⟨he was sitting ~ up in the . . . taxi —Saul Bellow⟩

²**gentlemanly** \"\ *adj* [ME *gentilmanly*, fr. *gentilman* + *-ly* (adj. suffix)] **:** having the character of or characteristic of a gentleman in nature, behavior, or appearance ⟨~ instincts⟩

gentleman of fortune : a gentleman seeking his fortune in daring or risky enterprises : ADVENTURER

gentleman-pensioner \ˌ≈≈≈ˌ≈(≈)≈\ *n, pl* **gentlemen-pensioners :** GENTLEMAN-AT-ARMS

gentleman-ranker \ˌ≈≈≈ˌ≈≈\ *n, pl* **gentlemen-rankers :** a gentleman serving in the British army as an enlisted man ⟨the *gentleman-ranker* that Kipling met from time to time in India . . . was in many cases an ex-officer who had been removed from his regiment —C.S.Jarvis⟩

gentleman's agreement *or* **gentlemen's agreement** *n* **:** an agreement secured only by the honor of the participants

gentleman's-cane \ˌ≈≈≈ˌ≈\ *n, pl* **gentleman's-canes :** PRINCE'S-FEATHER 2

gentleman's sorrel *n* **:** SHEEP SORREL 1

gentleman-usher \ˌ≈≈≈ˌ≈≈\ *n, pl* **gentlemen-ushers** [ME *gentilman husher*] **:** a gentleman who acts as usher to a person of rank

gentleman-usher of the black rod *often cap G&U&B&R* **:** BLACK ROD

gentlemen-and-ladies \ˌ≈≈≈≈ˌ≈≈\ *n pl but sing or pl in constr* **:** a shooting star (*Dodecatheon meadia*)

gen·tle·ness *n* -ES [ME *gentilnesse*, fr. *gentil* gentle + *-nesse* -ness — more at GENTLE] **:** the quality or state of being gentle; *esp* **:** mildness of manners or disposition

gentlepeople \'≈≈ˌ≈≈\ *n pl* **:** GENTLEFOLK

gentler *comparative of* GENTLE

gentles *pres 3d sing of* GENTLE, *pl of* GENTLE

gentle sex *n* **:** the female sex **:** women in general — used with *the* ⟨a member of the *gentle sex*⟩

gentlest *superlative of* GENTLE

gentle thistle *n* **:** a coarse European herb (*Cirsium anglicum*) with prickly-margined leaves

gentlewoman \'≈≈ˌ≈≈\ *n, pl* **gentlewomen** [ME *gentilwoman*, fr. *gentil* + *woman*] **1 a :** a woman of noble or gentle birth **:** a woman of quality ⟨a ~ of good and honorable stock —Francis Hackett⟩ ⟨a lady, as ladies went in Colombia . . . but she wasn't a ~ —Donn Byrne⟩ **b :** a woman attendant upon a lady of rank **2 :** a woman of refined manners or good breeding **:** LADY ⟨~ seeks part-time employment as companion or social secretary —*Saturday Rev.*⟩ **3 :** a woman member of a representative legislative body (as the U.S. House of Representatives) — used with *the* ⟨the chair recognizes the ~ from Connecticut⟩

gen·tle·wo·man·ly \'≈≈ˌ≈≈_lē, -li\ *adj* **:** having the appearance, traits, or character of a gentlewoman ⟨a valiant and ~ flourish —Rose Macaulay⟩

gentling *pres part of* GENTLE

gent·ly \'jentlē, -li\ *adv* [ME *gentilly*, fr. *gentil* gentle + *-ly* — more at GENTLE] **:** in a gentle manner: as **a** (1) **:** NOBLY, HONORABLY ⟨hated women ~ born —John Masefield⟩ (2) **:** COURTEOUSLY, SOFTLY, ELEGANTLY ⟨~ mannered family —G.B.Shaw⟩ ⟨a ~ spoken young man (3) **:** in an atmosphere of elegance or refinement **:** with much attention to good manners or deportment ⟨~ bred people who had never been forced to face much unpleasantness in the world —J.R.Chamberlain⟩ ⟨public schools were not to be considered for a ~ bred young girl —Maude Couch⟩ **b** (1) **:** QUIETLY, GRADUALLY, SLOWLY ⟨the wind whistling ~⟩ ⟨parkland that lifts ~ toward rolling hills —Frederick Nebel⟩ ⟨sway ~ back and forth —Fred Zimmer⟩ ⟨the slide in industrial production will continue ~ —D.M.Keezer⟩ ⟨the trout is ~ boiled —Jane Nickerson⟩ (2) **:** [2]EASY ⟨for the first two weeks I took things ~ —*Linguaphone Mag.*⟩ **c :** with gentleness **:** MILDLY, TENDERLY ⟨humorous and ~ satiric verses —*Encyc. Americana*⟩ ⟨rebuked him ~⟩

gen·too \'jen·ˌtü, ≈'≈\ *n* -S [Pg *gentio*, lit., Gentile, fr. LL *gentilis* — more at GENTILE] **1** *usu cap, archaic* **:** HINDU **2** *or* **gentoo penguin :** a penguin (*Pygoscelis papua*) of the subantarctic islands with a slaty gray back and throat, white underparts, and white spots above the eyes and on the back and side of the neck

gen·trice \'jen·trəs\ *n* -S [ME *gentrise*, fr. OF *genterise*, alter. of *gentilise, gentelise*, fr. *gentil* noble, gentle — more at GENTLE] *archaic* **:** gentility of birth **:** RANK

gen·try \'jen·trē, -ri\ *n* -ES [ME *gentrie*, alter. of *gentrise*] **1 a** *obs* **:** the qualities ascribed or appropriate to a man of gentle birth **:** good breeding **:** GENEROSITY, COURTESY ⟨show us so much ~ and goodwill —Shak.⟩ **b :** the condition or rank of a gentleman ⟨a favorite topic of discussion was whether apprenticeship to trade annulled ~ —A.R.Wagner⟩ **2 a :** people of quality or the class to which they belong **:** upper or ruling class **:** NOBILITY, ARISTOCRACY, ELITE ⟨retains the idea of the ~ versus the lower classes —Sinclair Lewis⟩ ⟨the two chief classes of New England: the yeomanry . . . and the ~, a group of capable merchants —V.L.Parrington⟩ ⟨a ~ . . . a class of rich people able to cultivate themselves with an expensive education —G.B.Shaw⟩ **b :** a class whose members are entitled to bear a coat of arms though not of noble rank; *esp* **:** the landed proprietors having such status ⟨the English ~ have never had the permanence of the Scottish landed families —L.G.Pine⟩ **c :** a class of landed proprietors marked by an aristocratic spirit and typically wielding large economic, social, and political influence; *also* **:** the persons making up such a class ⟨rural ~ from the 169 towns of Connecticut —*Amer. Guide Series: Conn.*⟩ ⟨no love was lost between . . . ~ and hillbilly commoners —C.V.Woodward⟩ **3 a :** people of a specified class or kind **:** FOLKS ⟨redingotes in the loud, colored checks, popular with the sporting ~ —*N.Y.Times*⟩ **b :** a particular group of people of doubtful, erroneous, or improper ideas, manners, or conduct ⟨they do a lot of damage . . . these ~ with their open diplomacy, openly arrived at —Howard Spring⟩ ⟨provide a wealth of . . . data on the activities of these ~ —*Amer. Polit. Sci. Rev.*⟩ **4** *dial chiefly Brit* **:** FAIRIES ⟨the ~ who harass travelers with tricks —James Reynolds⟩

gents *pl of* GENT

gen·ty \'jenti\ *adj* [prob. modif. of F *gentil* — more at GENTLE] **1** *chiefly Scot* **:** dainty and graceful **2** *chiefly Scot* **:** COURTEOUS, GENTEEL ⟨~ manners⟩

genu \'jē(ˌ)n(y)ü, 'je(-; 'ge(ˌ)nü\ *n, pl* **gen·ua** \'jenyəwə, 'genəwə\ [NL, fr. L, knee — more at KNEE] **:** KNEE 4c — **gen·u·al** \'jenyəwəl\ *adj*

gen·u·flect \'jenyəˌflekt\ *vi* -ED/-ING/-S [LL *genuflectere* to genuflect, fr. L *genu* knee + *flectere* to bend] **1 :** to bend the knee esp. in worship ⟨~ and walk out of the chapel —Joseph Dever⟩ **2 :** to be servilely or humbly obedient or respectful **:** KOWTOW ⟨each political party has ~*ed* before it —B.M. Bowie⟩ ⟨~*ed* before the . . . bureaucrats and rewrote their poems —Harvey Breit⟩

gen·u·flec·tion *also* **gen·u·flex·ion** \ˌ≈≈'flekshən, '≈≈ˌ≈≈\ *n* [LL *genuflexion-, genuflexio*, fr. *genuflexus* (past part. of *genuflectere*) + *-ion-, -io* -ion] **1 :** the act or an instance of bending the knee esp. in worship **2 :** the act or an instance of according servile or humble obedience or respect **:** a respectful gesture ⟨a ~ in the direction of Marxist orthodoxy —Alex Inkeles⟩

gen·u·flec·to·ry \ˌ≈≈ˌflekt(ə)rē\ *adj* **:** relating to or characterized by genuflection ⟨the tone of his mother's voice, sad, velvety, ~ —Mary McCarthy⟩

gen·u·ine \'jenyəwən *sometimes* ÷-ˌwīn\ *adj* [L *genuinus*, prob. irreg. (influence of *ingenuus* native, free-born) fr. *gen-* (stem of *gignere* to beget) + *-inus* -ine — more at INGENUOUS, KIN] **1** *obs* **:** not foreign **:** NATIVE, NATURAL **2 a :** actually having the reputed or apparent qualities or character **:** not adulterated or cheapened **:** PURE ⟨a ~ fine quality tea⟩ ⟨a ~ vintage wine⟩ **b :** actually produced by or proceeding from the reputed or alleged source or author **:** not faked or counterfeit **:** AUTHENTIC ⟨a ~ antique⟩ ⟨a ~ signature⟩ ⟨a ~ text⟩ **c :** sincerely and honestly felt or experienced **:** not forced but arising naturally **:** not feigned, factitious, or hypocritical ⟨the child of sinful but ~ love —H.O.Brogan⟩ **d :** having a real existence **:** conforming to reality **:** not abstract or frivolous ⟨the questions which are asked . . . are ~ questions —John Dewey⟩ ⟨~ confrontations of the human condition —Anthony Quinton⟩ **e :** conforming precisely to its name or description **:** properly so called **:** TRUE ⟨a ~ conservative⟩ ⟨a ~ idealist⟩ ⟨a slight sprinkling of ~ pickpockets —Joseph Conrad⟩ **3 :** of or relating to the original stock ⟨the ~ breed of mastiffs⟩ **4 :** free from hypocrisy or pretense **:** SINCERE, FRANK ⟨could [illegible] friends with anyone who was ~, not a snob, not a prig, not a pedant —H.S.Canby⟩ ⟨how much more ~ . . . their work than the pretentious efforts of our contemporaries —Henry Miller⟩ **syn** see AUTHENTIC

gen·u·ine·ly *adv* **:** in a genuine manner ⟨policies which will ~ serve the national interests —A.M.Schlesinger b.1917⟩ ⟨can be said ~ to aim at a scientific . . . treatment —M.R.Cohen⟩

gen·u·ine·ness \-n(n)əs\ *n* -ES **:** the quality or state of being genuine ⟨would hesitate on the threshold, mistrusting the ~ of the invitation —H.F.Ellis⟩

ge·nus \'jēnəs *sometimes* 'jen-\ *n, pl* **gen·era** \'jenərə\ [L, birth, race, class, kind — more at KIN] **1 :** a class, kind, or group marked by common characteristics or by one common characteristic **:** a group capable of including subgroups and also of being subsumed in a larger group ⟨such streams are a ~ by themselves and not miniature rivers —John Buchan⟩; *specif* **:** a taxonomic category ranking between the family and the species, comprising a group of structurally or phylogenetically related species or an isolated species exhibiting unusual differentiation, and being designated by a Latin or latinized capitalized singular noun which constitutes the first word of the technical name of a species or of any of its subdivisions and which is often used usu. uncapitalized and pluralized with a regular ending or sometimes a latinate plural as a vernacular name for plants or animals of the constituent species ⟨the species of oak collectively form the ~ *Quercus*⟩ — compare CLASSIFICATION 1a, NOMENCLATURE 4c **2** [NL, fr. L] **:** a class of objects divided into several subordinate species **:** a class more extensive than a species **3 :** MODE; *specif* **:** one of three basic tetrachords in Greek music **syn** see CLASS

genu val·gum \-'valgəm\ *n* [NL] **:** KNOCK-KNEE

genu va·rum \-'va(a)rəm\ *n* [NL] **:** BOWLEG

geny- *or* **genyo-** *comb form* [ISV, fr. Gk *genys* jaw, chin — more at CHIN] **:** lower jaw ⟨*genyo*plasty⟩

-ge·ny \jənē, -ni\ *n comb form* -ES [Gk *-geneia* act of being born, fr. *-genēs* born + *-ia* -y — more at -GEN] **:** generation **:** production **:** science of origin ⟨chondro*geny*⟩ ⟨morpho*geny*⟩ ⟨onto*geny*⟩

geo \'gyō\ *n* -S [of Scand origin; *akin* to ON *gjā* chasm, Norw dial. *gjo, jo;* akin to OE *geonian* to yawn — more at YAWN] *Scot* **:** a deep narrow rocky-sided coastal inlet — often used in place names

geo- — see GE-

geoanticline *var of* GEANTICLINE

ge·o·bi·ont \ˌjēōˌbīˌänt, jē'ōbēˌ-\ *n* [*ge-* + *-biont*] **:** an organism inhabiting the soil

geo·botanical \ˌjē(ˌ)ō+\ *adj* [*ge-* + *botanical*] **:** of or relating to phytogeography — **geo·botanically** \"+\ *adv*

geo·botanist \"+\ *n* [*ge-* + *botanist*] **:** PHYTOGEOGRAPHER

geo·botany \"+\ *n* [*ge-* + *botany*] **:** PHYTOGEOGRAPHY

ge·o·car·pic \ˌjēōˌkärpik\ *adj* [ISV *ge-* + *-carpic*] **:** producing or ripening the fruit beneath the surface of the ground ⟨the peanut is one of the few plants . . . which are ~ —W.P.Jacobs⟩ — **ge·o·car·py** \'≈≈ˌ≈pē\ *n* -ES

ge·o·cen·tric \ˌjēōˌsen·trik, -rēk\ *adj* [*ge-* + *-centric*] **1 :** relating to, measured from, or as if observed from the earth's center **:** having or relating to the earth as center — compare HELIOCENTRIC **2 :** taking or based on the earth as the center of perspective and valuation — **ge·o·cen·tri·cal·ly** \-rək(ə)lē, -rēk-, -li\ *adv*

ge·o·cen·tri·cism \ˌ≈≈'sen·trəˌsizəm\ *n* -S **:** a geocentric theory or belief

geocentric latitude *n* **1 :** the celestial latitude of a body as seen from the earth's center **2 :** the angle between the plane of the celestial equator and a line from the earth's center to a given point on the earth's surface — compare TERRESTRIAL LATITUDE

geocentric longitude *n* **1 :** celestial longitude based on or as seen from the earth's center — opposed to *heliocentric longitude* **2 :** GEOGRAPHICAL LONGITUDE

geocentric parallax *n* **:** the difference in direction of an astronomical body as measured from two points on earth **:** the angle subtended by the earth's radius at a member of the solar system (as the moon or sun)

ge·o·ce·rite \ˌjēō'siˌrīt\ *also* **ge·o·ce·rain** \-'siˌrān\ *n* -S [*geocerite* modif. (influenced by *-ite*) of G *geozerain*, fr. *geo-* ge- + L *cera* wax + G *-in; geocerain* fr. G *geozerain* — more at CEREOUS] **:** a mineral consisting of carbon, hydrogen, and oxygen occurring as a white waxy substance in brown coal

geo·chemical \ˌjēō+\ *adj* [*ge-* + *chemical*] **:** of, relating to, or using the methods of geochemistry — **geo·chemically** \"+\ *adv*

geochemical prospecting *n* **:** prospecting for minerals with portable chemical kits designed for rapid testing of metallic elements in surface waters

geo·chemist \ˌjēō+\ *n* [*ge-* + *chemist*] **:** a specialist in geochemistry

geo·chemistry \"+\ *n* [*ge-* + *chemistry*] **1 :** a science that deals with the chemical composition of and the actual or possible chemical changes in the crust of the earth **:** earth chemistry **2 :** the related chemical and geological properties of a substance ⟨the ~ of the rare earths⟩

geo·chronic \ˌjēō+\ *adj* [*ge-* + *chronic*] **:** of or relating to geochrony

geo·chronological *or* **geo·chronologic** \"+\ *adj* [*ge-* + *chronological, chronologic*] **:** of or relating to geochronology

geo·chronologist \"+\ *n* **:** a specialist in geochronology

geo·chronology \"+\ *n* [*ge-* + *chronology*] **:** the chronology of the past as indicated by geologic data rather than human records

geo·chronometric \"+\ *adj* [*ge-* + *chronometric*] **:** of or relating to geochronometry

geo·chronometry \"+\ *n* [*ge-* + *chronometry*] **:** the measurement of past time by geochronological methods, esp. those involving radioactive minerals or elements

ge·och·ro·ny \jē'äkrənē\ *n* -ES [*ge-* + Gk *chronos* time + E *-y*] **:** geologic chronology **:** a system of time divisions used in geology

ge·o·cline \'jēōˌklīn\ *n* [*ge-* + *-cline*] **:** the gradation in variation of any widespread polytypic group of organisms along geographical lines — compare ALLEN'S RULE, BERGMANN'S RULE

ge·o·coc·cyx \ˌjēō'käksiks\ *n, cap* [NL, fr. *ge-* + Gk *kokkyx* cuckoo — more at CUCKOO] **:** a genus of birds (family Cuculidae) comprising the roadrunners

ge·o·crat·ic \ˌjēōˌkrad·ik\ *adj* [ISV *ge-* + *-cratic* (as in *democratic*)] **:** of or relating to predominance or enlargement of land areas in relation to oceanic areas

ge·oc·ro·nite \jē'äkrəˌnīt\ *n* -S [G *geokronit*, fr. *geo-* ge- + *Kronos*, leader of the Titans in Greek mythology (fr. Gk) + G *-it* -ite] **:** a mineral $Pb_5(Sb,As)_2S_3$ consisting of a usu. massive lead-gray lead antimony arsenic sulfide

geo·cyclic \ˌjēō+\ *adj* [*ge-* + *cyclic*] **1 :** circling round the earth periodically **2 :** of, relating to, or illustrating the rotation of the earth ⟨a ~ machine⟩

ge·ode \'jēˌōd\ *n* -S [L *geodes*, fr. Gk *geōdēs* earthlike, fr. *gē* earth] **1 :** a nodule of stone having a cavity lined with crystals or mineral matter **2 :** the cavity in a geode

[1]ge·o·des·ic \ˌjēōˌdesik, -dēs-\ *adj* [F *géodésique*, fr. *géodésie* + *-ique* -ic, -ical] **1** *also* **ge·o·des·i·cal** \-səkəl\ **:** GEODETIC **2 :** constructed in the form of a geodesic dome ⟨a ~ house⟩

[2]geodesic \"\ *also* **geodesic line** *n* -S **:** the shortest line between two points on a mathematically derived surface (as a straight line on a plane or an arc of a great circle on a sphere)

geodesic dome *n* **:** a dome or vault made of light straight structural elements largely in tension ⟨the principle of the *geodesic dome* is an effort to reduce most structural stresses to tensions . . . and to reduce the weight of the structure to a point at which the building and the manufacture of building parts will be more economical —Peter Blake⟩

ge·od·e·sist *also* **ge·od·e·cist** \jē'ädəsəst\ *n* -S [*geodesist* fr. *geodesy* + *-ist; geodecist* alter. of *geodesist*] **:** a specialist in geodesy

ge·od·e·sy \-dəsē, -si\ *n* -ES [Gk *geōdaisia*, fr. *geō-* ge- + *daisia* (fr. *dais-*, stem of *daiesthai* to divide + *-ia* -y) — more at TIDE] **1 :** a branch of applied mathematics that determines by observation and measurement the exact positions of points and the figures and areas of large portions of the earth's surface, the shape and size of the earth, and the variations of terrestrial gravity and magnetism **2 :** GEODETIC SURVEYING

ge·o·det·ic \ˌjēəˌded·|ik, -et|, |ēk\ *also* **ge·o·det·i·cal** \|əkəl, |ēk-\ *adj* [fr. *geodesy*, after such pairs as E *genetic: genesis*] **1 :** of, relating to, or determined by geodesy **2 :** relating to the geometry of geodetic lines **3 :** employing metal strips built up in a basket-weave pattern in such a way that the material is distributed in proportion to the applied stresses — used of a type of airplane construction — **ge·o·det·i·cal·ly** \|ək(ə)lē, |ēk-, -li\ *adv*

geodetic latitude *n* **:** astronomical latitude corrected for station error

geodetic line *n* **:** a geodesic line on the earth

geodetic longitude *n* **:** GEOGRAPHICAL LONGITUDE

ge·o·det·ics \ˌ≈≈'ded·iks\ *n pl but sing in constr* **:** GEODESY

geodetic survey *n* **:** a survey of a large land area in which corrections are made for the curvature of the earth's surface

geodetic surveying *also* **geodetic engineering** *n* **:** surveying in which account is taken of and corrections made for the curvature of the earth's surface — compare PLANE SURVEYING

ge·o·dia \jē'ōdēə\ *n, cap* [NL, fr. Gk *geōdēs* earthlike + NL *-ia* — more at GEODE] **:** a genus (the type of the family Geodiidae) of large deep-sea sponges of the class Demospongiae with anchoring structures that resemble roots — **ge·od·i·id** \-dēəd\ *adj or n*

ge·od·ic \(')jēˌädik\ *or* **ge·o·dal** \(')jēˌōdᵊl\ *adj* [*geode* + *-ic* or *-al*] **:** of, relating to, or resembling a geode

ge·o·dif·er·ous \ˌjēˌōˌdif(ə)rəs\ *adj* [*geode* + *-i-* + *-ferous*] **:** containing geodes

Ge·o·dim·e·ter \ˌjēō'dimədˑə(r)\ *trademark* — used for an electronic-optical device that measures distance on the basis of the velocity of light

ge·od·ist \'jēˌōdəst\ *n* -S [*geode* + *-ist*] **:** a student of geodes

geo·duck *or* **go·e·duck** *or* **go·ey·duc** *or* **goo·ey·duck** *or* **gwe·duc** \'güēˌdək\ *n* -S [Chinook Jargon *go-duck*, of Chinookan origin; akin to Chinook *-tgwi-* neck and *-tk* something attached to something else] **:** a very large edible clam (*Panope generosa*) that weighs over five pounds, has siphons which when fully extended measure several feet in length and cannot be withdrawn into the shell, and is found burrowing deeply in sandy mud along the Pacific coast of No. America

geo·dynamic *or* **geo·dynamical** \ˌjēˌō+\ *adj* [ISV *ge-* + *dynamic, dynamical*] **:** of or relating to dynamic forces or processes within the earth

geo·dynamics \"+\ *n pl but sing in constr* [ISV *ge-* + *dynamics*] **:** a study of dynamic forces or processes within the earth

geo-economic \"+\ *adj* [*ge-* + *economic*] **:** of, relating to, or characterized by economic conditions or policies that are influenced by geographic factors and exist or are carried out on the international level ⟨a *geo-economic* atlas⟩ ⟨*geo-economic* study⟩

ge·o·gen \'jēəjən, -əˌjen\ *n* -S [ISV *ge-* + *-gen*] **:** a physical, biologic, or human environmental factor occurring in a particular region and favoring the development of particular diseases — distinguished from *pathogen*

ge·og·e·nous \(')jēˌäjənəs\ *adj* [*ge-* + *-genous*] **:** growing on or in the ground

ge·o·glos·sa·ce·ae \ˌjē(ˌ)ōˌglä'sāsēˌē\ *n pl, cap* [NL, *fr. Geoglossum*, type genus + *-aceae*] **:** a family (order Helotiales) of ascomycetous fungi having the hymenium covering the upper convex part of clavate or cap-shaped fruiting bodies

ge·o·glos·sum \ˌ≈≈'gläsəm\ *n, cap* [NL, fr. *ge-* + *-glossum* (fr. Gk *glōssa* tongue) — more at GLOSS] **:** the type genus of Geoglossaceae comprising the earthtongues

[1]geo·glyphic \ˌjēō+\ *adj* [*ge-* + *glyphic*] **:** of or relating to geoglyphics

[2]geoglyphic \"\ *n* -S **:** a mark (as an amphibian track or worm trail) found in rock and giving evidence of past geological events

ge·og·nost \'jēˌägˌnäst, 'jēəg-; jē'ägˌnäst, -ˌnəst\ *also* **ge·og·no·sist** \jē'ägnəsəst\ *n* -S [*geognost* fr. F *géognoste*, fr. *géo-* ge- + Gk *gnōstēs* one that knows, fr. *gignōskein* to know; *geognosist* fr. *geognosy* + *-ist*] **:** a specialist in geognosy

ge·og·nos·tic \ˌjēˌägˌnästik, ˌjēəg-\ *or* **ge·og·nos·ti·cal** \-təkəl\ *adj* **:** of or relating to geognosy — **ge·og·nos·ti·cal·ly** \-tək(ə)lē\ *adv*

ge·og·no·sy \jē'ägnəsē\ *n* -ES [ISV *ge-* + *-gnosy*] **:** a branch of geology that deals with the materials of the earth and its general exterior and interior constitution

ge·o·gon·ic \ˌjēəˌgänik\ *or* **ge·o·gon·i·cal** \-nəkəl\ *adj* [ISV *geogony* + *-ic, -ical*] **:** of or relating to geogony

ge·og·o·ny \jē'ägənē\ *n* -ES [*ge-* + *-gony*] **:** a science or a theory of the formation of the earth

ge·og·ra·pher \jē'ägrəfə(r) *also* ÷'jäg-, *chiefly in substand speech* -gəf-\ *n* -S [LL *geographus* (fr. Gk *geōgraphos*, fr. *geō-* ge- + *-graphos*, fr. *graphein* to write) + E *-er* — more at CARVE] **:** a specialist in geography

geographer cone *n* [so called fr. the resemblance of the blotches to the appearance of land masses upon a map] **:** a somewhat barrel-shaped venomous Indo-Pacific cone (*Conus geographus*) whose shell is mottled with brown blotches

ge·o·graph·ic \ˌjēəˌgrafik, -fēk\ *or* **ge·o·graph·i·cal** \-fəkəl, -fēk-\ *adj* [LL *geographicus*, fr. Gk *geōgraphikos*, fr. *geōgraphein* to describe the surface of the earth + *-ikos* -ic, -ical — more at GEOGRAPHY] **1 :** of or relating to geography ⟨~ field techniques —P.E.James⟩ **2 :** belonging to or characteristic of a particular region ⟨the special ~ and industrial perplexities in such industries as lumber, tool and die making —S.T. Williamson & Herbert Harris⟩ — **ge·o·graph·i·cal·ly** \-fək(ə)lē, -fēk-, -li\ *adv*

geographical biology *n* **:** BIOGEOGRAPHY

geographical botany *n* **:** PHYTOGEOGRAPHY

geographical coordinate *n* **:** either of the two lines of latitude and longitude whose intersection determines the geographical point of a place

geographical distribution *n* **:** the natural arrangement and apportionment of the various forms of animals and plants in the different regions and localities of the earth

geographical latitude *n* **:** the angle between the plane of the earth's equator and the line perpendicular to the standard spheroid at a given point on the earth's surface — compare TERRESTRIAL LATITUDE

geographical longitude *n* **:** terrestrial longitude based on the meridian defined by the perpendicular to the standard spheroid at the observer's position — called also *geodetic longitude*

geographical mile *n* **:** NAUTICAL MILE

geographical point *or* **geographical position** *n* **:** the point on the earth's surface for which a given celestial body is in the astronomical zenith

geographic race *n* **:** a subdivision of a biological species coincident with a geographic region and presumably the resultant of environmental peculiarities **:** a geographic subspecies — called also *geographical variety*

ge·o·graph·ics \ˌjēə'grafiks, -fēks\ *n pl but sing in constr* **:** GEOGRAPHY

geographic terrapin *or* **geographic tortoise** *n* [so called fr. the resemblance of its shell to a map] **:** MAP TURTLE

geographic tongue *n* [so called fr. the resemblance of the patches to land masses on a map] **:** a condition in which the tongue exhibits smooth patches surrounded by slightly elevated grayish margins — called also *wandering rash*

geographic variation *n* **:** the differentiation of distinctive subdivisions from geographically isolated parts of a potentially interbreeding population due to restriction of interbreeding between fractions and natural selection of locally valuable mutations **:** the primary mechanism of subspeciation

ge·og·ra·phize \jē'ägrəˌfīz *also* ÷'jäg-\ *vb* -ED/-ING/-S [*geography* + *-ize*] *vi* **:** to study geography ~ *vt* **:** to study or describe the geography of **:** treat geographically

ge·og·ra·phy \jē'ägrəfē, -fi *also* ÷'jäg-, *chiefly in substand speech* -gəf-\ *n* -ES *often attrib* [L *geographia*, fr. Gk *geōgraphia*, fr. *geōgraphein* to describe the surface of the earth (fr. *geō-* ge- + *graphein* to write) + *-ia* -y — more at CARVE] **1 :** a science that deals with the earth and its life; *esp* **:** the description of land, sea, air, and the distribution of plant and animal life including man and his industries with reference to the mutual relations of these diverse elements — see BIOGEOGRAPHY, COMMERCIAL GEOGRAPHY, ECONOMIC GEOGRAPHY, MATHEMATICAL GEOGRAPHY, PHYSICAL GEOGRAPHY, POLITICAL GEOGRAPHY **2 :** the geographic features of an area ⟨the ~ of Ohio⟩ **3 :** a treatise on geography **4 :** a delineation or systematic arrangement of constituent elements

: CONFIGURATION ⟨the philosophers . . . have tried to construct *geographies* of human reason —*Times Lit. Supp.*⟩
geography cone *n* **:** GEOGRAPHER CONE
geo·history \ˌjē(ˌ)ō+\ *n* [*ge-* + *history*] **:** history interpreted on the basis of geographic factors
geo·hydrologist \"+\ *n* **:** a specialist in geohydrology
geo·hydrology \"+\ *n* [*ge-* + *hydrology*] **:** a science that deals with the character, source, and mode of occurrence of underground water
ge·oid \ˈjēˌȯid\ *n* -s [G, fr. Gk *geoeidēs* earthlike, fr. *ge-* + *-oeidēs* -oid] **:** the surface within or around the earth that is everywhere normal to the direction of gravity, coincides with mean sea level in the oceans, and approximates to the shape of an ellipsoid of revolution — **ge·oi·dal** \(ˈ)jēˈȯidᵊl\ *adj*
geo·isotherm \ˌjē(ˌ)ō+\ *n* [ISV *ge-* + *isotherm*] **:** ISOGEOTHERM
ge·ol·o·ger \jēˈäləjə(r)\ *or* **ge·o·lo·gian** \ˌjēəˈlōj(ē)ən\ *n* -s [*geology* + *-er* or *-ian*] **:** GEOLOGIST
ge·o·log·ic \ˌjēəˈläjik, -jēk\ *or* **ge·o·log·i·cal** \-jəkəl, -jēk-\ *adj* [*geology* + *-ic, -ical*] **:** of, relating to, or based on geology **:** described or ascertained by geology ⟨~ strata⟩ ⟨a ~ lecture⟩ — **ge·o·log·i·cal·ly** \-jək(ə)lē, -jēk-, -li\ *adv*
geological age *n* **:** an age earlier than the postglacial and hence datable only by geology
geological survey *n* **1 :** a systematic examination of an area to determine the character, relations, distribution, and origin or mode of formation of its rock masses and mineral resources **2** *usu cap G&S* **:** a governmental bureau charged with making geological surveys
geologic column *n* **1 :** a columnar diagram that shows the rock formations of a locality or region and that is arranged to indicate their relations to the subdivisions of geologic time **2 :** the sequence of rock formations portrayed in a geologic column
ge·o·lo·gi·cian \ˌjēəlōˈjishən\ *n* -s **:** GEOLOGIST
geologic section *n* **:** the sequence of rock strata or lithologic units in a locality **:** the local geologic column
geologic thermometer *n* **:** a mineral or mineral aggregate that yields information concerning the limits of temperature within which it was formed
geologic time *n* **:** the long period dealt with by historical geology; *esp* **:** the period prior to human history
ge·ol·o·gist \jēˈäləjəst\ *n* -s [*geology* + *-ist*] **:** a specialist in geology
ge·ol·o·gize \-ˌjīz\ *vb* -ED/-ING/-s [*geology* + *-ize*] *vi* **:** to study geology or make geologic investigations ~ *vt* **:** to study geologically
ge·ol·o·graph \-ˌgraf, -ˌräf\ *n* [*geology* + *-graph*] **:** an automatic recorder of the rate of penetration of a bit during rotary drilling of wells
ge·ol·o·gy \jēˈäləjē, -ji\ *n* -ES *often attrib* [NL *geologia*, fr. *geo-* ge- + *-logia* -logy] **1 :** a science that deals with the history of the earth and its life esp. as recorded in the rocks — see DYNAMIC GEOLOGY, ECONOMIC GEOLOGY, ENGINEERING GEOLOGY, GEOGNOSY, HISTORICAL GEOLOGY, PALEONTOLOGIC GEOLOGY, PHYSICAL GEOLOGY, PHYSIOGRAPHIC GEOLOGY, STRATIGRAPHY, STRUCTURAL GEOLOGY **2 :** the geologic features of an area **:** the attributes of rocks, rock formations, or rock constituents of a district ⟨the ~ of Massachusetts⟩ **3 :** a treatise on geology
geo·magnetic \ˌjē(ˌ)ō+\ *adj* [*ge-* + *magnetic*] **1 :** dealing with, derived from, or relating to terrestrial magnetism **2 :** of or relating to the geomagnetic field
geomagnetic equator *n* **:** the great circle of the earth whose plane is perpendicular to the axis of the geomagnetic field — compare MAGNETIC EQUATOR
geomagnetic field *n* **:** a conventionalized symmetrical approximation of the earth's magnetic field having one diameter of the earth as its axis
geo·magnetician \"+\ *n* **:** a geophysicist who specializes in terrestrial magnetism
geomagnetic latitude *n* **:** a system of latitude reckoned like geographical latitude but along the geomagnetic meridians from the geomagnetic equator
geomagnetic meridian *n* **:** a great circle of the earth through the geomagnetic poles — compare MAGNETIC MERIDIAN
geomagnetic pole *n* **:** either of two spots on the earth's surface that are at the ends of the axis of the geomagnetic field and that do not coincide with the geographical poles or the magnetic poles
geo·magnetism \ˌjē(ˌ)ō+\ *n* [*ge-* + *magnetism*] **:** TERRESTRIAL MAGNETISM
ge·om·a·lic \jēˈäməˌlik, ˌjēōˈmalik\ *adj* [*ge-* + Gk *homalos* level, even (fr. *homos* common, same) + E *-ic* — more at SAME] **:** of or relating to geomalism
ge·om·a·lism \jēˈäməˌlizəm\ *n* -s [*ge-* + Gk *homalismos* action of leveling, fr. *homalos* + *-ismos* -ism] **:** a tendency of an organism to be influenced in growth by gravitation so that one side or lateral organ balances with another
ge·o·man·cer \ˈjēəˌman(t)sə(r)\ *n* -s [ME, fr. *geomancie* + *-er*] **:** one that practices geomancy ⟨went and found a ~ and asked him for a lucky day for burials —Pearl Buck⟩
ge·o·man·cy \-sē\ *n* -ES [ME *geomancie*, fr. MF, fr. ML *geomantia*, fr. LGk *geōmanteia*, fr. Gk *geō-* ge- + *-manteia* -mancy] **:** divination by means of figures or lines (as in natural or artificial configurations of earth or by connecting dots jotted at random on paper)
ge·o·man·tic \ˌjēəˈmantik\ *also* **ge·o·man·ti·cal** \-təkəl\ *adj* [ML *geomanticus*, fr. *geomantia* + L *-icus* -ic, -ical] **:** of or relating to geomancy — **ge·o·man·ti·cal·ly** \-tək(ə)lē\ *adv*
ge·o·mat·ic \ˌjēəˈmad·ik\ *or* **ge·o·mat·i·cal** \-d·əkəl\ *adj* [*ge-* + *mathematic, mathematical*] **:** of or relating to geomatics
ge·o·mat·ics \ˌ==ˈmad·iks\ *n pl but sing in constr* [*ge-* + *mathematics*] **:** the mathematics of the earth
geo·medical \ˌjē(ˌ)ō+\ *adj* [*ge-* + *medical*] **:** relating to or concerned with geomedicine
geo·medicine \"+\ *n* [*ge-* + *medicine*; trans. of G *geomedizin*] **:** a branch of medicine that deals with geographic factors in disease
ge·om·e·ter \jēˈäməd·ə(r), -ətə- *also* ÷ ˈjäm-\ *n* [ME, fr. MF or L; MF *geometre*, fr. L *geometres*, *geometra*, fr. Gk *geōmetrēs*, fr. *geōmetrein* to measure or survey land — more at GEOMETRY] **1 :** a specialist in geometry **2 :** a moth or moth larva of the family Geometridae **:** LOOPER
¹ge·o·met·ric \ˌjēəˈme·trik, -rēk\ *or* **ge·o·met·ri·cal** \-rəkəl, -rēk-\ *adj* [MF or L; MF *geometrique*, fr. L *geometricus*, fr. Gk *geōmetrikos*, fr. *geōmetrēs* + *-ikos* -ic, -ical] **1 :** of, relating to, or according to the methods or principles of geometry **:** determined by geometry ⟨the ~ solution of a problem⟩ **2** *usu cap* **:** of or relating to a style of Greek pottery made from the 10th century to about 700 B.C. and characterized by geometric decorative motifs (as bands, meanders, zigzags, chevrons, lozenges, or triangles) that were applied in black on a yellowish or buff surface **3 :** having or utilizing rectilinear or simple curvilinear motifs or outlines that bear little resemblance to natural forms ⟨a buffalo hide painted with ~ designs in red and black —Alice Marriott⟩ — **ge·o·met·ri·cal·ly** \-rək(ə)lē, -rēk-, -li\ *adv*
²geometric \"\ *n* -s **:** something (as a textile or rug) characterized by geometric design or decoration
geometrical clamp *n* **:** a clamp that holds a rigid body immovable by keeping it in six-point contact with an immovable rigid support
geometrical construction *n* **:** construction employing only straightedge and compasses or effected by drawing only straight lines and circles
geometrical optics *n pl but sing in constr* **:** a branch of optics that deals with those phenomena of reflection and refraction that can be mathematically deduced from simple empirical laws
geometrical pitch *n* **:** the distance an element of an airplane propeller would advance in one revolution if it were moving along a helix having an angle equal to the angle between the chord of the element and a plane perpendicular to the propeller axis
geometrical radius *n* **:** the pitch-circle radius of a gear
geometric design *n* **:** highway design in which the dimensions of the roadway are intended to promote safe, convenient, and economical movement of traffic
ge·om·e·tri·cian \(ˌ)jēˌämə'trishən\ *n* -s **:** GEOMETER
geometric isomerism *n* **:** stereoisomerism (as cis-trans isomerism) ascribed to different directional arrangements of specifically located groups in the molecule and usu. considered to be caused by prevention of free rotation in parts of the molecule (as by a double bond or a ring) — compare OPTICAL ISOMERISM
geometric lathe *n* **:** an instrument for engraving complicated patterns of interlacing lines (as on bank notes)
geometric mean *n* **1 :** a term between the first and last terms of a geometric progression — usu. used in pl. **2 :** the *n*th root of the product of *n* statistical variables
geometric plane *n* **:** GROUND PLANE
geometric progression *or* **geometric series** *n* **:** a progression or series in which the ratio of each term to the one immediately preceding it is always the same number ⟨1 + ½ + ¼ + ⅛ is a *geometric progression* in which the ratio is ½⟩
geometric spider *n* **:** any of numerous three-clawed eight-eyed sedentary spiders (family Epeiridae) that spin webs composed chiefly of radial and spiral threads (as the common garden spider *Miranda aurantia*)
geometric stairs *n pl* **:** continuous stairs that turn or wind about a central wellhole which has rounded corners or is circular or elliptical and that have the strings and rails arranged upon geometric principles and running continuously from top to bottom
geometric tortoise *n* [so called fr. the geometric patterns of the shells] **1 :** a common southern African tortoise (*Testudo geometrica* or *Psammobates geometrica*) with ornately sculptured dorsal shields raised into conical eminences and alternately streaked with yellow and black **2 :** any of several forms related to the geometric tortoise
geometric unit *n* **:** a unit of length, area, volume, or angular magnitude

GEOLOGIC TIME AND FORMATIONS

NORTH AMERICA

eras	periods and systems	epochs and series	principal mountain-making episodes
Cenozoic	Quaternary	Holocene (Recent) Pleistocene (Glacial)	
			Cascadian
	Tertiary	Pliocene Miocene Oligocene Eocene Paleocene	
			Laramide (Rocky mts.)
Mesozoic	Cretaceous (Upper Cretaceous)	Laramie Montana Colorado Dakota	
	Comanchean (Lower Cretaceous)	Washita Fredericksburg Trinity Arundel Patuxent	
			Nevadan
	Jurassic	Upper Middle Lower	
	Triassic	Upper Middle Lower	
Paleozoic	Permian	Ochoan Guadalupian Leonardian Wolfcamp	
			Appalachian
	Pennsylvanian	Virgilian Missourian Desmoinesian Atokan Morrowan	
	Mississippian	Chesterian Meramec Osagian Kinderhook	
			Acadian
	Devonian	Chautauquan Senecan Erian Ulsterian	
	Silurian	Cayugan Niagaran Medinan	
			Taconic
	Ordovician	Cincinnatian Champlainian Canadian	
	Cambrian	Croixan Albertan Waucobian	
			Killarney
Proterozoic	not divided into periods	Keweenawan — Beltian	
		Huronian — Grand Canyon	Algoman
Archeozoic		Timiskaming — Vishnu	
		Keewatin	Laurentian

EUROPE

eras	periods and systems	epochs and series	principal mountain-making episodes
Cenozoic	Quaternary	Holocene (Recent) Pleistocene (Glacial)	
	Tertiary	Pliocene Miocene Oligocene Eocene Paleocene	Alpine
Mesozoic	Cretaceous	Danian Senonian Turonian Cenomanian Albian Aptian Barremian Neocomian	
	Jurassic	Malm Dogger Lias	
	Triassic	Keuper Muschelkalk Bunter	
Paleozoic	Permian	Zechstein	
		Rothliegende	
			Hercynian *or* Armorican
	Upper Carboniferous ("Coal Measures")	Stephanian Westphalian Namurian	
	Carboniferous		Culmide
	Lower Carboniferous ("Mountain Limestone")	Dinantian *or* Culm	
	Devonian ("Old Red Sandstone")	Fammenian Frasnian Givetian Eifelian Coblenzian Gedinnian	
			Caledonian
	Silurian	Downtonian Ludlovian Wenlockian Llandoverian	
	Ordovician	Bala Llandeilo Llanvirn Arenig	
	Cambrian	Tremadoc Lingulella Menevian Harlech	
Precambrian: Algonkian	not divided into periods	Torridonian, Jotnian, Dalradian, Gothian	
Precambrian: Archean		Moine, Sveco-fennian, Lewisian	

YEARS AGO (dates established by lead-uranium ratios)	EARLIEST RECORD OF ANIMALS	EARLIEST RECORD OF PLANTS
	mankind	
70,000,000	placental mammals	
		grasses and cereals
160,000,000	birds	
	mammals	flowering plants
		ginkgos
230,000,000		
		cycads and conifers
	insects	lepidodendrons, calamites, cordaites, etc.
	reptiles	
	amphibians	seed ferns
		vascular plants: lycopods, horsetails, ferns, etc.
390,000,000		
	fishes	
500,000,000		mosses
620,000,000	invertebrates	spores of uncertain relationship marine algae
1,420,000,000		
2,300,000,000		

[1]**ge·om·e·trid** \jē'ämə·trəd, ¦jē¦me·t-\ *adj* [NL *Geometridae*] **:** of or relating to the family Geometridae

[2]**geometrid** \"\ *n* -s **:** a geometrid moth **:** GEOMETER

ge·o·met·ri·dae \jēə'me·trə,dē\ *n pl, cap* [NL, fr. L *geometres, geometra* geometer + NL *-idae;* fr. the looping movement, suggestive of earth measurement — more at GEOMETER] **:** a family of chiefly medium-sized and slender-bodied moths with large wings and larvae that are loopers and that often feed destructively on various trees and cultivated plants

ge·om·e·trist \jē'ämə·trəst *also* ÷ 'jäm-\ *n* -s [*geometry* + *-ist*] **:** GEOMETER

ge·om·e·tri·za·tion \(,)jē,ämə·trə'zāshən, -,trī'z-\ *n* -s **:** the act or process of geometrizing

ge·om·e·trize \jē'ämə,trīz\ *vb* -ED/-ING/-s [*geometry* + *-ize*] *vi* **:** to work by or as if by geometric methods or laws **:** investigate and draw conclusions by using geometric constructions and principles ~ *vt* **1 :** to represent geometrically **2 :** to make conform to geometric principles and laws **:** apply geometric principles and laws to

ge·om·e·triz·er \-zə(r)\ *n* -s **:** one that geometrizes

ge·om·e·try \jē'ämə·trē, -ri *also* ÷'jäm-\ *n* -ES *often attrib* [ME *geometrie*, fr. MF, fr. L *geometria*, fr. Gk *geōmetria*, fr. *geōmetrein* to measure or survey the earth (fr. *geō-* ge- + *metrein* to measure, fr. *metron* measure) + *-ia* -y — more at MEASURE] **1 a :** a branch of mathematics that deals with the measurement, properties, and relationships of points, lines, angles, surfaces, and solids **b :** a particular type or system of geometry **c :** a treatise on geometry **2 a :** CONFIGURATION ⟨~ of an automotive steering linkage⟩ ⟨~ of an optical system⟩ **b :** surface shape (as of a mechanical part or a crystal) **3 :** an arrangement of objects or parts that suggests geometrical figures or outlines ⟨the picturesque ~ of spars, masts, ropes, pulleys, and all the busy trappings of a Vineyard fisherman —Samuel Chamberlain⟩ ⟨what is of interest to musicians in "Wozzeck" is its ~, its contrapuntal plan, its structure —Robert Craft⟩

ge·o·mor·phic \¦jēə¦mȯrfik\ *adj* [*ge-* + *-morphic*] **:** of or relating to the form of the earth or its surface features **:** resembling the earth **:** GEOMORPHOLOGIC ⟨classification of geologic structures for purposes of ~ description —*Jour. of Geol.*⟩

geomorphic cycle *n* **:** CYCLE OF EROSION

ge·o·mor·phist \-fəst\ *n* -s [*geomorphy* + *-ist*] **:** GEOMORPHOLOGIST

ge·o·morphogenic \¦jē(,)ō+\ *adj* **:** of or relating to geomorphogeny

ge·o·mor·phog·e·nist \,jē(,)ō,mȯr'fäjənəst\ *n* -s **:** a specialist in geomorphogeny

geo·morphogeny \¦jē(,)ō+\ *n* [ISV *ge-* + *morphogeny;* orig. formed as F *géomorphogénie*] **:** a science that deals with the genesis of earth forms

geo·morphography \"+\ *n* [*ge-* + *morphography*] **:** the descriptive phase of geomorphology

geo·morphologic *or* **geo·morphological** \"+\ *adj* **:** of or relating to geomorphology

geo·morphologist \"+\ *n* **:** a specialist in geomorphology

geo·morphology \"+\ *n* [ISV *ge-* + *morphology*] **1 :** a science that deals with the land and submarine relief features of the earth's surface and seeks a genetic interpretation of them through using the principles of physiography in its descriptive aspects and of dynamic and structural geology in its explanatory phases **2 a :** the features dealt with in geomorphology ⟨the ~ of the Black hills⟩ **b :** a treatise on geomorphology

ge·o·mor·phy \'jēə,mȯrfē\ *n* -ES [ISV *ge-* + *morph-* + *-y*] **:** GEOMORPHOLOGY

[1]**ge·o·my·id** \¦jēō¦mīəd\ *adj* [NL *Geomyidae*] **:** of or relating to the family Geomyidae

[2]**geomyid** \"\ *n* -s **:** a rodent of the family Geomyidae

ge·o·my·i·dae \,jēō'mīə,dē\ *n pl, cap* [NL, fr. *Geomys*, type genus (fr. *ge-* + Gk *mys* mouse) + *-idae* — more at MOUSE] **:** a family of No. American sciuromorph burrowing rodents comprising the pocket gophers and extinct related forms

[1]**ge·o·my·oid** \¦jēō¦mī,ȯid\ *adj* [NL *Geomyoidea*] **:** of or relating to the superfamily Geomyoidea

[2]**geomyoid** \"\ *n* -s **:** a rodent of the superfamily Geomyoidea

ge·o·my·oi·dea \¦jē(,)ō,mī'ȯidēə\ *n pl, cap* [NL, fr. *Geomys* genus of rodents + *-oidea*] **:** a superfamily of rodents comprising those with external cheek pouches (as the pocket gophers and the kangaroo rat)

geo·navigation \¦jē(,)ō+\ *n* [*ge-* + *navigation*] **:** navigation by reckoning the course from other places on the earth's surface (as in piloting and dead reckoning)

geo·negative \"+\ *adj* [*ge-* + *negative*] **:** characterized by negative geotropism or geotaxis

ge·on·ic \(')gā¦ōnik, -¦än- *or* **ga·on·ic** \(')gā¦ōn-\ *adj, often cap* [*Geonim* or *Gaon* + *-ic*] **:** of or relating to the geonim

geonim *pl of* GAON

ge·on·o·ma \jē'änəmə\ *n* [NL, fr. Gk *geōnomos* colonist, fr. *geō-* ge- + *-nomos* (fr. *nemein* to distribute) — more at NIMBLE] **1** *cap* **:** a genus of tropical American palms with nearly entire or pinnately cleft leaves and a small fruit like a berry **2** -s **:** any palm of the genus *Geonoma*

geo·pathology \¦jē(,)ō+\ *n* [*ge-* + *pathology*] **:** a science that deals with the relation of geographic factors to peculiarities of specific diseases ⟨~ of hypertension⟩

ge·o·pha·gia \,jēō'fāj(ē)ə\ *n* -s [NL, fr. *ge-* + *-phagia*] **:** GEOPHAGY

ge·oph·a·gism \jē'äfə,jizəm\ *n* -s [ISV *ge-* + Gk *phagein* to eat + ISV *-ism* — more at BAKSHEESH] **:** GEOPHAGY

ge·oph·a·gist \-jəst\ *n* -s [*geophagy* + *-ist*] **:** one that eats earth

ge·oph·a·gous \(')jē¦äfəgəs\ *adj* [*ge-* + *-phagous*] **1 :** eating earth ⟨a ~ tribe⟩ **2 :** feeding on soil ⟨~ worms⟩

ge·oph·a·gy \jē'äfəjē\ *n* -ES [ISV *ge-* + *-phagy*] **:** the practice of eating earthy substances (as clay) that is widespread among primitive or depressed peoples and is held to represent an attempt to supply elements lacking in a scanty or unbalanced diet

ge·oph·i·la \jē'äfələ\ *n pl, cap* [NL, fr. *ge-* + *-phila*] *in some classifications* **:** a group of pulmonate gastropods including the land snails and slugs

ge·o·phil·o·morph \¦jē(,)ō¦filə,mȯrf\ *adj* [NL *Geophilomorpha*] **:** of or relating to the order Geophilomorpha

ge·o·phil·o·mor·pha \,=(,)=,==='mȯrfə\ *n pl, cap* [NL, fr. *Geophilus* + *-o-* + *-morpha*] **:** an order of small extremely elongate centipedes living in soil and under stones and having more than 30 pairs of legs

ge·oph·i·lous \(')jē¦äfələs\ *adj* [*ge-* + *-philous*] **:** living or growing in or on the ground ⟨~ insects⟩ ⟨~ plants⟩

ge·oph·i·lus \jē'äfələs\ *n, cap* [NL, fr. *ge-* + *-philus*] **:** a cosmopolitan genus (the type of the family Geophilidae) of geophilomorph centipedes

Ge·o·phone \'jēə,fōn\ *trademark* — used for an instrument designed to detect vibrations passing through rocks, soil, or ice

geo·photo \¦jēə+\ *n* [*ge-* + *photo*] **:** a photograph usu. taken from an airplane for use in geologic investigations

geo·physical \"+\ *adj* [*ge-* + *physical*] **:** of, relating to, or based on geophysics ⟨financing a ~ survey of its properties —*Wall Street Jour.*⟩ — **geo·physically** \"+\ *adv*

geophysical engineering *n* **:** a branch of engineering that deals with scientific methods of locating and studying underground deposits of ores, minerals, oil, gas, or water

geo·physicist \"+\ *n* [*geophysics* + *-ist*] **:** a specialist in geophysics

geo·physics \"+\ *n pl but sing in constr* [ISV *ge-* + *physics*] **1 :** the physics of the earth including the fields of meteorology, hydrology, oceanography, seismology, volcanology, magnetism, radioactivity, and geodesy **2 :** GEOPHYSICAL ENGINEERING

ge·o·phyte \'jēə,fīt\ *n* -s [*ge-* + *-phyte*] **:** a perennial plant that bears its overwintering buds below the surface of the soil — compare CHAMAEPHYTE, PHANEROPHYTE

ge·o·plana \,jēō'plānə, -lanə, -länə\ *n, cap* [NL, fr. *ge-* + L *plana*, fem. of *planus* flat, level — more at FLOOR] **:** a large genus (the type of the family Geoplanidae) of chiefly tropical terrestrial triclad turbellarian worms having a marginal band of eyes about the body

geo·polar \¦jē(,)ō+\ *adj* [*ge-* + *polar*] **:** of or relating to a pole of the earth

geo·political \"+\ *adj* [*ge-* + *political;* trans. of G *geopolitisch*] **:** of, relating to, or based on geopolitics ⟨the weakest link . . . is his tendency to ignore the ~ relationship of Western Europe to the worldwide situation —J.S.Roucek⟩ — **geo·politically** \"+\ *adv*

geo·politician \"+\ *n* [*ge-* + *politician;* trans. of G *geopolitiker*] **:** a specialist in geopolitics

geo·politics \"+\ *n pl but sing in constr* [*ge-* + *politics;* trans. of G *geopolitik*] **1 :** a study of the influence of such physical factors as geography, economics, and demography upon the politics and esp. the foreign policy of a state ⟨the present tendency to study ~ in colleges —Thomas Woody⟩ — compare POLITICAL GEOGRAPHY **2 :** a Nazi expansionist doctrine that emphasized strategic frontiers, lebensraum, and racial, economic, and social pressures as factors demanding reallocation of the earth's surface and resources ⟨made ~ into an effective organ of propaganda —G.H.Sabine⟩ **3 :** a governmental policy guided by geopolitics ⟨the ~ of the Japanese government⟩ **4 :** the combination of political and geographic factors characterizing a particular state or region ⟨a study of the ~ of the United Kingdom and the rest of the empire —*Armed Forces Talk*⟩

ge·o·po·li·tik \,gāō,pōlē'tēk\ *n* -s *usu cap* [G, fr. *ge-* + *politik* politics — more at REALPOLITIK] **:** GEOPOLITICS

ge·o·po·li·ti·ker \,gā(,)ōpō'lētikər\ *n* -s *sometimes cap* [G, fr. *geo-* ge- + *politiker* politician, fr. *politik* + *-er*] **:** GEOPOLITICIAN

ge·o·pon·ic \¦jēə¦pänik\ *also* **ge·o·pon·i·cal** \-nəkəl\ *adj* [Gk *geōponikos*, fr. *geōponein* to till the soil (fr. *geō-* ge- + *ponein* to toil) + *-ikos* -ic, -ical] **:** of or relating to tillage **:** AGRICULTURAL

ge·o·pon·ics \,=='päniks\ *n pl but sing in constr* [MGk *geōponika*, fr. Gk, neut. pl. of *geōponikos*] **:** an art or science of cultivating the earth **:** HUSBANDRY

geo·positive \¦jē(,)ō+\ *adj* [*ge-* + *positive*] **:** characterized by positive geotropism or geotaxis

geo·potential \"+\ *n* [*ge-* + *potential*] **:** the work that must be done at a given altitude in raising a unit mass from sea level to that altitude against the earth's gravitational field

ge·o·prum·non \,jēō'prəm,nän\ *n, cap* [NL, fr. *ge-* + Gk *proumnon* plum] **:** a small genus of herbs (family Leguminosae) bearing fleshy indehiscent pods — see EARTH PLUM, MILK VETCH

ge·o·rama \,jēə'ramə, -rämə\ *n* -s [F *géorama*, fr. *gé-* ge- + *-orama* (as in *panorama*)] **:** a hollow globe whose inner surface contains a map of the world for examination by one standing inside

geor·die \'jȯrdē\ *n* -s *usu cap* [fr. Sc *Geordie*, dim. of the name *George*] **1** [fr. the image of St. George such coins once bore] *chiefly Scot* **:** GUINEA ⟨jingling the *Geordies* in his hand —Neil Munro⟩ **2** *chiefly Scot* **a :** a coal miner esp. from the region around Tyneside **b :** a native of Scotland or northern England **3** *chiefly Scot* **:** a collier brig **4** *chiefly Scot* **:** a coal miner's safety lamp

[1]**george** \'jȯ(ə)rj, 'jō(ə)j\ *n* -s *usu cap* [after St. George †*ab* A.D. 303 Cappadocian martyr, patron saint of England] **1 :** either of two of the insignia of the British Order of the Garter: **a :** a jewel appended to the collar of the order — called also *Great George* **b :** a jewel appended to the ribbon of the order — called also *Lesser George* **2 :** a British half crown or guinea bearing the image of St. George

[2]**george** \"\ *usu cap* [fr. the name *George*] — a communications code word for the letter *g*

georg·es bank flounder \¦jȯr¦jəz-, ¦jō(ə)|\ *n, usu cap G&B* [fr. *Georges Bank*, elevation under the sea east of Cape Cod, Mass.] **:** a brownish yellow flounder (*Pseudopleuronectes americanus dignabilis*) — called also *lemon sole*

george town \¦jȯrj,taůn, ¦jō(ə)j-\ *adj, usu cap G&T* [fr. *George Town*, Federation of Malaya] **:** of or from the city of George Town, Federation of Malaya **:** of the kind or style prevalent in George Town

Geor·gette \(')jȯr¦jet, (')jō(ə)¦-\ *trademark* — used for a thin strong clothing crepe woven from hard twisted yarns to produce a dull pebbly surface

geor·gia \'jȯr|jə, 'jō(ə)-\ *sometimes* |jēə\ *adj, usu cap* [fr. *Georgia*, state in the southern U. S., fr. *George* I †1727 king of England] **:** of or from the state of Georgia **:** of the kind or style prevalent in Georgia **:** GEORGIAN

georgia bark *n, usu cap G* **:** the bitter bark of a fever tree (*Pinckneya pubens*) used as a tonic and vermifuge

geor·gia·des·ite \jō(r)'jādə,sīt\ *n* -s [F *georgiadésite*, fr. *Georgiades*, 20th cent. Greek mine director + F *-ite*] **:** a mineral $Pb_3(AsO_4)Cl_3$ consisting of a lead chloro-arsenate and occurring in white or brownish yellow orthorhombic crystals

georgia heart pine *n, usu cap G* **:** LONGLEAF PINE

[1]**geor·gian** \'jȯr|jən, 'jō(ə)| *sometimes* |jēən\ *n* -s *cap* [ME *Georgyen*, fr. MF *georgien*, fr. *Georgie* Georgia, region in the southern Caucasus + MF *-en* -an] **1 :** a native or inhabitant of Georgia in the Caucasus **2 :** the South Caucasic language of the Georgian people

[2]**georgian** \"\ *adj, usu cap* **1 a :** of, relating to, or characteristic of Georgia in the Caucasus **b :** of, relating to, or characteristic of the Georgians **2 :** of, relating to, or characteristic of the Georgian language

[3]**georgian** \"\ *n* -s *cap* [*Georgia*, state + E *-an*] **:** a native or resident of the state of Georgia

[4]**georgian** \"\ *adj, usu cap* **1 :** of, relating to, or characteristic of the state of Georgia **2 :** of, relating to, or characteristic of the people of Georgia

[5]**georgian** \"\ *adj, usu cap* **1** [after *George* I †1727, *George* II †1760, *George* III †1820, and *George* IV †1830, kings of England] **:** of, relating to, or characteristic of the reigns of the first four Georges of Great Britain ⟨the *Georgian* age having been . . . the most momentous age of our history —Robert Southey⟩ ⟨gracious *Georgian* beauty of Mount Vernon —Howard Fast⟩ **2** [after *George* V †1936 king of England] **:** of, relating to, or characteristic of the reign of George V of Great Britain ⟨the *Georgian* poets . . . wrote about their own personal relationships with trivial objects —C.D. Lewis⟩

[6]**georgian** \"\ *n* -s *usu cap* **1 :** one belonging to either of the Georgian periods; *specif* **:** a poet of the second decade of the 20th century ⟨the *Georgians*' general recommendations were the discarding of archaistic diction . . . and of pomposities generally —Lawrence Durrell⟩ **2 :** Georgian taste or style esp. in architecture

georgian architecture *n, usu cap G* [[5]*Georgian*] **:** architecture of or in the style of the Georgian era, esp. the period 1714–60

georgian furniture *n, usu cap G* **:** furniture of or in the style of the Georgian era, esp. the period 1750–90 — compare ADAM, CHIPPENDALE, HEPPLEWHITE, SHERATON

georgia pine *or* **georgia pitch pine** *or* **georgia yellow pine** *n, usu cap G* **:** LONGLEAF PINE

georgia stock *n, usu cap G* **:** a plow beam with handles and a standard to which a moldboard, shovels, teeth, or sweeps are attached

[1]**geor·gic** \'jȯr|jik, 'jō(ə)|, |jēk\ *n* -s [after the *Georgics*, a poem dealing with agriculture by Vergil (Publius Vergilius Maro) †19 B.C. Roman poet, fr. L *Georgica*, fr. Gk *geōrgika* lands under cultivation (title of a poem about agriculture by Nicander, 2d cent. B.C. Greek poet), fr. neut. pl. of *geōrgikos* agricultural, fr. *geōrgos* farmer (fr. *geō-* ge- + *-ergos*, fr. *ergon* work) + *-ikos* -ic — more at WORK] **:** a poem dealing with agriculture and rural affairs

[2]**georgic** \"\ *also* **geor·gi·cal** \|jəkəl, -jēk-\ *adj* [L *georgicus*, fr. Gk *geōrgikos*] **:** of or relating to agriculture and rural affairs **:** RUSTIC

geor·gi·na gidgee \(')jȯ(r)¦jēnə-\ *n, usu cap 1st G* [fr. *Georgina river*] **:** a scrubby Australian acacia (*Acacia georginae*) of the Georgina river district that much resembles and is sometimes considered a hybrid of the common gidgee and that has been implicated as a causative factor of Georgina River disease in animals that feed on its seed pods

georgina river disease *also* **georgina disease** *n, usu cap G&R* [fr. *Georgina river*, Northern Territory and Queensland, Australia] **:** a severe intoxication of Australian sheep and cattle due to ingestion of poisonous plant material believed to be the seeds of Georgina gidgee

geos *pl of* GEO

geo·science \¦jē(,)ō+\ *n* [*ge-* + *science;* trans. of G *geowissenschaft*] **1 :** the sciences (as geology, physical geography, geomorphology, geophysics, geochemistry) dealing with the earth **2 :** any of the geosciences

ge·o·scop·ic \¦jēə¦skäpik\ *adj* [*geoscopy* + *-ic*] **:** of or relating to geoscopy

ge·os·co·py \jē'äskəpē\ *n* -ES [*ge-* + *-scopy*] **:** knowledge of the earth, ground, or soil gained by inspection

geo·selenic \¦jē(,)ō+\ *adj* [*ge-* + *selenic*] **:** of or relating to the earth and the moon

geo·sere \'jē(,)ō,si(ə)r\ *n* [*ge-* + *sere* (cycle)] **:** a sequence of ecological climax communities following one another through geologic time in response to repeated physical and climatic alteration of a habitat

geo·sphere \'jē(,)ō+,-\ *n* [*ge-* + *sphere*] **1 :** the solid earth — distinguished from *atmosphere* and *hydrosphere* **2 :** one of the shells or spherical layers within the earth delimited above and below by discontinuities

ge·o·spi·za \,jēō'spīzə, jē'äspəzə\ *n, cap* [NL, fr. *ge-* + Gk *spiza*, a kind of finch] **:** a genus of finches of black or dark color confined to the Galápagos islands and commonly considered to form a distinct subfamily of Fringillidae

geo·static \¦jēō+\ *adj* [ISV *ge-* + *static*] **:** relating to pressure exerted by earth or a similar substance

geo·strategic \¦jē(,)ō+\ *adj* **:** of or relating to geostrategy

geo·strategist \"+\ *n* **:** a specialist in geostrategy

geo·strategy \"+\ *n* [*ge-* + *strategy*] **1 :** a branch of geopolitics that deals with strategy **2 :** the combination of geopolitical and strategic factors characterizing a particular geographic region ⟨after a preliminary briefing . . . on the ~ of the Pacific basin —*Jour. of Geol.*⟩ **3 :** the use by a government of strategy based upon geopolitics ⟨German ~ soon gave rise to the first clear exposition of the nature and main features of total war —Andrew Gyorgy⟩

ge·o·stroph·ic \¦jēō¦sträfik\ *adj* [*ge-* + Gk *strophikos* turned, fr. *strophē* action of turning + *-ikos* -ic — more at STROPHE] **:** of or relating to deflective force due to the rotation of the earth

geostrophic wind *n* **:** a wind whose direction and speed are determined by a balance of the pressure-gradient force and the force due to the earth's rotation

geo·synclinal \¦jē(,)ō+\ *adj* **:** of or relating to a geosyncline

geo·syncline *or* **geo·synclinal** \"+\ *n* [*ge-* + *syncline*, *synclinal*] **:** a great downward flexure of the earth's crust — opposed to *geanticline*

ge·o·tac·tic \¦jēō¦taktik\ *adj* [*ge-* + *-tactic*] **:** of or relating to geotaxis — **ge·o·tac·ti·cal·ly** \-tək(ə)lē\ *adv*

ge·o·tax·is \¦jēō¦taksəs\ *or* **ge·o·taxy** \'==,=sē\ *n, pl* **geotax·es** \-k,sēz\ *or* **geotaxies** [*geotaxis*, NL, fr. *ge-* + *taxis; geotaxy* fr. *ge-* + *-taxy*] **:** a taxis in which the force of gravity is the directive factor

geo·technic \¦jēō+\ *adj* [*ge-* + *technic*] **:** of or relating to geotechnics

geo·technics \"+\ *n pl but sing in constr* [*ge-* + *technics*] **:** a science of making the earth more habitable

geo·technology \¦jē(,)ō+\ *n* [*ge-* + *technology*] **:** the application of scientific methods and engineering techniques to the exploitation and utilization of natural resources (as mineral resources)

ge·o·tec·tol·o·gy \,jēō,tek'täləjē\ *n* -ES [*geotectonic* + *-logy*] **:** a study of structural geology

geo·tectonic \¦jēō+\ *adj* [*ge-* + *tectonic*] **:** of or relating to the form, arrangement, and structure of rock masses of the earth's crust **:** STRUCTURAL

geotectonic geology *n* **:** STRUCTURAL GEOLOGY

geo·tectonics \"+\ *n pl but sing in constr* [*ge-* + *tectonics*] **:** STRUCTURAL GEOLOGY

ge·o·teu·this \,jēō'tüthəs, -ō'tyü-\ *n, cap* [NL, fr. *ge-* + Gk *teuthis* squid] **:** a genus of extinct cuttlefishes abundant in the Upper Liassic formations of Europe

ge·o·therm \'jēō,thərm\ *n* -s [*ge-* + *-therm*] **:** a geothermal isopleth

geo·thermal *or* **geo·thermic** \¦jēō+\ *adj* [ISV *ge-* + *thermal*, *thermic*] **:** of or relating to the heat of the earth's interior ⟨economic development of ~ energy —M.P.McIntyre⟩

geothermal gradient *n* **:** the increase in the temperature of the earth from the surface downward averaging about 1°F for each 70 feet

geo·thermometer \¦jē(,)ō+\ *n* [ISV *ge-* + *thermometer*] **1 :** GEOLOGIC THERMOMETER **2 :** a thermometer designed to measure temperatures in deep-sea deposits or in bore holes deep below the surface of the earth

ge·ot·ri·cho·sis \jē,ä·trə'kōsəs\ *n* -ES [NL, fr. *Geotrichum* genus of fungi (fr. *ge-* + *-trichum*, fr. Gk *trich-*, *thrix* hair) + *-osis* — more at TRICHINA] **:** infection of the bronchi or lungs and sometimes the mouth and intestines by certain fungi (genus *Geotrichum*)

ge·o·trop·ic \¦jēə¦träpik\ *adj* [*ge-* + *-tropic*] **:** characterized by, exhibiting, or relating to geotropism — **ge·o·trop·i·cal·ly** \-pək(ə)lē\ *adv*

ge·ot·ro·pism \jē'ä·trə,pizəm\ *n* [ISV *ge-* + *-tropism;* orig. formed as G *geotropismus*] **1 :** tropism in which gravitational attraction is the orienting factor (as in roots growing down, shoots growing up, and the climbing, swimming, or right-side-up orientation of certain animals) **2 :** tropism in which turning or movement is toward rather than away from the earth — compare APOGEOTROPISM

ge·ot·ro·py \jē'ä·trəpē\ *n* -ES [*ge-* + *-tropy*] **:** GEOTROPISM

ge·o·tru·pes \,jēō'trü(,)pēz\ *n, cap* [NL, irreg. fr. *ge-* + Gk *trypē* hole] **:** a genus of bronze or black dung beetles that dig vertical tunnels in the soil and provision them with dung in which their larvae feed and grow

ge·phyr·ea \jə'firēə, jefə'rēə\ *n pl, cap* [NL, fr. Gk *gephyra* bridge; perh. akin to Arm *kamurj* bridge] **:** a prob. artificial group of marine worms variously regarded as a phylum or as a class of Annelida, including Echiuroidea, Sipunculoidea, and Priapuloidea, and comprising worms that are unsegmented as adults and have coeloms and separate sexes and typically a single pair of nephridia — **ge·phyr·e·an** \jə'firēən, ¦jefə¦rēən\ *adj or n*

geph·y·ro·cer·cal \¦jefə(,)rō¦sərkəl\ *adj* [Gk *gephyro-* (fr. *gephyra*) + E *-cercal*] **1 :** having the dorsal and anal fins confluent at the aborted end of the vertebral column of a fish's tail **2 :** having or relating to a gephyrocercal tail — **geph·y·ro·cer·cy** \'===,sərsē\ *n* -ES

gep·i·dae \'jepə,dē, 'ge-\ *or* **gep·ids** \-pədz\ *n pl, cap* [LL *Gepidae*] **:** a Germanic people akin to the Goths and eventually absorbed by the Lombards

ger \'ge(ə)r\ *n, pl* **ge·rim** \'gerəm\ [Heb *gēr*] **1 :** an alien resident in Hebrew territory protected in accordance with early Hebrew law by a native patron from oppression **2 :** PROSELYTE 2

ger *abbr* gerund; gerundial; gerundive

ge·rah *or* **ge·ra** \'girə\ *n* -s [Heb *gērāh*, lit., grain, bean] **:** an ancient Hebrew unit of weight equal to 1/20 shekel

ge·ra·ni·a·ce·ae \jə,rānē'āsē,ē\ *n pl, cap* [NL, fr. *Geranium*, type genus + *-aceae*] **:** a family of mostly herbaceous plants (order Geraniales) having chiefly opposite or whorled leaves and flowers with one-seeded carpels that separate individually from a central column when ripe — **ge·ra·ni·a·ceous** \-;=='āshəs\ *adj*

[1]**ge·ra·ni·al** \jə'rānē,al\ *n* -s [ISV *gerani-* (fr. NL *Geranium*) + *-al* (aldehyde)] **:** the trans form of citral

[2]**ge·ra·ni·al** \-nēəl\ *adj* [NL *Geraniales*] **:** of or relating to the order Geraniales

ge·ra·ni·a·les \jə,rānē'ā(,)lēz\ *n pl, cap* [NL, fr. *Geranium* + *-ales*] **:** an order of mostly herbaceous or shrubby dicotyledonous plants that have 5-parted regular flowers with stamens usu. a multiple of the number of sepals and a syncarpous ovary and that include the geraniums and cranesbills, wood sorrels, jewelweeds, flaxes, and a large but variable number of related plants — see EUPHORBIACEAE, GERANIACEAE

ge·ran·ic acid \jə'ranik-\ *n* [ISV *geraniol* + *-ic*] **:** a liquid unsaturated acid $C_9H_{15}COOH$ formed by oxidation of citral or geraniol

ge·ra·ni·ol \jə'rānē,ȯl, -,ōl\ *n* -s [ISV *gerani-* (fr. NL *Geranium*) + *-ol*] **:** a fragrant liquid unsaturated alcohol $C_{10}H_{17}OH$ that occurs both free and combined in many essential oils (as geranium, palmarosa, and citronella oils) and is used chiefly in rose and other perfumes and in soap — compare CITRAL, NEROL

ge·ra·ni·um \jə'rānēəm, -nyəm\ *n* [NL, fr. L *geranion*, *geranium*, any of several plants of the family Geraniaceae, fr. Gk *geranion*, dim. of *geranos* crane — more at CRANE] **1 a** *cap* **:** a widely distributed genus of plants (family Geraniaceae) having regular flowers without spurs and with glands that alternate with the petals — see WILD GERANIUM **b** -s **:** the dried rhizomes of the wild geranium (*G. maculatum*) formerly used as an astringent **2** -s **a :** any plant of the genus *Geranium* **b :** PELARGONIUM 2 — see FISH GERANIUM **3** -s **a :** a strong red that is yellower and lighter than geranium red, paler than Goya, and bluer and lighter than average cherry red **b** *of textiles* **:** a vivid red that is bluer, lighter, and slightly stronger than apple red and bluer, lighter, and stronger than carmine or scarlet

geranium lake *n* **1 :** any of various brilliant red lakes made from eosin **2 :** a vivid red that is lighter and slightly yellower and stronger than apple red, yellower, lighter, and stronger than carmine, and bluer, lighter, and stronger than scarlet — called also *spark*

geranium oil *n* **1 :** a pale yellow or greenish essential oil that has an odor like that of roses, that is obtained from various plants of the genus *Pelargonium*, and that is used chiefly in perfumes and soap **2 :** PALMAROSA OIL

geranium pink *n* **1 :** a variable color averaging a moderate to strong pink that is redder than nymph pink and bluer and darker than peachblossom **2 :** a deep pink that is bluer, lighter, and stronger than average coral (sense 3b) and bluer and deeper than fiesta — called also *Bermuda*

geranium red *n* **:** a strong red that is bluer and darker than geranium (sense 3a) or average cherry red and bluer, less strong, and slightly lighter than Goya

geranium rose *n* **:** a variable color averaging a moderate red that is bluer, lighter, and stronger than cerise or claret, bluer and lighter than average cherry, and yellower, lighter, and stronger than carnation red

ge·ra·nyl \jəˈrānᵊl, -ā,nil, ˈjerə,nil\ *n* -s [*geraniol* + *-yl*] **:** a univalent radical $C_{10}H_{17}$ that is derived from geraniol ⟨~ acetate⟩

ge·rar·dia \jəˈrärdēə\ *n* [NL, fr. John *Gerard* †1612 Eng. botanist + NL *-ia*] **1** *cap* **:** a genus of annual or perennial herbs (family Scrophulariaceae) that are often root-parasitic and have showy pink, purple, or yellow flowers with the corolla often distended on the lower side **2** -s **:** any plant of the genus *Gerardia* — see FALSE FOXGLOVE

geras *pl of* GERA

ger·a·sene \ˈgerə,sēn, ˈje-, ,==ˈ=\ *or* **ger·ge·sene** \ˈgərgə,-, ,==ˈ=\ *n* -s *cap* [LL *Gerasenus, Gergesenus*, fr. Gk *Gerasēnos, Gergesēnos*, fr. *Gerasa, Gergesa* ancient town in Palestine] **:** an inhabitant of the ancient Palestinian town Gerasa

ger·ate \ˈje,rāt\ *vt* -ED/-ING/-S [ME *geratten*] **:** to powder or spot (a shield) with such heraldic charges as mullets or roundels

ge·rat·ic \jəˈrad·ik\ *adj* [Gk *gērat-, gēras* old age + E -ic — more at CORN] **:** of or relating to old age **:** GERONTIC

ger·a·to·log·ic \,jerətəˈläjik\ *or* **ger·a·tol·o·gous** \,jerəˈtäləgəs\ *adj* **:** of or relating to geratology

ger·a·tol·o·gy \,jerəˈtäləjē\ *n* -ES [Gk *gērat-, gēras* + E *-logy*] **:** a scientific study of aging and its phenomena esp. as exhibited in biological groups nearing extinction

gerbe *or* **gerb** \ˈjərb\ *n* -s [F *gerbe*, lit., sheaf, fr. OF *jarbe*, of Gmc origin; akin to OHG *garba* sheaf — more at GARB] **:** a firework throwing a shower of sparks

ger·bera \ˈgərbərə, ˈjərb-, jərˈberə\ *n* [NL, after Traugott *Gerber* (*Gerberus*) †1743, Ger. naturalist] **1** *cap* **:** a genus of southern African or Asiatic herbs (family Compositae) having basal tufted leaves and solitary heads of yellow, pink, or orange flowers with prominent rays — see TRANSVAAL DAISY **2** -s **:** any plant or flower of the genus *Gerbera*

ger·ber convention \ˈgərbər-\ *n, usu cap G* [after John *Gerber*, 20th cent. Am. who devised it] **:** a bidding method in contract bridge that is based on the Blackwood convention and that uses a bid of four clubs instead of four no-trump as the asking bid, with responses of four diamonds to show no ace, four hearts one ace, four spades two aces, four no-trump three aces, and five clubs four aces

ger·bil \ˈjərbəl\ *or* **ger·bille** \", jərˈbē\ *n* -s [F *gerbille*, fr. NL *Gerbillus*] **:** any of numerous Old World burrowing desert rodents of *Gerbillus* and related genera that have long hind legs well adapted for leaping

ger·bil·lus \jərˈbiləs\ *n, cap* [NL, dim. of *gerboa, jerboa*, fr. Ar *yarbūʽ*] **:** a genus of rodents that constitutes with various related genera a subfamily of Cricetidae and comprises typical gerbils of Africa and Asia

ge·re·fa \yeˈrā(,)vä\ *n* -s [OE *gerēfa* — more at REEVE] **:** an administrative officer in Anglo-Saxon England

ge·rent \ˈjirənt\ *n* -s [L *gerent-, gerens*, pres. part. of *gerere* to bear, wage, cherish, manage — more at CAST] **:** one that rules or manages

ger·e·nuk \ˈgerə,nu̇k, gəˈrenək\ *n* -s [Somali *garanug*] **:** a long-necked antelope (*Litocranius walleri*) native to eastern Africa

gerfalcon *var of* GYRFALCON

gergesene *cap, var of* GERASENE

ger·hardt·ite \ˈger,härd·,īt\ *n* -s [Charles F. *Gerhardt* †1856 Fr. chemist + E *-ite*] **:** a mineral $Cu_2(NO_3)(OH)_3$ consisting of an emerald-green basic copper nitrate

ger·i·at·ric \,jerēˈa·trik, -rēk\ *adj* [Gk *gēras* old age + E *iatric* — more at CORN] **1 :** of or relating to geriatrics ⟨the ~ department of the hospital⟩ **2 :** of or relating to the aged or the process of aging ⟨significant ~ disorders⟩

ger·i·a·tri·cian \,jerēəˈtrishən\ *or* **geri·atrist** \,jerēˈa·trəst, ˈ==,== *also* jəˈrīə·t-\ *n* -s [*geriatrics* + *-ian* or *-ist*] **:** a specialist in geriatrics

ger·i·at·rics \,jerēˈa·triks, -rēks\ *n pl but sing in constr* [Gk *gēras* + E *-iatrics*] **:** a branch of medicine that deals with the problems and diseases of old age and aging people — compare GERONTOLOGY

gerim *pl of* GER

gerio·psychosis \ˈjiˌrē(,)ō, ˈjeˌ\ *n* [NL, fr. *gerio-* (fr. *gēras* old age) + *psychosis*] **:** SENILE PSYCHOSIS

gerkin *var of* GHERKIN

[1]**germ** \ˈjərm, ˈjəm, ˈjəim\ *n* -s *often attrib* [F *germe*, fr. L *germin-, germen*, alter. of (assumed) OL *genmin-, genmen*, fr. L *gen-*, stem of *gignere* to beget — more at KIN] **1 a :** a small mass of living substance capable of developing into an animal or plant or into an organ or part **:** BUD, SEED ⟨supernumerary tooth ~s may cause formation of supernumerary teeth —K.H. Thoma⟩ **b :** the embryo with the scutellum of a cereal grain that usu. is separated from the starchy endosperm during the milling ⟨the ~ of the wheat grain is very rich in oil content — Leslie Smith⟩ **2 a :** something from which development takes place or that serves or may serve as an origin **:** BEGINNING, RUDIMENT ⟨the Rule of St. Benedict . . . already contains the small ~ of that freedom and movement which developed in every branch of life —R.W.Southern⟩ **b :** HOMOEOMERY 1 **3 :** MICROORGANISM ⟨pathogenic bacteria are ~s⟩ ⟨virus ~⟩ **:** MICROBE, DISEASE GERM ⟨the cecal worm carries the ~ of blackhead in turkeys —B.F.Kaupp & R.C.Surface⟩ **syn** see MICROORGANISM

[2]**germ** \"\ *vb* -ED/-ING/-S **:** GERMINATE

[1]**ger·man** \ˈjərmən, ˈjəm-, ˈjəim-\ *archaic var of* GERMANE

[2]**german** \"\ *n* -s [MF *germain* brother, cousin, fr. *germain*, adj., having the same parents, fr. L *germanus*, irreg. fr. *germin-, germen* + *-anus* -an] *obs* **:** a near relative ⟨you'll have coursers for cousins, and gennets for ~s —Shak.⟩

[3]**german** \"\ *n* -s [ML *Germanus*, fr. L, any member of the Germanic peoples that inhabited western Europe in Roman times] **1** *cap* **a :** a native or inhabitant of Germany **b :** a person of German descent **2** *cap* **a :** the West Germanic language spoken mainly in Germany, Austria, and parts of Switzerland — see HIGH GERMAN, LOW GERMAN; INDO-EUROPEAN LANGUAGES table **b :** the literary and official language of Germany — called also *High German;* see MIDDLE HIGH GERMAN, OLD HIGH GERMAN **3** *cap* **:** one who speaks the German language or its dialectal variants outside Germany (as a Swiss German) **4** *sometimes cap* **a** *or* **german cotillion :** a dance consisting of capriciously involved figures intermingled with waltzes **b** *chiefly Midland* **:** a dancing party; *specif* **:** one at which the german is danced **5** *usu cap* **:** ALBACORE 1

[4]**german** \"\ *adj, usu cap* [L *Germanus* of or relating to the Germanic peoples that inhabited western Europe in Roman times] **1 a :** of, relating to, or characteristic of Germany **b :** of, relating to, or characteristic of the Germans **2 :** of, relating to, or characteristic of the German language — **ger·man·ly** *adv, usu cap*

[1]**german–american** \ˈ===ˈ===\ *n, usu cap G&A* **:** an American of German ancestry

[2]**german–american** \"\ *adj, usu cap G&A* **:** of, relating to, or having the characteristics of a German-American

german band *n, usu cap G* **:** a street band

german baptist brethren *n pl, usu cap G & both Bs* **:** DUNKERS — not used officially since 1908

german bee *n, usu cap G* **:** BLACK BEE

german bezoar *n, usu cap G* **:** a bezoar composed of interlaced fibers of hair with organic cementing matter

german brown *or* **german brown trout** *n, usu cap G* **:** BROWN TROUT

german carp *n, usu cap G* **:** CARP 1a

german catchfly *n, usu cap G* **:** a Eurasian perennial herb (*Lychnis viscaria*) with red or purple flowers that has viscid patches on the stem below the flower clusters and is used as an ornamental

german chamomile *n, usu cap G* **:** a wild chamomile (*Matricaria chamomilla*) with a fragrance like that of a pineapple

german chamomile oil *n, usu cap G* **:** CHAMOMILE OIL b

german coach *n, usu cap G&C* **:** a German breed of large rather coarse heavy harness horses that are bay, brown, or black in color

german cockroach *n, usu cap G* **:** CROTON BUG

ger·man·der \jərˈmandər, ˈjər,m-\ *n* -s [ME *germaunder*, fr. MF *germandree*, fr. ML *germandrea*, alter. of L *chamaedrys*, fr. Gk *chamaidrys*, fr. *chamai* on the ground + *drys* oak, tree — more at HUMBLE, TREE] **1 :** a plant of the genus *Teucrium* — see AMERICAN GERMANDER, WALL GERMANDER **2 :** any of several plants of the genus *Veronica; esp* **:** GERMANDER SPEEDWELL 1

germander sage *n* **:** WATER GERMANDER

germander speedwell *n* **1 :** an Old World speedwell (*Veronica chamaedrys*) with leaves resembling those of the wall germander **2** *also* **germander chickweed :** FIELD SPEEDWELL

[1]**ger·mane** \jə(r)ˈmān, ˈjər,m-, (ˈ)jə̄ˌm-, (ˈ)jəiˌm-\ *adj* [ME *germain, germane*, lit., having the same parents, fr. MF *germain* — more at GERMAN] **1** *archaic* **:** true or complete **:** GENUINE **2** *obs* **:** closely akin **3 :** having a close relationship **:** APPROPRIATE, PERTINENT ⟨their bizarre ideas . . . were scarcely ~ to the central lines of medieval thought —H.O. Taylor⟩ **syn** see RELEVANT

[2]**germane** \"\ *n* -s [ISV, fr. NL *germanium* + ISV *methane*] **1 :** a compound of germanium and hydrogen; *specif* **:** the tetrahydride GeH_4 obtained as a colorless gas of nauseating odor by reducing other germanium compounds **2 :** a derivative (as trichloro-germane $GeHCl_3$) of a germane

ger·mane·ly *adv* **:** in a germane manner

ger·mane·ness \-ānnəs\ *n* -ES **:** the quality or state of being germane

german fingering *n, usu cap G* **:** marking on piano music that indicates the thumb by the figure 1 and the fingers by the figures 2, 3, 4, and 5 — compare AMERICAN FINGERING

german flute *n, usu cap G* **:** the modern flute

german fried potatoes *n pl, usu cap G* **:** raw or cooked potatoes sliced and fried in a skillet

german gold *n, usu cap G* **:** DUTCH METAL

[1]**ger·man·ic** \jə(r)ˈmanik, ˈjərˌm-, (ˈ)jə̄ˌm-, (ˈ)jəiˌm-, -nēk\ *adj, usu cap* [ML & L; ML *Germanicus* German, fr. L, of the Germanic peoples in western Europe in Roman times, fr. *Germanus* member of such people + *-icus* -ic] **1 a :** GERMAN **b :** of a more or less German nature **:** having characteristics that are somewhat German **2 :** of, relating to, or characteristic of the Teutons **:** TEUTONIC **3 :** of, relating to, or constituting Germanic

[2]**germanic** \"\ *n* -s *cap* **:** a branch of the Indo-European language family containing English, German, Dutch, Afrikaans, Flemish, Frisian, the Scandinavian languages, and Gothic — called also *Teutonic;* see INDO-EUROPEAN LANGUAGES table

[3]**germanic** \", -mān-\ *adj* [NL *germanium* + E *-ic*] **:** of, relating to, or containing germanium — used esp. of compounds in which this element is tetravalent

germanic consonant shift *n, cap G* **:** CONSONANT SHIFT 1

ger·man·ics \(,)=ˈmaniks, -nēks\ *n pl but sing in constr, usu cap* **:** a study of Germanic languages **:** Germanic philology

ger·man·i·fy \-nə,fī\ *vt* -ED/-ING/-ES *often cap* [[4]*German* + *-ify*] **:** to make German in quality or character **:** GERMANIZE 2

ger·ma·nin \-ˈmānən\ *n* -s [ISV *german-* (fr. NL *germanium*) + *-in*] **:** SURAMIN

german iris *n, usu cap G* **1 :** any of several Old World bearded irises: as **a :** a large purple-flowered to white-flowered iris (*Iris germanica*) native to central and southern Europe **b :** any of several chiefly European irises (as *I. kochii* and *I. flavescens*) usu. considered to be closely related to or sometimes varieties of the German iris (*I. germanica*) **2 :** any of numerous tall bearded horticultural irises derived from the wild German irises (esp. *Iris germanica*) by hybridization and selection

ger·man·ish \ˈjərmənish\ *adj, usu cap* **:** GERMANIC 1b

ger·man·ism \ˈjərmə,nizəm, ˈjəm-, ˈjəim-\ *n* -s *usu cap* **1 :** a characteristic feature of German occurring in another language or dialect **2 :** allegiance to or partiality for Germany or German customs and culture **3 :** the policies, practices, or objectives believed to be distinctive of Germany or the German people

ger·man·ist \-nəst\ *n* -s *usu cap* [G, fr. L *Germania* land occupied by the Germanic peoples in western Europe in Roman times + G *-ist*] **1 :** a specialist in the German language, Germanics, or German literature and culture **2 :** an historian who magnifies the influence of Germanic institutions in the development of European civilization — compare ROMANIST

ger·man·is·tic \ˈ=məˈnistik, -tēk\ *adj, usu cap* **:** of or relating to Germanistics or Germanists

ger·man·is·tics \,==ˈ=stiks, -tēks\ *n pl but sing in constr, usu cap* [G *Germanistik*, fr. *Germanist* + *-ik* -ics] **:** GERMANICS

ger·ma·nite \ˈ==,nīt\ *n* -s [ISV *germ-* (fr. NL *germanium*) + *-ite;* orig. formed as G *germanit*] **:** a mineral $Cu_3(Ge,Fe,etc.)(S,As)_4$ consisting of a copper iron germanium sulfide occurring in metallic reddish gray masses

[1]**germanity** *n* -ES [*germane* + *-ity*] *obs* **:** KINSHIP

[2]**ger·man·i·ty** \jə(r)ˈmanəd·ē, ,jərˈ-, jə̄ˈ-, jəiˈ-, -nətē, -iˈ\ *n* -ES *usu cap* [[4]*german* + *-ity*] **:** the quality or spirit characteristic of Germany or the Germans ⟨an Aryan God who is no more than a concept of composite *Germanity* —Theodore Maynard⟩

ger·ma·ni·um \jə(r)ˈmānēəm, ,jərˈ-, jə̄ˈ-, jəiˈ-\ *n* -s [NL, fr. ML *Germania* Germany (fr. L, land inhabited by the Germanic peoples in Roman times) + NL *-ium*] **:** a grayish white hard brittle metalloid element resembling silicon but with a valence of 2 as well as 4 that occurs combined esp. in rare minerals (as germanite and argyrodite), in the ash of some lignites and coals, and in zinc-refinery residues from which it is recovered by conversion to its volatile tetrachloride, and that is used as a semiconductor (as in transistors) — symbol *Ge;* see ELEMENT table

german ivy *n, usu cap G* **:** a twining or creeping southern African plant (*Senecio mikanioides*) with yellow flowers and leaves resembling those of ivy

ger·man·iza·tion \,jərmənəˈzāshən, ,jəm-, ,jəim-, -,nīˈz-\ *n* -s *often cap* **:** the act or process of germanizing or the state of being germanized

ger·man·ize \ˈ==,nīz\ *vb* -ED/-ING/-S *often cap* [[4]*german* + *-ize*] *vt* **1** *archaic* **:** to translate into German **2 a :** to cause to acquire German customs or attitudes; *esp* **:** to force into conformity with German cultural patterns or governmental policies ⟨cities of the Polish Corridor . . . were *germanized* when the Nazis took over —Mario Pei⟩ **b :** to give a German quality to (speech or writing) by the use of German words or grammatical constructions ~ *vi* **:** to adopt German customs and manners or become German in sympathies and predilections

german knot *n, usu cap G* **:** a figure-eight knot

german knotgrass *n, usu cap G* **:** KNAWEL

german lilac *n, usu cap G* **:** RED VALERIAN

german madwort *n, usu cap G* **:** a low hairy annual herb (*Asperugo procumbens*) of the family Boraginaceae with blue flowers and a root used as a substitute for madder

german measles *n pl but sing in constr, usu cap G* **:** RUBELLA

german millet *n, usu cap G* **:** a foxtail millet (*Setaria italica stramineofructa*) with yellow fruits in large drooping often lobed spikes — called also *golden wonder millet;* compare SIBERIAN MILLET

[1]**germano-** *comb form, usu cap* [NL, fr. ML *Germanus* German, fr. L, any member of the Germanic peoples inhabiting western Europe in Roman times] **:** German ⟨*Germanophile*⟩ **:** German and ⟨*Germano-*Russian⟩

[2]**germano-** *comb form* [ISV, fr. NL *germanium*] **:** germanium — esp. in names of compounds containing germanium in place of carbon ⟨*germano*chloroform $GeHCl_3$⟩

[1]**ger·man·o·phile** \jə(r)ˈmanə,fīl, ,jərˈ-, jə̄ˈ-, jəiˈ-\ *or* **ger·man·o·phil** \-,fil\ *adj, usu cap* [[1]*Germano-* + *-phile, -phil*] **:** approving or favoring the German people and their institutions and customs

[2]**germanophile** \"\ *or* **germanophil** \"\ *n, usu cap* **:** one who is Germanophile

ger·man·o·phobe \-,fōb\ *n* -s *usu cap* [[1]*Germano-* + *-phobe*] **:** one having Germanophobia

ger·mano·pho·bia \(,)=,==ˈfōbēə; ,jərmanōˈf-, ,jəm-, ,jəim-\ *n, usu cap* [NL, fr. [1]*Germano-* + *-phobia*] **:** an intense dislike or fear of Germany and German characteristics, customs, and governmental activities ⟨~ . . . continues extremely strong in France —D.F.Schoenbrun⟩

ger·ma·nous \(ˈ)jərˈmānəs\ *adj* [NL *germanium* + E *-ous*] **:** of, relating to, or containing germanium in the bivalent state

german pancake *n, usu cap G* **:** a pancake oven-cooked in a skillet until brown and puffy

german process *n, usu cap G* **1 :** the process of reducing copper ore in a blast furnace after roasting **2 :** the discontinuous or batch method of cupeling lead bullion

german reformed *adj, cap G&R* **:** of or relating to the Reformed Church in the United States that derives from the Reformed Church of Germany and whose first synod was organized in 1747

german roach *n, usu cap G* **:** CROTON BUG

german rum *n, usu cap G* **:** a Jamaica rum very highly flavored esp. for export to Europe

germans *pl of* GERMAN

german script *n, usu cap G* **:** a cursive handwriting used extensively in German-speaking countries since the 15th century

german sesame oil *n, usu cap G* **:** CAMELINE OIL

german shepherd *or* **german shepherd dog** *or* **german police dog** *n, usu cap G* **:** a shepherd dog of a breed originating in northern Europe at an uncertain date that has a long well-muscled body, a long wedge-shaped head, powerful jaws, a long bushy tail, and a smooth coat varying in color from white through all the shades and mixtures to black but with wolf coloring, tans, mixed brown, brindle, and black predominating, is 22 to 26 inches in height, is intelligent and responsive and trains well, and is often used as a guard dog, in police work, and as a guide dog for the blind — called also *Alsatian*

german shorthaired pointer *n, usu cap G* **:** a liver or liver-and-white hunting dog of a breed developed in Germany by crossing the Spanish pointer with the bloodhound and mating the offspring with the common pointer

german silver *n, usu cap G* **:** NICKEL SILVER

german sixth *n, usu cap G* **:** an augmented sixth chord consisting of a musical tone with its major third, perfect fifth, and augmented sixth above the lowest tone (as A♭, C, E♭, F♯)

german tamarisk *n, usu cap G* **:** a Eurasian shrub (*Myricaria germanica*) of the family Tamaricaceae that resembles the tamarisk

ger·man·town \ˈjərmən·,tau̇n, ˈjəm-,ˈjəim-\ *n* -s *usu cap* [fr. *Germantown*, Pa.] **1** *or* **germantown wagon :** a four-wheeled one-horse covered wagon **2 :** a lightly twisted yarn usu. of 4-ply worsted used esp. for knitting and crocheting

ger·ma·ny \-mənē, -ni *also* -mn-\ *adj, usu cap* [fr. *Germany*, country in central Europe] **:** of or from Germany **:** of the kind or style prevalent in Germany **:** GERMAN

ger·mar·i·um \(,)jərˈma(a)rēəm\ *n* -s [NL, fr. *germen* + *-arium*] **:** the egg-producing part of the ovary in many flatworms and rotifers; *also* **:** the corresponding part of a testis — distinguished from *vitellarium*

germ band *n* **:** the thickening of the blastoderm of an insect egg from which the embryo proper arises

germ cell *n* **:** a cell set apart from the rest of the body to develop usu. after union with another of the opposite sex into a new individual **:** an egg or sperm cell or one of their antecedent cells — distinguished from *somatic cell*

germ center *n* **:** the lightly staining central proliferative area of a lymphoid follicle

germ disc *n* **:** GERMINAL DISC

germed *past of* GERM

ger·men \ˈjərmən, -,men\ *n* -s [L — more at GERM] **1** *archaic* **a:** the rudiment of an organism **:** GERM **b :** a young branch **:** SHOOT **2** [NL, fr. L] **a :** GONAD **b :** the germ cells and their precursors

germfree \ˈ=ˌ=\ *adj* [*germ* + *free*] **:** free of microorganisms **:** AXENIC

germ gland *n* **:** GONAD

ger·mi·ci·dal \ˌjərməˌsīdᵊl, ˌjəm-, ˌjəim-\ *adj* **:** of or relating to a germicide **:** destroying germs

ger·mi·cide \ˈ==,sīd\ *n* -s [[1]*germ* + *-i-* + *-cide*] **:** an agent that destroys germs (as disease germs) **:** BACTERICIDE — compare ANTISEPTIC, DISINFECTANT

germier *comparative of* GERMY

germiest *superlative of* GERMY

ger·mi·na·bil·i·ty \,==nəˈbiləd·ē, -ətē, -i\ *n* -ES **:** the capacity to germinate ⟨the ~ of the seed⟩

ger·mi·na·ble \ˈ==nəbəl\ *adj* [*germinate* + *-able*] **:** capable of germination

ger·mi·nal \ˈ=mənᵊl\ *adj* [F, fr. L *germin-, germen* + F *-al*] **1 a :** being in the germ or earliest stage of development **:** INCIPIENT, EMBRYONIC ⟨the ~ philosophical ideas underlying western culture —*Bull. of Bates Coll.*⟩ **b :** creative or productive esp. of new ideas or forces ⟨a highly original and ~ critic —Malcolm Ross⟩ **2 a :** of, relating to, or having the characteristics of a germ or germ cell **b :** of, relating to, or resembling the cells or tissues characteristic of the early stage of an embryo — **ger·mi·nal·ly** \-ᵊlē, -ᵊli\ *adv*

germinal apparatus *n* **:** EGG APPARATUS

germinal area *n* **:** the part of the blastoderm that forms the embryo proper of an amniote vertebrate

germinal cell *n* **:** an embryonic cell of the early vertebrate nervous system that is the source of neuroblasts and neuroglial cells

germinal center *n* **:** GERM CENTER

germinal disc *n* **1 :** BLASTODISC **2 :** GERMINAL AREA

germinal epithelium *n* **:** the epithelial covering of the genital ridges and of the gonads derived from them — see PRIMORDIAL OVUM

germinal layer *n* **1 :** GERM LAYER **2 :** a layer of cells from which new tissue is constantly formed; *specif* **:** the innermost layer of the epidermis

germinal membrane *n* **:** BLASTODERM

germinal vesicle *n* **:** the enlarged nucleus of the primary oocyte prior to completion of the reduction divisions

ger·mi·nant \ˈjərmənənt, ˈjəm-,ˈjəim-\ *adj* [L *germinant-, germinans*, pres. part. of *germinare*] **:** germinating or having the capacity to grow or develop ⟨the tendency to proselytize . . . was ~ in Israelitish religion —Moses Buttenwieser⟩

ger·mi·nate \-mə,nāt, *usu* -ād·+V\ *vb* -ED/-ING/-S [L *germinatus*, past part. of *germinare* to sprout, put forth, fr. *germin-, germen* bud, sprout, germ — more at GERM] *vt* **1 :** to cause to sprout or grow ⟨~ a broad bean on damp flannel — John Percival⟩ **2 :** to cause to originate or develop ⟨until recently the university presses *germinated* no ideas at all — M.S.Watson⟩ ~ *vi* **1** *archaic* **:** to shoot forth like a plant **:** EFFLORESCE ⟨the stone on which the native alum . . . ~s is black and shining —William Brownrigg⟩ **2 :** to begin to grow **:** SPROUT — used esp. of a spore or seed ⟨the seed . . . ~s on access of water, air, and warmth —W.F.Ganong⟩ **3 :** to come into being **:** EVOLVE ⟨before Western civilization began to ~ — A.L.Kroeber⟩

ger·mi·na·tion \,==ˈnāshən\ *n* -s [L *germination-, germinatio*, fr. *germinatus* + *-ion-, -io* -ion] **1 :** the beginning, process, or result of germinating: **a :** the initial development of a spore involving either production of a germ tube or internal breakup ⟨the first stage in ~ of a spore is the absorption of water —George Smith⟩ **b :** the resumption of growth by the embryo in a seed after planting that involves the development of a young plant from the embryo after a period of dormancy **:** SPROUTING ⟨~ starts when the seed coat is broken —F.S. Baker⟩ **c :** the development of a bud **d :** the production of a pollen tube by a pollen grain **2 :** the beginning of growth or development **:** EVOLUTION ⟨the ~ of newer and more tentative ideas —J.T.Edsall⟩

ger·mi·na·tive \'⸗⸗,nā|d·|iv, -,nə|, |t|, |ēv *also* |əv\ *adj* **:** of or relating to germination: **a :** having the power to germinate ⟨~ and virulent spores⟩ **b :** having the power to develop **:** EVOLVING ⟨afraid of falsifying his ~ perceptions by working over his drafts —*Brit. Bk. News*⟩ — **ger·mi·na·tive·ly** \|əvlē, -li\ *adv*

germinative vesicle *n* **:** GERMINAL VESICLE

ger·mi·na·tor \-,nād·ə(r), -ātə-\ *n* -s **1 :** one that germinates seeds **2 :** a cabinet or other container in which moistened seeds are tested for their ability to germinate

germing *adj* [fr. pres. part. of ²germ] **:** RUDIMENTARY, UNDEVELOPED

ger·mi·par·i·ty \,jərmə'parəd·ē\ *n* -ES [*germ* + *-i-* + L *parere* to produce + E *-ity* — more at PARE] **:** reproduction by germs — **ger·mip·a·rous** \(¦)jər¦mipərəs\ *adj*

ger·mis·ton \'jərməstən\ *adj, usu cap* [fr. *Germiston,* Union of So. Africa] **:** of or from the city of Germiston, Union of South Africa **:** of the kind or style prevalent in Germiston

germ layer *n* **:** any of the three primary layers of cells in the embryos of triploblastic animals that are differentiated during and immediately following gastrulation and that are precursors of the various tissues and organs of the adult — see ECTODERM, ENDODERM, MESODERM

germ·less \'⸗ləs\ *adj* **:** free from germs

germ line *or* **germ track** *n* **:** the sequence of cells from zygote to functional germ cell **:** GERM PLASM

germ·ling \'⸗liŋ\ *n* -s [¹*germ* + *-ling*] **:** a young gametophyte produced by the germination of a tetraspore; *also* **:** a young sporophyte

germ nucleus *n* **:** the nucleus of the egg or sperm cell

ger·mon \zhermōⁿ\ *n, pl* **germons** \-ōⁿ(z)\ [F] **:** ALBACORE 1

germ peg \'jərm-\ *n* [by folk etymology fr. *gem peg*] **:** GIM PEG

germ plasm *n* **1 :** germ cells and their precursors regarded as bearers of hereditary characters and as at all times fundamentally independent of other body cells **2 :** the hereditary material of the germ cells **:** GENES

germ pore *n* **:** a pore, pit, or thin area in the outer wall of a spore or pollen grain through which the germ tube or pollen tube makes its exit on germination

germproof \'⸗¦⸗\ *adj* **:** impervious to the penetration or action of germs

germs *pl of* GERM, *pres 3d sing of* GERM

germ separator *n* **:** a tank or other device for floating off the detached germs from the wet-milled grains of corn or sorghum in a starch factory

germ theory *n* **:** a theory in medicine: infections, contagious diseases, and certain other conditions (as suppurative lesions) result from the action of microorganisms

germ tube *n* **:** the slender tubular outgrowth first produced by most spores in germination

germ·ule \'jər(,)myül\ *n* -s [¹*germ* + *-ule*] **:** a small germ

germ warfare *n* **:** the use of germs or harmful bacteria as weapons in war ⟨charges about *germ warfare* which bacteriological experts have demonstrated to be false —*Foreign Policy Bull.*⟩

germy \'jərmē\ *adj, often* -ER/-EST [¹*germ* + *-y*] **:** full of germs ⟨the water in New York Harbor is oily, dirty, and ~ —Joseph Mitchell⟩

ger·o·der·ma \,jerō'dərmə\ *or* **ger·o·der·mia** \-mēə\ *n* -s [NL, irreg. fr. Gk *gerōn* old man + NL *-derma* or *-dermia*] **:** premature aging of the skin (as in Simmonds' disease)

ge·ron·i·mo \jə'ränə,mō\ *interj, usu cap* [after *Geronimo* †1900 Apache Indian chief] — used as a battle cry by paratroopers typically at the moment of jumping

geront- *or* **geronto-** *comb form* [F, *géront-, géronto-,* fr. Gk *geront-, geronto-,* fr. *geront-, gerōn* old man; akin to Gk *gēras* old age — more at CORN] **:** old age ⟨*gerontology*⟩

ge·ron·tal \jə'ränt°l\ *adj* [*geront-* + *-al*] **:** GERONTIC

ge·ron·tic \-tik\ *adj* [Gk *gerontikos* of or for old men, like an old man, fr. *geront-, gerōn* old man + *-ikos* -ic] **:** of or relating to decadence or old age

ger·on·toc·ra·cy \,jerən·'täkrəsē, -,rän-·\ *n* -ES [F *gérontocratie,* fr. *géronto-* geront- + *-cratie* -cracy] **:** rule by elders; *specif* **:** a form of social organization in which a group of old men or a council of elders dominates or exercises control — **ge·ron·to·crat** \jə'räntə,krat\ *n* -s — **ge·ron·to·crat·ic** \⸗¦⸗⸗¦krad·ik\ *adj*

ge·ron·to·ge·ous \jə¦räntō¦jēəs\ *adj* [*geront-* + *ge-* + *-ous*] **:** of or relating to the Old World or the eastern hemisphere

ge·ron·to·log·i·cal \jə¦räntō¦läjəkəl, ¦jeränt°l¦ä-\ *adj* **:** of or relating to gerontology ⟨~ research⟩

ger·on·tol·o·gist \,jerən·'täləjəst, -,rän-·\ *n* -s **:** a specialist in gerontology

ger·on·tol·o·gy \-jē,-ji\ *n* -ES [ISV *geront-* + *-logy*] **:** a scientific study of the phenomena of aging and of the problems of the aged — compare GERIATRICS

ge·ron·to·mor·phic \jə¦räntō¦mȯrfik\ *adj* [*geront-* + *-morphic*] **:** characterized by physical specialization most fully developed in the old male of a species ⟨~ traits⟩

ge·ron·to·mor·pho·sis \⸗,⸗⸗'mȯrfəsəs *sometimes* -,mȯr'fōsəs\ *n* -ES [NL, fr. *geront-* + *-morphosis*] **1 :** phylogenetic change involving specialization of the characters of adult organisms and accompanied by decreased capacity for further change **2 :** tendency toward racial senescence — compare FETALIZATION, PAEDOMORPHOSIS

ge·ron·to·phil·ia \jə,räntō'filēə\ *n* -s [NL, fr. *geront-* + *-philia*] **:** sex attraction toward old persons

-gerous \j(ə)rəs\ *adj comb form* [L *-ger* (fr. *gerere* to bear, wage, cherish) or F *-gère* (fr. L *-ger*) + E *-ous* — more at CAST] **:** bearing, producing — preceded by *i* ⟨crystalli*gerous*⟩ ⟨denti*gerous*⟩

ge·rou·sia *also* **ge·ru·sia** \jə'rüzh(ē)ə\ *n* -s *usu cap* [L & Gk; L *gerusia,* fr. Gk *gerousia,* fr. *geront-, geron* old, old man + *-ia* -y] **1 :** a council of elders in ancient Greece; *specif* **:** the Spartan senate **2 :** SANHEDRIN

ger·res \'je(,)rēz\ *n, cap* [NL, fr. L, a sea fish of little value] **:** the type genus of the family Gerridae comprising long-bodied compressed marine fishes with protrusible mouths and large silvery scales

ger·rho·no·tine \¦jerə¦nō,tīn\ *adj* [NL *Gerrhonotus* + E *-ine*] **:** of or relating to the genus *Gerrhonotus*

ger·rho·no·tus \,⸗⸗'nōd·əs\ *n, cap* [NL, fr. Gk *gerrho-* (fr. *gerrhon* hide-covered shield, anything made of wickerwork) + NL *-notus;* akin to ON *kjarr* bush, *kass* willow basket, Arm *car* tree] **:** a genus of long-tailed slow-moving chiefly terrestrial lizards (family Anguidae) that are widely distributed in western No. America — see ALLIGATOR LIZARD

ger·rho·sau·rid \,jerō'sȯrəd\ *n* -s [NL *Gerrhosauridae*] **:** a lizard of the family Gerrhosauridae

ger·rho·sau·ri·dae \-ȯrə,dē\ *n pl, cap* [NL, fr. *Gerrhosaurus,* type genus (fr. Gk *gerrho-* + NL *-saurus* + *-idae*] **:** a family of African and Malagasy lizards somewhat resembling the skinks

¹ger·ri·dae \'jerə,dē\ *n pl, cap* [NL, fr. *Gerris,* type genus + *-idae*] **:** a family of true bugs including the water striders

²gerridae \"\ *n pl, cap* [NL, fr. *Gerres,* type genus + *-idae*] **:** a family of chiefly tropical marine percoid fishes comprising various locally important food fishes — see GERRES, MOJARRA

¹ger·ry·man·der \'jerē,mandə(r), -ri,m-, -maan-, ,⸗⸗'⸗⸗ *also* 'ge- *or* ,ge-; *the "G" in the surname "Gerry" is pronounced* g\ *n* -s [Elbridge *Gerry* †1814 Amer. statesman + sala*mander;* fr. the fancied resemblance to a salamander (made famous by caricature) of the irregularly shaped outline of an election district in northeastern Mass. that had been formed for partisan purposes in 1812 during Gerry's governorship] **1 :** the act or method of gerrymandering ⟨the district was the product of a 1950 ~ —Gladwin Hill⟩ **2 :** a district or pattern of districts varying greatly in size or population as a result of gerrymandering ⟨three new ~s in New York City —Gus Tyler⟩

²gerrymander \"\ *vb* **gerrymandered; gerrymandered; gerrymandering** \-d(ə)riŋ\ **gerrymanders** *vt* **1 :** to divide (a territorial unit) into election districts in an unnatural and unfair way with the purpose of giving one political party an electoral majority in a large number of districts while concentrating the voting strength of the opposition in as few districts as possible ⟨California's Republican legislature ~*ed* the 26th . . . to make it overwhelmingly Democratic and turn four adjoining districts into Republican strongholds —*Time*⟩ **2 :** to divide (an area) into political units in an unnatural and unfair way with the purpose of giving special advantages to one group ⟨plans to ~ school districts so that de facto segregation could be maintained —Don Pryor⟩ ~ *vi* **:** to follow the practice of creating gerrymanders ⟨the electorate may punish them if they ~ too brazenly —W.K.Hancock⟩

gers \'gers\ *dial Brit var of* GRASS

gers·dorff·ite \'gerz,dȯr,fīt, 'gers,-\ *n* -s [G *gersdorffit,* fr. the von *Gersdorff* family, 19th cent. Austrian mine owners + G *-it* -ite] **:** a mineral NiAsS consisting of a silver-white to steel-gray nickel sulfarsenide that may also contain some iron and cobalt

ger·sum \'gersəm\ *n* -s [ME, jewel, costly gift, gersum, fr. OE *gærsum, gærsuma* jewel, costly gift, treasure, fr. ON *gersemi, görsemi,* fr. *görr* ready, equipped + *-semi* (fr. *-samr* -some) — more at YARE] **:** a fine paid by a vassal in feudal England to his superior usu. on taking a holding

ger·trude \'gər·,trüd\ *n* -s [fr. the name *Gertrude*] **:** an infant's slip usu. made of cotton and buttoned at each shoulder

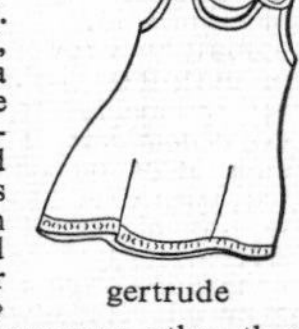
gertrude

ger·und \'jerənd\ *n* -s [LL *gerundium,* fr. L *gerundus,* gerundive of *gerere* to bear, act, perform — more at CAST] **1 :** a verbal noun in Latin that occurs in the genitive singular, dative singular, accusative singular, and ablative singular and that expresses the action of the verb as generalized or in continuance ⟨in Latin *ars vivendi* "the art of living" and *fratrem laudando* "in quoting your brother", *vivendi* and *laudando* are ~s⟩ **2 :** any of several linguistic forms in languages other than Latin that are felt to be analogous to the Latin gerund; *esp* **:** the English verbal noun in *-ing* that has the function of a substantive (as subject or object of a verb, object of a preposition, or complement of a verb) and at the same time shows the verbal features of tense and voice (as *choosing, having chosen, being chosen*), capacity to take adverbial qualifiers, and capacity to govern objects when the verb is transitive and that may have a subject in the objective or common case but often takes in place of a subject a possessive qualifier denoting the agent of its action esp. in literary use and when the agent is a pronoun or a noun denoting a person or persons ⟨in the sentences "I am surprised at his taking the matter so lightly" and "he left without anyone in the room noticing his departure", *taking* and *noticing* are ~s⟩ — see ³-ING

gerund-grinder \'⸗⸗,⸗⸗\ *n* **:** a pedantic teacher esp. of Latin grammar

gerund-grinding \'⸗⸗,⸗⸗\ *n* **:** pedantic instruction esp. in Latin grammar

ge·run·di·al \jə'rəndēəl, (')je¦r-\ *adj* [LL *gerundium* + E *-al*] **:** of, relating to, or like a gerund ⟨the ~ suffix⟩ — **ge·run·di·al·ly** \-əlē\ *adv*

ger·un·di·val \¦jerən¦dīvəl *sometimes* jə'rəndəvəl *or* -'rəndēv-\ *adj* **:** of, relating to, or like a gerundive

ge·run·dive \jə'rəndiv, -dēv *also* -dəv\ *n* -s [ME, fr. LL *gerundivus,* fr. *gerundium* + *-ivus* -ive — more at GERUND] **1 :** the Latin adjective that serves as the future passive participle, expresses necessity or fitness, and has the same suffix as the gerund **2 :** a verbal adjective in a language other than Latin analogous to the gerundive

gerusia *usu cap, var of* GEROUSIA

Ger·vais \(')zher¦vā\ *trademark* — used for cheese and milk products

ge·ryg·o·ne \jə'rigə(,)nē\ *n, cap* [NL, fr. Gk *gērygonē,* fem. of *gērygonos* born of sound, fr. *gērys* sound, voice + *gonos* that which is born, child, fr. *gignesthai* to be born — more at CARE, KIN] **:** a genus of small insectivorous Australasian warblers

ger·y·o·nia \,jerē'ōnēə\ *n, cap* [NL, fr. Gk *Geryon* (monster of Greco-Roman mythology having three bodies and powerful wings, fr. L, fr. Gk *Gēryōn*) + NL *-ia*] **:** a genus of craspedote medusae having six simple radial canals with corresponding tentacles

ger·ze·an \'gerzēən, 'gər-\ *adj, usu cap* [fr. *Gerzeh,* Egypt + E *-an*] **:** of or relating to an Aeneolithic culture of Upper Egypt characterized by the increased importance of agriculture, new techniques in industry, and expansion in the amount and area of foreign trade with a resulting influx of new materials and artifacts

ges *pl of* GE

ge·san \'zhäs°n\ *n* -s *usu cap* [irreg. fr. ²*ge* + *-an*] **:** a language stock in So. America including the Apinayé, Botocudo, Caingang, Cayapo, and Ge

ge·sell·schaft \gə'zel,shäft\ *n, pl* **gesellschafts** \-f(t)s\ *also* **gesellschaf·ten** \-tən\ [G, lit., company, society, fr. OHG *giselliscaft* companionship, fr. *gisellio* one that rooms with another, companion + (fr. *gi-,* perfective, associative, and collective prefix + *sal* hall) *-scaft* -ship — more at CO-, SALOON] **1 :** a rationally developed mechanistic type of social relationship characterized by impersonally contracted associations between persons — contrasted with *gemeinschaft* **2 :** a society characterized by the relationships existing in a gesellschaft

gesh·u·rite \'geshə,rīt, gə'shu̇,r-\ *n* -s *cap* [*Geshur,* region in ancient Palestine + E *-ite*] **1 :** a member of an Aramaean tribe in northeastern Palestine that was independent in David's time **2 :** a member of a tribe in southern Palestine

ge·sith \ye'sēth\ *n* -s [OE *gesīth,* lit., companion, one of a retinue of warriors; akin to OHG *gisind, gisindo* one of a retinue of warriors, ON *sinni,* Goth *gasinthja;* derivatives fr. the root of E *send*] **:** a wellborn companion or attendant of an Anglo-Saxon king **:** THANE — compare COMES

ge·sith·cund \-,kund\ *n* -s [OE *gesīthcund,* fr. *gesīth* + *-cund* (akin to OE *cynd* kind) — more at KIND] **:** the rank or class of the gesiths

ge·sith·cund·man \-n(d)mən\ *n, pl* **gesithcundmen :** a man of the rank of the gesiths

ges·nera \'gesnərə\ [NL, after K. *Gesner*] *syn of* GESNERIA

ges·ner·a·ce·ae \,gesnə'rāsē,ē\ [NL, fr. *Gesnera,* type genus + *-aceae*] *syn of* GESNERIACEAE

ges·ner·ad \'gesnə,rad\ *or* **ges·ne·ri·ad** \ge'snirē,ad\ *n* -s [NL *Gesnera* or *Gesneria* + E *-ad* (kind of plant)] **:** a plant of the genus *Gesneria* or of the family Gesneriaceae

ges·ne·ria \ge'snirēə\ *n* [NL, fr. Konrad *Gesner* †1565 Swiss naturalist + NL *-ia*] **1** *cap* **:** a large genus (the type of the family Gesneriaceae) of tropical American herbs having showy tubular flowers **2** -s **:** any plant of the genus *Gesneria*

ges·ne·ri·a·ce·ae \(,)ge,snirē'āsē,ē\ *n pl, cap* [NL, fr. *Gesneria* + *-aceae*] **:** a large family of tropical herbs or rarely woody plants (order Polemoniales) having chiefly opposite leaves and strongly zygomorphic flowers

ges·ne·ri·a·ceous \(¦)⸗¦⸗⸗¦āshəs\ *or* **ges·ner·a·ceous** \¦gesnə¦rā-\ *adj* [NL *Gesneriaceae* or *Gesneraceae* + E *-ous*] **:** of or relating to the family Gesneriaceae

gesneria family *n* **:** GESNERIACEAE

gesse \'jes\ *archaic var of* JESS

¹ges·so \'je(,)sō\ *n* -ES [It, lit., chalk, gypsum, plaster, fr. L *gypsum* — more at GYPSUM] **1 a :** plaster of paris or gypsum prepared with glue for use in painting or making bas-reliefs **b :** a paste prepared from mixing whiting with size or glue and spread upon a surface to fit it for painting or gilding **2 :** a surface prepared by spreading gesso upon it

²gesso \"\ *adj* **:** having gesso as a coating or constituent part ⟨some paintings are executed on ~ panels —Paul Ziff⟩ ⟨a kidney-shaped chest of ~ work —*New Yorker*⟩

³gesso \"\ *vt* -ED/-ING/-ES **:** to apply gesso to ⟨the article was to be ~*ed* all over —*N.Y. State Univ. Bull.*⟩

¹gest *or* **geste** \'jest\ *n* -s [ME *gest, jest, geste, jeste* deed, action, story, tale — more at JEST] **1 :** a notable deed or action **:** ADVENTURE, EXPLOIT ⟨knightly ~s and courtly pageantries —Elizabeth B. Browning⟩ **2 :** a tale of achievements or adventures; *esp* **:** a romance in verse ⟨~s and historic ballads written upon the story of Wallace —P.F.Tytler⟩

²gest *var of* GESTE

³gest *n* -s [alter. of earlier *gist,* fr. ME *giste* lodging for the night, fr. OF, fr. *gesir* to lie — more at GIST] *obs* **:** a stage or route in traveling esp. in a royal progress

ge·stalt \gə'shtält, -tält\ *n, pl* **gestalts** \-lts\ *also* **gestal·ten** \-lt°n,-ltən\ *often attrib* [G, shape, form, fr. MHG, appearance, nature, back-formation fr. *ungestalt* misshapen figure, fr. *ungestalt* ugly, fr. OHG, fr. *un-* ¹un- + *gestalt,* past part. of *stellen* to place, set up, shape — more at STALL] **1 :** a structure or configuration of physical, biological, or psychological phenomena so integrated as to constitute a functional unit with properties not derivable from its parts in summation **2 :** the pattern or figure assumed by a gestalt structure or system

ge·stalt·ist \-ltəst\ *n* -s *often cap* **:** GESTALT PSYCHOLOGIST

gestalt psychologist *n, sometimes cap G* **:** one who accepts or practices the principles of Gestalt psychology

gestalt psychology *n, usu cap G* **:** the study of perception and behavior from the standpoint of the organism's response to configurational wholes with stress on the identity of psychological and physiological events and rejection of atomistic or elemental analysis of stimulus, percept, and response — called also *configurationism*

ge·sta·po \gə'stä(,)pō, -tá(-\ *n* -s *often attrib* [G, secret-police organization in Nazi Germany, fr. *Ge*heime *Sta*ats*po*lizei, lit., secret state police] **:** a secret-police organization that operates esp. against persons suspected of treason or sedition and employs methods held to be underhanded and terrorist

ges·tate \'je,stāt, *usu* -ād·+V\ *vb* -ED/-ING/-S [back-formation fr. *gestation*] *vt* **1 :** to carry in the uterus during pregnancy ⟨enabling the mammal to ~ its young inside its body —G.B. Shaw⟩ **2 :** to conceive and gradually develop in the mind ⟨he was *gestating* quite another character, the hero of the next chapter —Florence B. Lennon⟩ ~ *vi* **:** to be in the process of gestation ⟨refusing to write a word of the proposed novel, the author declared that he was *gestating*⟩

ges·ta·tion \je'stāshən\ *n* -s [L *gestation-, gestatio,* fr. *gestatus* (past part. of *gestare* to bear, fr. *gestus,* past part. of *gerere* to bear, act) + *-ion-, -io* -ion — more at CAST] **1** *archaic* **:** exercise in which one is carried ⟨~ in a carriage or in a boat has . . . good effects —Thomas Watson †1882⟩ **2 a :** the carrying of young usu. in the uterus from conception to delivery **:** PREGNANCY ⟨other acute . . . illnesses occur in the early months of ~ —J.P.Greenhill⟩ **b :** the incubation of eggs **3 :** conception and development esp. in the mind ⟨this extraordinary book, thirty years in ~ —W.R.Parker⟩

ges·ta·tion·al \(')je¦stāshən°l, -shnəl\ *adj* **:** of or relating to gestation

gestation period *also* **gestation** *n* **:** the length of time during which gestation takes place ⟨the *gestation period* of a mare is about eleven months —F.A.Wrensch⟩ ⟨a new line of presses that would have a *gestation period* of about five years from drawing board to introduction —Joel Dean⟩

GESTATION PERIODS OF REPRESENTATIVE MAMMALS

ANIMAL	PERIOD OF GESTATION	
	average	limits
ass	365 days	340–385 days
bats (various)	35–50 days	uncertain
bear	208 days	180–225 days
camel	406 days	370–440 days
cat	63 days	52–69 days
chinchilla	110 days	105–115 days
cow	281 days	210–353 days
dog	63 days	53–71 days
elephant	624 days	510–720 days
goat	148 days	135–160 days
guinea pig	68 days	58–75 days
hamster (golden)	16 days	15–19 days
horse	336 days	264–420 days
kangaroo (giant)	38–40 days	uncertain
lion	108 days	105–113 days
man	267 days*	240–313 days**
mouse	19 days	18–31 days
opossum (Virginia)	12½ days	uncertain
rabbit	31 days	30–35 days
rat	21 days	21–30 days
sheep	151 days	135–160 days
swine	114 days	101–130 days
tiger	105–112 days	uncertain

*From last ovulation or 274–280 days from beginning of last menses

**The longest period of gestation in man that has ever been admitted in the law courts in Great Britain is 360 days.

ges·ta·tive \'jestəd·iv, -,stād·-\ *adj* **:** GESTATIONAL

¹geste *var of* GEST

²geste *also* **gest** \'jest\ *n* -s [MF *geste,* fr. L *gestus,* fr. *gestus,* past part. of *gerere*] **1** *archaic* **:** BEARING, DEPORTMENT ⟨his heroic grace and honorable *gest* —Edmund Spenser⟩ **2** *archaic* **:** GESTURE, MOVEMENT ⟨in the least ~ — the dropping low of the lid, the wrinkling of the brow —Elizabeth B. Browning⟩

ges·tic \-tik\ *adj* [²*geste* + *-ic*] **:** relating to or consisting of bodily movements or gestures ⟨artists who hold the most fantastically diverse theories as to what dancing is . . . — all recognize its ~ character —Susanne K. Langer⟩

ges·tic·u·lant \(')je¦stikyələnt *also* jə's-\ *adj* [L *gesticulant-, gesticulans,* pres. part. of *gesticulari*] **:** GESTICULATING

ges·tic·u·lar \-lə(r)\ *adj* [LL *gesticulus* + E *-ar*] **:** characterized or accompanied by gesticulation ⟨a ~ language⟩

ges·tic·u·late \je'stikyə,lāt *also* jə'-, *usu* -ād·+V\ *vb* -ED/-ING/-S [L *gesticulatus,* past part. of *gesticulari* to gesticulate, fr. (assumed) L *gesticulus* gesture (whence LL), dim. of L *gestus* gesture, deportment] *vt* **:** to express or indicate by gesture or gesticulation ⟨my mother *gesticulated* her wrath and despair —Hugh McCrae⟩ ~ *vi* **:** to make gestures or motions of the body or limbs esp. when speaking ⟨talking excitedly and *gesticulating* with her hands —Louis Auchincloss⟩ ⟨*gesticulated* to the waiter for the bill —Rebecca West⟩

ges·tic·u·la·tion \(,)je,stikyə'lāshən *also* jə,-\ *n* -s [L *gesticulation-, gesticulatio,* fr. *gesticulatus* + *-ion, -io* -ion] **1 :** the act of gesticulating ⟨~ . . . is not art; it is expression —Susanne K. Langer⟩ **2 :** an expressive motion of the body or limbs (as in emphasizing an argument) ⟨these people suddenly ceased muttering, but redoubled their ~s —*Encore*⟩ — compare GESTURE

ges·tic·u·la·tive \⸗'⸗kyə,lād·iv, ,ləd·-\ *adj* **:** inclined to or marked by gesticulation — **ges·tic·u·la·tive·ly** \-d·əvlē\ *adv*

ges·tic·u·la·tor \-,lād·ə(r)\ *n* -s [L, fr. *gesticulatus* + *-or*] **:** one that gesticulates; *esp* **:** ACTOR

gestic·u·la·to·ry \-,lə,tōrē\ *adj* **:** full of or characterized by gesticulations

ges·tion \'jes(h)chən\ *n* -s [L *gestion-, gestio,* fr. *gestus* (past part. of *gerere* to bear, act, manage) + *-ion, -io* -ion — more at CAST] **1 :** the act or process of carrying on **:** CONDUCT, MANAGEMENT ⟨that participation in the ~ of affairs which his office made incumbent on him —Thomas Jefferson⟩ **2** *Roman & civil law* **:** management of or interference with the business or affairs of another without authority **:** INTERMEDDLING

gestio pro hae·re·de \'gestē,ō,prō,hī'rā(,)dā\ *n* [L, behavior as heir] *Roman, civil, & Scots law* **:** conduct as an heir that makes one liable for the debts of an ancestor

ges·to·gen \'jestəjən\ *n* -s [*gestate* + *-o-* + *-gen*] **:** a progestational substance

gests *pl of* GEST

ges·tur·al \'jes(h)chərəl\ *adj* **:** of, relating to, or consisting of gestures ⟨the study of ~ communication⟩ ⟨acts with a ritual and ~ perfection —Walker Percy⟩

¹ges·ture \'jes(h)chə(r)\ *n* -s [ML *gestura* mode of action, fr. L *gestus* (past part. of *gerere* to bear, act) + *-ura* -ure — more at CAST] **1** *archaic* **:** the manner of carrying the body **:** CARRIAGE, BEARING ⟨the fashion of the countenance and the ~ of the body . . . is so correspondent to this state of mind —Edmund Burke⟩ **2** *obs* **:** the position or attitude of the body esp. in prayer ⟨as for their ~ or position, the men lay down leaning on their left elbow —Sir Thomas Browne〉 **3 :** the use of motions of the limbs or body as a means of intentional expression 〈we deduce motion from ~ —W.E.Allen〉 〈~ may be deliberate . . . or even symbolic —Susanne K. Langer〉 **4 :** a movement usu. of the body or limbs that symbolizes or emphasizes an idea, sentiment, or attitude 〈she gave a ~ of despair —H.G.Wells〉 〈the ability to find the appropriate ~*s* to convey the dramatic content of the work —*Encounter*〉 — compare GESTICULATION **5 :** a notable or expressive action: as **a :** something said or done by way of formality or courtesy 〈the invitation had been a ~ of sympathy toward a keen young officer without friends or relations —R.S.Porteous〉 **b :** something said or done to bring about a desired end (as in diplomacy) 〈diplomatic authorities brushed aside today the . . . proposal for an all-European security meeting as an insincere ~ and a propaganda appeal —W.H.Waggoner〉 〈the words were far more than a political ~ to draw popular support —V.L.Parrington〉 **c :** something said or done as a symbol or token 〈a ~ of royal authority〉 〈many members . . . deliberately invalidated their ballots as a protest ~ —*Current Biog.*〉

[2]**gesture** \"\ *vb* -ED/-ING/-S *vi* **:** to make gestures **:** GESTICULATE 〈*gesturing* vaguely with her full hands —Laura Krey〉 **~** *vt* **1 :** to indicate or express by gestures 〈what way is there of *gesturing* the cruelly impounded thought —Donald Davidson〉 **2 :** to direct by gestures 〈the policeman *gestured* him into the fork on the other side —Richard Llewellyn〉

gesture language *n* **:** communication by gestures; *esp* **:** SIGN LANGUAGE 〈*gesture languages* have not developed far because they occupy the hands —G.R.Harrison〉

ge·sund·heit \gə'zu̇nt,hīt\ *interj* [G, lit., health, fr. MHG *gesuntheit*, fr. *gesunt* healthy (fr. OHG *gisunt*) + *-heit* -hood (fr. OHG)— more at SOUND] — used to wish good health esp. to one who has just sneezed

geswarp *var of* GUESS-WARP

[1]**get** \(ˌ)gelt, *usu* \|d·+V; (ˌ)gi\|, *widely regarded as substandard, is quite frequent in educated speech when the verb does not have heavy stress as when a heavily stressed syllable immediately follows*\ *vb* **got** \(ˌ)gä\|\ *or archaic* **gat** \(ˌ)ga\|\ **got** \(ˌ)gä\|\ *or* **got·ten** \ˈgätᵊn\ **getting** \ˈged·iŋ, -etiŋ\ **gets** \(ˌ)ge\|, (ˌ)gi\|\ [ME *geten, getten*, fr. ON *geta* to get, beget, learn, name, speak; akin to OE *bigietan* to beget, OHG *pigezzan* to obtain, Goth *bigitan* to find, L *prehendere* to seize, grasp, Gk *chandanein* to hold, contain, Alb *gjet* to find, to get back; basic meaning: grasping, seizing] *vt* **1 a :** to gain possession of through one's own efforts 〈men are not born rich, and in *getting* wealth the man is generally sacrificed —R.W. Emerson〉 **b :** to earn from one's business or employment 〈what they ~ by day they spend by night —Daniel Defoe〉 **c :** to acquire or earn by or as if by labor or service 〈if I ~ your daughter's love, what dowry shall I have —Shak.〉 〈*got* an excellent reputation as an administrator〉 **d :** to become the recipient or possessor of 〈~*s* a check from his uncle every Christmas〉 **2 a** (1) **:** to obtain by way of advantage or superiority 〈~ the better of their opponents〉 〈~ the upper hand〉 〈*got* a good start and won the race〉 (2) **:** to receive by way of benefit or profit 〈is likely to ~ little for all his political activity〉 **b** (1) **:** to achieve as a result of military activity 〈having *gotten* the victory, pursued it to the utmost —Laurence Clarke〉 (2) **:** to gain possession of by military activity 〈and when the city Troy we shall have *got* —Thomas Hobbes〉 **3 a :** to obtain by or as if by concession or entreaty 〈*got* his father's consent to use the car〉 〈rapped vigorously on the door but could ~ no answer〉 **b :** to come to have 〈~ a good night's sleep〉 〈always ~*s* his own way〉 〈walked up the hill to ~ a view of the town〉 〈*got* the idea that he could do what he wanted to〉 **c :** to come down with (an illness) **:** CATCH 〈*got* measles from his brother〉 **4 a :** to cause to be provided or supplied **:** seek out and obtain 〈the officers *got* a search warrant〉 〈hoped to ~ dinner at the inn〉 **b :** to obtain for oneself or for another 〈in the spring the wanton lapwing ~*s* himself another crest —Alfred Tennyson〉 〈~ him his hat〉 〈sent the boy to ~ help from the neighbors〉 **c** *obs* **:** to obtain in marriage 〈I wonder why such a handsome . . . young gentleman as you do not ~ some rich widow —Jonathan Swift〉 **d** (1) **:** to obtain by hunting or fishing 〈went into the woods and *got* six squirrels in an hour〉 〈*got* several trout before breakfast〉 (2) **:** to obtain by harvesting **:** GATHER 〈*got* a good crop of wheat from the lower field〉 (3) **:** to obtain by mining 〈in proceeding to ~ the coal, the collier . . . works upon the face of the bed —*Collieries & Coal Trade*〉 **5 :** BEGET 〈~ you the sons your fathers *got*, and God will save the queen —A.E.Housman〉 **6** *obs* **:** to arrive at **:** REACH 〈if the wind blows strong and you cannot ~ the harbor, you must anchor —Woodes Rogers〉 **7 a :** to succeed in bringing or conveying **:** cause to come or go 〈*got* his luggage through customs in a few minutes〉 〈*got* his car to the garage before the gas ran out〉 **b :** to cause to move or be removed 〈~ thee out from this land and return unto the land of thy kindred —Gen 31:13 (AV)〉 〈~ the ladder away from the tree〉 〈~ the cat out of the house〉 **c :** to cause to be in a certain state, position, or condition 〈soon *got* the animal under control〉 〈*got* his feet wet〉 〈*got* the fender dented〉 〈will ~ himself into a jam if he's not careful〉 〈*getting* everything right that can by perseverance or expense be *got* right —Richard Mallett〉 **d :** to make ready **:** PREPARE 〈promised to ~ breakfast by eight o'clock〉 **8 a :** to take hold of **:** SEIZE 〈the dog *got* the thief by the leg〉 **b :** to make a captive of 〈have *got* your fellow tribune and hale him up and down —Shak.〉 **c :** to obtain the mastery of **:** OVERCOME 〈such practices will surely ~ you in the end〉 **d :** to have an emotional effect on **:** MOVE, TOUCH 〈you say that the music seemed to you very sad, that it *got* you —Olin Downes〉 **e :** to be a source of bafflement to **:** PUZZLE 〈this problem really ~*s* me〉 **f :** to cause annoyance to **:** IRRITATE 〈his conceit ~*s* me〉 **g :** to bring to retribution **:** take vengeance on; *specif* **:** KILL 〈she had not brought it along for fun; she was out to ~ her rival —Cabell Phillips〉 **9 a :** to be subjected to **:** meet with 〈*got* a bad fall from the horse〉 〈*got* a severe wound in battle〉 〈expects to ~ the worst of the bargain〉 **b :** to receive or suffer by way of punishment 〈~*s* a whipping at least once a week〉 〈*got* six months in jail〉 **c :** to suffer a specified injury to 〈*got* his nose broken playing football〉 **d :** to strike with force **:** HIT 〈the blow *got* him in the mouth〉 **10 a :** to acquire by study or experience 〈~ wisdom —Prov 4:5 (RSV)〉 〈*got* a good education at the university〉 **b :** to learn as a result of concentrated study 〈was told to ~ the poem by heart〉 〈~*s* his lessons faithfully〉 **c :** to ascertain through calculation or experiment **:** find out by arithmetical or other processes 〈worked the problem and *got* 46 as the answer〉 **d :** to learn by hearing 〈sorry, but I didn't ~ your name〉 **e :** to apprehend the meaning of **:** COMPREHEND, UNDERSTAND 〈the audience readily *got* the speaker's point〉 〈don't ~ me wrong〉 **11 :** to prevail on **:** PERSUADE, INDUCE 〈*got* the publisher to bring out a new deluxe edition〉 **12 a :** to come into or be in possession of — used in the past participle with the auxiliary *have* for emphasis 〈he has *got* ten dollars〉 **b :** to have as an obligation or necessity — used in the past participle with the auxiliary *have* 〈they've *got* to go to a funeral〉 〈you've *got* to eat more meat〉 **13 :** to succeed in finding 〈wondered what he could ~ to scold her about —William Black〉 **14 a :** to establish communication with 〈tried all afternoon to ~ them on the telephone〉 **b :** to receive by radio or on television 〈can ~ five stations since his new aerial was installed〉 **15** *chiefly Brit* **:** to hold out for **:** STAY 〈only a wonder of a horse can ~ those four miles and a half of ditches and fences —*London Daily Chronicle*〉 **16 :** to cause (an opposing player) to be put out **:** RETIRE 〈the shortstop's throw *got* the runner at first base〉 **~** *vi* **1 a :** to bring oneself **:** succeed in coming or going 〈hopes to ~ to New York for the holidays〉 〈*got* safely across the street〉 〈~ into the car〉 〈the car *got* through the mud〉 **b :** to come in the course of a journey 〈planned to ~ to the city before dark〉 〈they *got* home sooner than they had expected〉 **c :** to come in reaching a desired end or in attaining a state toward which progress has been made 〈finally *got* to sleep after midnight〉 **d :** to come into existence **:** APPEAR 〈dust *got* all over the books while we were away〉 **2 a :** to acquire wealth or property 〈whilst he was secretary . . . he had *gotten* vastly —John Evelyn〉 〈*getting* and spending we lay waste our powers —William Wordsworth〉 **b** *obs* **:** to derive profit **:** GAIN 〈gamesters are wont to . . . ~ by using false dice —William Penn〉 **3 a :** to have an opportunity **:** be able **:** CONTRIVE, MANAGE — used with following infinitive 〈he never *got* to go to college —Edmund Wilson〉 〈was lucky to ~ to see the new play〉 **b :** to come to be — used with following present participle 〈they *got* talking about old times and sat up half the night〉 **4 :** to succeed in becoming **:** make oneself **:** BECOME 〈how to ~ clear of all the debts I owe —Shak.〉 〈~ well soon〉 〈~*s* acquainted with the best people〉 — often used as a passive auxiliary 〈*got* caught in the rain〉 〈*got* married last week〉 〈behind every story there is another story that often never ~*s* told —Regina S. Jacobsen〉 **5 :** to go away at once **:** leave immediately 〈he presented a cocked revolver and told them to ~ —*Graceville (Minn.) Transcript*〉

syn OBTAIN, PROCURE, SECURE, ACQUIRE, GAIN, WIN: GET is very general in its meaning and simple and familiar in its use. OBTAIN is likewise rather general. It may suggest that the thing sought has been long desired or that it has come into possession only after the expenditure of considerable effort or the lapse of considerable time 〈the satisfaction *obtained* by the sentiment of communion with others, of the breaking down of barriers —John Dewey〉 〈in western New York where her early education was *obtained* —H.W.H.Knott〉 PROCURE is likely to suggest planning and contriving over a period of time and the use of unspecified or questionable means 〈the Duma laid claim to full power . . . and on March 15 *procured* the abdication of the frightened and despondent Nicholas II —F.A.Ogg & Harold Zink〉 〈some gifted spirit on our side *procured* (probably by larceny) a length of mine fuse —H.G.Wells〉 SECURE may suggest safe lasting possession or control 〈the large income and fortune which a prospering business *secures* for him is of his own making —J.A.Hobson〉 〈almost absolute safety against infection could be *secured* by the simple precaution of using safe, potable water —V.G. Heiser〉 ACQUIRE may suggest devious acquisition 〈the destruction of that ship by a Confederate cruiser, although it had *acquired* a British registry in order to avoid capture —H.W.H.Knott〉 It may also indicate continued, sustained, or cumulative acquisition 〈the habit of any virtue, moral or intellectual, cannot be assumed at once, but must be *acquired* by practice —C.H.Grandgent〉 GAIN often implies competition in acquiring something of value 〈if a London merchant, however, can buy at Canton for half an ounce of silver a commodity which he can afterwards sell at London for an ounce, he *gains* a hundred percent —Adam Smith〉 〈few men are placed in such fortunate circumstances as to be able to *gain* office —F.S.Oliver〉 WIN may suggest favorable qualities leading naturally to the acquisition of something desired despite competition or obstacles 〈the errors of his time were connected with his labors to remedy them and *win* a firmer knowledge than dialectic could supply —H.O.Taylor〉 〈Mrs. Woolf's fiction is too negligent of the requirements of the common reader to *win* a wide following —F.B.Millett〉

— **get after :** to subject to exhortation, reprimand, or attack 〈lax in *getting after* home-repair racketeers —*Wall Street Jour.*〉 — **get ahead :** to achieve success 〈struggles to *get ahead* as an interior decorator —J.W.Aldridge〉 — **get anywhere :** to be successful — usu. used with preceding negative 〈I don't think he will *get anywhere* with his plans〉 — **get around 1 :** to get the better of **:** CIRCUMVENT 〈a small group of aggressive citizens has managed to *get around* . . . the largest, richest, most powerful international combine in the history of the world —Fred Smith〉 **2 :** to escape the force of **:** EVADE 〈there is no *getting around* it: meaning implies convention —J.M.Barzun〉 — **get at 1 :** to reach with or as if with the hand 〈it is hard to *get at* the spark plugs without a proper wrench〉 **2 :** to acquire knowledge or understanding of 〈a fundamental method for *getting at* symbolism has been achieved —C.C.Walcutt〉 〈can *get at* the minds of companions only imaginatively —Bernard DeVoto〉 **3 :** to influence corruptly **:** BRIBE 〈take care she doesn't *get at* him —John Galsworthy〉 **4 a :** to make an attack on or do injury to 〈he hates us, and we are where he can *get at* us —Dorothy C. Fisher〉 **b :** to turn one's attention to **:** apply oneself to 〈a volume . . . which I long to *get at* but which must take its turn —O.W.Holmes †1935〉 **5 :** to try to prove or make clear 〈what he is *getting at* is continuity of experience —L.A. White〉 — **get behind :** to give active support or endorsement to 〈suggests that businessmen should *get behind* bond issues for school improvements —*Nation's Business*〉 — **get down on :** to develop dislike for 〈had no chance of promotion once the boss *got down on* him〉 — **get even :** to get even with someone **:** get revenge — **get even with :** to repay in kind 〈was determined to *get even with* him as soon as he could〉 — **get home :** to reach the final resting place or goal in a board game (as parchesi) — **get into :** to gain possession or control of **:** come over 〈can't understand what has *got into* that child〉 — **get it 1 :** to receive a scolding or punishment **2 :** to understand the meaning of what is seen or heard **:** COMPREHEND — **get nowhere :** to be unsuccessful 〈is likely to *get nowhere* with such a scheme〉 — **get on 1 :** ENTER, BOARD, MOUNT 〈*got on* the horse and rode away〉 **2 :** to produce an unfortunate effect on **:** DISTURB, UPSET 〈that sort of talk *gets on* my nerves〉 **3 :** to give attention or consideration to 〈doesn't know when to stop talking once he *gets on* music〉 **4 :** to subject to reprimand or punishment 〈promised to *get on* him for his negligence〉 — **get one's goat :** to make one angry, irritated, or annoyed 〈*gets my goat* to hear a man always grumbling —Adrian Bell〉 — **get one's hand in :** to regain one's skill in an activity by practice 〈after playing no tennis for some years, it took him time to *get his hand in*〉 — **get one's hooks on** *slang* **:** to obtain possession or control of **:** take over — **get out from under :** to escape impending danger or risk — **get over 1 a :** OVERCOME, SURMOUNT 〈once these difficulties were *got over* the work speeded up〉 **b :** to recover from 〈you can *get over* a disease by lying in bed —Charlton Laird〉 **c :** to become accustomed to **:** reconcile oneself to 〈the town will forget and forgive . . . and the parents will somehow *get over* it —Agnes S. Turnbull〉 **2 :** to move or travel across **:** COVER, TRAVERSE 〈was necessary for me to *get over* ground as fast as possible —A.W.Long〉 — **get religion :** to undergo religious conversion 〈she *got religion* and died in the odor of sanctity —Horace Wyndham〉 — **get somewhere :** to be successful 〈works so hard and so devotedly that he is sure to *get somewhere*〉 — **get the hook :** to be removed or discharged — **get there :** to be successful 〈he'll *get there* if hard work means anything〉 — **get through 1 :** to reach the end of **:** COMPLETE 〈*gets through* a greater amount of work with less expenditure of energy —James Hewitt〉 **2 :** to while away **:** succeed in passing 〈she found that there was . . . half an hour to be *got through* on a Friday afternoon —Robertson Davies〉 — **get to 1 :** to arrive at the point of **:** BEGIN 〈she *gets to* worrying if I leave her too long —Winifred Bambrick〉 **2 a :** to succeed in establishing contact with **:** REACH 〈adjusting the hours of our discussion groups so as to *get to* mothers who cannot afford baby-sitters —B.M.Beck〉 **b :** to have an effect on **:** INFLUENCE 〈it *got to* me until I couldn't think or sit still —Mickey Spillane〉 — **get together 1 :** to bring together **:** COLLECT, ACCUMULATE 〈in a few years he *got together* a good record collection〉 **2 :** to come together **:** ASSEMBLE 〈all the members of the family *get together* at least once a year〉 **3 :** to reach an agreement 〈the committee finally *got together* on its proposals〉 — **get up :** to cause oneself to climb, ascend, or mount 〈was hardly strong enough to *get up* the stairs〉 — **get wind of :** to become aware of **:** learn of through hints or rumors 〈*got wind of* the situation and came home〉 — **get with :** to pay attention to **:** become busy about 〈there were signs and sounds that television was about to *get with it* —*Newsweek*〉

[2]**get** \ˈget, *usu* -ed·+V\ *n* -S [ME, fr. *geten, getten*, v.] **1** *now dial Eng* **:** something that is gained; *esp* **:** EARNINGS **2 a :** something that is begotten: (1) **:** OFFSPRING 〈tries to make a hash of the lives of his innumerable ~ —John McCarten〉 (2) **:** the entire progeny of a male animal 〈a stallion's ~〉 — compare PRODUCE (3) *Scot* **:** CHILD; *specif* **:** BASTARD **b :** LINEAGE 〈a colt of champion ~〉 **3 :** a return of a shot in a game (as tennis) that usu. scores for an opponent

[3]**get** *also* **gett** \"\ *n, pl* **gittin** [Heb *gēṭ*] **1** *Jewish law* **:** a document of release from obligation; *specif* **:** BILL OF DIVORCE **2** *Jewish law* **:** a religious divorce

ge·ta \ˈge(ˌ)tä\ *also* **getas** \-äz\ *n pl* [Jap *geta*] **:** Japanese wooden clogs for outdoor wear

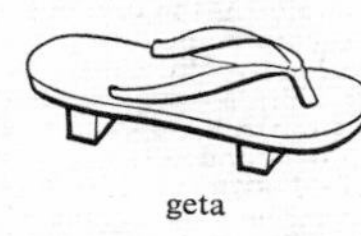
geta

getable *var of* GETTABLE

get about *vi* **1 a :** to be up and about **:** begin to walk 〈has recovered from his injuries and is *getting about* again〉 **b :** to come and go at will **:** be physically active 〈the students really *get about* on weekends〉 **2 :** to become current **:** CIRCULATE 〈the idea has *got about* that he's dangerous —Ellen Glasgow〉 〈the fear that it might *get about* among her acquaintances —Geoffrey Gorer〉

get across *vi* **:** to become clear or convincing 〈her thesis . . . would never *get across* if she didn't know how to make people in action both probable and interesting —H.C.Webster〉 **~** *vt* **:** to make clear or convincing 〈there will be cash to help *get* this point *across* —Helen Fuller〉

ge·tae \ˈjē,tē, ˈge,tī\ *also* **ge·tai** \ˈge,tī\ *n pl, usu cap* [L & Gk; L *Getae*, fr. Gk *Getai*] **1 :** a people of ancient times that lived in the region corresponding approximately to eastern Bulgaria, the Dobruja, Walachia, Moldavia, and Bessarabia **2 :** all the northern Thracian peoples, of whom the Dacians and Getae were the two main elements

get along *vi* **1 a :** to proceed toward a destination **:** move on 〈let's *get along* . . . and tell him about it —Marjory S. Douglas〉 **b :** to proceed with a series of acts or measures **:** PROGRESS 〈my mother was *getting along* with her housework —Maeve Brennan〉 **c :** to approach an advanced stage 〈it was *getting along* in the afternoon as we worked down this ridge —G.M. Dodge〉; *esp* **:** to approach old age 〈she's *getting along* and that's a big place for an old lady to handle —Ruth Moore〉 **2 :** to meet one's needs **:** FARE, MANAGE 〈books explaining how to *get along* in an uninhabited place —J.D.Hart〉 〈those who have hardly enough money to *get along* on —A.N.Whitehead〉 **3 :** to be or remain on congenial or harmonious terms 〈he is hard to *get along* with if you don't agree with him —O.W.Holmes †1935〉

[1]**ge·tan** \ˈjētᵊn\ *adj, usu cap* [*Getae* + *-an*] **:** GETIC

[2]**getan** \"\ *n* -S *usu cap* **:** a member of the Getae

get around *vi* **1 a :** to go from place to place 〈people . . . continued to *get around* in horse-drawn vehicles —*Amer. Guide Series: Wash.*〉 **b :** to travel or socialize extensively and so have wide knowledge or experience 〈is a good mixer and also *gets around* with the black-tie crowd —N.C.Stageberg〉 **2 :** to become known or current 〈sooner or later everybody's business *gets around* —Hamilton Basso〉 **3 a :** to find or take the necessary time or effort — used with *to* 〈those who never *got around* to reading the full work —R.E.Sherwood〉 **b :** to give attention or consideration usu. after considerable delay — used with *to* 〈knew we'd have to *get around* to the subject of seasickness sooner or later —Richard Joseph〉

get·at·able \(ˈ)ged·ˈad·əbəl\ *adj* [*get at* (phrase) + *-able*] **:** capable of being reached, attained, got, or known **:** APPROACHABLE, ACCESSIBLE 〈a very ~ man〉 〈both oil and coal are there but not in economical quantities or ~ locations〉

get away *vi* **1 :** to make one's escape **:** succeed in departing 〈went on, making straight for the road beyond, thinking only about *getting away* —Robert Westerby〉 〈something that's ingrained . . ., something that you can't *get away* from —Leslie Rees〉 **2 :** to start on a course **:** set out 〈the hikers planned to *get away* at dawn〉 **~** *vt* **1 :** to equip and send out **:** put into action 〈*got away* eight lifeboats and radioed a plea for more —*Time*〉 **2 :** to get rid of after brief possession 〈never saw anybody who could *get* the ball *away* faster —Ted Williams〉 — **get away with 1 :** to do (as a reprehensible act) without criticism or penalty **:** perform without suffering the consequences 〈can now *get away with* breaches of the rules and traditions which would never be allowed to others —Woodrow Wyatt〉 **2 :** to eat or drink **:** CONSUME 〈they *get away with* more alcohol than any other nation in the world —Emily Hahn〉

getaway \ˈ==,=\ *n* -S [*get away*] **:** an act or instance of getting away: as **a :** the making of or the ability to make a start from complete rest 〈a car with a good ~〉 **b :** ESCAPE 〈the thieves made their ~ in a stolen car〉

get back *vi* **1 :** to come or go again to a person, place, or condition **:** RETURN, REVERT, RETREAT 〈*getting back* to earth costs him all his balloons —Ellen L. Buell〉 **2 :** to gain revenge **:** RETALIATE — used with *at* 〈found an occasion for *getting back* at the First Consul by embroiling him with the Americans —Oscar Handlin〉 **~** *vt* **1 :** to regain possession of **:** RECOVER 〈*got back* nearly all the money he had lost〉

get by *vi* **1 :** to make ends meet **:** MANAGE, SURVIVE 〈*got by* for a time by hunting furs —M.C.Boatright〉 〈a marvel to me how all these . . . little two-by-four stores *get by* —John McNulty〉 **2 :** to succeed with the least possible effort or accomplishment 〈knew that with a little brushing up I could probably *get by* on an examination —Norman Cousins〉 **3 a :** to succeed without being discovered, criticized, or punished **:** pass unnoticed or unchallenged 〈a group of drivers is *getting by* with known violations —D.S.Buck〉 〈hold their jobs and *get by* socially . . . because they are easy to get along with —W.J.Reilly〉 **b :** to pass for a white person 〈all four grandparents were colored, but all could *get by* —W.L. White〉

get down *vi* **1 :** to alight esp. from a vehicle **:** DESCEND 〈the bus . . . was so jammed that I couldn't *get down* in time —Anna M. Ortese〉 **2 :** to give one's attention or consideration — used with *to* 〈having discussed the general theories . . . let's *get down* to cases —Richard Joseph〉 〈*get down* to business〉 **~** *vt* **1 :** to cause to be physically, mentally, or emotionally exhausted **:** DEPRESS 〈it did not *get* us *down*, but it got us thoroughly bored —A.L.Rowse〉 〈the heat was beginning to *get* her *down* —Mary Manning〉 **2 :** to bring oneself to eat **:** SWALLOW 〈one thing that he couldn't *get down* was baby octopus〉 **3 :** to commit to writing **:** DESCRIBE, DEPICT 〈she *gets* it all *down:* the real ruins, the fake ruins, . . . the litter in the fountains —Sean O'Faolain〉

gete \ˈjēt\ *n* -S *usu cap* [L *Getae*, n. pl.] **:** GETAN

geth·er *dial var of* GATHER

geth·sem·a·ne \geth'semənē, -ni\ *n* -S *usu cap* [fr. the Garden of *Gethsemane* on the Mount of Olives near Jerusalem where Christ was arrested (Mt 26), fr. Gk *Gethsēmanē, Gethsēmanei*] **:** a place or occasion of great esp. mental or spiritual suffering

[1]**ge·tic** \ˈjēd·ik, ˈjed-\ *adj, usu cap* [*Getae* + *-ic*] **:** of or relating to the Getae or their language

[2]**getic** \"\ *n* -S *usu cap* **:** the language of the Getae prob. belonging to the Thraco-Phrygian branch of the Indo-European family

get in *vi* **1 a :** to make or effect an entrance **:** ENTER 〈the burglar *got in* through an unlocked window〉 **b :** to reach one's destination **:** ARRIVE 〈the train *gets in* at noon〉 **c :** to succeed in having sexual intercourse; *specif* **:** to make an entrance at the beginning of coitus — usu. considered vulgar **2 a :** to become friendly **:** be on congenial terms 〈*got in* with a group of playboys and failed two freshman courses〉 **b :** to become involved 〈and now scamper . . . before you *get in* deeper with this bunch —Julian Maclaren-Ross〉 **3 :** to become accepted for membership or candidacy for office 〈the mayor *got in* by the slimmest of margins〉 **4 :** to reach the hawk as soon as the quarry has been killed **~** *vt* **1 a :** GATHER, HARVEST 〈hopes to *get* the hay *in* before the rainy season〉 **b :** PLANT, SOW 〈hopes to *get* the seed *in* by the end of the month〉 **2 a :** to include in one's schedule or routine 〈intended to *get in* some golf during the summer〉 **b :** to succeed in doing, making, or delivering 〈his dogs were badly mauled before he could *get* a shot *in* to kill the leopard —*Farmer's Weekly (So. Africa)*〉 **3 :** to cause to become involved **:** IMPLICATE 〈he'll *get* you *in* so deep you'll be lucky if you don't get a longer stretch than he does —Hartley Howard〉

get·ling \ˈgetliŋ\ *n* -S [[2]*get* + *-ling*] *Scot* **:** CHILD; *esp* **:** BASTARD

get off *vi* **1 :** to make a start **:** set out **:** DEPART 〈intended to *get off* on his vacation early in the morning〉 **2 :** to escape from a dangerous situation or from punishment 〈expected to *get off* with a light prison term —S.L.A.Marshall〉 **3 :** ALIGHT, DISMOUNT 〈the bus broke down and all the passengers had to *get off*⟩ **4 :** to leave work with the permission or knowledge of one's superior ⟨*got off* early and went to the ball game⟩ ~ *vt* **1 :** to bring about the departure of ⟨*got* him *off* on the evening train⟩ **2 :** to secure the release of or procure a modified penalty for ⟨his lawyers *got* him *off* with little difficulty⟩ **3 a :** to give expression to : UTTER ⟨*got off* a joke that none of his friends had heard before⟩ **b :** to write and send : DISPATCH ⟨plans to *get off* a long cable to the home office⟩

get-of-sire \ˈ=,=\ *n* [²*get*] **1 :** the entire progeny or a representative sample of the progeny of a sire **2 :** a class in a livestock show for judging the progeny of different sires

get on *vt* **:** to dress oneself in : DON ⟨*get on* thy boots: we'll ride all night —Shak.⟩ ~ *vi* **1 a :** to continue toward a destination : move along ⟨finished his drink and said that he had to be *getting on*⟩ **b :** to continue with one's work or business : PROCEED ⟨his desire to *get on* with his studies —T.B.Costain⟩ **c :** to draw near : come close ⟨it was *getting on* to four in the morning, and he had not yet closed an eye —F.W.Crofts⟩ **d :** to become late ⟨it was *getting on* in the afternoon and we were tired —L.A.Viereck⟩ **e :** to become old : AGE ⟨I am indeed *getting on* . . . and a helpmate would cheer my declining days —W.S.Gilbert⟩ **2 a :** to achieve success : PROGRESS, PROSPER ⟨watched every opportunity because he wanted to *get on* —Robert Westerby⟩ **b :** to carry on one's affairs : FARE, MANAGE ⟨the legacy . . . came after he was well started, and he always says he could have *got on* without it —Ellen Glasgow⟩ **3 :** to maintain a friendly relationship : be on good terms ⟨will she *get on* with your father's wife —Rose Macaulay⟩ **4 :** to gain knowledge or understanding : grasp the meaning : catch on — used with *to* ⟨he soon *got on* to the racket they were working⟩ **5** *chiefly Brit* **:** to make contact — used with *to* ⟨I'll *get on* to the telephone people first thing in the morning —Dorothy Sayers⟩

get out *vi* **1 a :** EMERGE, ESCAPE ⟨doubted that he would *get out* alive⟩ **b :** to leave a vehicle ⟨the passengers *got out* and walked across the bridge⟩ **c :** to go away at once — often used in the imperative as an interjection to express disbelief or amazement **2 :** to dispose of one's stock ⟨switched into the stock market, made a killing, and *got out* —Erle Stanley Gardner⟩ **3 :** to become known : leak out ⟨the remarks made at the secret hearing soon *got out*⟩ **4 :** to take part in social activities ⟨advise him not to read so much and to *get out* and mix more with people —Paul Woodring⟩ ~ *vt* **1 :** to cause to emerge or escape ⟨how can I *get* myself *out* of this muddle —C.W.H.Johnson⟩ **2 :** PUBLISH, PRODUCE ⟨*got out* an anthology of war poetry⟩ **3 :** to give forth with some effort : EMIT ⟨the lark could scarce *get out* his notes for joy —Alfred Tennyson⟩ **4 :** to cause to go to the polls ⟨party leaders worked hard to *get out* the vote⟩

get-out \ˈ=,=\ *n* -S [*get out*] **:** an escape from an awkward or difficult situation ⟨never uses in his own behalf the old *get-out* about being misreported by the press —*Punch*⟩ — compare ALL GET-OUT

get over *vi* **:** to become clear ⟨only if presented in that way can the ideas of industry *get over* to the workers —E.R.Smith⟩ ~ *vt* **1 :** to bring to an end : have done with : FINISH ⟨reckon I'll be glad to *get it over* —Ellen Glasgow⟩ **2 :** to make clear ⟨efforts were made to *get over* . . . the relationship of public officials toward individual citizens —P.P.Van Riper⟩

getpenny \ˈ=,==\ *n* [¹*get* + *penny*] *archaic* **:** a profitable venture or asset

get-rich-quick \(ˌ)=ˌ=ˈ=\ *adj* **:** characterized by or appealing to a desire for quick wealth and often lacking in financial stability or scruples ⟨*get-rich-quick* promoters⟩ ⟨the false prosperity of a *get-rich-quick* era⟩

get round *vb* **:** to get around

gets *pres 3d sing of* GET, *pl of* GET

get·sul \ˈget,sül\ *n* -S *usu cap* [Tibetan *getshul* (*dgetshul*)] **:** a Lamaist priest or monk not yet fully ordained

gett *var of* GET

get·ta·ble *also* **get·able** \ˈged·əbəl\ *adj* [¹*get* + *-able*] **:** capable of being got : ATTAINABLE, OBTAINABLE

¹**get·ter** \ˈged·ə(r)\ *n* -S [ME *geter, getter*, fr. *geten, getten* to get + *-er* — more at GET] **:** one that gets: as **a :** a chemically active substance (as metallic barium) introduced into a vacuum tube or incandescent electric lamp to remove traces of gas remaining after exhaustion of the enclosed space **b :** a sire esp. when a producer of superior progeny

²**getter** \"\ *vb* -ED/-ING/-S *vi* **:** to use a getter (as in evacuating a vacuum tube) ~ *vt* **:** to submit to the action of a getter

get through *vi* **1 :** to reach a destination ⟨the train failed to *get through* because of the floods⟩ **2 a :** to receive approval ⟨the bill *got through* by a margin of two votes⟩ **b :** to pass an examination or course ⟨many students *get through* with little study⟩ **3 a :** to become understood : make oneself clear ⟨our feelings must have *gotten through* to him quickly —E.L.Wallant⟩ **b :** to complete a telephone connection ⟨couldn't *get through* and . . . a surprised Sussex voice asked if he didn't know that the cable was down —Clemence Dane⟩ **4** *chiefly NewEng* **:** to resign or lose a job ⟨he *got through* at the mill last week⟩

getting *pres part of* GET

get-together \ˈ=,==\ *n* -S [fr. the phrase *get together*] **:** MEETING; *esp* **:** an informal social gathering

get-tough \=ˈ=\ *adj* [fr. the phrase *get tough*] **:** characterized by firmness and determination to act if and as necessary ⟨a *get-tough* international policy⟩

ge·tu·li·an \jēˈtülēən, jēˈtyü-\ *also* **ge·tu·lan** \-lən\ *adj, usu cap* [L *Gaetuli, Getuli* people inhabiting northwestern Africa in ancient times (fr. Gk *Gaitouli*) + E *-an*] **:** of or relating to the culture of any of the nomadic peoples of Libya and the eastern Sahara in Neolithic and Aeneolithic times

get up *vi* **1 a :** to arise from bed ⟨he *gets up* late on Sundays⟩ **b :** to rise to one's feet ⟨*got up* from the chair when the guests came in⟩ **c :** CLIMB, ASCEND, MOUNT ⟨*got up* on the roof to watch the eclipse⟩ **2 :** to increase in force or violence ⟨the added motion of the ship told him the sea was *getting up* —J.E.Macdonnell⟩ **3 :** to draw near : come close ⟨the batteries . . . opened on our approach and the fire was returned as our ships *got up* —Horatio Nelson⟩ **4 :** to go ahead or go faster — used in the imperative as a command to horses ~ *vt* **1 :** to cause to rise : RAISE ⟨finally *got* the anchor *up* and set sail⟩ **2 :** to make preparations for : set on foot : ORGANIZE ⟨*got up* a party for the newcomers⟩ ⟨*get up* a petition⟩ **3 :** to arrange as to external appearance : FINISH, DRESS ⟨the printed libretto . . . is handsomely and usefully *gotten up* —Herbert Weinstock⟩ ⟨he is *got up* for the artist's part — purple velvet coat, great flowing tie, black sombrero —H.J.Laski⟩ **4 :** to acquire a knowledge of : study for a special purpose ⟨was advised to *get up* German during the summer⟩ **5 :** to create in oneself : work up : GENERATE ⟨cannot *get up* an atom of sympathy for them⟩

getup \ˈ=,=\ *n* -S [*get up*] **1 a :** general composition or structure : manner in which the parts of a thing are combined : makeup and style (as of dress) : FORMAT **b :** OUTFIT, COSTUME, RIG ⟨you're never going to the party in that ~⟩ **2 :** act or time of getting up **3** *or* **get-up-and-go** *or* **get-up-and-get** \(ˌ)=ˌ==ˈ=\ **:** initiative and determination : SPUNK

ge·ul·lah *also* **ge·u·lah** \gə(ˌ)üˈlä, gəˈü(ˌ)lä\ *n* -S *usu cap* [Heb *gĕʼullāh* redemption] **:** the recital of the prayer of thanks to God for the redemption of Israel from Egypt in the Jewish ritual in the daily liturgy

ge·um \ˈjēəm\ *n* [NL, fr. L *gaeum, geum* herb bennet] **1** *cap* **:** a genus of perennial herbs (family Rosaceae) with pinnate or lyrate leaves and flowers with long plumose persistent styles **2** -S **:** AVENS

-geu·sia \ˈgyüzh(ē)ə\ *n comb form* -S [NL, fr. Gk *geusis* sense of taste, taste (fr. *geuesthai* to taste + *-sis*) + NL *-ia* — more at CHOOSE] **:** a (specified) condition of the sense of taste ⟨*parageusia*⟩

geu·si·o·lep·tic \ˌgyüzēōˈleptik\ *adj* [Gk *geusis* + E *-o-* + Gk *leptos* peeled, fine, delicate (fr. *lepein* to peel) + E *-ic* — more at LEPER] **:** having or characterized by pleasant flavor

gew·gaw \ˈgyü,gö *also* ˈgü,gö *sometimes* ˈjü,jö *or* ˈjü,gö\ *also* **gee·gaw** \ˈjē,gö, ˈgē,gö, ˈjē,jö\ *n* -S *often attrib* [origin unknown] **1 :** something lacking in substantial value : a thing of no account or worth : TRIFLE ⟨in such a society these accomplishments were no mere ~s⟩ **2 :** something showy or gaudy and usu. with little intrinsic worth ⟨decked out with all sorts of ~s⟩ — **gew·gawed** \-ōd\ *adj* — **gew·gaw·ish** \-ōish,-ōēsh\ *adj* — **gew·gawy** \-ōi,-ōē\ *adj*

gew·gaw·ry \-ōrē\ *n* -ES **:** cheap showiness

¹**gey** \ˈgāi\ *adj* [alter. of ¹*gay*] *chiefly Scot, of quantity and number* **:** CONSIDERABLE, FAIR ⟨waited a ~ while in the cold⟩

²**gey** \"\ *adv* [alter. of ³*gay*] *chiefly Scot* **:** VERY, QUITE, RATHER ⟨it's ~ dark and getting darker —John Buchan⟩

gey·an \ˈgāiən\ *adv* [¹*gey* + *an* (alter. of *and*)] *chiefly Scot* **:** TOLERABLY, CONSIDERABLY

gey·lies \ˈgāilēz\ *adv* [*geyly* + *-es*] *Scot* **:** tolerably well : very much

gey·ly \-lē\ *Scot var of* GAILY

¹**gey·ser** *in sense 1* ˈgīzə(r), *Brit also* ˈgāz- *or* ˈgēz-; *in sense 2 usu* ˈgēz-\ *n* -S [Icel *Geysir* (name of a geyser in Haukadal, Iceland), lit., gusher, fr. *geysa* to rush forward, gush, fr. ON; akin to ON *gjōsa* to gush, Goth *giutan* to pour — more at FOUND] **1** *also* **gey·sir** \"\ **:** a spring that throws forth intermittently escaping jets of heated water and steam as a result of the contact of subterranean water with rock hot enough to generate steam under conditions which prevent free circulation — see GEYSERITE **2** *Brit* **:** an apparatus for heating water rapidly esp. by injected steam (as for a bath or for washing dishes) — **gey·ser·al** \-zərəl\ *adj* — **gey·ser·ic** \ˈ=zərik, (ˈ)=ˈzerik\ *adj*

²**geyser** \"\ *vb* -ED/-ING/-S *vi* **:** to spurt like a geyser or cause spurting like that of a geyser ⟨blood ~*ed* from the cut⟩ ⟨the shells fell short and ~*ed* into the water⟩ ~ *vt* **:** to cause (something) to spurt like a geyser ⟨shells ~*ing* the water⟩

gey·ser·ine \ˈ=_zə,rīn, -rēn\ *adj* **:** of or relating to a geyser

gey·ser·ite \-rīt\ *n* -S [F *geysérite*, fr. *geyser* (fr. Icel *Geysir*) + *-ite*] **:** a hydrous form of silica that constitutes one variety of opal and is deposited around some hot springs and geysers in white or grayish concretionary masses which are porous, filamentous, or scaly

ge·ze·rah \gə,zäˈrä, gzä'-; gəˈzä(ˌ)rä, ˈgzä(-\ *n, pl* **geze·roth** *or* **geze·rot** \gə,zäˈrōt(h), gzä'-; gəˈzä(ˌ)rōs, ˈgzä(-\ [Heb *gĕzērāh*] **:** a temporary rabbinical decree issued as a preventive measure to meet the needs of the time

GFA *abbr* **1** general freight agent **2** good fair average

GFE *abbr* government furnished equipment

g flat *n, usu cap G* **1 :** the keynote of G-flat major **2 :** the tone a half step below G

g–flat major \ˈ=,=ˈ==\ *n, usu cap G* **:** the major musical key having a signature of six flats

GG *abbr* **1** gamma globulin **2** governor general **3** great gross

GH *abbr* growth hormone

GHA *abbr* Greenwich hour angle

ghaf·fir \(ˈ)gaˈfi(ə)r\ *n* -S [Ar *ghafīr*] **:** a native Egyptian guard or watchman

ghaist \ˈgāst\ *Scot var of* GHOST

gha·na \ˈgänə, ˈgä- *also* ˈga-\ *adj, usu cap* [fr. *Ghana*, country in western Africa] **:** of or from Ghana **:** of the kind or style prevalent in Ghana : GHANAIAN

¹**gha·na·ian** \-n(ə)yən,-nēən\ *adj, usu cap* [*Ghana* + *-ian*] **1 :** of, relating to, or characteristic of Ghana **2 :** of, relating to, or characteristic of the Ghanaians

²**ghanaian** \"\ *or* **gha·ni·an** \"\ *n* -S *cap* **:** a native or inhabitant of Ghana

gha·nese \(ˈ)=ˈnēz, -ēs\ *adj, usu cap* [*Ghana* + *-ese*] **:** GHANAIAN

gharial *var of* GAVIAL

ghar·ry *or* **ghar·ri** \ˈgarē, ˈgä-\ *n, pl* **gharries** *or* **gharris** [Hindi *gāṛī*] **:** a horse-drawn cab used esp. in India

gharry-wal·lah \ˈ=ˌ=ˈwälə\ *n* [Hindi *gāṛīwālā*, fr. *gāṛī* + *-wālā* (agent suffix)] **:** a gharry driver

ghasel *var of* GHAZEL

ghash·ghai \ˈgash,gī\ *n* -S *usu cap* **1 :** a people of southern Iran **2 :** a member of the Ghashghai people

ghas·sa·nid \gəˈsänəd, gaˈ-\ *n* -S *usu cap* [*Ghassan*, a 6th cent. A.D. people of northwestern Arabia + E *-id*] **:** one of an Arab dynasty governing under the suzerainty of the Roman and Byzantine empires the Arab tribes of Palestine and the region about Palmyra from the 5th century A.D. to A.D. 636

ghas·su·li·an \(ˈ)gaˈsülēən\ *adj, usu cap* [Teleilat *Ghassul*, site in Jordan + E *-ian*] **:** of, relating to, or being an Aeneolithic culture of Palestine

ghast \ˈgast, -aa(ə)-,-ai-,-á-\ *adj* [by shortening] *archaic* **:** GHASTLY

ghast·ful \-fəl\ *adj* [ME *gastful*, fr. *gast, gost* spirit, ghost + *-ful* — more at GHOST] **1** *obs* **:** full of fear : FRIGHTENED ⟨the prelate saw their fall with ~ eyes —John Ozell⟩ **2** *archaic* **:** giving rise to fear : FRIGHTFUL ⟨this ~ dream . . . soon awoke him —John Lane *fl*1620⟩ — **ghast·ful·ly** \-fəlē\ *adv, obs*

ghast·li·ly \-tləlē\ *or* **ghast·i·ly** \-tələ̄\ *adv* **:** in a ghastly manner

ghast·li·ness \-tlēnəs, -tlin-\ *n* -ES **:** the quality or state of being ghastly ⟨the ~ of the monster with its popeyes, gaping mouth, and horns —L.E.Schmeckebier⟩

¹**ghast·ly** \ˈgastlē, ˈgaas-,ˈgais-,ˈgás-, -li\ *adj*, -ER/-EST [ME *gastly*, fr. OE *gāstlīc* spiritual — more at GHOSTLY] **1 :** giving rise to terror : FRIGHTENING, TERRIFYING ⟨along the parapet rose great pyramids of German helmets, empty, ~, like . . . heaps of skulls —Louis Bromfield⟩ **2 :** resembling or suggestive of a ghost : DEATHLIKE, PALE, WAN ⟨his face was so ~ that it could scarcely be recognized —T.B.Macaulay⟩ ⟨her eyes are lighted up with a smile so ~ that people quake as they look at her —W.M.Thackeray⟩ **3** *obs* **:** filled with fear : TERRIFIED ⟨in great haste and fear with ~ . . . looks —Thomas Herbert⟩ **4 :** intensely unpleasant, disagreeable, or objectionable : TERRIBLE — often used as a generalized expression of disapproval ⟨such a life seems ~ in its emptiness and sterility —Aldous Huxley⟩ ⟨engaged in the ~ job of revising the curriculum —H.J.Laski⟩ **5 :** very great — used as an intensive ⟨the whole business is a ~ mistake —D.B.Chidsey⟩ ⟨the ~ waste of time that we indulge in —J.C.Powys⟩

²**ghastly** \"\ *adv* **:** in a ghastly manner ⟨her face was ~ pale —Washington Irving⟩

ghat *also* **ghaut** \ˈgót, ˈgät\ *n* -S [Hindi *ghāṭ*, fr. Skt *ghaṭṭa*] **1** *India* **a :** MOUNTAIN RANGE **b :** a mountain pass **2** *India* **a :** a landing place or platform on the bank of a river **b :** a passage or flight of steps leading from a landing place or platform to the water's edge (as for the convenience of bathers) — compare BURNING GHAT

ghat·ti gum \ˈgad·ē-\ *n* [native name in India] **:** an Indian gum obtained from the dhawa and related trees and used as a substitute for gum arabic

gha·wa·zee *or* **gha·wa·zi** \gəˈwä(ˌ)zē\ *n pl* [Ar *ghawāzī*, pl. of *ghāziyah*] **:** Egyptian dancing girls who usu. perform in the public streets

ghaz·el *or* **ghaz·al** *also* **gaz·el** *or* **gas·al** *or* **ghas·el** \ˈgazəl\ *n* -S [Ar *ghazal*] **:** an Arabic lyric poem that begins with a rhymed couplet whose rhyme is repeated in all even lines and that is esp. common in Persian literature

gha·zi *or* **ga·zi** \ˈgä(ˌ)zē\ *n* -S *often cap* [Ar *ghāzī*] **:** a Muslim warrior; *esp* **:** one victorious in battle with the opponents of Islam — often used as a title of honor

ghaz·na·vid *or* **ghaz·ne·vid** \ˈgäznə,vid\ *n* -S *usu cap* [irreg. fr. *Ghazni*, Afghanistan + E *-id*] **:** one of a Muslim dynasty ruling in southwestern Asia from the 10th to the 12th centuries

ghed·da wax \ˈgedə-\ *n, sometimes cap G* [prob. fr. Telugu *gedda* lump] **:** beeswax from Indian and African bees

ghee *or* **ghi** \ˈgē\ *n* -S [Hindi *ghī*, fr. Skt *ghṛta*; akin to MIr *gert* milk and perh. to Skt *jigharti* he besprinkles, Per *āgārdan* to mix] **1 :** a semifluid clarified butter made in India and neighboring countries usu. from buffalo milk **2 :** a fat made from vegetable oils

gheg *or* **geg** \ˈgeg\ *n* -S *usu cap* [Alb *geg*] **1 :** one of the northern Albanians — compare TOSK **2** *also* **gheg·ish** \-egish\ **:** the language of the Ghegs that constitutes the principal literary dialect of Albanian

ghent \ˈgent\ *adj, usu cap* [fr. *Ghent*, Belgium] **:** of or from the city of Ghent, Belgium **:** of the kind or style prevalent in Ghent

ghent azalea *n, usu cap G* **:** any of various rather hardy cultivated hybrid azaleas that have white to deep red flowers often marked with yellow or orange, result from interbreeding an Old World azalea (*Rhododendron flavum*) with one or more New World azaleas (as the complex hybrid *R.* × *mortieri*), and are commonly treated as forming a distinct hybrid group (*R.* × *gandavense*)

ghenting *n* -S [*Ghent*, Belgium + E *-ing*] *obs* **:** a linen cloth orig. made in Ghent

gher·kin *or* **ger·kin** \ˈgərkən, ˈgə̄k-,ˈgəik-\ *n* -S [D *gurken*, pl. of *gurk* cucumber, fr. *augurk*, fr. LG *augurke*, fr. MLG, fr. Pol *ogurek*, fr. MGk *agouros* watermelon, cucumber, prob. fr. MPer *angārah* watermelon] **1 a :** a small oblong prickly cucumber of West Indian origin that is used chiefly for pickling — called also *bur gherkin, West Indian gherkin* **b :** a slender annual trailing vine (*Cucumis anguria*) that bears gherkins **2 :** the immature fruit of the common cultivated cucumber esp. when used for pickling

¹**ghet·to** \ˈged·(ˌ)ō, ˈge(ˌ)tō\ *n, pl* **ghettos** *also* **ghettoes** [It] **1 a :** a quarter of a city (as in Italy) in which Jews were formerly required to live **b :** a quarter of a city in which the residents are chiefly Jews ⟨the tide of immigration from the ~s of Europe . . . streamed into New York —*Amer. Mercury*⟩ **2 :** a quarter of a city in which members of a minority racial or cultural group live esp. because of social, legal, or economic pressure ⟨there have long been self-imposed ~s in our big industrial centers —Charles Abrams⟩ ⟨the racial ~s which now shelter and set apart from the rest of the community Negroes and Chinese . . . are invariably located in the slum —R.E. Park⟩ **3 :** an isolated or segregated group ⟨they're in an economic ~, which . . . forces them to live in some cheap section —Morley Callaghan⟩

²**ghetto** \"\ *vt* -ED/-ING/-S **:** GHETTOIZE

ghet·to·iza·tion \ˌ=(ˌ)=əˈzāshən, -ˌīˈz-\ *n* -S **:** segregation in or as if in a ghetto

ghet·to·ize \ˈ=(ˌ)=ˌīz\ *vt* -ED/-ING/-S **:** to isolate in or as if in a ghetto

ghi *var of* GHEE

ghib·el·line \ˈgibə,lēn, -ˌlīn, -ˌlən\ *n* -S *usu cap* [It *ghibellino*, fr. OIt, fr. MHG *Wibeling*, appellative of the Salian emperors, fr. *Wibeling*, castle in Franconia, Germany] **:** a member of an aristocratic political party in Italy supporting the authority of the German emperors from the 12th to the 15th centuries — compare GUELF

ghib·el·lin·ism \-ˌnizəm\ *n* -S *usu cap* **1 :** the policy and principles of the Ghibellines **2 :** adherence to Ghibellinism

ghillie *var of* GILLIE

ghil·zai \ˈgil,zī\ *n* -S *usu cap* **:** an Afghan people believed to be of Turkish origin

ghimel *var of* GIMEL

ghior·des \gēˈórdəs, ˈgó-\ *n, pl* **ghiordes** *usu cap* [fr. Gördes (*Ghiordes*), town in Manisa, Turkey] **:** an Anatolian rug characterized by fine knotting, mellow colors, a wool pile, and a cotton web; *esp* **:** a fine prayer rug of the 17th and 18th centuries

ghiordes knot *n, usu cap G* [fr. Gördes (*Ghiordes*), Turkey] **:** a knot used in making carpets and rugs in which the two ends of pile yarn appear together at the surface between the two adjacent warp yarns around which they are twisted — called also *Turkish knot;* compare SEHNA KNOT

Ghiordes knot

ghobar numeral *var of* GOBAR NUMERAL

ghol \ˈgól, ˈgōl\ *n* -S [Hindi *ghol, gholā*] **:** a sciaenid fish (*Sciaena miles*) of the Indian coast whose liver is extremely rich in vitamin A

ghon tubercle \ˈgän-\ *also* **ghon focus** *n, usu cap G* [after Anton *Ghon* †1936 Czechoslovakian pathologist] **:** the primary tubercle occurring in the lung of a child as the initial lesion of tuberculous infection and appearing as a bean-shaped shadow in the roentgenogram

ghor·khar \ˈgór,kär\ *n* -S [Per] **:** a wild ass of northwestern India believed to be identical with the onager

¹**ghost** \ˈgōst\ *n* -S *often attrib* [ME *gost, gast*, fr. OE *gāst;* akin to OS *gēst* spirit, OHG *geist* spirit, ON *geiskafullr* full of terror, Goth *usgaisjan* to frighten, Skt *heḍa* anger] **1 a :** the life principle or vital spark **:** the soul regarded as the seat of life or intelligence — now used chiefly in the phrase *to give up the ghost* **b** *archaic* **:** the spirit of man as distinguished from the body **:** the conscious being ⟨knowledge of what the world ought to be to us who are body and ~ together —Nathaniel Fairfax⟩ **2 a :** a disembodied soul; *esp* **:** the soul of a dead person believed to be an inhabitant of the unseen world or to appear to the living in bodily likeness ⟨believe in the survival of the soul after death in the form of a ~ —Edward Sapir⟩ **b :** APPARITION, SPECTER **3 :** SPIRIT, DEMON ⟨that affable familiar ~ which nightly gulls him with intelligence —Shak.⟩; *esp* **:** a harmful or malevolent disembodied human spirit regarded as a power to be propitiated or averted by religious or magical rites **4** *obs* **:** PERSON ⟨no knight so rude . . . as to do outrage to a sleeping ~ —Edmund Spenser⟩ **5** *obs* **:** CORPSE ⟨a timely-parted ~ of ashy semblance, meager, pale, and bloodless —Shak.⟩ **6 :** a mark or visible sign left by something dead, lost, or no longer present : REMAINS ⟨the ~ of grandeur that lingers between the walls of abandoned haciendas —Mary Austin⟩ **7 a :** a faint shadowy outline or semblance : TRACE ⟨would search the white skies for the ~ of a cloud —Vicki Baum⟩ **b :** the least bit : IOTA, PARTICLE — usu. used with preceding negative ⟨hadn't . . . the ~ of a prospect of raising the money —Christopher Isherwood⟩ ⟨didn't have a ~ of a chance of defending himself against . . . this master killer —Frank Dufresne⟩ **8 a :** a false image : REFLECTION: **a** *or* **ghost image :** an unwanted or false image on a photographic negative caused by internal reflections in the camera lens **b :** a faint spurious line appearing in a grating spectrum as a result of a defect in the ruling of the grating **c** *or* **ghost image :** a faint double image appearing on a television screen (as a result of the reflection of signals from external objects (as buildings) before they reach the receiving antenna **9 :** one who does literary or artistic work for and in the name of another ⟨it is his lot to serve as ~ for successful comic-strip artists —John McCarten⟩; *specif* **:** GHOST-WRITER **10 :** a tissue, cell, or other structure that does not stain normally because of degenerative changes; *specif* **:** a red blood cell that has lost its hemoglobin **11 :** a light band that alternates with a dark one or runs through a dark mass, appears on a tooled or polished surface of steel, and indicates a zone of material made harder by a difference in composition **12 ghosts** *pl but sing in constr* [so called fr. the fact that the eliminated person is called a ghost] **:** a word game in which a player names a letter of the alphabet to which each succeeding player adds a letter that makes part of but does not complete a word, a player being eliminated from the game usu. after five instances in which he has either completed a word or been guilty of adding a letter that does not contribute to making a word **13 :** PHANTOM **14 :** an outline of a former crystal shape or rock structure bounded by inclusions that make it visible and outlined by bubbles or foreign substances

²**ghost** \"\ *vb* -ED/-ING/-S *vt* **1 :** to haunt like a ghost ⟨ask not . . . what madness ~s this old man —Robert Burton⟩ **2 :** to write for and in the name of another ⟨the common report that he ~*ed* the whole document —Bruce Bliven b. 1889⟩ ~ *vi* **1 a :** to move silently like a ghost ⟨the waiter ~*ed* up to the table —Hugh MacLennan⟩ **b :** to sail quietly with or as if with no apparent wind ⟨all day the fleet ~*ed* westward in light southerly airs —S.E.Morison⟩ **2 :** to engage in writing for and in the name of another ⟨you have no qualms about ~*ing* —E.C.Marston⟩

ghost crab *n* [so called fr. its color] **:** a pale yellowish crab (*Ocypode albicans*) common on sandy beaches from Rhode Island to Brazil

ghost dance *n* **:** a group dance for communication with the spirits of the dead; *specif* **:** a messianic cult and circle dance of Plains and Plateau Indians during the late 19th century

ghost·dom \ˈgōs(t)dəm\ *n* -S **:** the realm of ghosts

ghost·ess \-stəs\ *n* -ES [¹*ghost* + *-ess*] **:** a female ghost

ghostfish \ˈ=,=\ *n* **1 :** any of several whitish or transparent fishes (as the young of the ladyfishes) **2 :** the leptocephalus stage of an eel

ghostflower \ˈ=,==\ *n* **:** INDIAN PIPE

ghost fly *n* **:** GREENHOUSE WHITEFLY

ghost·i·ly \-tələ̄\ *adv* **:** in a manner resembling or suggestive of a ghost

¹**ghostlike** \ˈ=,=\ *adj* [¹*ghost* + *-like*] **:** resembling or sugges-

tive of a ghost ⟨an occasional ~ stand of dead oaks —*Amer. Guide Series: Fla.*⟩

[2]**ghostlike** \"\ *adv* **:** in a manner suggestive of a ghost ⟨gliding ~ about their subterranean apartments —W.H. Hudson †1922⟩

ghost·li·ness \ˈgōstlēnəs, -lin-\ *n* -ES [ME *gostlines*, fr. *gostly* + *-nes* -ness] **:** the quality or state of being ghostly

ghostlore \ˈ=,=\ *n* **:** lore dealing with ghosts

[1]**ghost·ly** \ˈgōstlē, -li\ *adj* -ER/-EST [ME *gostly*, fr. OE *gāstlic*, fr. *gāst* spirit, ghost + *-līc* -ly — more at GHOST, -LY] **1 :** of or relating to the soul **:** not carnal **:** SPIRITUAL ⟨many disorders, ~ and bodily, are transmitted to us by inheritance —John Tyndall⟩ **2 :** of or relating to the church **:** not secular **:** RELIGIOUS ⟨shall not be the worse for a ~ adviser —George Meredith⟩ ⟨snatching with ~ hands at scepters —Nathaniel Hawthorne⟩ **3 :** of, relating to, or having the characteristics of a ghost **:** SPECTRAL, SHADOWY ⟨a whole troupe of delightful but ~ spirits from another world —Scott Goddard⟩ ⟨startled to see the ~ silhouette of a submarine gliding under the railway bridge —Stewart Beach⟩ **4 :** of or relating to a ghost-writer ⟨a book written without ~ assistance⟩

[2]**ghostly** \"\ *adv* [ME *gostly*, fr. OE *gastlice*, fr. *gāstlic*] **:** in a ghostly manner ⟨two strips of snow shone ~ —Clive Arden⟩

ghost moth *n* [so called fr. the white color of the male and its habit of hovering in flight] **:** a moth of the family Hepialidae most American members of which are crepuscular

ghost·ol·o·gy \gōˈstäləjē\ *n* -ES [[1]*ghost* + *-o-* + *-logy*] **:** GHOSTLORE

ghost plant *n* **1 :** INDIAN PIPE **2 :** a tumbleweed (*Amaranthus graecizans*)

ghosts *pl of* GHOST, *pres 3d sing of* GHOST

ghost·ship \ˈgōs(t),ship, -ōsh,ship\ *n* [[1]*ghost* + *-ship*] **:** the state of being a ghost

ghost shrimp *n* **1 :** a mud-dwelling anomuran crustacean (*Callianassa californiensis*) with a long slender translucent body **2 :** any of various crustaceans similar to the ghost shrimp

ghost spot *n* **:** a disease of the tomato characterized by small whitish rings on the fruit surface

ghost story *n* **1 :** a story about ghosts **2 :** a tale based on imagination rather than fact

ghost surgery *n* **:** the practice of performing surgery on another physician's patient by arrangement with the physician but unknown to the patient

ghost town *n* **:** an abandoned town or village that is at least in part still standing

ghost word *also* **ghost name** *n* **:** an accidental word form never in established usage; *esp* **:** one arising from an editorial or typographical error or a mistaken pronunciation (as *phantomnation* or *dord*)

ghostwrite \ˈ=,=\ *vb* [back-formation fr. *ghost-writer*] *vi* **:** to write as a ghost-writer **~** *vt* **:** to write (as a speech) for another who is the presumed author

ghostwriter \ˈ=,==\ *n* **:** one that writes for and in the name of another

ghosty \ˈgōstē\ *adj* -ER/-EST [[1]*ghost* + *-y*] **:** of, relating to, or resembling a ghost

ghoul \ˈgül\ *n* -S [Ar *ghūl*, fr. *ghāla* to seize] **1 :** a legendary evil being held to rob graves and feed on corpses ⟨they are neither man nor woman, they are neither brute nor human; they are ~*s* —E.A.Poe⟩ **2 :** one resembling or suggestive of a ghoul ⟨that glamour ~, the lanky young witch with the chalk-white skin and the hearse-black gown and locks —John Mason Brown⟩; *specif* **:** one who preys upon the dead

ghou·lie \ˈgülē\ *n* -S [alter. (influenced by *ghoul*) of *goulash* (hand) + *-ie*] **:** contract bridge in which only goulash hands are played — usu. used in pl.

ghoul·ish \ˈgülish, -lēsh\ *adj* **:** of, resembling, or suggestive of a ghoul ⟨something ~ in the avidity with which they will pounce upon the misfortune of their friends —W.S.Maugham⟩ — **ghoul·ish·ly** *adv* — **ghoul·ish·ness** *n* -ES

GHQ *abbr* general headquarters

ghurkha *usu cap, var of* GURKHA

ghur·ry \ˈgərē\ *n* -ES [Hindi *gharī*, fr. Skt *ghaṭikā* water pot (used as a water clock), space of time, fr. *ghaṭa* pot, perh. of Dravidian origin; akin to Tamil *kuṭam* pot] **1** *India* **:** either of two periods of time: **a :** the 60th part of a day **:** 24 minutes **b :** HOUR **2** *India* **a :** TIMEPIECE; *specif* **:** WATER CLOCK **b :** a metal disk on which the hours are struck

ghuz *or* **ghuzz** \ˈgüz\ *n, pl* **ghuz** *or* **ghuzz** *usu cap* **:** a descendant of certain early Turkish invaders of Persia

ghyll *var of* [5]GILL

GHz *abbr* gigahertz

gi \ˈgē\ *n, pl* **gi** *usu cap* **:** [2]DAN

gi *abbr* gill

[1]**GI** \(ˈ)jē¦ī\ *adj* [fr. unofficial abbr. (used by U.S. Army quartermaster clerks in listing such articles as garbage cans) for *galvanized iron*, but taken to be abbr. for *government issue* or *general issue*] **1 :** carried or provided by an official supply department of the U.S. armed forces ⟨said the *GI* shoes hurt his feet —Jimmy Cannon⟩ **2 :** of, relating to, or characteristic of enlisted personnel of the U.S. armed forces ⟨that meal's scaled to a *GI* appetite —*Mademoiselle*⟩ **3 a :** conforming to military regulations or customs ⟨his fuzzy red-dyed hair cut in *GI* style —*Nat'l Geographic*⟩ **b :** devoted to or demanding strict military discipline ⟨he was, the men complained, too *GI* —a stickler for spit and polish —A.R.Matthews⟩ **4 :** designed for the use or benefit of military personnel ⟨more than 30 new *GI* training bills in the legislative hopper —*Time*⟩

[2]**GI** \"\ *n, pl* **GI's** *or* **GIs :** a member or former member of the U.S. armed forces; *esp* **:** an enlisted man ⟨many *GI's* showed an abysmal lack of knowledge —*Reporter*⟩

[3]**GI** \"\ *vt* **GI'd; GI'd; GI'ing; GI's** [[1]*GI*] **:** to prepare for or as if for military inspection ⟨the barracks . . . were in fine order — they'd been *GI'd* the night before —*New Republic*⟩

[4]**GI** \"\ *adv* [[1]*GI*] **:** in strict conformity with military regulations or customs ⟨men like to have everything run *GI* —R.V. Cassill⟩

GI *abbr* **1** galvanized iron **2** gastrointestinal **3** general issue; government issue

giai \ˈjī\ *n, pl* **giai** *usu cap* **:** a Tai affiliated people inhabiting the valley lands of the Claire, Song-Chay, and Red rivers of upper Tonkin in Vietnam — called also *Nhang*

gial·lo an·ti·co \ˌjä(ˌ)lō,an·ˈtē(ˌ)kō, -ˌän-\ *n* [It, lit., ancient yellow] **:** an ornamental marble found among Italian ruins and believed to have come orig. from Algeria

gial·lo·li·no \ˌjäləˈlē(ˌ)nō\ *n* -S [It, fr. *giallo* yellow] **:** any of various yellow pigments (as Naples yellow)

[1]**gi·ant** \ˈjīənt\ *n* -S [ME *geant, giaunt*, fr. MF *geant*, fr. (assumed) VL *gagant-, gagas*, alter. of L *gigant-, gigas*, fr. Gk] **1 :** a legendary manlike being of huge stature and great strength and of more than mortal but less than godlike power and endowment **2 a** (1) **:** a person of unusual stature or size ⟨a fair-haired young ~, slim and lean-faced —Liam O'Flaherty⟩ ⟨perceived the inner worth of the gaunt frontier ~ —Charles Lee⟩ (2) **:** a person exhibiting gigantism ⟨troupe of tiny people with a seven-foot ~ —*Amer. Guide Series: Wash.*⟩ **b :** a person of extraordinary powers or endowments ⟨one of the nation's journalistic ~*s* —J.A.Morris b.1904⟩ ⟨one of the ~*s* of his times . . . he imparted to his students his own contagious enthusiasm for literature —N.M. Pusey⟩ **3 :** something unusually large or powerful ⟨too small a crew to handle the clumsy ~ he commanded —Frank Yerby⟩ ⟨the tools needed . . . were among the ~*s* of the forging industry —E.A.Mossein⟩ ⟨imposes setbacks on its architectural ~*s* to let a little light and air into the city —Flora Lewis⟩ ⟨it rolls, with irresistible power, majestic and silent; a young ~ among rivers —Tom Marvel⟩ **4 :** GIANT STAR **5 :** a large nozzle used in hydraulic mining

[2]**giant** \"\ *adj* **1 :** resembling a giant **:** characterized by unusual size, proportion, scope, strength, power, or significance **:** extremely large ⟨the ~ corporation whose activities spread over many fields —R.B.Heflebower⟩ ⟨behind the local broadcasting station is the ~ network —Stuart Chase⟩ ⟨time has not staled his ~ intellect —*Saturday Rev.*⟩ ⟨they battle through bitter cold and ~ drifts —*Newsweek*⟩ **2** *of a plant or animal* **:** extremely large as contrasted with members of related species or varieties **syn** see HUGE

giant anteater *n* **:** ANT BEAR

giant arborvitae *n* **:** CANOE CEDAR

giant armadillo *n* **:** a large armadillo (*Priodontes giganteus*) measuring about three feet in length exclusive of the tail

giant bamboo *n* **:** a plant of the genus *Dendrocalamus*; *esp* **:** an immense Indo-Malayan grass (*D. giganteus*) with tough hollow stems that resemble tree trunks

giant bass *or* **giant black sea bass** *n* **:** a very large serranid fish (*Stereolepis gigas*) that is dark brown or black above and lighter below and is an important food and game fish of southern and Lower California — called also *black sea bass, jewfish*

giant book *n* **:** a large cardboard dummy of a book designed for display purposes

giant cabuya *n* **:** a Brazilian plant (*Furcraea gigantea*) that is closely related to and much resembles the agaves and is cultivated in warm regions for its hard fiber — see MAURITIUS HEMP

giant cactus *n* **:** SAGUARO

giant cane *n* **:** a tall grass (*Arundinaria gigantea*) of the southern U.S. — see CANEBRAKE

giant cedar *n* **:** RED CEDAR 2a

giant cell *n* **:** an unusually large cell; *esp* **:** a large multinuclear often phagocytic cell (as those characteristic of tubercular lesions, various sarcomas, or the megakaryocytes of the red marrow)

giant chinquapin *n* **:** a chinquapin (*Castanopsis chrysophylla*)

giant clam *n* **:** a very large clam; *specif* **:** a clam (*Tridacna derasa* or *T. gigas*) found on the coral reefs of the Indian and Pacific oceans that sometimes weighs more than 500 pounds

giant clover *n* **:** SWEET CLOVER

giant cockroach *n* **:** any of several large tropical American cockroaches constituting a genus (*Blaberus*) that is considered closely related to *Blattella* or sometimes made the type of a separate family

giant crab *n* **1 :** a Japanese deep-sea edible spider crab (*Macrocheira kaempferi*) that measures about a foot across the shell and has legs many feet in length **2 :** an immense Australian edible sea crab (*Pseudocarcinus gigas*) that attains a weight of 30 pounds and has the large claw 17 inches in length

giant daisy *n* **1 :** a tall European herb (*Chrysanthemum uliginosum*) resembling an aster **2 :** any of several herbs of the genus *Wyethia* of the western U.S.

giant danio *n* **:** a blue and yellow striped cyprinid fish (*Danio malabaricus*) of southeast Asia that attains a length of four inches and is often kept in tropical aquariums

gi·ant·esque \ˌjīənt·¦esk, -ən·¦te-\ *adj* **:** having the characteristics of a giant **:** IMMENSE

gi·ant·ess \ˈjīəntəs\ *n* -ES [ME *geauntesse, giauntesse*, fr. *geaunt, giaunt* giant + *-esse* -ess — more at GIANT] **:** a female giant; *esp* **:** an unusually large woman

giant fennel *n* **:** a tall Eurasian garden plant (*Ferula communis*)

giant fern *n* **:** either of two ferns: **a :** GOLDEN FERN **b :** a fern (*Acrostichum excelsum*) with smooth woody unarmed petioles

giant fiber *n* **:** a very large nerve fiber; *specif* **:** one formed by the confluence of processes from numerous segmental nerve cell bodies in the ventral chain of nerve ganglia of annelids and crustaceans

giant fir *n* **:** LOWLAND FIR

giant fish killer *n* **:** GIANT WATER BUG

giant flying squirrel *n* **:** a large brightly colored Asiatic flying squirrel of the genus *Petaurista*

giant forest mole *n* **:** FOREST MOLE

giant forget-me-not *n* **:** a Chatham Island herb (*Myosotidium nobile*) of the family Boraginaceae with large basal leaves and dense clusters of brilliant blue flowers

giant foxtail *n* **:** either of two coarse annual foxtails of the genus *Setaria* that are naturalized weeds in parts of the U.S.: **a :** an Asiatic foxtail (*S. faberii*) widely established in the eastern U.S. **b :** a West Indian foxtail (*S. magna*) established chiefly in the southeastern and southern U.S.

giant fulmar *n* **:** GIANT PETREL

giant granadilla *n* **1 :** a tropical American passionflower (*Passiflora quadrangularis*) **2 :** the oblong fruit of the granadilla

giant granite *n* **:** PEGMATITE

giant grouper *n* **:** any of several large groupers

giant helleborine *n* **:** STREAM ORCHID

giant hill *n* **:** a virus disease of the potato characterized by the formation of large tops and few tubers

giant holly fern *n* **:** a fern (*Polystichum munitum*) of western No. America with stiff auricled pinnae

gi·ant·hood \ˈjīənt,hu̇d\ *n* -S **:** HUGENESS, IMMENSITY

giant hornet *n* **:** a large black and orange European hornet (*Vespa crabro germana*) that is now established in the northeastern U.S. and is sometimes a pest because of its painful sting and its habit of gnawing the bark from twigs

giant hyssop *n* **:** a plant of the genus *Agastache*

gi·ant·ism \ˈjīənt,izəm, -ən,ti-\ *n* -S **1 :** the quality or state of being a giant **:** extreme or unusual largeness ⟨parallel to ~ in industry is the economic concentration of power into the hands of a relatively few corporations —R.J.Harris⟩ ⟨the new skyline . . . rose even above her, overwhelming the stars with the blatant ~ of the new New York —Booth Tarkington⟩ **2 a :** GIGANTISM 2 **b :** GIGANTISM 3

giant kangaroo *n* **:** a very large grayish brown kangaroo (*Macropus giganteus*) formerly abundant in open wooded areas in Australia but now greatly reduced in numbers

giant kelp *n* **:** any of several large Pacific kelps (esp. *Macrocystis pyrifera*)

giant kidney worm *n* **:** a blood-red nematode worm (*Dioctophyme renale*) that sometimes exceeds a yard in length and that invades the kidneys of dogs and occas. other mammals including man

giantlike \ˈ==,=\ *adj* **:** resembling a giant ⟨a man ~ in strength and stature⟩

giant lily *n* **1 a :** GIANT CABUYA **b :** an Australian amaryllid (*Doryanthes excelsa*) that is cultivated in warm regions for its tall spikes of brilliant red flowers **2 :** a tall Asiatic lily (*Lilium giganteum*) that bears long racemes of large white flowers in midsummer

gi·ant·ly *adj, sometimes* -ER/-EST *archaic* **:** GIANTLIKE ⟨aspire with such a ~ presumption —Christopher Marlowe⟩

giant moss *n* **:** a large erect moss of the genus *Dawsonia* (esp. *D. superba*)

giant nettle *n* **:** AUSTRALIAN NETTLE TREE

giant newt *n* **:** a newt (*Triturus torosus*) of western No. America that is six inches or more in length and is distinguished by a uniformly yellow or orange-red ventral surface

giant panda *n* **:** PANDA 2

giant pangolin *n* **:** a large scaly anteater (*Manis gigantea*) of western Africa

giant parsley *or* **giant parsnip** *n* **:** COW PARSNIP

giant perch *n* **:** BEGTI

giant petrel *n* **:** a large dusky brownish petrel (*Macronectes giganteus*) chiefly of antarctic seas that has a heavy pale-colored beak and approximates an albatross in size though not in wingspread

giant pig *n* **:** ENTELODONT

giant powder *n* **:** a blasting powder consisting of nitroglycerin, sodium nitrate, sulfur, rosin, and sometimes kieselguhr

giant puffball *n* **:** an edible puffball (*Calvatia gigantea*) that sometimes attains a diameter of two feet and may exceed 25 pounds in weight

giant pyramidal cell *n* **:** any of the large nerve cells in the fifth layer of the cerebral cortex that give rise to the fibers of the pyramidal tract

giant ragweed *n* **:** GREAT RAGWEED

giant rat *n* **1 :** a very large dull-brown Chinese rat (*Rattus edwardsi*) **2 :** any of several large coarse-furred West African cricetid rats (genus *Cricetomys*)

giant red-wing *n* **:** a large heavy-billed redwing blackbird (*Agelaius phoeniceus arctolegus*) that breeds in northern No. America and winters chiefly in the southern U.S.

giant reed *n* **1 :** a tall European grass (*Arundo donax*) with woody stems used in making organ reeds **2 :** DITCH REED **3 :** UVA GRASS

giant ryegrass *n* **:** a grass (*Elymus condensatus*) of the western U.S. with a thick spiky inflorescence

giants *pl of* GIANT

giant salamander *n* **1 :** a large edible salamander (*Megalobatrachus or Cryptobranchus maximus*) of Japan and China that attains a length of three to five feet **2 :** HELLBENDER

giant scallop *n* **:** a very large scallop (*Pecten magellanicus*) of the Atlantic coast of No. America

giant's cauldron *or* **giant's kettle** *n* **:** a large deep pothole formed in rock by the fall of a stream into the crevasse of a glacier

giant schnauzer *n* **:** a schnauzer that attains a height of 21½ to 25½ inches

giant sequoia *n* **:** BIG TREE

gi·ant·ship \ˈjīənt,ship\ *n* [[1]*giant* + *-ship*] **:** the quality or state of being giantlike

giant silkworm *n* **:** the larva of a moth of the family Saturniidae

giant skipper *n* **:** any of various large strong-flying butterflies that constitute the family Megathymidae

giant slalom *n* **:** a long zigzag downhill run in skiing

giant sloth *n* **:** a very large recently extinct So. American sloth (genus *Megatherium*) attaining the size of an elephant

giant snail *n* **:** a snail of the genus *Achatina*

giant squid *n* **:** any of several very large squids of *Architeuthis* and related genera

giant squirrel *n* **:** any of several very large reddish or black arboreal squirrels (genus *Ratufa*) of tropical Asiatic forests

giant star *n* **:** a star (as Capella or Arcturus) of great intrinsic luminosity and therefore of large mass

giant star grass *n* **:** a perennial grass (*Cynodon plectostachyum*) that has stems attaining a height of three to four feet and that is used esp. in Africa and India for pasture and hay

giant stride *n* **:** a gymnastic apparatus consisting of an upright pole surmounted by a revolving disk to which are hooked grips that when grasped enable one to take great strides around the pole

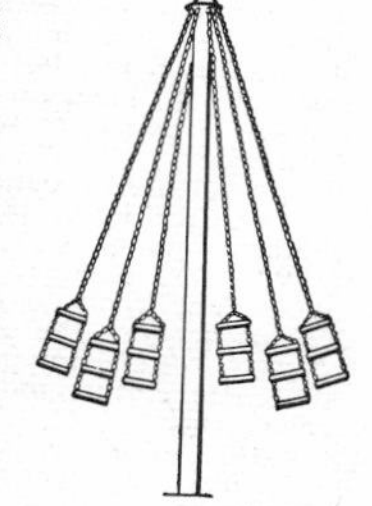
giant stride

giant sunflower *n* **:** a tall No. American sunflower (*Helianthus giganteus*) with edible tuberous roots — called also *Indian potato*

giant swing *n* **:** a complete swing of the body at full arms' length around a horizontal bar

giant tortoise *n* **:** any of numerous large long-lived slow-moving herbivorous land tortoises of the genus *Testudo* formerly abundant on the islands of the western Indian ocean and on the Galápagos islands but now largely exterminated by man

giant urticaria *n* **:** urticaria marked by an eruption of unusually large often confluent wheals

giant water bug *n* **:** any of several very large aquatic bugs (family Belostomatidae) having the hind legs flattened and fringed for use in swimming; *esp* **:** a very large dark No. American bug (*Lethocerus americanus*) often destructive to small freshwater fishes

giant water lily *n* **:** ROYAL WATER LILY

giant whortleberry *n* **:** HIGHBUSH BLUEBERRY

giant wild pig *n* **:** a large wild hog (*Sus barbatus*) of the Malay peninsula

giant wild rye *n* **:** a stout perennial grass (*Elymus condensatus*) of western No. America with short stout rhizomes and stiff erect flower spikes

giaour \ˈjau̇(ə)r\ *n* -S [Turk *gâvur*, fr. Per *gawr, gabr*] **:** one outside the Muslim faith **:** INFIDEL, UNBELIEVER ⟨an unadulterated Arab place of entertainment, seldom profaned by the presence of ~*s* —*Harper's*⟩

giar·dia \jēˈärdēə, ˈjär-\ *n* [NL, fr. Alfred M. *Giard* †1908 Fr. biologist + NL *-ia*] **1** *cap* **:** a genus of zooflagellates inhabiting the intestines of various mammals and including a species (*Giardia lamblia* syn. *Lamblia intestinalis*) that is associated with but not demonstrably the cause of diarrhea in man **2** -S **:** any flagellate of the genus *Giardia*

giar·di·a·sis \(ˌ)jē,ärˈdīəsəs, ˌjēər'-, jär'-\ *also* **giar·di·o·sis** \jē,ärdēˈōsəs, jär-\ *n, pl* **giardia·ses** \-ī,sēz\ *also* **giardio·ses** \-ēˈō,sēz\ [NL, fr. *Giardia* + *-iasis*] **:** infestation with or disease caused by flagellates of the genus *Giardia*

[1]**gib** \ˈgib\ *n* -S [ME *Gibbe, Gib*, a common name for cats, prob. by shortening & alter. fr. the name *Gilbert*] **1** *obs* **:** an old woman **2 :** a male cat; *specif* **:** a castrated male cat

[2]**gib** \"\ *n* -S [origin unknown] **1 :** a removable plate of metal or other material that is notched, tapered, or otherwise machined to hold other mechanical parts in place, bind them together, afford a bearing surface, or provide means for taking up wear **2 a :** a hooked projection that appears on the lower jaw of adult male salmon during or after the breeding season **b** *dial Eng* **:** GIB FISH

[3]**gib** \"\ *vt* **gibbed; gibbed; gibbing; gibs :** to secure or fasten with a gib

[4]**gib** \ˈgib\ *var of* GIP

[5]**gib** \ˈjib\ *var of* JIB

gibaro *var of* JIBARO

gibbed \ˈgibd\ *adj* [[1]*gib* + *-ed*] *of a cat* **:** CASTRATED

[1]**gib·ber** \ˈjibə(r) *sometimes* ˈgi-\ *or* **jib·ber** \ˈji-\ *vi* **gibbered** *or* **jibbered; gibbered** *or* **jibbered; gibbering** *or* **jibbering** \-b(ə)riŋ\ **gibbers** *or* **jibbers** [imit.] **:** to speak rapidly, inarticulately, and often foolishly **:** CHATTER ⟨the old hag . . . howled and ~*ed* with filthy gestures, calling for the thunderstorm —Charles Kingsley⟩ ⟨children were ~*ing* in their animal innocence —R.A.W.Hughes⟩ ⟨were as near ~*ing* idiots as men can get without being locked up —R.N. Ingersoll⟩

[2]**gibber** \"\ *n* -S **:** rapid, inarticulate, and often foolish utterance **:** GIBBERING ⟨have listened to ~ about . . . our present form or methods of governments —*Nation*⟩

[3]**gib·ber** \ˈgibə(r)\ *n* -S [native name in Australia] *Austral* **:** PEBBLE, STONE, BOULDER; *esp* **:** a desert stone polished or sculptured by sandblast

gibber bird *n* [[3]*gibber*] **:** a small grayish brown Australian warbler (*Ashbyia lovensis* or *Epthianura lovensis*) that frequents dry stone-covered plains

gib·ber·el·la \ˌjibəˈrelə\ *n, cap* [NL, dim. of L *gibber* hump on the back] **:** a genus of fungi (family Nectriaceae) having bluish perithecia cespitose or scattered on or around the stroma and occurring esp. on cereal grasses often in association with various abnormalities (as kernel scabs, foot rot, or seedling blight) — see EAR ROT, POKKAH BOENG

gib·ber·el·lic acid \¦==¦==lik-\ *n* [*giberellin* + *-ic*] **:** a crystalline acid $C_{18}H_{21}O_4COOH$ associated with the gibberellins and having similar effects on plants

gib·ber·el·lin \ˌ==ˈ=lən\ *n* -S [NL *Gibberella* (genus name of *Gibberella fujikuroi*) + E *-in*] **:** any of several plant-growth regulators that are produced by a fungus (*Gibberella fujikuroi*) and that act like auxins in promoting growth of shoots when applied in low concentrations but differ from auxins in some other effects (as in stimulating bud development under some conditions)

[1]**gib·ber·ish** \ˈjib(ə)rish, -rēsh *also* ˈgi-\ *n* -ES [prob. fr. [1]*gibber* + *-ish*] **1 :** confused, unintelligible, or meaningless speech or language ⟨sounded . . . like human language but was only such ~ as children may be heard amusing themselves with —Nathaniel Hawthorne⟩ **2 a :** a strange, barbarous, or outlandish language or dialect ⟨commenced talking in a ~ of which I understood very little but which he intended for French —George Borrow⟩ **b :** a technical or esoteric language used by workers in a particular activity or field of knowledge ⟨surrounded by a trainer, a jockey, and grooms speaking an impenetrable ~ —A.J.Liebling⟩ **3 :** pretentious or needlessly obscure speech or language ⟨deliberately confecting . . . ~ on the theory that the less the yokels understand, the more they will be impressed —C.J.Rolo⟩

[2]**gibberish** \"\ *adj, archaic* **:** lacking intelligibility or meaning

gibber plain *n, Austral* **:** a desert plain strewn with gibbers

[1]**gib·bet** \ˈjibət, *usu* -əd.+V\ *n* -S [ME *gibet* gallows, fr. OF, forked stick, gallows] **1** *or* **gibbet tree a :** an upright post with a projecting arm for hanging the bodies of executed criminals in chains or irons **b :** GALLOWS **2 :** the projecting arm of a crane **:** JIB

[2]**gibbet** \"\ *vt* -ED/-ING/-S **1 a :** to hang on a gibbet as a warning or for exposure to public scorn ⟨soon should I . . . be mangled on a wheel, then ~*ed* to blacken for the vultures —Samuel Rogers⟩ **b :** to expose to infamy or public scorn

⟨libel suits were successfully brought by men . . . who had been incidentally ~*ed* —*Times Lit. Supp.*⟩ **2 a :** to execute by hanging on a gibbet ⟨~*ed* the Covenanters because they denied the rights of a civil sovereign to frame liturgies —J.S. Blackie⟩ **b :** to hang as if on a gibbet ⟨half a dozen great cats hung ~*ed* there and rows of stoats —David Garnett⟩

³gibbet *n* -s [perh. alter. of MF *jupet* distance to which one can shout, fr. *juper* to shout, of imit. origin] *obs* **:** a hunting signal (as to a dog or hawk)

gibbing *pres part of* GIB

gib·ble-gab·ble \ˈgibəlˌgabəl\ *n* [redupl. of ²*gabble*] **:** GABBLE

gib·bles \ˈgibəlz\ *n pl* [origin unknown] *Scot* **:** TOOLS, GADGETS

gib·bon \ˈgibən\ *n* -s [F] **:** any of several apes of southeastern Asia and the East Indies that constitute the genera *Hylobates* and *Symphalangus*, are the smallest and most perfectly arboreal anthropoid apes, and have very long arms, small but distinct ischial callosities, and no cheek pouches or tail

gib·bon·oid \-ˌnȯid\ *adj* **:** of, relating to, or resembling the gibbons

gib·bose \jəˈbōs, giˈb-, ˈgi,b-\ *adj* [LL *gibbosus*, fr. L *gibbus* hump on the back + *-osus* -ose] **:** GIBBOUS

gib·bos·i·ty \jəˈbäsəd·ē, giˈb-\ *n* -ES [ME *gibbositee*, fr. MF *gibbosité*, fr. ML *gibbositat-, gibbositas*, fr. LL *gibbosus* + L *-itat-, -itas* -ity] **1 :** PROTUBERANCE, SWELLING; *specif* **:** KYPHOSIS **2 :** the quality or state of being gibbous; *specif* **:** the condition of being humpbacked

gib·bous \ˈjibəs, ˈgi-\ *adj* [ME, fr. MF *gibbeux*, fr. LL *gibbosus*] **1 a :** marked by convexity **:** ROUNDED, PROTUBERANT **b** *of the moon or a planet* **:** seen with more than half but not all of the apparent disk illuminated — see CONFIGURATION illustration, MOON illustration **c :** swollen or protuberant on one side **2 :** having a hump **:** HUMPBACKED ⟨these ~ human shapes —Thomas Hardy⟩ — **gib·bous·ly** *adv* — **gib·bous·ness** *n* -ES

gibbs-helm·holtz equation \ˈgibzˈhel|m,hōlts-, -ˈheu̇|\ *n, usu cap G&H* [after Josiah Willard *Gibbs* †1903 Am. mathematician and physicist and Hermann L. F. von *Helmholtz* †1894 Ger. scientist] **:** an equation in thermodynamics that is applicable to reversible chemical processes: the difference between the change in free energy and the heat of reaction at constant pressure equals the product of the absolute temperature and the rate of change of free energy with temperature

gibbs·ite \ˈgib,zīt\ *n* -s [George *Gibbs* †1833 Am. mineralogist + E *-ite*] **:** a mineral $Al(OH)_3$ consisting of light-colored translucent aluminum hydroxide occurring as monoclinic crystals and also in stalactitic and spheroidal forms — **gibbs·it·ic** \(ˈ)gibˈzid·ik\ *adj*

gibbs's mole \ˈgibz(əz)-\ *n, usu cap G* [George *Gibbs* †1873 Am. ethnologist] **:** a small mole (*Neurotrichus gibbsii*) of the western U.S.

gib·bus \ˈjibəs, ˈgi-\ *n* -ES [L] **:** HUMP; *specif* **:** the hump of the deformed spine in Pott's disease

gib-cat \ˈ=,=\ *n, dial Eng* **:** ¹GIB 2

¹gibe *or* **jibe** \ˈjīb\ *vb* -ED/-ING/-S [perh. fr. MF *giber* to shake, handle roughly] *vi* **:** to utter taunting sarcastic words **:** express scorn **:** SNEER — often used with *at* ⟨his friends *gibed* at him for his cowardice —B.L.K.Henderson⟩ ~ *vt* **:** to reproach with taunting sarcastic words **:** sneer at **:** MOCK ⟨you *gibed* each other . . . over the extent to which you found yourself shifted from the firm ground of reasoned conclusion —Mary Austin⟩ **syn** see SCOFF

²gibe *or* **jibe** \"\ *n* -s **:** a taunting sarcastic comment or expression **:** a scornful reproach **:** JEER ⟨was determined not to allow the young bloods' ~*s* to hurt him visibly —C.S.Forester⟩

³gibe *var of* JIBE

gi·bel \ˈgēbəl\ *n* -s [G *giebel* (formerly spelled *gibel*)] **:** CRUCIAN CARP

gib·e·on·ite \ˈgibēə,nīt\ *n* -s *cap* [*Gibeon*, city in ancient Palestine + E *-ite*] **:** one of the people of Gibeon in ancient Palestine condemned to be hewers of wood and drawers of water because of their deception of the Israelites

gib·er *or* **jib·er** \ˈjībə(r)\ *n* -s **:** one that gibes

gib fish *n* [²*gib*] *dial Eng* **:** a male salmon

gib-head key *n* [²*gib*] **:** a key with a projecting end that resembles the end of a gib and serves as a stop

gib·ing·ly \ˈjībinlē\ *adv* **:** in a gibing manner

gib·leh \ˈgiblə, -lē\ *n* -s [Ar *qiblīy* south wind] **:** a hot desert wind of northern Africa esp. Libya — compare HARMATTAN, SIROCCO

gib·let \ˈjiblət *also* ÷ ˈgi-, *usu* -əd·+V\ *also* **jib·let** \ˈji-\ *n* -s [ME *gibelet* entrails, garbage, fr. MF, stew of wildfowl, fr. OF (Picardy dial.), prob. irreg. dim. of *gibier, gebier* flesh of birds, of Gmc origin; akin to MHG *gebeize* hunt using falcons, fr. *beizen* to hunt birds with falcons, fr. OHG *beizzen*, causative of *bīzan* to bite — more at BITE] **1 :** an edible visceral organ of a fowl — usu. used in pl. **2 giblets** *pl, archaic* **:** odds and ends **:** TRIFLES ⟨the great ladies with their grace, lace, and ~*s* —Peter Hawker⟩

gi·boia \jəˈbȯi(y)ə\ *n* -s [Pg, fr. Tupi *giboia, jibóya*] **:** BOA CONSTRICTOR

gib plate *n* [²*gib*] **:** ²GIB 1

¹gi·bral·tar \jəˈbrȯltə(r)\ *adj, usu cap* [fr. *Gibraltar*, Brit. fortified colony on the Rock of *Gibraltar* in the south of the Iberian peninsula] **:** of or from the British colony of Gibraltar **:** of the kind or style prevalent in Gibraltar

²gibraltar \"\ *n* -s *usu cap* [fr. *Gibraltar*, Brit. colony] **1 :** an impregnable stronghold ⟨isolationist plea for retreat to the American *Gibraltar* —*Frontier*⟩ **2** *also* **gibraltar rock :** a hard white candy flavored usu. with peppermint or lemon

gibraltar candytuft *n, usu cap G* **:** an evergreen perennial herb (*Iberis gibraltarica*) used in rock gardens that has the flower stems branched above and the leaves usu. dentate toward their apex

gibraltar fever *n, usu cap G* **:** BRUCELLOSIS a

gi·bral·tar·i·an \jə,brȯlˈta(a)rēən, ,ji,b-\ *n* -s *usu cap* **:** a native or inhabitant of Gibraltar

gibs *pl of* GIB, *pres 3d sing of* GIB

gib·son \ˈgibsən\ *n* -s *usu cap* [fr. the name *Gibson*] **:** a cocktail consisting of gin and dry vermouth garnished with pearl onions

¹gibson girl *n, usu cap 1st G & often cap 2d G* [after Charles Dana *Gibson* †1944 Amer. illustrator] **1 :** an American girl regarded as representative of the fashions and manners of the 1890s **2** [so called from the curved shape of the transmitter] **:** a portable crank-operated radio transmitter orig. designed for use by aviators forced down at sea

²gibson girl *adj, usu cap 1st G & often cap 2d G* **:** of or relating to a style in women's clothing characterized by high necks, full sleeves, and wasp waists

gi·bus \ˈjībəs\ *also* **gibus hat** *n* -ES [F *gibus*, fr. *Gibus*, name of its 19th cent. Fr. inventor] **:** OPERA HAT

gid \ˈgid\ *n* -s [back-formation fr. ¹*giddy*] **:** a disease principally affecting sheep that is caused by the presence in the brain of the coenurus of a tapeworm (*Multiceps multiceps*) of the dog and related carnivores and is characterized by cerebral disturbances, dilated pupils, dizziness and circling movements, emaciation, and usu. death — called also *sturdy, turn-sick, waterbrain*

GI'd *past of* GI

gid·dap \giˈdap\ *v imper* [alter. of *get up*] — a command to a horse to go ahead or go faster

gid·di·fy \ˈgidə,fī\ *vt* -ED/-ING/-ES [¹*giddy* + *-fy*] **:** to make giddy **:** CONFUSE

gid·di·ly \ˈgidᵊlē, -dᵊli, -dəl-\ *adv* **:** in a giddy manner ⟨the lantern tossing ~ with the motion —T.B.Costain⟩ ⟨a very different crowd — mostly female, ~ hatted and all atwitter —Mollie Panter-Downes⟩

gid·di·ness \ˈgidēnəs, -din-\ *n* -ES [ME *gidinesse, gedinesse*, fr. *gidy, gedy* + *-nesse* -ness] **:** the quality or state of being giddy ⟨all the gaiety and spirits, but . . . little of the ~ of youth —Earl of Chesterfield⟩ ⟨a dimness and ~ crept over him —Charles Dickens⟩

¹gid·dy \ˈgidē, -di\ *adj* -ER/-EST [ME *gidy, gedy* mad, foolish, dizzy, fr. OE *gydig, gidig* possessed, mad, fr. the stem of *god* + *-ig* -y — more at GOD] **1 :** characterized by exuberance, impulsiveness, or thoughtlessness **:** lighthearted or harebrained ⟨he was no longer young and he had no wish to get entangled with a ~ girl —W.S.Maugham⟩ ⟨a ~, abandoned, hugely popular show —E.J.Kahn⟩ **2 a :** having a sensation of whirling or reeling about **:** affected with or as if with vertigo **:** DIZZY ⟨he was ~ . . . and the meadow swam like fishes under the high sun —Jean Stafford⟩ ⟨he paused, somewhat ~ from his quick descent of the stairs —Elinor Wylie⟩ **b :** causing a sensation of whirling or reeling about **:** tending to make dizzy ⟨staring down the coiling silvery barrel of his gun, down its circling and ~ bore —Eve Langley⟩ ⟨could almost feel . . . the lift as the car began its ~ rise into the air —*New Yorker*⟩ **c :** whirling or turning around with great rapidity **:** GYRATORY ⟨the ~ round of Fortune's wheel —Shak.⟩ ⟨swept me on before, ~ as a whirling stick —Edna S.V.Millay⟩ **3** *dial Eng* **:** crazed with anger **:** FURIOUS, WILD **4 :** suffering from gid — used esp. of sheep **5 :** extravagantly decorated or extremely ornate **:** GARISH, SHOWY ⟨a ~ organdy . . . apron festooned with ribbons and Christmas-tree balls —*New Yorker*⟩ ⟨long rococo halls, ~ with plush and whorled designs in gold —Djuna Barnes⟩

²giddy \"\ *vb* -ED/-ING/-ES *vt* **:** to make giddy ⟨the sight of so much that was growing and green *giddied* his senses —Gordon Webber⟩ ~ *vi* **:** to become giddy ⟨my head swims, my brain *giddies* —Sylvester Judd⟩

³giddy \"\ *n* -ES **:** GID

giddy gander *n* **:** MALE ORCHIS

gid·e·on \ˈgidēən\ *n* -s *usu cap* [after *Gideon*, Biblical leader of the Jews (Judg 6-8), fr. Heb *Gidh'ōn*] **:** a member of an interdenominational organization of laymen whose activities include the placing of Bibles in hotel rooms

gid·gee \ˈgijē\ *or* **gid·gea** *also* **gid·ya** *or* **gid·yea** \", -jə\ *n* -s [native name in Australia] **1 a :** a somewhat scrubby Australian acacia (*Acacia cambagei*) that grows chiefly in dry inland regions and has an extremely foul-smelling blossom **b :** GEORGINA GIDGEE **c :** YARRAN 1 **2 :** the dense hard dark wood of gidgee and various other small Australian acacias that is valued for turning and carving and used also for fencing and fuel

gie \ˈgē\ *vb* **gied** \-ēd\ **gied** \"\ *or* **gien** \-ēn\ **gieing; gies** [by alter.] *chiefly Scot* **:** GIVE

gi·em·sa stain \gēˈemzə-\ *also* **giemsa's stain** *or* **giemsa** *n, usu cap G* [after Gustav *Giemsa* †1948 Ger. chemotherapist] **:** a stain consisting of a mixture of eosin and methylene azure and used chiefly in differential staining of blood films

gier-eagle \ˈgi(ə)r, ˈgī(ə)r, ˈji(ə)r+,-\ *n* [D *gier* vulture, fr. MD; akin to OHG *gīr* vulture, *gīri* greedy, Norw dial. *gir* desire, passion, OE *geonian* to yawn — more at YAWN] **:** a bird pronounced unclean in ancient Jewish law ⟨and the pelican and the *gier-eagle* and the cormorant —Deut 14:17 (AV)⟩

gif \(ˌ)gif, ˌgəf\ *conj* [ME *gif, yif, if* — more at IF] *archaic* **:** IF

gif·blaar \ˈgif,blär\ *also* **gif** *n* -s [Afrik *gifblaar*, fr. *gif* poison + *blaar* leaf] **:** a perennial shrub (*Dichapetalum cymosum*) of southern Africa that is deadly poisonous to stock

¹giff-gaff \ˈgif,gaf\ *n* -s [prob. by alter. & redupl. fr. ¹*give*] **1** *dial Brit* **:** mutual assistance **:** fair exchange — often used in proverbs ⟨~ makes good fellowship⟩ **2** *dial Brit* **:** exchange of words **:** BANTER, REPARTEE ⟨the swift ~ that Kate and her lads were used to maintain —Neil Munro⟩

²giffgaff \"\ *vi* -ED/-ING/-S **:** to bandy words **:** BANTER

gif·o·la \ˈjifələ, ˈgi-; jəˈfōlə, gəˈ-\ *n, cap* [NL, anagram of *Filago*] *syn of* FILAGO

¹gift \ˈgift\ *n* -s *often attrib* [ME, fr. ON *gift, gipt;* akin to OE & OHG *gift*, Goth *fragifts* bestowal, betrothal; derivative fr. the root of OE *giefan* to give — more at GIVE] **1 :** a special or notable capacity, talent, or endowment either inherent, acquired, or given by a deity ⟨whatever physical ~*s* she may have are carefully cultivated —Lafcadio Hearn⟩ ⟨a sense for mathematics . . . is mainly a ~ of the gods —Bertrand Russell⟩ ⟨a ~ for pungent satire⟩ ⟨sight reading is an acquired ~⟩ **2 :** something that is voluntarily transferred by one person to another without compensation: as **a** (1) **:** a legal alienation with respect to real estate (2) **:** the conveyance of an estate tail as distinguished from a feoffment or from a demise or lease (3) **:** a voluntary transfer of real or personal property without any consideration or without a valuable consideration — distinguished from *sale* **b** *Christian relig* **:** one of the communion elements of bread and wine ⟨the Mass of the Presanctified ~*s*⟩ **c :** the point given in the game of seven-up to the eldest hand if he begs and the dealer insists upon the turnup for trump **3 :** the act, right, or power of giving or bestowing ⟨the office is not in his ~⟩ **4** *dial Eng* **:** a white speck on the fingernail which is supposed to portend a present

syn FACULTY, APTITUDE, TALENT, GENIUS, BENT, KNACK: GIFT indicates a special capacity inherent in one that facilitates doing, accomplishing, or knowing ⟨their excellent strategy and their *gift* for intrigue which brought many Indian tribes to their assistance —R.W.Murray⟩ ⟨anyone who happens to be blessed or cursed with the *gift* of humor —Sidney Alexander⟩ FACULTY in this sense simply indicates any distinct capacity or ability to do or accomplish; it lacks the connotative power of many of the others in this group ⟨there was mental *faculty* in those pliable brows to see through, and combat, an unwitting Wise Youth —George Meredith⟩ ⟨they . . . recover warmth and animation after the creative *faculty* has revived them —Ellen Glasgow⟩ APTITUDE may imply a natural liking for or an inherent potential ability at, without, however, implying anything more than promise ⟨many women . . . have no *aptitude* for domestic work —G.B.Shaw⟩ ⟨evidence is growing that the feminine mind has a special *aptitude* for detective fiction —*Times Lit. Supp.*⟩ TALENT indicates an inherent ability and may suggest an endowment which one should develop, a capacity for effective, facile execution or accomplishment, a less exalted power of accomplishment than is indicated by GENIUS ⟨he had . . . but to go forward to be supreme as soon as his *talent* could develop its full effect —Hilaire Belloc⟩ ⟨a surpassing *talent* for improvisation, an ability to call forth *genius* to flesh out his dreams —Henry Wallace⟩ ⟨what Goethe did really say was "the greatest *talent*", not "the greatest *genius*". The difference is important because, while *talent* gives the notion of power in a man's performance, *genius* gives rather the notion of felicity and perfection in it —Matthew Arnold⟩ GENIUS may indicate a strong aptitude for a particular matter, an aptitude ensuring successful execution ⟨has a *genius* for saying new and surprising things about old subjects —Aldous Huxley⟩ More generally, GENIUS is likely to designate a superior transcendent combination of intelligence, vision, and creative or interpretative power ⟨whose practical sense equaled his intuitive *genius* —Henry Adams⟩ ⟨a really great and successful writer must have a good deal of talent as well as a good deal of *genius* —J.W.Krutch⟩ BENT indicates an inherent inclination to some study or activity which militates toward successful execution ⟨he early showed a *bent* for journalism, and the year after he reached his majority . . . he became editor —W.B.Shaw⟩ KNACK may imply a ready dexterity or adroitness in execution hard to analyze, a dexterity independent of any great mental power ⟨improvisation was his *knack* and forte; he wrote rapidly and much — sometimes an entire novel in a month —Carl Van Doren⟩

²gift \"\ *vt* -ED/-ING/-S **1 :** to endow with some power, quality, or attribute **:** INVEST ⟨the Lord ~*ed* him with the power of forceful speech⟩ **2 a** *chiefly Brit* **:** to make a gift of ⟨~*ed* the money in memory of his uncle —*Brit. Agric. Bull.*⟩ ⟨I hear Her Excellency's ~*ed* the land —Kamala Markandaya⟩ **b :** to present with a gift **:** PRESENT ⟨generously ~*ed* us with a copy —*Saturday Rev.*⟩ ⟨~*ed* his parents with a television set —*Sydney (Australia) Sunday Telegraph*⟩ ⟨~*ed* her with a large heart-shaped diamond —Louella Parsons⟩

giftbook \ˈ=,=\ *n* **1 :** a book intended for giving away **2 :** an illustrated literary miscellany (as of verse, tales, and sketches) in vogue for gift purposes in the second quarter of the 19th century in the U.S. and published annually in ornamental format — called also *annual, keepsake*

gift cau·sa mor·tis \-,kau̇səˈmȯrd·əs, -,kau̇zə-, -,kȯzə-\ *n* [L *causa mortis* because of death] **:** a gift of personal property made by the donor in expectation of imminent death but revocable until his death

gift certificate *n* **:** a certified statement entitling the recipient to select merchandise in the amount stated thereon

gifted *adj* **1 :** endowed by nature or training with a gift: as **a :** having a special talent or other desirable quality ⟨~ with . . . spontaneous ease and charm —Dorothy Sayers⟩ ⟨~ in making coffee or chicken salad —Agnes S. Turnbull⟩ ⟨so much in love with the word and so little ~ for the deed —Lewis Galantiere⟩ ⟨a ~ linguist⟩ **b :** having superior intellectual capacity usu. with an intelligence quotient in the genius class ⟨a ~ child⟩ **2 :** reflecting or revealing a special gift or talent **:** OUTSTANDING, NOTABLE ⟨had a ~ voice —Jean Stafford⟩ ⟨two novels . . . were recognized as remarkably ~ —*Time*⟩ — **gift·ed·ly** *adv* — **gift·ed·ness** *n* -ES

gift·ie \ˈgifti\ *n* -s [¹*gift* + *-ie*] *Scot* **:** GIFT, FACULTY ⟨O wad some pow'r the ~ gie us to see oursels as others see us —Robert Burns⟩

gift of gab *or* **gift of the gab :** a talent for talking fluently

gift of tongues : ecstatic speech that is usu. unintelligible to hearers and is uttered in worship services of various contemporary religious groups laying great stress on religious excitation and emotional fervor

gift over *n* [fr. *gift over*, v.] **:** the transfer by will or other instrument of property upon the termination of the estate of one owner to the owner of the next succeeding estate therein

gifts *pl of* GIFT, *pres 3d sing of* GIFT

gift tax *n* **:** a tax that is imposed by the federal government and a number of states in the U.S. primarily as a supplement to and to prevent avoidance of death taxes through gifts of property before death inter vivos and that is assessed to the donor at graduated rates somewhat below death-tax rates and sometimes on a tax base which is cumulative during the lifetime of the donor with the tax rate on gifts in any one year being dependent upon the total amount of all prior gifts since adoption of the law

giftware \ˈ=,=\ *n* **:** wares or goods suitable for gifts

gift wrap *vt* **:** to wrap (merchandise intended as a gift) in specially attractive or fancy wrapping usu. with ribbons and bows

gi·fu \ˈgē(,)fü\ *adj, usu cap* [fr. *Gifu*, Japan] **:** of or from the city of Gifu, Japan **:** of the kind or style prevalent in Gifu

¹gig \ˈgig\ *n* -s [ME *gigg, gigge* giddy girl, top; perh. of Scand origin; akin to Dan *gig* top, ON *geiga* to turn aside; akin to OE *geonian* to yawn — more at YAWN] **1 :** something that whirls: as **a** *obs* **:** TOP, WHIRLIGIG **b** *or* **gig mill :** a rotary cylinder covered with teasels or wire teeth for napping fabrics (as wool) **c :** a three-number combination selected to appear among the numbers to be drawn from a lottery wheel **2 a** *archaic* **:** JOKE, WHIM **b** *dial Eng* **:** FUN, SPORT **c :** a person of odd or grotesque appearance **:** ODDITY, FOOL ⟨we would look like a lot of ~*s* in that rig-out —*Punch*⟩ **3 a :** a long light ship's boat for oars or sail usu. clinker-built and fast and usu. appropriated for the commanding officer ⟨the captain's ~⟩; *also* **:** a boat assigned for the captain's exclusive use **b :** a rowboat designed for speed rather than for work or carrying **4 :** a light carriage that has one pair of wheels and is drawn by one horse **:** CHAISE

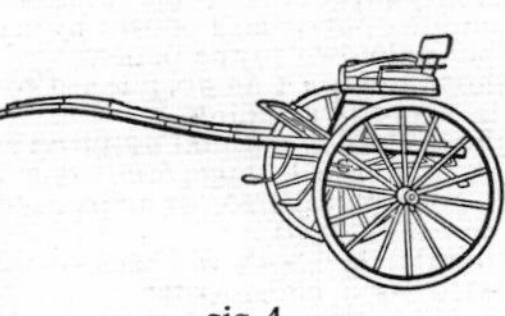
gig 4

²gig \"\ *vb* **gigged; gigged; gigging; gigs** *vt* **1 :** to nap (fabric) with the use of a gig **2 :** to move backwards and forwards ~ *vi* **:** to travel in a gig

³gig \"\ *n* -s [short for *fishgig*] **1 :** FISHGIG **2 :** an arrangement of hooks to be drawn through a school of fish when they will not bite in order to hook them in the bodies

⁴gig \"\ *vb* **gigged; gigged; gigging; gigs** *vt* **1 :** to spear with a fishgig ⟨~ a flounder⟩ **2 a** *chiefly West* **:** SPUR ⟨*gigged* him with the spurs —Ross Santee⟩ **:** PROD, JAB ⟨*gigged* him in the ribs —A.B.Guthrie⟩ **b :** HARASS, ANNOY ⟨~*s* . . . politicos with biting irony or refined ridicule —*Time*⟩ **c :** GOAD, PROVOKE, ROUSE ⟨~ his students into practice in the arts of thinking and analysis —*N.Y. Herald Tribune*⟩ ~ *vi* **:** to fish with a fishgig ⟨*gigging* for fish⟩

⁵gig \"\ *n* -s [origin unknown] *slang* **:** an official report of an infraction of military rules; *also* **:** demerits or light punishment resulting from such a report

⁶gig \"\ *vt* **gigged; gigged; gigging; gigs** *slang* **:** to report unfavorably for an infraction of military rules ⟨would be *gigged* by the first officer who saw him —*Life*⟩; *also* **:** to assign demerits or light punishment for such infraction ⟨gets *gigged* . . . for being eleven minutes late —J.G.Cozzens⟩

⁷gig \"\ *n* -s [origin unknown] **1 :** a single engagement; *esp* **:** ONE-NIGHT STAND ⟨graduate work in music, with as much sideline work, as many ~*s*, as the student can find time to develop his jazz skills —Barry Ulanov⟩ **2 :** JOB

gi·ga \ˈjēgə\ *n, pl* **gi·ghe** \-gā\ [It, fr. OIt, fiddle, of Gmc origin; akin to OHG *gīga* fiddle — more at JIG] **:** GIGUE

giga- \ˈjigə\ *comb form* [ISV, fr. Gk *gigas* giant] **:** billion ⟨*giga*cycle⟩ ⟨*giga*volt⟩

giga·hertz \ˈjigə + ,-\ *n* [ISV *giga-* + *hertz*] **:** a unit of frequency equal to one billion hertz — abbr. *GHz*

gigalira *var of* GIGELIRA

gigant- *or* **giganto-** *comb form* [Gk *gigant-, gigas*] **:** giant ⟨*gigant*ism⟩ ⟨*Giganto*pithecus⟩

gi·gant·an·thro·pus \,jī,gantˈan(t)thrəpəs, jə,g-, -,ganˈtan-; -,gant,anˈthrōp-\ [NL, fr. *gigant-* + *-anthropus*] *syn of* GIGANTOPITHECUS

gi·gan·te·an \,jī,ganˈtēən; (ˈ)jīˈgantē-, jəˈg-\ *adj* [L *giganteus* of the giants (fr. *gigant-, gigas* giant, fr. Gk) + E *-an*] **:** GIGANTIC ⟨a ~ granite altar —*Time*⟩ **syn** see HUGE

gi·gan·tesque \,jī,ganˈtesk; jīˈgan,t-, jəˈg-\ *adj* [F, fr. It *gigantesco*, fr. *gigant-* + *-esco* -esque] **:** of enormous or grotesquely large proportions **:** GIGANTIC ⟨Greek comedy is ~ buffoonery —J.J.Chapman⟩ ⟨a ~ novel⟩

gi·gan·tic \(ˈ)jīˈgantik, -gaan-, -tēk *also* jəˈg-\ *adj* [Gk *gigantikos*, fr. *gigant-* + *-ikos* -ic] **1** *obs* **:** of or relating to a giant **2 a :** like or suggesting a giant (as in size or strength) ⟨of a ~ stature . . . about eight feet in height and proportionally large —Mary W. Shelley⟩ ⟨wind and waves . . . were hurled with ~ force —*Encore*⟩ **b :** markedly larger than others of the same class or group **:** greater in size than the usual or expected ⟨a ~ fir⟩ ⟨a ~ wave⟩ ⟨a ~ tanker⟩ **c :** of extraordinary, towering, or superhuman intellectual or moral stature or force ⟨up in my mind rose the ~ artist of Rome in all his genius and glory —Eve Langley⟩ ⟨the ~ figures of Washington⟩ ⟨his personality became ~ . . . it overrode the man to whom he talked —Sherwood Anderson⟩ **d :** extremely large or great **:** ENORMOUS ⟨suffered a ~ setback⟩ ⟨possessed of a ~ hunger —Niccolò Tucci⟩ ⟨a ~ enterprise⟩ ⟨a ~ annual folk festival —J.A. Morris b. 1904⟩ **syn** see HUGE

gigantical *obs var of* GIGANTIC

gi·gan·ti·cal·ly \-tək(ə)lē, -tēk-, -li\ *adv* **:** in a gigantic manner **:** in the manner of a giant **:** ENORMOUSLY ⟨yawned ~⟩

gi·gan·tic·ness *n* -ES **:** the quality or state of being gigantic **:** extremely great size **:** HUGENESS

gigantic pine *n* **:** SUGAR PINE

gi·gan·tism \jīˈgan,tizəm, -gaan-, ˈ=,=,==; jəˈg-\ *n* -s [ISV *gigant-* + *-ism*] **1 :** GIANTISM 1 ⟨trade unions are as subject to ~ and centralization as are the industries to which they are related —Aldous Huxley⟩ ⟨the tendency toward ~ in American publishing —Howard M. Jones⟩ **2 :** development to abnormally large size from excessive growth of the long bones accompanied by muscular weakness and sexual impotence and usu. caused by overactivity of the pituitary gland before normal ossification is complete — compare ACROMEGALY **3 :** excessive vegetative growth frequently induced by the use of colchicine that results in the doubling of the number of chromosomes and is often accompanied by the inhibiting of reproduction

gi·gan·to·pi·the·cus \(,)jī,gantōpəˈthēkəs, jə,g-, -ōˈpithəkəs\ *n, cap* [NL, fr. *gigant-* + *-pithecus*] **:** a genus of giant fossil primates from the Pleistocene of China intermediate in a number of characters between the great apes and primitive man and sometimes placed in the Hominidae

gi·gan·tos·tra·ca \(,)jī,ganˈtästrəkə, jə,g-\ *n pl, cap* [NL, fr. *gigant-* + *-ostraca*] **:** a group of arthropods comprising the eurypteroids and sometimes related forms including the xiphosurans — compare MEROSTOMATA — **gi·gan·tos·tra·can** \ˌjīˌganˈtästrəkən; jīˈg-, jəˈg-\ *adj or n* — **gi·gan·tos·tra·cous** \-kəs\ *adj*

gig·ar·ti·na \ˌjigə(r)ˈtīnə, -tēnə\ *n, cap* [NL, fr. Gk *gigarton* grape seed + NL *-ina*; prob. akin to Gk *gēras* old age — more at CORN] : the type genus of Gigartinaceae comprising red algae mainly of the Pacific ocean having fleshy or cartilaginous compressed fronds with numerous outgrowths resembling teats on which the cystocarps are born

gig·ar·ti·na·ce·ae \ˌjigə(r)təˈnāsēˌē\ *n pl, cap* [NL, fr. *Gigartina*, type genus + *-aceae*] : a family of red algae (order Gigartinales) having procarps and large often unbranched fronds — see CHONDRUS GIGARTINA

gig·ar·ti·na·les \-ā(ˌ)lēz\ *n pl, cap* [NL, fr. *Gigartina* + *-ales*] : an order of red algae (subclass Florideae) in which the auxiliary cell arises as a vegetative cell of the gametophyte prior to fertilization — see GIGARTINACEAE

gi·gas \ˈjīˌgas\ *adj* [L, n., giant, fr. Gk] *of a polyploid plant* : having a thicker stem, taller growth, thicker and darker leaves, and larger flowers and seeds than a corresponding diploid plant

gig back *vt* [²*gig*] : to move back (a sawmill carriage) on the return stroke

gigback \ˈ=ˌ=\ *n* -s [*gig back*] : a mechanism for gigging back a sawmill carriage

gi·ge·li·ra *also* **gi·ga·li·ra** \ˌjēgəˈlirə\ *n, pl* **gigeli·re** *also* **gigali·re** \-rē\ [It *gigalira*, fr. *giga* fiddle + *lira* lyre] : XYLOPHONE

gi·ge·ri·um \jəˈjirēəm\ *n, pl* **gige·ria** \-ēə\ [NL, fr. L *gigeria*, pl., entrails of fowl, perh. of Iranian origin; akin to Per *jigar* liver] : GIZZARD 1

gigged *past of* GIG

gig·ger \ˈgigə(r)\ *n* -s [²*gig* + *-er*] : one that uses a gig; *specif* : a textile worker who raises nap on cloth by running it through a gig — called also *teaseler*

gigging *pres part of* GIG

¹**gig·gle** \ˈgigəl\ *vb* **giggled; giggled; giggling** \-ig(ə)liŋ\ **giggles** [imit.] *vi* : to laugh with continued short convulsive catchings of the voice or breath caused usu. by efforts at restraint : titter nervously : laugh in an affected or silly manner ~ *vt* : to express by or utter with a giggle

²**giggle** \ˈ"\ *n* -s : the act of giggling : a light silly laugh ⟨whispered . . . with a shocked ~ —Ruth Park⟩

gig·gler \ˈgig(ə)lə(r)\ *n* -s : one that giggles

gig·gling·ly *adv* : in a giggling manner

gig·gly \ˈgig(ə)lē, -li\ *adj* -ER/-EST : prone to giggling ⟨hospitable, faintly ~, and shy —*Harper's*⟩

gighe *pl of* GIGA

gig·let *also* **gig·lot** \ˈgiglət\ *n* -s [ME *gigelot, giggelot*, prob. fr. *giggi, gigge* silly girl — more at GIG] **1** *archaic* : a lascivious woman : WANTON ⟨set upon the ~ and beat her . . . soundly —S.H.Adams⟩ **2** : a giddy frivolous frolicsome girl ⟨that overgrown ~ —Osbert Sitwell⟩

gig mill *n* [¹*gig*] **1** : GIG 1b **2** : a textile mill using gigs

gig·o·lo \ˈjigəˌlō *sometimes* ˈzhig-, ˈzhēg-\ *n* -s [F, back-formation fr. *gigolette* girl who frequents public dances, prostitute, fr. *giguer* to dance, jig — more at JIG] **1** : a man living on the earnings of or supported by a woman **2** : a professional dancing partner or male escort

gig·ot \ˈjigət\ *n* -s [MF, dim. of *gigue* fiddle; fr. its shape — more at JIG] **1** : a leg (as of lamb or mutton) esp. when cooked **2** *also* **gigot sleeve** : a leg-of-mutton sleeve

gigs *pl of* GIG, *pres 3d sing of* GIG

gigue \ˈzhēg\ *n* -s [F — more at JIG] **1** : a medieval fiddle or viol **2** : JIG 1 **3** : a lively dance movement (as of the suite of the 17th and 18th centuries) having compound triple rhythm and consisting of two sections each of which is repeated

GI'ing *pres part of* GI

gi·jón *or* **gi·jon** \hēˈhōn, -ˈhōn\ *adj, usu cap* [fr. *Gijón*, Spain] : of or from the city of Gijón, Spain : of the kind or style prevalent in Gijón

gi·la·ki \gəˈläkē\ *n, pl* **gilaki** *or* **gilakis** *usu cap* **1 a** : a forest people of northern Persia inhabiting the southwestern shore of the Caspian sea **b** : a member of such people **2** : the Iranian language of the Gilaki people

gi·la monster \ˈhēlə-\ *also* **gila** *n* -s *usu cap G* [fr. *Gila* river, Arizona] : a large stout sluggish venomous lizard (*Heloderma suspectum*) that has venom glands in the lower lip, grooved teeth in the lower jaw, a thick tail, and a rough tuberculated skin pinkish or dull orange marked with black and that is found esp. in the arid regions of Arizona and New Mexico; *also* : a closely related lizard (*H. horridum*) of Mexico with an entirely black head — called also *beaded lizard*

gila trout *n, usu cap G* [fr. *Gila* river] : BONYTAIL

gila woodpecker *n, usu cap G* [fr. *Gila* river] : a large red-crowned woodpecker (*Melanerpes hypopolius uropygialis*) of southwestern No. America having the back finely barred with black and white and the underparts grayish brown

gil·bert \ˈgilbə(r)t, *usu* -d·+V\ *n* -s [after William *Gilbert* †1603 Eng. physicist] : the cgs unit of magnetomotive force equivalent to 10÷4π ampere-turn

gil·bert·ese \ˌgilbə(r)dˈēz, -ēs\ *n, pl* **gilbertese** *cap* [*Gilbert* islands in the central Pacific + E *-ese*] **1** : a Micronesian native or inhabitant of the Gilbert islands **2** : the Melanesian language of the Gilbertese

gil·ber·ti·an \(ˈ)gilˈbərd·ēən\ *adj, usu cap* [William S. *Gilbert* †1911 Eng. playwright + E *-ian*] : of, relating to, or suggesting the playwright Gilbert or the comic, wildly improbable, or topsy-turvy situations found in the Gilbert and Sullivan operas ⟨a *Gilbertian* world, peopled with foundlings and changelings —T.C.Worsley⟩ ⟨by various *Gilbertian* maneuvers . . . secured for himself the key positions —K.N.Cameron⟩

gil·bert's relief grass \ˈgilbə(r)ts-\ *n, usu cap G* [fr. the name *Gilbert*] : SOUTHERN CANARY GRASS

gil·christ's disease \ˈgilˌkri|s(t)s-, -ˌkrə|\ *n, usu cap G* [after Thomas C. *Gilchrist* †1927 Amer. dermatologist] : NORTH AMERICAN BLASTOMYCOSIS

¹**gild** \ˈgild\ *vt* **gilded** \-dəd\ *or* **gilt** \-lt\ **gilded** *or* **gilt; gilding; gilds** [ME *gilden*, fr. OE *gyldan*; akin to OHG *ubargulden* to gild all over, ON *gylla* to gild; causative-denominatives fr. the root of E *gold*] **1 a** : to overlay with a thin covering of gold ⟨~ a frame⟩ **b** : to tinge with a golden or yellowish light ⟨the night was ~*ed* by the streetlights —Marguerite Steen⟩ ⟨a gleam of sun ~*ed* the Abbey Towers —L.P. Smith⟩ **2 a** : to supply with money : give the attraction or prestige of wealth to ⟨money ~s the fool⟩ **b** (1) : to give an attractive but deceptive outward appearance to : EMBELLISH ⟨~ a lie⟩ ⟨~*ing* the future with the same old rose color —Virginia D. Dawson & Betty D. Wilson⟩ (2) : to make attractive : ADORN, BRIGHTEN ⟨~*ing* hardship with a saving grace —Bergen Evans⟩ ⟨glitter . . . and embroidery ~ femininity —*Fashion Digest*⟩ **c** *archaic* : to make bloody : smear with blood **d** *obs* : to make flushed (as with drinking) — often used with *over* — **gild the lily** : to add excessive or unnecessary ornamentation to something beautiful in its own right : paint the lily

²**gild** *var of* GUILD

gilded *adj* **1** : covered or tinged with gold or a golden color ⟨~ icons⟩ **2** : displaying a fine but deceptive outward appearance : superficially resplendent : ORNATE, MERETRICIOUS, TAWDRY ⟨the ~ and perfume but inwardly rotten nobility —R.A.Hall b.1911⟩ ⟨a conglomeration of ~ parasites —*N.Y. Times*⟩ ⟨slickly readable but ~ and thin —Nolan Miller⟩ **3** : having a background of wealth and luxury : PROSPEROUS, LUXURIOUS ⟨you'll see Rome's most ~ youth dancing by —P.E.Deutschman⟩ ⟨the ~ days of the twenties⟩ ⟨~ boys and girls —Carl Van Doren⟩ ⟨eating box lunches and staying away from the ~ dining rooms —*Wall Street Jour.*⟩

gilded flicker *n* : a flicker (*Colaptes chrysoides*) of the southwestern U.S. resembling the common eastern flicker in having the undersurface of the wings and tail yellow but lacking the red nape

¹**gil·der** \ˈgil(d)ə(r)\ *n* -s [ME, of Scand origin; akin to Norw dial. *gilder* trap, ON *gildra, gildri*; akin to ON *gilja* to entice, OSw *gælskap* lewdness and perh. to Gk *thelein* to wish, OSlav *želěti* to desire] *dial Eng* : SNARE; *esp* : one made of horsehair and used to catch birds

²**gild·er** \ˈgildə(r)\ *n* -s [¹*gild* + *-er*] : one that gilds; *esp* : one whose occupation is to overlay with gold or gilt

gilder's wax *n* : a preparation of wax, verdigris, and other substances for imparting a tint to gilding by burning off the wax so that the copper from the verdigris combines with the gold

gilder's whiting *n* : whiting ground to medium fineness

gildhall *var of* GUILDHALL

gilding *n* -s [ME, fr. gerund of *gilden* to gild — more at GILD] **1 a** (1) : the art or practice of overlaying or covering with gold (2) : the similar use of some other yellow metal (as brass) **b** : the surface so decorated **c** : the material used for such decoration **2** : a superficial prettifying or embellishment ⟨his great story needs no ~ —Burke Wilkinson⟩

gilding metal *n* **1** : a brass rich in copper from which articles to be gilded were formerly made **2** : brass containing 95 percent copper and 5 percent zinc or a similar alloy

gil·e·ad·ite \ˈgilēəˌdīt\ *n* -s *usu cap* [*Gilead*, region in Jordan + E *-ite*] **1** : a member of a branch of the ancient Israelite tribe of Manasseh **2** : an inhabitant of ancient Gilead

gi·le·ño \gəˈlān(ˌ)yō\ *n, pl* **gileño** *or* **gileños** *usu cap* [Sp, fr. the *Gila* river + Sp *-eño* (suffix added to place names to form names of inhabitants)] **1** : a group of Athapaskan peoples comprising the Chiricahua, Mimbreño, Mogollon, and Warm Spring Apaches of the Gila river headwaters in New Mexico and Arizona **2** : a member of the Gileño peoples

gi·let \zhēˈlā\ *n* -s [F, fr. Sp *gileco, jaleco, chaleco*, fr. Ar *jalīkah*, a garment worn by slaves in Algeria, fr. Turk *yelek* waistcoat, vest] : WAISTCOAT; *specif* : a woman's dickey resembling a waistcoat or blouse

gil·gai \ˈgilˌgī\ *n* -s [native name in Australia] : MELON HOLE

gil·gul \ˈgilˌgül\ *n, pl* **gil·gu·lim** \gilˈgüləm\ [Heb *gilgūl* (*nephesh*) metempsychosis, lit., turning over of the soul] : DYBBUK

gil·guy \ˈgilˌgī\ *n* -s [origin unknown] **1** : a rope temporarily used as a guy or lanyard **2** : GADGET — used esp. by sailors

gil·ia \ˈjilēə\ *n* [NL, fr. Felipe *Gil* 18th cent. Sp. botanist + NL *-ia*] **1** *cap* : a genus of No. American herbs (family Polemoniaceae) with often dissected leaves and campanulate to infundibuliform flowers of various colors **2** -s : any plant of the genus *Gilia* — see STANDING CYPRESS

giliak *usu cap, var of* GILYAK

¹**gill** \ˈjil\ *n* -s [ME *gille*, perh. fr. MF *gille, gelle* vat, tub, fr. L *gerulus* bearer, carrier, fr. *gerere* to bear — more at CAST] **1** : either of two units of capacity: **a** : a British unit equal to ¼ imperial pint or 8.669 cubic inches **b** : a U. S. liquid unit equal to ¼ U. S. liquid pint or 7.218 cubic inches — see MEASURE table **2** *dial Eng* : half a pint

²**gill** \ˈ"\ *vi* -ED/-ING/-S *dial Brit* : TIPPLE

³**gill** \ˈgil\ *n* -s [ME *gile, gille*, prob. of Scand origin; akin to OSw *geel* gill, Sw *gäl* gill, jaw, ODan *gæln* gill, ON *gjlnar* lips; akin to Gk *chelynē* lip, jawbone, *cheilos* lip, Arm *jelun* palate, ceiling] **1** : an organ for obtaining oxygen from water: as **a** : one of the highly vascular lamellar or filamentous processes of the pharynx of fishes and many larval amphibians by which oxygen dissolved in the surrounding water is absorbed through a thin enclosing membrane and certain wastes are given up **b** : any of various functionally comparable but structurally dissimilar organs of invertebrates (as the ctenidia within the mantle cavity of a bivalve mollusk or the branching respiratory tree that arises from the cloaca of a sea urchin) **c** (1) : the entire respiratory apparatus of a water-breathing animal (2) **gills** *pl* : the gills of a fish together with supporting branchial arches, branchial clefts, gill covers, and associated structures **2 a** : the fleshy flap below the beak of a fowl : WATTLE **b** : the flesh under or about the chin or jaws — usu. used in pl. ⟨decidedly pink about the ~s —Norman Douglas⟩ **c** : one of the radiating gill-shaped plates forming the undersurface of the pileus of various basidiomycetes **d** : one of the fallers which comb and arrange fibers or filaments in parallel order prior to spinning **e** : a corrugation or series of lips or fins usu. for promoting radiation of heat from a tube or plate (as in a heating system) — **to the gills** *adv* : as full as possible ⟨old cars loaded *to the gills* with household furniture —Meridel Le Sueur⟩

⁴**gill** \ˈ"\ *vb* -ED/-ING/-S [ME *gillen*, fr. *gile, gille*, n.] *vt* **1** : to remove the insides of (fish) **2** : to catch (fish) by the gills in a gill net **3** : to treat (fibers or filaments) in a gill box ~ *vi* : to become entangled in a gill net — used of fish

⁵**gill** \ˈ"\ *n* -s [ME *gille, gylle*, fr. ON *gil*; akin to MLG *gil* throat, OHG *gil* hernia, OE *gǣlan* to hinder, impede, ON *gīna* to yawn — more at YAWN] **1** *Brit* : a narrow steep-sided rocky valley sometimes containing a stream : RAVINE **2** *Brit* : a narrow stream or rivulet; *esp* : one flowing through a gill

⁶**gill** *or* **jill** \ˈjil\ *n* -s *often cap* [ME *gill*, short for the name *Gillian*] **1** : GIRL, SWEETHEART — usu. used in conjunction with *Jack* ⟨every Jack must have his *Gill*⟩ **2** *dial Eng* : GROUND IVY

⁷**gill** \ˈ"\ *n* -s [origin unknown] *dial Eng* : a two-wheeled frame for moving timber

gil·lar \gəˈlär\ *n* -s [native name in India] : a disease of East Indian sheep marked by loss of appetite, weakness, and diarrhea, usu. found fatal within a few days, and caused by infestation with immature paramphistome flukes

gill arch *n* [³*gill*] : BRANCHIAL ARCH

gil·la·roo \ˌgiləˈrü\ *n* -s [IrGael *giolla ruadh*, fr. *giolla* boy + *ruadh* red] : an Irish trout (*Salmo stomachicus*) in which the distal part of the stomach has thickened walls resembling a gizzard and serving to crush the shells of freshwater mollusks

gill bailer *n* [³*gill*] : a flat membranaceous expansion of the second maxilla in the crayfish and other decapod crustaceans by which water is scooped out of the gill cavity — called also *gill scoop*

gill basket *n* [³*gill*] : BRANCHIAL BASKET

gill box *n* [³*gill*] : a machine containing gills for drafting and combing fibers or filaments

gill cavity *or* **gill chamber** *n* [³*gill*] : the space between the gill arches and the gill cover into which the gill filaments project

gill cleft *n* [³*gill*] : BRANCHIAL CLEFT

gill cover *n* [³*gill*] : the fold of skin usu. stiffened by bony plates and often covered with scales that protects externally the gill apparatus of most fishes — compare OPERCULUM

gill disease *n* [³*gill*] : a destructive disease of trout and other fishes (as in hatcheries) marked by swollen eroded gills and usu. anemia and severe general debility and considered due to an unidentified bacterium or to a dietary deficiency

gilled \ˈgild\ *adj* [³*gill* + *-ed*] : provided with gills ⟨a ~ tadpole⟩ ⟨a ~ tube⟩

gil·le·nia \jəˈlēnēə, gə-\ *n, cap* [NL, fr. Arnold Gill (*Gillenius*) 17th cent. Ger. botanist + NL *-ia*] : a genus of American herbs (family Rosaceae) having trifoliolate leaves and white or pale rose flowers — see FALSE IPECAC, INDIAN PHYSIC

gill·er \ˈgilə(r)\ *n* -s [⁴*gill* + *-er*] **1** : one that guts fish; *esp* : a member of a fish-dressing gang who cuts out the gills and entrails of fish **2** : one that catches fish with a gill net **3** : one that supplies slivers to a gill box

gil·les·pite \gəˈleˌspīt\ *n* -s [Frank *Gillespie*, 20th cent. Am. collector of mineralogical specimens + E *-ite*] : a mineral $BaFeSi_4O_{10}$ consisting of a micaceous silicate of barium and iron

gill filament *or* **gill leaflet** *n* [³*gill*] : one of the filamentous or laminar processes making up a gill

gillflirt \ˈ=ˌ=\ *n* [⁶*gill* + *flirt*] *archaic* : a giddy or shameless girl

gill fungus *n* [³*gill*] : a basidiomycete having gills

gill-go-by-the-ground \ˌ=ˌ===ˌ=\ *n* [⁶*gill*] : GROUND IVY

gill helix *n* [³*gill*] : a spiral accessory branchial organ resembling a gill in certain characinids and clupeids

gillhooter \ˈ=ˌ==\ *n* [⁶*gil* + *hooter*] *dial Eng* : OWL; *esp* : BARN OWL

gil·lie *or* **gil·ly** *or* **ghil·lie** \ˈgilē\ *n, pl* **gillies** *or* **ghillies** [ScGael *gille* & IrGael *giolla* boy] **1** : a male attendant or servant to a Scottish Highland chief **2** *Scot & Irish* : a fishing and hunting guide **3** : a low-cut shoe with a decorative lacing; *esp* : a shoe tied by means of a cord that runs through loops or slots instead of eyelets and often winds around the ankle

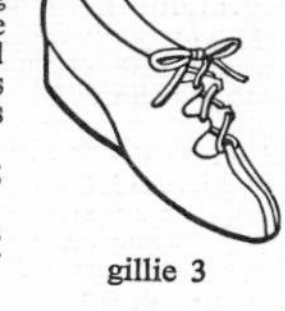
gillie 3

²**gillie** \ˈ"\ *vi* **gillied; gillied; gillying; gillies** : to serve as a gillie

³**gill·ie** \ˈjilē\ *n* -s [⁶*gill* + *-ie*] **1** *dial* : a stupid person **2** *dial* : a woman of easy virtue

⁴**gill·ie** \ˈ"\ *n* -s [¹*gill* + *-ie*] *Scot* : a gill of liquor

gil·lie cal·lum \ˌgiliˈkaləm\ *n, pl* **gillie callums** *usu cap G&C* [¹*gillie* + *callum*, of unknown origin] : a solo sword dance of the Scottish Highlands

gilliflower *var of* GILLYFLOWER

gilling *n* -s [fr. gerund of ⁴*gill*] : the process of laying fibers or filaments parallel by combing

gilling thread *n* [fr. pres. part. of ⁴*gill*] : a fine twisted cord used in making gill nets

gil·li·ver \ˈjiləvə(r)\ *dial Eng var of* GILLYFLOWER

gill·more needles \ˈgilˌmō(ə)r-\ *n pl, usu cap G* [fr. the name *Gillmore*] : two needles used in determining the rate of setting of cement paste

gill net *n* [³*gill*] : a flat net suspended vertically in the water with meshes that allow the head of a fish to pass but entangle its gill covers as it seeks to withdraw

gillnet \ˈ=ˌ=\ *vt* [*gill net*] : to catch (fish) with a gill net ⟨*gillnetted* over 5 tons of herring⟩

gill-netter \ˈ=ˌ==\ *n* : one that fishes with a gill net; *also* : a boat equipped for or engaged in such fishing

gill-over-the-ground \ˌ=ˌ===ˌ=\ *or* **gill-over-ground** \ˌ=ˌ==ˌ=\ *n* [⁶*gill*] : GROUND IVY

gill raker *also* **gill rake** *n* [³*gill*] : one of the bony processes on the inside of the branchial arches of fishes that help to prevent solid substances from being carried out through the branchial clefts

gill rod *n* [³*gill*] : one of the oblique supporting rods of the pharynx in lancelets

gills *pl of* GILL, *pres 3d sing of* GILL

gill scoop *n* [³*gill*] : GILL BAILER

gill slit *n* [³*gill*] **1** : BRANCHIAL CLEFT **2** : the external opening of the gill cavity when a gill cover is present

¹**gilly** *var of* GILLIE

²**gil·ly** \ˈgilē\ *n* -ES [⁷*gill* + *-y*] : a lumber wagon or any local wagon or truck hired for hauling circus or carnival paraphernalia

³**gilly** \ˈ"\ *vb* -ED/-ING/-ES *vt* : to transport by means of a gilly ~ *vi* : to be transportable on a gilly

gil·ly·flow·er *also* **gil·li·flow·er** \ˈjilē, -li + ˌ-\ *n* [by folk etymology fr. ME *gilofre, gelofer*, fr. MF *girofle, gilofre*, fr. L *caryophyllum*, fr. Gk *karyophyllon*, fr. *karyon* nut + *phyllon* leaf — more at CAREEN, BLADE] **1 a** *obs* : ⁴CLOVE 1a **b** : CLOVE PINK 1; *broadly* : any of several plants of the genus *Dianthus* **c** : STOCK 24a **d** : WALLFLOWER 1 **2** *dial Eng* : an aging Jezebel

gil·ly·gau·pus \ˌgiliˈgōpəs, -ˈgäp-\ *n* -ES [¹*gillie, gilly* + *-gaupus* (fr. ²*gawp*)] *dial Brit* : a stupid awkward person

gil·py *or* **gil·pey** \ˈgilpi\ *n, pl* **gilpies** *or* **gilpeys** [origin unknown] *chiefly Scot* : a lively frolicsome boy or girl ⟨I was a *gilpey* . . . na past fifteen —Robert Burns⟩

¹**gil·rav·age** \gəlˈravij\ *vi* [origin unknown] **1** *chiefly Scot* **a** : to live riotously and intemperately; *esp* : to practice intemperate eating and drinking **b** : to be noisy and boisterous in merrymaking **2** *chiefly Scot* : GAD, GALLIVANT

²**gilravage** \ˈ"\ *n, chiefly Scot* : UPROAR, COMMOTION

Gil·son·ite \ˈgilsəˌnīt\ *trademark* — used for uintaite

¹**gilt** \ˈgilt\ *adj* [ME, fr. past part. of *gilden* to gild — more at GILD] : covered with gold or gilt : of the color of gold : GILDED

²**gilt** \ˈ"\ *n* -s **1** : gold or something that resembles gold laid on the surface of a thing : GILDING **2** *slang* : MONEY **3** : superficial or shoddy prettiness or brilliance : false glitter ⟨the ~ has worn off some of these sparkling aphorisms —M.D.Geismar⟩

³**gilt** \ˈ"\ *or* **yilt** \ˈyilt\ *n* -s [ME *gilte, gylte*, fr. ON *gyltr, gylta* sow; akin to OE *gelte* young sow, MLG *gelte* spayed sow — more at GELD] : an immature female swine; *also* : a young sow usu. prior to production of her first litter but sometimes until bred to produce a second litter

gilt bronze *n* : bronze gilded and used in decoration (as for moldings or scrollwork) esp. in 17th and 18th century France — called also *bronze-doré*

gilt-edged *or* **gilt-edge** \ˈ=ˈ=\ *adj* **1** : having a gilt edge **2** : of the best quality ⟨a *gilt-edged* theatrical cast⟩ — used esp. of securities (as government obligations) of the safest character

gilthead \ˈ=ˌ=\ *n* : any of several marine fishes: as **a** : a valuable sparid food fish (*Sparus auratus*) common in the Mediterranean **b** : a cunner (*Crenilabrus melops*) of the British coasts

gil·yak \(ˈ)gilˈyak\ *or* **gil·iak** \", ˈgilēˌak\ *n, pl* **gilyak** *or* **gilyaks** *or* **giliak** *or* **giliaks** *usu cap* **1 a** : a people of hunters and fishers of Siberia that have classical pure Mongolian traits, are related to the Tungus, Goldi, and Buryats, and are found in the lower course of the Amur river and in adjacent northern Sakhalin Island **b** : a member of such people **2** : the language of the Gilyak **3** : a language family consisting only of Gilyak

gim \ˈjim\ *adj* [origin unknown] *dial Eng* : NEAT, TRIM

gim·bal \ˈgimbəl, ˈji-\ *or* **gimbal ring** *n* -s [alter. of *gemel*] : a contrivance that permits a body to incline freely in any direction or suspends something (as a barometer or a ship's compass) so that it will remain level when its support is tipped and that consists of a ring in which the body can turn on an axis through a diameter of the ring while the ring itself is so pivoted to its support that it can turn about a diameter at right angles to the first — usu. used in pl.

gimbals supporting a compass

gim·baled \-ld\ *adj* : provided with or supported on gimbals

gim·ber·nat's ligament \ˈh|imbə(r)ˌnäts-, ˈg|\ *n, usu cap G* [after Antonio de *Gimbernat* y Arbós †1816 Span. surgeon] : the portion of the aponeurosis of the external oblique muscle that is reflected from Poupart's ligament along the iliopectineal line

gim·ble \ˈgimbəl, ˈji-\ *vi* -ED/-ING/-S [origin unknown] : to make a face : GRIMACE

¹**gim·crack** *or* **jim·crack** \ˈjimˌkrak\ *n* -s [origin unknown] **1 a** : something usu. characterized by flimsy or tricky ingenuity rather than substance or worth : DOODAD, GADGET **b** : TOY, GEWGAW, KNICKKNACK, TRIFLE **2** *archaic* : a showily fashionable or affected person : FOP

²**gimcrack** *or* **jimcrack** \ˈ"\ *adj* **1** : hastily or shoddily constructed : having an improvised air or appearance : FLIMSY, UNSUBSTANTIAL ⟨a mess of ~ bungalows —J.B.Priestley⟩ ⟨~ stands for the sale . . . of ice-cream cones —Jean Stafford⟩ ⟨they were terrible ~ planes we flew in —W.S.Maugham⟩ **2** : TRIVIAL, FRIVOLOUS ⟨you expect me to pay for this ~ excursion of yours —Katherine Mansfield⟩

gim·crack·ery \-kərē, -ri\ *n* -ES **1** : a quantity of gimcracks ⟨colored candles and ~ . . . of odd origin —Kathryn Hulme⟩ **2** : cheap, contrived, or shoddy effects or expedients ⟨his interpretations are quite without sentimental ~ —Virgil Thomson⟩

¹**gim·el** *or* **gim·mel** *also* **ghim·el** \ˈgiməl *sometimes* ˈgēm-\ *n* -s [Heb *gimel*, lit., camel] **1** : the 3d letter of the Hebrew alphabet — symbol ג; see ALPHABET table **2** : the letter of the Phoenician or of any of various other Semitic alphabets corresponding to Hebrew gimel

²**gimel** *var of* GYMEL

¹**gim·let** \ˈgimlət, *usu* -əd·+V\ *n* -s [ME *gimlet, gimelot*, modif. of MF *guimbelet*, prob. modif. of MD *wimmelkijn* gimlet, fr. *wimmel* auger + *-kijn* -kin — more at WIMBLE, -KIN] : a small woodworking tool with a screw point, grooved shank, and cross handle for boring holes

gimlet

²**gimlet** \ˈ"\ *adj* : having a piercing, penetrating, or driving quality ⟨one of the ~ characters who, by diligence and memory . . . gain prizes in their school days —G.D.Brown⟩

³**gimlet** \ˈ"\ *vb* -ED/-ING/-S : to pierce or penetrate with or as if with a gimlet ⟨~*ing* through her inquisitor with her eyes —Elizabeth Bowen⟩

⁴**gimlet** \ˈ"\ *n* -s [¹*gimlet*; fr. the fluted structure of the stem] : an Australian gum tree (*Eucalyptus salubris*)

⁵**gimlet** \ˈ"\ *n* -s [prob. fr. ¹*gimlet*] : a cooling drink esp. of the British Pacific colonies (as Hong Kong) consisting usu. of sweetened lime juice, gin, and water either carbonated or plain

gimlet bit *n* : a bit with a spiral flute and a sharp threaded point for boring small holes in wood
gimlet eye *n* [¹gimlet] : a piercing or watchful eye ⟨a man with a *gimlet eye* for the future —*Newsweek*⟩ — **gimlet-eyed** \'≈,≈\ *adj*
gim·lety \-əd-lē, -ət|, |i\ *adj* [¹gimlet + -y] : like a gimlet : PIERCING, PENETRATING ⟨~ eyes⟩
¹**gim·mal** \'giməl, 'ji-\ *n* -s [alter. of ¹gemel] **1 gimmals** *pl* : joined work (as clockwork) whose parts move within each other **2** *or* **gimmal ring** : a pair or series of interlocked rings
²**gimmal** \"\ *also* **gim·maled** \-ld\ *adj* : made or consisting of gimmals or interlocked rings or links
¹**gim·me** \'gimē, -mi\ [by contr.] *slang* : give me
²**gimme** \"\ *adj, slang* : expecting or requesting a money contribution, a handout, or a special privilege ⟨on the list of countless ~ organizations —*Printer's Ink Monthly*⟩ ⟨the ~ concept of government which is held by so many citizens —Harold Zink⟩
³**gimme** \"\ *n* -s *slang* : extreme desire for presents — usu. used in pl. ⟨a bad case of the ~s —Eric Soames⟩
gimmel *var of* GIMEL
¹**gim·mer** \'gimər\ *n* -s [ME *gymbyre, gymmer*, fr. ON *gymbr* a live lamb one year old — more at CHIMERA] **1** *chiefly Scot* : a yearling female sheep : a two-tooth ewe **2** *dial Brit* : a woman friend : CRONY
²**gim·mer** *or* **gim·mor** \'jimə(r)\ *n* -s [prob. alter. of ¹gemel] **1** *dial* : HINGE, CLASP **2** *obs* : GIMMAL — usu. used in pl.
¹**gim·mick** \'gimik, -mēk\ *n* -s [origin unknown] **1 a** (1) : a mechanical device by which a gambling apparatus (as a roulette wheel) can be secretly and dishonestly controlled (2) : a mechanical device used to cheat or deceive **b** : an ingenious or novel mechanical device : GADGET ⟨a new ~ . . . claimed to unscrew the stickiest container —*Wall Street Jour.*⟩ ⟨no experimental ~s were installed —*N.Y. Herald Tribune*⟩ ⟨we have . . . radios, washing machines, bathtubs, and ~s of all sorts —H.F.Peters⟩ **c** : a decisive or strategic element or feature that is purposely hidden, unobtrusive, or not immediately apparent : CATCH, JOKER ⟨in some states ~s in the law make it almost impossible to successfully prosecute —*Best True Fact Detective*⟩ ⟨what's the ~ . . . what's in it for you —Maxwell Griffith⟩ ⟨you look for the ~ in innocent queries like that —*Ring*⟩ **2** : a new and ingenious device, scheme, or idea for solving a problem or achieving an end : a new angle of approach : a novel or unconventional twist ⟨the ~ was simple . . . we would take great historical moments and place microphones on the scene as if the network had . . . commentators covering the events —Goodman Ace⟩ ⟨commercial promotional ~s —Dwight MacDonald⟩ ⟨any ~ or glimmer of an amusing idea is a suitable substitute for professional talent —Elsa Maxwell⟩ ⟨a new book on Hamlet must have a new ~ —Robert Halsband⟩
²**gimmick** \"\ *vt* -ED/-ING/-S **1** : to alter or influence by means of a gimmick or similar device or method ⟨~*ing* up some difficult padlocks —W.L.Gresham⟩ **2** : to provide with a gimmick (as with an attention-catching device, a novel twist, or a gadget) ⟨one of the stories . . . is ~*ed* up —Gilbert Millstein⟩ ⟨now the show has been ~*ed* . . . with flashing lights and bad jokes —John Crosby⟩ ⟨the mechanism was ~*ed* . . . to prove what the missile could do —*Time*⟩
gim·mick·ery *or* **gim·mick·ry** \-k(ə)rē, -ri\ *n* -ES : an array or profusion of gimmicks ⟨carried an incomprehensible mass of miniature coils . . . and other electronic *gimmickry* —*N.Y. Times*⟩
gim·micky \-məkē, -ki\ *adj* : having or being like a gimmick ⟨a ~ side to stereo — recordings deliberately souped up and distorted —Roland Gelatt⟩
¹**gimp** \'jimp\ *var of* JIMP
²**gimp** \'gimp\ *n* -s [perh. fr. D] **1 a** : a flat narrow braid often with a wire or coarse cord running through it used as a trimming or decorative finish for upholstery and clothing **b** : a thread or yarn for embroidery or knitting made by twisting a heavy thread around a core thread **c** : a coarse thread for outlining a design in a piece of lace; *sometimes* : the pattern as opposed to the ground **2** : a silk fishline strengthened with wire
³**gimp** \"\ *vt* -ED/-ING/-S : to trim or make with gimp
⁴**gimp** \"\ *n* -s [origin unknown] : SPIRIT, VIM ⟨she does get some ~ into her characters —J.R.Chamberlin⟩ ⟨if I had an ounce of ~ in me —*Atlantic*⟩
⁵**gimp** \"\ *n* -s [origin unknown] : CRIPPLE ⟨the ~ swayed to one side —Jerry McClung⟩; *also* : a limping walk ⟨walks with a ~ in one leg —Damon Runyon⟩
⁶**gimp** \"\ *vi* -ED/-ING/-S : LIMP, HOBBLE ⟨came ~*ing* across the floor on three legs —Nelson Algren⟩ ⟨~*ing* along to the bus station —W.C.Williams⟩
gim peg \'jim-\ *or* **gem peg** \'jem-\ *n* [*gim* alter. of *gem*] : a cranked iron support in a lapidary's mill for the block into which the gem stick is stuck
gimp nail *or* **gimp tack** *n* [²gimp] : a small nail with a rounded head used to fasten gimp to furniture
gimpy \'gimpē, -pi\ *adj* -ER/-EST [⁵gimp + -y] : CRIPPLED, LAME, LIMPING ⟨threw himself again into his burlesque ~ gait —L.A.Fiedler⟩ ⟨a grizzled old veteran with a ~ leg —I.S. Cobb⟩
¹**gin** \'gin\ *vb* **gan** \'gan\ **gun·nen** \'gənən\ **ginning; gins** [ME *ginnen*, short for *onginnen* to begin (fr. OE *onginnan*) & *beginnen* to begin — more at BEGIN] *archaic* : BEGIN
²**gin** \'jin\ *n* -s [ME *gin*, modif. of OF *engin* skill, mechanical contrivance — more at ENGINE] : any of several machines, tools, or mechanical devices: as **a** : a snare or trap for game **b** : a machine for raising or moving heavy weights (as a tripod formed of poles united at the top, with a windlass, pulleys, and ropes) **c** : a cotton gin or any similar device used for separating seed or foreign matter from fiber to be used commercially; *also* : a building where cotton is ginned
³**gin** \"\ *vt* **ginned; ginned; ginning; gins 1** : to catch in a gin : SNARE **2** : to separate (cotton fiber) from seeds and waste material
⁴**gin** \(,)gin\ *conj* [perh. alter. of *gif*] *dial* : IF ⟨~ a body meet a body —Robert Burns⟩
⁵**gin** \'jin\ *n* -s [by shortening and alter. fr. ²geneva] **1 a** : a strong alcoholic liquor extensively made in the Netherlands by distilling a mash of grain (as rye) in pot stills with juniper berries — called also *Hollands* **b** : a similar liquor made from plain spirit flavored with an aromatic (as juniper berries, aniseed, coriander, fennel, or turpentine) and usu. containing about 40 percent of alcohol by weight **2 a** : GIN RUMMY **b** : the act of going gin : the act of laying down a full hand of matched cards in gin rummy; *also* : the bonus of usu. 20 or 25 points for doing so
⁶**gin** \"\ *adj* : having all 10 of one's cards in gin rummy matched in sets
⁷**gin** \"\ *adv* : with all 10 of one's cards in gin rummy matched in sets
⁸**gin** \(,)gin\ *prep* [by shortening & alter. fr. ²again] *dial* : BEFORE, BY ⟨I'll be home ~ midnight⟩
⁹**gin** *conj, dial* : by the time that : WHEN ⟨~ daylight came he had gone⟩
¹⁰**gin** \'gin\ *dial past of* GIVE
¹¹**gin** \'jin\ *n* -s [native name in Australia] *Austral* : an aboriginal woman
gin and it \'jinə'nit\ *n* [⁵gin + *and* + *it*, short for *Italian vermouth*] *chiefly Brit* : a drink of sweet vermouth and gin
gin and tonic *n* : a cooling drink consisting of dry gin and quinine water flavored and garnished with lime or lemon peel
gin block *n* [²gin] : an iron or steel tackle block containing one or more pulleys
gin buck *n* : a cocktail with a gin base to which are added lime or lemon juice and ginger ale served iced and garnished with lime or lemon peel
ginep *var of* GENIP
ging \'giŋ\ *n* -s [ME, alter. of *genge*, fr. OE, troop, fr. *gangan* to go — more at GANG] *archaic* : CREW, COMPANY, TROOP, GANG
gin·gel·ly *also* **jin·ji·li** \'jinjəlē\ *n, pl* **gingellies** *also* **jinjilis** [Hindi & Marathi *jinjalī*, fr. Ar *juljulān*] : SESAME SEED
gingelly oil *n* : SESAME OIL
¹**gin·ger** \'jinjə(r)\ *n* -s *often attrib* [ME *ginger, gingere*, alter. of *gingivere*, alter. (influenced by OF *gingembre, gingibre* ginger, fr. ML *gingiber*) of OE *gingifer*, modif. of ML *gingiber*, alter. of L *zingiber*, fr. Gk *zingiberi*, prob. modif. of Skt *śṛṅgavera*] **1** : a thickened irregular rhizome that is extremely pungent and aromatic, is widely used as a spice and sometimes in medicine as a carminative, stimulant, or counterirritant, and is usu. prepared by drying and grinding to a fine brownish powder — see BLACK GINGER, CANTON GINGER, JAMAICA GINGER, LIMED GINGER, WHITE GINGER **2** : a tropical perennial herb (*Zingiber officinale*) that is prob. native to the Pacific islands but is widely cultivated for its rhizome which constitutes most of the ginger of commerce; broadly : any plant of the genus *Zingiber* **3** : any of various plants of which some part (as root or juice) has a pungency or flavor suggestive of ginger (as various tansies and sedums or the wild gingers) **4** : high spirit : METTLE, PEP, VIGOR ⟨written . . . with the wit, bounce, and ~ that characterize the dances she has composed —*New Yorker*⟩ ⟨you've got an awful lot of ~ to you —Joseph Hergesheimer⟩ ⟨the only capital he had was the ~ to care hard and work hard —Willa Cather⟩ **5** : a strong brown that is stronger and slightly yellower and darker than average russet, deeper and slightly yellower than rust, and very slightly darker than gypsy — called also *Kaiser brown*
²**ginger** \"\ *vt* **gingered; gingered; gingering** \-nj(ə)riŋ\ **gingers 1** : to make lively or animated : stir to activity : pep up : REVIVE ⟨loyalty at home . . . is always ~*ed* by state executions —Francis Hackett⟩ — often used with *up* ⟨~ up the tourist trade —*N.Y.Times*⟩ ⟨~*ing* up the flow of revenue —Leslie Charteris⟩ **2** : ⁴FIG 2
³**ginger** \"\ *adj* : having the color of ginger ⟨with a youthful figure and ~ hair —A.J.Liebling⟩
⁴**ginger** \"\ *adj, chiefly dial* [back-formation fr. *gingerly*] : GINGERLY
⁵**ginger** \"\ *adv, chiefly dial* : GINGERLY ⟨got up, handling myself kind of ~ —Helen Eustis⟩
gin·ger·ade \,jinjə'rād\ *n, Brit* : a beverage flavored with ginger ⟨bought a bottle of ~ —Flora Thompson⟩
ginger ale *n* : a sweetened carbonated beverage flavored mainly with ginger extract — called also *ginger pop*
ginger beer *n* : a sweetened carbonated beverage heavily flavored with ginger or capsicum or both
¹**gin·ger·bread** \'jinjə(r),bred\ *n, often attrib* [ME *gingerbreed*, by folk etymology (influence of ME *ginger, gingere* ginger) fr. *gingebreed* gingerbread, ginger paste, by folk etymology (influence of ME *breed* bread) fr. *gingebras* ginger paste, fr. OF *gingembraz, gingebraz*, fr. *gingembre, gingibre* ginger — more at GINGER] **1** : a cake made with molasses, flavored with ginger, often cut in fancy shapes, and frosted **2** : something showy but unsubstantial or tasteless; *esp* : tawdry, gaudy, or superfluous ornament or embellishment in architecture ⟨interiors from which ~ and plush were banished —Edgar Kaufmann⟩
²**gingerbread** \"\ *adj* : adorned with, characterized by, or being gingerbread : showily, tawdrily, or elaborately ornamented ⟨a ~ clubhouse⟩ ⟨a frame dwelling with ~ trim —*Amer. Guide Series: N.C.*⟩ ⟨the ~ style of the Victorian era⟩ ⟨~ scrollwork⟩
gingerbread palm *n* [so called fr. the flavor of the fruit] : DOOM PALM
gingerbread plum *n* **1** : a West African tree (*Parinarium macrophyllum*) that has a strong light-brown wood and edible fruit **2** : the fruit of the gingerbread plum having a soft mealy edible pulp, a kernel rich in oil, and a cottony protective layer around the seeds that is used locally for tinder
gin·ger·bready \-dē,-di\ *adj* [¹gingerbread + -y] : like fancy gingerbread : tawdrily showy : overly ornamented ⟨~ architecture⟩
ginger brown T-5902 *n, usu cap G&B* : an organic pigment — see DYE table I (under *Pigment Brown 5*)
ginger cake *n* : GINGERBREAD
ginger coral *n* : SEA GINGER
ginger family *n* : ZINGIBERACEAE
ginger grass *n* **1** : any of various East Indian grasses of the genus *Cymbopogon* (esp. *C. martinii* var. *sofia*) **2** : a coarse grass (*Panicum glutinosum*) of the West Indies and tropical America useful as fodder
ginger-grass oil *n* : an essential oil that resembles palmarosa oil but has an odor like that of common ginger and that is obtained esp. from a ginger grass (*Cymbopogon martinii* var. *sofia*)
ginger group *n, chiefly Brit* : a group or element that serves as a driving, stimulating, or energizing force within a larger body (as a political party) ⟨a new body was formed to act as a high-level *ginger group* or steering committee —Richard Scott⟩
ginger lily *n* : BUTTERFLY LILY 1
gin·ger·li·ness \'jinjə(r)lēnəs, -lin-\ *n* -ES : the quality of being gingerly ⟨koala bears . . . show by their ~ how indispensable tails are to carefree tree living —Alan Devoe⟩
¹**gin·ger·ly** \-lē,-li\ *adj* [perh. fr. ¹ginger + -ly] : very cautious or tentative ⟨the issue . . . was handled only in a ~ way —W.S.White⟩ ⟨~ footwork suggested house guests trying to decide whether the lawn is too damp for croquet —*New Yorker*⟩
²**gingerly** \"\ *adv* [prob. fr. ¹gingerly] : with extreme care concerning the result of a movement or act : very cautiously ⟨tread their way ~ over the jagged stones —Brian Murtough⟩ ⟨~ laid the packages down —John Steinbeck⟩ ⟨handles the subject ~ —H.G.Merriam⟩
ginger nut *n* : a cookie spiced with ginger : GINGERSNAP
ginger oil *n* : a yellowish thick aromatic essential oil obtained from ginger and used chiefly as a flavoring material
ginger pine *n* : PORT ORFORD CEDAR
ginger plant *n* **1** : GINGER 2a **2** : a tansy (*Tanacetum vulgare*)
ginger pop *n* : GINGER ALE
gingerroot \'≈,≈\ *n* **1** : the unpulverized ginger rootstock **2** : COLTSFOOT a
gingers *pl of* GINGER, *pres 3d sing of* GINGER
gingersnap \'≈,≈\ *n* : a thin brittle cookie flavored with ginger and usu. sweetened with molasses
gingerspice \'≈,≈\ *n* : RUSTIC BROWN
ginger wine *n* : a ginger-flavored beverage sometimes fermented or effervescent
gin·gery \'jinj(ə)rē, -ri\ *adj* [¹ginger + -y] **1** : having the characteristics or color of ginger : flavored with ginger : SHARP, SPICY **2** : full of vigor : HIGH-SPIRITED, PEPPY, METTLESOME ⟨the high quick ~ ways of thoroughbreds —John Masefield⟩ ⟨in ~ good health —*Newsweek*⟩
ging·ham \'giŋəm\ *n* -s [modif. of Malay *genggang* checkered cloth] : a clothing fabric usu. of yarn-dyed cotton in plain weave made in solid colors, checks, plaids, and stripes and in various weights and qualities
gingiv- *or* **gingivo-** *comb form* [L *gingiv-*, fr. *gingiva* gum] **1** : gum : gums ⟨*gingiv*ectomy⟩ ⟨*gingiv*itis⟩ **2** : of the gums and ⟨*gingivo*stomatitis⟩ : gingival and ⟨*gingivo*labial⟩
gin·gi·va \jin'jīvə\ *n, pl* **gingi·vae** \-,vē\ [L — more at CONGER] : ¹GUM
gin·gi·val \(')jin;jīvəl, 'jinjəv-\ *adj* [L *gingiva* + E *-al*] : of or relating to the gums: as **a** : ALVEOLAR **b** : being between alveolar and dental
gingival crevice *n* : a narrow space between the free margin of the gingival epithelium and the adjacent enamel of a tooth
gin·gi·vec·to·my \,jinjə'vektəmē\ *n* -ES [ISV *gingiv-* + *-ectomy*] : the excision of a portion of the gingiva
gin·gi·vi·tis \,jinjə'vīd·əs\ *n* -ES [NL, fr. *gingiv-* + *-itis*] : inflammation of the gingival tissue
gingivostomatitis \jin;jīvō, ;jinjə(,)vō+\ *n* [NL, fr. *gingiv-* + *stomatitis*] : inflammation of the gums and of the mouth
gin·gly·form \'jiŋglə,fȯrm, 'gi-\ *adj* [ISV *gingly-* (fr. NL *ginglymus*) + *-form*] : GINGLYMOID
gin·glymo·arthrodia \'≈(,)mō+\ *n* [NL, fr. *ginglymo-* (fr. *ginglymus*) + *arthrodia*] : a composite anatomical joint of which one element has an axial or hinge motion and the other a simple gliding motion — **gin·glymo·arthrodial** \"+\ *adj*
gin·gly·mo·di \,jiŋglə'mō,dī, ,gi-\ *n pl, cap* [NL, irreg. fr. Gk *ginglymos*] : an order of ganoid fishes coextensive with the family Lepisosteidae and comprising the gars of fresh waters of No. America — compare HOLOSTEI — **gin·gly·mo·di·an** \≈≈'mōdēən\ *adj or n*
gin·gly·moid \'≈≈,mȯid\ *adj* [Gk *ginglymoeidēs* like a hinge, fr. *ginglymos* hinge + *-oeidēs* -oid] : of, relating to, or resembling a ginglymus
gin·gly·mos·to·ma \,≈≈'mästəmə\ *n, cap* [NL, fr. *ginglymo-* (fr. *ginglymus*) + *-stoma*] : a genus of galeoid sharks of shallow tropical seas in which more than one series of teeth are functional at a time — **gin·gly·mos·to·moid** \,≈≈;≈stə,mȯid\ *adj*
gin·gly·mus \'jiŋgləməs, 'gi-\ *n, pl* **gingly·mi** \-,mī, -,mē\ [NL, fr. Gk *ginglymos* hinge, joint] : a hinge joint (as between the humerus and ulna) admitting of motion in one plane only
ginhouse \'≈,≈\ *n* [²gin + *house*] : a building where cotton is ginned
gink \'giŋk\ *n* -s [origin unknown] *slang* : PERSON, GUY, FELLOW ⟨a calm, responsible-looking ~ —Saul Bellow⟩ ⟨deceased was a dashed unpleasant old ~ —Dorothy Sayers⟩
gink·go \'giŋ(,)kō *sometimes* 'ji- *or* -ŋk(,)gō *or* -ŋk(,)yō\ *n* [NL, fr. Jap *ginkyo*, fr. *gin* silver (fr. Chin *yin²*) + *kyo* apricot, fr. Chin *hsing⁴*] **1** *cap* : a monotypic genus of broad-leaved gymnospermous trees (family Ginkgoaceae) that are native to eastern China, have apparently been preserved as temple trees being very rare in the wild, and are distinguished by fan-shaped deciduous leaves and yellow fruits resembling drupes **2** *or* **ging·ko** \"\ *also* **gin·ko** \"\ *pl* **ginkgos** *or* **ginkgoes** *or* **gingkos** *or* **gingkoes** *also* **ginkos** *or* **ginkoes** : a tree (*Ginkgo biloba*) that is the sole representative of the genus *Ginkgo* — called also *maidenhair tree*
gink·go·ace·ae \,≈≈'āsē,ē\ *n pl, cap* [NL, fr. *Ginkgo*, type genus + *-aceae*] : a family of gymnospermous plants that is coextensive with the order Ginkgoales and includes the genus *Ginkgo* and certain form genera of extinct plants — **gink·go·aceous** \;≈≈;āshəs\ *adj*
gink·go·ales \,≈≈'ā(,)lēz\ *n pl, cap* [NL, fr. *Ginkgo* + *-ales*] : an order of gymnospermous trees that first appeared in the Permian and is represented by a single surviving species (*Ginkgo biloba*)
gink·go·ites \,≈≈'īd·(,)ēz\ *n, cap* [NL, fr. *Ginkgo* + L *-ites*] : a form genus of the family Ginkgoaceae comprising Mesozoic plants with the leaves usu. indented but not deeply divided into segments and with distinct petioles
ginkgo nut *n* : the fruit of the ginkgo
gin mill *n, slang* : a commercial establishment where alcoholic liquor is served : BAR, SALOON
ginned *past of* GIN
gin·ner \'jinə(r)\ *n* -s : an operator of a cotton gin or linter
gin·nery \'jinərē\ *n* -ES : an establishment where cotton is ginned
gin·ney \'ginē, -ni\ *n* -s [alter. of *guinea*] *slang* : ITALIAN — usu. used disparagingly
¹**gin·ning** \'gi-\ *pres part of* GIN
²**gin·ning** \'ji-\ *n* -s [fr. gerund of ³gin] **1** : the process or an instance of separating cotton fiber from seeds and waste plant material **2** : cotton as it comes from the cotton gin
ginny \'jinē, -ni\ *adj, often* -ER/-EST [⁵gin + -y] : of, suggesting, or affected with gin ⟨a ~ smell⟩ ⟨~ hilarity⟩ ⟨reports of ~ Village parties —Joseph Mitchell⟩
gino·rite \'jinə,rīt, jə'nōr,īt\ *n* -s [It, fr. Piero *Ginori*-Conti †1939 Ital. scientist + It *-ite*] : a mineral $Ca_2B_{14}O_{23}.8H_2O$ consisting of hydrous borate of calcium
gin pole *n* **1** : any one of the three poles of a hoisting gin **2** : a single pole held in a nearly vertical position by guys that supports a block and tackle used for lifting loads
gin rummy *n* [⁵gin (suggested by the identity in sound of *rum* meaning an alcoholic drink and *rum* meaning a card game) + *rummy*] : a card game for two players who are each dealt 10 cards from a 52-card pack similar to knock rummy except that a player may knock only if his unmatched cards count 10 or less
gins *pres 3d sing of* GIN, *pl of* GIN
gin saw *n* : the saw used to draw fibers through a cotton gin
gin·seng \'jin,saŋ, -,saiŋ, -,seŋ, -,siŋ; -in(t)siŋ, -in(t)seŋ\ *also* **gen·seng** \", jen-\ *n* -s [Chin (Pek) *jen²-shen¹*] **1** : a Chinese herb (*Panax schinseng*) having 5-foliolate leaves and umbels of small greenish flowers succeeded by scarlet berries **2** : any of several plants (genus *Panax*) related to or used as substitutes for the Chinese ginseng; *esp* : a No. American woodland herb (*P. quinquefolius*) with 5-foliolate leaves **3** : the aromatic root of either Chinese or American ginseng that has a sweetish taste suggestive of licorice and is highly valued as a medicine in China though of value chiefly as a demulcent
ginseng family *n* : ARALIACEAE
gin·shang \'jin,shaŋ, -shaiŋ\ *dial var of* GINSENG
gin trap *n* [²gin] *chiefly Brit* : a trap used esp. for catching rabbits
gin·zo \'gin(,)zō\ *n* -ES [prob. alter. of *guinea*] : a person of Italian extraction — usu. taken to be offensive
gio \'gyō\ *var of* GEO
gio·co·so \jō'kō(,)sō\ *adj* (*or adv*) [It, jocose, fr. L *jocosus* — more at JOCOSE] : LIVELY, HUMOROUS — used chiefly as a direction in music
gio·jo·so *also* **gio·io·so** \jō'yō(,)sō\ *adj* (*or adv*) [It *gioioso* joyous, fr. OIt, fr. OF *joios* — more at JOYOUS] : JOYOUS, GAY — used as a direction in music
gior·gio·nesque \,jȯrjō'nesk\ *adj, usu cap* [It *giorgionesco*, fr. *Giorgione* (Giorgio Barbarelli) †1511 Venetian painter + It *-esco* -esque] : characteristic of or resembling the style of the Italian painter Giorgione Barbarelli ⟨the whole sheet overflows with *Giorgionesque* motifs —*Art in America*⟩
gior·gi system \'jȯr(,)jē-\ *n, usu cap G* [after Giovanni *Giorgi* †1950 Ital. physicist] : the mks system of units
giot·tesque \(')jȯ;tesk, jē;ȯt-\ *adj, usu cap* [It *giottesco*, fr. *Giotto* di Bondone †1337? Florentine painter + It *-esco* -esque] : resembling the broad and simple style of the painter Giotto
¹**gip** *interj* [origin unknown] *obs* — used to express anger, impatience, surprise, or contempt
²**gip** \'gip\ *also* **gib** \-ib\ *vt* **gipped** *also* **gibbed; gipped** *also* **gibbed; gipping** *also* **gibbing; gips** *also* **gibs** [prob. of Scand origin; akin to Norw dial. *gipa* to cause to gape; akin to L *hiare* to gape, yawn — more at YAWN] : to remove the insides of (fish) — **gip·per** \-pə(r)\ *n* -s
gipon \ji'pän, '≈,≈\ *n* -s [ME *gipoun*, fr. MF *jupon* — more at JUPON] : JUPON
gipsy *var of* GYPSY
gir \'gi(ə)r\ *n* [fr. *Gir* Forest, near Veraval, western India] **1** *usu cap* : a breed of medium-sized Indian cattle of dairy type usu. having a distinctive dull red or brown speckling on a white background, widely distributed in tropical regions, and much used for crossbreeding **2** -s *often cap* : an animal of the Gir breed
gir *abbr* girder
gi·raf·fa \jə'rafə\ *n, cap* [NL, fr. It, giraffe] : a genus of artiodactylous mammals comprising the giraffes which together with the okapis and extinct related forms constitute a family and sometimes a superfamily of Artiodactyla — **gi·raf·fid** \-fəd\ *adj or n* — **gi·raf·foid** \-,fȯid\ *adj*
gi·raffe \jə'ra|f, -raa(ə)|, -rai|, -rà|\ *n, pl* **giraffes** \|fs *also* |vz\ [It & Ar; It *giraffa*, fr. Ar *zirāfah, zarāfah*, prob. of African origin; akin to Egypt *sr* giraffe] **1** : a large fleet African ruminant mammal (*Giraffa camelopardalis*) that is the tallest of living quadrupeds and has a very long rather stiff neck with only the usual seven vertebrae, long front legs, a pair of short skin-covered horns and a median frontal protuberance in both sexes, and a short coat of fawn or cream-colored hair marked with large reddish or brown blotches — called also *camelopard* **2** : a wing-shaped upright piano of the 18th and early 19th centuries **3** : a car higher at one end than at the other for use on inclines in mining

giraffe

giraffe camel *n* : any of several long-necked No. American fossil camels of the Miocene
gi·raff·ine \-fən, -,fīn\ *adj* [*giraffe* + *-ine*] : like a giraffe
gi·raff·ish \-fish, -fēsh\ *adj* : like a giraffe ⟨a roguish, ~ expression —May L. Becker⟩

gir·an·dole \ˈjirən,dōl\ n -s [F & It; F, fr. It *girandola*, fr. *girare* to turn, fr. LL *gyrare* — more at GYRE] **1 :** a radiating and showy or ornamental composition (as a cluster of skyrockets fired together or a fountain with rising column of water which spreads) — compare ANTHEMION **2 a :** an ornamental branched candle holder; *esp* **:** a brass figural candelabrum ornamented with glass prisms **b :** a mirror having attached candle holders **c :** an often convex circular mirror framed in a deep gilt molding and typically trimmed with gilt balls **3 :** a pendant earring usu. with three ornaments or stones hanging from a central piece

girandole 2c

girandole clock n **:** a clock similar to a banjo clock but having a large circular base resembling a girandole

gi·rard reagent \jəˈrärd-\ or **gi·rard's reagent** \-dz-\ n, usu cap G [after André Girard, 20th cent. Fr. chemist] **:** any of several hydrazides that contain a quaternary ammonium radical and are useful esp. in separating aldehydes or ketones (as some steroid hormones) from mixtures by forming soluble hydrazones: as **a :** a crystalline compound $(CH_3)_3N(Cl)CH_2CONHNH_2$ derived from trimethylamine or betaine — called also *Girard T reagent* **b :** a crystalline compound $C_5H_5N(Cl)CH_2CONHNH_2$ derived from pyridine — called also *Girard P reagent*

gir·a·sol \ˈjirə,sȯl, -sōl, -säl\ or **gir·a·sole** \-sōl\ n -s [It *girasole*, fr. *girare* to turn + *sole* sun, fr. L *sol* — more at SOLAR] **1 :** JERUSALEM ARTICHOKE **2 :** an opal of varying color which gives out fiery reflections in a bright light — called also *fire opal*

girasol thorn n **:** JERUSALEM THORN 2

gir·bo·tol process \ˈgərbə,tōl-, -tȯl-\ n, usu cap G [*girbotol* fr. *Girdler* Corporation, Louisville, Kentucky, company where the process was developed + Robert R. *Bottoms* b1890 Am. chemist that devised the process + E *-ol*] **:** a process used industrially for removing acidic impurities (as hydrogen sulfide or carbon dioxide) from gases by passing them through a solution of an ethanolamine

1gird \ˈgərd, ˈgə̄d, ˈgəid\ vb **girded** \|dəd\ also **girt** \|t, usu |d.+V\ **girded** also **girt; girding; girds** [ME *girden*, fr. OE *gyrdan*; akin to OHG *gurten* to gird, ON *gyrtha* to gird, OE *geard* yard — more at YARD] vt **1 a :** to encircle or bind with any flexible band (as a belt) ⟨the waist is ~*ed* by a purple . . . sash —*New Yorker*⟩ **b :** to make fast or secure (as a sword by a belt or clothing with a cord) **:** GIRDLE **c :** SURROUND, ENCIRCLE ⟨no castellated ramparts ~ Madrid —E.O.Hauser⟩ ⟨~*ed* round by an open porch —A.W.Turnbull⟩ **d** *chiefly Scot* **:** to put a rim or hoop on (a barrel or cask) **2 a :** PROVIDE, EQUIP ⟨~*ed* himself with an amulet . . . and a short stabbing spear —Charles Beadle⟩; *esp* **:** to invest with the sword of knighthood ⟨the marshal ~*ed* him, kissed him, "and so he was a knight" —R.W.Southern⟩ **b :** to invest with powers or attributes ⟨thou hast ~*ed* me with strength unto the battle —Ps 18:39 (AV)⟩ ⟨hast ~*ed* me with gladness —Ps 30:11 (AV)⟩ **3 :** to prepare (oneself) for a struggle, test of strength, or other action **:** BRACE ⟨the men ~*ed* themselves for the coming final blow⟩ ⟨the reader ~*s* himself for yet another disappointment —Charles Lee⟩ ~ *vi* **:** to prepare for a struggle, test of strength, or other action ⟨he ~*ed* for a rough fight —John Kobler⟩ ⟨~*ing* to repulse a new challenge to his powers —*N.Y. Times*⟩ **syn** see SURROUND — **gird one's loins :** to prepare for a test of strength or other trial **:** muster up one's resources **:** set to work — often used with *up* ⟨can the British gird up *their loins* and move ahead —Samuel Van Valkenburg & Ellsworth Huntington⟩

2gird \", dial Brit " or ˈgird\ vb -ED/-ING/-S [ME *girden*, *gurden* to strike, move rapidly, thrust] vt **1** *dial Brit* **:** STRIKE, SMITE **2 :** to sneer at **:** MOCK, GIBE ⟨the British public has never ceased ~*ing* him —Augustine Birrell⟩ ~ *vi* **1** *dial Brit* **:** to move or act quickly or energetically **:** RUSH **2 :** GIBE, JEST, RAIL — usu. used with *at* ⟨~*s* at your preoccupation . . . with bodily games —A.T.Quiller-Couch⟩ ⟨I shall not ~ at realism —W.T.Stace⟩ ⟨~*ing* at the wrongheadedness of . . . officials —*Times Lit. Supp.*⟩ **syn** see SCOFF

3gird \"\ n -s [ME (Sc), stroke, blow, fr. ME *girden*, *gurden* to strike] **:** a sarcastic remark **:** GIBE, SNEER, DIG ⟨trenchant ~*s* inspired by strong and genuine feeling against the modern changes —*Times Lit. Supp.*⟩

4gird \ˈgir(d)\ n -s [alter. of obs. *girth* hoop for a barrel or tub, fr. ME *girth* hoop for a barrel or tub, strap round the body of an animal to fasten something on its back — more at GIRTH] *Scot* **:** a hoop esp. for a barrel or tub; *also* **:** a hoop used as a child's plaything

girded var of GIRT

gird·er \ˈgərdər; ˈgə̄də(r, ˈgəidə(r\ n -s [1*gird* + *-er*] **1 a :** a horizontal main member supporting vertical concentrated loads (as from beams) **b :** BEAM; *esp* **:** an iron or steel beam either made in a single piece or built up typically of plates, flitches, latticework, or bars and often of very large proportions — compare BOWSTRING BEAM, BOX GIRDER, LATTICE GIRDER, PLATE GIRDER, TRUSS **c :** a structure built of reinforced concrete for a similar purpose **2 :** a rolled metal unit of I section or other section or a built-up unit of rolled members and plate that may be transverse or longitudinal depending on the structure to be supported

girder bridge n **:** a bridge in which the supporting members are girders

girder rail n **:** a heavy railroad rail having a deep web and used in a street where paving is laid

girding n -s [ME *girdinge*, *girding*, fr. *girden* to gird, encircle + *-inge*, *-ing*] **:** something with which one is girded; *specif*, *Scot* **:** a saddle girth

1gir·dle \ˈgərdəl, ˈgə̄d-, ˈgəid-\ n -s [ME *girdel*, fr. OE *gyrdel*; akin to OHG *gurtil* girdle, ON *gyrthill* girdle, OE *gyrdan* to gird — more at GIRD] **:** something that girds, encircles, confines, or restrains: as **a** (1) **:** a belt, sash, or article of dress encircling the body usu. at the waist to fasten or confine garments or to furnish a means of carrying things (as keys or a sword) ⟨her fingers playing . . . at the ~ of her frock —Donn Byrne⟩ (2) **:** a cord, narrow band, or belt worn as an ecclesiastical vestment around the waist to confine the alb (3) **:** a woman's close-fitting undergarment often boned and usu. partly or wholly elasticized and extending from the waist to just above or below the hips for figure control **b :** either of the two more or less complete bony rings at the anterior and at the posterior ends of the vertebrate trunk supporting the arms and legs respectively — see PECTORAL GIRDLE, PELVIC GIRDLE **c :** an architectural band **:** CINCTURE **d :** the edge of a brilliant that is grasped by the setting — see BRILLIANT illustration **e** (1) **:** either of the two bands resembling a hoop and forming the sides of the two valves of a diatom **:** CINGULUM (2) **:** the part of the shell lying between the epivalve and hypovalve in certain dinoflagellates (3) **:** the muscular and spicule-bearing peripheral part of the mantle of a chiton encircling the shell plates **f :** a belt or ring made by the removal of the bark and cambium around a tree, stem, or twig **g :** a plant disease characterized by girdling of the stem or branches

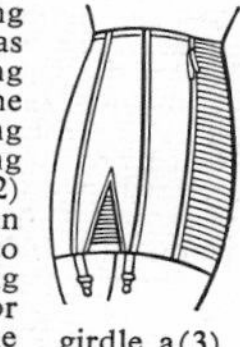
girdle a(3)

2girdle \"\ vt **girdled; girdled; girdling** \-d(ə)liŋ\ **girdles** **1 :** to put a girdle on **:** encircle or bind about with a girdle or sash **2 a :** to encircle as if with a belt or mesh ⟨50,000 miles of track in operation in 1870, enough to ~ the earth twice —R.H.Brown⟩ **b :** to move or travel around **:** make the circuit of ⟨two times *girdled* the world —Horace Sutton⟩ ⟨these engines . . . *girdled* the earth —*Amer. Guide Series: Conn.*⟩ ⟨a satellite *girdling* the moon⟩ **3 a :** to make a circular cut around (as a tree) through the outer bark and cortex in order to produce death by interrupting the circulation of water and nutrients **b :** to remove a ring of bark from (as a tree) for the purpose of increasing productivity and size of fruit by preventing passage to the roots of food elaborated by the leaves **c :** to destroy a ring of bark and conducting tissues about or remove one from (a plant stem) — used of a gnawing animal (as a rodent or an insect) and of disease ⟨raspberry canes *girdled* by crown rot⟩ **syn** see SURROUND

3gir·dle \", ˈgird(ə)l\ n -s [ME (Sc) *girdill*, *girdil*, alter. of ME *gridel* — more at GRIDDLE] *chiefly Scot* **:** GRIDDLE

girdle band n **:** GIRDLE e(1)

girdlecake \ˈ==,=\ n, *dial Brit* **:** GRIDDLE CAKE

girdle of ve·nus \,==ˈvēnəs\ usu cap G&V [after *Venus*, Italian goddess identified by the Romans with Aphrodite, Greek goddess of love] **:** a line that appears on the palm at the base of the fingers, that forms a semicircle beginning between the first and second fingers and ending between the third and fourth fingers, and that is held by palmists to indicate a high-strung nervous temperament and sometimes a tendency toward hysteria or despondency

gir·dler \ˈgərd(ə)lər; ˈgə̄d(ə)lə(r, ˈgəid-\ n -s [ME *girdeler*, fr. *girdel* girdle + *-er*] **1 :** a maker of girdles **2 :** one that girdles; *esp* **:** an insect that feeds on bark and gnaws grooves about stems and twigs

girdle-tailed lizard \ˈ==,=-\ n [so called fr. its practice of rolling its spiny tail over its soft belly as a protection when threatened] **:** a lizard of the family Cordylidae — called also *zonure*; see KLIPSALAMANDER

girds *pres 3d sing of* GIRD, *pl of* GIRD

gi·rel·la \jəˈrelə\ n, cap [NL, fr. F *girelle*] **:** the type genus of the family Girellidae

gi·rel·li·dae \-lə,dē\ n pl, cap [NL, fr. *Girella*, type genus + *-idae*] **:** a family that comprises herbivorous marine fishes with movable incisors and is closely related to Kyphosidae

gir·ga·shite \ˈgərgə,shīt\ or **gir·ga·site** \-,sīt\ n -s usu cap **:** a member of one of the ancient Canaanite tribes conquered by the Israelites

girl \R ˈgərl, *chiefly before pause or consonant* ˈgər·əl; –R ˈgə̄l or ˈgəil; *Brit sometimes* ˈgeəl or ˈgaəl or ˈgiəl\ n -s *often attrib* [ME *girle*, *gerle*, *gurle* young person of either sex] **1 a :** a female child ⟨announced the birth of a ~⟩ ⟨a study of the performance of primary-school boys and ~*s*⟩ **b :** a young unmarried woman **:** MAIDEN ⟨a ~ of striking beauty⟩ **c :** a single or married woman of any age ⟨gossipy old ~*s* of about seventy —J.B.Clayton⟩ **2 a** (1) **:** a female servant **:** MAID ⟨the ~ brought in and cleared away the dishes —Flora Thompson⟩ (2) **:** a female employee (as a secretary) ⟨I'll get my ~ to have a look through the card index —Nevil Shute⟩ **b :** PROSTITUTE **c :** SWEETHEART ⟨took his ~ to the movies⟩ **d :** DAUGHTER ⟨entered his ~ at a fashionable school⟩

girl·een \(ˈ)gərˈlēn\ n -s *Irish* **:** a young girl

girl friday n, *often cap G & usu cap F* [*girl* + *Friday* (as in *man Friday*)] **:** a valued private secretary or other female employee or assistant who gives efficient and devoted service and is usu. entrusted with a wide range of tasks ⟨the firm's *girl friday* — the head bookkeeper, scourge of the clerks, chief worrier —*Wall Street Jour.*⟩

girl friend n **1 :** a female friend **2 :** a favorite female companion of a boy or man **3 :** the female partner in an intimate or esp. an illicit relationship

girl guide n **:** a girl member of the Girl Guides organized in Great Britain in 1910 for carrying out a program of social and educational activities among young girls and for developing good citizenship and healthy useful living — compare BOY SCOUT, GIRL SCOUT

girlhood \ˈ=,hu̇d\ n -s **:** the condition or time of being a girl

1girl·ie *pronunc at* GIRL +ē *or* i\ n -s [*girl* + *-ie*] **1 :** GIRL — often used to indicate affection or intimacy **2** *slang* **:** PROSTITUTE

2girlie var of GIRLY

girl·ish *pronunc at* GIRL +ish *or* ēsh\ adj **:** of, relating to, or having the characteristics of a girl or girlhood **:** MAIDENLY ⟨~ hesitancies . . . delays and refusals —S.H.Adams⟩ — **girl·ish·ly** adv — **girl·ish·ness** n -ES

girls-and-boys \ˈ=;=;=\ n pl but sing or pl in constr **:** either of two plants of the genus *Dicentra*: **a :** DUTCHMAN'S-BREECHES **b :** SQUIRREL CORN

girl scout n **1 :** a member of the Girl Scout movement founded in the U.S. in 1912 on the plan of the British Girl Guides for developing good citizenship and healthy useful living among girls from 7 through 17 — compare BOY SCOUT, GIRL GUIDE **2 :** a girl scout approximately 10 through 17 years old as distinguished from a brownie

girly *pronunc at* GIRL + ē *or* i\ adj [*girl* + *-y* (adj. suffix)] **1 :** GIRLISH ⟨silly ~ sugary crudity has given way to womanly suavity —George Meredith⟩ **2** *or* **girl·ie** \"\ [*girlie*] **:** featuring scantily clothed girls ⟨~ shows⟩ ⟨slick ~ magazines⟩

girly-girly \ˈ==;==\ adj [redupl. of 1*girly*] **:** exaggeratedly or affectedly girlish ⟨manages to give sensible guidance without being prissy or *girly-girly* —*Newsweek*⟩

1girn \ˈgirn\ vi -ED/-ING/-S [ME *girnen*, alter. of *grinnen* — more at GRIN] **1** *chiefly Scot* **a :** to show the teeth **:** GRIMACE, SNARL **b :** to whimper and whine **:** complain peevishly **2** *chiefly Scot* **:** GRIN, SNEER

2girn \"\ n -s **1** *chiefly Scot* **a :** a snarl of rage **b :** a whining peevish tone **:** WHIMPER **2** *chiefly Scot* **:** GRIMACE, GRIN

3girn \"\ n -s [ME (Sc), alter. of ME *grin* — more at GRIN] *chiefly Scot* **:** SNARE, NOOSE, TRAP

4girn \"\ vt -ED/-ING/-S *chiefly Scot* **:** SNARE, TRAP

gir·nel or **gir·nal** \ˈgirnəl\ n -s [ME (Sc), prob. alter. of ME *garner*, *gerner* garner — more at GARNER] **1** *obs*, *Scot* **:** GRANARY **2** *Scot* **:** a meal chest or barrel ⟨sitting on a ~ in the stable —Ian MacLennan⟩

girn·ie \ˈgirni\ adj [1*girn* + *-ie*] *chiefly Scot* **:** ILL-TEMPERED, PEEVISH

gi·ro \ˈjī(,)rō\ n -s **:** AUTOGIRO

giron var of GYRON

girr \ˈgir\ n -s [by alter.] *Scot* **:** GIRD

girs pl of GIR

1girse \ˈgirs, ˈgərs\ *dial Brit var of* GRASS

2girse \ˈgi(r)s, ˈgərs\ *dial Eng var of* GIRTH

gir·sle \ˈgirsəl\ *chiefly Scot var of* GRISTLE

1girt \ˈgər|t, ˈgə̄|, ˈgəi|, usu |d.+V\ adj [fr. past part. of 1*gird*] **1** *also* **gird·ed** \|dəd\ **:** bound by a cable — used of a ship moored with such short cables that it strikes against one of them **2 :** PREPARED, READY, GEARED ⟨is it ~ for a supreme test —*Christian Science Monitor*⟩ ⟨~ for speed and action —F.L.Mott⟩

2girt \"\ vb -ED/-ING/-S [partly fr. ME *girten*, alter. of *girden* to gird, encircle; partly fr. 3*girt* — more at GIRD] vt **1 :** GIRD: as **a :** ENCIRCLE **b :** EQUIP, INVEST **2 :** to fasten by means of a girth ⟨a farmer's saddle had been ~*ed* on him —*Country Gentleman*⟩ **3 :** to surround with a line or cord to measure the girth **:** measure the girth of ⟨~ a tree⟩ ~ *vi* **:** to measure in girth

3girt \"\ n -s [alter. of *girth*] **1 :** GIRTH; *esp* **:** a measure around or across a curved or broken surface (as a molding) ascertained by following its profile **2 :** GIRDER: as **a :** a heavy timber framed into the second-floor corner posts as a footing for the roof rafters in housebuilding **b :** a horizontal member running from column to column or from bent to bent of a building frame or a trestle to stiffen the framework and to carry siding material

4girt \ˈgirt, ˈgərt\ *dial Brit var of* GREAT ⟨~ white birds —Llewelyn Powys⟩

1girth \ˈgər|th, ˈgə̄|, ˈgəi|; |t, usu |d.+V\ n -s [ME *girth*, *gerth*, fr. ON *gjǫrth*, *gerth* belt; akin to MD *gerde* belt, Goth *gairda* belt, OE *gyrdan* to gird, encircle — more at GIRD] **1 a :** a band or strap that encircles the body of a horse or other animal to fasten a saddle, pack, blanket, or other article upon its back — see HARNESS illustration **2 a :** a measure round the body of something **:** CIRCUMFERENCE ⟨the ~ of a tree trunk⟩ ⟨the ~ of a ship⟩; *esp* **:** the measure round a human body (as at the waist or belly) ⟨for the man of more than average ~ —Agnes M. Miall⟩ **b :** SIZE, DIMENSIONS ⟨the river was twice its usual ~⟩ ⟨when one looks at the ~ of standard works —*Times Lit. Supp.*⟩ **3 :** a horizontal longitudinal brace; *esp* **:** such a brace in square-set mine timbering **4 :** either of two thongs of leather or bands of webbing attached to the rounce of a hand printing press to move the carriage back and forth

2girth \"\ vb -ED/-ING/-S [ME *girthen* to gird, encircle, fr. *girth*, *girth*, n.] vt **1 :** to extend around **:** ENCIRCLE **2 :** to bind or fasten with a girth **:** put a girth on **3 :** to measure the girth of; *specif* **:** to determine the approximate weight of (an animal) by measuring the girth with a tape that converts linear measure to normal or average weight ~ *vi* **:** to measure in girth

girtline \ˈ=,=\ n [prob. fr. 4*girt* + *line*] **:** GANTLINE

gis n, cap [by alter. and shortening] *obs* **:** JESUS — used in the phrase *by Gis*

GIs pl of GI

GI's pl of GI, *pres 3d sing of* GI

gi·sant \zhēzän\ n, pl **gisants** \-än(z)\ [F, fr. pres. part. of *gésir* to lie, lie flat, fr. L *jacēre* to lie] **:** a recumbent sculpture of a deceased person shown sometimes with arms crossed over the chest

gi·sarme \gēˈzärm, jē-,zhē-\ n -s [ME, fr. OF *gisarme*, *guisarme*, of Gmc origin; akin to OHG *getīsarn* weeding tool, fr. *jetan*, *getan* to weed + *īsarn* iron — more at IRON] **:** a medieval weapon mounted on a long staff and carried by foot soldiers

gism var of JISM — usu. considered vulgar

gismo var of GIZMO

gis·mon·dite \jizˈmän,dīt, ˈjizmən-\ or **gis·mon·dine** \-,dēn\ n -s [*gismondite* fr. *gismondine* + *-ite*; *gismondine* fr. G *gismondin*, fr. C. G. *Gismondi* †1824 Ital. mineralogist + G *-in* -ine] **:** a mineral $CaAl_2Si_2O_8.4H_2O$ consisting of a light-colored hydrous calcium aluminum silicate occurring in pyramidal crystals

gist \ˈjist\ n -s [AF, it lies (said of a legal action), fr. MF, 3d pers. sing. pres. indic. of *gesir* to lie, fr. L *jacēre* to lie, fr. *jacere* to throw — more at JET (to spout)] **1 :** the ground or foundation of a legal action without which it would not be sustainable **2 :** the main point or material part (as of a question or debate) **:** the pith of a matter **:** ESSENCE ⟨the ~ of a question⟩ ⟨the ~ of all that can be said upon the matter —R.L. Stevenson⟩

git \(ˈ)git, usu -id.+V\ *dial var of* GET

gi·tal·in \jəˈtalən, ˈjid·ələn; *sometimes* jəˈtāl- or -ˈtäl- or -ˈtȧl-\ n -s [ISV *gital-* (fr. NL *digitalis*) + *-in*] **1 :** a crystalline water-soluble glycoside $C_{35}H_{56}O_{12}$ obtained from digitalis **2 :** an amorphous water-soluble mixture of glycosides of digitalis used similarly to digitalis

gi·ta·na \hēˈtänə\ n -s [Sp, fem. of *gitano*] **:** a Spanish gypsy girl or woman

git·a·ne·muk \,jid·əˈnēmək\ n, pl **gitanemuk** or **gitanemuks** usu cap **:** SERRANO

gi·ta·no \hēˈtä(,)nō\ n -s [Sp, prob. modif. of (assumed) ML *aegyptanus*, fr. L *Aegyptus* Egypt, country in northeastern Africa formerly reputed to be the homeland of the gypsies (fr. Gk *Aigyptos*) + *-anus* -an] **:** a Spanish male gypsy

gite var of GYTE

git-fid·dle \ˈgit,==\ n [*git-* (by shortening & alter. fr. *guitar*) + *fiddle*] *slang* **:** GUITAR

gi·tog·e·nin \jəˈtäjənən, -,nēn; ,jid·əˈjenən\ n [ISV *gito-* (fr. *gitonin*) + *-genin*] **:** a crystalline steroid sapogenin $C_{27}H_{44}O_4$ obtained esp. by hydrolysis of gitonin

gi·to·nin \jəˈtōnən, ˈjid·ənən\ n -s [ISV, fr. *digitonin*] **:** a crystalline steroid saponin $C_{51}H_{82}O_{23}$ occurring with digitonin

gi·tox·i·gen·in \jə,täksəˈjenən; (,)ji,täkˈsijənən, -,nēn\ n [ISV *gitoxi-* (fr. *gitoxin*) + *-genin*] **:** a crystalline steroid lactone $C_{23}H_{34}O_5$ obtained by hydrolysis of gitoxin

gi·tox·in \jəˈtäksən\ n [ISV, fr. *digitoxin*; orig. formed in G] **:** a poisonous crystalline steroid glycoside $C_{41}H_{64}O_{14}$ that is obtained from digitalis and from lanatoside B by hydrolysis

git·tar \ˈgi,tär, -tȧ(r\ *dial var of* GUITAR

git·ter cell \ˈgid·ə(r)-\ n [G *gitter* lattice, grating, prob. alter. of MHG *geter*, fr. OHG *getiri*; akin to OHG *gataro* door and prob. to OE *gaderian* to gather — more at GATHER] **:** an enlarged phagocytic cell of microglial origin having the cytoplasm distended with lipid granules and being characteristic of certain organic brain lesions

git·tern \R ˈgid·ərn or -itərn, –R -id·ən or -itən or -itən\ n -s [ME *giterne*, fr. MF *guiterne*, fr. OF, modif. of OSp *guitarra* — more at GUITAR] **:** a medieval stringed instrument of the guitar family played with a plectrum

gittern of the early 14th century

gittin pl of GET

git·tite \ˈgi,tīt, ˈgid-,īt, usu -id·+V\ n -s usu cap **:** an inhabitant of ancient Gath in Palestine, one of the chief cities of the Philistines

git-up \ˈgid-,əp\ n -s [alter. of *getup*] **:** DRIVE, ENERGY, AGGRESSIVENESS ⟨can always find something to do if he has a little *git-up* —Calder Willingham⟩

giulio var of JULIO

giust \ˈjüst\ *archaic var of* JOUST

giu·sta·men·te \,jüstəˈmentē\ adv [It, fr. *giusto* correct, just] **:** with precision **:** in strict tempo — used as a direction in music

giu·sto \ˈjü(,)stō\ adj (or adv) [It, correct, just, fr. L *justus* just — more at JUST] **:** in strict tempo **:** with exactness — used as a direction in music

1give \ˈgiv\ vb **gave** \ˈgāv\ or *substand* **give** \ˈgiv\ or *dial* **gin** \ˈgin\ or **guv** \ˈgəv\ **giv·en** \ˈgivən also -ivəm or -ibəm\ or *substand* **give** or *dial* **gin** or **guv**; **giving; gives** [ME *given*, of Scand origin; akin to OSw *giva* to give; akin to OE *giefan* to give, OHG *geban*, ON *gefa*, Goth *giban* to give, *gabei* wealth, L *habēre* to have, hold, OIr *gaibid* he takes, Lith *gabenti* to take away, Skt *gabhasti* hand] vt **1 a :** to confer the ownership of without receiving a return **:** make a present of ⟨*gave* him a watch on his birthday⟩ ⟨*gave* his books to the college⟩ **b :** to assign the future ownership of by will **:** BEQUEATH, DEVISE ⟨*gave* and bequeathed a larger sum to the college than any other person in its history —B.F.Wright⟩ **c :** to contribute without compensation ⟨did no more than a . . . citizen might be expected to do — bought bonds, *gave* blood, served as a civil-defense warden —H.N.Fairchild⟩ **2 a :** to grant or bestow by or as if by formal action ⟨has just been *given* two new honors —Harvey Breit⟩ ⟨responsible for the law *giving* women . . . equal pay with men —Laura M. Berrien⟩ **b :** to let have in or as if in answer to a prayer — used with *me* as indirect object ⟨as for me, ~ me liberty or ~ me death —Patrick Henry⟩ ⟨~ me the good old days⟩ **c :** to accord or yield to another ⟨had never *given* him her confidence —Ellen Glasgow⟩ **3 a :** to put into the possession of another for his use **:** HAND ⟨I'll ~ you a card to him and you go in there . . . and pick out what you want —S.H.Adams⟩ **b :** to provide or supply one with (food or drink) ⟨~ me a slab of that pie —K.M.Dodson⟩ **c** (1) **:** to administer as a sacrament ⟨*giving* extreme unction⟩ (2) **:** to administer as a medicine ⟨*gave* her spirits of ammonia and put ice on her forehead —Scott Fitzgerald⟩ **d :** to commit to the trust or keeping of another for a definite purpose ⟨*gave* him a letter to mail⟩ ⟨*gave* his suitcase to the porter⟩ ⟨~ the deck to the exec and get all the officers in the wardroom —Wirt Williams⟩ **e** (1) **:** to transfer from one's authority, custody, or responsibility ⟨*gave* the prisoner to the officials from the federal penitentiary⟩ (2) **:** to transfer from parental authority and care ⟨who giveth this woman to be married to this man —*Bk. of Com. Prayer*⟩ **f :** to execute and deliver ⟨all new employees must ~ bond⟩ **g :** to offer (something immaterial) for conveyance or transmittal ⟨~ my regards to your family⟩ ⟨~ our greetings to all our friends⟩ **4 a :** to offer to the action of another **:** PROFFER, EXPOSE ⟨I *gave* my back to the smiters —Isa 50:6 (RSV)⟩ ⟨he got up and *gave* his hand to the visitor⟩ ⟨~ the sails to the wind⟩ **b :** to yield (oneself) to a man in sexual intercourse ⟨a wild, harum-scarum woman who would have *given* herself to him . . . without marriage —Erle Stanley Gardner⟩ **c :** to perform the action appropriate or necessary to a public presentation or production of ⟨the orchestra ~*s* 10 concerts . . . each season —Claudia Cassidy⟩ ⟨a serious effort to ~ us a real puppet show —R.L.Shayon⟩ ⟨asked the soprano to ~ the group a song⟩ **d :** to present to view or observation ⟨the injured man *gave* a few signs of life⟩ ⟨*gave* evidence of promising intellectual gifts —C.A.Duniway⟩ ⟨*gave* them a good example⟩ **e :** to have or show as an armorial bearing or emblem, badge, or livery ⟨all his successors . . . may ~ the dozen white luces in their coat —Shak.⟩ **f :** to provide by way of entertainment **:** serve as host at ⟨*gave* a dinner in honor of his guests⟩ ⟨*gave* a ball for his nieces⟩ ⟨~ weekly teas⟩ **g :** to propose as a toast ⟨I rise to ~ . . . the memory of a man well known to all —John Wilson †1854⟩ ⟨gentlemen . . . I'll ~ you the ladies —Charles Dickens⟩ **h** *archaic* **:** to impart a tendency or propensity to **:** INCLINE **5 a :** to designate as a share or portion **:** ALLOT ⟨all the earth to thee and to thy race I ~ —John Milton⟩ ⟨immediate and infallible revelation of this kind is not *given* to man —W.R. Inge⟩ ⟨*gave* him the best room available⟩ **b :** to make assignment of (a name) ⟨the term Bushmen . . . was *given* in the 17th century by the Dutch settlers to the diminutive hunting peoples —C.D.Forde⟩ ⟨*gave* the child the name John⟩ **c :** to set forth as an actual or hypothetical datum **:** ASSUME ⟨three points of a circle are *given*⟩ **d :** to attribute in thought or speech **:** ASCRIBE ⟨*gave* all the glory to God⟩ ⟨*gave* full weight to the evidence⟩ ⟨a sound argument for *giving* the painting to Rembrandt⟩ **e** *obs* **:** to appoint a person to the office or function of ⟨and he *gave* some, apostles; and some, prophets; and some, evangelists; and some, pastors and teachers —Eph 4:11 (AV)⟩ **f** *obs* **:** to set down **:** REGARD, CONSIDER, DEEM ⟨men's reports ~ him much wronged —Shak.⟩ — usu. used with *for* ⟨*gave* him for drowned in one of the canals —Joseph Addison⟩ **6 a :** to yield or furnish as a product, consequence, or effect **:** PRODUCE, EMIT ⟨the gas *gave* its final flicker and went out —Jack McLaren⟩ ⟨the can, now quite empty and resonant, *gave* forth a hollow clatter —C.G.D.Roberts⟩ ⟨bushes . . . ~ forth a pungent aroma when the sun beats upon them —Norman Douglas⟩ ⟨cows ~ milk⟩ ⟨flints ~ sparks⟩ ⟨a compound that ~*s* a red color with iodine —Henry Tauber⟩ **b :** to yield or exhibit as a result of calculation or measurement ⟨84 divided by 12 ~*s* 7⟩ ⟨the amount of lead . . . would by simple calculation ~ the age of the material —W.E.Swinton⟩ ⟨a thermometer ~*s* the temperature of the room —James Jeans⟩ **c :** to bring forth **:** BEAR ⟨the largest ewe *gave* triplets —*Breeder's Gazette*⟩ **7 a :** to yield possession of by way of exchange **:** hand over in exchange for something or in discharge of a debt or obligation **:** PAY ⟨what shall a man ~ in return for his life —Mt 16:26 (RSV)⟩ **b :** to dispose of for a price **:** hand over for a consideration **:** SELL ⟨I can ~ you a jade necklace for five rupees —Robert Sherrod⟩ **c** *archaic* **:** to procure in exchange **:** be worth **:** FETCH ⟨the country . . . so much overstocked with timber that it would ~ no price —James Robertson⟩ **8 a :** to deliver or deal by some bodily action ⟨*gave* him a push down the stairs⟩ ⟨*gave* her a kiss⟩ **b :** to carry out (a movement of or as if of the body) **:** EXECUTE, MAKE ⟨he *gave* a cryptic smile —Hallam Tennyson⟩ ⟨could feel the ship ~ a convulsive lurch —T.B.Costain⟩ **c :** to inflict or impose as punishment ⟨*gave* the slave 20 lashes⟩ ⟨*gave* the boy a whipping⟩ **d :** to cause to be fired **:** DISCHARGE ⟨*gave* a short burst and damaged the enemy plane⟩ ⟨*gave* a salute of 21 guns⟩ **9 a :** to put forth (a sound) **:** VOICE ⟨he hesitated and *gave* a nervous laugh —Haldane Macfall⟩ ⟨*gave* a hiss to attract the attention of the others —T.B.Costain⟩ **b :** to deliver verbally **:** UTTER ⟨has never *given* me a cross word in his life —Ellen Glasgow⟩ ⟨the student raised his hand and *gave* the right answer⟩ ⟨his uncle *gave* him sound advice⟩ ⟨the sergeant *gave* the command to the troops⟩ ⟨the old man *gave* his blessing to the bride and groom⟩ **c :** to express as a wish **:** BID ⟨I *gave* him good day and he stopped and looked at me —S.H.Adams⟩ ⟨*gave* us good night and went sedately away —Eve Langley⟩ **d** (1) **:** to award by formal verdict **:** deliver by appropriate legal authority ⟨the judge *gave* him 10 years⟩ ⟨the judgment was *given* against the plaintiff⟩ (2) *cricket* **:** to rule on a fielder's appeal ⟨the umpire *gave* the batsman out⟩ **e :** to offer, suggest, or imply in the course of speaking ⟨the top kick always *gave* us that old business —Tom Shehan⟩ ⟨don't ~ me that legal double-talk —Louis Auchincloss⟩ **10 a :** to offer for the consideration, acceptance, or use of another ⟨can ~ several explanations of the passage⟩ ⟨~*s* no really good reason for his absence⟩ ⟨after several years' work he finally *gave* his novel to the world⟩ **b :** to provide a description of **:** REPRESENT, PORTRAY ⟨show me something of hers, something that seems to ~ her —H.G.Wells⟩ ⟨an artist who *gave* a scene as it must have happened —Roger Fry⟩ **c :** to make known **:** impart knowledge of or information about ⟨can ~ only a hint of the treasures to be found —Dana Burnet⟩ ⟨the results were *given* in a long paper⟩ ⟨the soldier *gave* his name, rank, and serial number⟩ ⟨will you ~ me the right time⟩ **11 a :** to suffer the loss of **:** SACRIFICE ⟨had *given* two legs in the Second World War —Marya Mannes⟩ ⟨gallantly *gave* his life for his country⟩ **b :** to offer by or as if by way of dedication or devotion **:** CONSIGN, COMMEND ⟨a resolution to ~ to God the half of his services . . . and the half of his money —M.J.Guest⟩ ⟨*gave* Mr. Dorrit to the devil with great liberality —Charles Dickens⟩ **c :** to apply freely or fully **:** DEVOTE ⟨children were *giving* themselves wholeheartedly to some raucous game —Maeve Brennan⟩ ⟨he *gave* his youth to literature, languages, and mechanics —Edward Clodd⟩ **d :** to offer as a pledge ⟨I ~ you my word of honor that it's true⟩ **12 a :** to cause to have or receive **:** OCCASION ⟨what dreams may come . . . must ~ us pause —Shak.⟩ ⟨it *gave* his views a foundation of solid fact which was impressive —H.J.Laski⟩ ⟨was buried in sight of the mountains which always *gave* him pleasure —Broadus Mitchell⟩ **b :** to cause a person to catch by or as if by contagion, infection, or exposure ⟨she *gave* him her cold⟩ ⟨the draft *gave* him a sore throat⟩ **c :** to produce (as a feeling) in a person or thing **:** bring about ⟨you do not ~ self-respect and self-reliance by censorship —Joyce Cary⟩ ⟨we ought not to ~ ourselves airs —Benjamin Jowett⟩ ⟨the stage sets ~ charm to the production⟩ **d :** to be the source or origin of ⟨this group ~*s* some of our really vicious criminals —R.L.Jenkins⟩ **e** *obs* **:** PUT, SET ⟨~ some stop to those atheistical and epicurean opinions —Matthew Hale⟩ **f :** to allow to have or take **:** PERMIT, CONCEDE ⟨~ me a day to think the problem over⟩ ⟨*gave* him 10 yards and still won the race⟩ ⟨the patients are *given* a long rest every afternoon⟩ ⟨was willing to ~ his opponent that point in the debate⟩ **g :** to be the cause of **:** be responsible for — used with an infinitive phrase as object ⟨a novelist of experience . . . ~*s* us to share his swift insight —*Nation*⟩ ⟨you *gave* me to believe that the school meant more to you than anything —Lael Tucker⟩ **13 :** to care to the extent of — usu. used with negative ⟨bewitched, bothered, and bewildered by life, he doesn't ~ a damn —Moore Raymond⟩ ⟨didn't ~ a hang —Nelson Algren⟩ **14 :** to make a telephone connection with ⟨asked central to ~ him the long-distance operator⟩ ~ *vi* **1 :** to make gifts or presents **:** CONTRIBUTE, DONATE ⟨it is more blessed to ~ than to receive —Acts 20:35 (RSV)⟩ **2** *archaic* **:** to deliver a blow or make an attack ⟨furiously *giving* upon the enemy with a great shout —Henry Holcroft⟩ **3 a :** to yield to physical force or strain **:** respond to pressure ⟨the dummy . . . has a breakable shoulder bone built to ~ when its human counterpart would —R.M.Yoder⟩ **b :** to collapse from the application of force or pressure **:** break down ⟨the rail of the fence *gave* suddenly under his weight —R.L.Stevenson⟩ **c :** to undergo or submit to a change through the modification of an inflexible attitude or the withdrawal from a rigid position **:** accept or make a concession ⟨if something does not ~ . . . the whole North Atlantic fare structure could be thrown wide open —Richard Witkin⟩ **4** *obs* **:** to become moist **:** WEEP ⟨flinty mankind whose eyes do never ~ but thorough lust and laughter —Shak.⟩ **5 a** *of weather* **:** to become mild **b** *of frozen ground* **:** THAW **6 :** to afford a view or passage **:** OPEN, LEAD ⟨a venerable lane *giving* on the cathedral close —Russell Kirk⟩ ⟨a cluster of stores and boatyards *giving* onto the harbor —Pete Barrett⟩ ⟨a cheerful compartment on the main deck with . . . a porthole *giving* out to sea —Horace Sutton⟩ ⟨flung open the door which *gave* upon the landing —Dorothy Sayers⟩ **7 a :** to enter wholeheartedly into an activity **:** get into the spirit of things ⟨if the teacher himself is . . . skillful in inspiring his pupils they will let go and ~ —F.R.Rogers⟩ **b :** to impart information **:** TALK ⟨he just won't ~; he glares straight ahead and keeps his mouth closed —Bennett Cerf⟩ **8** [trans. of G *gibt* (in the expression *was gibt's?* what is going on?), 3d pers. sing. pres. indic. of *geben* to give, fr. OHG *geban*] **:** to take place **:** HAPPEN, OCCUR — usu. used in the phrase *what gives* ⟨you poor dewy-eyed academics don't know what ~*s* in the rough-and-tumble —Frances G. Patton⟩ — **give a good account of :** to acquit (oneself) well ⟨able to *give a good account of* himself in a street brawl —W.J.Ghent⟩ — **give and take :** to engage in give-and-take ⟨faculty members will have to *give and take* in creating new courses or revising old ones —M.L.Wardell⟩ — **give battle :** to engage in a determined fight ⟨threw up log and earthwork defenses and *gave battle* —*Amer. Guide Series: La.*⟩ ⟨public opinion . . . against which Congress was not prepared to *give battle* —H.J.Laski⟩ — **give birth :** to bear a child ⟨she *gave birth* last Friday⟩ — **give birth to 1 :** to bring forth **:** BEAR ⟨*gave birth to* a son⟩ **2 :** to be the source of **:** ORIGINATE ⟨*gave birth . . . to* a smoldering feeling of discontent, an inarticulate desire for change —G.G.Coulton⟩ — **give ground :** to withdraw before or as if before superior force **:** RETREAT ⟨as the Roman legions advanced to the attack, this center *gave ground* slowly —Tom Wintringham⟩ ⟨the bond market is *giving ground* before the advance of the economy —Paul Heffernan⟩ — **give guard :** to inform a batsman if his bat is at guard — used of an umpire in cricket — **give it to :** to administer a beating or scolding to **:** attack vigorously ⟨looked at his colleagues . . . and *gave it to* them right between the eyes —*New Republic*⟩ — **give one his head :** to allow (as a horse) free rein ⟨the advanced students often are *given their heads* and allowed to launch scientific programs of their own —Karl Detzer⟩ — **give or take :** to add or subtract (a specified small unit) without material alteration ⟨a man 80 years old, *give or take* a year⟩ **:** allow a small inaccuracy of **:** accept a tolerance of — **give place 1 :** to yield precedence or superiority ⟨a house and garden of the king's *giving place* to few —Thomas Herbert⟩ **2 :** to yield by way of being succeeded or replaced ⟨fields of sugar beets . . . *give place* to wheat and grazing lands —*Amer. Guide Series: Oreg.*⟩ ⟨uneasiness *gave place* to alarm —Osgood Hardy⟩ — **give rise to :** to bring about **:** PRODUCE, OCCASION ⟨has exercised the skill of . . . scholars and *given rise to* an enormous body of literature —Edward Clodd⟩ ⟨a watershed that *gives rise to* two large river systems —*Amer. Guide Series: N.H.*⟩ — **give suck** *archaic* **:** SUCKLE — **give thanks :** to express gratitude; *specif* **:** to say grace ⟨and he took bread, and when he had *given thanks* he broke it and gave it to them —Lk 22:19 (RSV)⟩ — **give the gun 1 :** to open the throttle of ⟨the motor began to cough and die so he *gave* it *the gun*⟩ **2 :** to increase the speed of markedly ⟨on the open highway he *gave* the car *the gun*⟩ — **give the lie to 1 :** to accuse of falsehood ⟨they *gave* the queen *the lie* —Richard Bancroft⟩ **2 :** to show the falsity of ⟨the record . . . seems to have *given the lie to* ancient creeds —W.L.Sperry⟩ — **give voice 1 :** SING ⟨he emerged, pink and scrubbed, still *giving voice* —C.B.Kelland⟩ **2 :** to express strong feelings usu. of objection or displeasure — used with *to* — **give way 1 a :** to retreat before an advancing force ⟨our troops . . . *gave way* on the right —William Tennant⟩ **b** *archaic* **:** to make way **:** clear the way ⟨respect induced passengers to *give way* to the father and daughter —Sir Walter Scott⟩ **c :** to yield the right of way ⟨if it is your duty to *give way*, never leave your alteration of course until the last moment —Peter Heaton⟩ ⟨drivers *give way* to traffic coming in on the right —*Meet New Zealand*⟩ **2 a** *archaic* **:** to allow free scope, opportunity, or liberty of action ⟨they who through weakness *gave way* to the ill designs of bad men —Edmund Burke⟩ **b :** to yield oneself without check, restraint, or control **:** abandon oneself ⟨she horrified the young man by *giving way* to tears, publicly —F.A.Swinnerton⟩ **c :** to lose control of oneself ⟨courage kept her from quite *giving way* —Edna Lyall⟩ **3 a :** to yield to or as if to physical force or pressure **:** break down **:** COLLAPSE, FAIL ⟨bridges . . . can *give way* under the pounding hooves of a herd of bawling, jostling longhorns —S.E.Fletcher⟩ ⟨his fragile health *gave way* under the stress of study —H.W.Wiley⟩ **b :** to yield under entreaty or insistence **:** CONCEDE ⟨argued until, with a shrug of his shoulders, he *gave way* —Francis King⟩ **4 :** to yield place ⟨the desert landscape . . . had *given way* everywhere to abundant green vegetation —Rex Moorfoot⟩ ⟨discussion of specific issues *gave way* to very broad generalities —Walter Goodman⟩ **5 :** to begin to row or to row with increased energy ⟨the coxswain ordered the crew to *give way*⟩ **6 :** to decline in value — used of stocks

[2]**give** \"\ *n* -s **1 :** capacity or tendency to yield to force or strain ⟨placing their saddles a little farther back . . . they say the horse's spine has more ~ or bend at this point —S.E. Fletcher⟩ **2 :** the quality or state of being springy **:** ELASTICITY, RESILIENCE ⟨the ~ . . . of the knitted fabric makes it ideal for uses where any variables of conformation or stress exist —G.A.Urlaub⟩

give-and-go \¦==¦=\ *n* **:** a basketball maneuver in which the player in possession of the ball makes a short pass to a teammate and then cuts for the basket

[1]**give-and-take** \¦==¦=\ *adj* [[1]*give* + *and* + *take*, v.] **1** *Brit* **:** of or relating to a race in which the horses carry weights that vary according to their heights **2** [[2]*give-and-take*] **:** characterized by give-and-take ⟨*give-and-take* methods of adjustment —Dexter Perkins⟩

[2]**give-and-take** \"\ *n* [[1]*give* + *and* + *take*, v.] **1 :** the practice of making mutual concessions **:** COMPROMISE ⟨negotiation in the nature of things entails *give-and-take* —G.W.Johnson⟩ **2 :** good-natured exchange of ideas ⟨the *give-and-take* of conversation⟩ ⟨prefers the *give-and-take* of the committee room to the fanfare of the forum —*Today*⟩

give away *vb* [ME *given away*, fr. *given* to give + *away*] *vt* **1 :** to make a present of **:** DONATE ⟨a beautiful streamlined television set . . . is being practically *given away* —Stuart Chase⟩ **2** *obs* **:** to make a sacrifice of ⟨be merry, Cassio, for thy solicitor shall rather die than *give* thy cause *away* —Shak.⟩ **3 :** to perform the ceremony of delivering (a bride) to the bridegroom at a wedding **4 a :** to expose to detection or ridicule **:** BETRAY ⟨it would be useless to call him a cad for *giving* a woman *away* —O.S.J.Gogarty⟩ ⟨no prisoner would *give* a fellow prisoner *away* —Rex Ingamells⟩ **b :** to allow (as a secret) to be known **:** DISCLOSE, REVEAL ⟨the incident . . . also *gives away* an essential point —*Times Lit. Supp.*⟩ ⟨a chef does not *give away* all his culinary secrets —Darius Milhaud⟩ **5 :** to give an advantage by competing under a handicap of ⟨the thirty-year-old welterweight *gave away* six and a quarter pounds to his . . . middleweight arch foe —Jesse Abramson⟩ ~ *vi* **:** to yield to or as if to physical force or strain ⟨accidents are caused by the safety belt not being fastened or by the seat itself *giving away* —H.G.Armstrong⟩

giveaway \'==,=\ *n* -s *often attrib* [*give away*] **1 :** a game or a method of playing a game in which the object is to lose **2 :** an unintentional revelation or betrayal ⟨your approach to her is a ~ with respect to your theater comprehension —Stark Young⟩ **3 :** something given away free; *specif* **:** an item of merchandise presented as a gift or premium ⟨a rash of all types of gimmicks, ~*s*, and novel promotion ideas introduced . . . to bring in the customers —Dolores Plested⟩ **4 :** a radio or television program on which prizes are given away

give back *vi* **:** to withdraw from a position or place **:** RETIRE, RETREAT ⟨militiamen around the door *gave back* to let . . . the judges through —H.L.Davis⟩ ~ *vt* **:** to send in return or reply **:** RESTORE, RETURN ⟨*gave* her *back* the looks she was sending him —Mary Deasy⟩

give down *vt* **:** to let (milk) flow — used of a cow ⟨his cows didn't recognize him clean shaven and wouldn't *give down* their milk —Ross Wurm⟩

give in *vt* **1 :** to hand in **:** DELIVER, SUBMIT ⟨I desire to *give in* my notice —Henry Green⟩ **2 :** to make a formal announcement of **:** DECLARE ⟨*gave in* their adherence to the peace —Charlotte Yonge⟩ ~ *vi* **:** to yield under pressure, insistence, or entreaty **:** SURRENDER ⟨it's weakness in me to *give in*, but he broke my will when I was a child —Ellen Glasgow⟩ ⟨have *given in* to the whims of their betters —Isabelle Mallet⟩

[1]**given** *adj* [ME, fr. past part. of *given* to give] **1 :** presented as a gift **:** bestowed without compensation ⟨the millionaire . . . finds that ~ goods never prosper —*London Daily News*⟩ **2 :** marked by an inclination or disposition **:** PRONE — used with *to* ⟨armies everywhere and in all ages have been ~ to swearing —Burges Johnson⟩ **3** *of an official document* **:** having been executed **:** DATED ⟨~ under my hand and seal this 30th day of June⟩ **4 a :** definitely stated **:** FIXED, SPECIFIED ⟨the number of musicians to be engaged for a ~ concert —Robert Lawrence⟩ **b :** assumed as actual or hypothetical **:** set forth as or as if known **:** DETERMINED, GRANTED ⟨~ the national panickiness . . . liberals have to be very careful of the company they keep —H.J.Muller⟩ **5 :** immediately presented specif. without interpretation or elaboration ⟨the ~ element is this incorrigible presentational element; the criticizable and dubitable element is the element of interpretation —C.I. Lewis⟩ — used esp. in philosophy

[2]**given** *n* -s **:** something given **:** DATUM ⟨it is taken as a ~ that language is the principal mode of communication for human beings —G.L.Trager⟩; *esp* **:** the component of the knowing process that is distinguished from what is supplied by thought or inference or from the hypothetical ⟨in a sense the ~ is ineffable; it is that which remains untouched and unaltered, however it is construed by thought —C.I.Lewis⟩

given name *n* **:** CHRISTIAN NAME, FORENAME

giv·en·ness \-ən(n)ə̇s,-ᵊmnə̇s\ *n* -ES **:** the quality or state of being given ⟨the ~ of the environment dominates everything —A.N.Whitehead⟩

give off *vt* **1** *obs* **:** to put an end to **:** QUIT ⟨was persuaded to *give off* riding —Robert Peirce⟩ **2 :** to send out as a branch ⟨antlers with their . . . branches pointing forward and *giving off* short tines, like twigs —D.C.Peattie⟩ **3 :** to throw off **:** EMIT ⟨as the blood passes through the lungs it . . . *gives off* its excess nitrogen —H.G.Armstrong⟩ ⟨antique tapestries which . . . *gave off* a sickening odor of mold —L.C.Douglas⟩ ~ *vi* **1** *obs* **:** to come to an end **:** CEASE **2 :** to send out a branch **:** branch off

give on *vi* **1** *obs* **:** to make an attack ⟨the Trojans first *gave on* —George Chapman⟩ **2 :** to pay contango

give out *vb* [ME *given out*, fr. *given* to give + *out*] *vt* **1 a :** to make known to or as if to the public **:** DECLARE, PUBLISH ⟨*giving out* that the doctor was not well and required a few days of complete rest —Charles Dickens⟩ ⟨some . . . reader would *give out* at the top of his voice the war news and the racing —C.E.Montague⟩ **b** (1) **:** to read the words of (a hymn or psalm) for congregational singing (2) *archaic* **:** to play (a hymn tune) over so as to facilitate congregational singing **2 :** to send forth **:** EMIT ⟨an elaborate afternoon dress of cream-colored chiffon which *gave out* a continual rustle —Scott Fitzgerald⟩ **3 :** to make distribution of **:** ISSUE ⟨the sergeant *gave out* new uniforms to the troops⟩ ~ *vi* **1 a :** to become physically exhausted **:** COLLAPSE ⟨when one of his oxen *gave out*, he pushed it aside and stepped into the yoke himself —Meridel Le Sueur⟩ **b :** to break down **:** FAIL ⟨his voice *gave out* before he reached his most dramatic moment —*Sydney (Australia) Bull.*⟩ **c :** to come to an end **:** run short ⟨the food at last began to *give out* —O.E.Rölvaag⟩ **2 a :** to enter freely or unrestrainedly into an activity **:** let oneself go — used with following *with* ⟨his orchestra *gave out* with Latin rhythms that made staying in your seat difficult —P.T. Hartung⟩ **b :** to give expression to one's feelings or thoughts — used with following *with* ⟨*gave out* with the smile and the V-sign —*N.Y. Times*⟩ ⟨removed his false teeth in his eagerness to *give out* with a really untrammeled yell —Ben Crisler⟩

give over *vb* [ME *given over*, fr. *given* to give + *over*] *vt* **1 :** to bring to an end **:** put a stop to **:** CEASE, QUIT ⟨I resolved to *give over* all thoughts of you —Mary W. Montagu⟩ ⟨you'll have to *give over* that hammering —Rex Ingamells⟩ **2 a :** to yield (oneself) without check, restraint, or control **:** ABANDON ⟨she *gave* herself *over* to laughter before she could go on —H.D.Skidmore⟩ **b :** to set apart for or give up to a particular purpose or use **:** DEVOTE — usu. used in passive ⟨the area is now *given over* to a children's playground —*Amer. Guide Series: Oreg.*⟩ ⟨the second meeting . . . will probably be *given over* to the consideration and adoption of the constitution —A.T.Weaver⟩ **3** *archaic* **:** to pronounce incurable ⟨had been ill of a fever and *given over* by her physician —Anna Jameson⟩ **4 :** to put in charge or keeping **:** ENTRUST ⟨took him to the apartment and *gave* the old man *over* to his housekeeper —Nevil Shute⟩ **5** *archaic* **:** to despair of finding or seeing ⟨was now almost *given over*, the ponds and even the river . . . having been dragged —S.T.Coleridge⟩ ~ *vi* **:** to bring an activity or a course of action to an end **:** STOP ⟨mother told him to *give over* and let me alone —Brendan Behan⟩

giv·er \'givə(r)\ *n* -s [ME *giver*, *givere*, fr. *given* to give + *-er*, *-ere* -er] **:** one that gives **:** DONOR ⟨God loves a cheerful ~ —2 Cor 9:7 (RSV)⟩ — often used in combination ⟨alms*giver*⟩

gives *pres 3d sing of* GIVE, *pl of* GIVE

gi·ve·tian \zhə̇'vēshən, -vāsh-\ *adj, usu cap* [F *givétien*, fr. *Givet*, commune in Ardennes, France + F *-ien* -ian] **:** of or relating to the European Devonian — see GEOLOGIC TIME table

give up *vb* [ME *given up*, fr. *given* to give + *up*] *vt* **1 :** to hand over to or as if to another **:** RELINQUISH, SURRENDER ⟨the death of his wife a few years later caused him to *give up* his . . . home —J.M.Phalen⟩ ⟨things went from bad to worse until finally he had to *give up* his position —Scott Fitzgerald⟩ **2 :** to breathe forth **:** EMIT — now used esp. in the phrase *give up the ghost* **3** *obs* **:** to deliver verbally **:** PRESENT ⟨how he may be brought to *give up* the clearest evidence —Francis Atterbury⟩ **4 :** to have done with **:** desist from **:** FORSAKE, SACRIFICE ⟨men will never *give up* seeking to influence one another —R.M.Weaver⟩ ⟨you wouldn't *give up* science or your career —Susan Ertz⟩ ⟨*gave* the idea *up* in sheer weariness —T.B.Costain⟩ **5 a :** to yield (oneself) to a particular feeling, influence, or activity **:** ABANDON ⟨*gave* himself *up* completely to despair⟩ ⟨shutting himself away from the world and *giving* himself *up* to writing his novel —Edmund Wilson⟩ **b :** to set apart or devote to a particular purpose or use — usu. used in passive ⟨Mondays and Tuesdays were often *given up* to drink, cockfights, bearbaiting —J.H.Plumb⟩ **6 :** to declare incurable or insoluble ⟨the patient was *given up* by the doctors⟩ ⟨couldn't answer the riddle and so *gave* it *up*⟩ **7 a :** to make public **:** REVEAL ⟨we do not *give up* the names of our contributors —*Lippincott's Mag.*⟩ **b :** to make known (the name of a principal) in the process of completing a transaction on a stock exchange **8 :** to despair of seeing ⟨it's so late we *gave* you *up* —Charles Dickens⟩ ~ *vi* **:** to withdraw from an activity or course of action often as an admission of failure **:** STOP ⟨had lost flies and broken leaders until he had *given up* —Alexander MacDonald⟩ ⟨doctor tried to get your father to *give up* for a while —Ellen Glasgow⟩

give-up \'=,=\ *n* -s [*give up*] **:** a transaction on an exchange in which the broker reveals the name of his principal who is under obligation to complete the transaction

giv·ey *or* **givy** \'givē\ *adj* **givier**; **giviest** [[1]*give* + *-y*] **:** inclined to give ⟨the ground was soft and ~ —Conrad Richter⟩

giving *n* -s [fr. gerund of [1]*give*] **:** something given **:** GIFT ⟨their total ~*s* . . . have probably yielded a dividend of another $750,000,000 —Bernard Kalb⟩

giz·mo *or* **gis·mo** \'giz,mō\ *n* -s [origin unknown] **:** something whose name is unknown or forgotten **:** GADGET ⟨a ~ which blends the images of two cameras on the screen at once —Arthur Rankin⟩

gizz \'jiz\ *n* -ES [prob. by shortening & alter. fr. *jasey*] *chiefly Scot* **:** WIG

giz·zard \'gizə(r)d\ *n* -s [earlier *gysard*, alter. of *gysar*, fr. ME *giser*, *gyser*, fr. ONF *guisier* liver (esp. of a fowl), gizzard, modif. of L *gigeria* (neut. pl.) cooked entrails of poultry, perh. of Iranian origin; akin to Per *jigar* liver; akin to Gk *hēpat-*, *hēpar* liver — more at HEPATIC] **1 a :** the muscular enlargement of the alimentary canal of birds that immediately follows the crop, is best developed in seed-eating birds, typically has thick muscular walls and a tough horny lining, and serves to grind the food, its muscular action being commonly assisted by gravel swallowed by the bird **b :** a thickened part of an alimentary canal similar in function to the crop of a bird (as the proventriculus of an insect or the enlargement immediately in front of the intestine of an earthworm) **2 :** INNARDS ⟨it warms my ~ . . . and I am proud of you —O.W.Holmes †1935⟩ ⟨this notion has long stuck in my ~ —W.S.Maugham⟩

gizzard erosion *n* **:** an obscure dietary-deficiency disease of young chickens marked by local lesions or extensive sloughing of the gizzard lining

gizzard shad *n* **1 :** a forage fish (*Dorosoma cepedianum*) of eastern and central No. America — called also *hickory shad* **2 :** any of several fishes related to the gizzard shad

gizzard stone *n* **:** a fossil gastrolith

gizzard trout *n* **:** GILLAROO

gizzard worm *n* **:** any of various nematode worms parasitic in the gizzard of birds: as **a :** a spiruroid worm of the genus *Acuaria* that is a destructive parasite of chickens, turkeys, and related game birds **b :** a spiruroid worm (*Amidostomum anseris*) sometimes fatal to ducks and geese

giz·zen \'gizᵊn\ *or* **giz·zened** \-ᵊnd\ *adj* [*gizzen* of Scand origin (akin to Norw dial. *gisen* dried out, leaky); *gizzened* fr. past part. of Sc *gizzen*, v., to dry out, become leaky, of Scand origin; akin to Norw dial. *gisna* to dry out, become leaky, fr. *gisen* dried out, leaky; akin to L *hiare* to gape, yawn — more at YAWN] **1** *chiefly Scot* **:** dried out **:** leaky because of dryness — used of wood products **2** *chiefly Scot* **:** WIZENED, SHRIVELED — used of a person

giz·zern \ˈgizə(r)n\ *n* -s [ME *gisarn*, alter. of *giser, gyser* gizzard] *dial* : GIZZARD

gjet·ost *also* **gjed·ost** \ˈyed·ˌōst, ˈyā|, |ād-·, -ˌōst\ *n* -s [Norw *gjetost*, fr. *gjet* goat (fr. ON *geit*) + *ost* cheese, fr. ON *ostr* — more at GOAT, JUICE] : a hard dark brown cheese usu. made of goat's milk but sometimes made of a combination of cow's and goat's milk

gl *abbr* **1** gill **2** glass **3** glaze **4** gloria **5** gloss **6** glossary

GL *abbr* **1** Gothic letter **2** grand lodge **3** grid leak **4** ground level **5** gunlaying

gla·bel·la \glə'belə\ *n, pl* **glabel·lae** \-ˌlē, -ˌlī\ [NL, fr. L, fem. of *glabellus* hairless, smooth, fr. *glaber* bald — more at GLAD] **1** : the smooth prominence of the forehead between the eyebrows; *also* : the part of the frontal bone that lies immediately above the root of the nose or a point in the midsagittal plane of this area — see CRANIOMETRY illustration **2** : the median convex lobe of the cephalic shield of a trilobite — **gla·bel·lar** \-lə(r)\ *adj*

gla·bel·lo-occipital length \glə¦be(ˌ)lō+ . . . -\ *n* [*glabello-occipital* fr. *glabella* + *-o-* + *occipital*] : the distance between the glabella and the opisthocranion

gla·bel·lum \glə'beləm\ *n, pl* **glabel·la** \-lə\ [NL, fr. L, neut. of *glabellus*] : GLABELLA

gla·brate \ˈglāˌbrāt, -brət\ *adj* [L *glabratus*, past part. of *glabrare* to make bald, fr. *glabr-, glaber* bald] : GLABROUS, GLABRESCENT

gla·bres·cent \(ˈ)glā¦bresᵊnt\ *adj* [L *glabrescent-, glabrescens*, pres. part. of *glabrescere* to become bald, fr. *glabr-, glaber*] : glabrous or tending to become glabrous

gla·brous \ˈglābrəs\ *adj* [L *glabr-, glaber* bald + E *-ous*] : having a smooth even surface : free of roughness; *specif* : having an epidermal covering that is totally or relatively devoid of hairs or down ⟨the ~ leaves of some plants⟩ ⟨the ~ skin of the American Indian⟩ — **gla·brous·ness** *n* -ES

¹gla·cé \(ˈ)gla¦sā\ *adj* [F, past part. of *glacer* to glaze, cover with icing, freeze, fr. L *glaciare* to freeze, fr. *glacies* ice — more at GLACIER] **1** : made or finished so as to have a smooth glossy effect : having a lustrous surface — used of leathers or fabrics ⟨~ kid gloves⟩ ⟨~ silk⟩ **2** : coated with a glaze : GLAZED, CANDIED ⟨~ fruits⟩

²glacé \"\ *n* -s **1** : a glacé material ⟨a gown of black ~⟩ **2** : a glacé finish

³glacé \"\ *vt* **glacéed; glacéed; glacéing; glacés** **1** : to give a glacé finish to **2** : to coat with a glaze : CANDY

⁴glace \ˈglas\ *n* -s [F, lit., ice, fr. LL *glacia* — more at GLACIER] **1** : a frozen dessert (as ice cream or sherbet) **2** : a coating of glaze (as on candied fruits)

¹gla·cial \ˈglāshəl\ *adj* [L *glacialis*, fr. *glacies* ice + *-alis* -al] **1 a** : having the nature of ice : suggestive of ice : ICY: (1) : extremely cold : FRIGID, FREEZING, CHILLING ⟨a ~ wind⟩ ⟨the air in the cave was ~, penetrated to the very bones —Willa Cather⟩ (2) : devoid of warmth and cordiality ⟨a ~ handshake⟩ : chillingly hostile ⟨froze him in his tracks with a ~ stare —Roger Butterfield⟩ (3) : coldly immobile or imperturbable ⟨~ conservatism⟩ ⟨preserved a ~ calm⟩ **b** (1) : of, relating to, or produced by glaciers ⟨~ erosion⟩ ⟨~ deposits⟩ ⟨~ lakes⟩ : characterized by the presence of glaciers ⟨the ~ ages of the earth⟩ (2) : suggestive of the movement of glaciers : moving with extreme slowness : moving slowly and irresistibly or relentlessly ⟨the ~ pace of European integration —A.E. Stevenson b. 1900⟩ **c** : of or relating to a time or region of glaciation ⟨~ man⟩ : of, relating to, or produced by the Glacial epoch or one of the glacial ages ⟨~ climates⟩ **2** : tending at freezing temperature to form crystals resembling ice if pure but not if in aqueous solutions ⟨~ acrylic acid⟩ ⟨~ phosphoric acid⟩ — **gla·cial·ly** \-əlē, -əli\ *adv*

²glacial \"\ *n* -s : one of the glacial ages or stages of the Pleistocene epoch

glacial acetic acid *n* : acetic acid containing usu. less than 1 percent of water and obtained as a pungent caustic hygroscopic liquid that crystallizes readily and is a good solvent (as for oils and resins)

glacial boulder *n* : a boulder carried by glaciers to a point far beyond its original location

glacial drift *n* : DRIFT 2g(2)

glacial epoch *n* **1** : any of those parts of geologic time from Precambrian onward in both the northern and southern hemispheres during which a much larger portion of the earth was covered by glaciers than at present **2** *usu cap G & often cap E* : the Pleistocene epoch

GLACIAL EPOCHS

EPOCHS	AGES AND STAGES					APPROXIMATE TIME
	North America			Europe		
Recent	Postglacial					
	Wisconsin	*Mankato *Cary *Tazewell *Iowan		Würm	*Würm IV " III " II " I	5000–15000 B.C.
Pleistocene	Sangamon		III Interglacial	Riss-Würm		125,000 B.C.
	Illinoian			Riss		275,000 B.C.
	Yarmouth		II Interglacial	Mindel-Riss		375,000 B.C.
	Kansan			Mindel		675,000 B.C.
	Aftonian		I Interglacial	Günz-Mindel		750,000 B.C.
	Nebraskan			Günz		900,000 B.C.
Pliocene	Preglacial					1,000,000 B.C.

*Substage

gla·cial·ism \-əˌlizəm\ *n* -s : GLACIATION

gla·cial·ist \-ələst\ *n* -s **1** : GLACIOLOGIST **2** : one that supports the glacier theory

gla·cial·ize \-əˌlīz\ *vt* -ED/-ING/-S : GLACIATE

glacial meal *n* : ROCK FLOUR

glacial period *n* **1** : GLACIAL EPOCH **2** *usu cap G & often cap P* : the Pleistocene epoch

glacial theory *n* : GLACIER THEORY

gla·ci·ar·i·um \ˌglāshē'a(a)rēəm\ *n* -s [L *glacies* ice + E *-arium*] : a skating rink with a floor of artificial ice

gla·ci·ate \ˈglāshēˌāt *also* -sē-\ *vb* -ED/-ING/-S [L *glaciatus*, past part. of *glaciare* to freeze, fr. *glacies* ice] *vt* **1** : to convert into ice : FREEZE **2 a** : to cover with or as if with ice or snow; *specif* : to cover with glaciers ⟨no greenery could be seen in the whole *glaciated* region⟩ **b** : to subject to or alter by the action of glaciers : produce glacial effects (as erosion or the deposition of glacial drift) in or upon — usu. used in passive ⟨a valley which has been vigorously *glaciated* —W.J.Miller⟩ ⟨striated rocks found in that widely *glaciated* area⟩ ~ *vi* **1** : to become ice : become frozen **2** : to become covered with or as if with ice or snow; *specif* : to become covered with glaciers ⟨the poles *glaciated* —Martin Gardner⟩

gla·ci·a·tion \ˌglās(h)ē'āshən\ *n* -s [prob. fr. (assumed) NL *glaciation-, glaciatio*, fr. L *glaciatus* + *-ion-, -io* -ion] **1 a** : the action or process of becoming ice : FREEZING ⟨the ~ of clouds⟩ **b** : the formation of ice sheets; *specif* : the formation of glaciers ⟨an age of extensive ~⟩ **2 a** : the condition of being covered by ice sheets or glaciers; *specif* : GLACIAL ⟨deposits laid down during the period of the second ~ —*Amer. Anthropologist*⟩ **b** (1) : subjection to the action of glaciers ⟨cycles of weathering and ~ —Russell Lord⟩ (2) : the effects produced by the action of glaciers ⟨~ that is clearly evident throughout the area⟩

gla·cier \ˈglāshə(r) *sometimes* -āzhə- *or* -āshēə-, *Brit usu* ˈglasiə(r *or* -asyə-\ *n* -s [F dial. (Savoy), fr. MF dial. (Savoy, Vaud, Valais), fr. MF *glace* ice, fr. LL *glacia*, alter. of L *glacies*; akin to L *gelu* frost — more at COLD] : a large body of ice moving slowly down a slope or valley or spreading outward on a land surface and usu. carrying, pushing, or depositing loose rock and other debris and eroding land forms and having a perennial snowfield on which falling snow is converted to a granular icy mass which through the pressure of successive snowfalls and through the freezing of seasonal meltwater becomes solid ice and flows plastically downward to form the body of the glacier which grows or shrinks according to whether snowfall exceeds the rate of melting or not

glacier bear *n* : a small bluish gray bear of the glacier region of southern Alaska that is prob. a color variant of the black bear although sometimes considered a distinct species (*Ursus emmonsi* or *Euarctos emmonsi*)

glacier cataract *n* : the passage of a glacier over a declivity in its bed

gla·ciered \-ə(r)d\ *adj* : covered with glaciers : GLACIATED

gla·cier·et \ˌglāsh(ē)ə¦ret, -āzhə¦-\ *n* -s **1** : a miniature alpine glacier **2** : a small accumulation of névé that resembles a glacier

gla·cier·ist *pronunc at* GLACIER + əst\ *n* -s : GLACIALIST

gla·cier·iza·tion \ˌglāshərə'zāshən, -ˌrī'z- *sometimes* -lāzhə- *or* -lāshēə-\ *n* -s [*glacier* + *-ize* + *-ation*] : GLACIATION

gla·cier·ize \'=(=)=ˌrīz\ *vb* -ED/-ING/-S *see -ize in Explan Notes* [*glacier* + *-ize*] : GLACIATE

glacier lily *n* : a Rocky mountain dogtooth violet (*Erythronium grandiflorum*) with light yellow flowers — called also *snow lily*

glacier mill *n* [*mill* trans. of F *moulin*] : MOULIN

glacier table *n* : a block of stone supported above the surface of a glacier on a pedestal of ice

glacier theory *n* : a theory in glaciology: drift was deposited through the agency of glaciers in the Glacial epoch

glac·i·fi·ca·tion \ˌglāsəfə'kāshən\ *n* -s [L *glacies* ice + E *-fication*] **1** : GLACIATION 1 **2** : GLACIATION 2a

glacio- *comb form* [ISV, fr. *glacier*] **1** : glacier ⟨*glaciology*⟩ **2** : glacial and ⟨*glaciomarine*⟩

gla·cio·fluvial \¦glās(h)ē(ˌ)ō+\ *adj* : of, relating to, or coming from streams deriving much or all of their water from the melting of a glacier ⟨~ deposits⟩

gla·cio·lacustrine \"+\ *adj* : of, relating to, or coming from lakes deriving much or all of their water from the melting of a glacier ⟨~ clays and silts⟩

gla·ci·o·log·i·cal \¦glās(h)ēə¦läjəkəl\ *adj* : of or relating to glaciology

gla·ci·ol·o·gist \ˌglās(h)ē'äləjəst\ *n* -s [ISV *glaciology* + *-ist*] : a specialist in glaciology

gla·ci·ol·o·gy \-jē\ *n* -ES [ISV *glacio-* + *-logy*] **1** : a science concerned with the causes and modes of ice accumulation and with ice action on the earth's surface; *specif* : a branch of geology that treats of glacial epochs, glaciation, and the effects of ice in modifying the earth's surface and in affecting the life and distribution of plants and animals **2** : the glacial features of a region ⟨the ~ of Greenland⟩

gla·ci·om·e·ter \-'ämәd·ə(r)\ *n* : an instrument that measures glacial motion

gla·cio·natant \¦glās(h)ē(ˌ)ō+\ *adj* : of, relating to, or derived from masses of floating ice usu. glacial in origin

gla·cis \ˈglasē, -si, gla'sē, ˈglasəs, ˈglāsəs\ *n, pl* **glacis** \-sēz,-siz\ *also* **glacises** \-səsəz\ [F, fr. MF, fr. *glacer* to freeze, slide, fr. OF *glacier*, fr. L *glaciare* to freeze, fr. *glacies* ice — more at GLACIER] **1 a** : a gentle slope : INCLINE **b** : a slope used for defense against attack; *specif* : a natural or artificial slope that runs downward from the top of a counterscarp or covered way so as to expose attackers to firing from ramparts **2 a** : an area lying beyond the borders of a country and used as a buffer against an enemy : a protective barrier; *specif* : BUFFER STATE **b** : a combat area ⟨the ~ on which the future of mankind will be decided —H.W.Weigert⟩

glacis plate *n* : sloping armor plate formerly often used on the deck of naval vessels (as about hatches or turrets)

glack \ˈglak\ *n* -s [ScGael *glac* valley, hollow, palm of the hand, fr. MIr *glacc* hand; prob. akin to L *galla* gall on a plant — more at GALL (excrescence)] *Scot* : a narrow valley : RAVINE

gla·con \(ˈ)gla¦sōⁿ\ *n, pl* **glacons** \-ōⁿ(z)\ [F *glaçon* piece of ice, fr. OF, fr. *glace* ice — more at GLACIER] : a piece of sea ice ranging in size from a small fragment to a floe of medium dimensions

¹glad \ˈglad, -aa(ə)-,-ai-\ *adj, usu* **gladder**; *usu* **gladdest** [ME, shining, glad, fr. OE *glæd*; akin to OHG *glat* shining, smooth, ON *glathr* glad, sunny, L *glaber* bald, smooth, Russ *gladkiĭ* smooth, and perh. to OE *geolu* yellow — more at YELLOW] **1** *archaic* : having a cheerful or happy disposition by nature **2 a** : experiencing pleasure, joy, or delight through some immediate cause : made happy : filled with joy ⟨if you are happy, I am ~⟩ ⟨~ that they succeeded⟩ ⟨~ at the announcement⟩ ⟨were ~ to meet him⟩ **b** (1) : GRATIFIED, SATISFIED, PLEASED ⟨both his high-school friends were ~ of his company —William Du Bois⟩ (2) : not at all sorry : quite without regret or remorse ⟨they got what they deserved and I'm ~ of it⟩ **c** : very willing : quite content ⟨~ to do anything you say⟩ **3 a** (1) : marked by, expressive of, or caused by happiness and joy ⟨a ~ countenance⟩ ⟨up we climb with ~ exhilaration —John Muir †1914⟩ ⟨the others gave a ~ shout —Francis Shean⟩ (2) : surrounded by or attended with happiness and joy ⟨a ~ occasion⟩ **b** : causing happiness and joy ⟨the ~ news was flashed through the encampment —F.V.W.Mason⟩ : PLEASANT, CHEERING ⟨the same ~ assurance of meeting again —W.W. Howells⟩ **4** : full of brightness and cheerfulness : having a beautiful radiance ⟨a ~ spring morning⟩

syn HAPPY, CHEERFUL, LIGHTHEARTED, JOYFUL, JOYOUS: GLAD is generally the opposite of *sad* and *gloomy;* it indicates a degree of pleasure ranging from pleased satisfaction to elation ⟨always gleeful and jocular, even as afterward his entire saintly life was *glad* with an invincible gaiety of spirit —H.O.Taylor⟩ In cursory conventional expressions it indicates gratification or lack of reservation or regret ⟨I shall be *glad* of your company —G.B.Shaw⟩ HAPPY, often interchangeable with GLAD, may imply a more positive and demonstrative sense of well-being, satisfaction, and enjoyment ⟨like most men with a *happy* family life, it was no hardship for him to be alone —H.S. Canby⟩ ⟨all the delightful signs of their *happy* intimacy —Morley Callaghan⟩ CHEERFUL suggests lively, hearty, and optimistic good spirits arising from a naturally sanguine disposition or from some particular cause of happiness ⟨they [suicidal attempts] could not enter the *cheerful*, sanguine, courageous scheme of life . . . in part natural to her —Havelock Ellis⟩ ⟨as *cheerful* as could be expected, for his broken leg was knitting nicely —Jack London⟩ LIGHTHEARTED suggests a carefree, debonair, easygoing freedom from concern giving rise to lively mirth ⟨the gayest of worried people in Europe . . . they can be *lighthearted* in the midst of misery and joke at their own expense —H.J.Forman⟩ ⟨*lighthearted* optimistic libertarianism —M.R.Cohen⟩ JOYFUL and JOYOUS are very close together in indicating joy, marked happiness, high pleasure, elation; JOYOUS may hint a more lasting or more certain elated happiness, JOYFUL a more demonstrative happiness arising from a particular cause ⟨a bright and happy Christian, a weeping optimist who laughed away sin and doubt, a *joyful* Puritan —Sinclair Lewis⟩ ⟨thou with the smile on thy face and the *joyful* eyes and clear —William Morris⟩ ⟨that *joyous* serenity we think belongs to a better world than this —Sir Winston Churchill⟩ ⟨a *joyous*, lighthearted, and hilarious mode of life which offered a strong contrast to the more sober lives of New England —C.A. & Mary Beard⟩

²glad \"\ *vb* **gladded; gladded; gladding; glads** [ME *gladen*, fr. OE *gladian*, fr. *glæd*] *vt, archaic* : to make glad ~ *vi, obs* : to be glad

³glad \"\ *adv* [¹*glad*] *archaic* : GLADLY

⁴glad \"\ *n* -s [by shortening] : GLADIOLUS 1b

glad·den \-dᵊn\ *vb* **gladdened; gladdened; gladdening** \-d(ᵊ)niŋ\ **gladdens** [¹*glad* + *-en*] *vt* : to make glad ⟨something that will ~ your eyes —S.M.Crothers⟩ ~ *vi, archaic* : to be glad **syn** see PLEASE

gladder *comparative of* GLAD

gladdest *superlative of* GLAD

glad·don \ˈgladᵊn\ *n* -s [ME *gladen, gladene*, fr. OE *glædene*, perh. modif. of L *gladiolus* small sword, gladiolus] **1** *dial Eng* : IRIS; *esp* : STINKING IRIS **2** *dial Eng* : CATTAIL 1

glad·dy \ˈgladi\ *n* -ES [origin unknown] *dial Eng* : YELLOWHAMMER 1

glade \ˈglād\ *n* -s [perh. fr. ¹*glad*] **1 a** (1) : an open space surrounded by woods : CLEARING (2) : a wooded or open area lying between wooded slopes (3) *archaic* : an open stretch or group of interconnected openings forming a passage through woodland **b** : GROVE; *esp* : an open grove of tall old trees **2** : a marshy and usu. low-lying area: as **a** *South* : a periodically inundated grassy marsh often running between adjacent slopes **b** : a marshy area bounding or forming the headwaters of a stream **3** *obs* : a bright streak or patch of light

glade mallow *n* : a tall American herb (*Napaea dioica*) of the family Malvaceae with palmate leaves and small white dioecious flowers

gladey *var of* GLADY

glad eye *n* : a pleasant friendly glance : a welcoming glance ⟨giving the *glad eye* to voters of every persuasion —C.L. Becker⟩; *usu* : a glance indicating sexual interest and usu. intended to encourage sexual advances ⟨girls giving sailors the *glad eye*⟩

glad·ful \'=fəl\ *adj* [ME, fr. *glad*, n., gladness (fr. *glad*, adj.) + *-ful*] *archaic* : full of happiness and joy : GLAD

glad hand *n* [¹*glad* + *hand*] **1** : a warm friendly handshake ⟨moving among his patrons with a welcoming smile and a *glad hand* —Edwin Corle⟩ **2** : a warm welcome, greeting, or reception ⟨an affable people always ready to give strangers a *glad hand*⟩; *esp* : an effusive welcome, greeting, or reception usu. basically insincere and often marked by a display of obnoxious familiarity ⟨potential customers getting the *glad hand*⟩ ⟨master of the *glad hand* and the soft soap —H.A. Burton⟩

glad-hand \'=¦=\ *vb* [*glad hand*] *vt* : to extend a glad hand to ⟨political candidates *glad-handing* everyone they met⟩ ~ *vi* : to extend a glad hand ⟨you'll never find him *glad-handing* if he can help it⟩

glad-hander \"ə(r)\ *n* **1** : one given to glad-handing : one ready to extend a glad hand ⟨the home-loving, comfort-loving, rotund *glad-hander* —Christopher Rand⟩ ⟨this big, friendly fellow — a *glad-hander* who really seemed to mean it —R.M.Yoder⟩ **2** : one who is appointed to meet or greet others and win their goodwill ⟨a shy *glad-hander*, a public-relations man with a highly developed sense of privacy —Dwight Macdonald⟩

glad·i·ate \ˈgladēˌāt, -ēət\ *adj* [NL *gladiatus*, fr. L *gladius* sword + *-atus* -ate] : shaped like a sword : ENSIFORM ⟨the ~ leaves of a gladiolus⟩

glad·i·a·tor \ˈgladēˌād·ə(r), -ātə-\ *n* -s [L, fr. *gladius* sword, of Celt origin; akin to W *cleddyf* sword; akin to L *clades* destruction, defeat, Gk *klados* sprout, twig, branch, OSlav *kladivo* hammer, Gk *klan* to break — more at HALT (lame)] **1 a** : one (as a professional combatant or a captive, slave, or condemned criminal) equipped with some means of attack and defense and pitted against another or against a wild animal in a fight to the death for the entertainment of the public (as in the arena of the ancient Roman amphitheater) **b** : one that opposes another in a usu. public controversy : DISPUTANT, CONTROVERSIALIST ⟨the debates of the House were substantially carried on by some score of chosen ~s — Christopher Hollis⟩ **c** : a trained fighter; *specif* : PRIZEFIGHTER ⟨whether you consider it from his worth as a ~ or from the point of view of the box office —Gene Tunney⟩ **2** *obs* : a professional swordsman

glad·i·a·to·ri·al \ˌgladēə¦tōrēəl, -tȯr-\ *adj* **1** : of, relating to, or suggestive of gladiators or the combats of gladiators ⟨bloody ~ spectacles⟩ **2** : inclined toward controversy or contention : QUARRELSOME ⟨~ newspaper columnists⟩ ⟨those ~ contests in which the participants are encouraged to let their hostilities run riot —R.H.Wittcoff⟩

gladiatorian *adj, obs* : GLADIATORIAL

glad·i·a·tor·ship \'==,==,ship\ *n* : a display of gladiatorial skill

gladiatory *adj* [L *gladiatorius*, fr. *gladiator*] *obs* : GLADIATORIAL

glad·i·o·la \ˌgladē'ōlə\ *n* -s [back-formation fr. *gladiolus*, taken as a plural] : GLADIOLUS 1b

gladi·o·lar \ˌgladē'ōlə(r) *sometimes* glə'dīəl-\ *adj* [*gladiolus* + *-ar*] : of or relating to the gladiolus (sense 3)

glad·i·ole \ˈgladēˌōl\ *n* -s [ME *gladiol*, fr. L *gladiolus*] : GLADIOLUS 1b

gladi·o·lus \ˌgladē'ōləs *sometimes* glə'dīələs\ *n* [NL, fr. L, small sword, gladiolus, dim. of *gladius* sword] **1 a** *cap* : a genus of plants (family Iridaceae) native chiefly to Africa with a few native to Europe and Asia that have erect sword-shaped leaves and spikes of brilliantly colored irregular flowers arising from flattened corms **b** *pl* **gladiolus** \"\ *or* **gladio·li** \-ē'ōˌlī, -ē'ō(ˌ)lē; -ˈīəˌlī\ *also* **gladioluses** : any plant of the genus *Gladiolus* **2** -ES : a strong red that is bluer and paler than Goya, bluer than average cherry red, and bluer and darker than geranium (sense 3a) **3** *pl* **gladioli** : the large middle portion of the sternum lying between the upper manubrium and the lower xiphoid process — called also *mesosternum*

gladiolus 1b

gladiolus thrips *n* : a small thrips (*Taeniothrips simplex*) lemon-yellow when a nymph and grayish black when adult that feeds on all parts of the gladiolus causing bleaching and browning of leaves and whitening and blasting of flowers

glad·ite \ˈglaˌdīt\ *n* -s [Sw *gladit*, fr. *Gladhammar*, Sweden, its locality + Sw *-it* -ite] : a mineral $PbCuBi_5S_9$ consisting of a complex sulfide of lead, copper, and bismuth

gla·di·us \ˈglādēəs\ *n, pl* **gla·dii** \-ēˌī\ : PEN 5

glad·less \ˈgladləs, -aad-,-aid-\ *adj* [obs. E *glad*, n., gladness (fr. ME, fr. *glad*, adj.) + E *-less*] : devoid of happiness and joy ⟨a ~ life⟩

¹glad·ly *adj* -ER/-EST [ME, fr. OE *glædlīc* pleasant, shining] *archaic* : GLAD

²glad·ly *adv, sometimes* -ER/-EST [ME, fr. OE *glædlīce*, adv. fr. *glædlīc* pleasant, shining, fr. *glæd* shining, glad + *-lic* -ly (adj. suffix)] : in a glad manner: **a** : with happiness and joy : JOYFULLY ⟨~ welcomed him home again⟩ **b** : very willingly : CHEERFULLY ⟨your money will be ~ refunded⟩

glad·ness *n* -ES [ME *gladnesse*, fr. OE *glædnes*, fr. *glæd* glad + *-nes* -ness] : the quality or state of being glad : happiness and joy ⟨days filled with ~⟩ ⟨his voice . . . had such a warm, infectious ~ running through it —O.E.Rölvaag⟩

glad rags *n pl, slang* : dressy clothes : clothes worn at parties or on other festive social occasions : best clothes; *often* : formal dress (as evening clothes) ⟨were all there in their *glad rags*⟩

glads *pres 3d sing of* GLAD, *pl of* GLAD

glad·some \'=səm\ *adj, sometimes* -ER/-EST [ME *gladsom*, fr. *glad*, n., gladness (fr. *glad*, adj.) + *-som* -some] *archaic* : GLAD — **glad·some·ly** *adv* — **glad·some·ness** *n* -ES

glad·stone \ˈgladˌstōn, -d,st-, *chiefly Brit* -ˌtən\ *or* **gladstone bag** *n* -s *often cap G* [after William E. *Gladstone* †1898 Brit. statesman] **:** a traveling bag typically of leather and about two feet long with flexible sides on a rigid steel frame and opening flat into two equal compartments

gladstone

glad·sto·ni·an \(ˈ)gladz¦tōnēən, -d¦st-\ *adj, usu cap* [William E. *Gladstone* †1898 + E *-ian*] **:** of, relating to, or characteristic of W.E.Gladstone, his political policies, or the party that supported him

glady *also* **glad·ey** \ˈglādē\ *adj* **gladier; gladiest** [*glade* + *-y*] **1 a :** having glades; *esp* **:** full of glades ⟨a ~ countryside⟩ **b :** resembling a glade ⟨it was a ~ place, and ferns and moss grew all around —H.E.Giles⟩ **2 :** having a shallow soil and limestone outcrops ⟨extensive ~ areas wherein well-preserved fossils are abundant —*Jour. of Geol.*⟩

gla·gah *or* **gla·ga** \ˈglägə\ *n* -s [Malay *gĕlagah*] **:** KANS

glag·o·lit·ic \ˌglagə¦lid·ik\ *also* **glag·o·lith·ic** \-lithik\ *adj, usu cap* [irreg. fr. Serbo-Croatian *glagolica* Glagolitic alphabet + E *-ic*] **:** written in, constituting, or belonging to an alphabet of which the invention is attributed to St. Cyril in the 9th century A.D. and which was formerly used in writing various Slavic languages but is now used only in Catholic liturgical books in a limited area along the eastern coast of the Adriatic — compare CYRILLIC ALPHABET

gla·go·li·tsa \glə¦gōlyētsə, -ˌsä\ *n* -s *usu cap* [Serbo-Croatian *glagolica;* akin to OSlav *glagolŭ* word, *glasŭ* voice — more at CALL] **:** the Glagolitic alphabet

glaik \ˈglāk\ *n* -s [origin unknown] **1 glaiks** *pl, chiefly Scot* **:** derisive deception **:** MOCKERY **2** *chiefly Scot* **:** a flash of light

glai·kit *or* **glai·ked** \ˈglākət, -əd\ *adj* [ME (Sc) *glaikit, glakit*] *chiefly Scot* **:** showing a lack of common sense and good judgment **:** FOOLISH, SILLY, GIDDY

¹glair *or* **glaire** \ˈgla(a)(ə)r, -le\, |ə\ *n* -s [ME *gleyre* white of an egg, fr. MF *glaire,* fr. OF, modif. of (assumed) VL *claria,* fr. L *clarus* clear — more at CLEAR] **1 :** a sizing liquid made from egg white beaten with vinegar and applied to book covers before laying on gold leaf or to book edges before gilding **2 :** a viscid or slimy substance suggestive of the white of an egg

²glair *or* **glaire** \ˈ"\ *vt* -ED/-ING/-S **:** to apply glair to ⟨~*ed* book edges⟩

glair·e·ous \|rēəs\ *adj* [¹*glair* + *-eous*] *archaic* **:** GLAIRY

glair·i·ness \|rēnəs\ *n* -ES **:** the quality or state of being glairy

glairy \|rē\ *adj* -ER/-EST [¹*glair* + *-y*] **1 :** having the characteristics of glair **:** VISCID, SLIMY ⟨~ mucus⟩ **2 :** overlaid with or as if with glair ⟨a sticky ~ surface⟩

glais·tig *or* **glas·tig** \ˈglashtig\ *n* -s [ScGael *glaistig*] **:** a female sprite in Celtic mythology

glaive \ˈglāv\ *n* -s [ME *glaive, gleyve,* fr. OF *glaive* javelin, modif. of L *gladius* sword — more at GLADIATOR] **1** *obs* **:** HALBERD **2** *archaic* **:** SWORD; *esp* **:** BROADSWORD

glaiz·ie \ˈglāzi\ *Scot var of* GLAZY

glam \ˈglam\ *var of* GLAUM

gla·mor·gan·shire \glə¦mȯrgən,shi(ə)r, -ˌshər\ *or* **glamorgan** *adj, usu cap* [fr. *Glamorganshire, Glamorgan,* county in Wales] **:** of or from the county of Glamorgan, Wales **:** of the kind or style prevalent in Glamorgan

glam·or·iza·tion \ˌglamərəˈzāshən, -ˌrīˈz-\ *n* -s **:** the act of glamorizing or the process of being glamorized

glam·or·ize *also* **glam·our·ize** \ˈ==ˌrīz\ *vt* -ED/-ING/-S **1 :** to make glamorous **:** add glamour to **:** make more attractive esp. in a superficial illusory way ⟨*glamorizing* a living room⟩ **2 :** to attribute glamour to **:** look upon as glamorous **:** view or treat (as in writing) romantically **:** IDEALIZE, ROMANTICIZE, GLORIFY ⟨*glamorizing* war⟩ ⟨poverty *glamorized* into something alluring —Rose Thurburn⟩ — **glam·or·iz·er** \-zə(r)\ *n* -s

glam·or·ous *also* **glam·our·ous** \ˈglam(ə)rəs\ *adj* **:** characterized by or full of glamour **:** FASCINATING, ENCHANTING, ALLURING ⟨~ movie stars⟩ — **glam·or·ous·ly** *adv* — **glam·or·ous·ness** *n* -ES

¹glam·our *or* **glam·or** \ˈglamə(r)\ *n* -s [Sc *glamour, glamer,* alter. of E *grammar;* fr. the popular association of erudition with occult practices] **1 :** a magic spell **:** BEWITCHMENT ⟨the girls appeared to be under a ~ —Llewelyn Powys⟩ ⟨casting a ~ over the affairs of merchant princes —O.S.J.Gogarty⟩ **2 :** an elusive mysteriously exciting and often illusory attractiveness that stirs the imagination and appeals to a taste for the unconventional, the unexpected, the colorful, or the exotic ⟨the ~ of the French Foreign Legion⟩ **:** a strangely alluring atmosphere of romantic enchantment ⟨a beautifully decorated room that was filled with ~⟩ **:** a bewitching intangible irresistibly magnetic charm ⟨it was simply the ~ of the unknown that she had felt in him —Ellen Glasgow⟩; *often* **:** personal charm and poise combined with unusual physical and sexual attractiveness ⟨an actress radiant with ~⟩

²glamour \ˈ"\ *vt* **glamoured; glamoured; glamouring** \-m(ə)riŋ\ **glamours** [Sc, fr. *glamour, glamer,* n.] **1 :** to cast a magic spell upon **:** BEWITCH ⟨soon created such a realm of gorgeous marvel as ~*ed* the age with fantasy —H.B.Alexander⟩ **2 :** GLAMORIZE ⟨*glamoured*-up blondes were a dime a dozen — Raymond Chandler⟩

glamour boy *n* **:** a man (as an actor or adventurer) with whom glamour is esp. associated

glamour girl *n* **:** a woman (as an actress or model) with whom glamour is esp. associated

glam·ou·rie *or* **glam·ou·ry** \-mərē\ *n, pl* **glamouries** [Sc, alter. of *glamour, glamer,* n.] *archaic* **:** GLAMOUR 1

glam·our·less \-mə(r)ləs\ *adj* **:** devoid of glamour ⟨she was handsome in her ~ way —Edmund Wilson⟩

glamour puss *n, slang* **:** one that has a glamorously attractive face ⟨some *glamour puss* with two expressions and eighteen changes of costume —Raymond Chandler⟩

¹glance \ˈglan(t)s, -aa(ə)-,-ai-,-ȧ-\ *vb* -ED/-ING/-S [alter. of ME *glencen, glenchen,* perh. alter. of *glenten* to move quickly esp. in an oblique direction, strike something obliquely and glance aside, look sideways at something, gleam — more at GLENT] *vi* **1 a** (1) **:** to strike a surface obliquely so as to be deflected and go off at an angle **:** RICOCHET — usu. used with *off* ⟨the spear *glanced* off the heavy metal shield⟩ ⟨the bullet *glanced* off the stone wall and smashed through a window⟩ (2) **:** to strike a surface obliquely and bound onward at an angle often following with one or more additional oblique impacts and forward bounds **:** SKIP ⟨threw the small flat stone so that it *glanced* lightly across the pond⟩ (3) *of a ray of light* **:** to strike a reflecting surface obliquely and dart out at an angle ⟨light from the setting sun *glanced* off the oil tanks — Malcolm Lowry⟩ **b** (1) *obs* **:** to move swiftly (as in springing or dodging) esp. in an oblique or crosswise direction (2) **:** to make a glance in cricket **c** *archaic* **:** to move swiftly (as in speaking or writing) from one subject to another **2 a** (1) **:** to flash or gleam with quick intermittent rapidly successive rays of light (as those produced by sudden quick movements of a reflecting surface) **:** SPARKLE, SCINTILLATE, CORUSCATE ⟨clear mountain brooks *glancing* brightly in the morning sun⟩ (2) **:** to make sudden quick movements that cause quick intermittent flashes of light (as from a moving reflecting surface) ⟨dragonflies *glancing* and zigzagging over the pond⟩ **b :** to shine with a steady dazzling radiance **:** BEAM ⟨the *glancing* sun⟩ **3 a :** to touch briefly or indirectly on a subject (as in speaking or writing) **:** make an incidental reference **:** make an allusion — usu. used with *at* ⟨a book on contemporary civilization that often ~*s* at the customs of ancient cultures⟩ **b :** to refer briefly to something by way of censure or satire **:** cast discredit on something in a passing reference ⟨full of sly, glancing allusions to life as it is lived today —Gerald Bullett⟩ **4 a** *of the eyes* (1) **:** to move swiftly from one thing to another ⟨his eyes *glanced* from the judge to the jury and back again⟩ (2) *archaic* **:** to light upon something by or as if by chance ⟨her eye *glanced* on something which made her change color —T.L.Peacock⟩ **b :** to take a quick look at something ⟨*glancing* at the morning headlines⟩ **:** look briefly, hurriedly, or cursorily ⟨*glanced* about as though fearful of being overheard —Sherwood Anderson⟩ **:** look around here and there **:** make a quick inspection ⟨the bar, where we *glanced* first, was crowded —Scott Fitzgerald⟩ **~** *vt* **1 a** *obs* **:** to turn (the eyes or gaze) quickly aside or away **b** *archaic* **:** to turn (the eyes or gaze) quickly or briefly toward something **c** *archaic* (1) **:** to take a quick look at **:** view quickly **:** survey rapidly (2) **:** to catch a glimpse of **2** *obs* **a :** to allude to **b :** to barely touch **:** GRAZE **3 :** to give an oblique path of direction to: **a :** to throw (as a spear or stone) or shoot (as a bullet) so that the object thrown or shot glances from a surface **b** *archaic* **:** to aim (as an innuendo) indirectly **:** INSINUATE **4** *archaic* **:** to cause the reflection of ⟨*glanced* back the flame of the lamp merrily —Sir Walter Scott⟩ **5 :** to play (a bowled cricket ball) with a glance

²glance \ˈ"\ *n* -s **1 a** (1) **:** a quick intermittent flash or gleam of light (as one produced by sudden quick movements of a reflecting surface) ⟨the ~ of a brightly polished sword⟩ (2) *archaic* **:** a sudden quick movement (as of a reflecting surface) that produces flashes or gleams of light **b :** a ray of light shining with a steady radiance **:** BEAM ⟨the first ~ of sunlight sends the snow slithering in soft cascades —Adrian Bell⟩ **2 a** *archaic* **:** a rapid oblique or crosswise movement **b** *archaic* **:** a deflected impact or blow **c :** a stroke in the game of cricket made with a slanted bat that deflects the ball to leg **3 a :** a swift movement of the eyes from one thing to another ⟨the suspect's shifting ~⟩ **b :** a quick, brief, hurried, or cursory look ⟨the two old ladies darting ~*s* at us and smiling secretively —William Thornton⟩ ⟨museums in which pictures of a single style or artist can be compared and enjoyed at a ~ —R.J.Goldwater⟩ ⟨it was clear at first ~ that his condition was serious —T.B.Costain⟩ **4** *archaic* **a :** a brief satirical or censorious reference to something **:** GIBE **b :** a brief incidental reference **:** ALLUSION

³glance \ˈ"\ *n* -s [G *glanz* mineral sulfide, luster, shine] **:** any of several mineral sulfides that are mostly dark colored and that have a metallic luster

⁴glance \ˈ"\ *vt* -ED/-ING/-S [prob. fr. D *glanzen* to polish, gleam, fr. MD *glansen* to gleam, fr. *glans,* n., luster, shine, fr. MHG *glanz,* fr. OHG, fr. *glanz,* adj., bright — more at GLENT] **:** to give a high luster to (as by burnishing)

glance coal \ˈ"-ˌ\ *n* [trans. of G *glanzkohle,* fr. *glanz* luster, shine + *kohle* coal] **:** a hard lustrous coal; *esp* **:** ANTHRACITE

glance pitch *n* [²*glance*] **:** a pure asphalt — compare MANJAK

glanc·er \-sə(r)\ *n* -s [¹*glance* + *-er*] **:** FENDER SKID

glancing *adj* [fr. pres. part. of ¹*glance*] **1 :** INCIDENTAL, INDIRECT ⟨the book has a variety of ~ references to prominent personalities⟩ **2 :** CASUAL, UNSTUDIED, OFFHAND ⟨a citizen of the world who knew the Near East with the same ~ familiarity —H.V.Gregory⟩ ⟨he evoked the town and its surrounding countryside with his habitual ~ art —*Times Lit. Supp.*⟩ — **glanc·ing·ly** *adv*

glancing angle *n* [*glancing* fr. gerund of ¹*glance*] **:** the angle between an incident beam (as of X rays or electrons) and the surface upon which it is incident **:** the complement of the angle of incidence

glancing boom *n* **:** FENDER BOOM

¹gland \ˈgland, -aa(ə)-\ *n* -s [F *glande* gland (organ of secretion), glandular swelling esp. on the neck, fr. MF, acorn, gland (organ of secretion), glandular swelling esp. on the neck, fr. OF, acorn, glandular swelling esp. on the neck, fr. *glant, gland* acorn, fr. L *gland-, glans;* akin to Gk *balanos* acorn, Lith *gilė*] **1 a :** a cell or group of cells that selectively removes materials from the blood, concentrates or alters them, and secretes them for further use in the body or for elimination from the body and that typically consists of columnar or cuboidal epithelium resting on a basement membrane that is surrounded by a plexus of blood vessels — see ENDOCRINE, EXOCRINE, HOLOCRINE, MEROCRINE **b :** any of various animal structures suggestive of glands though not glandular in function: as (1) **:** LYMPH GLAND (2) **:** GLANS **c glands** *pl* **:** a diseased or inflamed condition of glands (as the lymph or salivary glands of the neck) **2 a :** any of various special secreting organs of plants: as (1) **:** one or more of the hairs on the leaves of sundew (2) **:** one or more of the extrafloral nectaries of many plants **b :** any of certain small protuberances of plants (as on the petiole of a peach leaf)

²gland \ˈ"\ *n* -s [origin unknown] **1 :** a device (as a series of carbon rings or of interlocking teeth) for preventing leakage of steam, water, gas, or other fluid past a joint (as in machinery); *specif* **:** the movable part of a stuffing box by which the packing is compressed **2 :** a short tube fitted to the envelope of a balloon or airship so that a rope may slide through without causing leakage

glan·dered \ˈglandə(r)d, -laan- *sometimes* -lȧn-\ *adj* **:** affected with glanders ⟨a ~ horse⟩

glan·der·ous \-d(ə)rəs\ *adj* **1 :** GLANDERED **2 :** produced by or resembling the effects of glanders ⟨a ~ condition⟩

glan·ders \-də(r)z\ *n pl but sing or pl in constr* [MF *glandres,* pl. of *glandre* glandular swelling esp. on the neck, fr. OF, fr. L *glandula,* dim. of *gland-, glans* acorn] **:** a highly contagious and very destructive disease of horses and other equines or sometimes of other animals (as dogs, guinea pigs, or man) that is caused by a bacterium (*Actinobacillus mallei* syn. *Malleomyces mallei* or *Pfeifferella mallei*) and that is characterized by caseating nodular lesions which tend to break down and form ulcers in mucous membranes, skin, and visceral organs and esp. in lymph nodes and along the course of lymphatic vessels and which may be accompanied by fever and edema and secondary symptoms referable to pulmonary, gastrointestinal, or other special organ involvement — compare FARCY

glandes *pl of* GLANS

gland·less \ˈglandləs, -laan-, *rapid* -nl-\ *adj* **:** devoid of glands

gland of bar·tho·lin \-ˌbärˈtōlən\ *usu cap B* [after Kaspar *Bartholin* †1738 Dan. physician] **:** either of two oval racemose glands lying one on each side of the lower part of the vagina and secreting a lubricating mucus

gland of bow·man \-ˈbōmən\ *usu cap B* [after Sir William *Bowman* †1892 Eng. ophthalmic surgeon] **:** any one of the tubular and often branched glands occurring beneath the sensory epithelium of the nose

gland of brunner *usu cap B* **:** BRUNNER'S GLAND

gland of cowper *usu cap C* **:** COWPER'S GLAND

gland of external secretion : EXOCRINE GLAND

gland of internal secretion : ENDOCRINE GLAND

gland of lieberkühn *usu cap L* **:** LIEBERKÜHN'S GLAND

gland of moll \-ˈmōl, -ȯ-,-ä-\ *usu cap M* [after Jacob A. *Moll* †1914 Du. ophthalmologist] **:** any of the small glands near the free margin of each eyelid regarded as modified sweat glands

gland of ty·son \-ˈtīsᵊn\ *usu cap T* [after Edward *Tyson* †1708 Eng. anatomist] **:** any of the small glands at the base of the glans penis that secrete smegma

glands *pl of* GLAND

glan·du·la \ˈglanjələ\ *n, pl* **glandu·lae** \-ˌlē, -ˌlī\ [NL, fr. L, glandular swelling esp. on the neck] **:** ¹GLAND 1; *esp* **:** a small gland

glan·du·lar \-lə(r)\ *adj* [F *glandulaire,* fr. *glandule* glandula, fr. L *glandula*] **1 a** (1) **:** of, relating to, or involving glands or gland cells ⟨~ cancer⟩ ⟨~ functions⟩ (2) **:** derived from glands or gland cells ⟨~ secretions⟩ **b :** having the characteristics or function of a gland ⟨~ tissue⟩ **c :** containing, bearing, or made up of glands or gland cells ⟨~ organs⟩ **2 a :** controlled or influenced by the secretions of glands; *esp* **:** resulting from abnormal functioning of glands ⟨the theory of ~ criminal behavior⟩ **b :** INNATE, INHERENT, INSTINCTIVE ⟨he had grown up with a ~ dislike for everything pretentious⟩ **c :** EARTHY, PHYSICAL; *esp* **:** SEXUAL ⟨he has adopted, as an interim substitute for love, an entirely ~ relationship with the proprietress of his café—W.M.Frohcok⟩ — **glan·du·lar·ly** *adv*

glandular epithelium *n* **:** the epithelium that forms the secreting surface of a gland

glandular fever *n* **:** INFECTIOUS MONONUCLEOSIS

glan·du·lif·er·ous \ˌglanjə¦lif(ə)rəs\ *adj* [obs. E *glandule* glandula, glandular swelling esp. on the neck (fr. MF, glandula) + E *-i-* + *-ferous*] **:** bearing small glands

glan·du·los·i·ty \ˌglanjəˈläsəd·ē\ *n* -ES [L *glandulosus* glandulous + E *-ity*] **:** the quality or state of being glandulous

glan·du·lous \ˈglanjələs, -laan-\ *adj* [ME *glandelous,* fr. MF *glanduleux,* fr. L *glandulosus,* fr. *glandula* + *-osus* -ose] **:** GLANDULAR — **glan·du·lous·ness** *n* -ES

gla·nen·che·li \glə¦neŋkə,lī\ *n pl, cap* [NL, fr. *glan-* (fr. Gk *glanis* sheatfish) + *-encheli* (fr. Gk *enchelys* eel) — more at ANGUIS] *in some classifications* **:** a suborder of Ostariophysi comprising the electric eels

glan·i·os·to·mi \ˌglanēˈästəˌmī\ *n pl, cap* [NL, fr. *glanio-* (fr. Gk *glanis*) + *-stomi*] *in some esp former classifications* **:** an order of fishes consisting of the sturgeons

glans \ˈglanz, -aa(ə)-\ *n, pl* **glan·des** \-nˌdēz\ [L *gland-, glans* acorn, glans penis — more at GLAND] **1 a** *or* **glans pe·nis** \-ˈpēnəs\ **:** a conical vascular body forming the extremity of the penis **b** *or* **glans cli·to·ri·dis** \-klə'tȯrədəs, -ˌklī'-\ **:** a conical vascular body forming the extremity of the clitoris **2 :** a nut enclosed by or seated in an involucre

glar \ˈglär\ *var of* GLAUR

¹glare \ˈgla(a)(ə)r, ˈgle|, |ə\ *vb* -ED/-ING/-S [ME *glaren;* akin to MD & MLG *glaren* to gleam, glare, OE *glæs* glass — more at GLASS] *vi* **1 a :** to shine esp. by reflection with a harsh uncomfortably brilliant light ⟨the heat was terrific, the pavements *glared* —Aldous Huxley⟩ ⟨the town was baking and *glaring* in the somniferous New York heat —Edmund Wilson⟩ **:** shine with an intense disagreeable brightness ⟨the sun *glared* down relentlessly⟩ ⟨a single naked bulb *glared* pitilessly in the center of the room⟩ **:** shine blindingly ⟨shielding our eyes as we crossed the white sand beach that blazed and *glared*⟩ ⟨miles of frozen snow that *glared* in the morning sunlight⟩ **b** *archaic* **:** to stand out offensively **:** be unpleasantly conspicuous **:** OBTRUDE **2 :** to stare with intense hostility, annoyance, or dislike **:** stare angrily or fiercely **:** GLOWER, SCOWL ⟨where two armies ~ at each other across a geographical line —Lindesay Parrott⟩ ⟨*glared* at him as he walked in late⟩ **~** *vt* **1 :** to express (as hostility) by glowering or scowling ⟨*glaring* defiance at each other —J.B.Priestley⟩ **2** *archaic* **:** to cause to be sharply reflected **syn** see BLAZE, GAZE

²glare \ˈ"\ *n* -s **1 a** (1) **:** a harsh uncomfortably bright light or reflection of light **:** intense disagreeable brightness ⟨the unshaded bulbs threw a cheap yellow ~ over the walls —A.P. Gaskell⟩ ⟨the ~ of publicity⟩; *specif* **:** painfully bright sunlight ⟨the ~ on the meadows was as blinding as if it shone on tin —Jean Stafford⟩ (2) *archaic* **:** the quality or state of being lustrous or glistening **:** SHININESS **b :** cheap showy brilliance **:** GARISHNESS, GAUDINESS ⟨art was partly corrupted by the fondness for ~, expensiveness, and size —F.W.Farrar⟩ **2 :** a fixed glowering look **:** a look expressive of intense hostility, annoyance, or dislike **:** an angry or fierce stare **:** SCOWL ⟨the baleful ~ of their eyes⟩ ⟨gave the jury a ~⟩

³glare \ˈ"\ *n* -s [prob. fr. ²*glare*] **:** a surface, sheet, or glaze of glare ice

⁴glare \ˈ"\ *archaic var of* GLAIR

glare ice *n* [prob. fr. ²*glare*] **:** ice that has a smooth slippery glassy surface ⟨sidewalks covered with *glare ice*⟩

glare·less \ˈ=ləs\ *adj* **:** free from glare ⟨opaque ~ paper⟩

gla·re·o·la \gləˈrēələ\ *n, cap* [NL, dim. of L *glarea* gravel; prob. akin to L *granum* grain — more at CORN] **:** a genus (the type of the family Glareolidae) of Old World shorebirds that comprises the pratincoles which are closely related to the coursers

glar·e·ole \ˈgla(a)rēˌōl\ *n* -s [NL *Glareola*] **:** PRATINCOLE

¹glareous *var of* GLAIREOUS

²glar·e·ous \ˈgla(a)rēəs\ *adj* [L *glarea* gravel + E *-ous*] **:** growing in gravelly soil ⟨~ plants⟩

glar·i·ness \ˈgla(a)rēnəs\ *n* -ES **:** the quality or state of being glary ⟨the ~ of the dusty roads⟩

glar·ing \ˈgla(a)riŋ, -ler-, -rēŋ\ *adj* [ME *glaringe,* fr. *glaren* to glare + *-inge, -ing* -ing] **1 :** marked by a fixed look of hostility, fierceness, or anger **:** GLOWERING, SCOWLING ⟨trembled at the sight of their ~ eyes⟩ **2 a :** shining with or reflecting a harsh uncomfortably bright light **:** blindingly bright ⟨~ spotlights⟩ ⟨the still surface of the ~ sea⟩ **b** (1) **:** showily brilliant **:** GARISH, GAUDY ⟨~ colors⟩ (2) **:** vulgarly ostentatious **:** blatantly crude ⟨the more raffish and ~ manners of the Regency —R.E. Roberts⟩ **3 :** painfully obvious **:** too apparent not to be noticed **:** FLAGRANT ⟨the gullibility with which we perpetuate ~ errors —Joseph O'Connor⟩ ⟨the self-assurance I have mentioned appears at its most ~ in a stupid man —Albert Dasnoy⟩ **:** unavoidably noticeable **:** inescapably evident **:** CONSPICUOUS ⟨the contrast between their words and their deeds today is ~ —O.M.Green⟩ **syn** see FLAGRANT

glar·ing·ly *adv* **:** in a glaring manner ⟨the need is ~ apparent⟩

glar·ing·ness *n* -ES **:** the quality or state of being glaring ⟨embarrassed by the ~ of this error⟩

glary \ˈgla(a)rē, -ler-, -ri\ *adj, usu* -ER/-EST [²*glare* + *-y*] **:** shining with or reflecting a harsh uncomfortably bright light **:** full of glare **:** GLARING ⟨sun-scorched, ~, waterless pieces of rock —Harry Luke⟩

glase *obs var of* GLAZE

gla·se·ri·an fissure \glə¦zirēən-, glä|\ *n, usu cap G* [*glaserian* fr. Johann Heinrich *Glaser* †1675 Swiss anatomist + E *-ian*] **:** PETROTYMPANIC FISSURE

glas·gow \ˈgla|(ˌ)skō, -laa|, -lai|, -lȧ|, |s(ˌ)gō *also* ˈglaz(ˌ)gō *or* -lȧz-\ *adj, usu cap* [fr. *Glasgow,* city in Scotland] **:** of or from the city of Glasgow, Scotland ⟨the *Glasgow* shipyards⟩ **:** of the kind or style prevalent in Glasgow

glasite *usu cap, var of* GLASSITE

¹glass \ˈglas, -aa(ə)-,-ai-,-ȧ-\ *n* -ES [ME *glas,* fr. OE *glæs;* akin to OHG *glas* amber, OE *glær* amber, ON *gler* glass, OE *geolu* yellow — more at YELLOW] **1 a :** an amorphous inorganic usu. transparent or translucent substance consisting typically of a mixture of silicates or sometimes borates or phosphates formed by fusion of sand or some other form of silica or by fusion of oxides of boron or phosphorus with a flux (as soda, potash) and a stabilizer (as lime, alumina) and sometimes metallic oxides or other coloring agents so that a mass is produced that cools to a rigid condition without crystallization and that may be blown, cast, pressed, rolled, drawn, or cut into various forms — see CROWN GLASS, FIBER GLASS, FLINT GLASS; compare CULLET, FRIT **b :** any of various inorganic or organic substances resembling glass esp. in transparency, hardness, and amorphous nature ⟨sodium phosphate ~⟩ ⟨organic ~*es* made from plastics⟩ — compare ²GLAZE 2a **c :** a substance (as obsidian, pumice) produced by the quick cooling of an igneous magma **2 a :** something made wholly or almost wholly of glass: as (1) **:** a glass container; *esp* **:** a glass drinking vessel (as a tumbler or a goblet) (2) **:** a glass mirror **:** LOOKING GLASS (3) **:** a sheet of glass (as a windowpane, the plate-glass front of a display case, the glass covering of a picture) (4) **:** a shaped hollow protective glass covering (as the bell-shaped covering set over some clocks or plants, the chimney of most oil lamps) (5) **:** a slightly curved or flat piece of glass covering the dial of a watch or clock **:** CRYSTAL (6) **:** OPTICAL GLASS (7) **:** either piece of glass or other transparent material in a pair of glasses (8) **:** an hourglass or half-hour glass (9) **:** WEATHERGLASS **b** (1) **:** an optical instrument (as a telescope or microscope) or device that has one or more lenses and that is designed to aid in the viewing of objects otherwise wholly or partly incapable of being seen by the average eye ⟨the captain kept his ~ fixed on the nearby shore⟩; *specif* **:** BINOCULARS ⟨stole the captain's ~*es*⟩ (2) **glasses** *pl* **:** a device used to correct defects of vision (as nearsightedness) or to protect the eyes (as from glare, dust, flying sparks) and consisting typically of two pieces of glass designed to bend light rays or of two pieces of ordinary colored or plain glass or other transparent material that are supported by a bridge resting on the nose and by sidepieces extending over the ears ⟨she put her ~*es* on the table⟩ — often used with *pair* ⟨bought a new pair of ~*es*⟩; called also *eyeglasses, spectacles;* compare GOGGLES, PINCE-NEZ **3 a :** the quantity held by a glass container (as a drinking glass) **:** GLASSFUL ⟨drank two ~*es* of water⟩ **b :** the time required for one end of an hourglass or half-hour glass to empty ⟨the ship had been sighted two ~*es* earlier⟩ **4 :** articles made of glass **:** GLASSWARE ⟨a sparkling new set of dinner ~⟩ **:** glass products ⟨famous for the manufacture of beautiful ~⟩ **5** *obs* **:** GLOSS **6** *obs* **:** the organ of sight **:** EYE

²glass \ˈ"\ *vb* -ED/-ING/-ES *vt* **1 a** (1) **:** to fit, set, or equip (as a window frame) with glass ⟨only three windows had been ~*ed*⟩ ⟨peered in through the ~*ed* upper half of the fruitshop door —I.S.Cobb⟩ (2) **:** to fit or equip with eyeglasses ⟨had been ~*ed* at an early age⟩ **b :** to cover or protect with glass ⟨~*ed* the picture before framing it⟩ **:** enclose, case, or wall with glass ⟨sunlight streamed into the porch which had been ~*ed* in⟩ **c :** to pack and seal hermetically in glass containers for preservation or transportation ⟨~*ed* fruits⟩ ⟨~*ed* coffee⟩ — compare ³CAN 1a **2 a :** to cause to have a glassy surface or appearance **:** make glassy ⟨boredom ~*ed* his eyes⟩ **b :** to smooth or polish (leather) with a glass burnisher ⟨~*ing* the hides⟩ **3 a :** to cause to be mirrored : REFLECT ⟨a solitary tree that was ~*ed* by the pool's still surface⟩ **b :** to see mirrored : see the reflection of ⟨considered her shining nails, as if ~*ing* her indolent beauty in them —Edith Wharton⟩ **4 :** to scan (as a terrain) with an optical instrument (as a pair of binoculars) esp. in an effort to discover game ⟨went out that afternoon and ~*ed* the country from the hills —Ernest Hemingway⟩ ⟨he may not notice you at a distance; you can ~ him, watch him, study him —Paul Schubert⟩ **~** *vi* **:** to become glassy ⟨the river is ~*ing* in a breathless calm —A.N.Whitehead⟩

[3]**glass** \"\ *adj* **1 a** (1) **:** made wholly or nearly wholly of glass ⟨a ~ bottle⟩ (2) **:** having walls or sides and often top or bottom made wholly or nearly wholly of glass panes, panels, or blocks ⟨a ~ porch⟩ ⟨a ~ recording studio⟩ **b :** resembling or suggestive of glass : GLASSY ⟨the ~ surface of the water⟩ **2 :** set or fitted with glass ⟨the plants were kept under a ~ frame⟩

glass arm *n* **:** an arm the muscles of which too easily become stiff and sore in use ⟨he's a good fielder but he's got a *glass arm*⟩

glass bell *n* **:** a bell jar made of glass

glass bender *n* **1 :** a worker who shapes glass disks in molds or under forming presses to make lenses for clocks, speedometers, headlights **2 :** a worker who heats and bends glass tubing for neon signs and fuses the electrodes into place

glass block *n* **:** a hollow translucent block usu. with ribbed exterior made by fusing two sections of clear pressed glass at high temperature and used as a building material chiefly for wall panels

glassblower \ˈ=,==\ *n* **:** one skilled in the art of glassblowing — compare LAMPWORKER

glassblowing \ˈ=,==\ *n* **:** an art of shaping a mass of glass by inflating it through a tube after the glass has been heated to a viscid state — compare LAMPWORKING

glass catfish *n* **:** a small transparent catfish (*Kryptopterus bicirrhus*) of southeast Asia

glass cement *n* **:** a binding mixture used to affix glass to glass or to some other material (as metal)

glass cloth *n* **1 :** an absorbent lintless plain-weave cloth (as of linen) used for wiping glass and china — called also *glass toweling* **2 :** a fabric formed of woven fiber glass

glass crab *n* **:** a transparent crustacean larva (as a phyllosoma) — called also *glass shrimp*

glass curtain *n* **:** a usu. sheer translucent or transparent window curtain hung immediately over the glass of a window or over a window shade and usu. not extending much beyond the sides of the window frame

glass cutter *n* **:** one that cuts or scores glass: as **a** (1) **:** a worker who cuts sheets of glass into specific sizes (as for windowpanes, mirrors) (2) **:** a worker who decorates the surface of glass by cutting, scoring, grinding, and polishing **b :** a tool (as a metal hand tool equipped with a small wheel of hardened steel or a tool with a diamond point) used for cutting or scoring glass

glass cutters b

glass cutting *n* **:** the art or process of cutting glass **:** the art of the glass cutter

glassed *past of* GLASS

glass eel *n* [so called fr. its transparency in its early stages] **:** ELVER

glass electrode *n* **:** an electrode that consists typically of a glass tube sealed at the bottom with a thin-walled glass bulb containing a solution of constant pH (as a chloride buffer) and a silver-silver chloride reference electrode and that is immersed in an unknown solution usu. along with a calomel electrode for determining the pH of this solution

glass·en \-sᵊn\ *adj* [ME, fr. *glas* glass + *-en*] **1** *archaic* **:** made of glass **2** *archaic* **:** resembling glass : GLASSY

glass·er \-sə(r)\ *n* -s **:** a machine used for glassing leather

glas·ser's disease \-sə(r)z-\ *n, usu cap G* [prob. fr. the name *Glasser*] **:** swine influenza marked by arthritis

glasses *pl of* GLASS, *pres 3d sing of* GLASS

glass eye *n* [[3]*glass* + *eye*] **1 a glass eyes** *pl, obs* **:** GLASSES **b :** an artificial eye made of glass **2 a** (1) **:** a condition of impaired eyesight or blindness in horses marked by a bright glassy eye and dilated pupil (2) **:** a horse affected with this condition **b** (1) **:** lymphomatosis of the eyes in chickens (2) **:** a chicken affected with this condition **3 a :** an eye having a pale, whitish, or colorless iris **b :** one that has such an eye

glasseye \ˈ=,=\ *n* [[3]*glass* + *eye*] **:** WALLEYED PIKE

glass-eye \ˈ=,=\ *n* [[3]*glass* + *eye*] **:** any of several African forest warblers constituting a genus (*Camaroptera*) of the family Sylviidae

glass-eyed \ˈ=ˌ=\ *adj* **1 :** having a glass eye **2 :** affected with the condition of glass eye

glass fiber *n* **:** a strong continuous filament or staple fiber made from molten glass; *esp* **:** a variety of such a filament or fiber that is extremely fine and pliable

glassfish \ˈ=,=\ *n* **:** any of several small Old World fishes constituting a genus *Ambassis* of the family Centropomidae, having a transparent body that allows the bones and viscera to be clearly visible, and being often kept in the tropical aquarium

glass·ful \-s,fu̇l\ *n* -s **:** the quantity held by a glass container (as a drinking glass)

glass gall *n* **:** a saline whitish scum sometimes cast up from glass in fusion

glass garden *n* **:** a small glass container (as a bowl) in which plants are grown : TERRARIUM — compare WARDIAN CASE

glass-glazed \ˈ=ˌ=\ *adj* **:** having a heavy glaze coating that gives a noticeably glassy appearance ⟨*glass-glazed* pottery⟩

glass green *n* **:** a light yellow green that is greener, lighter, and stronger than reed green and yellower and paler than sky green

glass-hard \ˈ=ˌ=\ *adj* **:** having a maximum degree of hardness ⟨*glass-hard* steel⟩

glass harmonica *n* **:** a musical instrument of the 18th and 19th centuries consisting of a series of hemispherical glasses turning on an axis and played by touching the edges with a dampened finger

glasshouse \ˈ=,=\ *n* [ME *glashous,* fr. *glas* glass + *hous* house] **1 a :** GLASSWORKS **b :** the part of a glassworks in which the glass is melted and shaped **2** *chiefly Brit* **:** GREENHOUSE

glass·ie *or* **glassy** \ˈglasē, -laas-,-lais-,-lȧs-, -si\ *n, pl* **glass·ies** [[1]*glass* + *-ie, -y*] **1 :** a playing marble made of glass **2 :** a transparent diamond crystal

glassier *comparative of* GLASSY

glassiest *superlative of* GLASSY

glass·i·ly \-sə̇lē, -li\ *adv* **:** in a glassy manner

glass·ine \(ˈ)=ˌsēn\ *n* -s [[1]*glass* + *-ine*] **:** a thin dense transparent or semitransparent paper that is highly resistant to the passage of air and grease ⟨doughnuts packaged in ~ bags⟩ ⟨reading the address through the envelope's ~ window⟩

glass·i·ness \ˈ=sēnə̇s, -sin-\ *n* -ES **1 :** the quality or state of being glassy **2 :** WATER CORE 2

glassing *pres part of* GLASS

glass·ite *or* **glas·ite** \-,sīt\ *n* -s *usu cap* [John *Glass* (or *Glas*) †1773 Scot. clergyman who founded the sect + E *-ite*] **:** a member of a Christian sect founded about 1730 and holding that there is no authority in the New Testament for giving the civil magistrate as such any function in the church — called also *Sandemanian*

glass jaw *n* **:** a jaw (as of a boxer) that is highly vulnerable to punches

glass·less \-slə̇s\ *adj* **:** devoid of glass

glassmaker \ˈ=,==\ *n* **:** one that makes glass

glassmakers' soap *n* **:** a substance (as manganese dioxide) used by glassmakers to remove a green color produced in glass by iron salts

glassmaking \ˈ=,==\ *n* **:** the art or process of manufacturing glass

glassman \-mən, -,man\ *n, pl* **glassmen 1 :** a dealer in glass products **2 :** GLASSMAKER

glass paper *n* [[1]*glass* + *paper*] **1 :** a strong paper faced with pulverized glass and used in abrading or smoothing slight irregularities in surfaces (as of wood) **2 :** a paper made from extremely fine glass fibers and marked by high resistance to moisture, heat, light, and vermin

glass-paper \ˈ=,==\ *vt* [*glass paper*] **:** to abrade or smooth with glass paper

glass pot *n* **:** a small fireclay crucible in which are fused the materials for making glass in small-scale operations—compare TANK FURNACE

glass run *n* **:** one of the grooves in which a glass window (as of an automobile) moves

glass sensation *n* **:** a consciousness of filled space evoked by transparent nonselective media (as glass) — compare BULKY COLOR

glass shot *n* **:** a motion-picture or television shot in which a part of a scene is made through a glass plate having other parts of the scene painted on its surface

glass shrimp *n* **:** GLASS CRAB

glass silk *n* **:** FIBER GLASS; *esp* **:** fiber glass in the form of continuous filaments used in textiles

glass snail *n* **:** any of numerous small transparent land snails constituting *Vitrina* and related genera and resembling slugs

glass snake *n* **1 :** a limbless lizard (*Ophisaurus ventralis*) of the southern U.S. superficially resembling a snake and having a tail capable of being broken off completely into one or more small pieces and replaced by a new tail **2 :** any of several lizards similar to the No. American glass snake that are found in the Old World

glass soap *n* **:** GLASSMAKERS' SOAP

glass sponge *n* [so called fr. the glassy spicules] **:** a siliceous sponge of the class Hyalospongiae

glass toweling *or* **glass towel** *n* **:** GLASS CLOTH 1

glassware \ˈ=,=\ *n* **:** articles made of glass; *esp* **:** tableware of glass used in serving food and drink

glass wool *n* **:** glass fibers in a mass resembling cotton batting or wool and used esp. for thermal insulation and air filters or fabricated into various products (as acoustic tile or wallboard)

glasswork \ˈ=,=\ *n* **1** *also* **glassworking** \ˈ=,==\ **a :** the making of glass or of glass articles **b :** work involving working with or on glass or glass articles: as (1) **:** the work of fitting or equipping with glass (as in fitting window frames with glass, equipping display cases with glass) (2) **:** the work of a glassblower, glass bender, or glass cutter **2 a :** articles made of glass : GLASSWARE **b :** sheets of glass cut into specific sizes (as for windowpanes, mirrors)

glassworker \ˈ=,==\ *n* **:** one that does glasswork; *specif* **:** GLAZIER

glassworks \ˈ=,=\ *n pl but usu sing in constr* **:** an establishment (as a factory) in which glass is made

glass worm *n* [so called fr. its transparency] **:** ARROWWORM

glasswort \ˈ=,=\ *n* [so called fr. its former use in the manufacture of glass] **1 :** a plant of the genus *Salicornia* (esp. *S. europaea*) **2 :** a saltwort (*Salsola kali*) with awl-shaped stiff leaves — called also *kelpwort*

[1]**glassy** \ˈglasē, -laas-, -lais-, -lȧs-, -si\ *adj, usu* -ER/-EST [[1]*glass* + *-y*] **1 a :** having the characteristics or appearance of glass : VITREOUS ⟨~ porcelain⟩ **b :** resembling or suggestive of glass (as in shininess, smoothness or slipperiness, fragility, transparency) ⟨the pavement was wet, ~ with water —Willa Cather⟩ ⟨the ~ surface of the lake⟩ **2 a :** marked by or having a dull fixedness of expression (as from boredom, shock, or stupidity) : LACKLUSTER, APATHETIC : FISHY ⟨his explanation awoke no response in their ~ eyes⟩ ⟨moonishly amused at anything that passed before their ~ eyes —Rebecca West⟩ **b :** cold and unsympathetic : devoid of cordiality : FORBIDDING ⟨gave him a disdainful ~ stare⟩ ⟨unable to penetrate their ~ reserve⟩ **c :** HARD, UNYIELDING, UNWAVERING ⟨a ~ determination to win⟩ ⟨staring at the floor with a rather ~ concentration —Louis Auchincloss⟩ **d :** lacking overtones : SHARP, SHRILL, STRIDENT ⟨a good recording except for the ~ quality of the strings⟩ **e :** smoothly superficial ⟨approached the problem with a ~ assurance⟩ **f :** breathlessly calm and bright ⟨a good many desert areas have this feeling of ~ stillness in the late afternoon —H.L.Davis⟩ ⟨a ~ quiver of heat —Eve Langley⟩ ⟨sun-drenched, ~ days —W.H.Hale⟩

[2]**glassy** *var of* GLASSIE

glass yarn *n* **:** yarn composed of glass fibers twisted from continuous filament strands or from staple fiber sliver

glassy-eyed \ˈ=ˌ=\ *adj* **:** marked by or having glassy eyes ⟨a book so dull it makes anyone *glassy-eyed* in five minutes⟩

glassy feldspar *n* **:** SANIDINE

glastig *var of* GLAISTIG

glas·ton·bury chair \ˈglastən,berē- *also* -sᵊn-\ *n, usu cap G* [*Glastonbury,* Somersetshire, England; so called fr. its having been designed in imitation of the abbot of Glastonbury's chair preserved in the bishop's palace at Wells, Somersetshire] **:** a small light folding chair with sloping arms and back and two crossed straight legs at the right and left sides

glastonbury thorn *n, usu cap G* [*Glastonbury,* Somersetshire, England; so called fr. a popular belief that it sprang up at Glastonbury from the staff of Joseph of Arimathea (Mt 27:57–60)] **:** a hawthorn that is a variety (*Crataegus monogyna praecox*) of a common Old World hawthorn

Glastonbury chair

[1]**glas·we·gian** \glaˈswēj(ē)ən\ *n* -s *cap* [irreg. (influence of *Galwegian, Norwegian*) fr. *Glasgow,* city in Scotland + E *-ian*] **:** a native or resident of Glasgow

[2]**glaswegian** \(ˈ)=ˌ=(=)=\ *adj, usu cap* **1 :** of, relating to, or characteristic of Glasgow **2 :** of, relating to, or characteristic of Glaswegians

glau·ber·ite \ˈglau̇bə,rīt *also* ˈglȯb-\ *n* -s [F *glaubérite,* fr. Johann R. *Glauber* †1668 Ger. chemist + F *-ite;* so called fr. its resemblance in chemical composition to Glauber's salt] **:** a light-colored brittle sodium calcium sulfate $Na_2Ca(SO_4)_2$ having a vitreous luster and saline taste

glauber's salt \-bə(r)(z)-\ *also* **glauber salt** *n, usu cap G* [after Johann R. *Glauber* †1668] **:** the crystalline decahydrate $Na_2SO_4.10H_2O$ of sodium sulfate occurring naturally as mirabilite, obtained also from salt cake, and used chiefly in dyeing and in medicine as a laxative; *sometimes* **:** anhydrous sodium sulfate — sometimes used in pl.

glauc- *or* **glauco-** *comb form* [L *glauc-* gleaming, gray, fr. Gk *glauk-, glauko-,* fr. *glaukos* — more at GLAUCOUS] **:** glaucous ⟨*glauc*ochroite⟩ ⟨*glauc*ope⟩

glau·ces·cence \glȯˈsesᵊn(t)s\ *n* -s [prob. fr. (assumed) NL *glaucescentia,* fr. *glaucescent-, glaucescens* glaucescent + L *-ia* -y] **:** the quality or state of being glaucescent

glau·ces·cent \(ˈ)=ˈsesᵊnt\ *adj* [prob. fr. (assumed) NL *glaucescent-, glaucescens,* fr. L *glauc-* + *-escent-, -escens* -escent] **:** slightly glaucous **:** becoming glaucous

glau·cid·i·um \glȯˈsidēəm\ *n, cap* [NL, fr. Gk *glaukidion* small owl, dim. of *glauk-, glaux* owl] **:** a genus of small owls comprising the pygmy owls

glau·cine \ˈglȯ,sēn, -ōsᵊn\ *n* -s [ISV *glauc-* (fr. NL *Glaucium*) + *-ine*] **:** a crystalline alkaloid $C_{21}H_{25}NO_4$ found esp. in the horned poppy

glau·ci·o·net·ta \,glȯsēəˈned·ə\ [NL, fr. Gk *glaukion,* a duck, fr. *glaukos*] *syn of* BUCEPHALA

glau·ci·um \ˈglȯsēəm\ *n, cap* [NL, perh. fr. Gk *glaukion* juice of a papaveraceous plant, fr. *glaukos*] **:** a small genus of Eurasian herbs (family Papaveraceae) with yellow flowers and a yellow acrid juice

glau·co·cer·i·nite \,glȯ(,)kōˈserə,nīt\ *n* -s [G *glaucokerinit,* fr. *glauc-* + Gk *kērinos* made of wax (fr. *kēros* wax) + G *-it* -ite — more at CEREUS] **:** a mineral perhaps $Zn_3Cu_2Al_8(SO_4)_2(OH)_{60}.4H_2O$ consisting of a hydrous basic sulfate of copper, zinc, and aluminum

glau·cochro·ite \,glȯkəˈkrō,īt, glȯˈkäkrə,wīt\ *n* -s [*glauc-* + Gk *chrōs* color + E *-ite* — more at CHROMATIC] **:** a mineral $CaMnSiO_4$ that consists of calcium manganese silicate, occurs in bluish green prismatic crystals, and is related to monticellite

glau·co·dot \ˈglȯkə,dät\ *also* **glau·co·dote** \-,dōt\ *n* -s [G *glaukodot,* fr. *glauk-* glauc- + *-dot* (fr. Gk *dotēr* giver, fr. *didonai* to give) — more at DATE] **:** a mineral (Co,Fe)AsS consisting of a grayish white metallic-looking cobalt iron sulfarsenide occurring in orthorhombic crystals or massive (hardness 5, sp. gr. 5.9–6.0)

glau·co·ma \glȯˈkōmə, glau̇ˈ-\ *n* -s [L, cataract (of the eye), fr. Gk *glaukōma,* fr. *glaukos* gleaming, gray] **:** a disease of the eye marked by increased pressure within the eyeball that damages the optic disk and results in gradual loss of vision and ultimate blindness

glau·coma·tous \(ˈ)=ˈkōməd·əs, -ˈkäm-\ *adj* [L *glaucomat-, glaucoma* + E *-ous*] **:** of, relating to, or affected with glaucoma

glau·co·mys \ˈglȯkə,mis\ *n, cap* [NL, fr. *glauc-* + *-mys*] **:** a genus of mammals comprising the No. American flying squirrels

glau·co·nia \glȯˈkōnēə\ [NL, perh. irreg. fr. L *glaucus* gleaming, gray, fr. Gk *glaukos*] *syn of* LEPTOTYPHLOPS

glau·co·nif·er·ous \,glȯkəˈnif(ə)rəs\ *adj* [ISV *glauconite* + *-i-* + *-ferous*] **:** containing glauconite

glau·co·nite \ˈglȯkə,nīt\ *n* -s [G *glaukonit,* fr. Gk *glaukon* (neut. of *glaukos*) + G *-it* -ite] **:** a mineral approximately $K_{15}(Fe,Mg,Al)_{4-6}(Si,Al)_8O_{20}(OH)_4$ consisting of a dull green earthy and micaceous iron potassium silicate occurring abundantly in greensand

glau·co·nit·ic \ˌ=ˌ=ˈnid·ik\ *adj* [ISV *glauconite* + *-ic*] **:** containing or resembling glauconite ⟨~ limestone⟩

glau·co·nit·iza·tion \ˌ=ˌ=,nīd·əˈzāshən\ *n* -s [*glauconite* + *-ize* + *-ation*] **:** formation of or conversion into glauconite

glau·cope \ˈglȯ,kōp\ *n* -s [*glauc-* + *-ope* (as in *cyanope*)] **:** a person with fair hair and blue eyes — compare CYANOPE — **glau·co·pi·an** \(ˈ)=ˈkōpēən\ *adj*

glau·co·phane \ˈglȯkə,fān\ *n* -s [G *glaukophan,* fr. *glauk-* glauc- + *-phan* -phane] **:** a mineral $Na_2(Mg,Fe)_3Al_2Si_8O_{22}(OH)_2$ consisting of a blue, bluish black, or grayish silicate of sodium, aluminum, iron, and magnesium occurring in certain crystalline schists

glau·coth·oe \glȯˈkäthə,wē\ *n* -s [NL, perh. irreg. fr. L *glaucus* or Gk *glaukos*] **:** a young hermit crab that has completed the swimming larval stages

[1]**glau·cous** \ˈglȯkəs\ *adj* [L *glaucus* gleaming, gray, fr. Gk *glaukos;* perh. akin to OE *clǣne* pure, clear — more at CLEAN] **1 a :** of a pale yellow green color **b :** of a light bluish gray or bluish white color **2 :** having a powdery or waxy coating that gives a frosted appearance and tends to rub off ⟨~ plums⟩ ⟨~ stems⟩ ⟨~ cabbage leaves⟩ ⟨~ grapes⟩ — **glau·cous·ness** *n* -ES

[2]**glaucous** \"\ *n* -ES **:** a pale yellow green that is yellower and stronger than smoke gray, greener and deeper than oyster gray, and yellower than average Nile

glaucous blue *n* **:** a grayish blue that is greener and paler than electric or copenhagen and greener and lighter than Gobelin

glaucous gray *n* **:** a light bluish gray to light gray that is redder and darker than skimmed-milk white and very slightly greener than cinerous

glaucous green *n* **:** a very pale green that is yellower and slightly less strong than tourmaline and yellower and duller than emerald tint

glaucous gull *n* **:** a large boreal gull (*Larus hyperboreus*) that is pure white with a bluish mantle when adult — called also *burgomaster*

glaucous honeysuckle *n* **:** a No. American vine (*Lonicera dioica*) having glaucous leaves and purplish flowers

glaucous willow *n* **:** a pussy willow (*Salix discolor*)

glaucous-winged gull \ˌ=ˌ=,=-\ *n* **:** a white gull (*Larus glaucescens*) having a pale gray mantle and pale gray wing tips and ranging from the Bering sea to California and Japan

glau·cus \ˈglȯkəs\ *n, cap* [NL, fr. L, gleaming, gray] **:** a genus of slender elongate pelagic nudibranchs with three pairs of lateral lobes — see SEA LIZARD

glaum \ˈglȧm, -ō-\ *vb* -ED/-ING/-S [prob. fr. ScGael *glàim* to handle awkwardly, seize voraciously] *dial chiefly Brit* **:** GRAB, CLUTCH, GROPE

glaur \ˈglȯr\ *n* -s [origin unknown] *chiefly Scot* **:** soft slimy mud **:** MIRE

glaux \ˈglȯks\ *n, cap* [NL, fr. L, a plant, fr. Gk *glaux, glax* swine cress] **:** a cosmopolitan genus of fleshy perennial herbs (family Primulaceae) having opposite leaves and small whitish flowers — see SEA MILKWORT

glave *obs var of* GLAIVE

glaver *vi* -ED/-ING/-S [ME *glaveren*] *obs* **:** to talk in a deceitfully kind or pleasant manner : FLATTER

gla·ver·ing \ˈglāv(ə)riŋ\ *adj* [ME *glaveringe,* fr. *glaveren* + *-inge, -ing* -ing] *archaic* **:** deceitfully kind, pleasant, or flattering ⟨a ~ smile⟩

[1]**glaze** \ˈglāz\ *vb* -ED/-ING/-S [ME *glasen,* fr. *glas* glass — more at GLASS] *vt* **1 a :** [2]GLASS 1a(1) **b :** [2]GLASS 1b **2 a :** to cover or coat with or as if with a glaze ⟨the storm *glazed* roads and trees with ice⟩ ⟨a new process for *glazing* pottery⟩ **:** apply a glaze to ⟨*glazing* doughnuts⟩; *specif* **:** to cover (as frozen fish) with an ice coating to prevent dehydration in storage and shipping **b :** to vitrify the surface of ⟨stones that the blast had *glazed*⟩ **3 a** (1) **:** to cause to shine like glass **:** give a smooth glossy or lustrous surface or finish to (as by calendering) : GLOSS ⟨*glazed* paper⟩ ⟨*glazed* textiles⟩ ⟨*glazing* fur coats⟩ ⟨*glazed* leather⟩ **:** cause to shine brightly (as by rubbing) : POLISH, BURNISH ⟨*glazing* metal surfaces⟩ (2) **:** to make smooth and even (as the walls of a house) by filling in depressions on the surface with a hard-drying putty before painting **b :** FERROTYPE **4 :** to dull the abrasive particles of (a grinding wheel) so that they no longer cut freely **~** *vi* **1 :** to become glazed or glassy ⟨his eyes *glazed,* his body twitched spasmodically —Gerald Beaumont⟩ ⟨then put in the sweetbreads to ~ —Hannah Glasse⟩ **2 :** to form a glaze ⟨ice *glazed* over each clear wedge of grass —P.M.Swatek⟩

[2]**glaze** \"\ *n* -s **1 a :** a smooth slippery coating of thin ice; *esp* **:** an ice coating that forms when cold rain comes into contact with objects (as rocks, pavements) that are below the freezing point — called also *sleet* **b :** a stretch of smooth slippery ice ⟨hiked over the ~ that lay between them and the camp⟩ **2 a :** material usu. applied to something as a solution or suspension in order to provide a distinctive surface coating; as (1) **:** a liquid preparation (as sugar syrup, gelatine dissolved in meat stock) brushed over or otherwise applied to food (as meat, fish, pastry) on which after application it hardens or becomes firm and adds flavor and a glossy appearance (2) **:** a glassy silica-containing mixture of oxides that is applied and fused to the surface of clayware for decoration or to make it nonporous (3) **:** a usu. dark transparent or semitransparent color applied to a lighter painted surface or to another color so as to achieve a decorative, unifying, or enriching effect **b** (1) **:** a thin smooth glossy or lustrous surface or finish consisting of or resembling glass (as the coating produced by application of a glaze, the smooth glossy finish produced on paper or cloth by calendering) ⟨staring at window reflections in the ~ of the teapot —Elizabeth Bowen⟩ : SHEEN ⟨chintz with a beautiful ~⟩ (2) **:** a bright shininess : GLOW ⟨her skin had the healthy ~ that comes from sunshine —Harold Brodkey⟩ **3 :** a fine transparent or translucent glassy film ⟨the senile ~ of his eyes —Fred Majdalany⟩ ⟨the ~ that had come over the dead man's eyes⟩

[3]**glaze** \"\ *vi* -ED/-ING/-S [prob. blend of *gaze* and *glare*] *archaic* **:** STARE, GLARE

glazed *adj* [fr. past part. of [1]*glaze*] **1 a :** covered or coated with a glaze ⟨~ food products⟩ **b :** having a surface made smooth and glossy or lustrous (as by calendering) ⟨~ paper⟩ ⟨~ cloth⟩ ⟨~ leather⟩ **c :** covered with or as if with a glassy film **:** marked by glassiness ⟨the ~ vacancy of his eyes —Stephen Crane⟩ ⟨his eyes wore that ~, unseeing expression which is the outward token of vague thinking —Carl Van Vechten⟩ **d :** rigidly fixed in expression : lacking mobility or vitality of expression : grimly set ⟨the ~ faces of survivors —W.H.Hale⟩ **2 :** fitted, set, or equipped with glass (as windowpanes) ⟨four ~ walls⟩

glazed frost *n, Brit* **:** GLAZE 1a

glaze kiln *n* **:** a kiln in which glazed pottery is fired

gla·zen \ˈglāzᵊn\ *adj* [ME *glasen,* fr. OE *glæsen,* fr. *glæs* glass + *-en*] *archaic* **:** GLASSEN

glaz·er \-zə(r)\ *n* -s [ME *glaser* one whose work is cutting and setting glass (as windowpanes), fr. *glasen* to glaze + *-er*] **1 :** one that glazes: as **a :** an operator of a machine that puts a gloss on leather by rubbing it with a hard roller after it has been oiled **b :** one that coats pottery, brick, or tile by dipping the product into a glaze solution **c :** one that gives furs a glossy finish **d :** PANMAN **2 :** a tool, machine, or other device used for glazing

glazes *pres 3d sing of* GLAZE, *pl of* GLAZE

gla·zier \'glāzhə(r), -zēə-\ *n* -s [ME *glasier*, fr. *glas* glass + *-ier*] **1 :** one whose work is cutting and setting glass (as windowpanes) — called also *glassworker* **2 :** one that heats and glazes the tapered ends of glass tubes (as used in making hypodermic syringe cylinders)

glazier's point *n* **:** a small triangular or diamond-shaped piece of thin sheet metal used to hold a pane of glass in a wooden sash while the putty is hardening or in case the putty loosens

gla·ziery \-zhərē, -zēərē, -ri\ *n* -ES [*glazier* + *-y*] **:** GLASSWORK

glaz·i·ly \'glāzəlē\ *adv* **:** in a glazy manner

glaz·i·ness \-zēnəs\ *n* -ES **:** the quality or state of being glazy

glazing *n* -s [ME *glasinge, glasing*, fr. *glasen* to glaze + *-inge, -ing* -ing] **1 :** the act or process or trade of using or applying or providing with glaze **2 a :** GLASSWORK **b :** GLAZE

glazing compound *n* **:** a caulking compound used esp. for holding window glass in place because it remains soft underneath the surface

glazing jack *n* **:** a device consisting of a glass or agate roller attached to the arm of a power-driven machine and used to glaze leather

glazy \-zē\ *adj* -ER/-EST [2*glaze* + *-y*] **:** having the appearance or suggestive of a glaze **:** resembling a glaze ⟨a ~ surface⟩ **:** GLAZED, GLASSY ⟨looked at them with an uncomprehending, ~ stare⟩

gld *abbr* guilder

1glead *var of* GLEDE

2glead *obs var of* GLEED

1gleam \'glēm\ *n* -s [ME *glem, gleem*, fr. OE *glǣm*; akin to OHG *gleimo* glowworm, ON *glja* to glitter, Gk *chliein* to luxuriate, OE *geolu* yellow — more at YELLOW] **1 a** *obs* **:** a brilliantly bright radiance of light (as of the sun) **:** dazzling splendor **b :** a transient appearance or occurrence of emitted or reflected light that is subdued (as when seen through darkness or water or some other intervening medium or as when seen at a distance) ⟨through the swirling fog they glimpsed the ~ of the white sand beach⟩ ⟨the silvery ~ of trout in the brook⟩ ⟨the ~ of the far-off lanterns⟩ or that is slowly changing (as from faintness to greater intensity) ⟨the ~ of dawn in the east⟩ or that has a merely relative brightness (as by contrast with a dark background) ⟨the ~ of many lights reflected in the dark waters of the river⟩ **:** a transient brightness ⟨she read the closely written sheets by the last ~ of daylight —Ellen Glasgow⟩ or a shifting play of subdued diffused reflected light ⟨the rich ~ of the polished mahogany⟩ **c** (1) **:** a small bright light ⟨the quick ~ of a match⟩ **:** a pinpoint of light **:** GLINT ⟨the ~ of anticipation in his eye⟩ (2) **:** a small beam or flash of emitted or reflected light ⟨a ~ of sunlight fell on the page he was reading⟩ ⟨the ~ of helmets in the sun⟩ **2 :** a brief or faint appearance, occurrence, or manifestation (as of a quality) ⟨a ~ of hope⟩ ⟨the ~ of gratitude in the eyes of an old man —H.M.Lydenberg⟩ ⟨a ~ of understanding in the prisoner's face —C.S.Forester⟩ **:** a faint trace ⟨there are perhaps ~*s* of truth in it here and there —G.B.Shaw⟩ ⟨a ~ of resemblance between the two⟩

2gleam \"\ *vb* -ED/-ING/-S [ME *glemen*, fr. *glem, gleem*, n.] *vi* **1 :** to shine with subdued emitted or reflected light ⟨the sun ~*ed* on the water —Robert Keable⟩ ⟨the firelight is ~*ing* and flashing from the polished brass —Osbert Lancaster⟩ **:** send out gleams ⟨a light ~*ed* through the chinks in the wall —Charles Dickens⟩ **:** become lighted up with gleams ⟨his eye ~*ing* at the sight of the two women —Louis Bromfield⟩ **2 :** to appear briefly, faintly, or transiently ⟨amusement ~*ed* swiftly at her from the boy's eyes —Harriet La Barre⟩ ⟨a light ~*ed* suddenly in the night⟩ ~ *vt* **:** to cause to gleam **:** emit or reflect by gleaming ⟨his monocle ~*ed* polite hostility —Christopher Isherwood⟩

gleam·ing·ly *adv* [*gleaming* (pres. part. of 2*gleam*) + *-ly*] **:** in a gleaming manner ⟨lights shining ~⟩

gleam·less \-ləs\ *adj* **:** that does not gleam **:** having no gleam **:** lacking brightness **:** DULL, LACKLUSTER ⟨~ wit⟩

gleamy \-mē\ *adj* -ER/-EST [1*gleam* + *-y*] **:** marked by gleams **:** GLEAMING

glean \'glēn\ *vb* -ED/-ING/-S [ME *glenen*, fr. MF *glener*, fr. LL *glenare, glennare*, of Gaulish origin; akin to MIr *digliunn* I glean; akin to Russ *glyadet'* to look — more at GLENT] *vi* **1 :** to pick up or gather together the scattered remainder of grain or other produce dropped or left lying by reapers or other regular gatherers ⟨spent hours ~*ing* in the wheat fields⟩ **2 :** to pick up, gather together, or acquire information or other material bit by bit from some source **:** gradually scrape together facts or other material found here and there in some source ⟨they learned what they wanted to know by ~*ing* through the library⟩ ~ *vt* **1 a :** to pick up or gather together (scattered grain or other produce left by reapers or other regular gatherers) ⟨~*ing* stray ears of corn⟩ **b :** to strip (as a grain field) by gleaning **:** leave bare by gleaning ⟨~*ing* a vineyard⟩ **2 a :** to pick up or scrape together (information, facts, or other material) in piecemeal fashion **:** acquire bit by bit from some source ⟨many stimulating ideas can be ~*ed* from that magazine⟩ **:** manage to get ⟨later on I ~*ed* an idea of your mother's strong character —Clemence Dane⟩ ⟨~*ed* a little hope from that —H.A.Chippendale⟩ ⟨some money can be ~*ed* from the venture⟩ **b :** to go over or through carefully so as to discover and pick up bits of information or other material ⟨the writings of our bolder ancestors are ~*ed* for signs of conformity —Philip Edwards⟩ **3 :** to find out in a superficial way or gain a cursory knowledge of by piecing together bits of information or other material picked up from some source ⟨I will call again to ~ your views —H.J.Laski⟩ **:** make out **:** LEARN, ASCERTAIN ⟨I could not ~ what he really meant⟩ ⟨~*ing* their whereabouts from what they had said before leaving⟩ **syn** see REAP

glean·er \-nə(r)\ *n* -s **:** one that gleans ⟨the ~*s* must follow the reapers if full profit is to be realized —E.E.Pratt⟩

glean·ings \-niŋz, -nēŋz\ *n pl* [fr. *gleaning*, gerund of *glean*] **:** things acquired by gleaning ⟨the ~ of long hours of research⟩

gle·ba \'glēbə\ *n, pl* **gle·bae** \-ē,bē\ [NL, fr. L *gleba, glaeba* clod] **:** the sporogenous tissue forming the central mass of the sporophore in some basidiomycetes (as the puffballs, stinkhorns) — **gle·bal** \-bəl\ *adj*

glebe \'glēb\ *n* -s [L *gleba, glaeba* clod, land — more at CLIP] **1** *archaic* **:** EARTH, LAND, SOIL, SOD; *specif* **:** a plot of cultivated land **2** [AF or ML; AF *glebe*, fr. ML *gleba*, fr. L *gleba, glaeba*] **a** *or* **glebe land :** the land belonging or yielding revenue to a parish church or ecclesiastical benefice **b :** a parsonage with or without the land appurtenant

glebe house *n, archaic* **:** PARSONAGE

gleby \-bē\ *adj* -ER/-EST [*glebe* + *-y*] **1** *archaic, of soil* **:** RICH, FERTILE **2** *obs* **:** abounding in rich soil

gle·cho·ma \glē'kōmə\ *syn of* GLECOMA

gle·co·ma \"\ *n, cap* [NL, irreg. fr. Gk *glēchōn, blēchōn* pennyroyal] **:** a small genus of creeping Eurasian herbs (family Labiatae) having orbicular or reniform leaves and axillary clusters of blue flowers

1gled \'gled\ *Scot var of* GLAD

2gled \"\ *chiefly Scot var of* GLEDE

1glede *also* **glead** \'glēd\ *n* -s [ME *glede*, fr. OE *glida*; akin to ON *gletha* kite; derivative fr. the root of OE *glīdan* to glide — more at GLIDE] **:** any of several birds of prey (as the common European buzzard or the osprey); *esp* **:** the common European kite (*Milvus milvus*)

2glede *obs var of* 1GLEED

gle·ditsch·ia \glə'dichēə\ [NL, fr. Johann G. Gleditsch †1786 + NL *-ia*] *syn of* GLEDITSIA

gle·dit·sia \-itsēə\ *n, cap* [NL, irreg. fr. Johann G. *Gleditsch* †1786 Ger. botanist + NL *-ia*] **:** a genus of thorny trees (family Leguminosae) with pinnate or bipinnate leaves and inconspicuous greenish spikes of flowers succeeded by large flat pods — see HONEY LOCUST

1glee \'glē\ *n* -s [ME, fr. OE *glēo* entertainment, fun, music; akin to ON *glȳ* joy, Gk *chleuē* joke, Russ *glum*] **1 :** high-spirited joy typically accompanied by exuberant outward display ⟨dancing with ~⟩ ⟨shouting with boyish ~⟩ ⟨a gasp of surprised ~ —*Newsweek*⟩ ⟨he appeared to be almost choking with ~ —Rex Ingamells⟩ and often mixed with or wholly prompted by maliciously delighted and exultant satisfaction over another's misfortune, predicament, or failure ⟨rubbing their hands in ~ over his discomfiture⟩ ⟨grinning with diabolical ~⟩ ⟨it betrayed the ~ felt by the meanspirited when they see people who do not deserve humiliation forced to suffer it —Rebecca West⟩ **:** delighted or triumphant happiness **:** REJOICING, GLADNESS, MIRTH, MERRIMENT **2 :** an unaccompanied song for three or more solo usu. male voices that was esp. popular in the 18th and 19th centuries

2glee \"\ *vi* **gleed; gleed; gleeing; glees** [ME *gleen, gleyen, glien*] **1** *chiefly Scot* **a :** SQUINT **b :** to take a sidelong look **2** *chiefly Scot* **:** to take a look with one eye; *specif* **:** AIM

3glee \"\ *n* -s **1** *chiefly Scot* **a :** SQUINT **b :** a sidelong look **2** *chiefly Scot* **:** a look with one eye; *specif* **:** AIM

4glee \"\ *adj, chiefly Scot* **:** SQUINT-EYED

glee club *n* **:** a group organized for singing glees, part-songs, ballads, choral pieces

1gleed \'glēd\ *n* -s [ME *gleed, glede*, fr. OE *glēd*; akin to OHG *gluot* fire, glow, ON *glōth* ember, glowing coal; derivative fr. the root of OE *glōwan* to glow — more at GLOW] **1** *dial Brit* **:** a burning or glowing coal **:** EMBER **2** *dial Brit* **:** FIRE, FLAMES

2gleed \"\ *adj* [ME (Sc) *gleid*, fr. ME *gleyen* to squint + *-ed*] **1** *chiefly Scot* **:** affected with squint in one or both eyes **:** SQUINT-EYED **2** *chiefly Scot* **:** CROOKED, ASKEW

glee·ful \'glēfəl\ *adj* **:** full of glee **:** exuberantly or exultantly joyful **:** delightedly or triumphantly happy **:** GLAD, MIRTHFUL, MERRY ⟨a ~ romp in the countryside⟩ ⟨~ over the downfall of their enemies⟩ — **glee·ful·ly** \-fəlē, -li\ *adv* — **glee·ful·ness** *n* -ES

1gleek \'glēk\ *n* -s [MF *glic*, fr. MD *gelijc* equal, alike; akin to OE *gelic* equal, alike — more at ALIKE] **1 :** a card game popular in England throughout the 16th to 18th centuries **2** *obs* **:** a group of three **:** TRIO

2gleek \"\ *n* -s [origin unknown] **1** *archaic* **a :** GIBE, JEST **b :** a practical joke **2** *archaic* **:** a flirtatious glance

3gleek \"\ *vb* -ED/-ING/-S *vt, obs* **:** to gain an advantage over (as by trickery) ~ *vi, archaic* **:** GIBE, JEST

glee·man \'glēmən\ *n, pl* **gleemen** [ME, fr. OE *glēoman*, fr. *glēo* entertainment, music + *man*] **:** a medieval usu. itinerant professional entertainer (as in England or Scotland) who sang songs often to his own accompaniment on a stringed instrument (as a harp), chanted or recited poetry, or related stories

glee·some \'glēsəm\ *adj, archaic* **:** GLEEFUL — **glee·some·ly** *adv, archaic* — **glee·some·ness** *n* -ES *archaic*

1gleet \'glēt, *usu* -ēd·+V\ *n* -s [ME *glet, glette* slimy or mucous matter, fr. MF *glete*, fr. L *glittus* sticky, viscous; akin to L *glut-, glus* glue — more at CLAY] **:** a chronic inflammation of a bodily orifice in man or animals usu. accompanied by an abnormal discharge from the orifice ⟨nasal ~⟩; *specif* **:** the discharge itself (as the urethral mucous discharge in gonorrhea)

2gleet \"\ *vi* -ED/-ING/-S *archaic* **:** to vent an abnormal discharge **:** discharge gleet

gleety \-ēd·|ē, -ēt|, |i\ *adj* -ER/-EST [1*gleet* + *-y*] **:** having the appearance or characteristics of gleet ⟨a ~ discharge⟩

gleg \'gleg\ *adj* [ME, quick in perception, fr. ON *glǫggr* clear, clear-sighted; akin to OE *glēaw* wise, OHG *glou* clever, Goth *glaggwo* exactly, and prob. to OE *glōwan* to glow — more at GLOW] **1** *chiefly Scot* **:** quick in perception and action **:** alert and nimble **2** *chiefly Scot* **:** having a keen edge **:** SHARP — **gleg·ly** *adv, chiefly Scot* — **gleg·ness** *n* -ES *chiefly Scot*

glei *var of* GLEY

glei·che·nia \glī'kēnēə\ *n, cap* [NL, fr. W. F. von Gleichen †1783 Ger. naturalist + NL *-ia*] **:** a genus (the type of the family Gleicheniaceae) of leptosporangiate ferns having sessile sporangia that lack an indusium and dehisce by a transverse annulus

gleich·schal·tung \'glīk,shäl(,)tůŋ, -,təŋ\ *n, pl* **gleich·schaltung·en** \-,tůŋən, -,təŋ-\ *usu cap* [G, coordination, fr. *gleichschalten* to coordinate, fr. *gleich* equally, alike (fr. OHG *gilīcho*, adv. of *gilīh* equal, alike) + *schalten* to govern, direct, fr. OHG *scaltan* to push; akin to OS *skaldan* to shove (a boat), OHG *scalta* boathook, ON *skalda* ferryboat, Gk *skallein* to hoe — more at LIKE, SHELL] **:** the act, process, or policy of achieving rigid and total coordination and uniformity (as in politics, culture, communication) by forcibly repressing or eliminating independence and freedom of thought, action, or expression **:** forced reduction to a common level **:** forced standardization or assimilation ⟨brutal *Gleichschaltung* by police methods⟩ ⟨the political *Gleichschaltung* of a reluctant adult population —Reinhard Bendix⟩

gleid \'glēd\ *var of* 1GLEED

glei·za·tion \glā'zāshən\ *n* -s [*gley* + *-ize* + *-ation*] **:** the development of gley **:** conversion into gley

glen \'glen\ *n* -s [ME (Sc), valley, fr. (assumed) obs. ScGael *glenn* (whence ScGael *gleann*); akin to MIr *glend, glenn* valley, W *glyn*] **:** a secluded narrow valley **:** a narrow depression between mountains or hills

glen·gar·ry \glen'garē, -ri\ *or* **glengarry bonnet** *also* **glen·garry cap** \(')=¦==-\ *n* -ES *often cap G* [*Glengarry*, valley in Inverness-shire, Scotland] **:** a woolen cap of Scottish origin typically having a crease in the crown from front to back and edges bound with ribbon that ends at the back in two small streamers

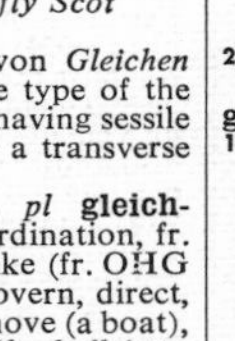

glengarry

glen·liv·et *or* **glen·liv·at** \glen'livət\ *n* -s *usu cap* [*Glenlivet*, Banffshire, Scotland, where it is manufactured] **:** a Scotch whiskey

glenn pepper *or* **glenn weed** \'glen-\ *n, usu cap G* [prob. fr. the name *Glenn*] **:** FIELD CRESS

gleno·humeral \¦gle(,)nō, -lē-(+\ *adj* [*gleno-* (fr. *glenoid*) + *humeral*] **:** of, relating to, or connecting the glenoid cavity and the humerus

glenoid \'gle,nȯid, -lē-,\ *also* **glenoi·dal** \(')=¦nȯidᵊl\ *adj* [*glenoid* fr. Gk *glēnoeidēs*, fr. *glēnē* socket of a joint, eyeball + *-oeidēs* -oid; *glenoidal* fr. *glenoid* + *-al*; perh. akin to OHG *kleini* delicate, dainty — more at CLEAN] **1 :** having the form of a smooth shallow depression — used chiefly of skeletal articulatory sockets **2 :** of or relating to the glenoid cavity or glenoid fossa

glenoid cavity *n* **:** the shallow cavity of the upper part of the scapula by which the humerus articulates with the shoulder girdle

glenoid fossa *n* **:** the depression in each lateral wall of the skull with which the mammalian mandible articulates

glen plaid *also* **glen check** \'glen,-\ *n, often cap G* **:** a twill pattern of broken checks in which stripes of two dark and two light yarns alternate with stripes of four dark and four light yarns and in which the same colors and design are used crosswise and lengthwise; *also* **:** a fabric that is woven in this pattern

1glent \'glent, 'glint\ *vi* -ED/-ING/-S [ME *glenten* to move quickly esp. in an oblique direction, strike something obliquely and glance aside, look sideways at something, gleam, of Scand origin; akin to ON *glettask* to utter taunts, Norw dial. *gletta* to look, Sw dial. *glänta* to clear up; akin to OHG *glanz* bright, Russ *glyadet'* to look, OE *geolu* yellow — more at YELLOW] **1** *dial Brit* **a :** to move quickly esp. in an oblique direction **b :** to strike something obliquely and glance aside **2** *dial Brit* **:** to look askance **:** look sideways at something **3** *dial Brit* **:** GLEAM, FLASH, SHINE

2glent \"\ *n* -s [ME, fr. *glenten*] **1** *dial Brit* **a :** a quick look **b :** a quick movement **2** *dial Brit* **:** GLEAM, FLASH

glen·ur·quhart \gle'nərkərt\ *or* **glenurquhart plaid** *also* **glenurquhart check** \(')=¦==-\ *n* -s *often cap G* [*Glen Urquhart*, valley in Inverness-shire, Scotland] **:** GLEN PLAID

gless \'gles\ *Scot var of* GLASS

gles·site \'gle,sīt\ *n* -s [G *glessit*, fr. L *glaesum, glesum, glessum* amber + G *-it* -ite; L *glaesum, glesum, glessum* of Gmc origin; akin to OHG *glas* glass — more at GLASS] **:** a fossil resin resembling amber

glew *obs var of* GLUE

1gley \'glǝi, 'glē\ *Scot var of* GLEE

2gley *also* **glei** \'glā\ *n* -s [Russ *gleĭ* clay; akin to Pol *glej* muddy ground, OE *clǣg* clay — more at CLAY] **:** a bluish gray or olive-gray sticky layer of clay formed under the surface of certain waterlogged soils

gleyd \'glēd, 'glād\ *var of* 2GLEED

gleyde \'glīd\ *n* -s [origin unknown] **1** *dial Brit* **:** a decrepit old horse **:** NAG **2** *dial Brit* **:** a disagreeable old man **:** CURMUDGEON

gli- *or* **glio-** *comb form* [NL, fr. MGk *glia* glue — more at CLAY] **1 :** gliomatous ⟨*glio*blastoma⟩ ⟨*glio*myoma⟩ **2 :** neuroglial ⟨*glio*some⟩ ⟨*glio*cyte⟩ ⟨*gli*osis⟩ **3 :** embedded in a gelatinous matrix ⟨*glio*bacteria⟩ **4 :** substance resembling glue ⟨*gli*ode⟩

glia \'glīə, 'glēə\ *n* -s [NL, fr. MGk, glue] **:** NEUROGLIA — **gli·al** \-əl\ *adj*

-glia \,glēə, 'glīə, 'glēə\ *n comb form* -s [NL, fr. MGk *glia* glue] **:** neuroglia made up of a (specified) kind or size of element ⟨astro*glia*⟩ ⟨micro*glia*⟩

gli·a·din \'glīədᵊn\ *n* -s [It *gliadina*, fr. *gliad-* (fr. MGk *glia* glue + *-ina* -in] **:** PROLAMIN; *usu* **:** a prolamin found esp. in wheat and rye and obtained as a soft sticky material by extracting gluten with dilute alcohol

1glib \'glib\ *n* -s [IrGael] **:** a mass of hair worn thickly matted so as to overhang the forehead and eyes and constituting a manner of hair arrangement at one time customary among the men of Ireland

2glib \"\ *adj, usu* **glibber;** *usu* **glibbest** [prob. modif. of LG *glibberig* slippery, fr. MLG *glibberich*] **1** *archaic* **:** having a smooth or slippery surface ⟨the snow lies ~ as glass —Robert Browning⟩ **2 a :** marked by lack of constraint, stiffness, or formality **:** free and easy **:** UNFORCED, CASUAL, NONCHALANT ⟨the ~ congeniality of college life⟩ ⟨~ manners⟩ **b** (1) **:** marked by little or no forethought or preparation **:** OFFHAND, UNSTUDIED, IMPROMPTU ⟨quick ~ answers⟩ ⟨an account which poured from her lips with such ~ alacrity that it might have been memorized —Erle Stanley Gardner⟩ (2) **:** marked by hastiness and lack of requisite forethought and preparation **:** UNTHINKING, UNREFLECTING ⟨jumping to ~ conclusions⟩ **c** (1) **:** lacking depth and substance **:** SUPERFICIAL, SHALLOW, EMPTY ⟨~ generalizations⟩ (2) **:** too easily arrived at and basically inadequate **:** PAT ⟨mouthing ~ solutions to the problem⟩ (3) **:** too easily made, done, or produced **:** SLICK ⟨a ~ frothy comedy⟩ ⟨turning out one ~ book after another⟩ ⟨the tale is ~, preposterous —Anthony Boucher⟩ **3 a :** characterized by a propensity for, ability to use, or production of a smooth ready flow of words **:** VOLUBLE ⟨a ~ tongue⟩ ⟨a ~ speaker⟩; *esp* **:** facile in the use of words to a degree indicative of superficiality, trickery, or deceitfulness ⟨a ~ writer on economics⟩ ⟨~ politicians⟩ **b :** spoken or written in an overly smooth easy manner ⟨~ phrases⟩ **syn** see VOCAL

3glib \"\ *vt* **glibbed; glibbed; glibbing; glibs** *archaic* **:** to make smooth or slippery **:** LUBRICATE; *esp* **:** to cause (as the tongue) to move freely as if by oiling

4glib *vt* **glibbed; glibbed; glibbing; glibs** [prob. alter. of *lib*] *obs* **:** CASTRATE

glib·bery \'glibərē\ *adj* [prob. fr. LG *glibberig*] **1** *now chiefly dial* **:** SMOOTH, SLIPPERY **2** *now chiefly dial* **:** not trustworthy **:** UNRELIABLE

glib-gab·bet \'glib,gabət\ *adj* [2*glib* + Sc *-gabbet* having (such) a mouth, -mouthed, fr. *gab* mouth + *-et* -ed (vb. suffix or adj. suffix), fr. ME (Sc) *-it, -ed*, fr. ME *-ed* — more at GAB] *Scot* **:** GLIB-TONGUED

glib·ly *also* **glib** *adv* **:** in a glib manner: **a :** EASILY, SMOOTHLY, READILY **b :** VOLUBLY

glib·ness *n* -ES **:** the quality or state of being glib

glib-tongued \'=¦=\ *adj* **:** having a glib tongue **:** VOLUBLE

1glid·der \'glidə(r)\ *vt* -ED/-ING/-S [obs. *glidder*, adj., slippery, fr. (assumed) ME *glidder*, fr. OE *glidder, glider*; akin to OE *glīdan* to glide] *dial Eng* **:** to glaze over (as with ice)

2glidder \"\ *n* -s [fr. or akin to obs. *glidder*, adj.] *dial Brit* **:** a loose stone (as on a hillside)

glid·dery \-dəri\ *adj* [1*glidder* + *-y*] *dial Eng* **:** SLIPPERY

1glide \'glīd\ *vb* **glided** \-dəd\ *or archaic* **glid** \'glid\ *also archaic* **glode** \'glōd\ **glided** *or archaic* **glid** *also archaic* **glode; gliding** \'glīdiŋ\ **glides** [ME *gliden*, fr. OE *glīdan*; akin to OHG *glītan* to glide, ON *gleithr* standing with legs far apart, and prob. to OE *geolu* yellow — more at YELLOW] *vi* **1 a :** to move smoothly, continuously, and effortlessly ⟨a canoe *gliding* over the still lake⟩ ⟨silvery fish *gliding* about in the depths of the pool⟩ ⟨snowy gulls *glided* through the blue of the sky⟩ **:** move with a quiet smoothness marked by little or no perceptible or distracting extraneous motion ⟨began *gliding* about with a tray full of glasses —Willa Cather⟩ ⟨watched the skiers ~ swiftly and silently down the slope⟩ **:** move lightly and silently ⟨*glided* out of the room as noiselessly as she had entered⟩ **b :** to move stealthily **:** move cautiously and furtively **:** SLIP, STEAL, CREEP ⟨*gliding* along the wall until they were out of sight⟩ **2 a :** to elapse gradually and imperceptibly ⟨hours *gliding* tranquilly by⟩ **b :** to pass or taper off into something different gradually and imperceptibly by slight progressive changes **:** MERGE ⟨feelings of hostility . . . ~ into those of peculiar courtesy —Archibald Alison⟩ **:** slip gradually into something ⟨*glided* into telling you the secret —Charles Dickens⟩ **3** *of an airplane* **:** to descend at a normal angle of attack with little or no thrust **4** *of the tongue* **:** to change position in the articulation of a glide **5 :** GLANCE *vi* 1b (2) ~ *vt* **1 :** to cause to glide ⟨*gliding* the airplane to a safe place to land⟩ ⟨*gliding* the boat over the water⟩ **2 :** to fly over in or as if in a glider ⟨wondered whether, if I got up enough momentum, I could . . . ~ the Atlantic —Richard Joseph⟩

2glide \"\ *n* -s **1 :** the action of gliding **:** a gliding movement; *specif* **:** the flight of a gliding aircraft ⟨saw the long ~ of the airplane⟩ **2 :** a calm stretch of shallow water flowing smoothly and gently ⟨fishing in the ~*s* of a stream⟩ **3 a :** PORTAMENTO 1 **b :** a nonsignificant sound produced by the passing of the vocal organs to or from the articulatory position of a speech sound; *specif* **:** the less prominent vowel or sound like a vowel in the articulation of two consecutive vowel sounds unequal in prominence (as the very brief \ē\ or \i\ sound of \y\ in \'yel\ *yell*) — see OFF-GLIDE, ON-GLIDE **4 a :** a fencing attack in which the forte of the weapon is pressed against the foible of the antagonist's weapon and the point then slid along his blade **b :** GLANCE 2c **5 :** a circular typically dome-shaped usu. metal button attached to the bottom of furniture legs or supports so as to provide a low-friction surface for easy movement of the furniture

glide-bomb \'=,=\ *vt* [1*glide* + *bomb*, v.] **:** to bomb (a target) with a bomb released from a gliding airplane

glide bomb *also* **glider bomb** *n* [*glide bomb* fr. 1*glide* + *bomb*, n.; *glider bomb* fr. *glider* + *bomb*, n.] **:** a bomb fitted with airfoils so that it glides toward its target with or without a guidance system

glide·less \'glīdləs\ *adj* **:** having no glide ⟨a ~ sound⟩

glide path *also* **glide slope** *n* **:** the path of descent of an airplane as marked out by a radio beam along which a pilot may bring an airplane to a safe landing when flying on instruments; *also* **:** the radio beam that marks out such a path

glide plane *n* **:** a crystallographic plane of symmetry that requires identity of the structure of the crystal with its original configuration following the combination of reflection of the crystal across the plane with movement of the structural configuration parallel to the plane

glid·er \'glīdə(r)\ *n* -s [ME *glydare*, fr. *glyden, gliden* to glide + *-are, -er, -ere* -er] **1 :** one that glides: as **a :** an aircraft similar to an airplane but without an engine — compare SAILPLANE **b :** a flat powerboat of shallow draft and high speed **c :** a porch seat or lounge suspended from uprights of an underframe by means of short chains or metal straps at the corners so as to permit its swinging smoothly back and forth **2 :** something that aids gliding ⟨an anterior pair of wings used as a ~⟩; *specif* **:** GLIDE 5

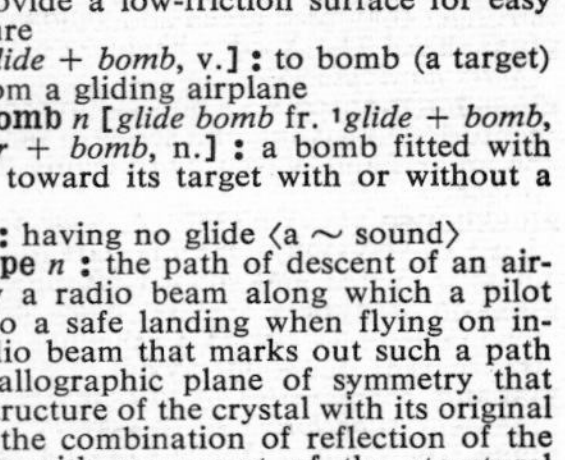

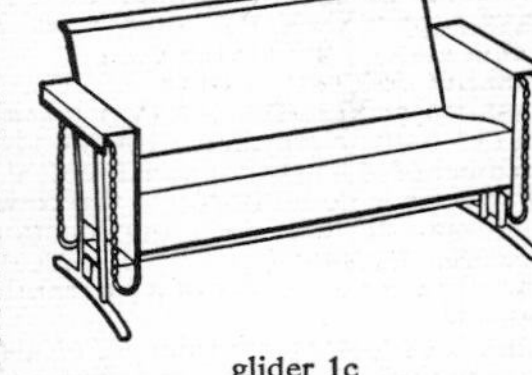
glider 1c

gliderport \'=,=,=\ *n* **:** a landing place for gliders

gliding *adj* [ME *glidinge, gliding*, fr. *gliden* to glide + *-inge, -ing* -ing] **:** that glides **:** marked by gliding ⟨a ~ way of walking⟩ — **glid·ing·ly** *adv*

gliding angle *n* [*gliding* fr. gerund of 1*glide*] **:** the angle between the plane of the horizon and the path of a glider or airplane; *esp* **:** the least angle at which a glider or airplane will glide to earth in still air

gliding growth *n* **:** plant growth marked by the sliding of a cell wall over the surface of a cell or cells adjacent to it (as in the formation of new initials in the cambium) — called also *sliding growth;* compare INTRUSIVE GROWTH, SYMPLASTIC GROWTH

gliding joint *n* **:** ARTHRODIA

1gliff \ˈglif\ *vt* -ED/-ING/-S [ME *gliffen* to look quickly, glance] *dial Brit* **:** FRIGHTEN

2gliff \"\ *n* -S [E dial. (northern) *gliff*, v., to look quickly, glance, fr. ME *gliffen*] **1** *chiefly Scot* **a :** GLIMPSE **b :** a faint trace **:** SUGGESTION **2** *chiefly Scot* **:** a sudden fright **:** SCARE **3** *chiefly Scot* **:** a brief moment **:** INSTANT

gliff·ing \-fiŋ\ *n* -S [fr. gerund of E dial. (northern) *gliff*, v.] *Scot* **:** INSTANT

1glim \ˈglim\ *n* -S [perh. short for *2glimmer*] **1 :** GLIMMER ⟨not a ~ of hope —P.E.Green⟩ **2** *slang* **:** a brief look **:** GLANCE **3 a** (1) **:** something (as a lamp, flashlight, candle) that furnishes light (2) **:** ILLUMINATION; *esp* **:** illumination from a particular source of light ⟨~s from a half dozen hurricane lamps spotted a path to the far door —Richard Llewellyn⟩ **b** *archaic* **:** EYE

2glim \"\ *vt* **glimmed; glimmed; glimming; glims** *slang* **:** to take a look at **:** glance at **:** WATCH

gli·ma \ˈglēmə\ *n* -S [Icel *glíma*, fr. OIcel] **:** a wrestling technique whose object is to throw an opponent to the floor on his back

1glime \ˈglīm\ *vi* -ED/-ING/-S [origin unknown] *dial chiefly Brit* **:** to look obliquely at something **:** steal a glance

2glime \"\ *n* -S *dial chiefly Brit* **:** an oblique glance

1glim·mer \ˈglimə(r)\ *vi* **glimmered; glimmered; glimmering** \-m(ə)riŋ\ **glimmers** [ME *glimeren, glemeren;* akin to MHG *glim* spark, *glimmen* to glow, *glimmern* to glow, ON *gljā* to glitter — more at GLEAM] **1 a :** to emit feeble or intermittent rays of light **:** shine faintly or unsteadily ⟨flickering candles ~*ed* in the windows of the old inn⟩ ⟨just below the intruder's pockmarked face ~*ed* the barrel of an automatic pistol —F.V.W.Mason⟩ **b :** to shimmer softly ⟨her white satin dress ~*ed* in the dusk⟩ **2 :** to appear indistinctly with or as if with a faintly luminous quality ⟨the chalk cliffs ~*ed* far off in the night⟩

2glimmer \"\ *n* -S **1 a :** a feeble or intermittent light **:** a faint or unsteady shining ⟨the space beyond the ~ of her lantern —Ellen Glasgow⟩ ⟨the first ~ of dawn⟩ **b :** a soft shimmer ⟨the moonlit ~ of the pool⟩ **2 a :** a dim perception **:** a faint idea ⟨the interview gave them a ~ of what they could expect⟩ **b :** a vague manifestation or indication **:** INTIMATION, INKLING ⟨had given the world only a ~ of her potential as a gay slaughterer of convention —Bernard Kalb⟩ **c :** an indistinct appearance marked by or as if by a faintly luminous quality ⟨he saw the ~ of her face in the shadow —R.P.Warren⟩ **3 :** a small amount or degree **:** a faint trace **:** BIT ⟨a ~ of hope showing in his eyes —T.B.Costain⟩ ⟨a ~ of intelligence⟩

3glimmer \"\ *n* -S [G, back-formation fr. *glimmern* to glow, fr. MHG] **:** MICA

glimmer gowk *n, dial Eng* **:** OWL

glimmer ice *n* **:** ice newly formed in cracks, holes, or surface puddles of other ice

1glimmering *adj* [ME *glimeringe, glimering*, fr. *glimeren* to glimmer + *-inge, -ing* -ing (v. suffix or adj. suffix)] **:** that glimmers ⟨the ~ mist of a spring rain splashed by sun and streaked by rainbow —Claudia Cassidy⟩ — **glim·mer·ing·ly** *adv*

2glimmering *n* -S [ME *glimeringe, glimering*, fr. *glimeren* to glimmer + *-inge, -ing* -ing (n. suffix)] **:** GLIMMER ⟨the last faint ~s of twilight —T.L.Peacock⟩ ⟨a ~ of happiness —W.R. Burnett⟩ ⟨~s of economic theory in the writings of the Greeks —Leo Fishman⟩

glim·mery \-m(ə)rē\ *adj* [*1glimmer* + *-y*] **:** tending to glimmer or having an effect suggestive of glimmering ⟨a peculiar ~ color⟩

1glimpse \ˈglim(p)s\ *vb* -ED/-ING/-S [ME *glimsen;* akin to MHG *glimsen* to glimmer, *glim* spark] *vi* **1** *archaic* **:** GLIMMER **2 :** to take a brief look **:** give a passing glance ⟨he *glimpsed* at the letter, then threw it impatiently aside⟩ ~ *vt* **1** *archaic* **:** to furnish a brief look at **2 :** to get a brief look at **:** see momentarily or incompletely ⟨*glimpsed* the man as he sped through the forest⟩ ⟨from the fragments of sculpture that remain we can ~ the strength and beauty of the figures that adorned the temples —W.K.Ferguson⟩ — **glimps·er** \-sə(r)\ *n* -S

2glimpse \"\ *n* -S **1** *archaic* **:** GLIMMER **2 :** a brief fleeting look **:** a momentary or incomplete view ⟨an occasional ~ of her husband's face behind the morning newspaper —Grace Nagle⟩ ⟨had interesting ~s of them as they went in and out of the various cabins —Joseph Conrad⟩

1glint \ˈglint\ *vb* -ED/-ING/-S [ME *glinten*, alter. of *glenten* — more at GLENT] *vi* **1 a** *archaic* **:** to move rapidly and usu. obliquely; *specif* **:** to glance off an object struck ⟨the majority of the shells struck armor and simply ~*ed* off —W.A.M. Goode⟩ **b** *of rays of light* **:** to strike a reflecting surface obliquely and dart out at an angle ⟨light gleaming and sparkling on the sea . . . ~*ing* from the sand—J.L.Lowes⟩ **2 a :** to shine usu. by reflection: (1) **:** to shine with tiny bright flashes **:** SPARKLE ⟨the slightly ruffled surface of the lake was ~*ing* brilliantly in the morning sunlight⟩ ⟨little tin cups that ~ like bright money —Lillian Smith⟩ ⟨you can see the rocks and pebbles ~*ing* under the shimmering veil of water —William Goyen⟩ (2) **:** to shine with a hard bright metallic luster of scattered light **:** GLITTER ⟨eyes ~*ing* with anger⟩ ⟨sunlight ~*ed* on the vicious edges of the bottle fragments —Harriet La Barre⟩ (3) **:** to shine with a subdued scattered light **:** GLEAM ⟨moonlight ~*ed* on the brass bed —Sloane Wilson⟩ **b :** to emit scattered rays of light ⟨held a magnifying glass over my hand and let the sun ~ through —Charles Spielberger⟩ **3 :** to look quickly or briefly **:** PEEP **4 :** to appear briefly, faintly, or transiently ⟨across the river the village . . . ~*ed* through the palms —H.O.Forbes⟩ ~ *vt* **:** to cause to glint **:** reflect in tiny flashes or gleams ⟨the dark surface of the water caught the lights of the boat and ~*ed* them brightly back⟩

2glint \"\ *n* -S **1 a** (1) **:** a tiny bright usu. reflected flash of light **:** SPARKLE ⟨watched the twin ~s of his eyeglasses⟩ (2) **:** a hard bright metallic point of light ⟨the singularly venomous ~ in her eye —Ngaio Marsh⟩ (3) **:** a small point of subdued light **:** GLEAM ⟨~s of ruddy light playing over the polished dark mahogany⟩ **b :** a ray of scattered light ⟨the little room was dusky, save for a narrow ~ streaming through the not quite closed door of the room —Charles Dickens⟩ **c** (1) **:** a shining appearance produced by tiny bright scattered flashes **:** sparkling brightness ⟨the ~ of unshed tears blurring the clear bright blue of his eyes —Marcia Davenport⟩ ⟨the ~ of spring and autumn sunlight —Donn Byrne⟩ (2) **:** a glittering metallic luster ⟨his bright eyes burning with a sharp wild ~ of madness —Thomas Wolfe⟩ (3) **:** a subdued radiance **:** GLEAMING ⟨the ~ of moonlight through the leaves⟩ **2** *archaic* **:** GLANCE, GLIMPSE **3 :** a brief, faint, or transient appearance or manifestation (as of a quality) ⟨thought I detected a ~ of recognition in her expression⟩

glint o' gold : a moderate yellow that is slightly stronger than mustard yellow and duller than colonial yellow

glio- — see GLI-

glio·blas·to·ma \ˌglī(ˌ)ō͟ˌblaˈstōmə\ *n, pl* **glioblastomas** \-məz\ *or* **glioblastoma·ta** \-məd·ə\ [NL, fr. *gli-* + *blast-* + *-oma*] **:** SPONGIOBLASTOMA

gli·o·cla·di·um \ˌglīōˈklādēəm\ *n, cap* [NL, fr. *gli-* + *-cladium* (fr. Gk *klados* branch) — more at GLADIATOR] **:** a genus of molds resembling those of the genus *Penicillium* but with the conidia of a spore head becoming surrounded by a slimy deposit that binds them into a rounded mass

gli·o·cyte \ˈglīōˌsīt\ *n* -S [*gli-* + *-cyte*] **:** a neuroglial cell

gli·o·ma \glīˈōmə\ *n, pl* **gliomas** \-məz\ *or* **glioma·ta** \-məd·ə\ [NL, fr. MGk *glia* glue + NL *-oma* — more at CLAY] **:** a tumor arising from neuroglia — **gli·o·ma·to·sis** \(ˌ)glīˌōməˈtōsəs\ *n, pl* **glioma·to·ses** \-ōˌsēz\ — **gli·oma·tous** \(ˈ)glīˈämədəs, -ˈōm-\ *adj*

gli·o·sis \glīˈōsəs\ *n, pl* **glio·ses** \-ōˌsēz\ [NL, fr. *gli-* + *-osis*] **:** excessive development of neuroglia esp. interstitially — compare GLIOMA — **gli·ot·ic** \(ˈ)glīˈäd·ik\ *adj*

glio·toxin \ˈglīō+\ *n* [ISV *glio-* (fr. NL *Gliocladium*) + *toxin*] **:** a crystalline antibiotic $C_{13}H_{14}N_2O_4S_2$ that is toxic to higher animals as well as to animal and plant pathogens and that is produced by various fungi esp. of the genus *Gliocladium*

gli·res \ˈglīˌrēz\ *n pl, cap* [NL, fr. L, pl. of *glir-, glis* dormouse] **:** a superorder or other division of Eutheria comprising the typical rodents and the lagomorph rodents and including the orders Rodentia (sense 1) and Lagomorpha

glir·i·cid·ia \ˌglirəˈsidēə\ *n, cap* [NL, fr. *gliri-* (fr. NL *Glires*) + L *-cida* -cide + NL *-ia*] **:** a genus of low-branching trees (family Leguminosae) with odd-pinnate leaves having 7 to 15 large leaflets, pink flowers borne in great profusion, dark durable wood, and roots that together with the leaves are believed to be poisonous to mice and rats

1glirid \ˈglirəd, -lir-\ *adj* [NL *Gliridae*] **:** of or relating to the Gliridae

2glirid \"\ *n* -S **:** a rodent of the family Gliridae **:** DORMOUSE

glir·i·dae \ˈglirəˌdē\ *n pl, cap* [NL, fr. *Glir-, Glis*, type genus + *-idae*] **:** a family of widely distributed Old World myomorph rodents including the dormice

glir·i·form \ˈglirəˌfȯrm\ *adj* [*glir-* (fr. NL *Glires*) + *-iform*] **1 :** resembling a rodent **2** *of incisor teeth* **:** having the form characteristic of the rodents

gli·rine \ˈglīˌrīn\ *adj* [*glir-* (fr. NL *Glires*) + *-ine*] **:** of or relating to the Glires

glis \ˈglis\ *n, cap* [NL *Glir-, Glis*, fr. L *glir-, glis* dormouse — more at GALEA] **:** a genus comprising the common Old World dormouse and being the type of the family Gliridae

1glisk \ˈglisk\ *n* -S [origin unknown] **1** *chiefly Scot* **:** GLIMPSE **2** *chiefly Scot* **:** GLEAM **3** *chiefly Scot* **:** a brief moment **:** INSTANT

2glisk \"\ *vb* -ED/-ING/-S *vt, chiefly Scot* **:** to glance at **:** look at cursorily ~ *vi, chiefly Scot* **:** to get a glimpse

gliss \ˈglis\ *n* -ES [by shortening] *slang* **:** GLISSANDO

1glis·sade \gləˈsäd, glēˈ-, -ˈsād *sometimes* -ˈsad\ *vi* -ED/-ING/-S [F *glissade*, n.] **1 a :** to slide by design or with control; *specif* **:** to make a controlled slide in a standing or sitting position without skis, toboggans, or other similar devices down a snow-covered slope ⟨the exhilaration of *glissading* down the side of a mountain⟩ **b :** to slide or slip haphazardly or without control ⟨rock rubble *glissading* down from the crumbling heights —C.A.Cotton⟩ **2 :** to move along smoothly and effortlessly **:** GLIDE ⟨the boat was light and buoyant, *glissading* gracefully over each swell in the lake⟩; *specif* **:** to perform a ballet glissade — **glis·sad·er** \-də(r)\ *n* -S

2glissade \"\ *n* -S [F, social error, slip, action of glissading, landslide, gliding step in ballet, glissando, fr. MF, social error, fr. *glisser* to slip, slide (fr. OF *glicier*, alter. of *glier*, fr. an OFrk verb akin to OHG *glītan* to glide) + *-ade* — more at GLIDE] **1 a :** the action of glissading ⟨a long ~ to the foot of the mountain⟩ **b :** a mass of glissading material ⟨her foot sent a tiny ~ of snow slithering down the bank —Victor Canning⟩ **c :** a slope suitable for glissading ⟨at last discovered a good ~⟩ **2 :** a gliding step in ballet **3 :** GLISSANDO

1glis·san·do \gləˈsän(ˌ)dō, glēˈ-\ *n* [prob. modif. (influenced by It *-ando* as in *accelerando*) of F *glissade*, n.] **1** *pl* **glissan·di** \-ˌdē\ *or* **glissandos a :** a rapid series of consecutive notes played on a piano, harp, or other similar instrument by sliding one or more fingers across adjacent keys or strings **b** (1) **:** a rapid series of chromatic notes played on a violin or other similar instrument by minute interruptions in sliding the finger along the string being bowed (2) **:** a series of notes (as on a clarinet) forming a nearly unbroken change of pitch **c :** PORTAMENTO 1 **2** -S **:** the technique of gradually increasing the electric current in the application of electroshock so as to minimize the shock of the total current applied

2glissando \"\ *adv (or adj)* **:** in the manner of a glissando — used as a direction in music

glis·sé \gləˈsā, glēˈ-\ *n* -S [F, fr. past part. of *glisser* to slip, slide] **:** GLISSADE

glis·sile \ˈglisəl\ *adj* [F *glisser* to slip, slide + E *-ile*] **:** capable of gliding — used esp. of a dislocation or other fault in a crystal — compare SESSILE

glis·son's capsule \ˈglisᵊnz-\ *n, usu cap G* [after Francis *Glisson* †1677 Eng. physician] **:** an investment of loose connective tissue entering the liver with the portal vessels and sheathing the larger vessels in their course through the organ

1glis·ten \ˈglisᵊn\ *vi* **glistened; glistened; glistening** \-s(ᵊ)niŋ\ **glistens** [ME *glistnen, glisnen*, fr. OE *glisnian;* akin to OE *glisian* to glitter, Sw dial. *glisa* to peep out, W *glwys* beautiful, OE *geolu* yellow — more at YELLOW] **:** to shine brightly usu. by reflection with a sparkling radiance ⟨early-morning dew ~*ing* on the grass⟩ ⟨a crust of snow ~*ing* in the sun⟩ or with the sleek shininess of or suggestive of a wet or oiled surface ⟨the drenched streets of the brightly lit city ~*ed* in the night⟩ ⟨the ~*ing* bodies of the swimmers⟩ ⟨her eyes were ~*ing* with happiness⟩ or with a glossy lustrousness ⟨brushed the dog's coat until it ~*ed*⟩

2glisten \"\ *n* -S **:** the quality or state of glistening ⟨the brass of the clock was polished to a mirrorlike ~ —J.C.Lincoln⟩

glis·ten·ing·ly *adv* [*glistening* (pres. part. of *1glisten*) + *-ly*] **:** in a glistening manner ⟨black hair that shone ~⟩

1glis·ter \ˈglistə(r)\ *vi* **glistered; glistered; glistering** \-t(ə)riŋ\ **glisters** [ME *glistren;* akin to OE *glisian* to glitter] **:** GLISTEN

2glister \"\ *n* -S **:** GLISTEN

glis·ter·ing·ly *adv* [*glistering* (fr. pres. part. of *1glister*) + *-ly*] **:** GLISTENINGLY

1glit·ter \ˈglid·ə(r), -itə-\ *vb* -ED/-ING/-S [ME *gliteren, gleteren*, fr. ON *glitra;* akin to OE *glitenian* to glitter, OHG *glīzan* to shine, ON *glita* to glitter, Goth *glitmunjan* to glisten, Gk *chlidē* luxury, effeminacy, OE *geolu* yellow — more at YELLOW] *vi* **1 :** to shine resplendently usu. by reflection with many quick small flashes of brilliant light ⟨a crown of jewels ~*ed* on her head⟩ ⟨a landscape ~*ing* with sun and rain —Ambrose Bierce⟩ or with a hard bright often metallic luster made up of many small scattered rapidly appearing and disappearing points of light ⟨dragonflies darting about and ~*ing* iridescently in the bright sunlight⟩ ⟨the horses tossed their heads, their well-oiled hooves ~*ing* as they shifted their feet nervously —Dorothy C. Fisher⟩ ⟨the sun of the late summer ~*ed* on the gold cups —Edith Sitwell⟩ or with a dazzling brilliance marked by stabbing rays of light ⟨shields and swords polished like mirrors ~*ed* in the morning sun⟩ ⟨sequins ~*ing* under the spotlights⟩ and often with a showy or gaudy effect ⟨the tree was lavishly hung with tinsel that quivered and ~*ed*⟩ **:** sparkle with twinkling points of light ⟨myriads of stars that ~*ed* in the dark and frigid lonesomeness of the sky⟩ ⟨far off they could see the lights of the city ~*ing* in the night⟩ **:** shine with a hard cold glassy brilliance marked by quick intermittent rapidly successive points of intense light ⟨her little eyes ~*ed* cruelly —Haldane Macfall⟩ **2 :** to be brilliantly or compellingly attractive usu. in a superficial way **:** make a brilliant appearance or impression ⟨the possibility of fame in the theater ~*ed* before them⟩ ~ *vt* **1 :** to cause to glitter ⟨brilliant stars ~*ing* the sky⟩ **2 :** to trim, sprinkle, or cover with something that glitters ⟨a belt that was ~*ed* with rhinestones⟩

2glitter \"\ *n* -S **1 a :** glittering brilliancy ⟨a great ~ of sunlight on the blue water —Ira Wolfert⟩ **:** glittering showiness or gaudiness ⟨the ~ of opening night at the opera⟩ ⟨the ~ of costume jewelry⟩ **:** glittering brightness ⟨the ~ of icicles⟩ ⟨the unnerving ~ of a glass eye —Weston La Barre⟩ **b :** glittering attractiveness ⟨the ~ of a career in the foreign service⟩ **2 :** small glittering objects (as sequins, rhinestones) or tiny glittering bits (as of tinsel, glass) used for ornamentation ⟨a neckline trimmed with ~⟩ or decoration ⟨at the base of the Christmas tree was a snowy sheet sprinkled with ~⟩

glit·ter·ance \-ərən(t)s\ *n* -S [*1glitter* + *-ance*] **:** GLITTER

glittering *adj* [fr. pres. part. of *1glitter*] **1 :** that glitters: **a :** RESPLENDENT, BRILLIANT ⟨a ~ costume⟩ ⟨~ society⟩ **b :** SPARKLING, TWINKLING ⟨a ~ sky⟩ **c :** shining glassily with a play of shifting points of intense light ⟨feverish ~ eyes⟩ **d :** SHOWY, GAUDY ⟨~ ornaments⟩ **2 a :** brilliantly or compellingly attractive usu. in a superficial way ⟨a ~ personality⟩ **b :** superficially convincing in a smoothly misleading or deceptive way **:** misleadingly or deceptively appealing ⟨the ~ generalities of propaganda⟩ — **glit·ter·ing·ly** *adv*

glit·tery \-ərē, -ərī\ *adj* [*2glitter* + *-y*] **:** GLITTERING; *esp* **:** having much glitter ⟨~ chandeliers⟩

gli·wi·ce \gləˈvētsə\ *adj, usu cap* [fr. *Gliwice*, city in Poland] **:** of or from the city of Gliwice, Poland **:** of the kind or style prevalent in Gliwice

1gloam \ˈglōm\ *vi* -ED/-ING/-S [back-formation fr. *gloaming*] *chiefly Scot* **:** to become twilight **:** grow toward dark **:** become dusk

2gloam \"\ *n* -S *archaic* **:** TWILIGHT, DUSK

gloam·ing \ˈglōmiŋ, -mēn\ *n* -S [ME (Sc) *gloming*, fr. OE *glōmung*, fr. *glōm* twilight; akin to OE *glōwan* to glow — more at GLOW] **:** TWILIGHT, DUSK ⟨leaving the robin to sing in the ~ —C.G.Glover⟩

1gloat \ˈglōt, *usu* -ōd·+V\ *vi* -ED/-ING/-S [prob. of Scand origin; akin to ON *glotta* to grin scornfully, Sw *glutta* to peep; akin to MHG *glotzen* to stare wide-eyed, OE *geolu* yellow — more at YELLOW] **1** *obs* **a :** to look or gaze at something indirectly or furtively **b :** to look or gaze at something admiringly or affectionately **2 :** to look at, gaze at, or think about something with great self-satisfaction or intense often passionate gratification or gleefully triumphant joy ⟨a miser ~*ing* over his gold⟩ ⟨always ready to ~ over a new victory⟩ **:** linger over or dwell upon something with extreme often evil delight **:** REVEL ⟨a vision of demons ~*ing* over the tortures of the damned⟩ ⟨~*ing* over every detail of the murder⟩ **:** exult over something with intense often malicious pleasure ⟨~*ed* at his discomfiture⟩ ⟨used to make wax images of the vital organs of a hated person, and hold them over a fire, ~*ing* to see them drip —Emma Hawkridge⟩ **syn** see GAZE

2gloat \"\ *n* -S **1 a :** the act of gloating ⟨the accomplishments of a great hunter, told without ~, without passion —Robert Bean⟩ **b :** an outward indication of gloating ⟨to watch the ~ in his eye —John Galsworthy⟩ **2 :** a feeling of triumphant often malicious satisfaction or joy ⟨enjoying a ~ over his success⟩

gloat·ing·ly *adv* [*gloating* (pres. part. of *1gloat*) + *-ly*] **:** in a gloating manner ⟨spoke ~ of the number of people he had swindled⟩

glob \ˈgläb\ *n* -S [perh. blend of *globe* and *blob*] **1 a :** a small drop **:** GLOBULE, BLOB ⟨tiny ~s of mercury⟩ ⟨spattered ~s of ink⟩ **b :** a lumpish usu. rounded mass of usu. large size ⟨threw ~s of mud at them⟩ ⟨a ~ of rice⟩ ⟨heaped the shortcake with great ~s of whipped cream⟩ **2 :** a touch, smear, or splash esp. of paint ⟨warm and appetizing ~s of color on the otherwise bleak and functional walls —Irwin Shaw⟩

glob·al \ˈglōbəl\ *adj* **1 :** having the shape of a globe **:** SPHERICAL ⟨the earth is a ~ mass⟩ **2 a** (1) **:** of, relating to, or involving the entire world ⟨~ economic problems⟩ ⟨~ health conditions⟩ ⟨~ warfare⟩ (2) **:** including or adapted to the entire world ⟨~ plans for peace⟩ ⟨a ~ point of view⟩ ⟨~ strategy⟩ **:** not narrow or provincial **:** unrestricted in outlook or application **:** BROAD, UNIVERSAL ⟨a philosophy which takes a ~ view —Alan Gewirth⟩ (3) **:** distributed over or extending throughout the entire world **:** WORLDWIDE ⟨~ airlines⟩ ⟨a system of ~ communication⟩ **:** ranging over or around the entire world ⟨~ travelers⟩ ⟨~ bombers⟩ **b :** of, relating to, or involving the globe of the eye ⟨~ anesthesia in cataract surgery⟩ **3 a** (1) **:** COMPREHENSIVE, ALL-INCLUSIVE, GRAND ⟨the ~ total of national income in the U. S.⟩ **:** OVERALL, TOTAL ⟨limiting the ~ tonnage of that country's navy⟩ ⟨the ~ output of a factory⟩ (2) **:** 3BLANKET 1 ⟨a ~ allocation of funds⟩ (3) **:** exhaustively complete ⟨a catalog noted for its ~ coverage of new recordings⟩ **b** (1) **:** of, relating to, or constituting an organic whole **:** not divided into parts **:** not fractionalized **:** UNIFIED, ORGANISMIC ⟨the newer psychiatry seeks to understand in a ~ way the dynamic structure of the patient's personality —*Psychological Abstracts*⟩ **:** emphasizing a totality rather than the constitutive elements of a totality ⟨the ~ method of reading that aims at immediate recognition of whole words⟩ (2) **:** of, relating to, or consisting of similar or identical parts **:** HOMOGENEOUS ⟨a country trying to perfect a ~ form of social community⟩ (3) **:** not admitting a choice **:** solidly uniform **:** MONOLITHIC ⟨confronted with a ~ list of political candidates⟩ **c :** marked by absence of particularizing detail **:** simple and highly undifferentiated **:** GENERALIZED ⟨~ perceptions of the world outside the self⟩ ⟨the typically ~ nature of primitive art⟩ — **glob·al·ly** \-bəlē, -li\ *adv*

glob·al·ism \-bəˌlizəm\ *n* -S **1 :** GLOBALIZATION **2 :** a policy or system favoring or promoting globalization ⟨proponents of ~ as a means of safeguarding national security⟩

glob·al·ist \-ˌləst\ *n* -S **:** one that favors or advocates globalism

glo·bal·i·ty \glōˈbaləd·ē\ *n* -ES **:** the condition of being global ⟨the ~ of the war —Frank Gervasi⟩

glob·al·iza·tion \ˌglōbələˈzāshən, -ˌlīˈz-\ *n* -S **:** the act of globalizing or condition of being globalized

glob·al·ize \ˈ=ˌlīz\ *vt* -ED/-ING/-S **:** to make global; *esp* **:** to make worldwide in scope or application ⟨*globalizing* democracy —O.L.Reiser & Blodwen Davies⟩

glo·bate \ˈglōˌbāt\ *adj* [L *globatus*, past part. of *globare* to make into a ball, fr. *globus* ball] **:** GLOBULAR 1a

glo·bat·ed \-ˌād·əd\ *adj* [L *globatus* + E *-ed*] *archaic* **:** formed into a globe

glob·by \ˈgläbē\ *adj, usu* -ER/-EST [*glob* + *-y*] **:** full of globs ⟨the paint would not spread evenly and the finished product looked ~⟩

1globe \ˈglōb\ *n* -S [MF, fr. L *globus* — more at CLIP] **1 :** something that is spherical or rounded **:** SPHERE, BALL: as **a** (1) **:** a round typically hollow and metal ball that has a map of the earth drawn on it and that is usu. set so as to be rotatable at an angle corresponding to the inclination of the earth's axis ⟨rotated the terrestrial ~ until the crimson triangle of India was opposite their eyes —Aldous Huxley⟩ (2) **:** a similar ball that shows the configurations of the heavens (as the location and arrangement of the constellations) ⟨referring to a celestial ~ during the lecture⟩ **b :** PLANET ⟨still undiscovered ~s in space⟩; *esp* **:** EARTH — usu. used with *the* or *this* ⟨journeys over much of the ~ —R.A.Cordell⟩ ⟨every habitable part of this ~⟩ ⟨airglow appears to be present at all times and is distributed over the entire ~ —C.T.Elvey⟩ **c :** a golden ball carried by sovereigns as an emblem of authority **:** ORB 1c(3) ⟨His the scepter, crown, and ~ —P.B.Shelley⟩ **d :** a spherical or rounded typically glass vessel (as a fishbowl) or covering (as a lampshade) or housing (as an electric light bulb) **e :** EYEBALL **2 :** a closely massed group or compact body

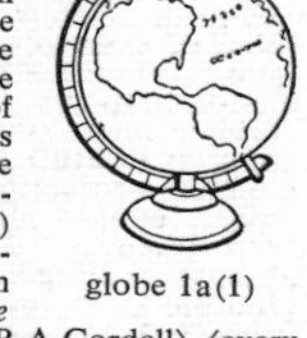

globe 1a(1)

2globe \"\ *vb* -ED/-ING/-S *vt, archaic* **:** to form into a globe ~ *vi, archaic* **:** to appear as a globe **:** take the form of a globe

globe amaranth *n* **:** an Indian herb (*Gomphrena globosa*) often cultivated for its globose flower heads that can be dried with nearly full retention of their color

globe animalcule *n* **:** an organism of the genus *Volvox*

globe artichoke *n* **:** ARTICHOKE 1, 2

globed *adj* [fr. past part. of *2globe*] **1 :** having the form of a globe ⟨the rocket burst into ~ masses of fire⟩ **2 :** provided with a globe ⟨~ lamps burning with a yellow glow⟩

globe daisy *n* **:** a plant of the genus *Globularia*

globefish \ˈ=ˌ=\ *n* **1 :** any of numerous chiefly tropical marine fishes forming the family Tetraodontidae of the order Plectognathi which can distend themselves to a globular form and float belly upward on the surface and most species of which are highly poisonous because of a powerful gastrointestinal irritant contained esp. in the skin and viscera — called also *balloonfish, puffer* **2 :** OCEAN SUNFISH

globeflower \ˈ=ˌ=\ *n* **:** a plant with globose flowers or flower clusters: as **a :** a plant of the genus *Trollius* with globose yellow flowers **b :** GLOBE DAISY **c :** BUTTONBUSH **d :** JAPANESE ROSE 1

globe joint *n* **:** BALL-AND-SOCKET JOINT

globe lichen *n* **:** a lichen having globular fruiting bodies

globe lightning *n* **:** BALL LIGHTNING

globe mallow *n* **:** a plant of the genus *Sphaeralcea*

globe sight *n* **:** a front sight (as for a rifle) consisting of a small ball or a disk with a hole in it placed on the top of a pin

globe thistle *n* **1 :** ARTICHOKE 1 **2 :** a plant of the genus *Echinops*

1globe–trot \ˈ=ˌ=\ *vi* [back-formation fr. *globe-trotter*] **:** to do globe-trotting ⟨an economical way to *globe-trot* —*Better Homes & Gardens*⟩

2globe–trot \"\ *n* **:** a globe-trotting journey ⟨nearing the end of a three-month *globe-trot* —*Time*⟩

globe–trotter \ˈ=ˌ=ˌ=\ *n* [*1globe* + *trotter*] **:** one that does globe-trotting esp. often or habitually ⟨a confirmed adventurer and *globe-trotter*⟩

¹globe–trotting \'ˌ=ˌ==\ *n* [¹*globe* + *trotting*, fr. gerund of *trot*, v.] **:** traveling about to many or widely separated countries esp. in a hurried or cursory manner and typically for the sake of sightseeing **:** traveling widely throughout the world ⟨travel bureaus that emphasize the joys of *globe-trotting*⟩

²globe–trotting \"\ *adj* **:** marked by, inclined toward, or given to globe-trotting ⟨long *globe-trotting* trips⟩ ⟨*globe-trotting* authors —Bennett Cerf⟩

globe tulip *n* **:** an herb of the genus *Calochortus*

globe valve *n* **:** a valve enclosed in a globular chamber

globical *adj* [¹*globe* + *-ical*] *obs* **:** GLOBULAR 1a

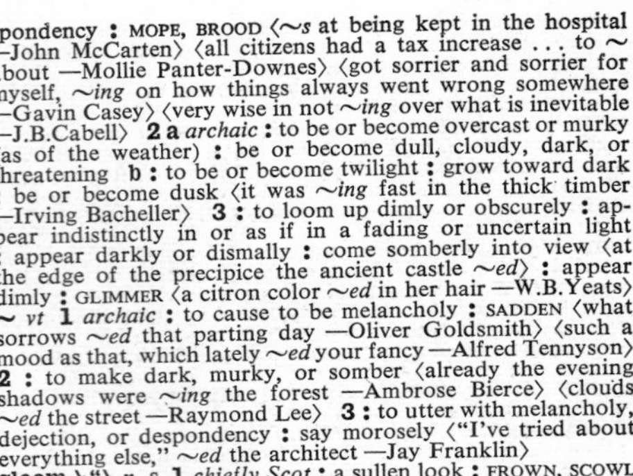

globe valve

glo·bi·ceph·a·la \ˌglōbə'sefələ\ *n, cap* [NL, fr. *globi-* (fr. L *globus* ball) + *-cephala* (fr. Gk *kephalē* head) — more at GLOBE, CEPHALIC] **:** a genus of rather small dark-colored toothed whales related to the grampus and killer whale and comprising the blackfish

glo·bid·i·al \(')glō¦bidēəl\ *adj* [NL *Globidium* + E *-al*] **:** of, relating to, or produced by parasites of the genus *Globidium* ⟨~ cysts⟩

glo·bid·i·o·sis \(ˌ)=ˌ=ē'ōsəs\ *n, pl* **globidio·ses** \-ōˌsēz\ [NL, fr. *Globidium* + *-osis*] **:** infection with or disease caused by parasites of the genus *Globidium*

glo·bid·i·um \glō'bidēəm\ *n, cap* [NL, fr. L *globus* ball + NL *-idium*] **:** a genus of microscopic parasites of the intestinal mucosa of herbivorous mammals that are commonly regarded as protozoans related to the Sarcosporidia, that form membranous cysts enclosing fusiform spores, and that sometimes produce severe symptoms of gastrointestinal disorder

glo·big·e·ri·na \(ˌ)glōˌbijə'rīnə, -rēnə\ *n* [NL, fr. *globi-* (fr. L *globus* ball) + *ger-* (fr. L *gerere* to carry, bear) + *-ina* — more at CAST] **1** *cap* **:** a genus (the type of the family Globigerinidae) of foraminifers having calcareous shells and living near the surface of the sea **2** *pl* **globigeri·nae** \-ī(ˌ)nē, -ēˌnī\ *also* **globigerinas a :** a foraminifer of the genus *Globigerina* **b :** the shell of a globigerina

glo·big·er·i·nal \=¦==¦rīnᵊl, -rēnᵊl\ *adj* [NL *Globigerina* + E *-al*] **:** GLOBIGERINE

globigerina ooze *n* **:** a layer of soft mud made up in large part of the shells of dead globigerinae and covering great areas of the sea bottom at depths of 1000 to 3000 feet

glo·big·er·ine \glō'bijəˌrīn, -rēn, -ˌrən\ *adj* [NL *Globigerina*] **:** of, relating to, or derived from *Globigerina* or globigerinae ⟨~ muds⟩

glo·bin \'glōbən\ *n* -s [ISV *glob-* (fr. L *globus* ball) + *-in*; orig. formed in G] **:** a colorless protein obtained by removal of heme from a hemoglobin or similar conjugated protein

globing *pres 3d sing of* GLOBE

globin zinc insulin *n* **:** a preparation for treating diabetes mellitus that contains insulin modified by the addition of zinc chloride and globin obtained from beef blood and is intermediate in duration of action between regular insulin and protamine zinc insulin

glo·bi·o·ceph·a·la \ˌglōbē(ˌ)ō'sefələ\ *or* **glo·bi·o·ceph·a·lus** \-ləs\ [NL, fr. *globi-* (fr. L *globus* ball) + *-o-* + *-cephala* (fr. Gk *kephalē* head) *or -cephalus*] *syn of* GLOBICEPHALA

globo- *comb form* [NL, fr. L *globus* ball] **1 a :** global **:** spherical ⟨*globo*cell⟩ **:** globular ⟨*globo*sphaerite⟩ — often joined to second element with a hyphen ⟨*globo*-cumulus⟩ **b :** world-wide ⟨*globo*-historical⟩ **2 :** globe **:** sphere ⟨*globo*ferous⟩

glo·boid \'glōˌbȯid\ *n or adj* [ISV *glob-* (fr. L *globus* ball) + *-oid*] **:** SPHEROID

glo·bose \'glōˌbōs, =¦=\ *adj* [L *globosus*, fr. *globus* + *-osus* -ose] **:** GLOBULAR 1a — **glo·bose·ly** *adv*

glo·bos·i·ty \glō'bäsəd·ē\ *n* -ES [LL *globositat-, globositas*, fr. L *globosus* globose + *-itat-, -itas* -ity] **:** the quality or state of being globose ⟨the ~ of the earth⟩

glo·bous \'glōbəs\ *adj* [obs. F or L; obs. F *globeux*, fr. L *globosus*] *archaic* **:** GLOBULAR 1a

globs *pl of* GLOB

glob·u·lar \'gläbyələ(r)\ *adj* [L *globulus* globule + E *-ar*] **1 a :** having the shape of a globe or globule **:** round like a ball **:** wholly or approximately spherical **:** GLOBOSE ⟨little ~ houses, like mud-wasp nests —Zane Grey⟩ **b :** fully rounded out **:** having nothing lacking **:** WHOLE, ENTIRE ⟨for the sake of ~ completeness —H.J.Mackinder⟩ **c :** worldwide in extent or range **:** GLOBAL ⟨~ air travel⟩ **2 :** having globules **:** made up of globules ⟨~ masses of fish eggs⟩ — **glob·u·lar·ly** *adv* — **glob·u·lar·ness** *n* -ES

globular chart *n* **:** a chart made on the globular projection

globular cluster *n* **:** a cluster of stars, galaxies, or supergalaxies that is usu. approximately spherical with compactness apparently increasing toward the center

glob·u·lar·ia \ˌgläbyə'la(a)rēə\ *n, cap* [NL, fr. L *globulus* + NL *-aria*] **:** a genus (the type of the family Globulariaceae) of European herbs or shrubs with blue flowers in globose heads

glob·u·lar·i·a·ce·ae \-ˌla(a)rē'āsēˌē\ *n pl, cap* [NL, fr. *Globularia*, type genus + *-aceae*] **:** a family of perennial herbs or small heathlike shrubs of the order Polemoniales with obovate entire often radical leaves and flowers in dense usu. globular heads — **glob·u·lar·i·a·ceous** \¦==ˌ==¦āshəs\ *adj*

glob·u·lar·i·ty \ˌgläbyə'larəd·ē\ *n* -ES **:** the quality or state of being globular ⟨the ~ of the planets⟩

globular lightning *n* **:** BALL LIGHTNING

globular projection *n* **:** a perspective projection of a hemisphere upon a plane parallel to its base sometimes used in cartography

globular sailing *n* **:** SPHERICAL SAILING

glob·ule \'gläˌbyül\ *n* -s [F, fr. L *globulus*, dimin. of *globus* globe] **1 :** a small often minute spherical mass (as of a liquid or semiliquid substance) **:** a small globular body (as a drop of water or a bead of sweat) **:** a tiny globe or ball ⟨~s of mercury⟩ ⟨~s of fat⟩; *specif* **:** a small spherical pill of compressed sugar usu. saturated with an alcoholic tincture and used in homeopathy **2 :** the male reproductive organ of a plant of the family Characeae

glob·u·let \'gläbyələt\ *n* -s [*globule* + *-et*] **:** a very small globule ⟨~s of water shone on her taut young skin —G.A. Wagner⟩

glob·u·lif·er·ous \¦==¦lif(ə)rəs\ *adj* [*globule* + *-iferous*] **:** SPHERULITIC

glob·u·lin \'gläbyələn\ *n* -s [ISV *globul-* (fr. L *globulus* globule) + *-in*] **:** any of a class of simple proteins (as myosin, edestin, gamma globulin) that are characterized by their almost complete insolubility in pure water or usu. in half-saturated ammonium sulfate or sodium sulfate solutions and by their solubility in dilute salt solutions, that are coagulable by heat, and that occur widely in plant and animal tissues (as blood plasma or serum); *specif* **:** SERUM GLOBULIN — see EUGLOBULIN, PSEUDOGLOBULIN

glob·u·lite \-ˌlīt\ *n* -s [F, fr. *globule* + *-ite*] **:** a tiny globular body of mineral crystallite — **glob·u·lit·ic** \¦==¦lid·ik\ *adj*

glob·u·lous \'gläbyələs\ *adj* [F *globuleux*, fr. *globule* + *-eux* -ous] **:** GLOBULAR

glo·bus hys·ter·i·cus \¦glōbəs·hə'sterəkəs\ *n* [NL, lit., hysteric ball] **:** a choking sensation (as of a lump in the throat) commonly experienced in hysteria

globus pal·li·dus \-'palədəs\ *n* [NL, lit., pale globe] **:** the median portion of the lenticular nucleus consisting chiefly of large bulliform cells

globy \'glōbē\ *adj* [¹*globe* + *-y*] *archaic* **:** GLOBULAR

glo·chid \'glōkəd\ *n* -s [NL *glochidium*] **:** GLOCHIDIUM 1

glo·chid·e·ous \glō'kidēəs\ *adj* [NL *glochidium* + E *-eous*] **:** GLOCHIDIATE

glo·chid·i·al \-ēəl\ *adj* [NL *glochidium* + E *-al*] **:** of or relating to glochidia

glo·chid·i·ate \-ēət, -ēˌāt\ *adj* [NL *glochidium* + E *-ate*] **1 :** having glochidia **2 :** having barbed tips ⟨~ leaves⟩

glo·chid·i·um \-ēəm\ *n, pl* **glochid·ia** \-ēə\ [NL, fr. Gk *glōchis* projecting point + NL *-idium* — more at GLOSS (explanation)] **1 :** a barbed hair or spine (as on the massulae of a water fern or on some cacti) **2 :** a larval freshwater mussel of the family Unionidae that hatches in the gill cavity of the parent mussel, is subsequently discharged into the water, and attaches itself as an external parasite to the gills or fins or other parts of fish

glo·chis \'glōkəs\ *n, pl* **glochi·nes** \glō'kī(ˌ)nēz\ [NL *glochin-, glochis*, fr. Gk *glōchin-, glōchis* projecting point] **:** GLOCHIDIUM 1

glock·en·spiel \'gläkənˌs(h)pēl\ *n* -s [G, fr. *glocke* bell (fr. OHG *glocka*, of Celt origin; akin to MIr *clocc*) + *spiel* play, fr. OHG *spil* — more at CLOCK, SPIEL] **1 :** CARILLON **2 a :** a percussion musical instrument consisting of a series of graduated metal bars tuned to the chromatic scale and played with two hammers **b :** any of various similar instruments with tubes or bells instead of bars **3 :** a pipe-organ percussion stop that imitates the tone quality of the glockenspiel

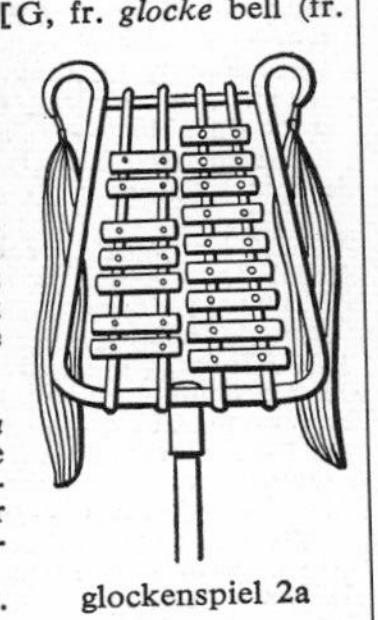

glockenspiel 2a

glode *archaic past of* GLIDE

gloea \'glēə\ *n* -s [NL, fr. LGk *gloia* glue; akin to L *glut-, glus* glue — more at CLAY] **:** an adhesive mucoid substance that some protozoans and other low organisms secrete about themselves — **gloe·al** \-əl\ *adj*

gloeo- *or* **gloio-** *comb form* [NL, fr. Gk *gloio-*, fr. *gloios* glutinous substance, gum; akin to L *glut-, glus* glue] **:** sticky **:** glutinous ⟨*Gloeo*capsa⟩ ⟨*Gloio*peltis⟩

gloe·o·cap·sa \ˌglēō'kapsə\ *n, cap* [NL, fr. *gloeo-* + L *capsa* case — more at CASE (box)] **:** a genus of unicellular blue-green algae (family Chroococcaceae) inhabiting both fresh and salt water, colonies of some species forming a characteristic dull bluish green film on damp soil (as in tropical greenhouses)

gloe·o·din·i·um \-'dinēəm\ *n, cap* [NL, fr. *gloeo-* + *din-* (fr. Gk *dinos* rotation, whirling, whirlpool) + *-ium* — more at DINO-] **:** a genus of subspherical greenish brown freshwater algae (order Dinocapsales) that form compact colonies within homogeneous or stratified envelopes

gloe·o·spo·ri·um \-'spōrēəm\ *n, cap* [NL, fr. *gloeo-* + *-sporium*] **:** a form genus of several hundred imperfect fungi (family Melanconiaceae) having no setae around the acervuli and often causing anthracnoses of cultivated plants — compare COLLETOTRICHUM

gloff \'gläf\ *n* -s [origin unknown] *Scot* **:** a sudden fright **:** SCARE

glo·ger's rule \'glōgə(r)z-\ *n, usu cap G* [after C. W. L. *Gloger* †1863 Ger. zoologist] **:** a statement in zoology: within a species of warm-blooded animals the degree of melanin pigmentation tends to vary directly with the mean environmental temperature

glogg \'glu̇g, 'gləg\ *n* -s [Sw *glögg*, fr. *glödga* to burn, mull, fr. OSw, fr. *glödhoger*, adj., glowing, fr. *glöth* ember, glowing coal; akin to OE *glēd* ember, glowing coal — more at GLEED] **:** a Swedish hot punch served usu. as a Christmas drink and made from a sweetened highly spiced mixture of wines and whiskey or brandy and containing almonds, raisins, and usu. orange peel

gloi·o·pel·tis \ˌglȯiō'peltəs\ *n, cap* [NL, fr. *gloeo-* + *-peltis* (prob. fr. Gk *peltē* small shield); prob. akin to L *pellis* skin — more at FELL (skin)] **:** a small genus of red algae closely related to *Gloiosiphonia* and furnishing a glue — see FUNORI, GLUE PLANT

gloi·o·si·pho·nia \-ōˌsī'fōnēə\ *n, cap* [NL, fr. *gloeo-* + L *siphon-, sipho* siphon, tube + NL *-ia* — more at SIPHON] **:** a small genus (the type of the family Gloiosiphoniaceae) of gelatinous red algae of the order Cryptonemiales — compare GLOIOPELTIS

¹glom \'gläm, -ö-\ *vt* **glommed; glommed; glomming; gloms** [prob. alter. of *glaum*] **1** *slang* **:** STEAL ⟨*glommed* a pile of money⟩ **2** *slang* **:** SEIZE, CATCH; *specif* **:** ARREST ⟨*glommed* the thugs⟩ — **glom on to 1** *slang* **:** to grab hold of **:** take possession of **:** appropriate to oneself ⟨she *glommed on to* every cent I'd saved —John McPartland⟩ **2** *slang* **:** to catch on to **:** UNDERSTAND ⟨*glomming on to* an idea⟩

²glom \"\ *vt* **glommed; glommed; glomming; gloms** [origin unknown] *slang* **:** to take a look at ⟨*glommed* her as she walked by⟩

³glom \"\ *n* -s *slang* **:** LOOK, VIEW ⟨got a good ~ at them⟩

glo·mal \'glōməl\ *adj* [NL *glomus* + E *-al*] **:** of or relating to a glomus

glome \'glōm\ *n* -s [L *glomus* ball, clew] **1** *archaic* **:** the center on which something is or is felt to be wound ⟨this is your last hour, this the butt, the ~ of all your days —Llewelyn Powys⟩ **2 :** a prominent rounded part of the frog of a horse's hoof on each side of the cleft

¹glom·er·ate \'gläməˌrāt, *usu* -ād·+V\ *vb* -ED/-ING/-S [L *glomeratus*, past part. of *glomerare* to form into a ball, fr. *glomer-, glomus* ball — more at CLAM (clamp)] **:** AGGLOMERATE, CONGLOMERATE — **glom·er·a·tion** \¦==¦rāshən\ *n* -s

²glom·er·ate \-mərət, -məˌrāt, *usu* ¦d+V\ *adj* [L *glomeratus*] **:** AGGLOMERATE, CONGLOMERATE

glom·er·el·la \ˌglämə'relə\ *n, cap* [NL, fr. L *glomer-, glomus* ball + NL *-ella*] **:** a genus of fungi closely related to *Gnomonia* and characterized by one-celled hyaline ascospores in rostrate perithecia borne in or on a stroma — see BITTER ROT, COTTON ANTHRACNOSE

glomerul- *or* **glomerulo-** *comb form* [NL, fr. *glomerulus*] **:** glomerulus of the kidney ⟨*glomerul*ar⟩ ⟨*glomerulo*nephritis⟩

glo·mer·u·lar \glä'mer(y)ələ(r), glə'-\ *adj* **:** of, relating to, or produced by a glomerulus ⟨~ nephritis⟩ ⟨~ filtration⟩

glo·mer·u·late \-lət, -ˌlāt\ *adj* [prob. fr. (assumed) NL *glomerulatus*, fr. *glomerulus* + L *-atus* -ate] **1 :** arranged in small compact clusters ⟨~ inflorescences⟩ ⟨~ capillaries⟩ **2 :** having glomeruli ⟨a ~ organ of the body⟩

glom·er·ule \'gläməˌrül, -ərˌyül\ *n* -s [NL *glomerulus*] **1 :** a compacted or sessile cyme (as of a boxtree) that resembles the flower head of a composite **2 :** GLOMERULUS

glo·mer·u·lo·nephritis \glä¦mer(y)ə(ˌ)lō+, glə¦-\ *n* [NL, fr. *glomerul-* + *nephritis*] **:** nephritis marked by inflammation of the capillaries of the renal glomeruli caused by toxins from infectious processes elsewhere in the body and accompanied by changes in other renal structures and by edema, albuminuria, and other symptoms

glo·mer·u·lo·sa \gläˌmer(y)ə'lōsə, glə-, -ōzə\ *n, pl* **glo·merulo·sae** \-ˌsē, -ˌzē, ¦ī\ [NL, fr. fem. of *glomerulosus* glomerulose] **:** a narrow outer zone of columnar cells arranged in loops and ovoids in the adrenal gland — called also *zona glomerulosa* — **glo·mer·u·lo·sal** \=¦==¦=səl, -zəl\ *adj*

glo·mer·u·lo·sclerosis \glä¦mer(y)ə(ˌ)lō+, glə¦-\ *n* [NL, fr. *glomerul-* + *sclerosis*] **:** nephrosclerosis involving the glomeruli

glo·mer·u·lose \=¦==ˌlōs\ *adj* [prob. fr. NL *glomerulosus*, fr. *glomerulus* + L *-osus* -ose] **:** GLOMERULATE 1

glo·mer·u·lus \-ləs\ *n, pl* **glomeru·li** \-ˌlī, -ˌlē\ [NL, glomerulus, glomerule, fr. L *glomer-, glomus* ball + NL *-ulus*] **:** a small convoluted or intertwined mass (as of organisms, nerve fibers, or capillaries): as **a :** a tuft of capillaries that is covered by epithelium, is situated at the point of origin of each vertebrate nephron, and normally passes a protein-free filtrate from the blood into the proximal convoluted tubule **b :** the convoluted secretory part of a sweat gland **c :** a dense entanglement of nerve fibers situated in the olfactory bulb and containing the primary synapses of the olfactory pathway **d :** a compact body of terminal fibers of neurons within an insect nerve center

glo·mus \'glōməs\ *n, pl* **glom·era** \'glämərə\ *also* **glo·mi** \'glōˌmī, -ˌmē\ [NL, fr. L *glomer-, glomus* ball] **1 :** a small arteriovenous anastomosis together with its supporting structures: as **a :** a vascular tuft that suggests a renal glomerulus and that develops from the embryonic aorta in relation to the pronephros **b** *or* **glomus caroticum** \-kə'rädəkəm\ **:** CAROTID BODY **c :** a tuft of the choroid plexus protruding into each lateral ventricle of the brain

¹gloom \'glüm\ *vb* -ED/-ING/-S [ME *gloumen, gloumben*; akin to MHG *beglūmen* to make turbid, deceive, Norw dial. *glome* to stare somberly and suspiciously, OSw *glūna* to look askance, OE *geolu* yellow — more at YELLOW] *vi* **1 a :** to be, look, or act sullen, displeased, or annoyed **:** FROWN, LOWER, SCOWL, GLOWER ⟨~ing over his coffee at the way he had been tricked⟩ **b :** to be, look, or act low in spirits **:** feel or show dejection or cheerlessness **:** feel or show melancholy or despondency **:** MOPE, BROOD ⟨~s at being kept in the hospital —John McCarten⟩ ⟨all citizens had a tax increase . . . to ~ about —Mollie Panter-Downes⟩ ⟨got sorrier and sorrier for myself, ~ing on how things always went wrong somewhere —Gavin Casey⟩ ⟨very wise in not ~ing over what is inevitable —J.B.Cabell⟩ **2 a** *archaic* **:** to be or become overcast or murky (as of the weather) **:** be or become dull, cloudy, dark, or threatening **b :** to be or become twilight **:** grow toward dark **:** be or become dusk ⟨it was ~ing fast in the thick timber —Irving Bacheller⟩ **3 :** to loom up dimly or obscurely **:** appear indistinctly in or as if in a fading or uncertain light **:** appear darkly or dismally **:** come somberly into view ⟨at the edge of the precipice the ancient castle ~ed⟩ **:** appear dimly **:** GLIMMER ⟨a citron color ~ed in her hair —W.B.Yeats⟩ ~ *vt* **1** *archaic* **:** to cause to be melancholy **:** SADDEN ⟨what sorrows ~ed that parting day —Oliver Goldsmith⟩ ⟨such a mood as that, which lately ~ed your fancy —Alfred Tennyson⟩ **2 :** to make dark, murky, or somber ⟨already the evening shadows were ~ing the forest —Ambrose Bierce⟩ ⟨clouds ~ed the street —Raymond Lee⟩ **3 :** to utter with melancholy, dejection, or despondency **:** say morosely ⟨"I've tried about everything else," ~ed the architect —Jay Franklin⟩

²gloom \"\ *n* -s **1** *chiefly Scot* **:** a sullen look **:** FROWN, SCOWL **2 a :** partial or total darkness ⟨the ~ of the night⟩ ⟨difficult for the most practiced eye to pierce far into the ~ —J.L. Motley⟩ **:** glimmering obscurity **:** DIMNESS ⟨the cool ~ of the cathedral⟩ ⟨the light coming through the windows set high in the walls had darkened to the sudden ~ of the summer storm —Mary Deasy⟩ **:** deep shadowiness or shadiness ⟨resting for a moment in the quiet ~ of the forest⟩; *esp* **:** a dismally depressing darkness or murkiness ⟨a raw and detestable winter day and the ~ and noise of the huge town oppressed the soul —Leonard Bacon⟩ **b :** a partially or totally darkened place, spot, or region ⟨in this Italian glare I pine for the ~s of London —Aldous Huxley⟩ **:** a shadowy or shady place ⟨within the green ~s of the shadowy oak —J.R.Lowell⟩ **3 a :** a state of melancholy or depression **:** lowness of spirits **:** DEJECTION, DESPONDENCY ⟨the results of the Rome meeting were rather inconclusive and discouraging as the delegates departed in ~ —S.B.Fay⟩ **b :** an appearance or atmosphere of melancholy and despondency ⟨constant repinings at the dullness of everything around them threw a real ~ over their domestic circle —Jane Austen⟩ **4 :** one who is depressingly melancholy ⟨I'd have been a ~ in all that commencement gaiety —Mark Reed⟩ **:** KILLJOY ⟨a set of ~s called censors —H.C.Witwer⟩ **syn** see SADNESS

gloom·ful \-fəl\ *adj, archaic* **:** GLOOMY

gloom·i·ly \-məlē, -li\ *adv* **:** in a gloomy manner ⟨~ staring at nothing —G.G.Carter⟩

gloom·i·ness \-mēnəs, -min-\ *n* -ES **:** the quality or state of being gloomy ⟨hating ~ like the plague⟩

¹glooming [fr. pres. part. of ¹*gloom*] *adj* **:** dimly glimmering **:** DARK, GLOOMY ⟨the ~ interior of an old inn⟩ — **glooming·ly** *adv*

²gloom·ing \'glümiŋ, -mēŋ\ *n* -s [prob. fr. gerund of ¹*gloom*] *archaic* **:** GLOAMING

gloom·less \-mləs\ *adj* **:** devoid of gloom ⟨~ joy⟩

glooms \'glümz\ *n pl* [pl. of ²*gloom*] **:** BLUES 1 — usu. used with *the* ⟨the sick morning ~ of debauchees —George Eliot⟩

gloomy \'glümē, -mi\ *adj, usu* -ER/-EST [¹*gloom* + *-y*] **1 a :** full of gloom **:** partially or totally dark ⟨the ~ night⟩ **:** SHADOWY ⟨the ~ center of the forest⟩ **:** dimly or murkily glimmering ⟨the ~ depths of the lake⟩; *esp* **:** dismally and depressingly dark ⟨~ weather⟩ ⟨oppressed by the squalor of the ~ tenements⟩ **b :** having an appearance of gloom **:** having a frowning or scowling appearance ⟨~ sullen savages⟩ **:** FORBIDDING, BLACK-BROWED ⟨tried to avoid the ~ stare of his wife⟩ **c :** low in spirits **:** MELANCHOLY, DOWNCAST, DEJECTED ⟨~ at the thought of what they had to face⟩ **2 :** causing gloom **:** DEPRESSING ⟨a sordid ~ story⟩ **:** devoid of brightness, color, and joy **:** SOMBER, DREARY ⟨a ~ landscape⟩ **:** DISHEARTENING, CHEERLESS ⟨a ~ report on the spread of crime⟩ **:** marked by little or no hopefulness **:** DESPONDENT, PESSIMISTIC ⟨contrary predictions are being made, some ~, some optimistic —J.T. Farrell⟩ **syn** see DARK, SULLEN

glop·pen \'gläpən\ *vt* -ED/-ING/-S [ME *glopnen*, fr. ON *glūpna* to be surprised, frightened, or downcast; akin to Sw dial. *glūpa* to gape, swallow, OFris *glūpa* to look, MLG *glūpen* to look with half-closed eyes, and perh. to OE *geolu* yellow — more at YELLOW] *now dial Eng* **:** SURPRISE, ALARM, ASTONISH

glore \'glō(ə)r\ *vi* -ED/-ING/-S [ME *gloren*, prob. of Scand origin; akin to ON *eldsglōr* glow of fire, Icel *glóra* to stare, gleam, Norw *glore* to gleam, glitter, Sw dial. *glora* to shine faintly; akin to MD *gloren* to gleam, Gk *chlōros* greenish yellow — more at YELLOW] *dial Eng* **:** to look fixedly **:** STARE

glo·ria \'glōrēə, -ȯr-\ *n* -s [LL, fr. L, glory] **1** *often cap* **:** a Christian doxology sung or recited in liturgies and worship services **2** [prob. fr. It, lit., glory, fr. L] **a :** AUREOLE 2, NIMBUS **b :** a representation (as in a painting) of dazzling light bursting from the opened heavens **3** [prob. fr. Sp, lit., glory, fr. L] **:** a lightweight closely-woven fabric usu. in plain weave made orig. with silk warp and a worsted or cotton filling and used chiefly for umbrellas or dresses

glo·ri·a·tion \ˌ==ˈāshən\ *n* -s [L *gloriation-, gloriatio*, fr. *gloriatus* (past part. of *gloriari* to boast, glory, fr. *gloria*, n., glory) + *-ion-, -io* -ion] *archaic* **:** the action of glorying

gloried *past of* GLORY

glories *pres 3d sing of* GLORY, *pl of* GLORY

glo·ri·fi·ca·tion \ˌglōrəfə'kāshən, -ȯr-\ *n* -s [LL *glorification-, glorificatio*, fr. *glorificatus* (past part. of *glorificare* to glorify) + L *-ion-, -io* -ion] **:** the act of glorifying or the state of being glorified

glo·ri·fi·er \'==ˌfī(ə)r, -īə\ *n* -s **:** one that glorifies

glo·ri·fy \-ˌfī\ *vb* -ED/-ING/-ES [ME *glorifien*, fr. MF *glorifier*, fr. LL *glorificare*, fr. L *gloria* glory + *-ficare* -fy] *vt* **1 a** (1) **:** to make glorious **:** surround with glory **:** secure honor, praise, or admiration for ⟨~ing the achievements of the nation⟩ (2) **:** to exalt to a state of glory; *esp* **:** to exalt to the glory of heaven ⟨Jesus was not yet *glorified* —Jn 7:39 (RSV)⟩ **b :** to throw a resplendent light upon **:** make splendid with light **:** light up brilliantly ⟨sparkling chandeliers *glorified* the entire room⟩ **c :** to cause to have great beauty, charm, or appeal ⟨a book that *glorifies* the apparently trivial incidents of everyday life⟩; *esp* **:** to cause to be or seem to be in some way superior to what would be or is the actual condition of the thing so acted upon ⟨a recipe for ~ing pancakes⟩ **d :** to express hearty approval of **:** engage in praise of **:** EXTOL ⟨~ing everything they did without exception⟩ **2 :** to give worshipful praise, honor, and thanksgiving to ⟨~ing God for all their blessings⟩ **3** *archaic* **:** VAUNT ~ *vi, obs* **:** GLORY

glo·ri·ole \-rēˌōl\ *n* -s [prob. blend of *glory* and *aureole*] **:** AUREOLE 2

glo·ri·o·sa \ˌglōrē'ōsə, -ȯr-, -'ōzə\ *n* [NL, fr. L, fem. of *gloriosus* glorious] **1** *cap* **:** a genus of tropical African and Asiatic climbing tuberous herbs (family Liliaceae) with flowers that are red or yellow and that resemble typical lilies **2** -s **:** any plant of the genus *Gloriosa* — called also *climbing lily*

glo·ri·ous \'glōrēəs, -ȯr-\ *adj* [ME, glorious, vainglorious, fr. MF & L; MF *glorieus, glorios* glorious, fr. L *gloriosus* glorious, vainglorious, fr. L *gloria* glory, vainglory + *-osus* -ose] **1 a :** possessing or deserving glory **:** ILLUSTRIOUS, PRAISEWORTHY ⟨a country that is ~ in the wealth of its literature⟩ ⟨a long and ~ career of service⟩ **b :** conferring or entitling to glory ⟨a struggle that was ~ to all that took part in it⟩ **2 :** marked by great beauty or splendor **:** RESPLENDENT, MAGNIFICENT ⟨a ~ spring morning⟩ ⟨a ~ work of art⟩ **3** *obs* **:** VAINGLORIOUS **4 :** extremely pleasant **:** WONDERFUL **:** intensely delightful **:** highly enjoyable ⟨enjoyed a ~ weekend⟩ **5** *archaic* **:** hilariously drunk **syn** see SPLENDID

glo·ri·ous·ly *adv* [ME, fr. *glorious* + *-ly*] **:** in a glorious manner

glo·ri·ous·ness *n* -ES [ME *gloriousnesse*, fr. *glorious* + *-nesse* -ness] **:** the quality or state of being glorious

¹glo·ry \'glōrē, -ȯrē, -ri\ *n* -ES [ME *glorie* glory, vainglory, fr. MF & L; MF *glorie, gloire* glory, fr. L *gloria* glory, vainglory] **1** *obs* **:** VAINGLORY **2 a :** lofty praise, honor, or admiration extended by common consent **:** high renown ⟨the ~ and riches they expect may never come —R.L.Stevenson⟩ **b :** worshipful praise, honor, and thanksgiving ⟨giving ~ to God⟩ **3 a :** something that merits or secures lofty praise, honor, or admiration ⟨the ~ of a brilliant career⟩ : a cause for or occasion of jubilant pride and boasting ⟨her children were a ~ to her⟩ : a source of intense joy or satisfaction ⟨pianissimos that were a ~ to hear —Winthrop Sargeant⟩ **b** : a highly distinguished, splendid, or renowned quality, attribute, possession, or action ⟨a place to visit . . . for the sake of its ancient *glories* —John Buchan⟩ : a resplendent asset or ornamentation ⟨the intellectual *glories* of the time —H.O.Taylor⟩ ⟨a ~ to the medical profession —Carson McCullers⟩ **4 a** (1) : great beauty or splendor : RESPLENDENCE, MAGNIFICENCE ⟨the grandeur of the wild wintry seas is matched only by the ~ of the summer combination of blue sea, golden-sanded bay, and purple cliffs —L.D.Stamp⟩ (2) : something marked by great beauty or resplendence ⟨a grand, red, rosy, crimson day — a perfect ~ of a day —John Muir †1914⟩ **b** : the splendor and beatific happiness of heaven : eternal life in heaven ⟨thou dost guide me with thy counsel, and afterward thou wilt receive me to ~ —Ps 73:24 (RSV)⟩; *broadly* : ETERNITY **5** : a condition of supreme exaltation or splendor ⟨an epoch of ~ for all the arts⟩ : a state of unhindered gratification, self-satisfaction, or enjoyment ⟨when he's teaching, he's in his ~⟩ : height of prosperity, power, or achievement ⟨ancient Greece in its ~⟩ **6 a** : a ring of light: as (1) : AUREOLE, NIMBUS (2) : CORONA 2a (3) : the head portion of a Brocken specter (4) : a set of concentric colored rings of light (as often surrounding the head portion of a Brocken specter) **b** : an emanation or play of light : a luminous glow : RADIANCE ⟨the dying *glories* of evening —George Meredith⟩ : a soft brightness ⟨wild flowers made a ~ on the hillside —Edith Hamilton⟩ **c** (1) : a dazzling illumination : a burst or blaze of blindingly bright light ⟨rockets rushed upward in a complete fiery encirclement and burst into ~ against the night sky —L.C.Stevens⟩; *specif* : a representation (as in a painting) of dazzling light bursting from the opened heavens (2) : SHEKINAH **syn** see FAME

²**glory** \ˈ"\ *vb* -ED/-ING/-ES [ME *glorien*, fr. L *gloriari* to boast, glory, fr. *gloria*, n.] *vi* **1 a** : to rejoice proudly : EXULT ⟨~*ing* in their strength⟩ ⟨*gloried* in their country's success⟩ **b** : to experience intense delight or self-satisfaction : REVEL ⟨~*ing* in this unaccustomed independence, she told herself that she intended . . . to have a wonderful time —Aurelia Levi⟩ **2** *obs* : BOAST **3** *archaic* : to shine radiantly or brilliantly ⟨a low sea sunset ~*ing* around her hair —Alfred Tennyson⟩ ~ *vt, archaic* : to give glory to : make glorious

³**glory** \ˈ"\ *or* **glory be** \ˌ==ˈ=\ *interj* [*glory* fr. ¹*glory*; *glory be* fr. ¹*glory* + *be*, 3d pers. sing. pres. subj. of *be*, v.; fr. the use of the words "glory" or "glory be" at the beginning of doxologies] — used to express surprise, wonder, or delight

glory-bower \ˈ==ˌ=\ *n* : a vine of the genus *Clerodendron*

glory-bush \ˈ==ˌ=\ *n* : TIBOUCHINA 2; *esp* : a Brazilian spiderflower (*Tibouchina semidecandra*) that is widely grown in warm regions for its terminal clusters of large purple flowers with conspicuous yellow anthers on crooked filaments

glory-flower \ˈ==ˌ=\ *n* : GLORY PEA

glory hole *n* **1 a** : a furnace for softening glass when it becomes stiff in offhand working and for fire-polishing glass **b** : an opening directly into the interior of such a furnace; *specif* : BOTTOMING HOLE **2** : a receptacle (as a box or cupboard) or area into which odds and ends are put haphazardly and in no particular order **3 a** : LAZARETTO 3 **b** : the quarters of stewards or stokers on board a ship **4** : an opencut or funnel-shaped excavation formed by drawing off soft or broken ore through an underground passage — called also *mill hole*

glory-lily \ˈ==ˈ==\ *n* : GLORIOSA 2

glory-of-the-snow \ˈ====ˈ=\ *n, pl* **glory-of-the-snows** : any of several hardy spring-flowering Old World bulbous herbs of the genus *Chionodoxa*; *esp* : a widely cultivated plant (*C. luciliae*) with intensely blue white-centered or occas. pink or solid-white flowers

glory-of-the-sun \ˈ====ˈ=\ *n, pl* **glory-of-the-suns** : a small bulbous scapose Chilean perennial herb (*Leucocoryne ixioides*) of the family Amaryllidaceae often cultivated for its lavender flowers that are borne in few-flowered umbels and have an involucre of two linear bracts

glory pea *n* : either of two clianthuses that are sometimes cultivated in warm climates for their racemes of large predominantly bright red flowers: **a** : STURT'S DESERT PEA **b** : KAKA BILL

glose \ˈglōz\ *archaic var of* GLOZE

¹**gloss** \ˈgläs, -ȯ-\ *n* -ES [prob. of Scand origin; akin to Icel *glossi* flame, spark, *glossa* to glow, flame, Norw dial. *glosa* to glow; akin to MHG *glosen* to glow, OE *geolu* yellow — more at YELLOW] **1** : a superficial soft glowing luster or glistening brightness : a smooth soft surface shininess ⟨the ~ of satin⟩ ⟨the yellowish ~ of old ivory —Willard Robertson⟩ : SLEEKNESS ⟨brushed the dog's coat to a beautiful ~⟩ **2 a** [prob. influenced in meaning by ³*gloss* and ¹*gloze*] : something (as a motive alleged) designed to veil or hide what would otherwise be objected to : a plausible pretext : SHOW, PRETENSE, SEMBLANCE, DODGE, EXCUSE ⟨giving national aggrandizement the ~ of moral sanction⟩ **b** : a deceptively attractive external appearance ⟨selfishness that had a ~ of humanitarianism about it⟩

²**gloss** \ˈ"\ *vt* -ED/-ING/-ES **1 a** : to give a deceptively attractive external appearance to : WHITEWASH : make appear right or acceptable (as by minimizing or playing down obviously objectionable features) — usu. used with *over* ⟨endeavored to ~ the matter over —Dorothy Sayers⟩ ⟨no attempt is made to ~ over discreditable behavior —Philip Friedman⟩ **b** : to veil or hide (something that would otherwise be objected to or to prove a source of difficulty) by some plausible pretext, subterfuge, pretense, or excuse — usu. used with *over* ⟨not wish to ~ over the fragmentary state of our present knowledge —A.S.Eddington⟩ ⟨a tendency to ~ over inadequacies in the data with generalizations —R.M.Adams⟩ **2** : to give a soft glowing luster or glistening brightness to : make glossy ⟨the tarred road was ~*ed* by the noonday sun⟩ ⟨feathers that were ~*ed* by much preening⟩ **syn** see PALLIATE

³**gloss** \ˈ"\ *n* -ES [alter. (influenced by L *glossa*) of *gloze*, fr. ME *glose*, fr. OF, fr. ML *glosa*, alter. of L *glossa* difficult word requiring explanation, fr. Gk *glōssa* difficult word requiring explanation, language, tongue; akin to Gk *glōchin-*, *glōchis* projecting point and perh. to OSlav *glogŭ* thorn] **1 a** (1) : a brief explanation or a translation or definition (as one appearing in the margin or between the lines of a text or in a wordbook based on the text) of a textual word or expression felt to be difficult or obscure (2) : an expanded interpretation of or commentary on a textual word or expression (3) : a usu. willfully misleading or otherwise false explanation or interpretation of or commentary on a textual word or expression : an interpretation marked by usu. conscious sophistry **b** (1) : GLOSSARY (2) : a continuous interlinear translation (3) : a continuous explanation or commentary accompanying a text; *specif* : a commentary (as made at Bologna from the 12th century to the 14th century) on the texts of Roman or Civil law **2** : a poetical composition consisting of an amplification of a stanza of a poem into several stanzas so that each of the new stanzas ends with a line or couplet of the text stanza

⁴**gloss** \ˈ"\ *vb* -ED/-ING/-ES *vi* **1** : to make glosses : introduce or furnish glosses ⟨spent much time in reading and ~*ing*⟩ **2** *archaic* : to make usu. unfavorable remarks : comment adversely ~ *vt* **1** : to make glosses on : introduce glosses into : furnish glosses for ⟨medieval scholars, when they found in a Latin text a word not familiar to them, were accustomed to ~ it —J.W.Krutch⟩ **2** : to make a false or perverse interpretation of; *specif* : to dispose of or reduce to nothing (as a difficult problem) by false or perverse interpretation ⟨trying to ~ away the irrationalities of the universe —Irwin Edman⟩

gloss- *or* **glosso-** *comb form* [L, tongue, fr. Gk *glōss-*, *glōsso-*, fr. *glōssa*] **1 a** : tongue ⟨*glossalgia*⟩ : glossal and ⟨*glossohyal*⟩ **b** : structure or organ like a tongue ⟨*Glossophora*⟩ **2** : language ⟨*glossology*⟩

gloss *abbr* glossary

glos·sa \ˈgläsə, -lȯsə\ *n, pl* **glos·sae** \-ˌsē, -ˌsī\ *also* **glossas** [NL, fr. Gk *glōssa* tongue] : a tongue or lingual structure esp. in an insect: as **a** : the median distal lobe of the labium of many insects : LINGUA; *also* : either of the two segments of which this lobe is often formed **b** : the long spirally coiled tongue of many butterflies and moths

-glossa \ˈ"\ *n comb form, pl* **-glossa** [NL, fr. Gk *glōssa*] : one or ones having (such) a tongue or part like a tongue — in taxonomic names in biology ⟨*Eriglossa*⟩ ⟨*Cheiroglossa*⟩

glos·sal \-səl\ *adj* [*gloss-* + *-al*] : of or relating to the tongue ⟨~ inflammation⟩

glos·sal·gia \gläˈsalj(ē)ə, glȯˈ-\ *n* -S [NL, fr. *gloss-* + *-algia*] : pain localized in the tongue; *esp* : neuralgic pain in the tongue

glos·sar·i·al \(ˈ)=ˈsa(a)rēəl\ *adj* : of, relating to, or having the characteristics of a glossary ⟨a ~ index⟩ ⟨~ notes⟩

glos·sa·rist \ˈ=ˌsərəst\ *n* -S **1** : one that makes textual glosses **2** : a compiler of a glossary

glos·sa·ry \ˈgläsərē, -ri *also* ˈglȯs-\ *n* -ES [ML *glossarium*, fr. L *glossa* difficult word requiring explanation + *-arium* -ary] : a collection of textual glosses ⟨an edition of Shakespeare with a good ~⟩ or of terms limited to a special area of knowledge ⟨a ~ of technical terms⟩ or usage ⟨a ~ of dialectal words⟩

glos·sate \ˈgläˌsāt, ˈglȯ-\ *adj* [NL *glossa* + E *-ate*] **1** : having a glossa **2** : HAUSTELLATE

glos·sa·tor \ˈgläˌsād·ə(r), ˈglȯ,-, =ˈ==\ *n* -S [ME *glosatour*, fr. ML *glosator*, fr. *glosatus* (past part. of *glosare* to gloss, fr. *glosa*, n., gloss) + L *-or* — more at GLOSS (explanation)] : GLOSSARIST

glossed *past of* GLOSS

glos·se·mat·ic \ˌgläsəˈmad·ik, ˌglȯs-\ *adj* [ISV *glossemat-* (fr. *glosseme*) + *-ic*] : of or relating to glossematics or a glosseme ⟨~ theory⟩

glos·se·ma·ti·cian \ˌ==məˈtishən\ *n* -S [ISV *glossematics* + *-ian*] : a specialist in glossematics

glos·se·mat·ics \-ˈmad·iks\ *n pl but sing in constr* [ISV *glossemat-* (fr. *glosseme*) + *-ics*] : linguistic analysis based on the distribution and interrelationship of glossemes

glos·seme \ˈgläˌsēm, ˈglȯ,-\ *n* -S [ISV *gloss-* + *-eme*] : the smallest unit (as a word, a stem, a grammatical element, an intonation, or an order of words) that signals a meaning in a language — **glos·se·mic** \(ˈ)=ˈsēmik\ *adj*

glosses *pl of* GLOSS, *pres 3d sing of* GLOSS

-glos·sia \ˈgläsēə, ˈglȯs-\ *n comb form* -S [NL, fr. Gk *-glōssia*, fr. *glōssa* tongue + *-ia* -y — more at GLOSS (explanation)] : condition of having (such) a tongue or (so many) tongues ⟨*diglossia*⟩ ⟨*pachyglossia*⟩

glossier *comparative of* GLOSSY

glossies *pl of* GLOSSY

glossiest *superlative of* GLOSSY

gloss·i·ly \ˈgläsəlē, ˈglȯs-, -li\ *adv* : in a glossy manner

glos·si·na \=ˈsīnə, -ˈsēnə\ *n* [NL, fr. *gloss-* + *-ina*] **1** *cap* : an African genus of two-winged flies with a long slender sharp proboscis and plumose aristae comprising the tsetse flies — compare SLEEPING SICKNESS; see GLOSSINIDAE **2** -S : any insect of the genus *Glossina* : TSETSE FLY

gloss·i·ness \ˈ=sēnəs, -sin-\ *n* -ES : the quality or state of being glossy

glossing *pres part of* GLOSS

glos·sin·i·dae \glāˈsinəˌdē, glȯˈ-\ *n pl, cap* [NL, fr. *Glossina*, type genus + *-idae*] *in some classifications* : a family of two-winged flies that is closely related to Muscidae and includes *Glossina* and a few closely related genera usu. included among the Muscidae

glos·si·pho·nia \ˌgläsəˈfōnēə, ˌglȯs-\ *n, cap* [NL, fr. *glos-* (fr. Gk *glōssa* tongue) + L *siphon-*, *sipho* siphon, tube + NL *-ia* — more at GLOSS (explanation), SIPHON] : the type genus of the family Glossiphoniidae comprising common often brightly colored freshwater leeches with one or more pairs of simple eyes

¹**glos·si·pho·ni·id** \ˈ==ˈ=nēəd\ *adj* [NL *Glossiphoniidae*] : of or relating to the Glossiphoniidae

²**glossiphoniid** \ˈ"\ *n* -S [NL *Glossiphoniidae*] : a leech of the family Glossiphoniidae

glos·si·pho·ni·idae \ˌ== fəˈnīəˌdē\ *n pl, cap* [NL, fr. *Glossiphonia*, type genus + *-idae*] : a family of rhynchobdellid leeches having the posterior sucker sharply demarked

gloss·ist \ˈgläsəst, ˈglȯs-\ *n* -S *archaic* : GLOSSARIST

glos·si·tis \=ˈsīd·əs\ *n* -ES [NL, fr. *gloss-* + *-itis*] : inflammation of the tongue

gloss·less \ˈgläsləs, ˈglȯs-\ *adj* : devoid of gloss

gloss·me·ter \-ˌsmēd·ə(r)\ *n* : a photometer for measuring the gloss of test surfaces

glosso- — see GLOSS-

glos·so·dyn·ia \ˌgläsōˈdinēə, ˌglȯs-\ *n* -S [NL, fr. *gloss-* + *-odynia*] : GLOSSALGIA

glos·sog·ra·pher \gläˈsägrəfə(r), glȯˈ-\ *n* -S [Gk *glōssographos* writer of explanations of difficult words (fr. *glōsso-* — fr. *glōssa* difficult word requiring explanation — + *-graphos* -grapher) + E *-er* — more at GLOSS (explanation), -GRAPHER] : GLOSSARIST

glos·sog·ra·phy \-fē\ *n* -ES [prob. fr. *glossographer*, after such pairs as E *geographer: geography*] : the writing or compilation of glosses

glos·so·hy·al \ˌgläsōˈhīəl, ˌglȯs-\ *adj* [*gloss-* + *hy-* (fr. *hyoid*) + *-al*] : of or relating to the hyoid arch and tongue; *specif* : of or relating to the median basihyal or an anterior extension or segment of it extending into and supporting the tongue

glos·soid \ˈ=ˌsȯid\ *adj* [Gk *glōssoeidēs*, fr. *glōss-* gloss- + *-oeidēs* -oid] : resembling a tongue ⟨a ~ proboscis⟩

gloss oil *n* [¹*gloss*] : a spirit varnish consisting of a solution of rosin partially neutralized with lime in mineral spirits or other paint thinner

glos·so·kinesthetic \ˌgläsō, ˌglȯsō+\ *adj* [*gloss-* + *kinesthetic*] : of or relating to sensations of tongue movement ⟨~ centers⟩

glos·so·la·lia \ˌ==ˈlālēə\ *n* -S [NL, fr. *gloss-* + *-lalia*] : GIFT OF TONGUES

glos·so·log·i·cal \ˈ=səˈläjəkəl\ *adj* [*glossology* + *-ical*] *archaic* : LINGUISTIC

glos·sol·o·gist \=ˈsäləjəst\ *n* -S [*glossology* + *-ist*] *archaic* : LINGUIST

glos·sol·o·gy \-jē\ *n* -ES [*gloss-* + *-logy*] **1** *archaic* : LINGUISTICS **2** *archaic* : NOMENCLATURE

glos·so·palatine arch \ˌglä|(ˌ)sō, ˌglȯ|+. . .-\ *n* [*glossopalatine* fr. NL *glossopalatinus* of the tongue and palate, fr. *gloss-* + (assumed) NL *palatinus* of the palate — more at PALATINE] : either of the anterior pillars of the fauces; *also* : the arch formed by both

glossopalatine nerve *n* : the branch of the facial nerve that supplies the anterior tongue and parts of the palate and fauces — called also *nerve of Wrisberg, nervus intermedius*

glos·so·pal·a·ti·nus \ˌ=(ˌ)=ˌpalaˈtīnəs, -tēn-\ *n, pl* **glossopalati·ni** \-tīˌnī, -tēˌnē\ [NL, fr. *glossopalatinus*, adj., of the tongue and palate] : a thin muscle arising from the soft palate on each side and inserted into the side and dorsum of the tongue

glos·sop·a·thy \gläˈsäpəthē\ *n* -ES [*gloss-* + *-pathy*] : tongue disease

glos·so·pet·ra \ˌ=ˌsōˈpe·trə\ *n, pl* **glossopet·rae** \-ˌtrē, -ˌtrī\ [NL, fr. L, tongue-shaped gem, fr. *gloss-* + *petra* rock, fr. Gk] : any of certain isolated fossil shark teeth

glos·soph·a·ga \=ˈsäfəgə\ *n, cap* [NL, fr. *gloss-* + *-phaga*] : a genus of small So. American bats (family Phyllostomatidae) having a long extensile tongue apparently used to scoop out the inside of fruits

glos·soph·a·gine \-fəˌjīn, -ˌjən\ *adj* [NL *Glossophaga* + E *-ine*] : of or relating to the *Glossophaga*

glos·so·pharyngeal \ˌglä|(ˌ)sō, ˌglȯ|+\ *adj* [prob. fr. NL *glossopharyngeus* glossopharyngeal (fr. *gloss-* + *pharyngeus* pharyngeal) + E *-al* — more at PHARYNGEAL] **1** : of or relating to both tongue and pharynx **2** : of or relating to the glossopharyngeal nerve ⟨~ lesions⟩

glossopharyngeal nerve *also* **glossopharyngeal** *n* : a mixed nerve that is either of the 9th pair of cranial nerves, that has sensory fibers arising from the superior and petrosal ganglia and motor fibers arising with those of the 10th nerve from the lateral wall of the medulla, and that supplies chiefly the pharynx, posterior tongue, and parotid gland with motor and sensory fibers including gustatory and autonomic secretory and vasodilator fibers

glos·soph·o·ra \=ˈsäfərə\ *n pl, cap* [NL, fr. *gloss-* + *-phora*] *in some classifications* : a division of mollusks consisting of those having a radula

glos·so·pode \ˈgläsəˌpōd, ˈglȯs-\ *n* -S [NL *glossopodium*] : GLOSSOPODIUM

glos·so·po·di·um \ˌ==ˈpōdēəm\ *n, pl* **glossopo·dia** \-ēə\ *or* **glossopodiums** [NL, fr. *gloss-* + *-podium*] : the sheathing leaf base in the quillworts

glos·sop·ter·is \=ˈsäptərəs\ *n* [NL, fr. *gloss-* + *-pteris*] **1** *cap* : a genus of chiefly Permian and Triassic fossil ferns or fernlike plants characterized by thick entire fronds with anastomosing veins **2** -ES : any plant of the genus *Glossopteris*

glos·so·py·ro·sis \ˌgläsōˌpīˈrōsəs, ˌglȯs-\ *n* [NL, fr. *gloss-* + Gk *pyrōsis* burning, inflammation — more at PYROSIS] : a burning sensation in the tongue

glos·so·the·ri·um \-ōˈthirēəm\ *n, cap* [NL, fr. *gloss-* + *-therium*] : a genus of large So. American Pleistocene ground sloths related to the genus *Mylodon* that have the nostrils completely enclosed by the premaxillae so that the skull has a superficial likeness to that of a turtle

gloss white *n* [¹*gloss*] : an extender pigment made by coprecipitation of blanc fixe and a hydrate of alumina and used chiefly in printing inks

¹**glossy** \ˈgläsē, ˈglȯs-, -si\ *adj, usu* -ER/-EST [¹*gloss* + *-y*] **1** : having a superficial soft glowing luster ⟨rich ~ leather⟩ or glistening brightness ⟨~ green foliage⟩ or smooth shininess ⟨the ~ pages of those magazines⟩ ⟨photographs printed on ~ paper⟩ or glowing sleekness ⟨the horse's ~ coat⟩ : LUSTROUS, SHINING, SILKY **2 a** : having a superficial largely deceptive or artificial attractiveness typically marked by apparent opulence ⟨a ~ nightclub⟩ or sophistication ⟨a ~ gathering of celebrities⟩ or smoothly captivating display ⟨a ~ musical⟩ : smoothly pretentious : SHOWY **b** : marked by urbanity and usu. only apparent conviction and sincerity : SUAVE, SMOOTH, GLIB ⟨the ~ commercials of radio and television⟩ ⟨~ salesmen⟩

²**glossy** \ˈ"\ *n* -ES **1** : SLICK 6 **2** : a photograph printed on smooth shiny paper

glossy ibis *n* : any of several ibises having dark-colored plumage with a more or less metallic luster and constituting the genus *Plegadis* of the family Threskiornithidae

glost \ˈglȯst, -ä-\ *n* -S [alter. of ¹*gloss*] : ²GLAZE 2a(2); *also* : clayware with glaze applied but not yet fired — called also *glostware*

glost fire *n* : the fire used for fusing a glaze to biscuit

glost firing *n* : a separate firing by which glaze is fused to clayware

-glot \ˌglät, *usu* -ād·+V\ *adj comb form* [Gk *-glōttos*, *-glōssos*, fr. *glōtta*, *glōssa* language, tongue — more at GLOSS (explanation)] : having knowledge of or using (a specified number of) languages ⟨*monoglot*⟩ ⟨*tetraglot*⟩

glott- *or* **glotto-** *comb form* [Gk *glōtt-*, *glōtto-*, *glōss-*, *glōsso-* tongue, fr. *glōtta*, *glōssa*] : language ⟨*glottology*⟩

glot·tal \ˈgläd·ᵊl, -ätᵊl\ *adj* [*glottis* + *-al*] : of, relating to, or produced in or by the glottis ⟨~ constriction⟩

glot·tal·ic \(ˈ)gläˈtalik\ *adj* : GLOTTALIZED

glot·tal·iza·tion \ˌgläd·ᵊləˈzāshən, -ätᵊl-, -ᵊlˌīˈz-\ *n* -S : the act of glottalizing

glot·tal·ize \ˈ==ˌīz\ *vt* -ED/-ING/-S : to articulate or accompany the articulation of with whole or partial glottal closure ⟨*glottalized* consonants⟩

glottal stop *also* **glottal catch** *or* **glottal plosive** *n* : complete closure of the glottis under breath pressure recognized by the ear chiefly by the occlusion or by the explosive release ⟨in New York City the *tt* in *bottle* is sometimes pronounced as a *glottal stop*⟩

¹**glot·tic** \ˈgläd·ik\ *adj* [Gk *glōttikos* of the tongue, fr. *glōtta*, *glōssa* tongue + *-ikos* -ic] *archaic* : LINGUISTIC

²**glottic** \ˈ"\ *adj* [ISV *glott-* (fr. NL *glottis*) + *-ic*] : GLOTTAL

glot·tis \ˈgläd·|əs, -ät|\ *n, pl* **glottises** \|əsəz\ *or* **glotti·des** \|əˌdēz\ [NL, fr. Gk *glōttis*, fr. *glōtta*, *glōssa* tongue] : the space between the vocal fold and arytenoid cartilage of one side of the larynx and those of the other side; *also* : the structures that surround this space — compare EPIGLOTTIS

glot·to·chronological \ˌgläd·(ˌ)ō, -ä(ˌ)tō +\ *adj* : of or relating to glottochronology

glot·to·chronology \ˈ"+\ *n* [*glott-* + *chronology*] **1** : the study of the time during which two or more languages have evolved separately from a common source **2** : a technique for estimating by statistical comparison of vocabulary samples the time during which two or more languages have evolved separately from a common source

glot·to·gon·ic \ˌgläd·ōˈgänik, -lätō-\ *adj* [*glott-* + Gk *gonē* generation + E *-ic*; akin to Gk *gignesthai* to be born — more at KIN] : of or relating to the origin of language ⟨~ problems⟩

glot·to·log·i·cal \ˌgläd·ᵊlˈäjəkəl, -ätᵊl-\ *adj* [*glottology* + *-ical*] : LINGUISTIC

glot·tol·o·gist \gläˈtäləjəst\ *n* -S [*glottology* + *-ist*] : LINGUIST

glot·tol·o·gy \-jē\ *n* -ES [*glott-* + *-logy*] : LINGUISTICS

¹**glouces·ter** \ˈglästə(r), ˈglȯs-\ *adj, usu cap* [fr. *Gloucester*, county and county borough in England] **1** : of or from the county borough of Gloucester, England : of the kind or style prevalent in Gloucester **2** : GLOUCESTERSHIRE

²**gloucester** \ˈ"\ *or* **gloucester cheese** *n* -S *usu cap G* [fr. *Gloucester*, county in England, where it was originally made] : a hard cheese resembling derby

gloucester old spots \-ˈōl(d)zˌpäts, -)ˌsp-\ *n pl but sing or pl in constr, usu cap G&O&S* [fr. *Gloucester*, county in England, where the breed was developed] : an old British breed of hardy black-and-white-spotted swine now chiefly used for crossbreeding

glouces·ter·shire \ˈglästə(r)ˌshi(ə)r, ˈglȯs-, -ˌshər\ *or* **gloucester** *adj, usu cap* [fr. *Gloucestershire* or *Gloucester*, county in England] : of or from the county of Gloucester, England : of the kind or style prevalent in Gloucester

gloup \ˈglüp\ *n* -S [prob. of Scand origin; akin to Norw dial. *glūp* hole, gorge, abyss; akin to Sw dial. *glūpa* to gape, swallow, OFris *glūpa* to look, MLG *glūpen* to look with half-closed eyes, and perh. to OE *geolu* yellow — more at YELLOW] : an opening in the roof of a sea cave through which incoming waves may force air to rush upward or water to spout intermittently : BLOWHOLE 3

glout \ˈglüt, ˈglau̇t\ *vi* -ED/-ING/-S [ME *glouten*, prob. of Scand origin; akin to ON *glotta* to grin scornfully, Sw *glutta* to peep — more at GLOAT] *archaic* : FROWN, SCOWL

¹**glove** \ˈgləv\ *n* -S [ME, fr. OE *glōf*; akin to ON *glōfi* glove; both prob. fr. a prehistoric NGmc-WGmc compound whose first constituent is represented by OE *ge-* (perfective, associative, and collective prefix) and whose second constituent is represented by ON *lōfi* palm of the hand, Goth *lofa*; akin to OHG *laffa* palm of the hand, Lith *lopa* claw, Russ *lapa* paw — more at CO-] **1 a** : a covering for the hand having separate sections or merely separate openings for each of the fingers and the thumb and often extending part way up the arm and made of various materials (as leather, wool, rubber) either with or without a snap or button or other fastening at the wrist and used to protect the hand against cold ⟨a bitter day and they were wool-lined ~*s*⟩ or intense heat ⟨asbestos ~*s*⟩ or irritation ⟨wore a pair of rubber ~*s* while washing the dishes⟩ or superficial injury ⟨a falconer's ~⟩ ⟨an archer's ~⟩ or to avoid contamination ⟨surgeons wearing sterile ~*s*⟩ ⟨~*s* for handling radioactive materials⟩ or as a dress accessory ⟨a pair of silk evening ~*s*⟩ — often used with *pair*; distinguished from *mitt* and *mitten* **b** : GAUNTLET 1a ⟨a ~ of mail⟩ **c** : GAUNTLET 2 ⟨threw down the ~ to skeptical critics —C.R.Anderson⟩ **2 a** : a usu. leather covering for the hand padded and reinforced at the palm and fingers and often having sections designed to cover more than one finger instead of having separate finger sections and used by defending players in the game of baseball to protect the hand when catching a thrown or struck ball — compare MITT **b** : BOXING GLOVE ⟨getting rusty in his boxing, hasn't put the ~*s* on for six months⟩ — **with gloves** *or* **with kid gloves** *or* **with velvet gloves** *adv* : with gentleness, consideration, or tact : CAUTIOUSLY, GINGERLY ⟨they've

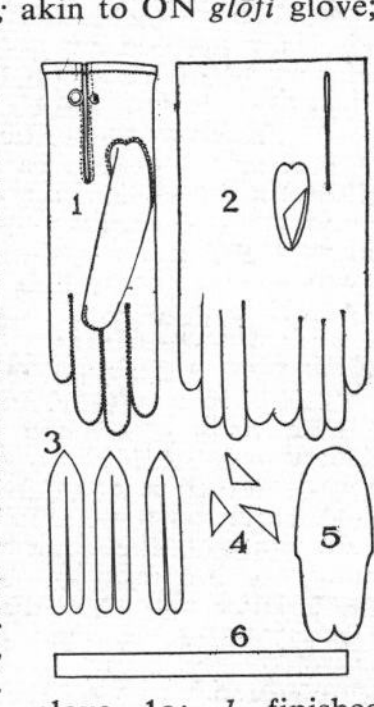

glove 1a: *1* finished glove, *2* trank, *3* fourchettes, *4* gussets, *5* thumb, *6* slit binding

got to be handled *with kid gloves*〉 — **with gloves off** *or* **without gloves** *adv* **1 :** without restraint **:** UNSPARINGLY, UNMERCIFULLY **2 :** without caution or ceremony **:** boldly and directly 〈attacked the problem *with gloves off*〉

²glove \"\ *vt* -ED/-ING/-S **1 a :** to cover with or as if with a glove **:** draw a glove over 〈*gloving* his right hand as he spoke〉 **b :** to furnish with gloves 〈warmly bundled up and *gloved* for the trip〉 **2 :** to catch (a baseball) in one's gloved hand 〈*gloved* a stinging line drive and fired it to first base〉

glove-and-stocking anesthesia *n* **:** glove anesthesia accompanied by anesthesia in the foot sometimes extending farther up the leg and usu. associated with hysteric states

glove anesthesia *n* **:** anesthesia in the hand sometimes extending farther up the arm and usu. associated with hysteric states

glove box *n* **:** a sealed protectively lined compartment having ports to which are attached gloves for use in handling materials inside the compartment

glove compartment *n* **:** a small storage cabinet in the dashboard of an automobile

glove doll *or* **glove puppet** *n* **:** HAND PUPPET

glove grain *n* **:** GRAIN 4b(1)

glove·less \ˈgləvləs\ *adj* **:** devoid of gloves

glove·man \-mən\ *n, pl* **glovemen :** FIELDER a

glov·er \-və(r)\ *n* -S [ME, fr. ¹*glove* + *-er*] **:** one that makes or sells gloves

glov·er scale \"-\ *also* **glover's scale** *n, usu cap G* [after Townend *Glover* †1883 Am. entomologist] **:** a widespread tropical armored scale (*Lepidosaphes gloverii*) esp. destructive to citrus

glover tower *n, usu cap G* [after John *Glover*, 19th cent. Eng. chemist] **:** a large packed tower that is situated before the chambers in the chamber process of making sulfuric acid and that serves esp. to cool the hot mixture of sulfur dioxide and air on its way to the chambers, to supply water vapor, to remove the nitrogen oxides from nitrous vitriol entering at the top from the Gay-Lussac tower, and to concentrate sulfuric acid also entering at the top from the chambers

glove silk *n* **:** a fine knit fabric of silk or artificial fiber used esp. for women's gloves and underwear

glove sponge *n* [so called fr. its shape] **:** a soft inferior commercial sponge of the Bahamas and Florida

glov·ing \ˈgləviŋ\ *n* -S [¹*glove* + *-ing*] **:** the making of gloves

¹glow \ˈglō\ *vb* -ED/-ING/-S [ME *glowen*, fr. OE *glōwan*; akin to OHG *gluoen* to glow, ON *glōa* to glow, OE *geolu* yellow, and perh. to Gk *chloos* green, light green, light green color — more at YELLOW] *vi* **1 a** (1) **:** to be or become hot to the point of radiating a suffused often slowly and unevenly pulsating light and an intense flameless heat **:** become heated to red heat or white heat **:** be or become incandescent 〈heated the metal until it ~*ed*〉 〈coals still ~*ing* in the fireplace〉 (2) **:** to shine with a suffused radiance as if intensely heated **:** emit or become lit up with an incandescent light **:** gleam in a suffused manner 〈gaily lighted houses ~*ed* in the dark〉 〈her eyes ~*ed* with pleasure〉 〈saw the harbor lights ~*ing* in the distance〉 **b** (1) **:** to have a rich warm suffused coloration typically reddish in hue or touched by reddish highlights 〈his troubled face ~*ing* in the firelight —Guy McCrone〉 〈paintings that ~*ed* with color〉 〈the leaves of the maple trees ~*ed* red and yellow in the sunlight —J.P. Marquand〉 (2) **:** to have a radiant warm typically ruddy coloration of the kind associated with youthfulness and physical well-being 〈cheeks ~*ing* with health〉 (3) **:** to have a markedly heightened reddish coloration (as that arising from strong emotion or embarrassment) **:** FLUSH, BLUSH 〈she was filled with excitement and her face ~*ed*〉 **2 a** (1) **:** to experience a sensation of tingling pervasive warmth 〈rubbed themselves with Turkish towels until they ~*ed* all over〉 〈a drink that makes the whole body ~〉 (2) **:** to experience a sensation as if of intense heat **:** burn with emotion or passion 〈~*ing* with rage and resentment〉 〈~*ing* with fervor〉 **b :** to be full of or show exuberance, elation, joyous good spirits 〈~*ing* with maternal pride —Carleton Beals〉 **:** be buoyant and vibrantly alive 〈every page of the book ~*s* with good humor〉 ~ *vt, obs* **:** to cause to glow 〈fans whose wind did seem to ~ the delicate cheeks which they did cool —Shak.〉

syn see BLAZE

²glow \"\ *n* -S **1 :** the quality or state of having a glowing coloration 〈the rich ~ of the mahogany table〉 〈the bright ~ in her cheeks〉 **2 a** (1) **:** considerable warmth of feeling or intensity of emotion or passion 〈the ~ of new love〉 (2) **:** tingling pervasive warmth or a sensation of such warmth 〈a ~ of happiness〉 〈walked away satisfied and all in a ~〉 〈they started pouring the stuff down steadily, feeling the warm ~ rising inside —D.M.Davin〉 **b :** a feeling or outward display of exuberance, elation, joyous good spirits 〈the good news left them with a ~ in their hearts〉 〈there was no mistaking the happy ~ on his face〉 〈the ~ of success〉 **3 a :** the state of glowing with heat and light 〈the ~ of dying embers〉 **:** INCANDESCENCE; *specif* **:** a relatively faint luminosity due to luminescence 〈the cathode ~ in a Crookes tube〉 — compare AFTERGLOW 2 **b :** glowing radiance **:** suffused gleaming 〈happy to see the ~ in her eyes〉 〈the ~ of the lighted Christmas tree〉

glow discharge *n* **:** a silent luminous electrical discharge without sparks through a gas

¹glow·er \ˈglau̇(ə)r, -au̇ə, *chiefly in southern US* -au̇wə(r, *chiefly in substand speech* -lō(ə)r *or* -lōə\ *vi* -ED/-ING/-S [ME (Sc) *glowren*, perh. of Scand origin; akin to ON *glyrna* eye, Norw dial. *glȳra* to look askance; akin to MLG *glūren* to watch, D *gluren* to peep, MHG *glosen* to glow — more at GLOSS (luster)] **1** *dial Brit* **:** to look intently; *esp* **:** to stare in amazement **2 :** to look or stare with sullen brooding annoyance or anger **:** gaze blackly **:** SCOWL, LOWER

²glower \"\ *n* -S **1** *dial Brit* **:** an intent look; *esp* **:** an amazed stare **2 :** a sullen brooding look of anger **:** SCOWL

³glow·er \ˈglō(ə)r, -ōə\ *n* -S [¹*glow* + *-er*] **:** the luminous element in a Nernst lamp

glow·er·ing·ly *adv* [*glowering* (pres. part. of ¹*glower*) + *-ly*] **:** in a glowering manner 〈looked ~ at the morning headlines〉

glowing *adj* [ME *glowinge, glowing*, fr. *glowen* to glow + *-inge, -ing* -ing] **:** that glows: **a :** burning incandescently **b** (1) **:** marked by a rich warm coloration 〈~ colors〉 (2) **:** marked by a radiant healthfully ruddy coloration 〈~ good health〉 **c** (1) **:** ARDENT, FERVID, IMPASSIONED 〈~ devotion〉 (2) **:** highly enthusiastic **:** WARM, EXUBERANT 〈a ~ account of the trip〉 〈~ praise〉 〈a ~ description〉 — **glow·ing·ly** *adv*

glowing cloud *n* **:** a mixture of hot volcanic gas and particles of lava erupted explosively from a volcano

glow lamp *n* **:** a gas-discharge hot-cathode electric lamp in which most of the light proceeds from the cathode glow and which is used esp. in stroboscopes and in variable-density sound-film recording

glow plug *n* **:** a small electric heating element placed inside a diesel-engine cylinder to preheat the air and facilitate starting

glowr *var of* ²GLOWER 1

glows *pres 3d sing of* GLOW, *pl of* GLOW

glow switch *n* **:** an inert-gas discharge tube in which one electrode is a bimetallic strip that bends as the tube warms up and contacts the other electrode thus short-circuiting the tube and which is used as a starting switch in fluorescent lamps

glow tube *n* **:** a gas-discharge tube (as of the cold-cathode type) that gives light due to electric discharge through a rarefied gas

glowworm \ˈ=,=\ *n* [ME, fr. *glowen* to glow + *worm*] **1 :** any of various luminous insects with wings rudimentary or lacking: as **a :** one of the wingless females or larvae of beetles of the family Lampyridae which emit light from some of the abdominal segments **b :** one of the web-making larvae of a New Zealand fungus gnat (*Bolitophila luminosa*) — compare FIREFLY **2 :** SEARED GREEN

glox·in·ia \gläkˈsinēə *also* -sēn-\ *n* [NL, fr. Benjamin P. *Gloxin*, 18th cent. Ger. physician and botanist + NL *-ia*] **1** *cap* **:** a small genus of tropical American herbs (family Gesneriaceae) with leafy stems and axillary flowers **2** -S **:** a greenhouse herb of the genus *Sinningia*; *esp* **:** a Brazilian herb (*S. speciosa*) that is the source of many horticultural varieties

gloy \ˈglói\ *n* -S [ME, modif. of MF *glui*] *Scot* **:** STRAW

¹gloze \ˈglōz\ *n* -S [ME *glose* flattery, plausible pretext, explanation of a difficult word — more at GLOSS (explanation)] **1** *archaic* **:** smooth empty talk; *esp* **:** FLATTERY **2** *archaic* **:** ¹GLOSS 2 **3** *archaic* **:** ³GLOSS 1

²gloze \"\ *vb* -ED/-ING/-S [ME *glosen* to use flattery, flatter, make glosses, make glosses on, fr. OF *gloser* to make glosses, make glosses on, fr. *glose*, n., explanation of a difficult word — more at GLOSS (explanation)] *vi* **1** *archaic* **:** to use smooth empty talk **:** FAWN; *esp* **:** to use flattery **2** *archaic* **:** ⁴GLOSS *vi* 1 ~ *vt* **1** *archaic* **:** to address with smooth empty talk **:** fawn upon; *esp* **:** FLATTER **2** *archaic* **:** ⁴GLOSS *vt* 1 **3 :** ⁴GLOSS *vt* 2

³gloze \"\ *vt* -ED/-ING/-S [²*gloze* (influenced in meaning by ²*gloss*)] **:** ²GLOSS 1 〈the spent, though *glozed* beyond all semblance of truth —Joseph Furphy〉 — often used with *over* 〈saw everything and *glozed* over nothing —William Irvine〉

syn see PALLIATE

⁴gloze \"\ *vt* -ED/-ING/-S [¹*gloss*] *archaic* **:** to light up **:** BRIGHTEN

glozing *adj* [ME *glosinge, glosing*, fr. *glosen* to flatter + *-inge, -ing* -ing] *archaic* **:** FAWNING, FLATTERING

glt *abbr* gilt

¹glub \ˈgləb\ *n* -S [imit.] **:** a gurgling, bubbling, or gulping sound (as of water running down a drain) — often reduplicated 〈listened to the ~, ~, ~ of the milk bottle as it sank below the surface of the pond〉 **:** an inarticulate strangled sound (as of someone attempting to speak while under water)

²glub \"\ *vi* **glubbed; glubbed; glubbing; glubs :** to make a glub — often reduplicated 〈like cold molasses *glub-glubbing* from a barrel —James Street〉

gluc- *or* **gluco-** *comb form* [ISV, fr. *glucose*] **1 a :** glucose 〈*glucogenic*〉 **:** related to or containing glucose 〈*glucomannans*〉 **b** *gluco-, usu ital* **:** having the stereochemical arrangement of atoms or groups found in glucose 〈D-*gluco*=pentahydroxy-pentyl〉 **2 :** GLYC- 1 〈*glucoproteins*〉 — not now in frequent use

glu·ca·gon \ˈglükə,gän\ *n* -S [*gluc-* + *-agon* (perh. fr. Gk *agōn*, pres. part. of *agein* to lead, drive) — more at AGENT] **:** a crystalline protein that is obtained from the islets of Langerhans of the pancreas, is present in some preparations of insulin, and increases the content of sugar in the blood by increasing the rate of breakdown of glycogen in the liver — called also *hyperglycemic-glycogenolytic factor*

glu·ca·mine \ˈglükə,mēn, -,mən\ *n* [ISV *gluc-* + *amine*] **:** an amine $HOCH_2(CHOH)_4CH_2NH_2$ obtained by reduction of glucosyl-amine or of glucose oxime; glucityl-amine

glu·car·ic acid \(ˈ)glü¦karik-\ *n* [*gluc-* + *-aric* (as in *saccharic*)] **:** SACCHARIC ACID

glu·cide \ˈglü,sīd\ *n* -S [ISV *gluc-* + *-ide*] **:** any of a class of carbohydrates comprising both the glycoses and the glycosides

glu·cin·i·um \glüˈsinēəm\ *or* **glu·ci·num** \-ˈsīnəm, -ˈsēn-\ *n* -S [NL, fr. *glucina* beryllium oxide (fr. F *glucine*, irreg. fr. Gk *glykys* sweet + F *-ine*) + *-ium* or *-um* (as in *aluminum*) — more at DULCET] **:** BERYLLIUM

glu·ci·tol \ˈglüsə,tȯl, -tōl\ *n* -S [*gluc-* + *-itol*] **:** a hexahydric alcohol $C_6H_8(OH)_6$ formed by reduction of glucose — see SORBITOL

glu·ci·tyl \-,til\ *n* -S [*glucitol* + *-yl*] **:** a univalent radical $HOCH_2(CHOH)_4CH_2$— derived from glucitol by removal of the hydroxyl group from the carbon atom at position one — compare GLUCOSE illustration

¹gluck \ˈglək\ *vi* -ED/-ING/-S [imit.] **:** GLUG — often reduplicated

²gluck \"\ *n* -S **:** GLUG — often reduplicated

glucke \ˈglükə\ *also* **gluck** \-k\ *n* -S [G *glucke*, lit., clucking hen, of imit. origin] **:** a roller-canary tour suggestive of a hen's clucking

glu·co·corticoid \¦glü(,)kō+\ *n* [*gluc-* + *corticoid*] **:** a corticoid (as cortisone) that affects chiefly carbohydrate metabolism

glu·co·genesis \,glükō+\ *n* [NL, fr. *gluc-* + L *genesis*] **:** formation of glucose within the animal body from any product of glycolysis — compare GLUCONEOGENESIS

glu·co·lipide *or* **glucolipid** \¦glükō+\ *n* [*gluc-* + *lipide, lipid*] **:** a glycolipide that yields glucose on hydrolysis

glu·co·nate \ˈglükə,nāt\ *n* -S [*glucon-* (fr. *gluconic acid*) + *-ate*] **:** a salt of gluconic acid (as calcium gluconate)

glu·co·neogenesis \¦glükō\ *n* [NL, fr. *gluc-* + *ne-* + L *genesis*] **:** formation of glucose within the animal body esp. by the liver from proteins, fats, and substances other than carbohydrates — compare GLUCOGENESIS — **gluconeogenetic** *adj*

glu·con·ic acid \(ˈ)glü¦känik-\ *n* [*gluconic* ISV *gluc-* + *-onic*] **:** a crystalline acid $HOCH_2(CHOH)_4COOH$ that is obtained by oxidation of glucose (as by fermentation with molds), that readily dehydrates to form lactones, and that is used chiefly in cleaning metals

glu·co·protein \¦glü(,)kō+\ *n* [*gluc-* + *protein*] **:** GLYCOPROTEIN

glu·co·pyranose \"+\ *n* [*gluc-* + *pyranose*] **:** one of the modifications of glucose characterized by a pyranose ring

glu·co·py·ran·o·side \,glü(,)kō,pīˈranə,sīd\ *n* -S [*glucopyranose* + *-ide*] **:** a glucoside that contains a pyranose ring in its structure

glu·co·py·ran·o·syl \-,sil\ *n* -S [*glucopyranose* + *-yl*] **:** a glucosyl radical that contains a pyranose ring in its structure

glu·co·sa·mine \glüˈkōsə,mēn, -ōzə-\ *n* [ISV *glucose* + *amine*] **:** a crystalline amino derivative $HOCH_2(CHOH)_3CH(NH_2)CHO$ of glucose occurring in the D-form as chitosamine and obtainable as the *N*-methyl derivative of the L-form by hydrolysis of streptomycin; 2-deoxy-2-amino-glucose

glu·co·san \ˈglükə,san\ *n* -S [ISV *glucose* + *-an*] **1 :** any of several intramolecular anhydrides $C_6H_{10}O_5$ of glucose — compare LEVOGLUCOSAN **2 :** a hexosan (as dextran or starch) that yields essentially only glucose on hydrolysis

glu·co·sa·zone \glüˈkōsə,zōn, -kōzə-\ *n* [*gluc-* + *osazone*] **1 :** the osazone of glucose, mannose, or fructose **2 :** GLUCOSE PHENYLOSAZONE

glu·cose \ˈglü,kōs *also* -ōz\ *n* -S [F, modif. of Gk *gleukos*

	open-chain form	cyclic forms	
1	CHO	HCOH	HOCH
2	HCOH	HCOH	HCOH
3	HOCH	HOCH	HOCH
4	HCOH	HCOH	HCOH
5	HCOH	HCO—	HCO—
6	CH₂OH	CH₂OH	CH₂OH
	D-glucose	α-D-glucose	β-D-glucose

must, sweet wine; akin to Gk *glykys* sweet — more at DULCET] **1 :** an aldose sugar $HOCH_2(CHOH)_4CHO$ known in dextrorotatory, levorotatory, and racemic forms; *esp* **:** the sweet colorless soluble dextrorotatory D-form that is readily obtained crystalline in both the alpha and beta modifications, that occurs esp. in plant saps and fruits, normally in blood, pathologically in the urine (as in diabetes mellitus), and combined in many disaccharides, trisaccharides, polysaccharides, and glucosides in most plant and animal tissues, and that is a chief source of protoplasmic energy and in its simple state is the usual form in which carbohydrate is assimilated into the animal body — see DEXTROSE, INVERT SUGAR, SUCROSE; compare GLYCERALDEHYDE, STRUCTURAL FORMULA **2 :** STARCH SYRUP — used chiefly commercially

glucose phenylosazone *n* **:** a yellow insoluble compound $C_6H_{10}O_4(=NNHC_6H_5)_2$ formed by reaction of glucose or mannose or fructose with phenylhydrazine and used as a derivative for identifying glucose

glucose phosphate *n* **:** a phosphoric derivative of glucose: as **a :** an acylal $C_6H_{11}O_5(OPO_3H_2)$ that reacts in the presence of phosphorylase with aldoses and ketoses to yield disaccharides (as with fructose yielding sucrose and phosphoric acid) or with itself in liver and muscle to yield glycogen and phosphoric acid; glucose 1-phosphate — called also *Cori ester* **b :** an ester $C_6H_{11}O_5(OPO_3H_2)$ formed from glucose and adenosine triphosphate in the presence of hexokinase and regarded as the essential first stage in the metabolism of glucose, subsequent changes being its enzymatic transformations into the corresponding fructose phosphate, glucose phosphate (sense a), and related compounds; glucose 6-phosphate — called also *Robison ester*

glu·co·si·dal \¦glükə¦sīdᵊl\ *adj* **:** GLUCOSIDIC

glu·co·si·dase \glüˈkōsə,dās, -ōzə-, -āz\ *n* -S [ISV *glucoside* + *-ase*] **:** an enzyme (as maltase) that hydrolyzes a glucoside

glu·co·side \ˈglükə,sīd\ *n* -S [ISV *glucose* + *-ide*] **:** GLYCOSIDE; *usu* **:** a glycoside that yields glucose on hydrolysis 〈methyl ~〉 — **glu·co·sid·ic** \¦glükə¦sidik\ *adj* — **glucosidically** *adv*

glu·co·sone \ˈglükə,sōn\ *n* [ISV *gluc-* + *osone*] **:** the osone $C_6H_{10}O_6$ of glucose

glu·co·sul·fone \¦glü(,)kō+\ *n* [*gluc-* + *sulfone*] **:** a drug derived from glucose and *para*-amino-phenyl sulfone and used chiefly in treating leprosy in the form of the sodium salt $[C_6H_{12}O_5(SO_3Na)NHC_6H_4]_2SO_2$

glu·cos·uria \,glü-\ *n* -S [NL, fr. ISV *glucose* + NL *-uria*] **:** GLYCOSURIA

glu·co·syl \ˈglükə,sil\ *n* -S [*glucose* + *-yl*] **:** a glycosyl radical $C_6H_{11}O_5$ derived from glucose — compare MALTOSE

glu·cu·ron·ic acid \,glükyə¦ränik-\ *n* [*glucuronic* fr. *gluc-* + Gk *ouron* urine + E *-ic* — more at URINE] **:** a crystalline aldehyde-acid $HOOC(CHOH)_4CHO$ obtainable from gum arabic by hydrolysis or from methyl glucoside by oxidation and occurring naturally esp. in the urine combined as glucuronides with toxic metabolic products (as phenols or indoxyl) or with steroid hormones

glu·cu·ron·i·dase \,glükyəˈränə,dās, -āz\ *n* -S [*glucuronide* + *-ase*] **:** an enzyme that hydrolyzes a glucuronide; *esp* **:** an enzyme that occurs widely (as in liver and spleen) and is active toward a beta-glucuronide 〈the physiological role of beta=*glucuronidase*〉

glu·cu·ro·nide \glüˈkyu̇rə,nīd\ *n* -S [*glucuron-* (fr. *glucuronic acid*) + *-ide*] **:** a glycosidic compound that yields glucuronic acid on hydrolysis 〈beta-*glucuronides* of estrogenic hormones〉

glu·cu·rono·lactone \glü¦kyu̇rə(,)nō, ¦glükyə¦ränə+\ *n* [*glucuron-* (fr. *glucuronic acid*) + *-o-* + *lactone*] **:** a crystalline aldehydic lactone $C_6H_8O_6$ made from glucuronic acid by heating and used in medicine

glu·cu·ron·o·side \,glükyəˈränə,sīd\ *n* -S [*glucuron-* (fr. *glucuronic acid*) + *-ose* + *-ide*] **:** GLUCURONIDE

¹glue \ˈglü\ *n* -S [ME *glu, glew*, fr. MF *glu* birdlime, glue, fr. OF, fr. LL *glut-, glus* glue — more at CLAY] **1 a** (1) **:** a hard protein substance that absorbs water to form a jelly or a viscous solution with strong adhesive properties that is obtained like gelatin by cooking down materials (as hides, bones) yielding collagen and is usu. considered to contain gelatin along with other products and is used for sticking together relatively heavy materials (as wood) — see ANIMAL GLUE, FISH GLUE; compare MUCILAGE, PASTE; CEMENT 2a (2) **:** a viscous solution of animal glue or fish glue — compare LIQUID GLUE **b :** any of various other strong adhesive substances (as casein glue, vegetable glue) **2 :** something that binds together 〈patriotism is the psychological ~ which helps to hold people of the same country together —R.S.Ellery〉 or holds tightly 〈his plunging spirit had got stuck in the ~ of convention and hypocrisy —Victoria Sackville-West〉 in a manner suggestive of glue

²glue \"\ *vb* **glued; glued; gluing** *also* **glueing; glues** [ME *gluen, glewen*, fr. MF *gluer*, fr. OF, fr. *glu*, n.] *vt* **1 :** to join or fix or cause to stick tightly with or as if with glue 〈*gluing* the wings onto the model airplane〉 〈reading with concentration, keeping his eyes *glued* to the page〉 **2 :** to daub, smear, or cover with glue 〈got their hands all *glued* up〉 ~ *vi* **:** to become glued **:** undergo gluing 〈a wood that *glues* easily〉

glue cell *n* **:** ADHESIVE CELL

glued-up stock \ˈ=,=-\ *n* [*glued* fr. past part. of ²*glue*] **:** edge=glued or laminated wood

glue·man \ˈglümən\ *n, pl* **gluemen 1 :** GLUER **2 :** one who makes glue

glue off *vt* **:** to apply glue to (the spine of a book) during the process of binding

glue plant *n* **:** an alga of the genus *Gloiopeltis* used chiefly in Japan and China for making glue or as a food

glue pot *n* [ME *glew pot*, fr. *glu, glew* glue + *pot*] **1 :** a double boiler designed esp. for melting glue **2** *Austral* **:** a stretch of deep sticky mud on a bush road

glu·er \ˈglüə(r), -ü(ə)r, -üə\ *n* -S [ME *glewer*, fr. *glewen* to glue + *-er*] **:** one that glues; *specif* **:** a worker who glues articles — called also *cementer*

glue up *vt* **:** to glue off

glu·ey \ˈglüē, -üi\ *adj, usu* **gluier**; *usu* **gluiest** [ME *gluwy, glewy*, fr. *glu, glew* glue + *-y*] **1 :** having the quality of glue 〈what we call a colloid, a ~ mass —W.E.Swinton〉 **:** resembling or suggestive of glue (as in stickiness or viscous consistency) 〈he thought how much he would like a beer to wash down the last gob of ~ rice —Earle Birney〉 **:** STICKY, GUMMY **2 :** daubed, smeared, or covered with glue 〈a ~ surface〉

¹glug \ˈgləg\ *n* -S [imit.] **:** a gurgling sound (as of liquid issuing from a bottle with intermittent partial air blockage) **:** GLUB — often reduplicated

²glug \"\ *vi* **glugged; glugged; glugging; glugs :** to make a glug — often reduplicated 〈glasses clinked . . . and the wine bottles *glugged* —Gerald Durrell〉

glu·gea \ˈglüj(ē)ə\ *n, cap* [NL] **:** a large genus of intracellular parasitic microsporidians related to *Nosema* that attack various insect larvae and fishes

glüh·wein \ˈglüe,vīn\ *n* -S [G *glühwein*, fr. *glühen* to mull, glow (fr. OHG *gluoen* to glow) + *wein* wine, fr. OHG *wīn* — more at GLOW, WINE] **:** mulled wine

glu·i·ly \ˈglüəlē, -li\ *adv* **:** in a gluey manner

glu·i·ness *or* **glu·ey·ness** \ˈglüēnəs, -üin-\ *n* -ES **:** the quality or state of being gluey

¹glum \ˈgləm\ *vi* **glummed; glummed; glumming; glums** [ME *glomen*, prob. alter. of *gloumen* — more at GLOOM] *chiefly dial* **:** to look glum **:** FROWN

²glum \"\ *adj, usu* **glummer**; *usu* **glummest 1 a :** broodingly morose **:** sullenly ill-humored or displeased 〈looked ~ when they heard the news〉 **b :** DISMAL, DREARY, GLOOMY 〈with a countenance as ~ as an undertaker's —W.M.Thackeray〉 **2** *dial Eng* **:** OVERCAST, THREATENING 〈the weather looks ~ today〉 **syn** see SULLEN

glu·ma·ceous \(ˈ)glü¦māshəs\ *adj* [prob. fr. (assumed) NL *glumaceus*, fr. NL *gluma* + L *-aceus* -aceous] **:** consisting or having the character of glumes 〈~ flowers〉

glume \ˈglüm\ *n* -S [NL *gluma*, fr. L, hull, husk; akin to L *glubere* to peel — more at CLEAVE] **:** a chaffy bract; *specif* **:** one of the two empty bracts at the base of the spikelet in grasses

glume blotch *n* **:** any of several fungous diseases causing diffuse dark spots on the glumes

glu·mif·er·ous \(ˈ)glü¦mif(ə)rəs\ *adj* [*glume* + *-iferous*] **:** bearing glumes

glu·mi·flo·rae \,glüməˈflōr,ē\ *n pl, cap* [NL, fr. *glumi-* (fr. *gluma* glume) + *-florae* (fr. L *flor-, flos* flower) — more at BLOW (to bloom)] *syn of* GRAMINALES

glum·ly *adv* **:** in a glum manner

glum·ness *n* -ES **:** the quality or state of being glum

glump \ˈgləmp\ *vi* -ED/-ING/-S [prob. alter. of ¹*glum*] *dial* **:** to look glum **:** FROWN

glump·ish \-pish\ *adj, archaic* **:** somewhat grumpy

glump·y \-pē\ *adj, usu* **glumpier**; *usu* **glumpiest** [*glump* + *-y*] *archaic* **:** GRUMPY

¹glunch \ˈglənch\ *vi* -ED/-ING/-ES [perh. alter. of ¹*glum*] *chiefly Scot* **:** to look sour or glum **:** FROWN 〈glowered and ~*ed* at me —John Buchan〉

²glunch \"\ *n* -ES *chiefly Scot* **:** a sour or glum look 〈a ~ of sour disdain —Robert Burns〉

glu·side \ˈglü,sīd\ *n* -S [NL *glusidum*, perh. irreg. fr. Gk *glykys* sweet + NL *-idum* -ide — more at DULCET] **:** SACCHARIN

¹glut \ˈglət, *usu* -əd·+V\ *vb* **glutted; glutted; glutting; gluts** [ME *glotten, glouten*, prob. fr. MF *glotir, gloutir* to swallow, fr. L *glutire* — more at GLUTTON] *vt* **1 :** to feed, fill, or gratify to the fullest possible extent **:** indulge to the point of satiety or revulsion **:** SATIATE, GORGE, SURFEIT 〈*glutting* themselves with food and drink〉 〈before he had quite *glutted* his great appetite —C.G.D.Roberts〉 〈the crowd, perhaps *glutted* with blood, is ominously silent —Claudia Cassidy〉 **2 :** to flood (the business market) with goods so that supply exceeds demand 〈selling *glutted* the market and cracked it —Lewis Nordyke〉 ~ *vi* **:** to feed upon something without restraint and to the point of satiety or revulsion **:** become gorged 〈sat by to ~ and laugh —J.H.Allen〉 **syn** see SATIATE

²glut \"\ *n* -S **1** *archaic* **:** the act of glutting or state of being glutted : full or excessive gratification : SURFEITING **2 :** an excessive quantity; *specif* **:** OVERSUPPLY ⟨when there is a ~ in the wheat market —M.R.Cohen⟩ ⟨the mounting ~ of indifference —Claudia Cassidy⟩

³glut \"\ *n* -s [perh. fr. ¹*glut*] *archaic* **:** DRAFT, SWALLOW

⁴glut \"\ *vt* **glutted; glutted; glutting; gluts** *archaic* **:** to swallow greedily **:** gulp down **:** WOLF

⁵glut \"\ *n* -s [origin unknown] **1 :** a block (as metal, wood) that is often tapered and that is used as a wedge or shim or lever fulcrum **2 :** material (as a piece of canvas with a thimble or pieces of rope with a thimble or becket) which is sewed or spliced near the center of the head of a square sail and to which a bunt jigger is hooked in hauling up the bunt for furling **3 :** a small brick used to fill out a course

glut·acon·ic acid \ˌglüd·əˌkänik-\ *n* [*glutaconic* prob. ISV *glut-* (fr. *gluten*) + *aconic* (in *aconic acid*)] **:** a crystalline unsaturated dicarboxylic acid $HOOCCH_2CH{=}CHCOOH$ isomeric with citraconic acid

glu·ta·mate \ˈglüd·əˌmāt\ *n* -s [*glutam-* (fr. *glutamic acid*) + *-ate*] **:** a salt or ester of glutamic acid; *esp* **:** MONOSODIUM GLUTAMATE

glu·tam·ic acid \(ˈ)glüˌtamik-\ *n* [*glutamic* ISV *glut-* (fr. *gluten*) + *amic* (in *amic acid*)] **:** a crystalline amino dicarboxylic acid $HOOCCH_2CH_2CH(NH_2)COOH$ that exists in three optically isomeric forms and occurs usu. as the dextrorotatory L-form both free and combined in glutamine and many proteins in plants and animals, that is usu. obtained by hydrolysis of gluten or from the waste waters of beet-sugar manufacture or by fermentation, and that takes part in transaminations and related metabolic reactions in the living organism; α-amino-glutaric acid

glu·ta·min·ase \ˈglüd·əmə,nās, glüˈtam-, -āz\ *n* -s [ISV *glutamine* + *-ase*] **:** an enzyme that hydrolyzes glutamine to glutamic acid and ammonia

glu·ta·mine \ˈglüd·ə,mēn, -,mən\ *n* -s [ISV *glut-* (fr. *gluten*) + *amine*] **:** a crystalline amino acid $H_2NOCCH_2CH_2CH(NH_2)COOH$ that occurs both free and combined in proteins in plants and animals and that yields glutamic acid and ammonia on hydrolysis; L-glutamic acid monoamide

glu·ta·min·ic acid \ˌglüd·əˌminik-\ *n* [*glutaminic* ISV *glutamine* + *-ic*] **:** GLUTAMIC ACID

glu·tam·o·yl \glüˈtamə,wil\ *or* **glu·tamyl** \ˈglüd·ə,mil, glüˈtaməl\ *n* -s [ISV *glutam-* (fr. *glutamic acid*) + *-oyl* or *-yl*] **:** the bivalent radical $-OCCH_2CH_2CH(NH_2)CO-$ of glutamic acid

glu·tar·ic acid \(ˈ)glüˌtarik-\ *n* [*glutaric* prob. ISV *glut-* (fr. *gluten*) + *-aric* (as in *tartaric acid*)] **:** a crystalline dicarboxylic acid $HOOC(CH_2)_3COOH$ made usu. by oxidation of cyclopentanone — compare KETOGLUTARIC ACID

glu·ta·ryl \ˈglüd·ə,ril, glüˈtarəl\ *n* -s [*glutar-* (fr. *glutaric acid*) + *-yl*] **:** the bivalent radical $-OC(CH_2)_3CO-$ of glutaric acid

glu·ta·thi·one \ˌglüd·əˈthīˌōn, -ˌthīˈōn\ *n* -s [ISV *gluta-* (fr. *glutamic acid*) + *thi-* + *-one*] **:** a crystalline tripeptide $C_{10}H_{17}N_3O_6S$ of glutamic acid, cysteine, and glycine that occurs in blood and other animal and plant tissues and that plays an important role in the activation of some enzymes and in biological oxidation-reduction processes

glu·te·al \ˈglüd·ēəl, (ˈ)glüˈtē-\ *adj* [NL *gluteus* + E *-al*] **:** of, relating to, or in the region of the gluteus muscles

gluteal artery *n* **:** one of the arteries supplying the gluteal muscles on each side of the body

gluteal nerve *n* **:** one of the nerves arising from the sacral plexus and supplying the gluteal muscles and adjacent parts

glu·telin \ˈglüd·ᵊlən, glüˈtel-\ *n* -s [ISV, irreg. fr. *gluten*] **:** any of a group of simple proteins (as glutenin) that occur esp. in the seeds of cereals and that are insoluble in neutral solvents and soluble in dilute acids or alkalies

glu·ten \ˈglütᵊn\ *n* -s [MF or L; MF *gluten*, fr. L, glue; akin to LL *glut-*, *glus* glue — more at CLAY] **1** *archaic* **a :** a sticky substance **:** ADHESIVE **b :** an albuminous element found in animal tissues **2 a :** a tenacious tough elastic protein substance characteristic of flour (as from wheat) that gives to bread dough cohesiveness and ability to retain gas, that is usu. obtained by washing the starch out of wheat flour, and that consists chiefly of gliadin and glutenin **b :** CORN GLUTEN — **glu·ten·ous** \-t(ᵊ)nəs\ *adj*

gluten bread *n* **:** bread made of wheat flour of high gluten and low starch content

gluten feed *n* **:** CORN GLUTEN FEED

glu·te·nin \ˈglütᵊnən\ *n* -s [*gluten* + *-in*] **:** a glutelin found esp. in wheat and obtained by extracting gluten with dilute alkali

gluten meal *n* **:** CORN GLUTEN MEAL

gluteo- *comb form* [NL *gluteus*] **:** gluteal and ⟨*gluteo*femoral⟩

glu·te·us \ˈglüd·ēəs, glüˈtē-\ *n, pl* **glu·tei** \-ē,ī\ [NL *glutaeus, gluteus*, irreg. fr. Gk *gloutos* buttock — more at CLOUD] **:** any one of certain muscles of the buttocks — see GLUTEUS MAXIMUS, GLUTEUS MEDIUS, GLUTEUS MINIMUS

gluteus max·i·mus \-ˈmaksəməs\ *n, pl* **glutei maxi·mi** \-sə,mī\ [NL, lit., largest gluteus] **:** the outermost muscle of three muscles found in each of the human buttocks that arises from the sacrum, coccyx, back part of the ilium and adjacent structures and that is inserted into the fascia lata of the thigh and the gluteal tuberosity of the femur

gluteus me·di·us \-ˈmēdēəs\ *n, pl* **glutei me·dii** \-dē,ī\ [NL, lit., middle gluteus] **:** the middle muscle of three muscles found in each of the human buttocks that arises from the outer surface of the ilium and that is inserted into the great trochanter of the femur

gluteus mi·ni·mus \-ˈminəməs\ *n, pl* **glutei mini·mi** \-nə,mī\ [NL, lit., smallest gluteus] **:** the innermost muscle of three muscles found in each of the human buttocks that arises from the outer surface of the ilium and that is inserted into the great trochanter of the femur

glut herring *n* **:** an anadromous herring (*Pomolobus aestivalis*) of the coast from New England to the Carolinas that appears in great numbers esp. southward later than the alewife and shad — called also *summer herring*

glu·ti·nin \ˈglütᵊnən\ *n* -s [prob. fr. *agglutinin*] **:** BLOCKING ANTIBODY

glu·ti·nize \-tᵊn,īz\ *vt* -ED/-ING/-S [*glutinous* + *-ize*] **:** to make glutinous

glu·ti·nose \-tᵊn,ōs\ *adj* [L *glutinosus*] **:** GLUTINOUS

glu·ti·nos·i·ty \ˌglütᵊnˈäsəd·ē\ *n* -ES [ME *glutinosite*, fr. (assumed) NL *glutinositat-, glutinositas*, fr. L *glutinosus* + *-itat-, -itas* -ity] **:** the quality or state of being glutinous

glu·ti·nous \ˈglüt(ᵊ)nəs\ *adj* [MF or L; MF *glutineux*, fr. L *glutinosus*, fr. *glutin-, gluten* glue + *-osus* -ose] **:** having the quality of glue esp. in physical properties ⟨a ~ substance⟩ **:** GLUEY, STICKY, GUMMY, ROPY ⟨all had ~ chipped beef on rocklike toast —Sloan Wilson⟩; *specif* **:** having a sticky surface ⟨~ plant leaves⟩ — **glu·ti·nous·ly** *adv* — **glu·ti·nous·ness** *n* -ES

glu·ti·tion \glüˈtishən\ *n* -s [LL *gluttition-, glutitio*, fr. L *glutitus*, past part of *gluttire* to swallow] **:** DEGLUTITION

glu·toid \ˈglü,tȯid\ *n* -s [ISV *glut-* (fr. *gluten*) + *-oid*] **:** gelatin hardened with formaldehyde and used in making enteric capsules and as a coating for enteric pills

glu·tose \ˈglü,tōs *also* -ōz\ *n* -s [ISV *glu-* (fr. *glucose*) + *-tose* (fr. *fructose*)] **:** an unfermentable carbohydrate fraction formed by the action of alkali on glucose or fructose or found in cane molasses

gluts *pres 3d sing of* GLUT, *pl of* GLUT

glutted *past of* GLUT

glutting *pres part of* GLUT

glut·ting·ly *adv, archaic* **:** GLUTTONOUSLY

¹glut·ton \ˈglətᵊn\ *n* -s [ME *glotoun*, fr. OF *gloton*, fr. LL *glutton-, glutto*; akin to OE *ceole* throat, OHG *kela*, L *gula* throat, *gluttire* to swallow, Gk *delear* bait, Russ *glotat'* to swallow, gulp] **1 a :** one that eats too much **:** one given to excessive eating and drinking **:** one that gluts **b** (1) **:** one that greedily or excessively indulges in something as if voraciously devouring it ⟨~*s* of morning air —Christopher Morley⟩ ⟨a ~ of books⟩ ⟨a literary ~⟩ (2) **:** one that has a great capacity for accepting or enduring something ⟨a ~ for work⟩ ⟨a ~ for punishment⟩ **2** [trans. of G *vielfrass*] **a :** a carnivorous mammal (*Gulo gulo*) of the family Mustelidae of the northern parts of Europe and Asia that is related to the marten and the sable and is about 2½ feet long and has a heavy build and long shaggy fur **b :** WOLVERINE 1a **syn** see EPICURE

²glutton \"\ *adj* [ME *glotoun*, fr. *glotoun*, n.] *archaic* **:** GLUTTONOUS

³glutton \"\ *vb* -ED/-ING/-S [¹*glutton*] *archaic* **:** GLUT

⁴glutton \"\ *also* **glutton bird** *n* -s [¹*glutton*] **:** GIANT PETREL

glut·ton·ize \ˈglətᵊn,īz\ *vb* -ED/-ING/-S *vi, archaic* **:** to feast gluttonously ~ *vt, archaic* **:** to feast gluttonously on

glut·ton·ous \ˈglət(ᵊ)nəs\ *adj* [ME *glotonous*, fr. *gloton, glotoun* glutton + *-ous*] **:** marked by or given to gluttony **syn** see VORACIOUS

glut·ton·ous·ly *adv* [ME *glotonously*, fr. *glotonous* + *-ly*] **:** in a gluttonous manner

glut·ton·ous·ness *n* -ES **:** the quality or state of being gluttonous

glut·tony \ˈglət(ᵊ)nē, -ni\ *n* -ES [ME *glotonie*, fr. OF, fr. *gloton* glutton + *-ie* -y] **1 :** excess in eating and drinking esp. when habitual **2 :** greedy or excessive indulgence of any desire or faculty

glyc- *or* **glyco-** *comb form* [ISV, fr. Gk *glyk-* sweet, fr. *glykys* — more at DULCET] **1 :** sugar ⟨*glyco*genic⟩ **:** related to or containing a sugar ⟨*glyc*emia⟩ ⟨*glyco*alkaloid⟩ ⟨*glyc*itol⟩ **:** sweet ⟨*glyco*gen⟩ **2 a :** glycerol ⟨*glyco*gelatin⟩ **b :** glycogen ⟨*glyco*static⟩ **c :** glycol ⟨*glyco*stat⟩ **d :** glycine ⟨*glyc*yl⟩ — used also to indicate other compounds spelled with initial *glyc-* **3 :** GLUC- 1a

gly·can \ˈglī,kan\ *n* -s [*glyc-* + *-an*] **:** POLYSACCHARIDE

gly·ce·mia *also* **gly·cae·mia** \glīˈsēmēə\ *n* -s [NL, fr. *glyc-* + *-emia*] **:** the presence of glucose in the blood — **gly·ce·mic** \(ˈ)glīˌsēmik\ *adj*

glycer- *or* **glycero-** *comb form* [ISV, fr. *glycerin*] **1 :** glycerol ⟨*glycer*yl⟩ **:** related to glycerol or glyceric acid ⟨*glycero*phosphoric acid⟩ ⟨*glycer*aldehyde⟩ **2** *glycero-, usu ital* **:** having the stereochemical arrangement of atoms or groups found in glyceraldehyde ⟨2-(D-*glycero*-1-hydroxyethyl)-benzimidazole⟩

glyc·era \ˈglisərə\ *n, cap* [NL, fr. L *Glycera* (feminine proper name)] **:** a common widely distributed genus (the type of the family Glyceridae) of usu. brightly colored burrowing marine polychaete worms having simple parapodia and an extremely large introvert armed with four chitinous jaws suggestive of hooks — **glyc·er·id** \-rəd\ *adj or n*

glyc·er·aldehyde \ˌglisər+\ *n* **:** a sweet crystalline compound that exists in solution as the monomeric dihydroxy aldehyde $HOCH_2CHOHCHO$ in dextrorotatory, levorotatory, and racemic forms but in the anhydrous state only as the crystalline dimer $C_6H_{12}O_6$, that is formed as an intermediate in carbohydrate metabolism by the breakdown of sugars, that yields glycerol on reduction, and that may be regarded as a triose and the simplest aldose capable of existing in both D- and L-stereoisomeric forms, which serve as reference standards for differentiating the stereoisomeric forms of all other sugars and also of other stereoisomeric compounds — called also *glyceric aldehyde, glycerose;* compare GLUCOSE 1, STRUCTURAL FORMULA

```
  CHO            CHO
  |              |
H-C-OH        HO-C-H
  |              |
  CH2OH          CH2OH

dextrorotatory     levorotatory
D-glyceraldehyde   L-glyceraldehyde
```

glyc·er·ate \ˈglisə,rāt\ *n* -s [ISV *glycer-* + *-ate*] **:** a salt or ester of glyceric acid

gly·ce·ria \gləˈsirēə, glīˈ-\ *n, cap* [NL, fr. Gk *glykeros* sweet + NL *-ia*] **:** a genus of chiefly No. American perennial paludal or aquatic grasses having lemmas very prominently 5- to 9-nerved

gly·cer·ic acid \gləˈserik-, (ˈ)gliˈserik-, ˈglisərik-\ *n* [*glyceric* ISV *glycer-* + *-ic*] **:** a syrupy hydroxy acid $HOCH_2CHOHCOOH$ obtainable by oxidation of glycerol or glyceraldehyde

glyceric aldehyde *n* **:** GLYCERALDEHYDE

glyc·er·ide \ˈglisə,rīd, -,rəd\ *n* -s [ISV *glycer-* + *-ide*] **:** any of a large class of compounds that are esters of glycerol esp. with fatty acids, that occur naturally as fats and fatty oils or are made synthetically, and that are classed as monoglycerides, diglycerides, and triglycerides according to the number of hydroxyl groups of glycerol esterified or as simple glycerides or mixed glycerides according as one or more than one kind of acid radical is present — **glyc·er·id·ic** \ˌglisəˌridik\ *adj*

¹glyc·er·in \ˈglis(ə)rən\ *or* **glyc·er·ine** \" *sometimes* ˈglisə,rēn *or* ,glisəˈrēn\ *n* -s [F *glycérine*, fr. Gk *glykeros* sweet + F *-ine*; akin to Gk *glykys* sweet — more at DULCET] **1 :** GLYCEROL — used esp. of the products for industrial and pharmaceutical uses **2 :** GLYCERITE

²glycerin \"\ *or* **glycerine** \"\ *vt* -ED/-ING/-S **:** GLYCERINATE

glyc·er·in·ate \ˈglis(ə)rə,nāt\ *vt* -ED/-ING/-S **:** to treat with or preserve in glycerin — **glyc·er·in·ation** \ˌglis(ə)rəˈnāshən\ *n* -s

glycerinated gelatin *n* [*glycerinated* fr. past part. of *glycerinate*] **:** a jellylike preparation made from glycerin, gelatin, and water and used as a base for suppositories and ointments

glyc·er·in·ize \ˈglis(ə)rə,nīz\ *vt* -ED/-ING/-S **:** GLYCERINATE

glycerin jelly *n* **:** a mixture of gelatin and glycerin used in the mounting of microscopic material

glycerin soap *n* **:** transparent toilet soap having glycerin as an ingredient

glyc·er·ite \ˈglisə,rīt\ *n* -s **:** a medicinal preparation made by mixing or dissolving a substance in glycerin

glyc·er·ize \-,rīz\ *vt* -ED/-ING/-S **:** GLYCERINATE

glyc·ero·gelatin \ˌglisə(,)rō+\ *n* **:** any of several medicated dermatologic preparations made from glycerin and glycerinated gelatin

glyc·er·ol \ˈglisə,rȯl, -rōl\ *n* -s [*glycer-* + *-ol*] **:** a sweet syrupy hygroscopic trihydroxy alcohol $HOCH_2CHOHCH_2OH$ that occurs combined as glycerides and is formed by alcoholic fermentation of sugars, that is usu. obtained as a by-product in the manufacture of soap or fatty acids by the saponification of fats or as a synthetic product from propylene or allyl alcohol, and that is used chiefly as a solvent and plasticizer, as a moistening agent, emollient, and lubricant, and as a starting material in the manufacture of many derivatives; 1,2,3-propane-triol — called also *glycerin;* see ALKYD, CHLOROHYDRIN, ESTER GUM, NITROGLYCERIN

¹glyc·er·o·late \ˈglis(ə)rə,lāt\ *n* -s [*glycerol* + ¹*-ate*] **:** GLYCERITE

²glycerolate \"\ *vt* -ED/-ING/-S [*glycerol* + ⁴*-ate*] **:** GLYCERINATE

glyc·er·ole \ˈglisə,rōl\ *n* -s [irreg. fr. *glycer-*] **:** GLYCERITE

glyc·er·o·lize \ˈglis(ə)rə,līz\ *vt* -ED/-ING/-S [*glycerol* + *-ize*] **:** GLYCERINATE

glyc·ero·phosphate \ˌglisə(,)rō+\ *n* [ISV *glycer-* + *phosphate*] **:** a salt or ester of either of the glycerophosphoric acids

glyc·ero·phosphoric acid \ˌglisə(,)rō+ . . . -\ *n* [*glycerophosphoric* ISV *glycer-* + *phosphoric*] **:** either of two syrupy isomeric dibasic acids $C_3H_5(OH)_2OPO_3H_2$ occurring naturally in combined form as lecithin and cephalin, obtained usu. as a mixture of the two by reaction of glycerol and phosphoric acid, and used in medicine in the form of salts: **a :** the alpha isomer existing in dextrorotatory, levorotatory, and racemic forms; glycerol 1-phosphate — called also *alpha-glycerophosphoric acid* **b :** the optically inactive beta isomer; glycerol 2-phosphate — called also *beta-glycerophosphate*

glyc·er·ose \ˈglisə,rōs *also* -ōz\ *n* -s [ISV *glycer-* + *-ose*] **:** GLYCERALDEHYDE — used esp. in relation to other sugars

glyc·er·oxide \ˌglisər+\ *n* **:** a derivative of glycerol in which a metal (as sodium) replaces hydroxylic hydrogen

glyc·er·yl \ˈglis(ə)rəl\ *n* -s [ISV *glycer-* + *-yl*] **:** a trivalent radical CH_2CHCH_2 derived from glycerol by removal of all three hydroxyl groups; *sometimes* **:** a univalent or bivalent radical derived from glycerol by removal of hydroxyl ⟨~ mono-stearate⟩

glyceryl triacetate *n* **:** ACETIN c

glyceryl trinitrate *n* **:** NITROGLYCERIN

gly·cid·ic acid \gləˈsˌidik-, (ˈ)gliˌs|\ *n* [*glycidic* ISV *glycid-* (as in E *glycidol*) + *-ic*] **:** a volatile mobile liquid C_2H_3OCOOH used in the form of derivatives in perfumes; α,β-epoxy-propionic acid

glyc·i·dol \ˈglisə,dȯl, -dōl\ *n* -s [obs. E *glycide* glycidol (fr. E *glyc-* + *-ide*) + E *-ol*] **:** a liquid alcohol $C_2H_3OCH_2OH$ obtained from glycerol by indirect dehydration; 2,3-epoxy-1-propanol

gly·cin \ˈglīsᵊn\ *also* **gly·cine** \", -ī,sēn\ *n* -s [prob. fr. ¹*glycine*] **:** a poisonous compound $HOC_6H_4NHCH_2COOH$ used in photography as a fine-grain developer; *N-(para-hydroxy-phenyl)glycine*

¹gly·cine \"\ *n* -s [ISV *glyc-* + *-ine*] **:** a sweet crystalline amino acid NH_2CH_2COOH that is formed by the hydrolysis of many proteins (as gelatin), hippuric acid, and glycocholic acid but is usu. made by reaction of chloroacetic acid and ammonia — called also *aminoacetic acid, glycocoll*

²glyc·i·ne \ˈglisᵊn,ē\ [NL, irreg. fr. Gk *glykys* sweet — more at DULCET] *syn of* APIOS

glyci·nin \ˈglīsᵊnən, ˈglis-\ *n* -s [NL *Glycine* + E *-in*] **:** a globulin found in the seeds of the soybean

glyciphagus *syn of* GLYCYPHAGUS

glyco- — see GLYC-

gly·co·chol·ate \ˌglīkōˈkä,lāt, -ˈkō,lāt; glīˈkäkə,lāt\ *n* -s [ISV *glycochol-* (fr. *glycocholic acid*) + *-ate*] **:** a salt or ester of glycocholic acid

gly·co·cholic acid \ˌglīkōˌkōlik-, -ˌkälik-\ *n* [*glycocholic* ISV *glyc-* + *cholic* (as in *cholic acid*)] **:** a crystalline acid $(HO)_3C_{23}H_{36}CONHCH_2COOH$ that occurs in bile esp. of man and herbivorous animals and that yields glycine and cholic acid on hydrolysis

gly·co·coll \ˈglīkō,käl\ *n* -s [ISV *glyc-* sweet (fr. Gk *glyk-*, fr. *glykys*) + *-o-* + *-coll*] **:** GLYCINE

gly·co·cy·a·mine \ˌglīkō,sīˈa,mēn, -,sīˈamən\ *n* [ISV *glyc-* + *cy-* (fr. *cyan-*) + *amine*] **:** a crystalline amino acid $NH_2C({=}NH)NHCH_2COOH$ that is produced enzymatically in the animal body from glycine and arginine and that yields creatine on methylation — called also *guanidoacetic acid*

gly·co·gen \ˈglīkəjən, -,jen\ *n* -s [ISV *glyc-* + *-gen*] **:** a white amorphous tasteless polysaccharide $(C_6H_{10}O_5)n$ constituting the principal form in which carbohydrate is stored in animal tissues, occurring esp. in the liver and in muscle and also in fungi and yeasts, and resembling starch in molecular structure and in the formation of only glucose on complete hydrolysis — called also *animal starch*

gly·co·gen·e·sis \ˌglīkəˈjenəsəs\ *n* [NL, fr. *glyc-* + L *genesis*] **1 :** formation of sugar from glycogen (as in the liver) **2 :** formation of glycogen (as from sugars or some amino acids)

gly·co·ge·net·ic \ˌglīkəjəˈned·ik\ *adj* [fr. NL *glycogenesis*, after E *genesis: genetic*] **:** of, relating to, or produced by glycogenesis

gly·co·gen·ic \ˌglīkəˈjenik\ *adj* [ISV *glycogen* + *-ic*] **1 :** of, relating to, or involving glycogen **2** [ISV *glyc-* + *-genic*] **:** GLYCOGENETIC

gly·co·gen·ol·y·sis \ˌglīkəjəˈnäləsəs\ *n, pl* **glycogenoly·ses** \-ə,sēz\ [NL, fr. *glycogeno-* (fr. ISV *glycogen*) + *-lysis*] **:** the breakdown of glycogen esp. to glucose in the animal body

gly·co·gen·o·lyt·ic \ˌglīkə,jenᵊlˈid·ik\ *adj* [ISV *glycogen* + *-o-* + *-lytic*] **:** of, relating to, or inducing glycogenolysis ⟨~ enzymes⟩ ⟨a ~ agent⟩

gly·co·gen·o·tropic \-nəˈträpik, -rōp-\ *adj* [ISV *glycogen* + *-o-* + *-tropic*] **:** tending to induce glycogenolysis ⟨a ~ hormone⟩

gly·cog·e·nous \(ˈ)glīˈkäjənəs\ *adj* [*glyc-* + *-genous*] **:** GLYCOGENETIC

gly·col \ˈglī,kȯl, -kōl\ *n* -s [ISV *glyc-* + *-ol*] **1 :** ETHYLENE GLYCOL **2 :** any of the large class of dihydroxy alcohols (as propylene glycol) of which ethylene glycol is the simplest member — compare DIOL

gly·col·aldehyde \ˌ≈·≈+\ *n* [ISV *glycol* + *aldehyde*] **:** a compound that in solution exists as the monomeric hydroxy aldehyde $HOCH_2CHO$ and as such is the simplest monosaccharide but that in the anhydrous state exists only as the crystalline dimer $C_4H_8O_4$; hydroxy-acetaldehyde — compare DIOSE

gly·co·late \ˈglīkə,lāt\ *or* **gly·col·late** \", glīˈkälˌāt\ *n* -s [*glycol* + *-ate*] **:** a salt or ester of glycolic acid

gly·col·ic acid *or* **gly·col·lic acid** \(ˈ)glīˌkälik-\ *n* [*glycolic, glycollic* ISV *glycol* + *-ic*] **:** a translucent crystalline compound $HOCH_2COOH$ found esp. in unripe grapes and in sugar beets, made usu. by hydrolysis of chloroacetic acid or as an intermediate in the manufacture of ethylene glycol, and used chiefly in processing textiles and leather and in cleaning metals

gly·co·lipide *or* **gly·co·lipid** \ˌglīkō+\ *n* [*glyc-* + *lipide, lipid*] **:** any of a class of lipides that yield on hydrolysis a sugar (as galactose or glucose), sphingosine or a related amino alcohol, fatty acids, and sometimes other acids and that include the cerebrosides and the gangliosides

gly·col·y·sis \glīˈkäləsəs\ *n, pl* **glycoly·ses** \-ə,sēz\ [NL, fr. *glyc-* + *-lysis*] **:** the enzymatic breakdown of glucose, glycogen, or other carbohydrate by way of phosphate derivatives with the production esp. of lactic acid in animals and of pyruvic acid in plants and with the release of energy — see ADENOSINE DIPHOSPHATE; compare FERMENTATION 1, RESPIRATION 2

gly·co·lyt·ic \ˌglīkəˈlid·ik\ *adj* [ISV *glyc-* + *-lytic*] **:** of, relating to, or inducing glycolysis ⟨a ~ enzyme system⟩ ⟨the ~ pathway⟩ — **gly·co·lyt·i·cal·ly** \-d·ək(ə)lē\ *adv*

gly·co·neogenesis \ˌglīkō+\ *n* [NL, fr. *glyc-* + *ne-* + L *genesis*] **:** GLUCONEOGENESIS

¹gly·con·ic \glīˈkänik\ *n* -s *sometimes cap* [*Glycon*, Greek poet of unknown date to whom the invention of this verse was ascribed in the 2d century A.D. + E *-ic*] **:** a variable verse or rhythmic system typically of the form ⏑⏑–⏑⏑–⏑– that may have a choriambus or dactyl at the beginning, middle, or end

²glyconic \(ˈ)≈ˌ≈≈\ *adj, sometimes cap* **:** of, relating to, or consisting of glyconics

glyconic acid *n* [*glyconic* ISV *glyc-* + *-onic*] **:** ALDONIC ACID

gly·co·peptide \ˌglī(,)kō+\ *n* [*glyc-* + *peptide*] **:** GLYCOPROTEIN

gly·co·protein \ˌ≈(,)≈+\ *n* [*glyc-* + *protein*] **:** any of a group of complex compounds containing sugar units or polysaccharides combined usu. covalently with amino acid units or polypeptides and including many common albumins and globulins (as egg albumin, some serum albumins, and some serum globulins) — called also *glycopeptide;* compare MUCOPROTEIN

gly·cose \ˈglī,kōs *also* -ōz\ *n* -s [F, alter. (influenced by Gk *glykys* sweet) of *glucose*] **1** *archaic* **:** GLUCOSE 1 **2 :** a simple sugar (as arabinose, glucose, or fructose) existing structurally in either its open-chain aldehyde or ketone modification or in its cyclic hemiacetal forms that contain furanose or pyranose rings **:** MONOSACCHARIDE

gly·co·si·dase \glīˈkōsə,dās, -ōzə-, -āz\ *n* -s [ISV *glycoside* + *-ase*] **:** an enzyme that hydrolyzes a glycoside, esp. a simple glycoside or an oligosaccharide

gly·co·side \ˈglīkə,sīd\ *n* -s [ISV *glycose* + *-ide*] **:** any of a large class of natural or synthetic compounds (as anthocyanins) that are acetal derivatives of sugars and that on hydrolysis (as by the action of enzymes or dilute acids) yield one or more molecules of a sugar and often a noncarbohydrate **:** a mixed acetal of which a cyclic form of a glycose is the hemiacetal and which may be classified as a furanoside or pyranoside according to the size of the ring of the glycose or as an alpha glycoside or a beta glycoside according to the optical rotation ⟨methyl ~*s*⟩ — see AGLYCON; compare GLUCOSE illustration, GLUCOSIDE, OLIGOSACCHARIDE, POLYSACCHARIDE — **gly·co·sid·ic** \ˌglīkəˈsidik\ *adj* — **gly·co·sid·i·cal·ly** \-d·ək(ə)lē\ *adv*

gly·cos·uria \ˌglī(,)kōˈs(h)u̇rēə, -ōsˈyu̇-\ *n* -s [NL, fr. ISV *glycose* + NL *-uria*] **:** the presence in the urine (as in diabetes mellitus) of abnormal amounts of sugar (as glucose) — compare GLYCURESIS — **gly·cos·uric** \ˌ≈(,)≈ˈ≈rik\ *adj*

gly·co·syl \ˈglīkə,sil\ *n* -s [*glycose* + *-yl*] **:** a univalent radical derived from a cyclic form of glycose by removal of the hemiacetal hydroxyl group — compare GLUCOSYL

gly·co·trop·ic \ˌglīkōˈträpik\ *also* **gly·co·trophic** \-ˈräfik, -rōf-\ *adj* [*glyc-* + *-tropic* or *-trophic*] **:** antagonizing the action of insulin esp. with regard to the production of hypoglycemia ⟨a ~ anterior-pituitary fraction⟩

glycu·re·sis \ˌglikyəˈrēsəs, ˌglīk-\ *n, pl* **glycure·ses** \-ē,sēz\ [NL, fr. *glyc-* + *uresis*] **:** physiologic excretion of large amounts of sugar in the urine following excessive carbohydrate intake — compare GLYCOSURIA

glycu·ron·ic acid \ˌglik|yəˈränik-, ˌglīk|\ *n* [*glycuronic* ISV *glyc-* + *uron-* (fr. Gk *ouron* urine) + *-ic* — more at URINE] **1** *archaic* **:** GLUCURONIC ACID **2 :** a uronic acid (as galacturonic acid) derived from a glycose (as galactose)

glycyl \ˈglīsəl, ˈglis-, -,sēl\ *n* -s [ISV *glyc-* + *-yl*] **:** the univalent acyl radical NH_2CH_2CO- of glycine

glyc·y·mer·i·dae \ˌglisəˈmerə,dē\ *n pl, cap* [NL, fr. *Glycymeris*, type genus (fr. L, a shellfish, prob. modif. of Gk *glykymaris* cockle) + *-idae*] **:** a family of bivalve mollusks (suborder Myacea) comprising the dog cockles

gly·cyph·a·gus \glī'sifəgəs, glə'-\ *n, cap* [NL, fr. *glycy-* (fr. Gk *glykys* sweet) + *-phagus* -phagous (fr. Gk *-phagos*) — more at DULCET] **:** a genus (the type of the family Glycyphagidae) of broad-bodied mites that are often abundant in stored organic material (as dried fruits, hides, and grain) and that sometimes cause a form of grocer's itch in persons handling infested material

glyc·yr·rhi·za \,glisə'rīzə\ *n* [NL, fr. L, licorice root — more at LICORICE] **1** *cap* **:** a genus of widely distributed perennial herbs or subshrubs (family Leguminosae) with odd-pinnate leaves, racemose or spicate flowers, and leathery often prickly pods — see LICORICE **2** -s [L] **:** LICORICE 1a

glyc·yr·rhi·zic acid \¦glisə¦rīzik-\ *n* [*glycyrrhizic* ISV *glycyrrhiz-* (fr. NL *Glycyrrhiza*) + *-ic*] **:** GLYCYRRHIZIN

glyc·yr·rhi·zin \,glisə'rīzᵊn\ *n* -s [ISV *glycyrrhiz-* (fr. NL *glycyrrhiza*) + *-in*] **:** a crystalline glycosidic acid $C_{42}H_{62}O_{16}$ constituting the sweet constituent of licorice root

glyde \'glīd\ *var of* GLEYDE

gly·ox·al \glī'äk,sal, ¦==¦=\ *n* -s [ISV *gly-* (fr. *glycol*) + *ox-* (oxal-) + *-al*] **:** a reactive yellow low-melting aldehyde CHOCHO made by catalytic oxidation of ethylene glycol and usu. handled in aqueous solution because of its ease of polymerization to an amorphous white solid

gly·ox·a·lase \glī'äksə,lās, -āz\ *n* -s [*glyoxal* + *-ase*] **:** an enzyme that accelerates reversibly the conversion in the presence of glutathione of pyruvaldehyde to lactic acid

gly·ox·al·ic acid \¦glī,äk¦salik-\ *n* [*glyoxalic* ISV *glyoxal* + *-ic*] **:** GLYOXYLIC ACID

gly·ox·al·i·dine \,glī,äk'salə,dēn, -ələdᵊn\ *n* -s [*glyoxal* + *-idine*] **:** IMIDAZOLINE

gly·ox·a·line \glī'äksə,lēn, -,lən\ *n* -s [ISV *glyoxal* + *-ine*] **:** IMIDAZOLE

gly·ox·ime \(')glī¦äk,sēm, -,səm\ *n* [ISV *gly-* (fr. *glyoxal*) + *oxime*] **:** a white crystalline compound $(CH{=}NOH)_2$ that is the oxime of glyoxal — compare DIMETHYLGLYOXIME

gly·ox·yl·ic acid \¦glī,äk¦silik-\ *n* [*glyoxylic* ISV *glyox-* (fr. *glyoxal*) + *-yl* + *-ic*] **:** a syrupy or crystalline aldehyde acid CHOCOOH or $CH(OH)_2COOH$ that occurs esp. in unripe fruits

glyph \'glif\ *n* -s [Gk *glyphē* carved work, fr. *glyphein* to carve — more at CLEAVE] **1 :** an ornamental vertical groove (as in a triglyph) **2 :** a symbolic figure or a character usu. incised or carved in relief; *specif* **:** the basic unit in the Maya system of writing consisting of a pictorial or conventionalized sign or of two or more such signs enclosed in a frame line having typically the form of a square with rounded corners ⟨many of the ~*s* represent, not Maya words or constructions, but universal ideas —A.A.Hill⟩

glyph·ic \'glifik\ *adj* **:** of, relating to, consisting of, or resembling glyphs ⟨a ~ system of writing⟩ ⟨~ inscriptions⟩

glypt- *or* **glypto-** *comb form* [F, fr. Gk *glypt-*, fr. *glyptos* carved, fr. *glyphein* to carve] **1 :** engraving ⟨*glyptology*⟩ **2 :** carved ⟨*Glyptodon*⟩

Glyp·tal \'gliptᵊl\ *trademark* — used for an alkyd

¹**glyp·tic** \'gliptik\ *n* -s [prob. fr. F *glyptique*, fr. Gk *glyptikē*, fr. *glyptos* carved] **:** the art or process of carving or engraving esp. on gems ⟨one of the most beautiful types of ~ ornamentation —Dorothy Daniel⟩

²**glyptic** \"\ *adj* **:** of or relating to glyptic

glyp·to·don \'gliptə,dän\ *n* [NL, fr. *glypt-* + *-odon*] **1** *cap* **:** a genus of large extinct mammals (order Edentata) that are related to the armadillos, have a head shield, have the back covered by a large rigid carapace composed of small 5-sided or 6-sided bony plates covered with horny plates and the tail encircled by rings of bony plates, and are represented by numerous remains in the Pleistocene of So. America and of southern No. America **2** -s **:** GLYPTODONT

glyp·to·dont \-nt\ *n* -s [NL *Glyptodont-, Glyptodon*] **:** a mammal of the genus *Glyptodon*

glyp·to·graph \-tə,graf, -āf\ *n* [prob. back-formation fr. *glyptography*] **:** a glyptic carving or engraving — **glyp·to·graph·ic** \¦==¦grafik\ *adj*

glyp·tog·ra·phy \glip'tägrəfē\ *n* -ES [F *glyptographie*, fr. Gk *glypt-* + F *-graphie* -graphy] **:** GLYPTIC

glyp·to·lith \'gliptə,lith\ *n* -s [*glypt-* + *-lith*] **:** VENTIFACT

glyp·tol·o·gy \glip'täləjē\ *n* -ES [ISV *glypt-* + *-logy*] **:** the study of glyptic

glyp·tos·tro·bus \glip'tästrəbəs, ,gliptə'strōbəs\ *n, cap* [NL, fr. *glypt-* + L *strobus* tree yielding an odoriferous gum] **:** a genus of conifers (family Taxodiaceae) having awl-shaped leaves, pear-shaped long-stalked cones with obovate scales, and small winged seeds

gm *abbr* gram

GM *abbr* **1** Geiger-Müller **2** general manager **3** general merchandise **4** general mortgage **5** gold medal **6** grand master **7** Greenwich meridian **8** guided missile **9** gunmetal

g major *n, usu cap G* **:** the major musical key having a signature of one sharp

g–man \'jē,man, -maa(ə)n\ *n, pl* **g–men** *usu cap G* [prob. fr. *g* (initial letter of *government*) + *man*] **:** a special agent of the Federal Bureau of Investigation of the U.S. Department of Justice

g–m counter \(')jē¦em-\ *n, usu cap G&M* [fr. Geiger-Müller *counter*] **:** GEIGER COUNTER

GME *abbr* gilt marbled edges

gmeli·na \gə'melənə, -māl-\ *n, cap* [NL, fr. Johann Georg *Gmelin* †1755 Ger. botanist] **:** a small genus of Australasian trees and shrubs (family Verbenaceae) with simple leaves and panicled tubular flowers — see QUEENSLAND BEECH

gmelin·ite \-,nīt\ *n* -s [Christian G. *Gmelin* †1860 Ger. chemist + E *-ite*] **:** a mineral $(Na_2,Ca)Al_2Si_4O_{12}{\cdot}6H_2O$ consisting of a colorless or light-colored zeolite isomorphous with chabazite (hardness 4.5, sp. gr. 2–2.2)

gme·lin's blue \gə'māl**ə**nz-, -,lēnz-\ *n, often cap G* [after Christian G. *Gmelin*] **1 :** ULTRAMARINE 1b **2 :** TURNBULL'S BLUE **3 :** FRENCH BLUE

gmelin's test *or* **gmelin's reaction** *n, usu cap G* [after Leopold *Gmelin* †1853 Ger. chemist] **:** a test for bile pigments (as in the urine) that is made by carefully mixing the solution to be tested with nitric acid containing some nitrous acid and that shows a positive result when a series of colors appears at the juncture of the solution and the acid

g minor *n, usu cap G* **:** the minor musical key having a signature of two flats

GMT *abbr* Greenwich mean time

g–m tube \(')jē¦em-\ *n, usu cap G&M* [fr. Geiger-Müller *tube*] **:** GEIGER-MÜLLER TUBE

GMV *abbr* gram-molecular volume

gn *abbr* **1** general **2** green **3** guinea **4** gun

GN *abbr* golden number

gnam·ma hole (gə)'namə-\ *n* [*gnamma* fr. native name in Australia] **:** a hollow or hole eroded or indented in solid rock of Australian deserts that sometimes contains water

¹**gnap** \'nap\ *vi* **gnapped; gnapped; gnapping; gnaps** [ME *gnappen*, prob. of imit. origin] *Scot* **:** BITE, SNAP

²**gnap** \"\ *n* -s *Scot* **:** MORSEL, BITE

gna·pha·li·oid \nə'fālē,ȯid\ *adj* [NL *Gnaphalium* + E *-oid*] **:** of or relating to the genus *Gnaphalium*

gna·pha·li·um \-lēəm\ *n, cap* [NL, alter. of L *gnaphalion* cudweed, modif. of Gk *gnaphallion*, fr. *gnaphallon* flock of wool, fr. *gnaptein* to card, alter. of *knaptein*; akin to OE *hnæppan* to strike, ON *hnaja* to cut, Lith *knabėti* to peel, L *cinis* ashes — more at INCINERATE] **:** a large genus of hoary or woolly-tomentose widely distributed herbs (family Compositae) having whitish persistent involucres — see BALSAMWEED 1

gnaphalium green *n, often cap 1st G* **:** a pale green that is lighter and stronger than celadon gray and yellower and darker than spray green

gnar *or* **gnarr** \'när, 'nä(r\ *vi* **gnarred; gnarred; gnarring; gnars** *or* **gnarrs** [imit.] **:** SNARL, GROWL — used chiefly of dogs

¹**gnarl** *R* 'närl, *chiefly before pause or consonant* -rəl, *–R* 'näl\ *vi* -ED/-ING/-S [prob. freq. of *gnar*] **1 :** GROWL, SNARL ⟨and wolves are ~*ing* who shall gnaw thee first —Shak.⟩ **2** *dial Eng* **:** GNAW, NIBBLE

²**gnarl** \"\ *vt* -ED/-ING/-S [back-formation fr. *gnarled*] **:** to twist or contort into or as if into a state of deformity ⟨the wind seems to have ~*ed* the dispositions of men and women as it has ~*ed* the apple trees —Carl Van Doren⟩ **syn** see DEFORM

³**gnarl** \"\ *n* -s **:** a knot in wood **:** a hard protuberance with twisted grain on a tree

gnarled \-ld\ *adj* [prob. alter. of *knurled*] **1 :** warped or twisted with or as if with gnarls **:** CROSS-GRAINED, KNOTTY ⟨the hand all ~ with work —D.H.Lawrence⟩ ⟨three ~ cedars stand at the entrance —*Amer. Guide Series: La.*⟩ **2 :** crabbed in disposition, aspect, or character **:** HARD-BITTEN ⟨public life abounds in ~ and striking figures; and the literary scene presents a splendid row of great eccentrics —*Times Lit. Supp.*⟩ ⟨a prose . . . knotty and ~ —D.L.Morgan⟩ ⟨in an environment tightly ~, among unimaginative folk, dependent upon agriculture for a living —*Saturday Rev.*⟩

gnarly \-ärlē, -äl-, -li\ *adj* -ER/-EST [³*gnarl* + *-y*] **:** GNARLED

¹**gnash** \'nash, -aa(ə)-,-ai-\ *vb* -ED/-ING/-ES [alter. of ME *gnasten, gnaisten*, prob. of imit. origin] *vi* **1 :** to grind or strike the teeth together ⟨he ~*ed* and kept me awake for hours⟩ **2 :** to grind together — used of the teeth ⟨his teeth ~*ed* audibly⟩ ~ *vt* **1 :** to strike or grind (the teeth) together esp. in anger or pain **2 :** to grind the teeth on **:** bite with grinding teeth ⟨the tiger ~*ed* the fox, the ermine, and the sloth —W.S. Landor⟩

²**gnash** \"\ *n* -ES **:** GNASHING, BITE ⟨the ~ and clash of cutlery on china —James Jones⟩

gnat \'nat, *usu* -ad.+V\ *n* -s [ME, fr. OE *gnætt*; akin to MHG *gnaz* scurf, ON *gnōtra* to rattle, OE *gnagan* to gnaw — more at GNAW] **1 a :** any of various small two-winged flies: as **a** *Brit* **:** MOSQUITO **b :** any of certain tiny biting flies (as a midge, blackfly, or sand fly) **c :** FUNGUS GNAT **2 :** any of various artificial flies tied as fishing lures

gnatcatcher \'=,==\ *n* **:** any of several very small No. and So. American insectivorous warblers constituting a genus (*Polioptila*) of the family Sylviidae

gnatflower \'=,=\ *n* **:** BEE ORCHIS

gnath- *or* **gnatho-** *comb form* [NL, fr. Gk *gnath-*, fr. *gnathos*; akin to Gk *genys* jaw — more at CHIN] **:** jaw ⟨*gnath*itis⟩ ⟨*gnatho*plasty⟩

-gna·tha \gnəthə\ *n comb form, pl* **-gnatha** [NL, fem. sing. and neut. pl. of *-gnathus* -gnathous] **:** one or ones having (such) a jaw — in taxonomic names in zoology ⟨*Agnatha*⟩ ⟨*Chaetognatha*⟩

-gna·thae \gnə,thē\ *n pl comb form* [NL, fem. pl. of *-gnathus* -gnathous] **:** ones having (such) a jaw — in taxonomic names in zoology ⟨*Desmognathae*⟩

gnat hawk *n* **:** the common European nightjar (*Caprimulgus europaeus*)

gnath·ic \'nathik\ *or* **gnathal** \'nathəl, 'nath-\ *adj* [*gnath-* + *-ic* or *-al*] **:** of or relating to the jaw

gnathic index *n* **:** the anthropometric ratio of the distance from the nasion to the basion to that from the basion to the alveolar point multiplied by 100

gnathi·on \'nathē,än, 'nath-\ *n* -s [NL, irreg. fr. Gk *gnathos* jaw] **1 :** the midpoint of the lower border of the human mandible — see CRANIOMETRY illustration **2 :** the most anterior point of the premaxillae on or near the middle line in various lower mammals

gnathism \'nā,thizəm, 'na,th-, *in combination* gnə,th-\ *n* -s [ISV *gnath-* + *-ism*] **:** the projection of the upper jaw beyond the general plane of the face — often used in combination ⟨*mesognathism*⟩ ⟨*orthognathism*⟩ ⟨*prognathism*⟩; compare FACIAL ANGLE

gnathite \'nā,thīt, 'na,th-\ *n* -s [*gnath-* + *-ite*] **:** a mouth appendage (as a mandible, maxilla, or maxilliped) of an arthropod

gnatho·base \'nāthə,bās, 'nath-\ *n* [*gnath-* + *base*] **:** a joint or process of the proximal part of the appendage of an arthropod modified to aid in carrying or masticating food — **gnatho·ba·sic** \¦==¦bāsik\ *adj*

gnathob·del·lae \,=,thäb'de(,)lē\ [NL, fr *gnath-* + *-bdellae* (fr. Gk *bdella* leech)] *syn of* GNATHOBDELLIDA

gnathob·del·lid \¦=¦=¦deləd\ *adj* [NL *Gnathobdellida*] **:** of or relating to the Gnathobdellida

gnathob·del·li·da \-,lədə\ *n pl, cap* [NL, fr. *gnath-* + *bdell-* + *-ida*] **:** an order or other division of leeches comprising those lacking a proboscis and having 2-toothed or 3-toothed chitinous jaws (as the medicinal leech, the horseleech, and the land leeches)

gnatho·ceph·a·lon \,=(,)thō'sefə,län, -,lən\ *n* [NL, fr. *gnath-* + *cephalon*] **:** the part of the insect head that lies behind the protocephalon, consists of several fused segments, and bears the mandibles and maxillae

gnatho·chi·lar·i·um \-,kī'la(a)rēəm\ *n* -s [NL, fr. *gnath-* + *chil-* + *-arium*] **:** the lower lip of certain arthropods usu. considered to consist of the fused maxillae; *sometimes* **:** LABIUM

gna·thon·ic \(')nā¦thänik\ *adj* [L *gnathonicus*, fr. *Gnathon*, *Gnatho* (sycophant in the comedy *Eunuchus* by Terence †*ab* 159B.C. Roman playwright) + L *-icus* -ic] **:** SYCOPHANTIC, TOADYING ⟨somewhat of a ~ and parasitic soul —Charles Kingsley⟩

¹**gnatho·pod** \'nāthə,päd, 'nath-\ *adj* [NL *Gnathopoda*] **:** of or relating to the Gnathopoda

²**gnathopod** \"\ *n* [ISV *gnath-* + *-pod*] **:** GNATHOPODITE

gna·thop·o·da \nə'thäpədə\ *n pl, cap* [NL, fr. *gnath-* + *-poda*] *in some esp former classifications* **:** a group that comprises invertebrate animals whose jaws are modified limbs and that is coextensive with or a subdivision of Arthropoda — **gna·thop·o·dous** \-dəs\ *adj*

gna·thop·o·dite \-,dīt\ *n* [*gnath-* + *-podite*] **:** a segmental appendage of an arthropod when modified wholly or in part to serve as a jaw; *esp* **:** MAXILLIPED

gnatho·so·ma \,nāthə'sōmə, ,nath-\ *also* **gnatho·some** \'==,sōm\ *n* [NL *gnathosoma*, fr. *gnath-* + *-soma*] **:** CAPITULUM 2e

gna·thos·te·gite \nə'thästə,jīt\ *n* -s [*gnath-* + *-stegite*] **:** one of a pair of broad plates that are developed from the outer maxillipeds of some crustaceans (as crabs) and that serve to cover the other mouthparts

¹**gna·thos·to·ma** \nə'thästəmə\ *n pl, cap* [NL, fr. *gnath-* + *-stoma*] *in some classifications* **:** a division of Crustacea comprising the Branchiopoda, Ostracoda, and Copepoda

²**gnathostoma** \"\ *n, cap* [NL, fr. *gnath-* + *-stoma*] **:** a genus (the type of the family Gnathostomatidae) of spiruroid nematodes comprising parasites living in tumors of the stomach wall of various Old World carnivorous mammals and occas. invading the subcutaneous tissues of man

gnatho·sto·ma·ta \,nāthə'stōmədə, ,nath-\ *n pl, cap* [NL, fr. *gnath-* + *-stomata*] **:** a superclass or other division of Vertebrata comprising those with jaws — compare AGNATHA

gnatho·stoma·tous \¦==¦stämədəs, -töm-\ *or* **gna·thos·to·mous** \nə'thästəməs\ *adj* [NL *Gnathostomata, Gnathostoma* + E *-ous*] **:** of or relating to Gnathostomata or Gnathostoma

gnatho·stome \'nāthə,stōm, 'nath-\ *n* -s [NL *Gnathostomi*] **:** a vertebrate animal that possesses true jaws

gna·thos·to·mi \nə'thästə,mī\ [NL, fr. *gnath-* + *-stomi*] *syn of* GNATHOSTOMATA

gna·thos·to·mi·a·sis \nə,thästə'mīəsəs\ *n* -ES [NL, fr. ²*Gnathostoma* + *-iasis*] **:** infestation with or disease caused by worms of the genus *Gnathostoma*

gnatho·thoracic \¦nāthō, ¦nathō+\ *adj* [fr. *gnathothorax*, after E *thorax: thoracic*] **:** of, relating to, or constituting a gnathothorax

gnatho·thorax \"+\ *n* [*gnath-* + *thorax*] **:** the thorax and the part of the head bearing the feeding organs of an arthropod regarded as one of the primary body regions — compare PROTOCEPHALON

-gna·thous \gnəthəs\ *adj comb form* [NL *-gnathus* -gnathous, fr. Gk *gnathos* jaw; akin to Gk *genys* jaw — more at CHIN] **:** having (such) a jaw ⟨*oxygnathous*⟩

-gna·thus \gnəthəs\ *n comb form* [NL, fr. *-gnathus* -gnathous] **:** one having (such) a jaw — in generic names of animals ⟨*Desmognathus*⟩

gnat·ling \'natliŋ\ *n* -s [*gnat* + *-ling*] **:** a small or insignificant person or thing; *specif* **:** a small gnat

gnatsnap \'=,=\ *or* **gnatsnapper** \'=,==\ *n* **:** a small bird that feeds on insects

gnat·ter \'natə(r)\ *vb* -ED/-ING/-S [prob. imit.] *vt, dial Brit* **:** NIBBLE ~ *vi* **1** *dial Brit* **:** to talk rapidly and idly **2** *dial Brit* **:** to be peevish **:** GRUMBLE

gnat·ty \'nad·ē\ *adj* -ER/-EST [*gnat* + *-y*] **:** infested with gnats

gnaw \'nȯ\ *vb* **gnawed** \-ȯd\ **gnawed** \"\ *also* **gnawn** \-ȯn\ **gnawing; gnaws** [ME *gnawen*, fr. OE *gnagan*; akin to OHG *gnagan, nagan* to gnaw, ON *gnaga* to gnaw, and perh. to Russ *gnit'* to rot] *vt* **1 a :** to bite or chew on with the teeth **:** wear away or remove a part from by persistent or repeated biting or nibbling ⟨the dog was ~*ing* a bone⟩ ⟨sheep ~ the tough grass off the range and leave it barren —Green Peyton⟩ **b :** to make by persistent or repeated biting or nibbling ⟨rats ~*ed* a hole in the floor⟩ **2 a :** to be a source of annoyance, worry, or vexation to **:** HARASS, PLAGUE ⟨the restraints of censorship . . . ~*ed* every correspondent —*Atlantic*⟩ ⟨her brain was ~*ed* by savage and distorted thoughts —James Boyd⟩ **b :** to cause (as the stomach) to feel discomfort similar to that produced by persistent biting ⟨hunger ~*ed* his vitals⟩ **3 :** to wear away by or as if by erosion or corrosion ⟨time shall ~ the proudest towers —Phineas Fletcher⟩ ~ *vi* **1 :** to bite persistently or repeatedly with the teeth ⟨the dog ~*ed* away at the bone⟩ ⟨he ~*ed* nervously at his underlip —Oscar Wilde⟩ ⟨a thousand men that fishes ~*ed* upon —Shak.⟩ **2 :** to produce an effect of or as if of gnawing **:** EAT ⟨the waves are ~*ing* away at the soft cliffs —Richard Joseph⟩ ⟨some of the roads ~ at the tires —Claudia Cassidy⟩ ⟨strange truths that have ~*ed* on her lonely heart —Lillian Smith⟩ ⟨inflation and taxation ~ increasingly at the savings of the people —*Freedom & Union*⟩

gnaw·er \'nȯ(ə)r, -ȯə\ *n* -s **:** one that gnaws; *esp* **:** RODENT

gnawing *n* -s **1 :** a persistent pain esp. in the stomach or bowels resembling that caused by gnawing **2 gnawings** *pl* **:** PANGS ⟨~*s* of hunger⟩

gnaw·ing·ly *adv* **:** in the manner of something that produces gnawing ⟨a ~ persistent sensation in the stomach⟩

gnd *abbr* ground

gneiss \'nīs\ *n* -ES [G *gneis*, prob. alter. of MHG *gneiste*, *ganeiste* spark, fr. OHG *gneisto*; akin to OE *gnāst* spark, ON *gneisti*] **:** a laminated or foliated metamorphic rock corresponding in composition to granite or some other feldspathic plutonic rock and often named for a conspicuous mineral constituent ⟨biotite ~⟩ ⟨hornblendic ~⟩ or for the plutonic or sedimentary rock of origin ⟨syenitic ~⟩ ⟨conglomerate ~⟩ — see ORTHOGNEISS, PARAGNEISS — **gneiss·ic** \-sik\ *adj* — **gneiss·ose** \-,sōs\ *adj*

gneiss·oid \-,sȯid\ *adj* **:** resembling gneiss **:** having the laminated structure of gneiss

gnesio–lutheran \¦nēzē(,)ō+\ *n, usu cap G&L* [Gk *gnēsios* genuine, born in wedlock + E *lutheran*; akin to Gk *genos* race, kin — more at KIN] **:** a Lutheran extremist opposed to the moderation of Melanchthon

gne·ta·ce·ae \nə'tāsē,ē\ *n pl, cap* [NL, fr. *Gnetum*, type genus + *-aceae*] **:** a family of plants (order Gnetales) having small unisexual flowers and fleshy or winged fruits — see EPHEDRA, GNETUM, WELWITSCHIA — **gne·ta·ceous** \-āshəs\ *adj*

gne·ta·le·an \-ālēən\ *adj* [NL *Gnetales* + E *-an*] **:** of, relating to, or characteristic of the order Gnetales

gne·ta·les \-ā(,)lēz\ *n pl, cap* [NL, fr. *Gnetum* + *-ales*] **:** an order of chiefly tropical or xerophytic woody gymnospermous plants that have two cotyledons, opposite leaves, vessels in the wood, and compound male and female strobili, consist of a single family (Gnetaceae), and are practically unknown as fossils but are sometimes considered on structural grounds to be near or on the ancestral line of the angiosperms

gne·tum \'nēd·əm\ *n, cap* [NL, alter. of *gnemon*, modif. of Moluccan Malay *ganemu*] **:** a genus (the type of the family Gnetaceae) of tropical shrubs or small trees usu. having climbing jointed stems and terminal spikes of flowers, the fruit being usu. drupaceous and aggregated in a rough cone

gnib \'nib\ *adj* [origin unknown] *Scot* **:** quick in response **:** READY, SHARP

gnoc·chi \'näkē, 'nōkē, *It* 'nʸȯkkē\ *n pl* [It, pl. of *gnocco*, alter. of *nocchio* knot in wood, perh. of Gmc origin; akin to MHG *knoche* bone, knot in wood; akin to OE *cnocian*, *cnucian* to knock — more at KNOCK] **:** dumplings of a pasta often made with cheese or potato and served with a sauce

¹**gnome** \'nōm, -ō,mē\ *n, pl* **gnomes** \-ōmz, -ō,mēz\ *or* **gno·mae** \-ō,mē\ [Gk *gnōmē* maxim, opinion, intelligence, fr. *gignōskein* to know — more at KNOW] **:** a brief reflection or maxim **:** APHORISM, PROVERB

²**gnome** \'nōm\ *n* -s [F, fr. NL *gnomus*] **1 :** an ageless often deformed dwarf creature of folklore conceived as living in the earth and usu. guarding precious ores or treasure **2 :** a dry wizened little old man ⟨a gnarled, unshaven ~ —Truman Capote⟩

gnome owl *n* [²*gnome*] **:** PYGMY OWL

gno·mic \'nōmik\ *adj* [LL *gnomicus*, fr. Gk *gnōmikos*, fr. *gnōmē* maxim + *-ikos* -ic] **1 a :** characterized by or expressive of aphorism or sententious wisdom esp. concerning human condition or conduct ⟨a ~ wisdom which appealed both to the intelligence and to the emotions —John Buchan⟩ ⟨a ~ and oracular tone —J.C.Powys⟩ ⟨~ poetry⟩ **b** *of a poet* **:** given to the composition of gnomic poetry **2 :** expressive of what is true generally, universally, or always — used of certain tenses ⟨"day follows night" is an example of the ~ present⟩ ⟨~ aorist⟩

gnom·ish \'nōmish\ *adj* [²*gnome* + *-ish*] **:** resembling a gnome ⟨that ~ nobleman with the abbreviated legs and a great genius —John Mason Brown⟩

gno·mo·log·ic \¦nōmə¦läjik\ *also* **gno·mo·log·i·cal** \-jəkəl\ *adj* [*gnomologic* fr. Gk *gnōmologikos*, fr. *gnōmologia* + *-ikos* -ic; *gnomological* fr. *gnomology* + *-al*] **:** characterized by or consisting of gnomes or precepts **:** GNOMIC

gno·mol·o·gy \nō'mäləjē\ *n* -ES [Gk *gnōmologia* anthology of gnomes, sententious style, fr. *gnōmo-* (fr. *gnōmē* maxim) + *-logia* -logy] **1 :** an anthology of gnomes **2 :** gnomic writing

gno·mon \'nō,män, -,mən\ *n* -s [L, fr. Gk *gnōmōn* interpreter, discerner, pointer on a sundial, carpenter's square, fr. *gignōskein* to know — more at KNOW] **1 :** an object that by the position or length of its shadow serves as an indicator esp. of the hour of the day: as **a :** the style, pin, or vertical plate of an ordinary sundial usu. set parallel to the earth's axis **b :** a column or shaft erected perpendicular to the horizon and formerly used to find the sun's meridian altitude **2 :** the remainder of a parallelogram after the removal of a similar parallelogram containing one of its corners **3** *archaic* **:** NOSE **4** *obs* **:** a rule of faith or conduct **:** CANON, TENET

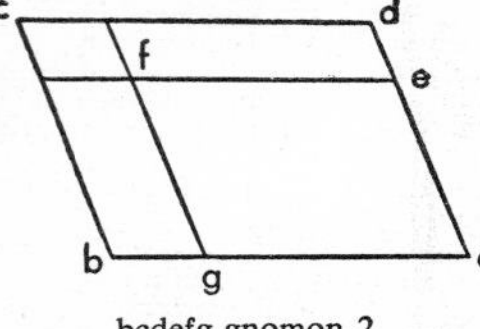

bcdefg gnomon 2

gno·mo·nia \nō'mōnēə\ *n, cap* [NL, fr. Gk *gnōmōn* carpenter's square + NL *-ia*; fr. the shape of the ostiole] **:** a genus (the type of the family Gnomoniaceae) of ascomycetous fungi having rostrate perithecia and hyaline 2-celled to 4-celled ascospores

gno·mon·ic \(')nō¦mänik\ *also* **gno·mon·i·cal** \-ənəkəl\ *adj* [*gnomonic* fr. L *gnomonicus*, fr. Gk *gnōmonikos*, fr. *gnōmon-*, *gnōmōn* pointer on a sundial + *-ikos* -ic; *gnomonical* fr. L *gnomonicus* + E *-al*] **1 :** of or relating to the gnomon of a sundial or its use in telling time **2 :** GNOMIC

gnomonic chart *n* **:** a chart on the gnomonic projection

gnomonic projection *n* **:** an azimuthal projection of a part of a hemisphere showing the earth's grid as projected by radials from a point at the center of the sphere onto a tangent plane so that all straight lines represent arcs of great circles thereby making this projection valuable for navigation when used in conjunction with the Mercator projection — called also *great-circle chart*

gno·mo·nics \nō'mäniks\ *n pl but sing in constr* **:** the art of using or making dials, esp. sundials

-gno·my \gnəmē, -mi\ *n comb form* -ES [LL *-gnomia*, fr. Gk *-gnōmia*, alter. of *-gnōmonia*, fr. *gnōmon-*, *gnōmōn* interpreter, discerner + *-ia* -y — more at GNOMON] **:** science, art, or means of judging ⟨*pathognomy*⟩

gno·ri·mo·sche·ma \,nōrəmō'skēmə\ *n, cap* [NL, fr. *gnorimo-* (fr. Gk *gnōrimos* well known) + L *schema* shape, form; akin to Gk *gignōskein* to know — more at SCHEME] **:** a genus of small dull narrow-winged moths related to the pink bollworm and including larvae that cause galls in plants, others that are leaf miners, and still others that are borers — see POTATO TUBERWORM

gno·se·o·log·i·cal *or* **gno·si·o·log·i·cal** \ˌ==ə;läjəkəl\ *adj* **:** of or relating to gnoseology — **gno·se·o·log·i·cal·ly** *or* **gno·si·o·log·i·cal·ly** \-k(ə)lē\ *adv*

gno·se·ol·o·gy *or* **gno·si·ol·o·gy** \ˌnōsē'äləjē, -ōzē-\ *n* -ES [NL *gnoseologia*, fr. *gnoseo-* (fr. Gk *gnōsis* knowledge) + L *-logia* -logy] **:** the philosophic theory of knowledge **:** inquiry into the basis, nature, validity, and limits of knowledge ⟨~ became coextensive with the whole of metaphysics —C.A. Hart⟩

-gno·sia \g'nōzh(ē)ə\ *n comb form* -S [NL, fr. Gk *-gnōsia*, fr. *gnōsis* knowledge] **:** -GNOSIS ⟨pharmaco*gnosia*⟩

gno·sis \'nōsəs\ *n, pl* **gno·ses** \-ō,sēz\ [Gk *gnōsis*, lit., knowledge, fr. *gignōskein* to know] **1 :** immediate knowledge of spiritual truth; *esp* **:** such knowledge as professed by the ancient Gnostics and held to be attainable through faith alone **2 :** the act or process of cognition or knowing

-gno·sis \(g)'nōsəs\ *n comb form, pl* **-gno·ses** \-ō,sēz\ [L, fr. Gk *gnōsis* knowledge] **:** knowledge **:** cognition **:** recognition ⟨baro*gnosis*⟩ ⟨psycho*gnosis*⟩

¹gnos·tic \'nästik\ *n* -S *usu cap* [LL *gnosticus*, fr. Gk *gnōstikos*, adj.] **:** an adherent of gnosticism or of a philosophy or theology influenced by gnosticism; *esp* **:** an adherent of any of several Gnostic sects of the 2d to 6th centuries adjudged heretical by the early Christian church

²gnostic \"\ *adj* [Gk *gnōstikos*, fr. *gnōstos* known (fr. *gignōskein* to know) + *-ikos* -ic — more at KNOW] **1 :** of, relating to, or characterized by knowledge or cognition **:** INTELLECTUAL, KNOWING **2** [¹*gnostic*] *usu cap* **:** of or relating to gnosticism or the Gnostics **3 :** SHREWD, CLEVER — **gnos·ti·cal·ly** \-tək(ə)lē\ *adv*

-gnos·tic \g'nästik, -tēk\ *or* **-gnos·ti·cal** \-təkəl, -tēk-\ *adj comb form* [-*gnostic* fr. ML *-gnosticus* knowing, fr. Gk *gnōstikos*, adj.; *-gnostical* fr. ML *-gnosticus* + E *-al*] **:** knowing **:** characterized by or relating to (such) knowledge ⟨geo*gnostic*⟩ ⟨geo*gnostical*⟩

gnos·ti·cism \'nästə,sizəm\ *n* -S *often cap* [¹*gnostic* + *-ism*] **:** the thought and practice of any of various cults of late pre-Christian and early Christian centuries declared heretical by the church and distinguished chiefly by pretension to mystic and esoteric religious insights, by emphasis on knowledge rather than faith, and by the conviction that matter is evil

gnos·ti·cize \-tə,sīz\ *vb* -ED/-ING/-S [¹*gnostic* + *-ize*] *vi* **:** to embrace or propound Gnostic views ~ *vt* **:** to make Gnostic **:** give Gnostic color or quality to ⟨threatened for a time to ~ Christianity⟩

-gno·sy \gnəsē, -si\ *n comb form* -ES [NL *-gnosia*, fr. Gk *-gnōsia*, fr. *gnōsis* knowledge] **:** -GNOSIS ⟨astro*gnosy*⟩

GNP *abbr* gross national product

gnr *abbr* gunner

gnu \'n(y)ü\ *n, pl* **gnu** *or* **gnus** [modif. of Bushman *nqu*] **:** any of several rather large but compact and blocky African antelopes (genera *Connochaetes* and *Gorgon*) having a large head like that of an ox, short mane, long and flowing tail, and horns in both sexes that curve downward and outward and then up with the bases forming a frontal shield in old individuals

gnu

gnu goat *n* **:** TAKIN

¹go \(ˈ)gō, *when followed without pause by a stressed syllable sometimes* gə *or* +V gəw\ *vb* **went** \(ˈ)went\ *or dial* **goed** \(ˈ)gōd\ **gone** \(ˈ)gȯn *also* (ˈ)gän\ *or substand* **went; going** \ˈgōiŋ, (ˈ)gōl, |ēn; *"going to" followed without pause by a verb is often* |gōənə *or* |gōnə\ *or dial* **gwine** \(ˈ)gwī(ə)n\ *or dial Brit* **gaun** \(ˈ)gȯn\ **goes** \(ˈ)gōz\ [ME *gon, goon, gan*, fr. OE *gān*; akin to OFris & OS *gān* to go, OHG *gān, gēn*, OSw & ODan *gā*, Crimean Goth *geen* to go, Gk *kichanein* to reach, attain, Skt *jahāti* he leaves, abandons] *vi* **1 a :** to move on a course **:** pass from point to point or station to station **:** proceed by any of several means ⟨~ by train⟩ ⟨a good day to ~ for a ride⟩ ⟨*went* as fast as he could through the snow⟩ ⟨held the rail as he *went* down the stairs⟩ ⟨the wheel *~es* round and round⟩ **b :** to be in motion — used esp. in a sentry's challenge ⟨halt! who *~es* there?⟩ **c :** to move away from something or thitherward **:** pass from one point to or toward another that is regarded as farther away **:** LEAVE, DEPART ⟨the lobby was filled with people coming and *~ing*⟩ ⟨had to ~ so as to catch the train⟩ ⟨*went* two by two into the dining room⟩ ⟨~ from one city to another⟩ ⟨told the dog to ~ get the ball⟩ ⟨~ and catch a falling star —John Donne⟩ ⟨the men ~ and cut bamboos in the jungle and bring them to the beach —J.G.Frazer⟩ **d :** to ride to hounds **2 a :** to take a certain course or follow a certain procedure ⟨people who want to know how . . . they can help to make the world ~ —Victor Reynolds⟩ **b :** to pass in a course determined by established procedure ⟨reports ~ through channels to the president⟩ **c :** to pass by a process felt to resemble journeying ⟨the message *went* by wire⟩ ⟨my eyes *went* into all corners of the stable —Owen Wister⟩ **d :** to proceed by or as if by a mental process or operation ⟨was determined to ~ to the bottom of the mystery⟩ **e :** to proceed without delay — used esp. to intensify a complementary verb ⟨if that infernal young fool hadn't *gone* and got killed —Dorothy Sayers⟩ ⟨told him to ~ hang himself⟩ **f** (1) **:** to extend from point to point or in a certain direction **:** RUN ⟨a new road that *~es* from the north shore to the south shore⟩ ⟨his land *~es* almost to the river⟩ ⟨dates back as far as our records ~ —T.B.Costain⟩ (2) **:** to give access **:** LEAD ⟨that door *~es* to the cellar⟩ ⟨a path *~ing* to the barn⟩ **3** *obs* **:** to move or travel on one's feet at an ordinary pace **:** WALK ⟨but when he could not ~, yet forward would he creep —Phineas Fletcher⟩ ⟨I have resolved to run when I can, to ~ when I cannot run —John Bunyan⟩ **4 a :** to be habitually in a certain state or condition ⟨children like to ~ bareheaded⟩ ⟨were advised to ~ armed after dark⟩ **b :** to be pregnant ⟨the fruit she *~es* with I pray for heartily, that it may find good time, and live —Shak.⟩ ⟨the elephant *~es* with young nearly two years⟩ **5 a** (1) **:** to come to be taken away, lost, or consumed ⟨a large part of the market for Welsh coal had *gone* forever —L.D.Stamp⟩ ⟨reserves to be brought up when the poet's youth is *~ing* —Max Beerbohm⟩ (2) **:** to come to be spent ⟨the money that he inherited *went* in a few years⟩ **b** (1) **:** to come to the end of life **:** DIE ⟨the doctor says he may drag on this way for several weeks, or he may ~ suddenly at any time —Ellen Glasgow⟩ (2) **:** to pass by **:** slip away **:** ELAPSE ⟨the trip . . . *went* much more quickly than I had expected —A.N.Whitehead⟩ ⟨the evening *went* pleasantly enough⟩ **c :** to come to be given up, rejected, or abolished ⟨if a day on the links left dad too tired . . . it really looked as if the golf had better ~ —Dorothy Barclay⟩ ⟨one-room schools devoid of plumbing . . . had to ~ —*Saturday Rev.*⟩ **d :** to pass by sale ⟨many items at the auction *went* for less than their true value⟩ ⟨*~ing, ~ing, gone*⟩ **e** *cricket* (1) **:** FALL ⟨three wickets *went* during the afternoon⟩ (2) **:** to have one's innings ended by dismissal ⟨the batsman *went* with his score at 50⟩ **f :** to become impaired or weakened **:** lose strength or effectiveness ⟨his hearing started to ~ —George Kent⟩ **g :** to give way esp. under great force or pressure **:** BREAK ⟨the starboard boat did ~, taking with it both davits and part of the starboard rail —H. A.Chippendale⟩ **h :** to cease to have an effect or influence ⟨the pain has finally *gone*⟩ **6 a :** to take place **:** HAPPEN, OCCUR ⟨you seem to try and get me into any . . . trouble that's *~ing* —Robert Westerby⟩ **b :** to have course or issue **:** FARE ⟨at the end of her first day on the job, he asked her how it *went* —Burnham Carter⟩ ⟨I only keep my eyes open and see how life *~es* —Eden Phillpotts⟩ **c :** to be in general or on an average **:** furnish a usual standard or measure ⟨an old town as American towns ~ —Dana Burnet⟩ ⟨the modest price makes it quite a bargain as handsomely illustrated books ~ —*Nation*⟩ **d :** to be or become esp. as the result of a contest **:** turn out to be ⟨a second election *went* in favor of his opponent —Broadus Mitchell⟩ ⟨the size of the Democratic margin in those cities . . . determines whether these states ~ Democratic —*Newsweek*⟩ **e :** to come to be performed or executed **:** proceed in a certain manner ⟨ the play . . . had been *~ing* none too well —S.H. Adams⟩ **f :** to accomplish what is attempted or intended **:** turn out well **:** SUCCEED ⟨successful novelists whose first plays failed to ~ —Henry Hewes⟩ ⟨when there was a party he wanted to make it ~ —W.S.Maugham⟩ **7 a :** to apply or set oneself ⟨*went* to fighting among themselves⟩ **b :** to put or subject oneself ⟨~ to a great deal of trouble⟩ ⟨*went* to unnecessary expense⟩ **c** *chiefly South & Midland* **:** to have a mind **:** INTEND — usu. used in the negative and with a following infinitive ⟨I didn't ~ to do it⟩ **8 :** to have recourse to another as a recognized authority for corroboration, vindication, or decision **:** carry an action or interest **:** RESORT ⟨decided to ~ to court to recover damages⟩ ⟨the government will ~ to the country with this issue⟩ ⟨one must ~ to the original documents for an account of the colony's early years⟩ **9 a :** to begin an action or motion ⟨here *~es*⟩ ⟨~ when the light turns green⟩ — often used in the imperative as a signal to start a race ⟨on your mark, get set, ~⟩ **b :** to maintain or perform a certain action or motion ⟨the music *~es* round and round⟩ ⟨all day the drums and the flutes had been *~ing* strong —John Berry⟩ ⟨his pulse *~es* quite rapidly⟩ **c :** to function in the proper or expected manner ⟨finally succeeded in getting the motor to ~⟩ **d :** to keep time ⟨a clock that will ~ a week without winding⟩ **e** (1) **:** to make a clear resonant sound **:** RING ⟨it was midnight when the bell *went* and I came up to his room —Ngaio Marsh⟩ (2) **:** to make a characteristic noise **:** SOUND ⟨as soon as the starting gun *went* the contestants began the race⟩ **10 a :** to pass at or as if at face value **:** have currency ⟨traveler's checks ~ everywhere⟩ ⟨a bit of gossip that once *went* for truth⟩ **b :** to pass from person to person **:** be current **:** CIRCULATE ⟨the report *~es* that the expedition was a failure⟩ **c :** to become known ⟨herring residues . . . ~ as a manure under the name of fish guano —S.J.Watson⟩ ⟨*went* by an alias for two years⟩ **11 a :** to come to be guided, governed, or regulated **:** act in accordance or harmony ⟨a good rule to ~ by⟩ ⟨was criticized for refusing to ~ with the times⟩ **b :** to come to be allotted or determined ⟨hanging and wiving *~es* by destiny —Shak.⟩ ⟨the crushing . . . realization that this is how things ~ —Bosley Crowther⟩ **c :** to come to be applied or appropriated ⟨a large part of the budget *~es* for military purposes⟩ **d** (1) **:** to pass by or as if by award, assignment, or lot ⟨the prize *went* to a sophomore⟩ ⟨nearly all the estate *went* to the creditors of the deceased⟩ (2) **:** to pass by inheritance or succession ⟨the farm *went* to the eldest son⟩ ⟨the title *~es* to the late duke's nephew⟩ **e** (1) **:** to contribute to an end **:** be among the constituents necessary for achieving a purpose or result ⟨the qualities that ~ to make a hero⟩ (2) **:** to be equivalent **:** AMOUNT ⟨100 cents ~ to a dollar⟩ **12 :** to be about, intending, or expecting something — used in a progressive tense with infinitive ⟨may be *~ing* to have a relapse⟩ ⟨is *~ing* to leave town⟩ ⟨is *~ing* to be a doctor⟩ ⟨was *~ing* to sing a solo⟩ **13 a :** to carry one's action to a certain point of progress or completeness ⟨*went* to great lengths in order to meet the deadline⟩ **b :** to reach a certain point **:** ATTAIN, EXTEND ⟨his knowledge fails to ~ very deep⟩ ⟨the differences ~ further than is commonly believed⟩ **c** (1) **:** to come or arrive at a certain state or condition — usu. used with *to* ⟨the flowers have *gone* to seed⟩ ⟨~ to sleep⟩ (2) **:** to come or arrive at a certain amount or sum — usu. used with *to* ⟨the bidding *went* to $50 before the chair was sold⟩ **14 a :** to come to be **:** BECOME ⟨*went* sound asleep⟩ ⟨the tire *went* flat⟩ ⟨he felt his hands ~ clammy as he spoke —Marcia Davenport⟩ ⟨serious matters and noble conventions get out of hand and ~ pompous —Virgil Thomson⟩ **b :** to undergo a change or transformation **:** TURN ⟨the light from the autumn afternoon was fading and the sky . . . was *~ing* from blue to gray —C.B.Flood⟩ **15 a :** to be in phrasing or expression **:** appear esp. in writing or print **:** READ ⟨the great mass of the public or, as the phrase *~es*, the man in the street —A.B. Walkley⟩ ⟨when he was eight years old, so the story *~es*, he began preaching to the barnyard fowl —H.H.Reichard⟩ **b :** to flow or glide rhythmically ⟨these poems ~ with a lilt⟩ **c :** to be capable of being sung or played ⟨a merry ballad . . . *~es* to the tune of "Two maids wooing a man" —Shak.⟩ ⟨the tune *~es* like this⟩ **16 a :** to be compatible, suitable, or becoming **:** HARMONIZE — usu. used with *together* or *with* ⟨the colors blue and gray ~ together⟩ ⟨claret *~es* with beef⟩ ⟨his tie doesn't ~ with his suit⟩ **b :** to be congenial **:** fit in — usu. used with *with* ⟨the sort of person who can ~ with any group⟩ **17 a :** to be capable of passing ⟨the piano will barely ~ through the door⟩ **b :** to be capable of being contained or inserted ⟨will these clothes ~ in your suitcase?⟩ ⟨the rod *~es* into a small hole near the top⟩ **c :** to be capable of extending ⟨a belt long enough to ~ around his waist⟩ ⟨enough cotton to make a rope that would ~ from coast to coast⟩ **d :** to have a usual or proper place or position **:** BELONG ⟨these books ~ on the top shelf⟩ **18 :** to have a tendency **:** serve as a means **:** CONDUCE ⟨the incident *~es* to show that he can be trusted⟩ **19 :** to admit of being played by all the players — used of a suit in cards ⟨led a spade and hoped that it would ~⟩ **20 a** (1) **:** to pass as accepted or authorized **:** carry authority ⟨what she said, *went*; when she summoned, prior engagements were to be broken —DeLancey Ferguson⟩ (2) **:** to be acceptable, satisfactory, or adequate **:** meet with or as if with approval ⟨you make up your own rules today and anything *~es* —Huntington Hartford⟩ **b :** to hold true **:** be valid ⟨the old saying that it takes all kinds of people to make a world *~es* for our train —F.J.Taylor⟩ **c :** to be of interest or concern ⟨as far as his speech *~es*, my point about it is this —Arthur Cavanaugh⟩ **21 :** to empty the bladder or bowels ⟨don't ask for the bedpan during the night unless you really have to ~ —Betty Smith⟩ ~ *vt* **1 :** to proceed along or according to **:** FOLLOW ⟨from the outset he *~es* his own pace —H.S. Bennett⟩ ⟨asked me if I was *~ing* his way⟩ **2 :** to pass or travel through **:** TRAVERSE ⟨to ~ its length . . . with the old houses on one side finally giving way to modern stores . . is to experience the meeting of old and new —R.W.Hatch⟩ **3 :** to set out on **:** UNDERTAKE ⟨I am very tired and I oughtn't to ~ another journey —Mrs. Patrick Campbell⟩ **4 a :** to make a wager of **:** BET ⟨was willing to ~ a dollar on the outcome of the game⟩ **b :** to make an offer of **:** BID ⟨was willing to ~ $50 for the clock⟩ ⟨~ four no-trump⟩ **5 a :** to serve in the capacity of **:** assume the function or obligation of ⟨promised to ~ bail for his friend⟩ **b :** to participate to the extent of ⟨decided to ~ halves if either of them found the treasure⟩ **6 a :** to indicate by sounding **:** STRIKE ⟨the clock on the mantel *went* nine⟩ **b :** to cause (a characteristic sound) to exist or occur ⟨the gun *went* bang⟩ ⟨the bell *~es* dingdong⟩ **7 :** YIELD, PRODUCE, WEIGH ⟨*went* a considerable amount⟩ ⟨a gigantic striped bass that would ~ a hundred pounds —*Saturday Rev.*⟩ **8 a :** to put up with **:** ENDURE, TOLERATE — usu. used with a negative ⟨it's that stink of caribou about them that I can't ~ —Gontran de Poncins⟩ **b :** to bear without serious financial detriment **:** AFFORD — usu. used with a negative ⟨insisted that he couldn't ~ $20,000 for a house⟩ **9 a :** to occupy oneself with **:** engage in ⟨didn't like anybody to ~ smelling his rose —Eudora Welty⟩ ⟨don't ~ shooting at moose —S.H.Holbrook⟩ **b :** to take pleasure in or receive satisfaction from **:** ENJOY ⟨I could ~ a soda —Hal Ellson⟩

syn LEAVE, DEPART, QUIT, WITHDRAW, RETIRE: GO is a general term indicating moving out or away; it is a neutral opposite for *come*. LEAVE centers attention on the fact of separation from a person, place, or thing ⟨*leaving* his family with their relatives⟩ ⟨*leaving* his boyhood town⟩ ⟨*leaving* the company after 10 years⟩ ⟨he is *leaving* on the noon plane⟩ DEPART is a slightly formal antonym for *arrive* ⟨cheers for the ex-president *departing* for his home⟩ ⟨*departing* from the country⟩ ⟨*departed* on the adventure late in 1523 —C.L.Jones⟩ QUIT may suggest a separating and going off or away attended by disengaging, freeing, ridding, or disentangling ⟨had given him a disgust to his business, and to his residence in a small market town; and, *quitting* them both, he had removed with his family —Jane Austen⟩ ⟨hesitating to spread its wings and *quit* forever the body which had been its home —Arnold Bennett⟩ WITHDRAW may suggest a deliberate removal for good reason ⟨constrained by the strength of his convictions to *withdraw* from the Catholic Church —W.L.Sullivan⟩ ⟨the family swarmed about her, shaking hands, pecking her on the cheek, then *withdrawing* to survey her from a distance —Olive H. Prouty⟩ ⟨spent three years in Paris with scientific friends; but feeling the need of solitude, he *withdrew* to Holland —Frank Thilly⟩ RETIRE may indicate a removal attended with renunciation, relinquishment, retreat, recession, or recoil ⟨prose has had the stage pretty much to itself for the past hundred years largely because poetry has refused to compete with it, preferring instead to *retire* to a private literary world of its own —Archibald MacLeish⟩ ⟨the British *retired* from Augusta, and loyalism in Georgia and South Carolina was severely checked —H.B.Fant⟩ ⟨had been moving forward into a narrower and narrower space as the enemy's center *retired* —Tom Wintringham⟩ — **go about :** to busy oneself with **:** take upon oneself **:** set about **:** UNDERTAKE ⟨the committee *went about* its assignment in a serious manner —Harold Zink⟩ — **go after :** to set out in pursuit or quest of **:** try to get ⟨are now urging their members to *go after* increases from their employers —Harry Conn⟩ — **go against 1 :** to run counter to **:** be or act contrary to **:** OPPOSE ⟨don't want you children to *go against* your mother's wishes —Dorothy C. Fisher⟩ **2 :** to turn out unfavorably for ⟨the umpire's decision *went against* the home team⟩ — **go ahead 1 :** to move forward **:** make one's way to the front (as in a race) **2 :** to continue without delay or hesitation **:** PROCEED ⟨*go ahead* with the job without bothering me —W.F. Davis⟩ **3 :** to develop to a higher, better, or more advanced stage **:** PROGRESS ⟨dairying has *gone ahead* rapidly —*Amer. Guide Series: Ind.*⟩ — **go all the way 1 :** to enter into complete agreement **2 :** to engage in sexual intercourse — **go at 1 a :** to make an attack on ⟨picking up a chair . . . and *going at* her with smashing blows —Glenway Wescott⟩ **b :** to make an approach to ⟨not every succeeding critic has *gone at* the book in this general fashion —R. R. Von Abele⟩ **2 :** to engage in vigorously or energetically **:** UNDERTAKE ⟨curious to know for what . . . reason we have *gone at* organizing with such abandoned enthusiasm —C.W.Ferguson⟩ — **go back on 1 :** to recede or withdraw from **:** ABANDON ⟨to do so would be to *go back on* our own first principles —A.W.Griswold⟩ **2 :** to be disloyal to **:** BETRAY ⟨refused to believe that his friend had *gone back on* him⟩ **3 :** to prove inadequate for **:** FAIL ⟨in advanced years a man's mind might *go back on* him at some unpredictable moment —Elmer Davis⟩ — **go before :** to precede esp. in time ⟨was greatly indebted to those who had *gone before* him⟩ — **go begging :** to be in little demand ⟨fish *went begging* when the cannery went out of business⟩ — **go bush 1** *Austral, of an animal* **:** to go wild **:** revert to a wild state ⟨they're good horses . . . descendants of stud horses *gone bush* —*Sydney (Australia) Bull.*⟩ **2** *Austral, of a person* **:** to live in the bush ⟨has *gone bush* for long periods, dressing and living much like the aborigines he knows so well —C.P.Mountford⟩ — **go down the drain :** to come to be outmoded, discarded, or lost ⟨our opinions . . . will have either *gone down the drain* or become every man's private conviction —Virgil Thomson⟩ — **go down the line :** to give wholehearted support — usu. used with *for* ⟨*went down the line* for a civil-rights program backed by the full power of the federal government —*Springfield (Mass.) Daily News*⟩ — **go far :** to be successful ⟨told him he was a great fellow and would *go far* —H. W. Van Loon⟩ — **go for 1 :** to pass for or serve as ⟨the bits of silvered glass that *went for* mirrors in those days —Charlotte Upton⟩ **2 :** to try to secure **:** aim at ⟨in money matters he *went for* the last penny —V.S.Pritchett⟩ **3 a :** to give support or approval to **:** FAVOR, ACCEPT ⟨I can *go for* no such resolution as this —B.F. Wade⟩ **b :** to have or display an active interest in or liking for ⟨she *went for* him in a big way —Chandler Brossard⟩ **4 :** to attack or assail physically or verbally ⟨his opponent *went for* him when his back was turned⟩ — **go for broke :** to put forth all one's strength or resources ⟨would *go for broke* in organizing textile employees —*Wall Street Jour.*⟩ — **go glimmering :** to pass from or as if from existence ⟨by this time the hope of a short war had *gone glimmering* —J.P.Baxter b. 1893⟩ — **go great guns :** to achieve great success ⟨the book was *going great guns* in twelve countries —George Thomas b. 1892⟩ — **go hang :** to cease to be of interest or concern **:** pass from memory or thought ⟨those who would take care of themselves and let the rest of the world *go hang* —H.M.Wriston⟩ — **go into 1 :** to dress oneself in **:** WEAR ⟨*went into* mourning⟩ **2 :** to pass into or let oneself be given up to ⟨*went into* hysterics⟩ **3 :** to take part or a place in; *esp* **:** to enter as a profession or occupation ⟨finally decided to *go into* law⟩ **4** *obs* **:** to agree or concur with ⟨we will all *go into* your opinion —Joseph Addison⟩ **5 :** to subject to examination or discussion **:** look into ⟨insisted that the problem be *gone into* carefully⟩ **6 :** to be capable of being contained in ⟨5 *goes into* 60 12 times⟩ — **go it 1 :** to behave esp. in a reckless, excited, or improper manner **:** carry on ⟨he had been *going it* a bit too hard —Angus Mowat⟩ **2 :** to proceed esp. in a rapid or furious manner ⟨was delighted to hear a Cockney call out above the cheering crowd "*go it*, old girl" —R.T.B.Fulford⟩ **3 :** to conduct one's affairs **:** ACT ⟨had casually toyed with the idea of *going it* alone —John McNulty⟩ — **go one better :** OUTDO, SURPASS ⟨all of his tone poems demand an orchestra of at least ninety players, and in at least one . . . he *goes* Wagner *one better*, calling for an orchestra of one hundred and sixteen —Deems Taylor⟩ — **go over 1 a :** to subject to careful consideration ⟨*went over* all the arguments before making up his mind⟩ **b :** to subject to careful inspection ⟨*went over* the house and grounds before deciding to buy⟩ **2 a :** REPEAT ⟨*goes over* the same story again and again⟩ **b :** STUDY ⟨*goes over* his lessons every night⟩ **3 :** to be suitable for covering **:** be capable of being put over ⟨bought an awning to *go over* the doorway⟩ **4 :** to examine carefully and revise ⟨students were told to *go over* their essays before handing them in⟩ — **go places :** to be on the way to success or achievement ⟨it is that kind of mechanic who *goes places* —C.B.Rawson⟩ — **go steady :** to have frequent dates exclusively with one member of the opposite sex ⟨argued that all the other girls were *going steady* and that this was the only way to be in on the fun —Geraldine Roberts⟩ — **go through 1 :** to subject to thorough examination, consideration, or study ⟨*went through* the items one by one⟩ **2 :** EXPERIENCE, UNDERGO ⟨*go through* hell and high water⟩ **3 :** to carry out **:** PERFORM ⟨the children *went through* their part of the program without a hitch⟩ **4 :** to appear in published form in ⟨the book has *gone through* six editions⟩ — **go to bed 1 :** to go to press ⟨when the paper *went to bed* at midafternoon he relaxed —T.W.Duncan⟩ **2 :** to engage in sexual relations ⟨is in the habit of *going to bed* with practically anybody who asks her to —Wolcott Gibbs⟩ **3 a** *of a card* **:** to fail to win through being withheld during early play **b** *of a cardplayer* **:** to lose the opportunity to win by withholding a winning card from early play — **go to one's head 1 :** to cause one to become confused, excited, or dizzy ⟨the wine *went to his head*⟩ **2 :** to cause one to become conceited or overconfident ⟨success *went to his head*⟩ — **go to pieces :** to become shattered in or as if in nerves or health — **go to sea :** to adopt the occupation of a sailor ⟨*went to sea* as a boy of 12⟩ — **go to town 1 :** to work or act rapidly, efficiently, or enthusiastically ⟨your friends were *going to town* on me properly when you arrived —Hartley Howard⟩ **2 :** to be successful ⟨military-aircraft production . . . has really begun to *go to town* in the last few months —*Popular Science Monthly*⟩ **3 :** to indulge oneself excessively ⟨his ability to enlarge an emotional experience without *going to town* sentimentally about it —Virgil Thomson⟩ — **go with 1 a :** ACCOMPANY ⟨*went with* me to the library⟩ **b :** DATE ⟨has been *going with* her for two years⟩ **2** *chiefly dial* **:** to become of **:** happen to ⟨my folks don't know what *went with* me —Archie Binns⟩ — **go without saying :** to be self-evident — **to go 1 :** REMAINING, LEFT ⟨there was only five minutes *to go* before the organist started the first hymn —Evelyn Waugh⟩ **2 :** available for taking out or suitable to be taken out ⟨ordered two toasted limburger-cheese sandwiches *to go* —James Jones⟩

²go \'gō\ *n* -ES **1 :** the act or manner of going ⟨a great come and ~ of officials, with district commissioners arriving and departing in a flurry of uniforms and salutes —Alan Moorehead⟩ **2 :** the height of fashion **:** RAGE ⟨elegant shawls labeled . . . "quite the ~" —R.S.Surtees⟩ **3 :** a turn of affairs that is often unexpected **:** INCIDENT, OCCURRENCE ⟨funniest ~ you ever did see —Ngaio Marsh⟩ **4 a :** the quantity used or furnished at one time ⟨you can obtain a ~ of brandy for sixpence —C.B.Fairbanks⟩ **b :** the vessel containing such a quantity ⟨a pewter ~⟩ **5 a :** a situation in cribbage when a player has no card that will not carry the count over 31 **b :** the score given to the cribbage player who brings the count exactly to or nearest to 31 **6 :** ENERGY, VIGOR, SPIRIT ⟨all sapped of ~ and foresight and perseverance by a cruel providence —John Galsworthy⟩ ⟨a play abounding in freshness, vitality, essential theatrical ~ —E.J.West⟩ **7 a :** a turn esp. in a game ⟨told his opponent that it was his ~⟩ **b :** ATTEMPT, TRY ⟨poets . . . who produce perfect results at the first ~ —W.H.Auden⟩ ⟨was going to have a ~ at setting down my observations of public life —A.W.Barkley⟩ **c :** CHANCE, OPPORTUNITY ⟨was given a ~ at building up the savings department —N.M.Clark⟩ **8 a :** a spell or period of activity ⟨it makes a lot of difference in the drying if one can get a large amount into the sheds in one ~ —Eve Langley⟩ **b :** an attack of illness ⟨I shall never forget her kindness to me when I had a bad ~ of pneumonia —Richard Rhodes⟩ **9 a :** SUCCESS ⟨figure out a new type vampire or werewolf yarn and it's a sure ~ —Dallas Ross⟩ **b :** BARGAIN, DEAL ⟨we've got opium to sell and your people want to buy it and it's a ~ —W.H. Smith⟩ **10 :** MATCH, CONTEST ⟨didn't want him to have a hard ~ the first time out because he wasn't sure how well his leg would stand up —G.F.T.Ryall⟩; *specif* **:** a boxing match — **from the word go :** from the very beginning ⟨he was a drag and a brake on me *from the word go* —W.D.Howells⟩ — **no go :** to no avail **:** USELESS, HOPELESS ⟨nobody'll ever know all the things I tried before I finally decided it was *no go* —Saul Bellow⟩ — **on the go 1** *archaic* **:** in a state of decline ⟨as to poor old England, I never see a paper but I think . . . that she is *on the go* —Edward FitzGerald⟩ **2 :** in a state of constant or restless activity ⟨a typical society woman — always *on the go* —Hiram Haydn⟩

³go \"\ *n* -ES [Jap] **:** a Japanese game that is played with black and white stones on a board marked by nineteen intersecting lines into 361 crosses and that has as its object the possession of the larger part of the board and the capturing of the opponent's stones

GO *abbr* **1** general office; general officer **2** general order **3** grand organ; great organ

¹goa \ˈgōə\ *adj, usu cap* [fr. *Goa,* region in India] **:** of or from Goa, India **:** of the kind or style prevalent in Goa **:** GOANESE

²goa \"\ *n* -S [Tibetan *dgoba*] **:** a common gazelle (*Gazella picticaudata*) of Tibet

³goa \"\ *n* -S [fr. *Goa,* India] **:** ²MUGGER

goa ball *n, usu cap G* [¹*Goa*] **:** a mixture of drugs made up in the form of a ball and formerly used as a remedy for fever

goa bean *n, usu cap G* [¹*Goa*] **:** a tropical Old World herbaceous annual vine (*Psophocarpus tetragonolobus*) bearing purplish or blue flowers in a close raceme and pods with four jagged wings **2 :** the edible seed of the Goa bean

go about *vi* **1 a :** to pass from one place to another **:** go here and there ⟨*went about* with a gang of people I don't care about —Dorothy Sayers⟩ **b :** to have currency **:** CIRCULATE ⟨there's not that kind of money *going about* now —George Macbean⟩ **2 :** TACK ⟨in . . . sailing there are two ways of *going about* — a right way and a wrong way —Peter Heaton⟩

go–about \ˈ==,=\ *n* -S [*go about*] **:** VAGRANT

goa butter *n, usu cap G* [¹*Goa*] **:** KOKUM BUTTER

goa cedar *or* **goa cypress** *n, usu cap G* [¹*Goa;* fr. the belief that it was native to India] **:** PORTUGUESE CYPRESS

¹goad \ˈgōd\ *n* -S [ME *gode,* fr. OE *gād* goad, arrowhead, spear point; akin to Lombard *gaida* spear, OHG *Gaido,* a personal name, ON *gedda* pike (fish), Skt *hinvati, hinoti* he urges on, throws] **1 :** a rod pointed at one end or fitted with a spike and used to urge on an animal — see OXGOAD **2 a :** something that wounds or pricks like a goad **:** STING, THORN ⟨French forts and . . . armies so near us will be everlasting ~*s* in our sides —Benjamin Franklin⟩ **b :** something that urges or stimulates like a goad **:** SPUR, STIMULUS ⟨insecurity, considered by some management people as the indispensable ~ for workers' efficiency —*Dun's Rev.*⟩ **syn** see MOTIVE

²goad \"\ *vt* -ED/-ING/-S **1 :** to drive with a goad or some other pointed instrument ⟨bound them to the plow and ~*ed* them onward with his lance —Charles Kingsley⟩ **2 :** to drive, incite, or rouse as if with a goad ⟨his editorials were so skillfully written that he often ~*ed* the opposition to madness —W.E.Smith⟩ ⟨knows what it is like to be ~*ed* by technical problems into achieving new insights —J.L.Stewart⟩ **syn** see URGE

goad·man \-dmən\ *or* **goads·man** \-dzm-\ *n, pl* **goadmen** *or* **goadsmen :** one who drives an animal or team by means of a goad

goad stick *n* **:** a stick used as a goad ⟨they banged the donkeys with their *goad sticks* —Mark Twain⟩

¹go-ahead \ˈ==,=\ *adj* [fr. the phrase *go ahead*] **1 :** marked by energy and enterprise **:** PROGRESSIVE ⟨helps spread prosperity and promotes *go-ahead* communities —N.M.Clark⟩ ⟨possessors of the *go-ahead* spirit essential to men —A.E. Rodway⟩ **2 :** indicating that one may proceed ⟨the committee's vote was the *go-ahead* signal . . . to make final plans —W.M.Blair⟩

²go-ahead \"\ *n* -S [fr. the phrase *go ahead*] **1 a :** ENERGY, SPIRIT, ENTERPRISE ⟨you're a bright youngster with lots of *go-ahead* —S.V.Benét⟩ **b :** a person possessing go-ahead ⟨the child'll be a *go-ahead* —A.T.Quiller-Couch⟩ **2 :** a sign, signal, or authority to proceed **:** GREEN LIGHT ⟨planes were waiting . . . for the *go-ahead* on the hazardous 2400-mile overwater hop —R.E.Byrd⟩ ⟨the first to mass-produce automobiles after the government *go-ahead* becomes effective —*Newsweek*⟩

go-ahead·ative·ness *or* **go-ahead·itive·ness** \ˌgōəˈhedəd-ivnəs\ *n* -ES [*go-ahead* + *-ative* or *-itive* + *-ness*] **:** PROGRESSIVENESS

go·ai \ˈgō,ī\ *var of* KOWHAI

go·a·ji·ro \ˌgōəˈhi(,)rō\ *n, pl* **goajiro** *or* **goajiros** *usu cap* [Sp *guajiro, goajiro,* of AmerInd origin] **1 a :** an Arawakan people of the peninsular region northwest of Lake Maracaibo **b :** a member of such people **2 :** the Arawakan language of the Goajiro people

¹goal \ˈgōl, *chiefly in dial or substand speech* ˈgül\ *n* -S [ME *gol* boundary, limit; perh. akin to OE *gǣlan* to hinder, impede — more at GILL (ravine)] **1 a :** the mark to which the contestants in a race run **:** the terminal point of a race ⟨runners who run well from the starting place to the ~ —Benjamin Jowett⟩ **b :** the conical column that marks each of the two turning points in a chariot race ⟨the space between the two . . . ~*s* was filled with statues and obelisks —Edward Gibbon⟩ **2 :** the end toward which effort or ambition is directed **:** AIM, PURPOSE ⟨leisure is a real commodity, a prize of life, a ~ to strive for —C.C.Furnas⟩ **:** a condition or state to be brought about through a course of action **3 a :** a station, area, cage, basket, or pair of uprights with or without a crossbar toward which the players in various games (as football, basketball, polo, lacrosse, hockey) attempt to advance the ball or puck and usu. through or into which it must go in order to score points — see FIELD HOCKEY illustration **b :** the act of causing the ball or puck to go through or into such a goal **c :** the score resulting from such an act **4 :** GOALKEEPER **5 :** the object complement of a verb **syn** see INTENTION — **in goal :** in one of the two parts of the ground immediately at the ends of the field of play in rugby and between the touchlines produced to the dead-ball lines

²goal \"\ *vi* -ED/-ING/-S **:** to seek or score a goal

go·ala \gōˈälə\ *n* -S *usu cap* [Hindi *goālā,* fr. Skt *gopālaka* cowherd, fr. *go* cow, bull + *pālaka* protector — more at COW, WALLAH] **:** a member of a Hindu caste employed chiefly in dairying

goal crease *n* **:** CREASE 3b

goal–directed *adj* **:** aimed toward a goal or toward completion of a task **:** having an object or anticipated reward **:** PURPOSEFUL, MEANINGFUL, NONRANDOM ⟨*goal-directed* behavior⟩ ⟨repetition must always be *goal-directed* —J.B.Carroll⟩

goal·ie \ˈgōlē, -li\ *n* -S [¹*goal* + *-ie*] **:** GOALKEEPER

goalkeeper \ˈ=,==\ *n* **:** a player who defends the goal in various games (as hockey, lacrosse, soccer)

goal kick *n* **:** a kick-in awarded a defending soccer player when the ball is driven by a member of the opposing team over the end line but not between the goalposts

goal·less \ˈgōlləs\ *adj* **:** having no goal scored by either team ⟨a ~ draw⟩

goal line *n* **:** a line marking each end of the field of play in various games and extending from one side of the field to the other or from one goalpost to the other — see FOOTBALL illustration

go along *vi* **1 :** to move along **:** CONTINUE, PROCEED ⟨the car *went along* at a moderate speed⟩ ⟨had to teach himself and his . . . assistants as they *went along* —Robert Berkelman⟩ **2 :** to go or travel as a companion ⟨having no particular interest in antiques, he *went along* for the ride —R.M.Hodesh⟩ — often used with *with* ⟨invited him to *go along* with us on the trip⟩ **3 :** to act in cooperation or express agreement ⟨were unwilling to take the gamble and declined to *go along* —Freeman Lincoln⟩ — often used with *with* ⟨were glad enough to *go along* with his tentative theory —Robert Shaplen⟩

goalpost \ˈ=,=\ *n* **:** one of two vertical posts that with a crossbar constitute the goal in various games

goal set *n* **:** a preparatory set oriented toward a goal

goaltender \ˈ=,==\ *n* **:** GOALKEEPER

¹go·an \ˈgōən\ *adj, usu cap* [*Goa,* region in India + E *-an*] **:** GOANESE

²goan \"\ *n* -S *cap* **:** GOANESE

¹go·a·nese \ˌgōəˈnēz, -ēs\ *adj, usu cap* [*Goa* + *-nese* (as in *Chinese*)] **1 :** of, relating to, or characteristic of Goa **2 :** of, relating to, or characteristic of the people of Goa

²goanese \"\ *n, pl* **goanese** *cap* **:** a native or inhabitant of Goa

go·an·na \gōˈanə\ *n* -S [alter. of *iguana*] *chiefly Austral* **:** any of several large monitor lizards of the family Varanidae — compare IGUANA

goa powder *n, usu cap G* [¹*Goa*] **:** a bitter powder found in the wood of a Brazilian tree (*Vataireopsis araroba*) and valued as the chief source of the drug chrysarobin

go around *vi* **1 a :** to pass from place to place **:** go here and there ⟨friends of your own age to *go around* with —Caroline Slade⟩ **b :** to have currency **:** CIRCULATE ⟨an amusing story is *going around* these days⟩ **2 :** to satisfy the demand **:** fill the need ⟨hardly enough food to *go around*⟩

go–around \ˈ==,=\ *n* -S [*go around*] **1 a :** ROUND ⟨apparent agreement . . . during the first *go-around* doesn't necessarily mean they'll see eye to eye indefinitely —*Newsweek*⟩ **b :** a heated argument, dispute, or struggle ⟨tried to tell them that this was a lousy way to treat a member of the family, and after a real *go-around* he had won —Don Tracy⟩ **2 :** RUNAROUND ⟨he's been giving us the *go-around* —Del Carnes⟩ **3 :** an act or instance of going around (as in a traffic pattern) ⟨cockpit work load is highest in a *go-around* from a missed instrument approach —E.W.Norris⟩

goas *pl of* GOA

go–ashore \ˈgōə,shō(ə)r\ *n* -S [prob. by folk etymology fr. Maori *'kōhua* cooking pot] *NewZeal* **:** a 3-footed iron caldron

goa stone *n, usu cap G* [¹*Goa*] **:** GOA BALL

go–as–you–please \ˌ===ˈ=\ *adj* **:** not bound by rule, law, or convention **:** EASYGOING ⟨bewildered by the old *go-as-you-please* liberty of alliterative rhythm —George Saintsbury⟩

¹goat \ˈgōt, *usu* -ōd.+V\ *n* -S *often attrib* [ME *gote, goot, gat,* fr. OE *gāt;* akin to OHG *geiz* goat, ON *geit,* Goth *gaits* goat, L *haedus* kid] **1 a :** any of various alert agile Old World hollow-horned ruminant mammals (genus *Capra*) closely related to the sheep and like them often domesticated but of lighter build and with backwardly arching horns that often form a closely twisted spiral, a short tail, and comparatively straight hair, the male usu. having a distinct beard — compare IBEX, MARKHOR **b :** any of several related animals of similar habits or characteristics — see GOAT ANTELOPE, MOUNTAIN GOAT **2 :** CAPRICORN **3 :** a licentious or lustful man **:** LECHER ⟨the doctor is . . . an old ~ and has ideas about spiriting his lovely client off to a little hideout —Wolcott Gibbs⟩ **4 :** GOATSKIN ⟨a book bound in ~⟩ **5 :** SCAPEGOAT ⟨dairy farmers have been made the ~ for all that's to be criticized in the government support program —Richard Lewis⟩ **6** *slang* **a :** a West Point cadet having the lowest academic rank in his class **b :** one who is being initiated into a fraternity or sorority **7 :** BROCCOLI BROWN **8 :** a yard locomotive

²goat \"\ *var of* GOTE

goat antelope *n* **:** any of several bovid mammals (as the chamois, goral, Rocky Mountain goat) related to the goats but in some respects resembling the antelopes

goatbrush \ˈ=,=\ *n* **:** OREGON BOX

goatbush \ˈ=,=\ *n* **:** a spiny shrub (*Castela texana*) of the family Simaroubaceae of Mexico and the southwestern U.S. having a bitter bark

goa·tee \(,)gōˈtē\ *n* -S [¹*goat* + *-ee;* fr. the resemblance to the beard of a he-goat] **:** a small trim pointed or tufted beard on a man's chin

goatee

goa·teed \-ēd\ *adj* **:** having a goatee ⟨a courtly ~ scholar⟩

goat fever *n* **:** BRUCELLOSIS

goat fig *n* **:** any of several wild figs; *esp* **:** CAPRIFIG

goatfish \ˈ=,=\ *n* **:** a fish of the family Mullidae **:** MULLET 2

goat grass *n* **:** any of various grasses of the genus *Aegilops; esp* **:** a European grass (*A. triuncialis*) naturalized as a weed in No. America whose sharp-pointed fruits cause injury when eaten by livestock

goat·herd \ˈgōt,hərd\ *n* [ME *gootherde,* fr. OE *gāthyrde,* fr. *gāt* goat + *hyrde* herder — more at GOAT, HERD] **:** one who tends goats

goatier *comparative of* GOATY

goatiest *superlative of* GOATY

goat·ish \ˈgōd·|ish, -ōt|, |ēsh\ *adj* **1 :** of, relating to, or having the characteristics of a goat **2 :** LASCIVIOUS, LECHEROUS — **goat·ish·ness** *n* -ES

goat–kneed \ˈgōtˌnēd\ *adj* **:** KNEE-SPRUNG

goatlike \ˈ=,=\ *adj* **:** resembling that of a goat ⟨a ~ odor⟩

goat·ling \ˈgōtliŋ\ *n* -S *Brit* **:** a young goat; *esp* **:** a female goat between one and two years old

goat moth *n* [so called fr. the fact that its larva exhales an odor suggestive of a he-goat] **:** any of the large stout-bodied moths of the family Cossidae; *esp* **:** a European moth (*Cossus cossus*) whose larva bores in the wood of living trees

goat nut *n* **:** JOJOBA

goat pepper *also* **goat's pepper** *n* **:** any of various small-fruited hot peppers

goat–pox \ˈ=,=\ *n* **:** a virus disease of goats that resembles cowpox and is either localized in the udder or occurs over the surface of the body

goats *pl of* GOAT

goatsbeard \ˈ=,=\ *n* **1 :** a plant of the genus *Tragopogon* **2 :** any of several plants of the genus *Aruncus; esp* **:** an herb (*A. sylvester*) cultivated for its small white flowers **3 :** a fungus of the genus *Clavaria*

goat's chico·ry *n* **:** PILEWORT 3

goats·foot \ˈgōts,fu̇t\ *n* -S **1 :** a southern African plant (*Oxalis caprina*) with bluish yellow flowers **2 :** GOUTWEED

goatsfoot convolvulus *n* **:** a tropicopolitan vine (*Ipomoea pes-caprae*) having coarse succulent leaves and showy purple flowers

goat's hair *n* **:** a bundle of short white hairy cirrus clouds believed to portend rain

goat's horn *n* [so called fr. the shape of the pod] **:** an herb (*Astragalus aegiceras*) of southern Europe

goat·skin \ˈ=,=\ *n* **1 :** the skin of a goat **2 :** leather made from goatskin

goat's rue *n* **1** *or* **goat rue :** a tall bushy blue-flowered European perennial plant (*Galega officinalis*) sometimes grown in flower gardens **2 :** CATGUT 3a

goat's thorn *n* **:** any of several thorny shrubs of the genus *Astragalus* (as *A. tragacanthus* and *A. poterium*) native to southern Europe and the Levant

goat·stone \ˈ=,=\ *n* **1 :** a bezoar from a goat **2 goatstones** *pl* **:** the clustered growths of any of several Old World orchids of the genus *Orchis*

goatsucker \ˈ=,==\ *n* [so called fr. the belief that it sucks the milk from goats] **:** any of various medium-sized long-winged crepuscular or nocturnal birds (as the whippoorwills and nighthawks) constituting the family Caprimulgidae, having a short wide bill, short legs, and soft mottled plumage, and feeding on insects which they catch on the wing — called also *nightjar;* see FROGMOUTH

goat·weed \ˈ=,=\ *n* **1 :** GOUTWEED **2 :** either of two West Indian plants (*Capraria biflora* and *Stemodia durantifolia*) of the family Scrophulariaceae **3 :** BILLY-GOAT WEED **4 :** a plant of the genus *Croton* **5 :** KLAMATH WEED

goatweed emperor *n* **:** a common brown and orange butterfly (*Anaea andria*) of the central U.S. that has larvae which feed on plants of the genus *Croton*

goat willow *n* **:** a sallow (*Salix caprea*)

goaty \ˈgōd·|ē, -ōt|, |i\ *adj* -ER/-EST **:** GOATISH

goave *var of* GOVE

go–away bird \ˌgōˈwā-\ *also* **go·way bird** \(ˈ)gōˌwā-\ *n* [imit.] **:** any of several African and Australian birds; *esp* **:** any of various African touracos

goa yam *n, usu cap G* [¹*Goa*] **:** KAAWI YAM

¹gob \ˈgäb\ *n* -S [ME *gobbe,* fr. MF *gobe* large morsel of food, large mouthful, back-formation fr. *gobet* mouthful, bite, piece — more at GOBBET] **1 :** a lump or mass of indefinite or variable shape ⟨the mud was thick . . . and clung to our shoes like huge ~*s* of discolored dough —H.D.Skidmore⟩ ⟨high fat clouds like ~*s* of whipped cream —William Faulkner⟩ **2 :** a large amount — usu. used in pl. ⟨he has ~*s* of money —P.B. Kyne⟩ ⟨they will certainly find in it ~*s* . . . of unadulterated narrative —C.J.Rolo⟩ **3 a :** a large mouthful of food ⟨a beer to wash down the last ~ of gluey rice —Earle Birney⟩ **b :** a large lump of some substance that is chewed and not swallowed (as tobacco) **4 :** a mass of molten glass gathered on a blowpipe or in a feeder as the initial step in forming a glass object **5 a :** the broken waste or filling left or placed in old mine workings **b :** a space from which material (as coal) has been mined

²gob \"\ *n* -S [IrGael & ScGael, beak, protruding mouth] **:** MOUTH ⟨a short stumpy man with a pipe perpetually in his ~ —Walter Macken⟩

³gob \"\ *n* -S [origin unknown] **:** SAILOR — usu. used of an enlisted man in the U.S. Navy

go·bar numeral *or* **gho·bar numeral** \(ˈ)gōˌbär-\ *or* **gu·bar numeral** \(ˈ)güˌbär-\ *n* [Ar *ghubār* dust, board with sand used for writing] **:** one of a set of ancient numerals which the Arabs developed from Hindu numerals and from which the modern arabic numerals are derived — see NUMBER table

gobbe \ˈgäb\ *n* -S [native name in the Caribbean] **:** BAMBARRA GROUNDNUT

¹gob·bet \ˈgäbət, *usu* -əd.+V\ *n* -S [ME *gobet,* fr. MF, mouthful, bite, piece, fr. *gober* to gulp down, swallow, prob. of Celt origin; akin to IrGael & ScGael *gob* beak, snout, protruding mouth] **1 a :** a piece or portion of food or raw meat **:** MORSEL ⟨smoking ~*s* of ready-cooked fish, chicken, and turkey —H.L. Davis⟩ ⟨slice them into ~*s* and fling their flesh to the dogs —Henry Taylor⟩ **b :** a mouthful of food ⟨slices of bread covered with honey which he was shoveling into himself in dripping gouts and ~*s* —Kenneth Roberts⟩ ⟨the masses of raw immigrants . . . were unwelcome ~*s* to the Brahmin stomach —V.L.Parrington⟩ **2 :** a lump or mass usu. of indefinite or variable shape **:** GOB ⟨a ~ of gold —Amy Lowell⟩ ⟨some revolting ~*s* of cotton —Jean Stafford⟩ ⟨watching the volcano throw up its ~*s* of smoke —Wallace Stegner⟩ **3 :** a fragment or extract of literature or music ⟨snippets and ~*s* of information culled from the classics —*Listener*⟩ ⟨unrelated ~*s* of quantitative knowledge —A.W.Griswold⟩ **4 :** a small quantity of liquid **:** DROP ⟨~*s* of oil —William Beebe⟩ ⟨she shipped a ~ of sea, only a thin little runnel that escaped at once through the open scuppers —Victoria Sackville-West⟩

²gobbet \"\ *vt* -ED/-ING/-S [ME *gobeten,* fr. *gobet,* n.] **1** *archaic* **:** to cut up (as a trout) **2** *obs* **:** to swallow in gobbets ⟨they ~ down his flesh —Robert Stapylton⟩

¹gob·ble \ˈgäbəl\ *vb* **gobbled; gobbled; gobbling** \-b(ə)liŋ\ **gobbles** [prob. fr. ¹*gob* + *-le* (freq. suffix)] *vt* **1 :** to eat greedily or swallow hastily and noisily in large mouthfuls **:** GULP ⟨they *gobbled* what was left of the breakfast —S.H. Adams⟩ ⟨turned themselves into tigers and *gobbled* up human beings —*Newsweek*⟩ **2 :** to seize or capture greedily or hastily **:** take eagerly **:** GRAB — usu. used with *up* ⟨permitting the three small countries to be *gobbled* up individually by their aggressive neighbor⟩ ⟨a bond issue was quickly *gobbled up* —E.O. Hauser⟩ **3 :** to read rapidly or greedily ⟨many bright girls can ~ up such books —Louise S. Bechtel⟩ ~ *vi* **:** to eat greedily and hastily

²gobble \"\ *vb* -ED/-ING/-S [imit.] *vi* **1 :** to make the natural guttural noise of a turkey cock ⟨the older toms ~ and strut to attract the attention of the females⟩ **2 :** to make a sound resembling the gobble of a turkey ⟨a tiny geyser *gobbled* —Rudyard Kipling⟩ ~ *vt* **:** to utter or emit by or as if by gobbling ⟨the obscenities that poured out of him were *gobbled* so that their point was lost —Walter Macken⟩

³gobble \"\ *n* -S **:** a noise made by or as if by gobbling

gob·ble·de·gook *or* **gob·ble·dy·gook** \ˈgäbəldēˌgu̇k, -di̇ˌ-, -ˌgük\ *n* [irreg. fr. ³*gobble*] **:** wordy and generally unintelligible jargon: **a :** inflated, involved, and obscure verbiage usu. associated with bureaucratic pronouncements ⟨the current law is a masterpiece of complexity and ~ —Roswell Magill⟩ **b :** the specialized language of a group or organization that is usu. wordy and complicated and often unintelligible to an outsider ⟨I don't get all this real-estate ~: twenty-seven-five, five down, exclusive development, unspoiled area, last frontier —Steve McNeil⟩ ⟨writing in a linguistic ~ unintelligible to everyone except the specialist —G.S.Lane⟩ **c :** a meaningless jumble of words ⟨only the teachers in the English department teach English; the others let their students get by with any old ~ —S.E.Morison⟩

¹gob·bler \ˈgäb(ə)lə(r)\ *n* -S [¹*gobble* + *-er*] **:** one that gobbles; *esp* **:** one that reads rapidly or greedily ⟨a great ~ of books⟩

²gobbler \-blə(r)\ *n* -S [²*gobble* + *-er*] **:** TURKEY-COCK

gobbo *var of* GOBO

¹gobe·lin \ˈgōbələn, ˈgäb-\ *adj, usu cap* [fr. the *Gobelin* dyehouse and tapestry works, Paris, France, established by the *Gobelin* family, 15th cent. Fr. dyers] **:** of, relating to, or being a French tapestry noted for its handworked pictorial designs

²gobelin \"\ *n* -S *usu cap* **1 a :** a Gobelin tapestry **b :** a handmade or machine-made imitation of a Gobelin **2** *or* **gobelin blue :** a grayish blue that is greener and paler than electric or average shadow blue, greener and duller than copenhagen, and greener and less strong than old china

gobelin green *n, usu cap 1st G* **:** a moderate green that is yellower and slightly duller than sea green (sense 1a) and yellower and paler than myrtle (sense 3a)

gobelin stitch *n, usu cap G* **:** any of several small vertical or slanting stitches worked over one or more threads of canvas to form a solid ground of stitches

gobe·mouche \(,)gōbˈmüsh\ *n, pl* **gobe·mouches** \-sh(əz)\ [F, fr. *gober* to gulp down, swallow + *mouche* fly, fr. L *musca* — more at GOBBET, MIDGE] **:** a credulous person; *esp* **:** one who believes everything he hears ⟨as words here cost nothing, the gulping ~ is plentifully supplied —Richard Ford⟩

go·ber·na·do·ra \ˌgōbə(r)nəˈdōrə\ *n* -S [MexSp, fr. Sp, wife of a governor, fem. of *gobernador* governor, fr. *gobernar* to govern, fr. L *gubernare* to pilot, steer, govern — more at GOVERN] **:** CREOSOTE BUSH

go–between \ˈ==,=\ *n* -S [fr. the phrase *go between*] **1 :** one that goes between: as **a :** one who promotes a love affair esp. by carrying messages and arranging meetings ⟨enjoying his mysterious importance as . . . *go-between* with the man she loves —Elizabeth Janeway⟩ **b :** one who negotiates a marriage **:** MARRIAGE BROKER ⟨conduct of negotiations . . . by parents through a *go-between* —G.P.Murdock⟩ **c :** an intermediate agent between two individuals or groups (as in politics) **:** EMISSARY, INTERMEDIARY ⟨the *go-between* taking messages from mother to son —Mary Webb⟩ ⟨the *go-between* who arranged the compromise between the two rival factions in the legislature⟩ **2 :** a connecting link or bridge ⟨the Crimea formerly played the part of *go-between* with the Mediterranean world —E.D.Laborde⟩ **3 :** one that belongs in part to each of two groups or classes ⟨these children of the wilds . . . could pass either as white or red and were in truth *go-betweens* —*Amer. Guide Series: Minn.*⟩

go·bi \ˈgōbē, -bi\ *n* -S [fr. the *Gobi* desert, Mongolia] **:** the lenticular mass of sedimentary deposits that occupies a tala or downwarp basin

gobies *pl of* GOBY

¹go·bi·e·soc·id \gōˌbīəˈsäsəd, ˌgōbēə-\ *adj* [NL *Gobiesocidae*] **:** of or relating to the Gobiesocidae

²gobiesocid \"\ *n* -s : a gobiesocid fish

go·bi·e·soc·i·dae \(,)gō,bīəˈsäsə,dē, ,gōbēə-\ *n pl, cap* [NL, fr. *Gobiesoc-, Gobiesox,* type genus + *-idae*] : a family of small marine teleost fishes that have soft dorsal and anal fins and a large sucker formed in part by the pelvic fins located well forward on the throat and that form an order Xenopterygii or in some classifications a highly specialized suborder of Percomorphi — compare CLINGFISH

go·bi·e·soc·i·form \gōˈbīəˈsäsə,fȯrm, ¦gōbēə-\ *adj* [NL *gobieosocidae* + E *-form*] : resembling the Gobiesocidae

go·bi·e·sox \gōˈbīə,säks, ˈgōbē-\ *n, cap* [NL, fr. L *gobius* gudgeon + *esox* pike — more at GOBY, ESOX] : the type genus of Gobiesocidae

¹go·bi·id \ˈgōbēəd\ *adj* [NL *Gobiidae*] : of or relating to the Gobiidae

²gobiid \"\ *n* -s : a gobiid fish

go·bi·idae \gōˈbīə,dē\ *n pl, cap* [NL, fr. *Gobius,* type genus + *-idae*] : a family of bony fishes that consists of the gobies and with a few related families constitutes a suborder Gobioidea of the order Percomorphi

go·bi·iform \ˈgōbēə,fȯrm\ *adj* [NL *Gobiiformes*] **1** : GOBIOID **2** : resembling a goby

go·bi·ifor·mes \,⸗⸗⸗ˈfȯr,mēz\ [NL, fr. *Gobius* + *-iformes*] *syn of* GOBIOIDEA

go·bi·nism \ˈgōbə,nizəm\ *n* -s *usu cap* [F *gobinisme,* fr. Comte Joseph A. de *Gobineau* †1882 Fr. orientalist + F *-isme* -ism] : the theory or doctrine that the white and esp. the Germanic race is the superior race among men

go·bio \ˈgōbē,ō\ *n, cap* [NL, fr. L gudgeon — more at GOBY] : a genus of freshwater cyprinid fishes that contains the true gudgeons

¹go·bi·oid \ˈgōbē,ȯid\ *adj* [NL *Gobioidea*] : of or relating to the Gobioidea

²gobioid \"\ *n* -s : a gobioid fish

go·bi·oi·dea \,⸗⸗ˈȯidēə\ *n pl, cap* [NL, fr. *Gobius* + *-oidea*] : a suborder of Percomorphi comprising the gobies and related fishes

go·bi·oi·dei \-dē,ī\ [NL, fr. *Gobius* + *-oidei*] *syn of* GOBIOIDEA

go·bi·us \ˈgōbēəs\ *n, cap* [NL, fr. L, gudgeon — more at GOBY] : the type genus of Gobiidae

¹gob·let \ˈgäblət, *usu* -əd.+V\ *n* -s [ME *gobelet, goblett,* fr. MF *gobelet,* prob. of Celt origin; akin to IrGael & ScGael *gob* beak, snout, protruding mouth] **1** *archaic* **a** : a bowl-shaped cup or drinking vessel without handles and sometimes footed and covered **b** : a wine cup **2** : a drinking glass with a foot and stem — compare TUMBLER

goblet 2

²goblet *n* -s [by alter.] *obs* : GOBBET

goblet cell *n* [¹*goblet;* fr. its shape] **1** : a mucus-secreting epithelial cell (as of columnar epithelium) that is distended at the free end with secretion or precursors **2** : a freshwater choanoflagellate (genus *Monosiga*) that is commonly attached to aquatic plants by a slender stalk — called also *chalice cell*

gob·lin \ˈgäblən\ *n* -s *often attrib* [ME *gobelin,* fr. MF, fr. ML *gobelinus,* fr. (assumed) ML *gobelus* goblin, modif. of Gk *kobalos* rogue, spirit resembling a satyr] : an ugly or grotesque sprite sometimes conceived as evil and malicious and sometimes as merely playful and mischievous ⟨~s haunt from fire or fen —William Collins †1759⟩ ⟨an amiable ~ attached to the old house from time immemorial —*Brit. Book News*⟩

gob·line \ˈgä,blīn\ *n* [*gob* (origin unknown) + *line*] : a backrope from the dolphin striker

gob·lin·esque \¦gäblə¦nesk\ *adj* : GOBLINISH

goblin fish *n* : a small Australian scorpion fish (*Glyptauchen panduratus*) noted for its grotesque appearance

gob·lin·ish \ˈgäblənish\ *adj* : resembling or suggestive of a goblin in appearance or behavior ⟨a fantastic ~ wink —J.C. Powys⟩

gob·lin·ry \-nrē\ *n* -ES : the acts or practices of goblins ⟨~ intended to deceive you —Lafcadio Hearn⟩

goblin scarlet *n* : CASTILIAN RED

goblin shark *n* : a galeoid shark (genus *Scapanorhynchus*) that has protrusible jaws and a greatly elongate snout and is found off the coasts of Japan and Portugal

¹go·bo \ˈgō(,)bō\ *n* -s [Jap *gobō*] **1** : a burdock (*Arctium lappa*) cultivated in Japan as a vegetable **2** *or* **gob·bo** \ˈgä·(-\ : OKRA

²gobo \"\ *n, pl* **gobos** *also* **goboes** [origin unknown] **1** : a portable black cloth-covered screen or dark strip of wallboard used in television and motion pictures to shield the camera from unwanted light **2** : a portable screen covered with sound-absorbing material that is used to protect (as a microphone) from unwanted sound

gob·o·nat·ed \ˈgäbə,nād·əd\ *adj* [prob. fr. obs. *gobon* slice (fr. ME *goboun, gobin,* fr. — assumed — AF *gobon,* fr. OF *gobet* mouthful, bite, piece) + E *-ate* + *-ed*] : COMPONY

go·bo·ny \gəˈbōnē\ *adj* [obs. *gobon* + *-y* (fr. F *-é* -ate, fr. L *-atus*)] : COMPONY

go·boon \(ˈ)gä¦bün, gəˈb-\ *var of* ²GABOON

gobs *pl of* GOB

gobstick \ˈ⸗,⸗\ *n* [²*gob* + *stick*] : a stick for removing the hook from the gullet of a fish

go by *vi* **1** : PASS ⟨as time *goes by*⟩ **2** : to make a brief visit : CALL ⟨all the family was at home when he *went by* yesterday⟩

go–by \ˈgō,bī\ *n* -s [*go by*] : intentional disregard or avoidance : RUNAROUND — usu. used in the phrase *give the go-by* ⟨I was good enough to see after they gave you the big *go-by,* wasn't I —Thomas Wolfe⟩

go·by \ˈgōbē, -bi\ *n, pl* **gobies** *also* **goby** [L *gobius, cobius, gobio* gudgeon, fr. Gk *kōbios,* prob. of non-IE origin] : any of numerous spiny-finned fishes constituting the family Gobiidae, usu. having a broad depressed head, large mouth, no lateral line, and the pelvic fins thoracic and often united to form a sucking disk, and occurring chiefly in shallow coastal waters — see MUDSKIPPER, MUDSUCKER

go–bye *or* **go–by** \ˈgō,bī\ *n* -s [*go by*] : the act of a greyhound that has gained a length's lead over an opponent after having started a length behind and passed him in a straight run

GOC *abbr* general officer commanding

go–cart \ˈ⸗,⸗\ *n* **1** : WALKER ⟨as much a prisoner as a child in a *go-cart* —Maria Edgeworth⟩ **2** : HANDCART ⟨pushing his belongings in a *go-cart* —*Johannesburg Rand Daily Mail*⟩ **3** : a light open carriage **4** : STROLLER ⟨wheeling my brother . . . in his *go-cart* —Willard Price⟩

go·cle·ni·an sorites \gōˈklē¦nēən-, -lā¦\ *n, usu cap G* [Rudolf *Goclenius* †1628 Ger. logician + E *-an*] : a sorites in which the order of the premises is reversed

¹god \ˈgäd *sometimes* ˈgȯd\ *n* -s [ME, fr. OE; akin to OFris & OS *god,* OHG *got,* ON *goth, guth,* Goth *guth* god and prob. to OIr *guth* voice, Gk *kauchasthai* to boast, Skt *havate* he calls, invokes; basic meaning: to call, invoke] **1** : a being of more than human attributes and powers; *esp* : a superhuman person conceived as the ruler or sovereign embodiment of some aspect, attribute, or department of reality and to whom worship is due and acceptable ⟨ancestor worship . . . occurs where ~s are thought once to have been human beings —E.A. Hoebel⟩ ⟨the grim wrath of the ~s on high —J.B.Noss⟩ ⟨the Greek ~s of love and war⟩ — often used interjectionally esp. as a cap. oath **2** : an artificial or natural object (as a carved idol or an animal or tree) that is thought to be the seat of divine powers, the expression of a divine personality, or itself a supernatural or divine agency ⟨also he makes a ~ and worships it —Isa 44:15 (RSV)⟩ ⟨not . . . every mummified and carefully buried animal had been a ~ —S.A.B.Mercer⟩ **3** : a person or thing that is honored as a god or deified : something held to be of supreme value ⟨his father — the adored ~ who had unjustly condemned him —Douglas Hubble⟩ ⟨power for power's sake was his mastering ~ —Hodding Carter⟩ **4** : one who wields great or despotic power ⟨the ruling ~s of the circulating libraries —Frederick Pollock⟩ **5 a** : an occupant of the gallery of a theater ⟨one young ~ between the acts favored the public with a song —W.M.Thackeray⟩ **b gods** *pl* : the gallery of a theater ⟨the applause . . . came mainly from a crowd of youngsters in the ~s —Frank Clune⟩ **6** : a human being of extraordinarily attractive physical stature ⟨a ~ . . . with great broad shoulders and a magnificent chest —W.S.Maugham⟩ — **ye gods and little fishes** — used to express surprise or indignation

²God \"\ *n* : the supreme or ultimate reality : the Deity variously conceived in theology, philosophy, and popular religion: as **a** (1) : the holy, infinite, and eternal spiritual reality presented in the Bible as the creator, sustainer, judge, righteous sovereign, and redeemer of the universe who acts with power in history in carrying out his purpose ⟨the Hebraic thought of ~ as the living sovereign Jehovah —O.C.Quick⟩ ⟨~ in Three Persons, blessed Trinity —Reginald Heber⟩ (2) : the eternal, invisible, arbitrarily omnipotent Lord of the worlds and final judge of all men presented in the Koran as all-knowing, just, compassionate, merciful, and unchangeable ⟨Allah hath said: Choose not two gods; there is only One ~ —*Koran*⟩ **b** (1) : the unchangeably perfect Being that is the first and final cause of the universe ⟨it is necessary that there should be as the first cause of the series of motions an unmoved mover or ~ —Frank Thilly⟩ — compare DEISM (2) : the whole of the universe in its unity ⟨religion is not forced to choose . . . the pantheistic ~ of idealism —James Collins⟩ — compare PANTHEISM (3) : reality opposed to appearance : ABSOLUTE ⟨Hegel claims that . . . religion is the self-consciousness of ~ . . . how the Absolute Spirit is conscious of itself in finite spirit —John Baillie⟩ (4) : the creative, integrative, and redemptive process at work in the world that is the supremely worthful actuality of all existence and upon which all other forms of existence depend for life, meaning, freedom, purpose, value, and the realization of their highest destiny ⟨we are invited to behold a growing universe and to discern at its heart . . . a finite growing ~ —T.B.Kilpatrick⟩ (5) : the one ultimate infinite reality that is pure existence, consciousness, and bliss without distinctions (as of time and space) ⟨~ in Hinduism is not the creator of individual selves and other eternal entities — Satischandra Chatterjee⟩ (6) *Christian Science* : infinite Mind : the incorporeal divine Principle ruling over all as eternal Spirit ⟨~ . . . the all-knowing, all-seeing, all-acting, all-wise, all-loving, and eternal; Principle; Mind; Soul; Spirit; Life; Truth; Love; all substance; intelligence —Mary B. Eddy⟩ **c** (1) : the Being supreme in power, wisdom, and goodness that men worship and to whom they pray ⟨turn to ~ in time of trouble⟩ (2) : the ideal or essence of what is best in human life ⟨to them ~ became a symbol for the highest human aspirations and without reality apart from the minds of men —K.S. Latourette⟩ — **for God's sake** — used typically to express surprise, disgust, or indignation — **God forbid** — used as a mild invocation ⟨if he should fail, *God forbid,* all will be lost⟩ — **with God** : in heaven — used of one who has died

³god \"\ *vt* **godded; godded; godding; gods** : to treat as a god : WORSHIP, IDOLIZE, DEIFY ⟨how the good priest ~s himself —Alfred Tennyson⟩ ⟨this last old man . . . loved me above the measure of a father; nay, godded me indeed —Shak.⟩

god–a–mercy \¦⸗əˈmərsē\ *interj, usu cap G* [ME *God a mercy* God have mercy] *archaic* — used to express gratitude or thanks ⟨*God-a-mercy* . . . what a happy thing —*Bystander*⟩

god–awful \(ˈ)⸗¦⸗\ *adj, often cap G* : extremely unpleasant, disagreeable, or objectionable : ABOMINABLE ⟨the *god-awful* mess I'm in —Dorothy Baker⟩

godchild \ˈ⸗,⸗\ *n* [ME, fr. *god* + *child*] **1** : one for whom a person becomes sponsor at baptism and whom he promises to see brought up as a Christian : GODSON, GODDAUGHTER ⟨both the bride and bridegroom were *godchildren* of the king and queen —*N.Y. Times*⟩ **2** : a child of another religious or cultural group having a relationship to a man or woman similar to that of a Christian godchild to his sponsor

¹god·damn *or* **god·dam** \ˈgäd¦dam, -daa(ə)m\ *n* -s *often cap* : DAMN ⟨they were in no mood to give a good ~ about anything —Robert Lowry⟩

²goddamn *or* **goddam** \(ˈ)⸗¦⸗\ *vb, sometimes cap, vt* : DAMN *vt* 5 ⟨I'll be ~*ed* —T.H.Martin⟩ ⟨he ~*ed* himself because he was getting soft —J.T.Farrell⟩ ~ *vi* : DAMN *vi* ⟨you feel like swearing and ~*ing* worse and worse —Ernest Hemingway⟩

¹god·damned \ˈ⸗,dam(d), -,daa(ə)m(d), *before "-est"* (ˈ)⸗¦⸗\ *or* **god·damn** *or* **god·dam** \-m\ *adj* : ¹DAMNED ⟨put that in your ~ notebook —Martha Gellhorn⟩

²goddamned \"\ *or* **goddamn** *or* **goddam** \"\ *adv* : ²DAMNED ⟨you're ~ right I want to go —John Steinbeck⟩

goddaughter \ˈ⸗,⸗⸗\ *n* [ME *goddoughter,* fr. OE *goddohtor,* fr. *god* + *dohtor* daughter — more at DAUGHTER] : a girl or woman whom one sponsors at baptism ⟨his responsibility for the religious education of his ~⟩

god·dess \ˈgädəs\ *n* -ES [ME *godesse, goddesse,* fr. *god* + *-esse* -ess] **1** : a female god : a divinity or deity of the female sex ⟨the Hindu assassins used hashish as devotees of the ~ Thuggee —Weston La Barre⟩ ⟨the ~ of mercy⟩ **2 a** : a woman who is the object of adoration ⟨like the lover whose imagination makes a ~ of some commonplace young woman —C.E.Montague⟩ **b** : something personified as a woman that is honored as a goddess, deified, or held to be of supreme value ⟨that characteristic middle-class ~ . . . — the English Common Law —Roy Lewis & Angus Maude⟩ **3** : a woman of great charms; *esp* : a woman of extraordinary physical beauty **4** : a female occupant of the gallery of a theater

god·dess·hood \-s,hu̇d\ *n* -s : the quality or state of being a goddess

god·dess–ship \-də(sh),ship, -dəs,sh-\ *n, often cap* [*goddess* + *-ship*] *archaic* : GODDESSHOOD — used with preceding possessive pronoun ⟨in all thy perfect *goddess-ship* —Lord Byron⟩ ⟨her *Goddess-ship* approves the air —Thomas Moore⟩

go·det \gōˈdet\ *n* -s *often attrib* [F, lit., drinking cup, mug, prob. of Gmc origin; akin to MLG *kodde* cylindrical piece of wood, MD *codde* chunk of wood, club] **1** : a triangular inset of cloth placed in a seam or slash to give fullness at the bottom edge of a skirt or sleeve **2** : a usu. glass or plastic roller around which synthetic filaments are passed under tension for stretching

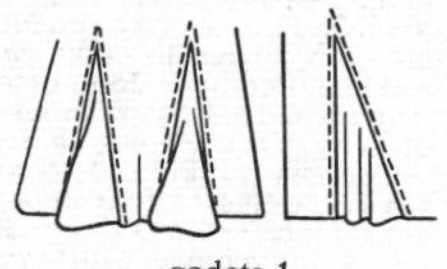

godets 1

go·de·tia \gōˈdēsh(ē)ə\ *n* [NL, fr. C. H. *Godet* †1879 Swiss botanist + NL *-ia*] **1** *cap* : a small genus of western American plants (family Onagraceae) having flowers in leafy racemes or spikes, the calyx often colored, and lilac or white petals that are often spotted with crimson or purple — see FAREWELL-TO-SPRING **2** -s : any plant of the genus *Godetia*

go–devil \ˈ⸗,⸗⸗\ *n* : any of various machines or devices: **a** : a weight formerly dropped into a borehole (as of an oil well) to explode a cartridge previously lowered; *also* : a small torpedo dropped in for the same purpose **b** : a cleaning scraper that is rotated and propelled through a pipeline by the force of the flowing oil **c** : ALLIGATOR 6b **d** : BUCK RAKE **e** : a cultivator having wooden sled runners equipped on each side with curved knives or discs that is designed to follow listed furrows and is used esp. for the first two cultivations of corn — called also *sled cultivator* **f** : a handcar or small gasoline-powered car used by railroad section gangs for transporting laborers and supplies

¹godfather \ˈ⸗,⸗⸗\ *n* [ME *godfader,* fr. OE *godfæder,* fr. *god* + *fæder* father — more at FATHER] **1** : a man who sponsors a child at baptism ⟨there shall be for every male child to be baptized . . . two ~s and one godmother —*Bk. of Com. Prayer*⟩ **2** : a man who assists in the Jewish rite of circumcision by holding the child upon his knees and may thereafter take an interest in the child's upbringing and welfare **3** : one having a relation to someone or something analogous to that of a male sponsor to his godchild: **a** *archaic* : a person who gives a name to someone or something ⟨these earthly ~s of heaven's lights that give a name to every fixed star —Shak.⟩ **b** : one primarily responsible for the care and development of someone or something ⟨the editor had been ~ to many an unknown young writer⟩ ⟨these two museums have long been benevolent ~s to contemporary painting⟩ **c** : one held to be the principal creator or original exponent of a school of thought or mode of behavior ⟨the spiritual ~ of the . . . demagogue in his addiction to reckless attacks for political purposes —*New Republic*⟩

²godfather \"\ *vt* : to act as godfather to; *esp* : to assume responsibility for the care or development of ⟨a novice writer is sometimes ~*ed* by a prominent editor⟩ ⟨proud that their company helped ~ this new industry —*Service*⟩

god–fear·er \ˈ⸗,firə(r)\ *n, cap G* : a devoutly religious person

god–fearing \ˈ⸗,⸗⸗\ *adj, usu cap G* : having a reverential and loving feeling toward God : devoutly religious : PIOUS ⟨a *God-fearing* and law-abiding people —H.L.Mencken⟩

god·for·sak·en \ˈgädfə(r)¦sākən\ *adj, sometimes cap* **1** : situated in a remote or desolate place ⟨another winter . . . in that ~ wilderness crossroads —H.L.Davis⟩ **2** : neglected in appearance : WRETCHED, DISMAL — used chiefly of places or objects ⟨the toughest, dreariest, most ~ looking country —Richard Bissell⟩ **3** : pitiable in circumstances : MISERABLE, UNFORTUNATE — used chiefly of persons ⟨for teaching poor ~ school children to write before they can read —H.L.Mencken⟩

god·ful \-fəl\ *adj, usu cap* : DIVINE, AWE-INSPIRING ⟨endless inspiring *Godful* beauty —John Muir †1914⟩

god–given \ˈ⸗,⸗⸗\ *adj, usu cap 1st G* **1** : given directly by God ⟨a *God-given* victory⟩ **2** : ordained by God in the nature of something : NATURAL ⟨we are so accustomed to our own slowly altering division of powers between the nation and the states that it seems to us . . . *God-given* —*Yale Rev.*⟩

god·head \-,hed\ *n* [ME *godhed,* fr. *god* + *-hed, -hede* -hood (akin to ME *-hod, -had* -hood)] **1** : the quality or state of being divine : DEITY 1a, DIVINITY ⟨a denial of our Lord's equality with the Father in ~ —B.J.Kidd⟩ ⟨life has not measured the success of its attempts at ~ by the beauty . . . of the result —G.B.Shaw⟩ **2** *cap* **a** : ²GOD, DEITY 1b — usu. used with *the* ⟨the devil and anathema of our forefathers hides the *Godhead* which we seek —D.H.Lawrence⟩ ⟨the Hindu, with Rama as the *Godhead,* accepts a pantheon of divinities —Andrew Mellor⟩ **b** : the nature of God esp. when regarded as triune : TRINITY ⟨the external relations within the *Godhead* itself —O.C.Quick⟩ ⟨the beginning and the end is the hidden darkness of the eternal *Godhead* —Frank Thilly⟩ **3** *sometimes cap* : ¹GOD 1 ⟨he was deliberately deified; . . . made the ~ of a creed —Frank Gorrell⟩ ⟨the nymphs and native ~s yet unknown —John Dryden⟩

god·hood \-,hu̇d\ *n* -s *sometimes cap* [ME *godhod,* fr. *god* + *-hod* -hood] **1** : GODHEAD 1 ⟨millions venerate the cow as a symbol of life and ~ —*N.Y. Times*⟩ **2** : the state or position of being God or a god ⟨bred to believe that ~ comes . . . to those killed in battle —*Time*⟩ ⟨implies for God that absolute ~ which makes worship imperative —O.J.Baab⟩

god·kin \-dkən\ *n* [*god* + *-kin*] : GODLING

god–king \ˈ⸗¦⸗\ *n* : a human ruler believed to be a god or to possess godlike powers or qualities ⟨the absolutist *god-kings* of Asia Minor and Egypt —Weston La Barre⟩

god·less \-ləs\ *adj* **1** : refusing to acknowledge God : lacking reverence for God ⟨the center of ~ world communism —*Newsweek*⟩ **2** : refusing to obey God's laws : UNGODLY, IMPIOUS, WICKED ⟨the Romans were ~, full of the grossest thoughts, and void of natural affection —Leslie Stephen⟩ ⟨she is a ~ woman of the world —W.M.Thackeray⟩ — **god·less·ly** *adv* — **god·less·ness** *n* -ES

god·let \-lət\ *n* -s : GODLING ⟨scores of lesser ~s who haunt the streams and forests —Kenneth Roberts⟩

godlike \ˈ⸗,⸗\ *adj, sometimes cap* **1** : resembling or having the qualities of God or a god : DIVINE ⟨venerated by them as a ~ man —*Times Lit. Supp.*⟩ **2** : appropriate to or befitting God or a god ⟨man must play God, for he has acquired certain ~ powers —R.H.Rovere⟩ ⟨a man of ~ sagacity —V.L.Parrington⟩ — **god·like·ness** *n* -ES

god·li·ly \-dləlē, ¦li\ *adv, sometimes cap, archaic* : in a godly fashion ⟨we should live soberly, righteously and ~ —John Norris †1711⟩

god·li·ness \-dlēnəs, -lin-\ *n* -ES : the conforming of one's life to the revealed character and purpose of God : RIGHTEOUSNESS

god·ling \-liŋ, -lēŋ\ *n* -s [ME, fr. *god* + *-ling*] **1** : an inferior or purely local deity : a supernatural being midway between a god and a fetish ⟨the friendly little ~s who presided over the routing of daily life —John Buchan⟩ ⟨as futile as the petty ~s . . . which they worship —N.H.Snaith⟩ **2** : the image of a godling ⟨the magic that he carries in his calabash is a ~ —Padraic Colum⟩

¹god·ly \-lē, -li\ *adj* -ER/-EST [ME, fr. *god* + *-ly*] **1** : of, relating to, or emanating from God : DIVINE ⟨everything is black or white, evil or good, satanic or ~ —*Saturday Rev.*⟩ **2** : reverencing God : obedient to the will of God from love and reverence for his character : PIOUS, RIGHTEOUS, DEVOUT ⟨that we may hereafter lead a ~, righteous, and sober life —*Bk. of Com. Prayer*⟩ ⟨gifted and ~ men —F.S.Mead⟩

²godly *adv, archaic* : in a godly fashion : PIOUSLY, DEVOUTLY, RIGHTEOUSLY ⟨all that will live ~ in Christ Jesus shall suffer persecution —2 Tim 3:12 (AV)⟩

godmamma *pronunc at* GOD + *pronunc at* MAMMA\ *n* : GODMOTHER

god–man \ˈ⸗¦man\ *n* **1** *usu cap* : one who is both God and man : CHRIST 1 ⟨when man prays, the sacred image of the *God-man* is with him —H.O.Taylor⟩ **2** *pl* **god–men** : one who is both a god and a man or who has the qualities of both : DEMIGOD, SUPERMAN ⟨their safety . . . is bound up with the life of one of these *god-men* —J.G.Frazer⟩

god–manhood \(ˈ)⸗¦⸗,hu̇d\ *n, usu cap* [*god-man* + *-hood*] : the quality or state of being both God and man ⟨through men the whole of the material universe is elevated to a certain participation in *God-manhood* —G.A.Ellard⟩

godmother \ˈ⸗,⸗⸗\ *n* [ME *godmoder,* fr. OE *godmōdor,* fr. *god* + *mōdor* mother — more at MOTHER] : a woman who sponsors a child at baptism ⟨for each male child to be baptized the rubric . . . requires two godfathers and one ~ —R.P.Crum⟩

go down *vi* **1 a** : to proceed or move to or as if to a lower place ⟨some *went down* to the sea in ships —Ps 107:23 (RSV)⟩ ⟨*went down* to the cellar to check the furnace⟩ **b** : to lead to or as if to a lower place ⟨a path *goes down* to the village⟩ **c** : to fall to or as if to the ground ⟨the plane *went down* in flames⟩ ⟨the boxer *went down* for a count of eight⟩ **d** *of a heavenly body* : to go below the horizon : SET **e** : to become submerged : SINK ⟨the ship *went down* with all hands aboard⟩ ⟨saved as he *went down* for the third time⟩ **f** *of mumps* : to descend into the testes **2** : to admit of being swallowed ⟨the medicine *went down* smoothly enough⟩ **3** : to undergo defeat or overthrow ⟨if America *goes down* we take the entire free world down with us —Sidney Hyman⟩ **4 a** : to find acceptance ⟨had an instinct . . . of knowing what answers *went down* well —Elizabeth Taylor⟩ **b** : to come to be considered or remembered esp. in posterity ⟨that story will *go down* as the best fairy tale I ever wrote —T.E.N.Driberg⟩ ⟨would *go down* in history as a nice try —R.M.Yoder⟩ **5 a** : to undergo a decline or decrease ⟨his temperature *went down* this morning⟩ ⟨the stock market is *going down*⟩ ⟨the number of members has *gone down*⟩ **b** : to become less violent : SUBSIDE ⟨the wind *went down* during the night⟩ **6** *Brit* **a** : to leave a college or university **b** : to graduate from a college or university **7** : to extend in time ⟨the first volume *goes down* to the end of the war⟩ **8** : to become sick ⟨are always *going down* . . . with that malaria —Eve Langley⟩ **9 a** : to fail to make one's contract in a card game **b** : to lie legally exposed on the table — used of the dummy hand in contract bridge **c** : to meld some or all of one's cards in rummy

go–down \ˈgō,dau̇n\ *n* -s [*go down*] *archaic* : a swallow or draft esp. of water or liquor ⟨a bottle of wine apiece, kept down by large *go-downs* of brandy —*Sporting Mag.*⟩

go·down \"\ *n* -s [Malay *gudang*] : a warehouse or storeroom in an oriental country ⟨traders whose ~s were crammed with U.S. goods . . . have no way of replenishing their stocks —*Time*⟩ ⟨the ~s in which were stored the families' food supplies —Christine Weston⟩

godpapa *pronunc at* GOD + *pronunc at* PAPA\ *n* : GODFATHER

godparent \ˈ⸗,⸗⸗\ *n* : GODFATHER, GODMOTHER, SPONSOR ⟨in case the parents die, the ~s will see to the welfare of the child —R.P.Crum⟩

god·par·ent·hood \ˈ⸗,⸗⸗,hu̇d\ *n* -s [*godparent* + *-hood*] : the state or condition of being a godparent ⟨~ inaugurates a set of enduring mutual obligations —Sol Tax⟩

gods *pl of* GOD, *pres 3d sing of* GOD

god's acre *n, cap G* [trans. of G *gottesacker*] : CHURCHYARD, BURYING GROUND, CEMETERY ⟨*God's acre* let out to the dead for so much per square foot —Sean O'Casey⟩

god's country *n, usu cap G* : a place conceived of as esp.

favored by God: as **a :** an area of civilization (as a city) away from the frontier ⟨music heard long before . . . in *God's country* in the East —*Springfield (Mass.) Republican*⟩ **b :** a place away from a city; *esp* **:** the open country ⟨out of the slums into *God's country*⟩ **c :** one's native or home state or region ⟨boosters go so much to the other extreme, talking about *God's country* —Sinclair Lewis⟩

god·send \ˈgäd,send\ *n* -s [back-formation fr. *god-sent*] **1 :** some desirable or needed thing that comes unexpectedly as if sent by God ⟨what a ~ your inexpensive books have been —R.J.Crohn⟩ ⟨the rain after the long drought was a ~⟩ **2 :** a happy or welcome event ⟨the experience was a ~ to a mind that was growing torpid —V.L.Parrington⟩

god–sent \-nt\ *adj* **:** sent by or as if by God

god's–eye \ˈ=,=\ *n, pl* **god's–eyes** *usu cap G* **:** GERMANDER SPEEDWELL

god·ship \ˈ=,ship\ *n* [*god* + *-ship*] **:** the rank, character, or personality of a god **:** DEITY, DIVINITY ⟨your name and mine were used with less reverence than became our ~*s* —John Dryden⟩

god–smith \ˈ=,=\ *n, archaic* **:** one that creates gods or idols usu. from metal ⟨gods . . . of every shape and size that *god-smiths* could produce —John Dryden⟩

godson \ˈ=,=\ *n* [ME *godsone*, fr. OE *godsunu*, fr. *god* god + *sunu* son — more at SON] **:** a boy or man whom one has sponsored at baptism

god's peace *n, cap G* **:** PEACE OF GOD

god·speed \ˈgädzˈpēd, -d,sp-\ *n, usu cap* [ME *god speid*, fr. the phrase *God spede* (*the*, etc.) may God prosper (you, etc.)] **1 :** a prosperous journey **:** SUCCESS ⟨wished him *Godspeed* and a safe return —Bruce Marshall⟩ ⟨bid the fliers *Godspeed* —A. R.Griffin⟩ **2** *archaic* **:** the nick of time **:** CONCLUSION — usu. used in the phrase *in the Godspeed* ⟨a devil came in just in the *Godspeed* —Roger L' Estrange⟩ **3 :** a wish for success given at parting ⟨the captain also received a hearty *Godspeed* —Mary S. Watts⟩

god's penny *n, often cap G* [ME *godes peny*] **:** a penny or small sum paid as earnest money esp. on concluding a purchase or hiring a servant ⟨among merchants the *god's penny* binds the contract of sale —Frederick Pollock & F.W.Maitland⟩ — called also *argentum dei, denarius dei, denier à dieu*

god's plenty *n, usu cap G* **1 :** a quantity larger than human need or desire **:** SUPERABUNDANCE ⟨since critics were . . . praising the use of symbols novelists determined to furnish the symbols, and in *God's plenty* —Malcolm Cowley⟩ **2 :** a very large number or amount ⟨the book was issued in *God's plenty* —J.D.Hart⟩

god's truce *n, cap G & usu cap T* **:** TRUCE OF GOD

god's word *n, cap G & usu cap W* **:** BIBLE 1a

god tree *n, usu cap G* **1 :** CEIBA 2a **2 :** DEODAR

1**god·ward** \ˈgädwə(r)d\ *or* **god·wards** \-)dz\ *adv, usu cap* [ME *godward*, fr. *god* + *-ward*] **1 :** with reference to God ⟨you are the most temperate man *Godward* and the most intemperate yourselfward —Jonathan Swift⟩ **2 :** toward God ⟨as if, being in the world, their tendency was *Godward* —Elizabeth B. Browning⟩ ⟨any heart, turned *Godwards*, feels more joy in one short hour of prayer —P.J.Bailey⟩

2**godward** \"\ *adj, usu cap* **:** directed or tending toward God ⟨the student of theological questions is actually living either a *Godward* or a godless life —Walter Moberly⟩

god·win·i·an \(ˈ)gäˈdwinēən\ *adj, usu cap* [William *Godwin* †1836 Eng. philosopher + E *-ian*] **:** of, relating to, or having the characteristics of William Godwin or his writings

god·wit \ˈgä,dwit\ *n* -s [origin unknown] **:** any of several long-billed wading birds that constitute a genus (*Limosa*) of the family Scolopacidae and that are much like the curlews but have the bill slightly curved upward — see BAR-TAILED GODWIT, BLACK-TAILED GODWIT, HUDSONIAN GODWIT, MARBLED GODWIT, PACIFIC GODWIT

goed *dial past of* GO

goeduck *or* **goeyduc** *var of* GEODUCK

go·el \ˈgō,el, -,äl\ *n* -s *often cap* [Heb *gō'ēl*] **:** REDEEMER, RECLAIMANT; *esp* **:** a next of kin upon whom according to ancient Hebrew custom devolved certain family rights and duties including the avenging of a murdered kinsman's blood and the redemption of the person or property of a kinsman in debt or helpless circumstances

go·er \ˈgō(ə)r, -ōə\ *n* -s [ME, fr. *gon* to go + *-er* — more at GO] **:** one that goes: **a :** something that moves (as a horse or vehicle) considered in reference to its gait or speed ⟨the mare was a pretty good ~ —F.M.Ford⟩ **b :** a departing traveler or guest — used chiefly in the phrase *comers and goers* ⟨all these comers and ~*s* lodge at the inn⟩ **c :** one that attends regularly or frequents — used chiefly in combination ⟨a strange and rich tonal world . . . alien to contemporary concert*goers* —R.D.Darrell⟩ ⟨less than one fifth of the agricultural population are weekly film*goers* —*Irish Digest*⟩

goes *pres 3d sing of* GO, *pl of* GO

goe·the·an *also* **goe·thi·an** \ˈgər|d-ēən, ˈgə|, |tē- *also* -gā| *sometimes* ˈgē\ *adj, usu cap* [Johann Wolfgang von *Goethe* †1832 Ger. poet + E *-an* or *-ian*] **:** of, relating to, or having the characteristics of Goethe or his works ⟨the *Goethean* insistence on the inseparability of mind and matter —H.W. Pfund⟩

goe·thite *or* **gö·thite** \|d-īt, |,tīt\ *n* -s [G *göthit*, fr. J. W. von *Goethe* + G *-it* -ite] **:** a mineral $HFeO_2$ consisting of an iron hydrogen oxide that occurs massive and in prismatic crystals with a fibrous, reniform, or stalactic structure and that is the commonest constituent of many forms of natural rust or limonite esp. in the gossans of sulfide-bearing ore deposits — compare LEPIDOCROCITE

go·et·ic \(ˈ)gō|ed·ik\ *adj* [Gk *goētikos*, fr. *goēt-*, *goēs* wizard, juggler (fr. *goan* to groan, weep, lament) + *-ikos* -ic — more at KITE] *archaic* **:** of or relating to goety

go·ety \ˈgōəd·ē\ *n* -ES [Gk *goēteia*, fr. *goēt-*, *goēs* + *-eia* -y] *archaic* **:** black magic or witchcraft in which the assistance of evil spirits is invoked **:** NECROMANCY

go·fer \ˈgōfə(r)\ *n* -s [F *gaufre* — more at GOFFER] *dial* **:** WAFFLE

1**goff** \ˈgäf\ *n* -s [MF *goffe* clumsy, awkward] *now dial Eng* **:** a stupid fool **:** DOPE, SIMPLETON

2**goff** \"\ *archaic var of* GOLF

1**gof·fer** *also* **gauf·fer** \ˈgäfə(r), ˈgȯf-, ˈgōf-\ *vt* -ED/-ING/-S [F *gaufrer*, fr. *gaufre* honeycomb, waffle, of Gmc origin; akin to MD *wafel* honeycomb, waffle — more at WAFFLE] **1 :** to crimp, plait, or flute (as linen or lace) esp. by means of a heated iron ⟨took pleasure in perfectly ~*ing* the frill on her father's shirts⟩ **2** *usu gauffer* **:** to indent or emboss (the gilt edges of a book) for decorative effect — compare 3CHASE 1a

2**goffer** *also* **gauffer** \"\ *n* -s **1 :** a tool or device (as a heated iron or a press) used in goffering **2 :** GOFFERER

gof·fered *also* **gauf·fered** *or* **gauf·fred** \-fə(r)d\ *adj* **1 :** dressed or finished with crimps or frills **:** CURLED, CRIMPED ⟨a stiff ~ ruff⟩ **2** *usu gauffered, of a book or its margin* **:** ornamented by gauffering **:** patterned (as by tooling or stenciling) over gilt

gof·fer·er *also* **gauf·fer·er** \-fərə(r)\ *n* -s **:** one that goffers (as linens or books) — usu. *gaufferer* in book-trade use

gof·fer·ing *also* **gauf·fer·ing** \-f(ə)riŋ\ *n* -s **1 :** the practice of one that goffers **2 :** a product of goffering **:** an embossed design **:** CRIMP, FRILL; *broadly* **:** something ornamented or finished with goffering

gof·fle \ˈgäfəl\ *vt* -ED/-ING/-S [by alter.] *dial Eng* **:** 1GOBBLE 1 ⟨as long as the fish ~*s* the bait —H.G.Tapply⟩

1**gog** *n* -s [back-formation fr. *agog*] *obs* **:** STIR, EXCITEMENT, EAGERNESS

2**gog** \ˈgäg\ *n* -s [origin unknown] *now dial Eng* **:** BOG, QUAGMIRE

go gage *n* **:** a limit gage that will just go in or on the part being tested — compare NO-GO GAGE

go–getter \ˈ=ˌ=\ *n, often attrib* **:** an enterprising person who goes after and gets what he wants **:** HUSTLER ⟨a nation of doers and *go-getters* —Telford Taylor⟩ ⟨live wires and *go-getters* are . . . heroes to the bulk of the people —*School & Society*⟩

1**go–getting** \ˈ=ˌ=\ *adj* **:** ENTERPRISING, AGGRESSIVE ⟨the *go-getting* materialism of the American environment —M.J. Adler⟩ ⟨a red-blooded, *go-getting*, two-fisted American he-man —Weston La Barre⟩

2**go–getting** \"\ *n* -s **:** AGGRESSIVENESS, ENTERPRISE ⟨admired as an example of successful *go-getting* —*Harper's*⟩ ⟨the current American psychology emphasizes *go-getting* —*Amer. Rev. of Reviews*⟩

1**gog·gle** \ˈgägəl\ *vb* **goggled; goggled; goggling** \-g(ə)liŋ\ **goggles** [ME *gogelen*] *vi* **1 a** *archaic* **:** to turn the eyes to one side or the other **:** look obliquely **:** SQUINT ⟨wink and ~ like an owl —Samuel Butler †1680⟩ **b :** to stare with wide or protuberant eyes usu. as a result of amazement, fright, or surprise ⟨the lieutenant *goggled* . . . like a fish in a glass jar —Kenneth Roberts⟩ ⟨sold . . . for sums that make one ~ in retrospect —J.T.Soby⟩ **2** *of the eyes* **a** *archaic* **:** to turn to one side or the other **:** take an oblique position ⟨mark on which side . . . the eyes do ~ —Thomas Raynalde⟩ **b :** to become wide or protuberant usu. as a result of amazement, fright, or surprise ⟨the frog's hideous large eyes were *goggling* out of his head —W.M.Thackeray⟩ **3 :** to fish underwater with a spear **:** SPEARFISH ~ *vt* **:** to turn (the eyes) to one side or from side to side **:** ROLL ⟨the stranger *goggled* about his eyes in an attempt to fix them steadily —T.L.Peacock⟩

2**goggle** \"\ *adj, of the eyes* **:** full and rolling **:** PROTUBERANT, STARING ⟨a rather moony, flat brat . . . with those ~ eyes gazing bluely at you —F.M.Ford⟩

3**goggle** \"\ *n* -s **1 :** a rolling or protuberance of the eyes **:** a wide-eyed stare ⟨the child's ~ at the room full of toys⟩ **2 goggles** *pl* **a :** eye coverings resembling spectacles but with shields at the sides and short projecting eye tubes with the glass fixed in the front end used to protect the eyes (as from water, light, dust, or cold) — often used with *pair* ⟨a pair of ~*s*⟩; see EYECUP 1b **b :** colored spectacles for relief from intense light ⟨got their sun ~*s* from the rucksacks —J.R.Ullman⟩ **3 :** a single framed protective device usu. of glass or plastic that is worn in front of the eyes and held in place by a headband

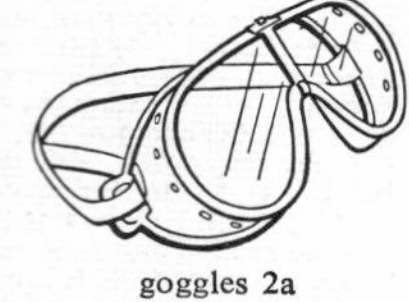

goggles 2a

goggled *adj* **1** *archaic* **:** GOGGLE ⟨one eye . . . was bigger and more ~ than the other —G.W.Dasent⟩ **2 :** wearing goggles ⟨the ~ men . . . turning iron rivets into so many showers of sparks —J.B.Priestley⟩

goggle–eye \ˈ=ˌ=\ *n* [ME *gogeleye*, fr *gogelen* + *eye*] **:** a fish having relatively large and prominent eyes: as **a :** WHITE CRAPPIE **b :** ROCK BASS 1 **c** *or* **goggle–eye jack :** BIG-EYED SCAD **d :** BLACK CRAPPIE **e :** WARMOUTH

goggle–eyed \ˈ=ˌ=\ *adj* [ME *gogeleyed*, fr. *gogelen* + *eyed*] **:** having or marked by bulging or rolling eyes often as a result of amazement or wonder ⟨the visitors seem to loiter with particularly *goggle-eyed* wonder in front of . . . the fabulous objects of lapis and rock crystal —Mollie Panter-Downes⟩

goggle–eyed perch *n* **:** CRAPPIE

goggle fish *vi* **:** GOGGLE 3, SPEARFISH

goggle–nose \ˈ=ˌ=\ *n* [so called fr. the dark spots on its bill] **:** SURF SCOTER

gog·gler \ˈgäg(ə)lə(r)\ *n* -s **1 :** one that goggles; *esp* **:** one that spearfishes ⟨most experienced ~*s* have their own favorite fishing holes —*Nat'l Geographic*⟩ **2 :** BIG-EYED SCAD

gog·gly \-lē\ *adj* -ER/-EST **:** GOGGLING ⟨she seemed in . . . the same excited ~ state —J.B.Priestley⟩ ⟨insects with their ~ eyes —*Dial*⟩

gog·let \ˈgäglət\ *also* **gug·let** \ˈgəg-\ *n* -s [Pg *gorgoleta*, dim. of *gorja* throat, fr. LL *gurga* — more at GORGE] **:** a long-necked water vessel usu. of porous earthenware that is used esp. in India for cooling water by evaporation ⟨~*s* cooling among walls —James Merrill⟩

1**go·go** \ˈgōˈgō\ *n* -s [Tag *gugò*] **:** a vine (*Entada scandens*) found in the Philippines the bark of which is macerated to produce a substitute for soap

2**go·go** \ˈgō(,)gō\ *n, pl* **gogo** *or* **gogos** *usu cap* **1 :** a Bantu people of the Unyamwezi highlands in Tanganyika who are similar to the Masai in manners and customs **2 :** a member of the Gogo people

gogs *pl of* GOG

go·han·na \gōˈhanə\ *var of* GOANNA

goi *var of* GOY

goi·del \ˈgȯidᵊl\ *n* -s *cap* [MIr *Gōidel*] **1 :** a member of the Gaelic branch of Celts **:** GAEL **2 :** a speaker of one of the Goidelic languages — compare BRYTHON

1**goi·del·ic** \(ˈ)gȯiˈdelik\ *adj, usu cap* [*Goidel* + *-ic*] **1 :** of, relating to, or characteristic of the Goidels **2 :** of, relating to, or characteristic of the division of the Celtic languages that includes Irish, Gaelic, and Manx — compare BRYTHONIC

2**goidelic** \"\ *n* -s *cap* **:** the Goidelic branch of the Celtic languages — see INDO-EUROPEAN LANGUAGES table

go in *vi* **1 a :** to make or effect an entrance **:** ENTER ⟨asked him to **go in** and wait⟩ **b :** to move forward **:** ADVANCE ⟨the officer was not long in *going in* on the whale —H.A. Chippendale⟩ **2 a :** to take part in a game or contest **b :** to go to bat in cricket **c :** to call the opening bet in poker **:** STAY **3** *of a heavenly body* **:** to become obscured by a cloud **4 :** to form a union or alliance **:** JOIN — often used with *with* ⟨they outlined the plan and asked the rest of us to *go in with* them⟩ — **go in for 1 :** to give support to or express approval of **:** ADVOCATE ⟨an overwhelming majority of the . . . candidates have *gone in for* disestablishment —*Manchester Examiner*⟩ **2 a :** to make one's particular interest or specialty ⟨so you think you'd like to *go in for* farming —Adrian Bell⟩ ⟨these big uniform people . . . *go in for* policemen's and firemen's uniforms and regalia for lodges —*Amer. Fabrics*⟩ **b :** to have or show an interest in or liking for ⟨lives more in the present than in the past and *goes in for* sports in a big way —Richard Joseph⟩ **3 :** to seek to acquire ⟨ought to *go in for* a better place to live in —Rex Ingamells⟩ ⟨she *goes in for* freedom and they both end in difficulties —John Erskine †1951⟩ **4 :** to engage or participate in **:** take part in ⟨it is pleasant to toy with the idea of New York's *going in for* similar salutes to its heritage —Cornelia O. Skinner⟩ **5 :** to have as a striking characteristic **:** FEATURE ⟨the . . . four-door sedan *goes in for* the longer, lower appearance —*Car Life*⟩ — **go in to** *or* **go in unto :** to have sexual intercourse with ⟨*go in to* your father's concubines whom he has left to keep the house —2 Sam 16:21 (RSV)⟩

1**going** *n* -s [ME, fr. gerund of *gon*, *goon* to go — more at GO] **1 a :** the act or action of going ⟨had to restrict myself to a careful routine of one hour's ~ and ten minutes' halt —D.L.Bush⟩ — often used in combination ⟨play*going*⟩ ⟨sea*going*⟩ **b :** DEPARTURE ⟨stand not upon the order of your ~, but go at once —Shak.⟩ **c :** the manner or style of going ⟨erect his port and firm his ~ —William Wordsworth⟩ **2 a :** a way (as a path or road) that leads from one place to another ⟨the . . . rail, which keeps horses from the inner ~, altered the layout of the course —*Sydney (Austral.) Sun and Guardian*⟩ **b :** a run of stairs **3 goings** *pl* **:** course of life **:** BEHAVIOR **:** ACTIONS ⟨for his eyes are upon the ways of man, and he seeth all his ~*s* —Job 34:21 (AV)⟩ **4 :** the condition of the ground (as for walking or racing) ⟨the surface of the cotton patch was baked hard, and climbing the fence we found the ~ better —Joseph Nelson⟩ **5 :** advance toward or as if toward an objective **:** PROGRESS ⟨wanted to build up enough capital to start farming . . . but the ~ was slow —John Bird⟩ ⟨in the new world he found it rough ~ —W.L.Gresham⟩

2**going** *adj* [ME, fr. pres. part. of *gon*, *goon*] **1 a :** that goes — often used in combination ⟨easy*going*⟩ ⟨out*going*⟩ **b :** MOVING, OPERATING, WORKING ⟨the interior of the shop was in ~ order —Arnold Bennett⟩ **2 a :** EXISTING, LIVING ⟨the finest crime novelist ~ —Anthony Boucher⟩ **b :** available for use or enjoyment ⟨watched his movements with the eyes of a hungry dog which believes that there is provender ~ —John Buchan⟩ **3 :** commonly or widely current or accepted **:** PREVAILING ⟨when you marketed your crops abroad, you sold in free markets for the ~ price —A.E.Stevenson b. 1900⟩ ⟨his fee was about five times larger than the ~ rate of our native talent —E.A. Weeks⟩ **4 :** conducting business, operations, or activities with the likelihood of indefinite continuance **:** actively carried on ⟨were not going to throw away their interest in a ~ concern for a hazardous new venture —Elmer Davis⟩ — **going and coming :** lacking a way out **:** having no escape ⟨they've got you now *going and coming* —Meridel Le Sueur⟩ — **going on :** drawing near to **:** APPROACHING ⟨it's *going on* eight —J.B.Clayton⟩ ⟨my son is six *going on* seven⟩

going–away \ˌ=ˈ=ˌ=\ *adj* [fr. pres. part. of *go away*] **:** designed for wear when leaving on a honeymoon ⟨had just decided how to have my *going-away* dress made —*Lippincott's Mag.*⟩

going barrel *n* **:** a mainspring barrel in a watch or clock that has teeth on its periphery for driving the train and that is mounted on an arbor which is stationary except during winding

going–concern value *n* **:** the value of the assets of an enterprise considered as an operating business and therefore based on its earning power and prospects rather than on the value of the same assets in the event of liquidation

going forth *n* [fr. the phrase *go forth*] **1** *archaic* **:** a way or place of exit ⟨mark well the entering in of the house, with every *going forth* of the sanctuary —Ezek 44:5 (AV)⟩ **2** *archaic* **:** BOUNDARY ⟨and the *going forth* thereof shall be from the south to Kadesh-barnea —Num 34:4 (AV)⟩

going light *n* [fr. the phrase *go light*] **:** any of various diseases of poultry marked by loss of weight; *specif* **:** AVIAN TUBERCULOSIS

going–over \ˌ=ˈ=ˌ=\ *n, pl* **goings–over** [fr. the phrase *go over*] **1 :** a careful or thorough inspection, examination, or investigation ⟨price control has weathered six thorough congressional *goings-over* —Bruce Bliven b. 1889⟩ **2 a :** a severe scolding **:** DRESSING DOWN ⟨got a good *going-over* in the morning . . . on account of my clothes —Mark Twain⟩ **b :** BEATING ⟨someone sure gave her a mean *going-over* —A.C.Tudor⟩

goings–on \ˌ=ˈ=\ *n pl* [fr. pres. part. of *go on*] **:** ACTIONS, EVENTS, HAPPENINGS ⟨there's some of the awfullest *goings-on* at her house —Sinclair Lewis⟩ ⟨gives her main attention to studying the *goings-on* in the . . . world around her —Jean C. Jones⟩ ⟨the present cry for change is a revulsion from the *goings-on* between wars —C.H.Grattan⟩

going to Jerusalem *usu cap J* **:** MUSICAL CHAIRS

going train *n* **:** the gearing in a striking or chiming timepiece that drives the hands

goit \ˈgȯit\ *var of* GOTE

goi·tcho \ˈgȯi(,)chō\ *n* -s [native name in northern Queensland, Australia] **:** a low weedy tropical herb (*Boerhavia diffusa*) used in Australia as forage

goi·ter *also* **goi·tre** \ˈgȯid·ə(r), -ȯitə-\ *n* -s [F *goitre*, fr. MF, back-formation fr. *goitron* throat, fr. (assumed) VL *guttrion-*, *guttrio*, fr. L *guttur* throat, crop of a bird + *-ion-*, *-io* -ion — more at COT] **:** an enlargement of the thyroid gland that is commonly visible as a swelling of the anterior part of the neck, that often results from insufficient intake of iodine and then is usu. accompanied by hypothyroidism, and that in other cases is associated with hyperthyroidism usu. together with toxic symptoms and exophthalmos — called also *struma*

goi·tered *also* **goi·tred** \-ə(r)d\ *adj* **:** affected with goiter

goiter stick *n* **:** the stalk of any of several brown algae (as of the genera *Sargassum* and *Laminaria*) used in So. America as a remedy for goiter

goi·tro·gen \ˈgȯitrəjən, -,jen\ *n* -s [*goitro-* (fr. *goiter*) + *-gen*] **:** a substance (as thiourea or thiouracil) that induces goiter formation

goi·tro·genesis \ˌgȯi·trə+\ *n* [NL, fr. *goitro-* + *genesis*] **:** the action or process of inducing goiter formation

goi·tro·gen·ic \ˌgȯi·trəˈjenik\ *also* **goi·ter·o·gen·ic** \", ˌgȯid·ərō-\ *adj* [*goitre* or *goiter* + *-o-* + *-genic*] **:** producing or tending to produce goiter

goi·tro·ge·nic·i·ty \ˌgȯi·trəjəˈnisəd·ē\ *n* -ES **:** the property of inducing goiter formation **:** the state of being a goitrogen

goi·trous *also* **goi·ter·ous** \ˈgȯitrəs; -ȯid·ər-,-ȯitər-\ *adj* [F *goitreux*, fr. MF *goitre* + *-eux* -ous] **:** relating to, affected with, or resembling goiter

gol \ˈgäl\ *interj* [euphemism for *God*] — a mild oath ("~," said the peddler, "I believe it" —*Atlantic*)

1**go·la** \ˈgōlə\ *n* -s [It, lit., throat, fr. L *gula* — more at GLUTTON] **:** CYMA

2**go·la** *or* **go·lah** \ˈgōlə, -(,)lä\ *n* -s [Hindi *golā*] **:** a warehouse for grain in India **:** STOREROOM, GRANARY

3**go·la** \ˈgōlə\ *n, pl* **gola** *or* **golas** *usu cap* **1 a :** an African people of Liberia and Sierra Leone **b :** a member of such people **2 :** the West-Atlantic language of the Gola people

gol·ach \ˈgäläk, -ək\ *n* -s [ScGael *gaillseach*] *Scot* **:** any of various small arthropods (as a beetle or centipede)

go·lah \gōˈlä, ˈgōlə\ *n* -s *sometimes cap* [Heb *gōlāh* exile] **:** DIASPORA, GALUTH

gol·con·da \gälˈkändə\ *n* -s *usu cap* [fr. *Golconda*, city in Hyderabad, India, formerly the center of the diamond trade] **:** a source of great wealth ⟨this means a *Golconda* for makers and sellers of accessories —*Newsweek*⟩; *esp* **:** a rich mine

1**gold** \ˈgōld\ *n* -s [ME, fr. OE; akin to OFris, OS, & OHG *gold*, ON *gull*, Goth *gulth* gold, OE *geolu* yellow — more at YELLOW] **1 a :** a very malleable, ductile, yellow trivalent and univalent metallic element that occurs chiefly in the free state but also in a few minerals as sylvanite or nagyagite, is indifferent to most chemicals but attacked by chlorine and aqua regia, and is hardened or changed in color for commercial use (as in coins, jewelry, dentures) by alloying with copper, silver, zinc, cadmium, and other metals — symbol *Au*; see ELEMENT table **b :** the heraldic metal or **2 a** (1) **:** gold coins (2) **:** a gold piece **b :** MONEY, RICHES **c :** a monetary standard linked directly to the value of the metal gold ⟨England went off ~ —A.M.Young⟩ **3 a :** thread or fabric made wholly or partly of gold **b :** decoration in gold leaf on gold color **:** GILDING **4 a :** a variable color averaging deep yellow **b :** a light olive brown **5 :** something resembling gold; *esp* **:** something treasured as the essence or finest exemplification of its kind ⟨taking bits of this and that and transmuting them into culinary ~ —Harold Sinclair⟩ ⟨a heart of ~⟩ **6 a :** the gilded or golden bull's-eye of an archery target **b :** a hit on such a bull's-eye ⟨you've made a ~⟩

2**gold** \"\ *adj* -ER/-EST [ME, fr. *gold*, n.] **1 a :** made or consisting of gold ⟨the gleaming ~ band ring —Carson McCullers⟩ **b :** of the heraldic metal or **2 :** having the color of gold **:** GOLDEN ⟨russet and ~ chrysanthemums —Louis Bromfield⟩ **3 a :** of, relating to, or payable in gold coin — see GOLD BOND **b :** of or relating to a monetary gold standard **4 :** of outstanding value, quality, or excellence ⟨the ~ tones of an alpine horn —Willa Cather⟩ **5** [so called fr. the practice during the construction of the Panama canal of paying skilled white labor in gold and unskilled colored labor in silver] **:** of or for the white population in the Panama Canal Zone

3**gold** \"\ *n* -s [ME *golde*, fr. OE, fr. 1*gold*] **1** *dial Brit* **:** POT MARIGOLD **2 :** CORN MARIGOLD

4**gold** *usu cap, var of* GOLDI

gold–and–silver flower \ˌ=ˈ=ˌ=-\ *n* **:** the flower of the European honeysuckle

gold–and–silver plant *n* **:** HONESTY

gold apple *n* **:** TOMATO

1**gol·darn** \(ˈ)gälˈdärn, -dän\ *or* **gol·durn** \-dərn, -dən, -dəin\ *vb* [euphemism for *goddamn*] *vt* **:** DAMN *vt* 5 ~ *vi* **:** DAMN *vi*

2**goldarn** \ˈ=ˌ=\ *or* **goldurn** \"\ *adj* [euphemism for *goddamned*] **:** 1DAMNED 2a, 2b

3**goldarn** \"\ *or* **goldurn** \"\ *adv* [euphemism for *goddamned*] **:** 2DAMNED

4**goldarn** \ˈ=ˌ=\ *or* **goldurn** \"\ *n* [euphemism for *goddamn*] **:** 2DAMN ⟨I don't give a ~ what your terms are —Erskine Caldwell⟩

1**goldarned** *or* **goldurned** \ˈ=ˌ=, *before* "-est" (ˈ)=ˌ=\ *adj* **:** 1DAMNED 2a, 2b

2**goldarned** *or* **goldurned** \"\ *adv* **:** 2DAMNED

goldback *var of* GOLDENBACK

gold–ball \ˈ=ˌ=\ *n* **:** GOLDCUP

goldband lily \ˈ=ˌ=-\ *n* **:** a highly scented lily (*Lilium auratum*) having wide trumpet-shaped white flowers with strongly recurved segments each of which has a median yellow band — called also *golden-banded lily*

gold bar *n* **:** a bar of gold; *specif* **:** ASSAY BAR

gold basis *n* **:** a financial basis with prices adjusted to the gold standard

gold bass *n* **1 :** SMALLMOUTH BLACK BASS **2 :** YELLOW BASS

goldbeater \ˈ=ˌ=\ *n* [ME *goldbeter*, fr. *gold* + *beter* beater] **:** one that beats gold into gold leaf

goldbeater's skin *n* **:** the prepared outside membrane of the large intestine of cattle used for separating the leaves of metal in goldbeating and sometimes as the moisture-sensitive element in hygrometers

goldbeating \ˈ=ˌ=\ *n* **:** an act, art, or process of hammering gold into thin leaves

gold·berg·ian \(')gōl(d)¦bərgēən\ *adj, usu cap* [Rube *Goldberg* b1883 Am. cartoonist + E *-ian*] **:** grotesquely complex **:** contrived with inept and excessive intricacy ⟨a strange *Goldbergian* contraption resembling a birdcage —*Newsweek*⟩
gold beryl *n* **:** CHRYSOBERYL
gold bloc *n* **:** a group of countries basing their currencies on a gold standard
gold blocking *n* **:** gold stamping (as of book covers) with an engraved block
gold–bloom \'=,=\ *n, dial Eng* **:** a marsh marigold (*Caltha palustris*)
gold bond *n* **:** a bond payable in gold coin of a specified weight and fineness — compare CURRENCY BOND
gold book *n* **:** a paper book usu. 3¼ inches by 3½ inches containing 25 sheets of gold leaf between the chalked leaves
gold braid *n* **1 :** any of various gold-colored braids used esp. on uniforms **2 :** ²BRAID 3
¹gold·brick \'gōl(d),brik\ *n* **1 a :** a worthless brick that appears to be made of gold **b :** something that appears to be valuable but is actually worthless **2** *also* **gold·brick·er** \-kə(r)\ -s [*goldbrick* fr. ²*goldbrick; goldbricker* fr. ²*goldbrick* + *-er*] **a :** a soldier free from regular military routine because of assignment to special duty **b :** a soldier who evades or halfheartedly performs assigned work ⟨would have a ~ court-martialed —R.O.Bowen⟩ **3** *also* **goldbricker** -s [*goldbrick* fr. ²*goldbrick; goldbricker* fr. ²*goldbrick* + *-er*] **:** one who evades work for which he is responsible **:** LOAFER, SHIRKER ⟨~s are turning up in offices and factories —*Tomorrow*⟩
²goldbrick \"\ *vb* [¹*goldbrick;* fr. a form of swindle in which worthless goldbricks are passed off as being actually made of gold] *vt* **:** SWINDLE ~ *vi* **:** to evade or halfheartedly perform assigned work **:** shirk duty or responsibility **:** goof off ⟨a man who ~s on work details and lets the others carry the load —Gregor Felsen⟩
gold bronze *n* **1 :** a powdered copper alloy used in printing to simulate gold and in the manufacture of gold paint **2 :** a grayish brown to yellowish brown that is very slightly deeper than soot brown and stronger and slightly darker than mummy brown (sense 2b) — called also *Vienna brown*
gold brown *n* **:** a strong brown that is yellower and paler than rust or average russet and yellower and paler than average copper brown — compare GOLDEN BROWN
goldbug \'=,=\ *n* **:** an advocate or supporter of the gold standard
gold bullion standard *n* **:** a gold standard under which the coinage and circulation of gold is usu. prohibited but the shipment of gold in international transactions is permitted and a gold bullion reserve is maintained as a support for the currency
gold cake *n* **:** a butter cake in which the yolks but not the whites of eggs are used
gold carp *n* **:** GOLDFISH
gold certificate *n* **:** a paper certificate issued by a public treasury against deposited gold; *specif* **:** a certificate first issued in 1934 by the U.S. Treasury to be held only by Federal Reserve banks and exchanged under treasury license for gold at the rate prevailing at the time of exchange — compare GOLD BULLION STANDARD, GOLD STANDARD, MANAGED CURRENCY; SILVER CERTIFICATE
gold–chain \'=,=\ *n* **1 :** a stonecrop (*Sedum acre*) **2 :** LABURNUM 2
gold chloride *n* **1 :** a chloride of gold; *esp* **:** the trichloride $AuCl_3$ or Au_2Cl_6 obtained as a dark red crystalline mass by the action of chlorine on heated gold and used chiefly in photography and in gilding and coloring ceramic ware and glass **2 :** CHLOROAURIC ACID — used chiefly commercially
gold clause *n* **:** a provision in a contract requiring payment to be made in gold coin or its equivalent
gold cloth *n* **1 :** CLOTH OF GOLD **2 :** LAMÉ
¹gold coast *adj, usu cap G&C* [fr. the *Gold Coast* (now *Ghana*), region in western Africa] **1 :** of, relating to, or characteristic of the Gold Coast, now Ghana, western Africa **2 :** of, relating to, or characteristic of the people of the Gold Coast
²gold coast *n, often cap G&C* [fr. *Gold Coast,* nickname for an exclusive residential section in Chicago] **:** an exclusive residential district
goldcrest \'=,=\ *n* **:** GOLDEN-CRESTED KINGLET; *specif* **:** a tiny European kinglet (*Regulus regulus*) having a bright yellow crown patch bordered with black
goldcup \'=,=\ *n* **1 :** BUTTERCUP 1 **2 :** a marsh marigold (*Caltha palustris*)
gold cure *n* **:** CHRYSOTHERAPY
gold cushion *n* **:** a wooden frame with a padded top surface on which gold leaf is laid out for cutting
gold democrat *n, usu cap G&D* **:** a member of the Democratic party favoring the gold standard; *esp* **:** one of a group of dissident Democrats supporting an independent ticket in the presidential election of 1896 — compare NATIONAL SILVER
gold–dig \'=,=\ *vb* [back-formation fr. *gold digger*] *vt* **:** to extract money or gifts from by coaxing or flattery ⟨why did you coax him, tease him, *gold-dig* him —Sinclair Lewis⟩ ~ *vi* **:** to extract money or gifts from men by coaxing or flattery ⟨she went with him wherever he wanted to go, and she never tried to maneuver him or *gold-dig* —Ann Chidester⟩
gold digger *n* **1 :** one that digs gold esp. in alluvial deposits **2 :** an avaricious woman; *esp* **:** one who uses her feminine charms to extract money or gifts from men ⟨found out the truth . . . called her a *gold digger* and walked out —Erle Stanley Gardner⟩
gold digging *n* **1 :** a gold placer mine **2 gold diggings** *pl* **:** a district containing gold placer mines
gold dust *n* **1 :** particles and sometimes flakes and pellets of gold obtained in placer mining **2 a :** BASKET-OF-GOLD **b :** a common stonecrop (*Sedum acre*)
gold–dust tree *or* **gold dust** *n* **:** an aucuba (*Aucuba japonica variegata*) with yellow-spotted leaves
gold dust twins *n pl* [so called fr. the twin Negro boys depicted on the box of *Gold Dust,* a trademarked soap powder] **:** a pair of inseparable and indefatigable workers
¹gold·en \'gōldən\ *adj, usu* -ER/-EST [ME, fr. ¹*gold* + *-en*] **1 a :** consisting of or relating to gold **:** made of gold ⟨a purse with a ~ frame —F.M.Stenton⟩ **b :** containing, bearing, or abounding in gold **:** AURIFEROUS **2 a :** having the color of gold ⟨~ grain⟩ **b :** BLOND — used of the color of hair **3 :** having the luster or sheen of gold **:** SHINING, AUREATE ⟨there is a ~ brightness in the air —Amy Lowell⟩ **4 :** characterized by a high degree of excellence **:** approaching a standard of perfection **:** SUPERB ⟨there was a quality of ~ goodness about him —Willa Cather⟩ **5 :** characterized by great prosperity, happiness, and achievement **:** FLOURISHING, SPACIOUS ⟨the world's great age begins anew, the ~ years return —P.B. Shelley⟩ ⟨the ~ days of river steamboats —*Amer. Guide Series: Ark.*⟩ **6 a :** radiant, youthful, or vigorous in person or manner ⟨~ lads and girls all must, as chimney sweepers, come to dust —Shak.⟩ **b :** colorful and successful esp. in athletics **:** possessed of a variety of talents that promise worldly success **:** popular and charming **:** WHITE-HEADED — often used with *boy* ⟨the ~ boys of the airlines⟩ ⟨a ~ boy who comes to dust —*New Republic*⟩ **7 :** constituting or yielding wealth **:** PROFITABLE ⟨Pakistan's ~ fiber, jute —William Costello⟩ **8 :** highly favorable **:** opportunely advantageous ⟨the first affirmative speaker in a debate has a ~ opportunity to influence the audience —A.T.Weaver⟩ ⟨if management fails to step in to fill their needs it passes up a ~ opportunity —Bruce Payne⟩ ⟨had the ~ opportunity to utilize a famous squelch —Bennett Cerf⟩ ⟨~ opportunities for anyone with some originality —W.H.Dowdeswell⟩ **9 :** of, relating to, or marking a 50th anniversary **10 :** rich and mellow in timbre or resonance ⟨the song of the wood thrush is more ~ and leisurely —John Burroughs⟩ ⟨had a smooth ~ tenor —*Current Biog.*⟩ — **gold·en·ly** *adv*
²golden \"\ *vb* -ED/-ING/-S *vt* **:** to make golden in color ⟨a full moon . . . ~*ed* the road —Edward Kimbrough⟩ ~ *vi* **:** to take on a golden color ⟨the pumpkin ripened and ~*ed* —J.M.Neale⟩
golden age *n, often cap G&A* **:** a period of great happiness, prosperity, and achievement: **a :** an idyllic state of nature held to have existed in the past and regarded as man's original condition ⟨believes that mankind in their development down from the *golden age* are destined to degenerate —K.R.Popper⟩ **b :** a time of ideal perfection regarded as attainable in the future ⟨a *golden age* of the human community is a distinct promise —*Saturday Rev.*⟩ **c :** the most flourishing period in the history of something **:** the time of highest achievement or greatest development ⟨the *golden age* of the novel⟩ ⟨the *golden age* of the political cartoonist⟩ ⟨the *golden age* of Spain⟩ — compare SILVER AGE
golden agouti *n* **:** a common tropical American rodent (*Dasyprocta aguti*) — compare AGOUTI
golden alexander *n, often cap A* **:** any of several herbaceous plants of the family Umbelliferae esp. of the genera *Zizia* and *Taenidia; usu* **:** a showy yellow-flowered perennial herb (*Z. aurea*) of moist meadows and swamps — usu. used in pl.
golden anniversary *n* **:** a 50th anniversary
golden apple *n* **1 :** BEL **2 :** TOMATO **3 :** HOG PLUM 1
golden aster *n* **:** an American plant of the genus *Chrysopsis* (esp. *C. mariana*)
goldenback \'=,=\ *or* **goldback** \'=,=\ *n* **:** a gold fern (*Pityrogramma triangularis*) of the Pacific coastal region of No. America that has erect fronds with dark brown shining stipes and broad coriaceous blades with the segments broadly rounded
golden balls *n pl* **:** three gilt balls used as a pawnbroker's sign
golden bamboo *n* **:** a grass (*Bambusa vulgaris aureo-variegata*) with yellow-striped leaves
golden–banded lily \'==,==-\ *n* **:** GOLDBAND LILY
golden barb *n* **:** a small golden-yellow Indian fish (*Barbus gelius*) sometimes kept in the tropical aquarium
golden bat *n* **:** SUCKER-FOOTED BAT
golden bell *n* **:** a shrub of the genus *Forsythia* — often used in pl.
golden bough *n* **:** MISTLETOE 1a
golden brown *n* **:** a variable color averaging a strong brown that is yellower and slightly darker than gold brown, yellower and paler than average russet, and yellower and less strong than rust
golden buck *n* **:** welsh rabbit topped with poached egg
goldenbush \'==,=\ *n* **1 :** a heathlike New Zealand shrub (*Cassinia fulvida*) of the family Compositae with evergreen yellowish foliage and white flowers **2 :** RABBIT BRUSH **3 :** a plant of the genus *Haplopappus*
golden calf *n* [so called fr. the golden calf made by Aaron for the Israelites to worship (Exod 32)] **:** an object of materialistic or unworthy worship; *esp* **:** MONEY ⟨this . . . material age when everything goes down before the *golden calf* —Eliot Gregory⟩
golden calla *n* **:** any of several callas of the genus *Zantedeschia* having yellow spathes
golden cat *n* **:** either of two small reddish or yellowish wildcats: **a :** a rather pale solid-colored cat (*Felis aurata*) of northwestern Africa **b :** a variably marked cat (*F. temminckii*) of southeastern Asia
golden chain *also* **golden chain tree** *n* **:** LABURNUM 2
golden chestnut *n* **:** a moderate brown that is redder, lighter, and stronger than chestnut brown and yellower, lighter, and stronger than bay — called also *pecan brown*
golden chinquapin *n* **:** a Pacific coast tree (*Castanopsis chrysophylla*) having evergreen tapering leathery leaves with golden yellow scales on the lower surface
golden clematis *n* **:** a clematis (*Clematis tangutica*) with serrate leaves and large yellow flowers
golden club *n* **:** an American aquatic plant (*Orontium aquaticum*) of the family Araceae with a spadix of minute yellow flowers
golden corydalis *n* **:** a diffusely branched herbaceous annual or biennial (*Corydalis aurea*) with golden-yellow flowers
golden cottonwood *n* **:** GOLDENBUSH 1
golden cress *n* **:** GOLDEN PEPPERGRASS
golden crest *n* **:** a woolly bog herb (*Lophiola americana*) of eastern No. America with loose panicles of yellowish flowers
golden–crested kinglet *also* **golden–crested wren** \'==,==-\ *n* **:** any of several kinglets having the crown patch golden yellow — see GOLDCREST
golden crown *n* **1 :** GOLDFLOWER 1b **2 :** a low perennial spreading grass (*Paspalum dilatatum*) of So. America
golden crownbeard *n* **:** a coarse annual yellow-flowered herb (*Ximenesia encelioides*) of the family Compositae
golden–crowned \¦==¦=\ *adj* **:** having the top of the head yellow — used of birds
golden–crowned accentor *n* **:** OVENBIRD 2
golden–crowned kinglet *n* **:** the American golden-crested kinglet (*Regulus satrapa*)
golden–crowned sparrow *n* **:** a rather large sparrow (*Zonotrichia coronata*) of the Pacific coast of No. America having a plain yellow crown bordered on each side by black
golden cudweed *n* **:** either of two composite plants (*Helichrysum orientale* and *Pterocaulon virgatum*) having golden-yellow flower heads that are sometimes used as everlastings
golden cup *n* **1 :** GOLDCUP 1 **2 :** a poppy (*Hunnemannia fumariaefolia*) having yellow flowers with separate sepals — called also *Mexican tulip poppy*
golden–cup oak *n* **:** CANYON LIVE OAK
golden currant *n* **1 :** a fragrant yellow-flowered ornamental shrub (*Ribes aureum*) of the western U.S. **2 :** BUFFALO CURRANT 1
golden cypress *n* **:** any of several ornamental trees or shrubs of the genus *Cupressus* having yellowish foliage
golden dewdrop *n* **:** a tropical American shrub (*Duranta repens*) sometimes planted for hedges in the southern and central U.S.
golden dock *n* **:** an American dock (*Rumex maritimus*)
golden eagle *n* **:** a large and powerful eagle (*Aquila chrysaëtos*) of the northern hemisphere that has brownish yellow tips on head and neck feathers
golden eardrops *n pl but usu sing in constr* **:** a stout California herb (*Dicentra chrysantha*) with glaucous bipinnate leaves and yellow irregular flowers
goldened *past of* GOLDEN
golden eggs *n pl but usu sing in constr* **:** SUNCUP
golden elder *n* **:** a common European elder (*Sambucus nigra aurea*) with yellow foliage and white flowers
goldener *comparative of* GOLDEN
goldenest *superlative of* GOLDEN
goldeneye \'==,=\ *n* **1 a :** a large-headed swift-flying diving duck (*Bucephala clangula* or *Glaucionetta clangula*) of Eurasia and No. America having the male strikingly marked in black and white and the female mottled gray with brown head, white collar, and white wing patches **b :** BARROW'S GOLDENEYE **2** *also* **golden–eyed fly** \'==,=-\ **:** a lacewing of the family Chrysopidae **3 :** a golden aster (*Chrysopsis villosa*) of central No. America with hairy foliage and golden-yellow flower heads
golden–eyed \¦==¦=\ *adj* **:** having the eye or iris yellow or golden
golden–eyed duck *n* **:** GOLDENEYE 1
golden–eyed grass *n* **:** a yellow-flowered California herb (*Sisyrinchium californicum*) with leaves that resemble blades of grass
golden feather *n* **:** an ornamental feverfew with yellow foliage
golden–feather yellow *n* **:** PYRETHRUM YELLOW
golden fern *n* **:** a stout tropical American fern (*Acrostichum aureum*) with large fronds that are golden yellow beneath
golden fig *n* **:** STRANGLER FIG b
golden fir *n* **:** CALIFORNIA RED FIR
golden fizz *n* **:** a fizz made from lemon juice, gin, egg yolk, and sugar
golden flax *n* **:** a European flax (*Linum flavum*) commonly cultivated for its bright yellow flowers
goldenfleece \'==,=\ *n* **:** a rayless goldenrod (*Chrysothamnus arborescens*)
golden flower *n* **1 :** any of several plants of the genus *Chrysanthemum; esp* **:** CORN MARIGOLD **2 :** a moss of the genus *Polytrichum* **3 :** GOLDENROD
golden glow *n* **1 :** a tall branching herb (*Rudbeckia laciniata hortensia*) with showy yellow much-doubled flower heads **2 :** a moderate orange yellow to strong yellow
golden gram *n* **:** MUNG BEAN
golden green *n* **:** a grayish to dark grayish yellow that is very slightly greener than light stone — called also *cloudy amber*
golden grouper *n* **:** either of two Pacific groupers that have both a dark and a yellow color phase: **a :** a grouper (*Mycteroperca pardalis*) of the Gulf of California that is greenish gray to brown with brown spots or golden yellow more or less splashed with black **b :** a closely related fish of the Galápagos islands that is greenish brown with purple to brown spots or a solid brilliant orange-yellow and that is placed in a separate species (*M. olfax*) or considered a geographical variety of the more northerly fish
goldenhair \'==,=\ *n* **:** a southern African shrub (*Chrysocoma coma-aurea*) of the family Compositae with golden-yellow flowers
golden hamster *n* **:** a small tawny hamster (*Mesocricetus auratus*) native to Asia Minor but kept as a pet in many parts of the world
golden hardhack *n* **:** SHRUBBY CINQUEFOIL
golden hawkweed *n* **1 :** KING DEVIL **2 :** ORANGE HAWKWEED 1
golden hedge hyssop *n* **:** GOLDENPERT
golden hop *n* **:** a pistillate hop (*Humulus lupulus*) with yellow foliage
golden horde *n, usu cap G&H* [trans. of Tatar *altūn ordū;* fr. the golden tent of Batu Khan †1255 Mongol ruler] **:** a body of Mongol Tatars overrunning eastern Europe in the 13th century, establishing the Kipchak khanate, and keeping Russia in subjection until 1486
golden horse *n* **:** PALOMINO
golden horseshoe bat *n* **:** a small Australian leaf-nosed bat (*Rhinonycteris aurantia*) with fur of a delicate tawny hue
goldening *pres part of* GOLDEN
golden ironweed *or* **golden honey plant** *n* **:** a perennial composite herb (*Actinomeris alternifolia*) of the eastern U.S. with showy yellow flowers
golden jerusalem *n, usu cap J* **:** CONEFLOWER a
golden jubilee *n* **:** GOLDEN ANNIVERSARY
golden larch *n* **:** a Chinese coniferous tree (*Pseudolarix amabilis*) with golden-yellow deciduous leaves
golden leaf *n* **:** a golden-leaved tree of the genus *Chrysophyllum*
golden lip *var of* GOLD LIP
goldenlocks \'==,=\ *n pl but sing or pl in constr* **:** WALL FERN
golden loosestrife *n* **:** LOOSESTRIFE 1
golden lungwort *n* **:** WALL HAWKWEED
golden maidenhair *n* **1 :** WALL FERN **2 :** HAIRCAP MOSS
golden marguerite *n* **:** YELLOW CHAMOMILE
golden meadow parsnip *n* **:** an American herb (*Zizia aurea*) with serrate leaflets
golden mean *n* **:** the way of wisdom and reasonableness between extremes **:** the happy medium between excess and defect
golden millet *n* **:** FOXTAIL MILLET
golden mole *n* **:** any of several fossorial insectivores of southern Africa constituting *Chrysochloris* and related genera and having iridescent guard hairs mingled with the underfur
golden monkey *n* **:** a monkey (*Rhinopithecus roxellanae*) of the high uplands of Tibet and China having a brilliant blue face and a dark coat overlaid with long silvery hairs that is greatly prized by the Chinese and commands extremely high prices
golden moss *n* **:** a stonecrop (*Sedum acre*)
golden mouse *n* **:** a tawny white-footed mouse (*Peromyscus nuttalli*) of the southeastern U.S.
goldenmouthed \¦==¦=\ *adj* **:** distinguished for lofty or persuasive utterance **:** ELOQUENT
golden nematode *n* **:** a small yellowish Old World nematode worm (*Heterodera rostochiensis*) established locally as a serious pest of potatoes in eastern No. America
gold·en·ness \'gōldən(n)əs\ *n* -ES **:** the quality or state of being golden
golden net *n* **:** a virus disease of peaches, plums, and apricots that causes marginal yellowing of the leaf veins
golden number *n* **:** the number of a particular calendar year in the Metonic cycle used to fix the date of Easter — compare DOMINICAL LETTER, EPACT; see EASTER table
golden oak *n* **1 :** DOWNY FALSE FOXGLOVE **2 :** oak furniture finished in a very light color
golden ocher *n* **:** OCHER BROWN
golden olive *n* **:** a variable color averaging a light olive that is greener and deeper than citrine, redder and deeper than grape green, and redder and stronger than old moss green
golden orange *n* **:** a strong orange that is deeper and slightly yellower than pumpkin and redder and duller than cadmium orange
golden oriole *n* **:** an Old World oriole (*Oriolus oriolus*) having the male brilliant yellow with black tail and wings and the female largely greenish yellow, breeding in central and southern Europe and western Asia, and wintering chiefly in Africa and southern Asia
golden osier *n* **1 :** GOLDEN WILLOW **2 :** SWEET GALE
golden palm civet *n* **:** a Ceylonese paradoxure (*Paradoxurus aureus*)
golden pea *n* **:** FALSE LUPINE
golden peppergrass *n* **:** an annual European herb (*Lepidium sativum*) naturalized in No. America and cultivated for its pungent foliage
golden perch *n* **:** CALLOP
gold·en·pert \'==,pərt\ *n* -s **:** a small yellow-flowered No. American herb (*Gratiola aurea*)
golden pheasant *n* **:** a brilliantly colored pheasant (*Chrysolophus pictus*) of China and Tibet often raised in captivity as an ornamental bird
golden pileolated warbler *n* **:** a Pacific coast warbler (*Wilsonia pusilla chryseola*) similar to but brighter in color than the pileolated warbler
golden pine *n* **:** GOLDEN LARCH
golden plover *n* **:** any of several gregarious migratory plovers breeding chiefly in the Arctic and wintering far south of the equator that as adults in summer plumage are speckled golden-yellow and white above with the lower parts being black and that are usu. placed in a distinct genus (*Pluvialis*) of the family Charadriidae
golden polypody *n* **1 :** WALL FERN **2 :** SERPENT FERN
golden poppy *n* **1 a :** ICELAND POPPY **b :** CALIFORNIA POPPY **2 :** a vivid reddish orange that is yellower and much lighter than international orange and stronger and slightly redder and lighter than chrome orange
golden ragwort *n* **:** a ragwort (*Senecio aureus*) of the U.S. having basal cordate leaves, lyrate or clasping stem leaves, and an open cluster of yellow-rayed flowers
golden rain *n* **:** LABURNUM 2
goldenrain tree \'==,=\ *also* **goldenrain** \'==,=\ *n* **:** a round-headed tree (*Koelreuteria paniculata*) having very long showy clusters of yellow flowers — called also *varnish tree*
golden rectangle *n* **:** a rectangle whose width is to its length as the length is to the sum of the width and length — compare GOLDEN SECTION
golden red *n* **:** a yellowish red
golden retriever *n* **:** a medium-sized golden-coated retriever developed chiefly in England by interbreeding Russian shepherd dogs with bloodhounds
golden robin *n* **:** BALTIMORE ORIOLE
goldenrod \'==,=\ *n* **1 :** any of numerous chiefly No. American composite plants mostly of the genus *Solidago* that are summer-blooming and fall-blooming perennials or biennials with stems resembling wands, variously shaped leaves, and heads of small yellow or sometimes white flowers often clustered in panicles — compare RAYLESS GOLDENROD **2 a :** a vivid yellow **b :** a strong yellow
goldenrod tree *n* **:** a Canary island shrub (*Bosea yervamora*) of the family Amaranthaceae with greenish yellow flowers
golden rule *n* **1 :** a rule stating that one should do to others as he would have others do to him — with reference to Mt 7:12 and Lk 6:31 **2 :** a first consideration or guiding principle ⟨the *golden rule* for eating and drinking is moderation —K.A. Henderson⟩
golden rust *n* **:** a rust fungus (*Puccinia glumarum*) that bears its urediospores in bright yellow sori
goldens *pres 3d sing of* GOLDEN
golden samphire *n* **:** a European maritime plant (*Inula crithmoides*) with bright yellow flowers
golden saxifrage *also* **golden spleen** *n* **:** any of several low aquatic herbs of the genus *Chrysosplenium; specif* **:** a plant (*C. americanum*) with yellowish flowers
goldenseal \'==,=\ *n* **1 :** a perennial American herb (*Hydrastis canadensis*) with a thick knotted yellow rootstock and large rounded leaves **2 :** the dried rhizome and roots of goldenseal used as an alterative and tonic

golden section *n* **:** the division of a line or the proportion of a geometrical figure in which the smaller dimension is to the greater as the greater is to the whole ⟨the *golden section* has for centuries been regarded as . . . a key to the mysteries of art —Herbert Read⟩ — called also *extreme and mean ratio*
golden shad *n* **1 :** ALEWIFE 1a **2 :** a skipjack (*Pomolobus chrysochloris*)
golden shiner *n* **:** a common cyprinid fish (*Notemigonus crysoleucas*) of eastern No. America having silvery sides with bright golden reflections
golden shower *n* **:** any of several leguminous shrubs or trees having drooping racemes of bright yellow flowers; *esp* **:** DRUMSTICK TREE
golden slipper *n* **:** any of several lady's slippers having yellow flowers (esp. *Cypripedium calceolus pubescens* and *C. calceolus parviflorum*)
golden spider lily *n* **:** a Chinese bulbous plant (*Lycoris aurea*) cultivated for its yellow flowers
golden spoon *n* **:** a usu. shrubby tropical American tree (*Byrsonima crassifolia*) that is sometimes cultivated for its sweet edible yellow fruits; *broadly* **:** [1]NANCE
golden star *n* **1 :** GOLDEN ASTER **2 :** GOLD JOINT **3 :** a plant of the genus *Bloomeria* (esp. *B. crocea*) **4 :** a tunicate of the genus *Botryllus* having zooids grouped like stars in the greenish yellow tunic
golden stool *n* **:** a wooden stool partly covered with gold that serves as the symbol of authority of Ashanti kings
golden syrup *n, chiefly Brit* **:** TREACLE 2b
golden text *n* **:** a brief passage of Scripture chosen as embodying the thought of a Sunday-school lesson
golden thistle *n* **:** any of several erect somewhat spiny composite herbs of the Mediterranean region that constitute the genus *Scolymus* and have sessile yellow flower heads of ligulate flowers — see SPANISH OYSTER PLANT
golden thread *n* **1 :** LOVE-IN-A-MIST 1 **2 :** GOLDTHREAD 1
golden–tongued \ˈ≈ˌ≈\ *adj* **:** gifted with superior powers of utterance or persuasion **:** ELOQUENT
goldentop \ˈ≈ˌ≈\ *n* **:** a European grass (*Lamarckia aurea*) with showy one-sided yellow panicles
golden trout *n* **1 :** a variable and brilliantly colored trout (*Salmo agua-bonito*) native to the high Sierras but introduced in other upland waters of western No. America — see ROOSEVELT TROUT, STEWART WHITE TROUT **2 :** SUNAPEE TROUT
golden tuft *n* **1 :** BASKET-OF-GOLD **2 :** GOLDEN CUDWEED
goldentwig \ˈ≈ˌ≈\ *also* **goldentwig dogwood** *n* **:** a red osier dogwood (*Cornus stolonifera flaviramea*) with yellow branchlets
golden warbler *n* **:** YELLOW WARBLER 1a
golden wasp *n* **:** CUCKOO WASP
golden wattle *n, Austral* **:** any of several yellow-flowered acacias; *esp* **:** a medium-sized tree (*Acacia pycnantha*) with very fragrant intensely yellow flowers in globular heads that is widely distributed in New South Wales and So. Australia, has a bark used in tanning, and is cultivated as an ornamental in mild climates
golden wave *n* **:** a Texas annual herb (*Coreopsis drummondii*) with a profusion of yellowish purple flowers
golden wedding *n* **:** a golden anniversary of a wedding
golden willow *n* **:** a European willow (*Salix vitellina*) whose yellow twigs are used in basketmaking
golden willow herb *n* **:** LOOSESTRIFE 1
goldenwing \ˈ≈ˌ≈\ *also* **golden–winged woodpecker** \ˈ≈ˌ≈-\ *n* **:** a flicker (*Colaptes auratus*)
golden–winged warbler *also* **goldenwing** *n* **:** a small No. American warbler (*Vermivora chrysoptera*) with a patch of bright yellow on the wing
golden wolf *n* **:** CHANCO
golden wonder millet *n* **:** GERMAN MILLET
golden yellow *n* **1 :** a variable color averaging a vivid yellow that is redder and duller than average buttercup or goldenrod (sense 2a) **2 :** a moderate to strong orange yellow that is very slightly yellower and stronger than Indian yellow and very slightly yellower and paler than Dutch orange
[1]**golder** *comparative of* GOLD
[2]**gol·der** \ˈgäl(d)ə(r)\ *var of* GOLLAR
goldest *superlative of* GOLD
gold–exchange standard *n* **:** a monetary standard under which gold does not circulate domestically and international debts are settled primarily in currency of nations that maintain a gold and esp. a gold bullion standard
gold export point *n* **:** the point of variation in the price of foreign exchange at which the export of gold becomes preferable to the use of exchange in settlement of international obligations — called also *gold point;* compare GOLD IMPORT POINT
goldeye \ˈ≈ˌ≈\ *n* **1 :** YELLOW STAR GRASS **2 :** a small isospondylous edible fish (*Amphiodon alosoides*) widely distributed in lakes and streams of northern and western No. America
gold fern *n* **:** any of several ferns (as members of the genera *Notholaena* and *Pityrogramma*) having the lower surfaces of the fronds covered with a golden yellow spore mass or group of sori
gold fever *n* **:** the contagious excitement of a gold rush
goldfield \ˈ≈ˌ≈\ *n* **:** a gold-mining district
gold fields *n pl but sing or pl in constr* **:** any of several yellow-flowered composite herbs constituting the genus *Baeria* and occurring along the western coast of No. America
gold–filled \ˈ≈ˌ≈\ *adj* **:** covered with a layer of gold so as to constitute filled gold — used esp. of jewelry
goldfinch \ˈ≈ˌ≈\ *n* [ME, fr. OE *goldfinc,* fr. *gold* + *finc* finch — more at FINCH] **1 :** a small brightly colored European finch (*Carduelis carduelis*) that has the front of the head and throat bright red, the nape with part of the wings and tail black, and the wings marked in bright yellow and that is often kept as a cage bird **2 :** YELLOWHAMMER 1 **3 :** any of several small American finches of the genus *Spinus* typically having the male in summer plumage variably yellow with black wings, tail, and crown
goldfinny \ˈ≈ˌ≈≈\ *n* -ES [prob. alter. of *goldsinny*] **1 :** a small brightly colored European wrasse (*Ctenolabrus rupestris*) **2 :** any of several European wrasses related to the goldfinny
[1]**goldfish** \ˈ≈ˌ≈\ *n* [[1]*gold* + *fish*] **1 a :** a small usu. golden yellow or orange cyprinid fish (*Carassius auratus*) that is native to China, closely related to the common carp, and much used as an aquarium and pond fish **b :** GARIBALDI **2** *slang* **:** canned salmon
[2]**goldfish** \"\ *adj* **:** resembling that of a goldfish; *specif* **:** exposed to public view ⟨patiently endured this ~ life —*Time*⟩
goldfish bowl *n* **1 :** a transparent glass bowl used as an aquarium for goldfish **2 :** a place or situation offering no privacy or secrecy ⟨the *goldfish bowls* in which an actor and his wife dwell —James Cagney⟩
goldflower \ˈ≈ˌ≈\ *n* **1 :** any of several yellow-flowered or predominantly yellow-flowered composite plants: as **a :** either of two European everlastings (*Helichrysum stoechas* and *H. orientale*) **b :** any of various bristly leaved annual herbs of southern Africa that constitute the genus *Gorteria* and have solitary or corymbose flower heads with ligulate orange-yellow ray flowers marked with brown **c :** a biennial herb (*Hymenoxys biennis*) of dry uplands of the southwestern U.S. that has yellow flower heads with fertile ray flowers **2 :** a shrubby hybrid St.-John's-wort (*Hypericum* × *moserianum*) with large golden yellow flowers
gold flux *n* **:** gold aventurine
gold foil *n* **:** gold beaten or rolled out very thin; *specif* **:** gold in sheets thicker than gold leaf
gold glass *n* **:** glassware ornamented with designs engraved on gold foil that is attached to the glass and then covered with a thin film of glass
gold–green \ˈ≈ˌ≈\ *adj* **:** dark green
gold heather *n* **:** BEACH HEATHER
gol·di \ˈgōldē, ˈgōl-\ *or* **gold** \-ld\ *n, pl* **goldi** *or* **goldis** *or* **golds** *usu cap* **1 a :** a group of Tungus peoples living along the Amur river **b :** a member of any of such peoples **2 :** the Tungusic language of the Goldi peoples
goldier *comparative of* GOLDY
gol·die's fern \ˈgōldēz-\ *or* **goldie–fern** *or* **goldie's shield fern** *or* **goldie's wood fern** *n, usu cap G* [after John *Goldie* †1886 Scot. traveler in the U.S., its discoverer] **:** a No. American fern (*Dryopteris goldiana*) with a blackish lustrous stipe

goldiest *superlative of* GOLDY
gold·i·locks *or* **goldy·locks** \ˈgōldēˌläks, -di,-\ *n pl but sing or pl in constr* [*goldy* + *locks,* pl. of *lock* (curl)] **1 :** a European herb (*Linosyris vulgaris*) of the family Compositae with heads of flowers resembling those of goldenrod **2 :** any of several shrubby southern African composite plants (genus *Chrysocoma*) that have bright yellow flower heads **3 :** a European buttercup (*Ranunculus auricomus*)
gold import point *n* **:** the point of variation in the price of foreign exchange at which the import of gold becomes preferable to the use of exchange in settlement of international obligations — called also *gold point;* compare GOLD EXPORT POINT
gold·ish \ˈgōldish\ *adj* [ME, fr. [1]*gold* + *-ish*] **:** somewhat golden **:** having a tinge of gold
gold·ite \ˈgōlˌdīt\ *n* -S [[1]*gold* + *-ite*] **:** an advocate of a gold monetary standard ⟨they were ~s to the last coin in the sock —John Gunther⟩
gold joint *n* **:** a perennial herb (*Chrysogonum virginianum*) of the family Compositae of the southeastern U.S. that has long-stalked leaves and radiate yellow flowers
gold knife \ˈ≈ˌ≈\ *n* **:** a long-bladed roundnosed knife for cutting gold leaf
gold lace *n* **:** lace or braid formerly made of gold wire but now usu. of gold silk or gold silk and cotton and used on uniforms or official robes to denote rank
gold–laced \ˈ≈ˌ≈\ *adj* **:** adorned with gold lace
gold leaf *n* **:** a sheet of gold ordinarily varying from four to five millionths of an inch in thickness that is used esp. for gilding and lettering on glass
gold·less \ˈgōldləs\ *adj* **:** lacking gold ⟨the ~ age, where gold disturbs no dreams —Lord Byron⟩
gold lip *or* **golden lip** *n* **:** a very large pearl oyster (*Pinctada maxima*) having the inner shell margin yellowish — see SILVER LIP
gold mine *n* [ME] **1 :** a place where gold is obtained by mining operations **2 :** a rich source of something desired or sought for ⟨that fantastic *gold mine* of early Americana —A.O. Vietor⟩ ⟨the Haydn piano sonatas . . . represent a *gold mine* of melody and of instrumental imagination —Virgil Thomson⟩
goldmist \ˈ≈ˌ≈\ *n* **:** a grayish yellow that is greener and very slightly lighter than chamois and greener, lighter, and stronger than old ivory or crash
gold mohur tree *n* [by folk etymology fr. *gulmohur*] **:** ROYAL POINCIANA
gold moss *also* **goldmoss stonecrop** *n* **:** a stonecrop (*Sedum acre*)
gold number *n* **:** a measure of the protective power of a lyophilic colloid expressed as the amount of the dry material that just protects a red gold sol under specified conditions — compare PROTECTIVE COLLOID
gold of pleasure *n* **:** an annual European false flax (*Camelina sativa*) that was formerly cultivated for its oil-rich seeds and is widely naturalized in No. America
gold pheasant *n* **1 :** GOLDEN PHEASANT **2 :** a brownish orange that is redder and duller than leather and slightly yellower and lighter than prairie brown, Windsor tan, Titian, or amber brown — called also *platina yellow, Prussian brown*
gold plate *n* **1 :** vessels or tableware of gold **2 :** gold electroplate — compare ROLLED GOLD
gold–plate \ˈ≈ˌ≈\ *vt* **:** to electroplate with gold
gold point *n* **1 :** GOLD EXPORT POINT **2 :** GOLD IMPORT POINT
gold premium *n* **:** the excess of purchasing power or exchange value of gold currency over another form of money (as paper dollars) of nominally equal value
gold reserve *n* **:** a fund of gold coin or bullion: as **a :** the fund of gold held by the U. S. Treasury **b :** the gold held by the central bank and the stabilization fund of a country
gold rocker *n* **:** CRADLE 3a
gold room *n* **:** a room in the N. Y. Stock Exchange formerly used for trading in gold
gold ruby glass *or* **gold ruby** *n* **:** RUBY GLASS
gold rush *n* **1 :** a rush to newly discovered goldfields in pursuit of riches ⟨the *gold rush* to Alaska⟩ **2 :** the headlong pursuit of sudden wealth in some new or lucrative field ⟨led the *gold rush* of the comic artists, whose output is minted daily —*N.Y. Herald Tribune*⟩ ⟨that *gold rush* of frightened businessmen toward higher prices —T.W.Arnold⟩
golds *pl of* GOLD
gold·schmidt·ine \ˈgōl(d)ˌshmidˌēn\ *n* -S [Victor *Goldschmidt* †1933 Ger. crystallographer + E *-ine*] **:** a mineral Ag_2Sb consisting of a silver antimonide that occurs in thin gray-white orthorhombic crystals
gold·schmidt·ite \-dˌīt\ *n* -S [V. *Goldschmidt* + E *-ite*] **:** SYLVANITE
gold·schmidt's process \ˈgōl(d)ˌshmits-\ *n, usu cap G* [after Hans *Goldschmidt* †1923 Ger. chemist] **:** ALUMINOTHERMY
gold shell *n* **:** a jingle shell (esp. *Anomia simplex*) of the Atlantic coast of No. America with a shell sulphur yellow to coppery red or sometimes silver gray or black
gold·sin·ny \ˈgōl(d)ˌsinē\ *n* -ES [origin unknown] **:** GOLDFINNY
gold size *n* **:** any of several adhesive compositions used for attaching gold leaf to surfaces
gold·smith \ˈgōl(d)ˌsmith\ *n* [ME, fr. OE, fr. [1]*gold* + *smith*] **1 :** an artisan who makes vessels, jewelry, or other articles of gold **2 :** a manufacturer of and dealer in articles of gold
goldsmith beetle *n* **:** any of several large bright yellow scarabaeid beetles with adults that feed on foliage and larvae that live in the soil and feed on roots: as **a :** a widely distributed European beetle (*Cetonia aurata*) **b :** a No. American beetle (*Cotalpa lanigera*) that is sometimes a locally important defoliator of deciduous trees
gold·smith·ery \-thərē\ *or* **gold·smith·ry** \-thrē\ *n* -ES [ME *goldsmithrie,* fr. *goldsmith* + *-rie* -ry] **1 :** the work, art, or trade of a goldsmith **2 :** articles manufactured by goldsmiths
gold·smith·ing \-thiŋ\ *n* **:** GOLDSMITHERY 1
gold sodium thiosulfate *n* **:** a soluble compound of gold $Na_3Au(S_2O_3)_2.2H_2O$ administered by intravenous injection in the treatment of rheumatoid arthritis and lupus erythematosus — called also *sodium aurothiosulfate*
gold solder *n* **:** a solder containing about 60 percent gold, 20 percent silver, and 20 percent copper
gold sol test *n* **:** a test of the ability of the globulins of an individual's cerebrospinal fluid to precipitate gold from colloidal solution, a positive result usu. being indicative of neurosyphilis
gold·spink \ˈ≈ˌ≈\ *n* **1** *chiefly Scot* **:** the European goldfinch **2** *chiefly Scot* **:** the European yellowhammer
gold spring *n* **:** a thin spring of gold that is attached to a chronometer detent and serves to unlock the escape wheel — called also *passing spring*
gold stamp *or* **gold stamping** *n* **:** genuine gold lettering or ornamentation on book covers
gold standard *n* **:** a monetary standard under which the basic unit of currency is defined by a stated quantity of gold and that is usu. characterized by the coinage and circulation of gold, unrestricted convertibility of other money into gold, and the free export and import of gold for the settlement of international obligations — compare GOLD BULLION STANDARD, GOLD-EXCHANGE STANDARD, MANAGED CURRENCY, STANDARD OF VALUE
gold star *adj* **:** entitled to display a gold star on a service flag as a symbol of a soldier killed in war ⟨a *gold star* mother⟩
gold stick *n* **1 :** the gold-headed staff presented by the British sovereign to the colonel of a regiment of Life Guardsmen or to the captain of the gentlemen-at-arms **2** *usu cap G&S* **:** one entitled to carry the gold stick on state occasions ⟨*Gold Sticks* and Silver Sticks have waited closely upon the persons of their sovereign —Elizabeth II⟩
goldstone \ˈ≈ˌ≈\ *n* **:** aventurine spangled close and fine with particles of gold-colored material
gold–tail \ˈ≈ˌ≈\ *or* **gold–tail moth** *n* **:** either of two white moths of the family Lymantriidae having yellow abdominal tufts: **a :** a European moth (*Euproctis similis*) that is closely related to the brown-tail moth **b :** an Australian moth (*Acyphas chionitis*)
gold therapy *also* **gold treatment** *n* **:** CHRYSOTHERAPY
goldthread \ˈ≈ˌ≈\ *n* **1 :** a plant of the genus *Coptis; esp* **:** a low smooth perennial No. American herb (*C. groenlandica*) with

alternately divided leaves and a bright yellow rootstock **2 :** DODDER
goldtit \ˈ≈ˌ≈\ *n* **:** VERDIN
goldurn *var of* GOLDARN
gold washer *n* **:** one that recovers gold by washing (as in a cradle); *also* **:** an apparatus for this purpose
gold washing *n* **1 :** the act or process of washing auriferous soil for gold **2 gold washings** *pl* **:** a place where gold washing is done
goldwasser *n* -S *often cap* [G, fr. *gold* (fr. OHG) + *wasser* water, fr. OHG *wazzer* — more at GOLD, WATER] **:** DANZIGER GOLDWASSER
gold watch *n* **:** SPATTERDOCK 1
goldwater \ˈ≈ˌ≈≈\ *n* [trans. of G *goldwasser*] **:** DANZIGER GOLDWASSER
goldweed \ˈ≈ˌ≈\ *n* **:** any of several plants of the genus *Ranunculus; esp* **:** CORN CROWFOOT
gold weight *n, obs* **:** the accuracy required in weighing gold
gold–winged woodpecker \ˈ≈ˌ≈-\ *n* **:** a flicker (*Colaptes auratus*)
goldwork \ˈ≈ˌ≈\ *n* **1 :** the act or art of working in gold **2 :** work done in gold (as by a smith)
goldworker \ˈ≈ˌ≈≈\ *n* **:** a person whose occupation is the obtaining or working of gold
goldworkings \ˈ≈ˌ≈≈\ *n pl* **:** a place where mining or washing for gold is done
gold·wyn·ism \ˈgōldwəˌnizəm\ *n* -S *usu cap* [Samuel *Goldwyn* *b*1882 Am. motion-picture producer + *-ism*] **:** a phrase or expression (as "include me out") involving a grotesque use of a word — compare IRISH BULL, MALAPROPISM
goldy \ˈgōldē\ *adj* -ER/-EST [ME, fr. [1]*gold* + *-y*] **:** GOLDEN
gold yellow *n* **:** GOLDEN YELLOW
goldylocks *var of* GOLDILOCKS
go·lem \ˈgōləm, ˈgāl-, ˈgȯil-\ *n* -S [Yiddish *goylem,* fr. Heb *gōlem* something shapeless] **1** *Jewish folklore* **:** an artificial figure constructed to represent a human being and endowed with life; *specif* **:** such a figure created by the cabalist Rabbi Löw of Prague in the 16th century **2 :** a senseless mechanical creature **:** AUTOMATON, ROBOT ⟨a total machine civilization is at best but a ~ —*Jewish Weekly News*⟩ **3 :** BLOCKHEAD 2
goles \ˈgōlz\ *n, cap* [euphemism] *dial Eng* **:** [2]GOD — used in oaths
[1]**golf** \ˈgälf, ˈgȯlf *also* ˈgäf *or* ˈgȯf *sometimes* ˈgəlf\ *n* -S *often*

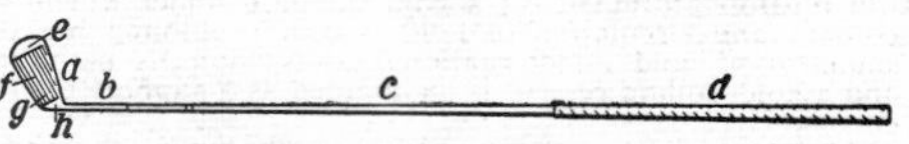

golf club (iron): *a* head, *b* hosel, *c* shaft, *d* grip, *e* toe or nose, *f* face, *g* heel, *h* neck

attrib [ME (Sc), prob. modif. of MD *colf, colve* club, stick used in a game resembling golf or field hockey; akin to OHG *kolbo* club, ON *kōlfr* clapper of a bell, bulb, arrow, L *galla* gallnut — more at GALL] **1 :** a game whose object is to sink a golf ball into each of the 9 or 18 successive holes on a golf course by using as few strokes of a golf club as possible and avoiding various natural or artificial hazards or obstacles — compare APPROACH, DRIVE, FAIRWAY, MATCH PLAY, MEDAL PLAY, PUTT, PUTTING GREEN, ROUGH, TEE **2** *or* **golf red :** BLOOD RED
[2]**golf** \"\ *vb* -ED/-ING/-S *vi* **:** to play golf ~ *vt* **:** to hit as if with a golf club **:** LOFT ⟨the batter ~*ed* a pop fly⟩
[3]**golf** \"\ *usu cap* — a communications code word for the letter *g*
golf bag *n* **:** a bag for carrying golf clubs and golf balls
golf ball *n* **:** a tough-covered ball used in golf and made of rubber thread wound about a center
golf club *n* **:** a long-shafted club with a head of wood or iron used to hit the ball in golf — see BRASSIE, DRIVER, NIBLICK, PUTTER, SPOON
golf course *n* **:** an area of land laid out for the game of golf with a series of 9 or 18 holes each including tee, fairway, and green and often one or more natural or artificial hazards — called also *golf links*
golf·er \-fə(r)\ *n* -S **:** one that golfs
golf green *n* **:** a dark yellowish green that is yellower and paler than holly green (sense 1), greener, lighter, and stronger than deep chrome green, and yellower, lighter, and stronger than average hunter green
golf hose *n* **:** knee-length woolen socks worn with knickers or shorts for sports
golf links *n pl* **:** GOLF COURSE

golf bag

golf shoe *n* **:** an oxford shoe of waterproof leather with sole spikes or hobnails that is worn esp. for golfing
golf widow *n* **:** a woman whose husband spends much time on the golf course
gol·gi \ˈgōljē\ *adj, usu cap* [after Camillo *Golgi* †1926 Ital. physician] **:** of, relating to, or constituting the Golgi apparatus ⟨the *Golgi* net of a nerve cell⟩
golgi apparatus *n, usu cap G* [after C. *Golgi*] **:** a cytoplasmic component esp. of functionally active cells that prob. plays a part in elaboration and secretion of cell products and when differentiated by special staining appears either as a net or as discrete particles although both appearances are prob. more or less artifactual — see CELL illustration
golgi body *n, usu cap G* [after C. *Golgi*] **:** a discrete mass of Golgi material as observed in certain stained preparations — called also *dictyosome*
golgi cell *n, usu cap G* [after C. *Golgi*] **:** a neuron with short dendrites and with either a long axon or an axon that breaks into processes soon after leaving the nerve-cell body
golgi material *or* **golgi substance** *n, usu cap G* [after C. *Golgi*] **:** specialized cytoplasm that constitutes the Golgi apparatus
golgi method *n, usu cap G* [after C. *Golgi*] **:** a method of preparing tissues for the study of nerves by using potassium bichromate and silver nitrate
golgi's organ *n, usu cap G* [after C. *Golgi*] **:** a spindle-shaped sensory end organ within a tendon
gol·go·tha \ˈgälgəthə, ˈgōl- *also* ≈ˈgäthə *or* ≈ˈgȯthə\ *n* -S [fr. *Golgotha,* the hill near Jerusalem where Christ was crucified, fr. LL, fr. Gk, fr. Aram *gulgultha,* fr. Heb *gulgoleth,* lit., skull] **1 :** a place of burial **:** CEMETERY, CHARNEL **2 :** a place of torment or martyrdom
gol·iard \ˈgōlyərd, -ˌyärd\ *n* -S *often cap* [F, fr. OF *goliart, goliard* glutton, drunkard, trickster, prob. fr. *gole* throat, gullet (fr. L *gula*) + *-art, -ard* — more at GLUTTON] **:** a wandering student of the 12th or 13th century given to the writing of goliardic verse and to convivial living and minstrelsy
gol·iar·dic \(ˈ)gōlˌyärdik\ *adj, often cap* **1 :** of, relating to, or being a type of medieval satirical poetry written in Latin **2 :** written in a manner suggestive of goliardic verse
go·li·ath \gəˈlīəth\ *n* -S *often cap* [after *Goliath,* biblical giant of the Philistines slain by David (1 Sam 17)] **:** GIANT ⟨slug it out with business ~s or that multitentacled giant squid, the U.S. government —Warner Olivier⟩
goliath beetle *n, sometimes cap G* **:** any of several very large African beetles of the family Cetoniidae commonly reddish brown marked with white and attaining a length of four inches
goliath crane *also* **goliath** *n* -S **:** a powerful traveling crane mounted on a movable gantry of large span
goliath frog *n* **:** a frog (*Rana goliath*) of the Cameroons and Gabon that attains a length of 1 foot and a weight sometimes exceeding 10 pounds
goliath heron *also* **goliath** *n* **:** a very large chiefly African heron (*Ardea goliath*) having the head, neck, and underparts brown and the back slaty gray
go·li·lla \gəˈlē(y)ə, -ēlyə\ *n* -S [Sp, dim. of *gola* throat, fr. L *gula* — more at GLUTTON] **:** a starched white collar worn by some Spanish magistrates

gollila

goll *n* -S [origin unknown] *obs* **:** HAND
[1]**gol·lar** *or* **gol·ler** \ˈgälə(r)\ *vi* -ED/-ING/-S [imit.] **1** *dial Brit*

: to call out in a loud voice **:** SHOUT, ROAR **2** *dial Brit* **:** to make a gurgling sound

²gollar *or* **goller** \"\ *n* -s **1** *chiefly Scot* **:** YELL, ROAR **2** *chiefly Scot* **:** an outburst of hasty words

gol·li·wog *or* **gol·li·wogg** \ˈgälē,wäg, -li,-\ *n* -s [after *Golliwogg,* an animated doll in books for children written by Bertha Upton †1912 Am. writer and illustrated by Florence Upton †1922 Am. portrait painter and illustrator] **1 :** a grotesque black doll ⟨among the dappled rocking horses and ~s —Osbert Sitwell⟩ **2 :** a grotesque person

gol·lop \ˈgäləp\ *dial var of* GULP

gol·ly \ˈgälē, -li\ *interj* [euphemism for *God*] — a mild oath

goloch *var of* GOLACH

go·los *or* **go·lus** \ˈgōləs\ *n* -ES *usu cap* [Yiddish *goles,* fr. Heb *gālūth* exile] **:** GALUTH

go·losh \gəˈläsh\ *chiefly Brit var of* GALOSH

golpe *or* **golp** \ˈgälp\ *n* -s [prob. fr. Sp *golpe* blow, bruise, fr. LL *colpus* — more at COPE] **:** a heraldic roundel purpure

gom \ˈgäm\ *var of* ⁶GAUM

go·ma·ri·an \gōˈmarēən, -ma(a)r-\ *also* **go·ma·rist** \-ˈmärəst\ *or* **go·ma·rite** \-ˈmä,rīt\ *n* -s *usu cap* [Franciscus *Gomarus* (Gommer) †1641 Dutch Calvinistic theologian + E *-ian* or *-ist* or *-ite*] **:** a follower of the Calvinist Gomarus

gom·been \gämˈbēn\ *n* -s [IrGael *gaimbín*] *Irish* **:** USURY

gombeen–man \-,man\ *n, pl* **gombeen–men** *Irish* **:** USURER

¹gombo *var of* GUMBO

²gom·bo \ˈgäm(,)bō\ *also* **gombo hemp** *n* -s [Pg *gombó*] **:** KENAF

gom·broon \(ˈ)gämˈbrün\ *n* -s [fr. *Gombroon* (Bandar Abbas), Iran] **:** a white semiporcelain often with a design pierced through the body but filled with the glaze

go·mel \ˈgōməl, ˈgóm-\ *adj, usu cap* [fr. *Gomel,* U.S.S.R.] **:** of or from the city of Gomel, U.S.S.R. **:** of the kind or style prevalent in Gomel

gom·er·al *or* **gom·er·el** *or* **gom·er·il** \ˈgäm(ə)rəl\ *n* -s [origin unknown] *dial chiefly Brit* **:** SIMPLETON, FOOL ⟨he's a liar and you're a ~ to hearken till him —Sir Walter Scott⟩

gom–gom *var of* GUM-GUM

gom·mi·er \ˈgämē,ā, ˈgəm-, -m,yā\ *n* -s [F, fr. *gomme* gum — more at GUM] **:** a Caribbean tree (*Pachylobus excelsa*) of the family Burseraceae that exudes a gum resembling incense

go·mon·tia \gōˈmänch(ē)ə\ *n, cap* [NL, fr. Maurice *Gomont,* 19th cent. Fr. botanist + NL *-ia*] **:** a genus of branching green algae (family Trentepohliaceae) including an alga (*G. polyrhiza*) that bores into marine mussel shells or dead algae and one (*G. lignicola*) that penetrates wood

gom·paauw *also* **gom paw** *or* **gom·pow** \ˈgäm,paů, -,pō\ *n* -s [Afrik *gompaauw, gompou,* fr. *gom* gum (fr. MD, fr. OF *gomme*) + *paauw, pou* peafowl, fr. MD *pau;* akin to OE *pēa* peafowl — more at GUM, PEACOCK] **:** a large bustard (*Choriotis kori*) of southern Africa that feeds chiefly on acacia gum — called also *kori bustard*

gom·pho·car·pus \ˌgäm(p)fōˈkärpəs\ *n, cap* [NL, fr. Gk *gomphos* tooth, peg, bolt, bond + NL *-carpus* — more at COMB] **:** a large genus of herbs and shrubs (family Asclepiadaceae) of southern Africa having showy flowers with corolla hoods that lack appendages

gom·pho·dont \ˈgäm(p)fə,dänt\ *adj* [Gk *gomphos* + E *-odont*] **:** having the teeth implanted in sockets

gom·pho·lo·bi·um \ˌgäm(p)fəˈlōbēəm\ *n, cap* [NL, fr. Gk *gomphos* + *lobos* pod, capsule, lobe + NL *-ium* — more at LOBE] **:** a genus of Australian shrubs (family Leguminosae) having alternate simple trifoliate leaves and showy flowers with the stamens all free — see POISON BUSH

gom·pho·sis \gämˈfōsə̇s\ *n* -ES [NL, fr. Gk *gomphōsis,* lit., a bolting together, fr. *gomphoun* to fasten with bolts (fr. *gomphos*) + *-sis*] **:** a union or immovable articulation in which a hard part is received into a bone cavity (as the teeth into the jaws)

gom·pho·the·ri·idae \ˌgäm(p)fōthəˈrīə,dē\ *n pl, cap* [NL, fr. *Gomphotherium,* type genus + *-idae*] **:** a family of widely distributed fossil elephants extinct since the Pleistocene

gom·pho·the·ri·um \ˌgäm(p)fōˈthirēəm\ *n, cap* [NL, fr. Gk *gomphos* + NL *-therium*] **:** a large genus (the type of the family Gomphotheriidae) of extinct elephants widely distributed in the Miocene and Pliocene and distinguished by a greatly elongated lower jaw bearing broad flat terminal tusks shaped like shovels

gom·phre·na \gämˈfrēnə\ *n, cap* [NL, alter. of L *gromphaena,* a kind of amaranth] **:** a genus of tropical herbs or low shrubs (family Amaranthaceae) having opposite leaves and flowers in close heads — see GLOBE AMARANTH

go·mu·ti \gōˈmüd·ē\ *n* -s [Malay (*pohon*) *gĕmuti*] **1** *also* **gomuti palm :** a Malayan feather palm (*Arenga pinnata*) that has large leaves with the bases densely clothed with fibers, yields a sweet sap from which jaggery and palm wine are made, and has a pith that furnishes a sago **2 :** the black wiry fiber obtained from gomuti used esp. for marine cordage and cable

gon \ˈgän\ *n* -s [short for *gondola*] **:** a railroad gondola

gon- *or* **gono-** *comb form* [LL *gono-,* fr. Gk *gon-, gono-,* fr. *gonos* offspring, procreation, seed, genitals, fr. the stem of *gignesthai* to be born — more at KIN] **:** sexual **:** generative **:** semen **:** seed ⟨*gon*angium⟩ ⟨*gono*duct⟩

-gon \,gän *sometimes* ,gən\ *n comb form* -s [NL *-gonum,* fr. Gk *-gōnon,* fr. *gōnia* angle; akin to Gk *gony* knee — more at KNEE] **:** figure having (so many) angles ⟨*nonagon*⟩

go·nad \ˈgō,nad *sometimes* ˈgä,-\ *n* -s [NL *gonad-, gonas,* fr. Gk *gonos*] **:** a primary sex gland **:** OVARY, TESTIS — **go·nad·al** \(ˈ)gō¦nadᵊl, (ˈ)gä¦-\ *adj*

go·nad·ec·to·mize \ˌgō,naˈdektə,mīz, |,nəˈd- *sometimes* ,gä|\ *vt* -ED/-ING/-S **:** to remove the gonads from

go·nad·ec·to·my \-təmē\ *n* -ES [*gonad* + *-ectomy*] **:** surgical removal of ovary or testis

gonado·trophic \(ˌ)gō¦nadə¦träfik, -rōf-, (ˌ)gä¦-, ˌgänədō¦-\ *or* **gonado·trop·ic** \-¦träpik\ *adj* [ISV *gonad* + *-o-* + *-trophic* or *-tropic*] **:** acting on or stimulating the gonads ⟨the ~ hormone of the anterior lobe of the pituitary gland⟩

go·nad·o·tro·phin \(ˌ)gō,nadəˈtrōfə̇n, (ˌ)gä,-, ˌgänədō-ˈ-\ *or* **go·nad·o·tro·pin** \-ˈrōpə̇n\ *n* -s [ISV *gonadotrophic, gonadotropic* + *-in*] **:** a gonadotrophic substance ⟨chorionic ~⟩

gon·a·duct \ˈgänə,dəkt\ *var of* GONODUCT

gon·a·ke *or* **gon·a·ke** \ˈgänə,kē\ *n* -s [native name in western Africa] **:** BABUL; *esp* **:** the pods of babul

go·nan·gi·al \(ˈ)gō¦nanjēəl\ *adj* [NL *gonangium* + E *-al*] **:** of or relating to a gonangium

go·nan·gi·um \-ēəm\ *n, pl* **gonan·gia** \-ēə\ *or* **gonangiums** [NL, fr. *gon-* + *-angium*] **1 :** a reproductive member of a hydrozoan colony producing gonophores or medusa buds **2 :** GONOTHECA

gon·apophysal \¦gan+\ *or* **gon·apophysial** \(ˌ)gän+\ *adj* [NL *gonapophysis* + E *-al*] **:** of, relating to, or constituting a gonapophysis

gon·apophysis \¦gän+\ *n, pl* **gonapophyses** [NL, fr. *gon-* + *apophysis*] **:** an organ or process of the anal region of an insect that serves in copulation, oviposition, or stinging — used chiefly of such structures when paired and regarded as modified appendages

gon·ca·lo al·ves \gən,salōˈalvəs\ *n* [Pg *gonçalo-alves*] **1 :** a tall tropical American timber tree (*Astronium fraxinifolium*) of the family Anacardiaceae that is esp. abundant in eastern Brazil **2 :** the hard strong durable heavy wood of the goncalo alves that has a straight grain and dark stripes on a yellowish to pinkish ground and is widely used for veneer, fine furniture, and heavy construction where its durability is important — called also *kingwood, zebrawood*

gond \ˈgänd\ *n* -s *usu cap* **1 :** a member of a Dravidian or pre-Dravidian people of central India **2 :** GONDI

gon·dang \ˈgän,daŋ\ *n* -s [Jav *gondang*] **:** a Javanese fig tree (*Ficus subracemosa*) the latex of which yields a wax

gondang wax *n* **:** the hard cream-colored wax obtained from the gondang — called also *fig wax*

gondi \ˈgändē\ *n* -s *usu cap* **:** the language of the Gonds

gon·do·la \ˈgändələ, ÷ gänˈdōlə, ÷ gənˈdō-; *some speakers who use* ˈ== *for sense 1 use* =ˈ== *for some of the other senses*\ *n* -s [It, fr. Venetian dial., fr. ML *gondula,* dim. of (assumed) VL *condua,* perh. fr. Gk *kondya,* pl. of *kondy* drinking vessel] **1 :** a long narrow flat-bottomed boat with a high prow and stern used on the canals of Venice and usu. propelled by a gondolier who stands at the stern facing the prow and usu. sculls with a single long oar **2** *or* **gun·da·low** *or* **gun·de·low** \ˈgəndə,lō, -n(d),lō\ **:** a heavy flat-bottomed boat used on New England rivers as a gunboat in the Revolutionary War and subsequently in the barge traffic there and on the Ohio and Mississippi rivers **3** *or* **gondola car :** a railroad car with no top, flat bottom, fixed sides, and sometimes demountable ends that is used chiefly for hauling steel, rock, or heavy bulk commodities **4 a :** an elongated car attached to the underside of an airship **b :** a metallic often spherical airtight enclosure suspended from a balloon for carrying passengers or meteorological or other instruments **5** *or* **gondola chair :** an upholstered chair whose back curves forward at both sides to form the arms **6 :** an island fixture used in self-service retail stores to display merchandise **7 :** a motor truck or trailer having a large hopper-shaped container for transporting mixed concrete

gondola 1

gon·do·let \ˌgändəˈlet\ *n* -s [It *gondoletta,* dim. of *gondola*] **:** a small gondola

gon·do·lier \ˌgändəˈli(ə)r, -iə\ *n* -s [F, fr. It *gondoliere,* fr. *gondola* + *-iere* -er] **:** one who propels a gondola

¹gone \ˈgón *also* ˈgän\ *adj* [fr. past part. of *go*] **1 a :** PAST ⟨sweet memories of ~ summers —John Cheever⟩ **b** *of an arrow* **:** having passed above the mark **2 a :** ADVANCED, INVOLVED, ABSORBED ⟨had expected to find her . . . far ~ in hysteria —Frank Yerby⟩ **b :** INFATUATED ⟨in love! she is so far ~ she does not know which way to sail —Edna S. V. Millay⟩ — often used with *on* ⟨was real ~ on that man —Pete Martin⟩ **c :** PREGNANT ⟨a woman seven months ~⟩ **3 a :** DEAD ⟨the stupid inanimate limbs of the ~ wretch —George Meredith⟩ **b :** done for **:** LOST, RUINED ⟨if he loses the steam and blacks out the ship we're ~ ducks —R.F.Mirvish⟩ **c** *obs* **:** DRUNK **d :** EXHAUSTED, FATIGUED ⟨nothing like cold spring water to put life back into a poor ~ body —Rebecca Caudill⟩ **e :** SINKING ⟨the empty or ~ feeling in the abdomen so common in elevators —H.G.Armstrong⟩ **4** *slang* **:** GREAT — used as a generalized expression of approval ⟨the duke qualifies as a real ~ fashion reporter —Inez Robb⟩

²gone \ˈgōn\ *n* -s [Gk *gonē* seed, offspring, fr. the stem of Gk *gignesthai* to be born — more at KIN] **:** GERM CELL

gone–by \ˈ=,=\ *adj* **:** long past or gone **:** BYGONE ⟨her gown of a *gone-by* century —Winston Churchill⟩

gonecium *var of* GONOECIUM

gon·ef \ˈgänəf\ *var of* GANEF

gone feeling *or* **gone sensation** *n* **:** a feeling of faintness or weakness

gone goose *also* **gone gosling** *n* **:** a person who is doomed **:** one in a hopeless predicament ⟨they got me now, boy . . . I'm a *gone goose* —Nathaniel Burt⟩ ⟨when she goes after a man he's a *gone goose* —W.H.Rudkin⟩

gone·ness \ˈgȯnnəs *also* ˈgänn-\ *n* -ES **:** a state of exhaustion **:** FAINTNESS

gon·er \ˈgȯnə(r) *also* ˈgän-\ *n* -s [*gone* + *-er*] **:** one that is irrevocably lost or ruined **:** one whose fate is sealed **:** a hopeless case ⟨this ship's a ~ —E.L.Beach⟩ ⟨if you fall behind . . . you're ~s —Kenneth Roberts⟩ ⟨felt is the surprise fabric of the season. Just when everybody thought it was a ~ it resurges in new strength —*Women's Wear Daily*⟩

goney *var of* GONY

gon·fa·lon \ˈgänfə,län, -,lən\ *n* -s [It *gonfalone,* fr. OIt, fr. OF *gonfanon, gonfalon* — more at GONFANON] **1 :** the ensign or standard in use by certain princes or states (as the medieval republics of Italy) **2 :** a flag that hangs from a crosspiece or frame ⟨the state flower was used by the candidate on his guidons and ~s⟩

gon·fa·lon·ier \ˌgänfə,läˈni(ə)r, -,lə¦n-\ *n* -s [It *gonfaloniere,* fr. OIt, fr. OF *gonfanonier, gonfalonier,* fr. *gonfanon, gonfalon* + *-ier* -er] **1 :** one who bears the gonfalon **:** STANDARD-BEARER; *specif* **:** a papal official at Rome who bears the standard of the church **2 :** the chief magistrate or other official of any of several republics in medieval Italy

gon·fa·lo·nie·re \,==,lənˈyerē, -,lən-, -e(,)rā\ *n, pl* **gonfa·lonie·ri** \-,rē\ [It] **:** GONFALONIER

gon·fa·non \ˈgänfə,nän, -,nən\ *n* -s [ME *gonfanoun,* fr. MF *gonfanon* gonfalon, of Gmc origin; akin to OHG *gundfano* war flag, fr. *gund-* battle, war + *fano* cloth — more at DEFEND, VANE] **:** GONFALON; *esp* **:** one beneath the head of a knight's lance

¹gong \ˈgäŋ, ˈgȯŋ\ *n* -s [Malay & Jav, of imit. origin] **1 :** a bronze plate with upturned rim that gives a subdued but very resonant penetrating sound when struck with a usu. padded hammer — called also *Chinese gong, tam-tam* **2 a** *or* **gong bell :** a flat bell resembling a saucer rung by striking it with a small hammer operated by some commonly electric mechanism **b :** a hardened wire rod wound in a flat spiral that is used in clocks and repeating watches to sound the time or chime or alarm

²gong \"\ *vi* -ED/-ING/-S **:** to make the sound of a gong ⟨the cemetery bells . . . ~*ed* in the air —Owen Dodson⟩

gong buoy *n* **:** a buoy equipped with a set of three or four gongs each having a different tone

gong 2a

gon·go·resque \¦gäŋgə¦resk, ,gȯŋ\ *adj, usu cap* [Luis de *Góngora* y Argote †1627 Span. poet + E *-esque*] **:** of or relating to the poet Góngora or to Gongorism ⟨putting into verses of *Gongoresque* lineage . . . the authentic qualities of an entirely contemporary emotion —Pedro Salinas⟩

gon·go·rism \ˈ==,rizəm\ *n* -s [Sp *gongorismo,* fr. Luis de *Góngora* y Argote + Sp *-ismo* -ism] **1** *usu cap* **:** a Spanish literary style esp. associated with the poet Góngora and his imitators characterized by a studied obscurity of meaning and expression and by extensive use of metaphorical imagery, exaggerated conceits, paradoxes, neologisms, and other ornate devices — compare EUPHUISM **2 a :** an excessively involved, ornate, and artificial style of writing ⟨her sheer virtuosity as a creator of images seems on the verge of ~ —*Saturday Rev.*⟩ **b :** an instance of such a style ⟨a swaggering rhetorician who . . . has to stop and search for the appropriate ~ —Malcolm Cowley⟩ — **gon·go·ris·tic** \¦==¦ristik\ *adj*

gon·gy·lo·ne·ma \ˌgänjəlōˈnēmə\ *n, cap* [NL, fr. Gk *gongylos* round + NL *-nema*] **:** a genus of spiruroid nematodes (family Thelaziidae) infesting the tissues of the digestive tract of various mammals and birds including man

goni- *or* **gonio-** *comb form* [Gk *gōnia* — more at -GON] **1 :** corner **:** angle ⟨*goniometer*⟩ **2 :** gonion

gonia *pl of* GONION *or of* GONIUM

go·ni·al \ˈgōnēəl\ *also* **go·ni·ac** \-ē,ak\ *adj* [*goni-* + *-al* or *-ac* (as in *maniac*)] **1 :** of or relating to the gonion **2 :** of or relating to gones or gonia

go·ni·as·ter \ˌgōnēˈastə(r)\ *n, cap* [NL, fr. *goni-* + *-aster*] **:** a common genus (the type of the family Goniasteridae) of cushion stars consisting of nearly pentagonal, rigid, and often brightly colored starfishes

go·ni·a·tite \ˈgōnēə,tīt\ *n* -s [NL *Goniatites*] **:** an ammonoid of the genus *Goniatites* or family Goniatitidae

go·ni·a·ti·tes \,===ˈtīd·(,)ēz\ *n, cap* [NL, irreg. fr. Gk *gōnia* angle] **:** a genus (the type of the family Goniatitidae) of ammonoids widespread in the Devonian and the Carboniferous and having a discoidal coiled shell with angular-lobed sutures — **go·ni·a·tit·ic** \,===¦tid·ik\ *adj* — **go·ni·a·ti·toid** \,===ˈtīd·əd\ *n* -s — **gon·i·a·ti·toid** \,===ˈtīd·,ȯid\ *adj* — **go·ni·ati·tid** \,===ˈtīd·əd\ *n* -s

gon·i·au·lax \,gōnēˈō,laks\ *syn of* GONYAULAX

gon·i·dan·gi·um \ˌgänəˈdanjēəm\ *n, pl* **gonidan·gia** \-ēə\ [NL, fr. *gonidium* + *-angium*] **:** a sporangium that contains or produces gonidia

gonidi- *or* **gonidio-** *comb form* [NL *gonidium*] **:** gonidium ⟨*gonidio*genous⟩

gonidia *pl of* GONIDIUM

go·nid·i·al \gōˈnidēəl\ *also* **go·nid·ic** \-dik\ *adj* [*gonidi-* + *-al* or *-ic*] **:** relating to, consisting of, or containing a gonidium

gonidial layer *n* **:** a layer of green chlorophyll-bearing cells found within the thallus of a lichen

go·nid·i·oid \-dē,ȯid\ *adj* [*gonidi-* + *-oid*] **:** resembling or having the nature of gonidia

go·nid·i·um \gōˈnidēəm\ *n, pl* **gonid·ia** \-ēə\ [NL, fr. *gon-* + *-idium*] **1 a :** an asexual reproductive cell or group of cells arising in or on the gametophyte usu. in special organs — see GONIDANGIUM **b :** one of the green chlorophyll-bearing cells found within the thallus of a lichen sometimes constituting a definite layer but often scattered — called also *brood cell;* see LICHEN **2 :** one of the supposed reproductive granules formed internally in certain bacteria (as of the genus *Azotobacter*)

-gonies *pl of* -GONY

gon·if *or* **gon·iff** \ˈgänəf\ *var of* GANEF

gon·i·mo·blast \ˈgänəmō,blast\ *n* [Gk *gonimos* productive (fr. stem of *gignesthai* to be born) + E *-blast* — more at KIN] **:** one of the sporogenous filaments which arise from the fertilized carpogonium in most red algae; *also* **:** the aggregation of such filaments

gon·i·mo·lobe \-,lōb\ *n* [*gonimo*blast + *lobe*] **:** the terminal cell of a gonimoblast that produces a carpospore

go·ni·o·co·tes \ˌgōnēəˈkōd·(,)ēz\ *n, cap* [NL, fr. *goni-* + *-cotes* (fr. Gk *kotis, kottis* occiput)] **:** a genus of bird lice attacking various wild and domestic birds — see FLUFF LOUSE

go·ni·o·des \ˌgōnēˈō(,)dēz\ *n, cap* [NL, fr. *goni-* + *-odes*] **:** a genus of biting lice attacking various wild and domestic birds

go·ni·om·e·ter \ˌgōnēˈämәd·ə(r)\ *n* [*goni-* + *-meter*] **1 :** an instrument for measuring angles (as in surveying, anthropometry, or mineralogy) **2 a :** a mutual inductor with a rotatable secondary coil connected to one or more antennas **b :** DIRECTION FINDER **3 :** an instrument with which the range of motion in a joint is measured

go·ni·o·met·ric \ˌgōnēə¦me·trik\ *also* **go·ni·o·met·ri·cal** \-rəkəl\ *adj* **:** of or relating to goniometry **:** relating to or determined with a goniometer — **go·ni·o·met·ri·cal·ly** \-rək(ə)lē\ *adv*

go·ni·om·e·try \ˌgōnēˈämə·trē\ *n* -ES [F *goniométrie,* fr. *gonio-* goni- + *-métrie* -metry] **:** measurement of angles

go·ni·on \ˈgōnē,än\ *n, pl* **go·nia** \-ēə\ [NL, fr. Gk *gōnia* angle — more at -GON] **:** the point at the angle of the human lower jaw on each side — see CRANIOMETRY illustration

go·ni·o·ne·mus \ˌgōnēəˈnēməs\ *n, cap* [NL, fr. *goni-* + *-nemus* (fr. *nēma* thread)] **:** a genus of small cosmopolitan hydrozoan jellyfishes (order Trachomedusae)

go·ni·oph·o·lis \ˌgōnēˈäfələs\ *n, cap* [NL, fr. *goni-* + Gk *pholis* horny scale — more at PHOLID-] **:** a genus of extinct crocodiles with amphicoelous vertebrae known from remains found in the Upper Jurassic of Europe and No. America

go·nio·photometer \ˌgōnē(,)ō+\ *n* [*goni-* + *photometer*] **:** a photometer for measuring the intensity of light specularly or diffusely reflected at different angles from a surface — **go·nio·photometric** \"+\ *adj*

go·ni·o·scope \ˈgōnēə,skōp\ *n* [*goni-* + *-scope*] **:** an instrument consisting of a contact lens to be fitted over the cornea and an optical system with which the interior of the eye can be viewed — **go·ni·o·scop·ic** \¦===¦skäpik\ *adj* — **go·ni·os·co·py** \,gōnēˈäskəpē\ *n* -ES

go·ni·o·stat \ˈgōnēə,stat\ *n* -s [*goni-* + *-stat*] **:** a device used in cutting gem facets

go·ni·tis \gōˈnīd·əs\ *n* -ES [NL, fr. Gk *gony* knee + NL *-itis* — more at KNEE] **:** inflammation of the knee

¹go·ni·um \ˈgōnēəm\ *n, cap* [NL, fr. Gk *gōnia* angle, corner — more at -GON] **:** a genus of colonial plantlike flagellates related to *Volvox* and forming small flat colonies of biflagellate cells

²gonium \"\ *n, pl* **go·nia** \-ēə\ *also* **goniums** [NL, fr. *gon-* + *-ium*] **:** an undifferentiated primitive germ cell **:** OOGONIUM, SPERMATOZOON — often used in combination ⟨archegonium⟩ ⟨spermatogonium⟩

gon·nard·ite \ˈgänə(r),dīt\ *n* -s [F *gonnardite,* fr. Ferdinand *Gonnard,* 19th cent. Fr. mineralogist + F *-ite*] **:** a mineral approximately $Na_2CaAl_4Si_6O_{20}.7H_2O$ consisting of a zeolite and occurring in radiating spherules (sp. gr. 2.3)

gono- — see GON-

gon·o·blas·tid·i·al \ˌgänə¦blaˈstidēəl\ *adj* [NL *gonoblastidium* + E *-al*] **:** of or relating to a gonoblastidium

gon·o·blas·tid·i·um \,==ˈ=ˈ=ēəm\ *also* **gon·o·blas·tid** \,gänōˈblastəd\ *n, pl* **gonoblastid·ia** \-ēə\ *also* **gonoblastids** [NL *gonoblastidium,* fr. *gon-* + Gk *blastos* sprout + NL *-idium*] **:** BLASTOSTYLE

gon·o·cho·ric \ˌgänə¦kȯrik\ *adj* **:** having the sexes separate **:** not hermaphroditic **:** DIOECIOUS

gon·o·cho·rism \ˌgänə¦kȯr,izəm\ *n* -s [ISV *gon-* + *-chorism* (fr. Gk *chōrismos* separation, fr. *chōrizein* to separate); orig. formed as G *gonochorismus* — more at CHORISIS] **1 :** DIOECISM **2 :** the development or evolution of sex — **gon·o·cho·ris·mal** \¦gänəkō¦rizməl\ *adj*

gon·o·cho·rist \ˈ¦gänə¦kȯrəst\ *n* -s [ISV *gon-* + *-chorist* (fr. Gk *chōristos* separable, fr. *chōrizein* to separate) orig. formed in G] **:** a dioecious individual or race; *esp* **:** one in which sex is determined by developmental rather than hereditary mechanisms — **gon·o·cho·ris·tic** \¦gänəkō¦ristik\ *adj*

gon·o·coc·cal \ˌgänə¦käkəl\ *or* **gon·o·coc·cic** \-ˈäk(s)ik\ *adj* [NL *gonococcus* + E *-al* or *-ic*] **:** of, relating to, or caused by gonococci

gon·o·coc·cus \,==ˈkäkəs\ *n, pl* **gonococ·ci** \-ä,kī, -ä(,)kē, -äk,sī, -äk,(,)sē\ *sometimes cap* [NL, fr. *gon-* + *-coccus*] **:** a pus-producing bacterium (*Neisseria gonorrhoeae*) that causes gonorrhea

gon·o·coel *or* **gon·o·coele** \ˈgänə,sēl\ *n* -s [*gon-* + *-coel, -coele*] **:** the body cavity that contains the gonads and that is sometimes considered the evolutionary precursor of the entire coelom of higher animals

gon·o·cox·ite \ˌgänəˈkäk,sīt\ *n* -s [ISV *gon-* + L *coxa* hip + E *-ite*] **:** the inner segment of a gonapophysis

gon·o·cyte \ˈgänə,sīt\ *n* -s [ISV *gon-* + *-cyte*] **:** a cell that produces gametes **:** GAMETOCYTE

gon·o·duct *also* **gon·a·duct** \ˈgänə,dəkt\ *n* [*gonoduct* fr. *gon-* + *duct; gonaduct* blend of *gonad* and *duct*] **:** the duct of a gonad being often coextensive in whole or in part with the excretory duct of a nephron

go·noe·ci·um \gəˈnēs(h)ēəm, gäˈ-,gōˈ-\ *also* **go·ne·ci·um** \-\ *n, pl* **gonoe·cia** \-ēə\ [NL, fr. *gon-* + Gk *oikia* house + NL *-ium* — more at VICINITY] **:** one of the modified reproductive zooecia of a bryozoan

gon·of *or* **gon·oph** \ˈgänəf\ *var of* GANEF

gono·genesis \¦gänō+\ *n* [NL, fr. *gon-* + *genesis*] **:** the maturation of germ cells **:** OOGENESIS, SPERMATOGENESIS

go no–go gage *or* **go not–go gage** \ˈ=ˈ=,=-\ *n* **:** a set of two complementary limit gages consisting of a go gage and a no-go gage

go·nol·o·bus \gōˈnäləbəs\ *n, cap* [NL, fr. *gon-* + *-lobus*] **:** a genus of American herbaceous vines (family Asclepiadaceae) with opposite cordate leaves, small whitish flowers in axillary clusters, and erect follicles

gon·o·mere \ˈgänə,mi(ə)r\ *n* -s [ISV *gon-* + *-mere*] **:** a pronucleus retaining its identity for a time during cleavage — **gon·o·mer·ic** \¦gänə¦merik\ *adj*

go·nom·ery \gōˈnämərē\ *n* -ES [ISV *gon-* + *-mery*] **:** the state or condition in which gonomeres are present

gon·o·phore \ˈgänə,fō(ə)r\ *n* -s [ISV *gon-* + *-phore*] **1 :** a sporophyll-bearing prolongation of the axis **2 :** a reproductive zooid of a hydroid colony representing the free-swimming medusa stage but differing from a medusa in remaining attached to the hydroid stock — see SPOROSAC — **gon·o·phor·ic** \¦==¦fȯrik\ *adj* — **go·noph·o·rous** \gōˈnäf(ə)rəs\ *adj*

gon·o·plasm \ˈgänə,plazəm\ *n* [*gon-* + *-plasm*] **:** the part of the protoplasm of the antheridium that enters into zygote formation in fungi of the family Peronosporaceae — compare PERIPLASM

gon·o·pod \-,päd\ *n* -s [*gon-* + *-pod*] **:** an appendage in many arthropods modified to serve as a copulatory organ

gon·o·po·di·al \ˌgänə¦pōdēəl\ *also* **gon·o·po·dal** \-dᵊl, gəˈnäpədᵊl\ *adj* [NL *gonopodium* + E *-al*] **:** of, relating to, or being a gonopodium

gon·o·po·di·um \ˌgänəˈpōdēəm\ *n, pl* [NL, fr. *gon-* + *podium*] **:** the anal fin of a male fish when modified to serve as a copulatory organ

gono·poietic \¦gänə+\ *adj* [*gon-* + *-poietic*] **:** productive of germ cells

gon·o·pore \ˈgänə,pō(ə)r\ *n* [*gon-* + *pore*] **:** a genital pore

gon·o·rhyn·chus \ˌgänəˈriŋkəs\ *n, cap* [NL, irreg. fr. *goni-* + *-rhynchus*] **:** a genus of slender cylindrical marine fishes without adipose fin, air bladder, or teeth that constitutes a family (Gonorhynchidae) and is the sole surviving representative of a distinct suborder of the order Isospondyli

gon·or·rhea *also* **gon·or·rhoea** \ˌgänəˈrēə\ *n* -s [NL, fr. LL, spermatorrhea, blennorrhea, fr. Gk *gonorrhoia*, fr. *gon-* + *-rrhoia* -rrhea] **:** a contagious inflammation of the genital mucous membrane caused by the gonococcus — called also *clap* — **gon·or·rhe·al** *also* **gon·or·rhoe·al** \ˌ≡≡ˈ≡əl\ *adj*

gon·o·some \ˈgänəˌsōm\ *n* -s [*gon-* + *-some*] **:** the totality of reproductive zooids of a hydroid — compare TROPHOSOME

gon·o·sto·mat·i·dae \ˌgänəstōˈmadəˌdē\ *n pl, cap* [NL, fr. *Gonostomat-, Gonostoma*, type genus (fr. *gon-* + *stomat-, stoma* mouth) + *-idae* — more at STOMACH] **:** a small family of slender elongate deep-sea isospondylous fishes of the Pacific and Indian oceans — compare VIPERFISH

gon·o·the·ca \ˌgänəˈthēkə\ *n, pl* **gonothe·cae** \-ē(ˌ)sē\ [NL, fr. *gon-* + *-theca*] **:** the protective covering of a gonangium — **gon·o·the·cal** \ˌ≡≡ˈ≡kəl\ *adj*

go·not·o·kont *or* **go·not·o·cont** \gōˈnädəˌkänt\ *n* -s [*gon-* + Gk *tokont-, tokōn*, pres. part. of *tokan* to be near delivery; akin to Gk *teknon* child — more at THANE] **1 :** GONOCYTE **2 :** a cell or organ in which meiosis occurs

gon·o·tome \ˈgänəˌtōm\ *n* -s [ISV *gon-* + *-tome*] **:** the portion of a somite that participates in gonad formation

gon·o·tyl \ˈgänəˌtil\ *n* -s [*gon-* + Gk *tylos* knob, penis — more at THOLE] **:** a sucker surrounding the genital opening and often intimately associated with the acetabulum of certain trematode worms

gono·zooid \ˈgänə+\ *n* [*gon-* + *zooid*] **1 a :** a sexual zooid or medusa bud of a hydroid **:** GONOPHORE **b :** a sexual zooid of a tunicate **2 :** OVICELL

gons *pl of* GON

-gons *pl of* -GON

go·ny *or* **go·ney** \ˈgōni, ˈgō-\ *n, pl* **gonies** *or* **goneys** [origin unknown] **1** *dial chiefly Brit* **:** BOOBY, DUNCE **2 :** GOONEY

-go·ny \gənē, -ni\ *n comb form* -ES [L *-gonia*, fr. Gk *goneia*, fr. *gonos* offspring, procreation, seed + *-eia* -y — more at GON-] **:** generation, reproduction, or manner of coming into being of a (specified) thing ⟨cosmo*gony*⟩ ⟨sporo*gony*⟩ ⟨theo*gony*⟩

go·ny·au·lax \ˌgōnēˈȯˌlaks\ *n* [NL, fr. Gk *gony* knee + *aulax* furrow — more at KNEE] **1** *cap* **:** a large genus of phosphorescent marine dinoflagellates that when unusually abundant cause red tide and a serious mussel poisoning of man — see MUSSEL POISONING **2** -ES **:** any member of the genus *Gonyaulax*

go·nys \ˈgōnəs\ *n* -ES [NL, prob. modif. of Gk *genys* jaw, cheek — more at CHIN] **:** the prominent ridge along the line of union of the two halves of the lower mandible of certain birds (as the gulls)

go·ny·sty·lus \ˌgōnəˈstīləs\ *n, cap* [NL, fr. Gk *gony* knee + *stylos* pillar; fr. the geniculate styles — more at KNEE, STEER] **:** a small genus of East Indian trees (order Malvales) constituting a monotypic family, having alternate leathery leaves, regular paniculate flowers and woody fruits, and yielding fragrant timber resembling agalloch

¹goo \ˈgü\ *n* -s [F *goût* — more at GOÛT] **1** *chiefly Scot* **a :** a strong taste **b :** a disagreeable smell **2** *chiefly Scot* **:** LIKING, PREFERENCE, TASTE

²goo \ˈ"\ *n* -s [by shortening & alter. fr. *gaspergou*] **:** FRESHWATER DRUM

³goo \ˈ"\ *n* -s [perh. alter. of ¹*glue*] **1 :** a viscid or sticky substance ⟨wash that ~ off your hair —Nancy Rutledge⟩ ⟨whisks away dirt and ~ in seconds —*advt*⟩ **2 :** sickly or cloying sentimentality ⟨of all the silly ~ —J.U.Newman⟩ ⟨the mental and aesthetic ~ . . . remains a bad taste in the mouth —Jay Leyda⟩

goober \ˈgübə(r), ˈgub-\ *or* **goober pea** *n* -s [of African origin; akin to Kimbundu *nguba* peanut, Kongo, kidney, peanut] *South & Midland* **:** PEANUT

gooch crucible *or* **gooch filter** \ˈgüch-\ *n, usu cap G* [after Frank A. *Gooch* †1929 Am. chemist] **:** a small crucible with perforated bottom in which precipitates can be collected (as by the use of fine asbestos), dried, and weighed

¹good \ˈgu̇d, *in formulas of meeting & parting often* ˌgəd\ *adj* **bet·ter** \ˈbedə(r), -etə-\ **best** \ˈbest\ [ME, fr. OE *gōd*; akin to OHG *guot* good, ON *gōthr*, Goth *goths* good, OFris *gadia* to unite, OHG *bigatōn* to fit together, *gigat* fitting, Skt *gadh* to hold fast; basic meaning: uniting, fitting] **1 a** (1) **:** having a favorable or auspicious character **:** PROSPEROUS, BENEFICIAL ⟨sailed for France with a ~ wind⟩ ⟨when the moon is ~ . . . they often pursue the chase far into the night —James Stevenson-Hamilton⟩ ⟨the country is enjoying ~ times⟩ ⟨the company has had a ~ year⟩ (2) **:** conveying or reporting what is favorable or fortunate **:** WELCOME ⟨have you heard the ~ news⟩ (3) **:** producing, marked by, or favorable to a bountiful yield or a yield of high quality **:** FERTILE ⟨the land around here is not very ~⟩ ⟨wine of a ~ recent year⟩ (4) **:** favorably affecting one's interests **:** leading to or attended by a favorable or prosperous outcome ⟨as his ~ fortune would have it⟩ ⟨wished him ~ luck⟩ (5) **:** marked by or conveying approval or commendation ⟨sought to win my ~ opinion⟩ ⟨had a ~ report on his work⟩ ⟨had not one ~ word to say about him⟩ (6) **:** making a favorable impression with respect to moral character **:** inspiring trust ⟨he had a ~ face; I instinctively liked him⟩ (7) **:** making a favorable impression with respect to appearance or other physical traits **:** COMELY, ATTRACTIVE, BEAUTIFUL ⟨had a ~ face and figure⟩ ⟨she's certainly ~ to look at⟩ ⟨had lost her ~ looks⟩ ⟨an early Georgian manor of distinguished ~ looks —H.H.Johnston⟩ (8) **:** BECOMING, APPROPRIATE ⟨don't like that dress . . . it isn't ~ for you —Elizabeth Hardwick⟩ (9) **:** reserved for special occasions **:** not shabby or worn **:** BEST ⟨he's got one ~ suit —James Sheldrake⟩ ⟨she wore her ~ dress⟩ **b** (1) **:** adapted to the end designed or proposed **:** satisfactory in performance **:** free from flaws or defects **:** USEFUL, SUITABLE, FIT ⟨this light is ~ for reading⟩ ⟨a ~ car⟩ ⟨this liquor . . . will keep ~ for a long time —*Encyc. Americana*⟩ ⟨is this fruit ~ to eat⟩ (2) **:** not impaired **:** SOUND ⟨this missing eye had more expression than the . . . ~ one —Vicki Baum⟩ ⟨had to do everything with his one ~ arm⟩ ⟨your hearing is ~⟩ ⟨enjoying ~ health⟩ (3) **:** not downcast or dejected **:** amiably cheerful **:** SUNNY, SMILING ⟨found him in a ~ mood⟩ ⟨his ~ humor is infectious⟩ ⟨trying to put a ~ face on your wretchedness —William Black⟩ (4) **:** not counterfeit **:** GENUINE ⟨insisted the new car was financed with ~ money —*Springfield (Mass.) Union*⟩ **:** not depreciated ⟨bad money drives ~ money out of circulation⟩ (5) **:** commercially sound or reliable ⟨a ~ debt⟩ ⟨a ~ risk⟩ ⟨a ~ check⟩ (6) **:** having a useful life of a specified duration **:** certain to last or live for a specified term — used with *for* ⟨most swords . . . were ~ only for half a dozen hard blows —Tom Wintringham⟩ ⟨the old fellow is ~ for another 30 years⟩ ⟨from the feel of it, the storm would be ~ for three days —Robert Murphy⟩ (7) **:** having the assured capacity or willingness to pay or contribute a specified amount — used with *for* ⟨is ~ for a cool million⟩ ⟨confident his friend would be ~ for a few hundred —Henry Miller⟩ (8) **:** certain to elicit or produce a specified result — used with *for* ⟨the very sound of the word was always ~ for a laugh —Alfred Kazin⟩ ⟨that is ~ for a three months' debate by itself —*New Republic*⟩ (9) **:** PROFITABLE, LUCRATIVE, ADVANTAGEOUS ⟨made a very ~ deal⟩ — often used in the phrase *good thing* ⟨knew they were onto a ~ thing —Bryan Morgan⟩ and esp. in the phrase *make a good thing of* ⟨was supposed to be making a ~ thing out of it —Hamilton Basso⟩ ⟨British authors . . . made a ~ thing of coming over here —Richard Joseph⟩ **c** (1) **:** suited to give or giving pleasure **:** AGREEABLE, PLEASANT ⟨all had a ~ time⟩ ⟨a ~ dinner⟩ ⟨we enjoyed your ~ company⟩ (2) **:** tending to promote well-being or health **:** SALUTARY, WHOLESOME — used chiefly with *for* ⟨sunshine and fresh air are ~ for one⟩ ⟨this is ~ medicine for a cold⟩ (3) **:** entertaining by its wit or sparkle **:** AMUSING, CLEVER, FUNNY ⟨a ~ joke⟩ ⟨he got off some ~ cracks⟩ ⟨that's a ~ one⟩ **d** (1) **:** not small or insignificant **:** comfortably large **:** CONSIDERABLE ⟨quite a ~ crowd down here today —Greville Texidor⟩ ⟨outpointed the three-time national champion . . . by a ~ margin —*Current Biog.*⟩ ⟨made a ~ profit⟩ (2) **:** allowing enough time and usu. to spare **:** sufficiently early **:** AMPLE ⟨hoped to be . . . home in ~ time for 7:30 supper —Dorothy Sayers⟩ ⟨help came in ~ season⟩ (3) **:** FULL — used as a qualifier to indicate a quantity not less and generally greater than the stated figure ⟨the earrings are a ~ inch long —Lois Long⟩ ⟨she was making a ~ twenty-five knots —Wirt Williams⟩ ⟨weighs a ~ 200 pounds —*Current Biog.*⟩ ⟨a ~ four hours nightly —Eleanor S. Lowman⟩ (4) — used as an intensive ⟨took to reading in ~ earnest⟩ ⟨I have known him for a ~ many years⟩ ⟨dealt him a ~ stiff blow⟩ ⟨I didn't give a ~ continental —Eudora Welty⟩ (5) **:** half resolved or fixed upon ⟨I got a ~ mind not to tell you —J.G. Cozzens⟩ ⟨she had a ~ notion to thrash the boy⟩ **e** (1) **:** having a basis in fact or logic **:** WELL-FOUNDED, COGENT ⟨had ~ reason to distrust him⟩ ⟨offered some ~ arguments in debate⟩ ⟨gave a ~ excuse for his lateness⟩ (2) **:** not disproved or refuted — often used in the phrase *hold good* ⟨it will hold ~ when hundreds of cleverer . . . systems have vanished —J.C. Powys⟩ ⟨the same thing holds ~ for society at large —J.J. Chapman⟩ (3) **:** not potential or possible but actual **:** existing in fact **:** REAL ⟨the much-boosted prospect of oil . . . has not come ~ —*Sydney (Australia) Bull.*⟩ — often used in the phrase *make good* ⟨has made his promises ~⟩ (4) **:** having binding effect or force **:** RECOGNIZED, HONORED ⟨this offer is ~ only on orders sent direct to the publisher —*Current History*⟩ ⟨coupons ~ . . . at the local photographers —*Current Biog.*⟩ ⟨a refreshment coupon ~ for either a drink or a cigar —C.F. Wittke⟩ ⟨a union member in ~ standing⟩ (5) **:** valid or effectual for the transfer of title or the creation or vesting of rights ⟨a ~ deed⟩ ⟨a ~ tender⟩ ⟨a ~ delivery⟩ (6) **:** TRUE 3b(1); *also* **:** VALID 5 (7) **:** landing within the proper part of the court esp. in racket and net games and therefore in play — used esp. of a ball **f** (1) **:** conforming to the needs or requirements of the case **:** ADEQUATE, SUFFICIENT, SATISFACTORY ⟨took ~ care of his men⟩ ⟨gave a ~ account of himself in battle⟩ ⟨fetched him a ~ blow⟩ ⟨made ~ speed on the homeward journey⟩ ⟨sentimental history . . . revels in a ~ cry —Albert Guerard⟩ ⟨made ~ use of his time⟩ ⟨let me have a ~ look at you —T.B.Costain⟩ (2) **:** conforming to or attaining a certain standard of correctness, competence, skill, or excellence ⟨speaks ~ English⟩ ⟨plays a ~ game of tennis⟩ ⟨~ but not brilliant verse⟩ ⟨~ manners⟩ ⟨~ form⟩ (3) **:** DISCRIMINATING, CHOICE ⟨he shows unerring ~ taste⟩ (4) **:** better than average but short of excellent — used of scholastic work (5) **:** containing more lean muscle and less fat than higher grades — used of meat, esp. beef **2 a** (1) **:** conforming to a certain ideal or standard of morality or virtue **:** wholly commendable **:** VIRTUOUS, PURE ⟨~ works⟩ ⟨a truly ~ man⟩ ⟨a ~ conscience⟩ ⟨would only date ~ girls⟩ ⟨~ conduct is its own reward⟩; *specif* **:** possessing either absolute or intrinsic value (2) **:** conforming to some abstract standard or ideal (as of prudent conduct or proper condition) **:** RIGHT, DESIRABLE, WISE ⟨do what you think ~⟩ ⟨it is not ~ to fritter away one's time⟩ ⟨it is ~ to love and be loved⟩ (3) **:** directed or tending toward the welfare of another **:** BENEVOLENT, FRIENDLY, AMIABLE ⟨be ~ enough to answer this letter promptly⟩ ⟨did me a ~ turn⟩ ⟨~ intentions⟩ ⟨you have my ~ wishes⟩ ⟨sought to restore ~ feeling between England and her colonies⟩ (4) **:** well-regarded **:** being without stain **:** FAIR, HONORABLE ⟨a ~ name⟩ (5) **:** well-behaved **:** DECOROUS ⟨now, be a ~ boy⟩ (6) **:** not sulky **:** not rancorous nor given to complaint **:** not troublesome **:** GRACIOUS ⟨a ~ loser⟩ ⟨a ~ patient⟩ **b** (1) **:** belonging to the aristocracy or socially distinguished class **:** NOBLE, RESPECTABLE ⟨sardonic jabs at smug ~ families —Margaret Willis⟩ ⟨~ blood flowed in his veins —Frank Yerby⟩ **:** conferring or enhancing social prestige or respectability ⟨a comparatively new family . . . but had made ~ marriages —A.I.Macnaghten⟩ ⟨would need an apartment with a ~ address —Morley Callaghan⟩ (2) *archaic* **:** WORSHIPFUL, WORTHY — used as a conventional epithet in addressing persons of high rank (3) **:** DEAR, KIND, EXCELLENT — used as a conventional epithet in courteous address or respectful reference ⟨my ~ sir⟩ (4) — used of a ship or town as a conventional epithet ⟨the ~ town of Edinburgh⟩ ⟨sailed on the ~ ship *Enterprise*⟩ (5) *chiefly Scot* **:** standing in the relationship of an in-law of a specified kind ⟨~ brother⟩ ⟨~ sister⟩ **c** (1) **:** having or demonstrating the qualities or skills requisite or appropriate in a specified capacity or occupation ⟨a ~ doctor⟩ ⟨a ~ soldier⟩ ⟨a ~ housewife⟩ (2) **:** COMPETENT, SKILLFUL, ADROIT ⟨very ~ with children⟩ ⟨~ at tennis⟩ ⟨very ~ at dancing⟩ (3) **:** sound or faithful in doctrine or belief **:** ORTHODOX ⟨a ~ Catholic⟩ — **as good as** *prep* **:** faithful to ⟨a man *as good as* his word⟩ ⟨*as good as* his promise⟩ — **as good as gold 1 :** of the highest worth or reliability ⟨his promise is *as good as gold*⟩ **2 :** exemplary in deportment **:** well-behaved ⟨the child was *as good as gold*⟩ — **good and** *adv* **:** VERY, ENTIRELY, THOROUGHLY — used as an intensive ⟨was *good and* mad⟩ ⟨went up on deck when he was *good and* ready —William Irish⟩

²good \ˈ"\ *n* -s [ME, fr. OE *gōd*, fr. *gōd*, adj.] **1 a :** something that possesses desirable qualities, promotes success, welfare, or happiness, or is otherwise beneficial ⟨teach a child to know ~ from evil⟩ **b :** something that satisfies or commends itself to the ethical consciousness or is conceived as fitting in the moral order of the universe: (1) **:** something that is either an end in itself or a means to such an end ⟨among the concrete ~*s* traditionally nominated for the position of highest ~ of all . . . are happiness and self-realization —Lucius Garvin⟩ (2) **:** the character of human beings or of their attitudes, motives, and actions that is morally praiseworthy — compare ETHICS **c :** the good element or portion of anything ⟨cherished the ~ in him, overlooking the bad⟩ **2 :** advancement of interest or happiness **:** WELFARE, PROSPERITY, ADVANTAGE, BENEFIT ⟨worked for the ~ of the whole community⟩ ⟨what is the ~ of idle debate⟩ **3 a :** a particular advantage or benefit **:** an object of desire or endeavor **:** something beneficial; *specif* **:** something that has economic utility or satisfies an economic want **b goods** *pl* **:** tangible movable personal property having intrinsic value usu. excluding money and other choses in action but sometimes including all personal property and occas. including vessels and even industrial crops or emblements, buildings, or other things affixed to real estate but agreed to be severed **:** chattels, wares, merchandise, food products, chemical compounds, and agricultural products ⟨household ~*s*⟩ ⟨baked ~*s*⟩ **c goods** *pl but sometimes sing in constr* **:** CLOTH — compare DRESS GOODS, DRY GOODS **d goods** *pl, Brit* **:** FREIGHT ⟨heavier classes of ~*s* vehicles⟩ ⟨a ~*s* train⟩ **e goods** *pl* **:** the contents of the mash tub when the mashing process in brewing has been completed **f :** official grade for meat of medium quality **4 a :** good persons — used with *the* ⟨the ~ die young⟩ **b :** one that is good ⟨if it's any ~ you'll pay a lot for it⟩ ⟨she was no particular ~ —Ethel Wilson⟩ ⟨that's no ~; it won't work⟩ ⟨I have no use for him; he's no ~⟩ **5 goods** *pl but sometimes sing in constr* **a :** something that comes up to expectations or requirements **:** the genuine article ⟨a youthful work . . . but it is the ~*s* —Arnold Bennett⟩ **b :** the qualities required of one or necessary to accomplish a desired end ⟨that boy has the ~*s*⟩ **c :** evidence or proof of wrongdoing ⟨didn't have the ~*s* on him —T.G.Cooke⟩ — **for good** *also* **for good and all** *adv* **:** completely and finally **:** FOREVER, FULLY ⟨fearful of losing their jobs *for good* —Meridel Le Sueur⟩ — **in good with** *prep* **:** in a favored or preferred position with ⟨another effort . . . to get *in good with* their new masters —A.M.Schlesinger b.1917⟩ — **to the good 1 :** for the best **:** BENEFICIAL ⟨the government's efforts to restrict credit were all *to the good* —*Time*⟩ ⟨all this is *to the good* —Sir Winston Churchill⟩ **2 :** in a position of net gain or profit ⟨he wound up the game $10 *to the good*⟩ ⟨two wins in the home-and-home series put the team 4 points *to the good*⟩

³good \ˈ"\ *adv* [ME, fr. *good*, adj.] **1 a :** in a satisfactory, competent, or adequate manner **:** WELL ⟨he showed me how I was doing —Herbert Gold⟩ ⟨worked here once and did real ~⟩ ⟨don't you hear so ~, teacher —W.B.Marsh⟩ — not often in formal use **b :** PROSPEROUSLY, NICELY ⟨hope you . . . are well and getting along ~ —Walt Whitman⟩ **2** *chiefly dial* **:** TOTALLY, THOROUGHLY, COMPLETELY ⟨when it got ~ dark —F.B.Gipson⟩ — **as good :** equally well ⟨*as good* almost kill a man as . . . a good book —John Milton⟩ — **as good as** *adv* **:** in effect **:** APPROXIMATELY, PRACTICALLY, VIRTUALLY ⟨he is *as good as* dead⟩

good afternoon *interj* — used conventionally as an utterance on meeting or parting in the afternoon

good–afternoon \(ˌ)≡ˌ≡≡ˈ≡\ *n* [*good afternoon*] **:** a remark on meeting or parting in the afternoon

good and lawful *adj, of a member of a grand jury* **:** having every statutory as well as common-law qualification required

good behavior *n* **:** proper or correct conduct or deportment ⟨his sentence was reduced for *good behavior* —*N.Y. Times*⟩ ⟨shall hold their offices during *good behavior* —*U.S. Constitution*⟩ — **on one's good behavior** *or* **upon one's good behavior 1 :** in a state of trial with the final disposition dependent upon proper conduct **2 :** well-behaved

¹good–bye *or* **good–by** \gu̇dˈbī, gədˈbī, gəˈbī, ˈbī\ *interj* [contr. of *God be with you*] — used conventionally as a concluding utterance at parting or often at closing a telephone conversation

²good–bye *or* **good–by** \gu̇dˈbī, gəd-, *attrib* " *or* ˈgu̇dˌbī\ *n, pl* **good–byes** *or* **good–bys** *often attrib* **1 a :** a concluding remark at parting ⟨said *good-bye*⟩ ⟨the chorus of *good-byes* —David Wagoner⟩ **b :** a farewell gesture ⟨tearfully waving *good-bye* to a knot of friends —Winston Churchill⟩ ⟨nodding a casual *good-bye* —J.D.Beresford⟩ ⟨a *good-bye* kiss⟩ **2 a :** a taking of leave ⟨in wartime one can't afford emotional *good-byes* —Edita Morris⟩ ⟨kissed her grandmother in *good-bye* —Betty Smith⟩ **b :** a riddance to something left behind or finished with ⟨*good-bye* to all that⟩ ⟨*good-bye* to noisy blasts —*Boy Scout Handbook*⟩ ⟨the year to which we have just said *good-bye* —Harrison Smith⟩

good cause *n* **:** a cause or reason sufficient in law **:** one that is based on equity or justice or that would motivate a reasonable man under all the circumstances

good consideration *n* **1 :** a consideration of blood or of natural love and affection **2 :** a valuable consideration **:** a moral obligation founded on an antecedent legal obligation presently unenforceable **:** a consideration that will sustain a contract

good dame *n* [ME *gudame*, fr. *gud*, *good* + *dame*] *archaic* **:** GRANDMOTHER

good day *interj* [ME] — used conventionally as an utterance on meeting or parting during the day

good–day \gu̇(d)ˈdā, gəˈdā\ *n* [ME *good day*, fr. *good day*, interj.] **:** a remark on meeting or parting during the day

good deal \(ˈ)gu̇ˈdēl, *chiefly before pause or consonant* -ēəl\ *n* **:** GREAT DEAL — **a good deal** *adv* **:** a great deal

good doer *n* **:** an animal that with normal care produces or develops especially well

goo·de·nia \gu̇ˈdēnyə\ *n, cap* [NL, fr. Samuel *Goodenough* †1827 Eng. bishop and botanical writer + NL *-ia*] **:** the type genus of Goodeniaceae

goo·de·ni·a·ce·ae \(ˌ)gu̇ˌdēnēˈāsēˌē\ *n pl, cap* [NL, fr. *Goodenia*, type genus + *-aceae*] **:** a family of chiefly Australian herbs or shrubs (order Campanulales)

good evening *interj* — used conventionally as an utterance on meeting or parting in the evening

good–evening \gu̇ˈdēv-, gəˈdēv-\ *n* [*good evening*] **:** a remark on meeting or parting in the evening

good faith *n* **:** a state of mind indicating honesty and lawfulness of purpose **:** belief in one's legal title or right **:** belief that one's conduct is not unconscionable or that known circumstances do not require further investigation **:** absence of fraud, deceit, collusion, or gross negligence — usu. used with *in* ⟨the board need have no fear of being in contempt of court if it acted in *good faith* —J.B.Martin⟩

good father \ˈ≡ˌ≡≡\ *n, chiefly Scot* **:** FATHER-IN-LAW; *sometimes* **:** STEPFATHER

good fellow *n* **1 a** *archaic* **:** a drinking companion **:** ROISTERER, REVELER **b :** a jovial agreeable person typically radiating good humor and heartiness ⟨seeking to be *good fellows* at all costs —C.W.Ferguson⟩ **2** *obs* **:** THIEF, ROBBER

good–fellowship \(ˈ)≡ˈ≡≡ˌ≡\ *n* **:** a spirit existing among good fellows; *esp* **:** a spirit of friendship and goodwill

good folk *n pl* **:** FAIRIES — used with *the*

good–for–naught \ˈ≡≡ˌ≡\ *n* **:** GOOD-FOR-NOTHING

¹good–for–nothing \ˈ≡≡ˌ≡≡, ˌ≡≡ˈ≡≡\ *n* -s **:** an idle worthless person ⟨the meeting place of all the armed *good-for-nothings* of the district —*Atlantic*⟩

²good–for–nothing \ˈ"\ *adj* **:** of no value **:** USELESS, WORTHLESS ⟨could hear their two *good-for-nothing* canaries —Eudora Welty⟩

good–for–nothingness \ˌ≡≡ˈ≡≡≡, ˈ≡≡ˌ≡≡≡\ *n* -ES **:** the quality or state of being good-for-nothing

good friday *n, usu cap G&F* [ME] **:** the Friday before Easter celebrated in churches as the anniversary of the Crucifixion of Christ and observed as a legal holiday in some states of the U.S. and in many Christian countries

good–friday grass *n, cap 1st G&F* **:** a wood rush (*Luzula campestris*) with short stolons connecting small decumbent crowns

good god \ˈ≡ˌ≡\ *n, usu cap 2d G* **:** PILEATED WOODPECKER

good–hearted \ˈ≡ˈ≡≡\ *adj* **:** having a kindly beneficent nature or disposition ⟨a *good-hearted* man when he was sober —A. Conan Doyle⟩ **:** WELL-MEANING ⟨*good-hearted* but inept efforts —Douglass Cater⟩ — **good–heart·ed·ly** *adv* — **good–heart·ed·ness** *n* -ES

good–hen·ry \gu̇dˈhenrē\ *n, usu cap G&H* [fr. the name *Henry*] **:** GOOD-KING-HENRY

good–humored \ˈ≡ˈ≡≡\ *adj* **:** characterized by or indicating good humor **:** GOOD-NATURED — **good–hu·mored·ly** *adv* — **good–hu·mored·ness** *n* -ES

goodies *pl of* GOODY

good·ing \ˈgu̇dᵊn, -diŋ\ *n* -s [²*good* + *-ing*] **:** an asking of alms and wishing good to the donors in rural areas of England

good·ish \ˈgu̇dish, -dēsh\ *adj* **1 :** moderately good **:** rather good ⟨a ~ local white wine —G.A.Wagner⟩ **2 :** rather considerable (as in number or extent) ⟨a ~ walk —Mary Webb⟩

good joe \gu̇(d)ˈjō, ˈgu̇dˈjō\ *n, often cap J* **:** a kindly obliging good-hearted person ⟨my failure to answer his letter promptly . . . furnished proof that I was not, as he'd thought, a *good Joe* —Philip Wylie⟩ ⟨you can see he's a *good joe* —James Jones⟩

good–king–hen·ry \ˌgu̇dˌkiŋˈhenrē\ *n, usu cap G&K&H* [alter. (influenced by the name of *Henry* VII †1509 king of England) of *Good-Henry*] **:** a European plant (*Chenopodium bonus-henricus*) naturalized in No. America and formerly cultivated and often collected from the wild as a potherb

good lack *interj, archaic* — used to express surprise or objection

good life *n* **1 a :** a life lived in accordance with certain moral laws **:** a life of virtue ⟨most men will not attain the *good life*, and . . . for their sake it is necessary to institute the laws —Walter Lippmann⟩ ⟨felt most sincerely that they were trying to lead the *good life* —A.A.Cohen⟩ **b :** a life characterized by or tending toward the harmonious rounded many-sided cultural and material development of the individual **:** a life promoting individual self-realization ⟨editing a magazine is a form of the *good life*; it is creating when the world is destroying —*Time*⟩ ⟨preparing for . . . the *good life*, through one or two years of liberal studies at the graduate level —*Science*⟩ ⟨never . . . confused the *good life* with an efficient economy —Sidney Hook⟩ **2 :** a life marked by a high standard of living **:** a life of material well-being ⟨a tidy home, a new car, a television set . . . these are the measures of the *good life* for millions —A.H.Raskin⟩

goodlike \ˈ≡ˌ≡\ *adj* **1** *now dial Eng* **:** appearing to be good ⟨a ~ farmer⟩ **2** *now dial Eng* **:** GOOD-LOOKING, HANDSOME

good·li·ness \ˈgu̇dlēnəs, -lin-\ *n* -ES **:** the quality or state of being goodly

good liver *n* **:** a person who lives well or luxuriously **:** BON VIVANT

good–looker \(ˈ)≡ˈ≡≡\ *n* **:** a good-looking person ⟨didn't I tell you she was a *good-looker* —Christopher Isherwood⟩

good–looking \ˈ≡ˈ≡≡\ *adj* **1 :** having a pleasing or attractive appearance ⟨a *good-looking* car⟩ **:** HANDSOME, COMELY **:** not plain **:** not homely **:** not ugly ⟨not *good-looking* and yet not ugly, for his features were rather good —W.S.Maugham⟩ **2 :** serving to enhance one's appearance **:** BECOMING ⟨a *good-looking* coat⟩ ⟨her hairdo is *good-looking*⟩ **syn** see BEAUTIFUL

good–look·ing·ness *n* -ES **:** the quality or state of being good-looking

good·ly \ˈgu̇dlē, -li\ *adj* -ER/-EST [ME, fr. OE *gōdlīc*, fr. *gōd* good + *-līc* -ly — more at GOOD] **1 :** of pleasing appearance, character, or quality **:** COMELY, HANDSOME, EXCELLENT ⟨a ~ person⟩ ⟨~ houses⟩ **2 :** LARGE, CONSIDERABLE ⟨a ~ crowd was assembled —Sherwood Anderson⟩

good·man \ˈgu̇dmən\ *n, pl* **goodmen** [ME, fr. *good* + *man*] **1 a** *chiefly archaic & dial* **:** the head of a family or household **:** HUSBAND **b** *chiefly dial* **:** INNKEEPER, LANDLORD **2** *often cap, archaic* **:** MISTER — usu. used with a surname ⟨the roof on *Goodman* Hodge's barn —John Gay⟩ **3** *archaic Scot* **:** a well-to-do yeoman **:** a man of property

good morning *interj* — used conventionally as an utterance on meeting or parting in the morning

good–morning \ˌ=ˈ==\ *n* [*good morning*] **:** a remark on meeting or parting in the morning

good–morning–spring \ˌ=ˈ==ˈ=\ *n* **:** SPRING BEAUTY 1

good morrow *interj* [ME *good morwe*] *archaic* **:** GOOD MORNING

good–morrow *n* [*good morrow*] *archaic* **:** GOOD-MORNING ⟨then to come, in spite of sorrow, and at my window bid *good-morrow* —John Milton⟩

good nature *n* **:** pleasant cheerful disposition to please and be pleased, to accede to others' wishes, and to overlook slights, impositions, or causes for offense

good–natured \ˈ=ˈ==\ *adj* **1 :** showing or reflecting good nature ⟨as pleasantness, affability, geniality, and kindliness⟩ **:** marked by a disposition to please ⟨you've got such a nice *good-natured* face and way with you that I'm sure we'll agree —W.M.Thackeray⟩ ⟨a *good-natured* jest⟩ **2 :** possessed or indicative of a strong inclination to please or to accede to others' wishes to the extent of submitting to slights or impositions ⟨horseplay and practical jokes . . . require *good-natured* toleration —W.G.Sumner⟩ **3** *of glass* **:** retaining temperatures high enough to permit easy working or shaping — contrasted with *short-natured* **syn** see AMIABLE

good–na·tured·ly *adv* **:** in a good-natured manner

good–na·tured·ness *n* -ES **:** the quality or state of being good-natured

good–neighbor \(ˈ)=ˈ==\ *adj* **1 :** marked by the principles of friendship, cooperation, and noninterference in the internal affairs of another country ⟨the *good-neighbor* policy⟩ **2 :** of, relating to, or involving the Latin-American countries ⟨to avoid *good-neighbor* complications the nationality of the sailors . . . will be changed from Brazilian to Portuguese in the screen version —*Newsweek*⟩

good–neighborliness \(ˈ)=ˈ====\ *n* **:** friendship and cooperation with and noninterference in the internal affairs of another country

good–neighborly \(ˈ)=ˈ===\ *adj* **:** marked by good-neighborliness ⟨a wish for *good-neighborly* relations —Werner Levi⟩

good·ness \ˈgu̇dnə̇s, *in exclamatory phrases also* ˈgu̇nə̇s\ *n* -ES [ME *goodnesse*, fr. OE *gōdnes*, fr. *gōd* good + *-nes* -ness — more at GOOD] **1 :** the quality or state of being good: as **a :** moral excellence **:** VIRTUE, BENEVOLENCE, GENEROSITY ⟨extolled the ~ of God⟩ — often used interjectionally or in such phrases as *for goodness' sake, goodness gracious,* or *goodness knows* ⟨a smuggler and forger and ~ knows what else —C.L.Boltz⟩ **b :** excellence in respect to material quality ⟨the ~ of soil⟩ **2 :** the nutritious, flavorful, or beneficial portion or element of something ⟨boil all the ~ out of the coffee⟩

good night *in sense 1 with varying stress & intonation, in sense 2 with heavy or emphatic stress on each syllable*\ *interj* [ME] **1** — used conventionally as a concluding utterance on parting at night **2** — used esp. to express surprise

good–night \gu̇dˈnīt, gə(d)ˈn-, *usu* -īd.+V\ *n* [*good night*] **1 a :** a concluding remark on parting at night ⟨left him at the church . . . with conventional *good-nights* —Harry Sylvester⟩ **b :** a farewell gesture at night ⟨back-porch *good-night* kisses —Jan Struther⟩ **2 :** a ballad telling the story of an executed criminal

good now *interj, archaic* — used to express entreaty or surprise ⟨*good now*, say so but seldom —Shak.⟩

good offices *n pl* **:** services as a mediator esp. between belligerent or disputing states ⟨Soviet *good offices* for the repatriation of British civilian internees in North Korea —*N.Y. Times*⟩

good people *n pl* **:** FAIRIES — used with *the* ⟨you shouldn't speak like that of the *good people*, it will draw them on you —Robert Gibbings⟩

goods *pl of* GOOD

good samaritan *n, usu cap G&S* [after the *good Samaritan* in the Biblical parable (Lk 10:30–37)] **:** one who compassionately renders personal assistance to the unfortunate

goods and chattels *n pl* **:** animate or inanimate personal property that is visible, tangible, and movable and has intrinsic value in itself as distinguished from real estate or freehold property or from personal property of the class of choses in action; *sometimes* **:** all personal property esp. in wills sometimes including choses in action

goods and effects *n pl* **:** all movable personal property including usu. choses in action

good sense *n* **:** sound judgment often instinctive or unlearned ⟨had the *good sense* to save his money⟩ **syn** see SENSE

goodsire *var of* GUDESIRE

goods yard *n, Brit* **:** a yard where goods wagons are received, classified, and dispatched in trains

good–tempered \ˈ=ˈ==\ *adj* **:** having or reflecting a good temper **:** not wrathful, harsh, or bitter **:** not easily vexed ⟨*good-tempered* discussions of other work in this field —D.L.Olmsted⟩ ⟨very *good-tempered* people⟩ — **good–tem·pered·ly** *adv* — **good–tem·pered·ness** *n* -ES

good templar *n, usu cap G&T* **:** a member of a secret society organized in the 19th century for the promotion of total abstinence from the use of alcoholic beverages

good time *n* **:** a deduction for good behavior made from a convict's term of imprisonment

good–time char·lie *also* **good–time char·ley** \ˌ=ˈ=ˈchär\|lē, -ˈchȧ\|, \|li\ *n, usu cap C* [fr. the name *Charlie, Charley*, dim. of *Charles*] **:** a happy-go-lucky convivial man given to fun making, hilarity, and the general pursuit of amusement ⟨just a *good-time Charlie*, borrowing two bucks here and five bucks there —Walter Karig⟩ ⟨I couldn't be a *good-time Charlie* . . . when I was a kid I was taught not to talk or joke or laugh at the table —A.J.Liebling⟩

good·wife \(ˈ)gu̇ˌdwīf; (ˈ)gœˌdwəif, (ˈ)gɪ̄ˌ-,(ˈ)giˌd-\ *n, pl* **goodwives** [ME, fr. *good* + *wife*] **1** *chiefly Scot* **a :** the lady of the house **b :** the mistress of an inn **:** LANDLADY **2** *often cap, archaic* **:** MRS., MADAM 1 — usu. used with a surname ⟨~ Brown⟩

goodwill \(ˈ)=ˈ=\ *n, often attrib* [ME *good will*] **1 a :** kindly feeling **:** WELL-WISHING, BENEVOLENCE, FRIENDLINESS ⟨none of us have anything but ~ toward you personally —Ralph Ellison⟩ ⟨a happy man . . . is a radiating focus of ~ —R.L. Stevenson⟩ ⟨a ~ tour of seven European capitals —C.B. Palmer b.1910⟩ **b :** the custom of a trade or business **:** the favor or advantage in the way of custom that a business has acquired beyond the mere value of what it sells whether due to the personality of those conducting it, the nature of its location, its reputation for skill or promptitude, or any other circumstance incidental to the business and tending to make it permanent **c :** the capitalized value of the excess of estimated future profits of a business over the rate of return on capital considered normal in the related industry **d :** the excess of the purchase price of a business over and above the value assigned to its net assets exclusive of goodwill **2 a :** cheerful consent ⟨they accepted their new burdens with surprising ~⟩ **b :** HEARTINESS, ZEAL **:** willing effort ⟨the need is for mind to be applied . . . with the particular joy and ~ of creativeness —Lionel Trilling⟩ ⟨with a little ~, two other major philosophic strategies can be derived —K.D.Burke⟩ **3** *usu* **good will :** a will acting freely from pure disinterested motives ⟨the concept of the *good will* is ultimately the concept of the formal will —R.D. Mack⟩

good·will·it \gu̇dˈwilə̇t, gœˈ-,gɪ̄ˈ-,giˈ-\ *adj* [fr. earlier *gudewillit*, fr. *gudewill* (var. of *goodwill*) + *-it* (var. of *-ed*)] **:** GUIDWILLIE

¹goody \ˈgu̇dē, -di\ *n* -ES [alter. of *goodwife*] **1** *archaic* **:** a usu married woman of lowly station — often used as a title preceding a surname **2** *archaic* **:** a woman who takes care of students' rooms (as at Harvard university)

²goody \"\ *n* -ES [¹*good* + *-y* (n. suffix)] **1 a :** something (as a piece of candy) that is particularly good to eat — usu. used in pl. **b :** something that is peculiarly attractive, pleasurable, or good — usu. used in pl. ⟨other *goodies* include . . . a dance or beach dress —Lois Long⟩ ⟨such *goodies* as model trains, cameras, microscopes, and college educations —*Time*⟩ **2 :** SPOT 7 **3** *Midland* **:** the kernel of a nut

³goody \"\ *adj* [¹*good* + *-y* (adj. suffix)] **:** GOODY-GOODY

⁴goody \"\ *interj* [¹*good* + *-y* (adj. suffix)] — used esp. by children to express delight

goodyear *n, obs* — used esp. in the phrase *what the goodyear* as a mild expletive or expression of surprise, vexation, or emphasis ⟨what the ~, my lord! why are you thus out of measure sad —Shak.⟩

good·year welt \ˈgu̇d,yi(ə)r- *also* ˈgu̇,ji(ə)r-\ *n* [fr. *Goodyear Welt*, a trademark] **:** a method of shoe construction in which the insole, upper, and welt are sewed together and the welt is then stitched to the outsole so as to leave the upper surface of the insole free of tacks and stitches

good·yera \ˈgu̇dyərə, gu̇dˈyirə, ˈgu̇jə-, gu̇ˈji-\ *n, cap* [NL, after John *Goodyer* †1664 Eng. botanist] **:** a genus of small orchids of the northern hemisphere with creeping rhizomes, stalked ovate leaves, and small flowers in a twisted raceme — see RATTLESNAKE PLANTAIN

¹goody–goody \ˌ==ˈ==\ *adj* [redupl. of ³*goody*] **:** sentimentally, affectedly, or unctuously good ⟨a *goody-goody* boy —Havelock Ellis⟩

²goody–goody \"\ *n* **:** a person who is goody-goody ⟨her . . . generous nature had nothing in it of the *goody-goody* —Van Wyck Brooks⟩

goo·ey \ˈgüē, ˈgüi\ *adj* **goo·i·er; goo·i·est** [³*goo* + *-ey*] **1 :** VISCID, STICKY ⟨a geyser of coal-black, thick, ~ oil —H.A.Chippendale⟩ ⟨a ~ mess of grated cheese —Green Peyton⟩ **2 :** excessively effusive or sentimental **:** CLOYING ⟨gave me a big, ~ hello —Ethel Merman⟩ ⟨~ sentimentality⟩ ⟨~ romance and tear-jerking melodrama —*Time*⟩

gooey duck *var of* GEODUCK

¹goof \ˈgüf\ *n* -S [prob. alter. of ¹*goff*] **1 :** a ridiculous stupid person ⟨plays her as a simple country ~ —Harold Hobson⟩ **2 :** a blunder or mistake ⟨made a ~ —D.D.Eisenhower⟩

²goof \"\ *vb* -ED/-ING/-S *vi* **1 :** to make a mistake or blunder ⟨often misfired and ~*ed* —G.P.Crist⟩ ⟨somebody had ~*ed* —Ethel Merman⟩ **2** *slang* **a :** to spend time idly or foolishly **:** shirk work **:** kill time ⟨~*ed* on their way home from school —J.T.Farrell⟩ ⟨get into . . . jams because you were ~*ing* around —*Infantry Jour.*⟩ — often used with *off* ⟨somebody is ~*ing* off on the job —*Springfield (Mass.) Daily News*⟩ **b :** to have one's mind or attention wander **:** become abstracted — often used with *off* ⟨could see he wasn't drunk, he was ~*ing* off —Paul Monash⟩ **3** *slang* **:** to be in a state of euphoria induced by a narcotic substance ⟨bought some more stuff and ~*ed* around until night —Wenzell Brown⟩ **~** *vt* **1 :** to make a mess of (as a performance or operation) esp. through a stupid blunder **:** BUNGLE ⟨just ~*ed* it —C.B.Palmer b.1910⟩ — often used with *up* ⟨if I don't ~ up the situation —Calder Willingham⟩ ⟨you'd ~ things up good —Tom Walters⟩ **2** *slang* **:** to intoxicate or stupefy esp. with a narcotic substance — often used in the past participle with *up* ⟨pretty ~*ed* up that night —V.L.Preston⟩

goofa *or* **goofah** *var of* GUFA

goofball \ˈ=ˌ=\ *n* **1** *slang* **:** a barbiturate sleeping pill used esp. in alcoholic beverages to induce a transient euphoria **2** *slang* **:** a demented or abnormal person ⟨plenty ~*s* in this here town —Richard Bissell⟩

¹goof·er \ˈgüfə(r)\ *n* -S [¹*goof* + *-er*] **:** GOOF ⟨had a considerable understanding of ~*s* because . . . he was a little goofy himself —Esther Forbes⟩

²goo·fer \"\ *also* **guf·fer** \ˈgəfə(r)\ *n* -S [of African origin; akin to Mende *ngafa* spirit, ghost, Ewe *ga³fe³* shrine of a god, Fon *kafo* iron fetish] **1 :** a witch doctor among Negroes of the southern U.S.; *esp* **:** a voodoo doctor **2 :** a curse or spell ⟨put the ~ on us —J.S.Redding⟩

goofer dust *n* [²*goofer*] **:** a powder or dust used in conjuration; *esp* **:** earth from a grave used for such purpose

go off *vi* **1 :** to undergo removal **:** come to be taken off ⟨protesting that if he had him, his head should *go off* —John Davies †1693⟩ **2 a :** to undergo discharge or explosion **:** come to be discharged or exploded ⟨what happened when the hydrogen bomb *went off* must have surprised and astonished the scientists —A.P.Ryan⟩ **b :** to burst forth or break out in a sudden and often noisy manner ⟨*went off* into a . . . fit of laughter —M.V.Reidy⟩ **3 a :** to go forth or away **:** DEPART ⟨had to sit down and wait for her because I could not just *go off* like that without explaining —Francis Stuart⟩ **b :** to leave the stage ⟨the directions called for the heroine to *go off* left⟩ **4 a :** to pass into or as if into unconsciousness ⟨*went off* at the first whiff of ether —O.S.J.Gogarty⟩ **b :** DIE ⟨the doctors told me that he might *go off* any day —H.R.Haggard⟩ **5 :** to find a purchaser **:** SELL ⟨trade flourishes and his commodities *go off* well —John Locke⟩ **6 :** to undergo decline or deterioration ⟨those clarkias have *gone off* very quickly —F.A.Swinnerton⟩ ⟨a small quantity of water . . . *goes off* quickly and loses its freshness —Henry Wynmalen⟩ **7 :** to follow the expected or desired course **:** PROCEED ⟨I had the assignment of it, but it seemed to *go off* pretty well —O.W.Holmes †1935⟩ **8 :** to make a characteristic noise **:** SOUND ⟨around one in the morning the sirens had *gone off* —Irwin Shaw⟩ **:** RING — **go off the deep end 1 :** to enter recklessly upon a course **:** go off half-cocked **:** become rapidly involved (as in difficulties) **2 :** to lose self-control **:** become very much excited

go–off \ˈ=ˌ=\ *n* -S [*go off*] **:** the act or time of going off **:** BEGINNING, START ⟨awaiting the *go-off* of a bomb —Speed Lamkin⟩ ⟨we were correct at the first *go-off* —*Amer. Antiquity*⟩

goof·i·ly \ˈgüfəlē, -li\ *adv* **:** in a goofy manner

goof·i·ness \-fēnə̇s, -fin-\ *n* -ES **:** the quality or state of being goofy ⟨seems to detect in my remarks a slight ~ —P.G. Wodehouse⟩

goofy \ˈgüfē, -fi\ *adj* -ER/-EST [¹*goof* + *-y*] **:** CRAZY, SILLY ⟨it sounds ~, but I'll do it —Erle Stanley Gardner⟩ ⟨this guy's ~ —Earle Birney⟩

goog \ˈgüg, ˈgu̇g\ *n* -S [origin unknown] *Austral* **:** EGG

¹goo·gly \ˈgüglē, -li\ *n* -ES [origin unknown] **:** an offbreak in cricket with a leg-break action — called also *bosey, wrong 'un*

²googly \"\ *adj* [alter. of *goggly*] **:** BULGING, STARING ⟨a large scarecrow with ~ eyes —Evelyn Woodforde⟩

googly–eyed \ˌ==ˈ=\ *adj* **:** GOGGLE-EYED

goo·gol \ˈgü,gȯl\ *n* -S [coined by Milton Sirotta, nine-year-old nephew of Dr. Edward Kasner †1955 Am. mathematician] **:** the figure 1 followed by 100 zeroes equal to 10^{100}

goo·gol·plex \-,pleks\ *n* -ES [*googol* + *-plex* (as in *duplex*)] **:** the figure 1 followed by a googol of zeroes equal to $10^{10^{100}}$

¹goo–goo \ˈgü(,)gü\ *adj* [prob. alter. of ¹*goggle*] **:** LOVING, ENTICING, AMOROUS — used chiefly in the phrase *goo-goo eyes* ⟨make *goo-goo* eyes at each other —*New Republic*⟩

²goo–goo \"\ *n* -S [fr. the initials of *good government*] **:** a member or advocate of a reform movement in politics esp. in the era of Theodore Roosevelt — usu. used disparagingly ⟨this group was contemptuously dismissed by machine politicians as *goo-goos* —*Fortune*⟩

³goo–goo *var of* GUGU

gooier *comparative of* GOOEY

gooiest *superlative of* GOOEY

¹gook \ˈgu̇k, ˈgük\ *n* -S [origin unknown] **:** a native belonging usu. to a brown or yellow race — usu. used disparagingly ⟨a little South Korean boy whom he starts by calling a ~ and ends by loving as a son —Robert Hatch⟩

²gook \"\ *n* -S [perh. alter. of ³*goo*] **1 :** sticky or gooey stuff ⟨painted the resulting ~ on the backs of black mice —*Time*⟩ **2 :** TRASH, JUNK, NONSENSE ⟨that's a lot of ~⟩

¹gool \ˈgül\ *n* -S [MF *gole, goule* throat, narrow passage, fr. L *gula* throat — more at GLUTTON] *now dial Eng* **:** a ditch or channel for water **:** SLUICE

²gool \"\ *n* -S [by alter.] *dial* **:** GOAL ⟨use the big cedar tree for ~⟩

goold \ˈgüld\ *Scot var of* GOLD

goo·ly \ˈgülē\ *n* -ES [origin unknown] *Austral* **:** STONE ⟨someone's been bunging *goolies* through her window —Ruth Park⟩

goom \ˈgüm, ˈgu̇m\ *dial var of* GUM

goo·ma \ˈgümə\ *n* -S [native name in Australia] **:** an Australian shrub (*Bertya cunninghami*) of the family Euphorbiaceae used in arid regions as fodder

goom·bay \ˈgümˌbā, ˈgüm-, =ˈ=\ *n* -S [of Bantu origin; akin to Kongo *nkumbi* ceremonial drum, Tshiluba *nkumbi* drum] **:** calypso music as developed in the Bahamas

go on *vi* **1 a :** to continue with or as if with a journey ⟨*went on* by train after the plane was grounded⟩ **b :** to continue in or as if in a course of action ⟨despite the heat he *went on* with his work⟩ **2** *obs* **:** to engage in a military attack ⟨the sergeant in *going on* was shot through the body —Fynes Moryson⟩ **3 a :** to proceed by or as if by a logical step ⟨after discoursing at some length on pronunciation, the professor *goes on* to vocabulary —Nancy Mitford⟩ **b** *of time* **:** PASS ⟨new art forms developed as the century *went on*⟩ **4 :** to take place **:** HAPPEN, OCCUR ⟨learn what is *going on* elsewhere —Bernard DeVoto⟩ **5 a :** to get along **:** FARE, MANAGE ⟨wondered if he could *go on* alone after his partner's death⟩ **b :** to deport oneself **:** ACT, BEHAVE ⟨we plagued and *went on* with him shamefully —Emily Brontë⟩ **6 :** to be capable of being put on ⟨washed her gloves and found that they wouldn't *go on*⟩ **7 a :** to talk esp. in an effusive manner ⟨the way people *go on* about their ancestors —Hamilton Basso⟩ **b :** RAIL, STORM ⟨didn't you hear the canon *going on* at her this morning? —Margaret Kennedy⟩ **8 a :** to come into operation, action, or production ⟨the lights *went on* an hour after the storm had ended⟩ **b :** to appear on the stage ⟨the callboy knocked five minutes before the actor was to *go on*⟩ **c :** to begin bowling in cricket ⟨a good time for a slow left-hander to *go on*⟩ — **go on for :** APPROACH, NEAR ⟨it must be *going on for* nine —Archibald MacLeish⟩

goon \ˈgün\ *n* -S [partly short for E dial. *gooney* simpleton, var. of *gony, gawney*; partly after Alice the *Goon*, a subhuman creature appearing in the comic strip *Thimble Theatre* by E. C. Segar †1938 Am. cartoonist] **1 :** a man hired (as by a racketeer) to terrorize or eliminate opponents **:** THUG, HATCHET MAN **2** *slang* **a :** a dull or unattractive person lacking conversational ability, esprit, or other social graces ⟨I'm mad about my Fine Arts prof . . . I know he's a ~, but I can't help it —Herman Wouk⟩ **b :** DOPE, SAP, BOOB ⟨don't be a ~ . . . don't be positively medieval —Catherine Hutter⟩

goonch \ˈgünch\ *n, pl* **goonch** *or* **goonches** [Hindi *gūc*] **:** a large voracious Indian freshwater catfish (*Bagarius bagarius*) believed to attain a weight of 250 pounds and a length of 6 feet

goon·da \ˈgündə\ *n* -S [Hindi *gunḍā* rascal, crook] *India* **:** professional terrorist **:** HOOLIGAN, GOON, THUG

goon·die \ˈgündē\ *n* -S [native name in Australia] **:** an Australian aboriginal hut

goo·ney *also* **goo·ny** *or* **goo·nie** \ˈgünē\ *n, pl* **gooneys** *also* **goonies** [prob. fr. E dial. *gooney* simpleton, var. of *gony, gawney*] **:** ALBATROSS; *esp* **:** BLACK-FOOTED ALBATROSS

goon·gar·rite \gün'ga,rīt, ˈgüngə,r-\ *n* -S [Lake *Goongarrie*, Western Australia + E *-ite*] **:** a mineral $Pb_4Bi_2S_7$ that consists of a sulfide of lead and bismuth and is found at Lake Goongarrie, Western Australia

¹goop \ˈgüp\ *n* -S [coined *ab*1900 by Gelett Burgess †1951 Am. humorist and illustrator] **1 :** a bad-mannered child ⟨don't act like a ~⟩ **2** *slang* **:** a dull, graceless, or simple-minded person **:** BOOB, DOPE ⟨such a big nerveless ~ —G.R. Stewart⟩ ⟨he was a ~, anyway —J.T.Farrell⟩

²goop \"\ *n* -S [prob. alter. of ³*goo*] **:** a viscid or sticky substance **:** GOO ⟨the ~ that comes from the tube —Alfred Frankenstein⟩ ⟨glanced at the brownish ~ congealed around the can —Maxwell Griffith⟩

³goop \"\ *vi* -ED/-ING/-S [prob. blend of ³*goo* and *drip*] *of a pen* **:** to drop blobs of ink on paper

goor *var of* GUR

gooral *var of* GORAL

goora·nut \ˈgu̇rə,=\ *n* [*goora-* of West African origin; akin to Hausa *go³ro¹* kola nut, Bambara & Malinke *goro, guro*] **:** KOLA NUT

goos *pl of* GOO

goo·san·der \gü'sandə(r), ˈ=,==\ *n* -S [alter. of earlier *gossander*, prob. fr. *gos-* (as in *gosling*) + *bergander*] **:** the common merganser (*Mergus merganser*) of the northern hemisphere

¹goose \ˈgüs\ *n, pl* **geese** \ˈgēs\ *see senses 4 and 5* [ME *goos, gos*, fr. OE *gōs*; akin to OHG *gans* goose, ON *gās*, L *anser*, Gk *chēn*, Skt *haṁsa*] **1 a :** any of numerous birds constituting a distinct subfamily of Anatidae, being in many respects intermediate between the swans and ducks, having a high somewhat compressed bill, legs of moderate length, completely feathered lores, and reticulate tarsi, and being usu. larger and longer-necked than ducks; *esp* **:** a member of any of the several breeds developed in domestication for their flesh and feathers — see BARNACLE GOOSE, BRANT, SNOW GOOSE **b :** a female goose as distinguished from a gander **c :** the flesh of a goose used for food **2 :** a silly person **:** SIMPLETON ⟨such a ~ I have seldom seen —Rachel Henning⟩ **3 a :** an obsolete game played with counters on a board **b :** KENO GOOSE **4** *pl* **gooses :** a tailor's smoothing iron with a gooseneck handle **5** *pl* **gooses :** an instance of goosing; *specif* **:** a poke between buttocks

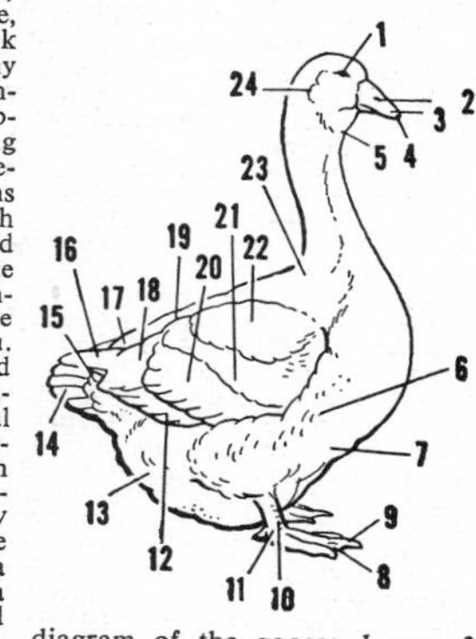

diagram of the goose: *1* eye, *2* nostril, *3* bill, *4* lobes, *5* dewlap, *6* breast, *7* keel, *8* web, *9* toes, *10* shank, *11* foot, *12* pinion coverts, *13* fluff, *14* tail feathers, *15* tail coverts, *16* wing flight feathers, *17* rump, *18* wing secondaries, *19* saddle, *20* wing coverts, *21* wing bow, *22* shoulder, *23* cape, *24* ear

²goose \"\ *vt* -ED/-ING/-S [prob. so called fr. the fancied resemblance of an upturned thumb to the outstretched neck of a goose] **1 :** to poke or dig (a person) in some sensitive spot; *esp* **:** to poke (a person) between buttocks with an upward thrust of a finger or hand from the rear **2 :** to feed gasoline to (an engine) in spurts

goose barnacle *n* **:** a barnacle of the family Lepadidae attached by a leathery stalk to rocks of the intertidal zone or to floating logs or the bottom of ships where they are sometimes important fouling organisms

goose·ber·ry \ˈgüs-, ˈgüz-, *chiefly Brit* ˈgu̇z- — see BERRY\ *n* **1 a :** the acid usu. bristly or spiny fruit of any of several shrubs of the genus *Ribes* **b :** a shrub bearing gooseberries **c :** CURRANT 2 **d :** any of numerous shrubs resembling the gooseberry — usu. used with an attributive ⟨American ~⟩ ⟨Barbados ~⟩ **2 :** a dark purplish red that is bluer and duller than pansy purple, bluer and less strong than raisin, and bluer and paler than Bokhara

gooseberry gourd *n* **:** GHERKIN

gooseberry mildew *n* **1 :** a mildew affecting gooseberries; *esp* **:** a mildew caused by a powdery mildew (*Sphaerotheca mors-uvae* or *Microsphaera grossulariae*) **2 :** a fungus that causes gooseberry mildew

gooseberry rust *n* **:** any of several diseases of gooseberries caused by true rust fungi (as *Cronartium ribicola*)

gooseberry tree *n* **:** OTAHEITE GOOSEBERRY

goose bumps *n pl* **:** GOOSEFLESH

goosecap \ˈ=,=\ *n, chiefly dial* **:** a silly person; *esp* **:** a flighty young girl

goose–drown·der \ˈ=,draundə(r)\ *n, chiefly Midland* **:** a heavy fall of rain **:** DOWNPOUR

goose egg *n* [so called fr. the egg-shaped numeral 0] **:** ZERO, NOTHING, FAILURE; *esp* **:** a score of zero in a game or contest

goosefish \ˈ=,=\ *n, pl* **goosefish** *or* **goosefishes :** ANGLER 2

gooseflesh \ˈ=,=\ *n* **:** a roughness of the skin produced by erection of its papillae and usu. caused by cold or fear — called also *goose bumps, goose pimples*

gooseflower \ˈ=,=\ *n* **:** PELICAN FLOWER

goosefoot \ˈ=,=\ *n, pl* **goosefoots 1 :** a plant of the family Chenopodiaceae and esp. of the genus *Chenopodium* **2 :** a southern African velvety shrub (*Aspalathus chenopoda*)

goosefoot family *n* **:** CHENOPODIACEAE

goosefoot maple *n* **:** STRIPED MAPLE

goosegirl \ˈ=,=\ *n* [trans. of G *gänsemädchen*] **:** a girl goose-herd

goose·gog \ˈgüz,gäg\ *n* -s [¹*goose* + *-gog* (origin unknown)] *dial Brit* : GOOSEBERRY

goose grass *n* **1 a** : CLEAVERS **b** : KNOTGRASS 1 **c** : SILVERWEED a(1) **d** : ARROW GRASS 1 **2 a** : YARD GRASS **b** : TEXAS MILLET **c** : SOFT CHEAT **d** : HORSETAIL 2

goose gray *n* : LAMA 2

goose gull *n* : GREAT BLACK-BACKED GULL

gooseherd \ˈ=,=, *chiefly dial* ˈgäzə(r)d\ *n* : one who tends geese

goose influenza *or* **goose septicemia** *n* : a usu. fatal disease of young geese marked by pulmonary inflammation, loss of appetite, and staggering gait and believed caused by a bacterium (*Shigella septicaemiae*)

gooseneck \ˈ=,=\ *n, often attrib* : something (as a faucet or pipe) curved like the neck of a goose or U-shaped: as **a** : a connecting pipe in a distilling apparatus **b** : the bar used to couple two logging trucks or sleds; *also* : the curved iron driven into the bottom of a slide to check descending logs **c** : an iron hook connecting a spar with a mast — **goose-necked** \ˈ=,=\ *adj*

gooseneck lamp *n* : an electric table lamp or desk lamp with a flexible shaft that permits control of the direction of the light

goose-neck lamp

gooseneck pediment *n* : a pediment formed of two balancing double-curved molded members ending in a scroll or rosette

gooseneck slicker *n* : an implement consisting of a long flat blade that is attached to the rear of sled runners with gooseneck arms and that runs under the soil surface to cut off weeds on fallow land

gooseneck trailer *n* : a truck trailer whose forward part is arched like a goose's neck and swiveled to the motor unit

goose pen *n* **1** : a pen for geese **2** : a hole burned in a standing tree

goose pimples *n pl* : GOOSEFLESH — **goose-pimply** \ˈ=,=(=)=\ *adj*

goose plant *n* : PELICAN FLOWER

goose plum *n* : an American wild plum (*Prunus americana*)

goose quill *n* : a quill of a goose; *also* : a quill pen

goose rump *n* : a rump (as of a horse) having considerable slope so that the tail is set down low

goose-rumped \ˈ=,=\ *adj* : having a goose rump

gooses *pl of* GOOSE, *pres 3d sing of* GOOSE

gooseskin \ˈ=,=\ *n* **1** : the skin of a goose **2** : GOOSEFLESH **3** : a pitted surface exhibited by some fossil copal

goose step *n* [trans. of G *gänseschritt*] : a straight-legged stiff-kneed step used by foot troops of some armies when passing in review

goose-step \ˈ=,=\ *vi* [*goose step*] **1** : to march in a goose step ⟨soldiers *goose-stepped* into the ancient capital⟩ **2** : to practice an unthinking conformity in thought or action : conform esp. under social pressure or from fear of reprisal ⟨a society *goose-stepping* to a set of taboos —W.W.Howells⟩ — **goose-stepper** \ˈ=,==\ *n*

goose tansy *n* : SILVERWEED a(1)

goosetongue \ˈ=,=\ *n* **1** *dial Eng* **a** : SNEEZEWORT 2 **b** : CLEAVERS **c** : BALM 3a **2** *dial Eng* : any of certain plantains (as *Plantago maritima* and *P. juncoides decipiens*)

¹**goosewing** \ˈ=,=\ *n* [¹*goose* + *wing*] : the weather lower corner of a course or topsail when the middle and lee parts of the sail are hauled up

²**goosewing** \"\ *vt* : to make goosewinged ~ *vi* : to sail with the wind aft, the jib out on one side, and the mainsail out on the other

goosewinged \ˈ=,wiŋd\ *adj* **1** : having the lee clew and middle of the sail hauled up and the weather part extended by the tack and drawing — used of a square sail **2** : having foresail set on one side and mainsail on the other : WING AND WING — used of a fore-and-aft-rigged ship

goos·ey *also* **goosy** \ˈgüsē, -si\ *adj* **goos·i·er**; **goos·i·est** **1 a** : belonging to or resembling a goose ⟨stretching out long ~ necks —D.C.Peattie⟩ **b** : FOOLISH, STUPID **2 a** : affected with gooseflesh : SCARED ⟨she had me quite ~ by her tales, weird and impossible as they were —Harry Lauder⟩ **b** : very nervous : SKITTISH ⟨a ~ horse . . . he hadn't been under saddle half a dozen times —F.B.Gipson⟩ **c** : susceptible to or reacting strongly (as by jumping in the air) to goosing : TICKLISH

goosing *pres part of* GOOSE

goote \ˈgüt\ *n* -s [native name in India] *India* : MARCOT

goo·tee \ˈgü,tē\ *n* -s [native name in India] *India* : AIR LAYERING, MARCOTTAGE

go out *vi* **1 a** : to go forth, abroad, or out of doors ⟨decided to *go out* to the stadium for the weigh-in and buy my ticket there —A.J.Liebling⟩; *specif* : to leave one's house ⟨induced me to *go out* for the evening —A.N.Whitehead⟩ **b** (1) : to take the field as a soldier ⟨there are other men fitter to *go out* than I —Shak.⟩ (2) : to participate as a principal in a duel **c** : to travel as or as if a colonist or immigrant ⟨a lad who *goes out* to the Canadian Rockies —*Brit. Book News*⟩ **d** : to work away from home ⟨is a workman's wife and has herself *gone out* as a char when things were difficult —*Saturday Rev.*⟩ **e** : to play the first nine holes of an 18-hole golf match ⟨*went out* in 38 and finished with 35 for a score of 73⟩ **2 a** : to come to an end ⟨March came in like a lion and *went out* like a lamb⟩ **b** : to become extinguished ⟨after a moment the hall light *went out* and she could hear . . . footsteps —Margaret A. Barnes⟩ **c** : to give up office : RESIGN ⟨an absolute certainty that the government will *go out* —Rachel M. Praed⟩ **d** : to become obsolete or unfashionable ⟨the sort of caricature that *went out* with twenty-three skiddoo —Charles Lee⟩ **e** *of the tide* : EBB, RECEDE **f** : to cease to operate or function : FAIL ⟨the men were ordered to jump when two of the plane's four engines *went out* —*Springfield (Mass.) Union*⟩ **g** : to end one's turn at bat (as in baseball) : make an out ⟨the batter *went out* on a fly to right field⟩ **h** (1) : to play the last card of one's hand (2) : to reach or exceed the total number of points required for game in cards **i** : DIE ⟨the patient caught pneumonia and *went out* shortly before midnight⟩ **3** : to take part in social activities ⟨the high-school set *went out* constantly during the holidays⟩ **4** : to take a B.A. degree at Cambridge University ⟨had *gone out* in honors, having been a second-class man —Anthony Trollope⟩ **5** : to become emotionally drawn or impelled : issue forth : flow out ⟨his sympathy *went out* to whoever suffered . . . from the injustice of society —V.L.Parrington⟩ **6** : to go on strike ⟨ready to *go out* also were 6000 textile workers —*Time*⟩ **7** : to become spread abroad : come to be issued or published ⟨an interoffice memo *goes out* in sixteen copies —J.M.Barzun⟩ **8** : to give way to pressure : BREAK, COLLAPSE ⟨a dam that might *go out* and drown many thousand people —F.D.Roosevelt⟩ **9** : to become a candidate : try out ⟨*went out* for the . . . team as a sixteen-year-old in his junior year —Stanley Frank⟩

go over *vi* **1** : to make one's way : go on or as if on a journey ⟨has *gone over* to the coast for a few days⟩ **2** : to become converted; *esp* : to turn from a religious or political belief ⟨a priest who *went over* to the Revolution and had much influence in those times —H.J.Laski⟩ **3** : to undergo postponement ⟨asked that the matter *go over* until tomorrow — and there it stands —A.H.Vandenberg⟩ **4** : to receive approval : SUCCEED ⟨the humor is rudimentary, but it *goes over* big in the wards —Hartzell Spence⟩ **5** : to make a touchdown in football ⟨the fullback *went over* from the 12-yard line⟩ — **go over the hill 1** : to leave one's military unit without authorization ⟨the boys would *go over the hill* their first shore leave —Frederic Wakeman⟩ **2** : to disappear without warning or explanation ⟨has *gone over the hill* with the ministry's payroll —*Time*⟩

goo·zle \ˈgüzəl\ *n* -s [by alter.] *dial* : GUZZLE 2

go·pak \ˈgō,pak\ *n* -s [Russ, fr. Ukrainian *hopak*, fr. *hop*, interj. used in lively dances, fr. G *hopp*; akin to MHG *hüpfen*, *hopfen* to hop — more at HOP] : a Ukrainian folk dance with heel beats

¹**go·pher** \ˈgōfə(r)\ *n* -s [short for earlier *megopher*, of unknown origin] **1 a** : a burrowing land tortoise (*Gopherus polyphemus*) of the coastal region of the southern U.S. whose shell attains the length of a foot or more and whose eggs and flesh are used as food **b** : any of several related land tortoises **2 a** : any of several burrowing rodents (family Geomyidae) of western No. America, Central America, and the southern U.S. east to Georgia that are the size of a large rat and have small eyes, short ears, strong claws on the forelimbs, and large cheek pouches opening beside the mouth — called also *pocket gopher* **b** (1) : any of numerous small ground squirrels of the prairie region of No. America that belong to the genus *Citellus* and are closely related to the chipmunks (2) : any of numerous related animals (as chipmunks, marmots, prairie dogs) **3** : GOPHER SNAKE **4** *also* **gopher rock cod** : any of various rockfishes of the genus *Sebastodes* **5** *usu cap* : MINNESOTAN — used as a nickname **6** : GOPHERMAN 2

²**gopher** \"\ *vi* -ED/-ING/-S : to mine haphazardly in irregular holes

gopher ball *n* : a pitched ball hit for extra bases; *specif* : one hit for a home run

go·pher·ber·ry \ˈgōfə(r)- — *see* BERRY\ *n* : BUSH HUCKLEBERRY

gopher frog *n* : a frog (*Rana aesopus*) of the southeastern U.S. often found in the burrows of the gopher tortoise

gopher hole *n* **1** : the hole of a gopher **2** : COYOTE HOLE

go·pher·man \-mən, -,man\ *n, pl* **gophermen 1** : a mine worker who extracts ore from pockets that are inaccessible to drilling machines **2** : a logger who digs earth from beneath logs at the point where the skidding chain is to be placed — called also *gopher, swamper*

gopher plant *n* : CAPER SPURGE

gopher plum *n* **1** : OGEECHEE LIME **2** *or* **gopher apple** : either of two plants of the genus *Chrysobalanus*: **a** : COCO PLUM **b** : a low spreading shrub (*C. oblongifolius*) of sandy soil of the southeastern U.S., Mexico, and the West Indies having a fruit that is important in the diet of many small animals (as the land tortoise)

gopher snake *n* **1** : INDIGO SNAKE **2** : BULL SNAKE

gopher tortoise *or* **gopher turtle** *n* : GOPHER 1

gopher wood \ˈgōfə(r),=\ *n* [Heb *gōpher*] : an unidentified wood used in the construction of Noah's ark ⟨make yourself an ark of *gopher wood* —Gen 6:14 (RSV)⟩

gopherwood \"\ *n* [¹*gopher* + *wood*] : YELLOWWOOD 1a

go·pu·ra \ˈgōpərə\ *also* **go·pu·ram** \-rəm\ *n* -s [Skt *gopura*, fr. *go* cow, bull + *pura* city, abode — more at COW, POLICE] : the gateway of a temple in southern India; *often* : the massive tower resembling a pyramid above the gateway

go-quick \ˈ=,=\ *n* : FLOWERING SPURGE

gor \ˈgȯ(ə)r, -ȯ(ə)\ *interj* [euphemism] *dial Brit* : GOD — usu. used as a mild oath ⟨by ~, he determined to improve his luck —Samuel Lover⟩

go·ra *or* **go·rah** \ˈgōrə\ *also* **gou·ra** \ˈgůrə\ *n* -s [Hottentot] : a Hottentot musical bow having its string attached to a quill or reed fixed at one end of the stick and made to vibrate by the breath of the player and combining the qualities of a stringed and a wind instrument

go·rac·co \gəˈrä(,)kō, -ra(-\ *n* -s [Hindi *gurākū*, fr. *gur* molasses — more at GUR] : a tobacco paste smoked in hookahs

go·ral \ˈgōrəl\ *or* **goo·ral** \ˈgůr-\ *n, pl* **gorals** *or* **goral** *or* **goorals** *or* **gooral** [perh. fr. a modern Indic word derived fr. Skt *gaura* gaur — more at GAUR] : any of several goat antelopes (genus *Naemorhedus*) occurring from the southern Himalayas to northern parts of China and being closely related to the Rocky Mountain goat

go·ran \gəˈrän\ *n* -s [Bengali *garān*] : either of two Indian mangroves (*Ceriops roxburghiana* and *C. candolleana*) of the family Rhizophoraceae valued for a tanning extract derived from the bark

gor·ble \ˈgȯrbəl\ *vi* [prob. by alter.] *chiefly Scot* : GOBBLE

gor·bli·mey \gȯ(r)ˈblīmi\ *interj, usu cap* [euphemism for *God blind me*] *Brit* — used to express amazement, surprise, or perplexity ⟨*Gorblimey* . . . it's fourteen feet long! —Guy Gilpatric⟩

gor·ceix·ite \ˈgȯ(r)sək,sīt\ *n* -s [G *gorceixit*, fr. Henrique *Gorceix* †1919 Brazilian mineralogist + G *-it* -ite] : a mineral $BaAl_3(PO_4)_2(OH)_5.H_2O$(?) consisting of a hydrous basic phosphate of barium and aluminum

gor·cock \ˈgȯr,käk\ *n* [*gor-* (origin unknown) + *cock*] *dial chiefly Brit* : a male red grouse

gor·crow \-,krō\ *n* [¹*gore* (filth) + *crow*] : CARRION CROW

gor·di·a·cea \,gȯ(r)dēˈāsh(ē)ə\ [NL, fr. *Gordius* genus of roundworms (after *Gordius* of Phrygia) + *-acea*] *syn of* NEMATOMORPHA

gor·di·a·cean \ˌ==ˈāsh(ē)ən\ *adj or n* [NL *Gordiacea* + E *-an*] : NEMATOMORPHAN

gordiaceous *adj* [NL *Gordiacea* + E *-ous*] : of, relating to, or being a member of the Nematomorpha

¹**gor·di·an** \ˈgȯ(r)dēən\ *n* -s [*Gordius* of Phrygia + E *-an* (n. suffix)] **1** *usu cap, archaic* : GORDIAN KNOT **2** [NL *Gordius* genus of roundworms + E *-an*] : a member of the Gordioidea

²**gordian** \"\ *adj* [*Gordius* of Phrygia + E *-an* (adj. suffix)] **1** *sometimes cap* : INTRICATE, COMPLICATED **2** [NL *Gordius* + E *-an*] : of or relating to the Gordioidea

gordian knot *n, often cap G* [*Gordius*, mythological founder of Phrygia, who tied an intricate knot in a chariot thong the untying of which was pronounced by oracle to be possible only to one destined to be master of Asia (fr. L, fr. Gk *Gordios*) + E *-an*] **1** : a problem most difficult of solution : an extreme difficulty ⟨this problem of slavery was to me a *gordian knot* —C.W.Garrison⟩ — usu. used in the phrase *cut the gordian knot* ⟨the temptation to cut the *gordian knots* of meaning by essentialist definitions —H.D.Aiken⟩; compare *cut the knot* at ¹CUT **2** : a knot so involved as not to be easily unraveled : an extremely intricate knot

¹**gor·di·id** \ˈgȯ(r)dēəd\ *adj* [NL *Gordiidae*] : of or relating to the Gordiidae or to the hairworms

²**gordiid** \"\ *n* -s : a member of the family Gordiidae : HAIRWORM

gor·di·idae \gȯ(r)ˈdīə,dē\ *n pl, cap* [NL, fr. *Gordius*, type genus (after *Gordius* of Phrygia) + *-idae*; fr. the knots into which such worms twist] : the chief family of Gordioidea coextensive with its type genus (*Gordius*) and including a number of long slender smooth-bodied worms (as hairworms or horsehair snakes)

¹**gor·di·oid** \ˈgȯ(r)dē,ȯid\ *adj* [NL *Gordioidea*] : of or relating to the Gordioidea; *also* : resembling a member of this group

²**gordioid** \"\ *n* -s : one of the Gordioidea : HAIRWORM

gor·di·oi·dea \,gȯ(r)dēˈȯidēə\ *n pl, cap* [NL, fr. *Gordius* + *-oidea*] : an order of Nematomorpha comprising freshwater forms parasitic as larvae in terrestrial or aquatic arthropods, lacking natatory bristles, and having the body cavity largely obscured by mesenchyme

¹**gor·do·nia** \gȯ(r)ˈdōnēə\ *n, cap* [NL, fr. G. *Gordon*, 19th cent. Scot. naturalist + NL *-ia*] : a genus of extinct reptiles from the New Red Sandstone of Scotland related to but smaller than those of *Dicynodon*

²**gordonia** \"\ *n* [NL, fr. James *Gordon* †1781 Eng. gardener + NL *-ia*] **1** *cap* : a genus of Asiatic and No. American shrubs or small trees (family Theaceae) with evergreen foliage and large white flowers — see LOBLOLLY BAY **2** -s : any tree of the genus *Gordonia* — called also *franklinia*

gor·don·ite \ˈgȯ(r)dᵊn,īt\ *n* -s [Samuel G. *Gordon* b1897 Am. mineralogist + E *-ite*] : a mineral $MgAl_2(PO_4)_2(OH)_2.8H_2O$ consisting of a hydrous basic phosphate of magnesium and aluminum found near Fairfield, Utah

gor·don setter \ˈgȯ(r)dᵊn-\ *n* [after Alexander, 4th Duke of *Gordon* †1827 Scot. nobleman and sportsman who was prominent in the development of the breed] **1** *usu cap G&S* : a breed of large long-haired showy bird dogs originating in Scotland about 1820 and distinguished from other setters only by their deep black color with tan, chestnut, or mahogany markings **2** *usu cap G, often cap S* : a dog of the Gordon Setter breed

gor·du·ra grass \gȯ(r)ˈdůrə-\ *n* [Pg *gordura* fat, fatness, fr. *gordo* fat (fr. L *gurdus* dull, stupid) + *-ura* -ure] : MOLASSES GRASS

¹**gore** \ˈgō(ə)r, -ō(ə)r,-ōə,-ȯ(ə)\ *n* -s [ME, fr. OE *gor*; akin to OHG *gor* dung, ON *gor* cud, OE *gearu* ready — more at YARE] **1** *now dial Brit* : a caked mass of filth or dirt of any kind **2 a** : BLOOD; *esp* : thick or clotted blood ⟨sacrificial altars stained with ~⟩ **b** *archaic* : a pool or mass of blood

²**gore** \"\ *n* -s [ME, fr. OE *gāra*; akin to OE *gār* spear, OHG *gēr* spear, *gēro* wedge-shaped object, ON *geirr* spear, *geiri* gore, OIr *gae* spear, Gk *chaios* shepherd's staff, Skt *heṣas* missile] **1 a** : a small usu. triangular piece of land ⟨the narrow lots, the ~s and dead ends that invite congestion —A.L.Guérard⟩ **b** : a relatively small unassigned or disputed tract of land lying between larger political divisions (as townships) **c** : a minor unorganized and usu. sparsely settled or uninhabited part of a county (as in Maine and Vermont) **2 a** (1) : a tapering or triangular piece of cloth (2) : one of several flared lengthwise sections of a garment (as a skirt) **b** : GUSSET 1c (1) **3 a** : one of the triangular pieces of the covering of a dome, umbrella, balloon, or similar object **b** : one of the series of related sections of a map that is applied to the surface of a sphere in the making of a terrestrial globe **4** : a heraldic bearing imagined as two curved lines drawn respectively from the sinister or dexter chief and from the lowest point of the shield to meeting in the fess point

gore 2a (2)

³**gore** \"\ *vt* -ED/-ING/-S : to cut into a tapering triangular form : provide (a skirt) with a gore

⁴**gore** \"\ *vt* -ED/-ING/-S [ME *goren*, prob. fr. *gore*, *gare* spear, fr. OE *gār* — more at ²GORE] **1** : to pierce or penetrate with a pointed instrument ⟨~ herself with a kitchen knife —Henry Jordan⟩ **2** : to pierce or wound with the horns or tusk ⟨before the bull can ~ the man on the ground —Barnaby Conrad⟩

gore·fish \ˈgō(ə)r,fish\ *n* [alter. of *garfish*] : NEEDLEFISH

gor·e·van \,gȯrəˈvän\ *n* -s [fr. *Gorevan*, town in northern Iran] **1** *usu cap* : a Persian rug of carpet size made with cotton warp and characterized by a medallion field covered with large angular designs and usu. bordered by three to five stripes, the prevailing colors being shades of terracotta, apricot, and blue **2** : AUBURN

¹**gorge** \ˈgȯrj, -ȯ(ə)j\ *n* -s [ME, fr. MF, fr. LL *gurga*, alter. of L *gurges* whirlpool, throat; akin to OHG *querka* throat, ON *kverk* throat, Skt *gargara* whirlpool, L *vorare* to devour — more at VORACIOUS] **1** : THROAT ⟨the strong, dark golden color of her hair, her shoulder bones and ~ —John Cheever⟩ ⟨full to the ~ with misery —Djuna Barnes⟩ — often used to indicate a strong feeling of repugnance or revulsion sometimes accompanied by a physical sensation of blockage or constriction, esp. with the verb *rise* ⟨when he tried to eat the flesh of his ox his ~ rose —Pearl Buck⟩ ⟨my very ~ rises at the thought —Agnes S. Turnbull⟩ **2 a** : a hawk's crop **b** : STOMACH, MAW, BELLY, GULLET ⟨thy ~ ever cramming —P.B.Shelley⟩ **c** : a full meal : a large amount of food ⟨~s o' wild plums . . . clean up to his elbows —J.W.Riley⟩ ⟨if it fails to get a real ~, it . . . cannot grow or mature —H.B. Glass⟩ **3** : the entrance into a bastion or other outwork of a fort — see BASTION illustration **4 a** : a band or fillet round the shaft just under the capital at the top in some orders of columnar architecture **b** : a concave molding : CAVETTO **c** : a small groove under a coping for carrying the drip **5** : a primitive device used instead of a fishhook consisting of an object (as a piece of bone attached in the middle to a line) easy to swallow but difficult to eject **6** : a narrow passage or entrance: as **a** : a defile between mountains **b** : a ravine with steep rocky walls **c** : a narrow steep-walled canyon or a particularly narrow steep-walled part of a canyon **7** : the groove in a pulley sheave **8** : an aggregation of matter that fills or chokes up a passage or channel : MASS ⟨an ice ~ in a river⟩ **9** : the line on the front of a coat or jacket formed by the crease of the lapel and collar

²**gorge** \"\ *vb* -ED/-ING/-S [ME *gorgen*, fr. MF *gorger*, fr. *gorge*, n.] *vi* : to eat greedily : eat to repletion ⟨~ throughout the day on delicacies —Jean Stafford⟩ ~ *vt* **1** : to stuff to capacity (as with food) : GLUT, SATIATE, CRAM ⟨people *gorging* themselves under the eyes of others who are starving —Hans Kohn⟩ **2** : FILL : choke up ⟨a vein *gorged* with blood⟩ **3** : to swallow greedily : DEVOUR ⟨~ the bait⟩ ⟨~ one's fill⟩ **syn** see SATIATE

³**gorge** \"\ *n* -s : the act or an instance of gorging ⟨lions alternate heavy ~s with . . . periods of fasting —James Stevenson-Hamilton⟩

¹**gorged** \-jd\ *adj* [fr. past part. of ²*gorge*] : GLUTTED — **gorgedly** \-j(ə)dlē\ *adv*

²**gorged** \"\ *adj* [¹*gorge* + *-ed*] *heraldry* : having the neck encircled (as with a coronet or ring) ⟨a lion ~ with a collar⟩

gorge hook *n* **1** : GORGE 5 **2** : a hook having two barbs : two hooks with shanks joined together

gor·geous \ˈgȯrjəs, -ȯ(ə)j-\ *adj* [alter. (influenced by *-ous*) of ME *gorgayse*, fr. MF *gorgias* elegant, fond of dress, fr. *gorgias* neckerchief, wimple, fr. *gorge* throat — more at GORGE] **1 a** : dressed in splendid or vivid colors : resplendently beautiful : MAGNIFICENT, SHOWY ⟨~ in the robes of worldwide academic distinction —R.M.Lovett⟩ ⟨the costumes were ~ enough to be put into museums —Mollie Panter-Downes⟩ **b** : characterized by brilliance or magnificence of any kind : DAZZLING, FLAMBOYANT, RESPLENDENT, COLORFUL ⟨related several stories of the ~ past —Elinor Wylie⟩ ⟨poetry . . . of weighted phrase and ~ adjective —Edith Hamilton⟩ ⟨often they believed their own ~ lies —Russell Lord⟩ **2** : supremely good or delightful : TERRIFIC, SPLENDID, SUPERB ⟨really ~ — a great human book —H.J.Laski⟩ ⟨a ~ meal⟩ ⟨had a ~ time⟩ **syn** see SPLENDID

gor·geous·ly *adv* : in a gorgeous manner

gor·geous·ness *n* -ES : the quality or state of being gorgeous

gor·ger·in \ˈgȯ(r)jərən\ *n* -s [F, fr. *gorge* throat] : the part of the capital in some columns between the termination of the shaft and the annulet of the echinus; *also* : the space between two neck moldings — called also *hypotrachelium, necking*

gor·get \ˈgȯrjət\ *n* -s [ME, fr. MF, dim. of *gorge* throat] **1** : a piece of armor defending the throat — see ARMOR illustration **2** : a covering for the throat: as **a** : an ornamental collar **b** : a part of the medieval wimple covering the throat and shoulders **c** : a usu. perforated primitive artifact of bone, stone, or shell prob. used as a neck or breast ornament or as an insignia **3** : a small ornamental plate worn on a chain about the neck by officers in full uniform in some armies **4** : a specially colored patch on the throat

gor·gia \ˈgȯrjə\ *n* -s [It *gorgia*, lit., throat, fr. OIt, fr. MF *gorge* — more at GORGE] : the improvised coloratura used in 16th century singing

gor·gio \ˈgȯr(,)jō\ *n* -s [Romany *gorjo*] : one who is not a gypsy ⟨it isn't like a gypsy to take unnecessary chances or do anything foolish in entertaining the ~s —W.L.Gresham⟩

gor·gon \ˈgȯrgən, -ȯ(ə)g-\ *n* -s [L *Gorgon-*, *Gorgo*, fr. Gk *Gorgon-*, *Gorgō*] **1** *usu cap* : one of three sisters in Greek mythology having snake-entwined hair and glaring eyes capable of turning the beholder to stone **2** : one resembling a gorgon; *esp* : an ugly, repulsive, or terrifying woman

gor·go·na·cea \,gȯ(r)gəˈnāshēə\ *n pl, cap* [NL, fr. *Gorgonia* + *-acea*] : an order of Alcyonaria distinguished from Alcyonacea chiefly by an axial skeleton covered and secreted by a cellular coenenchyme extending between the zooids or polyps that is usu. rather horny and commonly of branching form — **gor·go·na·cean** \ˌ==ˈnāshən\ *adj or n* — **gor·go·na·ceous** \-shəs\ *adj*

gor·go·nei·on \,gȯ(r)gəˈnī,än, -nē|, -nā|\ *or* **gor·go·ne·um** \-ˈnēəm\ *n, pl* **gorgo·neia** \|ə\ *or* **gorgo·nea** \-ēə\ [*gorgoneion* fr. Gk, fr. neut. of *gorgoneios* of a Gorgon, fr. *Gorgon-, Gorgō*; *gorgoneum* fr. NL, fr. Gk *gorgoneion*] : a representation of the face of a Gorgon frequent as an apotropaic symbol in Greek art

gor·go·nia \gȯ(r)ˈgōnēə\ *n, cap* [NL, fr. L, coral, fr. *Gorgon-*, *Gorgo* + *-ia* -y] : a genus of gorgonians (the type of the family Gorgoniidae) comprising the common sea fans with flexible horny axes — **gor·go·nid** \ˈgȯ(r)gənəd\ *adj or n*

gor·go·ni·a·cea \(,)gȯ(r),gōnēˈāshēə\ [NL, fr. *Gorgonia* + *-acea*] *syn of* GORGONACEA

¹**gor·go·nian** \(ˈ)gȯ(r)ˈgōnēən, -ōnyən\ *adj* [*gorgon* + *-ian*] **1** *often cap* : of, relating to, or resembling a Gorgon : TERRIFYING **2** [NL *Gorgonia* + E *-an*] : of or relating to the Gorgonacea

²**gorgonian** \"\ *n* -s : a member of the Gorgonacea

gor·go·nin \'gȯ(r)gənən\ *n* -s [NL *Gorgonia* + E *-in*] **:** a complex protein frequently containing appreciable quantities of iodine and bromine that makes up the horny skeleton of typical gorgonians

gor·gon·ize \'gȯ(r)gə,nīz\ *vt* -ED/-ING/-s *see -ize in Explan Notes* [*gorgon* + *-ize*] **:** to have a paralyzing or mesmerizing effect upon **:** STUPEFY, PETRIFY ⟨could with a look ~ or melt an audience —J.E.Agate⟩ ⟨*gorgonizing* him with her opaque yellow eyes —O.Henry⟩

gor·gon·zo·la \,gȯ(r)gən'zōlə, *attrib* ¦==¦==\ *or* **gorgonzola cheese** *n, usu cap G* [It *gorgonzola*, fr. *Gorgonzola*, town near Milan, Italy] **:** a blue cheese usu. made of cow's milk and having blue-green marbling after curing

gor·go·sau·rus \,gȯ(r)gə'sȯrəs\ *n, cap* [NL, fr. L *Gorgo* Gorgon + *-saurus*] **:** a genus of large carnivorous dinosaurs from the Upper Cretaceous strata of Alberta

gorier *comparative of* GORY

goriest *superlative of* GORY

go·ril·la \gə'rilə\ *n* -s [NL (specific epithet of *Troglodytes gorilla*, former binomial designation for the gorilla), fr. Gk *Gorillai*, an African tribe of hairy women] **1 :** an anthropoid ape (*Gorilla gorilla* syn. *G. savagei*) that inhabits a small part of the forest region of equatorial West Africa, is closely related to the chimpanzee but less arboreal, less erect, and much larger, sometimes exceeding five and one half feet in height and 500 pounds in weight, and has massive bones, broad shoulders, very long arms, strong jaws with prominent canine teeth, a nose with a low median ridge, small ears, and a face covered with black skin **2 a :** an ugly brute of a man **b** *slang* **:** a strong-arm man **:** THUG, GOON ⟨the employment of ~s for purposes of intimidation —C.A.Madison⟩

go·ril·li·an \gə'rilēən\ *or* **go·ril·line** \-,līn, -,lən\ *adj* **:** of, relating to, or resembling a gorilla

go·ril·loid \-,lȯid\ *adj* **:** like a gorilla

gor·i·ly \'gōrəlē, 'gȯr-, -li\ *adv* **:** in a gory manner

[1]**goring** *n* -s [fr. gerund of [4]*gore*] **:** the act of goring **:** an instance of goring or of being gored ⟨his terrible ~s . . . had no effect on his valor at all —Ernest Hemingway⟩

[2]**goring** *n* -s [fr. gerund of [3]*gore*] **1 :** the act of cutting (as cloth) into a triangular piece; *also* **:** a piece so cut **2 a :** [2]GORE 3 **b :** an elastic fabric used for inserts esp. in slip-on shoes

gor·ki \'gȯrkē, 'gō(ə)k-, -ki\ *adj, usu cap* [fr. *Gorki*, U.S.S.R.] **:** of or from the city of Gorki, U.S.S.R. **:** of the kind or style prevalent in Gorki

gor·lic acid \'gȯrlik-\ *n* [ISV *gorli* (*oil*) + *-ic; orig. formed as* F *gorlique*] **:** a liquid unsaturated acid $C_5H_7(C_{12}H_{22})COOH$ occurring as the glyceride esp. in gorli oil and chaulmoogra oil

gor·lin \'gȯrlən\ *n* -s [E dial. *gor* unfledged bird + *-lin* (alter. of *-ling*)] **1** *dial Brit* **:** an unfledged bird **2** *dial Brit* **:** a callow immature person

gor·li oil \-li-\ *n* [*gorli* fr. native name in Africa] **:** a fatty oil obtained from the seeds of African trees of a genus (*Caloncoba*) of the family Flacourtiaceae and similar in composition to chaulmoogra oil

gör·litz *or* **goer·litz** \'gerləts, 'gər-, 'gȯr-\ *adj, usu cap* [fr. *Görlitz*, Germany] **:** of or from the city of Görlitz, Germany **:** of the kind or style prevalent in Görlitz

gor·lov·ka \gȯ(r)'lȯfkə\ *adj, usu cap* [fr. *Gorlovka*, U.S.S.R.] **:** of or from the city of Gorlovka, U.S.S.R. **:** of the kind or style prevalent in Gorlovka

gorm \'gȯ(ə)m\ *var of* [4]GAUM

gormand *var of* GOURMAND

[1]**gormandize** *var of* GOURMANDISE

[2]**gor·man·dize** \'gȯ(r)mən,dīz\ *vb* -ED/-ING/-s *see -ize in Explan Notes vi* **:** to eat gluttonously or ravenously ~ *vt* **1 :** to eat greedily **:** DEVOUR **2** *archaic* **:** GLUT, SATIATE

gor·man·diz·er \-zə(r)\ *n* -s **:** GOURMAND, GLUTTON

gor·maw \'gȯ(ə)r,mȯ\ *n* -s [[1]*gore* + *maw* (gull)] *dial Brit* **:** CORMORANT

gorm·ing \'gȯ(ə)mən\ *or* **gormy** \'gȯ(ə)mi\ *var of* GAUMY

gorm·less \'gȯ(ə)mləs\ *var of* GAUMLESS

go round *vi* **:** to go around

go-round \'gō,=\ *n* [*go round*] **:** GO-AROUND

gorse \'gȯ(ə)rs\ *n* -s [ME *gorst*, fr. OE — more at HORROR] **1 :** FURZE **2 :** JUNIPER

gorsechat \'=,=\ *n, dial Eng* **:** WHINCHAT

gor·sedd \'gȯr,seth\ *n* -s *usu cap* [W, lit., mound, court, throne] **:** a mock druidical institution established in the late 18th century that assembles twice a year for the granting of bardic degrees and the conferring of bardic titles

gorse weevil *or* **gorse seed weevil** *n* **:** a small black European weevil (*Apion ulicis*) that feeds on gorse seed and has been introduced into New Zealand for use in biological control of this plant

gor·soon \(')gȯr¦sün\ *var of* GOSSOON

gorst \'gȯ(ə)rst\ *dial Brit var of* GORSE

gorsy *also* **gorsey** \'gȯrsē\ *adj* **gorsier; gorsiest** [*gorse* + *-y*] **:** of, relating to, characteristic of, or abounding in gorse ⟨windswept ~ earth —William Sansom⟩

gor·to·ni·an \gȯ(r)'tōnēən\ *n* -s *usu cap* [Samuel *Gorton* †1677 Am. religious leader + E *-ian*] **:** one of a short-lived sect composed of followers of Samuel Gorton orig. of Massachusetts and later of Rhode Island who rejected all outward forms and clergy and held that Christ was both human and divine and that heaven and hell exist only in the mind

gor·ton·ist \'gȯ(r)t°nəst\ *n* -s *usu cap* [S. *Gorton* + *-ist*] **:** GORTONIAN

gory \'gōrē, 'gȯr-, -ri\ *adj* -ER/-EST [ME, fr. [1]*gore* + *-y*] **1 a :** covered with gore **:** BLOODSTAINED ⟨never shake thy ~ locks at me —Shak.⟩ **b :** attended by much effusion of blood **:** MURDEROUS, SANGUINARY ⟨a lively and rather ~ prizefight —Wolcott Gibbs⟩ **2 :** of or relating to crimes, killings, or acts attended by much effusion of blood **:** BLOODCURDLING, SENSATIONAL ⟨ceremonials at which — according to a ~ legend — they made human sacrifices —*Amer. Guide Series: Calif.*⟩ ⟨~ exploitation of crime and mystery —V.L.Parrington⟩ ⟨a ~ narrative⟩

gory dew *n* **:** a gelatinous blood-red patch often seen on stones, soil, or walls and caused chiefly by a red alga (*Porphyridium cruentum*)

gos \'gäs\ *n* [by shortening] *Scot* **:** GOSHAWK

gosh \'gäsh *also* 'gärsh *or* 'gȯsh *or* 'gȯ(ə)rsh\ *interj* [euphemism for *God*] — used as a mild oath ⟨~, I was hungry —W.S. Maugham⟩

gosh-awful \'=¦==\ *adj* [euphemism] **:** GOD-AWFUL

gos·hawk *also* **gosshawk** \'gäs,hȯk\ *n* [ME *goshawke, goshauk*, fr. OE *gōshafoc*, fr. *gōs* goose + *hafoc* hawk — more at GOOSE, HAWK] **:** any of several long-tailed short-winged accipitrine hawks having powerful bills, long legs, and strong feet and being noted for their powerful flight, activity, and vigor — see ACCIPITER

go·shen·ite \'gōshə,nīt\ *n* -s [*Goshen*, Mass. + E *-ite*] **:** a colorless beryl

go·siute *also* **go·shute** \'gō,shüt\ *n, pl* **gosiute** *or* **gosiutes** *also* **goshute** *or* **goshutes** *usu cap* **1 :** a people of the Western Shoshoni living in northern Utah and eastern Nevada **2 :** a member of the Gosiute people

gos·lar·ite \'gäslə,rīt, -äzl-\ *n* -s [G *goslarit*, fr. *Goslar*, city in the Harz mts., Ger. + G *-it* ite] **:** a mineral $ZnSO_4.7H_2O$ that consists of white zinc sulfate formed by oxidation of sphalerite and that usu. occurs massive

gos·ling \'gäzliŋ, -lēŋ *sometimes* 'gȯz-\ *n* -s [ME, fr. *gos*, *goos* goose + *-ling* — more at GOOSE] **1 :** a young goose **2 :** a foolish or callow person **3** *dial Eng* **:** CATKIN

gosling grass *or* **gosling weed** *n* **:** CLEAVERS

gosling green *n* **:** a pale yellowish green

go-slow \(')=¦=\ *n* -s [fr. the phrase *go slow*] *Brit* **:** SLOWDOWN ⟨a serious threat to productivity from industrial strikes and *go-slows* —*Sydney (Australia) Bull.*⟩

gos·more \'gäs,mō(ə)r, -äz,m-\ *n* -s [perh. alter. of *gossamer*] **:** CAT'S-EAR 1

[1]**gos·pel** \'gäspəl *sometimes* 'gȯs-\ *n* -s [ME, fr. OE *godspel*, *gōdspel* (trans. of LL *evangelium*), fr. *gōd* good + *spell* tale — more at GOOD, SPELL, EVANGEL] **1** *sometimes cap* **a :** glad tidings; *esp* **:** the good news concerning Christ, the Kingdom of God, and salvation **b :** the teachings of Jesus and the apostles as a body or system **:** the Christian faith, revelation, or dispensation ⟨Jesus went about all Galilee . . . preaching the ~ of the kingdom —Mt 4:23 (AV)⟩ **c :** an interpretation of the gospel of Jesus Christ ⟨St. Paul's ~⟩ ⟨the social ~⟩ ⟨a highly revivalistic ~⟩ **2 a :** the story or record of Christ's life and teachings contained in the first four books of the New Testament **b** *usu cap* **:** one of the four New Testament books containing narratives of the life and death of Jesus Christ ascribed respectively to Matthew, Mark, Luke, and John; *also* **:** any of certain similar noncanonical ancient books — compare APOCRYPHA **c :** a book containing the four New Testament Gospels ⟨tracts and ~s were distributed by religious workers⟩ **3** *or* **gospel for the day** *usu cap G&D* **:** a lection taken from one of the New Testament gospels and forming part of a Christian liturgical service — called also *Holy Gospel* **4** *sometimes cap* **:** the message or teachings of a religious teacher **:** a doctrinal system of religious teachings ⟨the ~ of an Indian ascetic⟩ ⟨the first to bring the Buddhist ~ to China⟩ **5 a :** the message, teaching, doctrine, or course of action having certain efficacy or validity and held to or propounded with zeal **:** FAITH ⟨interested in spreading the ~ of conservation —R.M. Hodesh⟩ ⟨the ~ of progress⟩ ⟨the ~ of hard work⟩ ⟨the new proletarian ~ —J.C.Ransom⟩ **b :** something (as an assertion) of such an authoritative, infallible, or unimpeachable character or source as not to be questioned **:** absolute truth ⟨newspaper writers . . . are prone to regard it as ~ —C.J.Lovell⟩ ⟨you speak the ~ —Carl Van Vechten⟩ — often used in the phrase *gospel truth* ⟨stories like these were related as ~ truths —Herman Melville⟩

[2]**gospel** \"\ *vb* **gospeled** *or* **gospelled; gospeled** *or* **gospelled; gospeling** *or* **gospelling; gospels** [ME *gospellen*, fr. OE *godspellian*, fr. *godspel*, n.] *vt* **:** to instruct in or convert to the gospel **:** EVANGELIZE ~ *vi* **:** to preach the gospel

[3]**gospel** \"\ *adj, sometimes cap* [[1]*gospel*] **:** according with or relating to the gospel **:** filled with fervor **:** EVANGELICAL ⟨~ preaching⟩ ⟨~ song⟩

gos·pel·er *also* **gos·pel·ler** \-pələ(r)\ *n* -s [ME, fr. OE *godspellere*, fr. *godspellian* + *-ere* -er] **1** *obs* **:** one of the four Evangelists **2 :** one who preaches the gospel **:** EVANGELIST **3 :** one who reads or sings the liturgical Gospel at the communion service **4 :** one who propounds a gospel of any kind ⟨the ideal ~ of American success —*Saturday Rev.*⟩

gospel hall *n* **:** a building used for the worship services of a Christian sect ⟨the larger assemblies of Plymouth Brethren own *gospel halls*⟩

gos·pel·ize \-pə,līz\ *vb* -ED/-ING/-s *vt* **:** to instruct in the gospel **:** EVANGELIZE ~ *vi* **:** to preach the gospel **:** EVANGELIZE ⟨entertaining while he *gospelized* —T.M.Pearce⟩

gospel side *n, often cap G* **:** the left side of an altar or chancel as one faces it **:** north side — used esp. in churches in which the Epistle and the Gospel are read or sung from different sides

gospel team *n* **:** a group of evangelists who work together as a unit in conducting mass meetings, in leading the singing of gospel hymns, and in preaching the gospel for the purpose of converting their hearers

gospel tree *n, often cap G* **:** a tree set to distinguish a British parish or township boundary

gospel truth *n* **:** something infallibly or absolutely true

gos·po·din \,gäspə¦dēn, -əd¦yēn\ *n, pl* **gospo·da** \-ə¦dä\ [Russ; akin to OSlav *gospodĭ, gospodinŭ* lord, master, and prob. to L *hospit-, hospes* host — more at HOST] — used as a courtesy title in some Slavic countries

gos·port \'gä,spō(ə)rt\ *n* [fr. *Gosport*, England] **:** a flexible one-way speaking tube for communication between separate cockpits of an airplane usu. from flight instructor to student

[1]**gos·sa·mer** \'gäsəmə(r) *sometimes* -äz(ə)m-\ *n* -s [ME *gossomer* (prob. also "Indian summer", the period when geese were eaten extensively), fr. *gos*, *goos* goose + *somer* summer; fr. its prevalence at this season of the year — more at GOOSE, SUMMER] **1 a :** a fine filmy substance consisting of fragments or strands of cobweb often seen floating in air in calm clear weather or caught on grass or bushes **b :** a fragment or strand of gossamer **2 a :** a thin sheer fabric; *esp* **:** a delicate silk veiling resembling gauze **b** *Brit* **:** HAT **c :** a thin waterproof coat or cloak **3 :** something that is infinitely or exquisitely light, delicate, or tenuous ⟨a true gift for recapturing the ~ of youth's dreams —Andrea Parke⟩

[2]**gossamer** \"\ *adj* **:** infinitely or exquisitely light, delicate, or tenuous ⟨contrives a ~ delicacy wonderful to hear —*Atlantic*⟩ ⟨try to find justifications, however ~, for their behavior —Ben Karpman⟩

gossamer fern *n* **:** HAY-SCENTED FERN

gossamer spider *n* **:** a ballooning spider

gos·sa·mery \-mərē\ *adj* **:** like gossamer **:** FLIMSY

gos·san \'gäs°n\ *also* **goz·zan** \-äz°n\ *n* -s [Corn *gossen*, fr. *gōs* blood, fr. OCorn *guit;* akin to W *gwaed* blood, Bret *goad*] **:** decomposed rock or vein material of reddish or rusty color resulting from oxidized pyrites — called also *iron hat*

gosshawk *var of* GOSHAWK

[1]**gos·sip** \'gäsəp\ *n* -s [ME *godsib*, *gossib*, fr. OE *godsibb*, fr. *god* + *sibb* kinsman, fr. *sibb*, adj., related — more at GOD, SIB] **1** *now dial chiefly Brit* **:** a person spiritually related to another through being his sponsor at baptism **2 :** a friend or comrade **:** COMPANION, CRONY ⟨a ~ of his laughed when I refused the halfpenny —W.B.Yeats⟩ ⟨taking presents of . . . strawberries to the Queen and the Princess's other ~s —Edith Sitwell⟩ **3 :** a person who habitually retails facts, rumors, or behind-the-scenes information of an intimate, personal, or sensational nature **:** RUMORMONGER ⟨the worst ~ in town⟩ ⟨the syndicated movie ~s —*Newsweek*⟩ **4 a :** rumor, report, tattle, or behind-the-scenes information esp. of an intimate or personal nature ⟨common rumor or ~ profoundly influences the conclusions of many people —Edward Jenks⟩ ⟨~ columns . . . gleefully speculate upon prospective divorces among the well-known —D.L.Cohn⟩ **b** (1) **:** a conversation in which gossip is exchanged ⟨settled down for what she hoped would be a ~, but thought of as a nice chat —Monica Stirling⟩ ⟨a woman standing in her doorway for a ~ —Winefride Nolan⟩ (2) **:** light familiar chatty talk or writing ⟨these reminiscences of a once brilliant court are excellent ~⟩ ⟨certain recent ~ in intellectual circles —Eleanor M. Sickels⟩ ⟨I went back . . . in high hopes of hearing good hunting ~ —S.P.B.Mais⟩ **c :** the subject matter of gossip ⟨the power, ambition, and immense personal prestige of individuals like these . . . were common ~ —H.S.Bennett⟩ **5 :** a humorous party pastime in which a sentence or anecdote is whispered from one person to the next around the group and the final version compared with the original statement

[2]**gossip** \"\ *vb* **gossiped** *also* **gossipped; gossiped** *also* **gossipped; gossiping** *also* **gossipping; gossips** *vi* **:** to converse idly ⟨don't intend to ~ about my sickness —Lillian Hellman⟩ ⟨a group of students ~*ing* —John Berger⟩; *esp* **:** to retail facts, rumors, or behind-the-scenes information about other persons ⟨must have ~*ed* about the beauty of the Queen's daughter —J.E.M.White⟩ ⟨~s about the doings of the town —Cornelius Weygandt⟩ ~ *vt* **:** to tell or transmit by way of gossip ⟨~ed from one village to the next —Ernest Beaglehole⟩

gos·sip·er \-pə(r)\ *n* -s **:** a person given to gossip **:** GOSSIP

gos·sip·i·ness \-pēnəs, -pin-\ *n* -ES **:** the quality of being gossipy

gossiping *n* -s **1** *now dial Eng* **a :** a christening feast **:** CHRISTENING **b :** a meeting of gossips or friends (as at a lying-in) **2** *now dial Eng* **:** MERRYMAKING, CAROUSAL

gos·sip·ing·ly *adv* **:** in a gossiping manner

gossipmonger \'=,=,==\ *n* **:** one who retails gossip

gos·sip·red \'gäsə,pred, -,prəd\ *n* -s [ME *gossibrede*, fr. *gossib* + *-rede* state or condition — more at KINDRED] **:** the relationship between a person and his sponsors **:** spiritual affinity **:** SPONSORSHIP

gos·sip·ry \'gäsəprē, -ri\ *n* -ES **:** CHITCHAT, GOSSIP

gos·sipy \-pē, -pi\ *adj* **:** full of or given to gossip ⟨discuss the crops with some ~ farmer —V.L.Parrington⟩ ⟨a ~ chronicle⟩

gos·soon \(')gä¦sün\ *n* -s [modif. of F *garçon* — more at GARÇON] *chiefly Irish* **:** BOY, YOUTH; *esp* **:** a serving boy

gos·syp·e·tin \gä'sipət°n\ *n* -s [ISV *gossypin* + *-etin* (as in *quercetin*)] **:** a yellow crystalline flavone pigment $C_{15}H_{10}O_8$ occurring in cotton flowers and obtained by hydrolysis of gossypin and gossypitrin; 8-hydroxy-quercetin

gos·sy·pin \'gäsəpən\ *n* -s [ISV *gossyp-* (fr. NL *Gossypium*) + *-in*] **:** a glucoside $C_{21}H_{20}O_{13}$ occurring in cotton flowers and hibiscus flowers

gos·syp·i·trin \gä'sipə·trən\ *n* -s [ISV *gossyp-* (fr. NL *Gossypium*) + *-itrin* (as in *quercitrin*)] **:** a yellow crystalline glucoside $C_{21}H_{20}O_{13}$ occurring in cotton flowers and hibiscus flowers

gos·syp·i·um \gä'sipēəm\ *n, cap* [NL, fr. L *gossypion* cotton] **:** a genus of herbs or shrubs of the family Malvaceae yielding the cotton of commerce and having mostly palmately lobed leaves, showy flowers, and capsular fruits containing long-tailed seeds

gos·sy·pol \'gäsə,pōl, -pōl\ *n* -s [ISV *gossyp-* (fr. NL *Gossypium*) + *-ol*] **:** a phenolic pigment $C_{30}H_{30}O_8$ in cottonseed that crystallizes in both yellow and red forms and is toxic to some animals but is rendered harmless by processing of the seed for recovery of the oil

gos·ter \'gästə(r), 'gȯs-\ *var of* GAUSTER

gos·ther \'gästə(r), 'gȯs-\ *chiefly Irish var of* GAUSTER

got *past of* GET

[1]**gotch** \'gäch\ *n* -ES [origin unknown] *dial Eng* **:** a potbellied jug or pitcher usu. made of earthenware

[2]**gotch** \"\ *or* **gotched** \-cht\ *adj* [*gotch* fr. Sp *gacho* having horns that project downward, having floppy ears, back-formation fr. *agachar* to bow, lower, fr. L *coactare* to constrain, force, fr. *coactus*, past part. of *cogere* to collect, compel; *gotched* fr. Sp *gacho* + E *-ed* — more at COGENT] *West* **:** DROOPING, CROPPED ⟨the sorrel with a ~ ear —Agnes M. Cleaveland⟩

gote \'gōt\ *n* -s [ME; akin to MLG & MD *gote* channel or pipe for water, OE *gēotan* to pour — more at FOUND] *now dial Brit* **:** a channel for water **:** WATERCOURSE

gö·te·borg *or* **go·te·borg** \¦yəd·ə¦bȯr, *Swedish* ,yœtə'bȯry\ *adj, usu cap* [fr. *Göteborg*, Sweden] **:** GOTHENBURG

goth \'gäth, 'gȯth\ *n* -s [LL *Gothi*, pl., fr. Gk *Gothoi*, of Gmc origin; akin to Goth *Gutthiudai* (dat.) Gothic people, OE *Gotan* (pl.) Goths, ON *Gotar*] **1** *cap* **:** a member of a Germanic people that in ancient times dwelt between the Elbe and the Vistula and in the early centuries of the Christian era overran the Roman Empire — see OSTROGOTH, VISIGOTH **2** *cap* **:** a native of the Swedish provinces of Gotland and Vestergotland **3 :** a person totally lacking in culture or refinement **:** BARBARIAN

goth·am \'gäthəm *sometimes* 'gōth-\ *adj, usu cap* [fr. *Gotham*, nickname of the city of New York, fr. *Gotham*, a proverbial town in England noted for the folly of its inhabitants, fr. ME] *slang* **:** of or relating to the city of New York ⟨a *Gotham* hotel⟩

goth·am·ite \-thə,mīt\ *n* -s *usu cap* [*Gotham* (New York) + E *-ite*] **:** an inhabitant or resident of New York City

goth·en·burg \'gäthən,bərg *sometimes* -ät°n-\ *adj, usu cap* [fr. *Gothenburg* (Göteborg), Sweden] **:** of or from the city of Gothenburg, Sweden **:** of the kind or style prevalent in Gothenburg

gothi·an \'gäthēən, 'gȯth-\ *adj, usu cap* [F *Gothie*, Götaland, Sweden + E *-an*] **:** of, relating to, or constituting a division of the Precambrian — see GEOLOGIC TIME table

[1]**goth·ic** \'gäthik, -thēk *sometimes* 'gȯth-\ *adj* [LL *Gothicus*, fr. *Gothi* + L *-icus* -ic] **1** *usu cap* **a :** of, relating to, or resembling the Goths, their civilization, or their language **b :** TEUTONIC, GERMANIC ⟨in German they have a kind of *Gothic* eloquence that does not survive translation —Winthrop Sargeant⟩ ⟨the eclectic idiosyncrasy and studied barbarism of Carlyle's *Gothic* style —W.H.Gardner⟩ **c** (1) **:** of or relating to the middle ages **:** MEDIEVAL ⟨his face was calm and beautiful . . . above the *Gothic* splendor of his raiment —Elinor Wylie⟩ ⟨the monkish or *Gothic* ages . . . were therefore despised by the scholar and the philosopher —L.G.Pine⟩ ⟨a whole *Gothic* world had come to grief . . . there was now no armor glittering in the forest glades —Evelyn Waugh⟩ (2) **:** UNCOUTH, PRIMITIVE, BARBAROUS, UNCIVILIZED ⟨the *Gothic* obscurities and barbarities of the past —Ernest Barker⟩ ⟨the *Gothic* and barbarous self-complacency of his contemporaries —P.E. More⟩ (3) **:** SAVAGE, FEROCIOUS ⟨tetanus is a disease of *Gothic* ferocity —Berton Roueché⟩ **2** *usu cap* **a** (1) **:** of, relating to, or having the characteristics of a style of architecture developed in northern France and spreading through western Europe from the middle of the 12th century to the early 16th century that is characterized by the converging of weights and strains at isolated points upon slender vertical piers and counterbalancing buttresses with the building becoming essentially a stone skeleton of pillars, props, and ribs upon which rest shells of vaulting, with the enclosing walls made thin or sometimes almost wholly replaced by large windows of colored glass stiffened with metalwork and stone tracery, and with pointed arches and vaulting replacing the round of the Romanesque (2) **:** of or relating to an architectural style or an example of such style patterned upon or reflecting the strong influence of the medieval Gothic esp. in outward form ⟨a *Gothic* Presbyterian church⟩ ⟨*Gothic* buildings on an American campus⟩ ⟨the eye singles out the *Gothic* Woolworth Tower —*Ford Times*⟩ **b :** of or relating to an art style flourishing esp. in northern Europe from the 12th through the 19th centuries and distinguished by an austere verticality and a tendency toward naturalism **c** (1) **:** of or relating to a late 18th and early 19th century style of fiction characterized by the use of medieval settings, a murky atmosphere of horror and gloom, and macabre, mysterious, and violent incidents (2) **:** of or relating to a literary style or an example of such style characterized by grotesque, macabre, or fantastic incidents or by an atmosphere of irrational violence, desolation, and decay ⟨the foremost current . . . practitioner of the gruesomely *Gothic* weird tale —*Fantasy & Science Fiction*⟩ ⟨compounded of fantasy surrealism, allegory, and *Gothic* sensationalism —William Peden⟩ (3) **:** romantic in style or content as opposed to classical **3** *usu cap* **a** *of handwriting* **:** characterized by angularity and lateral compression — used specif. of a minuscule type of handwriting which developed in the 12th century in France from the Caroline minuscule and which in turn was the prototype of the modern black letter **b :** of or relating to this type of handwriting ⟨the characteristic *Gothic* features⟩ **4 :** FANTASTIC, UNREAL, EXTRAVAGANT, BAROQUE ⟨a world of spooks and goblins . . . a ~ world —Herbert Read⟩ ⟨allowing them lunch hours of ~ proportions —*New Yorker*⟩

[2]**gothic** \"\ *n* **1** *cap* **:** the East Germanic language of the Goths esp. as represented by the surviving fragments of a 4th century biblical translation made by Bishop Wulfila (*ab* A.D. 311–381) — see CRIMEAN GOTHIC, EAST GERMANIC; INDO-EUROPEAN LANGUAGES table **2** *usu cap* **:** Gothic art style or decoration; *specif* **:** the Gothic architectural style **3** *usu cap* **:** Gothic writing or lettering **4** *often cap* **a :** BLACK LETTER **b :** SANS SERIF

Gothic

Gothic 3

goth·i·cal·ly \-thək(ə)lē, -thēk-, -li\ *adv, sometimes cap* **:** in a Gothic manner ⟨~ elaborate —James Binder⟩

gothic alphabet *n, usu cap G* **:** an alphabet based principally on the Greek uncials and devised for the Gothic language by Bishop Wulfila in the 4th century A.D.

gothic arch *n, often cap G* **:** a pointed arch; *esp* **:** one with a joint instead of a keystone at its apex

gothic chasuble *n, usu cap G* **:** a chasuble of elbow length at the sides with the front and back shaped to a downward point — see CHASUBLE illustration

gothic chippendale *n, usu cap G&C* **:** 18th century furniture with pointed arches, clustered columns, and other medieval details

goth·i·cism \-thə,sizəm\ *n* -s *usu cap* **1** *archaic* **:** lack of taste or elegance **:** barbarous spirit or quality **2 :** Gothic spirit or principles **:** conformity to or practice of Gothic style

goth·i·cist \-thəsəst\ *n* -s *usu cap* **:** a practitioner of Gothic style (as in literature)

goth·i·cize \-thə,sīz\ *vt* -ED/-ING/-s *often cap* **:** to make Gothic **:** transform to the Gothic style

goth·ic·ness *n* -ES *usu cap* **:** the quality or state of being Gothic

gothic revival *n, usu cap G&R* **:** an artistic style or movement of the 18th and 19th centuries inspired by and imitative of the Gothic style esp. in architecture

goth·ish \-thish\ *adj, usu cap* [*Goth* + *-ish*] *archaic* **:** GOTHIC

göthite *var of* GOETHITE

go·thon·ic \(')gä¦thänik, (')gō¦-, (')gō¦-\ *adj, usu cap* [L *Gothones*, *Gotones* Goths (of Gmc origin; akin to OE *Gotan* Goths) + E *-ic* — more at GOTH] **:** GERMANIC, TEUTONIC

go through *vi* **1 :** to continue firmly or obstinately to the end **:** PERSIST, PERSEVERE — used with *with* ⟨I was *going through* with it if it killed me —A.W.Long⟩ **2 a :** to receive approval or sanction **:** PASS ⟨the proposed amendment failed to *go through*⟩

b : to come to be agreed on ⟨the deal *went through* and the house was sold⟩
goths *pl of* GOTH
got·land·er \'gät,landə(r), -lən-\ *n* -s *cap* [*Gotland*, island in the Baltic sea belonging to Sweden + E *-er*] : a native or inhabitant of the island of Gotland
go to *vi* **1** *archaic* — used interjectionally as an exhortation ⟨and they said one to another, *go to*, let us make brick —Gen 11:3 (AV)⟩ **2** *archaic* — used interjectionally to express disapproval or disbelief ⟨*go to*, you are a wag —Lord Byron⟩
go-to-meeting \,==ˈ==\ *adj* : suitable for churchgoing or other special occasions — used esp. of clothes ⟨dressed in *go-to-meeting* attire⟩
gotten *past part of* GET
göt·ter·däm·me·rung \,gə(r)|d-ə(r)'damərəŋ, ,gō|, ,ge|, ,gä|, |tə-, -dem-, -mə,ruŋ\ *n, pl* **götterdämmerun·gen** \-,ruŋən\ *usu cap* [G, twilight of the gods, fr. *götter* (pl. of *gott* god) + *dämmerung* twilight] : the stage or process of collapse and dissolution (as of a political or social order) typically attended by catastrophic violence and disorder ⟨two grandiose . . . novels describing the *Götterdämmerung* of the Nazi armies in Russia —*New Yorker*⟩
gou \'gü\ *n* -s [by shortening] : GASPERGOU
gouache \'gwäsh, gü'ä-,gə'wä-\ *n* -s [F, fr. It *guazzo*, lit., puddle, fr. a southern It. dial. word derived fr. L *aquatio* action of fetching water, watering, watering place, fr. *aquatus* (past part of *aquari* to fetch water, fr. *aqua* water) + *-io* -ion — more at ISLAND] **1** : a method of painting with opaque colors that have been ground in water and mingled with a preparation of gum **2 a** : a picture painted by gouache **b** : the pigment used in gouache
gouber \'gübə(r), 'gub-\ *var of* GOOBER
goud \'gaud\ *chiefly Scot var of* GOLD
gou·da \'gaudə, 'güdə, 'haudə\ *or* **gouda cheese** *n* -s *usu cap G* [fr. *Gouda*, Netherlands, where it was orig. made] : a whole-milk cheese of close texture and mild flavor shaped in flattened spheres and usu. covered with a red protective coating
¹**gouge** \'gauj, *Brit sometimes* 'güj\ *n* -s [ME *goodg, gowge*, fr. MF *gouge*, fr. LL *gubia, gulbia* hollow chisel, of Celt origin; akin to OIr *gulban* sting, MW *gwlf* notch, *gylf* beak, and prob. to Gaulish *galba* fat man — more at CALF] **1 a** : a chisel with a concavo-convex cross section used in its various forms esp. for scooping or cutting holes, channels, or grooves (as in wood or stone), for doing the roughing cuts in wood turning, or for removing portions of bone in surgery **b** : an incising tool that cuts forms or blanks (as for gloves or envelopes) from leather, paper, or other material **c** : a bookbinder's blind-tooling or gilding tool having a face that forms a curve; *also* : the impression made by it **2** [²*gouge*] **a** : the act of gouging with or as if with a gouge **b** : a groove or cavity scooped out (as with a gouge) **3** : an excessive or improper exaction : EXTORTION, SWINDLE, OVERCHARGE ⟨the only protection we have against a rubber-price ~ —*Newsweek*⟩; *also* : the amount extorted or overcharged ⟨the yearly ~ is closer to $200,000,000 —Lester David⟩ **4** : soft clayey material often present between a vein and a wall or along a fault — called also *selvage*

gouges 1a

²**gouge** \"\ *vb* -ED/-ING/-S *vt* **1** : to cut grooves, channels, or holes in with or as if with a gouge : scoop out with or as if with a gouge **2 a** : to force out (an opponent's eye) with the thumb **b** : to thrust the thumb or finger into (an opponent's eye) : thrust the thumb or finger into the eye of ⟨*gouged* one of his eyes so thoroughly that it bulged —John Lardner⟩ ⟨kick and ~ him into insensibility —*Time*⟩ **3** : to subject to extortion or undue exaction : OVERCHARGE, SWINDLE, EXPLOIT ⟨protect . . . the public against being *gouged* by ticket scalpers —M.R.Cohen⟩ ⟨unions and employers get together to ~ the consumer —C.R.Daugherty⟩ ⟨*gouged* for thousands . . . of dollars —*Newsweek*⟩ ~ *vi* **1** : to cut grooves, channels, or holes with or as if with a gouge ⟨such moving ice . . . scrapes, plucks, ~*s*, and scours —G.T.Renner & C.L.White⟩ : PIERCE, BORE ⟨his eyes *gouging* into mine —R.P.Warren⟩ **2** : to thrust the thumb or finger into the eye of an opponent ⟨still kicked and punched and *gouged* —Edwin Corle⟩ **3** : to practice extortion : OVERCHARGE ⟨doctors who were . . . *gouging* on patients —Milton Silverman⟩ ⟨began *gouging* on the price —Wenzell Brown⟩
gouge carving *n* : NICKING
gougelhof *var of* GUGELHUPF
goug·er \-jə(r)\ *n* -s : one that gouges: as **a** : a person who uses a gouge in shaping heels or toes of shoes **b** : a person who overcharges or takes unfair advantage of another ⟨rent ~*s* who objected to urban renewal programs⟩
gou·jon \'güjən\ *n* -s [LaF, fr. F, gudgeon — more at GUDGEON] : FLATHEAD CATFISH
gouk *var of* ²GOWK
goul *chiefly Scot var of* GOWL
gou·lard's extract \(')gü¦lärdz-\ *n, usu cap G* [after Thomas *Goulard* †1784 Fr. surgeon] : an aqueous solution of lead subacetate applied to bruises and sprains
gou·lash *also* **gu·lash** \'gü,läsh, -lash,-laa(ə)sh,-laish,-läsh\ *n* -ES [Hung *gulyás* herdsman, herdsman's stew] **1 a** : a beef stew with onion, paprika, and caraway — called also *Hungarian goulash* **b** : a stew of mixed ingredients **2 a** : a method of dealing in bridge in which each player arranges his 13-card hand into suits, the hands are stacked to reconstitute the pack, and this pack unshuffled is then dealt to the four players in lots of 5, 5, and 3 cards at a time, the object being to produce unusually long suits in the players' hands — called also *hollandaise, mayonnaise* **b** : a deal of the cards in this manner **c goulashes** *pl but sing in constr* : a bridge game in which a goulash is dealt whenever the bidding of a regular deal stops short of a game contract **d** : two-handed pinochle played with a 64-card pack **3** : a mixture of heterogeneous elements : MISHMASH, MEDLEY, JUMBLE ⟨a sort of linguistic ~ . . . made of many ingredients —Charlton Laird⟩
gould \'gau(l)d\ *Scot var of* GOLD
gould·ian finch \'güldēən-\ *also* **gouldian** *n* -s *often cap G* [John *Gould* †1881 Eng. naturalist + E *-ian*] : a small brilliantly colored Australian finch (*Poephila gouldiae*) often kept as a cage or aviary bird
goum \'güm\ *n* -s [F, fr. Ar dial. *gūm*, var. of Ar *qum* band, troop] **1** : a unit of native soldiers under French officers in No. Africa **2** : a member of a goum
gou·mi *or* **gu·mi** \'gümē\ *n* -s [Jap *gumi*] : a shrub (*Elaeagnus multiflora*) of Japan and China cultivated for its fragrant flowers and orange or reddish fruit
gou·mier \(')güm¦yā\ *n* -s [F, fr. *goum* + *-ier* -er] : GOUM 2
gound \'gaund\ *dial var of* GOWN
go under *vi* : to come to be overwhelmed, destroyed, or defeated : FAIL ⟨take the steps now to keep that country from *going under* —Norman Cousins⟩
goun·dou \'gün(,)dü\ *n* -s [F, fr. a native name in western Africa] : a tumorous swelling of the root of the nose involving the nasal bones, occurring in certain tropical areas, and often considered a late lesion of yaws — compare GANGOSA
go up *vi* **1 a** : to proceed or move to or as if to a higher place ⟨the elevator *went up* to the fourth floor⟩ ⟨*go up* in a plane for the first time⟩ **b** : to lead to or as if to a higher place ⟨a road *goes up* to the mountain lodge⟩ **2** : to become audible : come to be heard ⟨the roar that *went up*: I thought we'd burst the ribs of the roof —Gerard Perry⟩ **3** — used interjectionally esp. to express derision ⟨some small boys came out of the city and jeered at him, saying, "*Go up*, you baldhead" —2 Kings 2:23 (RSV)⟩ **4 a** : to come to ruin; *specif* : to become bankrupt **b** : to become destroyed ⟨caused his mansion to *go up* in flames —F.W.Saunders⟩ **5** *Brit* **a** : to enter a university **b** : to become a candidate **6 a** : to undergo construction ⟨new schools *go up* all the time —John Blofeld⟩ **b** : to come to be posted or put up ⟨placards declaring martial law were *going up* —J.P.O'Donnell⟩ **7** : to undergo an increase (as in price or number) : RISE ⟨medical costs have *gone up* —Vannevar Bush⟩ ⟨world population is *going up* —Ruth Douglass⟩ **8** : to become confused esp. with temporary loss of memory ⟨she *went up* in her lines in the third act and merely giggled —Irving Kolodin⟩
goup *var of* GAUP
¹**goura** *var of* GORA
²**gou·ra** \'gürə, 'gaurə\ *n, cap* [NL, fr. a native name in New Guinea] : a genus of birds (family Columbidae) including only the crowned pigeons
gou·ra·mi \gü'rämē\ *n, pl* **gourami** *or* **gouramis** *or* **gouramies** [Malay *gurami*] **1 a** : a large freshwater anabantid fish (*Osphronemus goramy*) that is an important food fish in southeastern Asia and the Malay archipelago **b** : any of several small brightly colored fishes of the same family that are often kept in the tropical aquarium — see CROAKING GOURAMI, THREE-SPOT GOURAMI **2** : YELLOW GROUPER 1
gourd \'gō(ə)rd, 'gō(-, 'gü(-; -ōəd, -ō(ə)d, -üəd\ *n* -s [ME *gourde*, fr. MF, fr. L *cucurbita*, prob. of non-IE origin like L *cucumer-, cucumis* cucumber — more at CUCUMBER] **1 a** *chiefly Brit* : a cucurbitaceous fruit (as a cucumber, watermelon, or squash) : PEPO **b** (1) : any of numerous hard-rinded inedible usu. large fruits (as a bottle gourd) of vines of the genus *Lagenaria* extensively used for vessels and utensils — called also *calabash* (2) : any of numerous hard-rinded inedible small fruits derived from a natural variety of the pumpkin (*Cucurbita pepo*) — called also *ornamental gourd* (3) : DISHCLOTH GOURD **c** *Brit* : PUMPKIN 1 a (3) **2** : a cucurbitaceous plant whose fruits are gourds **3** : any of various hard-rinded fruits (as of the calabash tree) resembling or used like gourds **4** : a cleaned dried shell of a gourd used as a dipper or water bottle
gourde \'gü(ə)rd\ *n* -s [AmerF, fr. F, fem. of *gourd* numb, dull, heavy, fr. L *gurdus* dull, stupid] **1 a** : the basic monetary unit of Haiti — see MONEY table **b** : a coin representing this unit **2** : DOLLAR — formerly used in Louisiana, Cuba, and Haiti
gourd family *n* : CUCURBITACEAE
gourdhead \'=,=\ *also* **gourdhead buffalo** *n* **1** : BIGMOUTH BUFFALO **2** : WOOD IBIS
¹**gour·mand** \'gü(ə)r,mänd, 'gō(ə)r,m-, 'gȯ(ə)r,m-, -üə,m-, -ōə,m-, -ȯ(ə),m-, -,mənd, =ˈmänd, (')=¦mäⁿ\ *also* **gor·mand** \'gȯ(ə)rmənd, -ȯ(ə)m-, -,mänd\ *n* -s [MF *gourmant*, adj. & n.] **1** : a greedy or ravenous eater : GLUTTON ⟨can a ~ ever appreciate rare and fragile flavors —E.J.Banfield⟩ **2** : a luxurious eater : EPICURE, GOURMET ⟨the French love good eating — they are all ~*s* —Laurence Sterne⟩ **syn** see EPICURE
²**gourmand** \"\ *also* **gormand** \"\ *adj* [MF *gourmant*] : fond of eating : GLUTTONOUS; *esp* : fond of dainty or luxurious food
gour·man·dise \'gürmən,dēz, 'gōrm-, 'gȯ(r)m-, -üəm-, -ōəm-, ,==ˈ=\ *also* **gor·man·dize** \'gȯ(r)mən,dīz, -dēz, ,==ˈdēz\ *n, pl* **gourman·dises** \-ēz(əz)\ *also* **gorman·diz·es** \-īzəz,-ēzəz\ [ME *gromandise*, fr. MF *gourmandise*, fr. *gourmant* + *-ise* -ice] : luxurious epicurean discrimination in eating and drinking
gour·man·diz·er \'==,dīzə(r)\ *n* -s : GOURMAND 1
gour·met \'gü(ə)r,mā, 'gō(ə)r,m-, 'gȯ(ə)r,m-, -üə,m-, -ōə,m-, =ˈ=\ *n* -s [F, fr. MF, alter. (perh. influenced by *gourmant* gourmand) of OF *gromet, grommes* boy servant, wine merchant's assistant] : a connoisseur in eating and drinking : EPICURE **syn** see EPICURE
gous *pl of* GOU
gousle *var of* GUSLA
gous·ty *or* **gous·tie** \'gausti, 'gəus-\ *adj* [origin unknown] **1** *dial Brit* : desolate and dismal **2** *dial Brit* : EERIE, GHOSTLY
¹**gout** \'gaut, *usu* -aud.+V\ *n* -s [ME *goute*, fr. OF, drop, gout (considered as caused by drops of diseased humors), fr. L *gutta* drop; perh. akin to Arm *kat', kat'n* drop, *kit', kt'an* milk] **1 a** : a metabolic disease occurring in paroxysms and marked by a painful inflammation of the fibrous and ligamentous parts of the joints, deposits of urates in and around the joints, and at times an excessive amount of uric acid in the blood **b** : a disease esp. of wheat characterized by swellings at the nodes — see GOUT FLY **2** : a mass or aggregate of something fluid, sticky, gaseous, or composed of fine particles : CLOT, BLOB, SPLASH, SPURT ⟨attacking snowy canvases with ~*s* of oil paint —*Times Lit. Supp.*⟩ ⟨the light ~ of sand the child's shovel . . . flung —William Faulkner⟩ ⟨hurled ~*s* of brown dust and gray smoke into the air —G.H.Johnston⟩ ⟨a great ~ of oil shot out of it —Ira Wolfert⟩ ⟨~ of water gushed forth —R.A.W. Hughes⟩ ⟨~*s* of blood⟩ **3 a** : waste fiber caught in yarn during spinning or accidentally woven into cloth **b** : a defect in cloth caused by gout
²**gout** \", 'gōt\ *n* -s [ME *goute*, alter. of *gote*] *now dial Eng* : an artificial water channel; *esp* : CULVERT
³**goût** \'gü\ *n* -s [F, fr. L *gustus*; akin to L *gustare* to taste, enjoy — more at CHOOSE] **1 a** : taste or flavor esp. of food **b** : RELISH, LIKING — used with *for* ⟨has no ~ for that sort of adventure⟩ **2** : artistic or literary good taste : DISCERNMENT ⟨the sting of having my ~ as a reader under attack —Peter De Vries⟩ ⟨has a very nice ~ in such matters⟩
goû·ter \(')gü¦tā\ *n* -s [F, fr. *goûter* to taste, enjoy, eat a snack, fr. L *gustare* to taste, enjoy — more at CHOOSE] : an afternoon snack ⟨sat on the sands to eat a childish ~ of bread and butter —Anne Green⟩
gout fly *n* [¹*gout*] : any of various chloropid flies (genus *Chlorops*) whose larvae feed in wheat, barley, and other grasses causing gout in infested plants
gout·i·ly \'gaud·ᵊlē, -aut|, |ᵊli, |əl-\ *adv* : in a gouty manner
gout·i·ness \|ēnəs, |in-\ *n* -ES : the quality or state of being gouty
gout·ish \|ish, |ēsh\ *adj* [ME *goutissh*, fr. *goute* + *-issh* -ish] : predisposed to gout : GOUTY
gout stool *n* : a stool with an adjustable top
¹**goutte** \'güt\ *n* -s [F, lit., drop, fr. OF *goute* — more at GOUT] : DROP 1c(5)
²**goutté** *or* **gouttée** *or* **goutty** *var of* GUTTÉE
gout tree *n* **1** : CLAMMY CHERRY **2** : a tree (*Varronia globosa*) of tropical America
goutweed \'=,=\ *n* : a coarse European plant (*Aegopodium podagraria*) with umbellate white flowers
gouty \'gaud·ē, -aut|, |i\ *adj, sometimes* -ER/-EST [ME *gowty*, fr. *goute* gout + *-y* — more at GOUT] **1 a** : diseased with gout ⟨a ~ person⟩ **b** : of or characteristic of gout ⟨a ~ paroxysm⟩ ⟨~ concretions⟩ **c** : causing or tending to induce gout ⟨some wines are distinctly ~⟩ **d** : used for or for use during an attack of gout ⟨~ shoes⟩ **2** : SWOLLEN, BULGING, OVERLARGE ⟨chairs with ~ legs —F.G.Roe⟩ **3** *archaic* : KNOBBY, KNOTTY
gouty stem *or* **gouty tree** *n* : BOTTLE TREE
gov *abbr* **1** government, governmental **2** governor
gove \'gōv\ *vi* -ED/-ING/-S [ME (Sc dial.) *goven*] *Scot* : to stare idly : GAPE ⟨~ away or sleep and loiter out the day —Allan Ramsay †1758⟩
gov·ern \'gəvə(r)n *sometimes* 'gəvᵊm *or* 'gəbᵊm\ *vb* **governed; governed; governing** \-və(r)niŋ, -*R sometimes* -vniŋ\ **governs** \-və(r)nz, -vᵊmz, -bᵊmz\ [ME *governen*, fr. OF *governer*, fr. L *gubernare* to steer, pilot, govern, fr. Gk *kybernan*, prob. of non-IE origin] *vt* **1 a** : to exercise arbitrarily or by established rules continuous sovereign authority over; *esp* : to control and direct the making and administration of policy in ⟨a cabinet which . . . is to ~ the land —C.J.Friedrich⟩ ⟨Europe was ~*ed* almost entirely by kings —Stringfellow Barr⟩ **b** : to rule without sovereign power : implement and carry into effect policy decisions over without having the power to determine basic policy : ADMINISTER ⟨the country is ruled but not ~*ed* —Frederick Puckle⟩ ⟨New York City is ~*ed* by its budget director . . . supported by department engineers, administrators —A.A.Berle⟩ **2 a** *archaic* : to control the workings or operation of : MANIPULATE ⟨~ these ventages with your fingers and thumbs . . . and it will discourse most eloquent music —Shak.⟩ **b** : to control the speed or power of (as a machine) esp. by automatic means — compare GOVERNOR 4 **3 a** : to control, direct, or strongly influence the actions and conduct of (as a person or a group) ⟨men are ~*ed* by memory rather than thought —John Dewey⟩ ⟨special students . . . are ~*ed* by the same scholastic regulations —*Bull. of Meharry Med. Coll.*⟩ **b** : DETERMINE, GUIDE, REGULATE ⟨a commission to ~ the union's business affairs⟩ ⟨deadlock and compromise largely ~*ed* the choice —B.K.Sandwell⟩ ⟨its agreements ~ working conditions in many ports —E.P.Hohman⟩ **c** : to hold in check : RESTRAIN ⟨this consuming passion for law made him ~ himself —H.E.Scudder⟩ ⟨I appeal to you to ~ your temper —Charles Dickens⟩ **4 a** *obs* : to require (a verb) to be in a certain person and number — used of the subject of a verb; compare AGREE *vi* 5 **b** : to require (a word) to be in a certain case or mood ⟨in English a transitive verb ~*s* a noun in the common case or a pronoun in the accusative case⟩ **c** : to call for (a certain case or mood) : REQUIRE ⟨the German preposition *mit* ~*s* the dative case⟩ ⟨the Greek conjunction *ean* ~*s* the subjunctive mood⟩ **5** : to constitute a rule or law for : serve as a precedent or deciding principle for ⟨policies . . . which should ~ the services of all libraries —Helen T. Geer⟩ ⟨the principles which should ~ the creation of proletarian literature —C.I.Glicksberg⟩ ~ *vi* **1** : to prevail or have decisive influence : CONTROL ⟨in all causes of passion admit reason to ~ —George Washington⟩ **2** : to exercise authority : perform the functions of government esp. in the making and execution of policy : RULE ⟨at the beginning of the seventeenth century our kings still ~*ed* as well as reigned —Ernest Barker⟩ — compare REIGN
gov·ern·able \-ə(r)nəbəl, -ᵊməb-\ *adj* : capable of being governed ⟨likely to be ~ by prudent counsel —George Meredith⟩ — **gov·ern·able·ness** *n* -ES
gov·ern·ance \'gəvə(r)nən(t)s\ *n* -s [ME *governaunce*, fr. MF *governance*, fr. *governer, gouverner* to govern + *-ance* — more at GOVERN] **1** : the act or process of governing : GOVERNMENT 2 ⟨the internal stresses and strains in the ~ of a nation —V.O.Key⟩ ⟨intelligence . . . in the ~ of men —Lewis Mumford⟩ **2 a** : the office, power, or function of governing ⟨invested with the ~ of the kingdom⟩ **b** : controlling or directing influence : AUTHORITY ⟨she disliked whatever did not yield to her ~ —Thomas Wolfe⟩ **3** : the state of being governed ⟨the colonies . . . passed through analogous stages from ~ to self-government —Alexander Brady⟩ **4 a** : the manner or method of governing : conduct of office ⟨her ironfisted ~ of her office is one of arbitrary whim and prejudice —H.L.Ickes⟩ ⟨inferred the nature of the governor from the observed mode of his ~ —I.R.Maxwell⟩ **b** *obs* : personal conduct, behavior, or manner of life ⟨the likest is to fall into mischance . . . regardless of his ~ —Edmund Spenser⟩ **5** : a system of governing : GOVERNMENT 7a ⟨the ancient ~ was sapped in its foundations —John Buchan⟩ ⟨a new world ~ enforced through power —*Yale Rev.*⟩
gov·er·nante \'gəvə(r)nənt, ¦==¦nänt\ *or* **gou·ver·nante** \'güv-, ¦güv-\ *n* -s [F *gouvernante*, fr. fem. of *gouvernant*, pres. part. of *gouverner* to govern, administer, bring up, fr. OF *governer* — more at GOVERN] **1** *archaic* : a woman having charge of a young person : CHAPERON 2, GOVERNESS 2 ⟨attended by . . . an old gentlewoman for her ~ —Jedidiah Morse⟩ **2** *archaic* : the mistress of a household : HOUSEKEEPER **3** *obs* : GOVERNESS 1 ⟨the government devolved upon the princess, as ~ during her son's minority —Tobias Smollett⟩
¹**gov·er·ness** \'gəvə(r)nəs\ *n* -ES [ME *governesse*, fr. MF *governeresse*, fr. *governeor* governor + *-esse* -ess — more at GOVERNOR] **1** : a woman that governs : a female governor ⟨his mother was named by the states *Governess* of the United Provinces —Charles Butler †1832⟩ ⟨a shining example to ~*es* of religious houses —Ann Radcliffe⟩ ⟨the moon, the ~ of floods —Shak.⟩ **2** : a woman entrusted with the care and supervision of a child or young person; *esp* : a female teacher employed in a private household ⟨my education and that of my brothers had been generally superintended . . . by a succession of ~*es* —Caroline Gilman⟩ **3** *archaic* : the wife of a governor ⟨introduced by the . . . *Governess* at Madras —Benjamin Heyne⟩
²**governess** \"\ *vb* -ED/-ING/-ES *vi* : to act or serve as a governess ⟨she's going to ~ in Winnipeg —Agnes Macdonald⟩ ~ *vt* **1** : to act as governess to : INSTRUCT ⟨and ~*es* her brother's rising family —*Tait's Mag.*⟩ **2** : to subject to or as if to the authority and instruction of a governess ⟨if you persist in ~*ing* people —G.B.Shaw⟩
governess cart *or* **governess car** *n* : a light two-wheeled cart entered from the rear with body partly or wholly of wickerwork and with a seat for two persons along each side — called also *tub-cart*
gov·er·nessy \-sē\ *adj* : having the characteristics of or suggesting a governess; *esp* : PRIM ⟨a big nunlike college girl with a ~ air —Frank O'Connor⟩

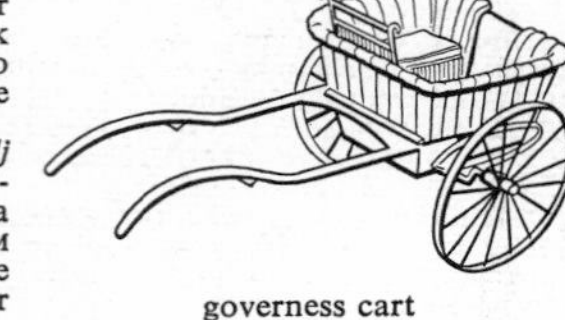
governess cart

governless *adj, obs* : lacking a government : UNGOVERNED
gov·ern·ment \'gə|və(r)mənt, |və(r)nm-, |v(ᵊ)m-, |b(ᵊ)m-\ *n* -s *often attrib* [MF *governement*, fr. *governer* to govern + *-ment*] **1** *obs* **a** : management of the limbs or the whole body ⟨shot many a dart at me . . . but I them warded all with wary ~ —Edmund Spenser⟩ **b** : moral conduct or behavior : DISCRETION ⟨harsh rage, defect of manners, want of ~ —Shak.⟩ **2** : the act or process of governing : authoritative direction or control ⟨to make rules for the ~ and regulation of the land and naval forces —*U.S. Constitution*⟩ ⟨unusual talent for the instruction and ~ of the young —S.P.Chase & J.K.Snyder⟩ **3 a** : the office, authority, or function of governing ⟨the ~ I cast upon my brother and to my state grew stranger —Shak.⟩ ⟨persuaded . . . to accept the ~ of Dover Castle —James Tyrrell⟩ **b** *obs* : the term during which a governing official holds office ⟨his fact, till now in the ~ of Lord Angelo, came not to an undoubtful proof —Shak.⟩ **4** *archaic* : an area organized as a political unit; *esp* : a territorial division ruled by a governor ⟨I pass'd through most of the Protestant ~*s* in Europe —Joseph Addison⟩ ⟨the czar . . . divided the empire into eight ~*s* —Charles Whitworth⟩ **5 a** : the influence of one word on another word that is required to be in a certain case or mood when it occurs in the same construction — called also *regimen* **b** : the effect of this influence **6 a** : the continuous exercise of authority over and the performance of functions for a political unit : RULE ⟨the end of ~ is the good of mankind —John Locke⟩ ⟨constitutional ~ does not exist unless procedural restraints are established —C.J.Friedrich⟩ ⟨before the fourteenth century . . . ~ had meant very largely the administration of justice —Christopher Morris⟩ ⟨he was active in school ~ —*Current Biog.*⟩ **b** : the political function of policy making as distinguished from the administration of policy decisions **7 a** : the organization, machinery, or agency through which a political unit exercises authority and performs functions and which is usu. classified according to the distribution of power within it ⟨the distinction between constitutional and absolute ~*s* —G.H.Sabine⟩ ⟨framing a ~ which is to be administered by men over men —James Madison⟩ ⟨the great growth of the national ~ —W.S.Sayre⟩ ⟨advanced through the ranks of his church's ~ —*Current Biog.*⟩ ⟨industrial capitalism . . . created clusters of private ~ —R.J. Harris⟩ — see ARISTOCRACY 2a, DEMOCRACY 1b, DICTATORSHIP 3, MONARCHY, OLIGARCHY, REPUBLIC, TYRANNY **b** : the complex of political institutions, laws, and customs through which the function of governing is carried out in a specific political unit ⟨the shifting of functions . . . which has characterized American ~ —C.F.Snider⟩ ⟨students of French ~⟩ ⟨an attempt to derive information about trade-union ~ —*Times Lit. Supp.*⟩ **8** : the body of persons that constitutes the governing authority of a political unit or organization: as **a** : the officials collectively comprising the governing body of a political unit and constituting the organization as an active agency ⟨a world in which ~*s* . . . are highly and effectively resolved to work together —F.D.Roosevelt⟩ ⟨the ~ had succeeded in transporting . . . tons of equipment inland —Wendell Willkie⟩ ⟨correspondence . . . that passed between the American ~ and the German ~ —*Chicago Daily News*⟩ **b** *usu cap* : the executive branch of the U.S. federal government including the political officials and usu. the permanent civil service employees : ADMINISTRATION 6a ⟨the senator's treatment of *Government* witnesses before the committee⟩ ⟨the *Government's* case was argued before the Supreme Court⟩ **c** *usu cap* : a small group of persons holding simultaneously the principal political executive offices of a nation or other political unit and responsible for the direction and supervision of public affairs: (1) : such a group in a parliamentary system constituted by the cabinet or by the ministry ⟨His Majesty's *Government* feel they have the right to know where they stand with the House of Commons —Sir Winston Churchill⟩ ⟨the typical opposition maneuver designed to embarrass the *Government*

—H.L.Bretton⟩ ⟨apart from providing a *Government*, the main functions of the New Zealand Parliament are firstly to legislate —Walter Nash⟩ (2) **:** ADMINISTRATION 6b **9 :** POLITICAL SCIENCE ⟨the other social sciences including economics and ~ —Weston La Barre⟩ **10 :** a security (as a bond) issued by or on behalf of the U.S. government — usu. used in pl. ⟨reserves in the form of cash or ~s —G.A.Mooney⟩

gov·ern·men·tal \ˌgə̇və(r)nˈment³l, \|və(r)ˌme-, \|vᵊmˌe-, \|bᵊm-ˌe-\ *adj* **:** of or relating to government or to the government of a particular political unit ⟨the core of a ~ system —C.J. Friedrich⟩ ⟨serious damage done . . . to public confidence and to ~ morale —G.F.Kennan⟩

governmental atonement *n* **:** the Grotian theory of atonement that Christ's death enables God as moral governor of the world to forgive sinners freely without encouraging disorder by signally revealing that suffering often of the innocent inevitably follows when sinners violate the divine world order

gov·ern·men·tal·ism \ˌ≈≈ˈ≈≈ˌizəm\ *n* -s **1 :** a theory advocating extension of the sphere and degree of government activity ⟨the keystone of ~ is the reduction of private enterprise⟩ — compare STATISM **2 :** the tendency toward extension of the role of government ⟨the growing ~ . . . of Switzerland was sanctioned —C.J.Friedrich⟩

gov·ern·men·tal·ist \-ˌəst\ *n* -s **:** one that advocates or implements governmentalism ⟨helps to perpetuate the ~s in office —*Fortune*⟩

gov·ern·men·tal·iza·tion \ˌ≈≈ˌ≈≈əˈzāshən, -ˌīˈz-\ *n* -s **:** the action or result of governmentalizing ⟨prevent the ~ of all international economic life —William Hard⟩

gov·ern·men·tal·ize \ˌ≈≈ˈ≈≈ˌīz\ *vt* -ED/-ING/-s **:** to subject to the regulation or control of a government ⟨the Federal government's effort to ~ medicine —Raymond Moley⟩

gov·ern·men·tal·ly \ˌ≈≈ˈ≈≈ē, -i\ *adv* **:** by or in terms of government or the government of a political unit ⟨not sufficiently popularly or ~ controlled —*World's Work*⟩

government bill *n, sometimes cap G* **:** a public or private bill prepared, introduced, and sponsored in the legislature by a member of the government ⟨in Great Britain a *government bill* . . . is in direct charge of a minister —F.A.Ogg & Harold Zink⟩ ⟨in France . . . *government bills* are drawn up in the departments —D.W.S.Lidderdale⟩ — compare PRIVATE MEMBER'S BILL

government bream *n* [so called fr. the fact that its markings suggest the broad arrow placed on government materials by the British Board of Ordnance] **:** a highly esteemed food fish (*Lutjanus sebae*) dwelling on the bottom of tropical Australian seas and marked when young by an arrangement of scarlet bands resembling a broad arrow

government corporation *n* **:** PUBLIC CORPORATION 2 ⟨the TVA is set up as a *government corporation* outside the executive departments —W.S.Sayre⟩

government depository *n, often cap G* **:** a bank that by law may receive deposits of government funds ⟨all member banks of the Federal Reserve system may . . . be designated as *government depositories* —G.G.Munn⟩

gov·ern·ment·ese \ˌgə̇və(r)mənˈtēz, \|və(r)nm-, \|v(ᵊ)m-, \|b(ᵊ)m-, -mənˌtēz\ *n* -s [*government* + *-ese*] **:** GOBBLEDYGOOK ⟨a tongue-in-cheek definition . . . given him in ~ —A.L. Hench⟩

government-general \ˈ≈(≈)≈ˈ≈(≈)≈\ *n, pl* **governments-general** *usu cap both Gs* **1 :** a territory over which a governor-general has jurisdiction ⟨Frenchmen have moved into the *Government-General* in large numbers —*N. Y. Herald Tribune*⟩ **2 :** a government headed by a governor-general ⟨administrative authority was vested in a *Government-General* —A.L. Grey⟩

government house *n* **1 :** a building containing the principal government offices esp. in a British colony or Commonwealth country **2 :** the official residence of a governor esp. of a British colony

government-in-exile \ˈ≈(≈)≈≈ˈ≈ˌ≈\ *n, pl* **governments-in-exile :** a government temporarily established on foreign soil following the occupation of its own territory by another authority ⟨breaking off relations with the Polish *government-in-exile* —W.H.Chamberlin⟩

government issue *adj, often cap G&I* **:** issued or provided by a government or a government agency ⟨standard *government-issue* equipment —A.Q.Maisel⟩

government man *n* **1 :** a government official; *esp* **:** G-MAN **2 :** a consistent supporter of the Government in power **3 :** a convict in 19th century Australia

government note *n* **:** a currency note issued by a government — compare BANK NOTE 1

government paper *n* **:** evidences of debt (as bonds or notes) issued by a government ⟨borrowings on *government paper* were as large as on commercial bills and notes —H.G. Moulton⟩

government security *n* **:** a security (as a bond or certificate) issued by or on behalf of a government — usu. used in pl. ⟨Federal Reserve Bank holdings of *government securities*⟩

gov·er·nor *R* ˈgəv(ə)nər *also* -vərnər, -*R* -v(ə)nə(r)\ *n* -s [ME *governour*, fr. MF *governeor*, fr. L *gubernator* steersman, fr. *gubernatus* (past part. of *gubernare* to steer) + *-or* — more at GOVERN] **1 :** one that governs: as **a :** one that exercises authority esp. over an area or group ⟨the kings, princes and ~s of the world —*Times Lit. Supp.*⟩ ⟨the American people . . . ~s of us all —H.S.Truman⟩ ⟨the sun . . . was the ~ of the heavens —S.F.Mason⟩ **b** *often cap, archaic* **:** GOD ⟨the Deity . . . which is the supreme *governor* of all things —Ralph Cudworth⟩ **c :** an official elected or appointed to act as ruler, chief executive, or nominal head of a political unit (as a colony, state, or province) ⟨each colony has its own government headed by the ~ who represents the crown —W.E.Simnett⟩ ⟨the office of ~ in the American states —W.S.Sayre⟩ ⟨Australian . . . state ~s act on the advice of their ministers —Geoffrey Sawer⟩ **d :** COMMANDANT ⟨the ~ of the besieged fortress⟩ **e :** the managing director and usu. the principal officer of an institution or organization ⟨is ~ of the Bank of France —Harrison Smith⟩ ⟨past ~ of the local lodge —*Springfield (Mass.) Union*⟩ ⟨assistant ~ of a large English prison⟩ ⟨the ~ of an Edinburgh hospital —H.A.Albert⟩ **f :** a member of a group of persons that directs or controls an institution or society **:** DIRECTOR ⟨the board of ~s of the Federal Reserve System . . . consists of seven members —E.W.Kemmerer⟩ ⟨the board of ~s of the National Press Club —*Newsweek*⟩ ⟨a ~ of the University of British Columbia —*Current Biog.*⟩ **g :** the chief of an Indian tribe or pueblo ⟨the party executing the order of the . . . ~s of the pueblos —*Weekly New Mexican*⟩ **2** *archaic* **:** one that has charge of the education of a young man usu. of royal or noble birth ⟨at the age of seven he was . . . handed over to a ~ —Nancy Mitford⟩ **3 a** *slang* **:** one looked upon as governing (as a father, guardian, or employer) ⟨my old ~ sent me to Eton —Angela Thirkell⟩ **b :** MISTER, SIR — usu. used in informal address ⟨come and look at 'em, ~ —Henry Mayhew⟩ **4 a :** an attachment to a machine (as a gasoline or steam engine) designed to afford automatic control or limitation of speed or power; *esp* **:** such an attachment actuated by the centrifugal force of whirling weights opposed by gravity or by springs **b :** a contrivance giving automatic control (as of pressure or temperature) — called also *regulator*

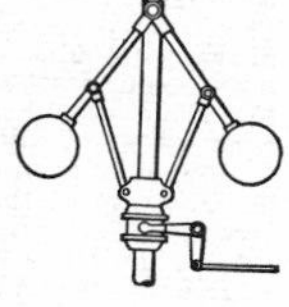
governor 4a

gov·er·nor·ate \-nərət, -ˌrāt\ *n* -s **:** an administrative division ruled by a governor ⟨Egypt is divided into . . . five ~s —*Egypt Almanac*⟩

governor-general \ˈ≈(≈)≈ˈ≈(≈)≈\ *n, pl* **governors-general** *or* **governor-generals :** a governor of high rank; *esp* **:** one who governs a large territory (as a country) or has lieutenant or deputy governors under him ⟨the *governor-general* is . . . appointed by the queen on the advice of the prime minister of Canada —*Canadian Citizenship Series*⟩ ⟨as early as 1548 a royal decree created the office of *governor general* . . . of Brazil —A.N.Christensen⟩

governor-general-in-council \ˈ≈(≈)≈ˈ≈(≈)≈ˈ≈≈\ *n, pl* **governors-general-in-council** *or* **governor-generals-in-council :** the governor-general in a member nation of the British Commonwealth acting with the advice and consent of the nation's Privy Council usu. as a formal means of giving legal effect to cabinet decisions ⟨in South Africa . . . all provincial ordinances must be assented to by the *governor-general-in-council* —Alexander Brady⟩

governor-generalship \ˌ≈(≈)≈ˈ≈(≈)≈ˌ≈\ *n* **1 :** the office of governor-general ⟨the *governor-generalship* of India . . . at which he aimed —T.E.Hook⟩ **2 :** the period of incumbency of a governor-general ⟨the two years of his *governor-generalship* —*Athenaeum*⟩

governor-in-council \ˌ≈(≈)≈≈ˈ≈≈\ *n, pl* **governors-in-council 1 :** the governor of a British colony acting with the advice and usu. in the presence of the executive council but not always with its consent ⟨referred to and decided by the *governor in council* —*Nigeria Order in Council, 1946*⟩ **2 :** GOVERNOR-GENERAL-IN-COUNCIL ⟨Canadian statutes . . . confer many and varied powers directly upon the *governor-in-council* —Alexander Brady⟩

governor's council *n* **:** an executive or legislative council elected (as in some states of the U. S.) or appointed (as in some former British colonies) to advise a governor or share in the functions of the office of governor ⟨only Maine, New Hampshire, and Massachusetts still have a *governor's council* —*Amer. Guide Series: Mass.*⟩

gov·er·nor·ship \ˈ≈(≈)≈ˌship\ *n* **1 a :** the office of governor ⟨the ~ was held for long periods by one man —*Amer. Guide Series: Conn.*⟩ ⟨the only man in Indiana's history to have held its ~ twice —*Current Biog.*⟩ **b :** the conduct of the office of governor ⟨his ~ of Bristol was the foundation of the impeachment —William Prynne & Clement Walker⟩ **2 :** the period of incumbency of a governor ⟨during his ~ many new laws were enacted⟩

governor's plum *or* **governor plum** *n* [so called fr. the fact that the genus *Flacourtia* was named after Etienne de Flacourt †1660 governor and historian of Madagascar] **:** a small often shrubby dioecious tree (*Flacourtia indica*) native to Madagascar and southern Asia and cultivated in tropical regions as a hedge plant and for its deep red somewhat acid fruits that resemble small plums — called also *ramontchi*

governor win·throp desk \-ˈwin(t)thrəp-\ *n, usu cap G&W* [after *Governor* John *Winthrop* †1649 governor of Mass. Colony] **:** a desk with an oxbow front and usu. claw-and-ball feet

Governor Winthrop desk

governs *pres 3d sing of* GOVERN

goves *pres 3d sing of* GOVE

goving *pres part of* GOVE

govt *abbr* government

gow·an \ˈgau̇ən\ *n* -s [prob. alter. of ME *gollan*] **1** *chiefly Scot* **:** DAISY 1 ⟨as fresh as ~s —Jane W. Carlyle⟩ **2** *chiefly Scot* **:** a white or yellow field flower — used chiefly in combination ⟨horse ~⟩

gow·any \-ni\ *adj, Scot* **:** abounding in gowans ⟨sweeter than ~ glens —Allan Ramsay †1758⟩

goway bird *var of* GOAWAY BIRD

gowd \ˈgau̇d\ *chiefly Scot var of* GOLD

gowd·en \ˈgau̇dᵊn\ *chiefly Scot var of* GOLDEN

gow·en cypress \ˈgau̇ən-\ *n* [after James R. *Gowen*, 19th cent. Brit. horticulturist] **:** a small tree or shrub (*Cupressus goveniana*) with erect or stiff branches, spherical cones, and light green to yellowish leaves that is native to California and used as an ornamental

gow·ers's tract \ˈgau̇(ə)rz(əz)-\ *n, usu cap G* [after Sir William R. *Gowers* †1915 Eng. neurologist] **:** a crescent-shaped tract of fibers in the anterior lateral part of the spinal cord

¹gowf \ˈgau̇f\ *Scot var of* GOLF

²gowf \"\ *n* -s [perh. fr. ¹*gowf* (also, "golf club")] *Scot* **:** a dull blow **:** CUFF, BUFFET

³gowf \"\ *vt* -ED/-ING/-s *Scot* **:** STRIKE, CUFF

go·wid·die \gōˈwidē\ *n* -s [origin unknown] **:** LABRADOR TEA a

go without *vi* **:** to deprive oneself ⟨those who *go without* to pay their doctor —S.B.Pettengill⟩

¹gowk \ˈgau̇k, ˈgük, ˈgōk\ *n* -s [ME *goke, gowke* fr. ON *gaukr* cuckoo; akin to OE *gēac* cuckoo, OHG *gouh*] **1** *dial Brit* **:** CUCKOO **2** *dial Brit* **:** SIMPLETON, FOOL, GAWK ⟨sat there all evening like a great ~ —Flora Thompson⟩

²gowk \ˈgau̇k\ *vi* -ED/-ING/-s [ME (Sc dial.) *gowken*, perh. fr. *gowk*, n.] *chiefly Scot* **:** to gaze or stare vacantly

gowk·ed \ˈgau̇kəd, -ət\ *or* **gowk·it** \-ət\ *adj* [¹*gowk* + *-ed* or *-it* (Sc var of *-ed*)] *chiefly Scot* **:** FOOLISH, GIDDY

gowk storm *n* [so called fr. the typical occurrence of short storms in the spring at the time of the cuckoo's return] *Scot & Irish* **:** a brief storm or period of adversity

¹gowl \ˈgau̇(ə)l, ˈgül\ *vi* -ED/-ING/-s [ME *goulen, gowlen*, fr. ON *gaula*; akin to ON *geyja* to bark and perh. to Gk *chaos* abyss — more at GUM] *dial Brit* **:** HOWL, YELL ⟨the hound dog ~*ed*⟩ ⟨wind ~s in the chimney —R.L.Stevenson⟩

²gowl \"\ *n* -s *dial Brit* **:** a loud cry **:** HOWL, YELL ⟨burst out in kind o' ~ o' anger —S.R.Crockett⟩

¹gown \ˈgau̇n\ *n* -s [ME *goun*, fr. MF *gone, goune*, fr. LL *gunna*, a fur or leather garment] **1 :** an outer garment: **a** *archaic* **:** a usu. loose and flowing outer garment worn by men ⟨the men wore ~s in the middle ages —F.W.Fairholt⟩ **b :** the official or distinctive robe worn by men and women in certain professions (as law, education, the church, and medicine); *esp* **:** a long loose usu. black garment worn by students, graduates, and officers of colleges and universities and varying in material, cut, and trimming with the academic degree of the wearer ⟨one of the barristers . . . hitched his ~ up on his shoulder —F.W.Crofts⟩ ⟨the medieval context surviving in these ~s and hoods —A.W.Griswold⟩ — see ACADEMIC COSTUME, GENEVA GOWN **c :** a loose garment draped in soft folds worn by the ancients (as the Roman toga) **:** the dress of peace ⟨the Mars deposed and arms to ~s made yield —John Dryden⟩ **d :** a woman's dress; *esp* **:** one suitable for afternoon or evening wear ⟨her faded calico ~ —Hamlin Garland⟩ ⟨the bride's . . . ~ and veil —*Mademoiselle*⟩ **e :** a loose informal garment esp. for lounging or resting (as a nightgown or a dressing gown) ⟨at first the baby will wear a ~ both day and night⟩ **f :** the cotton coverall worn by a surgeon in the operating room ⟨dressed in hospital ~s and masks —Grace Reiten⟩ **2 a :** the office or profession indicated by the wearing of distinctive robes ⟨men of the ~ and men of the sword⟩ **b :** the students and faculty of a college or university considered as a group distinct from the nonacademic world ⟨powerful rivalry in . . . society between town and ~ —Robertson Davies⟩

²gown \"\ *vt* -ED/-ING/-s [ME *gounen*, fr. *goun*, n.] **:** to dress in or invest with a gown ⟨to ~ herself in the latest Paris fashions —Margaret W. Hungerford⟩ ⟨capped and ~*ed* dignitaries in the commencement procession⟩

gown boy *n* **:** a boy of a foundation school ⟨the artless *gown boy* from Grey Friars —W.M.Thackeray⟩

gownd \-nd\ *dial var of* GOWN

gowns·man \-nzmən\ *n, pl* **gownsmen :** one that wears a gown: **a** *archaic* **:** one that wears the dress of peace **:** CIVILIAN ⟨military men are seldom disposed to take counsel with *gownsmen* on military matters —T.B.Macaulay⟩ **b :** one that wears a professional, official, or scholastic habit (as a lawyer, clergyman, or member of a university) ⟨the distance between the *gownsmen* and the townsmen —Charles Lamb⟩ **c** *Scot* **:** BEADSMAN 2b

gowp \ˈgau̇p\ *var of* GAUP

gow·pen \ˈgau̇pən\ *n* -s [ME *goupyne*, fr. ON *gaupn* (in plural only) cupped hand; akin to OHG *coufana* hand, OE *gēap* open, wide, *gōma* palate — more at GUM] **1** *chiefly Scot* **a :** the hollow of two hands held together as if forming a bowl **b** *also* **gow·pen·ful** \-ˌfu̇l\ *pl* **gowpenfuls :** a double handful ⟨gathered a *gowpenful* of flinty arrowheads —John Service⟩ **2** *Scots law* **:** the perquisite of meal from tenants by thirlage that is allowed to a miller's servant

goy *also* **goi** \ˈgȯi\ *n, pl* **goy·im** \-ȯi(y)əm\ *or* **goys** [Yiddish *goy*, fr. Heb *gōy* people, nation] **1 :** GENTILE 1a — often used disparagingly ⟨sure that any Jew is . . . superior to any ~ — Charles Angoff⟩ ⟨our children won't fall into the hands of the *goyim* —Isaac Metzker⟩ **2 :** a Jew who does not observe Jewish precepts — used esp. by Jews ⟨time enough for you to eat pork and be a ~ —Charles Angoff⟩

goya \ˈgȯi(y)ə\ *or* **goya red** *n* -s *often cap G* [after Francisco de *Goya* y Lucientes †1828 Span. painter] **:** a strong red that is deeper than geranium (sense 3a), yellower and deeper than geranium red, and bluer and deeper than average cherry red — called also *cadmium carmine, currant, English red, English vermilion, minium, oriental red, orient red, red currant, vermilion*

goy·a·zite \ˈgȯi(y)əˌzīt\ *n* -s [F *goyazite*, fr. *Goyaz* (Goiaz), state in Brazil + F *-ite*] **:** a mineral $SrAl_3(PO_4)_2(OH)_5.H_2O$ consisting of a granular yellowish white hydrous strontium aluminum phosphate

goy·ish \ˈgȯiish\ *adj* [*goy* + *-ish*] **:** of, relating to, or having the characteristics of a goy **:** GENTILE 1a ⟨in your ordinary ~ delicatessen —Ruth Glazer⟩ ⟨the general atmosphere was ~ —Charles Angoff⟩

goyle \ˈgȯi(ə)l\ *n* -s [origin unknown] *dial Eng* **:** a steep narrow valley **:** RAVINE, GULLY

gozzan *var of* GOSSAN

goz·zard \ˈgäzə(r)d\ *n* -s [alter. of ME *gosherde*, fr. *gos, goos* goose + *herde* herdsman — more at GOOSE, HERD] **:** GOOSEHERD

gp *abbr* group

GP *abbr* **1** general paresis **2** general pause **3** general practitioner **4** general purpose **5** geographic position **6** glide path **7** [L *Gloria Patri*] Glory be to the Father **8** great primer

GPA *abbr* general passenger agent

GPD *abbr, often not cap* gallons per day

GPH *abbr, often not cap* gallons per hour

GPI *abbr* **1** general paralysis of the insane **2** ground position indicator

GPM *abbr* **1** *often not cap* gallons per minute **2** geopotential meter

GPO *abbr* **1** general post office **2** government printing office

GPS *abbr, often not cap* gallons per second

GQ *abbr* general quarters

gr *abbr* **1** grade **2** grain **3** gram **4** grammar; grammatical **5** grand **6** graphite **7** gravity **8** gray **9** great **10** grind **11** groschen **12** gross **13** grosz **14** group

GR *abbr* **1** general reconnaissance **2** general reserve

gra \ˈgrō\ *n* -s [IrGael *grādh* love, fr. L *gratus* pleasing, beloved, dear — more at GRACE] *now dial Brit* **:** DEAR

graaf·ian follicle \ˈgrä\|fēən-, ˈgra\|\ *n, sometimes cap G* [Regnier de *Graaf* †1673 Dutch anatomist + E *-ian*] **:** a vesicle in the ovary of a mammal enclosing a developing egg and consisting in the typical form of an outer fibrous sheath and an inner cellular and vascular sheath derived from the ovarian stroma and separated by a hyaline basement membrane from an epithelial zone derived from the germinal epithelium and made up of several layers of small usu. polyhedral cells that are heaped at one point into a mound which projects into the fluid-filled cavity of the vesicle and encloses the growing egg

¹grab \ˈgrab, -aa(ə)b\ *vb* **grabbed; grabbed; grabbing; grabs** [obs. D or LG *grabben*, fr. MD & MLG, respectively; akin to OE *græppian* to seize, ME *graspen* to grasp, Sw *grapsen* to seize, grasp, Sw *grabba*, ON *grāpa* to snatch, Skt *gṛbhṇāti, gṛhṇāti* he seizes] *vt* **1 a :** to take or take hold of by a sudden motion or grasp **:** SEIZE, CLUTCH **b :** CAPTURE, RESTRAIN, ARREST **2 :** to get or appropriate to oneself unscrupulously ⟨~ public lands⟩ ⟨managed to ~ three or four millions of money selling bad whiskey or forestalling the wheat harvest and selling it at three times its cost —G.B.Shaw⟩ or with a complete unconcern for another's rights or desires ⟨spend all its energy *grabbing* world markets —*Time*⟩ **3 :** to get hold of, take, or avail oneself of with dispatch or haste ⟨*grabbed* a driver and cleanly smacked a drive 225 yards —*Time*⟩ ⟨drove home, *grabbed* a bath, a shave, clean linen and city clothes —H.A.Callahan⟩ ⟨after *grabbing* a bite of food he will have to leave —Philip Hamburger⟩ **~** *vi* **1 :** to make a grab **:** SNATCH — usu. used with *at* **2** *of a horse* **:** OVERREACH **3** *of an automobile clutch or brake* **:** to engage with abnormal abruptness causing a jolt **4 :** to impede or otherwise affect as if grabbing or momentarily holding ⟨concussions were *grabbing* at his plane steadily —Ira Wolfert⟩ **syn** see TAKE — **grab hold of :** to seize or grasp firmly and usu. suddenly ⟨*grabbed hold of* the door handle and yanked the door open⟩

²grab \"\ *n* -s **1 a :** the act of grabbing: as (1) **:** a sudden grasp or attempt to grasp ⟨the child made a ~ for the candy bar⟩ (2) **:** an appropriating of something or an attempt to appropriate by unscrupulous methods ⟨a ~ for power —*Frontier*⟩ ⟨the ~ for offshore oil rights⟩ **b :** something grabbed **2 :** a device for clutching an object (as for hauling or hoisting): as **a :** any of various implements for gripping and withdrawing (as a drill or broken cable) from a borehole or well **b :** CLAMSHELL 2a **c :** SKIDDING HOOKS — **up for grabs** *slang* **:** available for anyone who takes or is able to take ⟨the prize was *up for grabs* to anyone under 16 years of age⟩

³grab \"\ *adj* **1 :** intended to be grabbed or taken hold of (as for steadying oneself) ⟨a ~ rail by the door of the bus to assist passengers in getting on or alighting⟩ **2 :** taken or to be taken at random ⟨a ~ sample⟩

⁴grab \"\ *n* -s [Ar *ghurāb*, lit., raven] **:** an oriental coasting ship of light draft and broad beam and square raking stern, sharp bow with long overhang, lateen sails, and usu. two masts

grab-all \ˈ≈ˌ≈\ *n, Austral* **:** a setnet used for marine fishing near the shore

grab bag *n* **1 :** a bag or other receptacle holding small articles which are to be drawn (as at a party or fair) without being seen often on payment of a small sum **2 :** something resembling a grab bag: as **a :** something providing a miscellany of often choice items ⟨a *grab bag* of miscellaneous specimens, some of which may catch the reader's fancy —Dwight MacDonald⟩ ⟨the revue . . . is a cornucopia, a *grab bag*, a hash —Wolcott Gibbs⟩ ⟨the *grab bag* of good and bad that goes into the making of a happy and lasting marriage —Mollie Panter-Downes⟩ **b :** an assemblage or collection of often valuable things from which one may take or appropriate whatever he can grab ⟨reversing the public purse into a private *grab bag* —J.R.Aswell & E.J.Michelson⟩

grab bar *n* **:** a graspable bar attached to the wall in a shower or near a bathtub as an assistance to a bather in steadying himself

grab·ber \-bə(r)\ *n* -s **:** one that grabs esp. unscrupulously or inconsiderately ⟨horrified at the greed of the pension ~s —W.H.Upson⟩ ⟨unscrupulous land ~s —L.S.B.Leakey⟩

grab·ble \ˈgrabəl\ *vb* **grabbled; grabbled; grabbling** \-b(ə)liŋ\ **grabbles** [D *grabbelen*, fr. MD, freq. of *grabben* to grab — more at GRAB] *vi* **1 a :** to move the hand (as in searching) in a groping fashion **:** GROPE ⟨*grabbled* about in her bag —Angela Thirkell⟩ **b** *South* **:** to remove full grown potatoes without disturbing the plant, the soil being replaced to allow other tubers to develop **c** *South* **:** to catch fish by hand by groping (as along a riverbank) **2 :** to lie or fall prone **:** SPRAWL, GROVEL **~** *vt* **1** *South* **:** to harvest by grabbling **2** *South* **:** to catch (fish) by hand — **grab·bler** \-b(ə)lə(r)\ *n* -s

grab·bots \ˈgrabəts\ *n pl* [origin unknown] **:** refuse cotton separated from the seed in cottonseed oil mills

grab bucket *n* **:** CLAMSHELL 2a

grab·by \ˈgrabē, -aab-, -bi\ *adj* -ER/-EST **:** tending to grab all one can get **:** GRASPING, GREEDY

grab crane *n* **:** a hoisting machine fitted with a clamshell

grab dredge *or* **grab dredger** *n* **:** a dredger that operates with a clamshell

gra·ben \ˈgräbən\ *n* -s [G, ditch, fr. OHG *grabo*, fr. *graban* to dig — more at GRAVE] **:** a depressed segment of the earth's crust bounded on at least two sides by faults and generally of considerable length as compared with its width — compare HORST

grab game *n* **:** a scheme, ruse, or action marked by an unscrupulous usu. sudden appropriating of money or property

grabhook \ˈ≈ˌ≈\ *n* **:** a hook (as a grapnel) for grabbing (as the links of a chain)

grab iron *n* **:** a metal bar attached to the sides of railroad cars and locomotives for use as a handhold

grab link *n* **:** SLIP GRAB

grabman \ˈ≈ˌman, -ˌmən\ *n, pl* **grabmen :** a clipper in a coal mine

grab off *vt* **1 :** to take or appropriate forcefully or with haste or forthrightness ⟨dash in and *grab off* choice pieces of land —F.P.Gipson⟩ ⟨two Swiss

grabhook

mountaineers . . . had *grabbed off* the honors for the first ascent —*Time*⟩ **2 :** to choose for a partner (as in marriage) ⟨why is it that such a beauty . . . has not long ago been *grabbed off* —Walter O'Meara⟩

grab rope *n* **:** GUEST ROPE 2

grabs *pres 3d sing of* GRAB, *pl of* GRAB

grab skipper *n* **:** a short iron pry or hammer used in logging for removing the skidding hooks from a log

¹grace \\'grās\\ *n* -s [ME, fr. OF, fr. L *gratia* charm, favor, thanks, fr. *gratus* pleasing, beloved, grateful + *-ia* -y; akin to OHG *queran* to sigh, Skt *gṛṇāti* he praises] **1 a :** beneficence or generosity shown by God to man ⟨the very earthy problems that must be dealt with makes one rely heavily upon God for ~ and wisdom —*Guatemala News*⟩ ⟨a God who . . . works to bring his purposes to fruition through the willing response of men to his ~ —Norman Goodall⟩; *esp* **:** divine favor unmerited by man **:** the mercy of God as distinguished from his justice ⟨a man repentant and asking God's ~⟩ **b :** a free gift of God to man for his regeneration or sanctification **:** an influence emanating from God and acting for the spiritual well-being of the recipient ⟨the Methodists, following the Baptists, appealed to the people for they preached free will and universal ~ —Van Wyck Brooks⟩ ⟨it may be that they have no one praying for them, and they have squandered all the ordinary and extraordinary ~*s* allotted to them by God —D.J.Corrigan⟩ **c :** a state of acceptance with or of being pleasing to God **:** enjoyment of divine favor ⟨be in a state of ~⟩ ⟨outward and visible signs of an inward and spiritual ~⟩ **d :** a virtue or moral excellence regarded as coming from God **:** a Christian virtue ⟨the ~*s* of self-denial, humility, and love⟩ **e** *cap* **:** God as the source of grace **2 :** a short prayer either asking a blessing before or giving thanks after a meal **3 a :** disposition to kindness, favor, clemency, or compassion **:** benign goodwill ⟨the victor's ~ in treating the vanquished⟩ **b :** the display of kindly treatment usu. on the part of a superior **:** ready granting or forgiving **:** clement judging or treating ⟨thankful for this ~ on her brother's part —Margaret Deland⟩ **c** *archaic* **:** MERCY, CLEMENCY; *also* **:** FORGIVENESS **d (1) :** an act of kindness, favor, or goodwill ⟨do me this ~, my child —Alfred Tennyson⟩ ⟨had been some years in prison . . . where she was kept without books till at last by some special ~ a friend was allowed to send her some —Gilbert Murray⟩ **(2) :** a special favor from a person in power **:** PRIVILEGE, DISPENSATION ⟨each in his place, by right, not ~, shall rule his heritage —Rudyard Kipling⟩ ⟨woman gains entrance into such societies only through a kind of ~ bestowed upon her, not legitimately like the male —H.M.Parshley⟩ **(3) :** the prerogative of mercy exercised by an executive of the law (as by granting pardon) **(4) :** the same prerogative when exercised in the form of equitable relief through chancery **(5) :** favor shown by permitting an action to be postponed or by granting a reprieve or a temporary exemption from a penalty ⟨granted the condemned man a day of ~ to wind up his worldly affairs⟩ ⟨she didn't like to be rushed so he gave her an extra half hour's ~ before he called for her⟩ **e :** favor and approval — often used in pl. ⟨tried to stay in his employer's good ~*s*⟩ ⟨after he had fallen from ~ —*Amer. Guide Series: Pa.*⟩ ⟨worm your way into my ~*s* —Hamilton Basso⟩ **4 :** the favor shown or the portion allotted by fortune or Providence **:** LOT, FATE, LUCK **5** *obs* **:** beneficent efficacy or power **6 a (1) :** a charming or attractive endowment, characteristic, quality, or feature ⟨among disagreeable qualities he possessed the saving ~ of humor⟩ ⟨the little ~*s* of speech —George Sampson⟩ ⟨that quiet but unabashed hospitality which is a common ~ in Mexican households —Willa Cather⟩ **(2) :** an activity or accomplishment that lends such grace ⟨a young girl trained early in the ~*s* of singing, dancing, and playing the harp⟩ ⟨more distinguished for his learning than for his conversational ~*s* —Charles Gordon⟩ ⟨rising to receive him, with every refinement of manner known to the time, and with all the engaging ~*s* and courtesies of life —Charles Dickens⟩ **b (1) :** a manner of acting or of appearance adopted or affected with the intention of charming or pleasing **(2) :** AFFECTATION ⟨laughing at the woman's airs and ~*s*⟩ **c :** ATTRACTIVENESS, CHARM ⟨all the ~ of youth —John Buchan⟩ ⟨old civilizations do breed corruption as well as ~ —Sean O'Faolain⟩ ⟨the ~ of her loose falling tresses —George Meredith⟩ ⟨given an old story a new lucidity and ~ —Sara H. Hay⟩; *esp* **:** the pleasing quality associated with a special and refined fitness of proportion combined with an ease and beauty of movement, action, line, or expression ⟨a curved . . . staircase of unusual ~, with marble steps and wrought-iron railings —*Amer. Guide Series: N.Y. City*⟩ ⟨the stables had dignity and ~ in a degree one rarely sees in a modern edifice —H.J.Laski⟩ ⟨have been able to convey through the coarser medium of English prose something of this aesthetic ~, this deftness of touch —P.E.More⟩ **d :** PROPRIETY, SEEMLINESS, COMELINESS ⟨performed the necessary task without fanfare and with a quiet ~⟩ **e** *obs* **:** a thing or part characterized by beauty **:** ORNAMENT **f :** a musical decoration consisting of notes not belonging to the basic melody or harmony (as the trill, turn, appoggiatura) indicated by special symbols or small notes **7** — used with *your* in addressing a duke, a duchess, or an archbishop and formerly the king or queen of England or with *his* or *her* as a periphrastic designation for one of these **8** *at an English university* **a :** permission of a congregation to take a degree **b :** a proposal, decree, act, or vote of the governing body of an institution **c :** permission to take a degree obtained from a candidate's college or hall **9 a :** sense of propriety or right **:** GRACIOUSNESS, DECENCY ⟨had the ~ to apologize for the insulting remark⟩ **b :** VIRTUE ⟨will have to make a ~ of necessity —H.L.Ickes⟩ **c :** CONSIDERATENESS, THOUGHTFULNESS ⟨geographers in their maps have the ~ to indicate the bed of the Paroo river —C.E.W. Bean⟩ **10 a** *usu cap* **:** one of three sister goddesses in Greek mythology represented as beautiful and graceful, as associates of the Muses, and as attendants usu. on Eros, Aphrodite, and Dionysus and regarded as the givers of charm and beauty — usu. used in pl. **b :** one that resembles or represents such a goddess ⟨from every ceiling nymphs, cherubs, and ~*s* gaze down —*Amer. Guide Series: Vt.*⟩ **11 graces** *pl but sing in constr* **:** a game in which players throw and catch a small hoop by means of two sticks — used with *the;* see GRACE HOOP **syn** see MERCY — **by grace of** *or* **by the grace of :** by virtue of **:** with the help of **:** by reason of ⟨the camp existed *by grace of* the few white miners who explored the district —*Amer. Guide Series: Oreg.*⟩ ⟨survived only *by the grace of* money an uncle had left him⟩ — **do grace** *obs* **:** do credit or honor to **:** ADORN — **of grace :** reckoned from the birth of Christ ⟨born in the year *of grace* 1729⟩ — **with a bad grace** *or* **with an ill grace** *or* **with bad grace** *or* **with ill grace :** with unconcealed reluctance and usu. rudeness **:** with marked lack of grace ⟨accepted his defeat *with bad grace* and became almost insulting⟩ ⟨needed help but accepted it only *with an ill grace*⟩ — **with good grace** *adv* **:** GRACIOUSLY ⟨the Protestants of Northern Ireland have accepted *with good grace* the modern trend toward public education —Paul Blanshard⟩ ⟨*with* as *good grace* as I could summon I capitulated —George Copeland⟩

²grace \\"\\ *vt* -ED/-ING/-S [ME *gracen* to thank, show favor to, fr. OF *gracier*, fr. *grace*] **1** *obs* **a :** to be gracious to **:** FAVOR, COUNTENANCE **b :** GRATIFY, DELIGHT **2 :** to dignify or honor by an act of favor **:** do credit to ⟨discoveries are made every year which, in the past, would have *graced* a century —Albert Guérard⟩ **3 a :** to endow with grace **:** ADORN, EMBELLISH, ORNAMENT ⟨the fine broad meadowlands that ~ the tranquil valley floor —*Amer. Guide Series: Vt.*⟩ ⟨a banquet *graced* by a speaker —*Pleasures of Publishing*⟩ ⟨want to think of their forebears as polished courtiers who would ~ a modern drawing room —L.B.Wright⟩ ⟨the fabulous one-horned animal which ~*s* the British royal coat of arms —R.W.Murray⟩ **b :** to constitute a notable addition to or part of ⟨switches, buttons, wheels, knobs, and gadgets that may ~ the interior of any modern aircraft cockpit —H.G.Armstrong⟩ ⟨*gracing* the living room were five small aquariums and a large one —P.A.Zahl⟩ ⟨the giants among the scores of others who *graced* 17th century Holland —William Petersen⟩; *specif* **:** to embellish (a musical composition) with ornaments

grace-and-favor \\ˌ≈≈'≈\\ *adj* **:** constituting a habitation granted rent-free (as to a retainer) by the English royal household ⟨her *grace-and-favor* cottage at Kensington Palace —*Newsweek*⟩

grace cup *n* **:** a cup used in drinking a final health after the grace at the end of a meal; *also* **:** a health drunk from such a cup

grace·ful \\'≈fəl\\ *adj, sometimes* **gracefuller**; *sometimes* **gracefullest** [ME, fr. *grace* + *-ful*] **1** *obs* **:** specially marked by divine grace **2 :** displaying grace in form or action **:** pleasing or attractive or marked by a comeliness, propriety, or fitness in line, proportion, or esp. movement ⟨a stairway rises in a ~ curve at the rear of the hall —*Amer. Guide Series: Oreg.*⟩ ⟨a ~ bend of road and river —S.H.Holbrook⟩ ⟨the most ~ tree in Europe is the silver birch —C.E.W.Bean⟩ ⟨the swifts are extraordinarily ~ in flight —*Amer. Guide Series: Wash.*⟩ ⟨the author is a ~ and disciplined writer —*New Yorker*⟩ ⟨a ~ and delicate lyricism —Joseph Frank⟩ — **grace·ful·ly** \\-fəlē, -li\\ *adv* — **grace·ful·ness** *n* -ES

graceful kelp crab *n* **:** a common variably colored but usu. greenish brown kelp crab (*Pugettia gracilis*) found from the Aleutians to California

grace hoop *n* **:** a hoop used in the graces

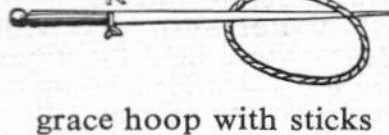

grace hoop with sticks

grace·less \\-ləs\\ *adj* [ME *graceles*, fr. *grace* + *-les* -less] **1 :** lacking grace: as **a :** UNREGENERATE, DEPRAVED, WICKED, IMPIOUS **b :** devoid of a sense of propriety or seemliness or befitting one devoid of such a sense ⟨a ~ and pushing person⟩ ⟨a ~ and rude remark⟩ **c :** devoid of qualities or endowments that give charm or attractiveness ⟨a lonely ~ factory girl —*Current Biog.*⟩ ⟨her body was thick and lumpish, as ~ as a bathtub —Ruth Park⟩ **:** UGLY ⟨a ~ statue⟩ **:** lacking graciousness ⟨a totally ~ hostess⟩ **d :** devoid of the special artistic quality of fitness or proportion combined with ease and beauty of movement or expression ⟨a ~ prose⟩ **2** *obs* **:** MERCILESS, CRUEL — **grace·less·ly** *adv* — **grace·less·ness** *n* -ES

grace note *n* **1 :** a musical note constituting or being part of an ornament; *esp* **:** APPOGGIATURA, ACCIACCATURA **2 :** something resembling or suggesting a grace note in forming a very small decorative unessential part of or addition to some large whole ⟨the literary contributions made by the President's collaborators . . . merely added *grace notes* to compositions that were the President's own —*New Yorker*⟩ ⟨the chanted songs . . . seem to have no real organic connection with the central theme but to be merely arbitrary and distracting *grace notes* —Wolcott Gibbs⟩

grace period *n* **:** a period of 30 days or one month during which premiums on insurance policies may be paid without penalty

graces *pl of* GRACE, *pres 3d sing of* GRACE

grace's warbler \\'grāsəz-\\ *also* **grace warbler** *n, usu cap G* [after *Grace* D. Coues †1925, sister of Dr. Elliott Coues †1899 Am. ornithologist who discovered it] **:** a gray-and-white warbler (*Dendroica graciae*) black-streaked above with a yellow throat and chest and common in the southwestern U.S. and adjacent Mexico

gra·ci·lar·ia \\ˌgrasə'la(a)rēə\\ *n, cap* [NL, fr. L *gracilis* slender + NL *-aria*] **:** a genus of gelatinous red algae (family Sphaerococcaceae) several species of which are important sources of agar-agar

gra·ci·lar·i·id \\ˌ≈≈'≈rēəd\\ *adj* [NL *Gracilariidae*] **:** of or relating to the Gracilariidae

gra·ci·la·ri·idae \\ˌ≈≈lə'rīəˌdē\\ *n pl, cap* [NL, fr. *Gracilaria*, type genus + *-idae*] **:** a family of small dull or metallic-colored tineoid moths having larvae that mine in the leaves of various plants

grac·ile \\'grasəl *also* -(ˌ)sil *or* -ˌsīl\\ *adj* [L *gracilis;* perh. akin to ON *horr* emaciation, L *cracent-, cracens* slender, Skt *kṛśa* emaciated, *kṛśyati* to become emaciated] **1 a :** SLENDER, THIN, SLIGHT ⟨the ~ hermit's lunch —James Merrill⟩ ⟨the human remains . . . indicate a ~ people with small teeth —D.A.Hooijer⟩ **b :** gracefully slender or slight ⟨her ~ and candid girlhood —Joseph Hergesheimer⟩ ⟨three ~, rosy-fleshed women —*Time*⟩ ⟨her red coarse little hands which did not seem to belong to those ~ arms —Arnold Bennett⟩ **2 :** GRACEFUL ⟨lifted her head high for an instant, with the ~ motion a seal has —R.P.Warren⟩ ⟨a ~ writer, thinker, and teacher —Lincoln Kirstein⟩ — **grac·ile·ness** *n* -ES

grac·i·lis \\'grasələs\\ *n* -ES [NL, fr. L, slender] **:** the most superficial muscle of the inside of the thigh arising from the lower part of the symphysis and the anterior half of the pubic arch and having its tendon inserted into the inner surface of the shaft of the tibia below the tuberosity

gra·cil·i·ty \\grə'silәd·ē, grə'-\\ *n* -ES [L *gracilitas*, fr. *gracilis* + *-itas* -ity] **:** GRACEFULNESS ⟨the ~ and speed of winged beauty —Clement Wood⟩; *esp* **:** grace of form **:** slightness

gra·ci·os·i·ty \\ˌgrāsh(ē)'äsəd·ē\\ *n* -ES [MF *gracieuseté*, fr. LL *gratiositat-, gratiositas*, fr. L *gratiosus* + L *-itat-, -itas* -ity] **:** GRACIOUSNESS

gra·ci·o·so \\ˌgräsē'ō(ˌ)sō\\ *n* -S [Sp, fr. *gracioso*, adj., agreeable, amusing, fr. L *gratiosus*] **:** a buffoon or a sportive and comic character in Spanish comedy

gra·cious \\'grāshəs\\ *adj* [ME, fr. MF *gracieus*, fr. L *gratiosus* enjoying favor, beloved, agreeable, fr. *gratia* favor, grace + *-osus* -ous — more at GRACE] **1 a** *obs* **:** marked by or having divine grace **:** PIOUS, GODLY **b** *archaic* **:** finding grace or favor **:** ACCEPTABLE ⟨but is he ~ in the people's eye —*Shak.*⟩ **2 :** marked by an attractive or pleasing character or appearance **:** characterized by grace in quality, traits, or nature: as **a :** marked by kindness and courtesy **:** markedly considerate of another's feelings or predilections ⟨a ~ and complimentary letter, encouraging him to continue his correspondence —W.M.Thackeray⟩ **b :** GRACEFUL ⟨the ~ sweep of fields shaded by stately elms —*Amer. Guide Series: Vt.*⟩ ⟨the ~ and comely form he had so skillfully mirrored in his art —Oscar Wilde⟩ **c :** marked by tact and delicacy in performance or execution **:** URBANE ⟨no more ~ yet telling caricature of the faults of a society —G.F.Kennan⟩ ⟨for austere and ~ allegory . . . the world is indebted to Spain —Helen Waddell⟩ **d (1) :** characterized by ease, good taste, and generosity of spirit and belonging to or suggesting the peace and tasteful leisure of wealth and good breeding ⟨a ~ and beautiful life for all who love peace and reflection, strength and youth —A.C.Benson⟩ **(2) :** befitting or associated with a life characterized in this way ⟨hansom cabs, ~ relics of a more leisurely epoch —*Amer. Guide Series: N.Y. City*⟩ ⟨a ~ plantation home⟩ **(3) :** artistically and esp. architecturally attractive in a way associated with a life or culture characterized in this way ⟨~ with carved interior cornices, mantelpieces, and dadoes —Bernard DeVoto⟩ **3 :** abounding in grace or mercy **:** characterized by marked beneficence **:** MERCIFUL, COMPASSIONATE ⟨after the insults and bad treatment of his former employer he was glad to find so ~ a master⟩ — often and esp. formerly used as a customary and courteous epithet ⟨asked if the ~ gentleman felt well —Guy McCrone⟩ esp. to royalty or those high in the scale of nobility ⟨His Most *Gracious* Majesty, the King⟩ ⟨my ~ lord, the Duke of Windsor⟩ **4** *obs* **:** LUCKY, FORTUNATE, HAPPY

syn CORDIAL, AFFABLE, GENIAL, SOCIABLE: GRACIOUS may apply to a pleasing, benign, or endearing kindliness and courtesy, esp. to inferiors ⟨seemed gratified by their excessive admiration, and gave most *gracious* smiles —Jane Austen⟩ ⟨*gracious* to everyone, but known to a very few —Willa Cather⟩ CORDIAL applies to hearty and sincere friendliness or, occas., to other deeply felt emotions ⟨the director was as *cordial* to the insignificant Martin Arrowsmith as though Martin were a visiting senator. He shook his hand warmly; he unbent in a smile —Sinclair Lewis⟩ ⟨we were friends in public, and saluted each other in the most *cordial* and charming manner —W.M.Thackeray⟩ AFFABLE applies to a smooth, benign approachability and ready friendliness and responsiveness ⟨don't find . . . that his wealth has made him arrogant and inaccessible; on the contrary he takes great pains to appear *affable* and gracious —Tobias Smollett⟩ ⟨easy of approach and *affable* in conversation. They seldom put on airs —W.S.Maugham⟩ GENIAL applies to blended cheer, warmth, and friendliness or other characteristics making one a good companion ⟨*genial* clergy of ample girth, stuffed with the buttered toast of a rectory tea —S.B. Leacock⟩ ⟨that atmosphere of peace and leisure which made his companionship so *genial* —L.P.Smith⟩ ⟨his face softened visibly, he became more and more *genial* and loquacious —W.H.Hudson †1922⟩ SOCIABLE applies to pleasure in social relationships and implies friendliness and readiness at pleasant conversation ⟨was genial and *sociable*, approachable at all times, and fond of social intercourse —J.S.Reeves⟩ ⟨a very *sociable* fellow, prone to talk as long as he can find a listener —Jack London⟩

gra·cious·ly *adv* [ME, fr. *gracious* + *-ly*] **:** in a gracious manner ⟨believed that God . . . had ~ bound himself in his covenant —J.G.Brauer⟩ ⟨writes ~, but does not cut deep —J.T.Flexner⟩ ⟨a philosopher who knows not how gracefully to leave the house in which he has lived so ~ all his life —F.J. Hoffman⟩

gra·cious·ness *n* -ES [ME *graciousnesse*, fr. *gracious* + *-nesse* -ness] **:** the quality or state of being gracious ⟨moved by the slim ~ of her figure —C.B.Kelland⟩ ⟨the courtly ~ of an old and gentle culture⟩

grack·le \\'grakəl\\ *n* -s [alter. of earlier *gracule*, fr. NL *Gracula*, genus of birds now limited to the hill mynas, alter. of L *graculus* jackdaw; perh. akin to OHG *krogil* gossipy, OE *crāwan* to crow — more at CROW] **1 :** any of various Old World birds of the family Sturnidae (as the hill mynas) **2 :** any of several rather large American blackbirds (family Icteridae) having black plumage that is glossy and iridescent or reflects metallic shades (as green, bronze, or purple) — see BRONZED GRACKLE, PURPLE GRACKLE

¹grad \\'grad, -aa(ə)d\\ *also* **grade** \\'grād\\ *n* -s [F *grade* degree, fr. L *gradus*] **:** the hundredth of a right angle in the centesimal system

²grad \\"\\ *n* -s [short for *graduate*] *slang* **:** GRADUATE, ALUMNUS, ALUMNA

grad *abbr* **1** gradient **2** graduate; graduated

grad·able \\'grādəbəl\\ *adj* **:** capable of being graded ⟨~ seed⟩

gradacol membrane *var of* GRADOCOL MEMBRANE

¹gra·date \\'grāˌdāt, ≈'≈, grə'd-\\ *vb* -ED/-ING/-S [back-formation fr. *gradation*] *vi* **:** to shade insensibly into another (as of a color) or each other (as of colors) **:** shade off **:** BLEND ~ *vt* **1 :** to cause (a color or colors) to gradate ⟨many layers of sheer material in *gradated* colors —Lois Long⟩ **2 :** to dispose or arrange in or into steps, grades, or ranks

²gradate \\"\\ *adj* [L *gradatus* furnished with steps, fr. *gradus* step, degree + *-atus* -ate] **:** occurring in or characterized by a serial arrangement with nearly equal variation between adjacent members **:** having a gradient or exhibiting gradation ⟨a ~ shell with regularly increasing whorls⟩ ⟨~ maturation of fern sori⟩ ⟨a ~ butterfly wing shading from deepest blue to pale yellow⟩

gra·da·tion \\grā'dāshən *also* grə'-\\ *n* -s [L *gradation-, gradatio*, fr. *gradus* step, degree + *-ation-, -atio* -ation — more at GRADE] **1** *obs* **:** CLIMAX 1 **2 a :** a series of things (as events or conditions) forming successive stages or steps (as in a course or action) **b :** a degree or relative position in an order or series **:** one of a series of intermediate varieties differing consecutively in form, character, or composition ⟨endless ~*s* in the balance between the denotation of words and their connotation —J.L.Lowes⟩ ⟨he grew into the scheme of things by insensible ~*s* —H.G. Wells⟩ ⟨through every ~ of increasing tenderness —Jane Austen⟩ **c** *obs* **:** RANK, POSITION **d :** the act or process of arranging in ranks, degrees, stages, or steps or the state of being so arranged **e :** a differing consecutively and often by minute differences in a way to form ranks, degrees, stages, or steps ⟨the wide range of ~ in these qualities —R.W.Murray⟩ **3 :** the act or process of progressing evenly or by regular steps **:** gradual advance ⟨the idea of progress or ~ from mineral to plant, from plant to animal, and from animal to man —*Times Lit. Supp.*⟩ **4 a :** a gradual passing from one tint or shade to another (as in painting or drawing) or a sequence or range of tints or shades that passes in this way ⟨a sequence of grays from black to white would be a ~ —S.C.Pepper⟩ **b :** the range of tones between the darkest and the lightest parts of a photographic image **c :** the rate at which the tones of a photographic image change with exposure **5 a :** change from one vowel to another accompanying a change in the degree of stress (as from the vowel of *ford* to the second vowel in *Oxford*) **b :** ABLAUT **6 :** a bringing of an area of land to a uniform or nearly uniform low grade or slope (as in the formation of plains by streams) — compare AGGRADATION, DEGRADATION **7 :** the frequency distribution of various sized grains in a soil, sediment, sedimentary rock, or other particulate material — **gra·da·tion·al** \\(ˈ)grā¦dāshənᵊl, grə'd-, -shnəl\\ *adj* — **gra·da·tion·al·ly** \\-nᵊlē, -nəlē, -li\\ *adv*

¹grada·to·ry \\'grādəˌtōrē, 'grad-\\ *n* -ES [prob. modif. of ML *gradatarium* stairway, fr. *gradatus* + *-arium* -ary] **:** a series of steps esp. from a cloister into a church

²gradatory \\"\\ *adj* [*gradation* + *-ory*] **:** progressing or advancing by gradations **:** arranged in a gradational series

grad·dan *or* **grad·den** \\'gradᵊn\\ *n* -s [ScGael *gradan*, *greadan* & IrGael *greadān*] *Scot & Irish* **:** parched grain

¹grade \\'grād\\ *n* -s [partly fr. L *gradus* step, degree; partly fr. F *grade*, fr. L *gradus;* akin to L *gradi* to step, go, OIr *in-grenn-* to pursue, Lith *gridyti* to go, wander, and perh. to Goth *grid* (acc.) step] **1 a :** a stage in a process ⟨passing through the ~*s* of growing up⟩ ⟨the highest ~ of development of the brain⟩ **b :** a position or level in a course of advancement or decline or in a scale of ranks, qualities, or orders ⟨the country gentlemen were of many different ~*s* of wealth and culture —G.M. Trevelyan⟩ ⟨a school of collegiate ~ —*Seton Hall Univ. Bull.*⟩: as **(1) :** one of the successive levels of a usu. elementary or secondary school course that usu. represents a year's work **(2) :** a military or naval rank ⟨a naval officer with the ~ of lieutenant commander⟩ **c :** a degree esp. of force or value ⟨the varying ~*s* of success with which a poem attains its end —Samuel Alexander⟩: as **(1) :** a degree of strength of an abrasive bond **(2) :** a relative value or content of an ore or mineral ⟨high-*grade* and low-*grade* ore⟩ **(3) :** a degree of severity in illness ⟨the patient had a carcinoma of ~ III⟩ **(4) :** a degree of plant food content in fertilizer expressed in percentages of nitrogen, phosphoric acid, and potash **(5) :** a degree of purity or concentration (as of a chemical) **2 a :** a class constituted by things that are at the same stage or have the same relative position, level, rank, or degree ⟨the nobles were a higher ~ of agriculturalists —John MacNeill⟩ ⟨guilty of a very low ~ of crime⟩; *esp* **:** a body of elementary school pupils at any one established level of advancement ⟨the fourth ~ was allowed to leave school early⟩ **b :** a mark indicating a particular grade (as of a student's accomplishment in general or of a particular piece of work) ⟨always got high ~*s* in school⟩ ⟨merited a ~ of B on his composition⟩ **c :** a standard of quality applied to foods ⟨prime-*grade* beef⟩ ⟨first-*grade* potatoes⟩ **d :** a standard of quality established as acceptable ⟨threw out all lumber that was below ~⟩ **3 a :** a rate of ascent or descent (as of a railroad, highway, conduit, or ground surface) **:** GRADIENT ⟨a heavy ~⟩ **:** deviation from a level surface to an inclined plane stated as so many feet per mile ⟨a ~ of 20 feet per mile⟩ or as one foot rise or fall in so many feet of horizontal distance ⟨a ~ of 1 in 264⟩ or as so much in a hundred feet or as a percentage of horizontal distance ⟨a 10 percent ~ is one of 10 feet to 100⟩ **b :** a graded ascending, descending, or level portion (as of a road, a railroad, or an embankment) **c :** level or elevation esp. of a land or water surface: as **(1) :** a datum or reference level **(2) :** the contemplated level of the ground when the work of erecting a building is completed **:** ground level ⟨the underpinning of the tower was above ~⟩ **(3) :** ELEVATION 1c **4** [trans. of G *stufe*] **:** any one of the phases of a root or of an affix that appear in an ablaut series and that are characterized by having different vowels **:** the characteristic vowel of such a phase **5 :** a domestic animal one of whose parents is purebred and the other either a scrub or an animal containing a considerable proportion of the blood of the same breed as the purebred parent **6 : grades** *pl* **:** elementary school — used with *the* ⟨taught in the ~*s* for 10 years⟩ **7 :** one of a series of patterns for clothing **8 :** one of the three forms of braille ranging from the fully spelled to the highly contracted — **at grade** *adv* **1 :** on the same level — used of highways, railroad tracks, pedestrian walks, or combinations of these at the point where they intersect **2 :** at such a level with relation to a slope that no perceptible erosion or deposition is effected — used of a stream bed that has been so established — **make the grade** : SUCCEED ⟨tried to pass the exam twice but didn't *make the grade*⟩ ⟨yearning to *make the grade* as a social leader⟩ — **over grade** *adv* : at a higher level — used of one highway, railroad track, or pedestrian walk where it crosses another — **under grade** *adv* : at a lower level — used of one highway, railroad track, or pedestrian walk where it crosses another

²grade \"\ *vb* -ED/-ING/-S *vt* **1** : to arrange in grades : divide into classes : CLASS, SORT: as **a** : to assign to a grade or assign a grade to ⟨~ pupils according to their reading ability⟩ ⟨~ lumber by its resistance to rot⟩ ⟨spent an evening *grading* papers the class had turned in⟩ **b** : to classify (a food) according to quality, size, purity, or other appropriate standard **c** : to arrange in an increasing or decreasing graduated and usu. proportional order (as of value, weight, intensity, difficulty) : GRADUATE ⟨purchased only *graded* reading material for use in the elementary grades⟩ ⟨necessary to ~ the weight of the hammers to correspond with the thickness of the strings —A.E.Wier⟩ ⟨a *graded* inheritance tax⟩ ⟨good works to be done in satisfaction for sins and *graded* according to the seriousness of the offense —K.S.Latourette⟩ **2** : to unite by evenly modulated or slight gradations : blend one shade of (as light or color) into another **3** : to reduce (as the line of a canal or roadbed) to an even grade whether on the level or in a progressive ascent or descent ⟨offered to ~ the remaining 26 miles of unfinished roadbed —*Amer. Guide Series: Texas*⟩ **4** : to alter (a vowel) by ablaut or vowel gradation — used chiefly in the passive **5** : to improve (as native stock) by breeding the females to purebred males — often used with *up* **6** : to make (a working pattern) from a standard pattern for clothing : make (a standard pattern) into a working pattern for clothing — compare GRADER 3 **~** *vi* **1 a** : to form a gradation or a series having only slight differences ⟨the colors *graded* gradually from red to orange to yellow⟩ ⟨anthracite ~*s* by imperceptible stages into bituminous coal —*Encyc. Americana*⟩ ⟨interrelated plant communities which *graded* from one to another through orderly transitions —R.W.Finley⟩ **b** : BLEND ⟨the colors *graded* into one another at the edges⟩ ⟨any further attempt here to segregate the two would serve no purpose, for . . . the one inevitably ~*s* into the other —W.H.Dowdeswell⟩ **2** : to proceed on an incline ⟨*grading* slowly downward —R.L.Stevenson⟩ **3** : to be of or merit a particular grade ⟨lambs *grading* choice to prime —*Chicago Daily Drovers Jour.*⟩ ⟨a story which ~*s* too low in reader interest —Richard Match⟩

³grade \"\ *adj* **1** : comprising the elementary grades : belonging to an elementary grade ⟨a ~ room⟩ : teaching the elementary grades ⟨a ~ teacher⟩ **2** *of a domestic animal* : of improved but not pure stock — distinguished from *crossbred* and *purebred;* compare SCRUB

-grade \ˌgrād\ *adj comb form* [F, fr. L *-gradus* going (fr. *gradi* to step, go) — more at GRADE] : walking ⟨digiti*grade*⟩ ⟨planti*grade*⟩ — chiefly in zoological terms

grade a \(ˈ)grā¦dā\ *adj, usu cap G&A* : of the highest grade : extremely good : FIRST-CLASS ⟨a *Grade A* movie⟩ ⟨a truly *Grade A* pie is now almost a museum piece —S.W.Dean⟩

grade·abil·i·ty \ˌgrādəˈbiləd·ē\ *n* : the steepness of grade that a motor vehicle is capable of climbing at efficient speed

grade beam *n* : a sill of structural steel or reinforced concrete atop the foundation of a building and supporting a wall at or near ground level

grade crossing *n* : an intersection or crossing of highways, railroad tracks, or pedestrian walks or combinations of these at grade

graded area *n* : a region that shows characteristic speech features reflecting different degrees of influence from one or more focal areas — called also *transition area;* compare FOCAL AREA, RELIC AREA

grade down *vt* : to decrease proportionally ⟨the wage earner postpones purchases or *grades down* his buying when uncertain about his future —*Biddle Survey*⟩

grade line *n* : a longitudinal reference line or slope to which a highway or railway is built

¹grade·ly \ˈgrādli\ *adj* [ME *greithly, graithly* ready, prompt, excellent, fr. ON *greithliga* ready, prompt, fr. *greithr* ready, free + *-ligr* -ly — more at READY] **1** *dial Eng* : fine, good, and desirable: **a** : upstanding and worthy ⟨how proud I am of Rochdale and of its ~ folks —Gracie Fields⟩ **b** : promising and likely ⟨a ~ lad⟩ **c** : physically well : being in good health ⟨Mama and Papa are . . . ~ —Charlotte Brontë⟩ **d** : physically attractive : GOOD-LOOKING **2** *dial Eng* : fitting and proper : APPROPRIATE

²gradely \"\ *adv* [ME *greithly, graithly* promptly, suitably, fr. ON *greithligr* promptly, fr. *greithligr*, adj.] **1** *dial Eng* : properly and suitably **2** *dial Eng* : WELL

grad·er \ˈgrādə(r)\ *n* -S **1** : one that grades: as **a** : a worker or machine that grades and sorts materials or products according to certain specifications (as of size, color, weight, condition, quality) **b** : a clerk who assists with the correction of students' test papers and the computation of grades **c** : a machine for grading and shallow excavating usu. having an adjustable blade for pushing material **d** : a worker who grades surfaces (as of roadbeds or excavation slopes) by means of hand tools or a grading machine **2** : a pupil in an elementary or secondary school grade — used with an ordinal numeral designating the grade ⟨a fifth ~⟩ ⟨a ninth ~⟩ **3** : a clothing worker who from a standard pattern size figures out and cuts out patterns for other sizes

grader man *n* **1** : a bulldozer operator **2** : an operator of a battery of machines for cleaning and grading seed corn

grades *pl of* GRADE, *pres 3d sing of* GRADE

grade school *also* **graded school** *n* **1** : ELEMENTARY SCHOOL : an elementary school system **2** : the elementary grades ⟨a young boy still in *grade school*⟩

grade separation *n* : a crossing of two highways or of a highway and pedestrian path or railroad utilizing an underpass or overpass

grade stake *n* : a stake driven in the ground so that the top has a predetermined elevation and used to establish the grade of an engineering work

grade up *vt* : to improve the quality or grade of by gradual degrees ⟨spent much money *grading up* his herd of cattle⟩ : IMPROVE, RAISE ⟨important that we *grade up* the standard of scholarship⟩

grad·grind \ˈgrad,grīnd\ *n* -S *usu cap* [after Thomas *Gradgrind*, a materialistic hardware merchant in the novel *Hard Times* (1854) by Charles Dickens †1870 Eng. novelist] : one that is patently and usu. as a matter of outspoken policy marked by a materialistic and philistine outlook : an uninspired and assiduous seeker after facts — **grad·grind·ian** \-dēən\ *adj, usu cap* — **grad·grind·ish** \-dish\ *adj, usu cap*

¹gra·di·ent \ˈgrādēənt\ *n* -S [L *gradient-, gradiens* (influenced in meaning by E ¹*grade*), pres. part. of *gradi* to step, go — more at GRADE] **1 a** : the inclination or the rate of regular or graded ascent or descent (as of a slope, roadway, or pipeline) **b** : a part (as of a road or pipeline) that slopes upward or downward : a portion of a way that is not level : SLOPE, GRADE, RAMP **2** : change in the value of a quantity (as temperature, pressure, or intensity of sound) per unit distance in a specified direction ⟨vertical temperature ~⟩ ⟨electric potential ~ along a wire⟩ **3** : the vector sum of the partial derivatives with respect to the three coordinate variables *x, y, z* of a scalar quantity whose value varies from point to point **4 a** : a graded difference in reactive capacity and metabolic activity along an embryonic axis or the radius of an embryonic field that constitutes a major effective agent in the organization of embryonic tissues and in the localization and differentiation of definitive structures and organs **b** : a graded difference in physiological activity esp. along the primary axis of the body

²gradient \"\ *adj* : being a gradient ⟨a ~ section of the road⟩ : constituting a gradient ⟨show definite ~ tendency — a tendency for the rate of delinquency and crime to decrease from the center outward —W.C.Reckless⟩

gradient concept *or* **gradient theory** *n* : a theory in embryology: embryonic differentiation is the result of gradation in the potentialities for development of various parts of the embryo of such nature that successful differentiation of a part inhibits the potentiality for similar change elsewhere in the system

gra·di·ent·er \-ē,entə(r)\ *n* -S : an attachment to an engineer's transit for measuring an angle of inclination in terms of the tangent of the angle and for measuring horizontal distances

gra·di·en·tia \ˌgrādēˈench(ē)ə\ *n pl, cap* [NL, fr. neut. pl. of L *gradient-, gradiens*] **1** *in former classifications* : the lizards and the caudate amphibians regarded as a natural group **2** *in former classifications* : CAUDATA

gradient velocity *or* **gradient wind** *n* : the velocity of the air that would cause it to move parallel to the current isobar if without friction

¹gra·dine \ˈgrā,dēn, grəˈdēn\ *or* **gra·din** \ˈgrādᵊn\ *n* -S [F *gradin*, fr. It *gradino*, dim. of *grado* step, degree, fr. L *gradus* — more at GRADE] **1** : one of a series of low steps or seats raised one above another **2** : a shelf at the back of an altar on which candlesticks and flowers are placed in a Christian church

²gra·dine \grəˈdēn\ *n* -S [F, fr. It *gradina*, fr. *grado* step] : a toothed chisel used by sculptors

grading *n* -S [fr. gerund of ²*grade*] : GRADE ⟨used several ~*s* of aggregate in making cement⟩

gra·di·no \grəˈdē(,)nō\ *n, pl* **gradi·ni** \-nē\ [It] **1** : GRADINE **2** : a painting or sculpture for ornamenting an altar gradine

gra·di·om·e·ter \ˌgrādēˈäməd·ə(r)\ *n* [¹*gradient* + -*o*- + -*meter*] : an instrument for measuring the gradient of a physical quantity (as of temperature, the earth's magnetic field, a slope)

grad·o·col membrane *also* **grad·a·col membrane** \ˈgradə,kōl-, -käl-\ *n* [G *gradokol*, fr. *grado-* (fr. ISV *grade*) + *kollodium* collodion] : a collodion membrane prepared from a solution of collodion in alcohol and ether in such a way as to have a predetermined average pore diameter and used esp. in ultrafiltration (as of a virus suspension)

grads *pl of* GRAD

¹grad·u·al \ˈgraj(ə)wəl, -jəl\ *also* **gradu·ale** \ˌgrädəˈwä(,)lā; ˈgraj(ə)wəl, -jəl\ *n* -S *often cap* [ML *graduale*, alter. of LL *gradale*, fr. L *gradus* step + -*ale* (neut. of -*alis* -al); fr. its being sung on the steps of the altar — more at GRADE] **1** : an antiphon or responsory sung or recited with the alleluia or the tract between the Epistle and Gospel originally from the steps of the altar in a Christian church **2** : a service book containing the musical portion of the mass sung by the choir

²gradual \"\ *adj* [ML *gradualis*, fr. L *gradus* step, degree + -*alis* -al] **1** : arranged in grades or degrees; *also* : admitting of such an arrangement **2 a** : proceeding by steps or degrees : advancing step by step (as in ascent or from one state to another) **b** (1) : moving, changing, or developing by fine, slight, or often imperceptible gradations or modulations ⟨a ~ change for the better in the patient's condition⟩ (2) *of an incline* : not steep or abrupt ⟨a ~ slope⟩ ⟨a ~ drop down to the town⟩

³gradual \"\ *adv, chiefly dial* : GRADUALLY

grad·u·al·ism \-j(ə)wə,lizəm, -jə,l-\ *n* -S **1** : the policy or practice of proceeding toward a desired end by gradual stages ⟨rejected pure Marxianism and developed a doctrine of gradualism —Alys Russell⟩ — compare IMMEDIATISM **2** : a theory in philosophy: between two apparently opposed notions (as analytic and synthetic truths) there is no sharp distinction or definite line of demarcation but a gradually altering continuity — compare DUALISM

¹grad·u·al·ist \-ˌləst\ *n* -S [²*gradual* + -*ist*] : an advocate of a policy, practice, or theory of gradualism

²gradualist \"\ *or* **grad·u·al·is·tic** \¦=(=)=¦listik\ *adj* : advocating, practicing, or based on gradualism

grad·u·al·i·ty \ˌgrajəˈwaləd·ē\ *n* -ES : the quality or state of being gradual or of coming about by gradual stages ⟨the ~ of significant reforms⟩

grad·u·al·ly \ˈgraj(ə)lē, -li, -j(ə)wəl-\ *adv* : in a gradual manner ⟨then the din ~ dies down, the music stops —Lafcadio Hearn⟩ ⟨~ aware of their intense significance —Matthew Arnold⟩

grad·u·al·ness \-lnəs\ *n* -ES : GRADUALITY

gradual psalm *n, usu cap G&P* : SONG OF ASCENTS

grad·u·and \ˈgrajə,wand\ *n* -S [ML *graduandus*, gerundive of *graduare*] *chiefly Brit* : one about to graduate : a candidate for a degree

¹grad·u·ate \ˈgraj(ə)wə¦t, -jə,wā|, *usu* |d.+V\ *n* -S [ME *graduat*, fr. ML *graduatus*, fr. past part. of *graduare*] **1 a** : one that has received an academic degree, a diploma, or a certificate ⟨a college ~⟩ ⟨a high school ~⟩; *also* : a graduate student ⟨in all courses open to ~*s* only —*Univ. of Minn. Bull.*⟩ **b** : one who has qualified in a particular field or for a particular position ⟨the expert planner, often an economist or a ~ of some branch of social service —M.B.Smith⟩ **c** : one who has passed through a significant or unusual and esp. powerful experience often associated with an institution ⟨a ~ of the Warsaw ghetto⟩ ⟨a reformatory ~⟩ **2** : a graduated cup, cylinder, or flask

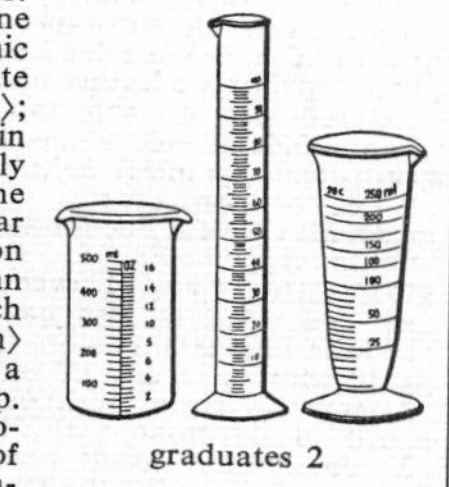
graduates 2

²graduate \"\ *adj* [ME *graduat*, fr. ML *graduatus*, past part. of *graduare*] **1 a** : holding an academic or professional degree, diploma, or certificate ⟨a ~ physician⟩ ⟨a ~ economist⟩ ⟨a ~ pilot⟩ **b** : of, relating to, or engaged in studies that go beyond the first or bachelor's degree and are usu. specialized or professional ⟨~ student⟩ ⟨~ course⟩ **2** : arranged by degrees : GRADUATED

³grad·u·ate \-jə,wāt, *usu* -ād.+V\ *vb* -ED/-ING/-S [ML *graduatus*, past part. of *graduare*, fr. L *gradus* step, degree — more at GRADE] *vt* **1 a** : to grant an academic or professional degree, diploma, or certificate to ⟨expect to ~ approximately 380,000 this year —A.W.Griswold⟩ : dismiss with such a degree, diploma, or certificate ⟨*graduated* from the university with honors⟩ **b** : to grant the right to go or concede the completion of the qualifications for going (as from an elementary school) at the end of the course or last grade ⟨many citizens were never *graduated* from high school⟩ **c** : to move up to the next school grade ⟨~ the boy from the third to the fourth grade⟩ **2** : to qualify as proficient or learned (as in a vice or other practice) **3 a** : to mark with degrees (as the scale of a thermometer) **b** : to divide into or arrange in regular or proportional steps, grades, gradations, or intervals (as punishments in relation to crimes) **4** *obs* : TEMPER, MODIFY : improve the grade of **5** : to concentrate (a liquid) by graduation **~** *vi* **1 a** : to receive from a university, college, or school an academic degree, a diploma, or a certificate denoting fulfillment of requirements leading to it : become a graduate ⟨~ from the university⟩ ⟨~ from divinity school⟩ ⟨~ with honors⟩ **b** : to qualify in a particular field or for a particular position (as after special training or experience) ⟨*graduated* as a seaman⟩ ⟨*graduated* as a chef⟩ **c** : to pass from one stage of experience, proficiency, or prestige to or into another usu. higher ⟨began as a boy to gather stamps, coins and butterflies, then *graduated* into a connoisseur of books in general —G.F.Whicher⟩ ⟨from the comics they soon ~ to *Treasure Island* and *Robinson Crusoe* —Eamon Ryan⟩ **2** : to pass by degrees : change gradually : shade off — **grad·u·a·tor** \-ād·ə(r), -ātə-\ *n* -S

graduated *adj* **1** : being a graduate **2 a** : marked with or divided into degrees : divided into or arranged in grades, steps, or successive levels usu. proportionally ⟨a ~ series of honors⟩ **b** *of a tax* : increasing in rate with increase in taxable base (as income or inheritance) : PROGRESSIVE **3** *of a bird's tail* : made up of feathers which become successively longer from the outer layer to innermost : TAPERED

graduate nurse *n* : a person who has completed the regular course of study and practical hospital training in nurses' training school — called also *trained nurse*

graduate school *n* : a school or division of a university or college devoted entirely to graduate studies, usu. having a dean and faculty of its own, and authorized to grant advanced degrees

grad·u·ate·ship *pronunc at* ¹GRADUATE +,ship\ *n, archaic* : the state of being a graduate or the period of one's life after graduation

grad·u·a·tion \ˌgrajəˈwāshən\ *n* -S [ML *graduation-, graduatio*, fr. *graduatus* + L *-ion-, -io* -ion] **1 a** : a division into degrees or quantity on a graduated scale ⟨faulty ~ of a thermometer⟩ **b** : a mark on an instrument or vessel indicating degrees or quantity; *collectively* : these marks **2 a** : the act of completing a phase of one's formal education; *esp* : the act of receiving a diploma, certificate, or degree from a school, college, or university ⟨went to extension classes after ~ from high school⟩ **b** : the act or ceremony of conferring academic diplomas, certificates, or degrees : COMMENCEMENT ⟨many visitors were on the campus for ~⟩ **3 a** : arrangement in or as if in degrees or gradations ⟨the abolition of the ~ of rank —Mark Pattison⟩ **b** : elevation to a higher stage of accomplishment, maturity, or prestige ⟨his ~ from . . . one of the most brilliant and lengthy childhoods on record —H.W.Wind⟩ **4** : the exposure of a liquid in large surfaces to the air so as to hasten its evaporation **5** : the smoothing of statistical data

gra·dus \ˈgrādəs\ *n* -ES [fr. *Gradus ad Parnassum* (L, lit., a step to Parnassus), a 17th cent. prosody dictionary long used in Brit. schools] **1** : a dictionary of Greek or Latin prosody and poetical phrases used as an aid in the writing of verse in Greek or Latin **2** : a handbook (as of law phrases or forms) or exercise book to assist in the mastering or performance of a difficult art or practice

graeco- — see GRECO-

¹graff \ˈgraf, -äf\ *vb* -ED/-ING/-S [ME *graffen*, fr. MF *grafier*, fr. *grafe*, n.] *archaic* : ¹GRAFT

²graff \"\ *n* -S [ME *graffe*, fr. MF *grafe*, fr. ML *graphium*, fr. L, stylus, fr. Gk *grapheion*, fr. *graphein* to write; fr. the resemblance of the scion inserted at an angle in the tree to a stylus poised for writing — more at CARVE] *archaic* : ²GRAFT

³graff \"\ *dial Brit var of* GRAVE

⁴graff \"\ *n* -S [D *graaf*, fr. MD *grave*, fr. *graven* to dig; akin to OHG *graban* to dig — more at GRAVE] : a trench, ditch, fosse, or canal used in fortification esp. as a moat

graf·fi·to \grəˈfēd·(,)ō\ *n, pl* **graffi·ti** \-d·(,)ē\ [It, dim. of *graffio* scratch, fr. *graffiare* to scratch, prob. fr. *grafio* stylus, fr. L *graphium* — more at GRAFF] : an inscription, figure, or design scratched on rocks or walls or on artifacts made of plaster, stone, or clay — compare SGRAFFITO

¹graft \ˈgraft, -aa(ə)-,-ai-,-á-\ *vb* -ED/-ING/-S [ME *graften*, alter. of *graffen* — more at GRAFF] *vt* **1 a** : to unite (plants or scion and stock) to form a graft ⟨impossible to ~ unrelated trees successfully⟩ : cause (a scion) to unite with a stock in a graft ⟨~*ed* a branch of white roses on his red rose tree⟩ **b** : to insert scions in (a plant) ⟨possible to cut back an old apple and ~ it with scions of a better variety⟩ **c** : to propagate (a plant) by grafting ⟨apples and most other fruits are ~*ed* to retain desirable qualities that do not come true from seed⟩ **d** : to perform the operation of preparing grafts on or of ⟨~ all our own replacement trees⟩ **2 a** : to join or fasten as if by grafting so as to bring about a close union ⟨the jute industry was also ~*ed* on to a local textile trade⟩ ⟨a hopeful ending ~*ed* on to the story —David Sylvester⟩ ⟨the level of industrial civilization ~*ed* on to a world of feudal manners —Frank Gibney⟩ ⟨the rail that was especially ~*ed* on to the grand staircase —Emily Hahn⟩ ⟨turn him adrift, ~*ing* upon him a sense of failure —Dixon Wecter⟩ **b** : to implant (living tissue) so as to form an organic union (as in a lesion) ⟨were able to ~ new skin over the badly burned area of the arm⟩ ⟨~*ed* a new piece of artery into the ruptured portion of the old artery⟩ **c** : to join or mend invisibly; *esp* : to weave together with a needle (two unfinished or broken edges of knitted fabric) **3** : to cover (as a rope, ringbolt, or stanchion on a boat) with a weaving of small cord **~** *vi* **1** : to become grafted ⟨many pears ~ well on quince rootstocks⟩ **2** : to perform grafting (as of a fruit tree or shrub) ⟨~*ing* is used especially to increase the numbers of a clonal plant or to improve the vigor of a plant of a weak-rooted variety⟩ **3** : to engage in graft

²graft \"\ *n* -S [ME *grafte*, alter. of *graffe* — more at GRAFF]

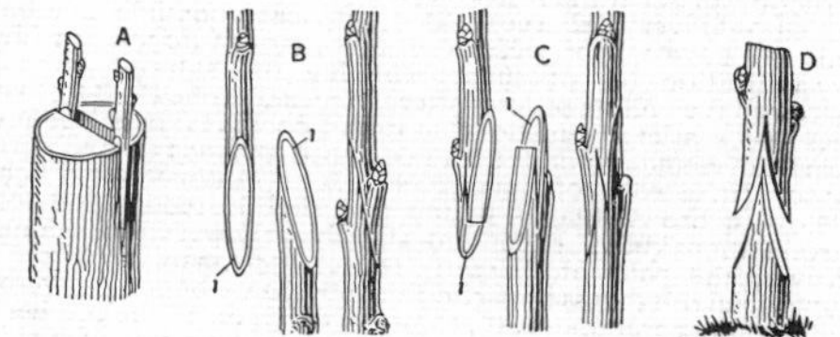

graft 1: *A* cleft, *B* splice, *C* whip or tongue, *D* saddle; *l* cambium

1 a : the growth or an individual resulting from the union of scion and stock : a grafted plant (as a rosebush) ⟨some excellent two-year-old ~*s* on dwarf rootstocks⟩ ⟨an expert can turn out a surprising number of ~*s* in a day⟩ **b** : SCION 1 **c** : the point of insertion of a scion upon a stock ⟨the ~ should be high enough to prevent the formation of scion roots⟩; *also* : the area of joining of scion and stock in grafting ⟨a poor ~ may break after several years satisfactory growth⟩ **2 a** : the act of grafting or of joining one thing to another as if by grafting ⟨a strange partial ~ of Nordic traits on broad-faced and broad-headed Mongolian physique —A.L.Kroeber⟩ **b** : something grafted in this way; *specif* : a piece of living tissue used in grafting — see AUTOGRAFT, HETEROGRAFT, HOMOGRAFT **3 a** : the acquisition of money, position, or other profit by dishonest or questionable means (as by actual theft or by taking advantage of a public office or a position of trust or employment to obtain fees, perquisites, profits on contracts, or pay for work not done or service not performed) : illegal or unfair practice for profit or personal gain ⟨tried to clear the ~, waste, and inefficiency out of government⟩ ⟨claimed that any large and complex business organization tended to breed ~ because of the inevitable towering hierarchy of command⟩ **b** : something gained in this way ⟨no matter how much ~ his subordinates may have garnered —Green Peyton⟩ **c** : something given as payment to one engaged in such a practice ⟨forced to pay out ~ to local politicians to avoid being annoyed by the police⟩ **d** : a means or method of making such gain or advantage ⟨systematic appropriation of public funds by lawless political groups . . . and the more honest ~ of special favors to real-estate or public-service interests —H.E.Davis⟩

³graft \"\ *n* -S [D *graft, gracht* ditch, canal, fr. MD; derivative fr. the stem of MD *graven* to dig, OHG *graban* — more at GRAVE] *now dial Eng* : DITCH, TRENCH

⁴graft \"\ *vi* -ED/-ING/-S [alter. of ¹*grave*] **1** *dial Eng* : DIG **2** *dial Eng* : WORK

⁵graft \"\ *n* -S *dial chiefly Brit* : WORK, LABOR; *also* : TRADE, OCCUPATION

graft·age \-tij, tēj\ *n* -S : the act or the principles and practice of grafting in horticulture : GRAFTING

¹graft·er \-tə(r)\ *n* -S [¹*graft* + -*er*] : one that grafts

²grafter \"\ *n* -S [⁴*graft* + -*er*] *chiefly Brit* : an industrious hardworking person

graft hybrid *n* : a chimeral hybrid produced by grafting in which tissue from scion and stock are intimately mingled in the new growth; *esp* : a shoot of a grafted plant exhibiting such mingling — compare CHIMERA 3

grafting *n* -S [ME, action of grafting, fr. gerund of *graften* to graft — more at GRAFT] : something grafted; *esp* : GRAFT 1, 2b

grafting tool *or* **grafting iron** *n* : an implement designed esp. for use in grafting that combines a handle, a blade for making the cut for a cleft graft and a wedge for holding it open while the scions are being inserted

grafting tool

grafting wax *n* : a composition of rosin, beeswax, and tallow used to protect the wounds and scions of newly grafted trees or to cover the wounds on pruned trees

graf·ton·ite \ˈgraftə,nīt\ *n* -S [*Grafton*, N.H. + E -*ite*] : a mineral $(Fe,Mn,Ca)_3(PO_4)_2$ consisting of an iron manganese calcium phosphate occurring in salmon-pink laminated intergrowths with triphylite (hardness 5, sp. gr. 3.7)

gra·ger \'grägə(r)\ *or* **greg·er** *or* **greg·ger** \-reg-\ *also* **grog·ger** \-räg-\ *n* -s [Yiddish *grager, greger*, fr. Pol *grzegarz* rattle] : a rattle or noisemaker traditionally used by children during the Purim festival at every mention of Haman's name during the reading in the synagogue of the scroll of the Book of Esther

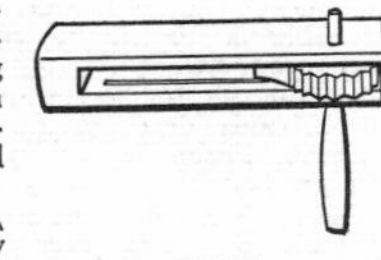
grager

gra·ham \'grāəm, 'gram, 'graa(ə)m\ *adj* [*graham (flour)*] : made wholly or largely of graham flour ⟨~ bread⟩ ⟨~ rolls⟩

graham cracker *n* [*graham (flour)*] : a dry slightly sweet square or rectangular cracker made mainly of whole wheat flour

graham flour *n* [after Sylvester *Graham* †1851 Am. advocate of dietary reform] : WHOLE WHEAT FLOUR

gra·ham·ism \-,mizəm\ *n* -s *usu cap* [S. *Graham* + E *-ism*] : a vegetarian dietary system advocated in the 19th century

¹gra·ham·ite \-,mīt\ *n* -s *usu cap* [S. *Graham* + E *-ite*] : an advocate of Grahamism

²grahamite \"\ *n* -s [J.A. and J.L. *Graham*, 19th cent. Am. mineowners + E *-ite*] : a lustrous pitch-black complex bituminous asphalt

graham's law *n, usu cap G* [after Thomas *Graham* †1869 Scot. chemist] : a statement in physics: under like conditions the diffusion rates of different gases are inversely proportional to the square roots of their densities

graham's salt *n, usu cap G* [after T. *Graham*] : sodium metaphosphate glass

¹grail \'grāl, *chiefly before pause or consonant* -āəl\ *n* -s [ME *graiel*, fr. MF *grael*, fr. ML *gradale* — more at GRADUAL] *archaic* : GRADUAL

²grail \"\ *n* -s [ME *graal, greal*, fr. MF, bowl, grail, fr. ML *gradalis*, perh. fr. L *gradus* step + *-alis* -al; perh. fr. its having consisted originally of a series of bowls or plates arranged one above the other — more at GRADE] **1** *usu cap* : the cup or platter which according to medieval legend was used by Christ at the Last Supper, was brought to Britain, and thereafter became the object of knightly quests that could be achieved only by those persons who were chaste in thought, word, and deed — called also *Holy Grail* **2** *sometimes cap* : an eminently desirable and ultimate object of an extended effort or quest ⟨the road we travel is long, but at the end lies the ~ of peace —A.E.Stevenson †1965⟩ ⟨at last on the track of his own elusive ~ —*Time*⟩

³grail \"\ *n* -s [perh. contr. of *gravel*] : GRAVEL ⟨silver globules and gold-sparkling ~ —Robert Browning⟩

¹grain \'grān\ *n* -s [ME *grain, grein*, partly fr. MF *grain* cereal plant, kernel, grain, fr. L *granum*; partly fr. MF *graine* seed, kermes, dye made from kermes, fr. L *grana*, pl. of *granum* — more at CORN] **1 a** (1) *obs* : a single small hard seed (2) : the seed or fruit resembling seed of any cereal grass (as wheat, oats, rice, millet) — compare CARYOPSIS **b** (1) : the unhusked or the threshed seeds or fruits of various food plants including the cereal grasses and in commercial and statutory usage (as in an insurance policy or trade list) other plants (as flax, peas, sugarcane) — compare CORN 3 (2) : the plants producing such seed or fruit **c** : one of the drupelets of a multiple fruit (as the raspberry) **d** : a rounded prominence on the back of a sepal (as in the common dock) **2 a** (1) : a small hard particle (as of sand, sugar, salt, gunpowder) (2) : one of the individual light-sensitive crystals of a photographic material or a particle resulting from the development of such a material; *collectively* : such crystals or particles (3) : an individual crystal in a metal; *collectively* : such crystals **b** (1) : a minute portion or particle ⟨a ~ of pollen⟩ ⟨the great structure of scientific knowledge to which his little ~ will be added —Oliver LaFarge⟩ (2) : the least possible amount ⟨did not have a ~ of sense⟩ ⟨left him no ~ of hope⟩ **c** : fine crystallization (as of sugar) ⟨boiling the solution to ~⟩ ⟨stopped the boiling process after the ~ had formed⟩ **3 a** : kermes or a scarlet dye made from it **b** : cochineal or a brilliant scarlet dye made from it **c** : a fast dye **d** *archaic* : COLOR, TINT, SHADE ⟨in a robe of darkest ~ —John Milton⟩ **e** : a light yellowish brown that is lighter and slightly redder and less strong than khaki, paler and slightly yellower than walnut brown, and paler and slightly redder than manila **4 a** : a superficial roughness imparting an appearance of being covered with grains : granulated appearance ⟨the ~ on a lithographer's plate⟩ **b** (1) *or* **grain side** : the outer or hair side of a skin or hide — compare FLESH 7 (2) : the markings on such a grain (3) : a surface artificially treated to resemble such a grain **c** : small pimply projections on the upper or outer surface of fully cured and fermented cigar leaf **5 a** : a unit of weight based on the weight of a grain of wheat taken as an average of the weight of grains from the middle of the ear and equal to .0648 gram — see CARAT GRAIN, MEASURE table **b** : a degree of hardness of water calculated by analysis of the number of such units of calcium carbonate per gallon of tested water — usu. used with a preceding number designating the number of units ⟨reduce the original 22-*grain* hardness —L.C.Huffman⟩ **c** *in Malta* : GRANO **6 a** : the appearance and texture of wood esp. as determined by the manner in which it is cut in relation to the cells, their size, shape, and orientation and their proportions and arrangement in annual rings : the appearance of the wood fibers in a piece of wood esp. as to their arrangement and direction of stratification; *also* : the direction of stratification of wood fibers **b** (1) : an appearance or texture that is due to the arrangement and esp. stratification of constituent particles or fibers and that is similar to or suggests the texture of wood ⟨the ~ of a rock⟩ ⟨the ~ of a metallic surface⟩ ⟨the ~ of a piece of meat⟩ (2) : a linear arrangement of roughly parallel ridges and valleys commonly displayed in regions of tilted sedimentary rocks; *also* : the direction of such linear features ⟨the ~ of the relief runs east and west⟩ **c** : a direction of cleavage of rock at right angles to and less conspicuous than the rift **d** : a direction of threads esp. in the warp of a fabric **e** : the fiber or yarn of a woven material that is dyed or is to be dyed ⟨dyed in the ~⟩ **f** : MACHINE DIRECTION **g** : the direction in which the blades of grass on a putting green tend to bend ⟨the average player never knows or cares whether he is putting with or against the ~ of a green —Paul Gallico⟩ **7 grains** *pl* : the remains of grain left in a mash tun after the completion of the mashing process **8 a** (1) : the arrangement of the particles of a body or of matter that determines its tactile quality esp. as to roughness or hardness ⟨the ~ of the freshly split piece of marble⟩ ⟨the fine ~ of her skin —Edna Ferber⟩ (2) : the roughness or hardness determined by this arrangement ⟨a soft-*grain* soap⟩ (3) : the coarseness or fineness of an abrasive expressed by a preceding number indicating the mesh of the finest screen through which the particles will pass ⟨a 24-*grain* grinding wheel⟩ **b** (1) : natural disposition : TEMPER, INCLINATION ⟨brothers similar in ~⟩ ⟨it went against the boy's ~ to tell lies⟩ (2) : basic quality or kind ⟨other poets of a tougher ~ —Van Wyck Brooks⟩ ⟨his work is . . . clearly in the American ~ —*Time*⟩ **c** : prevailing direction ⟨running against the ~ of the American polity —*Times Lit. Supp.*⟩ **9** : a piece of powder charge used in a rocket — **in grain** [ME, fr. MF *en graine* in kermes dye] **1** *of a dye* : RED, SCARLET **2** : COLORFAST **3** : DEEP-SEATED, INGRAINED ⟨anguish *in grain* —George Herbert⟩ ⟨a rogue *in grain* —Alfred Tennyson⟩ — **with a grain of salt** [trans. of L *cum grano salis*] : with some reservation or allowance : with caution ⟨take some of his more optimistic predictions *with a grain of salt*⟩

²grain \"\ *vb* -ED/-ING/-S *vt* **1** : INGRAIN 2 ⟨her hands were rough, broken, and ~*ed* with dirt —Rearden Conner⟩ **2 a** : to form (as powder) into grains : cause to separate in grains : GRANULATE **b** : to salt out — used esp. of soap **3** : to paint or otherwise decorate in imitation of a grain (as of wood or stone) **4** : to impart a granulated surface to (as paper, stone, or metal for lithographic work) : impress a grain upon (as a fabric) **5** : to feed with grain ~ *vi* : to form into grains : become granular : GRANULATE

³grain \"\ *n* -s [ME *grein, grain*, fr. ON *grein* branch, arm of the sea; akin to ON *grīna* to grin — more at GROAN] **1** *now dial Brit* **a** : an arm of the sea **b** : BRANCH, FORK ⟨a ~ of a river⟩ **c** : a branching fork in a tree **2 grains** *pl but sing in constr* : an iron fish spear or harpoon having two or more barbed points

⁴grain \"\ *vt* -ED/-ING/-S : to spear (fish) with a grains

⁵grain \"\ *vt* -ED/-ING/-S [fr. obs. *grane* trap, snare, noose, fr. ME — more at GRIN] *dial Eng* : STRANGLE, CHOKE

grain alcohol *n* : ETHYL ALCOHOL — used esp. in distinction from *wood alcohol*; see ALCOHOL 3

grain amaranth *n* : any of various amaranths grown esp. in So. America for their seed

grain beetle *n* : any of several small beetles whose larvae feed on and destroy stored grain

grain board *n* : plaster or gypsum wallboard bearing an imitation wood grain

grain borer *n* : an adult or larval insect that bores in grain

grain-burnt \'ˌ=,=\ *adj, of a horse* : having a digestive disturbance attributed to overfeeding with grain

grain-cut \'=,=\ *adj, of wood* : cut transversely to the grain

grain direction *n* : MACHINE DIRECTION

grain door *n* : a close-fitting removable device or partition used in boxcars hauling grain to seal openings around the lower part of permanent car doors and prevent leakage

grain drill *n* : a drill for sowing small grains (as of wheat) or fine seeds (as clover seed) — see CUP DRILL, SHOE DRILL

grained \'grānd\ *adj* [partly fr. ¹*grain* + *-ed*; partly fr. past part. of ²*grain*] **1 a** : having, consisting of, or producing grains — usu. used with a modifier specifying kind or quantity ⟨small-*grained* wheat⟩ ⟨a fine-*grained* gunpowder⟩ ⟨a many=*grained* grass⟩ **b** : GRANULAR ⟨boiled the sugar solution down to a ~ consistency⟩ **2 a** : having a grain — usu. used with a modifier specifying the kind ⟨a straight-*grained* wood⟩ ⟨an open-*grained* fibrous material⟩ ⟨a tough-*grained* writer⟩ **b** : treated (as by painting or staining) to exhibit a grain ⟨a painted and ~ commode⟩ **3 a** : having or treated so as to have a surface marked by a roughness or by distributed or stratified prominences or ridges ⟨~ leather⟩ **b** *of the edge of a coin* : MILLED — **grain·ed·ness** \ˌgrānədnəs\ *n* -ES

grain elevator *n* : ELEVATOR 1c

¹grain·er \'grānə(r)\ *n* -s [²*grain* + *-er*] **1** : a worker that grains: as **a** : an operator of a machine for graining lithographic printing plates **b** (1) : a worker who uses a graining comb, roller, sponge, or brush to decorate a metal or wooden surface with a simulated wood grain (2) : an operator of a machine for printing lines upon furniture parts to simulate the grain of wood **c** : a worker who softens and grains hides and skins by rubbing grain sides together with a graining board or by operating a graining machine — called also *boarder, dicer* **d** : a worker who melts TNT and drains it into graining kettles where it is crystallized by agitation and cooling **2** : a machine or device used in graining: as **a** : a machine that impresses a grain on boards **b** : a brush or tool used in graining wood or metal **c** : an instrument for graining skins **d** : an evaporating vat in which salt grains from brine

²grainer \"\ *n* -s [⁴*grain* + *-er*] : one that uses a grains

grain·ery \'grān(ə)rē, -ri\ *n* -ES [by alter.] : GRANARY

grainfield \'=,=\ *n* : a field where grain is grown

grain hay *n* : plants of any of the grain crops cut and cured for hay

grainier *comparative of* GRAINY

grainiest *superlative of* GRAINY

grain·i·ness \'grānēnəs, -nin-\ *n* -ES : the quality or state of being grainy

¹grain·ing \'grāniŋ, -nēŋ\ *n* -s [fr. gerund of ²*grain*] **1 a** *obs* : a ring of dots on a coin near the rim **b** : REEDING **2 a** : grain (as of wood, marble, or leather) or appearance of such a grain (as one achieved by painting, printing, or stamping) **b** : a process for producing an artificial grain (as in leather)

²grai·ning \"\ *n* -s [origin unknown] : a European freshwater cyprinoid fish (*Leuciscus leuciscus*)

³grain·ing \"\ *n* -s [fr. gerund of ⁴*grain*] : the action of fishing with a grains

graining board *n* : a cork-covered board that is strapped to the forearm and used in softening and graining hides or skins

grain itch *n* : an itching rash caused by the bite of the tarsonemid mite (*Pyemotes ventricosus*) that occurs chiefly on grain, straw, or straw products — compare GROCER'S ITCH

grainland \'=,=\ *n* : land on which grain grows or is grown

grain leather *n* : leather usu. heavier than buffing made from the grain side of a skin and in the case of cowhide often split from a hide already tanned and dried

grain·less \'grānləs\ *adj* : having no grain ⟨a ~ wood finish⟩ ⟨~ ear of corn⟩

grain mark *n* : a line on a gem facet resulting from imperfect polishing

grain mite *n* : any of several mites that frequent stored grain; *esp* : a small whitish hairy form (*Acarus siro*) sometimes causing unpleasant odors in imperfectly dry flour or grain

grain moth *n* : any of several small tineoid moths (as the Angoumois grain moth) whose larvae feed on stored grain

grain of paradise [ME, trans. of MF *graine de paradis*] **1** : one of the pungent seeds of a West African plant (*Aframomum melegueta*) of the family Zingiberaceae used as a spice — usu. used in pl. **2** : one of the dried fruits of an East Indian woody vine (*Anamirta cocculus*) — usu. used in pl.

grain raising *n* : irregularity in wood surfaces resulting from exposure to moisture or weathering

grain rust *n* : a rust that attacks a cereal grass; *esp* : a wheat stem rust (*Puccinia graminis*)

grains *pl of* GRAIN, *pres 3d sing of* GRAIN

grain screen *n* : an etched screen with an irregular stipple finish used in making mezzographs

¹grainsick \'=,=\ *n* -s : a sickness of cattle in which the rumen is excessively distended with food

²grainsick \"\ *adj* : suffering from grainsick — **grain·sick·ness** *n*

grain side *n* : GRAIN 4b(1)

grain smut *n* : a smut that attacks a cereal grass; *esp* : a kernel smut as distinguished from one invading the entire inflorescence

grain sorghum *n* : any of several sorghums that are cultivated primarily for grain — see DURRA, FETERITA, HEGARI, KAFFIR, KAOLIANG, MILO, SHALLU; compare SORGO

grain thief *n* : a device consisting chiefly of a long tube used for taking grain samples from various depths in a load of grain — compare THIEF 3

grain thrips *n* : any of several thrips feeding in cereal grains; *esp* : a cosmopolitan insect (*Limothrips cerealium*) common in developing flower stalks of oats and wild oats

grain weevil *n* : any of various small insects destructive of stored grain; *specif* : GRANARY WEEVIL

grainy \'grānē, -ni\ *adj* -ER/-EST [¹*grain* + *-y*] **1** : consisting of or resembling grains : GRANULAR ⟨soil of a ~ consistency⟩ ⟨a stone that is ~ in appearance⟩ **2 a** : having a usu. marked natural or artificial grain ⟨a ~ wood⟩ ⟨a floor of ~ plastic tile⟩ **b** *of paper* : showing on the surface the imprint of the felt used in its manufacture (as when the felt is coarse or worn) **3** *of a developed photographic image* : having a mottled appearance produced by the individual particles of silver of which it is composed

¹graip \'grāp\ *dial Brit var of* GROPE

²graip \"\ *n* -s [ME *grape*, of Scand origin; akin to Norw *greip* forked tool, ON *greip* hand spread out, grip; akin to OE *grāp* grasp, grip, OHG *greifa* fork, ON *grīpa* to grip, grasp — more at GRIPE] *dial Brit* : a usu. 3-tined garden fork or manure fork

graisse \'grās\ *or* **graisse disease** *n* -s [F *graisse*, lit., grease — more at GREASE] : a disease of white wines and cider caused by deficiency of tannin and the action of certain anaerobic bacteria

¹graith \'grāth, 'greth\ *vt* -ED/-ING/-S [ME *greithen, graithen*, fr. ON *greitha*, fr. *greithr* ready, prepared — more at READY] **1** *chiefly Scot* : to make ready and put in order **2** *chiefly Scot* : FURNISH, ARRAY

²graith \"\ *n* -s [ME, readiness, equipment, fr. ON *greithi*, fr. *greithr* ready, prepared] **1** *chiefly Scot* : equipment or apparel : accouterments for work, traveling, or war : GEAR **2** : POSSESSIONS, WEALTH

gral·lae \'gra,lē\ *n pl, cap* [NL, fr. L, stilts, fr. *gradi* to step, go — more at GRADE] **1** *in former classifications* : an order of birds including all the wading birds **2** *in former classifications* : a group of birds variously limited: as **a** : CHARADRII **b** : GRUIFORMES **c** : Charadrii and Gruiformes

gral·la·to·res \ˌgralə'tōr(,)ēz\ [NL, pl. of L *grallator* one who goes on stilts, fr. *grallae* stilts + *-ator*] *syn of* GRALLAE 1

gral·la·to·ri·al \ˌ==;tōrēəl\ *adj* [NL *Grallatores* + E *-ial*] : of or belonging to the wading birds

gral·li·na \grə'līnə, -lēnə\ *n* [NL, fr. L *grallae* stilts + NL *-ina*] **1** *cap* : a genus of passerine birds including the black-and-white magpie lark of Australia **2** -s : any bird of the genus *Grallina* : MAGPIE LARK

gral·line \'gra,līn\ *adj* [NL *Grallina*] : GRALLATORIAL

¹gral·loch \'graləḵ, -əḵ\ *n* -s [ScGael *greallach*] **1** *Brit* : the entrails of an animal (as a deer) **2** *Brit* : the act of gralloching

²gralloch \"\ *vt* -ED/-ING/-S *Brit* : to remove the entrails from (as a deer) : GUT

¹gram \'gram, -aa(ə)m\ *n* -s [Pg *grão* (formerly also spelled *gram*) grain, seed, chick-pea, fr. L *granum* grain — more at CORN] : any of several leguminous plants grown esp. for their seed: as **a** : CHICK-PEA **b** : HORSE GRAM **c** : MUNG BEAN

²gram *or* **gramme** \"\ *n* -s [F *gramme*, fr. LL *gramma*, a small weight, fr. Gk, letter, a small weight, fr. *graphein* to write — more at CARVE] **1** : a metric unit of mass and weight equal to 1/1000 kilogram and nearly equal to one cubic centimeter of water at its maximum density — see METRIC SYSTEM table **2** : the weight of the gram mass under standard gravity

³gram \"\ *n* -s [by shortening & alter.] : GRANDMOTHER

-gram \ˌgram, -aa(ə)m; *in "program" and in the southern US in "telegram" the preceding or* ˌgrəm\ *n comb form* -s [L *-gramma*, fr. Gk, fr. *gramma* letter, piece of writing] : drawing : writing : record ⟨chrono*gram*⟩ ⟨tele*gram*⟩ ⟨thermo*gram*⟩ ⟨spectro*gram*⟩

gram *abbr* grammar; grammatical

grama *or* **grama grass** *or* **gram·ma** *or* **gramma grass** \'gramə(-)\ *n* -s [Sp *grama* coarse grass, fr. L *gramina*, pl. of *gramen* grass — more at GRASS] : a pasture grass of the western U.S. belonging to the genus *Bouteloua* (as blue grama and black grama)

gram·a·rye *or* **gram·a·ry** \'gramərē\ *n, pl* **gramaryes** *or* **gramaries** [ME *gramarye, gramarie*, modif. of MF *gramaire* grammar, grammar book, book of sorcery — more at GRAMMAR] : NECROMANCY, MAGIC, ENCHANTMENT

gram atom \'=;==\ *or* **gram-atomic weight** \ˌ==;==-\ *n* : the quantity of a chemical element which has a weight in grams equal numerically to the atomic weight of the element ⟨a *gram atom* of oxygen is 16 grams⟩ — compare AVOGADRO NUMBER

gram calorie *n* : CALORIE a

gram-centimeter \'=;==,==\ *n* **1** : a unit of torque equal to that of a gram weight acting on a lever arm one centimeter long **2** : a unit of work in the cgs system equal to the work done in raising a weight of one gram against the force of gravity to a height of one centimeter

gram complex \'gram-\ *n, usu cap G* [after Hans Christian Joachim *Gram* †1938 Dan. physician] : the part of a gram-positive bacterial cell responsible for the characteristic staining by Gram's method and usu. considered to be a layer of ribonucleate in complex association with polysaccharides and protein immediately underlying the cell wall

grame \'grām\ *n* -s [ME, fr. OE *grama*, fr. *gram* angry, fierce, hostile; akin to OHG *gram* angry, hostile, ON *gramr* angry, hostile, OE *grimm* fierce, wild — more at GRIM] **1** *archaic* : ANGER **2** *archaic* : SORROW, HARM, MISERY

gram equivalent *n* : the quantity of a chemical element, radical, or compound which has a weight in grams equal to the equivalent

¹gra·mer·cy \grə'mərsē\ *interj* [ME *grand mercy, graunt mercy, gramercye*, fr. MF *grand merci* great thanks] *archaic* — used to express gratitude, surprise, or sudden strong feeling ⟨~! they for joy did grin —S.T.Coleridge⟩

²gramercy *n, obs* : THANKS ⟨works of compulsion are not worth ~ —Richard Montagu⟩

gram-fast \'=,=\ *adj, sometimes cap G* [after Hans C. J. *Gram* †1938 Dan. physician] : GRAM-POSITIVE

gram·i·ci·din \ˌgramə'sīdᵊn\ *n* -s [*gram*-positive + *-i-* + *-cide* + *-in*] : a crystalline antibiotic of a polypeptide nature produced by a soil bacterium (*Bacillus brevis*) that is active against most gram-positive disease-producing bacteria in local infections but when introduced into the blood stream is destructive of red blood cells — see TYROTHRICIN

gramied *past of* GRAMY

gramies *pres 3d sing of* GRAMY

gramin- *or* **gramini-** *comb form* [L *gramin-, gramen* — more at GRASS] : grass ⟨*gramini*vorous⟩ ⟨*gramini*ferous⟩

gram·i·na·ce·ae \ˌgramə'nāsē,ē\ [NL, fr. *gramin-* + *-aceae*] *syn of* GRAMINEAE

gram·i·na·ceous \ˌ==;nāshəs\ *adj* [*gramin-* + *-aceous*] : GRAMINEOUS

gram·i·na·les \ˌ==;nā(,)lēz\ *n pl, cap* [NL, fr. L *gramin-, gramen* grass + NL *-ales*] : an order of monocotyledonous plants including the grasses and sedges that is characterized by small flowers usu. arranged in spikelets with the perianth absent or reduced or represented by bristles or scales and with usu. ribbon-shaped leaves

gram·ine \'gra,mēn, -mən\ *n* -s [ISV *gram-* (fr. L *gramen* grass) + *-ine*] : a crystalline base ($C_8H_6N)CH_2N(CH_3)_2$ occurring esp. in the germ of Swedish barley and made from indole by reaction with formaldehyde and dimethylamine; 3-(dimethylamino-methyl)-indole

gra·min·e·ae \grə'minē,ē\ *n pl, cap* [NL, L, fr. fem. pl. of *gramineus*] : a large family of monocotyledonous plants (order Graminales) with culms hollow, leaves generally 2-ranked, and fruit a caryopsis — see GRASS; compare BAMBOO, CEREAL

gra·min·e·al \-nēəl\ *adj* [L *gramineus* + E *-al*] : GRAMINEOUS

gra·min·e·ous \-nēəs\ *adj* [L *gramineus*, fr. *gramin-, gramen* grass + *-eus* -eous — more at GRASS] **1** : resembling or relating to a grass **2** : belonging to the family Gramineae — **gramin·e·ous·ness** *n* -ES

gram·i·nic·o·lous \ˌgramə'nikələs\ *adj* [*gramin-* + *-colous*] : living upon grass ⟨a ~ parasite⟩ ⟨a ~ fungus⟩

gram·i·niv·o·rous \-ˌ;niv(ə)rəs\ *adj* [*gramin-* + *-vorous*] : feeding on grass

¹gram·i·noid \'gramə,nȯid\ *adj* [*gramin-* + *-oid*] : of or relating to grasses

²graminoid \"\ *n* -s : a graminoid plant

gram·i·nous \-nəs\ *adj* [L *graminosus*, fr. *gramin-, gramen* + *-osus* -ous] *archaic* : GRAMINEOUS

gramma *var of* GRAMA

gram·ma·log *or* **gram·ma·logue** \'gramə,lȯg *also* -läg\ *n* -s [Gk *gramma* letter + E *-log, -logue* — more at GRAM] **1** : a word represented in shorthand by a single stroke **2** : the stroke that represents a grammalog : LOGOGRAM 1

gram·mar \'gramə(r)\ *n* -s [ME *gramere, gramer, grammer*, fr. MF *gramaire*, modif. of L *grammatica*, fr. Gk *grammatikē*, fr. fem. of *grammatikos* skilled in grammar, fr. *grammat-, gramma* letter, piece of writing + *-ikos* -ic — more at GRAM] **1 a** : a branch of linguistic study that deals with the classes of words, their inflections or other means of indicating relation to each other, and their functions and relations in the sentence as employed according to established usage and that is sometimes extended to include related matter such as phonology, prosody, language history, orthography, orthoepy, etymology, or semantics — see ACCIDENCE, MORPHOLOGY, SYNTAX **b** : LINGUISTICS **c** : a study of what is to be preferred and what avoided in the inflections and syntax of a language **2** : that which is studied in grammar : those phenomena of language with which grammar deals : the characteristic system or the preferred system of inflections and syntax of a language **3 a** : a book in which grammar is methodically treated **b** : an elementary textbook for foreign language study **c** : a manner of speaking or writing that conforms to grammatical rules : speech or writing that is preferred to what should be avoided ⟨appalled at the bad ~ of college students⟩ **4 a** : the basic elements or principles of a science, art, discipline, practice ⟨the ~ of politics in Latin America is unfamiliar to the Anglo-Saxon mind —R.A.Humphreys⟩ ⟨the ~ of heraldry⟩ **b** : a treatise or book dealing with such elements or principles **c** : a set of such elements or principles ⟨music has universal appeal because it has a universal ~⟩

gram·mar·i·an \grə'merēən, -ma(a)r-, -mār-\ *n* -s [ME *gramarien, gramarian*, fr. MF *gramarien*, fr. *gramaire* grammar +

-ien -ian] **1 a :** a specialist in grammar or linguistics **:** PHILOLOGIST **b :** one who writes about or teaches grammar **2 :** one who writes on the basic elements or principles of any science, art, discipline, or practice

gram·mar·less \'gramə(r)ləs\ *adj* **1 :** lacking any marked analyzable grammatical forms and relationships ⟨a relatively ~ language⟩ **2 :** showing or marked by an ignorance of the approved forms or syntax of a language ⟨a man with a notably ~ speech and crudeness of manner⟩

grammar school *n* **1 a :** a secondary school providing instruction chiefly in Latin and often Greek usu. in preparation for college — called also *Latin grammar school* **b :** a chiefly British school providing a college preparatory course **2 a :** a school teaching the grades between the primary grades and high school **b :** the grades between the primary grades and high school

gram·mat·i·cal \grə'mad·ə̇kəl, -atˌ, |ēk-\ *also* **gram·mat·ic** \ik, |ēk\ *adj* [*grammatical* fr. LL *grammaticalis*, fr. L *grammaticus* grammatical (fr. Gk *grammatikos* skilled in grammar) + *-alis* -al; *grammatic* fr. L *grammaticus* — more at GRAMMAR] **1 a :** of or relating to grammar ⟨a ~ rule⟩ **b :** according to or following the words taken strictly in accordance with the rules of grammar **:** LITERAL ⟨~ sense⟩ ⟨a ~ interpretation⟩ **2 a :** according to the rules of grammar **:** correct as regards grammar ⟨strictly ~ use of the words⟩ **b :** of, relating to, or being in strict accordance with the grammar or methodic principles of an art or science, discipline, or practice ⟨the foremost ~ difference in the heraldry of the continent —D.L.Galbreath⟩ — **gram·mat·i·cal·ly** \|ə̇k(ə)lē, |ēk-, -li\ *adv* — **gram·mat·i·cal·ness** \|ə̇kəlnə̇s, |ēk-\ *n* -ES

grammatical change *n* [trans. of G *grammatischer wechsel*] **1 :** the system of consonant contrasts in the Germanic strong verb according to Verner's law (OE *cēosan*, choose; *coren*, chosen) **2 :** VERNER'S LAW

grammatical gender *n* **:** GENDER 2 — distinguished from *natural gender*

grammatical meaning *n* **1 :** the meaning expressed by a grammatical ending, word order, or intonation **:** a grammatical category (as plural, interrogative, subject, superlative) **2 :** the part of meaning which varies from one form of a paradigm to another (as from *plays* to *played* to *playing*) — compare LEXICAL MEANING

grammatical subject *n* **:** a term (as a pronoun) in a sentence that occupies the position of the subject in normal English word order and anticipates a subsequent word or phrase that specifies the actual substantive content (as *it* in the sentence "it is sometimes hard to do right") — called also *formal subject;* distinguished from *logical subject*

gram·mat·i·cism \grə'mad·əˌsizəm, -atə-\ *n* -S **:** a point or principle of grammar

gram·mat·i·cize \-ˌsīz\ *vb* -ED/-ING/-S *vt* **:** to make grammatical **:** reduce to rules of grammar ~ *vi* **:** to discuss points of grammar

gram·ma·tist \'gramədˌə̇st\ *n* -S [L *grammatista* schoolmaster, fr. Gk *grammatistēs*, fr. *grammatizein* to teach reading and writing, fr. *grammat-*, *gramma* letter, piece of writing + *-izein* -ize — more at GRAM] **:** a usu. pedantic grammarian — **gram·ma·tis·ti·cal** \ˌgramə¦tistə̇kəl\ *adj*

gram·ma·tol·a·try \ˌgramə'tälə·trē\ *n* -ES [Gk *grammato-* (fr. *grammat-*, *gramma*) + E *-latry*] **:** the worship of letters or words **:** devotion to the letter (as of Scripture)

gram·ma·to·phyl·lum \ˌgramədˌə'filəm\ *n, cap* [NL, fr. Gk *grammato-* + NL *-phyllum*] **:** a small genus of epiphytic Malayan orchids with long narrow leaves and drooping flower clusters often six feet long

gramme *var of* GRAM

gram–molecular \ˈ=¦==ˌ==\ *or* **gram–molar** \ˈ=¦=ˌ=\ *adj* **:** of, relating to, or containing a gram molecule

gram molecule *or* **gram–molecular weight** *n* **:** the quantity of a chemical compound or element that has a weight in grams numerically equal to the molecular weight — compare AVOGADRO NUMBER, MOLE

gram·my \'gramē, -mi\ *n* -ES [by shortening & alter.] **:** GRANDMOTHER

gram–negative \ˈ=¦===\ *adj, sometimes cap G* [after Hans C. J. *Gram* †1938 Dan. physician] **:** not holding the purple dye when stained by gram's method — used chiefly of bacteria

gram·o·phile \'graməˌfīl\ *n* -S [*gramophone* + *-phile*] **:** a lover and collector of phonograph records

Gram·o·phone \-ˌfōn\ *trademark* — used for a phonograph

gramp \'gramp, -aa(ə)mp, -aimp\ *or* **gramps** \-ps\ *n, pl* **gramps** [by shortening and alter. fr. *grandpa*] **:** GRANDFATHER

gram–positive \ˈ=¦===\ *adj, sometimes cap G* [after Hans C. J. *Gram*] **:** holding the purple dye when stained by gram's method — used chiefly of bacteria

gram·pus \'grampəs, -aam-, -aim-\ *n* -ES [alter. of earlier *graundepose*, *grampoys*, alter. of ME *grapay*, *graspey*, fr. MF *craspois*, *graspois*, *craspeis*, fr. *cras*, *gras* fat (fr. L *crassus*) + *pois*, *peis* fish, fr. L *piscis* — more at HURDLE, FISH] **1 a :** a cetacean (*Grampus griseus*) that is widely distributed in the seas of the northern hemisphere and that is related to the blackfish but has teeth in the lower jaw only **b :** any of various other cetaceans of similar size (as the blackfish or the killer whale) **2 :** the giant whip scorpion (*Mastigoproctus giganteus*) of the southern U.S. that is popularly but unjustifiably reputed to be exceedingly venomous

grams *pl of* GRAM

-grams *pl of* -GRAM

gram's method \'gramz-, -aa(ə)mz-\ *or* **gram method** *n, sometimes cap G* [after Hans C. J. *Gram*] **:** a method for the differential staining of bacteria by which they are treated with Gram's solution after being stained with gentian violet and are then treated with alcohol and washed in water with the result that certain species retain the dye while others are decolorized — see GRAM-NEGATIVE, GRAM-POSITIVE

gram's solution *n, usu cap G* [after H. C. J. *Gram*] **:** a solution of one part iodine, two parts potassium iodide, and 300 parts water used in staining bacteria by gram's method

gram stain *also* **gram's stain** *n, sometimes cap G* [after H. C. J. *Gram*] **:** GRAM'S METHOD; *also* **:** an instance of staining by this method ⟨did a *gram stain* on each specimen⟩

gram–variable \ˈ=¦====\ *adj, sometimes cap G* [*gram's (method)*] **:** staining irregularly or inconsistently by gram's method

gra·my \'grāmē\ *vt* -ED/-ING/-ES [*grame* + *-y* (as in *worry*)] *now dial* **:** to make angry **:** ANNOY

gran \'gran, -aa(ə)n\ *n* -S [by shortening] **:** GRANDMOTHER

¹gra·na \'grānə\ *or* **grana cheese** *n* -S [It (*formaggio di*) *grana* granular cheese, fr. *grana* grain, fr. L, pl. of *granum* — more at CORN] **:** PARMESAN

²gra·na \'grānə, -ānə\ *n pl* [NL, pl. of L *granum* grain] **:** minute organized bodies that make up most of the substance of plant chloroplasts and that are the actual seat of the chlorophyll

³grana *pl of* GRANUM

gra·na·da \grə'nädə, -nā-\ *adj, usu cap* [fr. *Granada*, Spain] **:** of or from the city of Granada, Spain **:** of the kind or style prevalent in Granada

gran·a·dilla \ˌgranə'dilə, -dē(y)ə\ *or* **gren·a·dilla** \ˌgren-\ *n* -S [Sp *granadilla*, dim. of *granada* pomegranate, fr. LL *granata* — more at GRENADE] **1 a :** GRANADILLA TREE **b :** GRANADILLA WOOD **2 :** the oblong fruit of various passionflowers (esp. *Passiflora quadrangularis* of tropical America) widely used as a dessert and for flavoring

granadilla tree *n* **:** a West Indian tree (*Brya ebenus*) of the family Leguminosae that furnishes a fine grade of green ebony

granadilla wood *n* **1 :** the wood of the granadilla tree — called also *cocuswood* **2 :** a dark red hardwood derived from a cocobolo (*Dalbergia retusa*) of northern So. America and used in making musical instruments (as clarinets) **3** *in Puerto Rico* **:** the yellow satiny wood of a tropical American tree (*Buchenavia capitata*) of the family Combretaceae **4 :** the chocolate-brown hardwood of a tropical American tree (*Caesalpinia granadillo*)

gran·a·dillo \-di(ˌ)lō, -dē(ˌ)(y)ō\ *n* -S [Sp, fr. *granadilla*] **1 :** GRANADILLA TREE **2 :** any tropical American passionflower yielding the fruit called granadilla **3 :** GRANADILLA WOOD 2

gra·na·ry \'grān(ə)rē, 'gran-, -ri\ *n* -ES [L *granarium*, fr. *granum* grain + *-arium* -ary — more at CORN] **1 :** a storehouse or repository for grain esp. after it is threshed or husked; *also* **:** a region producing grain in abundance **2 :** the chief source or storehouse esp. of grain ⟨Egypt as the ~ of the ancient world —Agnes Repplier⟩ ⟨became known as the ~ of the caravans that were moving up and down the country —L.S.B. Leakey⟩ ⟨the people remain the great ~ of vital spontaneity and nonpharisaic living force —Jacques Maritain⟩

granary weevil *n* **:** a small brown weevil (*Sitophilus granarius*) which feeds on and lays its eggs in the kernels of stored grain (as wheat, barley, maize) in which the larva develops and within the hull of which it pupates

gran·at \'granə̇t\ *n* -S [modif. of F *grenat* garnet — more at GARNET] **:** PONCEAU

gra·na·tum \grə'nād·əm, -nād·-\ *n* -S [NL, fr. L, pomegranate — more at GRENADE] **:** the bark or fruit rind of pomegranate which is high in tannin content

¹grand \'grand, -aa(ə)nd\ *adj* -ER/-EST [MF, fr. L *grandis* large, full-grown, old, great, grand; perh. akin to Gk *brenthos* pride, *brenthyesthai* to act proudly, swell up with pride, OSlav *grǫdĭ* breast; basic meaning: swelling] **1 a** *obs* **:** eminent or memorable in position or scale of operation **:** FAMOUS **b :** having more importance than others **:** PREEMINENT, FOREMOST, CHIEF ⟨remarking that death was the ~ mystery of all time⟩ **c :** having higher rank or more official dignity than others bearing the same general designation — used with titles indicating office, rank, or standing ⟨a ~ master⟩ ⟨a ~ champion⟩ ⟨a ~ duke⟩; *also* **:** having the highest or supreme rank of all the nation — used in the titles of sovereigns **2 a :** INCLUSIVE, COMPREHENSIVE ⟨the ~ total of all money paid out over the period⟩ ⟨three independent services, coordinated only to the extent necessary to have uniformity in ~ policy —T.K. Finletter⟩ **b :** DEFINITIVE, INCONTROVERTIBLE ⟨the Bible is the ~ proof in English that in the greatest writing literary beauty is not a main object but a by-product —Douglas Bush⟩ **3 :** MAIN, PRINCIPAL ⟨the ~ staircase leading up from the large front hallway⟩ ⟨the ~ ballroom⟩ ⟨to make expressive of the form within, of its volume and movement, this was the painter's ~ preoccupation —Laurence Binyon⟩ **4 a :** of large size, extent, value, or consequence **:** GREAT ⟨a ~ mistake⟩ ⟨a ~ imposture⟩ **b :** large in scope, grasp, or interest ⟨some ~ but impractical ideas about how to make money⟩ ⟨a ~ bringing together of a thousand details to make a clear and interesting lecture⟩ ⟨a ~ adventure among pirates and desperadoes⟩ **c :** being of a size or grade that confers distinction ⟨the ~ structure of the hippodrome⟩ ⟨a ~ chorus⟩ **5 a :** marked by great magnificence, display, ceremoniousness, or formality **:** SUMPTUOUS, GORGEOUS ⟨a ~ celebration in honor of the king's birthday⟩ ⟨a ~ exhibition of fireworks⟩; *also* **:** marked by a regal form and dignity ⟨the ~ manner of royalty descending from a coach —*Amer. Guide Series: Calif.*⟩ **b :** fine or imposing in appearance or impression **:** impressive because of physical, moral, or intellectual greatness **:** ILLUSTRIOUS, STATELY, NOBLE ⟨the ~ figure of the duchess at the head of the table⟩ ⟨the ~ totality of the author's literary output⟩ **:** MAJESTIC, SPLENDID, MAGNIFICENT ⟨a ~ regal ceremony⟩ ⟨made a ~ appearance in silk dress and jeweled tiara⟩ ⟨the worn, homely face, ~ in its utter simplicity —L.M.Angus-Butterworth⟩ **:** LOFTY, SUBLIME ⟨writing in the ~ style⟩ ⟨an epic poem around a ~ conception of heaven and hell⟩ **c :** pretending to or claiming social superiority **:** SUPERCILIOUS ⟨you were much too ~ to speak to us —Archibald Marshall⟩ **d :** designed to impress — used of actions ⟨a man given to ~ gestures and pretentious statements⟩ **6 :** very good **:** FINE, WONDERFUL ⟨got up in the morning feeling ~⟩ ⟨had a ~ time at the picnic⟩ **:** ADMIRABLE ⟨a ~ old man⟩ **7 :** of or relating to a grand lodge

syn MAGNIFICENT, IMPOSING, STATELY, MAJESTIC, AUGUST, NOBLE, GRANDIOSE: GRAND may apply to any sort of impressive greatness, ampleness, handsomeness, rank, dignity, or preeminence ⟨*grand* amid the hall floor was the Goth king in his gear —William Morris⟩ ⟨the *grandest* passages in the Bible —A.L.Guérard⟩ ⟨at the piano her mood exalted patriotism, uplifted in spirit by that *grand* song —Winston Churchill⟩ ⟨the great cathedral seemed so *grand* when one was all alone there with the music rolling away down the nave —J.R.Green⟩ MAGNIFICENT may apply to a most extreme and impressive scope, sumptuousness, splendor, stateliness, munificence, or handsomeness without loss of dignity or taste ⟨how *magnificent* was the sight of the royal escort, the brilliant uniforms of the troops, the marching bands —Edith Sitwell⟩ ⟨the *magnificent* marble town house, celebrated as a world's wonder, even in that age and country, in which so much splendor was lavished on municipal palaces —J.L.Motley⟩ ⟨perhaps the most *magnificent* manifestation of poetic mysticism is the last canto —G.G.Coulton⟩ IMPOSING may describe what is impressive through commanding size, dignity, or magnificence ⟨she came in, like a ship in full sail, an *imposing* creature, tall and stout, with an ample bust and an obesity girthed in —W.S.Maugham⟩ ⟨an *imposing* neoclassic structure in the form of a Greek cross with a Corinthian entrance portico —*Amer. Guide Series: Md.*⟩ ⟨an *imposing* appearance, with vast blocks or boulders of granite, sparkling with mica —*Amer. Guide Series: Texas*⟩ STATELY may suggest blended poised dignity and handsomeness, impressiveness, size and strength, or loftiness ⟨the picture of a regal and *stately* lady in court dress, with a high diamond tiara upon her noble head —A. Conan Doyle⟩ ⟨the long and *stately* flight of steps descending from the Capitoline Hill to the level of lower Rome —Nathaniel Hawthorne⟩ MAJESTIC, which blends the connotations of IMPOSING and STATELY, may also connote a lofty solemn thought-provoking or awe-inspiring grandeur ⟨calm and *majestic*, the very picture of courtly self-possession in his coat of gold brocade and black velvet breeches, with a jeweled order tangled in the rich laces upon his breast —Elinor Wylie⟩ ⟨the *majestic* movement of cosmic time —Aldous Huxley⟩ ⟨the *majestic* tradition of classic study gives to the old humanities a dignity that newer branches of learning can never attain —C.H.Grandgent⟩ AUGUST applies to an exalted impressiveness inspiring awe, wonder, reverence, or abashment ⟨a sight of the old heathen emperor is enough to create an evanescent sentiment of loyalty even in a democratic bosom, so *august* does he look, so fit to rule, so worthy of man's profoundest homage and obedience —Nathaniel Hawthorne⟩ ⟨for in the eternal city . . . a Power *august*, benignant and supreme shall then absolve thee of all farther duties —E.A. Poe⟩ NOBLE may imply illustrious, dignified excellence, stateliness, or loftiness ⟨the disinterested search for truth is certainly one of the highest and *noblest* careers that a man can choose —W.R.Inge⟩ ⟨the old artists, who attained their grand results by penetrating themselves with some *noble* and significant action —Matthew Arnold⟩ ⟨a *noble* building of rose-colored sandstone inlaid with white marble —Elinor Wylie⟩ GRANDIOSE may describe unusual largeness or scope or even majesty, but it commonly suggests an inflated pompous or preposterous pretension ⟨the *grandiose* complexities of the universe —J.W.Krutch⟩ ⟨a *grandiose* conception worthy of a feudal baron of commerce —V.L.Parrington⟩ All of these words lend themselves readily to hyperbole in application to trivial, mundane, or insignificant things being highly praised

²grand \"\ *n* -S **1** *usu cap* **a :** an officer of a fraternal society or other organization whose title contains the word *grand* ⟨a past ~⟩ **b :** the presiding officer of a club **2 :** GRAND PIANO **3** *slang* **:** a thousand dollars ⟨made about three ~ on a swindle⟩ **4 a :** one of the available bids or rounds in a card game: as (1) **:** a round in skat in which the four jacks are the only trumps (2) **:** a round in frog in which hearts are trumps — compare ¹CHICO **b :** GRAND SLAM

grand allemande *n* **:** a swing in square dancing once and a half around first grasping right forearms and then the left as each person is met in a grand right and left

gran·dam \'granˌdam, -dəm\ *n* -S [ME *graundam*, fr. OF *grant dame*, fr. *grant* grand + *dame* lady, mother] **1** *or* **grandame** \-ˌdām, -dəm\ **a :** GRANDMOTHER **b :** old woman **2** *also* **grand·dam** \-nˌdam, -ndəm\ **:** a dam's or sire's dam — used of an animal

grandaunt \ˈ=¦=\ *n* **:** the aunt of one's father or mother — called also *great-aunt*

grand·baby \'gran(d),==, -aan-\ *n* **:** an infant granddaughter or grandson ⟨have to put up with sons-in-law and two *grandbabies* —May L. Becker⟩

grand battement *n* [F, lit., great battement] **:** a battement in ballet executed with the free leg lifted high from the hip

grand canyon \ˈ=¦=\ *adj, usu cap G&C* [fr. the *Grand Canyon*, Ariz.] **:** of, relating to, or constituting a division of the Proterozoic — see GEOLOGIC TIME table

grand ca·pe \-'kā(ˌ)pē, -'kā(ˌ)pā\ *n* [AF *graunt cape* (part trans. of ML *cape magnum*), fr. *graunt*, *grand* large + *cape* any of several writs including the grand cape and the petit cape, fr. ML, fr. L *cape* (the first word in these writs), 2d pers. sing. imper. of *capere* to take — more at HEAVE] *Eng law* **:** a writ issued in the now obsolete real actions for the recovery of land on the failure of the defendant tenant in possession to make an appearance

grand chain *n* **:** GRAND RIGHT AND LEFT

grand·child \'gran(d),=, -aan-\ *n* **1 :** a son's or daughter's child **:** a child in the second degree of descent **2 :** something in a relationship analogous to or suggesting that of a grandchild

grand choeur \grāⁿkœr\ *adv* (*or adj*) [F *grand chœur*, lit., great chorus] **:** full organ — used as a direction in organ music

grand chop *n* **:** a customs clearance or receipt for dues and duties in the India and China trade

grand climacteric *n* **:** the sixty-third or the eighty-first year of a person's life

grand commander *n* **1 :** a member of one of the divisions of the highest grade in an order of knighthood **2 :** the chief fiscal officer in an order of knighthood (as the Knights Hospitalers) — **grand commandery** *n*

grand conjunction *n* **:** the occasional astrological configuration of the greater planets in a particular sign

grand cordon *n* **:** a cordon consisting of a broad ribbon usu. worn in the manner of a baldric and constituting a mark of high rank in an honorary order

grand council *n* **:** an executive council in a high or supreme position esp. as assistant to a governor or chief executive

grand council fire *n* **:** a ceremonial meeting of three or more groups of camp fire girls usu. including all the groups in a community

grand coup *n* **:** a coup in bridge or whist in which a player trumps a trick that his partner's card would otherwise have won

grand cross *n* **1 :** a decoration consisting of a cross that indicates the highest rank in many orders of knighthood **2 :** a person wearing a grand cross **:** KNIGHT GRAND CROSS

grand·dad *or* **gran·dad** \'gran,=, -raan-\ *n* [¹*grand* + *dad*] **:** GRANDFATHER

grand·dad·dy *also* **gran·dad·dy** \'gran,==, -raan-\ *n* [¹*grand* + *daddy*] **1 a :** GRANDFATHER **b :** one that is very old and venerable ⟨a cottonwood tree that was a real ~ —Richard Bissell⟩ **2 :** one that is the first, earliest, most ancient, or most venerable **:** one that has been in existence the longest ⟨the ~ of all the manufacturers of ready-built dwellings —*New Yorker*⟩ ⟨the ~ of midget-racing-car drivers⟩ ⟨the ~ of all reptiles —R.E.R.Hall⟩

granddaddy graybeard *n* **:** FRINGE TREE

granddaddy longlegs *n pl but sing or pl in constr* **:** DADDY LONGLEGS

granddam *var of* GRANDAM

grand·daugh·ter \'gran,==, -raan-\ *n* **:** the daughter of one's son or daughter — **grand·daugh·ter·ly** *adj*

granddaughter–in–law \'=,===,=\ *n, pl* **granddaughters–in–law :** the wife of one's grandson

grand day *n* **:** any of the four days Candlemas, Ascension, St. John the Baptist's, and All Saints' observed as holidays in the Inns of Court and Chancery and under English law as dies non juridici

grand dragon *n* **:** an officer of superior rank in the Ku-Klux or the Ku-Klux Klan hierarchy

grand drape *n* **:** a decorative narrow curtain hung along the top of a proscenium arch on the side toward the audience

grand–ducal \'gran¦==, -raan-\ *adj* **:** of, relating to, or befitting a grand duke or grand duchess

grand duchess *n* **1 :** the wife or widow of a grand duke **2 :** a woman who rules a grand duchy in her own right

grand duchy *n, often cap G&D* **:** the territory or dominion of a grand duke or grand duchess

grand duke *n* **:** the sovereign duke of a European state or country ranking immediately below a king and entitled to be called royal highness

grande cham·pagne \ˌgran(d)ˌsham¦pān, -raan(d)ˌshaam-, grāⁿdshāⁿpánʸ\ *n* [fr. *Grande Champagne*, vineyard area of Cognac, France] **:** FINE CHAMPAGNE

grande dame \grāⁿ(d)dám\ *n* [F, lit., great lady] **:** a lady usu. elderly and of great social or professional prestige, of high rank, or of extremely dignified or imposing manner

gran·dee \(')gran¦dē, -raan-\ *n* -S [Sp *grande*, fr. *grande*, adj., large, great, grand, fr. L *grandis* — more at GRAND] **:** a man of high rank or eminence; *esp* **:** a Spanish or Portuguese nobleman of the first rank

grande écaille \ˌgrändā'kī\ *also* **grand–ecoy** \ˌgrändā'kȯi\ *or* **grande és·caille** \-ā'kī\ *n, pl* **grande écailles** \-ī(z)\ *also* **grand–ecoys** \-ōi(z)\ *or* **grande éscailles** \-ī(z)\ [LaF *grande écaille*, lit., large or great scale] **:** TARPON

gran·dee·ship \='=ˌship\ *n* **:** the position or title of a grandee

grande passion *var of* GRAND PASSION

grander *comparative of* GRAND

grandest *superlative of* GRAND

gran·deur \'granjə(r), -raan- *also* -n,dyü(ə)r *or* -n,jü- *or* -ùə *sometimes* -ndyə(r) *or* -ndə(r) *or* -n,dü(ə)r *or* -n,düə *or* -n,dər(·) *or* -n,dō(r\ *n* -S [ME, fr. MF, fr. *grand* great + *-eur* -or — more at GRAND] **1** *archaic* **:** greatness of power or position ⟨exalted to this prodigious ~, Alexander was at the time of his death little more than thirty-two years old —George Grote⟩ **2 a :** personal greatness characterized chiefly by dignity of character, largeness of spirit, or significant scope of accomplishment ⟨in those rural epics . . . the descendants lose the ~ of those who first settled on the land —Sidney Alexander⟩ ⟨the moral ~ of the pioneer —C.I.Glicksberg⟩ **b :** dignity and sublimity (as of style) ⟨that lofty ~ of the diction of the English Bible—J.L.Lowes⟩ ⟨the sweetness or the ~ expected of religious music —*Time*⟩ ⟨the inability of men to sustain the ~ of their own ideal conceptions —*Times Lit. Supp.*⟩ **3 a :** the quality of being majestic, magnificent, splendid, stately, or imposing in an awe-inspiring way esp. to the view ⟨a scenic ~ in the wide view of mountains and valleys⟩ ⟨the ~ of the wild wintry seas —L.D.Stamp⟩ ⟨the former ~ of the queer castle-like homes of the Victorian era —*Amer. Guide Series: Tenn.*⟩ **b :** an instance of such a quality ⟨the most delightful of southern towns was almost certain to mix a little squalor with its ~*s* —Donald Davidson⟩

grandevity *n* -ES [L *grandaevitas*, fr. *grandaevus* aged (fr. *grandis* great + *aevum* time, eternity, age) + *-itas* -ity — more at GRAND, AGE] *obs* **:** great age

gran·dez·za \gran'detsə\ *or* **gran·de·za** \gran'dāsə\ *n* -S [It *grandezza* & Sp *grandeza*, fr. It & Sp *grande* large, great, grand (fr. L *grandis*) + It *-ezza* or Sp *-eza* (fr. L *-issa* -ess) — more at GRAND] *archaic* **:** grandeur or greatness esp. of manner or appearance

grand·fa·ther \'gran(d),==, -raan-\ *n* [ME *graund fader* (trans. of MF *grant pere*), fr. MF *grant* grand + ME *fader* father — more at GRAND, FATHER] **1 :** a father's or mother's father **:** an ancestor in the next degree above the father or mother in lineal ascent; *also* **:** FOREFATHER **2 :** one suggesting a grandfather in being a precursor in a line of similar things showing successive development, in being old and venerable, or in being the first or earliest in a line ⟨the church supper is the ~ of the country club —*Saturday Rev.*⟩ ⟨an old ~ of a tree⟩; *also* **:** something sizable or impressive in a way suggesting a long period of growth or development ⟨the ~ of all buttons —Ben Riker⟩

grandfather chair *or* **grandfather's chair** *n* **:** EASY CHAIR; *esp* **:** WING CHAIR

grandfather clause *n* **1 :** a clause exempting a class of persons (as from a regulatory law) because of circumstances applying before the clause takes effect; *specif* **:** a provision inserted in the constitutions of some southern states after the Civil War requiring high standards of literacy and substantial property qualifications of voters except for descendants of men voting before 1867 **2 :** one of numerous limitations on certain government regulations; *specif* **:** a provision by which an interstate carrier in bona fide operation prior to the effective date of regulation need not prove public convenience and necessity before it can be certified

grandfather clock *or* **grandfather's clock** *n* [fr. the song *My Grandfather's Clock* (1878) by Henry C. Work †1884 Am. songwriter] **:** a large pendulum clock having a long upright case usu. taller than 6½ feet

grandfather clock

grandfather graybeard *n* **1 :** FRINGE TREE **2 :** DADDY LONGLEGS

grand·father-in-law \ˈ=,===,=\ *n, pl* **grandfathers-in-law :** the grandfather of one's spouse

grand·fa·ther·ly \ˈ=,===\ *adj* **:** of, relating to, or befitting a grandfather ⟨an eminently human person of ~ years —Lewis Nichols⟩ **:** BENIGNANT ⟨looked on the child with ~ indulgence⟩ **:** old and venerable ⟨a ~ oak tree⟩

grandfather rights *n pl* **:** rights deriving from a grandfather clause

grandfather's-beard \ˈ=,==ˈ=\ *n, pl* **grandfather's-beards :** OLD-MAN'S-BEARD 1,4

grand·fer \ˈgranfə(r)\ *n* -S [by alter.] *dial Eng* **:** GRANDFATHER

grand finale *n* **:** a climactic finale (as of an opera or sports meet) marked by an imposing usu. colorful display or performance involving a large number of participants

grand fir *n* **:** LOWLAND FIR

grand·folks \ˈgran(d),=, -raan-\ *n pl* **:** GRANDPARENTS

grand guard *n* **1 :** a piece of plate armor of the 15th and 16th centuries used in tournaments as extra protection for left shoulder and breast **2 :** a former outpost of a military encampment

¹grand gui·gnol \ˌgräⁿgēnˈyȯl, -yōl\ *n, usu cap both Gs* [fr. *Le Grand Guignol*, a small theater in Montmartre, Paris, specializing in short plays full of sensationalism and horror] **:** a dramatic entertainment featuring the gruesome or horrible ⟨saw the play as a glorified *Grand Guignol* where story was the vital thing —*Theatre Arts*⟩

²grand guignol \"\ *adj, usu cap both Gs* **:** of, relating to, or having the characteristics of Grand Guignol ⟨a *Grand Guignol* program⟩ ⟨a *Grand Guignol* thriller⟩

grand hotel *n, often cap G&H* **:** a large well-equipped or imposing hotel usu. having an international clientele ⟨at Calvi . . . they would come to rest in their *grand hotel* of balconies and bathrooms —William Sansom⟩ ⟨New Delhi has become a sort of *Grand Hotel* for touring statesmen —Christopher Rand⟩

gran·di·flo·ra *or* **grandiflora rose** \ˌgrandəˈflōrə(-)\ *n* -S [NL, fr. L *grandis* great + NL *-flora* (fr. L *flor-, flos* flower) — more at GRAND, FLOWER] **:** a bush rose derived from crosses of floribunda and hybrid tea roses and characterized by production of blooms both singly and in clusters on the same plant

gran·dil·o·quence \granˈdiləkwən(t)s\ *n* -S [prob. fr. MF, fr. L *grandiloquus* (fr. *grandis* great, grand + *-loquus*, fr. *loqui* to speak) + MF *-ence* (as in *eloquence*) — more at GRAND] **:** the quality of being grandiloquent **:** the use of lofty words or phrases **:** BOMBAST

gran·dil·o·quent \(ˈ)=ˈ==kwənt\ *adj* [prob. back-formation fr. *grandiloquence*] **:** marked by a lofty, extravagantly colorful, pompous, or bombastic style, manner, or quality esp. in language ⟨a ~ and boastful speech about his great accomplishments⟩ ⟨danced to a rarely heard, ~ . . . score —Janet Flanner⟩ ⟨the latter's *Self Portrait* . . . was done in a more ~ manner —Wolfgang Stechow⟩ ⟨with a ~ gesture —Willard Robertson⟩ ⟨the ~ hero of a drama —Mary Webb⟩ ⟨~ summer estates —Bernard DeVoto⟩ — **gran·dil·o·quent·ly** *adv*

gran·dil·o·quous \-kwəs\ *adj* [L *grandiloquus*] *archaic* **:** GRANDILOQUENT

grand inquest *n* **:** GRAND JURY

grand inquisitor *n, often cap G&I* **:** the chief of a court of inquisition

gran·di·ose \ˈgrandē,ōs, ,==ˈ= *sometimes* -ōz\ *adj* [F, fr. It *grandioso*, fr. *grande* great (fr. L *grandis*) + *-oso* -ose — more at GRAND] **1 :** impressive because of uncommon largeness, scope, effect, grandeur, or majesty ⟨forget what more ~, noble, or beautiful character properly belongs to religious constructions —Matthew Arnold⟩ ⟨the ~ general scheme, unifying landscape, architecture, mural painting, and sculpture, was a revelation to the public —*Amer. Guide Series: Mich.*⟩ **2 :** characterized by affectation of grandeur, by pretense and pomp or overweeningness, or by absurd exaggeration ⟨have always been partial to ~ ideas about themselves —Irving Howe⟩ **syn** see GRAND

gran·di·ose·ly *adv* **:** in a grandiose manner ⟨the pompous absurdity so marked in many of our ~ ugly public monuments —D.L.Cohn⟩

gran·di·ose·ness *n* -ES **:** GRANDIOSITY

gran·di·os·i·ty \ˌ==ˈäsəd·ē, -ətē, -i\ *n* -ES [F *grandiosité*, fr. It *grandiosità*, fr. *grandioso* + *-ità* -ity (fr. L *-itat-, -itas*)] **:** the quality or state of being grandiose ⟨forgot his connubial incompetence in the *grandiosities* of his research projects —J.L.Davis⟩ ⟨feeling takes the place of comprehending, ~ the place of grandeur, pathos the place of understanding —R.H.Pearce⟩

gran·di·o·so \ˌgrandēˈō(,)sō, -raan-, -)zō\ *adv (or adj)* [It — more at GRANDIOSE] **:** in a broad and noble style — used as a direction in music

gran·dis·o·nant \(ˈ)granˈdisᵊnənt\ *or* **gran·dis·o·nous** \-ᵊnəs\ *adj* [*grandisonant* fr. LL *grandisonus* (fr. L *grandis* great + *-sonus*, fr. *sonare* to sound) + E *-ant*; *grandisonous* fr. LL *grandisonus* — more at GRAND, SOUND] *archaic* **:** giving the impression of grandeur

gran·di·so·ni·an \ˌgrandəˈsōnēən\ *adj, usu cap* [Sir Charles *Grandison*, a model gentleman portrayed in the novel of the same name (1753) by Samuel Richardson †1761 Eng. novelist + E *-ian*] **:** of, relating to, or befitting a model gentleman of the 18th century

gran·di·ty \ˈgrandəd·ē\ *n* -ES [L *granditas*, fr. *grandis* great, grand + *-itas* -ity — more at GRAND] *archaic* **:** grandness or an attribute or sign of it

grand je·té \ˌgräⁿzhəˈtā\ *n* [F] **:** a jeté in ballet with high kick or battement

grand jeu \gräⁿ ˈzhē, -ˈzhə, -ˈzhər, *F* gräⁿzhœ\ *adv (or adj)* [F, lit., grand play] **:** FULL ORGAN

grand juror \ˈ=ˈ==\ *or* **grand juryman** \ˈ=ˈ===\ *n* [*grand juror* fr. *grand jury*, after E *jury*: *juror*; *grand juryman* fr. *grand jury*, after E *jury*: *juryman*] **:** a member of a grand jury

grand jury \ˈ=ˈ==\ *n* [ME *graunde jurie*, lit., large jury, fr. AF *graund jurre*] **1 :** a body of from 12 to 23 good and lawful persons of a county who are returned in England by the sheriff to every session of the peace and of the assizes and in federal courts in the U. S. and in some state courts are impaneled usu. at intervals of a month or more to serve continuously until the next impanelment and whose duty it is to examine in private sessions accusations against persons charged with crime, to find bills of indictment against them to be presented to the court if they see just cause, and to act on such other public matters as may be brought before them — compare PETIT JURY **2 :** one that investigates crime in the manner of a grand jury ⟨appointed himself a one-man *grand jury* to bring the criminals to justice⟩

grand lama *n, often cap G&L* **:** DALAI LAMA

grand larceny *n* **1 :** larceny of property of a value greater than that fixed (as by a state) as constituting petit larceny **2 :** aggravated larceny of any amount

grand lecturer *n* **:** an officer appointed by a Masonic grand lodge to supervise an exemplification

grand lodge *n* **:** the chief lodge in a major division of lodges of Freemasons and some other fraternal orders

grand·ly \-ndlē, -li, *rapid* -nl-\ *adv* **:** in a grand manner ⟨singing more ~ than anyone else —Douglas Watt⟩ ⟨occupied a house which today would seem ~ large —F.L.Allen⟩

grand·ma \ˈgran(d)|(,)mä, -raan-, -ram|, -raam|, |(,)mȯ, |‿mə, |(,)mä\ *also* **grand·ma·ma** *or* **grand·mam·ma** \|,==, |=,=\ *n* **:** GRANDMOTHER

grand mal \ˈgranˈmäl, -raam-,-rän-, -mal,-mȧl, *F* gräⁿmȧl\ *n* [F, lit., *great illness*] **:** epilepsy due to an inborn usu. inherited dysrhythmia of the electrical pulsations of the brain as demonstrated by the electroencephalogram and characterized by attacks of violent convulsions, coma, constitutional disturbances, and usu. amnesia — compare PETIT MAL

grand·mam·my \ˈgran(d),==, -raan-\ *n* [¹*grand* + *mammy*] *dial* **:** GRANDMOTHER

grand manner *n* [trans. of F *grande manière*] **:** a dignified formal ceremonious manner, bearing, or mode of expression; *esp* **:** an elevated or grand style (as in music or literature)

grand march *n* **:** the opening ceremony at a large ball that consists of a march characterized by simple changes of pattern and is participated in by all the guests

grand master *n* **1 a :** the head of one of the former military orders of knighthood (as the Templars, Hospitalers) **b :** the chief officer of a Masonic grand lodge or of similar lodges in some other fraternal orders **2 :** an expert player (as of chess, checkers, bridge) whose superiority has been proved by frequent tournament victories

grandmaster key \ˈ=ˈ==-\ *n* **:** a master key designed to fit a number of different master-keyed systems of locks

grandmaternal \ˈ==ˈ==\ *adj* **:** GRANDMOTHERLY

grand mi·sère \ˌgräⁿmēˈze(ə)r\ *n* **:** a bid to lose all the tricks usu. at no-trump in a card game (as Boston)

grand·moth·er \ˈgran(d),==, -raan-\ *n* [ME *graundmoder* (trans. of MF *grant mere*), fr. MF *grant* grand + ME *moder* mother — more at GRAND, MOTHER] **1 a :** the mother of one's father or mother; *also* **:** FOREMOTHER **b :** an old or elderly and venerable woman **2 :** a woman or something thought of as female that is the earliest or oldest in a line of similar and usu. successively developing things ⟨the ~ of writers of modern verse⟩ ⟨the ~ of all suffragettes⟩ ⟨London . . . is the ~ of capitals —T.H.Fielding⟩

grandmother clock *n* **:** a clock that is about two thirds the size of a grandfather clock and sometimes has a repeat mechanism

grandmother-in-law \ˈ=,===,=\ *n, pl* **grandmothers-in-law :** the grandmother of one's spouse

grandmotherliness \ˈ=,====\ *n* **:** a grandmotherly quality **:** grandmotherly qualities

grand·moth·er·ly \ˈ=,===\ *adj* **:** of or belonging to a grandmother **:** like or befitting a grandmother (as in kindness or indulgence); *specif* **:** marked by great concern for trivial details of regulation **:** FUSSY

grand mufti *n* **:** ¹MUFTI

grand national assembly *n* **:** a unicameral parliament in a government (as the Turkish republic)

grand·neph·ew \ˈgran(d)ˈ=(,)=, -raan-\ *n* **:** a grandson of one's brother or sister

grand·ness \ˈgran(d)nəs, -raan-\ *n* -ES **:** the quality or state of being grand

grand·niece \ˈgran(d)ˈ=, -raan-\ *n* **:** a granddaughter of one's brother or sister

grand old man *n* **:** an elderly venerated practitioner or former practitioner of an art, profession, or sport ⟨the *grand old man* of twentieth century poetry —Babette Deutsch⟩ ⟨the *grand old man* of Italian conservative politics —Percy Winner⟩ ⟨the *grand old man* of cricket and the best batsman of his times —*Springfield (Mass.) Union*⟩

gran·do·ma·nia \ˌgrandōˈmānēə\ *n* [¹*grand* + *-o-* + *mania*] **:** a mania for elaborate, imposing, and showy buildings or furnishings

grand opera *n* **:** opera in which the plot is elaborated as in serious drama and the entire text set to music

grand organ *adv (or adj)* **:** FULL ORGAN

grand orgue \(ˈ)granˈdȯ(ə)rg, *F* gräⁿdȯrg\ *adv (or adj)* [F] **:** FULL ORGAN

grand·pa \ˈgran(d)|(,)pä, -raan-, -ram|, -raam|, |(,)pȯ, |‿pə, |(,)pȧ\ *also* **grand·pa·pa** \|,==, |=,=\ *n* **:** GRANDFATHER

grand·pap·py \|,==\ *n, dial* **:** GRANDFATHER

grand·par·ent \ˈgran(d),==, -raan-\ *n* **:** a parent's parent **:** a grandmother or grandfather — **grandparental** \ˈ==ˈ==\ *adj*

grand·par·ent·hood \ˈ=,==,hu̇d\ *n* -S **:** the state of being a grandparent

grand pas·sion *as grand* + *passion*, *or* gräⁿdpäsyōⁿ\ *also* **grande pas·sion** \"\ *n* [F *grande passion*, lit., great passion] **1 :** an overwhelming or vehement love **2 :** the object of a grand passion

grandpaternal \ˈ==ˈ==\ *adj* [*grand* + *paternal*] **:** GRANDFATHERLY ⟨taught, in deference to ~ feelings, to address his grandfather as "Mr. Wendell" —M.A.D.Howe⟩

grand pause *n* **:** GENERAL PAUSE

grand pawnee *n, usu cap G&P* **1 :** an Indian people of the Pawnee group **2 :** a member of the Grand Pawnee people

grand period of growth : the time during which a cell, organ, or organism is developing; *esp* **:** that period of development characterized by rapid increase in size

grand piano *n* **:** a wing-shaped piano in which the frame and strings are horizontal — contrasted with *upright piano*

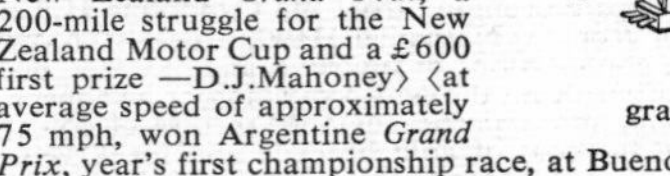

grand piano

grand prix \gräⁿ ˈprē\ *n, pl* **grand prix** *or* **grands prix** *or* **grand prixes** \-ē(z)\ *usu cap G&P* [fr. *Grand Prix de Paris* (F, lit., grand prize of Paris), an international horse race for three-year-olds established in 1863] **:** an international long-distance auto race over a tortuous course ⟨the New Zealand *Grand Prix*, a 200-mile struggle for the New Zealand Motor Cup and a £600 first prize —D.J.Mahoney⟩ ⟨at average speed of approximately 75 mph, won Argentine *Grand Prix*, year's first championship race, at Buenos Aires —*Sports Illustrated*⟩

grand quarter *n* **:** one of the four primary divisions of a heraldic shield which is divided quarterly; *esp* **:** a heraldic quarter that is itself quartered

grand quartering *n* **:** a quartering of a quartered coat with others in heraldic marshaling

grand rap·ids \ˈgranˈ(d)rapədz, ˈgraan-\ *adj, usu cap G&R* [fr. *Grand Rapids*, Mich.] **:** of or from the city of Grand Rapids, Mich. ⟨*Grand Rapids* furniture⟩ **:** of the kind or style prevalent in Grand Rapids

grand rapids disease *n* **:** TOMATO CANKER

gran·drelle \(ˈ)granˈdrel\ *n* -S *sometimes cap* [origin unknown] **:** a yarn usu. having two plies of different colors

grand right and left *n* **:** a circular weaving in and out in a square dance in which the men go in one direction and the women in the opposite, all dancers joining first their right hands and then left

grands *pl of* GRAND

grand-scale \ˈ=ˈ=\ *adj* **:** being or occurring on a large scale ⟨the *grand-scale* violence of a race determined to risk extinction —Anthony Boucher⟩ ⟨low water defeated hopes of *grand-scale* river navigation —*Amer. Guide Series: Minn.*⟩

grand sei·gneur \ˌgräⁿ,sānˈyər(·)\ *n, pl* **grand seigneurs** *or* **grands seigneurs** \-äⁿ,sānˈyərz,-ər(·)\ [F] **1 :** a great lord or nobleman ⟨the *grand seigneur* La Salle and his men glided through the . . . land —H.T.Kane⟩ **2 :** a man of dignity and aristocratic bearing ⟨described as a cultured country squire, a *grand seigneur* influential among his own people and a patron of the arts —A.D.Rees⟩

grand sei·gnior *or* **grand si·gnor** \ˈgran(d)ˈsēnyə(r), -raan-\ *n* **:** a former sultan of Turkey

grand sergeanty *or* **grand serjeanty** *n* [ME *graunte sergeaunte*, lit., large sergeanty, fr. AF *grand serjeanty*] **:** sergeanty requiring some special personal service to the king (as the carrying of his banner or his sword at coronation)

¹grand·sire \ˈgran(d),=, -raan-\ *n* [ME *grauntsire*, fr. OF *grant sire*, fr. *grant* grand + *sire*] **1 a** *or* **grand·sir** \-n(t)-sə(r)\ *now dial* **:** GRANDFATHER **b** *or* **grandsir** *Scot* **:** a great grandfather **c** *archaic* **:** ANCESTOR, FOREFATHER **d** *archaic* **:** an aged man **2 :** a dam's or sire's sire — used of an animal **3 :** a method of ringing changes on a set of church bells ⟨~ maximus⟩ — see CHANGE RINGING illustration

²grandsire \"\ *vt* **:** to be grandsire to ⟨*grandsired* the modern cult by preaching sanctification —*Amer. Mercury*⟩

grand slam *n* **1 a :** the winning of all the tricks of one hand in a card game (as bridge) **b :** the winning of all or specified tournaments in a sport at one time or in one season **2 :** a home run made with the bases loaded

grand·son \ˈgran(d),sən, -raan- *sometimes* -n(t)‿sən\ *n* **:** a son's or daughter's son

grandson-in-law \ˈ=(,)==,=\ *n, pl* **grandsons-in-law :** the husband of one's granddaughter

¹grand·stand \ˈgran(d),stand, -raan(d),staa(ə)nd\ *n* [¹*grand* + *stand*] **1 :** a usu. roofed structure serving as the principal spectator stand at a racecourse, stadium, or other place designed for spectator sports **2 :** the spectators (as at a sports event) or the audience (as at a festival)

grandstand

²grandstand \"\ *vi* -ED/-ING/-S **:** to play to spectators or to an audience **:** act or conduct oneself with a view to impressing onlookers ⟨chose to ~ in court —Erle Stanley Gardner⟩ ⟨the crazy ~*ing* of a glory-hungry major —Van Van Praag⟩ — **grand·stand·er** \-ə(r)\ *n*

³grandstand \"\ *adj* **1 a :** being in or as if in a grandstand ⟨join their neighbors on top of their houses where they had ~ seats for watching the next assault —F.B.Gipson⟩ **b :** resembling that provided by a grandstand ⟨a ~ view of the fight⟩ **2 :** designed or likely to impress or draw the applause of spectators ⟨behind-the-back dribbling and passing are strictly ~ stunts —Stanley Frank⟩

grand style *n* **1 :** a literary style marked by a sustained and lofty dignity, sublimity, and eloquence (as often attributed to epic poets) **2 :** an artistic style associated generally with 17th and early 18th century European works and characterized chiefly by the idealized representation of the human figure as noble and heroic in emulation of classical and Renaissance artistic prototypes

grand theft *n* **:** GRAND LARCENY

grand tier *n* **:** the tier immediately above the parterre

grand tour *n* **1 :** an extended European tour esp. through France, Germany, Italy, and Switzerland formerly commonly taken by youth of the British aristocracy as a part of their education **2 :** a tour resembling a grand tour: **a :** a tour through European capitals and places of significant historical or cultural interest **b :** a tour through a series of places of special interest ⟨a *grand tour* of the nightclubs of New York⟩ ⟨making the *grand tour* of the markets, quais, and parks —E.G. Robinson b. 1933⟩

grand trav·erse \ˈ=ˈtravə(r)s\ *or* **grand traverse disease** \ˈ=ˈ=-\ *n, usu cap G&T* [fr. *Grand Traverse* county, Mich.] *North* **:** pine of cattle

granduncle \ˈ=ˈ==\ *n* **:** a father's or mother's uncle — called also *great-uncle*

grand vicar *n* **:** a vicar-general of a diocese in France

grand vizier *n* **:** the chief officer of state of a Muslim country esp. formerly of the Ottoman Empire

grange \ˈgrānj\ *n* -S [ME *grange, graunge*, fr. MF *grange, granche*, fr. ML *granica*, fr. L *granum* grain + *-ica* (fem. of *-icus* -ic) — more at CORN] **1** *archaic* **:** GRANARY, BARN **2 a :** FARM; *esp* **:** a farmhouse or country house with barns or other buildings for farming **b :** an outlying farmhouse with its barns and other buildings belonging to a monastery or to a feudal lord **c** *obs* **:** a country house **3 a :** one of the lodges of an association of farmers joined with some secret rites to further their interests and particularly to bring producers and consumers, farmers and manufacturers, into direct commercial relations **b** *usu cap* **:** the association itself

grang·er \-jə(r)\ *n* -S [ME *graunger* tenant farmer, fr. MF *grangier*, fr. *grange* + *-ier* -er] **1** *archaic* **:** a farm steward **2 :** a member of a grange **3 :** FARMER — used esp. in the Northwest **4 a :** a grain-carrying railroad **b :** a stock or share in such a railroad

¹gran·ger·ism \ˈgrānjə,rizəm\ *n* -S [James *Granger* †1776 Eng. clergyman and biographer + E *-ism*] **:** the practice of grangerizing

²grang·er·ism \"\ *n* -S [*granger* + *-ism*] **:** the policy or methods of the grangers

gran·ger·ite \-jə,rīt\ *n* -S [J. *Granger* + E *-ite*] **:** one that grangerizes

gran·ger·iza·tion \ˌ==‿rəˈzāshən, -,rīˈz-\ *n* -S **:** an act or the result of grangerizing

gran·ger·ize \ˈgrānjə,rīz\ *vt* -ED/-ING/-S [James *Granger* + E *-ize*] **1 :** EXTRA-ILLUSTRATE **2 :** to mutilate (as a book or periodical) to obtain material for extra-illustration — **gran·ger·iz·er** \-zə(r)\ *n* -S

granger law *n* **:** one of the laws passed in various states of the middle west between 1869 and 1876 under influence of the Grange

grani *pl of* GRANO

grani- *comb form* [L, fr. *granum* — more at CORN] **:** grain ⟨*grani*form⟩ **:** grain or seeds ⟨*grani*vorous⟩

gra·ni·ta \grəˈnēd·ə\ *n* -S [It, fr. fem. of *granito*, past part. of *granire* to grain, granulate] **:** a coarse-grained sherbet

gran·ite \ˈgranət, *usu* -əd·+V\ *n* -S *often attrib* [It *granito*, fr. past part. of *granire* to grain, granulate, fr. *grano* grain, fr. L *granum* — more at CORN] **1 :** a natural igneous rock formation of visibly crystalline texture; *specif* **:** a usu. flesh-red whitish or gray very hard and durable holocrystalline-granular plutonic igneous rock consisting essentially of quartz, orthoclase or microcline, a smaller amount of acid plagioclase, usu. one or more members of the mica, amphibole, and less commonly pyroxene groups, and usu. accessories (as apatite, zircon, magnetite, and occas. topaz, tourmaline, garnet), the rock varying in texture from fine to very coarse and taking a fine polish — see APLITE, GRAPHIC GRANITE, PEGMATITE **2 :** unyielding firmness or endurance ⟨a man of ~, strong, able, and of inflexible integrity —H.S.Canby⟩ ⟨the cold ~ of Puritan formalism —V.L.Parrington⟩ **3** [It *granita*] **:** GRANITA **4** *or* **granite gray :** a purplish gray that is redder and slightly stronger than crane, darker than dove gray or cinder gray, and redder and deeper than zinc — called also *metallic gray*

granite blue *n* **:** PEARL 6 b

granite cloth *n* **:** a lightweight clothing fabric usu. of wool or worsted in various weaves and characterized by an irregular, pebbled, hard-finished surface

granite-gneiss \ˈ==ˈ=\ *n* **:** a rock consisting of an orthogneiss or paragneiss having the composition of a granite

granite paper *n* **:** a paper containing a small proportion of deeply colored fibers to produce a mottled appearance something like that of granite

graniteware \ˈ==,=\ *n* **1 a :** pottery with a speckled surface imitating that of granite **b :** a very hard pottery resembling ironstone china **2 :** ironware coated with an enamel suggestive of granite in appearance

gra·nit·ic \(ˈ)graˈnid·|ik, grəˈn-, -it|, |ēk\ *adj* **1 :** of or belonging to granite; *specif* **:** having a holocrystalline-allotriomorphic texture **2 :** resembling granite in hardness ⟨a ~ fist⟩ or in austere inflexibility ⟨a ~ and Puritanic personality⟩ ⟨a ~ morality⟩

gra·nit·i·cal \|əkəl, |ēk-\ *adj, archaic* **:** GRANITIC

gran·it·iza·tion \ˌgranəd·əˈzāshən, -d‿,īˈz-\ *n* -S **1 :** the development of granite from other rocks rich in alkalies, silica, and alumina by selective fusion or metasomatism **2 :** the condition of having developed by granitization

gran·it·ize \ˈgranəd·,īz\ *vt* -ED/-ING/-S [*granite* + *-ize*] **:** to cause to undergo granitization

gran·it·oid \ˈ=əd,ȯid\ *also* **gran·it·oi·dal** \ˌ==‿ˈȯidᵊl\ *adj* **:** resembling granite **:** GRANITIC

grani·vore \ˈgranə,vō(ə)r, -ran-\ *n* -S [back-formation fr. *granivorous*] **:** a granivorous animal or bird

gra·niv·o·rous \grəˈniv(ə)rəs, (ˈ)graˈn-, (ˈ)graˈn-\ *adj* [*grani-* + *-vorous*] **:** feeding on seeds or grain

gran·je·no \gränˈhā(,)nō\ *n* -S [MexSp] **:** a densely spiny shrub (*Celtis pallida*) occurring in Mexico and the adjacent U. S. and having edible berries

gran·nam \ˈgranəm\ *n* -S [alter. of *grandam*] *archaic* **:** GRANDMOTHER

¹gran·ny *or* **gran·nie** \ˈgranē, -ni\ *n, pl* **grannies** [by shortening & alter. fr. *grandmother*] **1 a :** GRANDMOTHER **b :** one that is markedly fussy or overly concerned about trivial details **2** *also* **granny woman** *South & Midland* **:** MIDWIFE **3 :** GRANNY KNOT

²granny \"\ *vb* -ED/-ING/-ES *vi, South & Midland* **:** to act or practice as a midwife ⟨*grannied* for over 50 years⟩ ~ *vt, South & Midland* **:** to act as a midwife for ⟨*grannied* all the babies⟩

granny knot *or* **granny's bend** *or* **granny's knot** *n* **:** an easily jammed and insecure knot often made by the inexperienced instead of a square knot

granny knot

gra·no \'grä(,)nō\ *n, pl* **gra·ni** \-(,)nē\ [It, lit., grain — more at GRANITE] **:** an old unit of monetary value of Naples and Malta equal to ⅓ of a farthing; *also* **:** a copper coin representing this value

grano- *comb form* [G, fr. *granit* granite, fr. It *granito* — more at GRANITE] **1 :** granite or a granitic substance ⟨*grano*blastic⟩ ⟨*grano*lith⟩ **2 :** granitic ⟨*grano*gabbro⟩

gran·o·blas·tic \¦granō¦blastik\ *adj* [ISV *grano-* + *blastic;* orig. formed as G *granoblastisch*] *of a rock* **:** having a texture in which the fragments are irregular and angular and appear like a mosaic under the microscope

grano·diorite \¦gra(,)nō+\ *n* [ISV *grano-* + *diorite*] **:** a granular intrusive quartzose igneous rock intermediate between granite and quartz diorite with plagioclase predominant over orthoclase

grano·gabbro \"+\ *n* [*grano-* + *gabbro*] **:** a plutonic rock intermediate between a granite and a gabbro and consisting of quartz, basic plagioclase, potash-feldspar, and one or more ferromagnesian minerals

gran·o·lith \'granə,lith\ *n* -s [*grano-* + *-lith*] **:** an artificial stone of crushed granite and cement — **gran·o·lith·ic** \¦==¦lithik\ *adj*

gran·o·phyre \'granə,fī(ə)r\ *n* -s [ISV *grano-* + *-phyre;* orig. formed as G *granophyr*] **:** a porphyritic igneous rock chiefly composed of alkalic feldspar and quartz and having a granular groundmass; *also* **:** a similar rock with the quartz and feldspar of the groundmass in micropegmatite intergrowths

gran·o·phyr·ic \¦==¦firik\ *adj* **:** of, belonging to, or like granophyre

grans *pl of* GRAN

¹grant \'grant, -aa(ə)-,-ai-,-á-\ *vb* -ED/-ING/-S [ME *graunten, granten*, fr. OF *creanter, greanter, graanter*, fr. (assumed) VL *credentare*, fr. L *credent-, credens*, pres. part. of *credere* to believe — more at CREED] *vt* **1 a :** to consent to carry out for a person **:** ALLOW, ACCORD ⟨after a conference the judge ~*ed* counsel his request⟩ ⟨~ a child his wish⟩ **b** *obs* **:** AGREE, ASSENT — used with a following infinitive with *to* **c :** to permit as a right, privilege, indulgence, or favor ⟨~ himself a quick view of the treasured letter⟩ ⟨~ a few moments' conversation to his admirers⟩ ⟨the sixty-six-pound free luggage allowance ~*ed* by the transatlantic airlines —Richard Joseph⟩ ⟨seek the seclusion that a cabin ~*s* —W.S.Gilbert⟩ **2 :** GIVE, BESTOW, CONFER ⟨~*ed* a sum of $2000 to the student to help him continue his education⟩ ⟨~*ed* a large acreage to deserving settlers⟩ ⟨~ a doctor's degree to a graduate student⟩ ⟨save every drop of rain the heavens ~ —Russell Lord⟩ ⟨~ a loan to an applicant⟩ ⟨the government ~*ed* full diplomatic recognition to the new nation⟩; *specif* **:** to make a conveyance of **:** give the possession or title of esp. by a deed or formal writing **3 a** *obs* **:** ACKNOWLEDGE, CONFESS **b :** be willing to concede **:** ADMIT, CONCEDE ⟨~ a proposition is true⟩ ⟨~ that the man was lying⟩ ⟨I ~ I was wrong⟩ ⟨the government is ~*ing* no preference as between types of small business in applying for financial assistance —W.B.Barnes⟩ **c :** to assume to be true **:** deem unquestionable ⟨~*ed* that the novelist has talent, he can nevertheless sometimes expect a hard time finding a publisher⟩ ~ *vi, obs* **:** ASSENT, CONSENT

syn AWARD, CONCEDE, ACCORD, VOUCHSAFE: GRANT may apply to giving to a petitioner or claimant, often a subordinate, something that has been sought and that could be withheld ⟨*granted* leave of absence for a year, he went abroad —Allen Johnson⟩ ⟨at the close of the Civil War a bounty of $100 was *granted* to those who had served three years —J. W.Oliver⟩ ⟨was *granted* the triumphal insignia and the right to be consul before the legal age —John Buchan⟩ AWARD, often interchangeable with GRANT, may apply to giving something adjudged merited or condign ⟨*awarded* him a medal as champion⟩ ⟨his land, *awarded* him by the Indians in 1835 in acknowledgment of his long service in their behalf —*Amer. Guide Series: La.*⟩ ⟨a certain difficulty arises in writing about a book to which one *awards* an unreserved enthusiasm —Carl Van Vechten⟩ CONCEDE indicates a giving, giving in, or yielding to some rightful request or compelling claim ⟨because physics, history, and religion have their different valuations of experience, we are obliged to *concede* a large measure of autonomy to the different studies —W.R.Inge⟩ ⟨even his harshest critics *concede* him a rocklike integrity, boundless courage, and an immobile sort of dignity —*Time*⟩ ACCORD may indicate a granting, sometimes reluctant, of what is due ⟨treated bishops with the superficial deference that a sergeant-major *accords* to a junior subaltern —Compton Mackenzie⟩ ⟨children easily appreciate justice, and will readily accord to others what others *accord* to them —Bertrand Russell⟩ ⟨the central fact to which . . . prevailing creeds refuse to *accord* sufficiently serious attention is the obvious impossibility of attaining omniscience —M.R.Cohen⟩ VOUCHSAFE may indicate a grant, esp. in response to a petition or request, explicit or implicit, by a person in power ⟨the occasional answers that Stalin used to *vouchsafe* to inquiries from American correspondents —Elmer Davis⟩ ⟨a kindly Being, who, in return for due rites and offerings, will *vouchsafe* nourishing rains and golden harvests —L.P.Smith⟩

— take for granted 1 : to assume as true, accurate, real, unquestionable, or to be expected ⟨*took* it *for granted* that he would not get into trouble with the licensing authorities⟩ ⟨*taken for granted* that words have definite meanings —T.S. Eliot⟩ **2 :** to pay inadequate attention to or value too lightly (as a possession, right, or privilege) ⟨inclined to *take* one's liberties *for granted* if they are never challenged⟩ ⟨began to *take* her husband *for granted* until he threatened to leave her⟩

²grant \"\ *n* -s [ME *graunt, grant*, fr. OF *creant, greant, graant*, fr. *creanter, greanter, graanter*] **1 :** the act of granting: as **a** *obs* (1) **:** CONSENT, PERMISSION (2) **:** ACKNOWLEDGMENT, CONFESSION **b :** CONCEDING ⟨his ~ of the election to his opponent⟩ **:** ALLOWING ⟨opposed the ~ of absentee voting⟩ **:** a bestowing or conferring ⟨the ~ of exclusive privileges in a railroad station —O.W.Holmes †1935⟩ **2 :** something granted; *esp* **:** a gift (as of land or a sum of money) usu. for a particular purpose ⟨subsidized by a ~ of two million pounds yearly from the British government⟩ ⟨a ~ of land to any member who could establish a specific number of settlers —*Amer. Guide Series: N. J.*⟩ ⟨obtained a ~ to study abroad for a year⟩ ⟨the university gave the scholar a ~ of the sum of $2000 to continue his research⟩ **3 a :** a transfer of real or personal property by deed or writing — compare ASSIGNMENT 3a, GIFT 2a **b :** the instrument by which such a transfer is made; *also* **:** the property so transferred **c** *Eng law* **:** a former conveyance of an incorporeal hereditament that could pass only by deed **4 :** a minor territorial division of Maine, New Hampshire, or Vermont orig. granted by the state to an individual or institution **5** *in livestock judging* **:** a specified point in which an animal judged inferior surpasses the class winner **— lie in grant :** to be transferable legally only by grant

grant·able \-təbəl\ *adj* **:** capable of being granted ⟨a right only ~ with the consent of a court⟩

grant-aid·ed school \'=,==-\ *n* **:** AIDED SCHOOL

grant caribou \'gra\|nt-, -aa(ə)\|,-ai\|,-á\|\ *or* **grant's caribou** *n, usu cap G* [after Madison *Grant* †1937 Amer. lawyer, explorer, writer on zoology] **:** a small light-colored caribou (*Rangifer arcticus granti*) of the Alaska peninsula

granted *past of* GRANT

grant·ed·ly *adv* **:** beyond question **:** not to be doubted **:** ADMITTEDLY ⟨this ~ ancient predicament —Dudley Fitts⟩ ⟨a ~ silly thing to do⟩

grant·ee \(')grant·¦ē, -aan-,-ain-,-án-, -n·¦tē\ *n* -s [ME *graunte*, fr. *graunten, granten* to grant + *-e* -ee] **:** one to whom a grant is made ⟨in awarding scholarships the college picked its ~*s* carefully⟩

grant·er \'grantə(r), -aan-,-ain-,-án-\ *n* -s [ME *graunter*, fr. *graunten* to grant + *-er*] **:** one that grants

gran·tha alphabet \'grəntə-, -ran-\ *n, usu cap G* [Skt *grantha* knot, act of tying together, book — more at CRADLE] **:** a south Indian alphabet of which there are numerous varieties used in Sanskrit inscriptions in the Tamil country as early as the 5th century A.D. and still used by Tamil Brahmans for writing Sanskrit books

gran·ther \'gran(t)thə(r)\ *n* -s [by contr.] *chiefly NewEng* **:** GRANDFATHER

gran·thi \'grəntē, -ran-\ *n* -s [Hindi *granthī*, fr. *Granth*, the sacred scripture of the Sikhs] **:** a reader of the sacred scriptures of the Sikhs whose function is to lead worship services in Sikh temples and gurdwaras

gran·tia \'granch(ē)ə, -ntēə\ *n, cap* [NL, fr. Robert E. *Grant* †1874 Scot. comparative anatomist + NL *-ia*] **:** a genus (the type of the family Grantiidae) of small cylindrical calcareous sycon sponges with triradiate spicules projecting into the cloacal cavity

grant-in-aid \¦==¦=\ *n, pl* **grants-in-aid 1 :** a grant or subsidy from public funds paid by a central to a local government in aid of some public undertaking (as education or highway construction) usu. conditional upon the maintenance of a specified standard or upon similar or proportional appropriations by the grantee **2 :** a grant or subsidy resembling a government grant-in-aid; *esp* **:** financial assistance extended by a public agency or private institution or foundation to an educational institution for particular educational projects or to an individual for educational purposes (as for furthering the individual's education or training or as assistance in the completion of a research project)

granting *pres part of* GRANT

grant·or \'grantə(r), (')grant·¦ó(ə)r, -n·¦tó-, -ó(ə), -raan-, -rain-,-rán-\ *n* -s **:** one that grants: **a :** the person by whom a grant, conveyance, or lease is made **b :** one that extends credit **:** GUARANTOR

grants *pres 3d sing of* GRANT, *pl of* GRANT

grant's gazelle *n, usu cap 1st G* [after James A. *Grant* †1892 Brit. explorer] **:** a large antelope (*Gazella granti*) of the East African plains distinguished by graceful diverging annulated horns

grant's zebra *n, usu cap G* [after James A. *Grant*] **:** a zebra that is a variety (*Equus burchelli granti*) of Burchell's zebra distinguished by complete lack of shadow striping and is widely distributed from Sudan and Ethiopia to Uganda and Kenya — compare CHAPMAN'S ZEBRA

granul- *or* **granuli-** *or* **granulo-** *comb form* [LL *granulum* — more at GRANULE] **:** granule ⟨*granuli*form⟩ ⟨*granulo*metric⟩ **:** granulation ⟨*granul*oma⟩

gran·u·lar \'granyələ(r)\ *adj* [LL *granulum* + E *-ar*] **1 a :** consisting of or appearing to consist of granules ⟨boil until the syrup becomes ~⟩ **:** having a structure or texture consisting of or appearing to consist of granules ⟨a ~ stone⟩ ⟨a very ~ sugar⟩ ⟨a ~ leather surface⟩ **b :** being a granule ⟨a ~ lump in an otherwise liquid-smooth salve⟩ **2 :** having or marked by granulations ⟨~ tissue⟩ **3** *of a sound or voice* **:** giving the impression of roughness or impurity ⟨a veiled ~ tone which sounds as though emanating from a mouthful of marbles —J.W.Freeman⟩ ⟨the famous ~ twang —*Newsweek*⟩ — **gran·u·lar·ly** *adv*

granular conjunctivitis *n* **:** TRACHOMA

granular hypothesis *n* **:** a statement in cytology: the visible and submicroscopic granular content of protoplasm constitutes the essential living matter — not much used by modern cytologists; compare BIOPHORE

gran·u·lar·i·ty \¦==¦larəd·ē, -ətē, -i\ *n* -ES **1 :** the quality or state of being granular ⟨a rock with medium to coarse ~⟩ **2 :** nonuniformity in light-transmitting or reflecting properties of a developed photographic image produced by its individual particles

granular layer *n* **:** the deeper layer of the cortex of the cerebellum containing numerous small closely packed cells

granular leukocyte *n* **:** a blood granulocyte; *esp* **:** a polymorphonuclear leukocyte

granular snow *n* **:** small pellets or grains of precipitation resembling snow

gran·u·lary \'granyə,lerē\ *adj* [LL *granulum* + E *-ary*] *archaic* **:** GRANULAR

¹gran·u·late \'granyə,lāt, *usu* -ād·+V\ *vb* -ED/-ING/-S [LL *granulum* granule + E *-ate* (v. suffix) — more at GRANULE] *vt* **:** to form or crystallize (as sugar) into grains, granules, or small masses **:** make granular ~ *vi* **1 :** to collect or become formed into grains or granules **2 :** to undergo granulation

²gran·u·late \-,lət, *usu* -əd·+V\ *adj* [NL *granulatus*, fr. LL *granulum* + L *-atus* -ate] **:** GRANULATED

granulated sugar *n* **:** a pure sugar that has been crystallized and centrifuged and then sent through a granulator where the crystals are dried, separated, and screened

gran·u·lat·er \-,lād·ə(r), -ātə-\ *n* -s **:** GRANULATOR

gran·u·la·tion \,==¦lāshən\ *n* -s [LL *granulum* + E *-ation*] **1 a :** the act or process of granulating ⟨the ~ of sugar⟩ **b :** the condition of being granulated ⟨the ~ of the leather was rough to the touch⟩ **2 a :** one of the small elevations of a granulated surface: (1) **:** a minute mass of tissue projecting from the surface of an organ (as on the eyelids in trachoma) (2) **:** one of the minute red granules made up of loops of newly formed capillaries that form on a raw surface (as of a wound) and that with fibroblasts are the active agents in the process of healing — see GRANULATION TISSUE **b :** the act or process of forming such elevations or granules **3 a :** GRANULE 2 **b :** the appearance of the sun's surface caused by the presence of granules **4 a :** an abnormal condition of a citrus fruit usu. left on the tree late in the season in which the juice sacs are hard and firm and the fruit tasteless **b :** the process by which this condition comes about

granulation tissue *n* **:** tissue made up of granulations that temporarily replaces lost tissue in a wound or lesion and forms a vascular protective framework during the healing process

gran·u·la·tor \'==,lād·ə(r), -ātə-\ *n* -s **:** one that granulates; *specif* **:** a large revolving cylinder in which sugar is dried and granulated

gran·ule \'gran(,)yül\ *n* -s [LL *granulum*, dim. of L *granum* grain — more at CORN] **1 a :** a little grain (as of sugar) **:** a small particle (as of pollen); *esp* **:** one of a number of particles forming a larger unit ⟨the ~*s* of the rock⟩ ⟨the carbon ~*s* in the dry-cell battery⟩ **b :** a small sugar-coated pill **2 :** one of the small, short-lived, brilliant spots on the sun's seething photosphere that are of irregular shape and several hundred miles in diameter **3 :** a clump of actinomycetes in a lesion

granule cell *n* **:** a connective tissue cell containing cytoplasmic granules that stain intensely with aniline dyes

granuli- — see GRANUL-

gran·u·lif·er·ous \¦granyə¦lif(ə)rəs\ *adj* [*granul-* + *-ferous*] **:** bearing, producing, or full of granules

gran·u·lite \'==,līt\ *n* -s [ISV *granul-* + *-ite*] **:** a banded or laminated whitish granular rock consisting of alkalic feldspar, quartz, and small red garnets and occurring with crystalline schists — **gran·u·lit·ic** \¦==¦lid·ik\ *adj*

granulo- — see GRANUL-

gran·u·lo·blast \'granyəlō,blast\ *n* [*granul-* + *-blast*] **:** a cellular precursor of a granulocyte **:** MYELOBLAST, MYELOCYTE — **gran·u·lo·blas·tic** \¦===¦blastik\ *adj*

gran·u·lo·blas·to·sis \,===,bla'stōsəs\ *n, pl* **granuloblastoses** \-ō,sēz\ [NL, fr. ISV *granuloblast* + NL *-osis*] **:** a disorder of the avian leukosis complex characterized by the presence of excessive numbers of immature blood granulocytes in affected birds

gran·u·lo·cyte \'granyəlō,sīt\ *n* -s [ISV *granul-* + *-cyte*] **:** a cell with granule-containing cytoplasm; *specif* **:** a polymorphonuclear leukocyte — **gran·u·lo·cyt·ic** \¦===¦sid·ik\ *adj*

gran·u·lo·cy·to·pe·nia \,===,sīd·ə'pēnēə\ *n* -s [NL, fr. ISV *granulocyte* + NL *-o-* + *-penia*] **:** deficiency of blood granulocytes; *specif* **:** an acute febrile condition marked by severe depression of the granulocyte-producing bone marrow and by prostration, chills, swollen neck, and sore throat sometimes with local ulceration and believed to be basically a response to the side effects of certain drugs of the coal-tar series (as amidopyrine) — called also *agranulocytic angina, agranulocytosis* — **gran·u·lo·cy·to·pe·nic** \¦====¦nik\ *adj*

gran·u·lo·cy·to·poi·e·sis \,===,pȯi'ēsəs\ *n, pl* **granulocytopoieses** \-ē,sēz\ [NL, fr. ISV *granulocyte* + NL *-o-* + *-poiesis*] **:** the formation of blood granulocytes typically in the bone marrow

gran·u·lo·cy·to·sis \,===,sī'tōsəs\ *n, pl* **granulocytoses** \-ō,sēz\ [NL, fr. ISV *granulocyte* + NL *-osis*] **:** an increase in the number of blood granulocytes — compare LYMPHOCYTOSIS, MONOCYTOSIS

gran·u·lo·ma \,granyə'lōmə\ *n, pl* **granulomas** \-ōməz\ *or* **granuloma·ta** \-ōməd·ə\ [NL, fr. *granul-* + *-oma*] **:** a mass or nodule composed of chronically inflamed tissue marked by the formation of granulations and usu. associated with an infective process — **gran·u·lom·a·tous** \¦==¦lämədəs, -¦lōm-\ *adj*

granuloma in·gui·na·le \-,iŋgwə'na(,)lē, -ā(,)lē, -ä(,)lā\ *or* **granuloma ve·ne·re·um** \-və'nirēəm\ *n* [*granuloma inguinale*, NL, lit., inguinal granuloma; *granuloma venereum*, NL, lit., venereal granuloma] **:** a chronic condition characterized by ulceration and formation of granulations beginning in the groin and spreading to the buttocks and genitals and caused by infection with a Donovan body (*Calymmatobacterium granulomatis*)

granuloma py·o·gen·i·cum \-,pīō'jenəkəm\ *n* [NL, lit., pus-forming granuloma] **:** a granuloma that develops usu. at the site of an injury and is believed to result from infection

gran·u·lo·ma·to·sis \,granyə,lōmə'tōsəs\ *n, pl* **granulomatoses** \-ō,sēz\ [NL, fr. *granulomat-, granuloma* + *-osis*] **:** a chronic condition marked by the formation of numerous granulomas

gran·u·lo·pe·nia \,granyəlō'pēnēə\ *n* -s [NL, fr. *granul-* + *-penia*] **:** GRANULOCYTOPENIA

gran·u·lo·poi·e·sis \-(,)lō,pȯi'ēsəs\ *n, pl* **granulopoieses** \-ē,sēz\ [NL, fr. *granul-* + *-poiesis*] **:** GRANULOCYTOPOIESIS

gran·u·lo·sa cell \¦granyə¦lōsə-, -ōzə-\ *n* [NL *granulosa*, fr. *granul-* + L *-osa* (fem. of *-osus* -ous)] **:** one of the cells of the epithelial lining of a graafian follicle

gran·u·lose \'granyə,lōs\ *adj* [*granul-* + *-ose*] **:** GRANULAR; *esp* **:** having the surface roughened with granules

gran·u·lo·sis \,==¦lōsəs\ *n, pl* **granulo·ses** \-ō,sēz\ [NL, fr. *granul-* + *-osis*] **:** a virus disease of larval insects distinguished by the presence of minute granular inclusions in infected cells and marked by sluggishness, loss of appetite, and whitish discoloration of the body

gran·u·lous \'==,ləs\ *adj* [LL *granulum* granule + E *-ous* — more at GRANULE] **:** GRANULAR

gra·num \'grānəm, -ran-,-rän-\ *n, pl* **gra·na** \-nə\ [L, grain, seed — more at CORN] **:** GRANULE

gran·ville wilt \'gran,vil-, *chiefly in southern US* -,vəl-\ *n, usu cap G* [fr. *Granville* co., N.C.] **:** a wilt of tobacco caused by a bacterium (*Pseudomonas solanacearum*)

grape \'grāp\ *n* -s [ME, fr. OF *crape, grape* hook, grape stalk, bunch of grapes, grape, of Gmc origin; akin to MD *crappe* hook, OHG *krapfo, krāpfo* — more at CRAVE] **1 a :** a smooth-skinned juicy berry ranging in color from green or white to deep red, purple, or black and in shape from globose to narrowly oblong that since ancient times has been eaten both dried and fresh as a fruit and has been fermented to produce wine — see RAISIN **b :** the fermented juice of the grape **:** WINE ⟨their hearts were expanding under the ~ —L.D.Lewis⟩ **2 :** any of numerous woody plants that constitute the genus *Vitis*, usu. climb by means of tendrils, produce clustered fruits that are grapes, are nearly cosmopolitan in cultivation, and include many cultivated hybrids and horticultural varieties derived from New and Old World species (as *V. vinifera, V. rotundifolia*, and *V. labrusca*) — called also *grapevine;* see FOX GRAPE, MUSCADINE, WINE GRAPE **3 a grapes** *pl* **:** a cluster of raw red nodules of granulation tissue in the hollow of the fetlock of horses that is characteristic of advanced or chronic grease heels **b grapes** *pl but usu sing in constr, also* **grape disease :** tuberculous disease of the pleura in cattle **4 :** GRAPESHOT **5 :** PLUM PURPLE 2

grapes 1a

grape anthracnose *n* **:** BIRD'S-EYE ROT

grape-berry moth \'=,==-\ *n* **:** a small slate-colored moth (*Paralobesia viteana*) whose larvae feed in grape flowers and fruit

grape co·las·pis \-kə'laspəs\ *n* [NL *Colaspis* genus of leaf beetles, fr. ²*col-* + *-aspis*] **:** a small pale brown elliptical leaf beetle (*Colaspis flavida* or a closely related form) whose larva is a short-legged grub that feeds on the roots of many cultivated plants and is sometimes esp. destructive to soybeans and corn planted after clover — called also *clover rootworm*

grape cure *n* **:** treatment of disease (as tuberculosis) by the free use of grapes as food

graped \'grāpt\ *adj* **:** having the grapes — used of horses or cattle

grape family *n* **:** VITACEAE

grape fern *n* **:** a fern of the genus *Botrychium*

grapefruit \'=,=\ *n* [so called fr. its growing in clusters] **1 :** a large typically globose citrus fruit with a bitter yellow rind and inner skin and a highly flavored somewhat acid juicy pulp varying in color from pale yellow to deep reddish pink — called also *pomelo* **2** *also* **grapefruit tree :** a small round-headed tree (*Citrus paradisi*) that produces grapefruit, is probably derived from the shaddock from which it differs chiefly in fruit characters, glabrous leaves and twigs, clustered growth of flowers and fruits, and solidity of the plant axis, and is widely cultivated in subtropical areas

grapefruit knife *n* **:** a small knife with serrated blade curved at the end

grapefruit league *n* [so called fr. the games' being played in warm regions where citrus fruits are grown] **:** major-league baseball teams playing exhibition games during spring training ⟨the championship of the *grapefruit league*⟩

grapefruit spoon *n* **:** ORANGE SPOON

grape green *n* **:** a light olive color that is greener and paler than citrine, paler than old moss green, and redder, less strong, and slightly lighter than average willow green

grape house *n* **:** a greenhouse devoted to the culture of grapes

grape hyacinth *n* **:** any of several small bulbous spring-flowering perennial herbs of the genus *Muscari* that have narrow linear leaves and blue, pink, or white drooping urn-shaped flowers closely set in a terminal raceme and that are native to the Mediterranean area but cosmopolitan in cultivation

grape ivy *n* **:** an evergreen tendril-climbing vine (*Cissus rhombifolia*) that is native to northern So. America, has trifoliate leaves with reddish hairy lower surfaces, and is used widely as a house plant

grape juice *n* **:** the usu. sterilized and often diluted juice of grapes used as a beverage

grape leaf folder *n* **:** a black moth (*Desmia funeralis*) with a white border and white spots on the wings whose grass-green caterpillar rolls up and feeds in the leaf of the grapevine

grape leafhopper *n* **:** any of several small yellowish leafhoppers that constitute the genus *Erythroneura*, are marked with red or brown bands, and suck the juices of the leaves of the grapevine thereby often causing them to wither and fall off

grape·less \'grāpləs\ *adj* **:** lacking grapes or the flavor of grapes **:** made without grapes ⟨~ wine⟩

grape·let \-lət\ *n* -s **:** a small grape

grape mealybug *n* **:** a widely distributed mealybug (*Pseudococcus maritimus*) that feeds on many economic plants

grape mildew *n* **1 :** a powdery mildew caused by an ascomycetous fungus (*Uncinula necator*) **2 :** a downy mildew caused by a phycomycetous fungus (*Plasmopara viticola*)

grape phylloxera *or* **grape louse** *n* **:** a small yellowish green No. American phylloxera (*Phylloxera vitifoliae*) that lives and forms galls on the leaves and roots of various grapes being relatively harmless to native forms but extremely destructive to European vinifera grapes

grape plume moth *n* **:** a common slender tan moth (*Pterophorus periscelidactylus*) whose larva makes a nest on grape leaves

graperoot \'=,=\ *n* **1 :** the bitter tonic root of any plant of the genus *Mahonia* (as Oregon grape) **2 :** a plant that yields graperoot

grape rootworm *n* **:** a grub that is the larva of a small yellowish brown chrysomelid beetle (*Fidia viticida*) of the eastern U.S. and that attacks the roots of the grapevine — see WESTERN GRAPE ROOTWORM

grape rot *n* **:** any of several fungous diseases of the grape; *esp* **:** a black rot caused by an ascomycetous fungus (*Guignardia bidwellii*)

grape rust *n* **:** a foliage rust of grapes caused by a rust fungus (*Phakopsora vitis*)

grap·ery \'grāp(ə)rē, -ri\ *n* -ES **:** an area or building in which grapes are grown

grape scale *n* **:** either of two scales (*Aspidiotus uvae* and *Eulecanium persicae*) that attack the grapevine and various fruit trees

grape-seed oil *n* **:** a pale to yellow usu. semidrying fatty oil obtained from grape seeds and used in foods, soap, and paint

grapeshot \'=,=\ *n* [so called fr. the resemblance to a bunch of grapes] **:** a cluster consisting usu. of nine small iron balls put together by means of cast-iron circular plates at top and bottom with two rings and a central connecting rod and used as a charge for a cannon

grapes of wrath [fr. *The Grapes of Wrath* (1939), novel by John Steinbeck *b*1902, Am. novelist, fr. the line "He is trampling out the vintage where the *grapes of wrath* are stored", fr. *The Battle Hymn of the Republic* by Julia W. Howe †1910 Am. writer and reformer] **:** an unjust or oppressive situation, action, or policy that may inflame desire for vengeance **:** an explosive condition ⟨will the *grapes of wrath* come to another harvest —Stuart Chase⟩

grape stake *n* **:** a post used for supporting wires to which grapevines are tied in vineyards

grapestone \'=,=\ *n* **:** a grape seed

grape sugar *n* **:** DEXTROSE

grape tree *n* **1 :** GRAPE 2 **2 :** SEA GRAPE 1b

grapevine \'=,=\ *n* **1 :** GRAPE 2 **2** [prob. so called fr. the grapevine's being thought of as a humble substitute for a telegraph line] **a :** RUMOR, REPORT; *esp* **:** one without foundation in fact ⟨it's all a nightmare, all a humbug and a bore; just another foolish ~ —*Atlantic*⟩ **b** *or* **grapevine telegraph** (1) **:** an informal means of circulating information, news, rumor, or gossip ⟨was logical to suppose that the neighborhood ~ would have had the story —Harold Sinclair⟩ ⟨the ~ had carried the news of their victory into every shop and home —Russell Whelan⟩ (2) **:** a means of spreading information obtained secretly or from private sources ⟨the workers hear by ~ a lot of the secrets of management —*Kiplinger Washington Letter*⟩ **3 :** a figure-skating pattern traced by both skates **4 :** a wrestling hold in which one or both arms or legs are twined about those of an opponent **5 :** a sidewise waltz step in which one foot keeps crossing first before and then behind the other

grapevine knot *n* **:** BARREL KNOT b

grapevine moth *n* **:** an Australian moth (*Phalaenoides glycine*) having a greenish yellow black-marked caterpillar that feeds on grape leaves and fruits

grapevine knot

grapevine phylloxera *n* **:** PHYLLOXERA

grapevine twist *n* **:** a square dance in which the dancers move between successive couples of a set and then circle the woman and the man of each set in turn

grape wine *n* **:** a variable color averaging a dark reddish purple that is less strong than royal purple (sense 1), redder, lighter, and stronger than average plum (sense 6a), and redder and less strong than imperial or violet carmine

grapey *var of* GRAPY

¹graph \'graf, -aa(ə)f, -aif, -âf\ *n* -S [short for *graphic formula*] **1 :** a diagram (as a series of points, a line, a curve, an area) that represents the variation of a variable in comparison with that of one or more other variables ⟨a ~ showing the increase of population during the last 100 years⟩ **2** *of a mathematical function* **:** the collection of all points whose coordinates satisfy the given functional relation

²graph \"\ *vt* -ED/-ING/-S **1 :** to represent or record by a graph **2 :** to plot (as a curve from its equation) on a graph

³graph \"\ *n* -S [prob. fr. *-graph*] **1 :** a spelling of a word **2 :** a single occurrence of a letter of an alphabet in any of its various shapes (as D, d, *D*, *d*) **3 :** a letter or combination of letters taken as a minimum unit in determining the phonemes of a language from written records — compare ALLOGRAPH 2, GRAPHEME

-graph \,graf, -aa(ə)f, -aif, -âf\ *n comb form* -S [MF *-graphe*, fr. L *-graphum*, fr. Gk *-graphon*, fr. neut. of *-graphos* written, writing (fr. *graphein* to write) — more at CARVE] **1 :** something written ⟨crypto*graph*⟩ ⟨holo*graph*⟩ **2 :** instrument for making or transmitting records ⟨chrono*graph*⟩ ⟨phono*graph*⟩ ⟨tele*graph*⟩

graph·eme \'gra,fēm\ *n* -S [³*graph* + *-eme*] **1 :** a letter of an alphabet — compare ALLOGRAPH 2a, ³GRAPH 2 **2 :** the sum of all written letters and letter combinations that represent one phoneme ⟨the *p* of *pin*, the *pp* of *hopping*, and the *gh* of *hiccough* are members of one ~⟩ — compare ALLOGRAPH 2b, ³GRAPH 3 — **gra·phe·mic** \(')gra¦fēmik\ *adj* — **gra·phe·mi·cal·ly** \-mək(ə)lē\ *adv* — **gra·phe·mics** \-miks\ *n pl but usu sing in constr*

-grapher \grəfə(r), *sometimes* ,graf- *when there is a corresponding verb form in "-graph"*\ *n comb form* -S [LL *-graphus* one that writes (such) material or in (such) a way (fr. Gk *-graphos*, fr. *-graphos* written, writing) + E *-er*] **:** one that writes about (specified) material or in a (specified) way ⟨cranio*grapher*⟩

-graph·ia \'grafēə\ *n comb form* -S [L — more at -GRAPHY] **1 :** writing on a (specified) topic **:** representation of a (specified) object ⟨blasto*graphia*⟩ ⟨stomato*graphia*⟩ **2 :** writing characterized by a (specified) psychological abnormality ⟨dys*graphia*⟩ ⟨pseuda*graphia*⟩

¹graph·ic \'grafik, -fēk\ *also* **graph·i·cal** \-fəkəl, -fēk-\ *adj* [graphic fr. L *graphicus*, fr. Gk *graphikos*, fr. *graphein* to write + *-ikos* -ic; *graphical* fr. L *graphicus* + E *-al*] **1 :** written, drawn, or engraved ⟨reproduction of the letters in ~ form —F.W.Goudy⟩ ⟨did not multiply with ~ symbols as we do —E.O.Winzerling⟩ **2 a** (1) **:** marked by clear and lively description or striking imaginative power ⟨its most ~ and beautiful stanzas —J.L.Lowes⟩ (2) **:** having the gift of clear and lively description ⟨a ~ writer⟩ **b :** sharply outlined or delineated ⟨plush buildings . . . which I saw as a ~ contrast to the slums —Ben Burns⟩ **3 a :** of or relating to the pictorial arts **:** pictorial or symbolic rather than verbal ⟨the natural distinction between literary and ~ art —Bliss Perry⟩ **b :** of, relating to, or involving such reproductive methods as those of engraving, etching, lithography, photography, serigraphy, and woodcut ⟨the etchings, drypoints, lithographs and engravings which together form his ~ work —*Brit. Book News*⟩ **c :** of or relating to the art of printing or the techniques associated with book production and communication by the printed word ⟨books considered as ~ rather than literary products —*Publishers' Weekly*⟩ **4 :** of, relating to, or used for writing ⟨the ~ system of the Maya⟩ **5 :** having mineral crystals resembling written or printed characters **:** exhibiting on the surface or in transverse section the appearance of such characters **:** having or displaying a rock fabric in which two minerals enclose each other by mutual intercrystallization **6 :** of, relating to, or represented by graphs, diagrams, lines, or similar means **:** DIAGRAMMATIC ⟨chart a trend in ~ fashion —L.W. Hall⟩ **7 :** of or relating to the written or printed word or the symbols or devices used in writing or printing to represent sound or convey meaning — **graph·i·cal·ly** \-fək(ə)lē, -fēk-, -li\ *adv* — **graph·ic·ness** \-fiknəs, -fēk-\ *n* -ES

²graphic \"\ *n* -S **1 a :** a product of graphic art (as a painting, watercolor, print) ⟨the ~s . . . include Chagall's original illustrations —Howard Devree⟩ **b graphics** *pl* **:** the graphic media ⟨~s and photography, the multiple arts; film, stage, and dance, the theatrical arts —*Museum of Modern Art Bull.*⟩ **2 a :** a picture, map, or graph used for illustration or demonstration ⟨these ~s embody widely accepted principles of visual education⟩ ⟨today, more and more, ~s are being used in company reports —*Jour. of Accountancy*⟩ **b graphics** *pl but sing in constr* **:** the art or science of representing a three-dimensional object on a two-dimensional surface according to mathematical rules of projection

-graph·ic \¦==\ *or* **-graph·i·cal** \¦===\ *adj comb form* [*-graphic* fr. LL *-graphicus*, fr. Gk *-graphikos*, fr. *graphikos* written; *-graphical* fr. LL *-graphicus* + E *-al*] **1 :** written or transmitted in a (specified) way ⟨steno*graphic*⟩ ⟨tele*graphic*⟩ **2 :** of or relating to writing in a (specified) field or on a (specified) subject ⟨bio*graphical*⟩ ⟨hagio*graphic*⟩

graphic accent *n* **:** ACCENT 5a

graphic arts *n pl* **:** the fine and applied arts of representation, decoration, and writing or printing on flat surfaces together with the techniques and crafts associated with each: as **a :** painting and drawing **b :** engraving, etching, lithography, photography, serigraphy, and woodcut **c :** writing and printing and the arts connected with bookmaking and other forms of publication

graphic formula *n* **:** STRUCTURAL FORMULA

graphic granite *n* **:** a light-colored intrusive rock having the quartz crystals so arranged in the feldspar as to appear in a transverse section like written characters — called also *Hebraic granite, pegmatite, runite*

graphic tellurium *n* **:** SYLVANITE

graphies *pl of* GRAPHY

-graphies *pl of* -GRAPHY

graphing *pres part of* GRAPH

graphis \'grafəs, -rāf-\ *n, cap* [NL, fr. L, drawing, design, fr. LGk, painting, embroidery, fr. Gk, stylus, fr. *graphein* to write; fr. the appearance of the apothecia] **:** a genus (the type of the family Graphidaceae) of grayish white crustaceous lichens that occur on bark

¹graph·ite \'gra,fīt, *usu* -īd.+V\ *n* -S [G *graphit*, fr. Gk *graphein* to write + G *-it* -ite] **1 :** a mineral consisting of soft black lustrous carbon that occurs both in hexagonal crystals and as foliated or granular massive, conducts electricity, and is used in lead pencils, crucibles, electrolytic anodes, as a lubricant, and as a moderator in atomic-energy plants (hardness 1–2, sp. gr. 2.09–2.23) — called also *black lead, plumbago*; see ELECTROGRAPHITE **2 :** a dark grayish blue to dark bluish gray

²graphite \"\ *vt* -ED/-ING/-S **:** to coat or impregnate with graphite **:** GRAPHITIZE 2

graphite blue *n* **:** a blackish blue that is stronger than midnight and greener than Romany

gra·phit·ic \(')gra¦fid·|ik, -fit|, |ēk\ *adj* **:** relating to, containing, derived from, or resembling graphite

graphitic carbon *n* **:** the portion of the carbon in iron or steel that is present as graphite — distinguished from *combined carbon*

graph·itiza·tion \,gra,fīd·ə'zāshən, -,fəd-·\ *n* -S **:** the process of graphitizing

graph·itize \'=,fə,tīz, -,fīd·,īz\ *vb* -ED/-ING/-S *vt* **1 :** to convert into graphite; *specif* **:** to anneal (cast iron or steel) so that some or all of the combined carbon is transformed into free carbon as graphite **2 :** to impregnate or coat with graphite **3 :** to cause graphite to form in; *specif* **:** to corrode and weaken (structural steel or cast-iron pipe) in service by heat so that combined carbon becomes graphite with resultant risk of metal failure ~ *vi* **1 :** to become converted into graphite **2 :** to cause graphite to form in a substance

graphitized carbon *n* **:** ELECTROGRAPHITE

graph·itoid \'gra,fīd·,ȯid, -,fə,tȯid\ *also* **graph·itoi·dal** \¦gra-,fīd·¦ȯid^{ə}l, -fə¦tȯi-\ *adj* **:** resembling graphite

graph·i·um \'grafēəm\ *n, cap* [NL, fr. L, stylus, fr. Gk *grapheion* pencil, paintbrush, fr. *graphein* to write — more at CARVE] **:** a form genus of imperfect fungi (family Stilbellaceae) with dark-colored coremia many of which (as the parasite of Dutch elm disease) have been determined to be conidial stages of members of the genus *Ceratostomella*

grapho- *comb form* [F, fr. MF, fr. Gk, fr. *graphē* writing, fr. *graphein* to write] **:** writing ⟨*grapho*logy⟩

graph·o·litha \,grafə'lithə\ *n, cap* [NL, fr. *grapho-* + *-litha* (fr. Gk *lithos* stone)] **:** a genus of rather small moths (family Olethreutidae) having larvae that feed in various fruits or flower heads — see ORIENTAL PEACH MOTH

graph·o·log·i·cal \¦==¦läjəkəl\ *adj* **:** of or relating to graphology

gra·phol·o·gist \gra'fäləjəst\ *n* -S **:** a specialist in graphology

gra·phol·o·gy \-jē\ *n* -ES [F *graphologie*, fr. *grapho-* + *-logie* -logy] **:** the study of handwriting esp. for the purpose of character analysis ⟨if taken away from fortunetellers . . . ~ may yet become a useful handmaiden of psychology —*Time*⟩

graph·o·met·ric \¦grafə¦me·trik\ *or* **graph·o·met·ri·cal** \-rəkəl\ *adj* **:** of or relating to graphometry

gra·phom·e·try \gra'fämə·trē\ *n* -ES [F *graphométrie*, fr. *grapho-* + *-métrie* -metry] **:** the science of determining constants in handwritings

Graph·o·phone \'grafə,fōn\ *trademark* — used for a phonograph using wax records

graph·or·rhea \,grafə'rēə\ *n* -S [NL, fr. *grapho-* + *-rrhea*] **:** a symptom of motor excitement consisting in continual and incoherent writing

grapho·spasm \'grafə + ,-\ *n* [ISV *grapho-* + *spasm*] **:** WRITER'S CRAMP

grapho·type \"+,-\ *n* [*grapho-* + *type*] **:** a form of chalk engraving — **grapho·typ·ic** \¦==¦tipik\ *adj*

graph paper *n* **:** paper ruled into small squares or other forms for drawing graphs, plotting curves, or making diagrams

graphs *pl of* GRAPH, *pres 3d sing of* GRAPH

-graphs *pl of* -GRAPH

graphy \'grafē, -fi\ *n* -ES [F *graphie* system of writing, fr. Gk *graphein* to write + F *-ie* -y] **1 :** MATER LECTIONIS **2 :** a variant spelling

-gra·phy \grafē, -fi\ *n comb form* -ES [L *-graphia*, fr. Gk, fr. *graphein* to write + *-ia* -y — more at CARVE] **1 :** writing or representation in a (specified) manner or by a (specified) means or of a (specified) object ⟨calli*graphy*⟩ ⟨carto*graphy*⟩ ⟨photo*graphy*⟩ ⟨steno*graphy*⟩ **2 :** writing on a (specified) subject or in a (specified) field ⟨bio*graphy*⟩ ⟨geo*graphy*⟩ ⟨metallo*graphy*⟩

grap·nel \'grapnəl\ *n* -S [ME *grapenel*, fr. (assumed) MF *grapinel*, dim. of MF *grapin*, dim. of *grape*, *crape* hook — more at GRAPE] **1 :** GRAPPLE 1a **2 :** a small anchor with four or five flukes or claws used in dragging or grappling operations and for anchoring a dory or skiff

grapnel 2

grap·pa \'grä(,)pä\ *n* -S [It, fr. It dial. (Tuscany) *grappa* grape stalk, of Gmc origin; akin to MD *crappe* hook, OHG *krapfo*, *krāpfo* — more at CRAVE] **:** a dry usu. colorless Italian brandy made from the distilled residue of a wine press — compare MARC

grap·pi·er cement \'grapē,ā-\ *n* [F *grappier*, fr. *grappe* cluster, bunch of grapes (fr. OF *grape* hook, grape stalk, bunch of grapes, grape) + *-ier* -er — more at GRAPE] **:** a cement made by grinding fine the lumps of underburned and overburned material left when a hydraulic lime is slaked

¹grap·ple \'grapəl\ *n* -S [MF *grappelle*, dim. of *grappe*, *grape* hook — more at GRAPE] **1 a :** an instrument with iron claws designed to be thrown by a rope and formerly used esp. to fasten an enemy ship alongside before boarding **b :** GRAPNEL 2 **2** [²*grapple*] **a :** the act of grappling or the state of being grappled ⟨such scathful ~ did he make with the most noble bottom of our fleet —Shak.⟩ **b :** a hand-to-hand struggle ⟨rose . . . fresh from his fall and fiercer ~ joined —John Milton⟩ **c :** a contest for superiority or victory ⟨a final ~ with ecclesiastical tyranny —Edward Miall⟩ **3 :** a bucket similar to a clamshell but having three or more jaws

²grapple \"\ *vb* **grappled; grappled; grappling** \-p(ə)liŋ\ **grapples** *vt* **1 :** to seize, hold, or drag with or as if with a grapple ⟨wished to ~ this vessel and take it —Charlotte M. Yonge⟩ ⟨*grappled* the river bottom for broken chains —James Dugan⟩ **2 :** to come to grips with **:** grasp with the hands **:** take hold of ⟨Junior, aged four, *grappling* the family mutt with a wrestler's stranglehold —*Springfield (Mass.) Daily News*⟩ ⟨*grappled* me to him with both arms . . . and hugged me —R.P.Warren⟩ **3 :** to fasten, join, or bind with a close bond ⟨those friends thou hast, and their adoption tried, ~ them to thy soul with hoops of steel —Shak.⟩ ~ *vi* **1 a :** to fasten oneself firmly with or as if with a grapple ⟨the piece of ice we *grappled* to —Francis Smith⟩ **b :** to make fast one's ship by means of a grapple — used with *with* ⟨~ with the enemy's ships and board them —Edward Edwards⟩ **2 :** to come to grips **:** engage in hand-to-hand encounter **:** contend in close combat ⟨*grappled* and commenced wrestling —John Doran⟩ ⟨*grappling* wildly with a big tough —Robert Westerby⟩ **3 :** to move the hands in or as if in grasping **:** GROPE ⟨*grappled* about the floor among the dead bodies —Thomas Lodge⟩ **4 :** to attempt to deal **:** COPE — used with *with* ⟨didn't ~ with any national problem until it was forced upon his attention —F.L. Allen⟩ ⟨many poets, playwrights and novelists have *grappled* with the subject —Howard Taubman⟩ **5 :** to use a grapple (as in searching) ⟨*grappled* in deep water for the missing safe⟩ **syn** see WRESTLE

grapple dredge *n* **:** a dredger that operates with a clamshell, orange-peel, or other bucket

grapple fork *n* **:** HAYFORK

grapple plant *n* **:** an herb (*Harpagophytum procumbens*) of southern Africa having woody fruits with hooked or barbed thorns

grap·pler \'grap(ə)lə(r)\ *n* -S **:** one that grapples: as **a :** GRAPPLE 1 **b :** WRESTLER

grapple shot *n* **:** a projectile used in lifesaving that has hinged claws designed to catch in a ship's rigging or to hold in the ground — called also *anchor shot*

grappling *n* -S **1 a :** GRAPPLE 1a **b :** GRAPNEL 2 **2** *archaic* **:** ANCHORAGE 3c

grappling iron *or* **grappling hook** *n* **:** a hooked iron for anchoring a boat, grappling ships to each other, or recovering sunken objects

grap·sid \'grapsəd\ *adj* [NL *Grapsidae*] **:** of or relating to the family Grapsidae

grap·si·dae \-sə,dē\ *n pl, cap* [NL, fr. *Grapsus*, type genus + *-idae*] **:** a cosmopolitan family of crabs including pelagic and littoral and shore crabs as well as a few that have adapted to a strictly terrestrial or to a freshwater mode of life — see GRAPSUS

¹grap·soid \-,sȯid\ *adj* [NL *Grapsus* + E *-oid*] **:** resembling or related to the family Grapsidae

²grapsoid \"\ *n* -S **:** a grapsoid crab

grap·sus \-səs\ *n, cap* [NL, modif. of Gk *grapsaios* crab] **:** a genus (the type of the family Grapsidae) of crabs having a somewhat quadrilateral carapace, wide postabdomen, and short eyestalks

grap·to·lite \'graptə,līt\ *n* -S [Gk *graptos* painted, written (fr. *graphein* to write) + E *-lite*] **:** any of numerous extinct colonial animals (group Graptolitoidea) that are known only as carbonized fossils from Upper Cambrian through Devonian rocks and that have zooids housed in small cups spaced along a chitinous support — compare GRAPTOLITOIDEA

grap·to·lith·i·da \,graptə'lithədə\ [NL, fr. *Graptolithus* + *-ida*] *syn of* GRAPTOLITOIDEA

grap·to·li·thi·na \-p(,)tōlə'thīnə, -thēnə\ [NL, fr. *Graptolithus* + *-ina*] *syn of* GRAPTOLITOIDEA

grap·to·li·toi·dea \-lə'tȯidēə\ *n, cap* [NL, fr. *Graptolitus*, genus of Graptolitoidea (alter. of *Graptolithus*, fr. Gk *graptos* painted, written + *lithos* stone) + *-oidea*] **:** a group of extinct animals of uncertain systematic rank and position formerly regarded as a division of Hydrozoa but now often placed in the Bryozoa or even associated with the pterobranchs in Hemichordata — see GRAPTOLITE

grap·to·zoa \,graptə'zōə\ [NL, fr. Gk *graptos* written, painted + NL *-zoa*] *syn of* GRAPTOLITOIDEA

grapy *or* **grap·ey** \'grāpē\ *adj* **grapier; grapiest 1 a :** of or relating to grapes or the vine ⟨~ clusters⟩ **b** *usu* **grapey :** having a grape taste as well as a wine taste — used esp. of some wines made from native American grapes; compare FOXY **2 :** affected with grapes

¹grasp \'grasp, -aa(ə)-, -ai-, -â-\ *vb* -ED/-ING/-S [ME *graspen* — more at GRAB] *vi* **1 :** to make the motion of seizing or trying to seize **:** CLUTCH — usu. used with *at* or *for* ⟨~*ing* for any support⟩ ⟨ready to ~ at straws⟩ **2** *obs* **:** EMBRACE, GRAPPLE — used with *with* or *about* ~ *vt* **1 :** to clutch at **:** take or seize eagerly **2 :** to seize and hold by clasping or embracing with or as if with the fingers or arms **:** take possession of ⟨thy hand is made to ~ a palmer's staff —Shak.⟩ ⟨~*ed* this moment to say —Edward Bok⟩ **3 :** to lay hold of with the mind **:** COMPREHEND, UNDERSTAND ⟨failed to ~ the importance of the undertaking⟩ **syn** see TAKE

²grasp \"\ *n* -S **1 a :** something intended for grasping or to be grasped (as a handle or a fluke of an anchor) ⟨a sturdy shaft with the ~ roughened to keep the hand from slipping⟩ **b :** the handle of an oar **2 :** an act or instance of grasping: as **a :** a hand grip **b :** EMBRACE **3 :** forcible holding **:** POSSESSION, HOLD, CONTROL ⟨the whole space that's in the tyrant's ~ —Shak.⟩ **4 a :** the reach of the arms **b :** the power of seizing and holding ⟨success was almost within his ~⟩ **5 :** mental hold or comprehension esp. when broad ⟨had a remarkable ~ of this complex subject⟩

grasp·able \-pəbəl\ *adj* **:** capable of being grasped **:** COMPREHENSIBLE, UNDERSTANDABLE ⟨a smooth ~ analysis of the situation⟩ — **grasp·able·ness** \-nəs\ *n* -ES — **grasp·ably** \-pəblē\ *adv*

grasp·er \-pə(r)\ *n* -S **:** one that grasps; *esp* **:** a grasping person

grasping *adj* **1 :** being accustomed or used to grasp ⟨~ tongs⟩; *broadly* **:** tending to hold firmly **:** TENACIOUS ⟨~ roots that bind the soil⟩ **2 :** desiring material possessions excessively or to such a degree as to overshadow propriety and fairness in dealings **:** urgently seeking wealth **:** AVARICIOUS **syn** see COVETOUS

grasp·ing·ly *adv* **:** in a grasping manner

grasp·ing·ness *n* -ES **:** the quality or state of being grasping

grasp·less \-pləs\ *adj* **1 :** lacking the power of grasping **:** unable to seize and hold **:** relaxed as from weakness or fear ⟨the message slipped from her ~ hand⟩ — compare NERVELESS **2 :** INCOMPREHENSIBLE

¹grass \'gras, -aa(ə)-, -ai-, -â-\ *n* -ES *often attrib* [ME *gras*, fr. OE *græs*; akin to OHG, ON, & Goth *gras* grass, OE *grōwan* to grow, and perh. to L *gramen* grass — more at GROW] **1 a :** green herbage that affords food for grazing animals and that usu. consists predominantly of narrow-leaved monocotyledonous plants of the families Gramineae, Cyperaceae, and Juncaceae often intermixed with various dicotyledonous herbs ⟨the moist spring has brought on a good growth of ~⟩ **b** *now chiefly dial* **:** a small herb; *esp* **:** one used medicinally **c :** a plant of the family Gramineae ⟨the bamboos include the largest ~*es* some of which attain a height of 120 feet⟩ **d :** any of various herbaceous plants with narrow linear foliage — used in combination; see BLUE-EYED GRASS **e** (1) **:** ASPARAGUS (2) *slang* **:** a leafy vegetable; *esp* **:** LETTUCE **2 a :** GRAZING ⟨~ enough to keep a cow⟩ **:** land set apart or available for grazing **b :** land on which grass is grown for hay or pasture **:** PASTURE, MEADOW, LEA **3** *obs* **:** the vegetative condition of a cereal before the ear of grain is developed **4 :** a leaf or plant of grass — now used only in pl. ⟨hair tangled with ~*es* and twigs⟩ **5 :** ground covered with growing grass ⟨keep off the ~⟩ ⟨dropped his bundles on the ~⟩ **6** *now dial* **:** the season at which grass springs into growth **:** SPRING **7 :** a state or place of retirement (as from cares, responsibilities, or privileges) ⟨would like to go to ~ for a month or so⟩ ⟨has been at ~ for several years⟩ **8 :** GRASS SPONGE **9 :** electronic noise on a radarscope that takes the form of vertical lines resembling lawn grass

²grass \"\ *vb* -ED/-ING/-ES *vt* **1 a :** to provide (as cattle) with grass for food **:** furnish with pasture **:** GRAZE ⟨pasture to ~ 30 head⟩ **b :** to feed (livestock) on grass without grain or other concentrates **2 a :** to cover with grass ⟨it is easier but more expensive to ~ a lawn with turfs⟩; *esp* **:** to seed to grass ⟨decided to ~ the north 40 that year⟩ — often used with *down* ⟨~*ed* down the newly cleared land with rye grass and white clover⟩ **b :** to lay with turfs **3 :** to spread (as linen for bleaching) on the grass **4 :** to bring or knock to the ground **:** FELL ⟨~*ed* his opponent with a well-placed blow⟩; *esp* **:** to shoot (a game bird) down or land (a fish) on the bank of a stream ~ *vi* **1 :** to produce grass — often used with *up* ⟨the new lawns are ~*ing* up well⟩ **2** *Brit, of a compositor* **:** to do temporary or casual work **:** SUB

grassation *n* -S [L *grassation-, grassatio*, fr. *grassatus* (past part. of *grassari* to go about, attack, rage against) + *-ion-, -io* -ion; akin to L *gradi* to step, go — more at GRADE] *obs* **:** an act of attacking violently; *also* **:** a lying in wait to attack

grass bass *n* **:** LARGEMOUTH BLACK BASS

grass beef *n* **:** beef from grass-fed animals

grass-bird \'=,=\ *n* **:** any of numerous birds associated with open grassy country: as **a :** SANDPIPER; *esp* **:** PECTORAL SANDPIPER **b** (1) **:** FERNBIRD (2) **:** a closely related Australian bird (*Megalurus gramineus*) **c :** a small warbler (*Sphenoeacus afer*) of southern Africa

grass-blade \'⸗,⸗\ *n* **:** one of the elongated linear leaves of a typical grass
grass bug *n* **:** any of numerous true bugs (as members of the family Miridae) that feed chiefly on grasses
grass bur *n* **:** BUR GRASS
grass captain *n, dial* **:** an aboveground supervisory employee of a mine
grass cattle *n* **:** cattle for beef that are finished on grass
grass character *n* [trans. of Chin (Pek) *ts'ao³ tzŭ⁴*] **:** one of the irregular cursive characters of a style of Chinese and Japanese writing for business and private use
grasschat \'⸗,⸗\ *n* [¹*grass* + *chat* (bird)] **:** WHINCHAT
grass cloth *n* [trans. of Chin (Pek) *hsia⁴ pu⁴*] **:** a lustrous, plain, and usu. loosely woven textile made chiefly in the Orient from various grass or other vegetable fibers and used chiefly for garments and table linens; *esp* **:** such a cloth woven from ramie fibers
grass court *n* **:** a lawn-tennis court with a playing surface of turf — compare HARD COURT
grass crab *n* **:** a shallow-water spider crab (*Macrocoeloma trispinosum*) brownish in color, covered with short velvety hairs, and common alongshore from No. Carolina to Brazil — called also *sponge crab*
grasscut \'⸗,⸗\ *n* [trans. of Hindi *ghāskhodā, ghāskātā*] **:** a servant attached to a party traveling in India who is responsible for cutting fodder for the animals of the party
grass cut *vb, slang* **:** HEDGEHOP
grass cutter *n* **1 :** one that cuts grass: as **a :** GRASSCUT **b :** a machine or device for cutting grass (as a lawn mower or a scythe) **2** *slang* **a :** a hard-hit baseball that skims the ground ⟨sent a *grass cutter* to the shortstop who fumbled it⟩ **b :** a low-flying airplane
grass cutting *n, slang* **:** HEDGEHOPPING
grass dance *n* **:** a strenuous male Indian show dance in which the dancers sometimes wear a bunch of grass at their belts
grass drake *n* **:** CORNCRAKE
grass egg *n* **:** an egg with a dark or greenish yolk that results when a hen feeds too freely on grasses or other green foods
grass·er \-sə(r)\ *n* -s **1 :** a beef animal marketed direct from the pasture or range without supplementary feeding **2 :** a calfskin or kip taken from an underfed animal and characterized by coarseness of grain
gras·se·rie \ˌgras(ə)ˈrē, ˈgräs-, ˈ⸗sərē\ *n* -s [F, fr. *gras* fat (fr. L *crassus*) + *-erie* -ery — more at HURDLE] **:** a destructive polyhedrosis disease of silkworms that is related to wilt and is marked by spotty yellowing of the skin and internal liquefaction — called also *jaundice*
grasses *pl of* GRASS, *pres 3d sing of* GRASS
gras·set \graˈsā\ *n, pl* **grassets** \-ā(z)\ [LaF, fr. F, chubby, plump, fr. *gras* fat] *Louisiana* **:** any of several small plump songbirds formerly used for food; *esp* **:** CHEWINK
gras·se·yé \ˌgrasəˈyā, -sēˈā\ *adj* [F, fr. past part. of *grasseyer* to use a uvular *r*, fr. MF, fr. *gras* fat] *of r* **:** pronounced as a uvular fricative; *broadly* **:** pronounced as either a uvular fricative or trill — **gras·seye·ment** \ˌgra,sāˈmäⁿ\ *n* -s
grass family *n* **:** GRAMINEAE
grass-fat \'⸗,⸗\ *adj, of livestock* **:** fattened only on pasture **:** not finished in a drylot or with supplementary feeding
grass-feed \'⸗,⸗\ *vi* **:** to feed on herbage **:** use or require a diet primarily made up of grasses ~ *vt* **:** to feed (as cattle) on grass; *esp* **:** to finish (beef cattle) for market on pasture
grass fern *n* **:** an epiphytic tropical American fern (*Vittaria lineata*) with narrow linear fronds in pendent tufts; *broadly* **:** any of several other ferns of the genus *Vittaria*
grass finch *n* **1 :** VESPER SPARROW **2 :** any of various weaverbirds; *esp* **:** an Australian member of the genus *Poephila*
grassflower \'⸗,⸗\ *n* **1 :** SPRING BEAUTY **2 :** BLUE-EYED GRASS
grass frog *n* **:** any of several frogs of semiterrestrial habits: as **a :** a common European frog (*Rana temporaria*) **b :** PICKEREL FROG
grass green *n* **1 :** a variable color averaging a strong yellowish green that is yellower and duller than shamrock green or Cyprus green **2 :** a moderate yellow green that is greener, lighter, and stronger than average moss green, yellower and deeper than average pea green, and yellower and darker than apple green (sense 1)
grass-grown \'⸗,⸗\ *adj* **:** overgrown with grass
grass-grub \'⸗,⸗\ *n* **1 :** a small shiny brown New Zealand cockchafer (*Odontria zealandica*) that feeds on grass; *specif* **:** its root-eating larva that is a very destructive pest of turf **2 :** CORBIE
grass gum *n* **:** GRASS TREE 1
grass hand *n* **1** *Brit* **:** a compositor on casual or job work **:** SUB **2** [trans. of Chin (Pek) *ts'ao³ shon³*] **:** the style of Chinese and Japanese writing that uses grass characters
grass hare *n* **:** an African steppe hare (*Poelagus marjorita* or *Lepus marjorita*) of the uplands of Uganda
grass hook *n* **:** a sickle with a smooth blade
grass·hop \'⸗,häp\ *vi* [back-formation fr. *grasshopper*] **:** to move erratically from place to place
¹**grasshopper** \'⸗,⸗⸗\ *n* [ME *grasshopper*, fr. *gras* grass + *hopper*] **1 :** any of numerous plant-eating orthopterous insects (suborder Saltatoria) having the hind legs adapted for leaping, biting and chewing mouthparts, stridulating organs in the males and rarely in the females, incomplete metamorphosis, and usu. wings as adults and being serious pests of plant life both because of their relatively large size and great numbers and in some areas because of their habit of engaging in migratory flights in which whole regions may be stripped of vegetation — see ACRIDIDAE, TETTIGONIIDAE; KATYDID, LONG-HORNED GRASSHOPPER, SHORT-HORNED GRASSHOPPER **2 :** a small firework that jumps about **3 :** an early locomotive with a vertical boiler and cylinders **4 :** a light unarmed scouting and liaison airplane used esp. for helping to direct field⸗ artillery fire
²**grasshopper** \"\ *vi* -ED/-ING/-S **1 :** to fish with a natural or artificial grasshopper for bait **2 :** to move a riverboat over shallows or sandbars by means of poles suggesting stilts
³**grasshopper** \"\ *adj* **1 :** suggesting the grasshopper in appearance or action ⟨a ~ plow⟩ ⟨a ~ type of counterbalance⟩ **2 :** light and frivolous **:** untouched by care for the future ⟨a ~ brain⟩
grasshopper hawk *n* [so called fr. the fact that it feeds on grasshoppers] **:** SPARROW HAWK
grasshopper indian *n, usu cap G&I* **:** UTE
grasshopper lark *n* **:** a grasshopper warbler (*Locustella naevia*)
grasshopper mouse *n* **:** a mouse of a genus (*Onychomys*) of stoutly built short-tailed insectivorous mice of western No. America that are closely related to the white-footed mice
grasshopper plow *n* **:** a shallow-set plow formerly used for breaking sod in the prairie regions of No. America
grasshopper sparrow *n* **:** any of several small American sparrows constituting the genus *Ammodramus*; *esp* **:** a common sparrow (*A. savannarum pratensis*) of eastern No. America having a yellow patch on the front edge of the wing and a song that resembles the stridulation of grasshoppers
grasshopper warbler *n* **:** any of several Old World warblers constituting the genus *Locustella*; *esp* **:** a common European warbler (*L. naevia*)
grasshouse \'⸗,⸗\ *n* **1** *obs* **:** a grassman's cottage **2** *or* **grass hut :** a habitation constructed mainly or largely of grass
grass·ie \'grasē, -raas-,-rais-,-räs-\ *n* -s [¹*grass* + *-ie*] *Austral* **:** RED-BACKED PARROT
grassier *comparative of* GRASSY
grassiest *superlative of* GRASSY
grass ill *n* **:** a digestive disorder of young lambs caused by too suddenly starting full feeding on grass
grass·i·ness \-sēnəs, -sin-\ *n* -ES **:** grassy quality; *also* **:** an expanse of grass or turf ⟨the shady ~ beneath the old hickories⟩
grassing *pres part of* GRASS
grass itch mite *n* **:** an Australian trombiculid mite (*Acomatacarus australiensis*) that lives on grasses and bites man and domestic animals and that sometimes becomes a serious pest in suburban areas
grassland \'⸗,⸗\ *n, often attrib* **1 :** farmland occupied chiefly by grasses and other forage plants (as clovers), used chiefly for grazing and hay, and often made a part of the regular cultural rotation — compare LEA **2 a :** land on which the natural dominant plant forms are grasses and forbs — often used in pl. ⟨the ~*s* of the West⟩; compare PRAIRIE, SAVANNA, TUNDRA **b :** an ecological community in which the prevailing or characteristic plants are grasses and similar plants
grassland buttercup *n* **:** a New Zealand crowfoot (*Ranunculus multiscapus*) with one-flowered scapes
grassland daisy *n* **:** a New Zealand herb (*Brachycome sinclairii*) with purplish or whitish flowers — compare SWAN RIVER DAISY
grassland farming *n* **:** a system of farming in which grass is the basic crop taken from the land whether as a direct cash crop or as a source of income through further processing (as by feeding cattle)
grass-leaved \'⸗,⸗\ *also* **grassy-leaved** \'⸗⸗,⸗\ *adj* **:** having long narrow leaves that resemble blades of grass ⟨a *grass⸗ leaved* orchid⟩
grass·less \'⸗ləs\ *adj* **:** lacking grass and usu. bare and barren ⟨shabby ~ yards⟩
grasslike \'⸗,⸗\ *adj* **:** resembling a grass esp. in having long slender leaves
grass lily *n* **:** an Australian herb (*Dichopogon strictus*) of the family Liliaceae with grasslike leaves and blue flowers
grass line *n* **:** a coir rope
grass linen *n* **:** grass cloth woven of ramie
grass·man \'⸗mən, -,man\ *n, pl* **grass·men** [ME *grasman*, fr. *gras* grass + *man*] **1** *obs Scot* **:** COTTER **2 :** an officer formerly in charge of grassland in the north of England
grass·mann's law \'gra|smənz, -raa|, -rai|, -rä|, -rå|\ *n, usu cap G* [after Hermann G. *Grassmann* †1877 Ger. mathematician & Sanskritist] **:** a statement of certain regular changes exhibited by Indo-European voiced aspirates in Sanskrit and Greek: when the aspirates occur at the beginning of successive syllables one of them, usu. the first, loses its aspiration and becomes in Greek a voiceless stop and in Sanskrit a voiced stop — compare GRIMM'S LAW
grass mat *n* **:** a woven mat simulating trimmed grass and used esp. to form backgrounds for displays or theatrical scenery
grass mildew *n* **:** a powdery mildew (*Erysiphe graminis*) that frequently attacks cereals and other grasses
grass moth *n* **:** any of several whose moths of the family *Pyralididae* including several whose larvae are destructive pests on lawn grasses — see GRASS WEBWORM
grass mouse *n* **1 :** a meadow mouse (*Microtus agrestis*) **2 :** a striped mouse (*Lemniscomys striatus*) of the African veldt
grassnut \'⸗,⸗\ *n* **1 :** PEANUT **2 :** a California brodiaea (*Brodiaea laxa*) with purplish blue or rarely white funnel⸗ shaped flowers borne in clusters on a tall scape, linear leaves, and a deep-seated edible corm
grass-of-par·nas·sus \-,pärˈnasəs,-(,)pä'-\ *n, often cap P* [fr. *Parnassus*, mountain in Greece] **:** a plant of the genus *Parnassia*
grass onion *n, dial* **:** CHIVE 1 — usu. used in pl.
grass owl *n* **:** a rather large long-legged owl (*Tyto longimembris*) that lives in tall grass and is widely distributed from India and southern China to northern Australia and Fiji
grass parrakeet *n* **:** any of numerous small Australian parrots; *esp* **:** BUDGERIGAR
grass parrot *n* **:** GRASS PARRAKEET; *esp* **:** any of several small brightly marked parrots (genera *Psephotus* and *Neophema*) — compare RED-BACKED PARROT
grass pea *n* **1 :** an Old World pea (*Lathyrus sativus*) grown in some warm areas chiefly for forage **2 :** the white wedge⸗ shaped seed of the grass pea used as food for man in India and for stock elsewhere
grass pickerel *n* **1 :** a small dark-banded pickerel (*Esox vermiculatus*) of quiet weedy waters esp. of central No. America — called also *little pickerel, mud pickerel* **2 :** CHAIN PICKEREL
grass pike *n* **1 :** ⁴PIKE 1a **2 :** CHAIN PICKEREL
grass pink *n* **1 :** a European pink (*Dianthus plumarius*) that is often cultivated for its very fragrant usu. pink or rosy flowers **2 :** DEPTFORD PINK **3 :** an orchid of the genus *Calopogon* (esp. *C. pulchellus*)
grassplot *also* **grassplat** \'⸗,⸗\ *n* **:** a plot of ground covered with grass
grass plover *n* **:** UPLAND PLOVER
grass poly *n* **:** a glabrous annual loosestrife (*Lythrum hyssopifolia*) with small solitary pink flowers that is prob. native to Europe but is widely naturalized in moist areas — called also *hyssop loosestrife*
grass pondweed *n* **:** a No. American submerged aquatic plant (*Potamogeton foliosus*) with slender grasslike leaves
grass porgy *n* [so called fr. its living in eelgrass] **:** a small sparid fish (*Calamus arctifrons*) of the Florida coast
grassquit \'⸗,⸗\ *n* [¹*grass* + *quit* (bird)] **:** any of several very small tropical American and West Indian finches of *Tiaris* and certain closely related genera
grass rooter \'⸗'rü|d·ə(r), -'rů|, |tə-\ *n* **:** one that belongs to or is concerned with the grass roots
grass roots \'⸗|⸗\ *n pl but sing or pl in constr* [¹*grass* + *roots*] **1 :** soil at or near the surface ⟨ore was found at the *grass roots*⟩ **2 a :** the farming and rural districts of a country as distinguished from the industrial and urban **b :** the people of these districts when constituting or acting as a fundamental politico-economic group and a source of independent popular opinion **3 :** the very foundation or source ⟨attack a problem at the *grass roots*⟩ **:** the fundamental part **:** BASIS ⟨the *grass roots* of political organization⟩
grass rope *n* **:** a rope made of any vegetable fiber other than cotton — compare GRASS LINE
grass rug *n* **:** a floor covering woven from strands of a tough slender marsh grass with a cotton warp and usu. decorated with stenciled patterns
grass sack *n, Midland* **:** a burlap bag **:** GUNNYSACK
grass sandwort *n* **:** a Rocky mountain sandwort (*Arenaria formosa*) with narrow grasslike leaves
grass shears *n pl* **:** shears designed primarily for clipping grass neatly in difficult spots (as along the edges of walks, flower beds, borders)

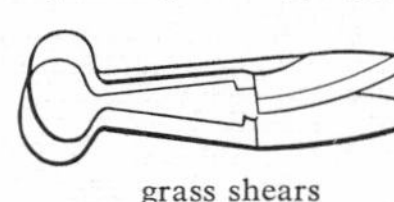
grass shears

grass shrimp *n* **1 :** any of several slender shrimps (genus *Hippolyte*) common among eelgrass along the Pacific coast of No. America **2 :** a small transparent freshwater shrimp (genus *Palaemonetes*) of the southeastern U. S. that is often used as bait by fishermen
grass sickness *also* **grass disease** *n* **:** a frequently fatal disease of grazing horses that is characterized by more or less complete interruption of normal gastrointestinal functioning with difficulty in swallowing, interruption of peristalsis, and fecal impaction and that is held to be caused by a poisonous plant or insect consumed with the forage or by an atypical form of botulism
grass silage *n* **:** silage made from young grasses or legumes and rich in protein but commonly requiring addition of acid or of a supplementary source of carbohydrate to ensure proper fermentation
grass skirt *n* **:** a skirt worn by women of some Pacific islands and made of native grasses or split leaves that hang loosely from a band; *also* **:** an imitation of this skirt
grass snake *n* **1 :** a common European ringed snake (*Natrix natrix*) **2 :** SMOOTH GREEN SNAKE **3 :** GARTER SNAKE; *esp* **:** one with indistinct or no stripes **4 :** BROWN SNAKE
grass snipe *n* **:** PECTORAL SANDPIPER
grass sorghum *n* **:** a leafy sorghum (as Sudan grass) cultivated esp. for hay or green feed
grass spider *n* **:** any of various spiders that spin concave webs on grass which are conspicuous when covered with dew; *esp* **:** a common No. American spider (*Agalena naevia*)
grass sponge *n* **:** a brittle usu. dark brown often very large inferior commercial sponge (*Spongia graminea*) occurring in the Gulf of Mexico, in the West Indies, and off the Florida coast
grass tetany *or* **grass staggers** *n* **:** a disease of cattle (as milch cows) marked by tetanic staggering, convulsions, coma, and frequently death and caused by reduction of blood calcium and magnesium when overeating on lush pasture — compare MILK FEVER
grass thrips *n* **:** a cosmopolitan thrips (*Anaphothrips obscurus*) esp. destructive to the developing inflorescence of grasses
grass tree *n* **1 :** any of several Australian arborescent plants (genus *Xanthorrhoea*) that yield acaroid resins; *esp* **:** a plant (*X. hastilis*) with a short woody stem crowned by a crowded tuft of long leaves **2 :** AUSTRALIAN GRASS TREE 2 **3 :** any of several Australasian trees with grasslike foliage: as **a :** a ti (*Cordyline australis*) **b :** LANCEWOOD **c :** a Tasmanian evergreen tree (*Richea pandanifolia*) with tapering slender leaves 3 to 5 feet long
grass-tree gum *n* **:** ACAROID RESIN; *esp* **:** the red variety of it
grassveld \'⸗|⸗\ *n* [Afrik *grasveld*, fr. *gras* grass + *veld* field] **:** natural grassland of southern Africa
grass vetch *or* **grass vetchling** *n* **:** an annual European vetch (*Lathyrus nissolia*) with minute stipules and crimson flowers
grass warbler *n* **:** any of various small brownish Old World warblers esp. of the genera *Cisticola* and *Locustella*
grass webworm *n* **:** any of numerous small grubs that are the larvae of grass moths and that spin webs around the base and roots of the grasses on which they feed
grassweed \'⸗,⸗\ *n* **:** EELGRASS 1
grass whip *n* **:** a long-handled grass cutter usu. having a straight blade at right angles to the handle and being used instead of a sickle to avoid stooping
grass widow *n* **1** *chiefly dial* **a :** a discarded mistress or common-law wife **b :** a woman who has had an illegitimate child **2 a :** a woman divorced or separated from her husband **b :** a woman whose husband is temporarily away from her — **grass·wid·ow·hood** \(')⸗'⸗⸗,⸗\ *n*
grass widower *n* **1 :** a man divorced or separated from his wife **2 :** a man whose wife is temporarily away from him
grasswork \'⸗,⸗\ *n* **1** *obs* **:** LAWN **2** *dial Eng* **:** mine work done at the surface **3 :** craftwork (as mats or basketry) made of grass
grassworm \'⸗,⸗\ *n* **:** any of various moth larvae that are destructive to grass; *specif* **:** FALL ARMYWORM
grasswort \'⸗,⸗\ *n* **:** a perennial mouse-ear chickweed (*Cerastium arvense*) widespread in Europe, Asia, and No. America and often cultivated for its large white flowers — called also *starry grasswort*
grass wrack *n* **:** EELGRASS 1
grass-wren \'⸗,⸗\ *n* **:** any of several small Australian warblers
grassy \'grasē, -raas-,-rais-,-räs-, -si\ *adj* -ER/-EST **1 a :** covered or abounding with grass ⟨a ~ lawn⟩ **b :** consisting of, relating to, or having a flavor or odor of grass ⟨~ fare⟩ ⟨~ butter⟩ **2 :** fed on grass ⟨~ sheep⟩ **3 :** resembling grass in color
grassy death camas *n* **:** a death camas with narrow leaves like blades of grass and racemes of greenish yellow flowers that is a source of livestock poisoning in parts of the northwestern U. S. and is considered a variety of the common death camas (*Zigadenus venenosus*) or made a separate species (*Z. gramineus*)
grassy-leaved *var of* GRASS-LEAVED
grat *past of* GREET
¹**grate** \'grāt, *usu* -ād·+V\ *n* -s [ME, fr. ML *grata, crata*, modif. of L *cratis* latticework, hurdle — more at HURDLE] **1 a** *archaic* **:** an enclosing railing often of ornately wrought iron **b** *obs* **:** CAGE, PRISON **2 :** a frame containing parallel or crossed bars forming an open latticework, permitting the passage of light, air, liquid, or sound, and commonly used to prevent unwanted ingress or egress (as of persons to or from a building) or passage (as of solids into a conduit for liquids) ⟨beautifully wrought ~*s* over the lower windows⟩ ⟨dislodging a heavy sewer ~⟩ **3 a :** a frame, bed, or basket of iron bars for holding fuel while it is burning **b :** FIREPLACE **c :** an open latticed or barred frame for cooking over a fire **4 :** a screen or sieve for use with stamp mortars for grading ore

grate 3a

²**grate** \"\ *vt* -ED/-ING/-S **1** *obs* **:** IMPRISON **2 :** to furnish with a grate ⟨~ a furnace⟩ **:** protect with a grating or bars ⟨~ an opening⟩
³**grate** \"\ *vb* -ED/-ING/-S [ME *graten*, fr. MF *grater* to scratch, scrape, of Gmc origin; akin to OHG *krazzōn* to scratch — more at SCRATCH] *vt* **1** *archaic* **:** to scrape or rub roughly or harshly **:** ABRADE — sometimes used with *down* or *away* **2 :** to reduce to small particles by rubbing with something rough or indented ⟨~ a nutmeg⟩ **3 a :** FRET, IRRITATE, OFFEND ⟨news, my good lord, from Rome . . . ~*s* me —Shak.⟩ **b** *obs* **:** to get by importunity or by extortion **4 a :** to gnash or grind (one's teeth) so as to produce a harsh discordant sound **b :** to cause to make such a sound ⟨*grated* the car into gear⟩ **c :** to utter (as speech) in a harsh voice ⟨*grating* an angry reply as he turned aside⟩ ~ *vi* **1 :** to rub roughly against something so as to produce harsh discordant sound ⟨the gears *grated* into place⟩ ⟨footsteps *grating* on the gravel⟩ **:** CREPITATE, RASP, GRIND **2 a** *obs* **:** to make unreasonable or burdensome demands **:** give offense by oppressive demands or importunity — usu. used with *upon* **b** *obs* **:** to dwell irritatingly — used with *upon* **c :** to produce an irritating effect **:** PERTURB, DISTRESS, ANNOY — used with *on* or *upon* ⟨such language ~*s* upon me⟩ ⟨his harsh voice *grated* on our ears⟩
⁴**grate** *n* -s [ME, fr. *graten*, v.] *obs* **:** a device for grating something **:** GRATER
grate·ful \'grātfəl\ *adj, sometimes* **gratefuller**; *sometimes* **gratefullest** [obs. E *grate* pleasing, thankful (fr. L *gratus* pleasing, beloved, worthy of thanks, grateful) + *-ful* — more at GRACE] **1 a :** appreciative of benefits received **:** willing or anxious to acknowledge and repay or give thanks for benefits ⟨a ~ heart⟩ **b :** expressing or induced by gratitude ⟨a ~ word of thanks⟩ ⟨a ~ acknowledgment⟩ **2 a :** affording pleasure or contentment **:** PLEASING ⟨such doctrines are only ~ to the abstruse scholar⟩ **b :** pleasing by reason of comfort supplied or discomfort alleviated ⟨glad to rest under the ~ shade of the elms⟩ ⟨the fire threw a ~ warmth into the room⟩ **syn** see PLEASANT
grate·ful·ly \-fəlē, -li\ *adv* **:** in a grateful manner
grate·ful·ness *n* -ES **:** the quality or state of being grateful ⟨~ for such a favor⟩
grate·less \-ləs\ *adj* [¹*grate* + *-less*] **:** having no grate ⟨a ~ heater⟩
grat·er \'grād·ə(r), -ātə-\ *n* -s [ME *gratere*, fr. *graten* to grate + *-ere* -er — more at GRATE] **:** one that grates; *esp* **:** a machine or device used for reducing material (as a nutmeg or a turnip) to small bits by rubbing or abrading
grate room *n* [¹*grate*] **:** a fire chamber below a glass-manufacturing furnace
gratewise \'⸗,⸗\ *adv* [¹*grate* + *-wise*] **:** in the manner or form of a grate ⟨steel bars piled ~⟩
gra·tic·u·la·tion \grə,tikyəˈlāshən\ *n* -s [F *graticuler* to make graticules (fr. *graticule*) + E *-ation*] **:** the division of a design or draft into squares to facilitate enlargement or reduction
grat·i·cule \'grad·ə,kyül\ *n* -s [F, fr. L *craticula* fine latticework, dim. of *cratis* latticework, hurdle — more at HURDLE] **1 :** a design or draft prepared by graticulation **2 a :** a scale on glass or other transparent material in the focal plane of a telescope or other optical instrument for the location and measurement of objects **b :** the network of lines of latitude and longitude upon which a map is drawn

grater

grat·i·fi·able \'grad·ə,fīəbəl, -atə-, ,⸗⸗'⸗⸗⸗\ *adj* **:** capable of being gratified **:** suitable for gratification ⟨such a wish is perfectly reasonable and ~⟩
grat·i·fi·ca·tion \,grad·əfəˈkāshən, -atə-\ *n* -s [MF or L; MF, fr. L *gratification-, gratificatio*, fr. *gratificatus* (past part. of *gratificari* to gratify) + *-ion-, -io* -ion] **1 a :** an act or instance of gratifying **b :** the state of being gratified **2** *archaic* **:** REWARD, RECOMPENSE; *esp* **:** GRATUITY **3 :** a source of gratification **:** something that pleases ⟨his success is a great ~ to me⟩ **4** *obs* **:** expression of gratification (as by prayer or worship)

grat·i·fied·ly \'ˌˌˌfīədlē, -li, ˌˌˌˌˌ, 'ˌˌˌfīd·\ *adv* **:** in a gratified manner **:** with gratification

grat·i·fi·er \'ˌˌˌfī(ə)r, -īə\ *n* -s **:** one that gratifies

grat·i·fy \'grad·ə,fī, -atə-\ *vt* -ED/-ING/-ES [MF *gratifier*, fr. L *gratificari*, fr. *gratus* pleasing, grateful + *-ificari* -ify — more at GRACE] **1 a** *obs* **:** to show gratitude to (a person) or for (as a service) **:** REQUITE **b** *archaic* **:** REMUNERATE, FEE **2 :** to give or be a source of pleasure or satisfaction to ⟨beauty *gratifies* the eye⟩: as **a :** to confer a favor on **:** OBLIGE ⟨the rulers *gratified* the people with subsidies and circuses⟩ **b :** to give rein to **:** INDULGE ⟨determined to ~ his whim⟩ **3** *obs* **a :** to receive or greet with pleasure **:** WELCOME **b :** GRACE, ADORN **syn** see PLEASE

gratifying *adj* **:** tending or able to gratify **:** PLEASING, SATISFYING ⟨received a very ~ reception⟩ ⟨found their praise ~⟩ **syn** see PLEASANT

grat·i·fy·ing·ly \'ˌˌˌˌˌ, ˌˌˌ'ˌˌˌ\ *adv* **:** in a gratifying manner ⟨~, such cases have been the exception —Gerda Luft⟩

gra·til·li·ty *also* **gra·til·i·ty** \grə'tilədē\ *n* -ES [by alter.] *archaic* **:** GRATUITY

grat·in \'grat°n, -ăt-\ *n* -s [F, fr. MF, fr. *grater* to scratch, scrape — more at GRATE] **:** a brown crust formed upon a gratinated dish; *also* **:** a dish with such a crust

grat·i·nate \'grat°n,āt\ *vt* -ED/-ING/-S [F *gratiner* (fr. *gratin*) + E *-ate*] **:** to cook with a covering of buttered crumbs or grated cheese until a crust or crisp surface forms

gra·ti·né \ˌgrat°n'ā, -ăt-\ *adj* [F, fr. past part. of *gratiner*] *of a food* **:** having a covering or crust (as of buttered crumbs or grated cheese)

grat·ing \'grād·iŋ, -ăt|, |ēŋ\ *n* -s [¹*grate* + *-ing*] **1 :** a partition, covering, or frame of parallel bars or crossbars **:** a latticework resembling a window grate **:** GRATE 2 **2 a :** a strong usu. wooden lattice used on shipboard in fair weather to cover a hatch and still admit light and air **b :** a movable lattice used for flooring (as of a boat) **c gratings** *pl* **:** the openwork metal floors and platforms of an engine room and boiler room in a ship **3 :** a system of close equidistant and parallel lines or bars (as ruled on a polished surface) used for producing spectra by diffraction

grat·ing·ly *adv* [fr. pres. part. of ³*grate* + *-ly*] **:** with a grating sound or effect **:** so as to grate ⟨his voice fell ~ on our ears⟩

gra·ti·o·la \grə'tīələ, -tēə-\ *n, cap* [NL, dim. of L *gratia* grace; fr. its alleged healing qualities — more at GRACE] **:** a genus of small widely distributed herbs (family Scrophulariaceae) with opposite sessile leaves and usu. two bracts at the base of the calyx — see HEDGE HYSSOP

gratis \'gra|d·ǝs, -rā|, |tǝs\ *adv (or adj)* [ME, fr. L *gratis*, *gratiis*, ablative pl. of *gratia* favor, kindness — more at GRACE] **:** without charge or recompense **:** FREE — often used in combination as an intensive ⟨got it free ~⟩ ⟨free ~ for nothing⟩

grat·i·tude \'grad·ə,tüd, -at|, |ə,tyüd\ *n* -s [ME (Sc dial.), fr. MF or ML; MF, fr. ML *gratitudo*, fr. L *gratus* pleasing, thankful + *-i-* + *-tudo* -tude — more at GRACE] **1** *obs* **:** FAVOR, GIFT, GRATUITY **2 :** the state of being grateful **:** warm and friendly feeling toward a benefactor prompting one to repay a favor **:** THANKFULNESS ⟨let us express our ~ positively⟩

grat·on·ite \'grat°n,īt\ *n* -s [Louis C. *Graton* b1880 Am. geologist + E *-ite*] **:** a mineral $Pb_9As_4S_{15}$ consisting of sulfide of lead and arsenic in rhombohedral crystals

grat·tage \grä'täzh, grə'-\ *n* -s [F, fr. *gratter* to scratch, scrape (fr. MF *grater*) + *-age* — more at GRATE] **:** the removal of granulations (as in trachoma) by scraping or by friction

grat·ten *or* **grat·ton** \'grat°n\ *n* -s [origin unknown] *dial Eng* **:** a stubble field **:** STUBBLE

grat·ters \'gratəz\ *n pl* [by alter.] *Brit* **:** CONGRATULATIONS

grat·toir \(')gra¦twär, -at-¦w-\ *n* -s [F, fr. *gratter* to scratch, scrape, fr. MF *grater* — more at GRATE] **:** THUMB FLINT

gratuital *adj* [L *gratuitus* + E *-al*] *obs* **:** GRATUITOUS

gra·tu·i·tous \grə'tüəd·|əs, grə·'tyü-, -üət|\ *adj* [L *gratuitus*, fr. *gratus* pleasing, grateful — more at GRACE] **1 a :** given freely or without recompense **:** granted without pay or without claim or merit ⟨the ~ blessings of Heaven —Roger L'Estrange⟩ **b :** costing the recipient or participant nothing **:** FREE ⟨homemade fun is ~ —Aldous Huxley⟩ **c :** not involving a return benefit, compensation, or consideration — opposed to *onerous;* see GRATUITOUS BAILMENT, GRATUITOUS CONTRACT **2 :** not called for by the circumstances ⟨a ~ insult⟩ **:** adopted or asserted without good ground ⟨a ~ assumption⟩ — **gra·tu·i·tous·ly** *adv* — **gra·tu·i·tous·ness** *n* -ES

gratuitous bailment *n* **:** a bailment for the sole benefit of the bailor

gratuitous contract *n* **:** a contract for the sole benefit of one of the parties

gra·tu·i·ty \|ē, |i\ *n* -ES [MF *gratuité*, fr. L *gratuitus* + MF *-té* -ty] **1 a :** graciousness esp. of manner or conduct **:** courteous consideration ⟨her manner completely lacking in ~⟩ **b :** an act of graciousness **:** a graceful courtesy ⟨all sorts of little *gratuities* of behavior —Elizabeth Bowen⟩ **2 :** something given voluntarily or over and above what is due usu. in return for or in anticipation of some service: as **a** *chiefly Brit* (1) **:** a cash sum given a soldier when he reenlists, retires, or is honorably discharged (2) **:** a lump sum paid in addition to pension to a retiring employee esp. under civil service **b :** ⁸TIP **c :** a payment intended to influence a person in the payer's behalf usu. improperly **:** BRIBE **d :** a payment made to a released convict in order to help him reestablish himself in society and sometimes in lieu of wages for labor performed in prison **e :** DEATH BENEFIT **3** *obs* **:** payment made or due for services **:** WAGES **4 :** the quality or state of being gratuitous

grat·u·lant \'grachələnt\ *adj* [L *gratulant-*, *gratulans*, pres. part. of *gratulari*] **:** showing gratification **:** CONGRATULATORY

¹**grat·u·late** \-,lāt\ *vb* -ED/-ING/-S [L *gratulatus*, past part. of *gratulari*, fr. *gratus* pleasing, thankful — more at GRACE] *vt* **1** *archaic* **:** to salute with declarations of joy **:** CONGRATULATE **2** *obs* **:** to show thankfulness for or to **:** GRATIFY, REPAY, RECOMPENSE ~ *vi, archaic* **:** to express sympathetic pleasure or satisfaction

²**gratulate** *adj* [L *gratulatus*, past part.] *obs* **:** GRATIFYING, PLEASING

grat·u·la·tion \,grachə'lāshən\ *n* -s [ME *gratulacyon*, fr. L *gratulation-*, *gratulatio*, fr. *gratulatus* + *-ion-*, *-io* -ion] **1 a :** GRATIFICATION, SATISFACTION, PLEASURE **b :** expression of gratification (as by ceremonial rejoicings) — usu. used in pl. **2 a :** CONGRATULATION **b :** words of congratulation **:** a congratulatory address **3** *obs* **a :** expression of gratitude **:** THANKS **b :** REWARD

grat·u·la·to·ri·ly \¦grachələ¦tōrəlē\ *adv* **:** in a gratulatory manner **:** with gratulation

grat·u·la·to·ry \'ˌˌˌˌ,tōrē\ *adj* [LL *gratulatorius*, fr. L *gratulatus* + *-orius* -ory] **:** expressing or characterized by gratulation; *esp* **:** CONGRATULATORY

grau·pel \'graùpəl\ *n* -s [G, dim. of *graupe* peeled grain, groat, prob. of Slavic origin; akin to Pol, Slovak, Serbo-Croatian, Russ, & Ukr *krupa* peeled grain, groat; akin to OE *hrēof* rough, scabby, leprous — more at DANDRUFF] **:** granular snow pellets — called also *soft hail*

grau·stark \'graù,stärk, 'gró,s-\ *n* -s *usu cap* [fr. *Graustark*, an imaginary country in the romantic novel *Graustark* (1901) by George B. McCutcheon †1928 Am. novelist] **1 :** an imaginary place of high romance ⟨a *Graustark* located on the old Spanish invasion route where the Christians and Moslems fought it out in the Dark and Middle Ages —Alva Johnston⟩ **2** [fr. the novel *Graustark*] **:** a highly romantic piece of writing ⟨his trip through the West had a coloration of *Graustark* —Bernard DeVoto⟩ ⟨pure *Graustark* —Wolcott Gibbs⟩ — **grau·stark·ian** \(')ˌˌ¦stärkēən\ *adj, usu cap*

gra·va·men \grə'vāmən, -'vām-; 'gravəm-, 'gravəm-\ *n, pl* **gravamens** \-nz\ *or* **gra·vam·i·na** \-'vamənə, -'vām-, -'vām-\ [LL, fr. L *gravare* to burden, fr. *gravis* heavy — more at GRIEVE] **:** GRIEVANCE: as **a** *obs* **:** a formal complaint **b :** a grievance laid in convocation by the lower house before the upper house; *also* **:** the writing embodying it **c :** the material part or basis (as of a grievance or charge)

gravaminous *adj* [LL *gravamin-*, *gravamen* + E *-ous*] *obs* **:** OPPRESSIVE, GRIEVOUS

gra·vat \'gravət\ *chiefly Scot var of* CRAVAT

grav·a·ta \¦gravə¦tä\ *n* -s [Pg *gravatá*, *caravatá*, fr. Tupi *caravatá*, *curuwatá*] **:** a tough resistant cordage fiber obtained from the leaves of a So. American bromeliad (*Ananas sagenaria*) that is closely related to the cultivated pineapple

¹**grave** \'grāv\ *vb* **graved** \-vd\ **grav·en** \-vən\ *or* **graved; graving; graves** [ME *graven*, fr. OE *grafan;* akin to OHG & Goth *graban* to dig, ON *grafa*, OSlav *pogreti* to bury] *vt* **1** *archaic* **:** DIG, EXCAVATE **2 a :** to carve out or give shape to by cutting with a chisel **:** SCULPTURE ⟨they *graved* the figure of a calf⟩ **b :** to carve or cut (as letters or figures) on some hard substance **:** ENGRAVE ⟨*graved* the date of his death on the blank space on the stone⟩ **c :** to remove (some portion of a printing surface) by cutting (as with a burin) — used with *out* ⟨~ out the redundant comma⟩ **3 :** to impress (as a thought) deeply **:** fix indelibly ⟨you could do worse than ~ his noble words in your mind⟩ ~ *vi* **1** *archaic* **:** EXCAVATE, DIG **2 a :** CARVE 2 **b :** to practice engraving

²**grave** \"\ *n* -s [ME, fr. OE *græf;* akin to OHG *grab* grave, ON *gröf;* derivatives fr. the root of OE *grafan* to dig] **1 a :** an excavation in the earth for use as a place of burial; *broadly* **:** a place of interment **:** TOMB, SEPULCHER **b :** a final ending (as by death or destruction) ⟨the ~ comes to all men⟩ ⟨the ~ of all our hopes⟩ **2 a** *obs* **:** an excavated pit, ditch, or trench **b** *now dial Eng* **:** a storage clamp; *esp* **:** one dug partly into the ground

³**grave** \"\ *n* -s [ME, fr. MD *grāve*, *grēve* — more at BURGRAVE] **1** *obs* **:** STEWARD, OVERSEER **2 :** a former elective township officer in Yorkshire and Lincolnshire, England

⁴**grave** \"\ *vt* -ED/-ING/-S [ME *graven*] **:** to clean (the bottom of a wooden ship) of encrusting growths and treat with pitch — see GRAVING DOCK

⁵**grave** \", *in sense 6* " *or* 'gräv *or* 'gräv\ *adj* -ER/-EST [MF, fr. L *gravis* heavy — more at GRIEVE] **1 a** *obs, of a person* **:** occupying a position of consequence and dignity **b** *obs* **:** based on knowledge and understanding **:** AUTHORITATIVE **c :** deserving serious consideration or thought **:** IMPORTANT, WEIGHTY ⟨a ~ issue⟩ **d** (1) **:** involving or resulting in serious consequences **:** likely to produce real harm or damage ⟨a ~ wrong⟩ ⟨ran a very ~ risk⟩ (2) **:** very serious **:** dangerous to life — used of an illness or its prospects ⟨a ~ disease⟩ ⟨a ~ prognosis⟩ **2 :** having a serious, sedate, and dignified appearance or demeanor ⟨watching his ~ face⟩ ⟨a ~ man little given to anger⟩ **3** *archaic* **:** of great weight **:** HEAVY **4 :** dull in color **:** SOMBER, SOBER, DRAB ⟨the ~ plain dress of the countryfolk⟩ **5** *of a sound* **:** low in pitch — contrasted with *acute* **6 a** *of an accent mark* **:** having the form ` **b :** marked with a grave accent ⟨a ~ *e* in caffè⟩ **c :** of the variety indicated by a grave accent ⟨a ~ intonation⟩ **syn** see SERIOUS

⁶**grave** \'gräv, -ä-,-à-\ *n* -s **:** a grave accent used to show that a vowel is pronounced with a fall of pitch (as in ancient Greek), that a vowel has a certain quality (as over *e* in French), that a final *e* is stressed and close and that a final *o* is stressed and open (as in Italian), that a syllable has a degree of stress between maximum and minimum (as in phonetic transcription), or that the *e* of the English ending *-ed* is in a line of poetry not silent but is to be pronounced \ə\ for the sake of the meter (as in "this cursèd day")

⁷**gra·ve** \'grä(,)vā, -rā(-\ *adv (or adj)* [It, heavy, grave, fr. L *gravis*] **:** slowly and solemnly — used as a direction in music

grave blanket *n* [²*grave*] **:** a grave covering that consists of evergreen plant material on a flexible wire frame and that is used chiefly in winter

grave box *n, dial* **:** COFFIN 2

gravecloth \'ˌ,ˌ\ *n* **:** SUDARIUM

graveclothes \'ˌ,ˌ\ *n pl* **:** the clothes in which a dead person is buried

graved *past of* GRAVE

gravedigger \'ˌ,ˌˌ\ *n* **1 a :** one that digs graves esp. as a means of livelihood **b :** one that is responsible for the end of something ⟨~s of modern civilization⟩ **2 a :** BURYING BEETLE **b** an Asiatic ratel (*Mellivora indica*)

gra·ve·do \grə'vē(,)dō\ *n* [L, fr. *gravis* heavy — more at GRIEVE] *archaic* **:** cold in the head

grave goods *n pl* **:** objects (as weapons, ornaments, tools) that are found buried with the dead in prehistoric graves

¹**grav·el** \'gravəl\ *n* -s *often attrib* [ME, fr. MF *gravele*, fr. OF, dim. of *grave*, *greve* pebbly ground, pebbly shore, perh. of Celt origin; akin to MBret *grouanenn* sand, W *gro* — more at GRIT] **1** *obs* **:** SAND **2 a :** loose or unconsolidated material consisting wholly or chiefly of rounded fragments of rock ranging in size from 2 millimeters to a meter or more in diameter — compare CONGLOMERATE, SAND **b :** a stratum of such material or a surface (as of a walk) covered with such material **3 :** a light grayish yellowish brown that is yellower and paler than almond brown and stronger than Cuban sand — called also *meerschaum* **4 a :** a deposit of small calculous concretions in the kidneys and urinary bladder **b :** the condition of having such a deposit

²**gravel** \"\ *vb* **graveled** *or* **gravelled; graveled** *or* **gravelled; graveling** *or* **gravelling** \-v(ə)liŋ\ **gravels** *vt* **1 :** to cover or spread with gravel **2 a :** to put at a loss **:** PERPLEX, CONFUSE, NONPLUS ⟨completely ~*ed* by his sister's reasoning⟩ **b :** IRRITATE, ANNOY, EMBARRASS, BOTHER ⟨those recurrent minor frictions that ~ the soul⟩ ⟨used to ~ her by saying that no great poet ever had such a loyal friend —Christopher Morley⟩ **3 :** to lame (a horse) by gravel lodged between the shoe and foot ~ *vi* **1** *dial* **:** to dig in gravel ⟨a dog ~*ing* for a bone⟩ **2** *of a bird* **:** to replenish the crop with gravel **3** *of rock* **:** to wear down to gravel

³**gravel** \"\ *adj* **:** harsh and usu. irritating — used chiefly of the human voice

gravel-bind \'ˌˌ,ˌ\ *n* **:** FIELD BINDWEED

gravel-blind \'ˌˌ,ˌ\ *adj* **:** having very weak vision **:** being almost blind — compare SAND-BLIND

gravel chickweed *n* **:** KNAWEL

gravel culture *n* **:** the growing of plants in an artificial medium using fine gravel to support the roots and supplying mineral nutrients in an aqueous solution

grave·less \'grāvləs\ *adj* [²*grave* + *-less*] **:** lacking a grave: **a :** lacking usual interment **:** UNBURIED ⟨these ~ bones⟩ **b :** not requiring graves **:** DEATHLESS ⟨the ~ home of the blessed⟩

gravel-grass \'ˌˌ,ˌ\ *n* **:** CLEAVERS

grav·el·ish \'grav(ə)lish\ *adj* **:** somewhat gravelly **:** resembling or containing an admixture of gravel ⟨a barren ~ soil⟩

grav·el·li·ness \-lēnəs, -lin-\ *n* -ES **:** the quality or state of being gravelly

grav·el·ly \-lē, -li\ *adj* [ME *gravely*, fr. ¹*gravel* + *-ly*] **1 :** abounding with, consisting of, or containing gravel ⟨a ~ soil⟩ **2 :** like or caused by gravel (sense 4) ⟨a ~ paroxysm⟩ **3 :** harsh and usu. irritating or unpleasant **:** GRAVEL — used esp. of the human voice

gravel plant *n* **:** ARBUTUS 3

gravelrash \'ˌˌ,ˌ\ *n* **:** abrasion of the skin by gravel or other rough surface

gravel roofing *n* **:** built-up roofing covered with gravel embedded in a bituminous surface

gravelroot \'ˌˌ,ˌ\ *n* **1 :** MARSH MILKWEED **2 :** HORSE BALM 1

gravel stop *n* **:** a metal flashing shape attached to roof structure to protect the roof edge against water penetration and to contain a built-up roof and prevent its gravel surface from falling over the roof edge

gravelweed \'ˌˌ,ˌ\ *n* **1 :** an American herb (*Verbesina helianthoides*) **2 :** BUSH HONEYSUCKLE 1 **3 :** CLEAVERS **4 :** a false gromwell (*Onosmodium virginicum*)

grave·ly \'grāvlē, -li\ *adv* [⁵*grave* + *-ly*] **1 :** in a grave manner **:** with sober serious mien ⟨thanked him ~⟩ ⟨quietly and ~ reviewing our situation⟩ **2 :** to a grave degree **:** so as to cause distress, harassment, suffering **:** SERIOUSLY ⟨a ~ impaired heart⟩ ⟨in the midst of plenty millions of people remain ~ underfed⟩

grave marker *n* **:** a marker (as of metal or stone) placed on a grave to identify the person buried there

gra·ve·men·te \,grävə'men·(,)tā\ *adv* [It, adv. of *grave* heavy, grave — more at GRAVE] **:** GRAVE — used as a direction in music

grave mixture *n* [⁵*grave*] **:** a compound pipe-organ stop sounding the lower harmonics and somber in effect

graven *past part of* GRAVE

grave·ness \'grāvnəs\ *n* -ES [⁵*grave* + *-ness*] **:** the quality or state of being grave **:** SOBERNESS, SEDATENESS, SERIOUSNESS

graven image *n* [ME] **:** an object of worship carved usu. from wood or stone **:** IDOL

graveolence *also* **graveolency** *n, pl* **graveolences** *also* **graveolencies** [L *graveolentia*, fr. *graveolent-*, *graveolens* + *-ia* -y] *obs* **:** a strong and offensive smell

gra·ve·o·lent \grə'vēələnt\ *adj* [L *graveolent-*, *graveolens*, fr. *gravis* heavy + *olent-*, *olens*, pres. part. of *olēre* to smell — more at GRIEVE, ODOR] **:** having a rank smell

grave plant *n* [²*grave*] **:** THORN APPLE 2

grave-post \'ˌ,ˌ\ *n* **:** a post set up at a grave in memory and honor of the dead esp. among primitive peoples — compare GRAVESTONE

¹**grav·er** \'grāvə(r)\ *n* -s [ME, fr. *graven* to dig, carve, engrave + *-er* — more at GRAVE] **:** one that graves: as **a :** ENGRAVER, SCULPTOR **b :** any of various cutting or shaving tools (as an engraver's burin) used in graving or in hand metal turning **c :** a small prehistoric tool of stone or bone used for working or marking stone, bone, ivory, horn, or pottery

²**graver** *comparative of* GRAVE

grave robber *n* **:** one that breaks open a grave to obtain interred valuables or to remove the body (as for illicit dissection) **:** a body snatcher **:** GHOUL

¹**graves** *pres 3d sing of* GRAVE, *pl of* GRAVE

²**graves** \'grāvz\ *archaic var of* GREAVES

³**graves** \'gräv\ *n, pl* **graves** \-vz\ *usu cap* [fr. *Graves*, district in Gironde dept., France] **:** a red or white table wine produced in Graves, France

graves' disease \'grāvz(əz)-\ *n, usu cap G* [after Robert J. *Graves* †1853 Ir. physician] **:** HYPERTHYROIDISM; *specif* **:** EXOPHTHALMIC GOITER

graveside \'ˌ,ˌ\ *n* **:** the space beside a grave; *esp* **:** the point at which mourners gather by the grave at the time of a burial ⟨only ~ services were held⟩

gravest *superlative of* GRAVE

gravestone \'ˌ,ˌ\ *n* [ME, fr. *grave* + *stone*] **:** a stone laid over or erected near a grave and usu. bearing an inscription to identify and preserve the memory of the dead **:** TOMBSTONE

gra·vette \grə'vet\ *or* **gravette point** *n* -s [fr. La *Gravette*, France, where it was found] **:** a small sharp prehistoric flint tool consisting of a blade like that of a knife with a very sharp point, a straight back, and a groove following one entire margin

gra·vett·ian \grə'ved·ēən\ *adj, usu cap* [La *Gravette*, rock shelter in the Couze valley of the Dordogne, France + E *-ian*] **:** of or relating to an Upper Paleolithic culture widespread in Europe and typified by a narrow pointed-blade tool with a straight blunted back edge

grave·ward \'grāvwə(r)d\ *or* **grave·wards** \-dz\ *adv (or adj)* [²*grave* + *-ward*, *-wards*] **:** toward or directed toward the grave

grave wax *n, archaic* **:** ADIPOCERE

graveyard \'ˌ,ˌ\ *n, often attrib* [²*grave* + *yard*] **1 :** a yard or enclosure for the interment of the dead **:** CEMETERY **2 a :** an organization or situation that brings something to an end ⟨the Ministry of Agriculture (that ~ of English political reputations) —Roy Lewis & Angus Maude⟩ ⟨a bill lost in one of the ~ committees of the legislature⟩ **b :** a place where disused, obsolete, or worn-out equipment is stored or held in reserve for emergency use; *esp* **:** a yard where old automobiles are stored or broken up for parts and scrap **3 a :** a melancholy and romantically gloomy place ⟨a ~ school of poetry⟩ **b :** a dull or unpleasing place

graveyard shift *n* **:** a work shift beginning late at night (as 12 o'clock) and being usu. the third and last of a business day; *also* **:** the workers on such a shift

graveyard stew *n, slang* **:** toast and milk

graveyard vote *n* **:** a vote improperly cast in the name of a person who has died or who is ineligible (as by having moved away) to vote

graveyard watch *n* **1 :** MIDWATCH **2 :** GRAVEYARD SHIFT

graveyard weed *also* **graveyard spurge** *n* **:** CYPRESS SPURGE

gravi- *comb form* [MF, fr. L, fr. *gravis* — more at GRIEVE] **:** heavy ⟨*gravi*grade⟩ ⟨*gravi*portal⟩

gravi·cembalo \,gravə, -rävə+\ *n, pl* **gravicembali** [It, alter. (influenced by *grave* heavy, grave) of *clavicembalo* — more at CLAVICEMBALO] **:** HARPSICHORD

grav·id \'gravəd\ *adj* [L *gravidus*, fr. *gravis* heavy — more at GRAVE] **1 a :** PREGNANT ⟨a ~ woman⟩; *esp* **:** distended by pregnancy ⟨the ~ uterus⟩ **b :** full of eggs ⟨a ~ tapeworm proglottid⟩ **:** having the body distended with ripe eggs ⟨stripping the eggs from ~ salmon⟩ **2 :** FILLED, DISTENDED — usu. followed by *with* ⟨physics is ~ with metaphysics —V.C. Aldrich⟩ ⟨~ with middle-class proprieties⟩ **3 :** awaiting or indicating the approach of something (as an ominous or distressing event) **:** PORTENTOUS ⟨clouds . . . going from white at the blue-sky edge to a ~ indigo —T.H.White b.1906⟩ — **grav·id·ly** *adv* — **grav·id·ness** *n* -ES

grav·i·da \'gravədə\ *n, pl* **gravidas** \-dəz\ *also* **gravi·dae** \-,dē\ [L, fr. fem. of *gravidus*] **:** a pregnant woman — often used in combination with a term or figure to indicate the number of pregnancies a woman has had ⟨a 4-*gravida*⟩ ⟨a ~ four⟩ ⟨a quadri*gravida*⟩; compare PARA — **gra·vid·ic** \(')gra¦vidik, grə'v-\ *adj*

gravidation *n* -s [ME *gravidacioun*, fr. LL *gravidatus* (past part. of *gravidare*, to impregnate, fr. L *gravidus*) + ME *-ioun* -ion] *obs* **:** PREGNANCY

gra·vid·i·ty \gra'vidəd·ē, grə'v-\ *n* -ES [L *graviditas*, fr. *gravidus* pregnant + *-itas* -ity] **:** PREGNANCY, PARITY

gra·vied \'grāvēd, -vid\ *adj* **:** covered or dressed with gravy ⟨~ beef and onions⟩ ⟨helped himself to another mound of well-*gravied* potatoes⟩

gravies *pl of* GRAVY

gra·vif·ic \(')gra¦vifik, grə'v-\ *adj* [*gravi-* + *-fic*] **:** able or tending to produce weight — used of a hypothetical ethereal fluid formerly postulated to explain gravitation

gra·vig·ra·da \grə'vigrədə, ,gravə'grädə\ *n pl, cap* [NL, fr. *gravi-* + *-grada* (fr. *gradi* to step, go) — more at GRADE] *in some classifications* **:** a division of the Edentata consisting of the ground sloths

grav·i·grade \'gravə,grād\ *n* [*gravi-* + *-grade*] **:** any of several large heavy-footed mammals (as an elephant); *esp* **:** GROUND SLOTH

gravilea *var of* GREVILLEA

gra·vim·e·ter \grə'vimǝd·ə(r), grə'v-, 'gravə,mēd·-\ *n* [F *gravimètre*, fr. *gravi-* + *-mètre* -meter] **1 :** a device similar to a hydrometer for determining the specific gravity of liquid or solid substances **2 :** a sensitive weighing instrument that measures the variation in the gravitational field by detecting small differences in the weight of a constant mass at different points (as on the earth or sea)

grav·i·met·ric \¦gravə¦me·trik\ *also* **grav·i·met·ri·cal** \-rəkəl\ *adj* [*gravi-* + *-metric*, *-metrical*] **1 :** of, involving, or relating to measurement by weight **:** measured by weight ⟨a ~ assay of a drug⟩ **2 :** of or relating to variations in the gravitational field determined by means of a gravimeter — **grav·i·met·ri·cal·ly** \-rək(ə)lē\ *adv*

gravimetric analysis *n* **:** chemical analysis in which the amounts of the constituents are determined by weighing

gravimetric density *n* **:** the mean density of the total contents including the air in the interstitial spaces of any volume filled with a granular substance (as gunpowder)

gra·vim·e·try \grə'vimətrē, grə'v-\ *n* -ES [*gravi-* + *-metry*] **:** the measurement of weight or density

grav·ing \'grāviŋ\ *n* -s [ME, fr. gerund of *graven* to dig, to grave — more at GRAVE] **1** *archaic* **:** the act of one that graves **2 :** something graved; *esp* **:** ENGRAVING

graving dock *n* [fr. gerund of ⁴*grave*] **:** a dry dock consisting of an enclosure openly adjoining a waterway from which it may be separated by a watertight barrier which is capable of being pumped dry when so separated and which is used esp. for cleaning the underwater parts of a ship; *broadly* **:** DRY DOCK

graving piece *n* [fr. gerund of ⁴*grave*] **:** a piece of wood for insertion in a plank of a ship to replace a defective part

graving tool *n* [fr. gerund of ¹*grave*] **:** GRAVER b

gravi·portal \¦gravə+\ *adj* [*gravi-* + *-portal* (fr. L *portare* to carry + E *-al*) — more at FARE] **:** having the body supports adapted to the bearing of great weights ⟨the elephant is a ~ mammal⟩

gravis \'gravəs, -āv-, -äv-\ *adj* [L, heavy, grave, severe — more at GRIEVE] **:** tending to be more than averagely virulent — used esp. of strains of diphtheria bacilli; compare INTERMEDIUS, MITIS

gravit- *or* **gravito-** *comb form* [ISV, fr. *gravity*] **:** gravity ⟨*gravito*chemical⟩

grav·i·tate \ˈgravə,tāt, *usu* -ād.+V\ *vb* -ED/-ING/-S [NL *gravitatus*, past part. of *gravitare*, fr. L *gravitas* weight — more at GRAVITY] *vi* **1 :** to obey the law of gravitation **:** exert a force or pressure or tend to move under the influence of gravitation **2 a :** to tend in a direction or toward an object ⟨the conversation *gravitated* toward politics⟩ **b :** to move casually but inexorably as though under an external force ⟨the boys *gravitated* together while the girls sat waiting⟩ **:** become attracted ⟨as children ~ toward home at dusk⟩ ~ *vt* **:** to move by gravitation: as **a :** to agitate (as gravel in diamond mining) so that the weighty parts settle to the bottom **b :** to cause or allow to flow by gravity ⟨the oil is *gravitated* through a pipeline⟩

grav·i·tat·er \-ād.ə(r)\ *n* -S **:** one that gravitates

grav·i·ta·tion \,gravəˈtāshən\ *n* -S [NL *gravitation-, gravitatio*, fr. *gravitatus* + L *-ion-, -io* -ion] **1 :** an action or a process of gravitating ⟨delivery of irrigation water under ~⟩ **2 :** a tendency toward or state of being drawn to something ⟨universal ~ to quantitative, statistical, numerical description —Hugh Miller b. 1891⟩ **3 :** a force manifested by acceleration toward each other of two free material particles or bodies or of radiant-energy quanta as if they were particles (as in the bending of rays of starlight passing close to the sun), these effects being attributed in relativity theory to the physical property of space according to which moving bodies follow minimum space-time tracks that are sensibly concave toward nearby massive bodies and that apparently constrain the motions of smaller bodies encompassed by them **:** an attraction between two bodies that is proportional to the product of their masses, inversely proportional to the square of the distance between them, and independent of their chemical nature or physical state and of intervening matter

grav·i·ta·tion·al \¦≈≈ˈtashənᵊl, -shnəl\ *adj* **:** of, relating to, or caused by gravitation ⟨sufficient energy to escape from the sun's ~ field —J.G.Davies⟩ — **grav·i·ta·tion·al·ly** \-ᵊlē, -əlē, li\ *adv*

gravitational astronomy *n* **:** CELESTIAL MECHANICS

gravitational constant *n* **:** CONSTANT OF GRAVITATION

gravitational field *n* **:** a region associated with any distribution of mass in which gravitational forces due to that mass may be detected

gravitational intensity *n* **:** a vector quantity related to the condition at any point under gravitational influence the measure of which is the gravitational force exerted upon a unit mass placed at the point in question — compare GRAVITATIONAL POTENTIAL

gravitational potential *n* **:** the scalar quantity characteristic of a point in a gravitational field whose gradient equals the intensity of the field and equal to the work required to move a body of unit mass from given point to a point infinitely remote

gravitational system *n* **:** a system of physical units based upon a unit of force that is the weight of a unit mass under a specified standard of gravity

gravitational water *n* **:** FREE WATER c

grav·i·ta·tive \ˈgravə,tād|iv, -,tə|, |t|, |ēv\ *adj* **:** of, caused by, or relating to gravity or gravitation ⟨high mountains on the borders of the present continents, through their local ~ attraction, raise the sea level on their borders —P.G. Worcester⟩

grav·i·tom·e·ter \,gravəˈtämәd.ə(r)\ *n* [*gravit-* + *-meter*] **:** a direct-reading instrument for the measurement of specific gravities of solids, liquids, or gases

¹grav·i·ty \ˈgravəd.ē, -ətē, -i\ *n* -ES [MF or L; MF *gravité*, fr. L *gravitat-, gravitas*, fr. *gravis* heavy, grave + *-tat-, -tas* -ty — more at GRIEVE] **1 :** the quality or state of being grave: as **a :** sobriety or seriousness of character or demeanor ⟨men of ~ and learning —Shak.⟩ **b :** IMPORTANCE, SIGNIFICANCE, DIGNITY; *esp* **:** SERIOUSNESS ⟨the ~ of an offense⟩ **c** *obs* **:** INFLUENCE, AUTHORITATIVENESS **d** *obs* — used as a title of respect or honor **e :** SOLEMNITY ⟨the ~ of the ceremony⟩ **2** *archaic* **:** something serious **:** a matter of importance **3 :** PONDERABILITY **4 :** WEIGHT, HEAVINESS — now used chiefly in the phrase *center of gravity* **5** [NL *gravitas*, fr. L] **a :** terrestrial gravitation **:** the gravitational attraction of the earth's mass for bodies at or near its surface as modified by the centrifugal force due to the earth's rotation; *broadly* **:** GRAVITATION **b :** ACCELERATION OF GRAVITY **c :** SPECIFIC GRAVITY

²gravity \"\ *adj* **1 :** using gravity **:** working or operated by gravity ⟨~ irrigation⟩ **2 :** utilizing thermal convection currents instead of a fluid circulated by mechanical means ⟨a ~ hot-air heating system⟩ ⟨~ ventilation⟩

gravity anomaly *n* **:** a difference between the locally observed and the theoretically calculated value of gravity that reflects local variations in density of underlying rocks and is often helpful in geophysical prospecting

gravity band *n* **:** BALANCING BAND

gravity cell *n* **:** a voltaic cell with a zinc electrode in zinc sulfate solution at the top and a copper electrode in copper sulfate solution at the bottom, the two liquids being kept from mixing by difference in specific gravity

gravity dam *n* **:** a dam so proportioned that it will resist overturning and sliding forces by its own weight

gravity fault *n* **:** NORMAL FAULT

gravity feed *n* **:** the supplying of a material (as oil to a bearing or gasoline to a carburetor) by gravity alone; *also* **:** a device or system for such supplying ⟨a carburetor with a *gravity feed*⟩

gravity hinge *n* **:** a hinge used esp. with shutters or blinds that because of gravity locks in the open position

gravity knife *n* **:** a switchblade knife in which the blade is sprung by a downward snap of the wrist

gravity meter *n* **:** GRAVIMETER 2

gravity railroad *or* **gravity railway** *n* **:** a railroad on which the cars run by gravity down slopes after being hauled up shorter but steeper inclines by stationary engines

gravity spring *n* **:** a spring in which the water issues solely in response to the direct action of gravity

gravity wave *n* **:** a wave propagated in the surface layers of water or other liquid because of the tendency of gravity to maintain a uniform level; *also* **:** a wave in a fluid (as the atmosphere) in which gravity is the restoring force

gravity wind *n* **:** a katabatic wind

gravity yard *n* **:** HUMP YARD

gra·vure \grəˈvyu̇(ə)r, grāˈv-, -u̇ə\ *n* -S [F, fr. *graver* to engrave (fr. MF, of Gmc origin; akin to OHG *graban* to dig, engrave) + *-ure* — more at GRAVE] **1 a :** a process for producing an intaglio printing plate on wood, copper, or other material (as by means of a burin) ⟨the process of ~, including in that generic term all forms of art which get their effect from the incision of a groove on some resistant material . . . thus includes drypoint and mezzotint, burin engraving and all forms of etching —Herbert Read⟩ — often used in combination **b :** a plate made by such a process or a print from it **2** [by shortening] **:** PHOTOGRAVURE

gra·vy \ˈgrāvē, -vi\ *n* -ES *often attrib* [ME *gravey, grave*, fr. MF *gravé*] **1 a** *obs* **:** a dressing for fish or other seafood or for vegetables usu. consisting of the liquid (as beer or wine) in which the food is cooked together with pulverized almonds and spices **b :** the juices that exude from meat during or after cooking esp. when thickened (as with flour) and seasoned for use as a sauce ⟨a helping of potatoes and ~⟩ ⟨a rich turkey ~⟩ **c :** any of several thickened sauces (as milk gravy) served esp. with meat or potatoes **d** *dial* **:** a savory juice (as from a berry pie) esp. when suitable for sopping **2 a :** something pleasing or valuable that occurs or is acquired over and above what would ordinarily be expected ⟨such a job is pure ~⟩ **b :** unforeseen profits or income **:** profits from special or unexpected sources **:** WINDFALL **c** *slang* **:** improper profits or a source of such profits (as political patronage or graft) **3** — used in the phrases *by gravy* and *good gravy* as a mild oath

gravy boat *n* **:** a low boat-shaped pitcher usu. with a long lip at one end and a handle at the other and often with a footed base or a separate or attached tray that is used chiefly for serving gravies and sauces — called also *sauceboat*

gravy train *also* **gravy boat** *n, slang* **:** a situation providing abnormal or excessive profits, advantages, or benefits for those occupying it usu. at the expense of some larger group

¹gray *or* **grey** \ˈgrā\ *adj* -ER/-EST [ME, fr. OE *grǣg*; akin to OHG *grāo* gray, ON *grār*, OSlav *zĭrěti* to see, look] **1 a :** of the color gray **:** of a color formed by a blending of white and black **b :** tending toward gray ⟨a *gray*-red⟩ **c :** dull in color **:** lacking brightness ⟨a ~ cloudy day⟩ **d** *of textiles* **:** being in an unbleached undyed state as taken from the loom **:** UNFINISHED ⟨finisher of ~ goods⟩ **2 a :** having the hair gray **:** HOARY ⟨a ~ old man⟩ **b :** ELDERLY, MATURE **:** characteristic of age ⟨~ wisdom⟩ **3 a :** clothed in gray **:** wearing a gray costume **b** *of an animal* **:** having a coat of mingled black and white hairs **4 :** lacking cheer or brightness ⟨a dim ~ report⟩ **:** dull in mood or outlook ⟨the ~ office routine⟩ **:** DISMAL, MISERABLE ⟨~ prospects of success⟩ **5 :** intermediate in position, condition, or character; *esp, of a marketing method* **:** evading the spirit of legal controls without being overtly illegal — **gray·ly** *or* **grey·ly** *adv*

²gray *or* **grey** \"\ *n* -S [ME, fr. *gray, grey*, adj.] **1 :** an animal or thing of gray color (as a horse, garment, cloth, spot) **2 a** *obs* **:** gray fur prob. of the badger **b** *archaic* **:** BADGER **3 a :** a color formed by blending black and white **b :** one of the series of neutral or achromatic object colors ranging between black and white and characteristically perceived to belong to objects that reflect diffusely to the same degree all parts of the spectrum **c :** an object color of low saturation **4** *slang Brit* **:** a halfpenny with both sides the same used by sharpers

³gray *or* **grey** \"\ *vb* -ED/-ING/-S [¹*gray, grey*] *vt* **:** to make or cause to become or appear gray or grayish ⟨~ the paint with a little lampblack⟩ ⟨~*ed* her mother's hair with worry⟩ ⟨clouds ~*ing* the sky⟩ ~ *vi* **:** to become gray

gray alder *n* **:** an alder (*Alnus incana*) that is native to Europe but introduced into and often an escape in No. America and that has whitish gray bark and doubly toothed leaves with the undersurface whitish and often heavily pubescent

gray antimony *n* **:** STIBNITE

grayback \ˈ≈,≈\ *n* **1 :** a Confederate soldier **2 :** any of various animals: as **a :** GRAY WHALE **b :** ³KNOT **c :** DOWITCHER **d :** SCAUP DUCK **e :** BODY LOUSE **f :** LAKE HERRING **3** *dial* **a :** a very large wave **b :** a large boulder

grayback beetle *n* **:** a large Australian scarab beetle (*Lepidoderma albohirtum*) having larvae that destroy sugarcane roots

graybeard \ˈ≈,≈\ *n* **1 :** one whose beard is gray; *specif* **:** an old man ⟨~*s* sunning themselves on marble steps —*Atlantic*⟩ **2 :** BELLARMINE **3** [so called fr. the feathery seed vessels that suggest gray hair or beard] *dial Eng* **:** VIRGIN'S BOWER

graybeard tree *n* **:** FRINGE TREE

gray birch *n* **1 :** AMERICAN GRAY BIRCH **2 :** WESTERN PAPER BIRCH **3 :** YELLOW BIRCH

gray bird *n* **:** any of numerous birds with more or less gray plumage: as **a :** any of several American finches; *esp* **:** JUNCO **b :** an immature swan in gray plumage **c :** any of several cuckoo shrikes of the southwest Pacific

gray blight *n* **:** a very common disease of the tea plant esp. in India and Ceylon that is caused by a fungus (*Pestalozzia theae*) which produces black dots on the leaves

gray body *n* **:** a body that emits radiant energy and has the same relative spectral energy distribution as a blackbody at the same temperature but in smaller amount

gray box *n* **:** any of several gray-barked Australian eucalypts (as *Eucalyptus hemiphloia* and *E. bicolor*)

gray brant *n* **:** WHITE-FRONTED GOOSE

gray-brown podzolic soil *n* **:** any of a group of zonal soils developed under deciduous forest in a temperate moist climate and characterized by a comparatively thin organic covering and an organic-mineral layer above a grayish brown leached layer which in turn rests upon an illuvial brown horizon

gray cast iron *n* **:** GRAY IRON

gray-cheeked thrush \ˈ≈,chēk(t)-\ *n* **:** a thrush (*Hylocichla minima*) of No. America

graycoat \ˈ≈,≈\ *n* **:** one that wears a gray coat (as a Confederate soldier in the American Civil War)

gray cobalt *n* **:** SMALTITE

gray column *n* **:** COLUMN 6c(3)

gray copper *or* **gray copper ore** *n* **:** TETRAHEDRITE

gray crane *n* **:** the common crane (*Grus grus*) of Europe and Asia

gray-crown *n* **:** HOODED CROW 1

gray-crowned babbler \ˈ≈,≈-\ *n* **:** an Australian babbler (*Pomatostomus temporalis*) largely dark to sooty brown with chestnut breast, white throat and tail tip, and a grayish white streak over each eye

gray cutting *n* **:** the decoration of glass with incised designs that are left unpolished to give a frosted or grayish effect

gray dawn *n* **:** ZINC 2

gray dipper *n* **:** the American water ouzel (*Cinclus mexicanus*)

gray dogwood *n* **:** an erect white fruited gray-twigged dogwood (*Cornus racemosa*) of northeastern No. America

gray drab *n* **:** QUAKER GRAY

gray drum *n* **:** BLACK DRUM

gray duck *n* **:** any of various ducks having more or less gray plumage: as **a :** GADWALL **b :** the female mallard **c :** PINTAIL 1 **d :** the black duck (*Anas superciliosa*) of Australia and New Zealand

grayed \ˈgrād\ *adj* **:** DULLED, DIMMED, DIMINISHED — used chiefly of colors

gray eminence *n* [trans. of F *éminence grise* — more at ÉMINENCE GRISE] **:** a person that exercises power behind the scenes

grayer *comparative of* GRAY

grayest *superlative of* GRAY

gray eye *n* **:** ocular lymphomatosis of the chicken

gray-faced \ˈ≈¦≈\ *adj* **1 :** having the face gray ⟨*gray-faced* ewes⟩ **2 :** having the face dull, drawn, and worn (as from grief or fatigue)

gray falcon *n* **1 :** PEREGRINE FALCON **2 :** HEN HARRIER

grayfish \ˈ≈,≈\ *n* **1 :** POLLACK; *esp* **:** a young pollack **2 :** DOGFISH — used esp. as a market name

gray fox *n* **:** a No. American fox (*Urocyon cinereoargenteus*) with a coarse grizzled or yellowish gray outer coat, a long full tail, furry soles of the feet, and elliptical pupils in the eyes that is most common in the southeastern U.S.

gray friar *often cap G&F, var of* GREY FRIAR

gray goldenrod *n* **:** a dyer's-weed (*Solidago nemoralis*)

gray goose *n* **:** any of various gray or grayish geese: as **a :** GREYLAG **b :** CANADA GOOSE

gray grunt *n* **:** a silvery dark-striped grunt (*Haemulon macrostomum*) of the tropical western Atlantic

gray gum *n* **:** any of several Australian eucalypts (as *Eucalyptus propinqua, E. tereticornis*, and *E. punctata*)

gray gurnard *n* **:** a small European gurnard (*Trigla gurnardus*)

grayhead \ˈ≈,≈\ *n* **:** an elderly person

gray-headed woodpecker \ˈ≈,≈≈-\ *n* **:** a common European woodpecker (*Picus canus*) with the front of the head red, the remainder of the head and throat gray, and the upper parts of the body green

gray hen *n* [ME] **:** the female black grouse

gray horn *n* **:** COLUMN 6c(3)

grayhound *var of* GREYHOUND

graying *pres part of* GRAY

gray iron *n* **:** pig or cast iron containing much graphitic carbon which causes its fracture to be dark gray

gray ironbark *n* **:** a large eucalyptus (*Eucalyptus paniculata*) with heavy dark gray furrowed bark and very hard strong durable wood that varies in color from pale gray to chocolaty brown and is much used for heavy framing

gray·ish \ˈgrāish, -āesh\ *adj* **1 :** somewhat or moderately gray ⟨the friars wear ~ robes⟩ **2** *of a color* **:** low in saturation **:** approaching the gray scale in the object-color solid ⟨eyes of ~ blue⟩

gray jay *n* **:** a Canada jay (*Perisoreus canadensis griseus*) of western No. America resembling but larger and grayer than the typical Canada jay; *broadly* **:** CANADA JAY

gray jumper *n* **:** APOSTLE BIRD b

gray kangaroo *n* **:** GIANT KANGAROO

gray kingbird *n* **:** a kingbird (*Tyrannus dominicensis dominicensis*) that breeds in the southeastern U.S. and winters in Mexico and Central America and is similar to but larger than the eastern kingbird

gray lady *n, usu cap G&L* [so called fr. the gray uniform worn on duty] **:** a volunteer worker of the American Red Cross who provides nonprofessional care and services for the sick and convalescent usu. in hospitals

graylag *var of* GREYLAG

gray leaf *n* **:** GRAY SPECK

gray-leaf pine *n* **1 :** DIGGER PINE **2 :** TORREY PINE

gray leaf spot *n* **:** a disease of tomatoes caused by the fungus (*Stemphylium solani*) and characterized by regular water-soaked brown leaf spots that become gray with age

gray lemming *n* **:** a member of a genus (*Myopus*) of short-footed Old World lemmings — called also *red-backed lemming*

gray·ling \ˈgrāliŋ, -lēŋ\ *n, pl* **grayling** *also* **graylings** [ME, fr. *gray* + *-ling*] **1 :** any of several salmonoid fishes (genus *Thymallus*) related to the trouts but having a broad high dorsal fin, inhabiting cold swift streams, and valued as food and sport fishes; *esp* **:** a common European fish (*T. thymallus*) found chiefly in northern Europe and the Alps and locally in England and Scotland — see ARCTIC GRAYLING **2 :** either of two salmonoid fishes (genus *Prototroctes*) of the southern hemisphere that in many respects resemble those of the genus *Thymallus*: **a :** a fish (*P. muraena*) of Australia and Tasmania **b :** a New Zealand fish (*P. oxyrhynchus*) **3 :** any of numerous grayish or brownish butterflies of the family Satyridae

graymalkin *var of* GRIMALKIN

gray mallard *n* **:** MALLARD 1

gray manganese ore *n* **:** MANGANITE 1

gray market *n* **:** a market using irregular channels of trade or undercover methods not actually or explicitly illegal and chiefly in scarce materials at excessive prices — **gray marketeer** *n* — **gray-marketing** \ˈ≈¦≈≈≈\ *n*

gray matter *n* **1 :** neural tissue esp. of the brain and spinal cord that contains nerve-cell bodies as well as nerve fibers, has a brownish gray color, and forms most of the cortex and nuclei of the brain, the columns of the spinal cord, and the bodies of ganglia — distinguished from *white matter* **2 :** BRAINS, INTELLECT

gray minyan ware *n, usu cap M* **:** GRAYWARE

gray mold *also* **gray mold rot** *n* **1 a :** any of various fungous diseases of fruits, vegetables, or herbaceous plants characterized by a grayish color of the affected surfaces **b :** a fungus causing such a disease (as members of the genera *Botrytis* and *Cercospora*) **2 :** downy mildew of the grape

gray moss *n* **:** SPANISH MOSS

gray mullet *n* **:** a mullet of the family Mugilidae — distinguished from *red mullet*

gray nerve fiber *n* **:** a nonmedullated nerve fiber

gray·ness *or* **grey·ness** *n* -ES [ME *graynes*, fr. ¹*gray* + *-nes* -ness] **1 :** the quality or state of being gray **2 :** the impression of unrelieved gray color given to the eye by a newspaper page or a large portion of one consisting largely of body type without relief (as by headlines, boxes)

gray nun *often cap G&N, var of* GREY NUN

gray nurse *or* **gray nurse shark** *n* **:** an Australian sand shark (*Carcharias arenarius*) attaining a length of 15 feet and reputed to be a man-eater; *also* **:** a closely related Indo-Pacific shark

gray oak *n* **1 :** SCARLET OAK **2 :** RED OAK 1a **3 :** a low scrubby live oak (*Quercus grisea*) of the southwestern U.S. having dark gray furrowed bark and entire dusty gray-blue leaves

grayout \ˈ≈,≈\ *n* -S **:** a transient dimming or haziness of vision resulting from temporary impairment of cerebral circulation

gray out *vi* **:** to experience a grayout

gray parrot *n* **:** AFRICAN GRAY

graypate \ˈ≈,≈\ *n* **:** a young goldfinch (sense 1) before development of crimson head feathers

gray perch *n* **:** FRESHWATER DRUM

gray pike *n* **1 :** SAUGER **2 :** WALLEYE 4

gray pine *n* **:** any of several American pines with grayish green foliage: as **a :** DIGGER PINE **b :** a piñon (*Pinus monophylla*) **c :** JACK PINE 1

gray plover *n* **1 :** BLACK-BELLIED PLOVER **2 :** ³KNOT

gray polypody *n* **:** a No. American fern (*Polypodium polypodioides*) growing on rocks or tree trunks and having the fronds grayish and scurfy below

gray poplar *n* **:** a rapidly growing tree (*Populus canescens*) that is native to Europe but introduced and naturalized elsewhere and that has faintly lobed dentate leaves which are gray on their lower surface

gray powder *n* **:** a moist gray powder consisting essentially of finely divided mercury and chalk occas. used as a mild cathartic for children

gray rabbit *n* **:** COTTONTAIL

gray rot *n* **:** a rot caused by a gray mold (*Botrytis cinerea*)

grays *pl of* GRAY, *pres 3d sing of* GRAY

gray sage *n* **:** SILVER SAGEBRUSH

gray sassafras *n* **:** an Australian timber tree (*Cryptocarya australis*) with bright scarlet fruits

grays·by \ˈgrāzbē\ *n* -ES [origin unknown] **:** a serranid fish (*Petrometopon cruentatus*) of the tropical western Atlantic typically reddish gray with vermilion spots but sometimes darker with brown spots or pale and banded

gray scab *n* **:** a disease of willow caused by the fungus (*Sphaceloma murrayae*) and characterized by irregular somewhat raised leaf spots with grayish white centers and narrow dark brown margins often merging to form large patches

gray scale *n* **:** a series of regularly spaced tones ranging from white to black through intermediate shades of gray used as a reference scale for control purposes in both color and black-and-white photography

gray seal *n* **:** a large grayish seal (*Halichoerus gryphus*) of the north Atlantic

gray shark *n* **:** any of several grayish sharks: as **a :** SAND SHARK a **b :** REQUIN SHARK **c :** COW SHARK

gray shrew *n* **:** a common and widely distributed shrew (*Crocidura attenuata*) of southeastern Asia

gray snapper *n* **:** a long-bodied typically grayish snapper (*Lutjanus griseus*) that is a valuable food fish and widely distributed in the tropical western Atlantic

gray·son lily \ˈgrāsᵊn-\ *n, usu cap G* [fr. *Grayson* co., Ky.] **:** a bulbous herb (*Hymenocallis occidentalis*) of the southeastern U.S. with lanceolate leaves and showy white flowers

gray sour *n* **1 :** treatment (as of cotton) with dilute hydrochloric or sulfuric acid after scouring and before bleaching **2 :** the bath or solution used in the gray sour

gray speck *n* **:** a disease of oats caused by manganese deficiency and characterized by light green to grayish spots on the leaves and esp. the blades that later turn buff or light brown

gray spot *n* **1 :** GRAY SPECK **2 :** GRAY LEAF SPOT

gray squeteague *n* **:** GRAY TROUT 1

gray squirrel *n* **:** a common rather large squirrel (*Sciurus carolinensis*) that is usu. light gray but may be very dark or even black in parts of its range which includes most of eastern No. America and by introduction England where it is largely replacing the native squirrel

gray stone *n* **:** PIPING ROCK

gray trout *n* **1 :** a common weakfish (*Cynoscion regalis*) of the Atlantic coast of the U.S. **2 :** LAKE TROUT

gray ultramarine ash *n* **:** a light bluish gray

gray vervet *n* **:** GRIVET

gray·wacke \ˈgrā+,-ə\ *n* -S [trans. of G *grauwacke*] **:** a coarse sandstone or fine-grained conglomerate that is usu. dark gray and is composed of subangular to rounded fragments of quartz, feldspars, and bits of other dark-colored minerals or rocks firmly cemented

gray wagtail *n* **:** a common wagtail (*Motacilla cinerea*) of Europe and northern and central Asia having a gray back

graywall \ˈ≈,≈\ *n* [so called fr. the discoloration of the skin] **:** a disease of tomatoes prob. caused by excess sunlight and characterized by translucent grayish brown streaks or blotches on the outer surface of the fruit and browning of the vascular strands

gray walnut *n* **:** BUTTERNUT 1

gray warbler *n* **:** a small rather plainly colored warbler (*Gerygone igata*) of New Zealand

grayware \ˈ≈,≈\ *n* **1 :** ancient gray pottery; *esp* **:** a usu. undecorated ware of fine gray body and good technique found in Greece — called also *gray Minyan ware* **2 :** one-coat enameled metalware : GRANITEWARE 2

gray wedge *n* **:** a nonselective light-absorbing screen having transmittance progressively decreasing in one direction transverse to the light rays

gray whale *n* **:** a rather large whalebone whale (*Rhachianectes glaucus*) of the northern Pacific formerly much hunted though of fierce active disposition and difficult to capture

gray widgeon *n* **1 :** GADWALL **2 :** PINTAIL 1

gray wildcat *n* **:** KAFFIR CAT

gray willow *n* **1 :** SILKY WILLOW 2 **2 :** a Eurasian shrubby willow (*Salix cinerea*) with whitish tomentose twigs

gray wolf *n* **:** a timber wolf of northern and western No. America

graz \'gräts\ *adj, usu cap* [fr. *Graz*, Austria] **:** of or from the city of Graz, Austria **:** of the kind or style prevalent in Graz

graz *abbr* [It *grazioso*] graceful

¹graze \'grāz\ *vb* -ED/-ING/-S [ME *grasen*, fr. OE *grasian*, fr. *græs* grass — more at GRASS] *vi* **1 a :** to feed on growing herbage **:** crop and eat grass ⟨cattle *grazing* on the slopes⟩; *often* **:** to feed while moving along a more or less definite course ⟨the heifer slowly *grazed* out of sight⟩ ⟨antelopes *grazing* toward the water hole⟩ **b :** to feed in the manner of a grazing animal esp. by nibbling at a surface growth ⟨parrot fishes *grazed* among the coral trees⟩ **2** *dial Eng* **:** to yield herbage for grazing **3 :** to put cattle to graze ⟨we used to ~ on the upland flush in late spring⟩ **~** *vt* **1 :** to crop and eat (growing herbage) **:** feed on the herbage of (as a pasture) — compare BROWSE **2 a :** to cause or put (as cattle) to graze ⟨*grazed* his stock on the water meadow⟩ **b :** to cause or put cattle to graze on (as herbage or a pasture) ⟨*grazed* the upper field after taking an early crop of hay⟩ — often used with *down* ⟨planned to ~ down the aftermath⟩ **c** *obs* **:** to have charge of (grazing cattle) **3 :** to supply herbage for the grazing of ⟨count on that pasture to ~ 30 head during August⟩ **syn** see FEED

²graze \"\ *n* -S **1 :** an act of grazing ⟨nothing better for a horse than a good ~ on fresh young grass⟩ **2 :** herbage for or suitable for grazing

³graze \"\ *vb* [perh. fr. ¹*graze*] *vt* **1 :** to rub or touch lightly in passing **:** touch and glance off **:** barely touch ⟨the falling tree just *grazed* his chair⟩ **2 :** to scratch or abrade by or as if by rubbing on a rough surface ⟨we got through, though we *grazed* both fenders slightly⟩ ⟨fell and *grazed* her knee⟩ **~** *vi* **:** to touch or rub against something in passing or so as to produce a scratch or abrasion ⟨our fenders just *grazed*⟩

⁴graze \"\ *n* **:** a scraping along a surface or an abrasion made by such scraping: as **a :** ²GLIDE 4a **b :** a burst of an artillery projectile on impact with the ground or other material object **c :** a superficial abrasion of the skin

graze·able *or* **graz·able** \-zəbəl\ *adj* [¹*graze* + *-able*] **:** fit or suitable for grazing ⟨~ pastures⟩

graz·er \-zə(r)\ *n* -S [¹*graze* + *-er*] **:** one that grazes; *esp* **:** an animal that feeds by grazing — compare BROWSER

gra·zier \'grāzhə(r), *chiefly Brit* -ziə(r\ *n* -S [ME *grasyer*, fr. *gras* grass + *-ier* — more at GRASS] **1 :** a person who grazes cattle; *broadly* **:** an owner or rancher of cattle **2** *Austral* **:** a sheep raiser; *esp* **:** one occupying government-owned land

gra·ziery \-ərē\ *n* -ES **:** the business of grazing cattle

¹grazing *n* -S [ME *grasing*, fr. gerund of *grasen* to graze] **1 :** the feeding or the method of feeding of animals that graze ⟨heavy ~ may kill out the better grasses⟩ ⟨the ~ of snails left clear tracks among the algae on the aquarium wall⟩ **2 :** herbage or land for grazing ⟨nomads seeking ~ for their herds⟩ ⟨an excellent property to be leased with all ~s and cropland⟩

²grazing *adj* [fr. pres. part. of ¹*graze*] **1 :** feeding by grazing ⟨~ animals⟩ **2 :** of, for, or relating to grazing ⟨~ land⟩ ⟨a ~ permit⟩ — **graz·ing·ly** *adv*

grazing angle *n* [fr. pres. part. of ³*graze*] **:** the glancing angle occurring in grazing incidence

grazing capacity *n* **:** the carrying capacity of a pasture or area of range usu. expressed as the number of animals (as cattle or deer) that it will support for a specified length of time or indefinitely

grazing fire *n* [fr. pres. part. of ³*graze*] **:** artillery fire approximately parallel to the ground

grazing incidence *n* [fr. pres. part. of ³*graze*] **:** incidence (as of X rays) at a very small glancing angle — see GRAZING ANGLE

gra·zi·o·so \,grätsē'ō(,)sō, -)zō\ *adj (or adv)* [It, fr. L *gratiosus* enjoying favor, beloved, agreeable — more at GRACIOUS] **:** graceful, smooth, or elegant in style — used as a direction in music

grd *abbr* **1** grind **2** ground **3** guaranteed

¹grease \'grēs\ *n* -S [ME *grese*, *grees*, fr. OF *craisse*, *graisse*, *cresse*, *gresse*, fr. (assumed) VL *crassia*, fr. L *crassus* fat + *-ia* -y — more at HURDLE] **1 a :** rendered animal fat esp. when softer than tallow, inedible, and obtained from waste products **b :** fatty tissue **:** FATNESS ⟨put some ~ on those thin bones of yours —S.H.Adams⟩ **c :** oily matter or a thick oily or buttery preparation esp. when not fine or pure **d :** a thick lubricant (as a petroleum oil thickened with a metallic soap) ⟨axle ~⟩ ⟨silicone ~s⟩ **2 a :** GREASE HEEL **b :** cutaneous horsepox of the pasterns **3** *or* **grease wool :** wool as it comes from the sheep retaining the natural oils or fats — **in grease** *or* **in the grease 1** *of a game animal* **:** fat and fit for food **2** *of wool or fur* **:** in the natural condition with grease and other impurities not removed

²grease \-ēs,-ēz — *for -s/-z regional differences see* GREASY\ *vb* -ED/-ING/-S [ME *gresen*, fr. *grese*, *grees*, n.] *vt* **1 a :** to smear or daub with grease ⟨~ a cake pan⟩ **b :** to lubricate with grease **c :** to soil with grease **2 :** to influence or persuade by gifts or bribes ⟨long-striking soft-coal miners would return to the pits in a two-week truce, *greased* by retroactive pay —*Newsweek*⟩ **3 :** to smooth or make easy of passage ⟨bribes *greased* their path⟩ **:** FACILITATE, EXPEDITE ⟨this ~s the decline in department store sales —*Wall Street Jour.*⟩ **4** *slang* **:** to land (a plane) smoothly ⟨*greased* the plane down the rain-slick runway —B.M.Bowie⟩ **~** *vi, slang* **:** to make a smooth landing with a plane ⟨he *greased* in on the first hundred feet of runway —Hugh Fosburgh⟩ — **grease the hand** *or* **grease the palm :** BRIBE, TIP — **grease the wheels :** to expedite matters **:** cause matters to go more smoothly to a desired end

greaseball \'ˌ=ˌ=\ *n* **:** LATIN AMERICAN; *esp* **:** MEXICAN — usu. taken to be offensive

grease band *n* **:** a band of sticky material placed around a tree trunk to prevent insects from climbing up the tree

greasebush \'ˌ=ˌ=\ *n* **:** GREASEWOOD

grease cup *n* **:** a cylindrical receptacle communicating with a bearing and having a deep screw top which may be packed full of lubricating grease and which when screwed on forces the grease into the bearing

greased \-ēst,-ēzd\ *adj, of a horse* **:** affected with grease heel

greased line fishing *n* **:** angling in which a fly line made buoyant with grease dressing is floated on the surface of the water

greased pig *n* **:** a small pig smeared with grease and set free for contestants to catch

greased pole *or* **greasy pole** *n* **:** a pole smeared with grease and erected vertically for a climbing contest or horizontally for a walking contest

grease gun *n* **1 :** a small hand pump for forcing grease under pressure into bearings **2 :** a submachine gun that resembles a grease gun

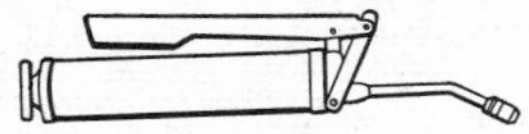

grease gun 1

grease heel *or* **greasy heel** *n* **:** a chronic inflammation of the skin of the fetlocks and pasterns of horses marked by an excess of oily secretion, ulcerations, and in severe cases general swelling of the legs, nodular excrescences, and a foul-smelling discharge and usu. affecting horses with thick coarse legs kept or worked under unsanitary conditions — compare GRAPE 3

greasehorn \'ˌ=ˌ=\ *n, dial Eng* **:** FLATTERER, SYCOPHANT ⟨smooth-faced, sniveling ~ —Charlotte Brontë⟩

grease·less \'grēsləs\ *adj* **:** having no grease ⟨a medicated ~ cream — won't stain clothes⟩

grease monkey *n* **1 :** a greaser of machinery; *specif* **:** an automobile serviceman who lubricates working parts of the engine and the chassis **2 :** an airplane mechanic

grease-nut \'ˌ=ˌ=\ *n* **1 :** the oily nut of an Australian tree (*Hernandia bivalvis*) **2 :** the tree that bears grease-nuts and furnishes soft gray timber

greasepaint \'ˌ=ˌ=\ *n* **1 :** a melted tallow or grease used in theater makeup **2 :** theater makeup

grease pencil *n* **:** a drawing pencil in which the marking substance is pigment and grease and the casing is paper to be unraveled as needed; *also* **:** a lithographic pencil

greaseproof \'ˌ=ˌ=\ *adj* **:** resistant to penetration by grease, oil, or wax ⟨~ wrapping paper⟩

greas·er \'grēsə(r), -ēzə-, *in sense 2 usu* -z-\ *n* -S **1 :** one that greases: as **a :** a worker who lubricates the working parts of a machine or a vehicle **b :** a worker who greases unpainted metal surfaces of firearms to prevent corrosion in transit or storage **c :** DOPER a **2 :** LATIN AMERICAN; *esp* **:** MEXICAN — usu. taken to be offensive **3 a :** RUDDY DUCK **b :** CACKLING GOOSE **4 :** BULL COOK

greaser blackfish *n* **:** BLACKFISH 1b

greases *pl of* GREASE, *pres 3d sing of* GREASE

grease spot *n* **:** a disease of turf grasses caused by a fungus (*Pythium aphanidermatum*) and characterized by spots usu. under two inches in diameter but often coalesced into patches or streaks having a distinctive greasy border of blackened leaves and intermingled cottony mycelium — called also *spot blight*; compare DOLLAR SPOT

grease-spot photometer *n* **:** a photometer in which a grease spot on a piece of paper becomes invisible when a light on each side of the paper illuminates the spot equally

grease trap *n* **:** a trap in a drain or waste pipe to prevent grease from passing into a sewer system

greasewood \'ˌ=ˌ=\ *n* **1 a :** a plant of the genus *Sarcobatus*; *esp* **:** a low stiff shrub (*S. vermiculatus*) common in alkaline soils in the western U.S. — called also *black greasewood* **b :** any of several other shrubs of the family Chenopodiaceae that resemble greasewood: as (1) **:** ORACHE (2) **:** HOPSAGE (3) **:** IODINE BUSH **2 :** either of two California shrubs: **a :** CHAMISO 1 **b :** WHITE SAGE e

grease wool *n* **:** GREASE 3

greas·i·ly \'grēs|əlē, -ēz|, -li\ *adv* **:** in a greasy manner

greas·i·ness \|ēnəs, |in-\ *n* -ES **:** the quality or state of being greasy

greasing *pres part of* GREASE

greasy \'grēs|ē, -ēz|, |i; *chiefly* -s- *Northwest, Southwest, central North, eastern New Eng; chiefly* -z- *South (including mountain areas) & Brit; both* -s- *&* -z- *Midland, western Pa, Middle Atlantic, NYC; sometimes* -s- *for literal sense and neutral connotation,* -z- *to convey an unpleasant connotation*\ *adj* -ER/-EST **1 a :** smeared or soiled with grease **b :** physically or morally repulsive: as (1) **:** distastefully unctuous or oily in manner ⟨his . . . insinuating tones, his ~ smile —Jack London⟩ (2) **:** SHIFTY, UNRELIABLE ⟨with his low backstairs cunning, with his ~ good nature —A.L.Guérard⟩ (3) *obs* **:** GROSS, INDECENT — often used of language **2 :** being grease ⟨a ~ ointment⟩ **:** containing an unusual amount of grease ⟨~ wool⟩ ⟨~ food⟩ **3** *of a horse* **:** affected with grease heel **4 a :** having or giving the appearance or feel of greasiness **:** seemingly unctuous to the touch or view ⟨the ~ texture of a stone⟩ ⟨the quartz had a ~ luster⟩ ⟨~, gagging fogs —Berton Roueché⟩ **b :** SLIPPERY ⟨the rain made the road ~⟩ ⟨the bank was steep and ~ with sea moss —Irwin Shaw⟩ **c** *of paper stock* **:** that drains with great slowness — opposed to *free stock* **5 :** THREATENING, DIRTY — used of the weather, the day, or the sky

greasy cutworm *n* **:** BLACK CUTWORM

greasy grind *n, slang* **:** a student who studies extremely hard usu. to the exclusion of extracurricular activities

greasy spoon *n, slang* **:** a small esp. cheap and usu. more or less unsanitary restaurant or diner

greasy spot *n* **:** a disease of citrus trees of unknown cause producing dark oily spots on the leaves esp. of grapefruit

greasy wool *n, Brit* **:** GREASE 3

¹great \'grā|t, *South often* -re(ə)l| *or* -rāə|; *usu* |d.+V\ *adj* -ER/-EST [ME *grete*, fr. OE *grēat* coarse-grained, large, tall; akin to OFris *grāt* large, OS *grōt*, OHG *grōz* and prob. to OE *grēot* sand, grit — more at GRIT] **1 a :** large in spatial dimension **:** of notable size **:** BIG ⟨a boy of nine, ~ and heavy for his years —Arnold Bennett⟩ ⟨had eaten ~ juicy steaks —Bruce Marshall⟩ ⟨the ~ size of these figures — the largest man is 167 feet long and has an arm spread of 164 feet —*Amer. Guide Series: Calif.*⟩ ⟨the best forests had been reduced to ~ stretches of stump land —*Amer. Guide Series: Minn.*⟩ **b** *now dial* **:** PREGNANT **c :** of a kind characterized by relative largeness — used in plant and animal names **d** *archaic* **:** CAPITAL ⟨~ A⟩ **e** *chiefly Scot, of a stream or body of water* **:** HIGH, SWOLLEN **f :** ELABORATE, AMPLE ⟨a plan worked out in ~ detail⟩ **2 a :** large in number **:** NUMEROUS ⟨a ~ multitude of warriors⟩ ⟨a ~ company of men⟩ ⟨the respect due his ~*er* years⟩ **b :** PREDOMINANT, OVERRULING — used in such phrases as *the great majority*, *the great body* ⟨the ~ bulk of the populace favors peace⟩ ⟨written nearly a thousand letters about goats, the ~ majority in reply to people who have asked questions —Joan & Harry Shields⟩ **3 :** considerable or remarkable in magnitude, power, intensity, degree, or effectiveness ⟨~ bloodshed⟩ ⟨a ~ weariness⟩ ⟨with ~ difficulty⟩ ⟨the year of the ~ inflation —H.H.Martin⟩ **:** LOUD ⟨a ~ voice⟩ ⟨a ~ uproar⟩ **:** HEAVY, FORCEFUL ⟨a ~ blow with the fist⟩ **:** INTENSE ⟨a ~ pain shooting through the arm⟩ **:** FAR-REACHING **:** big in scope ⟨when once the ~ plans for power transmission have been realized —Samuel Van Valkenburg & Ellsworth Huntington⟩ **:** EXTREME, MARKED ⟨showed ~ good taste⟩ **:** very close ⟨a ~ friend of mine⟩ **:** markedly accomplished ⟨a ~ lover⟩ ⟨a ~ hater⟩ **4 a :** full or charged esp. with an emotion ⟨~ with anger⟩ ⟨~ with pride⟩ ⟨others who returned from overseas ~ with message —E.P.Snow⟩ ⟨when kings are reduced to thumb size and beasts are ~ with wisdom —*Time*⟩ **b** *archaic* **:** PROUD, ARROGANT **5 a :** PROMINENT, RENOWNED ⟨a ~ politician⟩ ⟨a ~ dictator⟩ ⟨a ~ creator of confusion in the political scene⟩ **:** EMINENT, DISTINGUISHED ⟨a ~ poet⟩ ⟨the ~ and aging father of modern electronics⟩ **:** IMPORTANT, SIGNIFICANT ⟨one of the ~ theories in Christian ethics⟩ **:** WEIGHTY, EFFECTIVE ⟨a ~ argument in criminal-law practice⟩ ⟨a ~ truth⟩ **b :** chief or preeminent over others ⟨the ~ work of his old age was the decoration of the chapel —*Encyc. Americana*⟩ ⟨defines the scope of some of the ~ questions that call for answers —W.H. Bucher⟩ ⟨the ~ novelist of the war years⟩ — often used in titles ⟨Lord *Great* Chamberlain⟩ **c** (1) **:** belonging to the aristocracy ⟨most people thought it quite natural that ~ folk should have great privileges —G.B.Shaw⟩ (2) **:** marked by an aristocratic, dignified, lofty bearing **:** GRAND ⟨~ ladies descending from their chauffeured cars⟩ **d :** being such to a notable degree ⟨a ~ beauty⟩ ⟨a ~ indignity⟩ **e :** on a large scale or with large holdings ⟨the ~ farmers of the area⟩ ⟨appealed to the ~ manufacturers for help⟩ **6 :** long continued **:** lengthened in duration ⟨a ~ while⟩ ⟨a ~ interval⟩ **7 :** FAVORITE ⟨a ~ trick of his⟩ ⟨a ~ word among the members of the club⟩ **8** *chiefly dial* **:** FRIENDLY, CHUMMY, THICK — often used with overtones of disapproval ⟨they've been mighty ~ lately, I expect it'll all blow up some day —Anna Doleshaw⟩ **9 :** MAIN, PRINCIPAL ⟨held the conference in the ~ hall of the abbey⟩ ⟨came down the ~ staircase⟩ **10 :** older or younger or more remote in a family relationship by a single generation than (a specified relative) ⟨a *great*-grandfather⟩ **11 :** markedly superior in character or quality to others of the same class ⟨a book that could be called good but not ~⟩ **:** of high purpose or nature **:** LOFTY, NOBLE, MAGNANIMOUS ⟨a big man who needed only a little feeling to be a ~ man —H.J.Laski⟩ ⟨a person committed to ~ ends⟩ ⟨~ of soul and generous in actions⟩ **12 a :** remarkably or unusually informed or skilled — used with *at*, *on* ⟨a man ~ at tennis⟩ ⟨a speaker ~ on international relations⟩ **b :** unusually addicted to or enthusiastic about — used with *at*, *for*, or *on* ⟨a person ~ at talking by the hour⟩ ⟨a person ~ for gallivanting all over town⟩ ⟨mother was always ~ on fantasy —Catherine Hubbell⟩ ⟨a ~ church worker and well-known for his philanthropies —*Amer. Guide Series: Ind.*⟩ **c :** ASSIDUOUS, PERSISTENT ⟨a ~ talker⟩ ⟨a ~ skier although he is not very good at skiing⟩ ⟨a ~ collector of books⟩ **13 :** WONDERFUL, ADMIRABLE — used as a generalized term of enthusiastic approval ⟨had a ~ time⟩ ⟨the attitude of all concerned was just ~⟩ **14** *Eastern Church* **:** of or relating to Holy Week ⟨~ Monday⟩

²great \"\ *adv* [ME *grete*, fr. *grete*, adj.] **:** in a great manner **:** SUCCESSFULLY, WELL ⟨things are going ~⟩

³great \"\ *n, pl* **great** *or* **greats** [ME *grete*, fr. *grete*, adj.] **1 :** one that is great **:** one that is particularly noted or notable for superiority of accomplishment esp. in a particular field of activity ⟨the music of Mozart and Beethoven and all the other ~s —Deems Taylor⟩ ⟨his playing is less monumental . . . than that of any of the other pianistic ~ —Virgil Thomson⟩ ⟨the golfing ~s of last season⟩ ⟨some of the scientific ~s —*Science Illustrated*⟩ ⟨the ~ of London society came to their receptions —*Fashion Digest*⟩ ⟨the galaxy of football ~s —S.M.Spencer⟩ **2** [by shortening] **:** GREAT ORGAN **3** *greats pl, usu cap* **a :** the final examination for the B.A. in classics esp. with honors at Oxford University **b :** the course taken in preparation for this examination — compare GREAT GO

great albacore *n* **:** BLUEFIN 2

great angelica *n* **:** a large coarse American angelica (*Angelica atropurpurea*) with a usu. purplish stem

great anteater *n* **:** ANT BEAR 1

great antiphon *n, usu cap G&A* **:** one of the seven anthems beginning with an invocation (as *O Adonai*) that are sung at vespers one each day from December 17 to Christmas — called also *O Antiphon*; usu. used in pl.

great ape *n* **:** any of the recent anthropoid apes **:** GIBBON, ORANGUTAN, CHIMPANZEE, GORILLA

great assize *n* **:** LAST JUDGMENT

great auk *n* **:** a large flightless auk (*Pinguinus impennis*) two or two and a half feet long but with very small wings and formerly abundant on the coasts of the northern parts of the No. Atlantic but now extinct

great-aunt \'ˌ=ˌ=\ *n* **:** GRANDAUNT

great barracuda *n* **:** a grayish brown barracuda (*Sphyraena barracuda*) that often attains a length of over six feet, may be dangerous to swimmers, and is highly regarded as a food and sport fish though the flesh is reputed poisonous in some areas

great beams *n pl, chiefly NewEng* **:** the loft or haymow of a barn

great bellflower *n* **:** CANTERBURY BELL

great bilberry *n* **:** BOG BILBERRY

great bindweed *n* **:** HEDGE BINDWEED 1

great black-backed gull *n* **:** a very large black-backed gull (*Larus marinus*) that is becoming increasingly abundant along both coasts of the Atlantic

great black cockatoo *n* **:** a very large black cockatoo (*Probosciger aterrima*) of New Guinea and northern Australia that has a tall erectile crest, patches of bright red naked skin on the cheeks, and an extremely large powerful bill with which it cracks the palm nuts on which it chiefly feeds — called also *palm cockatoo*

great blue cat *n* **:** BLUE CAT

great blue heron *n* **:** a large slaty-blue American heron (*Ardea herodias*) about 50 inches long and with crested head

great blue shark *n* **:** a blue shark (*Carcharhinus glaucus*)

great books *adj* **:** of, relating to, or centered in certain classics of literature, philosophy, history, and science that are believed to contain the basic ideas of western culture ⟨an experimental *great books* program for 50 selected students —*Time*⟩

great bowerbird *n* **:** a large Australian bowerbird (*Chlamydera nuchalis*) common about settled areas in northern Australia and noted for the skill with which it builds its bower

great bulrush *n* **:** any of several large plants of the genus *Scirpus*: as **a :** a tall Eurasian sedge (*S. lacustris*) with naked terete stems and a compound umbel of numerous capitate spikes **b :** a bulrush (*S. validus*) of tropical America and southern U.S. with a stout scaly reddish rhizome, thick pliable culm, and spikelets in close fascicles or glomerules; *also* **:** a bulrush chiefly of northern No. America that is a variety (*S. validus creber*) of the above distinguished esp. by lax panicles

great bur *or* **great burdock** *n* **:** a European burdock (*Arctium lappa*) naturalized in No. America

great burnet *n* **:** a perennial burnet (*Sanguisorba officinalis*) with ellipsoid to short cylindric flower heads native to Eurasia but cultivated and escaped elsewhere

great bustard *n* **:** a bustard (*Otis tarda*) that is the largest of European land birds, attaining a weight of over 30 pounds and a wingspread of 8 feet and occurring in southern and eastern Europe and in much of Asia but formerly also in England and other parts of western Europe where it is now extinct

great carpenter bee *n* **:** a large carpenter bee (*Xylocopa virginica*) of eastern and southern No. America about the size of a bumblebee but distinguished by a smooth shining abdomen

great cattle *n* **:** all types of cattle except sheep and yearlings

great celandine *n* **:** CELANDINE 1

great cerebral vein *n* **:** a broad unpaired vein formed by the junction of Galen's veins and uniting with the inferior sagittal sinus to form the straight sinus

great chair *n* **:** ARMCHAIR

great chickweed *n* **:** a large-flowered chickweed (*Stellaria pubera*) chiefly of the southeastern U.S. — called also *star chickweed*

great circle *n* **:** a circle formed on the surface of a sphere by the intersection of a plane that passes through the center of the sphere; *specif* **:** such a circle on the surface of the earth of which an arc constitutes the shortest distance between any two terrestrial points — compare SMALL CIRCLE

great-circle chart *n* **:** GNOMONIC PROJECTION

great-circle sailing *n* **:** the navigation or conducting of a ship on a great-circle track or on a course determined in relation to a great-circle track — compare SAILING

great-circle track *n* **:** the track of a ship following or navigating on or in relation to a great circle

great climacteric *n, obs* **:** GRAND CLIMACTERIC

greatcoat \'ˌ=ˌ=\ *n* **1 :** a heavy overcoat **2 :** a warm jacket

great council *n* [ME *grete counseil*] **:** a preeminent political council: as **a :** the principal council or assembly of England under the Norman kings composed of the sovereign's tenants in capite **b :** a municipal legislative body of former times in some Italian towns and cities **c :** a major council of No. American Indian chiefs

great crested grebe *n* **:** a large Old World grebe (*Podiceps cristatus* or *Colymbus cristatus*) with black projecting ear tufts

great dane *n* **1** *usu cap G&D* **:** a breed of smooth-coated dogs that is believed to have originated in Germany several centuries ago, that is of massive size, great strength, and 28 inches at minimum height, that ranges in color from fawn through brindle, blue, and harlequin, that was formerly used chiefly for hunting wild boar, and that has been much used for draft purposes **2** *often cap G & usu cap D* **:** a dog of the Great Dane breed

great deal \(')grā(t)¦dēl, *chiefly before pause or consonant* -ēəl\ *n* **:** a large quantity **:** LOT ⟨received a *great deal* of sympathy at his bereavement⟩ ⟨asked for little but received a *great deal*⟩ — **a great deal** *adv* **1 :** to a considerable degree or extent **:** by a considerable amount ⟨a *great deal* better⟩ **2 :** OFTEN, FREQUENTLY ⟨he runs *a great deal*⟩ — used with intransitive verbs **3 :** HIGHLY ⟨think *a great deal* of that book⟩

great dionysia *n, usu cap G&D* **:** DIONYSIA b

great divide *n* [fr. the *Great Divide* (*Continental Divide*), watershed of the No. American continent] **1 :** a watershed between major drainage systems **2 :** a sharp or significant point of division between two strongly opposed or markedly different juxtaposed things — **cross the great divide :** DIE ⟨men who *crossed the great divide* by the alcoholic route in middle life —A.W.Long⟩

great dog *n* **:** a dog large enough by English forestry law to kill or maim deer or other large game

great duckweed *n* **:** a plant of the genus *Spirodela* (esp. *S. polyrhiza*)

great·en \'grāt°n, -ret-\ *vb* -ED/-ING/-S [¹*great* + *-en*] *vt* **:** to make greater **:** ENLARGE, MAGNIFY, INCREASE; *also* **:** to make more distinguished **:** EXALT, ENNOBLE **~** *vi* **:** to become greater **:** increase in size or significance

great entrance *n, usu cap G&E* [trans. of MGk *megalē eisodos*] **:** an Entrance in the liturgy of the Eastern Church during which the eucharistic elements are brought in

greater *adj* [fr. comp. of ¹*great*] **1** *music, obs* **:** MAJOR **2** *usu cap, of a political or geographic unit* **:** consisting of an original unit together with adjacent or other areas that are naturally or administratively connected with it ⟨*Greater* London⟩ ⟨*Greater* New York⟩ ⟨*Greater* Tokyo⟩

greater celandine *n* **:** CELANDINE 1

greater curvature *n* **:** the long border of the stomach that is primitively dorsal but in man turned to the left

greater feria *n* **1 :** a feria of the Roman Catholic church calendar (as a weekday of Advent or Lent) which must at least be commemorated in the office of a feast falling on the same day and the office of which has precedence over that of simple feasts or if privileged (as Ash Wednesday and the first three days of Holy Week) over any feast — called also *major feria* **2 :** a feria of the Anglican church calendar with a service that takes precedence over feasts of low rank falling on the same day

greater omentum *n* **:** a fatty omentum attached to the stomach and colon and hanging down over the small intestine — called also *caul, gastrocolic omentum*

greater scaup *or* **greater scaup duck** *n* **:** a No. American diving duck (*Aythya marila nearctica*) resembling the lesser scaup duck but being slightly larger and having a greenish iridescence on the head of the adult male, breeding in arctic northwestern America, and wintering on both coasts of No. America

greater shearwater *n* **:** a rather large chiefly sooty brown and white shearwater (*Puffinus gravis* or *Procellaria gravis*) of the eastern coast of No. and So. America

greater stitchwort *n* **:** a Eurasian annual herb (*Stellaria holostea*) with small white flowers

greater wax moth *n* **:** BEE MOTH

greater yellowlegs *n pl but sing or pl in constr* **:** a common No. American marsh and shore bird (*Tringa melanoleuca*) of the family Scolopacidae largely gray above and white below with black or dark gray flecking and yellow legs — compare LESSER YELLOWLEGS

greatest *superlative of* GREAT

greatest common divisor *n* **:** the largest integer or polynomial of highest degree that is an exact divisor of each of two or more integers or polynomials respectively

greatest common factor *n* **:** HIGHEST COMMON FACTOR

greatest elongation *n* **:** the configuration in which one celestial body reaches its greatest apparent distance from another ⟨the *greatest* eastern *elongation* of Venus with respect to the sun⟩ — see CONFIGURATION illustration

greatest happiness principle *n* **:** a principle in Benthamism: right and wrong are to be judged by the degree to which the action judged achieves the greatest happiness of the greatest number — called also *utility principle;* compare UNIVERSALISTIC HEDONISM

great fan palm *n* **:** PALMYRA

great fast *n, usu cap G&F* [trans. of MGk *megalē nēsteia*] *Eastern Church* **:** LENT 1

great father *n, usu cap G&F* **:** GREAT WHITE FATHER

great fee *n, in feudal law* **:** a fee held in capite

great flounder *n* **:** STARRY FLOUNDER

great friday *n, usu cap G&F* [trans. of LGk *megalē paraskeuē*] *Eastern Church* **:** GOOD FRIDAY

great go *n, archaic* **:** the final examination for the bachelor's degree in classics and mathematics at Oxford University

great goose grass *n* **:** GERMAN MADWORT

great gray kangaroo *n* **:** GIANT KANGAROO

great gray owl *n* **:** a large round-headed owl (*Strix nebulosa*) having very full fluffy plumage that is gray mottled and barred with darker gray and white and being nearly circumpolar in northern forests

great gray shrike *n* **:** a large shrike (*Lanius excubitor*) chiefly gray above with black-and-white wings and tail

great green orchis *n* **:** a greenish-flowered No. American terrestrial orchid (*Platanthera orbiculata*)

great gross *n* **:** a unit of quantity equal to 12 gross

great gun *n* **:** BIG GUN

great guns *adv* **:** with unremitting vigor or energy ⟨reaching the age of 78 . . . and still going *great guns* —*N.Y. Times*⟩; *also* **:** eminently successfully ⟨an enterprise that began slowly but after a while began to go *great guns*⟩ — often used interjectionally to express astonishment

greathead \ˈ⸗,⸗\ *n* **:** AMERICAN GOLDENEYE

greatheart \ˈ⸗,⸗\ *n* **:** a greathearted person

great-hearted \ˈ⸗¦⸗⸗\ *adj* [ME *grete herted*] **1 :** having or characterized by bravery **:** COURAGEOUS, FEARLESS **2 :** having or characterized by largeness or generosity of spirit **:** MAGNANIMOUS

great·heart·ed·ly *adv* **:** in a greathearted manner

great·heart·ed·ness *n* -ES **:** MAGNANIMITY

great hedge bedstraw *n* **:** WILD MADDER 2a

great horde *n, usu cap G&H* [trans. of Kirghiz *ulu-juz*] **:** a subdivision of the Kirghiz living south of Lake Balkhash in Soviet Central Asia the chief divisions of which are the Kangli and the Dulat

great horned owl *n* **1 :** a large No. American owl (*Bubo virginianus*) with conspicuous ear tufts **2 :** an eagle owl (*Bubo bubo*)

great house *n, chiefly Brit & South* **:** the main house of an estate or plantation

great indian plantain : a tall perennial herb (*Cacalia reniformis*) of the southeastern U.S.

great kelp *n* **:** GIANT KELP

great lake trout *or* **great lakes trout** \¦⸗,⸗ˈ⸗\ *n, usu cap G&L* [fr. *Great Lakes,* chain of lakes in central No. America] **:** LAKE TROUT

great land crab *n* **:** a large swift-moving dull-grayish land crab (*Cardisoma guanhumi*) of the family Gecarcinidae that is widely distributed from southern Florida and the West Indies to Brazil, is chiefly nocturnal, and lives in deep burrows or the open fields or woods and returns to the sea only to breed — called also *guanhumi, juey, tourlourou, white land crab*

great laurel *n* **:** BIG LAUREL

great lent *n, usu cap G&L* [trans. of MGk *megalē tessarkostē*] **:** LENT 1

great-line \ˈ⸗¦⸗\ *adj, Brit* **:** using a long line in fishing **:** DEEP-WATER ⟨trawl and *great-line* catches . . . by steam vessels —*Report on the Fisheries of Scotland*⟩

great lobelia *n* **:** a tall herb (*Lobelia siphilitica*) of the eastern U.S. with showy irregular blue flowers

great·ly *adv* [ME *gretely*, fr. *grete* great + *-ly* — more at GREAT] **1 :** to a great extent or high degree ⟨contributed ~ to the improvement of international relations⟩ **:** VERY ⟨not ~ bothered by the rude remarks⟩ **:** very much ⟨said he liked her ~ —Arnold Bennett⟩ ⟨a ~ intensified sound⟩ ⟨~ in want of a friend —G.B.Shaw⟩ **2 :** in a great manner **:** NOBLY, MAGNANIMOUSLY ⟨a man may live ~ in the law —O.W.Holmes †1935⟩

great maple *n* **:** SYCAMORE 2

great marischal *n* **:** a marshal of medieval Scotland before the bestowal of the title Earl Marischal — compare MARISCHAL, MARSHAL 1

great master *n* **1 :** GRAND MASTER 1 **2 a :** one held to be among the greatest or most skilled in one of the arts **b :** a work of such a one esp. in painting

great mean *n, obs* **:** the third string of a bass viol or of a violin **:** the D string of a violin

great millet *n* **:** DURRA

great mogul *n, usu cap G&M* **:** the sovereign of the empire founded in India by the Moguls under Baber in the 16th century

great mullein *n* **:** a tall-stalked very woolly mullein (*Verbascum thapsus*) with yellow or occas. white flowers

great-nephew \ˈ⸗¦⸗(,)⸗\ *n* **:** GRANDNEPHEW

great·ness *n* -ES [ME *gretenes*, fr. *grete* great + *-nes* -ness] **:** the quality or state of being great

great nettle *n* **:** STINGING NETTLE

great-niece \ˈ⸗¦⸗\ *n* **:** GRANDNIECE

great northern diver *n* **:** COMMON LOON

great northern pike *n* **:** ⁴PIKE 1a

great octave *n* **:** the musical octave that begins on the second C below middle C — see PITCH illustration

great officer of state : one of the nine officers in England that were orig. officers of the royal household and include the lord high steward, lord high chancellor, lord high treasurer, lord president of the council, lord privy seal, lord great chamberlain, lord high constable, earl marshal, and lord high admiral

great one *n* **:** one esp. enthusiastic or clearly of a particular habit of mind or action — used with *for* ⟨a *great one* for skiing⟩ ⟨a *great one* for leaving things as they are —Louis Auchincloss⟩ ⟨a *great one* for the ladies —Jack Iams⟩

great organ *n* **1 :** a division of a pipe organ having the pipes of largest scale and loudest tone **2 :** the manual controlling the great organ

great panda *n* **:** PANDA 2

great park lily *n* **:** LILY OF THE VALLEY

great pastern bone *n* **:** the first phalanx of the functional digit of the foot of an equine

great pike *n* **:** MUSKELLUNGE

great plains cottonwood *n* [fr. the *Great Plains,* the continental slope of central No. America] **:** a poplar (*Populus sargentii*) of central No. America with coriaceous coarsely serrate leaves commonly broader than they are long

great pompano *n* **:** ³PERMIT 1

great power *n, usu cap G&P* **:** one of the nations that carry the greatest political influence, resources, and military strength and figure most decisively in international relations

great-power \ˈ⸗¦⸗\ *adj* [*Great Power*] **:** of or relating to the Great Powers ⟨the diplomatic test of a new *great-power* conference —W.H.Chamberlin⟩

great pox *n* **:** SYPHILIS

great prim·er \-rim-\ *n* **:** a size of type approximately 18 point

great pueblo *adj, usu cap G&P* **:** of or relating to the climax of the development of the Pueblo culture in the southwestern U.S. characterized by many-storied stone buildings set in recesses in the cliffs or in the open and by an advanced development of pottery, murals, and dryland agriculture

great pyr·e·nees \-ˈpirə(,)nēz *sometimes* -,⸗⸗ˈ⸗\ *n* [ˈ*great* (as in *Great Dane*) + *Pyrenees,* mountain range on the Spanish-French border] **1** *usu cap G&P* **:** a breed of very large heavy-coated white dogs that resemble the Newfoundland in conformation and are valued as herd dogs and guard dogs **2** *pl* **great pyrenees** *often cap G&P* **:** an animal of the Great Pyrenees breed

great ragweed *n* **:** a coarse annual (*Ambrosia trifida*) with some or all of the leaves usu. deeply and palmately 3-cleft or 5-cleft

great reed warbler *n* **:** a rather large olivaceous to bright brown reed warbler (*Acrocephalus arundinaceus*) that is widely distributed in warmer parts of the Old World from western Europe to southern Africa and Australia

great rhododendron *n* **:** BIG LAUREL

great russian *n, cap G&R* **1 :** a member of the Russian-speaking people largely of the central and northeastern areas of the U.S.S.R. constituting the country's largest ethnic group — compare BELORUSSIAN, LITTLE RUSSIAN **2 :** ²RUSSIAN 2a

greats *pl of* GREAT

great st.-john's-wort *n, usu cap S&J* **:** a large-flowered St.-John's-wort (*Hypericum pyramidatum*)

great sallow *n* **:** a sallow (*Salix caprea*)

great sanicle *n* **:** LADY'S-MANTLE

great scale *n* **:** the scale ascribed to Guido d'Arezzo that includes the seven hexachords and all notes recognized in medieval church music, its notes being named by letters combined with the syllables of the successive hexachords (as Gamma ut, A re, B mi, C fa ut) — compare SOLMIZATION

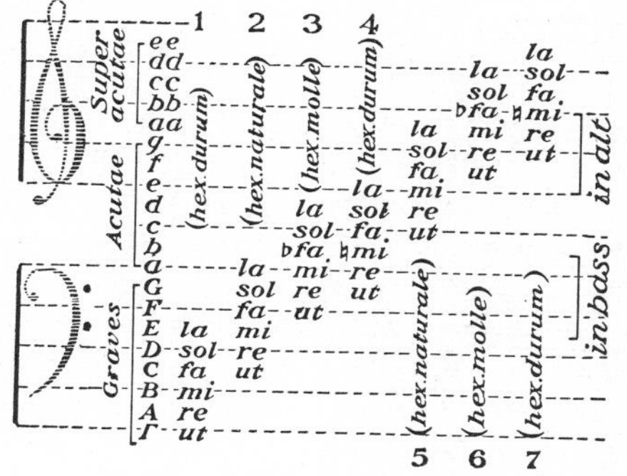

great scale

great scott \ˈ⸗ˈskät\ *interj, usu cap S* [fr. the name *Scott;* euphemism for *great God*] — a mild oath

great seal *n* [ME *grete seel*] **1 :** the personal seal of a monarch **2 :** the principal seal of a kingdom or state or of a bishop or of a corporation

great silver fir *n* **:** LOWLAND FIR

great skua *n* **:** a large stocky skua (*Catharacta skua*) having dusky plumage and broad rounded wings, breeding chiefly along arctic and antarctic shores, and foraging over most cold and temperate seas

great snipe *n* **:** an Old World snipe (*Capella media*) somewhat larger, darker, and more barred than the whole snipe

great soil group *n* **:** a group of soils having common characteristics usu. developed under the influence of environmental factors (as vegetation and climate) active over a considerable geographic range and comprising one or more families of soil

great solomon's-seal *n, usu cap 1st S* **:** a No. American perennial herb (*Polygonatum commutatum*) with smooth foliage and drooping axillary tubular greenish flowers

great spirit *n, usu cap G&S* **:** the chief deity in the indigenous religion of many No. American Indian tribes

great spotted woodpecker *n* **:** a common European and Asiatic woodpecker (*Dendrocopos major*) having a black back, white shoulder patches, crimson under tail coverts, and in the male a crimson patch on the nape

great spurred violet *n* **:** SELKIRK'S VIOLET

great sugar pine *n* **:** SUGAR PINE

great sunday *n, usu cap G&S* [trans. of LGk *megalē hēmera*] *Eastern Church* **:** EASTER SUNDAY

great-tailed grackle \ˈ⸗,⸗-\ *n* **:** BOAT-TAILED GRACKLE

great tit *n* **:** the largest common European tit (*Parus major*) distinguished by a glossy blue-black head and yellow underparts with a black stripe down the breast

great toe *n* **:** BIG TOE

great triangle *n, usu cap G&T* **:** a triangle formed on the palm by the lines of Life, Head, and Mercury that when well-developed is usu. held by palmists to indicate breadth of views, liberality, and generosity of spirit — called also *Triangle of Mars*

great tuna *or* **great tunny** *n* **:** BLUEFIN 2

great-uncle \ˈ⸗¦⸗⸗\ *n* **:** GRANDUNCLE

great vehicle *n, usu cap G&V* [trans. of Skt *mahāyāna*] **:** MAHAYANA

great water dock *n* **:** any of various plants of the genus *Rumex* (esp. *R. orbiculatus*)

great water parsnip *n* **:** a poisonous European herb (*Sium latifolium*) with divided leaves and tiny flowers

great week *n, usu cap G&W* [trans. of LGk *megalē hebdomas*] **:** HOLY WEEK — used in the early church and now esp. in the Eastern Church

great wheel *n* **:** the first wheel of a watch or clock train

great white father *also* **great father** *n, usu cap G&W&F* **1 :** the president of the U.S. **2 :** a person in a position of authority

great white heron *n* **1 :** a large white chiefly tropical egret (*Casmerodius albus*) that occurs in a number of varieties in both Old and New Worlds — compare AMERICAN EGRET **2 :** a large white heron (*Ardea occidentalis*) of Florida and Mexico

great white shark *n* **:** a large mackerel shark (*Carcharodon carcharias*) that is bluish gray when young but becomes dun or whitish in large specimens, that is widespread in warm and tropical seas, and that is a man-eater

great white trillium *n* **:** a perennial herb (*Trillium grandiflorum*) of eastern No. America with showy white petals

great white way *n, usu cap G&both Ws* [fr. the *Great White Way,* nickname for the theatrical section of Broadway in New York City] **:** a street brilliantly lighted at night and devoted chiefly to public amusements (as theaters) ⟨their *Great White Ways* flooded with pleasure-seekers —*Yale Rev.*⟩ ⟨theaters flanking a dozen *Great White Ways* —*Landscape*⟩

great willow herb *n* **:** FIREWEED b

great year *n* [ME *grete yere*, trans. of L *annus magnus*, trans. of Gk *megas eniautos*] **:** the period of about 25,800 years required for a complete cycle of precession of the equinoxes during which time the celestial pole describes a complete circle around the ecliptic pole

¹**greave** *n* -S [ME *greve*, fr. OE *grǣfa* — more at GROVE] *obs* **:** GROVE, THICKET

²**greave** \ˈgrēv\ *n* -S [ME *greve*, fr. MF, perh. fr. *greve* part in the hair, fr. *graver* to part the hair, of Gmc origin; akin to OHG *graban* to dig; fr. a comparison of the edge of the shinbone to a part in the hair — more at GRAVE] **:** armor for the leg below the knee — usu. used in pl.

³**greave** \"\ *vt* -ED/-ING/-S [by alter.] **:** ⁴GRAVE

greaved tortoise \ˈgrēv(d)-\ *n* [²*greave* + *-ed;* fr. the large plates on its front legs] **:** the largest of African tortoises (*Testudo calcarata*)

greaves \ˈgrēvz\ *n pl* [LG *greve* (pl. *greven*), fr. MLG *grēve;* akin to OHG *griobo* crackling, OE *grēot* sand, grit — more at GRIT] **:** CRACKLING 2a

grebe \ˈgrēb\ *n, pl* **grebe** *or* **grebes** [F *grèbe*] **1 :** any of various aquatic birds that constitute the family Colymbidae and order Colymbiformes, are closely related to the loons but with the toes lobate instead of webbed, have a rudimentary tail and narrow tarsi shaped like a blade, and are very expert divers and able to swim long distances under water — see GREAT CRESTED GREBE, RED-NECKED GREBE **2 :** a nearly neutral slightly reddish dark gray that is darker and slightly redder than lead

gre·bo \ˈgrā(,)bō\ *n, pl* **grebo** *or* **greboes** *usu cap* **1 :** a member of a Negro people of the Liberian coast **2 :** a Kwa language of the Grebo people

grecanic *adj, usu cap* [L *Graecanicus*, fr. *Graecus* — more at GREEK] *obs* **:** GRECIAN, GREEK

grece *or* **grice** \ˈgrēs\ *n* -S [ME *grece*, fr. OF *grez, greiz* steps, pl. (taken as sing.) of *gré, greit* step — more at GREE] **1** *now dial Eng* **:** a flight of steps; *also* **:** one of the steps in a flight **2** *or* **grece** \"\ **:** DEGREE 1b

¹**gre·cian** \ˈgrēshən\ *n* -S *cap* [L *Graecia* Greece (fr. *Graecus* + *-ia* -y) + E *-an*] **1 a :** a native of Greece **:** GREEK **b :** a hellenized Jew of the Diaspora **2 a** *archaic* **:** a specialist in the Greek language and Greek literature **b :** one skilled in Greek **3 :** a student in the sixth form of a school (as Christ's Hospital, London)

²**grecian** \"\ *adj, usu cap* **1 a :** of, relating to, or characteristic of Greece **b :** of, relating to, or characteristic of the Greeks **2** *of a woman's gown* **:** having flowing lines, layers of pleats, and many soft folds

grecian fire *n, usu cap G* **:** GREEK FIRE

gre·cian·ize \-shə,nīz\ *vt* -ED/-ING/-S *often cap* **:** GRECIZE

grecian rose *n, often cap G* **:** a dark yellowish pink

grecian sandal *n, usu cap G* **:** an open sandal consisting of a sole attached to the foot by an arrangement of interlaced straps crossing the toes and instep and fastening around the ankle

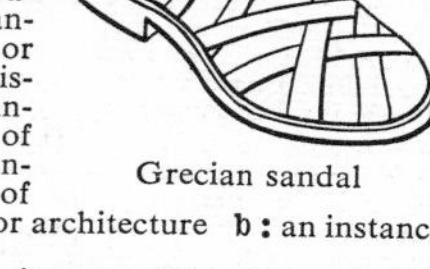
Grecian sandal

gre·cism \ˈgrē,sizəm\ *n* -S *usu cap* [ML *Graecismus*, fr. L *Graecus* Greek + *-ismus* -ism — more at GREEK] **1 :** a characteristic feature of Greek occurring in another language **2 a :** a quality or mode of thought or action distinctive of the Greeks esp. of ancient Greece **b :** the spirit of Greek art or culture esp. in ancient times **3 a :** imitation of Greek art, literature, sculpture, or architecture **b :** an instance of such imitation

gre·cize \-,sīz\ *vt* -ED/-ING/-S *often cap* [F *gréciser*, fr. LL *graecizare*, alter. of L *graecissare*, fr. Gk *graikizein* to speak Greek, fr. *graikos* Greek + *-izein* -ize] **1 :** to make Greek or Hellenistic in quality, traits, or cultural characteristics ⟨the *grecized* eastern capital of the Roman Empire⟩ ⟨steps toward *grecizing* the Jews of Asia Minor⟩ **2 :** to modify (as a word, phrase, language) to accord with characteristically Greek language forms esp. in spelling

greco- *or* **graeco-** *comb form, usu cap* [L *Graeco-*, fr. *Graecus* Greek — more at GREEK] **1 :** Greece or Greeks ⟨*Greco*phile⟩ ⟨*Greco*mania⟩ **2 :** Greek and ⟨*Greco*-Latin⟩ ⟨*Greco*-Persian⟩ ⟨*Graeco*-Roman⟩

greco-roman \¦grē(,)kō, -re(- *sometimes* -rā(-+\ *adj, usu cap G&R* [*Greco-* + *Roman*] **:** having characteristics that are partly Greek and partly Roman; *specif* **:** having the characteristics of Roman art done under strong Greek influence

greco-roman wrestling *n, usu cap G&R* **:** wrestling in which the use of the legs for attack or defense is forbidden and a fall is gained by the contestant who pins both his opponent's shoulders to the ground

¹**gree** \ˈgrē\ *n* -S [ME, fr. MF *gré*, fr. LL *gratum*, fr. neut. of L *gratus* pleasing, thankful — more at GRACE] *archaic* **:** GOODWILL, FAVOR, PLEASURE, SATISFACTION — **make gree** *archaic* **:** to give satisfaction (as for an injury)

²**gree** \"\ *n* -S [ME, fr. MF *gré* step, degree, fr. L *gradus* — more at GRADE] **1** *obs* **:** rank or position esp. in a social scale **2** *chiefly Scot* **:** MASTERY, SUPERIORITY; *also* **:** the reward for these qualities — **bear the gree** *chiefly Scot* **:** to carry off the prize

³**gree** \"\ *vb* -ED/-ING/-S [ME *green*, short for *agreen* — more at AGREE] *now dial* **:** AGREE

greece \ˈgrēs\ *adj, usu cap* [fr. *Greece*, country in southeastern Europe] **:** of or from Greece **:** of the kind or style prevalent in Greece **:** GREEK

greed \ˈgrēd\ *n* -S [back-formation fr. *greedy*] **1 :** inordinate or all-consuming and usu. reprehensible acquisitiveness esp. for wealth or gain **:** COVETOUSNESS, AVARICE ⟨a passionate ~ for other people's money⟩ **2 :** extreme or voracious desire esp. for food or drink; *also* **:** behavior motivated by such desire **syn** see CUPIDITY

greed·i·ly \-dᵊl|ē, -dəl|, |i\ *adv* [ME *grediliche, gredily*, fr. OE *grǣdilice*, fr. *grǣdig* + *-lice* -ly] **:** in a greedy manner **:** in a way that shows great desire or marked acquisitiveness; *esp* **:** in a way showing great hunger or thirst ⟨ate ~⟩ ⟨weakened by thirst, the party drank ~ —*Amer. Guide Series: Calif.*⟩

greed·i·ness \-dēnə̇s, -din-\ *n* -ES [ME *gredinesse*, fr. OE *grǣdignæsse*, fr. *grǣdig* + *-næsse*, *-ness* -ness] **:** the quality or state of being greedy: **a :** extreme or excessive desire for food or drink; *also* **:** behavior giving evidence of this **:** VORACITY **b :** extreme or excessive desire for wealth or gain **:** COVETOUSNESS **c :** strong desire or longing **:** EAGERNESS ⟨moved by a ~ for a more exciting existence⟩

greedy \-dē, -di\ *adj* -ER/-EST [ME *gredy*, fr. OE *grǣdig;* akin to OHG *grātag* greedy, ON *grāthr* greed, hunger, *grāthugr* greedy, Goth *gredus* hungry, *gredags* hungry, and perh. to OE *giernan* to long for — more at YEARN] **1 :** having or showing a very strong desire for food or drink **:** RAVENOUS, VORACIOUS — often used with *of* ⟨a lion ~ of his prey⟩ **2 :** having or marked by an intense usu. reprehensibly excessive or selfish desire esp. for possessions ⟨~ for money and power⟩ ⟨~ of her love⟩ ⟨so thoroughly mercenary, so frankly ~ —Dashiell Hammett⟩ ⟨the powerful depiction of the ~, obsessed, invalid love of the heroine —Anthony Quinton⟩ ⟨all who engaged in politics were ~ of office —G.M.Trevelyan⟩ **3 :** EAGER, KEEN ⟨went at the task with ~ interest⟩ ⟨elated and ~ for the future —Frances G. Patton⟩ **syn** see COVETOUS

greedy scale *n* **:** a scale (*Hemiberlesia rapax*) that is native to Europe but has been introduced into America and Australia and attacks many woody plants

greegree *var of* GRIS-GRIS

¹**greek** \ˈgrēk\ *n* -S [ME *Greke*, fr. OE *Grēcas*, pl., fr. L *Graecus*, fr. Gk *Graikos*] **1** *cap* **a :** a native or inhabitant of Greece **:** one of the Greek people; *specif* **:** a member of one of the races of ancient Greece — compare ACHAEAN, AEOLIAN, DORIAN, HELLADIC, HELLENE, HELLENISTIC 1, IONIAN, MYCENAEAN, PELASGIAN **b :** one that is of Greek descent **c :** one that is Grecian in physical form or beauty of face **:** one suggesting a figure of classical Greek sculpture ⟨the best athlete in our village, a young *Greek* in his movements —C.H.Towne⟩ **2** *cap* **a :** the language that has been used by the Greeks in its various stages of development from prehistoric times to the

present and that constitutes by itself a branch of the Indo-European language family — see AEOLIC, ARCADIAN, ATTIC, CYPRIOT, DORIC, IONIC, KOINE, LATE GREEK, MIDDLE GREEK, NEW GREEK; INDO-EUROPEAN LANGUAGES table **b :** ancient Greek as used from the time of the earliest records to the end of the 2d century A.D. **c** [trans. of L *Graecum* (in the medieval proverb *Graecum est; non potest legi* It is Greek; it cannot be read)] **:** something unintelligible; *esp* **:** GIBBERISH ⟨the theory of relativity is *Greek* to most people⟩ **3** *cap* **:** a member of an Eastern Orthodox church **:** ORTHODOX **4** *often cap* **a** *archaic* **:** SWINDLER, SHARPER; *esp* **:** CARDSHARPER **b** *obs* **:** a hail-fellow-well-met and reveler **5** *usu cap* **:** a member of a Greek-letter fraternity or sorority

²**greek** \"\ *adj, usu cap* [ME *greke*, fr. *Greke*, n.] **1 a :** of, relating to, or characteristic of Greece **b :** of, relating to, or characteristic of the Greeks **c :** of, relating to, or characteristic of the language of the Greeks **2** *of architecture* **:** of, relating to, or imitating the architecture of classical Greece **:** marked by pedimented structures that employ the Greek architectural orders **3 a :** Eastern Orthodox **b :** of, relating to, or being an Eastern church using the Byzantine rite in Greek **c :** of, relating to, or being the established Orthodox church of Greece autocephalous under a holy synod since 1833

greek alphabet *n, usu cap G* **:** an alphabet that has been used from ancient times for writing the Greek language, that is of Semitic origin but differs from Semitic alphabets in having characters for the vowels, and that has given rise directly or indirectly to various other alphabets (as the Latin, the Coptic, the Cyrillic)

greek calends *or* **greek kalends** *n pl, usu cap G* [trans. of L *kalendas graecas* (in *ad kalendas graecas solvere* to go without paying, lit., to pay at the Greek calends); fr. the fact that the Greeks did not reckon time by calends] **:** a time that will never arrive ⟨a bill he planned to pay at the *Greek calends*⟩

¹**greek catholic** *adj, usu cap G&C* **1 :** Eastern Orthodox **2 :** of, relating to, or being a Uniate church using the Byzantine rite

²**greek** \"\ *adj, usu cap* [ME *Greke*, fr. *Greke*, n.] **1 a :** of, church **2 :** a member of a Greek Catholic Uniate church

greek chorus *n, usu cap G* **1 :** a chorus in a classical Greek play typically serving to formulate, express, and comment on the moral issue that is raised by the dramatic action or to express an emotion appropriate to each stage of the dramatic conflict **2 :** a group of people who with persistence express esp. similar views or feelings about a particular action or series of actions

greek cross *n, usu cap G* **:** a cross having an upright and a transverse shaft equal in length and intersecting at their middles so that all four arms are equal in length

Greek cross

greek-cross plan *n, usu cap G* **:** a plan of a building having a square central mass and four equal arms

greek fir *n, usu cap G* **:** an ornamental Grecian evergreen tree (*Abies cephalonica*) with lustrous red-brown branches and stiff pointed leaves

greek fire *n, usu cap G* **1 :** an incendiary composition used in warfare by the Byzantine Greeks and said to have burst into flame on wetting **2 :** any of several flammable mixtures **:** WILDFIRE

greek foot *n, usu cap G* **:** an ancient Greek unit of length equal to 1.012 English feet

greek fret *or* **greek key** *n, usu cap G* **:** ⁴FRET 2

greek gift *n, usu cap G* [so called fr. the story of the Trojan horse — more at TROJAN HORSE] **:** a gift given or a favor done with a treacherous purpose

greek·ish \ˈgrēkish\ *adj, usu cap* [ME *grekissh*, fr. OE *grēcisc*, fr. *Grēcas*, pl., Greeks + *-isc* -ish — more at GREEK] **1** *archaic* **:** GREEK **2** [²*greek* + *-ish*] **:** Greek or somewhat Greek in quality or characteristics

greek·ish·ness *n* -ES *usu cap* **:** the quality or state of being somewhat Greek in characteristics

greek·ist \-kəst\ *n* -S *usu cap* **:** a specialist in Greek

greek·ize \ˈgrē,kīz\ *vt* -ED/-ING/-S *often cap* **:** GRECIZE

greek juniper *n, usu cap G* **:** an ornamental Eurasian tree (*Juniperus excelsa*) having a pyramidal shape, scaly leaves, and bluish black berrylike fruits

greek·less \ˈgrēklə̇s\ *adj, usu cap* **:** being without an ability to translate Greek **:** having no training in the Greek language ⟨writes for a *Greekless* reader —G.M.Messing⟩ — **greek·less·ness** *n* -ES *usu cap*

greek–letter fraternity *n, usu cap G* **:** a fraternity designated by usu. three Greek letters

greek–letter society *n, usu cap G* **:** a Greek-letter fraternity or sorority

greek–letter sorority *n, usu cap G* **:** a sorority designated by usu. three Greek letters

greek·ling \ˈgrēkliŋ\ *n* -S *cap, archaic* **:** a small, insignificant, or contemptible Greek

greek mode *n, usu cap G* **:** a descending musical scale based upon the tetrachord in which the octave species consists of two disjunct tetrachords

Dorian Hypodorian

Phrygian Hypophrygian

Lydian Hypolydian

Mixolydian [Hypomixolydian would be equivalent to Dorian.]

Greek modes

greek·ness *n* -ES *usu cap* **:** the quality or state of being Greek

greek orthodox *adj, usu cap G&O* **:** Eastern Orthodox; *specif* **:** GREEK 3c

greek partridge *n, usu cap G* **:** ROCK PARTRIDGE; *esp* **:** one of the varieties (*Alectoris graeca graeca*) of mountainous southern Europe with gray, black, and chestnut plumage

greek revival *n, cap G & usu cap R* **1 :** a style of architecture in the first half of the 19th century marked by the use or imitation of Greek orders **2 :** a style of decoration (as of furniture) using or imitating the decorative motifs of ancient Greece

greeks *pl of* GREEK

greek tea *n, usu cap G* **:** FRENCH TEA

greek tortoise *n, usu cap G* **:** EUROPEAN TORTOISE

greek valerian *n, usu cap G* **:** any of several plants of the genus *Polemonium*; *esp* **:** JACOB'S LADDER 1a

greek wave *n, usu cap G* **:** a curvilinear variant of the Greek fret

¹**green** \ˈgrēn\ *adj* -ER/-EST [ME *grene*, fr. OE *grēne*; akin to OHG *gruoni* green, ON *grænn* green, OE *grōwan* to grow — more at GROW] **1 a :** of the color green ⟨~ jade⟩ **b :** having the color of growing fresh grass or of the emerald ⟨~ lawns⟩ **2 a :** having abundant verdure **:** covered by green growth or foliage **:** VERDANT ⟨the hills are low and very beautiful because they are ~ —John Welman⟩ **b :** pleasant and alluring **:** exceedingly broad and fair ⟨an original scientist turns his feet ruinously into the wide ~ descent to popular science —Carl Van Doren⟩ **c** *of a season of the year* **:** characterized by mildness **:** TEMPERATE ⟨a ~ yule⟩ **d :** consisting of green plants, herbs, or vegetables ⟨a ~ salad⟩ ⟨gathered their ~ cargoes and returned to their rewarding trade —Anne Dorrance⟩ **3 a :** full of life and vigor **:** YOUTHFUL ⟨the Fates had ruled that he should reach a ~ old age —Robert Graves⟩ ⟨with his white head and his loneliness he remained young and ~ at heart —John Galsworthy⟩ **b :** strikingly alive **:** vivid despite the passage of time ⟨my memory of all of them is still ~ —J.J.Mallon⟩ ⟨hard to bring events into sharp and stable focus . . . while one's emotions about them are still ~ —Cabell Phillips⟩ **4 a** *of a plant* **:** YOUNG, FRESH, TENDER ⟨the burro . . . can subsist equally well on succulent ~ grasses or dry bark —*Amer. Guide Series: Ariz.*⟩ **b** *of a fruit or vegetable* **:** not ripened or matured **:** IMMATURE ⟨~ apples⟩ **5** *of a wound* **:** recently incurred **:** FRESH, UNHEALED ⟨like a ~ wound at first I felt it not —John Home⟩ **6 :** marked by a pale or sickly appearance ⟨is ~ with envy⟩ ⟨was scared ~⟩ ⟨wakes it now to look so ~ and pale —Shak.⟩ **7 a :** not fully processed or treated: as (1) *of coffee* **:** partly raw **:** RAW **:** not roasted (2) *of meat* **:** freshly killed **:** not dried or salted (3) *of market fish* **:** as taken from the water **:** not cleaned (4) *of liquor* **:** not aged (5) *of a bone* **:** not seasoned or dried and often containing marrow (6) *of a hide or pelt* **:** not dressed or tanned (7) *of lumber* **:** freshly sawed **:** UNSEASONED (8) *of ceramics* **:** not yet baked in an oven or kiln **:** not fired (9) *of metal powder* **:** not sintered **b :** not in condition for a particular use: as (1) *of concrete or mortar* **:** not sufficiently hardened (2) *of paper* **:** incompletely seasoned (3) *of an inking roller* **:** freshly cast (4) *of printer's proof* **:** not corrected **c** (1) *of a female fish* **:** not ready to spawn — compare RIPE, SPENT (2) *of a crab* **:** not quite ready to shed **8 a :** marked by inexperience or immaturity **:** lacking training, knowledge, or experience ⟨we are beginners and the humblest and ~*est* of the tribe —John Mason Brown⟩ ⟨shipped as a ~ hand on a vessel —W.J.Ghent⟩ **b :** lacking sophistication **:** unfamiliar with worldly ways **:** GULLIBLE, NAÏVE ⟨wasn't so ~ as to expect suspicious characters to look suspicious —G.K. Chesterton⟩ **c** *of a horse* **:** not fully qualified for or experienced in a particular function: (1) *of a workhorse* **:** broken but not trained (2) *of a Thoroughbred* **:** not yet raced for premiums or money or speeded against time (3) *of a hunter* **:** not previously exhibited or hunted **9** *obs* **:** recently buried ⟨where bloody Tybalt, yet but ~ in earth, lies festering in his shroud —Shak.⟩ **10** *of hemolytic streptococci* **:** tending to produce green pigment when cultured on blood media **syn** see RUDE

²**green** \"\ *vb* -ED/-ING/-S [ME *grenen*, fr. OE *grēnian*; akin to OHG *gruonēn* to become green, ON *grœnast*; inchoatives fr. the root of E ¹*green*] *vi* **:** to become or grow green ⟨my pea jacket had ~*ed* with wear —James Still⟩ ⟨in the soft moist air the grass was ~*ing* —Dorothy C. Fisher⟩ ~ *vt* **1 :** to make green **:** cause to acquire a green color ⟨the colors pouring down the balustrade and ~*ing* the floor —Richard Llewellyn⟩ ⟨white frock . . . which she had so carelessly ~*ed* about the skirt on the damping grass —Thomas Hardy⟩ **2 :** to make fun of by or as if by a hoax ⟨some witchcraft material which came to my attention seemed so extraordinary that I suspected my friends were ~*ing* me —Vance Randolph⟩

³**green** \"\ *n* -S [ME *grene*, fr. *grene*, adj.] **1 a :** a color whose hue is somewhat less yellow than that of growing fresh grass or of the emerald or is that of the part of the spectrum lying between blue and yellow **b :** the one of the four psychologically primary hues that is evoked in the average normal observer under normal conditions by radiant energy of the wavelength 530 millimicrons **c :** one of the six psychologically primary object colors **2 a :** clothing or cloth of a green color **b greens** *pl* **:** a green uniform ⟨a sergeant of marines, very snappy in his ~*s* —John Dos Passos⟩ **3 :** green vegetation ⟨new spring ~ mantled the hills⟩: as **a greens** *pl* **:** fresh foliage or leafy parts of plants for use as decoration; *esp* **:** evergreen branches for winter decorations ⟨always collected our own Christmas ~*s*⟩ **b greens** *pl* (1) **:** leafy herbs (as spinach, dandelions, Swiss chard) that are boiled or steamed as a vegetable **:** POTHERB 1 (2) **:** a vegetable whose foliage and foliage-bearing branches are the sole or chief edible part **:** GREEN VEGETABLE **4 :** a grassy plain or plot: as **a :** a common or park in the center of a town or village ⟨white clapboard and red brick Georgian homes and churches looking out on the placid village ~ —Budd Schulberg⟩ **b :** BOWLING GREEN **c :** PUTTING GREEN **d :** an archery shooting range **5 :** youthful vigor **:** VIRILITY — usu. used in the phrase *in the green* ⟨thy leaf has perished in the ~ —Alfred Tennyson⟩ **6 :** a pigment or dye that colors green **7 :** MONEY; *esp* **:** GREENBACKS **8 a :** the petticoat of an archery target **b :** a shot that hits in the petticoat **c :** an arrow that misses the target and hits the grass **9 :** a card belonging to one of the four suits in the German pack of playing cards and having a leaf as its symbol

⁴**green** \"\ *vi* -ED/-ING/-S [ME *grenen*, prob. modif. of ON *girna* — more at YEARN] *Scot* **:** YEARN, LONG

green·able \-nəbəl\ *adj* **:** capable of being made green

green acid *n* **:** any of various mixtures of water-soluble sulfonic acid derivatives of petroleum obtained as by-products in treating white oils with sulfuric acid

green adder's mouth *n* **:** a low No. American herb (*Malaxis unifolia*) having a solitary leaf and flowers with reflexed petals that resemble threads

green alder *n* **:** any of several alders: **a :** an alder (*Alnus crispa*) of northern No. America distinguished by the light green undersurfaces of the leaves and by the winged nuts **b :** a European alder (*A. viridis*) **c :** SPECKLED ALDER

green alga *n* **:** an alga in which the chlorophyll is not masked or characteristically obscured by other pigments; *specif* **:** any alga of the division Chlorophyta

green·a·lite \-nᵊl,īt\ *n* -S [¹*green* + connective *-a-* + *-lite*] **:** a mineral consisting of hydrous ferrous silicate of an earthy green color occurring as small granules in a cherty rock associated with the iron ores of the Mesabi range

green almond *n* **:** PISTACHIO 1a(2)

green aloe *n* **:** GIANT CABUYA

green amaranth *n* **:** PIGWEED a

green aphis *n, NewZeal* **:** GREEN PEACH APHID

green apple aphid *n* **:** APPLE APHID

green arrow arum *n* **:** an arrow arum (*Peltandra virginica*)

green ash *n* **:** a red ash (*Fraxinus pennsylvanica subintegerrima*) with branchlets, petioles, and lower leaf surfaces glabrous

greenback \ˈ=,=\ *n* **1 :** any of numerous animals variably greenish about the upper parts (as a green frog or various fishes) **2 a :** a legal-tender note issued by the U.S. government **b greenbacks** *pl* **:** MONEY

green–backed goldfinch \ˈ=,=-\ *n* **:** a goldfinch (*Spinus psaltria hesperophilus*) of western No. America having the upper parts olive green

green·back·er \ˈgrēn,bakə(r)\ *n* [*greenback* (money) + *-er*] **1** *usu cap* **:** a member of a post-Civil War American political party opposing any reduction in the amount of paper money in circulation **2 :** one who advocates a paper currency backed only by the U.S. government ⟨the silverites, the ~*s*, the price stabilizers, and others . . . are pledged to a central-bank scheme —*Harper's*⟩

green·back·ism \-a,kizəm\ *n* -S *usu cap* **:** the principles of the greenbackers

greenback mackerel *n* **:** PACIFIC MACKEREL

greenback shower *n* **:** a shower at which gifts of money are presented to the prospective bride

greenbark \ˈ=,=\ *or* **greenbark acacia** *n* **:** PALOVERDE

green bass *n* **:** LARGEMOUTH BLACK BASS

green bean *n* **:** any of numerous kidney beans that have the pods green when suitably matured for use as snap beans — compare WAX BEAN

greenbelt \ˈ=,=\ *n* **:** a belt of parkways, parks, or farmlands that encircles a town or community and is designed to prevent undesirable encroachments

green–blind \ˈ=,=\ *adj* **:** exhibiting or affected with deuteranopia

greenboard \ˈ=,=\ *n* **:** a chalkboard with a green surface **:** green blackboard

greenbone \ˈ=,=\ *n* **:** any of several fishes having the bones green esp. when cooked: as **a :** NEEDLEFISH **b :** EELPOUT 1a

green book *n, often cap G&B* **:** an official report of government affairs bound in green — used esp. of Italian, British, and British Indian reports

greenbottle fly \ˈ=,==-\ *also* **greenbottle** *n* **:** any of several brilliant coppery green-bodied flies of the family Calliphoridae; *esp* **:** a fly of the genus *Lucilia*

greenbrier \ˈ=,=\ *n* **:** a plant of the genus *Smilax*; *esp* **:** a prickly vine (*Smilax rotundifolia*) of the eastern U.S. with a yellowish green stem, thick leaves, and umbels of small greenish flowers

green bristle *or* **green bristlegrass** *n* **:** GREEN FOXTAIL

green broke *adj, of a horse* **:** incompletely broken or trained

green broom *n* **1 :** WOODWAXEN **2 :** SCOTCH BROOM

greenbug \ˈ=,=\ *n* **:** a green aphid (*Schizaphis graminum*) that is very destructive to wheat, oats, and other grains

green·bul \ˈgrēn,bu̇l\ *n* -S [short for *green bulbul*] **:** any of numerous variably greenish African bulbuls — called also *green bulbul*

green bulbul *n* **1 :** any of numerous predominantly green bulbuls of southeast Asia and the southwest Pacific that have rich silky plumage often varied with blue, black, or yellow and that feed chiefly on fruits and nectar — called also *fruitsucker, leafbird*; see CHLOROPSIS **2 :** GREENBUL

green charge *n* **:** a mixture of ingredients for gunpowder before the intimate mixing in the incorporating mill

green cheese *n* **1 :** cheese that is not ripened **:** new cheese **2 :** cheese (as sapsago) having a green color **3 :** cheese made of whey or skim milk

green cinnabar *n* **1 :** a green pigment consisting of fired oxides of cobalt and zinc **2 :** a pigment consisting of chrome yellow and Prussian blue

green citrus aphid *n* **:** a small green aphid (*Aphis spiraecola*) esp. abundant on citrus where it causes distorting and rosetting of the leaves — called also *spirea aphid*

green cloth *n* **1** *usu cap G&C* [so called fr. the green-covered table at which the board orig. carried on its business] **:** a board or court of justice of the British sovereign's household that is composed of the lord steward and his officers and has cognizance of matters of justice in the household with power to correct offenders and keep the peace within the palace **2 a :** a layout for gambling **b :** BILLIARD TABLE

green cloverworm \ˈ=ˈ==,=\ *n* **:** a small slender green larva of a noctuid moth (*Plathypena scabra*) destructive to clover and other legumes

green cod *n* **1 :** POLLACK **2 :** LINGCOD

green cormorant *n* **:** a shag (*Phalacrocorax aristotelis*)

green corn *n* **:** the young tender ears of Indian corn suitable for cooking as a vegetable — compare SWEET CORN

green crab *n* **:** a nearly cosmopolitan edible crab (*Carcinus maenas*) found along shores chiefly in the intertidal zone

green dragon *n* **1 :** a European arum (*Dracunculus vulgaris*) resembling the cuckoopint **2 :** an American arum (*Arisaema dracontium*) differing from the related common jack-in-the-pulpit by its digitate leaves, slender greenish yellow spathe, and elongated spadix

green drake *n* **1 :** any of various British mayflies **2 :** a fisherman's lure resembling a green drake

green duck *n* **:** a young duck; *esp* **:** a well-fattened young duck ready for market when 9 to 13 weeks old

green–ear disease *n* **:** a disease of pearl millet and other grasses in which part or all of the head becomes leafy from attacks of a downy mildew (*Sclerospora graminicola*)

green earth *n* [trans. of F *terre verte* or It *terra verde*] **1 :** TERRE VERTE **2 :** any of various naturally occurring silicates esp. of iron used chiefly as bases for green basic dyes — called also *terre verte*

green ebony *n* **1 a :** an ebony of a greenish color **b :** a tree of the genus *Diospyros* (as *D. melanoxylon*) yielding such ebony **2 :** COCUSWOOD

greened *past of* GREEN

¹**greener** *comparative of* GREEN

²**green·er** \ˈgrēnə(r)\ *n* -S [¹*green* + *-er*] **:** an unskilled or inexperienced workman; *esp* **:** one who is a recently arrived alien ⟨a ~ of the greenest order, having landed at the docks only a few hours ago —Israel Zangwill⟩

green·ery \ˈgrēn(ə)rē, -ri\ *n* -ES [¹*green* + *-ery*] **1 :** green foliage or plants **:** VERDURE ⟨the lake . . . reflects the ~ of hilly shores —*Amer. Guide Series: Oreg.*⟩ **2 :** decorations of green leaves and branches — compare ³GREEN 3a ⟨an awning-covered pavilion festooned for the occasion with ~ —Harriot B. Barbour⟩ **3 :** GREENHOUSE

greenest *superlative of* GREEN

green–eyed \ˈ=ˈ=\ *adj* **:** characterized by envy or distrust **:** JEALOUS ⟨beware, my lord, of jealousy; it is the *green-eyed* monster —Shak.⟩ ⟨the *green-eyed* locals who had spied on him —E.O.Schlunke⟩

green fee *also* **greens fee** *n* **:** a fee paid for the privilege of playing on a golf course

greenfeed \ˈ=,=\ *n, Austral* **:** succulent forage fed to livestock without ensiling

green felt *n* **1 :** an alga of the genus *Vaucheria* (esp. *V. terrestris*) **2 :** a dense green growth produced by green felt

greenfinch \ˈ=,=\ *n* **1 :** a very common European finch (*Chloris chloris*) having olive-green and yellow plumage **2 :** TEXAS SPARROW

green fingers *n pl* **:** GREEN THUMB

green fire *n* **:** a composition that burns with a bright green light produced usu. by barium nitrate

greenfish \ˈ=,=\ *n* **:** any of several variably greenish or bluish fishes: as **a :** POLLACK **b :** BLUEFISH 1 **c :** an opaleye (*Girella nigricans*)

green flash *n* **:** a momentary green appearance of the uppermost part of the sun's disk that results from atmospheric refraction when the sun sinks below or rises above the horizon

greenfly \ˈ=,=\ *n, Brit* **:** APHID; *esp* **:** GREEN PEACH APHID

green foxtail *n* **:** a European grass (*Setaria viridis*) naturalized in No. America where it is often a troublesome weed

green fringed orchis *n* **:** RAGGED ORCHIS

green frog *n* **:** a common frog (*Rana clamitans*) of the eastern and central U.S. and parts of Canada

green fruitworm *n* **:** the larva of any of several noctuid moths; *esp* **:** an orchard pest (*Lithophane antennata*) that feeds on leaves and fruits

green·gage \ˈgrēn,gāj, ˈ=ˈ=\ *n* -S [*green* + Sir William *Gage* †1820 Eng. botanist who imported it from France] **:** any of several rather small rounded greenish or greenish yellow cultivated plums of European origin grown chiefly for their superior dessert quality

green gall *n* **:** an oak apple collected before the escape of the enclosed wasp larva while very dark in color and rich in tannin

green gentian *n* **:** any of several plants of the genus *Swertia* found chiefly in the Rocky mountain region

greengill \ˈ=,=\ *n* **:** an oyster with gills or other parts tinged with a green pigment that results from its feeding on green vegetable organisms and that does not injure it as food — compare GREENING

green ginger *n* **:** undried ginger

green gland *n* **:** one of a pair of large green glands in crayfishes and related crustaceans that are believed to act as kidneys and that have outlets at the bases of the larger antennae

green glass *n* **1 :** a low grade of glass of soda-lime content whose natural green color is due to impurities in the raw materials **2 :** glass of any quality that has been colored green by the addition of coloring agents to the batch

green gold *n* **:** an alloy of 14 to 18 karat gold that is greenish in color and employs either silver or silver plus cadmium or zinc as the alloying metal

green goods *n pl* **1 :** counterfeit greenbacks **2 :** fresh vegetables

green goose *n* **:** a young goose; *esp* **:** a well-fattened young goose ready for market when 10 to 12 weeks old

green gown *n* [so called fr. the grass stains traditionally acquired when illicit love is made] *archaic* **:** a gown symbolically acquired at illicit loss of virginity ⟨many a *green gown* has been given, many a kiss, both odd and even —Robert Herrick †1674⟩

green gram *n* **:** MUNG BEAN

green grasshopper *n* **:** any of numerous green slender-bodied long-horned grasshoppers

greengrocer \ˈ=,==\ *n, chiefly Brit* **:** a retailer of fresh vegetables and fruit

greengrocery \ˈ=,=(=)=\ *n* **1** *chiefly Brit* **:** the wares of a greengrocer **2** *chiefly Brit* **:** a greengrocer's shop

green grosbeak *n* **:** GREENFINCH 1

green guenon *n* **:** GREEN MONKEY

green hand *n, dial* **:** GREEN THUMB

greenhead \ˈ=,=\ *n* **1** *archaic* **:** GREENHORN **2 a :** MALLARD **b :** GREATER SCAUP **3** *also* **greenhead fly :** any of several green-eyed biting flies of the family Tabanidae; *esp* **:** a large fly (*Tabanus nigrovittatus*) common near salt marshes **4 :** STRIPED BASS

green-headed *adj, obs* : marked by or based on inexperience ⟨the advice of his *green-headed* counselors —Francis Roberts⟩
greenheart \'⸗,⸗\ *n* **1** : any of several tropical American trees furnishing somewhat greenish usu. hard valuable wood: as **a** : BEBEERU **b** *West Indies* : a tree (*Colubrina ferruginosa*) used in general construction work **c** *Jamaica* : a tree (*Zizyphus chloroxylon*) with very hard durable wood **d** *in northeastern So. America* : BETHABARA **2** : the wood of a greenheart
green hellebore *n* **1** : AMERICAN HELLEBORE **2** : a hellebore (*Helleborus viridis*) with large pedate leaves and solitary nodding flowers
green heron *n* : any of various small herons (genus *Butorides*); *esp* : a small American heron (*B. virescens*) with mostly greenish back and chestnut neck
greenhew \'⸗,⸗\ *n* [³*green* + *hew*] : the right to cut vert
greenhide \'⸗,⸗\ *n, Austral* : RAWHIDE ⟨a long-lashed stock-whip and lariat of plaited ~ —I.L.Idriess⟩
greenhorn \'⸗,⸗\ *n* [obs. *greenhorn* animal with green or young horns, fr. ME *grenehorn*, fr. *grene* green + *horn*] **1** : an inexperienced or unsophisticated person ⟨an intellectual ~ from the provinces —Nigel Dennis⟩; *esp* : one easily duped or imposed upon **2** : a newcomer (as to a country) unacquainted with local manners and customs; *esp* : a recently arrived immigrant ⟨~*s* . . . looking half-starved after their long trip from the old country —Mary Deasy⟩
greenhouse \'⸗,⸗\ *n* **1** : a structure enclosed by glass and devoted to the cultivation or protection of tender plants or the production of plants out of season — compare CONSERVATORY, COOLHOUSE, HOTHOUSE **2** *chiefly Brit* : a place for drying ceramic ware before firing **3** : a plastic shell covering the cockpit, cabin, turret, or nose of an airplane
greenhouse leaf tier *n* : CELERY LEAF TIER
greenhouse thrips *n* : a thrips (*Heliothrips haemorrhoidalis*) that feeds on foliage and blossoms in greenhouses or in warm regions on citrus and other cultivated plants
greenhouse whitefly *n* : a tiny white 4-winged fly (*Trialeurodes vaporariorum*) that is related to the aphids and scale insects and has minute pale green larvae which together with the adults suck the juices from plants and thereby cause them to yellow and wilt
green hydra *n* : a cosmopolitan hydra (*Chlorohydra viridissima*) made green by the presence in its cells of chlorophyll-bearing plastids
greenie *var of* GREENY
greenier *comparative of* GREENY
greenies *pl of* GREENY
greeniest *superlative of* GREENY
green·ing \'grēniŋ, -nēŋ\ *n* -s [¹*green* + *-ing*] **1** : any of several green-skinned apples **2** : a green appearance of oysters caused by their feeding on minute green marine algae — compare GREENGILL **3** : SUNBURN 2a
green·ish \-nish, -nēsh\ *adj* [ME *grenissh*, fr. *grene* green + *-ish*] : somewhat green : having a tinge of green ⟨~ yellow⟩ ⟨~ fishes⟩ — **green·ish·ness** *n* -ES
green jack *n* : a West Indian cavalla (*Caranx ruber*)
green jay *n* : a jay (*Cyanocorax yucas*) that ranges from So. America to the Rio Grande and is brilliantly marked in green, blue, black, white, and yellow
green june beetle *n, usu cap J* : a large metallic green and brown scarabaeid beetle (*Cotinis nitida*) of the eastern U.S. whose grubs are turf pests
green·keep·er \'grēn,kēpə(r)\ *also* **greens·keep·er** \-nz,k-\ *n* : a person responsible for the upkeep of a golf course
green kurrajong *n* : a tall prickly Australian shrub (*Hibiscus heterophyllus*) that is sometimes cultivated for its large white purple-centered or crimson-centered flowers
green·land \'grēnlənd, -,land, -,laa(ə)nd\ *adj, usu cap* [fr. *Greenland*, largest island in the world, northeast of No. America, fr. Dan *Grønland*, fr. ON *Grænland*] : of or from Greenland : of the kind or style prevalent in Greenland : GREENLANDIC
greenland caribou *n, usu cap G* : BARREN GROUND CARIBOU
green·land·er \-də(r)\ *n* -s *cap* : a native or inhabitant of Greenland
greenland halibut *n, usu cap G* : a flatfish (*Reinhardtius hippoglossoides*) of the cold parts of the Atlantic that weighs 10 to 25 pounds and is colored on both sides
¹**green·land·ic** \(')grēn¦landik, -laan-, -dēk\ *adj, usu cap* [*Greenland* (the island) + E *-ic*] **1 a** : of, relating to, or characteristic of Greenland **b** : of, relating to, or characteristic of the Greenlanders **2** : of, relating to, or characteristic of the language of the Greenlanders
²**greenlandic** \"\ *n* -s *cap* : an Eskimo-Aleut dialect of Greenland often considered a language — compare YUPIK
green·land·ite \'grēnlən,dīt, -,lan-, -,laan-\ *n* -s [*Greenland* + E *-ite*] : COLUMBITE
greenland seal *n, usu cap G* : HARP SEAL
greenland shark *n, usu cap G* : a large shark (*Somniosus microcephalus*) of arctic seas having a small head, weak jaws, small teeth, very small fins, and skin covered uniformly with minute tubercles — called also *sleeper shark*
greenland spar *n, usu cap G* : CRYOLITE
greenland whale *n, usu cap G* : the whalebone whale of the Arctic (*Balaena mysticetus*) — called also *bowhead*
green laver *n* : SEA LETTUCE
green lead ore *n* : PYROMORPHITE
green leek *n* : an Australian parrakeet (*Polytelis swainsonii*) that is chiefly green with yellow on face and throat and the breast scarlet
green·less \'grēnlə̇s\ *adj* : lacking verdure
green·let \-lə̇t\ *n* -s : VIREO
green light *n* [so called fr. the color of traffic lights when traffic is allowed to proceed] : authority or permission to go ahead with a definite project ⟨got a message to leave town and stay lost until I got the *green light* to return —Polly Adler⟩ ⟨a city that has just given the *green light* to a program of progress —*Wall Street Jour.*⟩
green·ling \'grēnliŋ\ *n* -s [¹*green* + *-ling*] **1 a** (1) : any of several moderate-sized to large scorpaenoid food fishes (family Hexagrammidae) of the rocky coasts of the northern Pacific (2) : a common food and sport fish (*Hexagrammos decagrammus*) of the west coast of No. America — called also *kelp greenling* **b** : LINGCOD **2** : POLLACK
green linnet *n* : GREENFINCH 1
green lizard *n* : a common Eurasian lizard (*Lacerta viridis*) that becomes a foot long
green louse *n* : PLANT LOUSE
green·ly *adv, usu* -ER/-EST **1 a** : with a green color ⟨the . . . stream rushing between white crusts of frozen foam and washing ~ against ice-crowned boulders —Stephen Graham⟩ **b** : with green vegetation : VERDANTLY ⟨the earth broke ~ into spring —Millen Brand⟩ **2** : in an inexperienced manner : CLUMSILY ⟨we have done but ~ in hugger-mugger to inter him —Shak.⟩
green malt *n* : grain softened by steeping in water and allowed to germinate but not yet subjected to drying — compare MALT
green man *n* : JACK-IN-THE-GREEN 1
green mangle *n* : MARSH ELDER 2
green manure *or* **green-manure crop** *n* : an herbaceous crop (as clover) plowed under while green to enrich the soil
green-manure \¦⸗⸗¦⸗\ *vt* : to fertilize with green manure
green mealie *n, Africa* : CORN ON THE COB
green meat *n, Brit* : fresh green herbage for feeding animals
green milkweed *n* : a green-flowered herb (*Asclepias viridiflora*) of the eastern U.S. resembling the common milkweeds
green mold *n* **1** : a green or green-spored mold; *esp* : one belonging to the genus *Penicillium* or the genus *Aspergillus* — compare BLUE MOLD **2** : a disease caused by green mold
green monkey *n* : a West African long-tailed monkey (*Cercopithecus sabaeus*) that has greenish-appearing hair and is often tamed and trained
green mountain boy *n, usu cap G&M* [fr. *Green Mountain Boys*, a militia organized in Vermont during the Am. Revolution, fr. the *Green Mountains*, Vt.] : a male Vermonter — used as a nickname
green mud *n* : a deep-sea sediment consisting largely of the remains of Foraminifera and of glauconite
green muscardine *n* : a disease of silkworms and other caterpillars caused by a fungus (*Metarrhizium anisopliae*)
green·ness \'grēnnə̇s\ *n* -ES [ME *grennes, grennesse*, fr. OE *grēnnes*, fr. *grēne* green + *-nes* -ness — more at GREEN] : the quality or state of being green: as **a** : VERDANCY ⟨carried us past banks of soft ~ shaded by tall trees —Thomas Horgan⟩ **b** : green color ⟨~ of the sea⟩ ⟨~ of shutters against the white clapboards of the house⟩ **c** (1) : youth and immaturity ⟨the ~ of his years secured him from any suspicion —Tobias Smollett⟩ (2) : lack of training or knowledge : INEXPERIENCE ⟨soldiers without battle experience had shown ~ —A.J.Liebling⟩ (3) : GULLIBILITY, NAÏVETÉ ⟨betraying his ~ to the Yankees by his questions —H.D.Thoreau⟩ **d** : VITALITY, VIGOR ⟨the affection of a child gives a ~ to old age —Peter Parley⟩
green ocher *n* **1** : TERRE VERTE 2 **2** : a green pigment prepared from yellow ocher treated with potassium ferrocyanide
gree·nock·ite \'grēnə,kīt\ *n* -s [Charles M. Cathcart, Lord *Greenock* †1859 Eng. soldier + E *-ite*] : a mineral CdS consisting of native cadmium sulfide occurring in yellow translucent hexagonal crystals and as an earthy incrustation
green oil *n* : any of various oils that are green in color or that have not been refined: as **a** : ANTHRACENE OIL **b** : a fraction obtained from shale oil in the first distillation and chemical treatment
green onion *n* : a young onion pulled before the bulb has enlarged for its blanched base and lower stalk which are usu. eaten raw (as in salad)
green osier *n* : either of two dogwoods: **a** : BLUE DOGWOOD **b** : a coarse shrub (*Cornus rugosa*) with greenish branches, broadly ovate leaves, and bluish fruit — called also *round-leaved dogwood*
green out *vi* : to put forth green shoots ⟨after July's plentiful rainfall most of the state's cattle ranges were *greening out* —*Time*⟩ ~ *vt, Midland* : SWINDLE, CHEAT : make a fool of
gree·no·vite \'grēnə,vīt\ *n* -s [F *grenovite*, irreg. fr. George B. *Greenough* †1855 Eng. geologist + F *-ite*] : a sphene colored red or rose by manganese
green oyster *n* : GREENGILL
green paint *n* : the dirty blue-green deposit on wave-dashed rocks at the water's edge caused by certain blue-green algae (esp. of the genera *Coelosphaerium* and *Microcystis*)
green peach aphid *n* : a yellowish green aphid (*Myzus persicae*) native to Europe but now nearly cosmopolitan in distribution that feeds on numerous cultivated plants, is frequently a vector of virus diseases, and is esp. destructive to peaches, potatoes, and spinach — called also *greenfly, spinach aphid*
green peak *n, dial Eng* : GREEN WOODPECKER
green pepper *n* : SWEET PEPPER
green pigeon *n* : any of numerous chiefly tropical Old World fruit doves with green plumage and feathered tarsi — called also *fruit pigeon*
green pike *n* **1** : CHAIN PICKEREL **2** : WALLEYED PIKE **3** : SAUGER
green plover *n* **1** : LAPWING **2** : GOLDEN PLOVER
green poppy *n* : FOXGLOVE 1
green rein orchis *n* : a No. American terrestrial orchid (*Perularia flava*) with greenish yellow flowers
green river *n, usu cap G&R* [fr. *Green river*, a stream that flows through the region in Kentucky where it is produced] : a dark air-cured tobacco used chiefly for chewing tobacco
greenroom \'⸗,⸗\ *n* [prob. so called fr. its orig. being painted green] : a room in a theater or concert hall where actors or musicians relax esp. before going on stage and where they meet friends during intermissions or after performances
green rose *n* : a very large China rose (*Rosa chinensis viridiflora*) whose petals are represented by narrow green leaves
green rot *n* : a decay of fallen beech, oak, birch, or other deciduous trees in which the wood is colored a malachite green by a cup fungus (*Peziza aeruginosa*)
green rouge *n* : chromic oxide used as a polishing material esp. for platinum and stainless steel
greens *pres 3d sing of* GREEN, *pl of* GREEN
green salt *n* : coarse salt with about five percent impurities
green-salted \'⸗¦⸗⸗\ *adj* : salted while green — used esp. of hides
greensand \'⸗,⸗\ *n* **1** : a sedimentary deposit that consists largely of dark greenish grains of glauconite often mingled with clay or sand, occurs abundantly in the Cretaceous often little or not at all cemented, and is used as a water softener and as a source of potash **2** : highly siliceous sand that contains a little magnesia and alumina mixed with about one twelfth of its bulk of powdered coal or charcoal and is used when dampened for making foundry molds
green sandpiper *n* : a common Old World sandpiper (*Tringa ochropus*) related to the solitary sandpiper of America
greensauce \'⸗,⸗\ *n* **1** : SHEEP SORREL 1 **2** : a wood sorrel (*Oxalis montana*)
greenschist \'⸗,⸗\ *n* [¹*green* + *schist*] : a laminated metamorphic rock characterized by muscovite, quartz, and chlorite
green sea *n* : a solid wave of water coming aboard a ship ⟨rolling 30 degrees and taking *green seas* aboard —*Scientific American*⟩ — called also *green water*
green sea centipede *n* : a sea centipede (*Crabyzos longicaudatus*)
greens fee *var of* GREEN FEE
greenshank \'⸗,⸗\ *n* : an Old World sandpiper (*Tringa nebularia*) related to the yellowlegs of America
green-shaving \'⸗¦⸗⸗\ *n* : the process of scraping the flesh side of hides or skins
green shoulder *n* : a dominant genetic abnormality in the tomato characterized by lack of uniform coloration at maturity esp. about the shoulder of the fruit
green shrimp *n* **1** : a common edible shrimp (*Peneus setiferus*) of the south Atlantic coast of No. America that is whitish in color with dark antennae and with the telson edged with green **2** : an uncooked shrimp
greensick \'⸗,⸗\ *adj* [back-formation fr. *greensickness*] : affected with chlorosis
green·sick·ness *n* : CHLOROSIS
greenside \'⸗,⸗\ *n, dial Eng* : GRASSLAND, PASTURE
green silk *n* : any of various filamentous aquatic green algae esp. of the genus *Spirogyra* that have a silky touch when rubbed between the fingers
green singing finch *n* : a tropical African finch (*Serinus mozambicus*) that is largely green and black above and clear yellow below and is often kept as a cage bird
greenskeeper *var of* GREENKEEPER
green slate *n* : a grayish green that is yellower, less strong, and slightly lighter than slate green and yellower and duller than average bayberry or average blue spruce (sense 2a)
green sloke *n* : SEA LETTUCE
greens·man \'grēnzmən\ *n, pl* **greensmen** : one who decorates motion-picture sets with grass, flowers, shrubs, and other greenery
green smelt *n* : an unfrozen smelt
green smut *n* : a disease of rice characterized by enlarged grains covered by a green powder consisting of conidia and caused by a fungus (*Ustilaginoidea virens*) — called also *false smut*
green snail *n* **1** *also* **green shell** : a large turban shell (*Turbo marmoratus*) that is common in the Indian ocean and has a bright green shell with a nacreous lining **2** : a common greenish garden snail (*Helix aperta*) that is a pest in parts of southern California
green snake *n* **1** : either of two bright green harmless largely insectivorous No. American colubrid snakes: **a** : SMOOTH GREEN SNAKE **b** : ROUGH GREEN SNAKE **2** : any of numerous African colubrid snakes of *Chlorophis* and related genera
green snow *n* : snow colored by a growth of green algae
green soap *n* : a transparent to translucent soft soap that is yellowish white to brownish to greenish yellow and that is made from vegetable oils and used esp. in skin diseases — called also *medicinal soft soap*
green sorrel *n* : GARDEN SORREL
green spleenwort *n* : a small often many-crowned fern (*Asplenium viride*) with slender linear to lanceolate fronds and slim green stipes that is widely distributed in cool parts of the northern hemisphere
green spot *also* **greenspotting** *n* : a spotting of plant parts characterized by greenish color: as **a** : OLEOCELLOSIS **b** : a leaf spot of cured tobacco caused by a fungus (*Cercospora nicotianae*)
greenstick fracture *n* : a bone fracture in a young individual in which the bone is partly broken and partly bent
green stone *n* : a grayish yellow green that is yellower and paler than average sage green, yellower, lighter, and stronger than mermaid, and yellower, lighter, and slightly stronger than palmetto
greenstone \'⸗,⸗\ *n* **1** : any of numerous usu. altered dark green compact rocks (as diorite or diabase) **2** : NEPHRITE
green-striped mapleworm \'grēn,st¦rīpt-, -n,st¦\ *n* : a green caterpillar with black spines that is the larva of a cream and pink saturniid moth (*Anisota rubicunda*) and that occas. is a pest of maple trees
greenstuff \'⸗,⸗\ *n* : green vegetation used as foodstuff
green sturgeon *n* : a rather small sturgeon (*Acipenser acutirostris*) of the Pacific coast
green sulfur bacterium *n* : a member of the family Chlorobacteriaceae — see CHLOROBACTERIUM
green sunfish *n* : a sunfish (*Lepomis cyanellus*) of the Great Lakes region and southwestward to the Rio Grande that is largely greenish above with a blue spot on each scale
green·sward \'grēn,swȯ(ə)rd, -ȯ(ə)d\ *n* : turf that is green with growing grass ⟨went through the front door out onto a ~ hedged by boxwoods —J.M.Brinnin⟩
green table *n* [fr. *Green Tables*, nickname of the Committee of the Covenanting Government that ruled Scotland 1638-41; fr. the green cloth that covered the table where they transacted business] : COUNCIL BOARD
greentail \'⸗,⸗\ *n* : MENHADEN
green-tailed towhee \'⸗,⸗-\ *n* : a towhee (*Chlorura chlorura*) of the Rocky mountain region that is greenish above with chestnut crown and ashy underparts
green tea *n* : tea that is light in color from incomplete fermentation of the leaf before firing — compare BLACK TEA
greenth \'grēn(t)th\ *n* -s [¹*green* + *-th* (as in *warmth*)] : green growth : VERDURE ⟨the lovely ~ and blossoms of the horse chestnuts —George Eliot⟩
green thumb *n* : an unusual ability to make plants grow ⟨had the proverbial *green thumb* and the windows were full of plants and seed boxes —*Parents' Mag.*⟩
green thursday *n, cap G&T* [trans. of G *grüner donnerstag*] : MAUNDY THURSDAY
green-tip spray *n* : PREPINK SPRAY
green toad *n* : a Eurasian toad (*Bufo viridis*) with variable chiefly green coloring
green tody *n* : a tody (*Todus todus*) of Jamaica that is largely green with a crimson throat and whitish underparts
green tree-ant \'⸗'⸗,⸗\ *n* : a fiercely biting Old World tropical arboreal ant (*Oecophylla virescens*) that builds a nest of leaves sewn together with silk produced by the larval ants
green trout *n* : LARGEMOUTH BLACK BASS
green turtle *n* : a large sea turtle (*Chelonia mydas*) widely distributed in warm seas that has a smooth greenish or olive-colored shell and lays highly nutritious eggs and whose flesh is much used for food
gree·nuk \'grēnək\ *n* -s [by alter.] : GERENUK
green valley grass *n* : JOHNSON GRASS
green vegetable *n* : a vegetable having the edible parts rich in chlorophyll and forming an important source of vitamins and micronutrients
green vegetable bug *n* : a common and destructive cosmopolitan pentatomid bug (*Nezara viridula*) that is orange as a young nymph and bright green as an adult and that attacks many cultivated plants
green veratrum *n* : AMERICAN HELLEBORE
green verditer *n* **1** : a basic copper carbonate used as a green pigment — compare BREMEN GREEN 2 **2** : MALACHITE GREEN 3
green violet *n* : a leafy-stemmed herb (*Hybanthus concolor*) of the family Violaceae of eastern No. America having greenish white axillary flowers with petals of equal length
green vitriol *n* : ferrous sulfate heptahydrate
greenware \'⸗,⸗\ *n* : unfired pottery
green water *n* **1** : the water in shore on soundings — compare BLUE WATER **2** : GREEN SEA **3** : an opaque greenish condition of the water in an aquarium that is caused by excessive growth of algae and that is harmless and usu. healthful to fishes
green wattle *n* : any of several Australian wattles (esp. *Acacia decurrens*)
green wax *n* [ME *grenewax*; trans. of ML *viridis cera*] **1** : a seal of green wax attesting a document formerly issued from the exchequer to a sheriff **2 a** : a document attested by green wax **b** : the fines or amercements collected by virtue of such a document
greenweed \'⸗,⸗\ *n* : WOODWAXEN
green weight *n* : the weight of green lumber
green·wich hour angle *usu* 'grinij *in Greenwich, Eng, & in Great Britain as a whole, usu* 'grenich *or* 'grenēch *in Greenwich Village & in NYC as a whole, often in certain other places named Greenwich & usu by speakers unfamiliar with the local pronunc of any place named Greenwich* 'grēn,wich; *sometimes* 'grenij *or* 'grenēj *or* 'grinich *or* 'grinēch *or* 'grinēj *or* 'grēn,wich *or* 'grin,wich\ *n, usu cap G* [fr. *Greenwich, England*] : the hour angle of a celestial body at the meridian of Greenwich
greenwich meridian *n, usu cap G* [fr. *Greenwich*, England] : the prime meridian that passes through Greenwich
greenwich time *or* **greenwich civil time** *or* **greenwich mean time** *n, usu cap G* [fr. *Greenwich*, England] : the mean solar time of the meridian of Greenwich used as the prime basis of standard time throughout the world
greenwich village *n, usu cap G&V* [fr. *Greenwich Village*, bohemian section of New York City] : the bohemian quarter of a city
greenwing \'⸗,⸗\ *or* **green-winged teal** \'⸗,⸗-\ *n* : a small river duck (*Anas carolinensis*) the male of which has a chestnut head with a green eye patch and a metallic green area on the wing speculum
greenwithe \'⸗,⸗\ *n* **1** : a West Indian climbing orchid (*Vanilla claviculata*) **2** : a West Indian shrub (*Forsteronia floribunda*) of the family Apocynaceae having a milky juice that yields a rubber
¹**greenwood** \'⸗,⸗\ *n* [ME *grenewode*, fr. *grene* green + *wode* wood] **1** : a wood or forest green with foliage ⟨a yeoman in the ~ —Francis Hackett⟩ **2** : WOODWAXEN **3** : MOUNTAIN HOLLY 1 **4** : GREENHEART 1c
²**greenwood** \'⸗,⸗\ *adj* [¹*green* + *wood*] : SOFTWOOD 2
green woodpecker *n* : a common large European woodpecker (*Picus viridis*) that is chiefly green with a yellow rump and red on the head
greenwrap \'⸗,⸗\ *adj, of a tomato* : picked when immature and wrapped before packing
green wrasse *n* : a greenish Mediterranean wrasse (*Labrus viridis*) usu. with a silvery line along each side and unspotted fins
¹**greeny** \'grēnē\ *adj* -ER/-EST [¹*green* + *-y*] : having a tinge of green : GREENISH
²**greeny** \"\ *also* **green·ie** \"\ *n, pl* **greenies** : GREENHORN ⟨promised his daughter to . . . a ~, just come over, but rich —S.V.Benét⟩
greenyard \'⸗,⸗\ *n* **1** : a yard covered with turf **2** *Brit* : a pound for stray animals
grees *pl of* GREE, *pres 3d sing of* GREE
¹**greet** \'grēt\ *or* -ēd·+V\ *vb* -ED/-ING/-S [ME *greten*, fr. OE *grētan*; akin to OHG *gruozen* to address, attack, ON *græta* to cause to weep; causative fr. the root of E ³*greet*] *vt* **1** : to address with salutations or expressions of kind wishes : salute or accost in a friendly or courteous manner : pay respects or compliments to personally, through another, or by writing or token : HAIL, WELCOME ⟨my lord, the mayor of London comes to ~ you —Shak.⟩ **2** *obs* : to offer felicitations on **3** : to meet or receive with a salutation, demonstration, or other evidence of approbation or occas. of reproach ⟨the candidate was ~*ed* with cheers⟩ ⟨~*ing* their former hero with catcalls and boos⟩ **4** : to appear or present itself to : be perceived by ⟨offensive odors ~ the nose⟩ ⟨a surprising sight ~*ed* her eyes⟩ ~ *vi* **1** *obs* : to meet and give salutations **2** *obs* : MEET, ENCOUNTER
²**greet** *n* -s *obs* : GREETING
³**greet** \'grēt\ *vi* **grat** \'grat\ **grut·ten** \'grət°n\ **greeting; greets** [ME *greten*, fr. OE *grētan*; akin to ON *grāta* to weep, Goth *gretan*, and perh. to L *hirrire* to whimper, Skt *gharghara* crackling, rattling] **1** *chiefly Scot* : WEEP, CRY, LAMENT **2** *obs* : to call in entreaty or anger

[4]**greet** \"\ *n* [ME *gret, grete,* fr. *greten,* v., to weep] *now chiefly Scot* : WEEPING, SOBBING
[5]**greet** \"\ *n* [ME *gret, grete* — more at GRIT] *dial Eng* : finely crushed earth or rock
greet·er \'grēd·ə(r), -ētə-\ *n* -s [[1]*greet* + *-er*] : one that greets: as **a** : a person who welcomes esp. on behalf of another **b** : one that weeps
[1]**greeting** *n* -s [ME *greting,* fr. OE *grēting,* fr. *grētan* to greet + *-ing* — more at GREET] **1** : an expression of kindness or joy : a salutation at meeting or a compliment from one absent ⟨write to him . . . gentle adieus and ~s —Shak.⟩ **2** : a formal gesture of welcome often traditional ⟨pressed his palms together in the ancient Asian ~⟩
[2]**greeting** *adj* [ME *greting,* fr. *greting,* n.] : of, relating to, or used for greeting — **greet·ing·ly** *adv*
greeting card *n* : [3]CARD 6b
greet·ing·less \'==ləs\ *adj* : having or receiving no greeting
gref·fi·er \'grefē,ā\ *n* -s [MF, fr. *grefe, grafe* stylus (fr. ML *graphium*) + *-ier* -er — more at GRAFF] : REGISTRAR, RECORDER ⟨among the town officials is a ~⟩
gregal \'grēgəl, -reg-\ *adj* [L *gregalis,* fr. *greg-, grex* herd + *-alis* -al — more at GREGARIOUS] **1** *archaic* : belonging to or characteristic of a company or multitude **2** *obs* : GREGARIOUS
gre·ga·le \grā'gä(,)lā\ *n* -s [It *grecale, gregale,* fr. *grecale, gregale* Greek, fr. LL *Graecalis,* fr. L *Graecus* + *-alis* -al — more at GREEK] : a strong cold northeast wind of the central Mediterranean — called also *euroclydon*
greg·a·loid \'gregə,lȯid\ *adj* [*gregal* + *-oid*] : resulting from union of previously independent individuals — used of a protozoan colony
gre·gar·ia \grə'ga(a)rēə\ *n* -s [NL, fr. L, fem. of *gregarius*] : an irregularly recurrent phase in the life cycle of migratory or plague grasshoppers induced by crowded breeding conditions and marked by structural and color changes and the development of strongly gregarious behavior — compare SOLITARIA
greg·a·ri·na \,gregə'rīnə, -rēnə\ *n, cap* [NL, fr. L *gregarius* + NL *-ina*] : a genus of gregarines that are parasites in the alimentary canal of an arthropod
greg·a·ri·nae \,gregə'rī(,)nē\ *or* **greg·a·ri·nar·ia** \-,rə'na(a)rēə\ [*Gregarinae* fr. NL, fr. L *gregarius* + *-inae,* fem. pl. of *-inus* -ine; *Gregarinaria* fr. NL, fr. *Gregarina* + *-aria*] *syn of* GREGARINIDA
[1]**greg·a·rine** \'gregə,rīn, -,rēn, -,rən\ *adj* [NL *Gregarina*] : of or relating to the Gregarinida
[2]**gregarine** \"\ *n* -s [NL *Gregarina*] : a protozoan of the order Gregarinida — see MONOCYSTIS
greg·a·rin·i·an \,==rinēən\ *adj* : resembling a gregarine : GREGARINE
greg·a·rin·i·da \,=='rinədə\ *n pl, cap* [NL, fr. *Gregarina* + *-ida*] : a large order of parasitic vermiform telosporidian protozoans that usu. occur in insects and other invertebrates
greg·a·ri·ni·na \-,rə'nīnə, -nēnə\ [NL, fr. *Gregarina* + *-ina*] *syn of* GREGARINIDA
greg·a·ri·noi·dea \-'nȯidēə\ [NL, fr. *Gregarina* + *-oidea*] *syn of* GREGARINIDA
greg·a·ri·no·sis \-'nōsəs\ *n, pl* **gregarino·ses** \-ō,sēz\ [NL, fr. *Gregarina* + *-osis*] : a disease caused by the gregarines esp. in insects
gre·gar·i·ous \grə'ga(a)rēəs, grē'-, -'ger-,-'gār-\ *adj* [L *gregarius* of or relating to a herd or flock, fr. *greg-, grex* herd, flock + *-arius* -ary; akin to OIr *graig* herd of horses, Gk *ageirein* to collect, *agora* assembly, Lith *gurgulys* thickening] **1 a** : marked by an inclination to associate with others of one's kind : tending to live in a flock, herd, or community rather than alone ⟨fowl are ~⟩ ⟨man is a ~ animal, living in flocks with his kind, in order to face the common foe —Emil Brunner⟩ **b** : characteristic of or common throughout a group, flock, or community ⟨~ alarm at the intrusion⟩ **2** : marked by an instinctive or temperamental preference for a social rather than a solitary existence : wanting to be with others and disliking much solitude ⟨the American is sociable and ~: he does not like solitariness or the solitudes —W.L.Sperry⟩ **3 a** *of a plant* : growing in a cluster or a colony **b** : living in a community or in contiguous nests but not forming a true colony — used esp. of solitary wasps and bees **syn** see SOCIAL
gre·gar·i·ous·ly *adv* : in a gregarious manner
gre·gar·i·ous·ness *n* -ES : the quality or state of being gregarious
gregarious wave *n* : one of a constant series of waves formed by the regular movement of the sea at all times
grege *or* **greige** \'grāzh\ *n* -s [F *grège,* adj., raw (used of silk), fr. It *greggio*] **1** : RAW SILK **2 a** : BEIGE 2 **b** : NUTRIA 2
greger *or* **gregger** *var of* GRAGER
greg·gle \'gregəl\ *n* -s [origin unknown] *dial Eng* : WOOD HYACINTH
gre·go \'grē(,)gō, 'grā-(-\ *n* -s [Catal, lit., Greek, fr. L *Graecus* — more at GREEK] : a coarse warm jacket or coat with a hood formerly worn by seamen
[1]**gre·go·ri·an** \grə'gōrēən, gre'-,grā'-, -'gȯr-\ *adj, usu cap* [Pope *Gregory* XIII (Ugo Buoncompagni) †1585 + E *-an*] : of or relating to Pope Gregory XIII or to the Gregorian calendar
[2]**gregorian** \"\ *adj, usu cap* [Pope *Gregory* I †604 + E *-an*] : of or relating to Pope Gregory I : of, relating to, or having the characteristics of Gregorian chant
[3]**gregorian** \"\ *n, usu cap* **1** *obs* : one versed in the Gregorian chant **2** : GREGORIAN CHANT
[4]**gregorian** \"\ *n* -s [fr. the name *Gregory* + E *-an*] **1** *sometimes cap* : a 16th and 17th century wig **2** *usu cap* : a member of an 18th century English society similar to that of the Freemasons
[5]**gregorian** \"\ *adj, usu cap* [St. *Gregory* the Illuminator †332 + E *-an*] : of, relating to, or being the Armenian Church
gregorian calendar *n, usu cap G* [[1]*Gregorian*] : a revision of the Julian calendar introduced in 1582 and adopted in Great Britain and the English colonies in America in 1752 involving the suppression of the 10 days by which the vernal equinox had become displaced and providing that only those centesimal years divisible by 400 (as 1600) should be leap years — see MONTH table
gregorian chant *n, usu cap G* [[2]*Gregorian*] : one of the monodic and rhythmically free ritual melodies in one of the eight ecclesiastical modes comprising the liturgical chant of the Roman Catholic Church : PLAINSONG
gre·go·ri·an·ist \-nəst\ *n* -s *usu cap* [[2]*Gregorian* + *-ist*] : one who advocates using the Gregorian chants
gregorian mode *n, usu cap G* [[2]*Gregorian*] : ECCLESIASTICAL MODE
gregorian staff *n, usu cap G* [[2]*Gregorian*] : a 4-line staff with a C clef used for Gregorian music
gregorian telescope *n, usu cap G* [James *Gregory* †1675 Scot. mathematician and inventor + E *-an*] : a reflecting telescope that has a paraboloidal primary mirror with a perforation through which light is reflected to the eyepiece and an ellipsoidal secondary mirror set beyond the focus and that produces an erect image but a small field of view

Gregorian staffs

gregorian tone *n, usu cap G* [[2]*Gregorian*] **1** : one of the nine tunes with variants to which the psalms are sung in Gregorian music, eight of them being written in the eight most common ecclesiastical modes **2** : ECCLESIASTICAL MODE
gregorian year *n, usu cap G* [[1]*Gregorian*] : a year in the Gregorian calendar
greg·o·ry's powder \'greg(ə)rēz-, -rāg|, -riz-\ *n, usu cap G* [after James *Gregory* †1821 Scot. professor of medicine] : a laxative powder containing rhubarb, magnesia, and ginger
[1]**greige** *var of* GRÈGE
[2]**greige** \'grā(zh)\ *adj* [F *grège* raw (used of silk) — more at GRÈGE] : GRAY 1d
[3]**greige** \"\ *n* -s : a textile in the gray state of preparation
grei·sen \'grīz[ə]n\ *n* -s [G] : a crystalline rock consisting of quartz and mica that is common in the tin regions of Cornwall and Saxony and that is prob. a granite altered by magmatic exhalation
gre·king \'grēkən, -kiŋ\ *n* -s [ME *griking, greking;* akin to MD *grakinge* dawn, ON *grȳjandi* dawn, OE *grǣg* gray — more at GRAY] *now dial Brit* : DAWN
[1]**gre·mi·al** \'grēmēəl *sometimes* 'grāmē,äl\ *n* -s [L *gremium* lap, bosom + E *-al* — more at CRAM] **1** *archaic* : a full or resident member (as of a society or university) **2** *or* **gremial veil** : a lap cloth laid across the knees of a bishop seated at mass or other services
[2]**gre·mi·al** \'grēmēəl\ *adj* [L *gremium* + E *-al*] **1** : of or relating to the lap or bosom **2** *archaic* : having active or resident membership (as in a society or university)
gre·mio \'grāmē,ō\ *n* -s [Sp, lit., lap, fr. L *gremium*] : GUILD, UNION; *esp* : an employers' association in some European and Latin American countries
grem·lin \'gremlən\ *n* -s [perh. modif. (influenced by E *goblin*) of IrGael *gruaimin* ill-humored little fellow, fr. *gruaim* gloom, ill humor] : an impish little gnome reported by airmen as interfering with and disordering equipment (as motors, instruments, machine guns); *broadly* : an unaccountable disruptive influence
[1]**gre·nade** \grə'nād\ *n* -s [MF *granade, grenade,* fr. LL *granata* pomegranate, fr. pl. of L *granatum,* fr. neut. of *granatus* seedy, fr. *granum* grain, seed + *-atus* -ate — more at CORN] **1** *obs* : POMEGRANATE **2** : a missile consisting of a container fitted with a priming charge and a bursting charge and filled with a destructive agent (as gas, high explosive, incendiary chemicals) — see HAND GRENADE, RIFLE GRENADE **3** : a device that ejects poison gas or tear gas and is used esp. by police in dispersing mobs **4** : a glass bottle or globe that contains volatile chemicals and can be burst by throwing (as for extinguishing a fire)
[2]**grenade** \"\ *vt* -ED/-ING/-S : to use grenades against
grenade launcher *n* : a device attached to a rifle or carbine to permit the firing of a grenade
[1]**gre·na·di·an** \grə'nādēən\ *adj, usu cap* [*Grenada,* island in the West Indies + E *-ian*] : of or relating to Grenada, West Indies : of the style or kind typical of Grenada
[2]**grenadian** \"\ *n* -s *cap* : a native or resident of Grenada, West Indies
gren·a·dier \,grenə'di(ə)r, -iə\ *n* -s [F, fr. *grenade* + *-ier* -er] **1 a** : a soldier who carries and throws grenades **b** : one of a company attached to each regiment or battalion taking post on the right of the line and wearing a special uniform **c** : a member of a special regiment or corps ⟨a ~ of the guard of Napoleon I⟩ **2** : any of various deep-sea fishes that are related to the cods, that constitute a family Macruridae of the order Anacanthini, and that have an elongate tapering body and compressed pointed tail — called also *rattail*
gren·a·dier·ial \-irēəl\ *adj* : of, relating to, or characteristic of a grenadier
gren·a·dier·ly \,==di(ə)rlē, -iəl-, -li\ *adv* : like a grenadier
grenadilla *or* **grenadillo** *var of* GRANADILLA
[1]**gren·a·din** \'grenədən\ *also* **gren·a·dine** \,grenə'dēn\ *n* -s [F *grenadin,* fr. *grenade* pomegranate + *-in* -ine — more at GRENADE] : a small fricandeau ⟨seventeen ~s of prime beef . . . exquisitely interlarded with pork insertions —Joel Sayre⟩
[2]**grenadin** \"\ *or* **grenadine** \"\ *n* -s [F *grenadine,* fr. *grenade* pomegranate + *-ine*] : CLOVE PINK; *esp* : a strongly perfumed medium-sized carnation
gren·a·dine \,grenə'dēn\ *n* -s [F, fr. *grenade* pomegranate + *-ine*] **1 a** : a silk yarn of two or more threads that are twisted singly and again in the ply **b** : a plain or figured fabric of various fibers often in an open weave like that of gauze **2** *or* **grenadine red** : a moderate reddish orange that is yellower and paler than flamingo or crab apple **3** : a red sweet syrup of little or no alcoholic content flavored with pomegranates and used as a sweetening, flavoring, or coloring agent with carbonated water or cocktails
grenadine pink *n* : a strong yellowish pink that is redder and stronger than average salmon, yellower and deeper than melon, and yellower and stronger than peach red
gre·na·do \grə'nā(,)dō, -nä(-\ *n* -ES [modif. of Sp *granada,* lit., pomegranate, fr. LL *granata* — more at GRENADE] *archaic* : GRENADE
gren·a·tite \'grenə,tīt\ *n* -s [F, fr. *grenat* garnet + *-ite*] : STAUROLITE
gre·no·ble \grə'nōbəl, grə'nōbl(ə), -ōb(lə)\ *adj, usu cap* [fr. *Grenoble,* France] : of or from the city of Grenoble, France : of the kind or style prevalent in Grenoble
gren·ville series \'gren,vil-, *chiefly South* -,vəl-\ *n, usu cap G* [fr. *Grenville* co., Ontario, Canada] : a series of rocks consisting mainly of highly metamorphosed limestones and other sediments occurring in eastern Canada
grenz ray \'gren(t)s-\ *n, often cap G* [part trans. of G *grenzstrahl,* fr. *grenze* border (fr. MHG *grenize,* fr. Pol *granica*) + *strahl* ray] : a soft X ray with wavelength near the limit of extreme ultraviolet used esp. in treating skin lesions — called also *infraroentgen ray*
grès \'grā\ *n, pl* **grèses** \-āz\ [F, sandstone, stoneware, of Gmc origin; akin to OE *grēot* sand, grit — more at GRIT] : ceramic stoneware esp. when decorative in nature
grès de flan·dres \grādəflän[n]dr(ə), \d(rə)\ *n, usu cap F* [F, lit., stoneware from Flanders] : COLOGNE WARE
gresh·am's law \'greshəmz-\ *n, usu cap G* [after Sir Thomas *Gresham* †1579 Eng. financier] : an observation in economics: when two coins are equal in debt-paying value but unequal in intrinsic value, the one having the lesser intrinsic value tends to remain in circulation and the other to be hoarded or exported as bullion
gres·so·ri·al \(')gre'sōrēəl\ *adj* [L *gressus* (past part. of *gradi* to step, go) + E *-orial* (as in *cursorial*) — more at GRADE] : adapted for walking ⟨the ~ feet of some birds⟩
[1]**gret·na green** \,gretnə,=\ *n, often cap 1st G* [fr. *Gretna* parish, Scotland] : a moderate yellowish green to green that is less strong than Killarney green
[2]**gretna green** *n, usu cap both Gs* [fr. *Gretna Green,* Scottish village on the English border, famous for the runaway marriages performed there] : a place where many eloping couples are married
gre·vil·lea \grə'vilēə\ *n* [NL, after Charles F. *Greville* †1809 Scot. botanist] **1** *cap* : a large genus of Australian shrubs and trees (family Proteaceae) having usu. showy orange or red flowers with elongated curved style and woody follicles — see SILK OAK **2** *also* **gra·vil·ea** \"\ -s : a plant of the genus *Grevillea*
gré·vy's zebra \(')grā,vēz-\ *n, usu cap G* [after François P. J. *Grévy* †1891 president of France] : a zebra (*Equus grevyi*) with narrow and discontinuous stripes on the belly and the inner surface of the thighs
[1]**grew** *past of* GROW
[2]**grew** \'grü\ *n* -s [short for *grewhound*] *now dial Brit* : GREYHOUND
grew·hound \-ünd, -ü,haund\ *n* [ME, alter. of *grehound* — more at GREYHOUND] *dial Brit* : GREYHOUND
grew·ia \'grüyə, -üēə\ *n, cap* [NL, fr. Nehemiah *Grew* †1712 Eng. plant physiologist + NL *-ia*] : a large genus of chiefly tropical Old World shrubs and trees (family Tiliaceae) having alternate simple leaves, cymose flowers with colored sepals, and drupaceous sometimes edible fruits
grewsome *var of* GRUESOME
[1]**grex** \'greks\ *vi* -ED/-ING/-ES [PaG *greckse* & G dial. *greckse, grecksen* to groan, grumble, complain, fr. Early G *krachitzen* to cry hoarsely, freq. of *krachen* to crack, crash, roar, fr. OHG *krahhōn* — more at CRACK] *dial* : to grumble or complain often shrilly or scoldingly
[2]**grex** \"\ *n* -ES [*gram per X* (ten) *kilometers*] : a measuring unit for fibers, filaments, and yarns based on the weight in grams of 10,000 meters of fiber or yarn
grey \'grā\ *var of* GRAY
grey·cing \'grāsiŋ\ *n* -s [by contr.] *Brit* : greyhound racing
grey drake *n, Brit* : an adult female mayfly
grey friar *also* **gray friar** *n, often cap G&F* [ME *grey frere, gray frere*] : a Franciscan friar
[1]**grey·hound** *also* **gray·hound** \'grā,haund\ *n* [ME *grehound,* fr. OE *grīghund,* fr. *grīg-* (akin to ON *grey* bitch) + *hund* hound; perh. akin to OE *grǣg* gray — more at GRAY, HOUND] **1 a** : a tall slender graceful smooth-coated dog of a breed originating in the Near East that is characterized by swiftness and keen sight and has been used for coursing game for many centuries — see ITALIAN GREYHOUND **b** : any of several dogs (as a whippet or a saluki) related to or similar to the greyhound **2** : a swift steamer; *esp* : OCEAN LINER

greyhound

[2]**greyhound** \"\ *vi, of a hooked fish* : to alternate leaps and shallow dives at high speed
grey·lag \'grā,lag\ *or* **greylag goose** *also* **gray·lag** *n* [prob. fr. *gray* + *lag* (last)] : the common gray wild goose (*Anser anser* syn. *A. cinereus*) of Europe believed to be the chief wild ancestor of the common domestic geese
grey nun *also* **gray nun** *n, often cap G&N* : SISTER OF CHARITY OF MONTREAL
greyskin \'=,=\ *n, Africa* : a small percoid food fish (*Plectorhynchus griseus* or *Gaterin schotaf*) of the tropical Indo-Pacific from eastern Africa to Australia
grey wavey *n* : WHITE-FRONTED GOOSE
greywether \'=,==\ *n, dial Brit* : SARSEN
GRI *abbr* guaranteed retirement income
[1]**grib·ble** \'gribəl\ *n* -s [origin unknown] *dial Eng* : a young crab tree or blackthorn; *sometimes* : a cutting from one
[2]**gribble** \"\ *n* -s [prob. dim. of [2]*grub*] : a small marine isopod crustacean (*Limnoria lignorum* or *L. terebrans*) that burrows into and rapidly destroys submerged timber (as the piles of wharves) both in Europe and America
[1]**grice** \'grīs\ *n* -s [ME *grys, grise,* fr. ON *grīss* — more at GRIZZLE] *now chiefly Scot* : a young pig
[2]**grice** \'grēs\ *var of* GRECE
[1]**grid** \'grid\ *n* -s *often attrib* [back-formation fr. *gridiron*] **1** : GRATING, GRIDIRON **2** : something resembling or likened to a grating: as **a** (1) : a perforated or ridged metal plate used as a conductor and as a support for the active material of a storage-battery electrode (2) : an electrode consisting of a mesh or a spiral of fine wire interposed between two other elements of an electron tube (3) : NETWORK 4 (4) : a network of pipes (as for distributing gas or water) **b** : a network of uniformly spaced horizontal and perpendicular lines; *specif* : one used for locating points (as on a map, chart, or aerial photograph) by means of a system of coordinates **c** : a wooden framework into which a boat may be floated at high tide in order that repairs may be made when the tide falls **d** : a postal cancellation with a gridiron pattern (as on an early U.S. stamp) **e** : GRIDIRON 3c **f** : GRIDIRON 3d; *broadly* : FOOTBALL 1 ⟨forgotten ~ heroes⟩
[2]**grid** \"\ *vt* **gridded; gridded; gridding; grids** **1** : to equip or cover with a grid ⟨a map *gridded* with red lines⟩ **2** : to connect (as electric or gas lines) into a grid : distribute (as electricity or gas) by means of a grid
grid bias *n* : a small constant component of the grid potential in a vacuum tube usu. negative for ordinary triode control grids
grid cap *n* : a grid terminal (as on some amplifier tubes) that resembles a cap and is connected to the grid circuit by means of a spring clip
grid ceiling *n* : a perforated ceiling that allows light to shine through
grid circuit *n* : the electric circuit including the grid and cathode of an electron tube
grid condenser *n* : a capacitor connected in the grid circuit of an electron tube
grid current *n* : current flowing between the grid and cathode in an electron tube
grid·der \'gridə(r)\ *n* -s [[1]*grid* (gridiron) + *-er*] **1** : a football player **2** : a football fan
grid-dip meter *n* : a device for testing radio frequencies that consists of a vacuum-tube oscillator having in its grid circuit a current-indicating meter which indicates a decrease in current when the oscillator and the circuit to which it is coupled resonate at the same frequency
[1]**grid·dle** \'grid[ə]l\ *n* -s *often attrib* [ME *gredil, gridel,* fr. ONF *gredil,* fr. LL *craticulum* fine wickerwork — more at GRILL] **1 a** *now dial* : GRIDIRON 1, 2 **b** : any of various grids ⟨a ~ of sheep trails over the hill⟩ **2** : a flat surface (as of soapstone or metal) on which food (as batter or bacon) is placed to be cooked by dry heat (as from a fire or an electric element); *broadly* : a cooking device consisting of or incorporating a griddle ⟨got an electric ~ for her birthday⟩ — **on the griddle** : being subjected to examination or questioning ⟨we were *on the griddle* for several hours before we convinced the officials that we were not guilty⟩

griddle 2

[2]**griddle** \"\ *vt* **griddled; griddled; griddling** \-d(ə)liŋ\ **griddles** : to cook on a griddle
[3]**griddle** \"\ *vi* **griddled; griddled; griddling** \-d(ə)liŋ\ **griddles** [origin unknown] *slang Brit* : to sing as a beggar — **grid·dler** \-d(ə)lə(r)\ *n* -s
griddle cake *n* : a flat cake made of thin batter consisting basically of flour (as of wheat or buckwheat), liquid, and leavening and cooked on both sides on a griddle — called also *pancake*
griddle man *n* : a short-order cook
[1]**gride** \'grīd\ *vb* -ED/-ING/-S [ME *griden,* alter. of *girden* — more at GIRD] *vt* **1** *archaic* : to pierce or gash with a weapon **2** : to scrape or graze so as to produce a harsh rasping sound ~ *vi* : to scrape, graze, or rub against something so as to produce a harsh rasping sound
[2]**gride** \"\ *n* -s : a harsh scraping or cutting or the sound of it ⟨the ~ of leafless boughs in the blast of the wind⟩
grid·e·lin \'grid[ə]lən\ *n* -s [modif. of F *gris-de-lin,* lit., flax gray] : a dark purplish red that is bluer and paler than pansy purple, redder, lighter, and stronger than raisin, and bluer, lighter, and stronger than Bokhara — called also *gris-de-lin*
grid-glow tube *n* : a cold-cathode gas-filled electron tube in which glow discharge is started by a grid
[1]**grid·iron** \'grid,ī(ə)rn, -īən\ *n* [ME *gredire,* prob. by folk etymology (influence of *ire, iren* iron) fr. *gredil, gridel* — more at GRIDDLE] **1** : an iron grating formerly used for torture by fire **2** : a grated metal frame for broiling food over coals — compare GRIDDLE, GRILL **3** : something resembling a gridiron, grating, or lattice in structure or appearance: as **a** : a network of sections (as of pipes, railroad tracks, or roads) **b** : GRID 2c **c** : the arrangement of beams over a theater stage supporting the machinery for flying scenery **d** : a football field
[2]**gridiron** \"\ *vt* : to cover or mark with bars or lines suggestive of those of a gridiron
gridiron pendulum *n* : a compensation pendulum in which the unequal expansion of two different metals is utilized to maintain constant effective pendulum length
gridiron-tailed lizard \'=,=(=),=-\ *n* : a lizard of the genus *Callisaurus*
grid leak *n* : a resistor used in parallel with a capacitor in the grid circuit of a vacuum tube to limit grid bias by drawing off excess electrons that accumulate on the tube grid
grid line *n* : any of a series of numbered horizontal and perpendicular lines that divide a map into squares to form a grid by means of which any point may be located by a system of rectangular coordinates
grid man *n* : OVERHEAD MAN
grid metal *n* : ANTIMONIAL LEAD; *specif* : a lead containing about 9 percent antimony and sometimes a fraction of a percent of tin and used for storage-battery grids — compare HARD LEAD
grid modulation *n* : a system of modulation in which the modulating voltage is introduced into the grid circuit of the electron tube that provides the carrier
grids *pl of* GRID, *pres 3d sing of* GRID
grid voltage *n* : the instantaneous potential difference between the grid and the cathode of a vacuum tube
grie·ben \'grēbən\ *n pl* [G, pl. of *griebe* crackling, fr. OHG *griobo* — more at GREAVES] : cracklings from goose fat usu. salted
griece *var of* GRECE
grieced \'grēst\ *adj* : [2]DEGRADED
grief \'grēf\ *n* -s [ME *gref, grefe,* fr. OF *grief, gref,* adj., heavy, grave, difficult, troubled, fr. (assumed) VL *grevis,* alter. of L *gravis* — more at GRIEVE] **1** *obs* **a** (1) : SUFFERING, PAIN, DISTRESS; *also* : a cause of these (as a hurt, hardship, or

wound) (2) : a bodily injury : MALADY, DISEASE b : an aggrieved or angered state of mind : OFFENSE c : GRIEVANCE 3; *also* : a document setting forth a grievance 2 a : emotional suffering (as caused by bereavement, affliction, remorse, panic, despair) ⟨his deep ~ at his son's death⟩ ⟨a leaden ~ swept over her at thought of the past⟩ ⟨the ~ his loss in me had wrought —Alfred Tennyson⟩ b : a cause of such suffering ⟨such a child is a ~ to his parents⟩ 3 a : MISHAP, MISADVENTURE, ACCIDENT, BREAKAGE ⟨the day was marred by dozens of little ~s⟩ b : difficulty and vexation esp. from mishaps and accidents ⟨the ~s of a repairman's life⟩ c : hard usage : TROUBLE, ANNOYANCE ⟨enough ~ for one day⟩ d : an unpleasant end or condition : FAILURE, DISASTER — used chiefly in the phrase *come to grief* ⟨the expedition came to ~ when the supplies were accidentally lost⟩ **syn** see SORROW

grief·ful \'grēffəl\ *adj* [ME *greful*, fr. *gref, grefe* + *-ful*] : SORROWFUL, ANGUISHED — **grief·ful·ly** \-əlē\ *adv*

grief·less \'grēfləs\ *adj* : free from grief — **grief·less·ness** *n* -ES

grief stem *n* : a tube or rod of square cross section fitted into a square hole in the rotary-drill table and forming the top section of the rotary-drill shaft in an oil well

griege \'grāzh\ *n* -S [alter. of *grège*] : a variable color averaging a grayish yellow green that is yellower and paler than average sage green, mermaid, or palmetto and yellower and less strong than celadon

grien *var of* 4GREEN

grie·shoch \'grēshək, -ək\ *n* -S [ScGael *grìosach*] *Scot* : a bed of hot embers

gries·ly \'grēzlē\ *archaic var of* GRISLY

griev·ance \'grēvən(t)s\ *n* -S *often attrib* [ME *grevaunce*, fr. OF *grevance*, fr. *grever* to afflict, grieve + *-ance* — more at GRIEVE] 1 a : SUFFERING, GRIEF, DISTRESS ⟨~s illegally inflicted upon men by the king's ministers —J.G.Edwards⟩ b *archaic* : the infliction of a grievance 2 : aggrieved state : ANGER, ANNOYANCE, DISPLEASURE ⟨went their own way blithely, to the ~ of their leaders⟩ ⟨have long cherished a ~ against whistlers in public places⟩ 3 a : a cause of uneasiness or distress felt to afford rightful reason for reproach, complaint, or resistance ⟨the ~ of taxation without representation⟩ ⟨they had many ~s⟩ b : a working condition considered unsatisfactory and objected to by labor ⟨failure to respect seniority rights was a major ~⟩; *esp* : one involving violation of a collective agreement 4 : a complaint by an employee or a body of employees of unfair treatment by the employer ⟨a joint labor-management committee to act on ~s⟩

grievance committee *n* : a committee formed by a labor union or by employer and employees jointly to discuss and where possible eliminate grievances

grievance procedure *n* : the several stages or steps in which a labor grievance may be settled or to which it may be appealed

griev·ant \-nt\ *n* -S [*grieve* + *-ant*] : one who submits a grievance for arbitration ⟨order the ~ reinstated with back pay — *Labor Relations Reporter*⟩

1**grieve** \'grēv\ *n* -S [ME *greif, greff*, fr. OE (Northumbrian) *grǣfa*; akin to OE *gerēfa* reeve — more at REEVE] 1 a *archaic* : GOVERNOR, SHERIFF b *dial Eng* : 3GRAVE 2 *chiefly Scot* : a farm manager, steward, or overseer

2**grieve** \"\ *vb* -ED/-ING/-S [ME *greven*, fr. OF *grever*, fr. L *gravare* to burden, oppress, fr. *gravis* heavy, grave; akin to Goth *kaurjos* (nom. pl.) heavy, *kaurjan* to weigh upon, Gk *barys* heavy, *baros* weight, Skt *guru* heavy, important] *vt* 1 *archaic* : to injure, harm, or hurt esp. with disease 2 : to occasion grief to : cause to suffer : TRY, DISTRESS ⟨the children's conduct *grieved* their grandmother⟩ 3 : to feel or show grief over 4 *obs* a : PROVOKE, ANGER, ENRAGE b : to weigh or press heavily upon ~ *vi* 1 : to feel grief : be in pain of mind on account of an evil : SORROW, MOURN — often used with *at, for*, or *over* ⟨*grieving* over their mother's death⟩ ⟨must not ~ at such trifles⟩ 2 : to enter a grievance

syn MOURN, SORROW: GRIEVE may suggest lasting mental suffering, manifested or not, often with a tendency to concentrate on one's loss or distress ⟨he *grieved*, like an honest lad, to see his comrade left to face calamity alone —George Meredith⟩ ⟨last winter she died also, and my days are passed in work, lest I should *grieve* for her —Amy Lowell⟩ MOURN may more strongly imply demonstration of grief, often a deep grief, as at a bereavement ⟨national *mourning* for a dead sovereign⟩ ⟨his widow . . . *mourned* him —C.B.Flood⟩ SORROW may indicate deep distress tinged with regret and sadness ⟨I feel it when I *sorrow* most: 'tis better to have loved and lost —Alfred Tennyson⟩

grieved \'grēvd\ *adj* [ME *greved* vexed, fr. past part. of *greven*] : afflicted esp. with grief : vexed in mind — **grieved·ly** \-v(ə)dlē\ *adv*

griev·er \-və(r)\ *n* -S 1 : one that grieves 2 : a representative of labor on a grievance committee

grieves *pres 3d sing of* GRIEVE, *pl of* GRIEVE *or obs pl of* GRIEF

grieve·ship \'grēv,ship\ *n* [1*grieve* + *-ship*] *Brit* : the territory under a grieve

griev·ing·ly *adv* : with grief

griev·ous \'grēvəs, *chiefly in substand speech* -vēəs\ *adj* [ME *grevous*, fr. OF *greveus*, fr. *gref* grief + *-eus* -ous — more at GRIEF] 1 : weighing or falling heavily : BURDENSOME, OPPRESSIVE, ONEROUS ⟨the ~ cost of war⟩ 2 : causing, characterized by, or indicative of severe physical pain or suffering : HURTFUL, DISTRESSING, INJURIOUS ⟨a ~ wound⟩ ⟨~ lamentation⟩; *often* : INTENSE, SEVERE ⟨~ pain⟩ 3 : causing, characterized by, or indicative of great sorrow or severe emotional suffering ⟨a ~ loss⟩; *broadly* : extremely distressing or irritating ⟨a ~ insult⟩ 4 a : SERIOUS, DEPLORABLE ⟨his most ~ fault⟩ b *archaic* : outrageously bad : ATROCIOUS, HEINOUS 5 : expressing or full of grief, sorrow, or anguish ⟨a ~ cry⟩ **syn** see BITTER

griev·ous·ly *adv* [ME *grevously*, fr. *grevous* + *-ly*] : in a grievous manner or to a grievous degree : FLAGRANTLY, SERIOUSLY ⟨the prison population has ~ increased in the last fifteen years —*Times Lit. Supp.*⟩

griev·ous·ness *n* -ES [ME *grevousnesse*, fr. *grevous* + *-nesse* -ness] : the quality or state of being grievous

1**griff** \'grif\ *n* -S [origin unknown] *dial Eng* : a deep narrow glen or ravine

2**griff** \"\ *also* **grif·fin** \-fən\ *n* -S [origin unknown] *slang Brit* : an accurate account : a factually correct piece of information; *esp* : a bit of inside information : TIP

1**griffe** \'grif\ *n* -S [F, fr. AmerSp *grifo*, fr. Sp, adj., kinky-haired, fr. *grifo*, n., griffin, fr. L *gryphus* — more at GRIFFON] 1 : the offspring of a Negro and a mulatto : a person of three-quarter Negro and one-quarter white blood 2 : a person of mixed Negro and American Indian blood

2**griffe** *or* **griff** \"\ *n* -S [F *griffe*, lit., claw, fr. MF, of Gmc origin; akin to OHG *grīfan* to grasp, seize — more at GRIPE] 1 : an ornament resembling a claw that projects from the round base of an architectural column upon the angle formed by a corner of the plinth — called also *spur* 2 : an arrangement of parallel bars on a loom for lifting the hooked wires that raise the warp threads in weaving jacquard or dobby fabrics

1**grif·fin** \'grifən\ *also* **grif·fon** *or* **gryph·on** \-fən, -,fän\ *n* -S [ME *griffon, griffoun*, fr. MF *grifon*, fr. *grif*, fr. L *gryphus*, fr. Gk *gryp-, gryps*, fr. *grypos* curved, having a hooked nose; akin to OE *cradol* cradle — more at CRADLE] 1 a : a fabulous animal typically having head, forepart, and wings like those of an eagle but with visible usu. erect ears, forelegs like the legs of an eagle, and body, hind legs, and tail like those of a lion b : any of various fantastic animals in art that resemble the griffin or are considered to be ancestral or related to the typical griffin — see MALE GRIFFIN 2 : GRIFFON VULTURE

griffin 1b

2**griffin** \"\ *n* -S [origin unknown] 1 : a white person new to the East : one recently come from the Occident 2 a : an untried Chinese racing pony b : a tough hardy Mongolian pony used esp. for polo

3**griffin** \"\ *n* -S [by alter.] : 1GRIFFE 1

grif·fin·age \-nij\ *n* -S [2*griffin* + *-age*] : the state of being a white person recently come to the East

grif·fith·ite \'grifə,thīt\ *n* -S [*Griffith* Park, Los Angeles, Calif. + E *-ite*] : a chloritic mineral containing basic magnesium, iron, calcium, and aluminosilicate

1**grif·fon** \'grifən, -,fän\ *n* -S *usu cap* [ME *Griffoun*, fr. MF *Grifon*] *archaic* : GREEK

2**griffon** \"\ *n* [F, lit., griffin] 1 *usu cap* : a breed of small short-faced compact dogs of Belgian origin that occur in several varieties differing chiefly in length, color, or texture of coat 2 -S *sometimes cap* : a sporting dog of a breed originating in Holland but largely developed in France and comprising medium-sized long-headed dogs with downy undercoat and harsh wiry outer coat of gray or grayish white often with chestnut markings — called also *wire-haired pointing griffon*

grif·fo·nage \,grifə'näzh\ *n* -S [F, fr. MF *grifouner* to scribble (fr. *griffon* stylus, fr. *griffe* claw) + *-age* — more at GRIFFE] : careless handwriting : a crude or illegible scrawl

grif·fonne \(')gri¦fän\ *n* -S [F, fr. *griffe* — more at GRIFFE] : a woman of three-quarter Negro and one-quarter white blood

griffon vulture *n* : any of numerous large Old World vultures constituting a genus (*Gyps*); *esp* : a large squat light-colored vulture (*G. fulvus*) of mountainous parts in southern Europe, northern Africa, and eastward to India

griffs *pl of* GRIFF

1**grift** \'grift\ *n* -S [perh. alter. of 2*graft*] *slang* : methods or techniques of obtaining money illicitly (as in a confidence game or a crooked gamble) that depend primarily on adroitness and do not usu. involve the employment of physical force or violence — usu. used with *the* — **grift·er** \-tə(r)\ *n* -S

2**grift** \"\ *vb* -ED/-ING/-S *vi, slang* : to practice the grift : live by one's wits ~ *vt, slang* : to obtain (as money) by the grift

1**grig** \'grig\ *n* -S [ME *grege*] 1 : a small person or creature : DWARF: as a : CRICKET, GRASSHOPPER b : a small short-legged domestic fowl (as a bantam or a creeper fowl) c : a small or immature eel 2 : a gay lively light-hearted and usu. small or young person ⟨a ~ of a girl⟩ — often used as the typification of light-hearted easy happiness, gaiety, or content ⟨gathered about the table merry as so many ~s⟩ 3 *archaic* : FARTHING

2**grig** \"\ *vi* **grigged; grigged; grigging; grigs** : to fish for grigs

3**grig** \"\ *vt* [prob. fr. IrGael *griogaim* (I) tantalize, urge, incite] *dial* : TANTALIZE, IRRITATE, ANNOY ⟨the words *grigged* him a little⟩

4**grig** \"\ *n* -S [W *grug* or Corn *grig*] *dial Eng* : HEATHER

grig·gles \'grigəlz\ *n pl* [prob. fr. 1*grig* + *-le*, dim. suffix] *dial Eng* : small or inferior apples left on a tree after picking

gri·gnard reaction \(')grēn¦yär(d)-\ *n, usu cap G* [after Victor *Grignard* †1934 Fr. chemist] : the reaction of a Grignard reagent with any of several types of compounds (as an aldehyde, ketone, or ester) to yield any of a variety of compounds (as an alcohol)

grignard reagent *n, usu cap G* [after Victor *Grignard*] : any of various compounds of magnesium with an organic radical and a halogen (as ethyl-magnesium iodide C_2H_5MgI) that react readily (as with water, alcohols, amines, acids) in the Grignard reaction

grigri *var of* GRIS-GRIS

gri-gri *var of* GRUGRU

gri·has·tha \gər'hästə\ *n* -S [Skt *gṛhastha*] : the second stage in the Brahmanic ashrama in which a man assumes the duties and responsibilities of a householder

grike \'grīk\ *n* -S [alter. of ME *crike*, fr. ON *kriki* crack, bend, concavity — more at CREEK] : CREVICE, CRACK; *esp* : an opening in rock widened by natural forces (as weathering or solution)

1**grill** \'gril\ *vb* -ED/-ING/-S [F *griller*, fr. MF, fr. *gril*] *vt* 1 a : to broil on an open grill or a griddle ⟨wait to the last minute to ~ the steaks⟩ b *obs* : to cook by scalloping 2 a : to torment by or as if by broiling ⟨the sun beat down and ~*ed* them⟩ b : to distress with continued questioning in or as if in cross-examination : press with questions ⟨the police ~*ed* the suspect⟩ c : to afflict with difficulties, vexations, burdens, or onerous demands ~ *vi* 1 : to become grilled : BROIL ⟨lamb chops for ~*ing*⟩ 2 : to afflict a person with difficulties **syn** see AFFLICT

2**grill** \"\ *n* -S [F *gril* grill, gridiron, fr. MF, alter. of *gredil, gradil*, fr. LL *craticulum* fine wickerwork, alter. of L *craticula*, dim. of *cratis* wickerwork, hurdle — more at HURDLE] 1 *also* **grille** \"\ a : a cooking utensil on which food is exposed to red heat (as from charcoal or electricity) between bars b : GRIDDLE 2 c *Brit* : HOT PLATE 2 : food or a dish that is broiled usu. on a grill ⟨a piping hot ~ of oysters and bacon⟩ — see MIXED GRILL 3 : a grillroom or other usu. informal restaurant 4 [1*grill*] : an act or instance of grilling

grill 1a

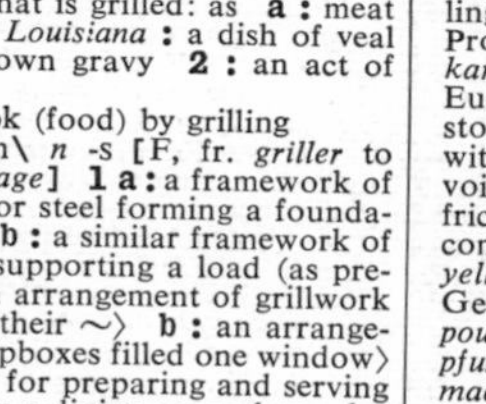

3**grill** \"\ *var of* GRILLE

4**grill** \"\ *vt* -ED/-ING/-S [3*grill*] : to impress (a stamp) with a grill

1**gril·lade** \grə'läd, grē'yäd\ *n* -S [F, fr. *griller* to grill + *-ade* — more at GRILL] 1 : something that is grilled: as a : meat broiled to order (as in a hotel) b *Louisiana* : a dish of veal cooked and served in a savory brown gravy 2 : an act of grilling

2**grillade** *vt* -ED/-ING/-S *obs* : to cook (food) by grilling

gril·lage \'grilij, grē'läzh, grē'yäzh\ *n* -S [F, fr. *griller* to supply with grillwork (fr. *grille*) + *-age*] 1 a : a framework of sleepers and crossbeams of timber or steel forming a foundation in marshy or treacherous soil b : a similar framework of stringers and crossbeams used for supporting a load (as precast concrete floor slabs) 2 a : an arrangement of grillwork ⟨glimpses of native women behind their ~⟩ b : an arrangement resembling a grille ⟨a ~ of soapboxes filled one window⟩

grill car *n* : a railroad car equipped for preparing and serving food and drinks less elaborately than a dining car and usu. for passengers on short runs

1**grille** *also* **grill** \'gril\ *n* -S [F *grille*, fr. MF, alter. of OF *greille, graille* grille, gridiron, griddle, fr. L *craticula* fine wickerwork — more at 2GRILL] 1 a : a grating (as of wrought iron, bronze, or wood) forming an often elaborate openwork barrier, screen, or cover (as to a door, window, or other opening): as (1) : an openwork barrier or grating in a heating or ventilating system : REGISTER (2) : an ornamental metal screen at the front of an automobile hiding the core of the radiator (3) : a mask with irregular perforations so arranged that when it is superimposed on a sheet of paper the words or other elements of a cryptographic message may be written through the perforations — see FLEISSNER GRILLE, TRELLIS CIPHER (4) : a grilled screen covering the outlet of a radio speaker or other amplifier b : an opening covered with a grille: as (1) : a window for the sale of tickets (2) : an air outlet (as of a ventilation system) covered with a protective or ornamental grille 2 : a square opening in the corner at the farther end of a court-tennis court on the hazard side 3 *usu* **grill** : a square or rectangular uninked pattern on a postage stamp (as on a U.S. 1867–71 issue) composed of rows of raised or sunken pyramidal bosses where the paper has been cut by corresponding bosses on a roller as a protection against illegal removal of cancellation marks

2**grille** *also* **grill** \"\ *adj, of table cutlery* : of a style characterized by unusual length of handle and shortness of blade or tine

3**grille** *var of* GRILL

grill·er \'grilə(r)\ *n* -S [1*grill* + *-er*] : one that grills; *usu* : a device for broiling : 2GRILL

grilling *pres part of* GRILL

grillroom \'=,=\ *n* [2*grill* + *room*] : an informal dining room esp. in a hotel or club

grills *pres 3d sing of* GRILL, *pl of* GRILL

grillwork \'=,=\ *n* [3*grill* + *work*] : work so constructed as to constitute or resemble a grille

grilse \'grils *also* -lts\ *n, pl* **grilse** *also* **grilses** [ME *grills, grilles*] 1 : a young mature Atlantic salmon returning from the sea to spawn for the first time when between 3 and 3½ years of age, being chiefly a small male of 4 to 12 pounds, and being very vigorous and active when compared with older fish 2 : any of various other salmon at a stage of development comparable to the Atlantic salmon grilse

1**grim** \'grim\ *adj* **grimmer; grimmest** [ME, fr. OE *grimm*; akin to OHG *grimm* savage, fierce, ON *grimmr* fierce, cruel, enraged, Gk *chromados* action of gnashing, Av *gram-* to get angry] 1 a : fierce in disposition or action : savage and merciless : cruel and pitiless ⟨gaunt ~ wolves descending into the valleys⟩ b : stern, fierce, and resolute : UNCOMPROMISING ⟨ready to do ~ battle for their rights⟩ 2 a : of harsh and forbidding aspect : stern or forbidding in action or appearance ⟨a ~ man loving duty more than humanity⟩ b : distressing or shocking to see : GRISLY, HORRIBLE ⟨the ~ row of traitors' heads over the gate⟩ 3 : unyielding and relentless : sternly determined ⟨~ purpose⟩ 4 : ghastly, repellent, or sinister in character or dealing with what is so ⟨a ~ task⟩ ⟨a ~ tale⟩ ⟨lectures seem to me a rather ~ treat —Willa Cather⟩ — **grim·ly** *adv* — **grim·ness** *n* -ES

2**grim** \"\ *vt* **grimmed; grimmed; grimming; grims** : to make grim and forbidding ⟨lurid clouds that ~ the silence⟩

1**grimace** \'griməs, grə'mās\ *n* -S [F, fr. MF, alter. of *grimache*, of Gmc origin; akin to OE *grīma* mask, helmet — more at GRIME] 1 : a deliberate or involuntary distortion of the countenance expressive of some feeling (as contempt, disapprobation, complacency) : a wry face ⟨gave a little ~ of disgust⟩ 2 a : artful show : AFFECTATION; *broadly* : SHAM, PRETENSE b *archaic* : an affected expression or attitude esp. of formal good manners or exaggerated gentility

2**grimace** \"\ *vi* -ED/-ING/-S [F *grimacer*, fr. *grimace*, n.] : to make grimaces : distort one's face : make faces — **grimac·er** \-sə(r)\ *n* -S

grimac·ing·ly *adv* : with grimaces

gri·mal·di·an \grə'maldēən, -mȯl-\ *adj, usu cap G* [*Grimaldi* (*race*) + *-an*] : of or relating to the Grimaldi race

gri·mal·di race *or* **grimaldi man** \-dē-\ *n, usu cap G* [fr. *Grimaldi* caves, Liguria, Italy, where remains were found] : an early Upper Paleolithic man somewhat resembling the Cro-Magnons but also showing some negroid characteristics and being known from buried skeletons of a woman and a boy

gri·mal·kin \grə'malkən, -mȯ(l)k-\ *also* **gray·mal·kin** \grā'-\ *n* [*grimalkin* alter. of *graymalkin*; *graymalkin* fr. *gray* + *malkin*] 1 : CAT 1; *esp* : an elderly queen 2 : an old and usu. cantankerous or otherwise unpleasant woman

1**grime** \'grīm\ *vt* -ED/-ING/-S [ME *grimen*, fr. MD, fr. *grime* mask, soot] : to sully or soil deeply : BESMEAR, BEGRIME

2**grime** \"\ *n* -S [Flem *grijm*, fr. MD *grime* soot, mask; akin to OE *grīma* mask, helmet, OS & ON, mask, OHG *grīmo* mask, Gk *chriein* to anoint, Lith *grieti* to skim off cream — more at CHRISM] : soil (as soot or dirt) usu. firmly adhering to or deeply embedded in a surface ⟨windows coated with ~⟩ ⟨the ~ of toil that no scrubbing could wholly remove from his hands⟩; *broadly* : accumulated dirtiness and disorder ⟨the ~ of the slums⟩

grime·less \-ləs\ *adj* : free from grime : CLEAN, IMMACULATE

grime's ditch *or* **grime's dyke** *usu cap G, var of* GRIM'S DITCH

grimes' grave \'grīmz(əz)-\ *n, usu cap both Gs* [origin unknown] : one of the pits sunk near Brandon, Suffolk, England, in Neolithic times for the mining of flint

grim·ful \'grim(p)fəl\ *adj* [ME, fr. *grim* + *-ful*] *archaic* : cruel and fierce : DREADFUL

grimgribber *n* -S [fr. *Grimgribber*, an imaginary estate subject of a legal discussion in the play *Conscious Lovers* (1722) by Sir Richard Steele †1729 Brit. essayist and dramatist] *obs* : technical jargon (as of legal matters)

grimier *comparative of* GRIMY

grimiest *superlative of* GRIMY

grim·i·ly \'grīməlē, -li\ *adv* : in a grimy condition or manner

grim·i·ness \-mēnəs, -min-\ *n* -ES : the quality or state of being grimy

grim·ly *adj* [ME, fr. OE *grimlīc*, fr. *grimm* grim + *-līc* -ly — more at GRIM] *archaic* : GRIM, HIDEOUS, STERN

grimme \'grim\ *n* -S [F, fr. NL *grimmia* (specific epithet of the Linnaean designation *Capra grimmia*), fr. Hermann N. *Grimm* †1711 Ger. scientist + NL *-ia*] : a small West African antelope (*Cephalophus rufilotus*) of a deep bay color

grimmer *comparative of* GRIM

grimmest *superlative of* GRIM

grim·mia \'grimēə\ *n, cap* [NL, fr. Johann F. K. *Grimm* †1821 Ger. botanist + NL *-ia*] : a widely distributed genus of tufted rock mosses that is the type of the family Grimmiaceae

grim·mi·a·ce·ae \,grimē'āsē,ē\ *n pl, cap* [NL, fr. *Grimmia*, type genus + *-aceae*] : a family of acrocarpous mosses that have the capsule on a short stalk and with a single peristome the teeth of which are often split or perforated and that form dark mats or cushions lacking chlorophyll except at the tips of stems and branches — **grim·mi·a·ceous** \,grimē¦āshəs\ *adj*

grim·mi·a·les \,grimē'ā(,)lēz\ *n pl, cap* [NL, fr. *Grimmia* + *-ales*] : an order of Musci comprising acrocarpous mosses that are usu. blackish green with branching stems and densely crowded leaves and that grow chiefly on rocks

grimming *pres part of* GRIM

grim·mish \'grimish\ *adj* : rather grim

grimm's law \'grimz-\ *n, usu cap G & often cap L* [after Jacob *Grimm* †1863 Ger. philologist] 1 a : a statement in historical linguistics: Proto-Indo-European voiceless stops became Proto-Germanic voiceless fricatives (as in Greek *pyr, treis, kardia* compared with English *fire, three, heart*), Proto-Indo-European voiced stops became Proto-Germanic voiceless stops (as in Old Slavic *jablŭko*, Greek *dyo, genos* compared with English *apple, two, kin*), and Proto-Indo-European voiced aspirated stops became Proto-Germanic voiced fricatives (as in Sanskrit *nābhi, madhya* "mid", Latin *helvus* compared with English *navel*, Old Norse *mithr* "mid", English *yellow*), and then Proto-Germanic voiceless stops became High German affricates or voiceless fricatives (as in English *pound, open, ten, eat, corn, make* compared with German *pfund, offen, zehn, essen*, Upper German *kchorn*, German *machen*), and Proto-Germanic voiced stops (coming from Proto-Germanic voiced fricatives) became High German voiceless stops (as in English *rib, middle*, Dutch *egge* "edge" compared with German *rippe, mittel* "means", *ecke* "corner") b : a statement in historical linguistics: Proto-Indo-European voiceless stops became Proto-Germanic voiceless fricatives (as in Greek *pyr, treis, kardia* compared with English *fire, three, heart*), Proto-Indo-European voiced stops became Proto-Germanic voiceless stops (as in Old Slavic *jablŭko*, Greek *dyo, genos* compared with English *apple, two, kin*), and Proto-Indo-European voiced aspirated stops became Proto-Germanic voiced fricatives (as in Sanskrit *nābhi, madhya* "mid", Latin *helvus* compared with English *navel*, Old Norse *mithr* "mid", English *yellow*) 2 a : CONSONANT SHIFT 3 b : CONSONANT SHIFT 1

grim·ness *n* -ES [ME *grimnesse*, fr. OE, fr. *grimm* + *-nesse* -ness] : the quality or state of being grim

gri·moire \grəm'wär\ *n* -S [F, fr. OF, alter. of *gramaire* grammar, grammar book, learned work, book of witchcraft — more at GRAMMAR] : a magician's manual for invoking demons and the spirits of the dead

grimp \'grimp\ *vi* -ED/-ING/-S [F *grimper*, fr. MF, alter. (prob. influenced by *ramper* to crawl) of *gripper* to climb, to seize with the claws or nails, of Gmc origin; akin to OS *grīpan* to grasp, seize — more at GRIPE] 1 : CLIMB 2 : to draw up ⟨the line ~*ed* into a hard knot⟩

grim reaper *n, often cap G&R* : death esp. when personified as a man or skeleton with a scythe

grims *pres 3d sing of* GRIM

grim's ditch *or* **grim's dyke** \'grimz-\ *also* **grime's ditch** *or* **grime's dyke** \'grīmz-\ *n, usu cap G* [origin unknown] : any of several ancient entrenchments found in the British Isles some of which are prehistoric

grim–the–collier \,grim-\ *n* -S [after *Grim the Collier*, character in the anonymous play *Grim the Collier of Croydon* (1662); fr. its black smutty involucre] : ORANGE HAWKWEED

grim·thorpe \'grim(p),thȯ(ə)rp\ *vt* -ED/-ING/-S [after Sir Edmund Beckett, first Baron *Grimthorpe* †1905 Eng. lawyer and architect whose restoration of St. Albans cathedral in England was severely criticized] : to remodel (an ancient building) without proper knowledge or care to retain its original quality and character

grimy \'grīmē, -mi\ *adj* **grimier; grimiest** [²*grime* + -*y*] **1 :** full of or covered with grime : BEGRIMED, DIRTY, FOUL; *also* : DUSKY, SWARTHY **2 :** mean and unpleasant : common and petty ⟨a ~ rascal⟩ ⟨told the whole story in all its ~ spite⟩

¹**grin** \'grin\ *n* -s [ME *grin, grine, grene,* fr. OE *grin;* akin to ME *grane* snare, noose] *chiefly Scot* : SNARE, NOOSE, TRAP

²**grin** \"\ *vt* **grinned; grinned; grinning; grins** [ME *grenen,* fr. *grin, grine, grene,* n.] : TRAP

³**grin** \"\ *vb* **grinned; grinned; grinning; grins** [ME *grennen, grinnen,* fr. OE *grennian;* akin to OHG *grennen* to snarl, ON *grenja* to howl, and prob. to OE *grānian* to groan — more at GROAN] *vi* **1 :** to draw back the lips from the teeth (as of a dog in snarling or a person in laughter or pain) so as to show them; *esp* : to do this in merriment or good humor (as in a broad smile) **2 a :** to gape open : PART **b :** to appear through interstices of a covering ⟨sometimes the paint checks and lets the undercoat ~ through⟩ ~ *vt* **1 :** to show (the teeth) usu. in a grin or snarl **2 :** to form or express by grinning ⟨*grinned* reassurance to the frightened children⟩ ⟨*grinning* a foolish grin⟩ — **grin like a cheshire cat** *usu cap 1st C* : to grin broadly — **grin on the other side of one's face :** to regret one's previous behavior in some matter that at the time seemed trivial or amusing ⟨you'll *grin on the other side of your face* if you have to pay for the damage you did⟩

⁴**grin** \"\ *n* -s **1 :** a facial expression produced by grinning ⟨a ~ of pain⟩; *esp* : a broad toothy smile **2 :** something exposed like the teeth in a grin: as **a :** an unfinished portion of baseboard exposed when a building settles **b :** a portion of the basic fabric of a rug exposed when the pile parts — compare GRIN *vi* 2b

¹**grind** \'grīnd\ *vb* **ground** \'grau̇nd\ *also archaic* **grinded; ground** *also archaic* **grinded** *or* **ground·en** \'grau̇ndən\ **grinding; grinds** [ME *grinden,* fr. OE *grindan;* akin to OHG *grint* scurf, ON *grandi* sandbar, Goth *grindafrathjis* faint-hearted, L *frendere* to crush, gnash, grind, Gk *chondros* grain, Lith *grendu* I rub, scrub, OE *grēot* sand, grit — more at GRIT] *vt* **1 a :** to reduce to powder by friction (as in a mill) or with the teeth : crush into small fragments **b :** to produce by or as if by the action of millstones **2 :** to wear down, polish, or sharpen by friction : make smooth, sharp, or pointed : WHET ⟨spent the morning ~*ing* axes and scythes⟩ **3 a :** to rub or press harshly ⟨~ the snake's head under his heel⟩ **b :** to rub together with a grating noise : GRATE, GRIT ⟨~ the teeth⟩ **4 :** to oppress by severe exactions : HARASS ⟨~ the subject or defraud the prince —John Dryden⟩ **5 :** to operate or produce by turning a crank ⟨~ a hand organ⟩ ⟨~ out a tune⟩ ~ *vi* **1 :** to perform the operation of grinding **2 :** to become ground or pulverized by friction ⟨corn ~*ing* slowly⟩ **3 :** to become polished or sharpened by friction ⟨glass ~*s* smooth⟩ ⟨steel ~*s* to a sharp edge⟩ ⟨pebbles ~*ing* on the beach⟩ **4 :** to move with difficulty or friction : GRATE ⟨the gears *ground* as he shifted into high⟩ ⟨frantically *ground* on the starter —Frank Schreider⟩ **5 :** to perform hard and distasteful service : DRUDGE; *esp* : to study hard ⟨~ for an examination⟩ **6 :** to rotate the hips in a suggestive manner in or as if in a burlesque striptease

²**grind** \"\ *n* -s [ME, fr. *grinden,* v.] **1 a :** an act of grinding (as of reducing to powder or sharpening by friction) **b :** a sound of grinding **2 a :** steady monotonous taxing labor, occupation, or routine ⟨sometimes life seems just a dull ~ without hope or future⟩ **b :** intensive and drudging study; *also* : a task or an assignment given by an instructor **3 :** a student who studies to the exclusion of all other activities often with more diligence than delight **4 :** the result of grinding; *esp* : the size of particle obtained by grinding ⟨there are several different ~*s* of coffee⟩ ⟨a fine ~ of meal is better for bread⟩ **5 :** an action of rotating the hips with a suggestive motion (as in a dance or in a burlesque striptease) — compare ²BUMP 5 **syn** see WORK

³**grind** \"\ *adj, of a motion-picture theater or other show* : exhibiting continuously or continuously between certain hours

⁴**grind** \'grind\ *n* -s [of Scand origin; akin to ON *grind* gate, lattice door; akin to OE *grindel* bar, bolt, OHG *grintil* bar, bolt, L *grunda* truss of a roof, Lith *grindis* floorboard; basic meaning: beam] *Scot* : a horizontal bar gate

⁵**grind** \"\ *n, pl* **grind** [Faroese *grindkval*] : BLACKFISH 2 — used chiefly in the Faroe islands ⟨the boats will be ready when the ~ come in⟩

grind·abil·i·ty \,grīndə'biləd·ē\ *n* : capacity for or resistance to being ground ⟨prepared an index of the ~ of various southern coals⟩

grind·able \'grīndəbəl\ *adj* : capable of being ground

grind down *vt* : to repress harshly : keep rigidly under control or in a state of submission ⟨the nobility *ground down* the peasants with an infinite variety of petty exactions⟩

grin·de·lia \grin'dēlyə, -lēə\ *n* [NL, fr. David Hieronymus *Grindel* †1836 Russ. botanist + NL -*ia*] **1 a** *cap* : a large genus of coarse gummy or resinous herbs (family Compositae) chiefly of western No. America that have flower heads with involucres consisting of phyllaries with spreading tips **b** -s : a plant of the genus *Grindelia* : GUMWEED **2** -s : the dried leaves and stems of various gumweeds (as *Grindelia camporum, G. cuneifolia,* and *G. squarrosa*) used internally as a remedy in bronchitis and as a local application in ivy poisoning

grind·er \'grīndə(r)\ *n* -s [ME, fr. *grinden* to grind + -*er* — more at GRIND] **1 a :** MOLAR 1 — distinguished from *cutter* **b grinders** *pl* : TEETH **2 :** a person that grinds: as **a :** a worker who crushes or pulverizes materials (as grain, stone, clay, scrap rubber) usu. by machine **b :** a worker who shapes, smooths, or cleans roughly finished articles by means of abrasives or grinding wheels; *esp* : one that sharpens tools by grinding (as on a grinding wheel) **c** *slang Brit* : a private tutor **d** *slang* : a carnival or sideshow barker who talks up a new crowd while one show is going on **e** *slang* : a burlesque performer specializing in grinds **3 :** a machine or device for grinding: as **a :** a machine for grinding with abrasives that typically takes the form of a grinding wheel and is used to cut hardened or tempered metals and to develop a smooth finish (as on metal, wood, stone) **b :** a pulverizing machine (as a ball mill or a wood-pulp grinding machine) **4** [so called fr. its whining call] : RESTLESS FLYCATCHER **5 :** an atmospheric disturbance that is heard by a radio listener as a rumbling and is caused by distant lightning **6 :** a large sandwich made of two slabs of bread cut lengthwise from the loaf or a whole small crusty loaf cut lengthwise and containing meat (as ham, salami, or meatballs), usu. cheese, tomato and lettuce, pickles or other appetizers, and sometimes (as with meatballs) a thick spicy sauce

grind·er·man \-mən, -,man\ *n, pl* **grindermen 1 :** one who tends an edge runner in papermaking **2 :** one who tends the grinders in preparing groundwood

grinder's green *n* : a chrome green containing usu. about 75 percent of extending pigments and commonly used for preparing green paints and pastes for tinting

grind in *vt* : to lap in (as a valve and valve seat) so that each surface serves as a lap for the other

¹**grinding** *n* -s [ME, fr. *grinden* to grind + -*ing* — more at GRIND] : an act or the sound of one that grinds

²**grinding** *adj* [fr. pres. part. of ¹*grind*] **1 :** used in or suitable for grinding ⟨the ~ teeth⟩ ⟨a good grade of white ~ corn⟩ **2** *of pain* **a :** extremely severe and wearing : EXCRUCIATING, AGONIZING **b :** of the type characteristic of the early stages of labor **3 :** burdensome and oppressive ⟨~ poverty⟩ ⟨a ~ suspicion⟩; *esp* : EXTORTIONATE ⟨~ levies and excessive taxes⟩ **4 a** *of sound* : harsh and strident ⟨a gritty ~ voice⟩ ⟨a bird with a peculiar ~ call⟩ **b :** characterized or accompanied by a grinding sound ⟨worn ~ gears⟩ — **grindingly** *adv*

grinding aid *n* : a material added in small amount to cement clinker to aid in the pulverizing of the clinker into powder

grinding mill *n* **1 :** any of various machines for grinding (as of grain or sugarcane) or for dressing by grinding (as of metal parts) **2 :** a lapidary's lathe

grinding wheel *n* : an abrasive wheel or disk used for cutting or smoothing hard materials

¹**grin·dle** \'grind°l\ *n* -s [ME *grendyll*] *dial Eng* : a small stream or ditch

²**grin·dle** *also* **grin·dal** *or* **grin·del** \'grind°l\ *or* **grin·nel** *or* **grin·nell** \-n°l\ *n* -s [G *gründel,* fr. *grund* bottom, ground, fr. OHG *grunt* — more at GROUND] : BOWFIN

grin·dle·stone \'grin(d)°lztən, -°lst-\ *n* [ME *grindelston,* fr. *grindel-* (fr. *grinden* to grind) + *ston* stone — more at GRIND, STONE] *dial* : GRINDSTONE

grin·dle·to·ni·an \,grind°l'tōnēən\ *n* -s *usu cap* [*Grindleton,* parish in Yorkshire, Eng. + E -*ian*] : a member of an English familist sect of the 17th century

grind out *vt* : to produce in a steady stream esp. more or less mechanically as though by turning a crank ⟨*ground out* his three novels a year for over 30 years⟩

grinds *pres 3d sing of* GRIND, *pl of* GRIND

grind·stone \'grīn(d)z,tōn, -),stōn, *archaic or dial* 'grinztən *or* -n(t)st-\ *n* [ME *grindston,* fr. *grinden* to grind + *ston* stone — more at GRIND, STONE] **1 a :** MILLSTONE 1 **b :** a flat circular stone of natural sandstone that revolves on an axle and is used for grinding tools or shaping or smoothing objects **2 :** stone suitable for grindstones

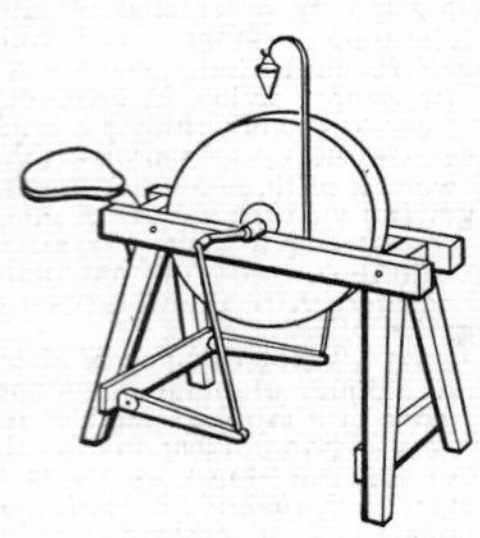

grindstone 1b

grind whale *n* [⁵*grind*] : BLACKFISH 2

grin·ga \'griŋgə, -ŋ(,)gä\ *n* -s [Sp, fem. of *gringo*] : a female gringo — sometimes used disparagingly

grin·go \-ŋ(,)gō\ *n* -s [Sp, alter. of *griego* Greek, unknown language, stranger, fr. L *Graecus* Greek — more at GREEK] : a white foreigner in Spain or Latin America esp. when of English or American origin — often used disparagingly

grin·go·lée \,griŋgə'lā\ *adj* [F *gringolé,* fr. *gringole* serpent's head] *of a cross* : having at the end of each arm a pair of serpent heads with each head turned outward ⟨a cross ~ in his heraldic escutcheon⟩

grinned *past of* GRIN

grin·nel·lia \grə'nelēə, -lyə\ *n, cap* [NL, fr. Henry *Grinnell* †1874 Am. merchant + NL -*ia*] : a genus related to *Delesseria* and comprising red algae with lanceolate fronds often 18 inches or more in length

grin·ner \'grinə(r)\ *n* -s [ME *grennare,* fr. *grennen, grinnen* to grin + -*are,* -*er* -er — more at GRIN] : one that grins

grin·nie *or* **grin·ny** \'grinē\ *n, pl* **grinnies** [origin unknown] *dial* : CHIPMUNK, GROUND SQUIRREL

grinning *pres part of* GRIN

grin·ning·ly *adv* : in a grinning manner : with a grin

grin·ny \'grinē, -ni\ *adj, usu* -ER/-EST : given to grinning

grins *pl of* GRIN, *pres 3d sing of* GRIN

grin·stone \'grinztən, -n(t)st-\ *obs or dial var of* GRINDSTONE

¹**grip** \'grip\ *vb* **gripped** *or* **gript; gripped** *or* **gript; gripping; grips** [ME *grippen,* fr. OE *grippan;* akin to OHG *gripfen* to grip, OE *grīpan* to seize, attack — more at GRIPE] *vt* **1 :** to seize or lay hold on tightly and tenaciously : grasp firmly **2** *archaic* : to take or get possession of : SEIZE, APPROPRIATE **3 :** to give a handclasp to **4 :** to fasten or attach by a grip or clutch **5 a :** to make a tenacious impression upon ⟨the pathos of the play *gripped* the beholders⟩ **b :** GRASP *vt* 3 ~ *vi* : to take firm hold ⟨the anchor ~*s*⟩ **:** close tightly ⟨his jaws *gripped*⟩ : rivet attention ⟨the story ~*s*⟩

²**grip** \"\ *n* -s [ME, partly fr. OE *gripe* grasp, seizure; partly fr. OE *gripa* handful, sheaf; akin to OE *grīpan* to seize, attack — more at GRIPE] **1 a :** an energetic or tenacious grasp : a seizing or clutching of something tightly (as with the hand) ⟨got a good ~ on his collar⟩ **b :** strength in gripping **c :** manner or style of gripping: as (1) : a peculiar mode of clasping the hand by which members of a group (as a secret order) recognize or greet one another (2) : arrangement of and muscular force applied through the hands in grasping something ⟨notice the balanced ~ of an expert golfer⟩ **2** *dial Eng* : as much as can be gripped : HANDFUL **3 :** a spasm of pain **4 a :** power or force of hold or domination : CONTROL, MASTERY ⟨unable to escape the ~ of his bad habits⟩ **b :** power of apprehension : GRASP ⟨he has a thorough ~ of his duty now⟩ ⟨no real intellectual ~ of the subject⟩ **5 :** a part or device for gripping; *esp* : an apparatus attached to a car for clutching a traction cable **6 :** a part or device by which something is grasped (as a handle): as **a** (1) : the portion of a firearm gripped by the trigger hand when firing (2) : either of the pieces (as of wood, plastic, mother-of-pearl) that are fitted one on either side to the portion of the frame of a handgun which forms the grip **b :** the plaited woolen covering on a bell rope — called also *sally* **7 :** a piece of hand luggage (as a suitcase) ⟨the bellboy carried the ~*s*⟩ **8 :** the total thickness of metal held between the two heads of a rivet in a riveted joint **9 :** SCENESHIFTER **10** [short for *gripgrass*] : CLEAVERS — **at grips** *adv* : in a relation resembling or involving a hand-to-hand struggle

³**grip** \'grip\ *also* **gripe** \'grīp\ *n* -s [ME *grippe, gripe, grip,* fr. OE *grȳpe;* akin to OE & MLG *grope* pot, MD *groepe, grope* ditch, *grope, groppe* pot, ON *greypa* to groove] *dial chiefly Eng* : a small ditch or furrow : GUTTER

⁴**grip** \"\ *vt, dial Eng* : TRENCH, DRAIN

⁵**grip** \"\ *n* -s [by alter.] : GRIPPE

grip car *n* : a car equipped with a device for gripping a traction cable by which the car is moved : CABLE CAR

¹**gripe** \'grīp\ *vb* **griped; griped; griping; gripes** [ME *gripen,* fr. OE *grīpan;* akin to OHG *grīfan* to seize, grasp, ON *grīpa,* Goth *greipan* to seize, grasp, Lith *griebti* to reach for, grasp] *vt* **1 a** *archaic* : to take, seize, or come forcibly into possession or control of **b :** to come to have and to hold tightly or penuriously ⟨*griping* his ill-gotten gains⟩ **c :** to grasp, clutch, or hold onto tightly ⟨*griping* his sword fast⟩ **d** *obs* : to enclose tightly **2 :** AFFLICT: as **a :** to distress, hurt, or grieve by or as if by grasping or seizing tightly ⟨may the fiend ~ his entrails —O.W.Holmes †1935⟩ **b :** to oppress by want, penury, or callous grasping exaction ⟨the poverty that ~*s* the very poor⟩ ⟨in the clutches of a *griping* sweatshop operator⟩ **c :** IRRITATE, ANGER, VEX ⟨a rookie *griped* by army regulations⟩ ⟨*griped* by the new income-tax provisions⟩ **3 :** to cause pinching and spasmodic pain in the bowels of ~ *vi* **1** *archaic* : to try to clutch : start to lay hold **2 :** to experience griping pains **3** *of a ship* : to tend to come up into the wind abnormally esp. so as to require the helm to be continually put up when sailing close-hauled **4 :** to complain usu. forcefully : object and criticize with sustained grumbling ⟨*griping* about food in the mess hall⟩ ⟨~ at the new regulations⟩ **syn** see COMPLAIN

²**gripe** \"\ *n* -s [ME, fr. *gripen,* v.] **1 :** the act of griping, clutching, or taking fast hold : firm seizure or grasp; *broadly* : CONTROL, MASTERY ⟨a barren scepter in my ~ —Shak.⟩ **2 a :** cruel exaction : OPPRESSION : pinching distress : AFFLICTION **b :** COMPLAINT, GRUMBLING **3 :** a pinching spasmodic intestinal pain — usu. used in pl. **4 :** something adapted to be grasped : HANDLE, GRIP **5 a :** something that can be grasped in the hand : HANDFUL **b** *obs* : the hand as a gripping instrument **6 :** a device (as a brake) for grasping or holding **7 a :** a timber sometimes scarfed into the forefoot and stem of a wooden ship for additional strength; *broadly* : FOREFOOT 2 **b :** the forward end of the dished keel of a steel ship to which the stem is attached **c gripes** *pl* : canvas bands and fastenings securing a lifeboat in its cradle

³**gripe** \"\ *n* -s [ME, fr. L *grypus, gryphus* — more at GRIFFIN] **1** *obs* : GRIFFIN 1a **2** *archaic* : VULTURE 1

grip·er \'grīpə(r)\ *n* -s : one that gripes

gripe's egg *n* [³*gripe*] *obs* : a vessel in size and shape like a very large egg used by alchemists

gripe water *n* [²*gripe*] : DILL WATER

gripey *var of* GRIPY

gripgrass \'=,=\ *n* : CLEAVERS

griph *or* **griphus** *n, pl* **griphs** *or* **griphuses** [L *griphus,* fr. Gk *griphos,* lit., fishing basket, creel] *obs* : PUZZLE, RIDDLE, ENIGMA

griph·ite \'gri,fīt\ *n* -s [Gk *griphos* enigma + E -*ite;* fr. its unusual composition] : a mineral $(Na,Al,Ca,Fe)_6Mn_4(PO_4)_5(OH)_4$ consisting of basic phosphate of sodium, calcium, iron, aluminum, and manganese with a crystal structure related to that of garnet

griping *adj* **1 :** causing or characteristic of gripe ⟨~ pains⟩ ⟨some foods are ~ when eaten to excess⟩ : PAINFUL, DISTRESSING **2 :** CLUTCHING, GRASPING; *broadly* : AVARICIOUS ⟨married a selfish, ~, spoiled woman⟩ — **grip·ing·ly** *adv*

grip·less \'gripləs\ *adj* : having no grip; *also* : lacking vigor : WEAK, LIFELESS

grip·man \-mən\ *n, pl* **gripmen :** a cable-car operator who makes the car's grip clutch or unclutch a moving cable to move or stop the car as desired

gripp·al \'gripəl\ *adj* [*grippe* + -*al*] : of, relating to, or associated with grippe ⟨~ pneumonia⟩

grippe \'grip\ *n* -s [F, lit., seizure, prob. fr. *gripper* to seize — more at GRIMP] : an acute febrile contagious virus disease identical with or resembling influenza

gripped *past of* GRIP

grip·per \'gripə(r)\ *n* -s **1 :** a device that holds something firmly: as **a :** a bookbinder's mechanism that grips and impels a book or other matter into a machine **b :** a device for holding a sheet being printed **2 a :** a worker who fashions or attaches grips (as on a handgun) **b :** a clipper in a coal mine

¹**grip·pi·ness** \'gripēnəs, -pin-\ *n* -ES [¹*grippy* + -*ness*] *chiefly Scot* : MISERLINESS, STINGINESS

²**gripp·i·ness** \"\ *n* -ES [²*grippy* + -*ness*] : the quality or state of being affected by or feeling as if one had the grippe

gripping *adj* : having the ability to grip; *esp* : taking a powerful hold upon one's interest or feelings — used esp. of a book or play ⟨a ~ tale of suspense⟩ — **grip·ping·ly** *adv* — **grip·ping·ness** *n* -ES

grip·pit \'gripət\ *adj* [fr. Sc var. of *gripped,* past part. of ¹*grip*] *Scot* : GRIPPED, CAUGHT, APPREHENDED ⟨it will be high treason if I'm *grippit* —John Buchan⟩

¹**grip·ple** \'gripəl\ *adj* [ME *gripel,* fr. OE *gripul,* fr. the stem of *gripan* to seize, attack — more at GRIPE] *dial Brit* : greedy and grasping : AVARICIOUS

²**gripple** *vb* [prob. blend of ¹*grip* and ¹*grapple*] *obs* : GRAPPLE, GRASP

¹**grip·py** \'gripē, -pi\ *adj* -ER/-EST [¹*grip* + -*y*] *chiefly Scot* : MISERLY, STINGY ⟨the wife is dreadful ~⟩

²**grippy** \'gripē, -pi\ *adj* -ER/-EST [*grippe* + -*y*] : affected with or like the grippe ⟨the *grippiest* time of the year —*Newsweek*⟩

grips *pres 3d sing of* GRIP, *pl of* GRIP

gripsack \'=,=\ *n* [²*grip* + *sack*] : TRAVELING BAG

grip safety *n* : a safety device on a firearm that prevents firing until it has been depressed by the pressure of the firer's hand upon the grip

gript *past of* GRIP

gripy *or* **grip·ey** \'grīpē, -pi\ *adj* **gripier; gripiest** [²*gripe* + -*y*] : resembling or tending to cause gripes ⟨~ pains⟩

griqua \'grēkwə, -rik-\ *n* -s *cap* [Afrik *Griekwa*] **1 :** one of a mixed people in Griqualand of Bushman and Hottentot descent **2 :** the mixed offspring of European, Bushman, and Hottentot ancestry esp. in Griqualand being mostly tall with dark curly hair and resembling Europeans — called also *Bastaard* **3 :** any person of mixed Caucasoid-Negroid descent — used chiefly in southwestern Africa

griqua·land·er \-,landə(r)\ *n* -s *cap* [Afrik *Griekwalander,* fr. *Griekwaland* Griqualand, region in southern Africa + -*er*] : a native or inhabitant of Griqualand

gris \'grē(s)\ *also* **grise** \-ēs\ *n, pl* **grises** \-rēsəz,-rēz\ [ME *gris,* fr. OF, fr. *gris,* adj., gray — more at GRIZZLE] : a costly gray fur used decoratively on medieval costumes

gri·saille \grə'zī, grē'-, -zāl,-zīl\ *n* -s [F, fr. *gris* gray, fr. OF] **1 a :** painting in monochrome usu. in shades of gray often as decoration to simulate sculptured relief or as underpainting for a glaze finish **b :** a covering of a dark base in porcelain and enamelwork with varying thicknesses of white so as to produce a cameo effect with the dark color showing through **c :** a coating of glasswork with white to produce an opalescent effect or as backing for a decorative pattern of colored glass **2 :** a fancy dress fabric orig. of silk with a fine crosswise rib and a grayish color resulting from interweaving black-and-white threads

grisamber *n* [by alter.] *obs* : AMBERGRIS

gris·ard \'grizə(r)d\ *n* -s [F, fr. *gris* gray + -*ard*] : a gray-headed person

gris·bet \'grizbət\ *var of* GRISTBITE

gris·de·lin \,grēd°l'an, 'grid°lən\ *n* -s [F, lit., flax gray] : GRIDELIN

grise \'grīs\ *var of* GRICE

gris·el·dy \'grizəldē\ *dial var of* GRISLY

gris·e·lin·ia \,grizə'linēə\ *n, cap* [NL, fr. Francesco *Griselini* †1783, Ital. botanist + NL -*ia*] : a small genus of New Zealand and So. American trees (family Cornaceae) that are occas. epiphytic in habit — see KAPUKA, PUKA

gris·eo·ful·vin \,grizēō'fu̇lvən, -'fəl-\ *n* -s [NL *griseofulvum* (specific epithet of *Penicillium griseofulvum*) + E -*in*] : a fungicidal antibiotic $C_{17}H_{17}ClO_6$ produced by molds of the genus *Penicillium*

gris·e·ous \'grizēəs\ *adj* [ML *griseus,* of Gmc origin; akin to OHG *gris* gray — more at GRIZZLE] : of a light color or white mottled with black or brown : GRIZZLED

gri·sette \grə'zet, grē'-\ *n* -s [F, fr. *grisette* inexpensive gray woolen cloth often used for dresses, fr. *gris* gray (fr. OF) + -*ette* — more at GRIZZLE] **1 :** a French girl of the working class **2 :** a young woman combining part-time prostitution with some other occupation ⟨the dusky ~*s* who sold love as well as flowers —H.S.Canby⟩ — **gri·set·tish** \-ed·ish\ *adj*

gris–gris *or* **gri·gri** *also* **gree·gree** \'grē(,)grē\ *n, pl* **gris-gris** *or* **grigris** *also* **greegrees** [of African origin; akin to Bulanda *grigri* charm, amulet] : a talisman, amulet, voodoo charm, spell, or incantation believed chiefly by people of African Negro origin or ancestry capable of warding off evil and bringing good luck to oneself or of bringing misfortune to another

gris·kin \'griskən\ *n* -s [*grice* + -*kin*] **1** *Brit* : a pork loin; *esp* : the lean part **2** *Brit* : a pork chop or other broiled meat : STEAK

gri·sle \'grizəl\ *archaic var of* GRIZZLE

gris·li·ness \'grizlēnəs, -lin-\ *n* -ES [ME *grislines,* fr. *grisly* + -*nes* -ness] : the quality or state of being grisly

¹**gris·ly** *or* **griz·zly** \'grizlē, -li\ *adj* -ER/-EST [ME, fr. OE *grislic,* fr. *gris-* (akin to OE *āgrīsan* to shudder, fear) + -*lic* -ly; akin to OHG *grisenlīh* terrible, MD & MLG *grisen* to shudder, and prob. to OE *grēot* sand, grit — more at GRIT] **1 a :** inspiring horror or intense fear : grim and ghastly ⟨these strange and ~ events⟩; *broadly* : harsh and forbidding ⟨a grim ~ winter's night⟩ **b :** being such as to inspire distaste or disgust ⟨a ~ account of the fire⟩ **2 :** caused by what is grim or horrible or marked by a sense of grim horror ⟨reason could not rid her of that ~ fear⟩

²**gris·ly** \"\ *adv, often* -ER/-EST [ME, fr. *grisly,* adj.] : DREADFULLY, TERRIBLY

³**grisly** *obs var of* GRISTLY

⁴**grisly** *var of* GRIZZLY

gris·on \'griz°n\ *n* [F, fr. *grison* gray, fr. MF, fr. *gris* — more at GRIZZLE] **1** -s : any of various So. American nearly plantigrade carnivorous mammals of the genus *Grison* (esp. *G. vittatus*) that resemble large weasels, are blackish below and gray above, and are often domesticated by the natives though very destructive to poultry **2** [NL, fr. F *grison*] *cap* : a genus of Mustelidae comprising the grisons

gris·sen \'gris°n\ *n* -s [ME *gressing,* fr. *grece* + -*ing* — more at GRECE] *now dial* : GRECE

gris·si·no \grə'sē(,)nō\ *n, pl* **grissi·ni** \-)nē\ [It, fr. It dial. (Piedmont) *grissin, ghersin,* fr. *ghersa* strip] : a long slender crusty breadstick usu. of Italian style or origin

¹**grist** \'grist\ *n* -s [ME, fr. OE *grīst;* akin to OE *grindan* to grind — more at GRIND] **1** *obs* : the act of grinding **2 a :** grain for grinding ⟨some wheats make better ~ than others⟩ **b :** a batch of grain taken to a mill for custom grinding ⟨farmers bringing their ~*s* of rye, buckwheat, and wheat to the mill⟩ **c :** the product obtained from a grist of grain including the flour or meal and the grain offals (as bran) **3 :** crushed or ground malt ready for use in brewing **4 a :** a large quantity : LOT, NUMBER ⟨got a ~ of lazy kinfolk out that way⟩ ⟨you never saw such a ~ of washing for three people⟩ **b :** a required or usual amount : STINT, OUTPUT ⟨the daily ~ of copy⟩ **5 a :** matter of interest or value forming the basis of a story, analysis, or other presentation or that can be assembled into such a basis ⟨consular records and trade-association reports form much of the ~ of the foreign market analyst⟩ ⟨local news ~ collected in police courts and schools⟩ **b :** something turned to one's own advantage esp. contrary to

ordinary expectation by one receiving or having to do with it — used esp. in the phrase *grist to one's mill*

²grist \"\ *vt* -ED/-ING/-S **:** to grind (grain) esp. as a custom operation

³grist \"\ *n* -S [origin unknown] **1 :** the count of a textile fiber or yarn **2** *chiefly Scot* **:** a size of rope ⟨a rope of common ~ is 3 inches in circumference with 20 yarns in each of the 3 strands⟩

grist·bite \'grizbət\ *vi* [ME *grisbiten,* fr. OE *gristbitian,* fr. *grist-bite* act of gnashing, fr. *grist* act of grinding + *bite* biting, fr. *bītan* to bite — more at GRIST, BITE] *dial chiefly Brit* **:** to grind or gnash the teeth

gris·thor·pia \gris'thȯ(r)pēə\ *n, cap* [NL, fr. *Gristhorpe,* Yorkshire, England + NL *-ia*] **:** a genus of fossil plants of the Jurassic formations of England that are usu. considered to be angiosperms and have pyriform carpels or carpellary fruits enclosing ovule or seed

gris·tle \'gris|əl *sometimes* -iz|\ *n* -S [ME *gristil,* fr. OE *gristle;* akin to OE *grost* gristle, OFris & MLG *gristel,* and prob. to OE *grindan* to grind — more at GRIND] **1 :** CARTILAGE; *broadly* **:** tough cartilaginous, tendinous, or fibrous matter esp. in table meats **2** *obs* **:** a young or delicate person visualized as having the bones soft and cartilaginous and not yet hardened into bone **3 :** strength of character **:** BACKBONE ⟨a hard-working man with some ~ —Erskine Caldwell⟩

gris·tli·ness \|(ə)lēnəs, -lin-\ *n* -ES **:** the quality or state of being gristly

gris·tly \|(ə)lē, -li\ *adj* -ER/-EST [ME *gristly,* fr. *gristil* gristle + *-y*] **:** consisting of or containing gristle ⟨tough ~ steak⟩

gristmill \'ˌ=,=\ *n* **:** a mill for grinding grain; *esp* **:** a custom mill that grinds for different customers — **gristmiller** \'ˌ=,==\ *n* — **gristmilling** \'ˌ=,==\ *n*

grisy *adj* [ME *gris* gray (fr. MF) + E *-y* — more at GRIS] *obs* **:** GRIZZLED

¹grit \'grit, *usu* -id·+V\ *n* -S [ME *gryt* bran, chaff, fr. OE *grytt;* akin to OHG *gruzzi* bran, OE *grēot* sand, grit — more at ²GRIT] **1** *obs* **:** milling offals **:** the coarse parts of meal **:** CHAFF **2 grits** *pl but sing or pl in constr* **a :** coarsely ground hulled grain (as maize, wheat, or rice) ⟨had boiled ~s fried with side meat for supper⟩ — compare HOMINY **b :** coarsely ground soybean oil cake used as a protein-rich supplement in animal rations and some commercial food products

²grit \"\ *n* -S *see sense 4b* [alter. (influenced by ¹*grit*) of ME *grete, greet,* fr. OE *grēot;* akin to OHG *grioz* gravel, sand, ON *grjōt* gravel, stone, L *furfur* bran, Gk *kenchros* millet, grain, Gk *chrōs* skin, Latvian *graûds* grain, Lith *graužas* gravel; basic meaning: rubbing] **1 a** *obs* **:** SAND, GRAVEL **b :** a hard sharp granule (as of sand); *also* **:** material (as many abrasives) composed of such granules **2 a :** a sandstone with grains of very unequal sizes **b :** a hard coarse-grained siliceous sandstone ⟨millstone ~⟩ — called also *gritrock* **c :** a finer sharp-grained sandstone ⟨grindstone ~⟩ **3** *now dial* **:** EARTH, SOIL **4 a :** the structure of a stone that adapts it to grind or sharpen ⟨quarried stones of excellent ~⟩ **:** hold of a grinding substance ⟨a hone of good ~⟩ **b** *pl* **grit :** the size of abrasive particles usu. expressed as their mesh ⟨diamond dust of 80 ~⟩ **5 :** firmness of mind or spirit **:** unyielding courage **6** *usu cap* **:** a Liberal in Canadian politics **syn** see FORTITUDE

³grit \"\ *vb* **gritted; gritted; gritting; grits** *vi* **:** to give forth a grating sound ⟨the dry snow *gritting* beneath our feet⟩ ~ *vt* **1 :** to cover or spread with grit; *esp* **:** to smooth (as marble) by means of a coarse abrasive preparatory to polishing **2 :** to cause (as one's teeth) to grind or grate ⟨*gritted* his gears when shifting into high⟩ **3 :** to utter harshly through or as if through gritted teeth

grit cell *n* **:** a stone cell esp. in leaves or fleshy fruits (as pears and quinces)

grith \'grith\ *n* -S [ME, fr. OE, fr. ON] **1 a** *obs* **:** assured security or protection (as by safe conduct) **b :** peace or security imposed or guaranteed in Anglo-Saxon and early medieval England by conditions arising out of associations of time and place: as (1) **:** the sanctuary or asylum afforded by the precincts of a church (2) **:** KING'S PEACE **2** *archaic* **:** a place of security **:** REFUGE, ASYLUM, SANCTUARY **3** *obs* **:** quarter in battle

grith·man \-mən\ *n, pl* **grithmen** [ME, fr. *grith* + *man*] *archaic* **:** a man who has taken sanctuary (as church grith)

grit·less \'gritləs\ *adj* **:** free from grit; *esp* **:** lacking firmness and stability of character

gritrock \'ˌ=,=\ *or* **gritstone** \'ˌ=,=\ *n* **:** GRIT 2b

grit·ti·ly \'grid·|ᵊl|ē, -it|, |əl|, |i\ *adv* **:** in a gritty manner ⟨our feet sounded ~ on the shale⟩ ⟨behaved very ~ for a youngster⟩

grit·ti·ness \'grid·|ēnəs, -it|, |in-\ *n* -ES **:** the quality or state of being gritty

grit·tle \'gritᵊl\ *vt* -ED/-ING/-S [¹*grit* + *-le*] *dial Brit* **:** to grind (grain) coarsely

grit·ty \'grid·|ē, -it|, |i\ *adj* -ER/-EST **1 a :** containing or resembling sand or grit **:** consisting of grit ⟨~ slopes⟩ **b :** suggestive of the presence of grit ⟨~ footsteps on the walk⟩ **2 :** courageously persistent **:** having grit **:** RESOLUTE, PLUCKY

gri·va·tion \grə'vāshən, grī'v-\ *n* -S [*grid variation*] **:** the angle between north as indicated by a grid on a map and magnetic north at any point — used esp. in aerial navigation

griv·et \'grivət, grə'vā\ *n* -S [F] **:** a monkey (*Cercopithecus aethiops*) of the upper Nile and Abyssinia having the back dull olive green and the lower parts white

gri·vois \grēvwä\ *adj* [F, fr. *grivois,* n., alert soldier, fr. *grive* thrush, war (in soldier slang)] **:** free and easy in tone **:** BROAD, INDECENT

gri·voi·se·rie \grēvwäzrē\ *n, pl* **grivoiseries** \-rē(z)\ [F, fr. *grivois* + *-erie* -ery] **:** bold licentious behavior **:** IMPROPRIETY; *often* **:** an act of impropriety

¹griz·zle \'grizəl\ *adj* [ME *grisel,* fr. MF, fr. OF, fr. *gris* gray, of Gmc origin; akin to OFris, OS, & OHG *gris* gray, ON *grīss* pig, and perh. to OE *grǣg* gray — more at GRAY] **:** GRAY, ROAN

²grizzle \"\ *n* -S **1** *archaic* **a :** gray hair **b :** a gray wig **2 a** (1) **:** GRAY 3a (2) **:** a roan coat pattern or color **b :** a gray or roan animal **3 :** a second-rate brick that is underburned, gray in color, and deficient in strength

³grizzle \"\ *vb* **grizzled; grizzled; grizzling** \-z(ə)liŋ\ **grizzles** *vt* **:** to make grayish ~ *vi* **:** to become grayish

⁴grizzle \"\ *vi* -ED/-ING/-S [origin unknown] **1** *Brit* **:** to complain vociferously ⟨always *grizzling* about the work being too much for him —Vance Palmer⟩ **:** GRIPE, GRUMBLE **2** *Brit* **:** FRET, WHIMPER ⟨children ~ a lot, get finicky over their food, and look pale and thin —*Auckland (New Zealand) Weekly News*⟩ **3** *Brit* **:** MOURN, LAMENT, GRIEVE ⟨*grizzling* over a corpse —Margery Allingham⟩

⁵grizzle \"\ *n* -S *Brit* **:** an irritable or lugubrious mood

griz·zled \-zəld\ *adj* [ME *griseled,* fr. MF *grisel* + ME *-ed*] **:** sprinkled, streaked, or mixed with gray ⟨~ hair hanging about her face⟩ ⟨~ chickens huddled in the rain⟩

griz·zler \-z(ə)lə(r)\ *n* -S [⁴*grizzle* + *-er*] *Brit* **:** a peevish person **:** a chronic griper

¹griz·zly *or* **gris·ly** \'grizlē, -li\ *adj* -ER/-EST [¹*grizzle* + *-ly*] **:** somewhat gray **:** GRIZZLED

²grizzly *or* **grisly** \"\ *n* -ES **1 :** GRIZZLY BEAR **2 a :** a coarse screening device used for ore, coal, gravel, or soil; *specif* **:** a heavy steel-bar screen for ore having moving chains **b :** a similar coarse grating (as for catching trash or large stones at a water inlet)

³grizzly *var of* GRISLY

grizzly bear *n* [¹*grizzly*] **1 :** a very large powerful typically brownish yellow bear (*Ursus horribilis*) of the uplands of western No. America that is closely related to the brown bear of Europe but much larger and heavier and that is very dangerous when brought to bay esp. because of its great strength and fierceness — compare SILVERTIP **2 :** a ragtime dance popular about the period of World War I

grizzly-bear cactus *also* **grizzly bear** *n* **:** a prickly pear (*Opuntia erinacea*) of the southwestern U.S. with very long flexible ashy gray spines

griz·zly·man \-mən\ *n, pl* **grizzlymen** [²*grizzly* + *man*] **:** a worker that screens ore in a grizzly

grm *abbr* **1** germination **2** gram

grn *abbr* green

gro *abbr* **1** gross **2** group

¹groan \'grōn\ *vb* -ED/-ING/-S [ME *gronen,* fr. OE *grānian;* akin to OHG *grīnan* to distort the mouth, mutter, grumble, growl, ON *grīna* to bare the teeth, sneer] *vi* **1 a :** to make a deep usu. inarticulate and involuntary often strangled sound typically abruptly begun and ended and usu. indicative of pain or grief or tension or desire or sometimes disapproval or annoyance ⟨the dying man *~ed* with every jolt of the ambulance⟩ ⟨men *~ing* under the weight of the loads they were carrying⟩ ⟨*~ed* with rage and frustration⟩ **b :** to make a harsh sound (as of heavy creaking, grating, rasping) upon subjection to sudden or prolonged strain (as of a heavy load) ⟨let himself fall into an armchair which *~ed* under him —H. M.Ledig-Rowohlt⟩ ⟨wagons that swayed and *~ed* up the hill⟩ **2 a :** to experience pain or grief enough to make one groan ⟨*~ed* when he read the telegram⟩ **b :** to undergo strain or oppression or overburdening enough to make one groan ⟨men who were once free now ~ in slavery⟩ ⟨tables which *~ed* under the weight of good things —Norman Douglas⟩ **c :** to desire something intensely enough to make one groan ⟨*~ing* to be with her again⟩ ⟨death *~ing* for fresh victims⟩ **d :** to disapprove of something or become annoyed with something enough to make one groan ⟨*~ing* over their stupidity⟩ ⟨one *~s* at the absence of an index —Sean O'Faolain⟩ ~ *vt* **1 :** to utter or express with groaning **:** breathe out with groaning ⟨will ~ out some prayer —William Barrett⟩ ⟨*~ing* their despair⟩ **2 :** to express disapproval of or annoyance with by groaning ⟨*~ing* them through the streets —Broadus Mitchell⟩ ⟨the consuls were *~ed* down —J.A.Froude⟩

²groan \"\ *n* -S [ME *gron, grone,* fr. *gronen,* v.] **1 :** a deep usu. inarticulate and involuntary often strangled sound typically abruptly begun and ended and usu. indicative of pain or grief or tension or desire or sometimes disapproval or annoyance **2 :** a harsh sound (as of heavy creaking, grating, rasping) produced by subjection to a sudden or prolonged strain (as of a heavy load)

groan·ful \-fəl\ *adj, archaic* **:** marked by groaning; *specif* **:** dismal and sad

groaning *n* -S [fr. gerund of ¹*groan*] *now chiefly dial* **:** LYING-IN; *specif* **:** LABOR 1b

groan·ing·ly *adv* **:** in a groaning manner

¹groat \'grōt, *usu* -ōd·+V\ *n* -S [ME *grotes,* pl., fr. OE *grotan;* akin to OE *grot* particle, *grēot* sand, grit — more at GRIT] **1** *usu* **groats** *pl but sing or pl in constr* **:** hulled grain broken into fragments larger than grits **2 a :** the part of a grain of oats or barley or buckwheat exclusive of the hull **b :** the hulled kernel of one of these grains

²groat \"\ *n* -S [ME *grote, groot,* fr. MD *groot, grot,* modif. (by false analogy of such pairs as MD *groot* large: MHG *grōz* large) of MHG *gros,* fr. ML (*denarius*) *grossus* — more at GROSCHEN] **1 :** one of several onetime European coins of varying chiefly small value; *esp* **:** a British coin worth fourpence **2 :** the bit of British Guiana

gro·bi·an \'grōbēən\ *n* -S [G, after *Grobian,* a fictional patron saint of vulgar people, fr. ML (*Sanctus*) *Grobianus,* fr. MHG *grob-, grop* coarse, vulgar (fr. OHG *gerob, grob* thick, coarse) + L *-ianus* -ian — more at GRUFF] **:** a slovenly crude often buffoonish individual **:** BOOR, LOUT

gro·bi·an·ism \-ə,nizəm\ *n* -S **:** behavior typical of a grobian **:** BOORISHNESS

gro·cer \'grōsə(r)\ *n* -S [ME *grocer, grosser* wholesale merchant, grocer, fr. MF *grossier* wholesale merchant, fr. *gros* thick, coarse, wholesale + *-ier* -er — more at GROSS] **:** a dealer in staple foodstuffs (as coffee, sugar, flour) and usu. meats and other foods (as fruits, vegetables, dairy products) and many household supplies (as soap, matches, paper napkins)

grocer's itch *n* **:** an itching dermatitis prob. allergic in nature that results from prolonged or repeated contacts with certain mites esp. of the family Acaridae, their products, or materials (as feeds, flour, or copra) infested by them — compare GRAIN ITCH

gro·cery \'grōs(ə)rē, -ri\ *n* -ES [ME *grocerie,* fr. *grocer* + *-ie* -y] **1 groceries** *pl* **a :** articles of food and other goods sold by a grocer ⟨went out to buy some *groceries*⟩ ⟨a bag of *groceries*⟩ — usu. sing. in Brit. usage ⟨had been sent with a parcel of ~ to the cottage —Sabine Baring-Gould⟩ **b** *dial* **:** intoxicating drink **:** LIQUOR **2** *or* **grocery store a :** the place of business of a retail grocer **:** a grocer's store **b** *dial* **:** BARROOM

gro·cery·man \-mən, -,man, -,maa(ə)n\ *n, pl* **grocerymen** **:** GROCER

gro·ce·te·ria \,grōsə'tirēə\ *n* -S [*grocery* + *-teria*] **:** a self-service grocery store

groe·nen·dael \'grünən,däl, -rōn-,-rän-,-ren-\ *n* -S *usu cap* [fr. *Groenendael,* village in Belgium where it was developed] **:** a black-coated Belgian sheepdog with a heavily plumed tail — compare MALINOIS

groff \'gräf\ *Scot var of* GRUFF

¹grog \'gräg *also* 'grȯg\ *n* -S [fr. *Old Grog,* nickname of Edward Vernon †1757 Eng. admiral who ordered the sailors' rum to be diluted; *Grog* short for *grogram;* fr. his habit of wearing a grogram cloak in bad weather] **1 :** spirituous liquor; *specif* **:** liquor (as rum) cut with water and now often served hot with lemon juice and sugar sometimes added **2 :** fired refractory material (as crushed pottery, firebricks) used in the manufacture of products (as crucibles) designed to resist extreme heat

²grog \"\ *vb* **grogged; grogged; grogging; grogs** *vi* **:** to drink grog ⟨had been *grogging* with the steward —Lyndall Hadow⟩ ~ *vt* **:** to soak (a liquor cask) with hot water so as to draw out the spirits from the wood

grog blossom *n* **:** RHINOPHYMA

grogger *var of* GRAGER

grog·gery \|g(ə)rē\ *n* -ES [¹*grog* + *-ery*] **1 :** a usu. low-class barroom **2 :** a liquor store **:** PACKAGE STORE

grog·gi·ly \|gəlē, -li\ *adv* **:** in a groggy manner **:** DAZEDLY ⟨~ opened his eyes⟩ **:** UNSTEADILY ⟨groped his way ~ across the room⟩

grog·gi·ness \|gēnəs, |gin-\ *n* -ES **:** the quality or state of being groggy

grog·gy \|gē, |gi\ *adj, usu* -ER/-EST [¹*grog* + *-y*] **1** *archaic* **:** INTOXICATED, DRUNK **2 a** *of a horse* **:** weakened (as from age, overwork, or disease) in the fetlock joints and entire forelegs so as to have a hobbling gait marked by the knuckling over of the fetlock joints **b** *of a boxer* **:** weakened from fighting and esp. from blows on the head so as to be unsteady on the feet or to stagger and to have an impaired consciousness **3 :** weak, sleepy, exhausted, ill, or otherwise physically affected in such a way as to be sluggish in one's reactions, torpid mentally, and usu. unsteady on the feet **:** LOGY, FOGGY, DAZED, MUDDLED **4 :** tending to wear away ⟨pumice and other soft ~ materials⟩ or crumble ⟨a ~ tooth⟩ or collapse ⟨a ~ old wooden tower⟩

gro·gnard \(,)grō;nyär\ *n* -S [F, fr. *grogner* to grunt, grumble (fr. OF *gronir, grogner,* fr. L *grunnire* to grunt) + *-ard*] **1 :** an old soldier **2** *often cap* **:** a soldier of the original imperial guard that was created by Napoleon I in 1804 and that made the final French charge at Waterloo

grog·ram \'grägrəm, -rōg-\ *n* -S [modif. of MF *gros grain* large grain, coarse texture] **1 :** a coarse loosely woven fabric of silk or of silk and mohair or orig. of silk and wool and often stiffened with gum **2 :** a garment (as a coat) made of grogram

grogshop \'ˌ=,=\ *n, chiefly Brit* **:** a usu. low-class barroom **:** GROGGERY

¹groin \'grȯin\ *n* -S [ME, fr. MF, fr. LL *grunium,* fr. L *grunnire* to grunt — more at GRUNT] *dial Brit* **:** the nose and sometimes the upper lip of an animal (as a swine)

²groin \"\ *n* -S [alter. (influenced by ¹*groin*) of ME *grynde,* fr. OE, abyss; akin to OE *grund* ground — more at GROUND] **1 :** the fold or depression marking the line between the lower part of the abdomen and the thigh; *also* **:** the region of this line — called also *inguen* **2 a** (1) **:** the projecting edge forming the curved line along which two intersecting vaults meet (2) **:** a rib (as of wood, stone) designed to cover this edge **b** (1) **:** the curved surface of a vault — not often in technical use (2) **:** the spandrel of a vault — not often in technical use **3** *also* **groyne** \"\ **:** a rigid structure built out at an angle from a shore to protect the shore from erosion by currents, tides, and waves or to trap sand (as for making a beach)

groins 2a(1)

³groin \"\ *vt* -ED/-ING/-S **:** to build or equip with groins ⟨a high corridor with a *~ed* ceiling⟩ ⟨*~ed* vaults⟩

groining *n* -S [fr. gerund of ³*groin*] **:** a set or series of groins **:** groined work ⟨lofty halls with beautiful ~⟩

gromet *var of* GRUMMET

gro·mia \'grōmēə\ *n, cap* [NL] **:** a genus (the type of the family Gromiidae) of testacean rhizopods widely distributed in fresh and salt water and in soil

¹grom·met \'grämət, 'grəm-, *usu* -əd·+V\ *also* **grum·met** \'grəm-\ *n* -S [perh. fr. obs. F *gormette* curb of a bridle] **1 :** a ring or loop of metal, rope, fabric, or other material that is passed through something (as the eyelet of a sail) to hold it in place or that fits around something (as an oar) to support or control it or that is built into something (as a machine belt) to reinforce it **2 a :** an eyelet of metal, plastic, or other material set into a perforation (as at the edge of a mailbag) so as to strengthen and protect the inner circumference of the perforation and the immediately surrounding area **b :** a device like a ring that is designed to protect or insulate something passed through it: as (1) **:** a bushing designed to protect from abrasion a cord or wire passing through a hole (2) **:** a washer designed to insulate an electric wire passing through a hole **3 :** a gasket or packing used to prevent leakage (as of steam) or entry (as of dust)

²grommet \"\ *vt* -ED/-ING/-S **1 :** to equip with grommets ⟨mailbags that have been properly *~ed*⟩ **2 :** to fasten, support, or reinforce with grommets ⟨the sail is *~ed* to its stay⟩

grommet nut *n* **:** a screw-thread nut with a blind hole and rounded head as used in connection with a machine screw for fastening a hinge to a door leaf

grom·well \'gräm,wel, -,wəl\ *n* -S [alter. of ME *gromil,* fr. MF *gromil, gremil,* fr. OF, fr. *gres* sandstone + *mil* millet — more at GRÈS, MILLET] **:** a plant of the genus *Lithospermum* (esp. *L. officinale*)

gro·ning·en \'grōniŋən\ *adj, usu cap* [fr. *Groningen,* Netherlands] **:** of or from the city of Groningen, Netherlands **:** of the kind or style prevalent in Groningen

¹groom \'grüm, -ü-\ *n* -S [ME *grom, grome;* perh. akin to OE *grōwan* to grow — more at GROW] **1 a** *obs* **:** a young male **:** BOY **b** *archaic* **:** an adult male **:** MAN, FELLOW **2 a** (1) *archaic* **:** a male attendant **:** MANSERVANT (2) **:** one of several officers of the English royal household — used with a specifying phrase ⟨served as ~ of the chamber⟩ **b :** a man or boy in charge of the feeding, conditioning, and stabling of horses **3** [by shortening] **:** BRIDEGROOM

²groom \"\ *vb* -ED/-ING/-S *vt* **:** to make presentable, acceptable, or attractive: as **a :** to attend to the cleaning of (as an animal); *esp* **:** to maintain the health and condition of the coat of (as a horse) by brushing, combing, currying, or similar attention ⟨*~ed* the horses until their coats shone sleekly⟩ **b :** to bring about or increase the acceptability or attractiveness of (as one's physical appearance) esp. by carefully attending to details of cleanliness and neatness **:** freshen up **:** spruce up ⟨spent a long time *~ing* himself before he ventured out⟩ make neat **:** make tidy ⟨a carefully *~ed* lawn⟩ **c :** to remove crudity or other objectionable features from **:** make smooth or elegant **:** POLISH, REFINE ⟨was master of the epigram which Wilde was later to ~ for the drawing room —Maurice Edelman⟩ **d :** to get into readiness for some specific objective **:** READY, PREPARE ⟨was being *~ed* as a presidential candidate⟩ ⟨*~ing* players for the Olympics⟩ ~ *vi* **:** to groom oneself ⟨is said to be *~ing* for the top position⟩ ⟨*~ing* for dinner⟩

³groom \"\ *n* -S [origin unknown] *dial Eng* **:** a forked stick used by thatchers

groom's cake *n* **:** a light fruitcake served at a wedding

grooms·man \-zmən\ *n, pl* **groomsmen** **:** a male friend who attends a bridegroom at his wedding

groop \'grüp, -ü-\ *n* -S [ME *grope, groupe,* fr. MD *grope, groepe* — more at GRIP] *dial Eng* **:** DITCH, DRAIN

¹groove \'grüv\ *n* -S [ME *grofe, groof;* akin to OHG *gruoba* pit, cave, ON *grōf,* Goth *groba* pit, cave, OE *grafan* to dig — more at GRAVE] **1** *dial Eng* **:** a mining shaft **:** MINE **2 a :** a long narrow hollow or channel made artificially in a surface: as (1) **:** the rectangular rabbet in the edge of a board designed to receive the tongue of another board in matching (2) **:** one of the spiral cuts of rifling (3) **:** the indentation on the bottom of a piece of printing type between the feet — compare NICK (4) **:** one of the cuts made across the back of an unbound hand-sewn book designed to receive the cords that secure the covers of the book — called also *kerf* (5) **:** the track on a phonograph record along which the stylus travels **b :** a long narrow depression occurring naturally on the surface of an organism or an anatomical part **c :** a long narrow furrow produced along a surface by a continuing erosive or otherwise wearing force (as of flowing water) **3 a** (1) **:** a fixed routine **:** settled course ⟨had hoped that the daily life on the farm would slip back into orderly *~s* —Ellen Glasgow⟩ **:** HABIT, CUSTOM, PRACTICE ⟨will get you into the writing ~ —Cy Lance⟩ (2) **:** an undeviating tiresomely predictable and often mechanical way of living or acting or thinking **:** RUT ⟨walled in by authority which saw to it that he moved in a prescribed ~ —W.P.Webb⟩ ⟨far too many of us feel safer in *~s* —F.A.Swinnerton⟩ ⟨fail to realize how often their thoughts revolve in ancient *~s* and circles —Thomas Munro⟩ **b :** a situation (as a profession, a way of living or acting) best suited to one's abilities or interests **:** NICHE ⟨found his ~ in advertising —*Newsweek*⟩ **4 :** an imaginary line from the pitcher to the catcher representing the course of a pitched ball in the game of baseball; *esp* **:** such a line passing over the center of the plate about waist high — usu. used with *the* ⟨hurled the ball right down the ~⟩ **5 a :** top form ⟨after a couple of measures the jazz trio really got into the ~⟩ ⟨a hot bath and a drink will put you back in the ~⟩ ⟨it made no difference, when he was in the ~, what he chose to talk about —Henry Miller⟩ **b :** currently favored style — usu. used in the phrase *in the groove* ⟨a new song that's right in the ~⟩

grooves 2a(1): *1* rectangular; *2* vee; *3* semicircular; *4* dovetail

²groove \"\ *vb* -ED/-ING/-S *vt* **1 a** (1) **:** to make a groove in **:** provide with a groove ⟨a set of scenery that is *grooved* and quickly movable⟩ (2) **:** to make a disc recording of ⟨*grooving* a popular song as soon as it is written⟩ **b** (1) **:** to join by a groove ⟨wide boards that had been *grooved* together⟩ (2) **:** to cause to be fixed into a groove **:** cause to be ingrained ⟨a deeply *grooved* habit of honesty⟩ **c :** to hollow out in the form of a groove **:** FURROW ⟨the experience that has been *grooved* into a person⟩ ⟨the years had *grooved* her mind that way —Bob Hope⟩ **2 :** to execute (as the delivery of a ball, the swing of a golf club) with maximum control and effect ⟨*grooved* the ball down the bowling alley⟩ ⟨developing a *grooved* swing⟩; *esp* **:** to pitch down the center of the groove ⟨*grooved* a fast ball past the batter⟩ ~ *vi* **1 :** to become settled into a groove **:** move in a groove ⟨*grooving* along in the routine of the job⟩ **2 :** to become joined or fitted by a groove ⟨elements of this rather intricate artistic pattern seem to ~ into each other —Scott Fitzgerald⟩ **3 :** to form a groove ⟨eyes with faint white wrinkles at the corners that *grooved* merrily when he smiled —Ernest Hemingway⟩

³groove \"\ *adj* **:** produced through a narrow deep opening formed at the free end of the tongue ⟨a ~ fricative such as \s\⟩ — compare SLIT

groove-billed ani \'ˌ=,=-\ *n* **:** a rather small ani (*Crotophaga sulcirostris*) having the upper mandible marked by several curved grooves and ridges

grooved ax *n* **:** a prehistoric stone ax typical of the woodland pattern in No. America with a groove in which the handle fits

groove diameter *n* **:** the width of the bore of a rifled arm that is measured between diametrically opposite grooves

grooved shrimp *n* **:** a shrimp with lateral grooves along the carapace; *esp* **:** BRAZILIAN SHRIMP

groove·less \-vləs\ *adj* **:** having no grooves

groov·er \-və(r)\ *n* -S [in sense 1, fr. ¹*groove* + *-er;* in other senses, fr. ²*groove* + *-er*] **1** *dial Eng* **:** MINER **2 a :** a device that makes grooves (as by cutting, punching) **b :** a worker

who makes grooves (as the operator of a machine that cuts tongues and grooves in box boards)
groov·i·ness \-vēnəs, -vin-\ *n* -ES **:** the quality or state of being groovy ⟨in the graduate . . . ~ is a grave defect, but it is also a common one —Walter Moberly⟩
grooving *n* -s **1 a :** a set of grooves **:** GROOVE **b :** the formation of grooves **2 :** a design made up of grooves
grooving saw *n* **:** a coarse-toothed circular saw used for cutting grooves in timber
groovy \-vē,-vi\ *adj, usu* -ER/-EST **1 :** settled into a fixed often tiresomely undeviating way of living or acting or thinking ⟨so-called leaders who have become ~ dolts⟩ **2 :** that is in the groove ⟨~ jazz⟩ ⟨a ~ recording⟩ — often a generalized expression of approval ⟨bought a ~ new convertible⟩
¹grope \'grōp\ *vb* -ED/-ING/-S [ME *gropen*, fr. OE *grāpian;* akin to OE *grīpan* to seize, attack — more at GRIPE] *vi* **1 a :** to feel about (as with the hands) blindly or uncertainly or hesitantly in an attempt to find something or touch something ⟨*groping* around in the shadowy room for a switch to turn on the light⟩ ⟨*groping* for her arm⟩ **:** reach out blindly ⟨tottered at the edge of the cliff, *groping* at the air⟩ **b :** to look for something blindly or uncertainly or hesitantly **:** search about blindly ⟨*groping* for the simplest ground rules of conduct —Gilbert Seldes⟩ ⟨*groped* confusedly for words —E.A. McCourt⟩ ⟨it was as though she *groped* after something which was vanishing —Victoria Sackville-West⟩ **2 :** to move or act blindly or uncertainly or hesitantly **:** feel one's way ⟨*groping* along through the darkness until they arrived at the door⟩ ⟨when her mind is *groping* about in this new attitude it will be easy for me to influence her —Liam O'Flaherty⟩ ⟨*groping* toward a solution to the problem⟩ **~** *vt* **1 a** (1) *obs* **:** TOUCH, HANDLE; *specif* **:** GRASP (2) **:** to pass the hands over (the person of another) for the sake of sexual pleasure **b** *now dial Brit* **:** to subject (as a criminal) to a manual search **2 :** to come upon, ascertain, or find (as one's way) by feeling about blindly or uncertainly or hesitantly **:** search out blindly ⟨the effort which it has cost our predecessors to ~ their way through the mists of ignorance and superstition —J.G.Frazer⟩ ⟨*groped* his way from the balcony to the bedroom door —Geoffrey Household⟩
²grope \"\ *n* -s **:** the action of groping
¹grop·er \-pə(r)\ *n* -s [¹*grope* + -*er*] **:** one that gropes
²gro·per \"\ *n* -s [modif. of Pg *garoupa* — more at GROUPER] **1 :** one of several groupers: as **a :** a very large voracious and dangerous fish (*Promicrops lanceolatus*) of tropical Indo-Pacific waters **b :** a food fish (*Polyprion oxygeneios*) of southern seas **2 :** a large Australian and Tasmanian labrid food fish (*Achoerodus gouldii*) having two well-marked color phases of purplish blue and red
groping *adj* [ME, fr. pres. part. of *gropen* to grope — more at GROPE] **:** blindly searching ⟨gazing up at her with a strange, ~ expression —Ellen Glasgow⟩ **:** moving or acting uncertainly **:** HESITANT ⟨a ~ uncertainty concerning the future forms of American life —Oscar Handlin⟩ — **grop·ing·ly** *adv*
gros \'grō\ *n, pl* **gros** \-ōz\ [F, fr. *gros*, adj., heavy, thick, coarse — more at GROSS] **:** a heavy durable fabric; *esp* **:** a cross-ribbed fabric of silk
gros·beak *also* **gross·beak** \'grōs,bēk\ *n* [part. trans. of F *grosbec*, fr. *gros* thick, coarse + *bec* beak] **:** one of several finches of Europe or America having large stout conical bills: as **a :** HAWFINCH **b :** EVENING GROSBEAK
gro·schen \'grōshən *also* -rōsh- *or* -räsh-\ *n, pl* **groschen** [G, fr. MHG dial. (Bohemia) *grosch, grosche*, fr. Czech *groš*, fr. ML (*denarius*) *grossus* thick (denarius) — more at GROSS] **1 :** a German coin worth a varying fraction of a taler and issued from the 13th century to the latter part of the 19th century **2 :** an Austrian coin worth $\frac{1}{100}$ schilling — see MONEY table
gros de lon·dres \,grōdə'lōⁿdr(ᵊ), -d(rə)\ *n, usu cap L* [F, lit., London gros] **:** a lightweight silk or rayon dress fabric with alternating wide and narrow crosswise ribs often of two different colors and often with a glossy finish
gro·ser \'grōzə(r)\ *n* -s [modif. of MF *grosele*, of Gmc origin; akin to MD *croeselbesie* gooseberry, G *kräuselbeere*, G dial. (Switzerland) *chrusel*] *dial Eng* **:** GOOSEBERRY
gro·set \'grōzət\ *also* **gros·sart** \-ōzə(r)t\ *n* -s [alter. of *groser*] *Scot* **:** GOOSEBERRY
gros·grain \'grō,grān\ *n* -s [F *gros grain* large grain, coarse texture] **:** a firm fabric in plain weave usu. with a silk or rayon warp and a heavy cotton filling that forms pronounced crosswise ribs
gros mi·chel \,grōmə'shel\ *n, pl* **gros michels** \-l(z)\ *usu cap G&M* [F, lit., big Michael] **:** JAMAICA BANANA
gros point \'grō,pȯint\ *n, pl* **gros points** [F, lit., large point] **1 :** RAISED POINT **2 a :** canvas work made with large tent stitches each of which crosses two vertical and two horizontal threads **b :** a stitch used in making such canvas work — compare PETIT POINT
¹gross \'grōs *sometimes* -ō-\ *adj, usu* -ER/-EST [ME, fr. MF *gros*, thick, coarse, fr. L *grossus;* perh. akin to MIr, W, Corn & Bret *bras* thick, large] **1 a** *archaic* **:** immediately obvious **:** PLAIN, EVIDENT ⟨'tis ~ you love my son —Shak.⟩ **b** (1) **:** glaringly noticeable **:** FLAGRANT ⟨one ~ error after another⟩ (2) **:** OUT-AND-OUT, COMPLETE, UTTER, UNMITIGATED, RANK ⟨a ~ traitor⟩ ⟨a ~ fool⟩ ⟨~ injustice⟩ **c :** visible without the aid of a microscope **:** large enough to be seen with the naked eye **:** MACROSCOPIC, MANIFEST ⟨~ lesions⟩ — compare OCCULT **2 a** (1) *archaic* **:** physically large **:** BIG, BULKY, MASSIVE ⟨the piers being extremely ~ —George Semple⟩ (2) **:** strongly and heavily built **:** STOCKY, BURLY ⟨a ~ giant of a man⟩ (3) **:** excessively fat or dumpy **:** excessively corpulent or lumpish ⟨a great, ~ girl with a fleshy face and small eyes —Margaret Long⟩ **b :** growing or spreading with excessive or abnormal luxuriance ⟨a ~ riot of vegetation⟩ **3 a** (1) **:** of, relating to, or dealing with general aspects or broad distinctions **:** not specific or closely detailed ⟨acquainted him with the ~ outlines of the matter⟩ **:** GENERAL, GENERALIZED, OVERALL ⟨important to understand the ~ behavior of the sexually responding animal —A.C.Kinsey⟩ (2) *archaic* **:** lacking clarity and precision **:** VAGUE, FOGGY **b :** consisting of an overall total exclusive of deductions ⟨~ earnings⟩ ⟨~ production⟩ ⟨~ annual profit⟩ — opposed to *net* **4 a :** made up of many closely compacted particles ⟨~ clouds of dust⟩ or drops ⟨a ~ fog⟩ ⟨~ vapors⟩ **:** DENSE, THICK **b :** made up of elements that are material or perceptible to the senses **:** EARTHY, CARNAL, ANIMAL ⟨both the intellectual and the ~*er* part of human nature⟩ **c** *archaic* **:** made up of or yielding relatively large or coarse parts or particles ⟨tarras or other ~ matter —John Smeaton⟩ **5** *archaic* **a :** undistinguished or poor in quality **:** COMMON, CHEAP, INFERIOR ⟨fish and oil and such ~ commodities —Daniel Defoe⟩ **b :** not fastidious in taste **:** UNDISCRIMINATING ⟨their diet is extremely ~ —E.W.Lane⟩ **c :** lacking delicacy of perception **:** slow to respond **:** DULL, STUPID, OAFISH **6 :** lacking knowledge or culture **:** IGNORANT, UNREFINED, RUDE, CLODDISH, PRIMITIVE, BARBARIC ⟨the ~ herd of the people⟩ **7 a :** coarse in nature, manner, or expression ⟨~ interests⟩ ⟨~ pleasures⟩ ⟨a ~ way of behaving⟩ **b :** lacking civility or decency **:** LOW, VULGAR, CRUDE, OFFENSIVE, OBSCENE ⟨a revoltingly ~ expletive⟩ ⟨habitually used ~ language⟩ **syn** see COARSE, FLAGRANT, WHOLE
²gross \"\ *n* -ES [ME, fr. *gross*, adj.] **1 a** *obs* **:** AMOUNT ⟨I cannot instantly raise up the ~ of full three thousand ducats —Shak.⟩ **b :** an overall total exclusive of deductions (as taxes, expenses) **:** sum total ⟨the company's ~ doubled in five years⟩ **2** *archaic* **:** main body **:** principal part **:** BULK, MASS ⟨the ~ of the army —Thomas Carlyle⟩ — **by the gross** *adv* **:** in large quantities and usu. at lower than retail prices **:** WHOLESALE ⟨bought bottle openers *by the gross*⟩ — **in gross 1** *obs* **:** in a general way **:** without going into details ⟨the unlettered Christian who believes *in gross* —John Dryden⟩ **2** *archaic* **:** by the gross **3** *of a right* **:** independently existing, belonging to a person, and not attached to land ⟨an advowson *in gross*⟩ — **in the gross** *archaic* **:** in totality **:** in entirety **:** as an undivided whole ⟨not to accept the past *in the gross* —R.C. Trench⟩
³gross \"\ *vt* -ED/-ING/-ES [¹*gross*] **:** to make, earn, or bring in (an overall total) exclusive of deductions (as taxes, expenses) ⟨a musical comedy that ~*ed* a million dollars⟩
⁴gross \"\ *n, pl* **gross** [ME *groos, groce*, fr. MF *grosse*, fr. fem. of *gros* thick, coarse — more at ¹GROSS] **:** an aggregate of 12 dozen things **:** an aggregate of 144 things; *specif* **:** a lot made up of 12 dozen usu. relatively small and substantially identical commercial objects ⟨ordered a ~ of pencils⟩ ⟨3 *gross* of can openers⟩
gross adventure *n* **:** the loan of money upon bottomry
gross anatomy *n* **:** a branch of anatomy that deals with the macroscopic structure of tissues and organs — compare HISTOLOGY
gross area *n* **:** the total area across a masonry unit including the hollow spaces
gross average *n* **:** GENERAL AVERAGE
grossbeak *var of* GROSBEAK
gross·en \'grōsᵊn *sometimes* -rōs-\ *vt* **grossened; grossened; grossening** \-s(ᵊ)niŋ\ **grossens** [¹*gross* + -*en*] **:** to make gross ⟨~*ed* faces . . . and thickened waists —J.G.Cozzens⟩
gross·er \-sə(r)\ *n* -s [³*gross* + -*er*] **1 :** PANMAN 3 **2 :** a product or production yielding a large volume of business ⟨top box-office ~⟩
gross·flö·te \'grōs,flœtə\ *n, pl* **grossflö·ten** \-tᵊn\ *often cap* [G, fr. *gross* large + *flöte* flute] **:** a labial pipe-organ stop of 8-foot pitch and powerful flute quality
gross income *n* **1 :** the total of all revenue or receipts usu. for a given period except receipts or returns of capital **2 :** all income derived from any source except for items specif. excluded by law and deductions of certain outlays (as cost of goods sold or expenses in connection with rental income)
gross·ly *adv* **:** in a gross manner
gross national product *n* **:** the total value of the goods and services produced in a nation during a specific period (as a year) and also comprising the total of expenditures by consumers and government plus gross private investment
gross negligence *n* **:** negligence marked by total or nearly total disregard for the rights of others and by total or nearly total indifference to the consequences of an act — compare ORDINARY NEGLIGENCE, SLIGHT NEGLIGENCE
gross·ness *n* -ES **:** the quality or state of being gross
gross premium *n* **:** the sum of the net premium in insurance and the load
gross ton *n* **:** TON 1a
gross tonnage *n* **:** TONNAGE 4a
¹gros·su·lar \'gräs(y)ələ(r)\ *n* -s [NL *Grossularia*] **:** GROSSULARITE
²grossular \"\ *adj* [NL *Grossularia*] **:** of, relating to, or resembling a gooseberry
gros·su·lar·ia \,==la(a)rēə\ *n* [NL, irreg. fr. F *groseille* gooseberry (fr. OF *groselle*) + NL -*aria* — more at GROSER] **1** *cap, in some classifications* **:** a genus of shrubs (family Saxifragaceae) now usu. included in the genus *Ribes* and characterized by spines at the nodes and by fruit that does not disarticulate from the stalk **2** -s **:** GROSSULARITE
gros·su·lar·i·a·ce·ae \,==,larē'āsē,ē\ *n pl, cap* [NL, fr. *Grossularia*, type genus + -*aceae*] *in some classifications* **:** a family of shrubs comprising those members of the family Saxifragaceae whose fruit is a berry and being usu. coextensive with the genus *Ribes* — **gros·su·lar·i·a·ceous** \'==,==¦āshəs\ *adj*
gros·su·lar·ite \'gräs(y)ələ,rīt\ *n* -s [G *grossularit*, fr. NL *Grossularia* + G -*it* -ite; fr. the color of some varieties that is reminiscent of the gooseberry] **:** a colorless or green, yellow, brown, or red garnet $Ca_3Al_2(SiO_4)_3$
gros ventre \'grō,väⁿt\ *n, pl* **gros ventre** \"\ *or* **gros ventres** \-ts\ *usu cap G&V* [F, lit., big belly] **1 :** ATSINA **2 :** HIDATSA
grosz \'grōsh\ *n, pl* **gro·szy** \-shē\ [Pol, fr. Czech *groš* — more at GROSCHEN] **:** a Polish monetary unit equal to $\frac{1}{100}$ zloty; *also* **:** a coin representing this unit — see MONEY table
grot \'grät\ *n* -s [MF *grotte*, fr. It *grotta* — more at GROTTO] **:** GROTTO
¹gro·tesque \(')grō¦tesk\ *n* -s [MF & OIt; MF *grotesque*, *crotesque*, fr. OIt *grottesca*, fr. (*pittura*) *grottesca*, lit., cave painting, ancient painting found in the ruins of Rome; *grottesca*, fem. of *grottesco*, adj.] **1 a :** decorative art (as in sculpture, painting, architecture) characterized by fanciful or fantastic representations of human and animal forms often combined with each other and interwoven with representations of foliage, flowers, fruit, wreaths, or other similar figures into a bizarre hybrid composite that is typically aesthetically satisfying but that may use distortion or exaggeration of the natural or the expected to the point of comic absurdity, ridiculous ugliness, or ludicrous caricature **b** (1) **:** a piece of decorative art done in this style (2) **:** one of the figures or designs in such a piece of decorative art (3) **:** something suggestive of or resembling such art or the figures or designs of such art ⟨his life was a ~, a mixture of sober realities and absurd incongruities⟩ **2 :** SANS SERIF
²grotesque \"\ *adj, sometimes* -ER/ -EST [F & It; F, fr. It *grottesco*, lit., of a cave, fr. *grotta* cave + -*esco* -esque — more at GROTTO] **:** of, relating to, having the characteristics of, or suggestive of the style of decorative art called grotesque: as **a :** FANCIFUL, FANTASTIC, BIZARRE ⟨a ~ Halloween costume⟩ **b :** comically incongruous or absurd **:** ridiculously ugly ⟨a wizened and ~ little old man⟩ **c :** having a quality of ludicrous caricature ⟨a ~ display of what was meant to be politeness⟩ **d :** departing markedly from the natural, the expected, or the typical (as by distortion, exaggeration) **:** ATYPICAL, ECCENTRIC ⟨a ~ form of animal life⟩ **syn** see FANTASTIC
gro·tesque·ly *adv* **:** in a grotesque manner
gro·tesque·ness *n* -ES **:** the quality or state of being grotesque
gro·tes·que·rie \grō'teskərē, -ri, (,)grō,teskə'rē\ *also* **gro·tes·que·ry** \='===\ *n, pl* **grotesqueries** [²*grotesque* + F -*erie* -ery or E -*ery*] **1 a** (1) **:** a grotesque figure or design (2) **:** a group of such figures or designs (3) **:** a piece of grotesque decorative art **b :** something suggestive of or resembling grotesque decorative art or the figures or designs of such art **:** something grotesque **2 :** GROTESQUENESS
groth·ite \'grōd,īt, -ō,thīt\ *n* -s [Paul von Groth †1927 Ger. mineralogist + E -*ite*] **:** SPHENE
gro·tian \'grōsh(ē)ən\ *adj, usu cap* [Hugo Grot*ius* †1645 Dutch statesman + E -*an*] **:** of or relating to Grotius or his legal and theological theories ⟨the *Grotian* conception of Christ's death —Williston Walker⟩ — **gro·tian·ism** \-,nizəm\ *n* -s *usu cap*
grott·huss–dra·per law \'grȯt¦,hüs¦'drāpə(r)-, 'grät¦, ¦,hüs¦\ *n, usu cap G&D* [after Theodor von *Grotthuss* †1822 Ger. physicist and John W. *Draper* †1882 Am. chemist] **:** a statement in physical chemistry: radiation produces photochemical action only through absorption of its energy by the substance affected
grot·to \'gräd·(,)ō, -ä(,)tō\ *n, pl* **grottoes** *also* **grottos** [It *grotta, grotto*, fr. L *crypta* vault, cavern — more at CRYPT] **1 a :** a natural covered opening in the earth: (1) **:** a cave typically picturesque and rocky and of limited size (2) **:** a recess in a cave (3) **:** a usu. arched recess or hollow place (as in the side of a hill) making a natural shelter and formed by or resembling the mouth of a cave **b :** an artificial recess or structure typically arched and rocky and made to resemble a natural grotto **2** *or* **grotto blue :** a strong greenish blue that is greener and paler than cobalt blue and greener, lighter, and stronger than average cerulean blue (sense 1a) or indigo carmine
grot·toed \-ōd\ *adj* **:** enclosed in or made into a grotto ⟨a shady ~ spot in the mountains⟩
grot·zen \'grōtsən\ *n* -s [G, lit., core of a fruit] **:** the center back strip of a fur pelt
¹grouch \'grau̇ch\ *n* -ES [prob. alter. of ²*grutch*] **1 a :** a fit of bad temper or irritability ⟨don't go near him, he has a ~ on this morning⟩ **b :** GRUDGE, COMPLAINT ⟨never nursed a ~ five minutes —W.A.White⟩ ⟨his chronic ~ at the press —*Newsweek*⟩ **2 :** an habitually irritable or bad-tempered or complaining person **:** GRUMBLER ⟨the irritable ~, the eternal quarreler — becomes such a nuisance —H.A.Overstreet⟩
²grouch \"\ *vi* -ED/-ING/-ES [prob. alter. of ¹*grutch*] **:** GRUMBLE, COMPLAIN, GROUSE ⟨finds every political and social situation a problem to be solved . . . instead of a cause for ~*ing* —E.K.Lindley⟩
grouch bag *n, slang* **:** PURSE
grouch·i·ly \-chəlē, -li\ *adv* **:** in a grouchy manner
grouch·i·ness \-chēnəs, -chin-\ *n* -ES **:** bad temper **:** SULKINESS, IRRITABILITY
grouchy \-chē,-chi\ *adj* -ER/-EST **:** given to grumbling and complaining **:** bad-tempered **:** PEEVISH, TOUCHY
grouf \'grüf\ *n* -s [ME (*one*) *gruff*, (*one the*) *groffe* on the face, prone, fr. ON *ā grūfu* — more at GROVELING (adv.)] *Scot* **:** the ventral surface of the body; *specif* **:** STOMACH
¹ground \'grau̇nd\ *n* -s *often attrib* [ME *ground, grund*, fr. OE *grund;* akin to OHG *grunt* ground, bottom, ON *grunnr* bottom, Goth *grundu*waddjus foundation wall, Gk *chrainein* to graze, touch slightly, and perh. to OE *grindan* to grind — more at GRIND] **1 a** *obs* **:** the lowest part **:** the surface that limits the downward extent of something **:** BOTTOM, FOUNDATION **b :** the bottom of the sea or a body of water **:** solid bottom — now used chiefly in nautical phrases ⟨had sufficient to anchor about a mile off shore and the holding ~ was not good —A.F.Ellis⟩ ⟨the boat struck ~⟩; compare AGROUND **c grounds** *pl* (1) **:** sediment at the bottom of a liquor or liquid (2) **:** ground coffee beans after brewing **d** *obs* **:** the pit of a theater **2 a :** the foundation or basis on which knowledge, belief, or conviction rests **:** a premise, reason, or collection of data upon which something (as a legal action or an argument) is made to rely for cogency or validity ⟨the reference to natural law as a ~ for the authority of civil law —Glenn Negley⟩ ⟨opposing divorce on religious ~*s*⟩ **b :** a sufficient and determining condition **:** a logical condition, physical cause, or metaphysical basis — used esp. of what is regarded as more fundamental than a merely natural cause ⟨the first principle or ~ of the universe —Frank Thilly⟩ **3 a :** the area surrounding and delimiting a figure or design **:** BACKGROUND **b :** the basic surface for figures in relief **c :** the surface upon which a picture or decoration is painted (as a preliminary coating laid on a canvas) **d :** the surface appearance of a fabric distinguished by a weave, color, texture; *specif* **:** the plain or background portion of a patterned fabric **e :** a stiff yet yielding substance (as wood or a pitch bed) on which a design is beaten into relief in repoussé work **f :** the pieces of net or the brides that support or hold together the patterns in lace; *also* **:** the net that serves as a foundation (as for appliqué) **g :** an acid-resistant liquid or paste that is made from varying proportions of wax, gum, and resin and that is used in etching to carry the design and to protect areas of the plate where no biting action is intended — see HARD GROUND, LIFT GROUND, SOFT GROUND **h :** a plain tinted coat which is applied to a wallpaper and over which a pattern is then printed **i :** wood or metal strips placed around all openings and along the top of the wall base to serve as guides in finishing the plaster **4 a :** a plainsong or other traditional tune used as the bass of a polyphonic musical composition **b :** GROUND BASS **c :** a composition making use of a ground bass **5 :** the surface on which man stands, moves, and dwells and on which objects naturally rest: as **a :** the surface of the earth ⟨deep under the ~⟩ ⟨a branch 60 feet above the ~⟩ ⟨uneven ~⟩ ⟨high ~⟩ **:** the earth as contrasted with the air ⟨~ troops⟩ ⟨~ attack⟩ or the water ⟨glad to feel firm ~ again after the rough voyage⟩ **b** *obs* **:** COUNTRY, LAND **c** *now dial* **:** a parcel of land enclosed for tillage or pasture **:** FIELD **d :** an area appropriated to or used for a particular purpose ⟨picnic ~⟩ ⟨parade ~⟩ ⟨camping ~⟩ **e grounds** *pl* **:** the gardens, lawn, and planted areas immediately surrounding and belonging to a house or other building ⟨hospital ~*s*⟩ **f :** an area to be won or defended in or as if in battle ⟨yielding ~ step by step⟩ ⟨shifting the ~ of his attack⟩ **g :** a topic or field of study or discourse **:** SUBJECT ⟨touch on forbidden ~⟩ ⟨cover a great deal of ~ in an hour's lecture⟩ **h** (1) **:** a cricket field (2) **:** the part of the field beginning at the popping crease and extending backward past the stumps ⟨a batsman may be stumped or run out only when he is out of his ~⟩ (3) *or* **ground staff :** the professional players employed by a cricket club **i** *chiefly Brit* **:** FLOOR ⟨kneeling on the ~ beside the couch he leaned over him —Aldous Huxley⟩ ⟨her gown swept the ~⟩ **6 a :** SOIL, EARTH ⟨till the ~ —Gen 2:5(AV)⟩ **b :** a special soil ⟨produce of each ~⟩ **c :** rock or formation through which mine workings are driven ⟨soft, wet, or loose ~⟩ **7 a :** a metal object buried in the earth to make electrical connection with it (as in a telephone or radio circuit) **b :** a large conducting body (as the chassis of a car or radio, the fuselage of a plane, or the earth itself) used as a common return for an electric circuit and as an arbitrary zero of potential **c :** electric connection with the earth or other ground **syn** see REASON — **from the ground up 1 :** entirely anew or afresh ⟨if one could begin *from the ground up* in each generation —Thomas Munro⟩ **2 :** from top to bottom **:** THOROUGHLY ⟨learning the business *from the ground up*⟩ — **into the ground** *adv* **:** beyond what is necessary or tolerable **:** to exhaustion **:** to death ⟨patiently labored an issue *into the ground* —*Newsweek*⟩ ⟨caution is no doubt a virtue but don't run it *into the ground*⟩ ⟨ran the other horses *into the ground* in the first half mile⟩ — **off the ground** *adv* **:** in or as if in flight ⟨the story . . . dramatically never gets *off the ground* —*New Republic*⟩ **:** off to a good start **:** under way ⟨difficult for his second-party movement to get *off the ground* —*Time*⟩ — **on the ground** *adv* **:** at the scene of action **:** on the spot ⟨already *on the ground*, energetically organizing —S.H.Adams⟩ — **take the ground :** to run aground ⟨choose a boat that is able to *take the ground* easily —Peter Heaton⟩ — **to ground** *adv* **:** into a burrow **:** into hiding ⟨the fox went *to ground* under a rocky escarpment —James Reynolds⟩ ⟨gone *to ground* in his country estate to avoid awkward questions⟩ ⟨till I have run the author *to ground* and exposed the whole shameful affair —John Buchan⟩ — **to the ground** *adv* **:** ENTIRELY, COMPLETELY, UTTERLY ⟨this life here suits me *to the ground* —Rose Macaulay⟩
²ground \"\ *vb* -ED/-ING/-S [ME *grounden, grunden*, fr. *ground, grund*, n.] *vt* **1 :** to bring to the ground **:** force down on the ground **:** FLOOR **2 a** *obs* **:** to set (a building) on a foundation **b :** to furnish a ground for **:** set on a basis (as of reason or principle or belief) ⟨sought to ~ the social good on the good of individuals —K.J.Arrow⟩ ⟨~*ed* their philosophy of life on logic as well as on metaphysics —Frank Thilly⟩ **c :** to instruct in elements or first principles **:** furnish (oneself or others) with a foundation of knowledge ⟨the study helped to ~ them in the mechanics of research⟩ ⟨must have every American citizen well ~*ed* in the classical ideals —Calvin Coolidge⟩ **3 :** to cover (a painting surface) with a ground **4 :** to place on or cause to touch the ground ⟨~ a rifle⟩ ⟨~ a ship on a sandbar⟩ **5 :** to prepare the surface of (leather) by scraping the flesh side with a moon knife **6 :** to connect electrically with a ground **7 a :** to restrict (a pilot, passenger, or airplane) to the ground to avoid accident (as from mechanical failure, ill health, or unfavorable flying weather) or to enforce a regulation (as of licensing or discipline) **b :** to bar (a jockey) from racing **c :** to bar (a licensed driver) from operating a vehicle **~** *vi* **1 :** to have a ground or basis **:** RELY — usu. used with *on* or *upon* ⟨the institutions . . . ~ on . . . four socializing forces —S.H.Chapman⟩ **2 :** to run aground **:** strike bottom ⟨the ship ~*ed* gently on a mud bank⟩ ⟨masses of ice had ~*ed* on the shore⟩ **3** *archaic* **:** to come to the ground **:** fall or light on the ground **4 :** to hit a grounder ⟨~*ed* into a double play⟩ ⟨~*ed* out to the shortstop⟩ **syn** see BASE — **ground arms :** to lay weapons on the ground in front of one esp. in token of surrender
³ground *past of* GRIND
ground·age \'grau̇ndij\ *n* -s *Brit* **:** a fee or charge for a ship to anchor in a port
ground almond *n* **:** CHUFA
ground angle *n* **:** the angle that an airplane's wing chord makes with the horizontal when the airplane is standing at rest
ground angling *n* **:** fishing with a floatless weighted line
ground annual \'grau̇nd-, 'grən(d)-\ *n* [ME *grund annuall*, fr. *grund* ground + *annuall*, *annual* annual — more at ANNUAL] *Scots law* **:** an annual duty or payment laid as a real burden upon land
ground an·nu·al·er \-'anyə(wə)lər\ *n, pl* **ground annualers** *Scots law* **:** one that pays a ground annual
ground ash *n* **1 a :** an ash sapling **b :** a walking stick made from ground ash **2 :** GOUTWEED **3 :** WILD ANGELICA **4 :** EUROPEAN ASH **5 :** WHITE ASH 1a
ground bait *n* **:** bait scattered on the water so as to attract fish
ground ball *n* **:** a batted ball in baseball that touches the ground before a fielder can field it; *esp* **:** GROUNDER
ground bass *n* **:** a bass passage usu. of four or eight measures continually repeated below constantly changing melody and harmony — called also *basso ostinato*
ground beam *n* **1 :** SLEEPER 2a **2 :** GROUND PLATE 1
ground beetle *n* **:** a beetle of the family Carabidae
ground·ber·ry \'grau̇n(d)- — *see* BERRY\ *n* **1 :** CHECKERBERRY 1a; *also* **:** the plant producing this berry **2** *Austral* **:** NATIVE CRANBERRY **3 :** a thick trailing evergreen shrub

(*Rubus hespidus*) of eastern No. America that is used as a ground cover esp. on banks and in rock gardens and that has hispid canes and glossy foliolate leaves
ground birch *n* **:** DWARF BIRCH
groundbird \ˈ⸗,⸗\ *n* **1 :** any of several Australian passerine birds constituting a genus (*Cinclosoma*) of the family Timaliidae and resembling thrushes **2 :** any of various small ground-nesting birds (as the field and vesper sparrows)
ground boss *n* **:** the captain of a mine
ground box *n* **:** DWARF BOX 3
groundbreaker \ˈ⸗,⸗⸗\ *n* **:** PIONEER, INNOVATOR
ground burnut *n* **:** PUNCTURE VINE
ground cable *n* **:** a mooring cable or chain that runs from a mooring anchor to a buoy
ground casing *n* **:** an unfinished casing for a window that serves as a plaster ground
ground cedar *n* **1 :** GROUND PINE 2 **2 :** a common highly variable juniper (*Juniperus communis*) that is cultivated in many varieties as an ornamental and esp. for foundation plantings
ground centaury *n* **1 :** AMERICAN COLUMBO **2 :** an annual herb (*Polygala nuttallii*) of the eastern U.S. with slender erect stems and greenish purple flowers
ground chain *n* **1 :** a length of chain attached along the first length of an anchor cable by which the anchor when weighed may be swung free of the ship — compare CAT CHAIN **2 :** GROUND CABLE
ground–cherry *n* **1 :** any of several shrubby European dwarf cherries (esp. *Prunus fruticosa*) **2 a :** a plant of the genus *Physalis* — called also *husk-tomato;* see CAPE GOOSEBERRY, CHINESE LANTERN PLANT, STRAWBERRY TOMATO **b :** the fruit of such a plant
ground circuit *n* **:** a telegraph or telephone circuit partly through the ground
ground clamp *n* **:** a metal strip for making electrical connection with a ground (as a water pipe)
ground cloth *n* **1 :** a canvas covering for the floor of a stage **2 :** GROUNDSHEET
ground coat *n* **1 :** the undercoat of paint in graining or scumbling **2 a :** PRIMING **b :** the first coat of enamel on a metal usu. with blue cobalt oxide added to promote adherence
ground–controlled approach *also* **ground–control approach** \ˈ⸗⸗,⸗-\ *n* **:** a blind landing in which the airplane is observed from the ground by means of radar and directed along a suitable glide path by radioed instructions to the pilot — abbr. *GCA*
ground–controlled interception *n* **:** an interception in air defense in which the fighter pilot is directed to his target by signals from a ground radar station — abbr. *GCI*
ground course *n* **:** the horizontal course of masonry next to the ground
ground cover *n* **1 :** all small plants (as mosses, ferns, grasses and other herbaceous plants and shrubs) in a forest except young trees **2 a :** a planting of prostrate or low plants (as ivy, pachysandra, myrtle) that covers the ground in place of turf **b :** a plant adapted for such use
ground crew *n* **:** a crew of mechanics and technicians who maintain and service aircraft
ground cuckoo *n* **:** ROADRUNNER
ground current *n* **:** EARTH CURRENT
ground detector *n* **:** a device for determining whether a circuit is well insulated from the ground
ground dove *n* **:** any of numerous very small chiefly tropical doves; *esp* **:** any of various tiny very tame American doves (genus *Columbigallina*) that nest on the ground or in low trees or bushes
grounded *past of* GROUND
ground·ed·ly *adv, archaic* **:** in a well-founded manner **:** FIRMLY, THOROUGHLY
ground effect *n* **:** the apparent increase in aerodynamic lift experienced by an aircraft when flying near the ground and observed up to a distance above the ground approximately equal to the wing span
ground elder *n, Brit* **:** GOUTWEED
grounden *archaic past part of* GRIND
ground·er \ˈgraùndə(r)\ *n* -S **:** one that grounds: as **a :** a ball (as in baseball, cricket, or soccer) that bounds or rolls along the ground; *esp* **:** a batted ball that strikes the ground almost immediately **b :** a worker who prepares a ground of surface or color (as on leather or paper)
ground fern *n* **:** MARSH FERN 1
ground fielding *n* **:** the fielding of grounders in cricket
ground finch *n* **1 :** TOWHEE **2 :** any of several dull-colored large-billed finches constituting a genus (*Geospiza*) that is restricted to the Galápagos islands
ground fir *n* **:** any of several club mosses (as *Lycopodium selago* and *L. obscurum*) having a stiff erect habit
ground fire *n* **1 :** a forest fire that burns the humus and usu. does not appear at the surface **2 :** SURFACE FIRE
groundfish \ˈ⸗,⸗\ *n* **:** a bottom fish; *esp* **:** any of the commercially important fishes (as cod, haddock, pollack, flounder) that live on the sea bottom
ground flax *n* **:** GOLD-OF-PLEASURE
ground flea *n* **1 :** FLEA BEETLE **2 :** SPRINGTAIL
ground floor *n* **1 :** the floor of a house most nearly on a level with the ground — compare FIRST FLOOR **2 :** a favorable position or privileged opportunity (as in making a speculative investment) usu. on terms obtained by the original or early participants — used chiefly in the phrase *in on the ground floor* ⟨he's heard of the boom along this coast, and wants to get in on the *ground floor* —O.Henry⟩
ground fog *n* **:** fog extending only a few feet from the ground; *specif* **:** one not exceeding the height of a man
ground form *n* [trans. of G *grundform*] **:** a root, stem, or word viewed as the common base from which various forms or words have developed **:** THEME
ground frost *n* **1 :** frozen ground **2 :** a temperature dropping below freezing at or near ground level and causing damage to vegetation
ground game *n, Brit* **:** game (as hares and rabbits) living on the ground — distinguished from *wing game*
ground gas *n* **:** gas including air held in openings or pores within the earth
ground gecko *n* **:** any of various small weak-limbed geckos of the southwestern U.S. and northern Mexico that constitute the genus *Coleonyx*, are strictly terrestrial in habits, and are variously barred and blotched with reddish or dark brown on a creamy or yellow ground
ground glass *n* **1 :** glass whose surface has been made light-diffusing by etching with hydrofluoric acid, sandblasting, or grinding with an abrasive; *specif* **:** a sheet of such glass used as a focusing screen in photography **2 :** glass reduced to powder by grinding or crushing for use as an abrasive
ground–glass \ˈ⸗ˈ⸗\ *adj* [*ground glass*] **:** relating to or characterized by ground glass: as **a :** having a surface polished **b :** having a surface ground or etched to a semi-transparency **c :** having a surface ground to fit ⟨*ground-glass* joint⟩
ground goldenrod *n* **:** a low velvety prairie goldenrod (*Solidago mollis*) of central No. America
ground goldflower *n* **:** a golden aster (*Chrysopsis falcata*) of the eastern U.S. with velvety foliage
ground hemlock *n* **:** any of several prostrate evergreen shrubs of the genus *Taxus* (esp. *T. canadensis* of eastern No. America) with low straggling stems, abruptly pointed leaves, and bright red fruits
groundhog \ˈ⸗,⸗\ *n* **1 :** WOODCHUCK **2 :** SANDHOG
groundhog case *n, South* **:** a desperate or critical situation **:** a situation with no alternative ⟨his was a *groundhog case;* it was take to the water or the dogs will get you —F.B. Gipson⟩
groundhog day *n, usu cap G&D* [so called fr. the belief that on that day the groundhog comes out of his burrow and if he casts a shadow returns for an additional period of winter weather] **:** February 2 in most parts of the U.S. or February 14 in some parts (as Missouri) which is popularly considered to indicate if sunny the continuance of wintry weather or if cloudy the early coming of spring
ground hold *n, obs* **:** GROUND TACKLE
ground holly *n* **1 :** PIPSISSEWA **2 :** WINTERGREEN 2a
ground honeysuckle *n* **:** BIRD'S-FOOT TREFOIL 1a
ground hornbill *n* **:** a hornbill of the African genus *Bucorvus* partly terrestrial in habits
ground ice *n* **1 :** ANCHOR ICE **2 :** clear ice in permanently frozen ground
groundier *comparative of* GROUNDY
groundiest *superlative of* GROUNDY
grounding *n* -S [fr. gerund of ²*ground*] **:** training or instruction esp. in the fundamentals of an art, science, or other field of knowledge **:** FOUNDATION ⟨a good ~ in chemistry⟩
ground itch *n* **:** an itching inflammation of the skin marking the entrance into the body of larval hookworms
ground ivy *n* [ME] **1 :** a trailing Eurasian mint (*Nepeta hederacea*) that is common as a weed in No. America and has rounded leaves and rather showy blue-purple flowers — called also *gill-over-the-ground* **2 :** any of several low-growing or trailing plants
ground jasmine *n* **:** an evergreen southern African shrub (*Passerina stelleri*) of the family Thymelaeaceae with white flowers
ground joint *n* **:** a joint (as between glass parts) of which the contacting surfaces are ground together to a close fit
ground joist *n* **:** SLEEPER 2a
ground juniper *n* **:** DWARF JUNIPER
groundkeeper \ˈ⸗,⸗⸗\ *n* **1 :** one that tends the grounds (as of a sports field, cemetery, park) **2 :** an undesired plant arising from self-sown seed or from roots in a planting of a desired species or variety
ground lag *n* **:** the horizontal distance by which the actual trajectory of a bomb in air lags behind the theoretical path in a vacuum
ground landlord *n* **:** the owner of a ground rent
ground lark *n* **:** PIPIT
ground laurel *n* **:** ARBUTUS 3
ground lead \-,lēd\ *n* **1 :** a contrivance for guiding a cable that hauls logs along the ground **2 :** GROUND WIRE
ground lease *n* **:** BUILDING LEASE
ground lemon *n* **:** MAYAPPLE
ground·less \ˈgraùndləs *rapid* -nl-\ *adj* [ME *groundeles* bottomless, unfathomable, fr. OE *grundlēas*, fr. *grund* ground + *-lēas* -less — more at GROUND, -LESS] **:** having no ground or foundation **:** lacking cause or reason for support ⟨~ fears⟩ ⟨a ~ charge of treason⟩ — **ground·less·ly** *adv* — **ground·less·ness** *n* -ES
ground level *n* **:** GROUND STATE
ground lily *n* **:** any of several plants of the genus *Trillium* (esp. *T. cernuum*)
groundline \ˈ⸗,⸗\ *n* **1 a :** strong hard-laid line that is used to form the main line of a setline and is usu. provided in bundles of 300 fathoms weighing 48, 40, or sometimes 32 pounds **b :** the main line of a setline consisting of one or more bundles of groundline **2 a :** the base line which represents a ground plane in pictures having no indication of spatial depth and upon which all figures and objects are placed irrespective of their real spatial relationship **b :** the bottom line of the picture plane of a drawing in linear perspective **c :** the bottom line of a photograph **d :** the line representing ground level in an architectural plan or drawing **3 :** FOUNDATION, BASIS
ground·ling \ˈgraùndliŋ, -lēŋ, *rapid* -nl-\ *n* -S [¹*ground* + *-ling*] **1 :** one that keeps close to the ground; *specif* **:** a fish (as the loach) that keeps at the bottom of the water **2 a :** a spectator in the cheaper part of a theater **b :** one of ordinary or unsophisticated taste or critical judgment **3 :** one that lives, works, or fights on the ground as distinct from in the air or on the sea
ground liverwort *n* **1 :** a common liverwort (*Marchantia polymorpha*) **2 :** a lichen (*Peltigera canina*) somewhat similar to the liverwort in appearance
ground lizard *n* **:** any of various small lizards of terrestrial habits; *esp* **:** a lizard (*Leiolopisma laterale*) of the southern U.S.
ground log *n* **:** a ship's log for use in shallow water and strong currents in which the chip is replaced by a sinker that rests on the bottom and measures speed over the ground rather than through the water
ground loop *n* **:** a sharp uncontrollable turn made by an airplane on the ground in landing, taking off, or taxiing
ground–loop \ˈ⸗ˈ⸗\ *vb* [*ground loop*] *vi, of an airplane or pilot* **:** to make a ground loop ~ *vt* **:** to cause (an airplane) to ground-loop
ground mahogany *n* **:** a Mexican mahogany tree (*Swietenia humilis*) that has harder, heavier, and darker-colored wood than the West Indian mahogany
ground mail *n, Scot* **:** the fee for interment in a graveyard
ground mallow *n* **:** DWARF MALLOW
ground·man \ˈgraùn(d)mən, -,man\ *n, pl* **groundmen** **1 a :** a strip-mine worker who moves dirt and coal within reach of power shovels **b :** a mine worker who deepens haulageways by digging out the bottom and lowering tracks **2 :** a member of a work crew who performs the tasks that can be done on or from the ground: as **a :** one who digs holes and raises poles for electric power or telephone lines and lifts equipment and tools to linemen **b :** one who assists with the erection of oil-well drilling rigs or power lines, the driving of piles, or the construction or wrecking of buildings **3 :** GROUNDKEEPER 1 **4 :** an electrician who attends to grounding connections
ground maple *n* **:** ALUMROOT
groundmass \ˈ⸗,⸗\ *n* **:** the fine-grained or glassy base of a porphyry in which the larger distinct crystals are embedded
ground meristem *n* **:** the part of the primary apical meristem of a plant that remains after the protoderm and procambium have been differentiated
ground mist *n* **:** GROUND FOG
ground moraine *n* **:** a moraine deposited beneath a glacier and back from its edge or end
groundneedle \ˈ⸗,⸗⸗\ *n* **:** a storksbill (*Erodium moschatum*) with short-stalked leaves
ground noise *n* **:** noise in reproduced or amplified sound caused by a source (as needle scratch, tube noise) other than the signal
ground note *n* **:** FUNDAMENTAL 2
ground·nut \ˈgraùn(d),nət, -aù,nət\ *n* **1 :** CHUFA **2 :** any of several plants having edible tuberous roots: as **a :** a No. American vine (*Apios tuberosa*) with pinnate leaves and clusters of brownish purple fragrant flowers **b :** DWARF GINSENG **c :** HARBINGER-OF-SPRING **d** *chiefly Brit* **:** PEANUT **3 :** the root of a groundnut
groundnut oil *n, chiefly Brit* **:** PEANUT OIL
ground oak *n* **1 :** DWARF OAK **2 :** GOPHER PLUM 2b
ground observer *n* **:** one that observes, tracks, and reports the movement of aircraft from an observation post
ground out *vi* **:** STRAND ⟨a small vessel could lie snug behind it, though she *grounded out* at low water —G.W.Brace⟩
ground owl *n* **:** BURROWING OWL
ground parrot *n* **1 :** KAKAPO **2 :** a formerly common ground-frequenting Australian parrot (*Pezoporus wallicus*) having green plumage barred with black and yellow and a scarlet patch on the forehead
ground pea *n* **1 :** PEANUT **2 :** GROUNDNUT 2a
ground pearl *n* **:** an encysted form of the female of various coccid insects of *Margarodes* and closely related genera in which a shelly covering is formed that in some regions is collected and strung into necklaces; *also* **:** a coccid having such an encysted form and sometimes being a serious pest of turf
ground pig *n* **:** CANE RAT 1
ground pigeon *n* **:** any of numerous pigeons that live largely on the ground (as the tooth-billed pigeon and the crowned pigeons)
ground pine *n* **1 :** a European bugle (*Ajuga chamaepitys*) with a resinous odor **2 :** any of several club mosses (esp. *Lycopodium clavatum* and *L. complanatum*) with long creeping stems and erect branches **:** GROUND FIR
ground pink *n* **:** MOSS PINK
ground pistachio *n* **:** PEANUT
ground plan *n* **1 :** a plan of the ground floor or of any floor of a building as distinguished from an elevation or perpendicular section **2 :** a first or basic plan **3 :** the pattern described on the ground by dancers
ground plane *n* **:** the horizontal plane of projection in perspective drawing
ground plate *n* **1** *archaic* **:** a timber laid horizontally on or near the ground to support the uprights of a building **:** SILL **2 :** a metallic plate buried in the ground to connect a circuit to earth
groundplot \ˈ⸗,⸗\ *n* **:** the determining of an aircraft's position by multiplying ground speed by time on course and measuring off the resultant distance from a previously known position
ground plum *n* **1 :** any of several milk vetches (esp. *Astragalus caryocarpus*) of the western U.S. **2 :** the fruit of a ground plum
ground–position indicator *n* **:** an instrument that indicates to the pilot of an aircraft his position relative to the ground
ground puppy *n* **1 :** CHANGA **2 :** HELLBENDER
ground quiver *n* **:** a device for holding arrows upright on the ground consisting of a metal rod with a horizontal ring at the top

ground quiver

ground raspberry *n* **:** GOLDENSEAL
ground rat *n* **:** CANE RAT 1
ground rattler *or* **ground rattlesnake** *n* **:** MASSASAUGA b
ground rent *n* **1 :** a price per year or term of years paid for the right to occupy and improve a piece of land; *also* **:** money or compensation so paid — compare ECONOMIC RENT **2 :** a rent charge reserved to himself and his heirs by the grantor of land in fee simple or on perpetual lease or lease for a term of years renewable forever and found chiefly in Pennsylvania and Maryland
ground robin *n* **:** TOWHEE
ground roller *n* **:** any of certain Madagascan birds (family Coraciidae) of terrestrial and crepuscular habits frequenting forests and feeding on insects, worms, or other small invertebrates
ground rope *n* **:** a weighted rope that keeps a trawlnet on the bottom
ground rose *n* **:** a low-growing prickly and often bristly shrub (*Rosa spithamaea*) of southern Oregon and California with creeping rootstocks and usu. corymbose flowers
groundrow \ˈ⸗ˈ⸗\ *n* [¹*ground* + *row*] **:** a low flat piece of scenery often representing a distant horizon and used to mask the lower part of a cyclorama or backdrop
ground rule *n* **1 :** a sports rule adopted to modify play on a particular field, court, or course (as because of space limitations or the encroachment of spectators on a playing field) ⟨if the backstop is less than 60 feet from home plate a *ground rule* will be necessary —Clement Wood & Gloria Goddard⟩ **2 :** a rule of procedure or a principle of action specified for or intended to apply to a particular event or situation ⟨having developed the primary purpose and general objectives of the company, a firm set of *ground rules* is therefore provided for the necessary detailed planning —C.F.Robinson⟩ ⟨the first fundamental change in labor-relations *ground rules* in nearly twelve years —*Time*⟩
grounds *pl of* GROUND, *pres 3d sing of* GROUND
ground school *n* **:** a school giving courses in aerodynamics, map making, photography, and other pertinent subjects for aviators
ground sea *n* **:** GROUND SWELL
ground seal *n* **:** BEARDED SEAL
¹**ground·sel** \ˈgraùn(d)səl\ *n* -S [ME *groundeswele*, fr. OE *grundeswelge*, fr. *grunde*, *grund* ground + *-swelge* (fr. *swelgan* to swallow, absorb), prob. by folk etymology fr. earlier *gundæswelge*, fr. *gund* pus + *-swelge;* akin to OHG *gund*, *gunt* pus, Norw dial. *gund* scab, Goth *gund* cancerous abscess, Gk *kanthylē* tumor, swelling — more at GROUND, SWALLOW] **:** an herb of the genus *Senecio* (esp. *S. vulgaris* in England and *S. aureus intercursus* in America) that is used sometimes as an emmenagogue
²**groundsel** \ˈ"\ *n* -S [ME *gronsell*, *ground sille*, fr. *ground* + *sille* sill — more at SILL] **1** *archaic* **:** a bed piece or foundation timber supporting a timber superstructure (as a wooden house or a set of mine timbers) **2** *archaic* **:** the lowest piece or the foundation of a structure **:** a fundamental principle **:** BASIS
groundsel bush *or* **groundsel tree** *n* **:** a No. American maritime shrub or small tree (*Baccharis halimifolia*) with leaves resembling those of groundsel; *broadly* **:** a plant of the genus *Baccharis*
ground shark *n* **1 :** any of numerous very active voracious sharks (genus *Carcharhinus*) found in shallow water along all warm coasts: as **a :** CUB SHARK **b :** BROWN SHARK **2 :** GREENLAND SHARK
groundsheet \ˈ⸗,⸗\ *n* **:** a waterproof sheet placed on the ground for protection from moisture ⟨slipped the newspaper . . . into my haversack thinking to use it as a ~ against the damp —Paul Roche⟩ — called also *ground cloth*
ground·sill \ˈgraùn(d)sәl, -,sil\ *n* [ME *ground sille*] *archaic* **:** ²GROUNDSEL
grounds keeper *n* **1 :** GARDENER; *esp* **:** one that cares for the grounds of a large property (as an estate) **2 :** GROUNDKEEPER 1
ground skidder *n* **:** a device that transports logs without lifting them clear of the ground
ground sloth *n* **:** any of various large and often very large extinct American edentate mammals related to the recent sloths and anteaters — compare MEGATHERIUM, MYLODON
ground sluice *n* **:** a channel or trough in the ground through which auriferous earth is sluiced for placer mining
grounds·man \ˈgraùn(d)zmən\ *n, pl* **groundsmen** **1 :** GROUNDKEEPER 1 **2** *chiefly Brit* **:** GROUNDMAN 2 **3 :** CRANE-FOLLOWER
ground snake *n* **:** any of numerous small terrestrial colubrid snakes: as **a :** any of a No. American genus (*Sonora*) of shy brightly ringed snakes **b :** a small reddish gray snake (*Haldea striatula* syn. *Potamophis striatula*) of the eastern U.S.
ground sparrow *n* **:** any of various small ground-nesting sparrows (as the song sparrow, vesper sparrow, or Savannah sparrow)
ground speed *n* **:** the velocity of an airplane with relation to the ground — compare AIRSPEED
ground squirrel *n* **1 :** any of various burrowing rodents (family Sciuridae): as **a** *chiefly South & Midland* **:** CHIPMUNK **b :** a member of the African genus *Xerus* **c :** any of numerous often striped rodents of western No. America that constitute *Citellus* and sometimes related genera, are often destructive pests of cultivated land, and in some areas serve as vectors of plague **2** *also* **ground–squirrel pea :** TWINLEAF
ground staff *n* **:** GROUND 5h (3)
ground state *n* **:** the energy level of an atomic electron system, atomic nucleus, or other systems of interacting elementary particles having the least energy of all its possible states — called also *ground level*
ground story *n* **:** GROUND FLOOR
ground–strafe \ˈ⸗,⸗\ *vt* **:** STRAFE
ground strake *n* **:** GARBOARD STRAKE
ground stroke *n* **:** a stroke made on a ball in tennis after it has rebounded from the ground — compare VOLLEY
ground substance *n* **:** a more or less completely homogeneous or apparently homogeneous matrix that forms the background in which the specific formed or differentiated elements of a system are suspended or enclosed: as **a :** the intercellular substance of tissues **b :** HYALOPLASM
ground sweet *n* **:** ARBUTUS 3
ground swell *n* **1 :** a broad deep swell or undulation of the ocean caused by a long-continued gale or seismic disturbance and felt even at a remote distance **2 :** a movement (as of political sentiment or political opinion) that is unmistakably evident but often lacking in visible leadership or overt expression ⟨by next year the *ground swell* of interest among veteran and labor groups may well push cooperative housing through Congress —Catherine Bauer⟩
ground table *n* **:** EARTH TABLE
ground tackle *or* **ground tackling** *n* **:** the anchors, cables, and other tackle used to secure a ship at anchor
ground thistle *n* **1 :** a stemless European thistle (*Carlina acaulis*) with crimson flower heads **2 :** CARDOON
ground thrush *n* **1 :** PITTA 2 **2 :** any of numerous Old World thrushes chiefly of a genus (*Geocichla*) of the family Turdidae

ground tier *n* **1 :** the lowest tier of articles stowed in a ship's hold **2 :** the lowest row of boxes in a theater or amphitheater
ground tissue *n* **:** PARENCHYMA 1
ground tone *n* **:** FUNDAMENTAL 2
ground vine *n* **:** TWINFLOWER
ground warbler *n* **:** any of various American warblers living or nesting chiefly on the ground
ground·ward \'graůndwə(r)d, *rapid* -nw-\ *also* **ground·wards** \-dz\ *adv* **:** toward the ground **:** DOWN
groundwater \'ˌ=,==\ *n* **:** water within the earth that supplies wells and springs; *specif* **:** water in the zone of saturation where all openings in rocks and soil are filled, the upper surface of which forms the water table
groundwater level *n* **1 :** WATER TABLE **2 :** the depth or elevation above or below sea level at which the surface of groundwater stands
ground wave *n* **:** a radio wave that is propagated along the surface of the earth
ground ways *n pl* **:** heavy timbers laid on the ground on each side of the keel of a ship under construction that form a track for launching and support the sliding ways that carry the ship into the water — called also *standing ways*
ground wire *n* **1 :** a wire making a ground connection **2 :** the part of a circuit formed by the earth
groundwood \'=,=\ *n* **:** wood ground into small particles by revolving grindstones and used in paper pulp ⟨~ pulp⟩ ⟨~ paper⟩; *also* **:** the pulp made from such wood
groundwork \'=,=\ *n* **:** something that forms a foundation or support **:** BASIS, GROUND
ground worm *n* **1 :** EARTHWORM **2 :** WORM SNAKE
ground wren *n* **1 :** WREN-TIT **2 :** HEATH-WREN
groundy \'graůndē\ *adj* -ER/-EST *of coffee* **:** having an earthy taste or aroma
ground yew *n* **1 :** CROWBERRY 1a **2 :** a ground hemlock (*Taxus canadensis*)
ground zero *n* **:** the point on the surface of the ground or water directly below which, above which, or at which the explosion of an atom bomb occurs
¹group \'grüp\ *n* -s [F *groupe*, fr. It *gruppo* group, knot, of Gmc origin; akin to OHG *kropf* craw — more at CROP] **1 :** two or more figures (as in sculpture or painting) forming a distinctive unit complete in itself or forming part of a larger composition ⟨the bronze ~ represents a mortally wounded southern soldier supported by Fame —*Amer. Guide Series: N.C.*⟩ ⟨a foreground ~ of satyrs and nymphs⟩ **2 a :** a relatively small number of individuals assembled or standing together ⟨a ~ of indifferent bystanders looked on⟩ ⟨~s of prisoners marching to their destination⟩ — compare CROWD **b :** an assemblage of objects regarded as a unit because of their comparative segregation from others ⟨a ~ of buildings⟩ ⟨a ~ of towns . . . were able to develop increasing commerce with the Near East —Stringfellow Barr⟩ ⟨a ~ of . . . highly finished, memorable stories —Paul Pickrel⟩: as (1) **:** a cluster of islands ⟨the ~ consists of four tiny islands⟩ ⟨contemplated the investigation of the South Sandwich ~ —R.N.Rudmose-Brown⟩ (2) **:** a cluster of hits on a target fired with the same sight setting and the same point of aim **3 :** a number of individuals bound together by a community of interest, purpose, or function: as **a** (1) **:** a social unit comprising individuals in continuous contact through intercommunication and shared participation in activities toward some commonly accepted end — see PRIMARY GROUP, SECONDARY GROUP (2) **:** CLASS 1a ⟨a government representative of all the great social ~s⟩ ⟨a small ~ of wealthy families virtually governed the province⟩ (3) **:** a relatively small number of persons associated formally or informally for a common end or drawn together through an affinity of views or interests **:** CIRCLE ⟨a dance ~⟩ ⟨a study ~⟩ ⟨a stamp ~⟩ ⟨a vanguard ~ of artists⟩ ⟨there grew up in the universities a ~ called the "New Critics" —F.O.Baker⟩ **b :** a number of students taking part in the same educational or extracurricular activities **:** CLASS 2b **c :** a combination of persons who are usu. employees of a single employer and are covered by a blanket or single insurance policy **d :** a combination of elected parliamentary representatives bound together by a common program or by a general identity of political views — used esp. of a grouping in the French National Assembly **e :** a combination of companies or other enterprises having interlocking interests or a single owner or management **:** SYNDICATE, TRUST, CHAIN ⟨vary in size from two-paper ~s to one which includes 20 papers —F.L.Mott⟩ ⟨the powerful hydroelectric ~⟩ **f** (1) **:** an administrative and tactical military unit consisting of a headquarters and two or more battalions not a permanent organic part of the group (2) **:** a unit of an echelon of the U. S. Air Force higher than a squadron and lower than a wing and composed of a headquarters and two or more squadrons **g :** the basic program unit of Camp Fire Girls consisting of no more than 20 Blue Bird members or camp fire girls and no more than 30 members in a Horizon Club plus a leader and often an assistant leader **4 a :** an assemblage of related organisms ⟨the A ~ of beta hemolytic streptococci⟩ — often used to avoid taxonomic connotations when the kind or degree of relationship is not clearly defined **b** (1) **:** an assemblage of atoms forming part of a molecule **:** RADICAL ⟨a methyl ~ (CH_3)⟩ ⟨the alcohol ~ (OH)⟩ — compare LIGAND (2) **:** an assemblage of elements forming one of the vertical columns of the periodic table **c** (1) **:** a stratigraphic division of the first order comprising the rocks deposited during an era — used in the system of nomenclature adopted by the International Geological Congress (2) **:** a stratigraphic division composed of two or more named formations — used in the system of nomenclature of the U. S. Geological Survey (3) **:** a consecutive series of beds or assemblage of related igneous rocks (4) **:** GREAT SOIL GROUP **d :** a syllable or series of syllables uttered with a single primary or quasi-primary stress **:** STRESS-GROUP **e :** a set of three or more cards of the same rank in the game of rummy **5 :** a mathematical aggregate in which the product of two elements is an element of the aggregate
²group \"\ *vb* -ED/-ING/-S [F *grouper* to group, fr. *groupe*, n.] *vt* **1 :** to form a group of **:** CLUSTER ⟨nine tennis courts are ~*ed* at one end of the field —*Bull. of Bates Coll.*⟩ ⟨with the other . . . pilots ~*ed* around him —Ed Cunningham⟩ **2 a :** to combine in a group or in groups **:** assign to a group **:** CLASSIFY ⟨the large class of barbaric ideas ~*ed* under sympathetic magic —Edward Clodd⟩ ⟨her mind was busily assorting and ~*ing* the faces before her —Ellen Glasgow⟩ ⟨~*ing* liberty of the press with trial by jury —Zechariah Chafee⟩; *specif* **:** to determine the blood group of ⟨after the patient and donor have been ~*ed* —R.L.Haden⟩ **b :** to arrange (as figures) in an artistic composition with regard to the aesthetic effect ⟨an oil painting . . . over the fire: horsemen ~*ed* apprehensively at midnight —Elizabeth Bowen⟩ ~ *vi* **1 :** to form a group **:** become a member of a group **:** BELONG, HARMONIZE ⟨he ~s with Tennyson and Spenser in contrast to Shakespeare and Donne —F.R.Leavis⟩ **2 :** to make well-defined groups of hits on a target
³group \"\ *adj* **1 :** of or relating to a group **:** belonging to or shared by the members of a group as a whole **:** COLLECTIVE ⟨an individual is not responsible for ~ acts⟩ ⟨a sad absence of ~ awareness —Julian Huxley⟩ ⟨~ discussion⟩ **2 :** constituting a unit of syntax composed of a word group ⟨*to be in need of* meaning "to need" is a ~ verb⟩ ⟨*impossible-to-be realized* in "an impossible-to-be realized wish" is a ~ adjunct⟩ ⟨*man of honor's* in "a man of honor's word" is a ~ genitive⟩
group agglutination *n* **:** CROSS AGGLUTINATION
group analysis *n* **:** the application of psychoanalysis to group psychotherapy
group annuity *n* **:** a pension plan providing annuities at retirement for all eligible persons under a single master contract usu. issued to an employer for the benefit of employees
group banking *n* **:** a system of control over two or more commercial banks by a holding company
group bonus *n* **:** an incentive wage divided among a number of workers cooperating on a task in proportion to time worked and rank held by each
group captain *n* **:** an officer (as in the British Royal Air Force) equivalent in rank to a colonel in the army
group dynamics *n pl but often sing in constr* **1 :** the forces and processes of interaction operating within a relatively small human group **2 :** the study of the forces and processes operating within a relatively small human group esp. within the theoretical framework of the view that the group is a sociological whole with dynamic properties of its own (as organization, stability, and goals) which can be objectively analyzed and accurately measured
grouped columns *n pl* **:** three or more columns placed upon the same pedestal or otherwise closely associated
¹grou·per \'grüpə(r)\ *n, pl* **groupers** *also* **grouper** [Pg *garoupa*, prob. of AmerInd origin; akin to Galibi *croupy*, a species of fish] **1 :** any of numerous fishes of the family Serranidae esp. of the genera *Epinephelus* and *Mycteroperea* that are typically solitary bottom fishes of warm seas and sometimes attain immense size — compare CABRILLA, HIND **2 :** TRIPLETAIL **3 :** any of several rockfishes (family Scorpaenidae)
²group·er \"\ *n* -s *usu cap* [Oxford *Group* + E *-er*] **:** a member of the Oxford Group **:** BUCHMANITE
group house *n* **:** ROW HOUSE
grouping *n* -s **1 :** the act, manner, or an instance of placing in groups ⟨~ should be considered by teachers . . . and administrators as primarily an instructional problem —Helen Heffernan⟩ ⟨achieve with ~ and composition . . . the impression of a great painting —*Ency. Britannica*⟩ ⟨the ~s of fact and argument and illustration so as to produce a cumulative and mass effect —B.N.Cardozo⟩ **2 a :** an assemblage of individuals grouped in a certain manner (as for utility or artistic effect) or naturally forming a distinct pattern or configuration ⟨jewelry designed to grow in size from a single diamond to a magnificent ~ of diamonds—*Jewelers' Circular-Keystone*⟩ ⟨a new type of population ~ . . . seen wherever a constellation of towns is clustered around a dominating metropolitan center —F.A.Ogg & P.O.Ray⟩ ⟨word ~s peculiar to advertising —W.H.Whyte⟩ ⟨the almost inevitable Vermont ~ of Civil War monument, cannon, and bandstand —*Amer. Guide Series: Vt.*⟩ **b :** pattern of organization or relationship **:** ALIGNMENT ⟨strict party lines were being replaced by sectional ~s —C.H. Lincoln⟩ ⟨clannish in their internal ~s, they are divided into many organizations —*Amer. Guide Series: Mich.*⟩ **c :** an assemblage of like individuals **:** GROUP ⟨the writings . . . fall into five well-defined ~s —E.M.Hinton⟩
group insurance *n* **:** insurance issued upon a group of persons under a single or blanket policy — compare GROUP LIFE INSURANCE
group·ism \'grü,pizəm\ *n* -s **:** the tendency to think and act as members of a group **:** the tendency to conform to the cultural pattern of a group at the expense of individualism and cultural diversity ⟨~ . . . rests not on obvious group emergencies but on the vague disquietude of lonely individuals —David Riesman⟩
group·let \'grüplət\ *n* -s **:** a small group
group life insurance *n* **:** insurance upon the lives of a number of persons under a blanket policy without medical examination and at low cost
group marriage *n* **1 :** COMMUNAL MARRIAGE **2 :** a system wherein common marital relations exist between a definite group of men and a definite group of women — compare PIRRAURA, PUNALUA
group·ment \'grüpmənt\ *n* -s [F *groupement*, fr. *grouper* to group + *-ment* — more at GROUP] **:** GROUP; *esp* **:** a group of military units
group mind *n* **1 :** the beliefs and desires common to a social group as a whole **2 :** a hypothetical psychic unity or collective consciousness of a group of individuals
group practice *also* **group medicine** *n* **:** medicine practiced by a group of associated physicians, (as specialists in different fields) working as partners or as partners and employees
group psychotherapy *n* **:** psychotherapy in which directive, inspirational, didactic, or analytic means are employed to bring about favorable personality changes in a group of patients; *esp* **:** psychotherapy in which a therapist leads or guides a group of emotionally ill patients in a discussion and sharing of their personal problems designed to promote relief from emotional conflict and tension and further social adjustment
group rate *n* **:** a uniform rate charged to or from any one of a group or block of points within a given territory — called also *blanket rate, block rate*
groups *pl of* GROUP, *pres 3d sing of* GROUP
group-specific \ˌ=ˌ=;==\ *adj* **:** having a specific relation to a particular blood group — used of polysaccharides found in red blood cells, tissues, and body fluids and usu. also in bodily discharges; compare ISOHEMAGGLUTINOGEN, NONSECRETOR, SECRETOR
group test *n* **:** a mental or achievement test (as the Army General Classification Test) designed to be administered to many individuals at once
group therapist *n* **:** a person who conducts group psychotherapy
group therapy *n* **1 :** therapy in which patients with the same diagnosis (as obesity) are brought together to share their difficulties in group discussions designed to build morale and stimulate interest **2 :** GROUP PSYCHOTHERAPY
group velocity *n* **:** the velocity with which some definite peculiarity of a composite wave train (as an interference maximum) advances through a medium — compare PHASE VELOCITY
group·wise \'grüp,wīz\ *adv* **:** with reference to the group **:** as a group ⟨the problem . . . is to help people see themselves and others ~ —Martin Chworowsky⟩
group work *n* **:** a technique within the field of social work wherein various groups (as educational and recreational) are guided by an agency leader to more effective personal adjustment and community participation
¹grouse \'graůs\ *n, pl* **grouse** *or* **grous·es** [origin unknown] **1 a :** any of numerous birds that constitute the family Tetraonidae, are mostly of medium to rather large size, have a plump body, strong feathered legs, and plumage less brilliant than that of pheasants and generally with reddish brown or other protective color, and include numerous important game birds (as the capercaillie, black grouse, and hazel hen of Europe and Asia or the ruffed grouse, prairie chicken, sage grouse, and others of America) **b** *Brit* **:** RED GROUSE **2 :** GAZELLE 2
²grouse \"\ *vi* -ED/-ING/-S **:** to seek or shoot grouse
³grouse \"\ *vi* -ED/-ING/-S [origin unknown] **:** to complain typically with sustained grumbling ⟨people ~ about excessive taxation, rationing —*Atlantic*⟩ **syn** see COMPLAIN
⁴grouse \"\ *n* -s **:** COMPLAINT, GROUCH ⟨a temporary outlet for ~s against the party in power —Mollie Panter-Downes⟩
grouse·ber·ry \'graůs- —*see* BERRY\ *n* **1 :** CHECKERBERRY 1a **2** *also* **grouse whortleberry :** a blueberry (*Vaccinium scoparium*)
grouse disease *n* **:** an infectious disease of grouse characterized by hoarseness, cyanosis of the conjunctiva, emaciation, and quick tiring on flying
grouse·less \'graůsləs\ *adj* [¹*grouse* + *-less*] **:** having no grouse
grouse locust *n* **:** a grasshopper of the family Tetrigidae
¹grou·ser \'graůzə(r)\ *n* -s [origin unknown] **1 :** a heavy pointed timber thrust down to serve as an anchor for a floating dredge or similar machine **2 :** one of a set of cleats on a tractor wheel or track for increasing traction
²grous·er \'graůsə(r)\ *n* -s [³*grouse* + *-er*] **:** a person who grouses; *specif* **:** one who habitually complains or grumbles
¹grout \'graůt, *usu* -aůd·+V\ *n* -s [ME, fr. OE *grūt*; akin to MD *grūte* malt, dregs, MHG *grūz* grain, sand, OE *grytt* grit — more at GRIT (coarse meal)] **1** *archaic* **a :** coarse meal **:** hulled grain **b grouts** *pl* **:** OATS **2** *now dial Eng* **a :** a malt infusion before or during fermentation **b :** SMALL BEER **3** *archaic* **:** porridge of grout or groats **4 :** LEES, DREGS, GROUNDS **5 a** (1) **:** thin mortar fluid enough to be poured and used for filling in spaces (as the joints of masonry, brickwork, brick or stone block pavements, forced under pressure as into prepacked graded stone to form concrete, into fissures in foundation rock, into railroad ballast or the subgrade, or into the space between tunnel lining and the surrounding earth) (2) **:** material used for a similar purpose; *specif* **:** a mixture of portland cement and water applied under pressure during oil-well drilling to prevent contamination of the oil by sealing off undesirable fluids and also to provide a protective wall around the metal casing **b** (1) **:** a coarse plaster or cement used for coating the wall of a building and usu. studded with small stones after application (2) **:** a fine plaster or cement used for finishing ceilings **c :** CONCRETE **d :** MORTAR
²grout \"\ *vt* -ED/-ING/-S **:** to fill up or finish with or as if with grout ⟨the material used in sealing or ~*ing* them —*U.S. War Dept. Technical Manual*⟩
³grout \"\ *vi* -ED/-ING/-S [perh. alter. of obs. E *grewt, grut* dry earth, soil, fr. ME *grut* mud, earth; akin to OE *grūt* grout, *grēot* grit, sand, earth — more at GRIT (sand)] *Brit* **:** ROOT, GRUB ⟨~*ing* in the grass —Virginia Woolf⟩
grout·er \'graůd·ə(r), -aůtə-\ *n* -s [²*grout* + *-er*] **1 :** a machine for grouting joints **2 :** a worker who operates a grouter
grouting *n* -s **1 :** the process of applying or using grout by flowing it into place by gravity or under pressure **2 :** GROUT 5
grout·ite \'graůd·,īt\ *n* -s [Frank F. *Grout* *b*1880 Am. geologist and mineralogist + E *-ite*] **:** a mineral $HMnO_2$ consisting of manganese, hydrogen, and oxygen, polymorphous with manganite, and belonging to the diaspore group
grout·man \'graůtmən, -,man\ *n, pl* **groutmen :** a worker who mixes grout and fills the joints between pavement blocks or bricks
grouty \'graůd·ē\ *adj* -ER/-EST [perh. fr. ¹*grout* + *-y*] **:** CROSS, SULKY, SULLEN ⟨those old warrior-priests were but gruff and ~ at the best —Herman Melville⟩ ⟨~, bad-tempered, and rude — Al Newman⟩
grouze \'graůz\ *vt* -ED/-ING/-S [perh. of imit. origin] *dial Eng* **:** to chew or crunch noisily
¹grove \'grōv\ *n* -s [ME, fr. OE *grāf*; akin to OE *grǣfa* grove, thicket, and perh. to Norw *greivla* to branch out] **1 a :** a smaller group of trees than a forest often without underwood and planted or growing naturally as if arranged by art **:** a wood of small extent ⟨a picnic ~⟩ **b** (1) **:** a planting of fruit or nut trees **:** ORCHARD ⟨a pecan ~⟩ ⟨a coffee ~⟩; *specif* **:** a planting of citrus trees ⟨an orange ~⟩ (2) **:** BED ⟨a ~ of kelp⟩ **2 :** a group resembling a grove ⟨had already set up a ~ of little shelter tents —John Buchan⟩
²grove \"\ *dial Eng var of* GRAVE
³grove \"\ *dial Brit var of* GROOVE
grov·el \'grävəl, 'grəv-\ *vi* **groveled** *or* **grovelled; groveled** *or* **grovelled; groveling** *or* **grovelling** \-v(ə)liŋ\ **grovels** [back-formation fr. ²*groveling*] **1 :** to creep on the earth or with the face to the ground as one's natural gait or manner of locomotion **:** CRAWL ⟨vampires can walk, rather than ~ like other bats —R.L.Ditmars & A.M.Greenhall⟩ **2 a :** to lie prone, go down on one's knees with the head bent, or drag oneself along with the body prostrate esp. in token of complete subservience or abasement or as an act of humiliation ⟨~*ed* across the floor to kiss the feet of the sultan —*Time*⟩ **b :** to abase or humble oneself **:** display servility **:** be abject **:** CRINGE ⟨he ~s and is polite to me —O.W.Holmes †1935⟩ ⟨~s in proud self-abasement —V.L.Parrington⟩ **3 :** to take delight in or give oneself over to what is base or unworthy **:** WALLOW ⟨here is the petty official ~*ing* in sentimentality — James Stern⟩ **syn** see WALLOW
grov·el·er *or* **grov·el·ler** \-v(ə)lə(r)\ *n* -s **:** a person who grovels
grove·less \'grōvləs\ *adj* **:** devoid of groves
¹grov·el·ing *or* **grov·el·ling** \'gräv(ə)liŋ, 'grəv-\ *or* **grov·el·ings** *or* **grov·el·lings** \-ŋz\ *adv* [ME *groveling, grufelinge, grovelings, gruflinges*, fr. *gruf, groffe*, adv., on the face, prone (fr. ON *á grúfu*) + *-ling, -lings*; akin to ON *grúfa* to grovel, *krjūpa* to creep — more at ON, CREEP] *archaic* **:** in prostrate position
²groveling *or* **grovelling** \"\ *adj* **1 a :** having the face or body on or toward the ground **:** not upright **:** PRONE ⟨the ~ creatures of the woods and fields⟩ **b :** having a creeping or crawling gait or locomotion ⟨the dominant creatures of the Cambrian seas were the . . . ~ arthropods —C.O.Dunbar⟩ **2 a :** ABJECT, SERVILE, CRINGING ⟨at once ~ and arrogant in the most peculiar fashion —Louis Bromfield⟩ ⟨without any ~ appeal for sympathy —Anthony West⟩ **b :** LOW, BASE ⟨who ever entertained so ~ a thought —Henry Fielding⟩
grov·el·ing·ly *or* **grov·el·ling·ly** *adv* **:** in a groveling manner
grovy \'grōvē\ *adj* -ER/-EST **:** relating to or resembling a grove **:** situated in or frequenting groves
grow \'grō\ *vb* **grew** \'grü\ *also dial* **growed** \'grōd\ **grown** \'grōn\ *also dial* **growed; growing; grows** [ME *growen*, fr. OE *grōwan*; akin to OHG *gruoen, gruowan* to grow, ON *grōa*] *vi* **1 a :** to spring up and come to maturity **:** have vegetal or animal life **:** exist as a living organism or one of its parts in a specified place **:** exist as native **:** THRIVE ⟨some plants will not ~ in sandy soils⟩ ⟨the mosquitoes . . . ~ in the swamps and marshy areas —Morris Fishbein⟩ ⟨unsightly hair ~s on his face⟩ ⟨immense beds of oysters ~ in the harbor —Joseph Mitchell⟩ ⟨rice ~s in warm countries⟩ **b :** to issue or become attached by or as if by a process of natural growth ⟨depicted with wings ~*ing* from his shoulders⟩ ⟨a plant ~*ing* out of a rock⟩ ⟨the vines *grew* together, concealing the naked stone⟩ **2 a :** to develop by natural processes: as (1) **:** to increase in size or substance by assimilation of new matter into the living organism ⟨the tree *grew* to an immense size⟩ ⟨the child stopped ~*ing* at an early age⟩ (2) **:** to increase in size by a natural inorganic process whereby material is added to the surface in such a way as to continue the established regular or periodic structure ⟨crystals, as well as plants, ~ —E.S.Dana⟩ **b :** to increase in any way **:** EXPAND, GAIN ⟨the wealth and power of the republic *grew*⟩ ⟨the city *grew* by leaps and bounds⟩ ⟨the saw making the woodpile ~ —Meridel Le Sueur⟩ ⟨~s in wisdom⟩; *specif* **:** to advance intellectually or morally ⟨at 90 he is still ~*ing* and helping others to ~ —H.A.Larrabee⟩ ⟨the subject should enable . . . the college student to ~ on several levels —Marion F. Stewart⟩ **3 a :** RESULT, ORIGINATE ⟨a lot of important business connections have *grown* from friendships between our wives and wives of executives of other companies —W.H.Whyte⟩ — usu. used with *out* ⟨a smile of polite incredulity which *grew* out of . . . ignorance —H.J.Laski⟩ **b :** to come into existence **:** become established **:** ARISE ⟨the original settlement . . . had *grown* on the Canberra site —H.W.H. King⟩ — often used with *up* ⟨a wicked practice had *grown* up⟩ ⟨a troublesome situation has *grown* up⟩ **4 a :** to pass by degrees into a state or condition **:** come to be **:** develop by degrees **:** BECOME ⟨*grew* pale at the sight⟩ ⟨have *grown* to like her⟩ ⟨*grew* bald⟩ ⟨the amount of land per person is ~*ing* constantly less —W.P.Webb⟩ ⟨his cold *grew* into pneumonia⟩ **b** *obs* **:** to come gradually or by degrees ⟨~ this to what adverse issue it can, I will put it in practice —Shak.⟩ **c** (1) **:** to obtain an increasing influence or command — used with *on* or *upon* ⟨a bad habit ~s on a man⟩ (2) *obs* **:** PRESUME (3) **:** to gain steadily in interest or attraction or in one's affection or estimation ⟨this seemingly artless music . . . ~s and ~s the more we listen —Roland Gelatt⟩ ⟨his poetry ~s in one's mind — Delmore Schwartz⟩ — usu. used with *on* or *upon* ⟨her looks were the kind that ~ on a man —Fred Majdalany⟩ **5** *of a ship's cable* **:** to stretch out **:** TEND, LEAD ~ *vt* **1 a :** to cause to grow **:** CULTIVATE, PRODUCE ⟨~ a crop⟩ ⟨~ wheat⟩ ⟨~ calves⟩ ⟨this cheese was *grown* . . . in Nottinghamshire — Joyce Warren⟩ ⟨Algeria ~s good wines —A.J.Liebling⟩ **b :** to let grow on the body **:** develop on the body ⟨decided to ~ a beard⟩ ⟨this prehistoric animal *grew* a thick protective covering⟩ **2 :** to cover or surround with vegetation of a specified kind ⟨all *grown* up to . . . bushes and grass — Dorothy C. Fisher⟩ ⟨*grown* up with cottonwood and birch — Corey Ford⟩ ⟨the house that was . . . *grown* about with weeds —Donn Byrne⟩ **3 :** DEVELOP 7 ⟨~s a craving to tell the world what he thinks of it —*Spectator*⟩ — **grow on trees :** to be so plentiful as to be easily acquired ⟨I was at Tours, where the girls *grew on trees* —K.S.Alling⟩ ⟨good jobs don't *grow on trees* —James Jones⟩
grow·able \'grōəbəl\ *adj* **:** capable of being grown
grow·er \-ō(ə)r, -ōə\ *n* -s **1 :** one that grows esp. in a specified way ⟨those trees are fast ~s⟩ **2 :** a person who grows a specified fruit or other product ⟨a trading center for apple ~s⟩ ⟨a supply point for livestock ~s⟩
growing *adj* **1 :** characterized by or displaying vegetal or animal life ⟨a broad window framed in ~ philodendron — *Monsanto Mag.*⟩ **2 :** increasing esp. in number, size, or degree ⟨~ evidence of a world depression —D.M.Fisher⟩ ⟨his ~ reputation for persuasive oratory⟩ ⟨made no attempt to cover the whole of a ~ subject —Harvey Graham⟩ **3 :** relating to or suitable for growth ⟨the ~ season for corn⟩ ⟨good ~ weather⟩ — **grow·ing·ly** *adv*

growing pains *n pl* **1 :** pains in the legs of children caused by fatigue, postural defects, emotional disturbances, or other factors having no demonstrable relation to growth **2 :** the stresses and strains attending the formative period (as of an industry) or any process of rapid or dynamic change or growth ⟨merely natural *growing pains* of a new economy —*Atlantic*⟩ ⟨the country's social and economic *growing pains* —J.H. Huizinga⟩ ⟨our fruit-canning industry . . . is still suffering from its *growing pains* —*Farmer's Weekly (So. Africa)*⟩

growing point *n* **1 :** the undifferentiated end of a plant shoot that is made up of a single apical cell or a group of cells and that produces primary meristematic tissue from which the tissues of the shoot differentiate **2 :** a point at which growth of any kind is generated or has its beginning ⟨the *growing points* of the economy must be invigorated —*Harper's*⟩ ⟨may be the *growing point* of philosophy in our time —C.W. Hendel⟩

growing zone *n* **1 :** a zone in front of the anus in certain annelid worms from which new segments are proliferated **2 :** a region behind the scolex in tapeworms similar in function to the growing zone in annelid worms

¹growl \ˈgrau̇l, *esp before pause or consonant* -au̇əl\ *vb* -ED/-ING/-S [prob. of imit. origin] *vi* **1 a :** RUMBLE ⟨it sounds like your guts are ~*ing* —Joseph Mitchell⟩ ⟨thunder faintly ~*ing* in the distance⟩ ⟨artillery ~*ed* and belched on the horizon —Earle Birney⟩ **b :** to utter a deep guttural threatening sound ⟨the dog ~*ed* at the stranger⟩ **c :** to make or move with a sound resembling or suggestive of the growl of an animal ⟨a truck . . . ~*ed* out onto the road —H.D.Skidmore⟩ ⟨listening to the water ~*ing* past —H.A.Calahan⟩ **2 :** to express oneself in an angry or surly manner : complain angrily : GRUMBLE ⟨hobnobbing together . . . and ~*ing* about the war —Zechariah Chafee⟩ ⟨~*ed* because the place . . . where they always parked, was taken —Greville Texidor⟩ ~ *vt* **:** to express with or by a growl : utter in a harsh, angry, or rasping tone or manner ⟨~*ing* out . . . lyrics in a hoarse contralto —J.S.Wilson b.1913⟩ ⟨~*ing* a deep and hollow roar —J.F.Dobie⟩ ⟨~*ed* out a stern warning⟩

²growl \"\ *n* -S **1 a :** a deep guttural inarticulate sound ⟨backed away as he heard the dog's warning ~⟩ ⟨broken now and then by . . . little bass ~*s* of laughter⟩ ⟨gave a ~ of amusement⟩ ⟨the full-throated ~ of an enraged lion⟩ **b :** a growling or rumbling sound resembling or suggestive of the growl of an animal ⟨the distant ~ of cannon⟩ ⟨the noisy, angry ~ of an aircraft engine —J.N.Bell⟩ **2 :** an utterance made in a harsh, rasping, or angry tone **:** a muttering complaint ⟨again the ~*s* began in the ranks —F.V.W.Mason⟩ ⟨~ that businessmen have replaced the clergy on governing boards —Perry Miller⟩ ⟨my letter of 31st December was a ~ against you —*Indian Information*⟩ **3 :** FLUTTER-TONGUING

growl·er \-au̇lə(r)\ *n* -S **1 :** one that growls ⟨the man was a notorious ~⟩ **2** *Brit* **:** CLARENCE **3 :** a container (as a can or pitcher) for beer bought by the measure **4 :** a small iceberg or mass of floe ice large enough to be a menace to ships **5 :** an electromagnetic device with two adjustable pole pieces used for finding short-circuited coils and for magnetizing and demagnetizing

growling *adj* **:** marked by a growl ⟨a low ~ voice⟩ ⟨listened to the ~ thunder⟩ — **growl·ing·ly** *adv*

growly \ˈgrau̇lē\ *adj* -ER/-EST **:** resembling a growl ⟨uttered a ~ sound⟩; *also* **:** IRRITABLE

grown \ˈgrōn\ *adj* **1 :** arrived at maturity **:** FULL-GROWN, MATURED, GROWN-UP ⟨children may do . . . that which would be ridiculous in a ~ maiden —Fred Whishaw⟩ ⟨a ~ man⟩ **2** *of grain* **:** having sprouted before reaping **3 :** roughly conforming to the required curvature in its natural shape — used of a shipbuilding timber of curved pattern **4 a :** cultivated or produced in a specified way or locality — used in combinations ⟨a home*grown* wine⟩ ⟨shade-*grown* tobacco⟩ **b :** overgrown with — used in combinations ⟨a cress-*grown* stream —*Amer. Guide Series: Ark.*⟩ ⟨the terrace . . . had been weed-*grown* for many years —Kathleen Freeman⟩

¹grown–up \ˈ=ˌ=\ *adj* [fr. past part. of *grow up*] **1 :** ADULT ⟨a *grown-up* woman —Hugh Walpole⟩ **2 :** of, for, or characteristic of adults ⟨the only *grown-up* way to keep peace in the world —Leverett Saltonstall⟩ ⟨began reading *grown-up* books at an early age⟩ ⟨insisted on wearing *grown-up* clothes⟩

²grown–up \"\ *n* -S **:** ADULT ⟨the attitude of *grown-ups* has changed —Pamela L. Travers⟩

grown–up·ness \(ˈ)=ˈ=nəs\ *n* -ES **:** the quality or state of being grown-up

grow out *vt* **:** to cause to grow toward or arrive at maturity ⟨*grow out* a steer⟩ — **grow out of :** OUTGROW ⟨the boy *grew out of* his clothes⟩ ⟨before Britain *grew out of* tyranny —P.L. Ritzema⟩

grows *pres 3d sing of* GROW

growth \ˈgrōth\ *n* -S [ME (Sc dial.) *grouth*, fr. ON *grōthr*, *grōthi*, fr. *grōa* to grow — more at GROW] **1 a** (1) **:** stage in the process of growing **:** SIZE ⟨the river reaches its greatest ~ a few miles above St. Louis⟩ ⟨the tree hasn't got its full ~⟩ **:** STATURE ⟨give added ~ and dimension to a book —Norman Cousins⟩ (2) **:** full growth ⟨by the looks of him he would be every inch of six feet when he attained his ~ —Archie Binns⟩ **b :** the process of growing: as (1) **:** an increase in the size of an organism or part esp. when involving increase in the amount of protoplasm — compare DEVELOPMENT, DIFFERENTIATION (2) **:** increase in size by a natural inorganic process whereby material is added to the surface in such a way as to continue the established regular or periodic structure ⟨~ or regrowth of mica under the influence of late solutions —*Economic Geology*⟩ (3) **:** a progressive development from lower or simpler to higher or more complex forms of organization **:** EVOLUTION ⟨the . . . history of the ~ of writing —A.N. Whitehead⟩ ⟨the ~ and decay of languages —G.R.Harrison⟩ (4) **:** progressive intellectual or moral advance or development **:** cultural or spiritual self-enrichment ⟨a lifetime of learning and continuous ~ is required of us —R.H.Wittcoff⟩ ⟨novels provide the basis for ~, experiences which can be rich and full —*Irish Digest*⟩ ⟨learning and ~ are always a result of what the individual brings to the learning situation —H.R.Douglass⟩ ⟨the theory that our native writers suffered from arrested ~ —C.I.Glicksberg⟩ (5) **:** RISE, EMERGENCE ⟨his lifetime encompassed the . . . ~ of the solidly Democratic South —*Current History*⟩ ⟨the first ~ and development of Macedonia . . . into the first of all known powers —George Grote⟩ (6) **:** qualitative or quantitative increase **:** EXPANSION ⟨the ~ of the oil industry⟩ ⟨the rapid ~ in luxury and sophistication —Carl Van Doren⟩ ⟨the ~ of urban population⟩ ⟨the ~ of illiteracy⟩ **2 a :** something that grows or has grown: as (1) **:** a stand of forest ⟨the road is bordered with close ~*s* of willow —*Amer. Guide Series: La.*⟩ ⟨a young ~ dedicated in 1926 —*Amer. Guide Series: Pa.*⟩ — see OLD GROWTH, SECOND GROWTH (2) **:** a cover of vegetation **:** VEGETATION ⟨a dense . . . ~ of European grasses which formed a thick sod —P.E.James⟩ ⟨the only other ~ here showing is a very little salt grass —G.R.Stewart⟩ (3) **:** PLANT ⟨this weed is a very noxious ~⟩ (4) **:** a lateral shoot or branch on the main stem of a plant **b :** abnormal proliferation of tissue (as a tumor) **c :** OUTGROWTH, OFFSHOOT ⟨a lovely phrase . . . which is really a ~ from the main tune —Herbert Wiseman⟩ **d :** the result of growth **:** PRODUCT, EFFECT, DEVELOPMENT ⟨Protestantism was a relatively recent ~⟩ ⟨this was the ~ of habit —Ellen Glasgow⟩ ⟨Virginia City and other Nevada towns were mushroom ~*s* from silver ore —*Dict. of Amer. History*⟩ **3 :** PRODUCTION, CULTIVATION, ORIGIN ⟨goods of foreign ~⟩ ⟨all his fruit and vegetables were of his own ~⟩

growth curve *n* **:** a graphic representation of the relative growth of an organism or population during a sequence of similar-length periods

growth factor *n* **:** a substance (as a vitamin, hormone, antibiotic, or metallic ion) exclusive of those used as sources of energy that when present in minute amounts promotes the growth of an organism — compare GROWTH REGULATOR

growth form *n* **1 a :** a structural category consisting of individuals or species of the same general habit of growth but not necessarily related **b :** a category of plants in Raunkiaer's system based on the degree of protection of their winter buds **2 :** the form assumed by an organism (as a plant) in immediate response to the interaction of a particular environment on its genetic potentialities

growth hormone *n* **:** a hormone that regulates growth

growth·less \ˈgrōthləs\ *adj* **:** having no growth

growth regulator *or* **growth substance** *n* **:** a substance that affects growth; *esp* **:** a synthetic substance (as naphthaleneacetic acid or dichlorophenoxyacetic acid) that resembles a naturally occurring hormone in producing a specific effect — compare AUXIN, GROWTH FACTOR

growth ring *n* **:** a layer of wood developed during any one continuous growth period; *usu* **:** ANNUAL RING

growth·some \-thsəm\ *adj* **:** conducive to growth **:** FERTILE ⟨life is greener, more ~ here —Frederic Morton⟩

growth stock *n* **:** investment shares of a company having a steady growth in business and profits over a long period of years

growthy \-thē\ *adj* -ER/-EST **1 :** favorable to growth ⟨the weather is unusually ~ —*Auckland (New Zealand) Weekly News*⟩ **2 :** capable of growth esp. to large size ⟨these bulls are ~ and rugged —*Pacific Stockman*⟩

grow up *vi* **:** to grow toward or arrive at full stature or physical or mental maturity ⟨just before she *grows up*, her mother tells her all about the . . . changes that are coming to her —Valeria H. Parker⟩ ⟨middle-aged children who had refused to *grow up* —Cyril Connolly⟩ ⟨*grew up* . . . in Brooklyn, getting good grades in school —Barbara B. Jamison⟩

growze \ˈgrau̇z\ *var of* GROUZE

groyne *var of* GROIN

gro·zart \ˈgrōzə(r)t\ *var of* GROSET

gro·zer *var of* GROSER

gro·zing iron \ˈgrōziŋ-\ *n* [part trans. of D *gruisijzer*, fr. *gruizen* (dial. *groezen*) to crush, trim glass (fr. *gruis* gravel, fragments, fr. MD *gruus*) + *yzer* iron; akin to MLG *grūs*, *grōs* crushed stone, gravel, OE *grēot* grit — more at GRIT (sand)] *archaic* **:** a steel tool for cutting glass

groz·ny \ˈgrōznē\ *adj, usu cap* [fr. *Grozny*, U.S.S.R.] **:** of or from the city of Grozny, U.S.S.R. **:** of the kind or style prevalent in Grozny

GR-S \ˌjēˌärˈes\ *also* **GR-S rubber** *n* [government rubber + styrene] **:** any of a class of general-purpose synthetic rubbers that are made by copolymerizing emulsions of butadiene and styrene commonly at a temperature of either 122°F or 41°F and that are used esp. in tires — see COLD RUBBER

gru *var of* ³GRUE

¹grub \ˈgrəb\ *vb* **grubbed; grubbed; grubbing; grubs** [ME *grobben*, *grubben*; akin to MD *grobben* to scramble, scrape, OHG *grubilōn* to dig, search, ON *gryfja* hole, pit, ditch, OE *grafan* to dig, grave — more at GRAVE (dig)] *vt* **1 :** to remove roots or stumps from **:** clear or break up the surface of by digging ⟨loggers cut off the virgin timber and farmers *grubbed* out their clearings —R.A.Billington⟩ ⟨women and children helped to ~ the land —E.H.Collis⟩ **2 a :** to dig up by the roots **:** root out by digging ⟨a palmetto was *grubbed* from the site —*Amer. Guide Series: Fla.*⟩ ⟨*grubbing* up bulbs and edible roots —E.J.Sawyer⟩ ⟨*grubbing* out stumps might be a long and costly business —*Amer. Guide Series: Minn.*⟩ **b :** to extract esp. by digging ⟨followed by sappers who *grubbed* up the mines —J.F.C.Fuller⟩ ⟨*grubbed* the mote as well as I could by the deficient light —Joseph Furphy⟩ **c :** to bring to light, assemble, or acquire by plodding, painful, or tedious effort ⟨barely *grubbing* a subsistence —Daniel Friedenberg⟩ ⟨the task of *grubbing* out new data —J.D.Hicks⟩ ⟨seems to have *grubbed* his materials together —A.S.Stein⟩ **3 :** to provide with food **:** FEED ⟨five children to ~⟩ ~ *vi* **1 a :** to dig in or under the ground esp. for an object that is difficult to reach or extricate ⟨*grubbing* in the earth for potatoes⟩ ⟨*grubbed* for clams on the mud flats⟩ ⟨scholars will ~ in the ruins for . . . records and fragments —W.P.Webb⟩ **b :** to search about esp. laboriously as if by digging **:** RUMMAGE ⟨*grubbed* hopelessly about the cupboard shelves —Arthur Morrison⟩ ⟨love to ~ through junk shops —Leo Lerman⟩ ⟨*grubbed* in the country-side for food and fuel —*Lamp*⟩ ⟨to ~ for origins is none of my business —Clive Bell⟩ **2 :** to lead a laborious or a drearily plodding life **:** TOIL, DRUDGE ⟨*grubbing* along from day to day⟩ ⟨have to begin *grubbing* all over again —Ellen Glasgow⟩ ⟨folks who ~ for money —James Street⟩ **3 :** to take food **:** EAT ⟨time to ~⟩ **syn** see DIG

²grub \"\ *n* -S [ME *grobbe*, *grubbe*, fr. *grobben*, *grubben*, v.] **1 :** a soft thick wormlike larva of an insect (as a beetle) **2 a :** a dull unattractive person **:** DRUDGE **b :** a person of grubby or slovenly appearance or of unpleasant or ill-bred manners **3 :** FOOD, VICTUALS ⟨time for ~⟩ ⟨a pot of coffee on the fire and warm ~ —F.B.Gipson⟩ **4 :** a root or stump in the ground

grub ax *n* **:** a mattock used in grubbing

grub·ber \ˈgrəbə(r)\ *n* -S [ME, fr. *grubben* to grub + *-er*] **1 :** one that grubs: as **a :** one that digs in the ground ⟨controlling her spinning maids and the ~*s* in the walled garden —Sinclair Lewis⟩ **b :** a laborious or plodding worker **:** DRUDGE ⟨the private browsing grounds of historical ~*s*⟩ **c :** MONEY-GRUBBER ⟨the ~*s* . . . almost unceasingly preoccupied with money —*New Republic*⟩ **d** (1) **:** a hand tool (as a grub ax) for use in grubbing (2) *Brit* **:** a cultivator that breaks up the surface of land by digging **:** ²CHISEL 2 **e** (1) **:** a person who grubs up trees, stumps, or brush (2) **:** an implement (as a grub hook) for grubbing up trees, stumps, or brush **2 :** BONEFISH 1

grub·bi·ly \-bəlē, -li\ *adv* **:** in a grubby manner ⟨~ dirty and poorly dressed —Cabell Phillips⟩

grub·bi·ness \-bēnəs, -bin-\ *n* -ES **:** the state of being grubby: **a :** the condition of being dirty, grimy, or slovenly **:** grubby look ⟨her occasional appearances in bare feet and her general look of ~ —*Life*⟩ **b :** SORDIDNESS, MEANNESS ⟨the ~ of being poor —Willa Cather⟩

grub·ble \ˈgrəbəl\ *vb* -ED/-ING/-S [prob. alter. (influenced by ¹*grub*) of *grabble*] *archaic* **:** GROPE

grub·by \ˈgrəbē, -bi\ *adj* -ER/-EST [²*grub* + *-y*] **1** *chiefly dial* **:** small and incompletely formed **b :** DWARFISH, STUNTED **2 :** infested with fly maggots **3 :** dirty, shabby, or slovenly in condition or appearance **:** GRIMY, MEAN ⟨their ~ little fingers —Roderick Finlayson⟩ ⟨colorless face, hair in curlers, clothes as ~ as the fog —Edith C. Rivett⟩ ⟨streets that looked as parched and ~ as I was —Thomas Wood †1950⟩ ⟨felt particularly ~ and unshaven —Robert Keable⟩ **4 :** low, sordid, or ignoble in character **:** BASE, CONTEMPTIBLE ⟨the pamphleteer's ~ motives —Albert Lynd⟩ ⟨a ~ lot of tax collectors, mortgage makers, moneylenders —J.R.Newman⟩ ⟨a ~ man of pleasure —C.J.Rolo⟩

grub hoe *or* **grubbing hoe** *n* **1 :** a heavy hoe for grubbing **2 :** GRUB AX

grub hook *n* **:** an implement resembling a plow for uprooting stumps

grub·less \-bləs\ *adj* **:** lacking food

grubroot \ˈ=ˌ=\ *n* **:** a blazing star (*Chamaelirium luteum*) with small white star-shaped flowers in a narrow raceme

grubs *pres 3d sing of* GRUB, *pl of* GRUB

grub screw *n* **:** a small headless screw that is slotted at one end to receive a screwdriver and when placed in a continuous threaded hole between two adjacent pieces prevents lateral movement

¹grubstake \ˈ=ˌ=\ *n* [²*grub* (*food*) + *stake*; fr. the lender's staking or risking the provisions so furnished] **1 :** supplies or funds furnished to a mining prospector on promise of a share in his discoveries **2 :** material assistance (as a gift, loan, advance) provided for a person in difficult circumstances or for the launching of an enterprise or project ⟨the ex-governor promised a . . . ~ for the unemployed —*Current Biog.*⟩ ⟨needed a ~ or he wouldn't have taken the job —Ross Santee⟩ ⟨meant to leave Cincinnati as soon as he could get a ~ —Arthur Krock⟩

²grubstake \"\ *vt* **:** to provide with a grubstake ⟨it is the public which pays . . . for the handsome profit to those who have *grubstaked* the candidates —P.H.Douglas⟩

grub·stak·er \-ə(r)\ *n* **1 :** one that gives a grubstake **2 :** one that receives a grubstake

grub street \ˈgrəb-\ *n, usu cap G&S, often attrib* [after *Grub Street* (now Milton Street), London, formerly inhabited by literary hacks] **:** the world or category of usu. mediocre, needy, and disdained writers who write for hire **:** the world of literary hacks ⟨*Grub Street* compilers —H.R.Warfel⟩ ⟨the translator . . . knows he'll always live on *Grub Street* —Richard Winston⟩ ⟨has done much to better the lot of *Grub Street* scribes —Thurston Macauley⟩

grubworm \ˈ=ˌ=\ *n* **:** GRUB

¹grudge \ˈgrəj\ *vb* -ED/-ING/-S [ME *gruggen*, *grudgen*, alter. of *grucchen*, *grutchen*, fr. OF *grucier*, *groucier*, of Gmc origin; akin to MHG *grogezen* to howl, lament] *vi* **:** COMPLAIN, GRUMBLE ⟨let us have parties and our friends in, and never *grudged* —Rose Macaulay⟩ ~ *vt* **:** to be unwilling to give or allow or to give or allow with reluctance or with resentment **:** BEGRUDGE ⟨~*s* you every morsel of food you eat —William Thornton⟩ ⟨surely you do not ~ him his superiority —G.B. Shaw⟩ ⟨you come to ~ even the sun for shining —Virginia Woolf⟩

²grudge \"\ *n* -S *often attrib* [ME *grugge*, fr. *gruggen*, v.] **:** a feeling of deep-seated resentment or ill will ⟨personal enemies against whom one has a ~ —R.F.Barton⟩ ⟨held no ~ against any . . . who had misused him —Willa Cather⟩ ⟨a ~ fence⟩ ⟨as we had never liked each other our collision would have elements of a ~ match —A.W.Turnbull⟩ ⟨fiction's ~ fights and revenges —Bernard De Voto⟩ **syn** see MALICE

grudge·ful \-fəl\ *adj* **:** harboring a grudge **:** full of resentment

grudge·less \-ləs\ *adj* **:** free of grudges or resentment

grudging *adj* **1 :** that grudges **:** UNWILLING, RELUCTANT **:** ILLIBERAL, UNGENEROUS ⟨conceived in a surly and ~ spirit —A.L.Guérard⟩ ⟨merit a larger recognition than has been accorded by a ~ posterity —V.L.Parrington⟩ **2 :** that is grudged **:** given, accorded, or permitted reluctantly, unwillingly, or stintingly **:** PARSIMONIOUS ⟨the basic biological sciences are given ~ governmental support —L.E.Hoyme⟩ ⟨his slow and ~ return to favor of a sort —*Encounter*⟩ ⟨lived on a ~ allowance from her father-in-law —G.F.Whicher⟩ — **grudg·ing·ly** *adv*

grudg·ing·ness *n* -ES **:** the quality or state of being grudging

¹grue \ˈgrü\ *vi* -ED/-ING/-S [fr. earlier *grow*, fr. ME *gruen*, *growen*, prob. fr. MD *grūwen*; akin to OHG *ingrūēn* to shiver, shudder, and prob. to OE *grēot* sand — more at GRIT] *now chiefly dial* **:** to shiver or shudder esp. with fear or cold ⟨exposed to the gruesome so extensively . . . we simply don't ~ any more —John Crosby⟩

²grue \"\ *n* -S **1 :** a fit of shivering **:** SHIVER ⟨the sound of wind in the rigging . . . gave him the chills and the ~*s* —R.B. Robertson⟩ ⟨impossible to read without a certain cold ~ —S.V.Benét⟩ **2 :** gruesome quality or effect ⟨a mystery novel . . . resolved with true ~ —Anthony Boucher⟩ ⟨serves the chilliest ~ with perfect elegance —J.S.Sandoe⟩

³grue \"\ *n* -S [ME] *now chiefly Scot* **:** PARTICLE, BIT ⟨hasn't a ~ of sense⟩

⁴grue \"\ *n* -S [origin unknown] *chiefly Scot* **:** thin floating ice **:** SNOW

gru·el \ˈgrü|əl, -ü|əl *also* -ü|l, *chiefly Brit* |(ˌ)il\ *n* -S [ME *grewel*, fr. MF *gruel*, fr. OF, of Gmc origin; akin to OE *grūt* grout — more at GROUT] **1 :** a liquid food made by boiling a cereal (as cornmeal, oatmeal, flour) in water or milk **:** thin porridge **2** *chiefly Brit* **:** PUNISHMENT, MEDICINE; *sometimes* **:** DEATH ⟨the Labor rank and file took their ~ wonderfully well —*Spectator*⟩

¹gru·el·ing *or* **gru·el·ling** *pronunc at* GRUEL + iŋ *or* ēŋ\ *n* -S [fr. gerund of obs. E *gruel* to punish, fr. *gruel*, n.] *Brit* **:** a severe beating or punishment **:** LICKING ⟨improved pastures . . . took a ~ from an adverse season —*Sydney (Australia) Bull.*⟩

²grueling *or* **gruelling** \"\ *adj* [fr. pres. part. of obs. E *gruel*, v.] **:** trying or taxing to the point of exhaustion **:** making severe demands **:** PUNISHING ⟨a ~ race⟩ ⟨delivering them to the . . . laboratories for ~ tests —*Monsanto Mag.*⟩ ⟨the labor that goes into building these terraces . . . is ~ —M.J.Herskovits⟩

gru·el·ly *pronunc at* GRUEL + ē *or* i\ *adj* **:** having the consistency of gruel **:** like gruel

gruen·ling·ite \ˈgrünliŋˌīt, -rēn-\ *n* -S [G *grünlingit*, fr. Friedrich *Grünling* †1919 Ger. mineralogist + G *-it* -ite] **:** a mineral Bi_4TeS_3 consisting of sulfide and telluride of bismuth

gru·es \ˈgrü(ˌ)ēz\ *n pl, cap* [NL, pl. of *Grus*] **:** a suborder of Gruiformes consisting of the cranes, limpkins, trumpeters, rails, and a few chiefly extinct related forms

grue·some *also* **grew·some** \ˈgrüsəm\ *adj, sometimes* -ER/-EST [*gruesome* alter. (influenced by ¹*grue*) of earlier *grewsome*, *growsome*; *grewsome* alter. of obs. E *growsome*, fr. *grow* (later, *grue*) + E *-some*] **:** inspiring horror or repulsion **:** FEARFUL, GRISLY, HIDEOUS ⟨~ scenes of battle and death —E.J.Fitzgerald⟩ ⟨a ~ little laugh⟩ ⟨the ~ details of a murder⟩

grue·some·ly *adv* **:** in a gruesome manner

grue·some·ness *n* -ES **:** the quality or state of being gruesome

¹gruff \ˈgrəf\ *adj* -ER/-EST [fr. earlier *grof*, *groiff*, fr. D *grof*, fr. MD; akin to OHG *grob*, *gerob* thick, coarse, *hruf* pock, scurf — more at DANDRUFF] **1** *now chiefly Scot* **:** having a coarse texture **:** COARSE-GRAINED **2 :** rough or stern in manner, speech, or aspect **:** SEVERE, HARSH, UNGRACIOUS ⟨a ~ burly man⟩ ⟨~ of manner and slow of speech —Ross Annett⟩ ⟨gave a ~, uneasy laugh —W.H.Wright⟩ ⟨covered his . . . friendly nature with a ~ exterior —Bruce Bliven b. 1889⟩ **3 :** deep and harsh **:** low-pitched and rough or hoarse ⟨spoke in a series of ~ barks —Dorothy Sayers⟩ ⟨heard the ~ voice of her father raised in anger —Christopher Bloom⟩ **syn** see BLUFF

²gruff \"\ *vt* -ED/-ING/-S **:** to utter in a gruff voice or manner ⟨"hurry it up," he ~*ed* at the hose tender —Wirt Williams⟩ ⟨~*ed*: "This is the first time I've ever been called a handmaiden" —*Time*⟩

gruff·ly *adv* **:** in a gruff manner

gruff·ness *n* -ES **:** the quality or state of being gruff

gruffs \ˈgrəfs\ *n pl* [pl. of obs. E *gruff*, fr. ¹*gruff*] **:** the tough parts not easily reducible to powder that remain in the process of powdering drugs — called also *tailings*

gru·gru \ˈgrü(ˌ)grü\ *n* -S [AmerSp (Puerto Rico) *grugrú*, of Cariban origin; akin to Yao *grugru*, lit., basket made of grugru] **1** *also* **grugru palm** *or* **gri-gri** \ˈgrē(ˌ)grē\ **:** any of several tropical American spiny palms (as the West Indian *Acrocomia aculeata* and the Brazilian *A. sclerocarpa*) **2** *or* **grugru grub** *also* **grugru worm :** a large edible grub that is the larva of certain tropical American weevils (genus *Rhynchophorus*) and that develops in and feeds on the pith of coconut and other palm trees and sometimes sugarcane

gru·idae \ˈgrüəˌdē\ *n pl, cap* [NL, fr. *Grus*, type genus + *-idae*] **:** a family (order Gruiformes) of long-legged wading birds comprising the cranes

gru·iform \-əˌfȯrm\ *adj* [in sense 1, fr. L *grus* crane + E *-iform*; in sense 2, fr. NL *Gruiformes* — more at GRUS] **1 :** resembling a crane **2 :** of or relating to the Gruiformes

gru·ifor·mes \ˌ==ˈfȯrˌmēz\ *n pl, cap* [NL, fr. *Grus* + *-iformes*] **:** a nearly cosmopolitan order of birds that are typically marsh-dwelling and wading birds with long legs, neck, and bill and rather heavy flight and that include the cranes, rails and coots, bustards, and a number of related tropical birds — see CARIAMA

gru·ine \ˈgrüˌīn, -üən\ *adj* [L *grus* crane + E *-ine*] **:** belonging to or resembling the cranes

gruing *pres part of* GRUE

gru·lla \ˈgrüyə\ *also* **gru·llo** \-ü(ˌ)yō\ *n* -S [MexSp, fr. Sp *grulla* crane, prob. alter. of OSp *gruya*, *grúa*, fr. L *grus*; fr. its crane color] *Southwest* **:** a mouse-dun horse

grum \ˈgrəm\ *adj* **grummer; grummest** [prob. blend of *grim* and *glum*] **:** MOROSE, GLUM, SOUR, SURLY ⟨a very ~ countenance —Mary S. Watts⟩ — **grum·ly** *adv* — **grum·ness** *n* -ES

¹grum·ble \ˈgrəmbəl\ *vb* **grumbled; grumbled; grumbling** \-b(ə)liŋ\ **grumbles** [prob. modif. of MF *grommeler*, fr. OF *grumeler*, fr. *gromer*, fr. MD *grommen*; akin to MLG *grummen* to grumble, OHG umbe*grummōn* to gnaw, *grimm* savage — more at GRIM] *vi* **1 :** to mutter in discontent **:** express dissatisfaction esp. in a low harsh voice and surly manner **:** COMPLAIN ⟨*grumbling* about no jobs, and no grub —Richard Llewellyn⟩ ⟨*grumbled* at her, continually muttering complaints —Kenneth Roberts⟩ **2 a :** to make low indistinct noises **:** GROWL **b :** to make a low heavy rumbling sound ⟨thunder *grumbled* in the distance⟩ ⟨heavy traffic *grumbling* along⟩ ⟨the anchor chain . . . began to ~ aboard —Victor Canning⟩ ~ *vt* **:** to express or utter with grumbling ⟨consumers *grumbled* their endless . . . complaints —B.F.Fairless⟩ ⟨*grumbled* his annoyance⟩ **syn** see COMPLAIN

²grumble \"\ *n* -S **1 a :** the act of expressing discontent esp. by muttering **:** COMPLAINT ⟨a final ~ . . . that the best part of this book has long been available at a much cheaper rate —*Times Lit. Supp.*⟩ **b** : a cause or reason for grumbling ⟨the high cost of living was his daily ~⟩ **2** : GROWL, RUMBLE ⟨creak and ~ of heavy trucks —Virginia A. Oakes⟩

grum·bler \-b(ə)lə(r)\ *n* -s : one that grumbles

grumbling *n* -s [fr. gerund of ¹*grumble*] **1** : a mutter of discontent : COMPLAINT ⟨the subject of general ~ —*Collier's Yr. Bk.*⟩ **2** : a growling or rumbling noise ⟨these whooshings and ~s . . . were apt to punctuate any time of the day —J.M. Brinnin⟩

grum·bling·ly *adv* [fr. pres. part. of ¹*grumble* + *-ly*] : in a grumbling manner

grume \'grüm\ *n* -s [F *grume, grumeau,* fr. MF *grumeau,* fr. OF, fr. L *grumus* hillock, pile of dirt — more at CRUMB] : a thick viscid fluid; *esp* : a clot of blood

gru·mi·cha·ma *also* **gru·mi·xa·ma** \,grüma'shäma\ *n* -s [modif. of Pg *grumixama, grumuchama*] : a Brazilian plant of the genus *Eugenia*; *esp* : a low-growing tree (*E. dombeyi* or *E. brasiliensis*) with glossy leaves and white flowers that is sometimes cultivated in mild climates for its dark red thin-skinned fruit which resembles the sweet cherry in appearance and flavor

grum·ly \'grəmlē\ *adj* -ER/-EST [prob. fr. obs. E *grummel* sediment, dregs (prob. of Scand origin) + E *-y*; akin to Sw *grummel* sediment, dregs] *now chiefly Scot* : turbid and troubled ⟨cold and watery grew the wind and ~ grew the sea —*Sir Patrick Spens*⟩

¹**grum·met** \'grəmət\ *n* -s [MF *gromet* cabin boy, servant — more at GOURMAND] **1** *also* **grom·et** \", 'gräm-\ : a cabin boy on a ship **2** *now dial Brit* : an awkward lad

²**grummet** *var of* GROMMET

gru·mose \'grü,mōs\ *adj* [*grumous* + *-ose*] : formed of clustered grains or granules

gru·mous \-məs\ *adj* [*grume* + *-ous*] **1** : resembling or containing grume : THICK, CLOTTED ⟨~ blood⟩ **2** : GRUMOSE

¹**grump** \'grəmp\ *n* -s [fr. obs. E *grumps* snubs, prob. of imit. origin] **1 grumps** *pl* : a fit of ill humor or sulkiness ⟨get out of one's seclusive ~s —H.A.Overstreet⟩ **2** : a person given to complaining : a sulky, ill-humored, or querulous person ⟨she's such a ~ lately —Mary Manning⟩

²**grump** \"\ *vb* -ED/-ING/-S *vi* **1** : SULK ⟨just ~*ed* around the house —Robie Macauley⟩ **2** : GRUMBLE, COMPLAIN ⟨~*ed* about the weather⟩ ⟨swore and stamped and ~*ed* —G.W. Brace⟩ ~ *vt* : to utter in a grumpy manner

¹**grumph** \'grəm(p)f\ *n* -s [imit.] *chiefly Scot* : GRUNT

²**grumph** \"\ *vb* -ED/-ING/-S *chiefly Scot* : GRUMP

grumph·ie \-m(p)fi, -mpi\ *n* -s [¹*grumph* + *-ie*] *chiefly Scot* : PIG; *specif* : SOW

grump·i·ly \'grəmpəlē, -li\ *adv* : in a grumpy manner

grump·i·ness \-pēnəs, -pin-\ *n* -ES : the quality or state of being grumpy

grump·ish \'grəmpish, -pēsh\ *adj* [¹*grump* + *-ish*] : GRUMPY

¹**grumpy** \'grəmpē, -pi\ *adj* -ER/-EST [¹*grump* + *-y*] : moodily cross : SURLY, ILL-HUMORED ⟨don't be surprised if the driver is ~ and rude —T.H.Fielding⟩

²**grumpy** \"\ *n* -ES : a grumpy person

¹**grun** \'grün, 'grən\ *vb* **grun**; **grun**; **grunning**; **gruns** [by alter.] *dial Brit* : ¹GRIND

²**grun** \"\ *dial Brit var of* GROUND

grund·riss \'grünt,ris\ *n, pl* **grundris·se** \-sə\ *usu cap* [G, fr. *grund* basis, foundation (fr. OHG *grunt* ground, bottom) + *riss* drawing, fr. OHG *riz* letter of the alphabet; akin to OHG *rīzan* to tear, write — more at GROUND, WRITE] : a comprehensive and systematic outline esp. of a science ⟨a severely technical *grundriss* of the many interrelated fields —L.M. Hollander⟩

¹**grundt·vig·ian** \(')grünt¦vigēən\ *adj, usu cap* [Nikolai F.S. *Grundtvig* †1872 Dan. theologian and poet + E *-ian*] : of or relating to Grundtvigians or Grundtvigianism

²**grundtvigian** \"\ *n* -s *usu cap* : an adherent or advocate of Grundtvigianism

grundt·vig·ian·ism \ˌ==ˌnizəm\ *n, usu cap* : a religious movement among Danish Lutherans that arose out of the activities of Nikolai Grundtvig in behalf of the principles of greater religious freedom for both laity and clergy and of the authority of the living Christ as opposed to formal creeds

grun·dy \'grəndē, -di\ *n* -ES *usu cap* [by shortening] : MRS. GRUNDY ⟨prudes in gumshoes and *Grundies* with head colds —D.C.Peattie⟩

grun·dy·ism \-dē,izəm, -di,iz-\ *n* -s *usu cap* : a narrow prudish intolerant conventionality esp. as to the proprieties

grun·dy–swal·low \'grəndē,==, -di-\ *n* [by folk etymology] : ¹GROUNDSEL

grü·ner·ite *or* **gru·ner·ite** \'grünə,rīt\ *n* -s [G *grünerit,* fr. E.L.*Grüner* 19th cent. German, who analyzed it + G *-it* -ite] : a variety of amphibole $Fe_7Si_8D_{22}(OH)_2$

gru·nion \'grənyən\ *n* -s [prob. fr. Sp *gruñón* grunter, fr. *gruñir* to grunt, fr. L *grunnire*] : a silversides (*Leuresthes tenuis*) of the California coast notable for the regularity with which it comes inshore to spawn at the time of a nearly full moon

grun·stane \'grənz,tān, -n,st-\ *chiefly Scot var of* GRINDSTONE

¹**grunt** \'grənt\ *vb* -ED/-ING/-S [ME *grunten, gronten,* fr. OE *grunnettan,* freq. of *grunian, grunnian*; of imit. origin like OHG *grunnizōn* to grunt, *grunzen* to grunt, ON *krytja* to murmur, L *grunnire* (OL *grundire*) to grunt, Gk *gry* grunt, *gryzein* to grunt, grumble] *vi* **1 a** : to make the natural throat noise of a hog **b** : to make a similar sound ⟨ferries ~*ing* . . . on the river —Robert Henderson⟩ ⟨only ~*ed* in answer —Kenneth Roberts⟩ **2** *dial* : to groan and complain : GRUMBLE ~ *vt* **1** : to express with a grunt ⟨~*ed* what might have been assent —S.E.White⟩ ⟨~*ed* his approval —Hugh Walpole⟩ **2** : to utter in a short, sharp, or surly manner ⟨~*ed* a few ungracious words in reply⟩

²**grunt** \"\ *n* -s **1 a** : the deep short sound characteristic of a hog **b** : a similar sound ⟨a ~ of satisfaction —Sherwood Anderson⟩ ⟨gave an offended ~ —Carolyn Hannay⟩ **2** [so called fr. the noise it makes when taken from the water] : any of numerous chiefly tropical marine percoid fishes of the family Pomadasidae related to the snappers — see FRENCH GRUNT, GRAY GRUNT, WHITE GRUNT, YELLOW GRUNT **3** [so called fr. the noise it makes when steaming] *chiefly New Eng* : a dessert made by dropping biscuit dough on top of boiling berries and covering and steaming ⟨blackberry ~⟩ **4** [prob. so called fr. the noise the helper emits under the load] : a groundman who assists in the erection of power lines

grunt·er \-tə(r)\ *n* -s [ME *gruntare,* fr. *grunten* + *-are,* -er -er] **1** : one that grunts; *specif* : HOG **2** : any of various fishes which make a grunting noise: as **a** : GRUNT **b** : DRUM; *esp* : FRESHWATER DRUM **c** : either of two sea breams of southern Africa **3** : a horse subject to grunting

¹**grunting** *n* -s [ME, fr. gerund of *grunten*] **1** : the act or an instance of grunting ⟨groanings and ~s on all sides⟩ ⟨a lot of ~ from the guys on crutches —R.O.Bowen⟩ **2** : abnormal respiration in a horse marked by a laryngeal sound emitted when it is struck or moved suddenly — compare ROARING

²**grunting** *adj* [fr. pres. part. of ¹*grunt*] : sounding like a grunt : resembling a grunt ⟨the breathing is shallow and ~ —Morris Fishbein⟩ ⟨a ~ mirthless laugh —Barnaby Conrad⟩ — **grunt·ing·ly** *adv*

¹**grun·tle** \'grənt³l, *dial Brit* " *or* 'grün-\ *vb* -ED/-ING/-S [ME *gruntlen,* freq. of *grunten* to grunt — more at GRUNT] *vi, now dial Brit* : GRUNT, GRUMBLE ~ *vt* [back-formation fr. *disgruntle*] : to put in good humor : SATISFY, SOOTHE, PLACATE ⟨were *gruntled* with a good meal and good conversation —W.P.Webb⟩ ⟨the warden was far from *gruntled* to find that the villagers had . . . pinched all the timber —Emrys Hughes⟩ ⟨was *gruntling* the cats —Christopher Morley⟩ — compare DISGRUNTLE

²**grun·tle** \'grənt³l\ *n* -s **1** *chiefly Scot* : the snout of a pig **2** *chiefly Scot* : FACE

grunt·ling \'grəntliŋ\ *n* -s [¹*grunt* + *-ling*] : a young pig

grup·pet·to \grü'ped·(,)ō\ *n, pl* **gruppet·ti** \-)ē\ [It, lit., small group, dim. of *gruppo*] : a 16th century musical ornamentation having the character of a trill

grup·po \'grü(,)pō\ *n, pl* **grup·pi** \-pē\ [It, group — more at GROUP] : GRUPPETTO

grus \'grüs, 'grəs\ *n, cap* [NL, fr. L, crane; akin to Lith *gervė* crane — more at CRANE] : the type genus of Gruidae consisting of the typical cranes

grush·ie \'grəshi\ *adj* [alter. of ¹*gross* + *-ie*] *Scot* : THRIVING

gruss \'grüs\ *n* -ES [G *grus,* fr. LG, fr. MLG *grūs, grōs*; akin to OE *grēot* grit — more at GRIT] : a rock that is finely granulated but not decomposed by weathering

¹**grutch** \'grəch, -ü-\ *vb* -ED/-ING/-ES [ME *grucchen, grutchen* — more at GRUDGE] *now chiefly dial* : MURMUR, COMPLAIN

²**grutch** \"\ *n* -ES [ME *gruch, grucche,* fr. *grucchen,* v.] *now dial* : GRUDGE

grutten *past part of* GREET

gru·yère cheese \(')grü¦ye(ə)r-, (')grē¦(y)|, |eə-\ *also* **gru·yère** *n* -s *usu cap G* [fr. *Gruyère* district, Fribourg canton, Switzerland, where it was orig. made] **1** : a pressed whole-milk cheese of a pale yellow color and nutty flavor and usu. with small holes **2** : a process cheese made in small forms and wrapped in foil

gryl·lid \'griləd\ *n* -s [NL *Gryllidae*] : a member of the Gryllidae : CRICKET

gryl·li·dae \-lə,dē\ *n pl, cap* [NL, fr. *Gryllus,* type genus + *-idae*] : a family of insects (order Orthoptera) consisting of the crickets

gryl·lo·blat·to·dea \,grilō(,)bla'tōdēə\ *n pl, cap* [NL, fr. *Grylloblatta,* a genus of insects (fr. *gryllo-* — fr. L *gryllus* cricket — + L *blatta* cockroach) + *-odea*] : a small extremely primitive suborder of Orthoptera often considered a separate order and comprising a few soft-bodied unpigmented wingless insects with long cerci and antennae and commonly no eyes or ocelli that occur near snow in mountains of western No. America and Japan and constitute a single family

gryl·lo·tal·pa \-lə'talpə\ *n, cap* [NL, fr. *gryllo-* (fr. L *gryllus* cricket) + L *talpa* mole] : a genus (the type of the family Gryllotalpidae) of large burrowing insects comprising the mole crickets that are related to the true crickets but have the forelimbs modified for digging

gryl·lus \'griləs\ *n* [NL, fr. L, cricket, grasshopper, a kind of comic figure, fr. Gk *gryllos* Egyptian dance, performer of an Egyptian dance, comic figure, caricature] **1** *cap* : a genus (the type of the family Gryllidae) of crickets once construed as including all known crickets but now restricted to certain typical Old World forms — compare ACHETA **2** *pl* **gryl·li** \-i,lī\ [L] : a comic combination of animals or of animal and human forms in Greco-Roman glyptic art esp. in intaglios

gryllus 2

gry·phaea \grə'fēə, grī'-\ *n, cap* [NL, fr. L *gryphus* or *gryph-, gryps* griffin — more at GRIFFIN] **1** : a genus of fossil mollusks related to the oyster but having the left valve arched with an incurved beak and the right valve flat **2** *in some classifications* : CRASSOSTREA — **gryph·ae·oid** \'grifē,ōid\ *adj*

gryphon *var of* GRIFFIN

gry·po·sis \grə'pōsəs, grī'-\ *n, pl* **grypo·ses** \-ō,sēz\ [LL, fr. LGk *grypōsis,* fr. Gk *grypousthai* to become hooked (fr. *grypos* hooked, curved) + *-sis* — more at GRIFFIN] : abnormal curvature esp. of the fingernail

grys·bok \'grīs,bäk, -rīs-\ *also* **grys·buck** \-,bək\ *n, pl* **grysbok** *also* **grysboks** [Afrik *grysbok,* fr. *grys* gray (fr. MD *grīs*) + *bok* male antelope] : a small reddish antelope (*Raphicerus melanotis*) of southern Africa

gs *abbr* gauss

GS *abbr* **1** general schedule **2** general secretary **3** general semantics **4** general service **5** general sessions **6** general staff **7** general superintendent **8** general support **9** gold standard **10** grammar school **11** grandson **12** ground speed

g's *or* **gs** *pl of* G

g salt *n, cap G* : a salt of G acid; *esp* : the dipotassium salt $HOC_{10}H_5(SO_3K)_2$

g sharp \'=,=\ *n, usu cap G* **1** : the keynote of G-sharp minor **2** : the tone a half step above G

g–sharp minor \'=,=ˌ=\ *n, usu cap G* : the minor musical key having a signature of five sharps

GSO *abbr* general staff officer

GST *abbr* Greenwich sidereal time

g star *n, usu cap G* : a star of spectral type G — see SPECTRAL TYPE table

g–string \'=,=\ *n, usu cap G* **1** *usu* **g string** : a string (as the lowest string of the violin) tuned to G **2** *also* **gee string a** : a breechcloth consisting usu. of a strip of cloth passed between the legs and supported by a waist cord **b** : a fancy between the legs and supported by a small pouch or strip of cloth used in the theatrical and burlesque costume of similar design **3** [fr. the initials of *Georg Goubou b*1906 Amer. physicist born in Germany, its inventor] : a high-frequency transmission line consisting of a wire covered by dielectric of such proportions and material that a large percentage of the propagated wave lies close to the wire

g suit *n, usu cap G* [gravity *suit*] : an aviator's suit having a built-in system of air bladders that become inflated in rapid aerial maneuvers and exert pressure on the body and legs of the wearer to counteract the physiological effects of acceleration greater than unity and prevent blackout

gt *abbr* **1** gilt **2** great **3** [L *gutta*] drop

GT *abbr* **1** *often not cap* gilt top **2** gross ton

GTC *abbr* good till canceled; good till countermanded

gtd *abbr* guaranteed

GTE *abbr* gilt top edge

GTM *abbr* **1** general traffic manager **2** good this month

gtt *abbr* [L *guttae*] drops

GTW *abbr* good this week

gu *abbr* **1** guarantee; guaranteed **2** guinea **3** gules

GU *abbr* genitourinary

guaca *var of* HUACA

gua·ca·coa \,gwäkə'kōə\ *n* -s [AmerSp, fr. Taino] : a Cuban tree (*Daphnopsis guacacoa*) of the family Thymelaeaceae that yields a strong white bast fiber

gua·ca·mo·le *also* **gua·cha·mo·le** \,gwäkə'mōlē\ *n* -s [AmerSp *guacamole,* fr. Nahuatl *ahuacamolli,* fr. *ahuacatl* avocado + *molli* sauce, stew] : a mixture of mashed avocado, tomato, and onion seasoned with condiments

gua·cha·ro \'gwächə,rō\ *n* -s [Sp *guácharo*] : OILBIRD

gua·chi·pi·lin \,gwächəpə'lēn\ *n* -s [AmerSp *guachipilin, guachipelin,* fr. (assumed) Nahuatl *cuauhchipilin,* fr. *cuahuitl* tree + *chipilin,* a species of Crotalaria] : a Central American timber tree (*Diphysa robinioides*) of the family Leguminosae that yields a fine-grained hard yellow wood and a yellow dye

guacho *var of* GAUCHO

gua·ci·mo \'gwäsə,mō\ *or* **gua·ci·ma** *or* **gua·si·ma** \-səmə\ *or* **hua·si·ma** \'wä-\ *n* -s [AmerSp *guácimo, guácima, guásima, guázuma,* fr. Taino *guácima, guaçūm*] : any of several tropical American timber trees esp. of the genus *Guazuma* (as *G. ulmifolia*) having inner bark that yields a mucilaginous substance used in medicine and a tough bast from which cordage is made

gua·co \'gwä(,)kō\ *n* -s [AmerSp] **1** : either of two plants believed to provide an antidote for snake bites: **a** : a tropical American vine (*Mikania guaco*) **b** : a birthwort (*Aristolochia maxima*) **2** : BEE PLANT a

gua·da·gni·ni \,gwädə'nēnē *also* -dən'yē-\ *n* -s *usu cap* [fr. *Guadagnini,* name of a noted family of 18th cent. Ital. violin makers] : a violin made by one of the Italian Guadagnini family in the 18th century

gua·da·la·ja·ra \,gwädələ'härə, -äthə-\ *adj, usu cap* [fr. *Guadalajara,* city in Mexico] : of or from the city of Guadalajara, Mexico : of the kind or style prevalent in Guadalajara

gua·dal·caz·a·rite \,gwäd³l'kazə,rīt\ *n* -s [G *guadalcazarit,* fr. *Guadalcázar,* San Luis Potosí state, Mex., its locality + G *-it* -ite] : a mineral (Hg,Zn)S consisting of a zincky metacinnabarite

gua·da·lupe caracara \'gwäd³l,üp-, ,==ˈ=-, ¦==¦üpē-\ *n, usu cap G* [fr. *Guadalupe,* a Mexican island off the western coast of Lower Calif.] : a caracara (*Polyborus lutosus*) formerly endemic on Guadalupe Island but now extinct

guadalupe cypress *n, usu cap G* : a low widely spreading evergreen tree (*Cupressus guadalupensis*) that is endemic on Guadalupe Island and is cultivated for its bluish foliage

guadalupe fur seal *n, usu cap G* : a fur seal (*Arctocephalus townsendi*) formerly common along the coast of California and Mexico but now limited to a small area where it is protected by the Mexican government

guadalupe palm *n, usu cap G* : a stout palm (*Erythea edulis*) of Guadalupe Island with edible buds and sweet pulpy fruit

guadalupe plum *n, usu cap G* : the fruit of the Guadalupe palm

gua·da·lu·pi·an \¦==¦üpēən\ *adj, usu cap* [*Guadalupe Basin,* west Texas and New Mexico + E *-ian*] : of, relating to, or constituting a subdivision of the American Permian — see GEOLOGIC TIME table

gua·de·loupe \'gwäd³l,üp, ,==ˈ=\ *adj, usu cap* [fr. *Guadeloupe,* island in the West Indies] : of or relating to the island of Guadeloupe : of the kind or style prevalent in Guadeloupe

gua·dua \'gwädəwə\ *n* -s [AmerSp] : a tropical American bamboo (*Guadua latifolia*) of the family Gramineae used esp. for construction and in paper manufacture

gua·guan·che \(g)wə'(g)wänchē\ *or* **gua·guan·cho** \-(,)chō\ *n* -s [AmerSp] : a barracuda (*Sphyraena guachancho*) of the Caribbean area and adjacent Atlantic coasts that is typically yellowish to olive above, silvery below, and spotted with black or dark brown

gua·ha·ri·bo \,gwä(h)ə'rē(,)bō, gwä'r-\ *n, pl* **guaharibo** *or* **guaharibos** *usu cap* [Sp, of AmerInd origin] **1 a** : a Shirianá people of the upper Orinoco valley, Venezuela **b** : a member of such people **2** : the language of the Guaharibo people

gua·hi·ban \gwä'(h)ēbən\ *adj, usu cap* : of or relating to the Guahibo people or their language

gua·hi·bo \-ē(,)bō\ *also* **gua·hi·vo** \-ē(,)vō\ *n, pl* **guahibo** *or* **guahibos** *usu cap* [Sp, of AmerInd origin] **1 a** : a group of peoples of eastern Colombia and southwestern Venezuela **b** : a member of any of such peoples **2** : the language of the Guahibo people

guai·ac \'g(w)ī,ak, -īək\ *also* **gai·ac** \'gī-\ *n* -s [NL *Guaiacum*] **1** : GUAIACUM 1b, 1c **2** *in French Guiana* **a** : TONKA BEAN **b** : a tree bearing the tonka bean

guai·a·col \'g(w)īə,kōl, -kōl\ *n* -s [*guaiacum* + E *-ol*] : a liquid or a crystalline solid $CH_3OC_6H_4OH$ with an aromatic odor ranging from colorless to yellowish in appearance and obtained by distilling guaiacum or from wood-tar creosote or synthetically and used chiefly as an expectorant and as a local anesthetic; *ortho*-methoxy-phenol

guaiac resin *n* : GUAIACUM 1c

guai·a·cum \'g(w)īəkəm\ *n* [NL, fr. Sp *guayaco, guayacán,* fr. Taino *guayacan*] **1 a** *cap* : a genus of tropical American trees and shrubs (family Zygophyllaceae) having pinnate leaves, mostly blue flowers, and capsular fruit **b** -s : the hard greenish brown wood yielded by trees of this genus (esp. *G. officinale*) — see LIGNUM VITAE **c** -s : a resin with a faint balsamic odor obtained as tears or masses from the trunk of either of two trees (*G. officinale* or *G. sanctum*) of this genus used formerly in medicine as a remedy for gout or rheumatism and now in various tests (as for peroxidases or blood stains) because of the formation of a blue color on oxidation **2** -s **a** : a tree (*Porlieria angustifolia*) of Texas and Mexico closely related to trees of the genus *Guaiacum* **b** : the wood of this tree **c** : the resinous exudate from this wood

guaiac wood *also* **guaiacum wood** *n* **1** : the heartwood of a palo santo (*Bulnesia sarmienti*) that yields an oil having an odor of tea or violets and used esp. as a fixative in perfumery **2** : the palo santo that yields guaiac wood

guai·can \(')gwī¦kän\ *n* -s [Sp *guaicán,* fr. Taino *guaican*] : REMORA

guai·cu·ru *or* **guay·cu·rú** \,gwīkə¦rü\ *n, pl* **guaicuru** *or* **guaicurus** *or* **guaycurú** *or* **guaycurús** *usu cap* [Sp *guaicurú, guaycurú,* of AmerInd origin] **1 a** : an Indian people living in southern Mato Grosso, Brazil **b** : a member of such people **2** : the language of the Guaicuru people

guai·cu·ru·an *or* **guay·cu·ru·an** \,==¦rüən\ *n* -s *usu cap* : a language family of the Chaco region in So. America

guaimi *usu cap, var of* GUAYMI

guai·ol \'g(w)ī,ōl, -,ōl\ *n* -s [ISV *guai-* (fr. NL *Guaiacum*) + *-ol*] : a crystalline sesquiterpenoid alcohol $C_{15}H_{25}OH$ found esp. in the oil of guaiacum wood

guai·ta·ca \,gwīd·ə'kä\ *n, pl* **guaitaca** *or* **guaitacas** *usu cap* [prob. fr. Pg *guaitacá,* of AmerInd origin] **1 a** : an extinct people of eastern Brazil **b** : a member of such people **2** : the language of the Guaitaca people

guaj·a·cum \'g(w)īəkəm\ [NL *Guaiacum*] *syn of* GUAIACUM

gua·ji·llo \gwä'hē(,)(y)ō\ *also* **gua·ji·lla** \-ē(y)ə\ *n* -s [MexSp] : a deep-rooted usu. spiny shrub (*Acacia berlandieri*) of the southwestern U.S. that has leaves with numerous leaflets and flowers in globose heads and that is an important honey plant when abundant

gua·ji·ra \gwä'hirə\ *n* -s [AmerSp (Cuba), lit., peasant woman] : a Cuban peasant dance tune or song whose rhythm shifts from 6/8 to 3/4 time while the eighth note retains the same time value

gua·ma \gwə'mä\ *n* -s [AmerSp *guamá,* fr. Taino *guama*] : any of several plants of the genus *Inga*; *esp* : a tropical American tree (*I. laurina*) used as a shade for coffee plantations

gua·ma·ni·an \gwä'mānēən, gwə'män-\ *n* -s *cap* [*Guam,* island in the Pacific ocean + E *-anian* (as in *Panamanian*)] : a native or inhabitant of Guam; *specif* : a Chamorro of Guam

gua·mo \'gwä(,)mō\ *n, pl* **guamo** *or* **guamos** *usu cap* [Sp, of AmerInd origin] **1 a** : a people of southwestern Venezuela **b** : a member of such people **2** : the language of the Guamo people

guamuchil *var of* HUAMUCHIL

guan \'gwän\ *n* -s [AmerSp] : any of various large tropical American birds (family Cracidae) that are highly regarded for sport and food, somewhat resemble turkeys in proportions and size, and are widely distributed in dense lowland forests

¹**guana** *var of* IGUANA

²**gua·ná** \gwə'nä\ *n, pl* **guaná** *or* **guanás** *usu cap* [Sp, of AmerInd origin] **1 a** : an Arawakan people or group of peoples of Mato Grosso, Brazil, and the Chaco region of Paraguay **b** : a member of any of such peoples **2** : the language of the Guaná people

³**gua·na** \'gwänə\ *n* -s [AmerSp (Cuba)] : MAJAGUA

gua·na·ba·na \gwə'näbənə\ *n* -s [Sp *guanábana* fruit of the soursop, fr. Taino, soursop] : SOURSOP

gua·na·cas·te \,gwänə'kastē\ *n* -s [Sp — more at CONACASTE] : CONACASTE

gua·na·co \gwə'nä(,)kō\ *or* **hua·na·co** \wə-\ *n, pl* **guanacos** *also* **guanaco** *or* **huanacos** *also* **huanaco** [Sp *guanaco, huanaco,* fr. Quechua *huanacu*] : a South American mammal (*Lama guanicoe*) that is related to the camel, lacks a dorsal hump, resembles a deer in appearance, and has a soft thick fawn-colored coat — compare ALPACA, LLAMA

gua·na·jua·tite \,gwänə'(h)wä,tīt\ *n* -s [*Guanajuato,* Mex., its locality + E *-ite*] : a mineral Bi_2Se_3 consisting of bismuth selenide occurring in bluish gray crystals or masses

gua·namine \'gwänə,mēn, ,==ˈ=, '== mən, gwə'namən\ *n* [*guanidine* + *amine*] : any of a series of bases formed by heating guanidine salts of the fatty acids and used to produce crystalline derivatives of fatty acids and in the manufacture of resins; a 2,4-diamino-6-alkyl-triazine

gua·na·qui·to \,gwänə'kē(,)tō\ *n* -s [Sp, lit., small guanaco, dim. of *guanaco*] : the pelt of a young guanaco

gua·nase \'gwä,nās, -āz\ *n* -s [*guanine* + *-ase*] : an enzyme present in most animal tissues that hydrolyzes guanine to xanthine and ammonia

gua·nay \gwə'nī\ *also* **guanay cormorant** *n, pl* **guanay·es** \-ī,ās\ *or* **guanays** \-īz\ [*guanay* fr. AmerSp (Peru), prob. fr. Quechua] : a white-breasted Peruvian cormorant (*Phalacrocorax bougainvillii*) that is a source of guano

guan·che \'gwän,(,)chā\ *n, pl* **guanches** *also* **guanche** *usu cap* [Sp] : one of a native people who formerly inhabited the Canary islands and who bore a superficial skeletal resemblance to the Cro-Magnon type — see HAMITE

guan·go \'gwäŋ(,)gō\ *n* -s [AmerSp] *West Indies* : RAIN TREE

gua·ni·dine \'gwänə,dēn, -dən\ *n* -s [ISV *guan-* (fr. *guanine*) + *-idine*] : a strong deliquescent crystalline base $NH{=}C(NH_2)_2$ found esp. in beet juice, vetch seedlings, or the embryo chick, formed by the oxidation of guanine but usu. made commercially by the reaction of dicyandiamide with ammonium nitrate, and used in the form of salts in organic synthesis and in medicine and in the form of organic derivatives as rubber accelerators

gua·ni·di·no \,gwänə'dē(,)nō\ *also* **gua·ni·do** \'gwänə,dō\ *adj* [*guanidino-, guanido-*] : relating to or containing the group $H_2NC({=}NH)NH-$ of guanidine

guanidino– *also* **guanido–** *comb form* [*guanidino-,* ISV, fr. *guanidine* + *-o-*; *guanido-* fr. *guanidine* + *-o-*] : containing the univalent group $H_2NC(=NH)NH-$ derived from guanidine by removal of one hydrogen atom

gua·ni·do·acetic acid \ˌgwänədō+. . .-\ *n* [*guanido-* + *acetic*] **:** GLYCOCYAMINE

gua·nif·er·ous \(ˈ)gwäˈnif(ə)rəs\ *adj* [*guano* + *-i-* + *-ferous*] **:** yielding guano

gua·nine \ˈgwäˌnēn, -ănən\ *n* -s [*guano* + *-ine*] **:** a crystalline purine base $C_5H_5N_5O$ found esp. in guano and other animal excrements and in many leguminous plants and obtained by hydrolysis of nucleic acids; 2-amino-6-hydroxy-purine

[1]gua·no \ˈgwä(ˌ)nō *sometimes* gyüˈanə\ *n* -s [Sp, fr. Quechua *huanu* dung] **1 :** a substance that is found on some coasts or islands frequented by sea fowl, is composed chiefly of their partially decomposed excrement, is rich in phosphates, nitrogenous matter, and other material for plant growth, and has been used extensively as a fertilizer **2 :** a product comparable to bird guano esp. as a fertilizer ⟨a ~ of fish-cannery refuse⟩

[2]guano \"\ *vt* -ED/-ING/-S **:** to enrich with or as if with guano

[3]guano *var of* IGUANA

[4]gua·no \ˈgwä(ˌ)nō\ *n* -s [AmerSp, fr. Taino] *West Indies* **:** BALSA 1

gua·no·phore \ˈgwänəˌfō(ə)r\ *n* -s [*guano-* (fr. *guanine*) + *-phore*] **:** a chromatophore that is characterized by pale granules or iridescent crystals of guanine and occurs notably in the skin of fishes and reptiles **:** LEUCOPHORE, IRIDOPHORE

guano sack *n* [*[1]guano*] *chiefly Midland* **:** GUNNYSACK

gua·no·sine \ˈgwänəˌsēn, -ˌsən\ *n* -s [ISV, blend of *guanine* and *ribose*] **:** a crystalline nucleoside $C_{10}H_{13}N_5O_5$ that is isolated esp. from vetch seedlings or coffee leaves and berries, that is obtained by partial hydrolysis of ribonucleic acid, and that yields on hydrolysis guanine and ribose

guans *pl of* GUAN

gua·nyl \ˈgwänᵊl\ *n* -s [*guan*idine + *-yl*] **:** the amidino group

gua·nyl·ic acid \(ˈ)gwäˌnilik-\ *n* [*guan*ine + *-yl* + *-ic*] **:** an amorphous nucleotide $C_{10}H_{14}N_5O_8P$ formed by partial hydrolysis of ribonucleic acid; an ester of guanosine and orthophosphoric acid

guao \ˈgwau̇\ *n* -s [AmerSp (Cuba), fr. Taino] **:** any of certain small tropical American trees constituting a genus *Comocladia* of the family Anacardiaceae, having odd-pinnate often spiny leaves, hard heavy reddish wood, and a caustic sap that poisons on contact, and yielding tannins and a dye extract — see MAIDEN PLUM

gua·pe·na \gwəˈpēnə\ *n* -s [AmerSp *guabina*, a kind of river fish, fr. Taino] **:** a West Indian ribbon fish (*Eques lanceolatus*)

gua·pi·lla \gwəˈpē(y)ə\ *n* -s [MexSp, istle (plant)] *Mexico* **:** ISTLE

gua·pi·nol \ˈgwäpəˌnōl, -nōl\ *n* -s [AmerSp, fr. Nahuatl *cuauh-pinolli*, lit., tree flour, fr. *cuahuitl* tree + *pinolli* flour, dust] **:** COURBARIL

guar \ˈgwär\ *n* -s [Hindi *guār*] **:** a drought-tolerant legume (*Cyanopsis psoralioides*) grown for forage and for its seeds which produce a gum used as a thickening agent and as a sizing material for paper and textiles

guar *abbr* guarantee; guaranteed; guarantor; guaranty

[1]gua·ra \gwəˈrä\ *n* -s [Pg *guará*, fr. Tupi] **:** SCARLET IBIS

[2]guara \ˈgwa(ə)rə\ [NL, fr. Pg *guará* scarlet ibis] *syn of* EUDOCIMUS

[3]gua·ra \gwəˈrä\ *n* -s [Pg *guará*, *aguara* — more at AGOUARA] **:** AGOUARA

[4]gua·ra \ˈgwärə\ *n* -s [AmerSp] **:** a tropical American tree of the genus *Cupania*

gua·ra·bu \ˌgwärəˈbü\ *n* -s [Pg *guarabú*, fr. Tupi] **:** any of several Brazilian timber trees of the genus *Astronium* (family Anacardiaceae) having heavy hard wood with close grain

gua·ra·cha \gwəˈrächə\ *n* -s [Sp, fr. OSp *guar* place, spot, site + *hacha* a dance performed with legs and feet only] **1 a :** a lively stamping Spanish solo dance **b :** music for this dance **2 a :** a lively Cuban dance tune in 6/8 time **b :** a ballroom dance with a box step developed in Cuba from the Spanish model

guarache *var of* HUARACHE

gua·ra·guao \ˌgwärəˈgwau̇\ *n* -s [AmerSp, fr. Taino] **:** any of several West Indian timber trees of the family Meliaceae; *esp* **:** a Puerto Rican timber tree (*Guarea guara*) that yields a wood resembling the related mahogany

gua·ra·na \ˌgwärəˈnä\ *n* -s [Sp & Pg *guaraná*, fr. Tupi] **1 :** a dried paste made from the seeds of a Brazilian climbing shrub (*Paullinia cupana*) containing tannin and caffeine and used in making an astringent drink **2 :** a drink flavored with guarana

gua·ra·ni \ˌgwärəˈnē\ *n, pl* **guarani** *or* **guaranis** *or* **guaranies** [Sp *guaraní*, of AmerInd origin] **1** *or* **guaraní** *usu cap* **a :** a Tupi-Guaranian people of Bolivia, Paraguay, and southern Brazil **b :** a member of such people **2** *or* **guaraní** *usu cap* **:** the language of the Guarani people **3 a :** the basic monetary unit of Paraguay — see MONEY table **b :** a note representing one guarani

gua·ra·ni·an \gwəˈränēən\ *adj, usu cap* **:** of or relating to the Guarani people

gua·ra·ño·ca \ˌgwärənˈyōkə\ *n, pl* **guarañoca** *or* **guarañocas** *usu cap* [Sp *Guarañoca*, of AmerInd origin] **1 a :** a Zamuco people of the Department of Santa Cruz, Bolivia **b :** a member of such people **2 :** the language of the Guarañoca people

[1]guar·an·tee \ˌgarənˈtē *also* ÷ˈgär- *or* ˈger- *or* ÷ˈgȧr-\ *n* -s [prob. alter. (influenced by such words as *assignee*, *lessee*) of *[1]guaranty*] **1 :** one who makes a guaranty **:** one who acts as a surety or gives security (as for a debt) **2 :** the act of one who makes a guaranty or acts as a surety **:** GUARANTY 1 **3 a :** an agreement by which one person undertakes to secure another in the possession or enjoyment of something **b :** an expressed or implied assurance of the quality of goods offered for sale or the length of satisfactory use to be expected from a product **c :** an expressed assurance of satisfaction with a definite promise of purchase money to be returned or goods to be replaced or other specified assurance **4 :** something given by way of security **:** something made or held as a security **:** GUARANTY 3

[2]guarantee \"\ *vt* **guaranteed; guaranteed; guaranteeing; guarantees 1 :** to be a guarantee, warranty, or surety for **:** undertake to answer for the debt, default, or miscarriage of (another) **:** become responsible for the fulfillment of (the agreement of another) **:** assume a suretyship for **2 :** to engage for the existence, permanence, or nature of (something) **:** undertake to do or secure (something) ⟨~ the winning of three tricks in a suit by losing the first trick⟩ **3 :** to give a guaranty to (another) **:** give or furnish security to **:** SECURE **4 :** to state or declare with conviction or an air of certainty ⟨he *guaranteed* that I had had appendicitis several times without knowing it —Arnold Bennett⟩

guaranteed annual wage *n* **:** an arrangement whereby an employer guarantees his employees a minimum amount of wages or employment during a year

guaranteed bond *n* **:** a bond on which payment of interest or principal or both are guaranteed by a corporation other than the issuer

guaranteed rate *n* **:** a minimum rate of pay assured to an incentive worker regardless of his output

guaranteed stock *n* **:** stock the dividends on which are guaranteed by a corporation other than the issuing corporation

guaranteed value *n* **:** NONFORFEITURE BENEFIT

guaranteed wage *n* **:** an assurance by an employer to qualified workers of continuing wage payments for a specified period of time

guar·an·tor \ˌ⸗rənˈtō(ə)r, -ō(ə), ˈ⸗rəntə(r)\ *n* -s [*[1]guaranty* + *-or*] **1 :** one that guarantees ⟨our Strategic Air Command is the ~ of our security —Carl Spaatz⟩ **2 :** one that makes or gives a guaranty or surety **:** one that enters in a guaranty

[1]guar·an·ty \ˈ⸗rəntē, -ti\ *n* -ES [MF *garantie*, *guarantie*, fr. OF, fr. (influenced by *garir*, *guarir* to protect, preserve, from a Gmc verb represented by OHG *werien* to defend) *garant*, *guarant* warrant, defender, protection, of Gmc origin; akin to OHG *werēnto* guarantor — more at WEIR, WARRANT] **1 :** an undertaking to answer for the payment of some debt or the performance of some duty of another in case of the failure of such other to pay or perform **:** a promise to answer for the debt, default, or miscarriage of another **2 :** GUARANTEE 3a **3 :** something given or possessed as security for the existence or continuance of something **:** something given or held as a means of securing the existence, performance, or fulfillment of something **:** SECURITY **4 :** a person who accepts or gives assurance of responsibility for something **:** GUARANTOR **5 :** the protection of a right afforded by legal provision (as in a constitution) ⟨constitutional *guaranties* of personal liberty⟩

[2]guaranty \"\ *vt* -ED/-ING/-ES **:** GUARANTEE

guaras *pl of* GUARA

gua·rau·no \gwəˈrau̇(ˌ)nō\ *n* -s *usu cap* [Sp, of AmerInd origin] **:** WARRAU

gua·ra·yo \gwəˈrī(ˌ)ō\ *n, pl* **guarayo** *or* **guarayos** *usu cap* [Sp, of AmerInd origin] **1 a :** a Tacanan people of northwestern Bolivia **b :** a member of such people **2 :** the language of the Guarayo people

gua·ra·yú \ˌgwärəˈyü\ *n, pl* **guarayú** *or* **guarayús** *usu cap* [Sp, of AmerInd origin] **1 a :** a Guaranian people of Bolivia **b :** a member of such people **2 :** the language of the Guarayú people

[1]guard \ˈgärd, ˈgȧd\ *n* -s [ME *garde*, fr. MF, fr. OF *garde*, *guarde*, fr. *garder*, *guarder*, v.] **1 :** one that defends against injury, danger, or attack ⟨his greatness was no ~ to bar heaven's shaft —Shak.⟩: as **a :** a bowl or stone played to a position where it protects another from attack in bowls or curling **b :** a low card held with a valuable higher card in the same suit **c** (1) **:** one of two players on either side of the center in the line in football (2) **:** either of two players stationed at the rear of the court in basketball whose play is primarily defensive **2 :** a man or body of men stationed to protect or control a person or position: as **a :** a soldier, sailor, marine, or airman or a number of them on guard duty ⟨~*s* were posted about the army camp⟩ ⟨slipped past the palace ~*s*⟩ **b guards** *pl* **:** troops attached to the person of a ruler (as a sovereign or governor) ⟨Royal Horse *Guards*⟩ ⟨Governor's Foot *Guards*⟩ ⟨Grenadier *Guards*⟩ ⟨Dragoon *Guards*⟩ **c :** a group loyal to a defeated person or to an outmoded principle ⟨an Old *Guard* Republican⟩ **d** (1) *Brit* **:** a railroad conductor (2) **:** a brakeman or gateman (as on a train of an elevated railroad or subway) **e :** one who is responsible for the safety and discipline of inmates of a prison, reformatory, or other place of detention while they are within the institution, in transit to or from the institution, or on work detail **f :** an officer of a society (as a secret order) whose duty it is to prevent intrusion by nonmembers **g :** a gateman or watchman of a building or plant **3** *obs* **:** an ornamental trimming of lace or embroidery on the edge of a garment **4 a :** a state of watchfulness and readiness against danger **:** state of standing in defense of a person or thing against possible injury, attack, or theft ⟨standing ~ over the treasure⟩ **b :** the service or duties of one who keeps military watch ⟨assigned to ~ duty on the border⟩ **5 a :** a posture of defense (as in fencing or boxing) **:** the position of the body or the arms in defense ⟨got a blow in under his ~⟩ ⟨caught him off ~⟩ ⟨kept his ~ up to protect his face⟩ **b :** the position of a cricketer's bat held perpendicularly at a point where it will stop a straight bowled ball that would otherwise hit the wicket **6 :** a fixture or attachment designed to protect or secure against injury, soiling, defacement, theft, or loss: as **a :** the part of a sword hilt that protects the hand **b :** a chain or band for holding in place or safeguarding from loss ⟨belt ~⟩ ⟨watch ~⟩ **c :** GUARD RING 1 **d :** TRIGGER GUARD **e :** FENDER **f** *Brit* **:** PILOT 4a **7 a :** a piece of protective body armor ⟨nose ~⟩ **b :** any of various devices worn by contestants as a protection against injury to some part ⟨shin ~⟩ **c :** the hard calcareous fusiform or subcylindrical piece which ensheathes the phragmacone and forms the rear end of the shell of belemnites — called also *rostrum* **8 a :** a fence or rail to prevent falling from the deck of a ship **b guards** *pl* **:** an extension of the deck of a ship beyond the hull; *esp* **:** the framework of timber in a side-wheel steamship protecting the paddle wheel and shaft **9 a :** a projecting paper or cloth strip bound with book leaves onto which an insert (as a map or folding plate) is fastened — called also *stub* **b :** a narrow leaf usu. ½ to ¾ inches wide that compensates for an object mounted to a full page (as in a scrapbook or album) — called also *stub* **c :** the supporting paper applied in rebinding to the broken folds of the leaves of a book before sewing **d :** a paper or cloth strip added to the fold of the first and last section of a book for additional strength

[2]guard \"\ *vb* -ED/-ING/-S [MF *garder*, fr. OF *garder*, *guarder* to ward, guard, of Gmc origin; akin to OHG *wartēn* to watch, take care — more at WARD] *vt* **1 :** to finish and protect an edge of with an ornamental border or lace edging **2 a :** to protect from danger **:** DEFEND, SHIELD **b :** to stand on the border or at the entrance of as if on guard ⟨lawns ~*ed* by stately elms⟩ or as a barrier ⟨rapids ~*ing* the lower reaches of the river⟩ **c :** to protect (a card or a man) in a game by safeguards or support ⟨forced to discard diamonds in order to ~ the king of clubs⟩ ⟨the separated pawns could not both be ~*ed*⟩ **3** *archaic* **:** to accompany for protection **:** ESCORT **4 a :** to watch over so as to prevent escape ⟨a closely ~*ed* secret⟩ ⟨~ a prisoner⟩ or restrain from violence or indiscretion ⟨warned her to ~ her tongue in the presence of these people —L.C. Douglas⟩ **b** *of a player in a goal game* **:** to maintain a position so as to prevent (an opponent) from playing effectively **5 :** to furnish with proper checks or corrections **:** SAFEGUARD ⟨~ an experiment⟩ **6 :** to equip (as a book, a machine, a window) with a guard **~** *vi* **:** to watch by way of caution or defense **:** be in a state or position of defense ⟨hitting with his right, ~*ing* with his left⟩ **:** stand guard **:** take precautions ⟨~ against mistakes by double-checking⟩ **syn** see DEFEND

guardage *n* -s *obs* **:** GUARDIANSHIP

[1]guar·dant \ˈgärdᵊnt\ *adj* [MF *gardant*, pres. part. of *garder*] **1** *also* **gar·dant** \"\ *heraldry* **:** having the head turned toward the spectator — used of a beast whose body is seen from the side ⟨a lion passant ~⟩ **2** *obs* **:** acting as a guard or guardian

[2]guardant *n* -s *obs* **:** GUARDIAN, KEEPER

guard boat *n* **:** a boat that is detailed on guard duty (as in a harbor)

guard book *n, Brit* **:** SCRAPBOOK, ALBUM, FOLDER

guard brush *n* **:** a metallic brush for picking up the current from the live rail of an electric railroad

guard cartridge *n* **:** a cartridge for guard purposes having a reduced powder charge and giving a low muzzle velocity to the bullet

guard cell *n* **:** one of the two crescent-shaped epidermal cells united at their ends whose changes in turgidity determine opening and closing of a stoma

guard chamber *n* **:** GUARDROOM

guard circle *n* **:** a final groove on a disc record that returns upon itself in order to protect the pickup from damage by being thrown toward the center of the record

guarded *adj* **1 :** PROTECTED, DEFENDED **2 :** CAUTIOUS, WARY, CIRCUMSPECT ⟨he was ~ in his expressions⟩ **:** framed or uttered with caution ⟨a ~ statement⟩ — **guard·ed·ly** *adv* — **guard·ed·ness** *n* -ES

guard·ee \ˈgärdˈē, ˈgȧd-, -di\ *n* -s [*[1]guard* + *-ee*] *Brit* **:** GUARDSMAN

guard·er \ˈgärdər, ˈgȧdə(r\ *n* -s **:** one that guards **:** WATCHMAN, WARDER, GUARD

guard flag *n* **:** a flag flown at anchor by a warship having the day's guard duty

guard hair *n* **:** any of the long coarse hairs forming a protective coating over the underfur of a furred mammal; *also* **:** the coat formed by these hairs

guardhouse \ˈ⸗,⸗\ *n* [*[1]guard* + *house*] **:** a building that serves as headquarters for the guard and as a lockup for military offenders

guardhouse lawyer *n* **:** a person in the military service who pretends to wide knowledge of regulations, military law, and his rights; *esp* **:** one who so pretends while in confinement

[1]guard·i·an \ˈgärdēən, ˈgȧd-\ *n* -s [ME *gardein*, fr. AF, fr. OF *gardenc*, fr. *garder*, *guarder* to ward, watch] **1 :** one that guards or secures **:** one to whom a person or thing is committed for protection, security, or preservation **2** [ME *gardian*, fr. MF *gardien*, fr. OF, fr. *garder* to guard + *-ien* -an — more at GUARD] **a :** a superior of a Franciscan monastery **3 :** one who has or is entitled or legally appointed to the care and management of the person or property of another (as a minor or a person incapable of managing his own affairs) — compare COMMITTEE, CURATOR, TUTOR; see GUARDIAN AD LITEM, GUARDIAN BY CUSTOM, GUARDIAN BY ELECTION, GUARDIAN BY STATUTE, GUARDIAN FOR NURTURE, GUARDIAN IN SOCAGE, NATURAL GUARDIAN, TESTAMENTARY GUARDIAN; WARD **4** *often cap* **:** the spiritual leader of the Bahais **5 :** an adult leader of a group of intermediate camp fire girls — compare ADVISER, LEADER

[2]guardian \"\ *adj* **:** performing or appropriate to the office of a protector ⟨the ~ lions by the entrance are strikingly rendered —*Amer. Guide Series: Vt.*⟩

guardian ad litem *n* **:** a guardian appointed by a court to represent in a particular lawsuit the interests of a party who is minor or an incompetent person or of a person unborn or unascertained who may become interested in property involved in the litigation

guardian angel *n* **:** an angel believed to have special care for a particular individual

guardian by custom 1 : a guardian according to a custom concerning lands of copyhold tenure where the right of guardianship falls to the next of blood incapable of inheriting the estate or may be claimed by special custom by the lord of the manor or his nominee **2 :** a guardian according to a now disused custom of London

guardian by election : a guardian elected by an infant himself having lands in socage upon attaining his 14th year

guardian by nature : NATURAL GUARDIAN

guardian by statute : a guardian appointed by a father by deed or will for his minor child under authority of a statute and sometimes having custody of both the person and the estate of the minor until he attains the age of 21

guard·i·ance *n* -s [*guardian* + *-ance*] *obs* **:** GUARDIANSHIP

guard·i·an·ess \ˈgärdēənəs, ˈgȧd-\ *n* -ES [*[1]guardian* + *-ess*] **:** a female guardian

guardian for nurture *or* **guardian by nurture** *Eng common law* **:** a father and upon his decease prob. the mother of children under 14 years of age having custody of their persons and not of their estates — compare NATURAL GUARDIAN

guardian in socage : the guardian of an infant who inherited lands held in socage under feudal tenure

guard·i·an·less \-ləs\ *adj* **:** lacking a guardian

guard·i·an·ly \-lē,-li\ *adj* **:** relating to a guardian

guardian of the poor : a member of a board appointed or elected to care for the relief of the poor or administer the poor laws within a township, parish, or district in England

guard·i·an·ship \-ˌship\ *n* **:** PROTECTION, CARE; *specif* **:** the relationship existing between guardian and ward

guardian spirit *n* **:** a tutelary being **:** GENIUS

guarding *n* -s [fr. gerund of *[2]guard*] **:** involuntary reaction to protect an area of pain (as by spasm of muscle on palpation of the abdomen over a painful lesion)

guard·ing·ly *adv* [fr. pres. part. of *[2]guard* + *-ly*] **:** in a protective or defensive manner

guard iron *n, Brit* **:** PILOT 4a

guard·less \ˈgärdləs, ˈgȧd-\ *adj* **1 a :** DEFENSELESS, UNPROTECTED **b :** UNWARY **2 :** lacking a guard ⟨~ swords⟩

guard line *n* **1 :** BEARER 5b (3) **2 :** a line constituting the inner side of the flangeway of a railroad crossing or switch and comprised of guardrails and wing rails — compare GAGE LINE

guard lock *n* **1 :** a tide lock at the mouth of a dock or basin or a lock for preventing flooding of a canal **2 :** a lock guarding the keyhole or bolt of another lock and having to be unlocked before the key of the main lock can be operated

guard mail *n* **:** mail delivered locally (as to a naval vessel) by messenger

guard mount *also* **guard mounting** *n* **1 :** the military ceremony of installing the new guard and relieving the old one **2 :** guard duty

guard of honor : a guard turned out to greet or accompany a distinguished person or to accompany the casket at a military funeral — compare COLOR GUARD

guard of the standard : the color guard of a cavalry regiment

guard pin *n* **:** a pin in a lever-escapement watch set into the pallet fork for preventing accidental unlocking of the escapement

guardrail \ˈ⸗,⸗\ *n* **1 :** a railing for guarding against danger or trespass **2 :** a timber bolted outside a ship along the plank-sheer to act as a fender **3 :** a rail placed on the inside of a main rail (as on a bridge or a curve or at a switch) as a safeguard against derailment

guard report *n* **:** a formal report submitted by the commander of a guard to higher authority at the close of each period of guard duty

guard ring *n* **:** a close-fitting finger ring worn outside another to keep the latter from slipping off

guardroom \ˈ⸗,⸗\ *n* **:** the room occupied by the guard during its term of duty

guards *pl of* GUARD, *pres 3d sing of* GUARD

guard·ship \ˈ⸗,ship\ *n* [*[1]guard* + *-ship*] **:** GUARDIANSHIP

guard ship \"\ *n* **:** a warship under way or at anchor assigned to a special administrative duty or required to maintain temporarily a higher degree of readiness than others of the squadron

guards·man \ˈgärdzmən, ˈgȧd-\ *n, pl* **guardsmen** [in sense 1, fr. *guard's* (gen. of *[1]guard*) + *man*; in sense 2, fr. *guards* (pl. of *[1]guard*) + *man*] **1** *archaic* **:** one who guards **:** GUARD, WARDER, WATCHMAN **2 :** a member of any military body called *guard* or *guards*

guard's van *n, Brit* **:** CABOOSE

guard tent *n* **:** a tent occupied by a military guard

guard timber *n* **:** a piece of timber used to maintain the spacing of ties in a railroad track

gua·rea \ˈgwärēə\ *n, cap* [NL, fr. AmerSp *guara*] **:** a genus of chiefly tropical American trees or shrubs (family Meliaceae) with pinnate leaves, small clustered flowers, and capsular fruits

guar gum *n* **:** a gum consisting of the ground endosperm of guar seeds that swells and disperses in water and is used chiefly as a thickening agent, in papermaking, and in ore dressing

gua·ri·ba \gwəˈrēbə\ *n* -s [Pg, fr. Tupi] **:** HOWLER MONKEY; *esp* **:** a monkey (*Alouatta caraya*) of Brazil

guar·ne·ri·us \gwärˈnērēəs, -wȧl, ˈner-, ˈnēr-, ˈnar-\ *or* **guar·ne·ri** \-rē,ri\ *also* **guar·nie·ri** \ˌnyer-, ˌnyär-\ *n, pl* **guarneriuses** *or* **guarneris** *also* **guarnieris** *usu cap* [NL *Guarnerius*, fr. It *Guarneri*, *Guarnieri*, name of a noted family of 17th & 18th cent. Ital. violin makers] **:** a violin made by one of the Italian Guarneri family in the 17th and 18th centuries

guar·nie·ri body \ˌnˈyerē-, -yärē-, -ri-\ *or* **guarnieri's body** *n, usu cap G* [after Giuseppe *Guarnieri* †1918 Ital. pathologist] **:** a minute inclusion body characteristic of variola and vaccinia

guar·ri \ˈgwärē\ *n* -s [native name in southern Africa] **:** the fruit of any of several African trees or shrubs of the genus *Euclea* (as *E. pseudebenus*) — compare CAPE EBONY

guars *pl of* GUAR

gua·sa \ˈgwäsə\ *n* -s [Sp] **:** a grouper (*Epinephelus guaza*) of Europe and the south Atlantic; *broadly* **:** any of various related fishes (as the spotted jewfish)

gua·sa·par \ˌgwäsəˈpär\ *n, pl* **guasapar** *or* **guasapars** *usu cap* [Sp *guazapar*, *guaziper*, of AmerInd origin] **1 :** a Varohío people of Chihuahua, Mexico **2 :** a member of the Guasapar people

gua·sa·ve \gwəˈsävē\ *n, pl* **guasave** *or* **guasaves** *usu cap* [Sp *guazave*, *guayave*, of AmerInd origin] **1 :** a Cahita people of Sinaloa, Mexico **2 :** a member of the Guasave people

guasima *var of* GUACIMO

gua·so \ˈgwä(ˌ)sō\ *n* -s [Sp, fr. Quechua *huasu*] **:** a Chilean agricultural laborer

guas·tal·line \ˈgwästəˌlēn, gwäˈstälən\ *n* -s *usu cap* [after Countess of *Guastalla* †ab 1569, who founded the sisterhood] **:** a member of a Roman Catholic sisterhood established in Milan about 1535 to manage an institute for the orphans of noble families — called also *Daughter of Mary*

gua·tam·bu \ˌgwädəmˈbü\ *n* -s [Pg *guatambú*, fr. Tupi] **1 :** a Brazilian timber tree (*Aspidosperma tomentosa*) **2 :** the bright yellow rather soft wood of the guatambu

gua·te·ma·la \ˌgwädəˈmälə, -wätə-, -mälə\ *adj, usu cap* [fr. *Guatemala*, country in Central America] **1 :** of or from Guatemala **:** of the kind or style prevalent in Guatemala **:** GUATEMALAN **2** *or* **guatemala city** *usu cap G&C* [fr. *Guatemala* or *Guatemala City*, capital of Guatemala] **:** of or from Guatemala City, the capital of Guatemala **:** of the kind or style prevalent in Guatemala City **:** GUATEMALAN

guatemala grass *n, usu cap 1st G* **1 :** TEOSINTE **2 :** a perennial grass (*Tripsacum laxum*) of the Caribbean area that is widely grown in warm regions for fodder and hay

1gua·te·ma·lan \-lən\ *adj, usu cap* [*Guatemala* + E *-an*] **1 a :** of, relating to, or characteristic of Guatemala **b :** of, relating to, or characteristic of the people of Guatemala **2 a :** of, relating to, or characteristic of Guatemala City **b :** of, relating to, or characteristic of the people of Guatemala City

2guatemalan \"\ *n* -s *cap* **:** a native or inhabitant of Guatemala

1gua·te·mal·tec·an \ˌ==ˌmälˈtekən, -ˌmäl-\ *adj, usu cap* [Sp *guatemalteco* + E *-an*] **:** GUATEMALA

2guatemaltecan \"\ *n* -s *cap* **:** GUATEMALAN

gua·te·mal·te·co \ˌ==ˌ=ˈte(ˌ)kō, -ˈtā(-\ *n* -s *cap* [Sp, fr. *Guatemala*] **:** GUATEMALAN

gua·ti·be·ro \gwäˈtēbəˌrō\ *or* **gua·ti·ve·re** \-ēvəˌrā\ *n* -s [AmerSp (Cuba) *guatibere*] **:** any of several groupers; *esp* **:** CONEY 5a

gua·tó \gwäˈtō\ *n, pl* **guató** *or* **guatós** *usu cap* [Sp & Pg, of AmerInd origin] **1 a :** a people of southwestern Mato Grosso, Brazil **b :** a member of such people **2 :** the language of the Guató people constituting the Guatoan language family

gua·to·an \-ōən\ *adj, usu cap* **:** of, relating to, or being the So. American Indian language family comprising Guató

gua·tu·san \gwäˈtüsᵊn\ *adj, usu cap* **:** of or relating to the Guatuso people or their language

gua·tu·so \gwäˈtü(ˌ)sō\ *n, pl* **guatuso** *or* **guatusos** *usu cap* [Sp *guatuso, guatuzo, huatuso,* of AmerInd origin] **1 a :** a Chibchan people of Costa Rica **b :** a member of such people **2 :** a language of the Guatuso people

gua·va \ˈgwävə *also* -wōvə\ *n, pl* **guavas** *also* **guava** [Sp, alter. of *guayaba,* of Arawakan origin; akin to Galibi *goyaba* guava, Tupi *guaiába, guayava*] **1 a :** a small shrubby tropical American tree (*Psidium guajava*) that is widely cultivated in warm regions for its sweet or somewhat acid usu. globular yellow fruit **b :** any of several other plants of the genus *Psidium* that bear edible fruit (as the strawberry guava or the Brazilian guava) **2 :** the fruit of a guava **3 :** INGA 2; *esp* **:** a West Indian tree (*Inga vera*) resembling the common guava and similarly used

gua·vi·na \gwäˈvēnə\ *n* -s [AmerSp *guabina,* fr. Taino] **1 :** a fish of the family Eleotridae **2 :** any of several gobies of the warmer parts of America

gua·xi·ma \gwäˈshēmə\ *n* -s [Pg *guaxima, guaxuma* caesar weed, fr. Tupi *aguaixima*] **:** a strong soft lustrous cordage fiber produced in parts of Africa and Brazil from Caesar weed

gua·ya·ba \gwəˈyäbə\ *n* -s [Sp — more at GUAVA] **:** GUAVA

gua·ya·bi \ˌgwīəˈbē\ *n* -s [AmerSp *guayabi, guayaibi,* fr. Guarani *guayavi*] **1 :** a large So. American timber tree (*Patagonula americana*) of the family Boraginaceae **2 :** the highly valued hard tough heavy wood of the guayabi: **a :** a thick whitish or pale brown sapwood that is used esp. for parts or articles (as tool handles and oars) subject to rough usage and recurrent strain **b :** a heartwood usu. variegated in shades of brown or blackish purple and capable of taking a high polish that is used for fine furniture, turning, and cabinetwork

gua·ya·bo \gwəˈyä(ˌ)bō\ *n* -s [Sp, guava (tree), fr. *guayaba* — more at GUAVA] **:** GUAVA

gua·ya·can \ˌgwīəˈkän\ *n* -s [Sp *guayacán* — more at GUAIACUM] **1 :** any of several So. and Central American timber trees typically with strong dense hard wood: as **a :** any of certain lignum vitae of the genus *Guaiacum* (esp. *G. sanctum*) **b :** any of certain trees of the genus *Tabebuia* **c :** an Argentine tree (*Caesalpinia melanocarpa*) yielding a timber used for railway ties, paving, and heavy construction **d :** GUAIACUM WOOD **2 :** GUAIACUM 2

gua·ya·ki \ˌgwīəˈkē\ *n, pl* **guayakí** *or* **guayakís** *usu cap* [Sp *guayaquí,* of AmerInd origin] **1 a :** a Guaranian people of Paraguay **b :** a member of such people **2 :** a language of the Guayakí people

gua·ya·quil \ˈgwīəˌkēl, -kil, ˌ==ˈ=\ *adj, usu cap* [fr. *Guayaquil,* city in Ecuador] **:** of or from the city of Guayaquil, Ecuador **:** of the kind or style prevalent in Guayaquil

guaycurú *usu cap, var of* GUAICURU

guay·mi *also* **guai·mi** \(ˈ)gwīˈmē\ *n, pl* **guaymi** *or* **guaymis** *usu cap* [Sp *guaymi, guaimi,* of AmerInd origin] **1 a :** a Chibchan people or group of peoples of Panama and Costa Rica **b :** a member of such people or group of peoples **2 :** a language of the Guaymi people

gua·yu·le \(g)wīˈülē\ *or* **hua·yu·le** \wī-\ *n* -s [AmerSp, fr. Nahuatl *cuauhuli,* lit., tree gum, fr. *cuahuitl* tree + *uli* gum] **1 :** a much-branched subshrub (*Parthenium argentatum*) with slender silvery leaves and small white flowers that is native to dry parts of Mexico and the adjacent southwestern U. S. and has been cultivated as a source of rubber **2** *or* **guayule rubber :** rubber obtained from guayule

gua·zu·ma \ˈgwäzəmə\ *n, cap* [NL, fr. AmerSp *guázuma* — more at GUACIMO] **:** a small genus of chiefly tropical American trees (family Sterculiaceae) with alternate toothed leaves, cymose flowers, and a woody capsule — see BASTARD CEDAR e

gua·zu·ti \ˌgwäzəˈtē\ *n* -s [AmerSp *guazuti,* fr. Guarani, lit., white deer, fr. *guazú* deer + *ti* white] **:** PAMPAS DEER

gubar numeral *var of* GOBAR NUMERAL

gub·ber·tushed \ˈgübə(r)ˌtüsht, ˈgəbə(r)ˌtəsht\ *adj* [*gubber,* of unknown origin + *tushed,* alter. of *toothed*] *now dial Eng* **:** having large projecting teeth **:** BUCK-TOOTHED

gub·bins \ˈgəbənz\ *also* **gub·bings** \", -biŋz\ *n pl but sing or pl in constr* [*gubbins,* pl. of *gubbin* fragment, paring, alter. of obs. E *gobone* gobbet, portion, fr. ME *gobyn, goboun; gubbings,* alter. of *gubbins*] **1** *dial Brit* **:** fish parings or refuse; *broadly* **:** any bits and pieces **:** SCRAPS **2** *Brit* **:** GADGETS, GADGETRY ⟨the ~ for changing a tire⟩ ⟨all the navigational ~ —J.L.Rhys⟩ **3** *Brit* **:** a foolish or futile person **:** SIMPLETON ⟨you silly ~⟩

guber *var of* GOOBER

gu·ber·nac·u·lar \ˌg(y)übə(r)ˈnakyələ(r), ˌgüb-\ *adj* **:** of, relating to, or constituting a gubernaculum

gu·ber·nac·u·lum \ˌ==ˈ==ləm\ *n, pl* **gubernacu·la** \-lə\ [NL, fr. L, rudder, fr. *gubernare* to steer + *-culum* -cle — more at GOVERN] **:** a part or structure that serves as a guide: as **a :** a fibrous cord that connects the fetal testis with the bottom of the scrotum and by failing to elongate commensurately with the rest of the fetus causes the descent of the testis **b :** a posterior flagellum of certain protozoans **c :** a sclerotized accessory structure associated with the copulatory spicules of various nematode worms

gu·ber·na·tion \ˌ==ˈnāshən\ *n* -s [ME *gubernacioun,* fr. L *gubernation-, gubernatio,* fr. *gubernatus* (past part. of *gubernare* to govern, steer) + *-ion-, -io* -ion] *archaic* **:** GOVERNMENT

gu·ber·na·tive \ˈ==ˌnād·iv, -ˌnəd-\ *adj* [ME, fr. MF or LL; MF *gubernatif,* fr. LL *gubernativus* governing, fr. L *gubernatus* (past part.) + *-ivus* -ive] **:** concerned with or devoted to government or governing — **gu·ber·na·tive·ly** \-d·əvlē\ *adv*

gu·ber·na·tor \-ˌnād·ə(r)\ *n* -s [L, fr. *gubernatus* (past part.) + *-or*] **:** RULER, GOVERNOR

gu·ber·na·to·ri·al *R & -R* ˌgübənəˈtōrēəl, -tȯr- *also* ˌgyüb- *or* ˌgüb- *sometimes* ˌgəb-, *R also* -bərn-\ *adj* [LL *gubernatorius* controlling, governing (fr. L *gubernator* governor) + E *-al*] **:** of or relating to a governor or to government

gubernatrix *n* -ES [L, fem. of *gubernator*] *obs* **:** a female ruler

gu·ber·ni·ya *or* **gu·ber·nia** \güˈbernēyə\ *n* -s [Russ *guberniya* government, guberniya, prob. fr. Pol *gubernja,* fr. L *gubernare* to govern] **1 :** a territorial subdivision of prerevolutionary Russia **2 :** a former provincial soviet — compare OBLAST

guck \ˈgək\ *n* -s [perh. blend of *goo* and *muck*] *slang* **:** something unpleasant or offensive ⟨an unbroken diet of custards and such ~⟩; *usu* **:** oozy sloppy dirt or debris ⟨beds of ~ from the cleaned sewers —Saul Bellow⟩

gu·dame \(ˈ)gœˈdām, (ˈ)gīē-, (ˈ)giˌ-, ˈ=ˌdəm\ *n* -s [ME (northern dial.) *gudame, goddame,* fr. *gud, gude* (var. of *good*) + *dame*] *Scot* **:** GRANDMOTHER

guddee *var of* 1GADDI

gud·dle \ˈgədᵊl\ *vb* -ED/-ING/-S [prob. of imit. origin] *vt* **:** to catch (fish) with the hands by groping (as under banks or stones) ~ *vi* **1 :** to grope for fish in their lurking places **2** *chiefly Scot* **:** to feel one's way with or as if with the hands **:** GROPE

1gude \ˈgœd, ˈgīēd, ˈgid\ *Scot var of* GOOD

2gude \ˈgüd\ *Scot var of* GOD

gude·sire \(ˈ)gœdˌsī(ə)r, (ˈ)gīēd-, (ˈ)gid-, ˈ=ˌs(h)ər, ˈgəchər\ *n* [ME (Scot. dial.) *gudsire,* fr. *gud* (var. of *good*) + *sire*] *Scot* **:** GRANDFATHER

gude·wife \(ˈ)gœdˌwəif, (ˈ)gīēˌ-, (ˈ)giˌ-\ *var of* GOODWIFE

1gud·geon \ˈgəjən\ *n* -s [ME *gudyon, gogoyne, goione,* fr. MF *gougon, goujon,* fr. OF *gogon, gojon,* perh. fr. LL *gubia, gulbia* hollow chisel — more at GOUGE] **1 :** PIVOT, JOURNAL: as **a :** an iron or steel pivot fixed in the end of a wooden shaft **b :** a crosshead pin on which a connecting rod turns **2 a :** a ring at the base of a hinge that encloses and turns on the pintle of the hinge **b :** a metal socket attached to the sternpost of a boat to receive the rudder pintle **c :** a notch in carrick bitts to receive a spindle bush **3 :** an iron pin for fastening together blocks of stone

2gudgeon \"\ *n* -s [ME *gojune, goion, gogyn,* fr. MF *gougon, gouvion,* fr. OF, fr. L *gobion-, gobio, cobion-, cobio* — more at GOBY] **1 a :** a small easily caught European freshwater fish (*Gobio gobio*) that is related to the carps and is often used for food and for bait **b** (1) **:** any of various gobies (2) **:** any of several Australian fishes of the family Eleotridae **c :** any of various killifishes **d :** BURBOT **2 a :** a person easily duped or cheated **b :** BAIT, ALLUREMENT

3gudgeon \"\ *vt* -ED/-ING/-S *archaic* **:** to deprive fraudulently **:** CHEAT, DUPE

gudgeon pin *n* **:** WRIST PIN

gud·mun·dite \ˈgüdmənˌdīt\ *n* -s [G *gudmundit,* fr. *Gudmundstorp,* Sweden, its locality + G *-it* -ite] **:** a mineral FeSbS that is a sulfide and antimonide of iron

gu·dok \(ˈ)güˈdük\ *n* -s [Russ, fr. *gudet'* to sound, drone, hum — more at GUSLA] **:** a primitive 3-stringed Russian viol instrument

gue \ˈgyü\ *n* -s [modif. of Norw (dial.) *gjija,* fr. ON *gīgja* fiddle — more at JIG] **:** a 2-stringed viol instrument formerly used in Shetland

guel·der rose \ˈgeldə(r)-\ *n* [fr. *Guelders* or *Guelderland* (D *Gelderland*), province, Netherlands] **:** CRANBERRY BUSH 2; *esp* **:** a cultivated form of the cranberry bush with large globose heads of sterile flowers — see SNOWBALL

guelf *or* **guelph** \ˈgwelf, -eüf\ *n* -s *usu cap* [It *Guelfo,* fr. ML *Guelphus,* fr. MHG *Welf,* name of a German princely family, fr. OHG *welf, hwelf* whelp — more at WHELP] **:** a member of a political faction in Italy from the 12th to the 15th centuries that opposed the authority of the German emperors in Italy and was made up of a church party asserting the papacy to be independent of the emperors and a party of principalities and city republics contending for their own rights and liberties — compare GHIBELLINE — **guelf·ic** *or* **guelph·ic** \-fik\ *adj, usu cap*

guelph keg \"-\ *n, usu cap G* [fr. the name *Guelph*] **:** a cylindrical wooden vessel made of two or three layers of veneer

gue·mal \ˈg(w)āməl\ *or* **gue·mul** \gwāˈmül\ *or* **ge·mul** \gāˈmül\ *or* **hue·mul** \wāˈmül\ *n* -s [AmerSp *güemul, guamul, huemul,* fr. Araucan *huemul*] **:** either of two small So. American deer (*Hippocamelus bisulcus* and *H. antisiensis*) having simple forked antlers

gue·non \gəˈnōⁿ, -nän\ *n* -s [F, fr. MF] **:** any of various long-tailed chiefly arboreal African monkeys of *Cercopithecus* and related genera (as the green monkey and grivet)

1guer·don \ˈgərdᵊn\ *n* -s [ME, fr. MF *guerdon, guerredon,* fr. OF, modif. (influenced by L *donum* gift) of OHG *widarlōn,* fr. *widar* again, against + *lōn* reward — more at WITH, LUCRE] **:** something that one has earned or gained **:** REWARD, RECOMPENSE, REQUITAL

2guerdon \"\ *vt* -ED/-ING/-S [ME *gerdonen,* fr. MF *guerredoner,* fr. OF, fr. *guerredon,* n.] **1 :** to give guerdon to **:** REWARD ⟨richly ~*ed* for his aid⟩ **2 :** to be a recompense for ⟨a gem to ~ faithful service⟩

guer·don·less \-ləs\ *adj* [ME *gwerdounles,* fr. *guerdoun, guerdon* + *-les* -less] **:** receiving no guerdon

gue·reza \gəˈrēzə\ *n* -s [native name in Ethiopia] **:** any of several African monkeys of the genus *Colobus* (esp. *C. guereza*) that have along the sides of the body and on the tail long white fringes of silky hair contrasting with the black or occas. reddish ground color of the coat

gue·ri·don \ˈgārēdōⁿ\ *n, pl* **gueridons** \-ōⁿ(z)\ [F *guéridon,* fr. the name *Guéridon*] **:** a small stand or table (as for a lamp or vase) usu. ornately carved and embellished

gue·rite \(ˈ)gāˈrēt\ *n* -s [F *guérite,* fr. MF, prob. alter. of OF *garite, guarite* watchtower — more at GARRET] **:** a turret or shelter for a sentry on an old fort

1guern·sey \ˈgərnzē, ˈgän-,ˈgain-, -zi\ *adj, usu cap* [fr. *Guernsey,* Channel islands] **:** of or from the island of Guernsey, Channel islands **:** of the kind or style prevalent in Guernsey

2guernsey \"\ *n* **1** -s **:** a heavy knitted garment usu. in the form of a shirt and worn esp. by sailors — compare JERSEY 2 **2 a** *usu cap* **:** a breed of fawn and white dairy cattle larger than Jerseys and producing rich yellowish milk that was developed on the island of Guernsey from stock of French origin **b** -s *often cap* **:** an animal of this breed

guernsey elm *n, usu cap G* **:** JERSEY ELM

guernsey lily *n, usu cap G* **:** a southern African bulbous plant (*Nerine sarniensis*) with bright red umbellate flowers that is naturalized on the island of Guernsey and widely cultivated as an ornamental

guernsey partridge *n, usu cap G* **:** RED-LEGGED PARTRIDGE

guer·ril·la *also* **gue·ril·la** \gəˈrilə\ *n* -s *often attrib* [Sp *guerrilla,* lit., small war, dim. of *guerra* war, fr. OHG *werra* discord, strife, quarrel — more at WAR] **1** *archaic* **:** irregular war carried on by independent bands **2 a :** one who carries on or assists in an irregular war or engages in irregular warfare in connection with a regular war; *esp* **:** a member of an independent band engaged in predatory excursions in wartime **b :** a member of a military detachment functioning in the rear of enemy lines esp. in guerrilla warfare

guer·ril·la·ism \-ləˌizəm\ *n* -s **:** the activities of guerrillas **:** GUERRILLA WARFARE

guerrilla warfare *n* **:** military actions carried out by small forces in the rear of an enemy with the object of harassing the enemy, interrupting his lines of communication, and destroying his supplies

guer·ri·lle·ro \ˌgerə(l)ˈye(ˌ)rō\ *n* -s [Sp, fr. *guerrilla*] **:** GUERRILLA 2a

gues *pl of* GUE

guesd·ism \ˈgeˌdizəm\ *n* -s *usu cap* [Jules B. *Guesde* †1922 Fr. political leader + E *-ism*] **:** Marxian socialism as advocated by Jules Guesde

guesd·ist \-ˌdəst\ *n* -s *usu cap* [J. *Guesde* + E *-ist*] **:** an advocate of or adherent to Guesdism

1guess \ˈges\ *vb* -ED/-ING/-ES [ME *gessen,* prob. of Scand origin; akin to Icel *gizka* to guess, Norw & Sw *gissa;* akin to MD *gissen, gessen* to guess, MLG *gissen* to guess, ON *geta* to get, guess — more at GET] *vt* **1 :** to form a judgment or opinion of without knowledge or often without means of knowledge: **a :** to form an opinion of from insufficient, uncertain, or ambiguous evidence or on grounds of probability alone **:** CONJECTURE, ESTIMATE, SURMISE ⟨could only ~ what the final result of this study would be⟩ ⟨~*ed* his age and missed by five years⟩ ⟨correctly ~*ed* the height of the building⟩ ⟨looked at the sky and ~*ed* that there would be rain before morning⟩ **:** ASSUME, DEDUCE, INFER ⟨the theory has first to be ~*ed,* and its consequences drawn out and tested afterwards —Maurice Cranston & J.W.N.Watkins⟩ ⟨what can be deduced and ~*ed* from these quaint and curious volumes of forgotten lore —A.M.Young⟩ **b :** to form an opinion of without evidence **:** make a random judgment or supposition concerning ⟨amused themselves by ~*ing* the identity of their fellow passengers⟩ ⟨a prize for ~*ing* correctly the number of beans in a beanbag⟩ ⟨~ which hand holds a coin⟩ **2 :** to conjecture correctly: **a :** to hit upon or solve by a conjecture **:** arrive at (a correct answer or solution) partly or solely by chance or intuition ⟨~*ed* my age the first time⟩ ⟨an amazing ability at ~*ing* riddles⟩ ⟨an attempt to ~ the acrostic with more than half the lines unsolved —J.E.S. Thompson⟩ ⟨new words can be ~*ed,* shades of meaning deduced from a second reading —J.M.Barzun⟩ **b :** to form a true or proper opinion of esp. without pertinent knowledge of one's own **:** CONCEIVE, DIVINE, GATHER ⟨an objective the full nature of which may not have been ~*ed* —Mary Austin⟩ ⟨enough is said for the reader to ~ something of what it must have meant to stand at last on the summit of the world —E.F.Norton⟩ **3 :** BELIEVE, IMAGINE, SUPPOSE, THINK — usu. used with an objective clause or with *so* ⟨~ I'll go to bed⟩ ⟨said he ~*ed* he knew as much as the next man⟩ ⟨thought for a moment and then answered that he ~*ed* so⟩ ⟨what saved him, I ~, was his unfaltering sense of the ridiculous —Giles Romilly⟩ ~ *vi* **:** to make a guess **:** form a random judgment **:** CONJECTURE ⟨if you don't know the answers, ~⟩ ⟨a matter we can only ~ about⟩ ⟨~*ed* wrong⟩ ⟨~*ed* at the probable outcome of the discussions⟩ **syn** see CONJECTURE

2guess \"\ *n* -ES [ME *gesse,* fr. *gessen,* v.] **:** an opinion formed without sufficient or decisive evidence or grounds **:** CONJECTURE, SURMISE ⟨when he had made his scientific ~, his hypothesis, he computed what ought to happen, if it were true, in certain definite cases —Josiah Royce⟩ — **by guess and by god** *also* **by guess and by gosh** *or* **by guess and by golly :** without employment of an ordinary degree of technical accuracy or knowledge (as in measuring or in formulating materials) ⟨some of these surveys were done completely *by guess and by god*⟩

3guess \"\ *adj* [prob. fr. D *gust,* fr. MD; akin to LG *güste* barren, EFris *güst, geste* barren, OHG *geisinī* barrenness — more at GEASON] *dial Eng, of a cow or ewe* **:** BARREN, DRY

guess·able \-səbəl\ *adj* **:** being such as may be guessed

guess·er \-sə(r)\ *n* -s [ME *gessare,* fr. *gessen,* v. + *-are, -er* -er] **:** one that guesses

guessing game *n* **:** a game in which the participants compete individually or in teams in the identification of something indicated obscurely (as in riddles or charades); *broadly* **:** a situation (as in politics or international relations) in which opposing factions attempt to gain advantages by each keeping its own intentions dark

guess·ing·ly *adv* [fr. pres. part. of 1*guess* + *-ly*] **:** by means of guessing **:** by guesswork

guess-rope \ˈgesˌrōp\ *n* [alter. (influenced by *guess-warp*) of earlier *guest rope*] **1 :** GUESS-WARP **2 :** GUEST ROPE

guess stick *n* **1** *slang* **:** SLIDE RULE **2** *slang* **:** SCALE RULE

1guess·ti·mate *or* **gues·ti·mate** \ˈgestəˌmāt\ *vt* -ED/-ING/-S [blend of 1*guess* and *estimate,* v.] *slang* **:** to form an estimate of (as future population, costs, employment) without adequate factual or statistical information

2guess·ti·mate *or* **gues·ti·mate** \-ˌmət\ *n* -s *slang* **:** an estimate arrived at solely or chiefly by guesswork

guess-warp *or* **ges·warp** \ˈgeˌswȯrp\ *n* [ME *gyes warp,* fr. *gyes* (origin and meaning unknown) + *warp*] **1 :** a line carried in a small boat from a ship to a buoy, an anchor, or the shore **2 :** GUEST ROPE **3 :** a line led from a ship through a fairlead on a boat boom for small boats to make fast to

guesswork \ˈ=ˌ=\ *n* [2*guess* + *work*] **:** work performed or results obtained by guess **:** CONJECTURE

1guest \ˈgest\ *n* -s *often attrib* [ME *gest, gist,* fr. ON *gestr;* akin to OE *gæst, giest* guest, stranger, OHG *gast,* Goth *gasts* guest, stranger, L *hostis* stranger, enemy] **1** *obs* **:** STRANGER **2 a :** a person entertained in one's house or at one's table ⟨had unexpected ~*s* for supper⟩ ⟨~ towels⟩ ⟨invited ~*s* for Christmas⟩ **b :** a person to whom hospitality (as of a home or club) is extended; *esp* **:** one invited to participate in some activity (as an excursion) at the expense of another ⟨played golf at the country club as the ~ of one of the members⟩ ⟨a theater party of six, the host and five ~*s*⟩ ⟨enjoyed ~ privileges at several clubs⟩ **c :** a person who lodges, boards, or receives refreshment for pay (as at a hotel, boardinghouse, restaurant) whether permanently or transiently **:** PATRON **d :** a traveler who in return for compensation receives from an innkeeper or hotelkeeper for an indefinite time board, lodging, and entertainment and for whose safety and comfort and the safeguarding of whose property the innkeeper or hotelkeeper is responsible under law — compare LODGER **e :** one who visits or travels in an area (as a state or province) beyond the boundaries of his established residence or work **f :** one who visits, travels or resides abroad by permission of a foreign country ⟨~ of Canada⟩ **g :** a person who accepts transportation (as in a motor vehicle) for which he makes no financial recompense **3 :** an organism sharing the dwelling of another; *usu* **:** an insect inhabiting or breeding in a nest or gall of another insect often without causing much inconvenience to the original owner except by consuming the supply of food **:** INQUILINE — compare MYRMECOPHILE **4 :** a mineral introduced into and usu. displacing a preexistent mineral or rock **5 a** *or* **guest artist** *or* **guest star :** a person usu. of prominence in the entertainment world who appears temporarily on a program (as a radio or television show) or with an organization (as an orchestra or theatrical stock company) ⟨a ~ announcer⟩ ⟨doubled his income by making ~ appearances⟩ **b :** a person not a regular member of a cast or company (as a member of a studio audience) who participates in a show

2guest \"\ *vb* -ED/-ING/-S [ME *gesten,* fr. *gest,* n.] *vt* **:** to receive or entertain as a guest ⟨local members ~*ed* most of the delegates⟩ ~ *vi* **1** *archaic* **:** to be or act the part of a guest **2 :** to appear as a guest (as on radio or television or in a theatrical performance)

guestchamber \ˈ=ˌ==\ *n* **:** GUEST ROOM

guest-conduct \ˌ=ˈ==\ *vt* **:** to lead or direct (a musical organization) as a guest — **guest conductor** *n*

guest·en \ˈgestən\ *adj* [ME *geston,* prob. fr. pl. of *gest*] *archaic* **:** for guests

guest·er \ˈgestə(r)\ *n* -s **:** one that guests

guest flag *n* **:** a blue rectangular flag with a diagonal white stripe flown on a yacht to indicate that the craft is being used by a guest of the owner in the owner's absence

guesthouse \ˈ=ˌ=\ *n* [ME *gest house,* fr. *gest* guest + *house*] **:** a building for guests: as **a :** a separate building in a monastic establishment provided esp. formerly for the reception of travelers **b :** a separate establishment on a private estate for the accommodation of guests **c :** a superior boardinghouse usu. providing for its guests recreational and social amenities as well as food and lodging

guest·ing \ˈgestiŋ\ *n* -s [ME *gesting,* fr. gerund of *gesten*] *archaic* **:** the action of lodging or entertaining a guest

guest·less \ˈgestləs\ *adj* **:** having no guests; *sometimes* **:** INHOSPITABLE

guest·ly \-lē\ *adj* **:** like a guest **:** suitable for guests

guestmaster \ˈ=ˌ==\ *n* **:** one whose duty it is to receive and entertain guests in a religious house **:** HOSTELER

guest of honor 1 : one in whose honor a social function or ceremony is held **2 :** an eminent person invited to a social function or ceremony

guest ranch *n* **:** DUDE RANCH

guest right *n* **:** a claim to a privilege (as entertainment or protection) to which a guest is entitled usu. for a brief period by custom or law; *also* **:** the right esp. among primitive peoples to make such a claim on the basis of blood or other relationship

guest room *n* **:** a room for the use of guests: as **a :** a bedroom in a home not regularly occupied by a member of the household and kept primarily for guests **:** a spare room **b :** a room in a hotel or lodging house for occupation by guests

guest rope \ˈgeˌstrōp\ *n* [prob. alter. of *guess* (as in *guess-warp*)] **1 :** a line that is supplementary to a towline and is used esp. to keep the tow steady **2 :** a line run along a ship's side or out to the end of a boom for small boats to hold to — called also *boat line, grab rope*

guestwise *adv, obs* **:** like a guest **:** in the manner proper to a guest

guet·a·pens \ˌged·əˈpäⁿ\ *n, pl* **guetapens** \-äⁿ(z)\ [F *guet-apens,* fr. MF, fr. *de guet apens* with premeditation, alter. of *de guet apensé*] **:** AMBUSH, SNARE, TRAP ⟨a trick to lure him into some ~ —Rafael Sabatini⟩

gue·tar *or* **gue·tare** \gwāˈtär\ *n, pl* **guetar** *or* **guetars** *or* **guetare** *or* **guetares** *usu cap* [Sp *Güetar,* of AmerInd origin] **1 a :** a Chibchan people of central Costa Rica **b :** a member of such people **2 :** the language of the Guetar people

gue·tre \ˈgād·ə(r)\ *archaic var of* GAITER

guet·tar·da \gəˈtärdə\ *n* [NL, after Jacques Étienne *Guettard* †1786 Fr. naturalist] **1** *cap* **:** a genus of tropical American shrubs or trees (family Rubiaceae) that have hard fine-grained yellowish brown to gray wood **2** -s **:** any plant of the genus *Guettarda*

gu·fa *or* **guf·fa** *also* **goo·fa** *or* **goo·fah** \ˈgüfə\ *or* **ku·fa** *or* **koo·fah** \ˈkü-\ *n* -s [Ar *quffah* basket] **:** a round boat made of wickerwork used in Mesopotamia from ancient times

gufa

guff \ˈgəf\ *n* -s [prob. of imit. origin] **:** utterances that are foolish, intended to mislead or deceive, and often truculent **:** HUMBUG, BALDERDASH; *broadly* **:** idle chitchat

[1]**guf·faw** \(,)gəˈfȯ, ˈ=,=\ *n* -s [imit.] **:** a loud or boisterous burst of laughter

[2]**guffaw** \"\ *vi* -ED/-ING/-s **:** to laugh noisily or coarsely

guf·fer \ˈgəfə(r)\ *n* -s [origin unknown] *Scot* **:** EELPOUT 1a

gu·gel·hupf \ˈgügəl,hu̇(p)f\ *or* **gu·gel·hof** *also* **gou·gel·hof** \-hōf\ *n* -s [G *gugelhupf, gugelhopf,* fr. *gugel* cowl, monk's hood (fr. MHG *gugel, gugele,* fr. OHG *cucula, cugelā,* fr. LL *cuculla*) + *hupf, hopf,* var. of dial. (Bavaria) *hepfen* yeast (fr. OHG *heffan* to raise, heave) — more at COWL (hood), HEAVE] **:** a semisweet cake usu. of yeast-leavened dough containing raisins, citron, and nuts and baked in a fluted tube pan

gug·gen·heim \ˈgügən,hīm, ˈgu̇g- *sometimes* ˈgəg-\ *n* -s *usu cap* [fr. the name *Guggenheim*] **:** CATEGORY 3

[1]**gug·gle** \ˈgəgəl\ *vb* **guggled; guggled; guggling** \-g(ə)liŋ\ **guggles** [imit.] *vi* **1 :** to make a sound like that of liquid poured from a flask **2 a :** to flow with a guggling sound **:** GURGLE ⟨water *guggling* over the stones⟩ **b :** to drink (as from a jug) with such a sound ~ *vt* **:** to pour or drink (as liquor) with a guggling sound

[2]**guggle** \"\ *n* -s **:** a sound of guggling **:** GURGLE

guglet *var of* GOGLET

gu·glia \ˈgülyə\ *or* **gu·glio** \-l(,)yō\ *n* -s [It *guglia,* alter. (resulting from incorrect division of *l'aguglia*) of obs. It *aguglia* (also, needle), fr. OProv *agulha,* fr. LL *acucula* ornamental pin — more at AGLET] **:** OBELISK

gu·gu *or* **goo–goo** \ˈgü(,)gü\ *n* -s [origin unknown] **:** a native of the Philippine islands — used chiefly in Hawaii and often disparagingly

guhr \ˈgu̇(ə)r\ *n* -s [G *guhr, gur;* akin to MHG *gern* to ferment, OHG *jesan* — more at YEAST] **1 :** a loose earthy deposit from water occurring in the cavities of rocks, being mostly white but sometimes red or yellow, and consisting of a varying mixture of clay or ocher **2** [by shortening] **:** KIESELGUHR

gui·ana \gēˈanə *also* -ˈänə *or* -ˈānə, *chiefly in British Guiana* gīˈanə\ *adj, usu cap* [fr. *Guiana,* region in northern So. America] **:** of or from Guiana, a region of northern So. America **:** of the kind or style prevalent in Guiana **:** GUIANESE

guiana chestnut *n, usu cap G* **:** the seed of the provision tree

gui·anan \-nən\ *adj or n, usu cap* [*Guiana,* the region + E *-an*] **:** GUIANESE

guiana plum *n, usu cap G* **1 :** any of several tropical American shrubs or small trees of the genus *Drypetes* (family Euphorbiaceae); *esp* **:** a shrubby tree (*D. lateriflora*) whose range extends northward into southern Florida — called also *Florida plum* **2 :** the usu. reddish rather dry drupaceous fruit of a Guiana plum

guiana tree *n, usu cap G* **:** a timber tree (*Helicostylis poeppigiana*) of the family Moraceae that has reddish brown hard heavy wood and is widely distributed in northern So. America

[1]**gui·a·nese** \,gēəˈnēz, ,gīə-, -ˈnēs\ *adj, usu cap* [*Guiana,* the region + E *-ese*] **1 :** of, relating to, or characteristic of the region of Guiana **2 :** of, relating to, or characteristic of the people of Guiana

[2]**guianese** \"\ *n* -s *usu cap* **:** a native or inhabitant of the region of Guiana

gui·ano–brazilian \gē,a(,)nō, -ˈä(-, -ˈā(-, ,gēə,nō, ,gīə,nō +\ *adj, usu cap G&B* [*Guiana,* the region + E *-o-* + [1]*Brazilian*] **:** of or relating to Guiana and Brazil; *broadly* **:** BRAZILIAN 3

guib \ˈgib\ *n* -s [native name in Africa] **:** a small harnessed antelope (*Tragelaphus scriptus*) of western Africa

gui·chet \gēˈshā\ *n* -s [F, fr. OF, of Gmc origin; akin to MD *wiket, winket* wicket — more at WICKET] **:** a grill opening (as a hatch or wicket); *esp* **:** a ticket window

guid \ˈgēd, ˈgied, ˈgid\ *Scot var of* GOOD

gui·da \ˈgwēdə\ *n* -s [It, guide, fr. OIt *guidare* to guide, direct, fr. OProv *guidar*] **1 :** the subject of a fugue or the antecedent of a canon **2 :** DIRECT 1 **3 :** a sign indicating the points of entry in a round or canon

guid·able \ˈgīdəbəl\ *adj* [[2]*guide* + *-able*] **:** capable of being guided **:** TRACTABLE

guid·ance \ˈgīdᵊn(t)s\ *n* -s *often attrib* **1 a :** an act of guiding **:** the superintendence or assistance rendered by a guide **:** DIRECTION, LEADING ⟨the blind boy depended on the ~ of his dog⟩ ⟨a manual for the ~ of home handymen⟩ **b :** advice in choosing courses, preparing for a vocation or further education, or coping with personal problems given to students by a teacher or a professional counselor ⟨a ~ specialist⟩ **2 :** a program or service functioning to promote the adjustment of special groups (as disturbed or delinquent children or prisoners) chiefly through psychological counseling and appraisal **3 :** the process of controlling the course of a projectile (as a missile or bomb) by a built-in mechanism ⟨~ system⟩ — compare GUIDED MISSILE

[1]**guide** \ˈgīd\ *n* -s [ME *gide,* fr. MF *guide,* fr. OProv *guida,* fr. *guidar* to guide, direct, of Gmc origin; akin to OE *witan* to look after, depart, *witan* to know — more at WIT] **1 a :** a person who leads or directs another in his way or course (as in a strange country or through difficult terrain) **b :** a person who exhibits and usu. discusses or explains points of interest (as of a city, a museum collection, or a building) to sightseers **c :** something (as a guidebook, signpost, or instruction manual) that provides a person with guiding information **d :** one (as a teacher) who directs a person in his conduct or course of life **:** DIRECTOR, SUPERVISOR ⟨no boy ever had a better ~ than I in the fundamental decencies of life⟩ **2 a :** a contrivance for directing the motion of something; *esp* **:** such a contrivance (as in a tool) having a directing edge, surface, or channel **b :** a device (as a ring or loop) made usu. of metal or agate and attached to a fishing rod to hold the line in position **c :** the groove in which the plow used in bookbinding moves **d :** a small device for guiding threads or strands of fiber on a spinning, winding, quilling, or other textile machine **e :** a device in a printing press or folding machine for holding and releasing a sheet **f :** a grooved director for a surgical probe or knife **g :** a sheet of metal or other material or a card with projecting edge or tab for labeling that is inserted in a card catalog, index, or other file to facilitate reference **3 a :** a person or vehicle upon whom the movements or alignments of a military command are regulated — used esp. in commands ⟨~ right⟩ ⟨~ center⟩ **b :** a warship on which others in a formation regulate their positions **4 a :** GIRL GUIDE **b :** an 11-year-old to 16-year-old girl guide — distinguished from *brownie*

[2]**guide** \"\ *vb* -ED/-ING/-s [ME *giden, guiden,* fr. MF *guider,* alter. (influenced by *guide,* n.) of OF *guier,* of Gmc origin; akin to OE *witan* to look after, depart, *witan* to know — more at WIT] *vt* **1 :** to act as a guide to **:** direct in a way **:** CONDUCT, PILOT ⟨*guided* us through the city⟩ **2 a :** to regulate and manage **:** direct or supervise esp. toward some desirable end, course, way, or development **b :** to superintend the training or education of **:** INSTRUCT, ADVISE, COUNSEL ⟨his studies were *guided* by one of the great educators of the day⟩ **3** *Scot* **:** to treat or handle esp. another person or an animal ⟨*guided* her ill⟩ ~ *vi* **:** to act or work as a guide

syn LEAD, STEER, PILOT, ENGINEER: GUIDE may apply to the act of conducting or directing along a course as performed by one with certain, specific, or intimate knowledge or by something equally trustworthy ⟨*guided* by a native on their expedition through the mountains⟩ ⟨*guide* patrons to their proper seats⟩ ⟨inspired and galvanized by the personality of a great man who was *guiding* them in their art —Stephen Williams⟩ ⟨be *guided* by good judgment —C.S.Kilby⟩ LEAD suggests preceding to show the way; sometimes, in addition, it indicates keeping those following in order; it may refer to taking initiative, determining procedure, or assuming a director's role ⟨*led* his men to safety⟩ ⟨*led* the caravan west⟩ ⟨*leading* the supporters of the amendment⟩ ⟨the man *leading* the research project⟩ STEER suggests the action of one planning or adhering to a course with concomitant controlling, governing, or maneuvering ⟨*steering* the ship past the sandbars into the harbor⟩ ⟨deftly *steered* the Council of the International Congress through its problems concerned with the place of the next session —A.L.Kroeber⟩ ⟨secure in the faith that his reasoned intelligence will *steer* him correctly at all times —H.N.Maclean⟩ PILOT suggests leading or steering over a dangerous, intricate, or complicated course or route ⟨*pilot* the ship through the channel⟩ ⟨wagon trains *piloted* by bearded scouts⟩ ⟨took his sister's arm and *piloted* her to a safe corner⟩ ⟨*piloting* important bills through the senate —*Current Biog.*⟩ ENGINEER may refer to planning and supervising construction; it often indicates carrying through, executing, or effectuating with contriving, maneuvering, manipulating, and calculating ⟨the influential Americans in Hawaii, with the connivance of U.S. Minister Stevens and the "moral" support of American marines, *engineered* a revolution, deposed the Queen —J.W. Ellison b.1891⟩ ⟨spokesman for the party when graceful adjustments were to be made or delicate compromises *engineered* —S.H.Adams⟩ ⟨behind it all was the Soviet leviathan skilfully, though at times crudely, pulling strings, *engineering,* manipulating, staging, and, if need be, intimidating and compelling —Alexander Dallin⟩

guideboard \ˈ=,=\ *n* **:** a board (as upon a guidepost) having upon it directions or information about the way

guide·book \ˈgīd,bu̇k\ *n* **:** HANDBOOK 1; *esp* **:** a book for tourists containing information about routes, accommodations, and places of historical or cultural interest — **guide·book·ish** \-kish\ *adj* — **guide·booky** \-kē\ *adj*

guide card *n* **:** GUIDE 2g

guided *adj* [fr. past part. of [2]*guide*] **1 :** accompanied or supervised by a guide ⟨a ~ tour⟩ ⟨~ groups⟩ **2 :** controllable as to direction of motion in the same way as a guided missile ⟨~ bomb⟩ ⟨~ plane⟩

guided missile *n* **:** a missile whose course toward a target may be altered during passage (as by means of a preset control, a built-in mechanism remotely controlled by radio, a target-seeking radar device, or a self-reacting device)

guide dog *n* **:** a dog trained to lead the blind

guide flag *or* **guide pennant** *n* **:** a flag or pennant flown on the ship that is to act as guide during a fleet maneuver

guide fossil *n* **:** INDEX FOSSIL

guide key *n* **:** HOME KEY

guide·less \ˈgīdləs\ *adj* **:** having no guide **:** lacking leadership or control — **guide·less·ness** *n* -ES

guideline \ˈ=,=\ *n* **:** a line by which one is guided: as **a :** a cord or rope to aid a passer over a difficult point (as on a trail) or to permit retracing a course (as in a cave) **b** (1) **:** an identifying number, letter, or word written on copy or set in a single line of type and placed above type matter for the guidance of copyreader and printer (2) **:** a line drawn from a typographical change to a mark in the margin **c :** an indication or outline of future policy or conduct (as of a government)

guide meridian *n* **:** a line that is marked by monuments, that runs north and south between other more carefully established meridians, and that is used for reference in surveying

guide mill *n* **:** a small roll train with guides on each side used in metalworking to prevent rolled bars from jamming

guide pin *n* **:** a pin or peg for aligning a tool or die properly with the work **:** PILOT — called also *leader pin*

guidepost \ˈ=,=\ *n* **1 :** a post (as at the fork of a road) with guideboards on it to direct travelers **2 :** GUIDE PIN **3 :** INDICATION, SIGN

guid·er \ˈgīdə(r)\ *n* -s [ME *gidour, gider,* fr. MF *guideor, guideur,* alter. (influenced by *guide*) of OF *guieor, guieur,* fr. *guier* to guide + *-eor, -eur* -or — more at GUIDE (v.)] **:** one that guides: as **a :** a device that functions as a guide (as in some production operation) **b :** an adult volunteer leader of a girl guide company in Britain, Canada, and various other countries

guidepost 1

guide rail *n* **:** a track or rail that serves as a guide; *specif* **:** one designed to guide a sliding door

guide rope *n* **:** a rope hung from a balloon or dirigible so as to trail along the ground for about half its length and used esp. to preserve altitude by variation of the length dragging without loss of ballast or gas

guides *pl of* GUIDE, *pres 3d sing of* GUIDE

guide·ship \ˈgīd,ship\ *n* -s [[1]*guide* + *-ship*] *Scot* **:** TREATMENT

guideway \ˈ=,=\ *n* **:** a channel, slot, or track in which something is fitted so that its line of motion is controlled

guide wheel *n* **:** either wheel of a pair of small wheels used to stabilize the rear of a bicycle for learners and young children

guide word *n* **:** CATCHWORD 1b

guiding *pres part of* GUIDE

guiding telescope *n* **:** a visual telescope mounted rigidly parallel to a photographic telescope and used by an observer to supplement the clock motion in maintaining immovable the image of a heavenly body on the photographic plate

guid·man \(ˈ)gœd,man, (ˈ)gied-, (ˈ)gid-\ *Scot var of* GOODMAN

gui·don \ˈgīdän, -īdᵊn\ *n* -s [MF, fr. OProv *guidoo,* fr. *guida* guide — more at GUIDE (n.)] **1 :** a flag resembling but smaller than a standard, cleft or rounded at the outward end, bearing a badge, arms, or other distinctive emblem, and borne as a personal cognizance of some person of rank orig. for military use but later chiefly for display at his funeral **2 a :** a small flag or streamer carried by mounted troops to indicate the side toward the guide when marching and to mark the line on which to make a formation **b :** a usu. swallow-tailed flag borne by a military unit (as of the U.S. armed forces) usu. as a unit marker **c :** a flag rounded and cleft at the outward end and borne as a unit marker (as by a British regiment of dragoons) **3 :** one who carries a guidon

gui·do·ni·an \gwēˈdōnēən\ *adj, usu cap* [*Guido* d'Arezzo (also called Fra *Guittone*) †*ab*1050 Benedictine monk and musical reformer + E *-ian*] **:** relating to the 11th century musician Guido d'Arezzo or his theory of movable hexachords

guidonian hand *n, usu cap G* **:** a figure representing the tones of the gamut on the joints of the left hand to which a singing master could point in teaching solmization

guidonian syllable *n, usu cap G* **:** one of the six syllables *ut* or *do, re, mi, fa, sol, la* used for the tones of the hexachord — compare SOLMIZATION

guid·sire *var of* GUDESIRE

guid·wife \(ˈ)gœd,wəif, (ˈ)giē-, (ˈ)gi-\ *var of* GOODWIFE

guid·willie \gœˈdwili, giē-, gi-\ *adj* [*guidwill* (var. of *goodwill*) + *-ie*] **1** *Scot* **:** LIBERAL, GENEROUS **2** *Scot* **:** CORDIAL, CHEERING ⟨we'll tak a right *guidwillie* waught for auld lang syne —Robert Burns⟩

guige \ˈgēj, ˈgēzh\ *n* -s [ME *gige,* fr. MF *guige, guiche,* fr. OF] **:** an extra leather strap by which the shield of a knight was slung

guignar·dia \gēnˈyärdēə, g(w)igˈnä-\ *n, cap* [NL, fr. Léon *Guignard* †1928 Fr. botanist + NL *-ia*] **:** a genus of fungi (family Sphaeriaceae) having single-celled or unequally 2-celled spindle-shaped hyaline ascospores — see BLACK ROT

guigne \ˈgēnʸ, -nyə\ *n, pl* **guignes** \-nʸ,-nyəz\ [F, fr. MF *guigne, guine*] **:** GEAN

gui·gnet's green \(ˈ)gēnˈyāz-\ *n, usu cap 1st G* [after C.E. *Guignet,* 19th cent. Fr. chemist who discovered the process] **1 :** a bluish green pigment of good brilliance and permanence consisting of a hydrated chromic oxide made by fusion of sodium dichromate and boric acid and hydrolysis of the product **2 :** a dark bluish green that is greener and stronger than average teal green and greener, lighter, and stronger than invisible green (sense 2) — called also *Mittler's green*

gui·gnol \gēnˈyȯl, -yōl\ *n* -s *sometimes cap* [F, prob. after *Guignol,* reputed name of a silkworker of Lyons and character of the puppet theater which Laurent Mourguet installed there for the earliest performance (in 1795) of French puppet shows] **1 :** PUPPET; *esp* **:** HAND PUPPET — compare MARIONETTE **2 :** PUPPET SHOW **3 :** a theatrical production featuring melodramatic tension, horror, and shock

gui·gno·let \,gēnyəˈlā\ *n* -s [F, dim. of *guigne*] **:** a French liqueur made from black sweet cherries

gui·jo \(ˈ)gēˈhō\ *n* -s [PhilSp, fr. Tag *gihò*] **1 :** a large Philippine timber tree (*Shorea guiso*) of the family Dipterocarpaceae having strong heavy hard wood with a striking figure and moderately fine texture **2 :** the wood of the guijo

guil·an·di·na \,gwilənˈdīnə, -ˈdēnə\ *n, cap* [NL, after *Guilandini* (Melchior Wieland) †1589 Prussian botanist in Italy] *in some classifications* **:** a genus that comprises tropical American woody vines, scrambling shrubs, and trees having seeds enclosed in large prickly pods and that is usu. included in the genus *Caesalpinia*

guild *also* **gild** \ˈgild\ *n* -s [ME *gilde,* fr. ON *gildi* guild, payment, tribute; akin to OE *gild, gield* service, tribute — more at GELD (tax)] **1 :** an association of men belonging to the same class, engaged in kindred pursuits, or having common interests or aims: as **a :** any of various medieval associations having both social and semireligious features **b :** a medieval association of merchants controlling local trade in some parts of Britain and sometimes constituting the local governing body **c :** a medieval association of members of a craft or trade established to promote the welfare of that craft and its members and sometimes replacing the merchants' guild as a governing body **d :** any of various modern associations, societies, or brotherhoods resembling the medieval guilds in their aims ⟨a ~ for charitable work⟩ ⟨the hospital ~ of our church⟩; *broadly* **:** FELLOWSHIP, SOCIETY **2** *obs* **:** the headquarters or meeting place of a guild **:** GUILDHALL **3 :** an ecological group of plants distinguished from ordinary herbs, shrubs, and trees by a special mode of life (as the saprophytic, parasitic, epiphytic, or twining) usu. involving some degree of dependence on other plants

guild church *n* **:** an English metropolitan church that has been freed from parish responsibilities in order to minister full time to nonresident city workers during their hours in the city

[1]**guil·der** \ˈgildə(r)\ *n* -s [modif. (influenced by E *-er*) of D *gulden* — more at GULDEN] **:** GULDEN, *esp* **:** a Dutch gulden — see MONEY table

[2]**guild·er** \"\ *n* -s [*guild* + *-er*] **:** a member of a modern guild

guild·hall \ˈgild,hȯl\ *n* [ME *gildhal, gildehalle,* fr. *gilde* guild + *hal, halle* hall — more at HALL] **:** the hall where a guild or corporation usu. assembles **:** TOWN HALL

guild·ite \ˈgil,dīt\ *n* -s [Frank N. *Guild* †1939 Am. mineralogist + E *-ite*] **:** a dark chestnut brown mineral $(Cu,Fe)_3(Fe,Al)_4(SO_4)_7(OH)_4 \cdot 15H_2O$ that is a basic hydrated sulfate of copper and iron

guild merchant *n* [*guild* + *merchant* (adj.)] **:** GUILD 1b

guild·ry \ˈgildri\ *n* -ES **1** *Scot* **:** guild membership **2** *often cap, Scot* **:** the municipal corporation of a royal Scottish burgh ⟨the ~ of Stirling⟩

guild·ship \ˈgild,ship\ *n* [*guild* + *-ship*] **1 :** GUILD 1a, 1b, 1c **2 :** the status of a guild member

guilds·man \ˈgil(d)zmən\ *n, pl* **guildsmen** [*guild's* (gen. of *guild*) + *man*] **1 :** a guild member **2 :** an advocate of guild socialism

guild socialism *n* **:** a socialistic theory advocating state ownership of all industries with monopolistic control and management in each by a guild composed of all its handworkers and brainworkers and restricted only by regulations safeguarding the consumers' interests; *esp* **:** such a theory developed in England early in the 20th century

guild tree \ˈgil(d)-\ *n* [obs. Sc. *guild,* alter. of [3]*gold*] **:** COMMON BARBERRY

[1]**guile** \ˈgīl, *esp before pause or consonant* -īəl\ *n* -s [ME *gile,* fr. OF *guile,* prob. of Gmc origin; akin to OE *wīgle* divination — more at WILE] **1 :** crafty or deceitful cunning **:** DUPLICITY, DECEIT, TREACHERY **2** *archaic* **:** STRATAGEM, DEVICE, TRICK **syn** see DECEIT

[2]**guile** \"\ *vt* -ED/-ING/-s [ME *gilen, guilen,* fr. OF *guiler,* fr. *guile,* n.] *archaic* **:** BEGUILE, DECEIVE

guile·ful \-fəl\ *adj* [ME *gileful,* fr. *gile* guile + *-ful*] **:** full of guile **:** characterized by cunning, deceit, or treachery **syn** see SLY

guile·ful·ly \-fəlē, -li\ *adv* [ME *gilefully,* fr. *gileful* + *-ly*] **:** in a guileful manner **:** with guile

guile·ful·ness *n* -ES [ME *gilefulnesse,* fr. *gileful* guileful + *-nesse* -ness] **:** guileful quality or state

guile·less \ˈgī(ə)lləs\ *adj* **:** free from guile; *broadly* **:** innocent, naive, and unsophisticated ⟨children raising their ~ eyes from play⟩ — **guile·less·ly** *adv* — **guile·less·ness** *n* -ES

guil·ery \ˈgīləri\ *n* -ES [ME *gilerie, gilrie,* fr. MF *gilerie,* fr. *giler, guiler* to guile + *-erie* -ery] *now dial Eng* **:** a trick or beguilement

guil·lain-bar·re syndrome \gē,yaⁿbəˈrā-\ *n, usu cap G&B* [after Georges *Guillain b*1876 Fr. physician and neurologist and Jean A. *Barré* 20th cent. Fr. neurologist] **:** a neurologic disorder of unknown cause characterized by sensory disturbances in the extremities and slight to severe locomotor impairment

guil·le·met \,gē(y)əˈmā, gilə,met\ *n* -s [F, irreg. dim. of *Guillaume* William, reputed name of its inventor] **:** either of the marks ⟨«or»⟩ used as quotation marks in French writing

guil·le·mot \ˈgilə,mät\ *n* -s [F, fr. MF, irreg. dim. of *Guillaume* William] **:** any of several narrow-billed auks of northern seas constituting two genera (*Uria* and *Cepphus*) of the family Alcidae and having skins, feathers, and eggs that are highly valued by natives of regions where they breed — see BLACK GUILLEMOT, MURRE

guil·loche \gəˈlōsh, gē(y)ō-\ *n* -s [F *guillochis,* fr. MF, perh. fr. the name *Guilloche,* fr. *Guillot,* familiar form of *Guillaume* William] **1 :** an architectural ornament in the form of two or more bands twisted over each other in a series leaving circular openings which are filled with round devices **2 :** a pattern (as on metalwork) made by interlacing curved lines

guilloche 1

[1]**guil·lo·tine** \ˈgilə,tēn, ˈ=,=; ,gē(y)əˈtēn, ˈ=,=\ *n* -s [F, after Joseph Ignace *Guillotin* †1814 Fr. physician who in 1789 proposed its use] **1 :** a machine for beheading by means of a heavy ax or blade that slides down in vertical guides **2 :** a shearing machine or instrument (as a paper cutter or metal cutter) that in action resembles a guillotine **3 :** a surgical instrument that consists of a ring bearing a sliding knife blade and is used for cutting out a tonsil or other protruding structure capable of being engaged by the ring **4 :** closure by the imposition of a predetermined time limit on the consideration of specific sections of a bill or portions of other legislative business ⟨announced that the Transport Bill was to pass — under a ~ — by 10 p.m. on Monday —*Punch*⟩ ⟨the New Zealand House has not had to adopt the ~ —Walter Nash⟩ **5 :** a window with a vertically sliding sash and without counterbalanced sash weights **6 :** something likened to a guillotine esp. in bringing about an abrupt termination (as of a former occupation) ⟨that ~ of joys, bedtime —Nadine Gordimer⟩ — compare AXE 3 **7 :** a wrestling fall in which from a cross-body ride the aggressor shifts his own arms and head under the opponent's locked arm and grasps the opponent's head in a reverse half nelson while retaining a scissors grip on his near leg

[2]**guillotine** \"\ *vb* -ED/-ING/-s [F *guillotiner,* fr. *guillotine*] *vt* **1 :** to behead with a guillotine **b :** to trim with a guillotine **2 :** to cut off or cut short as if with a guillotine ⟨*guillotining* needless waste⟩ **3 :** to subject (as a bill) to the guillotine ⟨the power to ~ bills in standing committee —Herbert Morrison⟩ ~ *vi* **:** to impose the guillotine ⟨the power to ~⟩

guillotine amputation *n* **:** a surgical amputation (as of a leg) in which the skin is incised circumferentially and allowed to retract, successive layers of muscle are then circularly divided, and finally the bone is divided and which is used esp. as an emergency procedure

guil·lo·tin·er \-nə(r)\ *n* -s **:** the operator of a guillotine

guillotine shears *n* **:** power shears in which the upper knife slides between vertical guides

[1]**guilt** \ˈgilt\ *n* -s [ME *gilt, gult,* fr. OE *gylt*] **1** *obs* **a :** delinquency or failure in respect to one's duty **:** OFFENSE, TRESPASS **b :** responsibility for an offense **:** FAULT **c :** state of deserving punishment **:** DESERTS **2 :** the fact of having com-

mitted a breach of conduct esp. violating law and involving a penalty; *broadly* **:** guilty conduct ⟨a life of ~ and shame⟩ **3 a :** the state of one who has committed an offense esp. consciously **:** CULPABILITY ⟨his ~ was written in his face⟩ **b :** feelings of culpability esp. for imagined offenses or from a sense of inadequacy **:** morbid self-reproach often manifest in marked preoccupation with the moral correctness of one's behavior **:** SELF-ACCUSATION ⟨aggressive responses originating in inner ~ and uncertainty⟩ **4 :** the state of being liable to penalty for offense against law — used in respect to persons and sometimes property that by reason of illegal usage has become liable to forfeiture or other burden

2**guilt** \"\ *archaic var of* GILT

guilt by association : moral guilt or unfitness presumed to exist on the basis of one's known associations ⟨the doctrine of *guilt by association* has on occasion been used to brand as currently disloyal persons who at some past time had been members of an organization not known to be or considered subversive at the time they were members⟩

guilt·i·ly \-tᵊlē, -li\ *adv* **:** in a guilty manner **:** with guilt

guilt·i·ness \-tēnəs, -tin-\ *n* -ES [ME *giltines*, fr. *gilty* guilty + *-nes*, *-ness* -ness] **:** the quality or state of being guilty

guilt·less \-tləs\ *adj* [ME *giltlesse*, fr. *gilt* guilt + *-lesse* -less] **1 :** free from guilt or evil **:** INNOCENT ⟨a ~ man⟩ ⟨~ of any evil intent⟩ **2 :** lacking experience, familiarity, or dealings — used postpositively and with *of* ⟨a bowed old house long ~ of paint⟩

guilt·less·ly *adv* **:** in a guiltless manner

guilt·less·ness *n* -ES **:** the quality or state of being guiltless

guilt offering *n* [so called fr. allusion to Num 5] **:** an animal sacrifice made in ancient Israel in atonement for trespass against the property of God or man following full restitution of property plus one fifth — called also *trespass offering*

guiltsick \'ˌ=ˌ=\ *adj* [1*guilt* + *sick*] **:** REMORSEFUL

guilty \'giltē, -ti\ *adj* -ER/-EST [ME *gilty*, fr. OE *gyltig*, fr. *gylt* guilt + *-ig* -y] **1 a :** having committed a breach of conduct **:** justly chargeable with or responsible for a delinquency, crime, or sin ⟨~ in the eyes of his fellowmen⟩ **b :** justly chargeable with or culpably responsible for a specified fault or crime ⟨~ of bad taste⟩ ⟨~ of larceny⟩ **2** *obs* **:** justly liable to or deserving of a penalty ⟨they answered and said, He is ~ of death Mt 26:66 (AV)⟩ **3 a :** suggesting, showing, or involving guilt ⟨~ looks⟩ ⟨~ acts⟩ **b :** filled with or suffering from guilt ⟨a ~ conscience⟩ ⟨~ minds⟩ **c :** resulting from a sense of guilt ⟨~ fears⟩ **4** *obs* **:** CONSCIOUS, COGNIZANT **syn** see BLAMEWORTHY

guim·bard \'gim,bärd, 'gam-\ *n* -S [F *guimbarde* jew's harp (formerly, a kind of dance), perh. fr. Prov *guimbardo*, a kind of dance, fr. *guimba* to leap, gambol, fr. OProv *guimbar*, *cembar* to leap, gambol, fr. *camba* leg — more at GAMBOL] **:** JEW'S HARP

gui·met's blue \(')gē¦māz-\ *n*, *often cap G* [after Jean Baptiste *Guimet* †1871 Fr. chemist] **1 :** ULTRAMARINE **2 :** FRENCH BLUE

guimpe \'gamp, 'gimp\ *n* -S [F, fr. OF *guimple*, *wimple* veil, pennant, wimple, of Gmc origin; akin to MD *wimpel* wimple, cloak — more at WIMPLE] **1 :** CHEMISETTE; *also* **:** a blouse worn under a jumper or pinafore **2 :** a wide usu. stiffly starched cloth used to cover the neck and shoulders by nuns of some orders **3** [by alter.] **:** GIMP 1

gui·nau \gē'naü\ *n*, *pl* **guinau** *or* **guinaus** *usu cap* [Sp *guinao*, of AmerInd origin] **1 a :** an extinct Arawakan people of Venezuela **b :** a member of such people **2 :** the language of the Guinau people

1**guin·ea** \'ginē, -ni\ *adj*, *usu cap* **1** [fr. *Guinea*, region in West Africa] **a :** of or from the region of Guinea, West Africa **:** of the kind or style prevalent in the region of Guinea **b :** trading with Guinea ⟨a *Guinea* merchant⟩ ⟨*Guinea* ships⟩ **2** [fr. *Guinea*, republic in West Africa] **:** of or from the Republic of Guinea **:** of the kind or style prevalent in the Republic of Guinea

2**guinea** \"\ *n* -S [after *Guinea*, region in West Africa] **1 a** [so called fr. the fact that it was supposedly first made out of gold from Guinea] **:** an English gold coin issued from 1663 to 1813 and fixed in 1717 as the equivalent of 21 shillings **b :** a unit of value equivalent to one guinea coin ⟨a five-*guinea* coin⟩ **c :** a unit of value equal to 21 shillings ⟨accounts are sometimes kept in and prices are sometimes quoted in *guineas*⟩ **d :** the Saudi Arabian sovereign first issued in 1951 **2 a :** a slave newly imported into the U. S. from Africa **b :** a person noticeably foreign **c** *slang* **:** ITALIAN — usu. used disparagingly **d** *usu cap* **:** one of a group of people of mixed white, Indian, and Negro ancestry who live chiefly in West Virginia and Maryland — often used disparagingly **3** [by shortening] **:** GUINEA FOWL **4 :** one who works in or about a stable; *specif* **:** a horse groom

guinea carmine B *n*, *usu cap G&C* [1*Guinea*] **:** an acid dye — see DYE table I (under *Acid Violet 12*)

guinea corn *n*, *usu cap G* **1 :** any of several grain sorghums; *esp* **:** DURRA **2 :** a variegated Indian corn

guinea duck *n*, *sometimes cap G* **:** MUSCOVY DUCK

guinea fast red *n*, *usu cap G&F&R* [1*Guinea*] **:** either of two acid dyes — see DYE table I (under *Acid Red 34* and *37*)

guinea fowl *n* **:** a West African bird (*Numida meleagris*) that is raised usu. on a small scale for food in most parts of the world and that has typically a bare neck and head, the latter surmounted by a bony casque, and slaty plumage speckled with white though pale and pure white varieties occur; *broadly* **:** any of several similar birds of continental Africa and Madagascar sometimes considered to constitute a subfamily of Phasianidae but now usu. made a separate family Numididae

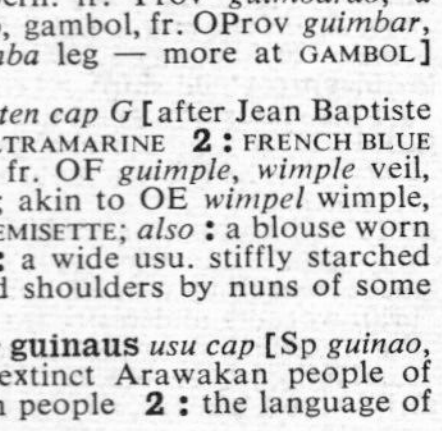

guinea fowl

guinea gold *n* **1 :** gold of 22 karats from which guineas were coined **2 :** an alloy containing 88 percent of copper and 12 percent of zinc that is used esp. for cheap jewelry — called also *red brass*

guinea gold vine *or* **guinea flower** *n* **:** any of several Australian evergreen vines constituting a genus (*Hibbertia*) closely related to *Dillenia* and widely cultivated for their large bright yellow single flowers

guinea grain *n* **:** GRAIN OF PARADISE 1 — usu. used in pl.

guinea grass *n* **1 :** a tall African forage grass (*Panicum maximum*) introduced into tropical America and the southern U. S. where it is used for hay **2 :** JOHNSON GRASS

guinea green *n*, *often cap 1st G* **:** a strong bluish green that is bluer and deeper than average emerald (sense 2c) and greener and deeper than average bright turquoise

guinea green B *n*, *usu cap both Gs* **:** an acid green triphenylmethane dye used chiefly in coloring foods — called also *Acid Green B*; *see* DYE table I (under *Acid Green 3*)

guinea hen *n* **:** a female guinea fowl; *broadly* **:** GUINEA FOWL

guinea–hen flower *n* **:** a Eurasian checkered lily (*Fritillaria meleagris*) that has in early spring pendent bell-shaped flowers usu. veined and checkered with purple or maroon on a paler ground and that is widely cultivated as an ornamental

guinea–hen weed *n* **:** a tropical American herb (*Petiveria alliacea*) having a strong odor suggesting the onion

guin·ea·man \-mən\ *n*, *pl* **guineamen** *usu cap* [1*Guinea* + *man*] **1** *archaic* **:** a merchant or a ship trading with Guinea **2 :** 1GUINEAN

1**guin·e·an** \'ginēən\ *n*, *cap* **1** [*Guinea*, region in West Africa + E *-an*] **:** a native or inhabitant of the region of Guinea, West Africa **2** [*Guinea*, republic in West Africa + E *-an*] **:** a native or inhabitant of the Republic of Guinea

2**guinean** \"\ *adj*, *usu cap* **1 a :** of, relating to, or characteristic of the region of Guinea, West Africa **b :** of, relating to, or characteristic of the people of the region of Guinea **2 a :** of, relating to, or characteristic of the Republic of Guinea **b :** of, relating to, or characteristic of the people of the Republic of Guinea

guinea negro *n*, *usu cap G&N* **:** a Negro from the Guinea coast of Africa; *broadly* **:** any newly arrived Negro slave in the southern U.S.

guinea peach *n*, *usu cap G* **1 :** COUNTRY FIG 1 **2 :** the fruit of the country fig somewhat resembling a large firm seedy strawberry and said to be emetic if eaten to excess

guinea pepper *n*, *usu cap G* **1 :** the pungent aromatic fruit of a tropical African tree (*Xylopia aethiopica*) that is used as a condiment and in folk medicine **2 :** any of various peppers usu. of moderate pungency that are cultivated or naturalized in Africa **3 :** GRAIN OF PARADISE 1 **4 :** a plant bearing Guinea peppers

guinea pig *n* **1** [prob. so called fr. the fact that *Guinea* represented the name of a distant country] **a :** a small stout-bodied short-eared nearly tailless domesticated hystricomorph rodent (genus *Cavia*) often kept as a pet and widely used in biological research, occurring in many combinations of black, white, and tawny red, having short or long hair, and being commonly considered a distinct species (*C. cobaya*) although probably a domesticated variety of some So. American species (as *C. porcellanus* or *C. cutleri*) — called also *cavy*; see APEREA **b :** an animal of *Cavia* or of related genera — often used with a qualifying term ⟨mountain *guinea pigs* of the genus *Microcavia*⟩ **2** *Brit* **a** [so called fr. the payment of guineas as fee to the vessel's captain] **:** MIDSHIPMAN **b :** a person receiving a guinea as a fee — often used of a doctor or clergyman substituting for another **3** [so called fr. the wide use made of guinea pigs in experimentation and research] **:** a subject of experimentation or testing designed to yield data for drawing scientific conclusions or large-scale calculations

guinea pig

guinea plum *n* **:** a large West African tree (*Parinarium excelsum*) with a rough-skinned reddish brown fruit that resembles a plum and is a locally important emergency food and a hard heavy durable wood that varies from yellowish white to reddish brown

guinea rush *n* **:** a widely distributed tropical sedge (*Cyperus articulatus*) with a rootstock that is used in folk medicine as a carminative or tonic and to check vomiting

guineas *pl of* GUINEA

guinea squash *n* **:** EGGPLANT

guinea worm *n*, *often cap G* **:** a slender nematode worm (*Dracunculus medinensis*) attaining a length of several feet, occurring as an adult in the subcutaneous tissues of man and various mammals in parts of Africa and other warm countries, and having a larva that develops in small freshwater crustaceans (as cyclops) and when ingested with drinking water passes through the intestinal wall and tissues to lodge beneath the skin of a mammalian host and there mature

gui·pure \gē'p(y)u̇(ə)r\ *n* -S [F, fr. MF, a kind of lace, fr. *guiper* to cover with silk or wool (of Gmc origin) + *-ure*; akin to MD *wippen* to swing, vibrate, OHG *wīfan* to reel, wind, Goth *weipan* to crown — more at VIBRATE] **:** any of various handmade or machine-made laces that lack a mesh background, consist of heavy or large pattern sections joined by brides or cutouts of cloth joined by bars, and are used esp. for women's dresses, trimmings, appliqués

gui·puz·co·an \gē·püthkōwən, -üsk-\ *n* -S *usu cap* [Sp *guipúzcoano*, fr. *guipuzcoano*, adj., of Guipúzcoa, fr. *Guipúzcoa*, province in northern Spain + Sp *-ano* (fr. L *-anus* -an)] **:** a dialect of the Basque language spoken largely in the province of Guipúzcoa in northern Spain

gui·ro \'(g)wē(,)rō\ *n*, *pl* **guiro** [AmerSp *güiro*, lit., bottle gourd, calabash, prob. fr. Taino] **:** a percussion instrument of Latin American origin made of a serrated gourd and played by scraping a stick along its surface

1**gui·sard** \(')gē¦zärd\ *n* -S *usu cap* [F, fr. *Guise*, name of a powerful 16th cent. ducal family of Lorraine + F *-ard*] **:** a partisan of the Guises in France in the 16th century

2**gui·sard** \'gīzərd\ *n* -S [fr. earlier *gysart*, *gyzard*, fr. obs. Sc *gys*, *gyse* to disguise (fr. ME *gysen* to dress, attire) + Sc *-art*, *-ard*] *Scot* **:** a masker or mummer

1**guise** \'gīz\ *n* -S [ME *gise*, *guise*, fr. OF *guise*, of Gmc origin; akin to OHG *wīsa* manner, style — more at WISE (manner)] **1 :** form or style of dress **:** COSTUME ⟨wondered if she should appear in such disordered ~⟩; *esp* **:** dress that is unexpected on or foreign to the wearer ⟨the lady clad in peasant ~⟩ **2** *archaic* **a :** MANNER, STYLE, FASHION, WAY ⟨it never was our ~ to slight the poor —Alexander Pope⟩ **b :** customary course or way (as of speaking or behaving) **3 a :** external appearance ⟨concerned more with the ~ than the inner worth of his product⟩; *broadly* **:** SHAPE, SEMBLANCE, ASPECT ⟨a fiend in frightful ~⟩ **b :** a superficial seeming **:** an artful or simulated appearance (as of propriety or worth) ⟨that such misconduct should take the ~ of religious ritual is shameful⟩ ⟨tricked the widow in the ~ of a friend of her late husband⟩ **4** *obs Scot* **:** a masked play or masquerade party

2**guise** \"\ *vb* -ED/-ING/-S [ME *gysen*, fr. *gyse*, *gise* (n.)] *vt* **:** DRESS, ARRANGE; *usu* **:** to provide with a foreign guise **:** DISGUISE ⟨the three younger children *guised* as angels⟩ ~ *vi*, *now dial Brit* **:** to appear in disguise esp. as a mummer **:** go mumming

guis·er \'gīzər\ *n* -S [ME (northern dial.) *gysar*, fr. *gysen*, v. + *-ar*, *-er* -er] *chiefly Scot* **:** a person in disguise **:** MUMMER; *esp* **:** a Christmas mummer

guis·quil \'gwē,skēl\ *var of* HUISQUIL

1**gui·tar** \gə'tär, -tå(r, *chiefly substand* 'gi,t- *also* 'gē,t-\ *n* -S [F *guitare*, fr. MF, fr. OSp *guitarra*, fr. Ar *qītār*, fr. Gk *kithara* cithara] **:** a flat-bodied stringed instrument that has a long fretted neck and usu. six strings, is played with a plectrum or plucked with the fingers, sounds an octave lower than written, and has a compass of over three octaves up from E in the great octave — called also *Spanish guitar*; compare ELECTRIC GUITAR, HAWAIIAN GUITAR

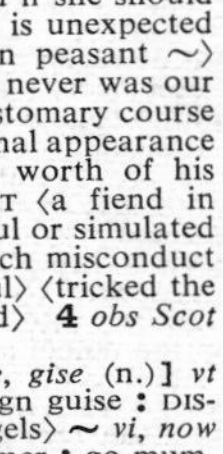

2**guitar** \"\ *vi* **guitarred; guitarred; guitarring; guitars :** to play the guitar

guitar fiddle *n* **:** VIELLE

gui·tar·fish \-tär,fish, -tå,f-\ *n* **:** any of several viviparous rays of the family Rhinobatidae somewhat resembling a guitar in outline when viewed from above

gui·tar·ist \-tärəst, -tär-\ *n* -S **:** one who performs on the guitar

guitar mandolin *n* **:** a guitar-shaped instrument strung, tuned, and played like a mandolin

guitar

guitar plant *n* **:** an Australian shrub (*Lomatia tinctoria*) of the family Proteaceae that furnishes a pink dye from the mealy dust of its seed coat

gui·tar–shaped \-tär,shāpt, -tå,sh-\ *adj* **:** having a strongly rounded lower portion separated from a comparable but often smaller upper portion by a smooth and gradual intermediate constriction so as to suggest the outline of the body of a guitar ⟨the hourglass figure was really more *guitar-shaped*⟩

guit·er·man·ite \'gid·ə(r)mə,nīt\ *n* -S [Frank *Guiterman* 19th cent. Am. metallurgist + E *-ite*] **:** a bluish gray mineral $Pb_{10}As_6S_{19}$ occurring in compact masses that is a compound of lead, arsenic, and sulfur (sp. gr., 5.94)

guit·guit \'gwit,gwit\ *n* -S [imit.] **:** any of several small tropical American honeycreepers

guit·to·ni·an \gwə'tōnēən\ *adj*, *usu cap* [*Guittone* d'Arezzo †1294 It. poet + E *-ian*] **:** of or relating to Guittone d'Arezzo, an Italian poet who is said to have devised the sonnet

gui·zard *var of* 2GUISARD

gu·jar \'güjə(r), 'gùj-, -,jär\ *n*, *pl* **gujar** *or* **gujars** *usu cap* [Hindi *Gūjar*, fr. Skt *Gurjara* Gujar, Gujarat] **1 :** a people of Kashmir that is divided into many subgroups, characterized by rather fair skin, and of uncertain relationship to other peoples of the area **2 :** a member of the Gujar people

gu·ja·ra·ti \,güjə'räd·ē, ,gùj-\ *n*, *pl* **gujarati** *usu cap* [Hindi *gujarātī*, fr. *Gujarāt* Gujarat, region in western India, fr. Skt *Gurjara*, *Gūrjara*] **1 :** the language of Gujarat, Baroda, and neighboring regions in northwestern India **2 :** an alphabet that is essentially a more carefully formed less cursive type of the Kaithi script and is now the principal alphabet used in writing the Gujarati language **3** *or* **guj·ra·ti** \güj'r-, gùj-\ [Hindi *Gujarātī*, *Gujrātī*, fr. *Gujarāt*, *Gujrāt* Gujarat] **:** one of a people chiefly of Gujarat speaking the Gujarati language and specializing in mercantile pursuits

gu·je·rat \¦gujə¦rät, ¦gùj-\ *n* -S *usu cap* [alter. of *Gujarati*] **1 :** GUJARATI 3 **2 :** a heavy wooden cart of India usu. drawn by oxen

guj·ran·wa·la \¦güjrən¦wälə, ¦gùj-\ *adj*, *usu cap* [fr. *Gujranwala*, city in Pakistan] **:** of or from the city of Gujranwala, Pakistan **:** of the kind or style prevalent in Gujranwala

gul \'gül, 'gùl\ *n* -S [Per — more at ROSE] **:** ROSE

gu·la \'g(y)ülə\ *n*, *pl* **gu·lae** \'g(y)ü,lē, 'gü,lī\ *or* **gulas** [ME, fr. L, throat, gullet — more at GLUTTON] **1 a :** the upper front of the neck next to the chin **:** the upper throat **b :** a plate in many insects including most beetles that forms the central part of the lower surface of the head and supports the submentum **2 a :** a molding or group of moldings having a large hollow **b :** OGEE

gu·la·man \gü'lämən\ *n* -S [Tag] **:** CEYLON MOSS

gu·lan·cha \gü'länchə\ *n* -S [Hindi *gulāca*, fr. Skt *gudacī*] **:** an East Indian woody vine (*Tinospora cordifolia*) of the family Menispermaceae with a bitter root believed to have tonic properties

1**gu·lar** \'g(y)ülə(r)\ *adj* [*gula* + *-ar*] **:** of, relating to, or situated on the gula

2**gular** \"\ *n* -S **:** a gular plate or scale (as on the throat of a fish)

gu·laris \g(y)ü'la(a)rəs, gü'lär-\ *n* -ES [NL, perh. fr. L *gula* gullet, throat + *-aris* -ar] **:** either of two West African top minnows: **a :** a topminnow (*Fundulopanchax gularis*) — called also *yellow gularis* **b :** a top minnow (*F. coeruleus*) — called also *blue gularis*

gulash *var of* GOULASH

1**gulch** \'gəlsh, 'gəl-, -lch\ *vb* -ED/-ING/-ES [ME *gulchen*; akin to Norw *gulka* to gulp, Sw dial. *gulka* to sob, Sw *gylka* to vomit, and prob. to Norw *gylpa* to gulp — more at GULP] *vt*, *now dial Eng* **:** to gulp or swallow greedily ~ *vi*, *now dial Eng* **:** to eat or drink with considerable noise and unbecoming haste

2**gulch** \"\ *n* -ES *now dial Eng* **:** a self-indulgent person (as a drunkard or glutton)

3**gulch** \"\ *n* -ES [perh. fr. 1*gulch*] *now dial Eng* **:** a heavy fall

4**gulch** \"\ *vi* -ED/-ING/-ES *now dial Eng* **:** to fall heavily

5**gulch** \'gəlch\ *n* -ES [perh. fr. 1*gulch*] **:** a deep or precipitous cleft in a hillside **:** a ravine or gully; *esp* **:** one that is short, steep-sided, and occas. occupied by a torrent

gul·den \'güldən *also* 'gùl- *or* 'gəl-\ *n*, *pl* **guldens** *or* **gulden** [ME (Sc dial.), Dutch gulden, fr. MD *gulden* (*florijn*), fr. *gulden* golden + *florijn* florin; akin to OE *gylden* golden, OHG *guldīn*; derivatives fr. the stem of E *gold*] **1 :** a German, Austrian, or Dutch gold coin patterned after the Florentine florin; *esp* **:** an old German coin issued from the 15th to the 17th centuries **2 :** any of various silver coins: as **a :** GULDENGROSCHEN **b :** an old Austrian silver coin worth 60 kreuzers before 1859 and 100 kreuzers from 1859 until its issue ceased in 1892 **3 :** any of various units of monetary value: as **a :** a unit of value equal to one gold or silver gulden **b** (1) **:** the basic monetary unit of the Netherlands — see MONEY table (2) **:** a coin or note representing this unit **c** (1) **:** the basic unit of value in Danzig 1920–39 (2) **:** a coin representing this value

guldengroschen \'==,==\ *n*, *pl* **guldengroschens** *or* **guldengroschen** [G, fr. *gulden* (fr. D) + *groschen*] **:** an old German silver coin that preceded the taler in the 15th century, was at first worth one gold gulden, and in the 17th century had the value of ⅔ of a taler — called also *guldentaler*

guldentaler \'==,==\ *n* -S [G, fr. *gulden* + *taler*] **:** GULDENGROSCHEN

gule of august \'gyül-\ *usu cap G&A* [part trans. of AF *goul de Aust*, *gule de Aust* (fr. *goul*, *gule* beginning, opening, lit., throat — fr. L *gula* — + *de* of + *Aust* August), trans. of ML *gula Augusti* — more at GLUTTON] **:** LAMMAS 1

1**gules** \'gyülz\ *n*, *pl* **gules** [ME *goules*, fr. MF *goules*, *gueules*, fr. OF, fr. *goles*, *gueules*, *gueules* fur neckpiece frequently dyed red, pl. of *gole*, lit., throat — more at GULLET] **1 :** the heraldic color red **2 a :** a red color **b :** something red

2**gules** \"\ *adj* **:** of the color gules — abbr. *gu*

1**gulf** \'gəlf, 'gəùf\ *n* -S *often attrib* [ME *goulf*, *golf*, fr. MF *golfe*, fr. OF, fr. OIt *golfo*, fr. LL *colpus*, *colfus*, fr. Gk *kolpos* bosom, bay, gulf; akin to OE *hwealf* vault, arch, OHG *walbo* vault, arch, *hwelben* to vault, arch, ON *hvalf* vault, Goth *hwilftrjom*, dat. pl., coffin] **1 :** a part of an ocean or sea extending into the land **:** a partially landlocked sea that is usu. larger than a bay ⟨the *Gulf* of Mexico⟩ **2 a :** a hollow place in the earth **:** a deep chasm or basin **:** ABYSS ⟨a ~ opened between the little town . . . and its suburbs —Charles Lyell⟩ **b :** a deep narrow pass ⟨the state's three central north-south ~s . . . are the natural gateways through mountains otherwise impassable by road —*N.Y.Times*⟩ **3 a :** a sucking eddy **:** WHIRLPOOL ⟨and whirl round the ~ before they sink —Samuel Johnson⟩ **b :** something that swallows up or devours ⟨the ~s . . . in which the population of the country is lost —Jeremy Bentham⟩ **4 :** an impassable or unbridgeable gap that serves as a means of separation **:** a wide interval ⟨the broad and deep ~ which . . . divides the living from the dead, the organic from the inorganic —W.R.Inge⟩ ⟨theory and reality, principles and practice — how many have fallen in the ~ between them —Theodore Draper⟩ **5** *archaic* **:** DRAFT 2

2**gulf** \"\ *vt* -ED/-ING/-S **1 :** to swallow up **:** ENGULF **2 :** to pass (a British university student) without honors

gulf coast tick *n*, *usu cap G & often cap C* [*Gulf Coast*, coastal area along the Gulf of Mexico] **:** a tick (*Amblyomma maculatum*) of the southern U. S. that is related to the lone star tick and that is often destructive to young game birds and also to the cattle of some regions

gulf flounder *or* **gulf fluke** *n*, *usu cap G* [*Gulf* of Mexico] **:** a flounder (*Paralichthys albiguttus*) of the southern Atlantic and Gulf coasts of the U. S.

gulf menhaden *n*, *usu cap G* [*Gulf* of Mexico] **:** a marine fish (*Brevoortia patronus*) of the Gulf of Mexico

gulf stream weed *n*, *usu cap G&S* [*Gulf Stream*, warm ocean current in the North Atlantic Ocean that flows out of the Gulf of Mexico] **:** GULFWEED

gulfweed \'=,=\ *n* [*Gulf* of Mexico + *weed*] **:** any of several seaweeds of the genus *Sargassum*; *esp* **:** a branching olive-brown seaweed (*S. bacciferum*) having numerous berrylike air vesicles and occurring in tropical American seas

gulf–weed crab *n* **:** a cosmopolitan pelagic crab (*Planes minutus*) common on gulfweed in the Sargasso sea and occas. found along the No. American shore

gulfy \-fē\ *adj*, *usu* -ER/-EST **:** full of whirlpools or hollows

gu·li hin·nai \¦gülēhi¦nī\ *or* **gu·li hen·na** \,==ˈhenə\ *n* [Per *guli ḥinnā*, fr. Per *gul* flower, rose + Ar *ḥinnā* henna] **:** a Persian rug design consisting of a plant with central stem and attached star flowers

1**gull** \'gùl, 'gəl\ *n* -S [ME *goll*, prob. fr. *gull*, *goule* yellow, fr. ON *gulr* — more at YELLOW] *now dial Eng* **:** an unfledged bird; *specif* **:** GOSLING

2**gull** \'gəl\ *n* -S [ME, of Celt origin; akin to W *gwylan* gull, OCorn *guilan*, Bret *gouelan*] **1 :** any of numerous long-winged web-footed aquatic birds that constitute the family Laridae; *esp* **:** any member of *Larus* or closely related genera all of which differ from the terns in their usu. larger size, stouter build, thicker bill somewhat hooked at the tip, less pointed wings, and short unforked tail, are largely white birds as adults with the back and upper surface of the wings mantled with some shade of gray, and usu. remain near shore or about inland waters where they feed largely on offal and are important harbor scavengers — see BLACK-BACKED GULL, HERRING GULL, KITTIWAKE, MEW **2 a :** a nearly neutral slightly yellowish medium gray that is darker than agate gray and lighter than flint gray or old silver **b** *of textiles* **:** a pinkish gray that is yellower and duller than pussywillow gray

3**gull** \"\ *n* -S [ME *golle* throat, gullet, fr. MF *gole*, *goule* throat, mouth — more at GULLET] **1** *now dial* **a :** a deep gully made by and containing a running stream **b :** RAVINE **2 :** a fissure filled with fragments of rock

4**gull** \"\ *vt* -ED/-ING/-S [fr. obs. E *gull* throat, gullet, fr. ME *golle*] **1** *obs* **:** to guzzle or gulp greedily **2 :** to make a dupe of : DECEIVE, CHEAT ⟨a subtle trick intended to ~ the unwary and naïve —R.C.Bone⟩ **3** [[3]gull] *now dial Eng* : to wash away : ERODE **syn** see DUPE

[5]**gull** \"\ *n* -s **1** : a person who is easily deceived or cheated : DUPE, SUCKER ⟨had been brought down to be the ~ of this intriguer —R.L.Stevenson⟩ **2** *obs* : TRICK, DECEPTION, FRAUD ⟨I should think this a ~ but that the white-bearded fellow speaks it —Shak.⟩

gull·able \'gələbəl\ *adj* [[4]gull + -able] : GULLIBLE

gul·lah \'gələ *sometimes* 'gülə\ *n* -s *usu cap* **1** : one of a group of Negroes inhabiting the sea islands and coastal districts of So. Carolina, Georgia, and a small part of northeastern Florida **2** : the language of the Gullahs

gull–billed tern \'≈,≈-\ *n* : a large tern (*Gelochelidon nilotica*) having a stout short bill like that of a typical gull

gull chaser *n* : POMARINE JAEGER

gul·ler \'gələr\ *Scot var of* GOLLAR

[1]**gull·ery** \'gələrē\ *n* -ES [[4]gull + -ery] *archaic* : TRICKERY, DECEPTION ⟨you think . . . that you may put any ~ you will on me —Sir Walter Scott⟩

[2]**gullery** \"\ *n* -ES [[2]gull + -ery] : a breeding place of gulls

[1]**gul·let** \'gələt, *usu* -əd.+V\ *n* -s [ME *golet*, fr. MF *goulet*, dim. of OF *gole, goule* throat, fr. L *gula* — more at GLUTTON] **1** : the tube by which food passes from the pharynx to the stomach : ESOPHAGUS; *broadly* : THROAT **2** : something that resembles a gullet in shape or function: as **a** : a variably tubular invagination of the cytoplasm of various protozoans that sometimes functions in the intake of food **b** : a channel for water **c** : DEFILE, RAVINE, GULLY **d** : the space between the tips of adjacent saw teeth **e** : a preparatory cut in excavations that is wide enough to allow the passage of earth in conveyors **3** : the dewlap of a goose or other bird

[2]**gullet** \"\ *vt* -ED/-ING/-S **1** : to make gullets in **2** : to excavate by means of gullets

gulleting file *n* : a blunt round file for deepening the gullets of large-toothed saws

gullet plate *n* : the iron arch under the pommel of a saddle

gullet worm *n* : a nematode worm infesting the gullet; *esp* : any of various worms (as *Gongylonema pulchrum* or *Syngamus laryngeus*) that invade the epithelial lining of the esophagus of ruminants

gull gray *n* : a purplish gray that is bluer, lighter, and slightly stronger than crane, bluer and lighter than granite, and bluer and slightly lighter than cinder gray

gull·ibil·i·ty \,gələ'biləd·ē, -ətē, -i\ *n* -ES : the quality or state of being gullible ⟨monstrous was the ~ of the people —Arnold Bennett⟩

gull·ible \'gələbəl\ *adj* [[4]gull + -ible] : easily deceived or cheated : readily duped ⟨the innocents of those days were certainly naïve; they were ~ —Bruce Bliven b. 1889⟩ — **gul·li·bly** \-blē, -li\ *adv*

gulling *pres part of* GULL

gul·li·on \'gúliən, 'gəl-\ *n* -s [prob. alter. of *cullion*] **1** *dial Eng* : a vile worthless person **2** *dial Eng* : STOMACHACHE

gull·ish \'gəlish\ *adj* [[5]gull + -ish] : FOOLISH, STUPID

gulls *pl of* GULL, *pres 3d sing of* GULL

gull wing *n* : an airplane wing slanting upward from the fuselage for a short distance and then leveling out

[1]**gul·ly** \'gúli, 'gəli\ *or* **gully knife** *n* -ES [*gully* short for *gully knife*, fr. *gully* (fr. obs. Sc. dial. *guly*, prob. alter. of ME *golet* gullet) + *knife*] **1** *dial Brit* : a large knife (as a butcher knife or carving knife) **2** *dial Brit* : SWORD

[2]**gul·ly** *or* **gul·ley** \'gəlē, -li\ *n, pl* **gullies** *or* **gulleys** [fr. obs. E *gully, gullye* gullet, prob. alter. of ME *golet* gullet — more at GULLET] **1 a** : a miniature valley or gorge worn in the earth orig. by running water through which water usu. runs only after rains **b** : a small ravine in the face of a precipice **2** *now dial* : a deep gutter : DRAIN **3** : a diminutive valley or gulch; *esp* : a wooded hollow with steep sides **4 a** : the part of a cricket field lying between point and third man **b** : a fielder placed in the gulley

[3]**gully** \"\ *vb* -ED/-ING/-ES *vt* : to make gullies in : erode so as to produce gullies in ~ *vi* : to undergo erosion : become gullied

[4]**gully** \'gúli, 'gəli\ *n* -ES [[1]gull + -y] *dial Eng* : [1]GULL

gully erosion *n* : soil erosion produced by running water esp. after heavy rains

gullygut *n* [*gully-* (prob. fr. [4]*gull*) + *gut*] *obs* : GLUTTON

gully–raker \'≈≈,≈≈\ *n* [[2]gully] **1** *Austral* : a thief who steals stray or unbranded cattle **2** *Austral* : a large stockwhip

gully root *n, West Indies* : the root of the guinea-hen weed

gully washer *n, dial* : an extremely heavy fall of rain usu. of short duration : CLOUDBURST

gul·mo·har \'gúlmə,här\ *also* **gul·mo·hur** \-hú(ə)r\ *n* -s [Hindi *gulmohur*, fr. Per *gul* rose, flower + *muhr* seal, gold coin] : ROYAL POINCIANA

gu·lo \'gyü(,)lō\ *n, cap* [NL, fr. L, glutton, epicure, fr. *gula* gullet, throat — more at GLUTTON] : the genus containing the glutton and wolverine

gulo- *comb form* [*gulose*] *usu ital* : having the stereochemical arrangement of atoms or groups found in gulose ⟨*gulo*≈saccharic acid⟩

gu·lose \'g(y)ü,lōs *also* -ōz\ *n* -s [ISV, irreg. fr. *glucose*] : a sugar $C_6H_{12}O_6$ stereoisomeric with glucose and obtainable by synthesis from xylose

gu·los·i·ty \gyü'läsəd·ē\ *n* -ES [ME (Sc. dial.) *gulosite*, fr. LL *gulositas*, fr. L *gulosus* gluttonous (fr. *gula* throat, gullet + *-osus* -ose) + *-itas* -ity — more at GLUTTON] : excessive appetite : GREEDINESS

[1]**gulp** \'gəlp\ *vb* -ED/-ING/-S [ME *gulpen*, fr. a MD or MLG word; akin to D & Fris *gulpen* to bubble forth, drink in large drafts, Norw *gylpa* to gulp, OE *gielpan* to boast — more at YELP] *vt* **1 a** : to swallow in large drafts or pieces hurriedly or greedily ⟨corrected me for ~*ing* my food —Rex Ingamells⟩ — often used with *down* ⟨~*ed* down the whiskey and put on our coats —Nevil Shute⟩ **b** : to consume in one swallow — often used with *down* ⟨raw meat is usually not chewed but ~*ed* down like an oyster —H.B.Collins⟩ **2 a** : to take in or absorb in any manner : DEVOUR — usu. used with *down* ⟨their attempts to ~ down knowledge and to regulate their lives by received ideas —*Atlantic*⟩ **b** : to accept without investigation or question : swallow whole — usu. used with *down* ⟨the old man . . . ~*ed* down the whole narrative —Henry Fielding⟩ **3** : to keep back as if by swallowing : SUPPRESS — often used with *down* ⟨~*ed* down her sobs and was resolved to be firm —Anthony Trollope⟩ ~ *vi* **1** : to catch the breath as if in taking a long drink ⟨the white settler ~*s* hard and smiles wanly —*Time*⟩ **2** : to swallow food or drink hurriedly or greedily ⟨should learn to taste rather than to ~ —*Current Biog.*⟩

[2]**gulp** \"\ *n* -s **1 a** : the act or an instance of gulping ⟨swallowed the medicine at one ~⟩ **b** : the amount taken in a single large swallow ⟨had time only for a ~ of hot coffee⟩ **2 a** : a spasmodic action of the throat made in or as if in swallowing **b** : the sound of such action ⟨eyes wide and luminous, cheeks flushed . . . she spoke in ~*s* —Murray Schumach⟩

gulp·er \-pə(r)\ *n* -s **1** : one that gulps **2** *also* **gulper eel** : any of several usu. small deep-sea fishes that resemble degenerate eels with greatly enlarged mouths, have a leptocephalus stage, and constitute the family Saccopharyngidae now usu. placed in the order Lyomeri

gulph *archaic var of* GULF

gul·pin \'gúlpən, 'gəl-\ *n* -s [perh. alter. of *galopin*] *dial Eng* : a gullible person : SIMPLETON

gulp·ing·ly *adv* : with a gulp

gulpy \'gəlpē\ *adj* -ER/-EST : marked by gulping

guls *pl of* GUL

gul·sach \'gəls(h)ə(k̟)\ *n* -s [ME *gowel sowght* (part trans. of ON *gulusótt*), fr. *gowel* yellow (fr. ON *gulr*) + *sowght, sought* sickness, fr. OE *suht*; akin to OHG *suht* sickness, ON *sótt*, Goth *sauhts* sickness, *siuks* ill — more at YELLOW, SICK] *now Scot* : JAUNDICE

guly *adj* [[1]gules + -y] *obs* : of the color gules : RED

[1]**gum** \'gəm, *dial* 'güm\ *n* -s *often attrib* [ME *gome*, fr. OE *gōma* palate; akin to OHG *guomo* palate, ON *gómr* gum, Gk *chaunos* loose, porous, *chaos* abyss] : the tissue that surrounds the necks of teeth and covers the alveolar parts of the jaws : the portion of it in either jaw or attached to a single tooth ⟨a ~ canker on the upper jaw⟩; *broadly* : the alveolar portion of a jaw with its enveloping soft tissues — usu. used in pl. ⟨a year later he could chew practically anything with his ~*s*⟩ — see TOOTH illustration

[2]**gum** \"\ *vb* **gummed**; **gummed**; **gumming**; **gums** *vt* **1** : to enlarge or deepen the spaces between the teeth of (a worn saw) — often used with *out* ⟨if you ~ out that saw it will probably go another year⟩ **2** *chiefly dial* : to chew (as food) with the gums ⟨can't find his store teeth half the time so he ~*s* his food⟩ ⟨*gummed* off a fresh portion of the fragment of plug tobacco —Noel Barker⟩ ~ *vi, dial* : to chew food or any other substance with the gums instead of teeth ⟨been *gumming* since he had his teeth drawn last month⟩

[3]**gum** \'gəm\ *n* -s *often attrib* [ME *gomme, gumme*, fr. OF *gomme*, fr. L *gummi, cummi*, fr. Gk *kommi*, fr. Egypt *qmy.t*] **1 a** : any of numerous colloidal polysaccharide substances that are gelatinous when moist but harden on drying, that are exuded by plants or extracted from them by solvents and either soluble in or swelling up with water, and that are salts of complex organic acids yielding hexuronic acids and aldoses on hydrolysis — compare MUCILAGE 1 **b** : any of various plant exudates (as a mucilage, oleoresin, or gum resin) **2** : a natural gum prepared for industrial or other use (as in pharmacy or cloth finishing or for adhesives or emollients) **3** : a substance in some respect resembling a natural plant gum: as **a** : a dextrin adhesive **b** : a gummy coating chiefly of sericin on the outside of a raw silk fiber **c** : thickened secretion (as at the corner of the eyes) **d** : a tarry deposit (as in a cylinder, bearing, or storage tank) left by an unsaturated hydrocarbon fuel (as gasoline) or lubricant **e** : a rubber composition containing only the ingredients essential for vulcanization — called also *high gum, pure gum* **4** *also* **gum tree a** : any of several trees that yield gums: as (1) : BLACK GUM (2) : SWEET GUM (3) : any of several West Indian laticiferous trees (as *Metopium toxiferum* and *Sapium laurifolium* (4) : SAPODILLA **b** *Austral* : a tree of the genus *Eucalyptus*; *esp* : any of various smooth-barked eucalyptus trees — compare [1]BOX 2a **5 a** *also* **gumwood** \'≈,≈\ : the wood or lumber of any gum; *esp* : that of the sweet gum **b** *chiefly Midland* : a vessel or container made of a hollow log — compare BEE GUM **6** : a rubber boot or overshoe **7** : CHEWING GUM — **in the gum** *of silk* : in a stage of manufacture before the gum has been removed by boiling

[4]**gum** \"\ *vb* **gummed**; **gummed**; **gumming**; **gums** [ME *gommen, gummen*, fr. *gomme, gumme*, n.] *vt* **1** : to smear or treat with gum : close or seal with gum : unite or stiffen by gum or a gummy substance **2** : to impede or clog with or as if with gum — often used with *up* ⟨*gummed* up the whole program⟩ ⟨the motor is all *gummed* up⟩ **3** [prob. fr. [3]*gum* (tree); prob. fr. the observation that opossums and raccoons often hide in a sweet-gum tree when hunted] : HUMBUG, TRICK, CHEAT **4** : to fill the spaces between the cutting particles of (as a file or an abrasive wheel) with the material being cut ~ *vi* **1 a** : to exude or form gum **b** : to become gummy (as by softening or thickening) ⟨some oils ~ readily⟩ **2** : to have the spaces between the cutting particles filled with the material being cut — used of an abrasive

[5]**gum** \"\ *interj, often cap* [alter. of *God*] — used as a mild oath

gum acacia *n* : GUM ARABIC; *esp* : gum arabic used in pharmacy

gum accroides *n* : ACAROID RESIN

gum aloes *n pl but sing or pl in constr* : ALOE 4

gum ammoniac *n* : AMMONIAC

gum arabic *n* [ME *gumme arabik*, part trans. of MF *gomme arabic*, fr. *gomme* gum + *arabic* Arabic, fr. L *Arabicus* — more at ARABIC] : a water-soluble gum obtained from several acacias (esp. *Acacia senegal* and *A. arabica*) used particularly in the manufacture of adhesives, inks, confectionery, in textile finishing, and in pharmacy — called also *gum acacia*

gum arabic tree *n* : a tree that yields gum arabic; *esp* : BABUL 1a

gum benjamin *or* **gum benzoin** *n* : BENZOIN 1

gum–bichromate *adj* : GUM-DICHROMATE

[1]**gum·bo** *also* **gom·bo** \'gəm(,)bō\ *n* -s [AmerF (Louisiana) *gombo*, of Bantu origin; akin to Umbundu *ochinggômbo* okra, Tshiluba *chinggômbô*] **1** : the okra plant or its edible pods **2 a** : a soup thickened with okra pods or with filé and usu. containing a variety of vegetables with meat (as chicken) or seafoods **b** : a thick conserve of one or more fruits **3 a** : any of various fine-grained silty soils common in the central U. S. that when saturated with water become impervious and soapy or waxy and very sticky **b** : a heavy sticky mud ⟨the track was sheer ~ after the rains⟩ **c** : something notably sticky or gummy ⟨brushes coated with a ~ of old oil and paint⟩ **4** *often cap* [AmerF *gombo*, perh. fr. Kongo *nkômbô* goat, runaway slave] : a patois used by Negroes and Creoles esp. in Louisiana **5** : MIXTURE, MÉLANGE ⟨New Orleans is a ~ — a composition of many peoples, many viewpoints, many riches —H.T.Kane⟩

[2]**gumbo** \"\ *adj* : of, relating to, or like gumbo

gumbo filé *n* [AmerF (Louisiana) *gombo filé*, fr. *gombo* gumbo + *filé*, n.] **1** : gumbo prepared with filé **2** : FILÉ

gumboil \'≈,≈\ *n* : an abscess in the gum : PARULIS

gumbo lily *n* : PRAIRIE LILY 2

gumbo–lim·bo \,≈≈'lim(,)bō\ *n* [perh. fr. [1]*gumbo* + *limbo*, of Bantu origin; akin to Kongo *edimbu* birdlime] **1** : a tropical American tree (*Bursera simaruba*) with smooth coppery bark that peels like that of some birches and a reddish resin used locally in cements and varnishes — called also *gum elemi* **2** : PARADISE TREE 1a

gum boot *n* : RUBBER BOOT

gum·boot·ed \'≈¦büd·əd, -ütəd\ *adj* : wearing gum boots

gum·bo·til \'gəmbō,til\ *n* -s [[1]*gumbo* + *till* (glacial drift)] : a dark leached nonlaminated very sticky clay that results from the weathering of glacial till

gum·by \'gümbē, 'güm-\ *also* **gum·bé** \-,bā, ≈'≈\ *n, pl* **gumbies** *also* **gumbés** [of Bantu origin; akin to Kongo *nkumbi* ceremonial drum, Tshiluba *nkumbi* drum] : a drum made by stretching a skin over a piece of a hollowed tree and used esp. by West Indian Negroes

gum camphor *n* : dextrorotatory camphor

gumchewer \'≈,≈≈\ *n* : a person that chews gum esp. habitually

gum copal *n* : COPAL

gum dammar *or* **gum damar** *n* : DAMMAR

gum–dichromate *adj* : relating to or constituting a photographic printing process that employs paper coated with a solution of gum or glue containing a pigment in suspension and sensitized with a dichromate, the print being developed and fixed by washing in water

gumdigger \'≈,≈≈\ *n, NewZeal* : one that digs fossil kauri resin

gum disease *n* : GUMMING DISEASE

gum drag·on \,gəm'dragən, -raig-\ *n* [by folk etymology (influence of *dragon*) fr. earlier *gum dragant*, part modif., part trans. of F *gomme adragante, gomme adragant*, fr. MF *gomme adragant*, fr. *gomme* gum + *adragant* tragacanth, alter. of *tragacanthe, tragacanth* — more at TRAGACANTH] : TRAGACANTH

gumdrop \'≈,≈\ *n, often attrib* : a candy made usu. from corn syrup with cornstarch, gelatin, or gum arabic according to the consistency desired, cast in molds that are typically nearly hemispherical, and coated with sugar crystals

gum·drop·py \-,dräpē\ *adj* [*gumdrop* + *-y*] : resembling a gumdrop esp. in texture

gum duct *or* **gum canal** *n* : an intercellular canal in a plant for the secretion or passage of gum

gum elastic *n* [prob. trans. of F *gomme élastique*] **1** : RUBBER 2a **2** : BUCKTHORN 2; *esp* : FALSE BUCKTHORN

gum elemi *n* [alter. of earlier *gumme elimi*, part trans. of NL *gumi elimi*, fr. *gumi* gum (fr. L *gummi, cummi*) + *elimi* elemi, prob. fr. Ar *al-lāmi* the elemi] **1** : ELEMI **2** : GUMBO-LIMBO 1

gum eraser *n* : a small gummy rubber block used esp. to remove smudges from paper

gumfield \'≈,≈\ *n* : an area where kauri resin occurs

gumflower \'≈,≈\ *n, Scot* : an artificial flower

gum flux *n* : GUMMOSIS

gum game *n* [prob. fr. [3]*gum* (tree) + *game*; prob. fr. the observation that opossums and raccoons often hide in a sweet≈gum tree when hunted] *slang* : a trick intended to cheat or swindle a victim

gum ghat·ti *or* **gum gat·tie** \,gəm'gad·ē\ *n* [*ghatti, gattie* native name in India] : GHATTI GUM

gum guaiac *or* **gum guaiacum** *n* : GUAIACUM 1c

gum–gum \'gəm,gəm\ *also* **gom–gom** \'gäm,gäm\ *n* [perh. native name in the Moluccas] : an iron bowl played as a musical instrument by striking with a stick; *also* : a graded set of such bowls

gum·har \'gəm,här\ *n* -s [prob. modif. of Beng *gāmārī*, fr. Skt *gambhārī*] : an Indian timber tree (*Gmelina arborea*) of the family Verbenaceae yielding a light brown lustrous wood that is highly resistant to moisture, easily worked, and used esp. for cabinetwork, carving, interior finishes, and boats and having roots, leaves, and fruits that are locally used in medicine — called also *gamari*

gumi *var of* GOUMI

gum juniper *n* : SANDARAC 3

gum ka·raya \,gəmkə'rīə\ *n* : STERCULIA GUM

gum kino *n* : KINO 1

gum·lah \gəm'lä\ *n* -s [Hindi *gamlā*] : a large pottery jar used in India for water

gum·less \'gəmləs\ *adj* : free from or lacking gum ⟨a ~ oil⟩ ⟨old ~ stamps⟩

gum·lie *or* **gum·ly** \'gəmli\ *adj* [alter. of *grumly*] **1** *Scot* : MUDDY, TURBID **2** *Scot* : GLOOMY

gumlike \'≈,≈\ *adj* : resembling gum : GUMMY

gum·ma \'gəmə\ *n, pl* **gum·mas** \-məz\ *also* **gum·ma·ta** \-məd·ə\ [NL, fr. LL, gum, fr. L *gummi, cummi* — more at GUM] : a tumor of gummy or rubbery consistency that resembles granulomatous tissue and is characteristic of the tertiary stage of syphilis — **gum·ma·tous** \-məd·əs\ *adj*

gum mastic *n* [ME *gumme mastyck*, fr. *gomme, gumme* gum + *mastyck, mastik* mastic] : MASTIC 1

gummed \'gəmd\ *adj* [ME *gommed*, fr. past part. of *gommen, gummen* to gum] : coated, smeared, stiffened, or mixed with gum ⟨~ labels⟩ ⟨hands all ~ with tar⟩

[1]**gum·mer** \'gəmə(r), *dial* 'güm-\ *n* -s **1** : a tool or machine for gumming a worn saw **2** : an old sheep that has lost all its teeth

[2]**gum·mer** \'gəmə(r)\ *n* -s [[4]*gum* + *-er*] **1** : one that applies gum or glue (as to envelopes, labels, or tape) **2** : a person that gathers gum from the trees that produce it

gum·mif·er·ous \,gə'mif(ə)rəs\ *adj* [ISV *gummi-* (fr. L *gummi* gum) + *-ferous*] : producing or bearing gum

gum·mi·ly \'gəməlē, -li\ *adv* : in a gummy manner

gum·mi·ness \-mēnəs, -min-\ *n* -ES : the quality or state of being gummy

gumming *n* -s [fr. gerund of [4]*gum*] **1** : an act of discharging gum or becoming gummy ⟨there was severe ~ of the cylinder walls with the new fuel⟩; *esp* : GUMMOSIS **2** : the application of a gummy preparation (as gum arabic) to a lithographic printing surface **3** : the gathering of gum (as spruce gum)

gumming disease *n* : any of various plant diseases characterized by gummosis (as mal di gomma of citrus trees or Cobb's disease of sugarcane)

gum·mite \'gə,mīt\ *n* -s [G *-gummit*, fr. *gummi* gum (fr. MHG, fr. L *gummi, cummi*) + *-it* -ite; fr. the gummy appearance of some specimens — more at GUM] : a yellow to reddish brown mixture of hydrous oxides of uranium, thorium, and lead consisting perhaps largely of curite — called also *uranium≈ocher*

gum·mo·sis \,gə'mōsəs\ *n, pl* **gummo·ses** \-ō,sēz\ [NL, fr. L *gummi* gum + NL *-osis*] : the pathological production of gummy exudates in plants (as various citrus and stone-fruit trees) as a result of cell degeneration usu. forming clear to amber hardened crusts or masses — see EXANTHEM; *broadly* : a plant disease marked by gummosis

gummosity *n* -ES [ME *gummosite* gummy substance, prob. fr. (assumed) ML *gummositat-, gummositas*, fr. L *gummosus* + *-itat-, -itas* -ity] **1** *obs* : a gummy substance **2** *obs* : the quality or state of being gummy

gum·mous \'gəməs\ *adj* [L *gummosus*, fr. *gummi, cummi* gum + *-osus* -ose] : resembling or composed of gum : GUMMY ⟨~ changes in tissue⟩

[1]**gum·my** \'gəmē, -mi\ *adj* -ER/-EST [ME, fr. *gomme, gumme* gum + *-y*] **1 a** : consisting of, containing, or producing gum ⟨a ~ mass⟩ **b** : covered with gum or a gumlike substance ⟨how did you get your hands so ~⟩ **c** : viscous and sticky ⟨the road had become a wallow of ~ mud⟩; *esp* : viscous and sticky but without lubricating value ⟨~ residues in motor oil⟩ **2 a** : having lumps as if of gum ⟨~ tumor⟩ ⟨a ~ ankle⟩ **b** *of a horse's leg* : lacking clear-cut lines : PUFFY **3** : lacking ease and smoothness : UNPLEASANT ⟨a very ~ state of affairs⟩ ⟨this ~ little essay⟩

[2]**gum·my** \", *dial* 'güm-\ *adj* -ER/-EST [[1]*gum* + *-y*] : showing the gums ⟨a ~ smile⟩; *esp* : TOOTHLESS ⟨a ~ old woman⟩

[3]**gum·my** \'gəmē, -mi\ *n* -ES **1** : GUMMY SHARK **2** *Austral* : [1]GUMMER 2

gummy shark *n* : any of several small sluggish Indo-Pacific sharks esp. of the genus *Mustelus* sometimes used for food

gum olibanum *n* : FRANKINCENSE 1

[1]**gump** \'gəmp\ *n* -s [origin unknown] *chiefly dial* : a foolish or dull-witted person

[2]**gump** \"\ *vb* -ED/-ING/-S [origin unknown] *chiefly Scot* : GUDDLE

gumphion *or* **gumpheon** *n* -s [ME (Sc) *gumfioun, gunfioun* gonfanon, alter. of ME *gonfanoun* — more at GONFANON] *obs Scot* : a funeral banner

gum plant *n* : GUMWEED

gum pocket *n* : a gum-filled cavity in the woody tissue of various plants

gump·tion \'gəm(p)shən\ *n* -s [origin unknown] **1** : shrewd common sense ⟨the business ~ that comes from experience⟩ **2** : courageous or ambitious enterprise : blended initiative, resolution, and effort ⟨the ~ to defend the position against odds⟩ **3 a** : the art of preparing painters' colors **b** : MEGILP **syn** see SENSE

gump·tious \-shəs\ *adj* [fr. *gumption*, after such pairs as E *ambition: ambitious*] : having gumption : ALERT, EAGER, VIGOROUS ⟨a ~ little helper⟩ — **gump·tious·ly** *adv*

gum resin *n* : a product consisting essentially of a mixture of gum and resin usu. obtained by making an incision in a plant and allowing the juice which exudes to solidify — **gum-resinous** \'≈¦≈≈≈\ *adj*

gum rosin *n* : rosin obtained from the oleoresin of living pine trees (as slash pine) by distilling off the volatile turpentine

gums *pl of* GUM, *pres 3d sing of* GUM

gum senegal *n, usu cap S* : SENEGAL GUM

gum shiraz *n* [*Shiraz*, city in southwest central Iran] : a gum similar to ghatti gum but insoluble in water

[1]**gumshoe** \'≈,≈\ *n* [[3]*gum* + *shoe*] **1 a** : a rubber overshoe **b** : a sneaker with a rubber sole **2** *also* **gumshoer** \'≈,≈≈\ : DETECTIVE, POLICEMAN, INVESTIGATOR

[2]**gumshoe** \"\ *adj* : carried on or behaving surreptitiously ⟨a ~ campaign⟩ ⟨a ~ man⟩

[3]**gumshoe** \"\ *vi* : to go stealthily; *broadly* : SNOOP, PRY

gum spirits *n pl but sing or pl in constr* : TURPENTINE 2a

gum spot *n* : a gummy streak or spot in lumber

gum succory *n* : a European biennial weed (*Chondrilla juncea*) with large pinnatifid basal leaves and branching wiry stems bearing yellow-rayed flowers; *broadly* : a plant of the genus *Chondrilla*

gumsucker \'≈,≈≈\ *n* [[3]*gum* + *sucker*; prob. fr. the children's habit of sucking gum exuded by eucalyptus trees] : an Australian esp. from Victoria — used as a nickname

gum thus *n* **1** : FRANKINCENSE 1 **2** : TURPENTINE 1b; *esp* : the oleoresin that hardens on the tree and is scraped off

gum tragacanth *n* : TRAGACANTH

gum tree *n* : [3]GUM 4

gum turpentine *n* : TURPENTINE 1, 2a

gumweed \'≈,≈\ *n* : a plant of the genus *Grindelia* (esp. *G. squarrosa* and *G. robusta*)

gumwood \'≈,≈\ *n* **1** : [3]GUM 5a **2** : a shrub (*Commidendron rugosum*) of the family Compositae that is endemic but rare on the island of St. Helena

[1]**gun** \'gən\ *n* -s [ME *gonne, gunne*, prob. irreg. fr. *Gonnilda, Gunnilda, Gunilda*, fem. proper name (sometimes applied to an engine of war), fr. ON *Gunnhildr*, fem. proper name] **1 a** : a piece of ordnance on a carriage or other mounting for throwing projectiles by the force of some explosive (as gunpowder) usu. with high muzzle velocity and with comparatively flat trajectory and consisting of a tube or barrel closed at one end where the projectile is placed in front of the explosive charge to be ignited : a piece of ordnance — distinguished from *howitzer* and *mortar* **b** : a portable firearm

(as a rifle, shotgun, carbine, pistol) — compare SMALL ARM **c** : a device (as an air rifle or a set gun) resembling such a piece of ordnance or such a firearm in that it throws or drives a projectile **2 a** : a discharge of a gun in a salute or as a signal ⟨a salute of 21 ~s⟩ ⟨the evening ~⟩ **b** : something serving as a signal of this kind esp. marking a beginning or ending of an enterprise ⟨his speech was the opening ~ of the campaign⟩ **3** [prob. by folk etymology fr. *ganef*] *slang* : THIEF **4 a** : one who shoots a gun : HUNTER **b** : a professional killer ⟨two loose ~s . . . who turn buffalo hunters in the last days of the burning West —Whitney Balliett⟩ **5** : something suggesting a gun in shape or function: as **a** : a small hand pump for projecting oil, grease, or other lubricating material : GREASE GUN **b** : an apparatus for forcibly spraying (as paint or caulking) or throwing on cement, concrete mixtures, or similar material **c** (1) : AIR HAMMER (2) : ELECTRIC HAMMER **d** : DUST GUN **e** : FLASHGUN **f** : TACKER 1f **g** : a stapling device **h** : an electric soldering tool with pistol grip **i** : ELECTRON GUN **6** : a throttle or throttle lever esp. of an airplane engine **7** *Austral* : an expert sheepshearer — **jump the gun** *or* **beat the gun** **1** : to start in a race before the starting signal ⟨disqualified for *jumping the gun*⟩ **2** : to act, move, or begin something before the approved, appropriate, or proper time ⟨were scheduled to be married in June but they *jumped the gun*⟩ — **under the gun** *or* **under the guns** **1** : under the surveillance of an armed guard **2** : called upon in a game of poker to bet or drop when several players not yet heard from may raise — used of the first and second players in turn after the deal

²gun \"\ *vb* **gunned; gunned; gunning; guns** *vi* **1** : to hunt with a gun : go hunting **2** : to move or progress usu. rapidly in a vehicle by gunning the motor ⟨*gunned* into the road, following the fresh tracks —Nard Jones⟩ ~ *vt* **1** : to equip with a gun **2 a** : to fire upon **b** : SHOOT ⟨he was . . . *gunned* down on the streets —*Time*⟩ ⟨famous anarchist, was *gunned* to death —Alexander Dallin⟩ **c** : to hunt in ⟨nonresidents who have *gunned* the Dakotas —Nash Buckingham⟩ **3** : to direct the fall of (a tree) in forestry **4 a** : to open up the throttle of (an engine) usu. rapidly so as to increase speed **b** : to increase the speed of (a motor-driven vehicle) markedly by opening the throttle or to drive by doing this ⟨*gunned* the car up the steep grade⟩ ⟨~ a motorboat⟩ — **gun for** **1** : to seek with determination the opportunity to catch (as a burglar) or bring to ruin or defeat (as an enemy) ⟨a malcontent *gunning for* his superior officer⟩ **2** : to turn all one's energy or efforts to acquire (as a position)

gu·na \ˈgünə, ˈgü-\ *n* -S [Skt *guṇa* thread, quality] **1** : one of three primal qualities or elements of matter according to Sankhya philosophy — see RAJAS, SATTVA, TAMAS **2** : a Sanskrit ablaut grade that strengthens the simple vowels by prefixing an *a* element to each so that *i* or *ī* becomes *e* (for earlier *ai*), *u* or *ū* becomes *o* (for earlier *au*), *r̥* becomes *ar*, and *l̥* becomes *al*, but *a* and *ā* remain unchanged

gu·nate \ˈ⸗ˌnāt\ *vb* -ED/-ING/-S [*guna* + *-ate*] *vt* : to subject to or change by guna (sense 2) ~ *vi* : to be subject to guna — **gu·na·tion** \⸗ˈnāshən\ *n* -S

gunboat \ˈ⸗ˌ⸗\ *n* **1** : an armed ship of shallow draft **2** : a small wheeled car for hauling coal or ore up an incline in a mine — called also *skip* **3** : CATAMARAN 4 **4** *slang* : one of a pair of markedly large shoes — usu. used in pl.

gun breech *n* : a mass of metal at the rear end of a cannon that extends from the rear face to the rifling

gun brig *n* : an armed 2-masted square-rigged sailing ship

gunbright \ˈ⸗ˌ⸗\ *n* -S [¹*gun* + *bright*, adj., fr. its use in scouring gun barrels] : a scouring rush (*Equisetum hyemale*)

gun burner *n* : a burner for oil-burning furnaces that atomizes the fuel as it escapes under pressure

gun camera *n* **1** : an aerial camera connected to and operated by the fire control mechanism of an airplane to photograph the effect of the fire on the target **2** : a camera mounted on a gun stock to be held and aimed like a gun

gun captain *n* : a petty officer in command of the crew of a gun on a ship

gun carriage *n* : a mechanism upon which a gun is mounted for maneuvering, firing, and sometimes being transported — see BARBETTE CARRIAGE; compare CASEMATE 2, TURRET 4b

gun chamber *n* : the part of a gun that receives the charge esp. in one using fixed ammunition

guncotton \ˈ⸗ˌ⸗⸗\ *n* : any of various cellulose nitrates; *esp* : an explosive consisting of a higher-nitrated product (as one containing at least 13.2% nitrogen) used chiefly in smokeless powder — compare PYROCELLULOSE, PYROXYLIN

gun crew *n* : the petty officers and men assigned to the service of a gun on a naval vessel

gun·da·low *or* **gun·de·low** \ˈgəndəˌlō\ *var of* GONDOLA

gun deck *n* [¹*gun* + *deck*] : a deck (as the first deck below the weather deck) on old-time warships carrying the ship's guns

gundeck \ˈ⸗ˌ⸗\ *vt* [*gun deck*] *slang* : to fake or falsify esp. by writing up (as a series of official reports) as if meeting requirements but actually without having carried out the required procedures

gun·di \ˈgəndē\ *n* -S [Maghrebi Ar *gundī*, perh. modif. of Berber *gerdi*, *gerda* rat] : a short-tailed northern African rodent (*Ctenodactylus gundi*) about eight inches long that with a few related African forms comprises the family Ctenodactylidae — see COMB RAT

gundog \ˈ⸗ˌ⸗\ *n* : a dog (as a pointer, setter, or retriever) that has been trained to accompany sportsmen when they hunt with guns

gun·dy \ˈgəndi\ *n* -ES [prob. alter. of *candy*] *Scot* : candy made with treacle

¹gunfight \ˈ⸗ˌ⸗\ *n* : a fight between two persons using guns

²gunfight \"\ *vi* : to engage in a gunfight

gunfighter \ˈ⸗ˌ⸗⸗\ *n* : one noted for taking part in gunfights or for his skill in gunfighting

gunfire \ˈ⸗ˌ⸗\ *n* **1 a** : the firing of guns **b** : the time of the firing of a gun **2** : the use of guns as weapons of war as distinguished from the use of other weapons or methods (as swords or shock tactics)

gunflint \ˈ⸗ˌ⸗\ *n* **1** : a small sharp flint for use in a flintlock to produce a spark of fire to ignite the priming **2** *usu cap* [so called fr. the use of old gunflints during Dorr's Rebellion in 1842] : RHODE ISLANDER — a nickname

gunge *or* **gunj** \ˈgənj\ *n, pl* **gunges** *or* **gunjes** [Hindi *gãj*, of Iranian origin; akin to Per *ganj* treasure] *India* : GRANARY, MARKET

gung ho \ˈgəŋˈhō\ *adj* [*Gung Ho*, slogan of certain U.S. forces in Asia in World War II, fr. Chin(Pek) *kung¹-ho²* (short for *ch'ing¹-kung¹-yeh² ho²-tso⁴ shê⁴* Light Industries Cooperative Society), taken to mean "work together"] : extremely or overly zealous or enthusiastic

gun glaze *n* : a surfacing glaze applied with a spray gun to a vehicle body as a preliminary to painting

gunhand \ˈ⸗ˌ⸗\ *n* : one hired by an individual to carry or handle a gun for the protection of the individual's property, workers, or enterprise or for the carrying on of his private warfare with other persons

gunhouse \ˈ⸗ˌ⸗\ *n* : a ship's gun enclosure made of relatively light armor for protection against weather and splinters

gunite \ˈgəˌnīt\ *vb* -ED/-ING/-S *vi* : to apply a Gunite mixture ~ *vt* : to apply a Gunite mixture to

Gun·ite \"\ *trademark* — used for a mixture of cement, sand, and water applied by compressed-air pressure through a specially adapted hose

gun·it·er \-ˌīd·ə(r)\ *n* -S **1** : one that applies a Gunite mixture with a cement gun **2** : GROUTER 2

gun·ja *or* **gun·jah** \ˈgənjə\ *var of* GANJA

gunk \ˈgəŋk\ *n* -S [prob. imit.] : filthy, sticky, or greasy matter usu. objectionably messy or smelly; *specif* : undesirable sludge or residue ⟨all fouled up with bananas, sweat, blood, and the ~ from the street —Vincent McHugh⟩ ⟨a sticky ~ to settle dusty cattle feed —*This Week Mag.*⟩

gunkhole \ˈ⸗ˌ⸗\ *n* : a shallow cove or channel nearly unnavigable because of mud, rocks, or vegetation

gunlayer \ˈ⸗ˌ⸗⸗\ *n, Brit* : a sailor who aims a ship's guns

gunlaying \ˈ⸗ˌ⸗⸗\ *n* [*laying*, fr. gerund of *lay*] : the process of aiming (as by determining range, azimuth, and elevation) a large gun at a target ⟨~ by radar⟩

gun·less \ˈgənləs\ *adj* : having or requiring no gun

gunline \ˈ⸗ˌ⸗\ *n* : a line or cable (as a towrope) one end of which can be shot (as from one ship to another) by a gun device

gunlock \ˈ⸗ˌ⸗\ *n* : a mechanism which is attached to or usu. integral with a firearm by which the charge is ignited — compare FLINTLOCK, MATCHLOCK, PERCUSSION LOCK, WHEEL LOCK

gunmaker \ˈ⸗ˌ⸗⸗\ *n* [ME *gonmaker*, fr. *gonne*, *gunne* gun + *maker*] : a maker or manufacturer of guns

gun·man \ˈgənmən, -ˌman, -ˌmaa(ə)n\ *n, pl* **gunmen** **1 a** : a man who is armed with or fires a gun; *also* : a guard armed with a gun **b** : a man noted for his speed or skill in handling a gun in gunplay or gunfights **2** : a criminal whose crimes involve the use of a gun : KILLER; *esp* : one hired to kill another with a gun

gunmetal \ˈ⸗ˌ⸗⸗\ *n* **1 a** (1) : a bronze ordinarily composed of nine parts of copper and one of tin and formerly much used as a material for cannon (2) : a metal or alloy used as a material for guns **b** : any of various alloys or metals treated so as to imitate nearly black tarnished copper-alloy gunmetal and used for the manufacture of metal novelties **2** *or* **gunmetal gray** : a nearly neutral slightly purplish dark gray that is darker and slightly redder than steel gray

gun moll *n* [¹*gun* (thief) + *moll*] **1** *slang* : a female thief **2** [influenced in meaning by ¹*gun* (firearm)] *slang* : the girl friend of a gangster; *also* : a female criminal noted for her carrying or use of a gun

gun money *n* : debased coins issued by James II in Ireland in 1689 and made partly of metal from old cannon

gun motor carriage *n* : a vehicle on which a gun is mounted

gun mount *n* : a structure that supports a gun

gunned *past of* GUN

¹gun·nel \ˈgənᵊl\ *n* -S [origin unknown] **1** : a small slimy elongate marine blenny (*Pholis gunnellus*) found on both sides of the north Atlantic — called also *butterfish* **2** : any of several blennies closely related to or resembling the gunnel

²gunnel *var of* GUNWALE

gunnen *past part of* GIN

gun·ner \ˈgənə(r)\ *n* -S [ME *gonner*, *gunner*, fr. *gonne*, *gunne* gun + *-er*] **1** : one who handles or works a gun: as **a** : a member of an artillery unit (as the Royal Artillery) **b** : an artillery corporal (as in the U.S. Army) whose specialty is the aiming of a gun **c** : one who shoots game **d** : one who shoots whales with a harpoon gun **2** : a warrant officer (as in the U.S. Navy) whose specialty is supervision of ordnance and ordnance stores

gun·nera \(ˌ)gəˈnirə, -nerə\ *n* [NL, fr. Johan Ernst *Gunnerus* †1773 Norw. botanist] **1** *cap* : a genus of widely distributed herbs (family Haloragaceae) several of which are used as garden ornamentals with large orbicular basal leaves and a thick spike of small flowers **2** -S : any plant of the genus *Gunnera*

gun·ne·ra·ce·ae \ˌgənəˈrāsēˌē\ *n pl, cap* [NL, fr. *Gunnera*, type genus + *-aceae*] *in some classifications* : a family coextensive with Haloragaceae

gunner's mate *n* : a petty officer (as in the U.S. Navy) responsible for the care and maintenance of a ship's weapons and ammunition

gunner's quadrant *n* : an instrument consisting of a graduated limb with a spirit level, and an arm by which it is applied to a cannon or mortar in adjusting the piece to the elevation for the desired range

gun·nery \ˈgən(ə)rē, -ri\ *n* -ES [¹*gun* + *-ery*] **1** : the use of or instruction in the use of guns; *specif* : a part of military science that deals with the flight of projectiles and with the manner of using guns so as to achieve the desired effect **2** *archaic* : the firing of guns

gunnery officer *n* : an officer (as in the U.S. Navy) who has general charge of the care and maintenance of the battery, ordnance material, and ammunition of a warship, superintends gun drills, and directs the gunnery training of the crew

gunnery sergeant *n* : a noncommissioned marine officer rating just below a first sergeant and above a staff sergeant

gunning *n* -S [fr. gerund of ²*gun*] : the shooting of a gun: **a** : hunting or shooting at game **b** : the criminal shooting or killing of a person

gunning stick \ˈ⸗⸗ˌ⸗\ *also* **gunstick** \ˈ⸗ˌ⸗\ *n* : a device made of wood strips several feet long crossed like a pair of scissors that is placed against an undercut in felling a tree to determine the direction of fall

gun·ny \ˈgənē, -ni\ *or* **gunny cloth** *n* -ES [Hindi *ganī*, *gonī*, fr. Skt *goṇī* sack, prob. of Dravidian origin; akin to Kanarese *gōni* sack] **1** : a strong coarse loosely woven material made from jute for bagging and sacking **2** : BURLAP

gunnysack *or* **gunny-bag** \ˈ⸗⸗ˌ⸗\ *n* : a sack made of gunny or burlap

gun·ny·sack·ing \-iŋ\ *n* : GUNNY

gun pendulum *n* : an apparatus used to determine ballistics data (as the initial velocity of a projectile or conditions existing in the bore of a gun during passage of the projectile) by means of measurement of the recoil caused by the discharge of a gun suspended as a pendulum — compare BALLISTIC PENDULUM

gun pit *n* : an excavation often with a parapet in front to protect a fieldpiece and its men from direct fire

gunplay \ˈ⸗ˌ⸗\ *n* : the shooting of small arms with intent to kill or scare : the action of men gunfighting

gunpoint \ˈ⸗ˌ⸗\ *n* : the point of a gun — **at gunpoint** *adv* : under a threat of death by being shot ⟨forced the bank president *at gunpoint* to open the safe —George Courson⟩

gunpointer \ˈ⸗ˌ⸗⸗\ *n* [¹*gun* + *pointer*] : a sailor who elevates, depresses, and fires a manually controlled gun aboard ship

gunport \ˈ⸗ˌ⸗\ *n* : an opening (as in a ship's side, a gun turret, a pillbox, or the nose, fuselage, or wing of an airplane) through which a gun can be fired

gunpowder \ˈ⸗ˌ⸗⸗\ *n* [ME *gonnepoudre*, fr. *gonne*, *gunne* gun + *poudre* powder] **1 a** : a black or brown explosive consisting of an intimate mechanical mixture of potassium nitrate, charcoal, and sulfur manufactured orig. as a powder and later usu. in grains of various sizes for different uses and used as the first and only military propellant until the introduction of smokeless powder — see BLACK POWDER, BROWN POWDER **b** : any of various powders used in guns as propelling charges ⟨smokeless ~⟩ — compare SMOKELESS POWDER **2** : GUNPOWDER TEA

gunpowder hammer *n* : a hammer or impact tool driven by the explosion of gunpowder

gunpowder tea *n* : a green tea each leaf of which is rolled into a small ball or pellet

gun·pow·dery \-ˌpaůd(ə)rē, -ri\ *adj* [*gunpowder* + *-y*] **1** *archaic* : VIOLENT, EXPLOSIVE **2** : smelling of gunpowder

gunpower \ˈ⸗ˌ⸗⸗\ *n* : the total weight of metal that can be thrown by the major battery of a battleship in one broadside

gun-rivet \ˈ⸗ˌ⸗⸗\ *vt* : to rivet with a pneumatic hammer

gun room *n* : an apartment on a British warship usu. aft of the berth deck orig. used by the gunner and his mates but now by the midshipmen and junior officers

gunrunner \ˈ⸗ˌ⸗⸗\ *n* : one engaged in gunrunning

gunrunning \ˈ⸗ˌ⸗⸗\ *n* : contraband traffic in arms and ammunition esp. when involving international relations or violation of customs laws

guns *pl of* GUN, *pres 3d sing of* GUN

gun·sel \ˈgən(t)səl\ *n* -S [prob. fr. Yiddish *genzel* gosling, fr. MHG *gensel*, dim. of *gans* goose, fr. OHG — more at GOOSE] **1** *slang* : a young, naïve, or stupid person **2** *slang* : a treacherous person **3** *slang* : CATAMITE **4** [influenced in meaning by ¹*gun*] *slang* : GUNMAN

gunshot \ˈ⸗ˌ⸗\ *n* [ME *gonneshot*, fr. *gonne*, *gunne* gun + *shot*] **1** : shot or a shot fired from a gun **2 a** : the distance to which shot can be thrown from a gun so as to be effective : the range of a gun

gun-shy \ˈ⸗ˌ⸗\ *adj* **1** : afraid of the sound of a gun or of other similar loud noises — used esp. of a dog **2** : afraid or markedly distrustful ⟨if you are a big-league player, you cannot very well afford to be *gun-shy* and duck away in panic from a ball —Paul Gallico⟩ ⟨was *gun-shy* of newspaper reporters —Charles Michelson⟩ ⟨the son of a bewildered age, *gun-shy* of propaganda —Dixon Wecter⟩

gunsight \ˈ⸗ˌ⸗\ *n* : ¹SIGHT 11a

gunsight lamp *n* : an optical sight permitting a gunner to aim at an airplane approaching directly down the glare from the sun's face

gunslick \ˈ⸗ˌ⸗\ *n, slang* : one who is noted for his fast handling of a gun esp. in gunfights

gun slide *n* : a fixed part of a gun mount on the upper surface of which the recoiling part travels

gunsling \ˈ⸗ˌ⸗\ *n* : SLING 3a (1)

gunslinger \ˈ⸗ˌ⸗⸗\ *n* [¹*gun* + *slinger*] : GUNMAN ⟨the three ~s who committed the crimes —Allan Bruce⟩ ⟨backed up his reputation as a ~ —Hoffman Birney⟩

gunslinging \ˈ⸗ˌ⸗⸗\ *n* [*slinging* fr. gerund of *sling*] : the shooting of a gun esp. in a gunfight ⟨irresponsible ~⟩

guns·man \ˈgənzmən\ *n, pl* **gunsmen** [*gun's* (gen. of ¹*gun*) + *man*] *archaic* : GUNMAN 1

gunsmith \ˈ⸗ˌ⸗\ *n* : one whose occupation is to design, make, or repair small firearms

gunsmithing \ˈ⸗ˌ⸗⸗\ *n* [¹*gun* + *smithing*] : the work of a gunsmith

gunsmithy \ˈ⸗ˌ⸗⸗\ *n* [¹*gun* + *smithy*] : the workshop of a gunsmith

gunstick *var of* GUNNING STICK

gunstock \ˈ⸗ˌ⸗\ *n* [ME *gonnestok*, fr. *gonne*, *gunne* gun + *stok* stock] : the stock to which the barrel and mechanism of a firearm are secured

gunstone \ˈ⸗ˌ⸗\ *n* [ME *gunneston*, fr. *gonne*, *gunne* gun + *stoon*, *ston* stone] **1** *obs* : CANNONBALL 1 **2** *heraldry* : a roundel sable : OGRESS, PELLET

gun tackle *n* : a block-and-tackle arrangement formerly used for running a gun carriage to and from a gun part or raising or lowering a gun — see GUNTACKLE PURCHASE; TACKLE illustration

guntackle purchase \ˈ⸗ˌ⸗⸗-\ *n* [*gun tackle* + *purchase*, n.] : a pulley tackle using two single blocks

gun·ter iron \ˈgəntə(r)-\ *n* : a fitting on a gunter rig consisting of two double eyes united by side bars so that one eye in each pair slides freely over a lower mast and the other serves as a step for a topmast

gunter rig *also* **gunter** *n* -S [after Edmund *Gunter* †1626 Eng. mathematician; fr. its resemblance to an instrument used in making mathematical calculations according to a system devised by Gunter] : a rig used on a small sailing boat consisting of an upper mast stepped in a gunter iron and moved up or down on a lower mast and supporting a yard to which is laced a triangular sail — called also *sliding gunter*

gunter's chain *n, usu cap G* [after Edmund *Gunter* †1626] : a chain 66 feet long consisting of 100 links of 7.92 inches that is the unit of length for surveys of U.S. public lands

gun-toting \ˈ⸗ˌ⸗⸗\ *adj* [*toting* fr. pres. part. of *tote*] : carrying and using a gun usu. for criminal purposes ⟨the *gun-toting* brothers wanted here for armed assault —*Springfield (Mass.) Union*⟩

gun toting *n* -S [*toting* fr. gerund of *tote*] : the carrying and use of a gun usu. for criminal purposes ⟨stiffer punishment for *gun toting* —W.T.Brannon⟩

gunter rig: *1* lower mast, *2* upper mast, *3* gunter irons, *4* halyard

guntub \ˈ⸗ˌ⸗\ *n* : the circular steel shield around a ship's gun

gun·wale *or* **gun·nel** *also* **gun·whale** \ˈgənᵊl\ *n* -S [*gunwale* & *gunnel* fr. ME *gonnewale*, fr. *gonne*, *gunne* gun + *wale*; *gunwhale* by folk etymology fr. *gunwale*; fr. its former use as a support for guns — more at WALE] **1 a** : the part of a vessel where topsides and deck meet **b** : the upper edge of the side or the rail of a small boat (as a canoe) **2** : a fore-and-aft member lying on or against the heads of the frames and inside the upper strake in boatbuilding — see INWALE — **gunwale down** *or* **gunwale to** : tipping or sinking until the gunwale is on a level with the water

gun·yah \ˈgənyə\ *n* -S [native name in Australia] **1** *Austral* : an aboriginal hut **2** *Austral* : a small hut or crude shelter built for use in the bush ⟨the camp consisted of dome-shaped bough ~s, roofed with sacks —Francis Ratcliffe⟩

gun·yang \ˈgənˌyaŋ\ *n* -S [native name in Australia] : the kangaroo apple of Australia

günz \ˈgin(t)s, -œ-\ *n* -ES *usu cap* [*Günz* river, Bavaria, Germany] : the earliest of four geologic stages marked by an advance of the ice during the Pleistocene glaciation of Europe — **günz·ian** \-sēən\ *adj, usu cap*

günz-min·del \-ˈmindᵊl\ *n, usu cap G&M* : the first geologic interglacial stage of the European Pleistocene between the Günz and Mindel stages of ice advance

¹gup *interj* [perh. contr. of *go up*] *obs* — used to express reproof, derision, or remonstrance

²gup \ˈgəp\ *n* -S [Hindi *gap*] *slang* : foolish talk : NONSENSE ⟨see what sort of ~ he's handed out —Ngaio Marsh⟩

¹gup·py \ˈgəpē, -pi\ *n* -ES [after R.J.Lechmere *Guppy* of Trinidad, who first presented specimens to the British Museum] : a small topminnow (*Lebistes reticulatus*) of the Barbados, Trinidad, and Venezuela frequently kept as an aquarium fish, the females reaching a length of about two inches and being plainly colored, the males being much smaller and having black, blue, and red markings

²guppy \"\ *n* -ES *sometimes cap* [greater underwater propulsive *power* + *-y*] : a submarine that has been streamlined (as by the removal of guns and the recessing of deck fittings) and equipped with snorkel

gup·ta \ˈgüptə, ˈgůp-\ *adj, usu cap* [*Gupta*, dynasty of kings of northern India] : of or relating to a dynasty of Brahman kings of northern India of the 4th to the 7th centuries and esp. to the art forms (as in religious sculpture or temple architecture) that characterized the period of that dynasty and spread from India into other eastern countries (as Ceylon and China)

¹gur *or* **goor** \ˈgů(ə)r\ *n* -S [Hindi *guṛ* coarse sugar, molasses, fr. Skt *guḍa*] : JAGGERY

²gur \"\ *n* -S *usu cap* : a branch of the Niger-Congo language family including Mossi, Dagomba, Senufo, Bariba, Gurma, and Gurunsi centered in the upper Volta river valley in Ghana and the Upper Volta territory, West Africa — called also *Mossi-Gurunsi*, *Voltaic*

gu·ra·ge \güˈrä(ˌ)gā\ *n* -S *cap* : a Semitic language or group of closely related languages spoken in southern Ethiopia

gur·dwa·ra \gůrˈdwärə\ *n* -S [Panjabi *gurduārā*, fr. Skt *guru* teacher + *dvāra* door; akin to Skt *dvār* door — more at GURU, DOOR] : a Sikh shrine or place of worship

gur·dy \ˈgərdē\ *n* -ES [short for *hurdy-gurdy*] : a revolving drum or large spool used in hauling nets and lines aboard commercial fishing boats

gurdy man *n* : a worker who coils fishing lines as they are pulled in and the fish removed

¹gurge \ˈgərj\ *vi* -ED/-ING/-S [L *gurges*, n.] : SURGE, SWIRL

²gurge \"\ *n* -S [L *gurges* whirlpool — more at GORGE] : a turbulent fountain : SURGE, EDDY

gur·geons \ˈgərjənz\ *n pl* [ME *gurgeones*] *now dial Eng* : coarse meal

gur·geon stopper \ˈgərjən-\ *n* [*gurgeon* perh. alter. of *gurjun*] : a small tree (*Eugenia buxifolia*) of southern Florida and the West Indies with hard wood — called also *Spanish stopper*

gur·ges \ˈgərˌjēz\ *n* -ES [L, whirlpool] : a heraldic charge consisting of a spiral made up of two narrow bands argent and azure and conventionally representing a whirlpool

gurges

gur·gi·ta·tion \ˌgərjəˈtāshən\ *n* -S [LL *gurgitatus* (past part. of *gurgitare* to engulf, fr. L *gurgit-*, *gurges* whirlpool) + E *-ion*] : a boiling or surging of a liquid : usu. violent ebullition

¹gur·gle \ˈgərgəl, ˈgəg-, ˈgəig-\ *vb* **gurgled; gurgled; gurgling** \-g(ə)liŋ\ **gurgles** [prob. imit.] *vi* **1** : to run or flow in a broken irregular chuckling current ⟨the brook *gurgled* over the rocks⟩ ⟨the water *gurgled* out of the narrow mouth of the bottle⟩ **2** : to make a sound like that of a gurgling liquid ⟨the baby *gurgling* in its crib⟩ ~ *vt* : to utter with a gurgling sound ⟨the woman *gurgled* her greetings to the children⟩

²gurgle \"\ *n* -S **1** : the act of gurgling ⟨the ~ of a brook over rocks⟩ **2** : the sound of gurgling or a single throaty chuckling sound like that of gurgling ⟨the ~s of the contented baby⟩

gurgling *n* -S [fr. gerund of ¹*gurgle*] : the sound of one that gurgles ⟨makes uncalled-for ~s of a bestial nature —Norman Douglas⟩

gur·gling·ly *adv* [*gurgling* (pres. part. of ¹*gurgle*) + *-ly*] : in the manner of one that gurgles ⟨the hostess approached them ~ and with a fatuous smile of joy⟩

gurgoyle var of GARGOYLE

gu·ri·an \'gu̇rēən\ n -s cap : a member of a Caucasian people closely related to the Georgians

gur·jun also **gur·jan** \'gərjən\ n -s [Bengali garjan] 1 : GURJUN BALSAM 2 a : a tree yielding gurjun balsam b : the wood of such a tree

gurjun balsam n : a thin oleoresin derived from several East Indian trees of the genus Dipterocarpus and resembling copaiba — called also wood oil

gurk \'gərk\ n -s [perh. fr. ScGael garrach] Scot : a stout well-built person

¹**gur·kha** or **ghur·kha** \'gu̇(ə)rkə, 'gər-\ n, pl **gurkha** or **ghurkha** or **gurkhas** or **ghurkhas** usu cap 1 : a member of a Rajput race that is Hindu in religion and Indo-European in speech and that settled in the province of Gurkha, Nepal, in the latter half of the 18th century and made themselves supreme 2 : a soldier from Nepal in the British and Indian armies

²**gurkha** \"\ adj, usu cap : of, relating to, or consisting of Gurkhas

gurl \'gərl\ vi -ED/-ING/-S [ME gurlen, of imit. origin] Scot : HOWL, GROWL, SNARL

gurly \-li\ adj -ER/-EST [gurl + -y] 1 Scot : rough and boisterous: a of weather : STORMY b of a person : uncouth and inclined to be surly ⟨the ~ brute —G.D.Brown⟩ 2 Scot : GURGLING ⟨the sounds of ~ burns⟩

gur·ma \'gu̇(ə)rmə\ n, pl **gurma** or **gurmas** usu cap 1 : a Negro people inhabiting the region adjacent to the White Volta river in West Africa 2 : a Gur language of the Gurma people

gur·mu·khi \'gu̇rmə(,)kē\ n -s usu cap [Panjabi gurmukhī, lit., from the mouth of the teacher, fr. Skt guru teacher + mukha mouth (prob. of Dravidian origin & akin to Tamil mukam); fr. the tradition that it was invented by the guru Angad in the 16th century — more at GURU] : the alphabet that the sacred texts of the Sikhs in whatever language are written in and that is also used by the Sikhs in secular writing in Panjabi

gur·nard \'gərnərd\ n, pl **gurnard** or **gurnards** [ME, fr. MF gornart, irreg. fr. grogner, grognier to grunt, grumble (fr. L grunnire to grunt) + -ard, -art -ard — more at GRUNT] 1 : any of various marine scorpaenid fishes constituting the family Triglidae, having the head armored and spined and three pairs of fingerlike processes which are modified ventral rays of the pectoral fins and are used as feelers and in crawling on the sea bottom, and including a few European forms that are used as food — see FLYING GURNARD, SEA ROBIN 2 : a dragonet (Callionymus draco)

gur·ney \'gərnē\ n -s [prob. fr. the name Gurney] West : a wheeled cot or stretcher

gur·ney·ite \-,īt\ n -s usu cap [Joseph J. Gurney †1847 Eng. Quaker minister + E -ite] : a follower of an English Friend who toured America preaching an evangelical Christianity that stressed biblical authority, the atonement, justification, and sanctification — compare WILBURITE

gu·ro \'gü(,)rō\ n, pl **guro** or **guros** usu cap : a people of the interior of the Ivory Coast now known chiefly for their wood carvings (as dancing masks) — called also Kweni

gurr \'gər\ vi -ED/-ING/-S [imit.] chiefly Scot : GROWL, SNARL

gur·ry \'gərē\ n -ES [origin unknown] : fishing offal: as a : the refuse from cutting up a whale and trying out the oil b : a slimy gummy substance (as that scraped off the back of a right whale or removed from a sponge in commercial processing) c : FISH OIL

gurs pl of GUR

gurt \'gərt\ dial Eng var of GREAT

gu·ru \gə'rü, 'gü(,)rü, 'gu̇(-\ n -s [Hindi gurū, fr. Skt guru, lit., heavy, weighty, venerable — more at GRIEVE] 1 a : a personal religious teacher and spiritual guide in Hinduism b often cap : one of a line of ten chief spiritual leaders in Sikhism recognized within the Sikh community as personal exemplars and temporal leaders as well beginning with Guru Nanak (1469-1538) and ending in 1708 with the death of Guru Govind Singh 2 : a person who acts as one's teacher and guide in matters of fundamental intellectual concern ⟨seeking the clique or the ~ essential to his soul —John Masefield⟩

gu·run·si \gə'rün(t)sē\ n, pl **gurunsi** or **gurunsies** usu cap 1 : a Negro people of the Ivory Coast of West Africa 2 : a Gur language of the Gurunsi people

gu·ru·ship \pronunc at GURU + ,ship\ n : the office or function of a guru

gur·witsch ray \'gu̇rvich-, -rwich-\ n, usu cap G [after Aleksandr G. Gurvich b1874 Russ. biologist] : MITOGENETIC RAY

¹**gush** \'gəsh\ vb -ED/-ING/-ES [ME guschen, gosshen, perh. of imit. origin] vi 1 : to pour, issue, flow, or spout copiously or violently ⟨the blood ~ed from the wound⟩ ⟨the spectacular fountains of lava that ~ for hundreds of feet into the air —Howel Williams⟩ — often used with forth or out ⟨the water ~ed forth from the hole in the tank⟩ ⟨words and yet more words ~ed out of him in an endless meaningless stream⟩ 2 : to give free rein to a sudden copious flow or issuing forth (as of blood or tears) — often used with forth or out ⟨the cut ~ed forth with blood⟩ ⟨always ~ing out in tears⟩ ⟨~ forth with a wondrous flow of eloquence⟩ 3 : to make an unrestrained and excessively sentimental usu. prolonged and often habitual display of affection or enthusiasm ⟨a woman who tended to ~ at the very mention of babies⟩ ⟨she would rush to him with all the girlish excitement . . . and ~ about everybody having a good time —E.A.Peeples⟩ ~ vt 1 : to emit or pour in a copious free flow ⟨the broken main ~ed a stream of water over the road⟩ — often used with forth or out ⟨the old man's eyes ~ed sudden tears —L.C.Douglas⟩ 2 : to say or utter in gushing ⟨"I'm dying to get to Europe," he ~ed. "It's positively the only, only place for those who wish to live the cultured life" —Rex Ingamells⟩ ⟨the woman ~ed maudlin greetings to everybody at the party⟩ syn see POUR

²**gush** \"\ n -ES 1 a : a gushing forth (as of a liquid) ⟨a sudden ~ of water from the hose nozzle⟩ b : the fluid emitted in such a gushing forth ⟨the ~ of oil spread out in a thin slippery film over the road⟩ c : a free usu. sudden outpouring : GUST, BURST ⟨a ~ of sound from the horns⟩ ⟨a ~ of feeling from the heart⟩ ⟨a ~ of flame⟩ ⟨a ~ of cheerful light —Charles Dickens⟩ ⟨a mighty ~ of energy —Science Yr. Bk.⟩ 2 : an unrestrained often prolonged display of sentiment ⟨a poem marked chiefly by ~⟩ ⟨a city which provides unusual opportunities for ~, for it has abundant superficial charm —Robertson Davies⟩ ⟨the insight of a cultivated mind and the ~ of the immature enthusiast —John Dewey⟩

gush·er \'gəshə(r)\ n -s 1 : one that gushes; specif : an oil well with a copious natural flow usu. sudden and violent in its initial uncontrolled stage 2 : something suggesting a gusher oil well in its flowing or spouting ⟨~s of critical applause⟩

gush·et \'gəshət\ n -s [ME (Sc) guschet piece of armor protecting the armpit, fr. MF gouchet, gousset piece of armor protecting the armpit — more at GUSSET] 1 Scot : the clock of a stocking 2 Scot : ¹GUSSET 2a

gush·i·ly \'gəshəlē, -li\ adv : in a gushy manner ⟨a rather ~ pleasant hostess⟩

gush·i·ness \-shēnəs, -shin-\ n -ES : the quality or state of a person that gushes or the quality of his expression ⟨a man of inexcusable ~ that poured sentiment like syrup over everyone⟩ ⟨the ~ of his prose writings⟩

gush·ing·ly adv [gushing (pres. part. of ¹gush) + -ly] : in the manner of one that gushes ⟨a ~ prolific writer of saccharine verse⟩ ⟨~ idealistic ladies —G.B.Shaw⟩

gushy \'gəshē, -shi\ adj -ER/-EST [²gush + -y] : marked by gushiness ⟨a laudation marked more by ~ sentiment than sincere admiration⟩ ⟨wrote particularly unrestrained and ~ poetry⟩

gus·la or **gus·le** or **gous·le** also **guz·la** \'güslə, 'gu̇, |zlə\ n -s [Serbo-Croatian gusle; akin to Bulg gŭsla gusla, Russ gusli gusli, OSlav gǫsli psaltery, Russ gudet' to sound, drone, Lith gausti — more at KITE] : a rudimentary musical instrument of the Balkans made with a round concave body, parchment sounding board, and one horsehair string and held between the knees and played with a curved bow

gus·li also **gus·lee** \-lē\ n -s [Russ] : a Russian musical instrument of the zither class having approximately 28 gut strings and played with a keyboard

¹**gus·set** \'gəsət, usu -əd·+V\ n -s [ME, fr. MF gouchet, gousset piece of armor protecting the armpit, armpit, fr. gousse pod + -et] 1 a : a piece of chain mail or plate at the openings of the joints in a suit of armor b : a usu. triangular or diamond-shaped insert (as of cloth or leather) placed in a seam (as of a sleeve, pocketbook, glove) to give ease or expansibility; also : a similar piece made by adding stitches at the heel of hose c : any V-shaped or triangular insert (as in a sail or skirt): as (1) : an elastic insert in a shoe upper (as for providing a snug fit) (2) or **gusset tongue** : BELLOWS TONGUE d : a pleat or fold esp. in bookbinding 2 : something resembling a gusset: as a : a gore of land b (1) or **gusset plate** : a connecting or reinforcing plate that joins the truss members in a truss joint or fits at a joint of a frame structure or set of braces (2) or **gusset stay** : a bracket or angular piece of iron for strengthening angles of a structure (as an airplane or a bridge) 3 : a pretended abatement in heraldry consisting of either side of a pall without the top opening

1 1

1,1 gussets 1b

²**gusset** \"\ vt -ED/-ING/-S : to provide with, connect, or reinforce with a gusset

¹**gust** \'gəst\ n -s [ME guste, fr. L gustus taste; akin to L gustare to taste — more at CHOOSE] 1 obs a : the sensation of taste b : INCLINATION, LIKING 2 a archaic : special flavor or taste (as of food or drink) b obs : FORETASTE 3 [prob. fr. Sp gusto delight, pleasure, taste, fr. L gustus taste] a obs : GRATIFICATION, ENJOYMENT b : great or keen delight — often used formerly with of, in, or to but now usu. with for ⟨~ of the things of the world —Jeremy Taylor⟩ ⟨a ~ for London —Samuel Johnson⟩ ⟨her father's early ~ for color and for amusement —E.K.Chambers⟩

²**gust** \'güst, 'gəst\ vt -ED/-ING/-S [ME gusten, fr. L gustare] now Scot : TASTE, RELISH

³**gust** \'gəst\ n -s [prob. fr. ON gustr; akin to OHG gussa flood, ON gjōsa to gush, MIr guss violence, anger, Goth giutan to pour — more at FOUND] 1 a : a sudden brief rushing or driving of wind b : a sudden change with respect to the earth in the speed or the direction or both of the wind of sufficient magnitude to produce a significant load upon the structure of an airplane encountering it 2 a : a burst, puff, outrush, or brief emission (as of rain, fire, smoke) suggesting a gust of wind ⟨a ~ of rain came down —Frank Taubes⟩ b : an outburst or quick venting esp. of temper or feeling ⟨unruly ~s of passion —William Black⟩ ⟨a ~ of laughter —John Wain⟩ ⟨his ~s of honest jocularity —Francis Hackett⟩ c : something that appears or comes into being or is experienced suddenly and usu. transiently : WAVE, SURGE ⟨a ~ of pain —Fred Majdalany⟩ ⟨a sudden ~ of frustration —Alan Moorehead⟩ ⟨a ~ of loneliness —Jean Stafford⟩ ⟨a ~ of personal concern —Janet Flanner⟩ syn see WIND

⁴**gust** \"\ vi -ED/-ING/-S : to blow or move in gusts ⟨the winds, now ~ing in the reverse direction —David Beaty⟩ ⟨the wind . . . ~ed in through the holes —Irwin Shaw⟩

gus·ta·ble \'gəstəbəl\ adj [LL gustabilis, fr. L gustare to taste + -abilis -able] 1 archaic : APPETIZING, SAVORY, TASTY 2 archaic : perceptible or distinguishable by taste ⟨an increased number of ~ differences —Herbert Spencer⟩

gus·ta·tion \,gə'stāshən\ n -s [L gustation-, gustatio, fr. gustatus (past part. of gustare) + -ion-, -io -ion] : the act or sensation of tasting

gus·ta·tive \'gəstəd·iv\ adj [ML gustativus, fr. L gustatus + -ivus -ive] : GUSTATORY — **gus·ta·tive·ness** n -ES

gus·ta·to·ri·al \¦gəstə¦tōrēəl, -tȯr-\ adj [gustatory + -al] : GUSTATORY

gus·ta·to·ri·ly \-rəlē, -li\ adv : in a gustatory manner

gus·ta·to·ry \'==,rē, -ri\ adj [L gustatus + E -ory] : of, relating to, affecting, associated with, or being the sense of taste ⟨~ nerves⟩ ⟨~ stimulation⟩

gustatory cell n : one of the sensory epithelial cells of a taste bud : TASTE CELL

gus·ta·vi·an \(,)gə'stāvēən, gu̇'s-, -täv-\ adj, usu cap [Gustavus (any of several kings of Sweden) + E -ian] : of or relating to the reign of the Swedish kings or any one of the Swedish kings named Gustavus (as III and IV)

¹**gust·ful** \'gəstfəl\ adj [¹gust + -ful] archaic : APPETIZING, SAVORY — **gust·ful·ly** \-fəlē\ adv

²**gustful** \"\ adj [³gust + -ful] : GUSTY, WINDY

¹**gust·i·ly** \'gəstəlē, -li, Scot " or 'güs-\ adv [²gusty + -ly] : with great relish ⟨picked up a long wrinkled-looking sausage . . . then crunched on it ~ —P.E.Deutschman⟩

²**gust·i·ly** \'gəs-\ adv [¹gusty + -ly] : in gusts ⟨the wind blew ~⟩ : in a manner suggesting a gust ⟨she sighed ~⟩

gust·i·ness \-tēnəs, -tin-\ n -ES [¹gusty + -ness] : the quality or state of being gusty; specif : the ratio of the maximum difference of wind velocity to its mean velocity in a given interval of time

gus·to \'gə(,)stō\ n -ES [Sp, delight, pleasure, taste, fr. L gustus taste; akin to L gustare to taste — more at CHOOSE] 1 a : TASTE, LIKING, APPRECIATION b : keen or intense appreciation : great usu. enthusiastic and vigorous enjoyment or delight ⟨describes the adventure . . . with enormous ~ —Robert Payne⟩ c : vitality marked by an overabundance of healthy positive and often unrefined vigor and enthusiasm ⟨the good animal ~ of a child of nature —Aldous Huxley⟩ ⟨its pioneering ~ and its tremendous physical energy —Green Peyton⟩ ⟨his gigantic ~, his delight in toil and struggle, his superb aliveness —H.L.Mencken⟩ 2 archaic : artistic style esp. marked by lofty spirit or taste

gus·to·so \gü'stō(,)sō,)zō\ adj (or adv) [It, adj., tasteful, fr. gusto taste, fr. L gustus] : with taste — used as a direction in music

gusts pl of GUST, pres 3d sing of GUST

gust tunnel n : an enclosed space within which a jet of air is made to impinge upon an airplane model in free flight for investigating the effects of atmospheric gusts upon the flight of airplanes

¹**gusty** \'gəstē, -ti\ adj -ER/-EST [³gust + -y] 1 a : blowing in gusts ⟨a ~ wind⟩ : marked by gusts ⟨a characteristic of hurricane winds is their irregular ~ nature —Amer. Guide Series: La.⟩ ⟨~ weather⟩ : giving forth gusts ⟨a series of ~ explosions⟩ : coming forth in a gust ⟨a ~ sigh⟩ ⟨~ squalls of rage —Edith Sitwell⟩ b : marked by outbursts of empty bombastic talk ⟨~ oratory —C.G.Bowers⟩ 2 : marked by gusto : exhibiting an overabundance of healthy positive often unrefined vigor and enthusiasm ⟨a ~, warmhearted woman —Time⟩ ⟨a lusty, ~ humor —N.Y.Times⟩ ⟨a ~ love of life —W.D.Edmonds⟩

²**gusty** \'güs-,'gəs-\ adj -ER/-EST [¹gust + -y] chiefly Scot : SAVORY, APPETIZING

¹**gut** \'gət, usu -əd·+V\ n -s [ME, fr. OE guttas (pl.); akin to OE gyte action of pouring, MD gote gutter, OHG guz action of pouring, OE gēotan to pour — more at FOUND] 1 a (1) : BOWELS, ENTRAILS — usu. used in pl. ⟨chicken ~s rank high among good catfish baits —J.R.Harlan & E.B.Speaker⟩ ⟨felt their ~s contract with fear —Barnaby Conrad⟩ (2) : INTESTINE ⟨see whether an amebicide acts directly on the amoeba or on commensal organisms in the ~ —Lancet⟩ (3) : the alimentary canal or cavity or the portion from the stomach down — usu. used in pl. ⟨would feel hunger nudging my ribs, twisting my empty ~s until they ached —Richard Wright⟩ (4) : STOMACH, BELLY — usu. used in pl.; not often in formal use ⟨his huge ~ hung far below his belt —L.M.Uris⟩ ⟨gave the man a poke in the ~s⟩ ⟨my stupidity in keeping that hustler's ~ filled with beer, T-bone steaks and whiskey —Frederic Wakeman⟩ b : CAT GUT 1 c : the inner usu. essential parts — usu. used in pl. ⟨working somewhere in the ~s of the machinery⟩ ⟨tear the word from the ~s of the dictionary —O.W.Holmes †1935⟩ ⟨land which has had its ~s mined out of it —A.J. Bruwer⟩ ⟨have you ever seen the ~s of a poem laid bare —F.J.Jennings⟩ d : a basic concept or consideration : ESSENCE — usu. used in pl. ⟨gets down to the very ~s of the matter⟩ ⟨getting in to the real ~s of the subject —H.J. Laski⟩ 2 a : a narrow sea passage (as a strait) : a small creek or narrow waterway (as in a marsh or on a tidal flat) ⟨inlets and ~s scoured by the rushing tides —R.W.Miner⟩ b : GULLY, RAVINE, VALLEY ⟨the deep ~ of the hills —Ian Hamilton⟩ 3 : the sac of fluid silk that is taken from a silkworm ready to spin its cocoon from which a coarse strong thread suitable for forming the leader of a fishline is produced 4 **guts** pl : strength or force of character : moral stamina : COURAGE, FORTITUDE : determined persistence ⟨he alone . . . has the ~s to grapple with the enemy on every political front —New Republic⟩ ⟨was a tower of strength, holding everything together by sheer unrelenting ~s —Nicholas Monsarrat⟩ syn see FORTITUDE — **hate one's guts** slang : to hate with extreme intensity ⟨I don't dislike him, I hate his guts —Erle Stanley Gardner⟩

²**gut** \"\ vt **gutted**; **gutted**; **gutting**; **guts** [ME gutten, fr. gut, n.] 1 a : to take out the bowels of : EVISCERATE ⟨his body opened and gutted, and the entrails burnt in the fire —J.H.Wheelwright⟩ ⟨found a dead rabbit, gutted it —Time⟩ b : to plunder of contents : remove the contents of ⟨a mob gutted the house⟩ c : to extract all the essential portions or passages from (as a book) 2 a : to destroy totally the inside of ⟨fire gutted the building⟩ b : to burn out ⟨a warehouse whose roof had been burned away and whose floors had been gutted —Time⟩ c : to destroy in essence ⟨the isolationist effort to ~ foreign aid —Atlantic⟩ ⟨inflation has already gutted the economy of country after country —U.S.Code⟩ 3 : to cause (as by wear) to develop ruts and holes ⟨a gutted road⟩

³**gut** \'güt, 'gət\ dial var of GOUT

gutbucket \'=,==\ n : hot jazz music played in a brash style with much improvisation and with a strong 2-beat rhythm : BARRELHOUSE

gut–hammer \'=,==\ n : the gong in a logging camp usu. consisting of a triangle of steel that is struck to summon lumberjacks to meals

gu·ti \'güd·ē\ n, pl **guti** or **gutis** usu cap 1 : a mountain people ruling Sumer and Akkad in the 24th century B.C. 2 : a member of the Guti people

gu·ti·an \-ēən\ n -s usu cap [Guti + -an] : GUTI 2

gu·ti·er·re·zia \,güd·ēə'rēzh(ē)ə\ n, cap [NL, fr. Gutiérrez, noble Span. family + NL -ia] : a genus of American herbs or low shrubs (family Compositae) with alternate linear entire leaves and yellow flower heads in corymbose clusters — see MATCHWEED

gut·less \'gətləs\ adj 1 : lacking courage, pluck, manliness, determination : being a moral weakling : COWARDLY ⟨the ~ captain wobbles, crosses up his men, plots to run out on the job —Time⟩ 2 a : lacking in vital physical qualities : lacking a substantial or human character ⟨~ spirit⟩ b : having no substance that is significant or worthy of respect ⟨a ~ profession⟩ ⟨a ~ enterprise⟩ — **gut·less·ness** n -ES

gut·nish \'gütnish\ also **gut·nic** \-nik\ n, pl **gutnishes** also **gutnics** usu cap [G gutnisch, fr. ON gotneskr, adj., of Gotland] : a Swedish dialect spoken on the island of Gotland

¹**gut out** vt [²gut + out] : to remove in the process of gutting ⟨the forests were gutted out and mined in the same fashion as the minerals —Lewis Mumford⟩

²**gut out** vb [prob. alter. (influenced by ¹gut out) of gutter out] vt : to snuff out ⟨burned so feebly and was so quickly gutted out —Van Wyck Brooks⟩ ~ vi : to gutter and go out

guts pl of GUT, pres 3d sing of GUT

gutshoot \'=,=\ vt [¹gut + shoot] slang : to shoot or wound in the stomach or abdomen

gutshot \'=,=\ n [¹gut + shot] slang : a wound in the stomach or abdomen from rifle fire or gunfire

gutstring \'=,=\ n : string made of sheep gut used esp. for surgical sutures

gutsy \'gətsē\ adj, usu -ER/-EST [guts (pl. of ¹gut) + -y] 1 slang : having guts : COURAGEOUS ⟨kids thought they were ~ to chuck a few stones through her windows —Ruth Park⟩ 2 slang : forceful, passionate, or lusty in quality : forthright and provocative in its effect upon the physical esp. sexual passions ⟨a ~ singer⟩

gutt abbr 1 [L gutta; guttae] drop; drops 2 guttural

¹**gut·ta** \'gəd·ə, 'gu̇d·ə\ n, pl **gut·tae** \-d·,ē, -üd·,ī\ also **guttas** [L, lit., drop — more at GOUT] : one of a series of ornaments in the Doric entablature that is usu. in the form of a frustum of a cone but is sometimes cylindrical — called also campana, drop, treenail

²**gutta** \'gəd·ə, -ətə\ n -s [Malay gĕtah sap, latex] 1 a : GUTTA-PERCHA b : the coagulated latex of any of various trees (esp. of the genera Palaquium and Payena) and vines that is used to adulterate gutta-percha and to mix with chicle in the making of chewing gum 2 : a white crystalline polymeric hydrocarbon $(C_5H_8)_x$ stereoisomeric with rubber hydrocarbon and constituting the principal ingredient of gutta-percha and balata

gutta balata n [²gutta] : BALATA 1

gutta gam·ba \¦==¦gambə\ n [perh. fr. Malay gĕtah sap, latex + E gamba (irreg. fr. Cambodia, region or country in southeast Indochina)] : GAMBOGE

gutta–gum tree n [gutta-gum prob. fr. ²gutta + gum] : a tropical American tree (Vismia guianensis) of the family Hypericaceae having red sap which yields American gamboge

gutta–per·cha \¦==¦pərchə, -pēch-,-pəich-\ n -s [Malay, fr. gĕtah sap, latex + pĕrcha tree producing gutta-percha] : a gray to brown tough plastic substance consisting essentially of gutta hydrocarbon with some resin that is obtained from the latex of several Malaysian sapotaceous trees of the genera Payena and Palaquium and is used esp. as electric insulation for submarine cables and in dentistry — compare BALATA

gutta ro·sa·cea \¦==rō'zās(h)ēə\ or **gutta ro·sea** \-'rōzēə\ n [ML, lit., rosy drop] : ACNE ROSACEA

gutta se·re·na \¦==,sə'rēnə\ n [NL, lit., clear drop] : AMAUROSIS

¹**gut·tate** \'gəd·,āt\ adj [L guttatus speckled, fr. gutta drop, spot — more at GOUT] : resembling a drop or having spots that resemble drops

²**guttate** \"\ vi -ED/-ING/-S [prob. back-formation fr. guttation] 1 : to lose moisture by guttation 2 : to exude in the process of guttation

gut·tat·ed \-ād·əd\ adj [L guttatus + E -ed] : GUTTATE

gut·ta·tim \,gə'tād·əm, gu̇'täd-\ adv [L, fr. gutta drop] : drop by drop — used in prescriptions

gut·ta·tion \,gə'tāshən\ n -s [ISV gutt- (fr. L gutta drop) + -ation; orig. formed in G] : the exudation of moisture from an uninjured surface of a plant (as from a hydathode)

gutted past of GUT

gut·té also **gut·té** or **gout·tée** or **gout·té** \(')gü¦tā, (')gə¦-\ or **gut·ty** or **gout·ty** \'güd·ē, 'gəd·ē\ adj [MF goutté spotted, speckled, fr. L guttatus speckled] heraldry : semé of drops

guttée d'eau \-'dō\ adj [guttée + F d'eau of water] heraldry : semé of drops argent

guttée de larmes \-,də'lärm\ adj [guttée + F de larmes of tears] heraldry : semé of drops azure

guttée de poix \-də'pwä\ adj [guttée + F de poix of pitch] heraldry : semé of drops sable

guttée de sang \-də'säⁿ\ adj [guttée + F de sang of blood] heraldry : semé of drops gules

guttée d'huile \-'dwēl\ adj [guttée + F d'huile of oil] heraldry : semé of drops vert

guttée d'olive \-,də'lēv\ adj [guttée + F d'olive of olive (color)] heraldry : GUTTÉE D'HUILE

guttée d'or \-'dȯ(ə)r\ adj [guttée + F d'or of gold] heraldry : semé of drops or

¹**gut·ter** \'gəd·ə(r), 'gətə-\ n -s [ME goter, guter, gotere, gutere, fr. OF gotiere, goutiere eaves, eaves trough, fr. gote, goute drop — more at GOUT] 1 a archaic : WATERCOURSE, BROOK b : a channel or gully worn by running water 2 : something forming or intended to form a channel: as a : a groove at an eaves or a usu. metal trough under an eaves to catch rainwater and carry it off (as to a downspout) b : a low area, course, ditch, or furrow (as at a roadside) to carry off surface water (as to a sewer) c : a V-shaped trough used in turpentining for guiding the turpentine into a cup d : a trough-shaped course behind the animals in a cattle barn into which dung and other wastes drop e : a grooved piece extending over the windows and doors of an automobile to catch and carry off water f : a depression or narrow trough on each side of a bowling alley to catch balls that roll off g : a depressed furrow between body parts (as on

the surface between a pair of adjacent ribs or in the dorsal wall of the body cavity on either side of the vertebral column) **h :** FIRELINE 2c **3 a :** GUTTER STICK **b :** a space between adjoining long sides at right angles to the foot of 4-page sections in a printing form **c :** the space in a form that produces the inside margins of a printed page; *also* **:** the white space formed by the adjoining inside margins of two facing pages (as of a book or magazine) **d :** RIVER 4 **4 :** the lowest most vulgar level or condition of usu. urban civilization ⟨raised in the ~ and condemned to a life of crime⟩ ⟨slang right out of the ~⟩ **5** *Austral* **:** the dry bed of a river of Tertiary age containing alluvial gold — called also *bottom* **6 :** the space between the barriers and sides of a cabinet in which electric wiring is concealed **7 :** BACKFLASH 3 **8 :** the wide space between the panes of an uncut sheet of stamps

[2]**gutter** \"\ *vb* -ED/-ING/-S [ME *guteren*, fr. *guter*, *gutere*, n.] *vt* **1 :** to cut or wear furrows or channels in ⟨a heavy rain ~*ing* the plowed field⟩ **2 :** to provide with a gutter ~ *vi* **1 a :** to flow in rivulets ⟨tears ~*ed* down her cheeks⟩ **b** *of a candle* **:** to melt away by reason of a channel forming on the side of the cup hollowed out by the burning wick so that the melted wax runs off rapidly **2 a :** to incline downward in a draft of wind — used of a candle or lamp flame **b :** to burn feebly ⟨torch of . . . liberty ~*ed* low —F.V.W.Mason⟩

[3]**gutter** \"\ *adj* [[1]*gutter*] **:** of, relating to, or befitting the gutter ⟨a ~ urchin⟩; *esp* **:** marked by extreme vulgarity, cheapness, or indecency ⟨~ profanity⟩ ⟨~ journalism⟩

[4]**gutter** \"\ *n* -S [[2]*gut* + *-er*] **:** a worker who cuts or pulls the guts from animals or fish or one who operates a machine that removes heads, tails, and guts from fish

gutter away *vi* **:** to disappear by degrees but usu. rapidly ⟨a brilliant orange flash split the darkness . . . and then *guttered away* to nothing —Nicholas Monsarrat⟩

guttering *n* -S [[1]*gutter* + *-ing*] **1 :** the material for or of gutters **2 a :** a length or section of a gutter **:** [1]GUTTER 2a ⟨saw a sparrow repeatedly slide down inside a short bent pipe from the ~ at the top —Alice E. Millard⟩ **b :** GUTTERS **3** [fr. gerund of [2]*gutter*] **:** the melted wax that runs down a candle

gutter ledge *n* [[1]*gutter*] **:** a bar fitting across a hatchway on a ship as a support for the hatch

gut·ter·man \-mən\ *n, pl* **guttermen** [[1]*gutter* + *man*] **:** SWAMPER 2a

gutter out *vi* **1 :** to become reduced to a small flame or glow and then become extinguished ⟨the candle *guttered out*⟩ **2 :** to come to an end or die feebly or undramatically ⟨another day of our life *gutters out* in . . . sleep —Ernest Beaglehole⟩ ⟨rebellion *guttered out* in the rain —*Time*⟩

gutters *pl of* GUTTER, *pres 3d sing of* GUTTER

guttersnipe \'==,=\ *n* -S **1 :** one belonging to or suited to the lowest moral or economic condition of usu. urban civilization **:** a street urchin **:** HOODLUM ⟨a pint-sized ~ whom he forces to pose as his son —*Time*⟩ ⟨now this bloodthirsty ~ must launch his mechanized armies upon new fields of slaughter —Sir Winston Churchill⟩ **2 :** a small poster; *also* **:** HANDBILL **3 a :** WILSON'S SNIPE **b :** SPOTTED SANDPIPER — **gut·ter·snip·ish** \-pish\ *adj*

gutter stick *n* **1 :** a length of wood furniture with a gutter running lengthwise used to separate adjoining pages imposed side by side in a chase **2 :** furniture used as a gutter stick

gut·tide \'gu̇t,tīd, 'gət,-\ *n* -S [alter. (influenced by [1]*gut*) of earlier *good tide* Shrove Tuesday, fr. [1]*good* + *tide*] *now dial Eng* **:** a time of feasting; *specif* **:** SHROVE TUESDAY

gut·tie \'gət,tī\ *n* -S [[1]*gut* + *tie*, n.] **:** colic in young cattle due to strangulation of a loop of intestine

gut·tif·er·ae \,gə'tifə,rē\ *n pl, cap* [NL, fr. fem. pl. of *guttifer* guttiferous] **:** a family of widely distributed chiefly tropical trees and shrubs (order Parietales) usu. having opposite or whorled leaves, unisexual flowers, resinous sap, and oil glands and including plants producing valuable fruits, oils, and resins, and some usable timber

gut·tif·er·a·les \,=,=='rā(,)lēz\ *n pl, cap* [NL, fr. *Guttiferae* + *-ales*] *in some classifications* **:** an order of plants coextensive with Parietales

[1]**gut·tif·er·ous** \ˌgəˈtif(ə)rəs\ *adj* [NL *guttifer* guttiferous (fr. *gutti-* — fr. L *gutta* drop — + L *-fer* -ferous) + E *-ous* — more at GOUT] **:** yielding gum or resinous substances

[2]**guttiferous** \"\ *adj* [NL *Guttiferae* + E *-ous*] **:** relating to the Guttiferae

gut·ti·form \'gəd·ə,fȯrm\ *adj* [prob. fr. (assumed) NL *guttiformis*, fr. NL *gutti-* (fr. L *gutta* drop) + L *-formis* -form] **:** having the shape of a drop (as a spot of color)

gut·ti·ness \-d·ēnəs\ *n* -ES *slang* **:** the quality or state of being gutty

gutting *pres part of* GUT

gut·tle \'gəd·ᵊl, -ətᵊl\ *vb* **guttled**; **guttled**; **guttling** \-d·ᵊliŋ, -t(ᵊ)l-\ **guttles** [irreg. fr. [1]*gut*] **:** to eat or drink greedily and noisily — **gut·tler** \-d·ᵊlə(r), -t(ᵊ)l-\ *n* -S

gut·tu·la \'gəchələ\ *n, pl* **guttu·lae** \-,lē\ [LL, dim. of L *gutta* drop] *biol* **:** a small spot shaped like a drop — **gut·tu·lar** \-lə(r)\ *adj* — **gut·tu·late** \-lət, -,lāt\ *adj*

gut·tule \'gə(,)chül\ *n* -S [LL *guttula*] **:** GUTTULA

[1]**gut·tur·al** \'gəd·ərəl, -ətər- *also* -ə·tr-\ *adj* [MF, prob. fr. ML *gutturalis*, fr. L *guttur* throat + *-alis* -al — more at COT] **1 :** of or relating to the throat **2 a :** being or belonging to a speech sound or a language or speaker having sounds that do not occur in standard English and that are articulated in the throat ⟨the glottal stop, uvular *r*, the sound of *ch* in German *Buch*, and the sound of *g* in *Wagen*, in some German speech are ~⟩ **b :** being or belonging to a sound or utterance or a language or speaker having sounds that are strange, unpleasant, or disagreeable **c :** VELAR, PALATAL — not often used technically **3 :** marked by or producing guttural sounds ⟨a ~ voice⟩ ⟨laughed in his quiet, ~ way —Julian Dana⟩ ⟨acres of ~ frogs —Marjory S. Douglas⟩ — **gut·tur·al·ism** \-rə,lizəm\ *n* -S — **gut·tur·al·i·ty** \,gəd·ə'raləd·ē, ,gətə-, -ətē, -i\ *n* -ES — **gut·tur·al·ly** \'gəd·ərəlē, -ətər-, -li *also* 'gə·tr-\ *adv* — **gut·tur·al·ness** *n* -ES

[2]**guttural** \"\ *n* -S **:** a guttural sound or symbol or guttural speech or utterance

gut·tur·al·iza·tion \,gəd·ərələ'zāshən, ,gətər-, -,lī'z- *also* ,gə·tr-\ *n* -S **:** the act or process of gutturalizing or the state of being gutturalized

gut·tur·al·ize \'gəd·ərə,līz, 'gətər- *also* 'gə·tr-\ *vb* -ED/-ING/-S [[1]*guttural* + *-ize*] *vt* **1 :** to pronounce or utter in a guttural manner **2 :** VELARIZE ~ *vi* **:** to speak in a guttural manner

[1]**gut·turo·nasal** \ˌgəd·ə(,)rō, -ətə-+\ *adj* [*gutturo-* (fr. [1]*guttural*) + *nasal*] **:** both velar and nasal — used of the sound \ŋ\

[2]**gutturonasal** \"\ *n* -S **:** a gutturonasal sound **:** the sound \ŋ\

[1]**gutty** *var of* GUTTÉE

[2]**gut·ty** \'gəd·ē\ *adj* -ER/-EST [[1]*gut* + *-y*] **1** *Scot* **:** fat-bellied and gross **2 :** having guts: as **a :** marked by vital and bold realism esp. in its physical detail ⟨a ~, scalp-raising account of the war . . . in southeast Asia —*Time*⟩ **b :** marked by or having courage or fortitude ⟨a ~ little kid —Oakley Hall⟩ ⟨the *guttiest* thing I ever saw a man do, in a life that has produced some fairly rugged moments —Philip Wylie⟩ **c :** having a significant or challenging substance or quality ⟨a ~ role in a play⟩ ⟨the ~, exciting pursuit of big or small game —Edison Marshall⟩ **d :** forthright and provocative in its effect upon the physical esp. sexual passions

gutweed \'=,=\ *n* [[1]*gut*] **:** a perennial sow thistle (*Sonchus aroensis*)

gut·zeit test \'gu̇t,sīt-\ *n, usu cap G* [after Max Adolf *Gutzeit* †1915 Ger. chemist] **:** a test for arsenic used esp. in toxicology that is based on the formation of arsine (as in the Marsh test) and the production by the arsine of a brown stain on filter paper moistened with mercuric chloride solution

guv *dial past of* GIVE

[1]**guy** \'gī\ *vt* -ED/-ING/-S [ME *gyen*, fr. MF *guier* — more at GUIDE] *archaic* **:** GUIDE

[2]**guy** \"\ *n* -S [prob. fr. D *gei* brail] **:** a rope, chain, or rod attached to something (as an object being hoisted or lowered) to brace, steady, or guide it **:** a cable connecting a suspension bridge with the land on either side to prevent lateral swaying

[3]**guy** \"\ *vt* -ED/-ING/-S **:** to steady or reinforce (as a vertical structure) or guide (as an object being hoisted) with a guy

[4]**guy** \"\ *n* -S [after *Guy* Fawkes †1606 Eng. conspirator] **1 a** *often cap* **:** a ragged and grotesque effigy of the English conspirator Guy Fawkes customarily paraded and burned in England on Guy Fawkes day ⟨dresses like a *Guy* —W.S. Gilbert⟩ **b :** an effigy of any person similarly treated **2 a** *chiefly Brit* **:** a person of grotesque appearance or dress **b :** LAUGHINGSTOCK ⟨they'd make a ~ of you in Latin, Greek and Hebrew —S.H.Adams⟩ **3 :** MAN, BOY, FELLOW ⟨a well-fed ~, wearing a gray sports jacket —Eli Waldron⟩ ⟨the greatest ~ he had ever known —T.O.Heggen⟩ **4** *Brit* **:** a hasty or secret departure **:** hurried decamping

[5]**guy** \"\ *vt* -ED/-ING/-S **:** to make fun of **:** ridicule often lightly or good-humoredly ⟨allows himself in one chapter to ~ the Court of King Arthur in a way of which few children will approve —*Times Lit. Supp.*⟩ ⟨the ~*ing* of authority is inherent in the English spirit —Kenneth Young⟩ ⟨. . . liked to ~ me and make me the subject of practical jokes —W.A.White⟩

guy·ana \(')gī'(y)anə, -ăn-, -ȧn-\ *adj, usu cap* [fr. *Guyana*, country in northeastern So. America] **:** of or from the country of Guyana **:** of the kind or style prevalent in Guyana

[1]**guy·a·nese** \ˌgīəˈnēz, -ēs\ *adj, usu cap* [*Guyana*, the country + E *-ese*] **1 :** of, relating to, or characteristic of Guyana **2 :** of, relating to, or characteristic of the people of Guyana

[2]**guyanese** *n, cap* **:** a native or inhabitant of Guyana

guy derrick *n* **:** a derrick whose mast is held upright by guy cables attached at the top

guy fawkes day \'gī'fȯks-\ *n, usu cap G&F&D* [after *Guy Fawkes* †1606 Eng. conspirator] **:** the anniversary of Nov. 5, 1605, when Guy Fawkes was seized for an attempt to blow up the House of Lords that is celebrated by bonfires

guy·ot \(')gēˈō\ *n* -S [after Arnold H. *Guyot* †1884 Am. geographer and geologist born in Switzerland] **:** a flat-topped submarine mountain or seamount, commonly found in the Pacific ocean where the flat summits are at depths below the surface of the water as great as 5000 feet

guy·trash \'gī·trash\ *n* -ES [origin unknown] *dial Eng* **:** a specter or ghost esp. in the form of an animal

guy·ver \'gīvə(r)\ *n* -S [origin unknown] *Austral* **:** fantastic talk or explanations

guze \'gyüz\ *n* -S [origin unknown] *heraldry* **:** a roundel sanguine

gu·ze·rat \ˌgüzəˈrät\ *n* [*Gujarat*, *Guzerat*, region of northwestern Bombay state, India] **1** *usu cap* **:** a breed of large heavy-boned Indian cattle widely used in crossbreeding to produce heat-resistant beef cattle **2** -S *often cap* **:** an animal of the Guzerat breed

guzla *var of* GUSLA

guz·man·ia \güz'manēə\ *n* [NL, fr. A. *Guzmán fl* 1800? Span. naturalist + NL *-ia*] **1** *cap* **:** a large genus of tropical American chiefly epiphytic herbs (family Bromeliaceae) resembling *Tillandsia* but having the perianth segments connate basally or closely connivent and the anthers on the perianth throat **2** -S **:** any plant of the genus *Guzmania*

[1]**guz·zle** \'gəzəl\ *vb* **guzzled**; **guzzled**; **guzzling** \-z(ə)liŋ\ **guzzles** [origin unknown] *vi* **:** to drink esp. liquor, beer, or wine greedily **:** drink habitually or frequently ⟨spent a weekend *guzzling* and playing cards⟩ ~ *vt* **1 :** to drink greedily, continually, or habitually ⟨~ beer⟩; *sometimes* **:** to eat greedily ⟨coming in here to ~ your muffins —Richard Blaker⟩ ⟨the monster *guzzled* its meal —C.G.D.Roberts⟩ **2 :** to use up (as money) in guzzling ⟨*guzzled* away the family fortune⟩

[2]**guzzle** \"\ *n* -S **1** *now dial* **:** a small stream often flowing through a marsh **2** *dial* **:** THROAT; *often* **:** ADAM'S APPLE

guz·zler \'gəz(ə)lə(r)\ *n* -S [[1]*guzzle* + *-er*] **1 :** one that guzzles **2 :** a device for preserving water for the use of game birds in arid regions

gvl *abbr* gravel

gwa·li·or \'gwälē,ȯ(ə)r\ *adj, usu cap* [fr. *Gwalior*, city in north central India] **:** of or from the city of Gwalior, India **:** of the kind or style prevalent in Gwalior

gwari *usu cap, var of* GBARI

gweduc *var of* GEODUCK

gwine \(ˈ)gwīn, 'gwīən\ *dial pres part of* GO

gwyn·i·ad \'gwinē,ad\ *also* **gwyn·i·ard** \-ē,ärd\ *n* -S [W *gwyniad*, fr. *gwyn* white — more at FINNOCK] **:** a fish (*Coregonus pennantii*) of Bala Lake in North Wales related to the lake whitefish

gy *abbr* **1** gray **2** gunnery **3** gyro

gy·a·ni \gē'änē\ *n* -S [Panjabi *gyānī*, fr. Skt *jñānin* one who has knowledge, fr. *jñāna* knowledge — more at JNANA] **:** a Sikh religious official who expounds religious lore and participates in gurdwara services

gya·rung \gē'ärəŋ\ *n* -S *usu cap* **:** a member of a people living on the eastern boundary of Tibet

gy·as·cu·tus \,gīə'sk(y)üd·əs, -'skəd·-\ *n* -ES [origin unknown] **:** an imaginary large four-legged beast with legs on one side longer than on the other for walking on hillsides

gy·as·sa \gī'asə\ *n* -S [Ar *qay(y)āsah*] **:** a flat-bottomed lateen-rigged seagoing barge used in the local coasting trade of the Gulf of Suez, the Red sea, and the eastern Mediterranean esp. for transporting cargoes of coal or rice

gybe *var of* JIBE

gy·gis \'jījəs, 'gī-\ *n, cap* [NL, fr. Gk *gygēs*, a water bird; perh. akin to Lith *gužùtys* stork] **:** a genus of tropical terns with pure white plumage

gyle \'gī(ə)l\ *or* **gail** \'gā(ə)l\ *n* -S [ME *gyle*, fr. MD *gijl*, fr. *gīlen* to boil, ferment] **1 :** wort in the process of fermentation added to a stout or ale **2 :** the beer produced at one brewing **:** BREWING 3

gym \'jim\ *n* -S *often attrib* [short for *gymnasium*] **1 :** GYMNASIUM ⟨played handball in the ~ twice a week⟩ **2 :** PHYSICAL EDUCATION ⟨~ is a required course for all freshmen⟩ **3 :** a metal frame supporting an assortment of outdoor play equipment (as a swing, seesaw, rings)

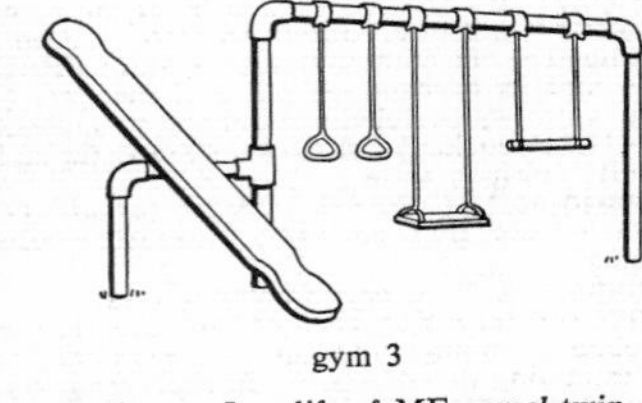
gym 3

gym·el *or* **gim·el** \'jiməl\ *n* -S [modif. of MF *gemel* twin — more at GEMEL] **1 :** vocal part writing in medieval music in which the voices usu. progress in parallel thirds **2 :** a direction for divisi singing used in 16th century choral music

gy·min·da \jə'mində\ *n, cap* [NL, anagram of *Myginda*, genus of trees or shrubs fr. Francis von *Mygind* 18th cent. Ger. botanist] **:** a small genus of tropical American shrubs and trees (family Celastraceae) with opposite leathery leaves and unisexual flowers in axillary cymes followed by small blue or black drupaceous fruits

gym·khana \jim'känə, -kanə, -kȧnə\ *n* -S [prob. modif. (influenced by E *gymnasium*) of Hindi *gend-khāna* racket court, fr. Per *khāna* house] **:** a meet or festival featuring sports contests or athletic skills: as **a :** a horseback-riding meet featuring games and novelty contests (as musical chairs, potato spearing, bareback jumping) **b :** a festival featuring gymnastics and athletic showmanship and often including pageantry **c :** an obstacle run for automobiles or a series of events designed to test driving skill

gymn- *or* **gymno-** *comb form* [NL, fr. Gk, fr. *gymnos* — more at NAKED] **:** naked **:** bare **:** uncovered ⟨*gymn*anthous⟩ ⟨*gymno*branchiate⟩

gym·na·de·nia \,jimnə'dēnēə\ *n, cap* [NL, fr. *gymn-* + Gk *adēn* gland + NL *-ia* — more at ADEN-] **:** a genus of European terrestrial orchids having greenish flowers with the lip of the corolla entire

gym·na·de·ni·op·sis \,==,=nē'äpsəs\ *n, cap* [NL, fr. *Gymnadenia* + *-opsis*] *in some classifications* **:** a genus of No. American terrestrial orchids that have appendages on the beak of the stigma and are now usu. included in the genus *Habenaria*

gym·nan·thes \jim'nan(,)thēz\ *n, cap* [NL, fr. *gymn-* + *-anthes*] **:** a small genus of tropical American shrubs or trees (family Euphorbiaceae) with alternate evergreen leaves, a milky juice, and a 3-lobed capsular fruit

gym·nan·thous \(')jimˈnan(t)thəs\ *adj* [*gymn-* + *-anthous*] **:** ACHLAMYDEOUS

gym·nar·chus \jim'närkəs\ *n, cap* [NL, fr. *gymn-* + Gk *archos* anus; fr. the absence of anal fins] **:** a monotypic genus (the type of the family Gymnarchidae) that contains a soft-finned African river fish having a sense organ in the tail that functions like radar

gym·na·sial \jim'nāzēəl, -āzh(ē)əl\ *adj* **:** of or relating to a gymnasium

gym·na·si·arch \-zē,ärk\ *n* -S [L *gymnasiarchus*, fr. Gk *gymnasiarchos*, fr. *gymnasion* gymnasium + *archos* chief, ruler — more at ARCHI-] **1 :** one responsible for the training of athletes in ancient Greece **2 :** the head or head tutor of a school or college

gym·na·si·ast \-zē,ast, -ēəst, -ē,aa(ə)st\ *n* -S [G, fr. NL *gymnasiasta*, fr. G *gymnasium* + NL *-asta* (fr. Gk *-astēs* -ast)] **1 :** a student in or graduate of a gymnasium **2** [*gymnasium* + *-ast*] **:** GYMNAST

gym·na·si·um \jim'nāzēəm *sometimes* -zhəm, *in sense 2* gim'näzēəm *or* -nȧz- *or* -ē,u̇m\ *n, pl* **gymnasiums** \-mz\ *or* **gymna·sia** \-zēə,-zhə\ [L, gymnastic school, school, fr. Gk *gymnasion*, fr. *gymnazein* to train naked, exercise, fr. *gymnos* naked — more at NAKED] **1 a :** a large room used for various indoor sports (as basketball, boxing, volleyball) and equipped with gymnastic apparatus **b :** a building (as on a college campus) containing appropriate space and equipment for various indoor sports activities associated with a program of physical education and typically including spectator accommodations, locker and shower rooms, a swimming pool, offices, and classrooms **2** [G, fr. L] **:** a secondary school designed to prepare students for the university; *esp* **:** a German secondary school whose curriculum stresses the classics, history, mathematics, and modern languages

gym·nast \'jim,nast, -nəst, -,naa(ə)st\ *n* -S [MF *gymnaste*, fr. Gk *gymnastēs* trainer of athletes, fr. *gymnazein*, v.] **:** one who is expert in gymnastics

[1]**gym·nas·tic** \jim'nastik, -aas-, -tēk\ *also* **gym·nas·ti·cal** \-təkəl, -tēk-\ *adj* [MF or L; MF *gymnastique*, fr. L *gymnasticus*, fr. Gk *gymnastikos*, fr. (assumed) *gymnastos* (verbal of *gymnazein* to train naked) + *-ikos* -ic] **:** of or relating to gymnastics **:** ATHLETIC — **gym·nas·ti·cal·ly** \-tək(ə)lē, -tēk-, -li\ *adv*

[2]**gymnastic** \"\ *n* -S [MF *gymnastique*, fr. Gk *gymnastikē*, fr. fem. of *gymnastikos*] **1 a :** physical exercise ⟨good ~ which will give health to the body —Benjamin Jowett⟩; *esp* **:** exercise that consists of calisthenics and performance on apparatus (as rings, bars) and is designed to promote strength, flexibility, agility, coordination, and body control — now usu. used in pl. ⟨~*s* have become one of the institutions of the country —James Grant⟩ **b gymnastics** *pl but sing in constr* **:** the art or practice of such exercise ⟨modern apparatus ~*s* was founded in the early 19th century —*Time*⟩ **2 :** something resembling gymnastics; *esp* **:** an exercise in intellectual or artistic dexterity ⟨my earlier philosophic study had been an intellectual ~ —John Dewey⟩ ⟨the pleasure that is derived from sheer mental ~*s* —Carlos Lynes⟩ **3 :** a physical feat, exercise, or contortion ⟨like a . . . wrestler about to embark upon some inexplicable ~ —Gordon Sager⟩ ⟨the ~*s* necessary for the killer to have swung from the fire escape —E.D.Radin⟩

gym·nic \'jimnik\ *adj* [L *gymnicus*, fr. Gk *gymnikos*, fr. *gymnos* naked + *-ikos* -ic] *archaic* **:** GYMNASTIC

gym·nics \-ks\ *n pl, archaic* **:** GYMNASTICS

gymno- — see GYMN-

gym·no·blast \'jimnə,blast\ *adj or n* [NL *Gymnoblastea*] **:** ANTHOMEDUSAN

gym·no·blas·tea \,jimnə'blastēə\ [NL, fr. *gymn-* + *-blastea* (fr. *-blastus* -blast)] *syn of* ANTHOMEDUSAE

gym·no·blas·tic \ˌjimnəˈblastik\ *adj* [*gymn-* + *-blastic*] **:** having naked medusa buds — used of anthomedusan hydroids

gym·no·ca·lyci·um \,jim(,)nōkə'lis(h)ēəm\ *n, cap* [NL, fr. *gymn-* + *calyc-* + *-ium*] **:** a genus of low globular So. American cacti with strongly tuberculate spiny ribs

gym·no·car·pe·ae \-'kärpē,ē\ *n pl, cap* [NL, fr. *gymn-* + *-carpeae* (fr. *-carpus* -carpous)] *in some classifications* **:** a group comprising those lichens whose fruiting body is open

gym·no·car·pous \ˌjimnəˈkärpəs\ *also* **gym·no·car·pic** \-pik\ *adj* [*gymnocarpous* fr. Gk *gymnokarpos*, fr. *gymn-* + *-karpos* -carpous; *gymnocarpic* fr. *gymn-* + *carp-* + *-ic*] **:** having the hymenium open or exposed on the surface of the thallus or fruiting body — used of lichens and fungi; compare ANGIOCARPOUS 2 — **gym·no·car·py** \'==,=pē\ *n* -ES

gym·no·cer·a·ta \,jim(,)nō'serəd·ə\ *n pl, cap* [NL, fr. *gymn-* + *-cerata* (fr. Gk *kerat-*, *keras* horn) — more at HORN] **:** a division of Heteroptera comprising true bugs with the antennae as long as or longer than the head and including most terrestrial bugs and the water striders — compare CRYPTOCERATA — **gym·no·cer·a·tous** \ˌ=(,)=ˈserəd·əs\ *adj*

gym·no·cid·i·um \,jimnə'sidēəm\ *n, pl* **gymnocid·ia** \-ēə\ [NL, fr. *gymn-* + *-ocidium* (prob. fr. Gk *oikidion* small house, dim. of *oikos* house) — more at VICINITY] **:** APOPHYSIS 2

gym·noc·la·dus \jim'näklədəs\ *n, cap* [NL, fr. *gymn-* + Gk *klados* sprout, branch — more at GLADIATOR] **:** a genus of trees (family Leguminosae) with twice-pinnate leaves, paniculate flowers, and thick pulpy pods — see KENTUCKY COFFEE TREE

gym·no·co·nia \,jimnə'kōnēə\ *n, cap* [NL, fr. *gymn-* + Gk *konis* dust + NL *-ia* — more at INCINERATE] **:** a genus of rusts (order Uredinales) having naked aecial sori and 2-celled teliospores and including a rust (*G. interstitialis*) of the raspberry and blackberry

gym·no·din·i·a·ce·ae \-,dinē'āsē,ē\ *n pl, cap* [NL, fr. *Gymnodinium*, type genus + *-aceae*] **:** a family of typically brownish algae (class Dinophyceae) that includes *Gymnodinium* and related genera when these are considered to be algae

gym·no·din·i·a·les \-ā(,)lēz\ *n pl, cap* [NL, fr. *Gymnodinium* + *-ales*] **:** an order of greenish brown algae (class Dinophyceae) having no cell wall but often a firm periplast that is longitudinally striated and comprising the naked dinoflagellates — compare PERIDINIALES

gym·no·din·i·um \-'dinēəm\ *n, cap* [NL, fr. *gymn-* + Gk *dinein* to whirl + NL *-ium*] **:** a large genus (the type of the family Gymnodiniidae) of marine and freshwater naked dinoflagellates that includes forms which are colorless or tinted yellowish to reddish brown, blue, or green by chromatophores and a few forms which cause red tide

gym·no·dont \'jimnə,dänt\ *adj or n* [NL *Gymnodontes*] **:** TETRAODONT

gym·no·don·tes \,jimnə'dän(,)tēz\ [NL, fr. *gymn-* + *-odontes*] *syn of* TETRAODONTOIDEA

gym·no·glos·sa \-'gläsə, -lȯsə\ *n pl, cap* [NL, fr. *gymn-* + *-glossa*] *in some classifications* **:** a division of Pectinibranchia comprising gastropods lacking jaws or radula — **gym·no·glos·sate** \ˌ=(,)=ˈgläsət, -ȯs-, -,sāt\ *adj*

gym·nog·y·nous \(')jimˈnäjənəs\ *adj* [*gymn-* + *-gynous*] *bot* **:** having a naked ovary

gym·no·gyps \'jimnə,jips\ *n, cap* [NL, fr. *gymn-* + Gk *gyps* vulture] **:** a genus of very large dark carrion-eating birds (family Cathartidae) containing solely the California condor

gym·no·lae·ma \,jimnə'lēmə\ [NL, prob. alter. of *Gymnolaemata*] *syn of* GYMNOLAEMATA

gym·no·lae·ma·ta \-məd·ə\ *n pl, cap* [NL, fr. *gymn-* + *laem-* (fr. Gk *laimos* throat, gullet) + *-ata*; prob. akin to Gk *laimos* greedy — more at LURE] **:** a class or other division of Bryozoa comprising chiefly marine bryozoans with a circular lophophore about the mouth and including most recent and extinct forms — compare PHYLACTOLAEMATA — **gym·no·lae·ma·tous** \ˌ==ˈ=məd·əs\ *adj*

gym·no·no·ti \,jimnə'nōd·,ī\ *n pl, cap* [NL, fr. *gymn-* + *-noti* (pl. of *-notus*); fr. the absence of a dorsal fin] *in some classifications* **:** a group of fishes including the electric eel and related forms

gym·no·pae·dia *or* **gym·no·pe·dia** \-'pēdēə\ *n* -S [NL, fr. Gk *gymnopaidia*, fr. *gymno-* gymn- + *paidia* childish play, amusement, game (fr. *paizein* to play, sport, fr. *paid-*, *pais* child) — more at FOAL] **:** a choral dance of religious origin performed by naked youths at ancient Greek festivals — **gym·no·pae·dic** \ˌ==ˈpēdik\ *adj*

gym·no·phi·o·na \-'fīənə\ *n pl, cap* [NL, fr. *gymn-* + *-ophiona* (fr. Gk *ophioneos* of a snake, serpentlike, fr. *ophis* serpent, snake) — more at ANGUIS] **:** an order of Amphibia that is coextensive with the family Caeciliidae and is distinguished by the limbless small-headed short-tailed form of its nearly eyeless members which are widely distributed in moist soil in tropical parts of the New and Old Worlds

gym·no·plast \'jimnə,plast\ *n* -S [*gymn-* + *-plast*] **:** a cell or mass of protoplasm devoid of a distinct cell wall

gym·no·rhi·na \ˌjimnəˈrīnə\ *n, cap* [NL, fr. *gymn-* + *-rhina*] : a genus of oscine birds that are included in Laniidae or placed in a distinct family and that include the piping crows of Australia

gym·no·so·ma·ta \ˌjimnəˈsōmәd·ə\ *n pl, cap* [NL, fr. *gymn-* + *-somata*] *in some classifications* : a division of Pteropoda comprising forms that lack shells — compare THECOSOMATA

gym·no·soph·i·cal \ˈjimnəˈsäfəkəl\ *adj* : NUDIST ⟨a ~ society⟩

gym·nos·o·phist \jimˈnäsəfəst\ *n* -s [L *gymnosophista*, fr. Gk *gymnosophistēs*, fr. *gymno-* gymn- + *sophistēs* wise man, philosopher (fr. *sophos* wise) — more at NAKED] **1** : one of a sect of ancient Hindu philosophers who went naked, lived ascetically, and practiced meditation **2** : one resembling a gymnosophist

gym·nos·o·phy \-fē\ *n* -ES : the doctrine of the gymnosophists; *esp* : NUDISM

gym·no·sperm \ˈjimnə,spərm\ *n* [NL *Gymnospermae*] : a plant of the class Gymnospermae

gym·no·sper·mae \ˌ==ˈspər(ˌ)mē\ *n pl, cap* [NL, fr. *gymn-* + *-spermae*] : a class of Pteropsida or in some classifications a subdivision of Spermatophyta comprising seed plants (as cycads and conifers) that produce naked seeds not enclosed in an ovary and in some instances have motile spermatozoids and including the subclasses Cycadophytae and Coniferophytae — compare ANGIOSPERMAE, FILICINEAE

gym·no·sper·mal \ˈ==ˈ=məl\ *also* **gym·no·sper·mic** \-mik\ *adj* [NL *gymnospermus* + *-al* or *-ic*] : GYMNOSPERMOUS

gym·no·sper·mous \ˈ==ˈ=məs\ *adj* [NL *gymnospermus* having naked seeds, fr. Gk *gymnospermos*, fr. *gymno-* gymn- + *-spermos* -spermous] : of, relating to, or characteristic of the class Gymnospermae; *esp* : having ovules and seeds naked and without an enclosing ovary — contrasted with *angiospermous* — **gym·no·sper·my** \ˈ==,=mē\ *n* -ES

gym·no·sporangium \ˈjim(ˌ)nō+\ *n, cap* [NL, fr. *gymn-* + *sporangium*] : a genus of heteroecious rusts (family Pucciniaceae) that have mostly 2-celled teliospores whose pedicels and walls form a gelatinous mass when wet, that in the telial stage produce galls on cedars and other conifers of the genera *Juniperus* and *Libocedrus*, and that in the aecial stage cause rust spots on the leaves and fruit of apples, pears, and other plants of the family Rosaceae — see APPLE RUST

gym·no·spore \ˈjimnə,spō(ə)r\ *n* [ISV *gymn-* + *spore*] : a spore not developing in a sporangium : a naked spore — **gym·nospo·rous** \ˈjimnəˈspōrəs, (ˈ)jimˈnäspərəs\ *adj*

gym·no·sto·ma·ta \ˌjimnəˈstōmәd·ə\ *n pl, cap* [NL, fr. *gymn-* + *-stomata*] : a suborder of holotrichous ciliates comprising holozoic forms with cytostome but without peristome or specialized oral cilia

gym·no·stoma·tous \ˈ==ˈstämәd·əs, -tōm-\ *or* **gym·nos·to·mous** \(ˈ)jimˈnästəməs\ *adj* [*gymn-* + *-stomatous* or *-stomous*] : having no peristome

gym·no·thorax \ˈjimnə+\ *n, cap* [NL, fr. *gymn-* + *thorax*] : a large genus of morays that have only the anterior nostrils provided with barbels and that may be poisonous when eaten

1**gym·no·tid** \jimˈnōtəd\ *adj* [NL *Gymnotidae*] : of or relating to the Gymnotidae

2**gymnotid** \"\ *n* -s : a fish of the family Gymnotidae

gym·noti·dae \jimˈnäd·ə,dē, -nōd-·\ *n pl, cap* [NL, fr. *Gymnotus*, type genus + *-idae*] : a family of So. American cyprinoid fishes that sometimes includes the electric eel but is usu. restricted to elongated forms lacking electric organs

gym·no·tus \-ˈnōd·əs\ *n, cap* [NL, fr. *gymn-* + *-notus*] : the type genus of the family Gymnotidae

1**gym·nu·ra** \-ˈ(y)u̇rə\ *n, cap* [NL, fr. *gymn-* + *-ura*] : a small genus of widely distributed stingrays that are usu. placed in Dasyatidae but sometimes made type of a separate family and that include several food fishes of tropical seas

2**gymnura** \"\ [NL, fr. *gymn-* + *-ura*] *syn of* ECHINO-SOREX

gym·nure \ˈjim,n(y)u̇(ə)r\ *n* -s [NL *Gymnura*] : MOONRAT

1**gym·nu·rine** \ˈjimn(y)ə,rīn, -ˌrən\ *adj* [NL *Gymnura* + E *-ine*] : of or relating to the genus *Echino-sorex*

2**gymnurine** \"\ *n* -s : a mammal of the genus *Echino-sorex*

gym·pie \ˈgimpē\ *or* **gympie nettle** *n* -s [fr. *Gympie*, Queensland, Australia] : an Australian nettle tree (*Laportea moroides*) having foliage and twigs covered with stinging hairs

gyms *pl of* GYM

gym shoe *n* : SNEAKER

gyn *abbr* gynecologic; gynecology

gyn- *or* **gyno-** *in words which contain this or a related comb form & in which the pronunc of "gy" is indicated by the symbol* =, *pronounce* ji (*when unstressed* jə), gī *sometimes* jī *or* gi (*or when unstressed* gə)\ *comb form* [Gk *gyn-*, fr. *gynē* — more at QUEEN] **1 a** : woman : of or relating to a woman ⟨*gyn*iatrics⟩ ⟨*gyno*cracy⟩ **b** : female : female and ⟨*gyn*androus⟩ : womanish **2** : female reproductive organ : ovary ⟨*gyno*phore⟩ : pistil ⟨*gyno*dioecious⟩

-gyn \jən, ˌjin\ *n comb form* -s [NL *-gynia*] : plant having (so many) pistils ⟨hexa*gyn*⟩

gynaec- *or* **gynaeco-** — see GYNEC-

gynae·can·drous \ˈ=nəˈkandrəs — *see* GYN-\ *adj* [*gynec-* + *-androus*] : bearing both staminate and pistillate flowers in the same cluster with the female flowers uppermost — compare ANDROGYNOUS 3a

gynae·ce·um \ˌ=nəˈsēəm — *see* GYN-\ *n* -s [L, fr. LGk *gynaikeion*, fr. neut. of Gk *gynaikeios* of women, feminine, fr. *gynaik-*, *gynē* woman, wife] **1** : the women's apartments in an ancient Greek or Roman house **2** [NL, fr. L, women's apartments] : GYNOECIUM

gy·nae·co·morph \=ˈnēkə,mȯrf — *see* GYN-\ *n* -s [*gynec-* + *-morph*] : a male resembling a female in appearance

gynae·co·ni·tis \ˌ=nəkōˈnīd·əs — *see* GYN-\ *n* -ES [L *gynaeconitis*, fr. Gk *gynaikōnitis*, fr. *gynaik-*, *gynē* woman] **1** : GYNAECEUM 1 **2** : the part of an Eastern Orthodox church reserved for women; *esp* : one side of the nave

gynae·co·phor·ic \ˈ===ˈfȯrik — *see* GYN-\ *also* **gyne·coph·o·ral** \ˈ==ˈkäfərəl — *see* GYN-\ *adj* [*gynecophore* + *-ic* or *-al*] : constituting the ventral groove in which a male schistosome clasps the female

gynaeo- — see GYNEO-

gy·nan·der \=ˈnandə(r) — *see* GYN-\ *n* -s [*gyn-* + *-ander* (fr. Gk *andr-*, *anēr*) — more at ANDR-] : a mosaic individual made up of diploid female portions of biparental origin and haploid male portions originating from an extra egg or sperm nucleus

gy·nan·drae \jəˈnan(ˌ)drē\ [NL, fr. *gyn-* + *-andrae*, pl. of *-andra*] *syn of* ORCHIDALES

gynan·drar·chy \=ˈnandrärkē, ˈ=ˌnən- — *see* GYN-\ *n* -ES [*gyn-* + *andr-* + *-archy*] : social organization among insects differing from gynarchy in that the male takes part in establishing the colony

1**gy·nan·dria** \=ˈnandrēə — *see* GYN-\ *n pl, cap* [NL, fr. Gk *gynandros* of doubtful sex, womanish (fr. *gyn-* + *andr-*, *anēr* man) + NL *-ia*] *in former classifications* : a class comprising plants with gynandrous flowers

2**gynandria** \"\ *n* -s [NL, fr. Gk *gynandros* + NL *-ia*] : GYNANDRY

gy·nan·drism \-ˌdrizəm\ *n* -s [*gyn-* + *andr-* + *-ism*] : GYNANDRY

gy·nan·dri·um \-ˌdrēəm\ *n, pl* **gynan·dria** \-ēə\ *also* **gynandriums** [NL, fr. *gyn-* + *andr-* + *-ium*] : COLUMN 5b

1**gy·nan·droid** \-ˌdrȯid\ *adj* [ISV *gynandr-* (fr. *gynandry*) + *-oid*] : exhibiting gynandry

2**gynandroid** \"\ *n* -s : a gynandroid person

gy·nan·dro·morph \-ˌdrə,mȯrf\ *n* -s [ISV *gyn-* + *andr-* + *-morph*] : an abnormal individual exhibiting characters of both sexes in various parts of the body : a sexual mosaic — compare HERMAPHRODITE, INTERSEX — **gy·nan·dro·mor·phic** \=ˈ==ˈmȯrfik\ *adj* — **gy·nan·dro·mor·phism** \=,==ˈ=,fizəm\ *n* -s — **gy·nan·dro·mor·phous** \=ˈ==ˈ=ˌfəs\ *adj* — **gy·nan·dro·mor·phy** \=ˈ==,=fē\ *n* -ES

gynan·dro·spor·ous \=ˈnandrəˈspōrəs, ˈ=ˌnənˈdräspərəs — *see* GYN-\ *adj* [*gyn-* + *andr-* + *-sporous*] : bearing androspores on the same filament as the oogonia and usu. near them — compare IDIOANDROSPOROUS

gynan·drous \(ˈ)=ˈnandrəs — *see* GYN-\ *adj* [Gk *gynandros* of doubtful sex, fr. *gynē* woman + *andr-*, *anēr* man] **1** : having the androecium and gynoecium united in a column **2** : characterized by gynandry

gynan·dry \-drē\ *n* -ES [2*gynandria*] : HERMAPHRODITISM, INTERSEXUALITY; *specif* : the condition of the pseudohermaphroditic female in which the external genitalia simulate those of the male

gynan·ther·ous \(ˈ)=,nan(t)thərəs — *see* GYN-\ *adj* [*gyn-* + *-antherous*] : having stamens abnormally converted into pistils

gynar·chy \ˈ=,närkē — *see* GYN-\ *n* -ES [*gyn-* + *-archy*] **1** : government by women **2** : a form of social organization among insects (as ants, bees, wasps) in which only the female parent takes part in establishing the colony

gyne \ˈjīn, ˈgīn\ *n* -s [Gk *gynē* woman — more at QUEEN] : FEMALE; *esp* : a functional female of one of the social insects

gyne- *comb form* [Gk *gynē* woman] : GYN- ⟨*gyne*cytology⟩

-gyne \ˌjīn\ *n comb form* -s [Gk *gynē* woman] **1** : woman : female ⟨pseudo*gyne*⟩ **2** : female reproductive organ ⟨tricho*gyne*⟩

gynec- *or* **gyneco-** *also* **gynaec-** *or* **gynaeco-** *comb form* [Gk *gynaiko-*, fr. *gynaik-*, *gynē* woman] : GYN- ⟨*gyneco*cracy⟩ ⟨*gyneco*logy⟩ ⟨*gyneco*id⟩

gynecium *var of* GYNOECIUM

gyne·co·cen·tric \ˈ=nəkō + — *see* GYN-\ *adj* [*gynec-* + *-centric*] : centering or centered on or in the female : dominated by or emphasizing feminine interests or point of view ⟨a ~ society⟩ — contrasted with *androcentric*

gyne·coc·ra·cy \ˌ=nəˈkäkrəsē — *see* GYN-\ *n* -ES [Gk *gynaikokratia*, fr. *gynaiko-* gynec- + *-kratia* -cracy] **1** : political and social supremacy of women — contrasted with *androcracy*; compare MATRIARCHY **2** : petticoat rule — usu. used disparagingly — **gyne·co·crat** \=ˈnēkə,krat, ˈ=nəkō,-\ *n* -s — **gyne·co·crat·ic** \=ˈnēkəˈkrad·ik, ˈ=ˌnəkōˈ-\ *also* **gyne·co·crat·i·cal** \-d·əkəl\ *adj*

gyne·co·gen·ic \ˈ=nəkōˈjenik — *see* GYN-\ *adj* [*gynec-* + *-genic*] : tending to induce female characteristics ⟨a ~ hormone⟩

1**gyne·coid** \ˈ=nə,kȯid — *see* GYN-\ *adj* [*gynec-* + *-oid*] **1 a** : having female characteristics : typical of a woman ⟨a ~ distribution of fat⟩ ⟨the ~ form of certain castrates⟩ **b** *of the pelvis* : having the rounded form typical of a well-built woman — compare ANDROID **2** : of, relating to, or exhibiting the characteristics of a gynecoid

2**gynecoid** \"\ *n* -s : an individual (as an egg-laying worker ant) that functions as a fully developed female although structurally incomplete

gyne·co·log·ic \ˈ=nəkəˈläjik, -nēk-, -jēk — *see* GYN-\ *also* **gyne·co·log·i·cal** \-jəkəl, -jēk-\ *adj* : of, relating to, or falling in the province of gynecology ⟨~ surgery⟩ ⟨~ patient⟩ ⟨~ tuberculosis⟩

gyne·col·o·gist \ˌ==ˈkäləjəst\ *n* -s : a physician who specializes in gynecology

gyne·col·o·gy \-jē,-ji\ *n* -ES [ISV *gynec-* + *-logy*] : a branch of medicine that deals with women, their diseases, hygiene, and medical care

gyne·co·mast \=ˈnēkə,mast, ˈ=nəkō- — *see* GYN-\ *n* -s [NL *gynecomastia*] : a male having a female degree of mammary development

gyne·co·mas·tia \ˌ=nəkōˈmastēə, =ˌnēkəˈ-\ *n* -s [NL, fr. *gynec-* + *-mastia*] : excessive development of the breast in the male

gyne·co·mor·phous \ˈ=nəkōˈmȯrfəs, -ˈnēkəˈ- — *see* GYN-\ *adj* [Gk *gynaikomorphos*, fr. *gynaiko-* gynec- + *-morphos* -morphous] : having the form of morphological characters of a female

gynecophoral *var of* GYNAECOPHORIC

gy·ne·co·phore \=ˈnēkə,fō(ə)r — *see* GYN-\ *n* -s [ISV *gynec-* + *-phore*] : gynaecophoric canal

gyneo- *or* **gynaeo-** *comb form* [Gk *gynaios* of women, fr. *gynē* woman — more at QUEEN] : GYN- ⟨*gyneo*cracy⟩

Gyner·gen \ˈ=nə(r)jən, -ˌjen — see GYN-\ *trademark* — used for ergotamine tartrate

gynes *pl of* GYNE

-gynes *pl of* -GYNE

gyne·type \ˈ=nə,tīp — *see* GYN-\ *n* [*gyne-* + *type*] : a designated female type specimen

-gyn·ia \ˈjinēə, ˈgi-\ *n pl comb form* [NL, fr. *-gynus* -gynous + *-ia*] : plants having (such or so many) pistils — in Linnaean botanical orders ⟨di*gynia*⟩ — **-gyn·i·an** \ˈ=nēən\ *adj or n comb form* — **-gyn·i·ous** \-ēəs\ *adj comb form*

gynic \ˈ=nik — *see* GYN-\ *adj* [*gyn-* + *-ic*] : of or relating to a female person — contrasted with *andric*

-gynies *pl of* -GYNY

gyno- — see GYN-

gyno·base \ˈ=nō+ — *see* GYN-\ *n* [*gyn-* + *-base*] : a prolongation of or from the receptacle bearing the gynoecium (as in the members of the Boraginaceae) — **gyno·ba·se·ous** \ˈ==-ˈbāsēəs\ *adj* — **gyno·bas·ic** \-ās|ik, |ēk *sometimes* -āz|\ *adj*

gyno·car·dia oil \ˈ=nəˈkärdēə- — *see* GYN-\ *n* [NL *Gynocardia*, genus of plants fr. which it is obtained, fr. *gyn-* + Gk *kardia* heart — more at HEART] **1** : a pale yellow drying oil obtained from the seeds of an East Indian tree (*Gynocardia odorata*) of the family Flacourtiaceae **2** : CHAULMOOGRA OIL

gy·noc·ra·cy \=ˈnäkrəsē — *see* GYN-\ *n* -ES [*gyn-* + *-cracy*] : GYNECOCRACY

gyno·dioecious \ˈ=nō+ — *see* GYN-\ *adj* [*gyn-* + *dioecious*] : dioecious but having some hermaphrodite or perfect flowers on an individual plant that bears mostly pistillate flowers — **gyno·dioeciously** \"+\ *adv* — **gyno·dioecism** \"+\ *n* -s — **gyno·dioecy** \"+\ *n* -ES

gy·noe·ci·um *also* **gy·ne·ci·um** \=ˈnēs(h)ēəm — *see* GYN-\ *n, pl* **gynoe·cia** *also* **gyne·cia** \-ēə\ [NL, alter. (influenced by Gk *oikion* house) of *gynaeceum*] **1** : the aggregate of carpels or megasporophylls in the flower of a seed plant : PISTILS **2** : the female inflorescence in liverworts

gyno·gamone \ˈ=nō+ — *see* GYN-\ *n* [ISV *gyn-* + *gamone*] : a gamone that occurs in an egg

gyno·genesis \"+\ *n* [NL, fr. *gyn-* + *-genesis*] : development in which the embryo contains only maternal chromosomes due to activation of an egg by a sperm that degenerates without fusing with the egg nucleus — compare ANDROGENESIS — **gyno·genetic** \"+\ *adj* — **gyno·genetically** \"+\ *adv* — **gyno·gen·e·tism** \ˌ==ˈjenə,tizəm\ *n* -s

gyno·gonidium \ˈ=nō+ — *see* GYN-\ *n, pl* **gynogonidia** [NL, fr. *gyn-* + *gonidium*] : a female germ cell of various colonial plantlike flagellates (as members of the genus *Volvox*)

gyno·monoecious \ˈ==(ˈ)=ˈ==\ *adj* [*gyn-* + *monoecious*] : having monoclinous and pistillate flowers on the same plant but no staminate flowers — **gyno·monoeciously** \"+\ *adv* — **gyno·monoecism** \"+\ *n* -s — **gyno·monoe·cy** \ˈ==ˈmä,nēsē, -ˈmō,-\ *n* -ES

gy·nop·a·ra \=ˈnäpərə — *see* GYN-\ *n, pl* **gynopa·rae** \-ə,rē\ [NL, fr. *gyn-* + *-para*] : a winged or wingless parthenogenetic viviparous aphid that produces the sexual generation of various aphids having a complex life cycle and host relations — **gy·nop·a·rous** \(ˈ)=ˈ===\ *adj*

gyno·phore \ˈ=nə,fō(ə)r — *see* GYN-\ *n* -s [*gyn-* + *-phore*] **1 a** : a prolongation of the receptacle that functions as a stalk and bears the gynoecium at its apex (as in the flowers of members of the Capparidaceae) — compare ANTHOPHORE, CARPOPHORE **b** : the developing multinucleate female reproductive structure in fungi (as those of the genus *Pyronema*) **2** : one of the branches bearing the female gonophores in siphonophores — **gyno·phor·ic** \ˈ==ˈfȯrik\ *adj*

gyno·sporangium \ˈ=nō+ — *see* GYN-\ *n* [NL, fr. *gyn-* + *sporangium*] : MEGASPORANGIUM

gyno·spore \"+,-\ *n* [*gyn-* + *spore*] : EMBRYO SAC

gyno·ste·gi·um \ˌ=nōˈstējēəm — *see* GYN-\ *n, pl* **gynostegia** \-jēə\ [NL, fr. *gyn-* + *steg-* + *-ium*] **1** : a covering of the gynoecium **2** : the staminal crown in plants of the genus *Asclepias*

gyno·ste·mi·um \-ˈstēmēəm\ *n, pl* **gynoste·mia** \-mēə\ [NL, fr. *gyn-* + Gk *stēmōn* warp, thread + NL *-ium* — more at STAMEN] : the column formed by the union of androecium and gynoecium (as in an orchid)

gyno·termone \ˈ=nō+ — *see* GYN-\ *n* [ISV *gyn-* + *termone*] : a female termone

-gy·nous \ˌjənəs, ˈjīn-, ˈgīn-\ *adj comb form* [NL *-gynus*, fr. Gk *-gynos*, fr. *gynē* woman — more at QUEEN] **1** : of, relating to, or having (such or so many) females ⟨poly*gynous*⟩ or female characteristics ⟨andro*gynous*⟩ : female ⟨ergato*gynous*⟩ : woman **2** : of, relating to, or having (such or so many) female organs, esp. pistils (in such a way or at such a time) ⟨hexa*gynous*⟩ ⟨proto*gynous*⟩

-gyns *pl of* -GYN

gy·nu·ra \=ˈn(y)u̇rə — *see* GYN-\ *n, cap* [NL, fr. *gyn-* + *-ura*] : a genus of tropical Asiatic and African herbs (family Compositae) having inconspicuous discoid heads of yellow flowers in loose terminal clusters — see VELVET PLANT

-gy·ny \jənē, -ni\ *n comb form* -ES [Gk *gynē* woman + E *-y*] **1** : existence of or condition of having (such or so many) females ⟨mono*gyny*⟩ **2** [*-gynous* + *-y*] : existence of or condition of having (such or so many) female organs, esp. pistils (in such a way or at such a time) ⟨epi*gyny*⟩

gyo·ku·ro \ˈgyȯkə,rō, ˌ==ˈ=\ *n* -s [Jap, lit., dew, pearly dew, fr. *gyoku* precious stone, gem + *ro* dew] : a high-grade tea made in Japan from the leaves of shaded bushes and used for domestic consumption

1**gyp** \ˈjip\ *n* -s [prob. short for 1*gypsy*] **1** : a male college servant (as at Cambridge University) ⟨the old ~ comes tapping at the door to learn my intentions for the evening —A.C.Benson⟩ — compare SCOUT 4 **2 a** : one who cheats : SWINDLER ⟨if any ~ does try to shake them down —A.H. Raskin⟩ **b** : an act or instance of cheating : FRAUD, SWINDLE ⟨have worked every tin-pot ~ you could think up to get a few dollars —*N.Y. Herald Tribune*⟩ **3** *chiefly South & Midland* : a female dog : BITCH ⟨as pretty a ~ as he'd ever laid eye on . . . a Walker hound with a brown streak running back from her ears —F.B.Gipson⟩ **4** : a small-scale racehorse owner who trains and often rides his own horses

2**gyp** \"\ *vb* **gypped**; **gypped**; **gypping**; **gyps** : CHEAT

3**gyp** \"\ *n* -s [origin unknown] : a hard time — used in the phrase *to give* (a person) *gyp* ⟨apart from weariness, hunger, and a fair mental strain, my leg was giving me ~ —*Yale Rev.*⟩

4**gyp** \"\ *n* -s [by shortening] : GYPSUM ⟨~ is very common in hard waters —W.F.Cloud⟩

5**gyp** \"\ *n* -s [by shortening] : GYPSOPHILA

gy·pa·etus \jəˈpāәd·əs\ *n, cap* [NL, fr. Gk *gyp-*, *gyps* vulture + *aetos* eagle — more at AETO-] : a genus of Old World vultures consisting of the lammergeiers

gyp corn \ˈjip-\ *n* [short for *Egyptian corn*] : SORGHUM; *esp* : DURRA

1**gype** \ˈgīp\ *n* -s [of Scand origin; akin to ON *geip* nonsense, *geipa* to talk nonsense, *gīpr* mouth, throat, Norw dial. *geipa* to talk nonsense; akin to MD *gīpen* to gasp, OE *gīpian*, *geonian* to yawn — more at YAWN] *Scot* : FOOL

2**gype** \"\ *vi* -ED/-ING/-S *Scot* : to stare like a fool

gyp joint *n* [1*gyp*] **1** : a crooked gambling establishment **2** : an establishment (as a store, restaurant, or bar) that cheats customers by charging excessive prices for shoddy goods or inferior service

gyp·per \ˈjipə(r)\ *n* -s [2*gyp* + *-er*] : one that gyps

gyp·pery \ˈjip(ə)rē, -ri\ *n* -ES [2*gyp* + *-ery*] : the act or practice of gypping : SWINDLING

gyp·po *also* **gypo** \ˈji(ˌ)pō\ *n* -s [by shortening & alter. fr. 1*gypsy*] **1** : a small logging operator who usu. works on a contract basis **2** : contract work done by a gyppo

gyps \ˈjips\ *n, cap* [NL, fr. Gk, vulture; akin to Gk *gypē* cave — more at COVE] : a genus of Old World vultures including the griffon vulture and related African and Asiatic vultures

gyp·se·ian *or* **gip·se·ian** \ˈjipsēən, =ˈ==\ *adj* : of or relating to gypsies

gyp·se·ous \ˈjipsēəs\ *adj* [LL *gypseus*, fr. L *gypsum*] : resembling, containing, or consisting of gypsum

gyp·sif·er·ous \(ˌ)jipˈsif(ə)rəs\ *adj* [*gypsi-* (fr. *gypsum*) + *-ferous*] : bearing gypsum

gyp·site \ˈjip,sīt\ *n* -s [*gyps*um + *-ite*] : earthy gypsum

gyp·sog·ra·phy \jipˈsägrəfē\ *n* -ES [*gyps*um + *-o-* + *-graphy*] : the art or practice of engraving on gypsum

gyp·soph·i·la \jipˈsäfələ\ *n* [NL, fr. *gypso-* (fr. L *gypsum*) + *-phila*] **1** *cap* : a large genus of Old World herbs (family Caryophyllaceae) having small delicate paniculate flowers with naked gamosepalous calyx and 5-clawed petals **2** -s : any plant of the genus *Gypsophila* — called also *baby's breath*

gyp·soph·i·lous \(ˈ)=ˈ==ləs\ *adj* [*gypso-* (fr. *gypsum*) + *-philous*] *of a plant* : flourishing in or on a substratum rich in gypsum — **gyp·soph·i·ly** \=ˈ==lē\ *n* -ES

gyp·so·plast \ˈjipsə,plast\ *n* -s [*gypso-* (fr. *gypsum*) + *-plast*] : a cast in plaster of paris or in white lime

1**gyp·sum** \ˈjipsəm\ *n* -s *often attrib* [L *gypsum*, *gypsus*, fr. Gk *gypsos* chalk, gypsum, cement, of Sem origin; akin to Ar *jibs* plaster, mortar] **1** : a widely distributed mineral $CaSO_4.2H_2O$ consisting of hydrous calcium sulfate that is colorless when pure, occurs massive or in the form of monoclinic crystals that easily split into folia, and is used chiefly as a soil amendment, as a retarder in portland cement, and in making plaster of Paris (hardness 2, sp. gr. 2.31-2.32) **2** : PLASTERBOARD ⟨~ lath⟩ ⟨~ sheathing⟩ ⟨~ wallboard⟩

2**gypsum** \"\ *vt* -ED/-ING/-S : to treat (as soil or water) with gypsum

gypsum block *n* : a gypsum building tile or block for use in nonbearing walls in the interior of a building

gypsum pink *n* : BABY'S BREATH 1a

gypsum plaster *or* **gypsum cement** *n* : a plaster produced from the basic material gypsum — compare CEMENT PLASTER, PLASTER OF PARIS

1**gyp·sy** *or* **gip·sy** \ˈjipsē, -si\ *n* -ES *often attrib* [by shortening & alter. fr. 2*Egyptian*] **1** *cap* : one of a dark Caucasoid people coming orig. from India and entering Europe in the 14th or 15th century that are now found chiefly in Turkey, Russia, Hungary, Spain, England, and the U.S., still maintain somewhat their itinerant life and tribal organization, and are noted as fortune-tellers, horse traders, metalworkers, and musicians **2** : one resembling a Gypsy esp. in appearance, manners, or mode of life ⟨dark of eye, tawny of skin, black as to her tangled hair, . . . a veritable ~ of a child —Richard Free⟩ ⟨oilmen . . . have been *gypsies* of the prairies, seeking, drilling, and never finding —*Lamp*⟩ **3** *cap* : ROMANY 2 **4** : a strong brown that is stronger and slightly yellower than average russet, deeper and slightly yellower than rust, and very slightly lighter than ginger — called also *Caledonian brown* **5** : an independent truck operator who has no regular route but hires his vehicle to others or follows seasonal or irregular sources of traffic **6** : GYP 4 **7** [by shortening] **a** : GYPSYHEAD **b** : GYPSY WINCH

2**gypsy** *or* **gipsy** \"\ *vi* -ED/-ING/-ES : to live or roam like a gypsy

gyp·sy·dom *or* **gip·sy·dom** \-dəm\ *n* -s : the realm of gypsies : gypsies and their life

gyp·sy·fy *or* **gip·sy·fy** \-sə,fī, -sē,-\ *vt* -ED/-ING/-ES : to make gypsylike esp. in appearance

gypsy hat *also* **gypsy bonnet** *n* : a simple broad-brimmed hat worn by women and children

gyp·sy·head \-sē,hed, -si,-\ *n* : a small auxiliary drum on the end of a winch or windlass

gyp·sy·ish *or* **gip·sy·ish** \-sēish, -si·ish\ *adj* : GYPSYLIKE

gyp·sy·ism *or* **gip·sy·ism** \-sē,izəm, -si,i-\ *n* -s : the life and ways of gypsies

gyp·sy·like *or* **gip·sy·like** \ˈ==,=\ *adj* : resembling or suggestive of a gypsy

gypsy moth *n* : an Old World tussock moth (*Porthetria dispar*) introduced about 1869 into the U.S. that has a brown male and a larger whitish female with wings marked by dark lines and that develops as a grayish brown mottled hairy caterpillar which is a very destructive defoliator of many trees

gypsy scale *n* : HUNGARIAN GYPSY SCALE

gypsyweed *or* **gipsyweed** \ˈ==,=\ *n* **1** : a water horehound (*Lycopus virginicus*) **2** : SPEEDWELL

gypsy winch *n* **1** : a small winch that may be operated by a crank **2** : a winch with a gypsyhead

gyr- *or* **gyro-** *comb form* [prob. fr. MF, fr. L, fr. Gk, fr. *gyros* — more at GYRE] **1** : ring : circle ⟨*gyro*mancy⟩ : spiral ⟨*Gyro*ceras⟩ **2** : gyral ⟨*gyro*scope⟩ ⟨*gyr*encephalate⟩ **3** : gyroscope ⟨*gyro*compass⟩

gyr·acan·thus \ˈjir, ˈjīr +\ *n, cap* [NL, fr. *gyr-* + *-acanthus*] : a genus of acanthodian fishes of the Carboniferous known solely from large round sculptured spines

1**gy·ral** \ˈjīrəl\ *adj* [2*gyre* + *-al*] **1** : GYRATORY **2** : of or involving a convolution of the brain — **gy·ral·ly** \-rəlē, -li\ *adv*

2**gyral** \"\ *n* -s : 2GYRE

1**gy·rate** \ˈjī,rā|t, -ˌrə|, *usu* |d·+V\ *adj* [L *gyratus* circular, rounded, fr. *gyrus* circle, ring + *-atus* -ate] **:** winding or coiled round **:** CURVED, RINGED, CONVOLUTED ⟨a ~ branch⟩

²gy·rate \ˈjīˌrāt, ⁼ˈ⁼, *usu* -ād·+V\ *vi* -ED/-ING/-S [LL *gyratus*, past part. of *gyrare* to gyrate, turn] **1 :** to revolve around a central point **:** move spirally about an axis ⟨the dory *gyrated* slowly and without direction near the marvelously still body of the plane —Kay Boyle⟩ **2 :** to turn or swing back and forth often rapidly with or as if with a circular or spiral motion ⟨seems to ~ wildly between the poles of sentimentalism and cold-blooded commercialism —Fredson Bowers⟩ ⟨the rain eddied and *gyrated* past them like a horizontal cataract —J. C.Powys⟩ **syn** see TURN

gy·ra·tion \jīˈrāshən\ *n* -S [MF or LL; MF *gyration, giration*, fr. LL *gyration-, gyratio*, fr. *gyratus* (past part.) + L *-ion-, -io* -ion] **1 :** the act or an instance of rotation in a circle or spiral **:** TURNING, WHIRLING, REVOLUTION **2 :** something that resembles gyration ⟨the first ~s of wishful thinking about the crash —Leo Gurko⟩ **3 :** the pattern of convolutions of the brain **4 :** one of the whorls of a spiral shell — **gy·ra·tion·al** \-shən³l, -shnəl\ *adj*

gy·ra·tor \ˈjīˌrād·ə(r), -ātə-, ⁼ˈ⁼⁼\ *n* -S **:** one that gyrates

gy·ra·to·ry \ˈjīrəˌtōrē, -tȯr-, -ri\ *adj* [*gyration* + *-ory*] **1 :** moving in a circle or spiral **:** REVOLVING **2** *Brit* **:** ROTARY — used of a system of traffic control

gyratory crusher *n* **:** a mill for crushing ore or rock or other materials that consists of a cone-shaped burr rotating in the throat of a broad stationary funnel

gy·rau·lus \jīˈrȯləs\ *n, cap* [NL, fr. *gyr-* + Gk *aulos* tube, groove, reed instrument like an oboe — more at ALVEOLUS] **:** a genus of freshwater snails (family Planorbidae) important in eastern Asia as intermediate hosts of the human intestinal fluke

¹gyre \ˈjī(ə)r\ *vb* -ED/-ING/-S [ME *giren*, fr. LL *gyrare*, fr. L *gyrus*, n.] *vt* **:** to cause to turn around **:** REVOLVE, SPIN, WHIRL ~ *vi* **:** to move in a circle or spiral ⟨the bomber was *gyring* and diving —Stephen Spender⟩

²gyre \"\ *n* -S [L *gyrus*, fr. Gk *gyros;* akin to Gk *gyros* round, curved — more at COWER] **1 :** a circular motion or a circle described by a moving body **:** REVOLUTION **2 :** a circular or spiral form **:** RING, VORTEX

³gyre \ˈgī(ə)r\ *n* -S [ON *gȳgr* witch, giantess; perh. akin to Skt *gūhati* he conceals, Lith *gužė* goddess of travel] *Scot* **:** a malignant spirit or spook

gyre carline *n, Scot* **:** WITCH, HAG

gy·rec·to·my \jīˈrektəmē\ *n* -ES [*gyrus* + E *-ectomy*] **:** excision of a cerebral gyrus

gyr·en·ceph·a·late \ˌjīˌrenˈsefəlāt, -ˌrən-\ *also* **gyr·en·ce·phal·ic** \ˌjīˌrensəˈfalik\ *or* **gyr·en·ceph·a·lous** \ˌjīˌrenˈsefələs, -ˌrən-\ *adj* [NL *Gyrencephala*, group of higher mammals (fr. *gyr-* + *encephala*) + E *-ate* or *-ic* or *-ous*] *of higher mammals* **:** having the surface of the brain convoluted

gy·rene \ˈjīˌrēn, ⁼ˈ⁼\ *n* -S [prob. by alter.] *slang* **:** MARINE ⟨a young fellow in a ~ uniform —MacKinlay Kantor⟩

gyr·falcon *or* **ger·falcon** *also* **jer·falcon** \ˈjər+ˌ-\ *n* [ME *gerfaucun*, fr. MF *girfaucon, gerfaut*, fr. OF, prob. fr. ON *geirfalki*, fr. *geirr* spear + *falki* falcon (prob. fr. MD *valke, valc*); akin to OHG *falcho* falcon — more at GORE (piece of land), FALCON] **:** any of various large falcons of the arctic regions of Europe, Asia, and America that commonly constitute a subgenus (*Hierofalco*) of the genus *Falco* and are about two feet long and more powerful though less active than the peregrine falcon — see BLACK GYRFALCON, WHITE GYRFALCON

gyri *pl of* GYRUS

gy·rin·i·dae \jəˈrinəˌdē, jī-\ *n pl, cap* [NL, fr. *Gyrinus*, type genus (fr. Gk *gyrinos* tadpole, fr. *gyros* round) + *-idae*] **:** a family of aquatic beetles comprising the whirligig beetles

¹gy·ro \ˈjī(ˌ)rō\ *n* -S **1** [by shortening] **:** GYROSCOPE **2 :** any of various devices whose operation depends on a gyroscope: as **a** [by shortening] **:** GYROCOMPASS **b** [by shortening] **:** GYROHORIZON

²gyro \"\ *adj* **:** GYROSCOPIC

gyro- — see GYR-

gy·ro·car \ˈjīrō+ˌ-\ *n* [*gyr-* + *car*] **:** a monorail car

gy·roc·era·cone \jīˈräsərə+ˌ-\ *n* [NL *Gyroceras* + E *cone*] **:** a nautiloid shell coiling like that of members of the genus *Gyroceras* — **gy·roc·era·conic** \⁼ˌ⁼⁼⁼+\ *adj*

gy·roc·er·an \jīˈräsərən\ *adj* [NL *Gyroceras* + E *-an*] **:** of or relating to the genus *Gyroceras*

gy·roc·er·as \-əs\ *n, cap* [NL, fr. *gyr-* + *-ceras*] **:** a genus of fossil nautiloid cephalopods having the shell in the form of a loosely coiled discoidal spiral

gy·ro·compass \ˈjīrō+\ *n* [*gyr-* + *compass*] **:** a compass consisting of a continuously driven gyroscope whose supporting ring confines the spinning axis to a horizontal plane so that the earth's rotation causes it to assume a position parallel to the earth's axis and thus point to the true north

gy·ro·cot·y·le \ˌjīrōˈkäd·³l(ˌ)ē\ *n, cap* [NL, fr. *gyr-* + Gk *kotylē* cup, small vessel — more at KETTLE] **:** a genus (the type of the family Gyrocotylidae) comprising cestodarian worms with a flattened body, an anterior sucker, and a posterior organ in the form of a frilled rosette and sometimes also including worms in which the rosette is replaced by a contractile cylindrical structure that ends in a strong sphincter — compare AMPHILINA

¹gy·ro·cot·y·lid \ˌ⁼⁼ˈ⁼⁼ə̇d\ *adj* [NL *Gyrocotylidae*, family of worms, fr. *Gyrocotyle*, type genus + *-idae*] **:** of or relating to the genus *Gyrocotyle* or the family Gyrocotylidae

²gyrocotylid \"\ *n* -S **:** a gyrocotylid worm

¹gy·ro·dac·ty·loid \ˌjīrōˈdaktəˌlȯid\ *adj* [NL *Gyrodactylus* + E *-oid*] **:** of or relating to the genus *Gyrodactylus* or to worms of this or related genera

²gyrodactyloid \"\ *n* -S **:** a gyrodactyloid worm

gy·ro·dac·ty·lus \ˌ⁼⁼ˈ⁼⁼ləs\ *n, cap* [NL, fr. *gyr-* + *dactylus*] **:** a genus (the type of the family Gyrodactylidae) of small monogenetic trematodes parasitic on fishes

gy·ro·dyne \ˈjīrōˌdīn\ *n* -S [*gyr-* + *-dyne* (as in *aerodyne*)] **:** an aircraft intermediate between the helicopter and the autogiro in that the total available engine power is divided in varying proportions between a lifting rotor and a propeller

Gyro Flux Gate *trademark* — used for an airplane compass that is horizontally stabilized by a gyroscope and that determines directions by means of a flux gate which responds to the earth's magnetic field

gy·ro·frequency \ˈjīrō+\ *n* [*gyr-* + *frequency*] **:** the frequency with which an electron or other charged particle executes spiral gyrations in moving obliquely across a magnetic field

gy·rog·o·nite \jīˈrägəˌnīt\ *n* -S [NL *Gyrogonites*] **:** a minute ovoid spiral-marked body that is the residue of the calcareous incrustation about the female sex organs of a fossil stonewort

gy·rogo·ni·tes \(ˌ)⁼ˌ⁼⁼ˈnīd·(ˌ)ēz, ˌgīrōgəˈ-\ *n, cap* [NL, fr. *gyr-* + *gon-* + L *-ites* -ite] **:** a form genus of stoneworts based on gyrogonites

gyro horizon *n* **:** ARTIFICIAL HORIZON 2

gy·roi·dal \(ˈ)jīˌrȯid³l\ *adj* [*gyr-* + *-oidal*] **:** spiral or gyratory in arrangement — used esp. of the planes of crystals — **gy·roi·dal·ly** \-d³lē\ *adv*

gy·ro·lite \ˈjīrəˌlīt\ *n* -S [*gyr-* + *-lite*] **:** a mineral $Ca_2Si_3O_7(OH)_2.H_2O$ consisting of hydrous calcium silicate in white concretions

gy·ro·lith \-ˌlith\ *n* -S [*gyr-* + *-lith*] **:** the fossil nutlet of a stonewort

gy·ro·ma \jīˈrōmə\ *n* -S [NL, fr. Gk *gyroun* to round, bend, fr. *gyros* ring, circle — more at GYRE] **:** CONVOLUTION: as **a :** the annulus of a fern **b :** a shield somewhat resembling a button in lichens of the genus *Gyrophora*

gy·ro·magnetic \ˌjīrō+\ *adj* [*gyr-* + *magnetic*] **:** of or relating to the magnetic properties of a rotating electrical particle

gyromagnetic ratio *n* **:** the ratio of the magnetic moment of a spinning electrical particle (as an electron) to its mechanical angular momentum

gy·ro·man·cy \ˈjīrəˌman(t)sē\ *n* -ES [prob. fr. MF *gyromancie*, fr. *gyro-* gyr- + *-mancie* -mancy] **:** divination in which one walking in or around a circle falls from dizziness and prognosticates from the place of the fall

gy·ro·mi·tra \ˌjīrōˈmī·trə\ *n, cap* [NL, fr. *gyr-* + *mitra*] **:** a genus of fungi (family Helvellaceae) forming large stipitate ascomata with folded ascus-bearing caps and including a form (*G. esculenta*) that produces edible fruiting bodies which may be poisonous if eaten raw

gy·ron *or* **gi·ron** \ˈjīrən, -ˌrän\ *n* -S [MF *giron* wedge-shaped piece of material, fr. OF, of Gmc origin; akin to OHG *gēro* wedge-shaped object — more at GORE] **:** a heraldic charge of triangular form having one side at the edge of the field and the opposite angle usu. at the fess point

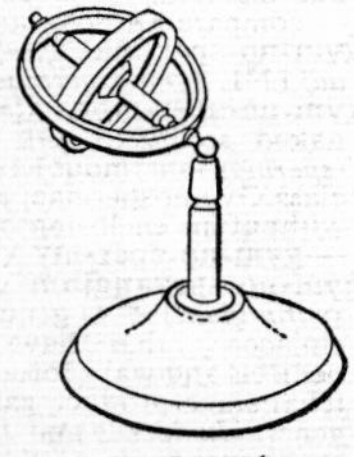
gyrons

gy·ron·ny \jīˈrānē, ˈjīrənē\ *adj* [ME *jerownde, gerundi*, fr. MF *gironné, geronné*, fr. OF, fr. *giron, geron*, n.] **:** divided so as to form a number of gyrons — used of a heraldic coat of arms

gy·roph·o·ra \jīˈräfərə\ *n, cap* [NL, fr. *gyr-* + *-phora*] **:** a genus (the type of the family Gyrophoraceae) of foliose rock-inhabiting lichens that includes the edible manna lichen (*G. esculenta*) of Japan — compare UMBILICARIA — **gy·roph·o·ra·ceous** \(ˌ)⁼ˌ⁼⁼ˈrāshəs\ *adj*

Gy·ro·pilot \ˈjīrō+ˌ-\ *trademark* — used for an automatic pilot

gy·ro·plane \ˈjīrōˌplān\ *n* [ISV *gyro-* (fr. *gyroscope*) + *-plane* (fr. *airplane*)] **:** an airplane balanced and supported by the aerodynamic forces acting on rapidly rotating horizontal or slightly inclined planes

gy·ro·scope \ˈjīrəˌskōp\ *n* [F, fr. *gyro-* gyr- + *-scope*] **1 :** a wheel or disk mounted to spin rapidly about an axis and also free to rotate about one or both of two axes perpendicular to each other and to the axis of spin so that a rotation of one of the two mutually perpendicular axes results from application of torque to the other when the wheel is spinning, the entire apparatus offering considerable opposition depending on the angular momentum to any torque that would change the direction of the axis of spin **2 :** something resembling a gyroscope **:** BALANCE WHEEL 2 ⟨systematic retirement programs can thus serve as a sort of economic ~ —*New Republic*⟩

gyroscope 1

gy·ro·scop·ic \ˌ⁼⁼ˈskäpik, -pēk\ *adj* **:** of, relating to, or having the characteristics of a gyroscope — **gy·ro·scop·i·cal·ly** \-pə̇k(ə)lē, -pēk-, -li\ *adv*

gyroscopic compass *n* **:** GYROCOMPASS

gy·ro·scop·ics \ˌ⁼⁼ˈ⁼piks, -pēks\ *n pl but sing in constr* **:** a branch of mechanics that deals with gyroscopes and their use in control and stabilization

gy·rose \ˈjīˌrōs\ *adj* [²*gyre* + *-ose*] **:** marked with wavy lines **:** UNDULATE, SINUATE

gy·ro·stabilization \ˌjīrō+\ *n* **:** the process of stabilizing or the condition of being stabilized by means of a gyrostabilizer

gy·ro·stabilized \"+\ *adj* **:** stabilized by means of a gyrostabilizer

gy·ro·stabilizer \"+\ *n* [¹*gyro* + *stabilizer*] **:** a stabilizing device (as for a ship or airplane) consisting of a continuously driven gyro spinning about a vertical axis and pivoted in trunnions so that its axis of spin may be tipped fore-and-aft in the vertical plane and serving to oppose sideways motion

gy·ro·stat \ˈjīrəˌstat\ *n* -S [ISV *gyr-* + *-stat*] **:** GYROSTABILIZER

gy·ro·stat·ic \ˌ⁼⁼ˈstad·ik\ *adj* **:** of or relating to a gyrostat or to its stabilizing effect — **gy·ro·stat·i·cal·ly** \-d·ə̇k(ə)lē\ *adv*

gyrostatic compass *n* **:** GYROCOMPASS

gy·ro·vague \ˈjīrōˌvāg\ *n* [F *gyrovague*, fr. LL *gyrovagus*, fr. L *gyro-* gyr- + *vagus* wandering — more at VAGARY] **:** a wandering and usu. dissolute monk of the early church

gy·rus \ˈjīrəs\ *n, pl* **gy·ri** \-ˌrī\ [NL, fr. L, circle — more at GYRE] **:** a convoluted ridge between grooves; *esp* **:** one of the characteristic ridges of superficial gray matter of the cerebral hemispheres

gyte \ˈgīt\ *adj, chiefly Scot* **:** DERANGED, MAD

gy·trash \ˈgīˌtrash\ *var of* GUYTRASH

gyt·tja \ˈyi(ˌ)chä\ *n* -S [Sw, fr. *gjuta* to pour, fr. OSw *giūta;* akin to ON *gjōta* to bear young, drop one's young — more at FOUND (pour)] **:** a lacustrine mud containing abundant organic material

¹gyve \ˈjīv\ *n* -S [ME] **:** FETTER, BOND, CHAIN — usu. used in pl.

²gyve \"\ *vt* -ED/-ING/-S [ME *gyven*, fr. *gyve*, n.] **:** to bind or restrain with fetters **:** SHACKLE, CHAIN

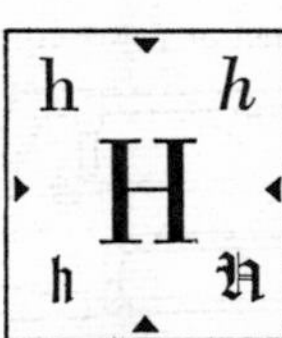

[1]h \'āch\ *n, pl* **h's** *or* **hs** \'āchəz\ *often cap, often attrib* **1 a :** the eighth letter of the English alphabet **b :** an instance of this letter printed, written, or otherwise represented **c :** a speech counterpart of orthographic *h* (as *h* in *hoe, ahead,* or German *hügel*) **2 :** a printer's type, a stamp, or some other instrument for reproducing the letter *h* **3 :** someone or something arbitrarily or conveniently designated *h* esp. as the eighth in order or class **4 :** something having the shape of the letter H ⟨grooved and slotted to receive H bronze members —Kenneth Cheesman⟩

[2]h *abbr, often cap* **1** hail **2** haler **3** half **4** hall **5** handily **6** harbor **7** hard; hardness **8** [Ger *hauch*] film **9** haze **10** headquarters **11** heat **12** hecto- **13** height **14** helicopter **15** heller **16** hence **17** henry **18** [L *heres*] heir **19** heroin **20** high **21** hit **22** holy **23** home **24** honor **25** horizon; horizontal **26** horn **27** horse **28** hot **29** hour **30** house **31** humidity **32** hundred **33** husband **34** hydrant

[3]h *symbol* **1** *cap* hydrogen **2** *cap* enthalpy **3** *cap* intensity of magnetic field **4** Planck constant

H^3 *or* **^{3}H** \(')āch¦thrē\ *symbol* tritium

H^2 *or* **^{2}H** \(')āch¦tü\ *symbol* deuterium

[1]ha *or* **hah** \'hä, 'hȧ\ *interj* [ME *ha*] — used to express surprise, joy, or grief or sometimes doubt or hesitation

[2]ha \"\ *vi* -ED/-ING/-S **:** to utter the exclamation *ha*

[3]ha *or* **hah** \"\ *n* -s **:** an utterance of the exclamation *ha*

[4]ha *or* **ha'** \hə, (¦)ha\ *var of* A

[5]ha *dial Brit pres 1st & 2d sing & pres pl of* HAVE

ha *abbr* hectare

HA *abbr* **1** heavy artillery **2** high-angle **3** *often not cap* [L *hoc anno*] in this year; [L *huius anni*] of this year **4** horse artillery **5** hot air **6** hour angle

ha' \'hȯ, 'hȧ\ *Scot var of* HALL

HAA *abbr* heavy antiaircraft

haab \'häb\ *n* -s [Maya] **1 :** TUN **2 :** the 365-day year of the Maya calendar — often distinguished from *tun*

haak-en-steek \'häkən,stēk\ *n* -s [Afrik, lit., hook and sting; fr. the fact that it has some curved and some straight thorns] **:** UMBRELLA THORN

haar \'(h)är\ *n* -s [prob. fr. a LG or D dial. word akin to D dial. *harig* damp, misty, MD *hare* sharp wind, piercing cold, Fris *harig* misty, ON *hārr* gray, hoary — more at HOAR] *dial Brit* **:** a cold wet sea fog

haar·der *var of* [2]HARDER

haar·lem \'härləm, 'hȧl-\ *adj, usu cap* [fr. *Haarlem,* Netherlands] **:** of or from the city of Haarlem, Netherlands **:** of the kind or style prevalent in Haarlem

haas·tia \'hästēə\ *n* -s [NL, fr. Sir John F. J. von *Haast* †1887 German-born geologist and explorer in New Zealand + NL *-ia*] **:** RAOULIA 2

hab *abbr* habitat

HAB *abbr* high-altitude bombing

ha·ba \'(h)äbə\ *n* -s [Sp, fr. L *faba* bean — more at BEAN] **:** BROAD BEAN

ha·bab \hə'bäb, 'hä,bäb\ *n, pl* **habab** *usu cap* **1 a :** a nomadic people of the Red sea region in Africa **b :** a member of such people **2 :** the Semitic language of the Habab

ha·ba·ne·ra \,(h)äbə'nerə, *often* ÷ -bən'ye- *although the fifth letter in Spanish is n not ñ*\ *n* -s [Sp (*danza*) *habanera,* lit., Havanan dance, fr. *danza* dance + *habanera,* fem. of *habanero* Havanan, fr. La *Habana,* Cuba + *-ero* -er] **1 :** a Cuban dance of voluptuous character in slow duple time **2 :** a slow Cuban dance tune in duple time with the distinctive rhythm of a dotted eighth note, a sixteenth note, and two eighth notes throughout

ha·ba·ne·ro \-e(,)rō\ *n* -s *cap* [Sp, fr. La *Habana* (Havana), Cuba + *-ero* -er] **:** a native or inhabitant of Havana, Cuba

hab·ble \'häbəl\ *Scot var of* HOBBLE

hab·da·lah *or* **hav·da·lah** \,hävdə'lä, häv'dȯlə\ *n* -s [Heb *habhdālāh* separation, division] **:** a Jewish religious ceremony marking the close of a Sabbath or of holidays and consisting of the recital by the head of a household of appropriate benedictions over a cup esp. of wine, a spice box, and a newly lighted special candle

ha·be·as cor·pus \'hābēə'skȯrpəs, -biə'-, -kȯ(ə)p-\ *n* [ME, fr. ML, lit., you should have the body (the opening words of the writ)] **1 :** any of several common-law writs that have for their object the bringing of a party before a court or judge and that are issued out of court or awarded by a judge in vacation; *esp* **:** HABEAS CORPUS AD SUBJICIENDUM ⟨the privilege of the writ of *habeas corpus* shall not be suspended, unless when in cases of rebellion or invasion the public safety may require it —*U.S. Constitution*⟩ **2 :** the right of a citizen to obtain a writ of habeas corpus as a protection against illegal imprisonment

habeas corpus ad fa·ci·en·dum et re·cip·i·en·dum \-ad-,fāshē'endəme·trȧ,sipē'endəm\ *n* [NL, lit., you should have the body for doing and receiving] **:** a writ issued from a superior court to an inferior court requiring that a defendant be produced with the cause of his being taken and held

habeas corpus ad pro·se·quen·dum \-,präsə'kwendəm\ *n* [NL, lit., you should have the body for prosecuting] **:** a writ for removing a prisoner for trial to the jurisdiction in which the offense was committed

habeas corpus ad sub·ji·ci·en·dum \-(,)səb,jisē'endəm\ *n* [NL, lit., you should have the body for submitting] **:** a writ for inquiring into the lawfulness of the restraint of a person who is imprisoned or detained in another's custody

habeas corpus ad tes·ti·fi·can·dum \-,testəfə'kandəm\ *n* [NL, lit., you should have the body for testifying] **:** a writ for bringing a person in custody into court as a witness

habeas corpus cum cau·sa \-(,)kəm'kȯzə\ *n* [NL, lit., you should have the body with the cause] **:** HABEAS CORPUS AD FACIENDUM ET RECIPIENDUM

hab·e·nar·ia \,habə'na(a)rēə\ *n* [NL, fr. L *habena* strap, thong (fr. *habēre* to have, hold) + NL *-aria;* fr. the shape of parts of the flowers — more at GIVE] **1** *cap* **:** a very large genus of somewhat glabrous orchids chiefly of the northern hemisphere with usu. small flowers having the lip lobed, entire, or fringed and borne in racemes or spikes — see FRINGED ORCHIS, REIN ORCHIS **2** -s **:** any plant of the genus *Habenaria* or its flower

ha·ben·dum \hə'bendəm\ *n* -s [NL, fr. L, to be had, neut. of *habendus,* gerundive of *habēre* to have, to hold (the first word of this part of the deed)] **:** the part of a deed that formerly limited and defined an estate and the extent of ownership granted and sometimes the type of tenancy by which the grantees would hold an estate but that is now rarely encountered or is merely formal in deeds in which a fee simple absolute is presumed granted

ha·ben·u·la \hə'benyələ\ *n, pl* **habenu·lae** \-yə(,)lē\ [L, dim. of *habena* strap, thong] **1** *also* **ha·ben·u·lar trigone** \-lə(r)-\ **:** an anatomic structure in the form of a band; *esp* **:** a small triangular area of the surface of the epithalamus on either side of the base of the pineal body **2** *also* **habenular nucleus :** a nucleus underlying each habenula and connected by commissural fibers that forms a correlation center for olfactory stimuli — called also *nucleus habenulae*

haber *var of* HAVER

haberah *var of* HAVERAH

hab·er·dash·er \'habə(r),dashə(r)\ *n* -s [ME *haberdassher,* fr. modif. of AF *hapertas* petty merchandise + ME *-er*] **1** *Brit* **:** a dealer in small wares or notions (as needles, thread, buttons, trimmings) **2 :** a dealer in men's furnishings (as shirts, ties, hats, gloves)

hab·er·dash·ery \-sh(ə)rē, -ri\ *n* -ES [ME *haberdassherie,* fr. *haberdassher* + *-ie* -y] **1 :** the goods sold by a haberdasher **2 :** a haberdasher's shop

haberdine *n* -s [ME, fr. MF *habordean,* by false division (the *l* being taken as the definite article) fr. *labordean,* fr. *Labourd,* Basque district in France] *obs* **:** a cod salted and dried

ha·be·re fa·ci·as pos·ses·si·o·nem \hə'birē'fāshēəspə,zesē'ō,nem\ *n* [ML, you should cause to have possession (the opening words of the writ)] **:** a writ of execution in ejectment orig. in England in cases of chattels real

habere facias sei·si·nam \-'sēzə,nam\ *n* [ML, you should cause to have seisin] **:** a common-law writ formerly used in real actions to recover seisin

hab·er·geon \'habərjən, hə'bərj(ē)ən\ *or* **hau·ber·geon** \'hȯb-, hȯ'-\ *n* -s [ME *haubergeoun,* fr. MF *haubergeon,* dim. of *hauberc* — more at HAUBERK] **1 :** a medieval jacket of mail shorter than a hauberk **2 :** HAUBERK

ha·ber process \'häbə(r)-\ *n, usu cap H* [after Fritz *Haber* †1934 Ger. chemist] **:** a catalytic process for synthesizing ammonia from nitrogen and hydrogen at elevated temperature and pressure

hab·ile \'habəl\ *adj* [F, fr. L *habilis* — more at ABLE] **1** *obs* **:** FIT, SUITABLE **2 :** ABLE, ADROIT, SKILLFUL ⟨that astonishing ~ use of his lean little hands —J.G.Cozzens⟩

ha·bil·i·ment \hə'biləmənt\ *n* -s [MF *habillement,* fr. *abillier, habiller* to prepare a log for working, prepare, dress (fr. *bille* log, trunk) + *-ment* — more at BILLET] **1 habiliments** *pl* **:** TRAPPINGS, EQUIPMENT, GEAR ⟨the disintegrative process of the frontier . . . stripping them of the ~*s* of civilization —W.P. Webb⟩ ⟨all the psychological trappings and ~*s* of a crusade —W.A.White⟩ **2 habiliments** *pl, archaic* **:** necessary equipment and material (as for war) **:** OUTFITTING **3 a :** the dress suited to or characteristic of a calling, occupation, or occasion **:** GARB, COSTUME, VESTMENT — usu. used in pl. ⟨dressed in shabby gaucho ~*s* —W.H.Hudson †1922⟩ ⟨~*s* of a priest⟩ ⟨the antique forms and ~*s* which their Roman ancestors had found congenial —G.C.Sellery⟩ **b :** CLOTHES, GARMENT, DRESS — usu. used in pl. ⟨pointed in silence to my torn and muddied ~*s* —Hugh McCrae⟩ ⟨seize a buttonhole, or any little bit of the ~*s,* of the man she was addressing —George Meredith⟩

ha·bil·i·men·ta·tion \hə,bilə(,)men·'tāshən\ *n* -s **:** the arts and industries connected with the manufacture and use of clothes

ha·bil·i·ment·ed \hə'bilə,mentəd\ *adj* **:** CLOTHED

ha·bil·i·tate \hə'bilə,tāt, *usu* -ād·+V\ *vb* -ED/-ING/-S [LL *habilitatus,* past part. of *habilitare,* fr. L *habilitas* aptness, ability — more at ABILITY] *vt* **1** *archaic* **:** QUALIFY, ENTITLE **2 :** to fit out (as a mine) **:** equip for working **3 :** CLOTHE, DRESS ~ *vi* **:** to qualify oneself (as for teaching in a university) ⟨had just *habilitated* as a privatdocent in the theological faculty —Jack Finegan⟩

ha·bil·i·ta·tion \hə,bilə'tāshən\ *n* -s [ML *habilitation-, habilitatio,* fr. LL *habilitatus* + L *-ion-, -io* -ion] **:** the act of habilitating **:** QUALIFICATION ⟨thesis for ~ as docent⟩ **:** CAPACITATION ⟨~ of cerebral palsy patients⟩

ha·bil·i·ty \hə'bilədē\ *n* -ES **:** the quality of being habile **:** EXPERTNESS

ha·bi·ru \'häbē,rü, hə'bē(,)rü\ *also* **ha·bi·ri** \-ē(,)rē\ *n pl, usu cap* [Bab *khabiru*] **:** a nomadic people mentioned in Assyro-Babylonian literature from 2000 B.C. on and often identified as the Hebrews of the Bible

[1]hab·it \'habət, *usu* -əd·+V\ *n* -s [ME *habit, abit,* fr. OF, fr. L *habitus* condition, appearance, attire, character, disposition, habit, fr. *habēre* to have, hold — more at GIVE] **1** *archaic* **a :** CLOTHING, APPAREL ⟨costly thy ~ as thy purse can buy —Shak.⟩ **:** mode of dress ⟨in the vile ~ of a village slave —Alexander Pope⟩ **b :** a garment or a suit of clothes **:** OUTFIT **2 a :** a costume indicative or characteristic of a calling, rank, or function ⟨monk's ~⟩ **b :** RIDING HABIT **3 :** BEARING, CONDUCT, BEHAVIOR — used esp. in Scots law in the phrase *habit and repute* ⟨marriage by ~ and repute⟩ **4 a :** bodily appearance or makeup **:** physical type **:** PHYSIQUE ⟨his corpulent ~ of body, natural both to the vigor of his type and to a sedentary way of life —Osbert Sitwell⟩ **b** *obs* **:** the body as a physiological organism **:** the system of bodily processes **c** *obs* **:** the body's surface **5 :** the prevailing disposition or character of a person's thoughts and feelings **:** mental makeup ⟨where he has gone to indulge a contemplative ~ —L.J.Halle⟩ ⟨a whole ~ of sensibility —F.R.Leavis⟩ **6 a** *of a person* **:** a settled tendency of behavior or normal manner of procedure **:** CUSTOM, PRACTICE, WAY ⟨contributed letters to the newspapers — a ~ that became a lifelong one —B.J.Hendrick⟩ ⟨the local ~ of building in perishable materials —Bernard Newman⟩ **b** *of a thing* **:** a usual manner of occurrence or behavior **:** TENDENCY ⟨black clouds there have a ~ of sitting right on the water —Ira Wolfert⟩ ⟨paste has a ~ of going hard and lumpy once opened⟩ **7 a :** a behavior pattern acquired by frequent repetition or developed as a physiologic function and showing itself in regularity ⟨the daily bowel ~⟩ or increased facility of performance or in a decreased power of resistance ⟨a drug ~⟩ **b :** an acquired or developed mode of behavior or function that has become nearly or completely involuntary ⟨put the keys back in his pocket through force of ~⟩ **8** *of an organism* **:** characteristic mode of growth or occurrence ⟨elms have a spreading ~⟩ ⟨a grass ubiquitous in its ~⟩ **9** *of a crystal* **:** characteristic or common assemblage of forms at crystallization leading to a usual appearance **10** *obs* **:** close acquaintance **:** FAMILIARITY ⟨he inclines to a sort of disgust . . . with the system and he has few . . . ~*s* with any of its professors —Edmund Burke⟩ **11 :** a generic entity occurring as an external or supernatural reality or force constitutive of or acting on an individual **12 :** ADDICTION 2a

syn HABITUDE, PRACTICE, USAGE, CUSTOM, USE, WONT: these all have in common the sense of a way of behaving that has become more or less fixed; in most cases they have the sense of such a way considered collectively or in the abstract. HABIT, usu. applying to individuals, signifies a way of acting or thinking done frequently enough to have become unconscious or unpremeditated in each repetition or to have become compulsive ⟨the *habit* of dawdling on the way to school⟩ ⟨a persistent *habit* of coughing⟩ ⟨*habits* of mind⟩ ⟨speech *habits*⟩ HABITUDE usu. suggests habitual or usual state of mind or attitude ⟨you who are so sincere with me are never quite sincere with others. You have contracted this bad *habitude* from your custom of addressing the people —W.S.Landor⟩ ⟨a confusion of assertions, viewpoints, personal motives and prejudices, and local *habitudes* can serve only to darken counsel —*Yale Rev.*⟩ PRACTICE suggests an act, often habitual, repeated with regularity and usu. by choice ⟨the team made a *practice* of leaving their scenarios unfinished until actual production —*Current Biog.*⟩ ⟨promised the people that he would establish democratic *practices* —*Collier's Yr. Bk.*⟩ ⟨the *practice* of supplementing poultry and hog feeds with antibiotics —*Americana Annual*⟩ ⟨the *practice* of self-examination —Anne Fremantle⟩ USAGE suggests more a customary action, a practice followed so generally that it has become a social norm ⟨an unwritten constitution comprising ancient British conventions and *usage* —*Americana Annual*⟩ ⟨earn a living in a business community without yielding to its *usages* —W.H.Hamilton⟩ ⟨better versed in diplomatic *usage* than any of his colleagues —F.A.Ogg & Harold Zink⟩ CUSTOM can apply to habit, practice, or usage that has become public and associated with an individual or group because of its long continuance, its uniformity, and often, its morally compulsive quality ⟨it is the Arabian *custom* to date, if possible, the birth of sons by unusual events —*Current Biog.*⟩ ⟨in contemporary society it is not a fashion that men wear trousers; it is the *custom* —Edward Sapir⟩ ⟨the *custom* — and this is all that it can be properly called — according to which Congress and the President tacitly agree to abide by the interpretation of the Court —M.R.Cohen⟩ USE, rare in current speech, signifies a customary act or practice more or less distinctive of an individual or particular group ⟨the polite *uses* of society⟩ ⟨the religious *use* and wont of the country people⟩ WONT applies to a habitual or customary manner, method, or practice distinguishing an individual or group; it differs from USE only in extending to manner ⟨intended to come oftener to church than had been his *wont* of late —William Black⟩ ⟨this nice balance between sovereignty and liberty is maintained by use and *wont* —V.L.Parrington⟩ ⟨a people living by *wont* in a natural atmosphere of suspicion and mistrust, and consumed by fantasies —V.S.Pritchett⟩ **syn** see in addition PHYSIQUE

[2]habit \"\ *vt* -ED/-ING/-S **:** CLOTHE, DRESS ⟨the nature of such pedantry to ~ itself in a harsh and crabbed style —R.M. Weaver⟩

[3]habit \"\ *vb* -ED/-ING/-S [ME *habiten* to dwell, reside, fr. MF *habiter,* fr. L *habitare* to have possession of, inhabit, dwell, abide, fr. *habitus,* past part. of *habēre* to have, hold — more at GIVE] *vi, obs* **:** LIVE, ABIDE ~ *vt* **1** *archaic* **:** INHABIT **2** *archaic* **:** ACCUSTOM, HABITUATE

hab·it·abil·i·ty \,habəd·ə'bilədē\ *n* **:** the state of being habitable

hab·it·able \'habəd·əbəl, -bətəb-\ *adj* [ME *abitable,* fr. OF *habitable, abitable,* fr. L *habitabilis,* fr. *habitare* + *-abilis* -able] **:** capable of being inhabited **:** that may be inhabited or dwelt in ⟨the ~ world⟩; *specif, of a dwelling* **:** reasonably fit for occupation by a tenant of the class for which it was let or of the class ordinarily occupying such a dwelling — **hab·it·able·ness** *n* -ES — **hab·it·ably** \-blē, -li\ *adv*

habitacle *n* -s [ME, fr. OF, fr. L *habitaculum* — more at BINNACLE] **1** *obs* **:** a dwelling place **2** *obs* **:** a niche in a wall (as for a statue)

hab·it·al·ly \'habəd·ᵊlē\ *adv* [irreg. fr. *habitat* + *-ly*] **:** with respect to habitat

hab·it·ancy \'habəd·ənsē\ *n* -ES **1 :** the fact of residence **:** INHABITANCY **2 :** the whole number of inhabitants **:** POPULATION

[1]hab·i·tant \'habəd·ənt\ *n* -s [MF, fr. pres. part. of *habiter* to dwell, inhabit — more at HABIT] **1 :** INHABITANT, RESIDENT **2** *or* **ha·bi·tan** \¦(h)abē¦täⁿ\ [CanF *habitant,* fr. F, inhabitant] **:** a settler or descendant of a settler of French origin belonging to the farming class in Canada

[2]ha·bi·tant \¦(h)abē¦täⁿ\ *adj* **:** relating to, characteristic of, or produced by the French farmers of Canada ⟨~ furniture⟩ ⟨~ homespun⟩

hab·i·tat \'habə,tat, *usu* -ad·+V\ *n* -s [L, it inhabits, 3d pers. sing. pres. indic. of *habitare* to inhabit (the initial word in Latin descriptions of species of fauna and flora in old natural histories) — more at HABIT] **1 a :** the place where a plant or animal species naturally lives and grows ⟨found as weeds throughout the tropics, but their original ~ has not been determined —Walter Bally⟩ **b :** the kind of site or region with respect to physical features (as soil, weather, elevation) naturally or normally preferred by a biological species ⟨provides three main kinds of ~, namely rocks, sand, and mud —W.H.Dowdeswell⟩ ⟨shell opaque and dull, varying in solidity according to the ~⟩ **c :** the purely physical environment of a locality occupied by a human group ⟨unable to maintain themselves as rulers in the steppe ~ of the nomads —Owen & Eleanor Lattimore⟩ **2 :** the place where something is commonly found ⟨has its natural ~ in university, in government, or in industrial laboratories —B.B.Watson⟩

habitat form *n* **:** ECAD

habitat group *n* **:** a museum exhibit showing plant and animal specimens in such attitudes and with their natural surroundings so reproduced as to picture their habits and habitat

hab·i·ta·tion \,habə'tāshən\ *n* -s [ME *habitacioun,* fr. MF *habitation,* fr. L *habitation-, habitatio,* fr. *habitatus* (past part. of *habitare* to inhabit, dwell) + *-ion-, -io* -io — more at HABIT] **1 a :** the act of inhabiting **:** state of inhabiting or dwelling or of being inhabited **:** OCCUPANCY **b :** the right of one with his family to occupy the residential property of another as a home **2 :** a dwelling place **:** HOUSE, HOME, RESIDENCE ⟨a map showing towns, villages, and scattered ~*s*⟩ ⟨his notebooks . . . gave his ideas a local ~ —Van Wyck Brooks⟩ **3 :** SETTLEMENT, COLONY ⟨their ~*s* were usually spoken of as camps, sometimes composed of 200 tents —Clark Wissler⟩ — **hab·i·ta·tion·al** \¦==¦tāshənᵊl, -shnəl\ *adj*

habit clinic *n* **:** a clinic dealing with the prevention and treatment of behavior problems in young children

habited *adj* **1** *obs* **:** fixed by habit **:** ACCUSTOMED **2** *archaic* **:** INHABITED **3 :** CLOTHED; *esp* **:** dressed in a habit ⟨the monasteries were gone, the ~ men and women were but memories —Sigmund Beale⟩

habit-forming \'==,==\ *adj* **:** inducing the formation of a habit or an addiction ⟨a *habit-forming* drug⟩

habiting *pres part of* HABIT

habits *pl of* HABIT, *pres 3d sing of* HABIT

habit spasm *n* **:** TIC 1

[1]ha·bit·u·al \hə'bich(ə)wəl, -chəl\ *adj* [ML *habitualis,* fr. L *habitus* condition, habit + *-alis* -al — more at HABIT] **1 :** of the nature of a habit **:** according to habit **:** established by or repeated by force of habit **:** CUSTOMARY ⟨~ smoking⟩ ⟨~ courtesy⟩ ⟨~ morning walk⟩ **2 :** doing, practicing, or acting in some manner by force of habit **:** customarily doing a certain thing ⟨a ~ drunkard⟩ ⟨~ playgoer⟩ ⟨his ~ position by the door⟩ **3 :** used or involved in the practice of a habit **:** USUAL ⟨~ topic⟩ **4 :** existing as a part of the inward constitution or habit **:** inherent in an individual ⟨~ faith⟩ ⟨~ grace⟩; *also* **:** NATIVE, INBORN ⟨~ tact⟩ **syn** *see* USUAL

[2]habitual \"\ *n* -s **:** an habitual offender; *esp* **:** an habitual drunkard, criminal, or user of drugs **:** ADDICT

habitual abortion *n* **:** recurrent abortion in successive pregnancies

habitual criminal *n* **:** one convicted of a crime who has a certain number of prior convictions for offenses of a character specified by statute (as felonies) and is thereby under some statutes subject to an increased penalty (as life imprisonment)

ha·bit·u·al·i·ty \hə,bichə'waləd·ē\ *n* -ES **:** the state of being controlled (as in thinking) by old habits

ha·bit·u·al·ly \-lē, -li\ *adv* **1 :** by habit **:** CUSTOMARILY, UNTHINKINGLY **2 :** CONSISTENTLY, PERSISTENTLY, REPEATEDLY, USUALLY

ha·bit·u·al·ness *n* -ES **:** the quality or state of being habitual

[1]habituate *adj* [LL *habituatus*] *obs* **:** formed by habit **:** HABITUAL

[2]ha·bit·u·ate \hə'bichə,wāt, *usu* -ād·+V\ *vt* -ED/-ING/-S [LL *habituatus,* past part. of *habituare,* fr. L *habitus* condition, appearance, habit — more at HABIT] **1 :** to make used to **:** ACCUSTOM, FAMILIARIZE ⟨*habituated* to courtly rhetoric —Francis Hackett⟩ ⟨trying to substitute coeducation, to ~ one sex to another so that difference of sex will be lost sight of —Margaret Mead⟩ **2** *obs* **:** to make (an action) habitual **3** *archaic* **:** to go to or be in frequently **:** FREQUENT

ha·bit·u·a·tion \=,=='wāshən\ *n* -s [ME *habituacioun,* fr. ML *habituation-, habituatio,* fr. LL *habituatus* + L *-ion-, -io* -ion] **1 :** the act or process of making habitual or accustomed ⟨the essence of the tragedy of Macbeth — the ~ to crime —T.S. Eliot⟩ **2 a :** tolerance to the effects of a drug acquired through continued use and manifested by decreasing effectiveness of the same amount of drug administered in successive doses ⟨cathartic ~⟩ ⟨narcotic ~⟩ **b :** the psychic or emotional counterpart of acquired tolerance that is manifested by psychologic dependence upon a drug after a period of use — often distinguished from *addiction*

[1]ha·bit·u·a·tive \='==,wād·iv\ *adj* [[2]*habituate* + *-ive*] *of a grammatical form* **:** expressing habitual action or condition — compare INCIPIATIVE

[2]habituative \"\ *n* -s **:** an habituative form

hab·i·tude \'habə,tüd, -ə·,tyüd\ *n* -s [ME *abitude,* fr. MF *habitude,* fr. L *habitudo,* fr. *habitus,* past part. of *habēre* to have, hold — more at GIVE] **1 a** *archaic* **:** native or essential character **:** normal constitution **b** *obs* **:** RELATION, RESPECT **2** *obs* **:** habitual association **:** FAMILIARITY **3 a :** habitual disposition or mode of behavior or procedure ⟨the sense of fitness and proportion that comes from years of ~ in the practice of an art —B.N.Cardozo⟩ **b :** HABIT, CUSTOM ⟨congressional investigation . . . has acquired the sanction of ~ —R.H.Rovere⟩ **syn** see HABIT

hab·i·tu·di·nal \¦habə¦tüd(ᵊ)nəl, -ə·¦tyü-\ *adj* [L *habitudin-, habitudo* + E *-al*] **:** relating to or associated with a habitude ⟨occupational and ~ diseases, such as . . . lead poisoning and extreme obesity —*Quarterly Rev.*⟩

ha·bit·ué \hə'bichə,wā, =,=='=\ *n* -s [F, fr. past part. of *habituer* to frequent, fr. LL *habituare* — more at HABITUATE] **1 :** one who frequents a place ⟨Paris ~*s*⟩ or class of places ⟨an ~ of the theater⟩ **2 :** a drug addict

hab·i·tus \'habəd·əs\ *n, pl* **habitus** [NL, fr. L, condition, appearance, character — more at HABIT] **1 a :** the body build and constitution esp. as related to predisposition to disease ⟨ulcer ~⟩ **:** HABIT 4a — see CONSTITUTIONAL TYPE **b :** HABIT 8 **2 a :** a mental power or faculty **b :** HABIT 6a

hab·nab \'(h)ab,nab\ *also* **hab or nab** \'(h)abə(r)'nab\ *adv* [fr. (assumed) ME dial. *habbe nabbe, habbe or nabbe* whether he (she, I) have or does (do) not have, fr. ME dial. *habbe,* 1st & 3d pers. sing. pres. subj. of *habben* to have (fr. OE *habban*) + ME *or* + ME dial. *nabbe,* 1st & 3d pers. sing. pres. subj. of *nabben* not to have, fr. OE *nabban,* fr. *ne* not + *habban* to have — more at HAVE, OR, NO] *now dial Brit* **:** in one way or another **:** by hook or crook

ha·boob \hə'büb\ *n* -s [Ar *habūb* violent wind] **:** a violent dust storm or sandstorm of northern Africa or India

habro- *comb form* [NL, fr. L, fr. Gk, fr. *habros*] **:** graceful — in generic names in zoology ⟨*Habronema*⟩

hab·ro·brac·on \ˌhabrōˈbrakən\ *n* [NL, fr. *habro-* + *Bracon* — more at BRACONIDAE] **1** *cap* **:** a genus of ichneumon flies — more at BRACONIDAE] **1** *cap* **:** a genus of very small wasps (family Braconidae) that are parasitic on caterpillars and that are valuable for laboratory studies of genetics **2** *-s often cap* **:** any insect of the genus *Habrobracon*

hab·ro·ne·ma \-ˈnēmə\ *n, cap* [NL, fr. *habro-* + *-nema*] **:** a genus of parasitic nematode worms (family Spiruridae) having developmental stages in flies of the genera *Musca* and *Stomoxys* and adult stages in the stomach of the horse or the proventriculus of various birds — see HABRONEMIASIS, SUMMER SORES

hab·ro·ne·mi·a·sis \ˌhabrōnēˈmīəsəs\ *also* **hab·ro·ne·mo·sis** \-ˈmōsəs\ *n* -ES [NL, fr. *Habronema* + *-iasis* or *-osis*] **:** infestation with or disease caused by roundworms of the genus *Habronema* and characterized in the horse by gastric tumors and inflammation or by summer sores

hab·ro·ne·mic \ˌhabrōˈnēmik\ *adj* [NL *Habronema* + E *-ic*] **:** relating to or caused by worms of the genus *Habronema*

ha·bu \ˈhä(ˌ)bü\ *n* -s [native name in the Ryukyu islands] **:** a dangerously venomous pit viper (*Trimeresurus flavoviridis*) common in the Ryukyu islands

ha·bu·ka \ˌhäˈbükə\ *var of* HAPUKU

ha·bu·tai *or* **ha·bu·tae** \ˈhäbəˌtī\ *n* -s [Jap *habutae*, lit., glossy silk] **:** a soft lightweight Japanese silk in plain weave

ha·ček \ˈhaˌchek\ *n* -s [Czech] **:** a diacritic ˇ placed over a letter (as in č, ě, ğ, š) to modify it **:** an inverted circumflex — called also *wedge*

ha·cen·da·do \ˌ(h)äsenˈdä(ˌ)dō\ *also* **ha·ci·en·da·do** \-sēe-\ *n* -s [Sp, fr. *hacienda*] **:** the owner or proprietor of a hacienda **:** rural landlord **:** LANDOWNER

ha·cen·de·ro \ˌ(h)äsenˈde(ˌ)rō\ *also* **ha·ci·en·de·ro** \-sēen-\ *n* -s [Sp, fr. *hacienda* + *-ero* -er] **:** HACENDADO

ha·ché \(h)äˈshā\ *adj* [F, fr. past part. of *hacher* to chop up, mince, hash, hatch (a map) — more at HASH] **:** MINCED, HASHED

[1]**ha·chure** \haˈshu̇(ə)r, ˈhashər\ *also* **hatch·ure** \ˈhachə(r)\ *n* -s [F, *hachure*, fr. *hacher* + *-ure*] **:** a short line used for shading and denoting surfaces in relief (as in map drawing) and drawn in the direction of sloping, being short, broad, and close together for a steep slope and long, narrow, and far apart for a gentle slope — compare CONTOUR LINE

[2]**hachure** \"\ *also* **hatchure** \"\ *vt* -ED/-ING/-S **:** to shade with or show by hachures — compare CROSSHATCH

h acid *n, usu cap H* **:** a crystalline acid $H_2NC_{10}H_4(OH)(SO_3H)_2$ made from naphthalene and used as a dye intermediate; 8-amino-1-naphthol-3,6-disulfonic acid

ha·ci·en·da \ˌ(h)äsēˈendə, ˌ(h)as-\ *n* -s [Sp, fr. L *facienda*, things to be done, neut. pl. of *faciendus*, fut. passive part. of *facere* to do, make — more at DO] **1 a :** a large estate (as a ranch or farm) in present or formerly Spanish-speaking countries **:** PLANTATION **b :** the main building of a farm or ranch **c :** the buildings of a mining or manufacturing establishment **2** *chiefly Southwest* **:** a ranch dwelling typically with low rambling lines and wide porches **3 :** the state revenue or its administration in a Spanish-speaking country ⟨was appointed minister of ~⟩

[1]**hack** \ˈhak\ *vb* -ED/-ING/-S [ME *hakken*, fr. OE *-haccian* (attested in *tōhaccian* to chop to pieces); akin to MLG *hacken* to hack, OHG *hacchōn*, OE *haca* door fastener, ON *haka* chin — more at HOOK] *vt* **1 a :** to cut with repeated irregular or unskillful blows ⟨was ~*ed* to pieces with swords⟩ ⟨plaster had been ~*ed* out of the wall⟩ **b :** to sever with repeated blows ⟨~*ed* off a bough with his hunting knife⟩ **c :** to mangle or mutilate with or as if with cutting blows ⟨we ~*ed* reputations to pieces —H.J.Laski⟩ ⟨the original story had been ~*ed* almost beyond recognition⟩ **d :** to trim or shape by or as if by crude or ruthless strokes ⟨lyrical expressions ~*ed* out with broad strokes of a brush charged with pure color —F.J.Mather⟩ ⟨huge sums were ~*ed* off the original appropriation⟩ **2 :** to clear (a path or area) by cutting away vegetation ⟨~*ed* their way through the jungle⟩ ⟨farms ~*ed* out of the wilderness⟩ **3 a :** to break up the surface of (land) **b :** to break up the soil and sow (seed) at the same operation — used with *in* ⟨~ in wheat⟩ **c :** to cut, trim, or uproot with a hack, hook, or sickle **4 :** CHIP *vt* 4 **5 a :** to roughen or dress (stone or concrete) with a hack hammer **b :** to tilt (a face brick) slightly in a wall so that the bottom is set in to prevent shadows **c :** to interrupt (a course of stones) by the use of two smaller courses in walling **6 :** to kick the shins of (an opposing player) in rugby **7** *chiefly Midland* **a :** ACHIEVE, MANAGE ⟨I can't quite ~ it⟩ **b :** to put up with **:** TOLERATE ⟨I can't ~ something like stealing —B.J.Friedman⟩ **8 :** to call out or give directions to (a bird dog) **9 :** to enter (a gamecock) in a single match **10** *chiefly Midland* **:** to disconcert and embarrass esp. by teasing **:** HECKLE ⟨he was so ~*ed* he could hardly talk⟩ ~ *vi* **1 :** to make cutting blows or rough cuts **:** CHOP ⟨~*ing* away at the vines and shrubs⟩ **2** *now dial Eng* **:** to speak haltingly **:** STAMMER **3 :** to cough in a short dry manner **:** cause short dry coughing ⟨a ~*ing* asthma⟩ **4 a :** to kick or kick at a rugby opponent's shins deliberately **b :** to strike or hold the arm of a basketball opponent with the hand **5** *slang* **:** LOAF, IDLE, KNOCK — used with *around* ⟨~*ing* around at the corner drugstore —Ruth McKenney⟩

[2]**hack** \"\ *n* -s [ME *hak;* akin to MHG & MD *hacke* mattock, hoe, pickax; derivatives fr. the root of E [1]*hack*] **1 :** a tool or implement for hacking (as a pick, mattock, or hoe) **2 :** CUT, NICK, NOTCH; *esp* **:** a blaze cut in a tree **3** *now dial Eng* **:** a stumbling or stammering in speech **4 :** a short dry cough **5 a :** a hacking blow ⟨a vicious ~ across the neck stunned him⟩ **b :** TRY, ATTEMPT, TURN, WHACK ⟨let me take a ~ at it⟩ **c :** an individual match of gamecocks **6 :** a kick on the shins in rugby **7 :** a foothold cut in the ice four yards behind the tee in curling **8 a** *chiefly Midland* **:** a state of embarrassed confusion — often used with *under* ⟨he put Joe under ~ teasing him about his girl⟩ **b :** restriction to quarters as punishment for naval officers — usu. used with *under* ⟨he had some of the officers under ~ and some of the crew grumbling —Fletcher Pratt⟩

[3]**hack** \"\ *n* -s [blend of [1]*hatch* and [1]*heck*] **1 a :** the board on which a falcon's meat is served **b :** the state of partial liberty in which a falcon is kept before training — used chiefly with *at* ⟨kept at ~⟩ ⟨flying at ~⟩ **2 :** FRAME, GRATING: as **a :** a frame for drying fish or cheese **b :** a rack for feeding cattle **c :** a grating in a millrace or above a dam **3 :** a long low pile into which bricks are built for drying after being molded

[4]**hack** \"\ *vt* -ED/-ING/-S **1 :** to keep (a hawk) in a state of partial liberty **2 :** to put (fish or cheese) on a frame for drying

[5]**hack** \"\ *n* -s [short for *hackney*] **1 a** (1) **:** a horse let out for common hire (2) **:** a horse used in all kinds of work **b :** a horse worn out in service **:** JADE **c :** a light easy saddle horse; *esp* **:** a three-gaited saddle horse **2 a :** a coach or carriage let for hire **:** HACKNEY ⟨on horse, on foot, in ~*s* and gilded chariots —Alexander Pope⟩ **b** *slang* **:** HEARSE **c** (1) **:** TAXICAB (2) **:** CABDRIVER **d** *slang* **:** CABOOSE **3 a :** one who hires out his professional service **:** one who forfeits individual freedom of action or initiative or professional integrity in exchange for wages or other assured reward **:** HIRELING, MERCENARY ⟨party ~*s* have replaced earnest New Dealers —*New Republic*⟩; *esp* **:** a writer who works on order from publishers **b :** a writer whose writings aim mainly at commercial success rather than literary quality **c** *slang* **:** a prison guard or custodian **4 :** a watch or inferior chronometer for use in place of the standard chronometer in marking time when taking observations at sea

[6]**hack** \"\ *adj* **1 :** working for hire ⟨~ attorney⟩ ⟨~ critic⟩ **2 :** performed by, suited to, or characteristic of a hack **:** MEDIOCRE, UNINSPIRED ⟨~ writing⟩ ⟨the staging and lighting were mostly on a ~ level —*New Republic*⟩ **3 :** HACKNEYED, TRITE ⟨~ dramatic scenes⟩

[7]**hack** \"\ *vb* -ED/-ING/-S *vt* **1 :** to make trite and commonplace by frequent and indiscriminate use ⟨the word "remarkable" has been so ~*ed* —J.H.Newman⟩ **2** *archaic* **:** to employ as a hack writer **3 :** to use as a hack **:** let out (as a horse) for hire ~ *vi* **1 :** to ride or drive at an ordinary pace or over the roads as distinguished from racing or riding across country **2 :** to become exposed or offered to common use for hire ⟨was then ~*ed* in the park for a year before going to stud —Dennis Craig⟩ **3 :** to live the life of a literary drudge or hack **:** do hack writing **4 :** to ride in a hackney coach or in a taxicab **5 :** to operate a taxicab

hackamatak *var of* HACKMATACK

hack·a·more \ˈhakəˌmō(ə)r, -ō(ə)r, -ōə, -ȯ(ə)\ *n* -s [by folk etymology fr. Sp *jáquima*, fr. OSp *xaquima*, fr. Ar *shakīmah*] **1 :** a bridle that consists of a halter often of soft rope or braided horsehair, has a loop capable of being tightened about the nose in place of a bit, and is used esp. in breaking and training horses **2 :** a primitive or emergency bridle consisting of a continuous length of rope or rawhide with a slip noose at one end that is passed over the lower jaw, the free end being looped over the head behind the ears and slipped through the noose on the opposite side so as to serve as a single rein

hackamore knot *n* **:** a knot that consists of a loop formed by concentric hitches and is used as a sling for a jug or bottle or as a rope bridle for a horse

hackamore knot

hackbarrow \ˈ=,=(,)=\ *n* [[3]*hack* + *barrow*] **:** a barrow for taking bricks from the molders to the hacks

hackberry \ˈhak- — *see* BERRY\ *n* [alter. of *hagberry*] **1 :** any of several No. American trees or shrubs of the genus *Celtis; esp* **:** a large round-headed tree (*C. occidentalis*) of eastern and central U.S. that has dark purple edible berries and is sometimes planted for shade or in shelterbelts — called also *sugarberry* **2 :** the pale to grayish or greenish yellow moderately hard tough wood of hackberry (esp. *C. occidentalis*)

hack·but \ˈhakˌbət\ *or* **hag·but** \-ag,-\ *n* -s [MF *haguebute, hacquebute*, modif. of MD *hakebusse* — more at HARQUEBUS] **:** HARQUEBUS

hack·but·eer \ˌhakbəˈti(ə)r\ *or* **hack·but·ter** \ˈhakˌbəd·ə(r)\ *n* -s [MF *haquebutier, hacquebutier*, fr. *haquebute, hacquebute* + *-ier* -er] **:** a soldier armed with a hackbut

hacked *past of* HACK

hacked bolt *n* [fr. past part. of [1]*hack*] **:** JAG BOLT

hack·ee \ˈhakē\ *n* -s [prob. of imit. origin] **:** CHIPMUNK

[1]**hack·er** \ˈhakə(r)\ *n* -s [[1]*hack* + *-er* (n. suffix)] **1 :** one that hacks: as **a** *dial Eng* **:** a hand implement or hooked fork for grubbing out roots **b :** one that handles green brick in ceramics manufacturing **c :** CHIPPER d **2 :** one who is inexperienced or unskilled in a sport ⟨an insouciance and grace in the man's movements which mean the difference between a willing courageous ~ . . . and a great artist —Barnaby Conrad⟩

[2]**hacker** \"\ *vi* -ED/-ING/-S [[1]*hack* + *-er* (v. suffix)] *dial Eng* **:** to hesitate in speaking **:** STAMMER

[3]**hacker** \"\ *n* -s [[5]*hack* + *-er*] **:** CABDRIVER

hack·ery \ˈhakərē\ *n* -ES [perh. fr. Bengali *hākārī* shouting (of drivers), fr. *hākā* shout] *India* **:** a bullock cart

hack hammer *n* [[2]*hack*] **:** a hammer that resembles an adz and is used in dressing stone and roughening

hack·ia \ˈhakēə\ *n* -s [fr. a native name in Brit. Guiana] **:** any of several tropical American trees (as of the genus *Tabebuia*) that yield notably hard heavy durable timber

hack·ie \ˈhakē, -ki\ *n* -s [[5]*hack* + *-ie*] **:** CABDRIVER

hacking *n* -s [fr. gerund of [1]*hack*] **:** the system of low cuts or scratches and grooves in a lap to hold diamond powder for cutting and polishing gems

hacking coat *or* **hacking jacket** *n* [fr. pres. part. of [7]*hack*] **:** a riding jacket with slits at the side or at the back and slanted flap pockets

hacking knife *n* [fr. pres. part. of [1]*hack*] **:** a knife with a short blade and stout handle used for rough work (as removing old putty)

hack·ing·ly *adv* **:** in a hacking manner

[1]**hack·le** \ˈ(h)akəl\ *n* -s [ME *hakel*, fr. OE *hacele* cloak; akin to OHG *hachul* mantle, ON *hökoll*, Goth *hakuls*, and prob. to OE *hēcen* kid, MLG *hōken* kid, OSlav *koza* goat] *now dial Eng* **:** any of various coverings: as **a :** the natural coat of an animal **b :** a bird's plumage **c :** a straw covering for a bee skep

[2]**hackle** \"\ *vt* -ED/-ING/-S *dial Eng* **:** to cover with a hackle

[3]**hack·le** \ˈhakəl\ *n* -s [ME *hakell, hekele* — more at HATCHEL] **1 :** a comb or board with long metal teeth for dressing flax, hemp, or jute **2 a :** one of the long narrow feathers on the neck or saddle of a bird (as the domestic fowl) **b :** the neck plumage of the male domestic fowl — see COCK illustration **3 hackles** *pl* **a :** erectile hairs along the neck and back of a dog or other animal **b :** TEMPER, DANDER ⟨don't get your ~*s* up about nothing⟩ **4 a** *or* **hackle fly :** an artificial fishing fly made chiefly of the filaments of a cock's neck feathers **b :** filaments of cock feather projecting downward from the head of an artificial fly — see FLY illustration

[4]**hackle** \"\ *vt* **hackled; hackled; hackling** \-k(ə)liŋ\ **hackles 1 :** to separate the long fibers of (flax, hemp, or jute) from waste material and from each other by combing with a hackle **2 :** to furnish (a fishing fly) with a hackle

[5]**hackle** \"\ *vt* -ED/-ING/-S [freq. of [1]*hack*] **:** to chop up or chop off roughly **:** HACK

[6]**hackle** \"\ *n* -s *often attrib* **:** fracture (as of glass) that results in hackly edges ⟨the coarser the ~ the more violent and sudden was the parting of the glass —C.J.Phillips⟩ ⟨~ marks⟩ ⟨~ structure⟩

hackleback \ˈ==,=\ *n* -s [[3]*hackle* + *back*] **1** *also* **hackleback sturgeon** [so called fr. the projecting scales on its back] **:** SHOVELNOSE STURGEON **2 :** an untrimmed barrel stave

hack·ler \ˈhak(ə)lə(r)\ *n* -s [[4]*hackle* + *-er*] **:** one that hackles; *esp* **:** a worker who hackles hemp, flax, or broomcorn

hacklog \ˈ=,=\ *n* [[1]*hack* + *log*] **:** CHOPPING BLOCK

hack·ly \ˈhak(ə)lē, -li\ *adj, sometimes* -ER/-EST [[5]*hackle* + *-y*] **:** looking as if hacked **:** ROUGH, JAGGED, BROKEN ⟨~ fracture surface of a mineral⟩

hack·man \ˈhakmən\ *n, pl* **hackmen** [[5]*hack* + *man*] **:** CABDRIVER

hack·man·ite \ˈhakməˌnīt\ *n* -s [Victor *Hackman*, 19th cent. Finnish scientist + E *-ite*] **:** a sodalite containing a little sulfur and usu. fluorescing orange or red under ultraviolet light

[1]**hack·ma·tack** \ˈhakməˌtak\ *n* -s [of Algonquian origin; akin to Abnaki *akemantak* snowshoe wood] **1 :** any of several coniferous trees: as **a :** a tamarack (*Larix laricina*) **b :** COMMON JUNIPER **2 :** the wood of hackmatack **3 :** BALSAM POPLAR

[2]**hackmatack** \"\ *also* **hack·a·ma·tak** \-kəm-\ *n* -s [alter. of *tacamahac*] **:** a tree (*Calophyllum tacamahaca*) that produces tacamahac

[1]**hack·ney** \ˈhaknē, -ni\ *n* [ME *hakeney, hakenai*, prob. fr. *Hakeneye* Hackney, formerly a town, now a metropolitan borough of London, England] **1** -s **a :** a horse suitable for ordinary riding or driving **:** NAG **b :** a trotting horse used chiefly for driving **2 a** *usu cap* **:** a breed of rather compact usu. chestnut, bay, or brown horses with a conspicuously high knee and hock flexion in stepping that originated in and about Norfolk, England as a result of interbreeding local trotting mares with Thoroughbred and Arabian sires **b** -s *often cap* **:** a horse of this breed **3** -s **a** *obs* **:** a horse or pony kept for hire **b** *obs* **:** one that works for hire **:** DRUDGE, SLAVE **c** *obs* **:** PROSTITUTE **4** -s **:** a carriage or automobile kept for hire **:** HACK, CAB

[2]**hackney** \"\ *adj* **1 :** kept for public hire ⟨~ cab⟩ ⟨~ carriage⟩ **2 :** HACKNEYED **3** *archaic* **:** done or suitable for doing by a drudge

[3]**hackney** \"\ *vt* -ED/-ING/-S **1 a :** to make common or frequent use of (as a horse) **:** wear out in common service **b :** to make trite, vulgar, or commonplace **2** *obs* **:** to drive hard **:** wear out by driving **3** *archaic* **a :** to make coarse (the sensibilities) **b :** to make sophisticated or jaded (as through worldly experience) ⟨~*ed* as he was in the ways of life —Tobias Smollett⟩

hackney coach *n* **:** a coach used as a hackney carriage; *esp* **:** a four-wheeled carriage drawn by two horses and having seats for six persons

hackneyed *adj* [fr. past part. of [3]*hackney*] **:** COMMONPLACE ⟨~ phrase⟩ ⟨~ metaphor⟩ ⟨histrionic rhetoric and ~ gesture —H.V.Gregory⟩ **syn** see TRITE

hack·ney·man \ˈhaknēmən, -nim-\ *n, pl* **hackneymen** [ME *hakeneyman*, fr. *hakeney* + *man*] **:** a man who hires out horses and carriages

hackney pony *n, often cap H* **:** a Hackney horse less than 14.2 hands high

hacks *pres 3d sing of* HACK, *pl of* HACK

hacksaw \ˈ=,=\ *n* [[1]*hack* + *saw*] **:** a hand or power-driven fine-tooth saw with blade under tension in a bow-shaped frame for cutting metal or other hard materials

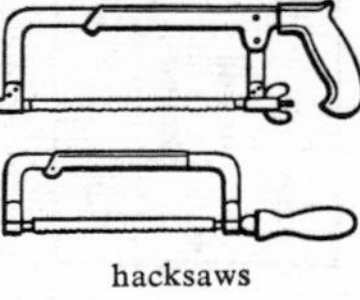
hacksaws

hackster *n* -s [[1]*hack* + *-ster*] **1** *obs* **:** RUFFIAN, ASSASSIN **2** *obs* **:** PROSTITUTE

hack·thorn \ˈhakˌthȯrn\ *n* [part modif., part trans. of Afrik *haak-doring*, fr. *haak* hook + *doring* thorn] **:** a southern African wattle (*Acacia detinens*)

hacktree \ˈ=,=\ *n* [*hack*berry + *tree*] **:** HACKBERRY 1

hack watch *n* [[5]*hack*] **:** a watch having a device for stopping the balance so that the hour, minute, and sweep-second hands may be reset at a desired instant — compare [5]HACK 4

hackwork \ˈ=,=\ *n* [[6]*hack* + *work*] **:** literary, artistic, or other professional work done on order or according to formula or conformity with commercial standards of quality; *esp* **:** work done by a hack writer ⟨the evil effect of ~ and two wars upon an outstanding talent —V.S.Pritchett⟩

hacky \ˈhakē\ *adj* -ER/-EST [[1]*hack* + *-y*] **:** HACKING ⟨a ~ cough⟩

hacqueton *var of* HAQUETON

had *past of* HAVE — see PAST PERFECT

ha·da·da \ˈhadədə\ *n* -s [Afrik *hadida*, of imit. origin] **:** HADEDAH IBIS

hadarim *pl of* HEDER

had·bot *or* **had·bote** \ˈhädˌbōt\ *n* -s [OE *hādbōt*, fr. *hād* person, degree + *bōt* remedy, recompense — more at -HOOD, BOOT] **:** recompense demanded under old English law for violence or insult to a person in holy orders

hadden *Scot past part of* HOLD

had·der \ˈhädər\ *chiefly Scot var of* HEATHER

haddest *archaic past 2d sing of* HAVE

had·die \ˈhädi\ *n* -s [by alter.] *Scot* **:** HADDOCK

had·ding·ton·shire \ˈhadiŋtənˌshi(ə)r, -ˌshər\ *or* **haddington** *adj, usu cap* [fr. *Haddingtonshire* or *Haddington* county (now usu. called *East Lothian*), Scotland] **:** EAST LOTHIAN

had·do \ˈha(ˌ)dō\ *n* -s [Nisqualli *huddoh*] **:** HUMPBACK SALMON

had·dock \ˈhadək\ *n, pl* **haddock** *also* **haddocks** [ME *haddok*] **1 :** an important food fish (*Melanogrammus aeglefinus*) of the family Gadidae that is usu. smaller than the common cod, has a black lateral line and a dark spot just behind the gills, and occurs on both sides of the Atlantic from Iceland south to the Mediterranean and Cape Hatteras **2 a :** HAKE **b :** ROSEFISH

had·dock·er \-kə(r)\ *n* -s **:** one that fishes for haddock

[1]**hade** \ˈ(h)ād\ *n* -s [origin unknown] *now dial Eng* **:** an unplowed strip left between plowed parts of a field

[2]**hade** \ˈhād\ *vi* -ED/-ING/-S [origin unknown] **:** to deviate from the vertical (as of a vein, fault, or lode)

[3]**hade** \"\ *n* -s **:** the angle made by a rock fault plane or a vein with the vertical

ha·de·an \(ˈ)hāˈdēən\ *adj, usu cap* **:** of, relating to, or characteristic of Hades

ha·de·dah ibis \ˈhadədə-\ *n* [Afrik *hadida*, of imit. origin] **:** a largely grayish brown African ibis (*Hagedashia hagedash*) having the wing coverts tinged with iridescent green

ha·den·doa *or* **ha·den·do·wa** \həˈdendəwə\ *n, pl* **hadendoa** *or* **hadendoas** *or* **hadendowa** *or* **hadendowas** *usu cap* **1 :** a chiefly nomadic Beja-speaking people of Nubia between the Nile and the Red sea related to the Beni Amer and Bisharin **2 :** a member of the Hadendoa people

ha·des \ˈhāˌdēz\ *n, pl* **hades** *usu cap* [fr. *Hades*, god of the underworld, abode of the dead in Greek mythology, fr. Gk *Haidēs, Aidēs*] **1 :** the abode or state of the dead **:** the place of departed spirits — compare NETHERWORLD, SHEOL **2 :** HELL ⟨go to ~⟩ ⟨hotter than ~ out on the firing range⟩ ⟨what in ~ are you doing here⟩

hadfield manganese steel \ˈhadˌfēl(d)-\ *n, usu cap H* [after Sir Robert *Hadfield* †1940 Eng. metallurgist] **:** a wear-resistant austenitic steel containing about 12 percent manganese and 1.2 percent carbon

[1]**ha·dhra·mau·tian** *or* **ha·dra·mau·tian** \ˌhädrəˈmȯshən\ *adj, usu cap* [*Hadhramaut, Hadramaut*, region of southeastern Arabia + E *-ian*] **:** of, relating to, or characteristic of the land, people, or dialect of Hadhramaut in southeastern Arabia

[2]**hadhramautian** *or* **hadramautian** \"\ *n* -s *usu cap* **:** HADHRAMI

ha·dhra·mau·tic \-ōd·ik\ *n* -s *usu cap* [*Hadhramaut* + E *-ic*] **:** the Arabic dialect of Hadhramaut

ha·dhra·mi *or* **ha·dra·mi** \ˈhädrəmē\ *n, pl* **hadhrami** *also* **hadhramis** *or* **hadrami** *also* **hadramis** *usu cap* **1 :** an Arabian theocratic people living in the region between Aden and Oman in southern Arabia **2 :** a member of the Hadhrami people

hading *n* -s [fr. gerund of [2]*hade*] **:** [3]HADE

ha·dith \həˈdēth\ *also* **ha·dit** \-ēt\ *n, pl* **hadith** *or* **hadiths** *also* **hadit** *or* **hadits** *often cap* [Ar *hadīth*] **1 :** a narrative record of the sayings or customs of Muhammad and his companions **2 :** the collective body of traditions relating to Muhammad and his companions

hadj *var of* HAJJ

hadj·e·mi *or* **haj·e·mi** \ˈhajəmē\ *n* -s *cap* [Per] **:** a Persian of mixed Iranian and Turkish or Turkic stock

hadji *var of* HAJI

had·land \ˈ(h)adlənd\ *dial Eng var of* HEADLAND

had·ley chest \ˈhadlē-\ *n, usu cap H* [fr. *Hadley*, Mass.] **:** an Early American chest that has three panels in the front, a well, and one, two, or rarely three drawers and that is ornamented over the entire front with flat carving usu. involving a tulip motif and sometimes including the initials of the owner

had·na \ˈhadnə\ [by alter.] *Scot* **:** had not

hadn't \ˈhadᵊn(t)\ [by contr.] **:** had not

hadn't ought *chiefly dial* **:** ought not — usu. used with *to* ⟨you really *hadn't ought* to do that⟩

had ought *chiefly dial* **:** OUGHT — usu. used with *to* ⟨I *had ought* to go but I don't want to⟩

hadr- *or* **hadro-** *comb form* [NL, fr. L, fr. Gk, fr. *hadros* thick, bulky; akin to Gk *hadēn* enough — more at SAD] **:** thick ⟨*hadrome*⟩ **:** heavy ⟨*Hadrosaurus*⟩

had·rome \ˈhaˌdrōm\ *also* **had·rom** \ˈhadrəm\ *n* -s [G *hadrom*, fr. *hadr-* + *-om* -ome] **1 :** the part of the mestome that conducts water **2 :** the somewhat rudimentary xylem in cryptogams

had·ro·me·ri·na \ˌhadrōməˈrīnə\ *n pl, cap* [NL, fr. *hadr-* + *mer-* (part) + *-ina*] **:** an order of Demospongiae including the boring sponges

had·ro·mycosis \ˈhadrō+\ *n* [NL, fr. *hadr-* + *mycosis*] **:** infestation of the xylem of a plant by a fungus; *also* **:** a plant disease due to such a cause

had·ro·my·cot·ic \ˌhadrō(ˌ)mīˈkäd·ik\ *adj* [fr. NL *hadromycosis*, after such pairs as NL *psychosis:* E *psychotic*] **:** relating to or caused by hadromycosis

had·ro·saur \ˈhadrəˌsȯ(ə)r, -ȯ(ə)\ *n* -s [NL *Hadrosaurus*] **:** a dinosaur of the genus *Hadrosaurus* or family Hadrosauridae **:** DUCK-BILLED DINOSAUR

had·ro·sau·rus \ˌ==ˈsȯrəs\ *n, cap* [NL, fr. *hadr-* + *-saurus*] **:** a genus (the type of a family Hadrosauridae) of heavy herbivorous dinosaurs found in the Cretaceous of No. America that attained a length of over thirty feet and had a large head with a broad bill like that of a duck and numerous small teeth

hadst *archaic past 2d sing of* HAVE

hae *chiefly Scot var of* HAVE *& chiefly Scot pres 1st sing & pres pl & Scot pres 2d sing of* HAVE

haec·ce·i·tas \hekˈsēəˌtas, hēk-\ *n* -ES [ML] **:** HAECCEITY

haec·ce·i·ty *or* **hec·ce·i·ty** \-əd·ē\ *n* -ES [ML *haecceitas*, fr. L *haec, haecce*, fem. of *hic, hicce* this + *-itas* -ity] **:** the status of being an individual or a particular nature **:** INDIVIDUALITY, SPECIFICITY, THISNESS; *specif* **:** what makes something to be an ultimate reality different from any other — compare QUIDDITY 2

[1]**haeck·e·li·an** \(ˈ)heˈkēlēən\ *adj, usu cap* [Ernst H. *Haeckel* †1919, Ger. biologist + E *-ian*] **:** relating to Haeckel or his theories — compare RECAPITULATION THEORY

[2]**haeckelian** \"\ *n* -s *usu cap* **:** a believer in Haeckel's theories

haeck·el·ism \'hekə,lizəm\ *n* -s *usu cap* [Ernst H. *Haeckel* + E *-ism*] **:** Haeckel's theories and speculations

haed *past of* HA, *Scot past of* HAVE

haeing *Scot pres part of* HAVE

haeltzuk *usu cap, var of* HEILTSUK

haem *var of* HEME

haem- *or* **haemo-** — see HEM-

haema- — see HEMA-

hae·ma·dip·sa \,hēmə'dipsə, ,hem-\ *n, cap* [NL, fr. *hem-* + Gk *dipsa* thirst] **:** a genus of small tropical land leeches that are troublesome to men and animals esp. because their bites result in prolonged bleeding

hae·ma·go·gus \-'gōgəs\ *n, cap* [NL, fr. LL, adj., drawing off blood, fr. Gk *haimagōgos*, fr. *haim-* hem- + *-agōgos* (fr. *agein* to lead, drive) — more at AGENT] **:** a genus of strong-flying diurnal Neotropical mosquitoes including several vectors of jungle yellow fever

hae·ma·moe·ba \-'mēbə\ [NL, fr. *hem-* + *amoeba*] *syn of* PLASMODIUM

hae·man·thus \hē'man(t)thəs\ *n, cap* [NL, fr. *hem-* + *-anthus*; fr. the color of some of the flowers] **:** a genus of African bulbous herbs (family Amaryllidaceae) comprising the blood lilies and having flowers in a dense head with a whorl of colored spathes

hae·ma·phy·sa·lis \,hēmə'fīsələs, ,hem-\ *n, cap* [NL, fr. *hem-* + Gk *physallis* bladder] **:** a cosmopolitan genus of small eyeless ticks (family Ixodidae) some of which are disease carriers

haemat- *or* **haemato-** — see HEMAT-

hae·mat·i·num \hē'madənəm\ *also* **hae·mat·i·non** \-d·ə,nän\ *n* -s [NL, fr. neut. of L *haematinus* blood-colored, fr. Gk *haimatinos* bloody, fr. *haimat-* hemat- + *-inos* -ine] **:** a hard opaque red glass made by the ancients; *also* **:** a modern imitation of this

hae·ma·to·bran·chia \,hēməd·ō'braŋkēə, ,hem-\ *n pl, cap* [NL, fr. *hemat-* + *-branchia*] *in some classifications* **:** a division of arthropods consisting of the trilobites, eurypterids, and king crabs — **haem·a·to·branch·i·ate** \¦≡≡≡¦braŋkēət, -ē,āt\ *adj*

hae·ma·to·do·cha \,hēməd·ō'dōkə, ,hem-, hē,mad·ə'-\ *n* -s [NL, fr. *hemat-* + Gk *dochē* receptacle] **:** a fibrous elastic sac in the palpus of male spiders that is distended with hemolymph during pairing

hae·ma·to·pi·nus \-'pīnəs\ *n, cap* [NL, fr. *hemat-* + *-pinus* (fr. Gk *pinein* to drink)] **:** a genus of sucking lice including various serious pests of domestic animals

hae·mat·o·pus \hē'madəpəs\ *n, cap* [NL, fr. *hemat-* + *-pus*] **:** a genus (the type of the family Haematopodidae) of shorebirds consisting of the oyster catchers

hae·ma·tox·y·lon \,hēmə'täksə,län, ,hem-\ *n* [NL, fr. *hemat-* + *-xylon*; fr. its red color] **1** *cap* **:** a genus of tropical American bushy and usu. thorny trees (family Leguminosae) having pinnate leaves and small yellow flowers borne in showy axillary racemes — see LOGWOOD **2** -s **:** the wood or dye of logwood

-hae·mia \'hēmēə\ — see -EMIA

haemin *var of* HEMIN

hae·mo·bartonella \¦hēmō, ¦hemō+\ *n* [NL, fr. *hemat-* + *Bartonella*] **1** *cap* **:** a genus of blood parasites (family Bartonellaceae) of various mammals believed to be rickettsiae related to the organism causing Oroya fever in man but not known to multiply in the host tissues or to cause any cutaneous eruption **2** *pl* **haemobartonellae :** any organism of the genus *Haemobartonella*

hae·mo·do·ra·ce·ae \,hēmōdə'rāsē,ē, ,hem-\ *n pl, cap* [NL, fr. *Haemodorum*, type genus (fr. *hem-* + Gk *dōron* gift) + *-aceae*] **:** a family of chiefly tropical plants (order Liliales) having flowers with three stamens and an inferior ovary arranged in a complex panicled inflorescence — **hae·mo·do·ra·ceous** \¦≡≡≡¦rāshəs\ *adj*

haemoglobin *var of* HEMOGLOBIN

hae·mo·gregarina \¦hēmō, ¦hemō+\ *n, cap* [NL, fr. *hem-* + *Gregarina*] **:** a genus (the type of the family Haemogregarinidae) of coccidia that are parasites at different stages of their life cycle in the circulatory system of vertebrates and of the digestive tract of invertebrates — **hae·mo·gregarine** *or* **he·mo·gregarine** \"+\ *adj or n*

hae·mon·cho·sis \,hē,mäŋ'kōsəs\ *or* **hae·mon·chi·a·sis** \,hē,mäŋ'kīəsəs\ *n* -ES [NL, fr. *Haemonchus* + *-osis* or *-iasis*] **:** infestation with or disease caused by worms of the genus *Haemonchus* (esp. *H. contortus*), being typically characterized by anemia, digestive disturbances, and emaciation resulting from the bloodsucking habits of the worms

hae·mon·chus \hē'mäŋkəs\ *n, cap* [NL, fr. *hem-* + *-onchus* (irreg. fr. Gk *onkos* barb of an arrow)] **:** a widely distributed genus of nematode worms (family Trichostrongylidae) comprising chiefly a parasite (*H. contortus*) of the abomasum of sheep and other ruminants and rarely in man — see HAEMONCHOSIS

hae·mop·is \hē'mäpəs\ *n, cap* [NL, fr. *hem-* + *-opis*] **:** a genus of large aquatic leeches (family Hirudinidae) that have few teeth or none and feed chiefly on small aquatic invertebrates

hae·mo·pro·te·id \,hēmō'prōd·ēəd, ,hem-\ *adj* [NL *Haemoproteidae*] **:** of or relating to the Haemoproteidae or to protozoans of this family

hae·mo·pro·te·i·dae \,hēmō(,)prō'tēə,dē, ,hem-\ *n pl, cap* [NL, fr. *Haemoproteus*, type genus + *-idae*] **:** a family of Haemosporidia related to the malarial parasites but having the schizogenous phases typically in visceral endothelium of various birds and including the two genera *Haemoproteus* and *Leucocytozoon*

hae·mo·proteus \¦hēmō, ¦hemō+\ *n, cap* [NL, fr. *hem-* + *Proteus*] **:** a genus of protozoan parasites occurring in the blood of certain birds (as pigeons)

haem·or·rha·gia \,hemə'rājēə\ *n* -s [L — more at HEMORRHAGE] **:** HEMORRHAGE

hae·mo·spo·rid·ia \,hēmōspə'ridēə, ,hem-\ *n pl, cap* [NL, fr. *hem-* + *-sporidia*] **:** an order of minute telosporidian protozoans parasitic at some stage of the life cycle in the blood cells of vertebrates that includes the malaria parasites (family Plasmodiidae), numerous bird parasites (family Haemoproteidae), and the piroplasms and related pathogens of cattle (family Babesiidae) — **hae·mo·spo·rid·i·an** \¦≡≡≡¦ridēən\ *adj or n*

hae·mu·li·dae \hē'myülə,dē\ [NL, fr. *Haemulon*, type genus (fr. *hem-* + Gk *oulon* gum) + *-idae*] *syn of* POMADASIDAE

haen *chiefly Scot past part of* HAVE

haereditas *var of* HEREDITAS

ha·e·re·mai \'häə,rä'mī(,)ē, 'häərə,mī\ *interj* [Maori, lit., come here] *Austral & NewZeal* — used to express welcome

haeres *var of* HERES

haes *Scot pres 3d sing of* HAVE

haet \'hāt\ *n* -s [contr. of *hae it* (in such phrases as *Deil hae it!* Devil take it!)] *chiefly Scot* **:** a small quantity **:** PARTICLE **:** WHIT

haff \'häf\ *n* -s [G, fr. LG, fr. MLG *haf* sea — more at HAVEN] **:** a long shallow lagoon separated from the open sea by a narrow sandbar or barrier beach (as on the Baltic coast of Germany)

haf·fet *or* **haf·fit** \'hafət\ *n* -s [ME (Sc dial.) *halfheid*, fr. *half* + *heid*, Sc var. of *hed* head — more at HEAD] *Scot* **:** CHEEK, TEMPLE; *esp* **:** the hair growing at the temple

haff·lins \'häflənz\ *var of* HALFLINGS

ha·fiz \'häfəz\ *n, pl* **hafiz** *or* **hafis** \-əs\ [Ar *ḥāfiẓ*, lit., one who remembers] **:** a Muslim who knows the Koran by heart — used as a title of respect

haf·ner ware \'häfnə(r)-\ *n, usu cap H* [G *hafnerware* pottery fr. *hafner* potter + *ware*] **:** mid-16th century German earthenware often in the form of stove tiles and heavy vessels

haf·ni·um \'hafnēəm\ *n* -s [NL, fr. *Hafnia* (Copenhagen), Denmark] **:** a high-melting gray tetravalent metallic element closely resembling zirconium chemically, occurring in most zirconium minerals, and useful because of its ready emission of electrons (as in filaments for incandescent lamps) — symbol *Hf*; see ELEMENT table

¹haft \'haft, 'häft\ *n* -s [ME, fr. OE *hæft*; akin to OE *hæft* bond, fetter, captive, OHG *haft* fetter, captivity, *hefti* handle, ON *hapt* fetter, *hepti* handle, Goth *hafts* burdened, *hafjan* to carry — more at HEAVE] **:** the handle of a weapon (as a sword or dagger) or tool (as a sickle, awl, file)

²haft \"\ *vt* -ED/-ING/-S [ME *haften*, fr. *haft*, n.] **:** to set in or furnish with a haft ⟨~ a dagger⟩

³haft \'(h)aft\ *vb* -ED/-ING/-S [prob. of Scand origin; akin to ON *heftha* to gain (land) by right of occupation, *hefth* possession, act of gaining by occupation, ON *hafa* to have — more at HAVE] *vt, dial Brit* **:** to accustom (sheep) to a different pasture ~ *vi, dial Brit* **:** to become settled or established esp. in a place of residence ⟨we are now nicely ~*ed* here⟩

⁴haft \"\ *n* -s **1** *dial Brit* **:** an established pasture **2** *dial Brit* **:** a dwelling place

haf·ta·rah *or* **haph·ta·rah** *or* **haf·to·rah** *or* **haph·to·rah** \,häftä'rä, häf'tōrə\ *n, pl* **haf·ta·roth** \,häftä'rōth\ *or* **haf·ta·rot** \-ōt\ *or* **haftarahs** *or* **haphtaroth** *or* **haphtarot** *or* **haphtarahs** *or* **haftoroth** *or* **haftorot** *or* **haftorahs** *or* **haphtoroth** *or* **haphtorot** *or* **haphtorahs** [Heb *haphṭārāh* conclusion] **:** one of the biblical selections esp. from the Books of the Prophets bearing on and read immediately after the parashah at the conclusion of the Jewish synagogue service on sabbaths, festivals, and fast days

¹hag \'hag, -aa(ə)g, -aig\ *n* -s [ME *hagge, hegge*, prob. fr. a shortened form of OE *hægtesse* harpy, witch; akin to MD *haghetisse* witch, OHG *hagzissa, hagazussa* harpy, witch; all fr. a prehistoric WGmc compound whose components are akin respectively to OE *haga* hedge and to G dial. (Westphalia) *dūs* devil; akin to Norw *tysja* elf, crippled woman, Gaulish *dusius* demon, incubus, Corn *dus, diz* devil, OE *dūst* dust — more at HEDGE, DUST] **1** *archaic* **a :** a female demon **:** FURY, HARPY **b :** an evil or frightening spirit **:** ELF, BOGEY, HOBGOBLIN ⟨blue meager ~, or stubborn unlaid ghost —John Milton⟩ **c :** NIGHTMARE **2 :** a woman who has compacted with the devil **:** WITCH ⟨you secret, black and midnight ~*s* —Shak.⟩ **3 a :** an ugly or evil-looking old woman **b :** a woman of haggard or slatternly appearance **c** *obs* **:** an old man **4 :** HAGFISH **5** [by shortening] **:** HAGDON

²hag \'(h)ag\ *vt* **hagged; hagged; hagging; hags 1** *dial Brit* **:** HARASS, HARRY **2** *dial Brit* **:** to urge on **:** GOAD **3** *dial Brit* **:** to tire out **:** FATIGUE

³hag \"\ *n* -s [ME, prob. fr. ON *hagi* enclosed pasture; akin to OE *haga* hedge] *dial Eng* **:** an enclosed wooded area **:** WOODS

⁴hag \"\ *vt* **hagged; hagged; hagging; hags** [ME *haggen*, of Scand origin; akin to ON *höggva* to chop — more at HEW] *dial Brit* **:** HACK, CHOP, HEW

⁵hag \"\ *n* -s [of Scand origin; akin to ON *högg* stroke (as of an ax or sword), blow, ravine, *höggva* to chop] **1** *dial Brit* **:** NOTCH, HACK **2** *dial Brit* **a :** a section of timber marked off for felling **b :** felled timber or brushwood **3** *dial Brit* **:** QUAGMIRE, MARSH, BOG **4** *dial Brit* **:** a firm spot in a bog **5** *dial Brit* **a :** the projection of peat where cutting has stopped **b :** the overhanging edge of a stream

hag·berry \'(h)agbəri\ *n* [*hag-* (of Scand origin; akin to ON *heggr* bird cherry, Sw *hägg*, Dan *hæg*) + berry — more at HEDGE] *dial Brit* **:** EUROPEAN BIRD CHERRY

hagborn \'≡,≡\ *adj* [¹*hag* + *born*] **:** born of a witch

hagbut *var of* HACKBUT

hag·don \'hagdən\ *n* -s [origin unknown] **:** any of several seabirds chiefly of the No. Atlantic: as **a :** SHEARWATER **b :** FULMAR

ha·gen \'hägən\ *adj, usu cap* [fr. *Hagen*, Germany] **:** of or from the city of Hagen, Germany **:** of the kind or style prevalent in Hagen

ha·ge·nia \hə'jēnēə\ *n, cap* [NL, fr. Karl Gottfried *Hagen* †1829 Ger. botanist + NL *-ia*] **:** a genus of pinnate-leaved Ethiopian trees (family Rosaceae) having large panicles of flowers — see BRAYERA

hagfish \'≡,≡\ *n* [¹*hag* + *fish*] **:** any of several marine cyclostomes (order Hyperotreta) that are related to the lampreys and in general resemble eels but have a round mouth surrounded by eight tentacles, a single nostril opening behind the pharynx, a tongue with horny teeth, and rudimentary eyes and labyrinthine apparatus and that feed upon fishes by boring into their bodies and consuming their viscera and flesh

hagg \'(h)ag\ *var of* ⁵HAG

hag·ga·da *or* **hag·ga·dah** \hə'gädə, -gō(\ *n, pl* **hagga·doth** *or* **hagga·dot** \-¦,dōt(h), -ōs\ *usu cap* [Heb *haggādhāh*, fr. *higgīdh* to tell] **1** *or* **ag·ga·da** \ə'g-\ **:** explanatory matter occurring in rabbinical literature, often taking the form of story, anecdote, legend, or parable, and treating such varied subjects as astronomy, astrology, magic, medicine, mysticism **2 :** explanatory matter in the Talmud interpreting the Scriptures as distinguished from that regulating religious practice — compare HALAKAH, MIDRASH — **hag·gadic** \-'gadik, -'gäd-\ *also* **hag·gadi·cal** \-dəkəl\ *adj, often cap*

hag·ga·dist \hə'gädəst\ *n* -s *often cap* **:** a haggadic writer **:** a student of the Haggada — **hag·ga·dis·tic** \,hagə¦distik\ *adj, often cap*

¹hag·gard \'hagə(r)d, 'haig- *sometimes* 'haag-\ *adj* [MF *hagard*] **1 a** *of a hawk* **:** caught after acquiring adult plumage **:** UNTAMED **b** *obs* **:** INTRACTABLE, WILLFUL **c** *obs* **:** WANTON, UNCHASTE ⟨if I do prove her ~ . . . I'll whistle her off —Shak.⟩ **2 :** wild in appearance: as **a** *of the eyes* **:** wild and staring **b** *of a person* **:** WILD-EYED ⟨staring his eyes, and ~ was his look —John Dryden⟩ **c :** having a worn or emaciated appearance caused by privation, suffering, anxiety, or age **:** HARROWED, GAUNT ⟨thin and worn, ~ from sleeplessness —Adria Langley⟩ — **hag·gard·ly** *adv* — **hag·gard·ness** *n* -ES

²haggard \"\ *n* -s **1 :** an adult hawk caught wild — compare EYAS **2** *obs* **:** an intractable person; *esp* **:** a woman reluctant to yield to wooing ⟨I have loved this proud disdainful ~ —Shak.⟩

³hag·gard \'(h)agəd\ *n* -s [of Scand origin; akin to ON *heygarthr* stockyard, fr. *hey* hay + *garthr* yard — more at HAY, YARD] *dial Brit* **:** a small plot of farm land; *esp* **:** an open area between the house and barn for keeping cattle or storing grain

hagged \'(h)agd\ *adj* [¹*hag* + *-ed*] **1** *dial Brit* **a :** BEWITCHED **:** ENCHANTED **b :** resembling a witch or a hag **2** *dial Brit* **:** HAGGARD, GAUNT

hagging *pres part of* HAG

hag·gis \'hagəs\ *n* -ES [ME *hagese, hagws, hagas*, prob. fr. *haggen* to hack, chop — more at HAG] **:** a pudding esp. popular in Scotland made of the heart, liver, and lungs of a sheep or a calf minced with suet, onions, oatmeal, and seasonings and boiled in the stomach of the animal

hag·gish \'hagish\ *adj* [¹*hag* + *-ish*] **:** resembling or characteristic of a hag — **hag·gish·ly** *adv* — **hag·gish·ness** *n* -ES

¹hag·gle \'hagəl, -aig-\ *vb* **haggled; haggled; haggling** \-g(ə)liŋ\ **haggles** [freq. of ⁴*hag*] *vt* **1 :** to cut roughly or clumsily **:** HACK ⟨~ a branch off⟩ **2** *archaic* **:** to annoy or exhaust with wrangling or heckling **:** NAG ~ *vi* **1 :** to cut roughly or make clumsily **:** HACK ⟨~ at a branch of the tree⟩ **2 :** to bargain or make difficulties in reaching a bargain **:** WRANGLE ⟨when it comes to making peace, we must not ~ over trifles —H.J.Laski⟩ **3** *now chiefly dial* **:** to go wearily or haltingly

²haggle \"\ *n* -s **:** an act or instance of haggling

³hag·gle \'(h)agəl\ *n* -s [ME *hagel* — more at HAIL] *dial Eng* **:** HAIL

hag·gler \'hag(ə)lə(r), -aig-\ *n* -s **1 :** one that haggles **2** *dial chiefly Brit* **:** HUCKSTER **1**

hag·gy \'hagi\ *adj* -ER/-EST [⁵*hag* + *-y*] *chiefly Scot* **:** boggy and uneven

ha·gi \'hägē\ *n* -s [Jap] **:** a Japanese bush clover (*Lespedeza bicolor*)

hagi- *or* **hagio-** *comb form* [LL, fr. Gk, fr. *hagios*] **1 :** holy ⟨*hagiographa*⟩ ⟨*hagioscope*⟩ **2 :** saints ⟨*hagiography*⟩

ha·gia \'hājēə\ *n pl* [LGk, fr. neut. pl. of Gk *hagios*] **:** consecrated eucharistic elements in the Eastern Church

ha·gi·gah \hə'gēgə\ *or* **cha·gi·gah** \kə'-\ *n pl* [Heb *ḥăghīghāh*] **:** the voluntary sacrifices offered with the paschal lamb at the Passover and on other festivals by Jews on their pilgrimages to the temple at Jerusalem

hag·i·oc·ra·cy \,hagē'äkrəsē, ,hājē-\ *n* -ES [*hagi-* + *-cracy*] **:** government by a body of persons regarded as holy; *also* **:** a state so governed

hag·i·og·ra·pher \-fə(r)\ *n* -s [ML *hagiographus* (fr. LGk *hagiographos*) + E *-er*] **1 :** one of the writers of the 13 books forming the third division of the Hebrew Scriptures **2 :** a writer of hagiography

hag·i·o·graph·ic \¦hagēə¦grafik, ¦hājē-\ *or* **hag·i·o·graph·i·cal** \-fəkəl\ *adj* **:** of or relating to the 13 books forming the third division of the Hebrew Scriptures **:** of or relating to hagiography

hag·i·og·ra·phist \,hagē'ägrəfəst, ,hājē-\ *n* -s [LL *hagiographus* + E *ist*] **:** HAGIOGRAPHER

hag·i·og·ra·phy \-fē, -fi\ *n* -ES [*hagi-* + *-graphy*] **:** biography of saints **:** saints' lives **:** biography of an idealizing or idolizing character ⟨the tone is one of personal affection rather than of ~ or impartial assessment —*Times Lit. Supp.*⟩

hag·i·ol·a·ter \,hagē'äləd·ə(r), ,hājē-\ *n* -s [*hagi-* + *-later*] **:** one that invokes or worships saints

hag·i·ol·a·trous \¦≡≡'älə·trəs\ *adj* **:** of or relating to the invocation or worship of saints

hag·i·ol·a·try \,≡≡'älə·trē\ *n* -ES [*hagi-* + *-latry*] **:** the invocation or worship of saints

hag·i·o·lith \'hagēə,lith, 'hājē-\ *n* -s [*hagi-* + *-lith*] **:** a stone monument or edifice (as a dolmen, a menhir, or an obelisk) erected for religious or ceremonial purposes — **hag·i·o·lith·ic** \¦≡≡≡¦lithik\ *adj*

hag·i·o·log·ic \¦hagēō¦läjik, ¦hājē-\ *or* **hag·i·o·log·i·cal** \-jəkəl\ *adj* **:** of or relating to hagiology

hag·i·ol·o·gist \,hagē'äləjəst, ,hājē-\ *n* -s **:** one skilled in hagiology

hag·i·ol·o·gy \-jē\ *n* -ES [*hagi-* + *-logy*] **:** the history or description of sacred writings or of sacred persons: as **a :** a narrative of the lives of saints **b :** a catalog of saints

hag·i·o·scope \'hagēə,skōp, 'hājē-\ *n* -s [*hagi-* + *-scope*] **:** an opening in the interior walls of a cruciform church so placed as to afford a view of the altar to those in the transept — called *also squint* — **hag·i·o·scop·ic** \¦≡≡≡¦skäpik\ *adj*

hag·let \'haglət\ *n* -s [origin unknown] **:** SHEARWATER

hag·me·na \,hägmə'nā\ *sometimes cap, var of* HOGMANAY

hag moth *n* [¹*hag*] **:** a No. American eucleid moth (*Phobetron pithecium*) whose larva feeds on trees and shrubs

hagride \'≡,≡\ *vt* [¹*hag* + *ride*] **1 :** to afflict with or as if with a nightmare **:** oppress with dread or anxiety **:** HARASS, TORMENT ⟨the great martian panic which showed how *hagridden* the American public had become —D.W.Brogan⟩ **2 :** to burden unduly ⟨families *hagridden* by poverty would find . . . a better life —Dixon Wecter⟩ **:** OBSESS ⟨*hagridden* by social prejudice and suspicion —J.E.P.Grigg⟩

hags *pl of* HAG, *pres 3d sing of* HAG

hagseed \'≡,≡\ *n* [¹*hag* + *seed*] **:** the offspring of a witch

hag's taper \'hagz-\ *also* **hagtaper** \'≡,≡\ *n, pl* **hag's tapers** *also* **hagtapers** [alter. of earlier *higgis taper, hickis taper, higtaper*, fr. *higgis, hickis, hig* (origin unknown) + *taper* (candle)] **:** MULLEIN **:** GREAT MULLEIN

hagstone \'≡,≡\ *n* **:** a naturally perforated stone used as an amulet against witchcraft

hague \'hāg\ *adj, usu cap* [fr. (*The*) *Hague*, Netherlands] **:** of or from The Hague, capital of the Netherlands **:** of the kind or of style prevalent in the Hague

hag·worm \'(h)ag,wərm, -,wəm\ *n* [ME, prob. fr. *hagge* hag + *worm*] **1** *dial Eng* **a :** a common snake (as an adder or viper) **2** *dial Eng* **:** BLINDWORM

hah *var of* HA

¹ha–ha \(')hä¦hä\ *interj* [ME, fr. OE *ha ha*, of imit. origin] — used to express amusement or derision

²ha–ha \'hä,hä, ≡'≡\ *also* **haw–haw** \'hȯ,hȯ, ≡'≡\ *n* -s [F *haha*, prob. fr. *haha*, interj. used to express surprise] **:** SUNK FENCE

haham *var of* HAKAM

hahn·e·mann·ism \'hänəmə,nizəm\ *n* -s *usu cap* [Samuel *Hahnemann* †1843 Ger. physician + E *-ism*] **:** HOMEOPATHY

hai·a·ri \hī'ärē\ *n* -s [native name in British Guiana] **1 :** FISH POISON **2 :** a plant of the genus *Lonchocarpus* that contains rotenone

hai·a·tha·lah \,hīə'tälə\ *n, pl* **haiathalah** *usu cap* **:** EPHTHALITE

hai·da \'hīdə\ *n, pl* **haida** *or* **haidas** *usu cap* **1 a :** a Skittagetan people of the Queen Charlotte islands, British Columbia, and Prince of Wales Island, Alaska **b :** a member of such people **2 :** the language of the Haida people **3 :** a language stock of the Na-dene phylum comprising Haida only — called *also Skittagetan* — **hai·dan** \-dᵊn\ *adj, usu cap*

hai·ding·er·ite \'hīdiŋə,rīt\ *n* -s [Wilhelm Karl von *Haidinger* †1871 Austrian mineralogist + E *-ite*] **:** a mineral $HCaAsO_4·H_2O$ consisting of white hydrous calcium arsenate

hai·duk \'hī,dük\ *n* -s [G *heiduck, haiduck*, fr. Hung *hajdúk*, pl. of *hajdú* robber] **1 :** a Balkan outlaw opposed to Turkish rule **2 :** a Hungarian mercenary foot soldier of a class eventually elevated to noble rank **3 :** a male attendant or servant in various European countries dressed in livery resembling the costume of Hungarian haiduks

hai·fa \'hīfə\ *adj, usu cap* [fr. *Haifa*, Israel] **:** of or from the city of Haifa, Israel **:** of the kind or style prevalent in Haifa

hai·gle \'hāgəl\ *var of* HAGGLE *vi* 3

¹haik *also* **haick** \'hīk, 'hāk\ *n, pl* **haiks** *or* **haika** *also* **haicks** [Ar *ḥā'ik, hayk*] **:** a voluminous piece of usu. white cloth worn as an outer garment by men and women in northern Africa

²haik *var of* HAKE

hai·kai \'hī,kī\ *n, pl* **haikai** [Jap] **:** an often playful type of Japanese verse or prose cultivated in the later feudal ages — compare HAIKU, HOKKU

hai·kal \'hī,kal, 'hā,-\ *n* -s [Syriac *haykal* & Heb *hēkhāl*, fr. Assyr-Bab *ēkallu*, fr. Sumerian *e gal* temple, palace, fr. *e* house + *gal* great] **1 :** a sanctuary of a Coptic church cut off from the nave by a screen and containing three altars **2 :** the main altar

hai·ku \'hī(,)kü\ *n, pl* **haiku** [Jap] **:** an unrhymed Japanese poem of three lines containing 5, 7, and 5 syllables respectively, referring in some way to one of the seasons of the year, and constituting a late 19th century development of the hokku

hai·kwan tael \'hī'kwän-\ *n* [*haikwan* fr. Chin (Pek) *hai³ kuan¹* maritime customs, lit., gate of the sea] **:** a unit of value used by the Chinese for reckoning customs duties **:** customs tael

¹hail \'hāl, *esp before pause or consonant* -āəl\ *n* -s [ME *hail, hagel, hawel*, fr. OE *hægl, hagol*; akin to OHG *hagal* hail, ON *hagl*, Runic Goth *haal* (name of a rune), Gk *kachlēx* pebble] **1 a :** precipitation in the form of small balls or lumps usu. consisting of concentric layers of clear ice and compact snow produced by the oscillation of raindrops within cumulonimbus clouds or by the freezing of raindrops from nimbus clouds **b** *archaic* **:** a shower of hail **:** HAILSTORM ⟨a very considerable portion of this country has been desolated by a ~ —Thomas Jefferson⟩ **2 :** something that gives the effect of falling hail ⟨a ~ of applause⟩ ⟨a ~ of shot kicked up river sand —F.B. Gipson⟩

²hail \"\ *vi* -ED/-ING/-S [ME *haylen, hawelen*, fr. OE *hagalian*, fr. *hagol*, n.] **1 :** to precipitate hail ⟨it rained and ~*ed*⟩ **2 :** to pour down like hail **:** strike in the manner of hail ⟨flak ~*s* upon the plane —*Science Yr. Bk.*⟩

³hail \"\ *interj* [ME *hail, heil*, fr. ON *heill*, fr. *heill*, adj., healthy — more at WHOLE] **1 —** used to express acclamation ⟨~ to the chief —Sir Walter Scott⟩ ⟨~, King of the Jews —Mk 15:18 (RSV)⟩ **2** *archaic* — used as a salutation ⟨all ~, sweet madam, and fair time of day —Shak.⟩ ⟨good morrow to you both. *Hail* to your grace —Shak.⟩ **3 :** HURRAH — used to express good feeling or enthusiasm ⟨*hail, hail*, the gang's all here⟩

⁴hail \"\ *vb* -ED/-ING/-S [ME *hailen, heilen*, fr. *hail, heil*, interj.] *vt* **1 a :** SALUTE, GREET, ACCOST ⟨~*ed* the report with undisguised satisfaction —J.B.Matthews⟩ ⟨~*ed* him and gave him her hand —P.B.Kyne⟩ **b :** to greet with enthusiastic approval **:** ACCLAIM ⟨~ him as a hero⟩ ⟨~ the advances audio has made —R.D.Darrell⟩ **2 :** to greet or summon by calling to ⟨~ a passing ship⟩ ⟨~ a taxi⟩ **3** *chiefly Scot* **:** to reach (the goal) esp. in a game of shinny ~ *vi* **1 :** to call out; *esp* **:** to call a greeting to a passing ship ⟨the ship ~*ed* as we passed⟩ — **hail from :** to have origin or home base in **:** come from ⟨he *hails from* the hill country⟩

⁵hail \"\ *n* -s **1 :** an exclamation of greeting **:** SALUTATION ⟨he heard a ~ and his own name called —George Meredith⟩; *specif* **:** a shout of acclamation ⟨greeted the emperor with a ~⟩ **2 :** a calling to attract attention **:** act of hailing ⟨after such ~, the windward yacht shall at once allow the leeward yacht room to tack —Guy Pennant⟩ **3** *chiefly Scot* **a :** the cry uttered when a goal is struck in a game (as shinny) **b :** GOAL ⟨defeated by four ~*s*⟩ — **within hail :** within hearing distance ⟨*within hail* of the telephone —Nevil Shute⟩

[6]**hail** \"\ *var of* HALE

hail columbia *n, usu cap H&C* [euphemism; fr. *Hail Columbia* (1798), patriotic song by Joseph Hopkinson †1842 Am. jurist] **:** HELL ⟨give them *Hail Columbia*⟩

hail·er \'hālə(r)\ *n* -s **:** one that hails

[1]**hail-fellow** \'ₛ,ₛ(,)ₛ\ *or* **hail-fellow-well-met** \'ₛ,ₛ(,)ₛ'ₛ'ₛ\ *adj* [fr. the archaic salutations *hail, fellow!* & *hail, fellow! well met!*] **:** heartily informal **:** COMRADELY ⟨extended a *hail-fellow* hand —Edith Wharton⟩ ⟨a giant of a man — rough, hearty, violent, *hail-fellow-well-met* —Kenneth Roberts⟩

[2]**hail-fellow** \"\ *or* **hail-fellow-well-met** \"\ *n, pl* **hail-fellows** *or* **hail-fellows-well-met** **1 :** a boon companion **:** PAL ⟨all were *hail-fellows-well-met* by the time the convention opened —*Typewriter Topics*⟩ **2 :** the quality or state of comradeship ⟨there was a *hail-fellow-well-met*, a camaraderie, a gregariousness about it —*N.Y. Times*⟩

hailing distance *n* [fr. gerund of [4]*hail*] **1 :** the limit to which a human voice is heard ⟨when a patron lives within *hailing distance* —*U.S. Post Office Manual*⟩ **2 :** a close proximity **:** short reach ⟨within *hailing distance* of knowledge —H.J. Muller⟩

hail insurance *n* [[1]*hail*] **:** insurance against loss resulting from damage by hail esp. to growing crops

hail mary *n, usu cap H&M* [ME *hail Marie, heil Marie;* trans. of ML *Ave Maria*] **:** AVE MARIA 1, 3

hailproof \'ₛ,ₛ\ *adj* **:** impervious to hail ⟨~ netting over tobacco plants⟩

hails *pl of* HAIL, *pres 3d sing of* HAIL

hailshot \'ₛ,ₛ\ *n, pl* **hailshot** [ME *hayle shotte*] *archaic* **:** small shot that scatters like hail

hailstone \'ₛ,ₛ\ *n* [ME, fr. OE *hagolstān* (akin to ON *haglsteinn* hailstone), fr. *hagol* hail + *stān* stone — more at HAIL, STONE] **:** a single ball or lump of ice falling from a cloud **:** a pellet of hail

hailstorm \'ₛ,ₛ\ *n* -s **1 :** a storm accompanied by hail **:** a shower of hail ⟨the rain changed to a violent ~ —*McClure's*⟩ **2 :** something that resembles a hailstorm in concentrated violence ⟨a ~ of contempt —William James⟩

haily \'hālē\ *adj* **:** made of or accompanied by hail

haim \'hām\ *chiefly dial var of* HAME

haim·suck·en \'hām,səkən\ *var of* HAMESUCKEN

[1]**hain** \'(h)ān\ *vt* -ED/-ING/-S [ME *hanen, haynen,* fr. ON *hegna* to enclose; akin to MLG *hegenen* to enclose, MHG *heinen* to enclose, OHG *hagan* thornbush, ON *hagi* enclosed pasture — more at HAG] *dial Brit* **1 :** to fence or enclose (a tract of land) for grass **2 :** to put aside **:** SAVE, SPARE

[2]**hain** \"\ *vt* -ED/-ING/-S [ME *heyen, heynen* to raise, fr. OE *hēan,* fr. *hēah* high — more at HIGH] *dial Eng* **:** to cause (a price or fee) to be increased **:** RAISE

hai·nai \'(h)ī,nī\ *n, pl* **hainai** *or* **hainais** *usu cap* **1 :** a Caddo people of the Texas panhandle **2 :** a member of such people — compare HASINAI

hai·nan·ese \,hīnə¦nēz, -ēs\ *n, pl* **hainanese** *cap* [*Hainan,* island in the So. China Sea + E *-ese*] **:** a native or inhabitant of the Chinese island of Hainan

hainch \'(h)änsh\ *dial Brit var of* HAUNCH

haing *pres part of* HA

hain't \'(')(h)ānt\ [partly contr. of *have not, has not;* partly alter. of *ain't*] **:** AIN'T

hai·phong \'hī'fȯŋ\ *adj, usu cap* [fr. *Haiphong,* northern Vietnam] **:** of or from the city of Haiphong, northern Vietnam **:** of the kind or style prevalent in Haiphong

[1]**hair** \'ha(a)(ə)r, 'he|, |ə\ *n* -s *often attrib* [ME *her, heer, hare, heir, hair,* fr. OE *hǣr;* akin to OFris *hēr* hair, OHG & ON *hār,* and perh. to MIr *carrach* scurfy, mangy, Lith *šerys* bristle, Skt *kapucchala* hair on the back of the head] **1 :** a slender threadlike outgrowth of the epidermis of an animal; *esp* **:** one of the usu. pigmented filaments that form the characteristic coat of a mammal, contain neither blood vessels nor nerves, and are composed chiefly of elongated and modified epidermal cells covered by a cuticle of flat imbricated cells that produce a rough surface — compare BRISTLE, HAIR FOLLICLE, ROOT, SPINE **2 a :** the hairy covering of an animal or of some particular part of him; *specif* **:** the coating of fairly coarse and relatively straight individual hairs on a human head — distinguished from *fur* and *wool* **b :** HAIRCLOTH **3 a** (1) **:** a minute distance or amount **:** TRIFLE ⟨won by a ~⟩ (2) **:** a precise degree **:** NICETY ⟨aligned to a ~⟩ **b :** something likened to hair ⟨~*s* of fire came up through the busted plates —Saul Bellow⟩ ⟨eucalyptus . . . tossed their purple-black ~ of leaves in the air —Eve Langley⟩ **4** *obs* **:** KIND, NATURE, CHARACTER ⟨the quality and ~ of our attempt brooks no division —Shak.⟩ **5 a :** a filamentous structure that resembles hair ⟨leaf ~⟩ **b :** BOW HAIR — **against the hair** *archaic* **:** contrary to the normal tendency **:** against the grain ⟨if you should fight, you go *against the hair* of your professions —Shak.⟩ — **hair of the dog :** a small amount of the cause of an ill used as a remedy for it; *specif* **:** a drink of liquor the morning after a drinking bout ⟨I'd fetched a bottle — a little of the *hair of the dog* would do me good —Ross Santee⟩ — **in one's hair :** persistently annoying ⟨people could be friendly without getting *in each other's hair* —J.R.Chamberlain⟩ — **in the hair 1** *of raw furs* **:** with the fur outward **2** *of hides* **:** with the hair on — **one's hair down :** one's normal reserve in abeyance ⟨management with *its hair down* —*Time*⟩ **:** one's guard down ⟨that doesn't mean you have to let *your hair down* and tell him all the innermost secrets of your business —Franklin Spier⟩ ⟨they took *their hair down* and we felt that we made progress . . . in getting the type of information we are after —J.P.Richards⟩ — **out of one's hair :** eliminated as an annoying factor ⟨keep the children of the guests occupied and *out of their mothers' hair* —Marvin Schwartz⟩

[2]**hair** \"\ *vb* -ED/-ING/-S *vt* **1 :** to remove hair from ⟨~ a hide⟩ **2 :** to apply hair to ⟨~ a doll⟩ ⟨~ a fiddlestick⟩ **:** cover with or as if with hair ⟨a thick, white hand . . . ~*ed* over with fine reddish fuzz —William Faulkner⟩ ~ *vi* **:** to produce hair or something resembling hair ⟨these woods would not ~ up —*Scientific American*⟩

hair ball \'ₛ,ₛ\ *n* **1 :** a compact mass of hair in the stomach occurring esp. during shedding in an animal (as a cat) that cleanses its coat by licking **2 :** PHYTOBEZOAR

hairbeard \'ₛ,ₛ\ *n* **:** a wood rush (*Luzula campestris*)

hairbell *n* **:** HAREBELL

hairbird \'ₛ,ₛ\ *n* [so called fr. its use of horsehair in its nest] **:** CHIPPING SPARROW

[1]**hairbrain** \'ₛ,ₛ\ *n* -s [by folk etymology] **:** HAREBRAIN

[2]**hairbrain** \"\ *adj* **:** HAREBRAINED

hairbrained \'ₛ,ₛ\ *adj* [by folk etymology] **:** HAREBRAINED

hair-branch tree *n* **:** an African shrub (*Trichocladus crinitus*) of the family Hamamelidaceae

hair brand *n* **:** a temporary cattle brand made by scorching or picking out the hair without scarring the skin and used esp. by rustlers

[1]**hairbreadth** *or* **hairsbreadth** \'ₛ,ₛ\ *n* **1 :** a narrow margin ⟨lost the governorship by a ~ —W.V.Shannon⟩ **2 :** HAIR 3a

[2]**hairbreadth** \"\ *adj* **:** having the breadth of a hair **:** very narrow ⟨~ escape⟩

hair brown *n* **:** a dark gray to brownish gray that is lighter and slightly redder than beaver gray — called also *argali, limestone, quail*

hairbrush \'ₛ,ₛ\ *n* **1 :** a brush for the hair **2 :** a brush made of hair

hair calf *n* **:** SLINK 1

haircap moss *n* **:** a moss of the genus *Polytrichum* (esp. *P. juniperinum*)

hair cell *n* **:** a cell with hairlike processes; *esp* **:** one of the sensory cells in the auditory epithelium of the organ of Corti

[1]**hair-check** \'ₛ,ₛ\ *n* **:** a fine crack resulting from shrinkage on the surface of concrete or paint — **hair-checking** \'ₛ,ₛₛ\ *n*

[2]**hair-check** \"\ *vi* **:** [1]CRAZE *vi* 3

haircloth \'ₛ,ₛ\ *n* -s **1 :** any of various stiff wiry fabrics having a hair weft esp. of horsehair or camel's hair and a cotton, linen, or wool warp and being used for upholstery or stiffening in garments **2 :** an article of haircloth; *esp* **:** HAIR SHIRT

haircomb \'ₛ,ₛ\ *n* **:** a way of combing the hair ⟨this form of ~ was almost a tradition among old-time bartenders —Herman Goodman⟩

hair compass *n* **:** a compass that permits of minute adjustment

haircut \'ₛ,ₛ\ *n* **1 :** the act or process of cutting and shaping the hair **2 :** a hairstyle achieved by cutting and shaping

haircutter \'ₛ,ₛₛ\ *n* **:** one that cuts hair

haircutting \'ₛ,ₛₛ\ *n* **:** the art or occupation of a barber

hair dividers *n pl* **:** HAIR COMPASS

hairdo \'ₛ,ₛ\ *n* -s **:** a way of dressing the hair ⟨go in for elaborate ~*s* —Agnes M. Miall⟩; *esp* **:** a modish coiffure for women ⟨season's favorite ~ —*N.Y. Times*⟩

hair-drawn \'ₛ,ₛ\ *adj* **:** HAIRSPLITTING ⟨impatient of such *hair-drawn* distinctions —S.H.Adams⟩

hairdress \'ₛ,ₛ\ *n* **:** COIFFURE

hairdresser \'ₛ,ₛₛ\ *n* **1 :** one whose business or occupation is hairdressing and giving beauty treatments **:** COSMETOLOGIST **2** *Brit* **:** BARBER ⟨having a shave at the *hairdresser's* —A.J. Liebling⟩

hairdressing \'ₛ,ₛₛ\ *n* **1 a :** the action or process of washing, cutting, curling, or arranging the hair **b :** the occupation of a hairdresser **c :** HAIRDO **2 :** a dressing (as a pomade) for the hair

haired \'ha(a)(ə)rd, 'he|, |əd\ *adj* [ME *hered,* fr. *her, heer* + *-ed*] **:** having hair — usu. preceded by a descriptive term ⟨corn ~⟩ ⟨fair-*haired*⟩ ⟨wavy ~⟩ ⟨sparsely ~ leaves⟩

hair·en \'harən\ *adj* [ME *heren,* fr. OE *hǣren,* fr. *hǣr* hair + *-en* — more at HAIR] *chiefly dial* **:** made of hair

hair fern *n* [short for *maidenhair fern*] **:** MAIDENHAIR

hair-fibered \'ₛ¦ₛₛ\ *adj, of plaster* **:** containing fiber as a binder

hair follicle *n* **:** the tubular epithelial sheath surrounding the lower part of a hair shaft and enclosing at the bottom a vascular papilla that supplies the growing basal part of the hair with nourishment — compare ROOT

hair grass *n* **1 :** any of several grasses having slender wiry stems or leaves: as **a :** ROUGH BENT **b :** any of several grasses of the genera *Deschampsia, Muhlenbergia,* and *Aira* **2 :** any of several fine-leaved strictly aquatic spike rushes including some that are popular as aerators for the balanced aquarium

hair grip *n, chiefly Brit* **:** BOBBY PIN

hairhound \'ₛ,ₛ\ *n* [by folk etymology] **:** HOREHOUND

hair hygrometer *n* **:** an absorption hygrometer with a sensitive element of human hair

hairier *comparative of* HAIRY

hairies *pl of* HAIRY

hairiest *superlative of* HAIRY

hair·i·ness \'ha(a)rēnəs, 'her-, -rin-\ *n* -ES [ME *heryness,* fr. *hery, heeri* hairy + *-ness*] **:** the quality or state of being hairy

hairing *pres part of* HAIR

hair kiln *n* **:** a kiln floor which consists of open-woven horsehair cloth supported on laths of wood and on which hops are placed to dry

hairlace *n* [ME *harlas,* fr. *har, heer* hair + *las* lace] *obs* **:** a fillet (as of net) for the hair

hair·less \'ha(a)(ə)rləs, 'he|, |əl-\ *adj* **:** lacking hair — **hair·less·ness** *n* -ES

hairlike \'ₛ,ₛ\ *adj* **:** resembling a hair **:** elongated, slender, and filamentous ⟨~ appendages of a crustacean⟩

[1]**hairline** \'ₛ,ₛ\ *n* **1** *archaic* **:** a cord (as a fishline) made of hair **2 a :** a very slender line ⟨faint ~ of light around the edges of the windows —Shirley A. Grau⟩; *specif* **:** a tiny line or crack on a surface (as of paint) **b :** a very small difference **:** narrow margin ⟨the ~ that divides the comic from the grotesque —Wolcott Gibbs⟩ **c** (1) **:** a fine line connecting thicker strokes in a printed letter — called also *thin stroke* (2) **:** a fine line on a printer's rule or ornament (3) **:** a fine line drawn or etched for reproduction (as on a steel engraving) (4) **:** a fine strand of surplus metal on the face of newly cast type or slugs **:** WHISKER **d** (1) **:** a printed or woven textile design consisting of lengthwise or crosswise lines usu. one thread wide (2) **:** a fabric with such a design **3 a :** the line at which the hair meets the scalp ⟨receding ~⟩ **b :** the way the hair frames the face ⟨has a nice ~⟩ — **to a hairline** *adv* **:** to a nicety **:** with exactitude ⟨matched *to a hairline*⟩

[2]**hairline** \"\ *adj* **1 :** of or relating to a very slender line **:** THIN ⟨~ mustache⟩ ⟨~ shading⟩ **2 a :** hinging on very small differences **:** CLOSE ⟨~ victory⟩ **b :** marked by exactitude **:** PRECISE ⟨~ accuracy⟩

hair man *n* **:** an operator of a machine in which cattle hair is washed, dried, and baled

hair moss *n* [by shortening] **:** HAIRCAP MOSS

hair moth *n* **:** a moth that destroys goods made of hair or fur; *esp* **:** WEBBING CLOTHES MOTH

hairn \'härn\ *var of* HARN

hairnet \'ₛ,ₛ\ *n* **:** an open-meshed net made usu. of human hair or silk and worn over the hair to keep it in place

hair orchid *n* **:** a Himalayan orchid (*Trichosma suavis*) with yellowish purple-streaked flowers

hair pencil *n* **1 :** a brush or pencil made of fine hair (as of a camel) and used in painting **2 :** a close tuft of hairs occurring on parts of the body of certain caterpillars

hairpiece \'ₛ,ₛ\ *n* **:** TOUPEE 2

[1]**hairpin** \'ₛ,ₛ\ *n* **1 :** a pin to hold the hair in place; *specif* **:** a two-pronged U-shaped pin made of wire, plastic, or bone **2 a :** something shaped like a hairpin; *specif* **:** a sharp turn in a road having relatively parallel approaches ⟨at the top of a long swinging ~ he looked back and saw the moving lights of a car —Wallace Stegner⟩ **b :** two closed slalom gates placed one immediately below the other on a ski slope

hairpins: *1* bone or plastic, *2* wire, *3* bobby pin

[2]**hairpin** \"\ *adj* **:** having the shape of a hairpin ⟨~ curve⟩

[3]**hairpin** \"\ *vb* [[1]*hairpin*] *vt, West* **:** to get up on (as a horse) **:** MOUNT ⟨*hairpinning* . . . at sight anything on four hoofs —P.A.Rollins⟩ ~ *vi* **:** to make a hairpin turn ⟨the road ~*s* up the mountainside —Tom Marvel⟩

hairpin lace *n* **:** a lace with looped edges made by crocheting around the prongs of a U-shaped needle

hair pyrites *n* [so called fr. its interwoven capillary crystals that suggest a wad of hair] **:** MILLERITE

hair-raiser \'ₛ,ₛₛ\ *n* **:** one that is hair-raising **:** CHILLER ⟨the ingredients for an old-fashioned *hair-raiser* —*Theatre Arts*⟩

hair-raising \'ₛ,ₛₛ\ *adj* **:** making the hair stand on end: **a :** causing fear or shock **:** TERRIFYING ⟨have listened to some *hair-raising* confessions in my time —Mary R. Rinehart⟩ **b :** causing surprise or excitement **:** THRILLING ⟨no vivid or brilliant or *hair-raising* item of song or dance —*Dance News*⟩ — **hair-rais·ing·ly** *adv*

hairs *pl of* HAIR, *pres 3d sing of* HAIR

hair salt *n* [trans. of G *haarsalz*] **1 :** ALUNOGEN **2 :** epsomite when in silky fibers

hairsbreadth *var of* HAIRBREADTH

hair seal *n* **1 a :** a seal whose coat lacks underfur **2 a :** the fur of the hair seal **b :** an article made of this fur

hairsheep \'ₛ,ₛ\ *n* [so called fr. the fact that the hide comes fr. a sheep that grows hair instead of wool] **:** a leather used in bookbinding — compare CABRETTA

hair shirt *n* **1 :** a shirt made of coarse rough animal hair worn next to the skin as a penance ⟨led him . . . to give himself to fasting, a *hair shirt,* and prayer —K.S.Latourette⟩ **2 :** one that flagellates **:** SCOURGE ⟨the *hair shirt* of duty —L.D.Lewis⟩ ⟨uncomfortable to live with — a regular *hair shirt* of a man —E.B.White⟩ — **hairshirted** *adj*

hair sieve *n* [ME *herseve,* fr. *her, heer* hair + *seve* sieve] **:** a strainer with a haircloth bottom

hairslip \'ₛ,ₛ\ *n* **:** loosening of the hair from a hide due to improper or inadequate curing

hair snake *n* **:** HORSEHAIR SNAKE

hair sofa *n* **:** a sofa upholstered in haircloth

hair space *n* **:** a very thin space used in printing (as the ½-point copper space or the 1-point brass space)

hairspace \'ₛ,ₛ\ *vt* [*hair space*] **:** to set with hair spaces

hairsplitter \'ₛ,ₛₛ\ *n* **:** one that indulges in hairsplitting **:** QUIBBLER

[1]**hairsplitting** \'ₛ,ₛₛ\ *adj* **:** making excessively fine or trivial distinctions in reasoning ⟨ancient ~ technicalities of special pleading —Charles Sumner⟩ ⟨tricky ~ statesmen —Weston La Barre⟩

[2]**hairsplitting** \"\ *n* **:** hairsplitting reasoning or argument ⟨an excessive penchant for intellectual and verbal ~ —J.W. Beach⟩

hairspring \'ₛ,ₛ\ *n* **:** a slender spiraled recoil spring that regulates the motion of the balance wheel of a timepiece — called also *balance spring*

hairst \'härst\ *chiefly Scot var of* HARVEST

hair·stane \'har,stan\ *Scot var of* HOARSTONE

hairstone \'ₛ,ₛ\ *n* [prob. trans. of G *haarstein*] **:** quartz thickly penetrated with hairlike crystals of rutile, actinolite, or other mineral

hair straightener *n* **:** an agent (as heat or a chemical preparation) used for straightening kinky hair

hairstreak \'ₛ,ₛ\ *n* **:** any of various small butterflies of *Strymon* and related genera usu. having striped markings under the wings and thin filamentous projections from the hind wings

hair stroke *n* **1 :** a delicate stroke in writing **2 :** SERIF

hairstyle \'ₛ,ₛ\ *n* **:** a way of wearing the hair **:** COIFFURE

hairstyling \'ₛ,ₛₛ\ *n* **:** the art or practice of a hair stylist

hair stylist *n* **:** one who designs individualized hairdos esp. for women and often dresses the hair in the suggested style

hairtail \'ₛ,ₛ\ *n* [so called fr. the fact that the tail ends in a hairlike filament] **:** CUTLASS FISH

hair trigger *n* **:** a gun trigger so delicately adjusted that it releases the cock at the slightest touch

hair-trigger \'ₛ,ₛₛ\ *or* **hair-triggered** \'ₛ,ₛₛ\ *adj* [*hair trigger*] **1 a :** disposed to react quickly ⟨*hair-trigger* children who needed only a leader . . . to break into happy riot —John Steinbeck⟩ **b :** immediately responsive to the slightest stimulus ⟨*hair-trigger* nerves⟩ ⟨there is a *hair-trigger* ferocity about leopards —Alan Moorehead⟩ **c :** marked by promptness **:** INSTANTANEOUS ⟨*hair-trigger* service on inquiries —J.J. Canavan⟩ **2 :** delicately adjusted or easily disrupted ⟨*hair-trigger* schedule⟩ ⟨*hair-trigger* balance⟩

hair-trigger flower *n* **:** an Australian plant of the genus *Stylidium* (esp. *S. graminifolium*) whose column of stamens reacts sensitively to the touch

hair trunk *n* **:** a trunk covered with hide from which the hair has not been removed

hairweed \'ₛ,ₛ\ *n* **1 :** a filamentous green alga **2 :** any of several plants of the genus *Cuscuta; esp* **:** CLOVER DODDER

hairwood \'ₛ,ₛ\ *n* [by alter.] **:** HAREWOOD 2

hairwork \'ₛ,ₛ\ *n* **1 :** the making of wigs, switches, and other articles from hair **2 :** articles made of hair

hair worker *n* **:** one that combs, sorts, and washes hair for use in hairwork

hairworm \'ₛ,ₛ\ *n* **:** any of various very slender elongated worms: as **a :** a worm of the nematode genus *Capillaria* **b :** a worm of the order Gordioidea **:** HORSEHAIR SNAKE

[1]**hairy** \'ha(a)rē, 'her-, -ri\ *adj* -ER/-EST [ME *heery,* fr. *heer* hair + *-y*] **1 :** covered with or as if with hair ⟨~ ape⟩ ⟨~ overcoat⟩; *specif* **:** having a downy fuzz on the stems and leaves ⟨~ lotus⟩ **2 :** made of or resembling hair ⟨~ gown and mossy cell —John Milton⟩ **3 a :** rough and broken **:** RUGGED ⟨we are getting into some ~ country —Adrian Bell⟩ **b :** CRUDE, FRIGHTENING, UNPLEASANT ⟨~ bodyguard⟩ ⟨had some pretty ~ moments —L.A.Viereck⟩

[2]**hairy** \"\ *n* -ES **:** one that is hairy; *specif* **:** a draft horse with heavy feathering on the legs

hairy armadillo *n* **:** a peludo (*Euphractus villosus*)

hairy arum *n* **:** a foul-smelling aroid (*Helicodiceros muscivorus*) of southern Europe with hairy purple spadix

hairy-bait \'ₛₛ,ₛ\ *n* **:** LUGWORM

hairy-chested \'ₛₛ¦ₛₛ\ *adj* **:** full of strength or vigor **:** ROBUST ⟨*hairy-chested* mining history —Phil Spelman⟩

hairy china cardamom *n, usu cap 1st C* **:** an aromatic seed of a Chinese herb (*Amomum villosum*) used as a substitute for true cardamom

hairy chinch bug *n* **:** a bug closely related to and possibly a short-winged variety of the chinch bug that is sometimes destructive to turf in the northeastern U.S.

hairy crab *n* **:** a subglobose crab of the group Dromiacea having the body partially covered with bits of algae and debris

hairy crabgrass *n* **:** CRABGRASS 1a

hairy-foot \'ₛₛ,ₛ\ *n, pl* **hairy-foots** [so called fr. the hairy down at the base of the stem] **:** an inedible mushroom (*Marasmius personatus*) related to the fairy-ring mushroom

hairy frog *n* **:** any of three large western African frogs of the genus *Astylosternus* (family Ranidae) having hairlike outgrowths of skin on the sides of the trunk and thighs

hairy grama *n* **:** a grama (*Bouteloua hirsuta*) having the rachis prolonged beyond the spikelets as a naked point and the leaf blades sparsely hairy — called also *black grama*

hairy greenweed *n* **:** a southern European shrub (*Genista pilosa*) cultivated as forage for sheep

hairy head *also* **hairy crown** *n* **1 :** HOODED MERGANSER **2 :** RED-BREASTED MERGANSER

hairy honeysuckle *n* **:** a twining shrub (*Lonicera hirsuta*) of moist woodlands of the northern and eastern U.S. and adjacent Canada with dull dark green leaves that are sessile or short-petioled and pubescent on both surfaces and with crowded terminal spikes of orange or yellow flowers

hairy indigo *n* **:** a shrubby perennial (*Indigofera hirsuta*) with hirsute stems and foliage, flowers in dense clusters, and the calyx lobes often nearly as long as the petal that is native to Asia, Africa, and Australia and has been introduced into the southern U.S. as a forage and soil-improvement crop

hairy lip fern *n* **:** WOOLLY LIP FERN

hairy-nosed wombat \'ₛₛ,ₛ-\ *n* **:** a southern Australian wombat (*Lasiorhinus latrifrons*) distinguished by an extremely hairy rhinarium

hairy pipewort *n* **:** a low herb (*Lachnocaulon anceps*) of the family Eriocaulaceae of the southeastern U.S. having a 3-angled hairy scape

hairy rat *n* **:** a long-tailed Australian rat (*Mesembryomys hirsutus*)

hairy root *n* **:** a phase of the crown-gall disease esp. in apples characterized by abnormal development of fine fibrous roots

hairy saki *n* **:** a tropical American monkey (*Pithecia monacha*) with a purplish brown face covered with short white hair and a body coat that varies from black to brown and yellowish white

hairy shore crab *n* **:** YELLOW SHORE CRAB

hairy solomon's seal *n, usu cap 1st S* **:** a pubescent alternate-leaved perennial herb (*Polygonatum pubescens*) of eastern No. America

hairy spurge *n* **:** a much-branched hirsute weed (*Euphorbia hirsuta*) that has decumbent or prostrate stems in a dense mat and is native to northeastern No. America

hairy sumac *n* **:** STAGHORN SUMAC

hairy-tailed mole \'ₛₛ,ₛ-\ *n* **:** BREWERS' MOLE

hairy vetch *or* **hairy tare** *n* **:** a European vetch (*Vicia villosa*) extensively cultivated as a cover and early forage crop

hairy willow herb *n* **:** a European willow herb (*Epilobium hirsutum*) with a stout hairy stem and rose-purple flowers

hairy woodpecker *n* **:** a common No. American woodpecker (*Dendrocopos villosus*) closely resembling but larger than the downy woodpecker

hais·la \'hīslə\ *n, pl* **haisla** *or* **haislas** *usu cap* **1 :** a Kwakiutl people of British Columbia — compare WAKASHAN **2 :** a member of the Kwakiutl people

hait \'hāt\ *interj* [ME] *chiefly Scot* — used to urge on an animal

haith \'hāth\ *interj* [prob. euphemism for *faith*] *chiefly Scot* — used as a mild oath

hai·thal \'hī,täl\ *n, usu cap* **:** EPHTHALITE

hai·ti \'hād·ē, -ātē, |i\ *adj, usu cap* [fr. *Haiti,* country in the West Indies] **:** of or from Haiti **:** of the kind or style prevalent in Haiti **:** HAITIAN

[1]**hai·tian** \'hāshən, 'hād·ēən, -āt|, |iən\ *adj, usu cap* [*Haiti* + E *-an*] **1 :** of, relating to, or characteristic of the island of Haiti **2 :** of, relating to, or characteristic of the people of Haiti

[2]**haitian** \"\ *n* -s **1** *cap* **:** a native or inhabitant of Haiti — compare TAINO **2** *or* **haitian creole** *usu cap H&C* **:** CREOLE 4b

hai·tsai \'hī'tsī\ *n* -s [Chin (Pek) *hai³-t'sai⁴,* fr. *hai³* sea + *t'sai⁴* herb, green vegetable] **1 :** a transparent gelatinous substance prepared from a red alga (*Gloiopeltis tenax*) and used by the Chinese for lanterns and windows and for stiffening cloth **2 :** the alga that yields haitsai

hai·ver \'hāvə(r)\ *var of* HAVER

ha·je \'hājē\ *n* -s [Ar *ḥayyah* snake] **:** an Egyptian cobra (*Naja haje*)

hajemi *cap, var of* HADJEMI

haji *or* **hadji** *or* **hajji** \'hajē\ *n* -S [Ar *ḥajjī*, fr. *ḥajj*] **:** one who has made a pilgrimage to Mecca — often used as a title

ha·jib \'hä,jib\ *n* -S [Ar *ḥājib*, lit., one who prevents from entering] **:** a Muslim court official often corresponding to a chamberlain or a prime minister

hajj *or* **hadj** *or* **haj** \'haj\ *n* -ES [Ar *ḥajj*] **:** the pilgrimage to Mecca prescribed as a religious duty for Muslims

ha·ka \'hä(,)kä\ *n* -S [Maori] **:** a Maori posture dance accompanied by rhythmic chanting

ha·ka·foth *or* **ha·ka·fot** *or* **hak·ka·foth** *or* **hak·ka·fot** \'häkə,fōth, -ōs, -ōt\ *n pl* [Heb *haqqāphōth*, pl. of *haqqāphāh* circuit] **:** a ceremony in the Jewish synagogue typically on Simhath Torah in which members of the congregation carrying the scrolls of the Torah make seven processional circuits around the bimah to the accompaniment of traditional hymns and songs

ha·kam *or* **ha·ham** \kä'käm\ *also* **cho·chem** \'kōkəm\ *n, pl* **haka·mim** *or* **haha·mim** \,käkä'mēm\ [Heb *ḥākhām* wise, wise man; *chochem* fr. Yiddish *khokhem*, fr. Heb *ḥākhām*] **1 :** one learned in Jewish law **:** WISE MAN; *specif, pl* **:** the rabbinical interpreters of biblical law of the first two Christian centuries whose interpretations are recorded in the Mishnah and contemporary works **2 :** a title given to a rabbi by the Sephardic Jews

¹hake \'hāk\ *n, pl* **hake** *also* **hakes** [ME] **1 :** any of several fishes (the genus *Merluccius*) that are related to the cods but often regarded as forming a separate family and several of which are of importance as food fishes **2 :** any of various marine fishes of *Urophycis* and related genera (family Gadidae) resembling the cod and having narrow filamentous pelvic fins placed under the throat — called also *codling*; compare SILVER HAKE, SQUIRREL HAKE, STOCKFISH, WHITE HAKE **3 :** NORTHERN WHITING

²hake \"\ *vi* -ED/-ING/-S **:** to fish for hake

³hake \"\ *vi* -ED/-ING/-S [ME *haken*] **1** *chiefly Scot* **:** to wander around idly **:** LOAF **2** *chiefly Scot* **:** to trudge or tramp — often used with *about* or *around*

⁴hake \"\ *n* -S **:** a person in the habit of haking

⁵hake \'(h)āk\ *n* -S [prob. of Scand origin; akin to Icel *haki* hook — more at HOOK] **1** *dial Eng* **:** HOOK; *esp* **:** POTHOOK **1** **2** *dial Eng* **:** a clevis of a plow

⁶hake *or* **haik** \'hāk\ *n* -S [prob. by alter.] **:** ³HACK 2

ha·kea \'häkēə, 'hāk-\ *n, cap* [NL, after C. L. von *Hake* †1818 Ger. horticulturist] **:** a genus of Australian shrubs and small trees (family Proteaceae) having evergreen often spiny leaves and showy flowers in dense clusters — see CUSHION-FLOWER

ha·ken·kreuz \'häkən,krȯits\ *n, pl* **hakenkreu·ze** \-tsə\ *or* **hakenkreuzes** *often cap* [G, fr. *haken* hook (fr. OHG *hācko, hāko*) + *kreuz* cross, fr. OHG *krūzi*, fr. L *cruc-, crux* — more at HOOK, CROSS] **:** the swastika used as a symbol of German anti-Semitism or of Germany under Nazi government

ha·ken·kreuz·ler \-tslə(r)\ *n, pl* **hakenkreuzler** *or* **hakenkreuzlers** *usu cap* [G, fr. *hakenkreuz*] **:** a member of any German-speaking organization in Europe after World War I using the swastika as an emblem of anti-Semitism or of extreme nationalist sentiment

¹ha·kim \hə'kēm\ *n, pl* **hakims** \-mz\ *also* **hu·ka·ma** \,həkə'mä\ [Ar *ḥakīm*, lit., wise one] **:** a Muslim physician

²ha·kim \'hä,kēm\ *n, pl* **hakim** *or* **hakims** [Ar *ḥākim*] **:** a Muslim ruler, governor, or judge

hak·ka \'häk'kä, 'hakə\ *n, pl* **hakka** *or* **hakkas** *usu cap* **1 a :** a people of the Yellow River plain that migrated into the hilly areas of southeastern China possibly during the T'ang dynasty **b :** a member of such people **2 :** a dialect of Chinese spoken in part of Kwangtung province

hakkafot *or* **hakkafoth** *var of* HAKAFOTH

ha·ko \'hä(,)kō\ *n* -S [Pawnee] **:** a Pawnee Indian ceremony representing the union of Heaven and Earth and the birth of life performed with prayers, invocation by pipe, and eagle dances to ensure long life and posterity to the participants

ha·ko·da·te \,häkə'däd·ā\ *adj, usu cap* [fr. *Hakodate*, Japan] **:** of or from the city of Hakodate, Japan **:** of the kind or style prevalent in Hakodate

hal- *or* **halo-** *comb form* [F, fr. Gk, fr. *hals* salt — more at SALT] **1 :** of or relating to a salt ⟨*halo*chromism⟩ **2** [ISV, fr. *halogen*] **a :** halogen ⟨*hal*ide⟩ **b** *now usu* **halo-** **:** containing halogen ⟨*halo*alkyl groups⟩ — compare CHLOR- 3

ha·la \'hälə\ *n* -S [Hawaiian] **:** a screw pine (*Pandanus odoratissimus* syn. *P. tectorius*) native from southern Asia west to Hawaii having a trunk supported by a clump of slanting aerial roots, branches ending in spiral tufts of long narrow leaves which are used for plaiting mats, baskets, and hats, and fruits resembling pineapples but falling apart on ripening into many wedge-shaped yellow to red sections which are used as food in Micronesia and for leis in Polynesia

hal·a·car·i·dae \,halə'karə,dē\ *n pl, cap* [NL, fr. *Halacarus*, type genus (fr. *hal-* + *Acarus*) + *-idae*] **:** a small family of leathery-bodied free-living mites (group Hydrachnellae) that frequent marine algae

ha·laf·ian \hə'läfēən\ *also* **ha·laf** \hə'läf\ *adj, usu cap* [fr. Tell *Halaf*, site in northeastern Syria on the Turkish border near the village of Ras el 'Ain] **:** of or belonging to an early Aeneolithic culture of Syria and north Mesopotamia characterized by the use of stone as well as copper, adobe buildings, and a fine polychrome pottery

ha·la·kah *or* **ha·la·chah** *or* **ha·la·cha** \hä'läkä, ,hälä'kä, hə'läkə\ *n, pl* **ha·la·kahs** \-käz, -kəz\ *or* **ha·la·koth** *or* **ha·la·choth** \hä'lä,kōth, ,hälä'kōth, -ōt, -ōs\ *often cap* [Heb *hălākhāh*, lit., way] **:** the body of Jewish oral laws supplementing written law or both oral and written law together or any particular law or custom prescribed by the legal codices

ha·lak·ic *or* **ha·lach·ic** \hə'lakik\ *adj, often cap* **:** of or relating to the halakah

ha·lal \hə'läl\ *vt* **halalled; halalled; halalling; halals** [Ar *ḥalāl* that which is lawful] **:** to slaughter for food according to Moslem law

ha·lal·cor \-,kō(ə)r\ *n* -S [Hindi *halālkhor*, fr. Per, fr. Ar *ḥalāl* + Per *khor* eating] **:** a person in Iran and India to whom any food is lawful

ha·la·pe·pe \,hälə'pāpē\ *n* -S [Hawaiian] **:** a tree (*Dracaena aurea*) of the Pacific islands having flowers resembling lilies and yielding a wood used for carving

hal·ate \'ha,lāt\ *n* -S [*hal-* + *-ate*] **:** a salt of chloric, bromic, or iodic acid

ha·la·tion \hā'lāshən, hə-, ha-\ *n* -S [*halo* + *-ation*] **1 :** the spreading of light beyond its proper boundaries in a developed photographic image (as around a window facing the sky in an interior view or around other bright objects) caused principally by reflection from the back of the film or plate **2 :** a bright ring that sometimes encompasses the point at which a bright light shows on a television screen

halavah *var of* HALVAH

hal·a·zone \'halə,zōn\ *n* -S [*hal-* + *az-* + *-one*] **:** a white crystalline powdery acid $C_6H_4(SO_2NCl_2)COOH$ used as a disinfectant for drinking water; *para-(N,N'*-dichloro-sulfamyl)-benzoic acid

hal·berd \'halbərd, 'hōlb-, 'häl-\ *or* **hal·bert** \-rt\ *n* -S [ME *haubert, halberd*, fr. MF *hallebarde*, fr. MHG *helmbarte*, fr. *helm* handle + *barte* ax, fr. OHG *barta*, fr. *bart* beard; akin to OHG *halb* handle — more at HELVE, BEARD] **:** a weapon used esp. in the 15th and 16th centuries that consists typically of a battle-ax and pike mounted on a handle about six feet long

hal·berd·ier \'⸗⸗'di(ə)r\ *n* -S [MF *hallebardier*, fr. *hallebarde* + *-ier* -er] **:** a person armed with a halberd; *esp* **:** a guard who carries a halberd as a symbol of his duty

heads of halberds

hal·chid·ho·ma \,halchə'dōmə\ *n, pl* **halchidhoma** *or* **halchidhomas** *usu cap* **1 :** an Indian people in the Colorado River valley near the mouth of the Gila allied with the Maricopa **2 :** a member of the Halchidhoma

¹hal·cy·on \'halsēən\ *n* [ME *alceon, alicion*, fr. L *halcyon, alcyon*, fr. Gk *halkyōn, alkyōn*] **1** -S **a :** a bird identified with the kingfisher that was fabled by the ancients to nest at sea in a floating nest about the time of the winter solstice and to calm the waves during incubation **b :** KINGFISHER **2** [NL, fr. L *halcyon, alcyon*] *cap* **:** a genus of large kingfishers widely distributed in warmer parts of the Old World

²halcyon \"\ *adj* **1 :** belonging to or suggestive of the period commonly reckoned as 14 days assumed by the ancients to occur at the time of the winter solstice during the nesting period of the halcyon ⟨the ~ calm⟩ **2 a :** pleasingly or idyllically calm or peaceful **:** SERENE ⟨a ~ atmosphere⟩ **b :** HAPPY, GOLDEN ⟨a ~ era⟩ ⟨the ~ days of youth⟩ **c :** PROSPEROUS, AFFLUENT ⟨the ~ days of the clipper-ship trade⟩ **syn** see CALM

hal·dane's law *or* **haldane's rule** \'hōl,dānz-\ *n, usu cap H* [after John B. S. *Haldane* b1892 Scottish geneticist] **:** a principle in genetics: when in an interspecific cross one sex is absent, rare, or sterile in the offspring, that sex is heterogametic

hal·dan·ite \'hōl(,)dā,nīt, -,də,-\ *n* -S *usu cap* [James Alexander *Haldane* †1851 and Robert *Haldane* †1842, his brother, Scot. clergymen and evangelists + E *-ite*] **:** a follower of an evangelical movement in Scotland led by the Haldane brothers

hal·du \'häl(,)dü\ *n* -S [Hindi *haldū*] **1 :** a timber tree (*Adina cordifolia*) of the family Rubiaceae with light-yellow even-grained wood **2 :** the wood of haldu

¹hale *also* **hail** \'hāl, *esp before pause or consonant* -āəl\ *adj* -ER/-EST [partly fr. ME (northern dial.) *hal, hale*, fr. OE *hāl*; partly fr. ME *hail, heil*, fr. ON *heill* — more at WHOLE] **1 :** free from defect, disease, or infirmity **:** SOUND, HEALTHY, ROBUST ⟨a ~ body⟩ ⟨~ in youth⟩ **2** *chiefly Scot* **:** WHOLE **syn** see HEALTHY

²hale \"\ *adv* [partly fr. ME *hal, hale*, fr. *hal, hale*, adj.; partly fr. ME *hail, heil*, fr. *hail, heil*, adj.] *now dial Brit* **:** WHOLLY

³hale \"\ *vb* -ED/-ING/-S [ME *halen*, fr. MF *haler* — more at HAUL] *vt* **1 :** HAUL, PULL, DRAW **2 :** to compel (a person) to go ⟨~ a vagrant into court⟩ **3** *obs* **:** VEX, ANNOY **~** *vi* **1** *obs* **:** to move briskly (as of a ship) **2** *now dial Brit* **:** to pour or flow copiously ⟨the sweat was *haling* off him⟩ **3 :** to pull or tug ⟨*haling* at the plow⟩ **syn** see PULL

⁴ha·le \'hä(,)lā\ *n* -S [Hawaiian] *in Hawaii* **:** HOUSE

hal·e·co·mor·phi \,halēkō'mȯr,fī\ *n pl, cap* [NL, fr. L *Halec*, genus of fish (fr. L *halec, hallec, alec, allec* fish brine) + NL *-o-* + *-morphi*] *syn of* CYCLOGANOIDEI

hal·e·cos·to·mi \,halə'kästə,mī\ *n pl, cap* [NL, fr. *Halec* + NL *-o-* + *-stomi*] **:** an order of extinct ganoid fishes resembling herrings

hale·ness *n* -ES **:** the quality or state of being hale ⟨the ~ of the old man at 90 was surprising⟩

ha·le·nia \hə'lēnēə\ *n, cap* [NL, fr. Johann *Halen*, 19th cent. Ger. botanist + NL *-ia*] **:** a genus of herbs (family Gentianaceae) with opposite leaves and spurred flowers — see SPURRED GENTIAN

¹hal·er \'hālə(r)\ *n* -S [³*hale* + *-er*] **:** one that hales

²ha·ler \'hälər, -,le(ə)r\ *n, pl* **halers** \-rz\ *or* **hale·ru** \-,lə,rü\ [Czech, fr. MHG *hallære, haller, heller* — more at HELLER] **:** a monetary unit of Czechoslovakia equal to 1/100 of the koruna — see MONEY table

hales \'ālz\ *n pl* [prob. of Scand origin; akin to ON *hali* tail, pointed end; akin to Gk *kēlon* arrow, MIr *cail* spear, Skt *śala* stick, porcupine quill] *dial Eng* **:** handles on an implement (as a plow or a wheelbarrow)

ha·le·sia \hə'lēzh(ē)ə, ha'-\ *n* [NL, fr. Stephen *Hales* †1761 Eng. physiologist + NL *-ia*] **1** *cap* **:** a genus of small trees (family Styracaceae) of southeastern No. America having alternate leaves and white bell-shaped flowers borne in great profusion before the leaves — see SILVER BELL **2** -S **:** any plant of the genus *Halesia*

hale·some \'hālsəm\ *adj* [ME (northern dial.) *halsum*, fr. *hal*, *hale* healthy + *-sum* -some — more at HALE] *chiefly Scot* **:** WHOLESOME

hale water *n, chiefly Scot* **:** a heavy rainfall

ha·ley-over \'hālē⸗⸗\ *n* [origin unknown] **:** ANTONY OVER

¹half \'haf, haa(ə)f, hai, hȧf, hä\; *in sense 2b the f is often lost when "past" follows*\ *n, pl* **halves** \|vz\ [ME, fr. OE *healf*; akin to OHG & Goth *halba* side, half, ON *halfa*, L *scalpere* to cut, scratch, Gk *skalops* mole (animal), OE *sciell* shell — more at SHELL] **1** *obs* **:** PART, SIDE **2 a :** one of two equal parts into which a thing is divisible ⟨~ of it⟩ ⟨~ of the profits⟩; *also* **:** a part of a thing approximately equal to the remainder ⟨the larger ~ of the fortune⟩ **:** a sizable portion ⟨the bottom ~ of the social pyramid —N.E.Eliason⟩ — often used without *of* esp. when a quantitative word follows ⟨~ the money⟩ **b :** half an hour — used in designation of time ⟨~ past ten⟩ ⟨~ after five⟩ **3 :** one of a pair: as **a :** PARTNER **b :** SEMESTER, TERM **c** (1) **:** one of the two playing periods usu. separated by an interval that together make up the playing time of certain games (as football) — see QUARTER 21b (2) **:** the turn of one team to bat in baseball ⟨first ~ of the eighth inning⟩ **4 a :** HALF CROWN **b :** HALF-DOLLAR **5 :** significant part **:** CRUX, WHOLE — used with a negative ⟨that's not the ~ of it⟩ **6** [by shortening] **:** HALFBACK **7 :** HALF TIME — **and a half** *slang* **:** of great size, importance, difficulty, or perplexity ⟨a job *and a half*⟩ — **by half** *adv* **:** by a great deal **:** far and away ⟨too stupid *by half*⟩ — **by halves** *adv* **:** inadequately or incompletely **:** HALFHEARTEDLY ⟨let's not do things *by halves*⟩ — **half a mind :** more or less of an intention ⟨have *half a mind* to go swimming⟩ **:** more or less intending ⟨am *half a mind* to go swimming⟩ — **in half** *adv* **:** into two equal or nearly equal parts ⟨cut an apple *in half*⟩

²half \"\ *adj* [ME, fr. OE *healf*; akin to OHG *halb* half, ON *halfr*, Goth *halbs*, OE *healf*, n.] **1 a :** being one of two equal parts ⟨a ~ share⟩ ⟨a ~ sheet of paper⟩ **b** (1) **:** amounting to nearly half **:** approximately a half (2) **:** PARTIAL, IMPERFECT ⟨~ knowledge of a subject⟩ **2 a :** reaching only half the normal distance ⟨a ~ gunshot away⟩ **b :** extending or covering only half (as of the regular or normal area) ⟨a ~ window⟩ ⟨a ~ mask⟩ **c :** covering the backbone and one quarter of the boards away from the backbone and sometimes the corners ⟨a book bound in ~ leather⟩ ⟨a *half*-vellum binding⟩ — compare FULL 12c **d :** PART-TIME ⟨working only ~ days⟩ ⟨~ shift⟩ **3** *chiefly dial Brit* **:** of a species of small size — used of birds and sometimes of fish

³half \"\ *adv* [ME, fr. *half*, adj.] **1 a :** in an equal part or degree **b :** only partially **:** not completely **:** IMPERFECTLY ⟨~ digested⟩ ⟨~ persuaded⟩ **2 a :** at all **:** REALLY — used with a negative ⟨a performance that wasn't ~ bad⟩ **b** — used with a negative and before a verb to imply the opposite of what is expressed ⟨didn't ~ beat up the policeman⟩ **3 a :** by half an hour less ⟨~ ten o'clock⟩ — used chiefly in Scotland and Ireland **b** — used before a numeral in designating soundings to add one half to the numeral ⟨~ six fathoms⟩ **c** — used in the nomenclature of points of the compass between the names of two points to designate a position or direction half a point from the first compass point in the direction of the second

hal·fa \'halfə\ *var of* ALFA

half-a-crown \¦⸗⸗¦⸗\ *n* **1 :** HALF CROWN **2 :** the sum of two shillings and sixpence

half a dollar *n* **:** HALF-DOLLAR

¹half-and-half \¦⸗⸗¦⸗\ *n* **:** something that is half one thing and half another: as **a :** a mixture of two malt beverages (as porter and ale or beer and stout) **b :** solder made of equal parts of lead and tin

²half-and-half \"\ *adj* **1 :** half one thing and half another ⟨a *half-and-half* mixture⟩ **2 a :** EQUAL ⟨a job demanding *half-and-half* cooperation⟩ **b :** demanding equal participation on the part of two persons ⟨a *half-and-half* proposition⟩ **3 :** PARTIAL ⟨*half-and-half* enthusiasm⟩

³half-and-half \"\ *adv* **1 :** into two equal parts ⟨divided *half-and-half*⟩ **2 :** EQUALLY ⟨a duty shared *half-and-half* by husband and wife⟩

half an eye *n* **:** partial vision; *esp* **:** a casual or careless glance

half-ape \'⸗,⸗\ *n* **:** one of the lower primates (as a lemur or tarsier)

half-armor \'⸗,⸗⸗\ *n* **:** armor protecting only a part of the body

half-assed \'⸗¦⸗\ *adj* **1** *slang* **:** lacking significance, adequacy, or completeness **:** DEFICIENT ⟨wasn't going to do a *half-assed* job —R.O.Bowen⟩ **2** *slang* **:** lacking intelligence, ability, or experience **:** STUPID ⟨those *half-assed* women on Quality Hill want to kick it out of town —Conrad Richter⟩

half aunt *n* **:** the half sister of a parent

halfback \'⸗,⸗\ *n* **1 :** one of the backs stationed near either flank in football **2 :** a player stationed immediately behind the forward line (as in field hockey or soccer or rugby)

half-baked \'⸗¦⸗\ *adj* **1 :** only imperfectly baked **:** UNDERDONE **2 a :** not well planned **:** poorly contrived ⟨a *half-baked* plan⟩ **b :** lacking judgment, intelligence, or common sense ⟨a *half-baked* individual⟩ ⟨dramatic ideas that are often trivial or *half-baked* —Winthrop Sargeant⟩

half-ball stroke *n* **:** a stroke in billiards in which the center of the striker's ball is made to hit the extreme edge of an object ball

half bat *n* **:** one half of a brick

halfbeak \'⸗,⸗\ *n* **:** any of a family (Hemiramphidae) of small elongate fishes resembling the gar, closely allied to the flying fishes and like these often moving some distance through the air above the water, having on the lower jaw an extension like a beak, and inhabiting chiefly warm seas

half-beam \'⸗,⸗\ *n* **:** a beam in a ship extending from one of the sides to a deck opening (as a hatchway)

half-bent \'⸗,⸗\ *n* **:** the first notch in the tumbler of a gunlock for the sear point to enter to half-cock the piece

half binding *n* **:** a book binding in which one kind of material (as leather, cloth, or vellum) covers the backbone, one quarter of the boards away from the backbone, and sometimes the corners while another kind of material covers the rest — compare FULL BINDING, QUARTER BINDING, THREE-QUARTER BINDING

half bishop *n* **:** an artist's canvas measuring 45 by 56 inches — compare BISHOP'S LENGTH

half blood *n* **1 a :** the relation between persons having one parent but not both in common — compare BLOOD 2, CONSANGUINEOUS, DEMISANG, UTERINE, WHOLE BLOOD **b :** a person so related to another **2 :** HALF-BREED 1 **3 :** a grade of wool next below fine in a descending scale of fineness — compare BLOOD 7, BRAID 2, QUARTER BLOOD **4 a :** an animal tracing from a pure breed or strain through one parent only **:** GRADE 5 **b :** an individual heterozygous for a specified character

half-blooded \'⸗¦⸗⸗\ *also* **half-blood** \'⸗,⸗\ *adj* **1 :** having half blood or being a half-breed **2 :** having one parent of good and one of inferior stock ⟨a *half-blooded* sheep⟩

half board *n* **:** a maneuver of luffing a boat sailing close-hauled so that it shoots into the wind but before it has quite lost headway of putting the helm up again and letting the boat fill away on the same tack

half bog soil *n* **:** an interzonal group of soils developed under swamp-forest types of vegetation, having mucky or peaty surface soil underlain by gray mineral soil, and appearing mostly in humid or subhumid climates

half boot *n* **:** a boot with a top reaching somewhat above the ankle

half-bound \'⸗¦⸗\ *adj* **:** having a half binding ⟨a *half-bound* book⟩

half-box \'⸗¦⸗\ *n* **:** a section of a page of a newspaper or periodical being usu. rectangular and marked off at the top and bottom by rules or an ornamental border — see BOX 9a

half-breadth plan *n* **:** a plan of one side of a ship showing by horizontal longitudinal sections the forms of the various waterlines, rail and deck lines at the side, the frame stations, and the buttock lines

¹half-bred \'⸗¦⸗\ *adj* **:** HALF-BLOODED

²half-bred \'⸗,⸗\ *n* -S **:** a half-blooded animal

¹half-breed \'⸗,⸗\ *n* -S **1 :** the offspring of parents of different races; *esp* **:** the offspring of an American Indian and a white person **2 a** *usu cap* **:** a member of the faction of the Republican party that supported President Garfield in his controversy in 1881 with Senators Conkling and Platt of New York State over a civil-service appointment **b :** an insurgent faction in a political party **3 :** an animal or plant produced by crossing two distinct forms — often used to distinguish the product of such a cross within a species; compare HYBRID

²half-breed \'⸗,⸗\ *adj* **:** HALF-BLOODED

half brother *n* [ME] **:** a brother by one parent only

half-bull \'⸗,⸗\ *n* **:** a male fur seal not fully adult

half cadence *or* **half close** \-¦klōz\ *n* **:** a musical chord sequence giving a sense of partial harmonic completion (as tonic to dominant) — see CADENCE illustration

¹half-caste \'⸗,⸗\ *n* **:** a person of mixed racial or cultural descent **:** HALF-BREED

²half-caste \"\ *adj* **:** of the rank of or relating to a half-caste

half-castrate \'⸗¦⸗⸗,⸗\ *vt* **:** to remove the descended testis of (a unilateral ridgeling) to prevent breeding

half-cell \'⸗,⸗\ *n* **:** a device consisting of a single electrode immersed in an electrolytic solution and thus developing a definite potential difference

half cent *n* **:** a coin representing one half a cent (as the copper half cent coined by the U. S. 1793–1857)

half chronometer *n* **:** a watch having an escapement compounded of the lever and chronometer escapements; *also* **:** a fine lever-escapement watch adjusted for temperature

half-close \'⸗¦klōs\ *adj* **:** MID 3

half cock *n* **1 :** the position of the hammer of a firearm when about half retracted and held by the sear so that it cannot be operated by a pull on the trigger **2 :** a state of inadequate preparation or mental confusion — used with *at* ⟨the whole project went off at *half cock*⟩

half-cock \'⸗¦⸗\ *vt* **:** to place the hammer of (a firearm) at half cock

half-cocked \'⸗¦⸗\ *adj* **1 :** being at half cock **2 :** lacking clear or rational preparation, knowledge, or intention ⟨go off *half-cocked*⟩; *also* **:** STUPID, FOOLISH ⟨*half-cocked* public officials⟩

half column *n* **:** an engaged column which projects from a wall by approximately half its diameter

half cone *n* **:** the part of a cone formed by half lines from the vertex — opposed to *double cone*

half-course \'⸗,⸗\ *n* **:** a course at a school, college, or university having fewer weekly meetings than the regular course and carrying correspondingly fewer credits

half cousin *n* **:** the child of a half uncle or half aunt

half-cracked \'⸗¦⸗\ *adj* **:** HALF-WITTED

half crown *n* **:** a British coin worth *2s 6d* being in the 16th cent. of gold, from 1601–1946 of silver, and then of cupronickel; *sometimes* **:** the sum of *2s 6d*

half deck *n* **1 :** an incomplete deck; *specif* **:** a portion of the deck of a sailing ship next below the spar deck between mainmast and cabin **2 :** a slipper limpet of the genus *Crepidula*

half-decked \'⸗¦⸗\ *adj* **:** partly decked and partly open ⟨*half-decked* craft . . . used by the later Vikings —C.I.Elton⟩

half-deck·er \'⸗¦dekə(r)\ *n* **:** a half-decked ship

half-diamond indention *n* **:** a style of display typesetting in which succeeding lines are indented at each end, each line being shorter than the preceding line — called also *inverted-pyramid indention*

half dime *n* **:** a silver five-cent coin struck by the U. S. mint in 1792 and from 1794 to 1873

half disme *n* **:** a half dime struck in 1792

half-dollar \'⸗¦⸗⸗\ *n* **1 :** a coin representing one half of a dollar ⟨a U. S. or Canadian *half-dollar*⟩ **2 :** the sum of fifty cents or one half of a dollar

half door *n* **1 :** either part of a Dutch door **2 :** a swing door that fills only a part of the doorway

half eagle *n* **:** the five-dollar gold piece issued by the U. S. 1795–1916 and in 1929 — compare EAGLE

half-evergreen \'⸗¦⸗⸗,⸗\ *adj, of a plant* **:** incompletely evergreen: **a :** having foliage that is functional and persistent during part of the winter or dry season **b :** tending to be evergreen in the milder but deciduous in the more rigorous part of the range

half-faced \'⸗¦⸗\ *adj* **1 :** showing a profile **2 :** closed or protecting on three sides but open on the front ⟨a *half-faced* tent⟩ ⟨a *half-faced* cabin⟩

half fare *n* **:** a reduced fare (as on railroads or buses) available to underage children, to employees, or to passengers who ride at a particular time or under certain circumstances

half gainer *n* **:** a gainer in which the diver executes a half-backward somersault and enters the water headfirst and facing the board

half gerund *n* **:** the gerund in *-ing* when taking certain constructions suggestive of the participle (as *coming* in "I don't like him coming here" and *climbing* in "he tears his shirt climbing trees")

half-hardy \'⸗¦⸗⸗\ *adj, of a plant* **:** able to withstand a moderately low temperature but injured by severe freezing and surviving the winter in cold climates only if carefully protected

half-hardy annual *n* **:** a plant that may endure a few degrees of frost but is killed at lower temperatures (as China aster or zinnia)

half hatchet *n* **:** a hatchet with a straight edge broader than the edge of a lathing hatchet and with a flat hammer face on the end opposite the cutting edge — see HATCHET illustration

halfhead bedstead \ˈ=,=-\ *n* **:** a bedstead with posts lower than the headboard

half header *n* **:** half a brick used to close a course

halfhearted \ˈ=¦==\ *adj* **:** lacking heart, spirit, or interest ⟨a ~ try⟩ — **half·heart·ed·ly** *adv* — **half·heart·ed·ness** *n* -ES

half hitch *n* **:** a knot usu. tied double and used for temporarily securing a rope to an object by making a turn around the object, around the standing part, under the turn, and when double, around the standing part again and through the last bight

half hitch

half-holiday \ˈ=,==,=\ *n* **:** a holiday limited to half a day

half hose *n* **:** men's socks reaching halfway to the knee

half hour *n* [ME] **1 :** thirty minutes **2 :** the midpoint of an hour — **half-hourly** \ˈ=¦=¦=\ *adv (or adj)*

half-hour glass \ˈ=¦=,=\ *n* **:** an instrument for measuring time in half-hour intervals

half hunter *n* **:** a watch having the outer half of the crystal protected by a metal casing

halfies *pl of* HALFY

half-inferior \ˈ=¦==¦===\ *adj* **:** borne below the androecium in a concave receptacle but free from the axis — used of the ovary (as in perigynous flowers)

half island *or* **half isle** *n* **:** PENINSULA

half joe \ˈ=¦jō\ *n, pl* **half joes** [*half* + *joe*, short for *johannes*] **:** JOHANNES

half-knot \ˈ=¦=\ *n* **:** a knot joining the ends of two cords and used in tying other knots (as the square knot); *also* **:** OVERHAND KNOT

half lap *n* **:** END LAP

half-length \ˈ=¦=\ *n* **:** something that is or represents only half the complete length (as a portrait showing only the upper half of a person)

half-life \ˈ=,=\ *also* **half-life period** *n* **1 :** the time required for half of the atoms of a radioactive substance present at the beginning to become disintegrated ⟨rays from uranium have a *half-life* of millions of years —F.B.Colton⟩ ⟨this isotope has *half-life* of twenty-three minutes —L.J.Levert⟩ ⟨there will still be one quarter of the element left at the end of two *half-life periods* —G.E.Owen⟩ **2 :** the time required for half the amount of a substance (as a drug or radioactive tracer) in or introduced into a living system to be eliminated whether by excretion, metabolic decomposition, or other natural process

half-light \ˈ=,=\ *n* **:** grayish light (as of dim interiors, evening, or mist); *also* **:** the portion of a work of art showing such light

half line *n* **:** a straight line in mathematics beginning at a given point and extending indefinitely in one direction only — called also *half ray*

¹half·ling *pronunc at* HALF + lən *or* liŋ\ *or* **half·lin** \-lən\ *n* -S [*half* + *-ling*] **1** *chiefly Scot* **:** a half-grown person **2** *chiefly Scot* **:** half of a silver penny

²halfling \"\ *or* **halflin** \"\ *adj, chiefly Scot* **:** not fully grown **:** IMMATURE

half·lings \-nz,-ŋz\ *adv* [ME *halfling, halflings*, fr. *half* + *-ling, -lings*] *Scot* **:** half or approximately half **:** PARTIALLY ⟨while Jennie ~ is afraid to speak —Robert Burns⟩

half-long \ˈ=¦=\ *adj, of a speech sound* **:** intermediate in duration between long and short

half-loop \ˈ=¦=\ *n* **:** a flight maneuver in which an aircraft pulls up in an inside loop but continues upside down in level flight in the direction from which it came

half·ly *adv* [ME, fr. *half* + *-ly*] **:** ³HALF

half-marrow \ˈ=¦=(,)=\ *n, now dial Brit* **:** a partner or mate; *specif* **:** SPOUSE

¹half-mast \ˈ=¦=\ *n* **:** a point some distance but not necessarily halfway down below the top of a mast or staff or the peak of a gaff ⟨a flag flown at *half-mast* as a token of mourning⟩

²half-mast \ˈ=¦=\ *adj* **:** located below the top of the mast ⟨a *half-mast* position⟩

³half-mast \"\ *vt* [¹*half-mast*] **:** to cause to hang at half-mast ⟨*half-mast* a flag⟩

half measure *n* **:** a partial, halfhearted, or weak line of action ⟨victory is seldom won by *half measures*⟩

half-mens \ˈhälf,men(t)s\ *n, pl* **halfmens** \"\ *or* **half·men·se** \-n(t)sə\ [Afrik, fr. *half* + *mens* human being, person] **:** a southern African plant (*Pachypodium namaquam*) of the family Apocynaceae having an upright naked stem surmounted by a crown of leaves and suggesting in outline the figure of a human

half-minded \ˈ=¦==\ *adj* **:** being of an undecided or partial intent, desire, or will ⟨*half-minded* to do something desperate⟩

half-monitor \ˈ=¦===\ *n* **:** a roof for hog or poultry houses shaped like a saw tooth

half-moon \ˈ=,=\ *also* **half moon** *n* **1 :** the moon at the quarters when half its disk appears illuminated — see MOON illustration **2 :** a figure or object that is pointed at both ends, is about a fourth as wide as it is long, and in plane outline is half of a circle with the straight section curved in so that one side is concave while the other is convex ⟨an island *half-moon*⟩ **3 :** the lunule of a fingernail **4 a :** a bluish black California marine food fish (*Medialuna californiensis*) of the family Scorpididae — called also *blue perch* **b :** SCALARE

half-mooned \ˈ=,münd\ *adj* **:** shaped like a half-moon ⟨in his *half-mooned* chair —Thomas Coryat⟩

half mourning *n* **1 :** a period of mourning succeeding that of deep mourning **2 :** mourning dress lightened by the use of white, gray, or lavender

half nelson *n* **:** a wrestling hold in which one arm is thrust under the corresponding arm of the opponent generally from behind and the hand placed upon the back of his neck — compare FULL NELSON, QUARTER NELSON, THREE-QUARTER NELSON

half nephew *n* **:** the son of a half brother or half sister

half·ness *n* -ES **:** the quality or state of being half

half niece *n* **:** the daughter of a half brother or half sister

half note *n* **:** a musical note of half the value of a whole note — called also *minim*

half nut *n* **:** a screw nut split lengthwise so that either one part may be arranged to ride on a screw or the two parts may be arranged to clamp about a screw

half notes

half-one \ˈ=¦=, *in sense 2* ˈ=,=\ *n* **1 :** a golf handicap of one stroke subtracted on alternate holes **2** *Irish* **:** a half a glass of whiskey

half-open \ˈ=¦==\ *adj* **:** MID 3

half-orphan \ˈ=¦==\ *n* **:** a child with only one parent living

half-pace *pronunc at* HALF + ,pās\ *n* [by folk etymology fr. MF *haut pas*, lit., high step] **1 :** a raised floor or dais or a platform or footpace at the top of steps (as for a throne or an altar) **2 :** a landing of a staircase like a broad step between two half flights — compare QUARTERPACE

half·pen·ny \ˈhāp(ə)nī\ *n, pl* **half·pence** \-pən(t)s\ *or* **halfpennies** \-p(ə)nīz\ [ME *halfpeny, halfpeni*, fr. *half* + *peny, peni* penny] **1 :** a coin or token representing one half of a penny (as a British coin issued from the time of Edward I) **2 :** the sum of half a penny **3 :** a small amount ⟨not a ~ less⟩

halfpenny post *n, Brit* **:** second-class mail

half·pen·ny·worth \-i,wərth, ˈhāpəth\ *n* **:** something that is worth or costs a halfpenny ⟨a ~ of fish⟩

half-pike \ˈ=¦=\ *n* **:** a pike with a short shaft — compare BOARDING PIKE, SPONTOON

half-pint \ˈ=¦=\ *n* **1 :** half a pint **2** *slang* **:** a short, small, or inconsequential person

half-pitch \ˈ=¦=\ *adj* **:** having a gradient of one to two ⟨a *half-pitch* slope⟩

half plane *n, math* **:** the part of a plane on one side of an indefinitely extended straight line drawn in it

half principal *n* **:** a principal roof rafter that does not extend to the ridge

half-rat·er \ˈ=¦==\ *n* **:** a small sailing yacht of about 15-ft. waterline built under the rating rule in use in Great Britain about the end of the 19th century

half ray *n* **:** HALF LINE

half rest *n* **:** a rest in music corresponding in value with a half note

half rhyme *n* **:** a terminal consonance other than rhyme in two or more words (as in the unstressed final syllables of *hollow* and *shallow* or the matching terminal consonant clusters of *stopped* and *wept*)

half ring *n* **:** one of the incomplete cartilaginous rings that support the upper part of the bronchial tubes of most birds and in singing birds form a part of the syrinx

half-ripe \ˈ=¦=\ *or* **half-ripened** \ˈ=¦==\ *adj* **:** of, relating to, or consisting of the current growth of a tree, shrub, or woody plant that has not yet reached the mature wood stage ⟨*half-ripe* part⟩

¹half-roll \ˈ=¦=\ *n* **:** a flight maneuver in which an airplane rolls halfway over and then flies upside down along its original line of flight

²half-roll \"\ *vi, of an airplane* **:** to perform a half-roll

half-round \ˈ=¦=\ *adj* **1 :** semicircular or approximately so; *also* **:** flat on one side and round on the other **2** *of veneer* **:** cut from a log placed off center in a lathe so that it comes into contact with the blade on rotation only when the projecting portion reaches the blade

half round \"\ *n* **:** something half-round (as a chisel or molding)

half-round file *n* **:** a file made flat on one side and convex on the other

half run *n* **:** a contract purchased from an advertising agency whereby a card of a type suitable for bus, subway, or train advertising is required to be placed in half of the cars in a specified district

half-saved \ˈ=¦=\ *adj, now dial Eng* **:** HALF-WITTED

half-seas over \ˈ=¦=¦==\ *adj, slang* **:** DRUNK

half sheet *n* **:** a sheet imposed and printed by the work-and-turn method

half shell *n* **:** either of the valves of a bivalve — **on the half shell :** in either of the halves of a shell ⟨oysters *on the half shell*⟩

half shirt *n* **:** a man's shirtfront or a woman's chemisette worn in the late 17th century; *also* **:** STOMACHER

half-shot \ˈ=¦=\ *adj, slang* **:** partially drunk

half-shrub \ˈ=,=\ *n* **:** a perennial plant in which the stems are more or less woody esp. at the base — **half-shrubby** \ˈ=¦==\ *adj*

half-sib \ˈ=¦=\ *also* **half-sibling** \ˈ=¦==\ *n* **:** a half brother or half sister — compare SIB

half-silvered \ˈ=¦==\ *adj, of a mirror or glass block* **:** having a metallic film backing of such thinness that only half the incident light is reflected with the remainder being transmitted through the backing

half sister *n* [ME] **:** a sister by one parent only

half size *n* **:** a size in suits, coats, or dresses for short or short-waisted women with full figures

half sleeve *n* **:** any of various sleeves that reach to a little above the elbow or to a little below the elbow

¹half-slip \ˈ=,=\ *n* **:** PETTICOAT 1c

²half-slip \ˈ=¦=\ *adj* **:** of or relating to the degree of ripeness of a melon when the peduncle is separated from the fruit by pulling or pressure

half-snap \ˈ=¦=\ *n* **:** a quick movement of a shotgun to the shoulder followed by a rapid check on the alignment of the piece before it is fired

half snipe *n* **:** JACKSNIPE

half sole *n* **:** a shoe sole extending from the shank forward **:** TAP

half-sole \ˈ=¦=\ *vt* [*half sole*] **:** to attach a half sole to esp. in repairing (a shoe)

half sovereign *n* **:** a British gold coin worth ten shillings or ½ pound sterling regularly issued up to 1916 and since then only occasionally (as in 1937)

half space *n* **:** a halfpace in a stair

half-staff \ˈ=¦=\ *n* **:** HALF-MAST — used of a flag on a flagpole

half step *n* **1 :** a walking step of 15 inches or in double time of 18 inches **2 :** the pitch interval in music between two adjacent keys on a keyboard instrument — called also *semitone*

half-stopped \ˈ=¦=\ *adj* **:** partly covered at the top — used of an organ pipe

half story *n* **:** an uppermost story which is usu. lighted by dormer windows and in which a sloping roof replaces the upper part of the front wall

half-stripe \ˈ=,=\ *n* **:** the narrow ¼-inch stripe which together with the full ½-inch stripe makes up the sleeve and shoulder-board rank insignia of naval officers below flag rank

half stuff *or* **half stock** *n* **:** paper pulp; *esp* **:** paper pulp from rags partly processed (as by washing, bleaching, and draining) and ready for the beater

half sweep *n* **:** a sweep with a blade on only one side for use in cultivating close to a crop row

half-sword *n* **1** *obs* **:** a sword of small size **2** *obs* **:** half the length of a sword — **at half-sword** *adv, obs* **:** at close quarters

half tester bed *n* **:** a bed with a low foot and a canopy projecting from the posts at the head

half tide *n* **:** the time or state halfway between flood and ebb

half timber \ˈ=¦==\ *or* **half-timbered** \ˈ=¦==\ *adj* **:** being of the Tudor or Elizabethan construction employing wood framing with spaces filled with masonry — **half-timbering** \ˈ=¦=(=)=\ *n*

half time *n* **:** time marking the completion of half of a game or contest; *also* **:** the intermission between the second and third quarters of a game (as football and basketball)

half-timer \ˈ=¦==\ *n* **1 :** one that spends only half the usual time at anything **2** *Brit* **:** a child who is permitted to work half his time at some employment

half tint *n* **:** DEMITINT

half title *n* **1 :** the title of a book usu. standing alone on a right-hand page directly preceding the title page — called also *bastard title* **2 :** the title of a book standing alone on a usu. right-hand page immediately preceding the first page of text or at the head of the first page of text

half-toe \ˈ=,=\ *n* **:** the ball of the foot as the base of support in a dance step

halftone \ˈ=,=\ *n, often attrib* **1 :** HALF STEP 2 **2 a :** any of the shades of gray between the darkest and the lightest parts of a photographic image — called also *middletone* **b** [so called fr. the fact that this process was the first that was successful in reproducing the halftones of a photo] **:** a photoengraving made from an image photographed through a screen having a lattice of horizontal and vertical lines and then etched so that the details of the image are reproduced in fine dots with the darker areas appearing as heavy and concentrated dots and the lighter areas as fine and diffused dots; *also* **:** a print made from a halftone — compare DROPOUT

half-tongue \ˈ=,=\ *n* [ME *half tong;* intended as trans. of ML *medietas linguae*] **:** a jury de medietate linguae in English law

¹half-track \ˈ=,=\ *n* -S **1 :** a chain-track drive system serving to propel a vehicle supported in front by a pair of wheels and consisting of an endless metal belt on each side of the vehicle driven by one of two inside sprockets, running on bogie wheels mounted on the frame, and laying down on the ground as it revolves a flexible track of cleated steel or hard-rubber plates **2 :** a motor vehicle equipped with half-tracks in the rear and wheels in the front; *specif* **:** such a vehicle lightly armored for military use

²half-track \ˈ=,=\ *also* **half-tracked** \ˈ=,=\ *adj* **:** equipped with half-tracks

half-truth \ˈ=,=\ *n* **:** a partially true or partially fabricated statement made to deceive or to escape censure ⟨a public led astray by the *half-truths* of a dictator⟩

half-turn \ˈ=,=\ *n* **:** reversal of direction (as in a staircase) either by one 180-degree turn or two right-angle turns

half twist *n* **1 :** a dive done in either pike or layout position from a springboard or platform in which the diver executes a half turn of the body on a longitudinal axis before entering the water — compare FULL TWIST **2 :** a half turn of the body in the air on a longitudinal axis executed alone or in conjunction with other maneuvers (as on a trampoline, from a springboard, or in vaulting)

half uncial *n* **:** a book hand formed by combining uncial characters with carefully written cursive forms and used as the typical book hand from the earliest times in Ireland and from the 7th century to the Norman Conquest in England

half uncials

half uncle *n* **:** the half brother of a parent

half-value layer *n* **:** the thickness of an absorbing substance necessary to reduce by one half the initial intensity of the radiation traversing it

half volley *n* **:** a ball that is stroked or batted at the instant it rebounds from the ground: as **a :** a kick in soccer taken on the run as a ball rebounds from the ground **b :** a dropkick in rugby **c :** a bowled cricket ball that lands near enough to the blockhole to be readily hit as soon as it leaves the ground

half-volley \ˈ=¦==\ *vb* [*half volley*] *vt* **:** to drive (a tennis ball) as a half volley ~ *vi* **:** to play a half volley in tennis

half-wave plate *n* **:** a crystal plate that reduces by ½ cycle the phase difference between the two components of polarized light traversing it — compare QUARTER-WAVE PLATE

half-wave rectifier *n* **:** a rectifier that utilizes one half cycle of alternating current and suppresses the other

¹halfway \ˈ=¦=\ *adv* [ME, fr. *half* + *way*] **1 :** at a point at or near the middle **:** MIDWAY ⟨two ships passing ~ across the ocean⟩ **2 :** with concessions **:** in a state of readiness to negotiate **:** AMENABLY ⟨the revolutionists met the national government ~⟩ **3 a :** PARTIALLY, ALMOST **:** very nearly ⟨the fighter ~ yielded⟩ **b :** MORE OR LESS ⟨a ~ kind remark⟩

²halfway \"\ *adj* **1 :** equally distant from the extremes of a space or course **:** midway between two points ⟨a ~ point⟩ **2 :** PARTIAL ⟨~ measures⟩

halfway covenant *n, cap H&C* **:** a form of church membership among the Congregational churches of New England allowed by decisions in 1657 and 1662 and permitting baptized persons of moral life and orthodox faith to enjoy privileges of full membership except the partaking of the Lord's Supper

halfway house *n* **:** an inn or place of call midway on a journey; *also* **:** any halfway place in a progress

half wellington *n, usu cap W* **:** a loose-topped leather boot similar to the Wellington but shorter and usu. worn under trousers

half-wit \ˈ=,=\ *n* **:** a foolish person **:** DOLT, BLOCKHEAD

half-witted \ˈ=¦==\ *adj* **1 :** SILLY, SENSELESS **2 :** mentally deficient **:** FOOLISH, IMBECILE — **half-wit·ted·ly** *adv* — **half-wit·ted·ness** *n* -ES

half-world \ˈ=,=\ *n* **1 :** HEMISPHERE ⟨will prevent economic development of our *half-world* —Hamish Hamilton⟩ **2 :** DEMIMONDE ⟨the painted hussies of the *half-world* . . . in pinchbeck finery —Donn Byrne⟩ **3 :** UNDERWORLD ⟨a criminal not previously connected with the *half-world* —Frank Mullady⟩

half Wellington

halfy *pronunc at* HALF + ē *or* i\ *n* -ES *slang* **:** a beggar who has had both legs amputated

half year *n* [ME] **1 :** one half of a year (as January to June or July to December) **2 :** one of two academic terms **:** SEMESTER — **half-yearly** \ˈ=¦==\ *adv (or adj)*

hali- *comb form* [NL, fr. Gk, fr. *hals* salt, sea — more at SALT] **1 :** sea ⟨*haliplankton*⟩ **2 :** salt **:** a salt ⟨*halisteresis*⟩

hal·i·ae·e·tus \,halēˈēədəs\ *n, cap* [NL, fr. Gk *haliaetos, haliaietos*, a bird (prob. the osprey), fr. *hali-* + *aetos, aietos* eagle] **:** a genus of eagles including the bald eagle and many sea eagles

hal·i·but \ˈhaləbət *also* ˈhäl-; *usu* -bəd·+V\ *n, pl* **halibut** *also* **halibuts** [ME *halybutte*, fr. *haly, holy* holy + *butte* flatfish, fr. its being eaten on holy days — more at HOLY, BUTT] **:** the largest of the flatfishes formerly regarded as forming a single species but now usu. divided into an Atlantic species (*Hippoglossus hippoglossus*) and a Pacific (*H. stenolepis*), being an inhabitant of all northern seas, and constituting one of the largest of teleost fishes, the female sometimes weighing several hundred pounds though the male rarely weighs over 50 pounds — see ARROW-TOOTHED HALIBUT, CALIFORNIA HALIBUT

hal·i·but·er \-(,)bəd·ə(r), -ətə-\ *n* -S **:** one that fishes for halibut; *also* **:** a boat used in such fishing

halibut-liver oil *n* **:** a yellowish to brownish fatty oil from the liver of the halibut used chiefly as a source of vitamin A

hal·i·car·nas·si·an *also* **hal·i·car·nas·se·an** \¦halə(,)kär¦nasēən\ *adj, cap* [*Halicarnassus*, ancient city in Asia Minor + E *-ian* or *-ean*] **:** of or belonging to ancient Halicarnassus

hal·i·choe·rus \,haləˈkirəs, -kēr-\ *n, cap* [NL, fr. *hali-* + Gk *choiros* young pig] **:** the genus comprising the gray seal

hal·i·clys·tus \-ˈklistəs\ *n, cap* [NL, fr. *hali-* + *-clystus* (prob. fr. Gk *klystēr* syringe)] **:** a widely distributed genus of stauromedusan jellyfishes (class Scyphozoa)

ha·lic·o·re \həˈlikə(,)rē\ [NL, fr. *hali-* + Gk *korē* girl] *syn of* DUGONG

ha·lic·ti·dae \həˈliktə,dē\ *n pl, cap* [NL, fr. *Halictus*, type genus + *-idae*] **:** a cosmopolitan family of small black or brightly metallic solitary bees including many pollinators valuable to agriculture — **ha·lic·tine** \-,tīn, -tən\ *adj*

ha·lic·tus \həˈliktəs\ *n, cap* [NL, irreg. fr. Gk *halizein* to gather, assemble, fr. *halēs* assembled, pressed together] **:** a cosmopolitan genus of gregarious but not social burrowing bees that provision the larval cells with pollen and nectar and include important pollinators of economic plants — see SWEAT BEE

halide \ˈha,līd,ˈhā,-,-,ləd\ *n* -S [*hal-* + *-ide*] **:** a binary compound of a halogen with a more electropositive element or radical

hal·i·dom \ˈhalədəm\ *or* **hal·i·dome** \-,dōm\ *n* -S [ME, fr. OE *hāligdōm*, fr. *hālig* holy + *-dōm* -dom — more at HOLY] *archaic* **:** a holy place or relic — often used in the phrase *by my halidom*

hal·i·eu·tic \,halēˈ(y)üd·ik\ *also* **hal·i·eu·ti·cal** \-d·əkəl\ *adj* [LL *halieuticus*, fr. Gk *halieutikos*, fr. (assumed) *halieutos* verbal of *halieuein* to fish, fr. *hals* salt, sea) + *-ikos* -ic — more at SALT] **:** of or relating to fishing — **hal·i·eu·ti·cal·ly** \-d·ək(ə)lē\ *adv*

hal·i·eu·tics \-d·iks\ *n pl but sing in constr* **:** the art or practice of fishing; *also* **:** a treatise on fishes or fishing

hal·i·fax \ˈhalə,faks\ *adj, usu cap* **1** [fr. *Halifax*, county borough in England] **:** of or from the county borough of Halifax, England **:** of the kind or style prevalent in Halifax **2** [fr. *Halifax*, N. S.] **:** of or from Halifax, the capital of Nova Scotia **:** of the kind or style prevalent in Halifax

¹hal·i·go·ni·an \,haləˈgōnēən\ *n* -S *cap* [ML *Haligonia* Halifax + E *-an*] **:** a native or inhabitant of Halifax, Nova Scotia or Halifax, England

²haligonian \"\ *adj, usu cap* **:** of or belonging to Haligonians

hal·i·me·da \,haləˈmēdə\ *n, cap* [NL, after *Halimede*, a nereid, fr. Gk *Halimēdē*] **:** a genus (family Codiaceae) of calcareous marine green algae remarkable for the jointed coenocytic thallus which in most of the species (as *H. tuna*) resembles a prickly-pear cactus in miniature

haling *pres part of* HALE

hal·ing hands \ˈhāliŋ,-\ *n pl* [*haling* fr. gerund of ³*hale*] **:** heavy woolen gloves or mittens worn esp. by sailors

hal·i·o·tis \,halēˈōd·əs\ *n* [NL, fr. *hali-* + Gk *ōt-, ous* ear] **1** *cap* **:** a genus (the type of the family Haliotidae) of gastropod mollusks comprising the abalones **2** *pl* **haliotis :** any mollusk of the genus *Haliotis* **:** ABALONE — **hal·i·o·toid** \ˈ===,tȯid, ,ōid\ *adj*

hali·plankton \¦halə+\ *n* [ISV *hali-* + *plankton*] **:** oceanic plankton

hal·i·se·ri·tes \,haləsəˈrīd·(,)ēz, hə,lis-\ *n, cap* [NL, fr. *hali-* + Gk *seris* endive + NL *-ites*] **:** a genus of Old World cretaceous fossil plants of uncertain relationship possibly related to the dicotyledonous genus *Fontainea* but by some considered thallophytes because of the dichotomous flat leaves

ha·lis·i·do·ta \hə,lisəˈdōd·ə\ *n, cap* [NL] **:** a genus of arctiid moths several of which have larvae that feed on the foliage of trees

hal·i·ste·re·sis \,haləstəˈrēsəs, hə,lis-\ *n, pl* **halistere·ses**

\-ē(,)sēz\ [NL, fr. *hali-* + Gk *-steresis* loss] : loss of salts esp. of lime from bone (as in osteomalacia)

hal·i·ste·ret·ic \ˌhaləstəˈred·ik, həˈlis-\ *adj* : affected with or constituting halisteresis

halite \ˈhaˌlīt, ˈhā-\ *n* -s [NL *halites*, fr. *hal-* + *-ites* -ite] : a mineral NaCl consisting of sodium chloride : native salt : ROCK SALT

hal·i·the·ri·um \ˌhaləˈthirēəm\ *n, cap* [NL, fr. *hali-* + *-therium*] : a genus of sirenians that is known from remains found in the Oligocene and Miocene of southern Europe and the Oligocene of Madagascar and is made type of a separate family or included in Dugongidae

hal·i·to·sis \ˌhaləˈtōsəs\ *n, pl* **halito·ses** \-ōˌsēz\ [NL, fr. L *halitus* breath (fr. *halare* to breathe) + NL *-osis* — more at EXHALE] : a condition of having fetid breath

hall \ˈhȯl\ *n* -s *often attrib* [ME *halle, hal*, fr. OE *heall;* akin to OHG *halla* hall, ON *höll*, L *cella* small room, Gk *kalia* hut, nest, Skt *śālā* hut, OE *helan* to conceal — more at HELL] **1 a** : the castle or house of a medieval king or noble **b** : the chief living room in such a structure used for eating, sleeping, and entertaining **c** *chiefly dial* : the living room or parlor of a house **2** : the manor house or residence of a landed proprietor — often used in proper names ⟨Locksley *Hall*⟩ ⟨Headlong *Hall*⟩ **3** *sometimes cap* : a large usu. imposing building used for public or semipublic purposes; *specif* : TOWN HALL — now used chiefly in proper names ⟨Westminster *Hall*⟩ ⟨Faneuil *Hall*⟩ **4 a** (1) : a building used by a college or university for teaching or research ⟨~s of learning⟩ — often used in proper names ⟨Goodheart *Hall*⟩ (2) : DORMITORY **b** : a college or a division of a college at some universities **c** (1) : the common dining room of an English college (2) : a meal served there **5 a** *archaic* : a cleared passageway through a crowd — used in the exclamation *a hall, a hall* **b** (1) : the entrance room or passageway of a residence or other building : FOYER, LOBBY ⟨the front ~ of the house⟩ ⟨left his rubbers in the back ~⟩ (2) : a corridor or passage in a building **6** : a large room for assembly usu. equipped with seats (as for lectures or concerts) : AUDITORIUM ⟨a lecture ~⟩ ⟨a concert ~⟩ **7** : a place used for public entertainment: as **a** : a building or room used for a particular kind of amusement or play ⟨a pool ~⟩ ⟨a gambling ~⟩ **b** : a building with an auditorium used for public musical entertainments; *specif* : MUSIC HALL **8** : a building belonging to or used as the place of assembly, social center, or headquarters of a fraternal society or trade union ⟨his office was the union ~ —R.F.Mirvish⟩ — often used in proper names ⟨Hungarian *Hall*⟩

hal·lah *or* **chal·lah** \ˈkälə, käˈlä\ *n, pl* **hal·loth** *or* **hal·lot** \ˈkäˌlōt(h), -ōs, ⸗ˈ⸗\ *or* **hal·lahs** \ˈkäləz\ [Heb *ḥallāh*] : a loaf of white bread often baked in braided or twisted form and used among Jews esp. at a Friday evening meal inaugurating the Sabbath and on holidays

hal·la·li \ˌhaləˈlē\ *n* -s [imit.] : a huntsman's bugle call ⟨his ~ rang high —George Meredith⟩

hal·lan \ˈhalən, ˈhäl-\ *n* -s [origin unknown] *dial Brit* : a partition in a cottage esp. between the door and the fireplace

hal·lan·shak·er \-ˌshākər, -ˌshak-\ *n* **1** *chiefly Scot* : a wandering beggar **2** *chiefly Scot* : RASCAL, SCOUNDREL

hall bedroom *n* : a small narrow bedroom formed by a partition at one end of a hall

hallboy \ˈ⸗ˌ⸗\ *n* **1** : CALLBOY **2** : a boy employed to clean the halls of a hotel

hall church *n* [trans. of G *hallenkirche*] : a Gothic church esp. in Germany in which in place of the clerestory the aisles are carried up to nearly the height of the nave

hallcist \ˈ⸗ˌ⸗\ *n* -s [*hall* + *cist* (grave)] : a large rectangular earth-covered corridor made of rock slabs and used in ancient times as a tomb

hall clock *n* : GRANDFATHER CLOCK

hall coefficient \ˈhȯl-\ *or* **hall constant** *n, usu cap H* [after Edwin H. *Hall* †1938 Am. physicist] : the quotient of the potential difference per unit width of metal strip in the Hall effect divided by the product of the magnetic intensity and the longitudinal current density

hal·le \ˈhälə\ *adj, usu cap* [fr. *Halle*, Germany] : of or from the city of Halle, Germany : of the kind or style prevalent in Halle

hall effect *n, usu cap H* [after Edwin H. *Hall*] : a potential difference observed between the edges of a strip of metal carrying a longitudinal current when placed in a magnetic field perpendicular to the plane of the strip

häl·le·flin·ta \ˌheləˈflintə\ *n* -s [Sw, fr. *hälle-* slab, rock (fr. OSw *hællo-, hælla*) + *flinta* flint, fr. OSw; akin to ON *hella* cliff, mountain, Goth *hallus* cliff, and to OE *flint* — more at HILL, FLINT] : a very compact banded rock resembling felsite and consisting of minute particles of feldspar and quartz with fine scales of mica and chlorite — **häl·le·flin·toid** \-ntˌȯid\ *adj*

hal·lel \häˈlāl, ˈhäˌlāl, ˈhaˌlel\ *n, usu cap* [Heb *hallēl* praise] : a selection of psalms of praise chanted on Passover, Shabuoth, Sukkoth, Hanukkah, and Rosh Hodesh

[1]**hal·le·lu·jah** \ˌhaləˈlüyə\ *interj, sometimes cap* [Heb *halălūyāh* praise (ye) the Lord] — used to express praise, joy, or thanks ⟨the mighty voice of a great multitude in heaven, crying, "*Hallelujah!*" —Rev 19:1 (RSV)⟩

[2]**hallelujah** \"\ *n* -s : a shout or song of praise or thanksgiving ⟨jubilant ~s for . . . the Minister of Housing —Mollie Panter-Downes⟩

[3]**hallelujah** \"\ *adj* [[2]*hallelujah*] : of or belonging to the Salvation Army ⟨~ lass⟩ ⟨~ bonnet⟩ ⟨~ meeting⟩

hal·len *var of* HALLAN

hal·len·kir·che \ˈhälənˌkirkə\ *n, pl* **hallenkir·chen** \-rkən\ *usu cap* [G, fr. *halle* hall + *kirche* church] : HALL CHURCH

hal·ley's method \ˈha|lēz- *also* ÷ˈhā|\ *n, cap H* [after Edmund *Halley* †1742 Eng. astronomer] : a method of finding the parallax of Venus and hence the sun's distance by observing the duration of a transit of Venus from stations widely separated in latitude

hallgirl \ˈ⸗ˌ⸗\ *n* : a girl employed to clean the halls of a hotel

hall house *n, chiefly Scot* : MANOR HOUSE

halliard *var of* HALYARD

hal·ling \ˈhäliŋ, ˈhal-\ *n* -s [Norw, fr. *Hallingdal* a valley in southern Norway] **1** : an acrobatic Norwegian dance in duple measure for one to three single dancers **2** : a lively dance tune written in a major key usu. in 2/4 time and usu. played on the Hardanger fiddle

hal·lion \ˈhalyən\ *n* -s [origin unknown] *chiefly Scot* : SCAMP, SCOUNDREL

[1]**hall·mark** \ˈhȯlˌmärk, -mȧk\ *n* [Goldsmiths' *Hall*, London, England, where gold and silver articles were assayed and stamped + E *mark*] **1 a** *in England* : an official mark stamped on gold and silver articles to attest their purity and comprised of the king's or queen's mark, the maker's mark, the assayer's mark, and a letter of the alphabet for the year, a new style being used when the alphabet in one style is exhausted **b** : a mark stamped on gold and silver articles consisting of the word "sterling" accompanied by the name or mark of the manufacturer **c** : a mark or device placed or stamped upon an article of trade to indicate origin, purity, or genuineness ⟨the ~ of a potter of the Ming dynasty⟩ **d** : the identifying mark or device (as of a company) ⟨the new ~ will be a small, bright spot on company letterheads —*Bull. Standard Oil of Calif.*⟩ **2** : a distinguishing or identifying characteristic, trait, or feature ⟨avoidance of such constructions . . . has become a ~ of social respectability —Thomas Pyles⟩ ⟨the ~ of the adult human being is responsibility —Weston La Barre⟩ ⟨his solicitude for the poor . . . is the ~ of his best stories —Hakon Stangerup⟩

[2]**hallmark** \"\ *vt* **1** : to stamp with a hallmark **2 a** : to constitute a distinguishing or identifying feature or trait of ⟨two great faults and two great virtues ~*ed* the work of the late . . . associate justice —Fred Rodell⟩ **b** : to have or display the distinguishing, validating, or identifying traits or features of ⟨a host of inconspicuous but ~*ed* spinsters —*Times Lit. Supp.*⟩ ⟨my one genuine ~*ed* ghost story —Rudyard Kipling⟩

hall·moot \ˈhȯlˌmüt\ *n* [ME *halimot*, fr. *hal* hall + *-imot* (fr. OE *gemōt* assembly) — more at HALL, GEMOT] : a private court of the lord of a manor : COURT BARON

[1]**hal·lo** *or* **hal·loa** \həˈlō, haˈ-, ˈha(ˌ)lō\ *or* **hal·loo** \-lü\ *or* **hul·loo** \(ˌ)həˈlü, ˈhə(ˌ)lü\ *interj* [origin unknown] **1** — used to attract attention **2** — used as a call of encouragement or jubilation

[2]**hallo** *or* **halloa** *or* **halloo** *or* **hulloo** \"\ *vb* -ED/-ING/-S *vi* : to cry *hallo* : call out : HOLLER ~ *vt* **1 a** : to call or cry *hallo* to : attract the attention of **b** : to call encouragement to **2** : to utter loudly : HOLLER

[3]**hallo** *or* **halloa** *or* **halloo** *or* **hulloo** \"\ *n, pl* **hallos** *or* **halloes** *or* **halloas** *or* **halloos** *or* **hulloos** : an exclamation or call of *hallo* : a halloing or shouting

[4]**hal·lo** \"\ *chiefly Brit var of* HELLO

hal·lock \ˈhalək\ *n* -s [after *Hallock*, 19th cent. Am. box manufacturer] : a rectangular wood veneer berry box with straight sides and a raised bottom

hall of fame *usu cap H&F* **1** : a hall, building, room, or other structure housing statues, busts, tablets, or other memorials commemorating famous or illustrious persons usu. selected for inclusion by a qualified group of electors ⟨a *Hall of Fame* honoring great merchants of America was inaugurated tonight —*Springfield (Mass.) Union*⟩ ⟨ground-breaking ceremonies were held today for the national cowboy *Hall of Fame* here —*N.Y. Times*⟩ **2** : a group of individuals in some particular category formally selected by a group of qualified electors or informally adjudged by popular opinion as most illustrious or meriting immortal fame ⟨earned herself a permanent place in the trotters' *Hall of Fame* —R.E.Meyer⟩

halloth *or* **hallot** *pl of* HALLAH

[1]**hal·low** \ˈha|(ˌ)lō, |ˌlə, *often* -ˌləw + V *sometimes* ˈhä|\ *vt* **hal·lowed** \|(ˌ)lōd, |ˌləd\ **hal·lowed** \", *in the Lord's Prayer* " *or* |ˌləwəd *or* |ˌlōəd\ **hallowing**; **hallows** [ME *halowen*, fr. OE *hālgian*, fr. *hālig* holy — more at HOLY] **1** : to make holy : set apart for holy or religious use : treat or keep as sacred : CONSECRATE ⟨~*ed* be thy name —Mt 6:9 (RSV)⟩ **2** : to respect greatly : VENERATE, REVERE ⟨institutions ~*ed* for their classical learning —*Loyola Univ. Bull.*⟩ ⟨the most ~*ed* of all law-enforcement agencies —Dwight MacDonald⟩

[2]**hal·low** \"\ *vb* -ED/-ING/-S [ME *halowen*, fr. MF *halloer*, fr. *hallo*, interj.] : HALLO ⟨~*ed* at several to explain himself —A.E.Fife⟩

[3]**hal·low** \ˈhalə, +V " *or* -ləw\ *dial var of* HOLLOW

hal·low·day \ˈhaləˌdā, -lōˌ-\ *n* [short for *All Hallow Day*, fr. ME *all halowen day*, lit., all the saints' day] **1** *dial Eng, usu cap* : ALL SAINTS' DAY **2** *dial Eng* : a saint's day : HOLIDAY

hallowed *see* [1]HALLOW\ *adj* [ME *halowed*, fr. past part. of *halowen* to hallow — more at HALLOW] **1** : CONSECRATED, BLESSED **2** : REVERED, VENERATED, SACRED ⟨the ~ heroes of the past —Oscar Fraley⟩ ⟨the ~ customs of our group —M.R. Cohen⟩

hal·lowed·ly *adv* : in a hallowed manner

hal·lowed·ness *n* -ES : the quality or state of being hallowed : HOLINESS

hal·low·een *also* **hal·low·e'en** \ˌhaləˈwēn, ÷ˌhäl-\ *n* -s *usu cap* [short for *All Hallow E'en*] : the evening preceding All Saints' Day : the evening of October 31 which is often devoted by young people to merrymaking (as with jack-o'-lanterns) and playing pranks sometimes involving petty damage to property

hal·low·mas \ˈhalō|ˌmas, -lə|, |ˌmaa(ə)s, |ˌmais, |ˌməs *sometimes* |ˌmȧs\ *n* -ES *cap* [short for *Allhallowmass*] : the feast of All Saints

hal·loy·site \həˈlȯiˌsīt, haˈ-, -ˌzīt\ *n* -s [F, fr. Omalius d'*Halloy* †1875 Belg. geologist + F *-ite*] : a clay mineral $Al_2Si_2O_5(OH)_4.nH_2O$ occurring in soft white or light-colored masses and in at least two states of hydration $n=2$, $n=4$

hall porter *n, chiefly Brit* : a porter or attendant who carries the luggage of patrons and performs other chores at a hotel

hall process \ˈhȯl-\ *n, usu cap H* [after Charles M. *Hall* †1914 Am. chemist] : the process by which aluminum is produced consisting of electrolysis of a molten solution of purified alumina in cryolite at a temperature of about 950°C

halls *pl of* HALL

hall scale *n, usu cap H* [after Maurice C. *Hall* *b*1886 Amer. zoologist] : an Asiatic scale (*Nilotaspis halli*) that has been introduced into California where it is a serious pest of stone fruit trees

hall's honeysuckle *n, usu cap 1st H* [after G. R. *Hall*, 20th cent. Am. physician who introduced the plant from China] : a honeysuckle (*Lonicera japonica halliana*) that is a vining variety of Japanese honeysuckle with flowers initially pure white but yellowing with age, is often used as an ornamental climber or ground cover, and has established itself as an aggressive escape in much of the southeastern U. S.

hallstand \ˈ⸗ˌ⸗\ *n* : a tall piece of furniture with a mirror, several pegs or arms for hats and other articles of clothing, a rack for umbrellas, and a compartment for storage

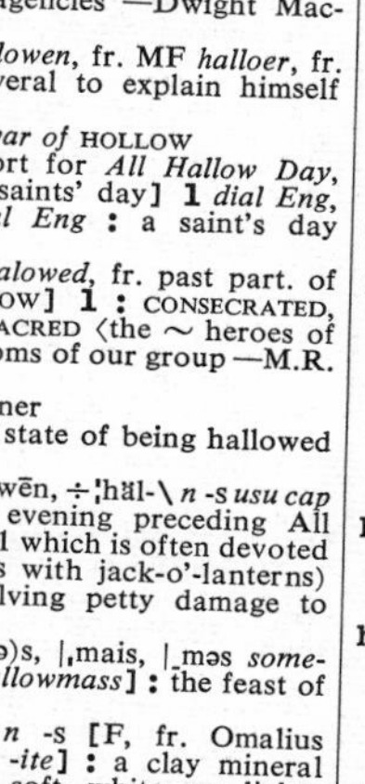

hallstand

hall·statt *or* **hall·stadt** \ˈhȯlˌstat, ˈhälˌshtät\ *adj, usu cap* [fr. *Hallstatt*, village in Austria] **1** : of or belonging to Hallstatt, Austria or the archaeological remains there **2** : of or relating to the earlier period of the Iron Age in Europe characterized by transition from the use of bronze to iron, possession of domestic animals, agriculture, and skill in the making of pottery and ornaments — compare LA TÈNE

hall·statt·an *also* **hall·stadt·an** \(ˈ)hȯlˌstad·ēən, (ˈ)hälˌshtäd·-\ *adj, usu cap* [*Hallstatt*, Austria + E *-an*] : HALLSTATT

hall tree *n* : CLOTHES TREE

hal·lu·ci·nate \həˈlüsᵊnˌāt *also* həlˈyü-\ *vb* -ED/-ING/-S [L *hallucinatus, alucinatus*, past part. of *hallucinari, alucinari* to talk idly, prate, dream, prob. fr. Gk *halyein, alyein* to be distraught, to wander] *vt* : to affect with visions or imaginary perceptions ⟨they are not *hallucinated*, they know that the object is not really there —R.S.Woodworth⟩ ⟨a poor *hallucinated* invalid —Marguerite Young⟩ ~ *vi* : to have hallucinations ⟨most normal persons have occasionally *hallucinated* —William McDougall⟩

hal·lu·ci·na·tion \⸗ˌ⸗⸗ˈāshən\ *n* -s [L *hallucination-, hallucinatio, alucination-, alucinatio*, fr. *hallucinatus, alucinatus* + *-ion-, -io* -ion] **1 a** : perception of objects with no reality : experience of sensations with no external cause usu. arising from disorder of the nervous system (as in delirium tremens or in functional psychosis without known neurological disease) **b** : the object of a hallucinatory perception **2** : a completely unfounded or mistaken impression or notion : DELUSION ⟨that popular ~, from which not even great scientists are . . . free —Lewis Mumford⟩ — **hal·lu·ci·na·tion·al** \⸗ˌ⸗⸗ˈāshənᵊl, -āshnəl\ *adj* — **hal·lu·ci·na·tive** \⸗ˈ⸗⸗ˌā‿·iv, ⸗ˈ⸗⸗ˌəd·iv\ *adj*

hal·lu·ci·na·to·ry \⸗ˈ⸗⸗ˌəˌtōrē\ *adj* : partaking of or tending to produce hallucination : not objectively perceived : IMAGINED, UNREAL ⟨fleeing in terror from a ~ wolf —Mark Kanzer⟩ ⟨succumbed to ~ rhetoric —Irving Howe⟩ ⟨the bizarre, ~ dreams of fever —Jean Stafford⟩

hal·lu·cino·gen \⸗ˈ⸗⸗ˌᵊˌjen, -ˌjən, ˌhalyəˈsinə-\ *n* -s [*hallucination* + *-o-* + *-gen*] : a substance that induces hallucinations; *esp* : one taken orally ⟨mescaline is a ~⟩ — **hal·lu·ci·no·gen·ic** \həˌlüsᵊnəˈjenik *also* həlˌyü-\ *adj*

hal·lu·ci·no·sis \həˌlüsᵊnˈōsəs *also* həlˌyü-\ *n, pl* **hallucino·ses** \-ōˌsēz\ [NL, fr. L *hallucinatio* + NL *-osis*] : a pathological mental state occurring esp. as a manifestation of alcoholism in which awareness consists largely or exclusively of hallucinations

hal·lux \ˈhaləks\ *n, pl* **hallu·ces** \-l(y)əˌsēz -ləˌs-\ [NL, fr. L *hallus, hallux* big toe] : the first or preaxial digit of the hind limb : BIG TOE

hallux val·gus \-ˈvalgəs\ *n* [NL, lit., wry big toe] : an abnormal deviation of the big toe toward the outside of the foot associated esp. with the wearing of ill-fitting shoes — compare BUNION

hall·wachs effect \ˈhälˌväks-\ *n, usu cap H* [after Wilhelm *Hallwachs* †1922 Ger. physicist] : a photoelectric effect in which a negatively charged body in a vacuum is discharged upon exposure to ultraviolet radiation

hallway \ˈ⸗ˌ⸗\ *n* : HALL; *esp* : an entrance hall

halm *var of* HAULM

Hal·ma \ˈhalmə\ *trademark* — used for a game played by two or four players on a board having 256 squares with the object being for each player to move or jump his men from their home corner to a corresponding position in the opposite corner

[1]**ha·lo** \ˈhā(ˌ)lō\ *n, pl* **halos** *or* **haloes** [L *halos* halo of the sun, fr. Gk *halōs* threshing floor, disk of the sun or the moon, halo around the sun or moon; akin to Gk *halōn* threshing floor, and perh. to *lyein* to loosen — more at LOSE] **1** : a circle, arc, or splotch of light either white or prismatically colored and definitely situated with reference to a luminous body and resulting from the reflection or refraction or both of its light; *specif* : circles round the sun or moon caused by the presence of ice particles in the atmosphere and differing from coronas in being of definite size usu. of about 22° or 46° radius and if colored in showing red on the side nearest to the luminary **2** : something resembling a halo: as **a** : NIMBUS **b** : a differentiated zone surrounding a central object ⟨the ~ around a boil⟩ ⟨the presence of a ~ of alteration has been used as a guide to ore finding —A.M.Bateman⟩; *specif* : a zone usu. of lighter colored tissue characteristically surrounding the lesions in certain plant diseases esp. of bacterial origin **c** : a circlet of flowers, a ribbon, or a small hat worn off the face and back on the head by women **3** : the aura of glory, veneration, prestige, or sentiment surrounding an idealized person or thing ⟨a . . . positive ~ surrounds scientific endeavors —John Dewey⟩ ⟨put a romantic ~ about the old plantation life —Oscar Handlin⟩ ⟨the exclusiveness of the institute . . . gave it a ~ —Romola Nijinsky⟩

[2]**halo** \"\ *vt* -ED/-ING/-ES : to form or surround with a halo : encircle as if with a halo ⟨red-gold hair . . . ~*ing* a slim face —Frank Yerby⟩ ⟨the ~*ed* lights burned her eyes —John Dos Passos⟩ ⟨~*ed* by publicity —F.L.Allen⟩

[3]**halo** \ˈha(ˌ)lō\ *adj* [*hal-*] : containing halogen — used esp. of organic compounds ⟨~ aldehydes⟩

halo- — see HAL-

ha·lob·a·tes \həˈläbəˌtēz\ *n, cap* [NL, fr. *hal-* + *-bates*] : a genus of small wingless marine water striders having the thorax large and the abdomen very small

hal·o·bi·ont \ˌhalōˈbīˌänt\ *n* -s *often attrib* [*hal-* + *-biont*] : an organism (as a plant) that flourishes in a saline habitat

halo blight *n* **1** *also* **halo spot** : a blight of beans and occas. other legumes that is caused by a bacterium (*Pseudomonas phaseolicola*) and typically produces on the leaves, stems, and pods round water-soaked lesions surrounded by a yellowish zonation, the lesions finally turning brick red **2** : blight affecting the leaves of oats and other grasses caused by a bacterium (*Pseudomonas coronafaciens*) characterized by oval water-soaked lesions turning gray to brownish and surrounded by a pale zonation

hal·o·chro·mism \ˌhaləˈkrōˌmizəm\ *n* -s [*hal-* + *chrom-* + *-ism*] : the phenomenon or property of the formation of strongly colored salts by addition of acids to colorless or faintly colored compounds

halo effect *n* : a tendency for a general opinion or attitude derived from rating an individual as high or low on one item of a test to exert an influence upon the rating of other and separate items, traits, or responses; *esp* : generalization from the perception of one outstanding personality trait to an overevaluation of the whole personality

hal·o·form \ˈhaləˌfȯrm\ *n* [*hal-* + *-form* (as in *chloroform*)] : a compound CHX_3 (as chloroform) derived from methane by replacement of three atoms of hydrogen by halogen

hal·o·gen \-ˌjən, -ˌjen\ *n* -s [Sw, fr. *halo-* hal- + *-gen*] : any of the five elements fluorine, chlorine, bromine, iodine, and astatine forming part of group VII A of the periodic table and existing in the free state normally as diatomic molecules — compare PSEUDOHALOGEN — **ha·log·e·nous** \(ˈ)haˈläjənəs\ *adj*

hal·o·gen·ate \ˈhaləjəˌnāt, haˈläj-\ *vt* -ED/-ING/-S : to treat or cause to combine with a halogen : introduce a halogen into (as an organic compound) — **hal·o·gen·a·tion** \ˌhaləjəˈnāshən, haˌläj-\ *n* -s

hal·o·gen·ide \ˈhaləjəˌnīd, haˈläj-\ *n* -s [ISV *halogen* + *-ide*] : HALIDE — used in the nomenclature adopted by the International Union of Pure and Applied Chemistry

hal·o·gen·oid \-ˌnȯid\ *n* -s : PSEUDOHALOGEN

hal·o·ge·ton \ˌhaləˈjētᵊn\ *n* [NL, fr. *hal-* + Gk *geitōn* neighbor] **1** *cap* : a small genus of Mediterranean and central Asian herbs and shrubs (family Chenopodiaceae) with fleshy semicylindrical leaves and axillary clusters of flowers — see BARILLA 1b **2** -s : any plant of the genus *Halogeton; esp* : a coarse annual herb (*H. glomeratus*) introduced into No. America from Siberia and now a noxious weed in western American rangelands dangerous to sheep and cattle because of its high oxalate content

hal·o·hy·drin \-ˈhīdrən\ *n* -s [ISV *hal-* + *-hydrin*] : any of a class of organic compounds derived from glycols or polyhydroxy alcohols (as glycerol) by substitution of halogen for part of the hydroxyl groups — compare CHLOROHYDRIN

halolike \ˈ⸗(ˌ)⸗ˌ⸗\ *adj* : resembling a halo

hal·o·lim·nic \ˌhalōˈlimnik\ *adj* [ISV *hal-* + *limn-* + *-ic*] *of a marine organism* : capable of living in fresh water

ha·lom·e·ter \haˈlämәd·ə(r)\ *n* [ISV *hal-* + *-meter*] : an instrument for measuring the forms of crystals of salts

hal·o·mor·phic \ˌhaləˈmȯrfik\ *adj* [*hal-* + *-morphic*] : of or relating to intrazonal soils characterized by the presence of either neutral or alkali salts or both — compare CALOMORPHIC, HYDROMORPHIC — **hal·o·mor·phism** \ˌ⸗⸗ˈ⸗ˌfizəm\ *n* -s

hal·o·phile \ˈhaləˌfīl\ *n* -s [ISV *hal-* + *-phile;* prob. orig. formed as Sw *halofil*] : a halophilic organism

hal·o·phil·ic \ˌ⸗⸗ˈfilik\ *or* **ha·loph·i·lous** \(ˈ)haˈläfələs\ *also* **hal·o·phile** \ˈhaləˌfīl\ *or* **hal·o·phil** \-ˌfil\ *adj* [*hal-* + *-philic* or *-philous* or *-phile, -phil*] *of an organism* : flourishing in a salty environment

hal·o·phyte \ˈhaləˌfīt\ *n* -s [ISV *hal-* + *-phyte*] : a plant that grows naturally in soils having a high content of various salts, that usu. resembles a true xerophyte and that occurs in many families (as Chenopodiaceae, Compositae, Plumbaginaceae) — compare MESOPHYTE — **hal·o·phyt·ic** \ˌ⸗⸗ˈfid·ik\ *adj*

hal·o·ra·ga·ce·ae \ˌhalərəˈgāsēˌē, həˌlȯr-\ *n pl, cap* [NL, fr. *Haloragis*, type genus + *-aceae*] : a family (order Myrtales) of usu. monoecious plants having predominantly unisexual flowers with 4 or 8 stamens and an inferior ovary

hal·o·rag·i·da·ce·ae *or* **hal·or·rhag·i·da·ce·ae** \ˌhaləˌrajəˈdāsēˌē\ [NL, fr. *Haloragid-, Haloragis* + *-aceae*] *syn of* HALORAGACEAE

hal·o·ra·gis \ˌhaləˈrājəs\ *n, cap* [NL, irreg. fr. *hal-* + Gk *rhag-, rhax* berry] : the type genus of Haloragaceae — see SEABERRY

halos *pl of* HALO

hal·o·saur \ˈhaləˌsȯ(ə)r\ *n* -s [NL *Halosaurus*] : a member of the Halosauridae

hal·o·sau·rid \ˌ⸗⸗ˈsȯrəd\ *adj* [NL *Halosauridae*] : of or relating to the Halosauridae

hal·o·sau·ri·dae \ˌ⸗⸗ˈ⸗rəˌdē\ *n pl, cap* [NL, fr. *Halosaurus*, type genus + *-idae*] : a family (order Heteromi) of mostly extinct deep-sea fishes having cycloid scales

hal·o·sau·rus \-rəs\ *n, cap* [NL, fr. *hal-* + *-saurus*] : the type genus of the Halosauridae

hal·o·sere \ˈhaləˌsi(ə)r\ *n* [*hal-* + *sere*] : an ecological sere originating in a saline habitat

halo spot *n* : HALO BLIGHT 1

halo·tolerant \ˌhalō+\ *adj* [*hal-* + *tolerant*] : HALOXENE

ha·lot·ri·chite \haˈlä·trəˌkīt\ *n* -s [G *halotrichit*, fr. *hal-* + *trich-* + *-it* -ite] **1** : a mineral $FeAl_2(SO_4)_4.22H_2O$ consisting of a hydrous iron aluminum sulfate **2** : any of several sulfates similar to halotrichite in construction and habit

halo·tyd·e·us \ˌhalōˈtīdēəs, -tid-, tīˌd(y)üs\ *n, cap* [NL, fr. *hal-* + *Tydeus*, genus of mites, after *Tydeus*, Greek mythological hero] : a genus of soft-bodied phytophagous mites that have the front pair of legs modified as sensory organs and that are destructive to legumes and certain other crops in southern Africa and Australia — see SANDMITE

hal·oxene \(ˈ)haˈläkˌsēn, ˈhaləˌzēn\ *adj* [*hal-* + Gk *xenos* foreign — more at XEN-] *of an organism* : tolerating but not preferring a saline habitat — compare HALOPHILIC

hals *or* **halse** \'hȯs, -ä-,-a-\ *n, pl* **halses** [ME *hals,* fr. OE *heals* — more at COLLAR] **1** *now dial Brit* : NECK **2** *now dial Brit* **a** : THROAT, WINDPIPE **b** : PASS, DEFILE, COL

halse \"\ *vt* -ED/-ING/-S [ME *halsen,* fr. *hals,* n.] *now dial Brit* : EMBRACE, HUG

hal·sen \'älzən, 'ȯzᵊn\ *vt* -ED/-ING/-S [ME *halsnen* to adjure, conjure, fr. *halsen* to adjure, conjure, entreat (fr. OE *hālsian*) + *-nen* -en; akin to OHG *heilisōn* to predict, adjure, conjure, ON *heilsa* to greet; derivatives fr. the root of OE *hāl* healthy, whole — more at WHOLE] *now dial Eng* : DIVINE, PREDICT

halsh \'(h)alsh\ *vt* -ED/-ING/-ES [ME *halchen* to embrace, tie, knot, prob. alter. of *halsen*] *dial Eng* : KNOT

¹**halt** \'hȯlt\ *adj* [ME, fr. OE *healt;* akin to OHG *halz* lame, ON *haltr,* Goth *halts* lame, L *clades* destruction, disaster, Gk *klan* to break, *kolos* docked, hornless, *kolobos* docked, curtailed, Lith *kalti* to beat, forge; basic meaning: beating, hewing] : having a halting walk : LAME ⟨gave alms to the ~ and . . . the poor —Jean Stafford⟩ ⟨a place for everyone . . . old and young, hale and ~ —Sir Winston Churchill⟩

²**halt** \"\ *vi* -ED/-ING/-S [ME *halten,* fr. OE *healtian;* akin to OHG *halzēn* to be lame, limp; derivatives fr. the root of E ¹*halt*] **1** : to walk or proceed lamely : LIMP ⟨so lamely . . . that dogs bark at me as I ~ by them —Shak.⟩ **2** : to stand in perplexity or doubt between alternate courses : WAVER **3** : to display weakness or imperfection (as in argument, development, or meter) : proceed raggedly or falteringly : FALTER, LAPSE ⟨the translation ~s now and then —*Brit. Book News*⟩ ⟨the verse that ~s in places⟩ ⟨the argument often ~s and sometimes breaks down completely⟩

³**halt** \"\ *n* -S [G, fr. MHG, fr. *halt!,* imp. of *halten* to hold, stop, fr. OHG *haltan* — more at HOLD] **1** : a temporary or definitive stop in marching or walking or in any action or process : arrest of progress ⟨the car came to a sudden ~⟩ ⟨economic progress was brought to a ~⟩ ⟨a ~, rather than a complete stoppage, in the flow of talent —*Irish Digest*⟩ ⟨time to call a ~ in a useless struggle⟩ **2** *chiefly Brit* : a stopping place for public transport; *esp* : a railway flag stop ⟨a slow train stopping at every station including ~s —*Punch*⟩

⁴**halt** \"\ *vb* -ED/-ING/-S [G *halten* to hold, stop, fr. OHG *haltan*] *vi* **1** : to cease marching or journeying : stop for a longer or shorter period : stand still ⟨ordered his troops to ~⟩ ⟨made two or three . . . paces about the room, and suddenly ~ed —W.J.Locke⟩ ⟨many families ~ed and took up land in the mountain valleys —*Amer. Guide Series: Tenn.*⟩ **2** : to discontinue temporarily or permanently : TERMINATE, END, SUSPEND ⟨hostilities ~ed while the generals conferred⟩ ⟨the project ~ed because of inadequate financial support⟩ ~ *vt* **1** : to cause to cease marching or journeying : bring to a stop ⟨~ed the wagon train at a small settlement⟩ ⟨~ed the advance of his troops⟩ ⟨slid the bowl back down the bar and ~ed it before the soldier —Kay Boyle⟩ ⟨marshes that would have ~ed any vehicle —*Amer Guide Series: N.C.*⟩ **2** : to cause the discontinuance of : terminate the existence or progress of : END ⟨did the best he could to ~ the erosion —D.L.Graham⟩ ⟨consumer spending . . . rose and ~ed the decline —*Dun's Rev.*⟩ ⟨~ hostilities⟩ ⟨sought to ~ corruption and increase efficiency⟩

¹**hal·ter** \'hȯltə(r)\ *n* -S *often attrib* [ME, fr. OE *hælftre;* akin to OHG *halftra* halter, MLG *halchter,* MD *halfter, halchter;* derivatives fr. the root of E *helve*] **1 a** : a rope or strap with or without a headstall for leading or tying a horse or other animal **b** : a headstall of rope or leather and usu. with noseband and throatlatch to which a lead may be attached **2** : a rope for hanging criminals : NOOSE; *also* : death by hanging **3 a** : a woman's or girl's waist typically held in place by bands or straps around the neck and across the back and leaving the back, arms, and midriff bare **b** : an adaptation of this style for the necklines of other garments (as blouses, dresses, bathing suits) **c** *or* **halter strap** : SLING 3a(3)

halter 1b

²**halter** \"\ *vt* **haltered; haltered; haltering** \-t(ə)riŋ, -ltriŋ\ **halters 1 a** : to catch with or as if with a halter : put a halter on (as a horse) **b** : to put a hangman's halter on : HANG **2** : to put restraint upon : BRIDLE, FETTER, HAMPER, RESTRAIN ⟨~ his conscience⟩ ⟨measures that had the effect of ~ing the daily press⟩

³**hal·ter** \", 'hal-\ *or* **hal·tere** \-,ti(ə)r, -iə\ *n, pl* **hal·teres** \ˌ=ˈti(ˌ)rēz; 'hȯl,ti(ə)rz, -iəz\ [NL, fr. L, jumping weight, fr. Gk *haltēr,* fr. *hallesthai* to jump — more at SALLY] : one of the modified second pair of wings in Diptera and the first pair in Strepsiptera that are reduced to club-shaped organs and that function as flight instruments — called also *balancer, poiser*

halterbreak \'=ˌ=ˌ=\ *vt* : to break (as a colt) to a halter

hal·te·rid·i·um \ˌhaltəˈridēəm\ [NL, fr. L *halter* + NL *-idium*] *syn of* HAEMOPROTEUS

hal·ti·ca \'haltikə\ [NL, prob. fr. Gk *haltikos* good at leaping — more at ALTICA] *syn of* ALTICA

halting *adj* [ME, fr. pres. part. of *halten* to limp — more at HALT] **1 a** : marked by a limp : LAME, LIMPING ⟨recognized the cripple's ~ walk⟩ **b** : slow and hesitant or reluctant : DRAGGING, UNCERTAIN ⟨walked home with heavy heart and ~ steps⟩ **c** : lacking smoothness, facility, verve, or display of easy command in delivery : marked by abrupt halts and starts : FALTERING, AWKWARD, UNGRACEFUL ⟨his speaking voice . . . is thin and ~ —*Current Biog.*⟩ ⟨too wise to let his ~ utterance weaken the impression of his facile pen —John Buchan⟩ ⟨his ~ delivery of the play's longest speech —Henry Hewes⟩ **2 a** : displaying weakness or imperfection (as in argument, development, or meter) : marked by lapses (as of grammar, interest, continuity) : proceeding raggedly or falteringly ⟨a very ~ argument⟩ ⟨the poem's weak and ~ rhymes⟩ ⟨the ~ development of this thin plot⟩ **b** : lacking in sureness (as of purpose, drive, or continuity) : proceeding by fits and starts : FUMBLING, INDECISIVE, VACILLATING, INEFFECTIVE ⟨development of the military intelligence service . . . was slow and ~ —G.F.Ashworth⟩ ⟨the season got off to a ~ start⟩ ⟨made ~ advance toward solving their difficulties —C.L.Jones⟩ — **halt·ing·ly** *adv*

halt·ing·ness *n* -ES : DEFECTIVENESS, FAULTINESS

halts *pres 3d sing of* HALT, *pl of* HALT

hal·uck·et \'haləkət\ *adj* [fr. past part. of Sc *hallock, haluck* to behave in a giddy or foolish manner, fr. *hallock, haluck* giddy, foolish girl] *Scot* : wild and giddy : HALF-WITTED

ha·luk·kah *or* **cha·lu·kah** *also* **ha·lu·kah** *or* **ha·lu·ka** *or* **cha·lu·ka** \ˌkälüˈkä, kəˈlükə\ *n* -S [Heb *ḥălūqqāh* portion, division] : a fund collected from Jews throughout the world for support of the needy in Palestine

ha·lutz *or* **cha·lutz** \kä'lüts\ *n, pl* **ha·lutz·im** *or* **cha·lutz·im** \ˌkä,lütˈsēm, kä'lütsim\ [NHeb *ḥālūṣ,* fr. Heb, warrior, vanguard] : a Jewish immigrant to Palestine who works in the Jewish settlements at tasks contributing to the development of the country as a Jewish homeland : PIONEER

ha·lutza *or* **cha·lutza** \ˌkäˈlütsə\ *n, pl* **halutz·oth** *or* **halutz·ot** *or* **chalutz·oth** *or* **chalutz·ot** \ˌkä,lütˈsōt(h), -ōs, ˌ=ˈ=\ [NHeb *ḥălūṣāh,* fem. of *ḥālūṣ*] : a female halutz

ha·lutz·i·ut *or* **cha·lutz·i·ut** \kä'lütsē,üt\ *n* -S [NHeb *ḥălūṣiut,* fr. *ḥālūṣ*] : PIONEERING; *specif* : the pioneer movement of the halutzim in Palestine

hal·vah *or* **hal·va** *or* **halavah** \h|äl'vä, k|, |äl'vä; 'häl(ˌ)vä, 'hál(ˌ)vä, -l(ə)və, -lə,v-; 'halvə\ *n* -S [Yiddish *halva,* fr. Romanian, fr. Turk *helva,* fr. Ar *ḥalwā* sweetmeat] : a flaky confection of crushed sesame seeds in a base of honey or other syrup

¹**halve** \'hav, -aa(ə)-,-ai-,-å-,-ä-\ *vt* -ED/-ING/-S [ME *halven, halfen,* fr. *half,* n. — more at HALF] **1 a** : to divide into two equal parts : separate into halves ⟨~ an apple⟩ ⟨ripe walnuts, *halved* and picked from the shell —Nora Waln⟩ **b** : to reduce to one half ⟨*halving* the purchase tax on cotton goods —*New Republic*⟩ ⟨doubling the profit by *halving* the cost⟩ **c** : to share equally ⟨was it the double of my dream . . . or did we ~ a dream? —W.B.Yeats⟩ ⟨it didn't much matter that he was here to ~ my triumph —Max Beerbohm⟩ **2** : to join two pieces of (timber) by cutting away each for half its thickness at the joining place and fitting together **3** : to play (as a hole, round, match) in the same number of strokes as one's opponent at golf

²**halve** \"\ *n* -S : a tie score on a hole or a round of golf ⟨salvaged a ~ on the 147-yard third —*N.Y. Herald Tribune*⟩

halved *adj* **1** : reduced to one half ⟨had to get along with a ~ income⟩ **2** : appearing as if one side or one half were cut away : DIMIDIATE

halv·ers \'ha-və(r)z\ *n pl* : half shares : HALVES ⟨went ~ on the price⟩

halves *pl of* HALF

hal·yard *or* **hal·liard** \'halyə(r)d\ *also* **haul·yard** \'hȯl-\ *n* -S [alter. of ME *halier,* fr. *halen* to pull — more at HALE] : a rope or tackle for hoisting and lowering (as a yard, spar, sail, flag) — see *ship* illustration

hal·yik·wa·mai \hal'yikwə,mī\ *n, pl* **halyikwamai** *or* **halyikwamais** *usu cap* **1** : an Indian people in the Colorado river valley below the mouth of the Gila allied with the Cocopa **2** : a member of the Halyikwamai people

hal·y·si·tes \ˌhaləˈsīd·(ˌ)ēz\ *n, cap* [NL, fr. Gk *halysis* chain + NL *-ites*] : a genus consisting of the chain corals

hal·zoun \(ˈ)halˈzün\ *n* -S [prob. fr. Ar *ḥalzūn* snail] : infestation of the larynx and pharynx by worms esp. of the genus *Fasciola* consumed in raw liver

¹**ham** \'am\ *n* -S [ME (attested only in place names), fr. OE *hamm;* akin to MLG *ham* enclosed land, OE *hemm* border — more at HEM] *now dial Eng* : a piece of grassland

²**ham** \'ham, -aa(ə)-\ *n* -S [ME *hamme,* fr. OE *hamm;* akin to OHG *hamma* popliteal space, thigh, haunch, ON *höm* haunch, Gk *knēmē* shinbone, OIr *cnāim* bone, leg] **1 a** : the part of the leg behind the knee : the hollow of the knee : POPLITEAL SPACE ⟨such a case as yours constrains a man to bow in the ~s —Shak.⟩ **b** : a buttock with its associated thigh or with the hinder part of a thigh — usu. used in pl. ⟨squatted submissively on his ~s —Joseph Conrad⟩ **c** : a hock or the hinder part of a hock **2 a** : the thigh of an animal prepared for food ⟨deer or elk ~s —R.R.Camp⟩; *esp* : the thigh of a hog either fresh or cured by salting and smoking ⟨~s . . . from . . . peanut-fed hogs —*U.S. Code*⟩ — see PORK illustration **b** : something that resembles such a ham in shape; *specif* : a cushion used esp. by tailors for pressing curved areas of garments **3** [short for *hamfatter*] **a** : an unskillful but flamboyant performer : EXHIBITIONIST, STRUTTER ⟨a wrestling match between a couple of ~s⟩ ⟨an oratorical ~⟩ ⟨the basset is a natural ~ —Charlotte Paul⟩; *esp* : an inept or ineffective actor esp. in an overtheatrical style ⟨a typical down-and-out vaudeville ~ —Bennett Cerf⟩ **b** : an inexperienced or incompetent telegraph operator **c** : a government-licensed operator of an amateur radio station ⟨once on the air, he got in touch with ~s on the mainland and they in turn warned ships away from the dangerous coast —R.B. Gehman⟩ **4 a** : melodrama or mawkish sentimentality : overdone theatricality ⟨a film scenario full of tears and ~ —V.S.Pritchett⟩ **b** : a tendency to histrionics : theatrical streak ⟨dignity may suffer as the ~ emerges in response to the camera's grinding —Walter Goodman⟩

³**ham** \"\ *adj* **1** : HAMMY ⟨~ actor⟩ ⟨less ~ than its rivals —William Empson⟩ ⟨in all his life he had never been in any situation so corny, so ~ —Charles Jackson⟩ **2** : of or relating to amateur radio ⟨~ operator⟩ ⟨~ radio band⟩ ⟨~ shack⟩

⁴**ham** \"\ *vb* **hammed; hammed; hamming; hams** *vt* **1** : to execute with exaggerated speech or gestures : OVERACT ⟨spoofed the story and *hammed* the action —Paul Jaretzki⟩ — often used with *up* ⟨~ it up in beer-hall fashion —*Metronome*⟩ **2** : to infuse with melodrama or mawkish sentimentality ⟨the narration was overly *hammed* in the writing —*Billboard*⟩ ~ *vi* : to overplay a part ⟨~s and mugs and . . . misses most of his best effects by underestimating his own simple power —Virgil Thomson⟩

hamada *var of* HAMMADA

¹**hama·dan** \ˌhaməˌdan, ˌhäməˈdän\ *n* -S *usu cap* [fr. *Hamadan,* Iran] **1** : a Persian rug made in and around Hamadan usu. of wool mixed with camels' hair, tied with the Ghiordes knot, and characterized by muted colors and small angular all-over patterns **2** : a Kurdish rug marketed in Hamadan

²**hamadan** \"\ *adj, usu cap* [fr. *Hamadan,* Iran] : of or from the city of Hamadan, Iran : of the kind or style prevalent in Hamadan

ham·a·dry·ad \ˌhaməˈdrīəd, -ī,ad\ *n* -S [L *Hamadryad-, Hamadryas,* fr. Gk, fr. Gk *hama* together with + *Dryad-, Dryas* Dryad — more at DRYAD] **1** : a nymph of trees and woods; *esp* : a nymph whose life begins and ends with that of a particular tree **2 a** [trans. of NL *hamadryas* (specific epithet of *Naja hamadryas*), fr. L *Hamadryas*] : KING COBRA **b** [trans. of NL *hamadryas* (specific epithet of *Papio hamadryas*), fr. L *Hamadryas*] : SACRED BABOON

ham·a·dry·as baboon \ˌ=ˌ=ˈdrīəs-\ *n* [NL *hamadryas,* specific epithet of *Papio hamadryas*] : SACRED BABOON

ha·mal *also* **ham·mal** \hə'mäl, -mȯl\ *n* -S [Ar *ḥammāl* porter] : a burden bearer in Turkey and other countries of the eastern Mediterranean : PORTER

ha·ma·ma·tsu \ˌhäməˈmät(ˌ)sü\ *adj, usu cap* [fr. *Hamamatsu,* Japan] : of or from the city of Hamamatsu, Japan : of the kind or style prevalent in Hamamatsu

ham·a·mel·i·da·ce·ae \ˌhamə,meləˈdāsē,ē\ *n pl, cap* [NL, fr. *Hamamelid-, Hamamelis,* type genus + *-aceae*] : a family of shrubs and trees (order Rosales) having small often clustered flowers and a bicarpellate bilocular ovary and comprising the witch hazels and related plants — see FOTHERGILLA, HAMAMELIS — **ham·a·mel·i·da·ceous** \ˌ=ˌ=ˌ=ˈdāshəs\ *adj*

ham·a·mel·i·dan·the·mum \ˌ=ˌ=ˌ=ˈdan(t)thəməm\ *n, cap* [NL, fr. *Hamamelid-, Hamamelis* + *-anthemum*] : a genus of fossil plants having flowers resembling those of the witch hazel and found in amber of Oligocene age in the region of the Baltic sea

ham·a·mel·i·dox·y·lon \-ˈdäksə,län\ *n, cap* [NL, fr. *Hamamelid-, Hamamelis* + *-o-* + *-xylon*] : a genus of fossil plants having wood identical with or similar to that of the witch hazel

ham·a·me·lis \-ˈmēləs\ *n, cap* [NL, fr. Gk *hamamēlis* medlar, fr. *hama* together with + *mēlon* apple, fruit — more at MELON] : a genus of shrubs or small trees (family Hamamelidaceae) having pinnately veined leaves and clustered flowers with elongated ribbon-shaped petals — see WITCH HAZEL

ham·a·mel·i·tes \ˌhaməˈmelə,tēz, -məˈlīd·(ˌ)ēz\ *n, cap* [NL, fr. *Hamamelis* + *-ites*] : a genus of fossil plants having leaves similar to those of the witch hazel

ha·man·tasch *also* **ha·man·tash** \ˈhämən,täsh, 'həm-\ *n, pl* **hamantaschen** \-shən\ [Yiddish *homentash,* fr. *Homen,* biblical chief minister of Ahasuerus and enemy of the Jews (Esth 3–7) + *tash* pocket, bag, fr. OHG *tasca,* fr. (assumed) VL *tasca* task, compensation, purse — more at TASK] : a three-cornered cake with a poppy-seed or prune filling traditionally eaten in Jewish households at Purim

ha·mar·tia \ˌhä,märˈtēə, həˈmärd·ēə\ *n* -S [Gk, fr. *hamartanein* to err] **1** : a defect of character : error, guilt, or sin esp. of the tragic hero in a literary work **2** : HAMARTOMA — **ha·mar·ti·al** \ˌhä,märˈtēəl, həˈmärd·ēəl\ *adj*

ha·mar·ti·ol·o·gy \hə,märd·ēˈäləjē\ *n* -ES [Gk *hamartia* sin + E *-o-* + *-logy*] : a part of theology treating the doctrine of sin — compare PONEROLOGY

ham·ar·to·ma \ˌhamə(r)ˈtōmə\ *n, pl* **hamartomas** *or* **hamartomata** [NL, fr. Gk *hamartia* + NL *-oma*] : a mass resembling a tumor assumed to represent anomalous development of tissue natural to a part or organ rather than a true tumor — **ham·ar·toma·tous** \ˌ;hamə(r)ˈtämədəs, -tōm-\ *adj*

ha·mate \'hā,māt\ *adj* [L *hamatus,* fr. *hamus* hook + *-atus* -ate; perh. akin to Gk *chamos* bent] : bent at the end into a hook : HOOKED

ha·mat·ed \-,mād·əd\ *adj* [L *hamatus* + E *-ed*] : HAMATE

¹**ha·math·ite** \'hāmə,thīt, -,ma,-\ *n* -S *usu cap* [*Hamath* (Hama), Syria + E *-ite*] : a native or inhabitant of the ancient city of Hamath in western Syria

²**hamathite** \"\ *adj, usu cap* **1** : of, relating to, or characteristic of Hamath **2** : of, relating to, or characteristic of the people of Hamath

ha·ma·tum \hə'mād·əm, -hā'-\ *n, pl* **hama·ta** \-d·ə\ *or* **hamatums** [NL, fr. neut. of L *hamatus* hooked] : a bone on the inner side of the second row of the carpus in mammals that apparently represents a fusion of the fourth and fifth carpal bones — called also *unciform*

ham beetle *n* : any of several small beetles that feed in cured or dried food products; *esp* : RED-LEGGED HAM BEETLE

ham·berg·ite \'ham(ˌ)bər,gīt\ *n* -S [Sw *hambergit,* fr. Axel *Hamberg* †1933 Swed. mineralogist + Sw *-it* -ite] : a mineral $Be_2(OH)BO_3$ consisting of beryllium borate and occurring as grayish white prismatic crystals (hardness 7.5, sp. gr. 2.35)

ham·ble \'ham(b)əl\ *vi* -ED/-ING/-S [perh. akin to LG *humpeln* to limp, OIr *camm* crooked — more at CHANGE] *dial Eng* : to limp or stumble in walking

ham·ble·to·nian \ˌhambəlˈtōnēən, -ōnyən\ *adj, usu cap* [after *Hambletonian,* 19th cent. Am. stallion from which this strain has descended] : a strain of American trotting horses

ham·bo \'häm(ˌ)bü\ *n* -S [Sw, fr. *Hambo,* parish in Hälsingland, Sweden] : a Swedish round danced to various melodies in triple time

hambone \'=ˌ=\ *n* [²*ham* + *bone*] *slang* : a performer using a spurious Negro dialect

ham·bro·line \'hambrə,līn, -ˌlən\ *also* **ham·ber·line** \-bə(r),-\ *or* **ham·ber** \-bə(r)\ *n* -S [*hambroline, hamberline* fr. E *hambro-, hamber-* (irreg. fr. *Hamburg,* Germany) + E *line; hamber* short for *hamberline*] : right-handed 3-strand usu. tarred hemp or jute marine cordage used for small seizings — compare ROUNDLINE

¹**ham·burg** \'ham,bərg, 'haam-, -bōg,-bəig\ *n* -S [fr. *Hamburg,* Germany] **1** *sometimes cap* : a machine-embroidered usu. fine cotton edging for trimming women's clothes **2** *usu cap* : a European breed of rather small domestic fowls with plumage usu. spangled or penciled with white, rose combs, and lead-blue legs **3** [short for *Hamburg steak*] : HAMBURGER

²**hamburg** \", 'häm,bùrg, 'hám-, -ùə|, |k\ *adj, usu cap* [fr. *Hamburg,* Germany] : of or from the city of Hamburg, Germany : of the kind or style prevalent in Hamburg

hamburg brandy *n, usu cap H* : an imitation grape brandy made by adding flavoring to potato or beet spirit

ham·burg·er \'ham,bərgər, 'haam-, -bōgə(r, -bəigə(r\ *n* -S *often attrib* [short for *Hamburger steak*] **1 a** : ground beef **b** : a cooked patty of ground beef — compare SALISBURY STEAK **2** : a sandwich made of a hamburger patty in a split round bun

hamburg parsley *n, usu cap H* : a parsley (*Petroselinum crispum* var. *tuberosum*) having smooth uncurled foliage and being cultivated primarily for its enlarged edible taproot which resembles a small very savory parsnip

hamburg steak *pronunc at* ¹HAMBURG +\ *or* **hamburger steak** *n, sometimes cap H* [²*Hamburg* or G *Hamburger* of Hamburg, fr. *Hamburg,* Germany] : HAMBURGER

¹**hame** \'hām\ *n* -S [ME, prob. fr. MD; akin to OE *ham* undergarment, *hame* covering, OHG *hama,* ON *hamr* covering, shape, Skt *śāmulya* woolen shirt] : one of the two curved wooden or metal projections which are attached to or form part of the collar of a draft horse and to which the traces are fastened

²**hame** \"\ *Scot var of* HOME

ha·meil \'hāməl\ *adj* [of Scand origin; akin to ON *heimill, heimall* domestic, at one's disposal, fr. *heimr* home, homeland — more at HOME] *Scot* : domestic and homelike

¹**hamel** *or* **hamil** \'aməl, '(h)ām-\ *n* -S [MF *hamel* — more at HAMLET] *now dial Eng* : HAMLET

²**ham·el** \'haməl\ *n* -S [Afrik, fr. MD; akin to OE *hamola* man with cropped hair, OHG *hamal* wether, *hamal* castrated, ON *hamla* to castrate, *skammr* short, Skt *śamala* error, damage; basic meaning: castrated] *Africa* : WETHER

ha·me·lia \hə'mēlyə\ *n* [NL, fr. Henri L. Du*hamel*-Dumonceau †1782 Fr. agriculturist + NL *-ia*] **1** *cap* : a genus (family Rubiaceae) of tropical American shrubs having flowers in scorpioid cymes with the corolla distinctly 5-ribbed **2** -S : any plant of the genus *Hamelia*

hame·suck·en *also* **haim·suck·en** \'hām,səkən\ *n* -S [ME *hamsoken,* fr. OE *hāmsōcn,* fr. *hām* home + *sōcn* attack; akin to ON *sōkn* attack, OE *sēcan* to attack, seek — more at HOME, SEEK] **1** *Scots law* : the assaulting of a person in his own house or dwelling place **2** *Old Eng law* **a** (1) : a franchise of trying persons charged with assaulting a person in his own home and receiving the fines or damages imposed (2) : such fines or damages **b** : BURGLARY, HOUSEBREAKING

ha·metz *or* **cha·metz** *or* **cho·metz** \kō'māts, 'kō,mets\ *n* -ES [Heb *ḥāmēṣ*] : leaven or leavened food banned during Passover

hame·with \'hāmwəth\ *adv (or adj)* [alter. of earlier *hameward,* fr. ²*hame* + *-ward*] *Scot* : HOMEWARD

ham·fare \'ham,fa(a)|(ə)r, -fe|\ *n* [ME *hamfare,* fr. *ham* home + *fare* journey, expedition — more at FARE] : HAMESUCKEN

ham·fat·ter \'ham,fad·ə(r)\ *n* -S [fr. "The *Ham-fat* Man," Negro minstrel song + E *-er*] *slang* : ²HAM 3a

ham-fisted \'=ˌ=ˌ=\ *adj, chiefly Brit* : HAM-HANDED 2

ham-handed \'=ˌ=ˌ=\ *adj* **1** : having especially large hands ⟨a *ham-handed* companion who looked like a heavyweight wrestler —W.M.Swann⟩ **2** : HEAVY-HANDED, CLUMSY ⟨*ham-handed* dramatist —J.C.Trewin⟩ ⟨teams made up of ponderous or *ham-handed* players —H.N.Maclean⟩

hami *pl of* HAMUS

ha·mi·form \'hāmə,fȯrm\ *adj* [L *hamus* hook + E *-iform* — more at HAMATE] : HOOKED 1

ha·milt \'hāməlt, -ld\ *var of* HAMEIL

ham·il·ton \'haməltᵊn, -tən\ *adj, usu cap* [fr. *Hamilton,* Ontario] : of or from the city of Hamilton, Ontario : of the kind or style prevalent in Hamilton

¹**ham·il·to·ni·an** \ˌ=ˌ=ˈtōnēən, -ōnyən\ *adj, usu cap* **1** [Alexander *Hamilton* †1804 Am. statesman + E *-ian*] **1** : of or relating to the statesman Hamilton or to his political and social doctrines or program characterized by advocacy of a strong central government of a unitary type, protection of industrial and commercial interests, and a general distrust of the political capacity or wisdom of the common man ⟨the *Hamiltonian* creed of selective suffrage —S.H.Adams⟩ ⟨the *Hamiltonian* tradition in the U.S. —Alexander Brady⟩ ⟨the clash of Jeffersonian and *Hamiltonian* America —R.M.Weaver⟩ ⟨the *Hamiltonian* realistic concern with . . . the protection of American industries —T.I.Cook & Malcolm Moos⟩ **2** [James *Hamilton* †1829 Brit. language teacher + E *-ian*] : of or relating to the scholar Hamilton or his system of language teaching **3** [Sir William *Hamilton* †1856 Scottish philosopher + E *-ian*] : of or relating to the philosopher Hamilton or his theories — compare HAMILTONISM **4** [Sir William R. *Hamilton* †1865 Brit. mathematician + E *-ian*] : of or relating to the mathematician Hamilton or his system of dynamics

²**hamiltonian** \"\ *n* -S *usu cap* : a follower or exponent of Hamiltonian doctrines or theories; *esp* : a follower or advocate of the social or political doctrines of Alexander Hamilton

ham·il·to·ni·an·ism \ˌhaməlˈtōnēə,nizəm, -ōnyə,-\ *n* -S *usu cap* [¹*Hamiltonian* + E *-ism*] : the body of social and political doctrines held by or associated with the statesman Hamilton : the Hamiltonian program or ideology

ham·il·ton·ism \'haməltᵊn,izəm, -ltə,ni-\ *n* -S *usu cap* [Sir William *Hamilton* + E *-ism*] : the philosophical and logical teachings of Sir William Hamilton esp. concerning the doctrine of natural realism and the quantification of the predicate

ham·i·noea \ˌhaməˈnēə\ *n, cap* [NL] : a common genus of bubble shells (family Akeridae) of the Pacific coast of No. America with a shell so thin that the pulsation of the heart of the translucent yellowish brown animal within is commonly visible through it

ham·ite \'ha,mīt, *usu* -īd·+V\ *n* -S *usu cap* [*Ham,* son of Noah, eponymous ancestor of the Hamites (Gen 10:6–20) + E *-ite*] **1** : a descendant of Ham, one of the sons of Noah **2 a** : a member of a group of African peoples including the Berber peoples north of the Sahara, the Tuaregs and Tibbu in the Sudan, possibly the extinct Guanches of the Canaries, the ancient Egyptians and their descendants, and the Galla of east Africa that are mostly Muslims, are highly variable in appearance but mainly Caucasoid, and are believed by many to be late-Paleolithic or post-Paleolithic colonists of western Europe **b** : a native speaker of a Hamitic language — compare COPT, ETHIOPIAN

ha·mi·tes \hə'mīd·(ˌ)ēz\ *n, cap* [NL, fr. L *hamus* hook + NL *-ites* — more at HAMATE] : a genus of extinct Cretaceous ammonoids with a shell forming repeated V-shaped loops in one plane

[1]**ham·it·ic** \(')ha¦mid·ik, hə'm-, -mitik\ *adj, usu cap* [*Hamite* + *-ic*] **1** : of, relating to, or characteristic of the Hamites **2** : of, relating to, or characteristic of one of the Hamitic languages

[2]**hamitic** \"\ *n* -s *usu cap* : HAMITIC LANGUAGES ⟨an authority on *Hamitic*⟩

ham·it·i·cized \ha'mid·ə,sīzd, hə'm-\ *adj, usu cap* : conjectured or presumed to have acquired through interbreeding certain traits hypothetically characteristic of the ancient ancestors of the Hamitic-speaking peoples

hamitic languages *n pl, usu cap H* : the Berber, Cushitic, and sometimes Egyptian branches of the Afro-Asiatic or Hamito-Semitic languages formerly regarded as constituting an independent language family or as constituting one of two coordinate subfamilies of the Hamito-Semitic languages

ham·i·tism \'hamə,tizəm\ *n* -s *usu cap* : the quality or state of being Hamitic

hamito- *comb form, usu cap* [*Hamitic*] : Hamitic and ⟨*Hamito*-Bantu⟩ ⟨*Hamito*-Semitic⟩ — usu. with hyphen

[1]**hamito-semitic** \¦hamə,tō+\ *adj, usu cap H&S* [*Hamito-* + *Semitic*] : of, relating to, or characteristic of the Hamito-Semitic languages

[2]**hamito-semitic** \"\ *n, usu cap H&S* : HAMITO-SEMITIC LANGUAGES

hamito-semitic languages *n pl, usu cap H&S* : AFRO-ASIATIC LANGUAGES

[1]**ham·let** \'hamlət, *usu* -əd·+V\ *n* -s [ME, fr. MF *hamelet*, dim. of *hamel*, dim. of *ham*, of Gmc origin; akin to OE *hām* homeland, village, house — more at HOME] **1** : a small village ⟨performances are being contemplated in cities, in towns, and even in ~s —Joseph Wechsberg⟩ ⟨a ~ in the town of Readsboro —J.H.Buffum⟩ **2** : the smallest incorporated unit of municipal government ⟨incorporation into a ~, the bottom rung of the municipal ladder —*N.Y.Times*⟩

[2]**hamlet** \"\ *n* -s [origin unknown] **1 a** : a large grouper (*Epinephelus striatus*) common from Florida to Brazil and in the Caribbean and important as a food fish — called also *Nassau grouper* **b** *Bahamas* : any young grouper **2** : a yellow and black thickly spotted moray (*Gymnothorax moringa*) used for food in the West Indies

[3]**hamlet** \"\ *n* -s *usu cap* [after *Hamlet*, chief character of the tragedy *Hamlet* (1600–1601) by William Shakespeare †1616 English dramatist] : a brooding indecisive person ⟨the very *Hamlet* of our age . . . a philosopher thrust into power at a time of violence —Michael Amrine⟩ ⟨tortured by indecision, a *Hamlet* in politics —*Newsweek*⟩

hamlike \'=,=\ *adj* : resembling a ham ⟨swung a ~ fist toward the west window of the kitchen —Kenneth Roberts⟩

ham·ma·da *or* **ha·ma·da** \hə'mädə\ *n* -s [Ar *hammādah*] : a rock-floored or rock-strewn desert region esp. in the Sahara

hammal *var of* HAMAL

ham·mar·ite \'hamə,rīt\ *n* -s [Sw *hammarit*, fr. Gladhammar, Sweden, its locality + Sw *-it* -ite] : a mineral prob. $Pb_2Cu_2Bi_4S_9$ consisting of lead, copper, and bismuth sulfide

hammed *past of* HAM

[1]**ham·mer** \'hamə(r)\ *n* -s *often attrib* [ME *hamer*, fr. OE *hamor*; akin to OHG *hamar* hammer, ON *hamarr* hammer, crag, Gk *akmōn* anvil, Skt *áśma* stone, Gk *akmē* edge — more at EDGE] **1 a** : a hand tool consisting of a solid head set crosswise on a handle and used for pounding (as in driving nails, breaking stone, beating metal surfaces) — see BALL PEEN HAMMER, CLAW HAMMER, SLEDGEHAMMER; compare MALLET **b** : a power tool that often substitutes a metal block or a drill for the hammerhead (as in driving posts, stamping or forging metal, or breaking up rock surfaces) — see AIR HAMMER, DROP HAMMER, JACKHAMMER; compare PILE DRIVER **2** : one that strikes like a hammer ⟨we need a concerted, vigorous voice; we need a ~ —Harvey Breit⟩ ⟨wielding this problem as the ~ with which they must smash the last vestiges of Christian thought —L.J. Shehan⟩ ⟨the ~ thrust of radio and television —*Saturday Rev.*⟩ **3** : something that resembles a hammer in form or action: as **a** : a lever with a striking head for ringing a bell or striking a gong (as in a clock or an electric bell) **b** *obs* : a door knocker **c** (1) : a steel cover for the powder pan of a flintlock gun against which the flint strikes to ignite the powder; *also* : an arm that holds the flint for striking : [1]COCK 4 (2) : an arm that strikes the cap in a percussion lock to ignite the propelling charge (3) : a part of the action of a modern gun that strikes the primer of the cartridge in firing or that strikes the firing pin to ignite the cartridge **d** : MALLEUS 1a **e** : GAVEL; *specif* : a gavel with which an auctioneer indicates that an article is sold to the last bidder **f** (1) : a padded mallet in a piano action for striking a string (2) : a hand mallet for playing on a percussion instrument of fixed pitch (as a dulcimer or a xylophone) **4** : a metal sphere hurled in the hammer throw that usu. weighs 16 pounds and together with its flexible wire handle measures not more than four feet in length — **under the hammer** *adv* : for sale at auction ⟨priceless heirlooms went *under the hammer*⟩

[2]**hammer** \"\ *vb* **hammered; hammered; hammering** \-m(ə)riŋ\ **hammers** [ME *hameren*, fr. *hamer*, n.] *vi* **1 a** : to strike blows esp. repeatedly with or as if with a hammer : POUND ⟨the impounded water ~s at the weak spots —Russell Lord⟩ ⟨his pulses ~ing in his head —Clive Arden⟩ **b** : WATER-HAMMER **2** : to become insistent or urgent : be in or keep up a state of agitation ⟨these thoughts . . . ~ed in her indignant consciousness —J.C.Powys⟩ **3** : to make repeated efforts as if shaping with a hammer: **a** : to reiterate an opinion or attitude repeatedly and emphatically : to place emphasis by constant repetition or discussion ⟨continually ~s on the danger of intrigue —O.M.Green⟩ — often used with *away* ⟨letters and pamphlets all ~ed away at the same point —Nathan Kelne⟩ **b** : to work persistently or tirelessly : TOIL, LABOR ⟨Beethoven thought of an air, ~ed at it, altered it again and again —C.W.H.Johnson⟩ **4** *now dial Eng* : to speak haltingly : STAMMER ~ *vt* **1 a** : to strike with a hammer : beat, drive, or shape with repeated blows ⟨~ a nail⟩ ⟨~ a horseshoe⟩ ⟨~ out a tray⟩ **b** : to fasten with a hammer (as by nailing) ⟨~ down a lid⟩ **c** : to build with hammer and nails — usu. used with *together* ⟨~ together a cold frame⟩ **2** : to strike as if with a hammer: **a** : to hit or drive with the force of a hammer ⟨~ed in three home runs in one game —Bob Broeg⟩ ⟨the incoming train ~ed the rear of the shorter train —*Springfield (Mass.) Union*⟩ **b** : to strike with repeated blows : POUND, THUMP ⟨~ a typewriter⟩ ⟨~ing a rather hard pillow into a more comfortable shape —Dorothy Sayers⟩ **c** : to bring or keep under attack : BELABOR ⟨the State Department is being badly ~ed on this issue —*New Republic*⟩ **3** : to produce or bring about as if by means of repeated blows: **a** : to shape or put together by persevering effort ⟨~ our words to fit a song —Charles Fox⟩ ⟨~ed together an alliance —*Newsweek*⟩ — often used with *out* ⟨~ out a policy⟩ ⟨~ out an empire⟩ ⟨sat at the piano for hours . . . trying to ~ out an original tune —Noel Coward⟩ **b** : to force or drive into the consciousness by reiteration ⟨~ing in day after day the same few and relatively simple beliefs —John Dewey⟩ — often used with *home* ⟨~s home the theme of freedom to think —Brooks Atkinson⟩ **c** : to level off : make smooth : ADJUST — usu. used with *out* ⟨differences are ~ed out in discussion —Walter Moberly⟩ **d** (1) : to force down the price of (a stock) by selling short ⟨told the broker whom I had been using to ~ down the stock to continue his operations —B.M.Baruch⟩ (2) : to declare (a member of the London stock exchange) to be a defaulter ⟨broke away to the stock exchange and at twenty-four was insolvent and ~ed —*Times Lit. Supp.*⟩

ham·mer-ai·toff projection \¦hämə'(r)ī,tóf-\ *n, usu cap H&A* [after Ernst von *Hammer* †1925 Ger. geographer and David *Aitoff* †1933 Russ. geographer] : AITOFF PROJECTION

hammer and sickle *n, sometimes cap H&S* [fr. its adoption (1923) by the U.S.S.R. on its national flag] **1** : an emblem consisting of a crossed sickle and hammer used as a symbol of peasant and worker **2** : a flag bearing the insignia of the hammer and sickle

hammer and tongs *adv* (*or adj*) : with the force and violence of a blacksmith pounding iron : with all one's strength : in a rough-and-tumble manner ⟨the wedding party going it *hammer and tongs* down the road —Richard Llewellyn⟩ ⟨go after a witness in the old *hammer-and-tongs* style —Mitchell Dawson⟩ ⟨has gone at his job in a *hammer-and-tongs* way that has annoyed — and offended — a good many businessmen —*Newsweek*⟩

hammer beam *n* : either of the short horizontal beams or cantilevers projecting from the top of a pair of opposite walls to support a roof principal for a Gothic roof and thus dispense with the necessity for a tie beam

hammerbird \'==,=\ *n* : HAMMERKOP

hammerblow \'==,=\ *n* : a stroke of or as if of a hammer; *specif* : a pounding of the rails by the driving wheels of a locomotive caused by the inertia of unbalanced parts

hammer brace *n* : a bracket under a hammer beam

hammer butt *n* : a block into which the base of a hammer shank in a piano action is fitted

1 hammer beams

hammercloth \'==,=\ *n* [ME *hamerclothe*] : an ornamented often fringed cloth hung over the coachman's seat esp. of a ceremonial coach

hammerdress \'==,=\ *vt* : to dress or face (stone) with a hammer

hammer drill *n* : a percussion rock drill in which a plunger or hammer strikes rapid blows on the shank of a loosely held drill — compare PISTON DRILL

hammered *adj* : having surface indentations produced or appearing to have been produced by hammering ⟨a bracelet of dark ~ metal —Douglass Wallop⟩

hammered glass *n* : rolled glass made nontransparent by embossing it on one side to resemble beaten metal

ham·mer·er \'hamərə(r)\ *n* -s : one that hammers

hammerhead \'==,=\ *n* **1** : the striking part of a hammer; *specif* : a part of a hammer in a piano action that strikes the strings **2** : one that is dense or stupid : BLOCKHEAD, NUMSKULL ⟨a big ~ but even if he had had a smart head, a no-good horse —Richard Wormser⟩ **3** : something that resembles the striking part of a hammer: as **a** : any of various medium-sized sharks that with the shovelheads constitute the family Sphyrnidae, have the eyes at the ends of lateral extensions of the flattened head, are active voracious fishes sometimes considered man-eaters, are widely distributed in warm seas, and include some (as *Sphyrna zygaena* and *S. fudes*) which are fished for their hides and vitamin-rich livers **b** (1) : HOG SUCKER (2) : HAMMERHEADED BAT (3) *or* **hammerheaded stork** \'==,==-\ : HAMMERKOP

hammerhead crane *n* : a heavy-duty crane with a horizontal counterbalanced jib

hammerheaded \¦==¦==\ *adj* **1** : having a head shaped like that of a hammer **2** : DENSE, STUPID, THICKHEADED

hammerheaded bat *n* : a West African epaulet bat (*Epomorphus monstrosus* or *Hypsegnathus monstrosus*) with greatly enlarged larynx and distinctive voice

hammerhead shark *also* **hammerheaded shark** *n* : HAMMERHEAD 3a

hammerhead stall *n* : a maneuver in which an airplane pulls up in a vertical climb until it almost stalls and then drops the nose in a wingover so that direction of flight is reversed

hammering *n* -s **1** : the act or process of beating or pounding with or as if with a hammer ⟨the art of silver ~⟩ ⟨slow ~ of heavy guns —Kenneth Roberts⟩ ⟨under ~s from me . . . the legislature passed a bill —F.D.Roosevelt⟩ **2** : a pattern of shallow indentations produced with a hammer

ham·mer·ing·ly *adv* : in a hammering manner

ham·mer·kop \'hamə(r),käp\ *also* **hammerkop bird** *or* **hammerkop stork** *n* -s [Afrik *hamerkop*, fr. *hamer* hammer + *kop* head] : a chiefly dusky brown African wading bird (*Scopus umbretta*) intermediate in some respects between storks and herons but distinguished by its large head with heavy bill and thick dorsal crest and by its huge domed nest

ham·mer·less \-ləs\ *adj* **1** : lacking a hammer **2** : having the hammer concealed — used of a gun having the hammer enclosed within the receiver

hammerlock \'==,=\ *n* : a wrestling hold in which an opponent's arm is held bent behind his back

ham·mer·man \-mən, -,man\ *n, pl* **hammermen** [ME, fr. *hamer* hammer + *man*] : one that works with a hammer; *esp* : an operator of a power-driven hammer (as a jackhammer)

hammer mill *n* **1** : a grinder in which feed and other products are pulverized by several rows of thin steel hammers revolving at high speed **2** : a crusher in which minerals (as ores, rock, coal) are broken up by the impact of swinging hammer bars hinged to a rapidly rotating shaft

hammer oyster *n* : any of several bivalve mollusks of *Malleus* and related genera of Chinese and Australian waters having elongated handle-shaped shells that resemble an oyster on the interior and that are prolonged in both directions at the dorsal margin to suggest the head of a hammer

hammer post *n* : a pendant in the shape of a pilaster that serves as impost to a hammer brace

hammer price *n* : the price at which a defaulter's contract is settled on the London stock exchange

hammer rail *n* : a padded strip of wood supporting the hammers in a piano action when at rest

hammers *pl of* HAMMER, *pres 3d sing of* HAMMER

hammer scale *n* : a scale that forms on heated metal when it is hammered

hammer shank *n* : a wooden dowel onto which a hammer in a piano action is fitted

hammer shell *n* : HAMMER OYSTER; *also*; its shell

hammersmith \'==,=\ *n* **1** : a smith who works with a hammer **2** : one who supervises work done with drop hammers or power presses

hammer spring *n* : a spring that actuates a hammer (as in a gun or a piano action)

hammer spur *n* : a projection on the hammer of a gun by which it is cocked

hammerstone \'==,=\ *n* : a prehistoric hammering implement consisting of a rounded stone

hammer throw *n* : a field event in which a metal sphere attached to a flexible handle is hurled for distance from inside a circle with a 7-foot diameter

hammertoe \¦==¦=\ *n* : a toe (as the second) deformed by permanent angular flexion of the second and third joints resulting in an incurved form resembling a claw

hammer tongs *n* : blacksmith's tongs having projecting lugs for engaging holes of hammerheads during forging

hammer-weld \¦==¦=\ *vt* : to weld by blows with a hammer

hammer welding *n* : forge welding by mechanical hammering

hammerwort \'==,=\ *n* : PELLITORY 1

hammer-wrought \¦==¦=\ *adj* : shaped with a hammer

hamming *pres part of* HAM

[1]**ham·mock** \'hamək *also* -mik *or* -mēk\ *n* -s *often attrib* [Sp *hamaca*, fr. Taino] **1** : a swinging couch or bed usu. made of netting or canvas and slung by cords from supports at each end ⟨two trees just wide enough apart to swing a ~⟩ **2** : something that resembles a hammock (as the suspended nest of an oriole); *specif* : a length of light twine netting hung along or across a sleeping-car berth to hold wearing apparel and other personal belongings

hammock 1

[2]**hammock** \"\ *vt* -ED/-ING/-S : to suspend in or as if in a hammock ⟨~ed him in her shawl in a loop that placed him close to her breast —John Steinbeck⟩ ⟨content to ~ himself passively in the amplitude of enveloping time —Victoria Sackville-West⟩

[3]**hammock** \"\ *n* -s *often attrib* [origin unknown] **1** : HUMMOCK **2** : a fertile area in the southern U.S. (as Florida) that is often somewhat higher than its surroundings and is characterized by hardwood vegetation and soil of greater depth and containing more humus than that of the flatwoods or pinelands; *specif* : an island of dense tropical undergrowth in the Everglades

hammock batten *n* **1** : one of the battens on a ship's beam from which a hammock is slung **2** : a bar used for spreading hammock clews

hammock clew *n* [[1]*hammock*] : CLEW 3b

hammock cloth *n* : a tarpaulin or piece of canvas used on a ship to cover stowed hammocks or to place over the openings in hammock nettings — called also *top cloth*

hammock hickory *n* [[3]*hammock*] : a Florida tree (*Carya floridana* or *C. magnifloridana*) having gray bark, reddish brown to gray twigs, leaves with 5 to 7 leaflets, and fruit that is broadly ellipsoid to pyriform

hammock netting *also* **hammock berthing** *n* : a net or a box trough to hold sailors' hammocks when not in use

ham·my \'hamē, 'haam-, -mi\ *adj* -ER/-EST **1 a** : flavored with or tasting of ham **b** : resembling ham in flavor or appearance **2** : like or characteristic of a ham actor : exaggeratedly and usu. self-consciously theatrical : OVERACTED ⟨children are not dismayed by ~ acting provided the story is good —Rose M. Daly⟩

ha·mo·tzi \hä'mōtsē\ *n* -s [Heb *hammōṣī*, lit., the one who brings forth; fr. the concluding words of the benediction] : the recital of the Hebrew benediction over bread before meals

[1]**ham·per** \'hampə(r), 'haam-, 'haim-\ *vt* **hampered; hampered; hampering** \-p(ə)riŋ\ **hampers** [ME *hamperen*; perh. akin to Flem *hampern* to stutter, MD *hāperen*] **1 a** : to restrict the movement of by bonds or obstacles : FETTER, IMPEDE ⟨elaborate ~ing clothes —James Laver⟩ ⟨icebergs ~ed the progress of the ship⟩ ⟨pitching . . . violently in the seaway, ~ed by her heavy tow —R.S.Porteous⟩ **b** : to interfere with the operation of : DISRUPT ⟨radio communications ~ed by static —*Globe & Mail*⟩ **2 a** : CURB, RESTRAIN, LIMIT ⟨the view . . . that rhyme and meter ~ the poet's free expression —J.L. Lowes⟩ ⟨did nothing to ~ the boisterousness of the occasion —Silas Spitzer⟩ **b** : to interfere with : ENCUMBER, HANDICAP, OBSTRUCT ⟨an obsolete ideology can ~ an economy —V.G. Childe⟩ ⟨~ed by lack of money as often as by lack of initiative —H.J.Hanham⟩

syn CLOG, TRAMMEL, FETTER, SHACKLE, MANACLE, HOG-TIE: HAMPER, the most general of these terms, can imply any impediment or restraining agent that encumbers, delays, or interferes with an action ⟨like other branches of science, history is now encumbered and *hampered* by its own mass —Henry Adams⟩ ⟨his principle was to choose competent lieutenants, and then to leave them to work without *hampering* interference —*Irish Digest*⟩ ⟨*hampered* in his progress by the weight of a large bundle on his back⟩ CLOG usu. implies a foreign useless impediment that clings, gums up, or obstructs ⟨all common ambitions, rank, possessions, power, the things which *clog* man's feet —John Buchan⟩ ⟨his mind is *clogged* with the strangest miscellany of truth and marvel —V.L. Parrington⟩ ⟨waved the traffic away from the *clogged* thoroughfare —Ralph Gustafson⟩ TRAMMEL suggests entanglement by or confinement within a net ⟨had now become *trammeled* in events —Ethel Wilson⟩ ⟨a landscape of increasing strangeness, replete with things shocking to a culture-*trammeled* understanding —B.L.Whorf⟩ FETTER suggests the total or almost total crippling restraint of chains or manacles ⟨a tendency toward introversion . . . had slowly mastered him, *fettering* his actions and segregating him in an unhappy little world —I.V.Morris⟩ ⟨watched a world prepare for war while he was *fettered* by the nation's propensity for isolationism —Estes Kefauver⟩ SHACKLE and MANACLE are very similar to although stronger than FETTER, usu. suggesting a total impeding of action ⟨if the power of the courts stereotypes legislation within the forms and limits . . . expedient in the 19th or perhaps the 18th century, it *shackles* progress and breeds distrust and suspicion of the courts —B.N.Cardozo⟩ ⟨keep Rome *manacled* hand and foot: no fear of unruliness —Robert Browning⟩ HOG-TIE implies a making completely helpless or a total thwarting ⟨as soon as the senator can get us *hog-tied* to that extent, he will . . . ram these unconstitutional measures down our throats —*Congressional Record*⟩ ⟨accuse Americans of being *hog-tied* to business —*advt*⟩

[2]**hamper** \"\ *n* -s **1** : something that impedes : OBSTRUCTION, SHACKLE ⟨if the Fourteenth Amendment is not to be a greater ~ . . . than I think was intended —O.W.Holmes †1935⟩ **2** : TOP-HAMPER

[3]**hamper** \"\ *n* -s [ME *hampere*, alter. of *hanaper* — more at *hanaper*] : a basket or box usu. with a cover for packing, storing, or transporting food and other articles: as **a** : a basket often of wickerwork for carrying food or drink ⟨a picnic ~⟩ ⟨helped . . . the yardman to pack the game in ~s —Adrian Bell⟩ **b** : a container of standardized capacity for shipping fruits and vegetables that is of splint, stave, or fiberboard construction and is circular, elliptical, or polygonal in shape with a top diameter usu. greater than the bottom, with slatted sides, and with a bottom that may be loose, stapled, or nailed in place or formed by a continuation of the sides — compare BASKET 1 **c** : a small ventilated receptacle for laundry made of wood, plastic, or metal and usu. having a flat side to fit against a wall **d** : a large canvas container on casters used for sorting and moving mail in a post office

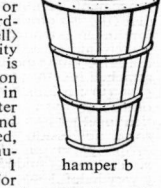

hamper b

[4]**hamper** \"\ *vt* **hampered; hampered; hampering** \-p(ə)riŋ\ **hampers** *chiefly Brit* **1** : to pack in a hamper ⟨trifles . . . ~ed up together —T.A.Browne⟩ **2** : to present with a hamper of food or wine ⟨something particularly charming about being ~ed at Christmas time —*Westminster Gazette*⟩

hamp·race \'ham,prās\ *n usu cap* [[1]*Hampshire* + Land*race*] : MONTANA 2a

[1]**hamp·shire** \'ham(p),shi(ə)r, 'haam-, -,shiə, -,shə(r)\ *n* [fr. *Hampshire*, England] **1** *usu cap* : an American breed of black, white-belted swine with white forelegs, rather long head, and straight face **2** -s *often cap* : an animal of the Hampshire breed

[2]**hampshire** \"\ *adj, usu cap* [fr. *Hampshire*, England] : of or from Hampshire, England : of the kind or style prevalent in Hampshire

[3]**hampshire** \"\ *also* **hampshire down** \¦=(,)=¦daůn\ *n* [[2]*Hampshire*] **1** *usu cap H&D* : a British breed of medium-wooled mutton-type sheep that are large, thick-fleshed, and hornless and have dark faces and legs **2** -s *usu cap H often cap D* : a sheep of the Hampshire breed

hams *pl of* HAM, *pres 3d sing of* HAM

ham·socn \'häm,sōkən\ *n* -s [OE *hāmsōcn* — more at HAMESUCKEN] : HAMESUCKEN

ham·ster \'hamztə(r), 'haam-, -m(p)st-\ *n* -s [G, fr. OHG *hamustro* (akin to OS *hamustra* hamster), of Slavic origin; akin to OSlav *chomĕstorŭ* hamster] : any of numerous Old World rodents of *Cricetus* and related genera having very large cheek pouches and somewhat resembling the American white-footed mouse but short-tailed and commonly larger and of burrowing habits — see GOLDEN HAMSTER

ham·stery \-tərē\ *n* -ES : an establishment for breeding and raising hamsters

[1]**hamstring** \'=,=\ *n* [[2]*ham* (popliteal space) + *string*] **1 a** : either of two groups of tendons bounding the upper part of the popliteal space at the back of the knee and forming the tendons of insertion of certain muscles of the back of the thigh **b** : the large tendon above and behind the hock of a quadruped : ACHILLES' TENDON **2** : a restrictive power : regulatory control ⟨fend for itself . . . among myriad regulations, restrictions, and government ~s —*Atlantic*⟩

[2]**hamstring** \"\ *vt* **hamstrung; hamstrung; hamstringing; hamstrings** **1 a** : to deprive of the power of locomotion by cutting the leg tendons : CRIPPLE, DISABLE ⟨wolf packs ~ and destroy many moose —Frank Dufresne⟩ **b** : to cut the muscle or tendons in the small of a whale ⟨it is sometimes the custom when fast to a whale more than commonly powerful and alert, to seek to ~ him —Herman Melville⟩ **2** : to make ineffective or powerless : limit or destroy the effectiveness of : HINDER, IMPAIR ⟨supporting rather than ~ing our negotiators —F.L. Allen⟩ ⟨talents *hamstrung* by respectability —Cyril Connolly⟩ ⟨~ . . . arms production by wresting away raw-material sources —Virginia Prewett⟩

ham·u·lar \'hamyələ(r)\ *adj* [L *hamulus* + E *-ar*] : HAMATE

ham·u·lus \-ləs\ *n, pl* **hamu·li** \-,lī\ [NL, fr. L, little hook, dim. of *hamus*] : a hook or hooklike process; *esp* : a little hook terminating the barbicel of a feather

ha·mus \'hāməs\ *n, pl* **ha·mi** \-,mī\ [NL, fr. L, hook — more at HAMATE] *biol* : a hook or curved process

ham·za *or* **ham·zah** \'hamzə\ *n* -s [Ar *hamzah*, lit., compression (as of the larynx)] **1 :** the sign for a glottal stop in Arabic orthography — usu. represented in English by an apostrophe **2 :** the sound for which the hamza stands

ham·zat·ed \-,zād·əd\ *adj* **:** bearing a hamza — used of a letter of the Arabic alphabet or of a word written in the Arabic alphabet ⟨a ~ alif⟩

¹han *dial Brit pres pl of* HAVE

²han \'hän, -a-\ *adj, usu cap* [*Han*, Chin. dynasty (206 B.C.–A.D. 220)] **1 :** of, relating to, or having the characteristics of the period of the Han dynasty ⟨*Han* pottery⟩ **2 :** of, relating to, or being a nationality group in China descended from the original Chinese and constituting an overwhelming majority of the population and the dominant cultural group **:** belonging to the Chinese proper as distinguished from other nationality groups (as the Manchu or Mongols) ⟨the *Han* race⟩

³han \"\ *n, pl* **han** *or* **hans** *usu cap* **1 :** an Athapaskan people of the Yukon river district in east central Alaska and the Yukon Territory of Canada **2 :** a member of the Han people

han' \'(h)an, 'hȯn\ *Scot var of* HAND

han·a·fi \'hanə(,)fē\ *n* -s *usu cap* [Ar *hanafīy*, after abu-*Hanifah* †767 Muslim jurist] **1 :** an orthodox school of Muslim jurisprudence predominating in Turkey and India — compare HANBALI, MALIKI, SHAFI'I **2** *or* **han·a·fite** \-,fīt\ **:** a follower of the Hanafi school

han·a·hill *or* **han·na·hill** \'hanə,hil\ *n* -s [origin unknown] **:** a sea bass (*Centropristes striatus*) of the Atlantic coast

han·ap \'ha,nap, -,nəp\ *n* -s [ME, fr. MF *hanap, henap*, of Gmc origin; akin to OE *hnæpp* bowl, drinking vessel, OS *hnapp*, MD & MLG *nap*, OHG *hnapf*, ON *hnappr*] **:** an elaborate medieval goblet or standing cup usu. having a cover

han·a·per \'hanəpə(r)\ *n* -s [ME (also, case to hold hanaps), fr. MF *hanapier* case to hold hanaps, fr. *hanap* + *-ier* -er] *Brit* **:** a small wicker case used as a repository for legal documents

han·a·ster \'hanəstə(r)\ *n* -s [ME *hanster*, fr. *hans* hansa + *-ster* — more at HANSA] **:** a person admitted to the merchant guild in Oxford, England

han·ba·li \'hanbə(,)lē\ *n* -s *usu cap* [Ar *hanbalīy*, after ibn-*Hanbal* †855 Arab jurist] **1 :** an orthodox school of Muslim jurisprudence predominating in Saudi Arabia — compare HANAFI, MALIKI, SHAFI'I **2** *or* **han·ba·lite** \-ə,līt\ **:** a follower of the Hanbali school

hance \'han(t)s\ *n* -s [obs. E *hance, haunce* lintel, fr. *hance, haunce* to raise, fr. ME *haunсen*, prob. short for *enhauncen* — more at ENHANCE] **1 :** a curved contour on a ship (as the fall of the fife rail to the deck) **2 a** (1) **:** the arc of minimum radius at the springing of an elliptical or similar arch (2) **:** the haunch of an arch **b :** a small arch joining a straight lintel to a jamb

hance arch *n* **:** an arch having greater curvature at its springings than at the crown

hanch \'hanch\ *vb* [ME *hanchen*, fr. MF *hancher*] *vt, now dial Eng* **:** to snap at noisily or greedily ~ *vi, now dial Eng* **:** to snap noisily and greedily

han·cock·ite \'han,kä,kīt\ *n* -s [E. P. *Hancock*, 19th cent. Am. mineralogist + E *-ite*] **:** a complex silicate that contains lead, calcium, strontium, and other metals and is isomorphous with epidote

¹hand \'hand, -aa(ə)-\ *n* -s *often attrib* [ME, fr. OE *hand, hond*; akin to OHG *hant* hand, ON *hönd*, Goth *handus*] **1 a** (1) **:** the terminal part of the vertebrate forelimb when modified (as in man) as a grasping organ being made up of wrist, metacarpus, terminal fingers, and opposable thumb or of these parts excluding the wrist and exhibiting unusual mobility and flexibility both of the digits and the whole organ (2) **:** the segment of the forelimb of a vertebrate above the fishes that corresponds to the hand (as the pinion of a bird) irrespective of its form or functional specialization ⟨a kangaroo's forearms seem undeveloped, but the powerful five-fingered ~*s* are skilled at feinting and clouting —*Springfield (Mass.) Union*⟩ **b :** a part serving the function of or resembling a hand: as (1) **:** the hind foot of an ape (2) **:** the chela of a crustacean (3) **:** the tarsus of either forelimb of an insect (as a fly) **c :** something resembling a hand in appearance, shape, function, or use or suggesting the fingers of a hand in shape, arrangement, or number: as (1) **:** an indicator or pointer on a dial ⟨the ~*s* of a clock⟩ (2) **:** a stylized figure of a hand with forefinger extended to point a direction or call attention to something; *specif* **:** INDEX 9 (3) **:** five articles (as oranges) of the same kind sold together (4) **:** a bunch of 8 to 20 bananas attached together on their stem (5) **:** a palmate form of ginger-root (6) **:** a bunch of large leaves tied together usu. with another leaf; *esp* **:** a bunch of 5 to 20 uniform leaves of tobacco tied together by a tie leaf at the butt end of the leaves **2 a :** personal possession — usu. used in pl. ⟨anxious not to let the property get out of his ~*s*⟩ **b** (1) **:** CONTROL, DIRECTION, SUPERVISION ⟨guided the proceedings from the front row with a very helpful ~ —*Sydney (Australia) Bull.*⟩ — usu. used in pl. ⟨kept the management of the firm in his own ~*s*⟩ ⟨the reception was already in the ~*s* of the florists and caterers⟩ (2) **:** right or privilege in controlling or directioning ⟨allowed the teacher a free ~ in her treatment of the children⟩ **3 a :** SIDE, DIRECTION ⟨armed men were running and fighting on either ~⟩ **b :** one of two sides of an issue or argument **:** one of two or more aspects of a subject or matter of consideration ⟨on the one ~ we can appeal for peace, or on the other declare war⟩ ⟨on the one ~ I should like to give the child a great deal of freedom but on the other ~ I don't want him totally out of my control⟩ **c** (1) **:** the manner of twisting or going round whether right-handed or left-handed ⟨the ~ of a spiral⟩ ⟨a right-*hand* screw⟩ (2) **:** the characteristic of a door determining whether it opens to the right or to the left as viewed from the outside (as of a cupboard or closet) or from the inside (as of a room) with door opening away — compare LEFT-HAND, LEFT-HAND REVERSE BEVEL, RIGHT-HAND, RIGHT-HAND REVERSE BEVEL (3) **:** the characteristic of a hinge determining whether it is to be fitted to a right-handed or left-handed door — compare LEFT-HAND, RIGHT-HAND (4) **:** the characteristic of a lock determining whether it throws to the right or left — compare LEFT-HAND, RIGHT-HAND **4 a :** a pledge or indication of agreement or of satisfaction with terms (as of a contract) ⟨without further talk he gave me his ~ on the deal and we closed it⟩ **b :** a pledge of betrothal or bestowal in marriage ⟨asked the man for his daughter's ~⟩ **5 hands** *pl* **:** skill in handling the reins in horsemanship ⟨he didn't ride well, he hadn't good ~*s* —H.G.Wells⟩ **6 a :** style of penmanship **:** HANDWRITING ⟨a handsome ~⟩ ⟨a crabbed ~⟩ ⟨left behind her twenty-six volumes written in her own ~ —Elizabeth Bowen⟩ ⟨in the cuneiform ~ —J.H.Breasted⟩ **b :** SIGNATURE ⟨some writs require a judge's ~⟩ **7 a :** SKILL, ABILITY ⟨wished to try his ~ at painting⟩ ⟨the comedienne tries her ~ at singing and dancing . . . for the first time —*Theatre Arts*⟩ **b :** an instrumental part ⟨several men had a ~ in the crime⟩ ⟨letting private industry have a bigger ~ in developing nuclear energy —*Wall Street Jour.*⟩ **8 :** a unit of measure equal to 4 inches used esp. for the height of horses — compare HANDBREADTH **9 a :** assistance or aid esp. involving physical effort ⟨gave the old man a ~ with his heavy bundles⟩ **b :** PARTICIPATION, INTEREST, CONCERN ⟨a project in which several people had a ~⟩ ⟨took a ~ in planning the new curriculum⟩ **c :** a round of applause ⟨won a good ~ for his acting⟩ ⟨gave the singer quite a ~⟩ **10 a** (1) **:** a player in a card game or board game (2) **:** the cards or pieces held by a player after a deal or distribution (3) **:** a set of cards or pieces in a player's possession at any point during a game (4) **:** the period of a game during which all cards or pieces distributed at one time are played (5) **:** a portion of undealt cards available for play in solitaire **b :** the force or solidity of one's position usu. as a negotiator against an opposing force ⟨these developments greatly strengthened the ~ of union policymakers —*Collier's Yr. Bk.*⟩ — often used in pl. **11 a :** one who performs or executes a particular work ⟨two portraits by the same ~⟩ ⟨essays by various ~*s* in praise of her work —*Collier's Yr. Bk.*⟩ **b** (1) **:** one employed at manual labor or general tasks ⟨a ranch ~⟩ (2) **:** WORKER, EMPLOYEE ⟨business was so successful the company soon was employing over a hundred ~*s*⟩ **c :** a member of a ship's crew ⟨all ~*s* on deck⟩ **d :** one relatively skilled in or disposed to perform a particular action or engage in a particular pursuit ⟨quite a ~ at figures⟩ ⟨a great ~ at carpentry⟩ **e :** a specialist in a usu. designated activity or region ⟨a Latin America ~⟩ — compare OLD HAND **12** *archaic* **:** one that is a source of information **13 a** *archaic* **:** a touch or stroke esp. of a brush on a painting **b :** HANDIWORK ⟨the destruction showed the ~ of vandals⟩ **c :** style of execution **:** WORKMANSHIP ⟨the very brushstrokes showed the ~ of a master⟩ **:** manner of handling **:** TOUCH ⟨in all the masques and pageants . . . his ~ was heavy and his invention flat —Francis Hackett⟩ ⟨treated the child with a light ~⟩ **14 :** the pawl that rotates the cylinder of a revolver **15** *dial* **:** the near horse **16** *dial Brit* **:** a locality or neighborhood ⟨he comes from over near Kendal ~⟩ **17** *or* **hand game :** a gambling game played by American Indians consisting of guessing the whereabouts of pieces of bone or other small objects which are passed rapidly from hand to hand **18** [trans. of L *manus*] **:** MANUS 2 **19 :** a turn of play in which there is an opportunity to score in a game **:** INNING **20 :** the feel of cloth or leather or tactile reaction to its textural qualities of smoothness, flexibility, softness ⟨the warm, dry, luxurious ~ of silk —*Collier's Yr. Bk.*⟩ **21** *also* **hand cheese :** any of several cheeses of a kind orig. molded by hand — **at close hand** *adv* **:** in close proximity **:** NEARBY ⟨as a personal friend he saw the great man *at close hand* on many occasions⟩ — **at first hand** *adv* **:** FIRSTHAND ⟨got the facts *at first hand* by going in person to the scene of the accident⟩ — **at hand :** near in time or place ⟨rather than buy more wood we used what was *at hand*⟩ ⟨the day of reckoning was *at hand*⟩ — **at second hand** *adv* **:** through an intermediary **:** INDIRECTLY ⟨got all his information *at second hand* rather than from original sources⟩ — **at the hands of** *or* **at the hand of :** by the act or instrumentality of ⟨the old way of life became totally outdated *at the hand of* the new technology and psychology⟩ **:** from the hands of ⟨received bad treatment *at the hands of* his master⟩ — **at third hand** *adv* **:** from a thirdhand source **:** in thirdhand condition **:** through more than one intermediary ⟨an account that was as unreliable as most information got *at third hand*⟩ — **by hand** *adv* **1 :** with the hands **:** by manual labor ⟨tilled the garden *by hand*⟩ **2 :** in handwriting ⟨a typewritten letter with a note added *by hand*⟩ **3 :** with personal care and attention ⟨bring a child up *by hand*⟩ **4 :** without the use of a machine that is usu. used for the purpose ⟨became disgusted with the adding machine so added the figures *by hand*⟩ — **for one's own hand :** for one's own advantage ⟨the group refused to work cooperatively, each member rather playing *for his own hand*⟩ — **from hand to hand :** from possession by one person to that of another **:** through successive possession by a number of people ⟨a bauble of little worth that went *from hand to hand*⟩ — **from hand to mouth :** with provision sufficient only for present needs **:** PRECARIOUSLY ⟨always poor and living *from hand to mouth*⟩ ⟨vagrants who live happily *from hand to mouth* —Brooks Atkinson⟩ — **in hand** *adv* **1 a :** in one's possession ⟨when he had enough money *in hand* he bought a car⟩ **b :** in control ⟨kept the children *in hand* by a system of rewards and punishments⟩ **c :** at one's disposal ⟨for a poor man he had a large amount of property *in hand* because of his position⟩ **:** to spare ⟨a race won with plenty of time *in hand*⟩ **2** *obs* **:** with one or accompanying one often on a leash **3 a :** in preparation ⟨a new play *in hand*⟩ **:** under consideration ⟨took the matter *in hand* at a board meeting⟩ **:** in course of transaction ⟨a business deal *in hand*⟩ **b :** under effective control or management ⟨got the business *in hand* before planning new sales campaigns⟩ **4 :** HAND IN HAND **5** *of a ball* **:** not yet in play or put out of play by the rules of the game — opposed to *in play* — **into hand** *adv* **:** into control or supervision ⟨the most troublesome children were taken *into hand* by special counselors⟩ — **lift a hand** *or* **raise a hand :** to make an effort **:** WORK — **of all hands** *obs* **:** on all sides **:** on every side — **off one's hands :** out of one's care or charge ⟨relieved to get so great a responsibility *off his hands*⟩ — **of one's hands** *obs* **:** of valor, skill, or ability esp. in fighting — **on all hands** *adv* **:** on every hand ⟨in the dark of the woods he could hear twittering and scurrying *on all hands*⟩ — **on every hand** *adv* **:** in or from every direction **:** EVERYWHERE ⟨as I . . . went into business, I found *on every hand* that quantity counted for more than quality —Edward Bok⟩ — **on hand** *adv* **1 :** in present possession and easily available ⟨a large stock of goods *on hand*⟩ **2 :** about to appear **:** PENDING, AFOOT ⟨reported there was trouble *on hand*⟩ **3 :** in attendance **:** PRESENT ⟨I will be *on hand* when you call⟩ — **on one's hands :** in one's possession, care, or management, often as a responsibility or a burden ⟨a lot of worthless property *on his hands*⟩ ⟨a problem child *on her hands* for a week⟩ ⟨a whole afternoon *on his hands* to do with as he wished⟩ — **out of hand** *adv* **1 :** without delay, hesitation, or preparation **:** FORTHWITH, PROMPTLY ⟨hanged the man *out of hand* without waiting for trial⟩ ⟨dismissed the traditional logic *out of hand* —J.A.Passmore⟩ **2 :** done with ⟨the business was finally *out of hand*⟩ **3 :** out of control ⟨let his temper get *out of hand*⟩ ⟨the children got *out of hand* and had to be spanked⟩ — **put one's hand on** *or* **lay one's hand on :** FIND, LOCATE ⟨arranged the files so he could *put his hand on* any fact he wanted in a moment⟩ — **put one's hand to** *or* **set one's hand to 1 :** to take hold of ⟨*put his hand to* the plow⟩ **2 :** to engage in **:** UNDERTAKE ⟨knew he would succeed in whatever he *put his hand to*⟩ — **to hand** *adv* **1 :** into possession ⟨used whatever came *to hand* and didn't cost anything⟩ **2 :** within reach **:** easily available ⟨weapons ready *to hand*⟩ ⟨convenient local ammunition lying *to hand* —Mollie Panter-Downes⟩ **3 :** into control or subjection ⟨the insurgents were brought quickly *to hand*⟩ — **to one's hand :** already prepared to appeal to one's taste or special talents ⟨a subject matter for a playwright just made *to his hand*⟩ — **under the hand of :** authenticated by the handwriting or signature of ⟨a deed executed *under the hand of* the owner⟩ — **with a heavy hand 1 :** with little mercy **:** STERNLY, RIGOROUSLY ⟨put down a revolt *with a heavy hand*⟩ **2 :** without grace, delicacy, or sensitivity **:** CLUMSILY ⟨went at the task *with a heavy hand* neglecting essential distinctions⟩ — **with clean hands :** UNCORRUPTED, INNOCENT ⟨although the opportunity to profit by dishonesty was always near he came out *with clean hands*⟩

²hand \"\ *vb* -ED/-ING/-S *vt* **1 a** *obs* **:** to manage with the hands **:** MANIPULATE; *also* **:** to lay hands on **b :** FURL ⟨~*ed* the mainsail —Thomas Horgan⟩ **2 :** to lead, guide, or assist with the hand **:** CONDUCT ⟨~ a lady into a bus⟩ ⟨~*ed* herself along the life line and followed her shipmates to the poop —Roland Barker⟩ **3 :** to give, pass, or transmit with the hand ⟨~ a person a letter⟩ **4 :** to make (one's way) by means of or by swinging with the hands ⟨an animal that ~*s* its way through the trees —Weston La Barre⟩ **5 :** to compel a person to submit to **:** administer forcefully to a person ⟨the smaller boy ~*ed* the bully a terrible beating⟩ ~ *vi* **:** to hand a sail — **hand it to :** to give credit to **:** concede the excellence of ⟨had to *hand it to* the committee for doing such a good job in getting out the vote⟩

hand–adz \'=,=\ *n* **:** a prehistoric celt-shaped tool usu. of stone having one flat and one curved surface and an adz type of cutting edge

hand alphabet *n* **:** MANUAL ALPHABET

hand and foot *adv* [ME, fr. OE *hand and fōt*] **1 :** in a way to prevent escape or totally impede action ⟨bound the prisoner *hand and foot*⟩ **2 :** TOTALLY, COMPLETELY, ASSIDUOUSLY ⟨a woman who waited on her husband *hand and foot*⟩

hand apple *n* **:** an apple suitable for eating without cooking

handarm \'=,=\ *n* **:** HANDGUN

hand ax *n* **:** a prehistoric stone implement consisting of a biface core having one end pointed for cutting and the other end rounded for holding in the hand

handbag \'=,=\ *n* **1 :** TRAVELING BAG **2 :** a woman's bag made in various shapes of fabric, leather, or plastic, held in the hand or looped by handles over the shoulder, and used for carrying usu. small personal articles and accessories

handball \'=,=\ *n* **1 :** a small hollow black rubber ball used in the game of handball **2 :** a game similar to squash played in a walled court or against a single wall or board by two or four players who use their hands to strike the ball

handbank \'=,=\ *vt* **:** to haul (logs) to be banked for further transportation — **hand·bank·er** \'=,=ə(r)\ *n*

handbarrow \'=,=(,)=\ *n* [ME *handberwe*, fr. *hand* + *berwe, barew, barowe* barrow — more at BARROW] **:** a flat rectangular frame with handles at both ends that is carried by two persons — compare WHEELBARROW

handbasin \'=,==\ *n* **:** WASHBOWL

handbell \'=,=\ *n* **:** a small bell with a handle; *esp* **:** one of a set tuned in a scale for musical performance

handbell

handbill \'=,=\ *n* **:** a small printed sheet to be distributed (as for advertising) by hand and often doubling as a poster

handbook \'=,=\ *n* [trans. of G *handbuch*] **1 a :** a book capable of being conveniently carried as a ready reference **:** MANUAL **b :** a concise reference book covering a particular subject or field of knowledge ⟨a ~ of geology⟩ ⟨a ~ of fungi⟩ ⟨a ~ of scouting⟩ ⟨a Milton ~⟩ **c :** a book of directions and information for travelers ⟨a ~ of France⟩ **2 a :** a bookmaker's book of bets **b :** a place where bookmaking is carried on

hand·book·ing \'=,=iŋ\ *n* **:** BOOKMAKING 2

handbow \'=,=\ *n* **:** a bow drawn by hand as distinguished from a crossbow

hand brake *n* **:** a brake (as on an automobile) operated by hand

hand·breadth \'han(d)\,=\ *or* **hands·breadth** \-n(d)z,=\ *n* **:** the breadth of a hand; *also* **:** any of various units of length based on the breadth of a hand varying from about 2½ to 4 inches — compare HAND 8

hand·breed \'han,brēd, 'hȯn-\ *n* [ME *handbrede*, fr. OE *handbred*, fr. *hand, hond* hand + *bred* surface, board; akin to OE *bord* piece of sawed lumber — more at HAND, BOARD] *chiefly Scot* **:** HANDBREADTH

hand breeding *n* **:** controlled mating in which both the time and the mating individuals are selected by the breeder — called also *hand mating*; opposed to *pasture breeding*

H and C *abbr, often not cap* hot and cold running water

handcar \'=,=\ *n* **:** a small four-wheeled car propelled by a hand-operated mechanism or by a small motor or fastened as a trailer to a motor-propelled car and used on railroad tracks for transporting men and materials in railroad-track construction and maintenance work

handcart \'=,=\ *n* **:** a cart drawn or pushed by hand

hand cheese *n* **:** HAND 21

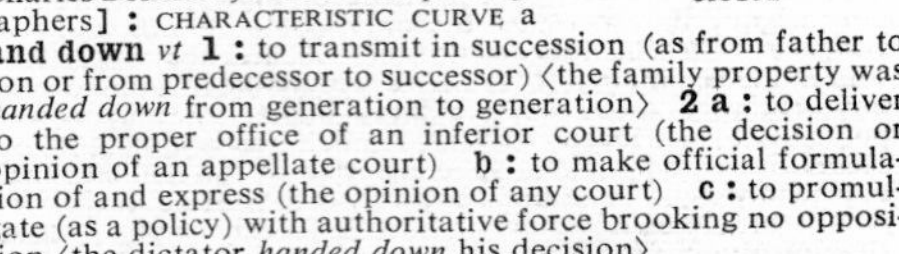
handcart

handclap \'=,=\ *n* **:** a clap of the hands in indication of approval or praise ⟨a flurry of ~*s* greeted his appearance as the featured pianist⟩

handclasp \'=,=\ *n* **:** a clasping of hands usu. by two people during an introduction of one to the other done as a formality upon meeting or parting or as a sign of friendship, affection, unanimity, or good wishes **:** HANDSHAKE

hand composition *n* **:** the work of a hand compositor

hand compositor *n* **:** one that sets type by hand esp. as contrasted with a typesetting-machine keyboard operator

¹handcraft \'=,=\ *n* [ME, fr. OE *handcræft*, fr. *hand* + *cræft*] **:** HANDICRAFT

²handcraft \"\ *vt* **:** to fashion by handicraft ⟨a distinguished weathervane ~*ed* of heavy aluminum —*House Beautiful*⟩ ⟨~*ed* dress materials —*New Yorker*⟩ ⟨a ~*ed* chassis that uses no production shortcuts —*advt*⟩

hand·craft·man \-f(t)smən\ *or* **hand·crafts·man** \-f(t)sm-\ *n, pl* **handcraftmen** *or* **handcraftsmen :** one who is skilled in handicraft

¹handcuff \'=,=\ *vt* **1 :** to apply handcuffs to **:** MANACLE **2 :** to restrain esp. completely or so as to prevent action by or as if by means of handcuffs ⟨the wording of the present charter would ~ the present parliament by preventing any revisions —*Current History*⟩

²handcuff \"\ *n* **:** a metal fastening that can be locked around a wrist and that is usu. connected by a chain or bar with another such fastening which can be locked about the other wrist of the same person or the wrist of another person **:** MANACLE — usu. used in pl. and often with *pair*

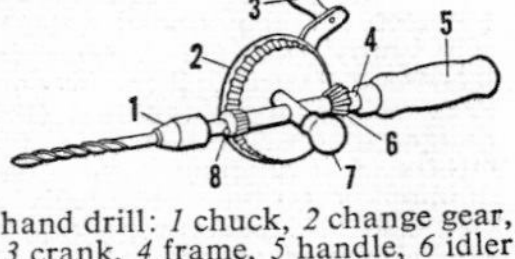
handcuffs, open and closed

hand cultivator *n* **:** WHEEL CULTIVATOR 2

h and d curve \,āchən'dē-\ *n, usu cap H&D* [after Ferdinand *Hurter* and Charles *Driffield* fl 1890 Brit. photographers] **:** CHARACTERISTIC CURVE a

hand down *vt* **1 :** to transmit in succession (as from father to son or from predecessor to successor) ⟨the family property was *handed down* from generation to generation⟩ **2 a :** to deliver to the proper office of an inferior court (the decision or opinion of an appellate court) **b :** to make official formulation of and express (the opinion of any court) **c :** to promulgate (as a policy) with authoritative force brooking no opposition ⟨the dictator *handed down* his decision⟩

hand–down \'=,=\ *n* -s [by shortening] **:** HAND-ME-DOWN

hand drill *n* **1 :** a small portable drilling machine resembling a breast drill but designed to be held and operated by hand **2 :** a primitive drill consisting of a shaft carrying a point of stone, bone, shell, or metal and revolved usu. by the palms of the hands

hand drill: *1* chuck, *2* change gear, *3* crank, *4* frame, *5* handle, *6* idler pinion, *7* detachable side handle, *8* pinion

h and d speed \,āchən-'dē-\ *n, usu cap H&D* [after Ferdinand *Hurter* and Charles *Driffield* fl 1890] **:** a number indicating the sensitivity of a photographic emulsion determined by the method of Hurter and Driffield

h and d system *n, usu cap H&D* [after Ferdinand *Hurter* and Charles *Driffield* fl 1890] **:** a system for determining the speed of photographic materials that is based on the characteristic curve and related to the inertia of the material

hand·ed \'handəd, 'haan-\ *adj* **1 :** having hands ⟨a ~, vertical, tree-living animal —Weston La Barre⟩ **2 :** being either right-hand, left-hand, right-hand reverse bevel, or left-hand reverse bevel — used of doors, hinges, locks, screws

hand·ed·ness *n* -ES **1 :** the quality or state of being handed **2 :** a tendency to use one hand rather than the other ⟨a test for ~⟩

han·de·lian \(')han'dēlyən, -lēən\ *adj, usu cap* [George F. *Handel*, (Händel) †1759 Ger. composer + E *-ian*] **:** of or relating to the German composer Handel or belonging to, befitting, or suggesting his music

hand·er \'handə(r), 'haan-\ *n* -s **1** *dial Brit* **:** a blow on the hand **2 :** one that drops tobacco hands to the prizer for packing in hogsheads

hander–in \'=;=\ *n, pl* **handers–in :** a textile worker who assists in the drawing-in of the warp

¹handfast \'=,=\ *vt* [ME *handfesten, handfasten*, fr. ON *handfesta*, fr. *hand-, hönd* hand + *festa* to fasten, fr. *fastr* fast — more at HAND, FAST] *archaic* **:** to bind in contract by joining hands; *esp* **:** BETROTH

²handfast \"\ *n, archaic* **:** a contract or covenant esp. of betrothal or marriage

³handfast \"\ *adj* [¹*hand* + *fast*] *archaic* **:** having a firm or close grasp **:** CLOSEFISTED

handfasting *n* -s **1** *archaic* **:** BETROTHAL **2 :** an irregular or probationary marriage contracted by joining hands and agreeing to live together as man and wife; *also* **:** the living together under such an agreement

hand–feed \'=,=\ *vt* **:** to provide and apportion rations to (animals) at regular intervals in quantities sufficient for a single feeding — compare SELF-FEED

hand file *n* **:** a file of rectangular section with parallel sides and slightly thicker than a mill file

¹handfish \'=,=\ *n* [¹*hand* + *fish* (n.); fr. the pectoral fins that resemble hands] **:** a fish of the family Brachionichthyidae

²handfish \'=;=\ *vi* [¹*hand* + *fish* (v.)] **:** to catch fish with the hands sometimes with bait as a lure **:** GUDDLE

hand–fives \'=,=\ *n pl but sing in constr* **:** FIVES

handflag \'=,=\ *n* **:** one of usu. two flags used in transmitting messages by semaphore

handflower tree \'⸗,⸗-\ *n* : HAND TREE

hand fly *n* [so called fr. its being nearest the angler's hand] : DROPPER 1a

hand frame *n* : a textile machine (as a knitting frame) worked by hand or foot power

hand·ful *also* **hand·full** \'han(d),fu̇l, 'haan-\ *n, pl* **hand·fuls** \-n(d),fu̇lz\ *or* **hands·ful** \-n(d)z,fu̇l\ [ME, fr. OE *handfull*, fr. *hand* hand + *full* full — more at HAND, FULL] **1 :** as much or as many as the hand will grasp or contain ⟨the child grabbed a ~ of jelly beans⟩ **2 :** a small quantity or number ⟨only a ~ of people have ever seen that great high region —*London Calling*⟩ ⟨bought for liquor and a ~ of pin money the huge tracts near the present Twin Cities —*Amer. Guide Series: Minn.*⟩ ⟨this figure had shrunk to only a ~ —Walter Sullivan⟩ ⟨only a few of our people are killers; only a ~ would take a man's life so greedily —Lillian Smith⟩ **3 :** as much as one can control or manage using all one's effort ⟨the rearing of the children and the keeping of the house proved to be a ~ for one of her frail constitution⟩ ⟨a snake as savage as this one would be a ~ —W.L.Gresham⟩

hand gallop *n* [so called fr. the fact that the horse is kept well in hand to control his speed] : a fast pace in horseback riding between a canter and a gallop : a very fast easy canter : a moderate gallop

hand game *n* : HAND 17

hand glass *n* **1 :** a small mirror with a handle **2 :** a 14-second or 28-second sandglass used in timing the running out of a nautical log line

handgrab \'⸗,⸗\ *n* : a bar or handle (as on a ship) used for steadying or supporting oneself

handgrasp \'⸗,⸗\ *n* : HANDLE

handgravure \'⸗⸗,⸗\ *n* : copperplate printing in which the inked plate is wiped by hand before each impression

hand grenade *n* : a grenade designed to be thrown by hand

handgrip \'⸗,⸗\ *n* [ME *hand grip*, fr. OE *handgripe*, fr. *hand* hand + *gripe* grip — more at HAND, GRIP] **1 :** a grasping with the hand : HANDCLASP **2 :** something that is attached to or forms part of an object and is designed to be grasped by the hand in lifting the object: as **a :** HANDLE ⟨the ~ of the revolver⟩ ⟨a pot with two small projecting ~*s*, one on each side⟩ **b :** HILT ⟨the ~ of a sword⟩ **c :** the outer usu. projecting end of the arm of an armchair ⟨it has nearly flat scrolled arms that . . . terminate in down-scrolled ~*s* —T.H.Ormsbee⟩ **3 handgrips** *pl* : close and usu. critical or desperate struggle : hand-to-hand combat — usu. used in the phrases *at handgrips* or *come to handgrips* ⟨before they lost the town the soldiers were at ~*s* with the enemy⟩ ⟨the struggle was so evenly matched the soldiers came to ~*s* before the issue was decided⟩

handguard \'⸗,⸗\ *n* **1 a :** a guard on a sword — compare CROSS GUARD **b :** a guard on a knife or dagger similar to that on a sword **2 :** a wooden piece above the barrel of a rifle

handgun \'⸗,⸗\ *n* [ME *handgunne*, fr. *hand* + *gunne* gun — more at GUN] : a firearm held and fired with one hand

¹hand·hab·end \'⸗,habənd\ *or* **handhaving** \'⸗,⸗⸗\ *adj* [*handhabend* fr. ME, fr. OE *handhabbend*, fr. *hand*, *hond* hand + *habbend*, pres. part. of *habben* to have — more at HAND, HAVE] : having possession of stolen goods — used in Old English law of a thief caught with the loot

²handhabend \"\ *or* **handhaving** \"\ *n* -s : the jurisdiction to try a handhabend thief

handhold \'⸗,⸗\ *n* **1 :** HOLD, GRIP ⟨got a ~ on the edge of the dock and pulled himself out of the water⟩ ⟨has a ~ on a rich chunk of the empire and he will not let go —*Time*⟩ **2 :** something to hold on to (as in mountain climbing) ⟨swinging from one ~ to the next in a line⟩; *specif* : the part of an implement fashioned for grasping with the hand

handhole \'⸗,⸗\ *n* **1 :** a hole large enough only for insertion of a hand (as for lifting) or of a hand and arm (as for cleaning out otherwise inaccessible places or giving access to enclosed parts) **2 :** a shallow form of manhole giving access to a top row of ducts in an underground electrical system

hand·hol·er \'⸗,⸗ə(r)\ *n* : an operator of a machine for cutting handholes in the ends of wooden boxes

hand horn *n* : a natural French horn whose pitch a player can modify or alter by inserting his hand in the bell

hand horse *n, dial* : the near horse

¹hand·i·cap \'handē,kap, 'haan-, -dȯ,-\ *n* -s *often attrib* [fr. obs. E, a game of forfeits and exchanges in which the players held forfeit money in a cap, alter. of *hand in cap*] **1 :** a race or any contest of agility, strength, or skill in which in order to equalize chances of winning an artificial disadvantage is imposed on a supposedly superior contestant or an artificial advantage is given to one supposedly inferior **2 a :** an advantage given a weaker contestant or a disadvantage imposed upon a stronger contestant in the form of points, strokes, weight to be carried, or distance from the target or goal in order to equalize chances of winning **b :** a disadvantage that makes achievement unusually difficult; *esp* : a physical disability that limits the capacity to work

²handicap \"\ *vb* **handicapped; handicapped; handicapping; handicaps** *vt* **1 a :** to give a handicap to **b :** to assign handicaps to in order to equalize chances of success ⟨the horses were admirably *handicapped* in the race⟩ **2 :** to put at a disadvantage ⟨*handicapped* in his job by worries over debts⟩ ~ *vi* : to engage in handicapping

hand·i·cap·per \-pə(r)\ *n* -s : one that handicaps in racing: **a :** the official (as of a jockey club) who assigns the weights to be carried by the horses in a handicap **b :** one whose job is handicapping ⟨earned some money as a ~ for a local newspaper⟩

handicapping *n* -s : the occupation of predicting winners in horse races usu. for publication

hand·i·craft \-,kraft, -aa(ə)-,-ai-,-á-\ *n* [ME *handie-crafte*, alter. (influenced by *handiwerk* handiwork) of *handcraft*, fr. *hand* + *craft*] **1 a :** an occupation in which articles are fashioned totally or chiefly by hand esp. with manual and often artistic skill usu. as either a trade or a hobby **b :** the articles fashioned by those engaged in such an occupation **2** *archaic* : one living by handicraft : HANDICRAFTSMAN

hand·i·craft·er \-tə(r)\ *n* -s : one that engages in a handicraft usu. as a hobby or avocation

hand·i·crafts·man \-f(t)smən\ *n, pl* **handicraftsmen** : one that engages in a handicraft : ARTISAN

hand·i·cuff \'⸗⸗,kəf\ *n* -s [¹*hand* + *-icuff*, as in *fisticuff*] *archaic* : a blow with the hand : FISTICUFF

handier *comparative of* HANDY

handiest *superlative of* HANDY

Handie–Talkie \'handē,tȯkē\ *trademark* — used for a small portable radio transmitter-receiver

hand·i·grips \'handē,grips\ *archaic var of* HANDGRIPS

hand·i·ly \'handəlē, 'haan-, -li\ *adv* [*handy* + *-ly*] **1 :** in a handy manner: as **a :** DEXTEROUSLY ⟨applied the brush ~ and finished the painting in a few minutes⟩ **b :** EASILY ⟨despite the handicap the horse won the race ~⟩ **c :** CONVENIENTLY ⟨kept the eraser ~ beside him as he wrote⟩ **2** *Midland* : JUSTLY, FAIRLY, RIGHTLY ⟨you can't ~ tell him to go home⟩

hand in *vt* : SUBMIT ⟨his thoughts were concentrated on *handing in* reports that would injure nobody —Alfred Burmeister⟩

hand–in \'⸗,⸗\ *n* -s [*hand in*] *in squash or badminton* : the player who serves the ball or his period of service

hand·i·ness \'handēnəs, 'haan-, -din-\ *n* -ES [*handy* + *-ness*] : the quality or state of being handy

handing *pres part of* HAND

hand in glove *or* **hand and glove** *adv* : in extremely close relationship or agreement esp. for nefarious purposes ⟨mass production is the outgrowth of the so-called industrial revolution and has had a part *hand in glove* with it —A.H.Compton⟩ ⟨the police were found to be working *hand in glove* with the racketeers⟩

hand in hand *adv* **1** *of two people* : with hands clasped usu. in affection or intimacy **2 :** in the manner of things that are inseparably interrelated : in union : CONJOINTLY ⟨freedom of speech and true democratic government go *hand in hand*⟩ ⟨more and more architecture and landscape architecture go *hand in hand* —*Collier's Yr. Bk.*⟩ ⟨illness and bad housing go *hand in hand* —*Times Lit. Supp.*⟩

hand–in–hand \'⸗⸗'⸗\ *adj* [*hand in hand*] **1** *of two people* : having the hands clasped usu. in affection or intimacy **2 :** being close or intimate : going side by side or in close relationship

handiron \'⸗,⸗\ *n* [by folk etymology] *dial* : ANDIRON

hand·i·work \'handē,⸗, 'haan-, -di,-\ *n* [ME *handiwerk*, fr. OE *handgeweorc*, fr. *hand* hand + *geweorc*, fr. *ge-* (collective and perfective prefix) + *weorc* work — more at HAND, CO-, WORK] **1 a :** work done by the hands ⟨occupied his time around the house with ~ of various kinds⟩ **b :** work done personally : personal or individual achievement ⟨his fortune is his own ~ —S.N.Behrman⟩ ⟨showed the ~ of a master criminal⟩ **2 :** the product of handiwork ⟨the fiddle was . . . the ~ of the great Italian master violin maker —*Fortnight*⟩ ⟨selling baskets, ~, and curios to tourists —*Amer. Guide Series: Maine*⟩

handjar *var of* KHANJAR

hand·ker·cher \'haŋkə(r)chə(r), 'haiŋ-\ *dial var of* HANDKERCHIEF

hand·ker·chief \'haŋkə(r)chəf, 'haiŋ-, -(,)chif, -,chēf\ *n, pl* **handkerchiefs** *also* **handkerchieves** \lfs, |vz; *many whose pl is* -ēvz *have* ə *or* i *as a last-syllable vowel in the sing*\ [*hand* + *kerchief*] **1 :** a piece of cloth usu. square and often printed, edged, or embroidered that is used for various usu. personal purposes (as the wiping of the nose or eyes) or as a costume accessory **2 :** KERCHIEF 1

handkerchief dance *n* : a dance in which kerchiefs are waved or in which dancers are linked by the kerchiefs they hold in their hands

handkerchief table *n* : a folding triangular table that becomes square when the drop leaf supported by a swinging leg is raised

hand–kissing \'⸗,⸗⸗\ *n* -s : the custom in some countries (as France) of a gentleman's pressing his lips to the back of a woman's hand as a gesture of courtesy (as in an introduction) or of affection

hand labor *n* : manual labor as distinct from machine work

handlaid \'⸗'⸗\ *adj* **1** *of paper* : HANDMADE **2** *of a rope or line* : laid by hand

hand language *n* : communication by means of a manual alphabet : DACTYLOLOGY

¹han·dle \'handᵊl, 'haan-, *rapid* -nᵊl\ *n* -s [ME *handel*, fr. OE *handle*; akin to MLG *hantel* handle; derivatives fr. the root of E ¹*hand*] **1 :** a part that is designed esp. to be grasped by the hand or that may be grasped by the hand (as for lifting or steering) **2 a :** something that resembles a handle in appearance, use, or function **b :** something (as a pretext or opportunity) that may be figuratively seized as a means of dealing with some larger abstract unit ⟨the only ~ he has for laying hold of the future —Dixon Wecter⟩ ⟨the ~ by which the writer grasps reality —Max Lerner & Edwin Mims⟩ **3 a** *slang* : NAME ⟨bore an odd ~⟩ ⟨with the heavenly ~ of St. Thomas —*Newsweek*⟩ : TITLE ⟨an Englishman with a ~ to his name—Baron or something⟩ **b** *dial* : a given name that is somewhat unusual ⟨what did they go and give the poor kid a ~ like that for —Edna Reynolds⟩ **4 :** HAND 20 ⟨a well-scoured acetate fabric will have a soft springy ~ —*Dyestuffs*⟩ **5** [²*handle*] : the total amount of money bet on a race, game, or event or over a period of time (as a season) **6** *chiefly NewZeal* : a measure of beer approximately one pint — **off the handle** *adv* : into a state marked esp. by sudden and violent anger ⟨her nerves were so bad that she flew *off the handle* at the least provocation⟩

²handle \"\ *vb* **handled; handled; handling** \-(ᵊ)liŋ\ **handles** [ME *handelen*, fr. OE *handlian*; akin to OHG *hantalōn* to take with the hands, ON *höndla* to handle, seize; derivatives fr. the root of E ¹*hand*] *vt* **1 a :** to touch, feel, hold, take up, move, or otherwise affect with the hand : use the hands upon ⟨~ a material to find out how rough it is⟩ ⟨please do not ~ the merchandise⟩ **b :** to manage in using with the hands (as a spade or a weapon) : PLY, MANIPULATE, WIELD ⟨~ a scythe⟩ ⟨~ a gun with precision⟩ ⟨excellent at *handling* a horse⟩ **c** *of a batsman in cricket* : to pick up or touch with the hand (a ball in play) except at the request of the fielding side — used esp. in the phrase *out, handled the ball* **2 a :** to deal with or treat of in writing or speaking or in the plastic arts (as a theme, subject, argument, or objection) ⟨the writer ~*s* the matter briefly and concisely⟩ ⟨told him how to ~ color in using oil paints⟩ **b :** to conduct oneself in relation to : assume an attitude to **c** (1) : MANAGE, CONTROL, DIRECT ⟨was asked to ~ the staff of researchers in the absence of the director⟩ ⟨a lawyer who ~*s* the affairs of several corporations⟩ (2) : to have immediate physical charge in the care and training of (an animal) ⟨a good man to ~ his stable of horses⟩; *also* : to hold and incite (a sporting animal or bird) in a match (3) : to train (a pugilist) and act as the second during a fight (4) : to engage professionally in showing or exhibiting (an animal) in a show-ring **d :** to supervise, oversee, or control (as a worker) in such a way as to encourage a maximum of work output or persuade to a particular course of action or conduct ⟨a boss whose special gift was an ability to ~ men⟩ **e :** to deal with : act upon : dispose of : perform some function with regard to ⟨a period in which to ~ the day's mail and clear up back business⟩ ⟨told how much freight was *handled* at the port of New York⟩ ⟨a disposal unit that could ~ the city's garbage⟩ **f :** to trade in : engage in the buying, selling, or distributing of (a commodity) ⟨will be *handling* new and used cars⟩ : have or cause to pass through one's hands in commercial transactions **g** (1) : to perform or do to the point of completeness or success ⟨a man who would really ~ the job⟩ (2) : to drink (intoxicating drinks) without losing the normal control of one's faculties or actions or acting in foolish ways ⟨could not ~ liquor and always began to giggle and get maudlin after two drinks⟩ **3** *in hunting* : KILL **4 :** to move up and down or draw out and replace (hides) in the pit in the process of tanning — see HANDLER 3 **5 :** to be competent enough or fit to act upon, perform, manage, direct, solve, or deal with successfully in some other way ⟨a singer unable to ~ the difficult passages of the score⟩ ⟨equal to *handling* any amount of business that came along⟩ ⟨unable to ~ the boys⟩ ⟨his inability to ~ so difficult a problem —Sherwood Anderson⟩ ⟨a faucet that ~*s* hot and cold water simultaneously⟩ ⟨a typewriter that can ~ almost any number of carbons⟩ **6 :** to have within its jurisdiction ⟨a court that ~*s* only probate matters⟩ ~ *vi* : to act, behave, or feel in a certain way when handled or directed ⟨bought a car that ~*s* well⟩ ⟨the schooner . . . ~*s* easily —Kenneth Roberts⟩ ⟨the dog ~*s* well in field trials⟩; *specif* : to submit obediently to direction or control ⟨the dog *handled* well in the trials⟩

syn HANDLE, MANIPULATE, WIELD, SWING, and PLY can mean in common to deal with as with the hands, esp. in an easy or dexterous manner. HANDLE implies at the least enough skill, and usu. a specified degree more, to accomplish one's end ⟨knew better than most men how to *handle* a blade —L.C. Douglas⟩ ⟨able to *handle* a foreign language with proficiency⟩ ⟨doubted that their economy could ever *handle* more than the natural population increase —*Time*⟩ MANIPULATE implies dexterity and adroitness in handling, esp. a mechanical or technical skill, and extends to suggest, in figurative use, a dealing with something in a crafty, artful, often fraudulent way ⟨the kind of courage required for mountaineering, for *manipulating* an aeroplane, or for managing a small ship in a gale —Bertrand Russell⟩ ⟨was able to *manipulate* sequences of words in blank verse in a manner which is quite his own —T.S.Eliot⟩ ⟨agencies by which some human beings *manipulate* other human beings for their own advantage —John Dewey⟩ ⟨a genius of legal dishonesty in *manipulating* stocks⟩ WIELD implies mastery and vigor in the handling of a tool, weapon, or other implement ⟨the longbow, which was so tall that the man *wielding* it had to pull the string back to his eye or ear —Tom Wintringham⟩ ⟨a past master in *wielding* a golf club⟩ ⟨*wield* the scalpel —G.B.Shaw⟩ ⟨*wield* tremendous political power —Green Peyton⟩ ⟨he *wields* . . . a very capable scholarship that gives backbone to his work —N.L.Rothman⟩ SWING in literal use implies a wide sweep of action ⟨*swing* a ball bat⟩ ⟨being able to *swing* an oar —H.A.Chippendale⟩ but in an extended figurative use it can imply the successful handling of something large or difficult in relation to one's capacities ⟨a task too hard for him to *swing*⟩ ⟨*swing* a big deal in high finance⟩ PLY is interchangeable with HANDLE or WIELD when great diligence or industry is implied ⟨tell them where it will best repay them to *ply* their pickaxes and spades —F.R. Leavis⟩ ⟨the experts *plied* their pens —R.F.Harrod⟩ **syn** see in addition TREAT

—handle with gloves on *or* **handle with kid gloves :** to treat with extreme care

han·dle·able \-ᵊləbəl\ *adj* : capable of being handled ⟨bucket feeding . . . makes the heifers gentle and ~ —*Australian Home Beautiful*⟩ ⟨a set of ~ . . . and inexpensive volumes —Margaret Marshall⟩

hand lead \-,led\ *n* : a small lead for sounding in shallow water

handlebar \'⸗⸗,⸗\ *n* **1 :** a straight or bent bar with a handle or serving as a handle **2 a** (1) *or* **handlebars** *pl* : the shaped bar that forms part of a cycle's steering mechanism and that is grasped by the hands — see BICYCLE illustration (2) : one end of such a bar usu. grasped by one hand while riding (3) : a part of a steering mechanism suggesting or shaped like such a bar or one end of such a bar **b handlebars** *pl* : HANDLEBAR MOUSTACHE

handlebar moustache *n* : a man's heavy moustache with long slightly curved sections at each end

handle blank *n* : a piece of dimension lumber often of hickory and suitable for making handles

han·dled \'handᵊld, 'haan-, *rapid* -nᵊld\ *adj* : having a usu. specified type of handle ⟨a pearl-*handled* penknife⟩ ⟨a long-*handled* knife⟩

handled cross *n* : ANKH

han·dle·less \'han(d)ᵊl(l)əs, 'haan-\ *adj* : having no handle

hand lens *n* : a magnifying glass designed to be held in the hand

han·dler \'hand(ᵊ)lə(r), 'haan-, *rapid* -n(ᵊ)l-\ *n* -s [ME, fr. *handelen* to handle + *-er*] **1 :** one that handles ⟨all ~*s* of food in restaurants require a health certificate⟩ ⟨the railroad was one of the largest ~*s* of coal in the world⟩: as **a :** a worker whose task it is to move, carry, stow, or arrange materials or objects by hand or chiefly by hand **b :** one in immediate physical charge of an animal **c :** one that holds and incites a dog, gamecock, or other sporting animal in a match or hunt **d :** one that helps to train a pugilist or acts as his second during a match **e :** one professionally engaged in exhibiting animals in the show ring **f :** one that guides, directs, and acts as publicity man and general agent for another (as for a political candidate during a campaign) **2 :** a worker who affixes handles (as to pottery or baskets) **3 :** a pit containing tanning liquor in which hides are worked over or handled in the tanning process

handles *pl of* HANDLE, *pres 3d sing of* HANDLE

hand·less \'handləs, 'haan-, *rapid* -nl-\ *adj* [ME, fr. ¹*hand* + *-less*] **1 :** having no hands ⟨a ~ war veteran⟩ **2 :** inefficient, clumsy, or incompetent in manual tasks ⟨could hardly empty a scuttle of ashes, so ~ was the poor creature —Mary H. Vorse⟩

hand letter *n* : a single letter usu. cut in brass that is applied by hand to the binding of a book

hand–letter \'⸗'⸗⸗\ *vb* [*hand letter*] *vt* **1 :** to print by hand ⟨a *hand-lettered* notice in chalk on the wall⟩ **2 :** to apply hand letters to (a book or its binding) ~ *vi* : PRINT

hand level *n* : a surveyor's level designed to be held in the hand and consisting of a telescope with a bubble tube so attached that the position of the bubble can be seen when looking through the telescope

h and l hinge *n, cap 1st H&L* : a door hinge resembling a ligature of a capital H and L

H and L hinge

handlike \'⸗,⸗\ *adj* : shaped like a hand or grasping in the manner of a hand

¹handline \'⸗,⸗\ *n* **1 :** a line managed chiefly by direct contact with the hands: as **a :** any of several comparatively simple arrangements of hooks and line designed for use in the hands of or under the immediate and continuous supervision of a fisherman — opposed to *setline* **b :** the line on a hand lead **c :** a line used without rod or reel for fishing **2 :** a fire hose of small diameter

²handline \'⸗,⸗\ *vi* : to fish with a handline — **hand·lin·er** \'⸗,⸗ə(r)\ *n*

handling *n* -s [ME, fr. OE *handlung*, fr. *handlian* to handle + *-ung* -ing — more at HANDLE] **1 a :** the action of one that handles something ⟨a child who needed a good deal of ~⟩ ⟨the horses seemed to thrive under his ~⟩ **b :** a process by which something is handled esp. in a commercial transaction ⟨the problem was not the sales but the ~ of the merchandise⟩; *esp* : the packaging and shipping of an object or a material (as to a consumer) ⟨made a small ~ charge for all deliveries of goods outside the city limits⟩ **2 :** the manner in which something is handled ⟨the coach liked his ball ~ and made him captain of the team⟩ ⟨improved in his ~ of language⟩; *esp* : the mode or style of treatment or presentation (as of a theme) in a musical, literary, or art work ⟨the dramatist's ~ of the climax of the action was ineffective⟩ **3 :** the manner in which something acts when handled ⟨the ~ of the automobile was smooth and effortless⟩

handling room *n* : a compartment opening into magazines and shell rooms in which ammunition is arranged and placed on hoists to be sent directly to the guns of a naval vessel

hand–lining \'⸗,⸗⸗\ *n* : fishing with a handline

handlist \'⸗,⸗\ *n* : a handy orig. fairly brief list (as of newspapers or manuscripts) for purposes of reference or check ⟨a ~ of 100 books on warfare⟩ ⟨a ~ of plays produced between 1850 and 1900⟩

¹handload \'⸗'⸗\ *vt* : to load (ammunition) by hand ~ *vi* : to handload ammunition — **handloading** \'⸗'⸗⸗\ *adj*

²handload \"\ *n* : a cartridge that has been loaded by hand

handloader \'⸗'⸗⸗\ *n* : one that loads his own cartridges

handlock \'⸗,⸗\ *vt* [fr. obs. E *handlock* handcuff (n.)] *archaic* : HANDCUFF, MANACLE

handloom \'⸗,⸗\ *n* : any of various looms or weaving devices operated wholly or partly by hand or foot power

handloomed \'⸗'⸗\ *adj* : woven on a handloom

¹handmade \'⸗'⸗\ *adj* **1 :** made by hand or a hand process esp. as distinguished from a machine or mechanical process ⟨~ paper⟩ ⟨~ furniture⟩ **2 :** simulating something that is handmade ⟨paper with a ~ finish⟩; *also* : used in the fabrication of such simulation ⟨~ felt⟩

²handmade \'⸗,⸗\ *n* -s : something that is handmade; *esp* : a handmade fabric or dress

handmaid \'⸗,⸗\ *n* [ME, fr. *hand* + *maid*] **1 :** a personal maid or female servant or attendant **2 :** something whose essential function is to serve and assist ⟨holds that the state . . . must become the servant or ~ of the church —*Times Lit. Supp.*⟩ ⟨even philosophy and logic . . . were in his eyes the mere ~*s* of the critical spirit —Richard Wollheim⟩

handmaiden \'⸗,⸗⸗\ *n* [ME, fr. *hand* + *maiden*] : HANDMAID ⟨good sense which . . . is the indispensable ~ of the critical art —Carlos Baker⟩ ⟨literature must never become the ~ of the history program or the science program —A.S.Artley⟩ ⟨ethics is not the ~ of theology —Brand Blanshard⟩ — **handmaid·en·ly** \-lē\ *adj*

handmaid moth *n* : a moth of the genus *Datana* (esp. *D. ministra*)

hand mast *n* : a mast made from one timber : POLE MAST

hand mating *n* : HAND BREEDING

¹hand–me–down \'⸗⸗,⸗\ *adj* **1** *of clothing* : ready-made and usu. cheap and shoddy ⟨cheap store clothes of the *hand-me-down* variety for export to the Southwest —Dixon Wecter⟩ **2 a :** put in use by one person or group after being already used and discarded by another : SECOND-HAND ⟨not just any old *hand-me-down* philosophy of education —*Atlantic*⟩ **b :** already having been worn or used and discarded by another (as an older brother) ⟨wearing their older sisters' *hand-me-down* evening dresses —Peter Taylor⟩

²hand–me–down \"\ *n* -s : something that is hand-me-down ⟨the terms . . . are *hand-me-downs* from former generations of businessmen —W.H.Whyte⟩ ⟨are our diet beliefs mere *hand-me-downs* from the previous generation —C.R.Stackhouse⟩; *esp* : a hand-me-down garment or suit ⟨uniforms . . . had the unmistakable fit of *hand-me-downs* —Hamilton Basso⟩ ⟨wore *hand-me-downs* until he was 16 and then was allowed to buy himself a new suit⟩

hand–minded \'⸗'⸗⸗\ *adj* : naturally disposed primarily to manual activities ⟨those who are so exclusively *hand-minded* as to suggest the wisdom of drawing them off into manual or technical schools —B.P.Fowler⟩ — **hand-mind·ed·ness** *n* -ES

hand money *n* : EARNEST MONEY

hand mower *n* : a lawn mower designed to be pushed by hand — distinguished from *power mower*

hand nut *n* : WING NUT, THUMB NUT

hand off *vt* **1** : to hand (the ball) to a nearby teammate during a football play **2** : to force (a tackler) away with the open palm of the hand while carrying the ball esp. in rugby

hand-off \'=,=\ *n* -S [*hand off*] **1** : a football play in which the ball is handed by one player to another nearby ⟨scored on a ~⟩; *also* : a ball that is transferred in this manner ⟨take a ~⟩ **2** : an act of handing off an opponent esp. in rugby

hand of pork *dial Eng* : a shoulder of pork without the blade bone

hand of write *Scot* : HANDWRITING

hand on *vt* : HAND DOWN 1 ⟨the father *handed on* his good reputation to his son⟩ ⟨*handed on* the tradition of French classical painting to the generation who followed him —Robert Richman⟩

hand orchis *n* [so called fr. the fingerlike tubers] : SPOTTED ORCHIS 1

hand organ *n* : a barrel organ operated by a hand crank

hand out *vt* **1** : to give free ⟨*handing out* free samples of a new breakfast food⟩ ⟨*handing out* passes to a movie⟩ or as a master or proprietor to an inferior or one he may patronize ⟨make a bow and accept anything the king wanted to *hand out* —Dorothy C. Fisher⟩ **2** : to give freely ⟨a politician *handing out* compliments to his constituents⟩ ⟨*handing out* advice to all prospective buyers⟩ **3** : ADMINISTER ⟨reconciled to any punishment *handed out* to him⟩

hand organ

handout \'=,=\ *n* -S [*hand out*] **1** : something handed out or designed to be handed out: as **a** : a portion of food, clothing, or money given to or as if to a beggar **b** : a folder or circular of information for free distribution (as an advertising throwaway) **c** (1) : a mimeographed or printed press release by a news service (2) : a prepared statement released to the press by advertisers, government agencies or officials, or publicity agencies **2** : ⁵DOWN 2c

hand over *vt* **1** : to yield control of : deliver up ⟨the thief *handed over* the stolen watch to the policeman⟩ **2** : hand on to another ⟨*handed over* the perquisites of office to his successor⟩ ⟨such privileges may be *handed over* as a dowry —Edward Sapir⟩

hand over fist *adv* : quickly and in large amounts ⟨began to make money *hand over fist*⟩

hand over hand *adv* : by grasping with the hands moving alternately one before or above the other ⟨climb a rope *hand over hand*⟩ ⟨haul in a line *hand over hand*⟩

hand over head *adv* [ME *hand ovyr hedd*] *archaic* : without heed of what one is really doing : RASHLY, RECKLESSLY

hand phone *n* : HANDSET

handpick \'=;=\ *vt* **1** : to pick by hand as opposed to a machine process ⟨machines supplanted the workers who ~*ed* the cotton⟩ ⟨~*ing* the insects from the plants⟩ **2 a** : to select with personal care for quality ⟨~ the man because of his education and training —T.M.Landy⟩ **b** : to select personally or to ensure the achievement of personal ends ⟨a party leader so strong he could ~ the political candidates⟩ ⟨a ~*ed* jury⟩

handpiece \'=,=\ *n* : the part of a mechanized device designed to be held or manipulated by hand; *esp* : the part of a mechanical shearer for sheep that is manipulated by the operator and that contains the shearing blades

hand-plant \'=,=\ *n* : the tobacco plant set in the starting hill at the beginning of a row in a tobacco field

hand plate *n* : a plate placed on a door to prevent its being soiled by the hands — called also *push plate;* compare FINGER PLATE

handplay \'=,=\ *n* **1** : an exchange of blows in hand-to-hand fighting **2** : the act of playing as high bidder in a game of skat with the cards dealt without using the skat

hand plow *n* : a light plow propelled by hand for use in gardens — called also *garden plow*

hand-pollinate \'=;==,=\ *vt* : to pollinate by hand usu. with a camel's-hair brush — **hand-pollination** \;=,==ˈ==\ *n*

handpress \'=,=\ *n* : a hand-operated printing or proving press

hand prop *n* : a small and movable property used by an actor during the performance of a play or a small property (as a cushion or drinking glass) capable of being carried on and off a set easily

hand pump *n* : a pump operated by hand; *esp* : one for emergency use when a power-operated pump fails

hand puppet *n* : a puppet constructed with a hollow head and arms attached to a costume fitting over the puppeteer's hand and activated by movements of the fingers and thumb inserted in the head and arms — called also *glove doll*

handrail \'=,=\ *n* : a narrow rail for grasping with the hand as a support

handrailing \'=,==\ *n* : HANDRAILS; *also* : material designed for a handrail

handreader \'=,==\ *n* : PALMIST

handreading \'=,==\ *n* : PALMISTRY

handrest \'=,=\ *n* : a rest or support for the hand or for a hand tool (as on a lathe)

hand puppet

hand ride *n* : an act of hand-riding; *also* : the ride in a race in which the jockey hand-rides

hand-ride \'=,=\ *vb* [*hand ride*] *vt* : to ride (a horse) without using a whip or spurs during a race ~ *vi* : to hand-ride a racehorse

hand rope *n* **1** : GUEST ROPE 2 **2** : a very flexible wire rope made up of usu. six strands about a hemp center and used for signal pulls, steering lines, elevator-controlling devices

hand-run \'=,=\ *adj, of lace* : machine-made but finished by hand

hand running *adv* : in unbroken succession : CONSECUTIVELY ⟨won three games *hand running*⟩ ⟨could chin a pole twenty times *hand running* —W.A.White⟩

hands *pl of* HAND, *pres 3d sing of* HAND

handsale \'=,=\ *n* **1** : a form of sale made binding by a handshake and customary among the early Teutonic races **2** : money paid as earnest money to bind a sale

hands around *n pl* : a movement in square dancing in which the dancers join hands and circle left

handsaw \'=,=\ *n* : a saw used with one hand and operated by a backward and forward drive of the arm; *esp* : the common saw consisting of a wide blade with a handle at one end — compare CROSSCUT SAW, HACKSAW, RIPSAW

handsaw fish *n* [so called fr. the finely serrated edge of the dorsal ray] : a fish of the genus *Alepisaurus*

handsbreadth *var of* HANDBREADTH

hand-schül·ler-chris·tian disease \ˌhan(d),shülə(r)'kris(h)chən-\ *n, usu cap H&S&C* [after Alfred J. *Hand* b1868 Am. physician + Artur *Schüller* b1874 Austrian neurologist + Henry *Christian* b1876 Am. physician] : an inflammatory histiocytosis associated with disturbances in cholesterol metabolism that occurs chiefly in young children and is marked by cystic defects of the skull, exophthalmos, and diabetes insipidus

¹**hand-screen** \'=,=\ *n* : a small usu. ornamented screen designed to be held in the hand and used formerly as a shade against heat or light

²**hand-screen** \'=,=\ *vt* : to print by the silk-screen process

hand screw *n* : a screw or screw device turned by hand — compare THUMBSCREW

hand-screw clamp *n* : a woodworker's clamp with two hardwood jaws joined by a pair of right-hand and left-hand threaded screws that maintain parallel adjustment of the jaws when their handles are turned in the same direction

hands down *adv* **1** : without much effort : EASILY ⟨won the race *hands down*⟩ **2** : without question or the possibility of dispute ⟨is *hands down* the most competent craftsman in his field⟩

hands-down \'=;=\ *adj* [*hands down*] **1** : achieved without great effort : EASY ⟨won a *hands-down* victory⟩ **2** : UNQUESTIONABLE, UNDISPUTED ⟨was the *hands-down* popular choice for the presidency⟩ ⟨books that were *hands-down* favorites of the editors and critics —Raymond Walters b.1912⟩

¹**handsel** *also* **han·sel** \'han(t)səl\ *n* -S [ME *hansell*, prob. fr. ON *handsal* obligation confirmed by a handshake, handshake, promise, fr. *hand-, hond* hand + *sal* payment, payday; akin to ON *selja* to give, sell — more at HAND, SELL] **1** *obs* **a** : a token of luck : LUCK **b** : AUGURY **2** : a gift made as a token of good wishes or luck esp. at the beginning of a new course of action or upon someone's entering upon a new condition: as **a** : a bridegroom's present to the bride on her wedding day **b** : money given at the new year **3** : something received first (as in a day of trading or at a shop newly opened) and taken to be a token of good luck **4 a** : a first installment or earnest money **b** : EARNEST, FORETASTE ⟨our present tears . . . are but the ~*s* of our joys hereafter —Robert Herrick †1674⟩

²**handsel** \"\ *also* **hansel** \"\ *vt* **handseled** *or* **handselled**; **handseled** *or* **handselled**; **handseling** *or* **handselling** \-s(ə)liŋ\ **handsels** [ME *handsellen*, fr. *handsel*, n.] **1** *chiefly Brit* : to give a handsel to **2** *chiefly Brit* : to celebrate the beginning of the existence or use of : inaugurate with a token or gesture of luck or pleasure ⟨~ a new house with a banquet⟩ **3** *chiefly Brit* : to use or do for the first time : be the first to try or experience

handsel monday *n, usu cap H&M* : the first Monday of the new year when handsels are given (as to servants, children) esp. in Scotland

handservant \'=,==\ *n* : HANDMAID

handset \'=,=\ *n* : a telephone mouthpiece and earpiece and the respective microphone and speaker mounted on a single handle — called also *French telephone*

hand-set \'=;=\ *adj* : consisting of or printed or cast from individual pieces of type assembled by hand

hand-setting \'=;==\ *n* : the setting or casting of hand-set printed matter

handshake \'=,=\ *n* : a grasping with the right hand of another's right hand or a grasping of right hands by two people often with a slight up and down shake of the hands usu. upon meeting or taking leave as a sign of friendship, affection, or good wishes or as a mere polite formality : HANDCLASP

handshaker \'=,==\ *n* **1** : one that makes capital of shaking hands or showing extreme politic friendliness ⟨money raisers, speechmakers, ~*s*, and official greeters —H.S.Commager⟩ **2** : one that is usu. naively fond of meeting people ⟨a natural ~ in the good sense of that abused word —S.H.Adams⟩

handsheet \'=,=\ *n* : a single sheet of paper made by a hand process for testing purposes (as to determine qualities of paper to be made from a given batch of pulp)

handshield \'=,=\ *n* : a welder's protective mask designed to be held up before the face by hand

handsled \'=,=\ *or* **handsleigh** \'=,=\ *n* : a sled that can be pulled by hand and that is usu. suitable for only one to ride : a small sled : a child's sled

hands-off \'=;=\ *adj* [*hands off*] : practicing noninterference ⟨preserved their *hands-off* policy toward the internal affairs of other countries⟩ : advocating or insisting upon noninterference ⟨showed a rather belligerent *hands-off* attitude when people came near his possessions⟩

hands off *v imper* : refrain from touching : refrain from interference : leave (one) alone

¹**hand·some** \'han(t)səm, 'haan-,'hain-\ *adj, usu* -ER/-EST [ME *handsom, handsum* easy to manipulate, perh. fr. (assumed) MD *handsaem* (whence D *handzaam*), fr. *hand* + *-saem* -some (akin to OHG *-sam*)] **1** *now dial* **a** : HANDY **b** : easy to handle or maneuver : suitable for handling **c** : conveniently near : ready and at hand **2** *chiefly dial* **a** : APPROPRIATE, SUITABLE **b** : of good quality ⟨~ vegetables⟩ **3 a** : of considerable value or of scope large enough to gratify highly : SIZABLE, AMPLE ⟨a very considerable, I may say a very ~, inheritance —Ngaio Marsh⟩ ⟨the soil, everywhere of ~ depth and finest quality —Thomas Carlyle⟩ ⟨winning the election by a ~ margin⟩ **b** : marked by or calling for skillful execution : ADROIT, ACCOMPLISHED, APT ⟨combining scholarship, imagination, literary flair, practical aptitude and personal gusto in the *handsomest* proportions —Richard Watts⟩ **4 a** : marked by or given with becoming graciousness, generosity, largess, magnanimity : not sparing : not merely equable or proper ⟨~ contributions to charities⟩ ⟨assuredly, the archbishop . . . leaves something ~ for the servants —George Borrow⟩ **b** : given to graceful commendation or laudation ⟨passed a ~ resolution in my favor —R.M.Lovett⟩ **5** : having an impressive and pleasing appearance: **a** : attractive, well-proportioned, and good-looking usu. in a way suggesting poise, dignity, and strength ⟨with reddish brown hair, bright brown eyes, fine forehead, and firm mouth and chin, he was exceptionally ~ —Allan Nevins & H.S.Commager⟩ ⟨though she had lost long ago her virginal loveliness, she had ripened . . . into a ~ and fruitful-looking woman —Ellen Glasgow⟩ **b** : imposing or noticeable through some combination of symmetry, proportion, size, or color ⟨a very ~ house with white marble steps . . . and a delicate silver knocker —Frances Trollope⟩ ⟨a very ~ . . . saddle, quilted on the seat with green plush, garnished with a double row of silver-headed studs —Laurence Sterne⟩ ⟨the red lizard, a ~ . . . form of the common olive-brown newt —*Amer. Guide Series: N.H.*⟩ **syn** see BEAUTIFUL, LIBERAL

²**handsome** \"\ *adv* -ER/-EST [ME *handsom*, fr. *handsom, handsum*, adj.] *now dial* : HANDSOMELY ⟨handsome is as ~ does⟩

handsome har·ry \ˌ==ˈharē\ *n, pl* **handsome harrys** *usu cap 2d H* : a deer grass (*Rhexia virginica*) having stems with pubescent internodes

hand·some·ly *adv* **1** : in a handsome manner ⟨a ~ bound book⟩ ⟨a ~ large donation to charity⟩ **2** *naut* **a** : slowly and carefully ⟨ease off a line ~⟩ **b** : in a shipshape manner ⟨the yacht hove alongside ~⟩

hand·some·ness *n* -ES : the quality or state of being handsome ⟨the man's ~ excused a slight slowness of wit⟩

hand·span \'=,=\ *n* : a distance equal to or an area equivalent in its circumference to a span ⟨a ~ waist⟩

hand·speak \'hanz,pēk, -n,sp-, -pik\ *dial var of* HANDSPIKE

hand specimen *n* **1** : a fragment of rock trimmed and shaped to dimensions of about 4x3x1 inches **2** : a fragment of rock with at least one freshly broken surface and small enough to be easily handled for megascopic study

¹**hand·spike** \'han(d)z,pīk, -),sp-, 'haan-\ *n* [by folk etymology fr. D *handspaak*, fr. *hand* + *spaak* pole] : a wooden bar or pole used as a lever (as in turning a windlass) or as a support (as for carrying timber)

²**handspike** \"\ *vt* **1** : to use a handspike on **2** : to move with a handspike

handspoke \'=,=\ *n, now dial Brit* : either of two bars used to carry a coffin at a funeral

handspring \'=,=\ *n* : an act or a feat esp. in tumbling in which the body turns forward or backward in a full circle from a standing position and lands first on the hands and then on the feet

hand stack *n, chiefly Midland* : a small pile of hay : HAYCOCK

¹**handstamp** \'=,=\ *n* **1** : a stamp (as of rubber) that is operated by hand **2** : a stamping (as a postal marking) that has been made by hand

²**handstamp** \'=,=\ *vt* **1** : to stamp by hand **2** : to impress (a marking) by means of a handstamp

handstamper \'=,==\ *n* : HANDSTAMP 1

handstand \'=,=\ *n* : an act of supporting the body on the hands with the trunk and legs balanced in air

handstick \'=,=\ *n, Midland* : HANDSPIKE

handstone \'=,=\ *n* **1** : COUP DE POING **2** : a stone held in the hand and applied to a milling stone for the grinding of seeds or grain

handstroke \'=,=\ *n* **1** : a blow with the hand **2** : a bell ringer's pull on the rope that swings a church bell to its mouth-up position : the sounding stroke — compare BACKSTROKE 2

handstruck \'=,=\ *adj, Brit* : HANDSTAMPED ⟨a ~ postage stamp or overprint⟩

hand's turn *n* : an act of manual labor; *esp* : a single usu. small expenditure of effort ⟨would not do a *hand's turn* to save himself from starvation⟩

hands up *v imper* : put (one's) hands up in the air and hold them up : SURRENDER

hand-tailor \'=;==\ *vt* **1** : to make chiefly by individual workmanship or by a specified number of hand operations to individual specifications ⟨a *hand-tailored* suit⟩ **2** : to make to order ⟨a truck or trailer *hand-tailored* to his own specifications —*Steelways*⟩

hand tap *n* : a tap for forming screw threads that is turned by hand

hand-tight \'=;=\ *adj* : being as tight as can be made by the hand alone : moderately tight

hand to hand *adv* [ME — more at HAND] : at very close quarters ⟨fought the bear *hand to hand* to the death —*Amer. Guide Series: Oreg.*⟩

hand-to-hand \;==;=\ *adj* [*hand to hand*] **1** : being at very close quarters ⟨*hand-to-hand* combat⟩ **2** : passed from person to person ⟨*hand-to-hand* delivery . . . of having of registered mail —*U.S. Post Office Manual*⟩

hand-to-mouth \;==;=\ *adj* : having or providing nothing to spare or having or providing barely enough esp. of money or the necessities of existence : PRECARIOUS ⟨leading a *hand-to-mouth* existence⟩ ⟨found employment in shoveling sidewalks, sawing wood, and other *hand-to-mouth* jobs —Dixon Wecter⟩ ⟨steel users . . . report that they are operating on a *hand-to-mouth* basis with less than a week's supply —*Newsweek*⟩

hand-tool \'=;=\ *vt* : TOOL *vt* 1

hand tooling *n* : the operation or product of hand-tooling

hand torch *n, Brit* : FLASHLIGHT

hand towel *n* : a small towel for the hands and usu. the face

handtrap \'=,=\ *n* : a mechanical device held in the hand and used to hurl clay targets into the air for shooting practice

hand-traverse \'=,==, '=;=,=, ;==;=\ *n* : a method used in mountaineering to cross a ledge that lacks standing room in which a climber grasps the ledge and moves along using his hands and allowing his body and legs to hang free

hand tree *n* : a tree (*Chiranthodendron pentadactylon*) of the family Sterculiaceae that is cultivated for its showy flowers whose spreading stamens suggest an open hand

hand truck *n* **1** : a small hand-propelled truck or wheelbarrow; *esp* : one consisting of a rectangular frame having at one end a pair of handles and at the other end a pair of small heavy wheels and a projecting edge or nose plate to slide under a load (as a trunk or box) and hold it in place **2** : a small truck having a motor for propulsion or lifting the load and controlled by a walking or riding operator

hand tub *n* : a fire-fighting apparatus consisting of an often tub-shaped reservoir of water pumped out through a hose by means of a pump with brakes that are rocked up and down by a number of men on each side of the apparatus; *also* : such an apparatus together with the wagon it is mounted on

hand truck 1

hand vise *n* : a small clamp or vise on a handle designed for holding small objects while they are being worked usu. by hand

hand vote *n* : a vote taken by counting the raised right hands of voters

hand wagon *n* : HANDCART

handwaled \'=;=\ *adj* [¹*hand* + *waled* past part. of *wale* (to choose)] *chiefly Scot* : individually selected : HANDPICKED

handweave \'=;=\ *vt* : to produce (fabric) on a handloom; *often* : to produce (fabric) on a loom on which the shuttle is actually thrown by hand — **handweaver** \'=;==\ *n*

handweaving \'=;==\ *n* : the occupation of one that hand weaves or the product of hand weaving

handwheel \'=,=\ *n* : a wheel worked by hand; *esp* : one whose rim serves as the handle by which a valve, lathe feed, or other part is operated

handwhile \'=,=\ *n* [ME, fr. OE *handhwīl*, fr. *hand, hond* hand + *hwīl* while — more at HAND, WHILE] *now Scot* : MOMENT, INSTANT

handwork \'=,=\ *n* [ME *handwerk*, fr. OE *hand-weorc*] : work done with the hands as distinguished from work done by a machine : HANDIWORK

handworked \'=;=\ *adj* : formed by hand or chiefly by hand processes ⟨~ lace⟩ ⟨a ~ iron railing⟩

handworker *or* **handworkman** \'=,==\ *n, pl* **handworkers** *or* **handworkmen** [¹*hand* + *worker* or *workman*] : one who is skilled at working with the hands

handwoven \'=;==\ *adj* : produced on a handloom on which the shuttle is often actually thrown by hand ⟨a ~ fabric⟩

handwrist \'=,=\ *n* [ME, fr. OE *hand-wyrst*, fr. *hand* + *wyrst* wrist — more at WRIST] *now dial Brit* : WRIST

handwrit \'=,=\ *n* [ME, fr. *hand* + *writ*] *now dial* : HANDWRITING

¹**handwrite** \'=,=\ *vt* [back-formation fr. *handwriting*] : to write by hand ⟨words in a written contract may be *handwritten* —E.M.Robinson⟩ ⟨these *handwritten* missives —Amy Lowell⟩

²**handwrite** \'=,=\ *n* -S **1** *now dial* : HANDWRITING **2** *now dial* : a person's signature

handwriting \'=,==\ *n* [¹*hand* + *writing*] **1** : writing in which the hand forms the letters with a pen, pencil, stylus, or similar writing implement; *also* : the cast or form of such writing peculiar to a particular person **2** : something written by hand : MANUSCRIPT — **the handwriting on the wall** [so called fr. the mysterious handwriting in the Bible that appeared on the wall of Belshazzar's palace to foretell his doom (Dan 5)] : a doom foreshadowed : an omen of one's fate usu. unpleasant

handwriting analysis *n* : GRAPHOLOGY

handwrought \'=;=\ *adj* : fashioned by hand or chiefly by hand processes ⟨~ nails⟩ ⟨~ silver⟩ ⟨~ details⟩

¹**handy** \'handē, 'haan-, -di\ *adj* -ER/-EST [¹*hand* + *-y*] **1** *obs* : performed by hand ⟨~ strokes —John Milton⟩ **2 a** : ready to the hand : conveniently near and accessible ⟨a ~ restaurant just around the corner⟩ ⟨kept his gun ~ as long as danger was near⟩ **b** : convenient for handling, for use, or for reference ⟨a ~ volume⟩; *also* : convenient for or adaptable to a variety of uses ⟨a ~ tool in the kitchen⟩ **c** *of a ship* : easily handled : obedient to the helm **3** : clever in using the hands esp. in a variety of convenient ways ⟨a man who is ~ around the house⟩ : ADROIT, DEXTEROUS ⟨~ with a paintbrush⟩ **syn** see DEXTEROUS

²**handy** \"\ *adv, dial* : HANDILY

handy-an·dy \ˌ==ˈandē, -'aan-, -di\ *n* -ES [after *Handy Andy* Rooney, hero of the novel *Handy Andy* by Samuel Lover †1868 Irish novelist] : HANDYMAN 1, 2

handy-bil·ly \ˌ==ˈbilē, -li\ *n* -ES **1** : WATCH TACKLE **2** : a small portable pump used chiefly aboard ship

handy boy *n* : a boy whose work is the doing of general tasks (as around a farm)

handycuff *var of* HANDICUFF

¹**handy-dan·dy** \ˌ==ˈdandē, -'daan-, -ndi\ *n* [ME, something held in a clasped hand, by redupl. fr. *hand*] *now dial Eng* : a child's game in which one child guesses in which closed hand another holds some small object

²**handy-dandy** \"\ *adv, dial Brit* : with quick alternation of place, circumstance, or condition

handy·man \-,man, -aa(ə)-\ *n, pl* **handymen** **1** : one whose work is the doing of general miscellaneous tasks; *esp* : one who performs miscellaneous or routine tasks (as about a home, public building, factory, laboratory) **2** : one that is competent in a variety of small skills or inventive or ingenious in repair or maintenance work (as around a house) or in the construction of handy devices **3** : one who has sufficient training to take responsibility for one or more phases of a trade (as in the shipbuilding industry) but who is not proficient enough to perform all its work phases **4** : JUMPER 1f

handy-pan·dy \ˌhandi'pandi\ *or* **handy-span·dy** \-'sp-\ *dial Brit var of* HANDY-DANDY

handy·weight \'==,=\ *adj, of a market animal* : intermediate in weight

handywoman \'==,==\ *n, pl* **handywomen** : a female handyman

handywork *archaic var of* HANDIWORK

[1]hang \ˈhaŋ, ˈhaiŋ *sometimes* ˈheŋ\ *vb* **hung** \ˈhəŋ\ *also* **hanged; hung** *also* **hanged; hanging; hangs** [partly fr. ME *hon* (past, *heng, hing, hang, hong;* past part. *hangen, hongen*), fr. OE *hōn* (vt); partly fr. ME *hangen, hongen,* fr. OE *hangian* (vi & vt); partly fr. ME *hengen, hingen,* fr. ON *hengja* (vt), causative fr. the root of ON *hanga* to hang; all akin to OHG *hāhan* to hang (vt), *hangēn* (vi), Goth *hāhan* to hang, and prob. to L *cunctari* to hesitate, Skt *śaṅkate* he wavers, doubts, fears, Hitt *ganki* he hangs] *vt* **1 a :** to fasten to some elevated point without support from below **:** SUSPEND ⟨~ a coat on a hook⟩ ⟨~ a pan from a beam over a stove⟩ ⟨~ meat to ripen⟩ ⟨a picture *hung* on the wall⟩ **b** (1) **:** to put to death by suspending from a cross, gibbet, or gallows — sometimes *hanged* in the past ⟨condemned to be *~ed* by the neck until dead⟩ (2) **:** to bring to justice or doom **:** expose in evil actions or objectionable ways in such a manner as to bring to punishment or an appropriate fate ⟨the criminal's very brazenness will ~ him sooner or later⟩ ⟨the chef's arrogant manner finally *hung* him and he lost his job⟩ — often used interjectionally as a mild imprecation ⟨I'll be *~ed*⟩ ⟨~ it all⟩ **c :** to fasten so as to allow free motion within given limits upon a point of suspension ⟨~ a pendulum⟩; *also* **:** to install by fastening in such a way ⟨can fit and ~ 20 doors in less than two hours —*Amer. Builder*⟩ **d :** to fit or fix in position or at a proper angle (a part of an implement that is swung in use) ⟨~ an ax to its helve⟩ **e :** to adjust the hem of (a skirt) so as to hang evenly and at a proper height when worn ⟨spent an hour *~ing* a skirt⟩ **2 :** to cover, decorate, or furnish by hanging pictures, trophies, drapery, or other decorations ⟨*hung* the room with evergreen boughs⟩ ⟨able to ~ themselves . . . with a variety of ostentatious ornaments —Jacquetta & Christopher Hawkes⟩ **3 :** to hold or bear in a suspended or inclined manner ⟨~ her head in embarrassment⟩ **4 a :** to fasten (as with glue or paste) to a wall ⟨~ wallpaper⟩ ⟨~ tile in the bathroom⟩ **b :** to cause (a name) to stick ⟨*hung* several nasty nicknames on him during the campaign⟩ **5 a :** to style or set (as a paragraph) in printing with a hanging indention ⟨~ each boldface entry word one em⟩ **b :** to place below the foot of a type page (overset type matter) **6 a :** to append or attach (as a rider) additionally to a legislative bill **b :** to impose (as an idea) upon a convenient form or medium for artistic expedience ⟨*hung* his sardonic and sometimes savage satire on romantic opera —*Time*⟩ **7 :** to prevent (as a jury) from reaching a decision (as by one member's refusal to join in a verdict which must be unanimous) **8 a :** to display (an exhibition of pictures) in a gallery or hall **b :** to display the works of (an artist) in a gallery **9 :** to catch (a fish) with a hook **10 :** to strike a blow with ⟨*hung* that left on the Dutchman's jaw —Ring Lardner⟩ **11 :** to give no further consideration to **:** neglect totally ⟨would ~ the responsibility and go fishing⟩ **~** *vi* **1 a :** to become suspended or fastened to some point above without support from below **:** DANGLE ⟨a purse *~ing* from a strap⟩ ⟨a sign *~ing* from a nail⟩ ⟨meat *~ing* to ripen⟩ ⟨a picture *~ing* on the wall⟩ **b** (1) **:** to die or become dead by hanging —sometimes *hanged* in the past ⟨he *~ed* for his crimes⟩ (2) **:** to come to justice **:** become subjected to an appropriate unpleasant doom **c** (1) **:** to remain poised or stationary in midair round about or overhead as if suspended ⟨a dim, oblong patch of light *~ing* slantwise in the darkness —Liam O'Flaherty⟩ ⟨clouds *~ing* low overhead⟩ ⟨the bird *hung* in the air a moment and then swooped⟩ ⟨musty air *hung* in the alleyway⟩ ⟨foggy weather had been *~ing* over the prairie —O.E.Rölvaag⟩ **:** HOVER ⟨around each *hung* a spirit, an emanation —Anton Vogt⟩ (2) **:** to have only a precarious hold ⟨meadows *~ing* on ridge and mountain slopes —John Muir †1914⟩ (3) **:** to stay with persistence ⟨the notion *hung* in his mind for days⟩ (4) **:** to await as if exposed ⟨that Indian property . . . *~s* as a rich prize for the taking —D'Arcy McNickle⟩ **d** (1) **:** to become fastened so as to allow free motion on the point of suspension ⟨the door *~s* on its hinges⟩ (2) **:** to be in a specified position on a point of suspension ⟨the casement window *hung* open over the street⟩ **e :** to be imminent **:** IMPEND ⟨evils ~ over the nation⟩ **f :** to be circumstantially relevant ⟨thereby *~s* a tale —Shak.⟩ **g :** to fall or droop from a usu. tense or taut position ⟨his lower lip *hung* open —J.D.Wall⟩ ⟨the reins *hung* loose on the horse's back⟩ **2 :** to rest or depend for authority or resolution ⟨an election often *~s* on one vote⟩ ⟨the question of unity *~s* on what the writer deems the veritable topic of his work —H.O. Taylor⟩ **3 :** to support things that are suspended or attached or that incline over or downward ⟨trees *~ing* with festoons of moss⟩ **4 a** (1) **:** to take hold for support **:** CLING, CLEAVE, ADHERE ⟨the woman seemed faint and *hung* on his arm⟩ ⟨*hung* to the trolley-car strap⟩ (2) **:** to keep persistent contact ⟨the dogs *hung* to the trail of the fox⟩ **b :** to be burdensome **:** act as an oppressive weight or care ⟨the worry *hung* on his mind until he was frantic⟩ ⟨time *~s* on his hands and he is unutterably bored⟩ **c :** LEAN ⟨*~ing* on the rail of the ship watching the sea⟩ **5 a :** to be indecisive or uncertain **:** be in suspense **:** suffer delay ⟨the decision is still *~ing*⟩ **b :** to occupy an uncertain mid-position ⟨his career *hung* for several years between law and medicine⟩ **6 :** to lean, incline, or jut over or downward ⟨high above it *~s* the rocky pinnacle —*Hot-Metal Magic*⟩ **7 :** to be in a state of rapt attention — usu. used with *on* ⟨*hung* on his every word⟩ **8 :** IDLE, LOITER ⟨found the boys *~ing* around poolrooms⟩ ⟨making the acquaintance of quiet gentlemen *~ing* about the fringes of tourist parties —Louis Bromfield⟩ — compare HANG AROUND **9 :** to have the charge stuck or arched in one part while the part underneath falls away so as to leave a gap — used esp. of a blast furnace for iron **10 :** to fit or fall from the figure in easy lines ⟨the coat *~s* loosely⟩ **11 a** *of a ball* **:** to rebound unexpectedly or unusually slowly (as in a game of cricket or tennis) **b** *of a racehorse* **:** to run at less than top speed **syn** see DEPEND — **hang fire 1 :** to be slow in the explosion of a charge after its primer has been discharged **2 :** to delay or be delayed usu. momentarily or temporarily ⟨the love of a young man who *hung fire* about carrying out his pledges —William de Morgan⟩ ⟨the plans had to *hang fire* until the city council approved them⟩ — **hang in the air :** to be uncompleted, unverified, or inadequately authorized ⟨something to be done, tested, made accurate, not left *hanging in the air* —A.N.Whitehead⟩ — **hang in the balance :** to be doubtful or uncertain ⟨the prisoner's fate *hangs in the balance*⟩ — **hang one on 1** *slang* **:** to inflict a heavy blow upon ⟨*hung one on* him and he was taken off in an ambulance⟩ **2** *slang* **:** to get very drunk — **hang over one's head :** to be an imminent threat or danger to one ⟨a charge of treason *hung over his head* for some time⟩ ⟨depression and insecurity *hanging over the head* of the entire nation⟩

[2]hang \"\ *n* -S **1 a :** the manner in which a thing hangs ⟨the ~ of the ax on its helve⟩ ⟨the ~ of the gown⟩ **b :** a position taken on any piece of gymnastics apparatus in which the center of gravity of a gymnast is below the point of support **2 :** DECLIVITY, SLOPE; *also* **:** DROOP ⟨the ~ of his lower lip⟩ **3 a :** the peculiar and significant order or meaning ⟨can't get the ~ of the discourse⟩ ⟨get the ~ of harmony singing —Dinah Shore⟩ **b :** the special method of doing, using, or dealing with something **:** KNACK ⟨took some time to get the ~ of driving the tractor⟩ **4 :** a hesitation, pause, or slackening in motion or in a course ⟨a marked ~ of the oar in the air before it dipped⟩ **5 :** the action of a furnace that hangs — called also *hanging* — **give a hang** *or* **care a hang :** to be concerned or worried ⟨does not *give a hang* whether he wins or not⟩

hang·able \-ŋəbəl\ *adj* **1 :** capable of being hanged esp. legally ⟨a person not ~ according to the law until he is of a certain age⟩ **2 :** punishable by hanging ⟨a ~ offense⟩

[1]hangar \ˈhaŋə(r), ˈhaiŋ-, -ŋgə- *sometimes* ˈheŋ- *or* -ŋˌgär *or* ŋˌgå(r\ *n* -S [F, fr. MF, prob. fr. ML *angarium* shed for shoeing horses, perh. fr. *angaria* carriage, wagon, fr. LL, compulsory service — more at ANGARIA] **:** SHELTER, SHED; *esp* **:** a covered and usu. enclosed area or a large shed for housing and repairing aircraft (as airplanes)

[2]hangar \"\ *vt* -ED/-ING/-S **:** to place or store in a hangar

hangar deck *n* **:** a deck on an aircraft carrier that is below the flight deck and that is used as a hangar

hang around *vi* **1 a :** to pass time or stay around a particular place aimlessly **:** loiter idly ⟨found nothing to do so spent his time just *hanging around* in the house⟩ ⟨*hanging around* in poolrooms⟩ **b :** to wait or occupy oneself in some adventitious way because of delay ⟨my ship was not ready to sail so that I was forced to *hang around* for several hours impatiently⟩ **2 :** to spend one's time in company esp. idly ⟨if you want to *hang around* with a bunch of football players that's your business —R.H.Newman⟩

hang back *vi* **1 a :** to drag behind others ⟨a small child following the older children but *hanging back* a little⟩ **b :** to delay purposely in advancing to a particular point ⟨we came almost alongside the ship but *hung back* until the captain's signal to come close⟩ **2 :** to be reluctant **:** HESITATE, FALTER

hang behind *vi* **:** to hang back

hangbird \ˈ=ˌ=\ *n* [so called fr. its habit of suspending its nest from a branch] **:** BALTIMORE ORIOLE

hang·by \ˈ=ˌbī\ *n* [fr. *hang by,* v.] *now dial Eng* **:** a flattering hanger-on **:** SYCOPHANT

hang·chow \ˈhaŋˈchau̇, ˈhäŋˈjō\ *adj, usu cap* [fr. *Hangchow,* China] **:** of or from the city of Hangchow, China **:** of the kind or style prevalent in Hangchow

[1]hangdog \ˈ=ˌ=\ *adj* [[1]*hang* + *dog*] **1 :** befitting a hangdog ⟨your manners have been of that silent and sullen and ~ kind —Charles Dickens⟩ **2 a :** ASHAMED, GUILTY ⟨had a ~ air about him even though he didn't get caught in the theft⟩ **b :** DEJECTED, COWED, PITIFUL ⟨the child's ~ look when told to go in the house⟩

[2]hangdog \"\ *n* [[1]*hang* + *dog*] **:** a despicable or miserable fellow

hange \ˈhanj\ *n* -S [ME *henge, hinge,* fr. *hengen, hingen* to hang — more at HANG] *dial Eng* **:** [2]PLUCK 2a

hanged *past of* HANG

hang·er \ˈhaŋə(r), ˈhaiŋ- *sometimes* ˈheŋ-\ *n* -S [ME, fr. *hangen* to hang + *-er* — more at HANG] **1 :** one that hangs: as **a :** HANGMAN **b :** a workman who hangs up articles to make them easily accessible or to position them for inspection or processing (as smoking, drying) **c :** a member of a hanging committee at an art exhibit **2 :** something that hangs, overhangs, or is suspended: as **a :** a decorative strip of cloth (as on a costume or a wall) **b :** a steep wooded declivity **c :** a depending part containing a bearing for a revolving piece; *esp* **:** a metal frame secured to the ceiling and carrying a bearing for overhead shafting **d :** a layer of tobacco leaves or stalks hung on sticks in a curing barn **3 :** a device or contrivance by which or to which something is hung or hangs: as **a :** a strap or loop on a sword belt by which a sword or dagger can be suspended **b :** a loop or chain (as on a collar) by which a garment is hung up **c :** a chain or S-shaped rod on which a pot is hung by a pothook **d :** a usu. metal or wooden device that fits inside a garment (as a suit) from shoulder to shoulder for hanging from a hook or rod (as in a closet) **e :** a metal strap used to hold an eaves in place **f :** a dangling leather loop or wooden handle that standing passengers in a moving trolley car, bus, or subway train may hold on to for keeping balance **g :** one of the devices upon which a sliding door is sometimes suspended **4 :** the written character ƨ resembling a pothanger and used as an exercise in teaching beginners to write — used chiefly in the phrase *pothooks and hangers* **5 :** a bobbin in bobbin lace holding a thread in one position **6 :** a vertical tension member receiving its stress only from the part of a structure directly attached to it **7 :** an iron box secured to and projecting from a wall or beam to carry one end of a joist or girder **8 :** [3]TANGLE **9 :** a metal frame for holding photographic film in tank development

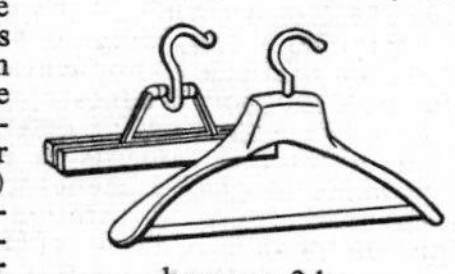

hangers 3d

hanger bolt *n* **:** a bolt made with a tapered lag-screw thread on one end and a machine-bolt thread on the other and used in timber construction

hanger bolt

hanger case *n* **:** a traveling bag with hangers and space for one or two suits

hang·er·man \-ˌman, -mən\ *n, pl* **hangermen :** one who installs hangers and brackets for supporting pipelines on ships — called also *bracketman*

hanger–off \ˈ=ˌ=ˈ=\ *n, pl* **hangers–off** *or* **hanger–offs** [*hang off,* v. + *-er*] **:** a slaughterhouse worker who suspends finished sheep carcasses from an overhead trolley and puts inspection stamps on them

hanger–on \ˈ=ˌ=ˈ=\ *n, pl* **hangers–on** *or* **hanger–ons** [*hang on* + *-er*] **:** one that hangs around a person, place, or institution in hope of personal gain (as patronage or preferment) ⟨soldiers became *hangers-on* of saloons and free-lunch bars —Dixon Wecter⟩ ⟨czars, princes and aristocracy, and their *hanger-ons* —F.D.Roosevelt⟩; *often* **:** one that hangs around in this manner with annoying persistence **syn** see PARASITE

hangersmith \ˈ==ˌ=\ *n* **:** one who makes hangers and brackets for supporting pipelines on ships

hanger wood *n* **:** drooping branches on a fruit tree (as peach)

hang–fair \ˈ=ˌ=\ *n, now dial Eng* **:** a public execution ⟨come to attend the *hang-fair* next day —Thomas Hardy⟩

hangfire \ˈ=ˌ=\ *n* [fr. the phrase *hang fire*] **:** a delay in the explosion of the charge of a gun after the primer has been fired **:** the temporary failure of a primer or igniter

hangi \ˈhäŋē\ *n* -S [Maori] **:** an underground oven used by the Maoris that consists of a pit in which stones are heated, wrapped food is placed on stones, and branches, wet sacks, and earth are used to cover the stones and food

hang·ie \ˈhaŋi\ *n* -S [[1]*hang* + *-ie*] *dial Brit* **:** HANGMAN

[1]hanging *n* -S [ME, fr. *hangen* to hang + *-ing* — more at HANG] **1 a :** the act of suspending something ⟨requested that the entire exhibition committee be at the ~ to assist in positioning the pictures⟩ **b :** a killing or execution in which a noose at the end of a suspended rope is placed around a person's neck and then the support under him quickly removed so that he drops or swings free and dies from a broken neck or from asphyxiation ⟨sentenced to ~⟩ — see GALLOWS; compare GIBBET 1 **2 :** something hung: as **a :** CURTAIN — usu. used in pl. **b :** a covering (as a tapestry or wallpaper) for a wall — usu. used in pl. **3 :** a downward slope or inclination **:** DECLIVITY ⟨the ~ of a ship's deck⟩ **4 :** HANG 5

[2]hanging *adj* **1 :** situated or lying on steeply sloping ground ⟨a ~ meadow on the mountainside⟩ or on top of some high place (as a wall or roof) ⟨a fine ~ garden aloft on breezy inaccessible heights —John Muir †1914⟩ **2 a :** leaning over or downward **:** drooping or jutting out and downward **:** OVERHANGING ⟨a ~ rock⟩ ⟨~ wood⟩ **b :** SUSPENDED, PENDENT **c :** supported only by the wall on one side ⟨a ~ staircase⟩ ⟨a ~ balcony⟩ **d :** situated at or having a discordant junction ⟨a ~ cirque⟩ **3** *obs* **:** being in suspense or abeyance **4** *archaic* **:** downcast or dejected in appearance **5 :** adapted for sustaining a hanging object **6 a :** deserving, likely to cause, or prone to inflict death by hanging ⟨a ~ crime⟩ ⟨a ~ judge⟩ **b :** being of great moment or significance ⟨not disposed to make a ~ matter of it —*Manchester Guardian Weekly*⟩ **7** *of a chess pawn* **:** connected and abreast

hanging barrel *n* **:** the going barrel in a watch whose arbor is supported by attachment to the upper plate only allowing the movement to be made very thin

hanging basket *n* **:** a container made (as of wood or wire) to resemble a basket to hold a plant hung up for decoration or for greenhouse cultivation (as of orchids)

hanging block *n* **:** a preparation like a hanging drop but with agar replacing the liquid medium

hanging bog *n* **:** QUAKING BOG

hanging buttress *n* **:** a buttress usu. supported on a corbel

hanging clamp *n* **:** a clamp that can be fixed to various parts of a ship to serve as a fixed iron for attachments (as for a tackle block or a stage)

hanging committee *n* **:** a committee having charge of the hanging of pictures in an exhibition

hanging drop *n* **:** a drop of liquid suspended from a cover glass usu. placed over the cavity of a depression slide and containing microorganisms or cells for microscopic study (as in an agglutination test)

hanging fly *n* **:** a mecopterous insect of the family Bittacidae

hanging glacier *n* **:** a body of ice or névé that breaks off abruptly at the edge of a precipice or steep slope

hanging indention *n* **:** indention in which the first word of the first line of a passage is set flush with the left-hand margin and the first words of the second and subsequent lines are set to the right of the left-hand margin

hanging keel *n* **:** BAR KEEL

hanging lie *n* **:** the position of a golf ball which comes to rest on ground sloping downward in the direction it is to be played

hanging moss *n* **1 :** a lichen of the genus *Usnea* **2 :** SPANISH MOSS

hanging paper *n* **:** partly processed paper that is to be converted (as by coating and printing) into wallpaper

hanging participle *n* **:** a participle that dangles syntactically

hanging rail *n* **:** the rail of a door or casement to which hinges are attached

hanging side *n* **:** the hanging-wall side of a geologic vein, fault, or bed

hanging sleeve *n* **1 :** an ornamental straight-hanging oversleeve of the 15th century usu. set in or tied on at the armhole **2 :** a loose open sleeve on a child's garment

hanging stairs *n pl* **:** stairs that are or appear to be supported along one side only (as by brackets projecting from an adjacent wall or by having one end of each step built into a wall, the front edge of each step being supported along the back edge of the step below)

hanging stile *n* **1** *also* **hanging head** *or* **hanging post :** the stile of a door to which hinges are secured **2 :** the upright of a window frame to which casements are hinged or in which the pulleys for sash windows are fastened

hanging valley *n* **:** a valley whose lower end is notably higher than the level of the valley or the shore to which it leads

hanging wall *n* **:** the upper or overhanging wall of an inclined vein, fault, or other geologic structure — opposed to *footwall*

hang·le \ˈhaŋəl\ *n* -S [[1]*hang* + *-le* (suffix denoting an instrument)] *dial Eng* **:** an iron pothook

hang·man \ˈhaŋmən, ˈhaiŋ-, -ˌman, -ˌmaa(ə)n *sometimes* ˈheŋ-\ *n, pl* **hangmen** [ME *hangeman,* fr. *hangen* to hang + *man*] **1 :** one who hangs another; *esp* **:** a public executioner **2 :** a game in which one player chooses a word and the others try to guess it one letter at a time, a part of a picture of a hanged man being drawn for each wrong guess

hangman's halter *or* **hangman's knot** *n* **:** a slip noose usu. made with eight or nine turns for hanging a condemned person

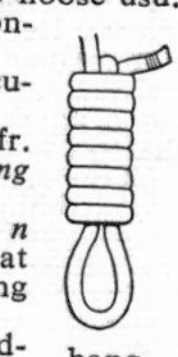

hangman's halter

hang·man·ship \ˈ==ˌship\ *n* **:** the office or the occupation of a hangman

hang·ment \ˈhaŋˌment\ *n* -S [ME *hangement,* fr. *hangen* to hang + *-ment*] *now dial chiefly Eng* **:** HANGING

hang·nail \ˈhaŋˌnāl, ˈhaiŋ- *sometimes* ˈheŋ-\ *n* [by folk etymology fr. *agnail, angnail* — more at AGNAIL] **:** a piece of skin from the nail fold hanging loose at the side or root of a fingernail

hangnest \ˈ=ˌ=\ *n* [so called fr. its habit of suspending its nest from a branch] **:** BALTIMORE ORIOLE

hang off *vi* **:** to hang back

hang on *vi* **1 a :** to keep hold **:** hold onto something usu. tightly ⟨the truck was bouncing so much we had to *hang on* to save ourselves from being thrown against the sides⟩ **b :** to persist tenaciously in an enterprise **:** refuse to give up ⟨even at the end of his life he was still *hanging on,* still seeking justice⟩ **2 :** to continue to cause suffering **:** resist getting better in health ⟨a winter cold that seemed to *hang on* all spring⟩ **3 a** *of a sound* **:** to continue to sound ⟨the strains of music *hung on* for a long time⟩ **b :** to continue listening on a telephone **:** keep a telephone connection open ⟨*hang on* a minute while I look it up⟩ — **hang on to :** to hold, grip, or keep tenaciously ⟨the child *hung on to* the lollipop for dear life⟩ ⟨swore he would *hang on to* the job until they fired him⟩

hang out *vi* **1** *obs* **:** to protrude in a downward direction **2 a** *slang* **:** LIVE, RESIDE ⟨*hung out* at a boardinghouse in town⟩ **b :** to spend one's time idly or in loitering around or in a particular place ⟨did a lot of *hanging out* in barrooms⟩ **~** *vt* **:** to suspend from something outside in order to display usu. to the public ⟨*hung out* a sign advertising his products⟩ ⟨*hung* Christmas decorations *out* around the windows⟩

hangout \ˈ=ˌ=\ *n* -S [*hang out*] **1 :** a place where one resides, stays, or tends to frequent or lounge around ⟨adopts the corner drugstore as his ~ —C.C.Scott⟩ **2 :** an often low-class place of entertainment ⟨got a beer at the ~ in the next block⟩

hang over *vi* **:** to remain to be handled or completed (as of unfinished business at the end of a meeting) ⟨the meeting adjourned and left the plans *hanging over*⟩ ⟨let the case *hang over* for the new administration —*Time*⟩

hangover \ˈ=ˌ==\ *n* -S [*hang over*] **1 :** something that remains from what is past (as a surviving trait or custom) ⟨manners that were really a ~ from an earlier day⟩ **2 a :** disagreeable physical effects (as headache, stupor, or nausea) following heavy consumption of alcohol **b :** disagreeable aftereffects from the use of drugs **c :** a letdown or deflation following great excitement or excess ⟨an exhausted silence seemed to come down over the capitol, a colossal election ~ —Mollie Panter-Downes⟩ **3 :** undue prolongation and indistinct articulation of bass notes from a loudspeaker because of poor design or inadequate damping

hangrod \ˈ=ˌ=\ *n* **:** a horizontal rod on which clothing is hung by means of coat hangers

hangs *pres 3d sing of* HANG, *pl of* HANG

hangtag \ˈ=ˌ=\ *n* **:** a tag attached to an article of merchandise giving information about the quality of its material and about its proper care

hang together *vi* **1 :** to remain united **:** stand by one another ⟨the boys felt a strong loyalty and *hung together* when in strange company⟩ ⟨the immigrant races had tended to *hang together,* united by language, a foreign-language press —F.L. Paxson⟩ **2 :** to form a consistent or coherent whole ⟨a set of facts that seem to *hang* well *together* —Edward Clodd⟩ **:** have unity (as of artistic construction) ⟨the story *hangs together* pretty well⟩

[1]han·gul \ˈhäŋgəl\ *n* -S [Kashmiri *hāṅgul*] **:** a deer (*Cervus cashmiriensis*) of Kashmir closely related to the red deer of Europe

[2]hangul *usu cap, var of* HANKUL

hang up *vt* **1 a :** to place on a hook or hanger designed for the purpose ⟨told the child to *hang up* his coat⟩ **b :** to place (a telephone receiver or earpiece) back on the hook or cradle so that the connection is broken **c** *Austral* **:** to tie (a horse) to a ring or post **d :** to cause (a tree) to catch in another tree in falling **2 :** to keep delayed, suspended, or held up ⟨the negotiations were *hung up* for a week by the illness of the prime minister⟩ **3 :** to cause (a record) to be set **:** ACHIEVE ⟨has *hung up* a record for the hundred-yard dash⟩ **4 :** to cause to stick or snag immovably ⟨the ship was *hung up* on a sandbar for two hours⟩ **~** *vi* **1 :** to hang up a telephone receiver or earpiece ⟨the speaker said goodbye and *hung up* abruptly⟩ **2 :** to become stuck or snagged so as to be immovable ⟨if the ship *hangs up* on a sandbar, we remove the passengers in lifeboats⟩ **3 :** to break a trip (as by automobile) for a night's rest

hang–up \ˈ=ˌ=\ *n* -S [*hang up*] **1 :** a tree caught in another tree in felling **2 :** an immovable obstacle (as a tree stump) in a skid road

ha·nif \haˈnēf, häˈ-\ *n* -S [Ar *ḥanīf,* prob. fr. Aram *ḥănēf* hypocrite, heretic] **:** a pre-Islamic hermit of Arabia that lived a wandering ascetic life and professed a vague form of monotheism

hani·fite \ˈhanəˌfīt, haˈnēˌf-\ *n* -S *usu cap* [Abū-*Ḥanīfah* †767 Muslim jurist + E *-ite*] **:** HANAFI 2

ha·nis \ˈhänə̇s\ *n, pl* **hanis** *or* **hanises** *usu cap* **1 :** a Kusan people on the shores of the Coos river and Coos Bay, Oregon **2 :** a member of the Hanis people

[1]hank \ˈhaŋk, ˈhaiŋk\ *vt* -ED/-ING/-S [ME *hanken,* of Scand origin; akin to ON *hanka* to coil, fasten, fr. *hank-, hönk,* n.] **1 :** to fasten with a hank **2 :** to fold, loop, or coil into a hank

[2]hank \"\ *n* -S [ME, of Scand origin; akin to ON *hönk* hank, coil, skein, clasp, *hanki* clasp; fr. or akin to MLG *hank* handle, fr. the stem of OHG *hengen, henken* to hang, causative fr. the root of *hāhan* to hang — more at HANG] **1 :** a coil, loop, or ring esp. of rope: as **a** *dial Eng* **:** a loop used to fasten or suspend something (as a strap on a door) **b :** a coiled or looped bundle (as of yarn, rope, wire) usu. containing a definite yardage ⟨a ~ of cotton yarn contains 840 yards⟩ —

see COUNT 8a; compare SKEIN 1 **c :** a ring (as of wood, iron, or rope) attached to the edge of a jib or staysail and running on a stay **2** *now chiefly dial* **:** ADVANTAGE, POWER, HOLD ⟨shouldn't let them get such a ~ over you⟩

1han·ker \'haŋkə(r), 'haiŋ-\ *vb* **hankered; hankered; han·kering** \-k(ə)riŋ\ **hankers** [prob. fr. Flem. *hankeren* (akin to D *hunkeren*), freq. of *hangen* to hang; akin to OHG *hāhan* to hang — more at HANG] *vi* **1** *now chiefly dial* **:** to linger or hang around esp. in anticipation or desire ⟨used to ~ around the stillroom —Thomas Hughes⟩ **2 a :** to desire strongly and yearn in distress ⟨a thirsty man ~*ing* for water⟩ **b :** to experience a controlled but persistent desire — usu. used with *for* or *after* ⟨~ to spend an evening in general conversation —Clifton Fadiman⟩ ⟨has always ~*ed* to do a bit of acting —Bennett Cerf⟩ ⟨spend a lot of time ~*ing* after forbidden pleasures⟩ ⟨~*ed* for a good cup of coffee⟩ **3** *chiefly Scot* **:** to hesitate or pause esp. in speaking ⟨he hums and he ~s —Robert Burns⟩ ~ *vt* **:** to yearn for **:** want badly ⟨it supplies what we have long ~*ed* —*Saturday Rev.*⟩ **syn** see LONG

2hanker \"\ *n* -S **:** HANKERING

han·ker·er \-kərə(r)\ *n* -S **:** one that hankers ⟨~s after pleasure⟩

hankering *n* -S **:** the experience of one that hankers **: a :** strong desire **:** great yearning ⟨the same ~ for swift success, the same hasty greed —*Times Lit. Supp.*⟩ **b :** a controlled but persistent desire ⟨push out of his consciousness the ~ to spend an evening alone⟩

han·ker·ing·ly *adv* **:** in the manner of one that hankers ⟨kept thinking ~ about seeing his family again⟩

hank for hank *adv, of boats* **:** on the same tack together and making equal speed ⟨sail *hank for hank*⟩

han·kie *or* **han·ky** *also* **han·key** \'haŋkē, 'haiŋ-, -ki\ *n, pl* **hankies** [by shortening & alter.] **:** HANDKERCHIEF

han·kle \'haŋkəl\ *vt* -ED/-ING/-S [freq. of 1*hank*] *now dial Eng* **1 :** TWIST, ENTANGLE **2 :** to involve (a person) in something by luring or enticing — usu. used with *in* or *on* ⟨didn't want to join but they *hankled* him in⟩

han·kow \'haŋ¦kau̇, 'han¦kau̇, -kō; 'hän¦kō\ *adj, usu cap* [fr. *Hankow*, China] **:** of or from the city of Hankow, China **:** of the kind or style prevalent in Hankow

hanks·ite \'haŋk,sīt\ *n* -S [Henry G. *Hanks* †1907 Am. mineralogist + E *-ite*] **:** a mineral $Na_{22}K(SO_4)_9(CO_3)_2Cl$ consisting of white or yellow sulfate-carbonate-chloride of sodium and potassium occurring in hexagonal crystals

han·kul \'hän,kül\ *also* **han·gul** \-ŋ,gül\ *n* -S *usu cap* [Korean] **:** the alphabet of 24, formerly 25, characters invented in the 15th century in which Korean is usu. written — called also *onmun*

han·ky-pank \¦haŋkē¦paŋk\ *adj* [short for *hanky-panky*] **:** marked by or derived from hanky-panky ⟨*hanky-pank* joints —*Life*⟩ ⟨their pockets full of *hanky-pank* money —Herbert Gold⟩

han·ky-pan·ky \-¦paŋkē\ *also* **hankey-pankey** *n, pl* **hanky-pankies** *also* **hankey-pankeys** [alter. (perh. influenced by *handkerchief*) of *hocus-pocus*] **1 :** questionable, deceitful, or fraudulent activity **:** TRICKERY **:** MISCHIEF ⟨there's been some *hanky-panky* going on, and we haven't got to the bottom of it —F.W.Crofts⟩ ⟨wanted things to be completely above board and no *hanky-panky*⟩ ⟨while the philandering physician was playing *hanky-panky* with his patients —Alan Hynd⟩ **2 :** meaningless or foolish activity or talk ⟨people went in for too much hullabaloo and *hanky-panky* —John Steinbeck⟩ ⟨had a thorough grasp of the political and social *hanky-panky* of his period —*Time*⟩

han·na \'hanə\ *dial Brit* **:** have not

hannahill *var of* HANAHILL

han·nay·ite \'hanē,īt\ *n* -S [G *hannayit*, fr. J. B. *Hannay*, 19th cent. Scot. chemist + G *-it* -ite] **:** a mineral $Mg_3(NH_4)_2H_4(PO_4)_4.8H_2O$ consisting of a hydrous acid ammonium magnesium phosphate occurring in guano

han·ni·bal·ic \¦hanə¦balik\ *also* **han·ni·ba·lian** \-¦bālyən, -lēən\ *adj, usu cap* [*Hannibal* †183 B.C. Carthaginian general who made war against Rome + E *-ic* or *-ian*] **:** of or relating to the Carthaginian general Hannibal

ha·no \'hä,nō, 'ha,-\ *n, pl* **hano** *or* **hanos** *usu cap* [Sp, of AmerInd origin] **1 :** a Tanoan people occupying a pueblo in Arizona **2 :** a member of the Hano people

ha·noi \(')ha¦nȯi *also* hə'n-\ *adj, usu cap* [fr. *Hanoi*, North Vietnam] **:** of or from Hanoi, the capital of North Vietnam **:** of the kind or style prevalent in Hanoi

hano·ver *or* **han·no·ver** \'ha(,)nōvə(r), -anəv-, *G* hä'nōvər *or* hä'nōfər\ *adj, usu cap* [fr. *Hanover* (Hannover), Germany] **:** of or from the city of Hanover, Germany **:** of the kind or style prevalent in Hanover

1han·o·ve·ri·an \¦hanō¦virēən, -anə¦- *also* -ver-\ *adj, usu cap* [*Hanover*, province of Prussia, Germany (fr. G *Hannover*) + E *-ian*] **1 a :** of, relating to, or subject to the Prussian province of Hanover **b :** of, relating to, or supporting the former ducal house of Hanover **c :** of, relating to, or supporting the British House of Hanover **2 :** of, relating to, or being a period of architectural development in western Europe usu. held to be equivalent to the 18th century

2hanoverian \"\ *n* **1** -S *cap* **a :** a native or inhabitant of Hanover, Germany **b :** a member of the former ducal house of Hanover **c :** a member or supporter of the British House of Hanover **2 a** *usu cap* **:** a breed of horses developed by crossing heavy cold-blooded German horses with Thoroughbreds **b** -S *often cap* **:** any animal of this breed

hans *pl of* HAN

han·sa \'han(t)sə, 'hän(,)zä\ *or* **hanse** \'han(t)s, 'hänzə\ *n* -S *usu cap* [*hansa*, fr. ML, fr. MLG *hanse*; *hanse* fr. ME *hans, hanze*, fr. MF & MLG; MF *hanse* fr. MLG; akin to OE *hōs* company, OHG *hansa* troop of warriors, Goth, company, multitude] **1 a :** a merchant guild in a medieval town **b :** an association for trading in foreign countries; *esp* **:** the league first constituted of merchants of various free German cities dealing abroad in the medieval period and later of the cities themselves and organized to secure greater safety and privileges in trading and mutual defense against foreign aggression either by law or arms **2 a :** the entrance fee to a merchant guild **b :** the tax levied upon traders not belonging to a guild

1han·sard \'han(t)sərd, -n,särd, -nzərd, -n,zärd\ *n* -S *usu cap* [*hansa* + *-ard*] **:** a merchant of one of the Hansa towns

2han·sard \'han(t)sərd, -n,särd\ *n* -S *usu cap* [after Luke *Hansard* †1828 Eng. printer who printed the journals of the House of Commons] **:** the official published report of proceedings in the British parliament

1han·se·at·ic \¦han(t)sē¦ad·ik, ¦haan-, -at|, |ēk *also* -nzē-\ *adj, usu cap* [ML *Hanseaticus*, fr. *hansa* — more at HANSA] **:** of or relating to the Hansa (sense 1b)

2hanseatic \"\ *n* -S *usu cap* **:** a member of the Hansa (sense 1b)

hansel *var of* HANDSEL

han·sen·osis \,han(t)sə'nōsəs\ *n* -ES [NL, fr. A. G. H. *Hansen* + NL *-osis*] **:** LEPROSY

han·sen·ot·ic \¦==¦näd·ik\ *adj* [fr. NL *hansenosis*, after such pairs as NL *neurosis: E neurotic*] **:** LEPROUS 1

han·sen's bacillus \'han(t)sənz-\ *n, usu cap H* [after Armauer G. H. *Hansen* †1912 Norw. physician who discovered the bacillus] **:** the bacterium (*Mycobacterium leprae*) that causes leprosy

hansen's disease *n, usu cap H* [after A. G. H. *Hansen*] **:** LEPROSY

hansh *var of* HANCH

han·som \'han(t)səm, 'haan-, 'hain-\ *or* **hansom cab** *n* -S [after Joseph Aloysius *Hansom* †1882 Eng. architect who designed such a vehicle] **:** a light two-wheeled covered carriage with the driver's seat elevated behind and with the reins passed over the top

hansom

hans·wurst \(')hän(t)s¦vu̇(ə)rst\ *n* -S *usu cap* [G, fr. LG *Hanswurst*, lit., Jack sausage] **:** a broadly farcical or burlesque stock character common in German comedy in the 16th to the 18th centuries

han't \(')(h)ānt, *chiefly Brit* (')(h)änt\ [by contraction] *dial* **:** have not **:** has not

hant \'hant, -aa(ə)-, -ai-, -ā-,-ä-\ *var of* HAUNT

h antigen *n, usu cap H* [G, fr. *hauchantigen*, fr. *hauch* breath + *antigen*] **:** FLAGELLAR ANTIGEN

han·tik \'hän.,tēk\ *n, pl* **hantik** *or* **hantiks** *usu cap* [native name on Panay] **1 a :** a Bisayan people inhabiting western Panay, Philippines **b :** a member of such people **2 :** an Austronesian language of the Hantik people that is sometimes considered a dialect of Bisayan

han·tle \'hant³l\ *n* -S [prob. alter. of *handful*] *chiefly Scot* **1 :** HANDFUL **2 :** QUANTITY, AMOUNT; *esp* **:** a sizable or considerable amount ⟨a ~ of money⟩ ⟨a good ~ of people⟩

ha·nuk·kah *or* **ha·nu·kah** *or* **cha·nu·kah** *also* **cha·nuk·kah** \'k¦änəkə, 'h|, |än-, -nük-, -,kä, -,kȧ, -nikə,-nēkə\ *n* -S *usu cap* [Heb *ḥănukkāh* dedication] **:** the eight-day Jewish festival of lights beginning on the 25th of Kislev and commemorating the victory of the Maccabees over Antiochus of Syria and their rededication of the defiled Temple of Jerusalem

hanum *var of* KHANUM

hanu·man \'hənü,män, 'hän-, ,==¦=\ *n* -S [Hindi *Hanumān*, a monkey god, hanuman, fr. nom. of Skt *hanumant*, lit., possessing (large) jaws, fr. *hanu* jaw — more at CHIN] **:** a common Indian monkey (*Presbytis entellus*) protected in its homeland as a protégé of a monkey god

ha·nu·nóo \¦hänə¦nō\ *n, pl* **hanunóo** *or* **hanunóos** *usu cap* **1 a :** a predominantly pagan people inhabiting southern Mindoro, Philippines **b :** a member of such people **2 :** an Austronesian language of the Hanunóo people

ha·nus·ite \'hänə,s(h)īt\ *n* -S [Czech *hanušit*, fr. Josef *Hanuš* †1956 Czech chemist + Czech *-it* -ite] **:** a mineral $Mg_2Si_3O_7(OH)_2.H_2O$ consisting of a hydrous basic silicate of magnesium that is a component of pectolite

ha·nus method \'hänəs(h)-, -,nüsh-\ *n, usu cap H* [after J. *Hanuš*] **:** a method for determining the iodine number of an oil or fat that consists in adding a mixture of iodine and bromine in glacial acetic acid and estimating the excess of unused halogen by titration with sodium thiosulfate

hao·le \'hau̇lē, -(,)lā\ *n* -S [Hawaiian] *Hawaii* **:** one who is not a member of the native race of Hawaii; *esp* **:** a member of the white race

hao·ma \'hau̇mə\ *n* -S [Av — more at SOMA (intoxicant)] **:** a sacred drink used ritually in Zoroastrianism and sometimes personified as a deified being — compare SOMA

hao·ri \'hau̇rē\ *n* -S [Jap] **:** a loose outer garment resembling a coat and extending to the knee and worn in Japan

1hap \'hap\ *n* -S [ME *hap, happe*, fr. ON *happ* good luck; akin to OE *gehæp* suitable, Sw dial. *happa* (*sig*) to take place, Norw *heppa* to take place, OIr *cob* victory, OSlav *kobi* augury] **1 :** something that happens or befalls without plan, apparent cause, or predictability ⟨odd little ~s and mishaps of domestic life⟩ **2 :** a force which shapes events unpredictably **:** CHANCE, LUCK, FORTUNE ⟨by some bad tide or ~ . . . the ill-made catamaran was overset —Herman Melville⟩ ⟨the fish of evil ~ . . . had been caught and frozen fast —Llewelyn Powys⟩ **syn** see CHANCE

2hap \"\ *vi* **happed; happed; happing; haps** [ME *happen*, fr. *hap, happe*, n.] **1 :** to have the fortune **:** HAPPEN, CHANCE ⟨what's to be done, if a man ~s to go wrong⟩ ⟨if ~ it must, that I must see thee lie —Robert Herrick †1674⟩ **2 :** to come by chance **:** LIGHT — used with *on* or *upon* ⟨*happed* upon the very book he was looking for⟩

3hap \"\ *vt* **happed; happed; happing; haps** [ME *happen*] *dial* **:** to wrap up for warmth **:** CLOTHE, COVER ⟨at the kitchen fire, *happed* in an old overcoat —Michael Murphy⟩

4hap \"\ *n* -S *dial* **:** something that serves as a covering or wrap (as a bed quilt or cloak)

ha·pa haole \¦häpə¦hau̇lē, -(,)lā\ *adj* [Hawaiian, fr. *hapa* half (fr. E *half*) + *haole* white person] *Hawaii* **:** of part-white ancestry or origin; *esp* **:** Hawaiian-Caucasian

hap·a·lo·nych·ia \,hapəlō'nikēə\ *n* -S [NL, fr. Gk *hapalos* soft + NL *-onychia*] **:** abnormal softness of the fingernails or toenails

hapax *n* -ES [by shortening] **:** HAPAX LEGOMENON

ha·pax le·go·me·non \¦ha,paksləˈgämə,nän, ¦hā,pak-, ¦hä-,pȧk-, -,nən\ *n, pl* **hapax legome·na** \-,nə, -,nä\ [Gk, something said only once] **:** a word or form evidenced by a single citation **:** a word or form occurring once and only once in a document or corpus

hapchance \'=,=\ *n* [1*hap* + *chance*] **:** a fortuitous or chance event or circumstance ⟨the ~ of a sounding word —Richard Llewellyn⟩ ⟨this ~ . . . enterprise is nothing to sneeze at —Dave Roberts⟩

ha'·pen·ny \'hāp(ə)ni\ *n* [by contr.] **:** HALFPENNY

hap–harlot \'=,==\ *n* [3*hap* + *harlot* (knave)] *now dial Eng* **:** a coarse coverlet

1haphazard \(')=¦==\ *n* [1*hap* + *hazard*] CHANCE, ACCIDENT, RANDOM ⟨this little remnant preserved by the ~ of chance —Edith Hamilton⟩ ⟨take our principles at ~ —John Locke⟩

2haphazard \"\ *adj* **:** marked by lack of plan, regularity, order, guidance, or direction **:** made, performed, or selected according to chance, whim, or speculation rather than on the basis of considered judgment or firm knowledge **:** AIMLESS, RANDOM ⟨his ~ untidy ways —Virginia Woolf⟩ ⟨not . . . a collection of ~ schemes, but rather the orderly component parts of a connected and logical whole —F.D.Roosevelt⟩ ⟨there must be some guidance unless selection is to be ~ —Muna Lee⟩ ⟨the room was . . . filled with ~ furniture —Howard Griffin⟩ ⟨~ ascriptions have been made —A.M.Young⟩ **syn** see RANDOM

3haphazard \"\ *adv* [2*haphazard*] **:** HAPHAZARDLY ⟨were built . . . without any regard to their situation, placed ~, wherever it was convenient —Edith Hamilton⟩

hap·haz·ard·ly *adv* **:** in a haphazard manner ⟨a little cluster of islands grouped ~ about a bigger green island —Louis Bromfield⟩

hap·haz·ard·ness *n* -ES **:** the quality or state of being haphazard

hap·haz·ard·ry \-rē\ *n* -ES **:** haphazard character or order **:** CHANCINESS, FORTUITY ⟨the good things in his work always have an air of ~ —*Manchester Guardian Weekly*⟩ ⟨whose forebears had known only the ~ of idol and fetish worship —Galbraith Welch⟩

haphtarah *or* **haphtorah** *var of* HAFTARAH

hapl- *or* **haplo-** *also* **apl-** *or* **aplo-** *comb form* [NL, fr. Gk *hapl-, haplo-*, fr. *haploos, haplous, haplos*, fr. *ha-* one (akin to Gk *homos* same) + *-ploos, -plous, -plos* multiplied by; akin to L *-plus* multiplied by — more at SAME, DOUBLE] **1 :** single **:** simple ⟨*haploscope*⟩ **2** [*haploid*] **:** of or relating to the haploid generation or condition

hap·less \'hapləs\ *adj* [1*hap* + *-less*] **:** marked by the absence of good luck **:** UNFORTUNATE ⟨~ beings caught in the grip of forces we can do little about —W.H.Whyte⟩ **syn** see UNLUCKY

hap·less·ly *adv* **:** in a hapless manner

hap·less·ness *n* -ES **:** the quality or state of being hapless

haplite *var of* APLITE

hap·lo·bi·ont \¦haplō¦bī,änt, ha'plōbē,änt\ *n* -S [*hapl-* + *-biont*] **:** a plant producing only sexual haploid individuals — compare DIPLOBIONT, HAPLONT — **hap·lo·bi·on·tic** \¦hap(,)lō,bī¦äntik, ha¦plōbē¦äntik\ *adj*

hap·lo·caulescent \¦ha(,)plō+\ *adj* [*hapl-* + *caulescent*] **:** having a simple axis — used of a plant (as the poppy) capable of developing reproductive organs on the primary axis; compare DIPLOCAULESCENT, TRIPLOCAULESCENT

hap·lo·chlamydeous \"+\ *adj* [*hapl-* + *chlamydeous*] **:** having rudimentary perianth leaves protecting the sporophylls (as in pistillate flowers of a walnut tree) — compare HOMOCHLAMYDEOUS

1hap·lo·diploid \"+\ *adj* [*hapl-* + *diploid*] **:** of, relating to, or characterized by haplodiploidy

2haplodiploid \"\ *n* **:** an individual produced by haplodiploidy

hap·lo·diploidy \"+\ *n* [*hapl-* + *diploidy*] **:** sex differentiation in which haploid males are produced from unfertilized eggs and diploid females from fertilized eggs (as in certain insects)

hap·lo·diplont \"+\ *n* [*hapl-* + *diplont*] **:** a haploid plant reproducing by spores

hap·lod·o·ci \ha'plädə,sī\ *n pl, cap* [NL, fr. *hapl-* + *-doci* (fr. Gk *dokos* beam, bar)] **:** an order of spiny-finned fishes comprising the toadfishes

hap·lo·dont \'haplə,dänt\ *adj* [*hapl-* + *-odont*] **:** having or constituting molar teeth with simple crowns without tubercles — **hap·lo·don·ty** \-ntē\ *n* -ES

hap·lo·dri·li \,haplə'drī,lī\ [NL, fr. *hapl-* + *-drili* (fr. Gk *drilos* worm)] *syn of* ARCHIANNELIDA

hap·log·ra·phy \ha'plägrəfē\ *n* -ES [*hapl-* + *-graphy*] **:** the omission in writing or copying of one of two or more adjacent and similar letters, syllables, words, or lines

1hap·loid \'ha,plȯid\ *adj* [ISV, fr. Gk *haploeidēs* single, fr. *hapl-* + *-oeidēs* -oid] **1 :** having the gametic number of chromosomes or half the number characteristic of the somatic cells **2 :** MONOPLOID

2haploid \"\ *n* -S **:** a haploid individual

hap·loi·dy \'ha,plȯidē\ *n* -ES **:** the condition of being haploid

1hap·lo·lep·id \¦haplə¦lepəd, ha'pläləp-\ *adj* [NL *Haplolepidae*] **:** of or relating to the family Haplolepidae

2haplolepid \"\ *n* -S **:** a fish of the family Haplolepidae

hap·lo·lep·i·dae \,haplə'lepə,dē\ *n pl, cap* [NL, fr. *Haplolepis*, type genus + *-idae*] **:** a family of small primitive Upper Carboniferous bony fishes with large scales

hap·lo·lep·is \,haplə'lepəs, ha'pläləp-\ *n, cap* [NL, fr. *hapl-* + Gk *lepis* scales of a fish] **:** the type genus of the family Haplolepidae

hap·lol·o·gy \ha'pläləjē\ *n* -ES [ISV *hapl-* + *-logy*] **:** contraction of a word by the omission of one or more similar sounds or syllables in pronunciation (as in \'lībrē\ for *library* or \'präblē\ for *probably*)

hap·lo·mi \ha'plō,mī\ *n pl, cap* [NL, fr. *hapl-* + *-omi* (fr. Gk *ōmos* shoulder)] **:** a small order of teleost fishes having cycloid scales, abdominal pelvic fins, a persistent air duct, and typically no mesocoracoid arch that is now usu. restricted to the pikes, the Alaska blackfish, and a few related forms but formerly included also the Microcyprini and some other fishes — **hap·lo·mous** \-məs\ *adj*

1hap·lo·mid \-məd\ *adj* [NL *Haplomi* + E *-id*] **:** of or relating to the order Haplomi

2haplomid \"\ *n* -S **:** a fish of the order Haplomi

hap·lo·mitosis \,ha(,)plō+\ *n* [NL, fr. *hapl-* + *mitosis*] **:** a primitive mitosis occurring in certain flagellates in which chromosomes are imperfectly differentiated and the endosome functions as a division center — compare MESOMITOSIS, PROMITOSIS

hap·lont \'ha,plänt\ *n* -S [ISV *hapl-* + *-ont*] **:** an organism having somatic cells with the haploid chromosome number and only the zygote diploid — compare DIPLONT, GAMETOPHYTE — **hap·lon·tic** \(')ha¦pläntik\ *adj*

hap·lo·pap·pus \,haplō'papəs\ *n, cap* [NL, fr. *hapl-* + *pappus*] **:** a genus of perennial herbs (family Compositae) of the western U. S. with mostly alternate rigid leaves and yellow flowers

hap·lo·peristomic *also* **hap·lo·peristomous** \¦ha(,)plō+\ *adj* [*hapl-* + *peristome* + *-ic* or *-ous*] **:** APLOPERISTOMATOUS

hap·lo·phase \'haplō,fāz\ *n* [ISV *hapl-* + *phase*] **:** the haploid phase (as the gametophyte) in the life cycle of certain plants

1hap·lo-polyploid \¦ha(,)plō+\ *adj* [*hapl-* + *polyploid*] *of a polyploid* **:** having the gametic number of chromosomes

2haplo-polyploid \"\ *n* **:** a haplo-polyploid individual

hap·lor·chis \ha'plȯrkəs\ *n, cap* [NL, fr. *hapl-* + Gk *orchis* testicle — more at ORCHIS] **:** a genus of minute digenetic trematodes (family Heterophyidae) infesting the intestines of flesh-eating birds and mammals and occas. man in tropical areas

hap·lo·scope \'haplə,skōp\ *n* [ISV *hapl-* + *-scope*] **:** a simple stereoscope used in the study of depth perception — **hap·lo·scop·ic** \¦==¦skäpik\ *adj*

hap·lo·sis \ha'plōsəs\ *n, pl* **haplo·ses** \-ō,sēz\ [NL, fr. *hapl-* + *-osis*] **:** the halving of the somatic chromosome number by meiosis — compare DIPLOSIS

hap·lo·spo·rid·ia \,hap(,)lōspə'ridēə\ *n pl, cap* [NL, fr. pl. of *Haplosporidium* genus of Acnidosporidia, fr. *hapl-* + *sporidium*] **:** a small order of Acnidosporidia comprising parasites in invertebrates and lower vertebrates and being of no known economic importance

1hap·lo·spo·rid·i·an \¦=(,)==¦ridēən\ *adj* [NL *Haplosporidia* + E *-an*] **:** of or relating to the order Haplosporidia

2haplosporidian \"\ *n* -S **:** a member of the order Haplosporidia

hap·lo·stemo·nous \¦haplō¦stēmənəs, -tem-\ *adj* [ISV *hapl-* + *-stemonous*] **:** ISOSTEMONOUS

hap·lo·thrips \'haplō,thrips\ *n, cap* [NL, fr. *hapl-* + L *thrips* — more at THRIPS] **:** a widespread genus of thrips including forms extremely destructive to cultivated plants

hap·lo·type \-,tīp\ *n* [*hapl-* + *type*] **:** the sole species included in the original description of a genus **:** ORTHOTYPE — **hap·lo·typ·ic** \¦=·¦tipik\ *adj*

hap·ly \'haplē, -li\ *adv* [ME, fr. *hap, happe* hap + *-ly* — more at HAP] **:** by chance, luck, or accident ⟨the sound of many a word in mocking echoes ~ overheard —George Santayana⟩

hap'orth *or* **ha'porth** *n* -S [by contr.] **:** HALFPENNYWORTH

happed *past of* HAP

1hap·pen \'hapən, -p°m\ *vb* **happened** \-pənd,-p°nd\ **happened** \"\ **happening** \-p(ə)niŋ\ **happens** \-pənz,-p°mz\ [ME *happenen, hapnen*, fr. *hap, happe*, n., hap + *-enen* -en — more at HAP] *vi* **1 a :** to occur fortuitously, casually, or coincidentally **:** come about without previous design — often used with impersonal *it* ⟨it ~s the 500-mile auto race is in progress —Bruce Westley⟩ ⟨as it ~s, I have the book right here⟩ **b :** to come into existence spontaneously or as if spontaneously without causal necessity, effort, or other process ⟨no success in life merely ~s —Katharine F. Gerould⟩ ⟨we were together and love ~*ed* —Galway Kinnell⟩ **2 a :** to present itself as an event or process **:** become a reality **:** come into being **:** take place **:** OCCUR ⟨a study of what ~s when we sleep⟩ ⟨accidents are continually ~*ing*⟩ ⟨cloudbursts do not ~ . . . often —G. W.Murray⟩ ⟨hurried to the scene . . . where the shooting ~*ed* —*Current Biog.*⟩ **b** (1) **:** to present itself as an experience or effect — used with *to* ⟨creep is what ~s to a hot metal when you pull it —R.P.Lister⟩ ⟨all sorts of pleasant things ~*ed* to him⟩ (2) **:** to present itself by way of injury or harm — used with *to* ⟨the tickbirds . . . make sure that nothing ~s to their rhino —Jule Mannix⟩ ⟨I'd have something ~ to me if I did —Rose Macaulay⟩ **3 :** to have the luck or fortune ⟨he ~s to be a very rich man⟩ ⟨forms of life which ~ to be adjusted to their environment —W.R.Inge⟩ ⟨I ~*ed* to hear it⟩ **4 :** to chance to come **:** FALL, LIGHT ⟨while leafing through a journal . . . I ~*ed* across this passage —R.A.Hall b.1911⟩ ⟨~*ed* on a cottage almost hidden in elm tree boughs —*Times Lit. Supp.*⟩ ⟨~*ed* upon a remarkable and neglected volume —Charlton Laird⟩ **5 :** to come or go casually **:** make an appearance **:** turn up **:** drop in ⟨he ~*ed* into the typists' room to borrow a stamp —Dorothy Sayers⟩ ⟨hoping that no wayfarer would ~ along the lane —Joseph Conrad⟩ ⟨any person who might ~ by was expected to . . . visit —*Amer. Guide Series: Texas*⟩ ~ *vt, dial* **:** to become of **:** occur to **:** BEFALL ⟨little I mind what ~s me —Augusta Gregory⟩ ⟨what would ~ my little business if I . . . married her —Frank O'Connor⟩

syn CHANCE, OCCUR, TRANSPIRE, BEFALL, BETIDE: HAPPEN is a general term without special connotation and signifies to take place either with or without plan, motivation, or apparent or assignable cause. CHANCE, perhaps somewhat archaic or literary in suggestion, stresses lack of plan or causation ⟨a novel that *chanced* to be local and concrete and true —Sinclair Lewis⟩ ⟨he *chanced* to sit banqueting with the mariners about the hour of tierce —G.G.Coulton⟩ OCCUR, often interchangeable with HAPPEN, has the additional meaning of be found, be met with, exist, may more strongly suggest an event which commands attention or consideration, and is more frequent than HAPPEN with negatives ⟨a sluggish, smoke-colored animal, *occurring* in shallow swamp waters —L.P.Schultz⟩ ⟨a bismuth bearing vein *occurs* on Charley Creek —*Encyc. Americana*⟩ ⟨when once a certain detachment from possessive vice and objective ambition has *occurred* in the mind —J.C. Powys⟩ ⟨this is possible in theory, but, actually, never seemed to *occur* —V.G.Heiser⟩ TRANSPIRE means to leak out and become known; by semantic change it has come to mean simply OCCUR, although it is likely to be used of events of some importance ⟨all memorable events . . . *transpire* in morning time and in a morning atmosphere —H.D.Thoreau⟩ ⟨no clear-cut issue developed and no real contest *transpired* —E.E.Robinson⟩ BEFALL and BETIDE, both rather literary, may suggest occurring because of destiny or fate and may be used esp. with reference to unpleasant matters ⟨a . . . piece of ill fortune, which about this time *befell* me —Charles Lamb⟩ ⟨the fate which Beria meted out to so many should now have *befallen* him —Malcolm Muggeridge⟩ ⟨woe *betide* a known traitor⟩

²**happen** \"\ *adv, now dial* : MAYBE, PERHAPS ⟨and ~ they'll tell him so too —Angus Wilson⟩

happenchance \ˈ==,=\ *n* [¹*happen* + *chance*] : HAPPENSTANCE

happening *n* -s : OCCURRENCE ⟨~s of major significance⟩

happen-so \ˈ==,=\ *n, dial* : chance occurrence : HAPPENSTANCE

hap·pen·stance \ˈhapənz(,)-, -pᵊmz(,)-, -ən(,)s-, -ᵊm(,)s- — *last syllable as at* CIRCUMSTANCE\ *n* -s [*happen* + *circumstance*] : a circumstance regarded as due to chance

hap·per \ˈhapər\ *Scot var of* HOPPER

happied *past of* HAPPY

happier *comparative of* HAPPY

happies *pres 3d sing of* HAPPY

happiest *superlative of* HAPPY

hap·pi·fy \ˈhapə,fī, -pē,f-\ *vt* -ED/-ING/-ES [*happy* + *-fy*] : to make happy ⟨~ existence by constant intercourse with those adapted to elevate it —Mary B. Eddy⟩

hap·pi·ly \-pəlē, -li\ *adv* [ME, fr. *happy* + *-ly*] **1** : by good fortune : FORTUNATELY, LUCKILY ⟨the date . . . has been ~ preserved for posterity —Sydney Race⟩ **2** *archaic* : by chance : HAPLY **3** : in a happy manner or state : with feelings of contentment ⟨I was driving ~ along —Richard Joseph⟩ **4** : in an adequate or fitting manner : APTLY, SUCCESSFULLY, APPROPRIATELY, FELICITOUSLY ⟨poetry writing and breadwinning do not go ~ together —Kenneth Mackenzie⟩ ⟨chances are he will mix the two very ~ —Leslie Check⟩ ⟨a matured poetic intelligence . . . ~ fused with the creative heat of poetic imagination —H.V.Gregory⟩

hap·pi·ness \-pēnəs, -pən-\ *n* -ES [*happy* + *-ness*] **1** *archaic* : good fortune : good luck : PROSPERITY ⟨all ~ bechance to thee —Shak.⟩ **2 a** (1) : a state of well-being characterized by relative permanence, by dominantly agreeable emotion ranging in value from mere contentment to deep and intense joy in living, and by a natural desire for its continuation (2) : a pleasurable or enjoyable experience ⟨I had the ~ of seeing you —W.S.Gilbert⟩ **b** *Aristotelianism* : EUDAEMONIA **3** : APTNESS, FELICITY ⟨his examples lack ~⟩ ⟨a striking ~ of expression⟩

syn FELICITY, BEATITUDE, BLESSEDNESS, BLISS: HAPPINESS is the general term denoting enjoyment of or pleasurable satisfaction in well-being, security, or fulfillment of wishes ⟨pleasures may come about through chance contact and stimulation; such pleasures are not to be despised in a world full of pain. But *happiness* and delight are a different sort of thing. They come to be through a fulfillment that reaches to the depths of our being — one that is an adjustment of our whole being with the conditions of existence —John Dewey⟩ FELICITY, a more bookish or elevated word, may denote a higher, more lasting, or more perfect happiness ⟨all the *felicity* which a marriage of true affection could bestow —Jane Austen⟩ ⟨*felicity* or continued happiness consists not in having prospered, but in the process of prospering —Frank Thilly⟩ BEATITUDE refers in this sense to the highest happiness, the felicity of the blessed ⟨the years of loving sacrifice in scraping that boxful without letting Patty go short were amply crowned for John by this one moment. He sat down again in the corner wrapped in *beatitude* —Mary Webb⟩ ⟨a sense of deep *beatitude* — a strange sweet foretaste of Nirvana —Max Beerbohm⟩ BLESSEDNESS suggests the deep joy of pure affection or of acceptance by a god ⟨the *blessedness* of the saints⟩ BLISS may apply to a complete and assured felicity ⟨all my life's *bliss* from thy dear life was given —Emily Brontë⟩ ⟨now safely lodged in perfect *bliss;* and with spirits elated to rapture —Jane Austen⟩

happing *pres part of* HAP

¹**hap·py** \ˈhapē, -pi\ *adj, usu* -ER/-EST [ME, fr. *hap, happe* hap + *-y* — more at HAP] **1** : favored by luck or fortune : FORTUNATE, PROSPEROUS, PROPITIOUS, FAVORABLE ⟨perennially ~ dice should be inspected to discover whether they are loaded —J.R.Newman⟩ ⟨scientific discoveries . . . seem to drop out of the blue, the gift of ~ chance —*Lamp*⟩ ⟨they experiment in color . . . with results sometimes ~, sometimes disastrous —Roger Fry⟩ **2** : notably well adapted or fitting : markedly effective : APT, FELICITOUS, APPROPRIATE, JUST ⟨he will seek to establish by law the ~ mean —G.L.Dickinson⟩ ⟨the ~ diction, and the graceful phrase —E.G.Bulwer-Lytton⟩ ⟨the passage in the finale was particularly ~ —Virgil Thomson⟩ ⟨television is an especially ~ medium —Irving Kolodin⟩ ⟨the attendants had a ~ thought —Jeremiah Dowling⟩ **3 a** : having the feeling arising from the consciousness of well-being ⟨would forbid any novelist to represent a good man as ever miserable or a wicked man as ever ~ —Havelock Ellis⟩ **b** : characterized or attended by happiness : expressing, reflecting, or suggestive of happiness : not tragic : PLEASANT, JOYOUS ⟨the ~ years of childhood⟩ ⟨a ~ family life⟩ ⟨a book with a ~ ending⟩ ⟨it had been a merciful passing, even a ~ one —S.H.Adams⟩ ⟨the ~ noises of prolonged mastication —C.H. Rickword⟩ ⟨paints a ~ picture of rural life⟩ ⟨past ~ brooks flashing to the sun —G.D.Brown⟩ **c** : GLAD, PLEASED ⟨I am ~ to meet you⟩ ⟨I would be ~ for the president to declare his policy —*Time*⟩ **d** : having or marked by an atmosphere of good fellowship or camaraderie : HARMONIOUS, CONGENIAL, FRIENDLY ⟨sailormen prefer a ~ to a taut ship, where strict discipline is the only diet —A.R.Griffin⟩ ⟨I know that they will find . . . a ~ welcome on the Canadian shore —F.D. Roosevelt⟩ ⟨its ~ industrial relations and the loyal spirit of its workers —Sam Pollock⟩ **4** *obs* : BLESSED **5** : having a feeling of well-being as a result of drink ⟨came home a bit ~⟩ **6 a** : characterized by a dazed irresponsible state — used as a terminal element in combination with the cause of the condition indicated ⟨a punch-*happy* prizefighter⟩ ⟨the gold-*happy* miners decided to have a horse race —J.A.Michener⟩ **b** : impulsively, nervously, or obsessively quick to use something — used as a terminal element in combinations with the object indicated ⟨they'll be gun-*happy* and . . . let go at anything that moves —William Wright⟩ ⟨trigger-*happy* soldiers⟩ **c** : enthusiastic to the point of obsession : OBSESSED — used as a terminal element in combination with the object of the feeling indicated ⟨I know your type . . . publicity-*happy* —Ellery Queen⟩ ⟨that guy is stripe-*happy* —Norman Mailer⟩ ⟨sailor-*happy* girls who move around after the fleet —Katharine T. Kinkead⟩ **syn** see FIT, GLAD, LUCKY

²**happy** \"\ *vt* -ED/-ING/-ES *now dial* : to make happy ⟨it don't ~ me up any —Howard Troyer⟩

happy dust *n, slang* : COCAINE; *also* : HEROIN

happy family *n, Austral* : an Australian babbler (genus *Pomatostomus*) of sociable habits; *esp* : GRAY-CROWNED BABBLER

happy-go-lucky \ˈ¦==,=¦==\ *adj* : marked by blithe lack of concern, care, plan, or serious forethought : disposed to accept cheerfully whatever happens : CAREFREE, EASYGOING ⟨on carefully prepared lines rather than as a *happy-go-lucky* venture —*Country Life*⟩ ⟨his amiable but *happy-go-lucky* household —*Amer. Guide Series: Fla.*⟩ **syn** see RANDOM

happy hunting ground *n* **1** : the No. American Indian paradise conceived as a region to which the souls of warriors and hunters pass after death for the purpose of spending a happy hereafter in hunting and feasting **2** : a choice or profitable area of operation or exploitation ⟨the reef limestones . . . have been the *happy hunting ground* for fossil collectors —*Jour. of Geol.*⟩ ⟨a *happy hunting ground* for crooks of all nationalities —David Masters⟩ ⟨junkyards . . . have become *happy hunting grounds* for the man in search of spare parts —G.H.Waltz⟩

happy jack *n, Austral* : HAPPY FAMILY

happy warrior *n* [so called fr. the use of the term in *Character of the Happy Warrior* (1807), poem by William Wordsworth †1850 Eng. poet] : one who is undaunted by difficulties : CRUSADER ⟨the *happy warrior* who . . . was to fight for all the revolution had stood for —Van Wyck Brooks⟩

¹**haps** *pl of* HAP, *pres 3d sing of* HAP

²**haps** \ˈhaps\ *dial Eng var of* HASP

hapt- *or* **hapto-** *comb form* [ISV, fr. Gk *haptein* to fasten — more at APSIS] : contact : combination ⟨*hapto*phore⟩

hap·ten \ˈhap,ten\ *also* **hap·tene** \-tēn\ *n* -s [G *hapten*, fr. *hapt-* + *-en* -ene] **1** : a nonantigenic or very weakly antigenic substance that reacts in vitro with an antibody **2** : a substance not antigenic in itself that in combination with a carrier antigen confers specificity or antigenicity or both — **hap·ten·ic** \(ˈ)hap¦tenik\ *adj*

hap·tere \ˈhap,ti(ə)r\ *n* -s [NL *hapteron*] : HAPTERON

hap·ter·on \ˈhaptə,rän\ *n, pl* **hap·tera** \-tərə\ [NL, fr. Gk *haptein* to fasten] : a discoid outgrowth or swelling of the stem by which a plant is fixed to its substratum (as in many rock-inhabiting seaweeds) : HOLDFAST

hap·tic \ˈhaptik\ *or* **hap·ti·cal** \-təkəl\ *adj* [ISV *hapt-* + *-ic, -ical*] **1** : relating to or based on the sense of touch ⟨~ impressions⟩ **2** : characterized by a predilection for the sense of touch ⟨a ~ person⟩

hap·to·phore \ˈhaptə,fō(ə)r\ *adj* [ISV *hapt-* + *-phore* (fr. Gk *-phoros* -phorous)] *immunol* : having an ability to enter into combination

hap·top·o·da \hapˈtäpədə\ *n pl, cap* [NL, fr. *hapt-* + *-poda*] : an order of extinct arachnids not closely related to any living group

hap·tor \ˈhaptər *also* -,tȯr\ *n* -s [NL, fr. *hapt-* + *-or*] : an organ of attachment in a parasitic worm; *esp* : a complex organ usu. with multiple suckers and strong hooks on the posterior end of many monogenetic trematodes — **hap·to·ral** \-,tərəl\ *adj*

hap·to·trop·ic \¦haptə¦träpik\ *adj* [ISV *hapt-* + *-tropic*] : exhibiting haptotropism — **hap·to·trop·i·cal·ly** \-pək(ə)lē\ *adv*

hap·tot·ro·pism \hapˈtä·trə,pizəm\ *n* [ISV *hapt-* + *-tropism*] : positive stereotropism esp. of plants

ha·pu \ˈhä(,)pü\ *n* -s [Maori] : a Maori clan or tribal subdivision

ha·pu·ku *or* **ha·pu·ka** \ˈhä,pükə\ *n, pl* **hapuku** *or* **hapuka** [Maori *hapuku*] *NewZeal* : GROPER 1b

haque·ton \ˈhaktən\ *n* -s [ME *hacton*, alter. of *aketoun* — more at ACTON] *archaic* : ACTON

har *var of* HAAR

har *abbr* harbor

ha·ra·ke·ke \ˈhärə,kākē\ *n* -s [Maori] : NEW ZEALAND FLAX

hara-kiri *also* **hari-kari** \,harēˈkirē, ,hariˈkiri, -arəˈk-, -ˈkar- *also* ,her- *or* -ˈker-\ *n* -s [Jap *harakiri*, fr. *hara* belly + *kiri* ending, cutting] **1** : suicide by disembowelment formerly practiced by the Japanese samurai or decreed to one of its members by the feudal court in consideration of his social status in lieu of the ordinary death penalty **2** : suicide by any means

haram *var of* HAREM

¹**ha·rangue** \həˈraŋ, -raiŋ\ *n* -s [ME *arang*, fr. MF *arenge, harengue, harangue*, fr. OIt *aringa, arenga* public address, fr. *aringare* to make a speech, fr. *aringo* public square, prob. fr. an (assumed) Gmc compound whose components are akin respectively to Goth *harjis* host and to OHG *hring* ring — more at HARRY, RING] **1 a** : a speech addressed to a public assembly : ORATION, DECLAMATION ⟨listening to his capacious ~ and its immaculate delivery —Sir Winston Churchill⟩ **b** : a bombastic ranting speech or writing ⟨found it a subject for rabble-rousing ~s —W.F.Jenkins⟩ ⟨embark on emotional and frequently violent ~s —K.E.Read⟩ ⟨the long, tiresome ~ so characteristic of . . . books on the subject —J.H.Donnelly⟩ **c** : a didactic, scolding, or hortatory talk or discussion : LECTURE ⟨launch into a brilliant ~ on the habits of trout —Honor Tracy⟩ ⟨gave me a ~ on the subject of my poor grades⟩ **2** : an animated discussion or conversation ⟨neglected to call up in the evening for our nightly ~ —Vli Beigel⟩ ⟨the morning ~s of husband-and-wife teams —M.G.Faught⟩

²**harangue** \"\ *vb* -ED/-ING/-S [F *haranguer*, fr. MF, fr. *harangue*] *vi* : to make a harangue : DECLAIM ⟨poets . . . and philosophers recited their works, and *harangued* for diversion —Tobias Smollett⟩ ~ *vt* : to address in a harangue ⟨that lady was still *haranguing* the girl —F.M.Ford⟩

ha·rangu·er \-ŋə(r)\ *n* -s : one that harangues

ha·rap·pa \həˈrapə\ *also* **ha·rap·pan** \-pən\ *adj, usu cap* [*Harappa* fr. *Harappa*, locality in West Punjab, Pakistan; *Harappan* fr. *Harappa* + E *-an*] : of or relating to a city culture of the Indus valley in the third and second millenniums B.C. characterized by a complex social and economic structure and an art largely concerned with the reproduction of animal forms

ha·ra·ri \həˈrärē\ *n, pl* **harari** *or* **hararis** *usu cap* [fr. *Harar*, region of Ethiopia] **1 a** : a people of eastern Ethiopia now mixed with the Somali but orig. Himyaritic Semites **b** : a member of such people **2** : a Semitic language of the Harari people

ha·ras \aˈrä, ˈaˈrä\ *n, pl* **haras** \-rä(z)\ [ME *harace, haras*, fr. OF *haraz*] **1** *archaic* : a horse-breeding establishment : stud farm **2** : HARRAS

¹**harass** \həˈras, ˈharəs, -raa(ə)s,-ˈrais *also* ˈherəs *or* haˈr-\ *vt* -ED/-ING/-ES [F *harasser*, fr. MF, fr. *harer* to set a dog on, fr. OF *hare*, interj. used to incite dogs, of Gmc origin; akin to OHG *hara, hera* hither; akin to OHG *hiar* here — more at HERE] **1 a** : to lay waste (as an enemy's country) : RAID, HARRY ⟨hostile Indians ~*ed* the frontier⟩ **b** : to worry and impede by repeated attacks ⟨his guerrilla forces cooperated with United States parachute troops in ~*ing* the Japanese —*Current Biog.*⟩ ⟨~*ed* the enemy retreat⟩ **2 a** : to tire out (as with physical or mental effort) : EXHAUST, FATIGUE ⟨I have been ~*ed* with the toil of verse —William Wordsworth⟩ **b** : to vex, trouble, or annoy continually or chronically (as with anxieties, burdens, or misfortune) : PLAGUE, BEDEVIL, BADGER ⟨sciatica occasionally ~*ed* her —Arnold Bennett⟩ ⟨~ the pilot and thus keep him in a constant state of . . . upset —H.G.Armstrong⟩ ⟨~*ed* . . . by lack of funds —Henry Miller⟩ **syn** see WORRY

²**harass** \"\ *n* -ES *archaic* : WORRY, HARASSMENT

harassed \-st\ *adj* **1** : WORN-OUT, EXHAUSTED, FATIGUED ⟨breathless and ~ at the end of the climb —Wyn Roberts⟩ **2 a** : sorely troubled, vexed, or burdened (as with cares, importunities, misfortune) : BADGERED ⟨looked like a ~ draper's clerk⟩ ⟨one of the . . . busiest and most ~ men in the country —S.H.Adams⟩ ⟨led a ~ life⟩ **b** : expressing or reflecting harassment ⟨wrote a series of ~ letters⟩ ⟨wore a ~ look on his face⟩

harassed·ly \-sədlē, -stlē, -li\ *adv* : in a harassed manner

harass·ing *adj* : causing or tending to cause harassment ⟨a series of ~ lawsuits —T.W.Arnold⟩ ⟨I've had many a ~ disappointment —E.B.Barrett⟩

harassing fire *n* : fire designed to disturb the rest, curtail the movement, or lower the morale of enemy troops; *esp* : artillery fire having these objects

harass·ing·ly *adv* : in a harassing manner

harass·ment \-smənt\ *n* -s **1** : the act or an instance of harassing : VEXATION, ANNOYANCE ⟨the ~ of unions . . . will become more difficult —T.W.Arnold⟩ ⟨chafed by the ~s of travel —R.L.Taylor⟩ ⟨the weather, taxes, . . . and various ~s of a more personal nature —*New Yorker*⟩ ⟨border incidents . . . no longer have the character of mere ~ —*Atlantic Monthly*⟩ **2** : the condition of being harassed ⟨showed signs of ~ —E.M.Lustgarten⟩ ⟨his continuing ~ may have been due in great part to his own . . . contentious personality —Stuart MacClintock⟩

harateen *var of* HARRATEEN

har·a·tin *also* **har·ra·tin** \¦harə¦tēn\ *n, pl* **haratin** *or* **haratins** *usu cap* **1 a** : a negroid Berber people of the southern slope of the Atlas mountains **b** : a member of such people **2** : a half-breed of Berber and Sudanese Negro parentage

har·bin \ˈhärbən, (ˈ)här¦bin\ *adj, usu cap* [fr. *Harbin*, Manchuria] : of or from the city of Harbin, Manchuria : of the kind or style prevalent in Harbin

¹**har·bin·ger** \ˈhärbənjər, ˈhȧbənjə(r\ *n* -s [ME *herbergere, herbergeour, herbengar* (also, one who provides lodging, host), fr. OF *herbergere, herbergeor* one that makes camp, one that provides lodgings, host, fr. *herberge* army encampment, hostelry, of Gmc origin; akin to OHG *heriberga* army encampment, hostelry — more at HARBOR] **1** : a person sent before to provide lodgings; *esp* : an officer of the English royal household formerly sent ahead to prepare lodgings (as on a royal progress) **2 a** *archaic* : a person sent before to announce the coming of someone : HERALD ⟨be myself the ~ and make joyful the hearing of my wife —Shak.⟩ **b** : one who pioneers in or initiates a major change (as in art, science, or doctrine) : PRECURSOR, FORERUNNER, TRAILBLAZER, APOSTLE ⟨the ~s of organized religion in Oregon were four . . . Indians —*Amer. Guide Series: Oregon*⟩ ⟨the great legal ~ of the New Deal revolution —*Time*⟩ ⟨the ~s of peace to a hitherto distracted . . . people —David Livingstone⟩ **c** : something that presages or foreshadows what is to come : PORTENT, OMEN, SIGN, INDICATION, SYMBOL ⟨robins are revered . . . as ~s of spring —E.A.Bauer⟩ ⟨the sinister white owl . . . the ~ of destruction —Alan Moorehead⟩ ⟨a proper wife is the surest ~ of success for the soldier —H.H. Arnold & I.C.Eaker⟩ ⟨winter's sad ~s, the yellow leaves —J.G.Frazer⟩

²**harbinger** \"\ *vt* -ED/-ING/-S : to be a harbinger of : PRESAGE

harbinger-of-spring \¦====¦=\ *n, pl* **harbingers-of-spring** : a small tuberous early-blooming No. American herb (*Erigenia bulbosa*) of the family Umbelliferae with ternate leaves and umbellate white flowers

¹**har·bor** \ˈhärbər, ˈhȧbə(r\ *n* -s *see -or in Explan Notes, often attrib* [ME *herberge, herberwe, herber, harborowe;* akin to OHG & OS *heriberga* army encampment, hostelry, MLG *herberge* hostelry, ON *herbergi;* all fr. a prehistoric WGmc-NGmc compound whose components are akin respectively to OHG *heri* army and to OHG *bergan* to shelter, hide — more at HARRY, BURY] **1 a** : a place of security and comfort : HAVEN, ASYLUM, REFUGE, SHELTER ⟨the . . . Loyalists found ~ in the same areas —W.G.Hardy⟩ ⟨a very ~ from the raging streets —Charles Dickens⟩ ⟨the beauty and the ~ of a snug house —Meridel Le Sueur⟩ **b** : the resting place or lair of a wild animal (as a deer) **2 a** : a small bay or other sheltered part of a considerable body of water usu. well protected either naturally or artificially (as by jetties) against high waves and strong currents and deep enough to furnish anchorage for ships or other craft; *esp* : such a place in which port facilities are provided ⟨Halifax ~⟩ ⟨a yacht ~⟩ **b** : INLET ⟨Pearl *Harbor*, Hawaii⟩ ⟨Otago *Harbor*, N. Z.⟩ ⟨Grays *Harbor*, Wash.⟩ ⟨Charlotte *Harbor*, Fla.⟩ ⟨Little Egg *Harbor*, N. J.⟩

syn HAVEN, PORT: HARBOR applies to a part of a body of water (as a sea or lake) partially or almost totally enclosed so that ships or boats entering it may be protected when they are moored, and by extension applies to any place of protection ⟨the boat arrived safely in the *harbor* by nightfall⟩ ⟨two promontories of land forming a natural *harbor*⟩ ⟨find a *harbor* until the financial panic had passed⟩ HAVEN, now chiefly literary except in names, adds to HARBOR the idea of refuge or place of peace ⟨a blessed *haven* into which convoys could slip from the submarine-infested Atlantic —Stewart Beach⟩ ⟨the colony acquired an unsavory reputation for providing a friendly *haven* for pirates —*Amer. Guide Series: R.I.*⟩ ⟨leave for a while their own crowded homes and find a calm cozy *haven* where they can talk without interruption —Ernest & Pearl Beaglehole⟩ ⟨an excellent *haven* for game birds and deer —*Amer. Guide Series: Minn.*⟩ PORT signifies a place, usu. both harbor and adjacent town or city, suitable for landing men or goods, and by extension applies to a destination or goal ⟨transatlantic steamers docked in the *port* of New York⟩ ⟨the home *port* of steamers formerly navigating the waters of the lake —*Amer. Guide Series: N.H.*⟩ ⟨steamboat *ports* on the Columbia —Dayton Kohler⟩ ⟨unload a damaged ship at the first available *port*⟩

²**harbor** \"\ *vb* **harbored; harbored; harboring** \-b(ə)riŋ\ **harbors** *see -or in Explan Notes* [ME *herbergen, herberwen, herberen, harborowen*, fr. *herberge, herberwe, herber, harborowe*, n.] *vt* **1 a** (1) : to give shelter or refuge to : take in ⟨benefited by ~*ing* and absorbing displaced European psychiatrists —Lauretta Bender⟩ ⟨~*ed* white renegades and strays from hostile tribes —*Amer. Guide Series: Tenn.*⟩ ⟨return of Greek children ~*ed* in other countries —*Americana Annual*⟩ (2) : to receive clandestinely and conceal ⟨a fugitive from justice⟩ (3) : to have (an animal) in one's keeping ⟨may not ~ a dog without a permit⟩ **b** (1) : to be the home or habitat of : CONTAIN ⟨the pool normally ~s several large trout —Alexander MacDonald⟩ ⟨her home . . . had ~*ed* her family for four generations —*Current Biog.*⟩ ⟨this structure ~s a mirror and bookrest —*New Yorker*⟩ ⟨the . . . buildings ~ a maze of ducts and pipes —Lewis Mumford⟩ ⟨caves which . . . certainly ~ bats —Thomas Barbour⟩ ⟨the same county that ~s the depressing cotton towns —L.D.Stamp⟩ (2) : to be the host of (a parasite) ⟨one of the pigs ~*ed* . . . kidney worms —J.E.Alicata⟩ **c** : to track (an animal) to lair or hiding place **2** : CHERISH, ENTERTAIN ⟨~ thoughts⟩ ⟨~ feelings⟩ ⟨~ a deep resentment against the U. S. —Winifred Raushenbush⟩ ⟨any power which might ~ aggressive designs —C.A.Fisher⟩ ⟨~*ed* a mistrust of expressed emotion —Stewart Cockburn⟩ **3** : to place (a ship) for shelter ~ *vi* **1 a** : to find or take shelter : be present ⟨it was quite thinkable that dreadful heresies might ~ there —G.W.Johnson⟩ **b** (1) *of an animal* : to rest or hide away esp. habitually ⟨fierce boars ~*ed* in the dense wood⟩ (2) : LIVE ⟨parasites that ~ in the blood⟩ **2** : to take shelter or come to anchor in a harbor **3** : to conceal a fugitive from justice ⟨you can be shot for ~*ing*, she thought —Ion Braby⟩

har·bor·age \-b(ə)rij\ *n* -s **1 a** : SHELTER, REFUGE ⟨talking as if he had a right to ~, attention, and affection —Clemence Dane⟩ ⟨for this ~ . . . hostility seemed to her a little price to pay —Katherine Freeman⟩ **b** : a place of shelter or refuge : RESTING-PLACE ⟨the island was a ~ for privateersmen and runaway slaves⟩ **c** : a place offering favorable environmental conditions for growth and life ⟨to reduce a rat population, competition must be increased by reducing food or ~ —*Wildlife Rev.*⟩ ⟨weedy hedgerows . . . are thus a ~ for many troublesome pests —F.D.Smith & Barbara Wilcox⟩ **2 a** : shelter for ships : harbor facilities ⟨the long indented coast offers excellent ~⟩ **b** : HARBOR ⟨the ship . . . was lifted over the sandbars into the safe ~ of Matanzas —J.B.Cabell & A.J. Hanna⟩

har·bor·er \-bərə(r)\ *n* -s **1** : one that harbors ⟨the ~ of suspicion does not inspire faith in himself —L.P.Stryker⟩ **2** : a person who tracks a deer to its harbor and keeps watch on it there

harbor gasket *n* : a canvas or sennit band used to secure a sail

harbor line *n* : a line defining the limits of a harbor

harbor master *n* **1** : an officer charged with the duty of executing the regulations respecting the use of a harbor esp. as to berthing and mooring **2** : an officer who directs the policing of a harbor area by members of a municipal police force

harbor porpoise *n* : a common porpoise (*Phocaena phocaena*) of the north Atlantic and Pacific

harbor seal *n* : a small seal (*Phoca vitulina*) about four feet long living along the north Atlantic coasts, occas. occurring as far south as the Mediterranean and New Jersey, usu. keeping near land, and often ascending rivers; *also* : a similar seal (*P. richardii*) of the north Pacific coasts

¹**har·bor·ward** \-b(ə)rwə(r)d\ *adv* [¹*harbor* + *-ward*] : toward the harbor ⟨a pleasant little frame house . . . looking ~ —*New Yorker*⟩

²**harborward** \"\ *adj* : facing the harbor ⟨lined on both the ~ and landward sides by residences —Lewis Mumford⟩

harbour *Brit var of* HARBOR

¹**hard** \ˈhärd, ˈhȧd\ *adj* -ER/-EST [ME, fr. OE *heard;* akin to OHG *hart* hard, ON *harthr* hard, Goth *hardus* severe, Gk *kratos* strength, *kratys* strong, and prob. to Skt *karkara* hard] **1 a** (1) : not easily penetrated, cut, or separated into parts : not easily yielding to pressure : FIRM, SOLID, COMPACT ⟨an extremely ~ stone⟩ ⟨wriggled uncomfortably in his ~ chair⟩ ⟨these apples are very ~⟩ (2) : having rigid boards on the sides covered in cloth or paper ⟨a ~ binding⟩ ⟨selling methods . . . to fit the ~ books —Henry Garfinkle⟩ (3) : HARDWOOD 2 **b** *of liquor* (1) : having a harsh, sharp, or acid taste ⟨a ~ wine⟩ (2) : STRONG, SPIRITUOUS, INTOXICATING; *specif* : having an alcoholic content of more than 22.5 percent **c** (1) : characterized by the presence of dissolved substances (as salts of magnesium and calcium) that prevent the formation of lather with soap — used of water and water solutions (2) *of oil* : too thick to pour at ordinary temperatures (3) : characterized by radiation of relatively high penetrating power ⟨~ X rays⟩; *also* : relating to or constituting a high-vacuum tube that produces such radiation ⟨~ tube⟩ (4) : having or producing relatively great photographic contrast ⟨a ~ negative⟩ ⟨~ paper⟩ (5) : difficult to fuse or soften ⟨a ~ glass⟩ ⟨a ~ enamel⟩ **d** (1) *of money* : metallic as distinct from paper ⟨the colonies suffered from a shortage of ~ money⟩ ⟨ranchers . . . who were known to keep their wealth in the form of ~ money —W.H.Breen⟩ (2) *of currency* : convertible into gold or heavily backed by a gold reserve and typically stable, high, or

appreciating in value ⟨the period of the eighteen-nineties witnessed a bitter struggle between the *hard*-money and the cheap-money groups —C.B.Swisher⟩; *also* **:** available to borrowers in limited supply and at high interest rates ⟨a *hard*-money policy⟩ (3) *of a currency* **:** soundly backed and usu. readily convertible into foreign currencies without restrictions or large discounts ⟨they require payment in dollars, pounds, or other ~ . . . currency —Joseph Wechsberg⟩ (4) **:** constituting currency as distinct from promissory notes or other documents of contingent value — often used as an intensive in the phrase *hard cash* ⟨he has to be paid in *hard* cash⟩ ⟨pay the writing schools ~ cash to liberate their muse —Edward Uhlan⟩ (5) *of prices* **:** high and firm **e** (1) **:** TIGHT — used esp. of yarns with many twists per inch (2) **:** NAPLESS — used esp. of woolen and worsted fabrics with a smooth clear finish (3) *of plumage* **:** close-fitting and firm in texture (4) *of individual feathers* **:** uniformly colored **2 a** (1) **:** capable of great physical exertion or endurance **:** not flabby or soft **:** physically fit ⟨nice animals in good ~ condition —R.M.Daw⟩ ⟨all likely lads in ~ condition —John Buchan⟩ (2) **:** resistant esp. to stress or disease **:** HARDY ⟨children of ~*er* stock —Ernest Beaglehole⟩ **b :** free of weakness or other flaw **:** STRONG, UNYIELDING, TEMPERED ⟨brought out of the war a character austere and not a little ~ —Edmund Wilson⟩ ⟨a man of ~ unbending will⟩ **c** (1) **:** not tentative or contingent **:** FIXED, DEFINITE, BINDING, CONCRETE ⟨failure . . . to make ~, firm decisions at high levels —*Science*⟩ ⟨the continuing lack of a ~ agreement with the U.S.—Benjamin Welles⟩ (2) **:** not speculative or conjectural **:** based on fact **:** objectively existent **:** FACTUAL, ACTUAL, RELIABLE ⟨backed by evidence which he considers ~ —*American Anthropologist*⟩ ⟨a comprehensive set of ~ figures emerged for the first time —*Time*⟩ ⟨most facts are independent of our volitions; that is why they are called ~ —Bertrand Russell⟩ ⟨~ evidence that the government's optimism is not unfounded —Sydney Gruson⟩ (3) **:** HARD-AND-FAST ⟨there can be no ~ line of division between these two groups of changes —Edward Sapir⟩ (4) **:** CLOSE, SEARCHING, CONCENTRATED ⟨took a last ~ look at the old homestead⟩ ⟨at a later date I will take a ~ look at my political future —*N.Y.Times*⟩ (5) *of news* **:** not trivial, diverting, or sensational **:** important in its economic, political, or other large bearing ⟨~ news refers to the less exciting and more analytical stories of public affairs, economics, social problems —F.L.Mott⟩ — compare SOFT **d :** free from sentimentality or illusions **:** viewing objectively or coolly **:** REALISTIC, PRACTICAL ⟨the ~ modern mind —*College English*⟩ ⟨the later version is ~*er*, less "poetic" in the Romantic sense, less sentimental —Louis MacNeice⟩ ⟨the most practical place to teach ~ practical thinking is in . . . sociology —*Nat'l Catholic Educational Assoc. Bull.*⟩ ⟨a Scotsman's ~, keen sense of the practical —R.W. Chapman⟩ ⟨notable for his ~ sense, frugality, and industry⟩ **3 a** (1) **:** difficult to bear or endure **:** not easy to put up with or consent to **:** GRIEVOUS, UNPLEASANT, DISTRESSING, BAD ⟨you've had very ~ luck⟩ ⟨the dory was . . . in ~ shape —G.W.Brace⟩ ⟨the ~ years dragged by⟩ ⟨too much reading is ~ on the eyes⟩ ⟨that traffic cop gave me a ~ time⟩; *specif* **:** economically depressed ⟨~ times followed, and domestic creditors suffered equally with the foreign —S.E.Morison & H.S.Commager⟩ ⟨the Alaska gold rush . . . put an end to ~ times —*Amer. Guide Series: Wash.*⟩ (2) **:** OPPRESSIVE, INEQUITABLE, UNJUST ⟨musicians also find it ~ that they must pay heavy duty . . . on orchestral instruments —*Report: (Canadian) Royal Commission on Nat'l Development*⟩ ⟨the ~ system of apprenticeship, virtual peonage, was failing rapidly —*Amer. Guide Series: Tenn.*⟩ **b** (1) **:** harsh or severe in one's dealings **:** lacking compassion or gentleness **:** UNFEELING, CALLOUS ⟨he was a stern, ~, cruel man —Anthony Trollope⟩ ⟨people who are ~, grasping, selfish —G.B.Shaw⟩ ⟨don't be too ~ on the boy⟩ (2) **:** INTRACTABLE, HARDENED, INCORRIGIBLE, TOUGH ⟨my first real assignment was as a sort of scoutmaster to a ~ gang of boys —R.M.Lovett⟩ ⟨a prison warden of long standing and accustomed to dealing with ~ cases⟩ (3) **:** devoid of fine or refined feelings **:** impudently bold **:** BRAZEN, SHAMELESS ⟨a ~, cheap, frightened floozy —Arthur Knight⟩ **c** (1) **:** harsh, severe, or offensive in tendency or effect **:** UNPALATABLE, CRUEL ⟨this is a ~ saying to people who have worked so much —Clement Attlee⟩ ⟨said some very ~ things to me⟩ **:** HOSTILE, RESENTFUL ⟨no ~ feelings, I'm sure⟩ **:** ROUGH, COARSE ⟨~ and frugal fare, yet we throve upon it⟩ **:** making no concession **:** STRICT, UNRELENTING ⟨he drives a very ~ bargain⟩ ⟨a credit to the ~ religious system under which they were bred —G.M. Trevelyan⟩ (2) **:** tending to put in a bad or sinister light **:** UNFAVORABLE, FORBIDDING ⟨~ stories too were told about him; something . . . concerning an hereditary propensity to eat men —Herman Melville⟩ (3) **:** RIGOROUS, INCLEMENT, VIOLENT ⟨one of the ~*est* winters in men's memories⟩ ⟨a ~, driving rain⟩ ⟨in ~ weather he stayed in his . . . house —Mary Webb⟩ **d** (1) **:** intense in force, manner, or degree **:** SHARP, PROFOUND, DEEP ⟨a ~ spell of coughing —Ellen Glasgow⟩ ⟨dealt him a ~ blow⟩ ⟨fell into a ~ sleep⟩ ⟨going at a ~ trot down that steep hill —Rachel Henning⟩ (2) **:** carried on, performed, or waged with great intensity, exertion, or energy **:** ARDUOUS, STRENUOUS, UNREMITTING ⟨got where he is by ~ work⟩ ⟨this question requires ~ thinking —W.H.Whyte⟩ ⟨with some the sell is ~, with big advertising budgets . . . and platoons of agents on the road —Blake Ehrlich⟩ (3) **:** performing or carrying on an activity or one's work with great energy, intensity, or persistence ⟨a ~ drinker⟩ ⟨one of the ~*est* workers on the floor⟩ ⟨a very ~ smoker —Tadhg Murphy⟩ (4) **:** subjecting to a severe strain **:** INTENSIVE, PUNISHING ⟨was nearing a century of ~ wear when it lost a cover —R.W.Chapman⟩ ⟨this garment will stand ~ use⟩ (5) **:** useful for a long time **:** DURABLE ⟨~ merchandise⟩ **e :** giving the impression of or suggesting hardness: as (1) **:** lacking in shading, delicacy, or subtlety **:** HARSH, STRIDENT ⟨this is for ~ big tone —Warwick Braithwaite⟩ ⟨it has a ~ but brilliant note —Robert Donington⟩ (2) **:** characterized by sharp or harsh outline, rigid execution, and stiff drawing ⟨exaggerated shadows to intensify crisp outlines and ~ forms —Katharine Kuh⟩ ⟨a portrait in the ~ but sincere and living fashion of the period —G.K.Chesterton⟩ (3) **:** sharply defined **:** STARK, CRISP, PRECISE ⟨looking . . . at the ~ shadows we cast on the ground —John Sköllе⟩ ⟨in the early twilight the outlines of the castle loomed ~ and clear⟩ (4) **:** not softened or shaded in any way **:** GLARING, VIVID ⟨~ bright sunlight at the water's edge —Oscar Handlin⟩ ⟨the light is so ~ and brilliant that . . . you have to screw up your eyes —Thomas Wood †1950⟩ ⟨had the ~ dull flush of the steady heavy drinker —Thomas Wolfe⟩ ⟨staring at the ceiling in the ~ light of the one unshaded lamp —Nevil Shute⟩ (5) **:** sounding as in *arcing* and *geese* respectively — used of *c* and *g* or their sound (6) *of a consonant* **:** VOICELESS (7) **:** constituting a vowel before which there is no \y\ sound and no \y\-like modification of a consonant or constituting a consonant in whose articulation there is no \y\-like modification and which is not followed by a \y\ sound (as in Russian) — compare PALATALIZE (8) **:** indicative or suggestive of severity, firmness, toughness, or insensitivity of temperament or character ⟨the same faint, ~ smile around the edges of her mouth —Thomas Wolfe⟩ ⟨with a rather ~ mouth and a supercilious manner —Scott Fitzgerald⟩ ⟨a fund of English openness and good nature legible in his ~ features —William Heath⟩ ⟨a ~ pair of eyes that belied his unmanly, almost effeminate face —Barnaby Conrad⟩ — often used in combination ⟨a *hard*-faced businessman who knows all the latest salacious limericks —Harold Wincott⟩ ⟨a *hard*-eyed little man⟩ **4 :** presenting difficulties, obstacles, or perplexities: as **a** (1) **:** difficult to accomplish, master, resolve, or acquire **:** not easy **:** TROUBLESOME, PERPLEXING ⟨this ailment is ~ to cure⟩ ⟨the American habit of tipping . . . is a ~ one to break —Richard Joseph⟩ ⟨of course all languages are ~ —Bernard Bloch⟩ ⟨a ~ decision⟩ ⟨she's playing ~ to get⟩ ⟨a distinctly ~ problem⟩ (2) **:** difficult to comprehend or explain **:** OBSCURE, DARK, THORNY ⟨a ~ saying, no doubt, . . . but it has its meaning —Havelock Ellis⟩ ⟨this is at first sight a very ~ saying, but a little consideration will show that it is only natural —J.A.Todd⟩ ⟨a book full of long, ~ words⟩ (3) **:** difficult to untie or unravel ⟨he tied his shoelaces in ~ knots —Erskine Caldwell⟩ **b** *archaic* **:** having difficulty in doing something **c :** attended or marked by drudgery, hardship, or other painful experience ⟨many perished on the long ~ march to safety⟩ ⟨fishing and lumbering . . . are ~ trades —Upton Sinclair⟩ ⟨the birth was ~ —Farley Mowat⟩

syn DIFFICULT, ARDUOUS: HARD is a general antonym for *easy* and is applicable to any activity requiring great exertion ⟨a *hard* task⟩ ⟨the *hard* work of digging the shaft⟩ ⟨a subject *hard* to teach⟩ ⟨inspirations such as these do not necessarily eliminate all the *hard* work that goes into developing them and putting them down on paper —J.D.Cook⟩ DIFFICULT may imply obstacles to be surmounted, problems to be solved, complications to be removed, simplifications to be made, or trials to be faced by skill, ingenuity, or resolution ⟨to climb a mountain which, as all who have climbed it testify, is long, steep, and *difficult* —W.R.Inge⟩ ⟨business of a delicate and *difficult* nature, which might get people into trouble —Charles Dickens⟩ ⟨trying to write things that have not been written before, and that were very *difficult* to write —Havelock Ellis⟩ ⟨the more *difficult* task of changing the ways of thinking, the habits, and the practices of the Japanese people —*Collier's Yr. Bk.*⟩ ARDUOUS may suggest need for perseverance and resolute exertion ⟨the local railways . . . worked their *arduous* ways up the mining valleys —O.S.Nock⟩ ⟨the *arduous* task of formulating legislation necessary to the country's welfare —F.D. Roosevelt⟩ ⟨the scientific spirit, like the spirit of sanctity, can be acquired only by the *arduous* methodical discipline —M.R. Cohen⟩ **syn** see in addition FIRM

— **hard up 1 :** short of money **:** economically distressed ⟨he managed to pay his way although awfully *hard up* at the time⟩ ⟨the region was perennially *hard up*⟩ **2 :** experiencing an acute want or deprivation of any kind ⟨far past the age when any woman, however *hard up*, would look at him twice —Ruth Park⟩ ⟨he's very *hard up* for friends⟩ — **the hard way** *adv* **1 :** in a manner difficult to bear or accomplish **:** RIGOROUSLY, LABORIOUSLY ⟨had come up *the hard way*, through modeling, the chorus line, dramatic school, little theaters and bit parts in screen and TV shows —Fergus McGill⟩ **2 :** by throwing a doublet in craps (as when the point is 4, 6, 8, or 10 and is made respectively by 2-2, 3-3, 4-4, or 5-5) ⟨to make 8 *the hard way* —C.B.Davis⟩

²hard \"\ *adv* -ER/-EST [ME *harde*, fr. OE *hearde*; akin to OHG *harto* extremely, ON *hartha*; derivative fr. the root of E ¹*hard*] **1 a :** with great or utmost effort or energy **:** VIGOROUSLY, STRENUOUSLY, EARNESTLY ⟨the men were ~ at work⟩ ⟨the lumbermen lived and played ~⟩ ⟨you've been going too ~ the last six months⟩ ⟨it forces one to think ~⟩ **b :** VIOLENTLY, FIERCELY ⟨drove the muzzle ~ into the gangster's face⟩ ⟨the rain came down ~⟩ ⟨the wind is blowing ~⟩ **c** (1) **:** to the full extent or the extreme limit — used in nautical directions esp. to the helmsman ⟨~ right⟩ ⟨~ alee⟩ ⟨~ aport⟩ (2) **:** to a considerable extent **:** MASSIVELY, LARGELY ⟨if . . . you wish to persevere with the present tree, cut it back ~ —*Sydney (Australia) Bull.*⟩ ⟨the strike cut production back ~⟩ **d :** in an immoderate manner **:** to an extreme degree **:** INTENSIVELY, UNREMITTINGLY ⟨he is hitting the bottle ~⟩ **e :** in a searching, close, or concentrated manner **:** INTENTLY ⟨looked ~ at him⟩ ⟨listen ~ to what I have to say⟩ **f :** in a sharp or emphatic manner **:** POINTEDLY ⟨the incident brought home to him ~ his inadequate grasp of the subject⟩ **2 a :** in such a manner as to cause hardship, difficulty, or pain **:** HARSHLY, SEVERELY, CRUELLY, BADLY ⟨the Stamp Act and other laws which bore ~ on colonial prosperity —H.E.Scudder⟩ ⟨such levies hit the poor ~*er* than the rich —*Collier's Yr. Bk.*⟩ ⟨things have gone very ~ with us⟩ **b :** with extreme rancor, bitterness, or grief **:** with animus or resentment of — often used with *take* ⟨this expansion of Russia's . . . was taken very ~ in the liberal Western world —*New Republic*⟩ ⟨it was his first taste of defeat . . . he took it ~ —S.H.Adams⟩ **c :** AUSTERELY, FRUGALLY ⟨they deserved to live ~ even if it deprived them of . . . leisure in which to think high —F.M.Ford⟩ **3 :** TIGHTLY, FIRMLY, FAST ⟨hold on ~⟩ **4 :** to the point of hardness ⟨like my eggs boiled ~⟩ ⟨the river froze ~⟩ **5 :** with difficulty **:** LABORIOUSLY ⟨breathing ~ after that long run⟩ **6 :** in close or immediate proximity in time or space ⟨caught the fish ~ in to the shore⟩ ⟨the house stood ~ by the river⟩ ⟨~ on the heels of the Supreme Court decision⟩ ⟨darkness was ~ at hand⟩ ⟨steamships berth ~ up against the main streets —William Sansom⟩

³hard \"\ *n* -S [ME, something that is hard, fr. *hard*, adj.] **1** *chiefly Brit* **:** a firm foreshore or landing place **2** *slang chiefly Brit* **:** HARD LABOR ⟨ten years ~ . . . for clouting some bloke —Richard Llewellyn⟩ **3 :** ERECTION 2 — used in the phrase *hard on*; usu. considered vulgar

hard-and-fast \ˌ=ˌ=ˈ=\ *adj* **:** not subject to deviation, revision, or modification **:** rigidly binding **:** FIXED, CATEGORICAL, ABSOLUTE ⟨*hard-and-fast* rules⟩ ⟨*hard-and-fast* distinctions⟩ ⟨a *hard-and-fast* line⟩

har·dang·er \här'däŋər\ *n* -S [*Hardanger*, district in Norway] **:** embroidery of Norwegian origin worked over counted threads in a geometrical design

hardanger fiddle *n, usu cap H* [trans. of Norw *hardangerfele*, fr. *Hardanger* + Norw *fele* fiddle] **:** a fiddle of Norwegian origin with four stopped and four sympathetic strings used to accompany the halling and other Scandinavian dances

¹hardback \'=,=\ *adj* **:** HARD 1a (2)

²hardback \"\ *n* **:** a book bound in hard covers

hardbake \'=,=\ *n, Brit* **:** a sweetmeat of sugar or molasses and almonds

hardball \'=,=\ *n* **:** BASEBALL

hard-bark hickory *n* **:** MOCKERNUT

hard beech *n* **:** a tall beech (*Nothofagus truncata*) with very hard wood found in south temperate regions esp. in New Zealand

hard-bill \'=,=\ *n* **:** any of numerous birds with a hard strong bill adapted to cracking seeds and nuts — compare SOFT-BILL

hard-bitten \'=¦==\ *adj* [¹*hard* + *-bitten* having (such) a bite (fr. *bitten*, past part. of *bite*)] **1 :** having a hard bite **:** inclined to bite hard ⟨so *hard-bitten* an animal that all the torture you can use will not make him leave his hold —Martin Hunter⟩ **2 a :** seasoned or steeled in battle **:** tough in fighting ⟨*hard-bitten* tribesmen, their . . . faces flecked with the blood of the fighting —T.E.Lawrence⟩ ⟨the rangers . . . were a *hard-bitten* lot, and they went after outlaws in a businesslike way —W.M. Raine⟩ **b** (1) **:** seasoned or steeled in struggle or experience of any kind **:** having the qualities appropriate to a veteran ⟨this genial but *hard-bitten* career diplomat —*Newsweek*⟩ (2) **:** CONFIRMED, INVETERATE ⟨*hard-bitten* amateur high-fidelity operators —R.S.Lanier⟩ ⟨*hard-bitten* bachelors complained that they were too shy to approach women —*Atlantic*⟩ **3 a** (1) **:** marked by severity or austerity of character **:** of tough moral fiber **:** UNYIELDING, INDOMITABLE, RUGGED ⟨a *hard-bitten*, granite-faced, Scotch-Irish Presbyterian —*Newsweek*⟩ ⟨his *hard-bitten* New England independence —Edwin Clark⟩ ⟨one of those *hard-bitten* ruggedly individualistic men —Pamela Taylor⟩ (2) **:** full of difficulties or hardships **:** HARSH ⟨the life of the farmer was all too often a lonely *hard-bitten* existence —*Amer. Guide Series: Ind.*⟩ **b :** lacking polish or refinement **:** rough or coarse in manner or appearance **:** TOUGH, HARD-BOILED ⟨patronized by roistering, *hard-bitten* seafarers —*Amer. Guide Series: Fla.*⟩ **c :** lacking sensitivity or compassion **:** CALLOUS, RUTHLESS, HARD ⟨the typical story of the *hard-bitten* man who clawed his way to the top —V.P.Hass⟩ **d :** free of sentimentality or illusions **:** not credulous or naive **:** TOUGH-MINDED, REALISTIC, PRACTICAL ⟨this *hard-bitten* gentleman has an aesthetic and romantic side —Stanley Walker⟩ ⟨a somewhat more *hard-bitten* scholarly segment . . . squared off for wordy battles with the faithful —M.W.Fishwick⟩ ⟨realistic, *hard-bitten*, and unrhetorical —*Saturday Rev.*⟩

hardboard \'=,=\ *n* **:** a composition board made by shredding wood chips by sudden release of high steam pressure and then compressing them with or without added binders or other materials at high temperatures

hard-boil \'=,=\ *vt* [back-formation fr. *hard-boiled*] **:** to cook (an egg) until hard-boiled

hard-boiled \'=¦=\ *adj* [²*hard* + *boiled*] **1 :** boiled until both white and yolk have solidified — used of an egg **2 :** heavily starched **:** STIFF ⟨wore a double-breasted, dark suit and a collar . . .; it was one of those *hard-boiled* old-timers —F.C. Othman⟩ — compare BOILED SHIRT **3 a :** devoid of sentimentality or weakness **:** CALLOUS, TOUGH ⟨I, a *hard-boiled* South Sea trader, was genuinely shocked —*Atlantic*⟩ ⟨*hard-boiled* politicians⟩ ⟨a *hard-boiled* outfit under a *hard-boiled* leader —E.J.Fitzgerald⟩ **b :** of or relating to a literary form or production characterized by impersonal matter-of-fact presentation of naturalistic or violent themes or incidents, by a generally unemotional or stoic tone, and often by a total absence of explicit or implied moral judgments ⟨the *hard-boiled* tradition of detective fiction —John Paterson⟩ ⟨the novels of the *hard-boiled* school —George Stevens⟩ **c :** DOWN-TO-EARTH, PRACTICAL, HARDHEADED, REALISTIC ⟨from the *hardest-boiled* examination of the American system, this is a blueprint for disaster —A.A.Berle⟩ ⟨handle aid programs on a friendly but *hard-boiled* business basis —*N.Y. Times*⟩ ⟨a fundamentally *hard-boiled* permanently businesslike people —*Times Lit. Supp.*⟩

hard-boiled·ness *n* -ES **:** the quality or state of being hard-boiled

hardboot \'=,=\ *n* **:** a person devoted to horse racing ⟨the local ~*s* tramped or rode trolleys —*Newsweek*⟩ — used esp. of Kentuckians

hardbought \'=¦=\ *adj* **:** gained or won by hard or intensive effort ⟨the ~ battle for political control —Allan Nevins⟩ ⟨lest the silent ~ knowledge show in his eyes —Ross Lockridge⟩

hardbound \'=,=\ *adj* **:** HARD 1a (2)

hard brick *or* **hard-burned brick** \'=,=-\ *n* **:** brick that has received the proper amount of burning in the kiln

hard candy *n* **:** candy made of sugar and corn syrup boiled without crystallizing and usu. fruit-flavored

hardcase \'=,=\ *n, often attrib* **1 :** a person by nature incorrigible or intractable **:** a tough customer; *esp* **:** a hardened criminal ⟨small-time ~ —Mickey Spillane⟩ ⟨ran with a ~ crowd —Luke Short⟩ ⟨remained at peace with local ~*s* by giving demonstrations of his . . . gunnery —W.L.Gresham⟩ **2 :** a person in a pitiful plight **:** a case of hardship ⟨my ~*s* were all of the literary sort —F.M.Ford⟩

hard cherry *n* **:** BIGARREAU CHERRY

hard cider *n* **:** fermented apple juice containing usu. less than 10 percent alcohol

hard clam *n* **:** a clam with a thick hard shell; *specif* **:** QUAHOG

hard coal *n* **:** ANTHRACITE

hard-coated \'=¦==\ *adj, of a dog* **:** having a crisp harsh-textured coat

hard core *n* **1** *usu* **hardcore** \'=,=\ *chiefly Brit* **:** brick rubbish, clinker, broken stone, or other hard material in pieces used as a bottom (as in making roads and in foundations) **2 :** an esp. resistant or enduring structural and usu. basic or central part of a larger entity: as **a :** the most militant, die-hard, or loyal element or nucleus of a group, organization, or movement ⟨this group, whose *hard core* . . . is the trade unions —C.J. Friedrich⟩ ⟨the party's *hard core* of stubborn ultraconservatives —*N.Y. Times*⟩ **b :** a group of refugees or displaced persons not readily sponsored or resettled because of physical or other incapacities; *specif* **:** a group of refugees requiring institutional care wherever they go ⟨*hard-core* cases — incurably sick people, bedridden old people, inevitable charges of the state —John Hersey⟩

hard court *n* **:** a lawn-tennis court with a paved surface (as of asphalt or concrete) — distinguished from *clay court* and *grass court*

hard-cover \'=,==\ *adj* **:** HARD 1a (2)

hard crab *n* **:** HARD-SHELL CRAB

hard-drawn \'=¦=\ *adj* **:** drawn so as to produce great hardness and strength — used esp. of copper wire and tubing

¹hard·en \'härdᵊn, 'hädᵊn\ *vb* **hardened; hardened; hardening** \-d(ᵊ)niŋ\ **hardens** [ME *hardnen*, fr. ¹*hard* + *-nen* -en] *vt* **1 :** to make hard or harder **:** make firm, tight, or compact: as **a :** to convert into solid or stiffer solid form ⟨~ an unsaturated oil by catalytic hydrogenation⟩ **b :** to make hard (as steel) by heat treatment, esp. heating and quenching in water, brine, or oil **c :** to compact (felt) by applying moisture, heat, friction, and pressure **d :** to decrease the swelling and raise the melting point of (the emulsion layer of a photographic material) by chemical treatment **2** *dial Eng* **a :** to make bold **:** urge on **:** ENCOURAGE **b :** to strengthen or confirm esp. in disposition, feelings, or a course of action **:** REINFORCE ⟨~*ed* him in his determination to leave at once⟩ ⟨a development that only ~*ed* his conviction that he was right⟩ **3 :** to make callous or unfeeling ⟨~*ed* his heart against me⟩ ⟨its influence did not ~ him; he has always risen above cynicism —L.A. Triebel⟩ **4 :** to make hardy or robust **:** INURE, TOUGHEN ⟨~ troops by long marches⟩ ⟨coarse foods . . . help to ~ the gums —Morris Fishbein⟩; *specif* **:** to inure to cold or other unfavorable environmental conditions (as by gradual exposure to lower temperatures or by decreasing the water supply) — often used with *off* **5 :** to signify that the pronunciation of (a consonant letter) is plosive rather than fricative ~ *vi* **1 :** to become hard or harder **:** acquire solidity, compactness, or rigidity ⟨mortar ~*s* by drying⟩ ⟨deviations ~ into modes of action —John Dewey⟩ **2 a :** to become confirmed or strengthened (as in feeling, disposition, or course of action) ⟨opposition began to ~ —L.S.B.Leakey⟩ **b :** to become hard in temper or disposition ⟨it was enough . . . to set up resistance in her: she ~*ed* —Elizabeth Bowen⟩ **c :** to assume an appearance or give an impression of harshness or severity ⟨her face ~*ed* instantly —Margaret Deland⟩ ⟨his face ~*ed* into anger —Liam O'Flaherty⟩ **3 :** to become higher or less subject to fluctuations downward **:** FIRM, STRENGTHEN, STIFFEN ⟨prices . . . ~*ed* quickly and drastically —R.F.Yates⟩ ⟨~*ing* commodity markets⟩

syn INURE, SEASON, ACCLIMATIZE, ACCLIMATE: HARDEN, in the sense pertinent here, is to habituate or toughen, usu. by degrees, to what generally causes pain or discomfort, or to make slowly callous to what usu. affects the feelings ⟨frontier life *hardened* most men quickly to rough conditions, often to extreme privations⟩ ⟨not yet *hardened* to the wicked world of international politics —Dexter Perkins⟩ To INURE one is to cause one to submit unwillingly, to harden one to patient endurance of the objectionable ⟨they were *inured* to hardship and unafraid of the wilderness —*Amer. Guide Series: Tenn.*⟩ ⟨an experienced judge is more or less *inured* to criticism —W.F. Brown b.1903⟩ SEASON suggests a gradual bettering of condition or increase in ability brought about by time or experience, a maturing (of a thing) to a sound, reliable condition, or a maturing (of a person or a talent) to a greater efficiency or perfection in a particular activity or calling ⟨old wood, *seasoned* by the sea wind for many decades —*Amer. Guide Series: N.Y. City*⟩ ⟨a soldier, *seasoned* by many campaigns⟩ ⟨the chapters which follow have all been tried out and *seasoned* with discussion —H.A.Overstreet⟩ To ACCLIMATIZE or to ACCLIMATE is to adapt or to accustom to new and hitherto alien conditions, ACCLIMATIZE more frequently suggesting a human agency ⟨to help *acclimatize* the new arrivals to conditions on the continent —Hanama Tasaki⟩ ⟨sheep . . . *acclimatized* to the hills —F.D.Smith & Barbara Wilcox⟩ ⟨they were *acclimatized* now to the cool atmosphere of professional life —Mary Lavin⟩ ⟨I became so well *acclimated* to German customs —David Fairchild⟩ ⟨*acclimating* the disabled veteran to the job and adjusting the job to the veteran —*Current Biog.*⟩

²harden \'(h)a(r)dən\ *n* -S *often attrib* [ME *herdyng, herden, harden*, irreg. fr. *herdes, hardes* hurds — more at HURDS] *dial Brit* **:** a fabric made of the coarser parts of flax or hemp

hard·en·abil·i·ty \ˌhärdᵊnə'bilədē\ *n* -ES **:** the property determining the depth to which a ferrous alloy can be hardened by quenching

har·den·ber·gia \ˌhärdᵊn'bərjēə\ *n, cap* [NL, fr. Franziska von *Hardenberg*, 19th cent. Austrian noblewoman + NL *-ia*] **:** a small genus of Australian woody climbers (family Leguminosae) with small violet-blue flowers

hardened *adj* [ME *hardned*, fr. past part. of *hardnen* to harden] **1 :** made hard or harder ⟨~ brass⟩ ⟨~ roads⟩ **2 a :** grown unfeeling or callous ⟨~ as I am, I felt a thrill of horror —Allen Upward⟩ **b :** CONFIRMED, INVETERATE, VETERAN ⟨many of the findings will hardly appeal except to ~ Johnsonians —*Times Lit. Supp.*⟩ ⟨~ fishermen protested —L.F. Ranlett⟩ ⟨a commercial or otherwise ~ traveler —W.C. Brownell⟩; *specif* **:** confirmed in error or vice ⟨a ~ little reprobate —W.M.Thackeray⟩ ⟨a ~ heretic⟩ ⟨~ criminals⟩ **c :** grown or become inured or steeled ⟨the duty was easy for a ~ horseman —S.H.Adams⟩ ⟨~ fighting men⟩

hard·en·er \'härd(ᵊ)nər, 'hàd(ᵊ)nə(r\ *n* -S **:** one that hardens: as **a** (1) **:** a worker who hardens steel objects by heating and quick cooling (2) **:** a preliminary alloy added to a melt in order to introduce alloying elements **b** (1) **:** a worker who hardens felt (2) **:** a machine for hardening felt **c :** a substance added (as to a paint or varnish) to impart greater hardness to the film **d :** a substance (as alum or formaldehyde) used in a gelatin film, emulsion, or processing bath to prevent swelling and softening during processing

hardening *n* -s [fr. gerund of ¹*harden*] **1 :** something (as a material used for converting the surface of iron into steel) that hardens **2 :** INDURATION 1d ⟨~ of the arteries⟩

hardens *pres 3d sing of* HARDEN

¹harder *comparative of* HARD

²har·der \ˈhärdə(r)\ *n* -s [Afrik, fr. D] *Africa* **:** GRAY MULLET

har·de·ri·an gland \(ˈ)här¦dirēən-\ *also* **harder's gland** *n, sometimes cap H* [after Johann J. *Harder* †1711 Swiss anatomist] **:** an accessory lacrimal gland on the inner side of the orbit in reptiles and birds but usu. degenerate in mammals

hardest *superlative of* HARD

hard-face \ˈ=,=\ *vt* **:** to weld a wear-resistant metal onto the surface of (a metal part)

hard-favored \ˈ=¦==\ *adj* **:** HARD-FEATURED — **hard-favored·ness** *n* -ES

hard-featured \ˈ=¦==\ *adj* **:** having coarse, unattractive, or stern features

hard fern *n* **:** DEER FERN; *broadly* **:** any of several ferns of the genus *Blechnum*

hard fescue *n* **:** a European fescue (*Festuca ovina duriuscula*) that is a variety of sheep fescue and is sometimes used in permanent pasture and lawn mixtures

hard-fiber \ˈ=,==\ *adj* [¹*hard* + *fiber*, n.] **:** vulcanized with zinc chloride — used of paper or boards

hard fiber *n* [¹*hard* + *fiber*, n.] **:** leaf fiber with heavily lignified walls that is hard and stiff in texture and is used in making cordage, twine, and textiles

hard finish *n* **:** a smooth finishing coat of hard fine plaster applied to the surface of rough plastering

hardfisted \ˈ=¦==\ *adj* **1 a :** having hard or strong hands esp. from labor **:** capable of hard physical labor **:** hardened to or by labor **:** STRONG ⟨had a ~ hired girl to help with the work —Floyd Dell⟩ ⟨~ sons of toil —Robert Grant †1940⟩ **b :** hard of will or temper **:** free of weakness **:** TOUGH, TOUGH-MINDED, RUTHLESS ⟨a ~ ruler and a demanding father —Diana Chang⟩ ⟨~ men of affairs⟩ **2 :** CLOSEFISTED, STINGY, MEAN ⟨as ~ . . . as any Boston landlord —G.W.Johnson⟩ — **hard·fist·ed·ness** *n* -ES

hard goods *n pl* **:** DURABLES

hard-grained \ˈ=¦=\ *adj* **1 :** having a close firm grain **2 :** of a hard nature **:** UNATTRACTIVE

hard grass *n* **:** any of several different grasses (as orchard grass and members of the genera *Sclerochloa* and *Glyceria*)

hard ground *n* **:** etching ground melted from a ball or cake onto a heated plate and spread while soft by means of a roller or dabber

hardhack \ˈ=,=\ *n* [¹*hard* + *hack*, v.] **1 :** an American shrub (*Spiraea tomentosa*) with rusty tomentose leaves and dense terminal panicles of pink or occas. white flowers **2 :** HOP HORNBEAM **3 :** SHRUBBY CINQUEFOIL

hardhanded \ˈ=¦==\ *adj* **:** HARDFISTED — **hard·hand·ed·ness** *n* -ES

hard hat *n* **1** *Brit* **:** DERBY **2 :** a protective hat usu. with a metal crown worn esp. by construction workers

hardhead \ˈ=,=\ *n* **1 a :** a shrewd practical hardheaded person ⟨a prospect that moves ~s as well as visionaries⟩ **b :** BLOCKHEAD **2 a :** any of several fishes: as (1) *also* **hardhead trout :** STEELHEAD TROUT (2) **:** ATLANTIC CROAKER (3) **:** a small cyprinid fish (*Mylopharodon conocephalus*) of California streams; *also* **:** the related greaser blackfish **b :** GRAY WHALE **3 a :** RUDDY DUCK **b** *or* **hardheaded duck** \ˈ=¦==-\ **:** WHITE-EYED DUCK **4 a :** KNAPWEED — usu. used in pl. **b :** RIBGRASS **c :** SNEEZEWORT 2 **d :** CORN COCKLE **5 :** HARDHEAD SPONGE **6 a :** a hard brittle white residue obtained in refining tin by liquation and containing tin, iron, arsenic, and copper **b :** a refractory lump of ore only partly smelted

hardheaded \ˈ=¦==\ *adj* [¹*hard* + *headed*] **1 :** STUBBORN, WILLFUL ⟨always was ~ about what she wanted —Erskine Caldwell⟩ **2 :** not moved by sentiment or impulse **:** having no illusions **:** PRACTICAL, SOBER, REALISTIC ⟨a ~ appraisal of our position in Asia today —*N. Y. Times*⟩ ⟨~ realists⟩ — **hard·head·ed·ly** *adv* — **hard·head·ed·ness** *n* -ES

hardhead sponge *n* **:** any of several commercial sponges having a harsh but elastic and fairly durable fiber that occur off the West Indies and Central America

hardhearted \ˈ=¦==\ *adj* [ME *hardherted*, fr. ¹*hard* + *herted* hearted] **:** UNSYMPATHETIC, UNFEELING, CALLOUS, CRUEL, PITILESS — **hard·heart·ed·ly** *adv* — **hard·heart·ed·ness** *n* -ES

hard-hitting \ˈ=,==\ *adj* **:** ENERGETIC, VIGOROUS, AGGRESSIVE, EFFECTIVE, INTENSIVE ⟨a *hard-hitting* advertising campaign⟩ ⟨writes a fast, *hard-hitting* prose —E.J.Fitzgerald⟩

har·die *or* **har·dy** \ˈhärdē\ *n, pl* **hardies** [prob. fr. ¹*hard* + *-ie* or *-y*] **:** a blacksmith's fuller or chisel having a square shank for insertion into a hole in the anvil

hardie hole *or* **hardy hole** *n* **:** a square hole in a blacksmith's anvil for insertion of the shank of a hardie

hardier *comparative of* HARDY

hardiest *superlative of* HARDY

har·di·head \ˈhärdē,hed\ *var of* HARDYHEAD

har·di·hood \ˈhärdē,hu̇d, ˈhȧd-, -di,-\ *n* [¹*hardy* + *-hood*] **1 a :** resolute courage and fortitude **:** strong will to prevail, withstand, or survive ⟨~ is the fisherman's talent by which he wins his living from the sea —Richard Jefferies⟩ **b :** self-assured resolute audacity or disdainful insolence ⟨no historian will have the ~ to maintain that he commands this . . . view —A.J.Toynbee⟩ **2 :** VIGOR, ROBUSTNESS ⟨a man of action . . . who greatly prized and honored physical ~ —J.D.Adams⟩ **syn** see TEMERITY

har·di·ly \-dəlē, -li\ *adv* [ME, fr. ¹*hardy* + *-ly*] **:** in a hardy manner **:** BOLDLY, STOUTLY ⟨stared back ~ —Clemence Dane⟩

har·dim \ˈhär,dim\ *n* -s [modif. of Ar *ḥirdhawn*] **:** STARRED LIZARD

har·di·ment \ˈhärdēmənt\ *n* -s [ME, fr. MF, fr. OF *hardiment*, *hardement*, fr. *hardi* bold + *-ment* — more at HARDY] **1** *archaic* **:** HARDIHOOD, BOLDNESS, COURAGE **2** *obs* **:** a bold deed

har·di·ness \ˈhärdēnəs, ˈhȧd-, -din-\ *n* -ES [ME *hardinesse*, fr. ¹*hardy* + *-nesse* -ness] **:** the quality or state of being hardy: as **a :** the condition of being inured to fatigue or hardship **:** capability of endurance or resistance ⟨a race of great ~⟩; *specif* **:** the ability of a plant to survive under adverse conditions esp. of low temperatures **b :** BOLDNESS, AUDACITY, TEMERITY ⟨somewhere ~ failed her —Elizabeth Bowen⟩

har·ding·grass \ˈhärdiŋ,gras\ *n, often cap* [prob. fr. the name *Harding*] **:** a perennial canary grass (*Phalaris tuberosa stenoptera*) of Australia and southern Africa introduced into No. America as a forage grass

hard·ish \ˈhärdish\ *adj* **:** rather hard ⟨the seats, though cushioned, were ~ —Lucien Price⟩

har·di·shrew \ˈhȧdi,shrü\ *n* [¹*hardy* + *shrew*] *Brit* **:** a common shrew (*Sorex araneus*)

hard labor *n* **:** compulsory labor imposed upon imprisoned criminals as a part of the prison discipline but not necessarily more severe nor greater in amount than that customarily performed by ordinary laborers

hard-laid \ˈ=¦=\ *adj, of rope* **:** twisted tightly so that the angle of the strands is about 45 degrees

hard lay *n* **:** a lay in which the strands of a rope are hard-laid for greater firmness and resistance to abrasive wear

hard lead *n* **1 :** unrefined lead made hard by impurities esp. of copper, antimony, and arsenic **2 :** ANTIMONIAL LEAD; *specif* **:** an alloy containing about 5 percent antimony — compare GRID METAL

hard lines *n pl, chiefly Brit* **:** hard luck ⟨it's damned *hard lines* to have a lot of planning . . . go for nothing —F.V.W.Mason⟩ — often used with *on* ⟨*hard lines* on the kid, I say —G.A. Wagner⟩

hard liquor *n* **:** DISTILLED LIQUOR

hard liver *or* **hard liver disease** *n* **:** a toxic hepatic cirrhosis of swine and cattle due to ingestion of the seeds of a tarweed (*Amsinckia intermedia*) in the northwestern U. S.

hard·ly *adv* [ME *hardely*, *hardly*, fr. OE *heardlice*, adv. of *heardlic* severe, bold, fr. *heard* hard + *-lic* -ly (adj. suffix)] **1 :** with force or energy **:** VIOLENTLY, VIGOROUSLY ⟨turquoise . . . earrings jangling down ~ on diminutive gold chains —Osbert Sitwell⟩ **2 a :** in a severe or harsh manner **:** ROUGHLY, UNFAIRLY, UNPLEASANTLY, BADLY ⟨things may go ~ with us . . . before the war is over —Nevil Shute⟩ **b :** with great or excessive grief or resentment ⟨had not believed that he would take it so ~⟩ **3 :** in a difficult manner **:** by hard work or struggle **:** with trouble **:** PAINFULLY ⟨the right to play croquet had been a ~ won concession —Osbert Lancaster⟩ ⟨wondering why the lesson had to be learned so ~ —Kamala Markandaya⟩ ⟨means of existence wrung so ~ from the soil —Sir Winston Churchill⟩ **4 :** only just **:** not quite **:** not altogether **:** BARELY, SCARCELY ⟨men who were ~ literate⟩ ⟨why, I ~ know him⟩ ⟨~ knew what to say⟩ ⟨this is ~ the time to discuss such matters⟩ — sometimes used in nonstandard construction with a superfluous negative ⟨horse thieves was so bad that a man couldn't ~ keep a . . . horse —J.F.Dobie⟩

hardly ever *adv* **:** almost never **:** very seldom ⟨we *hardly ever* see them anymore⟩

hard maple *n* **1 :** a maple with notably hard wood; *esp* **:** SUGAR MAPLE **2 :** the wood of a hard maple

hardmouthed \ˈ=¦=\ *adj* **1 a** *of a horse* **:** not sensitive to the bit **b :** OBSTINATE, STUBBORN ⟨~ women who laid down the law —John Galsworthy⟩ **2** *of a dog* **:** given to biting down hard on a retrieved bird

hard·ness *n* -ES [ME *hardnesse*, fr. OE *heardnes*, fr. *heard* hard + *-nes* -ness] **1 :** the quality or state of being hard: as **a** (1) **:** a property of solids, plastics, and very viscous liquids that is indicated by their solidity and firmness (2) **:** resistance of metal to indentation by an indenter of fixed shape and size under a static load or to scratching (as by a file or diamond cutting point) (3) **:** ability of a metal to cause rebound of a small standard object dropped from a fixed height (4) **:** the cohesion of the particles on the surface of a mineral as determined by its capacity to scratch another or be itself scratched — compare MOHS' SCALE **b :** a quality exhibited by water containing various dissolved salts (as of calcium and magnesium) that prevent soap from lathering by giving rise to an insoluble curdy precipitate and that cause incrustations in boilers or kettles — see PERMANENT HARDNESS, TEMPORARY HARDNESS; compare SOFTNESS **c :** a quality of radiation (as of X rays) that determines its penetrating power **d :** excessive contrast in a photographic negative or print **e** (1) **:** HARSHNESS, SEVERITY, CALLOUSNESS ⟨a ~ toward shop assistants by customers —Lucien Price⟩ ⟨free from all resentment, ~, and scorn —Oscar Wilde⟩ (2) **:** RIGOR, INCLEMENCY, DIFFICULTY ⟨the poverty of the country, the ~ of life —Felix Gilbert⟩ ⟨happier than the townsman . . . in spite of the ~ of his lot —G.E.Fussell⟩ (3) **:** freedom from sentimentality, weakness, or slackness ⟨it was Yeats's dryness and ~ that excited us —Louis MacNeice⟩ ⟨that doctrine of ~ which distinguishes the work of the best imagist poets —Jacob Isaacs⟩ **2 :** something hard to do or bear **:** HARDSHIP

hard-nosed \ˈ=¦=\ *adj* **:** HARD-BITTEN, STUBBORN ⟨a *hard-nosed* scrapping breed —Breck Porter⟩

hardock \ˈhär,dȧk\ *n* -s [origin unknown] **:** BURDOCK

hard-of-hearing *adj* **:** of, relating to, or characterized by a defective but functional sense of hearing

hard oil *n* **:** an interior varnish that dries with a relatively hard surface

hard pad *or* **hard pad disease** *n* **:** a serious and frequently fatal virus disease of dogs related to and sometimes indistinguishable from common distemper but typically involving bronchopneumonia, severe diarrhea, and a peculiar thickening and hardening of the skin of the pads and nose which commonly peels away as the acute stage of the disease subsides

hard palate *n* **:** a part of the human palate supported by the maxillary and palatine bones

hardpan \ˈ=,=\ *n* **1 :** a cemented or compacted and often clayey layer in soil that hampers root penetration and results from accumulation of cementing material or may be caused by repeated plowing to the same depth — compare PLOW SOLE **2 :** a firm substantial fundamental part or quality of something **:** BEDROCK ⟨gets down to the ~ of the question⟩

hard paste *n* **1 :** a ceramic body consisting of kaolin together with china stone or with feldspar and flint **2** *or* **hard-paste porcelain :** true high-fired porcelain made with a hard-paste body — compare SOFT PASTE

hard patch *n* **:** a plate riveted or welded over another to cover a break

hard pear *n* **1 :** a southern African shrub (*Olinia cymosa*) having square stems, cymose white flowers, red drupaceous fruit, and hard wood that is used for making musical instruments **2 :** a southern African tree (*Strychnos henningsii*) with elliptical leaves and spherical one-seeded fruit about ¾ inch in diameter

hard pine *n* **:** a pine (as longleaf pine or a pitch pine) having hard wood and leaves usu. in groups of two or three; *also* **:** the wood of a hard pine

hard put *adj* [*put* fr. past part. of *put*, v.] **:** faced with difficulty or perplexity **:** being in a quandary **:** barely or hardly able ⟨was *hard put* to find a satisfactory answer⟩ ⟨were *hard put* to meet mortgage payments —*Current Biog.*⟩ — often used in the phrase *hard put to it* ⟨*hard put to it* to account for the differences between the ancient Chinese and the ancient Egyptians —Bertrand Russell⟩

hard road *n* **:** a road that has been paved or otherwise hard-surfaced

hard-rock \ˈ=,=\ *adj, of a miner* **:** experienced in underground work in hard massive formations

hard rot *n* **:** any of several plant diseases characterized by lesions with hard surfaces and rotted tissue; *esp* **:** a disease of the gladiolus caused by a fungus (*Septoria gladioli*) that produces lesions on both leaves and corms

hard rubber *n* **:** a firm relatively inextensible rubber or rubber product: as **a :** a normally black substance having the texture of horn and made by vulcanizing natural rubber with high percentages (as about 30 to 50 percent) of sulfur and with or without other compounding ingredients **b :** a similar substance made from certain synthetic rubbers (as GR-S and nitrile rubber) and sulfur **c :** a similar substance made from natural or certain synthetic rubbers by the use of organic vulcanizing agents without elemental sulfur

hard rush *n* **:** a common rush (*Juncus effusus*)

¹hards \ˈhärdz\ *n pl* [ME *hardes*, *herdes* — more at HURDS] **:** HURDS

²hards *pl of* HARD

hard sauce *n* **:** a creamed mixture of butter and powdered sugar often with added cream and flavoring

¹hardscrabble \ˈ=¦==\ *adj* [¹*hard* + *scrabble*, n.] **:** yielding or gaining a bare or meager living with greatest difficulty or hardest labor **:** BARREN, IMPOVERISHED, MARGINAL ⟨ranges from ~ farms in the hilly portions . . . to productive farms on prairie land —*Social Forces*⟩ ⟨a rather ~ life . . . among people who had few comforts and amenities —Henry Beston⟩ ⟨a ~ farmer⟩ ⟨till their ~ acres . . . intensively —*Pa. Game News*⟩

²hardscrabble \ˈ"\ *n* **:** hardscrabble land ⟨homestead of field, stream, hayfield, and ~ —S.T.Williamson⟩

hard seed *n* **:** seed in which the testa is unusually hard and impervious to moisture and which is therefore slow in germinating unless treated mechanically or chemically

hard sell *n* **:** aggressive high-pressure selling or salesmanship — often used with *the* ⟨everyone had keyed himself up for the *hard sell* —*Business Week*⟩; compare SOFT SELL

hard-set \ˈ=¦=\ *adj* [ME *harde sette*, fr. *harde* hard (adv.) + *sette*, *set*, past part. of *setten* to set — more at SET] **1 :** hard pressed **:** HARD PUT ⟨it's *hard set* I am to walk —J.M.Synge⟩ **2 a :** fixed in rigidity **:** HARD, FIRM ⟨there is a *hard-set* line about his mouth —*Nation*⟩ **b :** subjected to the process of incubation by setting ⟨frightened a . . . gull from her *hard-set* eggs —E.A.Armstrong⟩

¹hard-shell \ˈ=¦=\ *adj* **1 a :** having a hard shell **b :** UNYIELDING, CONFIRMED, UNCOMPROMISING ⟨a *hard-shell* conservative⟩ **2** *often cap H&S* **:** of, relating to, or characteristic of the Hard-Shell Baptists

²hard-shell \ˈ=¦=\ *n* **1 :** HARD-SHELL CRAB **2** *often cap H&S* **:** a Hard-Shell Baptist

hard-shell baptist *n, usu cap H&S&B* **1 :** PRIMITIVE BAPTIST **2 :** a strict and uncompromising Baptist

hard-shell clam *also* **hard-shelled clam** *n* **:** QUAHOG

hard-shell crab *or* **hard-shelled crab** *n* **:** a crab that has not recently shed its shell and hence has the shell rigid — used chiefly of edible crabs (as the blue crab)

hard-shelled \ˈ=¦=\ *adj* [¹*hard* + *shelled*, adj.] **:** HARD-SHELL

hard·ship \ˈhärd,ship, ˈhȧd-\ *n* [ME *hardshipe*, fr. ¹*hard* + *-shipe* -ship] **1 a :** SUFFERING, PRIVATION ⟨years of danger and ~⟩ ⟨inflation was a cause of ~⟩ ⟨a life of ~⟩ **b :** a particular instance or type of suffering or privation ⟨the losses and ~s . . . entailed by war —Bertrand Russell⟩ ⟨enduring cold, hunger, and other ~s⟩ **2 :** something that causes or entails suffering or privation ⟨cannot help thinking it a ~ that more indulgence is allowed to men than to women —James Boswell⟩ ⟨one of the ~s of town life . . . is the absence of spring water —*Amer. Guide Series: N. C.*⟩ ⟨all the ~s of the northern passage — head winds, fog —L.B.Schmidt⟩ **syn** see DIFFICULTY

hard-sized \ˈ=¦=\ *adj, of paper* **:** sufficiently sized to be relatively impermeable by water — compare SLACK-SIZED

hard smut *n* **:** a disease of wheat caused by nematodes of the genus *Tylenchus* that transform the kernels into galls resembling the smut balls of bunt

hard soap *n* **:** soap made by using sodium hydroxide or sodium carbonate — compare CASTILE SOAP

hard solder *n* [¹*hard* + *solder*, n.] **:** a solder that contains copper, requires a red heat to melt, and is used for brazing

hard-solder \ˈ=¦==\ *vb* [*hard solder*] **:** to solder with hard solder **:** BRAZE

hard sponge *n* **:** ZIMOCCA

hardstand \ˈ=,=\ *also* **hardstanding** \ˈ=,==\ *n* **:** a hard-surfaced area (as at an airfield) for parking an airplane

hardstem bulrush *or* **hard-stemmed bulrush** \ˈ=,=-\ *n* **:** a widely distributed No. American bulrush (*Scirpus acutus*) that has hard rigid olive green culms and a rather stiff panicle; *also* **:** any of several closely related bulrushes

hard-surface \ˈ=¦==\ *vt* [¹*hard* + *surface*, v.] **1 :** to treat (as by paving or macadamizing) the surface of (as a road) to prevent muddiness **2 :** HARD-FACE

hardtack \ˈ=,=\ *n* **1 :** a hard biscuit or loaf bread made of flour and water without salt and baked in large or small forms — called also *pilot bread*, *ship biscuit* **2 :** any of several mountain mahoganies; *esp* **:** a spreading shrub or small tree (*Cercocarpus betuloides*) that has obovate distally serrate leaves dark green above and whitish below

hardtail \ˈ=,=\ *n* **1 a :** BLUE RUNNER **b :** a fish related to the blue runner **2 :** MULE

hard tick *n* **:** a tick of the family Ixodidae — compare SOFT TICK

hard-times token *n* **:** one of the tokens issued during the controversy between the Jacksonian administration and the Bank of the U. S. — called also *Jackson cent*

hardtop \ˈ=,=\ *n* [¹*hard* + *top*, n.] **1 :** an automobile with a metal roof **2** *also* **hardtop convertible :** an automobile similar to a convertible in lacking vertical posts between windows but differing in having a rigid top of metal or plastic that in some models is fixed and in others is either lowerable into the rear deck or demountable

¹hard-top \ˈ=,=\ *n* [¹*hard* + *top*, n.] **:** a hard-surfaced area or road

²hard-top \ˈ=,=\ *vt* **:** HARD-SURFACE

hard tussock *n* **:** a fescue (*Festuca novae-zealandiae*) common in New Zealand as a forage grass

hard wall plaster *n* **:** CEMENT PLASTER

hardware \ˈ=,=\ *n* **1 :** ware (as fittings, trimmings, cutlery, tools, parts of machines and appliances, metal building equipment, utensils) made of metal **2 a :** FIREARMS ⟨while the men spoke politely . . . most of them wore ~ —*Amer. Guide Series: Ariz.*⟩ ⟨riding up with plenty of ~ in sight —F.B.Gipson⟩ **b :** metal items of military equipment for combat use (as ships, guns, tanks, airplanes, and their parts) and major support items (as trucks, jeeps, radar)

hardware cloth *n* **:** galvanized screening of steel wire woven with a close mesh commonly ⅛ inch to ¾ inch

hardware disease *n* **:** traumatic damage to the viscera of cattle due to ingestion of a foreign body (as a nail or barbed wire)

hardwareman \ˈ=,=mən\ *n, pl* **hardwaremen :** a person who makes or deals in hardware

hard waste *n* **:** textile waste rejected during manufacturing processes after spinning and consisting usu. of twisted yarns

hard wheat *n* **:** a wheat with hard flinty kernels high in gluten and yielding a strong flour esp. suitable for bread and macaroni — compare DURUM WHEAT, SOFT WHEAT

hard·wick·ia \härˈdwikēə\ *n, cap* [NL, fr. Thomas *Hardwicke* †1835 Eng. artillery officer in India + NL *-ia*] **:** a small genus of Indian trees (family Leguminosae) having pinnate leaves and flowers in panicled racemes

¹hardwood \ˈ=,=\ *n* [¹*hard* + *wood*] **1 :** the wood of an angiospermous tree as distinguished from that of a coniferous tree, known orig. from hard European woods (as beech and oak) but including both the softest and the hardest of woods **2 :** a tree that yields hardwood **:** an arborescent angiosperm

²hardwood \ˈ"\ *adj* **1 :** having hardwood or made of hardwood **2 :** consisting of mature woody tissue ⟨~ cuttings⟩

hard-wooded \ˈ=¦==\ *adj* [¹*hard* + *wood* + *-ed*] **1 :** having hard wood that is difficult to work or finish **2 :** HARDWOOD 1

hardworking \ˈ=¦==\ *adj* **:** INDUSTRIOUS, LABORIOUS ⟨learned and ~ men —G.H.Turnbull⟩

¹har·dy \ˈhärdē, ˈhȧd-, -di\ *adj* -ER/-EST [ME *hardy*, *hardi*, fr. OF *hardi*, fr. past part. of (assumed) OF *hardir* to make hard, of Gmc origin; akin to OE *hierdan* to make hard, MD *harden*, *herden*, OHG *herten*, ON *hertha*, Goth *gahardjan*; causative denominative fr. the root of E ¹*hard*] **1 :** BOLD, DARING, BRAVE, RESOLUTE ⟨displayed a ~ intrepid spirit⟩ **2 :** full of assurance or presumption **:** AUDACIOUS, BRAZEN **3 a :** inured to fatigue or hardships **:** capable of endurance **:** STRONG, ROBUST ⟨the boys were ~, robust . . . little fellows —Samuel Butler †1902⟩ ⟨small and ~ ponies —*Amer. Guide Series: La.*⟩ **b :** capable of living outdoors over winter without artificial protection or of withstanding other adverse conditions (as insufficient or excessive light, excessive moisture, drought, lack of nourishing food) ⟨~ plants⟩ ⟨a ~ breed of cattle⟩ — compare HALF-HARDY, TENDER

²hardy *var of* HARDIE

hardy annual *n* **:** an annual (as radish or spinach) capable of resisting frosts or light freezing — compare TENDER ANNUAL

hardy border *n* **:** an ornamental or decorative planting of hardy herbaceous perennials (as peony, iris, phlox)

hardy catalpa *n* **:** WESTERN CATALPA

hardyhead \ˈ=,=,=\ *n* [prob. fr. ¹*hardy* + *head*, n.] *Austral* **:** SILVERSIDES

hardy orange *n* **:** TRIFOLIATE ORANGE

hardy perennial *n* **:** something that lasts from year to year or appears afresh from time to time ⟨the Borgias have been among the *hardy perennials* of historical literature —C.M.L. Beuf⟩ ⟨the climatic theory . . . one of those *hardy perennials* that the frosts of scholarship do not much discourage —Charlton Laird⟩

har·dy·ston·ite \ˈhärdēstə,nīt\ *n* -s [*Hardyston*, Sussex County, northern New Jersey + E *-ite*] **:** a mineral $Ca_2ZnSi_2O_7$ consisting of a zinc calcium silicate

¹hare \ˈha(a)(ə)r, ˈhel, |ə\ *n, pl* **hares** *also* **hare** [ME, fr. OE *hara*; akin to OHG *haso* hare, ON *heri*, W *ceinach*, Skt *śaśa* hare, OE *hasu* gray, OHG *hasan*, ON *höss* gray, L *canus* gray, white, hoary] **1 a :** any of various timid long-eared gnawing mammals (order Lagomorpha) with a divided upper lip, long strong hind legs adapted to leaping, and a short cocked tail that have soft usu. gray or brown fur turning white in some northern species in winter, usu. live in the open, feed chiefly on vegetation and bark, bear furred young with eyes open at birth, and are native to most parts of the world except Central and So. America, Australia, and Madagascar — compare COTTONTAIL, JACKRABBIT, RABBIT **b :** the fur or pelt of a hare often sheared and dyed to imitate more valuable furs **c :** a member of the family Leporidae — often used with a qualifying term ⟨African rock ~⟩ ⟨Asiatic harsh-furred ~⟩ **d :** an animal resembling a true hare in appearance or behavior **2 a :** one that is likened

European hare

to a hare: as (1) : a ridiculous person : FOOL ⟨made a ~ of him one time in my column —Sean O'Faolain⟩ (2) : the object of pursuit in a game of hare and hounds ⟨a flushed little ~ bounds past us, distributing the paper scent in his course —W.H.Rideine⟩ (3) *slang Brit* : a passenger traveling without a ticket ⟨the conductor came round and searched under the seats for ~*s* —Stephen Graham⟩ **b** : a topic for discussion or pursuit ⟨first raised this ~ about the decline of the novel —Harold Nicolson⟩ **3** *usu cap* **a** : an Athapaskan people west and northwest of Great Bear Lake, Canada **b** : a member of such people **c** : the language of the Hare people

2**hare** \"\ *vi* -ED/-ING/-S : to move swiftly : RUN ⟨scrambled down the wall and *hared* along the lane, my heart in my mouth —James Edwards⟩ — often used with *off* ⟨whichever team is called turns about and ~*s* off for base —J.B.Pick⟩

3**hare** \"\ *vt* -ED/-ING/-S [prob. alter. of 1*harry*] *archaic* : to tease or harass esp. by frightening

hare and hounds *n* : a game in which two or more of the players start out first, scatter bits of paper for a trail, and try to keep ahead of the others who try to catch them before they reach a designated place

harebell \'=,=\ *n* [ME *harebelle*, fr. 1*hare* + *belle* bell] **1** : a slender herb (*Campanula rotundifolia*) having blue flowers, cordate or ovate basal leaves, and linear stem leaves — called also *bluebell* **2** : WOOD HYACINTH

1**harebrain** \'=,=\ *n* [1*hare* + *brain*] : one who is flighty or foolish : CRACKPOT

2**harebrain** \"\ *adj* : HAREBRAINED

harebrained \'=¦=\ *adj* [1*hare* + *brained*] : FLIGHTY, FOOLISH, CRACKBRAINED — **hare·brained·ness** \'=¦brānnəs *also* -ndnəs\ *n* -ES

hared up *adj* [perh. alter. (influenced by 1*hair*) of *het up;* fr. the tendency of the hair on a person's head or an animal's back to stand on end as a result of extreme excitement] *dial* : being in a state of angry excitement : IRATE

hare–finder \'=,==\ *n, Brit* : one that goes ahead of a coursing party in order to start the hare ⟨you stare about like a *hare=finder* —Thomas Shadwell⟩

harefoot \'=,=\ *n* : a long narrow close-toed foot characteristic of some dogs, esp. the American foxhound

harefooted \'=¦==\ *adj* [1*hare* + *footed*] **1** : moving swiftly : FLEET **2** : having a harefoot

harehearted \'=¦==\ *adj* : easily frightened : TIMID

hare kangaroo *n* : HARE WALLABY

harelip \'=¦=\ *n* **1** : a lip congenitally cleft usu. in the center of the upper one but sometimes cleft both sides of center **2** : the deformity that a harelip exhibits

harelipped \'=¦=\ *adj* : having a harelip

harelipped bat *n* : a large tropical American fish-eating bat (genus *Noctilio*) exhibiting marked sexual dichromatism with the males orange-rufous and the females dark brown to drab

1**ha·rem** *or* **ha·ram** *also* **ha·rim** \'harəm, 'her- *sometimes* 'hār-, 'här-, hə'rēm\ *n* -S [Ar *ḥarīm* harem, anything forbidden or sacred & Ar *ḥaram* harem, sanctuary] **1 a** : a house or part of a house allotted to women in a Muslim household and usu. designed for maximum seclusion — called also *seraglio, zenana* **b** : the family of wives, concubines, female relatives, and servants occupying a harem **2** : a group usu. of women associated with one man ⟨a literary lion with his ~⟩ **3** : a Muslim sacred place (as a mosque) forbidden to non-Muslims **4** : a group of females controlled by one male — used of polygamous animals (as the fur seal, pheasant, wild horse)

2**harem** \"\ *adj* : of a style or design resembling that associated with a Turkish harem — used esp. of a woman's dress having a full skirt with the lower edge gathered on a narrow band and then turned under

ha·rem·lik \-m,lik\ *n* -S [Turk *haremlik*, fr. *harem* (fr. Ar *ḥarīm* & Ar *ḥaram*) + *-lik* place] : HAREM 1a

harem slipper *n* : BABOUCHE

ha·ren·gi·form \hə'renjə,fȯrm\ *adj* [*harengi-* (fr. NL *harengus* — specific epithet of the herring *Clupea harengus* —, fr. ML *harengus* herring, of Gmc origin and akin to MD *harinc*, *hareng* herring) + *-form* — more at HERRING] : having the shape of a herring

ha·ren·gu·la \hə'reŋgyələ\ *n, cap* [NL, fr. ML *harengus* herring + NL *-ula*] : a nearly cosmopolitan genus of small herrings (family Clupeidae)

hares *pl of* HARE, *pres 3d sing of* HARE

hare's apparatus \'ha(a)(ə)rz-\ *n, usu cap H* [after Robert *Hare* †1858 Am. chemist] : an apparatus for comparing the densities of liquids in two separate vessels by means of their rise in two graduated vertical tubes immersed at their lower ends in the liquids and connected at the top by a third tube to which suction is applied

hare's–beard \'=,=\ *n, pl* **hare's–beards** : MULLEIN

hare's–ear \'=,=\ *n, pl* **hare's–ears** **1** : a European annual herb (*Bupleurum rotundifolium*) with perfoliate leaves that resemble rabbit ears and small yellowish flowers **2** *also* **hare's=ear mustard** : a glabrous annual herb (*Conringia orientalis*) having sessile entire leaves with prominent basal lobes

hare's eye *n* : LAGOPHTHALMOS

hare's–foot \'=,=\ *or* **hare's–foot clover** *n, pl* **hare's–foots** *or* **hare's–foot clovers** : RABBIT-FOOT CLOVER

hare's–foot fern *n, pl* **hare's–foot ferns** **1** : a fern (*Davallia canariensis*) of the Canary islands and Madeira having a soft gray hairy rootstock **2** : an Australian fern (*Davallia pyxidata*) **3** : a bristle fern (*Trichomanes boschianum*) **4** : SERPENT FERN

hare's–foot trefoil *n, pl* **hare's–foot trefoils** : RABBIT-FOOT CLOVER

hare's–lettuce \'=,==\ *n, pl* **hare's–lettuces** : an annual sow thistle (*Sonchus oleraceus*)

hare's–tail \'=,=\ *n, pl* **hare's–tails** **1** : HARE'S-TAIL GRASS **2** : COTTON GRASS

hare's–tail grass *n, pl* **hare's–tail grasses** : a European grass (*Lagurus ovatus*) with florets in a spike that resembles a hare's tail naturalized in California and New Zealand and used for dry bouquets

hare's–tail rush *n, pl* **hare's–tail rushes** : COTTON GRASS

hare system \'ha(a)|(ə)r- 'he|, |ə-\ *n* [after Thomas *Hare* †1891 Eng. political reformer] : a system of proportional representation that aims to achieve party representation in the closest proportion to actual voting strength by transferring votes beyond those needed to elect a candidate from him to the next indicated choice — compare LIST SYSTEM, PREFERENTIAL VOTING, SINGLE TRANSFERABLE VOTE

hare wallaby *n* : any of several small Australian wallabies (genus *Lagorchestes*) that resemble hares and have hairy noses

harewood \'=,=\ *n* [alter. of earlier *aire-wood*, fr. obs. E *ayre*, *ayer* harewood (perh. fr. Friulian *ayar* maple tree, fr. L *acer*) + E *wood* — more at ACER] **1** : a greenish gray figured cabinet wood obtained by chemical treatment and dyeing of sycamore maple and sometimes other maples — called also *gray harewood* **2** : a strongly figured tropical American wood initially yellow but seasoning to silvery gray with greenish markings, obtained from a tree of the genus *Xanthoxylum*, and much used by 18th century cabinetmakers but now rarely available

har·fang \'här,faŋ\ *n* -S [Sw *harfång*, lit., hare catcher, fr. *hare* (fr. OSw *hari*) + *fånga* to catch, fr. OSw *fanga*, fr. MLG *vangen;* akin to OE *hara* hare and to OHG *fāhan* to catch — more at HARE, PACT] : SNOWY OWL

har·grave kite \'här,grāv-\ *n, usu cap H* [after Lawrence *Hargrave* †1915 Australian pioneer in aviation] : BOX KITE

ha·ri·a·li grass \,härē'älē-\ *also* **ha·ri·a·la grass** \-lə-\ *n* [Hindi *hariyālī*, fr. Skt *haritālikā*] *India* : BERMUDA GRASS

ha·ri·a·na \,härē'änə\ *n* [fr. *Hariana*, town in northwest India] **1** *usu cap* : an Indian breed of large rugged milk and draft cattle included among the Brahmans in American studbooks **2** -S *often cap* : an animal of the Hariana breed

1**har·i·cot** \'harə,kō, -,kät, *usu* -äd·+V\ *or* **haricot bean** *n* -S [F, perh. fr. *haricot* stew] : the ripe seed or the unripe pod of any of several beans of the genus *Phaseolus* (esp. *P. vulgaris*) used as a vegetable

2**haricot** \"\ *n* -S [F, fr. MF, prob. irreg. fr. *harigoter* to cut in pieces, fr. OF, perh. of Gmc origin; akin to OHG *heriōn* to lay waste — more at HARRY] : a stew esp. of mutton or lamb and vegetables

har·i·jan \'harə,jan\ *n* -S *often cap* [Skt *harijana* person belonging to the god Vishnu, fr. *Hari* Vishnu + *jana* person — more at KIN] : a member of the outcaste group in India : UNTOUCHABLE — used esp. by followers of Gandhi

hari–kari *var of* HARA-KIRI

harim *var of* HAREM

haring *pres part of* HARE

har·i·o·la·tion \,harēə'lāshən\ *n* -S [L *hariolation-, hariolatio* action of prophesying, fr. *hariolatus* (past part of *hariolari* to prophesy, divine) + *-ion-, -io* -ion; prob. akin to L *haruspex* soothsayer, diviner — more at YARN] : the act or process of deduction : GUESSWORK ⟨facts as distinguished from what classical scholars call ~*s* —George Saintsbury⟩

har·i·son's yellow rose \'harəsənz-\ *n, usu cap H* [after Mr. *Harison*, 19th cent. Am. horticulturist] : a hybrid rose (*Rosa harisonii*) with yellow flowers originating as a cross between the Scotch rose and the Austrian brier

1**hark** \'härk, 'hȧk\ *vb* -ED/-ING/-S [ME *herken;* akin to OFris *herkia, harkia* to listen, MD *horken, hoorken*, OHG *hōrechen*, and perh. to OHG *hōren* to hear — more at HEAR] *vt* **1** *archaic* : to give ear to : listen to ⟨~ what he himself here saith —William Beveridge⟩ **2** *Brit* : to urge to go ahead or to return — used with directional adverb ⟨~*ed* forward his pack of hounds —G.W.Dasent⟩ ⟨there is but one that ~*s* me back —Henry Taylor⟩ ~ *vi* **1** : to pay close attention : LISTEN ⟨when . . . some far cry came faintly through the wooded hills I have seen him lift his hand and bid us ~ —Irving Bacheller⟩ — often used with *to* ⟨only natural for them to ~ to him —G.G. Black⟩ **2** *chiefly Scot* : WHISPER

2**hark** \"\ *n* -S : a shout of encouragement or guidance to hounds

hark back *vi* **1** *of a hunting dog* : to retrace a course until a scent is regained **2 a** : to turn back to an earlier topic or circumstance ⟨*hark back* . . . to a passage already quoted —Susanne K. Langer⟩ ⟨don't *hark back* to the old days unless you can be amusing about them —Agnes Rogers⟩ **b** : to go back to something as an origin or source ⟨archaisms that *hark back* to the early days of colonialism —C.J.Crowley⟩ ⟨this proposition *harks back* to Locke and Smith —*Quarterly Jour. of Economics*⟩

hark–back \'=,=\ *n* -S [*hark back*] : a reversion or reference to something past ⟨this *hark-back* to the caveman code —Philip Gibbs⟩ ⟨*hark-backs* to the yesteryear lore of the theater —Abel Green⟩

harken *var of* HEARKEN

1**harl** *or* **harle** \'(h)ärl, '(h)ȧl\ *vb* -ED/-ING/-S [ME *harlen* to drag] *vt* **1** *dial Brit* : to drag, scrape, or pull (an object) usu. along the ground **2** *chiefly Scot* : to plaster (a surface) with roughcast ⟨the ~*ed* walls with which for many generations the Scots had finished their houses —Ian Finlay⟩ ~ *vi, chiefly Brit* : to troll for fish ⟨~*ing* for spring salmon —*Atlantic*⟩

2**harl** *or* **harle** \'hȧl\ *n* -S *Brit* : roughcast wall facing

3**harl** \'(h)ärl, '(h)ȧl\ *vt* -ED/-ING/-S [ME *harlen* to entangle] *dial Eng* **1** : to snarl up : ENTANGLE **2** *or* **harle** : to thread one leg of (a dead rabbit) through the other for ease in carrying

4**harl** \"\ *n* -S *dial Eng* : a tangled mass : SNARL

5**harl** \'härl\ *n* -S [ME *herle*, prob. fr. MLG *herle, harle*] **1** *or* **harle** : a fiber in a stalk of flax or hemp **2** : HERL

har·lan's hawk \'härlənz-\ *n, usu cap 1st H* [after Richard *Harlan* †1843 Am. physician and naturalist] : a hawk (*Buteo harlani*) of the southern U.S. that is similar to but darker than the red-tailed hawk

har·lech \'här,lek\ *adj, usu cap* [fr. *Harlech*, Wales] : of, relating to, or constituting a subdivision of the European Cambrian — see GEOLOGIC TIME table

har·lem blue \'härləm-\ *n, usu cap H* [*Haarlem*, city in the Netherlands] : ANTWERP BLUE

har·lem·ite \'härlə,mīt\ *n* -S *usu cap* [*Harlem*, a district of Manhattan borough, New York City + E *-ite*] : a native or resident of the district of Manhattan borough, New York City, north of Central Park between 8th Avenue and the East and Harlem rivers

1**har·le·quin** \'härlək(w)ən, 'hȧl-\ *n* -S [alter. (influenced by obs. F *harlequin*, fr. MF, fr. OIt *arlecchino*) of earlier *harlicken*, modif. of OIt *arlecchino*, fr. MF *Helquin, Hannequin, Hennequin*, leader of a troop of malevolent spirits popularly believed to fly through the air at night, fr. OF *Hellequin, Hielekin, Hierlekin*, prob. fr. (assumed) ME *Herle king* (whence ML *Herla rex*) King Herle, mythical figure who may orig. have been identical with Woden, chief god of the Germanic peoples] **1 a** *usu cap* : a quick-witted zany servant who is a stock character in commedia dell'arte, appears variously in European and American pantomime and ballet as a clown, a foppish simpleton, a magician, and the languishing lover of Columbine, and usu. wears a mask and parti-colored tights and carries a lath sword **b** : BUFFOON **2** : HARLEQUIN DUCK **3 a** : a variegated pattern (as of a textile) **b** : a combination of colors in patches on a solid ground (as in the coats of some dogs) ⟨a Great Dane's handsome ~⟩

harlequin 1a

2**harlequin** \"\ *vt* -ED/-ING/-S : to make a patchwork of : MOTTLE ⟨his face was ~*ed* with patches of some white cream he used for his complexion —Frederick Buechner⟩

3**harlequin** \"\ *adj* **1** : of a type or style inspired by or characteristic of Harlequin ⟨~ hat⟩ ⟨a ~ day, a strayed reveler from April, in glittering lozenges of blue and silver —Elinor Wylie⟩ **2** : of variegated usu. brilliant color and pattern ⟨~ fish⟩

har·le·quin·ade \,härlək(w)ə'nād, ,hȧl-\ *n* -S [modif. (influenced by *harlequin*) of F *arlequinade*, fr. *arlequin* harlequin (fr. MF, fr. OIt *arlecchino*) + *-ade*] **1 a** : a play or pantomime in which the harlequin has a leading role; *esp* : an introductory burlesque scene dominated by a clown and a harlequin **b** : an extravaganza ballet that features a dancing clown and other figures of fantasy **2** : a plotless comedy : FARCE ⟨incomparably at his best in the audacious ~ —*Atlantic*⟩ ⟨life is . . . a ~ written by a madman —H.J.Laski⟩

harlequin beetle *n* : a very large tropical American longicorn beetle (*Acrocinus longimanus*) having very long legs and antennae and intricately patterned red, black, and gray wing covers

harlequin bug *also* **harlequin cabbage bug** *n* : a black stinkbug (*Murgantia histrionica*) brilliantly marked with red, orange, and yellow that is destructive to cabbage and related plants in tropical America and the warmer parts of the U.S.

harlequin duck *n* : a small variegated sea duck (*Histrionicus histrionicus*) chiefly of northern No. America, Iceland, and Siberia with the male being chiefly blue with many white markings and red-brown sides

har·le·quin·ism \'härlək(w)ə,nizəm\ *n* -S : an action or expression characteristic of a harlequin

harlequin opal *n* : an opal with small angular patches of brilliant color on a reddish ground

harlequin pigeon *n* : FLOCK PIGEON

harlequin quail *n* **1** : a small African quail (*Coturnix delegorguei*) that frequents low-lying grassy tropical areas and is a highly regarded game and table bird **2** : any of various chiefly tropical American quails (genus *Cyrtonyx*) having the sides of the head conspicuously patterned in black and white

harlequin snake *n* : CORAL SNAKE; *esp* : BEAD SNAKE

harlequin table *n* [prob. so called fr. a resemblance between the movable set of drawers and some of the stage machinery of the commedia dell'arte] : a little 18th century English table convertible into a writing desk by means of a set of drawers pulled up from the level top

harling *n* -S [fr. gerund of 1*harl*] *Brit* : a method of angling for salmon in a large river by trailing a fly behind a boat while it is rowed back and forth from bank to bank

1**har·lot** \'härlət, 'hȧl-, *usu* -əd·+V\ *n* -S [ME *harlot, herlot*, fr. OF *herlot*] **1** *obs* : one of the riffraff : ROGUE, VAGABOND, KNAVE ⟨called him openly "beggarly ~ and cutthroat" —*Durham Depositions*⟩; *specif* : FORNICATOR ⟨the ~ king is quite beyond my arm —Shak.⟩ **2** : a disreputable woman; *specif* : PROSTITUTE

2**harlot** \"\ *adj* **1** : of or relating to a harlot ⟨~ house⟩ **2** : not subject to control : FICKLE ⟨pursuing the ~ goddess Fame —W.A.White⟩

3**harlot** \"\ *vi* -ED/-ING/-S : PROSTITUTE

har·lot·ry \-lətrē, -ri\ *n* -ES [ME *harlotrie*, fr. 1*harlot* + *-rie* -ry] **1** *obs* : coarse or ribald speech or action : OBSCENITY **2** : PROSTITUTION **3** : an unprincipled or immoral woman : BAGGAGE 4 ⟨he sups tonight with a ~ —Shak.⟩ **4** : tawdry attractiveness : VULGARITY ⟨brightly rouged and painted — but without ~, with a careful art —William Sansom⟩

harls *pres 3d sing of* HARL, *pl of* HARL

1**harm** \'härm, 'hȧm\ *n* -S [ME, fr. OE *hearm;* akin to OHG *harm* disgrace, injury, ON *harmr* grief, OSlav *sramŭ* shame] **1 a** : physical or mental damage : INJURY ⟨safety glass protects passengers from ~⟩ ⟨where the dune belt and the beach are both wide the sea did little ~ —J.A.Steers⟩ **b** : MISCHIEF, HURT, DISSERVICE ⟨his preelection declaration of independence had done him no ~ —Virginia Prewett⟩ **2** : an act or instance of injury ⟨guess at intents and assume ~*s* —Burges Johnson⟩; *specif* : a material and tangible detriment or loss to a person, whether or not the law grants a remedy — distinguished from *injury* **syn** see INJURY — **out of harm's way** : in a safe place : remote from sources of injury ⟨a loudspeaker set high *out of harm's way* —Evelyn Waugh⟩

2**harm** \"\ *vt* -ED/-ING/-S [ME *harmen*, fr. OE *hearmian*, fr. *hearm*, n.] : to cause hurt or damage to : INJURE ⟨the national interest . . . was gravely ~*ed* by this attack —Elmer Davis⟩ **syn** see INJURE

3**harm** \"\ *adj* [1*harm*] *South* : DISRESPECTFUL, UNKIND, HARMFUL ⟨never said a ~ word against your daddy —T.H.Phillips⟩

har·mal \'härməl\ *or* **har·ma·la** \-lə\ *or* **har·mel** \-məl\ *n* -S [NL *harmala*, fr. Gk, perh. of Sem origin; akin to Ar *ḥarmalah* harmal] : an herb (*Peganum harmala*) of India and the Levant with strong-scented seeds that yield several alkaloids and are used as a vermifuge and stimulant

har·ma·line \'härmə,lēn, -,lən\ *n* -S [ISV *harmal* + *-ine*] : a crystalline alkaloid $C_{13}H_{14}N_2O$ found in harmal seeds; dihydro-harmine

har·ma·lol \-,lȯl, -,lōl\ *n* -S [ISV *harmal* + *-ol*] : a brown crystalline phenolic alkaloid $C_{12}H_{12}N_2O$ found in harmal seeds

har·man \'härmən\ *also* **harman beck** *n* -S [origin unknown] *archaic* : CONSTABLE, BEADLE ⟨not the lad to betray anyone to the *harman beck* —Sir Walter Scott⟩

har·mat·tan \,härmə'tan, här'mad·ən\ *n* -S [Twi *haramata*, perh. fr. Ar *ḥarām* forbidden or evil thing; akin to Ar *ḥaram* harem] : a dry dust-laden wind blowing from the interior on the Atlantic coast of Africa in some seasons

harm·er \'härmər\ *n* -S : one that harms

harm·ful \'härmfəl, 'hȧm-\ *adj* [ME, fr. 1*harm* + *-ful*] : DAMAGING, TROUBLESOME, INJURIOUS ⟨~ drug⟩ ⟨~ influence⟩

harm·ful·ly \-f(ə)lē, -li\ *adv* : in a harmful manner

harm·ful·ness *n* -ES : the quality or state of being harmful

har·mine \'här,mēn, -,mən\ *n* -S [ISV *harmal* + *-ine*] : a white crystalline alkaloid $C_{13}H_{12}N_2O$ found in harmal seeds; harmalol methyl ether

harm·less \'härmləs, 'hȧm-\ *adj* [ME *harmles*, fr. 1*harm* + *-les, -lees* -less] **1** : free from harm : UNHURT **2** : free of guilt : INNOCENT ⟨any child or ~ thing —W.H.Davies⟩ **3** : free from liability or loss — often used in the phrase *to save harmless* or *to hold harmless* ⟨the company shall indemnify and save ~ each member of the committee against any and all expenses —C.M.Winslow⟩ **4** : free of or lacking capacity or intent to injure : INNOCUOUS ⟨the first ball was ~ —Dorothy Sayers⟩ ⟨~ craze for the small lions of literary society —W.S.Maugham⟩ ⟨~ joke⟩

harmless error *n* : a trivial technical error of law not requiring in the interests of justice a reversal of a judgment or the setting aside of a verdict or a new trial

harm·less·ly *adv* : in a harmless manner

harm·less·ness *n* -ES : the quality or state of being harmless

har·mol·i·ta \här'mäləd·ə\ *n, cap* [NL] : a genus of chalcid flies (family Eurytomidae) including numerous forms with larvae that feed in the stems of cereal grasses and weaken and distort them — see WHEAT JOINTWORM

har·mo·nia \här'mōnēə, -nyə\ *n* -S [NL, fr. Gk, harmonic suture, joint — more at HARMONY] : HARMONIC SUTURE

harmoniacal *adj* [LL *harmoniacus* musical (fr. L *harmonia* harmony) + E *-al*] *obs* : HARMONIOUS

har·mo·ni·al \här'mōnēəl\ *adj* [L *harmonia* + E *-al*] *archaic* : HARMONIOUS

1**har·mon·ic** \(')här¦mänik, (')hȧ¦-, -nēk\ *or* **har·mon·i·cal** \-nəkəl\ *adj* [*harmonic* fr. L *harmonicus*, fr. Gk *harmonikos*, fr. *harmonia* harmony + *-ikos* -ic; *harmonical* fr. L *harmonicus* + E *-al*] **1** *archaic* : of or relating to music : MUSICAL ⟨where the ~ meetings take place —Charles Dickens⟩; *specif* : relating to the melody of ancient music as distinct from its rhythm **2** : of or relating to harmony as distinguished from melody or rhythm ⟨subtleties of ~ change and tonality —Ralph Hill⟩ **3 a** : of agreeable musical consonance : HARMONIOUS ⟨~ chant⟩ **b** : pleasing to the ear : HARMONIZED ⟨great ~ orchestral effects of the older verse —J.L.Lowes⟩ **4** : expressible in terms of sine or cosine functions — see HARMONIC PROGRESSION **5** : of an integrated nature : CONGRUOUS ⟨a creative, ~, loving human being —M.F.A.Montagu⟩; *specif* : having the general proportions of the body in harmony with each other (as elongated face with elongated skull) **6** : of or relating to harmonics ⟨size of the resonating cavity cannot be the only determinant of the ~ response —Robert Donington⟩; *specif* : sounding an octave or more higher than another organ stop of similar length ⟨~ flute⟩

2**harmonic** \='==\ *n* -S **1 a** : one of a series of overtones or upper partials; *esp* : one produced by a vibration frequency which is an integral multiple of the vibration rate producing the fundamental ⟨the ear possesses the very odd characteristic of imagining the existence of the fundamental even when it is not present, if the ~*s* are strong —Oliver Read⟩ — compare NODE 5 **b** : a flutelike tone produced on a stringed instrument (as violin or harp) by touching a vibrating string at a nodal point causing one of the vibrating sections to determine the higher pitch in the harmonic series in direct proportion to the vibration frequency of the vibrating segment — called also *flageolet tone* **2** : a component frequency of a harmonic motion (as of an electromagnetic wave) that is an integral multiple of the fundamental frequency ⟨the second ~ has a frequency that is two times that of the fundamental⟩ ⟨if the current wave is analyzed mathematically, it is found to have a third ~ about one-third the amplitude of the fundamental 60-cycle wave —B.F.Bailey & J.S.Gault⟩ ⟨at the frequencies used for television signals, more so than on the broadcast bands, the second, third, and fourth ~*s* of the local oscillator in a superheterodyne receiver are liable to interfere with other sections of the receiver —*Television & Radar Encyc.*⟩

har·mon·i·ca \här'mänəkə, hȧ'-, -nēkə\ *n* -S [alter. (influenced by 1*harmonic*) of *armonica*] **1** : GLASS HARMONICA **2** : an instrument of graduated strips of glass or metal struck with hammers **3** : a small rectangular wind instrument with free metallic reeds recessed in adjacent air slots along its length from which alternate tones of the scale are sounded by exhaling and inhaling and chords or single notes are produced depending on the number of slots covered by the mouth — called also *mouth organ*

harmonica 3

har·mon·i·cal·ly \-nək(ə)lē, -nēk-, -li\ *adv* **1** *obs* : HARMONIOUSLY ⟨the same spirit ~ works in all believers through the world —John Flavel⟩ **2** : in respect to relations or properties bearing some resemblance to those of musical consonances **3** : in respect to harmony as distinguished from melody ⟨feels music melodically before he feels it ~ —Neville Cardus⟩ **4** : in harmonic progression or division

har·mon·i·cal·ness *n* -ES : the quality or state of being harmonic

harmonic analysis *n* : the approximate expression of a periodic function known only for some values of the independent variable in a finite series of sines and cosines

harmonic analyzer *n* : a machine for the automatic resolution of periodic curves into the component sine curves of which they may be regarded as the resultants

harmonic close *n* : CADENCE 2b

harmonic conjugates *n pl* : the two points that divide a line segment internally and externally in the same ratio

harmonic distortion *n* : distortion in which harmonics of an input signal are produced in an amplifier and appear in the output along with the amplified input signal

harmonic division *n* **:** the division of a line segment at two points internally and externally in the same ratio — compare HARMONIC CONJUGATES

har·mon·i·chord \här'mänə,kȯrd\ *n* -S [F *harmonicorde*, fr. *harmonie* harmony (fr. OF *armonie*) + *-corde* -chord — more at HARMONY] **:** a keyboard instrument in which a sustained string tone is produced by the action of a rotating wooden cylinder on the strings — compare SOSTINENTE PIANOFORTE

harmonic interval *n* **:** the pitch relation between simultaneous musical tones

har·mon·i·cism \här'mänə,sizəm\ *n* -S **:** the quality or state of being harmonic

harmonic law *n* **:** the third of Kepler's laws of planetary motion

harmonic mean *n* **1 :** the reciprocal of the arithmetic mean of the reciprocals of two or more quantities **2 :** one of the terms between the first and last terms of a harmonic progression

harmonic minor scale *n* **:** a minor scale like the natural form except that the 7th tone is raised by a half step (as A-B-C-D-E-F-G♯-A)

harmonic motion *n* **:** a vibratory motion that has one frequency or amplitude (as that of a sounding violin string or swinging pendulum) or a vibratory motion that is composed of two or more such simple vibratory motions— see SIMPLE HARMONIC MOTION

har·mon·i·con \här'mänəkən, hä'-, -nēk-\ *n, pl* **harmoni·ca** \-kə\ [Gk *harmonikon*, neut. of *harmonikos* musical — more at HARMONIC] **1 :** HARMONICA **2 :** ORCHESTRION

harmonic progression *n* **:** a progression the reciprocals of whose terms form an arithmetic progression

harmonic row *or* **harmonic range** *n* **:** a set of four collinear points — compare HARMONIC CONJUGATES

har·mon·ics \här'mäniks, hä'-, -nēks\ *n pl but usu sing in constr* **:** the doctrine or science of musical sounds

harmonic sequence of vowels : VOWEL HARMONY

harmonic series *n* **1 :** the divergent series 1+½+⅓+¼+⅕+ . . . **2 :** a series of partial tones consisting of a fundamental tone or first harmonic and all the overtones whose frequency ratio to it can be expressed in whole numbers, these harmonics usu. being consecutively numbered

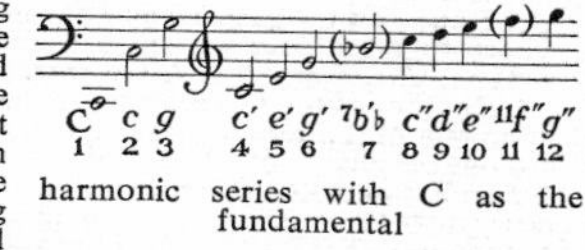

harmonic series with C as the fundamental

harmonic sign *or* **harmonic mark** *n* **:** a small circle ○ placed over a note in stringed-instrument music to indicate that it is to be played as a harmonic

harmonic stop *n* **:** a pipe-organ stop composed of pipes so constructed as to sound an octave or more higher than regular pipes of similar length

harmonic suture *n* **:** an immovable body joint formed by the contact of relatively smooth surfaces (as bones of the skull)

harmonic synthesizer *n* **:** a mechanical device (as a tide-predicting machine) that combines differing harmonics and graphs the result

harmonic theory *n* **:** a postulate in phonetics: the reinforcing vibrations produced in the superglottic cavities in vowel articulation are harmonics of the fundamental vocal-cord note — compare FORMANT, INHARMONIC THEORY

harmonies *pl of* HARMONY

har·mo·ni·ous \(')här'mōnēəs, (')hä'-, -nyəs\ *adj* [MF *armonieux*, *harmonieux*, fr. *armonie, harmonie* harmony — more at HARMONY] **1 :** musically concordant **:** agreeably consonant **2 :** having the component parts agreeably related to each other **:** CONGRUOUS ⟨~ medley of small vaulted chambers —Norman Douglas⟩ **3 :** marked by accord in sentiment or action **:** COMPATIBLE ⟨~ relationship between church and state —H.D.Hazeltine⟩ — **har·mo·ni·ous·ness** *n* -ES

har·mo·ni·ous·ly *adv* **:** in a harmonious manner **:** COMPATIBLY ⟨for such a large group of relatives to coexist ~ . . is an accomplishment —Freeman Lincoln⟩

har·mon·i·phon \här'mänə,fän\ *also* **har·mon·i·phone** \-,fōn\ *n* -S [prob. fr. F *harmoniphon*, fr. *harmonie* harmony (fr. OF *armonie*) + *-phon* (fr. Gk *phōnē* sound) — more at HARMONY, BAN] **:** an obsolete wind instrument consisting of a series of reed pipes blown with a single mouthpiece and controlled by means of a keyboard, the tone resembling that of the oboe

har·mo·nist \'härmənəst, 'häm-\ *n* -S [*harmony* + *-ist*] **1 a :** a member of a school of theorists in ancient Greece basing the principles of music on the subjective effects of tones rather than on their mathematical relations **b :** one who composes or performs music **c :** one skilled in harmony **2 :** one who shows the agreement or harmony of corresponding passages of different literary works (as the Gospels) ⟨editorial ~s of the Pentateuch —*Interpreter's Bible*⟩ **3 :** HARMONIZER **4** *usu cap* [*Harmony*, community in Pennsylvania + E *-ist*] **:** HARMONITE

har·mo·nis·tic \¦==¦nistik, -tēk\ *adj* **:** of, relating to, or characteristic of a harmony or harmonist ⟨~ methods⟩ — **har·mo·nis·ti·cal·ly** \-tək(ə)lē\ *adv*

har·mo·nite \'härmə,nīt\ *n* -S *usu cap* [*Harmony*, community in Pennsylvania founded in 1803 by the Harmonites + E *-ite*] **:** a member of an 18th century German communal religious sect that settled in Pennsylvania in 1803 — called also *Rappist*

har·mo·ni·um \här'mōnēəm, hä'-, -nyəm\ *n* -S [F, fr. *harmonie* harmony, fr. OF *armonie*] **:** REED ORGAN; *specif* **:** a keyboard instrument in which the tones are produced by forcing air through free metallic reeds by means of a bellows — contrasted with *American organ*

har·mo·niz·able \'härmə,nīzəbəl\ *adj* **:** capable of being brought into harmony

har·mo·ni·za·tion \,härmənə'zāshən, ,häm-, -nī-\ *n* -S **1 :** the quality or state of being in harmony ⟨style of ~⟩ **2 :** an act or instance of producing harmony ⟨has developed a wonderful faculty for ~ —Herbert Read⟩; *specif* **:** a piece of harmonized music ⟨~ for string quartet⟩

har·mo·nize \'härmə,nīz, 'häm-\ *vb* -ED/-ING/-S *see -ize in Explan Notes* [MF *harmoniser* to bring into harmony, fr. *armonie, harmonie* + *-iser* -ize] *vi* **1 :** to play or sing in harmony ⟨four small children who have been *harmonizing* in the next compartment since 6:00 a.m. —Bennett Cerf⟩ **2 a :** to be in accord **:** CORRELATE ⟨designed to ~ with normal feeding operations —W.F.Brown b.1903⟩ **b :** to become pleasingly related **:** BLEND ⟨furnishings and architecture ~ —Edgar Kaufmann⟩; *specif* **:** to unite in harmony ⟨the tenor and alto parts ~⟩ ~ *vt* **1 :** to bring into consonance **:** relate harmoniously ⟨~ the interests of his various properties —J.B. Hedges⟩ **2 :** to bring into accord **:** RECONCILE ⟨~ its practices . . . with its professed ideals —Vera M. Dean⟩ **3 :** to provide or accompany with harmony (as a melody) **syn** see AGREE

har·mo·niz·er \-zə(r)\ *n* -S **:** one that harmonizes

har·mon·o·graph \här'mänə,graf\ *n* [ISV *harmono-* (fr. Gk *harmonia* concord, harmony) + *-graph*] **:** an instrument for combining two or more vibrations usu. of two pendulums at right angles to each other and recording them in a single curve — compare LISSAJOUS FIGURE

har·mo·ny \'härmənē, 'häm-, -ni\ *n* -ES [ME *armonye*, fr. MF *armonie*, fr. OF, fr. L *harmonia*, fr. Gk, joint, concord, harmony, fr. *harmos* joint, fastening — more at ARM] **1 a** *archaic* **:** tuneful sound **:** MELODY ⟨ten thousand harps that tuned angelic *harmonies* —John Milton⟩ **b :** musicality of language ⟨tonal ~ of the poem —C.S.Kilby⟩ **2 a :** the combination of simultaneous musical notes into a chord (as a triad) **b :** the structure of a piece of music according to the composition and progression of its chords — compare MELODY, RHYTHM **c :** the science of the structure, relation, and progression of chords in homophonic composition **3 :** combination into a consistent whole **:** INTEGRATION ⟨~ of man and the machine in modern war —George Barrett⟩ **4 a :** CORRESPONDENCE, AGREEMENT, ACCORD ⟨the fullest freedom . . . comes when our desires are in ~ with those of our neighbors —A.H.Compton⟩ **b :** internal calm **:** TRANQUILLITY ⟨the moral task for man, if he is to achieve ~, is to . . . assure the supremacy of the good —Norman Kelman⟩ **5 :** a systematic arrangement of parallel literary passages (as of the Gospels) for the purpose of showing agreement or harmony **6 :** HARMONIC SUTURE **7 :** the arrangement of parts in pleasing relation to each other ⟨~ of his face —Alvin Redman⟩; *specif* **:** the orderly combination of colors resulting in an aesthetically pleasing general effect ⟨relations of contrast and ~ —John Dewey⟩ — compare COLOR BALANCE

harmony of the spheres : a doctrine promulgated by the Pythagoreans that the celestial spheres are separated by intervals corresponding to the relative lengths of strings that produce harmonious tones — compare MUSIC OF THE SPHERES

harmony of vowels : VOWEL HARMONY

har·most \'här,mäst\ *n* -S [Gk *harmostēs*, fr. *harmozein* to join together, govern; akin to Gk *harmos* joint, fastening — more at ARM] **:** a governor appointed by the Spartans over subject towns and peoples

har·mo·tome \'härmə,tōm\ *n* [F, fr. Gk *harmos* joint + *tomē* section, fr. *temnein* to cut; fr. its occurrence in crystalline form with an octahedron dividing parallel to the plane that passes through the terminal edges — more at TOME] **:** a mineral $(Ba,K)(Al,Si)_2Si_6O_{16}.6H_2O$ consisting of a hydrous silicate of aluminum, barium, and potassium

harms *pl of* HARM, *pres 3d sing of* HARM

¹harn \'härn\ *n* -S [ME *hernes, harnes* (pl.), of Scand origin; akin to ON *hjarni* brain; akin to OHG *hirni* brain, MD *hersene* brain, ON *hjarsi* crown of the head — more at CEREBRAL] *chiefly Scot* **:** BRAIN **:** BRAINS — usu. used in pl.

²harn \"\ *n* -S [by contr.] **:** ²HARDEN

¹har·ness \'härnəs, 'hàn-\ *n* -ES *often attrib* [ME *herneis, harneis* baggage of an army or of a group of travelers, gear of a riding horse, armor, furniture, equipment, fr. OF, prob. fr. (assumed) ON *hernest* provisions for an army, fr. ON *herr* army + *nest* provisions; akin to OE *nest* food, provisions, OHG *-nest* food, *ginesan* to survive — more at HARRY, NOSTALGIA] **1 a** (1) **:** the gear or tackle other than a yoke of a draft animal (as a horse, dog, or goat) (2) **:** TACKLE, GEAR, EQUIPMENT **:** the mounting or finishing parts (as of the mechanism and gear by which a large bell is suspended and rung) **b** (1) **:** occupational surroundings **:** work routine ⟨get back into ~ after a vacation⟩ ⟨many girls . . . take on the formidable task of running in double ~, embracing both marriage and a career —Robert Reid⟩ (2) **:** close association ⟨ability to work in ~ with others —R.P.Brooks⟩ **c :** something that resembles a harness ⟨knee ~⟩ ⟨parachute ~⟩ ⟨window-washer's ~⟩ ⟨toddler on a ~⟩; *specif* **:** a prefabricated system of wiring with the necessary insulation and terminals ready to be attached (as in an ignition or lighting system) **2 :** defensive military equipment for horse or man; *specif* **:** ARMOR ⟨smote the king of Israel between the joints of the ~ —I Kings 22:34 (AV)⟩ **3 :** clothing esp. of a specialized type ⟨a policeman's ~⟩ ⟨haven't seen her in anything but hospital ~ for a long time —L.C.Douglas⟩ **4 :** a part of the loom which holds the heddles and controls their motion and by which the warp threads are raised or depressed to form a shed — called also *leaf* — **in harness** *adv* **:** on duty ⟨constantly on call even when not *in harness*⟩ — compare *die in harness* at ¹DIE

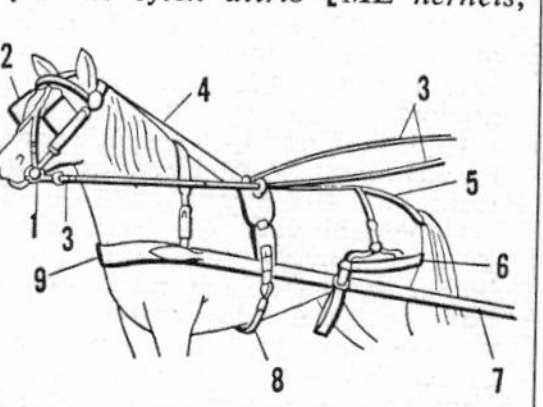

harness: *1* bit, *2* blinder, *3, 3* reins, *4* checkrein, *5* crupper, *6* breeching, *7* trace, *8* bellyband or girth, *9* breast collar

²harness \"\ *vt* -ED/-ING/-ES [ME *herneisen, harneisen*, fr. *herneis, harneis*, n.] **1** *archaic* **:** to dress or equip for battle **:** ARM ⟨~ yourselves for the war —John Bunyan⟩ **2 a :** to put a harness on ⟨~ a horse⟩ **b :** to attach by means of a harness ⟨the yellow wagon *~ed* to . . . two stout grays —Ellen Glasgow⟩ **c :** to tie together **:** YOKE ⟨must ~ his mechanical apparatus to his creative mind —Andrew Buchanan⟩ **3 :** to put to work **:** UTILIZE ⟨~ the atom for constructive purposes —*Mech. Engineering*⟩ ⟨~ words to convey ideas —*advt*⟩ ⟨they who have *~ed* contemporary social forces —W.H.Whyte⟩ ⟨*harnessing* the limitless power of the sun —*advt*⟩

harness bull *or* **harness cop** *n, slang* **:** a uniformed policeman ⟨the *harness bulls* just stood at attention —Mickey Spillane⟩

harness cask *n* **:** a tub on shipboard for storing or soaking salt meat preparatory to use

harnessed antelope *n* [*harnessed* fr. past part. of ²*harness*] **:** any of several antelopes of the genus *Tragelaphus* having striped markings that resemble a harness — see BUSHBUCK, GUIB

har·ness·er \-sə(r)\ *n* -S **:** one that harnesses

harness hitch *n* **:** MAN-HARNESS KNOT

harness horse *n* **1 :** a horse for racing in harness — compare PACER, TROTTER **2 :** DRAFT HORSE — distinguished from *saddle horse*

harness leather *n* **:** a strong pliable oil-finished leather made from cattle hides

harness plate *n* **:** electroplated hardware used on harness

harness race *n* **:** a trotting or pacing race between Standard-bred horses harnessed to 2-wheeled sulkies

harn·pan \'härn,pan\ *n* [ME *hernepanne, harnepanne*, fr. *herne-, harne-* (fr. *hernes, harnes* brains) + *panne* pan — more at HARN, PAN] *chiefly Scot* **:** casing for the brain **:** SKULL

harns *pl of* HARN

haro *var of* HARROW

ha·ro·seth *or* **ha·ro·set** *or* **ha·ro·ses** \hə'rōs(h)əth, -ət, -əs\ *or* **cha·ro·sety** *or* **cha·ro·set** *or* **cha·ro·ses** \kə'-\ *n pl but usu sing in constr* [Heb *ḥaroseth, ḥaroset*, fr. *ḥarsith, ḥarsit* clay or earthen pot] **:** a pastelike mixture of apples, nuts, cinnamon, and wine used during the seder meal on the Passover and symbolic of the clay from which the Israelites made bricks during their Egyptian slavery

¹harp \'härp, 'häp\ *n* -S [ME *harpe*, fr. OE *hearpe*; akin to OHG *harpha* harp, ON *harpa* harp, Gk *karphos* dry stalk, stick, Russ *korobit'* to bend, warp, and prob. to L *curvus* curved — more at CROWN] **1 a :** a musical instrument (as the clarsach, lyre) of ancient origin with strings set usu. in an open frame and plucked with the fingers **b :** an orchestral instrument with a triangular frame consisting of a large, hollow, and tapering back which is the sounding board, a vertical pillar, a curved neck to which the strings are attached by wrest pins, a base or pedestal equipped with seven pedals each of which when depressed one notch raises all strings of the same letter names one half step and when depressed two notches raises them a whole step, having usu. 46 strings tuned diatonically in C-flat major with a compass of 6½ octaves above C flat and with all C and F strings colored for ease of recognition **c :** JEW'S HARP 1 **d :** HARMONICA **e :** a percussion pipe-organ stop of metal or wooden bars with resonators sounded by electric hammer action **2 :** HARPER 2 **3 :** something that resembles a harp: as **a :** a forked fitting for holding a trolley wheel or shoe in contact with a power-supplying wire or cable **b :** a many-stringed implement used in cutting the curd of Swiss cheese **c :** a metal hoop or arch that supports a lampshade **4 :** HARP SEAL **5** *often cap* **:** a person of Irish birth or descent — often taken to be offensive

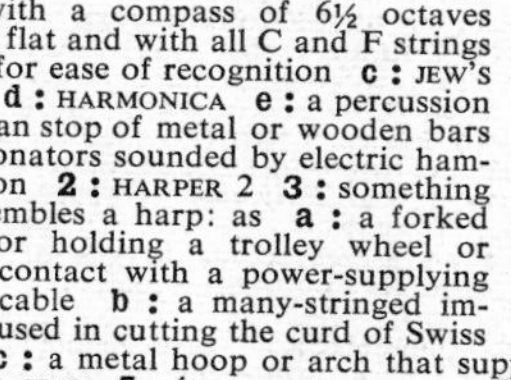

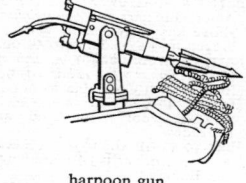

modern harp 1b: *1* base, *2* pillar, *3* neck, *4* body, *5* sound board, *6* pedals, *7* feet

²harp \"\ *vb* -ED/-ING/-S [ME *harpen*, fr. OE *hearpian*, fr. *hearpe*, n.] *vi* **1 :** to play on a harp **2 :** to dwell on a subject **:** repeat a theme with tiresome frequency ⟨continues to ~ on higher wages and shorter hours —G.W.Johnson⟩ ⟨if I seem to be *~ing* away at the value of variety —Alistair Cooke⟩ **3** *obs* **:** to form an opinion on insufficient evidence **:** GUESS ⟨only to ~ at the matter —John Cotgrave⟩ **4 :** to make a sound like a harp ⟨hear the wind ~ —E.J.Schoettle⟩ ~ *vt* **1** *obs* **:** to play on or recite to the accompaniment of a harp ⟨a tale . . . *~ed* in hall and bower —Thomas Warton⟩ **2** *archaic* **:** to attract or compel by playing sweetly on the harp ⟨could ~ his wife up out of hell —Alfred Tennyson⟩ **3** *archaic* **:** to discuss or refer to repeatedly and tediously **4** *archaic* **:** to guess at or give expression to ⟨thou hast *~ed* my fear aright —Shak.⟩ **5 :** to cut and mix curd of (Swiss cheese) with a harp

har·pa \'härpə\ *n, cap* [NL, fr. LL, harp, of Gmc origin; akin to OE *hearpe* harp] **:** the sole genus of the Harpidae

har·pac·toph·a·gous \¦här(,)pak¦täfəgəs\ *adj* [*harpacto-* (fr. Gk *harpaktos* stolen, got by plundering, fr. *harpazein* to snatch, seize) + *-phagous*; akin to Gk *harpagē* hook, rake — more at ASSART] **:** PREDATORY — used esp. of insects

har·pa·go \'härpə,gō\ *n, pl* **harpago·nes** \,härpə'gō,nēz\ [NL *harpagon-, harpago*, fr. L, grappling iron, irreg. fr. Gk *harpagē* hook, rake] **:** an element of the male copulatory apparatus of many insects that forms part of a clasper; *esp* **:** a modified stylus of the ninth segment forming one lateral half of a clasper — usu. used in pl.

har·pa·goph·y·tum \,härpə'gäfəd·əm\ *n, cap* [NL, fr. L *harpago* grappling hook + Gk *phyton* plant — more at PHYT-] **:** a small genus of southern African herbs (family Pedaliaceae) including the grapple plant

har·pa·gor·nis \,härpə'gȯrnəs\ *n, cap* [NL, fr. Gk *harpag-, harpax* rapacious + NL *-ornis*; akin to Gk *harpagē* hook, rake] **:** a genus of extinct birds (family Accipitridae) much larger than any existing eagle and found in the Pleistocene of New Zealand

harp·er \'härpər, 'häpə(r\ *n* -S [ME, fr. OE *hearpere*, fr. *hearpe* harp + *-ere* -er] **1 :** one that plays on a harp **2 :** any of several Irish coins of the 16th and 17th centuries having a harp on one side; *esp* **:** a silver shilling piece worth nine English pence — called also *harp shilling* **3 :** TOAD CRAB

har·pes \'här,pēz\ *n pl* [NL *harpe* (sing.), fr. Gk *harpē* sickle; akin to Gk *harpagē* hook, rake] **:** the claspers of a male moth or butterfly

harp guitar *or* **harp lute** *n* **:** a large guitar with triangular body and two extra bass strings — compare DITAL HARP

har·pi·dae \'härpə,dē\ *n pl, cap* [NL, fr. *Harpa* + *-idae*] **:** a family of tropical marine gastropod mollusks (suborder Stenoglossa) comprising the harp shells — see HARPA

harpies *pl of* HARPY

harp·in \'härpən\ *also* **harp·ing** \-piŋ\ *n* -S [prob. fr. ¹*harp* + *-ing*] **1** *archaic* **:** a wale around a ship's bow stouter than the rest of the strakes **2 :** one of the timbers used during construction of a ship to regulate and hold in place the cant frames

harping iron *or* **harping spear** *n* [*harping* prob. fr. MF *harper* to grapple, grasp + E *-ing*] *archaic* **:** HARPOON

harping johnny *n, usu cap J* [*harping* prob. fr. pres. part. of ²*harp*] **:** ORPINE

harp·ist \'härpəst, 'häp-\ *n* -S **:** a harp player

harp·less \-pləs\ *adj* **:** lacking a harp

¹har·poon \här'pün, hä'-\ *n* -S [prob. fr. D *harpoen*, fr. MD, fr. OF *harpon* brooch, fr. *harper* to grapple, grasp, prob. of Scand origin; akin to Icel *harpa* to pinch, squeeze together; prob. akin to ON *harpa* harp, OE *hearpe* — more at HARP] **1 :** a throwing weapon used in hunting large fish and sea animals; *specif* **:** a barbed whaling spear thrown by hand or shot from a gun that has a flat triangular head usu. detachable and sharpened at both edges, a long shaft, and a strong line for making the whale fast to the pursuing boat — compare TOGGLE IRON **2 :** a medical instrument with a barbed head used for removing bits of living tissue for examination

²harpoon \"\ *vt* -ED/-ING/-S **:** to strike or capture with or as if with a harpoon ⟨~ a whale⟩ ⟨~ an olive⟩

har·poon·er \-nə(r)\ *also* **har·poon·eer** \¦här(,)pü¦ni(ə)r\ *n* -S [¹*harpoon* + *-er* or *-eer*] **:** one that throws or fires a harpoon **:** BOATSTEERER

harpoon fork *n* **:** a fork for loading and unloading hay **:** HAYFORK

harpoon gun *n* **:** a machine for hurling a harpoon

harpoon line *n* **:** a light strong manila rope with a flexible lay now used principally for purse lines

harpoon log *n* **:** a log consisting of a rotator and a distance-registering device combined in a cylindrical case and towed astern — compare TAFFRAIL LOG

harpoon oar *n* **:** a forward oar pulled by the harpooner as a whaling ship approaches a whale

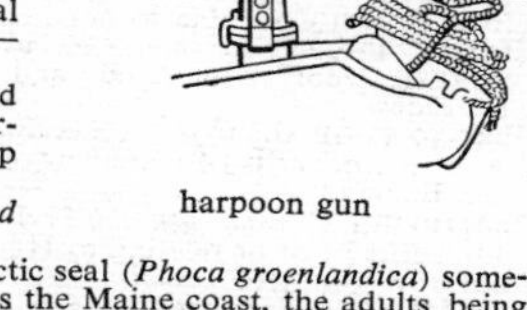
harpoon gun

harps *pl of* HARP, *pres 3d sing of* HARP

harp seal *n* **:** a common arctic seal (*Phoca groenlandica*) sometimes found as far south as the Maine coast, the adults being grayish above and white below, the male having a black crescent suggesting a harp along each side and a black face and throat, and the newborn young being all white

harp shell *n* **:** a tropical gastropod mollusk of the genus *Harpa* having a large variegated shell with prominent ribs

harp shilling *n* **:** HARPER

harpsical *also* **harpsicall** *n* -S [by alter.] *n, obs* **:** HARPSICHORD

harpsichon *also* **harpsicon** *n* -S [by alter.] *n, obs* **:** HARPSICHORD

harp·si·chord \'härpsə,kȯrd, 'häpsə,kȯ(ə)d\ *n* -S [modif. of It *arpicordo*, fr. *arpi-* (fr. *arpa* harp, fr. LL *harpa*) + *-cordo* (fr. *corda* cord, string, fr. L *chorda* cord) — more at HARPA, CORD] **:** a wire-stringed musical instrument resembling in shape the grand piano, usu. having two keyboards with one to four strings for each key and seven stops or pedals, and producing its tones by the plucking of its strings with quills or leather points set in jacks operated from the keyboards and capable of gradation of tone only by alternating the stops or keyboards

harpsichord

harp·si·chord·ist \-dəst\ *n* -S **:** one who plays the harpsichord

harp turtle *n* **:** LEATHERBACK

har·pu·la \'härpyələ\ *n* -S [native name in Bengal] **:** a fast-growing tree (*Harpullia cupanioides*) of India and the East Indies that yields a wood used esp. for building

har·pul·lia \här'pəlēə\ *n* [NL, fr. native name in Bengal] **1** *cap* **:** a genus of tropical Asiatic and African trees (family Sapindaceae) having pinnate leaves, panicles of greenish flowers and red or orange fruit **2** -S **:** any tree of the genus *Harpullia*

harpway tuning \'=,=-\ *n* [*harpway* fr. *harp* + *way*] **:** a tuning of a viol (as in fifths and fourths: A-E-A-E-A-D) to facilitate arpeggio playing

har·py \'härpē, 'häp-, -pi\ *n* -ES [L *Harpyia*, fr. Gk] **1 :** a predatory monster in chiefly classical mythology represented as having a woman's head and the body and claws of a vulture and as being an instrument of divine vengeance **2 a :** a predatory person **:** LEECH, SWINDLER ⟨homesteaders had managed to escape other *harpies* — such as land agents offering to hurry claims through —Dixon Wecter⟩ **b :** a shrewish or depraved woman ⟨gin shops . . . crowded by day as well as by night with screaming *harpies* —Kenneth Roberts⟩

harpy bat *also* **harpy** *n* -ES **1 :** any of various East Indian fruit bats having prominent tubular nostrils and constituting the genus *Nyctimene* **2 :** an East Indian insectivorous bat (*Harpiocephalus harpia*)

harpy eagle *also* **harpy** *n* -ES **:** either of two large eagles: **a :** a largely black-and-white eagle (*Harpia harpyja*) having a double crest on the head and remarkably strong bill and claws, found in northern So. and Central America where it is believed to prey on large forest birds and various mammals **b :** a rare eagle (*Pithecophaga jefferyi*) of the Philippines held to live chiefly on monkeys

har·que·bus *or* **ar·que·bus** \'(h)ärk(w)əbəs, '(h)äk-\ *n* -ES [MF *harquebuse, arquebuse,* modif. of MD *hakebusse,* fr. *hake* hook + *busse* box, tube, gun, fr. LL *buxis* box; akin to MD *hoec* corner — more at HOOK, BOX] **1 :** a portable but heavy matchlock gun invented about the middle of the 15th century and fired from a support to which it was attached by a fixed hook, later wheel-lock or flintlock modifications being lightened and provided with a bent stock and a longer butt so that they could be fired from the shoulder **2 harquebuses** *pl, obs* **:** soldiers armed with the harquebus

har·que·bus·ade \,==bə'sād\ *n* -S [MF, fr. *harquebuse* + *-ade*] **1** *obs* **:** a shot from a harquebus **2** *archaic* **:** a volley from harquebuses

har·que·bus·ier *or* **ar·que·bus·ier** \-'si(ə)r, -'siə\ *n* -S [MF, fr. *harquebuse, arquebuse* + *-ier* -er] **:** a soldier armed with a harquebus or sometimes with a musket or other gun ⟨at the head of a company of ~s —Frank Yerby⟩

harr \'(h)är\ *n* -S [ME *herre, harre,* fr. OE *heorra;* akin to ON *hjarri* hinge and perh. to L *cardin-, cardo* hinge — more at CARDINAL] **1** *obs* **:** a gate or door hinge **2** *now dial Eng* **:** an upright to which hinges are fastened and from which a door or gate swings

har·ras \'harəs\ *n* -ES [ME *haras* herd of stud horses, enclosure for a herd of stud horses, fr. OF *haras, haraz*] **:** a herd of stud horses

har·ra·teen *or* **har·a·teen** \'harə,tēn\ *n* -S [origin unknown] **:** an English fabric of linen or wool used chiefly for curtains and bed hangings in the 18th and early 19th centuries

harratin *usu cap, var of* HARATIN

harri *usu cap, var of* HURRI

har·ri·cane \'harə,kān\ *dial var of* HURRICANE

har·ri·dan \'harədən *also* 'her-, -dᵊn\ *n* -S [perh. modif. of F *haridelle* worn-out horse, tall lean ugly woman] **:** a haggard old woman **:** HAG; *esp* **:** a worn-out strumpet

harried *adj* [fr. past part. of ¹*harry*] **:** beset by disturbing problems or anxieties **:** HARASSED ⟨as ~ as innkeepers coping with a full house —Mary McGrory⟩ ⟨a rather ~ journalist trying to produce a maximum of copy —Edmund Wilson⟩

¹**har·ri·er** \'harēə(r), -riə- *also* 'her-\ *n* -S [irreg. fr. ¹*hare* + *-ier*] **1 :** a hunting dog from 19 to 21 inches high resembling a small foxhound and used for hunting rabbits and other small game **2 :** a runner on a cross-country team

²**harrier** \"\ *n* -S [¹*harry* + *-er*] **1 :** one that harries **2** [alter. (influenced by ¹*harry*) of earlier *harrower,* fr. ¹*harrow* + *-er*] **:** any of various slender hawks with long angled wings and long legs that constitute a genus (*Circus*), feed chiefly on small mammals, reptiles, and insects which they hunt by flying low over open ground, and usu. nest on the ground — see HEN HARRIER, MARSH HARRIER, MARSH HAWK

harrier eagle *n* **:** any of numerous rather large Old World hawks constituting a genus (*Circaetus*) and intermediate in some respects between typical hawks and typical eagles — called also *short-toed eagle*

harries *pres 3d sing of* HARRY, *pl of* HARRY

har·ring·ton \'hariŋtən\ *n* -S *usu cap* [after John, 1st Baron *Harington* of Exton †1613 Eng. nobleman who coined such tokens under a patent granted by James I] **:** a copper token worth a farthing in 17th century England

har·ris buck \'harəs-\ *n, usu cap H* [after Sir William C. *Harris* †1848 Eng. traveler] **:** SABLE ANTELOPE

har·ris·burg \'harəs,bərg, -,bəg *also* 'her-\ *adj, usu cap* [fr. *Harrisburg,* capital of Pennsylvania] **:** of or from Harrisburg, the capital of Pennsylvania ⟨*Harrisburg* residents⟩ **:** of the kind or style prevalent in Harrisburg

har·ris·ia \hə'risēə\ *n, cap* [NL, fr. William *Harris,* Jamaican botanist + NL *-ia*] **:** a genus of slender spiny tropical American cacti with solitary showy white or pink flowers

har·ri·son red \'harəsᵊn-\ *n, often cap H* [perh. after Birge *Harrison* †1929 Am. landscape painter] **:** CHINESE VERMILION

harris's hawk *or* **harris hawk** *n, usu cap 1st H* [after Edward *Harris* †1863 Am. naturalist] **:** a common hawk (*Parabuteo unicinctus harrisi*) of the deserts and prairies of southwestern U.S., Mexico, and Central America chiefly dark brown with conspicuous white markings on the tail

harris's sparrow *n, usu cap H* **:** a widely distributed No. American sparrow (*Zonotrichia querula*) largely dusky brown above and white below with a black cap and black bib prolonged into a median streak on the breast

harris's woodpecker *n, usu cap H* **:** a hairy woodpecker (*Dendrocopos villosus harrisi*) occurring along the Pacific coast from British Columbia to northern California

Harris Tweed *trademark* — used for a tweed made of Scottish wool spun, dyed, and handwoven in the Outer Hebrides

¹**har·ro·vi·an** \hə'rōvēən\ *n* -S *usu cap* [NL *Harrovia* Harrow + E *-an,* n. suffix] **:** a student of Harrow School in Middlesex, England

²**harrovian** \"\ *adj, usu cap* [NL *Harrovia* Harrow + E *-an,* adj. suffix] **:** of or relating to Harrow School

¹**har·row** \'ha(,)rō, -rə *also* 'he(-, *often* -,rəw+V\ *vt* -ED/-ING/-S [ME *harwen, herwen,* fr. OE *hergian* to harry — more at HARRY] **1** *archaic* **:** to descend into (hell) in order to bring away the souls of the righteous ⟨Christ hath ~*ed* hell —J.M. Neale⟩ **2** *archaic* **:** ROB, PILLAGE, PLUNDER ⟨long ~*ed* by oppressor's hand —Sir Walter Scott⟩

²**harrow** \"\ *n* -S *often attrib* [ME *harwe;* perh. akin to OSw *harf* harrow, Gk *keirein* to cut — more at SHEAR] **1 :** a cultivating implement used primarily for pulverizing or smoothing the soil and sometimes for mulching, covering seed, or removing weeds — compare BOG HARROW, BRUSH HARROW, DISC HARROW, DRAG 1d **2 a :** an implement that resembles a harrow; *specif:* a toothed framework drawn over an oyster bed to clear it of seaweed **b :** a formation that resembles a harrow — **under the harrow** *adv* **:** under constant threat of penalty or suffering ⟨every manifestation of initiative in the educated public was kept *under the harrow* —Bernard Pares⟩

³**harrow** \"\ *vt* -ED/-ING/-S [ME *harwen, harowen,* fr. *harwe,* n.] **1 a :** to cultivate with a harrow ⟨plowed and ~*ed* and laid his rows —Russell Lord⟩ **b :** to cultivate as if with a harrow ⟨~*ed* the ground for literature —Van Wyck Brooks⟩ **2 a :** to cut into as if with a harrow ⟨the whole thing looked ~*ed* in the pigment, rather than painted —F.J.Mather⟩ **b** *archaic* **:** to wound or tear physically **:** LACERATE ⟨~*ing* his cheeks with a few scratches —William Beckford⟩ **3 :** to cause distress or suffering to **:** AGONIZE ⟨has not set out to appall the reader with horrors nor to ~ him with miseries —Douglas Stewart⟩

⁴**har·row** *or* **har·o** \'ha(,)rō, hə'rō\ *interj* [ME *harrow, harow,* fr. MF *haro, harou,* fr. OF, prob. of Gmc origin; akin to OHG *hara* hither; akin to OE *hēr* here, OHG *hier* — more at HERE] — used to express alarm or distress

⁵**har·row** \'ha(,)rō\ *adj, usu cap* [fr. *Harrow* on the Hill, urban district, Middlesex, England] **:** of or from the urban district of Harrow on the Hill, England **:** of the kind or style prevalent in Harrow on the Hill

har·row·er \'harəwə(r), *also* 'her-\ *n* -S [ME *haroer, harower,* fr. *harwen, harowen* to cultivate with a harrow + *-er*] **:** one that harrows

harrowing *adj* [fr. pres. part. of ³*harrow*] **:** acutely distressing or painful **:** AGONIZING ⟨~ tales of unfortunates who had lost limbs or had been frozen to death —V.G.Heiser⟩ — **har·row·ing·ly** *adv*

harrow–plow \'=(,)=,=\ *n* [²*harrow*] **:** ONE-WAY DISC PLOW

harrs *pl of* HARR

har·rumph \hə'rəm(p)f\ *vi* -ED/-ING/-S [imit.] **1 :** to make a pompous throat-clearing sound ⟨several students chuckled and one or two professional alumni good-naturedly ~*ed* —W.H.Nelson⟩ **2 :** to comment disapprovingly **:** PROTEST ⟨the state department ~*ed* and . . . oil companies stood on their legal, unenforceable rights —*Time*⟩

¹**har·ry** \'harē, -ri *also* 'her-\ *vb* -ED/-ING/-ES [ME *harien, herien,* fr. OE *hergian;* akin to OHG *heriōn* to lay waste, ON *herja;* denominative fr. the noun represented by OE *here* army, OHG *heri,* ON *herr* army, Goth *harjis* host; akin to Gk *koiranos* commander, OPer *kāra* army] *vi* **:** to attack and loot **:** RAID ⟨had *harried* widely and laid siege to Paris —Charlton Laird⟩ ~ *vt* **1 a :** ASSAULT, DEVASTATE, RAVAGE ⟨ordered his troops to ~ the town⟩ ⟨shabby trees *harried* by fire —G.R. Stewart⟩ **b** *chiefly Scot* **:** to engage in robbing or plundering ⟨shame lassie for ~*ing* birds' nests —J.M.Barrie⟩ **2 a :** ATTACK ⟨~ a person⟩ ⟨the cat reached out a big fat paw and *harried* the boy —Erskine Caldwell⟩ **b :** to force (a person) to move along ⟨saga of migratory laborers *harried* across the continent —J.D.Hart⟩ **3** *now dial Brit* **:** to drag off as plunder — usu. used with *off* or *out* ⟨the devil came and *harried* off his soul —Emily Brontë⟩ **4 a :** to keep under constant attack or threat of attack **:** HARASS ⟨*harried* by guerrillas and occasionally invaded by organized forces —T.M.Spaulding⟩ **b :** to goad by constant demands or annoyances **:** TORMENT ⟨three renegade boys who came to ~ a couple of farm women —James Kelly⟩ ⟨*harries* the doctor by telephone —Mary B. Spahr⟩ **syn** see WORRY

²**harry** \"\ *n* -ES **1 :** harrying action ⟨teased and broken by the ~ of the following gale —J.D.Beresford⟩ **2 :** VEXATION ⟨cut off from the hurries and *harries* of the daily world —Roger Angell⟩

¹**harsh** \'härsh, 'hàsh\ *adj* -ER/-EST [alter. of earlier *harsk,* fr. ME, of Scand origin; akin to Norw *harsk* rancid, harsh, Sw *härsk* rancid; akin to MLG *harsch* rough, and prob. to L *carrere* to card — more at CHARD] **1 :** having a coarse or uneven surface **:** rough to the touch **:** SHAGGY ⟨a small terrier with a ~ dense coat —*Dict. of Sports*⟩ ⟨granite stones ~ with lichen —Nancy Hale⟩; *specif* **:** difficult to manipulate and finish because of too many large particles of aggregate in proportion to the amount of fine particles ⟨~ mortar⟩ ⟨~ concrete⟩ **2 a :** disagreeable to taste or smell **:** RAW, ACRID, IRRITATING ⟨the cognac was ~ —Winifred Bambrick⟩ ⟨a very irritating, pungent, ~ smoke —W.W.Garver⟩ **b :** disagreeable to the ear **:** GRATING, STRIDENT, JARRING ⟨her ~ voice was full of power and humor —G.W.Brace⟩ ⟨music . . . requires sounds of many contrasting kinds: as well as mellow —Robert Donington⟩ **c :** disagreeable to the eye **:** STARK ⟨~ dull greens and blacks —Roger Fry⟩ ⟨a ~, almost a violent, face —Claudia Cassidy⟩; *specif, photog* **:** HARD **d :** physically disagreeable **:** UNCOMFORTABLE ⟨wild and ~ country, full of hot sand and the cholla cactus —S.H.Adams⟩ ⟨~ north wind —Osbert Sitwell⟩ ⟨~ lives of toil in sweatshops and mines⟩ **3 a :** sharply unpleasant or rigorous **:** STERN ⟨the ~ facts of court delays in our city —S.H.Hofstadter⟩ ⟨could be done by a woman as easily as by a man . . . provided discipline were ~ enough —Lewis Mumford⟩ **b :** SEVERE, EXACTING, CRUEL ⟨as ~ and unlovable an old tyrant as one could well imagine —*Sat. Eve. Post*⟩ **4 :** lacking in aesthetic grace or refinement **:** CRUDE ⟨a ~ and sometimes unpleasant book, barren of pretty touches —Brendan Gill⟩ **syn** see ROUGH

²**harsh** \"\ *adv* **:** HARSHLY ⟨with *harsh*-resounding trumpets' dreadful bray —Shak.⟩

harsh·en \-shən\ *vb* -ED/-ING/-S *vt* **:** to make harsh ⟨a great gravity that ~*ed* his soft voice —*Scribner's*⟩ ~ *vi* **:** to become harsh ⟨saw the grain of his skin ~*ing* over face bones —Elizabeth Bowen⟩

harsh–furred hare \'=,=-\ *n* **:** a small hare (*Caprolagus hispidus* or *Lepus hispidus*) of the eastern Himalayan foothills with a massive skull, short ears, and a dull dark coat in which whitish bristly hairs are mingled

harsh·ly *adv* **:** in a harsh manner: **a :** coarsely to the touch **:** ROUGHLY ⟨rubbed herself ~ with a towel —I.V.Morris⟩ **b :** offensively to the senses **:** DISAGREEABLY ⟨houses on the far side, ~ white in this straight hard glare —Thomas Wood †1950⟩ **c :** unfeelingly to the sensibilities **:** RIGOROUSLY, CRUELLY ⟨~ limits the freedom of the creative imagination —Philip Toynbee⟩ ⟨he was made prisoner and ~ treated —E.M.Coulter⟩ **d :** ungracefully by aesthetic standards **:** CRUDELY ⟨a number of his canvases are slightly repellent — notably one of a ~ drawn, bedraggled mother and child —R.M.Coates⟩

harsh·ness *n* -ES [alter. of earlier *harsknes,* fr. ME, fr. *harsk* harsh + *-nes* -ness] **:** the quality or state of being harsh

hars·let \'härslət\ *dial var of* HASLET

hars·tig·ite \'härstə,gīt\ *n* -S [Sw *harstigit,* fr. *Harstig* mine, Sweden + Sw *-it* -ite] **:** a mineral $Be_2Ca_3Si_3O_{11}$ consisting of a silicate of beryllium and calcium (hardness 5.5, sp. gr. 3.05)

hart \'härt, 'hàt, *usu* -d·+V\ *n, pl* **harts** *also* **hart** [ME *hert,* fr. OE *heort, heorot;* akin to OHG *hiruz* hart, ON *hjörtr,* L *cervus* hart, stag, Gk *keras* horn — more at HORN] *chiefly Brit* **:** the male of the red deer esp. over five years old **:** STAG — compare HIND

har·tal \här'täl\ *n* -S [Hindi *haṛtāl,* fr. *hāṭ* shop + *tālā* lock] **:** concerted cessation of work and business esp. as a protest against a political situation or an act of government — compare NONCOOPERATION

har·te·beest \'härd·ə,bēst, 'hä|, |tə,-, |t,-\ *n, pl* **hartebeests** *also* **hartebeest** [obs. Afrik (now *hartbees*), fr. D *hartebeest, hertebeest* deer, fr. *hart, hert* deer, stag (fr. MD *hert*) + *beest* beast, fr. MD *beeste, beest,* fr. OF *beste;* akin to OE *heort, heorot* hart — more at HART, BEAST] **1 :** a large nearly exterminated African antelope (*Alcelaphus caama*) that is grayish brown in color with a yellow patch on the buttocks, black markings on the face, and ringed divergent horns bent back at the tips — compare SASSABY **2 :** any of several other African antelopes of the genus *Alcelaphus* — compare NORTHERN HARTEBEEST

hart·ford \'härtfərd, 'hàtfəd\ *adj, usu cap* [fr. *Hartford,* capital of Connecticut] **:** of or from Hartford, the capital of Connecticut ⟨*Hartford* insurance companies⟩ **:** of the kind or style prevalent in Hartford

hartford fern *n, usu cap H* **:** CLIMBING FERN

hart·ford·ite \-,dīt\ *n* -S *cap* **:** a native or resident of Hartford, Connecticut

hart·ite \'härd·,īt\ *n* -S [G *hartit,* fr. *Oberhart,* Austria + G *-it* -ite] **:** a white fossil resin perhaps $C_{19}H_{32}$ occurring in peat beds

hart·le·ian *also* **hart·ley·an** \'härtlēən, =ˈ==\ *adj, usu cap* [David *Hartley* †1757 Eng. philosopher, founder of the doctrine of associationism + E *-an*] **:** of or relating to the doctrine of associationism or its founder

hart·man·nia \härt'manēə\ *n, cap* [NL, fr. Emanuel *Hartmann,* 19th cent. Am. botanist + NL *-ia*] *in some classifications* **:** a small genus of American herbs (family Onagraceae) with alternate leaves and showy flowers in spikes or racemes that are usu. included in the genus *Oenothera*

¹**har·to·gia** \här'tōjēə\ [NL, fr. J. *Hartog,* 18th cent. Du. traveler + NL *-ia*] *syn of* AGATHOSMA

²**hartogia** \"\ *n, cap* [NL, fr. J. *Hartog* + NL *-ia*] **:** a genus of southern African plants (family Rutaceae) having white or purplish flowers with long-clawed petals, five stamens, and five conspicuous staminodia

hart's–eye \'=,=\ *n, pl* **hart's–eyes 1 :** CRETAN DITTANY **2 :** PARSNIP

harts·horn \'=,=\ *n* -S [ME *hertes horn,* fr. OE *heortes horn,* fr. *heortes* (gen. of *heort* hart) + *horn*] **1 :** a hart's horn or antler **2** *archaic* **a :** AMMONIA WATER **b :** AMMONIUM CARBONATE c **3** *or* **hartshorn plantain :** BUCKHORN 3b(1)

hartshorn bush *n* **:** ROYAL FERN

hartshorn plant *n* **:** an American pasqueflower (*Anemone patens*)

hart's–thorn \'=,=\ *n, pl* **hart's–thorns :** COMMON BUCKTHORN

hart's–tongue \'=,=\ *or* **hart's–tongue fern** *n, pl* **hart's–tongues** *or* **hart's–tongue ferns** [*hart's-tongue* fr. ME *hertestonge,* fr. *hertes* (gen. of *hert* hart) + *tonge* tongue; *hart's-tongue fern* fr. *hart's-tongue* + *fern;* fr. the shape of the fronds] **1 :** a chiefly Eurasian fern (*Phyllitis scolopendrium*) with simple lanceolate fronds often auriculate at the base **2 :** a tropical American fern (*Polybotria cervina*) of the family Polypodiaceae **3 :** STRAP FERN

hart's truffle *n* **:** an ascomycetous fungus of the genus *Elaphomyces* that resembles a puffball — compare LYCOPERDON NUT

har·um–scar·um \¦harəm¦skarəm, *also* ¦herəm¦skerəm\ *adv (or adj)* [perh. alter. (perh. influenced by ¹*helter-skelter*) **:** in a rash or heedless way **:** RECKLESSLY ⟨trucks whizzing *harum-scarum* along clay streets —Allan Ashbolt⟩ ⟨dashing *harum-scarum* from one rooftop to another⟩

²**harum–scarum** \"\ *n* -S **:** one that is rash or heedless **:** SCATTERBRAIN ⟨do you really expect those wild young *harum-scarums* to live up to their oath —S.H.Adams⟩ — **har·um–scar·um·ness** *n* -ES

ha·rus·pex *or* **arus·pex** \hə'rə,speks, '(h)arə-\ *n, pl* **haruspi·ces** *or* **aruspi·ces** \-'rəspə,sēz\ [L *haruspic-, haruspex,* fr. *haru-* (akin to Gk *chordē* gut, cord) + *-spic-, -spex* (fr. *spicere, specere* to look) — more at YARN, SPY] **1 :** one that foretells events by interpreting natural phenomena (as lightning) **:** SOOTHSAYER; *esp* **:** a diviner in ancient Rome basing his predictions on inspection of the entrails of sacrificial animals — compare AUGUR **2 :** one that prophesies **:** PROGNOSTICATOR ⟨our forecast has proved far more accurate than the divinations of the Democrat ~ —O.D.Heck⟩

ha·rus·pi·cal \-'rəspəkəl\ *adj* **:** of, relating to, or having the characteristics of an haruspex

ha·rus·pi·ca·tion \(h)ə,rəspə'kāshən\ *n* -S [L *haruspic-, haruspex* + E *-ation*] **1 :** HARUSPICY **2 :** an act or instance of foretelling events **:** PROPHECY ⟨it's the best job of social ~ that's been done in years —Christopher Morley⟩

ha·rus·pi·cy *or* **arus·pi·cy** \-'rəspəsē\ *n* -ES [L *haruspicium,* fr. *haruspic-, haruspex*] **:** the art or practice of divination — compare HARUSPEX

harvard beets *n pl, usu cap H* [*Harvard* University, Cambridge, Massachusetts] **:** diced or sliced cooked beets served in a vinegar sauce thickened with cornstarch

harvard crimson *n, often cap H* **1 :** a moderate red that is slightly darker than cerise, darker than claret, darker, very slightly bluer, and less strong than average strawberry (sense 2a), and bluer and very slightly darker than Turkey red — called also *jockey* **2** *of textiles* **:** a deep purplish red that is redder and paler than hollyhock or magenta (sense 2a) and stronger and slightly bluer and lighter than American beauty

har·ve·ian \'härvēən, =ˈ==\ *adj, usu cap* [William *Harvey* †1657 Eng. physician and anatomist + E *-an*] **:** of, relating to, or commemorating William Harvey

¹**har·vest** \'härvəst, 'hàv-\ *n* -S *often attrib* [ME *hervest* autumn, fr. OE *hærfest;* akin to OHG *herbist* autumn, ON *haust* autumn, L *carpere* to gather, pluck, Gk *karpos* fruit, Skt *kṛpāṇa* sword, Gk *keirein* to cut — more at SHEAR] **1 :** the season for gathering in agricultural crops ⟨he who has seen ten winters or ~s is ten years old —M.P.Nilsson⟩ ⟨considerable variation in the Territory as regards the date of the ~ —*Tanganyika Territory*⟩ **2 a :** the act or process of gathering in a crop ⟨the hay ~⟩ ⟨reduce the numbers of fish . . . through more intensive and efficient ~ by anglers —L.S. Marceau⟩ **b :** the gathering in of something other than a crop ⟨more to these poems than just the . . . ~ of a trained eye —*Times Lit. Supp.*⟩ **3 a :** a mature crop of grain or fruit **:** YIELD ⟨bountiful ~s of corn —John Bird⟩ **b :** the quantity of any natural product gathered usu. from a single area within a single season ⟨~ of elk⟩ ⟨~ of beaver skins⟩ ⟨salt ~⟩ ⟨ice ~⟩ **4 :** an accumulated store or productive result **:** ACHIEVEMENT, INGATHERING ⟨one's total ~ of thinking, feeling, living, and observing —T.S.Eliot⟩ ⟨the final ~ of the theocracy —V.L. Parrington⟩ ⟨~ of the guillotine —Alfred Cobban⟩ ⟨~ of half crowns —W.J.MacQueen-Pope⟩ **5** *or* **harvest brown :** a brownish orange to light brown that is lighter than sorrel or tawny, redder and lighter than raw sienna, and slightly yellower and lighter than caramel

²**harvest** \"\ *vb* -ED/-ING/-S [ME *hervesten,* fr. *hervest,* n.] *vt* **1 a :** to gather in (a crop) **:** REAP ⟨when all the beets are ~*ed* a steam shovel loads them on trucks —*Amer. Guide Series: Minn.*⟩ **b :** to gather (a natural product) as if by harvesting ⟨~ honey⟩ ⟨~ timber⟩ ⟨~ whales⟩ **2 a :** to accumulate a store of ⟨~ news leads and witticisms —Bennett Cerf⟩ **b :** to win as a result of achievements ⟨~*ed* rewards in fame and wealth . . . simply undreamed of —*N. Y. Herald Tribune*⟩ ~ *vi* **:** to gather in a food crop ⟨sold it standing in the field to save himself the trouble of ~*ing* —Pearl Buck⟩ ⟨the husky black bear ~s upon both soil and water —George Heinold⟩ **syn** see REAP

har·vest·able \-təbəl\ *adj* **:** capable of or subject to being harvested

harvest bug *n* **:** CHIGGER 2

harvest doll *or* **harvest mother** *or* **harvest queen** *n* **:** a doll decorated with grain and flowers or an image made from the last sheaf cut in the harvest and used in European celebrations of the harvest home — called also *kirn baby, mell-doll*

har·vest·er \-tə(r)\ *n* -S **:** one that harvests: as **a :** HARVESTMAN **b :** a machine for harvesting field crops — compare COMBINE 3, CORN BINDER, COTTON PICKER **c :** a gatherer of something other than crops ⟨semimonthly ~ of noteworthy pronouncements —*Official Catholic Yearbook*⟩

harvester ant *n* **:** an ant that gathers and stores up seeds for food: as **a :** a member of an Old World genus (*Messor*) common around the Mediterranean **b :** any of several western No. American ants; *esp* **:** a common ant (*Pogonomyrmex barbatus*) of southwestern U.S. — called also *agricultural ant*

harvester–thresher \'===ˈ==\ *n* **:** COMBINE 3

harvest fish *n* **:** any of various butterfishes of the family Stromateidae: as **a :** a small marine fish (*Peprilus paru*) having a narrow deep body and being found along the Atlantic coast of America from Brazil to Cape Cod **b :** DOLLARFISH 1

harvest fly *n* **:** CICADA; *specif* **:** DOG-DAY CICADA

harvest home *n* **1 :** the gathering and bringing home of the harvest; *also* **:** the time of harvest — see HARVEST DOLL **2 :** a feast made at the close of the harvest — called also *hockey, kirn, mell, mell supper* **3 :** the song sung by the reapers at the close of the harvest

harvesting *n* -S [fr. gerund of ²*harvest*] **:** an act or instance of gathering in a crop or store ⟨what crops survived the drought are rotted in the ~ —Oliver La Farge⟩ ⟨deer . . . are controlled by heavy ~ —Robert Crichton⟩

har·vest·less \'härvəstləs\ *adj* **:** lacking a harvest **:** UNPRODUCTIVE

harvest–lice \'=ˈ=,=\ *n pl but sing or pl in constr* **1 :** a hooked or barbed fruit that readily adheres to things (as clothing or the fur of an animal) which come in contact with it **2 :** a plant (as cleavers, agrimonia, or beggar-ticks of the genus *Bidens*) bearing fruits that are harvest-lice

har·vest·man \'==mən\ *n, pl* **harvestmen 1 :** one who harvests agricultural crops **:** harvest hand **2 :** an arachnid of the order Phalangida that superficially resembles a true spider but has a small rounded body composed of an indistinctly segmented cephalothorax to which the short broad abdomen showing nine dorsal plates is broadly joined, very long slender legs, chelate chelicerae, and rather short leglike pedipalpi — called also *daddy longlegs*

harvest mite *n* **:** CHIGGER 2

harvest moon *n* **:** the full moon nearest the time of the September equinox when for mid-northern latitudes its daily delay in rising is much shorter than usual by reason of the relatively small angle the moon's orbit makes with the eastern horizon

harvest mouse *n* **1 :** a small European field mouse (*Micromys minutus*) that builds a globular nest on the stems of wheat or other plants **2 :** any of several small field mice (genus *Reithrodontomys*) of the southern U.S.

harvests *pl of* HARVEST, *pres 3d sing of* HARVEST

harvest spider *n* **:** HARVESTMAN 2

harvesttime \'=ˈ=,=\ *n* [ME *hervest-time,* fr. *hervest* harvest, autumn + *time*] **:** the time during which an annual crop (as wheat) is harvested

harz·burg·ite \'härts,bər,gīt\ *n* -S [G *harzburgit,* fr *Harzburg,* Germany + G *-it* -ite] **:** a rock of the peridotite group consisting essentially of olivine and orthopyroxene

¹**has** *pres 3d sing of* HAVE

²**has** *pres 3d sing of* HA, *pl of* HA

has–been \'haz,bin\ *n* -S [fr. *has been,* 3d pers. sing. perf. indic. of *be*] **1 :** one that has passed the peak of effectiveness or popularity ⟨a seedy *has-been* of an actor traveling a comeback trail —Gordon Allison⟩ ⟨that little, dried-up *has-been* of a town —J.B.Benefield⟩ ⟨obsolete, a *has-been* as a warplane —*Springfield (Mass.) Daily News*⟩ **2 has–beens** *pl* **:** old times or past events ⟨just for *has-beens* I took him to lunch —W.H.Smith⟩

haschisch *var of* HASHISH

ha·sen·pfef·fer \'häzᵊn,(p)fefə(r)\ *or* **has·sen·pfef·fer** \'häs-\ *n* -S [G *hasenpfeffer,* fr. *hase* hare (fr. OHG *haso*) + *pfeffer* pepper, fr. OHG *pfeffar* — more at HARE, PEPPER] **1 :** a stew made of rabbit meat which has been soaked for two days in vinegar and pickling spices and to which sour cream is added before serving **2 :** a card game similar to euchre

¹**hash** \'hash, -aa(ə)sh, -aish\ *vb* -ED/-ING/-ES [F *hacher,* fr. OF *hachier,* fr. *hache* battle-ax, of Gmc origin; akin to OHG *happa* sickle, pruning knife; akin to Gk *koptein* to smite, cut off — more at CAPON] *vt* **1 a :** to chop to pieces; *specif* **:** to prepare for use in a meat and vegetable dish by cutting into

small pieces ⟨~ the leftover pot roast⟩ **b** : to make a confused muddle of : JUMBLE ⟨in both dates and geography he pretty well ~*es* the history of the . . . company —Bernard De Voto⟩ **2** : to cut with long strokes : SLASH ⟨they are . . . ~*ing* them down, and their blood is running down like water —Patrick Walker⟩ **3** : to talk about : REVIEW ⟨~ and rehash the evidence —D.W.Peck⟩ ~ *vi* **1** *slang* : to serve food in a restaurant : wait table ⟨got my job back ~*ing* —R.P.Warren⟩ **2** : to marshal facts : CONSIDER ⟨we've ~*ed* and rehashed enough —Hamilton Basso⟩

²hash \"\ *n* -ES **1 a** : chopped food; *specif* : a dish usu. consisting of leftover meat chopped into small pieces, mixed with potatoes, and browned by baking or frying **b** *slang* : a meal esp. in a cafeteria or at a lunch counter : FOOD ⟨called last week and took ~ with us —*Gringo & Greaser*⟩ ⟨waiter in a ~ joint —Scott Fitzgerald⟩ **2** : a restatement of something that is already known ⟨this much is old ~, but the . . . tabulation goes on to supply some curious verification —*N.Y. Herald Tribune*⟩ **3** : MIXTURE, JUMBLE, HODGEPODGE: as **a** : a confused muddle : MESS ⟨made rather a ~ of her life —Clive Arden⟩ ⟨one basic style of architecture with a ~ of every other style slapped on by successive owners —Sam Boal⟩ **b** : an undesired signal or combination of signals in a radio, radar, or television receiver due to set noise, radio noise, interference, or other cause **c** : a medley of miscellaneous steps and figures in square dancing **4** *chiefly Scot* : a careless or stupid person of slovenly speech or habits : worthless fellow

³hash \'(h)ash\ *dial var of* HARSH

hash·ab \'ha,shab\ *n* -S [Ar *khashab*] : a gray-barked acacia tree (*Acacia senegal*) found in the Sudan that is the source of a white or light-colored variety of gum arabic

hashed brown potatoes \'⸗,⸗-\ *also* **hash-browns** \'hash-,braünz\ *or* **hashed-browns** \-sht,-\ *n pl* : chopped cooked potatoes packed into a skillet and fried brown on both sides

hash·er \'hashə(r), -aash-, -aish-\ *n* -S **1** *slang* : WAITER, WAITRESS ⟨a ~ in the Shanghai Café —*N.Y. Times*⟩ **2 a** : COOKEE **b** : a worker who feeds into a hashing machine unmarketable meat that may be used for by-products

hash·ery \-shərē\ *n* -ES [²*hash* + -*ery*] *slang* : HASH HOUSE

hash house *n, slang* : an inexpensive eating place : BEANERY ⟨at an all-night *hash house* . . . he nurses a cup of coffee and a doughnut —Norman Mailer⟩

¹hash·im·ite *or* **hash·em·ite** \'hashə,mīt\ *n* -S *usu cap* [*Hashim*, great-grandfather of Muhammad (founder of the Muslim religion) + E -*ite*] : a member of an Arabic family having common ancestry with Muhammad and founding dynasties in countries of the eastern Mediterranean

²hashimite *or* **hashemite** \"\ *adj, usu cap* : of, relating to, or ruled by the Hashimites

hash·ish *also* **hash·eesh** *or* **hasch·isch** \'ha|(,)shēsh, 'haa|, 'hai|, |,shish *sometimes* ⸗'shēsh *or* hə'shēsh\ *n* -ES [Ar *ḥashīsh* dry herbage, hashish] **1** : a narcotic drug derived from the hemp (*Cannabis sativa*) that is smoked, chewed, or drunk for its intoxicating effect ⟨inhaled the ~ of his words with which he puffed dreamlike clouds about her head —Helen Howe⟩ — compare BHANG, CANNABIS, CHARAS, GANJA, MARIHUANA **2** : an intoxicating liquor prepared from cannabis

hash·ka·bah \häsh'käbə\ *n* -S *sometimes cap* [MHeb *hashkābhāh*, lit., lying down, fr. Heb *hashkībh* to lie down, die] : a recital of the memorial prayer for the dead esp. among Sephardic Jews

hash mark *n* : a military service stripe ⟨it takes a soldier or airman three years, and a sailor or marine four, to get a *hash mark* —*Armed Forces Talk*⟩

hash out *vt* : to thrash out ⟨invited by a faculty committee . . . to *hash out* their views on education theory —*Saturday Rev.*⟩

hash over *vt* : to talk over : DISCUSS ⟨*hash over* old times⟩ ⟨*hash over* a ball game⟩ ⟨plunged into the subject under discussion and *hashed it over* —E.J.Kahn⟩

hashslinger \'⸗,⸗⸗\ *n* : WAITER, WAITRESS

hash up *vt* **1** : to make a mess of : mutilate almost beyond recognition ⟨*hashed up* the account of the accident⟩ ⟨a concept that has *hashed up* remedial legislation⟩ **2** : to warm up : give fresh existence to : REANIMATE ⟨*hashing up* ancient quarrels —*Times Lit. Supp.*⟩ ⟨*hash up* novel interpretations of men and events based on little more than the findings of their predecessors —*Listener*⟩

ha·sid *or* **cha·sid** *or* **has·sid** *or* **chas·sid** \'hasəd, 'käs-\ *n, pl* **ha·sid·im** *or* **has·sid·im** \'hasədəm, kə'sēd-\ *usu cap* [Heb *ḥāsīdh* pious, one who is pious (pl. *ḥăsīdhīm*)] **1** : a member of a pious Jewish sect founded about the 3d century B.C. by opponents of Hellenistic innovations and devoted to the strict observance of the ritual of purification and separation — called also *assidean* **2** : a member of a Jewish sect devoted to mysticism and opposed to secular studies and Jewish rationalism that was founded in Poland about 1750 by Rabbi Israel ben Eliezer to revive the strict practices of the earlier Hasidim — **ha·sid·ic** *or* **cha·sid·ic** *or* **has·sid·ic** *or* **chas·sid·ic** \hə'sidik, kə'-\ *adj, usu cap*

hasidean *or* **hasidaean** *usu cap, var of* ASSIDEAN

has·i·dism *or* **chas·i·dism** *or* **hass·i·dism** *or* **chass·i·dism** \'hasə,dizəm, 'käs-\ *n* -S *usu cap* : the practices and beliefs of the Hasidim

ha·si·nai \'häsə,nī\ *n, pl* **hasinai** *usu cap* **1** : one of the three principal confederations of the Caddo Indians inhabiting northeastern Texas **2** : a member of the Hasinai Confederacy

hask \'(h)ask\ *adj* [ME, harsh, alter. of *harsk* — more at HARSH] **1** *now dial Eng, of weather* : cold and dry **2** *now dial Eng* **a** : rough and harsh to the touch **b** : harsh to the taste **3** *now dial Eng* : coarse and dry in texture

has·ka·lah \,haskə'lä, häs'kōlə\ *n* -S *usu cap, often attrib* [NHeb *haśkālāh*, lit., intellect, enlightenment] : an intellectual enlightenment movement among Jews of eastern Europe in the 18th and 19th centuries that attempted to acquaint the masses with European and Hebrew languages and secular education and culture to supplement talmudic studies — see MASKIL

has·let *or* **hass·let** \'haslət, 'häs-, -ăzl-\ *n* -S [ME *hastlet*, *hastelet*, fr. MF *hastelet* piece of meat roasted on a spit, dim. of *haste* piece of meat roasted on a spit, fr. OF, modif. (influenced by OF *haste* shaft of a spear, fr. L *hasta* spear) of a Gmc word represented by OHG *harsta* frying pan; akin to OE *hierstan*, *hyrstan* to fry, roast, MHG *harst* gridiron, OE *heorth* hearth — more at HEARTH, YARD] **1** : the edible viscera (as the heart or liver) of a butchered animal (as a hog) **2** : a braised dish made of edible viscera

has·mo·nae·an *or* **has·mo·ne·an** \¦hazmə¦nēən\ *or* **as·mo·nae·an** *or* **as·mo·ne·an** \¦az-\ *n* -S *usu cap* [LL *Asmonaeus* Hasmon, ancestor of the Maccabees (fr. Gk *Asamōnaios*) + E -*an*] : a member of a dynasty or family of Jewish patriots to which the Maccabees belonged

has·na \'haznə\ [by contr.] *dial Brit* : has not

hasn't \'haz'ən(t)\ [by contr.] : has not

¹hasp \'hasp, 'haa(ə)sp, 'haisp, 'hásp\ *n* -S [ME *hasp*, *haspe*, fr. OE *hæsp*, *hæpse*; akin to MHG *haspe* hasp, ON *hespa*, and perh. to L *capsa* chest, case — more at CASE] **1 a** : a fastener esp. for a door or lid consisting of a hinged metal strap that fits over a staple and is secured by a pin or padlock **b** : a similar strap having a projecting knob that snaps into a lock and that is much used on luggage **c** : any of several other devices (as a latch) for fastening a door or window ⟨the spring of the window ~ —G.M.Fenn⟩ **2** : a clasp for a book or an article of clothing ⟨a ledger bound with metal ~*s* —William Fifield⟩ ⟨cape with a ~ at the throat⟩ **3** *now dial Eng* **a** : a skein or hank of yarn, thread, or silk **b** : a fourth part of a spindle of such material

hasps 1

²hasp \"\ *vt* -ED/-ING/-S [ME *haspen*, fr. OE *hæpsian*, fr. *hæpse*, n.] **1** : to fasten with or as if with a hasp ⟨~ the door⟩ **2** *obs* : to confine in a small space — often used with *up* ⟨~*ed* up with thee in this small vehicle —*Spectator*⟩

hasp lock *n* **1** : a prison lock attached permanently to the hasp of a door and adapted to secure the door **2** : a detachable lock (as a padlock) to secure a hasp

has·sall's corpuscle *also* **has·sal's corpuscle** \'hasəlz-\ *n, usu cap H* : CORPUSCLE OF HASSALL

has·sar \'hasə(r)\ *n* -S [Arawak *asa*] : any of several armored catfishes (family Callichthyidae) of the Orinoco and its tributaries that are remarkable for their nest-building habits and for being able to leave the water and travel some distance on land

hassenpfeffer *var of* HASENPFEFFER

hassid *usu cap, var of* HASID

hassidean *or* **hassidaean** *usu cap, var of* ASSIDEAN

¹has·sle *also* **has·sel** \'hasəl, 'haas- 'hais-, 'hás-\ *n* -S [perh. blend of ²*haggle* and ²*tussle*] **1 a** : a heated argument : WRANGLE ⟨embroiling myself in a long, exasperating ~ with masons —S.J.Perelman⟩ **b** : a violent skirmish : FIGHT ⟨small units and small patrols, but for those in each ~ . . . it is still a tense, blood-curdling exchange of bullets —*N.Y. Times*⟩ **2** : a protracted debate : CONTROVERSY ⟨an extremely esoteric ~ over . . . ideas and concepts —Philip Hamburger⟩ **3 a** : a state of confusion or commotion : TURMOIL ⟨all ~ and hurly-burly —Ellery Queen⟩ **b** : a strenuous effort : STRUGGLE ⟨it's been a real ~ digging up new talent —Benny Goodman⟩

²hassle \"\ *vi* **hassled; hassled; hassling** \-s(ə)liŋ\ **hassles** : ARGUE, FIGHT, DISPUTE ⟨*hassled* with the umpires a time or two too many —Leo Durocher⟩ ⟨a lot of *hassling* back and forth over the telephone —*Sports Illustrated*⟩

hasslet *var of* HASLET

has·sock \'hasək, -aas-\ *n* -S [ME, fr. OE *hassuc*] **1** : a rank tuft of bog grass or sedge : TUSSOCK **2 a** : a small kneeling cushion or footstool ⟨an old-fashioned church ~ with flaps at the ends —Anna Kavan⟩ **b** : a bulky upholstered cushion used as an article of household furniture: as (1) : a large stuffed cushion that serves as a seat or leg rest — compare OTTOMAN, POUF (2) : a similar cushion or backless padded seat mounted on legs or having a hollow center for storage

hassocks 2b(1)

hassock fan *n* : an electric fan operating in a cylindrical hassock-shaped frame and propelling air upward from the floor

hassock grass *n* : TUFTED HAIR GRASS 2

has·socky \-kē\ *adj* : full of hassocks

has·su·na \hə'sünə\ *or* **has·su·nan** \-nən\ *adj, usu cap* [*hassuna* fr. *Hassuna*, archaeological site in northern Iraq; *hassunan* fr. *Hassuna* + E -*an*] : of or relating to an Aeneolithic culture of Mesopotamia earlier than the Halafian and characterized by the use of sometimes painted pottery, the manufacture of small clay figurines of women, and urn burial

hast *archaic pres 2d sing of* HAVE

has·ta \'hastə\ [contr. of *hast thou*] *dial Brit* : have you

has·tate \'ha,stāt\ *adj* [NL *hastatus*, fr. L *hasta* spear — more at YARD] **1** : shaped like an arrow with flaring barbs **2** *of a leaf* : triangular with sharp basal lobes spreading away from the petiole — see LEAF illustration — **has·tate·ly** *adv*

hastato- *comb form* [NL, fr. *hastatus*] : hastately : hastate and ⟨*hastato*lanceolate⟩ ⟨*hastato*sagittate⟩

¹haste \'hāst\ *n* -S [ME, fr. OF, of Gmc origin; akin to OE *hǣst* violence, OHG *heisti* violent, *heiftig* impetuous, ON *heipt*, *heifst* feud, war, hatred, Goth *haifsts* strife, conflict, fight; perh. akin to Skt *śibham* quickly] **1** : rapidity of motion : SPEED ⟨out of breath from ~ —Jane Austen⟩ **2** : rash or headlong action : PRECIPITATENESS ⟨~ makes waste⟩ ⟨the beauty of speed uncontaminated by ~ —*Harper's*⟩ **3** : overeagerness to act : HURRY ⟨I feel no ~ and no reluctance to depart —Edna S. V. Millay⟩

syn HURRY, SPEED, EXPEDITION, DISPATCH: HASTE indicates quickness or swiftness, often careless, on the part of persons impelled by urgency, pressure, eagerness ("Why this mad *haste*?" I asked. "Bandits", he shouted. —W.O.Douglas) HURRY may imply haste with confusion, agitation, and hustle ⟨there was a great *hurry* in the streets, of people speeding away to get shelter before the storm broke —Charles Dickens⟩ ⟨for whom all these women worked with such a sense of frantic *hurry* —Winifred Bambrick⟩ SPEED may focus attention on the fact of quickness, with very occasional implications of success ⟨such developments are bound to increase the *speed* of the social and economic revolution —R.W.Steel⟩ ⟨accused of slowness and undue deliberation, yet he built an adequate navy from nothing with surprising *speed* —H.K.Beale⟩ EXPEDITION and DISPATCH both designate efficient speed, the former with a suggestion of smooth efficiency, the latter of brisk promptness ⟨to move with reasonable *expedition* along the narrow pavements of Rotting Hill is impossible —Wyndham Lewis⟩ ⟨proceed with great *dispatch* and arrest the people involved —Dean Acheson⟩

²haste \"\ *vb* -ED/-ING/-S [ME *hasten*, fr. OF *haster*, fr. *haste*, n.] *vt, archaic* : to urge on : HASTEN ⟨with our fair entreaties ~ them on —Shak.⟩ ⟨~ thee, nymph, and bring with thee jest and youthful jollity —John Milton⟩ ~ *vi* : to move or act swiftly : HURRY ⟨~ to correct a seeming impression —O.W. Holmes †1935⟩ ⟨these minutes even now *hasting* into eternity —Winston Churchill⟩

haste·ful \-tfəl\ *adj* : full of haste : HASTY — **haste·ful·ly** \-fəlē\ *adv*

haste·less \-tləs\ *adj* : being without haste : UNHURRIED

has·ten \'hās°n\ *vb* **hastened; hastened; hastening** \-s(°)niŋ\ **hastens** [alter. of ²*haste*] *vt* **1 a** : to urge on : HURRY ⟨~*ed* her to the door —A.J.Cronin⟩ **b** : to speed up : ACCELERATE ⟨~ the coming of a new order —D.W.Brogan⟩ **2** *obs* : to send or bring quickly ⟨I pray . . . the king . . . to ~ his effectual letters —Edward Nicholas⟩ ~ *vi* : to move or act quickly : make haste : HURRY ⟨must ~ on to the bull ring —Mary Webb⟩ ⟨let me ~ to add that I do not mean absolute values —Kemp Malone⟩ **syn** see SPEED

has·ten·er \-s(°)nə(r)\ *n* -S : one that hastens

hast·er \'hāstə(r)\ *n* -S [²*haste* + -*er*] : HASTENER

has·ti·lude \'hastə,lüd\ *n, pl* **hastiludes** \-dz\ *or* **hastilu·dia** \,⸗⸗'lüdēə\ [ML *hastiludium*, fr. LL *hasti-* (fr. L *hasta* spear) + -*ludium* (fr. L *ludus* play, sport) — more at YARD, LUDICROUS] : a medieval joust : spear play ⟨one sport called ~*s* was no less dangerous than war itself —W.H.Dixon⟩

hast·i·ly \'hāstəlē, -li\ *adv* [ME, fr. *hasty* + -*ly*] **1** : rapidly and often with little attention to detail : HURRIEDLY ⟨read it ~⟩ ⟨wartime factories were ~ built⟩ **2** : without thorough consideration : RASHLY ⟨sold ~ and at a sacrifice —Raymond Weaver⟩

hast·i·ness \-tēnəs\ *n* -ES [ME *hastinesse*, fr. *hasty* + -*nesse* -*ness*] : the quality or state of being hasty

hast·ings \'(h)āstənz\ *n pl* [fr. pl. of obs. E *hasting* early fruit or vegetable, fr. *hasting*, adj., ripening early, fr. pres. part. of E ²*haste*] *now dial Eng* : early fruit or vegetables; *esp* : early peas

has·tings·ite \'hāstiŋ,zīt\ *n* -S [*Hastings* county, Ontario, Canada, its locality + E -*ite*] : a sodium-calcium-iron amphibole ideally $NaCa_2Fe_5Al_2Si_6O_{22}(OH)_2$ but generally containing a little potassium and magnesium

has·tu·la \'haschələ\ *n* -S [NL, fr. L, small spear, dim. of *hasta* spear] : a flat often triangular expansion at the upper surface of the petiole of a palm leaf where it joins the blade

hasty \'hāstē, -ti\ *adj* -ER/-EST [ME, fr. OF *hasti*, *hastif*, fr. *haste*, n. + -*if* -ive] **1 a** : rapid in action or movement : SPEEDY ⟨a ~ traveler⟩ **b** : made in a hurry : QUICK ⟨~ city-street snapshots —R.B.Heilman⟩ **c** : fast and often superficial : HURRIED ⟨a ~ smoke⟩ **2** : being in a hurry : EAGER, IMPATIENT ⟨too passionate and ~ to keep pace with the deliberate steps of his leader —Philip Marsh⟩ **3** : ill-considered : PRECIPITATE, RASH ⟨warning against ~ enterprises and partial solutions —M.R.Cohen⟩ **4** : prone to anger : IRRITABLE ⟨a man of ~ temper —G.B.Shaw⟩ **syn** see FAST, PRECIPITATE

hasty pudding *n* **1** *Brit* : a porridge or pudding made of oatmeal or flour boiled in water **2** *NewEng* : cornmeal mush usu. served hot with milk and maple sugar or molasses — compare INDIAN PUDDING

¹hat \'hat, *usu* -ad·+V\ *n* -S *often attrib* [ME, fr. OE *hæt*; akin to ON *hǫttr* head covering — more at HOOD] **1** : a covering for the head: as **a** : a head covering typically having a shaped crown and brim and made of felt, straw, or silk and worn by men — distinguished from *cap*; compare DERBY, FELT, STETSON, STRAW HAT **b** : a decorative accessory in a wide variety of shapes and materials worn by women — compare BONNET, CARTWHEEL, CLOCHE, PILLBOX, SAILOR, TOQUE **2 a** : a head covering of distinctive color or shape worn as a symbol of office ⟨cardinal's ~⟩ **b** : an office symbolized by or as if by the wearing of a special hat ⟨the two principal ~*s* a president wears are those of ceremonial head of state and chief executive —Cabell Phillips⟩ **3** : a layer of bark spread on the hides in a tanning pit **4** : a container used for taking up a collection of voluntary contributions (as of money) ⟨go round with the ~⟩ ⟨pass the ~⟩ — **have one's hat in the ring** *or* **throw one's hat in the ring** *or* **toss one's hat in the ring** : to announce one's entry or readiness to enter into a fight or contest (as for elective office) — **take one's hat off to** : to acknowledge the achievement or superiority of : COMPLIMENT ⟨he was colossal and I *take my hat off to* him —H.J.Laski⟩

²hat \"\ *vb* **hatted; hatted; hatting; hats** *vt* **1** : to furnish or provide with a hat ⟨smartly gowned, *hatted*, and gloved for the journey —A.N.Whitehead⟩ **2** : to bestow a cardinal's hat on ~ *vi* : to make or supply hats

³hat *dial past of* HIT

⁴hat *dial Eng var of* HIT

hatable *var of* HATEABLE

hat ball *n* : a game of roly-poly in which the ball is rolled into hats placed on the ground

hatband \'⸗,⸗\ *n* [ME, fr. ¹*hat* + *band*, n.] : a band of fabric, leather, or cord around the crown of a hat just above the brim

hatbox \'⸗,⸗\ *n* **1** : a box for holding hats **2** : a piece of hand luggage that is usu. round and deep, has a handle, and is designed esp. for carrying hats though it is often used as a traveling bag by women

¹hatch \'hach\ *n* -ES [ME *hache*, *hacche*, fr. OE *hæc*; akin to MD *hecke* trapdoor, grating, MLG *heck* fence] **1 a** *obs* : the lower half of a divided door ⟨in at the window or else o'er the ~ —Shak.⟩ **b** : a small door, wicket, or serving counter ⟨equipped with an escape ~ for use in case of fire —W.H. Goodenough⟩ ⟨shop through a ~ in the wall —*Time*⟩ ⟨snatched up two plates of cold tongue . . . from the serving-room ~ —Margaret Kennedy⟩ **2 a** *obs* (1) : movable planking over the cargo hold of a ship — usu. used in pl. (2) : DECK — usu. used in pl. ⟨upon the giddy footing of the ~*es* —Shak.⟩ **b** : a door or grated cover giving vertical access down into a compartment ⟨smoke rose through the same ~ where . . . men could climb to the cannon deck —J.H.Cutler⟩ ⟨luggage disappears through the big plane's ~⟩ ⟨the inspector lifts the ~ in the top of the oil storage tank⟩; *specif* : the cover of a tank turret ⟨one of the .50-caliber guns can be . . . fired from inside without opening the turret ~ —*Military Rev.*⟩ **c** : HATCHWAY **d** : an enclosed space : COMPARTMENT ⟨her ~*es* were enlarged and her lumber-carrying career . . . resumed —H.G.Peterson⟩ ⟨device . . . the airman is placing in its release ~ —*N. Y. Times Mag.*⟩ **3** : something that resembles a hatch: as **a** : FLOODGATE, SLUICE GATE **b** : an opening or door in the deck or fuselage of an airplane (as for a means of escape in an emergency or for loading cargo) **c** : a frame or weir in a river for catching fish

²hatch \'(h)ach\ *vt* -ED/-ING/-ES *now dial Eng* : to close (a door) with a hatch

³hatch \'hach\ *vb* -ED/-ING/-ES [ME *hacchen*; akin to MHG *hecken* to mate (said of birds)] *vi* **1** : to produce young from an egg by incubation ⟨the hen ~*ed* today⟩ **2** : to emerge from an egg or chrysalis ⟨watched the chickens ~⟩ ⟨begins to ~ from the chrysalis in early July —E.B.Ford⟩ — often used with *off* or *out* ⟨hens' eggs take 21 days to ~ out —*Jeyes' Poultry Bk.*⟩ **3** : to incubate eggs : BROOD ⟨the old hen is ~*ing*⟩ ~ *vt* **1** *archaic* : BREED, PROPAGATE ⟨what monsters now doth nature ~ —*Mirour for Magistrates*⟩ ⟨serving as a nursery bed to ~ . . . the infant plant —William Bartram⟩ **2 a** : to produce (young) from an egg by applying natural or artificial heat ⟨a duck . . . which ~*ed* chickens —Margaret Deland⟩ ⟨an incubator can ~ more eggs at a time than a hen⟩ **b** : to cause to incubate ⟨turtle eggs are ~*ed* by the sun⟩ **3** : to bring into being : ORIGINATE, PRODUCE ⟨~*ing* a program of economic aid —E.K.Lindley⟩ ⟨they repair to the little summer place to garden and smoke pipes, they ~ books, they go fishing —George Spelvin⟩; *esp* : to concoct in secret ⟨~ a conspiracy⟩ — often used with *up* ⟨when was all this ~*ed* up —Ann Bridge⟩

⁴hatch \"\ *n* -ES **1 a** : an act of hatching ⟨congregate in family groups soon after the ~ —W.W.Haines⟩ **b** : the transformation of a swarm of insects from a water-dwelling to a winged phase ⟨trout were rising freely to a ~ of small gray flies —F.C. Craighead b. 1916 & J.J.Craighead⟩ **2** : a product of hatching : brood of young ⟨the entire ~ in an incubator —J.E.Shillinger & L.C.Morley⟩

⁵hatch \"\ *vt* -ED/-ING/-ES [ME *hachen*, fr. MF *hacher*, fr. OF *hachier* to chop up — more at HASH] **1** : to inlay in fine lines : apply narrow bands of a different color or material to **2** : to mark with fine closely spaced parallel or crisscrossed lines in drawing or engraving chiefly to represent shading — see ³HATCHING

⁶hatch \"\ *n* -ES : STROKE, LINE; *esp* : one used in engraving or drawing to give the effect of shading

hatch·abil·i·ty \,hachə'bilədē\ *n* **1** : the quality or state of being hatchable ⟨low ~ generally means low vitality in the chicks that do hatch —*Reliable Poultry Jour.*⟩ **2** : the ability to produce hatchable eggs ⟨turkey hens which become broody during the laying season show higher . . . ~ than nonbroody hens —*Agric. Research in S. Dak.*⟩

hatch·able \'hachəbəl\ *adj* [³*hatch* + -*able*] *of an egg* : capable of being hatched

hatch bar *n* : a bar across a hatch to batten it down

hatch beam *n* : a heavy portable beam across a large hatch to support the cover

hatch deck *n* : a temporary deck of removable planking or covers over the hold

hatcheck \'⸗,⸗\ *adj* **1** : that checks hats and other articles of clothing ⟨~ girl⟩ **2** : used in the checking of hats and other articles of clothing ⟨~ stand⟩

¹hatch·el \'hachəl\ *also* **hetch·el** \'hech-\ *n* -S [*hatchel* alter. of *hetchel*, fr. ME *hechele*, *hekele*, *hakell*; akin to MD *hekele* hackle, MHG *hechel*, *hachel* hackle, OHG *hāko* hook — more at HOOK] : ³HACKLE 1

²hatchel \"\ *vt* **hatcheled** *or* **hatchelled; hatcheled** *or* **hatchelled; hatcheling** *or* **hatchelling; hatchels** [alter. of earlier *hetchel*, fr. ME *hechelen*, fr. *hechele*, n.] **1** : ⁴HACKLE 1 **2** : HECKLE 2

hatch·er \'hachə(r)\ *n* -S **1** : one that hatches; *specif* : a device to which eggs are transferred from the incubator shortly before they are due to hatch **2** : one that produces or originates

hatch·ery \-ch(ə)rē, -ri\ *n* -ES **1** : a place for hatching eggs (as of poultry or fish) **2** : a place for the large-scale production of weaning feeder pigs

hatch·ery·man \'⸗(⸗)⸗,⸗\ *n, pl* **hatcherymen** : one who operates a hatchery

hatches *pl of* HATCH, *pres 3d sing of* HATCH

¹hatch·et \'hachət, *usu* -əd·+V\ *n* -S *often attrib* [ME *hachet*, *hacchet* small ax, fr. MF *hachette*, fr. *hache* battle-ax + -*ette* — more at HASH] **1 a** : a short-handled ax with a hammerhead to be used with one hand either for cutting or hammering **b** : TOMAHAWK **2** : a dental excavator

²hatchet \"\ *vt* -ED/-ING/-S **1** : to cut or kill with a hatchet ⟨~ a tree⟩ ⟨~ an enemy⟩ **2** : to dispatch as if with a hatchet ⟨~ proposal⟩

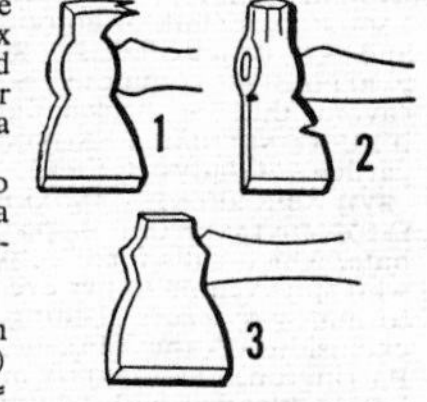

hatchets 1a: *1* claw, *2* half, *3* broad

hatchet cactus *n* : a small Mexican cactus (*Pelecyphora aselliformis*) with white flowers and hatchet-shaped tubercles

hatchet face *n* **1** : a long narrow face with sharp features **2** : a person having a thin sharp face — **hatchet-faced** \'⸗⸗¦⸗\ *adj*

hatchetfish \'⸗⸗,⸗\ *n* : any of several small So. American characin fishes with enlarged pectoral fins and thin wedge-shaped bodies that are often seen in tropical aquariums

hatchet job *n* : an act of defamation : malicious attack ⟨turned traitor to his class and performed a *hatchet job* on the commuting world —*Time*⟩

hatchet man *n* **1 :** a professional killer **:** TRIGGERMAN, HIGHBINDER ⟨the hooded cult retaliated and four . . . *hatchet men* were found dead in a ditch —W.M.Swann⟩ **2 a :** one who transmits orders or maintains discipline for a superior **:** HENCHMAN ⟨needed a competent and senior foreign service *hatchet man* to keep the . . . career boys under control —*Harper's*⟩; *specif* **:** an ideological watchdog or party disciplinarian ⟨served his party as chief *hatchet man* —Robert Bendiner⟩ **b** (1) **:** a writer who specializes in denunciation and invective often on orders from an employer and without regard to personal scruples ⟨our present journalistic *hatchet men* —B.R.Redman⟩ (2) **:** CRITIC ⟨a literary *hatchet man* —S.E.Hyman⟩

hatchet stake *n* **:** a sharp-edged stake on which to bend sheet metal — see STAKE illustration

hatch·ett·ine \'hachəd·,ēn, -d·ən\ *or* **hatch·ett·ite** \-d·,īt\ *n* -s [Charles *Hatchett* †1847 Eng. chemist + E *-ine* or *-ite*] **:** a mineral paraffin wax $C_{38}H_{78}$ melting at 55° to 65° C in the natural state and at 79° C when pure — called also *mineral tallow*

hatch·et·to·lite \-d·ō,līt\ *n* -s [Charles *Hatchett* †1847 + E *-o-* + *-lite*] **:** a uranium-bearing pyrochlore

hatchet work *n* **:** the work of a hatchet man

hatchgate \'≐,≐\ *n* **1 :** WICKET **2 :** ¹HATCH 3a

¹**hatching** *n* -s [ME *hacchynge*, fr. gerund of ME *hacchen* to produce young from an egg by incubation — more at HATCH (verb)] **:** ⁴HATCH

²**hatching** *n* -s [fr. gerund of ⁵*hatch*] **1 a :** the engraving or drawing of fine lines in close proximity to each other chiefly to give an effect of shading **b :** the pattern so created **2 :** the process or result of weaving threads of one color into an adjoining area of another color in a tapestry so as to produce an effect of shading or highlights **3 :** a fine concentric line of pores in the tangential section of some woods

hatching spine *n* **:** a spine on the unhatched young of various insects used to break the embryonic envelope

hatch·ite \'ha,chīt\ *n* -s [Frederick H. *Hatch* †1932 Eng. mining engineer and geologist + E *-ite*] **:** a mineral consisting of a sulfide of lead and arsenic that occurs in triclinic crystals but whose exact composition is unknown

hatch·ling \'hachliŋ\ *n* -s **:** a recently hatched animal

hatch·man \'≐mən\ *also* **hatch·mind·er** \'≐,≐≐\ *or* **hatch·way·man** \'≐,≐mən\ *n, pl* **hatchmen** *also* **hatchminders** *or* **hatchwaymen :** one who stands by a ship's hatch to assist with the loading and unloading

hatch·ment \'hachmənt\ *n* -s [perh. alter. of *achievement*] **:** a panel having the shape of a square placed cornerwise or of a lozenge, bearing the coat of arms of a deceased person, and displayed temporarily usu. on the outside wall of his dwelling

hatchure *var of* HACHURE

hatchway \'≐,≐\ *n* **:** an opening equipped with a hatch and giving access to a compartment, room, or cellar; *specif* **:** a passageway between the decks of a ship

hatch whip *n* **:** a block and tackle for hoisting cargo through a hatchway

hat dance *n* **:** a national courtship folk dance of Mexico performed by two people in which the man throws a sombrero on the ground and the girl signifies acceptance of him as her lover by dancing on its brim and then putting it on her head — compare JARABE

¹**hate** \'hāt, *usu* -ād·+V\ *n* -s *often attrib* [ME, alter. (prob. influenced by *haten*, v.) of *hete*, fr. OE; akin to OHG *haz* hate, ON *hatr* hate, Goth *hatis* wrath, Gk *kēdos* grief, mourning, Av *sādra* sorrow] **1 a :** intense hostility toward an object (as an individual) that has frustrated the release of an inner tension (as of a biological nature) ⟨quick dislike had ripened into ~ —I.V.Morris⟩ ⟨rid your mind of any hidden ~*s* or grudges —W.J.Reilly⟩; *specif* **:** a systematic esp. politically exploited expression of hate ⟨the forces of darkness, bigotry, and ~⟩ ⟨~ list⟩ ⟨~ bombings⟩ ⟨~ mail⟩ **b :** an habitual emotional attitude in which distaste is coupled with sustained ill will ⟨his life became increasingly dominated by ~⟩ **c :** a strong dislike or antipathy **:** DISTASTE ⟨developed a ~ for string quartets⟩ **2 :** an object of hatred ⟨a generation whose finest ~ had been big business —F.L.Paxson⟩

²**hate** \"\ *vb* -ED/-ING/-s [ME *haten*, fr. OE *hatian*; akin to OS *haton* to hate, OHG *hazzōn*, ON *hata*; denominative fr. the root of ¹*hate*] *vt* **1 :** to feel extreme enmity toward **:** regard with active hostility ⟨sit there *hating* one another and end up by cutting one another's throats —John Wain⟩ **2 a :** to have a strong aversion to **:** DETEST, RESENT ⟨~ what is evil, hold fast to what is good —Rom 12: 9 (RSV)⟩ ⟨they ~ being moved from one box to another —Henry Wynmalen⟩ **b :** to find distasteful **:** DISLIKE ⟨*hated* the cold and the snow —Harold Griffin⟩ ⟨so pretty she *hated* to get glasses when she needed them —John Steinbeck⟩ ⟨*hated* that young men should raise their hats to him out of respect for his superior age —Arnold Bennett⟩ ~ *vi* **:** to express or feel extreme enmity or active hostility ⟨harsh faces and *hating* eyes —Katherine A. Porter⟩

syn DETEST, LOATHE, ABHOR, ABOMINATE: HATE, the antonym of love, indicates an extreme of dislike, aversion, and enmity experienced often toward an equal with a possible accompanying feeling of grudging respect ⟨if there had been one atom of genuine passion in his duplicity, she might have despised him less even while she *hated* him more —Ellen Glasgow⟩ ⟨he *hates* Lucy Wales. I don't mean dislike, or find distasteful, or have an aversion for; I mean hate —Hamilton Basso⟩ Applied to things and qualities it indicates extreme dislike ⟨between the cruelty that we *hate* and the humor that we prize —Agnes Repplier⟩ DETEST indicates very strong aversion but may lack the actively hostile malevolence associated with HATE ⟨the boy glimpsed something of the system of slavery, and early came to *detest* it —C.E.Carter⟩ LOATHE may suggest disgust and revulsion rather than aversion and active antipathy ⟨except when I am listening to their music I *loathe* the whole race: great, stupid, brutal, immoral, sentimental savages —Rose Macaulay⟩ ⟨he is not hated, for in hate there is something of fear and something of respect, neither of which is present here. And you could not say *loathed*, for loathing is passive and this is an active feeling. Best say detested; vigorously disliked —T.O. Heggen⟩ ABHOR may suggest a revulsion or repugnance accompanied by a tendency to flinch from as though in fear or horror ⟨Rome had made herself *abhorred* throughout the world by the violence and avarice of her generals —J.A. Froude⟩ ⟨this temptation to *abhor* the flesh, which reached such a pitch that he was filled with a horror of all created life —Compton Mackenzie⟩ ⟨rats, who *abhor* light and crave privacy —V.G.Heiser⟩ ABOMINATE may indicate strong lasting hatred and loathing as of something foully unnatural ⟨the accused . . . protest, disclaim, *abominate* the honor —Robert Browning⟩ These words all weaken in hyperbolic usages.

— hate one's guts : to feel a particularly strong animosity or contempt for someone ⟨I don't dislike him, I *hate his guts* —E.S.Gardner⟩

³**hate** \"\ *var of* HAET

hate·able *or* **hat·able** \'hād·əbəl\ *adj* **:** subject to being hated **:** DETESTABLE

hate·ful \'hātfəl\ *adj* [ME, fr. ¹*hate* + *-ful*] **1 :** full of hate **:** MALICIOUS ⟨talk of an outbreak of the Sioux who were surly and ~ —Bruce Siberts⟩ **2 a :** exciting or deserving of hatred **:** REPULSIVE ⟨opinions ~ to the majority —M.R.Cohen⟩ ⟨avoid that ~ backslapping heartiness —R.B.McKerrow⟩ **b :** UNCONGENIAL, ANNOYING, DISTASTEFUL ⟨~ to be without a garden —Gladys B. Stern⟩

syn ABHORRENT, OBNOXIOUS, INVIDIOUS, REPUGNANT, REPELLENT, DISTASTEFUL: HATEFUL applies to that which arouses hate, which calls forth active hostility ⟨the *hateful* old cat . . . who spits venom in her every sentence —C.B.Tinker⟩ ⟨the war to him was a *hateful* thing, stupid and unjust, waged for the extension of the obscene system of negro slavery —V.L. Parrington⟩ ABHORRENT may characterize that which arouses hatred blended with feelings of horror or outrage ⟨to Greek thought the indefinite or limitless was as the monstrous and unformed, and therefore *abhorrent* to the classic ideals of perfection —H.O.Taylor⟩ ⟨they themselves consider sorcery as an *abhorrent* crime —W.J.Wallace & Edith S. Taylor⟩ OBNOXIOUS describes what is objectionable or extremely repulsive ⟨when mosquitoes grew *obnoxious* we packed up our dishes and went to the house —Della Lutes⟩ ⟨an opportunity to hang around the house and smoke too many cigars and aggravate his poor, patient wife, and exasperate his children, and make himself generally *obnoxious* to all —Simeon Ford⟩ ⟨resentment against the Stamp Act reached a climax . . . His Majesty's Ship Diligence was prevented from landing the *obnoxious* stamps —*Amer. Guide Series: N. C.*⟩ INVIDIOUS describes that which excites ill will, resentment, or hatred, and is likely to rankle ⟨bowed with an *invidious* curtness and insolently walked off the stage —Edmund Wilson⟩ ⟨the *invidious* task of improving other people's utterance —J.M.Barzun⟩ ⟨rogues, by which perhaps rather *invidious* name I designate persons who will do nothing unless they get something out of it for themselves —G.B.Shaw⟩ REPUGNANT applies to what is resisted, disliked, and shunned as incompatible with one's principles or tastes ⟨soon the pressures of male eyes, eyes expressing sex, the curious lamplike luminosity, became *repugnant* to her —Peggy Bennett⟩ ⟨the internationalism of the socialists found any barriers of race or nationality *repugnant* —Oscar Handlin⟩ ⟨the nonlegal methods of the magistrates in dispensing judgment, so *repugnant* to the spirit of the common law —V.L. Parrington⟩ REPELLENT, close to REPUGNANT, may apply to what is shunned as offensive to personal tastes and inclinations ⟨as *repellent* in form and abstract in substance as many of the German writers on aesthetics of the nineteenth century —Irving Babbitt⟩ ⟨as a cardinal's nephew he was accustomed to many and *repellent* smiles upon inimical lips —Elinor Wylie⟩ DISTASTEFUL, a somewhat less forceful term, applies to what one dislikes, usu. for strongly personal reasons ⟨don't like my letters shown about as curiosities: it is most *distasteful* to me —Oscar Wilde⟩ ⟨developed a keen interest in the purely scientific aspects of medicine, the more practical phases of a practitioner's routine being *distasteful* to him —J.F.Fulton⟩ ⟨plans to refurnish the bedrooms with her own personal belongings, since she finds it *distasteful* to think of using the personal belongings of its previous occupants —Kenneth Roberts⟩

hate·ful·ly \-fəlē, -li\ *adv* [ME, fr. *hateful* + *-ly*] **:** in a hateful manner

hate·ful·ness *n* -ES **:** the quality or state of being hateful

hate·less \'hātləs\ *adj* **:** being without hate — **hate·less·ness** *n* -ES

hatemonger \'≐,≐≐\ *n* **:** one who enjoys or makes a practice of stirring up enmity **:** AGITATOR ⟨local ~*s* were probably financed and directed from outside the state —*Associated Press*⟩

hatemongering \'≐,≐(≐)≐\ *n* **:** the act or practice of stirring up hatred or enmity

hate out *vt* **:** to drive out by hostility ⟨a common way of dealing with offenders was to *hate* them *out* of the community —C.M.Babcock⟩

hat·er \'hād·ə(r), -ātə-\ *n* -s [ME *hatere*, fr. *haten* to hate + *-ere* -er] **:** one that hates

hates *pl of* HATE, *pres 3d sing of* HATE

hate sheet *n* **:** a newspaper or periodical characterized by strong feelings against a race or a national or religious group ⟨the worst inflammatory *hate sheet* published —Walter Winchell⟩

hat·field yew \'hat,fēld-\ *n, sometimes cap H* [after T. D. *Hatfield* *fl*1900 Am. horticulturist] **:** an ornamental yew that is a variety (*Taxus cuspidata hatfieldii*) of Japanese yew with ascending branches and wide spreading leaves

hat·ful \'hat,fu̇l\ *n, pl* **hatfuls** *also* **hatsful** \-t,fu̇lz, ts,fu̇l\ **1 :** as much or as many as a hat will hold ⟨gathered a ~ of eggs⟩ **2 :** a considerable amount or number **:** PECK ⟨these dives can cost you a ~ of money —T.H.Fielding⟩ ⟨turned down a ~ of princes —Helen B. Woodward⟩

hath *archaic pres 3d sing of* HAVE

hatha–yoga \'həd·ə'yōgə\ *n* [Skt *haṭha* force, persistence + *yoga* disciplined activity — more at YOGA] **:** a system of physical exercises for the control and perfection of the body that constitutes one of the four chief Hindu disciplines — see YOGA

ha·thi gray \'häd·ē-\ *n* [Hindi *hāthī* elephant, fr. Skt *hastin*, fr. *hasta* hand, elephant's trunk; prob. akin to Lith *pažastė* armpit] **:** a greenish gray that is yellower, lighter, and slightly less strong than cabbage green

hath·or column \'hathə(r)-\ *n, usu cap H* [*Hathor*, ancient Egyptian goddess of love] **:** a type of Egyptian column usu. having a 4-faced capital carved with heads of the goddess Hathor

hathor–headed \¦≐≐¦≐≐\ *adj, usu cap H* **:** carved with masks of Hathor

ha·thor·ic \hə'thȯrik, -'thär-\ *adj, usu cap* [*Hathor* + E *-ic*] **:** of or relating to Hathor or to a column surmounted by her image

ha·ti \'had·ē\ *n* -s [Egypt *ḥati*] *often cap, Egyptian relig* **:** the physical heart — compare ²AB

hating *pres part of* HATE

hat in hand *adv* **:** in an attitude of respectful humility ⟨have to apologize *hat in hand*⟩

hat leather *n* **:** leather (as sheepskin or calf) for making hat or cap sweatbands

hat·less \'hatləs\ *adj* [ME *hatles*, fr. ¹*hat* + *-les* -less] **:** being without a hat — **hat·less·ness** *n* -ES

hat money *n* **1 :** PRIMAGE 1a **2 :** money in the form of truncated tin obelisks used in Pahang, Malay Peninsula in the 19th century

hat off *n, pl* **hats off :** ADMIRATION, CONGRATULATIONS ⟨end these memories with my *hat off* to the leaders —J.J.Mallon⟩ ⟨if you can do that and come up smiling — well, then, it's *hats off* all round —Myrtle R. White⟩

hat palm *n* **:** any of various palms or plants resembling palms whose leaves are used for making hats: as **a :** JIPIJAPA **b :** a palm (*Coccothrinax argentea*) of Panama **c :** CARNAUBA **d :** any of several West Indian fan palms of the genus *Thrinax*; *esp* **:** CHIP HAT PALM **e** *Philippines* **:** any of various palms of the genera *Areca*, *Corypha*, *Livistona*, and *Pandanus*

hat piece *n, obs* **:** a protective metal skullcap worn under a hat

hatpin \'≐,≐\ *n* **1 :** a long straight pin with an ornamented head that is used to keep a hat in place **2 :** a plant of the genus *Eriocaulon* (esp. *E. decangulare*)

hat rack *n* **1 a** (1) **:** a wooden framework with several projecting pegs that hangs against a wall and is used to hold hats and other articles of clothing (2) **:** CLOTHES TREE (3) **:** HALLSTAND **b :** a loop (as of wire) into which to slip the brim of a hat under a theater seat or shelf or against a wall **2 :** a thin low-quality meat animal

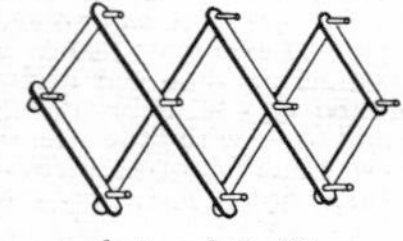
hat rack 1a(1)

ha·tred \'hā·trəd\ *n* -s [ME *hatred*, *hatered*, *hatereden*, fr. ¹*hate* + *-reden* (fr. OE *rǣden* condition) — more at KINDRED] **1 :** HATE **2 :** a general attitude of prejudiced hostility **:** group animosity ⟨the human race lives in a welter of organized ~*s* and threats of mutual extermination —Bertrand Russell⟩

hats *pl of* HAT, *pres 3d sing of* HAT

hat·sa \'hatsə\ *n, pl* **hatsa** *or* **hatsas** *usu cap* **1 a :** a Negro African people of northern Tanganyika **b :** a member of such people **2 :** the language spoken by the Hatsa people and related to Khoisan

hatsful *pl of* HATFUL

hatstand \'≐,≐\ *n* **1 a :** CLOTHES TREE **b :** HALLSTAND **2 :** an accessory for a closet shelf that consists of a short rod set in a base topped with a knob or disk and used to support a hat so that it will keep its shape while not in use

hatted *adj* [fr. past part. of ²*hat*] **:** wearing a hat ⟨two neatly ~ and gloved old ladies —Claudia Cassidy⟩ ⟨a bearskin-*hatted* sentry⟩

¹**hat·ter** \'had·ə(r), -atə-\ *n* -s [ME, fr. ¹*hat* + *-er*] **1 :** one that makes, sells, or cleans and repairs hats **2** [prob. so called fr. the presumed applicability of the proverbial expression "mad as a hatter"] *Austral* **a :** a solitary bush dweller **b :** a lone miner or prospector — often used of a person who has become eccentric from too much solitude **3 :** fur esp. of rabbits for making felt hats — usu. used in pl.

²**hatter** *vt* -ED/-ING/-s [ME (Sc) *hatteren*] **1** *now dial* **:** BATTER, BRUISE **2** *archaic* **:** to wear out **:** worry and harass — sometimes used with *out*

¹**hat·te·ria** \hə'tirēə\ [NL] *syn of* SPHENODON

²**hatteria** \"\ *n* -s **:** TUATARA

hat·ti \'had·ē\ *or* **khat·ti** \'kə-\ *n, pl* **hatti** *or* **hattis** *or* **khatti** *or* **khattis** *usu cap* [Akkadian *ḫatti*, *khatti*] **1 :** a pre-Hittite people of central Anatolia **2 :** a member of such people — **hat·ti·an** \'had·ēən\ *adj, usu cap*

¹**hat·tic** \'had·ik\ *adj, usu cap* [*Hatti* + *-ic*] **:** of or relating to the Hatti people

²**hattic** \"\ *n* -s *usu cap* **:** a language known from quotations in Hittite documents and assumed to be that of the Hatti

hatting *n* -s [fr. gerund of ²*hat*] **1 a :** the making of hats **b :** the material from which hats are made **2 :** HAT 3

hat·tock \'(h)ad·ək\ *n* -s [¹*hat* + *-ock*] **1** *obs* **:** a small hat **2** *dial Eng* **a :** a grain shock with the top protected by sheaves leaned slantingly against it heads down **b :** one of the two protecting sheaves

hat tree *n* **1 a :** CLOTHES TREE **b :** HALLSTAND **2 :** either of two Australian trees (*Sterculia discolor* and *S. lurida*) that produce strong bast fibers

hat trick *n* **1 a :** a sleight-of-hand trick performed with a hat **b :** a skillful maneuver ⟨a remarkable political *hat trick* —Mollie Panter-Downes⟩ **2 a** [prob. so called fr. a former practice of rewarding this feat with a present of a new hat] **:** the dismissal by a bowler of three batsmen with three consecutive balls in cricket **b :** a similar outstanding feat in another sport: as (1) **:** the winning of three consecutive horse races (2) **:** the scoring of three goals in one game by a hockey player (3) **:** the hitting by one player of a single, double, triple, and home run in a game of baseball

hau \'hau̇\ *n* -s [Hawaiian & Marquesan] **:** MAJAGUA a

haubergeon *var of* HABERGEON

hau·ber·get \¦hȯbə(r)¦jet\ *n* -s [ML *haubergettum*] **:** an early English woolen cloth

hau·berk \'hȯ(,)bərk\ *n* -s [ME, fr. OF *hauberc*, of Gmc origin; akin to OE *healsbeorg* neck armor, OHG *halsberg*, ON *halsbjǫrg*; all fr. a prehistoric WGmc-NGmc compound whose constituents are represented respectively by OE *heals* neck and OE *beorg* protection; akin to OE *beorgan* to preserve, defend — more at COLLAR, BURY] **1 :** a long tunic of ring or chain mail that with a close-fitting helmet and a shield constituted the main defensive armor of the 12th to 14th centuries **2 :** HABERGEON

hauberk

haud \'hȯd\ *chiefly Scot var of* HOLD

hau·er·ite \'hau̇ə,rīt\ *n* -s [G *hauerit*, fr. Franz von *Hauer* †1899 Austrian geologist + G *-it* -ite] **:** a mineral MnS_2 consisting of native manganese sulfide and occurring as reddish brown or brownish black octahedral or pyritohedral crystals or massive (sp. gr. 3.46)

hauf \'hȧf, 'hȯf\ *dial Brit var of* HALF

haugh \'hȯ(k̲), 'hä(k̲)\ *n* -s [ME (Sc dial.) *holch*, *hawch*, fr. OE *healh* corner of land; akin to OE *holh* cave, *hol* hollow — more at HOLE] *chiefly Scot* **:** a low-lying meadow by the side of a river **:** an alluvial plain

haught *adj* [alter. (influenced by such words as *caught*, *taught*) of ME *haute*, fr. MF *haut*, lit., high, fr. L *altus* — more at OLD] **1** *obs* **:** HAUGHTY ⟨thou ~ insulting man —Shak.⟩ **2** *obs* **:** NOBLE, HIGH-MINDED, LOFTY

haugh·ti·ly \'hȯd·ᵊl·ē, |t|, |ᵊli, |əl- *also* 'hä|\ *adv* **:** in a haughty manner

haugh·ti·ness \|ēnəs, |in-\ *n* -ES **:** the quality or state of being haughty **:** ARROGANCE

haugh·ty \|ē, |i\ *adj* -ER/-EST [*haught* + *-y*] **1 :** disdainfully proud or overbearing **:** ARROGANT ⟨~ young beauty . . . never deigned to notice us —Herman Melville⟩ **2** *obs* **:** exalted in nature **:** NOBLE ⟨words . . . equal unto this ~ enterprise —Edmund Spenser⟩ **3 :** imposing in aspect **:** LOFTY ⟨~ cathedral⟩

syn see PROUD

¹**haul** \'hȯl\ *vb* -ED/-ING/-s [ME *halen* to pull, draw, fr. OF *haler*, of Gmc origin; akin to MD *halen* to pull; akin to OE *geholian* to obtain, OHG *halōn*, *holōn*, *holēn* to call, fetch, OS *halōn*, and perh. to OE *hlōwan* to low — more at LOW] *vt* **1 a :** to change the course of (a ship) esp. so as to sail closer to the wind — often used with directional adverb ⟨told the chief officer to ~ her off four points —*Mercantile Marine Mag.*⟩ **b :** to sail or hold on a course ⟨~*ed* his skiff all the way north —A.B.Mayse⟩ **2 a** (1) **:** to exert traction on **:** PULL ⟨~ a wagon⟩ — often followed by directional adverb ⟨~ out a stump⟩ ⟨~ up a lobster pot⟩ ⟨~ in an anchor⟩ ⟨~ down a flag⟩ (2) **:** to take by drawing in or up (as with a net) ⟨~ herring⟩ **b :** to exert influence on so as to achieve a desired end **:** DRAG ⟨his wife . . . will ~ him to a highbrow play —Francis Fergusson⟩ **c :** to transport from one place to another in a vehicle **:** CART ⟨~ passengers⟩ ⟨~ coal from the mines⟩ ⟨cattle are ~*ed* by rail⟩ **3 :** to bring before (an authority) for interrogation or punishment **:** HALE ⟨~ traffic violators into court⟩ — often used with *up* ⟨~ up a . . . president of the United States to explain his conduct in office to a congressional committee —Elmer Davis⟩ ~ *vi* **1 a :** to change course so as to sail closer to the wind — often used with *up* ⟨she ~*ed* up 'til the sails began to shiver⟩ **b :** to sail on a course ⟨decided to ~ south⟩ **2 a** (1) **:** to exert traction **:** PULL ⟨~ on a rope⟩ — often followed by directional adverb ⟨~ back on the reins⟩ ⟨~*ed* over to put a pilot aboard —H.A.Chippendale⟩ (2) **:** to take or seek a catch esp. of fish by hauling a net ⟨go ~*ing* for herring⟩ **b :** to propel oneself **:** COME, GO ⟨about three o'clock we ~*ed* into Moonridge —Kenneth Clark⟩ ⟨the bull ~*ed* back for another lunge —F.B.Gipson⟩ **c :** to carry from one place to another **:** furnish transportation ⟨nominal charge for ~*ing*⟩ **3** *of the wind* **:** to change direction **:** SHIFT ⟨the wind has ~*ed* more to the south —William Willis⟩ — often used with *around* ⟨~*ed* around to the starboard quarter⟩ **syn** see PULL — **haul down one's colors :** SURRENDER ⟨saw she was beaten and *hauled down her colors*⟩ — **haul in one's horns :** retreat from an arrogant or aggressive position ⟨admitted his error and *hauled in his horns*⟩ — **haul one over the coals :** to criticize or reprimand **:** take to task **:** CENSURE ⟨*hauled him over the coals* for loafing on the job⟩ — **haul one's wind :** to head the bow of a ship closer into the wind **:** LUFF ⟨*hauled his wind* until the sail was trimmed in flat —Vincent McHugh⟩ — often used with *on*, *upon*, *or to*

²**haul** \"\ *n* -s **1 a :** an act of dragging **:** strong pull ⟨the rope stood up under the strain of the ~⟩ **b :** a mechanical device for pulling **:** CONVEYOR BELT ⟨mine cars on a car ~⟩ **2 :** the result of an effort to collect either legitimately or by theft **:** TAKE ⟨rich ~*s* of plankton —N.B.Marshall⟩ ⟨a mink coat ~ —Rose Thurburn⟩; *specif* **:** the fish taken in a single draft of a net **3** *ropemaking* **:** a bundle of yarns to be tarred **4 a :** an act of transporting ⟨a rail ~ meant that several hundred expensive . . . cars would have to be bought —N.M.Clark⟩ **b :** the distance or route over which a load is transported ⟨sand is normally taken from deposits within a reasonable ~ of the site of building —G.S.Brady⟩ ⟨ride first-class only on the short ~*s* —T.H.Fielding⟩ ⟨the long ~ round the Cape —Sir Winston Churchill⟩ **c :** the quantity of material transported **:** LOAD ⟨~*s* of unsifted ore —*Times Lit. Supp.*⟩

haulabout \'≐,≐,≐\ *n* -s [fr. *haul about*, v.] **:** a steel barge with large hatchways and coal transporters used for coaling ships

haul·age \'hȯlij\ *n* -s *often attrib* **1 :** the act or process of hauling **2 :** a charge made for hauling

haulage rope *n* **:** TRANSMISSION ROPE

haulageway \'≐≐,≐\ *n* **:** a passage in a coal mine along which coal is transported **:** GANGWAY 4

haulaway \'≐≐,≐\ *n* -s [fr. *haul away*, v.] **:** a motor truck designed for the transportation of new automobiles

haulaway

haulback \'≐,≐\ *n* -s [fr. *haul back*, v.] **1 :** a small wire rope used to pull the main cable back to the timber after each haulage in logging **2 :** COMEBACK 4

hauled *past of* HAUL

haul·er \'hȯlə(r)\ *n* -s **:** one that hauls; *specif* **:** a commercial establishment whose business is hauling

haul·ier \'hȯlyə(r), -liə-\ *Brit var of* HAULER

hauling *n* -s [fr. gerund of *haul*] **1 :** an act or instance of applying physical traction to move something **2 :** the act or occupation of transporting goods in a vehicle ⟨hired a trucker to do the ~⟩

hauling ground *n* **:** an area where young male seals congregate during the breeding season

[1]**haulm** \'hȯm, 'häm\ *n* -s [ME *halm*, fr. OE *healm*; akin to OHG *halm* straw, stem, ON *halmr* straw, stem, L *culmus* stalk, Gk *kalamos* reed, OSlav *slama* straw] **1** *Brit* **:** the stems or tops of cultivated plants (as peas, beans, potatoes, and cereals) esp. after the crop has been gathered **:** STRAW, LITTER **2** *Brit* **:** an individual plant stem (as the culm of a grass)

[2]**haulm** \"\ *vt* -ED/-ING/-S *Brit* **:** to arrange (straw) for thatching

haulmy \-mi\ *adj* -ER/-EST *Brit* **:** having haulms

haul off *vi* **:** to get ready often on the spur of the moment ⟨*haul off* and hit him⟩ ⟨what makes you think you can *haul off* and leave here without paying me? —Erskine Caldwell⟩

haulover \'=,==\ *n* -s [fr. *haul over*, v.] **:** PORTAGE 4

hauls *pres 3d sing of* HAUL, *pl of* HAUL

haul seine *n* **:** a long net for commercial fishing one end of which is usu. attached to the land and the other run around a school of fish which are then drawn ashore

haul seiner *n* **:** one that fishes with a haul seine

haul up *vi* **:** to come to a stop ⟨the child circled the room and *hauled up* in front of the visitor⟩

haul–up \'=,=\ *n* -s [fr. *haul up*, v.] **:** a jack ladder having a V-shaped trough up which logs are drawn by a jack chain

halyard *var of* HALYARD

haunch \'hȯnch, -ä-,-â-\ *n* -ES [ME *haunche*, fr. OF *hanche*, of Gmc origin; akin to MD *hanke* hip, haunch] **1 a :** the projecting region of the lateral parts of the pelvis and the hip joint **:** HIP ⟨his right arm resting forever on Eve's ~ —W.H.Auden⟩ **b :** the fleshy part of the buttock and top of the thigh **:** HINDQUARTER ⟨squatting first on one ~ and then on the other —William Humphrey⟩ — see HORSE illustration **2 :** a leg and loin of an animal for use as food ⟨~ of venison⟩ **3 :** either side of an arch between the springing and the crown **:** the part of an arch bounded by vertical lines drawn through the crown and the outer extremity of the extrados and by horizontal lines drawn through the crown and the spring point **4 :** the tapered end of a tenon **5 :** the shoulder of a highway — usu. used in pl.

haunch bone *n* **:** INNOMINATE BONE; *specif* **:** ILIUM

haunched \-cht\ *adj* **:** having haunches

haunch·less \-chləs\ *adj* **:** lacking haunches

haunchy \-chē\ *adj* -ER/-EST **:** having large haunches

[1]**haunt** \ hȯnt, -ä-,-â-\ *vb* -ED/-ING/-S [ME *haunten*, fr. OF *hanter*, prob. of Gmc origin; akin to OE *hāmettan* to domicile, ON *heimta* to bring home, fetch, pull, claim; derivatives fr. the stem of E *home*] *vt* **1 a :** to visit often **:** linger in the vicinity of (a place) **:** FREQUENT ⟨loved and ~*ed* the theater —Carlos Baker⟩ ⟨knew . . . what coverts the pheasants ~*ed* —Adrian Bell⟩ **b :** to continually seek the company of (a person) **:** hang around ⟨impostors that ~ the official in foreign ports —Van Wyck Brooks⟩ **2 a :** to have a disquieting or harmful effect on **:** TROUBLE, MOLEST ⟨the gnawing question . . . ~*ed* the uneasy royal heart —Francis Hackett⟩ ⟨crisis was to ~ her days —Charles Lee⟩ ⟨mysterious illness that . . . would not go until the being it ~*ed* lay dead —Edith Sitwell⟩ ⟨icebergs . . . which drift out to sea to ~ mariners —Glen Jacobsen⟩ **b** (1) **:** to linger in the consciousness of **:** recur constantly to ⟨the possibility of the dairy farm ~*ed* her mind —Ellen Glasgow⟩ ⟨single lines of poetry often ~ people who cannot trace them to their source —Bennett Cerf⟩ (2) **:** to reappear continually in **:** recur constantly in ⟨a certain type of . . . woman who has already ~*ed* his poetry —Edmund Wilson⟩ **3 :** to visit or inhabit as a disembodied spirit ⟨spirits are supposed to ~ the places where their bodies most resorted —Charles Dickens⟩ ⟨the river is ~*ed* by certain malevolent water spirits —J.G.Frazer⟩ ~ *vi* **1 :** to stay around or persist **:** LINGER ⟨likes to ~ around the firehouse⟩ ⟨scent that can ~ for a lifetime —Flora Thompson⟩ **2 :** to appear habitually as a disembodied spirit ⟨not far from . . . where she ~*ed* appeared for a short time a much more remarkable spirit —W.B.Yeats⟩

[2]**haunt** \"\ *n* -s [ME, fr. *haunten*, v.] **1** *now dial Brit* **:** PRACTICE, CUSTOM, HABIT **2** *obs* **:** an act of frequenting in numbers **:** CONCOURSE ⟨our life, exempt from public ~, finds tongues in trees —Shak.⟩ **3 a :** a place habitually frequented **:** favorite resort **:** HOME ⟨sages in their sequestered ~*s* —Laurence Binyon⟩ ⟨own their own ships and fly them to weekend ~*s* —Phil Gustafson⟩ ⟨quiet ~*s* of beauty —S.P.B. Mais⟩ **b** (1) **:** the lair or feeding ground of an animal **:** area where an animal is usu. to be found ⟨~ of the tiger⟩ ⟨herring are most plentiful when the water in their favorite ~*s* is a degree or two warmer than average —J.P.Tully⟩ (2) **:** the favorite environment of a plant ⟨~ of the cardinal flower⟩ **4** *or* **hant** \'hant, -aa(ə)-,-ai-,-â-,-ä-\ *chiefly dial* **:** a disembodied spirit **:** GHOST

haunted *adj* **1 :** FILLED, INFESTED — now usu. used in combination ⟨a sad, kindly, God-*haunted* man —S.N.Behrman⟩ ⟨seal-*haunted* isle —A.A.MacGregor⟩ ⟨moved . . . from one dust-*haunted* base to another —Martin Quigley⟩ **2 :** inhabited by or as if by apparitions **:** frequented by ghosts ⟨a ~ house⟩ ⟨as dusk comes on Kipling's study is the most ~ place I know —Christopher Morley⟩ **3 :** HARASSED, AFFLICTED, TROUBLED ⟨the deep ~ eyes of a man whose convictions have burned him hollow —T.H.White b. 1915⟩ — **haunt·ed·ness** *n* -ES

haunt·er \-tə(r)\ *n* -s [ME *hawntare*, fr. *hawnten*, *haunten* to haunt + *-are* -er] **:** one that haunts

[1]**haunting** *n* -s [ME, fr. *haunten* + *-ing*] **:** an act of frequenting esp. by a disembodied spirit ⟨simply not the case that all incumbents vouched for ~*s* —*A.G.N.Flew*⟩

[2]**haunting** *adj* [ME, fr. pres. part. of *haunten* to haunt — more at HAUNT] **:** that haunts: as **a :** lingering in the consciousness **:** not readily forgotten ⟨the cathedral organ and the distant voices have a ~ beauty —Claudia Cassidy⟩ **b :** having a disquieting effect **:** DISTURBING ⟨from two handsome and talented young men to two ~ horrors of disintegration —Charles Lee⟩ — **haunt·ing·ly** *adv*

haun·ty \'hȯnti, 'hän-,'han-\ *adj* -ER/-EST [origin unknown] *dial Eng* **:** UNRULY, RESTLESS

hau·pia \hau'pēə\ *n* -s [Hawaiian] **:** a Hawaiian pudding made of cornstarch and coconut cream

hau·ra·nit·ic \¦haurə¦nidˌik\ *adj*, *usu cap* [*Hauran*, region in southern Syria + E *-ite* + *-ic*] **:** of or relating to the region of Hauran

hau·ri·ant *also* **hau·ri·ent** \'hȯrēənt, 'haur-\ *adj* [L *haurient-*, *hauriens*, pres. part. of *haurire* to draw (as water), drain, devour — more at EXHAUST] *heraldry*, *of a fish or water animal* **:** being in pale with the head up as if rising for air — compare URINANT

haus *pl of* HAU

hau·sa *also* **haus·sa** \'hau̇|sə, |zə\ *n*, *pl* **hausa** *or* **hausas** *usu cap* **1 a :** a highly variable negroid people of the Sudan between Lake Chad and the Niger numbering in the millions and united primarily by language **b :** a member of such people **2 :** the Chad language of the Hausa people that is widely used in west Africa as a trade language

hause \'hȯs, 'häs\ *chiefly Scot var of* HALS

hau·sen \'hau̇zᵊn\ *n* -s [G, fr. MHG *hūse*, *hūsen*, fr. OHG *hūso* — more at HUSO] **:** BELUGA 1

haus·frau \'hau̇s,frau̇\ *n*, *pl* **hausfraus** \-au̇z\ *also* **haus·frau·en** \-au̇ən\ [G, fr. *haus* house (fr. OHG *hūs*) + *frau* wife, woman, fr. OHG *frouwa* lady, mistress — more at HOUSE, FROW] **:** the mistress of a household **:** HOUSEWIFE ⟨the women were dumpy, overworked ~*s* —Joanna Spencer⟩

haus·mann·ite \'hau̇smə,nīt\ *n* -s [J. F. L. *Hausmann* †1859 Ger. mineralogist + E *-ite*] **:** an opaque mineral Mn_3O_4 consisting of manganese tetroxide

hausse–col \(')(h)ōs¦käl\ *n* -s [F, by folk etymology (influence of F *hausser* to raise) fr. MF *housecol*, *hochecol*, *hauscol*] **:** GORGET 1

haust *abbr* [L *haustus*] draft — used in pharmacy

haus·tel·late \(')hȯ¦stelˌət, 'hȯstə,lāt\ *adj* [NL *haustellum* + E *-ate*] **:** having a haustellum **:** SUCTORIAL

haus·tel·lum \hȯ'steləm\ *n*, *pl* **haustel·la** \-lə\ [NL, fr. L *haustus* (past part. of *haurire* to draw, draw up) + *-ellum* (dim. suffix) — more at EXHAUST] **:** a proboscis adapted for sucking blood or the juices of plants

haus·to·ri·al \(')hȯ¦stōrēəl\ *adj* [NL *haustorium* + E *-al*] **:** HAUSTELLATE

haus·to·ri·um \=ˈ=rēəm\ *n*, *pl* **hausto·ria** \-rēə\ [NL, fr. L *haustus* + *-orium*] **:** a food-absorbing outgrowth of a hypha, stem, or other plant organ: as **a :** a projection from various fungous hyphae **b :** a cell of the embryo sac or embryo in some seed plants **c :** an outgrowth of the stem or root in a parasitic seed plant (as dodder)

haus·tral \'hȯstrəl\ *also* **haus·trat·ed** \-,strād·əd\ *adj* [NL *haustrum* + E *-al* or *-ated* (fr. *-ate* + *-ed*)] **:** of, relating to, or exhibiting haustra

haus·tra·tion \hȯ'strāshən\ *n* -s [NL *haustrum* + E *-ation*] **:** the quality or state of having haustra

haus·trum \'hȯstrəm\ *n*, *pl* **haus·tra** \-rə\ [NL, fr. L, machine for drawing water, fr. *haustus*, past part. of *haurire* to draw (as water) — more at EXHAUST] **:** a recess in the colon

haus·tus \'hȯstəs\ *n*, *pl* **haustus** [L, lit., action of drawing, fr. *haustus*, past part.] *Roman & civil law* **:** a right to draw water from a well or spring on another's land and a right of passage to and from the well or spring — compare SERVITUDE

haut·bois *also* **haut·boy** \'(h)ō,bȯi\ *n*, *pl* **hautbois** \-ȯiz\ *also* **hautboys** \"\ [MF *hautbois*, fr. *haut* high + *bois* wood, woods, of Gmc origin; akin to OHG *busc* bush, forest — more at HAUGHT, BUSH] **1 a :** OBOE **b :** a pipe-organ stop of 16, 8, and sometimes 4-foot pitch similar to an organ oboe **2 :** a strawberry (*Fragaria moschata*) native to Europe and early brought into cultivation having the calyx strongly recurved in fruit

haut·boist \-ȯist\ *also* **haut·boy·ist** \"\ *n* -s [F *hautboïste*, fr. *hautbois* + *-iste*] **:** OBOIST

haute cou·ture \,ōt,kü'tü(ə)r\ *n* [F, lit., high sewing] **1 :** the leading dressmaking establishments for the creation of exclusive often trend-setting fashions for women **2 a :** the art of creating high fashions for women **b :** the fashions created

haute école \,ōd·(,)ā'kōl\ *n* [F, lit., high school] **1 :** a method of training a horse in the more difficult feats of horsemanship **2 :** the technique of expert horsemanship

haute–lisse \(')ōt¦lēs\ *adj* [F] **:** HIGH-WARP

hau·teur \(')hō¦tər, (')(h)ō¦-\ *n* -s [F, fr. *haut* high, proud + *-eur* -or — more at HAUGHT] **:** an assumption of superiority **:** arrogant or condescending manner **:** HAUGHTINESS ⟨a cold ~ and disdain which infuriated his colleagues —J.H.Plumb⟩

haut monde \ō'mōⁿd, -ˈmänd\ *n* [F, lit., high world] **:** the socially elect **:** high society

haut pas \ō'pä\ *n* [ME *hautepase*, fr. MF *haut pas*, lit., high step] **:** a raised part of a floor **:** DAIS — compare HALFPACE

haut–relief \¦ō, ¦ō+=ˈ=\ *n* [F] **:** HIGH RELIEF

ha·uy·nite \ä'wē,nīt\ *or* **ha·uyne** \ä'wēn\ *n* -s [*hauynite* fr. *hauyne* + *-ite*; *hauyne* fr. F *haüyne*, fr. Abbé René Just Haüy †1822 Fr. mineralogist + F *-ine*] **:** an isometric silicate mineral $(Na,Ca)_{4-8}Al_6Si_6O_{24}(SO_4)_{1-2}$ consisting of sulfate of aluminum, calcium, and sodium and occurring commonly as rounded grains in various igneous rocks (hardness 5.5–6, sp. gr. 2.4–2.5)

hav *abbr* haversine

hav·age \'(h)avij\ *n* -s [¹*have* + *-age*] *dial Eng* **:** familial descent **:** LINEAGE

ha·vai·ki \hə'vīkē\ *n*, *cap* [Marquesan & Tuamotuan] **:** a fabled original homeland from which the Polynesians believe themselves to have come and to which their spirits return after death

[1]**ha·va·na** \hə'vanə\ *adj*, *usu cap* [fr. *Havana*, Cuba] **1 :** of or from Havana, the capital of Cuba ⟨a *Havana* cigar⟩ **2 :** of the kind or style prevalent in Havana **:** HAVANAN **2 a** *of tobacco* **:** grown in Cuba **b** *of a cigar* **:** made in Cuba or from Cuban tobacco

[2]**havana** \"\ *n* **1** -s *usu cap* [prob. fr. Sp *habano*, fr. *habano*, adj., of Havana, fr. La *Habana* (Havana), Cuba] **a :** a cigar made partly or wholly from Cuban tobacco ⟨a box of *Havanas*⟩ **b :** tobacco raised in Cuba ⟨*Havana* leaf⟩ **2** *or* **havana brown** -s *often cap H* **:** BISMARCK BROWN **3 a** *usu cap* **:** a breed of rather small brown rabbits originating in Holland **b** -s *often cap* **:** a rabbit of this breed

[1]**ha·van·an** \-nən\ *adj*, *usu cap* [*Havana*, Cuba + E *-an*] **1 :** of, relating to, or characteristic of Havana, the capital of Cuba **2 :** of, relating to, or characteristic of the people of Havana

[2]**havanan** \"\ *n* -s *cap* **:** a native or resident of Havana

havana seed *n*, *usu cap H* **:** any of several U. S. cigar tobaccos derived from seed orig. imported from Cuba

ha·va·su·pai \,hävə'sü,pī\ *n*, *pl* **havasupai** *or* **havasupais** *usu cap* **1 a :** an Indian people of Cataract Canyon, a tributary of Grand Canyon, Arizona **b :** a member of such people **2 :** a Yuman language of the Havasupai people

havdalah *var of* HABDALAH

[1]**have** \(¦)hav, (¦)hev; *as an auxiliary* " *or* ,(h)əv *or after a vowel* v; *before "to" usu* ¦haf *or* ¦hef\ *vb*, *past* **had** \(¦)had, (¦)hed; *as an auxiliary* " *or* (h)əd *or after a vowel* d\ *also archaic 2d sing* **hadst** \(¦)ha¦dzt, (¦)he¦, ,(h)ə¦, ¦dst, ¦tst\ *or* **had·dest** (with *thou*) \¦hadəst, ¦hed-\ *past part* **had** *also chiefly Scot* **haen** \(¦)hān\ *pres part* **hav·ing** \¦haviŋ, ¦hev-\ *pres 1st sing* **have** *also dial Brit* **ha** \(¦)ha, ,(h)ə\ *or chiefly Scot* **hae** \(¦)hā\ *2d sing* **have** *also archaic* **hast** (with *thou*) \(¦)hast, (¦)hest, ,(h)əst\ *or dial Brit* **ha**; *3d sing* **has** \(¦)haz, (¦)hez; *as an auxiliary* " *or* ,(h)əz *or after a vowel* z; *before "to" usu* ¦has *or* ¦hes\ *also archaic* **hath** \(¦)hath, (¦)heth, ,(h)əth\ *or dial Brit* **have**; *pl* **have** *also dial Brit* **ha** *or* **han** \(¦)han, (h)ən\ *or chiefly Scot* **hae** \(¦)hā\ [ME *haven*, *habben*, fr. OE *habban*; akin to OHG *habēn* to have, ON *hafa*, Goth *haban*, OE *hebban* to lift, raise — more at HEAVE] *vt* **1 a :** to hold in possession as property **:** OWN ⟨~ a cow⟩ ⟨~ a car⟩ ⟨~ a lot of money⟩ **b :** to hold, keep, or retain esp. in one's use, service, regard, or affection or at one's disposal ⟨can't ~ your cake and eat it too⟩ ⟨the chairman *has* all the tickets needed⟩ ⟨*has* some rare coins saved up⟩ ⟨~ him in fond remembrance⟩ ⟨~ no time to lose⟩ **c :** to consist of (as all one's elements or constituent parts) **:** CONTAIN, INCLUDE ⟨~ a subordinate part⟩ ⟨the car *has* a self-starter⟩ ⟨the lake *has* some large pickerel⟩ ⟨April *has* 30 days⟩ **d :** CARRY, BEAR, SUPPORT ⟨~ an essential part⟩ ⟨~ an attachment⟩ ⟨the house *has* a roof⟩ ⟨the dress *has* a label⟩ **:** WEAR ⟨*has* a blue suit⟩ ⟨*has* a tweed coat⟩ **e :** to be possessed by ⟨declaring she *had* a devil —Max Peacock⟩ **2 :** to feel compulsion, obligation, or necessity in regard to — used with a noun object followed by *to* and the infinitive ⟨~ a letter to write⟩ ⟨~ a task to perform⟩ ⟨~ nothing to do⟩ ⟨~ a deadline to meet⟩ **3 a :** to stand in any of several personal relationships to (as father to son, host to guest, friend to friend) ⟨the man *had* four daughters⟩ ⟨it is unpleasant to ~ enemies⟩ **b :** to be attended by or associated with often as an essential concomitant ⟨the king *has* many courtiers⟩ ⟨certain foods present special difficulties and so ~ rules of their own to make eating them easier —Agnes M. Miall⟩ ⟨the wine *had* no effect on me⟩ ⟨his proposal *had* many objections⟩ **c :** to stand or remain in any of several implicit physical, logical, or emotional relationships to ⟨as we sailed north we *had* Africa on our right⟩ ⟨*had* only six feet of water under the keel⟩ ⟨the word *has* no exact equivalent⟩ ⟨~ the voters on the right side⟩ **4 a** (1) **:** to acquire or get possession of **:** OBTAIN ⟨nothing to be *had* from the empty larder⟩ ⟨good meat could not be *had* at all during the food shortage⟩ (2) **:** GAIN ⟨*had* a lot from the trip⟩ ⟨*had* nothing from the experience⟩ (3) **:** to be able to avail oneself of or utilize (something already done or completed) ⟨in this field a student *has* many helpful monographs and handbooks⟩ (4) **:** WIN ⟨*had* the hole by two strokes⟩ ⟨ought to ~ the fight by the third round⟩ **b :** RECEIVE ⟨*had* news of the lost ship⟩ ⟨asked if the police *had* any information that might lead to an arrest⟩ ⟨*had* a letter from him⟩ **c :** ACCEPT ⟨so burnt no one would ~ a piece⟩; *specif* **:** to accept in marriage ⟨wished to marry but could find no one who would ~ him⟩ **d :** ACHIEVE ⟨believes a satisfactory peace can be *had* between the belligerent powers⟩ **e :** to copulate with ⟨rumor claimed he had never *had* a woman in his life —Norman Mailer⟩ **5 a :** to be marked, distinguished, or characterized by (as an attribute, quality, position, or a distinctive biographical fact) ⟨the cloth *has* a silky texture⟩ ⟨*had* a taste for exotic foods⟩ ⟨*has* a habit of nail biting⟩ ⟨the threat *had* the desired effect⟩ ⟨*had* a height of four feet⟩ ⟨the goods *had* a value of $1000⟩ ⟨the common law *had* its origin in a group of writs drawn from various uses —Curtis Bok⟩ **b :** EXHIBIT, SHOW, MANIFEST ⟨*had* the goodness to get a chair⟩ ⟨*had* the gall to refuse⟩ **c :** USE, EXERCISE ⟨~ a care what you say to him⟩ ⟨~ mercy on us⟩ **6 a :** to experience esp. by submitting to, undergoing, being affected by, enjoying, or suffering ⟨~ a rest⟩ ⟨~ a medical examination⟩ ⟨~ a cold⟩ ⟨the worst government they ever *had*⟩ ⟨~ an operation⟩ ⟨a book that will ~ a wide circulation⟩ **:** PASS ⟨~ a life full of suffering⟩ **b :** to carry on or engage in **:** PERFORM ⟨~ a standing feud with a political opponent⟩ ⟨~ a fight⟩ ⟨~ a talk with a friend⟩ ⟨~ a part in a play⟩; *also* **:** EXECUTE, TAKE ⟨*had* a punch at the assailant before he escaped⟩ ⟨*had* a look at the body⟩ **c :** to entertain in the mind or feelings **:** CHERISH ⟨*had* a great deal of affection for the children⟩ ⟨~ no doubt of success⟩ ⟨~ an opinion⟩ **7 a :** to cause to go **:** LEAD, CONVEY ⟨did not ~ the child anywhere where he could be exposed to measles⟩ ⟨the aunt *had* the child to live with her⟩ **b :** to cause to by persuasive or forceful means (as by inviting, ordering, compelling) — used with the infinitive without *to* ⟨*had* the chauffeur drive to town⟩ ⟨*had* the children go to bed early⟩ ⟨the court *had* him pay the man what he owed him⟩ ⟨you are going to pay for the damage and I'll ~ you know it⟩ **c :** to cause to be ⟨*has* people around at all times⟩ ⟨likes to ~ people in the office who are efficient⟩ ⟨*had* him sick with the details of the accident⟩ ⟨anxious to ~ you a satisfied customer —Richard Joseph⟩ ⟨nearly *had* the table over with her pushing and shoving⟩ ⟨*had* the tent poles down in a minute⟩ **d :** to cause to become ⟨I'll ~ him a good soldier before long⟩ **e** (1) **:** to cause to come by inviting ⟨~ friends over for an evening of bridge⟩ (2) **:** to receive as a guest ⟨I'll be over whenever you can ~ me⟩ **f :** to represent to be ⟨the author always *has* his characters doing foolish things⟩ **8 a :** to allow to or suffer to — used with the infinitive without *to* ⟨would not ~ him treat the dog so⟩ **b :** to allow to be or suffer to be ⟨will not ~ him chosen president⟩ ⟨~ women in the men's part of the building only once a month on visitors' day⟩ ⟨a strange man to ~ around⟩ **9 a** (1) **:** to be marked by an intellectual grasp of **:** KNOW, UNDERSTAND ⟨a student who *has* only a little French and no mathematics⟩ ⟨*having* no foreign language he was handicapped and ineffectual —Carl Van Doren⟩ (2) **:** to understand the character of ⟨you do not need to associate with him long before you ~ him⟩ (3) **:** to be able to handle adequately ⟨the job is so easy that in only a few days you ~ it⟩ **b :** to place in a scale of distinctions **:** CATEGORIZE ⟨sees with so many sense and other organs that you never know where to ~ him artistically —*Times Lit. Supp.*⟩ **10 a :** to maneuver into a position of disadvantage or cause to be at a disadvantage ⟨*had* his opponent at the point of defeat⟩ ⟨the criminal *had* the police nonplussed⟩ ⟨the team *had* their opponents beaten before the half⟩ **b :** to place or maneuver into a vulnerable or defenseless position or a position bringing certain defeat ⟨when he brought the charge before the court he *had* me since the evidence against me was in my own handwriting⟩ **c :** OUTWIT, OUTPLAY, OUTMANEUVER ⟨*had* his opponent in only three more moves of the chessmen⟩ **:** DEFEAT ⟨would like to play on but you ~ me steadily⟩; to get the better of or triumph over by finding, achieving, getting ⟨*had* the laugh on me⟩ ⟨*had* the goods on me⟩ ⟨*had* the jump on me⟩ **d :** TRICK, CHEAT, FOOL, BAMBOOZLE ⟨in this enterprise the partners *had* him and left him without a penny⟩ ⟨the size of this bill convinces me I've been *had*⟩ **11 a :** to be in a position to exercise (as a right or privilege) ⟨as a friend he *has* the freedom of my house⟩ ⟨*has* no right to go⟩ **b :** to be in control of **:** to be responsible for ⟨was put in charge and he *has* overall direction of the program — C.E.Black & E.C.Helmreich⟩ ⟨*has* the job of directing traffic⟩ **12 :** BEAR, BEGET ⟨she is going to ~ a baby⟩ ⟨the man *had* a son last week⟩ **13 :** to partake of **:** EAT, DRINK ⟨~ dinner at 7 o'clock⟩ ⟨~ coffee every morning⟩ **:** SMOKE ⟨~ a cigarette after breakfast⟩ **14 :** to give a job to **:** HIRE ⟨no shipowner will hire him, no captain will ~ him —P.J.Scharper⟩ **15 :** to associate oneself with **:** participate in ⟨won't ~ any part of the dirty business⟩ **16 a :** to cause to do one's bidding **:** CONTROL, DOMINATE ⟨the man with the money was always able to ~ him⟩ **b :** BUY 4, BRIBE, SUBORN ⟨as long as juries, judges and law enforcement officers can be *had* for a price —D.W. Maurer⟩ **17 :** to engage and hold (as the attention) ⟨the salesman *had* the interest of the buyer⟩ ⟨the political candidate *has* the ear of the farmers⟩ ~ *verbal auxiliary* **1 :** to be in a position or state marked by an action or state completed or ended or virtually completed or ended — used with the past participle to form the present perfect, past perfect, or future perfect ⟨*has* gone home⟩ ⟨~ been here already⟩ ⟨the army *had* already taken the town when we arrived⟩ ⟨will ~ finished dinner by the time the guests arrive⟩ **2 :** to be compelled or under obligation or necessity — used with the infinitive with *to* ⟨~ *to* see a doctor⟩ ⟨~ to pay taxes⟩ ⟨*had* to be home by six⟩ — compare ¹GET 12b

syn HOLD, OWN, POSSESS, ENJOY: HAVE is a very general term indicating any condition or action of control, retaining, keeping, regarding, or experiencing as one's own. HOLD suggests stronger control, grasp, or retention: *to hold to an opinion* suggests greater tenacity and resolution than *to have an opinion; to hold control* implies firm retention in contrast to *to have control*, which may imply the accidental or temporary; *to hold a job* suggests continuation, *to have one* occupation at the moment. OWN may suggest holding with power to use and dispose as a legal or natural right ⟨*own* one's own house⟩ ⟨the stockholders *own* the corporation, and the corporation *owns* the assets of the incorporated business —Harold Koontz & Cyril O'Donnell⟩ ⟨when a child is old enough, he should . . . be allowed to *own* books —Bertrand Russell⟩ POSSESS may be interchangeable with HAVE; similar to OWN, it may apply more widely to intangibles ⟨he *possesses*, through his experience, knowledge not possessed by those whose experience has been different —Bertrand Russell⟩ ⟨it must be a delightful city, and *possess* all the attractions of the next world —Oscar Wilde⟩ ENJOY implies having as one's own with all benefits and advantages, usu. pleasurable, or with other concomitants, perhaps unpleasant ⟨*enjoys* worldwide fame⟩ ⟨*enjoy* unlimited opportunities⟩ ⟨shorn of the remarkable privileges which he formerly *enjoyed* —J.G.Frazer⟩ **syn** see in addition OUGHT

— **had as good** *or* **had as well :** would benefit as much to **:** might as well — used with the infinitive without *to* ⟨*had as good* throw his money away as spend it foolishly⟩ — **had as lief** *or* **had as soon :** would just as gladly — used with the infinitive without *to* ⟨*had as lief* stay home as go gadding about⟩ — **had better** *or* **had best 1 :** would be wise to — used with the infinitive without *to* ⟨*had better* try slow walks to start building up his strength⟩ **2 :** should for one's own welfare ⟨*had better* pay what the court tells him to⟩ — **had liefer** *or* **had sooner** *or* **had rather :** would rather — used with the infinitive without *to* ⟨*had liefer* sit at home than go to the dance⟩ ⟨*had sooner* drink than sleep⟩ — **had liefest** *or* **had soonest :** would like best to — used with the infinitive without *to* ⟨*had liefest* have the least seasoned dishes⟩ — **have a go :** to hit a bowled cricket ball vigorously with intent to score — **have a hand in :** to exercise some control over ⟨*have a hand in* the management of the business⟩ **:** significantly influence or direct ⟨*having a hand in* the control of American domestic corporations —T.W.Arnold⟩ — **have at :** to go at or deal with usu. hostilely ⟨flops the morning bale of poetry manuscripts upon my desk and I pull up my chair to *have at* them —H.L. Mencken⟩ ⟨the two men *had at* each other with fists and feet⟩ ⟨have seen four . . . characters *have at* each other for two very powerful concluding acts —*Theatre Arts*⟩ — **have done :** STOP, CEASE, DESIST ⟨wish you would *have done* before I go mad⟩ — used chiefly in the imperative — **have done with :** to finish doing, using, dealing with, working on, or handling ⟨when he *had done with* the pen he laid it down⟩ ⟨will never *have done with* his persistent speechmaking⟩ — **have had it 1** *slang* **:** to have had or have done all one is going to be allowed to ⟨he's been cheating me for years but now he's *had it*⟩ **2** *slang* **:** to have experienced, endured, or suffered all one can or as much as one can ever expect to usu. of a particular kind of experience ⟨he felt he was capable of enduring pain but after that experience he'd *had it*⟩ ⟨if that's what it takes to make him happy, he *has had it* —*Nashville Tennessean*⟩ — **have it 1 a :** ASSERT, MAINTAIN, CLAIM ⟨rumor *has it* that there will be a marked change in women's fashions⟩ ⟨all their friends *have it* that they are secretly married⟩ — often used with *will* ⟨the enemy will *have it* that we are already defeated⟩ **b :** to conceive of and act in relation to a point under consideration ⟨which way do you want to *have it*⟩ ⟨*have it* your own way⟩ **2 :** to express or phrase it ⟨he was drunk as a lord, as his friends *have it*⟩ **3 :** to endure or suffer it — used with *will not* or *would not* ⟨tried to exploit him but he would not *have it*⟩ ⟨after his insult if he tries to explain I will not *have it*⟩ **4 :** to bring about : ARRANGE ⟨good fortune *had it* that we arrived early⟩ **5 a :** to gain or hold an advantage : WIN **b :** to gain the victory in a viva-voce vote ⟨the ayes *have it*⟩ **6 :** to receive or suffer a blow, punishment, or disaster ⟨the fighter let his opponent *have it* in the face⟩ **7 :** to have or have hit on a solution or a practicable or appropriate plan or method **8 :** to be so dealt with by fortune or circumstance that one's affairs or welfare are of a (particular favorable or unfavorable) character ⟨*had it* good in times of prosperity⟩ ⟨*has it* pretty tough since his wife died⟩ — **have it coming :** to deserve or merit what one gets, benefits by, or suffers ⟨so vicious a man that whatever evil things happen to him he will *have it coming*⟩ — **have it in for :** to intend to do harm to : wish evil to : plan to harm in some way ⟨*had it in for* all foreigners⟩ — **have it in one :** to have the capability or courage ⟨*has it in him* to do better than he did⟩ — **have it out :** to settle or clear up a matter of contention by free discussion or a fight — **have it over** *or* **have it all over :** to be in a more advantageous position than ⟨*has it over* one ignorant of the language⟩ — **have kittens :** to be in an agitated mood : become perturbed or upset ⟨company's coming and Ma's been *having kittens*⟩ — **have none of :** to refuse to allow, tolerate, or have anything to do with ⟨will *have none of* your sloppy ways around this house⟩ ⟨as soon as he found the business was dishonest he would *have none of* it⟩ — **have nothing on :** to have no advantage or superiority over ⟨the man was a crook but *had nothing on* the men he cheated who would have cheated him far more⟩; *esp* : to possess no incriminating or embarrassing information about ⟨felt at ease because he knew his opponents *had nothing on* him that they could use for blackmail⟩ — **have no use for :** to hold in contempt : DESPISE ⟨*has no use for* dishonest politicians⟩ : be unwilling to tolerate or deal with in any way — **have oneself :** to indulge in or go out of one's way to have (as a good time) : GET ⟨the boys *had themselves* a time while the parents were away⟩ — **have one's eye on :** to have marked intentions of acquiring or possessing ⟨*had his eye on* a little cottage up in the mountains⟩ ⟨*had his eye on* his neighbor's daughter⟩ — **have one's hands full :** to have in hand as much as or more than one can conveniently handle : be pressed with work, engagements, difficulties — **have one's head** *of a horse* **:** to move freely without restraint from the reins ⟨on the last stretch the trainer let the mare *have her head*⟩ — **have one's head** *or* **have one's hide :** to be extremely angry at or inflict severe punishment upon (as by beheading) ⟨he said that if I didn't stop bothering him he'd *have my hide*⟩ ⟨swore he'd *have the heads* of the outlaws⟩ — **have one's own back :** to get even — **have something on :** to possess incriminating or embarrassing information about ⟨*had something on* the police chief so that he felt safe from arrest⟩ — **have to do with 1 :** to have business or intercourse with : concern oneself with : deal with ⟨semantics *has to do with* the responses we have to words⟩ **2 :** to have (as something or nothing) in the way of connection or relation with, participation in, or effect on ⟨the lawyer would *have* nothing *to do with* the case⟩ ⟨your frame of mind *has* much *to do with* your physical wellbeing⟩ — **to have and to hold :** to possess by virtue of a lawful title (as under the habendum clause in a deed) — formerly used in deeds in English to introduce the tenendum

²have \ˈhav\ *n* -s **:** one that has material wealth as distinguished from one that is poor — compare HAVE-NOT ⟨conceived of war as a battle between the ~*s* and the have-nots for control of the world's wealth⟩ ⟨rich and poor, employer and employee, ~*s* and have-nots alike —*Engineering and Mining Jour.*⟩

have·lock \ˈhav,läk, -vlək\ *n* -s [after Sir Henry *Havelock* †1857 Eng. general in India] **:** a covering for a cap or hat with an extended back or back and sides to protect the neck from the sun or bad weather

¹ha·ven \ˈhāvən\ *n* -s [ME, fr. OE *hæfen, hæfene;* akin to OE *hæf* sea, MLG *haf* sea, *havene* harbor, MHG *hap, habe, habene* sea, harbor, ON *haf* sea, *höfn* harbor, OE *hebban* to raise, lift — more at HEAVE] **1 :** a bay, recess, or inlet of the sea or the mouth of a river that affords anchorage and shelter for shipping : HARBOR, PORT **2 :** a place of safety : SHELTER, ASYLUM **syn** see HARBOR

²haven \ˈ"\ *vb* -ED/-ING/-S *vi, obs* **:** to take refuge in a haven ~ *vt* **:** to shelter in a haven

ha·ven·less \-nləs\ *adj* [ME *havenlesse,* fr. *haven* + *-lesse* -less] **:** having no harbor or haven ⟨a ~ sea⟩ ⟨a ~ life⟩

have–not \ˈhav,nät\ *n* -s **:** one that is poor in material wealth as distinguished from one that is rich ⟨ownership of the natural resources of the earth by individuals, groups or nations, causing a struggle between the haves and *have-nots* which is the major cause of war and destruction —*Science News Letter*⟩

haven't \ˈhavənt, ˈhabᵊmt\ [by contr.] **:** have not

have on *vt* **1 :** WEAR ⟨the child *had* his best clothes *on* for the party⟩ ⟨*had on* a new suit⟩ **2 :** to plan to take part in : have (something) planned ⟨*have* a dance *on* for that night⟩ ⟨will see what he *has on* now⟩ ⟨if you don't *have* anything *on* tonight, come over⟩

¹hav·er \ˈhavə(r)\ *n* -s [ME, fr. ON *hafri;* akin to OHG *habaro,* OS *haboro;* prob. derivatives fr. the root of ON *hafr* male goat; fr. oats being used as food for goats — more at CAPRIOLE] **1** *chiefly Brit* **a :** OAT; *esp* **:** volunteer or uncultivated oats **b :** WILD OAT 1a **2** *chiefly Brit* **:** TALL OAT GRASS

²hav·er \ˈhävər\ *n* -s [ME, owner, fr. *haven* to have + *-er*] *Scots law* **:** the holder of a deed or other legal document

³ha·ver \ˈhāvə(r)\ *vi* -ED/-ING/-S [origin unknown] *chiefly Brit* **:** to hem and haw : stall for time (as by useless talk) ⟨waste no more time ~*ing* over a few missing guns —Marguerite Steen⟩

⁴ha·ver *or* **ha·ber** *or* **cha·ver** *or* **cha·ber** \ˈkävər\ *n, pl* **have·rim** *or* **habe·rim** \kä'vārim\ [Heb *ḥābhēr*] **:** COMRADE, ASSOCIATE

ha·ve·rah *or* **ha·be·rah** \ˈkävərə\ *n, pl* **have·roth** *or* **habe·roth** *or* **have·rot** *or* **habe·rot** \,kävə'rōth, -ōt\ [Heb *ḥābhērāh,* fem. of *ḥābhēr*] **:** a female haver

havercake \ˈ=,=\ *n* [¹*haver* + *cake*] *Scot* **:** OATCAKE

ha·ver·el \ˈhāv(ə)rəl\ *n* -s [³*haver* + *-el*] *chiefly Scot* **:** a garrulous half-wit

havergrass \ˈ=,=\ *n* [¹*haver* + *grass*] **:** any of several chiefly European wild oats

ha·ver·hill fever \ˈhāv(ə)rəl-\ *n, usu cap H* [fr. *Haverhill,* Mass., where the disease appeared in epidemic proportions in 1926] **:** rat-bite fever not always contracted from the bite of a rat but sometimes from contaminated food

ha·ver·ing \ˈhāv(ə)riŋ\ *adj* [fr. pres. part. of ³*haver*] *dial Brit* **:** equivocal and devious ⟨some ~ jargon that might mean anything —J.C.Powys⟩

ha·ver·ings \-ŋz\ *n pl* [fr. pl. of *havering,* gerund of ³*haver*] *Brit* **:** absurd, pointless, or maundering talk : BABBLINGS ⟨a tone of fatherly impatience with my moony ~ —H.H.Richardson⟩

havermeal \ˈ=,=\ *n* [¹*haver* + *meal*] *Scot* **:** OATMEAL

ha·vers \ˈhāvərz\ *n pl* [³*haver* + *-s*] *chiefly Scot* **:** stuff and nonsense : POPPYCOCK ⟨you're talking ~ —John Buchan⟩

hav·er·sack \ˈhavə(r),sak\ *n* [F *havresac* (formerly, bag for oats), fr. G *habersack* bag for oats, fr. *haber* oat, oats (fr. OHG *habaro*) + *sack* bag, fr. OHG *sac* — more at HAVER, SACK] **:** a bag or case similar to a knapsack but usu. worn over one shoulder

haversack

ha·ver·sian canal \hə'vərzhən-, (ˈ)hā¦v\ *sometimes* -rshən\ *n, sometimes cap H* [Clopton *Havers* †1702 Eng. physician and anatomist + E *-ian*] **:** any of the small canals through which the blood vessels ramify in bone

haversian system *n, sometimes cap H* **:** a haversian canal with the concentrically arranged laminae of bone that surround it

hav·er·sine \ˈhavə(r),sīn\ *n* [*half versed sine*] **:** half of the versed sine — abbr. *hav*

haves *pl of* HAVE

have up *vt* **1 :** to bring before an authority (as a court) to answer a charge ⟨the man *had* the writer *up* for libel⟩ ⟨the room where new boys were examined and old ones *had up* for rebuke or punishment —Samuel Butler †1902⟩ ⟨the man swore he would *have* them *up* for defamation of character⟩ **2 :** to be aroused in ⟨father *had* his temper *up* and swore loudly⟩ ⟨the revolutionaries *had* their blood *up* for some action⟩

¹ha·vey–ca·vey \ˈ(h)āviˈkāvi\ *adj* [origin unknown] *dial Eng* **:** precariously balanced : UNSTEADY

²havey–cavey \ˈ"\ *adv, dial Eng* **:** HELTER-SKELTER

hav·i·land \ˈhavələnd\ *n* -s *usu cap, often attrib* [after David *Haviland,* 19th cent. Am. manufacturer in France, its originator] **:** porcelain tableware designed for the American trade and made by a factory founded in 1839 at Limoges, France

hav·il·dar \ˈhavəl,där\ *n* -s [Hindi *ḥawāldār,* fr. Ar *ḥawāla* charge + Per *dār* having] **:** a noncommissioned officer in the Indian army corresponding to a sergeant

havildar major *n* **:** a sergeant major in the Indian army

¹having *n* -s [ME, fr. gerund of *haven* to have] **:** something one possesses or which belongs to one : PROPERTY — usu. used in pl.

²having *adj* [fr. pres. part. of ¹*have*] **:** GRASPING, AVARICIOUS ⟨she's got rather a ~ nature —John Galsworthy⟩

ha·vings \ˈhāviŋz\ *n pl but sing in constr* [ME, fr. pl. of *having,* gerund of *haven* to have] *Scot* **:** DEPORTMENT, BEHAVIOR, MANNERS; *specif* **:** good manners ⟨a lady of gentle ~⟩

hav·ior \ˈhāvyə(r)\ *n* -s [ME *haviour* possession, alter. of *havour,* alter. (influenced by ME *haven* to have) of *aver, avoir,* fr. MF *aveir, avoir,* fr. OF, fr. *aveir, avoir,* v., to have, fr. L *habēre* — more at GIVE] *chiefly dial* **:** BEHAVIOR

hav·la·gah \,hävlə'gä\ *n* -s [Heb *habhlāghāh*] **:** SELF-RESTRAINT ⟨as practiced by Zionist leaders for a policy of ~⟩

hav·na \ˈhavnə\ *dial Brit* **:** have not

¹hav·oc \ˈhavək, -vik, -vēk\ *n* -s [ME *havok,* fr. AF, modif. of OF *havot,* n., pillage & interj. used to signal start of pillage, perh. of Gmc origin; akin to Goth *hafjan* to lift — more at HEAVE] **1 :** wide and general damage or destruction : DEVASTATION, WASTE ⟨appalled by the ~ and loss of life caused by the earthquake —F.J.Crowley⟩ — see *cry havoc* at ¹CRY **2 :** great confusion and disorder ⟨several small children can create ~ in a house⟩ — **play havoc with** *or* **raise havoc with :** to do great damage to : render ineffectual : throw into disorder and confusion ⟨a weapon which could *play havoc with* land and sea defenses —Vera M. Dean⟩

²havoc \ˈ"\ *vb* **havocked; havocked; havocking; havocs :** to lay waste : DEVASTATE, DESTROY

havre *usu cap, var of* LE HAVRE

¹haw \ˈhȯ\ *n* -s [ME *hawe,* fr. OE *haga* hedge, hawthorn — more at HEDGE] **1 :** a piece of enclosed ground : YARD **2 a :** a hawthorn berry **b :** HAWTHORN **3 a :** the fruit of any of several shrubs or trees of the genus *Viburnum* **b :** a shrub or tree bearing such fruit

²haw \ˈ"\ *n* -s [origin unknown] **:** NICTITATING MEMBRANE; *esp* **:** an inflamed nictitating membrane of a domesticated mammal

³haw \ˈ"\ *vi* -ED/-ING/-S [imit.] **:** to inject a haw or a sound like it into one's speech during a hesitation or pause ⟨did a lot of hemming and ~*ing* during his talk⟩

⁴haw \ˈ"\ *n* -s **:** a sound often made by speakers during a pause while they are collecting their thoughts or trying to formulate them ⟨a long talk punctuated by hems and ~*s*⟩

⁵haw \ˈ"\ *v imper* [origin unknown] — used (1) as a command to a team or draft animal to turn to the left; (2) as a call in square dancing to progress to the left; compare ¹GEE ~ *vi* -ED/-ING/-S **1 :** to cry out the command *haw* to a draft animal ⟨we geed and ~*ed* until we were hoarse —A.M.Bailey⟩ **2 :** to turn to the near or left side ⟨the mare geed when she should have ~*ed*⟩ **3 :** to obey the command *haw* ⟨teaching a pair of young steers to ~⟩

ha·waii \hə'wä(,)(y)ē, -wī(,)(y)ē, -wȯ(,)(y)ē, -wä(,)(y)ē, -wäyə, -wȯyə, -wī(y)ə *also* hä'- *or* hä'- *or* -'vä(,)(y)ē *or* -vī-(,)(y)ē *or* -vä(,)(y)ē *sometimes* -'vȯ(,)(y)ē *or* -'wȯ(,)(y)ē; *a glottal stop often follows the 2d-syllable vowel when no y follows & when the last vowel is* ē\ *adj, usu cap* [*Hawaii,* state of the U.S., fr. Hawaiian *Hawaiʻi;* akin to Marquesan *Havaiki,* fabled original homeland of the Polynesians] **:** of or from Hawaii : of the kind or style prevalent in Hawaii : HAWAIIAN

¹ha·wai·ian \hə'wäyən, -wȯyən, -wī(y)ən\ *adj, usu cap* [*Hawaii* + E *-an*] **1 :** of or relating to Hawaii or the Hawaiian islands or the language of the Hawaiians **2 :** of or relating to a system of kinship terminology in which the terms for cross-cousins and parallel cousins are the same as those for sisters

²hawaiian \ˈ"\ *n* -s *cap* **1 :** a person of Hawaiian or part-Hawaiian ancestry **2 :** the Hawaiian language

ha·waii·ana *pronunc at* HAWAII *stressed* =,== + 'anə *or* 'änə *or* 'ānə *also* 'änə\ *n pl, usu cap* [*Hawaii* + E *-ana*] **:** objects relating characteristically to Hawaii or of Hawaiian origin (as books or curios)

hawaiian beet webworm *n, usu cap H* **:** a grub that is the larva of a pyralidid moth (*Hymenia recurvalis*) and is destructive to beets and other green crops in much of the U.S.

hawaiian crab *n, usu cap H* **:** a large Pacific swimming crab (*Portunus sanguinolentus*) that is related to the Atlantic blue crab and is an important market crab in Hawaii

hawaiian duck *n, usu cap H* **:** a small drab duck (*Anas wyvilliana*) prized for food in the Hawaiian islands that is prob. an offshoot of the mallard

hawaiian goose *n, usu cap H* **:** NENE

hawaiian guitar *n, usu cap H* **1 :** a flat-bodied stringed musical instrument that has a long fretted neck and usu. 6 to 8 strings, that is held in a horizontal position either on the knees of the player or on an adjustable stand, and that is played by plucking the strings with thimbles, the desired pitch being obtained by sliding a small metal bar across the raised strings **2 :** UKULELE

Hawaiian guitar 1

hawaiian mahogany *n, usu cap H* **:** KOA

haw·er \ˈhȯ(ə)r, -ȯə\ *n* -s [³*haw* + *-er*] **:** one that haws in speech ⟨one of your hemmers and ~*s*⟩

hawfinch \ˈ=,=\ *n* [¹*haw* + *finch*] **:** a common finch (*Coccothraustes coccothraustes*) of Europe and Asia having a large heavy bill and short thick neck, and a male that is marked with black, white, and shades of brown

¹haw–haw *var of* HA-HA

²haw–haw \(ˈ)hȯˈhȯ\ *n* -s [imit.] **:** a deep or esp. loud boisterous laugh : GUFFAW

³haw–haw \ˈ"\ *vi* -ED/-ING/-S **:** to laugh in haw-haws : GUFFAW

⁴haw–haw \ˈhȯ'hȯ\ *adj* [redupl. of ⁴*haw*] **:** marked by or given to the use of frequent haws as a habit or affectation of speech often associated with a southern British upper-class speech ⟨that famous *haw-haw* English accent —J.B.Priestley⟩ ⟨a kind of *haw-haw* way of talking —Clements Ripley⟩

¹hawk \ˈhȯk\ *n* -s [ME *hauk,* fr. OE *hafoc, heafoc;* akin to OHG *habuh* hawk, ON *haukr* hawk, Russ *kobets,* a kind of falcon] **1 a :** any of numerous diurnal birds of prey belonging to the suborder Falcones of the order Falconiformes: (1) **:** any of the smaller members of this group (as falcons, buzzards, harriers, kites, caracaras, and ospreys) as distinguished from the notably large eagles and Old World vultures (2) **:** any of various typical members of the family Accipitridae (as the New World Cooper's and sharp-shinned hawks and the Old World sparrow hawks) : ACCIPITER — see GOSHAWK; BILL illustration; compare OWL **b :** any of various birds that suggest hawks in appearance or behavior — used chiefly in combination; see NIGHTHAWK **2 :** one (as a swindler) who preys on his fellowmen **3 :** a small board or metal sheet with a handle on the underside used to hold mortar

hawk 3

²hawk \ˈ"\ *vb* -ED/-ING/-S [ME *hauken,* fr. *hauk,* n.] *vi* **1 :** to hunt birds by means of trained hawks : practice falconry **2 :** to soar and strike like a hawk ⟨birds ~*ing* after insects⟩ ~ *vt* **:** to hunt on the wing like a hawk ⟨the small bats ~ insects in midair —J.A.Thomson⟩

³hawk \ˈ"\ *vb* -ED/-ING/-S [back-formation fr. ²*hawker*] *vt* **:** to offer for sale by calling out or crying in the street : carry (merchandise) about from place to place for sale : PEDDLE : offer to various people for sale ⟨his works were ~*ed* in every street —Jonathan Swift⟩ ⟨small boys ~ large, luscious figs along the street —*Amer. Guide Series: N.C.*⟩ ⟨a dozen or so scripts which were currently being ~*ed* about town by various play agents —George Noble⟩ ~ *vi* **:** to peddle goods : hawk merchandise ⟨balloon-and-pennant man, ~*ing* by the grandstand gate —W.V.T.Clark⟩

⁴hawk \ˈ"\ *vb* -ED/-ING/-S [imit.] *vi* **:** to utter a harsh palatal or guttural sound in or as if in trying to clear the throat ~ *vt* **:** to raise (as phlegm) by hawking — often used with *up*

⁵hawk \ˈ"\ *n* -s **:** an audible effort to force up phlegm from the throat

hawkbell \ˈ=,=\ *n* [ME *haukes bell, hauk bell*] **:** a small hollow spherical bell containing a free pellet and often attached to a hawk's leg

¹hawkbill \ˈ=,=\ *or* **hawkbill turtle** *n* [¹*hawk* + *bill*] **:** HAWKSBILL TURTLE

²hawkbill \ˈ"\ *adj* [¹*hawk* + *bill*] **:** HAWK-BILLED

hawk–billed \ˈ=¦=\ *adj* **1 :** having a bill or jaws like a hawk's beak **2 :** shaped like a hawk's bill

hawkbit \ˈ=,=\ *n* [*hawkweed* + (*devil's*) *bit*] **:** any of various plants of the genus *Leontodon; esp* **:** FALL DANDELION

hawk cuckoo *n* **:** any of several Asiatic cuckoos of the genus *Cuculus* that outwardly resemble hawks — see BRAINFEVER BIRD

hawk eagle *n* **:** any of numerous eagles (as the African crowned eagle) exhibiting rather hawklike characters

¹hawk·er \ˈhȯkə(r)\ *n* -s [ME *hauker,* fr. OE *hafocere,* fr. *hafoc* hawk + *-ere* -er — more at HAWK] **1 :** FALCONER **2 :** an animal that captures its prey on the wing; *esp* **:** an insect that does this

²hawker \ˈ"\ *n* -s [by folk etymology fr. LG *hoker, höker* peddler, fr. MLG *hōker,* fr. *hōken, hūken* to peddle, bear on the back, squat + *-er;* akin to MD *hoken, hoeken* to peddle, squat, MHG *hūchen* to squat, ON *hūka* to squat, OE *hēah* high — more at HIGH] **1 :** one that hawks wares esp. in the streets : PEDDLER **2 :** one that hawks wares assisted by a beast of burden or private vehicle (as a carriage)

³hawker \ˈ"\ *n* -s [⁴*hawk* + *-er*] **:** one that hawks as if clearing his throat esp. constantly or habitually

hawk·ery \-kərē\ *n* -ES **:** a place where hawks are kept

hawke's bay \ˈhȯks-\ *adj, usu cap H&B* [fr. *Hawke's Bay,* provincial district in New Zealand] **:** of or from the provincial district of Hawke's Bay, New Zealand : of the kind or style prevalent in Hawke's Bay provincial district

hawkeye \ˈ=,=\ *n* **1 :** an unceasing minute scrutiny ⟨keeping . . . a ~ on all strangers riding in and out of the little village —Howard Troyer⟩ **2 :** one whose vision is markedly keen or who is esp. good in the perception of details (as errors) ⟨the ~*s* who trap printed mistakes before they get out to a critical public — *Trip through Brown and Bigelow*⟩ **3** *usu cap* **:** IOWAN 1 — a nickname

hawk–eyed \ˈ=¦=\ *adj* **:** having a keen eye : SHARP-SIGHTED

haw·kie *also* **haw·key** \ˈhȯki, ˈhäki\ *n, pl* **hawkies** *also* **hawkeys** [Sc dial. *hawkit, hawked* having white spots or streaks + *-ie, -ey*] *Scot* **:** a white-faced cow — often used as a pet name for any cow

hawking *n* -s [ME *hauking,* fr. gerund of *hauken* to hawk — more at HAWK] **:** FALCONRY

hawk·ish \ˈhȯkish, -kēsh\ *adj* **:** resembling or suggesting a hawk or the beak of a hawk in appearance ⟨a ~ face⟩ ⟨fishing boats with ~ prows —A.H.Leighton⟩

hawklike \ˈ=,=\ *adj* **:** resembling or suggesting a hawk in appearance or character ⟨a ~ nose —Louis Bromfield⟩ ⟨~ eagerness —*Wall Street Jour.*⟩ ⟨~ vision⟩

hawkmoth \ˈ=,=\ *n* **:** any of numerous rather large stout-bodied moths constituting a family (Sphingidae), having a long proboscis which at rest is kept coiled, long strong narrow fore wings more or less pointed at the ends, small hind wings, and stout antennae often hooked at the tip, and being usu. quiet in coloration but often handsomely patterned and graceful and hovering in flight — see HORNWORM

hawk nose *n* **:** a nose curved like a hawk's beak

hawk–nosed \ˈ=¦=\ *adj* **:** having a markedly curved and more or less pointed nose suggesting a hawk's beak ⟨the strength of the *hawk-nosed* face —Louis Bromfield⟩

hawk owl *n* **1 :** a largely diurnal owl (*Surnia ulula*) of northern forests that somewhat resembles a hawk in appearance, having a long rounded tail and rather short pointed wings **2 :** a wide-spread owl (*Ninox scutulata*) of eastern Asia and the Pacific islands having the facial disk little differentiated; *also* **:** any of several congeners (as the boobook owls)

hawk parrot *n* **:** a So. American parrot (*Deroptyus accipitrinus*) with a large erectile nuchal crest

hawks *pl of* HAWK, *pres 3d sing of* HAWK

hawk's–beard \ˈ=,=\ *n, pl* **hawk's–beards** [so called fr. the large bristly pappus] **:** a plant of the genus *Crepis*

hawksbill turtle \ˈ=,=-\ *or* **hawksbill** *n* **:** a carnivorous sea turtle (*Eretmochelys imbricata*) of tropical and subtropical seas, having a shell that rarely exceeds two feet in length and is covered with large overlapping horny plates of a brown color marbled with yellow that furnish the best tortoiseshell of commerce

hawk's–eye \ˈ=,=\ *n, pl* **hawk's–eyes 1 :** a blue variety of tigereye **2 :** GOLDEN PLOVER

hawk·shaw \ˈhȯk,shȯ\ *n* -s *usu cap* [after *Hawkshaw,* a detective in the play *The Ticket of Leave Man* (1863), by Tom Taylor †1880 Eng. dramatist and in the comic strip *Hawkshaw the Detective,* by Gus Mager †1956 Am. artist] **:** DETECTIVE

hawk swallow *n* **:** a common European swift (*Apus apus*)

hawkweed \ˈ=,=\ *n* **:** any of several composite plants esp. of the genera *Hieracium, Picris,* and *Erechtites*

hawky \ˈhȯkē\ *adj* -ER/-EST **:** HAWKLIKE

ha·wok \ˈhä,wäk\ *n, pl* **hawok** [Maidu *howok*] **:** Indian money of California consisting of shell disks or buttons

ha·wor·thia \hȯ'(w)ərthēə, -thēə\ *n* [NL, fr. Adrian H. *Haworth* †1833 Eng. botanist + NL *-ia*] **1** *cap* **:** a genus of succulent plants (family Liliaceae) from the Cape of Good Hope with thick fleshy leaves mostly crowded in a basal rosette and white or greenish flowers in a terminal spike **2** -s **:** any plant of the genus *Haworthia*

haws *pl of* HAW, *pres 3d sing of* HAW

hawse \ˈhȯz *also* -ȯs\ *n* -s [ME *halse,* fr. ON *hals* neck, part of the bow of a ship — more at COLLAR] **1 a :** HAWSEHOLE **b :** the part of a ship's bow that contains the hawseholes **2 :** the position or arrangement of the anchor cables of a ship when both a port and starboard anchor are used — see FOUL HAWSE, OPEN HAWSE **3 :** the distance or the space between a ship's bows and her anchor : the space spanned by the anchor cables ⟨the small boat anchored in the large ship's ~⟩

hawse bag *n* **:** a bag stuffed with sawdust, shavings, or oakum and used for closing a hawsehole — called also *jackass*

hawse bolster *n* **:** a wooden or iron guard at the end of or around a hawsepipe as protection against the chafing of the cable and to facilitate its movement

hawse–full \ˈ=,=\ *also* **hawse–fallen** \ˈ=,==\ *adj* **:** having the hawseholes under water : having the sea breaking through the hawseholes ⟨a ship riding *hawse-full* at anchor⟩

hawsehole \ˈ=,=\ *n* **:** one of the usu. steel-lined holes in the bow of a ship through which cables pass

hawse hook *n* **:** a breasthook above the hawseholes

hawsepiece \ˈ=,=\ *n* **:** one of the timbers in the bow of a wooden ship through which a hawsehole is cut

hawsepipe \ˈ=,=\ *n* **:** a cast-iron or steel pipe placed in the bows of a ship on each side of the stem for the anchor chains to pass through

haw·ser \ˈhȯzə(r) *also* -ȯsə-\ *n* -s [ME *haucer, hauser, hawser,* fr. AF *hauceour,* fr. MF *haucier* to raise, hoist (fr. — assumed — VL *altiare,* fr. L *altus* high) + *-our* -or — more at OLD] **:** a large rope for towing or mooring a ship or securing it at a dock

hawser bend *n* **:** a method of joining the ends of two heavy ropes by means of seizings

hawser clamp *n* **:** a device for gripping a hawser as it is paid out

hawser–laid \ˈ=,=¦=\ *adj* **:** CABLE-LAID

hawse timber *n* **:** HAWSEPIECE

hawsing iron *n* **:** CAULKING IRON

haw·thorn \ˈhȯ,thȯrn, -thȯ(ə)n\ *n* [ME *hawethorn,* fr. OE *hagathorn, haguthorn* fr. *haga* hedge, hawthorn + *thorn* thorn, thornbush — more at HEDGE, THORN] **:** a spring-flowering shrub or tree of the genus *Crataegus* (esp. the European *C.*

oxyacantha and the American *C. coccinea*) having usu. thorny branches, shining often lobed leaves, white or pink fragrant flowers, and small red fruits — see HAW, RED HAW

hawthorn china *n* **:** an oriental porcelain with a decoration of flowering plum-tree branches in white on a dark blue or black ground

hawthorn pattern *n* **:** the pattern on hawthorn china

hawthorn rust *n* **:** a rust fungus (*Gymnosporangium globosum*) in its aecial and pycnial stage

haw tree *n* **1** *obs* **:** HAWTHORN **2 :** WHITEBEAM **3 :** SERVICE TREE 1b

¹hay \'hā\ *n* -s [ME *haie, heie,* fr. OE *hege;* akin to OE *haga* hedge, hawthorn — more at HEDGE] **1** *archaic* **:** an enclosing fence **:** HEDGE **2** *archaic* **:** a place enclosed with a hay **:** PARK

²hay \"\ *n* -s [ME *hey,* fr. OE *hīeg, hīg, hēg;* akin to OHG *hewi* hay, ON *hey,* Goth *hawi* hay, OE *hēawan* to hew — more at HEW] **1 :** grass ready for mowing or esp. cut and cured for fodder; *specif* **:** the entire herbage sometimes including the seeds of grasses and other forage plants (as legumes) harvested and dried esp. for feed **2 :** a grayish greenish yellow that is slightly less strong and very slightly lighter than absinthe yellow, greener and duller than dusty yellow, and slightly deeper than yellow stone **3 :** a rewarding result of careful effort, industriousness, or cultivation (as of friendships) ⟨got some political ~ out of his association with underworld characters⟩ **4** *slang* **:** BED — used with *the* ⟨drag out of the ~ at six-thirty to dress and serve breakfast —Margaret Long⟩ ⟨caught him in the ~ with one of her maids —H.A.Smith⟩ **5 :** a trifling sum of money ⟨sells over $250,000 worth of them a year — and in the book trade that is anything but ~ —J.C.Furnas⟩

³hay \"\ *vb* -ED/-ING/-S *vi* **:** to cut and cure grass for hay and usu. haul it from the field and store it ~ *vt* **1 :** to dry (a cut grass) so as to make hay **2 :** to grow grass on for making hay ⟨~ the lower meadow⟩ **3 :** to give hay to ⟨~ the horses⟩

⁴hay \"\ *n* -s [ME *haye,* fr. AF *haie*] *archaic* **:** a net used for catching a wild animal (as a rabbit)

⁵hay *or* **hey** \"\ *n* -s [MF *haye*] **1 :** a rustic dance with much interweaving of couples **2 :** a right and left performed in a figure eight, straight line, or circular pattern in a dance

hay bacillus *n* [so called fr. the fact that isolations were formerly made from boiled hay infusions] **:** a rod-shaped spore-forming chiefly aerobic bacterium (*Bacillus subtilis*) widely distributed in soil and decaying organic matter

hay barrack *n* **:** BARRACK 4

haybird \'ˌ=ˌ=\ *n* **1 :** any of various small European birds (as the blackcap or the garden warbler) that build nests largely of grass **2 :** PECTORAL SANDPIPER

haybote \'=ˌ=\ *n* -s [ME *haybote, heybote,* fr. *haie, heie* hedge + *bote* profit, advantage, repair — more at ¹HAY, BOOT] **1 :** the wood or thorns allowed to a tenant or commoner in English law for repairing his hedges or fences — called also *hedgebote* **2 :** the right to take haybote

haybox \'=ˌ=\ *n* **:** a box packed with hay as insulation and used as a fireless cooker

hayburner \'=ˌ==\ *n, slang* **:** HORSE; *esp* **:** a second-rate racehorse

haycap \'=ˌ=\ *n* **:** a covering for a haycock

haycock \'=ˌ=\ *n* [ME *hay kock,* fr. *hay, hey* hay + *kock, cok* cock (pile) — more at HAY, COCK] **:** a small rounded somewhat conical pile of hay

hay cutter *n* **:** a machine for cutting or chopping hay into short lengths

hay·doo·dle \'hāˌdüdᵊl\ *n* [euphemism, *doodle* (as in *cock-a-doodle-do*) being substituted for ⁶*cock,* associated with ¹*cock* (penis)] *chiefly Midland* **:** HAYCOCK

hay down *vt* **:** to dry (tobacco) too rapidly during curing

haye \'hā, 'hī\ *n* -s [D *haai,* fr. MD *haey, haeye,* fr. ON *hār* thole, dogfish, shark; akin to OHG *huohili* small plow, Goth *hoha* plow, W *cainc* branch, OIr *cēcht* plow, Skt *śākhā* branch; basic meaning: branch] *archaic* **:** SHARK

hay·er \'hāə(r), 'he(ə)r, 'heə\ *n* -s **:** one that hays

hay fern *n* **:** HAY-SCENTED FERN

hay fever *n* **:** an acute allergic nasal catarrh and conjunctivitis that is sometimes accompanied by asthmatic symptoms; *specif* **:** POLLINOSIS

hay fe·ver·ite \hā'fēvəˌrīt\ *n* -s **:** one who is suffering from hay fever

hay-fever weed *n* **:** RAGWEED 2

hayfield \'=ˌ=\ *n* **:** a field where grasses or legumes for hay are grown

hayfork \'=ˌ=\ *n* **1 a :** a hand fork for pitching hay **b :** a mechanically operated fork for loading or unloading hay **2 :** an attachment to a hay tedder that stirs mowed hay

hay hook *n* **:** a steel hook held in the hand for dragging a bale of hay

haying *n* -s **:** the process or season of harvesting hay

hay jack *n* **:** HAYBIRD 1

hay knife *n* **:** a long-bladed knife with large rounded serrations on the edge for sawing off sections at the end of a stack or compact pile of hay

haylift \'=ˌ=\ *n* **:** an airlift engaged in dropping emergency food to farm animals isolated esp. by deep snow

hay-loader \'=ˌ==\ *n* **:** an implement for gathering hay from a windrow or swath and loading it into a wagon or trailer

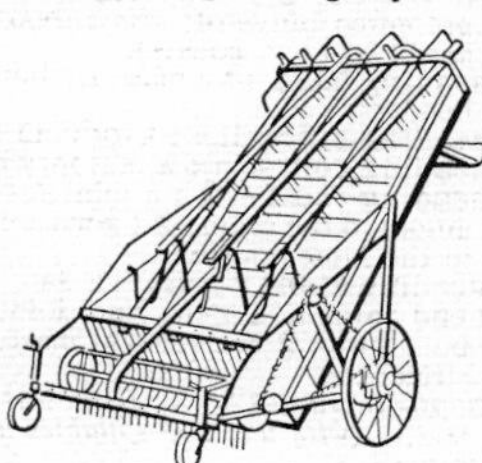
hay-loader

hayloft \'=ˌ=\ *n* **:** a loft or scaffold for hay **:** HAYMOW

haymaker \'=ˌ==\ *n* **1 a :** a worker who cuts and cures hay **b :** a machine for curing hay **2 a :** a powerful blow with the fist often resulting in a knockout **b :** an action or statement that is a stunning setback **:** an attack that overthrows or puts in a dangerous or extremely unpleasant position ⟨a leading coffee user today prepared a ~ for its coffee suppliers and announced that it plans to begin dispensing free tea with meals to discourage the use of coffee —*Springfield (Mass.) Daily News*⟩ ⟨traded ~s of innuendo and insult across the courtroom —*Time*⟩

haymaking \'=ˌ==\ *n* **1 :** the operation or work of cutting grass and curing it for hay **2 :** the act of taking full advantage of an easy opportunity ⟨the ~ of the profiteer after the war —W.R.Inge⟩

haymow \'=ˌ=\ *n* [ME *hay moghte* haystack, fr. *hay, hey* hay + *moghte, mowe* mow — more at HAY, MOW] **:** a part of a barn where hay is stored

hay plant *n* **:** WOODRUFF

hay press *n* **:** a baler for hay

hayrack \'=ˌ=\ *n* **1 :** a frame mounted on the running gear of a wagon and used in hauling hay or straw — called also *hayrig* **2 :** a feeding rack that holds hay for cattle or horses

hayrick \'=ˌ=\ *n* [ME *heyrek,* fr. *hey* hay + *rek, reke* rick — more at HAY, RICK] **:** a relatively large sometimes thatched outdoor pile of hay **:** HAYSTACK

hayride \'=ˌ=\ *n* **:** a pleasure ride usu. at night by a group in a wagon, sleigh, or open truck partly filled with straw or hay

hayrig \'=ˌ=\ *or* **hayrigging** \'=ˌ==\ *n* **:** HAYRACK

hays *pl of* HAY, *pres 3d sing of* HAY

hayscales \'=ˌ=\ *n pl* **:** large often public scales utilizing a platform for the weighing of hay on wagons or trucks

hay-scented fern \'=ˌ==-\ *n* **:** a No. American fern (*Dennstaedtia punctilobula*) with fragrant pale green fronds and an aroma like hay

hayseed \'=ˌ=\ *n* **1 a :** seed shattered from hay **b :** the bits of straw or chaff from hay that cling to clothes **2 :** a person who is markedly rustic and unsophisticated **:** YOKEL **3 :** any of various minute crustaceans (as the red feed) which live at the surface of the sea and upon which herrings and many other fishes feed

hay·sel \'hāsəl\ *n* -s [²*hay* + *sele*] *dial Eng* **:** the haying season

hayshaker \'=ˌ==\ *n, slang* **:** HAYSEED 2

hayshock \'=ˌ=\ *n, chiefly South & Midland* **:** HAYCOCK

haystack \'=ˌ=\ *n* [ME *haystak,* fr. *hay, hey* hay + *stak* stack — more at HAY, STACK] **:** a stack of hay **:** HAYRICK

hay sweep *n* **:** BUCK RAKE

hay-tal·let *or* **hay-tal·lat** \'hāˌtalət\ *n, dial Eng* **:** HAYLOFT

hay-time \'=ˌ=\ *n* **:** the period in which haying is usu. done

hayward \'=ˌ=\ *n* [ME *hayward, heyward,* fr. *haie, heie* enclosure, hedge + *ward* — more at HAY, WARD] **1 a :** an officer appointed to keep cattle from breaking through from a town common or roadway into enclosed fields and to impound strays **b :** the keeper of a town's common herd of cattle **2 :** FIELD DRIVER

¹haywire \'=ˌ=\ *n* [²*hay* + *wire*] **:** wire used to bind bales (as of hay or straw)

²haywire \"\ *adj* [so called fr. the frequent use of baling wire to make makeshift repairs] **1 a :** inadequately equipped ⟨a ~ outfit⟩ **:** FLIMSY **b :** put together inexpensively or patched up tentatively from available odds and ends **:** JURY-RIGGED ⟨a ~ plant hurriedly built of secondhand tank cars and salvaged equipment —*Monsanto Mag.*⟩ **2 a :** being out of order **:** BROKEN-DOWN ⟨luckily for us, their range-finding and director gear must have been ~ . . . so her fire wasn't very accurate —*Outspan*⟩ **b :** tangled up **:** mixed up **:** not running or working normally **:** acting in an odd way ⟨a ~ train that came and went at the worst possible hours —*N.Y. Herald Tribune Bk. Rev.*⟩ ⟨~ development of western industrial culture —Marston Bates⟩ — often used in the predicate with *go* ⟨magnetic compasses won't work, radios go ~, and ordinary engine oil freezes —*All Hands*⟩ ⟨psychologists have gone so ~ with this new freedom that many interpretations are wild and bizarre —P.M. Symonds⟩ **3 :** emotionally excited **:** gone to pieces **:** UPSET ⟨she's pretty much ~ just now, but she'll have settled down by the time you get here —Mary R. Rinehart⟩ — often used with *go* ⟨went completely ~ and in one mad, exotic moment she bought the red pocketbook —Mary D. Gillies⟩ ⟨many boxing champions have gone ~ after winning a title —D.M. Daniel⟩ ⟨the danger that men in responsible executive positions might go ~ —Elmer Davis⟩

³haywire \"\ *n* [¹*haywire;* fr. the appearance of the leaves] **:** a sporadic disease of potatoes that is of unknown cause but considered by some to be due to a virus or viruses but by others to be due to unfavorable conditions during tuber development and that is characterized by the production of dwarfed plants with elongated stiff sometimes rolled leaves which finally turn yellow with purplish discoloration esp. at the tips and margins

haz *abbr* hazard

ha·zan *or* **haz·zan** *or* **cha·zan** *or* **chaz·zan** \kə'zän, 'käzᵊn\ *n, pl* **haza·nim** *or* **hazza·nim** \kə'zänim\ [LHeb *ḥazzān*] **1 :** a synagogue official of the talmudic period **2 :** CANTOR 2

ha·zan·ic *or* **haz·zan·ic** *or* **cha·zan·ic** *or* **chaz·zan·ic** \-nik, -ᵊnik\ *adj* **1 :** belonging to or characteristic of a hazan **:** CANTORIAL 2 **2 :** connected with or relating to hazanuth

ha·za·nuth *or* **ha·za·nut** *or* **haz·za·nuth** *or* **haz·za·nut** *or* **cha·za·nuth** *or* **cha·za·nut** *or* **chaz·za·nuth** *or* **chaz·za·nut** \kə'zänət(h), -nəs\ *n* -s [LHeb *ḥazzānūth,* fr. *ḥazzan*] **1 :** cantorial singing or chanting **:** synagogal melodies **2 :** cantors of the synagogue; *collectively* **:** CANTORATE

ha·za·ra \hə'zärə\ *n, pl* **hazara** *or* **hazaras** *usu cap* **:** a Mongoloid people of Afghanistan

¹haz·ard \'hazə(r)d\ *n* -s [ME *hasard, hazard,* fr. MF *hasard,* fr. Ar *az-zahr* the die] **1 a :** a game of chance like craps played with two dice **b :** CHUCK-A-LUCK **2 a :** an adverse chance (as of being lost, injured, or defeated) **:** DANGER, PERIL ⟨the discovery of atomic fission brought into ~ the industrial potential of any state which could not destroy its enemy before it was itself destroyed —H.J.Laski⟩ **b :** a thing or condition that might operate against success or safety **:** a possible source of peril, danger, duress, or difficulty ⟨a coast visited by frequent dense fogs and mountains subject to violent storms constitute ~s to air travel —*Amer. Guide Series: Calif.*⟩ **c :** a condition that tends to create or increase the possibility of loss **3 a :** the effect of unpredictable, unplanned, and unanalyzable forces in determining events **:** CHANCE ⟨men and women danced together, women danced together, men danced together, as ~ had brought them together —Charles Dickens⟩ **b :** an event occurring without design, forethought, or direction **:** ACCIDENT ⟨looked like a fugitive, who had escaped from something in clothes caught up at ~ —Willa Cather⟩ **4 :** something risked (as stakes in gaming) **5 :** one of the winning openings in a court-tennis court — compare DEDANS, GRILLE, WINNING GALLERY **6 :** a stroke by which a pool ball is holed after contact with another ball — compare LOSING HAZARD, WINNING HAZARD **7 :** a golf-course obstacle restricting the player's stroke (as a bunker, sand trap, watercourse) **syn** see CHANCE, DANGER — **at hazard :** at stake

²hazard \"\ *vt* -ED/-ING/-S [ME *hasarden,* fr. *hasard*] **1 a :** to lay open to the risk of being lost, captured, or taken in or as if in a game of chance **:** GAMBLE, BET, VENTURE ⟨~*ed* a week's salary on a single turn of the cards⟩ ⟨asked him to ~ a small sum in a business venture⟩ **b :** to expose to possible risk of loss or damage ⟨so as not to ~ other buildings —*N.Y. City Fire Dept. Manual*⟩ **2 :** to take the risk of: **a :** to accept the chances and dangers of, venturing and daring to proceed or undertake despite them ⟨decided to ~ an open battle⟩ **b :** to have the courage to put forward or offer and expose to possible rebuff or censure (as a guess or suggestion) ⟨dares not ~ a prophecy —W.R.Sharp⟩ **syn** see VENTURE

haz·ard·er \-də(r)\ *n* -s [ME *hasardour, hasarder,* fr. MF *hasardeur,* fr. *hasarder* + *-eur* -or] **1 :** one that hazards **2** *archaic* **:** a player at hazard **:** GAMESTER

haz·ard·less \-dləs\ *adj* **:** not hazardous **:** marked by no hazard **:** involving no risk or danger

haz·ard·ous \-dəs\ *adj* [MF *hasardeux,* fr. *hasard* + *-eux* -ous] **1 :** depending on hazard or on chance; *specif* **:** ALEATORY **2 :** exposed or exposing one to hazard **:** involving risk of loss **:** RISKY **syn** see DANGEROUS

haz·ard·ous·ly *adv* **:** in a hazardous manner

haz·ard·ous·ness *n* -ES **:** the quality or state of being hazardous ⟨deterred by the ~ of the enterprise⟩

hazardry *n* -ES [ME *hasarderie, hasardrie,* fr. MF, fr. *hasarder* + *-erie* -ery] *obs* **:** GAMBLING

hazard side *n* **:** the side of a court-tennis court in which service is received — compare SERVICE SIDE

¹haze \'hāz\ *vb* -ED/-ING/-S [prob. back-formation fr. *hazy*] *vi* **1** *archaic* **:** to drizzle and fog **2 :** to become hazy or cloudy ⟨above the hotel the purple mountains *hazed* in the heat —William Sansom⟩ ~ *vt* **:** to make hazy **:** fog up **:** make dull or cloudy ⟨the purple night smoking up from the western water and *hazing* the world —Marjory S. Douglas⟩

²haze \"\ *n* -s [prob. back-formation fr. *hazy*] **1 a :** fine dust, salt particles, smoke, or particles of water finer and more scattered than those of fog causing lack of transparency of the air and making distant objects indistinct or invisible ⟨the fine ~ hanging lightly over the city and blurring its further outlines —Isolde Farrell⟩ ⟨a fog is likely soon to disappear by evaporation, while a ~ hangs on until washed out by rain, thinned by convection, or blown away by clear air —W.J.Humphreys⟩ **b :** a cloudy appearance in a transparent liquid or solid **c :** a dullness or cloudiness of finish (as on furniture) **:** BLOOM **2 :** something suggesting atmospheric haze: **a :** something giving the impression of clouds or cloudiness in the air or to the view ⟨the soft ~ of thickets of oaks —*Amer. Guide Series: Texas*⟩ ⟨a ~ of gnats danced under the bitten leaves —Elizabeth Taylor⟩ ⟨a ~ of greenery⟩ **b :** a state of mental dimness or obtuseness **:** haziness of mind or mental perception **c :** a state in which many things tend to merge and lose their separate identity ⟨looking back through the ~ of years —Allen Johnson⟩ **d :** a frame of mind vague or uncertain in its exact character but marked by strong generalized feeling dominating the reason ⟨a ~ of disbelief⟩ ⟨in a ~ of love⟩ or a set of conditions producing such a frame of mind ⟨its ~ of wine and waltz —Frederic Morton⟩

³haze \"\ *vt* -ED/-ING/-S [origin unknown] **1** *dial Eng* **:** to intimidate by physical punishment **2 a :** to harass (as a ship's crew) by exacting unnecessary, disagreeable, or difficult work **b** (1) **:** to harass or try to embarrass or disconcert by banter, ridicule, or criticism ⟨began to brood under the roughhouse play and built up a sullen resentment against the men who were *hazing* him —D.P.Mannix⟩ (2) **:** to subject (as a freshman or a fraternity pledge) to treatment intended to put in ridiculous or disconcerting positions **3** *West* **a :** to drive (animals) from horseback ⟨cowboys *hazed* herds slowly up north along an old Indian trail —S.E.Fletcher⟩ **b :** to separate (animals from a group) from horseback ⟨~ calves from a herd⟩ — often used with *out* ⟨~ out the dogies⟩

⁴haze \"\ *vt* -ED/-ING/-S [origin unknown] *dial Brit* **:** to season or mellow by drying in the sun

haze blue *n* **:** a pale purplish blue that is redder and paler than hydrangea blue, redder and slightly less strong than moonstone blue, and redder than starlight blue

haze gray *n* **:** a light gray similar to smoke gray

¹ha·zel \'hāzəl\ *n* -s [ME *hasel,* fr. OE *hæsel;* akin to OHG *hasal* hazel, ON *hasl,* OIr & OW *coll,* L *corulus*] **1 a :** a shrub or small tree of the genus *Corylus* (esp. *C. americana* and *C. cornuta* or in Europe *C. avellana*) — see FILBERT **b :** an Australian tree (*Pomaderris apetala*) grown for ornament and for its fine-grained wood **c :** the wood of either of these trees **d :** the wood of the sweet gum **2 a :** HAZELNUT 1 **b :** the fruit of the hawthorn **3 :** ASARABACCA **4** *also* **hazelnut :** a light brown to strong yellowish brown — called also *filbert, muffin, noisette*

²hazel \"\ *adj* [ME *hasel,* fr. *hasel,* n.] **1 :** consisting of hazels or of the wood of the hazel **:** relating to or derived from the hazel ⟨a ~ wand⟩ **2 :** of the color hazel **:** AVELLANEOUS

hazel alder *n* **:** SMOOTH ALDER

hazel hen *also* **hazel grouse** *n* **:** a European woodland grouse (*Tetrastes bonasia*) related to the American ruffed grouse

hazel hoe *n* **:** a large heavy grub hoe used in forests for trenching and clearing in fire fighting and for trimming small branches from tree trunks

ha·zel·ly \-zəlē\ *adj* **1 :** covered with or abounding in hazels **2 :** of the color hazel

hazel mouse *n* **:** a dormouse of the genus *Muscardinus*

hazelnut \'=ˌ=ˌ=\ *n* [ME *haselnutte,* fr. OE *hæselhnutu,* fr. *hæsel* hazel + *hnutu* nut — more at HAZEL, NUT] **1 :** any of several nuts that are produced by the hazel and that have a husk little or no longer than the nut **2 :** HAZEL 4

hazel pine *n* **:** the wood of the sweet gum **2 :** SWEET GUM

hazelwood \'=ˌ=ˌ=\ *n* **:** the wood of the sweet gum

hazelwort \'=ˌ=ˌ=\ *n* **:** an asarabacca (*Asarum europaeum*)

haz·er \'hāzə(r)\ *n* -s **:** one that hazes: as **a :** one of two cowboys who ride beside a bucking horse to protect both horse and broncobuster **b :** a rider who assists a cowboy bulldogging steers by riding on the opposite side of the steer to keep it from veering away

hazes *pres 3d sing of* HAZE, *pl of* HAZE

ha·zi·ly \'hāzəlē, -li\ *adv* **:** in a hazy manner ⟨saw the distant hills ~ through the field glasses⟩ ⟨remembered only ~ where he was going⟩

ha·zi·ness \-zēnəs, -zin-\ *n* -ES **:** the quality or state of being hazy ⟨the ~ of the smoky atmosphere⟩ ⟨a ~ in his mental processes⟩

hazing *n* -s **:** the action of one that hazes: **a :** the infliction of unnecessary or excessive work esp. on sailors in order to harass **b** (1) **:** an attempt to embarrass or disconcert by ridicule or persistent criticism (2) **:** the subjecting (as of a freshman or fraternity pledge) to treatment intended to put in ridiculous or disconcerting position

ha·zle \'hāzəl\ *vt* -ED/-ING/-S [freq. of ⁴*haze*] **:** HAZE

ha·zy \'hāzē, -zi\ *adj* -ER/-EST [fr. earlier *hawsey, heysey,* of unknown origin] **:** marked by haze: as **a :** obscured or made dim or cloudy with haze ⟨~ weather⟩ ⟨a ~ view of the mountains⟩ **b :** OBSCURE, VAGUE, INDEFINITE ⟨a ~ idea that he'd like to get married⟩ ⟨a somewhat ~ account of what he did⟩ ⟨~ logic⟩ **c :** CLOUDED ⟨a mirror ~ with steam⟩ ⟨some gasolines containing sulfur, when exposed to sunlight, become ~ —A.N.Sachanen⟩

hazy blue *n* **:** CAMEO GREEN

hazzan *var of* HAZAN

hazzanuth *or* **hazzanut** *var of* HAZANUTH

HB *abbr* **1** halfback **2** hard black **3** heavy bomber **4** His Beatitude; His Blessedness

Hb *symbol* hemoglobin

h bar *n, cap H* **:** a bar like an I bar but with wider flanges

h beam *n, cap H* **:** a beam like an I beam but with wider flanges

h-bomb \'=ˌ=\ *n, usu cap H* **:** HYDROGEN BOMB

h bone *n, cap H* **:** AITCHBONE

hbr *abbr* harbor

h-budding \'=ˌ==\ *n, cap H* **:** plate budding in which cuts in the bark of the stock are made in the form of an H

HC *abbr* **1** half calf **2** half chest **3** hand control **4** held covered; hold covered **5** high capacity **6** high church **7** high commissioner **8** high-compression **9** hockey club **10** Holy Communion **11** *often not cap* honoris causa **12** hot and cold **13** House of Commons **14** house of correction

hcap *abbr* handicap

HCF *abbr* highest common factor

HCL *abbr* high cost of living

hcp *abbr* handicap

hd *abbr* **1** hand **2** head **3** hogshead

HD *abbr* **1** harbor defense **2** heavy-duty **3** high density **4** home defense **5** horse-drawn

hdbk *abbr* handbook

hdg *abbr* heading

hdkf *abbr* handkerchief

hdl *abbr* **1** handle **2** headline

hdlg *abbr* handling

hdqrs *abbr* headquarters

hdw *abbr* hardware

hdwd *abbr* hardwood

hdwe *abbr* hardware

¹he \(ˈ)hē, ē, (h)i\ *pron* [ME, fr. OE *hē;* akin to OE *hēo, hīo* she, *hit* it, *hīe* they, OS *hē,* he, OHG *hē,* ON *hann* he, Goth *himma* (dat.) this, L *cis, citra* on this side, Gk *keinos, ekeinos* that (adj.), that person, Arm *sa* this, Hitt *ki;* basic meaning: this] **1 :** that male one ⟨I'll have no father, if you be not ~ —Shak.⟩ ⟨I spoke to the boy and ~ spoke to me⟩ **:** that one regarded as masculine (as by personification) ⟨last came Anarchy: ~ rode on a white horse —P.B.Shelley⟩ — used as nominative masculine pronoun of the third person singular usu. in reference to a previously specified subject or to someone indicated by some means (as pointing) ⟨~ heard me say it and so did ~⟩ ⟨~ with the beard is the one I mean⟩; sometimes in poetry and in substandard speech used pleonastically together with a noun as subject of a verb ⟨the Senator ~ said he'd have to have you —John Dos Passos⟩ ⟨Sir Oluf ~ rideth over the plain —H.W.Longfellow⟩ — see ¹HIM, ¹HIS; compare ³HIS, IT, SHE, THEY **2 :** that one whose sex is unknown or immaterial ⟨find out who is ringing the doorbell and what ~ wants⟩ ⟨~ that hath ears to hear, let him hear —Mt 11:15 (AV)⟩ — used as a nominative case form in general statements (as in statutes) to include females, fictitious persons (as corporations), and several persons collectively ⟨if a customer is dissatisfied ~ may return the goods⟩ ⟨one manufacturer is advertising . . . that ~ will sell cars freight-free —*Motor Trend*⟩ **3** *archaic* **:** the one **:** the other — used as a nominative masculine demonstrative pronoun in the expressions *he . . . he* and *he and he* **4 :** YOU — used as a nominative case form in speaking to or as if to a baby ⟨did ~ bump his little head⟩ and in some English dialects in addressing a boy or in addressing a person of higher or lower social status than the speaker **5 a** *substand* **:** HIM — used in a compound object ⟨between his wife and ~⟩ **b** *dial Eng* **:** HIM, IT — used emphatically as object of a verb or preposition ⟨don't give it to ~⟩

²he \'hē\ *n* -s *often attrib* [ME, fr. *he,* pron.] **1 :** a male person or animal ⟨the ~s would quarrel and fight with the females —Jonathan Swift⟩ — often used in combination ⟨a routine *he*-she plot⟩ ⟨*he*-goat⟩ **2 a :** one that is strongly masculine or virile — used chiefly in combination ⟨a real *he*-man⟩ ⟨that's what I call *he*-literature —Sinclair Lewis⟩ **b** *dial* **:** a large or powerful one of its kind — used chiefly in combination ⟨a regular old *he*-blizzard —Wallace Stegner⟩ **3** *Brit* **:** ³TAG 1; *also* **:** the player who is it

³he *also* **heh** \'hā\ *n* -s [Heb *hē',* perh. lit., window] **1 :** the fifth letter of the Hebrew alphabet — symbol ה; see ALPHABET table **2 :** the letter of the Phoenician alphabet or of any of various other Semitic alphabets corresponding to Hebrew he

HE *abbr* **1** high efficiency **2** high explosive **3** His Eminence **4** His Excellency; Her Excellency

He *symbol* helium

¹head \'hed\ *n* -s *see sense 6b* [ME *heved, hed,* fr. OE *hēafod;* akin to OHG *houbit* head, ON *hǫfuth,* Goth *haubith,* L *caput* head, Skt *kapucchala* hair at the back of the head] **1 :** the division of the human body that contains the brain, the eyes, the ears, the nose, and the mouth; *also* **:** the corresponding anterior division of the body of various animals including all vertebrates, most arthropods, and many mollusks and worms **2 a :** the seat of the intellect **:** the place where thought and inspiration originate **:** UNDERSTANDING, MIND ⟨two ~*s* are better than one⟩ ⟨he has some queer notions in his ~⟩ **b :** a person with respect to certain mental qualities ⟨let wiser ~*s* prevail⟩ **c :** natural aptitude or talent ⟨a good ~ for figures⟩ **d :** mental or emotional control **:** POISE ⟨can keep his ~ in a crisis⟩ ⟨level ~⟩ ⟨a situation calling for a cool ~⟩ **e :** HEADACHE ⟨it didn't give you a ~ like beer —R.O.Bowen⟩ **f :** the mouth as the organ of speech ⟨he'd better keep his ~ shut about this⟩ **3 a :** the hair on a head **b :** the hair as a head covering **:** COIFFURE, HEADDRESS **4 a :** a sculptured representation of a head ⟨a bronze ~ of Lincoln⟩ **b :** the obverse of a coin — compare HEAD OR TAIL **5 :** the antlers of a deer **6 a :** each one among a number **:** INDIVIDUAL ⟨count ~*s*⟩ ⟨a cost of $5 per ~⟩ **b** *pl* **head :** a unit of number (as of domestic animals) ⟨a thousand ~ of cattle⟩ **c** *Brit* **:** a herd or aggregation of game animals **7 a :** an end of something regarded as the upper or higher end ⟨~ of a valley⟩ ⟨~ of a slope⟩ ⟨~ of a staircase⟩ or as being the part most distant from an entrance ⟨~ of a bay⟩ or as being opposite the foot ⟨~ of a bed⟩ ⟨~ of a grave⟩ ⟨seated at the ~ of the table⟩ **b :** the source or beginning esp. of a stream ⟨the ~ of the Nile⟩ ⟨the ~ of navigation⟩ — compare FOUNTAINHEAD **c :** either end of something (as a bridge, cask, or drum) whose two ends may or need not be distinguished **d :** an underground passage or level in a coal mine **e :** a position or direction of the set of parallel planes in a massive crystalline rock along which fracture is most difficult, being normal to the direction of strongest cohesion **f :** a round or inning played from one end of a course to the other in certain games (as bowls and curling) **8 :** one who stands in relation to others somewhat as the head does to the other members of the body **:** DIRECTOR, CHIEF: as **a :** HEADMASTER **b :** one in charge of a division or department in an office or institution; *esp* **:** one in charge of a department in a school, college, or university **c :** an officer in charge of a hall or college (as at Oxford or Cambridge) **9 a :** CAPITULUM 3b **b :** the top or foliaged part of a plant consisting of a compacted mass of leaves ⟨~ of lettuce⟩ ⟨~ of a tree⟩ or close fructification ⟨~ of grain⟩ **c :** a bunch or hank of flax, hemp, or jute packed for marketing **10 :** HEADLAND, PROMONTORY, CAPE — now used chiefly in place names **11 a :** the leading element of a military column or a procession **b :** the leader or the leading position in dancing **c :** the hottest and most active portion of an advancing forest fire or grass fire **d :** freedom to proceed on one's course or to have one's way — used chiefly in the phrases *give one his head* and *let one have his head* **e :** HEADWAY ⟨often she had to fight for her ~ as the press of sail buried her bow —C.V.Reilly⟩ **12 :** the uppermost extremity or projecting part of an object **:** TOP ⟨~ of a cane⟩ ⟨~ of a bolt⟩ ⟨~ of a mast⟩ ⟨~ of a doorway⟩: as **a :** the striking part of a weapon (as an arrow, spear, ax) or tool (as a hammer, hatchet, ram) **b :** the striking end of a racket, club, stick, or paddle — see GOLF illustration **c :** the point of a violin bow — see BOW illustration **d** *of a bowed instrument* **:** the pegbox and scroll **e :** HEAD JOINT 1 **f :** the rounded proximal end of a long bone (as the humerus) **g :** the end of a muscle nearest the origin **h :** the anterior end of an invertebrate **:** SCOLEX **i :** the end of a cigar that is placed in the mouth **j :** a protective covering for the ends of roll paper **k :** the oval part of a printed musical note **13 a :** a body of water kept in reserve at a height (as for a mill or in a reservoir); *also* **:** the containing bank, dam, or wall **b :** a mass of water in motion (as in a rip current) **c :** a sudden rush of liquid (as water through an irrigation ditch or oil from a well) **d :** the flow of water used in irrigating a field **e :** unconsolidated earth material moved by solifluction — compare CONGELITURBATE **14 a :** the difference in elevation between two points in a body or column of fluid (as between the surface and a submerged orifice at which the fluid flows outward or when pumping into an elevated tank flows inward) **b :** the resulting pressure of the fluid at the lower point expressible as this height; *broadly* **:** pressure of a fluid ⟨an engine with a full ~ of steam⟩ **15 :** the front or foremost part of something: as **a :** the bow and adjacent parts of a ship ⟨brought her ~ into the wind⟩ **b :** a ship's toilet — compare BEAKHEAD 1b **c :** a portion of a hide in front of the flare of the shoulder — see HIDE illustration **d :** the approximate length of the head of a horse ⟨won the race by a ~⟩ **16 :** the place of leadership or of honor or command **:** the most important or foremost position ⟨at the ~ of his class⟩ **17 a (1) :** a word or words often in larger letters placed above or at the beginning of a passage of written or printed matter in order to introduce or categorize — called also *heading, headline;* compare RUNNING HEAD, SHOULDER HEAD, SIDEHEAD **(2) :** a separate part or topic of a discourse or writing **:** POINT ⟨~*s* of a sermon⟩ ⟨you may rest easy on that ~⟩ **b :** a portion of a page or sheet that is above the first line of printing; *also* **:** the corresponding blank part of an imposed form — compare PAGE 1d **18 a :** the topmost edge of a book standing upright — compare FOOT, TAIL; BINDING EDGE, FORE EDGE **b :** the upper edge of a sail — see SAIL illustration **19 a :** the foam or scum rising on a fermenting or effervescing liquid **b :** the cream that rises on standing milk **c heads** *pl* **:** the first runnings **d heads** *pl* **:** crude ore fed to a concentrating plant — compare CONCENTRATE, MIDDLING, TAILING **20 a :** the part of a boil, pimple, or abscess at which it is likely to break **b :** culminating point of action or of tension **:** CRISIS, CLIMAX, ISSUE **c** *archaic* **:** a gathered force (as in rebellion) ⟨to save our heads by raising of a ~ —Shak.⟩ **21 a :** a cover for an alembic or other distilling apparatus — see ALEMBIC illustration **b :** the hood of a carriage **c** *Brit* **:** the top of an automobile **22 a** *or* **head metal :** an extra piece of metal on a foundry casting made by filling up a riser after the mold is full in order to supply loss from shrinkage and to permit slag or dross and unsound metal to rise clear of the casting **b :** a riser filled in in this manner **c :** a part of a railroad rail supported by a web and base that guides and provides a running surface for the flanged wheels of cars and locomotives — see T RAIL illustration **23 :** a part or attachment of an apparatus, machine, or machine tool containing a device (as a cutter, grinder, polisher, drill) for acting mechanically on something ⟨turret ~ of a lathe⟩ ⟨milling ~⟩ ⟨sheep-shearing ~⟩ ⟨safety-*head* centrifuge⟩; *also* **:** the part of an apparatus that performs the chief function ⟨the ~ of a photographic enlarging camera⟩ ⟨a shower ~⟩ ⟨a sprinkler ~⟩ ⟨welding ~⟩ **24 a :** CYLINDER HEAD **b :** a movable mount for attaching a camera to a tripod or other support **c :** a device used in recording sound for converting electrical signals into the recorded form, for converting the recorded form into electrical signals, or for removing recorded material from a record — see ERASE HEAD, MAGNETIC HEAD, RECORDING HEAD, REPRODUCING HEAD **25 :** an immediate constituent of an endocentric compound or construction having the same grammatical function as the whole (as the terms *polite old man, old man,* and *man* in "a polite old man") **— by the head :** drawing the greater depth of water forward **— off one's head :** CRAZY, DISTRACTED **— out of one's head :** unable to command one's mental powers **:** DELIRIOUS **— over one's head 1 :** beyond one's comprehension ⟨liked pictures but art criticism was *over his head*⟩ ⟨the speech went *over the heads* of the audience⟩ **2 :** so as to pass over or ignore one's superior standing or authority ⟨quit when his juniors were promoted *over his head*⟩ ⟨went *over the head* of his boss to complain⟩ **3** *obs* **:** PAST, GONE-BY

²head \ˈ"\ *adj* [ME *heved, hed,* fr. *heved, hed,* n.] **1 :** of, relating to, or for a head or the head **2 :** PRINCIPAL, CHIEF, LEADING, FIRST ⟨~ chorister⟩ ⟨~ cook⟩ **3 :** situated at the head ⟨~ wall⟩ ⟨~ sails⟩ **4 :** coming from in front **:** meeting the head as it is moved forward ⟨~ sea⟩ ⟨~ tide⟩

³head \ˈ"\ *vb* -ED/-ING/-S [ME *hedden,* fr. *hed,* n.] *vt* **1 :** BEHEAD **2 a :** to lop off the top branches of **:** POLL ⟨~ a tree⟩ **b :** to cut back (the shoots of plants) to induce branching or check growth — often used with *in* or *back* **c :** to harvest (a crop) by cutting off the heads **3 a :** to put a head on **:** fit a head to ⟨~ an arrow⟩ ⟨~ a bolt⟩ ⟨~ a cask⟩ **b :** to form the head or top of ⟨the church tower was ~*ed* by a spire⟩ **4 :** to put oneself at the head of **:** act as leader to ⟨~ an expedition⟩ ⟨~ a revolt⟩ **5 a :** to face or oppose head on ⟨~ the waves⟩ ⟨~*ing* the driving rain⟩ **b :** to get in front of so as to hinder, stop, or turn back ⟨~ a herd of cattle⟩ **c :** to take a lead over (as in a race) **:** SURPASS **d :** to pass (a stream) by going round above the source **6 a :** to put something at the head of (as a list) **:** furnish with a heading ⟨each page was ~*ed* with the writer's name and the date⟩ **b :** to stand as the first or leading member of ⟨~*s* the list of local war heroes⟩ ⟨~*ed* his class all through school⟩ **7 :** to set the course or direct the progress of ⟨~ a ship northward⟩ ⟨~ a horse toward home⟩ **8 :** to drive or direct (as a soccer ball) by hitting with the head **~** *vi* **1 :** to form a head ⟨this cabbage ~*s* early⟩ ⟨the pimple ~*ed*⟩ **2 :** to point or proceed in a certain direction ⟨how does she ~, helmsman⟩ ⟨the fleet was ~*ing* out⟩ ⟨the dog ~*ed* for the woods⟩ ⟨the business seemed to be ~*ing* for trouble⟩ **3 a :** to have a source **:** ORIGINATE, RISE ⟨the more important rivers . . . ~ in the Rocky mountains or their foothills —*Scientific Monthly*⟩ **b :** to flow intermittently (as oil from a well)

head·ache \ˈheˌdāk *sometimes* -ˌdik *or* -ˌdēk\ *n* [ME *hedache,* fr. OE *hēafodece,* fr. *hēafod* head + *ece, ǣce* ache — more at HEAD, ACHE] **1 :** pain inside the head **:** CEPHALALGIA **2** [so called fr. the effect of their odor] **:** any of several poppies **3 :** a vexatious situation **:** a baffling problem **:** a source of trouble or worry ⟨the lack of funds for financing the educational needs of our communities sooner or later proves to be the principal ~ —C.A.Herter⟩

headache plant *n* [so called fr. its use as a remedy for headache] **:** AMERICAN PASQUEFLOWER

headache post *n* **:** a post placed on an oil-well derrick floor in order to prevent the walking beam from accidentally striking a workman

headache weed *n* **:** a West Indian plant of the genus *Hedyosmum* (family Chloranthaceae) held to be a remedy for headache

head–aching \-ˌdākiŋ, -kēŋ\ *adj* **:** causing headache

head·achy \ˈheˌdākē, -ki *sometimes* -ˌdik- *or* -ˌdēk-\ *adj* -ER/-EST **1 :** having headache **2 :** causing headache or attended by headache

head and front *n, archaic* **:** the foremost or essential feature or part ⟨the very *head and front* of my offending —Shak.⟩

head and shoulders *adv* **1** *archaic* **:** without good reason or excuse **:** by force **:** VIOLENTLY **2 :** beyond comparison **:** by far **:** OUTSTANDINGLY ⟨stood *head and shoulders* above the rest in character and ability⟩

head–and–tail–light \ˌ==ˈ=,=\ *also* **head–and–tail–light fish** *n* **:** a small So. American characin fish (*Hemigrammus ocellifer*) that is translucent green with orange-tinged black-tipped fins and shimmering red eyes and tail spots and is often kept in the tropical aquarium

¹headband \ˈ=,=\ *n* [¹*head* + *band*] **1 :** a band worn on or around the head: as **a :** an ornamental band (as of cloth, flowers, jewels) **b :** a band connecting two earphones **2 :** ARCHIVOLT 1 **3 :** a plain or decorative band printed or engraved at the head of a page or a chapter **4 :** a narrow strip of cloth sewn or glued by hand to a book at the extreme ends of the backbone — compare FOOTBAND

²headband \ˈ"\ *vt* **:** to fasten headbands on (a book)

head betony *n* **:** WOOD BETONY 2

head blight *or* **head blighting** *n* **:** a blighting of the heads of a cereal; *esp* **:** such a blighting caused by a fungus (*Gibberella zeae*) — compare WHEAT SCAB

headblock \ˈ=,=\ *n* **:** a block supporting the head of something: as **a :** a part of a sawmill carriage that supports the log **b :** a block of wood between the fifth wheel and the forward spring of a carriage or wagon **c :** one of a set of extra-long railroad ties used for supporting the operating mechanism of a point rail

headboard \ˈ=,=\ *n* **1 a (1) :** a board stretching between the headposts of a bed **(2) :** an upright structure forming a head for a bed **b :** a light partition that separates one berth in a sleeping car from that next to it **2 :** a wooden board at the upper corner of a Bermudian mainsail to which the halyard is shackled

headborough \ˈ=,=(,)=\ *n* [ME *hed borwe,* fr. *hed* head + *borwe* pledge, tithing — more at BORROW] **1 :** a chief of a frankpledge or tithing — compare TITHINGMAN **2 :** BORSHOLDER

headbox \ˈ=,=\ *n* **1 :** a receptacle in a papermaking machine that holds the stuff and regulates its flow onto the wire **2 :** a case covering the operating mechanism of a venetian blind

head boy *n* **:** a head prefect in a British school

head cabbage *or* **heading cabbage** *n* **:** CABBAGE 1

headcap \ˈ=,=\ *n* **:** the covering leather at the head and foot of the backbone of a hand-covered book shaped over the headbands

head capsule *n* **:** an exoskeleton of the head of an insect made up of fused chitinous plates in which the primitive segmentation is obscured

head–cavity \ˈ=,===\ *n* **:** one of the transitory somites of the head of an early vertebrate embryo

head cell *n* **:** CAPITULUM 3a

headcheese \ˈ=ˌ=\ *n* **:** the meat of the head, feet, and sometimes the tongue and heart esp. of a pig cut up fine, seasoned and boiled, and either made into a large sausage or pressed into a firm jellied mass

headchute \ˈ=,=\ *n* **:** a pipe for ejecting refuse from a ship's head

headcloth \ˈ=,=\ *n* **1 :** a cloth forming a covering or screen for the head of a bed **2 :** any of various cloth coverings for the head (as a kerchief, a kaffiyeh, a turban) **3 headcloths** *pl, obs* **:** the pieces of a woman's headdress

head cold *n* **:** a common cold in which the symptoms are primarily centered in the nasal passages and adjacent mucous tissues

head–collar \ˈ=,==\ *n, Brit* **:** HALTER 1b

head couple *n* **:** a couple in a square dance set whose backs are to the music or the caller; *also* **:** the couple opposite — compare FOOT COUPLE, SIDE COUPLE

head court *n* [ME *hed court*] **:** an obsolete Scottish county freeholders' court having charge for some time prior to 1832 of the registration of voters

head ditch *n* **:** an irrigation ditch across an upper slope from which water is drawn into basins or furrows

head·dress \ˈhe(d)ˌdres\ *n* **1 :** an often elaborate covering for the head (as for ceremonial or social occasions) **2 :** a manner of dressing the hair; *esp* **:** a fanciful arrangement of a woman's hair often with accessories (as flowers, veils, ribbons, combs)

head dropper *n* **:** a slaughterhouse worker who severs heads from carcasses and removes edible portions for processing

head·ed \ˈhedəd\ *adj* [ME *hedded,* fr. past part. of *hedden* to head — more at HEAD] **1 :** having a head or a heading ⟨a ~ bolt⟩ ⟨~ paragraphs⟩ **2 :** formed into a head **:** MATURED ⟨~ cabbage⟩ **3 :** having (such) a head or (so many) heads — often used in compounds ⟨curly-*headed* boy⟩ ⟨a cool-*headed* businessman⟩ ⟨a gold-*headed* cane⟩ **4** *of lumber* **:** tongued and grooved at the ends — usu. used in the phrase *dressed and headed*

head end *n* **1 :** the first few inches of fabric that are woven in a loom after new warp is started and that are often used for notations (as various marks of identification) **2 :** the cars of a passenger train that are immediately behind the locomotive and are commonly used for handling mail, express, and baggage

head·end·er \(ˈ)heˈdendə(r)\ *n* -S [*head end* + *-er*] **:** a head-on collision

head–end revenue *n* **:** revenue from railroad traffic (as mail, express, milk) carried at the head end

head–end system *n* **:** an arrangement whereby electricity for a complete railroad train is furnished by a single generating plant located on the locomotive or tender or on a separate car

head·er \ˈhedə(r)\ *n* -S [ME *heder,* fr. *hed* head + *-er*] **1** *obs* **:** HEADSMAN **2 a :** a worker or machine that removes heads; *esp* **:** a grain-harvesting machine that cuts off the grain heads and elevates them to a wagon **3 a :** a brick or stone laid in a wall with its end toward the face of the wall — opposed to *stretcher* **b :** a beam fitted between trimmers and across the ends of tail beams in a building frame **c :** a conduit or chamber (as the exhaust manifold of a multicylinder engine) into which a number of smaller conduits open **d :** a wall or barrier at either end of a motor truck or trailer body to prevent shifting of cargo on stopping or starting **4 a :** a worker or a machine that upsets rivets **b :** a cooper who puts heads on barrels by hand or by machine — called also *headerman* **5 :** an officer in charge of a whaleboat **6 :** a fall or dive head foremost ⟨tripped and took a ~ into a rosebush⟩ ⟨try a ~ off the high diving board⟩ **7 :** a dog trained to head cattle or sheep **8 :** a main shoot (as of a fruit tree) that tends to elongate with few side branches **9 :** SADDLE 12

header and thresher *n* **:** COMBINE 3

header bond *n* **:** a masonry bond in which all courses are header courses

header–box \ˈ==,=\ *or* **header barge** *n* **:** a large wagon box with one side higher than the other into which cut grain is elevated by header

header bond

header course *n* **:** a masonry course in which all the bricks are laid as headers

header fork *n* **:** a fork with three or four tines for pitching grain heads with attached straw harvested with a header

head·er·man \-mən, -ˌman\ *n, pl* **headermen 1 :** HEADER 4b **2 :** an operator of a machine for making steel bends, offsets, bolt blanks, bolt heads, and rivet heads **3 :** one who forges hot or cold metal on a bulldozer **4 :** a worker who rivets together the fitted-up metal plates of oil-storage tanks

header–up \ˈ==ˈ=\ *n* -S [*head up,* v. + *-er*] **1 :** HEADERMAN 2 **2 :** HEADER 4b

head fast *n* **:** a mooring hawser or chain at the head of a ship

headfirst \ˈ=ˈ=\ *adv* **:** with the head foremost **:** HEADLONG, ABRUPTLY, RECKLESSLY ⟨had plunged ~ into the statehood fight —Edna Ferber⟩

headfish \ˈ=,=\ *n* **:** OCEAN SUNFISH

head–flattening \ˈ=,=(=)=\ *n* **:** a practice dating from prehistoric times and formerly engaged in by various peoples of No. America and So. America whereby the skull is caused to develop with a flattened top by the application of pressure during infancy

head fold *n* **:** an anterior thickening of the blastoderm immediately anterior to the neural plate of an amniotic embryo from which the anterior part of the body develops

headforemost \(ˈ)=ˈ=(,)=\ *adv* **:** HEADFIRST, HEADLONG

head form *n* **:** the shape of a human head esp. with reference to the cephalic index

headframe \ˈ=,=\ *n* **:** a frame structure over a mine shaft to support the hoisting sheaves — called also *gallows*

head·ful \ˈ=ˌfu̇l\ *n* -S **:** a quantity (as of information) that fills the head

head gate *n* **1 :** a gate at the upper end of a canal lock **2 :** a gate for controlling the water flowing into a race, sluice, or irrigation ditch

headgear \ˈ=,=\ *n* **1 a :** a covering for the head (as a hat, cap, bonnet) **b :** a protective device for the head (as a soldier's helmet or a welder's helmet) **c :** HEAD HARNESS **2 :** hoisting or drilling gear at the top of a mine shaft or oil well

head harness *n* **:** a part of a horse's harness worn on or depending from the head and including bridle, checkrein, reins, bit, and blinders

headhouse *n* **1 :** a structure in which the headframe of a mine is housed **2 :** a part of a railroad passenger terminal providing accommodations for persons waiting for trains **3 :** a service area or building attached to a greenhouse usu. for housing the central temperature-control equipment and providing working and storage room

¹headhunt \ˈ=,=\ *n* **:** an expedition for securing heads as trophies

²headhunt \ˈ"\ *vi* **1 :** to kill and decapitate enemies and preserve their heads as trophies **2 :** to seek to deprive political enemies of position or influence ⟨an opportunity for local sniping and ~*ing* in individual states and districts —*N.Y. Times*⟩

headhunter \ˈ=,==\ *n* **:** one that practices headhunting

headier *comparative of* HEADY

headiest *superlative of* HEADY

head·i·ly \ˈhedˈlē, -ᵊli, -dəl-\ *adv* [ME *hedylyche,* fr. *hedy* heady + *-lyche, -liche* -ly] **1 :** RASHLY, HEADLONG **2 :** so as to cause exhilaration or dizziness

head in *vi* **:** to take a side track in order to give way to an approaching train

head·i·ness \-dēnə̇s, -din-\ *n* -ES [ME *hedinesse,* fr. *hedy* heady + *-nesse* -ness] **1 :** RASHNESS, HEADSTRONGNESS ⟨~ of youth⟩ **2 :** intoxicating quality ⟨the ~ of a spring morning⟩ ⟨a perfume with a ~ impossible to describe⟩

head·ing \ˈhediŋ, -dēŋ\ *n* -S [ME *hedding,* fr. gerund of *hedden* to head] **1** *archaic* **:** DECAPITATION **2 :** the compass direction in which the longitudinal axis of a ship or airplane points **3 :** something that forms or serves as a head: as **a :** HEAD 17a(1) **b :** a plain, colored, or patterned band woven at the beginning and end of a fabric **c (1) :** an edge of a ruffle above the line of gathering **(2) :** an edge of a curtain rising above a curtain rod **(3) :** FOOTING 8a **4 :** material for heads of casks or barrels **5 :** DRIFT 6a, 6b **6 :** an end of a stone or brick presented outward; *also* **:** HEADING COURSE **7** *South & Midland* **:** PILLOW, BOLSTER

heading bond *n* **:** a masonry bond that is formed by courses of headers

heading broccoli *n* **:** BROCCOLI 1

heading course *n* **:** a masonry course of headers only

heading joint *n* **1 :** a joint (as between two boards) at right angles to the grain **2 :** a masonry joint between two voussoirs in the same course

heading stone *n* **:** HEADER 3a

head joint *n* **1 :** the final joint of a flute containing the embouchure **2 :** a vertical masonry joint between the ends of stretchers

head·ker·chief \ˈ=,== (*with last two syllables like* KERCHIEF) *or* ˈ=(,)= (*with last two syllables as in* HANDKERCHIEF)\ *n* **:** KERCHIEF

head kidney *n* **1 :** PRONEPHROS **2 :** a nephridium often early developed in the cephalic segment of larval annelids and other invertebrates

head knee *n* **:** a timber in the frame of a ship fayed edgeways to the cutwater and stem

head lamp *n* **:** HEADLIGHT

head·land \ˈhedlənd, -ˌland, -ˌlaa(ə)nd\ *n* [ME *hedeland,* fr. OE *hēafodlond,* fr. *hēafod* head + *lond* land — more at HEAD, LAND] **1 :** a ridge or strip of unplowed land at the ends of furrows or near a fence **2 :** a point or portion usu. of high land jutting out into the sea, a lake, or other body of water

hea·dle \ˈhedᵊl\ *var of* HEDDLE

headledge \ˈ=,=\ *n* **1 :** either of the athwartship coamings of a hatchway or other deck opening **2 :** either of the upright end posts of a centerboard box

head·less \ˈhedlə̇s\ *adj* [ME *hevedles, hedles,* fr. OE *hēafodlēas,* fr. *hēafod* head + *-lēas* -less — more at HEAD] **1 a :** having no head **b :** BEHEADED ⟨~ corpse⟩ **c** *of a line of verse* **:** lacking the normal first syllable **2 :** having no chief or leader **3 :** lacking good sense or prudence **:** FOOLISH, STUPID **— headless·ness** *n* -ES

headletter \ˈ=,==\ *n* **:** type or lettering suitable for use in heads or display

head lettuce *n* **:** any of various cultivated lettuces that constitute a distinct variety (*Lactuca sativa capitata*) and are distinguished by leaves arranged in a dense rosette which ultimately develops into a compact head suggesting that of cabbage — compare LEAF LETTUCE

headlight \ˈ=,=\ *n* **1 :** a light usu. having a reflector and special lens and mounted on the front of a locomotive, streetcar, or motor vehicle for illuminating the road ahead

headlighting \ˈ=,==\ *n* **:** the illumination in front of a vehicle supplied by the headlights

head·like \ˈ=,=\ *adj* **:** resembling or suggesting a head in shape or function

head line *n, usu cap H* **:** LINE OF HEAD

¹headline \ˈ=,=\ *n* [¹*head* + *line*] **1 :** HEADROPE 2, 3 **2 :** HEAD FAST **3 a :** HEAD 17a(1) **b :** a head of a newspaper story or article usu. printed in large type and devised to summarize, give essential information about, or interest readers in reading the story or article that follows **c :** BANNER 4

²headline \"\ *vt* **1 :** to provide (as a news story) with a headline ⟨the editor *headlined* the story quickly⟩ — often followed by a specified headline as a complementary object ⟨*headlined* the story *Man Bites Dog*⟩ **2 :** to publicize highly in or as if in headlines ⟨a *headlined* hero of World War II⟩ **3 :** to be engaged as a leading performer in (a show) ⟨a blues singer *headlined* the floor show⟩

head·lin·er \ˈ=,līnə(r)\ *n* -s **:** a performer whose name is printed in a headline in the bill **:** STAR

headline schedule *n* **:** HEAD SCHEDULE

headlining \ˈ=ˌ==\ *n* [¹*head* + *lining*] **:** material that covers the ceiling of an automobile interior

headload \ˈ=ˌ=\ *n* **:** a load carried on the head ⟨women stagger under ~*s* that would shatter the spines of pack mules —*Time*⟩ ⟨the primitive method of ~*s* is still used to convey the cacao to road or rail —A.W.Knapp⟩

headlock \ˈ=ˌ=\ *n* **:** a wrestling hold in which one encircles his opponent's head with one arm and secures the grip by interlocking his fingers

head log *n* **:** a front bottom log on a skidway

¹head·long \ˈ=ˈlȯŋ *also* -ˈläŋ\ *adv* [ME *hedlong*, alter. of *hedling*, fr. *hed* head + *-ling*] **1 :** with the head foremost **:** HEADFIRST **2 :** without deliberation **:** RASHLY, RECKLESSLY, HEEDLESSLY **3 :** without delay or pause **:** in a rush **:** UNSWERVINGLY

²headlong \ˈ=ˌ=\ *adj* **1 :** IMPETUOUS, RASH, PRECIPITATE, RECKLESS ⟨her childlikeness, her ~ sympathies, the impulsive traits that endeared —W.R.Benét⟩ ⟨such personal possessions as they had been able to carry with them in their ~ flight —E.J. Phelan⟩ **2 :** plunging headforemost ⟨a ~ dive into the pool⟩ **3** *archaic* **:** STEEP, PRECIPITOUS ⟨like a tower upon a ~ rock —Lord Byron⟩ **syn** see PRECIPITATE

head·long·ness \ˈ=ˈ==\ *n* -ES **:** the quality or state of being headlong

head louse *n* **:** a sucking louse frequenting the head of its host; *esp* **:** a louse that is a variety (*Pediculus humanus capitis*) of the common louse of man, lives on the scalp, and attaches its eggs to hairs

head maggot *n* **:** the larva of the sheep botfly (*Oestrus ovis*)

head·man *in sense 1* ˈhedˌman *or* -maa(ə)n, *in sense 2* -ˌmən\ *n, pl* **headmen** [ME *hevedman, hedman*, fr. OE *hēafodman*, fr. *hēafod* head + *man* — more at HEAD, MAN] **1 a :** OVERSEER, FOREMAN, CHIEF **b :** a lesser chief or subleader of a primitive community (as a clan, tribe, or village) **2 :** HEADSMAN

headmark \ˈ=ˌ=\ *n* **1** *chiefly Scot* **:** the distinguishing characteristics esp. of the head that make one individual recognizable from another **2** *Midland* **:** a credit (as toward a prize to be awarded) given to a pupil for reaching the head position in an examination conducted with the pupils lined up and each pupil advancing toward the head of the line according to the proportionate number of his correct answers ⟨wanted to get the prize for the most ~*s* —J.H.Stuart⟩

headmaster \ˈ=ˈ==\ *n* **1 :** a man at the head of the staff of a private school usu. having some teaching duties but mainly concerned with administration, discipline, and counseling **2 :** the principal of a British secondary or elementary school

head·mas·ter·ly \-lē,-li\ *adj* **:** belonging to or characteristic of a headmaster

head·mas·ter·ship \-ˌship\ *n* **:** the post of a headmaster

head matter *n* [so called fr. its being obtained fr. the head of the whale] **:** the contents of the case of the sperm whale that yield spermaceti and clear oil

head metal *n* **:** HEAD 22a

head meter *n* **:** a flowmeter whose operation is dependent upon change of pressure head

headmistress \ˈ=ˈ==\ *n* **:** a woman at the head of the staff of a private school — compare HEADMASTER

head money *n* **1 :** HEAD TAX **2 :** money paid for killing or capturing a person (as an outlaw) **:** BOUNTY

head·most \ˈ=ˌmōst *also chiefly Brit* -ˌməst\ *adj* [¹*head* + *-most*] **:** most advanced **:** most forward **:** LEADING ⟨the ~ ship in the line⟩

headnote \ˈ=ˌ=\ *n* **1 :** a note of comment or explanation at the beginning (as of a page or chapter) **2 :** a summary prefixed to the report of a decided legal case stating the principles or rulings of the decision and usu. the main facts

head note *n* **:** HEAD TONE

head off *vt* **:** to turn back or turn aside **:** BLOCK, DIVERT, PREVENT ⟨a prime example of the way . . . troubleshooters *head off* strikes —*Time*⟩ ⟨police seemed to *head* me *off* in every direction —Adrian Bell⟩

head of horns *n* **:** HEAD 5

head on \(ˈ)=ˈ=\ *adv* **1 :** with the head or front pointing directly toward an object ⟨the ship struck the rocks *head on*⟩ ⟨the cars collided *head on*⟩ **2 :** in direct opposition or contradiction ⟨to let his wife settle this question without his meeting it *head on* —Herbert Gold⟩ ⟨what happens to the savage when he meets civilization *head on* —J.F.McComas⟩

head-on \ˈ=ˌ=\ *adj* [*head on*] **1 :** having the front facing in the direction of motion ⟨swerved to avoid a *head-on* crash⟩ or line of sight ⟨a *head-on* view of a building⟩ **2 :** directly opposite or opposing **:** FRONTAL ⟨a *head-on* attack on the committee's policy⟩

head or tail *n* **1 :** this side or that side — often used in pl. in tossing a coin to decide a choice, question, or stake — compare HEADS OR TAILS **2 :** beginning or end **:** one thing or another **:** something definite ⟨could not make *head or tail* of what he said⟩

head over ears *adv* **:** up to the ears **:** DEEPLY ⟨fell *head over ears* into English literature and history —Angela Thirkell⟩ ⟨*head over ears* in debt⟩

head over heels *adv* [alter. of *heels over head*] **1 a :** in or as if in a somersault ⟨fell *head over heels* down the hill⟩ ⟨a blow sent him *head over heels* into the pond⟩ **b :** upside down ⟨swung *head over heels* from the branch⟩ **2 :** HOPELESSLY, DEEPLY ⟨fell *head over heels* in love⟩ ⟨was *head over heels* in debt⟩

headpenny \ˈ=ˌ==\ *n* [ME *hed penny*, fr. *hed* head + *penny*] **1 :** HEAD TAX **2** *obs* **:** an individual or personal assessment or payment to church funds

headphone \ˈ=ˌ=\ *n* **:** an earphone held over the ear by a band worn on the head

headpiece \ˈ=ˌ=\ *n* **1 a :** a protective or defensive covering for the head; *esp* **:** any of the various helmets worn formerly by knights in armor and now by members of the armed forces, participants in some sports, and construction workers **b :** HAT, CAP **c :** HEADSTALL, HALTER **2 a :** HEAD **b :** UNDERSTANDING, BRAINS **3 a :** an ornament placed above the text matter of a page or at the beginning of a chapter — compare TAILPIECE **b :** HEADNOTE **4 :** a top part: as **a :** a headboard of a bed **b :** a lintel of a door or window

headphones

headpin \ˈ=ˌ=\ *n* **1 :** a bowling pin that stands foremost in the arrangement of pins — called also *kingpin* **2 :** KINGPIN 2

headpin bowling *n* **:** bowling in which a bowler aims directly at the 1-3 pocket when attempting to make a strike — compare SPOT BOWLING

headplate \ˈ=ˌ=\ *n* **:** a key plate for printing a design featuring a person's head

headpost \ˈ=ˌ=\ *n* **1 :** one of the posts at the head of a bed **2 :** the post nearest the manger in a stall

head post *n* **:** a movable post supporting an imitation head of leather used as an object for saber exercise in a cavalry riding school

head process *n* **:** an axial strand of cells that extends forward from the primitive knot in the early vertebrate embryo and is the precursor of the notochord

headquarter \ˈ=ˌ==, (ˈ)=ˈ==\ *vb* [back-formation fr. *headquarters*] *vi* **:** to make one's headquarters ~ *vt* **:** to place in headquarters

headquarters \ˈ=ˌ==, (ˈ)=ˈ==\ *n pl but often sing in constr* **1 a :** a place from which a military commander issues orders and performs the functions of command **b :** the personnel associated with and assisting the commander in performing his function **2 :** a chief or usual place of business **:** the administrative center of an enterprise or activity ⟨turned the archbishop's palace into a busy ~, organizing the duties of the clergy of all ranks —J.A.Gade⟩

headquarters company *n* **:** an administrative and tactical unit furnishing the necessary specialist personnel for headquarters of a battalion or higher unit

headrace \ˈ=ˌ=\ *n* **:** a race for conveying water to a point of industrial application (as a waterwheel or turbine)

¹head·rail \ˈheˌdrāl\ *n* **1 :** one of the elliptical rails at a wooden ship's head extending from the place of the figurehead to the bow **2 a :** the upper horizontal piece of a door **b :** a solid piece at the top of the back of a chair **c :** a crosspiece at the head of a bed

²headrail \"\ *n* [trans. of OE *hēafodhrægl*, fr. *hēafod* head + *hrægl* garment — more at HEAD, RAIL] **:** a medieval head covering for women consisting usu. of a cloth draped loosely over the head and hanging down in back

¹headreach \ˈ=ˌ=\ *vi* [¹*head* + *reach*] **:** to move ahead into the wind by momentum (as in tacking)

²headreach \"\ *n* **:** the distance covered by headreaching

head register *n* **:** the upper division in the pitch range of the human voice beginning at the point where the vocal cords readjust to produce the higher musical tone and characterized by a lighter tone quality

headrest \ˈ=ˌ=\ *n* **:** a shaped part or attachment (as on a barber's chair) for supporting the head

head rhyme *n* **:** BEGINNING RHYME

head rice *n* **:** unbroken grains of milled rice with the hull, bran, and germ removed

headrig \ˈ=ˌ=\ *n* **:** the main saw in a mill with or without other saws or associated equipment

headright \ˈ=ˌ=\ *n* **1 :** a grant (as of money or land) formerly given one who fulfilled certain conditions relating esp. to settling and developing land (as in Virginia in 1619 and in Texas in 1839) **2 :** a right belonging to an Indian member of a tribe to receive a per-capita share in the distribution of income earned by the tribal trust fund (as from the sale or lease of mineral rights) or a share of the fund on its termination; *also* **:** the right of a member to a share of tribal property

headring \ˈ=ˌ=\ *n* **1 :** an often decorated ring formed on the head by building up the hair with vegetable or animal fibers and worn by married warriors of some Kaffir tribes **2 :** a pad (as of vegetable fiber) worn to facilitate carrying a load on the head

head rod *n* **:** the switch rod nearest the point of a railroad switch

headroom \ˈ=ˌ=\ *n* **1 :** vertical space in which to stand or move **:** HEADWAY 2 **2 :** HEADSPACE 3

headrope \ˈ=ˌ=\ *n* [ME *hedrope*, fr. *hed* head + *rope*] **1** *obs* **:** rope leading from a masthead as a stay **2 a :** a part of a boltrope that is sewed along the upper edge of a sail **b :** a rope along the upper edge of a fishnet **3 a :** a rope at the head of an animal (as for tying or leading it) **b :** HEADFAST **4 :** AGAL

heads *pl of* HEAD, *pres 3d sing of* HEAD

head·sail \ˈhedsəl (*usual nautical pronunc*), -ˌsāl\ *n* **:** a sail (as a jib or fore staysail) set forward of the foremast

headsaw \ˈ=ˌ=\ *n* **:** a saw in a sawmill that cuts logs into planks, boards, and cants — compare RESAW

head scab *n* **:** sarcoptic mange of the head of sheep caused by a mite (*Sarcoptes scabiei* var. *ovis*)

head schedule *n* **:** a list of the type faces, type sizes, and headline forms approved for use in the headlines of a newspaper

head sea *n* **:** waves coming from directly ahead — compare FOLLOWING SEA, QUARTERING SEA

headset \ˈ=ˌ=\ *n* **1 :** an attachment for holding an earphone and transmitter in place at one's head **2 :** a pair of headphones

headshake \ˈ=ˌ=\ *n* **:** a shake of the head usu. signifying denial or distrust

headshaker \ˈ=ˌ==\ *n* **:** SKEPTIC, PESSIMIST ⟨adventurers . . . knowing before they began that the mockers and ~*s* would have the laugh of them —Clemence Dane⟩

headshaking \ˈ=ˌ==\ *n* **:** an act of shaking the head (as in disbelief or distrust)

head·ship \ˈhedˌship\ *n* **:** the position, office, or dignity of a head or chief **:** LEADERSHIP, PRIMACY

headshrinker \ˈ=ˌ==\ *n* **1 :** a headhunter who shrinks the heads of his victims **2** *slang* **:** PSYCHIATRIST

headsill \ˈ=ˌ=\ *n* **1 :** a horizontal member at the top of a doorframe or window frame **2 :** either of the pieces supporting the log at its ends in a saw pit

headskin \ˈ=ˌ=\ *n* **:** a tough elastic fatty mass covering the head of a sperm whale beneath the skin

heads·man \ˈhedzmən\ *n, pl* **headsmen 1 :** an executioner who cuts off heads **2 :** HEADER 5 **3 :** PUSHER 1e

head smut *n* **1 :** a covered smut of corn and sorghum caused by a fungus (*Sphacelotheca reiliana*) **2 :** any smut affecting the heads of grains or grasses

heads or tails *n pl but sing in constr* **:** a simple gambling game in which a coin is tossed and won by the player who successfully calls the side that lands upward — compare HEAD OR TAIL

head·space \ˈ=ˌ=\ *n* **1 :** a space between the breech and bolt face of a firearm using rimless ammunition **2 :** the space taken up by the cartridge rim in a firearm using rimmed ammunition **3 :** a space left between the contents and the ends or closure of a drum, barrel, can, or bottle in order to allow for variations in fill or expansion of contents — called also *outage*

headspring \ˈ=ˌ=\ *n* [ME *hedspring*, fr. *hed* head + *spring*] **1 :** FOUNTAINHEAD, SOURCE **2 :** a tumbling skill similar to a handspring except that the spring is made from the head and hands instead of from the hands alone

headstall \ˈ=ˌ=\ *n* [ME *hedstall*, fr. *hed* head + *stall*] **:** a part of a bridle or halter that encircles the head — see BRIDLE illustration

headstamp \ˈ=ˌ=\ *n* **:** numbers or letters stamped into the base of a cartridge case by the manufacturer in order to identify the cartridge and its original loading

headstand \ˈ=ˌ=\ *n* **:** an acrobatic feat of standing on one's head usu. with support from the hands

head start *n* [²*head*] **1 :** an advantage granted or achieved at the beginning of a race, a chase, or a competition **:** START ⟨a *head start* of 15 paces⟩ ⟨10-minute *head start*⟩ **2 :** a favorable or promising beginning **:** a good start

head stay *n* **:** FORESTAY

headstick \ˈ=ˌ=\ *n* **:** a short stick fitted to the headrope of a jib-headed sail or an ensign to prevent twisting

headstock \ˈ=ˌ=\ *n* **1 :** a bearing or pedestal for a revolving or moving part: as **a :** a part of a lathe that holds the revolving spindle and its attachments **b :** a part of a cylindrical grinding machine that rotates the work **c :** a part of a planing machine supporting the cutter **d :** a movable head in a measuring machine **e :** a framework containing a runway for the carriage in a spinning mule **f :** a headframe over a mine shaft **2 :** a pivoted crossbeam that supports a church bell

headstone \ˈ=ˌ=\ *n* **1 :** the principal stone in a foundation **:** chief stone **:** CORNERSTONE **2 :** the stone at the head of a grave

headstream \ˈ=ˌ=\ *n* **:** a stream that is the source or one of the sources of a river

head string *n* **:** a line connecting the second diamonds of the side rails at the head end of a billiard table that marks a limit on or within which the cue ball is placed in lagging for the break or beginning the game

headstrong \ˈ=ˌ=\ *adj* [ME *hedstrong*, fr. *hed* head + *strong*] **1 :** not easily restrained **:** UNGOVERNABLE, OBSTINATE ⟨~ youth⟩ **2 :** directed by ungovernable will **:** proceeding from obstinacy ⟨violent ~ actions⟩ **syn** see UNRULY

head·strong·ly *adv* **:** in a headstrong manner

head·strong·ness *n* -ES **:** the quality of being headstrong

heads up *interj* — used as a warning to look out for danger overhead or to clear a passageway

heads-up \ˈ=ˌ=\ *adj* [*heads up*] **:** ALERT, WIDE-AWAKE, RESOURCEFUL ⟨fast, aggressive, *heads-up* football⟩

head tax *n* **:** a tax usu. identical on every individual in a class or group: as **a :** POLL TAX **b :** a per-capita tax imposed on one (as a steamship company) bringing immigrants into the U.S.

head tie *n* **:** a kerchief for the head

headtire *n* [¹*head* + *tire* (headdress)] *obs* **:** HEADDRESS

head tone *n* **:** a vocal tone produced in the head register

head tree *n* **:** the spar tree nearest the donkey engine in a skyline logging system

head up *vt* **1 :** to close (as a barrel) at the head or with a head **2 :** HEAD *vt* 4 ~ *vi* **1 :** HEAD *vi* 3a **2 :** to come to an apex **:** find a head ⟨a bureaucracy that *headed up* in the king —W.P. Webb⟩

head voice *n* **:** the vocal tones of the head register

headwaiter \ˈ=ˈ==\ *n* **:** the head of the dining-room staff of a restaurant or hotel

headwall \ˈ=ˌ=\ *n* **1 a :** a precipice rising above the floor of a glacial cirque **b :** a steep slope forming the head of a valley **2 :** a wall of masonry or concrete built at the outlet of a drainpipe or culvert with the end of the conduit flush with the outer surface of the wall

¹head·ward \ˈhedw(ə)rd\ *also* **head·wards** \-dz\ *adv* [¹*head* + *-ward, -wards*] **:** toward the head **:** in the direction of the head ⟨a stream lengthens its course by eroding ~⟩

²headward \"\ *adj* **:** proceeding toward the head **:** occurring at or near the head ⟨~ erosion of a valley⟩ ⟨loss of consciousness caused by ~ acceleration of the body⟩

³head·ward \-ˌwȯrd, -ō(ə)d\ *n* -s [trans. of OE *hēafodweard*] **:** feudal service consisting in acting as a guard to the lord

head·wark \ˈ=ˌwärk\ *n* -s [ME *hedewerk*, fr. OE *hēafodwærc*, fr. *hēafod* head + *wærc* pain; akin to OE *weorc* work — more at HEAD, WARK] *chiefly dial Brit* **:** HEADACHE

headwater \ˈ=ˌ==\ *n* **:** the source and upper part of a stream — usu. used in pl.

headway \ˈ=ˌ=\ *n* **1 a :** motion or rate of motion in a forward direction (as of a ship) **b :** ADVANCE, PROGRESS ⟨make ~ in a profession⟩ ⟨a life in which the claims of spirit and emotion will make some ~ against the necessities of physical existence —Clive Bell⟩ **2 :** clear space (as under an arch or girder) sufficient to allow of easy passing underneath **:** HEADROOM **3 :** the time interval between two vehicles traveling in the same direction on the same route

headwear \ˈ=ˌ=\ *n* **:** apparel for the head **:** HEADGEAR 1a

head wind *n* **:** a wind blowing in a direction opposite to a course esp. of a ship or airplane ⟨delayed by strong *head winds*⟩

headword \ˈ=ˌ=\ *n* **1 :** a word or term often in distinctive type placed at the beginning of a chapter, paragraph, or entry (as in a dictionary or a catalog) **2 :** a word qualified by a modifier ⟨it is not always easy to state the precise kind of relation that exists between the modifier and its ~ —C.C.Fries⟩

headwork \ˈ=ˌ=\ *n* **1 :** mental labor; *esp* **:** clever thinking **2 :** ornamentation for an arch keystone **3 :** a structure for controlling the quantity of water entering a channel **4 headworks** *pl* **:** a platform or raft with tackle for warping or kedging a log raft through still water

headworker \ˈ=ˈ==\ *n* [²*head* + *worker*] **:** a director of a social agency or settlement

heady \ˈhedē, -di\ *adj* -ER/-EST [ME *hevedy, hedy*, fr. *heved, hed* head + *-y* — more at HEAD] **1 a :** WILLFUL, RASH ⟨the flow of the story is interrupted by . . . the giving of ~ opinions —S.L.A.Marshall⟩ **b :** VIOLENT, IMPETUOUS ⟨~ waters of the swollen river⟩ ⟨~ tempest⟩ **2 a :** tending to make giddy or light-headed **:** INTOXICATING ⟨~ perfume⟩ ⟨~ triumphs⟩ ⟨the ~ air of spring⟩ **b :** GIDDY, INTOXICATED, EXHILARATED ⟨students showing themselves ~ with ideas —*Time*⟩ **3 :** having or showing good judgment **:** SHREWD, CLEVER, SMART ⟨ran a ~ race⟩ ⟨one of the nimblest and *headiest* . . . quarterbacks —*Time*⟩

head yard *n* **:** a yard on a foremast

heaf \ˈhēf\ *n* -s [alter. of ⁴*haft, heft*] *dial Eng* **:** a piece of ground used as a sheep pasture

¹heal \ˈhēl, *esp before pause or consonant* -ēəl\ *vb* -ED/-ING/-S [ME *helen*, fr. OE *hǣlan*; akin to OHG *heilen* to heal, ON *heila*, Goth *hailjan*; causative denominatives fr. the root of OE *hāl* healthy, whole — more at WHOLE] *vt* **1 a :** to make sound or whole **:** restore to health **b :** to cure of disease or affliction ⟨a society to ~ convulsions or cramps —Ruth F. Kirk⟩ ⟨~ injured tissues⟩ **2 a :** to cause (an undesirable condition) to be overcome or eliminated **:** MEND ⟨the troubles . . . had not been forgotten, but they had been ~*ed* —William Power⟩ ⟨~ marital rifts and to ward off hasty divorce actions —*N.Y. Times*⟩; *specif* **:** to patch up (a rift or division) **:** CEMENT ⟨the conflicts between capital and labor . . . might temporarily be ~*ed* —J.A.Hobson⟩ ⟨~*ed* a breach between the two branches of the family —*Current Biog.*⟩ **b :** to restore to original purity or integrity **:** to make (a person) spiritually whole **:** to restore from evil ⟨~*ed* of his sins⟩ ⟨thus saith the Lord, I have ~*ed* these waters —2 Kings 2:21 (AV)⟩ ~ *vi* **1 :** to grow sound **:** return to a sound state ⟨the limb ~*s*⟩ ⟨the wound ~*s*⟩ **2 :** to effect a cure **syn** see CURE

²heal \"\ *vt* -ED/-ING/-S [ME *helen* to hide, conceal, cover, fr. OE *helan* — more at HELL] **1** *dial chiefly Eng* **:** to cover (as seeds) with earth **2** *dial chiefly Eng* **:** to cover with slates or tiles ⟨a leaky-roofed, tile-*healed* . . . cottage —F.M.Ford⟩

heal·able \ˈhēləbəl\ *adj* **:** capable of being healed

heal-all \ˈhēˌlȯl\ *n, pl* **heal-alls** \-ˌȯlz\ *also* **heals-alls** \-lz,ȯlz\ **1 :** SELF-HEAL **2 :** a plant of the genus *Scrophularia* **3 :** GREAT GREEN ORCHIS **4 :** YELLOW CLINTONIA

heald \ˈhēld\ *n* -s [ME *helde*, fr. OE *hefeld*; akin to MLG *hevelte* heddle, ON *hafald*; derivatives fr. the root of OE *hebban* to raise, lift — more at HEAVE] *chiefly Brit* **:** HEDDLE

heald·er \ˈhēldə(r)\ *n* -s *Brit* **:** DRAWER-IN

heal·er \ˈhēlə(r)\ *n* -s [ME *helere*, fr. *helen* to heal + *-ere* -er — more at HEAL] **1 :** one that heals ⟨time is a great ~⟩; *specif* **:** a person who engages in healing through means not requiring medical training or licensing **2 :** a Christian Science practitioner

¹healing *n* -s [ME *heling*, fr. OE *hǣling*, fr. *hǣlan* to heal + *-ing* — more at HEAL] **:** the act or process of curing or of restoring to health **:** the process of getting well

²healing *adj* [ME *heling*, fr. pres. part. of *helen* to heal] **:** tending to heal or cure **:** CURATIVE ⟨a ~ art⟩ — **heal·ing·ly** *adv*

healing blade *n* **:** BROAD-LEAVED PLANTAIN 1

healing herb *n* **1 :** COMFREY **2 :** HOARY PLANTAIN 1

heal·some \ˈhēlsəm\ *Scot var of* WHOLESOME

¹health \ˈhelth *also* -ltth\ *n* -s [ME *helthe*, fr. OE *hǣlth*, fr. *hāl* whole, healthy — more at WHOLE] **1 a :** the condition of an organism or one of its parts in which it performs its vital functions normally or properly **:** the state of being sound in body or mind ⟨nursed him back to ~⟩ ⟨he is the picture of ~⟩ ⟨dental ~⟩ ⟨mental ~⟩ — compare DISEASE **b :** the condition of an organism with respect to the performance of its vital functions esp. as evaluated subjectively or nonprofessionally ⟨how is your ~ today⟩ ⟨never in better ~⟩ ⟨her ~ is very delicate⟩ ⟨broken in ~⟩ ⟨went traveling for his ~⟩ **2 :** flourishing condition **:** WELL-BEING, VITALITY, PROSPERITY ⟨one more indication of the ~ of this pulsating . . . art form —Harriet Johnson⟩ ⟨expected the capitalist system to retain some degree of ~ —F.C.Barghoorn⟩ ⟨a serious menace to our economic ~ —F.L.Allen⟩ **3 :** a toast to someone's health, well-being, or prosperity ("to her Majesty!" he said . . . and drank a long ~ —Theodore Bonnet⟩ ⟨proposed the ~ of the ladies —B.A.Botkin & A.F.Harlow⟩

²health \"\ *adj* **1 :** of, relating to, or engaged in welfare work directed to the cure and prevention of disease ⟨a ~ center⟩ ⟨~ agencies⟩ **2 :** of, relating to, or conducive to health ⟨~ foods⟩ ⟨~ drinks⟩ ⟨~ education⟩

health department *n* **:** a division of a local or larger government responsible for the oversight and care of matters relating to public health

health·ful \-thfəl\ *adj* [ME *helthful*, fr. *helthe* health + *-ful*] **1 :** beneficial to health of body or mind **:** conducive to health **:** SALUTARY ⟨a ~ climate⟩ **2 :** HEALTHY ⟨a weird translation of Dickens' relatively ~ exuberance into a morbid . . . mysticism —*Writer*⟩ ⟨physical organization . . . which was at once ~ and exquisitely delicate —Nathaniel Hawthorne⟩

syn HEALTHY, WHOLESOME, SALUBRIOUS, SALUTARY, HYGIENIC, SANITARY: HEALTHFUL and HEALTHY are both used to mean conducive to or indicative of health or soundness, the former word being preferred in some quarters ⟨a *healthful* climate⟩ ⟨better nutrition, more *healthful* housing, sounder forms of recreation —Lewis Mumford⟩ ⟨one of the *healthiest* climates in England —Arnold Bennett⟩ ⟨extolled the *healthy* air of the hills as the best way to recover from fever —Hervey Allen⟩ ⟨*healthy* and normal outlets for youthful energies —Allan Nevins & H.S.Commager⟩ WHOLESOME may more strongly suggest beneficial, upbuilding, or sustaining capacities, physically, intellectually, or spiritually ⟨*wholesome* meats⟩ ⟨the warm rays of the sun, too, were *wholesome* for him in body and soul —Nathaniel Hawthorne⟩ ⟨one trade is healthier or cleanlier than another, that it is carried on in a more *wholesome* or pleasant locality —Alfred Marshall⟩ ⟨*wholesome*, fast-reading adaptations for teen-agers of the adult best sellers they want to read —*N.Y. Times Bk. Rev.*⟩ SALUBRIOUS may suggest the pleasantly invigorating or bracing ⟨these uplands are likewise often the most *salubrious* seat of living, with their fine scenery, their bracing ionized air, their range of recreation, from mountain-climbing and fishing to swimming and ice-skating —Lewis Mumford⟩ SALUTARY may describe something corrective, tonic, or otherwise beneficially effective although the thing in question may in itself be unpleasant ⟨in the open air, which is the most *salutary* of all things for both body and mind —R.L.Stevenson⟩ ⟨*salutary* was the tartness with which she protested, "You're the most conceited man that ever lived!" —Sinclair Lewis⟩ ⟨idle ladies and gentlemen are treated with *salutary* contempt, whilst the worker's blouse is duly honored —G.B.Shaw⟩ HYGIENIC is likely to suggest conformity with various health principles and laws ⟨anyone . . . who took the proper amount of balanced food, or consumed his excess heat units in regular exercise, and lived a reasonably *hygienic* life —V.G.Heiser⟩ SANITARY implies cleanly precaution against contamination, infection, or other unhealthful developments ⟨the *sanitary* appearance of the hospital kitchen⟩

health·ful·ly \-fəlē, -li\ *adv* [ME *helthfully*, fr. *helthful* + *-ly*] **:** in a healthful manner

health·ful·ness *n* -ES **:** the quality or state of being healthful

health·i·ly \-thəlē, -li\ *adv* **:** in a healthy manner

health·i·ness \-thēnəs, -thin-\ *n* -ES **:** the quality or state of being healthy

health insurance *n* **:** insurance against loss through illness of the insured

health·less \-thləs\ *adj* **1 :** lacking health of body or mind **:** INFIRM **2 :** not conducive to health **:** UNWHOLESOME

health line *n, usu cap H* **:** LINE OF MERCURY

health officer *n* **:** an officer charged with the enforcement of laws relating to health and sanitation **:** an executive officer under the direction of a health department or similar public body

health physicist *n* **:** a specialist in health physics

health physics *n pl but usu sing in constr* **:** physics dealing with the medical and hygienic aspects of and precautions against exposure to radioactive radiations

health·some \-thsəm\ *adj* **:** WHOLESOME, HEALTHFUL ⟨lent the street an air of good ~ quiet —William Sansom⟩

healthy \-thē, -thi\ *adj* -ER/-EST **1 a :** enjoying good health **:** free from disease **:** functioning properly or normally in its vital functions ⟨the examination revealed him to be a perfectly ~ man⟩ ⟨a ~ body⟩ ⟨~ eyes are a precious possession⟩ ⟨a ~ tree⟩ **b :** conducive to health **:** SALUTARY ⟨walk three miles every day . . . a beastly bore, but ~ —G.S.Patton⟩ ⟨his life recently had not been a ~ one —A. Conan Doyle⟩ ⟨the *healthiest* damned island in the Pacific —John Dos Passos⟩ **c :** indicating, reflecting, or suggestive of health ⟨a ~ color in his cheeks —Charles Dickens⟩ ⟨the ~ smell of grain —T.B. Costain⟩ ⟨stretched her arms over her head with a gesture of ~ fatigue —Ellen Glasgow⟩ **2 a :** morally or spiritually wholesome **:** not sickly, morbid, or sentimental **:** tending toward or indicating moral health ⟨their principal purpose of giving our children ~ entertainment —Coulton Waugh⟩ ⟨that's a good ~, cynical approach —James Street⟩ ⟨~ vulgarity inseparable from all vital human works —Albert Dasnoy⟩ ⟨in ~ reaction to the romantic fustian of the nineteenth century —Christopher Fry⟩ **b :** free from malfunctioning of any kind **:** VIABLE, PROSPEROUS, FLOURISHING, DESIRABLE ⟨the restoration of a ~ economy⟩ ⟨not a ~ state of affairs⟩ ⟨the negative plates are probably defective . . . requiring an extended period of charging and discharging to put them back in a ~ condition —A.L.Dyke⟩ ⟨a ~ book-publishing business —Harry Botsford⟩ **c :** productive of good of any kind **:** POSITIVE, BENEFICIAL ⟨showed his formidable ships of war . . . making a very ~ impression —C.S.Forester⟩ ⟨the creation of a ~ rivalry between the services —H.B.Hinton⟩ **d :** large in quantity or degree **:** CONSIDERABLE, MASSIVE ⟨repairs . . . account for a ~ bit of income —Bill Wolf⟩ ⟨the product carries a ~ price tag —*Printers' Ink*⟩ **e :** VIGOROUS, HEARTY ⟨a ~ appetite⟩ ⟨gives the boat a ~ shove . . . into deeper water —*All Hands*⟩ **3 :** SAFE — usu. used in negative construction ⟨not so ~ to be around . . . they might take a pop at us —Giorgio De Santillana⟩ ⟨not a ~ spot to be in at that time —H.A.Chippendale⟩

syn SOUND, WHOLESOME, ROBUST, HALE, WELL: HEALTHY can imply (1) the possession of full vigor of mind or body or (2) merely freedom from any sign of disease or morbidity ⟨a family with four *healthy*, active boys⟩ ⟨keep a child *healthy* during the winter⟩ ⟨a *healthy* outlook on life⟩ SOUND implies more strongly the absence of all defects of mind or body ⟨develop vigorous children, *sound* in mind and body⟩ ⟨*sound* of limb and healthy of mind⟩ WHOLESOME implies a healthiness that impresses others favorably, esp. as indicating physical, moral, or mental soundness or balance ⟨her hair carelessly pinned back, her eyes shining, her face aglow, looking oddly *wholesome* in a smeared white painter's smock —Herman Wouk⟩ ⟨a short, strongly made woman, *wholesome* and still youthful —C.B.Nordhoff & J.N.Hall⟩ ROBUST is the opposite of *delicate*, implying a vigor manifest in muscularity, solidity, strength of voice, power of endurance, and so on ⟨was looking *robust* and full of health and vigor —Samuel Butler †1902⟩ ⟨*robust* and tough in fiber —I.A.Gordon⟩ ⟨the giant zinnias are so *robust* here that you can transplant them in full bloom —Barrett McGurn⟩ HALE applies chiefly to elderly persons who still retain physical qualities of men in their prime ⟨this particular black panther was not old and sore, like many man-eaters. It was an exceedingly *hale* animal —David Walker⟩ ⟨his father, though an old man, was still *hale* —Sheila Kaye-Smith⟩ ⟨now in his 80th year but still alert, *hale* and hearty —*Wesfarmers News*⟩ WELL merely implies freedom from disease ⟨stay *well* amidst disease and poverty⟩ ⟨seemingly doomed to constant illness, only once in a while did he feel really *well*⟩ **syn** see in addition HEALTHFUL

healthy potato disease *n* **:** LATENT VIRUS DISEASE

¹heap \ˈhēp\ *n* -S [ME *heep, hepe*, fr. OE *hēap*; akin to OHG *houf, hūfo* heap, OS *hōp*, MLG *hūpe* heap, OE *hēah* high — more at HIGH] **1 :** a collection of things laid or thrown one on another **:** PILE ⟨small ~*s* of stones at which . . . sacrifices are offered —J.G.Frazer⟩ **2 :** a great number or large quantity **:** LOT ⟨there would be a ~ of noise and excitement —S.H. Holbrook⟩ ⟨it took a ~ of work —Meridel Le Sueur⟩ ⟨made a ~ of money⟩ ⟨there must be ~*s* of young poets who adore you —G.B.Shaw⟩ **3 :** the totality of rivals or competitors — used in the phrase *the top of the heap* ⟨it's getting to the top of the ~ that saves a man —Louis Auchincloss⟩ ⟨remain at the top of the concert ~ indefinitely —*Time*⟩ **4** *slang* **:** AUTOMOBILE; *esp* **:** an old beat-up automobile ⟨that ~ wasn't worth more than thirty dollars —C.L.Lamson⟩ ⟨my old tin ~ wouldn't start —Christopher Morley⟩ — **heap sight** *dial* **:** a great deal ⟨I'd a *heap sight* rather stay⟩ — **of a heap** *or* **all of a heap 1 :** so as to be stupefied, amazed, or overcome ⟨a lot of people were also struck *all of a heap* because . . . the favorite could do no better than finish third —G.F.T.Ryall⟩ ⟨struck him so completely *of a heap* that he was almost a broken man —H.L.Davis⟩ **2 :** all of a sudden ⟨*all of a heap* they had given her perplexity, immobility, and a dreadful thought —F.M.Ford⟩

²heap \"\ *vb* -ED/-ING/-S [ME *hepen*, fr. OE *hēapian*; akin to OHG *houfōn* to heap; denominatives fr. the root of E ¹*heap*] *vt* **1 a :** to throw or lay in a heap **:** pile or collect in great quantity **:** lay up **:** AMASS, ACCUMULATE ⟨stacks of firewood were ~*ed* all about the store —F.V.W.Mason⟩ **b :** to fill, load, or cover with a heap or heaps ⟨dishes ~*ed* high with food⟩ ⟨fields ~*ed* high with stacks of grain⟩ **2 a :** to accord, assign, or bestow lavishly or in large quantities ⟨~*ed* scorn and reproaches upon him⟩ ⟨~*ing* work upon his shoulders⟩ **b :** to bestow lavishly or in large quantities upon ⟨~*ed* him with stewardships and sinecures —Francis Hackett⟩ **3 :** to form or round into a heap (as in measuring) **:** fill (a measure) more than even full ~ *vi* **:** to form in a heap ⟨the tall clouds of deep July ~*ed* mountainous in the blue —C.G.Glover⟩

heaped measure *or* **heaping measure** *n* **:** dry measure obtained by filling the container heaping full

heap roasting *or* **heap roast** *n* **:** a process in which high-sulfur ore piled in the open is roasted without fuel other than for ignition, the heat being furnished by the combustion of the sulfur in the ore

heaps \ˈhēps\ *adv* [fr. pl. of ¹*heap*] **:** very much **:** EXTREMELY ⟨thanks just ~⟩ — not often in formal use

hear \ˈhi(ə)r, -iə\ *vb* **heard** \ˈhərd, ˈhə̄d\ *also dial* **heared** *or* **heerd** *or* **heered** \ˈhi(ə)rd, -i(ə)d\ *or* **hearn** *or* **heern** \ˈhi(ə)rn, -i(ə)n\ **heard** *also dial* **heared** *or* **heerd** *or* **heered** *or* **hearn** *or* **heern**; **hearing**; **hears** [ME *heren*, fr. OE *hieran, hȳran, hēran*; akin to OHG *hōren* to hear, ON *heyra*, Goth *hausjan* to hear, L *cavēre* to be on one's guard, Gk *akouein* to hear, *koein* to notice, hear, Skt *kavi* clever, wise] *vt* **1 :** to be made aware of by the ear **:** apprehend by the ear ⟨so great was the din that I could not ~ him⟩ ⟨he could ~ the distant rumble of the native drums⟩ **2 :** to be informed or gain knowledge of by hearing ⟨~ that business is picking up⟩ ⟨*heard* that you were ill⟩ ⟨*heard* nothing more about the affair⟩ — often used in the phrase *hear say* ⟨I've *heard* say that he has been married before⟩ and *heard tell* ⟨ain't *heard* tell of them since I don't know when —Hamilton Basso⟩ ⟨you may have *heard* tell of the wonder chemical, fluorine —*Amer. Girl*⟩ **3 a :** to listen to with favor or compliance **:** GRANT ⟨the Lord has *heard* my prayers⟩ **b :** to listen to with care or attention **:** give audience to ⟨won't you ~ my side of the story⟩ ⟨would not ~ the envoy, and angrily dismissed him⟩ ⟨would not ~ me through⟩ ⟨they *heard* him out, hiding their skepticism —F.D.Downey⟩ **c :** to attend and listen to ⟨~ a concert⟩ ⟨~ mass⟩ **d :** to listen to the recitation of ⟨he wants me to ~ him his part —Christopher Isherwood⟩ **4 a :** to give a legal hearing to ⟨~ a case⟩ ⟨the judge refused to ~ their claims⟩ **b** (1) **:** to take testimony from ⟨the committee *heard* 345 witnesses⟩ (2) **:** to take (testimony) usu. at a hearing ⟨the committee's decision to ~ testimony . . . on the condition of natives —*Current Biog.*⟩ ~ *vi* **1 :** to have the capacity of apprehending sound ⟨he can't ~ at all, poor fellow⟩ **2 a :** to gain information through oral communication **:** have a report **:** LEARN ⟨have *heard* about your doings⟩ ⟨who ever *heard* of such a thing⟩ **b :** to receive a message or letter ⟨haven't *heard* from him in two months⟩ **3 :** to entertain the idea **:** CONSENT, YIELD — used in negative construction with *of* ⟨will not ~ of my going⟩ or *to* ⟨would not ~ to it —Clyde Eagleton⟩ **4 :** to receive a scolding or tongue-lashing or punishment ⟨another complaint and you'll ~ from me⟩ **5** — often used in the expression *Hear! Hear!* during a speech to call attention to the words of the speaker or in applause

hear·able \ˈhirəbəl\ *adj* [ME *herable*, fr. *heren* to hear + *-able*] **:** capable of being heard

hear·er \-rə(r)\ *n* -S [ME *herere*, fr. *heren* to hear + *-ere* -er] **1 :** one that hears **:** AUDITOR **2 :** AUDIENT 2

hear·ing \ˈhiriŋ, -rēŋ\ *n* -S [ME *heringe*, fr. *heren* + *-inge* -ing] **1 a** (1) **:** the act or power of apprehending sound; *specif* **:** one of the special senses of vertebrates that is concerned with the perception of sound, is mediated through the organ of Corti of the ear in mammals or through corresponding sensory receptors of the lagena in lower vertebrates, is normally sensitive in man to sound vibrations between 16 and 27,000 cycles per second but most receptive to those between 2000 and 5000 cycles per second, is conducted centrally by the cochlear branch of the auditory nerve, and is coordinated esp. in the medial geniculate body (2) **:** an analogous perception of vibration in other animals ⟨the katydid . . . whose ~ is in slits on the front legs —C.D. & Mary Michener⟩ **b :** the extent within which sound may be heard **:** EARSHOT ⟨within ~ —Shak.⟩ **2 a** (1) **:** the act or an instance of actively or carefully listening (as to a speaker or performer) **:** AUDITION, AUDIENCE ⟨a powerful version . . . and you should give it a ~ —*Jazz Jour.*⟩ ⟨a man knows by instinct whether he'll get a tender ~ —Eden Phillpotts⟩ ⟨the orchestra did not impress me in one ~ as being quite up to Eastern . . . standards —Virgil Thomson⟩ (2) *dial Eng* **:** a church service **:** PREACHING (3) **:** opportunity to be heard or to present one's side of a case ⟨at least give me a ~⟩ ⟨the worst of men is entitled to a ~⟩ (4) **:** opportunity (as for a book or doctrine) to be generally known, evaluated, or appreciated **:** public attention or patronage ⟨no other book of equal seriousness ever had so quick a ~ —J.D.Hart⟩ ⟨a new trend which is struggling for a ~ —Edward Sapir⟩ ⟨numerous and fantastic theories of sleep continue to find a ~ —Webb Garrison⟩ **b** (1) **:** a trial in equity practice (2) **:** a listening to arguments or proofs and arguments in interlocutory proceedings (3) **:** a preliminary examination in criminal procedure (4) **:** a trial before an administrative tribunal **c :** a session (as of a congressional committee) in which witnesses are heard and testimony is taken ⟨the committee will hold ~*s* in a number of major cities⟩ **3** *chiefly dial* **:** a piece of news **:** RUMOR; *esp* **:** a choice bit of gossip **4** *Scot* **:** SCOLDING, LECTURE

hearing aid *n* **:** a device that amplifies the sound reaching an auditor's receptor organs; *specif* **:** an instrument for this purpose that consists of microphone, amplifier, and reproducer and is fundamentally comparable to a miniature telephone

hearing examiner *also* **hearing officer** *n* **:** a referee appointed by an agency of government to conduct an investigation or a public or private hearing and to report his findings of fact and sometimes his recommendations so that the agency may exercise its statutory powers (as by establishing rules and regulations or deciding controversies)

heark·en *also* **hark·en** \ˈhärkən, ˈhåk-\ *vb* -ED/-ING/-S [ME *herken*, fr. OE *heorcnian, hyrcnian*; akin to OFris *herkia, harkia* to listen — more at HARK] *vi* **1 :** to give ear **:** LISTEN ⟨~*ed* without much mental comment —Theodore Dreiser⟩ ⟨~*ed* to all they said night after night —Glenway Wescott⟩ ⟨stopped to ~ to the distant sound of another dog barking —Winnie Fitch⟩ **2 :** to listen with attention, sympathy, or acceptance of what is said **:** give respectful attention ⟨the boy was ~*ing* to another —Fanny Butcher⟩ ⟨how was it possible . . . that nobody ~*ed* to Goethe's voice —J.P.Hodin⟩ ⟨the humble folk who ~*ed* to these evangelists —G.M.Stephenson⟩ ~ *vt, archaic* **:** to give heed to **:** HEAR

hearken back *vi* **:** to hark back ⟨*hearken back* to the good old days of a century ago —Bernard Berelson⟩

hearn *dial past of* HEAR

hearsay \ˈ=,=\ *n* -S *often attrib* [fr. the phrase *hear say*] **1 :** something heard from another **:** REPORT, RUMOR ⟨like the ~*s* bandied about by the medievalists —S.N.Behrman⟩ ⟨the qualifications and doubts that distinguish critical science from ~ knowledge —M.R.Cohen⟩ ⟨places off the route, but known from ~ —G.F.Hudson⟩ **2 :** HEARSAY EVIDENCE

hearsay evidence *n* **:** legal testimony that consists in a narration by one person of matters told him by another; *broadly* **:** evidence that does not derive its value solely from the credit given to the witness himself as such but that rests in part on the veracity and competency of some other person or sometimes of the witness at another time

hearsay rule *n* **:** a rule barring the admission of hearsay evidence as testimony by reason of the unavailability of the sanctions of cross-examination to test the accuracy of the statement

¹hearse \ˈhərs, ˈhəs\ *n* -S [ME *herse*, fr. MF *herce* harrow, frame for holding candles, fr. L *hirpic-, hirpex* harrow, prob. of Oscan origin; akin to Oscan *hirpus* wolf; akin to L *hircus* he-goat] **1 a :** a usu. triangular frame of wood or metal designed to hold usu. 15 candles and used esp. in the Tenebrae service in Holy Week **b :** an elaborate temporary or permanent framework erected over a coffin or tomb of a royal, noble, or distinguished person and often decorated with lighted candles, banners, heraldic devices, and hangings and with memorial verses or epitaphs attached to it **2 a** *archaic* **:** COFFIN **:** GRAVE **:** TOMB **:** MONUMENT **b** *obs* **:** BIER 2 **3 :** a vehicle for conveying the dead to the grave

hearse 1a

²hearse \"\ *vt* -ED/-ING/-S **1 a** *archaic* **:** to place on a bier or in a coffin **b :** to convey in a hearse **2 :** BURY, ENTOMB **3 :** to shroud as if with a hearse

hears·ti·an \ˈhərstēən\ *adj, usu cap* [William Randolph *Hearst* †1951 Am newspaper publisher + E *-ian*] **:** of, relating to, or resembling the journalistic style or methods or the intense nationalism associated with the publisher William R. Hearst and his publications ⟨as chauvinistic, or *Hearstian*, as ever —Ted Oster⟩ ⟨the comic strip and other variegated features of the *Hearstian* type —*Vanity Fair*⟩

hearst·ling \ˈhərstliŋ\ *n* -S *usu cap* [W. R. *Hearst* + E *-ling*] **:** a journalist employed by or sharing the views of W. R. Hearst **:** a reactionary journalist ⟨how the *Hearstlings* will howl at the call for the repeal of the ban —K.N.Stewart⟩

¹heart \ˈhärt, ˈhåt, *usu* -d·+V\ *n* -S [ME *hert*, fr. OE *heorte*; akin to OHG *herza* heart, ON *hjarta*, Goth *hairto*, L *cord-, cor*, OIr *cride*, Gk *kardia*, Arm *sirt*, Hitt *karts*]

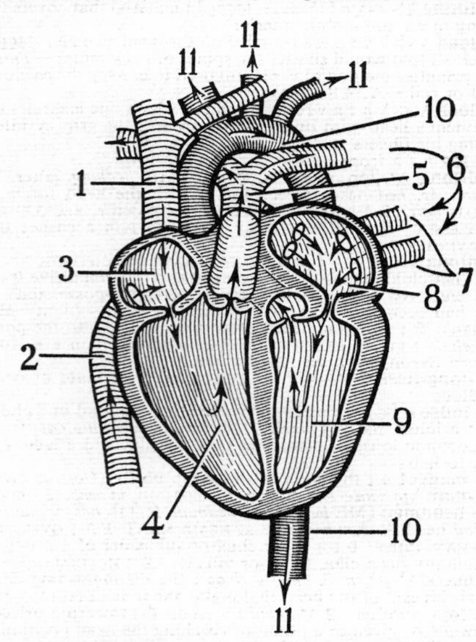

heart 1a, showing course of the blood coming from the extremities and entering from *1* superior vena cava and from *2* inferior vena cava; to *3* right auricle; to *4* right ventricle; to *5* pulmonary artery; to *6* lungs (not shown); to *7* pulmonary veins; to *8* left auricle; to *9* left ventricle; to *10* aorta; leaving by *11* to the extremities (not shown)

1 a : a hollow muscular organ of vertebrate animals that by its rhythmic contraction acts as a force pump maintaining the circulation of the blood, is in the human adult about five inches long and three and one half broad, of conical form, is placed obliquely in the chest with the broad end upward and to the right and the apex opposite the interval between the cartilages of the fifth and sixth ribs on the left side, is enclosed in a serous pericardium, and consists as in other mammals and in birds of four chambers divided into an upper pair of rather thin-walled auricles which receive blood from the veins and a lower pair of thick-walled ventricles into which the blood is forced and which in turn pump it into the arteries, back flow being prevented by valves, or in lower forms is less perfectly differentiated, having usu. two auricles and one ventricle in reptiles and amphibians and but a single auricle and ventricle in most fishes **b :** a structure in an invertebrate animal functionally analogous to the vertebrate heart: as (1) **:** a contractile ventricle with one to four thin-walled auricles that circulates the body fluid of most mollusks (2) **:** a contractile tube in most arthropods that receives blood from an investing pericardial sinus through openings provided with valves and circulates it forward and peripherally in the body (3) **:** any of a series of paired pulsating anterior blood vessels connecting the main dorsal and ventral blood vessels of certain annelids **c :** BREAST, BOSOM ⟨could have hugged him to my ~ —W.M.Thackeray⟩ **d :** something resembling a heart in shape: (1) **:** a conventionalized representation of a heart (as a decorative figure or a trinket) (2) **:** a red conventionalized figure of a heart stamped on a playing card (3) **:** a heart-shaped block through which a lanyard is reeved to extend stays (4) **:** the heart-shaped part of a pound net placed at the end of the leader to direct fish into the pot (5) **:** a foundry molder's heart-shaped trowel (6) **hearts** *pl but sing in constr* **:** a wood sorrel (*Oxalis montana*) **2 a :** a playing card marked with a conventionalized figure of a heart **b hearts** *pl* **:** the suit comprising cards so marked **c :** an odd bridge trick won or contracted for when hearts are trumps **d hearts** *pl but sing in constr* **:** a game resembling whist in which the object is to avoid taking tricks containing hearts and often other specified cards **3 a** (1) **:** the whole personality including intellectual as well as emotional functions or traits ⟨come from the ~ that is gay, warm, friendly, and enthusiastic —Constance Foster⟩ ⟨I say what is in my ~⟩ ⟨deep in your own ~, you share my prejudice —Walter de la Mare⟩ ⟨each man knew in his ~ that it was a lie —L.B.Salomon⟩ (2) *obs* **:** INTELLECT, UNDERSTANDING (3) **:** MEMORY, ROTE — used in the phrase *by heart* ⟨got the whole poem by ~⟩ ⟨knew the town's 500 telephone numbers by ~ —Peg Bracken⟩ (4) **:** OPINION, ATTITUDE, POSTURE — used chiefly in the phrase *change of heart* ⟨two aspects to the Soviet change of ~ on the Austrian treaty —T.P.Whitney⟩ **b** (1) **:** the emotional or moral as distinguished from the intellectual nature **:** CONSCIENCE, CHARACTER, SPIRIT ⟨has a good ~ but a weak head⟩ ⟨who can look into the ~ of a man⟩ ⟨his ~ dictated one course, his reason another⟩ (2) **:** generous disposition **:** SENSIBILITY, COMPASSION, FEELINGS ⟨have you no ~⟩ ⟨Oh, have a ~, lend me a dollar⟩ (3) **:** hardness or flintiness of character or temper **:** unfeeling disposition — usu. used with *have* in negative construction ⟨he loved his wife; he had not the ~ to deny her anything —Clara Morris⟩ ⟨hadn't the ~ . . . to refuse to come —Ellen Glasgow⟩ (4) **:** TEMPERAMENT, DISPOSITION, MOOD ⟨went home with a heavy ~⟩ ⟨are not inclined to regard free-trade agitation with a light ~ —*Dun's Rev.*⟩ (5) **:** GOODWILL, WILLINGNESS, SINCERITY, ZEAL — used chiefly in the phrase *with all my heart* ⟨will do it for you with all my ~⟩ **c :** LOVE, AFFECTIONS ⟨he lost his ~ to her at once⟩ ⟨laid his ~ at her feet⟩ ⟨a free public-school system . . . was one thing that lay near his ~ —A.W.Long⟩ ⟨his speeches won him ~*s* from coast to coast —William Clark⟩ **d :** COURAGE, ARDOR, ENTHUSIASM ⟨don't lose ~; all will turn out well⟩ ⟨felt some sinking of the ~⟩ ⟨an unsatisfactory . . . student, for my ~ was not in it —W.S.Maugham⟩ ⟨put ~ into me by what you say —O.W.Holmes †1935⟩ ⟨at the sight of reinforcements, the dispirited soldiers took ~⟩ ⟨still all ~ for my silly chase —Arthur Grimble⟩ ⟨many a people has kept itself in ~ when its statesmen have despaired —W.B.Adams⟩ **e** (1) **:** TASTE, LIKING ⟨likes music but has no ~ for grand opera⟩ — used chiefly in the phrase *after one's own heart* ⟨a man after his own ~⟩ (2) **:** fixed purpose or desire **:** ardent wish — now used chiefly in the phrase *set one's heart on* ⟨set his ~ on getting a new car⟩ (3) **:** intense concern, solicitude, or preoccupation — used chiefly in the phrase *at heart* ⟨people who are unaware of the issue which he has at ~ —J.H.Robinson⟩ ⟨with victory secured, there was one other thing that he had at ~⟩ **f :** one's innermost being **:** one's innermost or actual character, disposition, or feelings — used chiefly in the phrases *at heart* ⟨at ~ a

heart 1d(1)

sensitive high-strung man⟩ and *heart of hearts* ⟨assisting those who in their ~ of hearts are . . . implacably anti-American —Perry Miller⟩ ⟨in his ~ of hearts I do not think he ever really surrenders faith —Edward Wagenknecht⟩ **4** : PERSON ⟨two young ~s had been freed . . . from the burden of guilt and suspicion —Agnes S. Turnbull⟩ — usu. used with a qualifier ⟨poor ~! who would relieve her wants now⟩ ⟨farewell, dear ~⟩ **5** : the central or decisive part of something : CENTER: as **a** : an inner central area or region ⟨a system of waterways extending into the ~ of No. America⟩ **b** : an essential part : the part that determines the real nature of something or gives significance to the other parts : the determining aspect ⟨the discernment and understanding with which he penetrates to the ~ and essence of the problem —B.N.Cardozo⟩ ⟨those words of Jesus show us the ~ of Easter's meaning —W.F.Hambly⟩ **c** : the center of activity : a vital part on which continuing activity or existence depends ⟨Rome was the ~ and pulse of the empire —John Buchan⟩ **d** : HEARTWOOD **e** : CORE 1h **f** : a firm part (as of a head of lettuce); *also* : the center of a celery plant **6** *chiefly Brit* : condition for bearing crops : FERTILITY — used chiefly in the phrase *in good heart* ⟨the land has never been in better ~ —S.P.B.Mais⟩ **syn** see CENTER — **to heart** *adv* : under serious consideration : with deep concern : with hurt feelings ⟨took it *to heart*⟩ ⟨Sterne . . . laid the criticism *to heart* —Virginia Woolf⟩ — **to one's heart's content** : to the point of complete satisfaction or satiety : to the limits of one's will or pleasure ⟨eat *to your heart's content*⟩ ⟨printers imported any foreign books they thought would be popular . . . and reprinted them *to their heart's content* —Margaret Nicholson⟩

²heart \"\ *vb* -ED/-ING/-S [ME *herten*, fr. OE *hiertan*, fr. *heorte*, n.] *vt* **1** *archaic* : to give heart to : HEARTEN, ENCOURAGE, INSPIRIT **2** : to fix or seat in the heart **3** : to fill in (as a wall) with rubble or similar material ~ *vi* : to form a compact center or heart; *specif* : to develop a head (as of lettuce and cabbage)

³heart \"\ *dial var of* HEARTH

heartache \'=,=\ *n* : anguish of mind **syn** see SORROW

heart and soul *adv* : without reservations : COMPLETELY, WHOLLY ⟨count on me to help *heart and soul*⟩

heart attack *n* **1** : HEART FAILURE **2** : a seizure of weak or abnormal functioning of the heart

heart balm *n* : compensation for breach of promise to marry or alienation of affections ⟨two days after the marriage . . . was sued by another woman for two hundred thousand dollars' *heart balm* —Carey McWilliams⟩

heartbeat \'=,=\ *n* **1** : one complete pulsation of the heart **2** : the vital center or driving impulse ⟨the dining car is the real ~ and life of a train —Richard Barnitz⟩ ⟨the school is the ~ of our organic society —Agnes Meyer⟩

heart block *n* : incoordination of the heartbeat in which the auricles and ventricles beat independently due to defective transmission through the atrioventricular bundle and marked by decreased cardiac output often with cerebral ischemia

heart bond *n* : a masonry bond in which no header stone stretches across the wall but two headers meet in the middle and their joint is covered by another stone

¹heartbreak \'=,=\ *n* **1** : crushing grief ⟨the sorrow and the ~ which . . . abide in the homes of so many of our neighbors —H.S.Truman⟩ **2** : something that causes heartbreak ⟨proved a . . . ~ to the authors of his being —C.G.Glover⟩ ⟨the spectacle of his gentle fortitude was . . . a ~ —John Buchan⟩

²heartbreak \"\ *vt* [back-formation fr. *heartbroken*] : to break the heart of

heartbreaker \'=,==\ *n* : something that causes heartbreak ⟨arming merchant ships . . . has been another ~ —*Fortune*⟩

heartbreaking \'=,==\ *adj* : causing overpowering or intense sorrow, anguish, or distress ⟨made progress only with the most ~ efforts —Farley Mowat⟩ ⟨it is ~ to see new schools going up without proper . . . planning —Cecile Starr⟩ — **heart·break·ing·ly** *adv*

heartbroken \'=¦=\ *adj* [¹*heart* + *broken*] : overcome by sorrow — **heart·bro·ken·ly** *adv* — **heart·bro·ken·ness** \'härt¦brōkən(n)əs\ *n* -ES

heartburn \'=,=\ *n* **1** : a burning discomfort behind the lower part of the sternum usu. related to spasm of the lower end of the esophagus or of the cardia of the stomach — called also *cardialgia, pyrosis* **2** : HEARTBURNING

heartburning \'=,==\ *n* : intense or rancorous jealousy or resentment ⟨his promotion to ministerial rank is bound to cause much ~ —J.A.Stevenson⟩ ⟨the seniority rule . . . prevents bitter personal rivalries, factional sniping, and ~ —S.D. Bailey⟩

heart cherry *n* : any of several cultivated sweet cherries with rather soft-fleshed heart-shaped fruits — compare BIGARREAU CHERRY, DUKE 5

heart cockle *n* : ²COCKLE 1a; *esp* : a widely distributed burrowing cockle (*Isocardia cor*) with the umbones well separated giving the shell a heart-shaped appearance

heart disease *n* : an abnormal organic condition of the heart or of the heart and circulation

heart·ed \'härd·əd, 'hȧl, |təd\ *adj* [ME *herted*, fr. *hert* heart + *-ed* — more at HEART] **1** : having a (specified kind of) heart — often used in combination ⟨gave pleasure to lighter-*hearted* members of the staff —J.G.Cozzens⟩ **2** : seated or laid up in the heart

heart·ed·ness *n* -ES : the condition of having a heart esp. of a specified kind — often used in combination ⟨hard*heartedness*⟩ ⟨cold*heartedness*⟩

heart·en \'härt³n, 'hȧt-\ *vb* **heartened; heartened; hearten·ing** \-t(ᵊ)niŋ\ **heartens** [¹*heart-* + *-en*] *vt* **1** : to give heart to : inspire with fresh zeal, hope, or courage : rouse from indifference or discouragement ⟨people . . . whose presence either ~*ed* the spirit or kindled the mind —Jan Struther⟩ ⟨their supporters are enormously ~*ed* —Mollie Panter-Downes⟩ **2** *archaic* : to restore fertility or strength to (as land) ~ *vi* : to take courage : become imbued with fresh spirit and energy ⟨then the engine would ~ up and show off its paces —William Baucke⟩ **syn** see ENCOURAGE

heartening *adj* : tending or serving to hearten, inspire, or give fresh courage ⟨a ~ sign⟩ ⟨a ~ development⟩ — **heart·en·ing·ly** *adv*

heart failure *n* **1** : a condition in which the heart is unable to pump blood at an adequate rate or in adequate volume — see CONGESTIVE HEART FAILURE, CORONARY FAILURE **2** : cessation of the heartbeat : DEATH **3** : a sudden feeling of faintness (as at a surprise or sudden shock)

heartfelt \'=¦=\ *adj* : profoundly felt : EARNEST ⟨~ sympathy⟩ ⟨~ thanks⟩ **syn** see SINCERE

heart-free \'=¦=\ *adj* : not committed or engaged in one's affections ⟨quite *heart-free* —George Meredith⟩

heart·ful \'härtfəl\ *adj* [ME *hertful*, fr. *hert* heart + *-ful* — more at HEART] : full of heartfelt emotion : HEARTY ⟨~ prayers⟩ — **heart·ful·ly** \-fəlē\ *adv*

hearth \'härth, 'hȧth *sometimes* 'harth, 'hŏth\ *n* -S [ME *herth*, fr. OE *heorth*; akin to OHG *herd* hearth, ON *hyrr* fire, Goth *hauri* coal, Skt *kūḍayāti* he singes, and perh. to L *carbo* ember, charcoal, *cremare* to burn up] **1 a** : a brick, stone, or cement area of floor in front of a fireplace; *also* : a corresponding projection resembling a shelf on a stove **b** : the floor of a fireplace or of a brick oven on which a fire may be built **c** (1) : the lowest section of a blast furnace at and below the tuyeres where the molten metal and slag are collected (2) : the bottom of a refinery, reverberatory, or open-hearth furnace on which the ore or metal is exposed to the flame (3) : BLOOMERY (4) : the inside bottom of a cupola (5) : the fuel floor of a smith's forge (6) : the bottom of a heat-treating furnace that usu. supports the work **d** : the bed of a furnace on which pots rest in glass manufacturing **e** : a fire-hardened earth floor upon which primitive man built fires (as in an ancient rock shelter or campsite) **f** : a piece of wood against which a hardwood stick is rubbed or into which it is twirled to make fire by friction — compare FIRE DRILL **2** : HOUSE, HOME, FIRESIDE ⟨not rest . . . until every family has a ~ of its own —James Griffiths⟩ **3** : a nuclear area (as of high culture) : a vital or creative center : ECUMENE ⟨the small group of . . . nations that constitute the central ~ of occidental civilization —A.L. Kroeber⟩ ⟨the south and southwest of Mexico constitute one of the great culture ~s of the world —C.O.Sauer⟩

hearth·less \-thləs\ *adj* : not having a hearth

hearth money *n* **1** : PETER'S PENCE **2** : a 17th century English tax of two shillings on hearths in all houses paying the church and poor rates — called also *chimney money*

hearth-penny \'=,==\ *n* [ME *herthpeny*, fr. OE *heorthpenig*; fr. *heorth* hearth + *penig* penny — more at HEARTH, PENNY] : PETER PENNY

hearthrug \'=,=\ *n* : a rug for the front of the hearth

hearthside \'=,=\ *n* : FIRESIDE

hearthstone \'=,=\ *n* [ME *herthstone*, fr. *herth* hearth + *stone*] **1 a** : stone forming a hearth **b** : FIRESIDE, HOME **2** : a soft stone or composition of powdered stone and pipe clay used to whiten or scour hearths and doorsteps

heartier *comparative of* HEARTY

heartiest *superlative of* HEARTY

heart·i·ly \'härt³l·ē, 'hȧl, |tə-, -li\ *adv* [ME *hertily*, fr. *herty* hearty + *-ly*] **1** : in a hearty manner **2 a** : with all sincerity or goodwill : without reservations : WHOLEHEARTEDLY ⟨~ in sympathy with the essence of the liberal faith —M.R.Cohen⟩ **b** : with zest or gusto : VIGOROUSLY ⟨threw himself ~ into his work⟩ ⟨ate and drank ~⟩ **3** : COMPLETELY, THOROUGHLY, EXCEEDINGLY ⟨~ sick of this idle debate⟩

heart·i·ness \|d·ēnəs, |d·in-\ *n* -ES **1** : cordiality or geniality of manner : CHEERINESS, FRIENDLINESS ⟨detested his back-slapping ~⟩ **2** : ZEAL, ENTHUSIASM ⟨the music was sung with uninhibited ~ by the mountain folk —Herman Wouk⟩ ⟨enjoy themselves . . . with a ~ that makes the Londoner feel extremely envious —S.P.B.Mais⟩ **3** : VIGOR, STRENGTH ⟨an air of rugged outdoor ~ —J.J.Godwin⟩

hearting *n* -S [fr. gerund of ²*heart*] **1** : CORE 11 **2** : PUDDLE WALL **3** : BACKING 1a

heart·land \'härt,land, 'hȧt-, -laa(ə)nd, -,lənd\ *n* : an area of decisive importance : a pivotal or nuclear area ⟨the entire ~ of the country, the Mississippi Basin —A.W.Baum⟩ ⟨the German industrial ~ in the Ruhr valley —Henry Wallace⟩ ⟨the temperate highlands which are the ~ of the republic —A.P.Whitaker⟩ ⟨the ~ of Eastern duck and goose shooting —*Newsweek*⟩; *specif* : a central land area (as northern Eurasia from the Elbe to the Amur) conceived by geopoliticians to be capable of self-sufficiency as an economic and military unit, invulnerable to sea power, and therefore having strategic advantages for mastery of the world

heartleaf \'=,=\ *n* : any of several wild gingers that have distinctly cordate leaves and are usu. included in the genus *Asarum* but are sometimes segregated in a separate genus

heart-leaved aster \'=,=-\ *n* : a common blue aster (*Aster cordifolius*) of eastern No. America

heart-leaved willow *also* **heart-leafed willow** \'=,=-\ *n* : a common broad-leaved American willow (*Salix cordata*) with cordate leaves

heart·less \'härtləs, 'hȧt-\ *adj* [ME *hertles*, fr. *hert* heart + *-les* -less] **1** : devoid of heart **2 a** *archaic* : lacking courage or zeal : SPIRITLESS, DESPONDENT **b** : lacking feeling or affection : UNSYMPATHETIC, CRUEL ⟨it seems so ~ to leave her —G.B. Shaw⟩ ⟨a ~ mother, a false wife —W.M.Thackeray⟩ — **heart·less·ly** *adv* — **heart·less·ness** *n* -ES

heart line *n, usu cap H* : LINE OF HEART

heart liverleaf *or* **heart liverwort** *n* : a hepatica (*Hepatica triloba*)

heart-lung machine *n* : a mechanical pump that shunts the body's blood away from the heart and maintains the circulation during heart surgery

heart murmur *n* : MURMUR 4

heartnut \'=,=\ *n* : JAPANESE WALNUT

heart of palm : the edible young terminal bud of various palms (as a cabbage palmetto) usu. served raw and dressed as a salad

heartpea \'=,=\ *n* [so called fr. the shape of the seed] : BALLOON VINE

heart pine *n* : LONGLEAF PINE

heart rate *n* : a measure of cardiac activity usu. expressed as number of beats per minute

heartrending \'=,==\ *adj* : causing intense grief, anguish, or pain ⟨gives a ~ description of his own days under a private tutor —G.G.Coveton⟩ ⟨his untimely death was . . . ~ —*Nation*⟩

heart·rend·ing·ly *adv* : in a heartrending manner

heartrot \'=,=\ *n* : any of several rots involving the central part of a plant or plant organ: as **a** : disintegration of the heartwood of a tree (as by fungi of the genus *Fomes*) **b** : a disease of beets and rutabagas caused by a fungus (*Mycosphaerella tabifica*) that brings about decay of the heart and blighting of the leaves **c** : a rot of sugar beets caused by boron deficiency

hearts *pl of* HEART, *pres 3d sing of* HEART

heart sac *n* : PERICARDIUM

hearts-and-flowers *n pl but sing or pl in constr* : show of sentiment or sentimentality : cloying expressions of endearment ⟨cut out the *hearts-and-flowers* —Maritta Wolff⟩ ⟨I can't stand *hearts-and-flowers* stuff —Mary Miller⟩

heart-scalded \'härt¦skȯdəd\ *adj, dial Brit* : tormented by sorrow or remorse : TROUBLED

heart-searching \'=,==\ *n* : introspective analysis or self-examination ⟨the decision was reached only after prolonged *heart-searching* —*Times Lit. Supp.*⟩ ⟨of course these choices will not have been made without *heart-searchings* and contradictions —A.J.Toynbee⟩

hearts·ease \'härt,sēz, 'hȧt-\ *n* [ME *herts ese*, fr. *herts* (gen. of *hert* heart) + *ese* ease] **1** : peace of mind : TRANQUILLITY ⟨religion failed to bring him ~ —R.H.Bainton⟩ **2 a** : any of various violas: as (1) : WILD PANSY (2) : a common Old World viola (*Viola arvensis*) with creamy often violet-tinged flowers (3) : a violet (*V. ocellata*) of the Pacific coast of No. America with white petals tinged or marked with yellow and deep violet **b** : any of several smartweeds **3** : a strong violet that is redder and paler than pansy or clematis and redder and lighter than royal purple (sense 2)

heartseed \'=,=\ *n* [so called fr. the heart-shaped white spot on the black seed] : a plant of the genus *Cardiospermum*; *esp* : BALLOON VINE

heart shake *n* : a defect in timber consisting of shrinkage and separation of tissues across the annual rings usu. along the rays — compare RING SHAKE

heart shell *n* **1** : any of numerous bivalve mollusks esp. of the families Cardiidae and Carditidae with shells that are heart-shaped in outline when viewed from the end **2** : the shell of a heart-shell mollusk

heartsick \'=,=\ *adj* : very despondent : DEPRESSED ⟨was too ~ to rise and fight —W.A.White⟩ : reflecting or marked by a feeling of sickness ⟨longed with a ~ yearning for the first few days to be over —W.M.Thackeray⟩

heartsickening *adj* : causing depression or despondency

heartsickness \'=,==\ *n* : the quality or state of being heartsick ⟨died of . . . ~ after moving here and waiting for years for the man who never came —*Nat'l Geographic*⟩ ⟨the wild ~ of the desert —Lawrence Durrell⟩

heart snakeroot *n* [so called fr. the shape of the leaf] : WILD GINGER 2a

heart·some \'härtsəm\ *adj* [¹*heart* + *-some*] *chiefly Scot* : animating and enlivening : giving cheer ⟨a ~ thing, the smell of frying ham on a frosty morning —G.D.Brown⟩ — **heart·some·ly** *adv*

heartsore \'=,=\ *adj* : HEARTSICK ⟨a ~ lover⟩

heartstring \'=,=\ *n* [ME *hertstring*, fr. *hert* heart + *string*] **1** *obs* : a nerve or tendon supposed to support or sustain the heart **2** : the deepest emotions or affections — usu. used in pl. ⟨tore at the ~s of memory —William Beebe⟩ ⟨could touch the ~s of the audience —E.H.Collis⟩

heart-struck \'=¦=\ *adj* **1** : struck to the heart **2** *archaic* : driven to the heart : infixed in the mind

heartthrob \'=,=\ *n* **1** : the throb of a heart **2 a** : sentimental emotion : PASSION ⟨diary of ~s and rebuffs —*New Republic*⟩ **b** : SWEETHEART ⟨a girl on the . . . verge of giving her ~ the raspberry —P.G.Wodehouse⟩

heart tie *n* : a railroad crosstie with sapwood one fourth or less the width of the tie at the top measured at a point 20 inches to 40 inches from the middle of the tie

heart-to-heart \'==¦=\ *adj* : SINCERE, FRANK ⟨a *heart-to-heart* talk⟩

heart trefoil *n* [so called fr. the shape of the leaves] : SPOTTED MEDIC

heart urchin *n* : a heart-shaped sea urchin

heart wall *n* : CORE 11

heartwarming \'=,==\ *adj* : inspiring a glow of sympathetic feeling : pleasantly moving or stirring : CHEERING ⟨her story of their experiences is entertaining and ~ —*Hunting's Monthly List*⟩ ⟨most ~ literary event of the year —*New Internat'l Yr. Bk.*⟩

heartwater \'=,==\ *n* [so called fr. the accumulation of fluid in the pericardium] : a serious febrile disease of sheep, goats, and cattle in southern Africa caused by a rickettsial microorganism (*Cowdria ruminantium*) transmitted by a tick (*Amblyomma hebraeum*)

heartweed \'=,=\ *n* : LADY'S THUMB

heart-whole \'=¦=\ *adj* **1** : not broken or depressed in spirit : UNDISMAYED ⟨so many clowns have been small . . . pathetic; here is one large and *heart-whole* —G.W.Stonier⟩ **2** : having the affections free : not in love **3** : free from deceit or hypocrisy : SINCERE, GENUINE ⟨a *heart-whole* friendship —George Meredith⟩

heartwise \'härt,wīz\ *adv* [¹*heart* + *-wise*] : in the shape or manner of a heart ⟨her face . . . tapered ~ —T.B.Costain⟩

heartwood \'=,=\ *n* : the older harder nonliving central portion of wood usu. being darker in color, denser, less permeable, and more durable than the surrounding sapwood but in some woods (as white spruce) lacking distinctive color and then being difficult to distinguish — called also *duramen*

heartworm \'=,=\ *n* **1** : a filarial worm (*Dirofilaria immitis*) that is esp. common in warm regions, lives as an adult in the right heart of dogs and some other carnivores, and discharges active larvae into the circulating blood whence they may be picked up by mosquitoes and transmitted to other hosts **2** : infestation with or disease caused by the heartworm resulting typically in gasping, coughing, and nervous disorder and when severe commonly leading to death

¹hearty \'här|d·ē, 'hȧl, |tē, -i\ *adj* -ER/-EST [ME *herty*, fr. *hert* heart + *-y*] **1 a** : giving unqualified support : unreservedly loyal : THOROUGHGOING, ENTHUSIASTIC ⟨a ~ Federalist —F.J. Klingberg⟩ ⟨a ~ assumer of its full share of . . . responsibilities —F.S.C.Northrop⟩ ⟨my ~ concurrence in everything you've done —T.B.Costain⟩ **b** (1) : exuberantly or unreservedly cordial or genial : not reserved or ceremonious in manner : JOVIAL ⟨had a bluff and ~ bearing, but he was a rogue —Ross Annett⟩ ⟨being a shade too ~ about it —Angus Mowat⟩ ⟨a wonderful ~ manner with a boy —G.D.Brown⟩ (2) : giving exuberant or unrestrained expression to one's feelings ⟨a ~ burst of laughter greeted his arrival⟩ ⟨a string of ~ curses⟩ (3) : APPROVING ⟨no one but a Chancery lawyer had a ~ word for the Chancery —F.W.Maitland⟩ ⟨some colleagues are distinctly less ~ about the General —Hal Lehrman⟩ **2 a** : exhibiting vigorous good health ⟨the mate was as ~ as a young lion —Herman Melville⟩ ⟨is my friend ~, now I am thin and pine —A.E.Housman⟩ **b** (1) : having a good appetite : consuming abundantly or with gusto ⟨a ~ eater⟩ ⟨a ~ drinker⟩ (2) : ABUNDANT, AMPLE ⟨ate a ~ meal⟩ ⟨took a ~ swig⟩ **c** : NOURISHING, INVIGORATING ⟨almost a meal in itself, with 15 tender vegetables in ~ beef stock —*Better Homes & Gardens*⟩ ⟨has a ~ flavor that is much livelier than our refined . . . variety —Silas Spitzer⟩ : FULL-BODIED ⟨a ~ Rhone with a full bouquet —*New Yorker*⟩ **3** : vigorous or violent in manner or degree : VEHEMENT ⟨the breeze . . . was *heartier* . . . than before —Llewellyn Howland⟩ ⟨hooked a root and gave a ~ pull —C.S.Forester⟩ ⟨then came the rain in a ~ flood —John Muir †1914⟩ ⟨the wind had combed up some quite ~ waves —R.A.W.Hughes⟩ ⟨without any provocation at all give him a ~ kick —H.A.Chippendale⟩ **4** *chiefly Brit* : capable of bearing crops : FERTILE ⟨thistles so growing . . . signifieth the land to be ~ —Thomas Tusser⟩ **syn** see SINCERE

²hearty \"\ *n* -ES **1 a** : a bold brave fellow : COMRADE — used esp. in addressing sailors ⟨heave-ho, my *hearties*⟩ **b** : SAILOR ⟨the albatross mocked by the *hearties* —Stephen Spender⟩ **2** *chiefly Brit* : an individual of exuberant outgoing disposition or of athletic nonaesthetic tastes ⟨a Matisse reproduction could cause one's rooms to be wrecked . . . by rugger *hearties* —Jocelyn Brooke⟩

heart yarn *n* : yarn in the center of a rope

¹heat \'hēt, *usu* -ēd·+V\ *vb* **heated** \'hēd·əd, -ētəd\ *also dial* **het** \'het, *usu* -ed·+V\ **heated** *also dial* **het**; **heating; heats** [ME *heten*, fr. OE *hǣtan*; akin to OHG *heizen* to heat, MD *heten*, ON *heita*; causative-denominatives fr. the root of E *hot*] *vi* **1 a** : to become warm or hot : rise in temperature ⟨water ~*ing* in a large kettle⟩ ⟨the room slowly ~*ed*⟩ **b** : to become hot and spoil due to excessive or abnormal respiratory or fermentative activity ⟨grain containing excessive moisture may ~ seriously in the bin⟩ **2** : to become excited, moved, or inflamed in mind or spirit ⟨cannot see injustice without ~*ing*⟩ ~ *vt* **1** : to make warm or hot : raise the temperature of ⟨~ the oven to 350 degrees⟩ ⟨water ~*ed* by the sun⟩ **2** : to arouse the emotion or spirit of : excite, move, or inflame usu. intensely or to a course of action ⟨his arrogance ~s me beyond enduring⟩ ⟨these stirring words ~*ed* us all⟩ **3** : to make (as the human body) feverish or excessively hot ⟨wine ~s the blood⟩ ⟨he was ~*ed* by the long dry climb⟩ **4** *obs* : to run over (ground) : cover (ground) in or as if in a race

²heat \"\ *n* -S [ME *hete*, fr. OE *hǣte*, *hǣtu*; akin to OFris *hēte* heat, OHG *heizi*; derivatives fr. the root of E *hot*] **1 a** : the state of a body or of matter that is perceived as opposed to cold and is characterized by elevation of temperature : a condition of being hot : WARMTH, HOTNESS ⟨the iron lost its ~ in contact with the cold ground⟩; *usu* : a marked or notable degree of this state : high temperature ⟨the ~ was intense⟩ ⟨you'll need a good ~ to burn that damp rubbish⟩ ⟨midsummer ~⟩ ⟨a ~ of 500 degrees⟩ **b** (1) : a feverish state of the body : pathological excessive bodily temperature (as from inflammation) ⟨knew the throbbing ~ of an abscess⟩ ⟨sponged him with alcohol to relieve the ~ of the fever⟩ (2) : a warm flushed condition of the body (as after exercise) : a sensation produced by or like that produced by contact with or approach to heated matter ⟨felt the ~ rise in her face as she returned his look⟩ **c** : a hot place or situation (as a fire) ⟨the legendary salamander dallying at the heart of the ~⟩ ⟨out in the ~ all afternoon long⟩ ⟨dormant flies coming out into the ~⟩ **d** (1) : a period of heat or of exposure to heat ⟨requires a ~ of several hours to get out all the moisture⟩ ⟨had an unbroken ~ since the first of June⟩ (2) : a single complete operation of heating (as at a forge or in a furnace); *also* : the quantity of material so heated **e** (1) : a form of energy the addition of which causes substances to rise in temperature, fuse, evaporate, expand, or undergo any of various other related changes, which flows to a body by contact with or radiation from bodies at higher temperatures, and which can be produced in a body (as by compression) (2) : the energy associated with the random motions of the molecules, atoms, or smaller structural units of which matter is composed **f** : an indication of temperature attained as manifested by the condition, appearance, or color of a body ⟨when the rod is at the proper welding ~⟩ — compare RED HEAT **g** : one of a series of discrete rates or intensities of heating ⟨an electric iron may have three ~s⟩ **2 a** : intensity of feeling or reaction (as in fury, vehemence, or agitation of mind) ⟨answered with considerable ~⟩ ⟨such a ~ of eloquence flowed forth⟩ **b** : the height or stress of an action or condition ⟨in the ~ of battle⟩ ⟨during the first ~ of the epidemic⟩ **c** (1) : sexual excitement esp. in a female mammal : ESTRUS : a state in which a female will accept service by a male — usu. used with *in* or *into* or, esp. Brit., with *on* ⟨ewes come on ~ soon after flushing⟩ ⟨like a bitch in ~⟩ (2) : the time or duration of heat : an episode of heat ⟨a mare is most likely to settle during the foal ~ that occurs two or three weeks after parturition⟩ **3** : one of the fundamental qualities of bodies, elements, or humors recognized in medieval physiology **4** : pungency of flavor ⟨cherry peppers have greater ~ than most⟩ ⟨the tangy ~ of crystallized ginger⟩ **5** : a vigorous or violent uninterrupted action : a single continuous effort ⟨set down the outline of his paper at a single ~⟩: as **a** (1) : a single course in a race or other contest that consists of two or more courses for all contestants ⟨won two ~s out of three⟩ (2) : one of several preliminary races held to eliminate less competent contenders from the final race when contestants are too numerous to compete at once ⟨swam in the second ~ and won, but lost out in the final race⟩ **b** : a field trial event in which two dogs compete directly with each other and usu.

by comparison with other braces competing in the field trial **c** (1) *slang* **:** the intensification of law-enforcement activity or investigational pressure usu. with special concern for a particular kind of crime or criminal ⟨the bookies are out of business till the ~ is off⟩ (2) **:** pressure or coercion intended to influence a course of action or events ⟨taxpayers get relief by turning the ~ on their congressmen⟩ (3) **:** strain, tension, or difficulty resulting from the pressure of events ⟨weaken when the ~ is on⟩ **6 a :** a charge of metal made in a Bessemer converter or the steel scrap, pig, or molten iron, limestone, and fluxes in the open-hearth or electric furnace **b :** the resulting molten steel **c :** the ingots charged into the soaking pits or the blooms charged into the reheating furnace

heat·able \ˈhēd·əbəl, -ētəb-\ *adj* **:** capable of being heated **:** suitable for heating ⟨a compact ~ apartment⟩

heat balance *n* **:** the distribution of the heat energy supplied to a thermomechanical system (as a steam power plant) among the various drains upon it including both useful output and losses; *also* **:** an evaluation or record of such distribution

heat barrier *n* **:** THERMAL BARRIER

heat-body \ˈ=,==\ *vt* **:** to increase the viscosity of (an oil) by heating — compare BODIED OIL

heat budget *n* **:** the amount of heat required to raise the waters of a lake to their maximum summer temperature calculated from their minimum winter temperature of 0° C or 4° C and usu. expressed as gram calories of heat per square centimeter of lake surface

heat canker *n* **:** a canker of plant stems caused by high temperatures esp. of the surface soil ⟨flax is subject to *heat canker*⟩

heat capacity *n* **:** the quantity of heat required to raise the temperature of a body one degree — called also *thermal capacity*

heat center *n* **:** any of various areas in the central nervous system concerned with the regulation of the body temperature

heat content *n* **:** ENTHALPY

heat cramps *n pl* **:** a condition marked by the sudden development of cramps in skeletal muscles resulting from prolonged work in high temperatures accompanied by profuse perspiration with loss of sodium chloride from the body

heat death *n* **:** an ultimate state of thermal equilibrium implying conditions of maximum entropy and zero available energy that according to the laws of thermodynamics the material universe is apparently approaching

heat devil *n* **:** a shimmering appearance in the air above a heated surface

heated *adj* **1 :** made or become hot ⟨wiped his ~ face with a large bandanna⟩ **2 :** marked by emotional heat ⟨a ~ session of the conclave⟩ **:** IRATE, ANGRY ⟨an exchange of ~ words⟩

heat·ed·ly *adv* **:** in a heated manner **:** with heat ⟨denied the charges ~⟩

heated term *n* **:** the season of hot weather

heat engine *n* **:** a mechanism (as an external-combustion engine or an internal-combustion engine) for converting heat energy into mechanical energy

heat equator *n* **:** THERMAL EQUATOR

heat·er \ˈhēd·ə(r), -ētə-\ *n* -S [ME *heter*, fr. *heten* to heat + *-er* — more at HEAT] **1 :** something that heats **:** a contrivance that imparts heat or holds something to be heated: as **a :** a stove, furnace, radiator, or other device for giving off heat **b :** an iron core for heating box irons **c :** a wire or filament in an electron tube that heats the cathode indirectly **2 a :** one whose work is to heat something — often used in combination ⟨rivet ~⟩ ⟨tire ~⟩ **b :** one that heats metal billets to make them workable **c :** one that tends the burners that heat a petroleum-products still **3** *slang* **:** PISTOL

heater car *n* **:** a freight car with heating apparatus and insulation for transporting perishables in cold or freezing weather

heater piece *n* [*heater* (core for a box iron); fr. the shape] *NewEng* **:** a triangular plot of land

heater-shaped \ˈ==,=\ *also* **heater** *adj* [*heater* (core for a box iron)] **:** triangular or ogival in outline — used chiefly of a medieval shield

heat exchanger *n* **:** a device (as an automobile radiator, a regenerator, or an intercooler) for transferring heat from one fluid to another without allowing them to mix

heat exhaustion *n* **:** a condition characterized by faintness or fainting, palpitation, nausea, vomiting, headache, and profuse sweating and resulting from physical exertion in a hot environment — called also *heat prostration*; compare HEATSTROKE

heat·ful \ˈhētfəl\ *adj* **:** full of or producing heat; *esp* **:** capable of releasing abundant heat in combustion

heath \ˈhēth, *in Maine & adjacent Canada* ˈhath\ *n* -S [ME *heth, heeth*, fr. OE *hǣth*; akin to OHG *heida* heather, MHG *heide* heath (field), heather, ON *heithr* field, plateau, Goth *haithi* field, OW *coit* forest] **1 a** *obs* **:** any of various low-growing shrubby plants of open wastelands **b :** a plant of the family Ericaceae esp. of the genera *Erica* and *Calluna* typically growing on open barren rather acid and frequently ill-drained soil **c :** any of various heathlike plants: as (1) **:** POVERTY GRASS (2) **:** a tamarisk (*Tamarix gallica*) that is native to Western Europe but established as an escape in parts of No. America (3) **:** CROWBERRY 1a (4) **:** a desert plant that was probably the savin juniper — referring to Jer 17:6 (AV) (5) **:** AUSTRALIAN HEATH **2 a :** a tract of wasteland **b :** an extensive area of rather level open uncultivated land that usu. has poor coarse soil, inferior drainage, and a surface rich in peat or peaty humus and that characteristically has plants of the family Ericaceae as the dominant floral element **c :** a plant community typically occurring on heath in cool climates and being characterized by paucity or absence of trees and dominance of plants of the family Ericaceae — **one's native heath :** the region where one was born or brought up

heath aster *n* **:** either of two common much-branched pubescent perennial No. American asters (*Aster ericoides* and *A. arenosus*) with heathlike foliage and small white crowded flower heads

heat haze *n* **:** air rising above a hot surface (as of sand or rock) with a shimmering effect that tends to obscure details of the landscape

heath bell *n* **:** BELL HEATHER

heathbird \ˈ=,=\ *n* **:** BLACK GROUSE

heath-clad \ˈ=,=\ *adj* **:** covered with heath ⟨a *heath-clad* slope⟩

heath cock *n* **:** the male black grouse **:** BLACKCOCK

heath cypress *n* **:** any of various mosses; *esp* **:** a ground fir (*Lycopodium alpinum*) that resembles a miniature cypress tree

¹hea·then \ˈhēthən\ *adj* [ME *hethen*, fr. OE *hǣthen*, adj. & n.; akin to OHG *heidan*, adj., heathen, *heidano*, n., ON *heithinn*, adj., heathen, Goth *haithno* heathen woman, prob. derivatives fr. the root of E *heath* (land)] **1 :** of or relating to the heathen, their religions, or their customs **:** PAGAN, UNENLIGHTENED **2 :** STRANGE, UNFAMILIAR, FOREIGN

²heathen \ˈ"\ *n, pl* **heathens** *or* **heathen** [ME *hethen*, fr. OE *hǣthen*] **1 a :** an unconverted member of a people or nation that does not acknowledge the God of the Bible **:** PAGAN ⟨I shall give thee the ~ for thine inheritance —Ps 2:8 (AV)⟩ **b** *biblical* **:** IDOLATER, GENTILE **2 a :** a person whose culture or enlightenment is of an inferior grade; *esp* **:** an irreligious person **b :** a person felt to resemble a heathen (as in nonconformity or ignorance) ⟨a grand old ~ who made his own place in life⟩

hea·then·dom \-dəm\ *n* -S **1 :** the part of the world where heathenism prevails; *collectively* **:** HEATHEN **2 :** HEATHENISM

hea·then·esse \ˌhēthəˈnes\ *n* -S [ME *hethenesse*, fr. OE *hǣthennes*, fr. *hǣthen* heathen + *-nes*, -ness] **:** HEATHENDOM

hea·then·ish \ˈ==,nish\ *adj* **1 :** of or relating to the heathen **:** resembling or thought to be characteristic of heathens ⟨worse than ~ crimes — John Milton⟩ **2** *obs* **:** of heathen race or belief **:** HEATHEN **3 :** tending to be or somewhat heathen ⟨this ~ rhythm⟩ — **hea·then·ish·ly** *adv* — **hea·then·ish·ness** *n* -ES

hea·then·ism \-ˌnizəm\ *n* -S **:** the religious system or rites of heathens **:** IDOLATRY, PAGANISM; *also* **:** manners or morals like those of the heathen

hea·then·ize \-ˌnīz\ *vb* -ED/-ING/-S *vt* **:** to make heathen or heathenish ~ *vi* **:** to become heathen or heathenish

hea·then·ly *adj* [ME *hethenly*, fr. *hethen* heathen + *-ly*] **:** in a heathen manner **:** HEATHENISHLY

hea·then·ness \-ən(n)əs\ *n* -ES **:** the state or quality of being heathen

hea·then·ry \-ənrē, -ri\ *n* -ES **1 :** the state, quality, or character of the heathen **:** HEATHENISM **2 :** heathen nations or people **:** HEATHENDOM

¹heath·er \ˈhethə(r)\ *n* -S [ME (northern dial.) *hather, hadder*, prob. modif. of *heth, heeth* heath, heather — more at HEATH] **1 a :** HEATH 1b; *esp* **:** a common erect to almost prostrate evergreen heath (*Calluna vulgaris*) of northern and alpine regions that has small crowded sessile leaves and racemes of tiny usu. purplish pink flowers **b :** BEACH HEATHER **c :** CROWBERRY 1a **2 a** *also* **heather purple :** a grayish reddish purple that is bluer, stronger, and slightly lighter than campanula violet and bluer, lighter, and stronger than livid purple **b :** a grayish to moderate purplish red that is redder and darker than daphne red

²heather \ˈ"\ *adj* **1 :** of, relating to, prepared from, or like heather **2 :** having flecks or a mingling of various colors — used chiefly of woolen yarns and fabrics ⟨a soft ~ tweed⟩ **3 :** of the color heather

heather ale *n* **:** a Scottish traditional beverage brewed from an extract of heather blossoms with honey, spice, hops, and yeast

heather bell *n* **:** BELL HEATHER

heather-bleat \ˈ==,=\ *also* **heatherbleater** \ˈ==,==\ *or* **heather-blutter** \-ˌbləd·ər\ *n* -S *chiefly Scot* **:** a common Old World snipe (*Capella gallinago*)

heather cat *n, Scot* **:** VAGABOND, ROVER ⟨here today and gone tomorrow — a fair *heather cat* —R.L.Stevenson⟩

heather cow *n, chiefly Scot* **:** a tuft or twig of heath

heath·ered \ˈhethə(r)d\ *adj* **:** full of or covered with heather ⟨~ slopes⟩

heather grass *n* **:** HEATH GRASS

heath·ery \ˈheth(ə)rē, -ri\ *adj* **1 :** abounding in or covered with heather ⟨~ hillsides⟩ **2 :** suggesting or resembling heather ⟨a delicate ~ fragrance⟩; *esp* **:** HEATHER 2

heath family *n* **:** ERICACEAE

heath-fowl *or* **heath-game** \ˈ=,=\ *n* **1** *Brit* **:** BLACK GROUSE **2** *Brit* **:** RED GROUSE

heath grass *n* **:** a chiefly European perennial grass (*Sieglingia decumbens*) that grows commonly on heaths and moors and is indigenous in Newfoundland and in southwestern Nova Scotia

heath grouse *n* **:** BLACK GROUSE

heath hen *n* **1 :** the female black grouse **:** GRAY HEN **2 :** a grouse that was formerly abundant in the northeastern U.S. but is now completely extinct and that is usu. considered an eastern variety (*Tympanuchus cupido cupido*) of the prairie chicken

heath·land \ˈ=,land, -lənd\ *n* **:** HEATH 2a, MOOR 1

heath·less \-ləs\ *adj* **:** free from heath ⟨a ~ moor⟩

heathlike \ˈ=,=\ *adj* **:** resembling a heath; *usu* **:** similar to a plant of the genera *Erica* and *Calluna* in habits of growth or in having fine crowded leaves suggesting needles

heath pea *n* **:** a European leguminous herb (*Lathyrus tuberosus*) bearing small tubers used for food and in Scotland to flavor whiskey

heath peat *n* **:** peat formed chiefly from roots and stems of plants of the genera *Erica* and *Calluna*

heath poult *n* **:** the young of the black grouse

heaths *pl of* HEATH

heathwort \ˈ=,=\ *n* **:** HEATH 1b

heath-wren \ˈ=,=\ *n* **:** either of two warblers (*Hylacola pyrrhopygia* and *H. cauta*) that are shy ground-nesting birds of open rangelands of southern Australia and noted as songsters and mimics — called also *ground wren*

heathy \ˈhēthē, ˈhath-\ *adj* -ER/-EST [ME *hethy*, fr. *heth, heeth* heath + *-y* — more at HEATH] **:** of, relating to, or resembling heath **:** abounding with heath

heat hyperpyrexia *n* **:** HEATSTROKE

heating *pres part of* HEAT

heating element *n* **:** the part of an electric heating appliance in which the electrical energy is transformed into heat

heating furnace *n* **:** REHEATING FURNACE

heating load *n* **:** the quantity of heat per unit time that must be supplied to maintain the temperature in a building or portion of a building at a given level

heat·ing·ly *adv* **:** in a heating manner **:** so as to make hot

heating mantle *n* **:** an apparatus consisting of resistance wire stitched into glass cloth or asbestos cloth and tailored to surround a vessel to which it supplies heat

heating pad *n* **:** a flexible pad for applying heat (as to the body) consisting of electric heating elements embedded in insulating material

heating plant *n* **:** the whole system (as of boiler, pipes, and radiators or of furnace, ducts, and registers) used for heating an enclosed space (as a building or group of buildings)

heat lamp *n* **:** INFRARED LAMP

heat·less \ˈ=ləs\ *adj* **:** lacking heat; *esp* **:** having no artificial heat provided ⟨a ~ apartment⟩ ⟨observing ~ days to conserve fuel⟩

heat lightning *n* **:** vivid and extensive flashes of electric light without thunder that are seen near the horizon esp. at the close of a hot day and are ascribed to far-off lightning reflected by high clouds

heat of adsorption : the heat evolved when a given amount of a substance is adsorbed

heat of combustion : the heat of reaction resulting from the complete burning of a substance and expressed variously (as in calories per gram or per mole or esp. for fuels in British thermal units per pound or per cubic foot)

heat of condensation : heat evolved when a vapor changes to a liquid; *specif* **:** the quantity of heat that is evolved when unit mass of a vapor is changed at a specified temperature to a liquid and that equals the heat of vaporization

heat of decomposition : the heat of reaction resulting from the decomposition of a compound into its elements or into other neutral compounds; *esp* **:** the quantity involved in the decomposition of a mole

heat of dilution : the heat evolved per mole of solute when a solution is greatly diluted

heat of dissociation : the heat of reaction resulting from dissociation of molecules of a compound into smaller molecules, fragments, or atoms

heat of formation : the heat of reaction resulting from the formation of a compound by direct union of its elements, usu. expressed in calories per mole of the compound

heat of fusion : heat required to melt a solid; *specif* **:** the amount required to melt unit mass of a substance at standard pressure

heat of hydration : the heat evolved or absorbed when hydration occurs; *esp* **:** the amount involved when one mole is hydrated

heat of ionization : the heat required to ionize a substance; *esp* **:** the amount required to ionize one mole

heat of neutralization : the heat of reaction resulting from the neutralization of an acid or base; *esp* **:** the quantity produced when a gram equivalent of a base or acid is neutralized with a gram equivalent of an acid or base in dilute solution

heat of reaction : the heat evolved or absorbed during a chemical reaction taking place under conditions of constant temperature and of either constant volume or more often constant pressure; *esp* **:** the quantity involved when gram equivalents of the substances enter into the reaction

heat of solution : the heat evolved or absorbed when a substance dissolves; *specif* **:** the amount involved when one mole or sometimes one gram dissolves in a large excess of solvent

heat of sublimation : the heat absorbed when a solid sublimes; *specif* **:** the heat required to sublime unit mass at a specified temperature

heat of transition : the heat evolved or absorbed when a substance changes from one physical form to another

heat of vaporization : heat absorbed when a liquid vaporizes; *specif* **:** the quantity of heat required at a specified temperature to convert unit mass of liquid into vapor

heat of wetting : the heat evolved when an insoluble solid is wetted by a liquid (as water)

heat prostration *n* **:** HEAT EXHAUSTION

heat pump *n* **:** a device for transferring heat energy from a low-temperature locality to a high-temperature locality by mechanical means involving the compression and expansion of a fluid (as in mechanical refrigeration); *specif* **:** an apparatus for heating or cooling a building by transferring heat from or to a reservoir outside the building (as the ground, water, or air)

heat rash *n* **:** PRICKLY HEAT

heat ray *n* **:** a ray producing thermal effects; *specif* **:** an infrared ray

heat rigor *n* **:** rigor of living tissue caused by exposure to excessive but not immediately lethal temperatures

heat·ron·ic \(ˈ)hēˈtränik, -ētˈr-\ *adj* [blend of ²*heat* and *electronic*] **:** utilizing dielectric heating

heats *pres 3d sing of* HEAT, *pl of* HEAT

heat-seal \ˈ=,=\ *vt* **:** to unite (two or more thermoplastic surfaces) by heat and pressure to make a seam, closure, or attachment

heat seal *n* **:** a seal made by or a method of union involving heat-sealing

heat-set \ˈ=,=\ *vt* **:** to fix (as a plastic or pleats in fabric) in a permanent form through the action of heat

heatstroke \ˈ=,=\ *n* **:** a condition characterized by cessation of sweating with inadequate elimination of body heat, extremely high temperature, rapid pulse, hot dry skin, flaccid muscles, delirium, collapse, and coma and resulting from prolonged exposure to high environmental temperature which causes a breakdown of the temperature-regulating mechanism of the body — compare HEAT EXHAUSTION

heat-treat \ˈ=,=\ *vt* **:** to treat (as metals) by heating and cooling in a way that will produce desired properties (as hardness or ductility) — compare ANNEAL, HARDEN, NORMALIZE, PATENT, SPHEROIDIZE, TEMPER; MALLEABLEIZE; GRAPHITIZE

heat-treater \ˈ=,==\ *n* **:** one that heat-treats metals

heat treatment *n* **:** a process or an instance of heat-treating

heat unit *n* **1 :** BRITISH THERMAL UNIT **2 :** CALORIE

heat up *vt* **:** to cause to heat ~ *vi* **:** to become hot **:** HEAT

heat wave *n* **1 :** a wave of thermal radiation **2 :** HOT WAVE

heaume \ˈhōm\ *n* -S [MF, fr. OF *helme* — more at HELMET] **:** a large helmet chiefly of the 13th century worn over a hood of mail or close-fitting steel cap and supported by the shoulders rather than the head

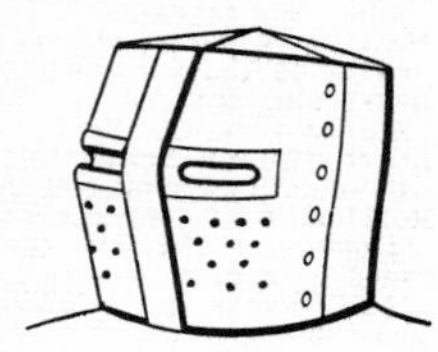

heaume

heaum·er \-mə(r)\ *n* -S **:** a maker of medieval helmets

heau·ta·rit \hōˈtärət, hyüˈt-\ *n* -S [Ar *ˈuṭārid*] *in alchemy* **:** MERCURY 1c

he·au·toph·a·ny \ˌhē,ȯˈtäfənē\ *n* -ES [Gk *heautou* of oneself (fr. *he* oneself + *autos* self) + E *-phany*] **:** manifestation of self

¹heave \ˈhēv\ *vb* **heaved** \-vd\ *or* **hove** \ˈhōv\ *or dial* **hoved** \ˈhōvd\ **heaved** *or* **hove** *or archaic & dial* **ho·ven** \ˈhōvən\ **heaving; heaves** [ME *hebben, heven*, fr. OE *hebban*; akin to OHG *heffen, hevan* to lift, raise, ON *hefja* to lift, raise, Goth *hafjan* to carry, L *capere* to take, seize, Gk *kaptein* to gulp down, *kōpē* handle, Alb *kap* I grasp, Skt *kapatī* two handfuls; basic meaning: grasping] *vt* **1** *obs* **a :** to raise or exalt in state or feeling **b :** BAPTIZE; *also* **:** to stand as sponsor for **c :** to offer or consecrate (a portion of a sacrifice) by symbolically lifting up or separating for special holy use — used of the action of an ancient Israelite priest **2 :** to cause to move upward or onward by a lifting effort **:** LIFT, RAISE; *usu* **:** to lift with exertion ⟨the wave *heaved* the boat on land⟩ **3** *obs* **:** to take up and remove **:** carry off **:** take away **4 :** THROW, CAST, TOSS, HURL ⟨he *hove* the lead⟩ ⟨*heaving* down the hay⟩ ⟨just ~ your books on the bed⟩ **5 a :** to utter with obvious effort or with a deep breath that causes the chest to heave visibly ⟨pulled off her shoes and *heaved* a sigh of relief⟩ **b :** VOMIT ⟨got carsick and *heaved* his lunch⟩ **6 a :** to cause to swell or rise ⟨the wind *heaved* the sea into mountainous waves⟩ ⟨a spent horse gasping and *heaving* his chest⟩ **b** *dial Brit* **:** to cause bloat in (a ruminant) ⟨sheep are often *hoven* by a sudden change to lush pasture⟩ **c :** to displace (as a mineral vein or a rock stratum) esp. by a fault; *usu* **:** to displace laterally or horizontally **7 a :** to draw, pull, or to haul on (as a rope) ⟨~ in the cable⟩ ⟨~ a line⟩ **b :** to cause (as a ship or sail) to move or to come into some position by or as if by hauling on a rope either as a means of propulsion or as a means of arranging for a particular kind of action ⟨~ a ship ahead, aback, or in stays⟩ ~ *vi* **1 a :** to rise or become thrown or raised up usu. as a result of the action of some external force (as pressure, wind, heat, or frost) ⟨the pavement *heaved* and buckled in the heat⟩ **b** *archaic* **:** to rise upward **:** TOWER, MOUNT **c** *of plants or roots* **:** to rise or become lifted out of the ground usu. by alternate freezing and thawing **2 :** to make an effort to raise, throw, or move something **:** strain to do something difficult **:** LABOR, STRUGGLE **3 a :** to rise and fall rhythmically or with alternate motions (as of waves, a ship at sea, or the chest in heavy breathing) ⟨waves *heaving* on a storm-tossed sea⟩ **b :** to pant for breath ⟨lay *heaving* from the strain of his effort⟩ **4 a :** GAG, RETCH ⟨could ~ from sheer disgust⟩ ⟨his stomach *heaved* at sight of the mess⟩ **b :** VOMIT — sometimes considered vulgar **5 a :** to haul or pull (as on a line) or push (as at a capstan); *specif* **:** to move a line or chain by the application of force through the interposition of a mechanical device (as a capstan) — compare HAUL **b :** to cause a ship to move in a specified direction or manner **c** *of a ship* **:** to move in an indicated way or direction ⟨the schooner *hove* alongside⟩ **6** *chiefly dial Brit, of livestock* **:** to become bloated **syn** see LIFT — **heave in stays** *of a sailing ship* **:** TACK — **heave one's gorge :** NAUSEATE **:** become nauseated — **heave the lead :** to make a sounding from a ship by means of a manual sounding line — **heave the log :** to cast the log over the stern to determine the speed of a ship

²heave \ˈ"\ *n* -S **1 a :** an effort to raise something (as a weight or oneself) or to move something heavy or resistant ⟨each ~ on the rope loosened the stump a bit more⟩ **b :** an act or instance of throwing **:** HURL, CAST ⟨skimmed the notice and gave it a ~ toward the wastebasket⟩ **2 :** an upward motion **:** RISING; *esp* **:** a rhythmical rising (as of the chest wall in difficult breathing or of the waves) **3 a :** the horizontal displacement by the faulting of a rock measured in a plane at right angles to the fault strike **b :** FROST HEAVE **4 heaves** *pl but usu sing in constr* **:** chronic pulmonary emphysema of the horse usu. associated with asthma, improper diet, or severe overexertion and marked by loss of elasticity of the lungs and distention of the air vesicles resulting in difficult expiration with heaving of the flanks and a persistent cough — called also *broken wind*

heave-and-haul \ˌ==ˈ=\ *vi* **heave-and-hauled; heave-and-hauled; heave-and-hauling; heave-and-hauls :** to fish with a handline by repeatedly throwing a hook out and drawing it back again

heave down *vt* **:** to careen (a ship) usu. for repairs or cleaning ~ *vi* **:** to careen a ship

heave ho \ˈ=ˈ=\ *interj* [¹*heave* + *ho*] — used esp. by sailors when heaving on a rope

heave-ho \ˈ=ˈ=\ *n* -S [*heave ho*] **:** DISMISSAL, REJECTION — used with *the* and often with *old* ⟨the voters finally got sick of the old guard and gave the mayor the old *heave-ho* at the polls⟩

heave·less \ˈ=ləs\ *adj* **:** free from heaves or heaving **:** QUIET ⟨a glassy ~ sea⟩

¹heav·en \ˈhevən *also* -evᵊm *or* -ebᵊm\ *n* -S [ME *heven, hevene*, fr. OE *heofon*; akin to OHG *himil*, OS *heban* sky, heaven, ON *himinn*, Goth *himins* sky, heaven, OE *hama* covering — more at HAME] **1 a :** the expanse of space surrounding the earth; *esp* **:** the expanse that seems to be over the earth like a great arch or dome **:** FIRMAMENT, CELESTIAL SPHERE — usu. used in pl. **b :** the part of the atmosphere in which clouds and winds occur and birds fly and from which rain and snow fall **:** the part of the atmosphere that is relatively dense and close to solid earth and that forms part of the biosphere ⟨a flock of geese crossing the bright ~⟩ **c** *archaic* **:** CLIMATE **d :** one of a series of realms represented (as in ancient and medieval cosmographies) as extending up or out from the earth **2** *often cap* **:** the dwelling place of the Deity **:** a celestial abode of bliss **:** the place or state of the blessed dead — compare ELYSIUM, HAPPY HUNTING GROUNDS, NIRVANA, PARADISE **3** *usu cap* **:** the sovereign of heaven **:** GOD; *also* **:** heavenly beings **:** the assembly of the blessed ⟨her prayers, whom *Heaven* delights to hear —Shak.⟩ **4 a :** a place or condition or period of utmost happiness, comfort, or delight **:** perfect felicity or contentment ⟨our week at the lake was ~ after the city's heat⟩ ⟨the mountain ~ to which we hope to retire one day⟩ ⟨this shabby proletarian ~⟩ **b** : a sublime or exalted condition ⟨the ~*s* of the imagination⟩ **c** : a transcendent cosmos or domain; *specif* : a realm of subsistent or eternal forms or entities ⟨a Platonic ~ of ideas⟩ **5 heavens** *pl but sing in constr* : a canopy or covering used over the stage in some Elizabethan theaters **6** : a divine state and condition of immortality in the doctrine of Christian Science in which sin is absent and all manifestations of Mind are harmoniously ordered under the divine Principle **7** *in Chinese religion* **a** : universal law **b** : NATURE **c** : cosmic ethical principle **d** : inexorable fate **e** : a supreme personal power — **heaven knows** : CERTAINLY, UNDOUBTEDLY — used as an intensive ⟨*heaven knows* we need advice⟩ ⟨our efforts, *heaven knows*, have accomplished little enough⟩ — **in heaven** *or* **under heaven** *adv* : among innumerable possibilities : EVER — used as an intensive ⟨where *in heaven* were you⟩ ⟨what *in heaven* happened⟩ ⟨what *under heaven* possessed you to do such a thing⟩ ⟨who *under heaven* would have done such a thing⟩ — **to heaven** *or* **to heavens** *or* **to high heaven** *or* **to high heavens** *adv* : to an unusual and often an exaggerated or excessive level or degree ⟨the muddy tide flat smelled *to high heavens*⟩ ⟨complained *to heaven* about the tax burden⟩

²heaven \"\ *vt* **heavened; heavened; heavening** \-v(ə)niŋ, -vᵊmiŋ, -bᵊmiŋ\ **heavens 1** *obs* : to place in happiness or bliss : BEATIFY **2** : to make heavenly or utterly happy in character

heaven-born \'ˌ=ˌ=\ *adj* : of heavenly birth or origin : CELESTIAL, DIVINE ⟨*heaven-born* compassion⟩

heaven-dust \'ˌ=ˌ=\ *n, slang* : COCAINE

heav·en·less \'==ləs\ *adj* : having no heaven : having no part or place in the heaven of the Deity ⟨heathens worshiping their ~ gods⟩

heavenlike \'==ˌ=\ *adv (or adj)* : HEAVENLY

heav·en·li·ness \-ˌlēnəs, -lin-\ *n* -ES : the quality or state of being heavenly

¹heav·en·ly \'hevənlē, -li *also* -evᵊml- *or* -ebᵊml-\ *adj, sometimes* -ER/-EST [ME *hevenly*, fr. OE *heofonlīc*, fr. *heofon* heaven + *-līc* -ly — more at HEAVEN] **1** : of or relating to the spatial heavens surrounding the earth **2** : of, relating to, or dwelling in the heaven of God or of a god : CELESTIAL ⟨~ spirits⟩ **3 a** : fit for or characteristic of the divine heaven : appropriate to heaven : SACRED, BLESSED, DIVINE ⟨the ~ music of an angel choir⟩ ⟨turn your thoughts to ~ matters⟩ **b** : eminently pleasing : DELIGHTFUL, ENCHANTING : remarkably pleasant ⟨a ~ day for a picnic⟩ ⟨had a ~ time⟩ ⟨what a ~ necklace⟩

²heavenly \"\ *adv* [ME *hevenly*, fr. OE *heofonlīce*, fr. *heofonlīc*] **1** : in a manner or to a degree resembling that of heaven : to the utmost : EXCEEDINGLY ⟨a maid most ~ pure⟩ ⟨were ~ happy there⟩ **2** : by the influence or agency of heaven ⟨our ~ guided soul shall climb —John Milton⟩

heavenly body *n* : CELESTIAL BODY

heavenly-minded \ˌ=ˌ==ˌ=\ *adj* : DEVOUT, GODLY, PIOUS —

heavenly-mindedness *n*

heavenly preceptor *n, usu cap H&P* [trans. of Chin (Pek) *t'ien¹ shih¹*] : a descendant of Chang Tao-ling chosen as the head of the Taoist organization — called also *celestial teacher;* used as a title

heaven-sent \'==ˌ=\ *adj* : sent from heaven : PROVIDENTIAL : peculiarly apt or appropriate ⟨a *heaven-sent* opportunity⟩

heaven tree *n* : TREE OF HEAVEN

heav·en·ward \'==wə(r)d\ *adv (or adj)* [ME *hevenward*, fr. *heven* heaven + *-ward*] : toward or directed or tending toward heaven — **heav·en·ward·ly** *adv* — **heav·en·ward·ness** *n* -ES

heav·en·wards \-dz\ *adv* : HEAVENWARD

heave offering *n* : a separated portion of an ancient Israelite religious offering that was ceremonially raised and lowered in dedication to God and that afterward was reserved for the officiating priest's use

heav·er \'hēvə(r)\ *n* -S : one that heaves: as **a** : a laborer employed in handling freight or bulk goods ⟨a coal ~⟩ **b** : a bar used as a lever (as in twisting rope)

heaves *pres 3d sing of* HEAVE, *pl of* HEAVE

heave to \'=ˈtü\ *vt* : to bring (a ship) by the wind with after sheets in and headsails aback so that it makes no headway but lies motionless except for drift ~ *vi* : to heave a ship to ⟨decided to *heave to* until daylight before attempting to pass the reef⟩

heavied *past of* HEAVY

heavier-than-air \ˌ====ˌ=\ *adj, of an aircraft* : having greater weight than displacement

heavies *pl of* HEAVY, *pres 3d sing of* HEAVY

heav·i·ly \'hevəlē, -li\ *adv* [ME *hevily*, fr. OE *hefiglīce*, fr. *hefig* heavy + *-līce* -ly] **1** : in a heavy manner : with great weight ⟨the weight bore ~ on the beams⟩ **2** : as if burdened with a great weight : slowly and laboriously : DULLY ⟨read the lesson ~⟩ **3** *archaic* : SORROWFULLY, DEJECTEDLY, GRIEVOUSLY ⟨why looks your grace so ~ today? —Shak.⟩ **4** : to a great degree : INJURIOUSLY, SEVERELY ⟨~ punished for his fault⟩ ⟨crops ~ damaged by frost⟩

heav·i·ness \-vēnəs, -vin-\ *n* -ES [ME *hevynesse*, fr. OE *hefignes*, fr. *hefig* heavy + *-nes* -ness] : the quality or state of being heavy ⟨a metal of surprising ~⟩ ⟨the produce markets exhibited a seasonal ~⟩

heaving *pres part of* HEAVE

heaving line *n* [fr. gerund of ¹*heave*] : a light line that has a weight on the free end and the other end attached to a heavier line (as a hawser) and that can be thrown across intervening space and used to draw the heavier line to a desired position (as for mooring a ship at a wharf)

heaving pile *n* : a heavy pile on a wharf to which are led tackles from the mastheads of a ship to be hove down

heav·i·side layer \'hevēˌsīd-\ *n, usu cap H* [after Oliver *Heaviside* †1925 Eng. physicist] : IONOSPHERE

¹heavy \'hevē, -vi\ *adj* -ER/-EST [ME *hevy*, fr. OE *hefig*, OS *hēbig*; akin to OHG *hebīc* heavy, ON *hǫfugr* heavy, OE *hebban* to lift, raise — more at HEAVE] **1 a** : having great weight : being such as may be lifted or moved only with effort : WEIGHTY, PONDEROUS ⟨a ~ load⟩ **b** : having a high specific gravity and great weight in proportion to bulk — opposed to *light* ⟨gold is one of the *heavier* metals⟩ **c** (1) *of an isotope* : having or being atoms of greater than normal mass ⟨carbon 13 and carbon 14 are both ~ carbons⟩ (2) *of a compound* : characterized by heavy isotopes ⟨~ ammonia⟩ ⟨~ ice⟩ **2 a** *obs* : HARSH, OPPRESSIVE **b** : hard to bear, endure, accomplish, or fulfill : BURDENSOME ⟨suffering under the ~ exactions of this tyrant⟩; *often* : GRIEVOUS, AFFLICTIVE ⟨a ~ sorrow⟩ **3** : of weighty import : SERIOUS, GRAVE, CONSEQUENTIAL ⟨~ news⟩ ⟨words ~ with meaning⟩ **4** : DEEP, PROFOUND, INTENSE ⟨a ~ silence⟩ ⟨~ late frosts destroyed the crop⟩ **5 a** : laden or borne down by something weighty or oppressive : ENCUMBERED, BURDENED ⟨returned with ~ spirit from the conference⟩ ⟨today's world is ~ with so-called celebrities —J.P.Jones⟩ : bowed down (as with care, grief, sorrow) ⟨a light wife doth make a ~ husband —Shak.⟩ **b** : PREGNANT, GRAVID; *esp* : approaching parturition — used chiefly in the phrase *heavy with young* **6 a** : slow or dull from or as if from loss of vitality or resiliency : SLUGGISH, INACTIVE ⟨a tired ~ step⟩ ⟨a ~ countenance⟩ **b** : lacking sparkle or vivacity : DRAB, STUPID, INERT ⟨a dull ~ style lacking liveliness and appeal⟩ ⟨a ~ writer⟩ **c** : lacking mirth or gaiety : DOLEFUL, LEADEN ⟨~ cheer⟩ ⟨made ~ work of the conversation⟩ **d** : characterized by declining prices ⟨the market was slow and ~⟩ ⟨government bonds have been ~ for some time⟩ **7 a** : overcome or dulled with weariness : DROWSY, SLEEPY ⟨eyes ~ from prolonged study⟩ **b** : dull and confused due to interruption of sleep : having a feeling of disorientation due to the relaxation of sleep ⟨the children were ~ with sleep⟩ **8** : greater in quantity or quality than the average of its kind or class: as **a** : unusually or exceptionally large ⟨a ~ fall of snow⟩ ⟨~ crops⟩ ⟨~ traffic⟩ **b** : of great force or momentum ⟨a ~ storm⟩ ⟨the *heaviest* sea in the last three seasons⟩ **c** : threatening to rain or snow : OVERCAST, LOWERING ⟨a ~ sky⟩ ⟨~ clouds⟩ **d** : impeding motion : CLOGGY, CLAYEY ⟨a ~ road⟩ ⟨cold ~ soils⟩ **e** : coming as if from a depth : LOUD, DEEP ⟨the ~ roll of thunder⟩ ⟨a ~ bass voice⟩ **f** : MASSIVE, COARSE ⟨a ~ scar⟩ ⟨a ~ growth of timber⟩ **g** : tending to produce dullness or sleepiness : OPPRESSIVE ⟨the ~ odor of tuberoses⟩ **h** : STEEP, ACUTE ⟨a ~ grade⟩ **i** : LABORIOUS, DIFFICULT ⟨a ~ task⟩ ⟨likely to be ~ sledding for a while⟩ **j** : being something specified to an exceptional degree ⟨a ~ drinker⟩ ⟨~ losers⟩ ⟨industry is a ~ user of electric power⟩; *broadly* : operating or dealing in large quantities ⟨~ buying of steel⟩ ⟨a ~ buyer⟩ **k** : having a high alcohol content : rich in malt and hop constituents and usu. dark in color ⟨~ ale⟩ **l** : of large capacity or output ⟨a ~ pump⟩ **m** : having a high boiling point — used esp. of distillates (as of petroleum) ⟨~ hydrocarbons⟩ ⟨~ ends present in gasoline⟩ **n** (1) : set or printed in boldface (2) : made with too much pressure of the sheet against the printing surface ⟨a ~ impression⟩ (3) : 11 points thick — used of the metal of an unmounted printing surface (as a copper engraving, stereotype, or electrotype) **o** *of a domino* : having a comparatively large number of pips ⟨the 6-6 is *heavier* than the 6-3⟩ **9 a** : digested slowly or with difficulty usu. because of excessive richness or seasoning ⟨a ~ fruitcake⟩ **b** : not properly raised or leavened ⟨~ bread⟩ : lacking in lightness ⟨rich dark cakes often tend to be ~⟩ **10 a** : belonging to or concerned with a class above a certain usual weight ⟨~ woolens⟩ ⟨~ trunk lines⟩ ⟨~ breeds⟩ **b** : producing metal, mineral, oil, or other basic substances and products derived from them ⟨~ industries⟩; *specif* : producing products on which other industries function **11 a** : heavily armed with guns of large caliber ⟨~ dragoons⟩ **b** : having maximally concentrated firepower often from a battery of medium-caliber guns ⟨~ antiaircraft emplacements⟩ **c** : heavily armored **12 a** : having stress or conspicuous sonority ⟨~ rhythm⟩ — used esp. of syllables in accentual verse; contrasted with *light* **b** : being the strongest of three degrees of stress in speech ⟨the ~ stress on the first syllable of *basketball*⟩ **c** *of a consonant* : VOICED — used esp. in connection with shorthand symbolization **13** : relating or assigned to theatrical parts or scenes of a grave or somber nature ⟨played ~ roles for years⟩

syn WEIGHTY, PONDEROUS, CUMBROUS, CUMBERSOME, HEFTY: HEAVY implies literally of greater weight than the average of its kind or class and figuratively more or less depressing, effort-taking, or unendurable to the mind or spirits, or depressed or dispirited ⟨a *heavy* bag⟩ ⟨a *heavy* child⟩ ⟨a *heavy* volume of literary criticism⟩ ⟨a *heavy* scent of lilacs⟩ ⟨a *heavy* heart⟩ WEIGHTY implies actually and not relatively heavy; figuratively it implies of serious import ⟨a boy carrying *weighty* packages⟩ ⟨a *weighty* series of international decisions⟩ ⟨*weighty* questions about our future domestic policy⟩ PONDEROUS implies literally a weighty massiveness, usu. difficult to maneuver, or figuratively something complicatedly labored, usu. suggesting a certain slow and dull deliberateness of mental effort ⟨a *ponderous* elephant⟩ ⟨heavy concentrations of troops and weapons for *ponderous* operations overland —H.H.Martin⟩ ⟨a sober and somewhat *ponderous* analysis of the police work —Anthony Boucher⟩ ⟨a book dealing with the necessity for world organization and the fundamentals of world law might be dull or at least *ponderous* reading —A.E. Stevenson b.1900⟩ CUMBROUS and CUMBERSOME imply literally a heaviness and bulkiness difficult to move, carry, or otherwise deal with; figuratively, they apply to what is ponderous and unwieldy ⟨*cumbrous* old-fashioned wagons —Eddie Doherty⟩ ⟨one long and *cumbrous* sentence after another —M.W.Straight⟩ ⟨the camel . . . that lumbering and *cumbersome* beast —*Story of Camel Hair*⟩ ⟨the *cumbersome* amendment procedure of the outworn constitution —F.L.Paxson⟩ HEFTY implies, literally, heaviness or solid weightiness usu. as estimated by picking up in one's arms, holding in one's hand, or measuring by the eye against an imagined norm, or, figuratively, weighty ⟨a *hefty* rock⟩ ⟨a *hefty* burden —A.J.Bruwer⟩ ⟨*hefty* peasants —*Time*⟩ ⟨*hefty* but handsome in her wedding dress —W.S.Maugham⟩ ⟨embodying so *hefty* a theme in a book —*Time*⟩

²heavy \"\ *vb* -ED/-ING/-ES [ME *hevyen*, fr. OE *hefigian*, fr. *hefig*, adj.] *vt, obs* : to make burdensome : weigh down : OPPRESS, BURDEN ~ *vi* : to play the role of a heavy : perform as a theatrical heavy

³heavy \"\ *adv* -ER/-EST [ME *hevy*, fr. OE *hefige*, fr. *hefig*, adj.] : in a heavy manner : HEAVILY ⟨time hung ~ on their hands⟩ ⟨a *heavy*-laden wagon⟩

⁴heavy \"\ *n* -ES [¹*heavy*] **1 heavies** *pl* **a** : heavy cavalry **b** : HEAVY ARTILLERY **c** : heavy tanks of an army or other military force **d** : HEAVY BOMBERS **2 a** : HEAVYWEIGHT 1a **b** : a theatrical role or an actor representing a dignified or imposing person **c** : VILLAIN 4 **3** : something (as underwear or cloth) heavy in comparison with typical members of its kind

⁵heavy \'hēvē, -vi\ *adj* -ER/-EST [¹*heave* + *-y*] *of a horse* : affected with heaves

heavy-armed \ˌ=ˌ=ˈ=\ *adj* : having or carrying heavy arms

heavy artillery *n* **1 a** : cannon of large caliber and great weight **b** *or* **heavy field artillery** : guns of 155 mm. or guns or howitzers of larger caliber **2** : troops that serve heavy guns

heavy bomber *n* : a large long-range bomber designed primarily to carry large and heavy bomb loads to distant strategic targets — compare LIGHT BOMBER, MEDIUM BOMBER

heavy chemical *n* : a chemical produced and handled in large lots (as a ton or more a day) and often in a more or less crude state — used esp. of acids (as sulfuric acid), alkalies, and salts (as aluminum sulfate) — compare FINE CHEMICAL

heavy concrete *n* : concrete in which the usu. rock aggregates are partially or wholly replaced by aggregates of metal (as steel) and which is used esp. for counterweights or in shielding nuclear reactors

heavy cream *n* : cream that is markedly thick; *esp* : cream that by law contains not less than 36 percent butterfat

heavy cruiser *n* : a large naval cruiser whose principal armament usu. consists of 8-inch guns — compare LIGHT CRUISER

heavy dactyl *n* : a spondee resulting from substitution of a long syllable for the two short syllables in the thesis of a dactyl

heavy-duty \ˌ=ˌ=ˈ=\ *adj* : able or designed to withstand unusual strain (as from heat, exposure, or wear) ⟨*heavy-duty* equipment⟩ ⟨a sturdy *heavy-duty* glove⟩

heavy-footed \ˌ=ˌ=ˈ=\ *adj* **1** : ponderous in or as if in movement ⟨a tired *heavy-footed* walk⟩ ⟨a *heavy-footed* literary style⟩ ⟨the conductor's rendering of the concerts was very *heavy-footed*⟩ **2** *dial* : PREGNANT **3** : inclined to drive an automobile at excessive speeds ⟨issuing a few tickets to *heavy-footed* drivers —Robert Latimer⟩

heavy going *n* : difficult travel or progress

heavy-handed \ˌ=ˌ=ˈ==\ *adj* **1** : awkward or clumsy in or as if in the use of the hands: as **a** : having the hands seem heavy esp. from fatigue **b** *dial, of a cook or server* : inclined to be overgenerous ⟨*heavy-handed* with the potatoes⟩ ⟨much too *heavy-handed* with salt⟩ **c** : lacking or deficient in lightness, grace, or sparkle ⟨a *heavy-handed* didactic style⟩ **2** : inclined to punish severely ⟨grandfather was *heavy-handed* with his own children but very indulgent with us grandchildren⟩; *broadly* : harshly oppressive ⟨*heavy-handed* tyranny⟩ — **heavy-handedly** *adv* — **heavy-handedness** *n* -ES

heavy-headed \ˌ=ˌ=ˈ==\ *adj* **1** : having a large or heavy head ⟨*heavy-headed* wheat⟩ **2 a** : DULL, STUPID **b** : DROWSY

heavyhearted \ˌ=ˌ=ˈ==\ *adj* [ME *hevy herted*] : SADDENED, DISPIRITED, MELANCHOLY — **heavy·heart·ed·ly** *adv* — **heavy·heart·ed·ness** *n* -ES

heavy hydrogen *n* : an isotope of hydrogen having a mass number greater than 1; *esp* : DEUTERIUM

heavy-laden \ˌ=ˌ=ˈ==\ *adj* : weighted down with or as if with a heavy burden : OPPRESSED, BURDENED ⟨a *heavy-laden* donkey⟩ ⟨*heavy-laden* with family cares⟩

heavy liquid *n* : a suspension of very fine particles of high specific gravity in water that forms a slurry with a specific gravity greater than that of water

heavy man *n, slang* : a professional criminal engaged in activities (as robbery or safecracking) that involve or may involve violence

heavy metal *n* : a metal of high specific gravity; *esp* : a metal having a specific gravity of 5.0 or over

heavy mineral *n* : a mineral of specific gravity higher than a standard (as 2.8 or 3.0) that commonly forms a minor component of a rock

heavy nitrogen *n* : an isotope of nitrogen having a mass number greater than 14; *esp* : nitrogen of mass 15

heavy oil *n* : an oil of high specific gravity; *specif* : a high-boiling distillate from tar

heavy oil of wine : a heavy yellow oily liquid obtained in the distillation of alcohol and sulfuric acid in making ether

heavy oxygen *n* : an isotope of oxygen having a mass number greater than 16; *esp* : oxygen of mass 18

heavy pine *or* **heavy-wooded pine** *n* : PONDEROSA PINE

heavy racket *n, slang* : a branch of crime that involves or may involve personal violence — compare HEAVY MAN

heavyset \ˌ=ˌ=ˈ=\ *adj* : stocky and compact and sometimes tending to stoutness in build ⟨a ~ man⟩

heavy solution *n* : a liquid of high density (as a solution of mercury iodide in potassium iodide or of the cadmium salt of a borotungstic acid) used esp. in determining the specific gravities of minerals and in separating them when mechanically mixed

heavy spar *n* : BARITE

heavy water *n* : water containing more than the usual proportion of heavy hydrogen, heavy oxygen, or both; *esp* : water that is enriched in deuterium so that it consists either wholly or in larger than normal proportion of deuterium oxide and that is used in tracer studies and as a moderator in nuclear reactors

heavy weapons company *n* : an infantry company usu. equipped with mortars, heavy machine guns, and recoilless rifles in addition to lighter weapons

heavyweight \'=ˌ=ˌ=\ *n, often attrib* **1** : one that is above average in weight: as **a** : a participant (as a boxer or wrestler) in a sport or athletic contest who belongs to the heaviest of the classes into which contestants are divided; *esp* : a boxer weighing not less than 175 pounds — compare FEATHERWEIGHT **b** : an exceptionally massive or heavy object (as a truck or naval vessel) **2** : one that carries unusual weight (as an outstanding writer or philosopher or a political leader) ⟨the ~*s* of the party gathered in New York⟩

hea·zle·wood·ite \'hēzəlˌwu̇ˌdīt\ *n* -S *usu cap* [*Heazlewood*, Tasmania, its locality + E *-ite*] : a mineral Ni_3S_2 consisting of sulfide of nickel

heb *abbr, usu cap* Hebrew

he-balsam \'=ˌ==\ *n* **1** : BLACK SPRUCE 1 **2** : RED SPRUCE

heb·do·mad \'hebdəˌmad\ *n* -S [L *hebdomad-*, *hebdomas*, fr. Gk *hebdomad-*, *hebdomas*, fr. *hebdomos* seventh (fr. *hepta* seven) + *-ad-*, *-as* fem. suffix denoting connection with or descent from — more at SEVEN] **1** : a group of seven ⟨a ~ of heavenly bodies⟩ **2** : a period of seven days : WEEK **3** *gnosticism* : a group of seven aeons derived from the seven planetary deities who in most systems were half-hostile powers that created the world

¹heb·dom·a·dal \(ˈ)hebˈdäməd^əl\ *adj* [LL *hebdomadalis*, fr. L *hebdomad-*, *hebdomas* + *-alis* -al] **1** *obs* : consisting of seven days : lasting seven days **2** : occurring every seven days : WEEKLY

²hebdomadal \"\ *n* -S : a weekly newspaper or magazine

heb·dom·a·dal·ly \-d^əlē\ *adv* : every week ⟨contributes ~ to the magazine⟩

¹heb·dom·a·dary \hebˈdäməˌderē\ *n* -ES [ME *ebdomadary*, fr. LL *hebdomadarius*, fr. L *hebdomad-*, *hebdomas* + *-arius* -ary (n. suffix)] : a member of a Roman Catholic chapter or convent appointed for the week to sing the chapter mass and lead the recitation of the canonical hours

²hebdomadary \"\ *adj* [ML *hebdomadarius*, fr. L *hebdomad-*, *hebdomas* + *-arius* -ary (adj. suffix)] : occurring every seven days

heb·dom·a·der \-ˌdə(r)\ *n* -S [alter. of ¹*hebdomadary*] : a member of a Scottish university formerly appointed for the week to superintend student discipline

¹he·be \'hē(ˌ)bē\ *n* [NL, after *Hebe*, goddess of youth, fr. Gk *Hēbē*, fr. *hēbē*, youth; akin to Lith *pajėgà* power, ability] **1** *cap, in some classifications* : a genus comprising the shrubby evergreen veronicas of the southern hemisphere **2** -S : any veronica that can be placed in the genus *Hebe* including several of considerable horticultural interest

²hebe \'hēb\ *n* -S *often cap* [short for ²*Hebrew*] : JEW — often taken to be offensive

hebe- *comb form* [Gk *hēbē* youth, pubes] : puberty ⟨*hebephrenia*⟩ : downy : hairy : pubescent ⟨*hebeanthous*⟩

he·be·phre·nia \ˌhēbəˈfrēnēə, ˌheb-\ *n* -S [NL, fr. *hebe-* + *-phrenia*] : a schizophrenic reaction that is characterized by silliness, delusions, hallucinations, and regression and that has an early insidious onset and a usu. unfavorable prognosis — **he·be·phre·nic** \ˌ==ˈfrenik *also* -rēn-\ *adj or n*

he·ber·den's node \'hebə(r)d^ənz-\ *n, usu cap H* [after William *Heberden* †1801 Eng. physician] : any of the bony knots at joint margins (as at the terminal joints of the fingers) commonly associated with degenerative arthritis

he·be·tate \'hebəˌtāt\ *vb* -ED/-ING/-S [L *hebetatus*, past part. of *hebetare* to make dull (lit. & fig.), fr. *hebet-*, *hebes* dull] *vt* : to blunt the sensitivity or keenness of : make dull or obtuse ⟨desultory reading . . . ~*s* the brain —J.R.Lowell⟩ ~ *vi* : to become dull or obtuse — **he·be·ta·tion** \ˌ=ˈtāshən\ *n* -S

he·be·tude \-əˌtüd, -əˌtyüd\ *n* -S [LL *hebetudo*, fr. L *hebēre* to be dull + *-tudo* -tude; akin to L *hebes* dull] : the absence of mental alertness or physical sensitivity : DULLNESS, LETHARGY ⟨her natural ~ must disgust him and eventually destroy all affection —Hugh McCrae⟩ — **he·be·tu·di·nous** \ˌ==ˈ=(ᵊ)nəs\ *adj*

he·brae·an \(ˈ)hēˈbrēən, hiˈb-, (ˈ)heˈb-, həˈb-\ *n* -S *usu cap* [L *Hebraeus* Hebrew + E *-an* — more at HEBREW] *archaic* : a Hebrew scholar

he·bra·ic \-ˈrāik, -rāēk\ *adj, usu cap* [ME *Ebrayke*, fr. LL *Hebraicus*, fr. Gk *Hebraikos*, fr. *Hebraios*, adj., Hebrew + *-ikos* -ic — more at HEBREW] **1** : of, relating to, or characteristic of the Hebrews or of their language, literature, or religion ⟨those early Christians who were of *Hebraic* blood instead of Greek or Roman —C.J.Bulliet⟩ ⟨a Jewish house of worship ought to be . . . *Hebraic* —A.R.Katz⟩ **2** : characterized by preoccupation with conscience and conduct ⟨was ardently *Hebraic*, exalting righteousness above love —V.L. Parrington⟩ ⟨the Hellenic and the *Hebraic* ways of looking at God, man, and the universe —Will Herberg⟩ — **he·bra·i·cal·ly** \-āək(ə)lē, -āēk-, -li\ *adv*

he·bra·i·ca \-ˈrāəkə, -ēkə\ *n pl, usu cap* [NL, fr. LL, neut. pl. of *Hebraicus*] : things Hebraic; *esp* : Hebraic literary or historical materials ⟨a collection of *Hebraica*⟩

hebraic granite *n, usu cap H* [so called fr. its supposed resemblance to letters of the Hebrew alphabet] : GRAPHIC GRANITE

he·bra·ism \'hē(ˌ)brāˌizəm, -ˌbrē|, -ˌbrə|\ *n* -S *usu cap* [*Hebraic* + *-ism*] **1** : a characteristic feature of Hebrew occurring in another language or dialect ⟨the first half of the book of Acts . . . is replete with *Hebraisms* —S.M.Gilmour⟩ **2 a** : the thought, spirit, or practice characteristic of the Hebrews ⟨*Hebraism* related itself to centuries of literary and philosophical creativity —J.L.Teller⟩ — compare HELLENISM 4 **b** : the moral theory of life held to be characteristic of the Hebrews ⟨the governing idea of Hellenism is spontaneity of consciousness; that of *Hebraism*, strictness of conscience —Matthew Arnold⟩

he·bra·ist \|ˌəst\ *n* -S *usu cap* [*Hebraic* + *-ist*] : a specialist in Hebrew and Hebraic studies

he·bra·is·tic \ˌ=(ˌ)=ˈistik, -tēk\ *adj, usu cap* **1** : HEBRAIC 1 ⟨*Hebraistic* culture⟩ **2** : characterized by or given to the use of Hebraisms ⟨the least *Hebraistic* writer in the New Testament —B.M.Metzger⟩

he·bra·iza·tion \ˌhēˌbrāəˈzāshən\ *n* -S *usu cap* : an act of hebraizing

he·bra·ize \'=(ˌ)=ˌīz\ *vb* -ED/-ING/-S *often cap* [*Hebraic* + *-ize*] *vi* **1** : to use Hebraisms ⟨must impeach him not only for atticizing but for *hebraizing* too —Richard Bentley †1742⟩ **2** : to follow Hebraism ⟨here he is *hebraizing* and introducing an element . . . foreign to the law of our race —Frederick Pollock & F.W.Maitland⟩ ~ *vt* : to make Hebraic: **a** : to cause to become adapted to Hebraism ⟨~ this fact, erect a cosmology upon it, and we have the vital principle of Calvinism —V.L.Parrington⟩ **b** : to adapt (a foreign word) to Hebrew usage; *specif* : to change (a name) to a Hebrew equivalent ⟨*hebraized* his name when Israel was reborn —*Hadassah Newsletter*⟩

¹he·brew \'hē(ˌ)brü\ *adj, usu cap* [ME *Ebreu*, *Hebru*, *Hebrewe*, fr. OF *ebreu*, *ebrieu*, *hebreu*, *hebrieu*, fr. L *Hebraeus*, fr. Gk *Hebraios*, fr. Aram *'Ebrai*] **1** : of, relating to, or characteristic of Hebrew **2** : of, relating to, or characteristic of the Hebrews

²hebrew \"\ *n* -S *cap* [ME *Ebreu*, *Hebru*, *Hebrewe*, fr. OF *ebreu*, *ebrieu*, *hebreu*, *hebrieu*, fr. LL *Hebraeus*, fr. L, adj.] **1** : a member or descendant from one of a group of tribes of the northern branch of the Semites that includes the Israelites, Ammonites, Moabites, and Edomites; *esp* : ISRAELITE — compare JEW **2 a** : the Semitic language of the ancient Hebrews in which most of the Old Testament was written — called also *Biblical Hebrew* **b** : any of various later forms of this language (as Mishnaic Hebrew, rabbinical Hebrew, or modern Hebrew)

hebrew alphabet *n, usu cap H* **1 :** a Semitic alphabet used since about the 5th century B.C. for writing Hebrew and in medieval and modern times used also for Yiddish and on occasion other languages — called also *Aramaic alphabet;* see ALPHABET table **2 :** the Semitic alphabet used in writing Hebrew until about the 5th century B.C. and on occasion as late as the 2d century A.D. — called also *ancient Hebrew alphabet, early Hebrew alphabet, old Hebrew alphabet*

he·brew·ism \'hē(,)brü,izəm\ *n* -s *usu cap* **:** HEBRAISM

he·bri·cian \hē'brishən\ *n* -s *usu cap* [*Hebrew* + *-ician*] *archaic* **:** HEBRAIST

¹**heb·ri·de·an** \,hebrə'dēən, he'brid-\ *or* **he·brid·i·an** \he'bridēən\ *adj, usu cap* [*Hebrides,* islands off the western coast of Scotland + E *-an, -ian*] **1 :** of, relating to, or characteristic of the Hebrides **2 :** of, relating to, or characteristic of the Hebrideans

²**hebridean** \"\ *or* **hebridian** \"\ *n* -s *cap* **:** a native or inhabitant of the Hebrides

he·bron·ite \'hēbrə,nīt\ *n* -s [*Hebron,* Maine, its locality + E *-ite*] **:** AMBLYGONITE

hec·ate \'hekə,tē, -kəd·ē, -kət\ *n* -s *usu cap* [after *Hecate,* Greek goddess of witchcraft, fr. L, fr. Gk *Hekatē*] *obs* **:** WITCH, HAG ⟨I speak not to that railing *Hecate* —Shak.⟩

hecato- *or* **hecaton-** *comb form* [Gk *hekato-,* fr. *hekaton* hundred — more at HUNDRED] **:** consisting of a hundred **:** having a hundred ⟨*hecato*phyllous⟩

hec·a·tomb \'hekə,tōm *sometimes* -tüm *or* -täm\ *n* -s [L *hecatombe,* fr. Gk *hekatombē,* fr. *hekaton* hundred + *-bē* (fr. stem of *bous* head of cattle, cow) — more at HUNDRED, COW] **1 :** an ancient Greek and Roman sacrifice consisting typically of 100 oxen or cattle **2 :** the sacrifice or slaughter of many victims ⟨make ourselves unhappy over the yearly ~ that follows the wake of the motor —Agnes Repplier⟩ **3 :** a large number or quantity ⟨the end of the war saw no ~s of officers slain by enfranchised privates —Dixon Wecter⟩

hec·a·ton·tar·chy \,hekə'tän,tärkē, '=,=,=\ *n* -ES [Gk *hekatont-* hundred (fr. *hekaton*) + E *-archy*] **:** government by 100 persons

hecceity *var of* HAECCEITY

hech \'hek\ *interj* [imit.] — used esp. in Scots to express surprise, contempt, sorrow, or pain

hechi·ma \he'chēmə, 'hechəmə\ *n* -s [Jap] **:** DISHCLOTH GOURD

hech·sher \'hekshər\ *n, pl* **hech·she·rim** \hek'shārəm, -,rēm\ *or* **hech·shers** \'hekshərz\ [LHeb *hekhshēr,* lit., fitting] **:** a rabbinical endorsement or certification esp. of food products that conform with traditional Jewish dietary laws — compare KASHRUTH

hecht \'hekt\ *Scot var of* ¹HIGHT

hech·tia \'hektēə, -kshēə\ *n, cap* [NL, fr. J. G. H. *Hecht* †1837 Prussian counselor + NL *-ia*] **:** a genus of Mexican desert herbs (family Bromeliaceae) with rosettes of spiny leaves and ornamental floral bracts

¹**heck** \'hek\ *n* -s [ME *hek,* fr. OE *hæc, -hec* — more at HATCH] **1** *dial Eng* **a :** the lower half of a divided door **b :** an inner door **2** *chiefly Scot* **:** a wooden rack for holding fodder **3 a :** a wooden grating set across a stream to obstruct the passage of fish **b** *chiefly Scot* **:** a grating in a millrace **4 a :** a device on a vertical frame for controlling warp threads in textile manufacturing **b :** any of various attachments on spinning wheels or warping mills for guiding thread in textile manufacturing

²**heck** \"\ *n* -s [euphemism] **:** ¹HELL 2 ⟨that's the ~ of it⟩ ⟨— he can't do that⟩ ⟨a ~ of a good fighter⟩

heck·el·phone \'hekəl,fōn\ *n* [G *heckelphon,* fr. Wilhelm *Heckel,* 20th cent. Ger. instrument maker, its inventor + G *-phon* -phone] **:** a woodwind instrument of the oboe family pitched an octave below the normal oboe

heck·er·ism \'hekə,rizəm\ *n* -s *usu cap* [Isaac Thomas *Hecker* †1888 Am. Roman Catholic clergyman + E *-ism*] **:** certain religious teachings (as the adaptation of traditional beliefs to the exigencies of modern culture, the exaltation of natural above supernatural virtues, the preference for active rather than passive virtue, the revision of traditional missionary technique) held to be erroneous by Pope Leo XIII — called also *Americanism*

heck-how \'hek,haù, -e,kaù\ *n* -s [origin unknown] **:** POISON HEMLOCK

¹**heck·le** \'hekəl\ *chiefly dial var of* HACKLE

²**heckle** \"\ *vt* **heckled; heckled; heckling** \-k(ə)liŋ\ **heckles** [ME *hekelen,* fr. *hakell, heckele* hackle — more at HATCHEL] **1 :** ⁴HACKLE 1 **2 a :** to harass with questions, challenges, gibes, or objections designed to embarrass and disconcert **:** BADGER ⟨would gather in front-row seats and ~ the performers with shouts —E.J.Kahn⟩ **b :** to interfere with unjustifiably or with hostile intent **:** meddle with so as to annoy, disturb, or injure **:** MOLEST ⟨*heckled* even by photographers who . . . set off flash bulbs as he was about to start —Claudia Cassidy⟩ ⟨seemed too harried and *heckled* by her life to spare love for the older children —John Dollard⟩ **syn** see BAIT

³**heckle** \"\ *var of* HICKWALL

heck·ler \-k(ə)lə(r)\ *n* -s **:** one that heckles ⟨spoke forcefully with a ready wit that took easy care of ~*s* —J.D.Hicks⟩

hec·o·gen·in \,hekō'jenən\ *n* [*heconin* saponin found in the juice of agaves (fr. *hec-* — fr. NL *Hectia,* genus name of *Hectia texensis* — + *-onin* — as in *saponin*) + *-genin*] **:** a crystalline steroid sapogenin $C_{27}H_{42}O_4$ obtained from a desert herb (*Hechtia texensis*) and many agaves and used in a synthesis of cortisone

hect- *or* **hecto-** *comb form* [F, irreg. fr. Gk *hekaton* — more at HUNDRED] **:** hundred ⟨*hect*are⟩ ⟨*hecto*graph⟩

hect·ar·age \'hek,ta(a)rij, -tär-\ *n* -s [*hectare* + *-age*] **:** area in hectares

hect·are \'hek,ta(a)(ə)r, -tär\ *n* -s [F, fr. *hect-* + *are*] **:** a metric unit of area equal to 100 ares or 10,000 square meters — see METRIC SYSTEM table

hec·ta·style \'hektə,stīl\ *n* [by alter.] **:** HEXASTYLE

hec·te \'hek(,)tē\ *n* -s [Gk *hektē,* fr. fem. of *hektos* sixth, fr. *hex* six — more at SIX] **:** an ancient Greek coin worth ⅙ stater; *esp* **:** an electrum coin of Phocaea and Lesbos

¹**hec·tic** \'hektik, -tēk\ *adj* [alter. (influenced by LL *hecticus*) of ME *etyk* (as in *fever etyk* hectic fever), fr. MF *etique,* fr. LL *hecticus,* fr. Gk *hektikos* habitual, habit-forming, consumptive, fr. *hekt-* (akin to *echein* to have) + *-ikos* -ic — more at SCHEME] **1 a :** HABITUAL, CONSTITUTIONAL, PERSISTENT; *specif, of a fever* **:** fluctuating but persistently recurrent ⟨~ fevers are characteristic of tuberculosis and septicemia⟩ **b :** characteristic of or habitually accompanying a hectic fever ⟨the ~ flush of tuberculosis⟩ **2 :** marked by a hectic condition **:** having a hectic fever **:** CONSUMPTIVE ⟨a ~ patient⟩ **3 :** having a glowing quality **:** FLUSHED, RED ⟨the ~ color had brightened in the boy's impatient face —Harriet La Barre⟩ **4 :** characterized by excitement, bustle, or feverish activity **:** RESTLESS ⟨the ~ years after oil was discovered —Harold Griffin⟩ ⟨~ travel through thirty different countries —Carveth Wells⟩ ⟨things were so ~ we couldn't even keep track of the people, let alone the material —N.O.Wahlstrom⟩ — **hec·ti·cal·ly** \-tək(ə)lē, -tēk-, -li\ *adv*

²**hectic** \"\ *n* -s [ME *etyk,* short for *fever etyk*] **1 :** a hectic fever **2 :** one affected by a hectic fever; *esp* **:** CONSUMPTIVE **3 :** hectic flush

hec·ti·cal \-təkəl, -tēk-\ *archaic var of* ¹HECTIC

hec·tic·ness *n* -ES **:** the quality or state of being hectic

hective *adj* [by alter.] *obs* **:** HECTIC

hec·to·cot·y·lif·er·ous \,hektə,käd·ᵊl¦if(ə)rəs\ *adj* [NL *hectocotylus* + E *-i-* + *-ferous*] **:** bearing hectocotyli

hec·to·cot·y·li·za·tion \,=,=,=,=ə'zāshən\ *n* -s **1 :** transformation into a hectocotylus **2 :** impregnation with a hectocotylus

hec·to·cot·y·lize \-'käd·ᵊl,īz\ *vt* -ED/-ING/-S [NL *hectocotylus* + E *-ize*] **1 :** to change into a hectocotylus **2 :** to impregnate with a hectocotylus

hec·to·cot·y·lus \-ᵊləs\ *n, pl* **hectocoty·li** \-ᵊl,ī\ [NL, fr. *hect-* + *-cotylus* (fr. Gk *kotylē* cup, anything hollow) — more at KETTLE] **:** a modified arm of a male cephalopod that is specially and variously adapted to effect the fertilization of the eggs; *esp* **:** an arm that in argonauts and some octopods receives the spermatophores, is inserted into the female mantle cavity, and then is broken free from the body of the male

hec·to·cot·y·ly \-ᵊlē\ *n* -ES **:** the quality or state of having or being converted into a hectocotylus

hec·to·gram *or* **hec·to·gramme** \'hektə,gram, -raa(ə)m\ *n* [F *hectogramme,* fr. *hecto-* hect- + *gramme* gram — more at GRAM] **:** a metric unit of mass and weight equal to 100 grams — see METRIC SYSTEM table

¹**hec·to·graph** *also* **hek·to·graph** \-,graf, -raa(ə)f,-raif,-răf\ *n* [G *hektograph,* fr. *hekto-* hect- + *-graph*] **:** a machine for making copies of a writing or drawing by transferring it to a slab of gelatin treated with glycerin and then taking impressions from the gelatin — **hec·to·graph·ic** \¦=='grafik, -fēk\ *adj*

²**hectograph** \"\ *vt* **:** to copy with a hectograph

hec·to·liter \'hektə + ,-\ *n* [F *hectolitre,* fr. *hecto-* hect- + *litre* liter — more at LITER] **:** a metric unit of capacity equal to 100 liters — see METRIC SYSTEM table

hec·to·meter \'hektə,med·ə(r), hek'täməd-\ *n* [F *hectomètre,* fr. *hecto-* hect- + *mètre* meter — more at METER] **:** a metric unit of length equal to 100 meters — see METRIC SYSTEM table

¹**hec·tor** \'hektə(r)\ *n* -s [after *Hector,* a Trojan warrior in Homer's *Iliad,* fr. L, fr. Gk *Hektōr*] **:** one that hectors **:** BULLY, BRAGGART

²**hector** \"\ *vb* **hectored; hectored; hectoring** \-t(ə)riŋ\ **hectors** *vi* **:** to play the bully **:** SWAGGER ~ *vt* **:** to harass, intimidate, bully, or domineer over by bluster, scolding, or personal pressure ⟨domineering wives who ~ their husbands and in-laws to her heart's content —Harrison Forman⟩ **syn** see BAIT

hec·tor·ing·ly *adv* **:** in a hectoring manner

hec·tor·ite \'hektə,rīt\ *n* -s [*Hector,* Calif., its locality + E *-ite*] **:** a mineral $(Mg,Li)_3Si_4O_{10}(OH)_2$ consisting of a hydrous silicate of magnesium and lithium — compare MONTMORILLONITE

hed \(¦)hed, (h)əd\ *chiefly Scot past of* HAVE

hed·dle *also* **hea·dle** \'hedᵊl\ *n* -s [prob. alter. of ME *helde* — more at HEALD] **1 :** one of the sets of parallel cords or wires that with their mounting compose the harness used to guide warp threads and raise and lower them in weaving **2 :** a metal blade or twisted wire with an eyelet in the center through which warp threads pass in weaving

hed·dler \-d(ᵊ)lə(r)\ *n* -s **:** DRAWER-IN

hed·e·bo \'hedə,bō\ *n* -s [Dan. *hedebobroderi,* fr. *hedebo* dwelling on the heath (fr. *hede* heath + *bo* dwelling) + *broderi* embroidery] **:** an embroidery characterized by drawnwork and decorative stitching

hed·en·berg·ite \'hedᵊn,bər,gīt\ *n* -s [Sw *hedenbergit,* fr. Ludwig *Hedenberg* 19th cent. Swed. mineralogist + Sw *-it* -ite] **:** a mineral $CaFeSi_2O_6$ consisting of a calcium-iron pyroxene

hede·o·ma \,hedē'ōmə, ,hēd-\ *n* [NL, prob. irreg. fr. Gk *hēdys* sweet + *osmē* smell; fr. the fragrant blossoms — more at SWEET, ODOR] **1** *cap* **:** a small genus of American herbs (family Labiatae) having small flowers in axillary clusters and with bilabiate corolla and two stamens — see PENNYROYAL 2 **2** -s **:** any plant of the genus *Hedeoma*

hedeoma oil *n* **:** PENNYROYAL OIL

¹**he·der** \'hēdə(r)\ *n* -s [prob. fr. ²*he* + *deer* (animal)] *dial Eng* **:** a male sheep; *esp* **:** one past eight or nine months old that has not been sheared

²**he·der** *or* **che·der** *also* **che·dar** \'kādər, 'ked-\ *n, pl* **ha·da·rim** \kə'därəm, -dōr-, -,rēm\ *or* **he·ders** \'kādərz, 'ked-\ [Yiddish *kheyder,* fr. Heb *hedher* room] **:** an elementary Jewish school in which children from about 7 to 13 years of age are taught to read the Pentateuch, the Prayer Book, and other books in Hebrew — compare TALMUD TORAH

hed·era \'hedərə\ *n, cap* [NL, fr. L, ivy; perh. akin to L *prehendere* to seize — more at GET] **:** a genus of Old World woody vines (family Araliaceae) usu. having palmate leaves but in adult form often becoming shrubby with unlobed leaves — see IVY

hed·er·a·gen·in \,hedərə'jenən; ,hedə'rajənən, -,nēn\ *n* -s [ISV *hedera-* (fr. NL *Hedera*) + *-gen* + *-in*] **:** a crystalline triterpenoid saponin $C_{30}H_{48}O_4$ obtained by hydrolysis of hederin and other saponins (as from soap nuts)

hed·er·in \'hedərən\ *n* -s [ISV *heder-* (fr. NL *Hedera,* genus name of *Hedera helix*) + *-in*] **:** a crystalline antibiotic glycoside $C_{41}H_{64}O_{11}$ active against fungi and bacteria that is found esp. in ivy — called also *alpha-hederin, helixin*

¹**hedge** \'hej\ *n* -s [ME *hegge,* fr. OE *hecg;* akin to OE *haga* hedge, hawthorn, OHG *hag* hedge, hedged-in enclosure, *heckis* hedge, ON *heggr* bird cherry (tree), L *caulae* sheepfold, *colum* sieve, W *cae* field, Corn *kē* hedge, fence] **1 a :** a fence or boundary formed by a row of shrubs or low trees planted close together ⟨white farmhouses with faded red barns and fields bordered with ~*s* of green —Gordon Webber⟩ **b :** any fence or wall marking a boundary or forming a barrier ⟨the high stone ~ . . . encircled the enclosure —A.L.Rowse⟩ **2 a :** a line or array forming a barrier or marking a boundary ⟨pikemen . . . present a ~ of metal points from which any cavalry would flinch —Tom Wintringham⟩ **b :** a protective or defensive barrier ⟨regarded it as the main function of their existence to raise a ~ around the law —F.W.Farrar⟩ **3 a :** a means of protection or defense — usu. used with *against* ⟨proponents of using fluorides as a ~ against tooth decay —*N.Y.Times*⟩ **b :** any of several means of protection against financial loss: as (1) **:** a bet made against the side or chance already bet on (2) **:** a purchase or sale made not primarily for income or profit but as protection against a known risk ⟨realization that common stocks are the best ~ against inflation —C.E.Merrill⟩ (3) **:** a purchase or sale of commodity futures made to offset the risk of loss from market fluctuations **4 :** a statement so qualified or calculated as to be noncommittal or ambiguous ⟨bureaucratic literature . . . festooned with ~*s* and qualifications —*Fortune*⟩ **5 :** OSAGE ORANGE

²**hedge** \"\ *vb* -ED/-ING/-S [ME *heggen,* fr. *hegge,* n.] *vt* **1 :** to enclose with or separate by a hedge **:** fence with a row of shrubs or low trees planted close together ⟨its modest lot is *hedged* by . . . hibiscus —Frederick Simpich⟩ **2 a :** to enclose as if with a hedge **:** ENCIRCLE ⟨meandering through an immense meadow *hedged* by forest —S.H.Holbrook⟩ ⟨a small dance floor crowded with couples and *hedged* with waiting men —Edmund Wilson⟩ **b :** to surround so as to form a protective barrier **:** GUARD, PROTECT ⟨remembered that no great divinity ~*s* this sovereign —Graham Greene⟩ **c :** to surround so as to prevent freedom of movement or action **:** FENCE, HEM, RESTRICT ⟨the bulk and pressure of the rules that ~ him on every side —B.N.Cardozo⟩ — often used with *about* or *in* ⟨are *hedged* about with many special conditions, limitations, and restrictions —F.L.Mott⟩ ⟨*hedged* themselves in with a thousand dos and don'ts —A.L.Kroeber⟩ **3 :** to obstruct with or as if with a hedge or barrier **:** HINDER ⟨the difficulties which *hedged* all approach —D.G.Mitchell⟩ **4** *obs* **:** to introduce and include within something larger or more important — used with *in* or *into* ⟨when you are sent on an errand, be sure to ~ in some business of your own —Jonathan Swift⟩ **5 a :** to reduce or eliminate the risk of (a bet) by making a bet against the side or chance already bet on ⟨is *hedging* its bets in the all-important diplomatic poker game —*Newsweek*⟩ **b :** to protect oneself against financial loss from ⟨were advising clients to ~ the imminent inflation by buying farmland —*Forum*⟩ **6 :** to form into a hedge or barrier ⟨ye are *hedged* on the borders of my path —Adah I. Menken⟩ **7 :** to qualify or modify so as to allow for contingencies or avoid rigid commitment ⟨when he states a position, he is apt to ~ it round with careful qualifications —Colm Brogan⟩ ~ *vi* **1 :** to plant or trim hedges **2 a :** to evade risk or responsibility by avoiding an open or decisive course **:** TRIM ⟨having found . . . every incentive to cower and cringe and ~ and no incentive whatever to stand upright as a man —Van Wyck Brooks⟩ **b :** to qualify or modify a statement or position so as to allow for contingencies or avoid rigid commitment ⟨the paper for which he was responsible never *hedged* on public questions —H.K.Rowe⟩ ⟨no mathematician is infallible; he may make mistakes; but he must not ~ —A.S.Eddington⟩ **3 a :** to protect oneself financially — usu. used with *against* ⟨in order to ~ against inflation and save . . . a part of one's possessions —George Katona⟩ **b :** to reduce or eliminate the risk of a bet by making a bet against the side or chance already bet on **c :** to buy or sell commodity futures as a protection against loss due to price fluctuations **d :** to buy or sell forward exchange as a protection against loss due to foreign-exchange fluctuations **4 :** to form a hedge or barrier ⟨invested with the sanctity that once *hedged* about a king —Dumas Malone⟩

³**hedge** \"\ *adj* [¹*hedge*] **1 :** of, for, or relating to a hedge ⟨a ~ corner⟩ ⟨a ~ plant⟩ ⟨~ selling on the commodity exchanges⟩ **2 :** born, living, or made near or as if near hedges **:** ROADSIDE ⟨a ~ parson⟩ ⟨a ~ marriage⟩ **3 :** belonging to an inferior grade or class **:** THIRD-RATE ⟨a ~ tavern⟩

hedge accentor *n* **:** HEDGE SPARROW

hedge apple *or* **hedge ball** *n* **:** OSAGE ORANGE

hedge-bet·ty \'=,bed·ē\ *n* [¹*hedge* + *Betty,* the name] *dial Eng* **:** HEDGE SPARROW

hedge bindweed *n* **1 :** a common Eurasian and American wild convolvulus (*Convolvulus sepium*) — called also *wild morning glory* **2** *also* **hedge buckwheat :** CLIMBING FALSE BUCKWHEAT

hedge bird *n* **:** VAGRANT, VAGABOND

hedge-bote \'=,bōt\ *n* -s [¹*hedge* + *bote,* obs. var. of ¹*boot*] **:** HAYBOTE

hedge cactus *n* **:** a So. American white-flowered cactus (*Cereus peruvianus*) widely grown for hedges in the tropics

hedge creeper *n, obs* **:** HEDGE BIRD

hedged *past of* HEDGE

hedge fence *n* **:** a hedge that serves as a fence

hedge fumitory *n* **:** FUMITORY

hedge garlic *n* **:** GARLIC MUSTARD

hedgehog \'=,=\ *n, often attrib* [ME *hegge hogge,* fr. *hegge* hedge + *hogge* hog — more at HEDGE, HOG] **1 a :** any of several nocturnal Old World insectivorous mammals that constitute the genus *Erinaceus* (esp. *E. europaeus*), have the hair on the upper part of the body mixed with prickles or spines, and are able to roll themselves up so as to present the spines outwardly in every direction **b :** any of various other spine-bearing animals (as the tenrecs or the porcupines) **2 a :** any of various prickly fruits or seed pods (as those of *Ranunculus arvensis* and *Medicago echinus*) **b :** a plant bearing such a fruit **3 :** any of various coarse variably spinose West Indian sponges **4 a** (1) **:** a military defensive obstacle made of barbed wire bound around three poles, logs, or lengths of metal (2) **:** a military defensive obstacle that is made of three 6-foot angle irons bolted together, sometimes wound with barbed wire, and usu. embedded in concrete and that is designed to damage tanks and boats in beach landings **b :** a military defensive stronghold securely entrenched or fortified with minefields and pillboxes and equipped with supplies for sustained resistance to encirclement **c :** a multiple rocket-propelled weapon used against submarines

hedgehog cactus *n* **:** any of several cacti with stout sharp spines: as **a :** a cactus of the genus *Echinocactus* **b** *or* **hedgehog cereus :** a cactus of the genus *Echinocereus*

hedgehog caterpillar *n* **:** the hairy larva of certain moths — compare WOOLLY BEAR

hedgehog fish *n* **:** PORCUPINE FISH

hedgehog fruit *n* **:** the prickly fruit of a maiden's-blush (*Echinocarpus australis*)

hedgehog fungus *also* **hedgehog mushroom** *n* [so called fr. the prickly hymenial surface] **:** a fungus of the genus *Hydnum* (esp. *H. erinaceum*)

hedgehog gourd *n* **:** an ornamental gourd (*Cucumis dipsaceus*) having a hairy fruit — called also *teasel gourd*

hedgehog grass *n* **:** BUR GRASS

hedge·hog·gy \'=,=ē, -i\ *adj* [*hedgehog* + *-y*] **:** tending to arouse aversion **:** FORBIDDING

hedgehog medic *n* **:** any of several plants of the genus *Medicago* (as *M. echinus*) having pods that resemble burs

hedgehog parsley *n* **:** a European herb (*Caucalis daucoides*) of the family Umbelliferae having fruit with prickly ribs

hedgehog rat *n* **:** SPINY RAT 1

hedgehog shell *n* **:** a spinose marine gastropod shell of *Murex* or related genera (as *M. tenuispina*)

hedgehog skate *n* **:** LITTLE SKATE

hedgehog tenrec *n* **:** a tenrec (*Setifer setosus*)

hedgehop \'=,=\ *vb* [back-formation fr. *hedgehopper*] *vi* **:** to fly an airplane at a low altitude; *specif* **:** to fly an airplane close to the ground and rise over obstacles as they appear ⟨went *hedgehopping* across Holland, dodging trees, telegraph poles and houses —*Life*⟩ ⟨~ over 12,000 miles of pipeline —*advt*⟩ ~ *vt* **1 a :** to transport by flying at a low altitude ⟨*hedgehopped* his passenger to the other end of the line —*Current Biog.*⟩ **b :** to fly an airplane close to the ground and rise so as to miss (an obstacle) ⟨was accused of *hedgehopping* three planes and a hangar and buzzing the control tower —*Newsweek*⟩ **2 :** to evade or elude as if by hedgehopping ⟨*hedgehopped* Soviet censors to carry a . . . message through the Iron Curtain —*N.Y. Times*⟩

hedgehopper \'=,==\ *n* **:** one that hedgehops: **a :** an airplane flying at a low altitude **b :** a pilot flying an airplane dangerously close to the ground

hedge hyssop *n* **1 :** an herb of the genus *Gratiola* (as the European *G. officinalis* or the American *G. aurea*) **2 :** any of several British plants resembling hedge hyssop (as *Scutellaria minor* and *Lythrum hyssopifolium*)

hedge·less \'hejləs\ *adj* **:** having no hedges

hedge maple *n* **:** a common low-growing Asiatic tree (*Acer campestre*) sometimes used as a hedge

hedge mushroom *n* **1 :** HORSE MUSHROOM **2 :** MEADOW MUSHROOM

hedge mustard *n* **:** a plant of the genus *Sisymbrium; esp* **:** a stiffly branching Old World annual herb (*S. officinale*) with pale yellow flowers that is widely naturalized in No. America and was formerly used in medicine as a diuretic and expectorant

hedge nettle *n* **:** a plant of the genus *Stachys:* as **a :** a perennial shade-loving Eurasiatic herb (*S. sylvatica*) with a green creeping rhizome having a foul odor when crushed **b :** a similar plant (*S. palustris*) with an odorless rhizome that is widespread in moist places in most of the northern hemisphere

hedge parsley *n* **:** any of several weedy plants of the family Umbelliferae with finely cut foliage resembling that of parsley; *esp* **:** an erect annual Eurasian weed (*Torilis japonica*) that has dense heads of white flowers, bristly fruits, and bipinnate leaves and is widely naturalized in eastern No. America

hedgepig \'=,=\ *n* **:** HEDGEHOG

hedge pink *n* **:** SOAPWORT 1

hedge-priest \'=,=\ *n* **:** an itinerant usu. uneducated priest

hedg·er \'hejə(r)\ *n* -s [in sense 1, fr. ¹*hedge* + *-er;* in sense 2, fr. ²*hedge* + *-er*] **1 :** one that plants or trims hedges **2 :** one that hedges (as in betting)

hedge rose *n* **:** any of various wild roses that tend to invade and thrive in hedgerows: as **a :** DOG ROSE **b :** SWEETBRIER **c :** MACARTNEY ROSE

hedgerow \'=,=\ *n* **:** a row of shrubs or trees enclosing or separating fields ⟨could see the white bursts of dogwood in the ~*s* —William Faulkner⟩

hedges *pl of* HEDGE, *pres 3d sing of* HEDGE

hedge school *n* [so called fr. the fact that in 17th and 18th cent. Ireland schools were held outside in out-of-the-way places to evade the law on Catholic education] **:** a school held out of doors esp. in Ireland

hedge sparrow *n* **:** a common European bird (*Prunella modularis* syn. *Accentor modularis*) that resembles a thrush, frequents hedges, and is reddish brown and ashen gray with the wing coverts tipped with white — called also *dunnock, hedge accentor*

hedge-sparrow egg *n* **:** a pale green to light yellowish green that is yellower and slightly lighter than cameo green

hedge violet *n* **:** a common European blue-flowered violet (*Viola sylvatica*) that grows in woods and hedgerows

hedge willow *n* **:** GREAT SALLOW

hedging *pres part of* HEDGE

hedg·ing·ly *adv* **:** in a hedging manner

hedgy \'hejē, -ji\ *adj* -ER/-EST **:** resembling or abounding in hedges ⟨~ growths⟩ ⟨a ~ countryside⟩

he·di·on·di·lla \,hedēən'dē(y)ə\ *n* -s [MexSp, fr. Sp *hediondo* stinking (fr. *heder* to stink, fr. L *foetēre, fetēre*) + *-illa* (dim. suffix) — more at FETID] **:** CREOSOTE BUSH

hed·ley·ite \'hedlē,īt\ *n* -s [*Hedley,* British Columbia, its locality + E *-ite*] **:** a mineral approximately Bi_7Te_3 consisting of an alloy of bismuth and tellurium

he·don·ic \(')hē¦dänik, -nēk\ *also* **he·don·i·cal** \-nəkəl, -nēk-\ *adj* [*hedonic* fr. Gk *hēdonikos,* fr. *hēdonē* pleasure +

-*ikos* -ic; *hedonical* fr. *hedonic* + *-al;* akin to Gk *hēdys* sweet — more at SWEET] **1 a :** of, relating to, or characterized by pleasure ⟨might have shocked them, had they been in a less ~ state —Herman Wouk⟩ **b :** involving the psychological range of feelings from pleasant to unpleasant ⟨any particular color may undergo an alteration of ~ . . . effect —Hunter Mead⟩ **2 :** HEDONISTIC **3 :** of or relating to hedonics or to the states of consciousness that it deals with ⟨the relative pleasurableness of an intent as a whole can be determined with the help of some ~ calculus —F.E.Oppenheim⟩ **4 :** concerned with the production of pleasure or pleasurable sensation — **he·don·i·cal·ly** \-nək(ə)lē, -nēk-, -li\ *adv*

hedonic gland *n* **:** any of several glands of various salamanders and reptiles that produce a secretion believed to function in sexual attraction and stimulation

he·don·ics \hē'däniks, -nēks\ *n pl but usu sing in constr* **1 :** a theory of ethics dealing with or based on the relation of duty to pleasure **2 :** a branch of psychology that deals with pleasant and unpleasant states of consciousness and their relation to organic life

he·do·nism \'hēdᵊn,izəm, -də,ni-\ *n* -s [Gk *hēdonē* pleasure + E *-ism*] **1 :** an ethical doctrine taught by the ancient Epicureans and Cyrenaics and by the modern utilitarians that asserts that pleasure or happiness is the sole or chief good in life — called also *ethical hedonism;* distinguished from *psychological hedonism;* compare EGOISTIC HEDONISM, EPICUREANISM, EUDAEMONISM, UNIVERSALISTIC HEDONISM **2 :** a way of life based on or suggesting the principles of hedonism ⟨she was a perfect specimen of selfish ~ —Donald Armstrong⟩

he·do·nist \-dᵊnəst, -dənə-\ *n* -s [Gk *hēdonē* + E *-ist*] **1 :** an adherent of ethical or psychological hedonism **2 :** one who practices hedonism

he·do·nis·tic \¦hēdᵊn¦istik, -də¦ni-, -tēk\ *also* **he·do·nis·ti·cal** \-tәkәl, -tēk-\ *adj* **1 :** of, relating to, or characterized by hedonism **2 :** of, relating to, or typical of hedonists — **he·do·nis·ti·cal·ly** \-tәk(ә)lē, -tēk-, -li\ *adv*

he·do·nom·e·ter \,hēdᵊn'ämәd·ә(r), -dә'nä-\ *n* [Gk *hēdonē* + E *-o-* + *-meter*] **:** a device for measuring pleasure

-he·dral \¦hēdrәl *sometimes chiefly Brit* ¦hed-\ *adj comb form* [NL *-hedron* + E *-al*] **:** having a (specified) number of surfaces ⟨*dihedral*⟩ **:** having a (specified) kind of surface ⟨*euhedral*⟩

hed·ri·oph·thal·ma \,hedrē,äf'thalmә\ [NL, irreg. fr. Gk *hedraios* sedentary, stationary (fr. *hedra* seat) + NL *-ophthalma*] *syn of* EDRIOPHTHALMA

-he·dron \¦hēdrәn *sometimes* ¦,drän *or chiefly Brit* ¦he\ *n comb form, pl* **-hedrons** \-nz\ *or* **-he·dra** \¦drә\ [NL, fr. Gk *-edron,* fr. *hedra* seat — more at SIT] **:** geometrical figure or crystal having a (specified) form or number of surfaces ⟨*holohedron*⟩ ⟨*trapezohedron*⟩

hedy- *comb form* [NL, fr. Gk *hēdy-,* fr. *hēdys* — more at SWEET] **:** pleasant ⟨*hedyphane*⟩

he·dych·i·um \hē'dikēәm\ *n* [NL, fr. *hedy-* + Gk *chiōn* snow; fr. the white fragrant flowers — more at CHION-] **1** *cap* **:** a genus of tropical Asiatic herbs (family Zingiberaceae) having showy labiate flowers in a spike or spiky cluster — see BUTTERFLY LILY 1 **2** -s **:** any plant of the genus *Hedychium*

hed·y·phane \'hedә,fān\ *n* -s [G *hedyphan,* fr. *hedy-* sweet + G *-phan* -phane] **:** a mineral $(Ca,Pb)_5Cl(AsO_4)_3$ consisting of a yellowish white monoclinic lead and calcium arsenate and chloride — compare APATITE

he·dys·a·rum \hē'disәrәm\ *n* [NL, fr. Gk *hēdysaron* goutweed, fr. *hēdy-* hedy- + *saron* broom] **1** *cap* **:** a genus of herbs (family Leguminosae) of the north temperate zone and northern Africa with racemose flowers and flat pods that separate into nearly orbicular joints **2** -s **:** any plant of the genus *Hedysarum*

hee·bie-jee·bies *also* **hee·by-jee·bies** \hēbē'jēbēz\ *n pl* [coined *ab* 1925 by Billy DeBeck †1942 Am. cartoonist] **:** a tense nervous jumpy condition produced by various causes (as strain, irritation, fear, worry) and sometimes marked by hallucinations **:** jangled nerves **:** JITTERS — used with *the* ⟨the unrelenting hollow beat of the jungle drums gave them the *heebie-jeebies*⟩

¹heed \'hēd\ *vb* -ED/-ING/-S [ME *heden, heeden,* fr. OE *hēdan;* akin to OHG *huoten* to protect, guard; causative-denominatives fr. the root of OHG *huota* guard, protection — more at HOOD] *vi* **:** to concern oneself with or take notice of something **:** have regard or pay attention ⟨no sound save for the anxious telegraph machine, which was saying something important, although no one would ~ —Jean Stafford⟩ ~ *vt* **:** to concern oneself with or take notice of **:** have regard to **:** pay attention to **:** MIND ⟨had ~*ed* the call of a poor farmer —H.F.Wilkins⟩ ⟨unless the lessons of the experience are ~*ed* —Carl Spaatz⟩ ⟨will ~ only force —Rupert Emerson⟩

²heed \"\ *n* -s [ME *hede,* fr. *heden,* v.] **:** ATTENTION, NOTICE, REGARD, CARE ⟨no one paid any ~ to him —Upton Sinclair⟩ ⟨take ~ of what you do⟩ ⟨while he gives ~ to public opinion he is not unduly swayed by it —Victor Lewis⟩

heed·ful \'hēdfәl\ *adj* **:** taking heed **:** ATTENTIVE, MINDFUL, CAREFUL, OBSERVANT ⟨~ of what they were doing⟩ ⟨so ~ a writer —W.S.Maugham⟩ — **heed·ful·ly** \-fәlē, -li\ *adv* — **heed·ful·ness** *n* -ES

heed·less \'hēdlәs\ *adj* **:** not taking heed **:** INATTENTIVE, UNMINDFUL, CARELESS, UNOBSERVANT, OBLIVIOUS ⟨~ of the younger lad's howling —Pearl Buck⟩ ⟨the ~ generosity and the spasmodic extravagance of persons used to large fortunes —Edith Wharton⟩ — **heed·less·ly** *adv* — **heed·less·ness** *n* -ES

¹hee-haw \'hē,hȯ\ *n, pl* **hee-haws** [imit.] **1 :** the bray of a donkey **2 :** a loud rude laugh **:** GUFFAW

²hee-haw \"\ *vi* **1** *of a donkey* **:** BRAY **2 :** to laugh loudly and rudely **:** GUFFAW

hee-hee *var of* HE-HE

¹heel \'hēl, *esp before pause or consonant* -ēәl\ *n* -s [ME *hele, heel,* fr. OE *hēla;* akin to OFris *hêl* heel, ON *hæll;* diminutives fr. the stem of OE *hōh* heel, hock — more at HOCK] **1 a :** the hind part of the foot of a human being below the ankle and behind the arch — opposed to *toe* **b :** the part of the hind limb of other vertebrates that is homologous with the human heel either occupying a similar situation (as in raccoons, bears, and other plantigrade animals) or relatively much raised above the ground (as in cows, horses, and other digitigrade animals) **:** HOCK **2 :** an anatomical structure suggestive of or associated with the hind part of the foot of a human being: as **a :** the hind part of a hoof **b :** the hind toe of a bird **c :** the spur of a cock **d :** either of the projections of a coffin bone **e :** the part of the palm of the hand nearest the wrist ⟨rubbed his eyes with the ~*s* of his hands —Warren Eyster⟩ **3 :** the foot as a symbol or instrument of violence or oppression ⟨even my bosom friend . . . has lifted his ~ against me —Ps 41:9 (RSV)⟩ ⟨under the ~ of a dictator⟩ **4 a :** one of the crusty ends of a loaf of bread **b :** one of the rind ends of a cheese **5 a :** the part of a shoe, boot, or slipper or of a sock or stocking that covers the heel of the human foot **b :** a solid part of a shoe or boot projecting downward and attached to or forming the back part of the sole under the heel of the foot — see SHOE illustration **6 a :** a latter or concluding part (as of a period of time) ⟨in the dismal ~ of . . . winter —Hamilton Basso⟩ **b :** REMAINDER, RESIDUE ⟨went to the nearest bottle of scotch and drained the ~ of it into his glass —Harry Sylvester⟩; *specif* **:** unburned and partially burned tobacco caked in the bowl of a pipe ⟨he knocked the ~ of his pipe of tobacco out on the palm of his hand —Seumas O'Kelly⟩ **7 :** a rear, low, or bottom part: as **a :** the after end of a ship's keel or the lower end of a mast **b :** the rear part of a plowshare **c :** the nut end of the bow of a musical instrument **d :** the part of a tool next to the tang or handle **e :** the crook of the head of a golf club where it joins the shaft — see GOLF illustration **f :** the base of a tuber or cutting or other part of a plant used for propagation of the plant **g :** the part of the rear extremity of a gun butt that is uppermost when the gun is held in firing position against the shoulder **h :** the rear end of a railroad frog **i :** a V-shaped piece of beef from the lower part of the round — called also *heel-of-round;* see BEEF illustration **j :** the base part of a ladder **k :** the lower end of a timber in a frame (as a post) **l :** the obtuse angle of the lower end of a rafter set sloping **8 :** a contemptible self-centered untrustworthy person **:** an altogether despicable individual; *esp* **:** a cheap double crosser ⟨a few ~*s* who appear to get away with it, but time eventually catches up with them —Frank Case⟩ **9** [²*heel*] **:** the act of heeling a ball in the game of rugby — **at heel** *adv* **:** close after **:** directly behind **:** in close pursuit ⟨the dog followed *at heel*⟩ — **by the heels :** in a tight grip **:** tightly constricted **:** securely confined ⟨the war, in which I'd hoped not to be caught, had me *by the heels* —Kenneth Roberts⟩ — **down at heel** *or* **down at the heel :** in or into a run-down, shabby, or slovenly condition ⟨old shoes which were *down at heel* —O.S.J.Gogarty⟩ ⟨they ran *down at the heel* somewhat as people will do anywhere when cut off from contact with a larger world —A.W.Long⟩ ⟨very *down at the heel* in appearance —Albert Hubbell⟩ — **on one's heels** *or* **upon one's heels :** following at heel — **on the heels of** *or* **upon the heels of :** close to the heels of **:** close after **:** immediately following ⟨*on the heels of* the news of what had happened —C.S.Forester⟩ **:** in close pursuit of ⟨stayed *on the heels of* the runaways⟩ — **to heel** *adv* **1 :** close to the heels **:** close behind ⟨at a word from his owner the dog moved *to heel*⟩ **2 :** into agreement, control, or subjection **:** into line ⟨the Commons, realizing that he was master still, came *to heel* —J.H.Plumb⟩ ⟨his disciplined mind, rejecting excuses, came heavily *to heel* —J.G.Cozzens⟩ ⟨it is hard to bring the eye *to heel* —D.L. Morgan⟩ — **under heel** *adv* **:** under control or subjection ⟨most of the continent was for a time brought *under heel* —A.L.Rowse⟩

²heel \"\ *vb* -ED/-ING/-S *vt* **1 a :** to furnish (as a shoe) with a heel **b** (1) **:** to fit (a gamecock) with a metal spur (2) **:** to arm (oneself) usu. with a gun ⟨wouldn't go through that territory without first ~*ing* himself⟩ **c** (1) **:** to supply or provide esp. with money or information ⟨a well-*heeled* customer⟩ ⟨better ~*ed* but still not flush⟩ ⟨I want to be ~*ed* when they book him —R.P.Warren⟩ (2) **:** to work for (a school newspaper or magazine) esp. as a reporter ⟨~*ed* the college paper —*Time*⟩ **2 :** to rope (as a steer) by the hind feet **3 a :** to follow closely after **:** follow at the heels of ⟨~*ed* them all the way up the ramp⟩ **b** *of a dog* **:** to urge (a lagging animal) onward by running after and nipping at the heels ⟨dogs ~*ed* the cattle and kept them on the move⟩ **4 a :** to exert pressure on with the heel: as (1) **:** to prod with the heel ⟨~*ed* his horse —A.B.Guthrie⟩ (2) **:** to crush with the heel ⟨~*ed* his cigarette out carefully —W.V.T.Clark⟩ **b :** to kick with the heel; *specif* **:** to pass (the ball) backward with the heel (as out of a scrum) in the game of rugby **5 :** to strike (a golf ball) with the heel of the club ~ *vi* **1 :** to move the heels rhythmically (as in dancing) **2 :** to move along at the heels of someone; *specif, of a dog* **:** to keep to heel ⟨a dog that ~*s* well⟩ **3 :** to move along rapidly **:** RUN ⟨~*ed* out of there as quick as he could⟩ **4 :** to heel a ball (as in the game of rugby) **5 :** to work for a school newspaper or magazine esp. as a reporter

³heel \"\ *vb* -ED/-ING/-S [alter. (prob. influenced by ¹*heel* and ²*heel*) of earlier *heeld, hield,* fr. ME *helden, heelden, hielden,* fr. OE *hieldan, heldan, hyldan;* akin to OE *heald* inclined, OHG *hald* inclined, *helden* to bow, ON *hallr* inclined, *hella* to pour out, Goth *hulths* inclination, favor, grace, Lith *šalis* side, region] *vi* **:** to tilt to one side **:** TIP, LEAN, CANT, LIST ⟨the sleigh was on one runner, ~*ing* like a yacht in a gale —Hamlin Garland⟩ — used esp. of a boat ⟨in such a strong wind the sailboat kept ~*ing* to the left⟩ and sometimes with *over* ⟨the subchaser ~*ed* over —C.F.Mitchell⟩ ~ *vt* **:** to cause (as a boat) to tilt **:** cause to list ⟨~*ing* the sloop well over and skimming her along to windward —K.M.Dodson⟩

⁴heel \"\ *n* -s **1 :** a tilt (as of a boat) to one side **:** LIST **2 :** the extent of a tilt (as of a boat) ⟨a ~ of six degrees to starboard⟩

heelaman *var of* HIELEMAN

¹heel-and-toe \¦=¦=\ *adj* **:** marked by the alternating use of the heel and toe ⟨a *heel-and-toe* dance routine⟩; *specif* **:** marked by the use of a stride in which the heel of one foot touches the ground before the toe of the other foot leaves it and in which the leg is straight and the knee locked as each foot touches or leaves the ground ⟨a *heel-and-toe* walking race⟩

²heel-and-toe \"\ *n* -s **:** a heel-and-toe stride or dance step

heel-and-toe watch *n* **:** a deck watch alternating with an equal period of rest

heelball \'=,=\ *n* **1 :** the underpart of the heel of the foot **2 :** a composition of wax and lampblack used by shoemakers for polishing and by antiquaries in copying inscriptions on stone

heel block *n* **1 :** a block or last to support a shoe which is being heeled or from which heel lifts are being driven out **2 :** a filler block at the heel end of a railroad frog between the frog rails that reinforces the frog and that also serves as a foot guard

heel bone *n* **:** CALCANEUS

heel boom *or* **heeling boom** *n* **:** a log-loading boom against which the end of a log being loaded bears and is steadied as it is lifted and swung into position

heeld *var of* HIELD

heel·er \'hēlә(r)\ *n* -s [²*heel* + *-er*] **1 :** one that heels **2 :** a worker that puts heels on shoes **3 :** a dog that heels animals **4 :** a local worker for a political boss — called also *ward heeler*

heel fly *n* **:** a warble fly that attacks cattle; *esp* **:** a common warble fly (*Hypoderma lineata*) of warm parts of America

heel in *vt* [²*heel*] **:** to cover temporarily (the roots of a plant or often of several plants in one hole) with soil before setting permanently

heeling error *n* [fr. pres. part. of ³*heel*] **:** a deviation of a compass due to a ship's heeling which causes vertical magnetic forces to have a horizontal component and transverse horizontal magnetic forces to have a vertical component

heel·less \'hēllәs\ *adj* **:** having no heel

heel-of-round \'==',=\ *n* **:** HEEL 7i

heel pad *n* **:** a pad (as of leather) fixed over an insole to provide a comfortable support for the heel of the foot

heelpath \'=,=\ *n* [¹*heel* + *path;* fr. its being contrasted to *towpath,* the homophones *tow* and *toe* being punningly equated] **:** BERM d

heelpiece \'=,=\ *n* **:** a piece designed for, situated at, or forming the heel of something; *specif* **:** a piece of leather or other material used in making or repairing the heel of a shoe

heel plate *n* **1 :** BUTT PLATE **2 :** a metal plate (as one designed to protect against wear) for the heel of a shoe

heelpost \'=,=\ *n* **1 :** a post to which a gate or door is hinged **2 :** the outer post of a stall partition in a stable

heel rope *n* **1 :** a rope fastened to the heel of a spar to control it **2 :** a rope used for hobbling a horse

heels *pl of* HEEL, *pres 3d sing of* HEEL

heel seat *n* **:** the part of a shoe to which the heel is attached

heel plates 2: *1* surface type, *2* insert type

heels over head *adv, archaic* **:** head over heels

heel spur *n* **:** the calcar of a bat's foot spreading the tail membrane

heel stay *n* **:** a piece of fabric or rough-surfaced leather cemented on the inside of the shoe at the back seam to prevent slipping at the heel

heel string *n, dial* **:** ACHILLES' TENDON

heeltap \'=,=\ *n* [¹*heel* + *tap*] **1 :** a lift for the heel of a shoe **2 a** (1) **:** a small quantity of liquor remaining in a drinking glass (2) **:** a small quantity of liquor remaining in a bottle, cask, or other storage vessel **b :** DREGS **3 :** an imperfection in the glass bottom of a bottle marked by inequalities of thickness

heeltree \'=,=\ *n* [¹*heel* + *tree*] **:** the whiffletree of a harrow

heelwork \'=,=\ *n* **:** dance technique emphasizing accents with the heels

heem·raad \'hām,räd, 'hem-\ *n, pl* **heemra·den** \-dᵊn\ *often cap* [Afrik, fr. *heem* farm, village, home + *raad* council, councilman] **1 :** a council assisting a local Boer magistrate in the government of rural districts in So. Africa prior to the establishment of British administration **2 :** a member of a heemraad

heer \'hi(ә)r\ *n* -s [ME (Sc dial.) *heir, hair,* lit., hair — more at HAIR] **:** an old unit of yarn measure of about 600 yards or 1/24 of a spindle

heerabol myrrh *var of* HERABOL MYRRH

heerd *or* **heered** *or* **heern** *dial past of* HEAR

heer·mann's gull \'her,mänz-\ *also* **heermann gull** *n, usu cap H* [after A. L. Heermann †1865 Am. naturalist] **:** a white-headed bluish gray gull (*Larus heermanni*) of the Pacific coast of No. America

heeze \'hēz\ *vt* -ED/-ING/-S [alter. of earlier *heise* — more at HOISE] **1** *dial Brit* **:** HOIST **2** *dial Brit* **:** EXALT

hef·ner candle \'hefnә(r)-\ *n, usu cap H* [after Friedrich von *Hefner*-Alteneck †1904 Ger. electrical engineer] **:** a German standard unit of luminous intensity equal to about 0.92 of the candela

¹heft \'heft\ *dial Brit var of* ³HAFT, ⁴HAFT

²heft \"\ *n* -s [fr. *heave,* after such pairs as E *weave: weft*] **1 :** WEIGHT, HEAVINESS ⟨his height and ~ varied a bit —A.J. Liebling⟩ ⟨plow horses of enormous ~ —Fannie Hurst⟩ **2** *archaic* **:** the greater part of something **:** BULK, MASS ⟨it's the ~ of their business —Mark Twain⟩

³heft \"\ *vb* -ED/-ING/-S *vt* **1 :** to heave up **:** HOIST, LIFT, RAISE ⟨~*ed* his pack higher on his broad shoulders —Norman Mailer⟩ **2 :** to test or ascertain the weight of by lifting or balancing ⟨picking the stone up and ~*ing* it —Emily Hahn⟩ ~ *vi* **:** to be heavy to a more or less clearly specified extent **:** WEIGH ⟨a box ~*ing* 15 pounds⟩ ⟨got an inch taller and ~*ed* heavier —C.T.Jackson⟩

heft·er \-tә(r)\ *n* -s **:** a worker who sorts and grades hides or leather

heft·i·ly \-tәlē\ *adv* **:** in a hefty manner **:** STRONGLY, MIGHTILY ⟨~ attacked the suggestion⟩

heft·i·ness \-tēnәs\ *n* -ES **:** the quality or state of being hefty

hefty \-tē, -ti\ *adj, usu* -ER/-EST [²*heft* + *-y*] **1 :** having considerable weight **:** quite heavy ⟨a couple of big ~ books⟩ **2 a** (1) **:** large or bulky and usu. strong **:** BIG, RUGGED ⟨a ~ six-footer —*Time*⟩ ⟨a ~ fellow, in the habit of standing no nonsense from his customers —W.S.Maugham⟩ (2) **:** exhibiting considerable strength or force **:** POWERFUL, MIGHTY ⟨struck a ~ blow⟩ **b :** having a size or extent that is by no means small or negligible **:** not insignificant in size ⟨had a ~ hill to climb over⟩ ⟨spent a ~ extent ⟨took a ~ hike⟩ **:** impressively large **:** good-sized ⟨a ~ majority —W.H.Whyte⟩ ⟨~ wage increases —*Time*⟩ ⟨paying up a pretty ~ sum for the settlement of certain debts —Claud Cockburn⟩ **:** IMPOSING ⟨tipped the scales at a ~ 224 pounds —Elizabeth Coatsworth⟩ **c :** quite rigorous or demanding by reason of size or extent ⟨received a ~ assignment that will take nearly all their time⟩ ⟨a ~ really tough job to do⟩ **3 :** generous in quantity **:** ABUNDANT, PLENTIFUL ⟨a ~ supply of ammunition —Clay Blair⟩ ⟨served up a ~ meal⟩ **syn** see HEAVY

he·gari \hә'garē, -'ger-, 'hegәrē\ *n* -s [Ar (Sudan) *hegiri,* fr. Ar *ḥajari, ḥijāri* stony, stonelike] **:** any of several grain sorghums native to the Sudan region of Africa that resemble kafir and have chalky white seeds and of which one variety is grown in the southwestern U.S.

¹he·ge·li·an \hā'gālēәn, hә'-, hā'jēl-, -'gēl-\ *adj, usu cap* [Georg W.F.*Hegel* †1831 Ger. philosopher + E *-ian*] **:** of or relating to Hegel or his objective idealism or dialectic

²hegelian \"\ *n* -s *usu cap* **:** a follower of Hegel or adherent of Hegelianism

he·ge·li·an·ism \-ә,nizәm\ *n* -s *usu cap* **1 :** Hegel's objective idealism according to which the rational and the real are equatable so that reason can arrive through dialectic at a comprehension of an absolute idea of which all phenomena are held to be partial representations **2 :** a philosophical system marked by the acceptance of Hegel's objective idealism and the revision of his dialectic or by rejection of his objective idealism and acceptance of his dialectic

he·ge·li·an·ize \-,nīz\ *vt* -ED/-ING/-S *often cap* **:** to bring into conformity with Hegel's objective idealism or dialectic

hegelian triad *n, usu cap H* **:** the three dialectical stages of thesis, antithesis, and synthesis often held to be Hegel's characterization of the progress of history or of logical thought

he·gel·ism \'hāgә,lizәm\ *n* -s *usu cap* [G.W.F.*Hegel* + E *-ism*] **:** HEGELIANISM

heg·e·mon \'hejә,män, 'hēj-\ *n* -s [Gk *hēgemōn* guide, leader] **:** one (as a political state) possessing hegemony

heg·e·mon·ic \¦==¦mänik\ *also* **heg·e·mon·i·cal** \-nәkәl\ *adj* [Gk *hēgemonikos,* fr. *hēgemon-, hēgemōn* + *-ikos* -ic, *-ical*] **:** of, relating to, or possessing hegemony ⟨~ states⟩

he·gem·o·nis·tic \hә¦jemә¦nistik\ *adj* [*hegemony* + *-istic*] **:** HEGEMONIC

he·gem·o·ny \hә'jemәnē, -ni *also* 'hejә,mōnē, -ni *sometimes* 'hegә,-\ *n* -ES [Gk *hēgemonia,* fr. *hēgemōn* guide, leader (fr. *hēgeisthai* to guide, lead) + *-ia* — more at SEEK] **1 :** preponderant influence or authority (as of a government or state) **:** LEADERSHIP, DOMINANCE ⟨aiming at world ~⟩ **2 :** a government or state possessing hegemony

he·gi·ra *also* **he·ji·ra** \hә'jīrә, 'hej(ә)rә\ *n* -s [fr. the *Hegira, Hejira,* the flight of Muhammad from Mecca in A.D. 622, fr. ML *hegira,* fr. Ar *hijrah,* lit., flight] **1** *usu cap* **:** the Muslim era **2 :** a journey or trip esp. when undertaken as a means of escaping from an undesirable or dangerous environment or as a means of arriving at a highly desirable destination ⟨the people wandered away on long ~*s* seeking new homesites near water —Frank Waters⟩; *specif* **:** a departure or flight made under such circumstances ⟨planning a ~ from the city to the cool peace of the mountains⟩ **3 :** EMIGRATION ⟨the ~ of many of the literati to Europe —C.I.Glicksberg⟩; *esp* **:** a mass exodus ⟨the ~ of farmers looking for new, cheap, fertile land —R.E.Riegel & G.D.Harmon⟩

he·gu·men \hә'gyümәn\ *n* -s [LL *hegumenus,* fr. LGk *hēgoumenos* leader, president, fr. Gk *hēgoumenos* fr. pres. part. of *hēgeisthai* to lead — more at SEEK] **:** the head of a religious community (as a small monastery) in the Eastern Church — used also as a title of honor for certain monks who are priests; compare ARCHIMANDRITE

¹heh *like* EH\ *interj* [imit.] — used typically to indicate interrogation and often to express scorn, amusement, or surprise

²heh *var of* HE

HEH *abbr* Her Exalted Highness; His Exalted Highness

he·he \'hā(,)hā\ *n, pl* **hehe** *or* **hehes** *usu cap* **1 a :** a Bantu-speaking people of Tanganyika Territory **b :** a member of such people **2 :** a Bantu language of the Hehe people

he-he *or* **hee-hee** \'hē'hē\ *interj* [imit.] — used to express or as an imitation of derisive laughter or a senile or foolish giggle

he-huckleberry \'=',== — *see* BERRY\ *n* **1 :** an ironwood (*Cyrilla racemiflora*) of the southern U.S. **2 :** PRIVET ANDROMEDA

HEI *abbr* high explosive incendiary

hei·au \'hā,aü\ *n* -s [Hawaiian] **:** a pre-Christian Hawaiian temple or other place of worship (as a stone platform or an earthen terrace)

heid \'hēd\ *dial var of* HEAD

¹hei·deg·ge·ri·an \,hī,de¦girēәn\ *adj, usu cap* [Martin *Heidegger* b1889 Ger. philosopher + E *-ian*] **:** of or relating to Heidegger or his existentialist philosophy

²heideggerian \"\ *n* -s *usu cap* **:** a follower of Heidegger or adherent of his existentialist philosophy

hei·del·berg \'hīdᵊl,bәrg, -,bәg\ *adj, usu cap* [fr. *Heidelberg,* Germany] **:** of or from the city of Heidelberg, Germany **:** of the kind or style prevalent in Heidelberg

heidelberg man *or* **heidelberg race** *n, usu cap H* **:** an early Pleistocene man that is known from a massive chinless fossilized jaw with distinctly human dentition, that is the earliest hominoid generally assigned to the genus *Homo,* that is usu. placed in a distinct species (*H. heidelbergensis*), and that is considered to be closely related to Neanderthal man

heif·er \'hefә(r)\ *n* -s [ME *hayfare, hayfre, heffre,* fr. OE *hēahfore,* perh. fr. *hēah* high + *-fore* (akin to OE *fearr* bull) — more at HIGH, PARE] **1 :** a young cow: **a :** one that is less than three years old and has freshened only once **b :** one that has never borne young or developed the proportions of a mature cow — used esp. in the meat trade **2 :** WOMAN; *esp* **:** a young woman

heif·er·ette \¦hefә¦ret\ *n* -s **:** a large heavy heifer having nearly the size and development of a mature cow

heigh \'hī, 'hā\ *interj* [origin unknown] — used to express cheeriness or exultation or to indicate interrogation or attract attention

[1]**heigh-ho** \'ˌ=ˌ=\ *interj* [*heigh* + *ho*] — used typically to express boredom, weariness, or sadness and sometimes to serve as a cry of encouragement

[2]**heigh-ho** \'ˌ=ˌ=\ *n* -s : [3]FLICKER

[1]**height** *also* **hight** \'hīt, *usu* -īd.+V *also* -ītth *sometimes* -īth\ *n* -s [ME *heighthe, heighte, heghte, heyeth*, fr. OE *hīehthu, hēhthu;* akin to OHG *hōhida* height, ON *hæth*, Goth *hauhitha;* derivatives fr. the root of E [1]*high*] **1 a :** the highest part of something material ⟨finally reached the ~ of the mountain⟩ **:** uppermost section or area or region **:** top part **:** SUMMIT, APEX, PINNACLE ⟨plunged down from the ~ of the tower⟩ **b :** the highest point of something not material ⟨at the ~ of fame⟩ **:** most advanced point **:** ZENITH ⟨the ~ of culture⟩ **:** most extreme degree ⟨the ~ of stupidity⟩ **:** fullest possible degree ⟨at the ~ of success⟩ **:** CULMINATION ⟨the ~ of all their desires⟩ ⟨the ~ of passion⟩ **:** most active or intense part **:** CLIMAX ⟨the ~ of an argument⟩ ⟨at the very ~ of the storm⟩ **2 a** (1) **:** the distance extending from the bottom to the top of something standing upright ⟨measured the ~ of the building⟩ or from the bottom to an arbitrarily chosen upper point ⟨the tree has a ~ of five feet at its first branch⟩ (2) **:** the distance extending from the lowest point to the highest point of an animal body esp. of a human being in a natural standing position ⟨a man who is six feet in ~⟩ or from the lowest point to an arbitrarily chosen upper point ⟨a dog two feet in ~ at the shoulder⟩ **:** STATURE **b** (1) **:** the extent of elevation above a level ⟨the land reaches a ~ of 600 feet above sea level⟩ **:** distance extending upwards **:** ALTITUDE ⟨impossible to know the exact ~ reached by the rocket⟩ (2) **:** the degree of approximation of the tongue to the palate in pronouncing a vowel **3 :** the quality of possessing sufficient or considerable or relatively great highness or stature or altitude ⟨a triumphal arch that would have been more impressive if it had had more ~⟩ **4 a :** an extent of land (as a hill, mountain, or plateau) rising to a considerable degree above the surrounding country **:** a lofty eminence **b :** a high place or point or position ⟨the ~s and depths of love⟩ **5 a** *obs* **:** an advanced degree of distinction (as in rank) **:** notable excellence **:** SUPERIORITY ⟨exceeded by the ~ of happier men —Shak.⟩ **b** (1) *obs* **:** HAUGHTINESS (2) *archaic* **:** loftiness of mind or spirit ⟨with something of the old Roman ~ about him —Charles Lamb⟩ **6** *obs* **a :** degree of geographical latitude **b :** position (as of a ship) off a coast

[2]**height** *also* **hight** \'hīt, 'hīkt\ *vt* -ED/-ING/-S *dial* **:** HEIGHTEN

height·en \'hīt°n\ *vb* **heightened; heightened; heightening** \-t(°)niŋ\ **heightens** [[1]*height* + *-en*] *vt* **1 a** (1) **:** to increase the amount or degree or detail or extent of **:** AUGMENT, AMPLIFY ⟨~*ing* his speed —Edith Sitwell⟩ ⟨conflict has ~*ed* citizens' awareness of what they want —Constance Green⟩ ⟨this only ~*s* our admiration —Edmund Wilson⟩ ⟨~*ed* their campaign against news censorship —*Americana Annual*⟩ (2) **:** to make (as a color, an emotional experience) brighter or more glowing or more intense **:** DEEPEN, INTENSIFY ⟨happiness ~*ed* the natural ruddiness of her cheeks⟩ (3) **:** to delineate more sharply **:** make more evident **:** bring out more strongly **:** point up **:** HIGHLIGHT ⟨shade ~*s* the brightness of light —Havelock Ellis⟩ ⟨the benevolent expression of his face was ~*ed* in later years by his white hair and beard —F.H.Dewey & E.S.Bates⟩ (4) **:** to make more acute **:** SHARPEN ⟨which had ~*ed* his appreciation of the more austere pleasures of the afternoon —Archibald Marshall⟩ (5) **:** to make more poignant ⟨their sorrow was ~*ed* by their forced absence from home⟩ (6) **:** to increase the impact of **:** STRENGTHEN ⟨rapid action ~*s* the effect of the drama⟩ **b** (1) **:** to give physical height to or increase the physical height of **:** raise high or higher **:** ELEVATE ⟨the building had been ~*ed* by the addition of a second story⟩ (2) **:** to raise above the ordinary or trite **:** make better by adding stature or distinction to ⟨how can we use this fact to ~ our civilization —C.A.Lindbergh b. 1902⟩ **2** *obs* **:** to cause to be elated or excited **:** EXALT ⟨being ~*ed* with this victory —James Ussher⟩ ~ *vi* **1** *archaic* **:** to become great or greater in physical height **:** GROW, RISE ⟨as we rode up the carriageway, the rock seemed to ~ marvelously —J.H. Newman⟩ **2 a :** to become great or greater in amount, degree, detail, or extent ⟨his youthful impatience ~*ed* —A.J.Cronin⟩ **b :** to become brighter (as of a color) or more glowing or more intense ⟨though the color had ~*ed* in his cheek, he did not flinch from his friend's gaze —James Joyce⟩ **syn** see INTENSIFY

height finder *n* **:** a device used to determine the height of an airborne object

height gauge *n* **1 :** a gauge having a micrometer or a vernier scale for measuring heights **2 :** a C-shaped metal device for measuring the foot-to-face height of printing type or mounted plates

heighth \'hī(t)th\ *chiefly dial var of* HEIGHT

height measure *n* **:** HYPSOMETER

height of burst : the vertical angle between the base of a target and the point of burst of artillery fire usu. as viewed from the firing point

height of land : [2]DIVIDE 2a

heights *pl of* HEIGHT, *pres 3d sing of* HEIGHT

height to paper : the height of printing type measured from foot to face and standardized at 0.9186 inch in English-speaking countries — called also *type height*

heil \'hī(ə)l\ *vb* -ED/-ING/-S [G, interj., hail (used frequently by the Nazis in such phrases as *Heil Hitler!* Hail Hitler! and *Sieg heil!* Hail victory!), fr. MHG, fr. *heil*, adj., healthy, fr. OHG — more at WHOLE] **:** to salute with the German exclamation *heil*

heilaman *var of* HIELEMAN

hei·li·gen·schein \'hīləgən,shīn\ *n* -s [G, lit., halo, fr. *heiliger* saint (fr. *heilig* holy, fr. OHG *heilag*) + *schein* shine, light, fr. OHG *scīn;* akin to OHG *skīnan* to shine — more at HOLY, SHINE] **:** a bright light around the shadow of a person's head (as on a field or lawn) caused by diffraction and reflection of sunlight by dewdrops

heils·ge·schich·te \'hīlzgə,shiktə\ *n* -s *usu cap* [G, fr. *heil* salvation + *geschichte* history] **:** an interpretation of history emphasizing God's saving acts and viewing Jesus Christ as central in redemption

heilt·suk *or* **haelt·zuk** \'hā(ə)lt,sùk, -,zùk\ *n, pl* **heiltsuk** *or* **heiltsuks** *or* **haeltzuk** *or* **haeltzuks** *usu cap* **1 :** a group of peoples including the Bellabella, China Hat, and Wikeno **2 :** a member of the Heiltsuk group

hei-mi·ao \'hāmē'aù\ *n, pl* **hei-miao** *or* **hei-miaos** *usu cap H&M* [Chin (Pek) *hei*[1] *miao*[2], fr. *hei*[1] black + *miao*[2] sprouts, shoots, descendants] **1 :** the principal division of the Miao peoples inhabiting the southeastern part of Kweichow province in southern China **2 :** a member of the Hei-Miao

hei·min \'hāmən\ *n, pl* **heimin** [Jap, fr. *hei* common + *min* people] **:** the class of commoners consisting of peasants and laborers and traders in the Japanese social scale — compare KWAZOKU, SHIZOKU

hei·nesque \(')hī¦nesk\ *adj, usu cap* [Heinrich *Heine* †1856 Ger. poet and writer + E *-esque*] **:** of, relating to, or resembling the style of Heine

[1]**hei·nie** *also* **hei·ne** *or* **hei·ney** \'hīnē, -ni\ *n* -s [G *Heinrich* Henry (a common German name) + E *-ie*] **:** GERMAN; *esp* **:** a German soldier — usu. used disparagingly

[2]**heinie** \"\ *n* -s [alter. of [4]*hinder*] *slang* **:** BUTTOCKS

hei·nous \'hānəs *sometimes* 'hēn- *or* 'hīn-\ *adj* [ME *heynous*, fr. MF *haineus* hateful, fr. *haine* hate (fr. *hair* to hate, of Gmc origin; akin to OS *haton* to hate) + *-eus* -ous — more at HATE] **:** hatefully or shockingly evil **:** grossly bad **:** enormously and flagrantly criminal **:** ABOMINABLE, EXECRABLE ⟨~ offenses⟩ ⟨a ~ act of treason⟩ ⟨a ~ accusation⟩ ⟨proposals of the most ~ nature —Elinor Wylie⟩ **syn** see OUTRAGEOUS

hei·nous·ly *adv* [ME *heynously*, fr. *heynous* + *-ly*] **:** in a heinous manner

hei·nous·ness *n* -ES **:** the quality or state of being heinous

[1]**heir** \'e(ə)r, 'a(ə)l, |ə\ *n* -s [ME *eir, heir*, fr. OF, fr. L *hered-, heres;* akin to Gk *chēros* left, bereaved, OE *gān* to go — more at GO] **1 a :** one who inherits or is entitled to succeed to the possession of property after the death of its owner: as (1) **:** HEIR AT LAW (2) **:** HERES (3) **:** one who in modern civil codes based upon the civil law (as in Europe) succeeds to the entire estate of a person by operation of law or by testament and has a right of renunciation and usu. a right of entry with the benefit of inventory (4) *Scots law* **:** one taking heritable property by destination **:** one who succeeds only to movable estate (5) **:** one who receives some of the property of a deceased person by operation of law, by virtue of a will, or in any of various other ways **b :** one who receives or is entitled to receive property during the lifetime of a former owner ⟨made his friend ~ of the farm after deciding to live elsewhere⟩ **2 :** one who inherits or is entitled to succeed to a hereditary rank, title, or office upon the death or removal from office by other cause (as abdication) of the holder ⟨~ to the principality of Monaco⟩ ⟨succession to the throne by the king's ~ following his abdication⟩ **3 :** one to whom something other than property (as a position of leadership, participation in a tradition or culture, a natural talent, a quality of character) is transmitted or seems to be transmitted in accordance with or apart from the wish of a predecessor and with or without the necessity of direct succession ⟨looked upon himself as the logical ~ of the slain dictator⟩ ⟨was the ~ of the two chief traditions of scholarship in Europe —R.W.Southern⟩ ⟨~ of his father's virtues and vices⟩

[2]**heir** \"\ *vt* -ED/-ING/-S *now chiefly dial* **:** INHERIT

heir apparency *n, pl* **heir apparencies :** APPARENCY 3

heir apparent *n, pl* **heirs apparent** [ME] **1 :** an heir whose right to an inheritance is indefeasible in law if he survives the legal ancestor ⟨became *heir apparent* to the throne when his grandfather . . . was killed —*Current Biog.*⟩ **2 :** HEIR PRESUMPTIVE — not used technically **3 :** one whose succession (as to a position or role) appears certain under existing circumstances ⟨*heir apparent* to Mr. Churchill as prime minister —*U.S. News & World Report*⟩ ⟨the Council of Europe, the parliamentary *heir apparent* of a federated Europe —J.R. Wike & A.Z.Rubinstein⟩

heir at law *n, pl* **heirs at law 1** *Eng common law* **:** an heir in whom an intestate's real property as distinguished from his personal estate is vested by operation of law and not by will or by curtesy or by right of dower — called also *legal heir;* compare DEVISEE, LEGATEE **2** *usu* **heir-at-law** *Scots law* **:** an heir in whom by operation of the law of intestate succession the heritable estate and part or all of the movables of a decedent are vested — called also *heir of line, heir whatsoever, legal heir*

heir·dom \-rdəm\ *n* -s **1** *archaic* **:** HERITAGE **2** *archaic* **:** HEIRSHIP

heir·ess \'erəs, 'ar-\ *n* -ES **:** a female heir; *esp* **:** a female heir to great wealth

heiress apparent *n, pl* **heiresses apparent 1 :** a female heir apparent **2 :** HEIRESS PRESUMPTIVE — not used technically

heiress presumptive *n, pl* **heiresses presumptive :** a female heir presumptive ⟨*heiress presumptive* to the British throne —*N.Y. Herald Tribune*⟩

heir general *n, pl* **heirs general** [ME *heire generall*] **:** HEIR AT LAW

heir in tail *n, pl* **heirs in tail :** one who expects to become or becomes a tenant in possession of a fee-tail estate in land upon the death of a tenant of the estate under special rules of common law or statute governing succession to such an estate as contrasted with the rules of inheritance under a statute of descent

heir·less \'ˌ=ləs\ *adj* **:** having no heir

heir·loom \'ˌ=,lüm\ *n* [ME *heirlome*, fr. *heir* + *lome* implement, tool — more at LOOM] **1 :** a piece of property (as a deed or charter) that is viewed by law or special custom or will or settlement as an inseparable part of an inheritance and is so inherited with the inheritance **2 :** something having special monetary or sentimental value or significance that is handed on either by or apart from formal inheritance from one generation to another ⟨the pin is a family ~⟩ ⟨a spiritual ~ that must, at all cost, be preserved intact —Edward Sapir⟩

heirmos *var of* HIRMOS

heir of entail *n, pl* **heirs of entail 1 :** HEIR IN TAIL **2** *Scots law* **:** an heir called to the succession by a destination **:** an heir of tailzie

heir of inventory *n, pl* **heirs of inventory** *Scots law* **:** BENEFICIARY HEIR

heir of line *n, pl* **heirs of line** *Scots law* **:** HEIR AT LAW 2

heir of provision *n, pl* **heirs of provision** *Scots law* **:** one who may or may not be an heir-at-law and who is called to succeed to property by the provisions of a deed or a contract or a bond **:** an heir by destination

heir of the body *n, pl* **heirs of the body :** a lineal heir esp. as contrasted with a collateral heir

heir portioner *n, pl* **heirs portioners 1** *Scots law* **:** one of two or more female heirs coming in the absence of male issue into a succession to an estate and sharing equally according to a succession to an estate and sharing equally according to degree of consanguinity, the share of any deceased female in the same degree going by representation to her heirs-at-law in the order of the eldest male, then other males, and finally the females **2** *Scots law* **:** one of two or more usu. female heirs in the same degree taking equal shares per capita

heir presumptive *n, pl* **heirs presumptive 1 :** an heir whose legal right to an inheritance may be defeated by the birth of a nearer relative ⟨*the heir presumptive* had been the king's brother —*Springfield (Mass.) Union*⟩ — compare HEIR APPARENT **2 :** one whose succession (as to a position or role) appears likely but not certain ⟨*heir presumptive* at the foreign office —*New Statesman & Nation*⟩

heirs *pl of* HEIR, *pres 3d sing of* HEIR

heir·ship \'ˌ=,ship\ *n* [ME *areschip*, fr. *are, eir* heir + *-schip, -ship* -ship] **1 a :** the condition of being an heir **b :** the right of inheritance **2** *archaic* **:** HERITAGE

heir whatsoever *n, pl* **heirs whatsoever** *Scots law* **:** HEIR AT LAW 2

hei·sen·berg's principle \'hīz°n,bərgz-\ *n, usu cap H* [after Werner K. *Heisenberg* b1901 Ger. physicist] **:** UNCERTAINTY PRINCIPLE

[1]**heist** \'hīst\ *vb* -ED/-ING/-S [alter. of [2]*hoist*] *vt* **1 :** *chiefly dial* **:** HOIST **2** *slang* **:** to appropriate unlawfully and usu. with violence **:** make off with **:** STEAL **3** *slang* **:** to commit armed robbery on **:** hold up; *specif* **:** to break into and rob ~ *vi, chiefly dial* **:** HOIST

[2]**heist** \"\ *n* -s **1** *slang* **a :** armed robbery **:** HOLDUP; *specif* **:** the act of breaking into and robbing an establishment (as a bank) **b :** THEFT **2** *slang* **:** something (as money, jewels) acquired by robbery or theft

heist·er \-tə(r)\ *n* -s **1** *chiefly dial* **:** one that hoists **2** *slang* **:** ROBBER, THIEF

heit \'hīt\ *var of* HAIT

hei-ti·ki \'hā'tēkē\ *n, pl* **hei-tiki** *or* **hei-tikis** [Maori, fr. *hei* to hang + *Tiki*, the first man in Maori legend] **:** a greenstone charm in the shape of a human figure worn as a neck pendant by the Maoris

hei-tiki

he·ja·zi \'hejəzē\ *n* -s *cap* [Ar *hijāzīy*, fr. *Hijāz* Hejaz, kingdom of western Arabia] **:** a native or inhabitant of the Hejaz

[2]**hejazi** \"\ *adj, usu cap* **1 :** of, relating to, or characteristic of the Hejaz **2 :** of, relating to, or characteristic of the people of the Hejaz

hejira *var of* HEGIRA

hektograph *var of* HECTOGRAPH

hel·arc·tos \he'lärktəs, -,täs\ *n, cap* [NL, irreg. fr. *heli-* + Gk *arktos* bear — more at ARCTIC] **:** a genus of mammals (family Ursidae)

hel·beh \'helbə\ *n* -s [Ar *ḥulbah*] **:** fenugreek seed that is mixed with durra in a flour commonly used in Egypt

held *past of* HOLD

held ball *n* **:** TIE BALL

hel·den·tenor \¦heldən'tā¦nō(ə)r, -tā¦nō(ə)r, -¦tenər\ *n, pl* **helden·te·no·re** \-¦tā'nōrə, -'nōrə\ *or* **heldentenors** [G, fr. *held* hero + *tenor*] **:** a tenor voice suited to heroic (as Wagnerian) roles **:** DRAMATIC TENOR

hele *var of* [2]HEAL

he·le·idae \hə'lēə,dē\ [NL, fr. *Helea*, genus of flies (fr. Gk *heleia*, fem. of *heleios* of a marsh, marsh-dwelling, fr. *helos* marsh) + *-idae* — more at HELODES] *syn of* CERATOPOGONIDAE

hel·e·na \'helənə\ *adj, usu cap* [fr. *Helena*, Mont.] **:** of or from Helena, the capital of Montana ⟨*Helena* businessmen⟩ **:** of the kind or style prevalent in Helena

hel·e·nalin \,helə'nalən, -nāl-\ *n* -s [*helen-* (fr. NL *Helenium*, genus name of the sneezeweed *Helenium autumnale*) + *-al-* (fr. NL *autumnale*, specific epithet of the sneezeweed *Helenium autumnale*) + *-in*] **:** a poisonous bitter crystalline compound $C_{15}H_{18}O_4$ that is the active principle of sneezeweed

hel·en flower \'helən-\ *also* **hel·en's flower** \-nz-\ *n, usu cap H* [NL *Helenium*] **:** a plant of the genus *Helenium*

hele·nin \'helənən, hə'lēnən\ *n* -s [NL *Helenium* + E *-in*] **1 :** alantolactone or a mixture from elecampane root containing it **2 :** HELENALIN

he·le·ni·um \hə'lēnēəm\ *n* [NL, fr. L, a plant, elecampane, fr. Gk *helenion*, perh. fr. *helenē* wicker basket; akin to Gk *helix* (adj.) twisted, (n.) spiral, anything of spiral shape, *helissein* to turn, wind, *eilein* to wind, roll, *eilyein* to enfold, enwrap — more at VOLUBLE] **1** *cap* **:** a genus of American herbs (family Compositae) with heads of yellow-rayed flowers and truncate-style branches — see SNEEZEWEED 1 **2** -s **:** any plant of the genus *Helenium*

hel·e·och·a·ris \,helē'äkərəs\ [NL — more at ELEOCHARIS] *syn of* ELEOCHARIS

hel·eo·plankton \¦helē(,)ō+\ *n* [ISV *heleo-* (fr. Gk *heleos*, gen. of *helos* marsh) + *plankton* — more at HELODES] **:** plankton typical of small bodies of still fresh water

hel·e·pole \'helə,pōl\ *also* **he·lep·o·lis** \hə'lepələs\ *n, pl* **helepoles** \'helə,pōlz\ *also* **helepolises** \hə'lepələsəz\ [F & L; F *hélépole*, fr. L *helepolis*, fr. Gk *helepolis*, fr. *helein* to take + *polis* city — more at SELL, POLICE] **:** an ancient siege engine composed of a movable tower covering a battering ram

helgramite *or* **helgrammite** *var of* HELLGRAMMITE

[1]**heli-** *or* **helio-** *comb form* [L, fr. Gk *hēli-, hēlio-*, fr. *hēlios* — more at SOLAR] **:** sun ⟨*Heli*ornis⟩ **:** the sun ⟨*helio*centric⟩ ⟨*helio*scope⟩ **:** sunlight **:** solar energy ⟨*helio*gravure⟩ **:** sun and ⟨*helio*lithic⟩

[2]**heli-** *comb form* [by shortening] **:** helicopter ⟨*heli*port⟩ ⟨*heli*mail⟩

he·li·a·cal \hə'līəkəl, hē'-,he'-\ *adj* [LL *heliacos, heliacus* (fr. Gk *hēliakos*, fr. *hēlios* sun) + E *-al*] **:** relating to or near the sun — used esp. of the last setting of a star before and its first rising after invisibility due to conjunction with the sun — **he·li·a·cal·ly** \-ək(ə)lē\ *adv*

heliacal cycle *n* **:** SOLAR CYCLE

heliacal year *n* **:** a Sothic year

he·li·am·pho·ra \,hēlē'am(p)fərə\ *n, cap* [NL, fr. *heli-* (fr. Gk *helissein* to roll, wind) + L *amphora*] **:** a genus of So. American pitcher plants (family Sarraceniaceae) native to the mountains of British Guiana and having scapes of nodding pink or white flowers

he·li·an·tha·ceous \¦hēlē,an¦thāshəs\ *adj* [NL *Helianthus* + E *-aceous*] **:** resembling, belonging to, or related to the genus *Helianthus*

he·li·an·thate \,hēlē'an,thāt\ *n* -s [*helianthin* + *-ate*] **:** a salt of helianthin ⟨the ~ of streptomycin⟩

he·li·an·the·mum \,hēlē'an(t)thəməm\ *n* [NL, fr. [1]*heli-* + *-anthemum*] **1** *cap* **:** a genus of Eurasian herbs or undershrubs (family Cistaceae) having showy variously colored flowers with fugacious petals **2** -s **:** any plant of the genus *Helianthemum* — called also *rockrose, sunrose*

he·li·an·thin \,hēlē'an(t)thən\ *also* **he·li·an·thine** \", -an-,thēn\ *n* -s [ISV *helianth-* (fr. NL *Helianthus;* fr. its color) + *-in, -ine*] **1 :** a red compound $(CH_3)_2N^+{=}C_6H_4{=}NNH{-}C_6H_4SO_3^-$ of quinone structure obtained by acidifying methyl orange **2 :** METHYL ORANGE

he·li·an·thus \-an(t)thəs\ *n* [NL, fr. [1]*heli-* + *-anthus*] **1** *cap* **:** a genus of tall erect or sometimes much-branched American annual or perennial herbs (family Compositae) comprising the sunflowers and having flower heads with purple or yellow disk flowers and showy yellow sterile rays — see JERUSALEM ARTICHOKE **2** -ES **:** any plant of the genus *Helianthus*

he·li·ast \'hēlē,ast\ *n* -s [Gk *hēliastēs* member of the Heliaea, fr. *hēliazesthai* to be a member of the Heliaea, fr. *Hēliaia* Heliaea, supreme court at Athens, public place in which the court was held] **:** DICAST — **he·li·as·tic** \¦hēlē¦astik\ *adj*

he·li·az·o·phyte \,hēlē'azə,fīt\ *n* -s [Gk *hēliazein* to bask in the sun (fr. *hēlios* sun) + E *-o-* + *-phyte* — more at SOLAR] **:** HELIOPHYTE

helic- *or* **helico-** *comb form* [Gk *helik-, heliko-*, fr. *helik-, helix* spiral — more at HELENIUM] **:** helix **:** spiral ⟨*helic*ine⟩ ⟨*helico*graph⟩

[1]**heli·cal** \'heləkəl, -lēk- *also* 'hēl-\ *adj* [*helic-* + *-al*] **1 :** of, relating to, or having the form of a helix; *broadly* **:** SPIRAL 1a ⟨the ~ thread of a bolt⟩ ⟨metal tubing with annular or ~ fins⟩ **2 :** having the angle of a helix formed about the pitch cylinder rather than being straight and parallel to the axis (as of a gear or milling cutter) ⟨~ teeth⟩ ⟨gears cut in a ~ rather than a spur shape for smoother operation⟩

[2]**helical** \"\ *n* -s **:** something helical in form (as a coil extension spring)

helical gear *also* **helical** *n* -s **:** a gear wheel having teeth set obliquely to the axis of rotation **:** SCREW WHEEL

heli·cal·ly \-k(ə)lē, -li\ *adv* **1 :** in a helical manner ⟨thread is wound ~ on the spool⟩ ⟨~ cut gear wheels⟩ **2 :** by use of a helical ⟨an iron cot with a link spring ~ attached to the angle-steel frame⟩

helical milling *n* **:** milling in which the work (as a helical gear) is given simultaneously a rotary motion and an endways motion — called also *spiral milling*

helical gears

heliced \'helәst, 'hel-\ *adj* **1 :** decorated with or having helices **2 :** having the form of a low conical spiral (as the shell of a snail of the genus *Helix*)

hel·i·cel·la \,helə'selə, ,hēl-\ *n, cap* [NL, fr. *helic-* + *-ella*] **:** a genus of land snails (family Helicidae) including several snails of veterinary importance as intermediate hosts of flukes and of some nematode lungworms of sheep and other ruminants

helices *pl of* HELIX

hel·i·chryse \'helə,krīs\ *n* -s [NL *Helichrysum*] **:** HELICHRYSUM 2

hel·i·chry·sum \,helə'krīsəm\ *n* [NL, fr. Gk *helichrysos*, fr. *helik-* helic- + *chrysos* gold — more at CHRYSALIS] **1** *cap* **:** a large genus of mostly African and Australian plants (family Compositae) with flower heads having shining involucres which retain their color when dried — see STRAWFLOWER **2** -s **:** any plant of the genus *Helichrysum*

he·lic·i·dae \hə'lisə,dē\ *n pl, cap* [NL, fr. *Helic-, Helix*, type genus + *-idae*] **:** a family of pulmonate land snails (suborder Stylommatophora) including the common edible snail and a number of pests — see [2]HELIX

he·lic·i·form \-sə,fȯrm\ *adj* [ISV *helic-* + *-iform*] **:** SPIRAL

hel·i·ci·na \,helə'sīnə\ *n* [NL, fr. *helic-* + *-ina*] **1** *cap* **:** a genus of operculate land snails (suborder Rhipidoglossa) that occur chiefly in warm regions and are distinguished by a short-spired shell, a single auricle, and a pulmonary chamber replacing the gill **2** -s **:** any mollusk shell of the genus *Helicina*

hel·i·cit·ic \¦helə¦sid·ik, ¦hel-\ *adj* [*helic-* + *-itic*] *of metamorphic rock* **:** marked by bands of inclusions showing the original bedding or schistosity of the rock and in many places cutting through the later formation

hel·i·cline \'helə,klīn\ *n* -s [*heli-* (fr. Gk *helix* spiral) + *-cline*] **:** a gradually ascending and curving ramp

helico- — see HELIC-

[1]**hel·i·coid** \'helə,kȯid\ *or* **hel·i·coi·dal** \¦helə¦kȯid°l\ *adj* [*helicoid* fr. Gk *helikoeidēs* of spiral form, fr. *helik-* helic- + *-oeidēs* -oid; *helicoidal* fr. *helicoid* + *-al*] **1 :** having the properties of a helicoid **2 :** forming or arranged in a spiral ⟨~ inflorescence⟩; *specif, of a gastropod shell* **:** having the form of a flat coil or flattened spiral ⟨*Planorbis* is characterized by a ~ shell⟩

[2]**helicoid** \"\ *n* -s **:** a surface resembling that of a screw thread that is generated by a curve which rotates about a straight line and moves in the direction of the line with a velocity whose ratio to the velocity of rotation is constant

helicoidal saw *n* **:** a stonecutter's saw consisting of an endless cable made of three steel wires twisted together, supplied with sand and water, and drawn along marble or other stone to cut it — called also *wire saw*

helicoid cyme *n* **:** BOSTRYX

hel·i·con \'helə,kän, -ləkən\ *n* -s [prob. fr. Gk *helik-, helix* spiral + E *-on* (as in *bombardon*)] **:** a very large bass tuba used in military bands that is made circular for carrying over the shoulder and around the body when marching

helicon

hel·i·co·nia \,helə'kōnēə, -nyə\ *n* [NL, fr. L, fem. of *Heliconius* of Helicon, fr. Gk *Helikōnios,* fr. *Helikōn* Helicon, mountain in Greece] **1** *cap* **:** a genus of tropical American perennial herbs (family Musaceae) that have inconspicuous flowers in terminal spikes often subtended by brightly colored bracts and large leaves often showily veined or mottled with red or yellow — see WILD PLANTAIN **2** -s **:** any plant of the genus *Heliconia*

1hel·i·co·nian \¦helə¦kōnēən, -nyən\ *adj, usu cap* [L *Heliconius* + E *-an*] **:** of or relating to the Boeotian mountain Helicon supposed by the ancient Greeks to be the residence of Apollo and the Muses

2heliconian \"\ *n* -s [NL *Heliconius* + E *-an*] **:** a butterfly of *Heliconius* or a related genus

hel·i·co·ni·idae \,helәkə'nīə,dē\ *n pl, cap* [NL, fr. *Heliconius,* type genus + *-idae*] *in some classifications* **:** a family of chiefly tropical American butterflies with long fore wings and small rounded hind wings that is commonly included in the family Nymphalidae

hel·i·co·ni·us \,helə'kōnēəs\ *n* [NL, fr. L, of Helicon] **1** *cap* **:** a large Neotropical genus of long-winged butterflies that are often brilliantly colored or mimetic and that with related American butterflies constitute a subfamily of Nymphalidae or in some classifications the separate family Heliconiidae **2** *pl* **helico·nii** \-ē,ī\ **:** any butterfly of the genus *Heliconius*

1heli·cop·ter \'helə,käptə(r), -lē,k- *also* 'hēl- *or sometimes* 'helēə,k- *or* 'hēlyə,k- *sometimes* ,==(=)'==\ *n* -s *often attrib* [F *hélicoptère,* fr. *hélico-* (fr. Gk *heliko-* helic-) + *ptère* (fr. Gk *pteron* wing) — more at FEATHER] **:** an aircraft whose support in the air is derived chiefly from the aerodynamic forces acting on one or more rotors turning about substantially vertical axes

2helicopter \"\ *or* **heli·copt** \-pt\ *vb* -ED/-ING/-S *vi* **:** to travel by or as if by helicopter ⟨can ~ from the station to the airfield⟩ ⟨winged seeds that . . . come *~ing* down —Richard Church⟩ ~ *vt* **:** to transport by helicopter ⟨*~ed* the officials aboard the ship⟩

hel·i·co·ru·bin \,helәkō'rübən\ *n* -s [*helico-* (fr. NL *Helic-, Helix,* genus name of *Helix pomatia*) + L *ruber* red + E *-in*] **:** a hemoprotein occurring in the intestine and hepatopancreas of pulmonate gastropods and in the hepatopancreas of the crayfish

hel·i·co·trema \-kō'trēmə\ *n* -s [NL, fr. *helic-* + *-trema*] **:** the minute opening by which the two scalae communicate at the top of the cochlea of the ear

helic·te·res \,helək'tirēz, hə'liktə,r-\ *n, cap* [NL, fr. Gk *heliktēres,* pl. of *heliktēr* anything twisted, fr. *helik-, helix* spiral — more at HELENIUM] **:** a large genus of tropical trees and shrubs (family Sterculiaceae) with axillary flowers and fruits consisting of five twisted carpels — see SCREW TREE

he·lic·tis \hə'liktəs\ *n, cap* [NL, fr. *hel-* (prob. fr. Gk *helos* marsh) + Gk *iktis* yellow-breasted marten] **:** a genus of mammals (family Mustelidae) comprising the ferret-badgers

he·lic·tite \hə'lik,tīt, 'helək-\ *n* -s [*helict-* (fr. Gk *heliktos* twisted, rolled, fr. *helik-, helix* spiral) + *-ite*] **:** an irregular stalactite with branching convolutions or spines

hel·i·go·land trap \'heləgō,land-\ *n, usu cap H* [fr. *Heligoland* (Helgoland), island in the North sea; fr. its original use there] **:** a large funnel-shaped structure of wire mesh opening into a smaller enclosure used for trapping birds (as for banding)

heling *pres part of* HELE

1he·lio \'hēlē,ō\ *n* -s [by shortening] **:** HELIOGRAPH

2helio \"\ *n* -s [by shortening] **:** HELIOTROPE

helio- — see HELI-

he·lio·centric \¦hēlēō+\ *adj* [1*heli-* + *-centric*] **:** referred to or measured from the sun's center or appearing as if seen from it **:** having or relating to the sun as the center (as of the planetary system) ⟨the ~ theory of Copernicus⟩ — compare GEOCENTRIC

heliocentric latitude *n* **:** the celestial latitude of a celestial body as if seen from the center of the sun

heliocentric longitude *n* **:** the celestial longitude of a celestial body as if seen from the center of the sun — opposed to *geocentric longitude*

heliocentric parallax *n* **:** the parallax of a celestial body measured with the earth's orbit around the sun as a baseline **:** the angle subtended at the celestial body by the radius of the earth's orbit — called also *annual parallax, stellar parallax*

he·lio·chrome \'hēlēə,krōm\ *n* -s [1*heli-* + *-chrome*] **:** a photograph in natural colors made orig. by use of a photohalide form of silver chloride

he·lio·chromy \-mē\ *n* -ES [F *héliochromie,* fr. *hélio-* 1heli- + *-chromie* -chromy] **:** COLOR PHOTOGRAPHY

he·li·o·don \'hēlēə,dän\ *n* -s [NL, fr. 1*heli-* + *-odon* (fr. Gk *hodos* way, path) — more at CEDE] **:** a device consisting of a pivoted platform and a spotlight on a vertical track used to simulate sun and shadow orientation for any latitude and day of year for a proposed building

he·li·o·dor \'hēlēə,dȯ(ə)r\ *n* -s [G] **:** a golden-yellow beryl found in southern Africa

he·lio·gram \-,gram\ *n* [1*heli-* + *-gram*] **:** a message transmitted by a heliograph

1he·lio·graph \-raf,-räf\ *n* [ISV 1*heli-* + *-graph*] **1 a :** PHOTOENGRAVING 2b **b :** PHOTOGRAPH **c :** PHOTOHELIOGRAPH **2 :** an apparatus for telegraphing by means of the sun's rays thrown from a mirror — compare HELIOTROPE 3

2heliograph \"\ *vb* **:** to signal by means of a heliograph

he·lio·graph·ic \¦hēlēə¦grafik\ *adj* **1** [F *héliographique,* fr. *hélio-* 1heli- + *-graphique* -graphic] **:** of, relating to, or by means of heliography or a heliograph ⟨~ communication⟩ **2** [1*heli-* + *-graphic*] **:** SOLAR 1 ⟨~ latitude⟩

he·li·og·ra·phy \,hēlē'ägrəfē\ *n* -ES **1** [F *héliographie,* fr. *hélio-* 1heli- + *-graphie* -graphy] **:** an early photographic process producing a photoengraving on a metal plate coated with an asphalt preparation; *broadly* **:** PHOTOGRAPHY **2** [1*heli-* + *-graphy*] **:** the system, art, or practice of signaling with a heliograph

he·lio·gra·vure \¦hēlēōgrə¦vyü(ə)r\ *n* [F *héliogravure,* fr. *hélio-* 1heli- + *gravure*] **:** PHOTOGRAVURE

he·li·ol·a·try \,hēlē'älətrē\ *n* -ES [1*heli-* + *-latry*] **:** sun worship

1he·li·o·lite \'hēlēə,līt\ *n* -s [NL *Heliolites,* genus of corals, fr. 1*heli-* + *-lites* (prob. fr. F *-lithe* -lite)] **:** a fossil coral of the family Heliolitidae

2heliolite \"\ *n* -s [F *héliolite,* fr. *hélio-* 1heli- + *-lite*] **:** aventurine feldspar

he·li·o·lith·ic \¦hēlēə¦lithik\ *adj* [1*heli-* + *-lithic*] **1 :** marked by, observing, or associated with practices (as sun worship and the erection of megaliths) held by some diffusionists to constitute a single widespread neolithic culture originating in Egypt ⟨~ culture⟩ ⟨~ peoples⟩ ⟨~ monuments⟩ **2 :** postulating an Egyptian origin for heliolithic traits found as the basis of higher culture in many parts of the world ⟨the ~ theory⟩

he·li·o·lit·i·dae \,hēlēō'lid·ə,dē\ *n pl, cap* [NL, fr. *Heliolites,* type genus + *-idae*] **:** a family of Paleozoic tabulate corals prob. related to the Helioporidae but having 12 radial septa in the large zooecia

he·li·om·e·ter \,hēlē'ämәd·ə(r)\ *n* [F *héliomètre,* fr. *hélio-* 1heli- + *-mètre* -meter] **:** a visual telescope that has a divided objective with two movable parts which give a double image and that was orig. designed for measuring the apparent diameter of the sun and later used for measuring angles between stars but is now largely replaced by photographic methods

he·lio·met·ric \¦hēlēō¦me·trik\ *adj* [F *héliométrique,* fr. *hélio-* 1heli- + *-métrique* -metric] **:** of, employing, or obtained by use of a heliometer ⟨~ observations⟩ ⟨~ results⟩ — **he·lio·met·ri·cal·ly** \-rək(ə)lē\ *adv*

he·li·om·e·try \,hēlē'ämə·trē\ *n* -ES **:** the art or practice of measuring with the heliometer

he·lio·micrometer \¦hēlē(,)ō+\ *n* [1*heli-* + *micrometer*] **:** an instrument for determining heliographic positions of spots and flocculi shown on direct photographs of the sun or on spectroheliograph plates

he·li·oph·i·la \,hēlē'äfələ\ *n, cap* [NL, fr. 1*heli-* + *-phila*] **:** a genus of southern African annual or partly woody perennial herbs (family Cruciferae) sometimes cultivated for their long showy racemes of bright blue flowers with white eyes

he·lio·phile \'hēlēə,fīl\ *n* -s [1*heli-* + *-phile*] **:** one attracted or adapted to sunlight ⟨*~s* flocking to the beach⟩; *specif* **:** an aquatic alga adapted to attain maximum exposure to sunlight

he·li·oph·i·lous \,hēlē'äfələs\ *also* **he·lio·phil·ic** \¦hēlēə¦filik\ *adj* [1*heli-* + *-philous* or *-philic*] **:** attracted by or adapted to sunlight

he·lio·phobe \'hēlēə,fōb\ *n* -s [1*heli-* + *-phobe*] **:** one that is abnormally sensitive to the effect of sunlight

he·li·oph·o·bous \,hēlē'äfəbəs\ *also* **he·lio·pho·bic** \¦hēlēə¦fōbik *also* -fäb-\ *adj* [1*heli-* + *-phobous* or *-phobic*] **:** avoiding the sun **:** shade loving ⟨~ plants⟩

he·li·o·phyl·lite \,hēlēō'fi,līt\ *n* -s [Sw *heliophyllit,* fr. 1*heli-* + *-phyll* + *-it* -ite] **:** a mineral approximately $Pb_6As_2O_7Cl_4$ consisting of oxychloride of lead and arsenic that is apparently dimorphous with ecdemite

he·li·o·phyte \'hēlēə,fīt\ *n* -s [1*heli-* + *-phyte*] **:** a plant thriving in or tolerating full sunlight

1he·li·o·pol·i·tan \¦hēlēə¦pälət°n\ *adj, usu cap* [LL *Heliopolitanus,* fr. L *Heliopolites* Heliopolitan (fr. Gk *Hēliopolitēs,* fr. *Hēliopolis* Heliopolis, ancient city in Lower Egypt) + *-anus* -an] **:** of or relating to ancient Heliopolis, esp. Heliopolis, Egypt

2heliopolitan \"\ *n* -s *cap* [L *Heliopolitanus,* fr. *Heliopolites* + *-anus* -an] **:** a native or inhabitant of the ancient city of Heliopolis

he·li·o·por·i·dae \,hēlēə'pȯrə,dē\ *n pl, cap* [NL, fr. *Heliopora,* type genus (fr. 1*heli-* + *-pora*) + *-idae*] **:** a family of tabulate corals (order Coenothecalia) comprising the blue coral and extinct related forms and having the corallum composed of large zooecia interspersed with more numerous smaller tubes occupied by simple polyps without tentacles or reproductive organs

he·li·op·sis \,hēlē'äpsəs\ *n, cap* [NL, fr. 1*heli-* + *-opsis*] **:** a small genus of American herbs (family Compositae) resembling a sunflower with fertile ray flowers and a conical receptacle

he·li·or·nis \-'ȯrnəs\ *n, cap* [NL, fr. *heli-* + *-ornis*] **:** the type genus of Heliornithidae including a single tropical American sun-grebe (*H. fulica*)

he·li·or·nith·i·dae \-,ȯr'nithə,dē\ *n pl, cap* [NL, fr. *Heliornith-, Heliornis,* type genus + *-idae*] **:** a family of tropical aquatic birds (order Gruiformes) comprising the sun-grebes and having a head and bill like those of a rail, a long body and tail, short legs, and lobed feet

1helios *pl of* HELIO

2he·li·os \'hēlē,äs, -ēəs\ *n* -ES [NL, fr. Gk *hēlios* sun — more at SOLAR] **:** LUMINANCE 2

he·li·o·sis \,hēlē'ōsəs\ *n, pl* **helio·ses** \-ō,sēz\ [NL, fr. LL, exposure to the sun, fr. Gk *hēliōsis,* fr. *hēliousthai* to be exposed to the sun, be sunburned (fr. *hēlios* sun) + *-sis*] **:** SUNSTROKE

he·li·o·stat \'hēlēə,stat\ *n* -s [NL *heliostata,* fr. 1*heli-* + *-stata* (fr. Gk *-statēs* -stat)] **1 :** an instrument consisting of a mirror mounted on an axis moved by clockwork by which a sunbeam is steadily reflected in one direction — compare COELOSTAT **2 :** a geodetic heliotrope — **he·li·o·stat·ic** \¦hēlēə¦stad·ik\ *adj*

he·lio·tactic \¦hēlēō¦taktik\ *adj* [1*heli-* + *-tactic*] **:** of or relating to heliotaxis

he·lio·tax·is \¦hēlēō¦taksəs\ *n* [NL, fr. 1*heli-* + *-taxis*] **:** phototaxis in which sunlight is the stimulus

he·lio·therapy \¦hēlēō+,-\ *n* [1*heli-* + *therapy*] **:** the use of sunlight or of an artificial source of ultraviolet, visible, or infrared radiation for therapeutic purposes

he·li·o·this \,hēlē'ōthəs\ *n, cap* [NL, irreg. fr. Gk *hēliōtis* (n.) dawn, (adj.) of the sun, fr. *hēlios* sun] **:** a genus of medium-sized noctuid moths including several forms having larvae that are destructive pests of cultivated crops — see CORN EARWORM

heliothis moth *n, Austral* **:** CORN EARWORM

he·lio·trope \'hēlēə,trōp, -lyə-, *Brit usu* 'hel-\ *n* -s [L *heliotropium,* fr. Gk *hēliotropion,* fr. *hēlios* sun + *-tropion* (fr. *tropos* turn) — more at SOLAR, TROPE] **1 a** *obs* **:** a plant of which the flower or stem turns toward the sun **b** [NL *Heliotropium*] **:** a plant of the genus *Heliotropium; esp* **:** GARDEN HELIOTROPE 2 **c :** GARDEN HELIOTROPE 1 **2 :** BLOODSTONE 1 **3 :** an instrument used in geodetic surveying for making long-distance observations by means of the sun's rays thrown from a mirror **4 a :** a variable color averaging a moderate purple that is bluer, lighter, and stronger than cobalt violet, manganese violet, or average amethyst, bluer and deeper than average lilac (sense 3a), and redder, stronger, and slightly lighter than mignon **b :** a moderate reddish purple that is redder and duller than bishop's violet **c :** any of various dyes imparting this color **5 :** a perfume imitating the scent of the garden heliotrope (sense 1)

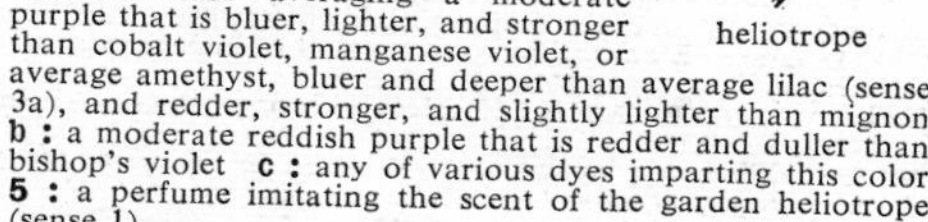

heliotrope

heliotrope gray *n* **:** a pale purple to purplish gray that is redder than plumbago gray

heliotropian *n* -s [modif. of Gk *hēliotropion*] *obs* **:** HELIOTROPE

he·lio·tropic \¦=(=)=¦trōpik, -räp-\ *adj* [ISV 1*heli-* + *-tropic*] **:** characterized by heliotropism ⟨spiders are negatively ~⟩ — **he·lio·tropi·cal·ly** \-pək(ə)lē\ *adv*

he·liotro·pin \,hēlēə,trōpən, ,hēlē'ä·trəp-\ *n* -s [ISV *heliotrop-* (fr. NL *Heliotropium*) + *-in*] **:** PIPERONAL

he·li·ot·ro·pism \,hēlē'ä·trə,pizəm, 'hēlēə,trō,p-\ *n* [ISV 1*heli-* + *-tropism*] **:** phototropism in which sunlight is the orienting stimulus (as in sunflower heads turning with the sun) — compare APHELIOTROPISM

he·li·o·tro·pi·um \,hēlēō'trōpēəm\ *n, cap* [NL, fr. Gk *hēliotropion* heliotrope — more at HELIOTROPE] **:** a genus of herbs and shrubs (family Boraginaceae) having small white or purple fragrant salver-shaped flowers in spikes — see HELIOTROPE 1b

he·lio·type \'hēlēə,tīp\ *n* [1*heli-* + *type*] **:** COLLOTYPE

he·lio·typography \¦hēlē(,)ō+\ *or* **he·lio·typy** \'hēlēə,tīpē\ *n* -ES [*heliotypography* fr. 1*heli-* + *typography; heliotypy* ISV 1*heli-* + *-typy*] **:** the collotype process

he·lio·zoa \,hēlēə'zōə\ *n pl, cap* [NL, fr. 1*heli-* + *-zoa*] **:** an order of Actinopoda consisting of free-living holozoic usu. freshwater protozoans that reproduce by binary fission or budding and comprise the sun animalcules — see ACTINOPHRYS, ACTINOPODA, ACTINOSPHAERIUM — **he·lio·zo·an** \¦hēlēə¦zōən\ *adj or n* — **he·lio·zo·ic** \-ōik\ *adj*

heli·port \'helə *also* 'hēlə+,-\ *n, often attrib* [2*heli-* + *port* (harbor)] **:** a landing and takeoff place for a helicopter (as on the roof of a building in the central area of a city)

he·lip·ter·um \hə'liptərəm\ *n, cap* [NL, fr. 1*heli-* + Gk *pteron* wing — more at FEATHER] **:** a genus of African and Australian herbs (family Compositae) having a plumose pappus and densely silky hairy achenes and grown as an everlasting

heli·so·ma \,helə'sōmə, ,hel-\ *n, cap* [NL, fr. *heli-* (prob. fr. Gk *helix* spiral) + *-soma* — more at HELENIUM] **:** a genus of freshwater snails (family Planorbidae) including intermediate hosts of echinostomes and possibly other flukes of medical or veterinary importance

he·li·um \'hēlēəm\ *n* -s *often attrib* [NL, fr. Gk *hēlios* sun + NL *-ium* — more at SOLAR] **:** a very light colorless inert gaseous element that is the most difficult of all gases to liquefy, that occurs throughout the universe but in economically extractable amounts only in certain natural gases (as in the Texas panhandle and Kansas), and that is used chiefly in inflating airships and balloons, in arc welding and other metallurgical and chemical processes as an inert gaseous shield, and in diluting oxygen for breathing (as by patients with respiratory ailments and by divers) — symbol *He;* see ALPHA PARTICLE; ELEMENT table

helium group *n* **:** the group of elements forming group zero of the periodic table **:** the group of inert gases

helium I \¦===¦wən\ *n* **:** normal liquid helium boiling at 4.2°K under a pressure of 1 atmosphere and capable of existing between the critical point of 5.2°K and 2.26 atmosphere and the lambda point of 2.19°K

helium II \¦===¦tü\ *n* **:** superfluid helium formed from helium I by cooling below the lambda point and characterized by a very low viscosity and very high thermal conductivity

1helix \'hēliks, 'hel-\ *n, pl* **heli·ces** \'helə,sēz, 'hēl-\ *also* **helix·es** \'hēliksəz, 'hel-\ [L, fr. Gk — more at HELENIUM] **1 :** something spiral in form: as **a :** an ornamental volute (as in an Ionic or Corinthian capital) **b :** a coil formed by winding wire around a uniform tube **2 :** the incurved rim of the external ear **3 :** a curve traced on a cylinder by the rotation of a point crossing its right sections at a constant oblique angle **:** a space curve with turns of constant slope from the base and constant distance from the axis **:** the curve described by the thread of a bolt or by a tubular coil spring; *broadly* **:** a three-dimensional curve with one or more turns around an axis (as the space curve described by a conical coil spring)

2helix \"\ *n, cap* [NL, fr. L, something spiral in form, volute] **:** a genus (the type of the family Helicidae) of orig. chiefly Eurasian and African pulmonate land snails having a coiled shell with a low conical spire and a wide reflexed lip and including the chief edible snails (as *H. pomatia*) as well as a number of pests of cultivated plants (as the brown snail)

helix angle *n* **:** the constant angle between the tangent to a helix and a generator of the cylinder upon which the helix lies

helix·in \'hēliksən, 'hel-\ *n* -s [NL *helix* (specific epithet of *Hedera helix*) (fr. L *helix* ivy, volute) + E *-in*] **:** HEDERIN

helix·om·e·ter \,==='sämәd·ə(r)\ *n* [*helix* + *-o-* + *-meter*] **:** a tubular instrument in which an electric light and a prism and lens system enable visual examination of a small-arms bore (as in criminal investigation)

1hell \'hel\ *n* -s *often attrib* [ME, fr. OE; akin to OE *helan* to conceal, OHG *hella* hell, *helan* to conceal, ON *hel* heathen realm of the dead, Goth *halja* hell, L *celare* to hide, conceal, Gk *kalyptein* to cover, conceal, Skt *śaraṇa* screening, protecting; basic meaning: concealing] **1 a :** a place or state of the dead or of the damned: as **(1) :** a place usu. under the ground in which the dead continue to exist **:** NETHERWORLD, HADES, SHEOL ⟨I will slay the last of them with the sword . . . though they dig into ~ —Amos 9:1-2 (AV)⟩ ⟨spake of the resurrection of Christ that his soul was not left in ~ —Acts 2:31 (AV)⟩ — compare LIMBO **(2) :** a netherworld in which the damned must suffer everlasting punishment (as by fire) and malevolent beings live under the rule of the devil — called also *Gehenna;* compare PURGATORY **(3) :** a spiritual state of lasting separation from God or of complete isolation **:** eternal death **b (1) :** a nether domain of the devil and the demons **(2) :** the fallen angels headed by Satan **:** the devil and the demons of hell **:** the powers of evil **c** *Christian Science* **:** ERROR 2b, SIN **2 a :** a place or state of misery, torment, or wickedness ⟨hundreds of gallons of spilled gasoline turn the . . . wreckage into a concentrated ~ of searing flames —H.G. Armstrong⟩ ⟨condemned to go through the ~ of war —F.L. Allen⟩ — used interjectionally to express irritation, irony, incredulity, or surprise ⟨oh ~⟩ ⟨expert, ~! — he's no more an expert than I am⟩; often used as a generalized term of abuse ⟨go to ~⟩ or as a mild oath ⟨to ~ with it⟩ or as an intensive ⟨~ yes⟩; often used with *in* ⟨what in ~ are you doing⟩ or *the* ⟨get the ~ out of here⟩ or *to* ⟨lives way to ~ out in the sticks⟩ ⟨hope to ~ you're right⟩ or *as* ⟨cold as ~⟩ ⟨serious as all ~⟩ ⟨he sure as ~ did it⟩ or in the phrases *hell of a* ⟨in a ~ of a mess⟩ ⟨heard a ~ of a crash⟩ ⟨a good singer and one ~ of an actor⟩ and *hell out of* ⟨scared the ~ out of him⟩ ⟨the big guns smashed ~ out of them⟩ **b :** a place or state of turmoil, disorder, or destruction **:** PANDEMONIUM ⟨all ~ broke loose⟩ **:** HAVOC ⟨raise ~ with the true shape of the facts —John Lardner⟩ ⟨the wind played ~ with the garden⟩ **:** RUIN ⟨said the country was going to ~ in a hack⟩ **c :** a cause of torment, tumult, or havoc; *specif* **:** severe verbal castigation ⟨got ~ from his boss for being late⟩ **d (1) :** unrestrained fun or sportiveness **:** TOMFOOLERY ⟨the children were full of ~ and the house was soon a shambles⟩ **(2) :** the vexations or adventurous satisfaction of an activity — usu. used in the phrase *just for the hell of it* ⟨broke all the windows just for the ~ of it⟩ ⟨hopped a freight just for the ~ of it⟩ **(3) :** the most vexing, pleasing, or notable feature — used with *the* ⟨the ~ of it was that nobody could understand him⟩ ⟨the ~ of the plan is that it works⟩ **3 a** *archaic* **:** a receptacle into which a tailor throws his pieces **b :** HELLBOX **4 :** GAMBLING HOUSE **:** a cheap place of public resort **:** HALL, HOUSE, JOINT ⟨dining . . . in the cheap obscurity of a Soho eating ~ —Aldous Huxley⟩ — **hell and gone :** an extreme or inaccessible distance ⟨no sooner does one build sluice boxes . . . than a freshet occurs and carries them to *hell and gone* —S.E. Morison⟩ — often used for emphasis ⟨he would be the *hell and gone* away from here by now —G.B.Whitlaw⟩ — **hell and high water** *or* **hell or high water :** difficulties of whatever kind or size ⟨will stand by his convictions come *hell or high water*⟩ ⟨led his men through *hell and high water*⟩ — **hell for :** extremely concerned with or insistent on ⟨he was *hell for* efficiency and made life miserable for any man who could not fulfill his duties —H.A.Chippendale⟩ — **hell on :** extremely hard on or destructive to ⟨such a life was *hell on* his digestion and soon brought on an ulcer⟩ — **hell to pay :** the devil to pay ⟨if he's late there'll be *hell to pay*⟩ — **what the hell** — used interjectionally to express carefree indifference or cynical resignation ⟨*what the hell,* I may as well go⟩

2hell \"\ *vi* -ED/-ING/-S **1 :** to behave in a noisy and often dissolute way **:** CAROUSE ⟨Saturday night was their night to ~ a little —H.E.Giles⟩ ⟨come down to the city to ~ around for a weekend —Merle Miller⟩ **2 :** to travel at high speed ⟨a police radio car came *~ing* down between the elevated pillars, siren blasting —Jack Jones b.1923⟩ ⟨with passengers numbering from two to nine, we *~ed* all over the countryside —Bill Mauldin⟩

hellaballoo *var of* HULLABALOO

hel·lad·ic \he'ladik\ *adj, usu cap* [L *Helladicus* Greek, fr. Gk *Helladikos,* fr. *Hellad-, Hellas* Greece + *-ikos* -ic] **:** of or relating to the Bronze Age culture of the Greek mainland lasting from about 2500 to 1100 B.C. — compare AEGEAN, GREEK 1

hel·la·do·the·ri·um \,helədō'thirēəm\ *n, cap* [NL, fr. Gk *Hellad-, Hellas* Greece + NL *-o-* + *-therium*] **:** a genus of extinct Pliocene giraffes of Greece and Asia Minor

hel·land·ite \'helən,dīt\ *n* -s [G *hellandit,* fr. Amund *Helland* †1918 Norw. geologist + G *-it* -ite] **:** a mineral consisting of a silicate of the cerium metals with aluminum, iron, manganese, and calcium

hell·ben·der \'hel,bendə(r)\ *n* **1 a :** a large voracious aquatic salamander (*Cryptobranchus alleganiensis*) that is common in the streams of the Ohio valley and that attains a length of 18 inches **b :** a related species (*C. bishopi*) of the Ozark region **2** *slang* **:** one that is exceedingly reckless or otherwise extreme

1hell–bent \'=¦=\ *adj* **1 :** stubbornly often recklessly determined **:** dead set ⟨they are *hell-bent* to cut taxes again before election —*New Republic*⟩ ⟨*hell-bent* on having his own way⟩ **2 :** moving at a reckless speed **:** going full tilt ⟨wonder if every next turn won't be good-bye after . . . meeting *hell-bent* trucks —Alfred Powers⟩; *broadly* **:** RECKLESS ⟨*hell-bent* adventure⟩ **3 :** moving willfully or speedily on the way to destruction ⟨a *hell-bent* civilization is about to slip its trolley —Christopher Morley⟩

2hell–bent \"\ *also* **hell-bent for election** *adv* **:** in a hell-bent manner **:** at full tilt ⟨the 15 . . . mares raced *hell-bent* for the first turn —G.F.T.Ryall⟩

hell–bind \'=,=\ *n* [1*hell* + *bind* (bine)] **:** DODDER

hell bomb *n, sometimes cap H* **:** HYDROGEN BOMB

hellbox \'=,=\ *n* **:** a receptacle into which a printer throws damaged or discarded type material

hellbroth \'=,=\ *n* **:** a brew for working black magic

hellcat \'=,=\ *n* **1 :** WITCH 1b(2) **2 :** one given to tormenting others; *esp* **:** SHREW

hell–diver \'=,==\ *n* **:** a pied-billed grebe or other rather small grebe

helldog \'=,=\ *n* **:** HELLHOUND

hell driver *n* **:** one that engages in hell driving esp. professionally

hell driving *n* **:** the performance of daredevil stunts with an automobile esp. for the entertainment of spectators

hel·le·bore \'helə,bō(ə)r\ *n* -s [L *helleborus, elleborus,* fr. Gk *helleboros,* perh. fr. *hellos, ellos* fawn + *-boros* (fr. *bibrōskein* to devour); akin to Gk *elaphos* deer — more at ELK, VORACIOUS] **1 a :** a plant of the genus *Helleborus* — see BEAR'S-FOOT 1 **b :** a poisonous herb of the genus *Veratrum* **2 a :** the dried rhizome and root of any medicinal herb of the genus *Helleborus* (as the black hellebores *H. niger* and *H. orientalis* and the green hellebore *H. viridis*) or a powder or extract of this used by the ancient Greeks and Romans in treating mental and other disorders **b :** the dried rhizome and root of a white hellebore (*Veratrum album* or *V. viride*) or a powder or extract of this containing alkaloids (as protoveratrine) used as a cardiac and respiratory depressant and also as an insecticide

hellebore green *n* **:** a moderate olive green that is yellower, lighter, and stronger than forest green (sense 2), cypress, or Lincoln green and greener and stronger than holly green (sense 2)

hellebore red *n* **:** a moderate purplish red that is bluer and darker than average rose, redder and duller than violine pink, and redder and paler than magenta rose

hel·lebo·rine \'helәbə,rīn, he'lebərən\ *n* -s [NL (in older classifications, a genus of orchids), fr. L, a kind of hellebore, fr. Gk *helleborinē,* fr. *helleboros* + *-inē* (fr. fem. of *-inos* -ine)] **:** any of several orchids: as **a :** a plant of the genus *Cephalanthera* (as *C. rubra*) **b :** a plant of the genus *Epipactis* (as *E. helleborine*) **c :** RATTLESNAKE PLANTAIN

hel·le·bo·rus \he'lebərəs\ *n, cap* [NL, fr. L, hellebore — more at HELLEBORE] **:** a genus of Eurasian perennial herbs (family Ranunculaceae) having deeply divided leaves and showy flowers with five petaloid sepals

helled *past of* HELL

hel·lene \'he,lēn\ *n* -s [Gk *Hellēn*] **1** *cap* **:** a Greek of the Hellenic period **2** *cap* **:** a Greek of the modern kingdom of Greece **3** *usu cap* **:** a person marked by intellectual or artistic Hellenism

¹hel·len·ic \he'lenik, -nēk *sometimes* -lēn-\ *adj, usu cap* [Gk *Hellēnikos,* fr. *Hellēn* + *-ikos* -ic] **1 :** GREEK; *specif* **:** of, relating to, or characteristic of Greek history or culture between the first Olympiad in 776 B.C. and the conquests of Alexander ending in 323 B.C. constituting a period of a growing sense of solidarity among the independent city states and of original and influential achievements in politics, art, literature, and philosophy **:** CLASSICAL ⟨the controlled intensity of thought and emotion of the *Hellenic* Athenians was not for the people of Hellenistic times —E.H.Short⟩ **2 :** marked by intellectual or artistic Hellenism ⟨the *Hellenic* temper of modern humanism⟩ — **hel·len·i·cal·ly** \-nək(ə)lē, -nēk-, -li\ *adv, often cap*

²hellenic \"\ *n* -s *usu cap* **:** classical Greek; *esp* **:** GREEK 2a

hel·le·nism \'helə,nizəm\ *n* -s *usu cap* [Gk *Hellēnismos* imitation of things Greek, use of pure Greek language, fr. *hellēnizein* to speak Greek, imitate the Greeks, fr. *Hellēn* + *-izein* -ize] **1 :** GRECISM 1 **2 a :** conformity to or imitation of ancient Greek thought, customs, or styles ⟨the *Hellenism* of some Seleucid Jews with their Greek hats and gymnasium exercises⟩ ⟨*Hellenism* in the art of the classical revival of the 18th century⟩ **b :** devotion to Greece or to Greek culture or ideals ⟨an Attic poet noted for his intense *Hellenism*⟩ **3 :** Greek civilization esp. as modified in the Hellenistic period by oriental influences **4 :** a body of humanistic and classical ideals associated with ancient Greece and including reason, the pursuit of knowledge and the arts, moderation, civic responsibility, and bodily development ⟨a revival of *Hellenism* fostered by some British Victorians⟩ — compare HEBRAISM 2 **5 :** the Greeks as a national or cultural group

¹hel·le·nist \-nəst\ *n* -s *usu cap* [Gk *Hellēnistēs,* fr. *hellēnizein*] **1 :** a person living in Hellenistic times not Greek in ancestry but Greek in language, outlook, and way of life; *esp* **:** a hellenized Jew ⟨the *Hellenists* murmured against the Hebrews because their widows were neglected —Acts 6:1 (RSV)⟩ **2 :** a specialist in the language or culture of ancient Greece

²hellenist \"\ *adj, usu cap* **:** of or relating to Hellenism or Hellenists

hel·le·nis·tic \,helə'nistik, -tēk\ *adj, usu cap* **1 :** of, relating to, or characteristic of the cosmopolitan culture that developed after the conquests of Alexander the Great and passed into Roman culture in about the 2d century A.D., blended Greek and eastern elements (as in art, literature, and philosophy), and used Koine Greek as a common language ⟨the *Hellenistic* belief in the unity of mankind⟩ **2 :** of, relating to, or being the empires of Alexander the Great, the Antigonids, the Seleucids, and the Ptolemies representing an expansion of Greek power and influence eastward as far as India and southward to Egypt during the three centuries between the conquests of Alexander and the eastern conquests of Rome ⟨the *Hellenistic* period⟩ ⟨*Hellenistic* Athens⟩ ⟨the *Hellenistic* monarchies⟩ — compare GREEK 1 **3 :** conforming to or essentially influenced by Hellenistic culture ⟨the Scriptures in Greek for *Hellenistic* Jews⟩ ⟨the conflicting viewpoints of Jewish and *Hellenistic* Christianity⟩ — **hel·le·nis·ti·cal·ly** \-tək(ə)lē, -tēk-, -li\ *adv, often cap*

hel·le·ni·za·tion \,helənə'zāshən, -,nī'z-\ *n* -s *often cap* **1 :** the act or process of hellenizing **2 :** the quality or state of being hellenized

hel·le·nize \'helə,nīz\ *vb* -ED/-ING/-S *often cap* [Gk *hellēnizein,* fr. *Hellēn* Greek + *-izein* -ize] *vi* **:** to become Greek or Hellenistic (as in cultural characteristics or language) ~ *vt* **:** to make Greek or Hellenistic in form or culture ⟨~ Roman sculpture⟩ ⟨~ a people⟩; *specif* **:** to alter (a word or phrase) so as to make conform to the distinctive language characteristics of Greek — **hel·le·niz·er** \-zə(r)\ *n* -s *often cap*

helleno- *comb form, usu cap* [Gk *hellēno-,* fr. *Hellēn* Greek] **1 :** the Greeks ⟨*Hellenocentric*⟩ ⟨*Hellenophile*⟩ **2 :** Greek and ⟨*Helleno*-Italic⟩

¹hel·ler \'helə(r)\ *n, pl* **hellers** *or* **heller** [G, fr. MHG *hallære, haller, heller,* fr. *Hall,* town in Swabia, Germany where they were first minted + MHG *-ære, -er* -er] **1 :** an old small silver coin first issued in Germany in the 13th century, later debased to billon and finally to copper, and spreading to Austria and Switzerland **2 :** an Austrian unit of value 1893-1925 equal to ¹⁄₁₀₀ of the krone; *also* **:** a coin representing this unit last issued in 1916 **3 :** HALER

²hell·er \"\ *n* -s [¹*hell* + *-er*] *chiefly dial* **:** one that is hard to handle; *esp* **:** a person inclined to make trouble ⟨used to be a ~ — drank a lot and threw his weight around till he got in jail —Warren Leslie⟩

hel·leri \'helə,rī, -,rē\ *n* -ES [NL (specific epithet of *Xiphophorus helleri*), after C. Heller, 20th cent. tropical fish collector] **1 :** SWORDTAIL **2 :** any of numerous brightly colored topminnows developed in the aquarium by hybridization between two tropical American fishes (*Xiphophorus helleri* and *Platypoecilus maculatus*)

hel·les·pon·tine \,helə'spänt³n, -än,tīn\ *adj, usu cap* [*Hellespont,* narrow strait between the Gallipoli peninsula in Europe and Turkey in Asia that connects the Sea of Marmara with the Aegean sea (fr. L *Hellespontus,* fr. Gk *Hellēspontos*) + E *-ine*] **:** of or relating to the Hellespont

¹hellfire \'=,=\ *n* [ME, fr. *hell* + *fire*] **1 :** the fire of hell **:** FIRE AND BRIMSTONE ⟨an old-fashioned Calvinist sermon on ~⟩ **2 :** something that torments like the fire of hell (as burning spite or resentment)

²hellfire \"\ *adj* **:** FIRE-AND-BRIMSTONE ⟨a ~ preacher⟩ ⟨preached on a ~ topic⟩

hell–fired \'=,=\ *adj* **:** DAMNED — used as an intensive ⟨is so *hell-fired* fussy⟩

hell·flö·te \'hel,flə(r)də, -lōl\ *n* -s [G, fr. *hell* bright, clear + *flöte* flute] **:** a clear-toned flute organ stop sounding at 8-foot pitch

¹hell–for–leather \'=='=\ *adv* **:** in a hell-for-leather manner **:** at full tilt **:** HELL-BENT ⟨galloped *hell-for-leather* down the trail⟩

²hell–for–leather \"\ *adj* [¹*hell-for-leather*] **:** marked by determined recklessness or great speed or force **:** RIP-ROARING ⟨she swept down the dizzying descent with the verve and *hell-for-leather* dash of a man —*Time*⟩

³hell–for–leather \"\ *n* **:** wild abandon or frantic haste ⟨became surer of his music . . . learned . . . to take it easy when the crowd did not demand *hell-for-leather* —Harold Sinclair⟩

hell·gram·mite *or* **hell·gra·mite** *or* **hel·gra·mite** *or* **hel·gram·mite** \'helgrə,mīt, *usu* -īd.+V\ *n* -s [origin unknown] **:** a long-lived carnivorous aquatic larva of a large North American insect (*Corydalus cornutus*) or of various related insects that is much used as a fish bait by anglers — called also *dobson, toe-biter*

hellhole \'=,=\ *n* **1 :** the pit of hell **2 :** a place of extreme discomfort or squalor **3 :** a place notorious for its wild or immoral activities

hellhound \'=,=\ *n* [ME *hellehound,* fr. OE *hellehund,* fr. *hell* hell + *hund* dog — more at HELL, HOUND] **1 :** a dog represented in mythology (as of ancient Greece and Scandinavia) as standing guard in the underworld **2 :** a fiendishly evil person

¹hel·li·cat \'helə,kat\ *n* [alter. (perh. influenced by E *hellcat*) of Sc *haloked,* fr. *halok* giddy girl + E *-ed*] *Scot* **:** an irresponsible and wild person

²hellicat \"\ *adj, Scot* **:** wild and giddy

hel·lier \'helyə(r)\ *n* -s [ME *helyer,* fr. *helen* to hide, conceal, cover + *-yer, -ier* -er — more at HEAL] *dial Eng* **:** a tiler or slater of roofs

helling *pres part of* HELL

hel·lion \'helyən\ *n* -s [prob. alter. (influenced by ¹*hell*) of *hallion*] **:** a disorderly, troublesome, or mischievous person ⟨the young ~s in my neighborhood are only interested in breaking windows and raising a row —*Camera*⟩ ⟨the difficult and usu. thankless work of teaching and mothering swarms of little ~s —J.A.MacEwen⟩

¹hell·ish \'helish, -lēsh\ *adj* [¹*hell* + *-ish*] **:** of, resembling, or befitting hell **:** causing torment **:** DEVILISH ⟨nothing more ~ than warfare within the soul —Frank Yerby⟩ — **hell·ish·ly** \-ləshlē, -li\ *adv* — **hell·ish·ness** \-lishnəs, -lēsh-\ *n* -ES

²hellish \"\ *adv* **:** in an execrable manner ⟨the child acted ~ all day⟩ — sometimes used as an intensive ⟨a ~ cold day⟩

hellkite \'=,=\ *n* **:** one that shows hellish cruelty

hellmouth \'=,=\ *n, often cap* **:** a property in a medieval mystery or miracle play representing the entrance of hell as the gaping jaws sometimes with moving joints of a monster resembling a whale

¹hel·lo \hə'lō, he'lō, 'he(,)lō, 'he'lō; *when a name follows, as in "Hello Bill", often* (,)=,=; *subject to wide intonational variation*\ *interj* [alter. of *hollo*] — used esp. as a familiar greeting or in answering the telephone or to express surprise

²hello \hə'lō, he'lō, 'he(,)lō\ *vi* -ED/-ING/-S **:** to call or say hello

³hello \"\ *n* -s **:** an expression or gesture of greeting ⟨just dropped in to say ~⟩ ⟨never failed to wave a cheery ~ as he passed⟩

hello girl *n* **:** a female telephone operator

hell on wheels : one noted for hell raising

hell–roaring \'=,==\ *adj* **:** marked by tumultuous violence or carousing

hellroot \'=,=\ *n* **:** SMALL BROOMRAPE

hells *pl of* HELL, *pres 3d sing of* HELL

hell's bells *interj* — used esp. to express impatience or irritation

hell ship *n* **:** a ship characterized by brutal discipline or inhumane living conditions

hell–vine \'=,=\ *n* **:** TRUMPET CREEPER

hell·ward \'helwə(r)d\ *adv* [short for earlier *to hellward,* fr. ME, fr. *to* + *hell* + *-ward*] **:** toward hell

hellweed \'=,=\ *n* **1 :** DODDER **2 :** CORN CROWFOOT **3 :** HEDGE BINDWEED

hell week *n* **:** a period of often rough initiation into a college fraternity

helly *adj, obs* **:** HELLISH

hel·ly's fluid \'helēz-\ *n, usu cap H* [after Konrad *Helly* *b*1875 Swiss pathologist] **:** a fixing fluid consisting of an aqueous solution of mercuric chloride, potassium dichromate, sodium sulfate, and neutral formalin used in microscopy esp. for preservation of the cytoplasm and mitochondria

¹helm \'helm, 'heùm\ *n* -s [ME, fr. OE — more at HELMET] **1 :** HELMET 1; *specif* **:** HEAUME **2** *dial Eng* **a** *or* **helm cloud :** a heavy cloud lying over a mountain top **b** *or* **helm wind :** a gale of wind from the mountains accompanying a helm cloud **3** *dial Brit* **:** a rough shed or shelter for cattle

²helm \"\ *vt* -ED/-ING/-S [ME *helmen,* fr. OE *helmian,* fr. *helm,* n., helmet] **:** to cover or furnish with a helmet

³helm \"\ *n* -s [ME *helme,* fr. OE *helma;* akin to OHG *helmo* tiller, MHG *helm, halm, halme* handle, ON *hjalm* rudder, helm, and prob. to OE *sciell* shell — more at SHELL] **1 a :** a lever or wheel controlling the rudder of a ship for steering **:** the tiller or the wheel of a ship; *broadly* **:** the entire apparatus by which a ship is steered **b :** a position of a tiller attached forward of the rudder or a corresponding position of a wheel ⟨gave the command "up ~"⟩ ⟨with ~ hard aport⟩ — compare RIGHT RUDDER, WEATHER HELM **c :** deviation of the position of the helm from the amidships position ⟨15-degree ~⟩ ⟨sometimes no amount of opposite ~ will straighten the boat —C.D.Lane⟩ **2 :** a position of control or of highest executive power (as in an organization) **:** HEAD

⁴helm \"\ *vt* -ED/-ING/-S **:** to direct with or as if with a helm **:** STEER

hel·met \'helmət, 'heùm-, *usu* -əd.+V\ *n* -s *often attrib* [MF *helmet, heaumet,* dim. of *helme, heaume* helmet, of Gmc origin; akin to OE & OHG *helm* helmet, ON *hjalmr,* Goth *hilms;* akin to OE *helan* to hide, conceal — more at HELL] **1 a :** a covering or enclosing headpiece of ancient or medieval armor — see ARMET, BASINET, MORION, SALLET; ARMOR illustration **b :** a piece of medieval head armor smaller than a heaume and resting on the head **:** CASQUE **c :** a heraldic representation of a helmet depicted above the shield in an achievement and supporting the crest **2 :** any of various protective head coverings usu. made of a hard material (as metal, heavy leather, fiber) to resist impact and supported by bands that prevent direct contact with the head for comfort and ventilation; *specif* **:** one covering the top, back, and sides of the head and often also the neck and having a window for the face and sometimes breathing or radio apparatus (as for a diver) — see CRASH HELMET, WELDER'S HELMET; compare GAS MASK, TOPEE **3 :** a variety of tumbler pigeon having a white ground color and a sharply defined cap and the tail of another color **4 :** something resembling a helmet in form or position: as **a :** a hood-shaped upper sepal or petal of some flowers (as monkshood or snapdragon) **b :** CASQUE 3 **c :** a galea of an insect **5 a :** a close-fitting cap (as of leather or knitted material) covering the top, back, and sides of the head and fastening under the chin — compare BALACLAVA **b :** a woman's small close-fitting brimless hat

helmets 2: *1* football, *2* lacrosse, *3* polo

helmet bird *n* **1 :** TOURACO **2 :** a Madagascan passerine bird (*Aerocharis prevostii*) having a swollen hooked beak and black-and-chestnut plumage

helmet crab *n* **:** KING CRAB 1

hel·met·ed \-məd.əd, -mət\ *adj* **1 :** wearing a helmet **2 :** having a helmet or a helmet-shaped form or structure

helmeted guinea fowl *n* **:** a guinea fowl (*Numida meleagris*) — used esp. of the wild African bird

helmetflower \'==,=\ *n* **:** a plant having flowers with helmet-shaped petals or sepals or a flower of such a plant: as **a :** MONKSHOOD **b :** SKULLCAP **c :** a tropical American orchid of the genus *Coryanthes*

helmetlike \'==,=\ *adj* **:** resembling a helmet in shape

helmet liner *n* **:** a stiff fabric or plastic headgear that fits inside a metal helmet and may be worn without the helmet

helmet orchid *n* **1 :** HELMETFLOWER c **2 :** an Australian orchid (*Pterostylis cucullata*) with a galeate lip

helmetpod \'==,=\ *n* **:** TWINLEAF

helmet quail *n* **:** any of several American partridges (as the valley quail and Gambel quail) constituting a genus (*Lophortyx*) distinguished by a forwardly curving crest

helmets *pl of* HELMET

helmet shell *n* **1 :** a gastropod mollusk of the family Cassididae **2 :** the thick-walled shell of the helmet shell often used for cameos

helmet shrike *n* **:** any of various chiefly tropical Old World passerine birds related to and resembling the shrikes but usu. isolated in a separate family (Prionopidae)

helm·holtz coil \'hel(m,hōlts, 'heù(\ *n, usu cap H* [after Hermann L.F. von *Helmholtz* †1894 Ger. physicist] **:** one of two equal parallel coaxial circular coils in series that are separated from each other by a distance equal to the radius of one coil for producing an approximately uniform magnetic field in the space between the coils

helmholtz double layer *n, usu cap H* [after H.L.F. von *Helmholtz*] **:** ELECTRIC DOUBLE LAYER

helmholtz resonator *n, usu cap H* [after H.L.F. von *Helmholtz*] **:** RESONATOR 1a

helming *pres part of* HELM

hel·minth \'hel,min(t)th, -,mən-\ *n, pl* **helminths** \-n(t)s, -n(t)ths\ [NL *Helminthes*] **:** a parasitic worm (as a roundworm, tapeworm, or leech); *esp* **:** one that parasitizes the intestine of a vertebrate

helminth- *or* **helmintho-** *comb form* [NL, fr. Gk, fr. *helminth-, helmis* intestinal worm, parasitic worm; akin to Gk *eulē* worm, maggot, Toch A *walyi* worms, Gk *eilein* to wind, roll — more at VOLUBLE] **1 :** helminth ⟨*helminth*iasis⟩ ⟨*helmintho*logy⟩ **2 :** shaped like a worm ⟨*helmintho*sporium⟩

hel·min·thes \hel'min(t)thēz, -n,thēz\ *n pl, cap* [NL, fr. Gk *helminth-, helmis*] **:** the parasitic worms — used as though a taxon but without taxonomic implications

hel·min·thi·a·sis \,hel,min'thīəsəs, -,mən-\ *n, pl* **helminthia·ses** \-ə,sēz\ [NL, fr. *helminth-* + *-iasis*] **:** infestation with or disease caused by parasitic worms

hel·min·thic \(')hel¦min(t)thik\ *adj* **:** of or caused by a helminth

hel·min·tho·clad·i·a·ce·ae \hel,min(t)thō,kladē'āsē,ē, -lād-\ *n pl, cap* [NL, fr. *Helminthocladia,* type genus (fr. *helminth-* + Gk *klados* branch + NL *-ia*) + *-aceae* — more at GLADIATOR] **:** a family of red algae (order Nemalionales) having no envelope of vegetative cells formed about the reproductive filaments

hel·min·thoid \hel'min,thȯid; 'helmən-, -,min-\ *adj* [*helminth-* + *-oid*] **:** resembling a helminth **:** WORMLIKE

hel·min·tho·log·i·cal \(;)hel¦min(t)thə¦läjəkəl\ *adj* **:** of or relating to helminthology ⟨~ abstracts⟩

hel·min·thol·o·gist \,helmən'thäləjəst, -,min-\ *n* -s **:** a specialist in helminthology

hel·min·thol·o·gy \-jē\ *n* -ES [*helminth-* + *-logy*] **:** a branch of zoology that is concerned with helminths; *esp* **:** the study of parasitic worms

hel·min·tho·spo·rin \(,)hel,min(t)thə'spōrən\ *n* -s [NL *Helminthosporium* + E *-in*] **:** a dark maroon crystalline phenolic pigment $C_{15}H_{10}O_5$ derived from anthraquinone and formed by the action of certain molds (as *Helminthosporium gramineum*) on sugar

hel·min·tho·spo·ri·um \-rēəm\ *n* [NL, fr. *helminth-* + *-sporium*] **1** *cap* **:** a form genus of saprophytic or parasitic imperfect fungi (family Dematiaceae) having erect conidiophores and elongate, clavate or cylindric, several-septate spores — see BARLEY STRIPE **2** *pl* **helminthospo·ria** \-rēə\ *or* **helminthosporiums :** any fungus of the genus *Helminthosporium* — **hel·min·tho·spo·roid** \(;)=¦==¦spōrȯid\ *adj*

helm·less \'helmləs, 'heùm-\ *adj* **:** lacking a helm

helm port *n* **:** an opening in the counter of a ship for the rudder stock

helm roof *n* [¹*helm*] **:** a 4-faced steeply pitched roof rising to a point from a base of four gables

helm roof

helms *pl of* HELM, *pres 3d sing of* HELM

helms·man \'helmzmən, 'heùm-\ *n, pl* **helms·men :** a man at the helm who steers a ship **:** STEERSMAN

helms·man·ship \-,ship\ *n* **:** the art or practice of steering a ship

¹helo- *comb form* [NL, fr. Gk *helos* — more at HELODES] **:** marsh **:** bog ⟨*helo*bious⟩ ⟨*helo*phyte⟩

²helo- *comb form* [NL, fr. Gk *hēlo-,* fr. *hēlos;* perh. akin to L *vallus* stake, palisade — more at WALL] **:** nail ⟨*Helo*derma⟩ ⟨*Helo*tium⟩

he·lo·bi·ae \he'lōbē,ē\ *syn of* NAIADALES

he·lo·bi·ous \-bēəs\ *adj* [¹*helo-* + *-bious* (fr. NL *-bius* having a — specified — mode of life) — more at -BIUS] **:** living in marshy places

helo·der·ma \,helō'dərmə, ,hel-\ *n, cap* [NL, fr. ²*helo-* + *-derma*] **:** the type genus of the family Helodermatidae comprising the American gila monsters

he·lo·der·mat·i·dae \,==(,)dər'mad.ə,dē\ *n pl, cap* [NL, fr. *Helodermat-, Heloderma,* type genus + *-idae*] **:** a small family of lizards having the dorsal scales replaced by rough tuberculated skin and including the American gila monsters and an obscure Bornean lizard

he·lo·des \he'lō(,)dēz\ *adj* [Gk *helōdēs,* fr. *helos* marsh; akin to Skt *saras* pond] **:** MARSHY

hel·o·dri·lus \,helō'drīləs\ *n, cap* [NL, fr. ¹*helo-* + Gk *drilos* worm] **:** a common No. American genus of earthworms (family Lumbricidae) found in rich soil or manure

he·lo·ni·as \hə'lōnēəs\ *n* [NL, irreg. fr. ¹*helo-* + *-ia*] **1** *cap* **:** a genus of bog herbs (family Melanthaceae) of the northeastern U.S. with basal leaves and purple racemose perfect flowers on a tall scape — see SWAMP PINK **2** -ES **:** the dried rhizome and roots of a blazing star (*Chamaelirium luteum*) formerly used as a vermifuge

hel·o·pel·tis \,helō'peltəs\ *n* [NL, fr. ¹*helo-* + *-peltis* (fr. Gk *peltē* shield)] **1** *cap* **:** a genus of tropical mirid bugs including several that attack economically important plants **2** -ES **:** any bug of the genus *Helopeltis; specif* **:** TEA MOSQUITO

hel·o·phyte \'helə,fīt\ *n* -s [¹*helo-* + *-phyte*] **:** a bog plant; *esp* **:** a perennial marsh plant having its overwintering buds under water — compare HYDROPHYTE

hel·ot \'helət\ *n* -s [L *Helotes,* pl., fr. Gk *Heilōtes*] **1** *usu cap* **:** a member of the lowest social and economic class of ancient Sparta thought to represent the conquered original population and constituting a body of serfs who were attached to the land, could not be sold, could be freed only by the state, were obliged to pay fixed portions of produce to the ruling Spartiates, and were required to serve in the armed forces — compare PERIOECI 2 **2 :** a member of any group of people deprived of rights and privileges and often exploited **:** SERF

he·lo·ti·a·les \hə,lōshē'ā(,)lēz, -ōd.ē-\ *n pl, cap* [NL, fr. *Helotium* + *-ales*] **:** an order of fungi (subclass Euascomycetes) that are characterized by inoperculate asci borne in a disk-shaped to goblet-shaped sessile or stalked apothecium which may be brilliantly colored or dark and dull and that include numerous saprophytes and a few parasites of economically important plants — compare PEZIZALES

hel·ot·ism \'helad.,izəm\ *n* -s **1 :** the quality or state of being a helot **:** SERFDOM **2 :** a symbiotic relation of plants or animals in which one functions as the slave of the other (as of that between certain species of ants) — compare COMMENSALISM, PARASITISM, SYMBIOSIS

he·lo·ti·um \hə'lōshēəm, -ōd.ē-\ *n, cap* [NL, fr. LGk *hēlōtos* nail-shaped (fr. Gk *hēlos* nail) + NL *-ium*] **:** a genus (the type of the family Helotiaceae) comprising fungi that have inoperculate asci arranged in a hymenial layer in a cup-shaped apothecium with a colored rim of elongate thin-walled hyphae

hel·ot·ry \'helətrē\ *n* -ES **1 :** the helots of a country or of an estate **2 :** the condition of a helot **:** SLAVERY, SERFDOM ⟨permanent white supremacy and permanent black ~ —Basil Davidson⟩

¹help \'help, 'heùp, *chiefly in southern U S* 'hep\ *vb* **helped** \-pt\ *or now chiefly dial* **holp** \'hō(l)p\ *or* **holped** \-pt\ **helped** *or now chiefly dial* **holp** *or* **holped** *or* **hol·pen** \'hō(l)pən\ **helping; helps** [ME *helpen,* fr. OE *helpan;* akin to OHG *helfan* to help, ON *hjalpa,* Goth *hilpan,* Lith *šelpti*] *vt* **1 a :** to give assistance or support to **:** AID ⟨agreed to ~ him with his biography —Ruth P. Randall⟩ ⟨from the beginning she had ~*ed* and abetted him —Stuart Cloete⟩ — often used interjectionally ⟨*Help!* I'm drowning⟩ **b :** to assist in attaining ⟨good pitching ~*ed* the team to the American league championship⟩ **2 a :** REMEDY, CURE, RELIEVE ⟨bright curtains ~ a drab room⟩ ⟨aspirin ~*s* a headache⟩ ⟨humor often ~*s* a tense situation⟩ **b** *archaic* **:** to rescue from harm or misfortune **:** SAVE ⟨~ beer that beginneth to sour —Hugh Plat⟩ ⟨~ us from famine —Alfred Tennyson⟩ **c :** to get (oneself) out of a difficulty **:** EXTRICATE ⟨sometimes I fought when I couldn't ~ myself —John Reed⟩ **3 a :** to be of use to **:** BENEFIT ⟨a good speech should either amuse or ~ an audience⟩ ⟨one-way sailing was ~*ed* by monsoons —Anne Dorrance⟩ **b :** to further the advancement of **:** PROMOTE ⟨this dispute certainly did not ~ the negotiations —Theodore Hsi-En Chen⟩ ⟨~*ing* industrial development with two loans —Paul Bareau⟩ **4 a :** to change for the better **:** MEND ⟨people get used to what they can't ~ quicker than they think they're going to —Mary Austin⟩ **b :** to keep oneself from **:** refrain from **:** AVOID ⟨neither of us could ~ laughing —Oscar Wilde⟩ ⟨couldn't ~ seeing it was stuffed with newspaper clippings —James Hilton⟩ **c :** to keep from occurring **:** PREVENT ⟨scolded him for something he couldn't ~⟩ **d :** to be kept from **:** fail in ⟨the campaign against industrial accidents cannot ~ producing results —F.D.Roosevelt⟩ **5 a :** to dispense esp. at a meal **:** SERVE ⟨a loop of gold thread hung down from her sleeve as she ~*ed* the soup —Virginia Woolf⟩ **b :** to serve with food or drink esp. at a meal — often used with *to* ⟨~*ed* his neighbor to the wine⟩ ⟨~*ing* himself . . . to a slice of beef —T.L.Peacock⟩ **6 :** to appropriate for the use of (oneself) ⟨the company had ~*ed* itself to a generous supply of bicycles —P.W.Thompson⟩ **~** *vi* **:** to give aid or support **:** be of use **:** ASSIST ⟨to ~ rather than to blame —A.C.Benson⟩ ⟨every little bit ~*s*⟩ — often used with a following infinitive ⟨this principle may at least ~ to explain —A.O.Wolfers⟩

syn AID, ASSIST: these three verbs are virtually interchangeable in meaning to furnish another person or thing with what is needed to fill an insufficiency or what is needed for the attainment of an end. HELP implies more frequently than the others, however, an advance toward an end ⟨only money could *help* her through the worst of her ordeal —Marcia Davenport⟩ ⟨*help* a team to win a game⟩ ⟨will *help* to combat inflation⟩ ⟨*help* a wounded soldier back to camp⟩ AID often suggests the need of help or relief, often stressing weakness or insufficiency in the one aided and strength in the one aiding ⟨his undergraduate work . . . was *aided* by tuition grants —*Current Biog.*⟩ ⟨a wide variety of literature . . . that will broaden their horizons and *aid* them to sound, democratic decisions —C.M. Wieting⟩ ⟨to *aid* families in distress⟩ ASSIST usu. stresses the secondary role of the one assisting or the subordinate character of the assistance ⟨to *assist* visitors in finding places in hotels and auto courts —*Amer. Guide Series: Nev.*⟩ ⟨the president . . . is *assisted* by an 11-man cabinet —*Americana Annual*⟩ **syn** see in addition IMPROVE

— **cannot help but :** cannot but — **so help me :** on my word of honor **:** believe it or not ⟨dressed, *so help me*, in pink and purple tights⟩

2**help** \"\ *n* -s [ME, fr. OE; akin to OHG *helfa, hilfa* help, ON *hjalp* help, OE *helpan* to help] **1 a :** an act or instance of giving aid or support **:** ASSISTANCE ⟨offered his ~ in unloading the baggage⟩ ⟨generous to all who needed ~⟩ ⟨making . . . decisions with the ~ of all significant facts —*College & Univ. Business*⟩ ⟨always tried to be of ~⟩ **b :** the strength or resources employed in giving assistance ⟨the ~ comprised food, clothing, and medicine —J.A.McVann⟩ **2 a :** a useful adjunct **:** source of aid ⟨printed ~*s* to the memory —C.S.Braden⟩ ⟨the singer is a ~ but he is not essential —Deems Taylor⟩ **b :** DEALER HELP **3 :** a possibility of preventing or curing **:** REMEDY ⟨a situation for which there was no ~⟩ **4 a :** one who is in the pay or service of another: (1) **:** ASSISTANT, ALLY ⟨I could get you three or four rupees a month as my ~ —Attia S. Hosain⟩ ⟨now if the ~ of Norfolk and myself . . . will but amount to five-and-twenty thousand —Shak.⟩ (2) *or pl* **help :** a domestic worker or farmhand ⟨I've . . . scrubbed the bathroom floor when the ~ has quit —Ethel Merman⟩ ⟨hired ~ sat at table with the rest of the family —Sherwood Anderson⟩ ⟨the two extra ~*s* we always get in for the birthday —Ngaio Marsh⟩ (3) *pl* **help :** an office or factory worker **:** EMPLOYEE ⟨ran an ad in the ~ wanted column⟩ ⟨one of the ~ in . . . government agencies —*Antioch Rev.*⟩ **b :** the services of a paid worker ⟨they were without ~ again and she had all the work to do —Hamilton Basso⟩ **5 :** HELPING

help·able \-pəbəl\ *adj* **:** capable of being helped

helped *past of* HELP

help·er \-pə(r)\ *n* -s [ME, fr. *helpen* + *-er*] **1 :** one that helps ⟨the most idiomatic class of verbs are the ~*s* —Frederick Bodmer⟩; *specif* **:** an extra locomotive to assist a train (as on a grade) **2 :** HELP 4a; *specif* **:** a relatively unskilled worker who assists another esp. by manual labor ⟨first a ~ and then a journeyman —Walter Bernstein⟩ **3** *usu cap, Islam* **:** a member of the ansar — compare COMPANION 4c

help·ful \-pfəl\ *adj* [ME, fr. *help* + *-ful*] **1 :** of service or assistance **:** USEFUL, SALUTARY ⟨certain ideas are not only agreeable to think about . . . but they are also ~ in life's practical struggles —William James⟩ ⟨to the stomach it is pleasant, wholesome, and ~ —E.J.Banfield⟩ **2 :** CONSTRUCTIVE, ENCOURAGING ⟨a price control picture that is ~ —T.W.Arnold⟩ — **help·ful·ly** \-fəlē, -li\ *adv*

help·ful·ness \-fəlnəs\ *n* -ES **:** the quality or state of being helpful ⟨the . . . ~ of reference books —C.B.Shaw⟩

1**helping** *n* -s [ME, fr. *helpen* to help + *-ing*] **1** *archaic* **:** an act or instance of giving aid **:** HELP ⟨the law of all true ~ —R.C. Trench⟩ **2 a :** a portion of food **:** SERVING ⟨sent his plate back for a second ~⟩ **b :** something compared to a serving of food **:** PORTION ⟨only bona fide settlers . . . deserved ~*s* from the public domain —Dixon Wecter⟩

2**helping** *adj* [ME, fr. pres. part. of *helpen*] **1 :** giving aid or support **2 :** AUXILIARY ⟨~ verbs⟩ — **help·ing·ly** *adv*

helping card *n* **:** a queen or jack led in whist in an effort to promote the value of a card in a partner's hand

helping hand *n* **1 :** AID, ASSISTANCE ⟨always ready to lend a *helping hand*⟩ **2 :** a bridge hand containing some strength (as a queen or king) in each of at least three suits but with no biddable suit of its own and with too little strength for a no-trump bid

help·less \-pləs\ *adj* [ME *helples*, fr. *help* + *-les* -less] **1 :** lacking protection or support **:** DEFENSELESS ⟨as ~ as a flock of shepherdless sheep —W.H.Mallock⟩ **2 :** lacking in effectiveness **:** FUTILE ⟨a ~ medley of indecisions —Hugh Walpole⟩ **3 a :** lacking in strength or vigor **:** incapable of action **:** POWERLESS ⟨fell ill and lay ~ at the mouth of the river —Francis Parkman⟩ ⟨the government . . . drifted ~ in the conflicting currents —Charles & Mary Beard⟩ **b :** lacking power to resist **:** INVOLUNTARY ⟨the tiny spill of pebbles in ~ fall —Richard Llewellyn⟩ **4 :** lacking in comprehension **:** BEWILDERED ⟨blinked at the candle in a ~ way, like a young barn owl —Mary Webb⟩

help·less·ly *adv* **:** in a helpless manner

help·less·ness *n* -ES **:** the quality or state of being helpless

help·mate \-p,māt, *usu* -ād·+V\ *n* [by folk etymology (influence of *mate*) fr. *helpmeet*] **:** one serving as a companion, partner, or assistant; *specif* **:** WIFE ⟨proved a good and faithful ~, assisted me much by attending the shop —Benjamin Franklin⟩

helpmeet \'=,=\ *n* [2*help* + *meet*, adj. (fitting) in *I will make an help meet for him* (Gen 2:18 AV)] **:** HELPMATE ⟨testify that their ~*s* retain that feminine tenderness and loyalty . . . no longer found in my own household —*Atlantic*⟩ ⟨chemistry . . . is the farmer's ~ —*Crops in Peace & War*⟩

help out *vi* **:** to render assistance **:** be of use ⟨won a scholarship which would *help out* —MacKinlay Kantor⟩ **~** *vt* **:** to give aid to ⟨agreed to *help* him *out*⟩

helps *pres 3d sing of* HELP, *pl of* HELP

hel–shoes \'hel,=\ *n pl, usu cap H* [part trans. of ON *helskōr*, fr. *hel* heathen realm of the dead + *skōr* shoes — more at HELL] *Norse mythol* **:** shoes placed on the dead before burial to aid them on the rough road to Hel

hel·sing·fors \'helsiŋ,fȯrz, -sēŋ-, -ȯ(ə)z\ *adj, usu cap* [fr. *Helsingfors* (Helsinki), Finland] **:** HELSINKI

hel·sin·ki \'hel,siŋkē, -ki, ='==\ *adj, usu cap* [fr. *Helsinki*, Finland] **:** of or from Helsinki, the capital of Finland **:** of the kind or style prevalent in Helsinki

1**hel·ter–skel·ter** \¦heltə(r)¦skeltə(r)\ *adv* [imit.] **1 :** in headlong disorder **:** PELL-MELL ⟨ran *helter-skelter*, getting in each other's way —F.V.W.Mason⟩ **2 :** in random order **:** HAPHAZARDLY ⟨magazines stacked *helter-skelter* on tables —T.H. White b. 1915⟩

2**helter–skelter** \"\ *n* -s **1 :** a disorderly confusion **:** TURMOIL ⟨the horses set off in a wild *helter-skelter* —J.M.Synge⟩ ⟨*helter-skelter* of conflict, emotion, and group activity —John Gould⟩ **2 :** an external spiral slide around a tower in an amusement park

3**helter–skelter** \"\ *adj* **1 :** confused and hurried **:** PRECIPITATE ⟨most companies are plagued with *helter-skelter* disorder when that five o'clock whistle blows —*Modern Industry*⟩ **2 a :** HIT-OR-MISS **:** HAPHAZARD ⟨shocked at the *helter-skelter* arrangement of the papers, all mussed and frayed —Jean Stafford⟩ ⟨the *helter-skelter* nondirectional nature of the discussion —John Withall⟩ **b :** FLIGHTY, SCATTERBRAINED ⟨*helter-skelter* attitude of the younger generation —Erle Stanley Gardner⟩

1**helve** \'helv, 'heu̇v\ *n* -s [ME, fr. OE *hielfe;* akin to OHG *halb* handle, OE *healf* half — more at HALF] **1 :** a handle of a tool or weapon (as an ax) **:** HAFT **2 :** a lever in a helve hammer that has the hammerhead at its end

2**helve** \"\ *vt* -ED/-ING/-S [ME *helven*, fr. *helve*, n.] **:** to furnish or fit with a helve

helve hammer *n* **:** a power hammer consisting essentially of a heavy head at one end of a lever lifted by power and dropping by its own weight on work that rests on an anvil — compare STRAP HAMMER, TRIP-HAMMER

hel·vel·la \hel'velə\ *n* [NL, fr. L, a small potherb, fr. *helvus* light-bay-colored + *-ella* (dim. suffix) — more at YELLOW] **1** *cap* **:** a genus (the type of the family Helvellaceae) comprising ascomycetous fungi with the ascocarps stalked, pileate, or saddle-shaped and often thrown into folds **2** -s **:** any fungus of the genus *Helvella* — **hel·vel·lic** \(')=¦velik\ *adj*

hel·vel·la·ce·ae \,helvə'lāsē,ē\ *n pl, cap* [NL, fr. *Helvella*, type genus + *-aceae*] **:** a family of fungi (order Pezizales) that includes various important edible fungi (as the morels) — see HELVELLA — **hel·vel·la·ceous** \¦==¦lāshəs\ *adj*

hel·vel·la·les \-'lā(,)lēz\ *n pl, cap* [NL, fr. *Helvella* + *-ales*] *in some classifications* **:** an order of fungi including the Helvellaceae and Geoglossaceae

hel·ve·tia blue \(')hel¦vēsh(ē)ə-\ *n, often cap H* [NL *Helvetia* Switzerland] **:** NAPOLEON BLUE

1**hel·ve·tian** \-shən\ *adj, usu cap* [NL *Helvetia* land of the Helvetii, Switzerland (fr. L *Helvetii*, ancient people of Switzerland + *-ia* -y) + E *-an*] **:** of or relating to the Helvetii or Helvetia **:** SWISS

2**helvetian** \"\ *n* -s *cap* **:** a native or inhabitant of Switzerland **:** SWISS; *specif* **:** a member of the ancient Helvetii

1**hel·vet·ic** \(')hel¦ved·ik\ *adj, usu cap* [L *Helveticus* of the Helvetii, fr. *Helvetii* + *-icus* -ic] **:** HELVETIAN

2**helvetic** \"\ *n* -s *usu cap* **:** a Swiss Protestant **:** a follower of Zwingli

hel·ve·tii \hel'vēshē,ī\ *n pl, usu cap* [L] **:** an early Celtic people of western Switzerland in the time of Julius Caesar

hel·vid·i·an \(')hel¦vidēən\ *adj, usu cap* [*Helvidius* *fl*A.D.380 Roman heretic + E *-an*] **:** of or relating to the teachings of the Roman layman Helvidius who held that Mary bore children after Jesus

hel·vite \'hel,vīt\ *also* **hel·vin** \-,vən\ *or* **hel·vine** \", -,vēn\ *n* -s [*helvite* alter. (influenced by *-ite*) of *helvin; helvin, helvine* fr. G *helvin*, fr. L *helvus* light-bay-colored + G *-in* — more at YELLOW] **:** a silicate mineral $(Mn,Fe,Zn)_8Be_6O_{24}S_2$ consisting of sulfide of manganese and beryllium and usu. containing also iron and zinc that is isomorphous with danalite and genthelvite

hel·volic acid \hel'vä\|lik-, -vō\|\ *n* [ISV *helvol-* (fr. L *helvolus, helveolus* pale yellow, fr. *helvus* light-bay-colored) + *-ic*] **:** FUMIGACIN

helxi·ne \helk'sīnē, -l'zī-\ *n, cap* [NL, fr. Gk *helxinē* pellitory, bindweed, fr. *helkein* to drag, pull — more at SULCUS] **:** a genus of plants (family Urticaceae) native to Corsica and Sardinia and cultivated elsewhere as pot plants with small leaves and tiny solitary flowers that form dense mossy mats — see BABY'S TEARS

hel·zel \'helzəl\ *n* -s [Yiddish, dim. of *hals* neck, fr. OHG — more at COLLAR] **:** a skin of the neck of poultry stuffed usu. with fat and flour

1**hem** \'hem\ *pron* [ME, fr. OE *him, heom*, dat. of *hīe* they — more at HE] **1** *dial* **:** THEM **2** *obs* **:** THEMSELVES

2**hem** \"\ *n* -s [ME *hem, hemm*, fr. OE; akin to ON *hemja* to hem in, restrain, OFris *hemma* to hinder, MHG *hemmen* to hem in, restrain, *hamen* to hem in, restrain, Arm *kamel* to press, squeeze, Russ *kom* lump, ball] **1 a :** a finished edge of a cloth article (as a skirt, sleeve, curtain, napkin, stocking) made by rolling or folding back an edge and stitching it down **b :** an edge usu. folded back and fastened down on articles of sheet metal, plastic, rubber, leather **2 a :** BORDER ⟨bright green ~ of reeds about the ponds —R.M.Lockley⟩ **b :** EDGE ⟨~ of the sea —Shak.⟩ ⟨the polar ~ —Emily Dickinson⟩ **3 :** the raised rim of a volute of an Ionic capital

3**hem** \"\ *vb* **hemmed; hemmed; hemming; hems** [ME *hemmen*, fr. *hem, hemm*, n.] *vt* **1 a :** to finish with a plain or decorative hem ⟨*hemmed* just above the ankle —*Women's Wear Daily*⟩ **b :** BORDER, EDGE **2 :** to enclose or confine with or as if with a ring around or arc before usu. preventing or hindering access, free activity, growth, or escape — usu. used with *in* ⟨body of water, *hemmed* in on all sides by evergreen forests —*Amer. Guide Series: N. H.*⟩ ⟨the regiment now found itself *hemmed* in by its own mine fields —P.W.Thompson⟩ **~** *vi* **:** to make hems in sewing **syn** see SURROUND

4**hem** \"; *as an interjection a throat-clearing sound*\ *n* -s [imit.] **:** a vocalized pause in speaking ⟨after clearing the husk in his throat with two or three ~*s* —T.L.Peacock⟩ **:** an instance of uttering this sound ⟨would use a peculiar rap at the door, and give four loud ~*s* —Oliver Goldsmith⟩ — often used interjectionally to call attention, to warn, or to express hesitation or doubt; compare 3HUM

5**hem** \'hem\ *vi* **hemmed; hemmed; hemming; hems :** to utter the sound represented by *hem* ⟨*hemmed* ominously as he always did when he was about to relieve his mind —W.A. White⟩ — often used with *haw* ⟨~ and haw and put it off, apparently in the hope that things will pick up —Clifford Aucoin⟩ ⟨*hemmed* and hawed, and then pointed out that the trouble was obviously connected with our consignment —F.W. Crofts⟩

6**hem** \"\ *archaic and dial var of* HIM

7**hem** \"\ *dial Eng var of* HAME

8**hem** \"\ *var of* HEME

hem- *or* **hemo-** *or* **hemi-** *or* **haem-** *or* **haemo-** *comb form* [MF *hemo-*, fr. L *haem-, haemo-*, fr. Gk *haim-, haimo-*, fr. *haima;* perh. akin to ON *seimr* honeycomb, OHG *seim* virgin honey, W *hufen* cream] **:** blood ⟨*hem*arthrosis⟩ ⟨*hem*agglutination⟩ ⟨*hemo*cyte⟩ — the forms *haem-* or *haemo-* are preferred in taxonomic names ⟨*Haema*canthus⟩ ⟨*Haemo*gregarina⟩

hema- *or* **haema-** *comb form* [NL, fr. Gk *haima* blood] **:** HEM- ⟨*hema*cytometer⟩ ⟨*hema*poiesis⟩ — *haema-* preferred in taxonomic names in biology ⟨*Haema*stoma⟩

hem·a·chate \'hemə,kāt\ *n* -s [L *haemachates*, fr. (assumed) Gk *haimachatēs*, fr. Gk *haima* blood + *achatēs* agate — more at AGATE] **:** a light-colored agate like bloodstone with red jasper spots

he·ma·cy·tom·e·ter \,hēmə(,)sī'tämәd·ə(r), ,hem-\ *n* [*hema-* + *cyt-* + *-meter*] **:** an instrument for counting blood cells

he·ma·cy·to·zo·on \-mə,sīd·ə'zō,än\ *n* [NL, fr. *hema-* + *cyt-* + *-zoon*] **:** HEMOCYTOZOON

he·mad \'hē,mad\ *adv* [*hem-* + 2*-ad*] **:** toward the hemal side

he·ma·dynamometer \¦hēmə, ¦hemə+\ *n* [*hema-* + *dynamometer*] **:** a device for measuring blood pressure

he·ma·fi·brite \,hēmə'fī,brīt, ,hem-\ *n* -s [ISV *hema-* + *fibr-* + *-ite*] **:** a mineral $Mn_3(AsO_4)(OH)_3.H_2O$ consisting of basic manganese arsenate

he·mag·glut·i·nate \,hēmə'glüd·ə,nāt, ,hem-\ *vt* [*hem-* + *agglutinate*] **:** to cause hemagglutination of

he·mag·glu·ti·na·tion \,==,=='nāshən\ *n* [ISV *hem-* + *agglutination*] **:** agglutination of red blood cells

he·mag·glu·ti·nin \,=='glüd·ənən\ *or* **he·mo·agglutinin** \¦hē(,)mō, ¦he(,)mō+\ *n* [ISV *hem-* + *agglutinin*] **:** an agglutinin that causes hemagglutination

he·mal \'hēməl\ *adj* [*hem-* + *-al*] **1 :** of or relating to the blood or blood vessels **2 :** situated on or belonging to the side of the spinal cord where the heart and chief blood vessels are placed **:** VENTRAL — used of vertebrate parts or organs

hemal arch *n* **:** a bony or cartilaginous arch extending ventrally from the spinal column: **a :** the arch formed by a vertebra and an associated pair of ribs **b** (1) **:** an arch on the ventral surface of each caudal vertebra of a lower vertebrate (as a fish or reptile) usu. considered to consist of the extended and ventrally fused parapophyses of the vertebra (2) **:** such an arch together with its dependent hemal spine forming a V-shaped or Y-shaped ventral prolongation of a caudal vertebra — called also *chevron bone*

he·mal·bu·men \,hēmal'byümən, ,hem-\ *n* [ISV *hem-* + *albumen*] **:** a preparation of blood containing iron albuminate and used in chlorosis and anemia

hemal node *or* **hemal gland** *n* **:** HEMOLYMPH GLAND

he·ma·moe·ba \,hēmə'mēbə, ,hem-\ *n* [NL, fr. *hem-* + *amoeba*] **1 :** an organism like an amoeba living in the blood; *esp* **:** MALARIA PARASITE **2 :** LEUKOCYTE

he–man \'=,=\ *n, pl* **he–men :** an obviously strong virile man ⟨the great open spaces, where red-blooded *he-men* still roam —H.L.Mencken⟩ ⟨peppy, poker-playing, sales-hustling *he-men* who are our most characteristic Americans —Sinclair Lewis⟩ ⟨the tough, assured, half-humorous *he-man* who can take his women or leave them alone —Arthur Knight⟩

he·man·gi·ec·ta·sis \hē¦manjē+\ *n* -ES [NL, fr. *hem-* + *angi-* + *ectasis*] **:** dilatation of blood vessels

he·man·gi·o·endothelioma \hē¦manjē(,)ō+\ *n* [NL, fr. *hemangio-* (fr. *hemangioma*) + *endothelioma*] **:** an often malignant tumor originating by proliferation of capillary endothelium

he·man·gi·oma \hē,manjē'ōmə\ *n, pl* **hemangiomas** *also* **hemangio·ma·ta** \-məd·ə\ [NL, fr. *hem-* + *angioma*] **:** a usu. benign tumor made up of blood vessels and typically occurring as a purplish or reddish slightly elevated area of skin overlying a network of intercommunicating capillaries — see PORT-WINE STAIN, STRAWBERRY MARK

he·man·gi·o·ma·to·sis \=,==,ōmə'tōsəs\ *n, pl* **hemangiomato·ses** \-ō,sēz\ [NL, fr. *hemangiomat-, hemangioma* + *-osis*] **:** a condition in which hemangiomas are present in several parts of the body

he·man·gi·o·sarcoma \hē¦manjē(,)ō+\ *n* [NL, fr. *hemangio-* (fr. *hemangioma*) + *sarcoma*] **:** a malignant hemangioma

he·ma·po·di·um \,hēmə'pōdēəm, ,hem-\ *or* **he·ma·pod** \'hēmə,päd, 'hem-\ *n, pl* **hemapodia** *also* **hemapodiums** *or* **hemapods** [*hemapodium*, NL, fr. *hema-* + *-podium; hemapod* fr. *hema-* + *-pod;* fr. its proximity to the dorsal blood vessel] **:** the dorsal lobe of a parapodium

he·map·o·dous \hē'mapədəs\ *adj* [*hema-* + *-podous*] **:** of or relating to a hemapodium **:** having hemapodia

he·ma·poi·e·sis \,hēmə(,)pȯi'ēsəs, ,hem-\ *n* [NL, fr. *hema-* + *-poiesis*] **:** HEMATOPOIESIS

he·mar·thro·sis \,hēmär'thrōsəs, ,hem-\ *n* [NL, fr. *hem-* + *arthrosis*] **:** hemorrhage into a joint

hemat- *or* **hemato-** *or* **haemat-** *or* **haemato-** *comb form* [L *haemat-, haemato-*, fr. Gk *haimat-, haimato-*, fr. *haimat-, haima* blood — more at HEM-] **:** HEM- ⟨*hemat*oid⟩ ⟨*hemato*crit⟩ — the forms *haemat-* or *haemato-* are preferred in taxonomic names ⟨*Haemato*zoon⟩ ⟨*Haemato*gaster⟩

he·ma·tal \'hēməd·əl, 'hem-\ *adj* [*hemat-* + *-al*] **:** relating to the blood or blood vessels

he·ma·te·in \,hēmə'tēən, ,hem-\ *n* -s [ISV *hemat-* + *-ein*] **:** a reddish brown crystalline phenolic quinonoid compound $C_{16}H_{12}O_6$ constituting the essential dye in logwood extracts — see HEMATOXYLIN

he·ma·tem·e·sis \-'teməsəs\ *n* -ES [NL, fr. *hemat-* + Gk *emesis* vomiting — more at EMESIS] **:** the vomiting of blood

he·ma·te·met·ic \¦hēməd·ə¦med·ik, ¦hem-\ *adj* [fr. NL *hematemesis*, after NL *emesis:* E *emetic*] **:** of or relating to hematemesis

he·ma·therm \'hēmə,thərm, 'hem-\ *n* -s [NL *Hematherma* (pl.), fr. *hema-* + *-therma* (fr. Gk *therma*, neut. pl. of *thermos* warm, hot) — more at WARM] **:** HOMOIOTHERM

he·ma·ther·mal \¦==¦thərməl\ *or* **he·ma·ther·mous** \-məs\ *adj* [*hematherm* + *-al* or *-ous*] **:** HOMOIOTHERMIC

1**he·mat·ic** \hē'mad·\|ik, -at\|, \|ēk\ *adj* [Gk *haimatikos*, fr. *haimat-* hemat- + *-ikos* -ic] **1 :** of or relating to blood **2 :** containing blood ⟨a ~ cyst⟩ **3 :** involving or affecting the blood ⟨a ~ crisis⟩ **4 :** having the color of blood **:** SANGUINEOUS

2**hematic** \"\ *n* -s **:** HEMATINIC

he·ma·tid \'hēməd·əd, 'hem-\ *n* -s [*hemat-* + *-id*] **:** a mature nonnucleated red blood cell

he·ma·ti·dro·sis \,hēməd·ə'drōsəs, ,hem-\ *n* -ES [NL, fr. *hemat-* + *-idrosis*] **:** the excretion through the skin of blood or blood pigments

hem·a·tin \'hemәd·ən, 'hēm-\ *n* -s [ISV *hemat-* + *-in*] **1** *or* **hem·a·tine** \-ə,tēn, -əd·ən\ **:** HEMATEIN ⟨~ extract crystals⟩ — used esp. of preparations for use in dyeing; see DYE table I (under *Natural Black 1*) **2 a :** a compound derived from oxidized heme and usu. obtained in aqueous alkaline solutions or as a brownish black or bluish black solid $C_{34}H_{32}N_4O_4FeOH$ by treatment of hemin chloride with alkali; ferriprotoporphyrin hydroxide **b :** any of several similar compounds regarded as formed by the breakdown of hemoglobin esp. in some pathological conditions **c :** any of various similar iron-porphyrin derivatives or closely related pyrrole derivatives — compare HEME 2

1**hem·a·tin·ic** \¦hemə¦tinik, ¦hēm-\ *n* -s [*hematin* + *-ic*] **:** an agent that tends to stimulate blood-cell formation or to increase the hemoglobin in the blood

2**hematinic** \"\ *adj* **:** functioning as a hematinic ⟨the ~ value of certain iron salts⟩

hem·a·tin·om·e·ter \,hemәd·ə'nämәd·ə(r), ,hēm-\ *n* [ISV *hematin* + *-o-* + *-meter*] **:** HEMOGLOBINOMETER — **hem·a·tin·o·met·ric** \¦==d·ənō¦me·trik\ *adj*

hem·a·tite \'hemə,tīt, 'hēm-\ *n* -s [L *haematites*, fr. Gk *haimatitēs* resembling blood, fr. *haimat-, haima* blood — more at HEM-] **:** a mineral Fe_2O_3 consisting of ferric oxide and constituting an important iron ore that occurs in splendent metallic-looking rhombohedral crystals, in massive forms, and in red earthy forms (hardness of crystals 5.5–6.5, sp. gr. of crystals about 5.20) — called also *specular iron;* see LIMONITE, RED OCHER

hematite red *n* **:** a dark to dark grayish red

hem·a·tit·ic \¦==¦tid·ik\ *adj* **:** of, containing, relating to, or resembling hematite in substance and color

he·ma·to·bic \¦==¦tōbik\ *or* **he·ma·to·bi·ous** \-bēəs\ *adj* [NL *hematobium* + E *-ic* or *-ous*] **:** living in blood **:** parasitic in blood

he·ma·to·bi·um \,hēmə'tōbēəm, ,hem-\ *n, pl* **hemato·bia** \-bēə\ [NL, fr. *hemat-* + *-bium* (fr. Gk *bios* mode of life) — more at QUICK] **:** an organism living in blood

hem·a·to·blast \'hemәd·ō,blast, 'hēm-\ *n* [ISV *hemat-* + *-blast*] **1 :** BLOOD PLATELET **2 :** an immature blood cell; *esp* **:** an immature red blood cell — **hem·a·to·blas·tic** \¦===¦blastik\ *adj*

hem·a·to·cele \'===,sēl\ *n* -s [ISV *hemat-* + *-cele*] **:** a blood-filled cavity of the body; *also* **:** the effusion of blood into a body cavity (as the scrotum)

hem·a·to·chrome \ ,krōm\ *n* [*hemat-* + *-chrome*] **:** an orange or reddish coloring matter found in various algae (as red snow)

hem·a·to·col·pos \,hemәd·ō'käl,päs, ,hēm-, -lpəs\ *or* **hem·a·to·col·pus** \-lpəs\ *n* -ES [NL, fr. *hemat-* + *-colpos* or *-colpus*] **:** an accumulation of blood within the vagina

he·mat·o·crit \hi'mad·əkrət, -,krit\ *n* -s [ISV *hemat-* + *-crit* (fr. Gk *kritēs* judge) — more at CRITERION] **1 :** an instrument for determining the relative amounts of plasma and corpuscles in blood usu. by means of centrifugation **2** *or* **hematocrit value :** a percentile ratio of volume of packed red blood cells to volume of whole blood centrifuged by a hematocrit

hem·a·to·cryal \,hemәd·ō¦krīəl, ,hēm-\ *adj* [*hemat-* + *cry-* + *-al*] **:** COLD-BLOODED

hem·a·to·cyte \'===,sīt\ *n* -s [*hemat-* + *-cyte*] **:** HEMOCYTE

hem·a·tog·e·nous \¦hemə¦täjənəs, ¦hēm-\ *adj* [*hemat-* + *-genous*] **1 :** concerned with the production of blood or of one or more of its constituents ⟨~ functions of the liver⟩ **2 a :** taking place by way of the blood ⟨~ metastasis of a tumor⟩ **b :** spread by way of the blood stream ⟨~ focal infection⟩ ⟨~ tuberculosis⟩

hem·a·to·gone \ˈhemədəˌgōn, ˈhēm-\ *or* **hem·a·to·go·nia** \ˌ==ˈgōnēə\ *n* -s [NL *hematogonia*, fr. *hemat-* + *-gonia* (fr. Gk *gonē* generation, offspring, seed) — more at GONE (germ cell)] : HEMOCYTOBLAST

he·ma·toid \ˈhēməˌtȯid, ˈhem-\ *adj* [Gk *haimatoeidēs*, fr. *haimat-* hemat- + *-eidēs* -oid] : resembling blood

he·ma·toi·din \ˌ==ˈtȯidᵊn\ *n* -s [ISV *hematoid* + *-in*] : BILIRUBIN

hem·a·to·lite \ˈhemədᵊˌlīt, ˈhēm-\ *n* -s [ISV *hemat-* + *-lite;* fr. its color; orig. formed as Sw or G *aimatolit*] : a mineral $(Mn,Mg)_4Al(AsO_4)(OH)_8$ consisting of a brownish red aluminum manganese arsenate in rhombohedral crystals (sp.gr. 3.3–3.4)

hem·a·to·log·ic \ˌhemədᵊˈläjik, ˌhēm-\ *or* **hem·a·to·log·i·cal** \-jəkəl\ *adj* : of, relating to, or involving blood

he·ma·tol·o·gist \ˌhēməˈtäləjəst, ˌhem-\ *n* -s : one that specializes in the study of the blood

he·ma·tol·o·gy \-jē\ *n* -ES [*hemat-* + *-logy*] : a branch of biology that deals with the blood and blood-forming organs

he·ma·tol·y·sis \-ˈtäləsəs\ *n* [NL, fr. *hemat-* + *-lysis*] : HEMOLYSIS — **hem·a·to·lyt·ic** \ˌhemədᵊlˈidik, ˌhēm-\ *adj*

he·ma·to·ma \ˌhēməˈtōmə, ˌhem-\ *n, pl* **hematomas** \-ōməz\ *also* **hematomata** \-ōmədə\ [NL, fr. *hemat-* + *-oma*] : a tumor or swelling containing blood

he·ma·tom·e·ter \-ˈtämədə(r)\ *n* [ISV *hemat-* + *-meter*] : HEMACYTOMETER

hem·a·to·metra \ˌhemədᵊˈmētrə, ˌhēm-\ *n* -s [NL, fr. *hemat-* + *-metra*] : an accumulation of blood or menstrual fluid in the uterus

hem·a·to·my·e·lia \-dᵊˌmīˈēlēə\ *n* -s [NL, fr. *hemat-* + *-myelia*] : a hemorrhage into the spinal cord

hem·a·to·pericardium \ˈhemədᵊ, ˈhēm-+\ *n* [NL, fr. *hemat-* + *pericardium*] : HEMOPERICARDIUM

hem·a·to·peritoneum \"+\ *n* [NL, fr. *hemat-* + *peritoneum*] : HEMOPERITONEUM

hem·a·toph·a·gous \ˌhēməˈtäfəgəs, ˌhem-\ *adj* [ISV *hemat-* + *-phagous*] : feeding on blood ⟨~ insects⟩ ⟨~ vampire bats⟩

he·ma·toph·a·nite \ˌ==ˈtäfəˌnīt\ *n* -s [ISV *hemat-* + *phan-* (prob. fr. Gk *phanos* light, bright) + *-ite;* orig. formed as G *hämatophanit*] : a mineral $Pb_5Fe_4O_{10}(Cl,OH)_2$ consisting of oxychloride lead and iron

hem·a·to·phyte \ˈhemədᵊˌfīt, ˈhēm-\ *n* -s [*hemat-* + *-phyte*] : a plant parasite (as a bacterium) of the blood

hem·a·to·plast \-ˌplast\ *n* -s [*hemat-* + *-plast*] : HEMATOBLAST

hem·a·to·poi·e·sis \ˌhemədᵊ(ˌ)pȯiˈēsəs, ˌhēm-\ *n* -ES [NL, fr. *hemat-* + *-poiesis*] : formation of blood or of blood cells within the living body

hem·a·to·poi·et·ic system \ˈ===(ˌ)=ˈed·ik-\ *n* [ISV *hemat-* + *-poietic*] : an organic system of the body consisting of the blood and the structures that function in its production

hem·a·to·porphyrin \ˈhemədᵊ, ˈhēm-+\ *n* [ISV *hemat-* + *porphyrin*] : any of several isomeric porphyrins $C_{20}H_6N_4$-$(CH_3)_4(CHOHCH_3)_2(CH_2CH_2COOH)_2$ that are hydrated derivatives of protoporphyrins; *esp* : the deep red crystalline pigment obtained by treating hematin or heme with acid

hem·a·to·por·phy·ri·nu·ria \ˌhemədᵊˌpȯrfərəˈn(y)u̇rēə, ˌhēm-\ *n* -s [NL, fr. ISV *hematoporphyrin* + NL *-uria*] : PORPHYRINURIA

hem·a·tor·rha·chis \ˌheməˈtȯrəkəs, ˌhēm-\ *n* -ES [NL, fr. *hemat-* + *-rrhachis*] : hemorrhage into the spinal canal

hem·a·to·salpinx \ˈhemədᵊ, ˈhēm-+\ *n* [NL, fr. *hemat-* + *salpinx*] : accumulation of blood in a fallopian tube

hem·a·to·scope \ˈhemədᵊˌskōp, ˈhēm-\ *n* [ISV *hemat-* + *-scope*] : an instrument for the spectroscopic examination of blood

hem·a·to·thermal \ˈhemədᵊ, ˈhēm-+\ *adj* [*hemat-* + *thermal*] : WARM-BLOODED

he·ma·tox·y·lin \ˌhēməˈtäksələn, ˌhem-\ *n* -s [ISV *hematoxyl-* (fr. NL *Haematoxylon*, genus of plants, fr. *haemat-* hemat- + *-xylon*) + *-in*] : a colorless to yellowish crystalline phenolic compound $C_{16}H_{14}O_6$ found in logwood and used chiefly as a biological stain because of its ready oxidation to hematein; hydroxy-brazilin

hem·a·to·zoal \ˈhemədᵊˈzōəl, ˈhēm-\ *adj* : of or relating to hematozoa; *also* : blood-dwelling

hem·a·to·zoan \ˌ===ˈzōən\ *n* -s [*hematozoon* + *-an*] : HEMATOZOON

hem·a·to·zo·on \-ōˌän\ *n, pl* **hemato·zoa** \-ōə\ [NL, fr. *hemat-* + *-zoon*] : a blood-dwelling animal parasite

he·ma·tu·ria \ˌhēməˈtu̇rēə, -əˈtyu̇-, ˌhem-\ *n* -s [NL, fr *hemat-* + *-uria*] : the presence of blood or blood cells in the urine — compare HEMOGLOBINURIA

he·mau·to·graph \hēˈmȯdəˌgraf, heˈ-\ *n* [*hem-* + *auto-* + *-graph*] : a curve that is obtained when a stream of blood from an artery strikes against a piece of moving paper and that is indicative of the variations in blood pressure — **he·mau·to·graph·ic** \=ˌ==ˈgrafik\ *adj* — **he·mau·tog·ra·phy** \ˌhēmȯˈtägrəfē, ˌhem-\ *n* -ES

heme \ˈhēm\ *also* **hem** \ˈhem\ *or* **haem** \ˈhēm, ˈhem\ *n* -s [ISV, fr. *hematin*] **1** : a deep red iron-containing pigment $C_{34}H_{32}N_4O_4Fe$ that is obtained from hemoglobin by treatment with acid to remove the globin, that is a ferrous derivative of protoporphyrin, and that readily oxidizes to hematin or hemin — called also *ferroprotoporphyrin, protoheme, reduced hematin* **2** : any of several compounds that are derived from protoporphyrin and iron in either the ferrous or ferric state and that constitute the nonprotein groups of some hemoproteins — compare HEMATIN 2c, HEMIN 2

hem·el·y·tral \heˈmelətrəl\ *adj* : of or relating to a hemelytron or to hemelytra

hem·el·y·tron \-əˌträn\ *also* **hem·el·y·trum** \-ətrəm\ *n, pl* **hemely·tra** \-ətrə\ [NL, fr. *hem-* (fr. *hemi-*) + *elytron* or *elytrum*] **1** : one of the basally thickened anterior wings of various insects (as of Hemiptera) **2** : one of the elytra of a chaetopod worm

hem·en \ˈhemən\ *pron* [ME, alter. of *hem* — more at HEM (them)] *now dial Brit* : THEM — compare ¹HEM

hem·era \ˈhemərə\ *n, pl* **hemerae** \-ə(ˌ)rē\ *also* **hemera** [NL, fr. Gk *hēmera* day; akin to Gk *ēmar* day, Arm *aur*] **1** : a stratigraphic zone comprising the time range of a particular fossil species **2** : a period of time during which a race of organisms is at the apex of its evolution

hem·er·a·lope \-rəˌlōp\ *n* -s [F *héméralope*, fr. Gk *hēmeralōp-, hēmeralōps*] : one affected with hemeralopia

hem·er·a·lo·pia \ˌ===ˈlōpēə\ *n* -s [NL, fr. Gk *hēmeralōp-, hēmeralōps* (fr. *hēmera* day + *alaos* blind + *ōp-, ōps* eye) + NL *-ia*] **1** : a defect of vision characterized by reduced visual capacity in bright lights — called also *day blindness* **2** : NYCTALOPIA — **hem·er·a·lopic** \ˌ===ˈläpik\ *adj*

hem·er·o·baptist \ˈhemərō+\ *n* [ML *Hemerobaptista*, fr. Gk *Hēmerobaptistēs*, fr. *hēmero-* (fr. *hēmera* day) + *baptistēs* baptizer — more at BAPTIST] *usu cap* : one who practices daily or frequent baptism or ceremonial ablution; *specif* : a member of an ancient Jewish sect

¹**hem·er·o·bi·id** \ˈhemərōˈbīəd\ *adj* [NL *Hemerobiidae*, family of flies, fr. *Hemerobius*, type genus + *-idae*] : of or relating to the genus *Hemerobius* or the family Hemerobiidae

²**hemerobiid** \"\ *n* -s : a hemerobiid fly

hem·er·o·bi·us \ˌheməˈrōbēəs\ *n, cap* [NL, fr. Gk *hēmerobios* living for a day, fr. *hēmero-* + *-bios* (fr. *bios* mode of life) — more at QUICK] : a genus (the type of the family Hemerobiidae) of small usu. dark-colored lacewings with wings mottled with smoky brown — compare APHIS LION

hem·er·o·cal·lis \ˌhemərōˈkaləs\ *n, cap* [NL, fr. Gk *hēmerokallēs*, a kind of lily, fr. *hēmero-* (fr. *hēmera* day) + *-kallēs* (fr. *kallos* beauty); fr. the fact that the blossoms close at night — more at CALLI-] : a genus of Eurasian herbs of the family Liliaceae with fibrous fleshy roots, basal linear leaves, and showy flowers in small clusters on leafless stems

he·me·ryth·rin \ˌhēməˈrithrən, ˌhem-\ *n* -s [*hem-* + *erythr-* + *-in*] : an iron-containing respiratory pigment in the blood of various invertebrates

¹**hemi-** *in pronunciations below*, ˈ==ˈhemē *or (usu not before vowels)* ˈhemə *sometimes* ˈheˌmī\ *prefix* [ME, fr. L, fr. Gk *hēmi-* — more at SEMI-] **1** : half of; *esp* : a lateral half of ⟨*hemi*centrum⟩ ⟨*hemi*cerebrum⟩ ⟨*hemi*cardia⟩ **2** : relating to or affecting a half (as a lateral half) of an organ or part or of the whole body ⟨*hemi*plegia⟩ ⟨*hemi*atrophy⟩ **3** *chem* **a** : half in respect to combining ratio ⟨*hemi*basic⟩ **b** : having one half of the molecular weight of a (specified) compound or class of compounds **c** : having one half the number of characteristic groups in a (specified) compound or class of compounds ⟨*hemi*cyanine⟩ **4** *crystallog* : having one half the number of faces ⟨*hemi*hedron⟩

²**hemi-** — see HEM-

-he·mia \ˈhēmēə, *esp Brit* ˈhēmyə\ — see -EMIA

hemi·acetal \ˈ== *at* HEMI-+\ *n* [¹*hemi-* + *acetal*] : any of a class of compounds characterized by the grouping >C(OH)-(OR) and usu. formed as intermediate products in the preparation of acetals from aldehydes or ketones ⟨an aldose is a favorable compound for the study of ~s —C.D.Hurd⟩ — see GLYCOSIDE, MONOSACCHARIDE

hemi·anatropous \"+\ *adj* [¹*hemi-* + *anatropous*] : AMPHITROPOUS

hemi·anesthesia \"+\ *n* [NL, fr. ¹*hemi-* + *anesthesia*] : loss of sensation in either lateral half of the body

hemi·a·nop·sia \ˌ==+əˈnäpsēə\ *also* **hem·i·a·no·pia** \-ˈnōpēə\ *n* -s [NL, fr. ¹*hemi-* + *an-* ²*a-* + *-opsia* or *-opia*] : blindness in one half of the visual field and affecting one or both eyes

hemi·a·nop·tic \ˈ===ˈnäptik\ *adj* [NL *hemianop*sia + E *optic*] : of or relating to hemianopsia

hemi·ascomycetes \ˈ== *at* HEMI-+\ *n pl, cap* [NL, fr. ¹*hemi-* + *Ascomycetes*] : a subclass of Ascomycetes comprising simple ascomycetous fungi that lack an ascocarp and have asci arising directly from the fertile ascogonium and each containing an indefinite number of spores — see ENDOMYCETALES, TAPHRINALES; compare PROTOASCOMYCETES

hemi·as·co·my·cet·i·dae \"+ˌa(ˌ)skōˌmīˈsedəˌdē\ *syn of* HEMIASCOMYCETES

hemi·atrophy \"+\ *n* -ES [NL *hemiatrophia*, fr. ¹*hemi-* + LL *atrophia* atrophy — more at ATROPHY] : atrophy of one half of an organ or part or of the whole body ⟨facial ~⟩ — opposed to *hemihypertrophy*

hemi·auxin \"+\ *n* [¹*hemi* + *auxin*] : an auxin precursor

hemi·azygous vein \"+ . . . -\ *n* [NL *hemiazygos*, fr. ¹*hemi-* + *azygos*] : the left azygous vein passing up on the left side, crossing ventral to the vertebral column, and joining the right azygous vein

hemi·ballism *also* **hemi·ballismus** \"+\ *n, pl* **hemiballisms** *also* **hemiballismuses** [NL *hemiballismus*, fr. ¹*hemi-* + *ballismus*] : violent uncontrollable movements of one lateral half of the body usu. due to hemorrhage in the opposite side of the brain

hemi·ba·sid·i·ae \ˌ==+bəˈsidēˌē\ [NL, fr. ¹*hemi-* + *-basidiae* (fr. *basidium*)] *syn of* HEMIBASIDII

hemi·ba·sid·i·a·les \ˌ===ˌsidēˈā(ˌ)lēz\ [NL, fr. *hemibasidium* + *-ales*] *syn of* USTILAGINALES

hemi·ba·sid·ii \ˌ===ˈsidēˌī\ *n pl, cap* [NL, fr. ¹*hemi-* + *-basidii* (fr. *basidium*)] *in some classifications* : a subclass of Basidiomycetes comprising fungi with the basidium produced from a resting spore and including the order Ustilaginales or this together with the Uredinales — compare EUBASIDII, HETEROBASIDIOMYCETES

hemi·basidiomycetes \ˈ== *at* HEMI-+\ [NL, fr. *hemi-* + *Basidiomycetes*] *syn of* HEMIBASIDII

hemi·basidium \"+\ *n* [NL, fr. ¹*hemi-* + *basidium*] : the transversely septate promycelium of a smut fungus — compare AUTOBASIDIUM, PROTOBASIDIUM

hemi·benthic *also* **hemi·benthonic** \"+\ *adj* [¹*hemi-* + *benthic* or *benthonic*] : having a planktonic stage or phase ⟨~ animals⟩

hemi·branch \ˈ==+ˌbraŋk\ *n* **1** [NL *Hemibranchii*] : one of the Hemibranchii **2** [¹*hemi-* + *-branch*] : a gill having lamellae or filaments only on one side; *collectively* : the lamellae or filaments on one side of a gill

hemi·branchiate \ˈ== *at* HEMI-+\ *adj* [¹*hemi-* + *branchiate*] **1** : having an incomplete or reduced branchial apparatus **2** : of or relating to the Hemibranchii

hemi·bran·chii \ˌ==+ˈbraŋkēˌī\ *n pl, cap* [NL, fr. ¹*hemi-* + *-branchii* (fr. L *branchia* gill) — more at BRANCHIA] *in some classifications* : a suborder of Thoracostei comprising fishes with an incomplete or reduced branchial apparatus and usu. including the sticklebacks, cornetfishes, bellows fishes, and shrimpfishes

he·mic \ˈhēmik, ˈhem-, -mēk\ *adj* [*hem-* + *-ic*] : of or relating to blood

hemi·car·dia \ˈ== *at* HEMI-+ˈkärdēə\ *n* -s [NL, fr. ¹*hemi-* + Gk *kardia* heart — more at HEART] : a lateral half of a 4=chambered heart

hemi·cellulose \ˈ==+\ *n* [ISV ¹*hemi-* + *cellulose*] : any of various polysaccharides that accompany cellulose and lignin in the skeletal substances of wood and green plants and that resemble cellulose in being insoluble in water and hydrolyzable to simple sugar units by acids but differ from it in being soluble in alkali and presumably of smaller molecular dimensions, in undergoing acid hydrolysis more easily, and in giving rise on hydrolysis not only to glucose but also to uronic acids, xylose, galactose, and other carbohydrates — compare CELLULOSAN, PENTOSAN, POLYURONIDE — **hemi·cellulosic** \"+\ *adj*

hemi·centrum \"+\ *n* [NL, fr. ¹*hemi-* + *centrum*] : a lateral half of the centrum of a vertebra

hemi·ceph·a·lous \"+ˈsefələs\ *or* **hemi·ce·phal·ic** \"+səˈfalik\ *adj* [¹*hemi-* + *-cephalous* or *-cephalic*] : having a poorly differentiated but distinct head — used of the larvae of various flies; compare EUCEPHALOUS

hemi·cerebrum \"+\ *n* [NL, fr. ¹*hemi-* + *cerebrum*] : a lateral half of the cerebrum : CEREBRAL HEMISPHERE

hemi·chorda \"+\ [NL, fr. ¹*hemi-* + *chorda* (notochord)] *syn of* HEMICHORDATA

hemi·chordata \"+\ *n pl, cap* [NL, fr. ¹*hemi-* + *chordata*] : a division of Chordata usu. considered both subphylum and class, including the Enteropneusta and Pterobranchia and in some classifications the Phoronidea, and comprising a group of vermiform marine animals that have in the proboscis an outgrowth of the pharyngeal wall which suggests and is probably homologous with the notochord of higher chordates — **hemi·chordate** \"+\ *n or adj*

hemi·cra·nia \ˌ==ˈkrānēə\ *n* -s [LL — more at MIGRAINE] : pain in one side of the head — opposed to *amphicrania*

hemi·cryptophyte \ˈ== *at* HEMI-+\ *n* [ISV ¹*hemi-* + *cryptophyte*] : a perennial plant having its overwintering buds located at the soil surface — **hemi·cryptophytic** \"+\ *adj*

hemi·crystalline \"+\ *adj* [ISV ¹*hemi* + *crystalline*] : partly crystalline : characterized by crystals embedded in an amorphous groundmass

he·mic·tic \hēˈmiktik\ *adj* [fr. NL *hemixis*, after such pairs as NL *apomixis*: E *apomictic*] : of or relating to hemixis

hemi·cy·cle \ˈ== *at* HEMI- + ˌsīkəl\ *n* [F *hémicycle*, modif. of L *hemicyclium*, fr. Gk *hēmikyklion*, fr. *hēmi-* ¹hemi- + *kyklos* circle + *-ion* -ium — more at CYCLE] **1** : a half circle : SEMICIRCLE **2** : a curved or approximately semicircular structure or arrangement (as in an arena) : a curving or semicircular form (as of a driveway) ⟨a simple ~ containing the altar —W.K.Sturges⟩ ⟨the ~ of our modern civilization, the horseshoe area where nomadic man first settled down to tend crops —*Nat'l Geographic*⟩

hemi·cyclic \"+\ *adj* [¹*hemi-* + *cyclic*] : having floral leaves partly in whorls and partly in spirals ⟨~ flowers⟩

hemi·dactylous \"+\ *adj* [NL *Hemidactylus* + E *-ous*] : of or relating to the genus *Hemidactylus*

hemi·dactylus \"+\ *n, cap* [NL, fr. ¹*hemi-* + *dactylus*] : a widely distributed genus of geckos having the digits dilated and provided with two rows of lamellae on the underside

hemi·demisemiquaver \"+\ *n* [¹*hemi-* + *demisemiquaver*] : SIXTY-FOURTH NOTE

hemi·dome \ˈ==+ˌdōm\ *n* [ISV ¹*hemi-* + *dome*] **1** : a pinacoid parallel to the orthoaxis and cutting the vertical axes and clinoaxes in a crystal **2** : a dome that has only two like faces (as an orthodome of a monoclinic crystal)

hemi·dystrophy \ˈ== *at* HEMI- +\ *n* [¹*hemi-* + *dystrophy*] : an unequal development of the two lateral halves of the body

hemi·elytral \"+\ *adj* [NL *hemielytron* + E *-al*] : HEMELYTRAL

hemi·elytron *also* **hemi·elytrum** \"+\ *n* [NL, fr. ¹*hemi-* + *elytron* or *elytrum*] : HEMELYTRON

hem·i·ep·es \ˌ==+ˈe(ˌ)pēz\ *n, pl* **hemiepe** [LL, fr. LGk *hēmiepes*, fr. Gk *hēmi-* ¹hemi- + *-epes* (neut. of *-epēs*, fr. *epos* verse, line, word) — more at VOICE] : a dactylic tripody having a spondaic third foot or lacking the two short syllables of the third foot

hemi·facial \ˈ== *at* HEMI- +\ *adj* [¹*hemi-* + *facial*] : involving or affecting one lateral half of the face ⟨~ spasm⟩

hemi·form \ˈ==+ˌ-\ *n* [¹*hemi-* + *form*] : a rust in which only the uredinial and telial stages are known

he·mig·a·lus \heˈmigələs\ *n, cap* [NL, fr. ¹*hemi-* + *-galus* (fr. Gk *galē* weasel) — more at GALEA] : a genus of East Indian civets comprising the banded palm civets (as *H. hardwickii*)

hemi·globin \ˈ== *at* HEMI- +\ *n* [*hem-* + *globin*] : METHEMOGLOBIN

hemi·glyph \ˈ==+ˌ-\ *n* [¹*hemi-* + *glyph*] : the half channel or groove on each edge of a triglyph

hemi·he·dral \ˌ==+ˈhēdrəl\ *or* **hemi·he·dric** \-rik\ *adj* [¹*hemi-* + *-hedron* + *-al* or *-ic*] **1** *of a crystal* : having half the faces required by complete symmetry — compare HOLOHEDRAL **2** : having the symmetry appropriate to a hemihedral form — **hemi·he·dral·ly** \-rəlē\ *adv*

hemi·he·drism \ˌ==+ˈhēˌdrizəm\ *also* **hemi·he·dry** \-ˈhēdrē\ *n, pl* **hemihedrisms** *also* **hemihedries** [¹*hemi-* + *-hedron* + *-ism* or *-y*] : the property of crystallizing hemihedrally

hemi·he·dron \-ˈhēdrən\ *n, pl* **hemihedrons** *or* **hemihedra** [NL, fr. ¹*hemi-* + *-hedron*] : a hemihedral form or crystal

hemi·holohedral \ˈ== *at* HEMI- +\ *adj* [¹*hemi-* + *holohedral*] *of a crystal* : having a hemihedral form in which half the octants have the full number of planes ⟨~ tetrahedron ⟨~ sphenoid⟩

hemi·hydrate \"+\ *n* [¹*hemi-* + *hydrate*] : a hydrate containing half a molecule of water to one of the compound forming the hydrate — compare PLASTER OF PARIS — **hemi·hydrated** \"+\ *adj*

hemi·hypertrophy \"+\ *n* [NL *hemihypertrophia*, fr. ¹*hemi-* + *hypertrophia* hypertrophy — more at HYPERTROPHY] : hypertrophy of one half of an organ or part or of the whole body ⟨facial ~⟩ — opposed to *hemiatrophy*

hemi·karyon \"+\ *n* [ISV ¹*hemi-* + *karyon;* orig. formed in G] : a cell nucleus containing the haploid number of chromosomes — opposed to *amphikaryon* — **hemi·kar·y·ot·ic** \"+ˌkarēˈäd·ik\ *adj*

hemi·lateral \"+\ *adj* [ISV ¹*hemi-* + *lateral*] : of or affecting one lateral half of the body

hemi·leia \ˌ==+ˈlīə\ *n, cap* [NL, fr. ¹*hemi-* + *-leia* (fr. Gk *leios* smooth, flat); fr. the shape of the spores — more at LIME] : a genus of rusts (order Uredinales) producing both urediospores and teliospores from a compound spore-bearing stalk

hemi·mel·li·tene \-ˈmeləˌtēn\ *n* -s [ISV ¹*hemi-* + *mellite* + *-ene*] : a liquid hydrocarbon $C_6H_3(CH_3)_3$ obtained from coal tar and petroleum; 1,2,3-trimethylbenzene

hemi·mellitic acid \ˈ== *at* HEMI- + . . . -\ *n* [ISV ¹*hemi-* + *mellitic*] : a crystalline acid $C_6H_3(COOH)_3$ derived from benzene and having half as many carboxyl groups as mellitic acid; 1,2,3-benzene-tricarboxylic acid

hem·im·er·id \heˈmimərəd\ *n* -s [NL *Hemimeridae*, family of insects, fr. *Hemimerus*, type genus + *-idae*] : an insect of the genus *Hemimerus*

hem·im·er·oi·dea \heˌmiməˈrȯidēə\ [NL, fr. *Hemimerus* + *-oidea*] *syn of* DIPLOGLOSSATA

hem·im·er·us \heˈmimərəs\ *n, cap* [NL, fr. ¹*hemi-* + *-merus* (fr. Gk *meros* part) — more at MERIT] : a genus (coextensive with the family Hemimeridae and the order or suborder Diploglossata) comprising small wingless viviparous African insects parasitic on rodents

hemi·metabola \ˈ== *at* HEMI- +\ *n pl, cap* [NL, fr. ¹*hemi-* + *Metabola*] : insects characterized by hemimetabolism

hemi·metabolism *also* **hemi·metabole** *or* **hemi·metaboly** \"+\ *n* [¹*hemi-* + *metabolism* or *metabole* or *metaboly*] : incomplete metamorphosis; *esp* : incomplete metamorphosis in various insects with aquatic larvae in which the young does not resemble the adult

hemi·metabolous *also* **hemi·metabolic** \"+\ *adj* **1** [¹*hemi-* + *metabolous* or *metabolic*] : of or relating to hemimetabolism **2** [NL *Hemimetabola* + E *-ous* or *-ic*] : of or relating to the Hemimetabola

hemi·metamorphic *or* **hemi·metamorphous** \"+\ *adj* [¹*hemi-* + *metamorphic* or *metamorphous*] : of, relating to, or being marked by hemimetamorphosis

hemi·metamorphosis \"+\ *n, pl* **hemimetamorphoses** [NL, fr. ¹*hemi-* + *metamorphosis*] : HEMIMETABOLISM

hemimixis *var of* HEMIXIS

hemi·morph \ˈ==+ˌmȯrf\ *n* -s [¹*hemi-* + *-morph*] : a hemimorphic form or crystal

hemi·mor·phic \ˈ==+ˈmȯrfik\ *adj* [ISV ¹*hemi-* + *-morphic*] : unsymmetrical in form as regards the two ends of an axis : having a singular and polar axis

hemi·mor·phism \ˌ==+ˈmȯrˌfizəm\ *or* **hemi·mor·phy** \ˈ==+ˌmȯrfē\ *n, pl* **hemimorphisms** *or* **hemimorphies** [ISV ¹*hemi-* + *-morphism* or *-morphy*] : the quality or state of being hemimorphic

hemi·mor·phite \ˌ==+ˈmȯrˌfīt\ *n* -s [ISV *hemimorphic* + *-ite;* orig. formed as G *hemimorphit*] **1** : a mineral $Zn_4Si_2O_7OH.H_2O$ consisting of a basic zinc silicate in usu. white or colorless transparent orthorhombic crystals **2** : SMITHSONITE

hemi·my·aria \"+mīˈa(a)rēə\ *n pl, cap* [NL, fr. ¹*hemi-* + *-myaria*] : a suborder of Thaliacea that is coextensive in recent classifications with the family Salpidae

he·min *also* **hae·min** \ˈhēmən\ *n* -s [ISV *hem-* + *-in*] **1 a** *also* **hemin chloride** : a red-brown to blue-black crystalline salt $C_{34}H_{32}N_4O_4FeCl$ derived from oxidized heme but usu. obtained in a characteristic crystalline form from hemoglobin by treatment with hot glacial acetic acid containing sodium chloride; ferriprotoporphyrin chloride — called also *protohemin;* compare BLOOD CRYSTAL, HEMATIN 2a, TEICHMANN'S CRYSTAL **b** : any of a series of salts of which hemin chloride is a member **2** : any of several iron-porphyrin derivatives similar to hemin chloride — compare HEME 2

hem·i·o·la \ˌhemēˈōlə\ *or* **hem·i·o·lia** \-lēə\ *n* -s [LL *hemiolia*, fr. Gk *hēmiolia* ratio of one and a half to one (3:2), fr. *hēmiolia*, fem. of *hēmiolios* in the ratio of one and a half to one (3:2), fr. *hēmi-* ¹hemi- + *-olios* (fr. *holos* whole) — more at SAFE] **1** : the interval of a fifth in medieval music **2** : the rhythmic alteration consisting of three notes in place of two or two notes in place of three

hem·i·ol·ic \ˌ==ˈälik\ *adj* [L *hemiolius* (fr. Gk *hēmiolios*) + E *-ic*] *in classical prosody* : of, relating to, or characterized by the proportion of three to two; *esp* : characterized by such a proportion between thesis and arsis ⟨a ~ foot⟩

hemi·o·pia \ˈ== *at* HEMI- + ˈōpēə\ *or* **hemi·op·sia** \-ˈäpsēə\ *n* -s [NL, fr. ¹*hemi-* + *-opia, -opsia*] : HEMIANOPSIA — **hemi·op·ic** \ˈ==+ˈäpik, -ˈōp-\ *adj*

hemi·orthotype \ˈ== *at* HEMI- +\ *adj* [*hemi-* + *orth-* + *type*] : MONOCLINIC

hemi·parasite \"+\ *n* [ISV ¹*hemi-* + *parasite*] **1** : a facultative parasite — compare HOLOPARASITE **2** : a parasitic plant that contains some chlorophyll and is therefore capable of photosynthesis (as the mistletoe) — **hemi·parasitic** \"+\ *adj*

hemi·paresis \"+\ *n* [NL, fr. ¹*hemi-* + *paresis*] : muscular weakness or partial paralysis restricted to one side of the body usu. of neural or psychic origin and often transitory — **hemi·paretic** \"+\ *adj*

hemi·penis \"+\ *n* [NL, fr. ¹*hemi-* + *penis*] : one of the paired copulatory organs of lizards and snakes

hemi·plankton \"+\ *n* [NL, fr. ¹*hemi-* + *plankton*] : plankton composed of predominantly plant organisms that at certain seasons come to rest on the bottom — compare HOLOPLANKTON

hemi·ple·gia \ˌ==+ˈplēj(ē)ə\ *n* -s [NL, fr. MGk *hēmiplēgia* paralysis, fr. *hēmi-* ¹hemi- + *-plēgia* -plegia] : paralysis of one lateral half of the body or part of it resulting from injury (as by hemorrhage or disease) to the motor centers of the brain

¹**hemi·ple·gic** \ˈ==+ˈplējik, -jēk\ *adj* [*hemiplegia* + *-ic*] : relating to or marked by hemiplegia

²**hemiplegic** \"\ *n* -s : a hemiplegic individual

hemi·pode \ˈ==+ˌpōd\ *also* **hemi·pod** \-ˌpäd\ *n* -s [NL *Hemipodius*, genus of birds, fr. Gk *hēmipod-, hēmipous* half foot, fr. *hēmi-* ¹hemi- + *pod-, pous* foot — more at FOOT] : BUTTON QUAIL

he·mip·pe \hēˈmipē\ *n* -s [NL *hemippus* (specific epithet of *Equus hemippus*), fr. ¹*hemi-* + *-ippus* (fr. Gk *hippos* horse) —

more at EQUINE] : a small wild ass (*Equus hemippus*) of Syria and Iraq

hemi·prism \ˈ== *at* HEMI- + ˌ-\ *n* [ISV ¹*hemi-* + *prism*] : a prism consisting of only two parallel faces (as in the triclinic system) : a pinacoid cutting two crystallographic axes

he·mip·tera \heˈmiptərə\ *n pl, cap* [NL, fr. ¹*hemi-* + *-ptera*] **1** : a large order of insects that comprise the true bugs (as the bedbug, squash bug, and chinch bug) and various related insects (as the aphids and mealybugs), that are generally more or less flattened, that have mouthparts adapted to piercing and sucking and usu. two pairs of wings of which the basal part of the anterior pair is thickened and coriaceous and the distal part membranous while the posterior pair is wholly membranous, that undergo an incomplete metamorphosis, and that include many important pests — see HETEROPTERA, HOMOPTERA **2 a** *in some classifications* : an order coextensive with Heteroptera **b** *in some esp former classifications* : an order including Hemiptera (sense 1) together with Anoplura and Thysanoptera

he·mip·ter·oid \-tə,rȯid\ *adj* [NL *Hemiptera* + E *-oid*] : characteristic of or resembling the Hemiptera ⟨~ insect⟩ ⟨~ mouthparts⟩

he·mip·ter·ol·o·gy \=,==ˈräləjē\ *n* -ES [NL *Hemiptera* + E *-o-* + *-logy*] : a branch of entomology that deals with Hemiptera

he·mip·ter·on \=ˈ==,rän\ *also* **he·mip·ter·an** \-rən\ *n* -S [*hemipteron*, NL, back-formation fr. *Hemiptera*; *hemipteran* fr. NL *Hemiptera* + E *-an*] : one of the Hemiptera

he·mip·ter·ous \-rəs\ *adj* [NL *Hemiptera* + E *-ous*] : of or relating to the Hemiptera

hemi·pyramid \¦== *at* HEMI- +\ *n* [ISV ¹*hemi-* + *pyramid*] : a crystallographic pyramid or inclined prism consisting of only two pairs of parallel faces (as in the monoclinic system)

hemi·quinonoid *or* **hemi·quinoid** \"+\ *adj* [¹*hemi-* + *quinonoid* or *quinoid*] : having or relating to a quinonoid arrangement of bonds but only one carbonyl group instead of two

hemi·ramph \ˈ==,ram(p)f\ *n* -S [NL *Hemiramphus*] : a halfbeak of the genus *Hemiramphus*

hem·i·ram·phid \¦==ˈram(p)fəd\ *adj* [NL *Hemiramphidae*, family of halfbeaks, fr. *Hemiramphus*, type genus + *-idae*] : HEMIRAMPHINE

hemi·ram·phine \-),fīn, -,fən\ *adj* [NL *Hemiramphus* + E *-ine*] : of or relating to the genus *Hemiramphus* or the family Hemiramphidae

hemi·ram·phus \,==ˈram(p)fəs\ *n, cap* [NL, fr. ¹*hemi-* + *-ramphus* (irreg. fr. Gk *rhamphos* crooked beak, beak)] : a widely distributed genus of halfbeaks now usu. made the type of a separate family (Hemirhamphidae) but sometimes esp. formerly included in the family Exocoetidae

hemirhamphus \"\ [NL, fr. ¹*hemi-* + Gk *rhamphos* crooked beak, beak] *syn of* HEMIRAMPHUS

hemi·saprophyte \¦== *at* HEMI- + *n* [ISV ¹*hemi-* + *saprophyte*] : a partial saprophyte: **a** : an organism usu. a saprophyte but capable of existing as a parasite — compare HOLOSAPROPHYTE **b** : a plant containing a small amount of chlorophyll but obtaining most of its food material from humus — **hemi·saprophytic** \"+\ *adj*

hemi·sect \,==+ˈsekt\ *vt* -ED/-ING/-S [¹*hemi-* + *-sect*] : to divide along the mesial plane

hemi·section \¦== *at* HEMI- + \ *n* [¹*hemi-* + *section*] : a division or dividing along the mesial plane

hemi·sphaeriales \"+\ [NL, fr. ¹*hemi-* + *Sphaeriales*] *syn of* MICROTHYRIALES

hem·i·spher·al \¦heməˈsfirəl, -fer-\ *adj* : HEMISPHERIC

hem·i·sphere \ˈheməˌsfi(ə)r, -iə\ *n* [alter. (influenced by MF *emisphere*) of ME *hemisphere*, *hemisperie*, fr. L *hemisphaerium*, fr. Gk *hēmisphairion*, fr. *hēmi-* ¹hemi- + *sphairion* small sphere (dim. of *sphaira* sphere, ball)] **1 a** : a half of the celestial sphere divided into two halves by the horizon, the celestial equator, or the ecliptic **b** *obs* : the sky above the horizon or overhead **c** : a projection on a plane surface of half of the celestial sphere **2** : REALM, PROVINCE ⟨a ~ of special knowledge⟩ ⟨a ~ of life heretofore unknown to us⟩ ⟨a discovery that was to have important repercussions in the ~s of French literary life —*Times Lit. Supp.*⟩ **3 a** : a half of the terrestrial globe esp. as divided by the equator ⟨sailed down over the equator into the southern ~⟩ or into halves one of which contains Europe, Asia, and Africa and the other the Americas ⟨sailed from Europe for the western ~⟩ **b** : a map or projection of one of these halves **c** : the inhabitants of one of these halves of the earth ⟨America's plans did not seem to interest the eastern ~⟩ **4** : either of two half spheres formed by a plane through a sphere's center **5** : CEREBRAL HEMISPHERE

hemi·spher·ec·to·my \,==,sfiˈrektəmē\ *n* -ES [*hemisphere* + *-ectomy*] : surgical removal of a cerebral hemisphere

hem·i·sphered \ˈhemə,sfi(ə)rd\ *adj* : having a hemisphere or hemispheric form

hem·i·spher·ic \¦heməˈsfirik, -fer-, -rēk\ *or* **hem·i·spher·i·cal** \-rəkəl, -rēk-\ *adj* [*hemisphere* + *-ic* or *-ical*] : of, relating to, or resembling a hemisphere ⟨a ~ bowl⟩ ⟨~ solidarity⟩ — **hem·i·spher·i·cal·ly** \-rək(ə)lē, -rēk-, -li\ *adv*

hemispherical scale *n* : a cosmopolitan soft scale (*Saissetia coffeae*) found in warm countries or as a greenhouse pest

hem·i·sphe·roid \,==ˈsfi,rȯid\ *n* [¹*hemi-* + *spheroid*] : one of the halves into which a plane of symmetry cuts a spheroid — **hem·i·sphe·roi·dal** \,==,sfiˈrȯidᵊl\ *adj*

hem·i·stich \ˈheməˌstik\ *n* [L *hemistichium*, fr. Gk *hēmistichion*, fr. *hēmi-* ¹hemi- + *stichos* line, verse + *-ion* -ium; akin to Gk *steichein* to go — more at STAIR] : half a poetic line usu. divided by a caesura (as a metrically independent colon or group of feet of less than regular length)

hem·i·stich·al \¦==ˈstikəl\ *adj* : of, relating to, or written in hemistichs ⟨a ~ division of a verse⟩

hemi·symmetrical \¦== *at* HEMI- +\ *adj* : HEMIHEDRAL

hemi·symmetry \"+\ *n* [¹*hemi-* + *symmetry*] : the quality or state of being hemisymmetrical

hemi·terpene \"+\ *n* [ISV ¹*hemi-* + *terpene*] : a compound C_5H_8 whose formula represents half that of a terpene; *esp* : ISOPRENE

hemi·thorax \"+\ *n* [NL, fr. ¹*hemi-* + *thorax*] : a lateral half of the thorax

he·mit·ro·pal \hēˈmi·trəpəl\ *adj* : HEMITROPOUS

¹hemi·trope \ˈ== *at* HEMI- + ˌtrōp\ *adj* [F *hémitrope*, adj. & n., fr. *hémi-* ¹hemi- + *-trope*] : half turned round : half inverted; *specif* : HEMITROPIC

²hemitrope \"\ *n* -S [F *hémitrope*] : a hemitropic crystal

hemi·trop·ic \,==¦träpik\ *adj, crystallog* : having a twinned structure such that one part would be parallel to the other if it were rotated 180 degrees

hemi·tro·pism \ˈ==,trō,pizəm\ *or* **he·mit·ro·py** \hēˈmi·trəpē\ *n, pl* **hemitropisms** *or* **hemitropies** [*hemitropism* fr. ¹*hemitrope* + *-ism*; *hemitropy* fr. F *hémitropie*, fr. *hémi-* ¹hemi- + *tropie* -tropy] : the quality or state of being hemitropic

he·mit·ro·pous \=ˈ==pəs\ *adj* **1** [¹*hemitrope* + *-ous*] : HEMITROPIC **2** [¹*hemi-* + *-tropous*] : AMPHITROPOUS

hemi·type \ˈ== *at* HEMI- + ˌ-\ *n* [¹*hemi-* + *type*] : one that is hemitypic

¹hemi·typic \¦==+\ *adj* [¹*hemi-* + *typic*] : imperfectly typical

²hemitypic \"+\ *n* -S : one that is hemitypic

he·mix·is \hēˈmiksəs\ *also* **hemi·mix·is** \,== *at* HEMI- + ˈmiksəs\ *n* -ES [*hemixis*, NL, contr. of *hemimixis*; *hemimixis*, fr. NL, fr. ¹*hemi-* + *-mixis*] : a reorganization process in various ciliated protozoans in which the macronucleus breaks up and a new macronucleus is reconstituted from the fragments without accompanying micronuclear changes — compare ENDOMIXIS

hemi·zo·ic \¦==+¦zōik\ *adj* [¹*hemi-* + *-zoic*] : having chlorophyll-bearing chromatophores but also ingesting solid food ⟨~ green flagellates⟩ — compare HOLOPHYTIC, HOLOZOIC

hemi·zygote \"+\ *n* [¹*hemi-* + *zygote*] : one that is hemizygous

hemi·zygotic \"+\ *adj* : HEMIZYGOUS

hemi·zy·gous \¦==+¦zīgəs, hēˈmizəgəs\ *adj* [¹*hemi-* + *-zygous*] : having or characterized by unpaired genes or a haploid organism or generation ⟨a ~ sex chromosome⟩

hemline \ˈ=,=\ *n* [²*hem* + *line*] : the line formed by the lower edge of a dress, skirt, or coat

hem·lock \ˈhem,läk\ *n, often attrib* [ME *hemeluc*, *hemlok*, *homelok*, fr. OE *hemlic*, *hymlic*, perh. fr. *hymele* hop plant; akin to MLG *homele* hop plant, ON *humli*; all prob. of Finno-Ugric origin akin to Finn *humala* hop plant & Vogul *qumlix*] **1 a** : any of several poisonous herbs having finely cut leaves and small white flowers; *esp* : any of the water hemlocks or the poison hemlock **b** : CONIUM 2 **2** *also* **hemlock fir** *or* **hemlock spruce a** : a tree of the genus *Tsuga* — see CAROLINA HEMLOCK, EASTERN HEMLOCK, MOUNTAIN HEMLOCK, WESTERN HEMLOCK; TREE illustration **b** : the soft coarse light splintery wood of a hemlock tree **3** : any of several prostrate evergreens of the genus *Taxus*

hemlock chervil *n* : a hedge parsley (*Torilis japonica*) that is native to Eurasia but naturalized widely in No. America

hemlock green *n* : a dark grayish green that is bluer and deeper than average ivy and bluer and darker than Persian green

hemlock leather *n* : leather tanned with hemlock bark or extract

hemlock looper *also* **hemlock spanworm** *n* : a greenish looper that is the larva of a rather plain buff or gray geometrid moth (*Lambdina fiscellaria*) of most of No. America, that feeds on hemlock and other conifers and oak, and that is sometimes a serious defoliator

hemlock parsley *n* : any of several plants of the genus *Conioselinum* (esp. *C. chinense*) that resemble the poisonous hemlocks but are themselves innocuous

hemlock pitch *n* : CANADA PITCH

hemlock sawfly *n* : a sawfly (*Neodiprion tsugae*) of western No. America having a larva that is a serious defoliator of western hemlock and occas. other conifers

hemlock storksbill *n* : ALFILARIA

hemmed *past of* HEM

hem·mel \ˈheməl\ *n* -S [perh. alter. of ¹*helm* (rough shed)] *dial Brit* : a simple shelter usu. in a field for cattle or hay

¹hem·mer \ˈhemə(r)\ *n* -S [ME, fr. *hemmen* to hem, border + *-er* — more at ³HEM] : one that hems: **a** : a worker who makes hems by hand or machine **b** : a sewing machine attachment for turning under and stitching hems **c** : a tool for turning over the edge of sheet metal

²hemmer \"\ *n* -S [⁵*hem* + *-er*] : one that hems in speech

hemming *n* -S [fr. gerund of ³*hem*] : the act or process of one that hems; *also* : HEM ⟨ran a wide ~ around the bottom of the cloth⟩

hemo- — see HEM-

he·mo·blast \ˈhēmə,blast, ˈhem-\ *n* [ISV *hem-* + *-blast*] : HEMATOBLAST

he·mo·chorial \¦hēmō, ¦hemō+\ *adj* [*hem-* + *chorial*] *of a placenta* : having fetal epithelium bathed in maternal blood ⟨the lower rodents, bats, some insectivores, and most primates including man are ~⟩ — compare ENDOTHELIOCHORIAL, EPITHELIOCHORIAL, SYNDESMOCHORIAL

he·mo·chromatosis \"+\ *n* [NL, fr. *hem-* + *chromatosis*] : a disease characterized by widespread deposition of iron-containing pigments (as hemosiderin) in the tissues resulting in bronzing of the skin, associated with cirrhosis of the liver and pancreas and frequently with diabetic symptoms, and occurring usu. in males — called also *bronze diabetes*

he·mo·chrome \ˈhēmə,krōm, ˈhem-\ *n* -S [ISV *hem-* + *-chrome*] : HEMOCHROMOGEN

he·mo·chro·mo·gen \,==ˈkrōmə,jen, -jən\ *n* -S [ISV *hemochromo-* (fr. *hemochrome*) + *-gen*] **1** : a colored compound formed from or related to hemoglobin; *esp* : a bright red combination of a nitrogen base (as globin or pyridine) with heme — compare HEMOPROTEIN **2** : a colored compound of a nitrogenous base with a metal-porphyrin derivative esp. when in the reduced form

he·mo·clas·tic crisis \¦==¦klastik-\ *n* [ISV *hem-* + *-clastic* (disintegrating)] : an acute transitory alteration of the blood that sometimes accompanies anaphylactic shock and is marked by intense leukopenia with relative lymphocytosis, alteration in blood coagulability, and fall in blood pressure

he·mo·coel *also* **he·mo·coele** \ˈhēmə,sēl, ˈhem-\ *n* -S [*hem-* + *-coele*] : a body cavity (as in arthropods) formed by the expansion of parts of the blood-vascular system — **he·mo·coe·lic** \¦==¦sēlik\ *adj* — **he·mo·coe·lous** \-ləs\ *adj*

he·mo·coelom \¦hēmō, ¦hemō+\ *n* [*hem-* + *coelom*] **1** : the part of the embryonic coelom in which the heart develops **2** : HEMOCOEL

he·mo·concentration \"+\ *n* [ISV *hem-* + *concentration*] : increased concentration of cells and solids in the blood usu. resulting from loss of fluid to the tissues — compare HEMODILUTION

he·mo·co·nia *also* **he·mo·ko·nia** \,hēməˈkōnēə, ,hem-\ *n* -S [NL, fr. *hem-* + Gk *konia* dust — more at INCINERATE] : small refractive colorless particles in the blood that are believed to be castoff granules from the cells in the blood or minute globules of fat — called also *blood dust*

he·mo·co·ni·o·sis \,==,kōnēˈōsəs\ *n, pl* **hemoconio·ses** \-ˈō,sēz\ [NL, fr. *hemoconia* + *-osis*] : a condition in which there is an abnormally high content of hemoconia in the blood

he·mo·culture \¦hēmō, ¦hemō+\ *n* [ISV *hem-* + *culture*] : a culture made from blood to detect the presence of pathogenic microorganisms by providing conditions likely to further their multiplication

he·mo·cu·pre·in \,hēməˈk(y)üprēən, ,hem-\ *n* -S [ISV *hem-* + *cupr-* + *-ein*] : a blue copper-containing protein obtained from red blood cells

he·mo·cy·a·nin \,==ˈsīənən\ *n* [ISV *hem-* + *cyan-* + *-in*] : a colorless copper-containing respiratory pigment found in solution in the blood plasma of various arthropods and mollusks and converted by oxygen to blue oxyhemocyanin

he·mo·cyte \ˈ==,sīt\ *n* -S [ISV *hem-* + *-cyte*] : a blood cell esp. of an invertebrate animal

he·mo·cy·to·blast \,==ˈsīd·ə,blast\ *n* -S [ISV *hemocyto-* (fr. *hemocyte*) + *-blast*] : a stem cell for blood-cellular elements; *esp* : one considered competent to produce all types of blood cell — **he·mo·cy·to·blas·tic** \¦==¦==¦blastik\ *adj*

he·mo·cy·to·blas·to·sis \,hēmə,sīd·ə,blaˈstōsəs, ,hem-\ *n, pl* **hemocytoblasto·ses** \-ō,sēz\ [NL, fr. ISV *hemocytoblast* + NL *-osis*] : lymphocytomatosis of chickens

he·mo·cy·to·gen·e·sis \-d·əˈjenəsəs\ *n* [NL, fr. *hemocyto-* (fr. ISV *hemocyte*) + L *genesis*] : the part of hematopoiesis concerned with the formation of blood cells

he·mo·cy·tol·y·sis \-,sīˈtäləsəs\ *n, pl* **hemocytoly·ses** \-ə,sēz\ [NL, fr. *hemocyto-* (fr. ISV *hemocyte*) + NL *-lysis*] : a breaking down or dissolution of red blood cells esp. by the action of hypotonic solutions

he·mo·cy·tom·e·ter \-ˈtäməd·ə(r)\ *n* [ISV *hem-* + *cyt-* + *-meter*] : HEMACYTOMETER

he·mo·cy·to·zo·on \-,sīd·əˈzō,än\ *n* -S [NL, fr. *hemocyto-* (fr. ISV *hemocyte*) + NL *-zoon*] : an animal parasite (as the plasmodium of malaria) living within a blood corpuscle

he·mo·dilution \¦hēmō, ¦hemō+\ *n* [*hem-* + *dilution*] : decreased concentration of cells and solids in the blood usu. resulting from gain of fluid from the tissues (as after hemorrhage) — compare HEMOCONCENTRATION

he·mo·dynamic \"+\ *adj* [ISV *hem-* + *dynamic*] **1** : of, relating to, or involving hemodynamics **2** : concerned with or functioning in the mechanics of blood circulation

he·mo·dynamics \"+\ *n pl but sing or pl in constr* [ISV *hem-* + *dynamics*] **1** : a branch of physiology that deals with circulatory movements and the forces involved in circulation of the blood **2 a** : the forces involved in circulation (as of a particular body part) ⟨renal ~⟩ **b** : hemodynamic effect (as of a drug)

he·mo·endothelial \"+\ *adj* [*hem-* + *endothelial*] *of a placenta* : having the fetal villi reduced to bare capillary loops that are bathed in maternal blood ⟨higher rodents are ~⟩

hemoflagellate \"+\ *n* [*hem-* + *flagellate*] : a flagellate (as a trypanosome) that is a blood parasite

he·mo·fus·cin \,hēməˈfəsən, ,hem-\ *n* [ISV *hem-* + *fusc-* (fr. L *fuscus* dark brown) + *-in* — more at DUSK] : a yellowish brown pigment found in small amount in some normal tissues and increased amount in certain pathological states (as hemochromatosis)

he·mo·glo·bic \¦==¦glōbik\ *adj* [*hemoglobin* + *-ic*] : HEMOGLOBINIC

he·mo·glo·bin *also* **hae·mo·glo·bin** \ˈ==,glōbən, ,==ˈ==\ *n* -S [ISV, short for earlier *hematoglobulin*, fr. *hemato-* (fr. *hematin*) + *globulin*] **1 a** : an iron-containing protein pigment occurring in the red blood cells of vertebrates and functioning primarily in the transport of oxygen from the lungs to the tissues of the body **b** : the dark purplish crystallizable form of this pigment that is found chiefly in the venous blood of vertebrates, that is a conjugated protein composed of heme and globin commonly in a ratio of four molecules of heme to one of globin but that may vary somewhat in different species and in different physiological and pathological states (as in some anemias), that combines loosely and reversibly with oxygen in the lungs or gills to form oxyhemoglobin and with carbon dioxide in the tissues to form carbhemoglobin, that in man is present normally in blood to the extent of 14 to 16 gm. in 100 ml. expressed sometimes on a scale of 0 to 100 with an average normal value (as 15 gm.) taken as 100, and that is determined in blood either colorimetrically or by quantitative estimation of the iron present — symbol *Hb*; called also *ferrohemoglobin, reduced hemoglobin*; compare CARBONYLHEMOGLOBIN, METHEMOGLOBIN **c** : any of numerous chemically similar iron-containing respiratory pigments that occur in cells or usu. free in the plasma of many annelid worms and certain other invertebrates, in some yeasts and other fungi, in the nodules formed on the roots of leguminous plants by nitrogen-fixing bacteria, and elsewhere — compare HEMOPROTEIN **2** : any of various respiratory pigments consisting of a conjugated protein that has as the nonprotein group either heme or an analogous compound containing a metal — compare MYOGLOBIN — **he·mo·glo·bin·ic** \¦==,glōˈbinik\ *adj* — **he·mo·glo·bi·nous** \¦==¦glōbənəs\ *adj*

hemoglobin A *n* : the hemoglobin in the red blood cells of normal adult human beings

he·mo·glo·bi·ne·mia \,==,glōbəˈnēmēə\ *n* -S [NL, fr. ISV *hemoglobin* + NL *-emia*] **1** : the presence of free hemoglobin in the blood plasma resulting from the solution of hemoglobin out of the red blood cells or from disintegration of the red cells **2** : AZOTEMIA

he·mo·glo·bi·nom·e·ter \-ˈnäməd·ə(r)\ *n* [ISV *hemoglobin* + *-o-* + *-meter*] : an instrument for the colorimetric determination of hemoglobin in blood ⟨visual and photoelectric ~s⟩ — **he·mo·glo·bi·nom·e·try** \-mə·trē\ *n* -ES

hemoglobin S *n* : the hemoglobin occurring in the red blood cells in sickle-cell anemia and sicklemia and differing from hemoglobin A in its lower solubility and lower isoelectric point

he·mo·glo·bi·nu·ria \-ˈn(y)u̇rēə\ *n* -S [NL, fr. ISV *hemoglobin* + NL *-uria*] : the presence of free hemoglobin in the urine — compare HEMATURIA — **he·mo·glo·bi·nu·ric** \¦==¦==¦n(y)u̇rik\ *adj*

he·mo·gram \ˈhēmə,gram, ˈhem-\ *n* [ISV *hem-* + *-gram*] : a systematic report of the findings from a blood examination

hemogregarine *var of* HAEMOGREGARINE

he·mo·his·ti·o·blast \,hēmōˈhistēō,blast, ,hem-\ *n* [ISV *hem-* + *histi-* + *-blast*] : a hemocytoblast that is a derivative of the reticuloendothelial system

he·moid \ˈhē,mȯid\ *adj* [ISV *hem-* + *-oid*] : resembling blood : HEMATOID

hemokonia *var of* HEMOCONIA

he·mo·lymph \ˈhēmə, ˈhemə+,-\ *n* [ISV *hem-* + *lymph*] : the circulatory fluid of various invertebrate animals that is functionally comparable to the blood and lymph of vertebrates

he·mo·lymphatic \¦==+\ *adj* [fr. *hemolymph*, after E *lymph: lymphatic*] : of, like, or relating to hemolymph or to a hemolymph gland

hemolymph gland *or* **hemolymph node** *n* : any of several small chiefly retroperitoneal nodes of tissue resembling lymph nodes but having the lymph spaces replaced in whole or in part by blood sinuses

he·mo·ly·sin \,hēməˈlīsᵊn, ,hem-\ *n* [ISV *hem-* + *lysin*] : a substance (as an antibody) that esp. in conjunction with complement causes the dissolution of red blood cells with liberation of the contained hemoglobin

he·mol·y·sis \hēˈmäləsəs\ *n, pl* **hemoly·ses** \-ə,sēz\ [NL, fr. *hem-* + *-lysis*] : liberation of hemoglobin from red blood cells; *specif* : such a liberation brought about by a specific hemolysin usu. interacting with complement

he·mo·lyt·ic \¦hēmə¦lid·ik, ¦hem-\ *adj* [ISV *hem-* + *-lytic*] : of, relating to, involving, or inducing hemolysis ⟨~ antigens⟩

hemolytic anemia *n* : anemia characterized by excessive destruction of red blood cells caused by chemical poisoning (as by certain sulfonamide compounds), infections (as malaria or sepsis), cell abnormalities (as sickle-cell anemia), or other agents or factors (as endogenous hemolysins)

hemolytic disease of the newborn : ERYTHROBLASTOSIS FETALIS

hemolytic jaundice *or* **hemolytic icterus** *n* : a condition characterized by excessive destruction of red blood cells accompanied by jaundice; *specif* : a rare familial anemia characterized by small thick fragile red blood cells which are extremely susceptible to hemolysis, by enlargement of the spleen, and by more or less marked jaundice

he·mo·lyze \ˈhēmə,līz, ˈhem-\ *vb* -ED/-ING/-S [fr. *hemolysis*, after such pairs as E *analysis: analyze*] *vt* : to cause (red blood cells) to dissolve : induce hemolysis of ~ *vi* : to undergo hemolysis

he·mom·e·ter \hēˈmäməd·ə(r)\ *n* [ISV *hem-* + *-meter*] : an instrument for measuring some quality of blood: as **a** : HEMOGLOBINOMETER **b** : HEMADYNAMOMETER **c** : HEMACYTOMETER — **he·mo·met·ric** \¦hēmə¦me·trik, ¦hem-\ *adj* — **he·mom·e·try** \hēˈmämə·trē\ *n* -ES

he·mo·parasite \¦hēmō, ¦hemō+\ *n* [*hem-* + *parasite*] : an animal parasite (as a hemoflagellate or a filarial worm) living in the blood of a vertebrate

he·mop·a·thy \hēˈmäpəthē\ *n* -ES [ISV *hem-* + *-pathy*] : a pathological state (as anemia or agranulocytosis) of the blood or blood-forming tissues

he·mo·pericardium \¦hēmō, ¦hemō+\ *n* [NL, fr. *hem-* + *pericardium*] : blood in the pericardial cavity

he·mo·peritoneum \"+\ *n* [NL, fr. *hem-* + *peritoneum*] : blood in the peritoneal cavity

he·mo·phage \ˈhēmə,fāj, ˈhem-\ *n* -S [*hem-* + *-phage*] : ERYTHROPHAGE

he·mo·pha·gia \,==ˈfājēə\ *n* -S [NL, fr. *hem-* + *-phagia*] **1** : an ingestion of blood **2** : phagocytosis of red blood cells — **he·moph·a·gous** \hēˈmäfəgəs\ *adj*

he·mo·phagocyte \¦hēmō, ¦hemō+\ *n* [*hem-* + *phagocyte*] **1** : HEMOPHAGE **2** : a phagocytic cell of the bloodstream — **he·mo·phagocytic** \"+\ *adj*

¹he·mo·phile \ˈhēmə,fīl, ˈhem-\ *adj* [*hem-* + *-phile*] : HEMOPHILIC

²hemophile \"\ *n* -S [ISV *hem-* + *-phile*] **1** : HEMOPHILIAC **2** : a hemophilic organism (as a bacterium)

he·mo·phil·ia \,==ˈfilēə\ *n* -S [NL, fr. *hem-* + *-philia*] : a tendency to uncontrollable bleeding; *esp* : a sex-linked hereditary blood defect of males characterized by delayed clotting of the blood and consequent difficulty in controlling hemorrhage even after minor injuries — compare PSEUDOHEMOPHILIA

¹he·mo·phil·i·ac \-lē,ak\ *n* -S [*hemophilia* + *-ac* (fr. Gk *-akos*, adj. suffix)] : one affected with hemophilia

²hemophiliac \¦==¦==,=\ *adj* [*hemophilia* + *-ac* (fr. Gk *-akos*, adj. suffix)] : HEMOPHILIC

he·mo·phil·ic \-¦filik\ *adj* **1** [*hemophilia* + *-ic*] : of, like, or affected with hemophilia **2** [*hem-* + *-philic*] : blood-loving — used of an organism (as a bacterium) that grows best in a medium containing blood

he·mo·phil·i·oid \-¦filē,ȯid\ *also* **he·moph·i·loid** \hēˈmäfə,lȯid\ *adj* [*hemophili-* or *hemophil-* (fr. *hemophilia*) + *-oid*] : resembling hemophilia esp. in exhibiting a tendency to uncontrollable bleeding ⟨a ~ state⟩

he·moph·i·lus \hēˈmäfələs\ *n, cap* [NL, fr. *hem-* + *-philus*] : a genus of minute nonmotile gram-negative strictly parasitic hemophilic bacteria (family Parvobacteriaceae) including several important pathogens (as *H. influenzae* associated with human respiratory infections, conjunctivitis, and meningitis, *H. suis* of swine influenza, or *H. ducreyi* of chancroid)

he·mo·poi·e·sis \,hēmō,pȯiˈēsəs, ,hem-\ *n* [NL, fr. *hem-* + *-poiesis*] : HEMATOPOIESIS — **he·mo·poi·et·ic** \¦==,pȯi¦ed·ik\ *adj*

he·mo·poi·etin \,==,pȯiˈētᵊn\ *n* -S [ISV *hemopoietic* + *-in*; prob. orig. formed as F *hémopoïétine*] : a hypothetical stimulant to blood-cell production possibly equivalent to the antianemic factor or one of its precursors

he·mo·proteidae \¦hēmō, ¦hemō+\ *syn of* HAEMOPROTEIDAE

he·mo·protein \"+\ *n* [*hem-* + *protein*] : a conjugated protein

(as hemoglobin, catalase, peroxidase, or cytochrome) whose nonprotein portion is heme or a heme : a hemochromogen with a protein combined with heme — compare CHROMOPROTEIN
he·mo·proteus \"+\ *syn of* HAEMOPROTEUS
he·mop·toe \hē'mäptəwē\ *n* -s [NL, alter. of *hemoptysis*] : hemorrhage from the lungs
he·mop·to·ic \-wik\ *adj* [prob. fr. LL *haemoptoicus* spitting blood, fr. LGk *haimoptoikos*, alter. of Gk *haimoptyikos*, fr. *haimo-* hem- + *-ptyikos* (fr. *ptyein* to spit + *-ikos* -ic) — more at SPEW] : of or produced by hemoptysis
he·mop·ty·sis \-təsəs\ *n, pl* **hemopty·ses** \-ə,sēz\ [NL, fr. *hem-* + *-ptysis*] : expectoration of blood from some part of the respiratory tract — compare HEMATEMESIS
he·mo·pyrrole \¦hēmō, ¦hemō+\ *n* [ISV *hem-* + *pyrrole*] : a low-melting solid or liquid homologue $C_8H_{13}N$ of pyrrole formed during reduction of hemin or phylloporphyrin with hydriodic acid; 2,3-dimethyl-4-ethyl-pyrrole
¹hem·or·rhage \'hem(ə)rij, -rēj\ *n* -s [F & L; F *hémorrhagie*, fr. L *haemorrhagia*, fr. Gk *haimorrhagia*, fr. *haimo-* hem- + *-rrhagia*] : a copious discharge of blood from the blood vessels
²hemorrhage \"\ *vi* -ED/-ING/-S : BLEED
hem·or·rhag·ic \¦hemə¦rajik\ *adj* [Gk *haimorrhagikos*, fr. *haimorrhagia* hemorrhage + *-ikos* -ic] : involving, associated with, or tending to cause hemorrhage ⟨~ retinitis⟩ ⟨~ toxemia⟩ ⟨~ agent⟩
hemorrhagic diathesis *n* : a constitutional tendency to spontaneous often severe bleeding — compare HEMOPHILIA, PURPURA HEMORRHAGICA
hemorrhagic septicemia *n* : pasteurellosis of domestic animals usu. due to a bacterium (*Pasteurella multocida*) and typically marked by internal hemorrhages, fever, mucopurulent discharges, and often pneumonia and diarrhea, typical forms being swine plague, shipping fever of cattle and lambs, and fowl cholera
hem·or·rhag·in \,==ˈrajən\ *n* -s [ISV *hemorrhage* + *-in*] : a toxic substance occurring usu. as a component of various snake venoms and capable of destroying the blood cells and the walls of small blood vessels — compare HEMOLYSIN
hem·or·rhoid \'hem(ə),rȯid\ *n* -s [MF *hemorrhoides*, pl, fr. L *haemorrhoidae*, fr. Gk *haimorrhoides*, fr. *haimorrhoos* flowing with blood, fr. *haimo-* hem- + *-rrhoos* (fr. *rhein* to flow) — more at STREAM] : a mass of dilated tortuous veins in swollen tissue situated at the anal margin or within the anal canal — usu. used in pl.; called also *piles*
¹hem·or·rhoi·dal \¦==¦rȯidᵊl\ *adj* [F *hémorrhoidal*, fr. MF, fr. *hemorrhoides* hemorrhoids + *-al*] **1** : of, relating to, or involving hemorrhoids **2** : RECTAL
²hemorrhoidal \"\ *n* -s : a hemorrhoidal part (as an artery or vein)
hemorrhoidal artery *n* : one of the arteries supplying the rectal and anal region that consists of a superior which is a continuation of the inferior mesenteric and a middle and inferior which are usu. branches of the hypogastric and pudendal respectively
hemorrhoidal vein *n* : any of the veins corresponding to the hemorrhoidal arteries and forming a plexus at the lower rectum and anus
hem·or·rhoid·ec·to·my \,hem(ə),rȯi'dektəmē\ *n* -ES [*hemorrhoid* + *-ectomy*] : surgical removal of a hemorrhoid
he·mo·salpinx \¦hēmō, ¦hemō+\ *n* [NL, fr. *hem-* + *salpinx*] : HEMATOSALPINX
he·mo·sid·er·in \,hēmō'sidərən, ,hem-\ *n* -s [ISV *hem-* + *sider-* + *-in*] : a yellowish brown granular pigment formed by breakdown of hemoglobin, found in phagocytes and in tissues esp. in disturbances of iron metabolism (as in hemochromatosis, hemosiderosis, or some anemias), and composed essentially of colloidal ferric oxide — compare FERRITIN
he·mo·sid·er·o·sis \,==,sidə'rōsəs\ *n, pl* **hemosidero·ses** \-ō,sēz\ [NL, fr. ISV *hemosiderin* + NL *-osis*] : a pathological condition marked by the deposition of hemosiderin in the tissues as a result of the breakdown of red blood cells — compare HEMOCHROMATOSIS — **he·mo·sid·er·ot·ic** \¦==,==¦räd·ik\ *adj*
he·mo·spo·rid·ia \,hēmōspə'ridēə, ,hem-\ *syn of* HAEMOSPORIDIA
he·mo·sta·sis \,hēmə'stāsəs\ *n, pl* **hemosta·ses** \-ə,sēz\ [NL, fr. Gk *haimostasis* styptic, fr. *haimo-* hem- + *-stasis*] **1** : stoppage or sluggishness of blood flow **2** : arrest of bleeding (as by a hemostatic agent)
he·mo·stat \'hēmə,stat, 'hem-\ *n* -s **1** [by shortening] : HEMOSTATIC **2** [*hem-* + *-stat*] : an instrument for compressing a bleeding vessel
¹he·mo·stat·ic \¦==¦stad·ik\ *n* -s [LGk *haimostatikos*, n. & adj.] : an agent that checks bleeding; *esp* : one that shortens the clotting time of blood — compare HEMOSTAT
²hemostatic \"\ *adj* [LGk *haimostatikos* good for stopping blood, fr. Gk *haimo-* hem- + *-statikos* -static] **1** : of or caused by hemostasis **2** : serving to check bleeding ⟨a ~ agent⟩
he·mo·thorax \¦hēmō, ¦hemō+\ *n* [NL, fr. *hem-* + *thorax*] : blood in the pleural cavity
he·mo·toxin \"+\ *n* [ISV *hem-* + *toxin*] : HEMOLYSIN
he·mot·ro·phe \hē'mä·trəfē\ *n* -s [*hem-* + *-trophe* (as in *embryotrophe*)] : the nutrients supplied to the embryo in placental mammals by the maternal bloodstream after formation of the placenta — compare EMBRYOTROPH, HISTOTROPH
he·mo·zo·on \,hēmə'zō,än, ,hem-\ *n, pl* **hemo·zoa** \-ōə\ [NL, fr. *hem-* + *-zoon*] : HEMATOZOON
hemp \'hemp\ *n* -s *often attrib* [ME *hemp, hempe*, fr. OE

hemp: flowering shoots of *1* staminate plant, of *2* pistillate plant; *3* staminate flower; *4* pistillate flower; *5* fruit

hænep, henep; akin to MD *hennep* hemp, OHG *hanaf, hanif*, ON *hampr*; prob. all of non-IE origin; akin to the source of Gk *kannabis* hemp & Arm *kanap*] **1 a** : a tall widely cultivated Asiatic herb (*Cannabis sativa*) with tough bast fiber that is used for making cloth, floor covering, and cordage — see BHANG, CANNABIDIOL, CANNABIN, CANNABINOL, CANNABIS, CHARAS, HASHISH; compare GANJA **b** : the fiber of this plant prepared for commercial use **c** : a narcotic drug (as hashish) from hemp **2** : the useful fiber of any of numerous plants (as jute, abaca, ramie) other than hemp; *also* : the plant producing such fiber **3** *archaic* **a** : a gallows rope **b** : HANGING **4** : a light grayish olive color that is redder and deeper than twine, Quaker gray, or average citron gray
hemp agrimony *n* : a coarse European herb (*Eupatorium cannabinum*) with reddish flower heads and sessile leaves
hemp-brake \'=,=\ *n* : ⁴BRAKE 1
hemp dogbane *n* : INDIAN HEMP 1
hem·pel column \'hempəl-\ *n, usu cap H* [after Walter *Hempel* †1916 Ger. chemist] : a vertical column for fractional distillation filled with glass beads and provided with a side tube for exit of the vapors
hemp·en \'hempən\ *adj* [ME, fr. *hemp* + ¹*-en*] **1** : of, relating to, made of, or like hemp **2** *archaic* : of or relating to a hangman's noose or a hanging
hemp family *n* : URTICACEAE
hemp nettle *n* : a plant of the genus *Galeopsis*; *esp* : a coarse bristly Eurasian herb (*G. tetrahit*) having foliage resembling that of the nettle and being common as a weed in the U. S.
hemp palm *n* : either of two dwarf fan palms (*Chamaerops humilis* of the Mediterranean region and *Trachycarpus excelsa* of China) the leaves of which yield the fiber African hair
hempseed \'=,=\ *n* [ME, fr. *hemp* + *seed*] : the seed of hemp
hempseed oil *n* : a light green to brownish yellow drying fatty oil obtained from hempseed and used chiefly in soft soap, paints, and varnishes and in Asia in foods
hemp tree *n* : AGNUS CASTUS
hempweed \'=,=\ *n* **1** : HEMP AGRIMONY **2** *also* **hemp vine** : CLIMBING HEMPWEED
¹hempy *or* **hemp·ie** \'hempi\ *n, pl* **hempies** [*hemp* + *-y* or *-ie*] **1** *chiefly Scot* : ROGUE, GALLOWS BIRD **2** *chiefly Scot* : a lively mischievous young person
²hempy *or* **hempie** \"\ *adj, Scot* : full of deviltry : MISCHIEVOUS
hems *pl of* HEM, *pres 3d sing of* HEM
¹hemstitch \'=,=\ *vt* [²*hem* + *stitch*] : to embroider (fabric) by drawing out parallel threads and stitching the exposed threads in groups to form various designs
²hemstitch \"\ *n* **1** *or* **hemstitching** \'=,==\ : decorative needlework similar to drawnwork that is often used on or near stitching lines of hems **2** : a stitch used in hemstitching

hemstitch 1

hemstitcher \'=,==\ *n* **1** : a worker who hemstitches by hand or machine **2** : a sewing-machine attachment for making hemstitching
hen \'hen\ *n* -s *often attrib* [ME, fr. OE *henn*; akin to OHG *henna* hen, OE *hana* rooster — more at CHANT] **1 a** : the female of the domestic fowl; *esp* : one that is more than a year old **b** : the female of any of various other birds (as most gallinaceous or domesticated birds) **c** : one who behaves like a hen ⟨there were younger children at home and Minnie was their devoted mother ~ —R.T.Moriarty⟩ **2 a** : the female of various marine animals (as the lobster) and some fishes **b** : HEN FISH **3** : an esp. older woman who is fussy or officious ⟨grown into a cantankerous old ~⟩ — **a hen on** : a secret plan in preparation : something hatching ⟨the higher officials knew there was *a hen on* —Jo Mora⟩
henad \'he,nad, 'hē,-\ *n* -s [Gk *henad-, henas*, fr. *hen*, neut. of *heis* one + *-ad-, -as* (fem. suffix denoting connection with); akin to Gk *homos* same — more at SAME, -AD] : MONAD 1a
hen and chickens *n, pl* **hens and chickens** : any of several plants having offsets, runners, or proliferous flowers: as **a** : HOUSELEEK **b** : GROUND IVY **c** : an English daisy with proliferous flowers **d** : a plant of the genus *Echeveria*
henbane \'=,=\ *n* [ME, fr. *hen* + *bane*] **1 a** : a fetid Old World herb (*Hyoscyamus niger*) having clammy-pubescent dentate leaves and yellowish brown flowers, containing a poison that is deadly esp. to fowls, and yielding from its leaves an extract that is used in medicine and has properties similar to those of belladonna — called also *black henbane* **b** : YELLOW HENBANE **2** : EGYPTIAN HENBANE
henbill \'=,=\ *n* **1** : PIED-BILLED GREBE **2** : AMERICAN COOT
henbit \'=,=\ *n* [*hen* + *bit* (morsel)] **1** : an annual dead nettle (*Lamium amplexicaule*) with reniform leaves and flowers that are arranged in whorls of 6 to 10 or more and have connivent calyx teeth — called also *bee nettle* **2** : IVY-LEAVED SPEEDWELL **3** : BLACK HOREHOUND
hence \'hen(t)s\ *adv* [ME *hennes, hens*, fr. *henne* hence (fr. OE *heonan*) + *-s* (adv. suffix); akin to OS *hinan, hinana* away from here, OHG *hina* & *hinnan, hinana*, OE *hēr* here — more at HERE] **1 a** : from this place : AWAY ⟨how churlishly I bid Lucretia ~ —Shak.⟩ ⟨get thee ~, Satan⟩; *specif* : from this world or life ⟨before I go ~ and be no more —Ps 39:13 (AV)⟩ **b** *obs* : at an interval in space : DISTANT ⟨three quarters of a mile ~ —Shak.⟩ — often used imperatively for *go hence* or *get (you) hence* ⟨*hence* with your little ones —Shak.⟩ **2 a** *archaic* : from now on : HENCEFORTH ⟨from ~ I'll love no friend —Shak.⟩ **b** : from this time : in the future ⟨a generation ~⟩ **3** : because of a preceding fact or premise : THEREFORE ⟨unorthodox and ~ unpopular doctrines —J.B.Conant⟩ **4** : from this source or origin ⟨~ the desire to impress public opinion —Hugh Gaitskell⟩ — **from hence** *adv, archaic* : HENCE : from this place ⟨a fortnight since we set out *from hence* upon a little excursion —Thomas Gray⟩ ⟨will not depart *from hence* —Robert Southey⟩
henceforth \(')=¦=\ *or* **henceforward** \(')=¦==\ *adv* [*henceforth* fr. ME *hennesforth*, fr. *hennes* + *forth*; *henceforward*, fr. ME *hennesforward*, fr. *hennes* + *forward*] : from this point on — **from henceforth** *or* **from henceforward** *adv, archaic* : HENCEFORTH ⟨*from henceforth* bear his name whose form thou bearest —Shak.⟩
henchboy *n* [*hench-* (as in *henchman*) + *boy*] *obs* : a boy attendant : PAGE
hench·man \'henchmən\ *n, pl* **henchmen** [ME *hengestman, henxtman, henxman* groom, squire, fr. *hengest* stallion, gelding (fr. OE) + *man*; akin to OFris *hanxt, hengst* horse, OHG *hengist* gelding, ON *hestr* stallion, horse, and perh. to W *caseg* mare, Gk *kēkiein* to gush forth, Lith *šokti* to jump, dance; basic meaning: jumping, bubbling] **1 a** *obs* : a squire or page to a person of high rank ⟨a little changeling boy to be my ~ —Shak.⟩ **b** : a household servant : RETAINER ⟨hear my ~ . . . about to ring the bell for luncheon —William Black⟩ **2 a** : the head gillie of a Scottish chief **b** : a subordinate who is heavily relied upon : RIGHT-HAND MAN ⟨the significant look that passes between the suave mastermind and his black-browed ~ —Richard Mallett⟩ **3 a** : a loyal supporter : ADHERENT ⟨the *henchmen* of German political and economic reaction —Hillel Silver⟩ **b** : a political follower giving active support; *esp* : one whose support is chiefly a matter of personal advantage ⟨a fat, easygoing minor ~ who held a judgeship —Hodding Carter⟩ **c** : an unscrupulous often violent member of a gang : HATCHET MAN ⟨a third car full of his armed *henchmen* following behind —F.L.Allen⟩
hen clam *n* [so called fr. the belief that such clams are female only] **1** : SURF CLAM **2** : PISMO CLAM
hen curlew *n* : a long-billed No. American curlew (*Numenius americanus*) now rare because of excessive hunting
hendeca- *or* **hendec-** *comb form* [Gk *hendeka-, hendek-*, fr. *hendeka*, fr. *hen* (neut. of *heis* one) + *deka* ten — more at HENAD, TEN] : eleven ⟨*hendeca*syllable⟩ ⟨*hendec*ane⟩
hen·deca·colic \(¦)hen¦dekə¦kōlik, -¦käl-\ *adj* [*hendeca-* + ²*colon* + *-ic*] *Greek & Latin prosody* : made up of eleven cola
hen·de·cane \'hendə,kān, hen'de,k-\ *n* -s [*hendeca-* + *-ane*] : UNDECANE
hen·deca·se·mic \(¦)hen¦dekə¦sēmik\ *adj* [*hendeca-* + Gk *sēma* sign + E *-ic*] *Greek & Latin prosody* : containing or equivalent to eleven short syllables — compare MORA
hen·deca·syllabic \(¦)hen¦dekə+\ *or* **en·deca·syllabic** \(¦)en-\ *adj* [L *hendecasyllabus* + E *-ic*] **1** : having eleven syllables **2** : composed of eleven-syllable lines
hen·deca·syllable \hen'dekə+,-, (,)hen,dekə+'-\ *n* [modif. (influenced by *syllable*) of L *hendecasyllabus*, fr. Gk *hendeka* eleven + *syllabē* syllable — more at SYLLABLE] : a line of eleven syllables ⟨the ~ is the principal verse in Italian poetry⟩
hen·decyl \(')hen¦desəl, -dēs-\ *n* -s [*hendecane* + *-yl*] : UNDECYL
hen·di·a·dys \hen'dīədəs\ *n* -ES [LL *hendiadys, hendiadyoin*, modif. of Gk *hen dia dyoin* one through two] : the expression of an idea by two nouns connected by *and* (as *cups and gold*) instead of by a noun and an adjective (as *golden cups*)
hen·don \'hendən\ *adj, usu cap* [fr. *Hendon*, England] : of or from the urban district of Hendon, England : of the kind or style prevalent in Hendon
hen·eicosane \(')hen+\ *n* -s [ISV *heneicos-* (fr. *hen-* — fr. Gk *hen*, neut. of *heis* one — + *eicosa-*) + *-ane*] : a paraffin hydrocarbon $C_{21}H_{44}$; *esp* : the white waxy normal heneicosane $CH_3(CH_2)_{19}CH_3$
hen·e·quen *also* **hen·i·quen** \'henəkən, ¦==¦ken\ *n* -s [Sp *henequén, heniquén, jeniquén*, prob. fr. Taino] **1** : a strong yellowish or reddish hard fiber derived from the leaves of a tropical American agave, produced chiefly in Yucatán, and used largely in the production of binder twine — see SISAL **2** : the agave (*Agave fourcroydes*) that yields henequen
hen feather *n* : a feather on the shaft of an arrow set at an angle of 120 degrees from the cock feather
hen-feathered \'=¦==\ *adj* : having plumage like that of a hen — used of a male bird that lacks sickle or hackle feathers; distinguished from *cock-feathered*
hen-feathering \'=,=(=)=\ *n* : plumage on a cock resembling that of the hen
hen fish *n* **1** : any of various marine fishes (as the pomfret) **2** : an adult female fish
hen flea *n* : STICKTIGHT FLEA

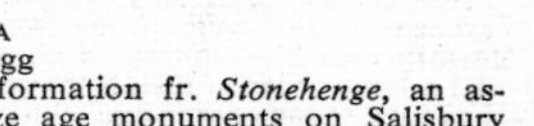

hen fruit *n, slang* : a hen's egg
henge \'henj\ *n* -s [back-formation fr. *Stonehenge*, an assemblage of upright bronze age monuments on Salisbury Plain, near Salisbury, England] : a circular Bronze Age structure (as of wood) with a surrounding bank and ditch found in England
hen gorse *n, dial Eng* : RESTHARROW
heng·yang \'həŋ¦yäŋ, 'heŋ-; 'heŋ¦yaŋ\ *adj, usu cap* [fr. *Hengyang*, China] : of or from the city of Hengyang, China : of the kind or style prevalent in Hengyang
hen harrier *n* : a common harrier (*Circus cyaneus*) of which the adult male is largely bluish gray and the female and young male brown above and buff with dark streaks below, the two types differing so much that they are sometimes mistaken for members of different species — compare MARSH HAWK
hen hawk *n* : any of several large buteonine hawks that sometimes attack poultry (as the red-tailed hawk and the red-shouldered hawk)
henhearted \'=¦==\ *adj* : TIMID, FEARFUL, COWARDLY
hen·ism \'he,nizəm\ *n* -s [G *henismus*, fr. Gk *hen* (neut. of *heis* one) + G *-ismus* -ism — more at HENAD] : SINGULARISM, MONISM 1a
henle's loop *n, usu cap H* : LOOP OF HENLE
henle's sheath *n, usu cap H* : SHEATH OF HENLE
¹hen·na \'henə\ *n* -s [Ar *ḥinnā'* alcanna (*Lawsonia inermis*)] **1** : an Old World tropical shrub or small tree (*Lawsonia inermis*) with small opposite leaves and axillary panicles of fragrant white flowers used by Buddhists and Muslims in religious ceremonies — called also *Egyptian henna* **2 a** : a reddish brown dye obtained from leaves of the henna plant and used in tinting or dyeing the hair red **b** : a liquid, powder, or paste made by mixing henna with other coloring agents (as metallic lakes, tannin, lampblack) — called also *compound henna* **3** : a variable color averaging a strong and moderate reddish brown to strong brown
²henna \"\ *vt* -ED/-ING/-S : to dye with henna
henne·bique \¦henə¦bēk, (')en¦b-\ *adj, usu cap* [after François *Hennebique* †1927 Fr. structural engineer] : relating to concrete reinforced with steel or iron
hen·nery \'henərē\ *n* -ES [*hen* + *-ery*] **1** : a poultry farm **2** : an enclosure or house for poultry
hen·nin \'henən\ *n* -s [MF] : a high cone-shaped headdress usu. with a thin veil pendent from the top worn by European women in the 15th century — called also *steeple headdress*
hen·ny \'henē\ *adj* [*hen* + *-y*] : HEN-FEATHERED
heno- *comb form* [Gk, fr. *hen-, heis* — more at HENAD] : one ⟨*heno*theism⟩
hen·o·the·ism \'henōthē,izəm, ¦==¦=,==\ *n* [G *henotheismus*, fr. *heno-* + *-theismus* -theism] : the worship of one god without denying the existence of other gods — called also *monolatry*; compare KATHENOTHEISM

hennin

hen·o·the·ist \'henō,thēəst\ *n* [*heno-* + *-theist*] : one who practices henotheism — **hen·o·the·is·tic** \¦==thē¦istik\ *adj*
hen party *n* : a party for women only
¹hen·peck \-k\ *vt* [back-formation fr. *henpecked*] : to subject (one's husband) to persistent nagging and attempts to dominate
²henpeck \"\ *n* **1** : a henpecked husband **2** : an act or instance of henpecking
hen·pecked \'hen,pekt\ *adj* : subject to domination or persistent nagging by a wife
hen pepper *n* : SHEPHERD'S PURSE
hen pigeon *n* : a long-legged erect pigeon with a short tail carried high
hen plant *n* : either of two common plantains: **a** : BROAD-LEAVED PLANTAIN 1 **b** : RIBGRASS
¹hen·ri·cian \hen'rishən\ *n* -s *usu cap* [in sense 1, fr. ML *Henricianus*, fr. *Henricus* (Henry of Lausanne), 12th cent. Fr. heresiarch + L *-ianus* -ian; in sense 2, fr. NL *Henricianus*, fr. *Henricus* (Henry VIII) †1547 king of England + L *-ianus* -ian] **1** : a member of a 12th century religious sect in Switzerland and southern France holding that the sacraments are valid only when administered by a priest who lives up to his monastic vows **2** : an advocate of secular supremacy over the church and of the ecclesiastical reforms instituted during the reign of Henry VIII of England
²henrician \(')=¦==\ *adj, usu cap* **1** : of, relating to, or associated with Henry of Lausanne **2** : of or relating to Henry VIII of England or the ecclesiastical measures taken during his reign
hen·ri deux faïence \¦äⁿ(,)rē¦də(r)¦-, -dē¦-, =¦=¦=-\ *n, usu cap H&D* [after Henry II (*Henri Deux*) †1559 king of France] : SAINT-PORCHAIRE FAÏENCE
hen·ri·et·ta \,henrē'edə\ *or* **henrietta cloth** \¦==¦==-\ *n* -s *usu cap H* [after *Henrietta* Maria †1669 queen consort of Charles I of England] : a fine soft twilled fabric for dresses made of wool and sometimes with a silk warp
henroost \'=,=\ *n* : a place where fowls roost
hen·ry \'henrē, -ri\ *n, pl* **henrys** *or* **henries** [after Joseph *Henry* †1878 Am. physicist] **1** : the practical mks unit of inductance equal to the self-inductance of a circuit or the mutual inductance of two circuits in which the variation of one ampere per second results in an induced electromotive force of one volt, the unit being taken as standard in the U. S. **2** : a unit of inductance that is equal to 1.00049 henries and that was formerly taken as the standard in the U. S. — called also *international henry*
henry's law *n, usu cap H* [after William Henry †1836 Eng. chemist] : a fact in physical chemistry: the weight of a gas dissolved by a liquid is proportional to the pressure of the gas
henry system *n, usu cap H* [after Sir Edward *Henry* †1931 Brit. government official] : a system of numerical and letter classification of fingerprint patterns that treats the ten fingers as a unit and forms the basis of the majority of identification systems employed in English-speaking countries
hens *pl of* HEN
hens·low's sparrow \'henz,lōz-\ *n, usu cap H* [after J. S. *Henslow* †1875 Am. botanist] : a common No. American sparrow (*Passerherbulus henslowii*) found in old fields
¹hent \'hent\ *vt* **hent; hent; henting; hents** [ME *henten*, fr. OE *hentan* — more at HUNT] **1** *dial* **a** : to lay hold on : SEIZE, CATCH **b** : to take away : carry off **2** *obs* : to arrive at : REACH ⟨have ~ the gates —Shak.⟩
²hent *n* -s [obs. E *hent* art of seizing, fr. ¹*hent*] *obs* : conception of an idea or plan : INTENT ⟨up, sword, and know thou a more horrid ~ —Shak.⟩
hen·te·ni·an \(')hen¦tēnēən\ *adj, usu cap* [John *Hentenius* (Henten) †1566 Fr. theologian who prepared the 1547 edition of the Vulgate + E *-an*] : of or relating to the 1547 edition of the Vulgate used for some time as the standard text of the Roman Catholic Church
hen track *or* **hen scratch** *n* : an illegible or scarcely legible mark intended as handwriting ⟨covering page after page of ruled yellow foolscap with his inky *hen tracks* —Bruce Bliven b. 1889⟩
hen·tri·a·con·tane \,hen·,trīə'kän·,tān, -,trēə-\ *n* -s [ISV *hentriacont-* (fr. *hen-* — fr. Gk *hen*, neut. of *heis* one — + *triacont-* — fr. Gk *triakonta* thirty) + *-ane*] : a solid paraffin hydrocarbon $C_{31}H_{64}$; *esp* : normal hentriacontane $CH_3(CH_2)_{29}CH_3$ found in many natural waxes
henware \'=,=\ *n* : BADDERLOCKS
henwife \'=,=\ *n, pl* **henwives** : a woman who raises poultry
he-oak \'=,=\ *n* : BEEFWOOD 1
he·or·to·log·i·cal \(¦)hē,ȯ(r)dᵊl¦äjəkəl\ *adj* : of or relating to heortology
he·or·tol·o·gy \,hē,ȯ(r)'täləjē\ *n* -ES [Gk *heortē* feast + E *-o-* + *-logy*] : a study of religious calendars; *esp* : a study of the history and the meaning of the seasons and festivals of the church year

[1]**hep** \ˈhep\ *var of* HIP

[2]**hep** \ˈhep, ˈhəp\ *interj* [origin unknown] — used to mark the cadence when troops are marching at attention

[3]**hep** \ˈhep\ *or* **hip** \ˈhip\ *adj* [origin unknown] **1 :** characterized by a keen informed awareness of or interest in what is new or smart **:** extremely alert and knowing ⟨astronautics, to which the small fry have been ~ for quite some time —C.J.Rolo⟩ ⟨you'll go crazy if you start using all that *hip* talk —Stanford Whitmore⟩ **2 :** characterized by a keen interest in and ready responsiveness to jazz ⟨each night after playing with his quintet before ~ audiences he studies classical compositions —Bob Thomas⟩ ⟨listening to recorded jazz with *hip* friends —*Metronome*⟩

HEP *abbr* hydroelectric power

he·par \ˈhē,pär\ *n* -s **1** [NL, fr. LL, liver (organ), fr. Gk *hēpar*] **:** LIVER 6 **2** [LL] **:** LIVER 1

hep·a·rin \ˈhepərən\ *n* -s [ISV *hepar* (organ) + *-in*] **:** a polysaccharide sulfuric acid ester found in liver, lung, and other tissues that prolongs the clotting time of blood by preventing the formation of fibrin and that is used in vascular surgery and in treatment of postoperative thrombosis and embolism

hep·a·rin·iza·tion \,hepərənəˈzāshən, -,nīˈz-\ *n* -s **:** the process of heparinizing

hep·a·rin·ize \ˈhepərə,nīz\ *vt* -ED/-ING/-S [*heparin* + *-ize*] **:** to treat with heparin so as to make the blood nonclotting

hepat- *or* **hepato-** *comb form* [ML, fr. L, fr. Gk *hēpat-, hēpato-*, fr. *hēpat-, hēpar*] **1 :** liver ⟨*hepat*ectomy⟩ ⟨*hepato*logy⟩ **2 :** liver and **:** hepatic and ⟨*hepato*colic⟩ ⟨*hepato*splenomegaly⟩

hep·a·tec·to·mize \,hepəˈtektə,mīz\ *vt* -ED/-ING/-S **:** to excise the liver of

hep·a·tec·to·my \-,mē\ *n* -ES [*hepat-* + *-ectomy*] **:** excision of the liver or of a part of the liver

[1]**he·pat·ic** \həˈpad·ik, -at|, |ēk\ *adj* [L *hepaticus*, fr. Gk *hēpatikos*, fr. *hēpat-, hēpar* liver + *-ikos* -ic; akin to L *jecur* liver, Skt *yakṛt*, Lith *jáknos, jeknos*] **1 a :** of, relating to, or affecting the liver ⟨~ cirrhosis⟩ **b :** resembling the liver in color or form ⟨~ aloes⟩ **2** *archaic* **:** of, relating to, or resembling a liver (sense 6) **3** [NL *Hepaticae*] **:** of or relating to the class Hepaticae

[2]**hepatic** \"\ *n* -s [NL *Hepaticae*] **:** a plant of the class Hepaticae **:** LIVERWORT

[1]**he·pat·i·ca** \|əkə, |ēkə\ *n* [NL, fr. ML, liverwort, fr. L *hepatica*, fem. of *hepaticus* of the liver; fr. the shape of the lobed leaves] **1 a** *cap* **:** a small genus of perennial herbs (family Ranunculaceae) of the north temperate zone that flower in the early spring and have lobed basal partly evergreen leaves and delicate white, pink, blue, or purplish flowers **b** -s **:** any plant or flower of the genus *Hepatica* **2** -s [ML] **:** a common liverwort (*Marchantia polymorpha*)

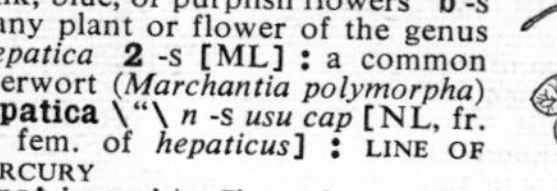
hepatica

[2]**hepatica** \"\ *n* -s *usu cap* [NL, fr. L, fem. of *hepaticus*] **:** LINE OF MERCURY

he·pat·i·cae \|ə,sē\ *n pl, cap* [NL fr. ML *hepaticae*, pl. of *hepatica* liverwort] **:** a class of Bryophyta comprising the liverworts and being distinguished from Musci by the presence of a usu. thalloid gametophyte that is not produced from a protonema, unicellular rhizoids and elaters, and antheridia and archegonia that are borne on the thallus and produce a short-lived and simple sporophyte — compare ANTHOCERATALES, JUNGERMANNIALES, MARCHANTIALES, SPHAEROCARPALES

hepatic artery *n* **:** the branch of the coeliac artery that supplies the liver with arterial blood

hepatic cell *n* **:** one of the polygonal epithelial cells of the liver that secrete bile

hepatic duct *n* **:** a duct conveying the bile away from the liver and in man and many other vertebrates uniting with the cystic duct to form the common bile duct — see DIGESTION illustration

hepatic line *n, usu cap H* **:** LINE OF MERCURY

he·pat·i·col·o·gist \hə,pad·əˈkäləjəst\ *n* -s **:** a specialist in hepaticology

he·pat·i·col·o·gy \-jē\ *n* -ES [NL *Hepaticae* + E *-o-* + *-logy*] **:** a branch of botany that deals with the Hepaticae

hepatic tanager *n* **:** a common tanager (*Piranga flava hepatica*) of the southwestern U. S. and Mexico

hepatic vein *n* **:** one of the veins that carry the blood received from the hepatic artery and from the portal vein away from the liver and that in man are usu. three in number and open into the inferior vena cava

hep·a·tite \ˈhepə,tīt\ *n* -s [G *hepatit*, fr. *hepat-* (fr. Gk *hēpat-* hepat-) + *-it* -ite; fr. its odor] **:** a barite that becomes fetid when rubbed or heated

hep·a·ti·tis \,hepəˈtīd·əs, -ītəs\ *n* -ES [NL, fr. *hepat-* + *-itis*] **:** inflammation of the liver or a condition characterized by such inflammation — see INFECTIOUS HEPATITIS

hep·a·ti·za·tion \,hepəd·əˈzāshən, -pə,tīˈz-\ *n* -s [*hepat-* + *-ization*] **:** conversion of tissue (as of the lungs in pneumonia) into a substance resembling liver tissue in which the affected tissue may become solidified

hep·a·tize \ˈhepə,tīz\ *vt* -ED/-ING/-S [*hepat-* + *-ize*] **:** to cause to undergo hepatization ⟨a *hepatized* area of lung tissue⟩

hepato- — see HEPAT-

hep·a·to·cellular \¦hepəd·ō+\ *adj* [*hepat-* + *cellular*] **:** of or involving hepatic cells ⟨~ jaundice⟩

hep·a·to·cu·pre·in \,hepəd·ōˈk(y)üprēən\ *n* -s [*hepat-* + *cupr-* + *-ein*] **:** a copper-containing protein isolated from ox liver

hep·a·to·fla·vin \-ˈflāvən *also* -lav-\ *n* [*hepat-* + *flavin*] **:** RIBOFLAVIN

hep·a·to·gen·ic \¦hepəd·ō¦jenik\ *or* **hep·a·tog·e·nous** \¦hepə¦täjənəs\ *adj* [*hepat-* + *-genic* or *-genous*] **:** produced or originating in the liver

hep·a·to·ma \,hepəˈtōmə\ *n, pl* **hepatomas** \-məz\ *or* **hepatoma·ta** \-məd·ə\ [NL, fr. *hepat-* + *-oma*] **:** a tumor of the liver that is usu. malignant — **hep·a·toma·tous** \¦==¦tämәd·əs, -¦tōm-\ *adj*

hep·a·to·me·gal·ic \¦hepəd·ōmə¦galik\ *adj* **:** of, relating to, or resembling hepatomegaly

hep·a·to·meg·a·ly \,==ˈmegəlē\ *n* -ES [*hepat-* + *-megaly*] **:** enlargement of the liver

hep·a·to·pancreas \¦hepəd·ō+\ *n* [NL *hepat-* + *pancreas*] **:** a glandular structure (as that of various crustaceans) that combines the digestive function of the vertebrate liver and pancreas — **hep·a·to·pancreatic** \"+\ *adj*

hep·a·to·portal \"+\ *adj* [*hepat-* + *portal*] **:** of or relating to the portal circulation of the liver as distinguished from that of the kidneys

hep·a·tos·co·py \,hepəˈtäskəpē\ *n* -ES [Gk *hēpatoskopia* inspection of the liver, fr. *hēpatoskopein* to inspect the liver (fr. *hēpat-* hepat- + *skopein* to inspect, contemplate, view) + *-ia* -y — more at SPY] **:** divination by inspection of the liver of animals

hep·a·to·splenomegaly \¦hepəd·ō+\ *n* [*hepat-* + *splenomegaly*] **:** coincident enlargement of the liver and spleen

hep·a·to·toxic \"+\ *adj* [*hepat-* + *toxic*] **:** causing injury to the liver ⟨~ drugs⟩

hepcat \ˈ=,=\ *n* [[3]*hep* + *cat*] **:** one who is extremely hep ⟨horn-rimmed intellectual ~*s* with wild black hair —Jack Kerouac⟩; *specif* **:** a player or devotee of hot jazz

hephthalite *usu cap, var of* EPHTHALITE

heph·the·mim·er·al caesura \¦hefthə¦mimərəl, ¦hepth-\ *n* [LL *hephthemimeris*, fr. Gk *hephthēmimerēs*, adj., containing seven halves, containing three feet and a half (fr. *hepta-* + *hēmi-* hemi- + *meros* part) + E *-al* — more at MERIT] **:** a caesura in classical verse occurring after the seventh half foot

hepi·al·i·dae \,hēpēˈalə,dē, ,hep-\ *n pl, cap* [NL, fr. *Hepialus*, type genus (irreg. fr. Gk *hēpiolos* moth) + *-idae*] **:** a family of lepidopterous insects comprising the ghost moths and having larvae burrow in wood or feed on roots

hepped up \ˈhep¦təp\ *adj* **1 :** marked by intense interest or enthusiasm **:** HIPPED — usu. used with *about* ⟨was all *hepped up* about buying some silverware —E.G.Grening⟩ **2 :** marked by lively motion or tempo **:** pepped up **:** JAZZED ⟨*hepped=up* dinner music —*Saturday Rev.*⟩

hep·pen \ˈhepən\ *adj, usu* -ER/-EST [of Scand origin; akin to ON *heppinn* lucky, *happ* good luck — more at HAP (chance)] **1** *dial Brit* **:** neat and comfortable **:** ATTRACTIVE **2** *dial Brit* **:** CLEVER, DEFT, HANDY

[1]**hep·ple·white** \ˈhepəl,(h)wīt\ *adj, usu cap* [after George *Hepplewhite* †1786 Eng. cabinetmaker] **:** of, relating to, or closely imitating a light and elegant style of furniture originating in the late 18th century England that is often distinguishable from Sheraton by its greater use of curves (as in the favored shield and heart backs of its chairs), in its preference for concave curves esp. at sideboard corners, in its characteristic detachment of chair backs from the seat rail except for short side posts, and in the sweep of the high arms of its chairs to meet the line of the front legs

[2]**hepplewhite** \"\ *n* -s *usu cap* **:** an article of Hepplewhite furniture

Hepplewhite chair

hep·ster \ˈhepstə(r)\ *or* **hip·ster** \ˈhip-\ *n* -s [[3]*hep* or *hip* + *-ster*] **1 :** a devotee of jazz ⟨the orchestra's free style in improvising has impressed at least one longhair as well as the ~*s* —*Newsweek*⟩ **2** *usu hipster* **:** one who professes hep attitudes or tastes ⟨the ladies and gentlemen of the late watch — the *hipsters* who take the sun as a personal affront —Billy Rose⟩ ⟨the colorful dialogue of the *hipster* —*Saturday Rev.*⟩

hepta- *or* **hept-** *comb form* [Gk, fr. *hepta* — more at SEVEN] **1 :** seven ⟨*hepta*gon⟩ **2** *chem* **:** containing seven atoms, groups, or equivalents ⟨*hepta*acetate⟩

hep·ta·chlor \ˈheptə,klō(ə)r\ *n* -s [*heptachloro-*, fr. *hepta-* + *chlor-*] **:** a solid insecticide $C_{10}H_5Cl_7$ similar to chlordane

hep·ta·chord \-,kȯrd\ *n* [LL *heptachordus* with seven strings, fr. Gk *heptachordos*, fr. *hepta-* + *-chordos* stringed — more at -CHORD] **1 :** a 7-stringed lyre of ancient Greece **2 :** a diatonic scale of seven notes or tones **3 :** the interval of a seventh

hep·tac·o·sane \hepˈtakə,sān\ *n* -s [ISV *heptacos-* (fr. *hepta-* + *-cos-* — fr. *eicosa-*) + *-ane*] **:** a solid paraffin hydrocarbon $C_{27}H_{56}$; *esp* **:** the normal hydrocarbon $CH_3(CH_2)_{25}CH_3$ occurring in many waxes

hep·tad \ˈhep,tad\ *n* -s [Gk *heptad-, heptas* the number seven, fr. *hepta* seven] **:** a group of seven ⟨a ~ of litanies⟩

hep·ta·dec·ane \,heptəˈde,kān\ *n* -s [ISV *heptadec-* (fr. *hepta-* + *deca-*) + *-ane*] **:** any of several isomeric paraffin hydrocarbons $C_{17}H_{36}$; *esp* **:** the low-melting crystalline normal hydrocarbon $CH_3(CH_2)_{15}CH_3$

hep·ta·dec·a·no·ic acid \¦heptə¦dekə¦nōik-\ *n* [ISV *heptadecane* + *-oic*] **:** MARGARIC ACID

hep·ta·decyl \,heptəˈdesəl, -dēs-\ *n* [*heptadecane* + *-yl*] **:** any of several univalent radicals $C_{17}H_{35}$ derived from the heptadecanes by removal of one hydrogen atom; *esp* **:** the normal radical $CH_3(CH_2)_{15}CH_2$–

hep·ta·gon \ˈheptə,gän *sometimes* -tәgәn\ *n* -s [Gk *heptagōnos* heptagonal, fr. *hepta* seven + *-gōnos* (fr. *gōnia* corner, angle) — more at -GON] **:** a plane polygon having seven angles and therefore seven sides

hep·tag·o·nal \(ˈ)hep¦tagənᵊl, -taig-\ *adj* **:** having seven angles or sides

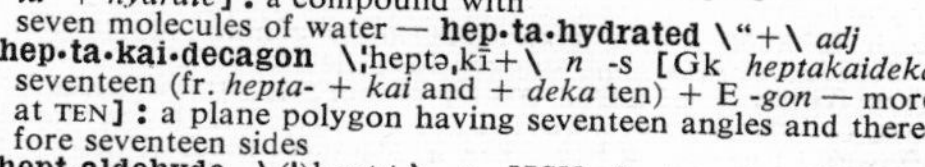
heptagons

hep·ta·hydrate \¦heptə+\ *n* [*hepta-* + *hydrate*] **:** a compound with seven molecules of water — **hep·ta·hydrated** \"+\ *adj*

hep·ta·kai·decagon \¦heptə,kī+\ *n* -s [Gk *heptakaideka* seventeen (fr. *hepta-* + *kai* and + *deka* ten) + E *-gon* — more at TEN] **:** a plane polygon having seventeen angles and therefore seventeen sides

hept·aldehyde \(ˈ)hept+\ *n* [ISV *hepta-* + *aldehyde*] **:** ENANTHALDEHYDE

hep·tam·e·ter \hepˈtaməd·ə(r)\ *n* [*hepta-* + *-meter*] **:** a poetic line of seven feet — **hep·ta·met·ri·cal** \¦heptə¦metrəkəl\ *adj*

hep·ta·nal \ˈheptə,nal\ *n* -s [*heptane* + *-al*] **:** ENANTHALDEHYDE

hep·tane \ˈhep,tān\ *n* -s [ISV *hepta-* + *-ane*] **:** any of nine isomeric paraffin hydrocarbons C_7H_{16}; *esp* **:** the liquid normal hydrocarbon $CH_3(CH_2)_5CH_3$ occurring in petroleum and as the chief constituent of some pine oils

hep·ta·no·ic acid \¦heptə¦nōik-\ *n* [*heptane* + *-oic*] **:** ENANTHIC ACID

hep·ta·none \ˈheptə,nōn\ *n* -s [ISV *heptane* + *-one*] **:** a ketone $C_7H_{14}O$ derived from normal heptane

hep·ta·phyllite \¦heptə+\ *n* [*hepta-* + *phyllite*] **:** any of a group of micas (as muscovite and other light-colored micas) with seven metallic ions per ten oxygen and two hydroxyl ions — compare OCTAPHYLLITE

[1]**hep·ta·ploid** \ˈheptə,plȯid\ *adj* [*hepta-* + *-ploid*] **:** having seven times the monoploid number of chromosomes

[2]**heptaploid** \"\ *n* -s **:** a heptaploid individual, group, or generation

hep·ta·ploi·dy \ˈ==,plȯidē\ *n* -ES **:** the condition of being heptaploid

hep·tarch \ˈhep,tärk\ *n* -s [*hepta-* + [1]*-arch*] **:** one of the rulers of a heptarchy

hep·tar·chal \(ˈ)hep¦tärkəl\ *or* **hep·tar·chic** \-kik\ *or* **hep·tar·chi·cal** \-kəkəl\ *adj* **:** of, relating to, or constituting a heptarchy

hep·tarchy \ˈhep,tärkē\ *n* -ES [*hepta-* + *-archy*] **1 :** a government by seven persons **2 :** a confederacy of seven Anglo-Saxon kingdoms held to have existed in the 7th and 8th centuries with each kingdom having its own ruler and one of the seven heptarchs sometimes being recognized as overlord

hep·ta·stich \ˈheptə,stik\ *n* -s [*hepta-* + *-stich*] **:** a group, stanza, or poem of seven lines

hep·ta·style \-,stīl\ *also* **hep·ta·sty·lar** \¦==¦stīlə(r)\ *adj* [*hepta-* + *-style, -stylar*] **:** marked by columniation with seven columns across the front — compare DISTYLE

hep·ta·sulfide \¦heptə+\ *n* [*hepta-* + *sulfide*] **:** a sulfide containing seven atoms of sulfur in the molecule

hep·ta·syllabic \¦heptə+\ *adj* [*hepta-* + *syllabic*] **:** consisting of or having seven syllables ⟨a ~ line⟩

hep·ta·syllable \"+\ *n* [*hepta-* + *syllable*] **:** a poetic line of seven syllables

hept·atomic \¦hept+\ *adj* [*hepta-* + *atomic*] **1 :** consisting of seven atoms **2 :** having seven replaceable atoms or radicals

hep·ta·tonic \¦heptə+\ *adj* [*hepta-* + *tonic*] **:** composed of seven musical tones

hep·ta·valent \¦heptə+\ *adj* [*hepta-* + *valent*] **:** having a valence of seven

hep·tene \ˈhep,tēn\ *n* -s [ISV *hepta-* + *-ene*] **:** any of the three straight-chain heptylenes

hep·ti·tol \ˈheptə,tōl, -,tōl\ *n* -s [*hepta-* + *-itol*] **:** a hepta-hydroxy alcohol that is obtained by reducing a heptose or that exists naturally

hep·tode \ˈhep,tōd\ *n* -s [ISV *hepta-* + *-ode*] **:** a vacuum tube with seven electrodes including a cathode, an anode, a control grid, and four additional grids or other electrodes

hep·to·ic acid \(ˈ)hep¦tōik-\ *n* [*heptane* + *-oic*] **:** any of the monocarboxylic acids $C_6H_{13}COOH$ (as enanthic acid) derived from the heptanes

hep·tose \ˈhep,tōs *also* -ōz\ *n* -s [ISV *hepta-* + *-ose*] **:** any of a class of monosaccharides $C_7H_{14}O_7$ containing seven carbon atoms in the molecule and obtainable in various ways from lower sugars

hept·ox·ide \hept+\ *n* [ISV *hepta-* + *oxide*] **:** an oxide containing seven oxygen atoms in the molecule

hep·tran·chi·as \hepˈtraŋkēəs\ *n, cap* [NL, prob. irreg. fr. *hepta-* + *branchiae*] **:** a genus of sharks (family Hexanchidae) having seven pairs of branchial clefts

hep·tu·lose \ˈheptə,lōs, -pchə- *also* -ōz\ *n* -s [*hepta-* + *-ulose*] **:** a ketose $C_7H_{14}O_7$ containing seven carbons in the molecule; *esp* **:** the isomer having the carbonyl group in the beta or 2-position ⟨D-*manno-heptulose* is found in avocados⟩

hep·tyl \ˈheptəl\ *n* -s [ISV *hepta-* + *-yl*] **:** any of several isomeric alkyl radicals C_7H_{15} derived from the heptanes; *esp* **:** the normal radical $CH_3(CH_2)_5CH_2$–

hep·tyl·ene \ˈheptə,lēn\ *n* -s [ISV *heptyl* + *-ene*] **:** any of several liquid isomeric hydrocarbons C_7H_{14} belonging to the ethylene series and including the heptenes

hep·tyl·ic acid \(ˈ)hep¦tilik-\ *n* [ISV *heptyl* + *-ic*] **:** HEPTOIC ACID

hep·tyne *also* **hep·tine** \ˈhep,tīn\ *n* -s [ISV *hepta-* + *-yne* or *-ine*] **:** any of three isomeric straight-chain liquid hydrocarbons C_7H_{12} of the acetylene series

[1]**her** [ME *hire*, fr. OE *hiere, hire, hyre*, gen. of *hēo, hīo* she — more at HE] *obs possessive of* [1]SHE

[2]**her** \R (h)ər, ˈhər, +V ˈhər·; -R (h)ə(r, ˈhə̄, +V ˈhər· *or* ˈhə̄ *also* ˈhər\ *adj* [ME *hire*, fr. OE *hiere, hire, hyre*, gen. of *hēo, hīo*] **1 a :** of or relating to her or herself as possessor **:** due to her **:** inherent in her **:** associated or connected with her ⟨before she has her ~ floor swept —Edna S. V. Millay⟩ ⟨you have not seen Maine until you have seen ~ islands —R.W. Hatch⟩ — compare [1]SHE **b :** of or relating to her or herself as author, doer, giver, or agent **:** effected by her **:** experienced by her as subject **:** that she is capable of ⟨~ paintings⟩ ⟨~ research⟩ ⟨the reason for ~ winning the game⟩ ⟨she did ~ best⟩ **c :** of or relating to her or herself as object of an action **:** experienced by her as object ⟨~ rescuer⟩ ⟨~ exclusion from the club⟩ **d :** that she has to do with or is supposed to possess or to have knowledge or a share of or some interest in ⟨she plays ~ waltzes beautifully⟩ **e :** that is esp. significant for her **:** that brings her good fortune or prominence — used with *day* or sometimes with other words indicating a division of time ⟨it's not only her birthday, it's ~ day⟩ **2** *now dial* **:** -'s — used after a noun or noun phrase designating a female person or something personified as female in place of the possessive ending *'s* ⟨Jane Doe ~ book⟩

[3]**her** \"\ *pron, objective case of* SHE [ME *hire*, fr. OE *hiere, hire, hyre*, dat. of *hēo, hīo*] **1** [1]SHE 1, 2, 3: **a** — used as indirect object of a verb ⟨tell ~ the news⟩ **b** — used as object of a preposition ⟨a gift for ~⟩ **c** — used as direct object of a verb ⟨lifted the skiff and slid ~ into the water —Ernest Hemingway⟩ **d** — used in comparisons after *than* and *as* when the first term in the comparison is the direct or indirect object of a verb or the object of a preposition ⟨the dress fits her sister as well as ~⟩ ⟨give me the book rather than ~⟩ ⟨this course of study would be more useful to you than ~⟩ **e** — used in absolute constructions esp. together with a prepositional phrase, adjective, or participle ⟨she was invited to go dancing two or three times a week, and ~ without half as many nice dresses as she really needed⟩ ⟨and ~ being my own child⟩ **f** — used by speakers on all educational levels and by many reputable writers, though disapproved by some grammarians, in the predicate after forms of *be*, in comparisons after *than* and *as* when the first term in the comparison is the subject of a verb, and in other positions where it is itself neither the subject of a verb nor the object of a verb or preposition ⟨it was not ~ one hated but the idea of her —Virginia Woolf⟩ ⟨her sister sings better than ~⟩ ⟨~ and her excuses⟩ **g** — used in substandard speech as the subject of a verb which it does not immediately precede or as part of the compound subject of a verb ⟨~ and John got married⟩ **h** — used with a gerund in combination with other pronouns (as *him*) in the objective case ⟨I can't imagine ~ doing that any more than I can imagine him doing it⟩ **2 :** HERSELF — used reflexively as indirect object of a verb ⟨she bought ~ a hat⟩, object of a preposition ⟨she took her son with ~⟩, or direct object of a verb ⟨she sat ~ down⟩

[4]**her** *like stressed pronunciations at* [2]HER\ *n* -s **:** WOMAN, GIRL ⟨four hims and a ~ —Charles Dickens⟩

her *abbr* **1** heraldic; heraldry **2** [L *heres*] heir

hera \ˈherə\ *n, pl* **hera** *or* **heras** *usu cap* **1 :** the peasant segment of the Nyoro people presumed to be cognate with the Bairu **2 :** a member of the Hera people

her·a·bol myrrh *or* **heer·a·bol myrrh** \ˈherə,bōl-\ *n* [origin unknown] **:** the true myrrh of commerce said to be obtained from an East African and Arabian tree (*Commiphora myrrha*)

her·a·cle·an \¦herə¦klēən\ *or* **her·a·cleian** \-lē(y)ən, -līən\ *adj, usu cap* [*Heraclean* fr. L *Heracleus*, (fr. Gk *Hērakleios*, fr. *Hēraklēs*, Heracles, legendary Greek hero) + E *-an*; *Heracleian* fr. Gk *Hērakleios* + E *-an*] **:** of or relating to the hero Heracles

he·rac·le·on·ite \həˈraklēə,nīt\ *n* -s *usu cap* [*Heracleon*, 2d cent. Gnostic Christian + E *-ite*] **:** a follower of the Gnostic Heracleon of Alexandria

[1]**her·a·cle·o·pol·i·tan** \¦herə,klēə¦pälətᵊn\ *or* **her·a·cle·op·o·lite** \,==,klēˈäpə,līt\ *adj, usu cap* [*Heracleopolit-*, *Heracleopolis*, ancient city of Egypt + E *-an* or *-ite*] **:** of or relating to the ancient city of Heracleopolis in northern Egypt — often used of the kings of the IXth and Xth dynasties in Egypt

[2]**heracleopolitan** \"\ *n* -s *usu cap* **:** a native or inhabitant of Heracleopolis in northern Egypt

her·a·cle·um \,herəˈklēəm\ *n, cap* [NL, irreg. fr. Gk *hērakleia*, a plant, fr. *Hēraklēs* Hercules] **:** a widely distributed genus of plants (family Umbelliferae) having wing-margined fruit and large umbels of white flowers — see COW PARSNIP

[1]**her·a·cli·te·an** \¦herə¦klīd·ēən, -,klīˈtēən\ *also* **her·a·clitic** \-¦klid·ik, -lī|\ *adj, usu cap* [L *Heraclite*us (fr. Gk *Hērakleiteios*, fr. *Hērakleitos* Heraclitus, 6th-5th cent. B.C. Greek philosopher) + E *-an* or *-ic*] **:** of or relating to the philosopher Heraclitus or his theories

[2]**heraclitean** \"\ *also* **heraclitic** \"\ *n* -s *usu cap* **:** a follower of Heraclitus

her·a·cli·te·an·ism \,==ˈklīd·ēə,nizəm, -,klīˈtē-\ *n* -s *usu cap* **:** a philosophy based on the theory that everything is in flux and nothing remains fixed except the logos which is at once law and a ruling element identified with fire and that the world is made of the four elements fire, water, earth, and air which are continually transmuted into one another in fixed measures

[1]**her·ald** \ˈherəld\ *n* -s [ME *heraud, herald*, fr. MF *hiraut, heraut*, fr. an (assumed) Gmc compound (akin to the name *Chariovalda* attested in Tacitus) whose first component is akin to OHG *heri* army, and whose 2d component is akin to OHG *waltan* to have power over, rule — more at HARRY, WIELD] **1 a :** an official at a tournament of arms whose duties consisting orig. of making announcements came to include keeping the scores, interpreting the rules, and marshaling the combatants **b :** an officer whose original duties of a tournament official came to include also the marshaling of other chivalric ceremonials, the making of official announcements, and the carrying of messages to or from rulers or commanders esp. in war with the status of ambassador **c :** such an officer of a monarch or government also having the responsibility for devising, granting, registering, and confirming armorial bearings, this responsibility coming to constitute his chief function as earlier functions became obsolete **:** OFFICER OF ARMS **d :** a member of the second of three grades of officers of arms ranking above a pursuivant and below a king of arms **2 a :** an official crier or messenger having duties similar in one or more respects to those of the herald of medieval and modern Europe ⟨Mercury was the gods' ~⟩ **b :** one (as a soldier) who signals with a trumpet ⟨more chieftains came, with ~*s* who blew on trumpets that were twelve feet long —Hector Bolitho⟩ **c :** AVANT-COURIER **3 a :** one that precedes or foreshadows **:** HARBINGER, FORERUNNER ⟨flights of ravens . . . are the sure ~*s* of the approach of the deer —Farley Mowat⟩ ⟨revolutions . . . were the ~*s* of social changes —R.W.Livingstone⟩ **b** (1) **:** one that conveys news or proclaims **:** ANNOUNCER ⟨hark the ~ angels sing —George Whitefield⟩ ⟨it was the lark, the ~ of the morn —Shak.⟩ (2) **:** one that supports or advocates **:** SPOKESMAN ⟨conspicuous ~ of this enfranchising movement —C.A. Dinsmore⟩ **4 :** a specialist in heraldry **:** HERALDIST **5 :** a European noctuid moth (*Scoliopteryx libatrix*) **6 :** the identifying symbol or monogram of a railroad usu. displayed on its freight cars

[2]**herald** \"\ *vt* -ED/-ING/-S **1 :** to give notice of **:** ANNOUNCE, SIGNAL ⟨the publisher ~*s* a second series —J.N.Hazard⟩ ⟨the approach of a cold air mass . . . is ~*ed* by a shift of the wind —P.E.James⟩ **2 a :** to bring to public notice **:** PUBLICIZE ⟨one of the most ~*ed* and most exciting events in the country —T.H.Fielding⟩ **b :** to greet esp. with enthusiasm **:** HAIL ⟨the show was ~*ed* with a glum essay —E.R.Bentley⟩ ⟨automation has been extravagantly ~*ed* by some as the threshold to a new Utopia —John Diebold⟩ **3 :** to signal the approach of **:** PRECEDE, FORESHADOW ⟨~*ed* by a man ringing a bell and

esquired by his clerk —Adrian Bell⟩ ⟨an increase in . . . local quakes in a volcanic region is fairly sure to ~ an eruption —Howel Williams⟩

he·ral·dic \he'raldik, hə'-, -dēk\ *adj* [F *héraldique*, fr. ML *heraldus* (fr. MF *hiraut, heraut*) + F *-ique* -ic] **:** of or relating to heralds or heraldry ⟨the ~ emblem of the emperor —Ethel Lewis⟩ ⟨the ~ procession moved on in gilded coaches —*Time*⟩ — **he·ral·di·cal·ly** \-dək(ə)lē, -dēk-, -lī\ *adv*

her·ald·ist \'herəldəst\ *n* -s **:** a specialist in heraldry

herald of arms *also* **herald at arms :** [1]HERALD 1

her·ald·ry \'herəldrē, -ri\ *n* -ES [[1]*herald* + *-ry*] **1 a :** the art or practice of an officer of arms including the devising, blazoning, and granting of armorial insignia, the investigation of persons' rights to use arms or particular armorial ensigns, the tracing and recording of pedigrees, the settling of questions of precedence, the marshaling of processions, and the supervision of public ceremonies **b :** pomp and elaborate ceremony esp. with display of armorial ensigns **:** PAGEANTRY ⟨historic ~ of a British coronation⟩ **c :** a branch of knowledge that deals with the history and practice of bearing and displaying armorial ensigns and with the art of describing them **:** ARMORY **2 a :** armorial ensigns ⟨methods of painting ~ have changed very little —G.W.Eve⟩ **b :** insignia (as military badges or Japanese mons) that resemble or are likened to armorial ensigns ⟨brands are the ~ of the range —J.F. Dobie⟩ **3** *archaic* **:** the office of an official crier or messenger ⟨I trust my next ~ will be to a more friendly court —E.G. Bulwer-Lytton⟩ **4** *obs* **:** social rank or precedence ⟨you are more saucy . . . than the commission of your birth and virtue gives you ~ —Shak.⟩ **5 :** advance notice or publicity ⟨the play opened with no ~ to speak of⟩

heralds' college *n, cap H&C* **:** COLLEGE OF ARMS

heralds' office *n, cap H & usu cap O* **:** COLLEGE OF ARMS

heraldy *n* -ES [ME *heraldie*, fr. *heraud, herald* + *-ie* -y] *obs* **:** HERALDRY

her·a·path·ite \'herə,pa,thīt, -pȧ,-\ *n* -s [William B. *Herapath* †1868 Eng. chemist + E *-ite*] **:** a salt of quinine that is obtained by treating the sulfate with iodine in the form of rhomboidal plates capable of polarizing light and that is used as a polarizing agent usu. in the form of small crystals oriented in the same direction in a transparent film

heras *pl of* HERA

he·rat \he'rät\ *or* **he·rati** \-ädē\ *n* -s *usu cap* [fr. *Herat*, Afghanistan, where such rugs are made] **1 :** a usu. heavy cotton, silk, or occas. wool Oriental rug of loose texture that is tied with the Ghiordes knot and characterized by a basic pattern of a rosette between two curved leaves that is often much elaborated — compare KHORASSAN **2 :** an Ispahan of the 16th and 17th centuries

herb \'(h)ərb, '(h)əb, '(h)əib\ *n* -s *often attrib* [ME *erbe, herbe*, fr. OF, fr. L *herba*] **1 :** a seed-producing annual, biennial, or herbaceous perennial that does not develop persistent woody tissue but dies down at the end of a growing season — compare SHRUB, TREE **2 :** a plant or plant part valued for its medicinal, savory, or aromatic qualities ⟨under ~s I have included laurel leaves —J.W.Parry⟩ **3** *archaic* **:** GRASS, VEGETATION ⟨underfoot the ~ was dry —Alfred Tennyson⟩ **4 :** the leafy top of an herbaceous plant considered separately from the root

her·ba·ce·ae \,(h)ər'bāsē,ē\ *n pl, cap* [NL, fr. fem. pl. of L *herbaceus*] *in some esp former classifications* **:** a phylum comprising all plants that are fundamentally herbaceous and remain so — compare LIGNOSAE

her·ba·ceous \(')(h)ər'bāshəs\ *adj* [L *herbaceus* grassy, fr. *herba* grass, herb + *-aceus* -aceous] **1 a :** of, relating to, or having the characteristics of an herb **b** *of a stem* **:** having little or no woody tissue and persisting usu. for a single growing season **2 :** having the texture, color, or appearance of a leaf ⟨~ sepals⟩ — **her·ba·ceous·ly** *adv* — **her·ba·ceous·ness** *n* -ES

herbaceous border *n* **:** a permanent flower border consisting primarily of hardy herbaceous perennials but frequently including annuals and biennials

herbaceous grafting *n* **:** grafting in which both stock and scion are herbaceous (as in grafting a scion of double-flowered gypsophila onto a stock of single-flowered gypsophila)

herbaceous perennial *n* **:** a plant whose top growth dies down annually but whose crowns, roots, bulbs, or rhizomes survive the winter

herb·age \'(h)ərbij, -əb-, -əib-, -bēj\ *n* -s [ME, fr. MF, fr. *herbe, erbe* herb + *-age*] **1 :** grass and other herbaceous vegetation esp. when used for grazing animals **:** PASTURE **2 :** the succulent parts (as the foliage and young stems) of herbaceous plants **3 :** an easement of pasturage on another's ground

her·ba im·pia \,(h)ərbə'impēə\ *n* [L, lit., undutiful or unfilial herb; fr. the fact that small branches shoot out from the top of the main stem and on top of the parent stem] **:** a cotton rose (*Filago germanica*)

[1]**herb·al** \'(h)ərbəl, -əb-, -əib-\ *n* -s [*herb* + *-al* (n. suffix)] **1 :** a book in which plants are named, described, and often pictured usu. with special reference to their officinal properties **2** *archaic* **:** HERBARIUM 1

[2]**herbal** \"\ *adj* [*herb* + *-al* (adj. suffix)] **:** of, relating to, or made of herbs

herb·al·ist \-ləst\ *n* -s **1 a :** one that collects, grows, or deals in herbs, esp. medicinal herbs **b :** HERB DOCTOR ⟨described herself as an ~ and dresser of sores —C.J.Brown⟩ **2** *obs* **:** BOTANIST

herb·al·ize \-,līz\ *vi* -ED/-ING/-S **:** to collect plants (as medicinal herbs)

her·ba·rism \-bə,rizəm\ *n* -s [L *herbaria* botany (fr. *herba* grass, herb + *-aria* -ary) + E *-ism*] *archaic* **:** BOTANY

herbarist *n* -s [L *herbaria* + E *-ist*] *obs* **:** HERBALIST

her·bar·i·um \,(h)ər'ba(a)rēəm, ,(h)ə'-, ,(h)əi'-, ,(h)ə(r)'-, -ber-, -bar-\ *n, pl* **herbaria** [LL, fr. L *herba* + *-arium* -ary] **1 :** a collection of dried plant specimens usu. mounted and systematically arranged for botanical reference **2 :** a room, building, or institution housing an herbarium

her·ba·rize \'hərbə,rīz\ *vi* -ED/-ING/-S [L *herbaria* + E *-ize*] *archaic* **:** BOTANIZE

[1]**her·bar·ti·an** \(')her¦bärdēən, ¦hər¦-\ *adj, usu cap* [Johann F. *Herbart* †1841 Ger. philosopher + E *-ian*] **:** of or relating to the German philosopher Herbart, his doctrines, or esp. the educational system outlined by him and developed by his disciples

[2]**herbartian** \"\ *n* -s *usu cap* **:** one who supports or believes in Herbartian doctrines

her·bar·ti·an·ism \(,)=¦==ə,nizəm\ *n* -s *usu cap* **:** the doctrines advocated by the German philosopher Herbart and his followers

herb·a·ry \'(h)ərbərē, -əb-, -əib-, -ri\ *n* -ES [*herb* + *-ary*] *archaic* **:** a garden of herbs or vegetables

herbbane \'=,=\ *n* **:** BROOMRAPE

herb bar·ba·ra \-'bärb(ə)rə, -'bȧb-\ *n, pl* **herbs barbara** *or* **herb barbaras** *usu cap B* [trans. of ML or NL *herba* (*Sanctae*) *Barbarae*, fr. *Barbara* (St. Barbara) 3d cent. Christian martyr] **:** WINTER CRESS

herb ben·net \-'benət\ *n, pl* **herbs bennet** *or* **herb bennets** [ME *herbe beneit*, fr. MF *herbe beneite, herbe benoite*, fr. ML *herba benedicta*, lit., blessed herb] **:** a European herb (*Geum urbanum*) with pinnatifid leaves and yellow flowers

herb chris·to·pher \-'kristəfə(r)\ *n, pl* **herbs christopher** *or* **herb christophers** *usu cap C* [trans. of NL or ML *herba* (*Sancti*) *Christophori*, after *Christophorus* (St. Christopher) 3d cent. Christian martyr] **1 :** a common European baneberry (*Actaea spicata*) **2 :** either of two American baneberries: **a :** WHITE BANEBERRY **b :** RED BANEBERRY **3 :** ROYAL FERN **4 :** FLEABANE a **5 :** MEADOWSWEET 2

herb doctor *n* **:** one who practices healing by the use of herbs — called also *herbalist*

her·bert river cherry \'hərbərt-\ *n, usu cap H&R* [fr. the *Herbert river*, Australia] **:** QUEENSLAND CHERRY

herb gerard \-jə'rärd, -'je,rärd\ *n, pl* **herbs gerard** *or* **herb gerards** *usu cap G* [trans. of ML or NL *herba* (*Sancti*) *Gerardi*, after *Gerardus* (St. Gerard) †1120 founder of the Knights of St. John] **:** GOUTWEED

her·bi·ci·dal \¦(h)ərbə¦sīdᵊl\ *adj* **1 :** of or relating to an herbicide **2 :** having the ability to destroy plants ⟨~ agents⟩

her·bi·cide \'=ə,sīd\ *n* -s [ISV *herbi-* (fr. L, fr. *herba* grass, herb) + *-cide*] **:** an agent (as a chemical) used to destroy or inhibit plant growth; *specif* **:** a selective weed killer that is not injurious to crop plants

herbier *comparative of* HERBY

herbiest *superlative of* HERBY

herb·ish \'(h)ərbish\ *adj, now dial* **:** of, relating to, or resembling herbs

her·biv·o·ra \(,)(h)ər'bivərə\ *n pl* [NL, fr. neut. pl. of *herbivorus*] **1** *cap, in former classifications* **:** a group of mammals nearly or exactly equivalent to Ungulata and feeding mainly on herbage **2 :** herbivorous animals; *esp* **:** members of the Herbivora

her·bi·vore \'(h)ərbə,vō(ə)r\ *n* -s [NL *Herbivora*] **:** a plant-eating animal; *esp* **:** one of the Herbivora

her·bi·vor·i·ty \,(h)ərbə'vȯrəd·ē\ *n* -ES [*herbivorous* + *-ity*] **:** the quality or state of being herbivorous ⟨the form of the molar teeth . . . is recognizable, but the ~ of the fossil is not thereby determined —Richard Owen⟩

her·biv·o·rous \¦(h)ər¦bivərəs, ,(h)ər'b-\ *adj* [NL *herbivorus*, fr. L *herbi-* (fr. *herba* grass, herb) + *-vorus* -vorous] **1 :** feeding on plants **:** PHYTOPHAGOUS — used esp. of mammals; compare CARNIVOROUS, OMNIVOROUS **2 :** having a stout body-build and a long small intestine **:** ENDOMORPHIC — opposed to *carnivorous* — **her·biv·o·rous·ly** *adv*

herb·less \'(h)ərbləs\ *adj* **:** lacking herbs or herbage

herb·let \-lət\ *n* -s *archaic* **:** a small herb

herblike \'=,=\ *adj* **:** resembling an herb

herb lily *n* **:** a plant of the genus *Alstroemeria*

herb mercury *n, pl* **herbs mercury** *or* **herb mercuries :** a Eurafrican annual herb (*Mercurialis annua*) widely naturalized as a weed and having inconspicuous greenish flowers

herb of grace *n, pl* **herbs of grace** [so called fr. the association of *rue* (plant) with *rue* (repentance)] **:** RUE

herb-of-the-cross \,===\ *n, pl* **herbs-of-the-cross :** EUROPEAN VERVAIN

her·bo·rist \'(h)ərbərəst\ *n* -s [MF *herboriste, herboliste*, irreg. fr. *herbe* herb (fr. L *herba*) + *-iste* -ist] **:** HERBALIST

her·bo·ri·za·tion \,==rə'zāshən, -,rī'z-\ *n* -s **:** an excursion for the study or collection of plants

her·bo·rize \'==,rīz\ *vi* -ED/-ING/-S [F *herboriser*, fr. *herboriste* + *-iser* -ize] **:** BOTANIZE

herb·ous \'(h)ərbəs\ *or* **her·bose** \-,bōs\ *adj* [L *herbosus*, fr. *herba* grass, herb + *-osus* -ous, -ose] **:** HERBY

herb par·is \-'parəs\ *n, pl* **herbs paris** *or* **herb parises** *usu cap P* [by folk etymology (influence of *Paris*, France) fr. ML or NL *herba paris*, lit., herb of a couple; fr. the resemblance of its four leaves on a stalk to a true lover's knot] **:** a European herb (*Paris quadrifolia*) resembling and closely related to the trilliums and commonly reputed to be poisonous

herb patience *n, pl* **herbs patience :** PATIENCE 3

herb rob·ert \-'räbə(r)t\ *n, pl* **herbs robert** *or* **herb roberts** *usu cap R* [trans. of ML *herba Roberti*, prob. fr. *Robertus* (St. Robert) †1067 Fr. ecclesiastic] **:** a sticky low herb (*Geranium robertianum*) with small reddish purple flowers

herbs *pl of* HERB

herb st. bar·ba·ra \-(,)sānt'bärb(ə)rə, -sənt-, -'bȧb-\ *n, pl* **herbs st. barbara** *or* **herb st. barbaras**, *usu cap S&B* [trans. of ML or NL *herba* (*Sanctae*) *Barbarae* — more at HERB BARBARA] **:** WINTER CRESS

herb she·rard \-shə'rärd\ *n, pl* **herbs sherard** *or* **herb sherards** [NL *Sherardia*] **:** FIELD MADDER

herb so·phia \-sə'fīə, -sō'-, -fēə\ *n, pl* **herbs sophia** *or* **herb sophias** *usu cap S* [prob. fr. NL *sophia* (specific epithet of *Descurainia sophia*), fr. the name *Sophia*] **:** a hedge mustard (*Descurainia sophia*) with long linear pods

herbst's corpuscle \'herps(ts)-\ *n, usu cap H* **:** CORPUSCLE OF HERBST

herb tobacco *n* **:** a mixture of herbs containing coltsfoot (*Tussilago farfara*) and smoked for relieving coughs

herb trinity *n, pl* **herbs trinity** *or* **herb trinities** [trans. of ML or NL *herba trinitatis*] **1** [so called fr. the three-colored flowers] **:** PANSY **2** [so called fr. the three lobes of the leaf] **:** HEPATICA 1b

herbwoman \'=,==\ *or* **herbwife** \'=,=\ *n, pl* **herbwomen** *or* **herbwives :** a woman who sells herbs

herby \'(h)ərbē\ *adj* -ER/-EST [*herb* + *y*] **1 :** abounding in herbaceous vegetation **2 :** relating to, resembling, or tasting like an herb ⟨a rich ~ flavor⟩

her·cog·a·mous \¦hər¦kägəməs\ *adj* [Gk *herkos* fence, barrier + E *-gamous*] **:** incapable of self-fertilization

her·cog·a·my \,hər'kägəmē\ *n* -ES [Gk *herkos* + E *-gamy*] **:** a state in which self-pollination is made impossible by structural obstacles (as in the flowers of orchids)

her·cu·la·ne·an \¦hərkyə¦lānēən\ *adj, usu cap* [*Herculaneum*, ancient city in southwestern Italy + E *-an*] **:** of or relating to the ancient Roman city of Herculaneum

her·cu·le·an \¦hər¦kyə¦lēən, ¦hər¦kyülēən, ¦hə¦, ¦həi¦, hə(r)'kyül-\ *adj, usu cap* [*Hercules* + E *-an*] **1 :** of or relating to Hercules or his feats ⟨*Herculean* labors⟩ **2 a :** of heroic proportions **:** very large and strong ⟨*Herculean* longshoreman⟩ ⟨the bed was a wide and *Herculean* piece —Ellery Queen⟩ **b :** of extraordinary might or tremendous difficulty **:** displaying or requiring the strength of a Hercules ⟨*Herculean* exertions⟩ ⟨*Herculean* task⟩ **syn** see HUGE

her·cu·les \'hərkyə,lēz, 'hək-,'həik-\ *n* -ES *usu cap* [after *Hercules*, Greco-Roman mythological hero noted for his great strength and for having accomplished twelve gigantic tasks imposed upon him, fr. L, fr. Gk *Hēraklēs*] **:** a man of great physical strength ⟨said of him that it was greedy and unfair to be an Adonis and a Hercules as well —E.V.Lucas⟩

hercules' allheal \-,lē'zȯl,hēl\ *n, usu cap H* **:** a European herb (*Opopanax chironium*) — compare WOUNDWORT

hercules beetle *n, usu cap H* **1 :** a very large beetle (*Dynastes hercules*) native to tropical America of which the male being prob. the largest existing insect attains a length of over five inches and bears a long forwardly projecting horn on the thorax and another on the head **2 :** RHINOCEROS BEETLE

hercules club *n, usu cap H* **:** a large Australian whelk (*Pyrazus ebeninus*) with a dark brown nodose shell

hercules'-club \'==,=¦=\ *n, pl* **hercules'-clubs** *usu cap* **1 :** any of several prickly shrubs or trees: **a :** an ornamental tree (*Zanthoxylum clava-herculis*) of the southeastern U. S. and the West Indies **b :** either of two shrubs of the Bahamas (*Zanthoxylum coreaceum* or *Caesalpinia bahamensis*) **2 :** a gourd (*Lagenaria vulgaris*) with fruit sometimes exceeding five feet in length **3 :** a small prickly tree (*Aralia spinosa*) of eastern U. S. — called also *angelica tree, devil's-walking-stick*

hercules stone *n, usu cap H* **:** LODESTONE

her·cyn·i·an \(¦)hər¦sinēən\ *adj, usu cap* [L *Hercynia* (*silva*) Hercynian forest + E *-an*] **1 :** of or relating to an extensive mountain range covered with forests in ancient Germany **2 :** of or relating to the folding and mountain building that took place in the eastern hemisphere in late Paleozoic time — see GEOLOGIC TIME table

her·cy·nite \'hərsə,nīt\ *n* -s [G *hercynit*, fr. L *Hercynia* (*silva*), its locality + G *-it* -ite] **:** a black mineral $FeAl_2O_4$ consisting of an oxide of iron and aluminum and constituting a member of the spinel series

[1]**herd** \'hərd, 'həd, 'həid\ *n* -s [ME *herde, herd*, fr. OE *heord*; akin to OHG *herta* herd, ON *hjörth*, Goth *hairda* herd, MW *cordd* troop, Gk *korthys* heap, Skt *śardha* herd, troop] **1 a :** a number of one kind of animal kept together under human care or control: as (1) **:** a company of one of the larger domestic animals ⟨a ~ of horses⟩ ⟨~s of swine⟩; *esp* **:** such a company of domestic oxen — often contrasted with *flock* ⟨patriarchs rich in ~s of cattle and flocks of sheep and goats⟩ (2) **:** a company of one kind of wild or semi-domesticated animals kept or bred for human use ⟨a ~ of ranch mink⟩ ⟨a ~ of laboratory mice⟩ **b :** a congregation of gregarious wild animals: as (1) **:** a group of one or more kinds of usu. large herbivorous mammals ⟨a ~ of elephants⟩ ⟨~s of antelopes darkening the African veldt⟩ or of marine mammals ⟨the dolphin ~ playing through the swell —Sacheverell Sitwell⟩ ⟨~s of seal coming ashore to bear young⟩ (2) **:** a school of large fish ⟨grazing on the bottom in ~s like the haddock —Rachel L. Carson⟩ (3) **:** a flock of large and usu. chiefly terrestrial or aquatic birds ⟨a ~ of swans⟩ ⟨a large ~ of wild turkeys⟩ **2 a :** a group of people usu. having a common bond ⟨entered the troop with the midwinter ~ of tenderfeet —MacKinlay Kantor⟩ **b :** the whole body of mankind **:** the undistinguished masses **:** MOB ⟨isolate the individual prophets from the ~ —Norman Cousins⟩; *esp* **:** society viewed as clinging to a blind conformity of standards and behavior ⟨the ~ of mankind can hardly be said to think; their notions are almost all adoptive —Earl of Chesterfield⟩ ⟨a boarding school where the thirteen-year-old . . . helplessly watches the ~ tearing to shreds the spirit of a nonconformist student —Rose Feld⟩ **3 :** a considerable quantity **:** large number ⟨~s of new cars from America —Christopher Rand⟩

[2]**herd** \"\ *vi* -ED/-ING/-S [ME *herden*, fr. *herde, herd*, n.] **1 a :** to come together in a herd **:** feed or run together ⟨animals are in general fond of ~*ing* and grazing in company —Oliver Goldsmith⟩ **b :** to assemble or move in a group ⟨New Yorkers . . . ~*ing* resignedly on subway platforms —Charlotte Devree⟩ ⟨when the bell rang they ~*ed* in together —Oliver La Farge⟩ **2 :** to place oneself in a group **:** ASSOCIATE ⟨it is desirable that young noblemen should ~ —Sir Walter Scott⟩

[3]**herd** \"\ *n* -s [ME *hierde, hirde, herde*, fr. OE *hyrde, hierde*; akin to OHG *hirti* herdsman, ON *hirthir*, Goth *hairdeis*; derivatives fr. the root of E [1]*herd*] **1 a :** one that herds domestic animals **:** HERDSMAN — now used chiefly in combination ⟨cow*herd*⟩ ⟨swine*herd*⟩ **b** *dial Brit* **:** SHEPHERD **2** [[4]*herd*] *West* **:** a tour of duty as a herdsman ⟨a new ranch hand, on ~ for the first time⟩ ⟨cook had flapjacks ready for the men coming off night ~⟩

[4]**herd** \"\ *vt* -ED/-ING/-S [ME *herden*, fr. *hierde, herde*, n.] **1 a :** to keep (animals) together **:** LEAD, DRIVE ⟨dogs are often trained to ~ sheep⟩ **b :** to gather, lead, or drive as if in a herd ⟨a nation that ~s fifteen millions of its own citizens into slave labor camps —James Burnham⟩ ⟨seventy-five boys and girls were ~*ed* by six or eight teachers —W.A.White⟩ **2 :** to place in a group **:** ASSOCIATE ⟨~ us with their kindred fools —Jonathan Swift⟩

herdbook \'=,=\ *n* **:** a book containing the records of one or more herds **:** an official record of the individuals and pedigrees of a recognized breed esp. of cattle or swine

herdboy \'=,=\ *n* **1 :** a boy who tends herd or assists a herder **2 :** COWBOY 3a

herd·er \-də(r)\ *n* -s [[4]*herd* + *-er*] **1 :** HERDSMAN **2 :** FLUME RUNNER **3 :** a worker who couples and uncouples locomotives in a railroad yard

her·der·ite \'hərdə,rīt, 'her-\ *n* -s [Baron Siegmund A. W. von *Herder* †1838 Ger. mining official + E *-ite*] **:** a mineral $CaBe(PO_4)(F,OH)$ consisting of phosphate and fluoride of beryllium and calcium

her·dic \'hərdik\ *n* -s [after Peter *Herdic* †1888 Am. inventor] **:** a small horse-drawn omnibus of late 19th century America having side seats and an entrance at the back ⟨a ~ load of boys from some dance in town —C.M.Flandrau⟩

herdic

herding *n* -s [fr. gerund of [4]*herd*] **:** the act or work of taking care of livestock

herd instinct *n* **:** an inherent tendency to congregate or to react in unison ⟨*herd instinct* of wild horses⟩ ⟨the startled cows obeyed the *herd instinct* to stampede⟩; *esp* **:** a theoretical human instinct toward gregariousness and conformity

herds *pl of* HERD, *pres 3d sing of* HERD

herd's-grass *also* **herd grass** \'=,=\ *n, pl* **herd's-grasses** [after John *Herd*, who in 1700 found timothy growing in N. H.] **1 :** TIMOTHY **2** [so called fr. its being frequently sown in mixtures with timothy] **:** REDTOP 1

herds·man \'hərdzmən, 'hədz-,'həid-\ *n, pl* **herdsmen** [alter. of earlier *herdman*, fr. ME *hirdman, herdman*, fr. OE *hyrdeman*, fr. *hierde, hyrde* herdsman + *man* — more at HERD] **:** a manager, breeder, or tender of livestock (as cattle or sheep)

herd·wick \'hər,dwik\ *n* [fr. obs. *herdwick* pasture ground, fr. ME, fr. *hierde, herde* herdsman + *wick*; fr. the breed's having been developed on the herdwicks of the Abbey of Furness in Lancashire, England] **1** *usu cap* **:** a British breed of very hardy coarse-wooled mountain sheep **2** -s *often cap* **:** an animal of the Herdwick breed

[1]**here** \'hi(ə)r, -iə; "*Come here!*" *is often* kə'mi-\ *adv* [ME, fr. OE *hēr*; akin to OHG *hiar, hier* here, ON & Goth *hēr*, OE *hē* he — more at HE] **1 a :** at this point in space **:** in this location ⟨turn ~⟩ ⟨if they mean to have a war, let it begin ~ —John Parker⟩ ⟨in this very spot ⟨he is not ~, for he has risen —Mt 28:6 (RSV)⟩ — opposed to *there*; often used interjectionally esp. in answering a roll call or in calling a domestic animal **b :** at this point in time **:** NOW ⟨~ it's August and summer's nearly over⟩ **2 a :** at this critical point esp. of an argument or development **:** at this juncture ⟨~ it becomes necessary to bring our concepts together —R.M.Weaver⟩ **b :** in the matter in question **:** in this case or particular ⟨the essential fact ~ was the division of the Roman empire —Gilbert Highet⟩ **3 :** in the present life or state **:** on earth ⟨happy ~, and more happy hereafter —Francis Bacon⟩ — often used with *below* ⟨implies some endeavor to improve conditions ~ below instead of a single-minded concentration on . . . the next world —Elmer Davis⟩ **4 :** to or into this place **:** HITHER ⟨bring the book ~⟩ **5 —** used interjectionally and often reduplicated as an admonitory rebuke ⟨~, that's enough⟩ or soothing encouragement ⟨~ ~, don't cry⟩ — **here goes —** used interjectionally to express resolution or resignation esp. at the beginning of a rash, difficult, or unpleasant undertaking — **neither here nor there :** having no interest or relevance **:** of no consequence ⟨matters of comfort and convenience that are *neither here nor there* to a real sailing fan⟩

[2]**here** \"\ *adj* [ME, fr. *here*, adv.] **1 —** used for emphasis esp. after a demonstrative pronoun or after a noun modified by a demonstrative adjective ⟨this boy ~ knows what happened⟩ **2** *now substand* — used for emphasis after a demonstrative adjective but before the noun modified ⟨with regard to this ~ robbery —Charles Dickens⟩

[3]**here** \"\ *n* -s [ME, fr. *here*, adv.] **1 :** the present location or juncture **:** this place ⟨where do we go from ~⟩ ⟨from ~ on the story gets more interesting⟩ — opposed to *there* **2 :** immediacy in space abstracted from the other qualities and relations of the immediate experience ⟨a ~ to which we relate all theres —James Ward⟩

[4]**he·re** \'he,re\ *n* -s [OE *here* army — more at HARRY] **:** an army in Anglo-Saxon times; *esp* **:** an army of invaders

hereabouts *or* **hereabout** \¦==¦=\ *adv* [ME *her abute*, fr. *her, here* here + *abute, about* about] **:** about or near this place **:** in this vicinity ⟨the countryside ~⟩ ⟨somewhere ~⟩

[1]**hereafter** \(')=¦==\ *adv* [ME *here after*, fr. OE *hēræfter*, fr. *hēr* here + *æfter* after — more at HERE, AFTER] **:** after this: **a :** after this in order or sequence ⟨here and ~ I am following . . . her own version —S.H.Adams⟩ **b :** after this in time ⟨devise the agencies . . . that will make them impossible ~ —B.N.Cardozo⟩ **c :** in some future time or state ⟨this life is a preparation for life ~ —F.B.Artz⟩ **d :** at the time of taking effect — used with this meaning in a statute and expressly so construed by law in some states of the U. S.

[2]**hereafter** \'=¦==\ *n* -s *sometimes cap* **1 :** a time to come **:** FUTURE **2 :** an existence or state beyond this life — often used with *the* ⟨a belief in the ~ is shown in gifts and articles left with the dead in many burials —P.I.Wellman⟩

[3]**hereafter** \(')=¦==\ *adj, archaic* **:** FUTURE ⟨that ~ ages may behold what ruin happened in revenge of him —Shak.⟩

here and now *n* **:** the immediately present space and time **:** this day and age — used with *the* ⟨although Omar was entirely negative in describing the joys of the hereafter, he was completely positive in enumerating the less doubtful joys of the *here and now* —H. W. Van Loon⟩ ⟨man's obligation is in the *here and now* —W.H.Whyte⟩

here and there *adv* [ME] **1 a :** in one place and another **:** IRREGULARLY ⟨hills topped *here and there* by white buildings —Fred Zimmer⟩ **b :** from time to time **:** now and then ⟨only caught a word *here and there*⟩ **2 :** hither and thither ⟨roamed *here and there* looking for blueberries⟩

hereat \=¦=\ *adv, archaic* [ME *here at*, fr. *here* + *at* (prep.)] **:** at or because of this

hereaway \¦==¦=\ *or* **here·aways** \¦==¦wāz\ *adv* [ME *hereaway*, fr. *here* + *away*] *now dial* **:** HEREABOUT

hereby \(')=¦=\ *adv* [ME, fr. *here* + *by* (prep.)] **:** by this

a *obs* **:** by this place **:** near here ⟨~ upon the edge of yonder coppice —Shak.⟩ **b :** by this means; *esp* **:** by means of this act or document ⟨the sum of $800 is ~ authorized to be appropriated for this purpose —*Congressional Record*⟩

heredes *pl of* HERES

he·red·i·ta·ble \hə'redədəbəl, he'-, ¦herə¦did-\ *adj* [MF, fr. LL *hereditare* to inherit (fr. L *hered-*, *heres* heir) + *-abilis* -able — more at HEIR] **:** HERITABLE

her·e·dit·a·ment \,herə'didəmənt; hə'redəd-, he'-\ *n* -s [ML *hereditamentum*, fr. LL *hereditare* + L *-mentum* -ment] *law* **:** heritable property **:** lands, tenements, any property corporeal or incorporeal, real, personal, or mixed, that may descend to an heir

he·red·i·tar·i·an \hə,redə'terēən, he,-\ *n* -s [*hereditary* + *-an*] **:** an advocate of hereditarianism

he·red·i·tar·i·an·ism \-ēə,nizəm\ *n* -s **:** a doctrine that individual differences may be accounted for primarily on the basis of genetics — compare ENVIRONMENTALISM

he·red·i·tar·i·ly \=¦==¦terəlē, -li\ *adv* **:** in an hereditary manner ⟨the members of society who are ~ predisposed toward mental illness —J.F.Cuber & R.A.Harper⟩

he·red·i·tar·i·ness \-rēnəs, -rin-\ *n* -ES **:** the quality or state of being hereditary

he·red·i·tary \hə'redə,terē, -ri *also* he'-\ *adj* [L *hereditarius*, fr. *hereditas* inheritance + *-arius* -ary — more at HEREDITY] **1 a :** genetically transmitted or capable of being genetically transmitted from parent to offspring ⟨~ factor⟩ ⟨~ disease⟩ — see HEREDITY 2; compare ACQUIRED, CONGENITAL, FAMILIAL **b :** characteristic of or fostered by one's predecessors **:** ANCESTRAL ⟨~ pride⟩ ⟨~ bravery⟩ ⟨~ feud⟩ **2 a :** descended or capable of descending from an ancestor to an heir at law **:** received or passing by inheritance or required to pass by inheritance ⟨~ wealth⟩ ⟨~ monarchy⟩ **b :** having title or possession through inheritance ⟨~ sovereign⟩ ⟨~ nobility⟩ **3 :** of a kind or status established by tradition ⟨~ enemy⟩ ⟨a ~ reputation for liberality and kindness —Louise P. Kellogg⟩ **4 :** of or relating to inheritance or heredity ⟨unless he had the ~ dispositions which he has, he would not behave the way he does —Arthur Pap⟩ ⟨the ~ principle, once a business has been founded, has proved . . . a serviceable method of ensuring fresh supplies of managerial talent —Roy Lewis & Angus Maude⟩ **syn** see INNATE

he·re·di·tas *also* **hae·re·di·tas** \hə'redə,tas\ *n, pl* **heredita·tes** \=,==¦tād·(,)ēz\ [L] *Roman & civil law* **:** inheritance or succession **:** the rights and liabilities to which an heir succeeds **:** an estate of a deceased person regarded as a juridical person

hereditas ja·cens \-'jā,senz\ *n* [L, lit., lying (inactive) inheritance] *Roman & civil law* **:** an inheritance not entered upon by the heir **:** a vacant succession

he·red·i·ty \hə'redədē, -ətē, -i *also* he'-\ *n* -ES [MF *heredité*, fr. L *hereditat-*, *hereditas*, fr. *hered-*, *heres* heir + *-itat-*, *-itas* -ity — more at HEIR] **1 a :** INHERITANCE ⟨their fathers were of yeoman rank, both by ~ and as large freeholders —Charles Partridge⟩ **b :** TRADITION ⟨Bretons are fishermen by ~⟩ **2 a :** the sum of the qualities and potentialities of an individual that are genetically derived from its ancestors **:** the germinal constitution of an individual **b :** the transmission of qualities from ancestor to descendant (as from parent to child) through a mechanism lying primarily in the chromosomes of the germ cells that in sexually reproducing organisms sorts out in meiosis the genes accumulated in past generations and recombines them during fertilization to produce a new individual conforming to the general pattern of its kind but exhibiting variations dependent both on specific recombination of factors and on interaction between the hereditary potentialities and the environment — compare GALTON'S LAW OF INHERITANCE, LAMARCKISM, MENDEL'S LAW, PANGENESIS, PHENOCOPY, WEISMANNISM

heredo- *comb form* [NL, fr. L *hered-*, *heres* heir — more at HEIR] **:** hereditary **:** hereditarily ⟨*heredo*ataxia⟩ ⟨*heredo*familial⟩

her·e·ford \'hərfərd, 'hēfəd, 'həifəd *sometimes* 'herəf-\ *n* [fr. county of *Hereford*, England] **1 a** *usu cap* **:** a breed of hardy red beef cattle with white faces and markings and either horned or polled that originated in Herefordshire, England, but are now extensively raised in the western U.S. and other grazing regions **b** -s *often cap* **:** an animal of this breed **2a** *usu cap* **:** an American breed of red and white swine typically having markings similar to those of Hereford cattle **b** -s *often cap* **:** a hog of this breed

hereford disease *n, cap H* **:** GRASS TETANY

her·e·ford·shire \'herəfərd,shi(ə)r, -fəd,shiə, -,shə(r), *US* " *or* 'hərf- *or* 'hēf- *or* 'həif-\ *or* **hereford** *adj, usu cap* [fr. *Herefordshire* or county of *Hereford*, Eng.] **:** of or from the county of Hereford, England **:** of the kind or style prevalent in Hereford

herefrom \(')=¦=\ *adv* [¹*here* + *from* (prep.)] *archaic* **:** from this: **a :** from this place **b :** from this source

he·re·geld \'herə,geld, -,ye-\ *n* -s [OE *heregeld*, *heregild*, fr. *here* army + *gield*, *geld*, *gild* payment, tribute — more at HARRY, GELD] **1 :** DANEGELD **2** [ME (Sc dial.) *heregeld*, *hereyeld*, *hereȝeld*, prob. fr. OE *heregeld*] *old Scots law* **:** a due or payment corresponding to the English heriot

herehence *adv* [¹*here* + *hence*] *obs* **:** from or away from this point or source

herein \(,)=¦=\ *adv* [ME *herinne*, *herin*, fr. OE *hērinne*, fr. *hēr* here + *inne* in — more at HERE, IN] **:** in this: **a :** in this place ⟨~ were many vaulted . . . walks hewn out of the rock —John Ray⟩ ⟨enclosed ~ you will find my check⟩ **b :** in this passage, book, or document ⟨all legislative powers ~ granted —*U.S.Constitution*⟩ **c :** in this fact or particular ⟨~ you war against your reputation —Shak.⟩

hereinabove \=¦=¦=, ¦=(,)==¦=\ *adv* [*herein* + *above*] **:** above this **:** at a prior point in this writing or document ⟨payments due said fund, as ~ described —*Nat'l Bituminous Coal Wage Agreement*⟩

hereinafter \¦==¦==\ *adv* [*herein* + *after*] **:** after this **:** in the following part of this writing or document ⟨a behavior to be ~ defined —Edward Sapir⟩ ⟨subject to conditions of this policy as ~ specified⟩

hereinbefore \=¦=¦=, ¦=(,)==¦=\ *adv* [*herein* + *before*] **:** before this **:** in the preceding part of this writing or document ⟨oaths ~ directed to be taken by the governor —Martin Wight⟩

hereinbelow \=¦==¦=, ¦=(,)==¦=\ *adv* [*herein* + *below*] **:** below this **:** at a subsequent point in this writing or document ⟨which report is ~ set forth in full —*U.S.Code*⟩

he·rem *or* **che·rem** \'kārəm, 'ker-\ *n* -s [Heb *ḥerem*] **:** one of three forms of ecclesiastical excommunication pronounced by a rabbi or by the officials of a synagogue or community

he·rend porcelain \'he,rend-\ *n, usu cap H* [fr. *Herend*, town in Hungary where it was made] **:** Hungarian hard-paste porcelain made since the 18th century and often imitative of other wares

here·ness *n* -ES [*here* + *-ness*] **:** the state of being here

her·eni·ging *also* **her·ee·ni·ging** \hə'rēnəkiŋ, -əkiŋ\ *n* -s *sometimes cap* [Afrik *hereniging* (formerly spelled *hereeniging*), lit., reunion, reuniting, fr. *herenig* to reunite + *-ing*] **:** an amalgamation of So. African political parties

hereof \(')=¦= *sometimes* -¦äf\ *adv* [ME *herof*, fr. OE *hērof*, fr. *hēr* here + *of* (prep.)] — more at HERE, OF] **:** of this ⟨the twigs ~ are physic —Thomas Fuller⟩; *specif* **:** of this writing or document ⟨shown in the schedule on the last page ~⟩

hereon \(')=¦=\ *adv* [ME *heron*, fr. OE *hēron*, fr. *hēr* here + *on* (prep.)] **:** on this: **a** *archaic* **:** on this fact or basis ⟨happiness grounded ~ —Nehemiah Grew⟩ **b :** on this writing or document ⟨endorsed ~⟩

hereout \(')=¦=\ *adv* [ME *herout*, *herut*, fr. *here* + *out*, *ut* out (prep.) — more at HERE, OUT] *archaic* **:** out of this: **a :** out of this place **:** from here **b :** out of this premise **:** HENCE

here–right \(')=¦=\ *adv*, *dial Eng* **:** on the spot **:** right here ⟨let's settle it *here-right* —F.T.Elworthy⟩

he·re·ro \hə're(,)rō, 'herə,rō\ *n, pl* **herero** *or* **hereros** *usu cap* **1 a :** a Bantu people of the central part of South-West Africa — compare DAMARA **b :** a member of the Herero people **2 :** the Bantu language of the Herero people

¹**heres** *pl of* HERE

²**he·res** \'hā,rās\ *or* **hae·res** \'hī,-\ *n, pl* **here·des** *or* **haere·des** \=¦rā,dās\ [L — more at HEIR] *civil law* **:** the universal successor of a deceased person — called also *heir*

he·re·si·arch \hə'rēzē,ärk, he'-, -rēsē-; 'herəsē,-\ *n* -s [LL *haeresiarcha*, fr. LGk *hairesiarchēs* leader of a sect, leader of a group of heretics, fr. Gk *hairesis* sect & LGk, heresy + Gk *-archēs* -arch — more at HERESY] **:** an originator or chief advocate of a heresy **:** leader of a group of heretics ⟨it is not only the lives of saints who leave their mark . . . but the lives of ~s and sinners as well —D.H.Wiest⟩ ⟨became the chief Communist ~ —E.J.Simmons⟩

he·re·si·mach \hə'rēzə,mak, he'-, -rēsə-; 'herəsē,-\ *n* -s [LGk *hairesimachos*, fr. *hairesis* heresy + Gk *-machos* (fr. *machesthai* to fight) — more at HERESY, -MACHY] **:** an active opponent of heresy and heretics

he·re·si·og·ra·phy \hə,rēzē'ägrəfē, he,-, -rēsē-; ,herəsē-\ *n* -ES [*heresio-* (fr. *heresy*) + *-graphy*] **:** a treatise on heresy

he·re·si·ol·o·gist \-'äləjəst\ *n* -s **:** a writer against heresies

he·re·si·ol·o·gy \-jē\ *n* -ES [*heresio-* (fr. *heresy*) + *-logy*] **1 :** the study of heresies **2 :** a treatise on heresies

he·res ne·ces·sa·ri·us \'hā,rā,snekə'sārēəs\ *n* [LL, lit., heir of necessity] *Roman law* **:** a slave who is instituted by his master as his heir and who upon his master's death automatically attains his freedom and becomes his heir

her·e·sy \'herəsē, -si\ *n* -ES [ME *eresie*, *heresie*, fr. OF, fr. LL *haeresis*, fr. LGk *hairesis*, fr. Gk, action of taking, choice, sect, fr. *hairein* to take + *-sis*; perh. akin to Gk *hormē* assault, attack — more at SERUM] **1 a :** adherence to a religious opinion that is contrary to an established dogma of a church **:** HETERODOXY ⟨was convicted of ~ . . . because of his belief in the preexistence of souls —H.E.Starr⟩ — opposed to *orthodoxy* **b :** a deliberate and obstinate denial of a revealed truth by a baptized member of the Roman Catholic Church — compare INQUISITION 3a **c :** an opinion or doctrine contrary to church dogma ⟨all the great *heresies* . . . in Christianity have been specifically concerned with the relationship of the Son to the Father —Weston La Barre⟩ **2 a :** dissent from a dominant theory or opinion in any field ⟨so much that used to be scientific ~ is now regarded as scientific truth —Elmer Davis⟩ ⟨preaching ~ to the good Jeffersonian progressives of his day —C.B.Forcey⟩ **b :** an opinion or doctrine contrary to the truth or to generally accepted beliefs ⟨our democratic ~ which holds that . . . truth is to be found by majority vote —M.W. Straight⟩ **3 :** a group or school of thought centering around a particular heresy ⟨favoring the German school of historians and other *heresies* of similar nature —A.G.Mayous⟩

¹**her·e·tic** \'herə,tik\ *n* -s [ME *eretik*, *heretik*, fr. MF *eretique*, *heretique*, adj. & n., fr. LL *haereticus*, fr. LGk *hairetikos*, fr. Gk, able to choose, fr. *hairetos* (verbal of *hairein* to take, *haireisthai* to choose) + *-ikos* -ic] **1 a :** a dissenter from established church dogma **:** DEVIATIONIST — distinguished from *infidel* **b :** a baptized member of the Roman Catholic Church who deliberately and obstinately disavows a revealed truth **2 :** one that dissents from an accepted belief or doctrine of any kind **:** INNOVATOR, NONCONFORMIST ⟨to delete from history its ~s and its radicals would be to deprive it of that rare quality known as independence of mind —F.C.Neff⟩ ⟨he who resists a mania may be trodden under foot like any other ~ —W.G. Sumner⟩

²**heretic** \", hə'red·|ik, he'-, -ret|, |ēk-\ *adj* [ME *eretik*, *heretik*, fr. MF *eretique*, *heretique*] **:** HERETICAL

he·ret·i·cal \hə'red·|əkəl, he'-, -ret|, |ēk-\ *adj* [ML *haereticalis*, fr. LL *haereticus* + L *-alis* -al] **1 :** of, relating to, or characterized by religious heresy **:** HETERODOX ⟨let a church member in good standing dare to utter ~ opinions on theology . . . his scalp is in danger —L.L.Rice⟩ — opposed to *orthodox* **2 :** of, relating to, or characterized by departure from accepted beliefs or standards **:** RADICAL, UNORTHODOX ⟨we must have a spirit of tolerance which allows the expression of all opinions, however ~ they may appear —J.B.Conant⟩ ⟨many critics regard individualism in art as an ~ innovation —John Dewey⟩ — **he·ret·i·cal·ly** \-k(ə)lē, -li\ *adv* — **he·ret·i·cal·ness** \-kəlnəs\ *n* -ES

he·ret·i·cate \-,kāt\ *vt* -ED/-ING/-S [ML *haereticatus*, past part. of *haereticare*, fr. LL *haereticus*] **1 :** to pronounce or denounce as heretical **2 :** to denounce as a heretic **:** make a heretic of — **he·ret·i·ca·tion** \=,=='kāshən\ *n* -s

he·ret·i·ca·tor \=¦==,kād·ə(r)\ *n* -s **:** one that hereticates

hereto \(,)=¦=\ *adv* [ME *herto*, fr. *her*, *here* here + *to* (prep.)] **:** to this writing or document ⟨the chart ~ attached⟩

¹**here·to·fore** \¦hir|d·ə¦fō(ə)r, ¦hiə|, |tə-, -fō(ə)r, -ōə, -ó(ə)\ *adv* [ME *heretofore*, *heretoforn*, fr. *here* + *tofore*, *toforn* before, fr. OE *tōforan*, fr. *tō* to + *foran* before, fr. *fore* — more at TO, FORE] **:** before this **:** up to this time **:** HITHERTO ⟨I tell you now what we have ~ kept secret from you —A.C. Whitehead⟩

²**heretofore** \"\ *adj* [ME *heretoforn*, fr. *heretoforn*, adv.] *archaic* **:** PREVIOUS ⟨in his ~ voyages —Nathaniel Hawthorne⟩

he·re·to·ga \,herə'tōgə, '==,==\ *also* **her·e·togh** \'herə,tōk\ *n* -s [ME & OE; ME *heretogh*, fr. OE *heretoga*; akin to OFris *hertoga* leader of an army, duke, OS *heritogo*, OHG *herizoho*, *herizogo*, ON *hertogi*; all fr. a prehistoric Gmc compound whose constituents are akin respectively to OE *here* army and to OE *togian* to draw, drag, and that is prob. a trans. of Gk *stratēlatēs* leader of an army — more at HARRY, TOW] **:** the leader of an army or commander of militia in Anglo-Saxon England

heretrix *var of* HERITRIX

hereunder \(,)=¦==\ *adv* [ME, fr. *here* + *under* (prep.)] **:** under this: **a :** under this written statement **:** subsequently in this writing or document **:** BELOW ⟨I subjoin ~ a brief description of the seven-year bean —*Farmer's Weekly*⟩ **b :** under this agreement **:** in accordance with the terms of this document ⟨registration of copyright . . . ~ shall not exempt the copyright proprietor from the deposit of copies —Richard Wincor⟩

hereunto \=¦=(,)=, ¦=(,)=¦=\ *adv* [¹*here* + *unto* (prep.)] **:** to this; *esp* **:** to this writing or document ⟨we ~ affix our signatures⟩

hereupon \¦==¦=\ *adv* [ME *herupon*, fr. *her*, *here* here + *upon* (prep.)] **:** on this **:** at or as a sequel to this **:** immediately after this ⟨the warning whistle sounded and ~ the last passengers scrambled aboard⟩

herewith \(,)=¦=\ *adv* [ME *herwith*, fr. OE *hērwith*, fr. *hēr* here + *with*] **:** with this: **a :** with this communication **:** accompanying this writing or document; *specif* **:** enclosed in this envelope ⟨you will find my check ~⟩ **b :** with this proof **:** by this **:** in this way ⟨~ the principle is established —A. L.Kroeber⟩

he·rez \hə'rez\ *n* -ES *usu cap* [fr. *Herez*, Iran, where such rugs are made] **:** a usu. large heavy cotton or wool Oriental rug of coarse texture and variable quality made in northwestern Iran and characterized by strong angular design and an ivory background

he·re·zeld \'herə,yeld\ *n* -s [alter. (*ȝ* being taken as *z*) of ME (Sc dial.) *heregeld*, *hereyeld*, *hereȝeld* — more at HEREGELD] **:** HEREGELD 2

heried *past of* HERY

heries *pres 3d sing of* HERY

herile *adj* [L *herilis*, *erilis*, fr. *herus*, *erus* master + *-ilis* -ile] *obs* **:** of or relating to a master

he·ring image \'hā|riŋ-, 'he|\ *n, usu cap H* [after Ewald *Hering* †1918 Ger. physiologist and psychologist] **:** a first positive afterimage in a succession of visual afterimages resulting from a brief light stimulus and appearing in the same hue as the original sensation

her·i·ot \'herēət\ *n* -s [ME *heriet*, *heriot*, fr. OE *heregeatwe*, *heregeatwa*, pl., military equipment, fr. *here* army + *geatwe*, *geatwa*, pl., equipment — more at HARRY] *Eng law* **:** a feudal duty or tribute due under English law to a lord upon the death of a tenant and consisting orig. of the horses and arms lent by the lord to his man, later of the best beast or chattel of the tenant, and in modern times (as surviving in copyhold tenures) of such a chattel as the custom of the manor enables the lord to take or of a money payment — distinguished from *relief*; compare HEREGELD 2, THIRDINGS

her·i·ot·able \-ēəd·əbəl\ *adj* **:** subject to payment of a heriot

heriot service *n* **:** a heriot reserved as an incident of the tenure of an estate in fee simple granted in free tenure before 1290

her·i·ta·bil·i·ty \,herəd·ə'bilədē, -rətə-, -lətē, -i\ *n* **:** the quality or state of being heritable

¹**her·i·ta·ble** \'herəd·əbəl, -rətə-\ *adj* [ME, fr. MF, fr. *heriter* to inherit + *-able*] **1 :** capable of being inherited or of passing by inheritance **:** INHERITABLE **2** *Scots law* **:** of or relating to heritage or heritables **3 :** HEREDITARY ⟨~ character⟩ ⟨~ office⟩ ⟨a viruslike agent transmitting ~ mammary tumors to young sucklings —*Lancet*⟩

²**heritable** \"\ *n* -s **1 :** a piece of heritable property — usu. used in pl.

heritable bond *or* **heritable security** *n, Scots law* **:** a form of bond or obligation carrying a yearly profit, secured upon land, treated as heritable, and now essentially like the English and American mortgage of real property

her·i·ta·bly \-blē, -bli\ *adv* **:** by right of inheritance

her·i·tage \'herəd·ij, -ətij *sometimes* -rə,tāj\ *n* -s [ME, fr. MF, fr. *heriter* to inherit (fr. LL *hereditare*, fr. L *hered-*, *heres* heir) + *-age* — more at HEIR] **1 a** *law* **:** real and other property that descends to an heir as distinguished from personal property that passes to an executor or administrator **:** PATRIMONY **b** *Scots law* **:** immovable property as distinguished from movable or personal property **2 a :** something transmitted by or acquired from a predecessor **:** INHERITANCE, LEGACY ⟨rich ~ of folklore⟩ ⟨a ~, a shrine, their history in stone —*Britain Today*⟩ ⟨war had left its ~ of poverty —Rose Macaulay⟩ ⟨the corn crop is a ~ from the Indians —*Annual Report of Ill. Power Co.*⟩ **b :** TRADITION ⟨a . . . party whose ~ is vision and boldness —M.W.Straight⟩ ⟨institutions . . . adapted to varying national ~s —S.P.Hayes b.1910⟩ **3 :** BIRTHRIGHT ⟨the ~ of natural freedom was long since cast away —V.L.Parrington⟩

her·i·tance \-rəd·ən(t)s, -ətə-\ *n* -s [ME *heritaunce*, fr. MF *heritance*, fr. *heriter* + *-ance*] *archaic* **:** HERITAGE, INHERITANCE

her·i·tie·ra \,herə'tirə\ *n, cap* [NL, after C.L.*L'Héritier* de Brutelle †1800 Fr. botanist] **:** a small genus of Australasian trees (family Sterculiaceae) yielding hard heavy durable wood

her·i·tor \'herəd·ə(r), -rətə-\ *n* -s [alter. of ME *heriter*, fr. MF *eretier*, *heritier*, fr. L *hereditarius*, hereditary — more at HEREDITARY] **1 :** INHERITOR **2** *Scots law* **:** the owner in fee of heritable property or in parochial law of such real property in a parish as is subject to public burdens

her·i·trix *or* **her·e·trix** \'herə·(,)triks\ *n, pl* **heritri·ces** \,herə·'trī(,)sēz\ *or* **heritrix·es** \'herə·,triksəz\ **:** a female heritor

herl \'hər(·ə)l\ *n* -s [ME *herle* — more at HARL] **1 :** a barb of a feather used in dressing an artificial fly **2 :** an artificial fly containing a herl

her·ling \'hərlən, 'her-, -liŋ\ *n* -s [origin unknown] *chiefly Scot* **:** SEA TROUT 1; *esp* **:** a young sea trout

herm \'hərm\ *n* -s [L *herma*, *hermes*, fr. Gk *hermēs* statue of Hermes, herm, fr. *Hermēs*, messenger of the gods] **:** a statue in the form of a square stone pillar surmounted by a bust or head ⟨a ~ of Themistocles which has been identified by its inscription —*New Internat'l Yr. Bk.*⟩; *esp* **:** a pillar surmounted by a usu. bearded head of Hermes — compare TERM

her·ma \'hərmə\ *n, pl* **her·mae** \-,mē, -,mī\ *or* **her·mai** \-,mī\ [L] **:** HERM

her·mae·an \,hər¦mēən\ *adj, often cap* [L *Hermaeus* (fr. Gk *Hermaios*, fr. *Hermēs*) + E *-an*] **:** of or relating to Hermes or a herm

her·ma·ic \-māik\ *adj, usu cap* [Gk *Hermaikos*, fr. *Hermaios* + *-ikos* -ic] **1 :** HERMETIC 1a **2 :** HERMAEAN

her·man·dad \,ermən'dä(th)\ *n, pl* **hermanda·des** \-ä(,)thās\ *sometimes cap* [Sp, brotherhood, fr. *hermano* brother (fr. L *germanus*, fr. *germanus*, adj., having the same parents) + *-dad* (fr. L *-tat-*, *-tas* -ty) — more at GERMAN] **:** one of several voluntary organizations formed in Spain during the 13th, 14th, and 15th centuries to maintain public order and resist the depredations of the nobles and later to exercise general police functions

her·mann's fluid \'hərmənz-, 'her,mänz-\ *n, usu cap H* [after Friedrich *Hermann* †1920 Ger. anatomist] **:** a fixing solution of platinic chloride, osmic acid, and acetic acid used in microscopy for cytological preparations

her·maph·ro·dism \hə(r)'mafrə,dizəm, ,hər'-, hə̄'-, həi'-\ *n* -s [F *hermaphrodisme*, fr. *hermaphrodite* (fr. L *hermaphroditus*) + *-isme* -ism] **:** HERMAPHRODITISM

¹**her·maph·ro·dite** \-dīt, *usu* -īd·+V\ *n* -s [ME *hermofrodite*, fr. L *hermaphroditus*, fr. Gk *hermaphroditos*, fr. *Hermaphroditos*, mythological son of Hermes and Aphrodite who became joined in body with the nymph Salmacis] **1 a :** an abnormal individual esp. among the higher vertebrates having both male and female reproductive organs — called also *androgyne* **b :** HOMOSEXUAL **2 :** a combination of diverse elements; *specif* **:** HERMAPHRODITE BRIG **3 :** an animal or plant that is normally equipped with both male and female reproductive organs **:** BISEXUAL ⟨the hydra . . . is a true ~ —Alpheus Hyatt⟩

²**hermaphrodite** \"\ *adj* **:** HERMAPHRODITIC

hermaphrodite brig *n* **:** a 2-masted vessel square-rigged forward and schooner-rigged aft — called also *brigantine*

hermaphrodite caliper *n* **:** a drawing instrument having one caliper and one divider leg

hermaphrodite duct *n* **:** a duct for the passage of both eggs and sperm in mollusks having an ovotestis

hermaphrodite brig

her·maph·ro·dit·ic \(,)=¦==¦did·|ik, ¦hər,m-, ¦hə̄,m-, ¦həi,m-, -¦dit|, |ēk\ *also* **her·maph·ro·dit·i·cal** \|əkəl, |ēk-\ *adj* **1 :** of, relating to, or characterized by hermaphroditism **2 :** MONOCLINOUS — **her·maph·ro·dit·i·cal·ly** \|ək(ə)lē, |ēk-, -li\ *adv*

her·maph·ro·dit·ish \-¦dīd·|ish, -īt|, |ēsh\ *adj* **:** HERMAPHRODITIC

her·maph·ro·dit·ism \(,)=¦==,dīd·,izəm, -,dī,tiz-\ *n* -s **:** the condition of being a hermaphrodite — compare DIOECISM

her·me·neut \'hərmə,n(y)üt\ *n* -s [Gk *hermēneutēs*, fr. *hermēneuein*] **:** an interpreter esp. in the early church

her·me·neu·tic \,hərmə¦n(y)üd·ik\ *or* **her·me·neu·ti·cal** \-d·əkəl\ *adj* [*hermeneutic* fr. Gk *hermēneutikos*, fr. (assumed) *hermēneutos* (verbal of *hermēneuein* to interpret, translate, fr. *hermēneus* interpreter, prob. of non-IE origin) + *-ikos* -ic; *hermeneutical* fr. Gk *hermēneutikos* + E *-al*] **:** of or relating to hermeneutics **:** INTERPRETATIVE ⟨use of the ~ principle in the sociology of religion⟩ — **her·me·neu·ti·cal·ly** \-d·ək(ə)lē\ *adv*

her·me·neu·tics \,hərmə'n(y)üd·iks\ *n pl but usu sing in constr, also* **her·me·neu·tic** [Gk *hermēneutikē*, fr. fem. of *hermēneutikos*] **:** the study of the methodological principles of interpretation and explanation; *specif* **:** the study of the general principles of biblical interpretation ⟨~ became a weapon in ecclesiastical controversies —J.H.Summers⟩

her·mes \'hər(,)mēz\ *n, pl* **her·mae** \-,mē, -,mī\ *or* **her·mai** \-,mī\ *usu cap* [L — more at HERM] **:** HERM

¹**her·met·ic** \hə(r)'med·|ik, ,hər'm-, (')hə̄'m-, (')həi'm-, -et|, |ēk\ *or* **her·met·i·cal** \|əkəl, |ēk-\ *adj* [NL *hermeticus*, fr. *Hermet-*, *Hermes Trismegistus* Thoth, the Egyptian god of wisdom, fabled author of a number of mystical, philosophical, and alchemistic writings, fr. Gk *Hermēt-*, *Hermēs trismegistos*, lit., thrice-great Hermes (with whom the Greeks identified Thoth) + L *-icus* -ic, *-ical*] **1** *sometimes cap* **a :** of or relating to the mystical and alchemical writings or teachings of Thoth, the Egyptian god of wisdom ⟨~ sciences⟩ **b :** relating to or characterized by occultism, alchemy, magic, or whatever is obscure and mysterious **:** RECONDITE ⟨~ poetry⟩ **2** [so called fr. the belief that Hermes Trismegistus invented a magic seal to keep vessels airtight] **a :** impervious to air **:** AIRTIGHT ⟨~ seal⟩ ⟨~ compass⟩ **b :** impervious to external influence ⟨as ~ as a nunnery —Eugene MacCown⟩ **3 :** of or relating to a herm **:** HERMAEAN

²**hermetic** \"\ *n* -s **1 :** ALCHEMIST **2 :** an expounder of hermetic teachings

her·met·i·cal·ly \|ək(ə)lē, |ēk-, -li\ *adv* **1 a :** in an airtight manner ⟨~ sealed suit for use in high-altitude flying —H.G. Armstrong⟩ **b :** in a manner that prevents entry or change ⟨doors ~ sealed to less illustrious callers —Marguerite Steen⟩

⟨two gentlemen of decided and ~ opposite views —Philip Hamburger⟩ **2 :** in an obscure or mystical manner ⟨~ painted in the Cubist discipline —Janet Flanner⟩

her·met·i·cism \(ˌ)=ˈmed·əˌsizəm, -etə-\ *n* -s *often cap* **:** HERMETISM

hermetic powder *n* **:** SYMPATHETIC POWDER

her·met·ics \(ˌ)=ˈmed·|iks, -et|, |ēks\ *n pl but usu sing in constr, usu cap* **:** HERMETISM

her·me·tism \ˈhərməˌtizəm\ *n* -s [*hermetic* + *-ism*] **1** *usu cap* **:** a system of ideas based on hermetic teachings **2 :** adherence to or practice of hermetic doctrine ⟨it is not . . . willful ~ if the message of their art is veiled and indirect —R.J. Goldwater⟩

her·me·tist \-məd·əst\ *n* -s *usu cap* **:** an adherent to hermetic doctrine or practices

her·mi·no·nes \ˌhərməˈnō(ˌ)nēz\ *or* **her·mi·o·nes** \-mēˈō-, -ˌmīˈō-\ *n pl, usu cap* [L] **:** a division of ancient Teutons described by Tacitus as occupying central and eastern Germany and including interior tribes (as the Hermunduri, Heruli, Suevians, Quadi, Lombards, Vandals)

her·mit \ˈhərmət, ˈhəm-, ˈhəim-, *usu* -əd·+V\ *n* -s *often attrib* [ME *ermite, eremite, hermite, heremite,* fr. OF, fr. LL *eremita,* fr. LGk *erēmitēs,* fr. Gk *erēmitēs,* adj., living in the desert, fr. *erēmia* desert (fr. *erēmos* desolate, lonely + *-ia* -y) + *-itēs* -ite — more at RETINA] **1 a :** one that retires from society and lives in solitude **:** ANCHORITE, RECLUSE ⟨seclusive ~*s* whether in mountain shacks or shuttered brownstone houses⟩ ⟨a ~ nation⟩; *specif* **:** a Christian ascetic living alone in an isolated place in order to devote himself to religious exercises ⟨Christian monasticism from the third century ~*s* of the Egyptian deserts⟩ — compare MONK **b :** a member of a monastic order (as the Carthusians) whose members lead a chiefly eremitical life or of the Hermits of St. Augustine **c** *obs* **:** BEADSMAN ⟨for . . . the late dignities heaped up to them we rest your ~*s* —Shak.⟩ **2 a** (1) **:** any of various plainly colored forest-dwelling tropical hummingbirds constituting the genus *Phaethornis* (2) **:** any of several related hummingbirds **b :** HERMIT CRAB **3 :** a spiced molasses cookie often containing chopped raisins and nuts

¹her·mit·age \-əd·ij, -ətij\ *n* -s [ME *ermitage, hermitage,* fr. OF, fr. *ermite, hermite* + *-age*] **1 a :** the habitation of a hermit ⟨some forlorn and naked ~ remote from all the pleasures of the world —Shak.⟩ **b :** a secluded residence or private retreat **:** HIDEAWAY ⟨retirement to some country ~ —John Buchan⟩ **c :** a house of various monastic orders **:** MONASTERY ⟨Carthusian ~⟩ **2 :** the life or condition of a hermit ⟨when public places like theaters and restaurants are an integral part of city life . . . it is sheer ~ to be forced to forgo both —Evelyn Barkins⟩

²her·mi·tage \ˈ(h)ermēˌtäzh\ *n* -s *usu cap* [fr. Tain-l'*Ermitage,* commune in Drôme dept., France] **1 :** a chiefly red Rhone Valley wine made from grapes grown above the commune of Tain-l'Ermitage **2 :** a wine similar to Hermitage made elsewhere

hermit crab *n* [so called fr. its living in the empty shells of gastropods, like a hermit in a cave] **1 :** any of numerous chiefly marine decapod crustaceans of the families Paguridae and Parapaguridae having somewhat elongated bodies and soft and more or less asymmetrical abdomens, occupying the empty shells of gastropods, and seeking larger shells as they increase in size — compare PURSE CRAB **2 :** one that behaves like a hermit crab ⟨creep out of that shell of gentility, you little *hermit crab* —W.J.Locke⟩

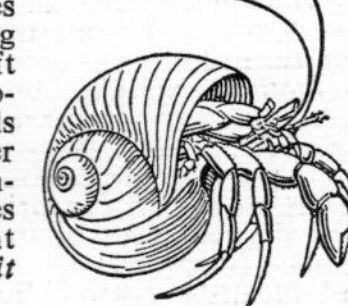
hermit crab in shell

hermit crow *n* [so called fr. its nongregarious habits] **:** CHOUGH

her·mit·ess \ˈhərməd·əs\ *or* **her·mi·tress** \-mə·trəs\ *n* -ES **:** a female hermit

her·mit·ic \(ˈ)hərˈmid·ik\ *or* **her·mit·i·cal** \-d·əkəl\ *adj* **:** of, relating to, or suited for a hermit — **her·mit·i·cal·ly** \-d·ək(ə)lē\ *adv*

her·mit·ize \ˈhərməd·ˌīz\ *vi* -ED/-ING/-S [*hermit* + *-ize*] **:** to live a solitary life

hermit of st. au·gus·tine \-əˈgəstən, -ˌȯˈg-, -ˈȯgəˌstēn\ *usu cap H&S&A* [after *St. Augustine* — more at AUGUSTINIAN] **:** a member of an order of friars established in 1256 by Pope Alexander IV

her·mit·ry \ˈhərmətrē\ *n* -ES [*hermit* + *-ry*] **:** the quality or state of being a hermit **:** ISOLATION

hermits *pl of* HERMIT

her·mit·ship \ˈ==ˌship\ *n* [*hermit* + *-ship*] **:** HERMITRY

hermit thrush *n* **:** a thrush (*Hylocichla guttata faxoni*) of eastern No. America that is dull brown above becoming rufous on the tail and spotted on the breast and is noted for its song; *broadly* **:** any of several related thrushes of western No. America

hermit warbler *n* **:** a warbler (*Dendroica occidentalis*) found from the Rocky mountains to the Pacific and having in the adult male a yellow head, black throat, and gray back

her·mo·dac·tyl \ˈhərməˌdaktᵊl, ˌ==ˈ==\ *or* **her·mo·dac·ty·lus** \ˌ==ˈ=tələs\ *n, pl* **hermodactyls** \-tᵊlz\ *or* **hermodactyli** \-təˌlī\ [ML *hermodactylus,* fr. Gk *hermodaktylon,* fr. *hermo-* (fr. *Hermēs,* messenger of the gods) + *-daktylon* (fr. *daktylos* finger)] **1 :** a root formerly used as a cathartic or for the relief of gout that was prob. derived from an Asiatic colchicum (*Colchicum luteum*) but has been often considered to be or confused with the root of the Mediterranean snake's-head iris **2 :** a plant producing hermodactyls; *broadly* **:** any of various colchicums — compare COLCHICINE

her·mo·ge·nian \ˌhərməˈjēnēən, -nyən\ *n, usu cap* [*Hermogenes,* 2d cent. A.D. Greek rhetorician (fr. L, fr. Gk *Hermogenēs*) + E *-ian*] **:** a disciple of Hermogenes in developing Marcion's doctrine of the eternity of matter

her·mo·glyph·ic \ˌhərməˈglifik\ *also* **her·mog·ly·phist** \(ˌ)hərˈmägləfəst; ˈhərməˌglif-, ˌ==ˈ==\ *n* -s [*hermoglyphic* fr. Gk *hermoglyphikos* of statuary, fr. *hermoglypheus* statuary (fr. *hermēs* herm + *-glypheus,* fr. *glyphein* to carve) + *-ikos* -ic; *hermoglyphist* fr. Gk *hermoglyphikos* + E *-ist* — more at HERM, CLEAVE] **:** one that carves statues; *esp* **:** one that engraves inscriptions on herms

her·mo·sa pink \(ˌ)hərˈmōsə-\ *n* [prob. fr. *hermosa* (*rose*) bourbon rose, fr. Sp *hermosa,* fem. of *hermoso* beautiful, fr. L *formosus* — more at FORMOSITY] **:** a moderate to strong pink that is yellower and lighter than nymph pink and bluer and darker than peachblossom (sense 1)

herms *pl of* HERM

¹hern \ˈhərn\ *n* -s [ME *herne, hirne,* fr. OE *hyrne;* akin to OFris *horne* corner, MLG *hörne,* ON *hyrni* corner, OE *horn* horn — more at HORN] *now dial Eng* **:** NOOK, CORNER

²hern \ˈhərn, ˈhər·ən\ *pron* [ME *hiren,* alter. (influenced by the *-n* in *min* mine, *thin* thine) of *hire* — more at HER] *dial* **:** HERS

³hern *also* **herne** \ˈhern, ˈhərn\ *dial Brit var of* HERON

her·nan·dia \(ˌ)hərˈnandēə\ *n, cap* [NL, fr. Francisco *Hernández* †1578 Span. botanist + NL *-ia*] **:** a genus (the type of the family Hernandiaceae of the order Ranales) of tropical trees having light combustible wood, alternate entire leaves, small paniculate flowers, and drupaceous fruits — **her·nan·di·a·ceous** \(ˌ)=ˌ==ˈāshəs\ *adj*

her·ne \ˈhe(ə)rnə\ *adj, usu cap* [fr. *Herne,* Germany] **:** of or from the city of Herne, Germany **:** of the kind or style prevalent in Herne

her·nia \ˈhərnēə, ˈhə̄n-, ˈhəin-, -nyə\ *n, pl* **herni·as** \-nēəz, -nyəz\ *or* **herni·ae** \-nēˌē\ [L — more at YARN] **:** a protrusion esp. of one of the abdominal viscera through connective tissue or through a wall of the cavity in which it is normally enclosed — called also *rupture* — **her·nial** \-nēəl, -nyəl\ *adj*

her·ni·ar·ia \ˌhərnēˈa(a)rēə\ *n, cap* [NL, fr. L *hernia* rupture + NL *-aria* — more at HERNIA] **:** a genus of small Old World herbs (family Caryophyllaceae) with minute green flowers — see RUPTUREWORT

her·ni·ar·in \-rən\ *n* -s [ISV *herniar-* (fr. NL *Herniaria,* genus name of *Herniaria hirsuta*) + *-in*] **:** a crystalline compound $C_{10}H_8O_3$ found esp. in a rupturewort (*Herniaria hirsuta*); the methyl ether of umbelliferone

¹her·ni·ary \ˈ==ˌerē, -ri\ *adj* [*hernia* + *-ary*] **:** of or relating to hernia or its treatment

²herniary \"\ *n* -ES [NL *Herniaria*] **:** a plant of the genus *Herniaria*

her·ni·ate \-ˌāt, *usu* -ˌād·+V\ *vi* -ED/-ING/-S [*hernia* + *-ate*] **:** to protrude through an abnormal body opening **:** RUPTURE

her·ni·a·tion \ˌ==ˈāshən\ *n* -s **1 :** the act or process of herniating **:** formation of a hernia **2 :** HERNIA

hernio- *comb form* [F, fr. L *hernia* — more at YARN] **:** hernia ⟨*hernio*rrhaphy⟩ ⟨*hernio*tomy⟩

her·ni·or·rha·phy \ˌhərnēˈȯrəfē\ *n* -ES [ISV *hernio-* + *-rrhaphy*] **:** an operation for hernia that involves opening the coverings, returning the contents to their normal place, obliterating the hernial sac, and closing the opening with strong sutures

her·ni·ot·o·my \-ˈäd·əmē\ *n* -ES [F *herniotomie,* fr. *hernio-* + *-tomie* -tomy] **:** the operation of cutting through a band of tissue that constricts a strangulated hernia

he·ro \ˈhē(ˌ)rō, ˈhi(-\ *n* -ES [back-formation fr. *heroes,* pl., fr. ME, fr. L, fr. Gk *hērōes,* pl. of *hērōs;* perh. akin to L *servare* to protect — more at SERVE] **1 a :** a mythological or legendary figure endowed with great strength, courage, or ability, favored by the gods, and often believed to be of divine or partly divine descent — compare CULTURE HERO, DEMIGOD **b :** a man of courage and nobility famed for his military achievements **:** an illustrious warrior **c :** a man admired for his achievements and noble qualities and considered a model or ideal **d :** the principal male character in a drama, novel, story, or narrative poem **:** PROTAGONIST **e :** the central figure in an event, action, or period **2** *New York* **:** POOR BOY

¹he·ro·di·an \həˈrōdēən, heˈ-\ *n* -s *usu cap* [ME, fr. LL *Herodianus,* fr. *Herodes* (Herod) †4 B.C. king of Judea + L *-ianus* *-ian*] **:** a member of a political party of biblical times consisting of Jews who were apparently partisans of the Herodian house and together with the Pharisees opposed Jesus

²herodian \"\ *adj, usu cap* **:** of or relating esp. to Herod the Great, king of Judea (37–4 B.C.)

he·rod·o·te·an \həˌrädəˈtēən\ *adj, usu cap* [*Herodotus,* 5th cent. B.C. Greek historian (fr. L, fr. Gk *Hērodotos*) + E *-ean*] **:** of, relating to, or suggestive of the historian Herodotus

heroess *n* -ES [*hero* + *-ess*] *obs* **:** HEROINE

¹he·ro·ic \həˈrōik, heˈ-, hēˈ-, -ōēk\ *also* **he·ro·i·cal** \-ōəkəl, -ōēk-\ *adj* [L *heroicus,* fr. Gk *hērōikos,* fr. *hērōs* hero + *-ikos* -ic, -ical] **1 a :** belonging to or representative or suggestive of the heroes of antiquity ⟨a ~ culture⟩ ⟨~ society⟩ ⟨the ~ age⟩ **b :** treating of or suitable to or used in the treatment of the heroes of antiquity ⟨~ legends⟩ ⟨~ material⟩ **2 a** (1) **:** arising from, exhibiting, or suggestive of boldness, spirit, or daring ⟨a ~ cavalry charge⟩ ⟨a ~ enterprise⟩ (2) **:** such as is likely to be undertaken only to save life ⟨~ surgery⟩ **:** EXTREME, RADICAL ⟨~ treatment⟩ **b :** supremely noble, altruistic, or self-sacrificing ⟨a ~ gesture⟩ ⟨~ deeds⟩ **3 a :** of impressively generous proportion, size, or volume ⟨a ~ voice⟩ ⟨~ contributions to charity⟩ **b :** larger than life but smaller than colossal ⟨a ~ statue⟩ **c :** having a pronounced effect **:** LARGE, POWERFUL — used chiefly of medicaments or dosage ⟨~ doses⟩ ⟨a ~ drug⟩ **4 :** belonging to or inspired by the literary conventions of Restoration England esp. as found in the works of John Dryden ⟨~ drama⟩

²heroic \"\ *n* -s **1 :** HEROIC VERSE, HEROIC POEM **2 heroics** *pl* **:** vainglorious, unnaturally extravagant, or shamelessly flamboyant conduct, behavior, or expression ⟨avoids all ~*s* . . . in its delineation of a man of dignity —*Newsweek*⟩

he·ro·i·cal·ly \-ōək(ə)lē, -ōēk-, -li\ *also* **he·ro·ic·ly** \-kl-\ *adv* **:** in a heroic manner ⟨struggling ~⟩ ⟨~ generous⟩

he·ro·i·cal·ness *n* -ES **:** the quality or state of being heroic **:** HEROICNESS

heroic couplet *n* **:** a couplet of rhyming iambic pentameters often forming a distinct rhetorical as well as metrical unit

he·ro·ic·ness *n* -ES **:** the quality or state of being heroic

he·ro·i·comic *or* **he·ro·i·comical** \həˈrōə, heˈ-, hēˈ-, -ōē+\ *adj* [F *héroïcomique,* blend of *héroïque* heroic (fr. L *heroicus*) and *comique* comic, comical, fr. L *comicus* — more at HEROIC, COMIC] **:** comic by being ludicrously noble, bold, or elevated

heroic poem *n* **:** an epic or a poem in epic style

heroic poetry *n* **:** epic poetry esp. celebrating the deeds of a hero

heroic stanza *or* **heroic quatrain** *n* **:** a rhymed quatrain in heroic verse with rhyme scheme *abab*

heroic verse *or* **heroic meter** *n* **1 :** dactylic hexameter — usu. used with special reference to epic verse of classical times **2** *or* **heroic line :** the verse form in which the heroic poetry of a particular language is or according to critical opinion should be composed (as the alexandrine in French and the hendecasyllabic line in Italian) **3 :** the iambic pentameter in rising rhythm used in epic and other serious English poetry during the 17th and 18th centuries

her·oin *also* **her·oine** \ˈhe|rəwən *sometimes* ˈhi| *or* |ˌrōin\ *n* -s [fr. *Heroin,* a trademark] **:** a bitter white crystalline narcotic $C_{21}H_{23}NO_5$ made from morphine but more potent than morphine and because of its addictive properties prohibited by law from being manufactured in or imported into the U. S. and many other countries — called also *diacetylmorphine, diamorphine*

¹her·o·ine \ˈherəwən *sometimes* ˈhir-\ *n* -s [L *heroina, heroine,* fr. Gk *hērōinē,* fem. of *hērōs* hero — more at HERO] **1 a :** a mythological or legendary woman having the qualities of a hero **b :** a woman admired for her achievements and noble qualities and considered a model or ideal **2 a :** the principal female character in a drama, novel, story, or narrative poem **b :** the central female figure in an event, action, or period

her·oin·ism \ˈhe|rəwəˌnizəm *sometimes* ˈhi| *or* |ˌrōiˌni-\ *n* -s [*heroin* + *-ism*] **:** addiction to heroin **:** habitual use of heroin

hero·ism \ˈherəˌwizəm *also* ˈhir- *or* ˈhēr-\ *n* -s [F *héroïsme,* fr. *héros* hero (fr. L *heros,* fr. Gk *hērōs*) *-isme* -ism — more at HERO] **1 :** heroic conduct ⟨the ~ of a regiment defending a position⟩ **2 :** the qualities (as courage, bravery, self-sacrifice, unselfishness) of a hero **:** heroic characteristics ⟨a nation famous for the ~ of its leaders⟩

hero·ize \ˈhē(ˌ)rōˌīz, ˈhi(-\ *vb* -ED/-ING/-S [*hero* + *-ize*] *vt* **:** to make heroic **:** treat or represent as a hero ⟨politicians *heroizing* themselves to their constituents⟩ ⟨*heroized* their leader⟩ ~ *vi* **:** to play the hero **:** represent oneself as a hero

he·ro·la \həˈrōlə\ *n* -s [origin unknown] **:** a large yellowish tawny African antelope (*Damaliscus hunteri*) with markings on face and tail

her·on \ˈherən\ *n, pl* **herons** *also* **heron** [ME *heiroun, heroun,* fr. MF *hairon, heron,* of Gmc origin; akin to OE *hrāgra* heron, OHG *heigaro, hreigaro,* ON *hegri;* akin to W *cryg* hoarse, Gk *krike* it creaked, Lith *krýkšti* to shriek, OHG *scrīan* to scream, cry — more at SCREAM] **:** any of various wading birds constituting the family Ardeidae that have a long neck and legs, a long tapering bill with a sharp point and sharp cutting edges, large wings and soft plumage, and the inner edge of the claw of the middle toe pectinate, that exhibit in some species dichromatism and develop in many species special plumes in the breeding season, that frequent chiefly the vicinity of water and feed mostly on aquatic animals which they capture by quick thrusts of the sharp bill, that usu. nest in trees often in communities, and that vary much in size among different species but are not as large as some of the cranes — see GREAT BLUE HERON, GREAT WHITE HERON, LITTLE BLUE HERON; compare EGRET

great blue heron

her·on·ry \-rē, -ri\ *n* -ES [*heron* + *-ry*] **:** a place where herons breed; *also* **:** a community of herons

heron's-bill \ˈ==ˌ=\ *also* **heronbill** \ˈ==ˌ=\ *n, pl* **heron's-bills** *also* **heronbills :** ERODIUM 2

her·on·sew \ˈherənˌsō, -süˌ\ *n* -s [ME *heronsewe,* fr. MF *heroncel, heronceau* young heron, dim. of *hairon, heron*] *dial Brit* **:** HERON

He·roult \(ˈ)āˌrü\ *trademark* — used for an arc furnace that heats both by radiation and by resistance of the bath and is widely used for making electric steel

hero worship *n* **1 :** veneration of heroes; *specif* **:** the recognition and just evaluation of illustrious individuals as the chief promoters of cultural advance **2 :** foolish or excessive adulation

hero-worship \ˈ=|=ˌ==\ *vt* [*hero worship*] **:** to feel, show, or express hero worship for — **hero-worshiper** \ˈ=ˌ=ˌ===\ *n*

her·pan·gi·na \ˌhərˌpanˈjīnə, ˌhərˈpanjənə\ *n* [NL, fr. *herpes* + *angina*] **:** a contagious disease of children characterized by fever, headache, and a vesicular eruption in the throat and caused by a strain of the Coxsackie virus

her·pes \ˈhər(ˌ)pēz\ *n* -ES [L, fr. Gk *herpēs,* fr. *herpein* to creep — more at SERPENT] **:** any of several virus diseases characterized by the formation of blisters on the skin or mucous membranes — see HERPES SIMPLEX, HERPES ZOSTER

herpes sim·plex \-ˈ==ˈsimˌpleks\ *n* [NL, lit., simple herpes] **:** a virus disease characterized by groups of blisters containing clear fluid formed on the skin or mucous membranes (as on the lips, mouth, genitals) — compare HERPES ZOSTER

her·pes·tes \ˌhərˈpe(ˌ)stēz\ *n, cap* [NL, fr. Gk *herpēstēs* animal that walks on all four feet, fr. *herpēstēs,* adj., creeping, fr. *herpein* to creep] **:** a genus of Old World carnivorous mammals (family Viverridae) comprising typical mongooses and sometimes placed in a separate family — **her·pes·tine** \-ˌstən, ˈhərpəˌstīn\ *adj or n*

her·pes·toi·dea \ˌhərˌpeˈstȯidēə\ [NL, fr. *Herpestes* + *-oidea*] *syn of* AELUROIDEA

herpes zos·ter \ˈ==ˈzōstər, -ˈzäs-\ *n* [NL, lit., girdle herpes; *zoster* fr. Gk *zōstēr* girdle; akin to Gk *zōnē* girdle, belt — more at ZONE] **:** an acute inflammation of the sensory ganglia of spinal and cranial nerves caused by a virus infection and associated with a vesicular eruption and neuralgic pains along the course of those nerves arising in the affected ganglia — called also *shingles;* compare HERPES SIMPLEX

herpet- *or* **herpeto-** *comb form* [partly fr. Gk *herpeton* animal that goes on all fours, snake, fr. neut. of *herpetos* creeping, fr. *herpein* to creep; partly fr. L *herpet-, herpes* herpes (also, a kind of animal, prob. a snake), fr. Gk *herpēt-, herpēs;* partly fr. Gk *herpetos* creeping — more at SERPENT] **1 :** reptile or reptiles ⟨*herpeto*fauna⟩ ⟨*herpeto*logy⟩ **2 :** herpes ⟨*herpet*iform⟩ **3 :** creeping ⟨*herpeto*monas⟩

her·pet·ic \(ˌ)hərˈped·ik\ *adj* [*herpet-* + *-ic*] **:** of or relating to herpes ⟨~ virus⟩ ⟨~ pain⟩ **:** resembling herpes ⟨~ lesions⟩

her·pet·i·form \-d·əˌfȯrm\ *adj* [ISV *herpet-* + *-iform*] **:** resembling herpes

her·pe·to·fauna \ˌhərpəd·ō+\ *n* [NL, fr. *herpet-* + *fauna*] **:** reptiles or reptile life esp. of a particular region

her·pe·to·log·ic \ˌhərpəd·əˈläjik\ *or* **her·pe·to·log·i·cal** \-jəkəl\ *adj* **:** of or relating to herpetology — **her·pe·to·log·i·cal·ly** \-jək(ə)lē\ *adv*

her·pe·tol·o·gist \ˌhərpəˈtäləjəst\ *n* -s **:** a specialist in herpetology

her·pe·tol·o·gy \-jē\ *n* -ES [*herpet-* + *-logy*] **:** a branch of zoology that treats of reptiles and amphibians

¹her·pe·tom·o·nad \ˌhərpəˈtäməˌnad\ *adj* [NL *Herpetomonad-, Herpetomonas*] **:** of or relating to the genus *Herpetomonas*

²herpetomonad \"\ *n* -s **:** a flagellate of the genus *Herpetomonas*

her·pe·tom·o·nas \-ˌnəs, -ˌnas\ *n* [NL, fr. *herpet-* + *-monas*] **1** *cap* **:** a genus of flagellates (family Trypanosomatidae) morphologically similar to *Trypanosoma* but exclusively parasites of the gut of insects **2** -ES **:** any flagellate of the genus *Herpetomonas; also* **:** any member of the Trypanosomatidae that appears to have two flagella due to precocious duplication of the locomotor apparatus

her·pob·del·li·da \ˌhərˌpäbˈdelədə\ [NL, fr. *Herpobdella* genus of leeches (fr. Gk *herpein* to creep + NL *-o-* + *-bdella*) + *-ida*] *syn of* PHARYNGOBDELLIDA

her·po·trich·ia \ˌhərpəˈtrikēə\ *n, cap* [NL, fr. Gk *herpein* to creep + NL *-o-* + *-trichia*] **:** a genus of fungi (family Sphaeriaceae) having perithecia on a brown mycelial layer and including a form (*Herpotrichia nigra*) that is a parasite on conifers

her·ren·volk \ˈherənˌfōk, -fōlk\ *n* -s *often cap* [G, fr. *herr* lord, master + *volk* people, nation] **:** a nationalistic group that believes itself to be racially preeminent and hence fitted to rule over inferior groups ⟨told the German people they were a *Herrenvolk* . . . destined to rule the inferior peoples of Europe —J.C.Harsch⟩

her·ring \ˈheriŋ, -rēŋ\ *n, pl* **herring** *or* **herrings** [ME *hering,* fr. OE *hǣring;* akin to OS *hering* herring, MD *harinc, hareng, herinc,* OHG *hārinc, hering*] **1 :** a valuable food fish (*Clupea harengus*) that reaches a length of about one foot, is extraordinarily abundant in the temperate and colder parts of the north Atlantic where it swims in great schools, feeds chiefly on small crustaceans, and approaches the coasts for spawning where it is caught and preserved in the adult state by smoking or salting and in the young state is extensively canned as sardines; *broadly* **:** a fish of the family Clupeidae — often used in combination ⟨California ~⟩; see ALEWIFE, FALL HERRING, GLUT HERRING **2 :** any of various fishes of families other than Clupeidae that resemble the north Atlantic herring — usu. used in combination; see FRESHWATER HERRING, LAKE HERRING, RAINBOW HERRING

¹herringbone \ˈ==ˌ=\ *n, often attrib* [*herring* + *bone*] **1 :** a pattern resembling the lateral skeletal configuration of a herring; *specif* **:** a pattern (as on a fabric) made up of adjacent rows of parallel lines where any two adjacent rows slope slightly in reverse directions **2 a :** a twilled fabric with a herringbone pattern; *also* **:** a suit made of such a fabric **b :** a herringbone arrangement of materials (as of bricks in a wall) **3 :** a method in skiing of ascending a slope by herringboning; *also* **:** a series of herringbone steps made by herringboning

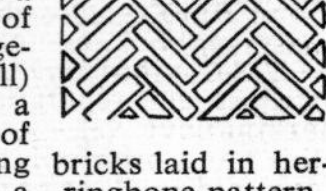
bricks laid in herringbone pattern

²herringbone \"\ *vt* **1 :** to produce a herringbone pattern on **2 :** to arrange in a herringbone pattern ~ *vi* **1 :** to produce herringbone configurations **2 :** to ascend a slope by toeing out with the ski tips and placing the weight on the inner border of the skis

herringbone bond *n* **:** a bond in masonry in which the bricks form a herringbone pattern

herringbone gear *n* **:** a gear with double helical teeth inclined in reverse directions and making a herringbone pattern

herringbone stitch *n* **:** an ornamental catch stitch

herringbone strutting *n* **:** crossed struts between floor joists

her·ring-cale *or* **her·ring-kale** \ˈ==ˌkāl\ *n* -s **:** a common fish (*Olisthops cyanomelas*) that resembles a wrasse and is found in Australian coastal waters

her·ring·er \-ŋə(r)\ *n* -s [*herring* + *-er*] **:** one that fishes for herrings

herring gull *n* **:** a common large gull (*Larus argentatus*) of the northern hemisphere that in the adult state is largely white with blue-gray mantle and dark wing tips and pink feet and in the immature state is mainly dark brown

herring gutted *adj, of a horse* **:** having a form usu. indicative of inferior quality where the abdomen or barrel narrows sharply toward the flanks

herring hog *n* **:** HARBOR PORPOISE

herring king *n* **:** OARFISH

herring oil *n* **:** a pale yellow to dark-colored fatty oil obtained from herring and used in making soap and fat-liquoring leather

herring pond *n* **:** a great body of water (as the Atlantic ocean or English channel) ⟨have been in perils on the great salt *herring pond* —David Humphreys⟩

herrn·hut·er \ˈhernˌhüd·ər, ˈ=ˈ==\ *n* -s *usu cap* [G, fr. *Herrnhut* (lit., Lord's protection), town near Dresden, Germany founded by the Moravians in 1722] **:** MORAVIAN

¹hers \ˈhərz, ˈhə̄z\ *pron, sing or pl in constr* [ME *hires, hirs,* fr. *hire* her + *-s* -'s — more at HER] **1 :** her one or her ones — used without a following noun as a pronoun equivalent in meaning to the adjective *her* ⟨what a stricken look was ~ —S.T.Coleridge⟩ ⟨the eternal years of God are ~ —W.C.Bryant⟩; often used after *of* to single out one or more members of a class belonging to or connected with a particular female person or animal ⟨a favorite dessert of ~⟩ ⟨some friends of ~⟩ or merely to identify something or someone as belonging to or connected with a particular female person or animal without any implication of membership in a more extensive class ⟨that face of ~ —Shak.⟩ ⟨those charming manners of ~⟩ **2 :** something that belongs to her **:** what belongs to her ⟨all that is his is ~⟩

²hers *pl of* HER
³hers \"\ *adj, obs* : ²HER 1 — used as the first of two possessive adjectives modifying the same noun ⟨~ and mine adultery — Shak.⟩
her·schel effect \'hərshəl-\ *n, usu cap H* [after John F.W. *Herschel* †1871 Eng. astronomer] : a partial destruction of the latent image in photography by action of long wave radiation which is either red or infrared
her·schelian \¦hər¦shelēən, -shēl-\ *adj, usu cap* [Sir William *Herschel* †1822 Eng. astronomer + E *-ian*] : of or relating to the astronomer Herschel
herschelian telescope *n, usu cap H* : a reflecting telescope in which the need for a secondary mirror is avoided by tilting the primary mirror slightly and thereby throwing the focused image to the side where it can be observed without obstruction to the incoming light rays — called also *off-axis reflector*
her·schel·ite \'hərshə,līt\ *n* -s [Sir John F. W. *Herschel* + E *-ite*] : a chabazite that consists of glassy crystals of complex twinned structure
herse *obs var of* HEARSE
her·self \(h)ə(r)'+\ *pron* [ME *hire self*, fr. OE *hiere self, hire self, hyre self*, dat. of *hēo self, hīo self* she herself — more at HE, SELF] **1** : that identical female one : that identical one regarded as feminine (as by personification) — compare ¹SHE 1; used (1) reflexively as object of a preposition or direct or indirect object of a verb ⟨she devotes a lot of time to her children and very little to ~⟩ ⟨she bought ~ some clothes⟩ ⟨she considers ~ lucky⟩ (2) for emphasis in apposition with *she, who, that*, or a noun ⟨she ~ painted the room⟩ ⟨she did it ~⟩ ⟨the housewife ~ bought the groceries⟩ ⟨the housewife bought the groceries ~⟩ ⟨armies threatened Rome ~⟩ ⟨my mother, who was young once ~⟩ (3) for emphasis instead of nonreflexive *her* as object of a preposition or direct or indirect object of a verb ⟨I looked beside me then, and I saw ~ —Padraic Colum⟩ (4) for emphasis instead of *she* or instead of *she herself* as subject of a verb ⟨she told me that neither her husband nor ~ could attend the meeting⟩ or as predicate nominative ⟨it's ~ she's trying to convince⟩ or in comparisons after *than* or *as* ⟨she met another woman as tall as ~⟩ (5) in absolute constructions ⟨~ an orphan, the authoress shows deep understanding of the problems of the orphan girl whose story she tells⟩ **2** : her normal, healthy, or sane condition ⟨she came to ~⟩ : her normal, healthy, or sane self ⟨ill for a week, she is now ~ again⟩ **3** *Scot* : MYSELF, YOURSELF, HIMSELF, ITSELF — used esp. in literary representations of the English spoken by Scottish Highlanders; compare ¹SHE 2 **4** *Irish & Scot* : a woman of consequence; *esp* : the mistress of the house ⟨where's ~⟩ **5** : YOURSELF ⟨did she hurt ~⟩ — compare HIMSELF 4
hership *n* [ME, fr. *herien* to harry + *-ship* — more at HARRY] **1** *obs* : a warlike raid esp. to steal cattle; *also* : the distress caused by such a raid **2** *obs* : the loot stolen in a hership
hert·ford·shire *Brit* 'hä(t)fədshiə(r, -shə(r), *US* " or 'härtfərd,shi(ə)r *or* -shər *or* 'hərt- *or* 'hōt- *or* 'həit-\ *or* **hertford** *adj, usu cap* [fr. *Hertfordshire* or county of *Hertford*, England] : of or from the county of Hertford, England : of the kind or style prevalent in Hertford
hertfordshire kindness *n, usu cap H* : a favor of the same kind in return
hertz \'hərts, 'hōts, 'həits; 'he(ə)rts, 'heəts\ *n, pl* **hertz** *or* **hertzes** [after Heinrich R. *Hertz* †1894 Ger. physicist] : a unit of frequency of a periodic process equal to one cycle per second — abbr. *Hz*
hertz·ian \-sēən\ *adj, sometimes cap* [H. R. *Hertz* + E *-ian*] : of, relating to, or developed by the physicist Hertz
hertzian telegraphy *n* : telegraphy by means of Hertzian waves : RADIOTELEGRAPH
hertzian wave *n, usu cap H* : an electromagnetic wave produced by the oscillation of electricity in a conductor (as a radio antenna) and of a length ranging from a few millimeters to many kilometers
hertz oscillator *or* **hertzian oscillator** *n* : an inductive and capacitive circuit in which electric oscillations resulting in the emission of Hertzian waves are set up by passage of a spark or otherwise
her·va ma·té \,ervə'mä(,)tā, -mäd·ə\ *n* [Pg *herva mate, erva mate*, lit., maté plant] : MATÉ
herx·hei·mer reaction \'herks,hīmər-\ *n, usu cap H* [after Karl *Herxheimer* †1944 Ger. dermatologist] : an increase in the symptoms of syphilis occurring in some persons when treatment with spirochetecidal drugs is instituted
hery *vt* -ED/-ING/-ES [ME *herien*, fr. OE *herian*; akin to OHG *harēn* to call, Goth *hazjan* to praise] *obs* : GLORIFY, PRAISE
her·ze·go·vinian \,hertsəgō'vēnēən, ,hər-, -vin-\ *n* -s *cap* [*Herzegovina*, region in the northwestern Balkan peninsula + E *-ian*] : a native of Herzegovina
hes *pl of* HE
hesh \'hesh\ *dial var of* HUSH
hesh·van *also* **hes·van** *or* **chesh·van** *or* **ches·van** \'keshvən\ *n* -s *usu cap* [Heb *ḥeshwān*, short for *marḥeshwān* Marheshvan] : the 2d month of the civil year or the 8th month of the ecclesiastical year in the Jewish calendar — see MONTH table
he·si·od·ic \¦hēsē¦ädik *sometimes* ¦hesē- *or* ¦hēzē-\ *adj, usu cap* [*Hesiod*, 8th cent. B.C. Greek poet (fr. Gk *Hēsiodos*) + E *-ic*] : of or relating to the poet Hesiod or his simple practical maxims or theology
he·si·o·ne \hə'sīə(,)nē\ *n, cap* [NL, after *Hesione*, Trojan princess of Greek mythology saved from a monster by Hercules, fr. L, fr. Gk *Hēsionē*] : a genus (the type of the family Hesionidae) of marine free-swimming polychaete worms having long peristomial cirri and two pairs of eyes
hes·i·tan·cy \'hezəd·ənsē, -zətən-, -si *also* -zət°n- *sometimes* -ztən- *or* 'hesə-\ *or* **hes·i·tance** \-n(t)s\ *n, pl* **hesitancies** *or* **hesitances** [LL *haesitantia*, fr. L, action of stammering, fr. *haesitant-, haesitans* + *-ia* -y] **1** : the quality or state of being hesitant: as **a** : INDECISION ⟨had lost that nervous ~ that had so troubled her —Elizabeth Goudge⟩ **b** : RELUCTANCE ⟨had no ~ in entering the field of composition —Fannie L. G. Cole⟩ **2** : an act or instance of hesitating : HESITATION ⟨her girlish *hesitancies*, her maidenly delays and refusals —S.H. Adams⟩
hes·i·tant \-nt\ *adj* [L *haesitant-, haesitans*, pres. part. of *haesitare*] : given to hesitation : tending to hold back (as from fear, indecision, or disinclination) ⟨a ~ fighter⟩ ⟨~ policies⟩
syn see DISINCLINED
hes·i·tant·ly *adv* : in a hesitant manner
hes·i·tate \'hezə,tāt *sometimes* 'hez,tāt *or* 'hesə,tāt, *usu* -ād·+V\ *vb* -ED/-ING/-S [L *haesitatus*, past part of *haesitare* to stick fast, stammer, hesitate, fr. the stem of *haerēre* to stick; akin to Lith *gaišti* to loiter, delay] *vi* **1 a** : to hold back in doubt or indecision : avoid facing a decision, encounter, or problem ⟨the government *hesitated* before each policy⟩ **b** : to hold back from or as if from scruple ⟨~ at treason⟩ **2** : to delay usu. momentarily : PAUSE ⟨a glimpse of a deer as it *hesitated* before disappearing into the underbrush⟩ **3** : STAMMER ~ *vt* : to express in a hesitant manner ⟨choose rather to ~ my opinion than to assert it roundly —J.R.Lowell⟩
syn HESITATE, WAVER, VACILLATE, and FALTER agree in meaning to show irresolution or uncertainty. HESITATE implies a pause or other sign of indecision before acting ⟨no properly qualified student should *hesitate* to apply —*Official Register of Harvard Univ.*⟩ ⟨the young second officer *hesitated* to break the established rule of every ship's discipline —Joseph Conrad⟩ ⟨she *hesitated* a minute and then she said, 'Yes.' —Dorothy Baker⟩ WAVER implies hesitation after having seemed to decide and usu. suggests weakness or retreat from a decision ⟨the great man, who never *wavered* in his faith —H.S.Canby⟩ ⟨he was a good student and possessed an un*wavering* will —Nora Waln⟩ ⟨Henry was in the grip of his own master-passion and he did not *waver* —Francis Hackett⟩ VACILLATE implies prolonged hesitation from inability to reach a decision ⟨the . . . government has been *vacillating* in its policies on such emigration —*Collier's Yr. Bk.*⟩ ⟨I have *vacillated* when I should have insisted; temporized when I should have taken definite action —Ngaio Marsh⟩ FALTER suggests a hesitation or wavering evident in some physical sign of nervousness, lack of courage, or outright fear, as an uncertainty or breaking of the voice ⟨kept the bright excited look upon her face without *faltering* —F. Tennyson Jesse⟩ ⟨his steps perceptibly *falter* —*Times Lit. Supp.*⟩ ⟨his eyes did not flinch and his tongue did not *falter* —Joseph Conrad⟩

hes·i·tat·er *also* **hes·i·ta·tor** \-ād·ə(r), -ātə-\ *n* -s : one that hesitates
hes·i·tat·ing·ly \'⸗⸗,⸗⸗⸗, ,⸗⸗'⸗⸗⸗\ *adv* : HESITANTLY
hes·i·ta·tion \,hezə'tāshən *sometimes* ,hesə-\ *n* -s [L *haesitation-, haesitatio*, fr. *haesitatus* + *-ion-, -io* -ion] **1** : the act or action of hesitating (as by holding back, pausing, or faltering) ⟨~ before decisions⟩ ⟨~ in accepting an offer⟩ **2** : a faltering in speech : STAMMERING **3** *also* **hesitation waltz** : a waltz in which the dancers intersperse at pleasure a gliding movement; *also* : the gliding movement in such a waltz
hesitation form *n* : a sound (as \ə\, \ə̄\, or \ä\ usu. prolonged) or word (as er, uh, mmm, what-you-may-call-it, well) involuntarily or deliberately used while a speaker is uncertain about the fitting expression of his thought or the correct name of a person or object
hes·i·ta·tive \'hezə,tā|d·|iv, -zətə|, -zəd·ə|, |t|, |ēv *sometimes* 'heztə| *or* 'hesə-\ *adj* : showing or characterized by hesitation — **hes·i·ta·tive·ly** \|əvlē, |ēv-, -li\ *adv*
hesp \'hesp\ *dial var of* HASP
hes·ped \'he,sped\ *n, pl* **hes·pe·dim** \he'spādəm, -,dēm\ [Heb *hespēdh*] : an oration or eulogy at a Jewish memorial service
hes·pe·ria \he'spirēə, -pēr-\ *n, cap* [NL, fr. L, west, fr. Gk, fr. *hesperos* of the evening, western (fr. *hesperos, hespera* evening) + *-ia* -y — more at WEST] : a genus of skipper butterflies that is the type of the family Hesperiidae and includes many small butterflies of the northern hemisphere that are mostly tawny with dark and pale markings
¹hes·pe·ri·an \(')⸗¦⸗rēən\ *adj, usu cap* [L *Hesperia* west + E *-an*] **1** : WESTERN, OCCIDENTAL **2** [NL *Hesperia* + E *-an*] : of or relating to the Hesperiidae
²hesperian \"\ *n* -s **1** *usu cap* : an inhabitant of the West : OCCIDENTAL **2** : a butterfly of the family Hesperiidae
¹hes·per·id \'hespərəd\ *or* **hes·pe·ri·id** \(')he¦spirēəd\ *adj* [NL *Hesperiidae*] : of or relating to the Hesperiidae
²hesperid *or* **hesperiid** *n* -s : an insect of the family Hesperiidae : a skipper butterfly
hes·per·i·date \he'sperə,dāt\ *or* **hes·per·id·e·ous** \¦hespə¦ridēəs\ *adj* [NL *hesperidium* + E *-ate* or *-eous*] : of, relating to, or being a hesperidium
hes·per·id·e·an *or* **hes·per·id·i·an** \¦hespə¦ridēən\ *adj, usu cap* [*Hesperides* mythological paradisiacal garden growing golden apples (fr. the *Hesperides*, the nymphs that guard it, fr. L, fr. Gk) + E *-an, -ian*] : of, relating to, or having the characteristics of the gardens of the Hesperides
hes·per·i·din \he'sperəd°n, -¦sperə¦din\ *n* -s [NL *hesperidium* + E *-in*] : a crystalline bioflavonoid glycoside $C_{28}H_{34}O_{15}$ found in most citrus fruits and esp. in orange peel that yields hesperitin, glucose, and rhamnose on hydrolysis — see CITRIN
hes·per·id·i·um \,hespə'ridēəm\ *n, pl* **hesperid·ia** \-ēə\ [NL, fr. the *Hesperides* + NL *-ium*; fr. the myth of the golden apples of the Hesperides] : a berry (as an orange or lime) having a leathery rind — see FRUIT illustration
hes·per·i·idae \,hespə'rīə,dē\ *n pl, cap* [NL, fr. *Hesperia*, type genus + *-idae*] : a large family of skipper butterflies (superfamily Hesperioidea) comprising the typical skippers — see HESPERIA; compare MEGATHYMIDAE
hes·per·i·nos \¦hespərə¦nȯs, -nōs\ *n* -ES [LGk, fr. Gk, adj., of the evening, fr. *hesperos, hespera* evening + *-inos* -ine — more at WEST] : the office in the Eastern Church corresponding to vespers in the Western Church
hes·pe·ri·oi·dea \(,)he,spirē'ȯidēə\ *n pl, cap* [NL, fr. *Hesperia* + *-oidea*] : a superfamily of Lepidoptera comprising insects often considered butterflies but usu. distinguished from the typical butterflies by the hooked tips of the widely separated antennae, peculiarities of the wing venation, and the erratic and often very swift flight — see HESPERIIDAE, MEGATHYMIDAE, SKIPPER
hes·per·is \'hespərəs\ *n, cap* [NL, fr. L, dame's violet, fr. Gk, fr. fem. of *hesperios* of the evening, fr. *hesperos, hespera* evening] : a genus of biennial or perennial Eurasian herbs (family Cruciferae) having large purple or white racemose flowers — see DAME'S VIOLET
hes·per·i·tin *also* **hes·per·e·tin** \he'sperət°n, -¦sperə¦tin\ *n* -s [prob. irreg. fr. *hesperidin*] : a crystalline compound $C_{16}H_{14}O_6$ derived from flavanone and obtained by hydrolysis of hesperidin; a monomethyl ether of eriodictyol
hes·per·or·nis \,hespə'rȯrnəs\ *n, cap* [NL, fr. Gk *hesperos* western + NL *-ornis*] : a genus of swimming birds (order Hesperornithiformes) from the Cretaceous of Kansas that resemble loons in form, that have teeth in each jaw implanted in a long groove, and that in some cases exceed five feet in length
hes·per·or·nith·i·for·mes \,hespə(,)rȯr,nithə'fȯr,mēz\ *n pl, cap* [NL, fr. *Hesperornith-, Hesperornis* + *-iformes*] : an order of extinct aquatic birds (superorder Odontognathae) including the genus *Hesperornis* and related Cretaceous forms
hesselbach's triangle *n, usu cap H* : TRIANGLE OF HESSELBACH
¹hes·sian \'heshən, *chiefly Brit* 'hesēən\ *adj, usu cap* [*Hesse*, region or state in southwestern Germany + E *-ian*] : of or relating to Hesse in Germany or the Hessians
²hessian \"\ *n* -s **1** *cap* **a** : a native of Hesse, a region or state in southwestern Germany **b** : a German mercenary often a native of Hesse serving in the British forces during the American Revolution **c** : a mercenary soldier **2 a** : HESSIAN BOOT **b** : HESSIAN ANDIRON **3** *chiefly Midland* **a** : SCAMP, RASCAL — used esp. of a child **b** : a troublesome or meddlesome person — used esp. of a woman **4** *also* **hessian cloth** : BURLAP
hessian andiron *n, usu cap H* : an andiron with an upright shaped to represent a Hessian soldier
hessian boot *n, usu cap H* : a high boot with a top extending to just below the knee and commonly ornamented with a tassel that was introduced into England by the Hessians early in the 19th century

Hessian boot

hessian crucible *n, usu cap H* : a cheap brittle fragile but very refractory crucible composed of the finest fireclay and sand and commonly used for a single heating
hessian fly *n, often cap H* [so called fr. the belief it was brought to America by Hessian soldiers] : a small two-winged fly (*Mayetiola destructor*) which is destructive to wheat in America and whose larvae live between the base of the lower leaves and the stalk and suck the juices of the plant
hess image \'hes-\ *n, usu cap H* [after Carl von *Hess* †1923 Ger. ophthalmologist] : a third positive afterimage in a succession of visual afterimages resulting from a brief light stimulus
hess·ite \'he,sīt\ *n* -s [G *hessit*, fr. Henry *Hess* †1850 Swiss chemist in Russia + G *-it* -ite] : a mineral Ag_2Te consisting of a lead-gray sectile silver telluride often auriferous and usu. massive
hessonite *var of* ESSONITE
hess's law \'hesəz-\ *n, usu cap H* [after Henry *Hess*] : a statement in chemistry: the heat change in a chemical reaction is the same regardless of the number of stages in which the reaction is effected
hest \'hest\ *n* -s [ME *hest, heste*, alter. of *hes*, fr. OE *hǣs*; akin to OE *hātan* to command, call, be called — more at HIGHT] *archaic* : COMMAND
hes·thog·e·nous \(')hes¦thäjənəs\ *adj* [irreg. fr. Gk *esthēs* clothing + E *-genous*] : having a covering of down when hatched : DASYPAEDIC
hesvan *usu cap, var of* HESHVAN
hes·y·chasm \'hesə,kazəm, 'hezə-\ *n* -s *often cap* [fr. *hesychast*, after such pairs as E *enthusiast: enthusiasm*] : hesychastic belief or practice
hes·y·chast \-kast\ *n* -s *often cap* [MGk *hēsychastēs*, fr. LGk, quietist, hermit, fr. Gk *hēsychazein* to be still, keep quiet, fr. *hēsychos* quiet; perh. akin to OE *sīd* long — more at SIDE] : one of an Eastern Orthodox ascetic sect of mystics originating among the monks of Mount Athos in the 14th century and practicing a quietistic method of contemplation for the purpose of attaining a beatific vision or similar mystical experience
hes·y·chas·tic \¦⸗⸗¦kastik\ *adj* [Gk *hēsychastikos*, fr. (assumed) Gk *hēsychastos* (verbal of *hēsychazein*) + Gk *-ikos* -ic] **1** : SOOTHING, CALMING — used esp. of a style of ancient Greek music **2** *often cap* [*hesychast* + *-ic*] : of or relating to the hesychasts or their solitary meditative mysticism

¹het *var of* HETH
²het \'het\ *n* -s *usu cap* : CHECHEHET
³het \'het, *usu* -ed·+V\ *dial var of* ²HEAT
⁴het \"\ *chiefly Scot var of* HOT
⁵het \"\ *dial past of* HEAT
he·tae·ra \-'tirə\ *or* **he·tai·ra** \-'tīrə\ *n, pl* **hetae·rae** \-i(,)rē\ *or* **hetaeras** *or* **hetairas** \-,rəz\ *or* **hetai·rai** \-ī,rī\ [Gk *hetaira*, lit., companion, fem. of *hetairos* comrade, companion] **1** : one of a class of highly cultivated courtesans in ancient Greece **2** : DEMIMONDAINE ⟨the lady in the canary-colored carriage was New York's first fashionable ~ —*Harper's*⟩ ⟨a hair-pulling fight between two drunken *hetaerae* over a free spender —*Amer. Mercury*⟩
he·tae·rism *or* **he·tai·rism** \-,rizəm\ *n* -s [Gk *hetairismos*, fr. *hetaira* + *-ismos* -ism] **1** : a general system of temporary or continued sexual relations outside wedlock : CONCUBINAGE **2** : a state of society conceived as existing in the past and characterized by the holding of women in common
he·tae·ro·lite \hə'tirə,līt\ *n* -s [Gk *hetairos* companion + E *-lite*] : a mineral $ZnMn_2O_4$ consisting of a zinc-manganese oxide found with chalcophanite
hetchel *var of* HATCHEL
heter- *or* **hetero-** *comb form* [MF or LL; MF, fr. LL, fr. Gk, fr. *heteros*; akin to Gk *heis*, *hen* one — more at SAME] **1** : other than usual : other : different ⟨*hetero*geneous⟩ ⟨*hetero*dox⟩ ⟨*Heter*anthera⟩ — opposed to *hom-, is-, orth-*, **2** : for, from, or to a different species ⟨*hetero*agglutinin⟩ **3 a** : containing atoms of different kinds ⟨*hetero*cyclic⟩ **b** : isomeric with or closely related to a (specified) compound ⟨*hetero*xanthine⟩
¹het·er·akid \¦hed·ə¦rakəd, -rak-\ *adj* [NL *Heterakidae*] : of or relating to the family Heterakidae; *esp* : caused by worms of the genus *Heterakis* ⟨~ transmission of blackhead⟩
²heterakid \"\ *n* -s : a worm of the family Heterakidae
het·er·aki·dae \,⸗⸗'ka,dē\ *n pl, cap* [NL, fr. *Heterakis*, type genus + *-idae*] : a somewhat variably limited family comprising nematode worms with three lips, a small buccal capsule, and usu. a posterior esophageal bulb and sometimes being included in the family Ascaridae — see HETERAKIS
het·er·a·kis \,⸗⸗'rakəs\ *n, cap* [NL, fr. *heter-* + Gk *akis* pointed object — more at ACIDANTHERA] : a genus (the type of the family Heterakidae) of nematode worms including the common cecal worm of chickens and turkeys
het·er·an·drous \¦hed·ə¦randrəs\ *adj* [*heter-* + *-androus*] : having stamens of different length or form — **het·er·an·dry** \'⸗⸗,⸗drē\ *n* -ES
het·er·an·gi·um \,⸗⸗'ranjēəm\ *n, cap* [NL, fr. *heter-* + *-angium*] : a genus of Devonian seed ferns having a protostelic stem resembling that of members of the genus *Gleichenia*
het·er·an·the·ra \-'ran(t)thərə\ *n, cap* [NL, fr. *heter-* + *-anthera*] : a genus of aquatic or marsh herbs (family Pontederiaceae) having flowers with a salverform perianth, three stamens, and a many-seeded capsule
het·er·atomic \¦hed·ər+\ *or* **het·ero·atomic** \¦hed·ə(,)rō+\ *adj* [*heter-* + *atomic*] : made up of atoms of different kinds
het·er·auxesis \¦hed·ər+\ *n* [NL, fr. *heter-* + *auxesis*] : allometric growth — compare ALLOMETRY — **het·er·auxetic** \"+\ *adj*
het·er·axial \"+\ *adj* [*heter-* + *axial*] : having three unequal axes perpendicular to each other (as in animals having biradial or bilateral symmetry)
heterecious *var of* HETEROECIOUS
het·er·ism \'hed·ə,rizəm\ *n* -s [*heter-* + *-ism*] : variability of animals and plants
het·er·i·za·tion \,hed·ərə'zāshən, -,rī'z-\ *n* -s [*heter-* + *-ization*] : a changing from one form into another
het·ero \'hed·ə,rō\ *adj* [*heter-*] : relating to or being an atom or element other than the predominating or significant one (as carbon) esp. in a ring of a molecule or compound ⟨~ atoms such as nitrogen or oxygen⟩
het·ero·agglutinin \¦hed·ə(,)rō+\ *n* [*heter-* + *agglutinin*] : a hemagglutinin found in serum and reacting with red cells of animals of other species than the one producing the serum
het·ero·autotroph \"+\ *n* [*heter-* + *autotroph*] : a heteroautotrophic organism
het·ero·autotrophic \"+\ *adj* [*heter-* + *autotrophic*] : requiring a simple organic source of carbon but utilizing inorganic nitrogen for metabolism
het·ero·auxin \"+\ *n* [G, fr. *heter-* + *auxin*] : INDOLEACETIC ACID
het·ero·ba·sid·i·ae \,hed·ərōbə'sidē,ē\ *n pl, cap* [NL, fr. *heter-* + *-basidiae* (fr. *basidium*)] *in some classifications* : a subclass of Basidiomycetes comprising fungi with a basidium that is transversely or vertically septate or forked or has four rounded terminal cells from each of which a sterigma and spore arise and including Tremellales and other orders or being restricted to the order Tremellales — compare EUBASIDIAE, TELIOSPOREAE
het·ero·basidiomycetes \¦hed·ə(,)rō+\ *n pl, cap* [NL, fr. *heter-* + *Basidiomycetes*] : a subclass of fungi (class Basidiomycetes) including the rusts, smuts, and jelly fungi that has septate or deeply divided basidia and basidiospores which often germinate to form conidia or similar spores — compare HOMOBASIDIOMYCETES — **het·ero·basidiomycetous** \"+\ *adj*
het·ero·ba·sid·io·my·cet·i·dae \¦⸗⸗(,)bə,sidē(,)ō,mī'sed·ə,dē\ *n pl, cap* [NL, fr. *heter-* + *Basidiomycetes* + *-idae*] *syn of* HETEROBASIDIOMYCETES
het·ero·basidium \"+\ *n* [NL, fr. *heter-* + *basidium*] : a basidium that is septate or with deep divisions (as in the subclass Heterobasidiomycetes)
het·ero·blas·tic \¦hed·ərō¦blastik\ *adj* [*heter-* + *-blastic*] **1** : having an indirect embryonic development — opposed to *homoblastic*; compare EMBRYOGENY **2** : arising from different germ layers — used of functionally similar organs of related animals **3** : having young and adult forms different ⟨~ leaves of flowering plants⟩ — **het·ero·blas·ty** \'⸗⸗⸗,blastē\ *n* -ES
het·ero·cap·sa·les \,hed·ə(,)rō,kap'sā(,)lēz\ *n pl, cap* [NL] : an order of yellowish to brownish green algae (class Xanthophyceae) that form amorphous or arborescent palmelloid colonies containing an indefinite number of cells which are capable of reverting to a motile state directly or through zoospore formation — compare HETEROCOCCALES, VOLVOCALES
het·ero·carpus \,hed·ərō'kärpəs\ *n, cap* [NL, fr. *heter-* + *carpus*] : a genus of bioluminescent prawns occurring in the Indian ocean
heterocaryon *var of* HETEROKARYON
heterocaryosis *var of* HETEROKARYOSIS
het·ero·cellular \¦hed·ə(,)rō+\ *adj* [*heter-* + *cellular*] : composed of more than one kind of cell
het·er·oc·era \,hed·ə'räsərə\ *n pl, cap* [NL, fr. *heter-* + *-cera*] : a division of Lepidoptera consisting of the moths — compare RHOPALOCERA — **het·er·oc·er·ous** \¦⸗⸗¦⸗⸗rəs\ *adj*
¹het·ero·cerc \'hed·ərō,sərk\ *n* -s [*heter-* + *-cerc* (fr. Gk *kerkos* tail)] : a heterocercal fish
²heterocerc \"\ *adj* : HETEROCERCAL
het·ero·cer·cal \¦⸗⸗⸗¦sərkəl\ *adj* [*heter-* + *-cercal*] **1** : having the upper lobe larger than the lower with the end of the vertebral column prolonged and somewhat upturned in the upper lobe — used of the tail fin of various fishes (as sharks) **2** : having or relating to a heterocercal tail fin — **het·ero·cer·cal·i·ty** \¦hed·ə(,)rō,sər'kaləd·ē\ *n* -ES
het·ero·charge \'hed·ərō+,-\ *n* [*heter-* + *charge*] : a charge on an electret that is of sign opposite to that of the electrode orig. in contact with it — compare HOMOCHARGE
het·ero·che·lous \¦hed·ərō¦kēləs\ *adj* [*heter-* + *chel-* + *-ous*] *of a crustacean* : having the chelae unlike in size and form — **het·ero·che·ly** \'⸗⸗⸗,kēlē\ *n* -ES
het·ero·chlamydeous \¦⸗⸗(,)⸗+\ *adj* [ISV *heter-* + *chlamydeous*] : having a perianth whose calyx and corolla are differentiated as to color and texture — compare HOMOCHLAMYDEOUS
het·er·o·chlo·ri·da·les \,⸗⸗(,)klōrə'dā(,)lēz\ *n pl, cap* [NL, fr. *Heterochlorid-, Heterochloris*, genus of algae + *-ales*] : an order of yellow-green algae including all members of the Xanthophyceae having flagellated vegetative cells
het·ero·chromatic \¦hed·ə(,)rō+\ *adj* [*heter-* + *chromatic*] **1** : of, relating to, or having different colors; *specif* : having a more or less complex pattern of colors — opposed to *homochromatic* **2** : made up of various wavelengths or frequencies : not monochromatic **3** [*heterochromatin* + *-ic*] : of or relating to heterochromatin — **het·ero·chromatism** \"+\ *n* -s

het·ero·chromatin \"+\ *n* [G, fr. *hetero-* heter- + *chromatin*] **:** densely staining chromatin appearing as nodules in or along chromosomes — compare EUCHROMATIN

het·ero·chro·ma·ti·za·tion \ˌhed·ərō,krōməd·əˈzāshən, -mə-,tīˈz-\ *n* -s [*heterochromat-* (fr. *heterochromatin*) + *-ization*] **:** the state of being or becoming heterochromatic **:** the transformation of genetically active euchromatin to inactive heterochromatin — **het·ero·chromatized** \ˌ⸗⸗⸗ˈ⸗mə,tīzd\ *adj*

het·ero·chrome \ˈ⸗⸗⸗,krōm\ *adj* [ISV *heter-* + *-chrome*] **:** HETEROCHROMATIC

het·ero·chro·mia \ˌ⸗⸗⸗ˈkrōmēə\ *n* -s [NL, fr. *heter-* + *-chromia*] **:** a difference in coloration in two anatomical structures or two parts of the same structure which are normally alike in color ⟨~ of the iris⟩

het·ero·chromomere \ˈhed·ə(,)rō+\ *n* [*heter-* + *chromomere*] **:** a chromomere of the heterochromatic region of a chromosome; *also* **:** a granule of heterochromatin

het·ero·chromosome \"+\ *n* [ISV *heter-* + *chromosome*] **:** a sex chromosome

het·ero·chro·mous \ˈhed·ərəˈkrōməs\ *or* **het·ero·chro·mic** \-mik\ *adj* [*heter-* + *chrom-* + *-ous* or *-ic*] **:** of different colors

het·er·och·ro·nism \ˌhed·əˈräkrə,nizəm\ *also* **het·er·och·ro·ny** \-ˌnē\ *n, pl* **heterochronisms** *also* **heterochronies** [*heterochronism* fr. NL *heterochronus* heterochronous (fr. *heter-* + Gk *-chronos* -chronous) + E *-ism; heterochrony* fr. NL *heterochronia,* fr. *heterochronus* + L *-ia* -y] **1 :** deviation from the typical embryological sequence of formation of organs and parts as a factor in evolution — compare FETALIZATION **2 :** irregularity in time relationships; *specif* **:** the existence of differences in chronaxies among functionally related tissue elements — **het·er·och·ro·nis·tic** \ˌ⸗⸗,⸗⸗ˈnistik\ *adj* — **het·er·och·ro·nous** \ˌ⸗⸗ˈräkrənəs\ *adj*

het·er·och·tho·nous \ˌ⸗⸗ˈräkthənəs\ *adj* [*heter-* + *-chthonous* (as in *autochthonous*)] **1 :** not indigenous **:** FOREIGN, NATURALIZED ⟨a ~ flora⟩ **2 a :** not formed in the place where it now occurs **:** TRANSPORTED ⟨~ rock⟩ **b :** removed from the original deposit (as by erosion) and reembedded (as certain fossils)

¹het·er·o·clite \ˈhed·ərə,klīt\ *n* -s [MF, n. & adj.] **1** *in the grammar of various languages* **:** a word irregular in inflection; *esp* **:** a noun irregular in declension (as Latin *pecus* having case forms of both third and fourth declensions) **2 :** one that deviates from the common rule or from common forms ⟨modern poetry is not a privilege of ~s —Wallace Stevens⟩

²heteroclite \"\ *adj* [MF or LL; MF, fr. LL *heteroclitus* irregularly inflected, fr. Gk *heteroklitos,* fr. *heter-* + (assumed) Gk *klitos* (verbal of Gk *klinein* to lean, incline, inflect) — more at LEAN] **:** deviating from ordinary forms or rules **:** IRREGULAR, ANOMALOUS, ABNORMAL ⟨a confusing, dusty, ~ accretion of objects —Janet Flanner⟩

het·er·o·clit·ic \ˌ⸗⸗⸗ˈklid·ik\ *adj* **:** marked by irregularity of inflection ⟨many nouns . . . are ~ in one or more cases —F.W. Householder⟩

het·ero·coc·ca·les \ˌhed·ə(,)rō,käˈkā(,)lēz\ *n pl, cap* [NL, fr. *Heterococcus,* genus of algae (fr. *heter-* + *-coccus*) + *-ales*] **:** an order of yellow-green algae including all members of the class Xanthophyceae having the immobile vegetative cells surrounded by a cell wall and incapable of returning to the motile state directly

het·ero·coe·la \ˌhed·ərōˈsēlə\ [NL, fr. *heter-* + *-coela,* neut. pl. of *-coelus* -coelous] *syn of* SYCONOSA

het·ero·coe·lan \ˌ⸗⸗⸗ˈ⸗lən\ *adj* [NL *Heterocoela* + E *-an*] **:** of or relating to the Syconosa

het·ero·coe·lous \-ləs\ *adj* [*heter-* + *-coelous*] **1 :** of or relating to vertebrae having saddle-shaped articular surfaces ⟨~ birds⟩ **2** [NL *Heterocoela* + E *-ous*] **:** of or relating to the Syconosa

het·er·o·cont \ˈhed·ərō,känt\ *adj* [NL *Heterocontae*] **:** of or relating to the Heterokontae

heterocontae *syn of* HETEROKONTAE

het·ero·co·tyl·ea \ˌhed·ə(,)rōkəˈtilēə, -ˌkädᵊlˈēə\ [NL, fr. *heter-* + *-cotylea* (fr. Gk *kotylē* cup, small vessel) — more at KETTLE] *syn of* MONOGENEA

het·ero·crine \ˈhed·ərə,krin, -rīn,-rēn; -ˌkrən\ *adj* [*heter-* + *-crine* (as in *endocrine*)] *of a gland* **:** having both an endocrine and an exocrine secretion **:** MIXED

het·ero·cy·cle \-ˌsīkəl\ *n* [*heter-* + *cycle*] **:** a heterocyclic ring system or a heterocyclic compound

¹het·ero·cyclic \ˌ⸗⸗⸗ˈsīklik, -lēk *also* -sik-\ *adj* [ISV *heter-* + *cyclic*] **:** relating to, characterized by, or being a ring composed of atoms of different elements ⟨furan and quinoline are ~⟩ — distinguished from *isocyclic*

²heterocyclic \"\ *n* **:** a heterocyclic compound or a heterocyclic ring system

het·ero·cyst \ˈhed·ərə,sist\ *n* [ISV *heter-* + *cyst*] **:** one of the large transparent thick-walled cells resembling spores occurring at intervals along the filament in certain filamentous blue-green algae

het·ero·dac·tyl \ˈhed·ərōˈdaktᵊl\ *adj* [ISV *heter-* + *-dactyl* (fr. Gk *daktylos* finger, toe)] **:** HETERODACTYLOUS

het·ero·dac·ty·lism \-tə,lizəm\ *n* -s [*heter-* + *-dactylism*] **1 :** unilateral polydactylism **2 :** a greater degree of polydactylism on one side than on the other

het·ero·dac·ty·lous \-tələs\ *adj* [*heter-* + *-dactylous*] **:** having the first and second toes turned backward ⟨trogons are ~⟩

het·er·od·era \ˌhed·əˈrädərə\ *n, cap* [NL, fr. *heter-* + *-dera* (fr. Gk *derē* neck) — more at DER-] **:** a genus (the type of the family Heteroderidae of the superfamily Tylenchoidea) of minute nematode worms many of which attack the roots and underground stems of various cultivated plants (as sugar beets, potatoes, peas) — compare GOLDEN NEMATODE, ROOT-KNOT NEMATODE

het·er·odon \ˈhed·ərə,dän\ *n, cap* [NL, fr. *heter-* + *-odon*] **:** a genus of small stocky colubrid snakes comprising the No. American hognose snakes

¹het·er·odont \-nt\ *adj* [ISV *heter-* + *-odont*] **1 :** having the teeth differentiated into incisors, canines, and molars ⟨~ mammals⟩ ⟨man is ~⟩ — opposed to *homodont* **2 :** having both cardinal and lateral teeth that fit into depressions on the opposite valve — compare HETERODONTA

²heterodont \"\ *n* -s **:** an animal with heterodont dentition

het·er·odon·ta \ˌ⸗⸗⸗ˈdäntə\ *n pl, cap* [NL fr. *heter-* + *-odonta*] *in some classifications* **:** an order of Lamellibranchia comprising bivalve mollusks with few hinge teeth but usu. with both lateral and cardinal teeth and with unequal adductor muscles

het·er·odon·ti·dae \-tə,dē\ *n pl, cap* [NL, fr. *Heterodontus,* type genus + *-idae*] **:** a family of small sharks (suborder Squaloidea) having a few recent representatives in warm parts of the Pacific and Indian oceans but known since Jurassic times, bearing two dorsal fins each armed with a spine, and having the posterior teeth arranged in a dense pavement adapted for crushing the shells of mollusks — see HETERODONTUS

het·er·odon·tus \-təs\ *n, cap* [NL, fr. *heter-* + *-odontus* (fr. Gk *odont-, odōn* tooth)] — more at TOOTH] **:** the type genus of Heterodontidae including most recent representatives of the family — see PORT JACKSON SHARK

het·er·o·dox \ˈhed·ərə,däks, ˈhetər-, ˈhe·tr-\ *adj* [LL *heterodoxus,* fr. Gk *heterodoxos,* fr. *hetero-* heter- + *doxa* opinion — more at DOXOLOGY] **1 :** differing from an established religious point of view: **a :** contrary to acknowledged religious opinion or belief **:** differing from a religious standard or official position **:** UNORTHODOX, HERETICAL ⟨~ sermon⟩ **b :** accepting or teaching heretical or unorthodox opinions or doctrines ⟨the ~ opponent of the established religion has often much more real faith than most of its followers —M.R.Cohen⟩ **2 :** lacking the usual content, qualities, or values **:** not following traditional form or procedure **:** UNCONVENTIONAL ⟨some ~ ideas on books —H.J.Laski⟩ ⟨the societies representing the orthodox practice of medicine have generally succeeded in keeping . . . ~ practitioners out —D.D.McKean⟩ — **het·er·o·dox·ly** *adv* — **het·ero·dox·ness** *n* -es

het·er·o·doxy \-sē,-si\ *n* [Gk *heterodoxia,* fr. *heterodoxos* + *-ia* -y] **1 :** the quality or state of being heterodox **:** departure from orthodoxy ⟨the unbridled ~ of the gay nineties —M.L. Bach⟩ **2 :** a heterodox opinion or doctrine ⟨revived the long-decaying . . . ~ and established it as the religion of the Persian state —H.A.R.Gibb⟩

het·er·od·ro·mous \ˈhed·əˈrädrəməs\ *adj* [*heter-* + *-dromous*] **:** having the genetic spiral of the branches reversed in its direction from that of the main stem ⟨~ leaf arrangement⟩ ⟨a ~ tendril⟩ — compare HOMODROMOUS — **het·er·od·ro·my** \ˌ⸗⸗ˈ⸗⸗mē\ *n* -ES

¹het·ero·dyne \ˈhed·ərə,dīn, ˈhetər-,ˈhe·tr-\ *adj* [*heter-* + *dyne*] **:** of or relating to the production of an electrical beat between two radio frequencies one of which usu. is that of a received signal-carrying current and the other that of an uninterrupted current introduced into the apparatus — compare SUPERHETERODYNE

²heterodyne \"\ *vt* -ED/-ING/-S **:** to combine (a radio frequency) with a different frequency so that a beat is produced ⟨a low value of signal frequency (generally about 100 kc), which is subsequently multiplied and *heterodyned* to produce the desired carrier frequency —*Radio Corp. of Amer. Rev.*⟩

¹het·er·oe·cious *or* **het·er·e·cious** \ˌhed·əˈrēshəs\ *adj* [*heter-* + *-oecious* or *-ecious* (fr. Gk *oikia* house + E *-ous*) — more at VICINITY] **:** passing through the different stages in its life cycle on alternate and often unrelated hosts ⟨~ rusts⟩ ⟨~ insects⟩ — contrasted with *homoecious;* compare AUTOECIOUS — **het·er·oe·cious·ly** *adv* — **het·er·oe·cious·ness** *n* -ES — **het·er·oe·cism** \ˌ⸗⸗ˈrē,sizəm\ *n* -s — **het·er·oe·cy** \ˈ⸗⸗,rēsē\ *n* -ES

²heteroecious *var of* HETEROICOUS

het·er·oe·cis·mal \ˌhed·əˈrē,sizməl; ˈhed·ərēˈs-, -rəˈ-\ *adj* [*heteroecism* (fr. ¹*heteroecious* + *-ism*) + *-al*] **:** HETEROECIOUS

het·ero·erotic \ˈhed·ə(,)rō+\ *adj* [*heter-* + *erotic*] **:** ALLOEROTIC

het·ero·erotism \"+\ *n* [*heter-* + *erotism*] **:** ALLOEROTISM

het·ero·fermentative \ˈhed·ə(,)rō+\ *adj* [*heter-* + *fermentative*] **:** producing a fermentation resulting in a number of end products — used esp. of lactic-acid bacteria that ferment carbohydrates and produce volatile acids and carbon dioxide as well as lactic acid

het·ero·fermenter \"+\ *n* [*heter-* + *fermenter*] **:** a heterofermentative organism

het·ero·fertilization \"+\ *n* [*heter-* + *fertilization*] **:** double fertilization in a seed plant (as maize) that results in phenotypically and probably genotypically different endosperm and embryo ⟨~ is considered to result when the polar nuclei and the egg fuse with male nuclei of differing genetic constitution⟩

het·ero·gamete \"+\ *n* [ISV *heter-* + *gamete*] **:** either of a pair of gametes that differ in form, size, or behavior, that are characteristic of most multicellular animals and many plants, and that occur typically as large nonmotile oogametes and small motile sperms — compare ISOGAMETE

het·ero·gametic \"+\ *adj* [*heter-* + *gametic*] **1 :** exhibiting heterogamety **:** DIGAMETIC **2 :** of or relating to a heterogamete or to heterogamety

het·ero·gam·e·tism \ˌ⸗(ˌ)⸗ˈgamə,tizəm\ *n* -s **:** HETEROGAMETY

het·ero·gam·e·ty \-məd·ē\ *n* -ES [*heter-* + *gamete* + *-y*] **:** the production by one sex of a species of two types of gametes of which one is destined to produce a male and the other a female

het·er·og·a·mous \ˈhed·əˈrägəməs\ *also* **het·ero·gam·ic** \ˈhed·ərōˈgamik\ *adj* [*heter-* + *-gamous* or *-gamic*] **:** exhibiting or characterized by diversity in the reproductive elements or processes: as **a** *of sexual reproduction* **:** characterized by fusion of unlike gametes; *esp* **:** OOGAMOUS 1 — often used of processes in higher organisms in contrast to *anisogamous;* compare ISOGAMOUS **b :** having heterogamous reproduction **c :** exhibiting alternation of generations in which two kinds of sexual generation (as dioecious and parthenogenetic) alternate **d :** bearing flowers of two kinds (as perfect and pistillate) — used esp. of sedges and composites and opposed to *homogamous*

het·er·og·a·my \ˌhed·əˈrägəmē\ *n* -ES [ISV *heter-* + *-gamy*] **1 :** the condition of being heterogamous — opposed to HOMOGAMY **2 :** heterogamous reproduction

het·ero·gangliate \ˈhed·ə(,)rō+\ *adj* [*heter-* + *gangliate*] **:** having the nerve ganglia more or less widely separated and unsymmetrically situated ⟨~ mollusks⟩

het·er·o·gen \ˈhed·ərəjən,-jen, ˈhe·tr-\ *n* -s [*heter-* + *-gen*] **:** a group of heterozygous hybrid organisms

het·er·o·gene \-ˌjēn\ *adj* [Gk *heterogenēs*] *archaic* **:** HETEROGENEOUS

het·er·o·ge·neal \ˈ⸗(⸗)⸗ˈjēnēəl, -nyəl\ *adj* [ML *heterogeneus* + E *-al*] *archaic* **:** HETEROGENEOUS

het·er·o·ge·ne·ity \ˌhed·ərəjəˈnēləd·ē, ˌhetər-, ˌhe·tr-, -rōj-, |əte, -i *sometimes* -nā| *or* ÷ -nī|\ *n* -ES [ML *heterogeneitas,* fr. *heterogeneus* heterogeneous + L *-itas* -ity] **:** the quality or state of being heterogeneous ⟨speaking by radio may vastly increase the number and ~ of your hearers —H.D.Scott⟩ ⟨the cultural ~ of the area —Mary Tew⟩ ⟨order which prevents variation from becoming a disordered ~ —John Dewey⟩

het·er·o·ge·neous \ˈ⸗(⸗)⸗ˈjēnēəs, -nyəs, *Brit sometimes* -ˈjen-\ *adj* [ML *heterogeneus,* fr. Gk *heterogenēs,* fr. *hetero-* heter- + *-genēs* born — more at -GEN] **1 :** differing in kind ⟨a ~ population —L.W.Doob⟩ ⟨genetically ~⟩ **2 :** consisting of dissimilar ingredients or constituents ⟨~ substances⟩ ⟨a town may be culturally or economically ~ —*Notes & Queries on Anthropology*⟩ ⟨having different values, opinions, or backgrounds ⟨the family is ~ enough to make quite a good party in itself —Rose Macaulay⟩ **3 a :** made up of parts or elements that are not unified, compatible, or proportionate ⟨no ~ hotchpotch but a book with an underlying unity —Roger Pippett⟩ **b :** incapable of comparison in respect to magnitude **:** being incommensurable ⟨volume and area are ~ quantities⟩ **4 :** having different genders in the singular and plural number ⟨Latin *locus* "place", which is masculine but has a neuter plural *loca,* is a ~ noun⟩ **5 :** possessed of unlike quality or meanings **:** DISPARATE ⟨not all the artists who painted . . . him from life were competent, and their results are ~ —J.C.Fitzpatrick⟩ **6 :** not uniform in structure or composition ⟨the ~ earth⟩ ⟨a ~ weld⟩ ⟨tumors which have a ~ composition by reason of structure and presence of necrosis —*Yr.Bk. of Endocrinology*⟩ ⟨the beam of x ray is not . . . monochromatic but ~, containing wavelengths over a large range —*Medical Physics*⟩ **7 :** relating to or occurring in or being a system that is not uniform throughout but consists of phases separated by boundaries (as solid-solid phases, solid-liquid phases, or solid-liquid-vapor phases) ⟨~ reaction⟩ — **het·er·o·ge·neous·ly** *adv* — **het·er·o·ge·neous·ness** *n* -ES

heterogeneous ray *n* **:** a vascular ray consisting of both upright and procumbent cells — compare HOMOGENEOUS RAY

het·ero·gen·er·a·tae \ˌhed·ə(,)rō,jenəˈrād·(,)ē, -ˈrād·(,)ē\ *n pl, cap* [NL, fr. *heter-* + L *generatae* (fem. pl. of *generatus,* past part. of *generare* to generate) — more at GENERATE] **:** a class of brown algae including those having two alternating generations unlike in vegetative structure, the larger sporophyte being often macroscopic and the smaller gametophyte usu. microscopic — compare ISOGENERATAE

het·ero·genesis \ˈhed·ərō+\ *n* [NL, fr. *heter-* + L *genesis*] **1 :** ABIOGENESIS **2 :** ALTERNATION OF GENERATIONS: as **a :** alternation of a dioecious and one or more parthenogenetic generations **b :** alternation of a haploid with a diploid generation

het·ero·genetic \ˈ⸗⸗(,)⸗+\ *adj* [*heter-* + *genetic*] **1 :** relating to or characterized by heterogenesis **2 :** HETEROPHILE

heterogenetic association *n* **:** the pairing in synapsis of genomes from diverse ancestors in a polyploid organism

heterogenetic induction *n, bot* **:** the union of two or more stimuli **:** complex stimulation

het·er·o·gen·ic \ˈhed·ərəˈjenik\ *adj* **1** [*heterogeny* + *-ic*] **:** HETEROGENETIC **2** [*heter-* + *gene* + *-ic*] **:** containing more than one allele of a gene — used of a cell or of population

het·er·og·e·nist \ˌhed·əˈräjənəst\ *n* -s [*heterogeny* + *-ist*] **:** ABIOGENIST

het·er·og·e·nous \ˌ⸗⸗ˈräjənəs\ *adj* **1** [*heter-* + *-genous*] **:** of other origin **:** not originating within the body — opposed to *autogenous* **2** [ML *heterogenus* diverse, fr. Gk *heterogenēs* — more at HETEROGENEOUS] **:** HETEROGENEOUS 2

heterogenous graft *n* **:** HETEROGRAFT

het·er·og·e·ny \-⸗ˈräjənē\ *n* -ES [*heterogenous* + *-y*] **1 :** a heterogenous collection or group ⟨the descendants of the ~ of Arab tribes that settled in Samaria —A.N.Williams b.1914⟩ **2** [*heter-* + *-geny*] **:** HETEROGENESIS **3 :** the application of different genders to neuter things

¹het·er·og·nath \ˈhed·ərəg,nath\ *adj* [NL *Heterognathi*] **:** of or relating to the Heterognathi

²heterognath \"\ *n* -s **:** ²CHARACIN

het·er·og·na·thi \ˌhed·əˈrägnə,thī\ *n pl, cap* [NL, fr. *heter-* + *-gnathi* (pl. of *-gnathus* -gnathous)] *in some classifications* **:** an order of teleost fishes that resemble members of the family Cyprinidae but have an adipose fin and teeth in the jaws and that comprise Characidae and related families now usu. included in a division of the suborder Cyprinoidea — compare OSTARIOPHYSI

het·er·o·gone \ˈhed·ərə,gōn\ *n* -s [back-formation fr. *heterogony*] **:** a heterogonous plant

het·er·o·gon·ic \ˈhed·ərəˈgänik\ *or* **het·er·og·o·nous** \ˈhed·əˈrägənəs\ *adj* [*heterogony* + *-ic* or *-ous*] **1 :** of, relating to, or characterized by heterogony; *esp* **:** ALLOMETRIC **2 :** being that course of development in which a generation of parasites is succeeded by a free-living generation — used of certain nematode worms; distinguished from *homogonic*

het·er·og·o·nism \ˌhed·əˈrägə,nizəm\ *n* -s [*heterogonous* + *-ism*] **:** HETEROGONY

het·er·og·o·nous·ly *adv* **:** in a heterogonous manner

het·er·og·o·ny \-nē\ *n* -ES [ISV *heter-* + *-gony*] **1 :** the state of having two or more kinds of perfect flowers varying in relative length of androecium and gynoecium — opposed to *homogony;* distinguished from *heteromorphism* **2 a :** ALTERNATION OF GENERATIONS; *esp* **:** alternation of a dioecious and hermaphroditic generation **b :** heterogamous reproduction **c :** ALLOMETRY

het·ero·graft \ˈhed·ərō+,-\ *n* [ISV *heter-* + *graft*] **:** a graft of tissue taken from a donor of one species to be grafted into a recipient of another species ⟨the use of ~s has proved impracticable in cosmetic surgery⟩ — compare AUTOGRAFT, HOMOGRAFT

het·ero·graph·ic \ˈhed·ərəˈgrafik\ *adj* **:** of, relating to, or characterized by heterography — opposed to *homographic*

het·er·og·ra·phy \ˌhed·əˈrägrəfē\ *n* -ES [*heter-* + *-graphy*] **1 :** spelling differing from standard current usage **2 :** spelling in which the same letters represent different sounds in different words or syllables (as in current English orthography)

het·er·og·y·nous \ˈhed·əˈräjənəs\ *or* **het·er·og·y·nal** \-nᵊl\ *adj* [*heterogynous* fr. *heter-* + *-gynous; heterogynal* fr. *heterogynous* + *-al*] **:** having females of more than one kind ⟨bees and ants are ~⟩

het·er·oi·cous \-ˈrȯikəs\ *also* **het·er·oe·cious** \-ˈrēshəs\ *adj* [*heter-* + *-oicous, -oecious* (fr. Gk *oikos* dwelling + E *-ous*) — more at VICINITY] **:** having archegonia and antheridia either on the same branch or on different branches of the same plant — compare PAROICOUS, POLYOICOUS

het·ero·karyon *also* **het·ero·caryon** \ˈhed·ərō+\ *n* -s [NL, fr. *heter-* + *karyon* or *caryon*] **:** a cell in the mycelium of a fungus that contains two or more genetically unlike nuclei — compare DIKARYON, HOMOKARYON

het·ero·kary·o·sis *or* **het·ero·cary·o·sis** \ˌ⸗⸗⸗,karēˈōsəs\ *n* -ES [NL, fr. *heter-* + *kary-* or *cary-* + *-osis*] **:** the condition of having cells that are heterokaryons

het·ero·kary·ot·ic *or* **het·ero·cary·ot·ic** \ˈhed·ə(,)rōˌkarēˈäd·ik\ *adj* [*heter-* + *kary-* or *cary-* + *-otic*] **:** of, relating to, or consisting of heterokaryons ⟨a ~ division⟩ ⟨~ mycelia⟩

het·ero·kinesis \ˈhed·ə(,)rō+\ *n* [NL, fr. *heter-* + *-kinesis*] **:** qualitative nuclear division — used of the meiotic reduction division in the heterogametic sex — **het·ero·kinetic** \"+\ *adj*

het·ero·kon·tae \ˌhed·ərōˈkän,tē\ *n pl, cap* [NL, fr. *heter-* + *-kontae* (fr. Gk *kontos* punting pole, fr. *kentein* to prick, goad); fr. the unequal length of the flagella — more at CENTER] *in some classifications* **:** a class of algae equivalent to Xanthophyceae that includes all the yellow-green algae having flagella of unequal length — compare ISOKONTAE

het·ero·lecithal \"+\ *adj* [*heter-* + Gk *lekithos* yolk of an egg + E *-al*] **:** having the yolk unequally distributed — opposed to *homolecithal*

het·er·ol·o·cha \ˌhed·əˈräləkə\ *n, cap* [NL, alter. of *Heteralocha,* fr. *heter-* + *-alocha* (fr. Gk *alochos* spouse, bedfellow, concubine)] *in some classifications* **:** a genus coextensive with *Neomorpha*

het·er·o·log·i·cal \ˈhed·ərəˈläjəkəl\ *also* **het·er·o·log·ic** \-jik\ *adj* [*heterology* + *-ical* or *-ic*] **:** of or relating to or characterized by heterology **:** HETEROLOGOUS — **het·er·o·log·i·cal·ly** \-jək(ə)lē\ *adv*

het·er·ol·o·gous \ˈhed·əˈräləgəs\ *adj* [*heter-* + Gk *logos* proportion, word + E *-ous* — more at LEGEND] **1 :** characterized by heterology **:** consisting of different elements or of like elements in different proportions **:** DIFFERENT **2 :** derived from a different species ⟨~ serum⟩ — compare AUTOLOGOUS, HOMOLOGOUS — **het·er·ol·o·gous·ly** *adv*

heterologous graft *n* **:** HETEROGRAFT

heterologous series *n* **:** a series (as ethane, ethyl alcohol, acetaldehyde, acetic acid) of related derivatives not homologous

heterologous stimulus *n* **:** a stimulus capable of affecting any available sensory end organ and thought to be further capable of being interpreted centrally as a stimulus of the kind to which the end organ is adapted to respond ⟨a blow on the eye acts as a *heterologous stimulus* seen as a flash of light⟩ — compare HOMOLOGOUS STIMULUS

het·er·ol·o·gy \ˌ⸗⸗ˈräləjē\ *n* -ES [ISV *heter-* + *-logy*] **:** the lack of correspondence of apparently similar bodily parts due to differences in fundamental makeup or origin — compare ANALOGY, HOMOLOGY

het·ero·lysin \ˈhed·ərō+\ *n* [ISV *heter-* + *lysin*] **:** a hemolysin from an animal of a different species

het·er·ol·y·sis \ˌhed·əˈräləsəs\ *n* [NL, fr. *heter-* + *-lysis*] **1 :** destruction by an outside agent; *specif* **:** solution (as of a cell) by lysins or enzymes from another source **2 :** decomposition of a compound into two oppositely charged particles or ions (as $X{:}Y \rightarrow X^{+} + {:}B^{-}$) — compare HOMOLYSIS — **het·er·o·lyt·ic** \ˈhed·ərōˈlid·ik\ *adj*

het·er·o·mal·lous \ˈhed·ərōˈmaləs\ *adj* [Gk *heteromallos* woolly, fr. *hetero-* heter- + *mallos* lock of wool] **:** spreading or turning in different directions — used of leaves of various mosses; opposed to *homomallous*

het·er·o·mas·ti·gote \ˌ⸗⸗⸗ˈmastə,gōt\ *or* **het·er·o·mas·ti·gate** \-ˌgāt\ *adj* [*heteromastigote,* alter. of *heteromastigate,* fr. *heter-* + *mastig-* + *-ate*] **:** having two unlike flagella ⟨~ dinoflagellates⟩

het·er·o·me·les \ˌ⸗⸗⸗ˈmē(,)lēz\ *n, cap* [NL, fr. *heter-* + *-meles* (fr. Gk *mēlon* apple)] *in some classifications* **:** a genus of plants including only the toyon — compare PHOTINIA

het·er·om·er·ous \ˌhed·əˈrämərəs\ *adj* [*heter-* + Gk *meros* part + E *-ous* — more at MERIT] **1 :** unrelated in chemical composition — used of homeomorphous substances **2** *of a flower* **:** having one or more whorls the number of whose members differs from that of the remaining whorls — opposed to *isomerous* **3 :** having a thallus with one or more layers of algal cells ⟨~ lichens⟩ — opposed to *homoeomerous*

het·ero·mesotroph \ˈhed·ərō+\ *n* -s [*heter-* + *mesotroph*] **:** a heteromesotrophic organism

het·ero·mesotrophic \"+\ *adj* [*heter-* + *mesotrophic*] **:** requiring a single organic source of nitrogen and carbon for metabolism

het·ero·metabolic \"+\ *or* **het·ero·metabolous** \"+\ *adj* [*heter-* + *metabolic* or *metabolous*] **:** of or relating to or exhibiting heterometabolism

het·ero·metabolism \"+\ *also* **het·ero·metaboly** \"+\ *n* [*heter-* + *metabolism* or *metaboly*] *of insects* **:** development with incomplete or direct metamorphosis in which the young nymph is fundamentally like the adult and no pupal stage precedes maturity — distinguished from *holometabolism;* compare HEMIMETABOLISM

het·ero·metatrophic \"+\ *adj* [*heter-* + *metatrophic*] **:** requiring complex organic sources of carbon and nitrogen for metabolism — compare HOLOZOIC

het·ero·met·ric \ˈhed·ərōˈme·trik\ *adj* [ISV *heter-* + *-metric*] **:** characterized by diversity of meter

het·er·o·mi \ˌhed·əˈrō,mī\ *n pl, cap* [NL, fr. *heter-* + *-omi* (fr. Gk *ōmos* shoulder) — more at HUMERUS] **:** a small order of eellike deep-sea teleost fishes with a spiny dorsal fin

het·er·o·mor·phic \ˈhed·ərōˈmȯrfik\ *or* **het·er·o·mor·phous** \-fəs\ *adj* [ISV *heter-* + *-morphic* or *-morphous*] **1 :** deviating from the usual form or exhibiting diversity of form: as **a :** having different forms at different stages of development ⟨holometabolic insects and certain plants with complex life cycles are ~⟩ **b :** having different forms in different members of a colony ⟨the polyps of many complex compound jellyfishes are highly ~ being chiefly specialized for feeding, defense, motility, or reproduction⟩ **c :** of irregular or unusual structure **:** of variable shape ⟨the leaves of emergent plants are commonly ~⟩ **d :** unlike in form or size — used specif. of synaptic chromosomes ⟨the X and Y chromosomes constitute a ~ pair⟩ ⟨~ bivalents⟩ **2 :** exhibiting or undergoing heteromorphosis

het·er·o·mor·phism \ˌ≈≈≈ˈmȯrˌfizəm\ *n* -s [ISV *heter-* + *-morphism*] **1 :** the quality or state of being heteromorphic **2 :** dissimilarity in crystal form shown by compounds of similar composition — contrasted with *homeomorphism* and *isomorphism* **3 :** HETEROGONY 1 **4 :** POLYMORPHISM

het·er·o·mor·phite \-ˌfīt\ *n* -s [ISV *heter-* + *morph-* + *-ite*] **:** a mineral $Pb_7Sb_8S_{19}$ consisting of a lead antimony sulfide related closely to fülöppite, plagionite, and semseyite

het·er·o·mor·pho·sis \ˌ≈≈≈ˈmȯrfəsə̇s\ *n* [NL, fr. *heter-* + *-morphosis*] **1 :** the production in an organism of an abnormal or misplaced part esp. in place of one that has been lost (as the regeneration of a tail in place of a head) — compare HOMOMORPHOSIS **2 a :** the production of a malformed or malplaced tissue or organ **b :** the formation of tissue of a different type from that from which it derives

het·er·o·mor·phy \ˈ≈≈≈ˌmȯrfē\ *n* -ES [ISV *heter-* + *-morphy*] **:** HETEROMORPHISM

het·ero·mya \ˌhed·ərōˈmīə\ [NL, fr. *heter-* + *-mya*] *syn of* HETEROMYARIA

het·ero·my·ar·ia \-ōmīˈa(a)rēə\ *n pl, cap* [NL, fr. *heter-* + *-myaria*] *in some classifications* **:** a division of Lamellibranchia comprising bivalve mollusks having two adductor muscles the anterior one of which is very small — compare ISOMYARIA, MONOMYARIA — **het·er·o·my·ar·i·an** \¦≈≈≈≈¦≈rēən\ *adj*

[1]**het·er·o·my·id** \¦hed·ərō¦mīə̇d\ *adj* [NL *Heteromyidae*] **:** of or relating to the Heteromyidae

[2]**heteromyid** \"\ *n* -s **:** one of the Heteromyidae

het·er·o·my·i·dae \ˌ≈≈≈ˈmīəˌdē\ *n pl, cap* [NL, fr. *Heteromys*, type genus + *-idae*] **:** a family of New World rodents having fur-lined external cheek pouches, large eyes, well developed ears, elongated hind limbs and tail adapted to leaping and balancing, and the ability to live on dry food and depending on metabolic water to survive under extreme desert conditions — see POCKET MOUSE 1

het·ero·mys \ˈ≈≈≈ˌmis\ *n, cap* [NL, fr. *heter-* + *-mys*] **:** the type genus of the family Heteromyidae

het·ero·nemertea \¦hed·ərō+\ *n pl, cap* [NL, fr. *heter-* + *Nemertea*] **:** an order of Nemertea (class Anopla) comprising long slender forms with cerebral organs and often with caudal cirri — **het·ero·nemertean** \"+\ *adj or n*

het·ero·nemertini \"+\ [NL, fr. *heter-* + *Nemertini*] *syn of* HETERONEMERTEA

[1]**het·er·o·ne·re·id** \¦hed·ərō¦nirēə̇d\ *adj* [NL *heteronereid-*, *heteronereis*] **:** of, relating to, or having the characters of a heteronereis

[2]**heteronereid** \"\ *n* -s **:** HETERONEREIS

het·ero·nereis \¦hed·ərō+\ *n* [NL, fr. *heter-* + *Nereis*] **:** a free-swimming dimorphic sexual individual of certain polychaete worms (family Nereidae) characterized by greatly enlarged eyes, enlarged and modified parapodia and other appendages, and more or less complete obliteration of the internal viscera by masses of developing germ cells

het·er·o·neu·ra \ˌ≈≈≈ˈn(y)u̇rə\ *n pl, cap* [NL, fr. *heter-* + *-neura*] *in some classifications* **:** a suborder of Lepidoptera including those forms in which the venation of the fore wings differs from that of the hind wings — compare HOMONEURA

het·er·on·o·mous \¦hed·ə¦ränəməs\ *adj* [G *heteronom* (fr. *heter-* + *-onom*, as in *autonom* autonomous, fr. Gk *autonomos*) + E *-ous* — more at AUTONOMOUS] **1 :** subject to or involving different laws of growth ⟨in most segmented animals . . . the segmentation is ~ —Libbie H. Hyman⟩ **2 :** subject to external controls and impositions **:** originating outside the self or one's own will ⟨nor is the Christian view ~, in the sense that the will is enslaved by the dictates of a despot alien to the self's will —W.W.Beach⟩ — **het·er·on·o·mous·ly** *adv*

het·er·on·o·my \ˌ≈≈ˈ≈≈mē\ *n* -ES [G *heteronomie*, fr. *heter-* + *-onomie* (as in *autonomie* autonomy, fr. Gk *autonomia*) — more at AUTONOMY] **1 :** a subjection to something else: as **a :** a subordination to the law or domination of another (as in political subjection) **b :** the condition of lacking moral freedom or self-determination ⟨in ~ the will . . . is obeying laws not of its own making —D.D.Runes⟩ — opposed to *autonomy* **2 :** the quality or state of being heteronomous

het·ero·nuclear \¦hed·ərō+\ *adj* [*heter-* + *nuclear*] **1 :** HETEROCYCLIC **2 :** of or relating to different rings in a chemical compound ⟨~ substitution in naphthalene⟩ **3 :** of or relating to a molecule composed of different nuclei ⟨hydrogen chloride HCl and deuterium hydride HD consist of ~ diatomic molecules⟩

het·er·on·y·mous \¦hed·ə¦ränəməs\ *adj* [LGk *heterōnymos*, fr. Gk *hetero-* heter- + *onyma*, *onoma* name — more at NAME] **:** having different designations ⟨parent and child are ~ relatives⟩ — opposed to *homonymous* — **het·er·on·y·mous·ly** *adv*

het·ero·ou·sia \¦hed·ərō¦üzēə, -üsēə, -üzh(ē)ə, -üsh(ē)ə\ *also* **het·er·ou·sia** \¦hed·ə¦rü-\ *n* [LGk, fr. Gk *hetero-*, *heter-* heter- + *ousia*] **:** difference in essence or substance

[1]**het·ero·ou·sian** *also* **het·er·ou·sian** \-ən\ *adj* [LGk *heteroousios*, *heterousios* (fr. Gk *hetero-*, *heter-* heter- + *ousia*) + E *-an*] **1 :** having different essential qualities **:** being of a different nature **2** *often cap* **:** of or relating to the heteroousians

[2]**heteroousian** \"\ *also* **heterousian** \"\ *n* -s *often cap* **:** an Arian holding that the Son was of a different substance from the Father — compare HOMOIOUSIAN, HOMOOUSIAN

het·er·o·path·ic \¦hed·ərō¦pathik\ *adj* [*heter-* + Gk *pathos* experience, suffering, emotion + E *-ic* — more at PATHOS] **1 :** different in operation or effect ⟨~ laws —J.S.Mill⟩ **2 :** identifying self with another

het·er·o·pel·mous \-¦pelməs\ *adj* [*heter-* + *-pelmous*] **:** having each of the two flexor tendons of the toes bifid with the branches of one going to the first and second toes and those of the other to the third and fourth toes

het·er·o·pet·al·ous \-¦ped·ᵊləs\ *adj* [*heter-* + *-petalous*] **:** having dissimilar petals

het·er·oph·a·gous \¦hed·ə¦räfə̇gəs\ *adj* [*heter-* + *-phagous*] **1 :** ALTRICIAL **2 :** feeding or living on two or more hosts at different stages of the life history ⟨digenetic trematodes are ~⟩

het·er·o·phe·my \ˈhed·ərəˌfēmē\ *n* -ES [*heter-* + Gk *phēmē* voice, speech (fr. *phanai* to say) + E *-y* — more at BAN] **:** unconscious use of words other than those intended

het·er·o·phil antibody \ˈ≈≈rəˌfil-\ *n* **:** an antibody characteristic of human blood during an attack of infectious mononucleosis that agglutinates sheep red blood cells

[1]**het·er·o·phile** \ˈ≈≈≈ˌfīl\ *also* **het·er·o·phil** \-ˌfil\ *or* **het·er·o·phil·ic** \¦≈≈≈¦filik\ *adj* [*heter-* + *-phile* or *-phil* or *-philic*] **:** reacting serologically with an antigen of another species

[2]**heterophile** \"\ *or* **heterophil** \"\ *n* -s [*heter-* + *-phile* or *-phil*] **:** NEUTROPHIL — used esp. in veterinary medicine

het·er·oph·o·ny \ˌhed·əˈräfənē\ *n* -ES [Gk *heterophōnia* diversity of note, fr. *heter-* + *-phōnia* -phony] **:** a singing or sounding of the same melody by two or more voices or instruments usu. with some modifications (as in rhythm or ornamentation) by one or both of the performers

het·er·o·pho·ria \ˌhed·ərōˈfōrēə\ *n* -s [NL, fr. *heter-* + *-phoria*] **:** latent strabismus in which one eye tends to deviate either medially or laterally — compare EXOPHORIA — **het·ero·phor·ic** \¦≈≈≈¦fȯrik\ *adj*

het·ero·phy·es \-ˈfī(ˌ)ēz\ *n, cap* [NL, fr. LGk *heterophyēs* of different nature, fr. Gk *heter-* + *phyē* growth, nature; akin to Gk *phyein* to bring forth — more at BE] **:** a genus (the type of the family Heterophyidae) of small digenetic trematode worms infesting the small intestine of dogs, cats, and man in Egypt and much of tropical Asia

[1]**het·er·o·phy·id** \¦≈≈≈¦fīə̇d\ *adj* [NL *Heterophyidae*, family of trematode worms, fr. *Heterophyes*, type genus + *-idae*] **:** of or relating to the genus *Heterophyes* or family Heterophyidae

[2]**heterophyid** \"\ *n* -s **:** a heterophyid worm

het·ero·phylesis \¦hed·ə(ˌ)rō+\ *n* [NL, fr. *heter-* + *phylesis*] **:** the quality or state of being heterophyletic

het·ero·phyletic \"+\ *adj* [*heter-* + *phyletic*] **:** of or relating to or possessing two or more lines of descent

het·er·o·phyl·lous \¦hed·ərō¦filəs\ *adj* [*heter-* + *-phyllous*] **1 :** having the foliage leaves of more than one form on the same plant or stem ⟨many eucalypts, pondweeds, and crowfoots are ~⟩ — opposed to *isophyllous* **2 :** having two or more forms of foliation of the septal margins ⟨~ ammonites⟩ — **het·er·o·phyl·ly** \ˈ≈≈≈ˌfilē\ *n* -ES

het·er·o·phyte \ˈhed·ərəˌfīt\ *n* -s [*heter-* + *-phyte*] **:** a plant that is dependent for food materials upon other living or dead plant or animal organisms or their products **:** PARASITE, SAPROPHYTE — compare AUTOPHYTE — **het·er·o·phyt·ic** \¦≈≈≈¦fid·ik\ *adj*

het·er·o·pi·idae \ˌhed·ərōˈpīəˌdē\ *n pl, cap* [NL, fr. *Heteropia*, type genus (fr. *heter-* + *-opia*) + *-idae*] **:** a family of sponges (order Heterocoela) with a distinct dermal cortex pierced by inhalant pores and with subdermal triradiate spicules

het·er·o·pla·sia \-ˈplāzh(ē)ə\ *n* -s [NL, fr. *heter-* + *-plasia*] **1 :** a development of a tissue from tissue of a different kind **2 :** a formation of abnormal tissue or of normal tissue in an abnormal locality

het·er·o·plasm \ˈhed·ərōˌplazəm\ *n* [ISV *heter-* + *-plasm*] **:** tissue formed or growing where it does not normally occur

het·er·o·plas·tic \¦≈≈≈¦plastik\ *adj* [ISV *heter-* + *-plastic*] **1 :** of or relating to heteroplasm or heteroplasty or heteroplasia **2 :** HETEROLOGOUS — **het·er·o·plas·ti·cal·ly** \-tə̇k(ə)lē\ *adv*

het·er·o·plas·ty \ˈ≈≈≈ˌplastē\ *n* -ES [ISV *heter-* + *-plasty*] **1 :** HETEROPLASIA **2 :** a grafting of tissue from an individual of one species into an individual of a different species

[1]**het·er·o·ploid** \-ˌplȯid\ *adj* [ISV *heter-* + *-ploid*] **:** having a chromosome number that is greater or smaller usu. by one than the somatic number characteristic of the species but not a simple multiple of the haploid chromosome number — compare POLYPLOID

[2]**heteroploid** \"\ *n* -s **:** a heteroploid individual

het·er·o·ploi·dy \-dē\ *n* -ES **:** the condition of being heteroploid

het·er·o·pod \-ˌpäd\ *n* -s [NL *Heteropoda*] **:** one of the Heteropoda

het·er·op·o·da \ˌhed·əˈräpədə\ *n pl, cap* [NL, fr. *heter-* + *-poda*] **:** a small division of Pectinibranchia (suborder Taenioglossa) formerly ranked as a separate order and comprising pelagic gastropod mollusks that swim at the surface with the ventral side up with a foot or a part of it forming a median fin and that have a transparent body and a transparent shell or none — **het·er·op·o·dous** \¦≈≈¦≈≈dəs\ *adj*

het·er·op·o·dal \¦≈≈¦≈≈dᵊl\ *adj* [*heter-* + *pod-* + *-al*] **:** of or relating to nerve cells having different kinds of branches

het·ero·polar \¦hed·ərō+\ *adj* [ISV *heter-* + *polar*] **1 :** of, relating to, or having unlike poles ⟨~ systems⟩ **2 :** POLAR 5b, IONIC — used esp. of chemical bonds or of crystals; distinguished from *homopolar* — **het·ero·polarity** \"+\ *n*

het·er·o·poly \¦hed·ərō¦pälē\ *adj* [ISV *heteropoly-*] **:** containing several groups or ions of different acid-forming elements

heteropoly- *comb form* [ISV *heter-* + *poly-*] **:** containing several groups or ions of different acid-forming elements — in names of complex inorganic acids and their salts ⟨*heteropoly*molybdates such as phosphomolybdates⟩; compare ISOPOLY-

heteropoly acid *n* **:** any of a large group of complex oxygen-containing acids derived from two or more different inorganic acids by elimination of water from two or more molecules of the acids; *esp* **:** an acid regarded as formed by combination of several molecules of an acid anhydride (as molybdenum trioxide or tungsten trioxide) with a second acid that furnishes the central atom (as phosphorus or silicon) of the complex — distinguished from *isopoly acid*

het·ero·polymer \¦hed·ərō+\ *n* [G, fr. *hetero-* heter- + *polymer*] **:** COPOLYMER

het·er·op·tera \ˌhed·əˈräptərə\ *n pl, cap* [NL, fr. *heter-* + *-ptera*] **:** a suborder of Hemiptera or sometimes a separate order comprising the true bugs — compare HOMOPTERA — **het·er·op·ter·ous** \¦≈≈¦≈≈rəs\ *adj*

het·ero·pycnosis \¦hed·ərō+\ *n* [NL, fr. *heter-* + *pycnosis*] **:** a differential degree of condensation that distinguishes various chromosomes (as sex) or parts of chromosomes in a nucleus — **het·ero·pycnotic** \"+\ *adj*

het·er·o·scope \ˈhed·ərəˌskōp\ *n* [*heter-* + *-scope*] **:** an apparatus for measuring the range of vision in strabismus — **het·er·os·co·py** \ˌhed·əˈräskəpē\ *n* -ES

[1]**het·ero·sexual** \¦hed·ərō+\ *adj* [ISV *heter-* + *sexual*] **1 :** of or relating to or characterized by heterosexuality ⟨sexual relationships between individuals of opposite sexes are ~ —A.C.Kinsey⟩ — opposed to *homosexual* **2 :** of or relating to different sexes ⟨~ twins⟩ ⟨a ~ flock of chickens —*Anatomical Record*⟩ ⟨the pairing off . . . is seldom ~ —A.J.Liebling⟩

[2]**heterosexual** \"\ *n* -s **:** a heterosexual individual

het·ero·sexuality \"+\ *n* [ISV *heter-* + *sexuality*] **:** the manifestation of sexual desire toward a member of the opposite sex ⟨the achievement of a healthy ~ —F.E.Williams⟩

het·er·o·side \ˈhed·ərōˌsīd, ˈ≈≈(ˌ)≈ˌsīd\ *n* -s [ISV *heter-* + *-oside*] **:** a glycoside that on hydrolysis yields a noncarbohydrate as well as a glycose — compare HOLOSIDE

het·er·o·si·pho·na·les \¦hed·ərōˌsīfəˈnā(ˌ)lēz\ *n pl, cap* [NL, fr. *heter-* + *siphon-* + *-ales*] **:** an order of yellow-green algae comprising the siphonaceous members of the class Xanthophyceae and including the single genus *Botrydium*

het·er·o·sis \ˌhed·əˈrōsə̇s\ *n, pl* **hetero·ses** \-ōˌsēz\ [NL, fr. Gk *heterōsis* alteration, alter. of *heteroiōsis*, fr. *heteroioun* to alter (fr. *heteroios* different in kind, fr. *heteros* other) + *-ōsis* -osis — more at HETER-] **:** a greater vigor or capacity for growth frequently displayed by crossbred animals or plants as compared with those resulting from inbreeding

het·er·o·site \ˈhed·ərəˌsīt\ *n* -s [F *hétérosite*, fr. Gk *heteros* other, different + F *-ite*] **:** a mineral isomorphous with purpurite and consisting of phosphate of iron and manganese

het·er·o·so·ma·ta \ˌhed·ərōˈsōməd·ə\ *n pl, cap* [NL, fr. *heter-* + *-somata*] **:** an order or other group of teleost fishes consisting of the flatfishes — **het·er·o·so·mate** \¦≈≈≈¦sōˌmāt\ *adj* — **het·er·o·so·ma·tous** \-ˌməd·əs\ *adj*

het·er·o·so·ma·ti \ˌ≈≈≈ˈsōməd·ˌī\ *or* **het·er·o·so·mi** \-ˈsōmī\ [NL, fr. *heter-* + *-somati* (fr. Gk *somata*) or *-somi* (pl. of *-somus*)] *syn of* HETEROSOMATA

het·er·o·some \ˈhed·ərəˌsōm\ *n* -s [*heter-* + *-some*] **:** HETEROCHROMOSOME

het·er·o·spo·re·ae \ˌhed·ərōˈspōrēˌē\ *n pl, cap* [NL, fr. *heter-* + *-sporeae* (fr. Gk *spora* seed) — more at SPORE] *in some classifications* **:** a primary subdivision of Pteridophyta including the Lycopodiaceae and Equisetaceae and producing two kinds of asexual spores

het·er·o·spo·ri·um \-rēəm\ *n, cap* [NL, fr. *heter-* + *-sporium*] **:** a form genus of imperfect fungi (family Dematiaceae) with echinulate and 2-septate to several-septate brown conidia

het·er·o·spor·ous \¦≈≈≈¦spōrəs, ¦hed·ə¦räspərəs\ *also* **het·er·o·spor·ic** \¦≈≈rō¦spōrik\ *adj* [*heter-* + *-sporous* or *-sporic*] **:** characterized by heterospory **:** reproducing asexually by heterospory ⟨~ plants⟩; *specif* **:** producing microspores and megaspores ⟨some pteridophytes and all spermatophytes are ~⟩

het·er·o·spo·ry \ˈ≈≈rōˌspōrē, ˌ≈≈ˈräspərē\ *n* -ES [*heter-* + *-spory*] **1 :** the production of asexual spores of more than one kind **2 :** the development of microspores and megaspores in some ferns and fern allies and in all seed plants — opposed to *homospory*

het·ero·static \¦hed·ərō+\ *adj* [ISV *heter-* + *static*] **:** of or relating to a method of electrostatic measurement in which one potential is measured by means of a different potential — **het·ero·statically** *adv*

het·er·os·tra·ca \ˌhed·əˈrästrə̇kə\ [NL] *syn of* HETEROSTRACI

[1]**het·er·os·tra·can** \¦≈≈¦≈≈kən\ *adj* [NL *Heterostraci* + E *-an*] **:** of or relating to the Heterostraci

[2]**heterostracan** \"\ *n* -s **:** an animal or fossil of the order Heterostraci

het·er·os·tra·ci \ˌ≈≈ˈ≈strəˌsī\ *n pl, cap* [NL, fr. *heter-* + Gk *ostrakon* shell, potsherd — more at OSTRACON] **:** a class or other division of ostracoderms with widely separated nares and eyes and with an exoskeleton which may consist of a few large plates or numerous placoid scales

het·er·o·stroph·ic \¦hed·ərō¦sträfik\ *adj* **1** [Gk *heterostrophos* + E *-ic*] **:** consisting of strophes differing in metrical form **2** [NL *heterostrophus* + E *-ic*] **:** relating to or marked by heterostrophy ⟨a shell with ~ whorls⟩

het·er·os·tro·phous \¦hed·ə¦rästrəfəs\ *adj* [NL *heterostrophus*] **:** HETEROSTROPHIC 1

het·er·os·tro·phy \ˌ≈≈ˈ≈≈fē\ *n* -ES [ISV *heter-* + *-strophy* (fr. Gk *strophē* turn)] **:** the quality or state of being coiled in a direction opposite to the usual one

het·er·o·styled \ˈhed·ərōˌstīld\ *adj* [*heter-* + *-styled*] **:** having styles of two or more distinct forms or of different lengths ⟨~ buckwheat⟩ — compare HOMOSTYLED

het·er·o·sty·lism \ˌ≈≈≈ˈstīˌlizəm\ *also* **het·er·o·sty·ly** \ˈ≈≈≈ˌstīlē\ *n, pl* **heterostylisms** *also* **heterostylies** [*heterostylism* fr. *heter-* + *style* + *-ism; heterostyly* fr. *heter-* + *-styly*] **:** HETEROGONY 1

het·er·o·sty·lous \¦≈≈≈¦stīləs\ *adj* [*heter-* + *-stylous*] **:** HETEROSTYLED

het·ero·suggestion \¦hed·ə(ˌ)rō+\ *n* [ISV *heter-* + *suggestion*] **:** suggestion used by one person to influence another

het·ero·syllabic \"+\ *adj* [*heter-* + *syllabic*] **:** belonging to another syllable or to different syllables

het·ero·syllis \"+\ *n, pl* **heterosylles** [NL, fr. *heter-* + *Syllis*] **:** a modified sexual form of an annelid of the family Syllidae comparable to a heteronereis

het·er·o·tac·tic \¦hed·ərō¦taktik\ *also* **het·er·o·tac·tous** \-təs\ *adj* [*heter-* + *-tactic* or *-tactous* (fr. Gk *taktos* ordered, fixed)] **:** characterized by or exhibiting heterotaxis

het·er·o·tax·ic \-¦taksik\ *adj* [NL *heterotaxis* + E *-ic*] **:** HETEROTACTIC

het·er·o·tax·is \ˌ≈≈≈ˈtaksə̇s\ *also* **het·er·o·tax·ia** \-ksēə\ *n, pl* **heterotax·es** \-kˌsēz\ *also* **heterotax·i·as** \-ksēəz\ [NL, fr. *heter-* + *-taxis* or *-taxia*] **:** abnormal arrangement (as of organs or parts of the body or of geological strata)

het·er·o·taxy \ˈ≈≈≈ˌtaksē\ *n* -ES [NL *heterotaxia*] **:** HETEROTAXIS

het·ero·telic \¦hed·ərō+\ *adj* [*heter-* + *telic*] **:** existing for the sake of something else **:** having an extraneous end or purpose — contrasted with *autotelic*

het·er·o·thal·lic \¦hed·ərō¦thalik\ *adj* [*heter-* + *thall-* + *-ic*] **1 :** having two or more genetically incompatible but morphologically similar haploid phases which function as separate sexes or strains — used esp. of certain algae and fungi or of the unisexual spores producing these strains — compare HOMOTHALLIC, MINUS, PLUS **2 :** DIOECIOUS — **het·er·o·thal·lism** \ˌ≈≈≈ˈthaˌlizəm\ *n* -s — **het·er·o·thal·ly** \ˈ≈≈≈ˌthalē\ *n* -ES

het·er·o·therm \ˈ≈≈≈ˌthərm\ *n* [*heter-* + *-therm*] **:** POIKILOTHERM

het·ero·ther·mic \¦hed·ərō¦thərmik\ *also* **het·ero·ther·mal** \-məl\ *or* **het·ero·ther·mous** \-məs\ *adj* [*heter-* + *thermic* or *thermal* or *-thermous*] **:** POIKILOTHERMIC

het·er·ot·ic \¦hed·ə¦räd·ik\ *adj* [fr. NL *heterosis*, after such pairs as NL *narcosis:* E *narcotic*] **:** of, relating to, or exhibiting heterosis ⟨~ tetraploids⟩ ⟨a ~ modification⟩

het·er·o·to·pia \ˌhed·ərōˈtōpēə\ *also* **het·er·ot·o·py** \ˌhed·əˈräd·əpē\ *n, pl* **heterotopias** *also* **heterotopies** [NL *heterotopia*, fr. *heter-* + *-topia* -topy] **:** displacement in or difference of position: as **a :** deviation of an organ from the normal position **b :** an abnormal habitat **c :** the grafting of tissue into an abnormal location (as skin into the anterior chamber of the eye) — **het·er·o·top·ic** \¦≈≈≈¦täpik\ *adj* — **het·er·ot·o·pous** \¦≈≈¦räd·əpəs\ *adj*

het·ero·transplant \¦hed·ərō+\ *n* [*heter-* + *transplant*] **:** HETEROGRAFT — **het·ero·transplantation** \"+\ *n*

het·er·o·trich \ˈ≈≈rōˌtrik\ *n* -s [NL *Heterotricha*] **:** one of the Heterotricha

het·er·ot·ri·cha \ˌhed·əˈrä·trə̇kə\ *n pl, cap* [NL, fr. *heter-* + *-tricha*] **:** a suborder of Spirotricha comprising ciliate protozoans that have uniform or reduced ciliation but no cirri and containing free-living organisms (as members of the genus *Stentor*) as well as commensals and parasites of vertebrate intestines — see BALANTIDIUM

het·er·o·tri·cha·les \ˌhed·ərō·trəˈkā(ˌ)lēz\ *n pl, cap* [NL, fr. *heter-* + *trich-* + *-ales*] **:** an order of yellow-green algae comprising all those with cells arranged in simple or branching filaments and including the single family Tribonemaceae

het·er·o·trich·i·da \-rō·ˈtrikədə\ [NL, fr. *heter-* + *trich-* + *-ida*] *syn of* HETEROTRICHA

het·er·o·tri·cho·sis \-rō·trəˈkōsə̇s\ *n* [NL, fr. *heter-* + *trich-* + *-osis*] **:** a condition of having hair of variegated color

het·er·ot·ri·chous \¦hed·ə¦rä·trə̇kəs\ *adj* [prob. fr. NL *heterotrichus*] **:** having the thallus differentiated into a prostrate portion and an upright or projecting system ⟨many algae are ~⟩ — **het·er·ot·ri·chy** \ˌ≈≈ˈrä·trə̇kē\ *n* -ES

het·er·ot·ro·pal \¦≈≈¦rä·trəpəl\ *adj* [Gk *heterotropos* of different sort, various + E *-al*] **:** AMPHITROPOUS

het·er·o·troph \ˈhed·ərō·ˌträf\ *also* **het·er·o·trophe** \-ˌtrōf\ *n* -s [*heter-* + *-troph* or *-trophe* (prob. fr. Gk *trophos* one that feeds)] **:** a heterotrophic individual — **het·er·ot·ro·phism** \ˌhed·əˈrä·trəˌfizəm\ *n* — **het·er·ot·ro·phy** \-ˌfē\ *n* -ES

heterotroph hypothesis *n* **:** a hypothesis in biology: the most primitive first life was heterotrophic — compare AUTOTROPH HYPOTHESIS

het·er·o·troph·ic \¦hed·ərō·¦träfik, -¦trōf-\ *adj* [*heter-* + *-trophic*] **:** obtaining nourishment from outside sources; *specif* **:** requiring complex organic compounds of nitrogen and carbon for metabolic synthesis ⟨most animals and those plants that do not carry on photosynthesis are ~⟩ — opposed to *autotrophic* — **het·er·o·troph·i·cal·ly** \-fə̇k(ə)lē\ *adv*

het·er·o·tro·pia \ˌ≈≈≈ˈtrōpēə\ *n* -s [NL, fr. *heter-* + *-tropia*] **:** STRABISMUS

het·er·ot·ro·pous \¦hed·ə¦rä·trəpəs\ *adj* [Gk *heterotropos* of different sort, various, fr. *hetero-* heter- + *-tropos* -tropous] **:** AMPHITROPOUS

het·ero·typic \¦hed·ərō+\ *also* **het·ero·typical** \"+\ *adj* [*heter-* + *typic* or *typical*] **1 :** of or being the reduction division of meiosis as contrasted with typical mitotic division — compare HOMEOTYPIC **2** *usu heterotypical* **:** of or being a genus containing groups of species showing various degrees of relationship **3 :** different in kind, arrangement, or form ⟨a ~ ecological community⟩ ⟨monkeys paralyzed with one poliomyelitis virus . . . show no . . . antibody . . . to a ~ virus — Isabel M. Morgan⟩ — **het·ero·typically** \"+\ *adv*

heterousia *var of* HETEROOUSIA

het·ero·xanthine \¦hed·ərō+\ *also* **het·ero·xanthin** \"+\ *n* [ISV *heter-* + *xanthine* or *xanthin*] **:** a crystalline compound $C_6H_6N_4O_2$ sometimes found in urine; 7-methyl-xanthine

het·er·ox·e·nous \¦hed·ə¦räksənəs\ *adj* [*heter-* + *-xenous*] **:** infesting more than one kind of host; *esp* **:** requiring at least two kinds of host to complete the life cycle — used of various parasites (as the malaria parasites or the liver flukes)

het·er·o·ze·te·sis \ˌhed·ərōzēˈtēsə̇s\ *n, pl* **heterozete·ses** \-tēˌsēz\ [NL, fr. *heter-* + Gk *zētēsis* search, inquiry (fr. *zētein* to seek, inquire)] **:** IGNORATIO ELENCHI

het·ero·zygosis \¦hed·ərō+\ *n* [NL, fr. *heter-* + *zygosis*] **1 :** a union of genetically dissimilar gametes to form a heterozygote **2 :** the state of being a heterozygote — compare HOMOZYGOSIS

het·ero·zy·gos·i·ty \"+zī¦gäsəd·ē\ *n* -ES **:** HETEROZYGOSIS 2

het·ero·zygote \"+\ *n* [*heter-* + *zygote*] **:** an animal or plant that contains genes for both members of at least one pair of allelomorphic characters and that segregates according to Mendel's laws and does not breed true to type with respect to the specified character **:** a heterozygous individual — compare HOMOZYGOTE — **het·ero·zygotic** \"+\ *adj*

het·er·o·zy·gous \¦hed·ərō¦zīgəs\ *adj* [*heter-* + *-zygous*] **1 :** of, relating to, or derived from a heterozygote **2 :** producing two types of gametes with respect to one or more allelomorphic characters — opposed to *homozygous* — **het·er·o·zy·gous·ly** *adv*

heth *also* **cheth** *or* **hheth** *or* **kheth** *or* **het** \ˈk̲āt, -āth, -ās, -et, -eth, -es\ *n* -s [Heb *ḥēth*] **1 :** the eighth letter of the Hebrew alphabet — symbol ח; see ALPHABET table **2 :** the letter of the Phoenician alphabet or of various other Semitic alphabets that corresponds to Hebrew heth

het·man \ˈhetmən\ *n* -s [Pol, fr. G *hauptmann* headman] **:** a cossack leader

het·man·ate \-əˌnāt\ *n* -s **:** the administration of a hetman

HETP \ˌāˌchēˌtēˈpē\ *abbr or n* -s hexaethyl tetraphosphate

Het·ra·zan \ˈhe·trəˌzan\ *trademark* — used for diethylcarbamazine citrate

hets *pl of* HET
het up *adj* [⁵*het*] *chiefly dial* **:** being in a state of excitement **:** worked up **:** ANGRY — used esp. to connote indignation or enthusiasm ⟨all *het up* over going⟩
HEU *abbr* hydroelectric unit
heu·chera \'hyükərə\ *n* [NL, after J. H. von *Heucher* †1747 Ger. botanist] **1** *cap* **:** a genus of No. American herbs (family Saxifragaceae) having basal cordate or orbicular leaves and small panicled flowers with petals entire or lacking **2** *-s* **:** any plant of the genus *Heuchera*
heu gase *or* **heu gaze** \hyü'gäz\ [origin unknown] — used as a view halloo in hunting otters
heugh *or* **heuch** \'kyük\ *n* -s [ME *hough, hogh, heuch*, fr. OE *hōh*] **1** *chiefly Scot* **a :** a steep crag or cliff **b :** a ravine or glen with overhanging sides **2** *chiefly Scot* **a :** a shaft of a coal mine **b :** an open coal pit
heu·land·ite \'hyülən,dīt\ *n* -s [Henry *Heuland* 19th cent. Eng. mineral collector + E *-ite*] **:** a zeolite $(Na,Ca)_{4\text{-}6}Al_6(Al,Si)_4Si_{26}O_{72}.24H_2O$ consisting of a hydrous aluminosilicate of sodium and calcium often occurring as foliated masses with pearly luster on the cleavage surfaces
¹**heu·ris·tic** \(')hyü'ristik, -tēk\ *adj* [G *heuristisch*, fr. NL *heuristicus*, fr. Gk *heuriskein* to discover, find] **:** serving to guide, discover, or reveal; *specif* **:** valuable for stimulating or conducting empirical research but unproved or incapable of proof — often used of arguments, methods, or constructs that assume or postulate what remains to be proven or that lead a person to find out for himself ⟨even vague and dubious assertions can render good services to empirical research as a ~ stimulus —Edgar Zilsel⟩ ⟨making the hypothesis more . . . completely understood as a ~ device —J.M.Yinger⟩ ⟨some wish to avoid the term . . . not deeming it a useful ~ tool —R.W.Firth⟩ — **heu·ris·ti·cal·ly** \-tək(ə)lē, -tēk-, -li\ *adv*
²**heuristic** \"\ *n* -s [G *heuristik*, fr. NL *heuristica*, fr. fem. of *heuristicus*] **1 :** the science or art of heuristic procedure **2 :** heuristic argument
heurt *or* **heurte** *var of* HURT
heus·ler alloy \'hyüslə(r)-\ *n, usu cap H* [after Conrad *Heusler* 19th cent. Ger. mining engineer and chemist] **1 :** a magnetic alloy composed of the nonmagnetic metals copper, manganese, and tin approximately in the proportions Cu_2Mn-Sn **2 :** any similar magnetic alloy (as one in which tin is replaced by aluminum, arsenic, antimony, bismuth, or boron, or copper is replaced by silver)
hev *dial var of* HAVE
he·vea \'hēvēə\ *n* [NL, fr. Sp *jebe* rubber plant, of AmerInd origin] **1** *cap* **:** a small genus of So. American trees (family Euphorbiaceae) which have trifoliolate leaves, small panicled apetalous flowers, and a capsular fruit and many of which yield latex used in rubber manufacture **2** *-s* **:** any plant of the genus *Hevea*
¹**hew** \'hyü\ *vb* **hewed; hewed** *or* **hewn; hewing; hews** [ME *hewen*, fr. OE *hēawan*; akin to OHG *houwan* to hew, ON *höggva* to hew, L *cudere* to beat, Toch (A) *kot* to split] *vt* **1 :** to cut with hard or rough blows of a heavy cutting instrument (as an ax, broadsword, or large chisel) ⟨the miners who ~ out the coal —G.B.Shaw⟩ **2 :** to fell (as a tree) by blows of an ax **:** cut down **3 :** to shape, form, create, or bring into being with or as if with hard rough blows or efforts ⟨my own grandparents ~*ed* their farms from the wilderness —J.T. Shotwell⟩ ⟨~ out a rock tomb⟩ ~ *vi* **1 :** to make rough heavy cutting blows (as with an ax) **2 :** ADHERE, CONFORM, STICK ⟨each of his . . . masterpieces ~*s* to its stanza form with meticulous accuracy —Clement Wood⟩ ⟨if he is elected . . . he will ~ to the constitutional law —*N.Y.Times*⟩ ⟨avoiding sentimentality by ~*ing* doggedly to domestic realism —Roger Pippett⟩ — often used in the phrase *hew to the line* ⟨I learned in a hard school and I know the importance of ~*ing* to the line —Archie Binns⟩ **syn** see CUT
²**hew** \"\ *now chiefly dial var of* HUE
hew·er \'hyüə(r), 'hyu̇(ə)r, 'hyu̇ə\ *n* -s [ME, fr. *hewen*, v. + *-er*] **:** a person whose work is hewing ⟨these skilled island ~*s* and masons work with primitive axes, chisels and saws —J.P. O'Donnell⟩ ⟨let them be ~*s* of wood and drawers of water unto all the congregation —Josh 9:21 (AV)⟩ ⟨deserve a better future than being mere ~*s* of wood and drawers of water for the highly industrialized countries —Emilio Abello⟩
hew·ett·ite \'hyüə,tīt\ *n* -s [D. Foster *Hewett* b1881 Am. geologist + E *-ite*] **:** a mineral $CaV_6O_{16}.9H_2O$ consisting of a hydrous calcium vanadate occurring in mahogany-red silky aggregates (sp. gr. 2.5)
hew·gag \'hyü,gag\ *n* [origin unknown] **:** a toy pipe of esp. the latter part of the 19th century resembling a kazoo ⟨sound the bull-roarers, and the ~*s* —W.A.White⟩
hew·let \'hyülət\ *var of* HOWLET
hewn \'hyün\ *adj* [fr. past part. of ¹*hew*] **1 :** felled, cut, or shaped by hewing (as with an ax) **:** roughly squared ⟨a house built of ~ logs⟩ **2** *of stone* **:** roughly dressed (as with a hammer)
¹**hex** \'heks\ *vb* -ED/-ING/-ES *vi* [PaG *hexe*, fr. G *hexen*, fr. *hexe*, n.] **:** to practice witchcraft ~ *vt* [PaG *verhexe*, fr. *ver-* for- + *hexe*, v.] **1 :** to practice witchcraft upon **:** put a hex on ⟨he can . . . ~ him, and he knows it —J.H.Allen⟩ **2 :** to affect as if by an evil spell **:** JINX, QUEER ⟨giving in to an unscientific fear of ~*ing* the whole project —Daniel Lang⟩ ⟨~*es* the acoustics —*Springfield (Mass.) Daily News*⟩
²**hex** \"\ *n* -ES *often attrib* **1 :** SPELL, ENCHANTMENT, JINX ⟨my grandmother used to say some families had a ~ on them —Sherman Kent⟩ ⟨sung to death in a musical ~ rendered by an enemy —*Newsweek*⟩ ⟨we came to the conclusion that he had put a ~ on the cars —Linda Braidwood⟩ **2** [PaG *hex* & G *hexe*, fr. MHG *hecse, häxe*; akin to OHG *hagzissa, hagazussa* harpy, witch — more at HAG (harpy)] **:** a person who practices witchcraft **:** WITCH ⟨I couldn't talk to you without twenty old ~*es* watching —Sinclair Lewis⟩
³**hex** \"\ *adj* [short for *hexagonal*] **:** hexagonal in shape ⟨a bolt with a ~ head⟩
hex *abbr* **1** hexachord **2** hexagon; hexagonal
hexa- *or* **hex-** *comb form* [Gk, fr. *hex* six — more at SIX] **1 :** six ⟨*hexatomic*⟩ **2 :** containing six atoms, groups, or equivalents ⟨*hexoxide*⟩ ⟨*hexaacetate*⟩
hex·a·bi·ose *or* **hex·o·bi·ose** \,heksə'bī,ōs\ *n* [*hexabiose* fr. *hexa-* + *biose*; *hexobiose*, ISV *hexo-* (fr. *hexa-*) + *biose*] **:** a disaccharide (as maltose) yielding two hexose molecules on hydrolysis
hexa·bromide \¦heksə+\ *n* [*hexa-* + *bromide*] **:** a bromide containing six atoms of bromine in the molecule
hex·a·canth \'heksə,kan(t)th\ *or* **hex·a·can·thous** \¦==¦kan(t)thəs\ *adj* [NL *hexacanthus*, fr. *hexa-* + *-acanthus* (fr. Gk *akantha* thorn) — more at ACANTH-] *zool* **:** having six hooks; *specif* **:** constituting the onchosphere of a tapeworm
hexachlor- *or* **hexachloro-** *comb form* [*hexa-* + *chlor-*] **:** containing six atoms of chlorine — compare CHLOR-
hexa·chloride \¦heksə+\ *n* [*hexa-* + *chloride*] **:** a chloride containing six atoms of chlorine in the molecule
hex·a·chlo·ro \¦heksə¦klō(,)rō, -lȯ(-\ *adj* [*hexachlor-*] **:** containing six atoms of chlorine
hex·a·chlo·ro·cyclohexane \¦==¦==+\ *n* [*hexachlor-* + *cyclohexane*] **:** a hexachloro derivative of cyclohexane; *esp* **:** BENZENE HEXACHLORIDE
hex·a·chlo·ro·ethane \"+\ *also* **hex·a·chlor·ethane** \¦heksə,klōr, -lȯr+\ *n* [ISV *hexa-* + *chlor-* + *ethane*] **:** a toxic crystalline compound C_2Cl_6 of camphoraceous odor made usu. by chlorinating tetrachloroethylene and used esp. in smoke bombs and in the control of liver flukes in ruminants
hex·a·chlo·ro·phene \,heksə'klōrə,fēn, -lȯr-\ *n* -s [*hexachlor-* + *-phene* (fr. *-phenol*)] **:** a crystalline phenolic antibacterial agent $CH_2(C_6HCl_3OH)_2$ made by condensing a trichlorophenol with formaldehyde and used esp. in soap
hexa·chloroplatinate \¦heksə+\ *n* [*hexa-* + *chloroplatinate*] **:** CHLOROPLATINATE
hex·a·chord \'heksə,kȯrd, -ȯ(ə)d\ *n* [*hexa-* + *-chord*] **1 :** a diatonic series of six tones having a semitone between the third and fourth tones that formed the basic unit of analysis from the 11th to the 18th centuries, seven such overlapping series beginning successively on G, C, and F comprising all of the recognized tones — compare GREAT SCALE, SOLMIZATION **2 :** a 6-stringed musical instrument — **hex·a·chord·ic** \¦==¦kȯrdik\ *adj*

hex·a·con·tane \,heksə'kän,tān\ *n* -s [ISV *hexacont-* (fr. Gk *hexēkonta* sixty) + *-ane*] **:** a solid paraffin hydrocarbon $C_{60}H_{122}$; *esp* **:** the normal hydrocarbon $CH_3(CH_2)_{58}CH_3$
hex·a·co·ral·lia \,heksəkə'ralēə\ *or* **hex·a·co·ral·lia** \-lēə\ [NL, fr. *hexa-* + L *coralla, corallia* (pl. of *corallum, corallium* coral) — more at CORAL] *syn of* ZOANTHARIA
hex·a·co·sane \,heksə'kō,sān\ *n* -s [ISV *hexacos-* (fr. *hexa-* + *-cos-* — fr. *eicosa-*) + *-ane*] **:** a solid paraffin hydrocarbon $C_{26}H_{54}$; *esp* **:** the normal hydrocarbon $CH_3(CH_2)_{24}CH_3$
hex·ac·ti·nal \¦hek(,)sak¦tīnᵊl, (')hek¦saktənᵊl\ *or* **hex·ac·tine** \(')hek¦sak,tīn, -,tən\ *adj* [*hexa-* + *-actinal* or *-actine*] **:** having six rays ⟨~ sponge spicules⟩
¹**hex·ac·ti·nel·lid** \¦hek(,)saktə¦neləd\ *adj* [NL *Hexactinellida*] **:** of, relating to, or characteristic of the Hyalospongiae
²**hexactinellid** \"\ *n* -s **:** one of the Hyalospongiae
hex·ac·ti·nel·li·da \,=(,)==ʹnelədə\ [NL, fr. *Hexactinella*, genus of sponges (fr. *hexa-* + *actin-* + *-ella*) + *-ida*] *syn of* HYALOSPONGIAE
hex·ac·ti·ni·an \¦hek(,)sak¦tinēən\ *adj* [*hexa-* + *actin-* + *-an*] **:** having the tentacles or mesenteries in multiples of six
hex·ad \'hek,sad\ *or* **hex·ade** \-,sād\ *n* -s [LL *hexad-, hexas* the number six, fr. Gk, fr. *hex* six + *-ad-, -as* -ad — more at SIX] **:** a group or series of six
hexa·decane \¦heksə+\ *n* -s [ISV *hexadec-* (fr. *hexa-* + *deca-*) + *-ane*] **:** any of numerous isomeric hydrocarbons $C_{16}H_{34}$; *esp* **:** CETANE
hex·a·dec·a·no·ic acid \¦heksə¦dekə¦nōik-\ *n* [*hexadecane* + *-oic*] **:** PALMITIC ACID
hex·a·dec·a·nol \,==ʹdekə,nōl, -,nȯl\ *n* -s [*hexadecane* + *-ol*] **:** any of several alcohols $C_{16}H_{33}OH$ derived from cetane; *esp* **:** CETYL ALCOHOL
hex·a·dec·ene \-ʹde,sēn\ *n* -s [ISV *hexadec-* (fr. *hexa-* + *deca-*) + *-ene*] **:** any of several straight-chain isomeric hydrocarbons $C_{16}H_{32}$ of the ethylene series; *esp* **:** CETENE
hexa·decyl \¦heksə+\ *n* [*hexadecane* + *-yl*] **:** an alkyl radical derived from a hexadecane; *esp* **:** CETYL
hex·ad·ic \(')hek¦sadik\ *adj* [*hexad* + *-ic*] **:** of or relating to a hexad
hex·a·di·ene \,heksə'dī,ēn\ *n* -s [ISV *hexa-* + *-diene*] **:** any of six straight-chain isomeric diolefins C_6H_{10}
hex·a·em·er·al \¦heksə¦emərəl\ *or* **hex·a·em·er·ic** \-rik\ *adj* [*hexaemeron* + *-al* or *-ic*] **:** of or relating to the hexaemeron
hex·a·em·er·on \,==ʹemə,rän\ *or* **hex·a·hem·er·on** \-ʹhe-\ *n* -s [LL *hexaēmeron*, fr. Gk *hexaēmeron*, fr. neut. of *hexaēmeros* of six days, fr. *hexa-* + *hēmera* day — more at HEMERA] **:** the six days of the creation
hexa·ethyl tetraphosphate \¦heksə+ . . . -\ *n* [*hexa-* + *ethyl*] **:** an insecticide $(C_2H_5)_6P_4O_{13}$ obtained synthetically usu. as a yellow liquid mixture containing tetraethyl pyrophosphate — called also *HETP*
hexa·fluoride \"+\ *n* [*hexa-* + *fluoride*] **:** a fluoride containing six atoms of fluorine in the molecule
hex·a·foos \'heksə,füs\ *n, pl* **hexafoos** [PaG *hexefuss*, fr. *hex* witch + *fuss* foot (fr. OHG *fuoz*) — more at HEX, FOOT] **:** a three-toed or triangular mark put on some Pennsylvania barns to keep evil spirits from the cattle or for decoration
¹**hex·a·gon** \'heksə,gän *sometimes* -səgən\ *n* -s [Gk *hexagōnon*, neut. of *hexagōnos* hexagonal, fr. *hexa-* six (fr. *hex*) + *-gōnos* -cornered, -angled (fr. *gōnia* angle, corner) — more at SIX, -GON] **1 :** a plane polygon of six angles and therefore six sides — see AREA table **2 :** a hexagonal object

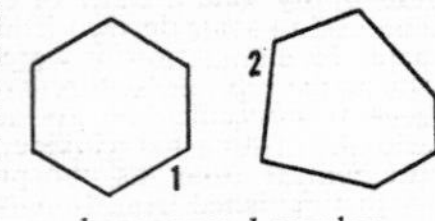
hexagons: *1* regular, *2* irregular

²**hexagon** \"\ *adj* **:** constituting a hexagon ⟨a ~ tower⟩
hex·ag·o·nal \(')hek¦sagənᵊl, -saig-\ *adj* **1 :** having six angles and six sides **:** six-sided **:** divided into hexagons **2 :** having a hexagon as section or base **3 :** relating or belonging to a hexagonal system — see SCALENOHEDRON illustration — **hex·ag·o·nal·ly** \-ᵊlē, -ᵊli\ *adv*
hexagonal system *n* **:** a crystal system characterized by three equal lateral axes intersecting at angles of 60 degrees and a vertical axis of variable length at right angles (as in the hexagonal prism) — see CRYSTAL SYSTEM illustration
hex·a·gram \'heksə,gram\ *n* [ISV *hexa-* + *-gram*] **:** a figure formed by completing externally an equilateral triangle on each side of a regular hexagon

hexagram

¹**hex·a·gram·mid** \¦==¦gra,mid\ *adj* [NL *Hexagrammidae*] **:** of or relating to the Hexagrammidae
²**hexagrammid** \"\ *n* -s **:** a member of the family Hexagrammidae
hex·a·gram·mi·dae \,heksə'gramə,dē\ *n pl, cap* [NL, fr. *Hexagrammos*, type genus + *-idae*] **:** a family of marine carnivorous fishes (order Scleroparei) of the northern Pacific ocean that includes several food fishes — see GREENLING
hex·a·gram·mos \-a,mäs\ *n, cap* [NL, fr. *hexa-* + *-grammos* (fr. Gk *gramma* line) — more at GRAMMAR] **:** the type genus of the family Hexagrammidae
hex·a·he·dral \¦heksə¦hēdrəl\ *adj* [NL *hexahedron* + E *-al*] **:** having the form of a hexahedron
hexahedral coordination *n* **:** the state or condition of being surrounded by eight atoms whose centers lie at the corners of a hexahedron
hex·a·he·dron \,==ʹ=drən\ *n, pl* **hexahedrons** \-rənz\ *also* **hexahe·dra** \-rə\ [NL, fr. LL, fr. Gk *hexaedron*, fr. neut. of *hexaedros* of six surfaces, fr. *hexa-* + *-edros* (fr. *hedra* base, seat)] **1 :** a polyhedron of six faces **2 :** ¹CUBE 5
hexahemeron *var of* HEXAEMERON
hexahydr- *or* **hexahydro-** *comb form* [ISV *hexa-* + *hydr-*] **:** combined with six atoms of hydrogen — in names of chemical compounds ⟨*hexahydro*benzene⟩
hexa·hydrate \¦heksə+\ *n* [*hexa-* + *hydrate*] **:** a chemical compound with six molecules of water — **hexa·hydrated** \"+\ *adj*
hex·a·hy·dric \¦heksə¦hīdrik\ *adj* [*hexa-* + *-hydric*] **:** HEXAHYDROXY — used esp. of alcohols and phenols
hex·a·hy·drite \,==ʹhī,drīt\ *n* -s [ISV *hexa-* + *hydr-* + *-ite*] **:** a mineral $MgSO_4.6H_2O$ consisting of a hydrous magnesium sulfate
hexa·hydroxy \¦heksə+\ *adj* [*hexahydroxy-*] **:** containing six hydroxyl groups in the molecule
hexahydroxy- *comb form* [ISV *hexa-* + *hydroxy-*] **:** containing six hydroxyl groups — in names of chemical compounds
hex·a·kis·octahedron \¦heksəkis+\ *n* [NL, fr. Gk *hexakis* six times (fr. *hex* six) + NL *octahedron* — more at SIX] **:** HEXOCTAHEDRON
hex·a·kis·tetrahedron \"+\ *n* [NL, fr. Gk *hexakis* six times + NL *tetrahedron*] **:** HEXTETRAHEDRON
hex·a·mer \'heksəmə(r)\ *n* -s [*hexa-* + *-mer*] **:** a polymer formed from six molecules of a monomer — **hex·a·mer·ic** \¦heksə¦merik\ *adj*
hex·am·er·al \(')hek¦sam(ə)rəl\ *adj* [*hexamerous* + *-al*] **:** HEXAMEROUS
hex·am·er·ous \-rəs\ *adj* [*hexa-* + *-merous*] **1** *bot* **:** consisting of six parts **:** having floral whorls composed of six members **2** *zool* **:** having six parts or parts in multiples of six arranged radially — used esp. of anthozoans in which the tentacles and mesenteries are in multiples of six
hexa·metaphosphate \¦heksə+\ *n* [*hexa-* + *metaphosphate*] **:** a metaphosphate glass; *esp* **:** SODIUM HEXAMETAPHOSPHATE — not used systematically
¹**hex·am·e·ter** \hek'samədə(r), -mətə-\ *n* [L, fr. Gk *hexametron*, fr. neut. of *hexametros*] **:** a line of six metrical feet or of six dipodies: as **a :** the six-foot dactylic line of Greek and Latin epic poetry in which the first four feet are dactyls or spondees, the fifth a dactyl, and the sixth a spondee (as in Vergil's "Arma virumque cano Trojae qui primus ab oris") **b :** the six-foot dactylic line of English poetry (as in Coleridge's "Strongly it bears us along on swelling and limitless billows")
²**hexameter** \(')¦===\ *adj* [L, fr. Gk *hexametros* of six meters, fr. *hexa-* + *-metros* (akin to *metron* measure) — more at

MEASURE] **1 :** having six metrical feet — used esp. of dactylic or spondaic verse **2 :** having six dipodies — used esp. of classical iambic, trochaic, or anapestic verse
hex·a·me·tho·ni·um \,heksəmə'thōnēəm\ *n* -s [NL, fr. *hexa-* + *methonium*] **:** the bivalent substituted ammonium ion $[(CH_3)_3N(CH_2)_6N(CH_3)_3]^{++}$ derived by methylation of hexamethylenediamine; *also* **:** any salt (as the chloride or bromide) containing this ion used as a ganglionic blocking agent in the treatment of hypertension
hexa·methyl \¦heksə+\ *adj* [ISV *hexa-* + *methyl*] **:** containing six methyl groups in the molecule
hexa·methylene \"+\ *n* [ISV *hexa-* + *methylene*] **1 :** CYCLOHEXANE **2 :** the bivalent radical $-CH_2(CH_2)_4CH_2-$ derived from normal hexane by removal of one hydrogen atom from each end carbon atom
hexamethylene·diamine \"+\ *n* [ISV *hexamethylene* + *diamine*] **:** a crystalline base $H_2N(CH_2)_6NH_2$ made by hydrogenation of adiponitrile and used in the manufacture of nylon; 1,6-hexane-diamine
hexa·methylene·tetramine \"+\ *n* [ISV *hexamethylene* + *tetramine*] **:** a crystalline tricyclic weak base $(CH_2)_6N_4$ made by the action of ammonia on formaldehyde and used chiefly as a source of formaldehyde (as in the manufacture of phenolic resins), as a vulcanization accelerator, and in medicine as a urinary antiseptic — called also *hexamine, methenamine*
hex·am·e·trist \hek'samə·trəst\ *n* -s [*hexameter* + *-ist*] **:** one who writes in hexameters
hex·a·mine \,heksə¦mēn, hek'samən\ *n* [by contr.] **:** HEXAMETHYLENETETRAMINE
hex·am·i·ta \hek'samədə\ *n, cap* [NL, fr. *hexa-* + *-mita* (fr. Gk *mitos* thread) — more at DIMITY] **:** a genus (the type of the family Hexamitidae) of binucleate zooflagellates having six anterior and two trailing flagella and including free-living forms as well as intestinal parasites of birds (as *H. meleagridis*) and of salmonid fishes (as *H. salmonis*) that are associated with enteritides — compare GIARDIA
hex·am·i·ti·a·sis \hek,samə'tīəsəs\ *n* -ES [NL, fr. *Hexamita* + *-iasis*] **:** infestation with or disease caused by flagellates of the genus *Hexamita*
¹**hex·am·i·tid** \(')hek¦samədəd\ *adj* [NL *Hexamitidae*, family of zooflagellates, fr. *Hexamita*, type genus + *-idae*] **:** of or relating to the genus *Hexamita* or family Hexamitidae
²**hexamitid** \"\ *n* -s **:** a member of the genus *Hexamita* or family Hexamitidae
hex·ammine \hek'sa,mēn, -,mən, ,heksə'mēn\ *n* [*hexa-* + *ammine*] **:** an ammine containing six molecules of ammonia
hex·a·nal \'heksə,nal\ *n* -s [*hexane* + *-al*] **:** a volatile liquid aldehyde $CH_3(CH_2)_4CHO$ of irritating odor obtained from several volatile oils (as eucalyptus oil and peppermint oil) — called also *caproaldehyde*
hex·an·chi·dae \hek'saŋkə,dē\ *n pl, cap* [NL, fr. *Hexanchus*, type genus + *-idae*] **:** a family of sharks consisting of many fossil forms and a few living forms that have one dorsal fin and a palatoquadrate which articulates with the postorbital part of the skull
hex·an·chus \hek'saŋkəs\ *n, cap* [NL, fr. *hexa-* + *anchus* (prob. fr. Gk *anchein* to strangle) — more at ANGER] **:** the type genus of the family *Hexanchidae* sometimes considered to include all living members of the family but sometimes restricted to those with six pairs of branchial clefts
hex·ane \'hek,sān\ *n* -s [ISV *hexa-* + *-ane*] **:** any of five isomeric volatile liquid paraffin hydrocarbons C_6H_{14} found in petroleum; *esp* **:** the normal hydrocarbon $CH_3(CH_2)_4CH_3$
hexa·nitrate \¦heksə+\ *n* [*hexa-* + *nitrate*] **:** a compound containing six nitrate groups in the molecule
hexa·ni·tro·diphenylamine \¦heksə¦nī·trō+\ *n* [ISV *hexa-* + *nitro-* + *diphenylamine*] **:** a light-yellow poisonous crystalline compound $[(NO_2)_3C_6H_2]_2NH$ made by nitrating diphenylamine and used as a high explosive — called also *dipicrylamine;* see AURANTIA
hex·a·no·ic acid \¦heksə¦nōik-\ *n* [ISV *hexan-* (fr. *hexane*) + *-oic*] **:** CAPROIC ACID — used in the system of nomenclature adopted by the International Union of Pure and Applied Chemistry
hex·a·no·yl \¦heksə¦nōəl; hek'sanə,wil, -,wēl\ *n* -s [ISV *hexan-* (fr. *hexanoic acid*) + *-oyl*] **:** CAPROYL
hexa·partite \¦heksə+\ *adj* [*hexa-* + *partite*] **:** SEXPARTITE
hexa·petaloid \"+\ *adj* [*hexa-* + *petaloid*] **:** having or being a perianth with six petaloid divisions
hexa·petalous \"+\ *adj* [*hexa-* + *-petalous*] **:** having or being a perianth with six petals
hex·a·pla \'heksəplə\ *n* -s *often cap* [LL, fr. Gk *hexapla*, fr. neut. pl. of *hexaplous, hexaploos* sixfold, fr. *hexa-* + *-plous, -ploos* -fold (as in *diploos* double) — more at DOUBLE] **:** an edition or work in six texts or versions in parallel columns — compare TETRAPLA — **hex·a·plar** \-lə(r)\ *adj, often cap*
hex·a·plar·ic \¦heksə¦plarik\ *also* **hex·a·plar·i·an** \¦==¦pla(a)rēən\ *adj, often cap* **:** of or relating to a hexapla; *esp* **:** of or relating to the edition of the Old Testament compiled by Origen in the 3d century A.D. and consisting of the Hebrew text, a transliteration in Greek, and the Greek versions of Aquila, Symmachus, the Septuagint, and Theodotion
¹**hex·a·ploid** \'heksə,plȯid\ *adj* [ISV *hexa-* + *-ploid*] **:** sixfold in appearance or arrangement; *specif* **:** having or being six times the monoploid chromosome number ⟨a ~ cell⟩ — compare DIPLOID, HAPLOID, POLYPLOID
²**hexaploid** \"\ *n* -s **:** a hexaploid individual
hex·a·ploidy \-dē\ *n* -ES **:** the condition of being hexaploid
¹**hex·a·pod** \'heksə,päd\ *n* -s [Gk *hexapod-, hexapous*, adj., six-footed, fr. *hexa-* + *pod-, pous* foot — more at FOOT] **:** INSECT 1b
²**hexapod** \"\ *adj* **1 :** six-footed **2 :** of or relating to insects
hex·ap·o·da \hek'sapədə\ *n pl, cap* [NL, fr. *hexa-* + *-poda*] *in some classifications* **:** a class or other division of Arthropoda coextensive with the class Insecta — used esp. when Collembola and Protura are considered with the typical insects
hex·ap·o·dous \-dəs\ *adj* **:** HEXAPOD
hex·ap·o·dy \-dē\ *n* -ES [ISV *hexa-* + *-pody* (as in *dipody*)] **:** a prosodic line or group consisting of six feet
hex·arch \'hek,särk\ *adj* [*hexa-* + *-arch*] *of a root* **:** having six radiating vascular strands ⟨the ~ roots of an onion⟩
¹**hex·a·so·mic** \¦heksə¦sōmik\ *adj* [*hexa-* + *-somic*] **:** having one chromosome or a few chromosomes hexaploid in otherwise diploid nuclei
²**hexasomic** \"\ *n* -s **:** a hexasomic individual
hex·as·ter \hek'sastə(r)\ *n* [NL, fr. *hexa-* + *-aster* (star)] **:** a triaxon sponge spicule usu. with equal rays
hex·as·ter·oph·o·ra \,hek,sastə'räf(ə)rə\ *n pl, cap* [NL, fr. *hexaster* + *-o-* + *-phora*] **:** an order of Hyalospongiae comprising sponges with hexasters but not amphidisks among the spicules
hex·a·stich \'heksə,stik\ *also* **hex·as·ti·chon** \hek'sastə,kän\ *n, pl* **hexastichs** *also* **hex·as·ti·cha** \-'=stəkə\ [NL *hexastichon*, fr. ML, prob. fr. Gk *hexastichon*, neut. of *hexastichos* of six rows, of six lines, fr. *hexa-* + *stichos* row, line; akin to Gk *steichein* to go — more at STICH] **:** a group, stanza, or poem of six lines — **hex·a·stich·ic** \¦heksə¦stikik\ *adj*
hex·a·sty·lar \¦heksə¦stīlə(r)\ *adj* **:** HEXASTYLE
¹**hex·a·style** \'heksə,stīl\ *n* [L *hexastylos*, adj., of six columns] **:** a portico with six columns
²**hexastyle** \"\ *adj* **:** marked by columniation with six columns across the front — compare DISTYLE
hex·a·sty·los \,heksə'stī,läs\ *n* -ES [NL, fr. L, adj., of six columns, fr. Gk, fr. *hexa-* + *stylos* column, pillar — more at STOIC] **:** a hexastyle building
hexa·syllabic \¦heksə+\ *adj* [Gk *hexasyllabos* (fr. *hexa-* + *syllabē* syllable) + E *-ic* — more at SYLLABLE] **:** comprising six syllables
hexa·syllable \"+\ *n* [*hexa-* + *syllable*] **:** a word of six syllables
hexatetrahedron *var of* HEXTETRAHEDRON
hex·a·teu·chal \¦heksə¦tükəl, -sə-¦tyü-\ *adj, usu cap* [*Hexateuch* the first 6 books of the Bible (fr. *hexa-* + *-teuch*, as in *Pentateuch* the first 5 books of the Bible) + E *-al* — more at PENTATEUCHAL] **:** of or relating to the first six books of the Old Testament
hex·atomic \¦heks+\ *adj* [*hexa-* + *atomic*] **1 :** consisting of six atoms **2 :** having six replaceable atoms or radicals
hex·a·tri·a·con·tane \,heksə,trīə'kän,tān\ *n* [ISV *hexatriacont-* (fr. *hexa-* + *triacont-* — fr. Gk *triakonta* thirty) + *-ane*]

HORSES

QUARTER HORSE
PALOMINO
BELGIAN
AMERICAN SADDLE HORSE
HACKNEY
MORGAN
SHETLAND PONY
THOROUGHBRED
PERCHERON
ARABIAN
STANDARDBRED

: a solid paraffin hydrocarbon $C_{36}H_{74}$; *esp* : the normal hydrocarbon $CH_3(CH_2)_{34}CH_3$
hexa·valent \¦heksə+\ *adj* [ISV *hexa-* + *valent*] : having a valence of six
hex·ax·on \'hek'sak,sän\ *n* [NL, fr. *hexa-* + Gk *axōn* axle, axis — more at AXIS] : HEXASTER
hexed *past of* HEX
hex·en·be·sen \'heksən,bāzᵊn\ *n* -s [G, fr. *hexen* (pl. of *hexe* witch) + *besen* broom, fr. OHG *besmo* — more at HEX, BESOM] : WITCHES'-BROOM
hex·ene \'hek,sēn\ *n* -s [ISV *hexa-* + *-ene*] : any of the three straight-chain hexylenes
hex·er \'heksə(r)\ *n* -s [¹*hex* + *-er*] : a person who hexes
hex·e·rei \,heksə'rī\ *n* -s [PaG, fr. G, fr. *hexen* to practice witchcraft + *-erei* -ery (fr. MHG *-erie*, fr. OF *-erie*) — more at HEX] : WITCHCRAFT
hexes *pres 3d sing of* HEX, *pl of* HEX
hex·es·trol *also* **hex·oes·trol** \hek'se,strōl, -rōl\ *n* -s [*hexane* + NL *estrus* or *oestrus* + E *-ol*] : a crystalline estrogenic diphenol $[HOC_6H_4CH(C_2H_5)-]_2$ derived from diphenylethane; dihydro-diethylstilbestrol
hex·ine \'hek,sīn\ *archaic var of* HEXYNE
hexing *pres part of* HEX
hex·i·tol \'heksə,tōl, -,tōl\ *n* -s [*hexose* + *-itol*] : any of the hexahydroxy alcohols $HOCH_2(CHOH)_4CH_2OH$ obtainable by reduction of the corresponding hexoses and in some cases (as mannitol and sorbitol) occurring naturally
hex mark *or* **hex sign** *n* : a usu. stylized often symbolic design placed on a structure (as a building or an enclosure for animals) for the purpose of warding off evil spirits or simply for its decorative effect — compare HEXAFOOS
hexo·barbital \¦heksō+\ *n* [*hexo-* (fr. *hexa-*) + *barbital*] : a crystalline barbiturate $C_{12}H_{16}N_2O_3$ used as a sedative and hypnotic and in the form of its soluble sodium salt as an intravenous anesthetic of short duration
hexo·barbitone \"+\ *n* [*hexo-* (fr. *hexa-*) + *barbitone*] : HEXOBARBITAL
hexobiose *var of* HEXABIOSE
hex·octahedral \(¦)heks+\ *adj* [NL *hexoctahedron* + E *-al*] : having the shape or symmetry of a hexoctahedron
hex·octahedron \"+\ *n* [NL, fr. *hexa-* + *octahedron*] : an isometric crystal having 48 equal triangular faces
hex·ode \'hek,sōd\ *n* -s [ISV *hexa-* + *-ode*] : a vacuum tube with six electrodes consisting of a cathode, an anode, a control grid, and three additional grids or other electrodes

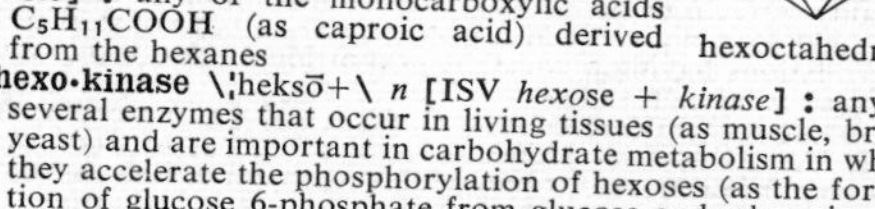

hexoctahedron

hex·o·ic acid \(')hek¦sōik-\ *n* [*hexane* + *-oic*] : any of the monocarboxylic acids $C_5H_{11}COOH$ (as caproic acid) derived from the hexanes
hexo·kinase \¦heksō+\ *n* [ISV *hexose* + *kinase*] : any of several enzymes that occur in living tissues (as muscle, brain, yeast) and are important in carbohydrate metabolism in which they accelerate the phosphorylation of hexoses (as the formation of glucose 6-phosphate from glucose and adenosine triphosphate in the presence of magnesium ions or similar cations)
-hex·ol \'hek,sōl, -,sōl\ *n suffix* -s [ISV *hexa-* + *-ol*] : containing six hydroxyl groups ⟨cyclohexane*-hexol*⟩
hex·one \'hek,sōn\ *n* -s [ISV *hexa-* + *-one*; orig. formed as G *hexon*] : METHYL ISOBUTYL KETONE — used esp. of the technical grade
hex·on·ic acid \(')hek¦sänik-\ *n* [ISV *hexa-* + *-onic*] : an aldonic acid (as gluconic acid) that contains six carbon atoms in a molecule
hex·os·a·mine \hek'säsə,mēn\ *n* [ISV *hexose* + *amine*] : an amine (as glucosamine) derived from a hexose by replacement of hydroxyl by the amino group
hex·o·san \'heksō,san\ *n* -s [*hexose* + *-an*] : any of a class of polysaccharides (as fructosans or glucosans) yielding only hexoses on hydrolysis
hex·ose \'hek,sōs\ *n* -s [ISV *hexa-* + *-ose*] : any of a class of monosaccharides $C_6H_{12}O_6$ (as glucose or fructose) containing six carbon atoms in the molecule
hexose phosphate *n* : a phosphoric derivative of a hexose (as glucose phosphate) of which two types have been found in living tissues as intermediates of carbohydrate metabolism: **a** *or* **hexose monophosphate** : a mono-phosphoric ester or acylal $C_6H_{11}O_5(OPO_3H_2)$ **b** *or* **hexose diphosphate** : a diphosphoric ester $C_6H_{10}O_4(OPO_3H_2)_2$
hex·oxide \(')heks+\ *n* [*hex-* + *oxide*] : an oxide containing six atoms of oxygen in the molecule
hex·partite \(')heks+\ *adj* [*hexa-* + *partite*] *archit* : SEXPARTITE
hex·tetrahedral \(¦)heks+\ *adj* [NL *hextetrahedron* + E *-al*] : having the shape or symmetry of a hextetrahedron
hex·tetrahedron \"+\ *n* [NL, fr. *hexa-* + *tetrahedron*] : a 24-faced crystalline form of the tetrahedral group of the isometric system
hex·u·lose \'heksyə,lōs\ *n* -s [*hexa-* + *-ulose*] : a ketose $C_6H_{12}O_6$ (as fructose or sorbose) containing six carbon atoms in the molecule; *esp* : the isomer having the carbonyl group in the beta or 2-position; compare GLUCOSE illustration
hex·u·ron·ic acid \¦heksyə¦ränik-\ *n* [*hexa-* + *-uronic*] **1** : ASCORBIC ACID — now little used **2** : a uronic acid (as glucuronic acid) derived from a hexose (as glucose)
hex·yl \'heksəl\ *n* -s [ISV *hexa-* + *-yl*] : an alkyl radical C_6H_{13} derived from a hexane; *esp* : the normal radical $CH_3(CH_2)_4CH_2-$
hex·yl·ene \'heksə,lēn\ *n* -s [ISV *hexyl* + *-ene*] : any of several liquid isomeric hydrocarbons C_6H_{12} belonging to the ethylene series and including the hexenes
hex·yl·ic acid \(')hek¦silik-\ *n* [ISV *hexyl* + *-ic*] : HEXOIC ACID
hexylresorcinol \¦==¦==,=\ *n* [*hexyl* + *resorcinol*] : a white or yellowish white crystalline phenol $C_6H_{13}C_6H_3(OH)_2$ used in medicine as an antiseptic and internally as an anthelmintic; 1,3-dihydroxy-4-*n*-hexyl-benzene
hex·yne \'hek,sīn\ *n* -s [*hexa-* + *-yne*] : any of three isomeric straight-chain hydrocarbons C_6H_{10} of the acetylene series
¹**hey** \'hā\ *interj* [ME *hei, hey*] — used to call attention or to incite, to express interrogation, surprise, or exultation, or with indefinite meaning in the burden of a song
²**hey** *var of* HAY
hey cockalorum *n* : HIGH COCKALORUM 1
¹**hey·day** \'hā,dā\ *interj* [fr. earlier *heyda*, alter. of ¹*hey*] *archaic* — used to express frolicsomeness, exultation, or sometimes wonder
²**heyday** *also* **heydey** \"\ *n* **1** *archaic* : high spirits : FROLICSOMENESS, WILDNESS, JOY **2** : a time of highest strength, vigor, or prosperity : ACME ⟨in the ~ of his power⟩ ⟨Athens and Venice in their commercial ~ —David Riesman⟩ ⟨during the ~ of the fur trade —Grace L. Nute⟩
¹**hey rube** *interj* [¹*hey* + *rube*] — used traditionally as a rallying cry among circus or carnival folk in a fight with townspeople
²**hey rube** *n* : a usu. free-for-all fight between circus or carnival folk and townspeople ⟨we found ourselves with an old-fashioned *hey rube* and obliged to move the show on that night —Herbert Gold⟩
hf *abbr* half
HF *abbr* **1** *often not cap* high frequency **2** home fleet **3** home forces
Hf *symbol* hafnium
HFC *abbr* high-frequency current
HFM *abbr* hold for money
hg *abbr* **1** hectogram **2** heliogram
HG *abbr* **1** Her Grace; His Grace **2** High German **3** home guard
Hg *symbol* [NL *hydrargyrum*] mercury
h girder *n, cap H* : a girder like an I beam but with wider flanges
hgm *abbr* hectogram
hgt *abbr* height
HH *abbr* **1** Her Highness; His Highness **2** His Holiness
hhd *abbr* hogshead
hheth *var of* HETH
HHG *abbr* household goods

h hinge *n, cap 1st H* : a hinge with leaves that when open resemble the letter H
h hour *n, usu cap 1st H* [*²h* (abbr. for *hour*)] : the hour set for launching a specific tactical operation — compare D DAY, ZERO HOUR
hi \'hī(ē), -ī(i)\ *interj* [ME *hy*] — used to express greeting or to attract attention
HI *abbr* high intensity
hi·a·tal \(')hī¦ādᵊl\ *adj* [*hiatus* + *-al*] **1** : having a rock texture in which the sizes of the individual crystals do not vary in a continuous series but are in two or more series of marked differences **2** : HIATUS
¹**hi·a·tus** \hī'ādəs, -ātəs\ *n* -ES [L, fr. past part. of *hiare* to gape — more at YAWN] **1 a** : a break in or as if in a material object : GAP : APERTURE ⟨the weedy ~ between the town and the railroad —Willa Cather⟩ ⟨the ~ between the theory and the practice of the party —J.G.Colton⟩ **b** : a gap or passage through an anatomical part or organ; *esp* : a gap through which another part or organ passes **2 a** : an interruption or lapse in or as if in time or continuity ⟨the programs that are to fill in during the summer ~ —Saul Carson⟩ ⟨if deposition of sediment should cease everywhere for a time, a natural . . . ~ in the stratigraphic record would result —C.O.Dunbar⟩ ⟨~*es* of thought when certain links in the association of ideas are dropped —Edmund Wilson⟩ **b** : the occurrence of or relationship between two vowel sounds without pause or intervening consonantal sound (as when *beyond* is pronounced without a \y\ sound) **syn** see BREAK

H hinge

²**hiatus** \"\ *adj* **1** : involving a hiatus **2** *of a hernia* : having a part that herniates through the esophageal hiatus of the diaphragm
hi·ba arborvitae \'hēbə-\ *n* [Jap *hiba*] : a large Japanese evergreen tree (*Thujopsis dolobrata*) that has glossy green leaves with a broad white band on the underside and is used as an ornamental
hi·ba·chi \hē'bächē\ *n* -s [Jap, fr. *hi* fire + *hachi* bowl] : a charcoal brazier
hib·ber·tia \hi'bərd·ēə, -rsh(ē)ə\ *n* [NL, fr. George *Hibbert* †1837 Eng. merchant and botanist + NL *-ia*] **1** *cap* : a genus of Australasian shrubs (family Dilleniaceae) having showy yellow or white flowers with numerous stamens and five fugacious petals **2** -s : any plant of the genus *Hibbertia*
hi·ber·na·cle \'hībə(r),nakəl\ *n* -s [NL *hibernaculum*] : HIBERNACULUM 2a ⟨brought forth a frog from his ~ in the leaves —John Burroughs⟩
hi·ber·nac·u·lum \,hībə(r)'nakyələm\ *n, pl* **hibernacula** \-lə\ [NL, fr. L, winter residence, fr. *hibernus* of winter, wintry + *-culum* -cle — more at HIBERNATE] **1** : the winter resting part of a plant (as a bud or underground stem) **2 a** : a shelter that is occupied during the winter by a dormant insect or other animal and that usu. has a characteristic structure for each species — called also *hibernacle* **b** : an encysted bud in a freshwater bryozoan that survives the winter and develops into a colony in the spring **c** : the epiphragm of a snail
hi·ber·nal \(')hī¦bərnᵊl\ *adj* [LL *hibernalis*, fr. L *hibernus* of winter + *-alis* -al] : of or relating to winter : WINTRY
¹**hi·ber·nant** \'hībə(r)nənt\ *adj* [L *hibernant-, hibernans*, pres. part. of *hibernare*] : HIBERNATING ⟨~ animals⟩
²**hibernant** \"\ *n* -s : an animal that hibernates
hi·ber·nate \'hībə(r),nāt, *usu* -ād.+V\ *vi* -ED/-ING/-S [L *hibernatus*, past part. of *hibernare*, fr. *hibernus* of winter, wintry; akin to L *hiems* winter, Gk *cheimōn*, OSlav *zima*, Skt *himā*] **1 a** : to pass the winter in a torpid or lethargic state; *specif* : to pass the winter in a torpid condition in which the body temperature drops to a little above freezing and metabolic activity is reduced nearly to zero — used esp. of various mammals; compare AESTIVATE **b** : to pass the winter in a resting state — used esp. of the spores and winter buds of various plants **2 a** : to pass the winter esp. in a milder climate ⟨six million farmers lived close enough to Florida to ~ there easily —Alva Johnston⟩ **b** : to be or become inactive or dormant ⟨a few mots survive, to ~ in the mind, and come out again on an early summer day —Osbert Sitwell⟩
hibernating gland *n* : a tissue found beneath the skin of the back or abdomen of various mammals that consists of brownish fat cells in a network of vascular connective tissue and serves as a storage for food
hi·ber·na·tion \,hībə(r)'nāshən\ *n* -s **1** : the act of hibernating ⟨a new concept of the relation between food and ~ of the black bear —R.E.Trippensee⟩ **2** : the state of one that hibernates ⟨came out of his comfortable ~ to make his first political pronouncement since his retirement —*Time*⟩ — opposed to *aestivation*
hi·ber·na·tor \'hībə(r),nād·ə(r), -ātə-\ *n* -s : one that hibernates
¹**hi·ber·nian** \(')hī¦bərnēən, -bən-,-bəin-, -nyən\ *adj, usu cap* [*Hibernia* Ireland (fr. L) + E *-an*] **1** : of, relating to, or characteristic of Ireland **2** : of, relating to, or characteristic of the Irish
²**hibernian** \"\ *n* -s *usu cap* : a native or inhabitant of Ireland : IRISHMAN
hibernian green *n, often cap H* : a dark yellowish green that is yellower and paler than holly green (sense 1), lighter and stronger than deep chrome green, and yellower, lighter, and stronger than average hunter green — called also *paradise green*
hi·ber·nian·ism \hī'bərnēə,nizəm, -bən-,-bəin-, -nyə-\ *n* -s *usu cap* : HIBERNICISM
hi·ber·ni·cism \-nə,sizəm\ *n* -s *usu cap* [ML *Hibernicus* Irish (fr. *Hibernia* + L *-icus* -ic) + E *-ism*] : something characteristically Irish; *specif* : IRISH BULL
hi·ber·ni·cize \-,sīz\ *vt* -ED/-ING/-S *often cap* [ML *Hibernicus* + E *-ize*] : to make Irish : express in an Irish way
hiberno- *comb form, usu cap* [*Hibernia*] **1** : Irish and ⟨*Hiberno*-Celtic⟩ **2** : Ireland ⟨*Hibernology*⟩
hi·bis·cus \hī'biskəs, hə'-\ *n* [NL, fr. L, *hibiscum, hibiscus* marshmallow] **1** *cap* : a large widely distributed genus of herbs, shrubs, or small trees (family Malvaceae) with dentate or lobed leaves and large showy flowers — see CHINA ROSE, KENAF, ROSE OF SHARON **2** -ES : any plant or flower of the genus *Hibiscus*
hi·bi·to \(h)ē'bē(,)tō\ *n, pl* **hibito** *or* **hibitos** *usu cap* [Sp, of AmerInd origin] **1 a** : an extinct Cholonan people of northwestern Peru **b** : a member of such people **2** : the language of the Hibito people
hibsch·ite \'hip,shīt\ *n* -s [Joseph E. *Hibsch* *b*1882 Czech mineralogist + E *-ite*] : a mineral $Ca_3Al_2(SiO_4)_2(OH)_4$ consisting of a calcium aluminum silicate-hydroxide
hic *often read as* 'hik\ *interj* [imit.] — used to express the sound of a hiccup
hicaco *var of* ICACO
hic·a·tee *or* **hic·o·tee** \'hikə,tē, ,==='=\ *or* **hic·o·tea** \,hikə'tāə\ *n* -s [Sp *hicotea, jicotea*, prob. fr. Taino *icotea, icota*] : a West Indian freshwater tortoise (*Chrysemys palustris*)
hic·can *also* **hi·can** \(')hī¦kan, -kän\ *n* -s [*hickory* + *pecan*] : the nut of a tree produced by hybridizing a hickory and a pecan
hic·cius doc·cius \¦hiksh(ē)əs'däksh(ē)əs, ¦hiksēəs'däksēəs\ *n* [perh. modif. of L *hic est doctus* this is a learned man] *archaic* : a juggler's formula
¹**hic·cup** *or* **hic·cough** \'hi|,kəp *sometimes* 'hē| *or* |,kəp *or* |,kōf *or* |,käf\ *n* -s [*hiccup* of imit. origin; *hiccough* by folk etymology (influence of *cough*) fr. *hiccup*] **1** : a spasmodic inspiratory movement of the diaphragm involuntarily checked by a sudden closure of the glottis that produces a characteristic sound **2** *or* **hiccups** *pl but sometimes sing in constr* : an attack of hiccuping ⟨severe ~*s* is sometimes seen after operation —*Lancet*⟩ ⟨intractable ~ . . . may be successfully treated —*Jour. Amer. Med. Assoc.*⟩
²**hiccup** *also* **hiccough** \"\ *vb* **hiccuped** *also* **hiccupped** *also* **hiccoughed**; **hiccuped** *also* **hiccupped** *also* **hiccoughed**; **hiccuping** *also* **hiccupping** *also* **hiccoughing**; **hiccups** *also* **hiccoughs** *vi* **1** : to have or suffer from hiccups : make a hiccup **2** : to make a sound suggestive of hiccups ⟨the locomotive ~*ed* and belched a gobbet of smoke into the air —S.H. Adams⟩ ~ *vt* : to speak with or as if with hiccups — usu. used with *out* ⟨was ~*ing* out the lines —W.M.Thackeray⟩
hic·cup-nut \'=(,)=,=\ *n* **1** : the seed of an ornamental southern African red-flowering shrub (*Combretum bracteosum*) **2** : the plant that bears hiccup-nuts
hicht \'hikt\ *Scot var of* HEIGHT
hichu *var of* ICHU
hic ja·cet \(')hik'jāsət, (')hēk'yäkət\ *n* -s [L, here lies] : an inscription on a tombstone : EPITAPH ⟨among the knightly brasses of the graves, and by the cold *hic jacets* of the dead —Alfred Tennyson⟩
¹**hick** \'hik\ *n* -s [fr. *Hick*, nickname for *Richard*] : an awkward, rude, unsophisticated, or provincial person ⟨their dullest gags, especially written down for the ~*s* —Edmund Wilson⟩ ⟨the immemorial game of luring ~*s*, tired businessmen and holidaymakers into their shows —Sheldon Cheney⟩ **syn** see BOOR
²**hick** \"\ *adj* : of, relating to, or having the characteristics of a hick : suggestive of hicks : COUNTRY ⟨a ~ town⟩
³**hick** \"\ *n* -s [imit.] : HICCUP 1
⁴**hick** \"\ *vi* -ED/-ING/-S : HICCUP 1
¹**hick·ey** *also* **hicky** \'hikē, -ki\ *n, pl* **hickeys** *also* **hickies** [origin unknown] **1 a** : a threaded coupling used to attach an electrical fixture to an outlet box **b** : a device for bending pipe and conduit **2** : a contrivance or device whose name is unknown or forgotten : GADGET ⟨that little ~ with the rubber roller on a handle —*Bagpipe*⟩
²**hickey** \"\ *n* -s [origin unknown] **1** : PIMPLE **2** : a defect in a negative or printing plate
hick joint *n* [perh. fr. the name *Hick*] : a joint finished flush with the surface of masonry
¹**hick·o·ry** \'hik(ə)rē, -ri\ *n* -ES [short for *pokahickory*, fr. Virginia *pawcohiccora* food prepared fr. pounded nuts and water] **1 a** : an American tree of the genus *Carya* — see HICKORY NUT; TREE illustration **b** : the valuable hard wood of various hickories **2** : a switch or cane used typically for punishing a child **3** : a rapid gait : CLIP **4 a** : any of various Australian trees (as the featherwood or various members of the genera *Acacia* and *Eucalyptus*) **b** : the wood of an Australian hickory
²**hickory** \"\ *adj* **1** : of, relating to, or made of hickory ⟨a ~ chair⟩ **2 a** : marked by firmness or toughness ⟨the old general, with all his ~ characteristics —Washington Irving⟩ **b** : marked by the absence of religious zeal or devotion : religiously indifferent or lukewarm
³**hickory** \"\ *vt* -ED/-ING/-ES : to give a whipping to : CANE, SWITCH
hickory acacia *n* : an Australian acacia (*Acacia leprosa*) with hard reddish brown wood
hickory bark beetle *also* **hickory bark borer** *n* : a small beetle (*Scolytus quadrispinosus*) that burrows beneath the bark of various hickories
hickory borer *n* : any of various beetles whose larvae live under the bark or in the wood of hickories
hickory elm *n* : ROCK ELM 1
hickoryhead \'=(=)=,=\ *n* : RUDDY DUCK
hickory horned devil *n* : a caterpillar that has a greenish body, red head, and four large curved anterior spines and is the larva of the regal moth
hickory midge *n* : a gallfly (*Caryomyia caryae*) that forms globular galls on the leaves of various hickories; *broadly* : a member of the genus *Caryomyia*
hickory nut *n* : the oblong or nearly orbicular nut or fruit of the hickory that is usu. compressed on the sides, sharp-pointed at the apex, and enclosed in a 4-valved husk
hickory oak *n* : CANYON LIVE OAK
hickory pine *n* **1** : BRISTLECONE PINE **2** : TABLE-MOUNTAIN PINE
hickory poplar *n* : TULIP TREE 1
hickory shad *n* [so called fr. the similarity of the stomachs to hickory nuts] **1** : FALL HERRING **2** : GIZZARD SHAD
hickory shirt *also* **hickory** *n* : a shirt made of a strong twilled cotton fabric with vertical stripes and used esp. for work clothing
hickory shuckworm *n* : a small white brown-headed grub that is the larva of an olethreutid moth (*Laspeyresia caryana*) and that feeds in the developing fruits of hickory and pecan
hickory wattle *n* : a Queensland acacia (*Acacia aulacocarpa*)
hicks *pl of* HICK, *pres 3d sing of* HICK
hicks·ite \'hik,sīt\ *n* -s *usu cap* [Elias *Hicks* †1830 Am. Quaker minister + E *-ite*] : a member of a liberal branch of Quakers who emphasize the Inner Light at the expense of historical Christianity and the Bible
hicks yew *or* **hicks' yew** \'hiks(əz)-\ *n, usu cap H* [fr. *Hicks* nurseries, Westbury, L.I.] : a hybrid yew (*Taxus media hicksii*) having a columnar shape and ascending branches
hick·wall \'hi,kwōl\ *n* [ME *hygh-whele*, prob. of imit. origin] *dial Eng* : GREEN WOODPECKER
hicky *var of* HICKEY
hi·co·ria \hi'kōrēə\ [NL, modif. of E *hickory*] *syn of* CARYA
hicotee *or* **hicotea** *var of* HICATEE
hid \'hid\ *adj* [ME, fr. past part. of *hiden* to hide — more at HIDE] : HIDDEN ⟨like the ~ scent in an unbudded rose —John Keats⟩
hid·abil·i·ty \,hīdə'biləd·ē\ *n* **1** : the quality or state of being hidable **2** : ability to obscure ⟨paints of superior durability, ~, and color-holding qualities —*Amer. Builder*⟩
hid·able \'hīdəbəl\ *adj* : capable of being hidden ⟨jewels are such ~ trifles —*English Digest*⟩
hid·age \'hīdij\ *n* -s [ML *hidagium*, fr. *hida* hide (fr. ME *hyde*) + *-agium* -age] *old Eng law* **1** : a tax or tribute paid to the royal exchequer for every hide of land **2** : the value or measure assessed as a basis for hidage
hi·dal·go \hi'dal(,)gō, ē'thäl-\ *n* -s *often cap* [Sp, fr. OSp *fijo dalgo*, lit., son of something, son of riches or property] : a member of the lower nobility of Spain
hid·at·ed \'hī,dād·əd\ *adj* [NL *hidatus* (past part. of *hidare* to measure in hides, fr. ML *hida* hide) + E *-ed*] : measured in hides
hid·a·tion \hī'dāshən\ *n* -s [NL *hidatus* + E *-ion*] : a measuring in or assessing by hides
hi·dat·sa \hi'dätsə, -dat-\ *n, pl* **hidatsa** *also* **hidatsas** *usu cap* **1 a** : a Siouan people of the Missouri River valley in No. Dakota related to the Crow — compare GROS VENTRE **b** : a member of such people **2** : the language of the Hidatsa people
hid·den \'hidᵊn\ *adj* [fr. past part. of ²*hide*] **1** : being out of sight or off the beaten track : CONCEALED ⟨pulling a ~ switch —D.J.Ingle⟩ ⟨a ~ Broadway restaurant —Scott Fitzgerald⟩ **2** : UNEXPLAINED, UNDISCLOSED, OBSCURE, SECRET ⟨rendering . . . apparent that which is ~ —Matthew Arnold⟩ ⟨rid your mind of any ~ hates or grudges —W.J.Reilly⟩; *specif* : not shown in the accounts or not shown on the books under the usual heading ⟨~ assets⟩ **3** : obscured by something that makes recognition difficult : covered up ⟨~ vowel⟩ ⟨clouds race across the ~ moon⟩ ⟨~ transfers of dollars, the largest item being the estimated $125 million spent by U. S. troops in Germany —*Americana Annual*⟩ — **hid·den·ly** *adv* — **hid·den·ness** \-ᵊn(n)əs\ *n* -ES
hidden fifth *n* : an unsounded musical interval of a fifth that is implied by the similar up or down motion of two voice parts and that if sounded would produce consecutive fifths
hidden hunger *n* : a nutritional deficiency caused by lack of balance in an otherwise full diet ⟨*hidden hunger* is suffered by cats . . . permitted to eat only liver —Doris Bryant⟩
hid·den·ite \'hidᵊn,īt\ *n* -s [William E. *Hidden* †1918 Am. mineralogist + E *-ite*] : a transparent yellow to green spodumene valued as a gem — compare KUNZITE
hidden octave *n* : an unsounded musical interval of an octave that is implied by the similar up or down motion of two voice parts and that if sounded would produce consecutive octaves
hidden pensioner *n* : an employee no longer performing at peak efficiency but retained in service at a wage exceeding his value to the employer
hidden quantity *n, Latin prosody* : the quantity of a hidden vowel so situated that its natural quantity is not determinable by scansion (as when it comes before a double consonant or before two or more consecutive consonants other than a mute and a liquid in the same word)
hidden reserve *n* : SECRET RESERVE
¹**hide** \'hīd\ *n* -s [ME *hyde*, fr. OE *hīgid, hīd*; akin to OE *hīwan* members of a household — more at HOME] : any of various old English units of land area; *esp* : a unit of 120 acres used in the Domesday Book — see CARUCATE, SULUNG

²hide \"\ *vb* **hid** \'hid\ **hidden** \'hidᵊn\ *or* **hid; hiding** \'hīdiŋ\ **hides** \'hīdz\ [ME *hiden,* fr. OE *hȳdan;* akin to MIr *codal* skin, Gk *keuthein* to conceal, Skt *kuhara* cave, OE *hȳd* hide, skin — more at ⁴HIDE] *vt* **1 a :** to deposit in a place of concealment : put out of sight : SECRETE ⟨a key under a doormat⟩ **b :** to conceal for shelter or protection : SHIELD ⟨Rock of Ages, cleft for me, let me ~ myself in thee —A.M. Toplady⟩ **2 :** to withhold from someone or from public knowledge : keep secret ⟨fled to her room to ~ her grief —Andrew Meredith⟩ ⟨to keep a secret, you must also ~ the fact that you have one to keep —Piero Compton⟩ **3 a :** to screen from view or from detection by the senses : cover up ⟨a thick mantle of glacial deposits ~*s* the solid rocks —L.D. Stamp⟩ ⟨the purling water was nearly *hidden* by the birr of wings —Sacheverell Sitwell⟩ ⟨sugar coating ~*s* the taste of pills⟩ **b :** to submerge in something that makes comprehension difficult : BURY 3b, OBSCURE ⟨pokes fun at some of his colleagues who ~ their important messages in language only intelligible to other professors —*Word Study*⟩ ⟨facts *hidden* in folklore⟩ ~ *vi* **1 a :** to remain out of sight : become concealed ⟨*hid* in the island bushes is a frigate —H.S.Canby⟩ ⟨spongy bogs . . . *hiding* here and there in the woods —John Muir †1914⟩ **b :** to go into or remain in concealment to evade authority or pursuit ⟨fewer places for violators to ~ —*Newsweek*⟩ — often used with *out* or *up* ⟨people who do not wish to have any contact with the military government authorities are . . . *hiding* out on farms —Nora Waln⟩ ⟨went back to the ranch kind of slow to give me time to ~ up —C.T.Jackson⟩ **2 :** to seek protection or evade responsibility : take refuge — usu. used with *behind* ⟨~*s* behind dark glasses, hoping to avoid being recognized⟩ ⟨heads of companies who are not . . . gift-minded ~ behind their boards of directors —*Saturday Rev.*⟩ **syn** see CONCEAL — **hide one's face from :** to turn away from : IGNORE ⟨I will forsake them and *hide my face from* them, and they will be devoured —Deut 31:17 (RSV)⟩ — **hide one's head 1** *obs* **:** to take shelter or refuge ⟨alack the heavy day when such a sacred king should *hide his head* —Shak.⟩ **2 :** to keep silent for fear of reproach ⟨the pessimists *hid their heads* at the opening of the new century —Oscar Handlin⟩ — **hide one's light under a bushel :** to be excessively modest : conceal one's abilities : shrink from public notice ⟨a fine poet who *hid her light under a bushel*⟩

³hide \"\ *n* **-s 1 :** a hiding place ⟨knew his ~ had to be very good to elude the scrutiny of the local liquor raiders —*Springfield (Mass.) Union*⟩ **2** *Brit* **:** ³BLIND 2 ⟨in shooting at driven lions it is best to wait until they have passed the ~ —James Stevenson-Hamilton⟩

⁴hide \"\ *n* **-s** *often attrib* [ME *hid, hide,* fr. OE *hȳd;* akin to OHG *hūt* skin, hide, ON *hūth* skin, hide, L *cutis* skin, Gk *kytos* hollow vessel, *skytos* skin, leather, OPruss *keuto* shell, covering, Skt *skunāti* he covers; basic meaning: to cover, conceal] **1 a :** the outer covering of an animal : COAT ⟨bald patches of rock like the ~ of a bison when it is shedding —Norman Mailer⟩ **b :** a raw or tanned pelt taken from an adult of one of the larger animals (as a cow) as distinguished from a skin of one of the smaller or younger animals (as a goat or calf) ⟨calfskins . . . produce a softer leather than cattle ~*s* —G.S. Brady⟩ **c :** a piece of dressed pelt used as material for a manufactured article : LEATHER ⟨ladies' luggage set, in English ~ —*advt*⟩ **2 a :** the skin of a human being ⟨he had a certain hard brownness of ~ . . . a horny quality in his face and hands —Arthur Morrison⟩ ⟨much of the industrial plant was doubtless built out of the ~*s* of the people —W.O. Douglas⟩ **b :** a covering aspect or front that gives protection against outside pressure ⟨too tough a ~ to have hurt feelings⟩ **c :** LIFE ⟨such strategy often saved the ~ of the Grand Old Party —Dixon Wecter⟩ — **hide or hair** *or* **hide nor hair :** a vestige or trace of a missing person or object ⟨a wife he hadn't seen *hide or hair* of in over 20 years —H.L.Davis⟩ ⟨turned the closet inside out but couldn't find *hide or hair* of the beach umbrella⟩ ⟨no one has seen *hide nor hair* of him since —*Time*⟩

hide 1b: *a b d c* butt; *A B d b, A B c a* bends; *a b f g* shoulder; *E, E,* belly; *D, D,* cheeks; *F* head

⁵hide \"\ *vt* -ED/-ING/-S **:** to give a beating to : FLOG ⟨victualed him and clothed him and *hided* him for his own good when he needed it —S.H.Adams⟩

hide and coop *n* [*coop* fr. *coop,* interj. used by players to call out from their hiding places] **:** HIDE-AND-SEEK

¹hide-and-seek \ˌ=ˌ=(ˌ)=ˈ=\ *n* **1** *or* **hide-and-go-seek** \ˌ=ˌ=ˌ=ˈ=\ **:** a children's game in which one player blinds his eyes and after giving the others time to hide goes looking for and tries to catch them — called also *hide-and-coop, hy spy, I spy* **2 :** a procedure resembling the game of hide-and-seek involving reciprocal deception or evasion ⟨rumrunners playing *hide-and-seek* with government agents —*Amer. Guide Series: Fla.*⟩

²hide-and-seek \"\ *vi* [¹*hide-and-seek*] **:** to play at hide-and-seek ⟨opposing planes *hide-and-seeking* in the darkness —F.V.Drake⟩

¹hideaway \'=ˌ=ˌ=\ *n* **-s** [fr. *hide away,* v.] **1 :** a place of retreat or concealment : REFUGE ⟨intimate, private ~*s* —P.E. Deutschman⟩ ⟨a ~ . . . used to secrete slaves on the Underground Railway —*Amer. Guide Series: Md.*⟩ **2 :** a small secluded restaurant or place of entertainment ⟨dine-and-dance places, exclusive ~*s* —*Emporia (Kans.) Gazette*⟩

²hideaway \"\ *adj* [fr. *hide away,* v.] **:** CONCEALED, SECLUDED ⟨~ bed⟩ ⟨~ restaurant⟩

hidebound \'=ˌ=\ *adj* [⁴*hide* + *bound*] **1 a :** having a dry skin lacking in pliancy and adhering closely to the underlying flesh and usu. also a rough and lusterless coat esp. as an accompaniment to disease — used of domestic animals **b :** having scleroderma — used of human beings **c :** having the bark so close and constricting that it impedes growth — used of trees **2 a** *obs* **:** sparing in expenditure : MISERLY **b :** having an inflexible or ultraconservative character : BIGOTED, NARROW ⟨a nature sometimes ~ and selfish and narrow to the last degree —G.G.Coulton⟩ ⟨the most ~ bureaucrat could not have been more obsoletely reactionary, uninventive, and obstructive —G.B.Shaw⟩ ⟨judicial proceedings should not be ~ by arbitrary rules handed down from the past —K. W.Colgrove⟩ — **hide·bound·ness** \'hīdˌbaùn(d)nəs *also* -ndnəs\ *n* **-ES**

hideland \'=ˌ=\ *n* [¹*hide* + *land*] **:** ¹HIDE

hide·less \'hīdləs\ *adj* [⁴*hide* + *-less*] **:** lacking a hide or skin

hid·eos·i·ty \ˌhidēˈäsəd·ē\ *n* **-ES** [fr. *hideous,* after such pairs as E *curious : curiosity*] **:** a hideous thing : HIDEOUSNESS ⟨the high-water mark of ~ —*Architectural Rev.*⟩ ⟨this vile incrustation of *hideosities* —Dan Wickenden⟩

hid·eous \'hidēəs *sometimes* ÷'hijəs\ *adj* [alter. (influenced by such words as *courteous*) of ME *hidous,* fr. OF *hisdos, hidous, hideus,* fr. *hisde, hide* terror] **1 a :** offensive to the sight : GRUESOME, UGLY ⟨one man still living in ~ squalor among the bones of his fellow travelers —Mabel R. Gillis⟩ ⟨a ~ congeries of fuming kilns —V.S.Pritchett⟩ ⟨writers concerning the warthog generally commence by enlarging upon its ~ appearance —James Stevenson-Hamilton⟩ ⟨a lampshade . . . too ~ for anyone in their senses to buy —W.H.Auden⟩ **b :** offensive to another of the senses : FRIGHTFUL, TERRIBLE ⟨the ~ gasping struggle the asthmatic woman was making to get her breath —Leslie Ford⟩ ⟨during the summer this southward-facing row of buildings must be ~ with heat —G.R. Stewart⟩ **c :** appallingly large : MONSTROUS ⟨the great scar on a mountainside left by the racing snow, and the ~ mass of snow and soil and rock . . . on the valley floor —Russell Henderson⟩ **2 a :** offensive to the mind or to the moral sense : HATEFUL, SHOCKING ⟨monstrous and ~ thoughts —J.C.Powys⟩ ⟨a ~ pattern of injustice —Paul Blanshard⟩ **b :** EMBARRASSING, LUDICROUS, DISMAYING ⟨I am in ~ straits about the . . . performance of a play of mine —G.B.Shaw⟩ ⟨a ~ accident attended the serving of the dessert —Jean Stafford⟩ **syn** see UGLY

hid·eous·ly *adv* **:** in a hideous manner ⟨~ snarling white plaster lions —Mollie Panter-Downes⟩

hid·eous·ness *n* **-ES :** the quality or state of being hideous

hideout \'=ˌ=\ *n* **-s** [fr. *hide out,* v.] **:** a place of refuge, retreat, or concealment ⟨spiriting his lovely client off to a little ~ that he has —Wolcott Gibbs⟩ ⟨had stopped to refuel their car while taking him to their ~ —*Fingerprint Identification*⟩

hideout gun *n* **:** a handgun that can be easily concealed upon the person

hide powder *n* **:** powdered hide usu. specially prepared and standardized for use in the analysis of tannins and tanning materials

hid·er \'hīdə(r)\ *n* **-s** [ME, fr. *hiden* to hide + *-er* — more at HIDE] **:** one that hides

hide rope *n* **1 :** a rope plaited from strips of green hide **2 :** a fiber rope used for tying baled goods (as hides)

hides *pl of* HIDE, *pres 3d sing of* HIDE

hide splitter *n* **:** one that separates the grain layer from the flesh layer of a hide

hide spreader *n* **:** one that spreads raw hides one on top of another to form a pack for curing

hidey-hole *or* **hidy-hole** \'hīdēˌhōl\ *n* [alter. of earlier *hiding-hole*] **:** HIDEAWAY 1

¹hiding *n* **-s** [ME *hidinge,* fr. *hiden* to hide + *-inge* -ing] **1 :** the act or action of hiding; *esp* **:** a withdrawal from one's usual haunts to evade authority or secure privacy ⟨having got into difficulties with the government for his press reports and cartoons, he went into ~ —*Irish Digest*⟩ **2 :** a place or means of concealment ⟨take me to that ~ in the hills —Alfred Tennyson⟩

²hiding *n* **-s** [fr. gerund of ⁵*hide*] **:** an infliction of physical punishment : BEATING ⟨a fighter . . . who had been taking ~*s* in the gymnasium —*Sporting Life*⟩ ⟨the roof of a van really takes a ~ in all weathers —Keith Winser⟩; *esp* **:** WHIPPING ⟨put her over my knee and gave her a ~ —Saul Bellow⟩

hiding power *n* **:** the ability of a paint or painting material to obscure the surface upon which it is applied — distinguished from *coverage*

¹hid·lings \'hidlənz, -liŋz\ *or* **hid·lins** \-lənz\ *adv* [ME *hidlinges,* fr. *hid* (past part. of *hiden* to hide) + *-linges* -lings — more at HIDE] *chiefly Scot* **:** in a clandestine manner : SECRETLY — usu. used with *in*

²hidlings \"\ *or* **hidlins** \"\ *adj, chiefly Scot* **:** SECRET, CLANDESTINE

hidr- *or* **hidro-** *comb form* [NL, fr. Gk *hidrōs* sweat — more at SWEAT] **:** of or by means of perspiration **:** of the sweat glands ⟨*hidr*adenitis⟩ ⟨*hidro*cystoma⟩

hidrad·e·ni·tis \ˌhiˌdradᵊnˈīdəs, ˌhī-\ *n* [NL, fr. *hidr-* + *adenitis*] **:** inflammation of a sweat gland

hi·dro·sis \hiˈdrōsəs, hī'-\ *n, pl* **hidro·ses** \-ōˌsēz\ [NL, fr. Gk *hidrōsis,* fr. *hidrōt-, hidrōs* sweat + *-sis*] **:** excretion of sweat : PERSPIRATION

hi·drot·ic \(ˈ)=ˈdräd·ik\ *adj* [Gk *hidrōtikos,* fr. *hidrōt-, hidrōs* sweat + *-ikos* -ic] **:** causing perspiration : DIAPHORETIC, SUDORIFIC

¹hie \'hī\ *vb* **hied; hied; hying** *or* **hieing** \'hīiŋ\ **hies** [ME *hien,* fr. OE *higian* to strive, be eager, hasten; akin to OSw *hikka* to pant, Norw, to sob, Russ *sigat'* to jump, Skt *śīghra* quick] *vi* **:** to go quickly : HASTEN ⟨thither we advise you to ~ —*New Yorker*⟩ ~ *vt* **:** to cause (oneself) to go quickly ⟨*hied* myself to the post office —H.A.Chippendale⟩

²hie \"\ *chiefly Scot var of* HIGH

hie·lan *or* **hie·land** \'hēlən(d), -nt\ *Scot var of* HIGHLAND

hield *vi* -ED/-ING/-S [ME *helden, heelden, hielden* — more at HEEL] *obs* **:** TILT, LEAN, HEEL ⟨let it be laid in a dish ~*ing* toward the one side —Peter Morwen⟩

hie·le·man *or* **hee·la·man** *or* **hei·la·man** \'hēləmən\ *n* **-s** [native name in Australia] **:** an elongated wooden shield used by Australian aborigines

hielmite *var of* HJELMITE

hi·emal \'hīəməl\ *adj* [L *hiemalis,* fr. *hiem-, hiems* winter + *-alis* -al — more at HIBERNATE] **:** of or relating to winter : WINTRY

hieng \hēˈeŋ\ *n, pl* **hieng** *or* **hiengs** *usu cap* **1 :** a mountain people of Cambodia **2 :** a member of the Hieng people

hie on *vt* **:** to rouse to quick action : urge on ⟨*hie on* a hound⟩

hier- *or* **hiero-** *comb form* [LL, fr. Gk, fr. *hieros* powerful, supernatural, holy, sacred — more at IRE] **:** sacred : holy ⟨*hier*archy⟩ ⟨*hiero*glyph⟩

hiera *pl of* HIERON

hi·er·a·cite \'hīərəˌsīt, hīˈerəˌs-, ˌhīəˈrāˌs-\ *or* **hi·er·a·cian** \ˌhīəˈrāshən\ *n* **-s** *usu cap* [*Hieracite* fr. LL *Hieracita,* fr. *Hieracas,* 4th cent. A.D. Egyptian ascetic + L *-ita* -ite; *Hieracian* fr. *Hieracas* + E *-ian*] **:** a follower of the ascetic Hieracas

hi·er·a·ci·um \ˌhīəˈrāshēəm\ *n* [NL, fr. Gk *hierakion* hawkweed, fr. *hierak-, hierax* hawk, fr. *hienai* to hurry — more at VIA] **1** *cap* **:** a very large and nearly cosmopolitan genus of weedy perennial herbs (family Compositae) having simple often basal leaves and heads of yellow or reddish orange ray flowers — see ORANGE HAWKWEED **2** *pl* **hieracia** *also* **hieraciums :** any plant of the genus *Hieracium*

hi·er·a·co·sphinx \ˌhīəˈrākə+ˌ-\ *n* [Gk *hierako-* (fr. *hierak-, hierax* hawk) + E *sphinx*] **:** a hawk-headed sphinx

hiera pic·ra \ˌhīərəˈpikrə\ *n* [ML, lit., powerful or sacred antidote] **:** a cathartic powder made of aloes and canella bark

hi·er·arch \'hīəˌrärk, -ˌräk *also* 'hīˌr-\ *n* **-s** [MF or ML; MF *hierarche,* fr. ML *hierarcha,* fr. Gk *hierarchēs,* fr. *hier-* + *-archēs* -arch] **1 :** a religious leader holding high office or vested with controlling authority : chief prelate : HIGH PRIEST ⟨the important central painting . . . shows the apostolic succession of ~*s* —W.E.Needham⟩ ⟨steps taken by the British East India Company to . . . establish relations with the Tibetan ~*s* —Beatrice D. Miller⟩ **2 :** one having authority or pontifical dignity resembling that of a hierarch ⟨former ministers, generals, blackshirt ~*s* —Janet Flanner⟩ ⟨proceed with the utmost decorum and in what the ~*s* . . . considered the best of Senate tradition —*N.Y. Times Mag.*⟩

hi·er·ar·chal \ˌhīəˈrärkəl, -ˈräk- *also* (ˈ)hīˈr-\ *or* **hi·er·ar·chi·al** \-kēəl\ *adj* **:** HIERARCHICAL — **hi·er·ar·chal·ly** \ˌ=ˈ=kəlē, (ˈ)=ˈ=kəlē, -li\ *or* **hi·er·ar·chi·al·ly** \-kēəlē, -li\ *adv*

hi·er·ar·chi·cal \-kəkəl, -kēk-\ *or* **hi·er·ar·chic** \-kik,-kēk\ *adj* [MF or ML; MF *hierarchique,* fr. ML *hierarchicus,* fr. *hierarchia* + L *-icus* -ic, -ical] **1 :** of, relating to, or controlled by a religious hierarchy ⟨the liturgy of the mass presupposes . . . the ~ order of church and society corresponds to the divine hierarchy —Jacob Taubes⟩ **2 a :** of an authoritarian or aristocratic character : STRATIFIED ⟨although the ~ federal arrangement is typical, there are many organizations which are unitary —D.D.McKean⟩ ⟨only a ~ society with a leisure class at the top can produce works of art —*Partisan Rev.*⟩ **b :** having the power to control : INFLUENTIAL ⟨a denial . . . due to pressure from a political or ~ source interfering with the due course of judicial proceedings —M.R.Cohen⟩ **3 :** of or relating to a classification of people according to artistic, social, economic, or other criteria ⟨a ~ feeling has grown up in Italy about the standings of the artists —R.M.Coates⟩ ⟨the ~ status of a child in relation to other members of the family —Norman Cameron⟩ ⟨the tailor, department head, and floor supervisor were summoned, appealed to, and appalled in *hierarchic* succession —Marvin Barrett⟩ **4 :** of, relating to, or constituting a related series : SEQUENTIAL ⟨the ~ arrangement of cultures constructed by the 19th century anthropologists —Henry Orenstein⟩ — **hi·er·ar·chi·cal·ly** \-k(ə)lē, -kēk-, -li\ *adv*

hi·er·ar·chism \'hīəˌrärˌkizəm, -ˌräk- *also* 'hīˌr-\ *n* **-s :** the system or authority of a hierarchy

hi·er·ar·chi·za·tion \(ˌ)=ˌ=ˌkəˈzāshən, -ˌkīˈz-\ *n* **-s 1 :** the act or process of establishing a hierarchy ⟨~ . . . leads to a clear-cut stratification of all members of any organized group —P.A.Sorokin⟩ **2 :** the quality or state of being a hierarchy ⟨the traditional ~ of the three orders of abstraction —F.G. Connolly⟩

hi·er·ar·chize \'hīəˌrärˌkīz, -ˌräk- *also* 'hīˌr-\ *vt* -ED/-ING/-S **:** to arrange hierarchically ⟨*hierarchized* systems of organization —C.H.Page⟩

hi·er·ar·chy \'hīəˌrärkē, -ˌräk-, -ki *also* 'hīˌr-\ *n* **-ES** [ME *ierarchie,* fr. MF *ierarchie, hierarchie,* fr. ML *hierarchia,* fr. LGk, fr. Gk *hierarchēs* + *-ia* -y] **1 :** a rank or order of holy beings — *see* CELESTIAL HIERARCHY **2 :** a form of government administered by an authoritarian group ⟨the company town implies a ~ despotically, if benevolently, guiding the lives of those beneath —W.H.Whyte⟩ ⟨the ~ relates all units in vertical levels of responsibility —J.E.Pate⟩; *esp* **:** control exercised by a priesthood ⟨unlimited centralization of ecclesiastical ~ —A.C.N.Gallenga⟩ **3 a :** an authoritarian body of religious officials organized by rank and jurisdiction ⟨the priest, with the ~ at his back, was in theory almost everything to his people —G.G.Coulton⟩ ⟨three cardinals and 65 bishops attended the annual meeting of the American ~ —*Official Catholic Yearbook*⟩ ⟨the power . . . of the great Buddhist ~ is nothing less than stupendous —Edith Hamilton⟩ **b :** a controlling group of any kind ⟨when all power is centered in the top ~ of a single party, there is none left over to serve as a check against the ruling class —A.M.Schlesinger b.1917⟩ ⟨officials at the pinnacle of the mobilization ~ —*Wall Street Jour.*⟩ ⟨the publisher who has . . . exceeded his proper function by becoming the head and dictator of the newspaper ~ —Alistair Cooke⟩ ⟨at the bottom of the ~ of managerial personnel are the foremen —Kurt Braun⟩ ⟨rising steadily in the ~ of the local Boy Scouts —Brendan Gill⟩ **4 a :** the classification of a group of people with regard to ability or economic or social standing ⟨the function of true criticism is to establish a definite ~ among the great artists of the past —C.W.Shumaker⟩ ⟨continuous waves of new immigrants, each pushing the preceding waves upward in the ethnic ~ —Richard Hofstadter⟩ ⟨the seating arrangement was an accurate index of the Hollywood ~ —Budd Schulberg⟩ **b :** a group of people so classified ⟨made his way into the ~ of business families in Montreal —Hugh MacLennan⟩ **c :** the status attaching to such a group ⟨the social ~ that may be associated with possessions —Ruth Benedict⟩; *specif* **:** a graded series of social statuses or class levels ⟨upper and lower class ~ in a community⟩ **5 a :** the arrangement of objects, elements, or values in a graduated series ⟨the ~ of occupations is based on the degree of skill and responsibility they entail⟩ ⟨government officials determine the ~ of importance of affairs of state⟩ **b :** a series of objects, elements, or values so arranged ⟨the Supreme Court is the head of a ~ of federal courts —Felix Frankfurter⟩ ⟨in the multicellular organism there is a ~ of levels — cells, tissues, organs —A.B.Novikoff⟩; *specif, logic* **:** a series the members of which are grouped in accordance with a principle (as of importance, perfection or priority) ⟨~ of values⟩ ⟨an ontological ~ in which the objects of knowledge are arranged in an ascending order of reality —George Boas⟩ **c :** the stratification so achieved ⟨a rigid ~ of clubs —R.M.Lovett⟩; *specif* **:** a table of statistical correlations having a constant proportional relationship and graded from high to low

¹hi·er·at·ic \ˌhīəˈrad·ik *also* (ˈ)hīˈr-\ *adj* [L *hieraticus,* fr. Gk *hieratikos,* fr. (assumed) *hieratos* (verbal of *hierasthai* to be a priest, fr. *hieros* powerful, supernatural, holy, sacred) + *-ikos* -ic — more at IRE] **1 :** written in, constituting, or belonging to a cursive form of ancient Egyptian writing simpler and less pictorial than the hieroglyphic ⟨only those who served in the temples knew the secret of the ~ writing —W.M.James⟩ — see DEMOTIC 2 **2** *also* **hi·er·at·i·cal** \-d·əkəl\ **:** of, relating to, or associated with priestly functions : SACERDOTAL ⟨the gestures ~ as if from some slow and ancient ritual —Hallam Tennyson⟩ ⟨~ art of the church —Herbert Read⟩ ⟨the powerful ~ sculpture of the Aztecs —B.D. Wolfe⟩ — **hi·er·at·i·cal·ly** \-ək(ə)lē\ *adv*

²hieratic \"\ *n* **-s :** a cursive form of ancient Egyptian writing ⟨the oldest dated papyrus . . . is written in ~ —H.B.Van Hoesen & F.K.Walter⟩

hi·er·a·tite \'hīərəˌtīt\ *n* **-s** [It, fr. *Hiera* (Vulcano), one of the Lipari islands, Italy + It *-ite*] **:** a mineral K_2SiF_6 consisting of potassium fluosilicate found as grayish concretions in the fumaroles of Vulcano

-hi·er·ic \ˌhīˈerik, -rēk\ *adj comb form* [Gk *hieron (osteon)* sacrum (fr. hieron — neut. of *hieros* powerful, sacred — + *osteon* bone) + E *-ic* — more at IRE] **:** having (such) a sacrum ⟨dolicho*hieric*⟩ ⟨platy*hieric*⟩

hiero- — see HIER-

hi·er·och·loe \ˌhīəˈräkləˌ(ˌ)wē\ *n, cap* [NL, fr. *hier-* + Gk *chloē* young grass] **:** a genus of aromatic perennial grasses native to temperate and cold regions having spikelets with a perfect terminal floret and two staminate florets — see HOLY GRASS

hi·er·oc·ra·cy \-krəsē\ *n* **-ES** [*hier-* + *-cracy*] **:** government by ecclesiastics : HIERARCHY

hi·er·o·crat·ic \ˌhī(ə)rəˈkrad·ik\ *or* **hi·er·o·crat·i·cal** \-d·əkəl\ *adj* [fr. *hierocracy,* after such pairs as E *democracy: democratic, democratical*] **:** of or relating to government by ecclesiastics (as priests or prelates)

hi·er·o·dule \'hī(ə)rəˌd(y)ül, hīˈer-\ *n* **-s** [LL *hierodulus,* fr. Gk *hierodoulos,* fr. *hier-* + *doulos* slave] **:** a slave attached to the service of a temple; *esp* **:** a sacred prostitute in ancient Greece

hi·er·o·du·lic \ˌhī(ə)rəˈd(y)ülik, (ˌ)hīˌer-\ *adj* **:** of or relating to a hierodule

¹hi·er·o·glyph \'hī(ə)rəˌglif, -rō-\ *n* **-s** [F *hiéroglyphe,* fr. MF *hieroglyphe,* back-formation fr. *hieroglyphique*] **1 :** a character used in a system of hieroglyphic writing ⟨Maya ~*s* were sculptured or . . . incised on stone stelae —J.E.S.Thompson⟩ esp. in ancient Egypt ⟨~*s* often occur on monuments written vertically and from left to right —J.E.M.White⟩ — compare IDEOGRAM **2 :** something that resembles a hieroglyph in form or symbolism ⟨the river glistened in a ~ across the country —D.H.Lawrence⟩ ⟨at the corners of her eyes and mouth were written the decipherable ~*s* of disillusion —Helen Howe⟩ ⟨symbolic ~*s* consisting of nothing more than a few brush strokes —*Times Lit. Supp.*⟩

²hieroglyph \"\ *vt* -ED/-ING/-S **:** to express in or inscribe with hieroglyphs ⟨the first ~*ed* sarcophagus we had yet seen —Amelia B. Edwards⟩

¹hi·er·o·glyph·ic \ˌ=(=)=ˈglifik, -fēk\ *or* **hi·er·o·glyph·i·cal** \-fəkəl, -fēk-\ *adj* [*hieroglyphic* fr. MF *hieroglyphique,* fr. LL *hieroglyphicus,* fr. Gk *hieroglyphikos,* fr. *hier-* + *glyphikos* of carving; *hieroglyphical* fr. MF *hieroglyphique* + E *-al* — more at GLYPHIC] **1 a :** written in, constituting, or belonging to that form of ancient Egyptian writing in which the characters are for the most part recognizable pictures of objects — compare DEMOTIC, HIERATIC **b :** written in, constituting, or belonging to any system of writing in which the characters are to a substantial degree recognizable pictures ⟨finest of the three surviving Maya ~ books —J.E.S.Thompson⟩ **2 :** inscribed with hieroglyphic characters ⟨~ obelisk⟩ **3 :** resembling hieroglyphic in form ⟨coleus mosaic — causing . . . ~ markings on leaves —*Experiment Station Record*⟩, symbolism ⟨~ emblem⟩, or illegibility ⟨the most ~ of prescriptions —H.V. Morton⟩ ⟨*hieroglyphical* entries in thick, half-obliterated pencil —Bram Stoker⟩ — **hi·er·o·glyph·i·cal·ly** \-fək(ə)lē, -fēk-, -li\ *adv*

²hieroglyphic \"\ *n* **-s 1 :** HIEROGLYPH 1 **2 :** a system of hieroglyphic writing ⟨a German philologist . . . started the decipherment of Hittite ~ —C.J.Rolo⟩; *specif* **:** the picture script of the ancient Egyptian priesthood ⟨the elaborate ~ . . . was too slow and laborious a method of writing for the needs of everyday business —J.H.Breasted⟩ — often used in pl. but sing. or pl. in constr. **3 :** something that resembles a hieroglyphic in form, symbolic content, or difficulty of decipherment ⟨the frightening ~*s* of . . . shorthand —*advt*⟩ ⟨the traditional ~ that was said to identify for tramps the houses where meals were certain —Ben Riker⟩ ⟨the *hieroglyphic*-covered blackboard —Philip Hamburger⟩

hieroglyphics (Egyptian)

³hieroglyphic *vt* [²*hieroglyphic*] *obs* **:** HIEROGLYPH

hieroglyphic hittite *n, usu cap both Hs* **:** a language related to cuneiform Hittite and known from inscriptions in the Hittite hieroglyphic script — see INDO-EUROPEAN LANGUAGES table

hi·er·o·glyph·ist \ˌ=(=)=ˈglifəst, ˈ=(=)=ˌ=; ˌhīəˈräglәf-, hīˈrä-\ *n* **-s :** a writer of hieroglyphics

hi·er·o·gram \'hī(ə)rə,gram\ *n* [*hier-* + *-gram*] **:** a sacred emblem or graphic symbol

hi·er·o·gram·mat \,hī(ə)rə'gramət, -,mat\ *or* **hi·er·o·gram·mate** \-‚mət, -,māt\ *n* -s [Gk *hierogrammateus*, fr. *hier-* + *grammateus* scribe, fr. *grammat-*, *gramma* letter, writing — more at GRAMMAR] **:** a writer of sacred records esp. in hieroglyphics

hi·er·o·gram·mat·ic \¦hī(ə)rəgrə¦mad·ik\ *or* **hi·er·o·gram·mat·i·cal** \-d·ə̇kəl\ *adj* [*hier-* + Gk *grammat-*, *gramma* letter, writing + E *-ic*, *-ical*] **:** of or relating to hierograms

hi·er·o·graph \'hī(ə)rə,graf, -,ráf\ *n* [*hier-* + *-graph*] **:** HIEROGRAM — **hi·er·o·graph·ic** \¦=(=)=¦grafik\ *or* **hi·er·o·graph·i·cal** \-fə̇kəl\ *adj*

hi·er·og·ra·phy \,hīə'rägrəfē, hī'r-\ *n* -ES [LGk *hierographia*, fr. Gk *hier-* + *-graphia* -graphy] **:** descriptive writing on sacred subjects **:** a treatise on religion

hi·er·ol·a·try \-älə·trē\ *n* -ES [*hier-* + *-latry*] **:** worship of saints or sacred things

hi·er·o·log·ic \¦hī(ə)rə¦läjik\ *or* **hi·er·o·log·i·cal** \-jə̇kəl\ *adj* **:** of or relating to hierology

hi·er·ol·o·gist \,hīə'räləjə̇st, hī'r-\ *n* -s **:** one skilled in hierology

hi·er·ol·o·gy \-jē\ *n* -ES [*hier-* + *-logy*] **1 :** a body of knowledge of sacred things **:** the literary or traditional embodiment of the religious beliefs of a people ⟨the ~ of Greece⟩ **2 :** HAGIOLOGY

hi·er·o·mon·ach \,hī(ə)rō'mänək, -ä,nak; ,hīə'rämə,nak\ *n* -s [LGk or MGk *hieromonachos*, fr. Gk *hier-* + *monachos* monk — more at MONK] **:** HIEROMONK

hi·er·o·monk \'hī(ə)rō,məŋk\ *n* [part. trans. of LGk or MGk *hieromonachos*] **:** a monk of the Eastern Church who is also a priest

hi·er·on \'hīə,rän\ *n*, *pl* **hi·era** \-ərə\ [Gk, fr. neut. of *hieros* holy, sacred — more at IRE] **:** a consecrated place (as a temple) in ancient Greece

hi·er·o·nym·ic \¦hī(ə)rə¦nimik\ *also* **hi·er·o·nym·i·an** \-mēən\ *adj*, *usu cap* [Eusebius *Hieronymus* (St. Jerome) †420 church father + E *-ic* or *-ian*] **:** of, relating to, or composed by St. Jerome ⟨the *Hieronymic* version of the Bible⟩

hi·er·on·y·mite \,hīə'ränə,mīt, hī'r-\ *also* **hi·er·o·nym·i·an** \,hī(ə)rə'nimēən\ *n* -s *usu cap* [Eusebius *Hieronymus* + E *-ite* or *-ian*] **:** a member of any of various hermit orders named in honor of St. Jerome

hi·er·o·phant \'hī(ə)rə,fant; hī'erə,fant, -‚fənt\ *n* -s [LL *hierophanta*, *hierophantes*, fr. Gk *hierophantēs*, fr. *hier-* + *-phantēs* (fr. *phainein* to reveal, show, make known) — more at FANCY] **1 :** a priest in ancient Greece ⟨a ~ . . . dressed in a fawn skin, with a crown of poplar leaves —L.P.Smith⟩; *specif* **:** the chief priest of the Eleusinian mysteries **2 a :** a spokesman or interpreter ⟨the ~ of Beauty, the dedicated poet of the cult —F.R.Leavis⟩ ⟨the molder and ~ of the national life —Van Wyck Brooks⟩ **b :** a leading advocate ⟨sociologists have long been ~*s* of methodology —R.K.Merton⟩

hi·er·o·phan·tic \¦hī(ə)rə¦fantik, (¦)hī¦er-\ *adj* [Gk *hierophantikos*, fr. *hierophantēs* + *-ikos* -ic] **:** of, relating to, or resembling a hierophant — **hi·er·o·phan·ti·cal·ly** \-tə̇k(ə)lē\ *adv*

hi·er·o·sol·y·mi·tan \,hī(ə)rō¦sälə¦mītᵊn\ *adj*, *usu cap* [LL *Hierosolymitanus*, fr. *Hierosolyma* Jerusalem (fr. Gk *Hierosolyma*) + L *-ita* -ite + *-anus* -an] **:** of or relating to the city of Jerusalem

hi·er·ur·gi·cal \¦hīə¦rərjə̇kəl, (')hī¦r-\ *adj* **:** of or relating to hierurgy

hi·er·ur·gy \'hīə,rərjē, -ī,rər-\ *n* -ES [Gk *hierourgia*, fr. *hierourgos* sacrificing priest (fr. *hier-* + *-ergos*, fr. *ergon* work) + *-ia* -y] **:** an act or rite of worship **:** LITURGY

hies *pl of* HIE, *pres 3d sing of* HIE

hifalutin *var of* HIGHFALUTIN

1hi-fi \'hī'fī\ *n* -s [*high fi*delity] **1 :** HIGH FIDELITY **2 :** the equipment needed to play high-fidelity recordings ⟨to own *hi-fi* is to join a community of music lovers —Brooks Atkinson⟩ **3 :** the practice of listening to high-fidelity recordings as a pastime ⟨up to the present, *hi-fi* has been largely . . . the hobby of the enthusiastic amateur —Thomas Heinitz⟩

2hi-fi \'=¦=\ *adj* **1 :** of or relating to hi-fi ⟨*hi-fi* fan⟩ ⟨*hi-fi* range⟩ **2 :** characterized by high fidelity ⟨*hi-fi* recording⟩ **3 :** designed to reproduce hi-fi recordings ⟨*hi-fi* phonograph⟩

hi-flash \'hī¦=\ *adj* [*high flash*] **:** having a high flash point — used esp. of solvents ⟨*hi-flash* naphtha⟩

hig·gle \'higəl\ *vi* **higgled**; **higgled**; **higgling** \-g(ə)liŋ\ **higgles** [prob. alter. of 1*haggle*] **:** to bargain for small advantages (as in buying and selling) **:** HAGGLE, CHAFFER ⟨the purchaser *higgling* about the odd cent —Walt Whitman⟩

1hig·gle·dy-pig·gle·dy *also* **hig·gle·ty-pig·gle·ty** \¦higəld|ē¦pigəld|ē, -lt| . . . lt|, |i¦ . . . |i\ *adv* [origin unknown] **:** in confusion **:** without order or coherence **:** TOPSY-TURVY ⟨everything was heaped *higgledy-piggledy* on the luggage racks —Leonide Zarine⟩

2higgledy-piggledy *also* **higglety-pigglety** \"\ *adj* **:** CONFUSED, JUMBLED ⟨a *higgledy-piggledy* patchwork of . . . overlapping powers —F.D.Roosevelt⟩

hig·gler \'hig(ə)lə(r)\ *n* -s **:** an itinerant peddler **:** HAWKER ⟨is as a rule sold to ~*s* —T.D.Marsh⟩ ⟨belonged to a local ~ . . . a man that used the roads buying poultry for resale —F.M. Ford⟩

1high \'hī\ *adj* -ER/-EST [ME *hegh*, *hey*, *high*, fr. OE *hēah*; akin to OHG *hōh* high, ON *hār*, Goth *hauhs* high, L *cacumen* top, point, OIr *cūar* bent, crooked, Skt *kucati* he contracts, bends, curves; basic meaning: bending] **1 a** (1) **:** having a relatively great upward extension **:** LOFTY ⟨a ~ tree⟩ ⟨a ~ mountain⟩ (2) **:** being at or rising to a considerable elevation above the ground or other base **:** ELEVATED ⟨a ~ leap⟩ ⟨a ~ plateau⟩ (3) **:** of, relating to, or located on highlands or a plateau ⟨*High* Asia⟩ (4) *of a person* **:** TALL (5) **:** having a specified altitude or elevation ⟨a new office building 10 stories ~⟩ — often used in combination ⟨knee-*high*⟩ ⟨sky-*high*⟩ (6) **:** articulated with some part of the tongue close to the palate ⟨\ē\, \i\, \ü\, and \u̇\ are ~ vowels⟩ (7) **:** pitched above shoulder height ⟨a ~ ball⟩ **b** (1) **:** advanced toward its acme or fullest extent ⟨it was now ~ June —Guy McCrone⟩ **:** advanced toward its most active or culminating period ⟨an Italian vacation during the ~ season —*N.Y. Times*⟩; *specif* **:** constituting the late, fully developed, or most creative stage or period (as of an artistic style or career or historical movement) ⟨*High* Baroque⟩ ⟨*High* Gothic⟩ ⟨the ~ period of William Faulkner's work —M.D.Geismar⟩ ⟨the ~ middle ages⟩ (2) none too early **:** verging on lateness — usu. used in the phrase *high time* ⟨~ time . . . that your mother came home —Isa Glenn⟩ (3) **:** acute in pitch **:** SHARP, SHRILL ⟨a ~ tone⟩ ⟨a ~ alto voice⟩ ⟨she heard the ~ giggles of the . . . young men —Louis Auchincloss⟩ **:** RAISED, LOUD ⟨"halt!" he called in a ~ voice⟩; *also* **:** of or relating to those musical notes or tones in the three-line or thrice-accented octave esp. in singing ⟨she sang a ~ C easily⟩ (4) **:** long past **:** ANCIENT, REMOTE ⟨the use of which goes back . . . to a ~ antiquity —Edward Clodd⟩ (5) **:** being far toward one of the poles with the equator as base — used chiefly in the phrase *high latitude* (6) **:** being near the wind — used of a ship or its head when pointing close to the wind (7) **:** being toward the middle or near the end of a series of compounds ⟨~*er* alcohols containing six or more carbon atoms⟩ (8) **:** having a complex organization **:** greatly differentiated or developed phylogenetically — usu. used in the comparative degree of advanced types of animals and plants ⟨the ~*er* algae⟩ ⟨the ~*er* apes⟩ (9) **:** sexually mature and active ⟨~ males of the species⟩ (10) **:** exhausted of nearly all air or gas ⟨~ vacuum⟩ **c** (1) **:** of relatively great degree, size, or amount ⟨gambling for ~ stakes⟩ ⟨unemployment was ~⟩ ⟨the ~ cost of living⟩ ⟨enjoyed a ~ standard of living⟩ ⟨moved at a ~ speed⟩ ⟨going into the market at the time of ~ business —Samuel Johnson⟩ ⟨an automobile engine having ~ compression⟩ (2) **:** dear in price **:** EXPENSIVE ⟨everything is so ~ nowadays⟩ (3) **:** VIOLENT, STRONG, VEHEMENT ⟨a ~ wind came up⟩ ⟨the ~ passions of this hour⟩ **:** marked by high waves ⟨a ~ sea⟩ (4) **:** containing a relatively great amount ⟨a food ~ in iron⟩ (5) **:** having more value than another card ⟨the queen is ~*er* than the jack⟩ **:** capable of taking a trick ⟨the nine is ~⟩ (6) **:** giving the highest ratio of propeller-shaft to engine-shaft speed and the lowest multiplication of torque ⟨a ~ transmission gear⟩ ⟨in ~ gear⟩ **d** (1) **:** INTENSE, EXTREME ⟨people of ~ anxiety —Vance Packard⟩ ⟨~ disfavor in her face —Edna Ferber⟩ ⟨the boys were in ~ glee —H.A. Chippendale⟩ ⟨the ~ brilliance of this gem⟩ ⟨my . . . uncle's ~ disapproval —Joyce Cary⟩ ⟨the ~ seriousness . . . and the sound scholarship which inform his work —C.I.Glicksberg⟩ ⟨his hopes were ~⟩ (2) **:** RICH, LUXURIOUS ⟨indulged in a brief but reckless period of ~ living —H.M.Skala⟩ (3) **:** marked by a pink or rosy glow or flush **:** FLORID ⟨a large, personable widow, with a . . . ~ complexion —Dorothy Sayers⟩ ⟨a sturdy, handsome, *high*-colored woman —Carl Van Doren⟩; *also* **:** BRIGHT, PRONOUNCED ⟨fall styles in ~ shades —*N. Y. Times*⟩ ⟨~ flesh tints play a major part in the tonal organization of the picture —Bernard Smith⟩ (4) **:** strong-scented **:** slightly tainted ⟨should cook game when it is ~⟩; *also* **:** MALODOROUS, STINKING ⟨dead . . . had been there since yesterday, and they were plenty ~ —Shelby Foote⟩ ⟨found their blankets a little ~ for civilized noses —Jackson Burgess⟩ (5) **:** INTENSIVE ⟨made their localities into symbols of ~ farming —A.W.Smith⟩ ⟨the first systematic efforts at ~ breeding —E.D. Ross⟩ **2 :** elevated or advanced in rank, quality, or character: as **a** (1) of exalted social or political standing **:** ARISTOCRATIC, POWERFUL ⟨~ society consisting of the Spaniards and Creoles of property —C.L.Jones⟩ ⟨mainly concerned with Roman ~ life —William Murray⟩ ⟨a ~ official of the government⟩ (2) **:** of the first or great consequence **:** IMPORTANT, SUPREME ⟨primarily a parliament is a ~ court of justice —A.F.Pollard⟩ ⟨~ preparations were necessary for this journey —Herbert Hoover⟩ **:** GRAVE, SERIOUS ⟨a ~ insult⟩ ⟨aroused ~ displeasure⟩ **:** CRITICAL, CLIMACTIC ⟨at this ~ hour of Australia's history —W.F.Hambly⟩ ⟨the ~ moments were the start in the freshness of morning —John Buchan⟩ ⟨the ~ point of the novel is the escape⟩ ⟨the ~ spot of the Republican doings will come Friday night —*Spokane (Wash.) Spokesman-Rev.*⟩ (3) **:** relating to matters of the first importance **:** conducted on an exalted political or social level ⟨offered a fertile field for ~ intrigue —Carl Bridenbaugh⟩ ⟨born into the world of ~ politics⟩ (4) **:** rating or ranking as best, first, or most eligible ⟨the ~ man among entrants in the tryout⟩ ⟨if a bidder should be the ~ bidder on a facility —*U. S. Code*⟩ **b** (1) **:** morally or spiritually exalted **:** NOBLE, EDIFYING ⟨a man of ~ character⟩ ⟨met his death in the ~ Roman fashion —John Buchan⟩ ⟨writing is a ~ calling —Cyril Connolly⟩ ⟨good intent and ~ purpose are not enough —D.D.Eisenhower⟩ ⟨~ thinking and plain living⟩ (2) **:** intellectually or artistically of the first order **:** EXCELLENT ⟨the ~ tradition of the European fairy story and folk tale —*Brit. Book News*⟩ ⟨a theatrical production of ~ quality⟩ (3) **:** preeminent among or surpassing other civilizations or societies by some criteria ⟨the ~ civilizations of Middle America and the Andean Highlands —Holger Cahill⟩ (4) **:** characterized by sublime, heroic, or stirring events or subject matter **:** intensely moving **:** EXCITING ⟨a tale of ~ adventure⟩ ⟨~ romance and profound sympathy for the proletariat appear side by side in the poetry —*Encyc. Americana*⟩ ⟨the act in which she faces her accusers is ~ drama⟩ ⟨the ~ tragedy ends with both . . . dying but clasping each other's hands —Leslie Rees⟩ (5) **:** depending not so much on situation as on fine characterization and witty dialogue ⟨~ comedy⟩ (6) **:** conforming to some standard of correctness or excellence in speech or grammar ⟨the ~ Arabic of the Koran —J.C.Swaim⟩ (7) **:** not of the ordinary or routine sort **:** EXTRAVAGANT, BOISTEROUS ⟨an hour for ~ . . . nonsense —Elinor Wylie⟩ ⟨held ~ revelry at the castle that night⟩ ⟨along with her went excitement and ~ occasion —Nadine Gordimer⟩ **c :** difficult to comprehend or master **:** RECONDITE, ABSTRUSE ⟨when it comes to philosophy, ~ thought, and the eternal verities —Bergen Evans⟩ **3 a** (1) **:** indicating or reflecting anger **:** WRATHFUL ⟨saw there were going to be ~ words —Dodie Smith⟩ ⟨threatening them in very ~ language —George Willison⟩ (2) **:** ARROGANT, OVERBEARING, IMPERIOUS ⟨carry things with a ~ hand —John Buchan⟩ ⟨you certainly take a very ~ tone —Louis Auchincloss⟩ (3) **:** PRETENTIOUS, AMBITIOUS ⟨a ~ boast, but it is true —W.R.Inge⟩ ⟨makes ~ claims for his invention⟩ **b** (1) **:** ZEALOUS, EAGER, FAVORABLE, KEEN — usu. used with *on* ⟨is unusually ~ on her next venture —Lewis Funke⟩ ⟨has been particularly ~ on him —*Newsweek*⟩ (2) **:** extreme, devoted, or rigid in advocacy or practice esp. in matters of doctrine or ceremony ⟨hated as the leader of ~ toryism —*Brit. Book News*⟩; *specif, usu cap* **:** HIGH CHURCH **c** (1) **:** ELATED, GAY, CHEERFUL ⟨she hadn't the ~ spirits which endear grown-ups to healthy children —Joseph Conrad⟩ ⟨had a ~ old time together⟩ ⟨his heart was ~ as he entered the old homestead⟩ ⟨those were the ~ days —Sinclair Lewis⟩ (2) **:** hysterically or feverishly excited or gay **:** keyed up ⟨so ~ from nervous tension . . . they need half a dozen drinks to sober down —Alfred Bester⟩ ⟨like a ~ patient after shock treatment —Joseph Hitrec⟩ (3) **:** INTOXICATED, DRUNK ⟨getting ~*er* all the time by nipping at . . . martinis —Daniel Curley⟩ ⟨~ as a kite⟩; *also* **:** excited or stupefied by a narcotic substance (as heroin)

syn TALL, LOFTY: HIGH, the most general of these terms, implies marked extension upward, usu. from a base or foundation, or placement at a conspicuous height above the ground or above some lower level taken as the norm ⟨a *high* building⟩ ⟨a *high* cliff⟩ ⟨a *high* cupboard⟩ In extension it is often used to indicate a great degree of what it modifies or to stress a certain moral elevation ⟨a *high* color⟩ ⟨a *high* volume of sound⟩ ⟨a *high* purpose⟩ TALL applies to what rises or grows high by comparison with others of its kind, esp. when it is small in breadth as compared to its height ⟨a *tall* man⟩ ⟨a *tall* flagpole⟩ LOFTY, suggesting a greater, more imposing altitude than HIGH or TALL, has a much wider figurative than literal application carrying the idea of moral grandeur, dignity, or stature or of superciliousness ⟨a *lofty* mountain⟩ ⟨a *lofty* position in the church⟩ ⟨a *lofty* plane of conversation⟩ ⟨a *lofty* attitude toward servants⟩

2high \"\ *adv* -ER/-EST [ME *heghe*, *heye*, *highe*, *high*, fr. OE *hēah*, *hēage*, fr. *hēah*, adj.] **:** in a high manner: as **a** (1) **:** at or to a great distance or altitude ⟨after a cup of tea we walked a little ~*er* —John Seago⟩ ⟨climbed ~ on the ladder⟩ ⟨the waves dashed ~⟩ — often used in combination ⟨a *high*-climbing vine⟩ (2) **:** far up toward the source ⟨allow passage of . . . vessels as ~ as Albany —Herman Beukema⟩ — usu. used with *up* ⟨lives ~ up the river⟩ **b :** in or to a high position, amount, or degree ⟨prices have gone too ~⟩ ⟨that young man is aiming ~⟩ ⟨how ~ can one rise in this organization⟩ ⟨delay had cost ~ in bitterness —*Time*⟩ — often used in combination ⟨a *high*-ranking official⟩ **c :** RICHLY, LUXURIOUSLY ⟨has gay reunions . . . and lives ~ —J.W.Krutch⟩ — often used in the phrases *high off the hog* or *high on the hog* ⟨the new America is eating too ~ on the hog for its own good —*Newsweek*⟩

3high \"\ *n* -s [ME *hegh*, *hey*, *high*, fr. *hegh*, *hey*, *high*, adj.] **1 :** an elevated place or region: as **a :** HILL, KNOLL ⟨flat as a table top, without a single ~ or low —Harold Sinclair⟩ **b :** the upper region **:** the space overhead **:** SKY — usu. used with *on* ⟨each lifted on ~ his knife —A.C.Whitehead⟩ ⟨watched the birds wheeling on ~⟩ **c :** HEAVEN — used with *on* ⟨a judgment from on ~ —C.S.Kilby⟩ **d :** a region of high barometric pressure **:** ANTICYCLONE **2 a :** a high point **:** a top level **:** HEIGHT, ACME ⟨carrying snobbery to new . . . ~*s* —Leslie Charteris⟩ ⟨a ~ of 38 was due today . . . the weatherman forecast —*Cleveland (Ohio) Plain Dealer*⟩; *specif* **:** the highest price paid for a security during a specified period ⟨the daily ~⟩ **b :** the transmission gear giving the highest ratio of propeller-shaft to engine-shaft speed and the lowest multiplication of torque and consequently the highest speed of travel of an automotive vehicle **c** (1) **:** the highest trump that has been dealt in any game of the all-fours family (2) **:** the highest-ranking combination of upcards in stud poker **3 :** people of a class regarded as socially superior ⟨you find scoundrels among both the ~ and the low⟩ **4 :** HIGH SCHOOL ⟨she learned bookkeeping in ~ —John O'Hara⟩ **5** *slang* **:** the excited or stupefied state produced by a narcotic substance (as heroin)

high altar *n* [ME] **:** the principal altar in a church

high analysis *adj*, *of a fertilizer* **:** containing more than 20 percent of total plant nutrients

high and dry *adv* **1 :** out of the reach of the current or tide **:** out of water — used of a ship aground above water **2 :** in a helpless or abandoned position **:** without recourse ⟨millions of old people were left *high and dry* —M.A.Abrams⟩ ⟨resting *high and dry* on a bed of concrete —Dana Burnet⟩

high and low *adv* **:** upstairs and downstairs **:** EVERYWHERE ⟨looked for it *high and low*⟩

high-and-mighty \¦==¦==\ *adj* **:** characterized by arrogance **:** IMPERIOUS ⟨rivermen . . . who had been *high-and-mighty* now were sitting on drift logs, literally, wondering what was coming next —Frederick Way⟩

high-angle fire *n* **:** cannon fire delivered at elevations greater than that for the maximum range

high-back \'=¦=\ *adj*, *of a vowel* **:** high and back

1highball \'=,=\ *n* [1*high* + *ball*] **1 a** [so called fr. the fact that in early RR practice a metal ball was raised on a pole as a go-ahead signal to the engineer] **:** a railroad signal for a train to proceed at full speed **b :** a fast train **2 :** a drink of spirituous liquor mixed with water or more often a carbonated beverage (as seltzer or ginger ale) and served in a tall glass usu. with ice ⟨applejack ~⟩ ⟨whiskey ~⟩

2highball \"\ *vi* **:** to go at full or high speed ⟨see how safely they ~ with a full load —*Civil Engineering*⟩ ⟨a ~*ing* express train⟩ ~ *vt* **:** to drive at full or high speed ⟨how we ~*ed* those camions up —Christopher Morley⟩

high·ball·er \"ə(r)\ *n* [1*highball* (signal) + *-er*] **:** SIGNALMAN

high bar *n* **:** a horizontal bar adjusted above head height and used as a support in some gymnastic exercises

high beam *n* **:** the focus of a vehicle headlight that sends the light forward for maximum long-range illumination of the road ahead and is intended for driving in open country — contrasted with *low beam*

high beams *n pl*, *New Eng* **:** LOFT

high·be·lia \hī'bēlyə, -lēə\ *n* -s [1*high* (in contrast to *lo-*, punningly taken as *low*) + lo*belia*] **:** any of various tall-growing American lobelias; *esp* **:** GREAT LOBELIA

high·bind·er \'hī,bīndə(r)\ *n* -s [fr. the *Highbinders*, a gang of vagabonds in New York City *ab*1806] **1 a :** THUG, GANGSTER, RUFFIAN ⟨this gang of ~*s* were supposed to be enforcing the law —Julien Hyer⟩ **b :** HATCHET MAN; *specif* **:** a member of an organized band of Chinese professional killers operating in the Chinese quarter of an American city **2 :** a person who engages in fraudulent or shady activities **:** CONFIDENCE MAN, SWINDLER ⟨employ the saliva test on horses to guard against ~*s* injecting stimulants —C.B.Davis⟩ ⟨the ~ boys of the last Florida boom —Robert Moses⟩; *specif* **:** a corrupt or scheming politician ⟨the county payroll has 2,200 experienced vote raisers, many of them ~*s* of the lowest degree —*Nation*⟩

high·bind·ing \-diŋ\ *n* **:** SKULDUGGERY, FRAUD ⟨the techniques of larceny and ~ —R.H.Rovere⟩ ⟨the aroma of ~ will not down —R.B.McKerrow⟩

high blood pressure *n* **:** HYPERTENSION

high blower *n* **:** a horse that produces blowing esp. during exercise

high-blown \'=¦=\ *adj* **:** inflated esp. with conceit **:** PRETENTIOUS ⟨*high-blown* but slightly mystifying verse —Stuart Keate⟩

high blueberry *n* **:** HIGHBUSH BLUEBERRY

high-boiling \'=¦==\ *adj* **:** boiling at a relatively high temperature

highborn \'=¦=\ *adj* **:** of noble birth

highboy \'=,=\ *n* **:** a high chest of drawers mounted on a base which has legs of considerable length and usu. several drawers esp. in style between 1690 and 1780 — compare BONNET TOP, LOWBOY

highboy

high-braced \'=¦=\ *adj*, *archery* **:** HIGH-STRUNG

high brass *n* **1 :** brass containing at least 33 percent zinc — compare LOW BRASS **2 :** high-ranking officers or officials ⟨the living honorees weren't always political or military or railroad *high brass* —B.A.Botkin & A.F.Harlow⟩ ⟨doesn't know enlisted men and their opinion of *high brass* —G.W.Johnson⟩

highbred \'=¦=\ *adj* **1 :** marked by high birth or breeding **:** coming from superior stock ⟨the ~ descendant of an ancient baron —Sir Walter Scott⟩ ⟨a ~ dog⟩ **2 :** having the characteristics of or associated with high birth or breeding **:** REFINED ⟨the grand manner and ~ ways of the society he frequented —J.R.Lowell⟩

1highbrow \'=,=\ *n* [1*high* + *brow*] **:** a person who possesses or has pretensions to strong intellectual interests or superiority **:** one who regards aloofly or contemptuously manifestations of mass culture **:** EGGHEAD ⟨~*s* . . . despise soap operas and are repelled by the success stories in popular magazines —W. O.Aydelotte⟩ ⟨~*s* who believe that . . . art is for art's sake —A.J.Toynbee⟩

2highbrow \"\ *adj* **:** of, relating to, or appropriate to a highbrow **:** having or giving the appearance of strong intellectual interests or superiority ⟨liking jazz or not liking jazz is almost equally ~ today —Roger Angell⟩ ⟨a Chinese scholar can be ineffably ~ —E.R.Hughes⟩ ⟨the magazine . . . will be uncompromisingly ~ —*Time*⟩

high-browed \'=¦=\ *adj* **1 :** having a high brow **2 :** HIGHBROW ⟨the *high-browed* literary critics⟩

high·brow·ism \'hī,brau̇,izəm\ *n* -s **:** the state of mind associated with a highbrow **:** self-conscious intellectual superiority **:** INTELLECTUALISM

high-brown \'=¦=\ *adj* **:** being a high yellow

highbush \'=,=\ *adj* **:** forming a notably tall or erect bush ⟨~ willows⟩ **:** borne on a highbush plant ⟨the ~ berries are larger and sweeter⟩

highbush blueberry *n* **1 :** any of several tall-growing blueberries of eastern No. America; *esp* **:** a highly variable moisture-loving shrub (*Vaccinium corymbosum*) that has deciduous ovate to broadly lanceolate leaves, whitish or pinkish flowers, and bluish to blackish edible fruit usu. with a distinct bloom and that is the source of most cultivated blueberries — compare EVERGREEN BLUEBERRY, RABBITEYE **2 :** the fruit of a highbush blueberry

highbush cranberry *n* **:** CRANBERRY BUSH 2

highbush huckleberry *n* **:** BLACK HUCKLEBERRY

high-card pool *n* **:** RED DOG 3

high-central \'=¦==\ *adj*, *of a vowel* **:** high and central

high chair \'=,=\ *n* **:** a child's chair with long legs, a feeding tray, and a footrest

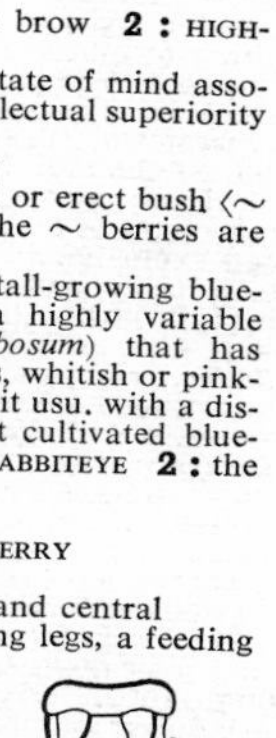

high church *adj*, *usu cap H&C* [back-formation fr. *high churchman*] **:** tending toward or stressing sacerdotal, liturgical, ceremonial, traditional, and Catholic elements as appropriate to the life of the Christian church — compare LOW CHURCH

high churchman *n*, *often cap H&C* **:** a person who adheres to High Church principles

high-class \'=¦=\ *adj* [fr. the phrase *high class*] **:** of a class rated as superior in high degree **:** FIRST-CLASS ⟨modern *high-class* accommodations⟩ ⟨a *high-class* mechanic⟩

high-climber \'=¦==\ *n* **1 :** CLIMBER 1a **2 :** HIGH RIGGER

high chair

high cockalorum *n* **1** *Brit* **:** a boys' game of leapfrog — used as a shout during the game **2 :** a person with pretensions to great importance **:** a high-and-mighty person **:** BIG SHOT ⟨placed himself as the *high cockalorum* of the universe —J.F.Stevens⟩

high command *n* **1 :** the supreme headquarters of a military force **2 :** the supreme leadership or decision-making group of any organization ⟨the Republican *high command* attempted to repair this damage —*New Yorker*⟩

high commission *n* **1 :** a group of persons delegated supreme authority and responsibility for the performance of some duty or the execution of some trust ⟨the Allied *High Commission* for Germany⟩ **2 :** the office or jurisdiction of a high commissioner ⟨the Western Pacific *high commission* includes the Gilbert and Ellice Islands Colony —Martin Wight⟩

high commissioner *n* **1 :** a representative of one country stationed in another; *esp* **:** a representative of the government of one British Commonwealth country in the capital of another with representational functions broadly similar to those of an ambassador — compare AGENT-GENERAL **2 a :** the chief officer of a colonial territory or dependency **b :** the chief representative officer in a mandate, protectorate, or trust territory **3 :** the chief officer of an international commission or other agency ⟨the United Nations *high commissioner* for refugees⟩

high council *n* **:** a body of 12 high priests in the Mormon Church presided over by the stake presidency and having executive and judicial authority within the stake — compare APOSTLE

high-count \ˈ=ˌ=\ *adj* **:** having a large number of warp and weft yarns to the square inch ⟨a *high-count* percale sheeting⟩ — compare THREAD COUNT

high court *n* **:** a superior court: as **a :** SUPREME COURT **b :** an Australian court that is the highest and has power of judicial review of legislation

high court of justice *usu cap H&C&J* **:** the system of superior courts having the highest general criminal and civil jurisdiction in England and Wales and including divisions corresponding to the formerly independent courts now constituting it — compare ADMIRALTY 3, CHANCERY 1a, COURT OF COMMON PLEAS 1, COURT OF KING'S BENCH, EXCHEQUER 2, PROBATE COURT

high court of justiciary *usu cap H&C&J* **:** the supreme court having jurisdiction over criminal cases in Scotland ⟨their trial began in the *High Court of Justiciary* in Edinburgh —David Masters⟩ — compare COURT OF SESSION

high cranberry *n* **:** CRANBERRY BUSH 2

high crime *n* **1 :** a crime of an infamous nature contrary to public morality but not technically constituting a felony; *specif* **:** an offense which the U.S. Senate deems to constitute adequate grounds for removal of the president, vice-president, or any civil officer as a person unfit to hold public office and deserving of impeachment **2 :** a crime of a serious or aggravated nature

¹high-cut \ˈ=ˈ=\ *adj* [*high* + *cut*] **1 :** cut high up **2 :** having a high top — used of a boot

²high-cut \ˈ=ˌ=\ *n* **:** a laced boot reaching well up the calf of the leg

high daddy *n* **:** HIGHBOY

high day *n* [ME] **:** HOLY DAY, FEAST DAY

highday *interj* [by alter.] *obs* **:** HEYDAY

high-dried \ˈ=ˈ=\ *adj* **:** deprived of an unusually high percentage of its moisture by drying or baking

highdried \ˈ=ˌ=\ *n* -s [*high-dried*] **:** RED HERRING

high dutch *n, cap H&D* **1 :** HIGH GERMAN **2 :** the literary Dutch of the Netherlands in contrast to Afrikaans or Low Dutch

high-duty \ˈ=ˈ==\ *adj* [fr. the phrase *high duty*] **1** *of a machine* **:** being capable of doing a large amount of work in a specified time ⟨a *high-duty* drill⟩ **2 :** constituting products subject to a relatively high tax ⟨*high-duty* goods⟩

high enema *n* **:** an enema in which the injected material reaches the colon — compare LOW ENEMA

high·er \ˈhī(ə)r, -īə\ *comparative of* HIGH

higher arithmetic *n* **:** the general theory of numbers

higher bacterium *n* **:** any of numerous bacteria of comparatively complex organization — often contrasted with *eubacterium*

higher certificate *n* **:** HIGHER SCHOOL CERTIFICATE

higher criticism *n* **:** the literary-historical study of the Bible that seeks to determine such factors as authorship, date, place of origin, circumstances of composition, purpose of the author, and the historical credibility of each of the various biblical writings together with the meaning intended by their authors — compare LOWER CRITICISM

higher degree *n* **:** ADVANCED DEGREE

higher education *n* **:** education beyond the secondary level **:** education provided by a college or university

higher functional calculus *n* **:** functional calculus in which quantification is applied not only to individual variables but also to functional and propositional variables — called also *functional calculus of the second order*

higher fungus *n* **:** any of numerous fungi with hyphae well-developed, septate, and usu. at some stage of development interwoven into a compact tissue esp. in the fruiting body (as in Ascomycetes, Basidiomycetes and Fungi Imperfecti) — compare LOWER FUNGUS

higher institution *n* **:** an educational institution of collegiate or more advanced grade

higher law *n* **:** a principle of divine or moral law that is considered to be superior to constitutions and enacted legislation

higher learning *n* **:** education, learning, or scholarship on the collegiate or university level

higher mammal *n* **:** any of the placental or eutherian mammals; *esp* **:** a member of the Educabilia

higher mathematics *n pl but sing in constr* **:** mathematics of more advanced content than ordinary arithmetic and algebra, geometry, trigonometry, and beginning calculus

higher school certificate *n* **:** a certificate awarded on the successful completion of an examination taken by British secondary-school students who are preparing to enter a university

higher thought *n, usu cap H&T* **:** NEW THOUGHT

higher-up \ˈ==ˈ=\ *n* -s [fr. the phrase *higher up*] **:** a superior officer or official **:** a chief leader or agent in an organization ⟨brought to the attention of the *higher-ups* in the . . . State Department —Lindsay Rogers⟩

high·est \ˈhīəst\ *superlative of* HIGH

highest common factor *n* **:** the largest integer or polynomial of highest degree that is an exact divisor of each of two or more integers or polynomials respectively

high explosive *n* **:** a detonating explosive (as trinitrotoluene) used for its shattering effect

¹high·fa·lu·tin \ˌhīfəˈlütᵊn\ *also* **high·fa·lu·ting** \", -üd·|iŋ, -üt|, |ēŋ\ *or* **hi·fa·lu·tin** *adj* [perh. fr. ¹*high* + alter. of *fluting*, pres. part. of ²*flute*] **1 :** characterized by or reflecting an attitude of self-importance or superciliousness **:** PRETENTIOUS ⟨~ people like the kind of fine ladies his wife was always playing bridge with —Nathaniel La Mar⟩ ⟨impress our correspondents by ~ letterheads —H.F.Ellis⟩ **2 :** expressed in or marked by the use of high-flown bombastic language **:** POMPOUS ⟨has written perhaps half a dozen excellent pieces . . . and a great deal of ~ bathos —H.L.Mencken⟩ ⟨a study of American adolescence done in a rather high-toned and ~ way —*Time & Tide*⟩ ⟨pretentious idealism or just ~ and pretentious talk —William Chomsky⟩

²highfalutin \"\ *n* -s **:** high-flown pretentious language **:** BOMBAST ⟨a medium . . . in which dramatic characters can express the purest poetry without ~ —T.S.Eliot⟩

high fashion *n* **:** HIGH STYLE

high festival *n* **:** a church festival observed in the more liturgical churches with full ceremonial

high fidelity *n* **:** the reproduction of sound with a high degree of faithfulness to the original (as by a radio or phonograph loudspeaker) — compare HI-FI

high finance *n* **:** large and complex financial operations or the major financial institutions that engage in them — sometimes used with an implication of unethical practice ⟨*high finance* is . . . Greek to most people —J.R.Aswell & E.J. Michelson⟩

high five *n* **:** ³CINCH

high flanker *n* **:** a male horse with incompletely descended testes

highflier *or* **highflyer** \ˈ=ˈ==\ *n* **1 :** one that flies high **2** *archaic* **:** one who is uncompromisingly orthodox or extreme in point of doctrine; *esp* **:** one who is extreme in supporting the claims to authority of the Church of England **:** HIGH CHURCHMAN **3 :** FLIER 6 ⟨took a ~ in watermelons that year —F.B.Gipson⟩

high-flown \ˈ=ˈ=\ *adj* **1 :** being high above the ordinary level of thought or sentiment **:** ELEVATED, EXALTED ⟨argue in terms of *high-flown* ideals —Oliver Franks⟩ **2 :** having a turgid or inflated character **:** BOMBASTIC, PRETENTIOUS ⟨*high-flown* talk of preserving the moral tone of the school —Leslie Rees⟩ ⟨the usual inflated rhetoric and *high-flown* vocabulary —James Yaffe⟩

high-flying \ˈ=ˈ==\ *adj* **1 :** rising to a considerable height ⟨displaying *high-flying* hoofs and thrashing tails —Court Paige⟩ **2 a :** inflated or pretentious in style, content, or ambition **:** HIGH-FLOWN ⟨a *high-flying* dissertation on the means to attain a social revolution —Wilfred Fienburgh⟩ ⟨*high-flying* proposals⟩ **b :** having an extremely lofty or metaphysical character **:** being too abstract or remote from human affairs **:** TRANSCENDENTAL ⟨directed against the institutional, or *high-flying* school —C.N.Feidelson⟩ ⟨mocked the *high-flying* . . . Platonists —P.D.Partner⟩

high forest *n* [trans. of G *hochwald*] **:** a forest from seed — compare COPPICE

high frequency *n* **:** a frequency that is relatively high; *specif* **:** a radio frequency in the middle range of the radio spectrum — see RADIO FREQUENCY table

high-frequency \ˈ=ˈ===\ *adj* [*high frequency*] **1 :** occurring very frequently ⟨drills based on the repetition of *high-frequency* words⟩ **2 :** relating to high frequency: as **a :** involving a radio wave of high frequency — used esp. of sound waves and vibrations **b :** SUPERSONIC 1

high-frequency telephony *n* **:** an art or process of telephonic communication by means of carrier currents over electric conductors (as transmission lines) through the use of transmitting and receiving equipment like those used in radio

high-front \ˈ=ˈ=\ *adj, of a vowel* **:** high and front

high gear *n* **1 :** ³HIGH 2b **2 :** a state of intense or maximum activity ⟨the political campaign will move into *high gear* —G.C.Wright⟩ ⟨operations went into *high gear* last year —*N.Y. Times*⟩

high german *n, cap H&G* [trans. of G *hochdeutsch*] **1 :** German as natively used in southern and central Germany — see MIDDLE HIGH GERMAN, OLD HIGH GERMAN; compare BENRATH LINE, LOW GERMAN **2 :** ³GERMAN 2b

high german consonant shift *n, usu cap H&G* **:** CONSONANT SHIFT 2

high grade *n* **:** something that is of superior grade: as **a :** ore of high value or of relatively high value as compared with the average ore in a specific mine **b :** a grade animal that in conformation and economic qualities approximates the breed to which its known purebred ancestors belong

¹high-grade \ˈ=ˈ=\ *adj* [*high grade*] **:** of superior grade or quality ⟨*high-grade* writing⟩ ⟨*high-grade* manganese⟩: as **a :** being securities or other investments involving little or no risk and affording a relatively assured income ⟨*high-grade* bonds⟩ **b :** being near the upper extreme of the range in which it may occur ⟨a *high-grade* moron approaches normality⟩ ⟨a *high-grade* hydrocephalic exhibits maximum deformity⟩ — compare LOW-GRADE

²high-grade \"\ *vt* [*high grade*] **:** to steal (rich ore) from a mine; *also* **:** to mine only (the rich ore) — **high-grader** \ˈ=ˌ==\ *n* — **high-grading** \ˈ=ˌ==\ *n*

high-ground willow oak *n* **:** TURKEY OAK c

high-grown \ˈ=ˈ=\ *adj* **1 :** grown tall **2 :** covered with tall vegetation ⟨a *high-grown* slope⟩ **3** *of coffee* **:** grown at a high altitude

high-handed \ˈ=ˈ==\ *adj* **:** OVERBEARING, ARBITRARY ⟨*high-handed* behavior⟩ — **high-hand·ed·ly** *adv* — **high-hand·ed·ness** *n* -ES

high hat *n* **1 :** BEAVER 3 **2** *usu* **high-hat** \ˈ=ˈ=\ **:** one who assumes an attitude of superiority **:** SNOB, SWELL ⟨amid the gasps of the *high-hats* he . . . threw in his lot with the British Labor Party —*New Republic*⟩

¹high-hat \ˈ=ˈ=\ *adj* [*high hat*] **:** supercilious or snobbish in attitude or manner **:** ARISTOCRATIC ⟨*high-hat* over the type of job she wants —*Springfield (Mass.) Union*⟩ ⟨cold, impersonal, a trifle *high-hat* —*Nation*⟩

²high-hat \"\ *vt* [*high hat*] **:** to look down one's nose at **:** treat snobbishly **:** SNUB ⟨*high-hatted* her . . . when they were sober —Edmund Wilson⟩ ⟨the literati tended to *high-hat* the first issues —Jay Franklin⟩

high heal-all *n* **:** WOOD BETONY 2

high-hearted \ˈ=ˈ==\ *adj* [ME *highe herted*] **1 :** full of courage or nobility **:** HIGH-SPIRITED ⟨*high-hearted* language —Archibald MacLeish⟩ **2 :** full of gaiety **:** INSOUCIANT, LIGHTHEARTED ⟨a *high-hearted* junket —*Huntting's Monthly List*⟩ — **high-heart·ed·ly** *adv* — **high-heart·ed·ness** *n* -ES

high-high \ˈ=ˈ=\ *adj, of tide* **:** higher than the normal high

high-hold·er \ˈ=ˌhōldə(r)\ *also* **high-hole** \ˈ=ˌhōl\ *or* **high-hol·er** \ˈ=ˌhōlə(r)\ *n* [by folk etymology fr. ME *hygh-whele*, prob. of imit. origin] *dial* **:** ³FLICKER

high holiday *or* **high holy day** *n, usu cap both Hs & D* **:** either of the Jewish religious holidays Rosh Hashanah and Yom Kippur observed respectively on the 1st and the 10th of Tishri with particular solemnity

high horse *n* **1 :** an unyielding, pretentious, or arrogant mood **:** a high and mighty air or attitude ⟨when he . . . saw the desperate need for more men, he came down off his *high horse* —J.F.Dobie⟩ ⟨wanted to get on her *high horse* and treat him as if he were nothing —William Heuman⟩ **2 :** a sulky or resentful mood, air, or attitude ⟨on your *high horse* because he didn't praise your mince —Arnold Bennett⟩

high-house \ˈ=ˌ=\ *n* **:** a trap house on the left side of a skeet range that projects the target from a point 10 feet from the ground — called also *hi-trap;* compare LOW-HOUSE

high hurdles *n pl but sing or pl in constr* **:** a track event of 120 yards or 110 meters distance with ten 3 ft. 6 in. hurdles to be surmounted — compare LOW HURDLES

high iron *n* **:** a main-line railroad track

high·ish \ˈhīish\ *adj* **:** rather high ⟨with a ~ collar and a black cord necktie —*New Yorker*⟩

high-jack *var of* HIJACK

high jinks *also* **hi·jinks** *or* **high jinx** \ˈhīˌjiŋ(k)s\ *n pl* **1 :** an old Scottish game of forfeits at drinking **2 :** boisterous or noisy sport **:** HORSEPLAY ⟨the juvenile *high jinks* of a college reunion —John Mason Brown⟩ ⟨the officers and men . . . were indulging in *high jinks* ashore —H.C.Ickes⟩

high jump *n* **:** a jump for height in a track or field contest either from a standing position or from a running start

high jumper *n* **:** an athlete who participates in the high jump

high jumping *n, pl* **high jumpings :** the act or action of performing the high jump

high-key \ˈ=ˈ=\ *adj* **:** having or producing light tones only with little contrast — used of a photographic print or subject or of the lighting of a photographic subject

¹high·land \ˈhīlənd *sometimes* -ˌland *or* -ˌlaa(ə)nd\ *n* [ME, fr. *high* + *land*] **1 :** elevated or mountainous land **2** *usu cap* [²*Highland*] **:** WEST HIGHLAND

²highland \"\ *adj* **1 :** of or relating to a highland **:** inhabiting or growing in a highland **2** *usu cap* [fr. the *Highlands*, northern part of Scotland] **:** of, related to, or typical of the Highlands of Scotland ⟨typically *Highland* . . . a strange mixture of pride and tenderness, of poverty and generosity —Ian Finlay⟩

high·land·er \-də(r)\ *n* -s **1 :** an inhabitant of a highland **2** *usu cap* **:** an inhabitant of the Highlands of Scotland — compare LOWLANDER

highland fling *n, usu cap H* **:** a Scottish folk dance that is performed usu. by three or four persons, with nimble footwork and low kicks

highland pony *n, usu cap H* **:** a comparatively large hardy pony native to the Highlands of Scotland and some adjacent islands

high-lead \ˈ=ˌlēd\ *n* **:** SPAR TREE

high-lead logging *n* **:** HIGH-LINE LOGGING

high-level \ˈ=ˈ==\ *adj* **1 :** carried out or engaged in at a high altitude ⟨were ordered to take to the slit trenches if the *high-level* attack developed —*Coast Artillery Jour.*⟩ **2 a :** of, involving, or engaged in by persons of high position, rank, or achievement ⟨a *high-level* staff to set up and supervise a political and operational training center —S.K.Padover⟩ ⟨time to push the proposal for a *high-level* conference —Drew Middleton⟩ ⟨*high-level* discussions of the control of atomic energy —C.L.Sulzberger⟩ **b :** holding high position or rank ⟨*high-level* government officials will meet . . . to discuss the outlook for aluminum —T.E.Mullaney⟩

¹highlight \ˈ=ˌ=\ *n* [¹*high* + *light*] **1 a :** the lightest spot or area (as in a painting or engraving) **:** a spot or any of several spots in a modeled drawing or painting that receives the greatest amount of illumination **b :** a bright part of a photographic picture or subject represented by a considerable density in the negative and by nearly clear paper or other support in the print **2 :** an event, detail, topic, or accomplishment of major significance or special interest ⟨one of the ~*s* of the fashionable London season —Emily Hahn⟩ ⟨more analysis will be written . . . later but here are some ~*s* —*Kiplinger Washington Letter*⟩ ⟨these are only ~*s:* he also wrote . . . several volumes of verse, numerous short stories —E.P. Earnest⟩

²highlight \"\ *vt* **1 :** to illuminate with vivid distinctness **:** throw a strong light upon ⟨designed for general store lighting and to ~ featured merchandise —*Electrical World*⟩ ⟨matches flared, momentarily ~*ing* the faces —*Nat'l Geographic*⟩ **2 :** to paint out the highlight areas of (a halftone negative); *also* **:** to etch away the light dots in the corresponding areas of (a printing plate) — compare DROP OUT **3 a :** to center attention upon **:** cause to loom large in importance or urgency **:** EMPHASIZE, STRESS ⟨these publications . . . ~*ed* the deficiencies of the current freshman program —T.F.Dunn⟩ ⟨~ a major factor in the Hemisphere's aid program —*Atlantic*⟩ **b :** to constitute a highlight or distinctive feature of ⟨the slang that ~*s* his dialogue —Bennett Cerf⟩ ⟨three new talents . . . ~*ed* the year —*Britannica Bk. of the Yr.*⟩

highlight halftone *n* **:** DROPOUT 3

highlighting \ˈ=ˌ==\ *n* **1 :** the act or effect of casting a highlight upon or giving prominence to something ⟨~ is accomplished by the use of high-powered . . . spotlights —H.F.Helvenston⟩ **2 :** additional illumination for enhancing the highlights on a photographic subject

high-line \ˈ=ˈ=\ *adj* **:** being a fisherman or fishing boat with a large or the largest catch ⟨*high-line* vessels sometimes average 400,000 pounds per man —*Commercial Fishing*⟩

highline \ˈ=ˌ=\ *n* **1 :** a high-voltage electric transmission line **2 :** a line or cable strung between ships or from ship to shore (as for the transfer of cargo or crew)

high-line logging *n* **:** logging in which the logs with one end in the air are hauled in by a highline cable

highliner \ˈ=ˌ==\ *n* **:** a high-line fisherman or fishing boat

high-lived \ˈ=ˈlīvd\ *adj, of a horse* **:** HIGH-SPIRITED ⟨a horse of kind disposition but very *high-lived* —J.L.Hervey⟩

high liver *n* **:** one that lives luxuriously

high·lone \ˈhīˌlōn\ *adv* [by alter.] *dial* **:** ALONE ⟨the baby has just learned to stand ~⟩

high lonesome *n, dial* **:** DRUNK, BENDER, SPREE ⟨got on a *high lonesome* and told the barkeeper his business —J.F.Dobie⟩

highlow \ˈ=ˌ=\ *n, dial chiefly Eng* **:** an ankle-high laced boot

high-low \ˈ=ˈ=\ *n* **1 :** a come-on or echo in bridge or whist in which the play of an unnecessarily high card is later confirmed by the play of a lower card of the same suit **2 :** a game of poker in which the highest ranking and lowest ranking hands divide the pot equally

high-low-jack \ˈ=ˌ=ˈ=\ *n* **:** any of several card games derived from all fours (as cinch, pitch, seven-up) in each of which there are special scoring values for winning the highest trump in play, the lowest trump in play, the jack of trumps, and either the ten of trumps or the most points with ace counting 4, king 3, queen 2, and jack 1

high·ly *adv* [ME *heghly, heyly, highly*, fr. OE *hēalīce*, fr. *hēah* high + *-līce* -ly — more at HIGH] **1 :** in or to a high place, level, or rank ⟨only a few ~ placed persons . . . know the entire story —H.L.Stimson⟩ **2 a :** in or to a high degree, amount, or extent **:** EXTREMELY, INTENSELY ⟨a ~ interesting article⟩ ⟨a ~ successful play⟩ ⟨a ~ educated woman⟩ **b :** at a high rate or wage ⟨a ~ paid skilled worker⟩ **3 a :** in a noble or elevated manner **:** SOLEMNLY ⟨let us now and here ~ resolve to . . . march along the path of real progress —F.D. Roosevelt⟩ **b :** with high approval or favor **:** FAVORABLY ⟨does not think ~ of many of his films —*Current Biog.*⟩

highly-strung \ˈ==ˈ=\ *adj* **:** HIGH-STRUNG

high mallow *n* **:** a common biennial hirsute mallow (*Malva sylvestris*) native to Europe and naturalized in the eastern U.S. having an erect stem, long-petioled leaves and rose-purple flowers with darker veins

high mass *n, often cap H&M* [ME] **:** a mass that is sung and not said by a priest with the assistance of a deacon and subdeacon and characteristically with incense, music, and greater ceremonial than in a low mass

high-melting \ˈ=ˈ==\ *adj* **:** melting at a relatively high temperature

high milling *n* **:** a process of making flour from grain by several successive grindings and intermediate sorting

high-minded \ˈ=ˈ==\ *adj* **1** *archaic* **:** PROUD, ARROGANT **2 :** of or marked by or reflecting elevated principles and feelings ⟨a *high-minded* man⟩ ⟨*high-minded* talk⟩ — **high-mind·ed·ly** *adv* — **high-mind·ed·ness** *n* -ES

high-mixed \ˈ=ˈ=\ *adj, of a vowel* **:** high and central

high moor *n* **:** a boggy acid upland area characterized by abundant heaths and sphagnum

high-muck-a-muck \ˈhīˌmək|ēˌmək, |ə-\ *or* **high-muckety-muck** \|əd·ē|-\ *n* [by folk etymology fr. Chinook Jargon *hiu muckamuck* plenty to eat] **:** a person of high station or importance; *esp* **:** such a person marked by arrogance or conceit

high·ness *n* -ES [ME *heghnes, heynes, highnes*, fr. OE *hēahnes*, *hēanes*, fr. *hēah* high + *-nes* -ness — more at HIGH] **1 :** the quality or state of being high **:** ELEVATION, LOFTINESS ⟨the ~ of a flooded river⟩ **2 :** a person of honor — used as a title given to kings, princes, or other persons of exalted rank ⟨His Royal *Highness* the Prince of Wales⟩

high noon *n* **1 :** precisely noon **2 :** the most advanced, flourishing, or creative stage or period ⟨the *high noon* of his genius —John Pfeiffer⟩ ⟨the *high noon* of mid-Victorian liberalism —*Times Lit. Supp.*⟩

high-octane \ˈ=ˈ==\ *adj* **1 :** having a high octane number (as at least 80) and hence good antiknock properties ⟨*high-octane* aviation gasoline⟩ **2 :** of extreme degree **:** HIGH-POWERED **:** high quality ⟨aquavit, that *high-octane* Swedish liqueur —Bill Hosakawa⟩ ⟨verbs produced by back-formation are usually challenged by *high-octane* purists —H.L. Mencken⟩

high-pass filter *n* **:** an electric-circuit filter that transmits only frequencies above a prescribed frequency limit

high-pitched \ˈ=ˈ=\ *adj* **:** having a high pitch: as **a** (1) **:** being lofty in tone or thought ⟨the magazine was a little *high-pitched* intellectually —R.G.Martin⟩ (2) **:** marked by or exhibiting strong feeling or intense sensibility **:** AGITATED ⟨*high-pitched* denunciations —James Gray⟩ ⟨a *high-pitched* religiosity —Roger Fry⟩ ⟨that restless *high-pitched* life —Gertrude Atherton⟩ **b :** pitched in a high key or register ⟨the composition was too *high-pitched* for the singer⟩ ⟨spoke in a *high-pitched* voice⟩ **c :** inclining steeply ⟨a *high-pitched* roof⟩

high place *n* [ME] **:** a temple or altar used by the ancient Semites and built usu. on a hill or elevation

highpockets \ˈ=ˌ==\ *n pl but sing in constr* **:** a very tall lank man

high polymer *n* **:** a macromolecular substance (as polystyrene or cellulose) consisting of molecules that are large multiples of units of low molecular weight

high port *n* **:** a cross-body position in which a rifle is carried while a soldier is charging or jumping

high-powered *also* **high-power** \ˈ=ˈ==\ *adj* **:** having high power or quality: as **a :** having great drive, energy, or capacity **:** DYNAMIC ⟨import *high-powered* professional talent to help him —T.H.White b. 1915⟩ ⟨many *high-powered* executives . . . work themselves to death —Bruce Bliven b. 1889⟩ **b** *usu* **high-power** using a cartridge with a bullet heavy enough and having a muzzle velocity high enough for hunting deer and larger game ⟨a *high-power* rifle⟩

¹high-pressure \ˈ=ˈ==\ *adj* [fr. the phrase *high pressure*] **1 a :** having, involving, or operating at a high or comparatively high pressure ⟨a *high-pressure* automobile tire⟩ **b :** having a high barometric pressure **2 a :** using or characterized by forceful methods of selling **:** AGGRESSIVE, INSISTENT ⟨a *high-pressure* salesman⟩ ⟨*high-pressure* blurbs about toothpaste —*Amer. Guide Series: N.Y.*⟩ — compare LOW-PRESSURE **b :** imposing or involving severe strain or tension ⟨the . . . stresses of *high-pressure* occupations —*Fortune*⟩ ⟨the *high-pressure* merry-go-round of big business administration —*Current Biog.*⟩

²high-pressure \"\ *vt* [fr. the phrase *high pressure*] **:** to urge to a course of action with insistent, importunate, or forceful arguments **:** overcome the resistance of by such methods ⟨don't try to *high-pressure* me —Edwin Corle⟩ ⟨beware of salesmen who seek to *high-pressure* you into precipitate purchases —*Assoc. of Better Business Bureaus*⟩ ⟨*high-pressuring* the elected representatives of the people —Karl Schriftgiesser⟩

high-pressure area *n* : [3]HIGH 1d

high priest *n* [ME *hege prest*] **1** : a chief priest; *esp* : the head of the Jewish priesthood in ancient times **2** : a priest of the Melchizedek priesthood in the Mormon Church **3** : a principal officer of a Masonic chapter **4** : the head of a movement or chief expounder of a doctrine ⟨the philosophical *high priests* of modern education —M.B.Smith⟩

high priestess *n* : a female high priest

high priesthood *n* : the priesthood of a high priest; *specif* : the Melchizedek priesthood of the Mormon Church

high-priestly \ˈ=ˈ=ˌ=\ *adj* [*high priest* + *-ly*] : of, relating to, or having the characteristics of a high priest

high-proof \ˈ=ˈ=\ *adj* : highly rectified : very strongly alcoholic ⟨*high-proof* spirits⟩

high relief *n* [trans. of F *haut-relief*] : sculptural relief in which half or more than half of the natural circumference of the modeled form projects from the surrounding surface — distinguished from *bas-relief*

high renaissance *n, usu cap H&R* : the artistic style of the first half of the 16th century in western Europe esp. as manifested in Rome and Florence and characterized by heroic centralized composition, technical mastery of drawing and conception, and a mature humanistic content

high rigger *n* **1** : a logger who rigs spar trees — called also *high-climber* **2** : a worker who erects high ladders for acrobatic performances

highroad \ˈ=ˌ=\ *n* **1** *chiefly Brit* : HIGHWAY **2** : the best approach : an easy way ⟨there is no one ~ to literary appreciation —Geoffrey Bullough⟩ ⟨the direct ~ to salvation —*New Republic*⟩

high roller *n* **1** : one who spends freely in fast or luxurious living ⟨one wealthy cowman . . . who was always a *high roller* in town —Ross Santee⟩ **2** : one who gambles recklessly or for high stakes ⟨round up some . . . *high rollers* to fade his bets —C.B.Davis⟩

highs *pl of* HIGH

[1]**high school** *n* **1** : a secondary school usu. public-supported and usu. organized on a 3-year or 4-year basis and comprising several divisions (as college preparatory, commercial, vocational, general) **2** *Brit* : a college preparatory school **3** : a school specializing in adult education often professional or technical but sometimes liberal — compare FOLK HIGH SCHOOL

[2]**high school** *n* [trans. of F *haute école*] : a system of advanced exercises in horsemanship

high school·er \ˈ=ˌskülə(r)\ *n* : a high school student

high sea *n* : the open part of the sea or ocean: as **a** : the sea or ocean lying outside the territorial waters or maritime belts of a country — usu. used in pl. **b** : the part of the sea or ocean within which transactions are subject to court of admiralty jurisdiction — usu. used in pl.

high-sighted *adj, obs* : looking upward : HAUGHTY

high sign *n* : SIGNAL; *esp* : a warning or informing signal given stealthily or with gestures — usu. used in the phrase *give the high sign* ⟨gave her the *high sign* when the plainclothes police . . . had gone off to supper —Ida A. R. Wylie⟩

high-sounding \ˈ=ˈ==\ *adj* : POMPOUS, IMPOSING ⟨*high-sounding* but barren title —J.L.Motley⟩

high-speed \ˈ=ˈ=\ *adj* **1** : operated or adapted for operation at high speed **2** : suitable for or relating to the production of short-exposure photographs of rapidly moving objects or events of short duration (as for analytical measurement or study) ⟨*high-speed* film⟩ ⟨*high-speed* photography⟩

high-speed steel *n* : an alloy tool steel which when heat-treated retains much of its hardness and toughness at red heat thus enabling tools made of it to cut at high speeds even though red-hot through friction

high-speed turn *n* : TEMPO TURN

high-spirited \ˈ=ˈ===\ *adj* : characterized by a bold, energetic, or lofty spirit : having ardor or fire : not dull or apathetic ⟨a *high-spirited* tomboy of a child —Katharine Scherman⟩ — **high-spirit·ed·ly** *adv* — **high-spirit·ed·ness** *n* -ES

high-step \ˈ=ˈ=\ *vi* [back-formation fr. *high-stepper*] : to move with a high step ⟨*high-stepping* across the sand —Nadine Gordimer⟩

high-stepper \ˈ=ˈ==\ *n* : one that steps high; *esp* : a spirited horse that moves with a high step

high-stepping \ˈ=ˈ==\ *adj* **1** : moving with a high step ⟨a *high-stepping* horse⟩ **2** : given to the pursuit of pleasure : living fast or wild ⟨a *high-stepping* town with plenty of fun for all —Helene Huff⟩

high-stick·ing \ˈ=ˈstikiŋ\ *n* : the act of carrying the blade of the stick at an illegal height in the game of ice hockey

high street *n* [ME *hege strete, heighe strete*, fr. OE *hēahstrǣt*, fr. *hēah* high + *strǣt* street — more at HIGH, STREET] *Brit* : a main or principal street

high-strung \ˈ=ˈ=\ *adj* **1** : being in a state of tense or extreme sensibility : highly sensitive or nervous ⟨a *high-strung* person⟩ ⟨dogs . . . are *high-strung* creatures —Joyce Cary⟩ **2** *of an archery bow* : having a distance greater than a fistmele between handle and bowstring

high style *n* : the newest in fashion or design often with extreme lines and usu. adopted by a limited number of people — called also *high fashion*

[1]**hight** \ˈhīt, *Scot* ˈhikt\ *vb past* [ME *highten*, fr. *hehte, heet, highte* (past of *hoten*), fr. OE *heht*, past of *hātan* to command, promise, call, be called; akin to OHG *heizzan* to command, promise, call, ON *heita*, Goth *haitan*, and prob. to L *ciēre* to put in motion, move, Gk *kiein* to go, goes away, travel, *kinein* to set in motion, Skt *cyavate* he moves, goes away; basic meaning: to set in motion] **1** *archaic* : CALLED, NAMED ⟨Childe Harold was he ~ —Lord Byron⟩ **2** *chiefly Scot* **a** : pledged as security **b** : PROMISED

[2]**hight** *var of* HEIGHT

high table *n* : an elevated table in the dining room of a British college for use by the master and fellows of the college and distinguished guests

hightail \ˈ=ˌ=\ *vi* : to move at full speed or rapidly esp. in making a getaway : clear out ⟨a young purse snatcher ~*ing* up a steep hill —Elgar Dolson⟩ — often used with *it* ⟨~*ed* it straight through town —Eudora Welty⟩ ⟨where Washington and his troops made their final stand before ~*ing* it across the Hudson —Bernard Kalb⟩ ⟨~*ed* it off with another man —Shelby Foote⟩

high tea *n, Brit* : a meal served between five and six o'clock usu. with meat, salad, stewed fruit, cakes or cookies, and with tea

high-temperature \ˈ=ˈ= . . .\ *adj* : operating or carried out at high temperatures ⟨*high-temperature* furnaces⟩ ⟨*high-temperature* carbonization of coal⟩

high-temperature cement *n* : a cement capable of resisting high temperatures without fusing, softening, or spalling and suitable for the bonding of refractory materials

high-temperature short-time method *n* : FLASH PASTEURIZATION

high-tension \ˈ=ˈ==\ *adj* : having a high voltage or relating to apparatus to be used at high voltage — used esp. to indicate thousands of volts

high-test \ˈ=ˈ=\ *adj* : passing a difficult test; *specif* : having a high volatility — used esp. of gasoline and naphtha

high-test hypochlorite *n* : CALCIUM HYPOCHLORITE b

high tide *n* **1** : the tide when it is high water **2** : the culminating point : CLIMAX ⟨it was, perhaps, *high tide* of the . . . movement, its greatest hour —J.B.Martin⟩

hightoby \ˈ=ˈ==\ *n* [short for earlier *hightobyman*, fr. thieves' argot *hightoby* highway, highway robbery (fr. [1]*high* + *toby*) + *man*] *Brit* : HIGHWAYMAN

high-toned \ˈ=ˈ=\ *also* **high-tone** \ˈ=ˌ=\ *adj* **1 a** : having a high moral or intellectual tone or quality : DIGNIFIED ⟨Jefferson's *high-toned* . . . and yet devastating reply —C.G. Bowers⟩ ⟨the London *Times* . . . and other *high-toned* publications —H.L.Mencken⟩ **b** : of superior social rank, manners, or breeding : ARISTOCRATIC ⟨the *highest-tone* plantation owners in this state —Lillian Hellman⟩ ⟨discreet, decorous, and *high-toned* establishments —Eugene Burr⟩ ⟨has just admitted to its *high-toned* studbook a new breed of dog —*New Yorker*⟩ **2** : marked by pretensions to superior social status : putting on airs : PRETENTIOUS, HIGH-FLOWN ⟨*high-toned* insincerity —David Gascoyne⟩

high treason *n* [ME *hye treasoune*] **1** : treason against the sovereign or the state being in old English law the highest offense against the state — compare PETIT TREASON **2** : TREASON

highty-tighty \ˌhīdēˈtīdē\ *adj* [by alter.] : HOITY-TOITY ⟨had a *highty-tighty* way that repulsed me —W.A.White⟩

[1]**high-up** \ˈ"ˌ=\ *adj* [[2]*high* + *up*] : of high rank or status ⟨*high-up* officers on both sides —M.A.Hancock⟩

[2]**high-up** \ˈ"\ *n, pl* **high-ups** : a person of high rank or status ⟨the *high-ups* in London and America —Frederick Howard⟩

highveld \ˈ=ˌ=\ *n* [part trans. of Afrik *hoogveld*, fr. *hoog* high + *veld* field, veldt] *southern Africa* : plateau land with an elevation of about 4000 feet used esp. for grazing

high-warp \ˈ=ˈ=\ *adj* : having the warp threads hung or strung vertically ⟨*high-warp* tapestry⟩

high water *n* **1 a** : water at its utmost flow or greatest elevation; *specif* : the water of the sea, a lake, or river at its ordinarily highest level or flow **b** : the time of such elevation **2** : FRESHET ⟨wanted a new house after a *high water* on the river carried her old one away —Shirley A. Grau⟩

high-water \ˈ=ˈ==\ *adj* [*high water*] : unusually short; *esp* : having or being trousers that are unfashionably short ⟨an ancient *high-water* suit —Sinclair Lewis⟩ ⟨bought me *high-water* pants —Calder Willingham⟩

high-water line *or* **high-water mark** *n* **1 a** : the line of the shore of the sea or of a lake or river to which the waters usu. reach at high water: (1) : the line that marks the limit of the rise of the medium tides of the sea between the spring and neap tides (2) : the line that marks the limit of the soil so affected by the water of a lake or river as to have a nature and vegetation distinct from that of the banks **b** : a mark showing the highest level reached by a body of water **2** *usu high-water mark* : the highest point : ACME ⟨the *high-water mark* of a girl's social career —Hamilton Basso⟩

high-water shrub *n* : MARSH ELDER 2

highway \ˈ=ˌ=\ *n* -S *often attrib* [ME *heghewei, highway*, fr. OE *hēiweg, hēahweg*, fr. *hēah* high + *weg* way — more at HIGH, WAY] **1 a** : a road or way on land or water that is open to public use as a matter of right whether or not a thoroughfare : a public road or way (as a footpath, road, or waterway) including the right-of-way — compare PRIVATE WAY **b** : such a road or way established and maintained (as by a state) in accordance with law **c** : a main direct road (as between one town or city and another) — sometimes contrasted with *byway* **2** : a primary or well-known aspect or field ⟨the ~s and byways of literature⟩

highway bond *n* : a bond issued by a taxing jurisdiction the proceeds of which are for the construction of highways

highway engineer *n* : an engineer whose training or occupation is in highway engineering

highway engineering *n* : a branch of civil engineering dealing with the planning, location, design, construction, and maintenance of highways and with the regulations and control devices employed in highway traffic operations

high·way·man \ˈ=ˌ=mən *sometimes* (ˈ)=ˈ==\ *n, pl* **highwaymen** : a person who robs on the public road : a highway robber

highway post office *n* : a bus carrying mail which is sorted in transit

highway robbery *n* **1** : robbery committed on or near a public highway esp. against travelers **2** : excessive profit or advantage derived from a business transaction

highwheeler \ˈ=ˈ==\ *n* : a steam locomotive with large driving wheels for high-speed passenger-train service

high wine *n* : distilled spirits containing a high percentage of alcohol — usu. used in pl.

high wire *n* : a tightrope considerably higher above ground than the one ordinarily used

high-wrought \ˈ=ˈ=\ *adj* **1** : wrought with fine art or skill : ELABORATE ⟨the recipient of these *high-wrought* epistles —*Times Lit. Supp.*⟩ **2** : worked up or agitated to a high degree ⟨a *high-wrought* passion⟩

high yellow *n* : a mulatto or colored person of light-yellow color

HIH *abbr* Her Imperial Highness; His Imperial Highness

hi·jack *or* **high-jack** \ˈhīˌjak\ *vt* [origin unknown] **1 a** (1) : to steal by stopping a vehicle carrying contraband, illicit, or stolen goods ⟨~ a truckload of bootleg whiskey —*Emporia* (*Kans.*) *Gazette*⟩ (2) : to stop in transit and steal the cargo of ⟨~ a truck near the foot of the mountain⟩ (3) : to hold up and rob in the manner of one who hijacks ⟨attempted to ~ us for the jewelry right in daylight —Frank O'Leary⟩ **b** : to steal or rob as if by hijacking ⟨accused of ~*ing* half a million marks' worth of textiles —Joseph Wechsberg⟩ ⟨connives against the republic and has to flee the country in a ~*ed* airplane —Harvey Swados⟩ ⟨reputedly ~*ed* the less intrepid gentry of their ill-got booty and their slaves —*N.Y. Herald Tribune*⟩ **c** : KIDNAP ⟨about sixty thousand Kanakas were enticed or ~*ed* to Australia —Alan Moorehead⟩ **2 a** : to subject to extortion or swindling ⟨has deliberately set out to . . . ~ the American people through uncontrolled profits and inflation —Philip Murray †1952⟩ **b** : COERCE, FORCE ⟨~*ing* buyers into purchasing unwanted accessories —N.K.Teeters & J.O.Reinemann⟩

hi·jack·er *or* **high-jack·er** \-kə(r)\ *n* : one that hijacks ⟨repair-bill ~s —*Road & Track*⟩ ⟨~s stole . . . over $20 million worth of cargo from trucks —*Business Week*⟩

hijinks *var of* HIGH JINKS

hij·ra *or* **hij·rah** \ˈhijrə\ *n* -S [Ar *hijrah*, lit., flight] : HEGIRA

[1]**hike** \ˈhīk\ *vb* -ED/-ING/-S [perh. akin to [1]*hitch*] *vt* **1 a** *dial chiefly Eng* : to raise or toss with the horns : GORE **b** *dial Brit* : to toss up and down : SWING **2** : to move, pull, or raise often with a jerk or other sudden motion ⟨*hiked* him out —Adrian Bell⟩ ⟨*hiked* himself onto my bed⟩ ⟨*hiking* their dresses above their knees —E.D.Radin⟩ ⟨sections *hiked* into place by cranes —*Newsweek*⟩ **3** : to increase in amount esp. sharply or suddenly ⟨~ taxes on luxury goods⟩ ⟨~ rents⟩ **4** : to cause to hike ⟨*hiked* himself off to work⟩ : guide or lead on a hike ⟨*hiked* them until their feet hurt⟩ ~ *vi* **1 a** : MARCH, TRAMP, WALK ⟨*hiked* 10 miles that day⟩ ⟨you have to park the car . . . and ~ in —Linda Braidwood⟩; *esp* : to go on a long walk or march for pleasure or exercise ⟨loves to ~⟩ ⟨arranged to spend the weekend *hiking*⟩ **b** *dial chiefly Eng* : to go away : DECAMP — usu. used with *off* or *out* **c** : to journey or travel by any means ⟨~ on skis through snow and dark —Carl Jonas⟩ ⟨borrowed some money and *hiked* over to Paris⟩ **2** *dial Brit* : to toss up and down : JOLT, JOUNCE, SWAY **3** : to rise or go up as if by being pulled : work upward out of place ⟨no shrinking, no sagging, no *hiking* —*N.Y.Times*⟩ —usu. used with *up* ⟨her skirt and slip had *hiked* up in back —Ralph Chapman⟩

[2]**hike** \ˈ"\ *n* -S **1** : TRAMP, MARCH; *esp* : a long walk undertaken for pleasure or exercise **2** : a lifting or a moving upward (as of a quantity, amount, degree) : INCREASE, RISE ⟨a 10 percent ~ in taxes⟩ ⟨called for a ~ in production⟩ ⟨wage ~s⟩ a hike for pleasure or exercise

hik·er \-kə(r)\ *n* -S : one that hikes; *esp* : a person who goes on a hike for pleasure or exercise

hi·ku·li \(h)iˈkülē\ *n* -S [Huichol] : PEYOTE

hila *pl of* HILUM

hi·lar \ˈhīlə(r)\ *adj* [NL *hilum* + E *-ar*] : of, relating to, or located near a hilum

hi·lar·ia \həˈla(a)rēə, hīˈ-\ *n* -S *usu cap* [L, fr. neut. pl. of *hilaris*] : an imperial Roman festival of the cult of Cybele held on the vernal equinox to celebrate the renewal of life on earth in the spring symbolized by the resurrection of the god Attis

[2]**hilaria** \ˈ"\ *n, cap* [NL, irreg. fr. Auguste de Saint-*Hilaire* †1853 Fr. botanist + NL *-ia*] : a small genus of grasses of the southwestern U. S. and Mexico having a terminal spike with the spikelets in threes — see CURLY MESQUITE

hi·lar·i·ous \həˈla(a)rēəs, -ler-, -lär- *also* (ˈ)hīˈl-\ *adj* [modif. (influenced by E *-ious*) of L *hilarus, hilaris*, fr. Gk *hilaros* — more at SILLY] : marked by hilarity : affording or given to hilarity : LUDICROUS, MERRY, MIRTHFUL ⟨serious plays . . . alternated with ~ broad comedy —W.P.Eaton⟩ ⟨a joyous, lighthearted, ~ mode of life —C.A. and Mary Beard⟩

hi·lar·i·ous·ly *adv* : in a hilarious manner

hi·lar·i·ous·ness *n* -ES : HILARITY

hi·lar·i·ty \həˈlarəd·ē, -ətē, -i *also* hīˈ- *or* -ler-\ *n* -ES [MF *hilarité*, fr. L *hilaritat-, hilaritas*, fr. *hilarus, hilaris* + *-itat-, -itas* -ity] **1** : temperate gaiety : CHEER, CHEERFULNESS ⟨wine gives not light, gay, ideal ~ but tumultuous, noisy, clamorous merriment —Samuel Johnson⟩ **2** : boisterous merriment : intense mirth or laughter ⟨in a continual gale of ~⟩

hil·a·ry·mas \ˈhil(ə)rēməs\ *n* -ES *usu cap* [ME *Hillarimesse*, fr. St. *Hilary* †*ab* A.D. 367 bishop of Poitiers + ME *messe* mass — more at MASS] : the feast of St. Hilary on January 13 in the Anglican calendar and January 14 in the Roman Catholic calendar

hil·a·ry term \ˈhilərē-\ *n, usu cap H* [after St. *Hilary*] **1** *chiefly Brit* **a** : the term from January 11 to 31 during which the superior courts of England were formerly open — compare EASTER TERM, MICHAELMAS TERM **b** *also* **hilary sitting** : the sitting of the High Court of Justice of England between January 11 and the Wednesday before Easter **2** *chiefly Brit* : the second academic term in a British university beginning in mid January and ending before Easter

hilch \ˈhilch, -lsh\ *vi* -ED/-ING/-ES [prob. alter. of Sc *hilt* to limp, alter. of [2]*halt*] *chiefly Scot* : to hobble along : LIMP

hil·de·brand·ine \ˌhildəˈbrandən, -n,dīn\ *also* **hil·de·brand·ian** \-ndēən\ *adj, usu cap* [*Hildebrand* (Pope Gregory VII), Ital. prelate + E *-ine* or *-ian*] **1** : of or relating to Hildebrand esp. with reference to his drastic reforms of church government and his assertion of papal supremacy over the lower clergy and civil authorities **2** : adhering to the principles of Hildebrand ⟨the *Hildebrandine* party⟩

[1]**hil·ding** \ˈhildiŋ\ *adj* [perh. fr. pres. part. of *hild, hyld*, obs. var. of *hield*] *archaic* : lacking moral principles, convictions, or courage : BASE

[2]**hilding** \ˈ"\ *n* -S *archaic* : a hilding person

hil·gard·ite \ˈhilˌgärˌdīt, -gər-\ *n* -S [Eugene W. *Hilgard* †1916 Amer. geologist + E *-ite*] : a mineral $Ca_8(B_6O_{11})_3Cl_4.4H_2O$ consisting of hydrous chloride and borate of calcium occurring in colorless monoclinic domatic crystals

hili *pl of* HILUS

hi·li·fer·ous \(ˈ)hīˈlif(ə)rəs\ *adj* [ISV *hili-* (fr. NL *hilum*) + *-ferous*] : bearing a hilum

hil·i·gay·non *also* **hil·i·gai·non** \ˌhiləˈgīnən\ *n, pl* **hiligaynon** *or* **hiligaynons** *also* **hiligainon** *or* **hiligainons** *usu cap* [native name on Panay] **1 a** : a Bisayan people inhabiting Panay and part of Negros, Philippines **b** : a member of the Hiligaynon people **2** : an Austronesian language of the Hiligaynon people related to but not mutually intelligible with Cebuan and frequently considered a dialect of Bisayan

[1]**hill** \ˈhil\ *n* -S *often attrib* [ME *hill, hul*, fr. OE *hyll*; akin to OE *holm* island, OS *holm* hill, ON *holmr* island, L *collis* hill, *culmen* top, *celsus* high, Gk *kolōnos* hill, Lith *kelti* to lift up, and perh. to OE *heall* stone, rock, ON *hallr* stone, Goth *hallus* rock, cliff, and perh. to Skt *kūṭa* hammer, mallet; basic meaning: rising, raising] **1** : a natural elevation of land of local area and well-defined outline: **a** : a more or less rounded elevation as contrasted with a peaked or precipitous one — compare BUTTE, MESA **b** : a conspicuous elevation in a comparatively flat country ⟨the seven ~s on which Rome was built⟩ **c** (1) : any of the inferior elevations of a rugged country : an elevation higher than a rise and lower than a mountain (2) **hills** *pl* : a range or group of hills ⟨visited the Black ~s and the Rocky mountains⟩ **d** : hilly country ⟨a ~ district⟩ ⟨~ people⟩ — often used in pl. ⟨lives in the ~s⟩ **2** : a heap or mound of earth or other material reared by human or animal agency ⟨the ~s of a prairie dogs' town⟩ **3** : a group of several seeds or plants planted in one hole ⟨sow five seeds to each ~⟩ ⟨a ~ of beans⟩ **4** : an incline esp. in a road : SLOPE ⟨trucks laboring up the long ~⟩ **5** *dial* : dry land surrounded by swamp, marsh, or water : solid ground **6** : an elevation on any surface : RIDGE ⟨the ~s and hollows of the cobblestone pavement⟩ — **over the hill** : past the peak : on the downgrade ⟨I was *over the hill* as far as moneymaking was concerned —W.A.White⟩ — compare *go over the hill* at GO OVER

[2]**hill** \ˈ"\ *vt* -ED/-ING/-S **1** : to form into a heap ⟨~ up soil around roses⟩ **2** : to heap or draw earth around or upon ⟨~*ed* the potatoes⟩

[3]**hill** \ˈ"\ *vt* -ED/-ING/-S [ME *hulen, hilen, hillen*, prob. fr. ON *hylja* to hide, cover; akin to OHG *hullen* to cover, Goth *huljan* to cover, OE *helan* to hide, conceal — more at HELL] *dial Eng* : to protect by covering : HIDE

hill-and-dale \ˌ==ˈ=\ *adj* [fr. the phrase (*over*) *hill and dale*] *of a phonograph record* : having a groove of varying depth

[1]**hill·bil·ly** \ˈhilˌbilē, -li, ˈ=ˌ==\ *n* -ES [[1]*hill* + *Billy*, nickname for *William*] **1** : a person from a backwoods area (as the mountains of the southern U. S.) — often used disparagingly **2** : a hillbilly song

[2]**hillbilly** \ˈ"\ *adj* **1** : of or relating to a hillbilly : suggestive of hillbillies **2** : relating to or characterized by hillbilly music

hillbilly music *n* **1** : folk songs and folk style of singing and playing of the southern U.S. **2** : any music deriving from or imitating folk style or the style of the western cowboy esp. as exploited commercially — called also *country music*

hillbird \ˈ=ˌ=\ *n* **1** : UPLAND PLOVER **2** : FIELDFARE

hill climb *n* : a road race over a hilly course held by an automobile or motorcycle club

hillcrest \ˈ=ˌ=\ *n* : the top line of a hill

hillculture \ˈ=ˌ==\ *n* -S [trans. of D *bergcultuur*] : agriculture utilizing erosion-preventing crops that are ecologically and economically best suited for sloping or hilly land

hill-drop \ˈ=ˌ=\ *adj* : planting a full hill at desired intervals ⟨a *hill-drop* corn planter⟩

hil·le·brand·ite \ˈhiləˌbranˌdīt, ˌ==ˈ=ˌ=\ *n* -S [William F. *Hillebrand* †1925 Amer. chemist + E *-ite*] : a mineral $Ca_2SiO_3(OH)_2$ consisting of a hydrous calcium silicate occurring in white masses

hil·lel·ite \ˈhiˌleˌlīt\ *n* -S *usu cap* [*Hillel* †A.D. 9 Jewish teacher + E *-ite*] : an adherent of the liberal and humanitarian principles of interpretation of the Jewish law developed by Rabbi Hillel and opposed by the Shammaites

hill·er \ˈhilə(r)\ *n* -S : an attachment to a cultivator or plow for hilling plants

hill fox *n* : a fox (*Vulpes himalaicus*) that has fur of a pale fulvous color and is found in the mountains of India

hill grub *n* : a larva of the antler moth (*Cerapteryx graminis*) that is often destructive to pasture grasses in England

hill holder *n* : a device other than a hand brake that keeps a motor vehicle from backing down an incline when the foot is removed from the brake pedal; *esp* : such a device connected to a clutch pedal to keep the brakes applied as long as the clutch pedal is depressed

hill indexing *n, pl* **hill indexings** : indexing by preplanting a potato of each hill

hill·i·ness \ˈhilēnəs, -lin-\ *n* -ES : the quality or state of being hilly

hill·man \ˈhilmən\ *also* **hills·man** \-lzm-\ *n, pl* **hillmen** *also* **hillsmen** : a man native to or inhabiting a hilly or mountainous often isolated area and typically differing markedly in outlook, customs, and speech from a man of the plains

hill myna *n* : an Asiatic starling (*Gracula religiosa*) that is black with a white spot on the wings and a pair of flat yellow wattles on the head and is often tamed and taught to pronounce words

hil·lo *or* **hil·loa** \həˈlō, ˈhi(ˌ)lō, ˈhiˈlō — *see* HELLO\ *archaic var of* HELLO

hil·lock \ˈhilək\ *n* -S [ME *hilloc*, fr. *hill* + *-oc* -ock] : a small hill : MOUND — **hill·ocked** \-kt\ *adj* — **hill·ocky** \-kē\ *adj*

hillock tree *n* : an Australian shrub (*Melaleuca hypericifolia*) with showy spikes of red flowers

hill of beans : something of negligible importance or value — used chiefly in negative constructions ⟨doesn't amount to a *hill of beans*⟩ ⟨not worth a *hill of beans*⟩

hill partridge *n* **1** : any of numerous partridges of southern Asia and the East Indies that constitute a genus (*Arborophila*) of the family Phasianidae — called also *tree partridge* **2** : SPUR FOWL

hill planter *n* : a machine that is used for planting seed (as corn) in hills

hill reaction \ˈhil-\ *n, usu cap H* [after Robin *Hill*, Brit. chemist] : a photochemical liberation of oxygen from water by cells or cell fragments containing chlorophyll that is equivalent to the photochemical phase of plant photosynthesis

hills *pl of* HILL, *pres 3d sing of* HILL

hillside \ˈ=ˌ=\ *n, often attrib* [ME *hulle syde*, fr. *hulle, hill* hill + *syde, side* side] : a part of a hill between the summit and the foot ⟨a green valley whose ~s . . . are a mass of yellow buttercups —*Amer. Guide Series: Minn.*⟩ ⟨pell-mell down the ~ streets —Sherwood Anderson⟩

hillside plow *n* : SWIVEL PLOW

hillslope \ˈ=ˌ=\ *n* : HILLSIDE

hills-of-snow \ˈ==ˈ=\ *n, pl* **hills-of-snow** : a Japanese hydrangea (*Hydrangea arborescens grandiflora*) with large clusters of snow-white sterile flowers

hill star *n* : any of several hummingbirds comprising the genus *Oreotrochilus* and inhabiting parts of the Andes

hill station *n* : a village or government post (as in India) situated in the hills or low mountain ranges and serving usu. as a health resort in the hot season

hill tit *n* : any of numerous small Asiatic singing birds of *Siva*, *Leiothrix*, and related genera

hilltop \ˈ=ˌ=\ *n* : the highest part of a hill

hi·lul ha·shem \kə̇ˈlülhəˈshām\ *n* -s [Heb *ḥillūl hashshēm* desecration of the name (of God)] : an act in contravention of Jewish religious or ethical principles that is regarded as an offense to God — compare KIDDUSH HASHEM

hillwort \ˈ=ˌ=\ *n* : WILD THYME

hilly \ˈhilē, -li\ *adj* -ER/-EST [ME, fr. *hill* + *-y*] **1** : abounding with hills **2** : inclining like a hill : of the character of a hill : STEEP

hi·lo grass \ˈhē(ˌ)lō-\ *n* [Hawaiian *hilo*] : a sour grass (*Paspalum conjugatum*) that is common in the Hawaiian islands and is often a troublesome weed because of its ability to cover vast areas in a short time

hil·sa \ˈhilsə *also* -l(t)sə\ *n* -s [Hindi *hilsā*, fr. Skt *ilīśa*, *illiśa*] : a valuable anadromous herring (*Clupea ilisha*) of India resembling a shad

1hilt \ˈhilt\ *n* -s [ME, fr. OE; akin to OS *helta* oar handle, OHG *helza* hilt, ON *hjalt* hilt, W *cleddyf* sword, OE *healt* lame — more at HALT] **1** : a handle of a sword or dagger **2** : the handle of any weapon or of a tool (as a miner's pick) — **to the hilt** *or* **up to the hilt** : to the very limit : FULLY, COMPLETELY ⟨mortgaged the farm *up to the hilt*⟩ ⟨proved its importance *to the hilt*⟩

hilt

2hilt \"\ *dial past of* HOLD

3hilt \"\ *dial var of* HOLD

hi·lum \ˈhīləm\ *n, pl* **hi·la** \-lə\ [NL, fr. L, trifle] **1 a** : a scar on a seed (as a bean) marking the point of attachment of the ovule to the funiculus **b** : the nucleus of a starch grain **c** : a small lateral outgrowth on a basidiospore near the point of its attachment to the sterigma on which it was borne **2** : a mark or notch in or opening from a bodily part suggesting the hilum of a bean: as **a** : the part of a gland or of certain other organs where the blood vessels, nerves, or ducts leave and enter ⟨the ~ of the kidney⟩ ⟨the ~ of the lung⟩ **b** : a small opening in the statoblast of a sponge

hi·lus \-ləs\ *n, pl* **hi·li** \-ˌlī\ [NL, alter. of *hilum*] : HILUM 2a

1him \ˌ(h)im, ˈhim, ˌēm\ *pron, objective case of* HE [ME, fr. OE, dat. of *hē* he — more at HE] **1** : 1HE 1, 2, 3, 4: **a** — used as indirect object of a verb ⟨friends who have given ~ the most sympathy —W.M.Thackeray⟩ **b** — used as object of a preposition ⟨we may not fight a duel with Death nor engage in controversy with ~ —W.L.Sullivan⟩ **c** — used as direct object of a verb ⟨I know ~⟩ **d** — used in comparisons after *than* and *as* when the first term in the comparison is the direct or indirect object of a verb or the object of a preposition ⟨the jacket fits you as well as ~⟩ ⟨give me the book rather than ~⟩ ⟨this treatment would be more beneficial to you than ~⟩ **e** — used in absolute constructions esp. together with a prepositional phrase, adjective, or participle ⟨I met him down near the river, at the height of the first run of fish, and ~ without his rod —Alasdair Carmichael⟩ ⟨~ being such a fool, the Fool Killer heard about him —Helen Eustis⟩ **f** — used by speakers on all educational levels and by many reputable writers though disapproved by some grammarians in the predicate after forms of *be*, in comparisons after *than* and *as* when the first term in the comparison is the subject of a verb, and in other positions where it is itself neither the subject of a verb nor the object of a verb or preposition ⟨it was ~⟩ ⟨she is as tall as ~⟩ ⟨~ and his promises!⟩ **g** — used in substandard speech and formerly also by reputable writers as the subject of a verb which it does not immediately precede or as part of the compound subject of a verb ⟨damned be ~ that first cries "Hold, enough!" —Shak.⟩ ⟨~ and his wife was real old-timers —Vance Randolph⟩ **h** — used like the adjective *his* with a gerund by speakers and writers on all educational levels though disapproved by some grammarians ⟨what do you think of ~ becoming a doctor⟩ **2** : HIMSELF — used reflexively as indirect object of a verb ⟨he went to his . . . tailor . . . and got ~ a . . . gray spring suit —W.A.White⟩, object of a preposition ⟨he couldn't decide whether to have the package delivered or take it with ~⟩, or direct object of a verb ⟨a child that . . . finds ~ suddenly in his mother's arms again —Nathaniel Hawthorne⟩

2him \ˈhim\ *n* -s : MAN, BOY ⟨four ~*s* and a her —Charles Dickens⟩

HIM *abbr* Her Imperial Majesty; His Imperial Majesty

hi·ma \ˈhēmə\ *also* **hu·ma** \ˈhümə\ *n, pl* **hima** *or* **himas** *also* **huma** *or* **humas** *usu cap* **1** : a Bantu-speaking pastoral people who constitute the ruling segment of the population of the Uganda kingdoms of Nyankole, Nyoro, and Toro and an inferior class among the Ganda people, are found also in Ruanda and on the western shore of Lake Albert in the Congo, and are supposed to be cognate in origin with the Tusi and perhaps the Galla and Somali **2** : a member of the Hima people

hima·laya berry \ˌhiməˈlāə-; həˈmäl(ə)yə-, -ˈmȧl, ǀlēə-; *sometimes* ˌhiməˈläyə- *or* -ˈlȧyə- *or* -ˈlīə-\ *n, usu cap H* [fr. the *Himalayas*, mountain range between Nepal and Tibet] : a European blackberry (*Rubus procerus*) introduced and naturalized in the U.S. and having leaves strongly whitened beneath with dense felty tomentum

himalaya honeysuckle *n, usu cap H* : a Himalayan shrub honeysuckle (*Leycesteria formosa*) of the family Caprifoliaceae with drooping spikes of purplish flowers

1hima·layan *pronunc at* HIMALAYA BERRY +n\ *adj, usu cap* [*Himalaya*s + E *-an*] **1** : of, relating to, or characteristic of the Himalayas **2** : extremely large ⟨was responsible for a *Himalayan* blunder⟩

2himalayan \"\ *n* **1** *or* **himalayan rabbit** *usu cap H* **a** : a breed of small white domesticated rabbits with black nose, feet, tail, and ear tips **b** -s *often cap H* : a rabbit of this breed **2** -s : total or partial restriction of pigmentation to the cooler parts of the body (as tail, paws, face, ears) occurring as one of a polygenic series of variants in mammalian coat color dominant to albinism but recessive to chinchilla and the wild type and exhibited in typical form in the Himalayan rabbit and less perfectly in the Siamese cat

himalayan barley *n, usu cap H* : an Asiatic barley (*Hordeum vulgare trifurcatum*) having the awns represented by short furcate branches

himalayan black bear *n, usu cap H* : BLACK BEAR 2

himalayan cedar *n, usu cap H* : DEODAR

himalayan cypress *n, usu cap H* : BHUTAN CYPRESS

himalayan fir *n, usu cap H* : a very large evergreen tree (*Abies spectabilis*) of the mountains of northern India that is cultivated for its majestic habit and luxuriant foliage

himalayan hare *n, usu cap H* : a large long-eared hare (*Lepus oiostalus*) that is usu. silvery brown with the tail white above and is found at high elevations in Tibet

himalayan lilac *n, usu cap H* : a shrub (*Syringa emodi*) of the mountains of northern India that has pale-lilac or white flowers

himalayan pine *n, usu cap H* : a Himalayan tree (*Pinus excelsa*) with wide-spreading branches and drooping bluish-gray leaves — called also *Asiatic white pine*

himalayan rhubarb *n, usu cap H* : an East Indian herb (*Rheum emodi*) that is one of the sources of emodin — called also *Indian rhubarb*

himalayan snow cock *n, usu cap H* : a snow cock (*Tetraogallus himalayensis*) having a chestnut pectoral band and a white chest with black bars

himalayan spruce *n, usu cap H* : a spruce (*Picea smithiana*) of the Himalayan region that is cultivated for ornament

hima·lo-chinese \ˌhimə(ˌ)lō, həˌmä(- +\ *adj, usu cap H&C* [*Himalo-*, fr. *Himalayas*] : BURMO-CHINESE

hi·man·to·pus \həˈmantəpəs\ *n, cap* [NL, fr. Gk *himantopous*, a kind of water bird, fr. *himant-*, *himas* thong, strap + *-o-* + *pous* foot] : a genus of wading birds comprising the stilts

hi·mat·i·on \həˈmad·ēˌän, -ēən\ *n* -s [Gk, dim. of *himat-*, *hima*, *heimat-*, *heima* garment, fr. *hennynai* to clothe — more at WEAR] : a long loose outer garment of ancient Greece consisting of a rectangular cloth worn by both men and women usu. with one end pulled over the left shoulder from the rear and the remainder going round the back, under the right arm and across the front and draped over the left arm or shoulder — compare CHITON, CHLAMYS, PEPLOS, TRIBON

himation

hi·me·ji \həˈmäjē\ *adj, usu cap* [fr. *Himeji*, Japan] : of or from the city of Himeji, Japan : of the kind or style prevalent in Himeji

hime·ne *also* **himi·ne** \ˈhēməˌnā, ˈhim-\ *n* -s [Tahitian, Hawaiian, & Marquesan *himene*, fr. E *hymn*] : a native song or hymn of French Oceania

himp \ˈhimp\ *vi* -ED/-ING/-S [prob. akin to G dial. *hümpen*, *himpen* to limp] *dial Eng* : LIMP

him·self \(h)imˈ=, ēmˈ=\ *pron* [ME, fr. OE *him selfum*, dat., him himself, fr. *him* + *selfum*, dat. of *self* — more at SELF] **1** : that identical male one : that identical one regarded as masculine (as by personification) : that identical one whose sex is unknown or immaterial — compare 1HE; used (1) reflexively as object of a preposition or direct or indirect object of a verb ⟨everyone must look out for ~⟩ ⟨in those days Providence was still busying ~ with everybody's affairs —Arnold Bennett⟩ ⟨he got ~ a new suit⟩; (2) for emphasis in apposition with *he*, *who*, *that*, or a noun ⟨he ~ informed me⟩ ⟨he informed me ~⟩ ⟨the composer ~ conducted the symphony⟩ ⟨the composer conducted the symphony ~⟩ ⟨criticizing the king's advisers and the king ~⟩ ⟨the judge, who had once been a lawyer ~⟩; (3) for emphasis instead of nonreflexive *him* as object of a preposition or direct or indirect object of a verb ⟨his income supports his wife and ~⟩; (4) for emphasis instead of *he* or instead of *he himself* as subject of a verb ⟨he was never influenced in art by any fashions save those ~ created —Osbert Sitwell⟩ or as predicate nominative ⟨he has only one loyal disciple and that is ~⟩ or in comparisons after *than* or *as* ⟨he associated mainly with people younger than ~⟩; (5) in absolute constructions ⟨~ simple, fair-minded, unhappy, he comes in contact with the more extravagant varieties of Americans abroad —Carl Van Doren⟩ **2** : his normal, healthy, or sane condition ⟨he came to ~⟩ : his normal, healthy, or sane self ⟨ill for some time, he is now ~ again⟩ **3** *Irish & Scot* : a man of consequence; *esp* : the master of the house ⟨she has . . . breakfast on the table before ~ is up —Cahir Healy⟩ **4** : YOURSELF — used in speaking to or as if to a baby ⟨did he hurt ~⟩; used in some English dialects in addressing a boy or a person of higher or lower social status than the speaker; compare 1HE 4

1him·yar·ite \ˈhimyəˌrīt\ *n* -s *usu cap* [*Himyar*, a legendary ancient king in Yemen + E *-ite*] **1 a** : an Arab people of antiquity dwelling in southern Arabia **b** : a member of such people **2** : an Arab of a group of related ancient peoples of southern Arabia that included besides the Himyarites proper the Sabaeans and Minaeans, that had a civilization of great antiquity, and that were completely absorbed by northern Arabs by the time of Muhammad

2himyarite \"\ *or* **him·yar·it·ic** \ˈ==ˈrid·ik\ *adj, usu cap* : of or relating to the ancient Himyarites or their language

himyaritic \"\ *or* **himyarite** \"\ *n* -s *usu cap* : the language of the Himyarites occurring in inscriptions ranging from about 700 B.C. to A.D. 550

1hin \ˌ(h)ən, ˌ(h)ēn\ *pron* [ME, fr. OE *hine*, accus. of *hē* he — more at HE] *dial chiefly Eng* : HIM

2hin \ˈhin, -ē-\ *n* -s [Heb *hīn*, fr. Egypt *hnw*] : an ancient Hebrew unit of measure for liquids equal to about a gallon and a half

hi·na·lea \ˌhēnəˈlāə\ *n* -s [Hawaiian] : a brilliantly marked convict fish (*Hepatus triostegus*) of the Hawaiian islands that is often used for food

hi·nau \ˈhēˌnaů\ *n* -s [Maori] : a New Zealand timber tree (*Elaeocarpus dentatus*) whose bark yields a useful dye

hi·na·ya·na \ˌhēnəˈyänə, -ēnēˈ(y)ä-\ *n* -s *cap* [Skt *hīnayāna*, lit., lesser vehicle, fr. *hīna* left behind, inferior, lesser (fr. *hīyate* he is left) + *yāna* action of going, vehicle, fr. *yāti* he goes; akin to *jahāti* he leaves — more at GO, JANITOR] : the smaller more conservative branch of Buddhism dominant in Ceylon, Burma, Thailand, and Cambodia and characterized by adherence to the Pali scriptures and to the nontheistic nonspeculative ideal of self-purification to nirvana through contemplative and moral effort esp. as an arhat — called also *Little Vehicle*, *Pali Buddhism*, *Southern Buddhism*, *Theravada;* compare MAHAYANA

hi·na·ya·nist \-nə̇st\ *n* -s *usu cap* : an adherent of Hinayana — **hi·na·ya·nis·tic** \ˈ==(ˌ)=ˈnistik\ *adj, usu cap*

1hind \ˈhīnd\ *n, pl* **hinds** *also* **hind** [ME *hinde*, fr. OE *hind;* akin to OHG *hinta* hind, ON *hind*, Gk *kemas* young deer, Skt *śáma* hornless; basic meaning: hornless] **1** : a female of the red deer — compare HART, STAG **2** : any of various typically spotted groupers — see RED HIND, ROCK HIND, SPECKLED HIND

2hind \"\ *n* -s [ME *hine* servant, farmhand, fr. OE *hīna*, gen. of *hīwan*, pl., members of a household — more at HOME] **1 a** : a farm laborer in northern England and Scotland; *esp* : a skilled farm worker who is provided with a cottage on the farm as a home for himself and his family **b** : an English farm manager : BAILIFF **2** : an unsophisticated countryman : HICK, RUSTIC

3hind \", *before consonants & in "hind end" often* -n\ *adj* [ME *hint*, prob. back-formation fr. OE *hinder*, adv., behind, & *hindema* last; akin to OHG *hintar*, prep., behind, *hintaro*, adj., rear, *hintana*, adv., from behind, behind, ON *hindri* last, Goth *hindana*, adv., behind, beyond, *hindar*, prep., behind, beyond, and prob. to OE *hē* he — more at HE] : of or forming the part that follows or is behind : BACK, REAR ⟨the dog's ~ legs⟩ ⟨the handkerchief in his ~ pocket⟩ — compare FORE — **on one's hind legs** : taking an indignant or determinedly independent attitude ⟨got up *on my hind legs* . . . and sounded off —Saul Bellow⟩

4hind \ˈhīnd\ *n* -s : HINDQUARTER ⟨a ~ of beef⟩

hind·ber·ry \ˈhīn(d)- — *see* BERRY\ *n* [fr. (assumed) ME *hindberie*, fr. OE (akin to OHG *hintberi* raspberry), fr. *hind* + *berie* berry — more at BERRY] : EUROPEAN RASPBERRY

hindbrain \ˈ=ˌ=\ *n* **1 a** : the posterior of the three primary divisions of the vertebrate brain or the parts developed from it including the cerebellum, pons, and medulla oblongata **b** : METENCEPHALON 1 — distinguished from *myelencephalon* **c** : MYELENCEPHALON **2** : the posterior segment of the brain of an invertebrate (as an insect) : TRITOCEREBRUM

hindcast \ˈ=ˌ=\ *n* : a statistical calculation determining probable past conditions (as of marine wave characteristics at a given place and time)

hind end *see* 3HIND\ *n* **1** : a part that follows behind : REAR ⟨the *hind end* of a train⟩ **2** : BUTTOCKS, RUMP

1hin·der \ˈhində(r)\ **hindered**; **hindered**; **hindering** \-d(ə)riŋ\ **hinders** *vb* [ME *hindren*, *hinderen*, fr. OE *hindrian;* akin to OHG *hintarōn* to hinder, ON *hindra*, and prob. to OE *hinder* behind — more at HIND] *vt* **1** *obs* : to do harm to : IMPAIR, DAMAGE ⟨fight against Jerusalem, and to ~ it —Neh 4:3 (AV)⟩ **2** : to make slow or difficult the course or progress of : RETARD, HAMPER ⟨policies that will further or ~ the cause of independence⟩ ⟨was greatly ~*ed* in his efforts by bad weather⟩ **3** : to keep from occurring, starting, or continuing : hold back : PREVENT, CHECK — often used with *from* ⟨machines are sometimes ~*ed* by speed from delivering their best performance —Edith Diehl⟩ ⟨could not ~ himself from dwelling upon it —Stephen Crane⟩ **4** : to interfere with the activity of (a group or molecule of a compound) esp. as a result of space relationships — compare BLOCK 1g, STERIC HINDRANCE ~ *vi* : to delay, impede, or prevent action : be a hindrance ⟨uncertain whether it would help or ~⟩

syn IMPEDE, OBSTRUCT, BLOCK, BAR, DAM: HINDER indicates a checking or holding back from acting, moving, or starting, often with harmful or annoying delay or interference ⟨shallow water and constantly shifting sandbars at the mouth of the Mississippi impeded navigation and *hindered* the full development of New Orleans as a port —*Amer. Guide Series: La.*⟩ ⟨after the war German physicists maintained that the Nazis *hindered* research on a bomb, permitting only work toward an atomic power plant —*Current Biog.*⟩ IMPEDE suggests checking motion or progress by or as if by clogging or fettering so that forward activity is difficult ⟨he looked at her, startled, and placed his hand on hers, *impeding* the rapidity of her embroidery needle —Rose Macaulay⟩ ⟨action is *impeded* by a multitude of rules and regulations drawn up by the agency itself —E.M.Eriksson⟩ OBSTRUCT indicates hindering free and easy passage by obstacles in the way or by interference ⟨at some point below the Danish camp he *obstructed* the course of the Lea, so that the Danish ships could not be brought downstream —F.M.Stenton⟩ ⟨charged with *obstructing* the military in the execution of duty —Francis Stuart⟩ ⟨the restriction of the power of the House of Lords to *obstruct* legislation —Alfred Plummer⟩ BLOCK indicates complete obstruction to egress, passage, or exit ⟨roads *blocked* by the storm⟩ ⟨the steamer Heilo, which, having run aground, was *blocking* the entrance to Corinto harbor —*Current Biog.*⟩ ⟨a polyglot of diagnostic labels and systems, effectively *blocking* communication and the collection of medical statistics —G.N.Raines⟩ BAR is often a close synonym for BLOCK; it may indicate a purposive blocking or suggest a prohibiting that renders a physical obstacle unnecessary ⟨streetcars that, if not quite medieval, *bar* the road to the hurrying traveler —*N. Y. Times*⟩ ⟨to *bar* further immigration of aliens⟩ DAM may apply to obstructing whatever flows or may be thought of as flowing ⟨*dam* up the waters⟩ ⟨instances in which the bile ducts are blocked so that the bile is *dammed* back —Morris Fishbein⟩ ⟨the nun in her cell lost in contemplation is but inspired by a desire which, *dammed* in its earthly course, rises and rises to unimaginable heights —Francis Stuart⟩

2hinder \"\ *n* -s : accidental interference esp. by an opponent in some games (as handball and squash) that prevents a fair and unobstructed chance to return a ball

3hind·er \ˈhīndə(r), *dial Brit* " *or* ˈhində- *or* ˈhin(t)ə-\ *adj* [ME, prob. fr. OE *hinder*, adv., behind — more at HIND] **1** : situated behind or at or in the rear : BACK, HIND ⟨a long oval forward part and a taillike ~ portion —R.E.Coker⟩ **2** *dial Brit* : YONDER

4hind·er \ˈhīndə(r), *Brit* " *or* ˈhində- *or* ˈhin(t)ə-\ *n* -s *chiefly dial* : BUTTOCKS

hindering impediment *n* : IMPEDIENT IMPEDIMENT

hin·der·ing·ly *adv* : in a hindering manner

hin·der·lands *or* **hin·der·lings** *or* **hin·der·lins** \ˈhindərlə̇nz, ˈhin(t)ə-\ *n pl* [*hinderlands* alter. of *hinderlins, hinderlings; hinderlins, hinderlings* fr. 3*hinder* + *-lings* or *-lins* (alter. of *-lings*)] *Scot* : BUTTOCKS

hind·er·most \ˈhīndə(r)ˌmōst, *chiefly Brit* -ˌməst\ *adj* [alter. (influenced by *most*) of ME *hindermest*, fr. 3*hinder* + *-mest* -most] *archaic* : HINDMOST

hin·der·some \ˈhində(r)səm\ *adj* [1*hinder* + *-some*] *now dial* : likely to hinder : TROUBLESOME

hind-foremost \ˈ=ˈ=(ˌ)=\ *adv* : with the hind part before : in reverse order

hindgut \ˈ=ˌ=\ *n* **1** : the posterior part of the alimentary canal of a vertebrate embryo **2** : the portion of the posterior intestine of an invertebrate formed by an infolding of the ectoderm

1hin·di \ˈhin(ˌ)dē\ *n* -s *cap* [Hindi *hindī*, fr. *Hind* India, fr. Per] **1 a** : a literary language of northern India usu. written in the Devanagari alphabet that is the official language of several states in India and is scheduled to become the official language of the republic **b** : a complex of vernacular dialects of northern India for which Hindi is the usual literary language **2** : a member of a cultural group inhabiting the middle and upper Ganges-Jumna valley, speaking a Hindi dialect, and characterized by dark skin, tall stature, and long head

2hindi \"\ *adj, usu cap* : of or relating to northern India or its language ⟨*Hindi* troops⟩ ⟨*Hindi* dialects⟩

hind kidney *n* : METANEPHROS

hind·ley's screw \ˈhīǀn(d)lēz-, ˈhiǀ\ *n, usu cap H* [after Henry *Hindley*, 18th cent. Eng. clockmaker] : an endless screw or worm shaped like an hourglass to fit a part of the circumference of a worm wheel so as to increase the bearing area and thereby diminish the wear — called also *hourglass screw*

hind·most \ˈhīn(d)ˌmōst, *chiefly Brit* -ˌməst\ *adj* [3*hind* + *-most*] : farthest in or toward the rear : most remote : LAST

hindneck \ˈ=ˌ=\ *n* : NAPE — used chiefly of birds

hindquarter \ˈ=ˌ==\ *n* **1** : the back half of a side of beef, veal, mutton, or lamb including a leg and usu. one or more ribs **2 hindquarters** *pl* : the hind biped of a quadruped; *broadly* : all the structures of a quadruped that lie posterior to the attachment of the hind legs to the trunk including the hind legs, rump, and posterior part of the back

hin·drance *also* **hin·der·ance** \ˈhind(ə)rən(t)s\ *n* -s [ME *hinderaunce*, fr. *hindren*, *hinderen* to hinder + *-aunce* -ance — more at HINDER] **1** : the state of being hindered ⟨his rebellion against . . . his tremor of knee and ~ of speech —Glenway Wescott⟩ **2** : the action of hindering ⟨~ of industry by too easily obtained patents —*Jour. of Patent Office Society*⟩ **3** : something that hinders : BLOCK, DRAWBACK ⟨sunken hulks that are a ~ to navigation⟩

hinds *pl of* HIND

hindsaddle \ˈ=ˌ==\ *n* : a wholesale cut of veal, lamb, or mutton consisting of undivided hindquarters and usu. including one pair of ribs — compare FORESADDLE

hind shank *n* : a cut of beef, veal, or mutton from the upper part of a hind leg

1hindside \ˈ=ˌ=\ *n* [3*hind* + *side*] *chiefly dial* : the back side ⟨she had her dress on ~ to⟩ ⟨put on his clothes ~ before⟩

2hindside \"\ *prep, chiefly dial* : BEHIND

hindsight \ˈ=ˌ=\ *n* **1** : a rear sight of a firearm **2** : perception of the nature and demands of an event after it has happened ⟨that ~ is better than foresight is axiomatic⟩

1hin·du *also* **hin·doo** \ˈhin(ˌ)dü\ *n* -s [Per *Hindū*, fr. *Hind* India, fr. OPer *Hindu* — more at INDIA] **1** *usu cap* : an adherent of Hinduism **2** *cap* : a native or inhabitant of India

2hindu *also* **hindoo** \"\ *adj, usu cap* **1** : of, relating to, or characteristic of the Hindus ⟨a *Hindu* poet⟩ **2** : of, relating to, or characteristic of Hinduism ⟨*Hindu* gods⟩

hin·du·ism \-üˌizəm\ *n* -s **1** *usu cap* : a complex body of social, cultural, and religious beliefs and practices evolved in and largely confined to the Indian subcontinent and marked by a caste system, an outlook tending to view all forms and theories as aspects of one eternal being and truth, a belief in ahimsa, karma, dharma, samsara, and moksha, and the practice of the way of works, the way of knowledge, or the way of devotion as the means of release from the round of rebirths : the way of life and form of thought of a Hindu — compare AVATAR, BHAKTI, BRAHMANISM, JNANA-MARGA, KARMA-MARGA **2** *usu cap* : a religious philosophy based on Hinduism **3** *cap* : the dominant cultic religion of India marked by participation in one of the bhakti sects (as Vaishnavism, Sivaism, Shaktism)

hin·du·ize \-üˌīz\ *vt* -ED/-ING/-S *often cap* : to bring into conformity with Hinduism : make Hindu (as in customs, outlook, or religion)

hindu numeral *or* **hindu-arabic numeral** *n, usu cap H&A* : ARABIC NUMERAL

1hin·du·stani \ˌhindüˈstanē, -dəˈ-, -tän-, -tȧn-, -ni\ *also* **hin·do·stani** \", -dōˈ-\ *n* -s *cap* [Hindi *Hindūstānī*, fr. Per *Hindūstān* India] **1** : Hindi, Urdu, and various vernacular dialects of northern India comprising a group of which literary Hindi and Urdu are considered diverse written forms **2** : the dialect of Delhi and the region to the northeast of Delhi **3** : a form of speech allied to Urdu but less divergent from Hindi, used in some urban areas and formerly in the British army, and commonly written in the Roman alphabet

2hindustani \ˈ==ˈ==\ *also* **hindostani** \ˈ==ˈ==\ *adj, usu cap* : of or relating to Hindustan or its people or Hindustani

hind wing *n* : a posterior wing of an insect

1hine *obs var of* HIND

²hi·ne \'hē(,)nä\ *n* -s [native name in Burma] **:** a male Indian elephant without tusks or tushes — compare TUSKER
hi·ney *var of* ²HEINIE
¹hing \'hiŋ\ *dial var of* HANG
²hing \"\ *dial past of* HANG
³hing \"\ *n* -s [Hindi *hīg*, fr. Skt *hiṅgu*] **:** ASAFETIDA
¹hinge \'hinj\ *n* -s *often attrib* [ME *heng, heeng, hyng;* akin to MD *henge, hengene* hook, handle, MLG *henge* hinge; derivatives fr. the root of E *hang*] **1 a :** a jointed or flexible device on which a door, lid, or other swinging part turns comprising typically a pair of metal leaves joined through the knuckles by a pin — see BUTT HINGE, CLEANING HINGE, H HINGE, HOOK-AND-EYE HINGE, PIANO HINGE **b :** a flexible ligamentous joint (as of a bivalve shell) **c** (1) **:** a paper or muslin joint, stub, or guard in a bound book that strengthens or permits the free flexing of a section, insert leaf, or map (2) **:** ¹JOINT 2d **d :** a small piece of thin gummed paper used in fastening a stamp in an album or on a sheet — called also *mount* **2** *obs* **a :** the earth's axis **b :** a cardinal point of the compass **3 :** something on which a development turns or depends **:** a basic issue or determining factor **:** TURNING POINT **4 :** a strategic point or line in the battle position of an army **5 :** HINGE LINE
²hinge \"\ *vb* -ED/-ING/-S *vt* **1 :** to attach by or furnish with hinges **2 :** to mount (a stamp) with a hinge **:** fasten a hinge to (a stamp) ~ *vi* **:** to be contingent or dependent on a single cardinal point or sole decisive consideration — used with *on* or *upon* ⟨a decision on which success or irrevocable failure *hinged* —Bernard De Voto⟩ **syn** see DEPEND
hingecorner \'=,==\ *n* **:** a hinged corner (as on a box or packing case)
hinged-back tortoise *n* **:** any of various grotesque tropical African tortoises that constitute a genus *Kinixys* of the family Testudinidae and have the posterior part of the carapace hinged
hinged frame *n* **:** a revolver frame hinged forward of the trigger to allow the forward portion of the frame to be rocked forward so as to expose the cylinder for loading and cleaning
hinged·ly \'hinj(ə)dlē\ *adv* **:** by means of hinging ⟨each of said inner panels being ~ connected to an end of one of the inner panels —*Modern Packaging*⟩
hinge fault *n* **:** a fault in the earth's surface in which displacement increases in one direction from a hinge line
hinge joint *n* **:** a joint that permits motion in one plane; *esp* **:** GINGLYMUS
hinge·less \'hinjləs\ *adj* **:** having no hinge
hinge line *also* **hinge** *n* **1 a :** an imaginary line on the earth's surface which can be regarded as a boundary between a stable region and one undergoing upward or downward movement **b :** a line around which one wall of a fault may appear to have rotated with respect to the other wall **2 :** the dorsal edge or border of a bivalve shell on which the hinge is situated
hinge plate *n* **1 :** the part of each valve that supports the hinge teeth in a bivalve mollusk **2 :** the part of a brachiopod that bears the sockets of the dorsal valve
hing·er \'hinjə(r)\ *n* -s **:** one that makes or puts on hinges
hinge tooth *n* **:** a projection of one valve of a bivalve shell that is located near the hinge line and that fits into a corresponding indentation in the other valve
hinging post *n* **:** GATEPOST
hin·gle \'hiŋgəl\ *n* -s [ME *hengle;* akin to MD *hengel* fishhook, MLG & MHG, hook, handle; derivatives fr. the root of E *hang*] *dial Eng* **:** the part (as a gate hinge or pot handle) by which something hangs
hink *n* -s [prob. of Scand origin; akin to ON *hinkr* hesitation, fr. *hinka* to limp, fr. MLG *hinken;* akin to OE *hincian* to limp, OHG *hinkan* to limp, ON *skakkr* crooked, askew — more at SHANK] *obs* **:** HESITATION, FALTERING
hin·kum·boo·by \'hiŋkəm,bübē\ *n* [fr. *hinkumbooby* (in the refrain *hinkumbooby round about*), prob. fr. Sc *hinkum* mischievous child + *booby*] *chiefly Scot* **:** a singing game similar to looby-loo
hin·most \'hinməst, -,mōst\ *dial Brit var of* HINDMOST
hin·na \'hinə\ [Sc *hin-* (fr. *hae*) + *na*] *Scot* **:** have not
hin·ner \'hinər\ *Scot var of* ³HINDER
hin·ney *or* **hin·ny** *or* **hin·nie** \'hini\ *dial Brit var of* HONEY
hin·ni·tes \hi'nīd·(,)ēz\ *n, cap* [NL, fr. L *hinnus* + NL *-ites*] **:** a genus of scallops (family Pectinidae) containing forms that become attached to the substrate with consequent thickening and modification of the shell to resemble that of an oyster and including the rock oyster (*H. giganteus*) of the Pacific coast of No. America
hin·ny \'hinē\ *n* -ES [modif. of L *hinnus*, prob. modif. (influenced by L *hinnire* to neigh, of imit. origin) of Gk *ginnos, innos*, prob. of non-IE origin] **:** a hybrid between a stallion and an ass that differs from the mule in having a more bushy tail, in having a body disproportionately large in comparison with the legs, and in being of a gentler disposition
hi·no·ki \hə'nōkē\ *or* **hinoki cypress** *n* -s [Jap *hinoki*, lit., fire tree] **1 :** SUN TREE **2 :** the wood or fiber of the hinoki
hins *pl of* HIN
hins·dal·ite \'hinz,dā,līt, -,dəl,-\ *n* -s [*Hinsdale* county, Colo., its locality + E *-ite*] **:** a mineral $(Pb,Sr)Al_3(PO_4)(SO_4)(OH)_6$ consisting of a basic lead and strontium aluminum sulphate and phosphate occurring in coarse crystals and masses
¹hint \'hint\ *n* -s [prob. alter. of obs. *hent* act of seizing — more at HENT] **1** *archaic* **:** an occasion that can be taken advantage of **:** OPPORTUNITY ⟨look about you ere the ~ be past —Alexander Ross⟩ **2 a :** a suggestion for action given in an indirect or summary manner ⟨a list of helpful ~*s* for new students⟩ **b :** a statement conveying by implication what it is preferred not to say explicitly ⟨dropping ~*s* . . . of something mysterious and important about to happen —Sherwood Anderson⟩ ⟨his failure for some years to declare himself definitely in the struggle against the Nazis laid him open to . . . ~*s* of cowardice —H.J.Muller⟩ **3 a :** a usu. slight indication of the approach, existence, or nature of something **:** SIGN, FOREWARNING, CLUE ⟨when the . . . beat of a tom-tom rose without ~ or introduction —William Beebe⟩ ⟨I can give only a ~ of the treasures to be found in the . . . museum —Dana Burnet⟩ **4 :** a very small amount **:** SUGGESTION ⟨friendly and cheerful with just the right ~ of respect —Margaret Kennedy⟩ **:** SUSPICION ⟨carry out this task . . . without ~ of favoritism —Peyton Boswell⟩ **:** DASH ⟨turnip greens seasoned with a ~ of vinegar⟩ ⟨a ~ of nutmeg and a suspicion of orange-flower water —Elinor Wylie⟩ **5** *Scot* **:** MOMENT, INSTANT
²hint \"\ *vb* -ED/-ING/-S *vt* **1 :** to seek to convey by a hint **:** to bring to mind by a slight reference or allusion rather than a full or explicit expression ⟨~ a suspicion⟩ ⟨~*ed* that he would like to be invited⟩ ⟨your father ~*ed* that the school wasn't good enough for you —Mary Austin⟩ **2 :** to indicate or reveal in the manner of a hint ⟨mighty ruins around the city ~ a better past —Curtis Dahl⟩ **:** PRESAGE, FORESHADOW, SUGGEST ⟨a cool, bright day, ~*ing* Indian summer —John Muir⟩ **3 :** to cause to go by hinting **:** send by a hint ⟨~ them along tactfully . . . toward the stuff that counts —Christopher Morley⟩ ~ *vi* **1 :** to make an indirect suggestion, allusion, or reference **:** give a hint ⟨~ broadly for the coveted invitation⟩ ⟨the face of the old retainer ~*ed* of things still untold —T.B.Costain⟩ — usu. used with *at* ⟨finally caught on to what he was ~*ing* at⟩ ⟨little gusts of wind ~*ed* at the storm to follow⟩ **2** *Scot* **:** to go about slyly or furtively esp. in order to further one's own interests **:** slink about or watch quietly **syn** see SUGGEST
³hint \"\ *adj* -ER/-EST [by alter.] *Scot* **:** HIND
⁴hint \"\ *prep, Scot* **:** BEHIND
⁵hint \"\ *n* -s **1** *Scot* **:** BACK, REAR **2** *Scot* **:** a furrow left between two ridges in plowing
⁶hint \"\ *vi* -ED/-ING/-S *Scot* **:** to plow up the furrow that is left to the last between two ridges **:** finish a ridge in plowing
hint·er \'hintə(r)\ *n* -s **:** one that hints
hin·ter·hand \'hintə(r)+,-\ *n* [G, fr. *hinter* rear, last + *hand*] **:** ENDHAND
hin·ter·land \'hintə(r),land, -laa(ə)nd\ *n* [G, fr. *hinter* rear + *land*] **1 a :** a region behind a coast or other usu. specified place ⟨the herdsmen have tended to avoid the immediate ~ of the coast —Walter Fitzgerald⟩; *specif* **:** the territory extending inland from a coastal colony (as along a river system or to the recognized boundary of another territory) over which the colonial power is sometimes held to possess sovereignty **b :** a region that provides supplies for the nation controlling it ⟨the vast ~ Nazi Germany has conquered in eastern and southern Europe —*New Republic*⟩ **c :** a region remote from cities and towns **:** WILDERNESS ⟨when this section, then a rough and rugged ~, was first being settled —*Amer. Guide Series: Minn.*⟩ **d :** a part of a country or region lying beyond any or all of its metropolitan or cultural centers **:** INTERIOR, STICKS ⟨by various profound thinkers in the ~ and by their counterparts in New York —G.J.Nathan⟩ ⟨steer the American out of the capital cities abroad and into the ~*s*, into the country pubs and . . . village taverns —Horace Sutton⟩ **2 :** the area often including satellites of which a city is the economic or cultural center **:** an urban zone of influence ⟨sometimes the ~*s* of different seaports overlap —W.G.Moore⟩ **3 :** a little-known sometimes contributory area of knowledge **:** FRONTIER ⟨a ~ of surgery hitherto neglected by the regular practitioner —W.T. Stead⟩ **:** BACKGROUND ⟨taught . . . to read around a subject, to understand its ~ —Hewlett Johnson⟩
hint·ing·ly *adv* **:** in a hinting manner
hin·ton test \'hint³n-, -ntən-\ *n, usu cap H* [after William A. *Hinton* b1883 Am. physician] **:** a blood-serum test for syphilis
hin·tze·ite \'hin(t)sə,īt\ *n* -s [G *hintzeit*, fr. Carl A. F. *Hintze* †1916 Ger. mineralogist + G *-it* -ite] **:** KALIBORITE
hi·o·don \'hīə,dän\ *n, cap* [NL, irreg. fr. *hy-* + *-odon*] **:** a genus (the type of the family Hiodontidae) of No. American freshwater fishes comprising the mooneyes — **hi·o·dont** \-nt\ *adj or n*
h ion *n, cap H* **:** HYDROGEN ION
hiort·dahl·ite \'yō(r)t,dä,līt, -,də,l-\ *n* -s [Norw *hiortdahlit*, fr. T. H. *Hiortdahl* †1925 Norw. chemist + Norw *-it* -ite] **:** a rare mineral $(Ca,Na)_{13}Zr_3Si_9(O,OH,F)_{33}$ consisting essentially of a sodium calcium zirconium silicate containing also fluorine and occurring as pale yellow tabular triclinic crystals
¹hip \'hip\ *also* **hep** \'hep\ *n* -s [ME *hepe, heppe, hipe*, fr. OE *hēope;* akin to OS *hiopo* bramble, OHG *hiafo, hiufa, hiefa* hip, bramble, Norw dial. *hjupa*, Dan *hyben*, and perh. to OPruss *kaäubri* thorn] **:** the ripened false fruit of a rosebush (as the dog rose) that consists of a fleshy receptacle enclosing numerous achenes
²hip \'hip\ *n* -s *often attrib* [ME *hip, hippe, hepe*, fr. OE *hype;* akin to OHG *huf* hip, Goth *hups* hip, L *cubitus, cubitum* elbow, *cubare* to lie down, Gk *kybos* cube, cubical die, vertebra, hollow before the hip (in cattle), OE *hēah* high — more at HIGH] **1 a** (1) **:** the laterally projecting region of each side of the lower or posterior part of the mammalian trunk that is formed by the lateral parts of the pelvis and upper part of the femur together with the fleshy parts covering them **:** HAUNCH (2) **:** HIP JOINT 1 **b :** COXA 2 **2 a :** the external angle formed by the meeting of two sloping sides or skirts of a roof that have their wall plates running in different directions **b** *also* **hip joint :** the junction between an inclined end post and the top chord of a truss **c :** HIP RAFTER — **on the hip** *archaic* **:** at a disadvantage ⟨feeling that she had the culprit *on the hip* —Anthony Trollope⟩
³hip \"\ *vt* **hipped; hipped; hipping; hips 1 :** to strain, injure, or fracture the hip of — usu. used of livestock **2 a :** to throw (an opponent) over one's hip in wrestling **:** throw by a cross-buttock **b :** to bump with one's hip (as in checking a sports opponent) ⟨I took a throw from the outfield, . . . *hipped* him, and he went sprawling to the right of the plate —G.R. Tebbetts⟩ **c :** to support or carry on the hip ⟨he loaded his small revolver and *hipped* it —Christopher Morley⟩ **3 :** to make (as a roof) with a hip
⁴hip \"\ *vb* **hipped; hipped; hipping; hips** [ME *hippen, huppen;* akin to OE *hoppian* to hop — more at HOP] *vi, now dial Brit* **:** to hop esp. on one foot ~ *vt, dial Brit* **:** to pass over **:** MISS, SKIP
⁵hip \"\ *n* -s [by shortening & alter.] *archaic* **:** HYPOCHONDRIA ⟨you have caught the ~ of your hypochondriac wife —Richard Cumberland †1811⟩
⁶hip \"\ *vt* **hipped; hipped; hipping; hips :** to make depressed, worried, or hypochondriac ⟨I rather would hearten than ~ thee —Elizabeth B. Browning⟩
⁷hip \"\ *interj* [origin unknown] — usu. used to begin a cheer ⟨~ ~ hooray⟩
⁸hip *var of* HEP
hip and thigh *adv* **:** OVERWHELMINGLY, UNSPARINGLY ⟨smote him *hip and thigh* with great slaughter —Judg 15:8 (RSV)⟩
hip-and-valley roof *n* **:** a roof so shaped as to have both hips and valleys — compare HIP ROOF
hip bath *n* **:** SITZ BATH
hip·ber·ry \'hip- —*see* BERRY\ *n* **:** ¹HIP
hipbone \'=,=\ *n* [ME *hipboon*, fr. *hip* + *boon* bone — more at BONE] **:** INNOMINATE BONE
hip boot *n* **:** a boot reaching to the hips that is worn esp. by fishermen
hip girdle *n* **:** PELVIC GIRDLE
hip joint *n* **1 :** the articulation between the femur and the innominate bone **2 :** ²HIP 2b
hip knob *n* **:** a finial, ball, or other ornament at the intersection of the hip rafters and the ridge of a roof
hiplength \'=,=\ *adj* **:** extending to or over the hips ⟨a ~ coat⟩
hip·less \'hipləs\ *adj* **:** having or seeming to have no hips
hipline \'=,=\ *n* **:** the line formed by the lower edge of a hiplength garment or by measuring the hip at its fullest part

hip boot

hip lock *n* **:** a cross-buttock in which a headlock is held throughout the maneuver
hipp- *or* **hippo-** *comb form* [L, fr. Gk, fr. *hippos* — more at EQUINE] **:** horse ⟨*hippo*gastronomy⟩ ⟨*hipp*uric acid⟩
hip·pa \'hipə\ [NL, alter. of L *hippus*, a sea fish, fr. Gk *hippos*, lit., horse] *syn of* EMERITA
hip·parch \'hi,pärk\ *n* -s [Gk *hipparchos, hipparchēs*, fr. *hipp-* + *-archos, -archēs* -arch] **:** a commander of cavalry in ancient Greece
hip·par·i·on \hi'pa(a)rē,än, -ēən\ *n* [NL, fr. Gk, pony, dim. of *hippos* horse] **1** *cap* **:** a genus of extinct Miocene and Pliocene three-toed mammals related to but not now considered direct ancestors of the horse **2** -s **:** any animal or fossil of the genus *Hipparion*
hip·pe·as·trum \,hipē'astrəm\ *n* [NL, fr. Gk *hippeus* horseman (fr. *hippos*) + *astron* star; fr. the equitant leaves and the star-shaped flowers — more at STAR] **1** *cap* **:** a genus of tropical American bulbous plants (family Amaryllidaceae) that are widely cultivated for their showy white to crimson flowers and that are sometimes included in the genus *Amaryllis* **2** -s **:** any amaryllis of the genus *Hippeastrum*
¹hipped \'hipt\ *adj* [²*hip* + *-ed*] **1 :** having hips ⟨a ~ roof⟩ — often used in combination ⟨a broad-*hipped* person⟩ **2 :** HIP-SHOT
²hipped \'hipt\ *adj* [⁵*hip* + *-ed*] **1 :** marked by worry, depression, or hypochondria ⟨with his bad habits and his domestic grievances he became completely ~ —H.W.Longfellow⟩ ⟨felt ~ because no one . . . bothered about his claret-colored ribbon —Philip Gibbs⟩ **2 :** absorbed or interested to an extreme or unreasonable degree **:** OBSESSED — usu. used with *on* ⟨married to a girl who is ~ on psychoanalysis —Bennett Cerf⟩
hip·pe·la·tes \,hipə'lad·(,)ēz\ *n, cap* [NL, fr. Gk *hippelatēs* horse driver, fr. *hipp-* + *elatēs* driver (fr. *elaunein* to drive); fr. the large spurs] **:** a genus of small black American eye gnats (family Chloropidae) including some that are held to be vectors of pinkeye and yaws
hip·pen *or* **hip·pin** \'hipən\ *n* -s [²*hip* + *-en* or *-in* (alter. of *-ing*)] *dial* **:** a baby's diaper
hip·pe·ty-hop *or* **hip·pi·ty-hop** \'hipəd·ē,häp\ *or* **hip·pe·ty-hop·pe·ty** *or* **hip·pi·ty-hop·pi·ty** \-äpəd·ē\ *adv (or adj)* [irreg. fr. ⁴*hip* + *hop*] **:** with a hopping rhythm or motion ⟨the rabbit went *hippety-hop* across the lawn⟩ ⟨rising and falling in their saddles, with a *hippity-hop* motion —Laura Krey⟩
hip·peu·tis \hi'pyüd·əs\ *n, cap* [NL, prob. fr. Gk *hippeutēs* horseman, fr. *hippos* horse — more at EQUINE] **:** a genus of freshwater snails (family Planorbidae) that are occas. the intermediate hosts of some medically important flukes
hip·pic \'hipik\ *adj* [Gk *hippikos*, fr. *hippos* horse + *-ikos* -ic] **:** of or relating to horses or horse racing ⟨the chief English ~ events of the season —*Punch*⟩
hip·pid·i·on \hi'pidē,än, -ēən\ *n, cap* [NL, fr. Gk *hippidion*, dim. of *hippos*] **:** a genus of extinct Pleistocene horses of Argentina and Brazil
hip·pid·i·um \-ēəm\ [NL, alter. of *Hippidion*] *syn of* HIPPIDION
hippier *comparative of* HIPPY
hippiest *superlative of* HIPPY
hipping *pres part of* HIP
hip·pio·spongia \,hipē(,)ō+\ *n, cap* [NL, alter. of *Hippospongia*] **:** a genus of sponges (family Spongiidae) containing numerous important commercial sponges
hip·pish \'hipish\ *adj* [⁵*hip* + *-ish*] **:** characterized by or suffering from worry, depression, or hypochondria **:** HIPPED
hip·ple \'hipəl\ *n* -s [ME *heepil, hypil*, dim. of *heep, hepe* heap — more at HEAP] *dial Eng* **:** a small heap; *esp* **:** a small haycock
hip·po \'hi(,)pō\ *n* -s [by shortening] **:** HIPPOPOTAMUS
hippo- — see HIPP-
hip·po·bos·ca \,hipə'bäskə\ *n, cap* [NL, fr. *hipp-* + *-bosca* (fr. Gk *boskein* to feed)] **:** the type genus of the family Hippoboscidae
¹hip·po·bos·cid \',==:bäs(k)əd\ *adj* [NL *Hippoboscidae*] **:** of or relating to the Hippoboscidae
²hippoboscid \"\ *n* -s **:** a fly of the family Hippoboscidae
hip·po·bos·ci·dae \,==:bäs(k)ə,dē\ *n pl, cap* [NL, fr. *Hippobosca*, type genus + *-idae*] **:** a family of winged or wingless dipterans that comprise the louse flies, are bloodsucking parasites on birds and mammals, and are larviparous bringing forth single advanced larvae from time to time which almost immediately pupate — compare SHEEP KED
hip·po·camp \'hipə,kamp\ *n* [Gk *hippokampos*] **:** HIPPOCAMPUS 1
hip·po·cam·pal \,==:kampəl\ *adj* [NL *hippocampus* + E *-al*] **:** of or relating to the hippocampus
hippocampal convolution *or* **hippocampal gyrus** *n* **:** a convolution of the cerebral cortex that borders the hippocampus and contains elements of both archipallium and neopallium
hippocampal fissure *n* **:** DENTATE FISSURE
hip·po·cam·pine \,==:kam,pīn, -pən\ *adj* [NL *Hippocampus* + E *-ine*] **:** of or relating to sea horses
hip·po·cam·pus \,==:kampəs\ *n* [NL, fr. Gk *hippokampos* sea horse, legendary sea monster, fr. *hippo-* hipp- + *kampos* sea monster] **1** *pl* **hippocam·pi** \-m,pī\ **:** a legendary creature with the head and forequarters of a horse and the tail of a dolphin or fish **2** *pl* **hippocampi :** a curved elongated ridge extending over the floor of the descending horn of each lateral ventricle of the brain, consisting of gray matter covered on the ventricular surface with white matter, and forming the larger part of the archipallium **3** *cap* **:** a genus of fishes (family Syngnathidae) consisting of the typical sea horses
hip·po·cas·ta·na·ce·ae \,hipə,kastə'nāsē,ē\ *n pl, cap* [NL, fr. *Hippocastanum*, type genus in former classifications (fr. *hipp-* + Gk *kastanon* chestnut) + *-aceae*] **:** a family of trees (order Sapindales) having opposite palmately lobed leaves, showy flowers in large clusters, and nutlike seeds encased in a leathery capsule and including the buckeyes
hip·po·centaur \,hipə+\ *n* [L *hippocentaurus*, fr. Gk *hippokentauros*, fr. *hippo-* hipp- + *kentauros* centaur] **:** CENTAUR
hip·po·cras \'hipə,kras, -krəs\ *n* -ES [ME *ypocras*, after *Hippocras, Hypocras, Ypocras* Hippocrates †ab377 B.C. Greek physician, its legendary inventor; prob. fr. his name's having been falsely analyzed as Gk *hypo* under + *krasis* mixture] **:** an aromatic highly spiced wine of medieval Europe
hip·po·crat·ea \,hipə'krad·ēə\ *n, cap* [NL, after *Hippocrates*] **:** a genus (the type of the family Hippocrateaceae) of tropical trees or twining shrubs having a 3-lobed capsule with winged seeds — see WOOD ALMOND
hip·po·crat·e·a·ce·ae \,==,krad·ē'āsē,ē\ *n pl, cap* [NL, fr. *Hippocratea*, type genus + *-aceae*] **:** a family of tropical shrubs or trees (order Sapindales) having opposite leaves and small 5-parted flowers — **hip·po·crat·e·a·ceous** \,==,==:āshəs\ *adj*
hip·po·crat·ic \,hipə;krad·|ik, -at|, |ēk\ *also* **hip·po·crat·i·cal** \|əkəl, |ēk-\ *adj, usu cap* [LL *Hippocraticus*, fr. *Hippocrates* (fr. Gk *Hippokratēs*) + *-icus* -ic, -ical] **:** of or relating to Hippocrates or to the school of medicine that took his name
hippocratic facies *n, usu cap H* **:** the face as it appears near death and in some debilitating conditions marked by sunken eyes and temples, pinched nose, and tense hard skin
hippocratic finger *n, usu cap H* **:** a clubbed finger
hippocratic oath *n, usu cap H* **:** an oath embodying a code of medical ethics that is usu. taken by those about to begin medical practice
hip·poc·ra·tism \hi'päkrə,tizəm\ *n* -s *usu cap* [*Hippocrates* + E *-ism*] **:** the medical doctrine of the Hippocratic school
hip·po·crene \'hipə,krēn, ,==:krēnē\ *n* -s *usu cap* [fr. *Hippocrene*, a fountain in ancient Greece that was fabled to have burst forth when the ground was struck by the hoof of the winged horse Pegasus and that was supposed to be a source of poetic inspiration, fr. L, fr. Gk *Hippokrēnē*, fr. *hippo-* hipp- + *krēnē* fountain] **:** poetic inspiration ⟨we shrink from a cup of the purest *Hippocrene* after the critics' solar microscope —J.R. Lowell⟩ ⟨a loiterer by the waves of *Hippocrene* —O.W.Holmes †1894⟩
hip·po·crep·i·form \,hipə;krepə,fȯrm\ *adj* [*hipp-* + Gk *krēpis* boot + E *-form* — more at CREPIDULA] **:** shaped like a horseshoe
¹hip·po·drome \'hipə,drōm\ *n* -s [MF, fr. L *hippodromos*, fr. Gk, fr. *hippo-* hipp- + *dromos* racecourse — more at -DROME] **1 :** an oval stadium for horse and chariot races in ancient Greece **2 a :** an arena for equestrian performances **b** (1) **:** a spectacle presented in a hippodrome (2) **:** an activity suggesting such a spectacle **3 :** a sports contest with a predetermined winner
²hippodrome \"\ *vi* -ED/-ING/-S **1 :** to arrange or fix a sports contest whose winner is predetermined **2 :** to act as if in a hippodrome **:** attract attention by or as if by spectacular performance
hip·po·drom·ic \,==:drämik, -rōm-\ *adj* **:** of, relating to, or having the characteristics of a hippodrome
hip·po·glos·sus \,hipə'gläsəs, -lȯs-\ *n, cap* [NL, fr. *hipp-* + *-glossus* (fr. Gk *glōssa* tongue) — more at GLOSS] **:** a genus of flatfishes containing the typical halibuts and sometimes being made to be the type of a separate family but usu. included in the Pleuronectidae
hip·po·griff \'hipə,grif\ *n* -s [F *hippogriffe*, fr. It *ippogrifo*, fr. *ippo-* (fr. L *hippo-* hipp) + *grifo* griffin, fr. L *gryphus* — more at GRIFFIN] **:** a legendary animal having the foreparts of a winged griffin and the body and hindquarters of a horse
hip·po·griffin \,hipə+\ *n* [by alter. (influenced by *griffin*)] **:** HIPPOGRIFF
¹hip·poid \'hi,pȯid\ *adj* [NL *Hippoidea*] **:** of or relating to the Hippoidea
²hippoid \"\ *n* -s **:** a mammal of the group Hippoidea
hip·poi·dea \hi'pȯidēə\ *n pl, cap* [NL, fr. *hipp-* + *-oidea*] *in some classifications* **:** a division of perissodactylous mammals comprising the Equidae and extinct related forms
hip·po·lith \'hipə,lith\ *or* **hip·po·lite** \-,līt\ *n* -s [NL *hippolithus*, fr. *hipp-* + *-lithus* -lith, -lite] **:** a concretion from the intestines of the horse
hip·pol·o·gy \hi'päləjē\ *n* -ES [ISV *hipp-* + *-logy*] **:** the study of the horse
hip·pol·y·te \hi'pälə(,)tē\ *n, cap* [NL, after *Hippolyte*, Amazon in Greek mythology, fr. Gk *Hippolytē*] **:** a common and widely distributed genus (the type of the family Hippolytidae) of small prawns having the abdomen sharply bent at the third segment — **hip·pol·y·tid** \-,təd\ *adj or n*
hip·pom·a·nes \hi'pämə,nēz\ *n* -ES [L, fr. Gk, fr. *hippo-* hipp- + *-manes* (fr. *mainesthai* to rage, be furious) — more at MIND] **:** a growth found on the forehead of a newborn foal and held in antiquity to be aphrodisiac
hip·po·mo·bile \,hipəmō,bē(ə)l, ,==:mō,b-\ *n* [*hipp-* + *-mobile* (as in *automobile*)] **:** a horse-drawn vehicle
hip·po·mor·pha \,hipə'mȯrfə\ *n pl, cap* [NL, fr. *hipp-* + *-morpha*] **:** a suborder of Perissodactyla comprising horses, asses, zebras, and many extinct related forms
¹hip·po·nac·te·an \,hipə,nak;tēən, -;naktē-\ *adj, usu cap* [L *Hipponacteus* of Hipponax (fr. *Hipponact-*, *Hipponax*, 6th cent. B.C. Greek poet reputed to have invented the choliamb, fr. Gk *Hipponakt-, Hippōnax*) + E *-an*] **:** of or relating to Hipponax or to the verse forms ascribed to him; *specif* **:** CHOLIAMBIC
²hipponactean \"\ *n* -s *usu cap* **:** a Hipponactean verse; *specif* **:** a hypercatalectic form of glyconic

hipponactean distich *n, usu cap H* : a distich composed of a catalectic trochaic dimeter and iambic trimeter

hip·po·pathology \¦hi(ˌ)pō+\ *n* [*hipp-* + *pathology*] : the pathology of the horse

hip·poph·aë \hiˈpäfəˌē\ *n, cap* [NL, fr. L *hippophaes*, fr. Gk, spurge] : a genus of thorny deciduous Old World shrubs (family Eleagnaceae) including the sea buckthorn

hip·poph·a·gism \hiˈpäfəˌjizəm\ *n* -s [*hipp-* + *-phagism*] : HIPPOPHAGY

hip·poph·a·gist \-jəst\ *n* -s [*hippophagy* + *-ist*] : one that eats horseflesh — **hip·poph·a·gis·ti·cal** \hi¦päfə¦jistəkəl\ *adj*

hip·poph·a·gous \(ˈ)hi¦päfəgəs\ *adj* [*hipp-* + *-phagous*] : eating horseflesh

hip·poph·a·gy \=ˈ=fəjē\ *n* -ES [*hipp-* + *-phagy*] : the act or practice of eating horseflesh

hip·po·pod \ˈhipəˌpäd\ *n, pl* **hippopods** \-dz\ *or* **hippop·o·des** \hiˈpäpəˌdēz\ [*hipp-* + *-pod*] : a legendary creature having the body of a man and the legs of a horse

hip·po·pot·am·ic \ˌhi(ˌ)pōpə¦tamik, ˌhipəpə¦-; ¦hipə¦päd·ə(ˌ)mik\ *or* **hip·po·po·ta·mi·an** \ˌhi(ˌ)pōpə¦tāmēən, ¦hipəpə¦-\ *adj* : of, relating to, or resembling the hippopotamus; *specif* : UNWIELDY

hip·po·pot·a·mus \ˌhipəˈpäd·əməs, -ätəm-\ *n* [L, fr. Gk, fr. *hippo-* hipp- + *potamos* river, fr. *petesthai* to fly, dart, rush — more at FEATHER] **1** *pl* **hip·popotamus·es** \-səz\ *or* **hippopota·mi** \-ˌmī, -(ˌ)mē\ : any of various large herbivorous four-toed chiefly aquatic mammals of the order Artiodactyla with an extremely large head and mouth, bare and very thick skin, and short legs; *esp* : a member of the genus *Hippopotamus* (as *H. amphibius*) formerly common in most rivers of Africa that is except for the elephant the bulkiest existing quadruped and has long canine and incisor teeth that yield a good quality of ivory **2** *cap* [NL, fr. L] : a genus (the type of the family Hippopotamidae) of mammals that includes the typical hippopotamuses

hippopotamus

hippos *pl of* HIPPO

hip·po·si·de·ros \ˌhi(ˌ)pōsəˈdirəs, -sīˈd-\ *n, cap* [NL, fr. *hipp-* + Gk *sidēros* iron, object made of iron] : a large genus (the type of the family Hipposideridae) of horseshoe bats comprising some 40 species and ranging from northwest Africa to the Philippines and Australia

hip·po·spongia \¦hipə+\ [NL, fr. *hipp-* + *Spongia*] *syn of* SPONGIA

hip·po·ti·grine \¦hipə¦tīgrən, -ˌgrīn\ *adj* [NL *Hippotigris*, subgenus of *Equus* containing the zebras (fr. *hipp-* + Gk *tigris* tiger) + E *-ine* — more at TIGER] : of or relating to the zebra

hip·pot·o·my \hiˈpäd·əmē\ *n* -ES [ISV *hipp-* + *-tomy* (as in *anatomy*)] : the anatomy of the horse

hip·pot·ra·gine \hiˈpä·trəˌjīn, -əˌgīn, -əjən, -əgən\ *adj* [NL *Hippotragus* + E *-ine*] : of or relating to the genus *Hippotragus* or to any of the antelopes belonging to it

hip·pot·ra·gus \-rəgəs\ *n, cap* [NL, fr. *hipp-* + Gk *tragos* he-goat] : a genus of large antelopes with long annulated backwardly curved horns that includes the sable and roan antelopes and the extinct blaubok

hip·pu·rate \hiˈpyúˌrāt, ˈhipyəˌr-\ *n* -s [ISV *hippuric* + *-ate*] : a salt or ester of hippuric acid

hip·pu·ric acid \(ˈ)hi¦pyúrik-\ *n* [*hipp-* + *-uric*] : a white crystalline nitrogenous acid $C_6H_5CONHCH_2COOH$ formed in the liver as a detoxication product of benzoic acid and present in the urine of herbivorous animals and in small quantity in human urine — called also *benzoylglycine*

hip·pu·ri·case \hiˈpyúrəˌkās, -āz\ *n* -s [ISV *hippuric* + *-ase*] : HISTOZYME

hip·pu·ris \hiˈpyúrəs\ *n, cap* [NL, fr. Gk *hippouris* horsetail fr. *hipp-* + *-ouris* (fr. *oura* tail)] : a widely distributed genus of small-flowered aquatic herbs (family Haloragaceae) with single erect stems and verticillate leaves

hip·pu·rite \ˈhipyəˌrīt\ *n* -s [NL *Hippurites*] : a mollusk or fossil of the genus *Hippurites*

hip·pu·ri·tes \ˌhipyəˈrīd·(ˌ)ēz\ *n, cap* [NL, fr. *hipp-* + *ur-* (tail) + *-ites*] : a genus (the type of the family Hippuritidae) of aberrant marine bivalve mollusks that are confined to the Cretaceous and whose lower valve is conical, usu. longitudinally ribbed, and attached by its apex and whose upper valve is depressed conic with a nearly central umbo — **hip·pu·rit·ic** \¦==¦rid·ik\ *adj* — **hip·pu·ri·tid** \-ˈrīd·əd\ *adj or n* — **hip·pu·ri·toid** \-ˈrīd·ˌȯid\ *adj*

hip·pus \ˈhipəs\ *n* -ES [NL, fr. Gk *hippos* horse, eye complaint — more at EQUINE] : a spasmodic variation in the size of the pupil of the eye caused by a tremor of the iris

-hippus \ˈ"\ *n comb form* [NL, fr. Gk *hippos*] : horse — in generic names esp. in paleontology ⟨*Eohippus*⟩

hip·py \ˈhipē\ *adj, usu* -ER/-EST : having or resembling large hips ⟨farthingales . . . to make the hips seem *hippier* and the waist tinier —*Britannica Bk. of the Yr.*⟩

hip rafter *n* : the rafter extending from the wall plate to the ridge and forming the angle of a hip roof

hip roll *n* : a tile or strip that covers the angle of a hip roof

hip roof *n* : a roof having sloping ends and sloping sides — compare HIP-AND-VALLEY ROOF

hips *pl of* HIP, *pres 3d sing of* HIP

hip·shot \ˈ=ˌ=\ *adj* **1** : having the hip dislocated **2** : having one hip lower than the other ⟨spun slowly toward the long mirror . . . and posed ~ like a model —Crary Moore⟩

hipster *var of* HEPSTER

hip tile *n* : a tile for covering the hip of a roof

hip vertical *n* : a vertical member whose upper end is at the hip of a truss

hip roof

hir·able *or* **hire·able** \ˈhīrəbəl\ *adj* : capable of being hired : available for hire

hi·ra·do ware \həˈrä(ˌ)dō-\ *n, usu cap H* [fr. *Hirado*, town and island of Japan where such porcelain is manufactured] : a Hizen porcelain characteristically decorated in underglaze blue with a design showing children playing under a fir tree

hi·ra·ga·na \¦hirə¦gänə\ *n* -s [Jap, lit., flat kana] : the cursive script that is one of two sets of symbols in which Japanese kana is written — compare KATAKANA

hir·car·rah \hərˈkarə\ *n* -s [Per *harkāra*, fr. *har* every, all (fr. OPer *haruva-*) + *kār* work, deed, fr. MPer, fr. OPer *kar-* to do, make] *India* : COURIER, SPY

hirch *var of* HIRTCH

hir·cine \ˈhərˌsīn, -ˌsᵊn\ *adj* [L *hircinus*, fr. *hircus* he-goat + *-inus* -ine; perh. akin to L *horrēre* to bristle — more at HORROR] : of, relating to, or suggestive of a goat; *esp* : resembling a goat in smell

hir·co·cer·vus \ˌhərkōˈsərvəs\ *n* -ES [LL, fr. L *hircus* he-goat + *cervus* stag; trans. of Gk *tragelaphos*, fr. *tragos* he-goat + *elaphos* stag] : a legendary creature that is half goat and half stag

hir·die-gir·die \¦hirdi¦girdi, ¦hərdi¦gər-\ *adv* [alter. of *hiddie-giddie*, fr. ME (Sc) *hiddy-giddy*, prob. redupl. (influenced by *hed*, head) of *giddy*] *dial Brit* : TOPSY-TURVY

hir·dum-dir·dum \¦hirdəm¦dirdəm, ¦hərdəm¦dər-\ *n* [prob. redupl. (influenced by *heard*) of *dirdum*] *dial Brit* : UPROAR

¹hire \ˈhī(ə)r, ˈhīə\ *n* -s [ME, fr. OE *hȳr*; akin to OFris *hēre* tax, lease, rent, OS *hūra*, *hūria*, MLG & MD *hūre*] **1 a** : payment for the temporary use of something ⟨the heaviest single item of government expenditure is . . . the ~ of the money we borrowed for the war —G.B.Shaw⟩ **b** : payment for labor or personal services : WAGES ⟨the laborer is worthy of his ~ —Lk 10:7 (AV)⟩ **2 a** (1) : the act of hiring ⟨the government office which controlled the ~ of coolies —Dillon Ripley⟩ (2) : an instance of such act ⟨the monthly base compensation payroll . . . is $70,000 as the result of new ~s and merit and length-of-service increases —*U.S.Code*⟩ **b** : the state of being hired : EMPLOYMENT ⟨men of every political leaning are in the ~ of big corporations —Robert Shaplen⟩ **syn** see WAGE — **for hire** *also* **on hire** : available for use or service in return for payment ⟨a coal lighter which plies *for hire* up and down the Meuse —H.J.Laski⟩ ⟨a thrashing machine went *on hire* from farm to farm —Flora Thompson⟩

²hire \ˈ"\ *vb* -ED/-ING/-S [ME *hiren*, fr. OE *hȳrian*; akin to OFris *hēra* to lease, MLG & MD *huren*; denominatives fr. the root of E ¹*hire*] *vt* **1 a** : to engage the personal services of for a fixed sum : employ for wages ⟨many clergy fought in person, and others *hired* substitutes —G.G.Coulton⟩ ⟨the leader . . . ~s staff people to think up the ideas —W.H.Whyte⟩ — sometimes used with *away* or *on* ⟨can ~ them away from any company . . . if you offer them a few more dollars —W.J.Reilly⟩ ⟨the crew was fully *hired on* —John Hersey⟩ **b** : to engage the temporary use of for a fixed sum ⟨came down with a hundred people in four private cars and *hired* a whole floor of the . . . hotel —Scott Fitzgerald⟩ ⟨*hired* a car for the afternoon —Elizabeth Bowen⟩ **c** *archaic* : BORROW ⟨she can ~ the money, and I know she will pay you —A.D.McFaul⟩ **2 a** : to grant the personal services of for a fixed sum — often used with *out* ⟨have been *hiring* themselves out as practical consultants —Vance Packard⟩ ⟨the colonel had *hired out* most of his slaves —Winston Churchill⟩ **b** : to grant the temporary use of for a fixed sum ⟨bored-looking camels which they ~ to visitors as props for exotic snapshots —Mollie Panter-Downes⟩ — often used with *out* ⟨the town council *hired out* chairs for visitors —B.L.K.Henderson⟩ **3** : to pay for having (something done) ⟨my father . . . had to ~ all his share of the farm work done —W.A.White⟩ ~ *vi* : to accept employment ⟨asked me if I would ~ with him to tend shop and keep books —John Woolman⟩ — **hire one's time** : to pay one's master for the right to use one's time for one's own gain

hired girl *n* : a woman employed as a domestic; *specif* : one living in a farm household who helps around the house and performs light farm chores

hired hand *n* : FARMHAND

hired man *n* : a man employed to do odd jobs about a house, estate, or farm; *esp* : FARMHAND

hire in *vi* : to accept employment and begin to work ⟨most of the guys . . . who've *hired in* over the past fourteen years —Warner Bloomberg⟩

hire·less \ˈhī(ə)rləs, -īəl-\ *adj* : receiving no payment or reward ⟨preaching . . . in most of the great towns as an ~ volunteer —S.T.Coleridge⟩

hire·ling \-liŋ, -lēŋ\ *n* -s *often attrib* **1** : one who is hired; *esp* : one whose motives and interests in serving another are chiefly gainful ⟨was murdered by ~s in the service of foreign powers —Stoyan Christowe⟩ **2** : one whose motives are venal or mercenary ⟨baser ~s who live by lies on good men's lives —Lord Byron⟩ **3** : a horse for hire ⟨went to a neighboring livery stable to look for ~s —Evelyn Waugh⟩

hire on *vi* : to find or accept employment ⟨doubtful that he could *hire on* as a Hollywood extra —F.B.Gipson⟩

hire out *vi* : to accept employment ⟨young Englishman who *hired out* as a photographer —Marcus Duffield⟩

hire purchase *n* **1** *chiefly Brit* : a contract of hire with an option of purchase in which a person hires goods for a specified period and at a fixed rent with the added condition that if he retains the goods for the full period and pays all the installments of rent as they become due the contract shall determine and the title vest absolutely in him and that if he chooses he may at any time during the term surrender the goods and be quit of any liability for future installments upon the contract — compare CONDITIONAL SALE **2** *chiefly Brit* : the practice of buying by hire purchase

hir·er \ˈhīrə(r)\ *n* -s [ME, fr. *hiren* to hire + *-er*] : one that hires

hiring *n* -s [ME, fr. gerund of *hiren* to hire — more at HIRE] : the contract or relationship between the parties to a transaction in which one hires the services or property of the other

hiring hall *n* : a union-operated employment agency or placement office where registered applicants are referred to jobs (as in the shipping industry) on a rotation basis — compare SHAPE-UP

hir·ling \ˈhərlən, ˈhir-, -liŋ\ *var of* HERLING

hir·mos *or* **heir·mos** \ˈirˌmōs\ *n, pl* **hir·moi** *or* **heir·moi** \-ˌmȯi\ [LGk *heirmos*, fr. Gk, series, sequence, connection; akin to Gk *eirein* to fasten together — more at SERIES] : a troparion, hymn, or canticle with a fixed rhythm and melody that is used as a standard rhythmic and melodic pattern for other troparia in the canon of the Eastern Church

hirn \ˈhərn, -i-\ *var of* ¹HERN

hir·ne·o·la \ˌhərˈnēələ\ [NL, dim. of L *hirnea* jug] *syn of* AURICULARIA

hiro·shi·ma \¦hirə¦shēmə, -rō¦-; həˈrōshəmə, -ˈräsh-, -ˈrōsh-; *Jap approximately* hiˈrō·shē(ˌ)mä\ *adj, usu cap* [fr. *Hiroshima*, Japan] : of or from the city of Hiroshima, Japan : of the kind or style prevalent in Hiroshima

¹hir·ple \ˈhirpəl\ *vi* -ED/-ING/-S [ME (Sc dial.) *hirplen*] *chiefly Scot* : to walk with a limp : HOBBLE

²hirple \ˈ"\ *n* -s *Scot* : LIMP

hirsch·sprung's disease \ˈhirshˌprúŋz-\ *n, usu cap H* [after Harold *Hirschsprung* †1916 Dan. physician] : congenital megacolon

¹hir·sel *also* **hir·sle** \ˈhirsəl\ *n* -s [ME *hirsill*, fr. ON *hirzla*, *hirthsla* safekeeping, custody, fr. *hirtha* to guard sheep, fr. *hirthir* shepherd — more at HERD] **1** *Scot* : a flock of sheep **2** *Scot* : the land grazed by a flock of sheep ⟨like a poor lamb that has wandered from its own native ~ —Sir Walter Scott⟩ **3** *Scot* : a large number or quantity : MULTITUDE

²hirsel *also* **hirsle** \ˈ"\ *vt* **hirseled** *or* **hirselled** *also* **hirsled**; **hirseled** *or* **hirselled** *also* **hirsled**; **hirseling** *or* **hirselling** *also* **hirsling**; **hirsels** *also* **hirsles** *Scot* : to arrange in or as if in flocks

³hirsel *also* **hirsle** \ˈ"\ *vb* **hirseled** *or* **hirselled** *also* **hirsled**; **hirseled** *or* **hirselled** *also* **hirsled**; **hirseling** *or* **hirselling** *also* **hirsling**; **hirsels** *also* **hirsles** [origin unknown] *vi* **1** *Scot* : to move along a surface awkwardly : SLITHER **2** *Scot* : to move clumsily or with difficulty : SCRAMBLE **3** *Scot* : to move with a rustling or grating noise ~ *vt, Scot* : to cause to move awkwardly or with difficulty

hirst \ˈhirst\ *n* -s [ME *hirst*, *hurst* grove, knoll — more at HURST] **1** *Scot* **a** : a barren unproductive plot of ground **b** : a sandbank in a river **2** *Scot* : a great number or quantity **3** *Scot* : the part of the floor of a mill where the millstones turn in their framework

hirst·ie \ˈhirsti\ *adj* [*hirst* + *-ie* (Sc var. of *-y*)] *Scot* : BARE, BARREN

hir·su·tal \(ˈ)hər¦süd·ᵊl\ *adj* [L *hirsutus* + E *-al*] : of or relating to the hair

hir·sute \ˈhərˌsüt, ˈhi(ə)rˌs-, ˈhə̄ˌs-, ˈhəiˌs-, ˈhiəˌs-, (ˌ)=ˈ=, *usu* -üd·+V\ *adj* [L *hirsutus*; akin to L *hirtus* rough, shaggy, *horrēre* to bristle — more at HORROR] **1 a** : rough with hair or bristles : HAIRY, SHAGGY ⟨the dog's master patted the ~ fellow —Horace Sutton⟩ **b** *biol* : pubescent with coarse stiff hairs **c** : covered with feathers that resemble hair **2** : of, relating to, or having the characteristics of hair — **hir·sute·ness** *n* -ES

hir·su·tel·la \ˌhər(ˌ)süˈtelə, ˌhir-\ *n, cap* [NL, fr. L *hirsutus* + NL *-ella*] : a genus of basidiomycetous fungi of uncertain taxonomic position that are associated with and believed to be parasitic upon various insects

hir·su·ti·es \(ˌ)hərˈsüshēˌēz, hir-\ *n, pl* **hirsuties** [NL, fr. L *hirsutus*] : HIRSUTISM

hir·sut·ism *pronunc at* HIRSUTE + ˌizəm\ *n* -s [ISV *hirsute* + *-ism*] : excessive growth of hair of normal or abnormal distribution : HYPERTRICHOSIS

hir·su·tu·lous \(ˌ)hər¦süchələs, ¦hir-\ *adj* [*hirsute* + *-ulous*] : minutely or slightly hirsute

¹hirtch \ˈhirch\ *vi* -ED/-ING/-ES [origin unknown] **1** *Scot* : to shudder with or as if with cold **2** *Scot* : to walk with a jerky hobbling motion

²hirtch \ˈ"\ *n* -ES *Scot* : HITCH

hir·tel·la \(ˌ)hərˈtelə, hir-\ *n, cap* [NL, fr. L *hirtus* + NL *-ella*] : a genus of chiefly tropical American shrubs or small trees (family Rosaceae) having axillary or terminal racemes of small white or purplish flowers with numerous stamens

hir·tel·lous \(ˌ)hər¦teləs, ¦hir-\ *adj* [L *hirtus* + *-ellus* (diminutive suffix)] : finely hirsute ⟨thickened ~ leaves⟩

hiru·din \ˈhir(y)ədən, həˈrüdᵊn\ *n* -s [fr. *Hirudin*, a trademark] : a preparation of the active principles of the buccal glands of a leech used to retard or prevent the clotting of blood

hir·u·din·ea \ˌhir(y)əˈdinēə\ *n pl, cap* [NL, fr. *Hirudin-*, *Hirudo*] : a class of hermaphroditic aquatic, terrestrial, or parasitic annelid worms distinguished by a coelom nearly obliterated by connective tissue and reduced to a series of vascular sinuses, by modification of the hindmost segments into a sucking disk, and by the absence of parapodia and setae — compare GNATHOBDELLIDA, PHARYNGOBDELLIDA, RHYNCHOBDELLIDA — **hir·u·din·e·an** \¦==¦dinēən\ *adj or n*

hir·u·din·ei \ˌ==ˈdinēˌī\ [NL, fr. *Hirudin-*, *Hirudo*] *syn of* HIRUDINEA

hir·u·di·ni·a·sis \ˌhir(y)ədəˈnīəsəs, həˌrüdᵊnˈī-\ *n, pl* **hirudi·nia·ses** \-īəˌsēz\ [NL, fr. *Hirudin-*, *Hirudo* + *-iasis*] : infestation with leeches

hir·u·din·i·dae \ˌhir(y)əˈdinəˌdē\ *n pl, cap* [NL, fr. *Hirudin-*, *Hirudo*, type genus + *-idae*] : a family of aquatic leeches that have 5-ringed segments, 5 pairs of eyes, and usu. 3-toothed jaws and that include the common medicinal leech

hi·ru·di·nize \həˈrüdᵊnˌīz\ *vt* -ED/-ING/-S : to retard or prevent the coagulation of (blood) by the injection of hirudin

hi·ru·do \həˈrü(ˌ)dō\ *n, cap* [NL, fr. L, leech] : a genus (the type of the family Hirudinidae) of the order Gnathobdellida that includes the common medicinal leech

¹hirun·dine \həˈrəndən, -ˌdīn; ˈhirənˌdīn\ *adj* [L *hirundo* swallow + E *-ine*] : of, relating to, or resembling the swallow

²hirundine \ˈ"\ *n* -s [NL *Hirundinidae*] : ¹SWALLOW 1

hir·un·din·i·dae \ˌhirənˈdinəˌdē\ *n pl, cap* [NL, fr. *Hirundin-*, *Hirundo*, type genus (fr. L, swallow) + *-idae*] : a family of passerine birds consisting of the swallows and martins — **hi·run·di·nous** \həˈrəndənəs\ *adj*

¹his [ME, fr. OE, gen. of *hē* he — more at HE] *obs possessive of* ¹HE

²his \(h)iz, ¦hiz, ˌēz\ *adj* [ME, fr. OE, gen. of *hē*] **1 a** : of or relating to him or himself as possessor : due to him : inherent in him : associated or connected with him ⟨a wise man who built ~ house upon the rock —Mt 7:24 (RSV)⟩ ⟨the western ocean in one of the very worst of ~ moods —Cicely F. Smith⟩ ⟨did he bump ~ little head⟩ — compare ¹HE **b** : of or relating to him or himself as author, doer, giver, or agent : effected by him : experienced by him as subject : that he is capable of ⟨reading Shakespeare's histories as well as ~ comedies and tragedies⟩ ⟨~ promise⟩ ⟨success attributed to ~ having been prompt⟩ ⟨he ran ~ fastest⟩ **c** : of or relating to him or himself as object of an action : experienced by him as object ⟨he awaited ~ confirmation by the senate⟩ ⟨a secret combination against a person with the object of ~ hurt or injury —H.E.Scudder⟩ **d** : that he has to do with or is supposed to possess or to have knowledge or a share of or some special interest in ⟨the boy who knows ~ baseball —David Dempsey⟩ ⟨he enthusiastically supports ~ local symphony —*Amer. Guide Series: Minn.*⟩ **e** : that is esp. significant for him : that brings him good fortune or prominence — used with *day* or sometimes with other words indicating a division of time ⟨this was ~ day and the treat was on him —H.A.Chippendale⟩ **2** *obs* : ITS — used as late as the 17th century with no implied personification ⟨if the salt have lost ~ savor, wherewith shall it be salted? —Mt 5:13 (AV)⟩ **3** *archaic* : 's — used after a noun or noun phrase in place of the possessive ending *'s* ⟨at the tide of Christ ~ birth —Thomas Fuller⟩ ⟨in George the First ~ time —W.M.Thackeray⟩ ⟨Billy Bones, ~ fancy —R.L.Stevenson⟩

³his \ˈhiz\ *pron, sing or pl in constr* [ME, fr. OE, gen. of *hē*] **1** : his one or his ones — used without a following noun as a pronoun equivalent in meaning to the adjective *his* ⟨if my brother had my shape, and I had ~ —Shak.⟩ ⟨my dog is large and ~ is small⟩ ⟨your eyes are blue and ~ are brown⟩; often used after *of* to single out one or more members of a class belonging to or connected with a particular male person or animal ⟨a friend of ~⟩ ⟨four or five books of ~⟩ or merely to identify something or someone as belonging to or connected with a particular male person or animal without any implication of membership in a more extensive class ⟨that overbearing manner of ~⟩ ⟨those big feet of ~⟩ **2** : something that belongs to him : what belongs to him ⟨all that is ~ is hers⟩

his *abbr* history

hish \ˈhish\ *dial var of* HISS

his heels *n pl but sing or pl in constr* : a jack that is turned up as the starter in cribbage and that scores two points for the dealer

his·ing·er·ite \ˈhisiŋəˌrīt, ˈhizi-\ *n* -s [G *hisingerit*, fr. Wilhelm *Hisinger* †1852 Swed. geologist + G *-it* -ite] : a mineral perhaps $Fe_2Si_2O_5(OH)_4.2H_2O$ consisting of a black amorphous iron ore that is a hydrous ferric silicate

his·lop·ite \ˈhizləˌpīt, ˈhisl-\ *n* -s [Stephen *Hislop* †1863 Eng. missionary to India and amateur geologist + E *-ite*] : a bright green Indian calcite

hisn *or* **his'n** \ˈhizᵊn\ *pron* [ME *hysene*, alter. (influenced by the *-n* in *min* mine, *thin* thine) of *his*] *dial* : HIS

his·pa \ˈhispə\ *n* [NL, irreg. fr. L *hispidus* rough, hairy, bristly] **1** *cap* : a genus (often the type of the family Hispidae) of spiny Old World beetles with larvae that are leaf miners **2** -s : a beetle of *Hispa* or various closely related genera

his·pan·ic \(ˈ)hi¦spanik, -nēk\ *adj, usu cap* [L *Hispanicus*, fr. *Hispania* Spain, Iberian peninsula + L *-icus* -ic] : relating to or derived from the people, speech, or culture of Spain or of Spain and Portugal; *often* : LATIN-AMERICAN ⟨the folklore of *Hispanic* groups⟩ — **hispanic-american** \ˈ"+\ *adj, usu cap H&A*

his·pan·i·cism \hiˈspanəˌsizəm\ *n* -s *usu cap* : a word, phrase, or mode of expression distinctive of Spanish esp. when it appears in an English context

his·pan·i·cist \-səst\ *n* -s *usu cap* : HISPANIST

his·pan·i·ci·za·tion \(ˌ)=¦==səˈzāshən, -ˌsīˈz-\ *n* -s *often cap* : the act or a process of hispanicizing

his·pan·i·cize \=ˈ==ˌsīz\ *vt* -ED/-ING/-S *often cap* : to make Spanish: **a** : to cause to acquire a quality, qualities, traits or outlook distinctive of Spanish culture or Spaniards ⟨to ~ the conquered Indians⟩ **b** : to modify (language or a particular word or expression) to conform to linguistic characteristics distinctive of Spanish ("beisbol" is *hispanicized* "baseball") **c** : to bring under the control of Spain or Spaniards ⟨the government was *hispanicized*⟩

his·pa·ni·dad \ˌēspänēˈthä(th)\ *n* -s *often cap* [Sp, fr. *hispánico* Hispanic (fr. L *Hispanicus*) + *-dad* -ty (fr. L *-tat-*, *-tas*)] : hispanism esp. as adapted to fascist purposes and used for the undermining of U.S. influence in Latin America

his·pan·io·lize \hiˈspanyəˌlīz, ˌhispənˈyōˌl-\ *vt* -ED/-ING/-S *often cap* [modif. (influenced by *Hispanic*) of Sp *españolizar*, fr. *español* Spanish (fr. — assumed — VL *Hispaniolus*, fr. L *Hispania* Spain) + *-izar* -ize] : HISPANICIZE

his·pa·nism \ˈhispəˌnizəm\ *n* -s *often cap* [Sp *hispanismo*, fr. *hispano* Spanish, Hispanic (fr. L *Hispanus*) + *-ismo* -ism] **1** : the Spanish and Latin-American movement to reassert the spiritual and cultural unity of Spain and the Latin-American countries and promote the return to classic Spanish culture and Spanish supremacy in Latin America — compare HISPANIDAD **2** : a linguistic feature of Spanish origin or due to Spanish influence

his·pa·nist \-nəst\ *n* -s *usu cap* [Sp *hispanista*, fr. *hispano* + *-ista* -ist] : a scholar specially informed in the Spanish or Portuguese languages or Spanish or Portuguese literature, linguistics, or civilization

his·pa·ni·za·tion \ˌhispənəˈzāshən, -ˌnīˈz-\ *n* -s *often cap* [Sp *hispanización*, fr. *hispanizar* + *-ación* -ation] : HISPANICIZATION

his·pa·nize \ˈhispəˌnīz\ *vt* -ED/-ING/-S *often cap* [Sp *hispanizar*, fr. *hispano* + *-izar* -ize] : HISPANICIZE

his·pano \hiˈspa(ˌ)nō, -pä(-, -pā(-; ˈhispəˌnō\ *n* -s *cap* [short for *Hispano-American*] : a native or resident of the southwestern U.S. descended from Spaniards settled there before annexation

hispano- *comb form, usu cap* [Sp *hispano*, fr. L *Hispanus*] : Spanish and ⟨*Hispano*-German⟩ : Spanish ⟨*hispanophile*⟩

hispano-moresque \=¦==(ˌ)=+\ *adj, usu cap H&M* **1** : of, relating to, or produced in the era of Moorish ascendancy in Spain — used chiefly of art or cultural objects (as pottery, textiles) **2** *of a rug* : antique and oriental and found in Spain

his·pan·o·phile \hiˈspanəˌfīl\ *also* **his·pano·phil** \-ˌfil\ *n* -s *often cap* [*Hispano-* + *-phile, -phil*] **:** one partial to Spain or esp. fond of Spanish culture or civilization

¹his·per·ic \(ˈ)hiˈsperik\ *adj, usu cap* [fr. *Hisperica famina*, 6th cent. Latin work written in Ireland in the Hisperic style] **:** belonging to or constituting a style of Latin writing that probably originated in Ireland in the 6th century and that is characterized by extreme obscurity intentionally produced by periphrasis, coinage of new words, and very liberal use of loanwords to express quite ordinary meanings

²hisperic \"\ *n* -s *cap* **:** Hisperic Latin

his·pid \ˈhispəd\ *adj* [L *hispidus*; prob. akin to L *horrēre* to bristle — more at HORROR] **:** rough or covered with bristles, stiff hairs, or minute spines ⟨a ~ leaf⟩ — **his·pid·i·ty** \hiˈspidəd·ē\ *n* -ES

his·pid·u·lous \(ˈ)hiˈspijələs\ *also* **his·pid·u·late** \-lət, -ˌlāt\ *adj* [*hispid* + *-ulous* or *-ulate* (fr. *-ulous* + *-ate*)] **:** minutely hispid

his·pine \ˈhiˌspīn, -ˌspən\ *adj* [NL *Hispa* + E *-ine*] **:** of or related to the genus *Hispa*

¹hiss \ˈhis\ *vb* -ED/-ING/-ES [ME *hissen*, of imit. origin] *vi* **:** to make a sharp sibilant sound: as **a :** to make the sound by which an animal (as a goose or snake) indicates alarm, fear, or irritation ⟨the kitten ~*ed* at sight of the dog⟩ **b :** to make such a sound as an expression of hatred, passion, or disapproval ⟨the crowd booed and ~*ed*⟩ **c :** to escape or move with a hissing sound ⟨the wind ~*ed* about the caves⟩ — used esp. of substances under pressure ⟨steam ~*ing* from the kettle's spout⟩ ⟨air ~*ed* from the faulty valve⟩ ~ *vt* **1 :** to condemn or express contempt or dislike for by hissing ⟨~*ed* the speaker from the stage⟩ **2 :** to utter with a hissing sound ⟨~ disapproval⟩ ⟨sibilants should be clearly ~*ed*⟩

²hiss \"\ *n* -ES **1 :** a prolonged sibilant sound like that of the speech sound \s\ or \z\: as **a :** any of various animal sounds usu. indicative of alarm, fear, or irritation ⟨the ~ of an aroused gander⟩ ⟨startled by the sharp ~ of a snake⟩ **b :** the sound made by steam or other gas escaping through a narrow opening **c** (1) **:** the friction that characterizes the utterance of a voiceless fricative consonant (2) **:** a voiceless fricative; *specif* **:** \s\ — compare BUZZ **2 :** a hiss used as an expression of dislike, disapprobation, or contempt ⟨~*es* rose from all parts of the audience⟩

³hiss \"\ *or* **hissing** *adj* **:** being or involving the sibilant \s\ or \z\ ⟨~ sibilants of Georgian speech⟩ — compare HUSH

hiss·able \ˈhisəbəl\ *adj* **:** fit for hissing ⟨a sibilant ~ malediction⟩ **:** deserving to be hissed ⟨a thoroughly ~ villain⟩

his·self \(h)i(z)ˈs, ē(z)ˈs\ *also* **his·sel** \-ˈsel\ *pron* [ME *his self*, fr. *his* + *self*] *substand* **:** HIMSELF ⟨when he come to ~ they told him it was a Union hospital —Helen Eustis⟩

hiss·er \ˈhisə(r)\ *n* -s [ME, fr. *hissen* + *-er*] **:** one that hisses

hissing *n* -s [ME, fr. gerund of *hissen* to hiss] **1 :** an act or instance of emitting a hiss **2 :** an occasion of contempt **:** an object of scorn ⟨the priests, because of their breaches of the restrictions . . . made their calling a reproach and a ~ —A.M. Young⟩

hissing adder *or* **hissing snake** *also* **hissing viper** *n* **:** HOGNOSE SNAKE

hiss·ing·ly *adv* **:** in a hissing manner **:** with a sound of hissing

hissy \ˈhisē\ *n* -ES [origin unknown] *Southwest* **:** a fit of temper **:** TANTRUM

¹hist \s *often prolonged and usu with* p *preceding and/or* t *or a glottal stop following; often read as* ˈhist\ *interj* [origin unknown] — used to demand attention or quietly to attract a person's attention

²hist \ˈhīst\ *dial var of* HOIST

hist- *or* **histo-** *comb form* [F, fr. Gk *histos* mast, beam of a loom, loom, web, fr. *histanai* to cause to stand — more at STAND] **:** tissue ⟨*hist*amine⟩ ⟨*histo*physiology⟩

hist *abbr* **1** historian; historic; historical; history

his·tami·nase \hiˈstamə̇ˌnās, ˈhistəm-, -āz\ *n* -s [ISV *histamine* + *-ase*] **:** a flavoprotein enzyme occurring widely in plant and animal tissues (as in the kidney and small intestine) and capable of oxidizing histamine and various diamines (as putrescine) — called also *diamine oxidase*

his·ta·mine \ˈhistəˌmēn, -mə̇n\ *also* **his·ta·min** \-ˌmə̇n\ *n* -s [ISV *hist-* + *amine*] **:** a crystalline base $C_3H_3N_2CH_2CH_2NH_2$ that is found in ergot and other plants and usu. combined in animal tissues, that is formed from histidine by decarboxylation, and that is held to be responsible for the dilation and increased permeability of blood vessels which play a major role in allergic reactions; 4(or 5)-imidazole-ethylamine — see ANTIHISTAMINE, GASTRIN — **his·ta·min·ic** \ˌ==ˈminik\ *adj*

histamine flare *n* **:** an allergic tissue reaction to histamine manifested by local flushing of the skin

his·ta·min·er·gic \ˌ==məˈnərjik\ *adj* [ISV *histamine* + *-ergy* + *-ic*] **1** *of autonomic nerve fibers* **:** liberating histamine **2** *of autonomic nerve fibers* **:** activated by histamine

his·tamino·lyt·ic \ˌ==ˌmēnəˈlid·ik, -ˌmin-; hiˌstamənōˈl-\ *adj* [ISV *histamine* + *-o-* + *-lytic*] **:** breaking down or tending to break down histamine ⟨~ action of blood plasma⟩

histe \ˈhīst\ *dial var of* HOIST

his·ter \ˈhistə(r)\ *also* **hister beetle** *n* -s [NL *Hister*, genus of beetles, fr. L *hister* actor, fr. Etruscan; fr. the fact that these beetles play dead when disturbed] **:** a beetle of the family Histeridae

¹his·ter·id \-tərə̇d\ *adj* [NL *Histeridae*] **:** of or relating to the Histeridae

²histerid \"\ *n* -s **:** HISTER

his·ter·i·dae \hiˈsterəˌdē\ *n pl, cap* [NL, fr. *Hister*, type genus + *-idae*] **:** a family of rather sluggish dark-colored and often shining beetles that live chiefly in decaying organic matter and have larvae which prey on other insects and insect larvae

histi- *or* **histio-** *comb form* [Gk *histion* web, cloth, sail, dim. of *histos* mast, beam of a loom, loom, web — more at HIST-] **1 :** sail ⟨*Histi*opterus⟩ **2 :** tissue ⟨*histio*cyte⟩

his·ti·dase \ˈhistəˌdās, -āz\ *n* -s [ISV *histid*in + *-ase*] **:** an enzyme occurring esp. in the liver of vertebrates that is capable of deaminating histidine to form urocanic acid

his·ti·dine \-ˌdēn, -ˌdə̇n\ *also* **his·ti·din** \-dən\ *n* -s [ISV *hist-* + *-idine, -idin*; orig. formed as G *histidin*] **:** a crystalline basic amino acid $C_3H_3N_2CH_2CH(NH_2)COOH$ that is essential in the nutrition of the rat, is synthesized by microorganisms and by plants, and is formed by the decomposition of most proteins (as globin); 4(or 5)-imidazole-alanine

hist·ie \ˈhistē\ *var of* HIRSTIE

his·ti·o·cyte \ˈhistēəˌsīt\ *n* -s [ISV *histi-* + *-cyte*] **:** a phagocytic tissue cell that may be fixed or freely motile, is derived from the reticuloendothelial system, and resembles the monocyte with which it is sometimes identified — called also *clasmatocyte, macrophage* — **his·ti·o·cyt·ic** \ˌ==ˈsid·ik\ *adj*

his·ti·o·cy·to·ma \ˌ==(ˌ)=ˌsīˈtōmə\ *n, pl* **histiocytomas** \-məz\ *also* **histiocyto·ma·ta** \-məd·ə\ [NL, fr. ISV *histiocyte* + NL *-oma*] **:** a tumor consisting predominantly of histiocytes, being usu. nonmalignant, and occurring esp. in young male dogs

his·ti·o·cy·to·sis \-ˈtōsə̇s\ *n, pl* **histiocyto·ses** \-ōˌsēz\ [NL, fr. ISV *histiocyte* + NL *-osis*] **:** abnormal multiplication of histiocytes; *broadly* **:** a condition characterized by such multiplication

his·ti·oid \ˈhistēˌȯid\ *adj* [ISV *histi-* + *-oid*] **:** HISTOID

his·ti·ol·o·gy \ˌhistēˈäləjē, -ji\ *n* -ES [by alter.] **:** HISTOLOGY

his·ti·oph·a·gous \ˌ==ˈäfəgəs\ *adj* [*histi-* + *-phagous*] **:** feeding on tissues ⟨~ protozoans⟩

his·ti·o·phor·i·dae \ˌhistēəˈfȯrəˌdē\ [NL, fr. *Histiophorus*, type genus (fr. *histi-* + *-phorus*) + *-idae*] *syn of* ISTIOPHORIDAE

his·ti·op·ter·i·dae \ˌ==ˌäpˈterəˌdē\ *n pl, cap* [NL, fr. *Histiopterus*, type genus (fr. *histi-* + *-pterus*) + *-idae*] **:** a family of deep-sea percoid fishes with compressed body, rough scales, and strong fin spines — see BOARFISH

histo- — see HIST-

his·to·blast \ˈhistəˌblast\ *n* [ISV *hist-* + *-blast*] **:** a cell or cell group possessing broad histogenetic capacity: as **a :** HISTIOCYTE **b :** IMAGINAL DISK

his·to·chemical \ˌhi(ˌ)stō+\ *adj* [*hist-* + *chemical*] **:** of, relating to, or by means of histochemistry — **his·to·chemical·ly** \"+\ *adv*

his·to·chemistry \"+\ *n* [ISV *hist-* + *chemistry*] **:** a science that deals with the chemical constitution of living cells and tissues by combining the techniques of biochemistry and histology

his·to·chem·o·graph \ˌhi(ˌ)stōkeməˌgraf, -ˌrȧf\ *n* [*hist-* + *chem-* + *-graph*] **:** a picture or pattern produced on a photographic plate by the chemical action of a histological specimen in contact with the emulsion — **his·to·che·mog·ra·phy** \-ˌkeˈmägrəfē, -ˌkəˈ-\ *n* -ES

his·to·cyte \ˈhistəˌsīt\ *n* -s [ISV *hist-* + *-cyte*] **1 :** HISTIOCYTE **2 :** a cell (as in various lower invertebrates) with highly developed capacity to form tissues

his·to·gen \-tə̇jən, -ˌjen\ *n* -s [ISV *hist-* + *-gen*] **:** a zone or clearly delimited region of primary tissue in or from which the specific parts of a plant organ are believed to be produced — see DERMATOGEN, PERIBLEM, PLEROME; HISTOGEN THEORY; compare CALYPTROGEN, CORPUS, TUNICA

his·to·genesis \ˌhistə+\ *n* [NL, fr. *hist-* + L *genesis*] **:** the formation and differentiation of tissues ⟨the ~ of floral organs⟩ ⟨~ of a neoplasm⟩

his·to·ge·net·ic \ˌhistəjəˈned·ik\ *adj* [*hist-* + *genetic*] **1 :** of or relating to histogenesis **2 :** of or relating to histogenetics — **his·to·ge·net·i·cal·ly** \-d·ə̇k(ə)lē\ *adv*

his·to·ge·net·ics \-d·iks\ *n pl but sing or pl in constr* **:** a branch of genetics concerned with the genetic significance and basis of somatic variation (as in the production of bud sports and graft hybrids)

his·to·gen·ic \ˌ==(ˌ)=ˈjenik\ *adj* [ISV *hist-* + *-genic*] **:** producing tissue

histogen theory *n* **:** a theory in botany: a growing point (as of a stem or root) consists of three histogens each of which gives rise to a different tissue — see DERMATOGEN, PERIBLEM, PLEROME

his·tog·e·ny \hiˈstäjənē\ *n* -ES [ISV *hist-* + *-geny*] **:** HISTOGENESIS

his·to·gram \ˈhistəˌgram\ *n* -s [*history* + *-gram*] **:** a graphical representation of a frequency distribution by means of rectangles whose widths represent the class intervals and whose heights represent the corresponding frequencies

his·tog·ra·phy \hiˈstägrəfē\ *n* -ES [ISV *hist-* + *-graphy*] **:** description of bodily tissue

his·toid \ˈhiˌstȯid\ *adj* [ISV *hist-* + *-oid*] **1 :** resembling the normal tissues ⟨~ tumors⟩ **2 :** developed from or consisting of but one tissue

his·to·log·i·cal \ˌhistəˈläjəkəl, -jēk-\ *also* **his·to·log·ic** \-jik,-jēk\ *adj* **:** of or relating to histology or to the microscopic structure of the tissues of organisms ⟨~ studies⟩ ⟨the ~ picture in Bright's disease⟩ — **his·to·log·i·cal·ly** \-jə̇k(ə)lē, -jēk-, -li\ *adv*

his·tol·o·gist \hiˈstäləjə̇st\ *n* -s **:** a specialist in histology

his·tol·o·gy \-jē, -ji\ *n* -ES [F *histologie*, fr. *hist-* + *-logie* -logy] **1 :** a branch of anatomy that deals with the minute structure of animal and vegetable tissues as discernible with the microscope **:** microscopic anatomy — compare CYTOLOGY **2 :** a treatise on histology **3 :** tissue structure or organization (as of an organism) ⟨the ~ of a fetus⟩ ⟨the ~ of the pancreas⟩

his·tol·y·sis \-ləsə̇s\ *n* [NL, fr. *hist-* + *-lysis*] **1 :** the breakdown of bodily tissues **2 :** the process by which in the pupa of a holometabolous insect many or most of the larval organs dissolve into a creamy material and leave intact only various groups of cells out of which new organs for the imago are formed

his·to·lyt·ic \ˌhistəˈlid·ik\ *adj* [fr. NL *histolysis*, after such pairs as E *analysis* : *analytic*] **:** of, relating to, or inducing histolysis

his·tol·y·zate \hiˈstäləˌzāt\ *n* -s [irreg. fr. NL *histolysis* + E *-ate*] **:** a product of tissue lysis

his·to·metabasis \ˌhi(ˌ)stō+\ *n* [NL, fr. *hist-* + *metabasis*] **:** fossilization in which the minute details of texture of the organism are retained

his·tom·o·nad \hiˈstäməˌnad\ *n* [NL *Histomonad-, Histomonas*] **:** a protozoan of the genus *Histomonas*

his·tom·o·nal \(ˈ)hiˈstämənᵊl\ *adj* **:** of, relating to, or caused by histomonads ⟨~ diarrhea⟩

his·tom·o·nas \ˌ=ˈ==ˌnəs, -ˌnas\ *n, cap* [NL, fr. *hist-* + *monas*] **:** a genus of zooflagellates (family Mastigamoebidae) that exhibit both amoeboid and flagellate phases, are parasites in the liver and intestinal mucosa of chickens, turkeys, and various other birds and are usu. considered to include a single species (*H. meleagridis*) that is the causative agent of blackhead

his·tomo·ni·a·sis \(ˌ)hiˌstäməˈnīəsə̇s, ˌhistəmə-\ *n* -ES [NL, fr. *Histomonas* + *-iasis*] **:** infection with or disease caused by protozoans of the genus *Histomonas* **:** BLACKHEAD 3

his·tone \ˈhiˌstōn\ *n* -s [ISV *hist-* + *-one*] **:** any of various simple proteins that are soluble in water but insoluble in dilute ammonia, that yield a high proportion of basic amino acids on hydrolysis but are less strongly basic than protamines, and that are found esp. in some glandular tissues (as thymus) combined with deoxyribonucleic acid

his·to·pathologic *or* **his·to·pathological** \ˌhi(ˌ)stō+\ *adj* **:** of or relating to histopathology ⟨a ~ process⟩ **:** involving the methods of histopathology ⟨a ~ examination⟩

his·to·pathologist \"+\ *n* **:** a pathologist who specializes in the detection of the effects of disease on body tissues; *esp* **:** one who identifies neoplasms by their histological characteristics

his·to·pathology \"+\ *n* [ISV *hist-* + *pathology*] **1 :** a branch of pathology concerned with the tissue changes characteristic of disease **2 :** the tissue changes that affect a part or accompany a disease ⟨~ of the eye⟩ ⟨~ of tuberculosis⟩

his·to·physiology \"+\ *n* [*hist-* + *physiology*] **1 :** a branch of physiology concerned with the function and activities of tissues **2 :** structural and functional tissue organization (as of a body part) ⟨the ~ of the thyroid gland⟩

his·to·plas·ma \ˌhistəˈplazmə\ *n* [NL, fr. *hist-* + *plasma*] **1** *cap* **:** a genus of fungi (family Coccidioidaceae) usu. considered to consist of a single widespread species (*H. capsulatum*) of fungi that cause histoplasmosis, live parasitically as heavily encapsulated yeastlike cells in blood, lymph, or various tissues, and grow saprophytically (as on nutritive media) as a mycelium that produces both conidia and chlamydospores **2** -s **:** any fungus of the genus *Histoplasma*

his·to·plas·min \-mən, ˈ==ˌ==\ *n* -s [ISV *histoplasm-* (fr. NL *Histoplasma*, genus name of *Histoplasma capsulatum*) + *-in*] **:** a sterile filtrate of a culture of a fungus (*Histoplasma capsulatum*) used in a cutaneous test for histoplasmosis

his·to·plas·mo·sis \-ˌplazˈmōsə̇s\ *n, pl* **histoplasmo·ses** \-ōˌsēz\ [NL, fr. *Histoplasma* (genus name of *Histoplasma capsulatum*) + *-osis*] **:** a disease that is endemic in the Mississippi and Ohio river valleys of the U.S., is caused by infection with a fungus (*Histoplasma capsulatum*), and is marked by benign involvement of lymph nodes of the trachea and bronchi usu. without symptoms or by severe progressive generalized involvement of the lymph nodes and the reticuloendothelial system with fever, anemia, leukopenia and often with local lesions (as of the skin, mouth, or throat)

his·to·ri·an \hiˈstōrēən, -tȯr- *sometimes* -tär-\ *n* -s [MF *historien*, fr. L *historia* narrative, history + MF *-en* -an — more at HISTORY] **1 :** a writer of history; *esp* **:** one that produces a work of scholarly synthesis as distinguished from a compilation or chronicle ⟨an ~ and not a mere chronicler —*Times Lit. Supp.*⟩ **2 :** CHRONICLER

his·to·ri·at·ed \-rēˌād·əd\ *adj* [ML *historiatus* (past part. of *historiare* to tell a story in pictures, fr. LL, to relate, fr. L *historia* narrative, history) + E *-ed* — more at HISTORY] **:** adorned with figures (as flowers, animals) having significance rather than purely decorative elements (as scrolls, diapers) — used orig. of the elaborately decorated initials of books and manuscripts and now chiefly of a symbolic representational manner of presenting supplementary information on a map or chart

¹his·tor·i·cal \hiˈstȯrə̇kəl, -tär-, -rēk-\ *or* **his·tor·ic** \-rik, -rēk\ *adj* [*historical* fr. L *historicus* (fr. Gk *historikos* exact, precise, historical, fr. *historia* inquiry, information, narrative, history + *-ikos* -ic) + E *-al*; *historic* fr. L *historicus* — more at HISTORY] **1** *usu historical* **a :** of, relating to, or having the character of history esp. as distinguished from myth or legend ⟨an ~ event⟩ ⟨the ~ middle ages were quite unlike those of fiction⟩ **b :** based on or dealing with history ⟨~ studies⟩ **:** true to history **:** accurate in respect to history ⟨reproducing the manners of the period with ~ fidelity⟩ **c :** used in the past and reproduced in historical presentations **d :** based on, resulting from, or acknowledged to be true because of past events or experiences ⟨the ~ necessity for space of growing populations⟩ **2** *usu historic* **a :** important, famous, or decisive in history ⟨*historic* battlefields⟩ ⟨*historic* buildings⟩ **b :** having considerable importance, significance, or consequence ⟨an *historic* occasion⟩ **3 a :** SECONDARY 1e **b** *usu historical* **:** DIACHRONIC ⟨~ grammar⟩ ⟨~ linguistics⟩

²historical \"\ *n* -s **:** a novel, play or motion picture based upon history

historical cost *n* **1 :** a cost computed after production from records made concurrently with various steps of production — contrasted with *predetermined cost* and *standard cost* **2 :** the value at which a capital asset is recorded on the books representing the outlay of money or its equivalent given in exchange at the time of acquisition ⟨depreciation is based on *historical cost* rather than on replacement value⟩ **3 :** the original cost of a property in a public utility

historical criticism *n* **:** criticism in the light of historical evidence — compare HIGHER CRITICISM

historical geology *n* **:** a branch of geology that deals with the chronology of the events in the earth's history

historical infinitive *n* **:** the present infinitive used with a subject nominative as a finite verb in place of a past indicative

his·tor·i·cal·ly \-rə̇k(ə)lē, -rēk-, -li\ *adv* **1 :** in accordance with or in respect to history ⟨an ~ accurate account⟩ **:** as a matter of history ⟨popular leaders have ~ appeared when the needs and tensions were great enough⟩ **2 :** in the course of history **:** in past times or previous dealings ⟨all employees whom an employer has ~ treated together —*U.S.Code*⟩

historical materialism *n* **:** the part of dialectical materialism dealing with the history of society and holding that ideas and institutions develop as the superstructure of a material economic base, that the course of history is dominated by the struggle of competing classes, and that the final dialectical stages comprise the development of capitalism, the dictatorship of the proletariat, and after the withering away of the state the emergence of a classless society

historical method *n* **:** a technique of presenting information (as in teaching or criticism) in which a topic is considered in terms of its earliest phases and followed in an historical course through its subsequent evolution and development

his·tor·i·cal·ness \-kəlnə̇s\ *n* -ES **:** the quality or state of being historical

historical novel *n* **:** a novel having as its setting a period of history and usu. introducing some historical personages and events

historical perfect *n* **:** the perfect tense when used in Latin to express action completed in an indefinite past

historical present *n* **:** the present tense used in telling of past events

historical school *n* **:** a school of economics developed in Germany in the middle of the 19th century that emphasizes institutional factors in society and pursues a systematic investigation of the development of economic institutions — compare CLASSICAL 3b(3) **2 :** a school of legal philosophy that emphasizes the relation of the evolution of law to the historical milieu and minimizes the importance of arbitrary human action and of natural processes to its development **3 :** a school of ethnology that emphasizes empirical study of the historical continuity of a specific culture or culture area as contrasted with comparative study of diverse or related cultures or culture areas

historical sociology *n* **:** a branch of sociology concerned with study of the origins, stages, and laws of social life and social institutions

his·tor·i·cism \hiˈstȯrəˌsizəm, -tär-\ *n* -s **1 a :** a theory that all sociocultural phenomena are historically determined, that all truths are relative, that there are no absolute values, categories, or standards, and that the student of the past must enter into the mind and attitudes of past periods, accept their point of view, and avoid all intrusion of his own standards or preconceptions **b :** the practice of writing or treating history in accordance with such a theory **c :** a theory of history holding that the development of human society is a process governed by inexorable laws of change operating independently of human wills or wishes **2 a :** a strong or exaggerated concern with or respect for the institutions and traditions of the past ⟨stands for ~ and empiricism in the tradition of Burke —*Times Lit. Supp.*⟩ **b :** the use of or undue reliance upon historical forms or styles in art esp. in architectural design

¹his·tor·i·cist \-sə̇st\ *n* -s [fr. *historicism*, after such pairs as E *baptism* : *baptist*] **:** an advocate of historicism

²historicist \"\ *adj* **:** of, relating to, or based on historicism

his·to·ric·i·ty \ˌhistəˈrisəd·ē, -ətē, -i\ *n* -ES [prob. fr. F *historicité*, fr. L *historicus* + F *-ité* -ity] **1 :** the quality or state of being historic esp. as distinct from the mythological or legendary **2 :** a condition of being placed in the stream of historical developments; *also* **:** a result of such placement

his·tor·i·cize \hiˈstȯrəˌsīz, -tär-\ *vb* -ED/-ING/-S *vt* **1 :** to render historic **:** give an appearance of historical verity or significance to ⟨the traditional myth of the god's victory over the dragon . . . is *historicized* as the triumph of Yahweh over the enemies of Israel —Philip Wheelwright⟩ **2 :** to make dependent on historicism esp. as a basis for action or an explanation of occurrences ⟨various disciplines also have been nationalized and over-*historicized* —Christian Gauss⟩ ~ *vi* **:** to use historical material or depend on historicism ⟨the nationalist and *historicizing* spirit of the 19th century —G.M.J. Moser⟩

historico- *comb form* [NL, fr. L *historicus* — more at HISTORICAL] **:** historical **:** historical and ⟨*historico*philosophical⟩ ⟨*historico*social⟩

his·tor·i·co·critical \hiˈstȯrə̇(ˌ)kō, -tär-, -rē(-+\ *adj* **:** based on or involving the use of techniques of both historian and critic ⟨an ~ examination of religion⟩ — **his·tor·i·co·critical·ly** \"+\ *adv*

his·to·ried \ˈhist(ə)rēd, -rid\ *adj* **:** related in or as history **:** having a history **:** HISTORICAL

his·to·ri·ette \hiˌstōrēˈet, -tȯr-, ˌ=ˌ==ˈ=\ *n* -s [F, fr. L *historia* narrative, history + F *-ette* (dim. suffix) — more at HISTORY] **:** a short history or story

his·tor·i·fy \hiˈstȯrəˌfī, -tär-\ *vt* -ED/-ING/-S [*history* + *-fy*] **:** to record in or as history

historio- *comb form* [MF, fr. LL, fr. Gk, fr. *historia* inquiry, information, narrative, history — more at HISTORY] **:** history ⟨*historio*metric⟩ ⟨*historio*grapher⟩

his·to·ri·og·ra·pher \(ˌ)hiˌstōrēˈägrəfə(r), -tȯr- *sometimes* -tär-\ *n* -s [MF *historiographeur*, fr. LL *historiographus* (fr. Gk *historiographos*, fr. *historio-* + *-graphos* writer, fr. *graphein* to write) + MF *-eur* -or — more at CARVE] **1 :** a writer of history **:** HISTORIAN **2 :** a person appointed to write a history or to record the continuing history of a country, group, or institution **:** an official historian ⟨since 1924 has been ~ of the Protestant Episcopal Diocese of Virginia —*Christian Century*⟩

his·to·ri·og·ra·pher·ship \-ˌship\ *n* **:** the office of historiographer

his·to·ri·o·graph·ic \hiˌstōrēəˈgrafik, -tȯr- *sometimes* -tär-\ *also* **his·to·ri·o·graph·i·cal** \-fə̇kəl\ *adj* **:** of or relating to historiography — **his·to·ri·o·graph·i·cal·ly** \-fə̇k(ə)lē\ *adv*

his·to·ri·og·ra·phy \(ˌ)hiˌstōrēˈägrəfē, -tȯr- *sometimes* -tär-\ *n* -ES [MF *historiographie*, fr. Gk *historiographia*, fr. *historio-* + *-graphia* -graphy] **1 a :** the writing of history; *esp* **:** the writing of history based on the critical examination of sources, the selection of particulars from the authentic materials, and the synthesis of particulars into a narrative that will stand the test of critical methods **b :** the principles, theory, and history of historical writing ⟨a course in ~⟩ **2 :** the product of historical writing **:** a body of historical literature ⟨no single work in our ~ has moved more Englishmen —*Times Lit. Supp.*⟩ ⟨for most of the 9th century northern ~ shrinks to a few disconnected annals —F.M.Stenton⟩

his·to·ri·ol·o·gy \-ˈäləjē\ *n* -ES [*historio-* + *-logy*] **:** the study or knowledge of history

his·to·rism \ˈhistəˌrizəm\ *n* -s [G *historismus*, fr. *historie* history (fr. L *historia*) + G *-ismus* -ism] **:** HISTORICISM 1

¹his·to·ry \ˈhist(ə)rē, -ri\ *n* -ES [L *historia*, fr. Gk *historia* inquiry, information, narrative, history, fr. *historein* to inquire into, examine, relate (fr. *histor-*, *histōr* judge) + *-ia* -y; akin to Gk *idein* to see — more at WIT] **1 :** a narrative of events connected with a real or imaginary object, person, or career **:** TALE, STORY; *esp* **:** such a narrative devoted to the exposition of the natural unfolding and interdependence of the events treated ⟨carefully recording the ~ of our vacation for father⟩ ⟨a ~ of passion, greed, and retribution⟩ **2 a :** a systematic written account comprising a chronological record of events (as affecting a city, state, nation, institution, science, or art) and usu. including a philosophical explanation of the cause and origin of such events — usu. distinguished from *annals* and *chronicle* **b :** a treatise presenting systematically related natural phenomena (as of geography, animals, or plants) ⟨an illustrated ~ of British birds⟩ **c :** an account of a sick person's family and personal background, his past health, and present illness **3 :** a branch of knowledge that records and explains past events as steps in the sequence of human activities : the study of the character and significance of events — usu. used with a qualifying adjective ⟨medieval ~⟩ ⟨European ~⟩ **4** [MF *histoire* story, history, picture, fr. L *historia*] **a** (1) *obs* : a pictorial representation of an historical subject (2) *or* **history painting :** painting esp. popular in the 17th and 18th centuries in which a complex of figures conveys a story or message usu. based on history or legend **b** (1) *obs* : DRAMA 1 (2) : a drama based on historical events **5 a :** the events that form the subject matter of a history : a series of events clustering about some center of interest (as a nation, a department of culture, a natural epoch or evolution, a living being or a species) upon the character and significance of which these events cast light **b :** the character and significance of such a center of interest — compare LIFE HISTORY **c** *broadly* : past events ⟨that's all ~ now⟩; *esp* : those events involving or concerned with mankind **d :** previous treatment, handling, or experience (as of a metal) ⟨the results of heat treating will depend in part on the previous ~ of the specimen⟩ ⟨thermal ~ may modify photoelectric reactivity of certain compounds⟩ ⟨there was a ~ of repeated exposure to near-freezing temperature that might explain the mutation⟩

²**history** \"\ *vt* -ED/-ING/-ES [ME *historien*, fr. MF *historier*, fr. LL & ML *historiare* — more at HISTORIATED] **1** *obs* : NARRATE, RECOUNT **2** *obs* : to decorate with an historical record or scenes from history

his·to·ry·less \-ləs\ *adj* : having no history or no recorded history or no history worthy of record

historymaker \ˈ=(=)=,==\ *n* : one that by acts, ideas, or existence modifies the course of history

history of religions : the objective study of the origin and historical development of the religions of mankind — compare COMPARATIVE RELIGION

history painting *n* **1 :** HISTORY 4a(2) **2 :** the practice or techniques of painting histories

his·to·toxic \ˌhistə+\ *adj* [ISV *hist-* + *toxic*] **1 :** toxic to tissues ⟨~ agents⟩ **2 :** of, relating to, or caused by a histotoxin ⟨the development of a ~ anoxia⟩

his·to·toxin \"+\ *n* [*hist-* + *toxin*] : any of various poisonous substances formed in specific body tissues and usu. deleterious to the body in which they are formed

his·to·troph \ˈhistəˌträf, -rōf\ *or* **his·to·trophe** \-rōf\ *n* -s [F *histotrophe*, fr. *hist-* + *-trophe* (fr. Gk *trophos* one that feeds or rears)] : all materials supplied for nutrition of the embryo in viviparous animals from sources other than the maternal bloodstream — compare EMBRYOTROPH, HEMOTROPHE

his·to·trop·ic \ˌhistəˈträpik\ *adj* [*hist-* + *-tropic*] : exhibiting or characterized by histotropism ⟨~ parasites⟩

his·tot·ro·pism \hiˈstä·trəˌpizəm\ *n* [*hist-* + *-tropism*] : attraction (as of a parasite) to a particular kind of tissue

his·to·zo·ic \ˌhistəˈzōik\ *adj* [*hist-* + *-zoic*] : living in the tissues of a host ⟨~ parasites⟩

his·to·zyme \ˈhistəˌzīm\ *n* [ISV *hist-* + *-zyme*] : an enzyme widely distributed in mammalian tissues that is capable of splitting acyl groups from hippuric acid and other acylated amino acids or from peptides — called also *hippuricase*

his·trio \ˈhistrēˌō\ *n* -s [L, alter. of *hister*, fr. Etruscan] : ACTOR

his·tri·ob·del·lea \ˌhistrēˌäbˈdelēə\ *n pl, cap* [NL, fr. L *histrio* actor + NL *-bdellea* (fr. Gk *bdella* leech)] : a small group of segmented invertebrate animals that are intermediate in some respects between the Aschelminthes and the Annelida and that are all parasitic on marine crustaceans

his·tri·on \ˈhistrēˌän\ *n* -s [MF, fr. L *histrion-*, *histrio*] : ACTOR

¹**his·tri·on·ic** \ˌhistrēˈänik, -nēk\ *also* **his·tri·on·i·cal** \-nəkəl, -nēk-\ *adj* [LL *histrionicus*, fr. L *histrion-*, *histrio* + *-icus* -ic] **1 :** of or relating to actors, acting, or the theater ⟨an able actor ever seeking ~ perfection⟩ **2 :** deliberately affected : THEATRICAL, STAGED ⟨her heart attacks were as ~ as her sister's fits of temper⟩ — **his·tri·on·i·cal·ly** \-nək(ə)lē, -nēk-, -li\ *adv*

²**histrionic** \"\ *n* -s **1 :** ACTOR **2 histrionics** *pl but sometimes sing in constr* **a :** theatrical performances **b :** staged or stagy conduct or exhibition of temperament usu. intended to produce some particular effect or response in others

his·tri·on·i·cus \ˌhistrēˈänəkəs\ *n, cap* [NL, fr. LL, adj., histrionic; fr. their handsome plumage] : a genus of ducks including only the harlequin duck

his·tri·o·nism \ˈhistrēəˌnizəm\ *n* -s : THEATRICALITY

his·trix \ˈhistriks\ [NL, alter. of *Hystrix*] *syn of* HYSTRIX

¹**hit** \ˈhit, *usu* -id·+V\ *vb* **hit; hit; hitting; hits** [ME *hitten*, fr. ON *hitta* to hit upon, meet up with, hit; perh. akin to OE *hentan* to pursue, attack, seize — more at HUNT] *vt* **1 a :** to reach or get at by striking with or as if with a sudden blow ⟨~ a ball⟩ ⟨be ~ by adversity⟩ **b :** to come in quick forceful contact with ⟨the ball ~ the house and bounced off⟩ **2 a :** to cause to come into sudden forceful contact ⟨~ his hand against the wall⟩ ⟨~ the stick against the railing⟩ **b :** to deliver (a blow) usu. in a vigorous or violent manner : STRIKE **c :** to strike a blow at or to ⟨~ the table suddenly⟩ ⟨~ the boy in the eye⟩ **3 a :** to affect esp. strongly and to the detriment or distress of ⟨life had never ~ her very hard —Nevil Shute⟩ ⟨drought ~ the range country early that year⟩ **b :** to criticize adversely : CENSURE ⟨no prime minister in our history has been ~ so hard by a biographer who knew him —*Times Lit. Supp.*⟩ **4 :** to make a request of or a claim or demand upon (as for a loan or a job) ⟨~ his friend for 10 dollars⟩ — often used with *up* ⟨~ up his father's friends for work⟩ **5 a :** to come upon, find, or discover by or as if by chance or accident ⟨spent years in prospecting without ever *hitting* gold⟩ **b :** to meet with, reach, or experience by or as if by chance or accident ⟨after several weeks of travel, we ~ our first snowstorm⟩ ⟨~ a run of bad luck⟩ **6 :** to reach or attain by or as if by hitting: as **a :** to accord with usu. exactly and purposely ⟨writing that ~s the public taste precisely⟩ **b :** to act in precise accord with ⟨~ a musical cue⟩ **c :** to reach as a rate, standard, or level ⟨a car that can ~ 100 mph.⟩ ⟨prices ~ an all-time high⟩ ⟨when you ~ the middle sixties⟩ **d** *of fish* : to bite at or on : TAKE ⟨in certain times of the season fish will only ~ live bait⟩ **e :** to appear in or on (as for public sale, consumption, use) ⟨sweet corn ~s the markets in New England in midsummer⟩ ⟨a magazine that ~s the newsstands early in the month⟩ ⟨morning papers often ~ the streets in the late evening⟩ ⟨this recording will ~ the jukeboxes soon⟩ **f** *of an author* : to achieve publication in ⟨took him some time to ~ the better magazines⟩ **g :** to be reported in ⟨~ the front pages⟩ **h :** to impinge on or command the attention of ⟨advertising techniques designed to ~ the subconscious mind⟩ **i :** STRESS, EMPHASIZE ⟨always ~ the message-bearing words firmly⟩ ⟨inclined to ~ the wrong syllable⟩ **j :** to arrive at, in, or on for a brief or transitory stay ⟨arranged to ~ town two days before his brother⟩ ⟨when the first forces ~ the beach⟩ ⟨planned on *hitting* all the new night spots⟩ **k** (1) : to reach or strike (as a target) for a score in a game or contest ⟨unbelievable ability to ~ the basket⟩ (2) : to succeed in making (a scoring play) ⟨~ three goals before their opponents were well warmed up⟩ (3) *slang* : to win in a lottery or game of chance or acquire as if by so winning ⟨~ first prize⟩ ⟨an act that didn't ~ the big money until he took it to New York⟩ — often used with *for* and the thing or the amount gained ⟨~ the numbers pool for $2000⟩ ⟨~ the company education fund for a year in technical school⟩ **l** *slang* (1) : to go, lie, or drop on or upon usu. suddenly or at once ⟨~ the deck⟩ (2) : to get onto and begin to move along or travel on ⟨~ the road⟩ ⟨~ the right path⟩ **7 :** to capture with precision (as a mood, an idea, a personal characteristic in a description or representation) ⟨none of these analyses seems quite to ~ the main characteristic —R.D.Ellmann⟩ **8 :** to set in operation or cause to function by or as if by striking or touching ⟨~ the lights⟩ ⟨*hitting* slow chords on a guitar⟩ ⟨had to ~ the brakes suddenly⟩ **9 :** to indulge in (as liquor) esp. excessively, habitually, or compulsively ⟨had been *hitting* the bottle for days⟩ **10 a :** to deal another card to (a player at blackjack) **b :** to have another card dealt to (a hand in blackjack) **c :** FILL *vt* 7 **~** *vi* **1 :** to strike or strike out at something with or as if with a sudden blow (as of the fist or a missile) ⟨in the third round he began *hitting* wildly⟩ ⟨*hitting* only about once in five shots⟩ **2 a :** to come into forcible contact with something ⟨when he fell, he ~ hard⟩ — often used with *against* ⟨tipped over and ~ against the wall and was damaged⟩ **b :** ATTACK ⟨guessed at where they would ~, and the date of D day —Dan Levin⟩ **c** *of a fish* : STRIKE *vi* 15b **d :** to arrive with a disturbing or damaging effect ⟨a heavy storm that ~ just at sundown⟩ ⟨had been still in school when the bad times ~⟩ ⟨the grippe ~ unusually severely that year⟩ **3 a :** to meet or reach something aimed at or desired : succeed in attaining or obtaining something often by or as if by chance — often used with *on* or *upon* ⟨~ on a solution⟩ ⟨~ upon a satisfactory explanation⟩ **b :** to draw or be dealt a valuable card in poker ⟨drew to an inside straight and ~⟩ **c :** to hit a blot **4** *of a crop, now dial* : to germinate, grow, or yield well **5** *obs* : to be in agreement : SUIT — used with *with* ⟨the scheme ~ so exactly with my temper —Daniel Defoe⟩ **6 :** to direct one's course : direct oneself ⟨~ for the nearest lunchroom⟩ ⟨in spring the peddlers ~ up the coast with packs and carts⟩ **7** *of an internal-combustion engine* : to fire the charge in the cylinders **8 a :** to be a winner (as in a lottery) **b :** to make a score (as in a game) **syn** see STRIKE — **hit a blot 1 :** to capture a man exposed on a point in backgammon **2 :** to find a flaw (as in a policy or argument) — **hit for six 1** *Brit* : to hit for six runs in cricket **2** *Brit* : to hit hard : DEFEAT, TROUNCE — **hit it off :** to associate agreeably : get along well : have a mutually congenial relationship ⟨had *hit it off* from the very start⟩ — **hit it up :** to work, play, or perform with speed, animation, or abandon ⟨the band was already *hitting it up* when we arrived⟩ — **hit one's stride :** to reach one's best speed or performance : exhibit maximum competence or capability — **hit the books** *or* **hit one's books :** to study esp. with intensity — **hit the bricks** *slang* : to go on strike : walk out — **hit the hay** *or* **hit the sack** *slang* : to go to bed — **hit the high points** *or* **hit the high spots :** to touch on or at the most important or salient points or places ⟨a lecture that *hit* only *the high points* of the subject⟩ ⟨with only three days in town the best we could do was *hit the high spots*⟩ — **hit the jackpot** *slang* : to be or become notably and usu. unexpectedly successful — **hit the nail on the head :** to perform effectively or be effective : be exactly right — **hit the roof** *also* **hit the ceiling :** to give vent to a burst of anger or angry protest — **hit the silk** *slang* : to parachute from an airplane — **hit the spot :** to give complete or special satisfaction — used esp. of food or drink

²**hit** \"\ *n* -s [ME *hete*, fr. *hitten*, v.] **1 a :** a blow striking an object aimed at — contrasted with *miss* ⟨scored a ~ on his first try⟩ ⟨two ~s and three misses out of five tries⟩ **b :** an impact of one thing against another : COLLISION **2 a :** a stroke of luck : a fortunate chance ⟨answered the questions correctly by a series of lucky ~s⟩ **b :** a theatrical production, book, or song that is conspicuously successful or popular; *broadly* : anything that is exceedingly popular, pleasing, or successful ⟨this new style is a big ~ with the high-school set⟩ **c :** a win in various gambling games ⟨a string of 20 ~s on a pinball machine⟩ **3 :** a censorious, sarcastic, or telling remark or statement ⟨took a sharp ~ at grasping politicians⟩ **4 :** a backgammon game won after the opponent has removed some of his men **5** *dial* : a bountiful crop — used esp. of fruit **6 :** a stroke in various games by which a ball is hit so as to result in a score, advancement of a runner, or some other advantage; *specif, in baseball* : BASE HIT **7** *printing* : IMPRESSION 6b ⟨even two ~s of white ink didn't quite seem to cover the green cloth —*Book Production*⟩

³**hit** \(ˌ)hit, *usu* -id·+V\ *obs or dial var of* IT

hit-and-miss \ˌ==ˈ=\ *adj* : sometimes hitting or corresponding in position and sometimes not : RANDOM, HIT-OR-MISS

hit-and-run \ˌ==ˈ=\ *adj* **1 :** being or relating to a baseball play in which a base runner starts for the next base as the pitcher starts to pitch and the batter attempts to hit the ball **2 a** (1) *of the driver of a vehicle* : guilty of leaving the scene of an accident without stopping to render assistance or to comply with legal requirements (2) : caused by, resulting from, or involving a hit-and-run driver ⟨increasing numbers of *hit-and-run* deaths⟩ ⟨a *hit-and-run* accident⟩ **b :** involving or intended for quick specific action or results rather than permanent use ⟨small *hit-and-run* units of troops⟩ ⟨*hit-and-run* merchandising⟩

hit-and-runner \"ə(r)\ *n* : one that hits and runs away; *esp* : a hit-and-run driver

¹**hitch** \ˈhich\ *vb* -ED/-ING/-ES [ME *hytchen*] *vt* **1 :** to move with jerks or jerkily ⟨~*ing* his chair closer to the table⟩ **2 a :** to catch or fasten by or as if by a hook or a knot ⟨~*ed* his horse to the top rail of the fence⟩ **b :** to connect (a vehicle or implement) with a source of motive power ⟨~ a rake to a tractor⟩ or to attach (a source of motive power) to a vehicle or instrument ⟨~ the horses to the wagon⟩ **c** *slang* : to join in marriage **3 :** to introduce into a literary work esp. irrelevantly or by obvious straining ⟨can't avoid ~*ing* in a word or two about personal responsibility⟩ **4 :** HITCHHIKE ⟨could ~ a ride on their trucks —Dillon Ripley⟩ **~** *vi* **1 :** to move interruptedly or with halts and jerks usu. due to an obstruction or impediment : HOBBLE ⟨~*ed* slowly along on his cane⟩ **2 a :** to become entangled or made fast : become linked or yoked ⟨presumably these infinitesimal particles ~*ed* together to become matter⟩ **b** *slang* : to become joined in marriage — often used with *up* ⟨decided to ~ up⟩ **3 :** HITCHHIKE ⟨could not risk ~*ing* back —James Jones⟩ — **hitch horses** *archaic* : to act or be in agreement : HARMONIZE — usu. used with *together*

²**hitch** \"\ *n* -ES **1 :** a sudden movement or pull : JERK, TWITCH ⟨gave his trousers a ~⟩ **2 a :** HOBBLE, LIMP ⟨a ~ in his gait⟩ **b** *dial* : CRICK ⟨had a ~ in his back⟩ **3 :** a sudden halt or stop (as from an accident) : ENTANGLEMENT, OBSTRUCTION, STOPPAGE, IMPEDIMENT ⟨a ~ in the performance⟩ **4 :** the act or fact of catching hold of or on something (as a hook) **5 :** a connection between a vehicle or implement and a detachable source of motive power (as a tractor or a horse) **6** *slang* : a period of military service; *broadly* : a sharply delimited period in one's life ⟨served a three-year ~ in prison⟩ ⟨put in a ~ with the diplomatic service after leaving the army⟩ **7 :** a recess cut in rock to support the end of a timber in mining or tunneling operations **8 :** any of various knots used to form a temporary loop or noose in a line or to secure a line temporarily to an object; *sometimes* : HALF HITCH **9 :** HITCHHIKE, LIFT 5b ⟨get a ~ into town —Irwin Shaw⟩

³**hitch** \"\ *n* -ES [origin unknown] : a minnow (*Lavinia exilicauda*) with silvery sides and dark back that occurs in streams about San Francisco and Monterey and reaches a length of 12 inches

hitch and kick *n* : a standing high jump in which the jumper springs from, kicks with, and alights on the same foot

hitch·cock chair *also* **hitchcock** \ˈhich,käk\ *n, usu cap H* [after Lambert H. *Hitchcock* †1852 Am. furniture manufacturer] : a turned usu. rush-seated chair with legs often and back always slightly bent with a top rail and back posts above the seat, and with a finish usu. of black paint and stenciled decoration

Hitchcock chair

hitch·er \ˈhichə(r)\ *n* -s : one that hitches or catches (as a boat hook)

¹**hitchhike** \ˈ=,=\ *vb* [²*hitch* + *hike*] *vi* : to travel by securing free rides from passing vehicles or in transport available by chance ⟨boys *hitchhiking* home from school⟩ ⟨soldiers *hitchhiking* back to their base in a military plane⟩ **~** *vt* **1 :** to proceed or progress on (as a course or way) by hitchhiking ⟨*hitchhiked* his way to the Pacific coast⟩ **2 :** to obtain (a ride) as a hitchhiker ⟨*hitchhiked* a lift on the next plane out⟩

²**hitchhike** \"\ *n* **1 :** a trip made by hitchhiking **2** *or* **hitch·hik·er** \"ə(r)\ : a brief commercial that follows a radio or television program and usu. advertises a secondary product of the sponsor

hitch·hik·er \"ə(r)\ *n* : one that hitchhikes

hitch·i·ly \ˈhichəlē, -li\ *adv* : in a hitchy manner : JERKILY

hitching *pres part of* HITCH

hitching bar *n* : HITCHRACK

hitching post *n* : a fixed and often elaborate standard to which a horse or team can be fastened to prevent straying — compare HITCHRACK

hitching post

hitch·i·ti \ˈhichədˌē\ *n, pl* **hitchiti** *or* **hitchitis** *usu cap* **1 a :** a Muskogean people of Georgia, member of the Creek confederacy **b :** a member of such people **2 :** the language of the Hitchiti people

hitch kick *n* **1 :** a running motion executed by a broad jumper while in the air to increase the distance of his jump **2 :** HITCH AND KICK

hitch pin *n* : one of a row of slanting metal pins in a piano action to which the strings are attached at the ends opposite the tuning pins

hitchrack \ˈ=,=\ *n* : a fixed horizontal rail to which a horse or team can be fastened to prevent straying — compare HITCHING POST

hitch up *vi* : to harness a draft animal or team and make it fast (as to a wagon or implement) ⟨we *hitched up* and were on our way before sunrise⟩

hitchy \ˈhichē, -chi\ *adj* -ER/-EST : having impeded movement : JERKY

hithe \ˈhīth, -th\ *n* -s [ME *hythe*, fr. OE *hȳth*; akin to OS *hūth* port] : a small port or harbor esp. on a river — now used chiefly in place names

¹**hith·er** \ˈhithə(r)\ *adv* [ME *hider*, *hither*, fr. OE *hider*; akin to ON *hethra* here, Goth *hidre* hither, L *citro* hither, *citra* on this side — more at HE] **1 :** to this place ⟨bring ~ your sick and sorrowful⟩ ⟨~ came the children to play⟩ — compare *hence*, *thither* **2** *obs* : to this point, source, conclusion, design : HERETO

²**hither** \"\ *adj* [ME *hider*, *hither*, fr. *hider*, *hither*, adv.] **1 :** being on the side next or toward the person speaking : NEARER ⟨on the ~ side of the hill⟩ — compare FARTHER, THITHER **2** *of time* : EARLIER

hither and thither *adv* [ME *hider and thider*, fr. OE] : to and fro : backward and forward : in various and usu. random directions ⟨roving *hither and thither*⟩

hither-and-thither \ˌ===ˈ==\ *vi* -ED/-ING/-S [*hither and thither*] : to move confusedly or at random

hither and yon *also* **hither and yond** *adv* : HITHER AND THITHER

hith·er·most \ˈ==,mōst *also chiefly Brit* -ˌməst\ *adj* [²*hither* + *-most*] : nearest on this side

¹**hith·er·to** \ˈ==,tü, ˌ==ˈ=\ *adv* [ME *hiderto*, fr. *hider* (adv.) + *to* (prep.)] **1 :** up to this time : as yet : until now ⟨~ unknown resources⟩ **2 :** to this place ⟨the appointed delegates shall come ~⟩

²**hitherto** \"\ *adj* : existing or done hitherto : PREVIOUS, PRIOR ⟨our ~ experience suggests⟩

hith·er·ward \ˈ==wə(r)d\ *also* **hith·er·wards** \-dz\ *adv* [ME *hiderward*, *hitherwarde*, fr. OE *hiderweard*, fr. *hider* hither + *-weard* -ward] : toward this place : HITHER

hit·le·ri·an \(ˈ)hitˈlirēən\ *adj, usu cap* [Adolf *Hitler* †1945 dictator of Germany + E *-ian*] : of, relating to, or suggestive of Adolf Hitler or his regime in Germany ⟨a *Hitlerian* disregard of human rights⟩

hit·ler·ism \ˈhitləˌrizəm\ *n* -s *usu cap* [A. *Hitler* + E *-ism*] : the extreme nationalistic doctrines of the German National Socialist party under the leadership of Adolf Hitler, from about 1930 : NAZISM

¹**hit·ler·ite** \-ˌrīt, *usu* -īd·+V\ *n* -s *usu cap* [A. *Hitler* + E *-ite*] : an adherent of Hitlerism

²**hitlerite** \"\ *adj, usu cap* : HITLERIAN

hit·less \ˈhitləs\ *adj, of a baseball player or team* : making no base hits

hit off *vt* : to characterize precisely and usu. satirically ⟨in a brilliant metaphor . . . *hits* himself *off* with terrible accuracy —V.S.Pritchett⟩ ⟨really *hits off* the contours and hierarchies of an English village with an amusing slyness —H.J.Laski⟩; *broadly* : IMITATE ⟨*hits off* an old turkey-gobbler to perfection⟩ **~** *vi* : to be in harmony or agreement : ACCORD ⟨soft shade that will *hit off* with anything⟩ ⟨his late arrival *hit off* perfectly with our plan⟩

hit-off \ˈ=,=\ *n* -s [*hit off*] : a clever imitation ⟨did an amusing *hit-off* of his brother⟩

hit or miss *adv* : without regard to accuracy or precision : at random : in a happy-go-lucky fashion

hit-or-miss \ˌ==ˈ=\ *adj* [*hit or miss*] : unpredictable and uncertain usu. through lack of care, forethought, system, or plan : marked by indifferent, ill-considered, or empirical expediency ⟨making all allowances for the *hit-or-miss* element in affirmations of a general kind —*Times Lit. Supp.*⟩; *broadly* : having no fixed or predetermined pattern ⟨a *hit-or-miss* carpet⟩ **syn** see RANDOM

hit out *vi* : to aim angry often random blows ⟨*hit out* and . . . caught him right between the eyes —H.A.Chippendale⟩ ⟨*hitting out* at injustice and prejudice⟩

hit parade *n* [fr. *Your Hit Parade*, a service mark] : a group or listing of transitorily most popular items of a particular kind (as popular songs)

hi-trap \ˈhī,=\ *n* [alter. of *high* + *trap*] : HIGH-HOUSE

hit-run \ˈ=ˈ=\ *adj* : HIT-AND-RUN 2

hits *pres 3d sing of* HIT, *pl of* HIT

hit-skip \ˈ=ˈ=\ *adj* : HIT-AND-RUN 2

hit·ta·ble \ˈhid·əbəl, -itə-\ *adj* : capable of being hit

hit·ter \ˈhid·ə(r), -itə-\ *n* -s : one that hits

hit theory *n* : a theory in genetics: the mutafacient action of mutagenically active radiations depends upon the taking up of an effective amount of the radiation by a sensitive region of the cell

hitting *pres part of* HIT

¹**hit·tite** \ˈhiˌtīt, ˈhid·ˌ|, *usu* |īd·+V\ *n* -s *usu cap* [Heb *Ḥittī* (fr. Hitt *ḫatti*) + E *-ite*] **1 :** a member of the aboriginal population of the ancient city or country of Khatti in eastern Asia Minor **2 a :** a member of a conquering people in Asia Minor and later in Syria whose origin is not certainly known, whose characteristic features, the sloping forehead and large aquiline nose, as preserved in Hittite and Egyptian reliefs, seem to have been derived from the autochthonous Hittites, and whose empire in the 2d millennium B.C. rivaled the Babylonian and Egyptian **b :** an Indo-European or Indo-Hittite language of this people known from a large body of texts in cuneiform writing largely found at Bogazköy in central Asia Minor — compare HIEROGLYPHIC HITTITE; see INDO-EUROPEAN LANGUAGES table

²**hittite** \"\ *adj, usu cap* : of or relating to the Hittites or their language

hittite hieroglyph *n, usu cap 1st H* **1 hittite hieroglyphs** *pl* : a system of writing known from inscriptions from Asia Minor and esp. northern Syria dating from about 1500 B.C. to about 600 B.C. and composed of pictorial symbols partly ideographic and partly phonetic in which the language Hieroglyphic Hittite was written **2 :** a character in the Hittite hieroglyphs

hittite hieroglyphic *n, usu cap 1st H* : HITTITE HIEROGLYPH

hit·tit·ol·o·gy \ˌhiˌtīdˈäləjē, ˌhid·ˌīd·ˈä-, ˌhiˌtīˈtä-\ *also* **hit·tol·o·gy** \hiˈtä-\ *n* -ES *usu cap* [*Hittito-* or *Hitto-* (fr. ¹*Hittite*) + *-logy*] : a branch of knowledge concerned with Hittite philology, archaeology, and history

hit·ty-mis·sy \ˌhid·ēˈmisē\ *adv (or adj)* [irreg. fr. *hit or miss* + *-y*] : HIT OR MISS

hit wicket *adj, of a batsman in cricket* : having broken the wicket with the bat or some part of the person in making a stroke at a ball — used in the phrase *out, hit wicket*; abbr *hw*

¹**hive** \ˈhīv\ *n* -s [ME *hive*, *heve*, fr. OE *hȳf*; akin to ON *hūfr* hull of a ship, L *cupa* tub, cask, Gk *kypellon* cup, *kypros*, a measure for grain, Skt *kūpa* hole, cave, OE *hēah* high — more at HIGH] **1 :** a container for housing honeybees now usu. consisting of a base, a lower rectangular hive body containing removable frames for brood, one or more upper supers that provide room for the storage honey, and a weather-

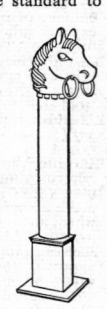

tight cover — called also *beehive;* compare BEE GUM, SKEP **2 :** the bees of one hive **:** a colony of bees **3 :** something resembling a hive: as **a** *obs* **:** a head covering suggesting a plaited skep **b :** a dwelling place **:** a center of family life ⟨forced out of the family ~ by the excess of hands and the deficiency of land —H.E.Scudder⟩ **c :** a center of activity or a place swarming with busy occupants ⟨the teeming ~ of a great railroad station⟩ ⟨a ~ of political unrest⟩ **d :** a source or point of origin ⟨the ~ from which these barbarians came lay far to the north⟩

²hive \"\ *vb* -ED/-ING/-S *vt* **1 a :** to collect into, place in, or cause to enter a hive ⟨*hived* 7 swarms of wild bees⟩ **b :** to shelter in or as if in a hive ⟨these rascals that the city ~*s*⟩ **2 a :** to store up in a hive ⟨a strong colony in a good season may ~ 100 pounds of honey⟩ **b :** to gather and accumulate for future need **:** lay up in store ⟨why did they penuriously ~ and distribute water —Norman Douglas⟩ — sometimes used with *up* or *away* ⟨*hiving* away the extra dollars⟩ ~ *vi* **1 a** *of bees* **:** to enter and take possession of a hive ⟨the swarm *hived* readily⟩ **b :** to reside or gather like bees in close association ⟨the multitudes that ~ in city apartments⟩ **2 :** to secrete oneself or shut oneself up — usu. used with *up* ⟨*hiving* up in an old camp to sit out the storm⟩

³hive \"\ *n* -S [back-formation fr. *hives*] **:** an urticarial wheal **:** a lesion of hives

hive bee *n* **:** a domestic honeybee

hive body *n* **:** the brood chamber of a hive

hive·less \'hīvləs\ *adj* **:** having no hive

hive off *vi* **:** to break away from a group like a swarm from a hive of bees ⟨a portion of a nation *hives off* to a new territory and builds a new nationalism of its own —R.M.MacIver⟩

hiv·er \'hīvə(r)\ *n* -S **:** one that hives

hives \'hīvz\ *n pl but sing or pl in constr* [origin unknown] **1 :** URTICARIA **2 :** an eruptive skin disease

hive syrup *n* **:** compound syrup of squill formerly employed as an emetic in croup and as an expectorant

hive tool *n* **:** a blunt metal chisel that has the end opposite the blade bent at right angles to the shaft and is used by beekeepers to separate supers and to scrape away propolis from parts of the hive

hive tool

hive vine *n* **:** PARTRIDGEBERRY

hive·ward \'hīvwə(r)d\ *or* **hive·wards** \-dz\ *adv* **:** toward a hive ⟨bees flying ~ in a straight line⟩

hi·vite \'hī,vīt\ *also* **hiv·vite** \'hi,v-\ *n* -S *usu cap* **:** a member of one of the ancient Canaanite peoples who were conquered by the Israelites

hi·wi hi·wi \,hēwē'hēwē\ *n* [Maori] **:** a small marine spiny-finned food fish (*Chironemus fergussoni*) of New Zealand

hi·ya \'hīyə\ *interj* [alter. of *how are you*] — used as an informal greeting

hi·zen porcelain \'hē,zen-, ='=-\ *n, usu cap H* [fr. *Hizen*, old province of Kyushu Island, Japan] **:** any of several Japanese porcelains noted for rich decoration, delicate coloring, and fine modeling

hizz \'hiz\ *obs or dial var of* HISS

hiz·zie \'hizi\ *Scot var of* HUSSY

HJ *abbr* [L *hic jacet*] here lies

hjelm·ite *also* **hielm·ite** \'(h)yel,mīt, hē'el-\ *n* -S [Sw *hjelmit*, fr. P. J. *Hjelm* †1813 Swedish chemist + Sw *-it* -ite] **:** a black mineral that contains yttrium, iron, manganese, uranium, calcium, columbium, tantalum, tin, and tungsten oxide, is often metamict, and has uncertain affinities — compare SAMARSKITE, TAPIOLITE

hjelm·slev·ian \(')(h)yelmz¦levēan, -eüm-,- m(p)¦sl-\ *adj, usu cap* [Louis *Hjelmslev* b1899 Dan. linguist + E *-ian*] **:** belonging to or characteristic of the linguistic methods or terminology of Louis Hjelmslev

HJR *abbr* House joint resolution

HJS *abbr* [L *hic jacet sepultus*] here lies buried

hkf *abbr* handkerchief

hl *abbr* hectoliter

HL *abbr* **1** height-length **2** *often not cap* [L *hoc loco*] in this place; [L *hujus loci*] of this place **3** horizontal line **4** House of Lords

h l hinge *n, cap 1st H&L* **:** H AND L HINGE

hm *abbr* hectometer

HM *abbr* **1** half morocco **2** handmade **3** harbor master **4** harmonic mean **5** headmaster; headmistress **6** heavy mobile **7** Her Majesty; His Majesty **8** *often not cap* [L *hoc mense*] in this month; [L *hujus mensis*] of this month **9** home missions

hmd *abbr* humid

HMD *abbr* hydraulic mean depth

HMG *abbr* **1** heavy machine gun **2** Her Majesty's Government; His Majesty's Government

hmlt *abbr* hamlet

HMP *abbr* **1** handmade paper **2** [L *hoc monumentum posuit*] he erected this monument

HMS *abbr* **1** Her Majesty's Service; His Majesty's Service **2** Her Majesty's Ship; His Majesty's Ship

hnd *abbr* **1** hand **2** hundred

hndbk *abbr* handbook

¹ho \'hō\ *interj* [ME] — used typically to express surprise or delight or indignation or derision or to attract attention and esp. postpositively to attract attention to something specified ⟨land ~⟩; often used postpositively as a rallying cry with a specified direction or destination ⟨westward ~⟩

²ho \"\ *v imper* [ME, fr. OF *ho* halt, stop] — a call intended to stop a movement or an action; compare WHOA

³ho \"\ *vi, dial Eng* **:** ³HONE

⁴ho \"\ *n, pl* **ho** *or* **hos** *usu cap* **1 a :** a people of the northeastern part of the Indian subcontinent south of the Ganges plain **b :** a member of such people **2 :** the Munda language of the Ho people

ho *abbr* house

HO *abbr* **1** head office; home office **2** holy day of obligation **3** hostilities only

Ho *symbol* holmium

hoactzin *var of* HOATZIN

¹hoar \'hō(ə)r, 'hȯ(ə)r, -ōə, -ȯ(ə)\ *adj* [ME *hor, hoor*, fr. OE *hār;* akin to OHG *hēr* gray, old, ON *hárr* gray, old, Gk *kirros* orange yellow, Skt *śiti* white] *archaic* **:** HOARY ⟨whose beard with age is ~ —S.T.Coleridge⟩

²hoar \"\ *n* -S [ME *hor, hoor*, fr. *hor, hoor*, adj.] **1** *archaic* **:** HOARINESS **2 a :** a hoary coating ⟨the thick ~ of dust which had accumulated on their shoes —Thomas Hardy⟩ **b :** HOARFROST, RIME

¹hoard \'hō(ə)rd, 'hȯ(ə)rd, 'hōəd, 'hȯ(ə)d\ *n* -S [ME *hord*, fr. OE; akin to OHG *hort* treasure, ON *hodd*, Goth *huzd* treasure, Gk *kysthos* vulva, OE *hȳdan* to hide — more at HIDE] **1 :** a collection or accumulation or amassment of something usu. of special value or utility that is put aside for preservation or safekeeping or future use often in a greedy or miserly or otherwise unreasonable manner and that is often kept hidden or as if hidden **:** a supply or stock or fund of something that is stored up and closely and often jealously guarded ⟨a ~ of money⟩ ⟨a ~ of provisions⟩ ⟨a ~ of facts⟩; *often* **:** TREASURE ⟨dug up a ~ of gold and jewels⟩ ⟨a ~ of coins⟩ **2** *obs* **:** the place where a hoard is kept **:** REPOSITORY; *specif, obs* **:** TREASURY

²hoard \"\ *vb* -ED/-ING/-S [ME *horden*, fr. OE *hordian*, fr. *hord*, n.] *vt* **1 :** to collect or accumulate or amass into a hoard **:** lay up a hoard of ⟨~*ing* their money and refusing to make even reasonable expenditures⟩ **2 :** to keep (as a desire) hidden and in reserve and allow to develop or become strengthened ⟨she ~*ed* her intention —Virginia Woolf⟩ ⟨the people outside disperse their affections, you ~ yours, you nurse them into intensity —Joseph Conrad⟩ ~ *vi* **:** to lay up a hoard; *esp* **:** to practice hoarding **syn** see ACCUMULATE

³hoard \"\ *n* -S [alter. of earlier *hourd*, prob. fr. F dial., scaffold, scaffolding, fr. OF *hourt* scaffold, scaffolding, platform, of Gmc origin; akin to OHG *hurd* hurdle — more at HURDLE] **:** ²HOARDING 1

¹hoard·ing \'hōrdiŋ, 'hȯr-, -dēŋ\ *n* -S [fr. gerund of ²*hoard*] **1 :** the greedy or miserly accumulation and storing or hiding of money or goods **2 :** something hoarded — usu. used in pl. ⟨the ~*s* of a lifetime⟩

²hoarding \"\ *n* -S [³*hoard* + *-ing*] **1 :** a temporary board fence put about a building being erected or repaired **2** *Brit* **:** BILLBOARD

hoard·ing·ly *adv* **:** in a manner marked by hoarding **:** in a greedy or miserly manner

hoarfrost \'=,=\ *n* [ME *horforst*, fr. *hor, hoor* hoar + *forst, frost* frost] **:** FROST 1c(1)

hoar–green \'=¦=\ *adj* **:** grayish white with greenish cast

hoarhead \'=,=\ *n* [ME *horheed*, fr. *hor, hoor* hoar + *heed* head] *archaic* **:** one having a hoary head

hoarhound *var of* HOREHOUND

hoar·i·ly \'hōrəlē, 'hȯr-, -li\ *adv* **:** in a hoary manner

hoar·i·ness \-rēnəs, -rin-\ *n* -ES **:** the quality or state of being hoary

hoarse \'hō(ə)rs, 'hȯ(ə)rs, -ōəs, -ȯ(ə)s\ *adj, usu* -ER/-EST [ME *hors*, alter. (perh. influenced by *harsk* harsh) of earlier *hos*, fr. OE *hās;* akin to OHG *heis* hoarse, ON *háss*, OE *hāt* hot — more at HOT] **1 :** marked by a relatively low harsh or husky often muffled or laboriously forced quality of sound having little or no resonance **:** not clear or smooth or musical in tone **:** rough-sounding **:** RAUCOUS, GRATING, RASPING, CROAKING ⟨the ~ voice of a person with a cold⟩ ⟨the ~ sound made by a frog⟩ ⟨the ~ cry of a crow⟩ **2 :** having a hoarse voice or cry **:** making hoarse sounds ⟨had caught a cold and was quite ~⟩ ⟨~ from too much talking⟩ ⟨~ with emotion⟩ **syn** see LOUD

hoarse·ly *adv* **:** in a hoarse manner **:** with a hoarse voice or cry or sound or tone

hoars·en \'hōrsᵊn, 'hȯr-, 'hōəs-, 'hȯ(ə)s-\ *vb* **hoarsened; hoarsened; hoarsening** \-s(ᵊ)niŋ\ **hoarsens** *vt* **:** to make hoarse ⟨it agitated their bodies and ~*ed* their voices —Walter O'Meara⟩ ~ *vi* **:** to become hoarse ⟨the deep voice ~*ed* — E.C.Marston⟩

hoarse·ness \-snəs\ *n* -ES [alter. (influenced by *hoarse*) of ME *hosnes*, fr. OE *hāsnys*, fr. *hās* hoarse + *-nys, -nes* -ness] **:** the quality or state of being hoarse

hoarstone \'=,=\ *n* [ME *horeston, harestan*, fr. OE *hār stān*, fr. *hār* hoar + *stān* stone] **1** *Brit* **:** a stone used anciently to mark boundaries **2** *Brit* **:** a stone erected anciently as a memorial (as of an event)

hoary \'hōrē, 'hȯr-, -ri\ *adj, usu* -ER/-EST **1 a :** gray or white; *specif* **:** gray or white with age ⟨nodded his ~ head⟩ **b** (1) **:** having hair that is gray or white with age ⟨a ~ old man⟩ (2) **:** CANESCENT **2** (3) *of a plant* **:** having grayish or whitish leaves **2 a** (1) **:** very old **:** ANCIENT ⟨~ legends⟩; *esp* **:** impressively or venerably old ⟨the ~ walls of the castle⟩ ⟨the ~ figure of the prophet⟩ (2) **:** so old or so familiar as to be without freshness and sparkle ⟨~ jokes⟩ or devoid of interest or ability to stimulate ⟨~ clichés⟩ ⟨~ half-truths⟩ **:** TRITE, STALE, HACKNEYED **b :** far removed in time past **:** REMOTE ⟨~ antiquity⟩

hoary alder *n* **:** SPECKLED ALDER

hoary alyssum *n* **:** a tall leafy perennial European plant (*Berteroa incana*) with gray-green foliage, entire leaves, and pubescent pods that is naturalized in No. America and is sometimes troublesome as a weed

hoary bat *n* **:** a rather large migratory bat (*Lasiurus cinereus*) having yellowish or brown hair tipped with white

hoary cinquefoil : SILVERWEED a(2)

hoary cress *or* **hoary peppergrass** *or* **hoary pepperwort** *n* **:** a perennial cruciferous European herb (*Cardaria draba*) with clasping stem leaves, clusters of small white flowers, and reniform or cordate depressed pods that is naturalized widely in America and often becomes a troublesome weed in the western U.S.

hoary–haired \'=¦=¦=\ *adj* **:** having hoary hair

hoary–headed \'=¦=¦=\ *adj* **:** having a hoary head

hoary marmot *n* **:** a large gray marmot (*Marmota pruinosa*) of northwestern No. America — called also *mountain badger*

hoary pea *n* **:** a plant of the genus *Tephrosia; esp* **:** GOAT'S RUE

hoary plantain *n* **1 :** a widely distributed Old World perennial plantain (*Plantago media*) that is naturalized in No. America and has a flat rosette of finely hirsute leaves and a tall scape bearing inconspicuous whitish fragrant flowers **2 :** a No. American annual or biennial plantain (*P. virginica*) with long soft hairs on the leaves

hoary puccoon *n* **:** a No. American perennial herb (*Lithospermum canescens*) with hairy foliage

hoary redpoll *n* **:** HORNEMANN'S REDPOLL

hoary vervain *n* **:** a densely white hairy perennial herb (*Verbena stricta*) of central No. America with showy purplish blue spicate flowers

hoary willow *n* **:** a white-leaved No. American shrub (*Salix candida*)

¹hoast \'hōst\ *n* -S [ME *host, hoost*, fr. ON *hōsti;* akin to OE *hwōsta* cough, OHG *huosto* cough, Skt *kāsate* he coughs] *dial Brit* **:** COUGH

²hoast \"\ *vb* -ED/-ING/-S [ME *hosten*, fr. ON *hōsta;* akin to ON *hōsti*, n.] *dial Brit* **:** COUGH

ho·a·tzin \wä(t)'sēn\ *or* **hoac·tzin** \wäk(t)'s-\ *also* **hoa·cin** \wä's-\ *n, pl* **hoatzins** \-ēnz\ *also* **hoatzi·nes** \-ē(,)nās\ *or* **hoac·tzins** \-ēnz\ *also* **hoactzi·nes** \-ē(,)nās\ [AmerSp, fr. Nahuatl *uatzin* pheasant] **:** a crested bird (*Opisthocamus hoazin*) of tropical So. America constituting the suborder Opisthocomi of the Galliformes that is somewhat smaller than a pheasant and that has olivaceous plumage marked with white above and that has a disagreeable strong musky smell and the young of which have a well-developed claw on the first and second fingers of the wing by means of which they climb about — called also *stinkbird*

¹hoax \'hōks\ *vt* -ED/-ING/-ES [prob. by contr. of *hocus*] **:** to trick into believing or accepting or doing something **:** play upon the credulity of so as to bring about belief in or acceptance of what is actually false and often preposterous **:** take in **:** DELUDE, DUPE, MISLEAD, VICTIMIZE ⟨~*ed* them into thinking the diamonds were genuine⟩ ⟨eager to ~ people into swallowing propaganda⟩ ⟨even the experts were ~*ed*⟩ **syn** see DUPE

²hoax \"\ *n* -ES **1 :** an act intended to trick or dupe **:** a piece of trickery **:** IMPOSTURE ⟨played a ~ on the miners —*New Republic*⟩ ⟨~*es* have occurred even in the present century —R.W.Murray⟩ **2 :** something accepted or believed in through trickery **:** something established by fraud or fabrication ⟨the book was once thought to be based on actual experience, but it is now recognized as a literary ~⟩ ⟨Piltdown man is one of the biggest ~*es* ever launched on the scientific world⟩

¹hob \'häb\ *n* -S [ME *hob, hobbe*, fr. *Hobbe*, nickname of *Robert* or *Robin*] **1** *now dial Eng* **a :** a clownish lout **b :** RUSTIC **2** *now dial Eng* **:** HOBGOBLIN, ELF **3 :** a male ferret — **play hob 1 :** to cause mischief **:** make trouble **:** cause an upset **:** cause confusion or disruption or havoc — usu. used with *with* ⟨would disorganize his life and *play hob* with his standard of living —John Lardner⟩ **2 :** to take liberties **:** make free — usu. used with *with* ⟨a biased book that *plays hob* with historical fact⟩ — **raise hob 1 :** to play hob — usu. used with *with* ⟨the war . . . *raised hob* with international trade —*Harper's*⟩ **2 a :** to show extreme irritation or wrath ⟨his . . . wife was getting on his nerves and he was *raising* unaccountable *hob* —V.B.Hass⟩ — often used with *with* ⟨*raised hob* with him for being late⟩ **b :** to be riotous (as with intoxication or glee) and cause a rumpus ⟨going to go out tonight and *raise hob*⟩

²hob \"\ *n* -S [origin unknown] **1 :** a level projection (as of brickwork, stone, or iron) at the back or side of an open fireplace on which something (as a kettle) can be placed to be kept warm **2** *archaic* **a :** a peg or stake used as a target in quoits and similar games **b :** a game in which such a peg or stake is used **3 :** HOBNAIL **4 a** (1) **:** a cutting tool consisting of a fluted steel worm that is used in a milling machine for cutting the teeth of worm wheels or screw chasers or other tool devices or used in a gear hobber for hobbing the teeth of gear wheels (2) **:** MASTER TAP (3) **:** SELLERS HOB (4) **:** an engraved steel block that is casehardened and used to impress an embossing die or a die-casting die — called also *hub* **b :** LEADER 1d

³hob \"\ *vt* **hobbed; hobbed; hobbing; hobs 1 :** to furnish with hobnails **2 a :** to cut (as the teeth of worm wheels) with a hob **b :** to impress (as an embossing die) with a hob

¹hob and nob \'häbə(n)¦näb\ *interj* [prob. alter. of earlier *hob or nob*, alter. of *hab or nab* — more at HABNAB] *archaic* — used as an informal toast in convivial drinking

²hob and nob \"\ *also* **hob a nob** \"\ *adv (or adj) archaic* **:** in a close and friendly relationship **:** in a warmly companionable relationship

³hob and nob \"\ *or* **hob–a–nob** \"\ *archaic var of* ¹HOBNOB

ho·bart \'hō,bärt\ *adj, usu cap* **:** of or from Hobart, the capital of Tasmania **:** of the kind or style prevalent in Hobart

hob·ba·de·hoy *or* **hob·ba·dy·hoy** \'häbədē¦hȯi\ *also* **hob·ber·de·hoy** \-bə(r)d-\ *archaic var of* HOBBLEDEHOY

hob·ber \'häbə(r)\ *n* -S **1 :** a machine used for hobbing; *also* **:** the operator of such a machine **2 :** a pitched horseshoe or quoit leaning against a stake or peg without ringing it — called also *leaner*

¹hobbes·ian \'häbzēən\ *adj, usu cap* [Thomas *Hobbes* †1679 Eng. philosopher + E *-ian*] **:** of or relating to Hobbes or Hobbism

²hobbesian \"\ *n* -S *usu cap* **:** HOBBIST

hobbied *past of* HOBBY

hobbies *pres 3d sing of* HOBBY

hob·bil \'häbəl\ *n* -S [alter. of obs *hoball*, prob. fr. ¹*hob*] *now dial Eng* **:** a stupid individual **:** DOLT

hob·bism \'hä,bizəm\ *n* -S *usu cap* **:** the philosophical system of Hobbes; *esp* **:** Hobbes' political theory maintaining that man has a natural right to self-preservation and happiness and that the clashing interests and desires of individuals must be controlled by a strong government esp. of a monarchist constitution

¹hob·bist \'häbəst\ *n* -S *usu cap* **:** a follower of Hobbes or advocate of Hobbism

²hobbist \"\ *adj, usu cap* **:** HOBBESIAN

¹hob·ble \'häbəl\ *vb* **hobbled; hobbled; hobbling** \-b(ə)liŋ\ **hobbles** [ME *hoblen;* akin to MD *hobbelen* to turn, roll] *vi* **1 :** to move along unsteadily or with great difficulty or uncertainty **:** advance waveringly or laboriously or painfully **:** limp along **:** move lamely **:** struggle along ⟨the crippled ship managed to ~ into port⟩ ⟨try to ~ along to the end of the school term⟩; *specif* **:** to walk with a halting labored typically up-and-down movement often marked by lurching or wobbling ⟨saw an old man *hobbling* down the street⟩ ⟨*hobbling* along on his crutches⟩ **2** *of an arrow* **:** to wobble in flight ~ *vt* **1 :** to cause to hobble **:** make lame **:** CRIPPLE ⟨was *hobbled* by an ankle injury⟩ **2** [prob. alter. of *hopple*] **a :** to tie or otherwise fasten together the legs of (as a horse) to prevent straying or to keep under control **:** FETTER ⟨*hobbled* the horses before turning them loose⟩ **b :** to interfere with the free movement or advance of **:** HAMPER, OBSTRUCT, IMPEDE ⟨felt himself *hobbled* by his parents' lack of understanding⟩ ⟨*hobbling* factory production by inefficient methods⟩

²hobble \"\ *n* -S **1 :** a hobbling movement or hobbling manner of walking ⟨had a bad ~ —Adrian Bell⟩ **2** *archaic* **:** an awkward or perplexing situation **3 a :** something used for tying the legs (as of a horse) esp. to prevent straying **:** FETTER **b :** something that restrains or hampers ⟨censorship and other ~*s* of free expression⟩ **4 :** HOBBLE SKIRT

hobblebush \'=,=\ *n* [²*hobble* + *bush;* fr. the hindrance caused by its drooping branches] **:** a shrub (*Viburnum alnifolium*) of northern No. America that has long straggling branches and opposite double-toothed leaves — called also *American wayfaring tree*

hobbled *adj* [fr. past part. of ¹*hobble*] *West* **:** tied together beneath the belly of a horse — used of stirrups

hob·ble·de·hoy \'häbəldē¦hȯi\ *n* -S [origin unknown] **:** a usu. awkward callow adolescent male **:** a gawky youth

hobble out *vt* **:** to attach hobbles to (as a horse) and allow to wander about esp. in a pasture ⟨had *hobbled out* some horses not far from his cabin —Ross Santee⟩ ⟨and *hobbled* the animals *out* to graze —Fred Gipson⟩

¹hob·bler \-b(ə)lə(r)\ *n* -S [¹*hobble* + *-er*] **:** one that hobbles

²hob·bler \'häb(ə)lə(r)\ *n* -S [alter. (perh. influenced by ¹*hobble*) of *hoveler*] **:** an unlicensed boat pilot or a freelance longshoreman in some parts of southern England

hob·ble·shew \'häbəl,shü\ *or* **hob·ble·show** \-,shō\ *var of* HUBBLESHEW

hobble skirt *n* [²*hobble*] **:** a skirt with bottom fullness constricted at the ankles by a band

hob·ble·te·hoy \'häbəltē¦hȯi\ *or* **hob·by·de·hoy** \-bēdē¦-\ *archaic var of* HOBBLEDEHOY

hob·bling·ly *adv* [*hobbling* (pres. part. of ¹*hobble*) + *-ly*] **:** with a hobbling movement **:** LAMELY

hob·bly \'häb(ə)li\ *adj* [*hobble* + *-y*] *dial Brit* **:** having a rough uneven surface

¹hob·by \'häbē, -bi\ *n* -ES [ME *hoby, hobyn*, perh. fr. *Hobbin*, nickname of *Robert* or *Robin*] **1** *or* **hobby horse** *archaic* **:** a small or medium-sized light horse esp. of Irish origin having a gentle ambling pace **2** *archaic* **:** HOBBYHORSE 1,3 **3 a :** HOBBYHORSE 4a **b :** a specialized pursuit (as stamp collecting, painting, woodworking, gardening) that is outside one's regular occupation and that one finds particularly interesting and enjoys doing usu. in a nonprofessional way as a source of leisure-time relaxation; *broadly* **:** any favorite pursuit or interest **4** *archaic* **:** DANDY HORSE

²hobby \"\ *vi* -ED/-ING/-ES **:** to follow a hobby **:** have a hobby ⟨*hobbied* in photography for many years⟩ ⟨now *hobbies* at painting⟩

³hobby \"\ *n* -ES [ME *hoby*, modif. of MF *hobé*, fr. OF, alter. of *hobel*, perh. fr. *hobeler* to skirmish, prob. fr. MD *hobbelen* to turn, roll — more at HOBBLE] **:** a small falcon (*Falco subbuteo*) widely distributed in the Old World and formerly trained for hawking and flown at small birds (as larks)

hobbyhorse \'=,=,=\ *n* **1 a :** a figure designed to resemble a horse and made of light material (as wickerwork) that is fastened about the waist of a dancer (as in the morris dance or in Spanish or Javanese dance rituals) who dances about imitating the movements of a high-spirited horse **b :** a dancer wearing this figure and performing a dance associated with it **2** *obs* **:** BUFFOON **3 a :** a child's plaything which consists typically of a stick having an imitation horse's head at one end and sometimes wheels at the other and which the child straddles and pretends to ride — called also *stick horse* **b :** one of the horses on a merry-go-round **c :** ROCKING HORSE **4 a :** something (as a pet idea or favorite topic or special object of concern) with which one is preoccupied or to which one constantly reverts ⟨this is one of his political ~*s*⟩; *specif* **:** a cranky obsession **b** *archaic* **:** HOBBY 3b **5 :** DANDY HORSE

hobbyhorse 3a

hob·by·ist \'häbēəst, -biə-\ *n* -S [¹*hobby* + *-ist*] **1** *archaic* **:** one that is preoccupied with a pet idea or cranky obsession **2 :** one that has one or more hobbies; *esp* **:** one that is particularly fond of cultivating hobbies

hobby lantern *n* [¹*hob* + *-y*] *dial Eng* **:** WILL-O'-THE-WISP

hob ferret *n* **:** ¹HOB 2

hobgoblin \'=,==\ *n* [¹*hob* + *goblin*] **1 :** a goblin esp. when conceived of as mischievous or impish **2 :** BOGEY 3 ⟨unreason has taken the place of evil as the ~ of a rational society —Albert Hubbell⟩ **:** BUGABOO ⟨a foolish consistency is the ~ of little minds —R.W.Emerson⟩

hobnail \'=,=\ *n, often attrib* [²*hob* + *nail*] **1 :** a short nail with a large head and a sharp point that is used esp. for studding soles of heavy shoes (as work shoes) **2** *archaic* **:** a countrified often loutish individual **:** CLODHOPPER ⟨troops of ~*s* clumping to church —W.M.Thackeray⟩ **3 a :** a pattern consisting of small tufts usu. closely spaced (as on some bedspreads) or of similarly spaced bosses often having the shape of diamonds (as in some vases and other objects made of pressed glass) **b :** one of the tufts or bosses used in such a pattern

hobnailed \'=,nāld\ *adj* **1 :** studded with or as if with hobnails ⟨~ boots⟩ **2 a :** marked by the wearing of heavy shoes or boots studded with hobnails ⟨~ laborers⟩ ⟨the ~ entry of investigating officialdom into the classroom —M.H.Bernstein⟩ **b :** countrified and often loutish ⟨too ~ to have much feeling⟩

hobnail liver *also* **hobnailed liver** *n* **1 :** the liver as it appears in one form of cirrhosis in which it is shrunken and hard and covered with small projecting nodules **2 :** the cirrhosis associated with hobnail liver **:** LAENNEC'S CIRRHOSIS

¹hob·nob \ˈhäb,näb\ *vi* **hobnobbed; hobnobbed; hobnobbing; hobnobs** [alter. of *habnab*] **1** *archaic* **:** to drink sociably or convivially — often used with *with* **2 a :** to associate familiarly **:** go about in an easy informal companionship **:** chum around — often used with *with* ⟨once *hobnobbed* with kings and princes⟩ ⟨have *hobnobbed* ever since they were boys⟩ **b :** to talk informally and freely to or with someone **:** speak familiarly — usu. used with *with* **:** CHAT ⟨officials have long enjoyed the practice of *hobnobbing* with newspapermen —Douglass Cater⟩ — **hob·nob·ber** \-näbə(r)\ *n* -s

²hobnob \"\ *n* -s **:** an informal sociable meeting and chat **:** GET-TOGETHER ⟨going to have a quiet little ~ with them⟩

¹ho·bo \ˈhō(,)bō\ *n, pl* **hoboes** *also* **hobos** [perh. alter. of

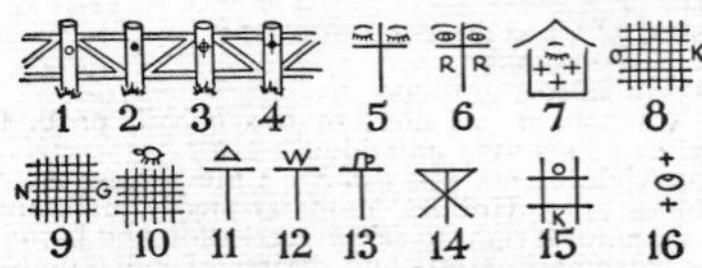

common symbols used by hoboes: *1* good for a handout, *2* cranky woman or bad dog, *3* not generous, *4* stay away, *5* police not hostile, *6* police hostile; *R R* used for railroad police, *7* jail good for a night's lodging, *8* clean jail, *9* jail food no good, *10* unclean jail, *11* jail has rock pile, *12* jail is a workhouse, *13* saloons in town, *14* town is hostile, *15* streets good for begging, *16* plainclothes detectives here

ho, boy, a call used in the northwestern U.S. in the 1880's by railway mail handlers when delivering mail] **1 :** a migratory worker **2 a :** one that is homeless and usu. penniless and that leads a largely vagrant life often by choice and that occas. works at odd jobs **:** TRAMP **b :** ⁷BUM 1a, 1b **syn** see VAGABOND

²hobo \"\ *vi* -ED/-ING/-ES **:** to live or travel in the manner of a hobo ⟨spent two years ~*ing* around the country⟩

ho·bo·he·mia \,hō(,)bōˈhēmēə\ *n* [blend of *hobo* and *bohemia*] **1 :** a usu. run-down urban district in which hoboes congregate **2 :** a fringe group of society made up of hoboes **:** the hobo realm — **ho·bo·he·mi·an** \¦==(,)=¦hēmēən\ *adj or n*

ho·bo·ism \ˈhō(,)bō,izəm\ *n* -s **:** the condition of being a hobo

¹hob or nob \¦häbə(r)¦näb\ *var of* ¹HOB AND NOB

²hob or nob *archaic var of* ¹HOBNOB

hobs *pl of* HOB, *pres 3d sing of* HOB

hob·son–job·son \¦häbsən¦jäbsən\ *n* -s *usu cap H&J* [Anglo-Indian modif. (influenced by the Eng. surnames *Hobson* and *Jobson*) of Ar *yā Ḥasan! yā Ḥusayn!* O Hasan! O Husain! (cry repeated at the Muharram festival as an expression of mourning for Hasan and Husain, grandsons of Muhammad, killed in the early struggles between the Sunni and Shi'a parties)] **:** assimilation of the sounds of a word or words foreign to a language into the sounds of a word or words coined or already existent in the language (as Spanish *cucaracha* has become English *cockroach* or as English *riding coat* has become French *redingote*) ⟨the law of Hobson-Jobson has played a great role in the evolution of surnames —R.F. Barton⟩ — compare FOLK ETYMOLOGY

hob·son's choice \¦häbsənz-\ *n, usu cap H* [after Thomas *Hobson* †1631 Eng. liveryman; fr. his practice of requiring every customer to take the horse which stood nearest the door] **1 :** an apparent freedom to take or reject something offered when in actual fact no such freedom exists **:** an apparent freedom of choice where there is no real alternative: **a :** the forced acceptance of something whether one likes it or not (as in a so-called free election where only one candidate is proposed) **b** (1) **:** the necessity of accepting something objectionable through the fact that one would otherwise get nothing at all (as an underpaid job rather than no job at all) (2) **:** the necessity of accepting one of two or more equally objectionable things (as enslavement or annihilation by a conquered people) **2 :** something that one must accept through want of any real alternative **:** the object of a Hobson's choice ⟨military unity . . . is . . . a *Hobson's choice* which all accept —V.D.Hurd⟩

hob tap *n* [²*hob*] **:** MASTER TAP

hob·thrush \ˈhäb,thrəsh\ *n* [prob. irreg. fr. ¹*hob* + obs. E *thurse* goblin, fr. ME *thirs* malevolent supernatural being, fr. OE *thyrs* demon; akin to OHG *duris* giant, ON *thurs*] *dial Eng* **:** HOBGOBLIN

hoc \ˈhäk\ *n* -s [F, perh. fr. L, this, neut. of *hic* this] **:** a card game in which the holder gives certain cards any value

¹hoch \ˈhäk, -ō-\ *chiefly Scot var of* HOCK

²hoch \ˈhōk\ *interj, often cap* [G, lit., high, fr. OHG *hōh* — more at HIGH] — used to express salutation and approval

hoche·laga \(,)h|äsh(ə)ˈlagə, |ōsh-, |ósh, -lä-\ *n, pl* **hochelaga** *or* **hochelagas** *usu cap* **1 :** an extinct Iroquoian people located on the site of present Montreal **2 :** a member of the Hochelaga people

hoch·moor \ˈhōk+,-\ *adj* [G *hoch* high + *moor* fen, swamp, fr. OHG *muor* — more at MOOR] **:** being or growing on various acid peats or peaty soils ⟨the ~ soils along the Baltic coast⟩ ⟨certain ~ plants⟩

höchst \ˈhə(r)kst, ˈhōk-, ˈhek- *Ger* ˈhœkst *or* -œk-\ *adj, often cap* [*Höchst*, former city (now part of Frankfurt am Main) in western Germany] **:** of or being a German porcelain made during the 18th century and largely influenced by the styles of Meissen porcelain

¹hock \ˈhäk\ *n* -s [ME *hocke*, fr. OE *hoc*] **:** any of several mallows of the genera *Althaea* and *Malva* — now used only in holly*hock*

²hock \"\ *vb* -ED/-ING/-S [ME *hocken* to celebrate Hocktide, fr. *hocke-, hoke-* (in *hockedai, hokeday* Hockday)] *vt, archaic* **:** to tease or harass after a manner formerly customary at Hocktide ~ *vi* **:** to behave in a brash rambunctious manner suitable to Hocktide

³hock \"\ *n* -s [prob. alter. of *hook*] *chiefly Brit* **:** a strong usu. handled hook used esp. for cargo handling or for hanging meat

⁴hock \"\ n -s [alter. of ME *hoch, hough*, fr. OE *hōh* heel; akin to ON *hāsin* hock, sinew, Skt *kankāla* skeleton] **1 a :** the tarsal joint or its region in the hind limb of a digitigrade quadruped (as the horse) that corresponds to the ankle of man but is elevated and bends backward and that is a compound joint containing a number of small bones and having a prominence at the back caused by the calcaneum and corresponding to the heel of man — see COW illustration **b :** the corresponding joint of a fowl's leg — called also *knee;* see COCK illustration **2 :** a small cut of meat from either the front or hind leg just above the foot — used esp. of pork ⟨pork ~*s* and sauerkraut⟩ **3** *chiefly dial* **:** the hip and thigh — often used in pl. ⟨so hipless . . . his pants . . . forever slipping down around his ~*s* —F.B. Gipson⟩

⁵hock \"\ *vt* -ED/-ING/-S **:** to disable by cutting the tendons of the hock **:** HAMSTRING

⁶hock \"\ *n* -s *often cap* [modif. of *Hochheimer* fr. *Hochheim*, Germany, its locality] *chiefly Brit* **:** RHINE WINE 1

⁷hock \"\ *n* -s [D *hok* pen (for animals), hovel, prison] **1 a :** restraint of goods usu. as a pledge for a loan ⟨put his winter overcoat into ~⟩ ⟨had difficulty getting the technical supplies out of ~ with the customs⟩ **b** *slang* **:** PRISON ⟨will be 10 years before he gets out of ~⟩ **2** [Afrik *hok*, fr. D] *Africa* **:** a small or temporary building or enclosure ⟨a chicken ~⟩ — **in hock :** PAWNED ⟨his watch was *in hock*⟩ **:** in debt ⟨the company was heavily *in hock* to the banks⟩

⁸hock \"\ *vt* -ED/-ING/-S **:** to pledge as security for a loan **:** PAWN

⁹hock \"\ *n* -s [perh. short for *hockelty*] **:** the last card in a faro dealing box

hock·day \ˈhäk,dā\ *or* **hoke·day** \ˈhōk-\ *n, usu cap* [ME *hockedai, hokeday*] **1 :** the second Tuesday after Easter celebrated in England before the 18th century with rough sport and humorous play orig. for the collection of funds for community purposes — called also *Hock Tuesday* **2 :** the second Monday after Easter — called also *Hock Monday*

hock disease *n* [⁴*hock*] **:** perosis of the young chicken or turkey

hock·el·ty \ˈhäkəltē\ *n* -ES [origin unknown] **:** ⁹HOCK

hock·er \ˈhäkə(r)\ *n* -s **:** one that hocks

²hocker \"\ *vi* -ED/-ING/-S [modif. of Norw dial. *hokra* to crouch, fr. ON *hūka* to squat] *dial Eng* **:** to behave or move in an awkward flustered manner

hock·et *or* **ho·quet** \ˈhäkət\ *n* -s [ME *hocket* obstacle, fr. MF *hoquet*, of imit. origin] **1 :** HICCUP **2** *in medieval music* **:** an interruption of a voice part by interjected rests resulting in a broken musical line; *also* **:** a composition using such an interruption as a contrapuntal device

¹hock·ey \ˈhäkē, -ki\ *n* -s *often attrib* [perh. fr. MF *hoquet* shepherd's crook, dim. of *hoc* hook, of Gmc origin; akin to MD *hoec* corner — more at HOOK] **1 :** a game in which two parties of players provided with sticks curved or hooked at the end seek to drive a ball or other small object through opposite goals: as **a :** FIELD HOCKEY **b :** ICE HOCKEY **2 :** HOCKEY STICK

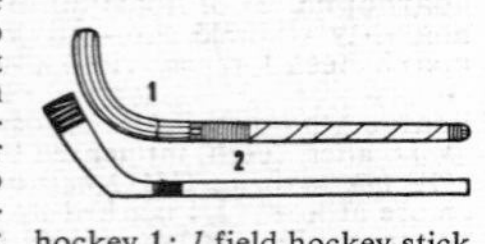

hockey 1: *1* field hockey stick, *2* ice hockey stick

²hockey \"\ *n* -ES [earlier *hocky*, prob. fr. LG *hokk* pile of sheaves (fr. MLG *hocke;* akin to MD *hocke*, ME *hock* pile, ON *hūka* to squat) + E *-y* — more at HAWKER] **1** *chiefly dial* **:** HARVEST HOME **2** *chiefly dial* **:** a harvest-home supper

³hock·ey \", ˈhök-, ˈhīk-\ *n* -ES [origin unknown] *chiefly Midland* **:** EXCREMENT, FECES

⁴hockey \"\ *vi* -ED/-ING/-S *chiefly Midland* **:** DEFECATE

hock·ey·ist \ˈhäkē|əst, -ki\ *also* **hock·ey·ite** \|,īt\ *n* -s **:** a hockey player

hockey skate *n* **:** a tubular skate made with a short curved blade and a shoe giving support and protection to the foot and ankle and worn esp. by ice hockey players

hockey stick *n* **:** a curved or angled stick used in playing hockey

hocking *pres part of* HOCK

hock·ing ale \ˈhäkiŋ-\ *n* [ME *hokyng*, gerund of *hoken, hocken* to celebrate Hocktide — more at HOCK] *archaic* **:** ale for the Hocktide festival

hock leg *n* [⁴*hock*] **:** a cabriole having a broken curve on the inner side of the knee — see LEG illustration

hockey skate

hock monday \ˈhäk-\ *n, usu cap H&M* [ME *hoc Monday*, fr. *hoc-, hocke-, hoke-* (in *hockedai, hokeday* Hockday) + *Monday*] **:** HOCKDAY 2

hock money \"+\ *n, usu cap H* [ME *hockemoney*, fr. *hocke-, hoke-* + *money*] *archaic* **:** money collected at Hocktide

hocks *pl of* HOCK, *pres 3d sing of* HOCK

hock shop *n* [⁷*hock*] **:** PAWNSHOP

hocktide \ˈ=,=\ *n, usu cap* [ME *hoketyde*, fr. *hoke-* + *tyde, tide* time, season — more at TIDE] **:** Hock Monday and Hock Tuesday

hock tuesday *n, usu cap H&T* [ME *hoke Tuesday*, fr. *hoc-, hocke-, hoke-* (in *hockedai, hakeday* Hockday) + *Tuesday*] **:** HOCKDAY 1

hocs *pl of* HOC

¹ho·cus \ˈhōkəs\ *n, pl* **hocuses** *or* **hocusses** [short for *hocus-pocus*] **1** *obs* **a :** CONJURER, CHEAT, DECEIVER **b :** CHEATING, TRICKERY, FRAUD **2 :** drugged liquor

²hocus \"\ *vt* **hocused** *or* **hocussed; hocused** *or* **hocussed; hocusing** *or* **hocussing; hocuses** *or* **hocusses 1 :** DECEIVE, CHEAT **2 a :** ADULTERATE, DRUG ⟨~*ed* liquor⟩ **b :** to ply with stupefying drugs

¹ho·cus–po·cus *also* **ho·kus–po·kus** \¦hōkə¦spōkəs\ *n* -ES [prob. invented by jugglers in imitation of Latin] **1 a** *obs* **:** JUGGLER, TRICKSTER **b** *archaic* **:** a juggler's trick or art **:** SLEIGHT OF HAND **2 :** words or a formula used (as by jugglers) in pretended incantations without regard to the usual meaning **3 :** nonsense or sham used or intended to cloak deception ⟨the *hocus-pocus* of city politics⟩; *broadly* **:** something that confuses, misleads, or is difficult to comprehend ⟨the tape recordings, through some electronic *hocus-pocus*, will retain all the visual quality of the original telecast —*Newsweek*⟩

²hocus–pocus \"\ *vb* **hocus-pocussed** *or* **hocus-pocused; hocus-pocussed** *or* **hocus-pocused; hocus-pocussing** *or* **hocus-pocusing; hocus-pocusses** *or* **hocus-pocuses** *vi* **:** to play the part of a conjurer; *broadly* **:** TRICK, CHEAT ~ *vt* **:** to play tricks on **:** TRICK, BEFOOL ⟨got through *hocus-pocussing* the jury —Shelby Foote⟩

¹hod \ˈhäd\ *n* -s [prob. fr. MD *hodde;* akin to MHG *hotte, hotze* cradle, G dial. *hotteln, hotzeln* to shake, Lith *kutėti* to shake up, ME *schuderen* to shudder — more at SHUDDER] **1 :** a tray or trough with a pole handle that is borne on the shoulder for carrying mortar, brick, or similar loads **2 :** a utensil for holding or carrying coal **:** COAL SCUTTLE

²hod \"\ *vi* **hodded; hodded; hodding; hods** [prob. imit.] *Scot* **:** to bob up and down **:** JOG

³hod \ˈhōd\ *vb* [by alter.] *Scot* **:** HIDE

⁴hod \ˈhäd, -ó-\ *dial Eng var of* HOLD

ho·dag \ˈhō,dag\ *n* -s [origin unknown] **:** a mythical animal reported chiefly from Wisconsin and Minnesota, noted for its ugliness, lateral horns, and hooked tail, and reputed to be outstanding in both ferocity and melancholy

hod carrier *n* **:** a laborer employed in carrying bricks, mortar, concrete, or plaster to supply bricklayers, stonemasons, cement finishers, or plasterers on the job

hod·den \ˈhädᵊn\ *n* -s [origin unknown] *chiefly Scot* **:** coarse cloth of undyed wool

hodden grey *n, dial Brit* **:** HODDEN; *esp* **:** hodden prepared from a mingling of white or light fleeces with a small proportion of natural black wool

hod·dle \ˈhädᵊl\ *vi* -ED/-ING/-S [prob. by alter.] *Scot* **:** WADDLE

hoddy–doddy \¦hädē¦dädē\ *n, pl* **hoddy–doddies** [prob. alter. and redupl. of *dodman, hodmadod*] **1** *dial Eng* **a :** GARDEN SNAIL **b :** a snail shell **2** *archaic* **a :** a short and stout person **b :** a henpecked man **:** CUCKOLD **c :** FOOL, BLOCKHEAD, SIMPLETON

hod·dy·poll \ˈ==,pōl\ *n* -s [*hoddy-* (fr. *hoddy-doddy*) + *poll*] **1 :** a fumbling inept person **2** *obs* **:** CUCKOLD

hod·ful \ˈhäd,fu̇l\ *n, pl* **hodfuls** *also* **hodsful :** the quantity that may be carried at one time in a hod ⟨a ~ of coal⟩; *broadly* **:** a considerable quantity **:** LOTS ⟨had ~*s* of fun⟩

hodge \ˈhäj\ *n* -s [ME *Hoge*, nickname of *Roger*] **:** an English rustic or farm laborer

¹hodge·podge \ˈhäj,päj\ *n* -s [alter. of *hotchpotch*] **1 :** a heterogeneous mixture often of incongruous and ill-suited elements **:** MIXTURE, MEDLEY **2 :** HOTCHPOTCH 1

²hodgepodge \"\ *vt* -ED/-ING/-S **:** to make into a hodgepodge

hodg·kin's disease \ˈhäjkənz-\ *n, usu cap H* [after Thomas *Hodgkin* †1866 Eng. physician] **:** a disease of unknown cause that is characterized by progressive enlargement of lymph glands, spleen, and liver and by progressive anemia and that in some respects suggests an inflammatory or tumorous process

hodg·kin·son·ite \ˈhäjkənsə,nīt\ *n* -s [H. H. *Hodgkinson* Am. mineralogist + E *-ite*] **:** a mineral $MnZn_2SiO_5.H_2O$ consisting of a hydrous zinc manganese silicate that occurs in the form of pink to reddish brown crystals

ho·di·er·nal \¦hōdē¦ərnᵊl, ¦häd-\ *adj* [obs. E *hodiern* hodiernal (fr. L *hodiernus*, fr. *hodie* today, contr. of *hoc die* this day) + E *-al*] **:** of this day

hodja *var of* KHOJA

hod·ma·dod \ˈhädmə,däd\ *n* -s [alter. and redupl. of *dodman*] **1** *dial Eng* **a :** SNAIL; *esp* **:** GARDEN SNAIL **b :** a snail shell **2** *dial Eng* **:** a deformed or clumsy person **3** *dial Eng* **:** SCARECROW

hod·man \ˈhädmən\ *n, pl* **hodmen** [¹*hod* + *man*] *chiefly Brit* **:** HOD CARRIER; *broadly* **:** one whose duties are mere routine assistance **:** HACK

hod·o·graph \ˈhädə,graf, -raf\ *n* [Gk *hodos* path + E *-graph* — more at CEDE] **:** a path described by the extremity of a vector drawn from a fixed origin and representing the linear velocity of a moving point — **hod·o·graph·ic** \¦==¦grafik\ *adj*

hod·o·scope \ˈ==,skōp\ *n* [Gk *hodos* path + E *-scope*] **:** an instrument for tracing the paths of cosmic-ray or other ionizing particles by means of ion counters in close array

hods *pl of* HOD, *pres 3d sing of* HOD

¹hoe \ˈhō\ *n* -s [ME *hoh*, fr. OE *hōh;* prob. akin to OE *hōh* heel — more at ⁴HOCK] *obs* **:** PROMONTORY, HILL, CLIFF — used in English place names ⟨on the *Hoe* at Plymouth⟩

²hoe \"\ *n* -s [ME *howe*, fr. MF *houe*, fr. OF, of Gmc origin; akin to MD *houwe* mattock, OHG *houwa;* derivative fr. the verb represented by OHG *houwan* to hew — more at HEW] **1 a :** an agricultural implement that usu. consists of a thin flat blade set transversely on a long handle and is used esp. for cultivating, weeding, or loosening the earth around plants **b :** an implement that functions like a hoe and is arranged with a wheel and one or two handles for more rapid cultivation **c :** a one-horse tillage implement for cultivating between rows (as of vines or bushes) ⟨a berry ~⟩ ⟨a grape ~⟩ **d :** any of various cultivating or weeding implements usu. for use with animal or mechanical draft — see ROTARY HOE, SPRING HOE, SPRING-TRIP HOE, WHEEL CULTIVATOR **2 :** an implement or tool felt to resemble or serving a purpose like that of a hoe: as **a :** a rake designed for stirring up a furnace fire **b :** an instrument for spreading and mixing mortar, concrete, or similar substances **c :** BACKHOE

hoe 1a

³hoe \"\ *vb* **hoed; hoed; hoeing; hoes** [ME *howwen*, fr. *howe*, n.] *vi* **:** to use a hoe **:** work with a hoe ⟨was ~*ing* in the field by the road⟩ ~ *vt* **:** to weed, cultivate, or thin (a crop) with a hoe ⟨~ out the strawberries⟩ **:** remove (weeds) by hoeing ⟨soon have to ~ the weeds from the corn⟩ **:** dress or cultivate (land) by hoeing ⟨*hoed* 7 acres with a spring hoe⟩

⁴hoe \"\ *n* -s [E dial. (Shetland) *ho*, of Scand origin; akin to ON *hār* dogfish, shark, tholepin — more at HAYE] *chiefly Scot* **:** SPINY DOGFISH

hoecake \ˈ=,=\ *n* [²*hoe* + *cake;* fr. its being baked on the blade of a hoe] **1** *chiefly South & Midland* **:** a small cake made of cornmeal, water, and salt usu. cooked before an open fire **2** *chiefly South & Midland* **:** a hoecake to which shortening has been added and which is usu. baked on a griddle or in an oven

hoe culture *also* **hoe agriculture** *or* **hoe cultivation** *n* **:** the growing of crops by hand methods including use of a hoe for stirring the soil

hoedown \ˈ=,=\ *n* -s [³*hoe* + *down*] **1 a :** a lively old-time dance; *esp* **:** SQUARE DANCE **b :** a lively hillbilly tune played usu. to accompany folk or square dancing **2 a :** an informal dancing party at which hoedowns are danced **b** *slang* **:** a loud or spectacular affair (as a social or theatrical event)

hoe drill *n* **:** a seed drill with hoeing devices for opening furrows

hoeg·bom·ite \ˈhōgbə,mīt, ˈhäg-\ *n* -s [Sw *högbomit*, fr. Arvid Gustaf *Högbom*, 20th cent. Swed. scientist + Sw *-it* -ite] **:** a mineral $Mg(Al,Fe,Ti)_4O_7$(?) consisting of an oxide of magnesium, aluminum, iron, and titanium

ho·er \ˈhōə(r), -ōr\ *n* -s **:** one that hoes

hoer·nes·ite \ˈhərnə,sīt, ˈhōr-\ *n* -s [G *hörnesit*, fr. Moritz *Hoernes* †1868 Austrian paleontologist + G *-it* -ite] **:** a mineral $Mg_3As_2O_8.8H_2O$ consisting of hydrous magnesium arsenate occurring as crystals resembling gypsum

hoff·man clamp \ˈhäf|mən, ˈhȯ|\ *n, usu cap H* [prob. fr. the name *Hoffman*] **:** a pinchcock for flexible tubing controlled by a screw

hoffmann's anodyne *n, usu cap H* [after Friedrich *Hoffmann* †1742 Ger. physician] **:** COMPOUND SPIRIT OF ETHER

hoffmann's drops *n pl, usu cap H* [after Friederich *Hoffmann* †1742] **:** SPIRIT OF ETHER

hof·mann reaction *or* **hofmann rearrangement** \ˈhäf|mən-, ˈhȯ|, ˈhō|\ *n, usu cap H* [after August Wilhelm von *Hofmann* †1892 Ger. chemist] **:** the conversion of an acid amide $RCONH_2$ to an amine RNH_2 with one less carbon atom by treatment with sodium hypobromite

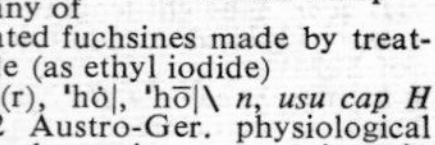

Hoffman clamp

hofmann's violet *n, usu cap H* **:** any of several violet dyes that are alkylated fuchsines made by treating rosaniline with an alkyl halide (as ethyl iodide)

hof·meis·ter series \ˈhäf,mīstə(r), ˈhȯ|, ˈhō|\ *n, usu cap H* [after Franz *Hofmeister* †1922 Austro-Ger. physiological chemist] **:** an arrangement of salts, anions, or cations in descending order of their effect upon a physical phenomenon (as the swelling of gelatin) — called also *lyotropic series*

¹hog \ˈhȯg, -äg-\ *n, pl* **hogs** *also* **hog** *often attrib* [ME *hogge*, fr. OE *hogg*, perh. of Celt origin; akin to W *hwch* hog, Corn *hoch* — more at SOW] **1 a :** a domestic swine **:** PIG, SOW, BOAR; *esp* **:** an adult or a growing animal weighing more than 120 pounds — compare PORK **b** *Brit* **:** ²BARROW **c :** a wild boar; *broadly* **:** any of various animals of the family Suidae — usu. used in combination ⟨the wart*hogs* and river ~*s* are tropical relatives of our domestic swine⟩ **2** *usu* **hogg** *Brit* **a :** a young sheep usu. less than or about a year in age and not yet shorn; *also* **:** wool from such a sheep **b :** a young domestic animal (as a bullock) of similar age — often used in combination ⟨several good *hogg* colts⟩ **3 :** a person felt to resemble a hog esp. in selfishness, gluttony, or filthiness — often used in combination **4** *or* **hogg** *slang* **a** *Brit* **:** SHILLING **b :** DIME **5 :** a curling stone that fails to pass the hog score **6 :** a machine with revolving cutters for reducing bulk material (as waste lumber or animal carcasses) to small bits — called also *hogger* **7 :** a frame of timber or a heavy flat rough broom hauled along a ship's bottom under water to clean it **8 :** an agitator for mixing and stirring pulp in papermaking **9** *slang* **:** a railroad locomotive — **on the hog** *slang* **:** having no funds **:** BROKE

²hog \"\ *vb* **hogged; hogged; hogging; hogs** *vt* **1 :** to cut (a horse's mane) short **:** ROACH **2 :** to clean the bottom of (a ship) with a hog **3 a :** to cause to arch like the back of a hog **b :** to cause (as a ship or timber) to bow up in the middle and sag at the ends usu. as a result of improper loading or supporting **4 a** *Brit* **:** to winter over (young sheep) **b :** to utilize (an unharvested crop) by turning in hogs to feed — often used with *down* or *off* ⟨got a drove of gilts to ~ down the corn⟩ ⟨it would be cheaper to ~ off that piece than to harvest it⟩ **5 a :** to take, grasp, or retain selfishly or in excess of one's due or need ⟨don't ~ the light, I want to read too⟩ ⟨*hogging* everything in sight⟩ **b :** to consume voraciously — usu. used with *down* ⟨*hogged* down his dinner and rushed out⟩ ⟨finished the book next day, *hogging* it down in great gulps —Bruce Marshall⟩ **6 :** to play (a curling stone) so as not to pass the hog score **7 :** to tear up or shred (bulk material) into bits with a hog ~ *vi* **1 :** to become curved upward in the middle like a hog's back — used esp. of a ship or its bottom or keel **2 :** to act like a hog esp. in taking more than one's share

ho gage \ˈā,chō-\ *n, usu cap H&O* [*half o gage*] **:** a scale of ⅛ inch to one foot used in model railroading for trains and track layout with a distance between rails of ⅝ inch

ho·gan \ˈhō,gän, -gàn, -gan\ *n* -s [Navaho *hogan*, fr. *ho-*, deictic prefix + *-gan* dwelling] **:** a conical, hexagonal, or octagonal dwelling characteristic of the Navaho Indian made with a door traditionally facing east and constructed of logs and sticks covered with mud, sods, or adobe or sometimes of stones — compare LODGE 8a

hog and hominy *n* **:** pork and Indian corn; *broadly* **:** meager or very plain and simple food

hogan–mogan *obs var of* HOGEN-MOGEN

ho·garth chair \ˈhō,gärth, -gàth-\ *n, usu cap H* [after William *Hogarth* †1764 Eng. painter] **:** any of certain 18th century English side chairs, usu. with hooped back and cabriole legs

ho·garth·ian \(ˈ)hō¦gärthēən, -gàth-\ *adj, usu cap* [William *Hogarth* + E *-ian*] **:** relating to, characteristic of, or suggesting Hogarth or his work ⟨a thoroughly *Hogarthian* attitude⟩ ⟨*Hogarthian* cartoons of the human scene —*Dial*⟩

hogarth's line *n, usu cap H* [after William *Hogarth*, who considered it the essence of beauty] **:** an S-shaped line used for decorative and compositional purposes esp. in painting and engraving

hogback \ˈ=,=\ *n* **1 :** an arched back suggesting that of a hog ⟨most of the sunfishes have ~*s*⟩ **2 :** something felt to resemble the back of a hog in outline or section: as **a :** a ridge of land formed by the outcropping edges of tilted strata; *broadly* **:** a ridge with a sharp summit and steeply sloping sides **b :** a sharp rise in the floor of a coal mine **c :** HOGFRAME

hog-backed \'=¦=\ *or* **hogback** \'=,=\ *adj* **:** having an arched back or prominence ⟨a *hog-backed* island in the channel⟩
hog badger *n* **:** HOG-NOSED BADGER
hog banana *n* **:** a rather large coarse-textured red-skinned banana that is usu. eaten cooked
hog bean *n* **:** HENBANE 1
hogbite \'=,=\ *n* **:** GUM SUCCORY 1
hog brace *n* **:** HOGFRAME
hog brake *n* **:** BRACKEN 1b
hog cane *n* **:** SALT REED GRASS
hog chain *n* **:** a chain or a tie rod used in a ship to prevent hogging
hogchoker \'=,==\ *also* **hogchoke** \'=,=\ *n* **:** a small American sole (esp. *Achirus fasciatus*) of no market value
hog cholera *n* **:** a highly infectious often fatal virus disease of swine characterized by fever, loss of appetite, diarrhea, petechial hemorrhages esp. in the kidneys and lymph glands, and in chronic cases intestinal ulceration often complicated by secondary infection with the necrotic enteritis bacterium
hog clover *n* **:** BUR CLOVER
hog constable *n* **:** HOGREEVE
hog corn *n* **:** poor quality Indian corn
hog-corn ratio *n* **:** CORN-HOG RATIO
hog cranberry *n* **1 :** CROWBERRY 1a **2 :** BEARBERRY 1
hog deer *n* **:** a white-spotted deer (*Axis porcinus* syn. *Hyelaphus porcinus*) of India about two feet high at the withers
hog-dressed \'=¦=\ *adj, of a meat animal* **:** bled and eviscerated but having the skin left on the carcass
[1]**hogen-mogen** \¦hōgən¦mōgən\ *n* -s *usu cap H&M* [prob. alter. of D *hoogmogend* all-powerful] **1** *obs* **:** a person of consequence or one who affects authority **2** *archaic* **:** HOLLANDER; *collectively* **:** the people of Holland — often used disparagingly
[2]**hogen-mogen** \"\ *adj, usu cap H&M* **1** *obs* **a :** HIGH-AND-MIGHTY **b** *of liquor* **:** STRONG **2** *archaic* **:** DUTCH
hog feeder *n* **:** an operator who feeds bulk material into and supervises a shredding or mincing hog — called also *hogger*
hog fennel *n* **:** a plant of *Oxypolis* or the closely related genus *Lomatium*
hogfish \'=,=\ *n* see PLURAL *note* **1 :** any of various fishes felt to resemble a hog: as **a :** a large West Indian and Florida wrasse (*Lachnolaimus maximus*) often used for food **b :** a pigfish (*Orthopristis chrysopterus*) **c :** LOG PERCH **d :** a large red spiny-headed European marine scorpion fish (*Scorpaena scorfa*) **2** *obs* **a :** PORPOISE **b :** MANATEE
hog flu *n* **:** SWINE INFLUENZA
hogframe \'=,=\ *n* **:** a trussed frame extending fore and aft esp. in American river and lake steamers, being usu. above deck, and reaching to the ends to increase longitudinal strength and stiffness and prevent hogging — called also *hogback, hogging frame*
hog fuel *n* **:** ground up or powdered wood used for fuel
hogg *var of* HOG
hog·gas·ter \'hȯgəstə(r), 'häg-\ *n* -s [ME *hogaster*, fr. *hogge* hog + L *-aster* (dim. suffix) — more at HOG] **1** *archaic* **:** a boar in its third year **2** *archaic* **:** HOG 2a
hogged \'hȯgd, -äg-\ *adj* **1 :** raised in the center or falling away at the ends or sides **:** HOG-BACKED — used esp. of a ship or of a road that is sharply convex in section **2** *of a horse's mane* **:** cut short **:** ROACHED
hoggee *var of* HOGGY
[1]**hog·ger** \'hägər, 'hȯg-\ *n* -s [origin unknown] **1** *chiefly Scot* **:** a stocking made without a foot and worn as a gaiter **2** *chiefly Scot* **:** an old stocking used for keeping money
[2]**hog·ger** \'hȯgə(r), 'häg-\ *n* -s [partly fr. [1]*hog* + *-er;* partly fr. [2]*hog* + *-er*] **1 a :** a machine tool that takes heavy cuts at high speed **b :** HOG 6 **2 a** *slang* **:** a locomotive engineer — called also *hoghead* **b :** HOG FEEDER
hog·ger·el \'häg(ə)rəl\ *n* -s [ME (Sc dial), dim. of *hogge* hog, sheep — more at HOG] *Brit* **:** a young sheep; *usu* **:** HOG 2a
hog·gery \'hȯg(ə)rē, 'häg-, -ri\ *n* -ES **1 :** a place where hogs are kept **:** PIGGERY, HOG HOUSE **2 :** hoggish character or manners **:** gross animality **:** GREED
hog·get \'hägət\ *n* -s [ME, fr. [1]*hog* + *-et*] *chiefly Brit* **:** HOG 2a
hog·gin *also* **hog·ging** \'hȯgən, 'häg-, ·giŋ\ *n* -s [origin unknown] **:** a material composed of screenings or siftings of gravel or of a mixture of loam, coarse sand, and fine gravel
hogging *pres part of* HOG
hogging frame *or* **hogging girder** *n* **:** HOGFRAME
hogging line *n* **:** a line or chain used to draw a collision mat into position over a damaged area of a ship's hull
hog·gish \'hȯgish, 'häg-, -gēsh\ *adj* **:** like a hog esp. in gluttony or selfishness — compare PIGGISH, SWINISH — **hog·gish·ly** *adv* — **hog·gish·ness** *n* -ES
hoggs *pl of* HOGG
hog gum *n* **1 a :** a gum resin obtained from a West Indian tree (*Moronobea coccinea*) of the family Guttiferae **b :** a similar product obtained from other trees (as *Rhus metopium*) **c :** TRAGACANTH; *also* **:** a similar gum (as bassora or kutira) **2 :** any of various tropical trees chiefly of the families Anacardiaceae and Guttiferae that produce hog gum or are associated or confused with trees producing hog gum
hog·gy *or* **hog·gee** \'hȯgē, 'häg-\ *n, pl* **hoggies** *or* **hoggees** [prob. fr. [1]*hog* + *-y* or *-ee* (alter. of *-y*)] **:** a towpath driver for the early 19th century barge transportation system in parts of the eastern U.S.
hog·head \'hȯg,hed, 'häg-\ *n, slang* **:** HOGGER 2a
hogherd \'=,=\ *n* [ME] **:** SWINEHERD
hog hook *n* **:** a hook with a transverse handle for handling a hog carcass while scalding it
hog house *n* **:** a building in which hogs are housed **:** PIGPEN, STY; *esp* **:** a building with facilities for housing a number of hogs under one roof
hog in *vi, of a cutting tool* **:** to dig in and take a bigger cut than intended with a possible stalling of the machine or breaking of the tool
hog in armor : one self-conscious or ill at ease in fine clothes
hog-killing \'=,==\ *or* **hog-killing time** *n, dial* **:** a jolly or riotous party
hog latin *n, usu cap L* **:** PIG LATIN
hogleg \'=,=\ *n, chiefly West* **:** a large single-action revolver of the type carried in the West by cowboys and frontiersmen
hoglike \'=,=\ *adj* **:** like or like that of a hog ⟨a heavy ~ face⟩
hog lily *n* **:** SPATTERDOCK
hog line *n* **:** HOG SCORE
hog·ling \'hȯgliŋ, 'häg-\ *n* -s [ME, fr. *hog* + *-ling*] **1** *obs* **:** PIGLET **2** *dial Brit* **:** LAMB
hog lot *n* **:** an enclosure usu. with housing in which hogs are reared or fattened for market
hog louse *n* **:** a large sucking louse (*Haematopinus suis*) that is parasitic on the hog and in some areas is associated with the transmission of swine pox
hog·man \'=mən\ *n, pl* **hogmen 1 :** a raiser of or attendant on hogs **:** a hog farmer **:** SWINEHERD **2 :** HOG FEEDER
hog·ma·nay *also* **hag·me·na** \¦hägmə¦nā\ *n* -s *sometimes cap* [origin unknown] **1** *Scot* **:** NEW YEAR'S EVE **2 :** a traditional Scottish celebration at New Year's Eve: **a :** the going about of children from house to house singing and asking for gifts usu. of cakes or nuts **b :** the going about from house to house with the intention of being the first visitor **3 :** a cake, gift, or treat given at New Year's Eve
hog-maned \'=¦mānd\ *adj* **:** having a short bristly mane **:** ROACHED
hog millet *n* **:** MILLET 1a
hog mol·ly \-,mälē\ *n* **1** *or* **hog mullet :** HOG SUCKER **2 :** LOG PERCH
hog money *n* **:** early 17th century copper coins of Bermuda bearing the image of a hog and valued from twopence to a shilling
hog-mouthed fry \'=,=-\ *n* **:** a small fish (*Anchoviella choerostomus*) that resembles an anchovy and is common at Bermuda
hognose \'=,=\ *adj* **:** having a rounded cutting edge — used of a cutting or boring tool
hog-nosed badger \'=,=-\ *n* **:** a large short-legged Asiatic badger (*Arctonyx collaris*) with white fur tipped with black and white markings on face, neck, tail, and ears — called also *sand badger*
hog-nosed skunk *n* **:** a large stocky white-backed skunk (*Conepatus mesoleucus*) of southwestern No. America with a short white tail and a naked muzzle; *also* **:** any of several closely related So. American skunks — called also *white-backed skunk*
hog-nosed viper *n* **:** any of several small tropical American pit vipers (genus *Bothrops*) related to the fer-de-lance but with short fangs and venom of low toxicity
hognose snake *or* **hog-nosed snake** *n* **:** any of certain moderate-sized stout-bodied No. American snakes that constitute the genus *Heterodon*, are perfectly harmless though often reputed deadly prob. because of the threatening way in which they dilate the neck, flatten the head, and hiss and blow when startled, and are noted for the habit of rolling over on the back and playing dead when their threatening display is ineffective — called also *blowing adder, flatheaded adder, puffing adder, sand viper*
hognut \'=,=\ *n* **1 :** EARTHNUT 1a **2 :** PIGNUT 2 **3 :** JAMAICA COBNUT
ho·go \'hō(,)gō\ *n* -s [modif. of F *haut goût* high savor or flavor] *now dial Eng* **:** a notably strong flavor or smell
hog oiler *n* **:** a device that automatically applies oil or insecticide to the skin of a hog that rubs against it
hog out *vt* **1 :** to cut (metal) out of a piece of work at very high speeds and very fast feeds **2 :** to machine (as a part) from a billet of size and shape such that the removal of much metal is necessary in order to achieve the shape desired
hog peanut *n* **:** a plant of the genus *Amphicarpa* that is usu. considered to constitute a single variable species (*A. bracteata*), is widely distributed in eastern and central No. America, and produces abundant subterranean fruits, each containing a single edible seed which resembles a peanut, is much relished by hogs, and was formerly important in Amerindian dietary — called also *wild peanut*
hogpen \'=,=\ *n* **:** PIGPEN 1
hog perch *n* **:** LOG PERCH
hog plum *n* **1 :** a tree of the genus *Spondias; esp* **:** a tropical American tree (*S. mombin*) sometimes cultivated for its edible yellow fruits which resemble plums **2 :** POISON-WOOD 1 **3 :** the Chickasaw plum or other wild plum of the southern U.S. **4 :** FALSE SANDALWOOD 1
hog potato *n* **1 :** a small or inferior potato often boiled for hog feed **2 a :** MAN-OF-THE-EARTH **b :** DEATH CAMAS
hog pox *n* **:** SWINE POX 2
hogreeve \'=,=\ *n* -s **:** a former New England town officer responsible for the impounding of stray hogs
hog ring *n* **1 :** a split metal ring usu. with beveled points that can be pushed through the median cartilage of the nose of a pig and there locked to prevent rooting or to serve as a means of leading the animal **2 :** an upholstery fastener resembling a hog ring — **hog-ringer** \'=,==\ *n*

hog rings 1

hog-round \'=¦=\ *adv (or adj)* **:** at a flat rate **:** without grading ⟨sometimes it is wiser to sell *hog-round*⟩ ⟨a common custom on southern cotton markets for buyers to take everything *hog-round* on a middling basis —Clarence Poe⟩
hogs *pl of* HOG, *pres 3d sing of* HOG
hog's-back \'=,=\ *n* **:** HOGBACK
hog's-bean \'=,=\ *n, pl* **hog's-beans 1 :** HENBANE **2 :** SEA STARWORT
hog score *n* **:** a line that is marked across a curling rink 7 yards in front of each tee and that a stone must pass or be removed from the ice — called also *hog line;* see CURLING illustration
hog scraper *n* **:** a circular concave metal disk with a sharp rim suitable for scraping the bristles from a hog carcass and a handle often in the form of a candle holder in the center of its convex surface; *also* **:** a candlestick with a hog-scraper base
hog's fennel *n* **1 :** a European sulphurweed (*Peucedanum officinale* or a closely related species) **2 :** MAYWEED 1
hog's-haw \'=,=\ *n, pl* **hog s-haws :** a hawthorn (*Crataegus brachyacantha*) of the southern U.S.
hogs·head \'hȯgz,hed, 'häg-, *sometimes* -zəd *dial* -zət\ *n* [ME *hoggeshed*, fr. *hogges* (gen. of *hogge* hog) + *hed* head — more at HOG, HEAD] **1 :** a large cask or barrel; *esp* **:** one containing from 63 to 140 gallons — abbr. *hhd* **2 :** any of various units of capacity equal to the amount a hogshead will hold: as **a :** a U.S. unit equal to 63 gallons **b :** a British unit equal to 54 imperial gallons or 64.85 U.S. gallons **3 :** something (as an unpleasing person) felt to resemble the head of a hog
hog's head cheese \'hȯ¦gz,hed-, 'hä¦, =='=-\ *n, dial* **:** HEADCHEESE
hog sheer *n* **:** the deck curve of a ship in which the middle portion of the deck is higher than the ends
hog·skin \'=,=\ *n* **1 :** PIGSKIN 1 **2 :** an article (as a saddle or a pair of gloves) made of pigskin
hog's-meat \'=,=\ *n, pl* **hog's-meats 1 :** a small chiefly tropical American herb (*Boerhavia coccinea*) with sticky foliage and reddish flowers **2 :** a tropical American ornamental vine (*Aristolochia grandiflora*) with poisonous roots
hog snake *n* **:** HOGNOSE SNAKE
hog's-potato \'==¦=(,)=\ *n, pl* **hog's-potatoes :** HOG POTATO 2
hogs·teer \'hȯgz,ti(ə)r, 'häg-, -g,st-\ *n* [alter. of *hoggaster*] **:** a wild boar in his third year
hog sucker *n* **:** a No. American fish (*Hypentelium nigricans*) of the family Catostomidae that is brassy olive marked with brown, is widely distributed in warm clear shallow streams, and in some areas is used as food — called also *hog molly*
hog-tie \'=,=\ *vt* **1 :** to make (a thrown animal) helpless by tying the hind legs together and then to one or both front legs with a short line ⟨*hog-tying* calves for branding⟩ **2 :** to make (as a person) helpless ⟨financial institutions . . . damned for *hog-tying* the region's economy —*Frontier*⟩ ⟨a police force *hog-tied* by graft and corruption⟩ **syn** see HAMPER
hog wallow *n* **1 a :** a depression in land made by the wallowing of swine **b :** a similar depression said to be due to heavy rains **2 :** a land surface characterized by numerous low rounded mounds — usu. used in pl.
hogwash \'=,=\ *n* [ME *hoggyswasch*, fr. *hoggys* (gen. of *hogge* hog) + *wasch* wash — more at HOG, WASH] **1 a :** SWILL 1a, SLOP 4a(1) **b :** poor or flavorless food or drink **2 :** something (as writing or propaganda) that is insipid, worthless, or lacking in real substance ⟨the ~ of political oratory⟩
hogweed \'=,=\ *n* **:** any of various weeds or coarse plants: as **a :** RAGWEED 2 **b :** KNOTWEED **c :** DOG FENNEL **d :** HORSEWEED **e** *Brit* (1) **:** COW PARSNIP (2) **:** HEDGE PARSLEY
hog-wild \'=¦=\ *adj* **:** free from restraint and often disorderly or foolish ⟨*hog-wild* enthusiasm⟩ **:** overenthusiastic and often extravagant or intemperate ⟨legislatures gone *hog-wild* on spending⟩
hog wire *n* **1 :** barbed wire having 4-pointed barbs and weighing about 400 pounds per mile **2 :** heavy woven fencing with the meshes smaller at the bottom and usu. with the bottommost wire barbed

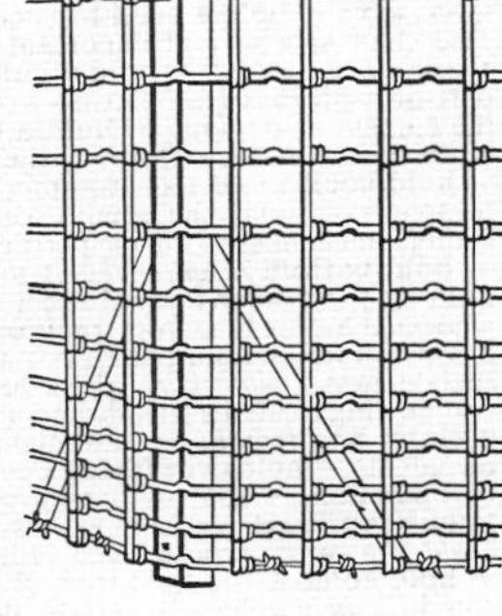
hog wire 2

hogwort \'=,=\ *n* **:** an annual silvery green weed (*Croton capitatus*) of the southeastern U.S. — called also *woolly croton*
hog-wrestle \'=,==\ *n, slang* **:** an informal dance (as a country dance) sometimes marked by coarse vulgar conduct
hoh \'hō\ *n, pl* **hoh** *or* **hohs** *usu cap* **1 :** an Indian people of the Olympic Peninsula, Washington, speaking the Quileute language **2 :** a member of the Hoh people
ho·he \'hō(,)hā\ *n, pl* **hohe** *or* **hohes** *usu cap* **:** ASSINIBOIN
[1]**ho·hen·stau·fen** \'hōən,s(h)taufən, ,=='==\ *adj, usu cap* **:** of or relating to a German princely family of Swabian origin that furnished sovereigns of the Holy Roman Empire from 1138–1254 and of Sicily from 1194–1266
[2]**hohenstaufen** \"\ *n* -s *usu cap* **:** a member of the Hohenstaufen family; *esp* **:** a Hohenstaufen sovereign
[1]**ho·hen·zol·lern** \'hōən,z¦älə(r)n, -ōən(t)s¦, ¦ōl-, ,=='==\ *adj, usu cap* **:** of or relating to a German princely family founded about the 11th century that furnished kings of Prussia from 1701–1918 and German emperors from 1871–1918
[2]**hohenzollern** \"\ *n* -s *usu cap* **:** a member of the Hohenzollern family; *esp* **:** a Hohenzollern sovereign
ho·hen·zol·lern·ism \-ə(r),nizəm\ *n* -s *usu cap* **:** Prussianism as developed under and exemplified by the Hohenzollern rulers of Germany
hohl·flö·te \'hōl,flād·ə, -lǣd·ə, *G* -lœtə\ *or* **hohl·flute** \-flüt, *usu* -üd·+V\ *n* -s [*hohlflöte* fr. G, fr. *hohl* hollow (fr. OHG *hol*) + *flöte* flute; *hohlflute* part trans. of G *hohlflöte* — more at HOLE, DOPPELFLÖTE] **:** a pipe-organ flute stop usu. in 8-foot pitch with a dull hollow quality
hoh·mann·ite \'hōmə,nīt\ *n* -s *usu cap* [G *hohmannit*, fr. Thomas *Hohmann*, its discoverer + G *-it* -ite] **:** a mineral $Fe_2(SO_4)_2(OH)_2 \cdot 7H_2O$ consisting of a hydrated basic ferric sulfate
ho·ho·kam \'hōhō,käm, hō'hōkəm\ *adj, usu cap* [Pima *húhukamJ* ancient one] **:** of or belonging to a prehistoric desert culture of southwestern U.S. centering in the Gila valley of Arizona and contemporaneous with the Anasazi culture to the north and characterized by irrigated agriculture, large pit houses, good pottery, decorative bone and shell ornaments, and use of cremation
ho-hum \'hō¦həm\ *adj* [imit.] **:** dull and routine **:** UNINTERESTED, UNINTERESTING ⟨looked on in *ho-hum* unconcern —*Springfield (Mass.) Union*⟩ — often used interjectionally
hoi *var of* HOY
[1]**hoick** \'hȯik\ *vt* -ED/-ING/-S [prob. alter. of [1]*hike*] **1** *chiefly dial* **:** to yank or pull with a jerk ⟨before you could have counted ten, I was ~*ed* out of my job —Vincent Sheean⟩ **2 :** to cause (an airplane) to climb steeply
[2]**hoick** \"\ *n* -s **:** a rough or jerky movement in rowing
[3]**hoick** \"\ *vi* -ED/-ING/-S [imit.] **:** to clear the throat **:** HAWK
hoicks \'hȯiks\ *also* **hoick** \-k\ *interj* [origin unknown] — used chiefly to urge on hounds
hoid *n* -s [prob. alter. of *hoy*] *obs* **:** a state of excitement
hoi pol·loi \¦hȯipə¦lȯi, *chiefly Brit* hȯi'pä,lȯi\ *n pl* [Gk *hoi polloi* the many] **1 :** ordinary people **:** the general populace **:** MULTITUDE, MASSES ⟨strain so hard in making their questions comprehensible to *hoi polloi* —S.L.Payne⟩ ⟨burlesque performance . . . for the *hoi polloi* —Henry Miller⟩ **2** *slang* **:** people of distinction or wealth or elevated social status **:** ELITE
hoise \'hȯiz\ *vt* **hoised** \-zd\ *or* **hoist** \-ȯist\ **hoised** *or* **hoist; hoising; hoises** [alter. of earlier *heise*, prob. fr. MD *hischen* or (assumed) MLG *hissen* (whence LG *hissen*), of imit. origin] **1** *dial* **:** to raise upward or into the air by means of a tackle **:** HOIST ⟨~ the mainsail⟩ **2** *dial* **:** to lift and carry off — **hoist with one's own petard** *or* **hoist by one's own petard :** blown up by one's own bomb; *usu* **:** victimized or hurt by one's own scheme
[1]**hoist** \'hȯist, *chiefly dial* 'hīst\ *vb* -ED/-ING/-S [alter. of *hoise*] *vt* **:** RAISE, LIFT, ELEVATE: as **a :** to raise into position by means of tackle ⟨~ all sails⟩ ⟨~*ed* the mate's boat aboard⟩ **b :** to raise (a flag or a hoist of flags) often as a formal indication of possession or sovereignty **c :** to move from one place to another by or as if by lifting ⟨groaned as they ~*ed* him into the ambulance⟩ ⟨~*ing* himself out of bed⟩ **d** *slang* **:** to pick up and drink ⟨decided to ~ a few with the boys⟩ **e :** to cause to be or become higher or greater ⟨the war ~*ed* prices⟩ **f** *slang* **:** STEAL **~** *vi* **1 :** to become hoisted **:** RISE ⟨the load ~*s* well with the new tackle⟩ ⟨let it ~ right up to the upper block⟩ **2 :** to pull on a rope in hoisting something ⟨~ until it's near the top⟩ — often used with *away* **syn** see LIFT
[2]**hoist** \"\ *n* -s **1 :** an act of hoisting **:** LIFT, BOOST ⟨gave him a ~ over the wall⟩ **2 :** an apparatus (as a mechanical tackle or hydraulic lift) by which things are hoisted: as **a** *chiefly Brit* **:** a freight or other service elevator **b :** CHAIN HOIST **3 a :** the extent to which something can be hoisted or its mass or dimension when hoisted ⟨a sail with a 30-foot ~⟩ ⟨a ~ of several tons⟩ **b** (1) **:** the perpendicular edge or height of a flag when viewed flying or as if flying from a staff — compare [2]FLY 6c (2) **:** the part of the field of a flag that adjoins the staff **c :** the height or depth of a square sail except a course **:** the length of a fore-and-aft sail or staysail as measured along the luff **4 a :** a string of flags hoisted or to be hoisted as a signal usu. from one ship to another **b :** a message or information conveyed by such a hoist
hoist·er \-tə(r)\ *n* -s **:** one that hoists; *esp* **:** a mechanical apparatus for hoisting or one who operates it
hoisting pad *n* [*hoisting* fr. gerund of [1]*hoist*] **:** metal fittings on a boat for attaching hoisting equipment
hoisting tower *n* **:** a temporary elevator shaft of scaffolding used to hoist materials on building-construction work
hoist·man \-tmən\ *n, pl* **hoistmen** [[2]*hoist* + *man*] **:** the operator of a hoist **:** ENGINEMAN
hoistway \'=,=\ *n* **:** a passage (as an elevator shaft) through or along which a thing may be hoisted
hoit \'hȯit\ *n* -s [E dial. *hoit*, v., to romp, play the fool] *dial Brit* **:** a lazy stupid person
[1]**hoi·ty-toi·ty** \¦hȯid·ē¦tȯid·ē, ¦hīd·ē¦tīd·ē\ *n* -ES [redupl. of *hoity*, fr. E dial. *hoit*, v.] **1 a** *obs* **:** thoughtless or frivolous or giddy behavior **b :** affectation of superiority **:** patronizing pomposity **2 :** a hoity-toity person
[2]**hoity-toity** \"\ *adj* **1 :** THOUGHTLESS, FRIVOLOUS, GIDDY, FLIGHTY ⟨very *hoity-toity* of me not to know that royal personage —W.S.Maugham⟩ **2 :** affecting superiority **:** haughty and patronizing **:** POMPOUS ⟨*hoity-toity* airs and graces⟩ ⟨an inflated *hoity-toity* manner⟩
ho·ja \'ō(,)hä\ *n* -s [Sp, leaf, fr. L *folia*, pl. of *folium* leaf — more at BLADE] *Southwest* **:** a piece of corn husk formerly used for rolling cigarettes
hok \'häk\ *n* -s [Afrik *hak*, fr. D *hok* hutch, hovel, fr. MD *hocke* corn, grain — more at HOCK] *Africa* **:** a small enclosure (as for storage) **:** PEN
ho·kal·tec·an \¦hō,kal'tekən, ,hōkəl-\ *n, pl* **hokaltecan** *or* **hokaltecans** *usu cap* [by alter.] **:** HOKAN-COAHUILTECAN
ho·kan \'hōkən\ *n, pl* **hokan** *or* **hokans** *also* **ho·ka** \-kə\ *n, pl* **hoka** *or* **hokas** *usu cap* [coined 1913 by Roland B. Dixon †1934 and Alfred L. Kroeber †1960 Am. anthropologists] **1 :** a language stock centering in California comprising the Chimarikan, Esselenian, Kulanapan, Quoratean, Shastan, Yuman, and Yanan families **2 :** a language phylum generally considered as comprising the Hokan stock plus Chumashan, Jicaquean, Salinan, Serian, Supanecan, Tequistlatecan, and Washoan
hokan-coahuiltecan \¦hōkən+\ *n, usu cap H&C* **:** the Hokan language phylum enlarged by the inclusion of Coahuiltecan and sometimes Karankawa and Tonkawan — called also *Hokaltecan*
hokan-siouan \"+\ *n, usu cap H&S* **:** a language phylum comprising the Hokan, Supanecan, and Coahuiltecan language stocks
[1]**hoke** \'hōk\ *n* -s [by shortening] **:** HOKUM
[2]**hoke** \"\ *vt* -ED/-ING/-S *slang* **:** to give a false quality or value to **:** FAKE — *usu. used with up* ⟨tired of these *hoked-up* excuses⟩
hokeday *usu cap, var of* HOCKDAY
[1]**ho·key** \'hōkē\ *interj* [origin unknown] — used as a mild oath
[2]**hok·ey** \"\ *adj* [irreg. fr. *hokum* + *-y*] *slang* **:** marked by hokum **:** being characterized by or the product of hoking **:** hoked up ⟨a ~ version of an old favorite⟩
hokey-pokey \¦hōkē¦pōkē\ *n* -s [prob. alter. of *hocus-pocus*] **1** *slang* **:** HOKUM, BUNKUM, MONKEY BUSINESS **2 :** ice cream packaged in small portions (as between sweet wafers or in a paper cup) and sold by street vendors or peddlers
hokh·mah *or* **hok·mah** *or* **chok·mah** \'kōk(,)mä, =='=\ *n* -s *usu cap, often attrib* [Heb *ḥokhmāh* wisdom] **:** WISDOM LITERATURE
hok·ku \'hō(,)kü, 'hä(-\ *n, pl* **hokku** [Jap, fr. *hok* beginning, first + *ku* hemistich] **1 :** a fixed lyric form of Japanese origin having three short unrhymed lines of five, seven, and five syllables and being typically epigrammatic or suggestive — compare HAIKU **2 :** a lyric in hokku form

hok–lo \ˈhȯ(ˌ)klō, ˈhä(-\ *n, pl* **hok–lo** *or* **hok–los** *usu cap* [Chin (Cant), man from Fukien, fr. *hok* Fukien + *lo* man, person] **:** a member of a people with a distinctive dialect that inhabit sectors of northeastern Kwangtung including Swatow and parts of adjacent southern Fukien including Amoy and that have migrated in large numbers to Formosa and various countries of southeast Asia

ho·kum \ˈhōkəm\ *n* -s [prob. blend of [1]*hocus-pocus* and *bunkum*] **1 :** a device found to elicit a display of mirth or sentimental emotion from an audience and therefore deliberately used to impel persons to a desired action **2 :** something worthless or untrue **:** BUNKUM

hokus–pokus *var of* HOCUS-POCUS

hol \ˈhäl\ *n* -s [by shortening] *Brit* **:** HOLIDAY

hol- *or* **holo-** *comb form* [ME *holo-*, fr. OF, fr. L *hol-*, *holo-*, fr. Gk, fr. *holos* — more at SAFE] **1 a :** complete **:** entire **:** total ⟨*holo*graph⟩ ⟨*holo*parasite⟩ **b :** completely **:** totally **:** throughout ⟨*hol*arthritic⟩ ⟨*holo*branchiate⟩ ⟨*holo*axial⟩ ⟨*holo*crystalline⟩ **c :** without division **:** forming one piece ⟨*holo*gnathous⟩ ⟨*holo*rhinal⟩ **2 a :** similar **:** homogeneous ⟨*holo*morph⟩ **b :** similarly **:** homogeneously ⟨*holo*gamous⟩ **3** *usu holo-* **:** containing the highest possible number of hydroxyl groups — in names of inorganic acids ⟨*holo*phosphoric acid $P(OH)_5$ or H_5PO_5⟩ ⟨*holo*quinonoid⟩

hol *abbr* hollow

ho·la \ˈō(ˌ)lä\ *interj* [Sp] — used esp. among Latin Americans to attract attention or to shout encouragement or exultation

hol·andric \(ˈ)häl, (ˈ)hōl+\ *adj* [ISV *hol-* + *andric*] **1 a :** inherited solely in the male line **b :** transmitted by a gene or genes in the nonhomologous portion of the Y chromosome **2 :** having the full number of testes characteristic of a group — compare METANDRIC

hol·an·dry \ˈhäˌlandrē, ˈhōˌ-\ *n* -ES **:** the quality or state of being holandric

hol·arctic \(ˈ)häl, (ˈ)hōl+\ *adj* [*hol-* + *arctic*] **1 :** of or relating to the arctic regions **2** *usu cap* **:** of, relating to, or being the biogeographic realm or region that includes the northern parts of the Old and the New World and comprises the Palaearctic and Nearctic regions or subregions

holard \ˈhäˌlärd, ˈhōˌ-\ *n* -s [*hol-* + Gk *ard*ein to water] **:** the entire water content of the soil — compare CHRESARD, ECHARD

hol·as·pid·e·an \ˌhäˌlaˌspidēən, ˌhōˌ-\ *adj* [*hol-* + *aspid-* + *-ean*] **:** having a single series of large scutes on the posterior side of the tarsus (as in the true larks)

hol·bein stitch \ˈhō|lˌbīn *sometimes* ˈhä|\ *n, usu cap H* [after Hans *Holbein* †1543 Ger. artist; fr. the kind of embroidery seen in his paintings] **:** a running stitch worked twice often in different colors on the same line to make a continuous reversible pattern

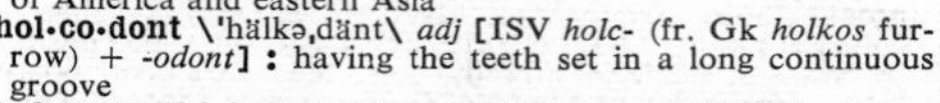

Holbein stitch

hol·boell's grebe \ˈhōlˌbu̇lz-\ *n, usu cap H* [after Carl P. *Holboell* †1856 Dan. civil servant] **:** a red-necked grebe (*Colymbus grisegena holboelli*) of America and eastern Asia

hol·co·dont \ˈhälkəˌdänt\ *adj* [ISV *holc-* (fr. Gk *holkos* furrow) + *-odont*] **:** having the teeth set in a long continuous groove

hol·co·no·ti \ˌhälkəˈnōd·ˌī, -d·(ˌ)ē\ *n pl, cap* [NL, fr. *holco-* (fr. Gk *holkos* furrow) + *-noti* (fr. Gk *nōton* back) — more at NATES] **:** the Embiotocidae regarded as an independent order of fishes

hol·cus \ˈhälkəs\ *n, cap* [NL, fr. L, wall barley (*Hordeum murinum*), fr. Gk *holkos* wall barley, furrow — more at SULCUS] **:** a genus of Old World grasses widely naturalized in America with velvety pubescence and deciduous spikelets — see VELVET GRASS

[1]**hold** \ˈhōld *dial sometimes* -lt\ *vb* **held** \ˈheld\ *or dial past* **hilt** \ˈhilt\ **held** *or archaic* **hold·en** \ˈhōldən\ **holding; holds** \ˈhōl(d)z\ [ME *holden*, fr. OE *healdan, haldan;* akin to OHG *haltan* to hold, ON *halda*, Goth *haldan* to tend cattle, L *celer* rapid, Gk *kellein* to run a ship to land, Skt *kālayati* he drives, holds, carries] *vt* **1 a :** to retain in one's keeping **:** maintain possession of **:** not give up or relinquish **:** POSSESS, HAVE ⟨*held* property worth millions⟩ ⟨~ several slaves as household servants⟩ ⟨~*s* the title to the property⟩ ⟨~*s* the power to hire or fire at will⟩ **b :** to retain or occupy by force **:** defend and not retreat from ⟨the soldiers *held* the bridge against all attacks⟩ **c :** to keep control of or authority or jurisdiction over ⟨wished to ~ the territory because of the fur trade⟩ **d :** to have power over **:** affect strongly and unremittingly ⟨a pleasurable excitement *held* him —D.G.Gerahty⟩ ⟨invalidism *held* him for eight years —J.C.Archer⟩ **e :** to have possession of the privileges, benefits, or perquisites of ⟨~*s* the eastern seaboard under an authorization granted by the manufacturer of the goods⟩ **f :** to use or keep as a threat or as a means of gaining advantage **2 :** to impose restraint upon or limit in motion or action ⟨the bushing *held* the drive shaft so that it had no play whatsoever⟩: as **a :** to refrain from producing (as speech or noise) ⟨~ your talk, man⟩ **b** (1) **:** to keep back **:** not loose **:** not let go ⟨~ the dogs so the strangers can pass⟩ (2) **:** STAY, ARREST ⟨~ him with a glance⟩ ⟨a strange compunction *held* his hand as he raised it to strike⟩ ⟨tried to ~ him from an action he would always regret⟩ (3) **:** DELAY ⟨*held* the curtain for an hour until the arrival of the royal carriage at the theater⟩ (4) **:** to stop the action of usu. temporarily ⟨time must be allowed . . . for ~*ing* the press while waiting for the sheet to dry —F.W.Hoch⟩ **c** (1) **:** to keep from advancing or succeeding in attack ⟨were able to ~ the enemy⟩ (2) **:** to keep (as an opposing team) from gaining an advantage ⟨the weaker team *held* the stronger during the first half⟩ **d :** to restrict or limit (as in amount of variation, advance, gain, loss) by acting to control or oppose ⟨*held* the sound to one level of loudness⟩ ⟨*held* the army to only a few miles' gain⟩ ⟨*held* the opposing team to only two runs⟩ **e :** to bind legally or morally **:** CONSTRAIN ⟨~ a man to his word⟩ — often used with an adjective complement ⟨~ a man responsible for his actions⟩ ⟨~ the men accountable for all money spent⟩ **f** *Scot* **:** to oppress by affliction **:** keep down **:** hold down **g :** DETAIN ⟨*held* him in conversation for ten minutes before letting him go⟩ **h :** RESTRICT, LIMIT ⟨bouts have been *held* to three 1½-minute rounds —Barrett McGurn⟩ **i :** to tense muscles in order to brace (oneself) ⟨had to ~ himself against the swaying and bumping of the coach⟩ **j :** to keep (a herd of cattle) together in a unit ⟨out ~*ing* the herd while the rest were eating⟩ **3** *obs* **:** to abide by (as a promise) or keep inviolate (as a faith) **4 a :** to have or keep in the grasp ⟨~ a child's hand⟩ ⟨~ a pocketbook tightly⟩ ⟨this volume is a joy to ~ as well as to read —J.M.Chase⟩ **b** (1) **:** to keep as if in a grasp **:** cause to be or remain in a particular situation, position, or relation, within certain limits, or of a particular quality ⟨~ a person in suspense⟩ ⟨~ an emotion under rigid control⟩ ⟨~ a ladder steady⟩ ⟨~ a child in check⟩ ⟨~ himself in readiness⟩ ⟨the stern demands of necessity *held* men in their grip —V.L.Parrington⟩ ⟨the searchlight . . . caught and *held* them in its glare —Nevil Shute⟩ (2) **:** to place and usu. not allow to move ⟨~ a pad of gauze to a wound⟩ ⟨~ your hand against my cheek⟩ **:** FIX ⟨*held* his eyes steadily on the picture⟩ **c** (1) **:** SUPPORT, SUSTAIN ⟨the building was *held* by concrete underpinning⟩ ⟨roof will ~ a deadweight of 94 inches of snow —*Monsanto Mag.*⟩ ⟨~*s* his seventy-two years easily⟩ (2) **:** to keep (as a bank of dirt) from eroding, collapsing, or washing away ⟨pines and other hardy trees were planted to ~ the sand —George Farwell⟩ **d** (1) **:** RETAIN ⟨struggling to ~, or to capture, the allegiance of the British people —F.A.Ogg & Harold Zink⟩ ⟨the parents still ~ the children's affection⟩ ⟨the suit ~*s* its press well⟩ ⟨a plastic that will ~ any shape you press it into⟩ **:** to retain by not vomiting ⟨unable to take a bite of food or ~ it on his stomach when it was forced upon him —F.B.Gipson⟩ **:** retain by not discharging ⟨the metal *held* the electrical charge for a long time⟩ (2) **:** to keep in custody **:** keep as a prisoner ⟨the cops agreed that the death was accidental, and did not ~ him —*Time*⟩ **e** (1) **:** to have in one's keeping **:** STORE ⟨another consideration was the cost of storing type — we certainly could not afford to ~ it forever —B.L.Stratton⟩ **:** keep on file or record ⟨the title is *held* at the registry of deeds⟩ (2) **:** RESERVE ⟨called the hotel and asked them to ~ a room for him⟩ ⟨*held* a few seats in case some visiting celebrities turned up⟩ **f :** BEAR, CARRY, COMPORT ⟨something unbending and strong, peasantlike, in the way he ~*s* himself —Madaleine Chapsal⟩ **g** (1) **:** to maintain in being or action **:** keep up without interruption, diminution, or flagging **:** SUSTAIN, PRESERVE ⟨~ one's course due north⟩ ⟨~ silence⟩ (2) **:** to maintain in a given condition (as of temperature, pressure, or humidity) or stage of processing (3) **:** to maintain a given condition in (4) **:** to maintain the articulation of (a speech sound) or the production of (as a note in music) ⟨the vowel in *feet* is not *held* as long as the vowel in *feed*⟩ **h :** to keep the uninterrupted interest, attention, or devotion of **:** keep from other interests, attractions, or places ⟨the play *held* the audience for over three hours⟩ ⟨a community that . . . ~*s* young people and offers inducements to them to stay and help build a greater hometown —J.C.Penney⟩ ⟨newspaper editing did not ~ him long —A.H.Meneely⟩ ⟨wants to ~ her husband while resisting his domination —H.M.Parshley⟩ **i :** to keep (as a letter or package) from being delivered usu. temporarily ⟨asked the post office to ~ his mail until he returned⟩ **j :** to cover (the ears) so as to prevent hearing ⟨when I spoke she *held* her ears —Eudora Welty⟩ **k :** to constitute or provide adequate satisfaction for ⟨enough food to ~ him for a week⟩ ⟨had had enough of high causes and noble sacrifice to ~ them for a long time —F.L.Allen⟩ **l** (1) **:** not to veer or alter from ⟨the car *held* 70 miles an hour for 20 miles⟩ ⟨prices had *held* the same level for a month⟩ ⟨had trouble ~*ing* his course⟩ (2) **:** to be free of marked bouncing, swerving, or skidding on ⟨a car that ~*s* the road well at any speed⟩ **m :** to make an exhibition of or call persistently to one's consciousness ⟨trying to entertain his audience by ~*ing* his betters to ridicule⟩ **n :** to fix on and not turn away from ⟨for a few minutes the flashlight *held* the canoe, then lost it —Erle Stanley Gardner⟩ **5 a** (1) **:** to receive and retain ⟨the can ~*s* gasoline⟩ **:** have within **:** CONTAIN ⟨the cemetery which *held* the bodies of his family for seven generations back⟩ ⟨the room *held* only Victorian furniture⟩ ⟨the envelope which *held* his ticket —J.P.Marquand⟩ (2) **:** to have or retain within its limits as if in a container ⟨throw into a word every trace of meaning it can ~ —C.S.Kilby⟩ ⟨the cast *held* some noted singers⟩ ⟨could ~ large quantities of verse in his mind without effort⟩ (3) **:** to keep within moderate bounds the characteristic intoxicating effects of (an alcoholic liquor) ⟨drank heavily but *held* it well⟩ **b** (1) **:** to be able or designed to receive and retain or contain ⟨a special container to ~ flammable liquids⟩ ⟨the basket that *held* outgoing mail was empty⟩ (2) **:** ACCOMMODATE ⟨the hotel could ~ over 300 guests⟩ ⟨sleeping platforms ran the length of the side walls in two tiers, ~*ing* eight men —Meridel Le Sueur⟩ **c :** to be marked or characterized by as an essential feature ⟨the volume *held* an historical rather than a literary interest⟩ ⟨its steeply pitched gable roof ~*s* one dormer —*Amer. Guide Series: Md.*⟩ ⟨a scene that *held* many fond memories for him⟩ ⟨the famous hymn of creation . . . ~*s* an awesome vastness of mood —Emma Hawkridge⟩ **d :** to provide or have in reserve as a reward ⟨the story ~*s* a happy ending for everybody⟩ ⟨the tournament ~*s* a nice prize for the winner⟩ ⟨would like to know what the future ~*s*⟩ **6 a :** HARBOR, EXPERIENCE ⟨~ a feeling⟩ ⟨a nation for whom we all ~ a good deal of admiration⟩ ⟨~*s* no sympathy for criminals⟩ **b :** ACCEPT ⟨~ a point of view⟩ **:** BELIEVE ⟨~ a theory⟩ ⟨~ opposing opinions⟩ **:** subscribe to ⟨the aesthetic philosophy we happen to ~ —C.I.Glicksberg⟩ **c** (1) **:** CONSIDER, REGARD, THINK, JUDGE ⟨*held* that the action was dishonest⟩ ⟨*held* calculus to be too difficult for that age group⟩ ⟨*held* by many to be the greatest contemporary tennis player⟩ ⟨the expression of those truths *held* to be self-evident —F.B. Millett⟩ (2) **:** to decide in a judicial ruling ⟨the court *held* that the man was sane⟩ (3) **:** ESTEEM, VALUE ⟨the story is that he *held* it so lightly that he lost the land on one turn of the cards —*Amer. Guide Series: N.C.*⟩ **d :** to have or maintain in judgment or regard ⟨~ someone in contempt⟩ ⟨~ a parent in honor⟩ **7 a :** to engage in with someone else or with others **:** do by concerted action ⟨the student body *held* games in the afternoon⟩ **b :** CONVOKE, CONVENE ⟨the king *held* an assembly of all his courtiers⟩ ⟨the second court session was *held* in the afternoon⟩ **:** arrange for and have in a united action ⟨the company *held* a feast to celebrate victory⟩ **:** schedule and assemble or meet ⟨some classes were *held* in the evening⟩ **8 a :** to be or stand in (as a relative position) ⟨~*s* second place in the city golf tournament⟩ ⟨urban redevelopment continues to ~ an important place in planning programs —*Collier's Yr. Bk.*⟩ **b :** to have earned or been appointed, promoted, or elected to and now occupy (as an office) ⟨~*s* a captaincy in the navy⟩ ⟨~*s* a secretaryship in the club⟩ ⟨*held* the presidency for two terms⟩ **c :** to have earned or been awarded (as an academic degree) ⟨~*s* an M.D. from one of the best medical schools⟩ ⟨~*s* a German Ph.D.⟩ ⟨~*s* a medal of honor⟩ **9** *now dial Brit* **:** BET, WAGER **10 a** *obs* **:** to handle so as to guide or manage (as reins or a gun) **b :** POINT, AIM, DIRECT — used with *on* ⟨*held* a gun on the grocer while an accomplice robbed the till⟩ **11** *obs* **:** to endure or bear up under (as rough handling or invidious comparison) **~** *vi* **1 a :** to maintain position **:** not retreat **:** remain unconquered or unsubdued ⟨the troops *held* in the face of repeated attacks⟩ **b** (1) **:** to continue or remain esp. as is or of the same kind or quality **:** LAST ⟨winter *held* until the middle of March⟩ ⟨his anger *held* for several days⟩ ⟨the output of copper *held* at the level of the year before⟩ ⟨hoping that the good weather would ~⟩ **:** not change or alter ⟨we can go if the present circumstances ~⟩ ⟨our luck *held* and we won⟩ ⟨the habit of a lifetime *held* —John Buchan⟩ — often used with *up* ⟨the good weather *held* up for several days⟩ (2) **:** to endure a test or trial ⟨their courage *held* against all odds⟩ — often used with *up* ⟨if his interest ~*s* up⟩ **2 a :** to maintain a grasp on or a connection with something **:** remain fastened to something (as by a strap) **:** keep hold ⟨the anchor *held* in the rough sea⟩ **:** not slip **:** not lose a grip **:** CLING ⟨felt his rubber soles grip and ~⟩ **b** *of a female mammal* **:** to hold to service **:** CONCEIVE **3 :** to derive right or title (as to the possession of lands or as land to be held) — usu. used with *of* or *from* ⟨*held* of the crown by an outright gift⟩ **4 :** to bear or carry oneself ⟨a man who *held* aloof from strangers⟩ ⟨asked the boy to ~ still⟩ **5 :** to be or remain valid **:** APPLY ⟨the rule ~*s* only in special cases⟩ **:** prove consistent or acceptable to reason or logic ⟨the theory does not ~ under analysis⟩ **6 :** to go ahead **:** continue as one has been going ⟨the travelers *held* on their way⟩ ⟨*held* south for several miles⟩ **:** not veer or fluctuate in progress or forward movement ⟨the plane *held* steadily on its course by automatic control⟩ **7 :** to restrain or withhold oneself **:** cease or forbear an intended or threatened action **:** HALT, STOP, PAUSE ⟨wished that he might ~ a while and stop his incessant chatter⟩ **8 :** to take place ⟨went . . . to the place where the funeral service was ~*ing* —John Bennett⟩ ⟨annual show and sale of highland ponies ~*s* on Monday —*Scotsman*⟩ **9 :** to pause in archery between drawing and loosing an arrow **10 :** to hold copy (as in proofreading) **syn** see CONTAIN, HAVE, KEEP — **hold a brief :** to act as or be a counsel in a legal case ⟨had *held* several important *briefs*⟩ — **hold a brief for :** ADVOCATE, DEFEND — **hold a candle to :** to qualify for comparison with ⟨asserted that no wrestler could *hold a candle to* the current champion⟩ — **hold a close wind** *or* **hold a good wind :** to sail very close to the wind making little leeway — **hold book :** to act as prompter during a rehearsal or a performance of a play ⟨help paint scenery, carry props, do a little acting, and *hold book* during performances —Maurice Zolotow⟩ — **hold bottom** *of an anchor* **:** to hold in holding ground — **hold by :** to remain faithful to **:** hold to or be devoted to ⟨those who *hold by* the humanist tradition⟩ — **hold copy :** to work as a copyholder — **hold court :** to act with marked and courtly sociableness ⟨*held court* whenever he was in public nodding and bowing to all his friends and acquaintances⟩ — **hold down a claim :** to remain on land claimed so as to establish one's ownership — **hold everything** *slang* **:** to stop or cease an action or operation — usu. used as a command or exhortation — **hold fire :** to refrain from expressing oneself or taking action ⟨*held fire* on specific foreign policy questions —*N.Y.Times*⟩ — **hold good 1 :** to hold true **2 :** to hold up **:** ENDURE, LAST ⟨his luck *held good* all year⟩ — **hold hands :** to go hand in hand esp. as an expression of affection — **hold in demesne** *law* **:** to hold in one's own possession or power — **hold one's breath 1 :** to cease breathing momentarily (as from fear) **2 :** to be in extreme suspense ⟨*held her breath* all during the examination for fear the child would not pass⟩ — **hold one's ground :** to maintain a position ⟨the speaker calmly *held his ground* in the face of angry opposition⟩ — **hold one's horses** *slang* **:** to stop action or talk for a moment **:** wait or be patient for a minute — usu. used as a command or exhortation — **hold one's own :** to maintain one's position **:** prove at least equal to opposition ⟨proved able to *hold their own* under heavy attack⟩ ⟨the lighter boy *held his own* well against the heavier boxer⟩ — **hold one's peace :** to keep silent **:** keep one's thoughts to oneself ⟨felt it would do no good to complain so *held his peace*⟩ — **hold one's tongue :** to keep silent ⟨told the boy sharply to *hold his tongue*⟩ — **hold tack with 1** *of a boat* **:** to keep on the same tacks as and change tacks with (another boat) **2 :** to keep up with (as in activity) — **hold the bag** *also* **hold the sack 1 :** to be or be left empty-handed or with only the most undesirable items of a group of apportioned items **2 :** to bear alone and in full a responsibility that should properly have been shared by others ⟨when the police began to investigate, five of the men left the country leaving the sixth *holding the bag*⟩ — **hold the boards :** to hold the stage — **hold the field 1 :** to maintain a position in a field of play or an arena of contest **2 :** to remain dominantly before the public ⟨a doctrine which *held the field* for quite five hundred years —R.W.Southern⟩ — **hold the fort 1 :** to maintain a firm position usu. against opposition ⟨found himself *holding the fort* against a solid block of opponents of the plan⟩ **2 :** to take care of usual affairs ⟨a skeleton staff was left to *hold the fort* at the office during the Saturday morning —Dorothy Sayers⟩ — **hold the line :** to keep things as they are without undesirable alteration ⟨*holding the line* on the price of electrical appliances despite increased costs⟩ ⟨*hold the line* on present taxes⟩ — **hold the market :** to buy or sell in order to maintain prices as they are — **hold the stage :** to continue to be produced — used of a play — **hold the wind :** to sail close to the wind without making much leeway — **hold to 1 a :** to remain steadfast, attached, or faithful to **:** adhere to ⟨*hold to* an established plan⟩ ⟨*hold to* one's purpose⟩ ⟨*hold to* one's family in all circumstances⟩ **b :** to subscribe to **:** BELIEVE ⟨those who *hold to* the doctrine of spontaneous generation —J.B.Conant⟩ **2 :** to stay close to or on (as a particular course) ⟨the new ships *hold* closely *to* the major trade lanes —R.H.Brown⟩ — **hold to account :** to hold responsible ⟨*hold* all salesmen *to account* for the money spent on company business⟩ — **hold to service** *of a domestic animal* **:** to become pregnant **:** SETTLE — **hold true :** to remain true or valid esp. under changed circumstances ⟨the theory *holds true* in all applications⟩ — **hold up one's head :** to conduct oneself in a normally unashamed manner ⟨if they found out that she had cheated, she would be unable to *hold up her head* again⟩ — **hold water 1 a :** to retain water without leaking **b :** to be whole, consistent, or valid **:** stand up under criticism or analysis ⟨an accusation which would *hold water* in a court of law —Michael Howard⟩ ⟨an explanation that would not *hold water* if the true facts were known⟩ **2 :** to hold oars steady in the water usu. at right angles to the direction of movement to check headway — **hold with :** to agree with (as a principle) or approve of (as a practice) ⟨political methods that few would *hold with*⟩

[2]**hold** \ˈhōld, *dial often* -lt\ *n* -s [ME *hold, holde* hold, possession, land that is held, property, fr. OE *heald, hald* protection, keeping, fr. *healdan, haldan* to hold] **1 a :** a place of temporary shelter or refuge; *also* **:** a lair or a lurking place (as of a fish) **b :** STRONGHOLD **2 a :** CONFINEMENT, CUSTODY **b :** a place of confining **:** PRISON **3 a** (1) **:** the act or the manner of holding or grasping (as in the hands or arms) ⟨released his ~ on the man's arm⟩ ⟨has a strong ~ for a small man⟩ **:** GRASP ⟨took a firm ~ on the club⟩ **:** CLASP, GRIP ⟨in his arms his ~ was tight and reassuring⟩ — often used idiomatically without an article as object of *catch, get, have, seize, take* ⟨got ~ of the oar and was pulled out of the water⟩ ⟨seized ~ as the rope brushed his fingers⟩ ⟨held out a hand and waited until the child took ~⟩ ⟨took ~ of the knob and opened the door⟩ ⟨the boy's sneakers suddenly took ~ and stopped him from sliding off the roof⟩ ⟨saw that the climber had ~ of the rope before he began to haul on it⟩ (2) **:** a manner of grasping an opponent in wrestling ⟨knee ~*s* and body presses⟩ **b** (1) **:** a nonphysical bond, grip, or clasp which attaches, restrains, or constrains or by or through which something is affected, controlled, dominated, or possessed — often used with *on, upon*, or *over* ⟨afraid they might lose their ~ on the domestic market —*Sydney (Australia) Bull.*⟩ ⟨yet the ~ of the public school upon the middle-class mind has not weakened —Roy Lewis & Angus Maude⟩ ⟨the father had a strong ~ over his children⟩ and often used idiomatically without an article as object of *catch, get, have, seize, take* ⟨the newspapers got ~ of the story⟩ ⟨after a moment of panic he got ~ of himself⟩ ⟨seized ~ and stepped up production 50 percent⟩ ⟨in the confusion of contradictory ideas we did not know what philosophy he had ~ of⟩ (2) **:** an action, expedient, or device for achieving an end ⟨arguing that in . . . politics no ~*s* are barred —*New Republic*⟩ **c :** conscious grasp **:** full comprehension — used with *on* or *upon* ⟨at the point of sleep one loses his ~ on the real world⟩ ⟨how weak was his ~ upon character —Roger Fry⟩ **4 :** something that may be grasped as a support ⟨climbed up the rock using some ledges and jutting pieces as ~*s*⟩ **5 :** a pause between the completion of the draw and the release of the arrow in archery **6 a :** FERMATA **b :** a rhythmic lengthening of a word or syllable or a symbol used to indicate this **c :** the time between the onset and the release of a vocal articulation **7 :** a sudden motionless posture at the end of a dance or dance phrase **8 a :** an order or indication that something is to be reserved ⟨put a ~ on all the hotel rooms still unoccupied⟩ **b :** an order or indication that some action is to be delayed ⟨announced a ~ on all takeoffs until the weather cleared⟩ **c :** a notation on a depositor's account to indicate that the balance or a portion thereof should not be paid out

[3]**hold** \"\ *n* -s [fr. (assumed) ME *hold*, alter. (prob. influenced by ME [2]*hold*) of ME [1]*hole*] **1 a :** the interior of a ship below decks; *esp* **:** the cargo deck of a ship **b :** the interior of a plane; *esp* **:** the cargo compartment of a plane **2 a :** a division of the interior esp. the cargo deck of a ship **b :** a division of the interior of a plane esp. for cargo

[4]**hold** \"\ *n* -s [OE, fr. ON *hölthr* free landowner, man; akin to OE *hæle, hæleth* man, hero, OS *helith* man, hero, ON *halr* man, and perh. to Skt *kalya* healthy — more at CALLI-] **:** an officer of high rank in the Danelaw corresponding to the high reeve of the Anglo-Saxons

hold·able \ˈhōldəbəl\ *adj* **:** capable of being held **:** of a size or character that makes holding convenient or desirable

holdall \ˈ=ˌ=\ *n* -s [[1]*hold* + *all*] **:** a container for miscellaneous articles; *esp* **:** an often cloth traveling case or bag

hold away *vi* **1** *Scot* **:** to remain at a distance **:** hold off **2** *chiefly Scot* **:** to continue on one's way

hold back *vb* [[1]*hold* + *back*] *vt* **1 a :** to keep in check **:** RESTRAIN, CURB ⟨had to *hold* the children *back* from running out into the street⟩ **b :** to keep from advancing to the next stage, grade, or level ⟨followed the policy of *holding* any child *back* who could not read adequately⟩ **2 a :** to retain in one's keeping ⟨*held* a large sum *back* to cover costs of handling⟩ **b :** to keep to oneself ⟨who is at liberty to speak and *hold* nothing *back* —F.L.Paxson⟩ **3 :** to shade (a portion of an image in photography) while printing to reduce the density **~** *vi* **:** to keep oneself from doing, feeling, or indulging in something **:** hold aloof ⟨*held back* from making a complete statement about his political position⟩ ⟨were asked to *hold back* on food deliveries during the shortage⟩ ⟨when they asked the child to come in he *held back*⟩ **syn** see KEEP

holdback \ˈ=ˌ=\ *n* [*hold back*] **1 :** a device (as an iron catch on a carriage shaft with a looped strap) to enable a horse to back or hold back a vehicle **2 :** one of several devices for holding something back or open: as **a :** a device (as a specially constructed hinge) for holding a door, shutter, or casement window open **b :** TIEBACK **3 a :** the act of holding something back or of holding back on something (as work or production) ⟨ordered a ~ until negotiations looked more auspicious⟩ **b :** something held back or withheld often temporarily ⟨a ~ of a week's salary to be paid on satisfactory completion of the job⟩

hold beam *n* **:** a beam placed in the hold of a ship to supply usu. transverse structural strength

hold–clear \ˈ=ˌ=\ *n* -s [fr. the phrase *hold clear*] **:** a device for holding a railroad signal in any position other than its most restrictive

hold down *vb* [¹*hold* + *down*] *vt* **1 a :** to keep in subjection ⟨conquered them but had no success in *holding* them *down*⟩ **b :** RESTRAIN, CURB ⟨noisy despite all efforts to *hold* them *down*⟩ **2 :** to retain continuously and handle competently (as a job) **:** hold and keep ⟨a man who had *held down* some significant political positions⟩ **3 :** to take care of ⟨some friends *held down* his grocery business while he was sick⟩ ~ *vi* **:** to limit oneself ⟨he is not stopping smoking but *holding down* to three cigarettes a day⟩ — **hold down on :** to keep down or low ⟨*held down on* the price he was willing to pay⟩

hold–down \ˈ≈,≈\ *n* -s [*hold down*] **:** a clamp or other device for holding a part down against another part (as a sheet against the bed of a press or a battery against the bottom of its container)

holden *archaic past part of* HOLD

hol·den·ite \ˈhōldə,nīt\ *n* -s [Albert F. *Holden* †1913 Am. mining engineer + E *-ite*] **:** a mineral $(Mn,Ca)_4(Zn,Mg,Fe)_2(AsO_4)(OH)_5O_2$ consisting of a basic manganese zinc arsenate with minor calcium, magnesium, and iron and occurring as red orthorhombic crystals at Franklin, New Jersey

¹**hold·er** \ˈhōldə(r)\ *n* -s [ME, fr. *holden* to hold + *-er*] **1 :** one that holds something: as **a** (1) **:** POSSESSOR, OWNER — often used in combination ⟨slave*holder*⟩ ⟨job*holder*⟩ (2) **:** one who holds any estate in land **:** a person in constructive possession of land having the right of immediate possession thereto which he can exercise without hindrance **:** a tenant in his own right or under another in actual possession of land **b :** a person in possession of and legally entitled to receive payment of a bill, note, or check **:** the payee, endorsee in possession, or the bearer of a bill, note, or check — compare HOLDER IN DUE COURSE **c :** a worker who holds articles during an industrial process **d :** one who has won or been awarded and reaps the benefits of a scholarship or fellowship **e :** one who has won, earned, or been awarded a trophy, title, or degree ⟨the ~ of a tennis championship⟩ ⟨was ~ of several swimming cups⟩ ⟨the ~ of a college degree in animal husbandry⟩ **2 :** a device or contrivance by which or a container in which something is held ⟨umbrella ~⟩ ⟨a flower ~⟩: as **a :** either of two loops attached to reins for holding a pulling horse **b :** a thick protective cloth pad for grasping hot utensils **c :** a narrow tubular device often used by smokers for holding a cigarette or cigar while smoking it **d :** a flat lightproof container in which photographic films or plates may be held for use in a camera **e :** a device that resembles a safety pin and is used in knitting for holding stitches temporarily to keep them from dropping **3 :** something (as a strap or rail) which one may grasp for support or for steadying oneself **4 :** a device by which something (as a door or shutter) is held back or open

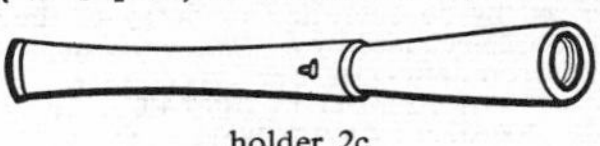
holder 2c

²**holder** \"\ *n* -s [ME, fr. (assumed) ME *hold* + ME *-er* — more at ³HOLD] **:** a worker in the hold of a ship

holder–forth \ˌ≈ˈ≈\ *n, pl* **holders–forth :** one that holds forth **:** PREACHER, RANTER

holder in due course : the holder of a negotiable instrument that is complete and regular on its face who takes it in good faith and for value before it is overdue and without notice of its dishonor or of any infirmity in it or of any defect in the title of the person negotiating it

holder–on \ˌ≈≈ˈ≈\ *n, pl* **holders–on** *or* **holder–ons 1 :** a worker who bucks rivets **2 :** a pneumatic tool used in place of a dolly to back up rivets while they are being headed

holder process *n* **:** HOLDING METHOD

holder–up \ˌ≈≈ˈ≈\ *n, pl* **holders–up** *or* **holder–ups :** one that holds something up; *specif* **:** a man who holds up the setting punch in riveting

holdfast \ˈ≈,≈\ *n* -s *often attrib* [fr. the phrase *hold fast*] **1 :** something that secures, holds in place, or supports: as **a** (1) **:** a rhizoidal base resembling a sucker but without absorption cells by which the thallus of many algae (as seaweeds) is attached to its support (2) **:** a discoid extremity of a tendril in certain plants (as the Virginia creeper) by which the vines fix themselves to flat surfaces **b :** an organ (as the acetabulum of a trematode or the scolex of a tapeworm) by which a parasitic animal attaches itself to its host **2 :** something to which something else (as a guy line or tackle) may be secured firmly **3 :** an actinomycotic tumor of the jaw — not used technically

hold·fast·ness \ˈhōl(d),fas(t)nəs, -faas-, -fais-, -fȧs-\ *n* -ES **:** the tendency to keep a firm often stubborn hold (as on a position or possession) **:** TENACITY, PERSISTENCE

hold forth *vb* [ME *holden forth*, fr. *holden* to hold + *forth*] *vt* **:** OFFER, EXHIBIT, PROPOUND ⟨*hold forth* the hopes of better times to come⟩ ⟨*hold* it *forth* that one can cure all ailments of the spirit⟩ ~ *vi* **1 :** to speak out in public esp. at length **:** HARANGUE, PREACH — often used disparagingly **2 :** to conduct one's affairs ⟨a group of nuclear physicists now *holding forth* at their annual convention⟩ **3 :** to take place **:** undergo performance ⟨a region in which every variety of winter sports *holds forth*⟩

hold in *vb* [ME *holden in*, fr. *holden* to hold + *in*] *vt* **:** to keep in check **:** RESTRAIN, CURB ⟨the rider had a hard time *holding* his horse *in*⟩ ~ *vi* **:** to restrain oneself **:** keep silent ⟨wanted to speak but thought better of it and *held in*⟩

¹**holding** *n* -s [ME *holdyng*, gerund of *holden* to hold] **1 :** the act of one that holds or takes hold **:** HOLD, GRIP, CLASP **2 :** something that is held: as **a :** land held esp. by a vassal of a superior **:** TENEMENT ⟨small ~*s* of less than 5 acres —*Americana Annual*⟩ **b :** an actual judgment or ruling of a court upon any issue of law raised in a case **:** the actual final decision of a court on the particular facts of a given case as distinguished from the dictum ⟨difficult to find a recent . . . enactment that equals in impact and scope this judicial ~ —J.P.Roche & M.M.Gordon⟩ **c :** any property that is owned or possessed — usu. used in pl. ⟨record-breaking frozen fish ~*s* totaled 179 million pounds —*Americana Annual*⟩ ⟨the ~*s* of American libraries —*Current Biog.*⟩ **3 :** something that holds **:** a means of holding **:** ATTACHMENT, CONNECTION **4 :** personal contact esp. with the hands or arms that retards or interferes with the movement of an opponent in some sports (as basketball, football, soccer) **5 :** a company or enterprise owned or controlled by a holding company

²**holding** *adj* [ME *holdyng*, pres. part. of *holden* to hold] **1 :** effecting a delay **:** being a hindrance or interference ⟨a ~ action to prevent the passage of more drastic control legislation —E.P.Hutchinson⟩ **2 :** designed for usu. temporary storage or retention ⟨a ~ refrigerator at a railhead⟩ ⟨a ~ pen for the horses⟩ ⟨shunted the cars onto the ~ track⟩

holding attack *n* **:** a secondary attack designed to hold an enemy in position in a military envelopment

holding company *n* **:** a company that owns part or all of one or more other companies for purposes of control — compare INVESTMENT COMPANY

holding fund *n* **:** a sum of money allotted or set aside for investment usu. for noncommercial purposes (as scholarships or grants-in-aid)

holding ground *n* **:** bottom that an anchor can hold in

holding method *n* **:** a method of pasteurization in which a fluid (as milk or fruit juice) is heated to not less than 143° F for at least 30 minutes

holding–out partner \ˌ≈≈ˈ≈-\ *n* **:** NOMINAL PARTNER

holding–up hammer \ˌ≈≈ˈ≈-\ *n* **:** a riveter's dolly

hold·man \ˈhōl(d)mən\ *n, pl* **holdmen :** a dock worker who works in a ship's hold in loading or unloading a ship

hold off *vb* [ME *holden of*, fr. *holden* to hold + *of* off] *vt* **1 a :** to keep at a distance ⟨a tendency to *hold* people *off*⟩ **b :** WITHSTAND ⟨*held* all enemy attacks *off*⟩ **2 :** POSTPONE, DELAY ⟨*held off* going to see a doctor⟩ ⟨tries to *hold off* making decisions⟩ ~ *vi* **1 a :** to keep aloof ⟨a tendency to *hold off* from people⟩ **b :** ABSTAIN ⟨*held off* from smoking for a month⟩ **2 :** to hold back **:** HESITATE ⟨*held off* from answering directly⟩

hold–off \ˈ≈,≈\ *n* -s [*hold off*] **:** the act or period of holding off **:** a delay or period of delay or postponement

hold on *vi* [ME *holden on*, fr. *holden* to hold + *on*] **1 a :** to go on **:** maintain a course **:** CONTINUE ⟨*held on* in their route until they arrived at a river⟩ **b :** to remain unconquered or undefeated ⟨felt they could *hold on* under siege for at least two months⟩ **2 a :** to maintain one's position **:** hold on to something **:** hang on ⟨a ledge where the tree roots could *hold on*⟩ **b :** to delay action (as in making a sale) ⟨wanted to sell but *held on*, hoping for a rise in price⟩ **3 :** to wait a minute **:** STOP, CEASE — used esp. in the imperative ⟨the man became irritated at the speaker and finally cried, "*Hold on!*"⟩ — **hold on to 1 a :** to keep in the grasp esp. with persistence ⟨the child *held on to* the man's hand tightly⟩ ⟨*held on to* what he had with desperation⟩ **b :** to keep control of ⟨*held on to* his temper⟩ ⟨had a hard time *holding on to* himself⟩ **2 a :** not to relinquish **:** not give up or abandon ⟨she *held on to* a quiet plan of her own —Margaret Deland⟩ **b :** to continue to produce (as a sound) or sing (as a note) ⟨*held on to* the final chord for a long time⟩

hold out *vb* [¹*hold* + *out*] *vt* **1 a :** to reach or stretch out ⟨the cook *held* a plate of food *out* to him⟩ ⟨*held* his hand *out* with a smile⟩ **b :** OFFER, PROFFER ⟨a job that seemed to *hold* many more opportunities *out* to him than his old one⟩ ⟨could *hold out* no hope of advancement⟩ **2 :** to make out to be **:** REPRESENT ⟨*held* himself *out* as a trained pharmacist⟩ **3 a** *archaic* **:** to keep up **:** CONTINUE, MAINTAIN **b** *obs* **:** SUSTAIN **c** *archaic* **:** to defend against a foe **4 :** to retain possession of (a card) secretly for the purpose of cheating or deceiving in a game (as poker) ~ *vi* **1 a :** to remain unsubdued by opposing forces **:** not yield or give way **:** LAST, ENDURE ⟨the garrison under siege *held out* for almost a month⟩; *also* **:** to continue to operate **:** not fail ⟨prayed the engine would *hold out* until we got home⟩ **b :** to refuse to come to an agreement or make a settlement until certain terms are met ⟨*held out* for a shorter working day⟩ **2 :** to hang out ⟨a gang of adolescents who *hold out* at the corner drug store⟩ — **hold out on 1 :** to withhold something from ⟨she didn't tell me she was rich; she's been *holding out on* me⟩ **2 :** to withhold a part or the whole of ⟨threatened to *hold out on* his sister's dividends if she didn't pose —*Fortune*⟩

holdout \ˈ≈,≈\ *n* -s [*hold out*] **1 :** the act or an instance of holding out: as **a :** a holding out by a negotiator to try to force concessions **b :** the act of secreting one or more cards of a pack for private use in a gambling game **2 :** a mechanism designed to assist a holdout in a game of cards **3 :** something held out **4 :** one that holds out (as in negotiations or an anticipated action) ⟨there was one ~ among the negotiators⟩ ⟨expected her to go from the movies to television but she remained a ~⟩

hold over *vb* [¹*hold* + *over*] *vi* **1 :** to continue in occupancy of land or exercise the powers of office beyond the limits of the term set or fixed **2 :** to continue into the succeeding beat or measure — used of a note or tone **3 :** to continue to exist **:** REMAIN, LAST, ENDURE ⟨no rancor *held over* through the years —W.A.White⟩ ~ *vt* **1 a :** to keep for future action **:** POSTPONE ⟨*held* the picnic *over* until better weather came⟩ ⟨*held over* several bills until the next session⟩ **b :** to keep in one's possession or as part of one's knowledge **:** RETAIN **:** not lose ⟨a conviction *held over* from school days —Robertson Davies⟩ **2 a :** to retain in possession or occupancy esp. of a post or office from an earlier term or period **:** keep on ⟨department heads who had been *held over* from the previous administration⟩ **b :** to renew or prolong the engagement of (as a performer or an act) **:** CONTINUE ⟨*held* the acrobats *over* for a second week⟩ ⟨a smash hit *held over* by popular demand⟩ **3 :** to continue (as the production of a note) into the succeeding beat or measure

¹**holdover** \ˈ≈,≈≈\ *n* -s [*hold over*] **1 :** one that holds over or is held over: as **a :** one that remains in office after the departure of his associates **b :** CARRY-OVER 2 **c :** a tree left in cutting as a reserve for a future crop or a tree remaining after fire or wind damage **d :** HANGOVER 2a **e :** an act or a performer whose engagement is immediately continued **f :** a team member remaining on a team from a past season ⟨a backfield consisting of a new man and three ~*s*⟩ **2 :** a cell where one is held for appearance before a court

²**holdover** \"\ *adj* **1 :** of, belonging to, or being a holdover ⟨a team with four ~ players⟩ ⟨the city has a ~ mayor although almost all other officials are new⟩ **2** *plant pathol* **:** permitting survival of a pathogenic organism under unfavorable conditions ⟨a ~ canker⟩ ⟨a ~ stage⟩

holds *pres 3d sing of* HOLD, *pl of* HOLD

hold together *vt* **1 :** to preserve as a unit **:** keep from separating into component parts ⟨only rubber bands *held* the toy *together*⟩ **:** preserve from disintegrating or failing ⟨only the force of the man's will *held* the company *together* in the last five years⟩ ⟨are of different inspirations but all *held together* by a remarkable unity —*Amer. Guide Series: Conn.*⟩ **2 :** to keep from nervous or mental collapse ⟨the novelist's attempt to *hold* himself *together* —Pat Frank⟩ ~ *vi* **:** to remain loyal to each other **:** preserve a unanimity of feeling or action ⟨we have only to *hold together* to go safely through the dark valley —Sir Winston Churchill⟩

hold up *vb* [ME *holden up*, fr. *holden* to hold + *up*] *vt* **1 a** (1) **:** RAISE, LIFT ⟨*hold* your hand *up* if you wish the chairman to recognize you⟩ ⟨*hold up* the object so it can be seen more clearly⟩ (2) **:** SUPPORT, SUSTAIN ⟨the underpinnings were not adequate to *hold* the house *up*⟩ ⟨the confiscated money *held* the toppling regime *up* for only a short time⟩ **b :** HOLD *vt* 4m **c :** to expose or call to attention as something one subscribes to, advocates, or lives by ⟨*held* a high standard *up* for his colleagues to follow⟩ ⟨*held up* the Old Testament in opposition to 18th century rationalism —William Petersen⟩ **2 a :** to rein in **:** CHECK, HALT ⟨*hold up* a horse⟩ **b :** to prevent (a fox or cub) from leaving a covert thus assuring a find and kill in fox hunting **c :** to stop, delay, or impede the course or advance of ⟨the accident *held* the traffic *up* for an hour⟩ ⟨a storm that *held* deliveries *up* for a day⟩ ⟨felt that she was *holding* her husband *up* in his career⟩ **3 :** to refuse to play (the winning card of a suit led) **4 :** to rob at gun's point ⟨*held* a gas station *up* and got away with several thousand dollars⟩ ⟨plotting to *hold up* a bank⟩ ~ *vi* **1 a** (1) **:** to remain undismayed or unsubdued (as under attack or misfortune) ⟨was determined to *hold up* for her children's sake⟩ ⟨*held up* under attack⟩ (2) **:** to keep from falling **:** not to collapse, crumble, or fall apart ⟨an industry that *held up* well in the depression⟩ **b :** to prove true, accurate, or valid ⟨much depends on how well the weather forecasts *hold up*⟩ ⟨wondered if the charges would *hold up* in court⟩ **c :** to prove effective **:** PREVAIL ⟨despite attempts to countermand them, the provisions of the old charter *held up*⟩ **2 a :** to keep up **:** not fall behind or lose ground **:** hold out ⟨even the smaller children *held up* pretty well until the last mile⟩ **b :** to retain interest or artistic effectiveness esp. over an extended period of time ⟨a book that *holds up* well⟩ **3 :** to stop an action or postpone an intended action ⟨planned a picnic but the rain forced us to *hold up*⟩ **4 :** to keep from raining **:** remain clear ⟨a beautiful day, if it only *holds up*⟩ — **hold up on 1 :** DELAY, POSTPONE ⟨ran out of money and had to *hold up on* all plans to travel⟩ **2 :** to hold back (sense 2a) ⟨the court *held up on* the money until the estate was totally settled⟩

holdup \ˈ≈,≈\ *n* -s [*hold up*] **1 :** the act or process of holding something up: as **a :** a robbery at the point of a gun **b :** a delay or a stopping of something ⟨a week's ~ in the completion of the plans⟩; *specif* **:** the delay or keeping back of a liquid during fractional distillation or reflex extraction with solvents or of a gas in fluidization **c :** the saving for later use of a card that could win the current trick in a bridge game **2 :** an instance of extortion **3 :** a place where livestock may be temporarily held on a range

holdup man *n* **:** a criminal who commits a holdup ⟨had mistaken the gendarme for a *holdup man* —H.A.Chippendale⟩

hold yard *n* **:** a yard for holding railroad cars or trains convenient for immediate use

¹**hole** \ˈhōl\ *n* -s [ME, hole, hollow place, hold (of a ship), fr. OE *hol* hole, hollow place (fr. neut. of *hol*, adj., hollow) & OE *holh* hole, hollow; akin to OHG *hol*, adj., hollow, ON *holr*, adj., hollow, Goth us*hulon* to hollow out, L *caulis* stalk of a plant, Gk *kaulos* stem, and perh. to Skt *kulyā* brook, ditch; basic meaning: hollow] **1 a :** an opening into or through anything **:** APERTURE, PERFORATION ⟨a ~ in a roof⟩ ⟨shot a ~ through a board⟩ ⟨entered the shed through a ~ in the side⟩ ⟨fishing through a ~ in the ice⟩ **b :** a pocket of a pool table ⟨dropped the eight ball in the corner ~⟩ **c :** an opening in a defensive football lineup (as a space between players or created by a player who is out of position or has been blocked) that offers an opportunity for an offensive player to advance the ball **2 a :** a hollow place **:** a cavity in a solid body or area ⟨a ~ in an apple⟩ ⟨a ~ in the hillside⟩: as (1) **:** a hollow in the ground **:** EXCAVATION, PIT, CAVE ⟨the steam shovel had dug a large ~⟩ (2) **:** a hollow in the ground filled with soft material (3) **:** a deep place in a body of water (4) **:** a mine, a well, or other shaft dug or drilled in the earth **b :** an unfilled or blank area (as in a page or column printed or to be printed) ⟨expand your story to fill an 18-line ~⟩ **c :** the hold of a ship **d :** a sense of loss or persistent yearning for something lost — usu. used in the phrase *to make a hole in* ⟨the loss of his daughter made quite a ~ in the man's life⟩ **e** (1) **:** a defect that exists in a crystal (as of a semiconductor) due to an electron having left its normal position in one of the crystal bonds and that is equivalent in many respects to a positively charged particle (2) **:** VACANCY 7 **f :** an air pocket as it affects an aircraft usu. causing it to drop suddenly **3 a :** an underground habitation or lurking place usu. excavated **:** DEN, BURROW ⟨the fox in his ~⟩ ⟨a rabbit ~⟩ **b :** a prison cell esp. for solitary confinement **4 a :** FLAW, FAULT ⟨looking for ~*s* in his character⟩ **b :** a weak spot or inconsistency (as in a line of reasoning) ⟨his stories are full of ~*s* since he does not explain how his characters get from one psychological state to another⟩ ⟨ingenious theory in which . . . there are many ~*s* —V.S.Pritchett⟩ **c :** an oversight or inadequate provision (as in a law, statute, treaty, or agreement) that permits significant evasions ⟨stop up the manifest ~*s* in the neutrality laws —R.M.Lovett⟩ **5 a :** a small cavity or perforation of significance in various games: as (1) **:** a small cavity into which a marble is to be played in any of various marble games (2) **:** a usu. lined cavity 4½ inches in diameter and 4 or more inches deep in a putting green into which the ball is to be played in a game of golf **b** (1) **:** the unit of play from a tee to its corresponding hole in a game of golf (2) **:** the fairway from a tee to its corresponding green on a golf course (3) **:** the score made in playing the ball from the tee into the hole in a game of golf **6 a :** a mean, dingy, or small and disreputable place esp. of lodging or habitation ⟨lived in some ~ or other across the tracks⟩ ⟨the ladies' cabin . . . is a dreadful ~ —Rachel Henning⟩ **b :** a place that one finds objectionable or offensive **7 :** a small bay **:** COVE **8 :** an awkward embarrassing position **:** FIX ⟨the loss of so competent an assistant put him in a ~ for a little while⟩ ⟨the noble heroes that got the rebels out of a ~ at the battle of Long Island —Kenneth Roberts⟩ **:** a losing position ⟨the ball team dropped the next two games which put them in the ~ by five games⟩; *esp* **:** a position of debt or financial loss ⟨in the ~ to the tune of several thousand dollars⟩ ⟨lent him some money to get him temporarily out of a ~⟩ **9** *West* **:** a level grassy mountain valley — usu. used in place names ⟨Jackson *Hole*⟩ **10 :** a side track branching from a main line of a railroad — **in the hole 1 a :** FACEDOWN — used of a hole card in stud poker **b :** having a score below zero **2 a :** next but one to bat in a ball game **b** *of a pitcher* **:** having pitched more balls than strikes to a batter **c** *of a batter* **:** having two strikes against him

²**hole** \"\ *vb* -ED/-ING/-S [ME *holen*, fr. OE *holian*; akin to OHG *holōn* to hollow out, ON *hola*, Goth *ushulon*; denominative fr. the root of OE *hol* hole] *vt* **1 :** to make a hole in (as by cutting, digging, boring, or shooting at) **:** PERFORATE, PIERCE ⟨*holing* the fence posts to take the crosspieces⟩ ⟨the ship was *holed* along the waterline by enemy fire⟩ **2 a :** to drive (as an animal or ball) into a hole ⟨the dogs *holed* the fox⟩ ⟨*holed* the ball in a single shot⟩ **b :** to place in a hole **3 :** to undercut (the coal) in a bed in coal mining ~ *vi* **1 :** to make a hole in something; *esp* **:** to excavate or undercut in coal mining **2 a :** to go or get into a hole **b** *of a train* **:** to take a side track so that an oncoming train can pass on the main track

hole·able \ˈhōləbəl\ *adj* **:** capable of being holed esp. in one stroke

hole–and–corner \ˌ≈≈ˈ≈≈\ *also* **hole–in–corner** \ˈ≈≈ˈ≈≈\ *adj* **1 :** hidden from public view esp. for reprehensible reasons **:** CLANDESTINE, UNDERHAND ⟨carrying on a *hole-and-corner* intrigue —*Times Lit. Supp.*⟩ ⟨done behind my back in a *hole-and-corner* fashion —Dorothy Sayers⟩ ⟨following a *hole-in-corner*, semiconspiratorial existence —*N. Y. Times*⟩ **2 :** belonging to the peripheral unimportant activities of life **:** INSIGNIFICANT ⟨marriage degenerated into a *hole-and-corner* existence in which spirit and intellect played no part —Olive Arden⟩ ⟨a *hole-and-corner* life in some obscure community —H.G.Wells⟩

hole board *n* **:** COMBER BOARD

hole card *n* **1 :** a card in stud poker that is properly dealt facedown and that the holder need not expose before the showdown — called also *down card* **2 :** a possession, action, or power that carries often unexpected weight in negotiations or other relationships and that is held in reserve or used to its most strategic advantage

ho·lec·ty·pi·na \hō,lektəˈpīnə\ *n pl, cap* [NL, fr. *Holectypus*, genus of sea urchins (fr. *hol-* + Gk *ektypos* worked in relief) + *-ina*] **:** a suborder of extinct sea urchins (order Exocycloida) having a central peristome, an excentric periproct, an Aristotle's lantern, and nonpetaloid ambulacra and found in Jurassic, Cretaceous, and Eocene strata

¹**ho·lec·ty·poid** \hōˈlektə,pȯid\ *adj* [NL *Holectypoida*] **:** of or relating to the Holectypina

²**holectypoid** \"\ *n* -s [NL *Holectypoida*] **:** a sea urchin of the suborder Holectypina

ho·lec·ty·poi·da \hō,lektəˈpȯidə\ [NL, fr. *Holectypus* + *-oida*] *syn of* HOLECTYPINA

hole–high \ˈ≈ˈ≈\ *adj* **:** stopping or resting on a line that is roughly even with the hole one is playing toward — used of an approach shot in golf

hole in *vi* **:** to take refuge or lodging **:** put up for the night ⟨stopped traveling and *holed in* at a motel⟩

hole in one : ¹ACE 4

hole–in–the–wall \ˈ≈≈≈ˈ≈\ *n, pl* **holes–in–the–wall :** a small and insignificant place esp. difficult to locate ⟨in the jewelry business and ran a *hole-in-the-wall* you could barely squeeze into⟩ ⟨a *hole-in-the-wall* patent-medicine manufacturer⟩

hole·less \ˈhōlləs\ *adj* [*hole* + *-less*] **:** having no hole or aperture

hole out *vt* **1 :** to play (the ball) into the cup in a game of golf **2 :** to complete a hole in golf for ⟨his second putt *holed* him *out* for a six⟩ ~ *vi* **:** to play one's ball into the cup in a game of golf

holeproof \ˈ≈ˈ≈\ *adj* **1 a :** designed to be proof against holes worn in by ordinary use ⟨~ stockings⟩ **b :** having no flaws or weak points ⟨the evidence against the prisoner was ~⟩ **2 :** designed to prevent evasion or subversion — used of a law, statute, provision, or system ⟨asked them to formulate laws that were ~ and would stop graft and corruption in the city⟩

hol·er \ˈhōlə(r)\ *n* -s [²*hole* + *-er*] **1 :** one that digs or fashions holes **2 :** one that has a specified number of holes — used in combinations ⟨the golf course was only a nine-*holer*⟩ ⟨the outhouse was a two-*holer*⟩

holes *pl of* HOLE, *pres 3d sing of* HOLE

hole saw *n* **:** CROWN SAW

hole through *vi* **:** to connect two underground tunnels by removing the rock that divides them

hole up *vi* **1 :** to take refuge or shelter in a hole or cave or as if in one **:** seek protection ⟨gone upstate to where her people were . . . figured on *holing up* with them for a while until she got over being afraid —R.F.Mirvish⟩ ⟨*holed up* in caves until they were blasted out by tommy gun and dynamite —*Newsweek*⟩ **2 :** to go into hiding ⟨breaks jail and *holes up* in an isolated turkey ranch —*Newsweek*⟩ ⟨badmen who *holed up* in badlands where others dared not venture —*Ford Times*⟩ ~ *vt* **1 a :** to place in or as if in a refuge, a shelter, or a hiding place ⟨during the wartime absence of her husband . . . she was *holed up* with two small sons on a farm —*New Yorker*⟩ **b :** IMPRISON ⟨the gunman *holed* them *up* in the house for two days⟩ **2 :** to hold up or delay esp. for a long time ⟨housing legislation is *holed up* in a Senate committee —*Time*⟩

holey \ˈhōlē, -li\ *adj* [ME *holly*, fr. *hole*, *hol* hole + *-y*] **:** having a hole or being full of holes ⟨wearing a ~ bathing suit —*Time*⟩

holey dollar *n* **:** a Spanish piece of eight or dollar having a round hole in its center, bearing the denomination 5 shillings, and current in Australia 1813–29 — called also *colonial dollar, pierced dollar, ring dollar*

hol·ger niel·sen method \'hōlgə(r)'nēlsən-\ *n, usu cap H&N* [after *Holger Nielsen* †1955 Dan. army officer who originated it] **:** BACK PRESSURE–ARM LIFT METHOD

hol ha·mo·ed *or* **chol ha·mo·ed** \ˌkōlhä'mōəd\ *n pl, sometimes cap* [Heb *ḥol ha-moed*, lit., the secular portion of the festival] **:** the four intermediate semiholidays between the first two and last two full festival days of Passover; *also* **:** the five intermediate days between the first two and last two days of Sukkoth

ho·li \'hōlē\ *n* -s *usu cap* [Hindi *holī*, fr. Skt *holikā*] **:** a Hindu spring festival characterized by boisterous and usu. ribald revelry including esp. the throwing of colored water and powder

ho·lia \'hōlēə\ *n* -s [origin unknown] **:** HUMPBACK SALMON

¹hol·i·day \'hälə,dā, *chiefly Brit* -,di\ *n* -s [ME, fr. OE *hāligdæg*, fr. *hālig* holy + *dæg* day — more at HOLY, DAY] **1 :** HOLY DAY **2 a :** a day on which one is exempt from one's usual labor or vocational activity ⟨had a ~ on the day the boss's daughter was married⟩ **b :** a time of release from work **:** FESTIVITY, CELEBRATION — usu. used in the phrase *to make holiday* ⟨the people who are making ~ flock to the beaches⟩ **c** *chiefly Brit* **:** VACATION ⟨everybody is on ~ in August —Joy Packer⟩ ⟨went on ~ for two weeks⟩ — often used in pl. with *the* ⟨worried about how to keep the child occupied for the ~*s*⟩ **d :** a period of exemption (as from a tax or from fear) ⟨tax ~*s* up to ten years —J.P.McEvoy⟩ ⟨gave myself a ~ from sad forebodings —Mary B. Chesnut⟩ **:** a period of relief ⟨a ~ from periodical literature —Aldous Huxley⟩ **3 a :** a day marked by a general cessation from work as an act of public commemoration of some event and often accompanied by public ceremonies and parades — see LEGAL HOLIDAY, NATIONAL HOLIDAY **b :** a good time **:** a festive occasion ⟨massacring soldiers to make a despot's ~ —H.R.G.Greaves⟩ **4 :** a spot accidentally left uncovered on a coated or painted surface

²holiday \"\ *adj* **:** of, belonging to, or befitting a holiday **:** FESTIVE, CAREFREE ⟨~ reading⟩ ⟨wearing ~ clothes⟩ ⟨a face with a ~ look⟩ ⟨~ atmosphere on the excursion boat⟩

³holiday \"\ *vi* **:** to take or spend a holiday esp. in a journey or at a resort ⟨~*ing* in the country⟩

holiday disease *n* [so called fr. its frequent occurrence after holidays as a result of overexertion] **:** azoturia of horses

hol·i·day·er \'hälə,dāə(r)\ *n* -s [³*holiday* + -*er*] **:** one on a holiday **:** VACATIONER ⟨~*s* who want to lead the fairly simple life for their all too short two-week break —Marvin Schwartz⟩

holiday flag *n* **:** the largest size of the national flag flown (as at U.S. Navy shore installations and Marine Corps posts) on national holidays and special occasions — compare GARRISON FLAG

holidaymaker \'⸗⸗(,)⸗,⸗⸗\ *n* **:** HOLIDAYER ⟨boatloads of ~*s* —*Nat'l Geographic*⟩

hol·i·days \'hälə,dāz\ *adv* **:** on holidays **:** on any holiday

holier *comparative of* HOLY

¹holier-than-thou \'⸗⸗⸗¦⸗\ *adj* [compar. of ¹*holy*] **:** marked by an objectionable air of usu. pious superiority ⟨preserved always an infuriating *holier-than-thou* attitude toward his erring younger brother⟩ ⟨loudly prayed with a *holier-than-thou* expression on his face —G.W.Benson⟩

²holier-than-thou \'⸗⸗⸗¦⸗\ *n* -s **:** one that is holier-than-thou ⟨his success in self-reform turned him into a *holier-than-thou* before his less successful friends⟩

holiest *superlative of* HOLY

ho·li·ly \'hōləlē\ *adv* [ME, fr. *holy* + -*ly*] **:** in a holy manner **:** PIOUSLY

¹ho·li·ness \'hōlēnəs, -lin-\ *n* -ES [ME *holynesse*, fr. OE *hālignes*, fr. *hālig* holy + -*nes* -ness — more at HOLY] **1 :** the quality or state of being holy **:** SANCTITY, SAINTLINESS ⟨the ~ of the saints⟩ ⟨the ~ of the consecrated place⟩ — often used as a title for various high religious dignitaries ⟨His *Holiness* Pope Pius XII⟩ ⟨His *Holiness* the Dalai Lama⟩ **2 :** a state of moral and spiritual perfection **:** complete sanctification **:** SINLESSNESS; *specif* **:** a state of sinlessness that according to some small religious groups is bestowed as a blessing on a Christian believer following conversion and is often a prerequisite of salvation

²holiness \"\ *adj, often cap* **:** emphasizing a perfectionist doctrine of holiness as a prerequisite of salvation ⟨the group was Arminian, Pentecostal, and *Holiness*⟩

holiness body *or* **holiness church** *n, often cap H* **:** one of numerous small religious groups in America emphasizing a perfectionist doctrine of holiness

holing *pres part of* HOLE

holis *pl of* HOLI

hol·ish·kes \'kälishkəz\ *n pl* [Yiddish] **:** stuffed cabbage

ho·lism \'hō,lizəm\ *n* -s [*hol-* + -*ism*] **1 :** the philosophic theory first formulated by Jan C. Smuts that the determining factors in nature are wholes (as organisms) which are irreducible to the sum of their parts and that the evolution of the universe is the record of the activity and making of these wholes **2 :** a theory or doctrine according to which a whole cannot be analyzed without residue into the sum of its parts or reduced to discrete elements — compare GESTALT PSYCHOLOGY, ORGANICISM

ho·list \'hōləst\ *n* -s [*hol-* + -*ist*] **:** an advocate of holism or holistic principles ⟨a ~ who denied that the English state, for example, is a logical construction out of individual people, and who asserted that it is an organism which develops, and responds to challenges, according to holistic laws —J.W.N. Watkins⟩

ho·lis·tic \(')hō¦listik\ *adj* **1 :** of, relating to, or based on holism **2 a :** in accordance with a theory of holism or conceptions advocated by holism ⟨the ~ strain in his thinking⟩ **b :** emphasizing the organic or functional relation between parts and wholes ⟨a ~ rather than an atomistic approach to the study of culture⟩ — **ho·lis·ti·cal·ly** \-tək(ə)lē\ *adv*

holk \'hōk\ *var of* ²HOWK

¹holl \'häl\ *adj* [ME, fr. OE *hol* — more at HOLE] *dial Eng* **:** HOLLOW

²holl \"\ *n* -s [ME, fr. OE *hol*, fr. neut. of *hol*, adj., hollow] **:** a hollow place: as **a :** *dial Eng* **:** DITCH **b** *obs* **:** a ship's hold

¹hol·land \'hälənd\ *n* -s *often cap* [ME *holand*, fr. *Holand*, county in the Netherlands, fr. MD *Holland*] **1 a :** a linen shirting of former times made in the Netherlands **b :** a cotton or linen fabric in plain weave usu. heavily sized or glazed and used for window shades, bookbinding, clothing **2 :** a smooth glazed or unglazed finish for cotton fabrics to make them opaque or semiopaque **3 :** ²DUTCH 1b

²holland \"\ *adj, usu cap* [fr. *Holland* the Netherlands, kingdom in northwestern Europe] **1 :** NETHERLANDS **2 :** of or belonging to a landholding company organized in Holland about 1791 to sell land in western New York state to settlers ⟨*Holland* purchase⟩

hol·lan·daise \¦hälən¦dāz\ *n* -s **:** GOULASH 2a

hollandaise sauce *also* **hollandaise** *n* -s [part trans. of F *sauce hollandaise*, lit., Dutch sauce, fr. *sauce* + *hollandaise*, fem. of *hollandais* Dutch, fr. *Hollande* Holland, country in northwestern Europe] **:** sauce made of butter, yolks of eggs, and lemon juice or vinegar

holland blue *n, often cap H* **:** a dark blue that is redder and duller than Peking blue or Flemish blue and greener and less strong than Japan blue — called also *canton, orion*

hol·land·er \'häləndə(r)\ *n* -s **1** *cap* **a :** a native or inhabitant of the Netherlands **b :** a Dutch ship **2** *often cap* **:** DUTCH CLINKER **3** *often cap* [so called fr. its invention in the Netherlands] **:** a paper-pulp beater typically consisting of an iron roll set with steel blades and revolving in an oval tub

holland gin *n, usu cap H* **:** HOLLANDS

hol·land·ite \'hälən,dīt\ *n* -s [Sir Thomas H. *Holland* †1947 Brit. geologist + E -*ite*] **:** a mineral $MnBaMn_6O_{14}$ consisting of a crystallized manganate of barium and manganese from central India

hol·lands \'hälən(d)z\ *n, usu cap* [modif. of D *hollandsch* Dutch, fr. *hollandsch genever* Dutch gin] **:** gin made in the Netherlands

hol·lan·tide \'hälən,tīd\ *n, usu cap* [by shortening & alter.] *dial Eng* **:** ALLHALLOWTIDE

¹hol·ler \'hälə(r)\ *vb* **hollered; hollered; hollering** \-l(ə)riŋ\ **hollers** [alter. of ²*hollo*] *vi* **1** *chiefly dial, of a bird or animal* **:** to utter its characteristic cry or call ⟨spring frogs were ~*ing* in the marsh last night⟩ **2 a :** to make a loud noise ⟨the children were seeing who could ~ the loudest⟩ **b :** to shout or cry out to attract attention or summon someone ⟨~ for help⟩ or in pain or fear ⟨heard his brothers ~*ing* as they were killed —G.F.Weisel⟩ or in enthusiasm or exuberance ⟨baseball fans ~*ing* for the team⟩ **3 :** GRIPE, COMPLAIN, GRUMBLE ⟨people will always ~ about an increase in taxes⟩ ~ *vt* **1 a :** to express by hollering ⟨~ encouragement⟩ **b :** to call out (a word or phrase) ⟨~ uncle⟩ ⟨~ bloody murder⟩ **2** *chiefly dial* **:** to call or summon by hollering — often used with *out* ⟨wake up first in the morning and ~ out the ranch hands⟩

²holler \"\ *n* -s **1 :** a shout or outcry esp. of joy or exuberance ⟨with a whoop and a ~ the winners left⟩ or to attract attention or summon aid **2 :** GRIPE, COMPLAINT ⟨the new law brought a ~ from the minority⟩ **3 :** an American Negro work song freely improvised usu. in terms of the particular occupation of the moment and often without words ⟨cornfield ~⟩ — compare JUBILEE 8

³holler \"\ *chiefly dial var of* HOLLOW

holler guy *n, slang* **:** a member of a team who unofficially but effectively assumes responsibility for the success of the team during a game by the direction of play or by constant encouraging chatter

hollering *adj* [fr. pres. part. of ¹*holler*] **:** marked by or as if by shouting ⟨~ headlines . . . were always about murder of one sort or another —William Saroyan⟩

hollering distance *n, dial* **:** HAILING DISTANCE

hol·ler·ith machine \'hälərəth-\ *also* **hollerith** *n* -s *usu cap H* [after Herman *Hollerith*, 19th cent. inventor] **:** a machine for tabulating and sorting punched cards and tabulating data from them

hollies *pl of* HOLLY

hol·lin *or* **hol·len** \'hälən\ *n* -s [ME *holen, holyn*, fr. OE *holen, holegn* — more at HOLLY] *dial Brit* **:** HOLLY

¹hol·lo \'hä(,)lō, hä'lō, hə'lō\ *or* **hol·la** \'hälə; hə'lä, hə'l-, -'lä\ *or* **hol·loo** \'hä(,)lü, hä'lü, hə'lü\ *also* **hol·loa** \'hä(,)lō, hä'lō, hə'lō\ *interj* [origin unknown] **1 —** used to attract attention **2 —** used as a call of encouragement or jubilation

²hollo \"\ *or* **holla** \"\ *or* **holloo** \"\ *also* **holloa** \"\ *vb* -ED/-ING/-ES *vi* **:** to cry hollo **:** call out **:** HOLLER ~ *vt* **1 a :** to call or cry hollo to **:** attract the attention of **b :** to call encouragement to **2 :** to utter loudly **:** HOLLER ⟨that reeling man . . . ~*ing* bawdy inanities —C.C.Morrison⟩

³hollo \"\ *or* **holla** \"\ *or* **holloo** \"\ *also* **holloa** \"\ *n, pl* **hollos** *or* **holloes** *or* **hollas** *or* **holloos** *also* **holloas :** an exclamation or call of hollo ⟨listening to the ~*s* of the fox hunters⟩ **:** HOLLOING, SHOUTING, HOLLER

hol·long \'hä,lȯŋ\ *n* -s [Assamese *holoṅ* large] **:** an East Indian timber tree (*Dipterocarpus pilosus*) having resinous decay-resistant wood

¹hol·low \'hä(,)lō, -lə *often* -ləw+V\ *adj, often* -ER/-EST [ME *holwe, holg, holh*, fr. *holg, holh* hole, den, fr. OE *holh* hole, hollow — more at HOLE] **1 a :** constituting a depression or a low or excavated place ⟨a ~ spot in the road⟩ ⟨the force of the meteor's fall made a ~ place in the open plain⟩ **:** curved or rounded inward **:** CONCAVE ⟨the dish was covered by a ~ piece of metal⟩ **:** SUNKEN ⟨~ temples⟩ **b :** marked by hollows or sunken areas ⟨his face became gaunter and more ~ with each passing year⟩ **c** *of the sea* **:** having deep-troughed waves **d :** having a concave face or surface — used of various tools esp. when designed for curved work ⟨~ adz⟩ ⟨~ auger⟩ ⟨~ punch⟩ **2 a** (1) **:** having an empty space or cavity within **:** not solid ⟨a ~ tree⟩ ⟨~ sphere⟩ (2) *of a two-dimensional figure* **:** being in outline only **:** not filled in **:** consisting partly of unfilled spaces ⟨~ letters⟩ **b :** EMPTY ⟨a ~ walnut⟩ ⟨a ~ feeling in the stomach⟩ **c** (1) **:** devoid of worth, value, significance, or substance ⟨a ~ victory⟩ ⟨a ~ gain⟩ ⟨the whole celebration seems strangely ~ and unreal —W.F.Hambly⟩ ⟨the ~ position taken by the opposition⟩ **:** lacking in qualities that give substance, worth, or moral or intellectual solidity ⟨men of social significance but essentially ~⟩ (2) **:** devoid of any significant ideas, principles, or purposes ⟨we are the ~ men —T.S.Eliot⟩ ⟨a ~ generation of youths⟩ **d :** having hollow spaces in the interior; *esp* **:** having a net area less than 75 percent of the gross area — used of a masonry unit (as a brick or building tile) **3 a :** sounding or reverberating like a sound made in a cave or large empty enclosure **:** muffled and sepulchral **:** breathy and lacking in overtones **:** producing confused echoes ⟨the car in the empty garage started with a ~ roar⟩ ⟨the ~ echo of the monkeys' call —M.P.O'Connor⟩ ⟨the ~ subdued sound of the wind outside —Robert Murphy⟩ **b :** making or being a sound of or as if of beating on a hollow enclosure ⟨the ~ drumming of horses' hooves on the bridge⟩ **4 :** marked by insincerity or lack of good faith ⟨a ~ greeting to an enemy⟩ ⟨a ~ promise⟩ **:** FALSE, DECEITFUL, TREACHEROUS ⟨a ~ heart⟩ ⟨a ~ truce⟩ ⟨talk about war aims sounded ~ to them —F.L. Allen⟩ **5 :** COMPLETE, THOROUGH **syn** see VAIN

²hollow \"\ *vb* -ED/-ING/-S [ME *holwen*, fr. *holwe*, adj.] *vt* **1 a :** to make hollow **:** form an indentation or concavity in — usu. used with *out* ⟨~ out half of a coconut shell⟩ ⟨~*ed* a place out in the cliffside where he could hide⟩ **b :** to make concave or cause to be curved or rounded inward ⟨the can cover must be cut in two, and each half so ~*ed* as to fit around the pipe —Emily Holt⟩ ⟨the short double woolly scarf which you could ~ into a cap —Fred Majdalany⟩ **c** (1) **:** to gouge, dig, or scrape the inside out of — usu. used with *out* ⟨~*ed* out a stump and filled it with concrete⟩ (2) **:** GUT — often used with *out* ⟨dozens of dead cities, their insides ~*ed* out by dynamite and fire —Norman Cousins⟩ **2 :** to form by hollowing something out ⟨rain barrels ~*ed* out from trees —Robert Shaplen⟩ **:** EXCAVATE — usu. used with *out* ⟨engineers ~*ed* out a tunnel through the mountain⟩ ~ *vi* **:** to become hollow ⟨her cheeks ~*ed* suddenly as she sucked in her breath⟩

³hollow \"\ *n* -s [¹*hollow*] **1 :** a low spot surrounded by elevations **:** a depressed or low part of a surface **:** CONCAVITY, CHANNEL, BASIN ⟨driving down through the ~ in the road⟩ ⟨the ~ of the hand⟩; *esp* **:** a small valley **:** RAVINE, NOTCH, DINGLE **2 a :** an unfilled space within anything **:** CAVITY, HOLE ⟨in the ~ of a tree⟩ **b :** an area marked by such a space or cavity ⟨the horse buses rumble by, dropping a note as their hooves strike the ~ of the bridge —*Times Lit. Supp.*⟩ ⟨pounding on the ~ of the wall⟩

⁴hollow \"\ *adv* [¹*hollow*] **:** HOLLOWLY ⟨the attacks on him rang ~ because he had proved his honesty and integrity⟩

holloware \'⸗(,)⸗,⸗\ *n* [by alter.] **:** HOLLOW WARE

hollow back *n* **:** a book back in which the backs of the sections are affixed to the backbone of the cover only at the joints, the separation sometimes being made by a flattened tubular lining of paper or cloth; *also* **:** a book so bound or a style of binding featuring this construction — called also *open back, spring back*; compare TIGHT BACKBONE; see SPINE illustration

hollow cabochon *n* **:** a cabochon with a concave back

hollow charge *n* **:** an explosive which concentrates its force in one direction (as in a projectile designed to blow a hole through armor plate)

hollow-cut \'⸗(,)⸗¦⸗\ *adj* **:** made with a pile cut in graduated lengths for a corded effect — used of normally even-pile fabrics (as velveteen)

hollow-faced bat \'⸗⸗,⸗-\ *n* **:** any of various Asiatic or African bats (genus *Nycteris*) with a basin-shaped depression in the front of the skull that is margined by fleshy foliate outgrowths

hollow-ground \'⸗(,)⸗¦⸗\ *adj* **:** ground so as to have a concave surface behind the cutting edge ⟨a *hollow-ground* razor⟩ ⟨a *hollow-ground* blade of a skate⟩

hollow handle *n* **:** a haft of a piece of silver flatware molded of two hollow halves soldered together and fastened to the shank of the object (as a knife or a serving fork or spoon)

hollow heart *n* **:** an abnormal condition of potato tubers which is usu. the result of rapid and uneven growth and in which the central tissue ruptures and leaves a cavity

hollow horn *n* **:** debility in cattle popularly attributed to the hollowness of their horns

hollow-horned \'⸗(,)⸗¦⸗\ *adj* **1 :** having permanent horns with a bony core into which the frontal sinuses often extend to form air spaces (as in cattle, sheep, goats, and true antelopes) **2** *of lumber* **:** HONEYCOMBED

hollow-horning \'⸗(,)⸗,⸗⸗\ *n, of lumber* **:** HONEYCOMBING

hollow leg *n, slang* **:** an unusual capacity for alcoholic drinks

hol·low·ly *adv* **:** in a hollow manner ⟨the sound echoed ~ in the cave⟩

hollow mill *n* **:** a milling cutter with three or more cutting edges enclosing and revolving around the cylindrical workpiece

hol·low·ness *n* -ES [ME *holownesse*, fr. *holwe, holowe* hollow + -*nesse* -ness] **:** the quality or state of being hollow ⟨testing the wall for ~ by tapping on it lightly⟩ ⟨the ~ and trickery of these appeals —F.D.Roosevelt⟩ ⟨the ~, the sham, the silliness of the empty pageant —Oscar Wilde⟩

hollow newel *n* **:** an opening in the center of a winding staircase in place of a newel-post, the stairs being supported each step by those below, and all held in place by the wall — called also *open newel;* distinguished from *solid newel*

hollow newel stair *n* **:** OPEN-NEWEL STAIR

hollow organ *n* **:** any visceral organ that has the form of a hollow tube or pouch (as the stomach or intestine) or that includes a cavity which subserves a vital function (as the heart or bladder)

hollow square *n* **:** a formation of troops in former military tactics in the shape of a square with the sides each usu. consisting of several ranks of soldiers and the middle holding the officers and the colors

hollow stalk *or* **hollow stem** *n* **:** any plant disease characterized by degeneration or decay of the pith of the stalk (as of tobacco caused by *Erwinia aroideae* or of cauliflower caused by boron deficiency)

hollow tail *n* **:** WOLF-IN-THE-TAIL

hollow wall *n* **:** CAVITY WALL

hollow ware *n* **:** articles (as of pottery, glass, or metal) that have volume and significant depth ⟨cups, bowls, and pots are typical *hollow ware*⟩ — distinguished from *flatware*

holls *pl of* HOLL

hol·lus·chick \'häləs,chik\ *n, pl* **holluschick·ie** \-kē\ [modif. of Russ *kholostyak* bachelor] **:** a young male fur seal

hol·ly \'hälē, -li\ *n* -ES *often attrib* [ME, fr. OE *holegn, holen;* akin to OHG *hulis* holly, ON *hulfr*, MIr *cuilenn*] **1 a :** a tree or shrub of the genus *Ilex* (as English holly or American holly) — see CHINESE HOLLY, INKBERRY 1; compare MATÉ **b :** the foliage or branches of this tree or shrub used for esp. Christmas decoration **2 :** a tree whose leaves resemble those of holly (as *Prunus ilicifolia* and *Photinia arbutifolia* of California, members of the genus *Olearia* of New Zealand, or the holm oak) **3 :** SEA HOLLY

European holly

holly bay *n* **1 :** LOBLOLLY BAY **2 :** EVERGREEN MAGNOLIA

holly family *n* **:** AQUIFOLIACEAE

holly fern *n* **:** any of certain ferns having fronds of a texture and glossy surface suggesting holly: as **a :** an evergreen fern (*Polystichum lonchitis*) of the north temperate zone **b :** a Californian fern (*Polystichum aculeatum*) that is often cultivated for ornament **c :** a tropical Old World fern (*Cyrtomium aculeatum*)

hollygrape \'⸗⸗,⸗\ *n* **:** OREGON GRAPE

holly green *n* **1 :** a dark yellowish green that is greener, stronger, and very slightly darker than average palm green, greener, lighter, and stronger than deep chrome green or average hunter green, and greener and deeper than golf green **2 :** a moderate olive green that is yellower and paler than forest green and yellower, lighter, and stronger than cypress or Lincoln green

hol·ly·hock \'hälē,häk, -li,-, -,hȯk\ *n* -s [ME *holihoc*, fr. *holi*, *holy* holy + *hoc* hock (mallow)] **1 :** a tall perennial Chinese herb (*Althaea rosea*) cultivated in gardens as a biennial with large coarse rounded leaves and showy flowers in a large terminal spike **2 :** a deep purplish red that is bluer and deeper than Harvard crimson (sense 2) or American beauty and redder and duller than magenta (sense 2a)

hollyhock delphinium *n* **:** any of various cultivated larkspurs with narrow flower clusters forming spires

hollyhock tree *n* **:** an Australian shrub (*Hibiscus splendens*) with showy rose-colored flowers

holly laurel *n* **:** ISLAY

holly leaf miner *n* **:** a small black fly (*Phytomyza ilicis*) having a yellowish larva that tunnels in the leaves of various hollies

holly-leaved barberry \¦⸗⸗¦⸗-\ *or* **hollyleaf barberry** \'⸗⸗,⸗¦⸗-\ *n* **:** OREGON GRAPE

holly-leaved cherry *or* **hollyleaf cherry** *n* **:** ISLAY

holly oak *n* **:** an oak (as the holm oak) with leaves like holly

holly rose *n* **:** a West Indian shrub (*Turnera ulmifolia*) with showy yellow flowers

¹hol·ly·wood \'hälē,wu̇d, -li,-\ *n, usu cap* [fr. *Hollywood*, district in the city of Los Angeles, California] **1 a :** the American motion-picture industry ⟨a lawyer speaking for *Hollywood* before an investigating committee⟩ **b :** a place constituting a center for a motion-picture industry ⟨there are many *Hollywoods* besides the one in California —*N.Y. Times*⟩ **2 :** something produced by or befitting the American motion-picture industry or its productions ⟨pure *Hollywood* —Will Irwin & T.M.Johnson⟩

²hollywood \"\ *adj, usu cap* **1 :** of or from Hollywood, a district of Los Angeles, Calif. **:** of the kind or style prevalent in Hollywood ⟨a *Hollywood* fashion⟩ **2 :** of, relating to, produced by, or characteristic of the American motion-picture industry esp. as centered in Los Angeles, Calif., and vicinity ⟨a *Hollywood* film technique⟩

hollywood bed *n, usu cap H* **1 :** a bed consisting of a mattress on a box spring supported by 4 or 6 low legs and sometimes having an upholstered headboard separately fastened to a wall **2 :** any bed on a low frame and without a footboard, corner posts, and sometimes a headboard

Hollywood bed

hollywood gin *or* **hollywood** *n, usu cap H* [so called fr. its introduction by the motion-picture colony in Hollywood] **:** a method of scoring in gin rummy whereby each deal is scored as though part of three different games

¹hol·ly·wood·ian \¦hälē¦wu̇dēən, -li¦-\ *n* -s *cap* **:** a native or resident of Hollywood, Calif.; *also* **:** a person employed in the Hollywood motion-picture industry

²hollywoodian \¦⸗⸗¦⸗⸗⸗\ *adj, cap* **:** of or befitting Hollywood or Hollywoodians

hol·ly·wood·ish \'hälē,wu̇dish\ *adj, usu cap* **:** HOLLYWOODIAN ⟨*Hollywoodish* klieg lights and grinding cameras —*Newsweek*⟩ ⟨a *Hollywoodish* sort of bombast —Moses Smith⟩

hol·ly·wood·ite \'⸗⸗,wu̇,dīt\ *n* -s *cap* **:** HOLLYWOODIAN

hol·ly·wood·ize \-,dīz\ *vt* -ED/-ING/-S *often cap* **:** to make (as an author or his writings) conform to standards set up by the American motion-picture industry ⟨does not believe that the author can be completely *Hollywoodized* —A.A.VanDuym⟩

hollywood palm *n, usu cap H* **:** a glabrous perennial (*Kalanchoe verticillata*) of southern Africa that is used as an ornamental pot plant and that has long linear leaves mottled with violet brown and terminal clusters of salmon to scarlet flowers

hol·ly·woody \-u̇dē\ *adj, usu cap* **:** characterized by the less desirable qualities attributed to motion pictures as produced by Hollywood ⟨the story was called thick and *Hollywoody* —Janet Flanner⟩

¹holm *or* **holme** \'hōm *also* -ōlm\ *n* -s [ME, fr. OE *holm*, fr. ON *hōlmr* small island; akin to OE *holm* sea, OS *holm* hill, OE *hyll* hill — more at HILL] **1** *Brit* **:** a small island in a river or lake or near the mainland — often used in place names **2** *chiefly Brit* **:** low flat land near a river **:** BOTTOMS

²holm \"\ *n* -s [ME, alter. of *holen* holly, fr. OE — more at HOLLY] **:** HOLM OAK

holm·berry \'⸗- — *see* BERRY\ *n* [²*holm* + *berry*] **:** the berry of the butcher's-broom

holmes·ian \'hōmzēən *also* -ōlm-\ *adj* [Sherlock *Holmes*, a detective in stories by Sir Arthur Conan Doyle †1930 Brit. writer + E -*ian*] *usu cap* **:** of, belonging to or suggesting the detective Sherlock Holmes

holmes light \'hōmz- *also* -ōlmz-\ *or* **holmes signal** *n, usu cap H* [prob. fr. the name *Holmes*] **:** a signaling device that consists of a case containing impure calcium phosphide and a float and that when thrown into water generates hydrogen phosphides that take fire spontaneously

holm·gang \'hō(l)m,gaŋ\ n [ON hólmganga, fr. hólmr small island + ganga act of going; akin to OE gang act of going — more at GANG] archaic : a duel esp. on an island

holm·gren yarn test \'hōm|grən, -,gren- also -ōlm|\ also **holmgren test** n, usu cap H [after Alarik Frithiof Holmgren †1897 Swed. physiologist] : a method of testing color vision by the use of colored wool yarns

holmi·um \'hō(l)mēəm\ n -s [NL, fr. Holmia (latinized form of Stockholm, Sweden) + NL -ium; fr. the locality near which minerals rich in yttrium are found] : a trivalent metallic element of the rare-earth group that occurs with yttrium (as in gadolinite) and that forms cream-colored or yellow compounds which are among the most highly magnetic known — symbol Ho; see ELEMENT table

holm oak n [²holm] **1** : an evergreen oak (Quercus ilex) of southern Europe with leaves resembling those of holly **2** : the hard wood of the holm oak

holm·quist·ite \'hōm,kwi,stīt also -ōlm-\ n -s usu cap [Sw hölmquistit, fr. Per Johan Hölmquist, Swed. scientist + Sw -it -ite] : a mineral $(Na,K,Ca)Li(Mg, Fe)_3Al_2Si_8O_{22}(OH)_2$ consisting of an alkali and a silicate of iron, magnesium, lithium, and aluminum and related to hornblende

holm tree n [ME holme tre, fr. ²holm + tree] : HOLM OAK

holo- — see HOL-

holo·axial \ˌhälō, ˌhōlō+\ adj [hol- + axial] of a crystal system : having all the axes of symmetry possible

holo·baptist \"+\ n [hol- + Baptist] : IMMERSIONIST

holo·basidium \"+\ [NL, fr. hol- + basidium] syn of AUTOBASIDIUM

holo·benthic \"+\ adj [hol- + benthic] : inhabiting the deep sea during all stages of life

hol·o·blas·tic \ˌhälōˌblastik, ˌhōl-\ adj [ISV hol- + -blastic] of an egg : undergoing complete cleavage as a result of the absence of an impeding mass of yolk material : having cleavage planes that divide the whole egg into distinct and separate though coherent blastomeres — opposed to meroblastic — **hol·o·blas·ti·cal·ly** \-tək(ə)lē\ adv

hol·o·branch \'hälə,braŋk, 'hōl-\ n -s [ISV hol- + -branch] : a fish gill in which the branchial arch has two rows of lamellae or filaments — compare HEMIBRANCH 2

hol·o·car·pic \ˌhäləˌkärpik, ˌhōl-\ adj [hol- + -carpic] **1** : having the whole thallus developed into a fruiting body or sporangium ⟨~ algae⟩ ⟨~ fungi⟩ **2** : lacking rhizoids and haustoria — compare EUCARPIC

hol·o·car·pous \-pəs\ adj [hol- + -carpous] : HOLOCARPIC 1

holo·caust \'hälə,kȯst, 'hōl- also 'hōl- or ˌ|kȧst sometimes -lē| or -li| or ˌ|kəst\ n -s [ME, fr. OF holocauste, fr. LL holocaustum, fr. Gk holokauston, neut. of holokaustos burnt whole, fr. hol- + kaustos burnt, fr. kaiein to burn — more at CAUSTIC] **1** : a burnt sacrifice : a sacrificial offering wholly consumed by fire **2** : a complete or thorough sacrifice or destruction esp. by fire ⟨burned all his books and paper in a giant ~⟩ ⟨thousands of enemy troops consumed in the ~ —Upton Sinclair⟩ ⟨an atomic global ~ —J.B.Conant⟩ — **holo·caus·tic** \ˌ≈≈ˈkȯstik, -tēk also -ˈkäs-\ adj

holo·cellulose \ˌhälō, ˌhōlō+\ n [ISV hol- + cellulose; orig. formed in G] : the total polysaccharide fraction of wood or straw and the like that is made up of cellulose and all of the hemicelluloses and that is obtained by removing the extractives and the lignin from the original natural material

hol·o·cene \'hälə,sēn, 'hōl-\ adj, usu cap [ISV hol- + -cene] : RECENT 3

hol·o·cen·trid \ˌhälō'sen·trəd, ˌhōl-\ n -s [NL Holocentridae] : a fish of the family Holocentridae

hol·o·cen·tri·dae \-rə,dē\ n pl, cap [NL, fr. Holocentrus, type genus + -idae] : a family of tropical marine fishes closely related to and in old classifications included in the Berycidae

hol·o·cen·trus \-rəs\ n, cap [NL, fr. hol- + -centrus (fr. Gk kentros sharp point, fr. kentein to prick, goad) — more at CENTER] : the type genus of the family Holocentridae containing certain typical squirrelfishes

hol·o·ceph·a·la \ˌhälō'sefələ, ˌhōl-\ [NL, fr. hol- + -cephala] syn of HOLOCEPHALI

¹hol·o·ceph·a·lan \ˌ≈≈ˈ≈≈lən\ or **hol·o·ce·pha·li·an** \ˌhälōsəˈfālēən, ˌhōl-\ adj [NL Holocephali + E -an or -ian] : of or relating to the subclass Holocephali

²holocephalan \"\ or **holocephalian** \"\ n -s : a fish of the subclass Holocephali

hol·o·ceph·a·li \ˌhälō'sefə,lī, ˌhōl-\ n pl, cap [NL, fr. hol- + -cephali] : a subclass of Chondrichthyes that is sometimes made a separate class, includes the recent chimaeras and certain chiefly extinct related fishes some of which date from Devonian time, and is distinguished by a cartilaginous skeleton, gill clefts covered by a fold of skin, high compressed head with small narrow mouth and the dentition reduced to broad flat plates, and a body tapering off into a long tail — **hol·o·ceph·a·lous** \ˌ≈≈ˈsefələs\ adj

hol·o·cho·a·nite \ˌhälōˌkōə,nīt, ˌhōl-\ n -s [NL Holochoanites, suborder of nautiloids in some classifications, fr. hol- + Gk choanē funnel (fr. chein to pour) + NL -ites -ite — more at FOUND] : a fossil nautiloid in which the funnels about the siphuncle extend from one septum to the next — **hol·o·cho·a·nit·ic** \ˌ≈≈ˈ≈nid·ik\ adj

ho·loch·ro·al \hə'läkrəwəl\ adj [hol- + Gk chrōs skin, color + E -al — more at GRIT] : having compound eyes with the visual area covered by a continuous cornea — used esp. of certain trilobites

hol·o·clas·tic \ˌhäləˌklastik, ˌhōl-\ adj [ISV hol- + -clastic] : being or belonging to ordinary sedimentary rocks as distinguished from tuffs or pyroclastic rocks

hol·o·coe·not·ic \ˌhäləsēˌnäd·ik, ˌhōl-\ adj [hol- + coen- + -otic] : acting in concert — used of the impact of a complex environment on living organisms

hol·o·crine \'hälə krən, 'hōl-, -ə,krīn\ adj [ISV hol- + -crine (fr. Gk krinein to separate, decide) — more at CERTAIN] : producing a secretion consisting of altered secretory cells; also : produced by a holocrine gland — compare MEROCRINE

holo·crystalline \ˌhälō, ˌhōlō+\ adj [ISV hol- + crystalline] : completely crystalline : made up wholly of crystals or crystalline particles — used of a rock (as granite)

hol·o·dac·tyl·ic \ˌhälō(,)dakˌtilik, ˌhōl-\ adj [MGk holodaktylos (fr. Gk hol- + daktylos dactyl) + E -ic] of a hexameter : having all the feet dactyls except the last

hol·o·dis·cus \ˌhälō'diskəs, ˌhōl-\ n, cap [NL, fr. hol- + -discus] : a small genus of shrubs (family Rosaceae) of western No. America that resemble spirea and have flowers in a pendant pyramidal panicle and achenes enclosed in the calyx

holo·enzyme \ˌhälō, ˌhōlō+\ n [ISV hol- + enzyme] : a complete active enzyme consisting of an apoenzyme combined with its coenzyme

holo·gamete \"+\ n [hol- + gamete] : a hologamous gamete

ho·log·a·mous \hə'lägəməs\ adj [hol- + -gamous] **1** : having gametes of essentially the same size and structural features as vegetative cells — used of various flagellates, ciliates, diatoms, and desmids **2** : having the entire thallus developing into a gametangium — used of thalloid plants, esp. fungi

ho·log·a·my \-mē\ n -ES [hol- + -gamy] : the condition of being hologamous

hol·o·go·nia \ˌhälə'gōnēə, ˌhōl-\ n pl, cap [NL, fr. hol- + -gonia (fr. Gk gonos offspring, procreation, genitals) — more at GON-] in some classifications : an order of Nematoda comprising forms in which the germinal area extends the whole length of the gonad — compare TELOGONIA — **hol·o·gon·ic** \ˌ≈≈ˈgänik\ adj

holo·gonidium \ˌhälō, ˌhōlō+\ n [NL, fr. hol- + gonidium] : SOREDIUM

¹hol·o·graph \'hälə,graf, 'hōl-\ n [LL holographus written entirely in one's own hand, fr. LGk holographos, fr. Gk hol- + -graphos written, writing (fr. graphein to write) — more at CARVE] : a document (as a letter, deed, or will) wholly in the handwriting of the person from whom it proceeds and whose act it purports to be

²holograph \"\ or **hol·o·graph·ic** \ˌ≈≈ˈgrafik\ or **hol·o·graph·i·cal** \-fəkəl\ adj : being a holograph : written entirely in one's own hand

holographic will n : a testamentary instrument that is written entirely by the testator in his own handwriting and signed by him and that even if unattested is usu. recognized as a valid will in most jurisdictions

holo·gynic \ˌhälō, ˌhōlō+\ adj [ISV hol- + gynic] : inherited solely in the female line, presumably through transmission as a recessive factor in the nonhomologous portion of the X chromosome — **ho·log·y·ny** \hə'läjənē\ n -ES

hol·o·he·dral \ˌhälōˈhēdrəl, ˌhōl-\ adj [hol- + Gk hedra seat + E -al — more at SIT] of a crystal : having all the faces required by complete symmetry — compare HEMIHEDRAL, TETARTOHEDRAL — **hol·o·he·drism** \ˌ≈≈ˈhē,drizəm\ n -s — **hol·o·he·dry** \-ēdrē\ n -ES

hol·o·he·dron \ˌ≈≈ˈhēdrən\ n, pl **holohedrons** or **holohedra** [NL, fr. hol- + -hedron] : a holohedral crystal form

holo·hemihedral \ˌhälō, ˌhōlō+\ adj [hol- + hemihedral] : belonging to, presenting, or being hemihedral crystal forms

holo·hyaline \"+\ adj [hol- + hyaline] of a rock : wholly glassy

ho·lo·ku \hō'lōkü\ n -s [Hawaiian holokū] : a woman's long one-piece gown usu. made with some fitting and a train and worn esp. in Hawaii

holo·mastigote \ˌhälō, ˌhōlō+\ adj [hol- + mastigote] : having many flagella scattered evenly over the body

holo·metabola \"+\ n pl, cap [NL, fr. hol- + Metabola] in some classifications : a group comprising all insects that have complete metamorphosis

holo·metabolic \"+\ adj [hol- + metabolic] : HOLOMETABOLOUS

holo·metabolism \"+\ n [hol- + Gk metabolē change + E -ism — more at METABOLISM] of an insect : development with complete metamorphosis — distinguished from heterometabolism; compare AMETABOLISM — **holo·metabolous** \"+\ adj

holo·metaboly \"+\ n [ISV hol- + metaboly] : HOLOMETABOLISM

hol·o·mic·tic \ˌhäləˌmiktik, ˌhōl-\ adj [hol- + -mictic (fr. Gk miktos mixed; akin to Gk misgein to mix) — more at MIX] of a lake : undergoing a complete circulation that extends to the deepest parts during overturn

hol·o·mor·pho·sis \ˌhälō'mȯrfəsəs, ˌhōl- sometimes -ō,mȯr'fōsəs\ n, pl **holomorpho·ses** \-,sēz\ [NL, fr. hol- + -morphosis] : the complete regeneration of a lost part

hol·o·my·ar·i·an \ˌhälō(,)mīˌa(a)rēən, ˌhōl-\ also **hol·o·my·ar·i·al** \-əl\ adj [NL Holomyaria, division of nematode worms in some classifications (fr. hol- + -myaria) + E -an or -al] of a nematode worm : having the muscle layer continuous or divided into two longitudinal zones without true muscle cells

holo·nephros \ˌhälō, ˌhōlō+\ n [NL, fr. hol- + -nephros] : a hypothetical generalized vertebrate kidney consisting of a single nephric tubule in each trunk segment of either side of the body

holo·parasite \"+\ n [ISV hol- + parasite; orig. formed as G holoparasit] : an obligate parasite — compare HEMIPARASITE — **holo·parasitic** \"+\ adj

hol·o·pho·tal \ˌhäləˌfōd·ᵊl, ˌhōl-\ adj [hol- + phot- + -al] : of or relating to a holophote; esp : reflecting the whole of the light from a light source in a given direction

hol·o·phote \'≈≈,fōt\ n -s [back-formation fr. holophotal] : an optical apparatus for collecting and throwing in a desired direction by means of lenses or reflectors a large amount of the light from a source (as a lighthouse lamp)

holo·phrase \'hälə,frāz, 'hōl-\ n [hol- + phrase] : a single word expressing a complex of ideas; also : HOLOPHRASIS

ho·loph·ra·sis \hə'läfrəsəs\ n, pl **holophra·ses** \-,sēz\ [hol- + Gk phrasis expression, phrase] : the expression of a complex of ideas by a single word; also : HOLOPHRASE

hol·o·phrasm \'hälə,frazəm, 'hōl-\ n -s [fr. holophrastic, after such pairs as E spasm: spastic] : HOLOPHRASE

hol·o·phras·tic \ˌ≈≈ˈfrastik\ adj [ISV hol- + -phrastic (fr. Gk phrastikos expressive, fr. phrazein to express) — more at PHRASE] : of or relating to holophrasis : equivalent to a whole phrase : expressing a complex of ideas in a single word

hol·o·phyt·ic \ˌhäləˌfid·ik, ˌhōl-\ adj [hol- + -phytic] : obtaining food after the manner of a green plant : PHOTOAUTOTROPHIC — opposed to holozoic; compare HEMIZOIC

hol·o·plank·ton \ˌhälō'plaŋktən, ˌhōl-\ n [ISV hol- + plankton] : plankton composed of organisms that pass their whole life floating, drifting, or swimming weakly in the water — compare HEMIPLANKTON — **hol·o·plank·ton·ic** \ˌ≈≈(,)plaŋkˈtänik\ adj

hol·o·plast \'hälō,plast, 'hōl-\ n -s [hol- + -plast] : paneling made of plastic-impregnated paper tubes with a variety of surfaces

hol·op·neus·tic \ˌhäləpˌn(y)üstik, ˌhōl-\ adj [ISV hol- + -pneustic (fr. Gk pneustikos of or for breathing, fr. — assumed — Gk pneustos — verbal of Gk pnein to breathe — + Gk -ikos -ic) — more at SNEEZE] : having all the spiracles or tracheal stigmata open — distinguished from apneustic; used of various insects

hol·optic \(')häl, (')hōl+\ adj [hol- + optic] of a two-winged fly : having the compound eyes contiguous in front — compare DICHOPTIC

¹hol·op·tych·i·an \ˌhäləpˌtikēən, ˌhōl-\ adj [NL Holoptychius + E -an (adj. suffix)] : ¹HOLOPTYCHIID

²holoptychian \"\ n -s [NL Holoptychius + E -an (n. suffix)] : ²HOLOPTYCHIID

¹hol·op·tych·i·id \-ēəd\ adj [NL Holoptychiidae] : of or relating to the Holoptychiidae

²holoptychiid \"\ n -s [NL Holoptychiidae] : a fish of the family Holoptychiidae

hol·op·ty·chi·idae \ˌhäləptə'kīə,dē, ˌhōl-\ n pl, cap [NL, fr. Holoptychius, type genus + -idae] : a family of Devonian fishes (order Rhipidistia) having unossified vertebrae, teeth of complicated structure, and the body covered with imbricating cycloid enameled scales

hol·op·tych·i·us \ˌ≈≈ˈtikēəs\ n, cap [NL, fr. hol- + -ptychius (fr. Gk ptych-, ptyx fold) — more at PTYCH-] : the type genus of Holoptychiidae

holo·rhinal \ˌhälō, ˌhōlō+\ adj [hol- + rhinal] of a bird : having the anterior border of the nasal bones not deeply cleft — opposed to schizorhinal

holo·saprophyte \"+\ n [ISV hol- + saprophyte; orig. formed in G] : a totally saprophytic organism : an obligate saprophyte — compare HEMISAPROPHYTE

holo·sericeous \"+\ adj [hol- + sericeous] : covered with silky hair : entirely sericeous

hol·o·side \'hälə,sīd, 'hōl-\ n -s [ISV hol- + -oside] : a glycoside that yields only glycoses on hydrolysis — compare HETEROSIDE

holo·siderite \ˌhälō, ˌhōlō+\ n [ISV hol- + siderite] : meteoric iron or a meteorite consisting of metallic iron without stony matter

holo·siphonate \"+\ adj [hol- + siphonate] : having a completely tubular siphon — used of the Dibranchia

hol·o·so·ma·ta \ˌhälō'sōməd·ə, ˌhōl-, -'säm-\ n pl, cap [NL, fr. hol- + Gk -somata] in some classifications : a division of ascidians comprising compound ascidians with zooids of which the bodies are not divided into regions and sometimes including the simple ascidians — **hol·o·som·a·tous** \ˌ≈≈ˈsäməd·əs, -ˈsōm-\ adj

hol·o·spondaic \ˌhälō, ˌhōlō+\ adj [hol- + spondaic] : made up wholly of spondees

¹ho·los·te·an \hə'lästēən\ or **ho·los·te·ous** \-ēəs\ adj [NL Holostei + E -an or -ous] : of or relating to fishes of the order Holostei

²holostean \"\ n -s : a fish of the order Holostei

ho·los·tei \-ē,ī\ n pl, cap [NL, fr. hol- + -ostei (fr. Gk osteon bone) — more at OSSEOUS] in many classifications : an order of ganoid fishes having a well-developed bony skeleton and approaching teleosts in structure now usu. restricted to the gars (family Lepisosteidae) and various extinct genera (as Lepidotes and Semionotus) but sometimes extended to include the bowfin and related fishes or made a superorder including the teleosts — compare CYCLOGANOIDEI, GINGLYMODI

holo·steric \ˌhälō, ˌhōlō+\ adj [ISV hol- + steric] : wholly solid — used of a barometer (as the aneroid) constructed without the use of liquids

ho·los·te·um \hə'lästēəm\ n, cap [NL, fr. Gk holosteon, a plant, fr. hol- + osteon bone] : a Eurasian genus of plants (family Caryophyllaceae) resembling chickweed and having the flowers in cymes like umbels — see JAGGED CHICKWEED

hol·o·sto·ma·ta \ˌhälō'stōməd·ə, ˌhōl-, -tām-\ n pl, cap [NL, fr. hol- + -stomata] in many classifications : a suborder of Digenea coextensive with the family Strigeidae

hol·o·stom·a·tous \ˌ≈≈ˈstäməd·əs, -tōm-\ adj [hol- + -stomatous] : having the margin of the aperture entire and more or less circular ⟨~ gastropod shells⟩

hol·o·stome \'hälə,stōm, 'hōl-\ adj or n [NL Holostomata] : STRIGEID

ho·los·to·mous \hə'lästəməs\ adj [hol- + -stomous] : HOLOSTOMATOUS

hol·o·sty·lic \ˌhäləˌstīlik, ˌhōl-\ adj [hol- + -stylic] : having the jaws connected directly with the cranium ⟨~ chimaeras⟩ — compare AUTOSTYLIC

holo·symmetric \ˌhälō, ˌhōlō+\ or **holo·symmetrical** \"+\ adj [hol- + symmetric, symmetrical] : HOLOHEDRAL — **holo·symmetry** \"+\ n

holo·systematic \"+\ adj [hol- + systematic] : HOLOHEDRAL

holo·systolic \"+\ adj [ISV hol- + systolic] : relating to an entire systole

holo·thecal \"+\ adj [hol- + thecal] : BOOTED 2

holo·thoracic \"\ adj [hol- + thorac- + -ic] : having the three parts of the thorax closely united ⟨~ insects⟩ — compare SCHIZOTHORACIC

hol·o·thu·ria \ˌhälō'thürēə, ˌhōl-\ n, cap [NL, fr. L, a water polyp, fr. Gk holothourion] **1** : a Linnaean genus containing various rather wormlike aquatic animals (as some gephyreans and holothurians) originally thought to be modified mollusks **2** : a large cosmopolitan genus of holothurians that is the type of the family Holothuriidae and is characterized by the presence of scattered more or less papillate pedicels — compare TREPANG

hol·o·thu·ri·ae \-ē,ē\ [NL, fr. Holothuria] syn of HOLOTHURIOIDEA

¹hol·o·thu·ri·an \ˌ≈≈ˈthürēən\ adj [NL Holothuria + E -an] : belonging to the Holothurioidea

²holothurian \"\ n -s : one of the Holothurioidea : SEA CUCUMBER

hol·o·thu·rid·ea \ˌhälōthə'ridēə, ˌhōl-\ or **hol·o·thu·roi·da** \-'rȯidə\ [NL, fr. Holothuria + -idea or -oida] syn of HOLOTHURIOIDEA

hol·o·thu·ri·idae \-'rīə,dē\ n pl, cap [NL, fr. Holothuria, type genus + -idae] : a large cosmopolitan family (order Aspidochirota) of holothurians that includes all those of economic importance — see HOLOTHURIA

¹hol·o·thu·ri·oid \ˌhälōˌthürē,ȯid, ˌhōl-\ adj [NL Holothurioidea] : ¹HOLOTHURIAN

²holothurioid \"\ n -s [NL Holothurioidea] : ²HOLOTHURIAN

hol·o·thu·ri·oi·dea \ˌ≈≈,≈≈ˈȯidēə\ n pl, cap [NL, fr. Holothuria + -oidea] : a class of echinoderms comprising the sea cucumbers and having a more or less elongate form usu. with well-marked bilateral symmetry and differentiated dorsal and ventral surfaces, a flexible but tough and muscular body with the skeleton reduced to scattered ossicles or spicules, a water-vascular system with radial ambulacral vessels and tube feet for creeping, respiratory trees, Cuvierian organs, and strong branched tentacles about the mouth — compare TREPANG

hol·o·thu·roi·dea \ˌhälōthə'rȯidēə, ˌhōl-\ [NL, irreg. fr. Holothuria + -oidea] syn of HOLOTHURIOIDEA

hol·o·trich \'hälə,trik, 'hōl-\ n -s [NL Holotricha] : a protozoan of the order Holotricha

ho·lot·ri·cha \hə'lä·trəkə\ n pl, cap [NL, fr. hol- + -tricha] : a large order of uniformly ciliated euciliate protozoans without adoral zone, usu. with a cytostome, and with holozoic or saprozoic nutrition — **ho·lot·ri·chal** \-kəl\ or **ho·lot·ri·chous** \-kəs\ adj — **ho·lot·ri·chous·ly** adv

hol·o·trich·i·da \ˌhälō'trikədə, ˌhōl-\ [NL, fr. Holotricha + -ida] syn of HOLOTRICHA

holo·type \'hälə,tīp, 'hōl-\ n [hol- + type] **1** : the single specimen designated by an author as the type of a species or lesser taxon at the time of establishing a group — compare LECTOTYPE **2** : the type of a species or lesser taxon designated at a date later than that of establishing a group or by another person than the author of the taxon — compare NEOTYPE — **holo·typ·ic** \ˌ≈≈ˈtipik\ adj

hol·o·zo·ic \ˌhäləˌzōik, ˌhōl-\ adj [hol- + -zoic] : obtaining food after the manner of most animals by ingesting complex organic matter : HETEROTROPHIC — opposed to holophytic; compare HEMIZOIC

holp now chiefly dial past of HELP

holped now chiefly dial past of HELP

holpen now chiefly dial past part of HELP

hols pl of HOL

hol·stein-friesian \'hōlz,tēn, -l,st- also -tīn or NewEng 'hälə(,)stēn\ or **holstein** n [fr. Holstein, region of NW Germany, its later locality + Friesian] **1** usu cap H&F : a breed of large dairy cattle orig. from northern Holland and Friesland that produce large quantities of comparatively low-fat milk and that are usu. black and white in irregular patches **2** -s often cap H&F : any animal of the Holstein-Friesian breed

¹hol·ster \'hōlztə(r), -l(t)st-\ n -s [D; akin to OE heolstor darkness, cover, ON hulstr case, Goth hulistr veil, OE helan to conceal — more at HELL] **1** : a usu. leather case for a pistol that is often open at the top to facilitate quick withdrawal, that often conforms to the pistol's shape, and that is usu. carried at the belt or under one arm or often at the front of a saddle **2 holsters** pl : housings or standards for a set of rolls in steel manufacturing

²holster \"\ vt **holstered**; **holstered**; **holstering** \-t(ə)riŋ\ **holsters** : to place in a holster

holster stock n : a pistol holster that can be attached to the pistol to form a shoulder stock

holster 1

¹holt \'hōlt\ n -s [ME, fr. OE; akin to OHG holz wood, ON holt, L clades destruction, Gk klados twig — more at GLADIATOR] **1** now dial **a** : a small woods : COPSE **b** : a wooded hill or rise **2** : a planted grove of osiers or willows

²holt \"\ n -s [ME, alter. of ²hold] **1** ²HOLD 3 **2** dial Brit : a den or lair esp. of a burrowing animal (as an otter)

ho·lus-bo·lus \ˌhōləsˈbōləs\ adv [prob. redupl. of bolus] : all at once : ALTOGETHER ⟨gulped it down, holus-bolus⟩ ⟨existing economic system was taken over holus-bolus —A.J.Brewer⟩

¹ho·ly \'hōlē, -li\ adj -ER/-EST [ME holy, hooly, haly, fr. OE hālig; akin to OHG heilag holy, ON heilagr, Goth hailags, OE hāl whole — more at WHOLE] **1 a** : set apart and dedicated to the service or worship of God or a god : HALLOWED, SACRED ⟨~ vessels⟩ ⟨the ~ priesthood⟩ **b** : dedicated to or laying claim to being dedicated to a sacred or selfless purpose ⟨gave money to various ~ causes⟩ **2 a** (1) : perfect in righteousness and divine love : infinitely good : worthy of complete devotion and trust : commanding one's fullest powers of adoration and reverence ⟨the ~ Lord God Almighty⟩ (2) : of or befitting something that is perfect or worthy in this way ⟨a smile of ~ sweetness —George Meredith⟩ **b** : spiritually whole, sound, or perfect : of unimpaired innocence or proved virtue : pure in heart : GODLY, PIOUS — often used in mild oaths ⟨my ~ aunt⟩ **3 a** : venerated because of association with someone or something holy ⟨~ relics⟩ ⟨the ~ cross⟩ **b** of a saint or saintly person : worthy of veneration ⟨~ martyrs⟩ **c** : to be treated with veneration or the utmost respect ⟨to him every action of the campaign was ~⟩ **d** : being awesome, frightening, or beyond belief ⟨the child was a ~ terror⟩ ⟨so frightened he had the ~ horrors⟩ **4** : not capable of being approached with impunity : filled with mysterious, superhuman, and potentially fatal power : dangerously powerful if violated ⟨some words are considered so ~ they must never be spoken aloud —Stuart Chase⟩

²holy \"\ n -ES [ME holi, adj., fr. OE] **1** [trans. of LL sanctus] : a holy place : SANCTUARY **2** obs : SAINT **3** cap : ²GOD 1 ⟨into the presence of the Holy⟩

holy ark n, often cap H&A : ARK 3

holy basil n : a basil (Ocimum sanctum) found in the tropics of the Old World that is extensively naturalized in tropical America and that in India is held sacred to Vishnu

holy bread n [ME holy brede] **1** : bread consecrated in the Eucharist **2** : bread provided for the Communion service **3** : ANTIDORON

holy cats interj — used as an exclamation of surprise, amazement, or bewilderment

holy clover n : SAINFOIN 1

holy communion n, usu cap H&C : COMMUNION 2

holy cow *interj* — used as an exclamation of surprise, amazement, or bewilderment
holy cross day *n, usu cap H&C&D* : HOLY-ROOD DAY 2
holy day *n* [ME *haly day*, fr. OE *hāligdæg* — more at HOLIDAY] **1 :** a day set aside as having special religious significance to be commemorated by religious services, feasting, or fasting; *specif* : HOLY DAY OF OBLIGATION **2** *archaic* : HOLIDAY
holy day of obligation 1 : one of the days on which Roman Catholics are obliged to hear mass and abstain from servile work ⟨Sunday is a common *holy day of obligation*⟩ **2 :** one of the days on which communicants of the Episcopal Church are obliged to take Communion
holy dollar *n* [by alter.] : HOLEY DOLLAR
holy doors *n pl, often cap H&D* : the doors and esp. the central doors in the iconostasis in an Eastern church that separate the bema from the main part of the church — called also *royal doors*
holy family *n, usu cap H&F* : a painting or piece of sculpture in which the infant Jesus and the Virgin are represented attended by sacred personages (as St. Joseph, the infant St. John Baptist, St. Elisabeth, and St. Anna or angels or fathers of the church)
holy father *n, usu cap H&F* : POPE 1a
holy fire *n* [ME *holy fuyre*, trans. of L *sacer ignis*] *archaic* : ERYSIPELAS
holy ghost *n, cap H&G* [ME *holi gost*, fr. OE *hālig gāst*, trans. of LL *spiritus sanctus*, trans. of Gk *pneuma hagion*, trans. of Heb *ruaḥ ha-godesh* holy spirit] : HOLY SPIRIT
holy ghost flower *also* **holy ghost orchid** *or* **holy ghost** *n, usu cap H&G* [so called fr. the resemblance of part of the flower to a dove, a symbol of the Holy Ghost] : DOVEFLOWER
holy grail *n, usu cap H&G* : 2GRAIL
holy grass *n* [so called fr. the custom in northern Europe of strewing it before church doors on saints' days] : any of several sweet-scented grasses of the genus *Hierochloe*; *esp* : SWEET GRASS
holy green *n* : TERRE VERTE 2
holy herb *n* [trans. of LGk *hierobotanē*] **1 :** YERBA SANTA **2 :** HOLY BASIL **3 :** VERVAIN 1
holy innocents' day *n, usu cap H&I&D* : the day of December 28 commemorating the children slain by Herod after he had been told by the Magi of the birth of a king of the Jews
holy joe *n, usu cap H&J, slang* : PARSON, CHAPLAIN
holy jumper *n, usu cap H&J* : JUMPER 1a
holy kiss *n* [trans. of LL *osculum sanctum*, trans. of Gk *philēma hagion*] : KISS OF PEACE
holy lamb *n, usu cap H&L* : AGNUS DEI 1
holy mackerel *interj* — used as an exclamation of surprise or amazement
holy moses *interj* — used as an exclamation of surprise or amazement
holy mysteries *n pl, usu cap H&M* : the liturgy in the Eastern Church
holy of holies [ME *holi of halowes*, trans. of LL *sanctum sanctorum*, trans. of Gk *to hagion tōn hagiōn*, trans. of Heb *qōdesh ha-qŏdāshīm*] **1 a :** the innermost chamber of a Jewish temple **b :** the bema in an Eastern Orthodox church : SANCTUARY **c :** a very sacred place ⟨father's study was always considered the *holy of holies* by the children⟩ **2 :** something considered as if very sacred ⟨defeated that legislative *holy of holies*, a veterans' pension bill —*Newsweek*⟩
holy oil *n* [ME *holi oylle*] **1 :** CHRISM 1a **2 :** olive oil blessed by a bishop or in an Eastern church by a priest — see OIL OF CATECHUMENS, OIL OF THE SICK **3 :** the oil taken from the grave of a saint or in an Eastern church from the lamps at the altar and used for various blessings
holy one *n* **1** *cap H&O* : 2GOD a(1) ⟨the Lord, the *Holy One* of Israel —Isa 10:20 (RSV)⟩ **2** *often cap H&O* : ANGEL ⟨and behold, a watcher, a *holy one*, came down from heaven —Dan 4:13 (RSV)⟩ **3** *cap H&O* : CHRIST 1 ⟨the *Holy One* of God —Mk 1:24 (RSV)⟩
holy order *n, often cap H&O* [ME] **1 :** MAJOR ORDER **2 holy orders** *pl* : ORDINATION **3 :** ORDER 1a(2) — usu. used in pl.
holy people *n, usu cap H&P* : the supernatural beings of the sacred world who in the religion of the Navahos have great power to help or harm humans — contrasted with *Earth People*
holy place *n* **1 :** a place set apart for religious rites; *specif* : the larger chamber of the Jewish tabernacle and temple separated from the holy of holies by a veil **2 :** a place made sacred by association : SHRINE; *specif* : one of various places (as of the birth, death, resurrection, and ascension of Jesus) of religious pilgrimage
holy pole *n* [prob. alter. of *holey pole*; fr. its hollow stems] : ANT TREE
holy roller *n, usu cap H&R* **1 :** one of a minor religious sect in the U. S. and Canada whose meetings are often characterized by frenzied excitement **2 :** one of various religious groups resembling or felt to resemble the Holy Rollers
holy-rood day *n, usu cap H&R&D* [ME *holi rode dei*] **1 :** the 3d day of May on which occurs the feast of the Invention of the Cross **2 :** September 14 — called also *Holy Cross Day*
holy sacrament *n, usu cap H&S* [ME] : SACRAMENT 2
holy saturday *n, usu cap H&S* [ME] : the Saturday immediately preceding the festival of Easter : the vigil of Easter
holy scripture *n, usu cap H&S* [ME] : BIBLE 1, 5
holy scriptures *n pl, usu cap H&S* : BIBLE 1, 5
holy smoke *interj* — used to express surprise or amazement ⟨*holy smoke*! You'd think a man 26 years old . . . would have more sense —E.J.Curran⟩
holy spear *n* : 1LANCE 2c
holy spirit *n, cap H&S* [ME *hooli spirit*, trans. of LL *spiritus sanctus*] : God as present and active in the spiritual experience of men : the third person of the Trinity — called also *Holy Ghost*
1holystone \ˈ==,=\ *n* [*1holy* + *stone*; prob. fr. the fact that seamen likened it to a prayer book or bible] : a soft sandstone used to scrub a ship's decks
2holystone \"\ *vb* : to scrub with a holystone
holy synod *n* : a governing body in an autocephalous church being composed usu. of several bishops representing the whole episcopate of the particular church under the presidency of the primate
holy table *n, usu cap H&T* : the altar or communion table
holy thistle *n* **1 :** BLESSED THISTLE 1 **2 :** MILK THISTLE 1
holy thursday *n, usu cap H&T* [ME, fr. OE *hālig thunresdæg*] **1** ASCENSION DAY **2 :** MAUNDY THURSDAY
holytide \ˈ==,=\ *n* [ME *halitide*, fr. *hali* holy + *tide*] : a time devoted to religion
holy tree *n* : CHINABERRY 2
holy unction *n, often cap H&U* [ME *hooly unctioun*] : a ceremonial in Eastern Orthodox and various Catholic non-Roman churches of anointing with oil the dead or those in imminent danger of dying
holy war *n* **1 :** a war waged for what is regarded as a holy purpose **2 :** JIHAD
holy water *n* [ME, fr. OE *hāligwæter*, fr. *hālig* holy + *wæter* water] : water blessed by a priest and used as a purifying sacramental in church and home
holy-water sprinkler *n* : MORNING STAR 2
holy week *n, usu cap H&W* [ME *hali wuca*] : the week before Easter in which the passion of Christ is commemorated among Christians
holy well *n* : a well or spring venerated often from pagan times for reputed healing properties
holy writ *n* [ME, fr. OE *hālige writu* holy writings] **1** *usu cap H&W* : BIBLE 1 **2 :** a writing that is taken to be as sacred as the Bible ⟨the potpourri of special nostrums . . . became a kind of political *holy writ* —N.E.Long⟩
holy year *n, usu cap H&Y* : a jubilee year
hom- *or* **homo-** *comb form* [L, fr. Gk, fr. *homos* — more at SAME] **1 :** one and the same : similar : alike ⟨*homo*geneous⟩ ⟨*hom*onym⟩ — opposed to *heter-* **2 :** homologous with a (specified) organic compound esp. with a formula containing one carbon and two hydrogen atoms CH_2 more than the compound to whose name the prefix is added ⟨*homo*serine $HOCH_2CH_2CH(NH_2)COOH$⟩ **3 :** from the same species : corresponding in type of structure ⟨*homo*graft⟩ ⟨*homo*lysin⟩
ho·ma \ˈhōmə\ *n* -s [Av *haoma* haoma, plant that is the source of haoma and is conceived as the tree of life — more at SOMA] **1 :** HAOMA **2** *or* **hom** \ˈhōm\ [*hom* fr. Per *hōm*, fr. Av *haoma*] : a stylized tree pattern originating in Mesopotamia as a symbol of the tree of life and used esp. in Persian textiles
1hom·age \ˈ(h)ämij, -mēj\ *n* -s [ME *omage, homage*, fr. OF *omage, hommage*, fr. *om, omme, homme* man, vassal (fr. L *homin-, homo* man) + *-age*; akin to OE *guma* man, OHG *gomo*, ON *gumi*, Goth *guma* man, OPruss *smoy* human being, Toch B *śaumo* human being, L *humus* earth — more at HUMBLE] **1 a :** a feudal solemn public ceremony by which in return for a fief (as a tenancy of land) a man acknowledges himself the man or vassal of a lord and recognizes the rights and duties inherent in this relationship — compare COMMENDATION 4, FEALTY 1, LIEGE **b :** the relationship between a feudal lord and his man **c :** an act done or payment made in meeting the obligations of vassalage **2 :** a body of persons bound under feudal law by homage; *specif* : the body of tenants attending a manorial court or those acting as jury **3 a :** reverential regard : RESPECT, DEFERENCE ⟨the ~ that matter pays to spirit —Clive Bell⟩; *esp* : respect shown by external action : OBEISANCE ⟨then the ~ of . . . peers; and again the air was lively with the trumpets and drums —Hector Bolitho⟩ **b :** flattering attention : TRIBUTE ⟨turned to look at the young woman . . . and permitted himself the ~ of a smile —Guy McCrone⟩ ⟨the present pamphlet is a modest . . . ~ to one of the leading linguists of our times —André Martinet⟩ **syn** see HONOR
2homage \"\ *vt* -ED/-ING/-S [MF *hommager*, fr. *hommage*] : to pay homage to
homage blue *n* : a dark purplish blue that is slightly less strong and very slightly darker than Scotch blue and slightly less strong and very slightly lighter than national flag blue
hom·ag·er \-jə(r)\ *n* -s [ME *omager*, fr. MF *omagier, hommagier*, fr. *omage, hommage* + *-ier* -er] **1 :** one that pays homage **2 :** one who holds land by fief; *specif* : one of the tenants of a manor
homal- *or* **homalo-** *comb form* [NL, fr. Gk, fr. *homalos*; akin to Gk *homos* same — more at SAME] **1 :** flat : even ⟨*homalo*sternal⟩ **2 :** equal ⟨*homalo*graphic⟩
ho·mali·um \hōˈmalēəm, -māl-\ *n, cap* [NL, fr. *homal-* + *-ium*] : a large widely distributed genus of tropical trees (family Flacourtiaceae) including several that yield hard heavy durable timber used for construction or cabinetwork — see ORANGHA
ho·mal·o·do·the·ri·um \hō,malədōˈthirēəm\ *n, cap* [NL, irreg. fr. *homal-* + Gk *odont-, odōn* tooth + NL *-therium* — more at TOOTH] : a genus of extinct So. American Miocene herbivorous mammals (order Notoungulata) the size of a small ox with the teeth comparatively undifferentiated, the 5-toed feet ending in heavy blunt claws, and the forefeet adapted for digging
homalographic *var of* HOMOLOGRAPHIC
hom·a·lo·no·tus \,häməloˈnōdəs\ *n, cap* [NL, fr. *homal-* + *-notus*] : a genus of Silurian and Devonian trilobites having long indistinctly 3-lobed bodies
1hom·a·lop·sid \,häməˈläpsəd\ *adj* [NL *Homalopsidae*] : of or relating to the Homalopsidae
2homalopsid \"\ *n* -s : a snake of the family Homalopsidae
hom·a·lop·si·dae \,==ˈsə,dē\ *n pl, cap* [NL, fr. *Homalopsis*, type genus (fr. *homal-* + *-opsis*) + *-idae*] : a family of venomous opisthoglyphous water snakes of southeastern Asia and northern Australia that are often included as a subfamily in the family Colubridae
ho·man's sign \ˈhōmənz-\ *n, usu cap H* [after John Homans †1954 Am. surgeon] : pain in the calf of the leg or dorsiflexion of the foot with leg extended diagnostic of thrombosis in the deep veins of the area
ho·mar·i·dae \hōˈmarə,dē\ *n pl, cap* [NL, fr. *Homarus*, type genus + *-idae*] : a family of decapod crustaceans (tribe Astacura) comprising the large-clawed lobsters
ho·ma·rus \ˈhämərəs\ *n, cap* [NL, fr. F *homard* lobster, fr. MF, of Scand origin; akin to ON *humarr* lobster — more at CAMBARUS] : a genus of decapod crustaceans including the common lobsters of Europe and No. America and the little Cape lobster (*H. capensis*) of southern Africa and with the related genus *Nephrops* constituting a family (Homaridae or Nephropsidae)
hom·atom·ic \ˌhōm, ¦häm+\ *adj* [*hom-* + *atomic*] : consisting of like atoms
hom·atro·pine \(ˈ)hōm, (ˈ)häm+\ *n* [ISV *hom-* + *atropine*] : a poisonous crystalline ester $C_{16}H_{21}NO_3$ of tropine and mandelic acid used (as in the form of its hydrobromide) for dilating the pupil of the eye
hom·axial \(ˈ)hōm, (ˈ)häm+\ *or* **hom·ax·o·ni·al** \¦=ˌak-ˈsōnēəl\ *also* **hom·ax·on·ic** \-ˈsänik\ *adj* [*hom-* + *axial* or *-axonial, -axonic* (fr. Gk *axon-, axōn* axle, axis + E *-ial* or *-ic*) — more at AXIS] *biol* : having all the axes equal
1hombre *var of* OMBRE
2hom·bre \ˈämbrē, ˈəm-, -m(,)brā\ *n* -s [Sp, man, fr. L *homin-, homo* — more at HOMAGE] : GUY ⟨that conceited ~ . . . will be riding in here —Zane Grey⟩ ⟨bad ~s held up the stagecoach⟩
hom·burg \ˈhäm,bərg, -bȯg,-bəig *also* -bu̇rg *or* -bu̇əg\ *n* -s [fr. *Homburg*, town near Wiesbaden, Germany, where such hats were first made] *often cap* : a man's hat of smooth-finished felt with a stiff curled ribbon-bound brim and a high tapered crown creased lengthwise

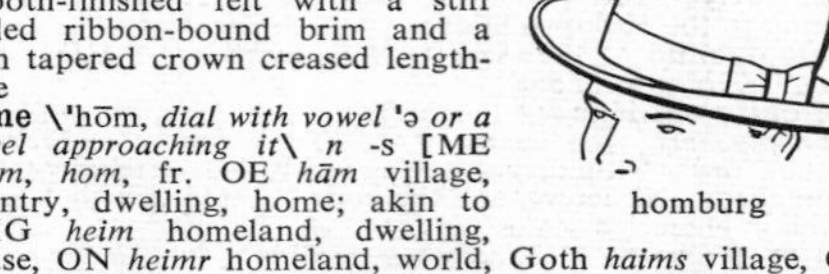

homburg

1home \ˈhōm, *dial with vowel* ˈə *or a vowel approaching it*\ *n* -s [ME *hoom, hom*, fr. OE *hām* village, country, dwelling, home; akin to OHG *heim* homeland, dwelling, house, ON *heimr* homeland, world, Goth *haims* village, Gk *kōmē*, Lith *kaimas* village, OE *hīwan* members of a household, L *civis* citizen, Gk *koiman* to put to sleep — more at CEMETERY] **1 a :** the house and grounds with their appurtenances habitually occupied by a family : one's principal place of residence : DOMICILE **b :** a private dwelling : HOUSE ⟨interpret . . . history through the architecture of its stores and ~s —R.W. Howard⟩ **c :** the refuge or usual haunt of an animal ⟨the pool at the foot of the rapids is . . . the ~ of big trout —Alexander MacDonald⟩ **2 :** one's abode after death ⟨I'm but a stranger here, heaven is my ~ —T.R.Taylor⟩ **3 a :** the social unit formed by a family living together in one dwelling ⟨a man establishes a ~ and makes use of a specific piece of land —P.E. James⟩ **b :** the family environment to which one is emotionally attached : focus of domestic affections ⟨~ is where the heart is⟩ **4 a :** a familiar or suitable setting : congenial environment ⟨finds no spiritual ~ in the gang —John Brooks⟩ ⟨the theater would have been the proper ~ for his characters and plots —L.O.Coxe⟩ **b :** normal environment : HABITAT ⟨California is the ~ of the redwood⟩ ⟨the ~ of petroleum is in sedimentary rocks —A.M.Bateman⟩ **c :** center of cultivation : FOCAL POINT ⟨concept of a university as the ~ of learning —J.B. Conant⟩ **5 a :** the country or place of origin ⟨Britain is the ~ of railroads —Richard Joseph⟩ ⟨in the ~ of the direct primary —F.L.Paxson⟩; *specif* : MOTHER COUNTRY ⟨people . . . from the old ~s moved into the same pursuits because they had brought across similar skills —Oscar Handlin⟩ **b :** center or base of operations : LOCATION, HEADQUARTERS ⟨the amphitheater . . . will be the ~ of one of two festival companies —E.B.Radcliffe⟩ ⟨the four largest national broadcasting networks . . . have their ~ in the city —*Amer. Guide Series: N. Y.*⟩ ⟨the pilot . . . heads for ~ —*Newsweek*⟩ **6 :** an establishment taking the place of a home — see NURSING HOME, TOURIST HOME; compare FUNERAL HOME **7 a :** the objective toward which a player progresses in certain active sports (as baseball) or toward which he moves his pieces in various board games (as backgammon) **b :** an area in which a player is safe from attack **c :** one's original position in a square-dance set **d** (1) : either of two lacrosse positions nearest the opponent's goal (2) : a player assigned to either of these positions — compare INSIDE HOME, OUTSIDE HOME — **at home** \ətˈhōm *sometimes chiefly Brit & NewEng* əˈtōm\ **1 a :** in one's own house or home ⟨generally to be found *at home* in the morning⟩ **b :** ready to receive callers ⟨the newly wed couple will be *at home* after June 15⟩ **2 a :** in the country of origin : on the domestic front ⟨totalitarianism is despotic *at home* and expansionist abroad —George Fischer⟩ **b :** in the mother country ⟨people . . . *at home* and throughout the Commonwealth —Wendell Willkie⟩ **3 a :** in a familiar or congenial relationship : relaxed and comfortable : at ease ⟨a pleasant manner that soon made me feel *at home*⟩ ⟨he is . . . *at home* among the diplomatic and fashionable circles —Peggy Durdin⟩ **b :** in harmony with the surroundings : acclimated to the environment ⟨in the universities where basic research is most *at home* —M.H.Trytten⟩ ⟨*at home* in surf, the young abound in rock pools —J.L.B.Smith⟩ **4 :** on familiar ground : COMPETENT, KNOWLEDGEABLE ⟨*at home* in Italian opera —George Jellinek⟩ ⟨the sciences of biology and psychology in which the author is masterfully *at home*⟩

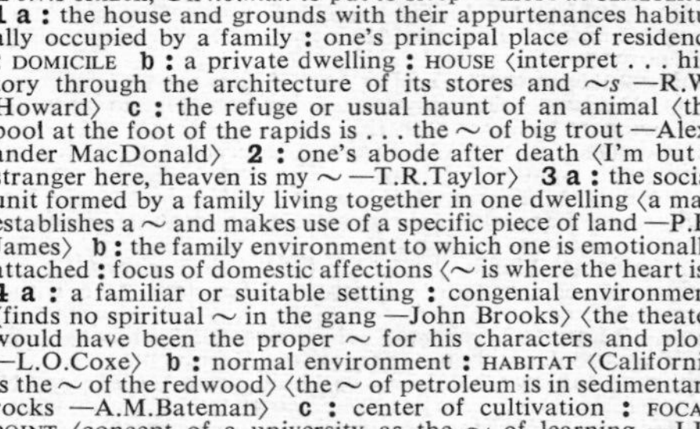

2home \"\ *adv* [ME *hoom, hom, home*, fr. OE *hām*, acc. of *hām*, n.] **1 a :** to or at one's principal place of residence ⟨go ~ on the bus⟩ ⟨stay ~ and practice the piano⟩ **b :** to one's family ⟨writes ~ once a week⟩ **c :** to or at the focus of one's sympathies ⟨has deserted the speculative heights . . . and is back ~ among the sweet and profound bums —Paul Pickrel⟩ **2 :** to or at the country or place of origin ⟨ordering diplomats ~ from various parts of the world⟩ ⟨customs differ from those back ~⟩; *specif* : to the mother country ⟨ordinances passed in the colonies are periodically transmitted ~⟩ **3 a :** to the final or closed position : to the full or ultimate limit ⟨drive a nail ~⟩ ⟨shove ~ a bolt⟩; *specif* : into position for loosing from a bow ⟨draw an arrow ~⟩ **b** (1) : to or toward a ship or its interior ⟨haul an anchor ~⟩ (2) : from the sea onto the shore ⟨the wind is blowing ~⟩ **c :** to an ultimate objective (as the finish line) in a game or sport : to the end of a course ⟨he had 33 on the outward nine and 35 coming ~ —*N. Y. Times*⟩ **d :** to a successful, rewarding, or winning end ⟨if the long shot comes ~ —Richard Scammon⟩ ⟨when my ship comes ~⟩ **4 a :** to the center of consciousness or sensitivity ⟨insights . . . whose truth strikes ~ to any candid and reflective mind J.H.Randall⟩ ⟨the full significance of this discovery was brought ~ to him —J.B.Conant⟩ **b :** to the point of uncovering underlying facts or truths ⟨questions are asked, parried, pressed ~ —R.W.Speaight⟩
3home \"\ *adj* [*1home*] **1 :** of, relating to, or adjacent to a home ⟨~ building⟩ ⟨~ cooking⟩ ⟨doctored my scratches with some of their ~ remedies —Bruce Siberto⟩ ⟨tramped with him over his ~ acres —Witmer Stone⟩ **2 a :** of or relating to the country or place of origin : DOMESTIC, NATIVE ⟨~ industry⟩ ⟨~ city⟩ ⟨~ language⟩; *specif* : of or relating to the mother country ⟨gap between the ~ and the Kenya points of view —Lionel Fleming⟩ **b :** of or relating to the vicinity of the home : LOCAL ⟨after finishing a preparatory course in the ~ academy . . . attended Yale College —F.L.Riley⟩ **c :** of or relating to a headquarters or base of operations ⟨~ territory⟩ esp. of an athletic team ⟨will close their ~ season today —*N.Y.Times*⟩ **3 a :** reaching the mark physically or emotionally : well-aimed and effective ⟨dispatched the bull with a dexterous ~ thrust⟩ ⟨this was a very ~ question —A.R. Smith⟩ **b :** being in proximity to or constituting the objective in a game or sport ⟨in Saturday's race he was forced . . . wide at the ~ turn —*Sydney (Australia) Bull.*⟩ ⟨the counter is moved around the board and up the path to the ~ space⟩ **4 :** ORIGINAL, NORMAL — used of the position of a machine or its parts ⟨the cylinder travels past the ~ position, and is then pushed back . . . against a catch —John Southward⟩
4home \"\ *vb* -ED/-ING/-S [*1home*] *vi* **1 a :** to go or return home ⟨a plane ~s to its carrier⟩ ⟨when school is out a boy ~s to his dog and his marbles⟩; *specif, of an animal* : to return accurately to its home or natal area from a distance ⟨a pigeon ~s to its loft⟩ ⟨a salmon ~s to the stream in which it was spawned⟩ **b :** to move toward an objective by following a beam or landmark — usu. used with *on* or *in* ⟨picked up a radio beam and *homed* on it toward the fiord —Sloan Wilson⟩ ⟨mariners . . . sought the dark spires of Oakland's redwoods to ~ on —J.W.Noble⟩ ⟨with one engine out of action, the aircraft turned back and *homed* in on the . . . radio beacon —*U.N.Bull.*⟩ **c :** to become guided to a target by an emanation from it — usu. used with *on* or *in* ⟨the new long-range electric torpedo . . . ~s on the noise of the target ship's propellers —*N.Y.Times*⟩ ⟨keep the missile *homing* in on the source of heat —*Newsweek*⟩ **2 :** to have a home or headquarters ⟨several fine publishers have *homed* in that marvelous city —H.G.Merriam⟩ **~** *vt* **1 :** to send to or provide with a home ⟨radar installations . . . *homed* friendly aircraft to land bases —*Crowsnest*⟩ ⟨hidden pools and much wider creeks each of which *homed* its cranes —I.L.Idriess⟩ **2 :** to teach (a pigeon) to return to a loft
home- *or* **homeo-** *or* **homoe-** *or* **homoeo-** *also* **homoi-** *or* **homoio-** *comb form* [L & Gk; L *homoeo-*, fr. Gk *homoi-, homoio-*, fr. *homoios*, fr. *homos* — more at SAME] : like : similar ⟨*homeo*pathy⟩ ⟨*homoeo*graphy⟩ ⟨*homoio*thermic⟩
home-and-home \¦==¦=\ *adj* : taking place alternately on the home grounds of competing teams or participants engaged in successive contests or contests related by being on the same schedule ⟨*home-and-home* series⟩
home base *n* **1 :** HOME PLATE **2 :** HOME 5b **3 :** HOME 7a
homebody \ˈ=,==\ *n* : one whose life centers around the home and its activities : STAY-AT-HOME ⟨he and his wife are *homebodies*: they love to read and listen to records —*Time*⟩
homeborn \ˈ=,=\ *adj* : home produced : INDIGENOUS ⟨~ hockey players breaking up the Canadian monopoly⟩
1homebound \ˈ=,=\ *adj* [*1home* + *4bound*] : confined to the home ⟨~ invalid⟩
2homebound \ˈ=¦=\ *adj* [*1home* + *1bound*] : going homeward ⟨~ traveler⟩ ⟨became eligible for redeployment and were shipped to ~ outfits —W.J.Statoff⟩
homebred \ˈ=¦=\ *adj* **1 :** HOMEBORN **2** *archaic* : having little experience outside the home : UNSOPHISTICATED
home brew *n* **1 :** an alcoholic beverage made at home or with homemade equipment usu. by trial-and-error methods **2 :** something formulated at home ⟨puritanism in rural England was never a *home brew*; it was always imported from the town —H.J.Massingham⟩
home car *n* : a freight car on the tracks of the railroad line to which it belongs — contrasted with *foreign car*
homecoming \ˈ=¦==\ *n* -s [ME *homcomyng*, fr. *hom* home + *comyng* coming] **1 :** a return to or arrival at one's home ⟨take off for Lisbon on his last ~ —Henry La Cossitt⟩ ⟨dramatic moment of the bride's ~ —Sinclair Lewis⟩ **2 a :** the return of a group of people to a place formerly frequented or regarded as home ⟨a holiday celebrating the ~ of . . . illustrious natives —Thomas Sugrue⟩ **b :** an occasion for or celebration of such a return ⟨traveled halfway across the continent to be present at his college ~⟩
homecraft \ˈ=,=\ *n* : the household arts (as cooking); *esp* : handcrafts (as weaving) that may be practiced at home
home demonstration *n* : a demonstration of a new or useful method of performing a household task; *specif* : a demonstration given to women in rural areas by an agent of a government extension service
home economics *n pl but usu sing in constr* : the theory and practice of homemaking; *specif* : a field of study and research forming part of an academic curriculum of formal subjects and practical skills (as in nutrition, clothing, child care, home furnishing and decoration, household accounts, family and community relationships) necessary for good home management and family life
home economist *n* : a specialist in home economics
home edition *n* : CITY EDITION
home factor *n* : DOMESTIC FACTOR
homefelt \ˈ=,=\ *adj, archaic* : felt in one's own breast : INWARD, PRIVATE
home folks *n pl* : the people of one's home locality; *esp* : the members of one's immediate family
home freezer *n* : FREEZER 1d(2)
home fried potatoes *n pl* : COTTAGE FRIED POTATOES
home front *n* : a sphere of civilian activity directly or indirectly supporting the armed forces of a nation at war by production and supply of war materiel, civilian defense, and the preservation of public order and morale ⟨in somber contrast to the tinsel prosperity of the *home front* —Oscar Handlin⟩
homegrown \ˈ=¦=\ *adj* **1 :** grown or produced at home or in the vicinity of the home : NATIVE, LOCAL ⟨~ corn⟩ ⟨~ bacon⟩ ⟨smoked bad ~ cigarettes —Upton Sinclair⟩ ⟨put up with ~ amateur talkers during most of the season —H.W. Wind⟩ **2 :** produced or located in or characteristic of the

home country or place of origin : DOMESTIC, INDIGENOUS ⟨~ politician⟩ ⟨~ literature⟩ ⟨~ industry⟩ ⟨a delightful mixture of ~ raffishness and imported elegance —Peggy Durdin⟩

home guard *n* : a force organized often on a volunteer basis for local defense or home protection esp. when the regular army is in a combat area — compare HOME RESERVE

home guardsman *n, pl* **home guardsmen** : a member of a home guard

home industry *n* : a gainful employment carried on in the home

homekeeping \ˈ=,==\ *adj* : STAY-AT-HOME

home key *n* : one of the eight keys for the characters *asdf* and *jkl;* on which the fingers normally rest in starting position for touch typing — called also *guide key*

home·land \ˈhōm,land, -aa(ə)nd *also* -ˌlənd\ *n* **1** : country of origin : native land ⟨represents his ~ in international competition⟩; *specif* : MOTHER COUNTRY ⟨urged to . . . support the ~ — although many of them never had been citizens —Oscar Handlin⟩ **2** : chief place of residence : region in which one's home is located ⟨appetizing dishes from her ~, the Pennsylvania Dutch country —V.O.Williams⟩

home·less \-ˌləs\ *adj* : having no home or permanent place of residence ⟨the ~, unhappy, uprooted look of a displaced person —John Mason Brown⟩ — **home·less·ly** *adv*

home·less·ness *n* -ES : the quality or state of being homeless

homelife \ˈ=,=\ *n* : the domestic routine or way of living ⟨television will change the ~ of America —L.A.Appley⟩

homelike \ˈ=,=\ *adj* : having the qualities associated with family living : simple and wholesome : INVITING ⟨a ~ meal⟩ ⟨the hotel tries to create a ~ atmosphere⟩ — **home·like·ness** *n*

home·li·ness \ˈhōmlēnəs, -lin-\ *n* -ES [ME *hoomlynesse*, fr. *hoomly* homely + *-nesse* -ness] : the quality or state of being homely: **a** : COZINESS, INTIMACY **b** : lack of elegance, beauty, or refinement **c** : SIMPLICITY ⟨voters attracted by his ~ of speech⟩

1**home·ly** \-lē,-li\ *adj* -ER/-EST [ME *hoomly, homly*, fr. *hoom, hom* home + *-ly* (adj. suffix) — more at HOME] **1** : HOMEY **2 a** : established on a friendly footing : INTIMATE — often used with *with* ⟨asked them to . . . dinner at our house and they came and were ~ with us —*Times Lit. Supp.*⟩ **b** : frequently encountered : COMMONPLACE, FAMILIAR ⟨translates the issue into ~ terms and makes the point beyond all doubt —Robert Bendiner⟩ ⟨an English garden full of the old ~ plants —David Ewen⟩ **3** : of a sympathetic character : KINDLY ⟨nature, the ~ nurse . . . has her own ways of comforting —G.G.Coulton⟩ **4 a** : natural and unaffected : SIMPLE ⟨~ courtesy⟩ ⟨a pastorale written in ~ muted prose about life on a farm —*New Yorker*⟩ **b** : free from ornament or complexity : PLAIN ⟨~ food⟩ ⟨shrines that are simple, quaint, ~ and common —J.C.Powys⟩ ⟨so many bizarre forms of dinosaur that these are almost ~ by comparison —W.E. Swinton⟩ **c** : free from ambiguity : DIRECT ⟨~ vigor of expression⟩ **d** : lacking in elegance or sophistication ⟨a ~ audience drawn from the surrounding farms⟩ **5** : lacking in physical beauty or proportion : plain-featured : UNATTRACTIVE ⟨an awkward, lanky giant whose ~ countenance was surmounted by a shock of rough black hair —Allan Nevins & H.S.Commager⟩ ⟨make possible retirement of at least two or three of the buildings . . . downright ~ to behold —B.F.Wright⟩ **syn** see PLAIN

2**homely** *adv* [ME *hoomly, homly*, fr. *hoom, hom* + *-ly* (adv. suffix)] *obs* : in a homely way : FAMILIARLY, KINDLY : RUDELY

home·lyn \ˈhōmlən, ˈhäm-\ *also* **homelyn ray** *n* -S [origin unknown] : a European ray (*Raja maculata*)

homemade \ˈhōˈmād *also* -ōmˈm-\ *adj* **1 a** : made or prepared in the home or on the premises ⟨~ bread⟩ ⟨~ skis⟩ **b** : constructed, produced, or acquired by one's own efforts ⟨~ jalopy⟩ ⟨used ~ apparatus in his experiments⟩ ⟨this obviously ~ memoir —*New Yorker*⟩ ⟨a major with . . . a ~ education —Mari Sandoz⟩ **2** : of domestic origin or manufacture : NATIVE ⟨~ Saturday Reviews and Yankee Athenaeums —H.L.Mencken⟩ ⟨~ typewriters⟩

homemaker \ˈ=,==\ *n* **1** : one that makes a home : one whose occupation is household and family management — usu. used of a wife and mother as distinguished from a paid housekeeper **2** : a welfare worker placed by a social agency to take care of a family during the absence or illness of the mother

homemaking \ˈ=,==\ *n* : the creation and maintenance of a wholesome family environment — compare HOME ECONOMICS

home mission *n* : a religious mission conducted within the nation or national territories of the sponsoring church or organization — called also *national mission;* compare FOREIGN MISSION

home missionary *n* : a missionary appointed to a home mission

homeo- — see HOME-

ho·meo·blas·tic \ˌhōmēōˈblastik, ˌhäm-\ *adj* [ISV *home-* + *-blastic;* orig. formed as G *homöoblastisch*] : having a texture corresponding to the equigranular in igneous rock and grains of approximately equal size — used of metamorphic rock

ho·meo·chromatic \ˌ=mē(ˌ)ō+\ *adj* [*home-* + *chromatic*] : of similar color

ho·me·och·ro·nous \ˌhōmēˈäkrənəs, ˌhäm-\ *adj* [*home-* + *-chronous*] : recurring at the same period of life in succeeding generations — used of organs, traits, or other characters; compare HETEROCHRONISM 1

ho·meo·crystalline \ˌhōmē(ˌ)ō, ˌhäm-+\ *adj* [ISV *home-* + *crystalline;* orig. formed as G *homöokrystallinisch*] : having the crystals of the constituent minerals equally developed : GRANITIC

home office *n* : principal business location or base of operations : HEADQUARTERS ⟨the branch manager had a telegram from the *home office* informing him of price changes⟩ ⟨the diplomat cables the *home office* for instructions⟩

ho·me·ol·o·gy \ˌhōmēˈäləjē, ˌhäm-\ *n* -ES [*home-* + *-logy*] : SIMILARITY, LIKENESS

ho·meo·morph \ˈ=mēə,mȯrf\ *n* -S [ISV *home-* + *-morph*] : an individual bearing a superficial resemblance to another; *specif* : a crystalline substance exhibiting homeomorphism

ho·meo·mor·phic \ˌ===ˈmȯrfik\ *adj* [*home-* + *-morphic*] **1** : characterized by homeomorphism; *specif* : topologically equivalent — used of geometric figures **2** : HOMOMORPHIC

ho·meo·mor·phism \-ˌfizəm\ *n* -S [ISV *homeomorphous* + *-ism*] **1** : a near similarity of crystalline forms between unlike chemical compounds — compare HETEROMORPHISM 2 **2** : topological equivalence between two geometric figures in which each can be transformed into the other by a continuous deformation

ho·meo·mor·phous \-ˌfəs\ *adj* [Gk *homoiomorphos* of like form, fr. *homoio-* home- + *-morphos* -morphous] **1** : manifesting homeomorphism **2** : HOMOMORPHOUS

ho·meo·mor·phy \ˈ===,=fē\ *n* -ES [*home-* + *-morphy*] : HOMOMORPHY

ho·meo·path \-ˌpath\ *n* -S [G *homöopath*, fr. *homöo-* home- + *-path*] : a believer in or practitioner of homeopathy

ho·meo·path·ic \ˌ===ˈpathik\ *adj* [G *homöopathisch*, fr. *homöo-* home- + *-pathisch* -pathic] **1** : of or relating to the belief in or practice of homeopathy ⟨~ remedy⟩ **2** : of a diluted or analogous nature ⟨a ~ abolitionist, intellectually persuaded rather than emotionally —W.A.White⟩ — **ho·meo·path·i·cal·ly** \-thək(ə)lē\ *adv*

homeopathic magic *n* : IMITATIVE MAGIC

ho·me·op·a·thy \ˌhōmēˈäpəthē, ˌhäm-\ *n* -ES [G *homöopathie*, fr. *homöo-* home- + *-pathie* -pathy] : a system of medical practice that treats a disease by the administration of minute doses of a remedy that would in healthy persons produce symptoms of the disease treated — compare ALLOPATHY

ho·meo·pla·sia \ˌ=mēōˈplāzh(ē)ə\ *n* -S [NL, fr. *home-* + *-plasia*] : a growth of tissue similar to normal tissue

ho·meo·plas·tic \ˌ===ˈplastik\ *adj* [*home-* + *-plastic*] : formed by or related to homeoplasia

homeosis *var of* HOMOEOSIS

ho·me·osmotic \ˌhōmē, ˌhämē+\ *adj* [*home-* + *osmotic*] : having a relatively constant bodily osmotic pressure that is maintained independent of the osmotic pressure of the external environment — compare POIKILOSMOTIC

ho·meosta·sis \ˌhōmēōˈstāsəs, ˌhäm-, -ˈstasəs; -mēˈästəsəs\ *n* -ES [NL, fr. *home-* + *-stasis*] **1** : a tendency toward maintenance of a relatively stable internal environment in the bodies of higher animals through a series of interacting physiological processes (as the maintenance of a fairly constant degree of body heat in the face of widely varying external temperatures) **2** : a tendency toward maintenance of a relatively stable psychological condition of the individual with respect to contending drives, motivations, and other psychodynamic forces **3** : a tendency toward maintenance of relatively stable social conditions among groups with respect to various factors (as food supply and population among animals) and to competing tendencies and powers within the body politic, to society, or to culture among men

ho·meo·stat·ic \ˌ=mēōˈstad·ik\ *adj* [*home-* + *-static*] : related to or characterized by homeostasis

homeothermic *var of* HOMOIOTHERMIC

homeotic *var of* HOMOEOTIC

ho·meo·transplant \ˌhōmē(ˌ)ō, ˌhäm-+\ *or* **ho·moio·trans·plant** \hōˌmȯiō+\ *n* [*home-* + *transplant*] : HOMOGRAFT

1**ho·meo·type** \ˈhōmēə, ˈhäm+,-\ *n* [*home-* + *type*] : a biological specimen that has been carefully compared with and identified with an original or primary type

2**homeotype** \"\ *adj* : HOMEOTYPIC

ho·meo·typic *also* **ho·meo·typical** \ˌ===+\ *adj* [*home-* + *typic, typical*] : being or relating to the second or equational meiotic division — compare HETEROTYPIC, MEIOSIS

homeowner \ˈ=,==\ *n* : one that owns a home

ho·meo·zo·ic \ˌhōmēōˈzōik, ˌhäm-\ *adj* [ISV *home-* + *-zoic*] : of, relating to, or being one or more biogeographic regions throughout which the forms of life are the same or similar

homeplace \ˈ=,=\ *n* : a family home or its location

home plate *n* : a 5-sided slab of whitened rubber that is 17 inches wide and anchored flush with the ground at the apex of the baseball diamond, that determines the width of the strike zone, and that must be touched by a base runner in order to score a run — called also *home, home base, platter, rubber;* see BASEBALL illustration

home port *n* **1** : the port from which a ship hails or from which it is documented **2 a** : the port from which a man-of-war normally operates **b** : the dockyard in which a ship in the British navy is commissioned and to which she returns for refits

home position *n* : HOME 7c

1**ho·mer** \ˈhōmə(r)\ *also* **cho·mer** \ˈkō-\ *n* -S [Heb *ḥōmer*] : an ancient Hebrew unit of capacity for dry or liquid measure equal to about 10½ or in later times 11½ bushels or about 100 gallons

2**hom·er** \ˈhōmə(r)\ *n* -S [1*home* + *-er*] **1** : HOMING PIGEON **2 a** : HOME RUN **b** *slang* : a sports official who favors the home team

3**homer** \"\ *vi* **homered; homered; homering** \-m(ə)riŋ\ **homers** : to hit a home run

home rails *n pl* : shares of domestic railroads offered on the London Stock Exchange

home range *n* : the area to which an animal confines his activities — compare TERRITORY

home reserve *n* : a part of the organized armed forces of a country whose members live at home, carry on their usual vocations, and except for occasional calls for drill or instruction are liable to call only in emergency — called also *militia, national guard, territorial reserve;* compare HOME GUARD

ho·me·ria \hōˈmirēə\ *n, cap* [NL, fr. *Homer*, Greek poet + NL *-ia*] : a genus of southern African herbs (family Iridaceae) that resemble tulips and are sometimes poisonous to cattle — see CAPE TULIP

ho·me·ri·an \hōˈmirēən, -mēr-\ *adj, usu cap* [*Homer* + E *-ian*] : HOMERIC

ho·mer·ic \hōˈmerik, -rēk\ *adj, usu cap* [L *Homericus*, fr. Gk *Homērikos*, fr. *Homēros* Homer, traditional Greek epic poet who prob. lived *ab* the 8th cent. B.C. + Gk *-ikos* -ic] **1** : of or relating to the Greek poet Homer, his age, or his writings ⟨classical *Homeric* conception of death —Alfred Einstein⟩ **2** : of epic proportions : HEROIC, GARGANTUAN ⟨*Homeric* feats of reporting —Stanley Walker⟩ ⟨~ laughter⟩ — **ho·mer·i·cal·ly** \-rək(ə)lē, -rēk-, -li\ *adv, often cap*

ho·mer·i·can \-rəkən\ *adj, usu cap* [L *Homericus* + E *-an*] *archaic* : HOMERIC

homeric simile *n, usu cap H* : EPIC SIMILE

ho·mer·ist \ˈhōmərəst\ *n* -S *usu cap* : a specialist in Homer and his epics

home road *n* : the railroad owning or leasing a car in freight-car interchange

ho·mer·ol·o·gist \ˌhōməˈräləjəst\ *n* -S *usu cap* : a specialist in Homerology

ho·mer·ol·o·gy \-jē\ *n* -ES *usu cap* [*Homer* + *-o-* + *-logy*] : a study of Homer's poems and of his life and times

homeroom \ˈ=,=\ *n* **1** : a schoolroom where pupils of the same class or grade but often with different academic programs report at the opening of school and meet informally under the guidance of a teacher to conduct class business, plan and organize group activities, and discuss individual and group problems **2** : a group of pupils assigned to the same homeroom

home row *n* : the bank of keys on a typewriter containing the home keys

home rule *n* **1 a** : self-government esp. with regard to local and internal legislation by the inhabitants of a dependent or federated country or territory or colony ⟨split the Liberal party over the issue of *home rule* for Ireland —C.J.Friedrich⟩; *specif, Brit* : dominion status **b** : the political theory or principle of self-government **2 a** : partial municipal autonomy granted to some cities whereby they are authorized to frame their own charters and manage their own affairs within limits set by the state esp. as to taxation, finance, police, and education **b** : limited authority granted by a state to a county esp. with regard to the determination of its organizational structure

home ruler *n* : one that advocates home rule; *specif, often cap H&R* : an advocate or supporter of Irish home-rule policy ⟨emphatically an Irishman . . . and a strong *home ruler* —H.H.Johnston⟩

home run *n* : a hit in baseball that enables the batter to make a complete circuit of the bases and score a run

homes *pl of* HOME, *pres 3d sing of* HOME

home scrap *n* : steel scrap that is utilized within the plant where it originates

homeseeker \ˈ=,==\ *n* : one that seeks a home; *esp* : a pioneer in search of land on which to settle ⟨excitement caused by the advent of ~*s* from the eastern states —*Atlantic*⟩

homesick \ˈ=,=\ *adj* [back-formation fr. *homesickness*] **1** : longing for home and family while absent from them ⟨the boy was ~ his first week at camp⟩ **2** : yearning for a familiar or sympathetic environment ⟨that stretch of blue water was the one thing he was ~ for —Willa Cather⟩ ⟨~ for their comparatively carefree nineteenth-century past —A.J.Toynbee⟩

home·sick·ness *n* -ES [trans. of G *heimweh*] : the quality or state of being homesick : NOSTALGIA

home signal *n* : a railroad signal placed at the beginning of a block to indicate whether or not the block is clear — compare DISTANT SIGNAL

homesite \ˈ=,=\ *n* **1** : a location suitable for a home ⟨divided the lakefront into ~*s*⟩ **2** : the location of a home ⟨stayed in their bombed-out ~*s* —M.W.Childs⟩

1**homespun** \ˈ=,=\ *adj* [1*home* + *spun*] **1 a** : spun or made at or as if at home ⟨~ cloth⟩ ⟨turn out woven and knitted goods on hand machines that preserve the ~ quality —J.M.Mead⟩ **b** : made of homespun or of a fabric resembling homespun ⟨yeomanry . . . turned out in their working clothes and ~ country garbs —Washington Irving⟩ ⟨other popular cotton suiting choices include . . . ~ types that have weave interest —*Women's Wear Daily*⟩ **2 a** : of or relating to the common people : PLEBEIAN, UNSOPHISTICATED ⟨~ tastes⟩ ⟨~ virtues⟩ ⟨both still assume the air of ~ country boys —T.H.White b.1915⟩ : FOLKSY ⟨oozed with idiosyncrasy, naïveté and ~ humor —E.S.Turner⟩ ⟨prose which varies from the movingly lyrical to the designedly ~ —Clifton Fadiman⟩ **b** : of unaffected simplicity : UNPRETENTIOUS ⟨dresses up his thoughts in very plain ~ garments —William Clark⟩ ⟨~, kindly, shrewd men whose strength resided in their neighborliness —Norman Cousins⟩ **c** : plain and direct : PRACTICAL, STRAIGHTFORWARD ⟨will make a good ~ wife —Thomas Hardy⟩ ⟨managed the affairs of local government with the same ~ skill that went to their farming —V.L.Parrington⟩ ⟨circumstances which brought forth . . . a ~ nationalism —A.G.Mazour⟩

2**homespun** \"\ *n* -S **1 a** : a loosely woven usu. woolen or linen fabric handloomed in the home from uneven hand-spun yarns **b** : a machine-made tweedy material of a plain weave and spongy texture usu. made from irregular woolen, cotton, rayon, or linen yarns and used for outer garments and upholstery **2** : a character or utterance possessing the rustic simplicity of homespun ⟨instead of the silken splendor of the upper middle classes he gives us the ~ of the poor —Grace Frank⟩

1**home·stead** \ˈhōmz,ted, -m,st- *also* -ˌtəd *or* -ˌstəd\ *n* [1*home* + *stead*] **1 a** : the home and land of a family; *esp* : ancestral home ⟨coming into possession . . . of the old Abbot ~ "Three Beeches" —Witmer Stone⟩ **b** : a private residence : HOUSE ⟨a seventeenth-century farm ~ with thatched roof —A.N. Whitehead⟩ **c** : the living quarters on a ranch in Australasia ⟨a good station to manage because the ~ is near the middle —Nevil Shute⟩ **2 a** : a tract of land usu. consisting of 160 acres acquired from U.S. public lands by filing a record and living on and cultivating the tract ⟨these fences marked the boundaries of the small ~*s* which had recently been claimed —Agnes M. Cleaveland⟩ **b** : the land and buildings on such a tract occupied as a home for the owner and his family and more or less legally protected in some jurisdictions from the claims of creditors against both the owner and his surviving spouse and minor children — see HOMESTEAD LAW

2**homestead** \"\ *vt* : to acquire or occupy as a homestead under a homestead law ⟨lacked the experience needed to ~ virgin territory —R.A.Billington⟩ ~ *vi* : to acquire or settle on land under a homestead law ⟨the original settler in the area . . . has lived there since he ~*ed* back in 1902 —Byron Fish⟩

home·stead·er \-də(r)\ *n* -S **1** : one who seeks or establishes a homestead under a homestead law ⟨announced that the lands ceded by the Cherokee tribes . . . would be thrown open to ~*s* —*Amer. Mercury*⟩ **2** : the possessor of a homestead

homestead law *n* **1** : a law conferring special privileges or exemptions upon owners of homesteads; *esp* : a law exempting a homestead from attachment or sale under execution for general debts **2** : any of several legislative acts authorizing the sale of public lands to settlers

homestead lease *or* **homestead selection** *n, Austral* : a leasehold tenure; *esp* : one created by the Crown Land Acts of 1884 and subsequent legislation

home·ster \ˈhōmztə(r), -mst-\ *n* -S [1*home* + *-ster*] *Brit* **1** : a member of the home team in an athletic contest **2** : HOMEBODY

homestretch \ˈ=ˈ=\ *n* **1** : the part of a racecourse between the last curve and the winning post — compare BACKSTRETCH **2** : the final stage (as of a project) ⟨reached the ~ on his thesis with two weeks to spare⟩

home study *n* : a course of instruction administered by mail and carried on in the student's home — compare CORRESPONDENCE SCHOOL

home table *n* : the side of the inner table in backgammon into which a player moves his stones before bearing off

hometown \ˈ=ˈ=\ *n, often attrib* : the city or town of one's birth or principal residence ⟨his ~ gave the new champion a rousing welcome⟩

home truth *n* **1** : an unpleasant fact that jars the sensibilities ⟨*home truths* demand utterance but not in a scolding voice or a tone edged with arrogance —H.M.Wriston⟩ **2** : a statement of undisputed fact

home visitor *n* : a caseworker who helps children to adjust to school and community life through individual guidance based on information gathered by visits with parents, teachers, and schoolmates

1**home·ward** \ˈhōmwə(r)d\ *or* **home·wards** \-dz\ *adv* [ME *homward, homwards*, fr. OE *hāmweard*, fr. *hām* home + *-weard* -ward — more at HOME] : in the direction of one's house or place of origin : toward home ⟨battling my way ~ one dark night against the wind and rain —L.P.Smith⟩

2**homeward** *adj* : being or going in the direction of home ⟨a few belated ~ figures were hurrying along —Michael Foster⟩

home·ward·ly *adv* : HOMEWARD

homework \ˈ=,=\ *n* **1** : work done at home; *specif* : remunerative employment carried on in the home usu. on a piecework basis ⟨the wife and mother . . . tries to eke out the scanty income by ~ —Mabel Elliott & Francis Merrill⟩ **2 a** : an assignment given to a student to be completed outside of the classroom ⟨hurried to finish his ~ so he could play ball⟩ **b** : preparatory reading or research (as for a discussion) ⟨put in . . . two days on ~ prior to each meeting —Dwight Macdonald⟩

homeworker \ˈ=ˈ==\ *n* : one that carries on remunerative employment in the home ⟨concealed the existence of ~*s* who were not paid proper overtime wages —*Progressive Labor World*⟩

hom·ey *also* **homy** \ˈhōmē, -mi\ *adj* -ER/-EST [1*home* + *-y*] **1** : having an air of comfortable intimacy or domesticity : COZY, FAMILIAR ⟨took a chair by the fire and looked round the ~ room with a sigh of relief —*Strand Mag.*⟩ ⟨just the right size teapot . . . in the regular old brownware, very ~ —*New Yorker*⟩ **2 a** : having an air of simple informality or hospitality usu. associated with home : FRIENDLY, UNPRETENTIOUS ⟨lends a ~ touch —*Vanity Fair*⟩ ⟨private power companies traveling under the ~ alias of "local interests" —Leland Olds⟩ **b** : of a family nature : INTIMATE ⟨like the candidate to answer a few ~ questions designed to elicit the lowdown on his wife and relatives —Claud Cockburn⟩ **c** : FOLKSY ⟨written in the excruciatingly ~ prose that is so often confused with the American vulgate —W.H.Whyte⟩ — **hom·ey·ness** *or* **hom·i·ness** \-mēnəs, -min-\ *n* -ES

homi·ci·dal \ˌhäməˈsīdᵊl *also* ˌhōm-\ *adj* : of, relating to, or having a tendency toward homicide : MURDEROUS — **homi·ci·dal·ly** \-dᵊlē, -dᵊli\ *adv*

homi·cide \ˈhämə,sīd *also* hōm-\ *n* -S [in sense 1, fr. ME, fr. MF, fr. L *homicida*, fr. *homi-* (fr. *homo* human being, man) + *-cida* -cide (killer); in sense 2, fr. ME, fr. MF, fr. L *homicidium*, fr. *homi-* + *-cidium* -cide (killing) — more at HOMAGE] **1** : a person who kills another person : MANSLAYER ⟨the ~ must observe a rigorous taboo —J.G.Frazer⟩ **2 a** : a killing of one human being by another ⟨tabloid headlines about the latest ~⟩; *specif* : a killing of a human being through human agency ⟨charged with drunken driving and vehicle ~⟩ **b** : a squad of detectives that specializes in solving murders ⟨the boys in ~ will get all the details —Thurston Scott⟩

homi·cid·i·ous \ˌ==ˈsidēəs\ *adj* [L *homicidium* + E *-ous*] *archaic* : HOMICIDAL

homi·culture \ˈhämə, ˈhōmə + ˌ-\ *n* [L *homi-* (fr. *homo* man) + E *culture*] : scientific physical improvement of mankind

hom·i·lete \ˈhämə,lēt\ *n* -S [Gk *homilētēs* disciple, scholar, fr, *homilein*] : HOMILIST

hom·i·let·ic \ˌ==ˈled·ik\ *adj* [LL *homileticus*, fr. Gk *homilētikos* affable, social, fr. *homilētos* (verbal of *homilein* to consort with, talk with, address, make a speech) + *-ikos* -ic — more at HOMILY] **1** : of the nature of a homily : resembling a sermon **2** : of or relating to homiletics : HORTATORY

hom·i·let·i·cal \-d·əkəl\ *adj* [in sense 1, fr. Gk *homilētikos* + E *-al;* in sense 2 fr. LL *homileticus* + E *-al*] **1** *obs* : of or relating to friendly companionship : SOCIAL **2** : HOMILETIC — **hom·i·let·i·cal·ly** \-k(ə)lē\ *adv*

hom·i·let·ics \ˌ==ˈled·iks\ *n pl but sing in constr* [Gk *homilētikē* art of conversation, fr. fem. of *homilētikos*] **1** : the art of preaching ⟨have on occasion made ~ a substitute for statecraft —J.M.Blum⟩ **2** : a branch of theology that deals with homilies or sermons ⟨a lecturer in ~⟩

ho·mil·i·ary \häˈmilē,erē\ *n* -ES [ML *homiliarium*, fr. LL *homilia* homily + L *-arium* -ary] : a book of homilies

hom·i·list \ˈhäməlǝst\ *n* -S [*homily* + *-ist*] : one who prepares or delivers a homily

hom·i·lite \-ˌlīt\ *n* -S [G or Sw *homilit*, fr. Gk *homilein* + G or Sw *-it* -ite] : a mineral $(Ca,Fe)_3Al_5B_2Si_2O_{16}$ consisting of a black or blackish brown iron calcium borosilicate

hom·i·lize \-ˌlīz\ *vi* -ED/-ING/-S [*homily* + *-ize*] : to deliver a homily : PREACH

hom·i·ly \ˈhäməlē, -li\ *n* -ES [alter. (influenced by LL *homilia*) of ME *omelie*, fr. MF, fr. LL *homilia*, fr. LGk, fr. Gk, conversation, discourse, fr. *homilein* to consort with, talk with, address, make a speech (fr. *homilos* crowd, assembly) + *-ia* — more at MILITATE] **1** : a discourse on a religious theme esp. delivered to a congregation during a church service

⟨ideas derived from *homilies* and the common teaching of the church —W.P.Ker⟩ **2 :** a lecture or discussion on a moral theme : ADMONITION ⟨the criminal of old was given copious drafts of exhortation and ~ administered . . . by reformers —B.N.Cardozo⟩

homin- or **homini-** *comb form* [L *homin-, homo* — more at HOMAGE] : man : human ⟨*hominine*⟩ ⟨*hominiform*⟩ ⟨*hominisection*⟩

hom·i·nal \ˈhämənᵊl\ *adj* [*homin-* + *-al*] : of, relating to, or constituted by man as a species : HUMAN ⟨the vegetable, animal, and ~ kingdoms⟩

hominess *var of* HOMEYNESS

¹homing *n* -s [fr. gerund of ⁴*home*] **1 a :** an accurate return of an animal to a known place (as a home range) **b :** a tendency to return to a known place as a facet of animal behavior ⟨~ is a well-known characteristic of salmon⟩ ⟨~ is an acquired skill operating through topographical memory —*Biol. Abstracts*⟩ **2 :** navigation toward an objective by maintaining a constant bearing on a radio beam or other point of reference ⟨for ~ a loop antenna located perpendicular to the center line of the aircraft is used —*Aircraft Navigation Manual*⟩

²homing *adj* [fr. pres. part. of ⁴*home*] **1 :** home-returning; *specif* : habitually returning to a known place ⟨shad are ~ fish⟩ **2 :** guiding or being guided to an objective ⟨~ beacon⟩ ⟨an acoustic ~ torpedo which, attracted by the submarine's noise, would follow it down and detonate on contact —R.S.Benson⟩

homing pigeon *n* : a racing pigeon sometimes used for carrying messages and trained to return to its loft from distances up to 500 miles or more by being released at gradually increased distances from home — compare CARRIER PIGEON

¹hom·i·nid *also* **hom·o·nid** \ˈhämənəd, -ˌnid\ *or* **ho·min·i·an** \hōˈminēən\ *n* -s [*hominid* fr. NL *Hominidae; homonid* alter. of *hominid; hominian* fr. NL *Homin-, Homo* + E *-ian*] : one of the Hominidae : a manlike creature : MAN ⟨fossil ~*s* . . . are already quite uniformly assignable to our present genus *Homo* —W.M.Krogman⟩

²hominid \"\ *also* **hominian** \"\ *adj* : of, relating to, or characterizing the Hominidae ⟨regarding man as emerging from a welter of genetically related ~ types —Weston LaBarre⟩

ho·min·i·dae \hōˈminəˌdē\ *n pl, cap* [NL, fr. *Homin-, Homo,* type genus + *-idae*] : a family of mammals (order Primates) to which man and his ancestors belong : a family of animals consisting of mankind — see HOMO, MAN 1b(2), PITHECANTHROPUS

hom·i·nine \ˈhäməˌnīn, -mən\ *adj* [*homin-* + *-ine*] : HUMAN

hom·i·nism \-ˌnizəm\ *n* -s [*homin-* + *-ism*] : pragmatic humanism that regards man as only a highly differentiated animal

hom·i·niv·o·rous \ˌ==ˈniv(ə)rəs\ *adj* [*homin-* + *-vorous*] : man-eating

¹hom·i·noid \ˈhäməˌnȯid\ *adj* [NL *Hominoidea*] **1 :** of, relating to, or characterizing the Hominoidea **2 :** resembling the Hominidae : MANLIKE

²hominoid \"\ *n* -s : one of the Hominoidea : an animal resembling man

hom·i·noi·dea \ˌ==ˈnȯidēə\ *n pl, cap* [NL, fr. *Homin-, Homo* + *-oidea*] **1** *in some classifications* : a major division of Primates segregating *Homo* and related fossil forms from the great apes **2 :** a superfamily of Anthropoidea comprising the great apes and the recent and fossil hominids as distinguished from the lower Old World monkeys — compare CERCOPITHECIDAE

hom·i·ny \ˈhämənē, -ni\ *n* -ES [prob. fr. a word of Algonquian origin whose 1st constituent is unknown and whose 2d constituent is akin to Natick *-minne* small fruit, grain (used in all names given to prepared corn)] : kernels of hulled corn (as white flint corn) with the germ removed and either whole or ground — see HOMINY GRITS; compare ¹GRIT 2a

hominy grits *n pl but sing or pl in constr* : hominy in uniform granular particles

hom·ish \ˈhōmish\ *adj* [¹*home* + *-ish*] : HOMEY — **hom·ish·ness** *n* -ES

hommock *var of* HUMMOCK

¹ho·mo \ˈhō(ˌ)mō\ *n, cap* [NL, fr. L, man, human being — more at HOMAGE] : the genus of man : a genus of mammals consisting of mankind that is the type and sole surviving member of the family Hominidae and is usu. held to include a single recent species (*H. sapiens*) comprising all surviving and various extinct men — see MAN 1b(2)

²homo \"\ *n* -s [by shortening] *slang* : HOMOSEXUAL

homo- *in pronunciations below,* ¦== = ¦hō(ˌ)mō *or* ¦hä(ˌ)mō *or* -ˌmə\ — see HOM-

homo alieni juris \ˈhō(ˌ)mō+\ *n* [L] : a man under the control of another — opposed to *homo sui juris*

homo·basidiomycetes *pronunc at* HOMO- +\ *n pl, cap* [NL, fr. *hom-* + *Basidiomycetes*] : a subclass of Basidiomycetes comprising fungi with nonseptate and nondivided basidia and basidiospores that usu. germinate directly to form a mycelium and including the gill fungi, pore fungi, coral fungi, and bird's-nest fungi and the puffballs and stinkhorns — compare HETEROBASIDIOMYCETES

homo·ba·sid·io·my·cet·i·dae \¦==(ˌ)bəˌsidē(ˌ)ōˌmīˈsed·əˌdē\ *syn of* HOMOBASIDIOMYCETES

homo·basidium \"+\ *n* [NL, fr. *hom-* + *basidium*] : AUTOBASIDIUM

homo·blas·tic \¦==¦blastik\ *adj* [*hom-* + *-blastic*] : having a direct embryonic development : arising from cells of the same kind; *specif* : having the embryo similar in appearance to the adult plant and developing directly from the fertilized seed — **homo·blas·ty** \ˈ==ˌ=tē\ *n* -ES

homocaryon *var of* HOMOKARYON

¹homo·centric *also* **homo·centrical** *pronunc at* HOMO- +\ *adj* [NL *homocentricus,* fr. Gk *homokentros* concentric (fr. *homo-* hom- + *-kentros,* fr. *kentron* center) + L *-icus* -ic — more at CENTER] : having the same center ⟨~ spheres⟩; *specif* : diverging from or converging toward a common center — used of light rays forming a pencil

²homocentric \"\ *adj* [L *homo* man, human being + E *-centric* — more at HOMAGE] : centered on man ⟨the universe is not ~ —Junjiro Takakusu⟩ — **homo·centrically** \"+\ *adv*

homo·cercal *pronunc at* HOMO- +\ *adj* [*hom-* + *-cercal*] **1 :** having the upper and lower lobes approximately symmetrical and the vertebral column ending at or near the middle of the base — used of the tail fin of various fishes (as most teleosts) **2 :** having or relating to a homocercal tail fin — compare ISOCERCAL

homo·charge \"+ˌ-\ *n* [*hom-* + *charge*] : a charge on an electret that is of the same sign as that of the electrode orig. in contact with it — compare HETEROCHARGE

homo·chlamydeous \"+\ *adj* [*hom-* + *chlamydeous*] : having a perianth whose inner and outer series are similar or not differentiated into calyx and corolla ⟨the lily has a typical ~ perianth⟩ — compare ACHLAMYDEAE

homo·chromatic \"+\ *adj* [*hom-* + *chromatic*] **1 :** of or relating to one color **2** *of an afterimage* : having approximately the same hues as an original image — opposed to *heterochromatic*

homo·chromosome \"+\ *n* [*hom-* + *chromosome*] : AUTOSOME

ho·moch·ro·nous \(ˈ)hōˈmäkrənəs, (ˈ)hä-\ *adj* [*hom-* + *-chronous*] : HOMEOCHRONOUS

homo·clime *pronunc at* HOMO- + ˌ-\ *n* [*hom-* + *clime*] : a climatically similar environment; *specif* : a region climatically similar to another specified region ⟨New World ~*s* of certain parts of Australia⟩

homo·cli·nal \¦==¦klīnᵊl\ *adj* : of or relating to a homocline

homo·cline \ˈ==ˌklīn\ *n* -s [*hom-* + *-cline*] : a layer of stratified rock (as one limb of an anticline or syncline) in which the strata dip consistently in one general direction though the angle of dip may vary greatly from place to place — compare MONOCLINE

homo·coe·la \¦==ˈsēlə\ [NL, fr. *hom-* + *-coela* (fr. neut. pl. of *-coelus* -coelous)] *syn of* ASCONOSA

homo·cyclic \¦==+\ *adj* [*hom-* + *cyclic*] : ISOCYCLIC

homo·cysteine \"+\ *n* [*hom-* + *cysteine*] : a crystalline amino acid $HSCH_2CH_2CH(NH_2)COOH$ held to be formed by demethylation of methionine in the animal organism; α-amino-γ-mercapto-butyric acid

homo·cystine \"+\ *n* [*hom-* + *cystine*] : a crystalline amino acid $[-SCH_2CH_2CH(NH_2)COOH]_2$ formed by oxidation of homocysteine

homo·dermic \"+\ *adj* [*hom-* + *dermic*] *biol* : originating from the same germ layer — **homo·der·my** \ˈ==ˌdərmē\ *n* -ES

homo·dont \ˈ==ˌdänt\ *adj* [ISV *hom-* + *-odont*] : having all the teeth similar in form ⟨the porpoise is a ~ animal⟩ — opposed to *heterodont*

ho·mod·ro·mal \hōˈmädrəməl, hä'-\ *adj* [NL *homodromus* + E *-al*] : HOMODROMOUS

ho·mod·ro·mous \-məs\ *or* **homo·drome** \ˈhōməˌdrōm, ˈhäm-\ *adj* [NL *homodromus,* fr. *hom-* + *-dromus* -dromous] : having the genetic spiral following the same direction in both stem and branches — compare HETERODROMOUS

ho·mod·ro·my \hōˈmädrəmē, hä'-\ *n* -ES [ISV *homodromous* + *-y*] : the quality or state of being homodromous

homo·dynamic *pronunc at* HOMO- +\ *adj* [*hom-* + *dynamic*] : producing a continuous succession of generations until interrupted by adverse circumstances (as cold or lack of food) — used of an insect

homo·dyne \ˈ==ˌdīn\ *adj* [*hom-* + *dyne*] : of or relating to the process of detecting a radio wave by the aid of a locally generated current or wave of exactly the same frequency as that of the incoming wave ⟨~ reception⟩ — see ZERO BEAT

homoe- *or* **homoeo-** — see HOME-

ho·moe·an \(ˈ)hō¦mēən, (ˈ)hä¦-, ˈ=ˌmē-\ *or* **ho·moi·an** \(ˈ)=¦mȯi(y)ən\ *n* -s *often cap* [*Homoean* fr. NL *Homoeus* (fr. Gk *homoios* like) + E *-an; Homoian* fr. Gk *homoios* + E *-an* — more at HOME-] : a member of an Arian party holding to the doctrine that the Son is like the Father though not in essence — compare ANOMOEAN, APOLLINARIAN, HOMOIOUSIAN

ho·moe·cious \(ˈ)hō¦mēshəs, (ˈ)hä¦-\ *adj* [*hom-* + Gk *oikia* house + E *-ous* — more at VICINITY] : having the same host during the entire life cycle — used esp. of a beetle parasitic in the nest of an ant — contrasted with *heteroecious;* compare AUTOECIOUS

ho·moe·om·er·al \¦hōmē¦ämərəl, ¦häm-\ *adj* [Gk *homoiomerēs* consisting of equal parts (fr. *homoio-* home- + *-merēs,* fr. *meros* part) + E *-al* — more at MERIT] *prosody* : having like or corresponding parts

ho·moeo·me·ria \hōˌmēəməˈrīə, hä,-, ˌ=ˌmē(ˌ)ōm-, -ˈmirēə\ *n, pl* **homoeomeri·ae** \-rīˌē, -rēˌē\ [L] : HOMOEOMERY — **ho·moeo·me·ri·an** \-rīən, -rēən\ *n* -s — **ho·moeo·me·ri·an·ism** \-əˌnizəm\ *n* -s

ho·moeo·mer·ic \ˌ=¦=¦merik, ¦===¦-, -mir-\ *or* **ho·moeo·mer·i·cal** \-rəkəl\ *adj* [*homoeomery* + *-ic, -ical*] **1 :** of or relating to homoeomery **2 :** consisting of homogeneous parts or particles **3** *usu* **homoeomeric** [Gk *homoiomerēs* + E *-ic*] : HOMOEOMERAL

¹homoe·om·er·ous \¦hōmē¦ämərəs, ˈhäm-\ *adj* [Gk *homoiomerēs* + E *-ous*] **1 :** having the algal cells scattered throughout the thallus ⟨~ lichens⟩ — opposed to *heteromerous* **2** [*homoeomery* + *-ous*] : HOMOEOMERIC 1, 2 **3 :** HOMOEOMERAL

²homoeomerous \"\ *adj* [*home-* + Gk *mēros* thigh + E *-ous*] : having the sciatic artery developed as the main artery of the thigh — used of a bird

ho·moe·om·ery \ˌ=ˈ=ˌrē\ *n* -ES [L *homoeomeria,* fr. Gk *homoiomereia,* fr. *homoiomerēs* + *-eia* -y] **1 :** one of an infinite number of homogeneous ultimate particles of matter constituting through their combination and separation everything in the world **2 :** an Anaxagorean theory postulating homoeomeries

ho·moe·o·sis *or* **ho·me·o·sis** \ˌhōmēˈōsəs, ˌhäm-\ *n* -ES [NL, fr. Gk *homoiōsis* assimilation, resemblance, fr. *homoioun* to make like, become like (fr. *homoios* like) + *-sis* — more at HOME-] *biol* : an assumption by one part or structure in a series of a form characteristic of another member of the series ⟨with a wing of the fore-wing type in place of one of the normal hind wings, it provides an extreme instance of ~ —G.E.Hyde⟩ — compare HETEROMORPHOSIS

ho·moeo·te·leu·tic \hōˌmēōtəˈlüd·ik, hä¦-; ¦hōmē(ˌ)ōtə-, ¦häm- *also* -təlˈyü-\ *adj* [Gk *homoioteleutos* having the same ending (fr. *homoio-* home- + *-teleutos,* fr. *teleutē* end) + E *-ic* — more at TELEUT-] **1 :** having the same or similar endings ⟨~ words⟩ **2** [*homoeoteleuton* + *-ic*] : due to homoeoteleuton ⟨~ error⟩

ho·moeo·te·leu·ton \=ˌ==təˈlüˌtän *also* -təlˈyü-\ *n* -s [LL, fr. Gk *homoioteleuton,* fr. neut. of *homoioteleutos*] : an occurrence in writing of the same or similar endings near together (as in neighboring clauses or lines) whether happening by chance or done for rhythmical effect ⟨~ is a frequent cause of omissions in copying⟩

homoe·ot·ic *also* **home·ot·ic** \¦hōmē¦äd·ik, ¦häm-\ *adj* [fr. NL *homoeosis, homeosis,* after such pairs as NL *hypnosis:* E *hypnotic*] : of or relating to homoeosis

ho·moe·ot·o·py \ˌ=ˈ=ˈäd·əpē\ *n* -ES [*home-* + *-topy*] : HOMOEOTELEUTON

homo·erotic \¦hō(ˌ)mō, ¦hä(ˌ)mō+\ *adj* [*hom-* + *erotic*] **1 :** involving or characterized by homoeroticism ⟨the ~ level of development⟩ **2 :** HOMOSEXUAL

homo·eroticism *also* **homo·erotism** \"+\ *n* [*hom-* + *eroticism* or *erotism*] **1 :** the tendency to obtain libidinal gratification from a member of one's own sex **2 :** HOMOSEXUALITY

ho·mo fa·ber \ˈhō(ˌ)mōˈfäbə(r), -ˌbe(ə)r; -ˈfābə-\ *n* [NL, lit., skillful man] **1 :** man the maker or creator **2** *in Bergsonism* : man as engaged in transforming both himself morally and material things — contrasted with *homo sapiens*

homo·fermentative \ˈhō(ˌ)mō, ¦hä(- +\ *adj* [*hom-* + *fermentative*] : producing a fermentation resulting wholly or principally in a single end product — used esp. of economically important lactic-acid bacteria that ferment carbohydrates to lactic acid

homo·fermenter \"+\ *n* [*hom-* + *fermenter*] : a homofermentative organism

homo·gametic *pronunc at* HOMO- +\ *adj* [*hom-* + *gametic*] : forming one kind of germ cell; *esp* : having an X chromosome in all gametes — compare DIGAMETIC, HETEROGAMETIC

ho·mog·a·mous \hōˈmägəməs, hä'-\ *or* **homo·gam·ic** *pronunc at* HOMO- + ¦gamik\ *adj* [*hom-* + *-gamous, -gamic*] : characterized by or relating to homogamy

ho·mog·a·my \hōˈmägəmē, hä'-\ *n* -ES [G *homogamie,* fr. *homo-* hom- + *-gamie* -gamy] **1 a :** a state of having flowers alike throughout (as in the heads of chicory and related plants or the spikes of many sedges) — opposed to *heterogamy* **b :** the maturing of the stamens and pistils at the same period — used of a perfect or monoclinous flower **2 a :** reproduction within an isolated group perpetuating qualities by which it is differentiated from the larger group of which it is a part — compare APOGAMY **b :** the mating of like with like whether selection is determined by physical or cultural similarities or both

homo·gangliate *pronunc at* HOMO- +\ *adj* [*hom-* + *gangliate*] : having symmetrically arranged nervous ganglia ⟨~ annelid worms⟩ ⟨~ arthropods⟩

ho·mo·gen \ˈ==jən, -ˌjen\ *n* -s [*hom-* + *-gen*] *biol* **1 :** a group having a common origin **2 :** one of two or more homogenous organs or parts

ho·mog·e·nate \hōˈmäjəˌnāt, hə'-, -ˌnət\ *n* -s [*homogenize* + *-ate*] : a substance that has been homogenized; *esp* : biological tissue that has been finely divided (as by a grinder) and thoroughly mixed ⟨liver ~⟩ — compare MACERATE

ho·mo·ge·neal \¦hōmə¦jēnyəl, -nēəl *sometimes* ¦häm-\ *adj* [ML *homogeneus* + E *-al*] : HOMOGENEOUS

homo·ge·ne·ity \ˌhōməjəˈnēəd·ē, -mōj-, -ətē, -i *sometimes* ˌhäm- *or* -nā- *or* ÷ -nīə-\ *n* -ES [ML *homogeneitas,* fr. *homogeneus* + *-itas* -ity] : the quality or state of being homogeneous

ho·mo·ge·neous \¦==¦jēnēəs, -nyəs, *Brit sometimes* -¦jen-\ *adj* [ML *homogeneus, homogenus,* fr. Gk *homogenēs,* fr. *homo-* hom- + *-genēs* (fr. *genos* kind, race) — more at SAME, KIN] **1 a :** of a similar kind or nature : COMPARABLE, EQUIVALENT ⟨the three schools . . . are relatively ~ —B.F.Wright⟩ **b :** having no discordant elements : CONSISTENT, COMPATIBLE ⟨everything about her was ~: her looks, her possessions, the way in which she dressed —Osbert Sitwell⟩ ⟨country people . . . whose manners and morals were ~ with those of the country itself —Van Wyck Brooks⟩ **2 a :** of uniform structure or composition throughout ⟨~ granite⟩ ⟨~ sand deposits . . . laid down under steady conditions of wind —R.A.Bagnold⟩; *specif* : relating to, occurring in, or being a system that contains no internal physical boundaries ⟨~ system⟩ ⟨~ catalysis⟩ **b :** of a single type : showing no variation ⟨bituminous coal is often treated as a ~ product —G.G.Somers⟩ ⟨customary to speak of the Asian mind as though it were ~ —Iqbal Singh⟩; *specif* : MONOCHROMATIC 2 **c :** consisting of uniform elements (as of people or groups with similar background) ⟨~ nation⟩ ⟨~ community⟩ ⟨the sound of a full consort of viols is rich and ~ —Robert Donington⟩ **3 :** of the same mathematical degree or dimensions in every term in the symbols considered ⟨a ~ equation⟩ **4 :** HOMOGENOUS 1 — **ho·mo·ge·neous·ly** *adv* — **ho·mo·ge·neous·ness** *n* -ES

homogeneous equilibrium *n* : equilibrium in a homogeneous system

homogeneous ray *n* : a vascular ray consisting of only upright or only procumbent cells — compare HETEROGENEOUS RAY

homogeneous reaction *n* : reaction in a homogeneous system

homogeneous reactor *n* : a nuclear reactor in which the fuel is distributed (as by being dissolved in a liquid) uniformly or approximately uniformly throughout the moderator material

homogeneous roof *n* : a roof (as a concrete dome) forming a solid shell of one material

homo·genesis *pronunc at* HOMO- +\ *n* [NL, fr. *hom-* + *genesis*] : production of offspring that resemble the parents — compare HETEROGENESIS 2

homo·genetic *or* **homo·genetical** \"+\ *adj* [*hom-* + *genetic, genetical*] : HOMOGENOUS

homo·gen·ic \"+\ *adj* [*hom-* + *genic*] **1 :** HOMOGENOUS **2 :** having only one allele of a gene or genes — used of a gamete or of a population

ho·mog·e·ni·za·tion \hōˌmäjənəˈzāshən, hə,-, hä,-, -ˌnīˈz-\ *n* -s **1 :** the quality or state of being homogenized **2 :** the act or process of homogenizing

ho·mog·e·nize \=ˈ==ˌnīz\ *vb* -ED/-ING/-S [*homogenous* + *-ize*] *vt* **1 a :** to blend (diverse elements) into a smooth mixture ⟨after these two main ingredients . . . have been thoroughly *homogenized* —D.A.Dearle⟩ **b :** to blend as if by homogenizing : make homogeneous ⟨trying to legislate decency or ~ social relations by law —Malcolm Moos⟩ **c :** to anneal (an alloy) for a long time at a high temperature to make more nearly uniform in chemical composition throughout **2 a :** to reduce to particles of uniform size evenly distributed ⟨~ peanut butter⟩ ⟨a fragment of cocoon . . . was cut into small pieces and *homogenized* into tiny fragments in water —*Science*⟩; *specif* : to grind (tobacco leaves) into a pulp and compress into a sheet for use as binder **b :** to reduce the particles of (a liquid) to uniform size and distribute them evenly ⟨~ paint⟩ — compare EMULSIFY **c :** to break up the fat globules and other solids of (milk or cream) by means of a homogenizer ~ *vi* : to attain a uniform state or consistency through reduction or blending ⟨heat causes the product to ~⟩

homogenized *adj* **1 :** reduced to small evenly distributed particles ⟨~ baby food⟩ ⟨~ cosmetics⟩ **2 :** of unvarying uniformity : HOMOGENEOUS ⟨Americans are anything but a standard ~ article —David Davidson⟩

ho·mog·e·niz·er \-zə(r)\ *n* -s : one that homogenizes; *esp* : a machine that forces a substance through fine openings against a hard surface for the purpose of blending or emulsification — compare COLLOID MILL, EMULSIFIER

ho·mog·e·nous \-ˌnəs\ *adj* [ML *homogenus* of the same kind — more at HOMOGENEOUS] **1 :** of, relating to, or exhibiting homogeny **2 :** HOMOPLASTIC 2 **3 :** HOMOGENEOUS

homo·gen·tis·ic acid *pronunc at* HOMO- +¦jen¦tizik-\ *n* [*homogentisic* ISV *hom-* + *gentisic* (in *gentisic acid*)] : a crystalline acid $C_6H_3(OH)_2CH_2COOH$ formed as an intermediate in the metabolism of phenylalanine and tyrosine and found esp. in the urine in cases of alkaptonuria

ho·mog·e·ny \hōˈmäjənē, hə'-, hä'-\ *n* -ES [Gk *homogeneia,* fr. *homogenēs* of the same kind + *-ia* -y — more at HOMOGENEOUS] : correspondence between parts or organs due to descent from the same ancestral type : HOMOLOGY — opposed to *homoplasy*

homo·gone *pronunc at* HOMO- +ˌgōn\ *adj* [*hom-* + *-gone*] : HOMOGONOUS

homo·gon·ic \¦==¦gänik, -¦gōn-\ *adj* [*hom-* + *-gonic* (fr. *-gone* + *-ic*)] : being that course of development in which one generation of parasites immediately succeeds another — used of various nematode worms; distinguished from *heterogonic*

ho·mog·o·nous \hōˈmägənəs, hə'-, hä'-\ *adj* : of or relating to homogony — **ho·mog·o·nous·ly** *adv*

ho·mog·o·ny \-nē\ *n* -ES [*hom-* + *-gony*] : a condition of having one kind of flowers with the androecium and gynoecium of uniform relative length — opposed to *heterogony*

ho·mo·graft *pronunc at* HOMO- +ˌ-\ *n* [*hom-* + *graft*] : a graft of tissue taken from a donor of the same species as the recipient — compare HETEROGRAFT

homo·graph \ˈhäməˌgraf, ˈhōm-, -raa(ə)f, -raif, -räf\ *n* [*hom-* + *-graph*] : one of two or more words spelled alike but differing in derivation or meaning or pronunciation (as *fair,* market and *fair,* beautiful; *lead,* to conduct and *lead,* metal) — called also *homonym*

homo·graph·ic \¦==¦grafik\ *adj* [*hom-* + *-graphic*] **1 :** of, relating to, or consisting of a homograph **2 :** employing a single and separate character to represent each sound : PHONETIC — opposed to *heterographic*

ho·mog·ra·phy \hōˈmägrəfē, hō'-, -fi\ *n* -ES [*hom-* + *-graphy*] : homographic spelling

homo·he·dral *pronunc at* HOMO- +¦hēdrəl *sometimes chiefly Brit* ¦hed-\ *adj* [*hom-* + *-hedral*] : having equal or corresponding faces; *also* : HOLOHEDRAL

homoi- *or* **homoio-** — see HOME-

homoian *often cap, var of* HOMOEAN

ho·moio·genetic \hōˌmȯiō+\ *adj* [*home-* + *genetic*] : having the ability to induce the formation of a similar part when grafted into an undetermined field ⟨the ~ inducing of a new neural tube by a neural tube graft⟩ — used of a determined part of an embryo

ho·moio·me·ria \hōˌmȯi(y)əməˈrīə, ˌhōmēōm-, ˌhämēōm-, -ˈmirēə\ *n, pl* **homoiomeri·ae** \-rīˌē, -rēˌē\ [Gk *homoiomereia* — more at HOMOEOMERY] : HOMOEOMERY — **ho·moio·me·ri·an** \-rīən, -rēən\ *n* -s — **ho·moio·me·ri·an·ism** \-əˌnizəm\ *n* -s

ho·moi·osmotic \(ˌ)hō¦mȯi, (ˌ)hä¦- +\ *adj* [*home-* + *osmotic*] : having a bodily osmotic regulating mechanism and having body fluids that differ in osmotic pressure from the surrounding medium or from sea water ⟨~ animals include all the land and freshwater vertebrates⟩ — compare POIKILOSMOTIC

ho·moio·te·leu·ton \hōˌmȯi(y)ōtəˈlüˌtän *also* -təlˈyü-\ *n* -s [Gk — more at HOMOEOTELEUTON] : HOMOEOTELEUTON

ho·moio·therm \hōˈmȯi(y)əˌthərm\ *or* **homeo·therm** \ˈhōmēə,-, ˈhäm-\ *n* -s [*home-* + *-therm*] : a homoiothermic organism

ho·moio·ther·mic \hōˌmȯi(y)əˈthərmik\ *or* **homeo·ther·mic** \¦hōmēō¦-, ¦häm-\ *also* **ho·moio·ther·mal** \hōˌmȯi(y)əˈthərməl\ *adj* [*home-* + *-thermic, thermal*] : having a relatively uniform body temperature maintained nearly independent of the environmental temperature : WARM-BLOODED

ho·moio·ther·my \hōˈmȯi(y)əˌthərmē\ *or* **homeo·ther·my** \ˈhōmēō,-, ˈhäm-\ *also* **ho·moio·ther·mism** \hōˌmȯi(y)əˈthərˌmizəm\ *n, pl* **homoiothermies** *or* **homeothermies** *also* **homoiothermisms** [*home-* + *-thermy* or *-thermism* (fr. *therm-* + *-ism*)] : the state of being homoiothermic : warm-blooded condition or state

homoiotransplant *var of* HOMEOTRANSPLANT

ho·moi·ou·sia \ˌhōˌmȯiˈüzēə, -üsēə, -üzh(ē)ə, -üsh(ē)ə\ *n* -s [NL, fr. LGk *homoiousios* + L *-ia* -y] : similarity but not identity in essence or substance : essential likeness

¹ho·moi·ou·sian \-ən\ *n* -s *often cap* [LGk *homoiousios* of like substance (fr. Gk *homoi-* home- + *-ousios,* fr. *ousia* substance, being) + E *-an* (n. suffix)] : one that accepts the homoiousian doctrine

²homoiousian \"\ *adj* [LGk *homoiousios* + E *-an* (adj. suffix)] **1 a :** holding to the doctrine that the Son is essentially like the Father but not of the same substance **b :** of or relating to the doctrine of homoiousia — distinguished from *homoousian;* compare HETEROOUSIAN **2 :** of or relating to the homoiousians **3 :** of or relating to homoiousia

ho·moi·ou·sian·ism \-əˌnizəm\ *n* -s : the doctrines and beliefs of the homoiousians

ho·moi·ou·sious \ˌ==ˈ==əs\ *adj* [LGk *homoiousios*] : HOMOIOUSIAN

homo·karyon *also* **homo·caryon** *pronunc at* HOMO- +\ *n* -s [NL, fr. *hom-* + *karyon*] : a cell in the mycelium of a fungus that contains two or more genetically identical nuclei — compare DIKARYON, HETEROKARYON

homo·kary·osis *or* **homo·cary·osis** \ˌ≠≠ˌkarēˈōsəs\ *n* -ES [NL, fr. *homokaryon, homocaryon* + *-osis*] **:** the condition of having homokaryons

homo·kary·ot·ic *or* **homo·cary·ot·ic** \¦≠≠¦≠≠¦äd·ik\ *adj* [irreg. fr. NL *homokaryon, homocaryon* + E *-ic*] **1 :** of, relating to, or being part of a homokaryon ⟨~ nuclei⟩ **2 :** involving or consisting of homokaryons **:** exhibiting homokaryosis ⟨a ~ mycelium⟩ ⟨~ development⟩

homo·lateral *pronunc at* HOMO- +\ *adj* [ISV *hom-* + *lateral*] **:** IPSILATERAL

homo·lecithal \"+\ *adj* [*hom-* + *lecithal*] **:** having the yolk small in amount and nearly uniformly distributed — used of an egg; opposed to *heterolecithal;* compare ALECITHAL

ho·mo le·ga·lis \¦hō(ˌ)mōlə'galəs, -gāl-,-gal-\ *n* [ML] **:** one whose status as a citizen or member of a community is recognized in law **:** a legal person

ho·mol·o·gate \hō'mäləˌgāt\ *vb* -ED/-ING/-S [ML *homologatus*, past part. of *homologare*, fr. Gk *homologein* to agree, fr. *homologos* agreeing — more at HOMOLOGOUS] *vt* **1 :** to agree with **:** SANCTION ⟨~ the act of an ally⟩ **2 :** APPROVE, ALLOW, CONFIRM ⟨a party to an adverse judgment ~s it by failure to appeal⟩ **3** *Scots law* **:** to cause (a document or transaction that is defective or informal) to be validated **:** RATIFY **4 :** to confirm officially (some aspect of the performance of an airplane, as speed, altitude, duration) ~ *vi* **:** to be or act in accord **:** AGREE, CONCUR — **ho·mol·o·ga·tion** \≠ˌ≠≠'gāshən\ *n* -S

homo·log·i·cal *pronunc at* HOMO- + ¦läjəkəl\ *also* **homo·log·ic** \-jik\ *adj* [*homology* + *-ical, -ic*] **:** relating to or characterized by homology **:** HOMOLOGOUS — **homo·log·i·cal·ly** \-jək(ə)lē\ *adv*

ho·mol·o·gize \hō'mäləˌjīz, hə'-\ *vb* -ED/-ING/-S [*homologous* + *-ize*] *vi* **:** to be homologous **:** CORRESPOND ⟨a man's arm ~s with a dog's foreleg⟩ ~ *vt* **1 :** to make homologous ⟨~ one set of rules with another⟩ **2 :** to demonstrate the homology of (as parts)

ho·mol·o·giz·er \-zə(r)\ *n* -S **:** one that homologizes

homolo·gou·me·na \ˌhämələ'gümənə, hōˌmäl-\ *also* **homolo·gu·me·na** \-'g(y)ü-\ *n pl* [LGk *homologoumena*, fr. Gk, neut. pl. of *homologoumenos*, pres. passive part. of *homologein* to agree, fr. *homologos*] **:** books of the New Testament acknowledged as authoritative and canonical from the earliest time — compare ANTILEGOMENA

ho·mol·o·gous \hō'mäləgəs, hə'-\ *adj* [Gk *homologos* agreeing, fr. *hom-* hom- + *-logos* (fr. *legein* to speak) — more at LEGEND] **1 :** of, relating to, or characterized by homology: as **a :** having the same relative position, proportion, value, or structure **:** CORRESPONDING ⟨~ constituents in logically equivalent . . . sentences —Arthur Pap⟩ **b** (1) **:** corresponding in structure or origin — compare ANALOGOUS 2a (2) **:** of like genic constitution — used of allelic chromosomes **c :** belonging to or consisting of a chemical series whose members exhibit homology **d :** showing geometrical homology **2 :** derived from or developed in response to organisms of the same species ⟨a ~ tissue graft⟩ ⟨bacteria suspended in a ~ serum⟩ — compare AUTOLOGOUS, HETEROLOGOUS — **ho·mol·o·gous·ly** *adv*

homologous graft *n* **:** HOMOGRAFT

homologous serum hepatitis *or* **homologous serum jaundice** *n* **:** INFECTIOUS HEPATITIS

homologous stimulus *n* **:** an agent (as light or sound) that is the normal stimulus of a sense organ and is able to produce its specialized stimulation only when acting on the organ adapted to receive it — compare HETEROLOGOUS STIMULUS

homologous theory *n* **:** a theory in botany: the sporophyte and gametophyte in plants are essentially alike, the sporophyte having developed by direct modification of the gametophyte — compare ANTITHETIC THEORY

homologous twin *n* **:** IDENTICAL TWIN

homolo·graph·ic \¦häməl¦grafik, hōˌmäl-\ *or* **hom·a·lo·graph·ic** \¦häməl-\ *adj* [modif. of F *homalographique*, fr. *homalo-* homal- + *-graphique* -graphic] **:** preserving the mutual relations of parts esp. as to size and form

homolographic projection *n* **:** an equal-area map projection — compare MOLLWEIDE PROJECTION

homo·logue *or* **homo·log** \'hōməˌlȯg, 'häm- *also* -läg\ *n* -S [fr. *homologous*, after such pairs as E *analogous: analogue*] **1 :** one that exhibits homology ⟨interlingual ~⟩ ⟨~s of the ethylene series⟩ ⟨corresponding sides of similar polygons are ~s of each other⟩ ⟨pectoral fin, wing, and arm are ~s⟩ **2 :** a homologous chromosome or pair of chromosomes

ho·mol·o·gy \hō'mäləjē, hə'-, -ji\ *n* -ES [Gk *homologia* agreement, fr. *homologos* agreeing + *-ia* -y — more at HOMOLOGOUS] **1 :** a similarity often attributable to common origin **:** AFFINITY ⟨the anthropologist is in the curious position of dealing with . . . striking *homologies* not necessarily due to historical contact —Edward Sapir⟩ **2 a :** likeness short of identity in structure or function between parts of different organisms due to evolutionary differentiation from the same or a corresponding part of a remote ancestor ⟨the structural relation between the wing of a bird and the pectoral fin of a fish is a familiar example of ~⟩ — distinguished from *analogy* **b :** correspondence in structure between different parts of the same individual **3 a :** the relation existing between chemical compounds in a series whose successive members have in composition a regular difference esp. of one carbon and two hydrogen atoms CH_2 (as in the series of alcohols beginning with methyl alcohol CH_3OH, ethyl alcohol C_2H_5OH, propyl alcohol C_3H_7OH) **b :** the relation existing among elements in the same group of the periodic table (as the elements of the halogen group) **4 :** a one-to-one correspondence of two coplanar geometrical figures whereby the junction lines of correspondent points are copunctal in the center of homology and the junction points of correspondent lines are collinear on the axis of homology

ho·mol·o·sine projection \hō'mäləˌsīn-\ *n* [*homolo*graphic + *sine*] **:** an equal-area map projection that combines the sinusoidal projection for latitudes up to 40° with the homolographic for areas poleward of these latitudes

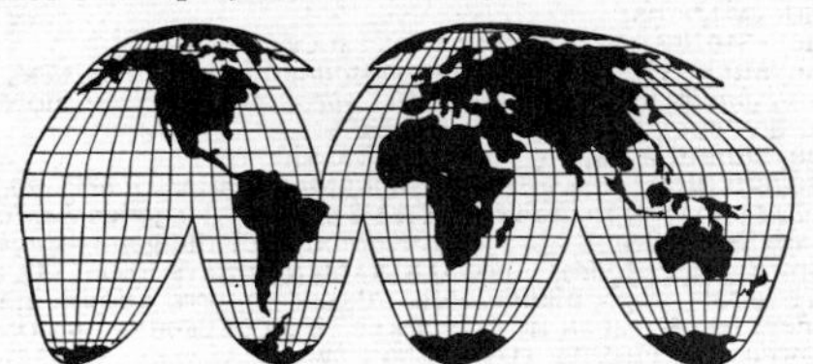

homolosine projection

ho·mol·y·sis \hō'mäləsəs\ *n* [NL, fr. *hom-* + *-lysis*] **:** the decomposition of a chemical compound into two neutral atoms or radicals (as X:Y → X· + Y·) — compare HETEROLYSIS — **homo·lyt·ic** \ˌhōmə¦lid·ik, ˌhäm-\ *adj*

homo·mal·lous *pronunc at* HOMO- + ¦maləs\ *adj* [*hom-* + *-mallous* (as in *heteromallous*)] **:** uniformly curving to one side — used of the leaves of mosses; opposed to *heteromallous*

ho·mo men·su·ra \¦hō(ˌ)mōˌmen'sürə\ *n* [L, lit., man the measure] **:** a doctrine first propounded by Protagoras holding that man is the measure of all things, that everything is relative to human apprehension and evaluation, and that there is no objective truth

homo·metrical *pronunc at* HOMO- +\ *adj* [*hom-* + *metrical*] **:** having the same meter — **homo·metrically** \"+\ *adv*

homo·mor·phic \"+¦mȯrfik\ *adj* [*hom-* + *-morphic*] **1 :** of, relating to, or characterized by homomorphism or homomorphy **2 :** alike in form or size — used specif. of synaptic chromosomes; compare HETEROMORPHIC d

homo·mor·phism \ˌ≠≠'≠ˌfizəm\ *n* -S [ISV *hom-* + *-morphism*] **:** likeness in form: as **a :** HOMOMORPHY **b :** the state of having perfect flowers of only one type — distinguished from *heterogony* — **homo·mor·phous** \¦≠≠¦≠fəs\ *adj*

homo·mor·pho·sis \ˌ≠≠'mȯrfəsəs *sometimes* -ˌmȯr'fōsəs\ *n* [NL, fr. *hom-* + *-morphosis*] **:** regeneration by an organism of a part similar to one that has been lost — compare HETEROMORPHOSIS

homo·mor·phy \'≠≠ˌ≠fē\ *n* -ES [ISV *hom-* + *-morphy*] **:** similarity of form (as in external characters) with different fundamental structure **:** superficial resemblance between organisms of different groups due to convergence — opposed to *homophyly;* compare HOMOLOGY 2a

homo·neu·ra \ˌ≠≠'n(y)ürə\ *n pl, cap* [NL, fr. *hom-* + *-neura*] **:** a suborder of primitive Lepidoptera including those forms in which the venation is alike in the two pairs of wings — compare HETERONEURA

homonid *var of* HOMINID

ho·mon·o·mous \(ˈ)hō¦mänəməs, (ˈ)hä¦-\ *adj* [Gk *homonomos* under the same laws, fr. *homo-* hom- + *-nomos* (fr. *nomos* usage, custom, law) — more at NIMBLE] **:** similar in function and structure and developed to a like degree — used of metameric parts and animals ⟨a few insects have nearly ~ legs and wings⟩ — **ho·mon·o·mous·ly** *adv*

homo·nuclear *pronunc at* HOMO- +\ *adj* [*hom-* + *nuclear*] **1 :** of or relating to the same ring in a chemical compound ⟨~ substitution in naphthalene⟩ **2 :** of or relating to a molecule composed of like nuclei (as hydrogen H_2 or nitrogen N_2)

homo·nym \'häməˌnim, 'hōm-\ *n* -S [L *homonymum* the same word used to denote different things, fr. Gk *homōnymon*, fr. neut. of *homōnymos* having the same name] **1 a :** HOMOPHONE **b :** HOMOGRAPH **c :** one of two or more words spelled and pronounced alike but different in meaning (as *pool* of water and *pool* the game) **2 :** NAMESAKE **3 :** a taxonomic designation rejected because the identical term has been used to designate another group of the same rank — compare SYNONYM

homo·nym·ic \¦≠≠¦nimik\ *adj* **:** of, relating to, or being homonyms — **homo·nym·i·ty** \ˌ≠≠'nimədˌē\ *n* -ES

ho·mon·y·mous \hō'mänəməs, hä'-\ *adj* [L *homonymus*, fr. Gk *homōnymos* having the same name, fr. *homo-* hom- + *-ōnymos* (fr. *onyma, onoma* name) — more at NAME] **1 a :** having two or more different significations **:** AMBIGUOUS — used chiefly of words **b :** having the same designation ⟨the state and its capital are ~⟩ — opposed to *heteronymous* **c :** HOMONYMIC **2 a :** standing in the same relation; *specif* **:** relating to or being a convergence of the eyes such that the object is beyond the fixation point resulting in double vision with the right-eye image to the right of the left-eye image ⟨~ diplopia⟩ **b :** UNILATERAL ⟨~ hemianopia⟩ — **ho·mon·y·mous·ly** *adv*

ho·mon·y·my \-mē\ *n* -ES [LL *homonymia* identity of name, fr. Gk *homōnymia*, fr. *homōnymos* + *-ia* -y] **:** the quality or state of being homonymous

homo·osis \ˌhōmō'ōsəs, ˌhäm-\ *n* -ES [NL, fr. *hom-* + *-osis*] **:** development in one part of an organism of a structure normally produced in another part

homo·ou·sia \¦≠≠¦üzēə, -üsēə, -üzh(ē)ə, -üsh(ē)ə\ *n* -S [NL, fr. LGk *homoousios* + L *-ia* -y] **:** identity in essence or substance

¹homo·ou·sian \-ən\ *n* -S *often cap* [modif. (influenced by LGk *homoousios*) of LL *homousianus*, adj. & n., fr. LGk *homoousios* of the same substance (fr. Gk *homo-* hom- + *ousios*, fr. *ousia* substance) + L *-anus* -an] **:** one that accepts the homoousian doctrine of the Nicene Creed

²homoousian \"\ *adj* **1 a :** holding to the doctrine of the Nicene Creed that the Son of God is of the same essence or substance with the Father **b :** of or relating to the doctrine of homoousia — distinguished from *homoiousian;* compare HETEROOUSIAN **2 :** of or relating to the homoousians **3 :** of or relating to homoousia

homo·ou·sian·ism \-əˌnizəm\ *n* -S **:** the doctrines and beliefs of the homoousians

homo·ou·si·on \-üz(h)ēˌän, -üs(h)-\ *n* -S *often cap* [Gk, acc. masc. sing. of *homoousios*] **:** a theological doctrine holding that Christ is of one substance with God ⟨the very existence of Christianity . . . was at stake over the *Homoousion* —C.H. Turner⟩

homo·pet·al·ous \¦≠≠¦ped·ᵊləs\ *adj* [ISV *hom-* + *-petalous*] **:** having petals alike

homo·phone \'häməˌfōn, 'hōm-\ *n* [ISV *hom-* + *-phone*] **1 :** one of two or more words pronounced alike but different in meaning or derivation or spelling (as *all* and *awl; to, too,* and *two; rite, write, right,* and *wright*) — called also *homonym* **2 :** a character or group of characters pronounced the same as another character or group ⟨η, ι, υ, ει, and οι are ~s in modern Greek, all being pronounced \ē\⟩

homo·phon·ic \¦≠≠¦fänik\ *adj* [Gk *homophōnos* + E *-ic*] **1 :** sounding alike or being of the same musical pitch **:** UNISONOUS **2 :** relating to homophony **:** MONOPHONIC — compare POLYPHONIC **3 :** having all musical parts moving in the same rhythm — **homo·phon·i·cal·ly** \-nək(ə)lē\ *adv*

ho·moph·o·nous \hō'mäfənəs, hä'-, hə'-\ *adj* [Gk *homophōnos*, fr. *homo-* hom- + *-phōnos* (fr. *phōnē* sound, voice) — more at BAN] **1 :** HOMOPHONIC **1 2** *also* **homo·phone** \'häməˌfōn, 'hōm-\ **:** being a homophone

ho·moph·o·ny \hō'mäfənē, hä'-, hə'-\ *n* -ES [Gk *homophōnia*, fr. *homophōnos* + *-ia* -y] **1 :** sameness of sound **:** the quality or state of being homophonous **2 a :** UNISON **b :** MONODY 4a — compare POLYPHONY **c :** composition in which the voice or instrumental parts move in one rhythm in chordal style

homo·phyletic *pronunc at* HOMO- +\ *adj* [ISV *hom-* + *phyletic;* orig. formed as G *homophyl*] **:** relating to homophyly **:** belonging to the same race

ho·moph·y·ly \hō'mäfəlē\ *n* -ES [ISV *hom-* + *phyl-* + *-y;* orig. formed as G *homophylie*] **:** resemblance due to common ancestry — opposed to *homomorphy*

homo·pla·sia \ˌ≠≠ *at* HOMO- + 'plāzh(ē)ə\ *or* **homo·pla·sis** \-'plāsəs\ *n, pl* **homopla·sias** \-āzh(ē)əz\ *or* **homopla·ses** \-āˌsēz\ [NL, fr. *hom-* + *-plasia, -plasis*] **:** HOMOPLASY

homo·plas·tic \¦≠≠¦plastik\ *adj* [ISV *hom-* + *-plastic*] **1 :** of or relating to homoplasy ⟨~ organ⟩ **2 :** of, relating to, or derived from another individual of the same species ⟨~ graft⟩ — **homo·plas·ti·cal·ly** \-tək(ə)lē\ *adv*

homo·plasy \'≠≠ˌplāsē, -lasē; hō'mäplasē, hä'-\ *n* -ES [*hom-* + *-plasy*] **:** correspondence between parts or organs acquired as the result of parallel evolution or convergence — opposed to *homogeny*

homo·ploid \'≠≠ˌplȯid\ *adj* [*hom-* + *-ploid*] **:** exhibiting similar degrees of ploidy

homo·polar \¦≠≠+\ *adj* [ISV *hom-* + *polar*] **1 :** having the poles of the primary axis alike **2 :** alike in both senses (as AB and BA) with respect to physical or other property — used of a direction in crystals; compare CENTER OF SYMMETRY 2 **3 a :** relating to, characterized by, or being a union of atoms of like state as regards polarity **:** NONPOLAR, NONIONIC — distinguished from *heteropolar;* compare IONIC, POLAR **b :** UNIPOLAR ⟨~ dynamo⟩ — **homo·polarity** \"+\ *n*

homopolar generator *n* **:** a generator producing direct current without reversals of potential or resort to commutation

homopolar machine *n* **:** ACYCLIC MACHINE

homo·polymer *pronunc at* HOMO- +\ *n* [*homo*geneous + *polymer*] **:** a polymer (as polyethylene, polyvinyl acetate) containing only units of one single monomer

homo·polymerization \"+\ *n* **:** the process of homopolymerizing

homo·polymerize \"+\ *vi* -ED/-ING/-S [*homopolymer* + *-ize*] **:** to form a homopolymer

ho·mop·tera \hō'mäptərə\ *n pl, cap* [NL, fr. *hom-* + *-ptera*] **:** a large and important suborder of Hemiptera (sometimes considered a separate order) comprising the cicadas, lantern flies, leafhoppers, spittle insects, treehoppers, aphids, psyllas, whiteflies, and scales all of which have a small prothorax and sucking mouthparts consisting of a jointed beak and undergo an incomplete metamorphosis — compare HETEROPTERA — **ho·mop·ter·an** \-rən\ *adj* — **ho·mop·ter·ous** \-rəs\ *adj*

ho·mop·ter·ist \-rəst\ *n* -S [NL *Homoptera* + *-ist*] **:** a specialist on or student of the Homoptera

ho·mop·ter·on \-ˌrän\ *n* -S [NL, back-formation fr. *Homoptera*] **:** one of the Homoptera

ho·mor·elaps \hō'mȯrəˌlaps\ [NL, prob. irreg. fr. *hom-* + *Elaps*] *syn of* ELAPS

hom·organic \ˌhōm, ˌhäm+\ *adj* [*hom-* + *organic*] **:** sharing one or more of the articulating vocal organs **:** articulated with the same basic closure or constriction but differentiated by one or more modifications ⟨\p\, \b\, and \m\ are ~, contact of the two lips being common to all three⟩

homos *pl of* HOMO

ho·mo sapi·ens \¦hō(ˌ)mō'sapēənz, -sāp- *also* -ēˌenz *or* -ēˌen(t)s\ *n* [NL, a biological species, fr. *Homo* + *sapiens* (specific epithet), fr. L, wise — more at SAPIENT] **1** *usu cap H* **:** MANKIND 1 **2** *pl* **homo sapiens :** sentient, conscious, thinking man — contrasted with *homo faber*

homo·sce·das·tic *pronunc at* HOMO- + s(k)ə¦dastik\ *adj* [*hom-* + LGk *skedastikos* able to scatter, fr. Gk *skedastos* capable of being scattered (fr. *skedannynai* to scatter) + *-ikos* -ic — more at SHATTER] **:** having equal standard deviations ⟨~ statistical distributions⟩ — **homo·sce·das·tic·i·ty** \¦≠(ˌ)≠-ˌs(k)ēˌda'stisəd·ē\ *n* -ES

¹ho·mo·sexual \¦hōmə, -mō +\ *adj* [*hom-* + *sexual*] **1 :** of, relating to, or being of the same sex ⟨~ twins⟩ **2 a :** of, relating to, or exhibiting homosexuality ⟨~ tendency⟩ ⟨~ act⟩ — opposed to *heterosexual* **b :** involving, characterized by, or based on homosexuality ⟨a child's ~ phase⟩

²homosexual \"\ *n* -S **:** one who is inclined toward or practices homosexuality

ho·mo·sexualist \ˌ≠≠+\ *n* **:** HOMOSEXUAL

ho·mo·sexuality \"+\ *n* **1 :** atypical sexuality characterized by manifestation of sexual desire toward a member of one's own sex **2 :** erotic activity with a member of one's own sex — compare LESBIANISM **3 a :** a stage in normal psychosexual development occurring during prepuberty in the male and during early adolescence in the female during which libidinal gratification is sought with members of one's own sex **b :** the extent to which one's libido is fixated at a homoerotic level

ho·mo sig·no·rum \¦hō(ˌ)mōsig'nōrəm\ *n* [NL, lit., man of signs] **:** a conventionalized figure often found in old almanacs showing a man surrounded by signs of the zodiac from which lines point to the parts of the body thought to be subject to their influence

ho·mo·spor·ous *pronunc at* HOMO- + ¦spōrəs; (ˈ)hō¦mäspərəs, (ˈ)hä¦-\ *adj* [*hom-* + *-sporous*] **:** characterized by homospory — compare PROTHALLIUM

homo·spory \'≠≠ˌspōrē, ≠'≠ˌspərē\ *n* -ES [*hom-* + *-spory*] **:** the production by various plants (as the club mosses and horsetails) of asexual spores of only one kind — opposed to *heterospory*

ho·mos·te·us \hō'mästēəs, hä'-\ *n, cap* [NL, fr. *hom-* + *-osteus*] **:** a genus of very large flattened Devonian fishes (subclass Arthrodira) having slender toothless jaws

homo·styled *pronunc at* HOMO- + ¦stīld\ *also* **homo·sty·lic** \¦≠≠¦stīlik\ *or* **homo·sty·lous** \-īləs\ *adj* [*homostyled* fr. *hom-* + *styled; homostylic* fr. *hom-* + *style* + *-ic; homostylous* fr. *hom-* + *-stylous*] **:** having styles all of one length — compare HETEROSTYLED

homo·sty·ly \'≠≠ˌstīlē\ *n* -ES [ISV *hom-* + *-styly;* orig. formed as G *homostylie*] **:** HOMOGONY

ho·mo sui juris \¦hō(ˌ)mō+\ *n* [L] **:** a man under his own control — opposed to *homo alieni juris*

homo·tac·tic *pronunc at* HOMO- + ¦taktik\ *adj* [*hom-* + *-tactic*] **:** HOMOTAXIAL

homo·tax·e·ous \-¦taksēəs\ *adj* [NL *homotaxis* + E *-eous*] **:** HOMOTAXIAL

homo·tax·ia \ˌ≠≠'taksēə\ *n* -S [NL, fr. *hom-* + *-taxia*] **:** HOMOTAXIS

homo·tax·i·al \¦≠≠¦taksēəl\ *adj* [NL *homotaxis* + E *-al*] **:** of or relating to homotaxis — **homo·tax·i·al·ly** \-əlē\ *adv*

homo·tax·is \¦≠≠¦taksəs\ *n* [NL, fr. *hom-* + *-taxis*] **:** similarity in arrangement; *esp* **:** similarity in fossil content and in order of arrangement of stratified deposits that are not necessarily contemporaneous

ho·mo·taxy \'≠≠ˌtaksē\ *n* -ES [NL *homotaxia*] **:** HOMOTAXIS

homo·thal·lic *pronunc at* HOMO- + ¦thalik\ *adj* [*hom-* + *thall-* + *-ic*] **1 :** having only one haploid phase producing genetically compatible gametes — used esp. of algae and fungi or of the spores producing such a phase; compare HETEROTHALLIC **2 :** MONOECIOUS

homo·thal·lism \ˌ≠≠'thaˌlizəm\ *n* -S **:** the quality or state of being homothallic

ho·mo·therm \'≠≠ˌthərm\ *n* -S [*hom-* + *-therm*] **:** HOMOIOTHERM

homo·ther·mous \¦≠≠¦thərməs\ *also* **homo·ther·mal** \-məl\ *or* **homo·ther·mic** \-mik\ *adj* [*hom-* + *-thermous, thermal, thermic*] **:** HOMOIOTHERMIC

homo·thet·ic \¦≠≠¦thed·ik\ *adj* [ISV *hom-* + Gk *thetikos* fit for placing; orig. formed as F *homothétique* — more at THETIC] **:** similar and similarly oriented — used of geometric figures

homo·top·ic \-¦täpik\ *adj* [*hom-* + Gk *topos* place + E *-ic*] **1 :** relating to the same or corresponding places or parts ⟨~ tumors⟩ **2 :** HOMEOMORPHIC — **ho·mot·o·py** \hō'mäd·əpē\ *n* -ES

homo·transplant *pronunc at* HOMO- +\ *n* [*hom-* + *transplant*] **:** HOMOGRAFT — **homo·transplantation** \"+\ *n*

ho·mot·ro·pous \hō'mä·trəpəs\ *or* **ho·mot·ro·pal** \-pəl\ *adj* [F *homotrope* (fr. *homo-* hom- + *-trope*) + E *-ous* or *-al*] **:** having the radicle directed toward the hilum ⟨~ seeds⟩

homo·typ·al *pronunc at* HOMO- + ¦tīpəl\ *adj* **:** of or relating to a homotype

homo·type \'≠≠ˌ≠\ *n* [*hom-* + *type*] **1 :** a part or organ of the same fundamental structure as another **:** HOMOLOGUE ⟨the right arm is the ~ of the right leg⟩ ⟨one arm is the ~ of the other⟩ **2 :** HOMEOTYPE

homo·typ·ic \¦≠≠¦tipik\ *or* **homo·typ·i·cal** \-pəkəl\ *adj* **1 :** of or relating to a homotype **2 :** being the equational division of meiosis — **homo·typ·i·cal·ly** \-pək(ə)lē\ *adv*

homo·typy \'≠≠ˌtīpē\ *n* -ES [ISV *hom-* + *-typy*] **:** the relation existing between homotypes **:** SERIAL HOMOLOGY

homo·zygosis \¦≠≠+\ *n* [NL, fr. *hom-* + *zygosis*] **1 :** the union of gametes identical for one or more pairs of genes **:** the act or process of becoming a homozygote **2 :** the quality or state of being a homozygote — compare HETEROZYGOSIS

homo·zygosity \"+\ *n* -ES **:** HOMOZYGOSIS 2

homo·zygote \"+\ *n* [ISV *hom-* + *zygote*] **:** an animal or plant containing either but not both members of at least one pair of allelomorphic characters **:** an individual that breeds true to type and is termed pure with respect to a specified character — compare HETEROZYGOTE, MENDEL'S LAWS — **homo·zygotic** \"+\ *adj*

homo·zy·gous \"+¦zīgəs\ *adj* **1 :** possessing genes for only one member of at least one pair of allelomorphic characters **2 :** producing only one type of gamete with respect to a specified character — opposed to *heterozygous* — **homo·zy·gous·ly** *adv*

hom·rai \'hōmˌrī, 'häm-\ *or* **homu·rai** \-məˌrī\ *n* -S [Nepali *hōgrāyo*] **:** a large hornbill (*Buceros bicornis*) of India and southeastern Asia

homs \'hōmz, -m(p)s\ *adj, usu cap* [fr. *Homs*, Syria] **:** of or from the city of Homs, Syria **:** of the kind or style prevalent in Homs

homuncio *n* -ES [L, dim. of *homin-, homo* man — more at HOMAGE] *obs* **:** HOMUNCULUS

ho·mun·cu·lar \(ˈ)hō¦məŋkyələ(r)\ *adj* [*homunculus* + *-ar*] **:** resembling or characteristic of a homunculus

ho·mun·cu·lus \≠'≠≠ləs\ *n, pl* **homuncu·li** \-ˌlī\ [L, dim. of *homin-, homo* man] **:** a little man **:** DWARF **:** MANIKIN; *specif* **:** a manikin that is artificially produced in a cucurbit by an alchemist

homy *var of* HOMEY

hon \'hən\ *n* -S [short for *honey*] **:** SWEETHEART, DEAR ⟨you're a great old girl, ~ —Sinclair Lewis⟩

hon *abbr* honor; honorable; honorary; honored

ho·nan \'hō'nan\ *n* -S [fr. *Honan*, province in China where it was originally made] **:** a lustrous lightweight silk material resembling pongee now widely imitated in other fibers

honble *abbr* honorable

hon·da \'händə\ *also* **hon·do** \-n(ˌ)dō\ *n* -S [Sp *honda* sling, fr. L *funda*, perh. fr. Gk *sphendonē*] **:** a metal, knotted, or spliced eye at one end of a lariat through which the other end is passed to form a running noose or lasso

hon·do \'hän(ˌ)dō\ *n* -S [Sp, bottom, fr. L *fundus* — more at BOTTOM] **:** a broad low-lying arroyo in the southwestern U.S.

¹hon·du·ran \(ˈ)hän¦d(y)ürən, -)ür-\ *adj, usu cap* [*Honduras* + E *-an* (adj. suffix)] **:** of, relating to, or characteristic of Honduras

²honduran \"\ *n* -S *cap* [*Honduras* + E *-an* (n. suffix)] **:** a native or inhabitant of Honduras

¹hon·du·ra·ne·an *also* **hon·du·ra·ni·an** \¦händ(y)ə¦rānēən\

adj, usu cap [irreg. fr. *Honduras* + E *-ean, -ian,* vars. of *-an* (adj. suffix)] **:** HONDURAN

²honduranean *or* **honduranian** \"\ *n* -s *usu cap* [irreg. fr. *Honduras* + E *-ean, -ian,* vars. of *-an* (n. suffix)] **:** HONDURAN

hon·du·ras \(ˈ)hän¦d(y)u̇rəs, -)ür-\ *adj, usu cap* [fr. *Honduras,* republic in Central Amer.; British *Honduras,* crown colony in Central Amer.] **:** of or from Honduras **:** of the kind or style prevalent in Honduras **:** HONDURAN

honduras bark *n, usu cap H* [fr. Rep. of *Honduras,* its locality] **:** CASCARA AMARGA

honduras cedar *n, usu cap H* **:** SPANISH CEDAR

honduras mahogany *n, usu cap H* **1 :** an important Central American timber tree (*Swietenia macrophylla*) closely related to true mahogany **2 :** MAHOGANY 1a(2)

honduras rosewood *n, usu cap H* **:** a valuable dark streaked wood from one or more Central American trees of the genus *Dalbergia* (as *D. stevensonii* and *D. cubilquitzensis*)

¹hone \ˈhōn\ *n* -s [ME, fr. OE *hān* stone; akin to ON *hein* whetstone, L *cos,* Gk *kōnos* cone, Skt *sisāti* he sharpens, *sana* whetstone] **1 a :** a fine-grit stone used for sharpening a cutting implement (as a razor) — compare OILSTONE, WHETSTONE **b :** an artificial stone consisting of an abrading substance and used for sharpening **2 :** a tool for enlarging holes to precise tolerances and controlling finishes esp. of internal cylindrical surfaces by means of a mechanically rotated and expanded abrasive **3 :** a drag for dressing and smoothing a road surface (as gravel)

²hone \"\ *vt* -ED/-ING/-S **1 :** to sharpen with or as if with a hone **:** WHET ⟨learned to ~ and strop his razor correctly —G.S.Perry⟩ ⟨*honed* his antlers sharp as knives —D.C.Peattie⟩ ⟨the Yankee character was *honed* sharp right here —Bernard DeVoto⟩ **2 :** to enlarge or smooth with a hone ⟨cylinder bodies are bored and then *honed* to a mirror finish —*Mechanical Engineering*⟩ ⟨the walls of the vestibule are lined with *honed* pink stone from Mankato —*Amer. Guide Series: Minn.*⟩

³hone \"\ *vi* -ED/-ING/-S [MF *hoigner* to murmur, grumble, perh. alter. (influenced by *groigner* to grumble, fr. L *grunnire* to grunt) of *honir, honnir* to dishonor, of Gmc origin; akin to OE *hīenan, hȳnan* to abase, OHG *hōnen* to revile, Goth *haunjan* to abase; causative-denominative fr. a Gmc adjective represented by OE *hēan* lowly, abject, Goth *hauns* humble; akin to OHG *hōna* scorn, ON *hāth* act of jeering, Gk *kauros* bad, Latvian *kauns* disgrace — more at GRUNT] **1** *now dial* **:** to grumble and moan **2** *now dial* **:** LONG, YEARN — usu. used with *for* or *after* ⟨'tis vain, 'tis vain, my dear young man, to ~ for Barbara Allen —*Barbara Allen*⟩

hon·er \-nə(r)\ *n* -s [²*hone* + *-er*] **:** one that hones

¹hon·est \ˈänəst\ *adj, sometimes* -ER/-EST [ME *honest, honeste,* fr. OF *honeste,* fr. L *honestus* honorable, decent, handsome, fr. *honos, honor* esteem, honor] **1 a :** free from fraud or deception **:** LEGITIMATE, TRUTHFUL ⟨make an ~ dollar⟩ ⟨an atmosphere still magically colored by gentility, culture and ~ wealth —Winston Brebner⟩ ⟨the first need is for ~ and candid presentation of the facts —Dean Acheson⟩ **b :** of unquestioned authenticity **:** GENUINE, REAL ⟨making ~ stops at stop signs —*Christian Science Monitor*⟩ ⟨when it's not making ~ rain . . . it's misting from the marshes or fogging from the sea —T.H.Fielding⟩ — often used intensively in hyphened combination with *to* and an object ⟨the first *honest*-to-God American beauty I had seen in four months —Tom O'Reilly⟩ ⟨a real *honest*-to-goodness Cape Cod lobster stew —M.F.Leonard⟩ **c** (1) **:** free of ostentation or pretense **:** HUMBLE ⟨younger sons . . . were often apprenticed to some ~ trade —Wallace Clare⟩ (2) **:** free of ornament or disguise **:** PLAIN ⟨a cafeteria which . . . serves really good ~ food —C.M.Smith⟩ **2 a** *obs* **:** of good repute **:** ESTIMABLE **b :** virtuous in the eyes of society **:** REPUTABLE ⟨the fortune . . . made the woman ~, as her second protector immediately married her —G.L.Phillips⟩ **c** *chiefly Brit* **:** GOOD, WORTHY ⟨an ~ fellow, who did his best to please⟩ ⟨I keep six ~ serving-men —Rudyard Kipling⟩ **3 a :** of a creditable nature **:** PRAISEWORTHY ⟨workers who would not take the trouble to turn out an ~ job —Roy Lewis & Angus Maude⟩ **b** *obs* **:** of good reputation **:** RESPECTABLE ⟨now let's go to an ~ alehouse and sing Old Rose —Izaak Walton⟩ **4 a :** characterized by integrity **:** adhering to principle **:** UPRIGHT ⟨~ merchants⟩ ⟨no ~ prostitute would have had the face to ask the prices they asked —Robert Graves⟩ **b :** frank and straightforward **:** SINCERE ⟨early in life I had to choose between ~ arrogance and hypocritical humility —F.L.Wright⟩ ⟨an ~ appeal to the people was the last thing desired by the Federalists —V.L.Parrington⟩ **c :** direct and uncomplicated **:** INNOCENT, SIMPLE ⟨the ~ sleep of any tired child —Alice Marriott⟩ ⟨the ~ average playgoer simply wants to be told what play is best worth going to—for him —C.E.Montague⟩ **syn** see UPRIGHT

²honest \"\ *vt* -ED/-ING/-S *obs* **:** to make honest or honorable **:** JUSTIFY

³honest \"\ *adv* **:** HONESTLY ⟨I have ever found thee ~ true —Shak.⟩ ⟨~ I won't tell⟩ — often used intensively in hyphened combination with *to* and an object ⟨knowing I was *honest*-to-goodness off and away —Helen Eustis⟩

honest injun *adv, usu cap I* **:** on my word of honor **:** HONESTLY

hon·est·ly *adv* [ME, fr. ¹*honest* + *-ly*] **:** in an honest manner **:** with honesty

hon·est·ness *n* -ES [ME *honestnes,* fr. ¹ *honest* + *-nes* -ness] **:** the quality or state of being honest

hone·stone \ˈ⸗,⸗\ *n* **:** a stone suitable for making hones for sharpening; *also* **:** a hone made from such a stone

hon·es·ty \ˈänəstē, -ti\ *n* -ES [ME *honeste* estimable character, honor, fr. OF *honesté,* fr. L *honestat-, honestas,* fr. *honestus* honorable] **1** *obs* **:** estimable character; *esp* **:** CHASTITY ⟨the honor of a maid is her name; and no legacy is so rich as ~ —Shak.⟩ **2 a :** fairness and straightforwardness of conduct **:** INTEGRITY ⟨was not greatly pleased with Lincoln, though admitting his ~ and fair capability —W.C.Ford⟩ **b :** adherence to the facts **:** freedom from subterfuge or duplicity **:** TRUTHFULNESS, SINCERITY ⟨~ is the best policy⟩ ⟨the field worker depends on the ~ of the people for correct replies —J.M.Mogey⟩ ⟨a film of rare ~ and heart —Arthur Knight⟩ ⟨peaceable life in all godliness and ~ —1 Tim 2:2 (AV)⟩ **3** [so called fr. the semitransparent pods] **:** a European plant of the genus *Lunaria* (esp. *L. annua*) — called also *satinpod*

honesty clause *n* **:** FULL REPORTING CLAUSE

hone·wort \ˈhōn,-\ *n* [*hone-* (of unknown origin) + *wort*] **:** any of several plants of the family Umbelliferae: as **a :** STONE PARSLEY **b :** a perennial herb (*Cryptotaenia canadensis*) with thin three-foliolate leaves and small white flowers — called also *wild chervil*

¹hon·ey \ˈhənē, -ni\ *n, pl* **hon·eys** *or* **hon·ies** \-nēz,-niz\ [ME *hony,* fr. OE *hunig;* akin to OHG *honag* honey, ON *hunang,* L *canicae* bran, Gk *knēkos* tawny, and perh. to Skt *kāñcana* gold] **1 a :** a sweet viscid material that is elaborated out of the nectar of flowers in the honey sac of various kinds of bees and stored in the nest for use during the winter as food for the larvae or esp. in the case of the honeybee for the colony and that has a flavor and color depending largely on the plants from which the nectar is gathered with that of clover being esp. esteemed by man for whom as for certain wild animals honey constitutes a favorite article of food — compare HONEYCOMB, INVERT SUGAR **b :** a sweet fluid resembling honey that is collected or elaborated by various other insects — compare HONEY ANT, HONEYDEW **2 a :** SWEETHEART, DEAR — often used as a term of endearment **b :** something superlative in appearance, excellence, complexity, or degree ⟨a ~ of a full-length coat . . . in white American broadtail —Lois Long⟩ ⟨incidental romance and a ~ of an Indian battle at the end —Muriel Burns⟩ ⟨it must have been a ~ with the complicated distilling columns, the automatic controls, the valves and pressure tanks —Joseph Starobin⟩ ⟨if there is a postwar depression . . . it will be a ~ —George Soule⟩ **3 :** the quality or state of being sweet **:** SWEETNESS **:** something that is sweet ⟨coaxed him with ~ in her voice⟩ ⟨seduced by the ~ of admiration⟩ **4** *pharmacy* **:** any of various preparations consisting of simple mixtures of medicaments with honey ⟨borax ~⟩ **5 :** a sweet syrupy liquid (as maple syrup) with a flavor resembling honey — see APPLE HONEY **6** *or* **honey yellow :** a dark grayish yellow that is redder, stronger, and slightly lighter than California green, redder, stronger, and slightly lighter than olivesheen, and very slightly redder than yellowstone — called also *middle stone* **7 :** HONEY LOCUST

²honey \"\ *vb* **hon·eyed** *also* **hon·ied** \-nēd,-nid\ **honeyed** *also* **honied; honeying; honeys** *also* **honies** [ME *honien,* fr. *hony,* n.] *vt* **1 :** to sweeten with or as if with honey **2 a :** to call one "honey" as a term of endearment ⟨their husbands were *~ing* . . . them all the time —Thomas Hart⟩ **b :** to speak ingratiatingly to **:** FLATTER ⟨the station master . . . *~ed* him up the steps of the last coach —Thomas Wood †1950⟩ **~** *vi* **1 :** to use blandishments or cajolery — often used with *up* ⟨by *~ing* up to his landlady got his socks darned and his buttons sewn on⟩ **2 :** to be flattering or obsequious **:** FAWN ⟨rough to common men but *~ing* at the whisper of a lord —Alfred Tennyson⟩

³honey \"\ *adj* **hon·i·er** \-nēə(r), -niə-\ **hon·i·est** \-nēəst, -niə-\ *adj* [ME *hony,* fr. *hony,* n.] **1 :** of or relating to honey or its production ⟨~ cake⟩ **2 a :** resembling honey (as in color or sweetness) ⟨among the walking shoes is one of ~ or black alligator —*New Yorker*⟩ ⟨the ~ peace in old poems —Robinson Jeffers⟩ **b** *archaic* **:** DEAR ⟨my good sweet ~ lord —Shak.⟩

honey agaric *n* **:** HONEY MUSHROOM

honey ant *n* **:** any of various ants some of whose workers serve as receptacles for the storage of honey which they are able to regurgitate from their greatly distended abdomens when it is needed to feed other members of the colony

honey badger *n* **:** RATEL

honey bag *n* **:** HONEY SAC

honeyballs \ˈ⸗⸗,⸗\ *n pl* **:** BUTTONBUSH

honey balm *n* **:** a sweet-scented mint (*Melittis melissophyllum*) of central and southern Europe

honey bear *n* **1 :** KINKAJOU **2 :** SLOTH BEAR

honeybee \ˈ⸗⸗,⸗\ *n* **:** any of certain social honey-producing bees of *Apis* and related genera; *esp* **:** a native European bee (*Apis mellifera*) that is kept for its honey and wax in most parts of the world, has developed into several races differing in size, color, disposition, and productivity, and has escaped to the wild wherever suitable conditions prevail — compare BLACK BEE, CARNIOLAN BEE, DRONE, HONEYCOMB, ITALIAN BEE, QUEEN BEE, WORKER

honeybees: *1* queen, *2* drone, *3* worker

honey beige *n* **:** DORADO 2

honey bell *n* **:** an African shrub (*Mahernia verticillata*) of the family Sterculiaceae having sweet honey-yellow flowers and used as an ornamental

hon·ey·ber·ry \ˈ⸗⸗- — *see* BERRY\ *n* **1 :** the fruit of either of two trees having sweetish berries: **a :** an Old World hackberry (*Celtis australis*) **b :** GENIP 2 **2 :** a tree that bears honeyberries

honeybind *also* **honeybine** \ˈ⸗⸗,⸗\ *n* **:** WOODBINE 1

honey bird *n* **1 :** HONEY GUIDE **2 :** HONEY EATER

honeyblob \ˈ⸗⸗,⸗\ *n, Brit* **:** GOOSEBERRY

honey-blonde \¦⸗⸗¦⸗\ *adj* **:** HONEY 2a

honeybloom \ˈ⸗⸗,⸗\ *n* **:** SPREADING DOGBANE

honey bread *n* **:** CAROB 1

honeybunch *or* **honeybun** \ˈ⸗⸗,⸗\ *n* **:** HONEY 2a

honey buzzard *n* **:** a European hawk (*Pernis apivorus*) related to the kites and feeding on insects and small reptiles and often tearing up nests of wasps and bumblebees to eat their larvae — called also *honey kite*

honey clover *n* **1 :** WHITE SWEET CLOVER **2 :** KURA CLOVER

¹honeycomb \ˈ⸗⸗,⸗\ *n, often attrib* [ME *honycomb,* fr. OE *hunigcamb,* fr. *hunig* honey + *camb* comb — more at ¹HONEY, COMB] **1 a :** a mass of hexagonal prismatic wax cells varying in size according to their use built by honeybees in their nest or hive to contain their brood and stores of honey — compare BEESWAX **b :** a mass of cells containing honey used as an article of food ⟨pats of butter stamped with a swan, and slabs of ~ —Mary Webb⟩ **2 :** a flaw in metal due to imperfect casting, corrosion, or the abrasive action of gunpowder ⟨a scratch or spot of ~ in the grooves renders the rifle completely useless for match-shooting —W.W.Greener⟩ **3 a :** something that resembles a honeycomb in structure or appearance ⟨a ~ of pigeonholes stuffed with old letters —Berton Rouechè⟩ ⟨a ~ of dark, roofed-in arcades —Mollie Panter-Downes⟩ ⟨is experimenting with metal ~ made of stainless steel —Reid Hale⟩ ⟨a red ~ of fire burning far into a great pine root —Eve Langley⟩; *specif* **:** a building facade having a multicellular pattern of repeated units **b** (1) **:** a weave with a small allover pattern of raised squares, oblongs, or diamonds with indented centers formed by long floats (2) **:** a reversible fabric of this weave made usu. of cotton or wool and used for clothing or towels — called also *waffle cloth* **c** *or* **honeycomb stomach :** RETICULUM 1 **d :** HONEYCOMB SPONGE

honeycomb 1a

²honeycomb \"\ *vt* **1 a :** to cause to be full of cavities like a honeycomb **:** make into a tissue of holes separated by thin walls or partitions **:** PIT ⟨both substances eat and ~ the pipe —Emily Holt⟩ ⟨the tunnels of the subways ~ rocks and rivers and skyscrapers —*Amer. Guide Series: N. Y. City*⟩ ⟨the limestone country hereabouts is *~ed* with caves and grottoes —Tom Marvel⟩ **b :** to make into a checkered pattern **:** FRET ⟨the 650,000-odd peasant settlements which ~ the countryside —Daniel & Alice Thorner⟩ ⟨blouses are ruched and *~ed* in alternating panels⟩ **2 a :** to penetrate into every part of **:** FILL, INFILTRATE ⟨a book that has been *~ed* with classical allusions⟩ ⟨the . . . government is *~ed* with spies —T.H.White b.1915⟩ **b :** SUBVERT, WEAKEN ⟨the gigantic edifice of prices was *~ed* with speculative credit —F.L.Allen⟩ **~** *vi* **:** to become pitted, checked, or cellular in structure or appearance ⟨acids cause boiler metal to ~⟩ ⟨the cliff opened . . . before the girl, *~ing* into archways and steep flights of stairs —Kay Boyle⟩

honeycomb coral *n* **:** a fossil coral of *Favosites* or a related genus

honeycombing *n* **:** internal cracking or checking in lumber due to imperfect seasoning and often not visible on the surface — called also *hollow-horning*

honeycomb ringworm *n* **:** FAVUS

honeycomb sponge *n* **:** a fine soft-fibered commercial sponge (*Hippospongia equina elastica*) of a massive form occurring in the Mediterranean and Red seas

honeycomb stitch *n* **:** any of various decorative stitches used in smocking, lacemaking, or knitting to form a honeycomb pattern

honeycomb tripe *n* **:** TRIPE 1a(2)

honeycreeper \ˈ⸗⸗,⸗⸗\ *n* **:** any of numerous small bright-colored oscine birds constituting the family Coerebidae found in tropical and subtropical America — see BANANA QUIT; compare CREEPER 4, HONEY EATER

honeycup \ˈ⸗⸗,⸗\ *n* **:** SENSITIVE PEA

hon·ey·dew \ˈhənē,d(y)ü, -ni,-\ *n* **1 :** a saccharine deposit found on the leaves of many plants that is secreted usu. by aphids or scales but sometimes by a fungus esp. of the genus *Claviceps* **2 :** something as sweet as honeydew or as honey ⟨on ~ hath fed, and drunk the milk of paradise —S.T.Coleridge⟩ ⟨a gentle ~ of a southern girl —Raymond Walters b.1912⟩ **3 :** tobacco moistened with molasses **4 :** a moderate orange that is redder and paler than Persian orange, redder and paler than ocher brown, and redder, stronger, and slightly darker than average apricot **5 :** HONEYDEW MELON

hon·ey·dewed \-üd\ *adj* **:** covered with honeydew ⟨~ foliage⟩

honeydew melon *n* **:** a smooth-skinned white, greenish white, or pale yellow muskmelon derived from the winter melon and having greenish very sweet flesh

honeydrop \ˈ⸗⸗,⸗\ *n* **:** a drop of honey or something like a drop of honey in sweetness

honey eater *n* **:** any of several oscine birds that constitute the family Meliphagidae, are found mostly in the south Pacific, and have a long protrusible tongue adapted for extracting nectar and small insects from flowers — called also *honeysucker;* see BELLBIRD, FLYING COACHMAN, FRIARBIRD, STITCHBIRD, WATTLEBIRD; compare HONEYCREEPER

hon·eyed *also* **hon·ied** \-nēd,-nid\ *adj* [ME *honied,* fr. past part. of *honien* to honey] **:** sweetened with or as if with honey ⟨stilling the ~ air —Walter de la Mare⟩ ⟨many a wily rogue beguiles with ~ tongue —Peggy Bennett⟩ — **hon·eyed·ly** *adv* — **hon·eyed·ness** *n* -ES

honey extractor *n* **:** EXTRACTOR 1c

honeyflow \ˈ⸗⸗,⸗\ *n* **:** a supply or period of availability of floral nectar suitable for bees to convert into honey ⟨some swarming was evident . . . due to the heavy ~ —*Canadian Bee Jour.*⟩ ⟨the ~ . . . began during the latter part of June —*Western Canada Beekeeper*⟩

honeyflower \ˈ⸗⸗,⸗⸗\ *n* **:** any of several flowers yielding nectar copiously: as **a :** a plant of the genus *Melianthus* **b :** either of two Australian shrubs (*Protea mellifera* or the related *Lambertia formosa*) **c :** BEE ORCHIS **d :** a sweet sultan (*Centaurea moschata*)

honeyflower family *n* **:** MELIANTHACEAE

hon·ey·fug·gle \ˈhənē,fəgəl\ *also* **hon·ey·fo·gle** \-fōg-\ *or* **hon·ey·fu·gle** \-f(y)üg-\ *vb* -ED/-ING/-S [perh. fr. ¹*honey* + E dial. *fugel* to cheat, trick] *vt* **1** *chiefly dial* **a :** DECEIVE, CHEAT, COZEN **b :** to obtain by cheating or deception **:** FINAGLE 2 **2** *chiefly dial* **:** FLATTER, CAJOLE, BLANDISH **~** *vi, chiefly dial* **:** to ingratiate or seek to ingratiate oneself so as to cheat or deceive

honey gland *n* **:** NECTARY

honey gold *n* **:** a moderate yellow that is redder and deeper than colonial yellow or mustard yellow and greener and stronger than brass

honey grass *n* **1 :** MOLASSES GRASS **2 :** MELIC GRASS

honey guide *n* **1 :** any of several small plainly colored nonpasserine birds of the family Indicatoridae esp. of the genera *Indicator* and *Prodotiscus* that inhabit Africa, the Himalayas, and the East Indies and include some that lead men or lower animals to the nests of bees — compare BARBET **2 :** a spot or stripe of a different color from the rest of the corolla that is found on the petals of many flowers and is assumed to act as a guide to insects in their quest of nectar

honeying *pres part of* HONEY

honey kite *n* **:** HONEY BUZZARD

hon·ey·less \ˈhənēləs\ *adj* **:** lacking honey

honey locust *n* **1 a** (1) **:** a tall usu. spiny No. American tree (*Gleditsia triacanthos*) that has bipinnate leaves, small greenish flowers in drooping racemes followed by long twisted pods containing seeds resembling beans and separated by a sweet edible pulp, and very hard durable reddish or reddish brown wood (2) **:** LOCUST 3a(2) (3) **:** CLAMMY LOCUST **b :** the wood of a honey locust **2 a :** MESQUITE 1a; *esp* **:** any of various large arborescent tropical American mesquites with strong heavy wood **b :** the wood of such a tropical American mesquite

honey mesquite *n* **:** MESQUITE 1a

¹hon·ey·moon \ˈhənē,mün, -ni,-\ *n, often attrib* [¹*honey* + *moon* (month); fr. the idea that the first month of marriage is the sweetest] **1 a :** a trip or vacation taken by a newly married couple ⟨has planned *~s* for more than 60,000 newlyweds —Walter Winchell⟩ ⟨a popular ~ resort⟩ ⟨obviously a ~ couple⟩ **b :** a period usu. of exceptional compatibility immediately following marriage ⟨made their ~ last a lifetime⟩ **2 :** a period of unusual harmony following the establishment of a new relationship ⟨today . . . congress thwarts the president, after a brief ~ in each administration —Irving Brant⟩ ⟨the ~ period of war alliance —Merle Fainsod⟩

²honeymoon \"\ *vi* -ED/-ING/-S **:** to spend a honeymoon ⟨had a fashionable wedding and *~ed* in Bermuda⟩ — **hon·ey·moon·er** \-ünə(r)\ *n* -s

honeymoon bridge *n* **:** any of several forms of auction or contract bridge for two players

honeymouthed *also* **honeylipped** \¦⸗⸗¦⸗\ *adj* **:** sweet or cajoling in speech ⟨cajoled him with ~ flattery until his suspicion was quieted —John Bennett⟩

honey mushroom *or* **honey fungus** *n* **:** an edible agaric (*Armillaria mellea*) commonly associated with the roots of trees **:** SHOESTRING FUNGUS — called also *honey agaric*

honeymyrtle \ˈ⸗⸗,⸗⸗\ *n* **:** an Australian tree of the genus *Melaleuca*

honey of rose *pharmacy* **:** a mixture of fluid extract of rose and purified honey

honey palm *n* **:** COQUITO PALM

honey plant *n* **:** any of numerous flowering plants that furnish nectar suitable for the making of honey by insects; *specif* **:** a plant of the genus *Hoya*

honeypod \ˈ⸗⸗,⸗\ *n* **1 :** MESQUITE 1a **2 :** a pod of a mesquite

honey possum *or* **honey mouse** *n* **:** a small chestnut-brown long-muzzled phalanger (*Tarsipes spencerae*) of southwestern Australia that feeds upon nectar and small insects

honeypot \ˈ⸗⸗,⸗\ *n* [ME *hony pot,* fr. *hony* honey + *pot*] **1 a :** a receptacle for honey: **a :** one of the isolated waxen vessels constructed by some wild bees **b :** a glass or crockery container for table use ⟨early blown *~s* or jam pots have high lids, deep rims, and solid finials —C.W.Drepperd⟩ **2 honeypots** *pl* **:** a game in which a child (called the *honeypot*) with his hands clasped under his hams is swung backward and forward by his arms until his grip relaxes in order to find his weight which is reckoned at a pound for each swing **3 :** a flower head of a southern African shrub (*Protea cynaroides*) which when open is shaped like a pot and consists of an involucre of showy bracts surrounding a head of small flowers **4 a :** HONEY ANT **b :** a replete of a honey ant

honeypot ant *n* **:** HONEY ANT

honeys *pl of* HONEY, *pres 3d sing of* HONEY

honey sac *or* **honey stomach** *n* **:** a distension of the esophagus of a bee in which the honey is elaborated **:** CROP 2c

honeyscented gum \ˈ⸗⸗,⸗⸗-\ *n* **:** YELLOW BOX

honey shucks *n pl but usu sing in constr, also* **honey shuck :** HONEY LOCUST

honey-stalks \ˈ⸗⸗,⸗\ *n pl* **:** HONEYSUCKLE CLOVER

honeysuck \ˈ⸗⸗,⸗\ *n* [ME *honysouke,* fr. OE *hunisūce,* fr. *huni-, hunig* honey + *-sūce* (fr. *sūcan* to suck) — more at ¹HONEY, SUCK] *now dial* **:** HONEYSUCKLE

honeysucker \ˈ⸗⸗,⸗⸗\ *n* **:** HONEY EATER

honeysuckle \ˈ⸗⸗,⸗⸗\ *n* -s [ME *honysoukel,* alter. of *honysouke*] **1** *obs* **:** clover or its flowers **2 a :** a plant of the genus *Lonicera* — see WOODBINE 1 **b :** a shrub or tree of the genus *Banksia* (esp. *B. integrifolia*) — see AUSTRALIAN HONEYSUCKLE **3 :** any of several other plants with tubular flowers abounding in honey: as **a :** BUSH HONEYSUCKLE **b :** COLUMBINE **c** HONEYFLOWER **d :** PINXTER FLOWER **e :** SWAMP AZALEA **4 :** REWA-REWA

honeysuckle apple *n* **:** SWAMP APPLE

honeysuckle clover *n, chiefly dial* **:** a clover (as red clover or white Dutch clover) that is rich in nectar

honeysuckled \ˈ⸗⸗,⸗⸗\ *adj* **:** covered with honeysuckle

honeysuckle family *n* **:** CAPRIFOLIACEAE

honeysuckle ornament *n* **:** ANTHEMION

honey-sweet \¦⸗⸗¦⸗\ *adj* [ME *hony sweete,* fr. OE *hunigswēte,* fr. *hunig* honey + *swēte* sweet] **:** sweet with or as if with honey ⟨*honey-sweet* blossoms⟩ ⟨*honey-sweet* voice⟩

honeysweet \ˈ⸗⸗,⸗\ *n* [*honey-sweet*] **:** a white woolly perennial herb (*Tidestromia oblongifolia*) of the desert region of the U.S. forming broad flat mats and having stems and involucral bracts that often turn reddish with age and honey-scented yellow flowers

honey-tongued \¦⸗⸗¦⸗\ *adj* **:** SMOOTH-TONGUED

honey tree *n* **1 :** a forest tree that harbors wild bees and honey **2 :** JAPANESE RAISIN TREE

honey tube *n* **:** either of a pair of small cornicles borne on the dorsal part of one of the abdominal segments of many aphids and formerly believed to secrete honeydew

honey vine *n* **:** SAND VINE

honeywood \ˈ⸗⸗,⸗\ *n* **:** a Tasmanian shrub (*Bedfordia salicina*) of the family Compositae having white foliage and heads of yellow flowers

honeywort \ˈ⸗⸗,⸗\ *n* **1 :** a European plant of the genus *Cerinthe* (esp. *C. retorta*) often cultivated for its flowers which yield much honey **2 :** a sweet-scented crosswort (*Galium cruciatum*)

honey yellow *n* **:** HONEY 6

hong \ˈhäŋ, ˈhȯŋ\ *n* -s [Chin (Cant) *hōng* row, mercantile

firm, guild] **:** a commercial establishment or house of foreign trade in China ⟨clippers . . . known equally in Canton ~s and European countinghouses —*Nat'l Geographic*⟩
hong kong \ˈhäŋ,käŋ, ˈhȯŋ,kȯŋ, (ˈ)=ˈ=\ *adj, usu cap H&K* [fr. *Hong Kong,* British crown colony in southeastern China] **:** of or from the British crown colony of Hong Kong **:** of the kind or style prevalent in Hong Kong
[1]**honied** *var of* HONEYED
[2]**honied** *past of* HONEY
honier *comparative of* HONEY
honies *pl of* HONEY, *pres 3d sing of* HONEY
honiest *superlative of* HONEY
honing *pres part of* HONE
hon·i·ton \ˈhänətᵊn, ˈhən-\ *or* **honiton lace** *n, usu cap H* [fr. *Honiton,* municipal borough in Devonshire, England] **:** any of various laces made orig. at Honiton, England; *esp* **:** a bobbin lace with designs of foliage, figures, or flowers, joined by brides or appliquéd to machine-made net
[1]**honk** \ˈhäŋk, -ȯ- *sometimes* -ə-\ *n* -s [imit.] **1 :** the cry of a goose **2 :** a sound resembling the cry of a goose
[2]**honk** \"\ *vb* -ED/-ING/-S *vi* **1 :** to utter the characteristic cry of a goose ⟨northbound geese ~ overhead —Corey Ford⟩ **2 :** to make a noise resembling the cry of a goose ⟨seals ~*ing* and splashing in a tank⟩ ⟨a fogbound ship ~*s* mournfully⟩ ~ *vt* **:** to cause (as a horn) to make a honk ⟨pulled up in front of the house and ~*ed* his horn⟩ ⟨finished her tears and ~*ed* her nose into the . . . handkerchief —Peggy Bennett⟩
honk·er \-kə(r)\ *n* -s **:** one that honks; *specif* **:** CANADA GOOSE
honky–tonk \ˈhäŋkē,täŋk, ˈhȯŋkē,tȯŋk, ˈhəŋkē,təŋk, -ki-, ,==ˈ=\ *n* -s *often attrib* [origin unknown] **:** a cheap nightclub or dance hall **:** DIVE 2 ⟨a row of brothels, gin mills and *honky-tonks* —Robert O'Brien⟩ ⟨a real *honky-tonk* joint, with hill-billy music and pinball machines going full blast —A.L.Davis⟩
hon·ni·a·sont \ˈhänēə,sänt\ *n, pl* **honniasont** *or* **honniasonts** *usu cap* **1 :** an Iroquoian people of the valley of the upper Ohio river and its tributaries **2 :** a member of the Honniasont people
hono·lu·lan \,hänᵊlˈülən, -nəˈlü- *also* ,hōn-\ *n* -s *cap* [*Honolulu,* Hawaii + E *-an*] **:** a native or inhabitant of Honolulu
hono·lu·lu \ˈ==ˈ=(,)lü *sometimes* -,lə\ *adj, usu cap* [fr. *Honolulu,* Hawaii] **:** of or from Honolulu, the capital of Hawaii **:** of the kind or style prevalent in Honolulu
[1]**hon·or** \ˈänə(r)\ *n* -s *see -or in Explan Notes, often attrib* [ME *onour, honour, honor* fr. OF *onur, honur, honeur, honor,* fr. L *honor-, honos* or *honor*] **1 a :** good name or public esteem **:** REPUTATION, GLORY ⟨a national administration of such integrity . . . that its ~ at home will ensure respect abroad —D.D.Eisenhower⟩ ⟨a prophet is not without ~ except in his own country —Mt 13:57 (RSV)⟩ **b :** outward respect or admiration **:** RECOGNITION, DEFERENCE ⟨a dinner in ~ of the football coach⟩ ⟨treat the clergy with ~⟩ **2 :** a special prerogative **:** PRIVILEGE ⟨I have the ~ to inform you⟩ ⟨the second artist . . . to be accorded the ~ of designing the annual Christmas seal —*Phoenix Flame*⟩ **3 :** a person of superior standing or importance — now used esp. as a title for and in a mode of address to certain holders of high office (as judges and mayors of cities) ⟨if Your *Honor* please⟩ ⟨His *Honor* presided⟩ **4 a :** one that is of intrinsic value **:** ASSET ⟨he is an ~ to his profession⟩ **b** *obs* **:** one that decorates **:** ORNAMENT ⟨the woods, in scarlet ~*s* bright —William Cowper⟩ **5 :** an evidence or symbol of distinction **:** mark of respect or admiration: as **a :** an exalted title or rank ⟨elected United States Senator in 1794 and governor of Maryland . . . he declined both ~*s* — *Amer. Guide Series: Md.*⟩ **b** (1) **:** BADGE, DECORATION ⟨among his ~*s* is the Order of the Golden Fleece⟩ (2) a ceremonial rite or observance ⟨the general was buried with full military ~*s*⟩ (3) **honors** *pl* **:** drum ruffles and trumpet flourishes and the national anthem or other music played during a ceremony when troops are presented **c** *archaic* **:** a gesture of deference **:** BOW ⟨they . . . made their ~*s* very prettily as they passed by us—Samuel Richardson⟩ **d honors** *pl* **:** social courtesies or civilities esp. as when rendered by a host ⟨the president did the ~*s* and the new club member acknowledged each introduction with a gracious nod⟩ ⟨handed him the carving knife, and asked him to do the ~*s* of the table⟩ **e** (1) **:** an academic grade, distinction, or award conferred on a superior student by a school or college ⟨received her B.A. with first class ~*s* from the University of London —B.F.Wright⟩ ⟨gained a first with ~*s* in mathematics —Lois I. Woodville⟩ (2) *or* **honors** *pl but sing in constr* **:** a course of study either supplementing or replacing a regular course, open to students of superior ability, and usu. culminating in an examination or thesis to determine eligibility for a degree with special distinction ⟨~ study gives to seniors . . . an opportunity to do independent study and research in their major field —*Bull. of Bates College*⟩ ⟨British universities offer two types of courses in the faculties of arts and science: an ~*s* course . . . and an ordinary, pass, or general course—I.L.Kandel⟩ **f :** an accolade for supremacy in a contest or field of competition ⟨the debating team won regional ~*s*⟩ ⟨airlines vie for commercial ~*s*⟩ **g :** an achievement award earned by a camp fire girl ⟨Camp Fire's method of giving individual recognition is the ~ bead —*Camp Fire Girl*⟩ **6 :** CHASTITY, PURITY, VIRGINITY — used of a woman ⟨fought fiercely for her ~ and her life —Barton Black⟩ **7 a :** a holding of a large amount of land including numerous manors **b :** the seignorial franchise or jurisdiction annexed to such a holding **8 a :** adherence to high standards of justice and responsibility **:** ethical conduct **:** INTEGRITY ⟨code of ~⟩ ⟨an acute sense of ~ in private and business matters —Edith Wharton⟩ — compare BUSHIDO, NOBLESSE OBLIGE **b :** one's word given as a guarantee of performance **9 a** (1) *or* **honor-card :** an ace, king, queen, jack, or ten (2) **:** the ace, king, queen, jack, or ten of the trump suit in bridge or any ace when the contract is no-trump considered from the standpoint of its scoring value (3) **:** the ace, king, queen, or jack of the trump suit in whist (4) **:** the scoring value of honors held in bridge or whist — usu. used in pl. (5) **honors** *pl* **:** HONOR SCORE **b :** the privilege of playing first; *specif* **:** the privilege of driving a golf ball first from the tee that is granted the winner of the previous hole or the last unhalved hole **c :** one of 28 special-value tiles in the game of Mah-Jongg
syn HONOR, HOMAGE, REVERENCE, DEFERENCE, and OBEISANCE agree in signifying respect or esteem shown to another or claimed by him as a right. HONOR can apply to the recognition of one's title to great respect or to the expression of that respect ⟨to hold a statesman in high *honor*⟩ ⟨some member of the family there to see you get your *honor* —Agnes S. Turnbull⟩ ⟨to accept the *honor* the university proffered him⟩ HOMAGE adds the idea of accompanying praise or tribute esp. from one owing allegiance ⟨the ostentatious *homage* paid by state officials to bishops —*Times Lit. Supp.*⟩ ⟨brought up in the veneration of a man so truly worthy of *homage* —Matthew Arnold⟩ ⟨the *homage* which man owes his Creator —M.W.Baldwin⟩ REVERENCE implies profound respect usu. colored by love, devotion, or awe ⟨a *reverence* for all things sacred⟩ ⟨they rather produce in man thoughtfulness, *reverence,* a sense, confused yet precious, of the boundless importance of the unseen world —Charles Kingsley⟩ ⟨a *reverence* for government —Sherwood Anderson⟩ DEFERENCE implies a yielding or submitting to another's judgment or preference out of respect or reverence ⟨the attitude of *deference* which Elizabethan children were taught to cultivate toward their fathers —G.E.Dawson⟩ ⟨the magistrate and the clergyman . . . were conceded a *deference* which superior education, and not superior birth, compelled —H.E.Scudder⟩ OBEISANCE implies a show of honor or reverence by or as if by bowing or kneeling, often applying to a self-humbling gesture in confession of defeat or subjection ⟨the court is also showing great *obeisance* to the wishes of the executive and administrative branches —*New Republic*⟩ ⟨continually making humble *obeisance* to supercilious superiors —A.E.Wier⟩ ⟨unfortunate growing things . . . found that they were clipped, mowed, segregated, pruned, espaliered and generally bullied into *obeisance* —T.H.Robsjohn-Gibbings⟩
syn see in addition FAME
[2]**honor** \"\ *vt* **honored**; **honored**; **honoring** \-n(ə)riŋ\ **honors** *see -or in Explan Notes* [ME *onouren, honouren,* fr. OF *onurer, honurer, honeurer,* fr. L *honorare,* fr. *honor-, honos* or *honor*] **1 a :** to show high regard or appreciation for **:** pay tribute to **:** EXALT, PRAISE ⟨~ your father and your mother —Exod 20:12 (RSV)⟩ ⟨he has been ~*ed* at half a dozen public luncheons and banquets —J.A.Morris b. 1904⟩ **b :** to confer a distinction upon ⟨the only Englishman in all history that the world ~*s* with the surname of Great —Kemp Malone⟩ ⟨in addition to his French decorations, he was ~*ed* by the governments of Great Britain, Italy, Belgium, Serbia, and Venezuela —J.J.Senturia⟩ **2 :** to be a credit to **:** ADORN ⟨the quality of his statesmanship would ~ any country⟩ **3 a :** to treat with consideration **:** RECOGNIZE, RESPECT ⟨federal bill . . . to ~ state commitments of addicts —D.W.Maurer & V.H. Vogel⟩ ⟨truck drivers were ~*ing* the picket line —*Springfield (Mass.) Union*⟩ **b :** to live up to or fulfill **:** carry out ⟨~ a treaty⟩ ⟨~ a contract⟩; *specif* **:** to accept and comply with the terms of ⟨~ a check⟩ ⟨~ a requisition . . . for the surrender of a violator —P.G.Auchampaugh⟩ **4 :** to salute with a bow usu. at the beginning or at the end of a square dance ⟨~ your partner⟩
[1]**hon·or·able** \ˈänər(ə)bəl, -nrəb-\ *adj, see -or in Explan Notes* [ME *honourable, honorable,* fr. MF, fr. L *honorabilis,* fr. *honorare* + *-abilis* -able] **1 a** *obs* **:** up to a standard of respectability (as in quality, size, amount) **:** DECENT, CONSIDERABLE ⟨when he plays at tables, chides the dice in ~ terms —Shak.⟩ **b :** deserving of honor **:** ADMIRABLE, DIGNIFIED ⟨judges are ~ for their high calling⟩ ⟨marriage is an ~ estate —*Bk. of Com. Prayer*⟩ **2 :** conferring honor ⟨won an ~ mention for verse⟩ **3 a :** of great renown **:** ILLUSTRIOUS ⟨comes of a family ~ for centuries⟩ **b** *usu cap* (1) **:** belonging to a family or having a rank entitled to honor — used as a courtesy title for the younger children of earls and for all children of viscounts and barons and for maids of honor and also given to the wife of any man having a courtesy title; abbr. *Hon.*; compare MOST HONORABLE, RIGHT HONORABLE (2) **:** being of high eminence or dignity — used in the U.S. as a title or in a mode of reference for members of congress and of state legislatures, cabinet officers and their assistants, commissioners of bureaus, heads of state departments, judges, mayors of cities, and various other high government officials; abbr. *Hon.* **4 a :** doing credit to the possessor ⟨~ wounds⟩ **b :** consistent with an untarnished reputation ⟨~ dismissal⟩ ⟨~ peace terms⟩ **5 :** characterized by integrity **:** ETHICAL, UPRIGHT ⟨Brutus is an ~ man —Shak.⟩ ⟨~ in all his dealings⟩ ⟨assured her that his intentions were ~⟩ **syn** see UPRIGHT
[2]**honorable** \"\ *n* -s *see -or in Explan Notes* [ME *honourable, honorable,* fr. *honourable, honorable,* adj.] **1 a :** any of various members of British noble families ⟨a host of little cousins, lords and ~*s* for playmates —*Time*⟩ **b :** any of various high British governmental officials to whom the title of Honorable is officially applied **2 :** a person of rank or distinction ⟨the guest list was studded with judges, congressmen, and other ~*s*⟩
honorable discharge *n* **:** a formal release given a member of the armed forces at the conclusion (as by expiration of his enlistment) of a period of honest and faithful service
hon·or·able·ness \-nəs\ *also* **hon·or·abil·i·ty** \,än(ə)rəˈbilədē\ *n* -ES **:** the quality or state of being honorable
honorable ordinary *n, heraldry* **:** an ordinary as distinguished from a subordinary
hon·or·ably \ˈänər(ə)blē, -nrəb-, -li\ *adv* [ME *honourably, honorably,* fr. *honourable, honorable,* adj. + *-y*] **:** in an honorable manner **:** with honor ⟨dealt ~ with his opponent⟩ ⟨was ~ discharged from the marine corps⟩
hon·or·and \ˈänə,rand, -raa(ə)nd\ *n* -s [fr. L *honorandus,* gerundive of *honorare* to honor — more at HONOR] **:** one that is awarded an honor (as an honorary degree)
hon·or·ar·i·ly \ˈänə,rerəlē, -li\ *adv* **:** in an honorary manner
hon·o·rar·i·um \,änəˈrerēəm, -ˈra(a)r-, -ˈrär-\ *n, pl* **honoraria** \-ēə\ *also* **honorariums** [L, fr. neut. of *honorarius* honorary] **:** an honorary payment or reward usu. given as compensation for services on which custom or propriety forbids any fixed business price to be set or for which no payment can be enforced at law ⟨supplementing his income by *honoraria* from speaking engagements⟩ ⟨the medal carries an ~ of $500⟩
[1]**hon·or·ary** \ˈänə,rerē, -eri\ *adj* [L *honorarius,* fr. *honor* honor + *-arius* -ary — more at HONOR] **1 a :** having or conferring distinction ⟨~ scholar⟩ ⟨~ bridesmaid⟩ ⟨~ engineering society⟩ **b :** COMMEMORATIVE ⟨~ plaque⟩ ⟨wrote an ~ ode for the centennial⟩ **2 a :** conferred in recognition of achievement or service without the usual prerequisites, duties, or obligations **:** TITULAR ⟨does not really tell us what it is like to hold an ~, though honorable, position in a domain where once his word was law —Richard Griffith⟩ ⟨two hard-earned degrees . . . and several ~ ones —A.W.Griswold⟩ **b :** UNPAID, UNREMUNERATIVE, VOLUNTARY ⟨~ secretary⟩ ⟨in the Australian theater play-writing remains very largely an ~ task and consequently a luxury —Leslie Rees⟩ **3 :** dependent on honor for fulfillment **:** MORAL — used esp. of an obligation
[2]**honorary** \"\ *n* -ES [L *honorarium*] **1** *archaic* **:** HONORARIUM **2** [by shortening] **:** an honorary society ⟨elected to . . . the senior men's ~ —Neil Stueck⟩ **3** [*honorary* (degree)] **:** an honorary degree or its recipient
honorary canon *n* **:** a cleric appointed to assist occas. in the services of a cathedral but not residentiary and not entitled to stipend or vote in the chapter — compare MAJOR CANON
honorary trust *n* **:** a transfer of property for a designated noncharitable purpose that empowers the transferee to apply the property to the designated purpose or else to surrender it to the one making the transfer or to his estate and that is not enforceable as a trust because it does not benefit a specific ascertainable existing person
honor attendant *n* **1 :** BRIDESMAID **2 :** MAID OF HONOR 2
honor camp *n* **:** a work camp of trusted prisoners conducted under an honor system
honor–card \ˈ==,=\ *n* **:** HONOR 9a(1)
honor court *n, Eng feudal law* **:** a court held for an honor as a whole
honored *adj* **1 :** held in honor **:** RESPECTED **2 :** accorded recognition
hon·or·ee \,änəˈrē\ *n* -s **:** one that receives an honor
hon·or·er \ˈänərə(r)\ *n* -s [ME *honurer,* fr. *onouren, honouren, honuren* to honor + *-er* — more at HONOR] **:** one that honors
honor guard *n* **:** GUARD OF HONOR
hon·o·ri·al \(ˈ)äˈnōrēəl\ *adj* [[1]*honor* + *-ial*] **:** of or relating to a seignorial holding under English feudal law
[1]**hon·or·if·ic** \,änəˈrifik, -fēk\ *also* **hon·or·if·i·cal** \-fəkəl, -fēk-\ *adj* [*honorific* fr. L *honorificus,* fr. *honorare* to honor; *honorifical* fr. L *honorificus* + E *-al*] **1 :** conferring or conveying honor ⟨~ social status commonly attaches to membership in a recognized profession —D.D.McKean⟩ ⟨a largely honorary but distinctly ~ post —*Time*⟩ ⟨the elaborate set of ~ words used to people of rank —Margaret Mead⟩ **2 :** belonging to or constituting a class of grammatical forms used in speaking to or about a social superior — **hon·or·if·i·cal·ly** \-fək(ə)lē, -fēk-, -li\ *adv*
[2]**honorific** \"\ *n* -s **1 :** an honorific term of address esp. when used by an Oriental to convey verbal respect ⟨a leader in the movement to abolish caste distinctions — he has officially repudiated the hereditary . . . ~ of "Pandit" before his name —Robert Trumbull⟩ **2 :** an honorific word or form
honoring *pres part of* HONOR
ho·no·ris cau·sa \(h)ä,nōrəˈskaủsə, (h)ə,n-, (h)ō,n-, (h)ȯ,n-, -nȯr-, -kaủ(,)sä, -kaủ(,)zä *sometimes* -kȯzə\ *adv (or adj)* [L] **:** as a token of respect or honor; *esp* **:** in recognition of distinctions or accomplishments not achieved in course ⟨degrees conferred *honoris causa*⟩ ⟨the degree of doctor of laws *honoris causa*⟩
hon·or·less \ˈänə(r)ləs\ *adj, see -or in Explan Notes* **:** lacking honor
honor point *n* **1 :** a point in an escutcheon of arms approximately midway between the middle chief point and the fess point — see POINT illustration **2 honor points** *pl* **:** HONOR SCORE 1
honor price *n* **:** a price paid by an offender or his kinsmen to the injured person or his kinsmen under ancient Irish law — compare CRO, ERIC, GALANAS
honor roll *n* **:** a roster of names of persons deserving honor: as **a :** a list of pupils achieving academic distinction **b :** a public memorial listing the names of local citizens who have served in the armed forces
honors *pl of* HONOR, *pres 3d sing of* HONOR
honor score *n* **1 :** a score that does not count toward game in contract bridge — called also *honor points, honors* **2 :** a space provided on a contract bridge score sheet for recording extra tricks, penalties, and bonuses
honor society *n* **:** a society for the recognition of scholarly achievement esp. at the undergraduate level in colleges and universities
honors of war : courtesies granted a vanquished enemy (as the privilege of marching out from a camp or town armed and with colors flying)
honor system *n* **:** a system granting freedom from customary surveillance (as to students or prisoners) with the understanding that those who are so freed will be bound by their honor to observe regulations ⟨prison farms operated under the *honor system*⟩; *specif* **:** a system of conducting examinations without faculty supervision
honor trick \ˈ==,=\ *n* **:** a high card or combination of high cards having a specified trick-winning expectancy and used as a basis for evaluating the strength of a contract bridge hand — called also *quick trick*
hon·our \ˈänə(r)\ *chiefly Brit var of* HONOR
hon·tish \ˈhäntish\ *adj* [origin unknown] *dial Eng* **:** HAUGHTY
hony *abbr* honorary
honyak *or* **honyock** *usu cap, var of* HUNYAK
[1]**hoo** *obs var of* HO
[2]**hoo** *dial var of* WHO
[3]**hoo** \ˈhü\ *interj* [origin unknown] — used chiefly to express an emotional reaction (as of surprise or triumph) or as a call
[4]**hoo** \(ˈ)hü\ *chiefly Scot var of* HOW
[5]**hoo** \"\ *var of* [4]HOW
[1]**hooch** \ˈhük\ *interj, chiefly Scot* [origin unknown] — used to express emotion (as excitement, elation)
[2]**hooch** \ˈhüch\ *n* -ES [short for *hoochinoo*] *slang* **:** alcoholic liquor esp. when inferior, obtained illicitly, or made surreptitiously
hoochie–coochie *or* **hoochy–koochy** *var of* HOOTCHY-KOOTCHY
hoo·chi·noo \ˈhüchə,nü, ,==ˈ=\ *n* -s [fr. the *Hoochinoo* Indians, a Tlingit people of Alaska that made such liquor, fr. Tlingit *Hutsnuwu,* lit., grizzly bear fort] **:** a distilled liquor made by Alaska Indians
[1]**hood** \ˈhủd\ *n* -s [ME *hood, hod,* fr. OE *hōd;* akin to OFris *hōd* head covering, *hōde* guard, protection, OHG *huot* head covering, helmet, *huota* guard, protection, ON *höttr* head covering, and perh. to L *cassis* helmet, MIr *cais* love; basic meaning: protecting, covering] **1 a** (1) **:** a covering usu. of cloth or leather for the head and neck and sometimes the shoulders that is attached to a garment or worn separately and is made with a loose or close-fitting opening for the face — see COWL 1, FRENCH HOOD (2) **:** a flexible covering of mail worn by an armored man usu. under a helmet or dependent from a steel cap esp. to protect the neck (3) **:** the head covering of an ecclesiastical garment; *esp* **:** a monk's cowl (4) **:** a protective covering for the head and face that often extends below the shoulders, is made of various resistant materials, and is used by persons exposed to special hazards (as heat, fumes, radiation) **b :** a covering for a hawk's head and eyes **c :** a covering for a horse's head; *also* **:** BLINDER **2 :** something felt to resemble a hood: as **a** (1) **:** an ornamental fold at the back of an ecclesiastical vestment (2) **:** an ornamental scarf that is worn over an academic gown so as to swathe the neck and hang loose or form a closed pouch in back and that indicates by its color the wearer's college and often his degree or field of specialization — see ACADEMIC COSTUME **b :** a color marking or crest on the head of an animal or an expansion of the head that occupies the position of or suggests a hood ⟨a cobra spreading his ~⟩ — compare HOODED **c** (1) **:** a cap of foam on water (2) **:** the upper fine-textured part of a batholith **d** (1) **:** a hood-shaped upper petal of some flowers (as of monkshood) — called also *helmet* (2) **:** a thickened structure that replaces the awn in barleys **e :** an unblocked usu. cone-shaped hat body of felt, straw, or other material **3 :** a covering that protects or obscures like a hood: as **a** *chiefly Brit* (1) **:** a covering of earth and hay or straw over a heap of produce (2) **:** a thatch or shelter of straw over a beehive (3) **:** CAPSHEAF 1 **b :** a cap over the top of a chimney; *esp* **:** a metal cap designed to secure constant draft by turning with the wind **c** (1) **:** a top cover for the body of a vehicle (as a carriage or perambulator) that is usu. flexible and designed to be folded back when desired (2) *Brit* **:** the top of an automobile; *esp* **:** a fabric top for a convertible **d** (1) **:** a projecting cover above a hearth forming the upper part of a fireplace and confining and directing smoke to its flue (2) **:** an enclosure or cover (as a canopy or booth) for exhausting by means of a draft disagreeable or noxious fumes, sprays, smoke, or dusts ⟨installed a ~ over the kitchen range⟩ (3) **:** the part of a furnace cupola shell above the charging hole (4) **:** BONNET 2e(4) **e :** a covering or porch for a companion hatch or other opening on a boat **f :** a projecting canopy on a building (as over a door or window) **g :** the endmost plank of a strake or plate of a shell strake, reaching the stem or stern of a wooden ship or both stem and stern **h** (1) **:** a protective cowl or cover for mechanical devices or parts of them (2) **:** the removable metal covering over the engine of an automobile — called also *bonnet* **i :** a covering over the front of a stirrup **j :** a covering that protects and supports the connections of a suspended electric lighting unit **k** (1) **:** an arched or rounded top on furniture (2) **:** the case enclosing the dial and works of some tall clocks **l :** a metal band that holds the reel of a fishing rod in position on the reel seat **m :** a protective cover (as of metal, paper, or plastic) fitted over the lip or top of a container and used esp. to maintain sterile or sanitary conditions of the unopened package **4 :** HOODED SEAL

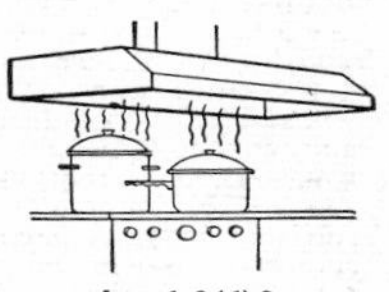
hood 3(d)2

[2]**hood** \"\ *vt* -ED/-ING/-S [ME *hooden, hoden,* fr. *hood, hod,* n.] **1 :** to cover or furnish with a hood ⟨one must ~ the young hawk early in his training⟩ **2 :** to cover over or obscure (as for protection or concealment) **:** HIDE ⟨~*ing* the flashlight with his hand⟩; *esp* **:** to partially close (the eyes or eyelids) ⟨~*ed* her eyes against the sun⟩
[3]**hood** \ˈhủd, -ü-\ *n* -s [short for *hoodlum*] *slang* **:** HOODLUM: as **a :** a gangster or racketeer **b :** a gunman or strong-arm man
-hood \,hủd, *after voiceless consonants sometimes* ,ủd *as in* ˈprē,stủd *one pronunciation of "priesthood"*\ *n suffix* -s [ME *-hod, -hode,* fr. OE *-hād;* akin to OFris&OS *-hēd,* suffix denoting state or condition, OHG *-heit;* all fr. a prehistoric Gmc word represented by OE *hād* person, rank, state, condition, OHG *heit* person, rank, state, condition, ON *heithr* honor, Goth *haidus* manner, way; akin to OE *hādor* bright, clear, OHG *heitar,* ON *heithr,* and prob. to L *caesius* bluish gray, *caelum* sky, heaven, Skt *citra* variegated, bright, *ketu* brightness, light; basic meaning: bright] **1 :** state **:** condition **:** quality **:** character ⟨boy*hood*⟩ ⟨girl*hood*⟩ ⟨hard*ihood*⟩ ⟨unlikeli*hood*⟩ **2 :** an instance of a specified state, condition, quality, or character ⟨false*hood*⟩ **3 :** individuals sharing a specified state, condition, quality, or character ⟨brother*hood*⟩
hoodcap \ˈ=,=\ *n* **:** HOODED SEAL
hood clock *also* **hooded clock** *n* **:** a wall or mantel clock having the movement enclosed in a case and the weights and pendulum if weight-driven exposed to view
hooded *adj* [ME *hoded, hooded,* fr. *hod, hood* + *-ed*] **1 a :** covered or furnished with a hood or something resembling a hood **b :** having the awn replaced by a trifurcate hood — used of some cereal grasses **2 a :** shaped like a hood **b :** rolled in expanded conical form with a reflexed tip **:** CUCULLATE — used of plant organs ⟨arums with ~ spathes⟩ **3 a :** having the head conspicuously different in color from the rest of the body — used chiefly of birds **b :** having a crest on the head that suggests a hood ⟨~ seals⟩ **c** *of a cobra* **:** having the skin at each side of the neck capable of expansion by movements of the ribs — **hood·ed·ness** *n* -ES
hooded crow *n* **1 :** a European crow (*Corvus cornix*) that is black with gray back and underparts and is closely related to the carrion crow **2** *India* **:** HOUSE CROW
hooded gull *n* **:** BLACK-HEADED GULL; *esp* **:** a common European gull (*Larus ridibundus*)

hooded ladies' tresses *n pl but sing or pl in constr* : a native orchid (*Spiranthes romanzoffiana*) that is widely distributed in northern No. America and occurs occas. in Ireland and eastern Asia and that has spikes of small creamy or straw-colored almond-scented flowers with sepals and petals partly fused into an upward arching hood
hooded merganser *or* **hooded sheldrake** *n* : a small No. American merganser (*Lophodytes cucullatus*) having a high vertical nearly circular crest on the head of the adult male
hooded milfoil *n* : PURPLE BLADDERWORT
hooded oriole *n* : an oriole (*Icterus cucullatus*) of the southwestern U.S. and Mexico that occurs in several races and is distinguished by the yellow head and black throat of the male
hooded pitcher plant *n* : a yellow-flowered pitcher plant (*Sarracenia minor*) of the southeastern U.S. having variegated trumpet-shaped leaves with green and purple veins and white or yellowish blotches and with the orifice closely covered by an arched hood
hooded rat *n* : a strain of the black rat developed in captivity and characterized by a white body and black head
hooded seal *n* : a large seal (*Cystophora cristata*) of the north Atlantic distinguished by a large inflatable sac upon the forepart of the head of the male
hooded snake *n* : COBRA
hooded tern *n* : LITTLE TERN
hooded top *n* : BONNET TOP
hooded violet *n* : a usu. purple-flowered tufted violet (*Viola cucullata*) of No. America having the young leaves rolled in and the lateral petals bearded
hooded warbler *n* : an American warbler (*Wilsonia citrina*) having in the male the forehead, ear coverts, and lower parts gamboge yellow and the rest of the head, neck, and chest black
hood·ie *also* **hoody** \'hu̇dē, 'hēdi, 'hēdi\ *n, pl* **hoodies** [1*hood* + *-ie, -y*] **1 a** *or* **hoodie crow** : HOODED CROW 1 **b** : CARRION CROW **2** *dial Brit* : a hooded gull (*Larus ridibundus*)
hooding *pres part of* HOOD
hooding end *or* **hood end** *n* : the end of a hood of a ship that enters the rabbet in the stempost or sternpost
hood·less \'hu̇dləs\ *adj* : lacking a hood ⟨an African ~ cobra⟩
hoodlike \'=,=\ *adj* : resembling a hood ⟨a ~ crest⟩ : enclosing like a hood ⟨a ~ upper petal⟩
hood·lum \'hüdləm *also* 'hu̇d-\ *n* -s [origin unknown] **1 a** : THUG, RUFFIAN, MOBSTER; *esp* : a small-time criminal whose crimes include acts of violence ⟨a gang of ~s had murdered four people —J.A.Michener⟩ ⟨a ~ . . . works for gangsters, and bumps guys off after they have been put on the spot —C.R.Cooper⟩ **b** : one who behaves in an uncouth or ruffianly manner ⟨some of the tenderest scenes . . . were spoiled by ~s in the gallery —*Amer. Guide Series: Wash.*⟩ **c** : a young ruffian or street loafer : a rowdy or misbehaved child or adolescent ⟨that kid was a real ~, . . . shot craps and everything —*Lamp*⟩ **2** *West* **a** *or* **hoodlum wagon** : a wagon used at roundup to carry bedding and miscellaneous supplies **b** : the driver of a hoodlum, usu. serving also as cook's helper
hood·lum·ish \-mish\ *adj* : like or typical of a hoodlum ⟨~ louts⟩ ⟨~ behavior⟩
hood·lum·ism \-lə,mizəm\ *n* -s : conduct typical of a hoodlum : rough rowdy behavior : delinquency or criminality marked esp. by gross disregard for the rights of others
hood·man-blind \,hu̇dmən'=\ *n, archaic* : BLINDMAN'S BUFF
hoodmold \'=,=\ *also* **hood molding** *n* : a molding that projects over the head of an arch and forms the outermost member of the archivolt : DRIPSTONE

hoodmold

1hoo·doo \'hü(,)dü\ *n* -s [of African origin; akin to Hausa *hu'du'ba'* to arouse resentment against someone] **1** : VOODOO **2 a** : something that brings or is associated with the occurrence of bad luck : JINX, JONAH — compare MASCOT **b** : bad luck **3 a** : a natural column or pinnacle of rock common in parts of western No. America that results from weathering or erosion and occurs in varied and often fantastic forms **b** : EARTH PILLAR
2hoodoo \"\ *adj* **1** : of, relating to, or being a hoodoo ⟨~ priests⟩ ⟨a ~ fetish⟩ **2 a** : persistently unlucky as if under a spell ⟨a ~ ship⟩ : JINXED **b** : bringing or associated with bad luck ⟨when that ~ planet crops up in a horoscope⟩
3hoodoo \"\ *vt* -ED/-ING/-S : to cast a spell on : bring to misfortune by occult means; *broadly* : be a source of misfortune to
hoo·doo·ism \-,izəm\ *n* -s : VOODOOISM
hoods *pl of* HOOD, *pres 3d sing of* HOOD
-hoods *pl of* -HOOD
hoodsheaf \'=,=\ *n* [*hood* + *sheaf*] : CAPSHEAF 1
1hood·wink \'hu̇d,wiŋk\ *vt* [1*hood* + *wink*] **1** *archaic* : to blind by covering the eyes : BLINDFOLD **2** *obs* : to hide out of sight or mind **3** : to deceive by false appearance : impose upon ⟨such an easy person to ~⟩ ⟨packages designed to ~ buyers⟩ **syn** see DUPE
2hoodwink \"\ *n* **1** : the act of hoodwinking **2** : a device for concealing or dissembling (as a mask or blindfold) : BLIND
hood·wink·er \-kə(r)\ *n* : one that hoodwinks
hoodwise \'=,=\ *adv* [1*hood* + *-wise*] : in the manner of or so as to serve the purpose of a hood ⟨held a newspaper ~ over her hat⟩
hoodwort \'=,=\ *n* : MAD-DOG SKULLCAP
hoo·ey \'hüē, -üi\ *n* -s [origin unknown] : something false or unacceptable : HOKUM, NONSENSE — often used interjectionally
1hoof \'hu̇f, 'hüf\ *n, pl* **hooves** \|vz\ *or* **hoofs** \|fs\ [ME, fr. OE *hōf*; akin to OFris & OS *hōf* hoof, OHG *huof*, ON *hōfr* hoof, Skt *śapha* hoof, claw, Av *safa-* horse's hoof] **1 a** : a curved covering of horn that protects the front of or more or less extensively encloses the ends of the digits of an ungulate mammal and that corresponds to a nail or claw — see COW illustration **b** : a hoofed foot esp. of a horse or other equine — compare CLOVEN FOOT **c** : FOOT; *esp* : a large, heavy, or ill-managed human foot ⟨heard those *hooves* on the stair⟩ **2** *now chiefly dial* : a hoofed animal; *usu* : a hoofed domestic mammal ⟨hadn't a ~ fit to dress⟩ **3** : one of the smaller and more angulate plates (as a marginal plate) of the shell of the hawksbill turtle; *also* : the tortoise shell composing these plates — used chiefly commercially — **on the hoof 1** *of meat animals* : LIVING, LIVEWEIGHT ⟨10 cents a pound *on the hoof*⟩ ⟨*on the hoof* meat is supplied —*Nat'l Geographic*⟩ **2** *of persons* : in ordinary condition : without an opportunity for any special show ⟨meeting people *on the hoof* across a sales counter⟩ ⟨executives expert at judging men *on the hoof*⟩
2hoof \"\ *vb* -ED/-ING/-S *vt* **1** : WALK ⟨~*ed* a mile to school each day⟩ ⟨~*ing* it to town⟩ **2** : KICK, TRAMPLE ⟨buffalo ~*ed* up the dust⟩ ⟨colts ~*ing* the sod⟩ **3** : to put out by or as if by kicking : throw out : EJECT, BOOT ⟨uncle got me ~*ed* out of that —F.M.Ford⟩ ~ *vi* : to move on the feet (as in walking, tramping, or dancing); *esp* : to execute noisy rhythmic footwork (as in tap-dancing)
hoof-and-mouth disease *n* : FOOT-AND-MOUTH DISEASE
hoofbeat \'=,=\ *n* : the sound of a hoof striking the ground or other hard surface ⟨~*s* fading in the distance⟩
hoofbound \'=,=\ *adj* : having a dry and contracted hoof that occasions pain and lameness
hoofed \'hu̇ft, -üft\ *adj* **1** : having hoofs : UNGULATE — often used in combination ⟨cloven-*hoofed*⟩ **2** *of a shoe* : having a broad rounded front
hoofed locust *n* [so called fr. the fact that sheep closely crop the vegetation when they graze] : SHEEP — usu. used disparagingly by cattlemen
hoof·er \'hu̇fə(r), -üf-\ *n* -s **1** : one that travels on foot **2** *slang* : DANCER; *esp* : a professional dancer (as in vaudeville or a chorus)
hoof foot *n* : a furniture foot in the form of a usu. cloven hoof
hoof·i·ness \-fēnəs, -fin-\ *n* -ES : the quality or state of being hoofed
hoof·less \-fləs\ *adj* : lacking hooves
hoof·let \-lət\ *n* -s [1*hoof* + *-let*] : a small hoof; *esp* : FALSE HOOF

hoof foot

hooflike \'=,=\ *adj* : resembling a hoof; *esp* : having the horny texture of a hoof ⟨~ calluses⟩
hoof-pick \'=,=\ *n* : a hooked implement used to remove foreign objects from a hoof
hoofprint \'=,=\ *n* : an impression or hollow made by a hoof
hoofrot \'=,=\ *n* : FOOT ROT 2
hoog·aars \'hō,gärs\ *n, pl* **hoogaars** \", -rz\ [D, fr. *hoog* high + *aars* buttocks] : a Dutch sloop
hoo-ha \'hü,hä\ *n* -s [origin unknown] : HULLABALOO
1hook \'hu̇k\ *n* -s [ME *hok, hook*, fr. OE *hōc*; akin to OFris *hōk* corner, MD *hoec* fishhook, corner, OE *haca* bolt, OHG *hāko* hook, Icel *haki* hook, ON *haka* chin, MIr *ailcheng* rake, stand for weapons, Lith *kengė* hook, latch] **1 a** (1) : an implement for cutting grass or grain : SICKLE, SCYTHE (2) : an implement for cutting or lopping : BILLHOOK **b** : a hand fork with the tines turned nearly at right angles to the handle ⟨a potato ~⟩ ⟨manure ~*s*⟩ **c** : a curved metal prong attached to a leather wristband for tearing the husks from an ear of corn **2 a** : a piece of metal or other hard or tough material formed or bent into a curve or at an angle for catching, holding, sustaining, or pulling something ⟨a ~ for fastening a gate⟩ ⟨a ~ for filing papers⟩ **b** : any of various hooked objects: as (1) : BREASTHOOK (2) : an artificial replacement for the hand made in the form of a hook (3) : an instrument used in surgery to take hold of tissue ⟨crypt ~⟩ ⟨chordotomy ~⟩ (4) : the part of a hook and eye that is bent over to form a finger that fits into the eye (5) : a long pole with a hooked end by which one in the wings can reach out and pull a performer off the stage — often used in the phrase *get the hook* (6) : FIRE HOOK **3 a** : FISHHOOK; *broadly* : any angling device or lure capable of taking but one fish at a time **b** : something designed to attract and ensnare **4** : a part of a hinge that is fixed to a post and on which the part that is fixed to a door or gate hangs and turns **5** : something felt to resemble a hook: as **a** : a sharp bend or curve (as in a stream) or a spit or narrow cape of sand or gravel turned landward at the outer end ⟨wave action may build spits into ~*s*⟩ **b** (1) : an angular or recurved mark (as a written character or an element in one) (2) : EAR ⟨the ~ of lower-case g or q⟩ (3) : 5FLAG 3a (4) : PARENTHESIS 3a — used in printing; usu. in pl. **c** (1) : a recurved part or appendage of a plant or animal ⟨burrs clinging by their ~*s*⟩ (2) *or* **hook bone** : the projecting angle of the hipbone of cattle — usu. used in pl. ⟨a good covering of flesh over the ~*s*⟩ **d** : the angle between the face of a tooth and a line to the center of a circular saw or to a line perpendicular to the back of a band saw **e** : ANCHOR **f hooks** *pl, slang* : FINGERS ⟨just let me get my ~*s* on him⟩ **g** : a lever by which a device (as a fire-alarm box) is actuated **h** : a mobile wrecking crane; *broadly* : a wreck train or car mounting a crane **6 a** : an act or instance of hooking ⟨the cow gave a sudden ~ and ripped his sleeve⟩ **b** : a flight of a ball (as in golf, cricket, bowling, baseball) that deviates from a straight course in a direction opposite to the dominant hand of the player projecting it; *also* : a ball following such a course — compare SLICE, SPIN **c** : a short blow delivered with a circular motion by a boxer while the elbow remains bent and rigid **7** : CROOK 2b — **by hook or by crook** *also* **by hook or crook** : by any means : fairly or unfairly ⟨determined to win *by hook or by crook*⟩ — **drop off the hooks** *or* **slip off the hooks** *Brit* : DIE — **off the hook** *adv (or adj)* : out of a difficulty or trouble ⟨counted on his friends to get him *off the hook*⟩ — **off the hooks** *obs* : disordered in mind or body : UNHINGED, DERANGED — **on one's own hook** : on one's own account or responsibility : without authorization or assistance : by oneself : INDEPENDENTLY

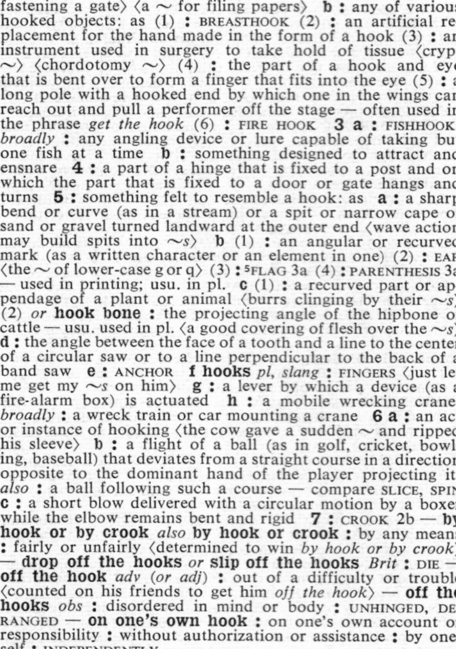
hooks 2a

2hook \"\ *vb* -ED/-ING/-S [ME *hoken*, fr. *hok, hook*, n.] *vt* **1** : to give the form of a hook to : CROOK ⟨~*ed* an arm about the stanchion⟩ **2 a** : to make fast with or as if with a hook or hooks ⟨~ a dress⟩ **b** : to seize, capture, or hold with a hook ⟨~*ed* a large trout⟩ **c** : to secure or catch as if with a hook ⟨~*ed* herself a husband⟩: as (1) *slang* : to reduce to a complete loss of self-control : make wholly dependent — usu. used in passive ⟨~*ed* by the morphine habit⟩ (2) *slang* : to entrap into improper, undesirable, or foolish activity ⟨when the sucker listens he's half ~*ed*⟩ (3) : to hold (a dancing partner) by interlocking feet or elbows; *also* : to interlock (feet or elbows) in dancing **3 a** : to seize and draw with or as if with a hook ⟨~*ed* the logs out of the channel⟩ **b** : to take by stealth : STEAL, PILFER ⟨~*ing* apples from the tree⟩ **4** : to strike or pierce with the points of the horns : GORE **5 a** : to make (as a rug) by drawing loops of thread, yarn, or cloth through a coarse fabric with a hook **b** : to so draw (as yarn) in forming a pattern ⟨~*ed* heavy woolen rags into an ombré pattern⟩ **6 a** : to strike (a boxing opponent) with a hook **b** : to strike or throw (as a golf ball or bowling ball) so that a hook results — compare FADE, SLICE **c** : to hit (a bowled cricket ball) to leg with a stroke in which the bat swings upward and in a leg direction **d** (1) : to intercept (the ball) in rugby and propel backward with the heel of the boot from the front line of the scrum (2) : to gain possession of (the ball) in soccer by reaching out, intercepting, and drawing with the foot ~ *vi* **1** : to bend sharply so as to form a hook : CURVE ⟨the beak ~*s* strongly downward⟩ **2** *slang* : to make off : LEAVE, DEPART ⟨~*ed* for home⟩ — usu. used with formulary *it* ⟨~ it, the cops are coming⟩ **3** : to secure or fasten by or as if by a hook ⟨a dress that ~*s* in back⟩ **4 a** : to make an attack with the horns ⟨the bull ~*ed* at his handler⟩ **b** : to deliver a hook in boxing ⟨~*ing* expertly but without much power⟩ **5 a** *of a ball* : to travel in or be a hook ⟨the ball ~*ed* badly but bounced onto the fairway⟩ **b** *of a player* : to hook a ball ⟨~*ed* into the rough⟩ **c** : to score or attempt to score in basketball with a hook shot
hookah *also* **hooka** \'hu̇kə, 'hükə\ *n* -s [Ar *huqqah* round box, casket, bottle of a water pipe] : a pipe for smoking that has a long flexible tube whereby the smoke is cooled by passing through water — compare NARGILEH
hook-and-butt joint *n* : a scarf joint formed to resist tension
hook and eye *n* : a two-part fastening device (as on a garment or a door) consisting of a wire hook that catches over a bar or into a loop of wire — see FASTENER illustration
hook-and-eye \'=,=\ *adj* [*hook and eye*] : having religious scruples against the wearing of buttons ⟨a *hook-and-eye* sect⟩
hook-and-eye hinge *n* : a hinge intended for use on a gate and consisting of an L-shaped hook secured to one member (as the gatepost) and fitted into an eye-shaped loop or screw hook secured to the other member (as the gate)

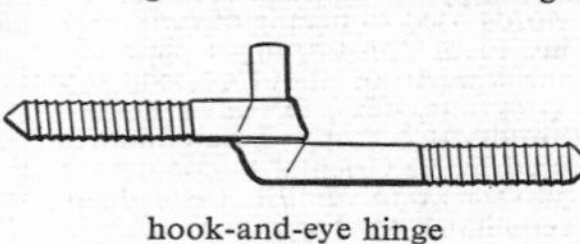
hook-and-eye hinge

hook and ladder *n* **1** *or* **hook-and-ladder truck** : LADDER TRUCK **2** *or* **hook-and-ladder company** : LADDER COMPANY
hook-and-liner \'=,=\ *n* : a boat (as a tuna clipper) for fishing with hook and line
hook·a·roon \,hu̇kə'rün\ *n* -s [1*hook* + *-aroon* (as in *pickaroon*)] : 2PICKAROON
hook-bill \'=,=\ *n* : a parrot or a closely related bird (as a cockatoo or parrakeet) esp. when domesticated
hook-billed \'=,bild\ *adj* : having a strongly curved bill or jaws ⟨a *hook-billed* salmon⟩
hook bolt *n* : a bolt hooked at one end and threaded at the other to receive a nut
hook bones *n* : HOOK 5c(2)
hook check *n* : a technique of gaining possession of an ice-hockey puck or diverting it to a teammate by hooking it away from the opponent with one's stick

hook bolts

hook climber *n* : a plant (as a climbing rose) that climbs by hooks or prickles
hooked \'hu̇kt\ *adj* **1** : having the form of a hook ⟨the ~ bill of a bird of prey⟩ **2** : provided with a hook or hooks ⟨a fireman's ~ ax⟩ **3** : made by hooking ⟨a ~ design⟩ ⟨~ carpets⟩ **4** *slang* : addicted to narcotics : having reached a state of physical dependence on narcotics — **hooked·ness** \'hu̇k(t)nəs, -kədn-\ *n* -ES
hooked rug *n* : a rug formed by hooking into a strong coarse fabric back loops (as of yarn or strips of cloth) to form a surface pile
1hookem-snivey \,hu̇kəm'snivi\ *n* -s [fr. earlier *hook and snivey*, prob. fr. *hook* (to steal)] *dial chiefly Eng* : TRICKERY, DECEIT
2hookem-snivey *adj, dial chiefly Eng* : DECEITFUL, TRICKY
1hook·er \'hu̇kə(r)\ *n* -s [2*hook* + *-er*] **1 a** : one that hooks esp. habitually ⟨that cow is a bad ~⟩ **b** *slang* : THIEF, PICKPOCKET **c** [fr. the fact that they fasten their clothes with hooks rather than buttons] *usu cap* : one of the Amish Mennonites **d** : a worker that uses a hook or hooking device to fasten, move, handle, or form articles with which he works: as (1) : a logger that fastens logs to hooks, cables, or tongs by which they may be skidded or loaded (2) : a steelworker that guides billets in a rolling mill (3) : a sponge fisher that detaches sponges with a sponge hook (4) : a maker of hooked rugs (5) : an operator of a machine for folding and measuring cloth **e** : a player in the front row of a rugby scrum who hooks the ball **2** *slang* : DRINK; *esp* : a copious drink of liquor ⟨a ~ of hard cider⟩ **3** [prob. fr. 2*hook* (to entrap) + *-er*] *slang* : PROSTITUTE
2hooker \"\ *n* -s [D *hoeker*, fr. earlier *hoeckboot*, fr. MD *hoecboot* fishing boat, fr. *hoec* fishhook + *boot* boat — more at HOOK] **1** : a Dutch boat with two masts **2** : a fishing boat with one mast used on the coasts of England and Ireland **3** : an old, outmoded, or clumsy boat
hooker cell \"-\ *n, usu cap H* [after Albert H. *Hooker* †1936 Am. electrochemist] : a cell that has graphite anodes and wire-screen cathodes covered with asbestos diaphragms and that is used for making sodium hydroxide and chlorine by electrolysis of sodium chloride
hoo·ke·ri·a·les \(,)hu̇r,kirē'ā(,)lēz\ *n pl, cap* [NL, fr. *Hookeria*, genus of mosses (fr. Sir William J. *Hooker* †1865 Eng. botanist + NL *-ia*) + *-ales*] : an order of usu. pleurocarpous mosses with branched prostrate gametophores, asymmetrical leaves often with two midribs, and capsules with a double peristome
hooker-out \'=,=\ *n, pl* **hookers-out** [*hook out*, v. + *-er*] **1** : a tonger in a wireworks **2** : STICKMAN 1c(1)
hooker's green *n, usu cap H* [after William *Hooker* †1832 Eng. botanical painter] **1** : a green pigment consisting of a mixture of Prussian blue and gamboge **2** : a moderate to strong green that is yellower and stronger than spearmint
hooker's orchid *n, usu cap H* [after Sir William J. *Hooker* †1865 Eng. botanist] : a long-spurred orchid (*Habenaria hookeri*) having basal leaves and petals connivent under the upper sepal
hooke's law \'hu̇ks-\ *n, usu cap H* [after Robert *Hooke* †1703 Eng. scientist] : a statement of elasticity: the stress within an elastic solid up to the elastic limit is proportional to the strain responsible for it
hookey *var of* HOOKY
hook gage *n* : an instrument for measuring the rise or drop in elevation of a liquid (as water in a reservoir) from a previously recorded level by means of a pointed hook that is directly connected to a fixed part containing a scale (as a vernier) and is submerged and moved gradually until its point just pierces the surface of the liquid from beneath when the measurement is taken
hook-headed spike \'=,==-\ *n* : a spike with extended head to hook over the base of a railroad rail and secure it to a tie
hookier *comparative of* HOOKY
hookiest *superlative of* HOOKY
hooking *pres part of* HOOK
hooking iron *n* : a hand tool with a pointed metal blade for removing caulking from seams (as of a boat)
hook·ish \'hu̇kish\ *adj* : somewhat hooked ⟨a prominent ~ nose⟩
hook ladder *n* : POMPIER LADDER
hook·less \-kləs\ *adj* : having no hooks
hook·let \-klət\ *n* -s [1*hook* + *-let*] : a small hook ⟨a circle of ~*s* on the tapeworm scolex⟩ — see ECHINOCOCCUS illustration
hooklike \'=,=\ *adj* : resembling a hook esp. in recurved form or in ability to grasp and hold ⟨~ thorns⟩
hook·man \'hu̇kmən, -,man\ *n, pl* **hookmen** : a worker that uses a gaff or a cant hook (as in handling logs or fish)
hook money *n* : Persian larin money
hooknose \'=,=\ *n* : an aquiline nose
hook order *n* : a pattern of social organization within a herd of cattle that is characterized by the right of any member to hook one of lower status without fear of retaliation and its submission to hooking by one of higher rank — compare PECK ORDER
hook pass *n* : a basketball pass executed in a manner similar to that of a hook shot
hook rope *n* : a rope with a hook on the end used esp. on shipboard for clearing and handling lines
hook rug *n* : HOOKED RUG
hooks *pl of* HOOK, *pres 3d sing of* HOOK
hook screw *n* : SCREW HOOK
hookshop \'=,=\ *n* [2*hook* (to entrap) + *shop*] *slang* : BROTHEL 2
hook shot *n* : a clear or bank shot in basketball in which a player shoots sideways for the basket by bringing the ball up over his head in an arc with the far hand and releasing it in a usu. flat trajectory
hook slide *n* : a foot-first slide to a base in a baseball game in which the runner with both legs extended throws his body to either side to avoid the baseman and hooks the base with the inside foot
hook squid *n* : any of certain squids (*Enoploteuthis* and related genera) in which the acetabula of the sessile arms are modified into a formidable armament of hooks
hook strip *n* : a horizontal strip or band of wood supporting a series of hooks (as for hanging hats and coats)
hookswinging \'=,==\ *n* : a voluntary ritual torture in which the individual is suspended by hooks inserted into the muscles of the back
hook tender *n* : a working foreman in charge of a crew yarding logs
hooktip \'=,=\ *or* **hook-tip moth** *n* : a moth of the family Drepanidae
hook·um \'hu̇kəm\ *n* -s [Hindi *hukm*, fr. Ar, decision, judgment] *India* : COMMAND, ORDER; *esp* : an official paper giving instructions
hook·um·pake \'hu̇kəm,pāk\ *n* -s [imit.] *Midland* : WOODCOCK 1a(2)
hookum-snivey *var of* HOOKEM-SNIVEY
hook up *vi* : to attach a horse or other source of draft to a vehicle ⟨*hooked up* and drove to the meadow⟩ ~ *vt* **1** : to attach (as a team) to a vehicle **2** : to install in or connect into a suitable environment to function as part of a system ⟨*hooked* the big parlor heater *up* each fall⟩ ⟨*hook* the gas *up*⟩ ⟨finished *hooking up* the new bathroom⟩ **3** *dial* : MARRY ⟨arranged to have the parson *hook* them *up*⟩
hookup \'=,=\ *n* -s [*hook up*] **1** : a group or number of items cooperating or acting together: as **a** : an assemblage (as of apparatus or circuits) used for a specific purpose (as radio transmission or reception); *also* : the general scheme or plan of such an assemblage **b** : a sequence or arrangement of communicating and usu. interacting parts (as the steering gear or brake mechanism of an automobile) ⟨the stoker ~ on the furnace⟩ **2** : the establishment of a hookup : a linking of two or more items into an interacting whole: as **a** : an assembling of parts into a functional whole ⟨finished the ~ of the new pump⟩ **b** : a midair recoupling of a parasite fighter airplane to the belly of the bomber from which it was previously launched **3** : the end of a line transposed to the line above and preceded by a left-hand bracket ⟨~*s* are sometimes necessary in narrow-measure setting⟩ **4** : a state of cooperation or alliance between diverse and often supposedly mutually antagonistic elements ⟨explaining the ~ between politics and crime⟩ ⟨a ~ designed to protect the sovereignty of small nations⟩

ho·oku·pu \ˌhōəˈkü(ˌ)pü\ *n* -s [Hawaiian *ho'okupu*] **:** a Hawaiian ceremonial presentation of gifts formerly offered as tribute to a chief

hookweed \ˈ=ˌ=\ *n* **:** SELF-HEAL

hookworm \ˈ=ˌ=\ *n* **1 :** any of numerous parasitic nematode worms (family Ancylostomatidae) having strong buccal hooks or plates for attaching to the host's intestinal lining and including serious bloodsucking pests of man, many domestic and wild mammals, and a few birds — see ANCYLOSTOMA **2 :** or **hookworm disease :** disease caused by hookworms **:** ANCYLOSTOMIASIS

hook·wormy \"ē\ *adj* **:** infested by hookworms

hook wrench *or* **hook spanner** *n* **:** a wrench having a hook at the end (as for turning a bolt head or nut)

[1]**hooky** \ˈhu̇kē, -ki\ *adj* -ER/-EST [[1]*hook* + *-y*] **1 :** full of or covered with hooks **2 :** resembling or having the form of a hook

[2]**hooky** \"\ *or* **hook·ey** \"\ *n, pl* **hookies** *or* **hookeys** [prob. fr. [2]*hook* (to make off) + *-y*] **:** TRUANT — used chiefly in the phrase *play hooky*

hool \ˈhœl, -üe-\ *Scot var of* HULL

ho·olau·lea \ˌhōəˌlau̇ˈlāə\ *n* -s [Hawaiian *ho'olaule'a*, fr. *ho'o* to make + *lau* much + *le'a* gaiety] **:** a Hawaiian celebration or festival

hoo·let \ˈhülət\ *chiefly Scot var of* HOWLET

hoo·ley \ˈhülē\ *n* -s [origin unknown] **:** an Irish party usu. with music

hoo·ley–ann \ˌhülēˈan\ *also* **hoo·li·an** \", (ˈ)hülˈyan\ *n* -s [origin unknown] *West* **:** a throw with a lariat in which the loop is well spread and settles from above on its objective

hoo·li·gan \ˈhüləgən, -lēg-\ *n* -s *often attrib* [perh. after an Irishman named *Hooligan fl* 1898 in Southwark, London, England] **1 :** HOODLUM 1 **2 :** a person that as a representative of some special interest (as a political or racial philosophy) attempts to override the legal and human rights of other people **3 :** a gambling game played with 10 dice in which a player attempts to throw a selected number 26 or more times in 13 throws

hoo·li·gan·ism \-gəˌnizəm\ *n* -s **:** lawless disorderly conduct typical of hooligans; *often* **:** VANDALISM

hoo·li·han \ˈhüləˌhan\ *vt* **hoolihanned; hoolihanned; hoolihanning; hoolihans** [prob. fr. the name *Hoolihan*] *West* **:** to bring down (a steer) in bulldogging by leaping well forward on the horns rather than by twisting

hoo·lock \ˈhüˌläk, -lək\ *n* -s [native name in Assam or Burma] **:** a small gibbon (*Hylobates hoolock*) of Assam and upper Burma; *broadly* **:** a gibbon of the genus *Hylobates*

[1]**hoo·ly** \ˈhœli\ *adv* [ME *holy*, of Scand origin; akin to ON *hōfliga* fairly, with moderation, fr. *hōfligr* moderate, fr. *hōf* moderation, proportion + *-ligr* -ly; akin to ON *hefja* to lift — more at HEAVE] *chiefly Scot* **:** in a slow, careful, or gentle manner

[2]**hooly** \"\ *adj* [ME (Sc dial.) *huly*, of Scand origin; akin to ON *hōfligr* moderate] *chiefly Scot* **:** SLOW, CAREFUL

ho·oma·li·ma·li \ˌhōəˌmäləˈmälē\ *n* -s [Hawaiian *ho'omalimali*] *Hawaii* **:** something designed primarily to attract favorable attention **:** SOFT SOAP

hoon \ˈhün, -ü-\ *n* -s [Hindi *hūn, hun*] *India* **:** PAGODA 2

hoondee *or* **hoondi** *var of* HUNDI

[1]**hoop** \ˈhüp, -ü-\ *n* -s *often attrib* [ME *hop, hoop*, fr. OE *hōp*; akin to OFris *hōp* ring, band, MD *hoep* ring, band, hoop, Lith *kabė* hook, and perh. to OIr *camm* crooked — more at CHANGE] **1 a :** a strip of wood or metal bent in a circular form and united at the ends that is used esp. for holding together the staves of containers (as casks, tubs, barrels) — see BARREL illustration **b :** such a hoop or a substitute used as a plaything — compare HULA HOOP **2 :** something felt to resemble a hoop **:** a circular figure or object esp. when serving or viewed as a retaining band **:** RING, CIRCLET: as **a :** FINGER RING **b :** either or both members of an embroidery hoop **c :** one of the cylindrical forgings that are concentric with the tube and that are shrunk in rows upon the tube, jacket, or inner layer in the construction of a built-up gun **d :** CHEESE HOOP **e :** a large circle of light material usu. supporting a sheet of paper through which performers leap in various spectacular shows (as in a circus) **f :** a piece of cane looped at one end for handing messages to the crew of a moving railroad train **g :** the rim of a basketball basket; *broadly* **:** the entire basket **3 :** a circle or series of graduated circles of whalebone, metal, or other flexible material inserted into a petticoat or joined by tapes and used to expand a woman's skirt ⟨wore ~s under ruffled white mull⟩ **4 a** *dial Eng* **:** an old unit of capacity (as for grain) varying from ¼ peck to 4 pecks **b** *obs* **:** the quantity of drink contained between any two adjacent hoops of a hooped quart pot **5 hoops** *pl* **:** light strip steel folded up like a skein of wool into lengths of 14 feet **6 :** a croquet wicket **7 :** a shoulder yoke used for carrying loads

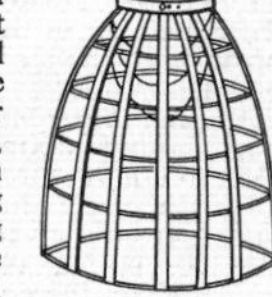

hoop 3

[2]**hoop** \"\ *vb* -ED/-ING/-S [ME *hoopen*, fr. *hop, hoop*, n.] *vt* **1 a :** to bind, enclose, or fasten (as a barrel) with hoops **b :** CLASP, ENCLOSE, SURROUND **2 a :** to place on or in a hoop ⟨~*ing* her embroidery⟩ ⟨~ curds in the making of cheese⟩ **b :** to score at basketball ⟨~*ed* 5 points to win the game⟩ **3 :** to give the form of a hoop or partial hoop to ⟨a measuring worm ~*ing* his back⟩ ⟨~*ed* the backs of the chairs in a graceful arch⟩ ~ *vi* **1 :** to assume the form of a hoop or partial hoop ⟨the cat's back ~*ed* under his hand⟩ **2 :** to keep a hula hoop revolving about the body

[3]**hoop** \ˈhüp, -ü-\ *archaic var of* WHOOP

[4]**hoop** *n* -s [MF *huppe*, fr. L *upupa*, of imit. origin like Gk *epop-, epops* hoopoe, G dial *huppupp*] *obs* **:** HOOPOE

hoop ash *n* **1 :** BLACK ASH 1 **2 :** HACKBERRY

hoop back \ˈ=ˌ=\ *n* **:** a back (as of a Windsor chair) formed by a bent piece of wood fitted with vertical spindles

hoop dance *n* **:** a male exhibition dance with hoops performed among Indian peoples and imitators from New Mexico to the Great Lakes

hoop driver *n* **:** a tool for setting and tightening hoops (as on a barrel)

hooped *adj* **1 :** made with or shaped like a hoop ⟨a ~ chair back⟩; *esp* **:** having a full rounded contour ⟨a horse with well-*hooped* ribs⟩ **2 :** having, wearing, or enclosed by a hoop ⟨a ~ skirt⟩ ⟨graceful ~ dancers⟩ ⟨~ curds ripening into cheese⟩

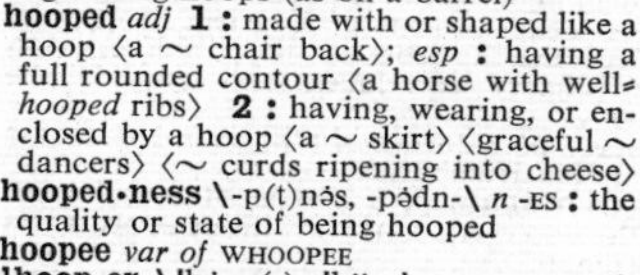

hoop back

hooped·ness \-p(t)nəs, -pəd-n-\ *n* -ES **:** the quality or state of being hooped

hoopee *var of* WHOOPEE

[1]**hoop·er** \ˈhüpə(r), ˈhüp-\ *n* -s **:** one that hoops: as **a :** a man or machine that makes or applies hoops (as to barrels or tubs) **b :** a worker that stretches skins (as sealskins) over a hoop-shaped frame for curing or processing **c :** HOOPSTER

[2]**hooper** *or* **hooper swan** *var of* WHOOPER SWAN

hoop·erat·ing *or* **hooper rating** \ˈhüpəˈrād·iŋ, ˈhüp-, -ātˌ|ēŋ\ *n* -s *usu cap H* [after Claude E. *Hooper* †1954 Am. statistician] **:** a percentage indication of the number of radios or television sets tuned to a particular program at a particular time ⟨rain on a Sunday raises *Hooperatings* —Saul Carson⟩ ⟨the most glamorous, high *Hooperating* show on the air —Frederic Wakeman⟩

hoop fastener *n* **:** a special nail for securing the hoops of a barrel

hoo·pid salmon \ˈhüpəd-, ˈhüp-\ *also* **hoopid** *n* -s [origin unknown] **:** SILVER SALMON

hoop·ing \ˈhüpiŋ, ˈhüp-\ *n* -s [[1]*hoop* + *-ing*] **1 :** stock for making hoops **2 :** HOOPS; *esp* **:** a set of hoops used together ⟨the ~ on this barrel is too slack⟩

hoop iron *n* **:** iron in thin strips used for or suitable for use as barrel hoops ⟨arrowheads of sharpened *hoop iron*⟩

hoop·la *also* **houp–la** \ˈhüˌplä, ˈhu̇-, -ˌlä\ *n* -s [F *houp-là*, interj.] **1 a :** excited commotion ⟨the ~ occasioned . . . by the report —C.J.Rolo⟩; *often* **:** gay or rowdy excitement ⟨holiday ~ and parties⟩ **b :** gaudy, artificial, or pretentious show **:** TO-DO ⟨opportunities for plenty of romantic ~ in a costume drama —John McCarten⟩ ⟨launched the new promotion in a blaze of ~⟩ **c :** something (as utterances) designed to bewilder or confuse ⟨official ~ about the back of organized crime being broken —Joseph LeBaron⟩ **:** BUNKUM, BALLYHOO **2** [influenced in meaning by [1]*hoop*] **:** a game in which novelty items are won by tossing rings over them

hoople \ˈhüpəl, ˈhüp-\ *n* -s [D *hoepel*, dim. of *hoep* hoop, fr. MD — more at HOOP] *dial* **:** HOOP; *esp* **:** a child's hoop for play

hoop·less \-pləs\ *adj* **:** lacking a hoop ⟨an old ~ barrel⟩

hooplike \ˈ=ˌ=\ *adj* **:** like a hoop **:** ARCHED, ROUNDED

hoop·man \ˈhüpmən, ˈhüp-\ *n, pl* **hoopmen :** a basketball player

hoop net *n* **:** an elongated cylindrical net supported by one or more hoops and fitted with one or more valves resembling funnels through which fishes may enter but not escape that is used esp. in rivers or other waters where fishes tend to move along regular paths

hoo·poe *also* **hoo·poo** \ˈhü(ˌ)pü, -pō\ *n* -s [imit. alter. of [4]*hoop*] **:** any of certain Old World nonpasserine birds (family Upupidae) having a slender decurved bill; *esp* **:** a widely distributed bird (*Upupa epops*) of Europe, Asia, and northern Africa that is of the size of a large thrush with a handsome erectile semicircular crest and cinnamon-colored and black plumage and feeds on insects and other small invertebrates found about decaying organic matter — see WOOD HOOPOE

hoop–petticoat daffodil *also* **hoop–petticoat narcissus** *n* **:** a small early-flowering narcissus (*Narcissus bulbocodium*) that has yellow conical to bell-shaped flowers borne singly, is native from southern France to Morocco, and is widely grown as a rock-garden plant

hoop pine *n* **:** an araucaria (*Araucaria cunninghamii*) of Australia and New Guinea that yields a valuable light soft even-textured wood

hoop pole *n* **:** a straight slender length of green sapling wood usu. of hickory or white oak that was formerly used as stock for barrel hoops

hoop ring *n* **:** a finger ring in the form of a plain or ornamented band or with low-mounted stones along the band

hoops *pl of* HOOP, *pres 3d sing of* HOOP

hoopskirt \ˈ=ˌ=\ *n* **1 :** an underskirt stiffened with or as if with hoops **2 :** a full outer skirt expanded by petticoats or hoops

hoop snake *n* **1** *chiefly South and Midland* **:** a fabled snake of extremely venomous character that rolls itself up with its tail in its mouth to proceed at great speed in the manner of a hoop and destroys both animal and plant life with a sting in the end of its tail **2 :** either of two harmless brightly colored burrowing colubrid snakes chiefly of the southeastern U. S.: **a :** a large snake (*Farancia abacura*) that is blue black above and largely red below and has a sharp nonvenomous spine at the end of its tail — called also *horn snake* **b :** RAINBOW SNAKE

hoop·ster \ˈhüpstə(r), ˈhüp-\ *n* -s [[1]*hoop* + *-ster*] **1 :** a basketball player **2 :** one that keeps a hula hoop revolving

hoopstick \ˈ=ˌ=\ *n* **1 a :** HOOP POLE **b :** a light framing member for a carriage or wagon hood **2 :** a stick for rolling a child's play hoop

hoop withe *or* **hoop withy** *n* **1 :** a tropical Old World shrub (*Colubrina asiatica*) the fruits of which are used as fish poison in the Philippines **2 :** a tropical American shrub of a genus (*Trichostigma*) of the family Phytolaccaceae (esp. *T. octandrum*)

hoopwood \ˈ=ˌ=\ *n* **1 :** BLACK ASH 1 **2 :** a winterberry (*Ilex laevigata*)

hoorah *or* **hooray** *var of* HURRAH

hoorah's nest *or* **hooraw's nest** *var of* HURRAH'S NEST

hoo·roosh \hə'rüsh\ *n* -ES [imit.] **:** a wild, hurried, or excited state or situation **:** CONFUSION ⟨such a ~ as we had getting to the docks⟩

[1]**hoose** \ˈhüs\ *chiefly Scot var of* HOUSE

[2]**hoose** *also* **hooze** \ˈhüz\ *n* -s [prob. akin to E *wheeze*] **1** *dial Eng* **:** a dry cough **:** WHEEZING, WHEEZE **2 :** verminous bronchitis of cattle, sheep, and goats caused by larval strongylid roundworms irritating the bronchial tubes and producing a dry hacking cough — called also *husk*

[3]**hoose** *or* **hooze** \"\ *vi* -ED/-ING/-S *dial Eng* **:** WHEEZE

hoose·gow *also* **hoos·gow** \ˈhüsˌgau̇\ *n* -s [Sp *juzgado* panel of judges, tribunal, courtroom, fr. past part. of *juzgar* to judge, fr. L *judicare* — more at JUDGE] *slang* **:** JAIL, LOCKUP, GUARDHOUSE, PRISON

[1]**hoosh** \ˈhüsh\ *interj* [origin unknown] — used esp. in driving away animals

[2]**hoosh** \"\ *vt* -ED/-ING/-ES [perh. alter. of *hoise*] *chiefly Irish* **:** BOOST, LIFT

[3]**hoosh** \"\ *n* -ES *chiefly Irish* **:** HOIST, BOOST

[4]**hoosh** \"\ *n* -ES [origin unknown] **:** a thick soup

hoo·sier \ˈhüzhə(r)\ *n* -s [perh. alter. of E dial. *hoozer* anything large of its kind] **1 :** an awkward, unhandy, or unskilled person; *esp* **:** an ignorant rustic **2** *usu cap* **:** INDIANAN — used as a nickname

[2]**hoosier** \"\ *adj, usu cap* **:** of or relating to Indiana or its people ⟨the *Hoosier* state⟩

[3]**hoosier** \"\ *vi* -ED/-ING/-S *slang* **:** to loaf on or botch a job

hoo·sier·ism \-zhəˌrizəm\ *n* -s *usu cap* **:** a turn of speech typical of or peculiar to natives of a geographic area centered on Indiana

[1]**hoot** \ˈhüt, *usu* -üd·+V\ *vb* -ED/-ING/-S [ME *houten, hoten*, of imit. origin] *vi* **1 :** to utter a loud shout; *usu* **:** to cry out or shout in contempt ⟨matrons and girls shall ~ at thee no more —John Dryden⟩ **2 a :** to make the natural throat noise of an owl **b :** to make a sound resembling the hoot of an owl — used esp. of other birds or mammals **3 :** to make a loud clamorous mechanical sound — used esp. of a siren and similar devices ⟨foghorns ~*ing* in the gloom⟩ ~ *vt* **1 a :** to assail with contemptuous cries or other expressions of disapproval or contempt ⟨men of goodwill ~*ed* by rowdies⟩ **b :** to check, interrupt, or drive out by hooting ⟨~*ed* down the speaker⟩ ⟨~*ing* unpopular actors off the stage⟩ **2 :** to express in or by hoots ⟨~*ed* his disapproval⟩

[2]**hoot** \"\ *n* -s **1 :** a loud inarticulate shout or noise; *esp* **:** a derisive cry ⟨gave a ~ of contempt⟩ **2 a :** the cry of an owl **b :** a sound (as of a motor horn) suggesting this cry **3 :** a very small amount **:** BIT, TRIFLE, WHIT — used chiefly in negative constructions and esp. with the indefinite article ⟨don't care a ~ what you decide⟩ ⟨she didn't really give two ~s about me —Eric Soames⟩

[3]**hoot** \"\ *or* **hoots** \-ts\ *interj* [origin unknown] *chiefly Scot* — used to express impatience, mild dissatisfaction, or objection and often in combination ⟨~ awa⟩ ⟨~ mon⟩

[4]**hoot** \"\ *n* -s [Maori *utu* price, requital] *slang Austral* **:** MONEY

hoo·ta·ma·gan·zy \ˌhüd·əməˌganzē\ *n* -ES [by alter.] **:** HOODED MERGANSER

hootch *var of* [2]HOOCH

hootchy–kootchy *or* **hootchie–kootchie** \ˌhüchēˈküchē, ˌhu̇chiˈkuchi\ *also* **hootchy–kootch** \-ˈkuch\ *or* **hoochie–coochie** *or* **hoochy–koochy** *n, pl* **hootchy–kootchies** *also* **hootchy–kootches** *or* **hoochie–coochies** *or* **hoochy–koochies** [perh. alter. of *hula-hula*] **:** COOCH

hoo·te·nan·ny *or* **hoot·nan·ny** *also* **hoo·ta·nan·ny** \ˈhütᵊnˌanē, ˈhütˌna-, =(=)ˈ=ˌ=\ *n* -ES [origin unknown] **1 a** *chiefly dial* **:** THING, GADGET; *usu* **:** a device or piece of mechanical equipment — used esp. when the standard name is unknown ⟨the ~ that goes on top of the carburetor⟩ **b** *usu hootnanny* **:** a device for holding a crosscut saw in position while sawing a log from the under side **2** *usu hootenanny* **:** a gathering at which folk singers entertain often with the audience joining in

hoot·er \ˈhüd·ə(r), -ütə-\ *n* -s **1 :** one that hoots: as **a** *chiefly Brit* **:** a whistle, siren, or other device (as an automobile or in a factory) for producing a loud hooting noise **b :** a bird (as an owl or blue grouse) that has a hooting call **2 :** [2]HOOT 3

hoot·ing·ly *adv* **:** in the manner of a hoot ⟨sounded ~ in the empty hall⟩ **:** to the point of hooting ⟨~ astonished⟩

hoot owl *n* **:** OWL; *esp* **:** any of various owls (as the tawny owl of Europe or the barred owl of America) having a loud hooting call

hooved \ˈhu̇vd, -ü-\ *adj* **:** having or characterized by hooves ⟨the ~ mammals⟩ **:** HOOFED — often used in combination ⟨strong-*hooved*⟩

hoo·ver apron \ˈhüvə(r)-\ *n* [after Herbert *Hoover* †1964 31st president of the U. S.; fr. its popularity among home gardeners when Hoover was food administrator in World War I] **:** a woman's coverall in the form of a dress that closes by a tie at the waist and has an overlapping reversible front

hoo·ver·crat \ˈhüvəˌkrat\ *n* -s *usu cap* [Herbert *Hoover* + E *democrat*] **:** a Democrat of the southern U.S. voting for or supporting Herbert Hoover in the presidential election of 1928 — **hoo·ver·crat·ic** \ˌ==ˈkrad·ik\ *adj, usu cap*

hoo·ver·ism \ˈhüvəˌrizəm\ *n* -s *often cap* [Herbert *Hoover* + E *-ism*] **:** a system or views formulated by or attributed to Herbert Hoover

hoo·ver·ize \-ˌrīz\ *vb* -ED/-ING/-S *often cap* [Herbert *Hoover* + E *-ize*; fr. his policy as U.S. food administrator 1917–19] *vi* **:** to economize esp. in the use of food ~ *vt* **:** to be saving of or sparing in the use of (food)

hoo·ver·ville \-vəˌvil\ *n, usu cap* [Herbert *Hoover* + E *-ville* (final constituent in many names of towns); fr. the prevalence of such housing during his presidency] **:** a collection of ramshackle dwellings erected upon a dump or urban wasteland and occupied by dispossessed, unemployed, or migratory persons

hooves *pl of* HOOF

[1]**hop** \ˈhäp\ *vb* **hopped; hopped; hopping; hops** [ME *hoppen*, fr. OE *hoppian*; akin to MLG *hupfen, hüpfen, hopfen* to hop, ON *hoppa* to hop, OE *hype* hip — more at HIP] *vi* **1 a :** to move by a quick springy leap or in a series of leaps **:** JUMP ⟨chalked out a hopscotch game and began to ~ around its squares —Dorothy C. Fisher⟩ ⟨~ on a fast-moving train⟩; *esp* **:** to move by leaping with all feet off the ground ⟨a . . . bird came *hopping* around —Francis Birtles⟩ **b :** to jump on one foot or move about in such manner ⟨requiring the applicant to ~ on the toes of each foot —H.G.Armstrong⟩ **c :** BOUNCE, REBOUND ⟨the ball *hopped* around the playing field⟩ **2 a :** to emerge with a quick elastic movement suggestive of a leap ⟨*hopped* out of bed bright and early⟩ ⟨*hopped* out of the car and opened the door for the lady⟩ **b :** to move or go quickly **:** make a quick trip **:** RUN ⟨do you want to ~ down to the store —Oakley Hall⟩ ⟨*hopped* down to the city for the day⟩; *specif* **:** to make a flight usu. of short duration ⟨Western Airlines . . . ~s all over the West —Gladwin Hill⟩ ⟨~s to Miami for Christmas —Phil Gustafson⟩ **c** *slang chiefly Brit* **:** to go away **:** SCRAM ⟨state your business and get *hopping* —Ruth Park⟩ — usu. used with *it* ⟨no, thanks . . . got to ~ it —Richard Llewellyn⟩ **3 :** to set about doing something — usu. used in the phrase *hop to it* ⟨lots of work to be done . . . you'd better ~ to it —Gordon Webber⟩ **4 :** to make a verbal attack **:** give a tongue-lashing ⟨expect them to make . . . mistakes and don't ~ all over them when they do —W.J.Reilly⟩ ~ *vt* **1 a :** to jump over ⟨the men *hopped* the rails and were in the boats —H.A.Chippendale⟩ **b :** to give a hopping motion to ⟨*hopped* the ball up and down⟩ **c :** to get upon by or as if by hopping **:** climb aboard ⟨~ a freight⟩ ⟨*hopped* a street car —John Dos Passos⟩ **d :** HITCHHIKE ⟨~ a ride⟩ **2 a :** to transport in an airplane from one point to another ⟨the heaviest machinery can be *hopped* over the Andes —*Skyways*⟩ ⟨save . . . travel time by *hopping* them for short distances —*Time*⟩ **b :** to cross by airplane ⟨fears about air armadas *hopping* the Atlantic —S.L.A.Marshall⟩ **3** *slang* **:** to attack physically or verbally **:** JUMP ⟨~ an enemy aircraft⟩ **4 :** to wait on **:** give service to **:** TEND, SERVE ⟨you're here to ~ bells —Calder Willingham⟩ ⟨young girls and boys in uniform *hopping* cars —Horace McCoy⟩ ⟨did you think I was going to . . . ~ bar for the rest of my life —Maritta Wolff⟩

[2]**hop** \"\ *n* -s **1 a :** an instance of hopping **:** a short brisk leap esp. on one leg **b** (1) **:** BOUNCE, REBOUND ⟨the shortstop took it on the first ~⟩ ⟨one mortar shell hit a tree, took a freak ~ —Mack Morriss⟩ (2) **:** a slight, sudden elevation taken by a fast pitched ball in its course of flight **2 :** DANCE, BALL ⟨formal and informal ~s —*Career for Tomorrow*⟩ ⟨going to the junior *hop*⟩; *also* **:** a party with dancing **3 a :** a flight in an airplane usu. of short duration ⟨made his dramatic ~ to Paris last week —*New Republic*⟩ **b :** a usu. short or quick trip or excursion ⟨supplement their rations with ~s across the border —Richard Joseph⟩ ⟨weekend ~s to Paris —Sinclair Lewis⟩ ⟨required long ~s on bad trains —Virginia D. Dawson and Betty D. Wilson⟩ **c :** a ride given by a passing vehicle ⟨~s most of the way, and a little walking —J.A. Michener⟩ — **on the hop** *adv (or adj), Brit* **:** in the act **:** with the goods **:** by surprise or unawares — usu. used in the phrase *catch on the hop* ⟨would never catch him *on the hop* —*Sydney (Australia) Bull.*⟩ ⟨that flood of customers caught them *on the hop* —Fred Majdalany⟩

[3]**hop** \"\ *n* -s *often attrib* [ME *hoppe*, fr. MD; akin to OS *feldhoppo* hop, OHG *hopfo* hop, Norw *hupp* tassel, OE *scēaf* sheaf — more at SHEAF] **1 a :** a twining Eurasian vine (*Humulus lupulus*) with 3-lobed or 5-lobed leaves and small greenish dioecious flowers that is widely cultivated in America, occurs often as an escape, and is sometimes confused with a native hop plant (*H. Americanus*) **b hops** *pl* **:** the ripened and dried pistillate cones of hop used chiefly to impart a bitter flavor to malt liquors and also in medicine as a tonic **2** *slang* **:** a narcotic drug; *esp* **:** OPIUM

[4]**hop** \"\ *vb* **hopped; hopped; hopping; hops** *vt* **1 :** to impregnate with hops **2 a** (1) **:** to drug or stimulate with drugs **:** DOPE ⟨I'm not drunk . . . I'm *hopped* to the eyes —Ernest Hemingway⟩ — usu. used with *up* ⟨maybe he was *hopped* up on dope of some sort —Shirley A. Grau⟩ (2) **:** to administer a stimulant to (a race horse) **b :** to stimulate or excite by any means **:** ROUSE — used with *up* ⟨used those alumni banquets to ~ everybody up —Millard Lampell⟩ ⟨*hopped* up by the music —Morley Callaghan⟩ **c :** to increase the power of (an engine) or the power of the engine of (a vehicle) beyond an original rating — used with *up* ⟨~ up the motor⟩ ~ *vi* **:** to gather or grow hops

ho·pak \ˈhōˌpak\ *n* -s [Ukrainian — more at GOPAK] **:** GOPAK

hop aphid *n* **:** a widely distributed aphid (*Phorodon humuli*) that feeds on the growing shoots of hops and other cultivated plants — called also *hop fly, hop louse*

hop back *n* **:** a brewing vat into which the wort is run after boiling in the copper and which has a perforated false bottom for straining off the hops — called also *hop jack*

hopbine *or* **hopbind** \ˈ=ˌ=\ *n* **:** BINE a

hopbush \ˈ=ˌ=\ *n* **:** a shrub or tree of the genus *Dodonaea* — see AKEAKE 1

Hop·cal·ite \ˈhäpkəˌlīt\ *trademark* — used for a granular mixture of specially prepared manganese dioxide with other oxides used as a catalyst esp. for removing carbon monoxide from air by oxidation or for detecting carbon monoxide in gas analysis

hop clover *n* **1 :** any of several plants of the genus *Trifolium* with heads of yellow flowers resembling hop **2 :** BLACK MEDIC

[1]**hope** \ˈhōp\ *vb* -ED/-ING/-S [ME *hopen*, fr. OE *hopian*; akin to OFris *hopia* to hope, MLG & MD *hopen*, MHG *hoffen* to hope, and perh. to OE *hoppian* to hop — more at HOP] *vi* **1 :** to cherish a desire with expectation ⟨~s for great things from his son⟩ **2** *archaic* **:** to place confidence or trust — usu. used with *in* ⟨I ~ in thy word —Ps 119:81 (RSV)⟩ ~ *vt* **1 a :** to desire with expectation or with belief in the possibility of obtaining **:** cherish hope of ⟨what I have been longing for, though I never *hoped* it —Rachel Henning⟩ **b :** DESIRE, TRUST ⟨~ and expect to be back in my laboratory —E.J.Simmons⟩ ⟨~ he'll let us in⟩ **2** *Midland* **:** WISH ⟨all *hoped* him well —H.E.Giles⟩ **syn** see EXPECT — **hope against hope :** to hope without any basis for expecting fulfillment

[2]**hope** \"\ *n* -s [ME, fr. OE *hopa*; akin to OFris, MLG, & MD *hope*, MHG *hoffe*; derivatives fr. the root of E [1]*hope*] **1 :** TRUST, RELIANCE ⟨all my ~ is in the Lord⟩ **2 a :** desire accompanied with expectation of obtaining what is desired or belief that it is obtainable ⟨wished but not with ~ —John Milton⟩ ⟨all ~ is dead⟩ ⟨are in ~s of an early recovery⟩ **b :** one on whom hopes are centered ⟨the team's only ~ for victory⟩ **c :** a source of hopeful expectation **:** PROMISE ⟨viewed America as the land of ~⟩ **d :** something that is hoped for **:** an object of hope ⟨the arrival of reinforcements was their last forlorn ~⟩ ⟨a healthy family is the ~ . . . of every homemaker —Mary S. Switzer⟩

[3]**hope** \"\ *n* -s [ME, fr. OE *hop*; akin to OE *hype* hip — more at HIP] **1** *now chiefly dial* **:** a piece of arable land surrounded by waste; *esp* **:** one surrounded by swamp or marsh **2** *dial chiefly Brit* **:** a broad upland valley sometimes rounded and often with a stream running through it **3** *now dial* **:** a small bay or inlet

ho·pea \'hōpēə\ *n, cap* [NL, after John *Hope* †1786 Sc. physician and botanist] **:** a genus of tropical trees (family Dipterocarpaceae) with simple leaves, usu. fragrant flowers with one-sided spikes or racemes, and often hard heavy wood — compare MERAWAN

hope chest *n* **1 :** a young woman's accumulation of clothes and domestic furnishings (as silver, linen) kept in or as if in a chest in anticipation of her marriage — compare BOTTOM DRAWER **2 :** a box for use as a hope chest

¹**hope·ful** \'hōpfəl\ *adj* [²*hope* + *-ful*] **1 :** full of hope or agreeable expectation **:** inclined to hope **:** happily expectant **2 :** having qualities which inspire hope **:** giving promise of good or of success ⟨a ~ prospect⟩ — **hope·ful·ly** \-fəlē, -li\ *adv* — **hope·ful·ness** *n* -ES

²**hopeful** \"\ *n* -s **:** a person who aspires hopefully or expectantly to become or achieve something ⟨before the convention . . . meets the various presidential ~*s* have set up headquarters —D.D.McKean⟩ ⟨not all who want to write can go to universities . . . a large army of ~*s* is scattered all over the land —Edward Uhlan⟩

hope·ite \'hō,pīt\ *n* -s [Thomas C. *Hope* †1844 Scot. chemist + E *-ite*] **:** a mineral $Zn_3(PO_4)_2.4H_2O$ consisting of a hydrous phosphate of zinc (sp. gr. 2.76–2.85)

hope·less \'hōpləs\ *adj* **1 a** (1) **:** devoid of hope **:** having no expectation of good **:** DESPAIRING ⟨girls feel ~ if they haven't a marriage at least in sight —Sidonie M. Gruenberg⟩ ⟨three lonely and ~ old women —Upton Sinclair⟩ ⟨was never ~ of anybody —Margaret Deland⟩ (2) **:** reflecting or indicating lack of hope ⟨gazed with lusterless, ~ eyes —Jack London⟩ **b :** not susceptible of remedy or cure **:** INCURABLE ⟨should be aware of his responsibility if he declares a . . . patient ~ —*Jour. Amer. Med. Assoc.*⟩ **c :** being beyond redemption **:** offering no prospect of change or improvement ⟨the dream of every magazine writer who is not a ~ hack —Raymond Chandler⟩ ⟨as an actor he is really ~⟩ ⟨a ~ extrovert, giving herself completely and trustingly to everyone —*Holiday*⟩ ⟨a ~ Anglophile —Richard Joseph⟩ **2 a :** giving no ground for hope **:** promising nothing desirable **:** DESPERATE ⟨the situation looked ~ indeed —C.B.Nordhoff & J.N.Hall⟩ **b :** incapable of solution, management, or accomplishment **:** IMPOSSIBLE, INSOLUBLE ⟨a ~ task⟩ ⟨had a ~ jumble of papers on my hands —*Phoenix Flame*⟩ ⟨the defective . . . whose redemption is ~ —B.N.Cardozo⟩ ⟨worked at depths that seemed ~ fifty years ago —Waldemar Kaempffert⟩ ⟨in ~ conflict with religion —R.W.Murray⟩ ⟨lucidity ~ to find amid all the cluttering detail of advanced works —*Geog. Journal*⟩ **syn** see DESPONDENT

hope·less·ly *adv* **:** in a hopeless manner

hope·less·ness *n* -ES **:** the quality or state of being hopeless

hop·er \'hōpə(r)\ *n* -s [ME, fr. *hopen* to hope + *-er*] **:** one that hopes

hopes *pres 3d sing of* HOPE, *pl of* HOPE

hope·well \'hōp,wel\ *or* **hope·well·ian** \(')hōp¦welēən\ *adj, usu cap* [after Cloud *Hopewell*, 19th cent. Am. farmer on whose Ohio farm type stations were found] **:** of or belonging to the most advanced of the mound-building cultures of No. America centered in the Ohio and Illinois river valleys and characterized by large complex earthworks and burial mounds, artistic excellence in artifacts, and frequent cremation of the dead

hop flea beetle *n* **:** a small flea beetle (*Psylliodes punctulata*) sometimes injurious to hops

hop flour *or* **hop meal** *n* **:** LUPULIN

hop fly *n* **:** HOP APHID

hophead \'ˌ=ˌ=\ *n* [³*hop* + *head*] *slang* **:** a drug addict

hop hornbeam *n* **:** a tree of the genus *Ostrya*; *esp* **:** an American tree (*O. virginiana*) with fruiting clusters resembling hops

ho·pi \'hō(,)pē, -,pi\ *n, pl* **hopi** *also* **hopis** *usu cap* [Hopi *Hópi*, lit., good, peaceful] **1 a :** a Shoshonean people of Pueblo Indians in northeastern Arizona **b :** a member of such people **2 :** the language of the Hopi people **3 :** FRENCH BEIGE

hoping *pres part of* HOPE

hop·ing·ly *adv* **:** in a hopeful manner ⟨regarded me ~⟩

hopi way *n, usu cap H&W* **:** the ethical and behavioral code of the Hopi people depicted dramatically in the annual ceremonial cycle and including rules for each of the roles which a person of either sex and at the various age levels is expected to assume throughout life

hop jack *n* **:** HOP BACK

hop kiln *n* **:** a kiln for drying hops

¹**hop·kins·ian** \häp'kinzēən\ *n* -s *usu cap* [Samuel *Hopkins* †1803 Am. clergyman + *-ian*] **:** a follower of the clergyman Samuel Hopkins who taught a rigorous form of Calvinistic theology

²**hopkinsian** \(')=¦==\ *adj, usu cap* **:** of or relating to Hopkinsians or to Hopkinsianism

hop·kins·ian·ism \=¦==ə,nizəm\ *n* -s *usu cap* **:** the theology taught by Samuel Hopkins holding that one must submit unconditionally to the will of God and be willing to be damned if the glory of God requires it

hop·lite \'hä,plīt\ *n* -s [Gk *hoplitēs*, fr. *hoplon* tool, weapon, piece of armor (fr. *hepein* to care for, prepare) + *-itēs* -ite — more at SEPULCHER] **:** a heavily armed infantry soldier of ancient Greece equipped with helmet, cuirass, greaves, shield, spear, and sword

hoplo- *comb form* [NL, fr. Gk *hopl-, hoplo-* tool, weapon, piece of armor, fr. *hoplon*] **:** heavily armed **:** having powerful offensive members — used chiefly in zoological taxa ⟨*Hoplo*nemertea⟩

hop·lo·car·i·da \,häplō'karədə\ *n pl, cap* [NL, fr. *hoplo-* + *-carida* (fr. Gk *karid-, karis* shrimp, prawn)] **:** a division of Malacostraca coextensive with an order Stomatopoda of tropical marine burrowing crustaceans comprising the mantis shrimps and having a reduced capelike carapace, a large powerful abdomen, five pairs of anteriorly directly thoracic maxillipeds of which the second pair form greatly enlarged raptorial arms, and enlarged swimming appendages on the abdomen with large branching gills on the exopodites

hop·lo·ceph·a·lus \-'sefələs\ *n, cap* [NL, fr. *hoplo-* + *-cephalus*] **:** a genus of moderately venomous Australian elapid snakes

hop·lo·nemertea \¦häplō+\ *n pl, cap* [NL, fr. *hoplo-* + *Nemertea*] **:** an order of Nemertea (class Enopla) comprising variable forms with the proboscis armed with stylets and with an intestinal cecum — **hop·lo·nemertean** \"+\ *adj*

hop·lo·nemertini \"+\ [NL, fr. *hoplo-* + *Nemertini*] *syn of* HOPLONEMERTEA

hop·lo·pho·ne·us \,häplə'fōnēəs\ *n, cap* [NL, fr. *hoplo-* + Gk *phonios* murderous] **:** a genus of primitive sabertooths from the Oligocene and Miocene of western No. America having the large heads and canines of later forms but small brains and a grasping forefoot

hop louse *n* **:** HOP APHID

hop marjoram *n* **:** CRETAN DITTANY

hop medic *n* **:** BLACK MEDIC

hop merchant *n* **:** a comma butterfly (*Polygonia comma*)

hop mildew *n* **1 :** either of two parasitic fungi attacking the hop: **a :** a powdery mildew (*Sphaerotheca humuli*) **b :** a downy mildew (*Peronoplasmopara humuli*) **2 :** disease of hops caused by a hop mildew

hop oil *also* **hops oil** *n* **:** a brownish yellow aromatic essential oil obtained from hops and used chiefly in flavoring cereal beverages

hop-o'-my-thumb \¦häpəmə'thəm, -,mī'-\ *n, pl* **hop-o'-my-thumbs :** a very diminutive person **:** DWARF, PYGMY

hopped *adj* **:** impregnated with hops

hopped-up \'=¦=\ *adj* [fr. past part. of *hop up*, v.] **1 a :** being under the stimulating or stupefying influence of a narcotic drug **:** DOPED ⟨when . . . not *hopped-up*, she had a certain pride in her bearing —Polly Adler⟩ **b** (1) **:** full of enthusiasm **:** ENTHUSIASTIC, EXUBERANT, AROUSED, ROUSED, EXCITED ⟨all *hopped-up* over the visit —Danton Walker⟩ ⟨squeaking past an obstinate, *hopped-up* . . . team —*Official Basketball Guide*⟩ (2) **:** dressed up **:** EMBELLISHED ⟨this *hopped-up* image of plantation life —Manny Farber⟩ ⟨*hopped-up* commonplaces about abstract evil and abstract good —A.M.Mizener⟩ **2 :** having its engine power increased beyond the original rating ⟨a *hopped-up* hot rod —*Science Newsletter*⟩

¹**hop·per** \'häpə(r)\ *n* -s [ME, fr. *hoppen* to hop + *-er* — more at HOP] **1 :** one that hops: as **a :** a leaping insect (as a leafhopper, grasshopper, or froghopper); *specif* **:** an immature hopping form usu. of an insect that is winged as an adult (as the larva of a cheese fly or a young grasshopper or locust) **b** (1) **:** a person who makes flights or trips of usu. short duration ⟨the first island-*hopper* in the Caribbean —*Newsweek*⟩ (2) **:** one who flits about from one place of a specified kind to another of the same kind — usu. used in combination ⟨a table*hopper*⟩ ⟨a bar*hopper*⟩ **c :** a batted ball which rebounds from the ground **2 a :** a chute, box, or receptacle usu. funnel-shaped with an opening at the lower part for delivering material (as grain, fuel, or coal) **b :** something like or likened to a hopper in form or function as: (1) **:** any of the compartments of a hopper frame or the hopper frame itself (2) **:** a feeder for animals; *esp* **:** one from which food flows automatically from an enclosed reservoir to the compartment from which it is eaten **c :** a box usu. on the desk of the clerk or other official of a legislative body into which a proposed bill is dropped **d :** the process of realization or preparation — used in the phrase *in the hopper* ⟨your show is in the ~ and you might just as well . . . not worry —E.J.Kahn⟩ ⟨a plan for exempting . . . small businesses from wage controls is in the ~ —*Washington Report*⟩ **3 a :** a ship used esp. to convey mud, gravel, or sand dredged from harbors out to sea and constructed with a full midship section from which the cargo is discharged through the bottom **b :** HOPPER CAR **c** (1) **:** a tank holding water or other liquid and having a device for releasing its contents through a pipe in the bottom (2) **:** a toilet bowl

²**hopper** \"\ *n* -s [³*hop* + *-er*] **1 :** a hop picker **2 :** a brewery worker who pours dried hops into casks **3 :** an inverted pyramid or cone through which malt passes to the grinding mill in the brewing process

hopper boy *n* **:** a revolving rake used in flour milling to spread and stir freshly ground flour for cooling before it is bolted

hopperburn \'==,=\ *n* **:** a browning and shriveling of potato foliage associated with the feeding of the potato leafhopper — compare TIPBURN

hopper car *n* **:** a freight car with a floor sloping to one or more hinged doors or hoppers for discharging bulk contents (as coal, ore, sand) by gravity and with a permanent roof and roof hatches when used for carrying bulk commodities (as cement) which must be kept dry

hopper car

hopper closet *n* **:** a toilet with a hopper

hopper crystal *n* **:** a funnel-shaped crystal

hop·per·doz·er \'häpə(r),dōzə(r)\ *n* [¹*hopper* + *-dozer* (as in *bulldozer*)] **:** a device for collecting and destroying insects (as grasshoppers) that is drawn on runners across a field and has a shield against which insects jump and fall into a pan containing kerosene or oil

hopper frame *n* **:** a window frame that has superimposed fanlights opening inward and is used esp. in hospitals — called also *hospital light*

hoppergrass \'==,=\ *n* [by alter.] *dial* **:** GRASSHOPPER

hop·per·man \'==mən\ *n, pl* **hoppermen 1 :** a member of the crew of a hopper barge **2 :** a worker who adjusts and attends hoppers

hop·pet \'häpət\ *n* -s [obs. E *hopper* basket, seed-basket (fr. ME, fr. *hoppen* to hop + *-er*) + *-et* — more at HOP] *dial Eng* **:** BASKET, BUCKET

¹**hop·ping** \'häpiŋ, -pēŋ\ *adj* **1 :** journeying or flitting about from one place of a specified kind to another place of the same kind — usu. used in combination ⟨thus began a frenetic show*hopping* existence —*N.Y.Times*⟩ **2 :** moving about busily **:** working hard **:** intensely active **:** BUSY ⟨intrigue and foul play keep the captain ~ —Andrea Parke⟩ ⟨the drivers were kept ~ to cover . . . 66 square miles —*Crowsnest*⟩ **3 :** extremely angry **:** FURIOUS

²**hopping** \"\ *adv* **:** EXTREMELY, VIOLENTLY — used in the phrase *hopping mad* ⟨apt to get ~ mad and bring suit —Margaret Nicholson⟩ ⟨~ mad when we discovered that barbed wire —W.A.White⟩

hopping dick *n, usu cap D* **:** a Jamaican thrush (*Turdus aurantius*) resembling a blackbird (*Turdus merula*)

hop·ping·ly *adv* **:** in a hopping manner ⟨flown ~ away —Israel Zangwill⟩

hoppin john \'häpən-\ *also* **hopping john** *n, usu cap J* **:** a stew made with cowpeas, rice, and bacon or salt pork esp. popular in the southern states and traditionally served on New Year's Day

¹**hop·ple** \'häpəl\ *vt* **hoppled; hoppled; hoppling** \-p(ə)liŋ\ **hopples** [prob. fr. ¹*hop* + *-le*] **:** to fetter the feet of (as a horse or cow) **:** HOBBLE

²**hopple** \"\ *n* -s **:** a fetter used for grazing horses or cattle or a leg harness usu. of leather to control the gait of trotting or pacing horses — used chiefly in pl.

¹**hop·py** \'häpē, -pi\ *adj* -ER/-EST [³*hop* + *-y*] **1 :** abounding in hops **2 :** having the bitter taste of hops — used esp. of ale or beer

²**hoppy** \"\ *n* -ES *slang* **:** a drug addict

³**hoppy** \"\ *adj* -ER/-EST [²*hop* + *-y*] **:** characterized by a hopping step or movement ⟨a restless, ~ Frenchman —Ludwig Bemelmans⟩ ⟨a lively little blue crane with a ~ leg —I.L. Idriess⟩

hops *pres 3d sing of* HOP, *pl of* HOP

hopsack \'=,=\ *n* [ME *hopsak* sack for hops, fr. *hoppe* hop + *sak* sack] **:** HOPSACKING 2

hopsacking \'=,==\ *n* [³*hop* + *sacking*] **1 :** material of hemp and jute used esp. as bagging by hop growers **2 :** a rough-surfaced clothing fabric loosely woven of various fibers in an open basket weave

hopsage \'=,=\ *n* [³*hop* + *sage*] **:** any of certain low shrubs of alkaline regions of western No. America that constitute the genus *Grayia* of the family Chenopodiaceae and are locally important native browse plants; *esp* **:** an erect much-branched shrub (*G. spinosa*) having the flowers in dense terminal spikes, the fruiting bracts broadly rounded and often tinged with red, and forming a cluster resembling the strobilus of a hopvine

¹**hopscotch** \'=,=\ *n* [¹*hop* + *scotch* (line)] **:** a child's game of many variations in which a player tosses a small flat stone or similar object consecutively into the lined and numbered areas of a figure outlined upon the ground, hops on one foot through the figure and back to the area in which the stone lies, picks up the stone, and hops on out trying to avoid errors (as stepping on a line or losing balance)

one form of hopscotch figure

²**hopscotch** \"\ *vi* **:** to move with or as if with the hopping step used in the game of hopscotch ⟨children ~ between the tables —Willie S. Ethridge⟩

hops oil *var of* HOP OIL

hop, step, and jump *n* **:** a field event in which the participants cover as much ground as possible by a hop, stride, and jump in succession usu. after a running start

hop·toad \'häp,tōd\ *also* **hop·py·toad** \-pē,-\ *n, chiefly dial* **:** TOAD

hop tree *n* [³*hop*] **:** a small American tree (*Ptelea trifoliata*) having 2-seeded samaras as fruits

hop trefoil *n* **:** HOP CLOVER

hopvine \'=,=\ *n* **1 :** the twining stem of the hop **:** HOPBINE **2 :** a hop plant

hopyard \'=,=\ *n* **:** a hop field

hoquet *var of* HOCKET

hor *abbr* **1** horizon; horizontal **2** horological; horology

¹**ho·ra** *also* **ho·rah** *or* **hor·ra** \'hōrə, 'hȯrə\ *n* -s [NHeb & Romanian; NHeb *hōrāh*, fr. Romanian *horă*, fr. Turk *hora*] **1 :** a folk dance of Romania and Israel in which dancers form a circle, lock arms, and dance to the left or right with grapevine steps and hops **2 :** music to which the hora is danced

²**hora** \"\ *n* -s [native name in Ceylon] **:** a tree (*Dipterocarpus Zeylanicus*) of Ceylon with reddish brown strong heavy wood

ho·ra·ry \'hōrərē\ *adj* [ML *horarius*, fr. L *hora* hour + *-arius* -ary — more at HOUR] *archaic* **:** of or relating to an hour **:** noting the hours

ho·ra·tian \hə'rāshən, hō'-,hȯ'- *also* -shēən\ *adj, usu cap* [L *Horatianus*, fr. *Horatius* Horace (Quintus Horatius Flaccus) †8 B.C. Latin poet + L *-anus* -an] **:** of or relating to the poet Horace or resembling his poetic style (as in finish of form and aptness of diction)

ho·ra·tio al·ger \hə¦rā(,)shō¦alj'ə(r), -āshē,ō-\ *adj, usu cap H&A* [after *Horatio Alger* †1899 Am. clergyman and author of juvenile fiction] **:** of, relating to, or resembling the works of Horatio Alger in which success is achieved through self-reliance and hard work ⟨their own *Horatio Alger* myth of honest poor boy rises to riches —James Jones⟩

horde \'hō(ə)rd, 'hȯ(ə)rd, -ōəd, -ȯ(ə)d\ *n* -s [MF, G & Pol; MF & G *horde*, fr Pol *horda*, of Mongolic origin; akin to Mongolian *ordu, orda* court, camp, horde, Kalmuck *orda*] **1 a** (1) **:** a clan or tribal group of Tatar or other Mongolian nomadic tent dwellers claiming exclusive hunting or grazing rights over a defined area (2) **:** a people or tribe of nomadic life **b :** a usu. small and typically nomadic social group composed of allied or related family groups occupying a common territory; *esp* **:** such a group among the Australian aborigines **c :** a hypothetical primordial social unit comprised of a number of families ⟨the primitive ~ posited by evolutionists⟩ **2 :** an unorganized or loosely organized mass of individuals **:** a vast number **:** CROWD, SWARM, AGGLOMERATION ⟨circling ~*s* of mixed insects —B.J.Haimes⟩ ⟨unpolluted . . . by their brief contact with the touristic ~ —Arnold Bennett⟩ ⟨~*s* of Irish . . . came to the American shore —*Amer. Guide Series: N.Y.*⟩ ⟨most companies today take ~*s* of pictures —W.B.Eidson⟩ **syn** see CROWD

hor·de·in \'hȯ(r)dēən\ *n* -s [F *hordéine*, fr. L *hordeum* barley + F *-ine*] **:** a prolamin found in the seeds of barley

hor·de·nine \-də,nēn, -,nən\ *n* -s [ISV *horden-* (fr. L *hordeum*) + *-ine*; orig. formed in F] **:** a crystalline alkaloid $HOC_6H_4CH_2CH_2N(CH_3)_2$ found in germinating barley and in mescal

hor·de·o·lum \hȯ(r)'dēələm\ *n, pl* **hordeo·la** \-lə\ [NL, alter. of LL *hordeolus*, dim. of L *hordeum* barley] **:** ⁴STY

hor·de·um \'hȯ(r)dēəm\ *n* [NL, fr. L, barley; akin to OHG *gersta* barley, Gk *kri*, Alb *drith*, and prob. to L *horrēre* to bristle — more at HORROR] **1** *cap* **:** a widely distributed genus of grasses having the flowers in dense spikes often with long-awned glumes and the one-flowered spikelets in clusters of two or three at each joint of the rachis — see BARLEY **2** -s **:** any grass of the genus *Hordeum*

hore·hound *or* **hoar·hound** \'hō(ə)r,hau̇nd, 'hȯ(ə)r-, 'hōə,h-, 'hȯ(ə),h-\ *n* [by folk etymology fr. ME *horhoune*, fr. OE *hārhūne*, fr. *hār* hoary + *hūne* horehound — more at HOAR] **1 a :** a European aromatic mint (*Marrubium vulgare*) that is naturalized in the U.S., has pubescent leaves and small axillary flowers, has a very bitter taste, and is used as a tonic and anthelmintic — called also *white horehound* **b :** an extract or confection made from this plant and used as a remedy for coughs and colds **2 :** any of several labiates resembling horehound in appearance — used with an attributive or qualifying adjective ⟨black ~⟩ ⟨water ~⟩

horehound bug *n* **:** a widespread orange and black Australian bug (*Agonoscelis rutila*) destructive to the foliage of horehound and other crop plants

ho·rite \'hōr,īt\ *n* -s *usu cap* **1 :** a cave-dwelling people of the biblical period prior to the time of Abraham that inhabited the Dead sea region of the eastern Mediterranean **2 :** a member of the Horite people

¹**ho·ri·zon** \hə'rīzᵊn\ *n* -s [alter. (influenced by LL *horizon*) of ME *orisonte, orizon*, fr. LL *horizont-, horizon*, fr. Gk *horizont-, horizōn*, fr. pres. part. of *horizein* to separate, part, bound, define, fr. *horos* boundary, limit + *-izein* -ize; akin to L *urvus* circumference of a city, Oscan *uruvú* boundary] **1 a :** a circle that bounds the part of the earth's surface visible from a given point **:** an apparent junction of earth and sky **b** (1) **:** a great circle 90 degrees from the zenith and constituting the equator of the horizon system of coordinates (2) **:** the circle in which a plane perpendicular to the direction of gravity intersects the celestial sphere (3) **:** the plane tangent to the earth's surface at the observer's position (4) **:** a level mirror (as the surface of mercury in a shallow vessel or a plane reflector adjusted to the true level artificially) used esp. in observing altitudes — called also *artificial horizon, false horizon* **c** *or* **horizon line :** an imaginary line in a picture on which is projected the point of sight or station point of the spectator and which in a landscape replaces the natural horizon — compare PERSPECTIVE **d** (1) **:** the fullest range or widest limit of perception, interest, appreciation, knowledge, or experience ⟨the ~ of the human intellect has widened wonderfully during the past hundred years —C.W.Eliot⟩ ⟨your ~ contracts, your mind's eye is focused upon a small circle of . . . details —Jan Struther⟩ (2) **:** the range or limit of hope or expectation or a visible and seemingly attainable end or object lying within or upon it **:** GOAL, PROSPECT ⟨youth . . . demands of life some hope and ~ —John Buchan⟩ ⟨China with its ~*s* of industrialization and trade —M.W.Straight⟩ **2 a :** the geological deposit of a particular time, usu. identified by distinctive fossils **:** a stratigraphic level or position in the geologic column **:** a natural soil layer; *also* **:** ZONE **b :** any of the reasonably distinct layers of soil or its underlying material seen in a vertical section or profile of land and gradually developed as a result of natural soil-forming processes (as the incorporation of organic matter with disintegrated rock material) — see A-HORIZON, B-HORIZON, C-HORIZON, D-HORIZON **c** (1) **:** a cultural area or level of development indicated by widely separated groups of artifacts showing cultural similarities (as in specific styles or objects) (2) **:** a period of time indicated by a particular level of development in an excavated site **3 :** HORIZON BLUE 2 **syn** see RANGE

²**horizon** \"\ *vt* -ED/-ING/-S **:** to limit by a horizon

ho·ri·zon·al \-z(ᵊ)nəl\ *adj* **:** of or relating to a horizon **:** having a horizon ⟨the functional significance of a ~ diffusion —*Amer. Antiquity*⟩ ⟨never has the opportunity for the individual career been so exalted . . . so ~ —S.N.Behrman⟩

horizon blue *n* **1 :** a variable color averaging a light greenish blue to blue **2** *also* **horizon :** a greenish white

horizon clubber *n* [*Horizon Club* + *-er*] **:** a member of Horizon Club, the senior program of the Camp Fire Girls for girls in the ninth grade through high school or about 15 through 18

horizon coordinate *n* **:** any member of a system of celestial coordinates based on the horizon of the observer with azimuth being the primary coordinate and altitude the secondary coordinate

ho·ri·zon·less \-zᵊnləs\ *adj* **:** devoid of a horizon **:** HOPELESS ⟨it was a ~ grind —Philip Hamburger⟩

horizon system of coordinates : a system of celestial coordinates based on the observer's horizon with its coordinates being altitude and azimuth

¹**hor·i·zon·tal** \¦hȯrə¦zäntᵊl, ¦här-\ *adj* [LL *horizont-, horizon* + E *-al*] **1 a :** of, relating to, or situated near the horizon **b :** parallel to the horizon **:** being on a level **:** FLAT ⟨a ~ line⟩ ⟨a ~ surface⟩ **c :** measured or contained in a plane of the horizon ⟨~ distance⟩ **d :** placed or operating chiefly along a plane parallel to the horizon — used esp. of machines and mechanical devices ⟨a ~ escapement⟩ **e** *bot* **:** situated in a plane at a right angle to the plane of the primary axis ⟨~ branches⟩ **f** *of a stamp* **:** having a rectangular shape with the longer sides forming the top and bottom **2 a :** applied equally or uniformly to all individuals in a group **:** OVERALL, GENERAL ⟨~ rate increases⟩ ⟨demands for ~ slashing of local government costs —O.K.Armstrong⟩ ⟨the increased ~ spread of buying power —Bud Wilson⟩ **b :** relating to, uniting, or consisting of individuals of similar type or on the same level: as (1) **:** consisting of two or more economic units on the same level of production or distribution ⟨his gigantic ~ and vertical combination of business ventures is efficiently run —Claire Sterling⟩ ⟨a ~ merger⟩ (2) **:** of, relating to, or comprising persons of similar status ⟨a union made up of meat cutters or railroad engineers . . . would be considered ~ —J.F.Cuber⟩ ⟨it must be . . . ~, in the sense of uniting students of similar ages —*General Education in a Free Society*⟩ ⟨~ strata . . . based upon the social values that are attached to occupation, education, place of residence in the community, and associations —August Hollingshead⟩ (3) **:** relating to the

motion of a succession of musical notes or tones forming a melodic line or part — **hor·i·zon·tal·ly** \-ᵊlē, -ᵊli\ *adv*

²horizontal \"\ *n* -s : something that is horizontal; *esp* : a horizontal line ⟨the mood of quiet is emphasized by the ~s of the lake —S.M.Green⟩

horizontal bar *n* **1** : a bar fixed in horizontal position for gymnastic exercise **2** : an event in gymnastic competition

horizontal engine *n* : an engine with horizontal line of stroke

horizontal fault *n* : a fault in the earth's crust with no vertical displacement

horizontal intensity *n* : the horizontal component of the intensity of the earth's magnetic field

hor·i·zon·tal·i·ty \ˌhȯrəˌzänˈtaləd·ē, ˌhär-\ *n* -ES : the quality or state of being horizontal ⟨his houses have a pronounced ~ —J.M.Richards⟩

hor·i·zon·tal·ize \ˌhȯrəˈzäntᵊlˌīz, ˌhär-\ *vt* -ED/-ING/-S : to arrange horizontally ⟨information with which to scale and ~ the model —*U.S. Army Tech. Manual*⟩

horizontal kiln *n* : a kiln that has its axis in a horizontal as opposed to a vertical position with the materials being processed moved through by the slight slope and rotation of the kiln itself or carried through on conveyors

horizontal ladder *n* : a ladder of wood or metal held in a horizontal position usu. by upright supports and used in a gymnasium or on a playground for suspension exercises esp. for the development of arm and shoulder-girdle strength

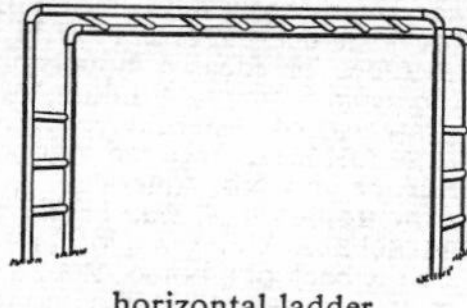
horizontal ladder

horizontal parallax *n* : the maximum geocentric parallax observed when the celestial body is at the horizon

horizontal pendulum *n* : a pendulum that oscillates in a horizontal plane (as a compass needle on its pivot)

horizontal section *n* : a section representing an object as cut horizontally through its center

horizontal structure *n* : POLYPHONY 1 — compare VERTICAL STRUCTURE

horizontal training *n* : the operation of training fruit trees or grapevines so that the branches will spread out laterally in a horizontal direction — compare ESPALIER

horizontal training of a tree

hor·key \ˈhȯrkē\ *var of* ²HOCKEY

horloge *var of* HOROLOGE

hor·me \ˈhȯr(ˌ)mē\ *n* -S [G, fr. Gk *hormē* impulse, attack, assault — more at SERUM] : vital energy as an urge to purposive activity

hor·mic \-mik\ *adj* : of or relating to horme; *specif* : purposively directed toward a goal ⟨~ activities of the organism⟩

hormic psychology *n* : psychology concerned with the purposive factor or force in behavior

hor·mi·go \(h)ȯ(r)ˈmē(ˌ)gō\ *n* -S [AmerSp, fr. Sp *hormiga* ant, fr. L *formica* — more at PISMIRE] **1** : ANT TREE **2** : QUIRA

hor·mism \ˈhȯ(r)ˌmizəm\ *n* -S [*horme* + *-ism*] : HORMIC PSYCHOLOGY

hor·mo·den·dron \ˌhȯ(r)məˈdendrən\ *syn of* HORMODENDRUM

hor·mo·den·drum \-rəm\ *n, cap* [NL, fr. Gk *hormos* chain, necklace (fr. *eirein* to fasten) + *dendron* tree — more at SERIES, DENDR-] : a form genus of imperfect fungi (family Dematiaceae) having dull brownish to black spores produced in chains resembling trees

hor·mo·gon \ˈhȯ(r)məˌgän\ *or* **hor·mo·gone** \-ˌgōn\ *n* -S [NL *hormogonium*] : HORMOGONIUM

hor·mo·go·na·les \ˌhȯ(r)məgōˈnā(ˌ)lēz\ *n pl, cap* [NL, fr. *hormogonium* + *-ales*] : an order of filamentous blue-green algae having the capacity to form hormogonia

hor·mo·go·ni·um \ˌhȯ(r)məˈgōnēəm\ *n, pl* **hormogo·nia** \-ēə\ [NL, fr. Gk *hormos* + *gonium*] : a portion of a filament between two heterocysts in many blue-green algae that becomes detached as a reproductive body — **hor·mog·o·nous** \(ˈ)hȯ(r)¦mägənəs\ *adj*

hor·mo·nal \(ˈ)hȯ(r)¦mōnᵊl\ *adj* [ISV *hormone* + *-al*] : of, relating to, or effected by hormones — **hor·mo·nal·ly** \-ᵊlē\ *adv*

hor·mone \ˈhȯrˌmōn, ˈhȯ(ə)-\ *n* -S [Gk *hormōn*, pres. part. of *horman* to stir up, set in motion, fr. *hormē* impulse, attack, assault — more at SERUM] **1** : a specific organic product of living cells that, transported by body fluids or sap, produces a specific effect on the activity of cells remote from its point of origin : internal secretion : AUTACOID; *esp* : such a product exerting a stimulatory or excitatory effect on a cellular activity — compare AUXIN, CHALONE, PLANT HORMONE **2** : a synthetic substance that resembles a naturally occurring hormone in producing a specific biological effect — compare GROWTH REGULATOR

hormonelike \ˈ=ˌ=ˌ=\ *adj* : resembling a hormone esp. in physiological action

hor·mon·ic \(ˈ)hȯ(r)¦mänik, -mōn-\ *adj* : HORMONAL

hor·mon·iza·tion \ˌhȯ(r)ˌmōnəˈzāshən\ *n* -S : the process of hormonizing

hor·mon·ize \ˈhȯ(r)ˌmōˌnīz\ *vt* -ED/-ING/-S [*hormone* + *-ize*] : to treat with a hormone; *specif* : to castrate chemically — compare CAPONETTE

hor·mo·noid \ˈhȯ(r)məˌnȯid, -ˌmōn-\ *adj* : resembling that of a hormone

hor·mo·spore \ˈhȯrməˌspō(ə)r\ *n* [NL *hormogonium* + E *spore*] : a terminally borne hormogonium in some blue-green algae with cells modified in shape and having exceptionally thick walls

¹horn \ˈhȯ(ə)rn, ˈhȯ(ə)n\ *n* -S [ME, fr. OE; akin to OHG & ON *horn*, Goth *haurn*, L *cornu* horn, *cerebrum* brain, Gk *keras* horn, Skt *śṛṅga*] **1 a** (1) : one of the paired bony processes that arise from the upper part of the head of many ungulate mammals, that function chiefly as weapons, and that in cattle and related forms are usu. present in both sexes and are unbranched and permanent with a bony core anchored to the skull and a sheath of horn and in deer are solid deciduous bony outgrowths usu. branching and usu. present only in the male — see ANTLER; COW illustration (2) : a horned animal (3) : a part like an animal's horn attributed to a divine or supernatural being and esp. to the devil **b** : a natural projection or excrescence from an animal that resembles or suggests a horn: as (1) : a projection (as the casque of a hornbill) from the beak of a bird (2) : a tuft of feathers on the head of a bird (as a horned owl) (3) : a projection from the head or thorax of an insect or from the head of a reptile or fish (4) : a sharp spine in front of the fins of a fish (as a horned pout) (5) : one of the tentacles of a snail **c** (1) : the tough fibrous material derived from epithelial tissue and consisting chiefly of keratin with which the horns of cattle and related animals are covered (2) : any similar substance (as that which forms the hoof crust of horses, sheep, cattle) (3) : a manufactured product (as a plastic resembling horn) (4) : a bow tip made of horn into which the bowstring nock is cut (5) : HORN SPOON 2 **d** : the hollow horn of an animal used as a drinking cup ⟨handed him a ~ filled with red Chilean wine —*Time*⟩ or for holding other liquid or substance (as ink or powder); *also* : DRINK ⟨did sometimes take a ~ when he thought it would do him good —*Atlantic*⟩ **e** : CORNUCOPIA **2** : something resembling or suggestive of a horn: as **a** : one of the curved ends of a crescent; *esp* : a cusp of the moon when crescent-shaped **b** (1) : a body of land or water shaped like a horn (2) : a sharp peak in a rugged mountain region **c** (1) : a horn-shaped part of a device or mechanism (as a blacksmith's anvil or a horning press); *specif* : a part of a shoemaking machine over which a shoe is placed when being tacked, nailed, pegged, and in some instances sewed (2) : one of the outer ends of a ship's crosstrees; *also* : one of the points of the jaws of a gaff or boom (3) : a high pommel of a saddle; *also* : either of the projections on a lady's saddle for supporting the leg — see STOCK SADDLE illustration (4) : a short lever attached to a control surface of an airplane by means of which it is operated (5) *or* **horn antenna** : a radio antenna in which a metallic envelope that is usu. a rectangular cross-section wave guide flares out to project a signal into space (6) : a tube of varying sectional area used in some types of loudspeaker **d** : an erect penis — usu. considered vulgar **e** : CORNU **3 a** : a musical wind instrument formed from the horn of an animal (as an ox or ram); *specif* : SHOFAR **b** (1) : a brass wind instrument employing the lips as the vibrating medium (as the trumpet, saxhorn, tuba) or a plastic, wood, or metal imitation used as a children's toy (2) : FRENCH HORN (3) : a wind instrument (as the saxophone, clarinet, trombone) used in a jazz band **c** (1) : a usu. electrically operated device (as on an automobile or a diesel locomotive or in a factory) that makes a noise like that of a horn and is used for sounding a warning signal (2) : AIR HORN **4 a** : a means of defense : source of strength : POWER, GLORY, PRIDE ⟨The Lord is ... the ~ of my salvation —Ps 18:2 (RSV)⟩ ⟨the election of a prominent layman ... will help to elevate the ~ of the church —A.W.Long⟩ **b** [so called fr. the old custom of cutting the spurs from cockerels when they were castrated and implanting them in the comb, where they would grow into hornlike members that made it easy to pick out the capons, capons being frequent symbols of cuckoldry] : an imaginary horn supposedly growing upon the head of a cuckold and regarded as an emblem of his state — usu. used in pl. **c** : one of the equally disadvantageous alternatives presented by a dilemma ⟨to get off the ~s of this dilemma will not be easy —*Atlantic*⟩

²horn \"\ *adj* [ME, fr. *horn*, n.] : of or resembling horn or a horn; *esp* : composed or made of horn or a similar substance (as a plastic) ⟨~ spectacles⟩

³horn \"\ *vb* -ED/-ING/-S [¹*horn*] *vt* **1** : CUCKOLD **2 a** : to butt or gore with the horns **b** : to drive with the horns — used with *out* or *off* ⟨the young bull who had come to ~ the old one out of the herd —*Omnibook*⟩ **3 a** (1) : to wedge or fasten (as a boom or spar of a ship) as if between horns ⟨~ the boom in a crotch⟩ (2) : to install (the frame of a ship) square to the keel after allowing for the keel's declivity **b** : to press or hammer (a piece of metal) on the horn of an anvil **4** *dial Eng* : to proclaim or spread the news of ~ *vi*, *dial Eng* : to talk in a gossipy manner

horn alligator *n* : leather from an alligator's back

horn angle *n* : a figure formed by two plane curves tangent to each other on the same side of their mutual tangent line

hornbeam \ˈ=ˌ=\ *n* [¹*horn* + *beam*; fr. its hard, smooth, close-grained wood — more at BEAM] **1** : a tree of the genus *Carpinus*: as **a** : an Old World tree (*C. betulus*) with smooth gray bark, hardy white wood, and leaves resembling those of the beech **b** : a similar tree (*C. caroliniana*) of America **2** : HOP HORNBEAM **3** : PLANER TREE

hornbill \ˈ=ˌ=\ *n* : any of various large bulky omnivorous chiefly arboreal birds of Africa, southern Asia, and the East Indies constituting the suborder Bucerotes and having plumage that is predominantly black and white and an enormous bill that is usu. surmounted by a horny casque

horn·blende \ˈhȯrnˌblend, ˈhȯ(ə)n-\ *n* [G, fr. *horn* horn (fr. OHG) + *blende* blende — more at HORN, BLENDE] **1** : a mineral approximately $Ca_2Na(Mg,Fe)_4(Al,Fe,Ti)_3Si_6O_{22}(O,OH)_2$ consisting of the common black, dark green, or brown variety of aluminous amphibole, containing considerable iron, and occurring as distinct crystals and in columnar, fibrous, and granular form **2** : AMPHIBOLE

horn·blen·dic \(ˈ)hȯ(r)n¦blendik\ *adj* : containing hornblende in quantity : resembling or relating to hornblende

horn·blend·ite \ˈ=ˌblenˌdīt\ *n* -S [*hornblende* + *-ite*] : a granular igneous rock composed almost entirely of hornblende

horn·blend·iza·tion \ˌhȯ(r)nˌblendəˈzāshən\ *n* -S : the transformation of a rock into hornblende by replacement processes

horn block *n* : PEDESTAL 3a

hornbook \ˈ=ˌ=\ *n* **1** : a child's primer formerly in use consisting typically of a sheet of parchment or later of paper mounted on a thin wooden board and protected by a sheet of transparent horn and having on it the alphabet and other rudiments such as the digits and often the Lord's Prayer — compare BATTLEDORE 3 **2** : a rudimentary treatise ⟨~s of political theory —V.O.Key⟩

horn cell *n* : a nerve cell lying in one of the gray columns of the spinal cord

horn chestnut *n* : WATER CHESTNUT

horn·church \ˈhȯrnˌchərch\ *adj, usu cap* [fr. *Hornchurch*, urban district, England] : of or from the urban district of Hornchurch, England : of the kind or style prevalent in Hornchurch

horn–core \ˈ=ˌ=\ *n* : the bony inner shaft of a typical horn (as that of a cow)

horn dance *n* : a dance of Abbots Bromley, Staffordshire, England, with characters and patterns similar to those of the morris and distinguished by men carrying antlers

horned \ˈhȯ(ə)rnd, ¦hȯ(ə)nd *sometimes when not in combination* -nəd\ *adj* [ME, fr. OE *horn* + *-ed*] **1** : having horns ⟨a mythical ~ beast, the unicorn⟩ — often used in combination ⟨long-*horned*⟩ **2** : having a process or appendage resembling a horn **3** : having a part shaped like a horn ⟨the ~ moon —S.T.Coleridge⟩

horned adder *n* : HORNED VIPER

horned bladderwort *n* : a No. American bog or aquatic herb (*Stomoisia cornuta*) with stems and minute linear leaves underground and solitary or few yellow showy irregular flowers on a slender naked scape

horned cattle *n* : cattle with horns; *specif* : bovine animals (as cows, bulls, steers)

horned crab *n* : a decorator crab (*Stenocionops furcata*)

horned dace *n* : a common No. American cyprinid fish (*Semotilus atromaculatus*)

horned frog *n* **1** : any of various So. American frogs constituting a genus (*Ceratophrys*) of the family Leptodactylidae and usu. having triangular processes on the eyelids **2** : HORNED TOAD

horned grebe *n* : a grebe (*Colymbus auritus*) that is widely distributed in northern parts of the northern hemisphere, is chiefly dark above and silky white below, and is distinguished when in breeding plumage by a glossy black head banded on either side with gold which encloses the eye and terminates in a brief ear tuft

horned hazel *n* : BEAKED HAZEL

horned hog *n* : BABIRUSA

horned hummer *n* : SUN GEM

horned iguana *n* : a Haitian iguana (*Metopoceras cornutus*) having three hornlike scales on the head

horned lark *n* : a small lark (*Eremophila alpestris*) and its subspecies widely distributed in the northern hemisphere

horned lizard *n* : HORNED TOAD

horned milfoil *n* : PURPLE BLADDERWORT

horned·ness \ˈhȯrnədnəs, -n(d)nəs, ˈhȯ(ə)n-\ *n* -ES : the quality or state of being horned

horned owl *n* : any of various owls (as the American great horned owl) having conspicuous tufts of feathers on the head

horned pheasant *n* : CRIMSON TRAGOPAN

horned pondweed *n* : a submerged aquatic weed (*Zannichellia palustris*)

horned poppy *n* : a yellow-flowered Eurasian herb (*Glaucium flavum*) adventive in the U. S.

horned pout *n* : BULLHEAD 1b; *esp* : a common bullhead (*Ameiurus nebulosus*) of the eastern U. S. which has been introduced into streams of the Pacific coast — called also *Sacramento cat*

horned puffin *n* : a puffin of the north Pacific having a small fleshy appendage resembling a horn on the eyelid

horned rattlesnake *n* : SIDEWINDER

horned ray *n* [so called fr. its cephalic fins or processes] : a ray of the family Mobulidae : DEVILFISH, MANTA

horned rush *n* : any of various sedges of the genus *Rhynchospora*; *esp* : a tall sedge (*R. corniculata*) of the eastern U. S. with a long-beaked achene

horned screamer *n* : a screamer (*Anhima cornuta*) of northern So. America with a long slender yellowish white process resembling a horn on the forehead — compare CRESTED SCREAMER

horned shark *n* : a small California shark (*Heterodontus francisci*) related to the bullhead of Australia

horned snake *n* **1** : HORNED VIPER **2** : HOOP SNAKE

horned toad *n* : any of various small harmless insectivorous lizards constituting the genus *Phrynosoma* (family Iguanidae) of the dry sandy plains of the western U. S. and Mexico and having several hornlike spines on the head and a broad flat body covered with spiny scales

horned violet *n* [so called fr. the elongated spur of the corolla] : TUFTED PANSY

horned viper *n* : a common desert-dwelling viper (*Aspis cornutus*) of Egypt and Asia Minor distinguished by a horny scale resembling a spike above each eye — compare ASP

horned wavey *n* : ROSS'S GOOSE

hor·ne·mann's redpoll \ˈhȯ(r)nəˌmänz-\ *n, usu cap H* [after Friedrich K. *Hornemann* †1801 Ger. explorer] : a redpoll (*Carduelis hornemanni*) of Europe with a small and pale breast and rump

hor·ne·oph·y·ton \ˌhȯ(r)nēˈäfəˌtän\ *n, cap* [NL, fr. *horneo-* (fr. E *horn*) + *phyton*] : a genus of Devonian fossil plants (family Rhyniaceae) similar to those of the genus *Rhynia* but smaller and lacking vascular tissue in the rhizome and considered to be one of the earliest forms of vascular land plants

horn·er \ˈhȯrnər\ *n* -S [ME, fr. ¹*horn* + *-er*] **1** : one who works or deals in horn **2** : one who blows a horn **3** *obs* : one who cuckolds another man **4** *slang* : one who inhales heroin

hor·ne·ro \(h)ȯ(r)ˈne(ˌ)rō\ *n* -S [AmerSp, fr. Sp, baker, fr. *horno* oven (fr. L *furnus*) + *-ero* -er; fr. the fact that its nest resembles an oven — more at FURNACE] : BAKER BIRD

hor·ner's method \ˈhȯrnərz-\ *n, usu cap H* [after William G. *Horner* †1837 Eng. mathematician] : a numerical method of successive approximations used for computing to any number of decimal places an approximate value of any real root of an algebraic equation with real coefficients

horner's syndrome *n, usu cap H* [after Johann F. *Horner* †1886 Swiss ophthalmologist] : a syndrome marked by sinking in of the eyeball, contraction of the pupil, drooping of the upper eyelid, and vasodilation and anhidrosis of the face, and caused by injury to the cervical sympathetic innervation

hor·net \ˈhȯrnət, ˈhȯ(ə)n-, *usu* -əd.+V\ *n* -S [ME *hernet, harnette*, fr. OE *hyrnet*; akin to OS *hornut* hornet, OHG *hurnuz, hornaz*, MD *horsel*, L *crabro* hornet, Lith *širšė* wasp, and prob. to OE *horn* — more at HORN] : any of the larger social wasps of the family Vespidae that are vigorous strong-flying insects with powerful stings, usu. construct nests of macerated wood pulp resembling paper, and feed on both animal and vegetable matter — see GIANT HORNET, WHITE-FACED HORNET; compare YELLOW JACKET

white-faced hornet

hornet's nest *n* : a troublesome situation : angry reaction ⟨must have known that his frank comments ... would stir up a *hornet's nest* —*U. S. Investor*⟩

horn·fels \ˈhȯrnˌfelz\ *n, pl* **hornfels** [G, fr. *horn* horn (fr. OHG) + *fels* cliff, rock, fr. OHG *felis, felisa* — more at HORN, FELL] : a fine-grained silicate rock produced by contact metamorphism

hornfish \ˈ=ˌ=\ *n* : a fish of the family Triacanthidae

horn fly *n* : a small black European blood-sucking two-winged fly (*Haematobia irritans*) introduced into No. America and other cattle-raising areas that clusters about the horns of cattle or hovers about their backs and causes great irritation by its bites

horn gap *n* : an arc gap formed by two horn-shaped electrodes that diverge so that the arc extinguishes itself

hornier *comparative of* HORNY

horniest *superlative of* HORNY

horn·i·fy \ˈhȯ(r)nəˌfī\ *vt* -ED/-ING/-ES [¹*horn* + *-ify*] : to make hard like horn; *specif* : to make keratotic ⟨*hornified* skin⟩

horn·i·ly \ˈhȯ(r)nəlē\ *adv* : in a horny manner

horn in *vi* : to participate without invitation or often consent : butt in : INTRUDE ⟨*horned in* with advice⟩ ⟨*horn in* on a deal⟩

¹horning *pres part of* HORN

²horn·ing \ˈhȯrniŋ\ *n* -S *chiefly North* : SHIVAREE

horning press *or* **horn press** *n* : a punch press with a horn by means of which the seams on hollow tinware are closed

horn·ist \ˈhȯrnəst\ *n* -S : a performer on a French horn

hor·ni·to \(h)ȯ(r)ˈnēd·(ˌ)ō\ *n* -S [Sp, dim. of *horno* oven — more at HORNERO] : a low oven-shaped mound in volcanic regions that emits smoke and vapors

horn knot *n* : SPIKE KNOT

horn·less \ˈ=ləs\ *adj* : having no horn

horn·less·ness *n* -ES : the condition of being hornless

horn lightning arrester *n* : a lightning arrester in which the spark gap is formed by two wires that diverge like a pair of horns — see LIGHTNING ARRESTER illustration

hornlike \ˈ=ˌ=\ *adj* **1** : having the form of a horn esp. in being elongated, pointed, and protruding ⟨a ~ process⟩ **2** : resembling horn : CORNEOUS, HORNY, KERATINOUS

horn mercury *n* [so called fr. its horny appearance when fused] : CALOMEL

horn of plenty : CORNUCOPIA

horn owl *n* : HORNED OWL

hornpie \ˈ=ˌ=\ *n* [¹*horn* + *pie*; fr. the tufted feathers on its head] *dial Eng* : LAPWING

hornpipe \ˈ=ˌ=\ *n* [ME fr. *horn* + *pipe*] **1 a** : a single reed wind instrument popular in England and thought to be of Celtic origin consisting of a wooden or bone pipe with holes at intervals along its length and with the bell and mouthpiece usu. made of horn — compare PIBGORN, STOCKHORN **b** : a lively country dance tune in 3⁄2, 3⁄4, or 4⁄4 time orig. played on this instrument **2** : a lively folk dance of the British Isles usu. performed by a single person and orig. accompanied by hornpipe playing **3** : a tune in the rhythm of a hornpipe

horn poppy *n* : HORNED POPPY

hornpout \ˈ=ˌ=\ *n* : HORNED POUT

horn quicksilver *n* [so called fr. its horny appearance when fused] : native calomel

horn–rimmed \ˈ=ˌ=\ *adj* : having rims of horn

horn–rims \ˈ=ˌ=\ *n pl* : spectacles with horn rims ⟨a stocky girl with *horn-rims* —William DuBois⟩

horns *pl of* HORN, *pres 3d sing of* HORN

horn shark *n* : HORNED SHARK

horn shell *n* : a snail of the genus *Cerithidea*

horn silver *n* [trans. of G *hornsilber*] : CERARGYRITE

horn snake *n* : HOOP SNAKE

horn socket *n* : a fishing tool consisting of a cone which seizes broken rods or tools in bored wells

horn spoon *n* **1** : a spoon made of horn — used chiefly interjectionally in the phrase *by the great horn spoon* ⟨cookies, by the great *horn spoon* —Hamlin Garland⟩ **2** *also* **horn** : a small receptacle like a trough made from a section of cow horn and used for careful washing tests in gold mining

hornstone \ˈ=ˌ=\ *n* [trans. of G *hornstein*] : a mineral consisting of a variety of quartz much like flint but more brittle

horn·swog·gle *also* **horn·swag·gle** \ˈhȯ(r)n¦swägəl\ *vt* -ED/-ING/-S [origin unknown] : BAMBOOZLE, HOAX ⟨continued to ~ the trading public right and left —F.L.Allen⟩

horn·swog·gled *also* **horn·swag·gled** \-ld\ *adj* : DAMNED 2a ⟨I'll be ~ if they didn't owe him $400 then —*N.Y. Sun*⟩

horntail \ˈ=ˌ=\ *n* : any of various insects constituting a family (Siricidae) of Hymenoptera related to the typical sawflies but having larvae that burrow in woody plants and on the females a stout hornlike ovipositor for depositing the egg within the plant

horn timber *n* : a timber extending aft from the sternpost to the transom of a ship and forming the central support of the stern

hornweed \ˈ=ˌ=\ *n* : HORNWORT

hornworm \ˈ=ˌ=\ *n* : a larva of various hawkmoths (as a tobacco worm) having a hornlike tail process

hornwort \ˈ=ˌ=\ *n* **1** : a plant of the genus *Ceratophyllum* **2** : a plant of the order Anthocerotales

horn wrack *n* : a bryozoan of the genus *Flustra*

horny \ˈhȯrnē, ˈhȯ(ə)nē, -ni\ *adj* -ER/-EST [ME, fr. ¹*horn* + *-y*] **1 a** : of or made of horn or of a hornlike substance ⟨after the ~ material has been cut away —Morris Fishbein⟩ **b** : HARD, CALLOUS ⟨his feet were ~ and scarred —W.S.Maugham⟩ — often used in combination ⟨*horny*-handed⟩ **c** : compact and homogeneous with a dull luster like that of flint or of an animal's horn — used of the texture of a mineral **2 :** having horns or hornlike projections **3** [¹*horn* (erect penis) + *-y*] **:** easily excited sexually **:** LASCIVIOUS — usu. considered vulgar

horny coral *n* **:** GORGONIAN

hornyhead chub *also* **hornyhead** \ˈ==,=\ *n* **:** a common chub (*Nocomis biguttatus*) of the larger streams from Pennsylvania to Wyoming and south to Alabama distinguished by the males having the head covered with conical hornlike processes during the breeding season

horny laminae *n pl* **:** laminae on the inside of the wall of an animal's hoof

horny sponge *n* **:** a sponge lacking spicules but having a spongin skeleton that is more or less horny

hor·o·ka·ka \,hȯrəˈkäkə\ *n* -s [Maori] **:** a prostrate woody Australasian herb (*Mesembryanthemum australe*)

hor·o·loge \ˈhȯrə,lōj, ˈhär-, -läj\ *or* **hor·loge** \ˈhȯr,l-\ *n* -s [ME *orloge, oriloge, horologe*, fr. MF, fr. L *horologium*, fr. Gk *hōrologion*, fr. *hōro-* (fr. *hōra* period of time, time of day) + *-logion* (fr. *legein* to gather, speak, tell) — more at HOUR, LEGEND] **:** a timekeeping device; *esp* **:** an early or primitive one (as a sundial or an early clock using a foliot)

ho·rol·o·ger \həˈräləjə(r)\ *n* -s [*horology* + *-er*] **:** HOROLOGIST

hor·o·log·ic \,hȯrəˈläjik, ,här-, -jēk\ *also* **hor·o·log·i·cal** \-jəkəl, -jēk-\ *adj* [ML *horologicus*, fr. MGk *hōrologikos*, fr. Gk *hōrologion* + *-ikos* -ic, -ical] **:** of or relating to a horologe or horology — **hor·o·log·i·cal·ly** \-jək(ə)lē, -jēk-, -li\ *adv*

ho·ro·lo·gion \,ȯrəˈlō,yȯn\ *n* [MGk *hōrologion*, fr. Gk, timepiece] **:** a liturgical book in the Eastern Church containing the daily offices corresponding to the Western breviary

ho·rol·o·gist \həˈräləjəst\ *n* -s **:** a person skilled in the practice or theory of horology **:** a maker of clocks or watches

hor·o·lo·gium \,hȯrəˈlōj(ē)əm\ *n, pl* **horolo·gia** \-ə\ [L] **1 :** TIMEPIECE **2** [ML, fr. MGk *hōrologion*] **:** HOROLOGION

¹**ho·rol·o·gy** \həˈräləjē\ *n* -ES [ME *horologie*, fr. L *horologium*] **:** TIMEPIECE

²**horology** \"\ *n* -ES [Gk *hōro-* + E *-logy*] **1 :** the science of measuring time **2 :** the principles and art of constructing instruments for indicating time

ho·rom·e·try \həˈrämə·trē\ *n* -ES [Gk *hōro-* + E *-metry*] **:** HOROLOGY 1

ho·ro·pi·to \,hȯrōˈpēd·(,)ō\ *n* -s [Maori] **:** NEW ZEALAND PEPPER TREE

ho·rop·ter \həˈräptə(r), ˈhȯ,r-\ *n* -s [F *horoptère*, fr. Gk *horos* boundary + *optēr* one that looks] **:** the locus of points in external space whose images are formed on corresponding places of the two retinas and which are therefore seen single — **hor·op·ter·ic** \ˈhȯ,räpˈterik\ *adj*

¹**hor·o·scope** \ˈhȯrə,skōp, ˈhär-\ *n* [MF, fr. L *horoscopus*, fr. Gk *hōroskopos*, fr. *hōro-* + *skopos* observer, fr. *skopein* to view, watch — more at SPY] **:** a diagram representing the twelve mundane houses and showing the relative positions of planets and signs of the zodiac at a particular time used by astrologers to foretell the events of a person's life or to answer horary questions ⟨cast a ~ in order to determine the exact day and hour at which a vessel should weigh anchor —G.L. Kittredge⟩; *specif* **:** NATIVITY

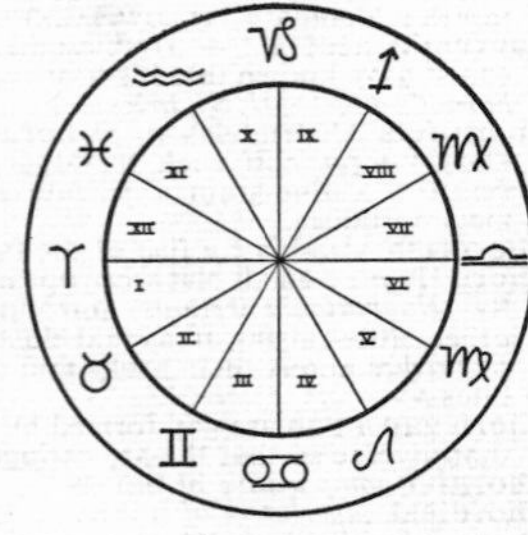
horoscope

²**horoscope** \"\ *vb* -ED/-ING/-S *vi* **:** to make horoscopes ~ *vt* **:** to cast the horoscope of — **hor·o·scop·er** \-pə(r)\ *n* -s

hor·o·scop·ic \ˈ==ˈskäpik, -kōp-, -pēk\ *adj* [L *horoscopicus*, fr. Gk *hōroskopikos*, fr. *hōroskopos* + *-ikos* -ic] **:** of or relating to a horoscope

hor·o·tel·ic \ˈhȯrəˈtelik\ *adj* **:** of or relating to horotely

hor·o·tely \ˈ==,=lē\ *n* -ES [Gk *horos* boundary, limit + *telos* end, consummation, degree of completion, state of maturity + E *-y*] **:** biological evolution at rates within the range or rate distribution usual for a given group of plants or animals — compare BRADYTELY, TACHYTELY

horra *var of* HORA

hor·ren·dous \hȯˈrendəs, hä-, hə-\ *adj* [L *horrendus*, fr. gerundive of *horrēre* to bristle, tremble — more at HORROR] **:** being such as to inspire horror **:** DREADFUL, FEARFUL, FRIGHTFUL, HORRIBLE ⟨began slapping some ~ taxes on these huge estates —A.C.Spectorsky⟩ ⟨a . . . ~ blending of Hollywood and history —Charles Lee⟩ — **hor·ren·dous·ly** *adv*

hor·rent \ˈhȯrənt, ˈhär-\ *adj* [L *horrent-, horrens*, pres. part. of *horrēre*] *archaic* **:** standing up like bristles **:** covered with bristling points **:** BRISTLED, BRISTLING ⟨~ with figures in strong relief —Thomas De Quincey⟩

hor·ri·bi·le dic·tu \hō,ribə(,)lēˈdik(,)tü, hä,-, hə,-\ [L] **:** horrible to say ⟨there is, *horribile dictu*, no mention of the fact that he was president of Harvard —*Times Lit. Supp.*⟩

¹**hor·ri·ble** \ˈhȯrəbəl, ˈhär-\ *adj* [ME *orrible, horrible*, fr. MF, fr. L *horribilis*, fr. *horrēre* to bristle, tremble, shudder + *-ibilis* -ible — more at HORROR] **1 :** marked by or conducive to horror **:** likely to arouse fear, dread, or abhorrence ⟨coconuts in the ~ likeness of a head shrunken by headhunters —Sinclair Lewis⟩ ⟨her hearers derived a ~ enjoyment from . . . her wrath —Charles Dickens⟩ **2 :** extremely unpleasant or disagreeable **:** conducive to feelings of acute dislike, disgust, or repulsion ⟨of all horrors in this blessed town, snow is the most ~ —W.M.Thackeray⟩ ⟨the weather is always ~ when I travel —Aldous Huxley⟩ **syn** see FEARFUL

²**horrible** \"\ *adv* [ME *orrible, horrible*, fr. orrible, horrible, adj.] **:** to an extreme degree **:** HORRIBLY, EXCEEDINGLY ⟨she was ~ mad⟩

³**horrible** \"\ *n* -s [¹*horrible*] **:** a horrible person or thing; *specif* **:** a person fantastically garbed (as for a masquerade or holiday parade) — usu. used in pl. ⟨the ~s, grotesquely costumed children, will parade along a few . . . streets —*Time*⟩ — see ANTIQUES AND HORRIBLES

hor·ri·ble·ness *n* -ES [ME *orriblenesse, horriblenesse*, fr. *orrible, horrible* + *-nesse* -ness] **:** the quality or state of being horrible

hor·ri·bly \-blē,-bli\ *adv* **:** in a horrible manner

hor·rid \ˈhȯrəd, ˈhär-\ *adj, sometimes* -ER/-EST [L *horridus*, fr. *horrēre*] **1** *archaic* **:** ROUGH, RUGGED, BRISTLING **2 a :** being such as to inspire horror **:** DREADFUL, HIDEOUS, SHOCKING ⟨performed a ~ . . . rite of that strange magic —Emma Hawkridge⟩ ⟨over the island a ~ stillness tarried —Jean Stafford⟩ **b :** inspiring disgust or repulsion **:** very offensive **:** NASTY ⟨gave her a loud . . . smack on the back, with ~ familiarity —Liam O'Flaherty⟩ ⟨he's a ~ person⟩ — **hor·rid·ly** *adv* — **hor·rid·ness** *n* -ES

hor·rif·ic \hȯˈrifik, hä-, hə-\ *adj* [MF *horrifique*, fr. L *horrificus*, fr. *horrēre* to bristle, tremble, shudder + *-ificus* -ific — more at HORROR] **:** dreadful to behold or contemplate **:** inspiring horror or fear **:** HORRIFYING, HORRIBLE ⟨this ~ picture of conditions in the mining industry —*Brit. Book News*⟩ ⟨~ black headlines in our daily papers —Charles Jackson⟩ **syn** see FEARFUL

hor·rif·i·cal·ly \-fək(ə)lē\ *adv* **:** in a horrific manner

hor·ri·fi·ca·tion \,hȯrəfəˈkāshən, ,här-\ *n* -s [L *horrificare* to horrify + E *-tion* — more at HORRIFY] **1 :** the act of horrifying or condition of being horrified **2 :** something that horrifies ⟨his two overcoats making him look like a mountain of ~ —Arthur Miller⟩

hor·ri·fied \ˈ==,fīd\ *adj* **:** filled with or marked or attended by a sensation, appearance, or attitude of horror **:** expressing or reflecting horror ⟨we were ~, frightened, and angry at the same time —W.A.White⟩ ⟨strained his eyeballs in a ~ stare at vacancy —G.D.Brown⟩ ⟨grip the reader with a . . . ~ fascination —Norman Birkett⟩ — **hor·ri·fied·ly** \-ī(ə)dlē, -li\ *adv*

hor·ri·fy \ˈhȯrə,fī, ˈhär-\ *vt* -ED/-ING/-ES [L *horrificare*, fr. *horrificus* horrific — more at HORRIFIC] **:** to cause to feel horror **:** strike with horror ⟨smoking right through soup, fish, meat, salad, and dessert in a way to ~ the epicure —Frances Perkins⟩ ⟨may ~ some employers who are still living in the nineteenth century —Roy Lewis & Angus Maude⟩ **syn** see DISMAY

hor·ri·fy·ing·ly *adv* **:** in a horrifying manner **:** so as to horrify

hor·rip·i·late \hȯˈripə,lāt\ *vt* -ED/-ING/-S [back-formation fr. *horripilation*] **:** to produce horripilation in (as by sudden fear) ⟨a strange, wild, *horripilating* tale —R.C.Lewis⟩

hor·rip·i·la·tion \(,)=,==ˈlāshən\ *n* -s [LL *horripilation-, horripilatio*, fr. L *horripilatus* (past part. of *horripilare* to bristle, be shaggy, fr. *horrēre* + *pilus* hair) + *-ion-, -io* -ion — more at PILE] **:** a bristling of the hair of the head or body (as from disease, terror, or chilliness) **:** GOOSEFLESH

¹**hor·ror** \ˈhȯrə(r), ˈhär-\ *n* -s [ME *orrour, horrour*, fr. MF *orror, horror, horreur*, fr. L *horror* action of trembling or shuddering, terror, horror, fr. *horrēre* to bristle, tremble, shudder + *-or*; akin to OE *gorst* gorse, Gk *chēr* hedgehog, *chersos* dry land, mainland, OIr *garb* rough, Skt *harṣate* he becomes stiff, resists, shudders; basic meaning: stiffening] **1 a :** a painful emotion of intense fear, dread, or dismay **:** CONSTERNATION ⟨I saw astonishment giving place to ~ on the faces of the people about me —H.G.Wells⟩ ⟨only to find to my ~ that the dealer knew its value as well as I —H.J.Laski⟩ **b :** intense aversion or repugnance ⟨shrank from the task with all the ~ of a well-bred English gentleman —Virginia Woolf⟩ ⟨the Spanish ~ of any taint of Moorish blood —A.H.Quinn⟩ **2 a :** the quality of inspiring horror **:** repulsive, horrible, or dismal quality or character ⟨statements emphasizing the ~ of this disclosure —Elmer Davis⟩ ⟨sat in silence . . . contemplating the ~ of their lives —Liam O'Flaherty⟩ **b :** something (as an experience, event, or object) that inspires horror **:** something that is horrible ⟨for him the reef was not a beautiful thing but a ~ —Alan Moorehead⟩ ⟨I know that this Nazi ~ has to be destroyed —Upton Sinclair⟩ ⟨made speeches, and hired lawyers, but was unable to avert the ~ —Alva Johnston⟩ **c horrors** *pl* (1) **:** a state of extreme nervous depression or apprehension **:** BLUES, NERVES ⟨smells and . . . sounds which could give one the ~s —Marcia Davenport⟩ ⟨his nervous breakdowns, the attacks of the ~s he is known to have suffered from —V.S.Pritchett⟩ ⟨one of their best batsmen was in the ~s —Ray Robinson⟩ (2) **:** DELIRIUM TREMENS ⟨came home roaring drunk and that night had the ~s⟩ **syn** see FEAR

²**horror** \"\ *adj* **:** specializing in or marked by themes or incidents of extreme violence, cruelty, or weird or macabre quality **:** calculated to inspire feelings of dread or horror **:** BLOODCURDLING ⟨some ~ stories from the Old Testament —J.C.Swaim⟩ ⟨an Elizabethan ~ play —Geoffrey Grigson⟩ ⟨has the strange fascination of a ~ novel —Alfred Frankfurter⟩ ⟨~ comics⟩

horror-struck \ˈ==,=\ *adj* **:** struck with horror ⟨stood *horror-struck* as they watched . . . their own city destroyed —*Nashville Tennessean*⟩

horror va·cui \ˈ==ˈvakyə,wī\ *n* [NL, horror of a vacuum] **:** horror of empty spaces; *esp* **:** an aversion to empty spaces in artistic designs ⟨the Germans share this *horror vacui*, but there is always a marked spatial curiosity in their ornament —Nikolaus Pevsner⟩

hor·ry \ˈhäri\ *adj* [ME *hory*, fr. OE *horig*, fr. *horh* filth, phlegm; akin to OFris *hore* mud, filth, OS *horu, horo* dirt, filth, OHG *horo* dirt, filth, ON *horr* nasal mucus — more at CORYZA] *now dial Eng* **:** disgustingly dirty **:** FOUL

¹**hors con·cours** \,ȯr,kōⁿˈkü(ə)r\ *adv* [F, outside of competition] **:** in the manner of one that does not compete ⟨finished too late to enter competition . . . and was shown *hors concours* —R.F.Hawkins⟩

²**hors concours** \"\ *adj* [F, outside of competition] **1 :** excluded from competition ⟨artists . . . who had already received a medal . . . were *hors concours* —John Rewald⟩ **2 :** being without equal or rival **:** SUPREME ⟨these practitioners of the art . . . salute her as *hors concours* —J.M.Murry⟩

hors de com·bat \,ȯrdəˌkōⁿˈbä\ *adv (or adj)* [F] **:** out of the combat **:** in a disabled condition ⟨the master of that art is able . . . to put an untrained antagonist completely *hors de combat* —Lafcadio Hearn⟩ ⟨with the president *hors de combat* and . . . on the verge of complete retirement —R.H.Rovere⟩

hors d'oeuvre \ȯrˈdərv, ȯ(ə)ˈdərv; ȯ(ə)ˈdōv, -dəiv; *sometimes* ȯrˈdəv\ *n, pl* **hors d'oeuvres** *also* **hors d'oeuvre** \-v(z)\ [F *hors-d'œuvre* something nonessential, sidedish, hors d'oeuvre, fr. the phrase *hors d'œuvre*, nonessential, lit., outside of work] **:** an appetizer usu. one of an assortment served on plates, shells, or compartmented dishes with crackers or toast bits on the side — usu. used in pl.; compare CANAPÉ 1

¹**horse** *R* ˈhȯ(ə)rs, *-R* ˈhȯ(ə)s, *dial R* ˈhȯs *or* ˈhä(r)s *-R* ˈhäs\

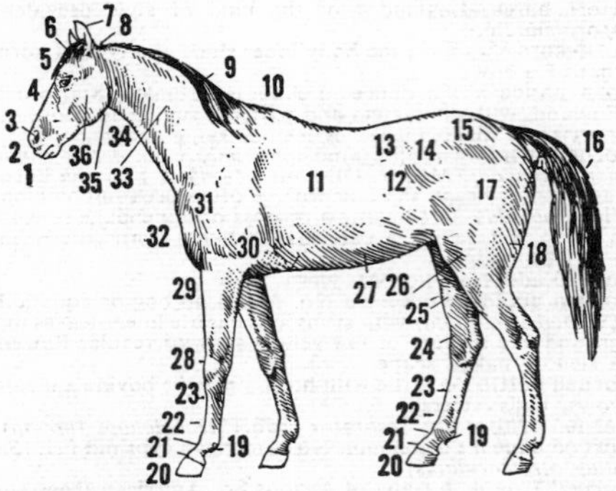

parts of the horse: *1* mouth, *2* nose, *3* nostril, *4* face, *5* forehead, *6* forelock, *7* ear, *8* poll, *9* mane, *10* withers, *11* ribs, *12* flank, *13* loin, *14* haunch, *15* croup, *16* tail, *17* thigh, *18* buttock, *19, 19* fetlocks, *20, 20* hooves, *21, 21* coronets, *22, 22* pasterns, *23, 23* cannons, *24* hock, *25* gaskin, *26* stifle, *27* belly, *28* knee, *29* forearm, *30* elbow, *31* shoulder, *32* breast, *33* neck, *34* throatlatch, *35* lower jaw, *36* cheek

n, pl **horses** *also* **horse** [ME *hors*, fr. OE; akin to OFris *hors, hars* horse, OS *hros, hers*, OHG *hros*, ON *hross*, and perh. to ON *hrata* to stagger, fall — more at CARDINAL] **1 a** (1) **:** a large solid-hoofed herbivorous mammal (*Equus caballus*) domesticated by man since a prehistoric period and used as a beast of burden, a draft animal, or for riding, and distinguished from the other existing members of the genus *Equus* and family Equidae by the long hair of the mane and tail, the usual presence of a callosity on the inside of the hind leg below the hock, and other less constant characters (as the larger size, larger hooves, more arched neck, small head, short ears) (2) **:** a horse over 14.2 hands tall — compare COLT, PONY (3) **:** RACEHORSE ⟨play the ~s⟩ **b** (1) **:** the male of the horse **:** STALLION; *sometimes* **:** a gelding as distinguished from an entire male (2) **:** a stallion four years old or older — used in the terminology of the U.S. Trotting Association **c** (1) **:** any of various extinct animals closely related to the horse (2) **:** any member of the family Equidae **2 :** any of several devices: as **a :** a hook-shaped tool used in making embossed or hammered work **b** (1) **:** FOOTROPE (2) **:** a breastband or similar protection for a sailor in an exposed position (3) **:** TRAVELER 3b (4) **:** JACKSTAY 1 **c :** a frame usu. with legs used for supporting something (as planks, a staging, clothing) **:** TRESTLE; *specif* **:** a sloping frame used in printing for holding paper about to be printed **d :** a notched board to support the steps of a staircase **e** (1) **:** SIDE HORSE (2) **:** LONG HORSE **3** *horse pl* **:** HORSEMEN ⟨the whole party of 1500 ~ —H.A.Shield⟩; *esp* **:** CAVALRY ⟨a regiment of ~⟩ **4 a :** a mass of the same geological character as the wall rock occurring within a vein; *esp* **:** a body of useless rock within an ore deposit **b :** a mass of rock enclosed between two branches of a fault or vein **5 a :** HORSEPOWER **b** *slang* **:** HEROIN ⟨went back on the ~ —*Police Dragnet*⟩ — **from the horse's mouth :** from the original source **:** from an unimpeachable source ⟨information he had just obtained . . . *from the horse's mouth* —*Newsweek*⟩

²**horse** \"\ *vb* -ED/-ING/-S [ME *horsen*, fr. *hors*, n.] *vt* **1 a :** to provide with a horse; *specif* **:** to provide horses for (a vehicle) **b :** to place on a horse **2 a :** to lift, pull, or push roughly or by main force ⟨*horsing* him around in the snow —Theodore Morrison⟩ ⟨sweating gunners *horsed* their pieces into action —Bruce Catton⟩ **b :** to hang (leather) on a horse to drain — often used with *up* **3 :** to subject to horseplay **:** play a joke on **:** KID ⟨if there was nothing else to do, you could ~ the . . . newspaper vendor —Wallace Stegner⟩ ~ *vi* **1** *of a mare* **:** to be in heat **:** be willing to take a stallion **2 :** to engage in horseplay **:** PLAY, FOOL — usu. used with *around* ⟨I ~ around quite a lot, just to keep from getting bored —J.D.Salinger⟩ ⟨I never ~ around much with the women —Norman Mailer⟩ **3 :** to read a proof by comparing it directly with copy

³**horse** \"\ *adj* [¹*horse*] **1 a :** relating to a horse **:** of or for a horse **b :** hauled or powered by a horse ⟨a ~ barge⟩ **2 :** large or coarse of its kind ⟨~ corn⟩ **3 :** mounted on horse ⟨~ dragoons⟩ **:** for mounted troops ⟨~ barracks⟩

horse aloes *n* **:** CABALLINE ALOES

horse-and-buggy \ˈ==ˈ==\ *adj* **1 :** of or relating to the era before the advent of the automobile and other socially revolutionizing major inventions ⟨devotes a lovingly lavish amount of space to *horse-and-buggy* days —A.W.Derleth⟩ ⟨having been born in the *horse-and-buggy* era —J.N.Hall⟩ **2 :** clinging to outworn attitudes or ideas **:** hopelessly outmoded **:** OLD-FASHIONED ⟨*horse-and-buggy* thinking⟩ ⟨the *horse-and-buggy* naval strategists of yesterday —F.H.Gervasi⟩

horse ant *n* **:** a large red mound-building ant (*Formica rufa*) of Europe and No. America

horse apples *n pl, chiefly dial* **:** dried horse droppings

¹**horseback** \ˈ=,=\ *n* [ME *horsback*, fr. *hors* horse + *back*] **1 :** the back of a horse **2 a :** a natural ridge of sand, gravel, or rock **:** HOGBACK **b :** a mound, ridge, bank, or parting of barren rock in a coal seam

²**horseback** \"\ *adv* **:** on horseback

horse·back·er \"ə(r)\ *n* **:** a person on horseback

horse balm *n* **1 :** an erect smooth perennial strong-scented herb (*Collinsonia canadensis*) of eastern No. America with serrate pointed leaves and a loose panicle of yellowish flowers — called also *horseweed* **2 :** a plant of the genus *Monarda*

horsebane \ˈ=,=\ *n* **:** a European water dropwort (*Oenanthe phellandrium*)

horsebean \ˈ=,=\ *n* **1 :** BROAD BEAN 1 **2 :** a West Indian bean of the genus *Canavalia* **3 :** JERUSALEM THORN 2

horse block *n* **:** a block or platform for use in mounting or dismounting from a horse or entering or leaving a vehicle

horse boat *n* **:** a boat for conveying horses and cattle

horse bot *also* **horse bee** *n* **:** HORSE BOTFLY; *specif* **:** the larval stage of a horse botfly

horse botfly *n* **:** any of several botflies chiefly attacking horses; *esp* **:** a cosmopolitan cloudy-winged form (*Gasterophilus intestinalis*) that glues its eggs to the hairs esp. of the forelegs whence they are taken into the mouth where they hatch into young bots and pass into the stomach and become attached to the lining

horse box *n* **:** a railroad car or trailer for transporting horses (as racers)

horseboy \ˈ=,=\ *n, Brit* **:** HOSTLER

horse brass *n* **:** a brass ornament fastened to a martingale

horsebreaker \ˈ=,==\ *n* **:** one who breaks or trains horses

horse brier *n* **:** GREENBRIER

horsebrush \ˈ=,=\ *n* **:** any of several plants of the genus *Tetradymia* (family Compositae) that occur on rangelands in the western U.S. and are a major cause of bighead of American sheep

horsebush \ˈ=,=\ *n, in the Bahama islands* **:** any of several plants: as **a :** a West Indian tree (*Peltophorum adnatum*) of the family Leguminosae with densely brown-tomentose foliage and racemose yellow flowers **b :** an annual weedy herb (*Heliotropium parviflorum*) with spicate white flowers **c :** a West Indian sticky shrub (*Gundlachia corymbosa*) of the family Compositae with alternate leaves and many small white flowers in corymbose heads

horse cane *n* **:** GREAT RAGWEED

horsecar \ˈ=,=\ *n* **1 :** a railroad car or streetcar drawn by horses **2 :** a car fitted for transporting horses

horse cassia *n* **1 :** an East Indian cassia (*Cassia marginata*) with long pods containing a black cathartic pulp used as a horse medicine **2 :** CANAFISTULA 2

horse cavalry *n* **:** cavalry mounted on horses as distinct from mechanized cavalry

horse chestnut *n* [so called fr. its having been used to treat respiratory ailments in horses] **1 a :** a large Asiatic tree (*Aesculus hippocastanum*) that was introduced into Europe in the 16th century and is widely cultivated as an ornamental and shade tree and naturalized as an escape in much of the temperate zone and that has a rough bark, coarse branches, opposite palmately compound leaves, and predominantly white flowers in showy terminal clusters which are followed by large glossy brown seeds enclosed in a coarsely prickly bur; *broadly* **:** any of several trees of the genus *Aesculus* — see BUCKEYE, TREE illustration **b :** the seed of a horse chestnut **2 :** a dark grayish brown that is deeper and very slightly redder than average chocolate brown and deeper and very slightly yellower than African brown

horse-chestnut family *n* **:** HIPPOCASTANACEAE

horsecloth \ˈ=,=\ *n* **:** a cloth for a covering or trapping of a horse

horse conch *n* **:** a massive conch (*Fasciolaria gigantea*) of the warm western Atlantic, the animal being bright red and enclosed in a yellowish spired shell as much as two feet in length

horse coper *n, Brit* **:** a horse dealer; *esp* **:** a dishonest one ⟨a timber buyer was thought to hold the same kind of reputation as a *horse coper* —F.D.Smith & Barbara Wilcox⟩

horse·cors·er *or* **horse·cours·er** \ˈ=,kōrsər, -,kōr-\ *n* [¹*horse* + obs. *corser, courser* horsedealer, fr. *corse* (to barter) or *course* (var. of *corse*) + *-er*] *archaic* **:** a dealer in horses; *esp* **:** a tricky dealer

horse crab *n* **1 :** KING CRAB **2 :** either of two very large crabs (*Telmessus cheiragonus* and *Erimacrus isenbeckii*) widely distributed in waters of moderate depths along the coasts of the northern Pacific ocean

horse crevalle *n* **:** BLUE RUNNER

horsed *past of* HORSE

horse daisy *n* **1 :** DAISY 1b **2 :** MAYWEED 1

horse dance *n* **1 :** a dance of No. American Indians imitating the rearing of a horse **2 :** a dance executed on either a hobbyhorse or a live horse

horse devil *n* **:** a wild indigo (*Baptisia lanceolata*) of the southern U.S. that when dried and withered is rolled about by the wind sometimes frightening horses

horse doctor *n* **1 :** one who doctors horses **:** VETERINARIAN **2 :** an inadequately trained or incompetent doctor

horse elder *n* **:** ELECAMPANE

horse-eye \ˈ=,=\ *or* **horse-eye bean** *n* **1 :** a seed of the cowhage (*Mucuna pruriens*); *also* **:** the plant itself **2 :** OXEYE BEAN **3 :** a seed of the hyacinth bean

horse-eye jack *also* **horse-eyed jack** \ˈ=,=-\ *n* **:** any of several carangid food fishes: as **a :** a blue and silver carangid fish (*Caranx latus*) of the tropical western Atlantic **b :** BIG-EYED SCAD

horseface \ˈ=,=\ *n* **:** a long homely face

horse family *n* **:** EQUIDAE

horsefeathers \ˈ=,==\ *n pl, slang* **:** NONSENSE, BALDERDASH — often used interjectionally

horse fiddle *n, chiefly dial* **:** a noisemaking device based on the principle of a rosined bow drawn across a string

horsefish \ˈ=,=\ *n, pl* **horsefish** *or* **horsefishes 1 a :** MOONFISH a **b :** SAUGER **c :** a sea horse (genus *Hippocampus*) **d :** a dusky rough-skinned southern African scorpaenid fish (*Congiopodus torvus*) **2 :** KING CRAB 1

horseflesh \ˈ=,=\ *n* **1 :** the flesh of a horse esp. when slaughtered for food **2 :** horses considered esp. with reference to riding, driving, or racing **3 :** any of several hard often reddish West Indian timbers: as **a :** SABICU **b :** the wood of a bully tree (*Manilkara bidentata*) **c :** the wood of black mangrove

horseflesh mahogany *n* **1 :** any of several hard mottled tropical American woods that somewhat resemble mahogany

2 : a tree (as *Peltophorum adnatum* or *Hieronyma caribaea*) that yields horseflesh mahogany

horseflesh ore *n* [so called fr. its reddish color when newly fractured] *dial Eng* : BORNITE

horsefly \ˈ=,=\ *n* **1** : any of numerous rather large stocky swift-flying two-winged flies constituting the family Tabanidae having in the female a piercing proboscis with which they suck the blood of animals (as horses and cattle) inflicting painful bites — compare CHRYSOPS, GREENHEAD **2** : any of several other flies annoying to horses (as the horse tick *Hippobosca equina*)

horsefly weed *n* [so called fr. its supposed ability to drive away horseflies] : INDIGO BROOM

horse gentian *n* : a plant of the genus *Triosteum; esp* : FEVERROOT

horse gowan *n* **1** : DAISY 1b **2** : CHAMOMILE **3** : DANDELION **4** : any of several plants of the genera *Crepis* and *Hypochaeris*

horse gram *or* **horse grain** *n* : a twining herb (*Dolichos biflorus*) of the tropics of the Old World that is cultivated in India for fodder with the seeds being used as food

horsehair \ˈ=,=\ *n, often attrib* [ME *hors her*, fr. *hors* horse + *her* hair — more at HAIR] **1 a** : a hair of a horse esp. from the mane or tail **b** : a quantity of such hairs **2** : HAIRCLOTH

horsehair blight *n* : a disease of tea and other tropical plants caused by a fungus (*Marasmius equicrinis*) the mycelium of which hangs in black festoons from the branches

horsehair lichen *n* : any of several lichens esp. of the genus *Alectoria* with a thallus consisting of filaments resembling hair — called also *horsetail lichen*

horsehair snake *or* **horsehair worm** *n* : a free-living adult gordioid worm

horsehead \ˈ=,=\ *n* : MOONFISH a

horse·heal *or* **horse·heel** \ˈ=,hē(ə)l\ *n* [by folk etymology fr. ME *horselne, horshelne, horshelyn*, fr. OE *horselene, horshelene*, fr. *hors* horse + *elene, eolone* elecampane, fr. ML *elena* (*campana*) — more at HORSE, ELECAMPANE] : ELECAMPANE

horsehide \ˈ=,=\ *n* **1** : the hide of a horse or colt or leather made from either — compare CORDOVAN **2** : BASEBALL 2

horse hoe *n* : a horse-drawn surface cultivator

horsehoof \ˈ=,=\ *n, pl* **horsehoofs** [ME *horshoof*, fr. *hors* horse + *hoof*] : COLTSFOOT

horsehoof clam *n* : a large tropical clam (*Hippopus hippopus*) related to and much resembling the giant clam (*Tridacna derasi*) — called also *horseshoe clam*

horsekeeper \ˈ=,==\ *n* [ME *horskepare*, fr. *hors* horse + *kepare, keper* keeper] : one who has charge of horses : GROOM

horse knacker *n* : KNACKER

horse knob *or* **horse knop** *n* : KNAPWEED

horse latitudes *n pl* : either of two belts or regions in the neighborhood of 30° N. and 30° S. latitude characterized by high pressure, calms, and light baffling winds; *esp* : that part of the northern belt which is over the Atlantic ocean

horselaugh \ˈ=,=\ *n* : a loud boisterous laugh : GUFFAW

horseleech \ˈ=,=\ *n* [ME *horsleche*, fr. *hors* horse + *leche* leech — more at LEECH] : a common European leech (*Haemopis gulo*) that feeds chiefly on worms; *also* : any of several related No. American leeches

horse·less carriage \ˈ=ləs-\ *n* : AUTOMOBILE — used esp. of early models

horselike \ˈ=,=\ *adj* : resembling a horse

horse louse *n* **1** : a sucking louse (*Haematopinus asini*) found on horses and other equines **2** : any of several biting lice infesting horses

horse mackerel *n* **1** : any of several large scombroid fishes: as **a** : BLUEFIN TUNA **b** : CHILE BONITO **2** : any of various large fishes of the family Carangidae; *esp* : a large Atlantic food fish (*Trachurus trachurus*)

horse·man \ˈ=mən\ *n, pl* **horsemen** [ME *horsman*, fr. *hors* horse + *man*] **1 a** : a rider on horseback **b** : one skilled in managing horses **2** : a breeder or raiser of horses

horse·man·ship \-,ship\ *n* : the art of riding horseback : equestrian skill : MANEGE

horsemeat \ˈ=,=\ *n* : the flesh of the horse esp. for use as food ⟨a ~ butcher⟩ ⟨~ is important in the diet of mink⟩

horsemint \ˈ=,=\ *n* [ME *horsminte* fr. *hors* + *minte* mint] : any of various coarse mints: as **a** : WATER MINT **b** : a plant of the genus *Monarda; esp* : a tall erect perennial herb (*M. punctata*) with petioled lanceolate leaves somewhat hairy beneath and heads of purple-spotted creamy flowers subtended by purplish or whitish bracts

horse-mule \ˈ=,=\ *n* : a male mule

horse mushroom *n* : a rather coarse edible mushroom (*Agaricus arvensis*) with a hollow stem, pale gills, and a broad white cap — compare MEADOW MUSHROOM

horse mussel *n* : a large coarse marine mussel (*Modiolus modiolus*) found on the shores of northern Europe and America; *also* : any similar closely related species

horse nettle *n* : a coarse prickly weed (*Solanum carolinense*) common in eastern and southern U.S., having white or pale-purple flowers and bright-yellow fruit resembling berries — called also *ball nettle, bull nettle*

horse opera *n* : a motion picture or radio or television play having its scene laid in the western U.S. and usu. having cowboys as its principal characters

horse parlor *n* : a place where betting on horses is carried on

horse piece *n* : one of the large pieces into which blubber is cut before mincing

horse pistol *n* : a large pistol formerly carried by horsemen

¹horseplay \ˈ=,=\ *n* [¹*horse* + *play*] : rough or boisterous play

²horseplay \ˈ"\ *vi* : to engage in horseplay ⟨~*ed* around with the boys —Betty Smith⟩

horseplayer \ˈ=,==\ *n* [¹*horse* + *player*] : one who habitually bets on horse races

horseplaying \ˈ=,==\ *n* [¹*horse* + *playing*] : betting on horse races

horse plum *n* **1** : AMERICAN PLUM **2** : CANADA PLUM

horsepond \ˈ=,=\ *n* : a pond for watering horses

horse post *n* **1** : a hitching post **2 a** : a mail carrier who makes his deliveries on horseback **b** : a mail service performed by such carriers

horsepower \ˈ=,==\ *n* **1 a** : the power that a horse exerts in pulling **b** : a machine worked by a horse **2** : a standard unit of power equal in the U.S. to 746 watts and nearly equivalent to the English gravitational unit of the same name that equals 550 foot-pounds of work per second — compare BRAKE HORSEPOWER, INDICATED HORSEPOWER

horsepower-hour \ˈ=,==ˈ=\ *n* : the work performed or energy consumed by working at the rate of one horsepower for one hour, being equal to 1,980,000 foot-pounds

horsepox \ˈ=,=\ *n* : a virus disease of horses related to cowpox and marked by a vesiculopustular eruption of the skin esp. on the pasterns and sometimes by a vesiculopapular inflammation of the buccal mucosa — called also *equine variola*

horse purslane *n* : a coarse tropical American fleshy weed (*Trianthema portulacastrum*) of the family Aizoaceae

horse racer *n* **1** : one who keeps horses for racing **2** : JOCKEY **3** : a devotee of horse racing

horse racing *n* : the racing of horses as a sport

horseradish \ˈ=,==\ *n* **1 a** : a tall coarse white-flowered herb (*Armoracia lapathifolia*) native to Europe and widely cultivated **b** : the pungent root of horseradish **c** : KERGUELEN CABBAGE **2** : a condiment made of the grated root of the horseradish plant often moistened with vinegar or a similar substance

horseradish tree *n* **1** : an East Indian tree (*Moringa oleifera*) that has a horseradish-flavored root and is cultivated throughout the tropics for its elongated capsular fruit which when young is pickled or cooked as a vegetable and for its seeds which yield ben oil **2** : any Australian tree of the genus *Codonocarpus* (family Phytolaccaceae) having pungent leaves suggesting the flavor of horseradish or mustard

horse rake *n* : a horse-drawn rake

horse room *n* : a bookmaker's establishment which provides information on horse races and opportunity to bet on them

horses *pl of* HORSE, *pres 3d sing of* HORSE

horse savin *n* : COMMON JUNIPER

horse sense *n* : plain shrewd unsophisticated common sense ⟨juries seldom accept purely scientific evidence if it seems in conflict with everyday *horse sense* —E.M.Lustgarten⟩ **syn** see SENSE

horseshit \ˈ=,=\ *n* **1** : horse droppings — usu. considered vulgar **2** : BUNK, NONSENSE — usu. considered vulgar

¹horseshoe \ˈ=,=\ *n* [ME *hors sho*, fr. *hors* + *sho* shoe] **1** : a shoe for horses usu. consisting of a narrow plate of iron conformed to the rim of a horse's hoof **2** : something (as a valley or other physical feature) shaped like a horseshoe ⟨the town . . . stood in the mouth of a ~ —John Buchan⟩ ⟨the vast ~ of hills surrounding the central plains —D.G.E.Hall⟩ **3 horseshoes** *pl* : a game like quoits played with horseshoes or with horseshoe-shaped pieces of metal which are thrown from one peg in the ground toward another 40 feet away with the object of ringing or coming close to the peg

underside of typical horseshoes: *1* plain shoe, *2* shoe with toe and heel calks

²horseshoe \ˈ"\ *vt* **1** : to furnish with horseshoes : put shoes on (a horse) **2** : to put in the shape of a horseshoe; *specif* : to make (an architectural arch) like a horseshoe

³horseshoe \ˈ"\ *adj* **1** : shaped like a horseshoe ⟨a ~ curve⟩ ⟨the ~ bend of a river⟩ **2** *of an arch* : having an intrados that widens above the springing before narrowing to a rounded or pointed crown — see ARCH illustration

horseshoe bat *n* : any of several bats of the Old World (families Rhinolophidae and Hipposideridae) having a more or less horseshoe-shaped leaf on the nose

horseshoe clam *n* : HORSEHOOF CLAM

horseshoe crab *n* : KING CRAB

horseshoe kidney *n* : congenital partial fusion of the kidneys resulting in a horseshoe shape

horseshoe nail *n* : a thin pointed nail with heavy flaring head that is used to fix a horseshoe to the hoof

horseshoe plate *n* : a plate around a ship's rudder stock that is shaped like a horseshoe and designed to prevent water from entering the rudder trunk

horseshoer \ˈ=,==\ *n* : one who makes horseshoes or shoes horses; *specif* : BLACKSMITH 1b

horseshoe snake *n* : a harmless colubrid snake (*Zamenis hippocrepis*) of Spain and Africa

horseshoe vetch *n* : a European herb (*Hippocrepis comosa*) of the family Leguminosae with yellow umbellate flowers succeeded by flattened pods that separate into horseshoe-shaped joints

horseshoe violet *n* : BIRD'S-FOOT VIOLET

horse show *n* : a competitive exhibition of horses and vehicles esp. as an annual fashionable event

horsesickness \ˈ=,==\ *n* : AFRICAN HORSE SICKNESS

horse's neck *n* : a tall drink consisting of ginger ale or ginger ale and a liquor served iced in a large tumbler with a spiral of lemon peel hanging over the rim

horse sorrel *n* **1** : a European water dock (*Rumex hydrolapathum*) **2** : SHEEP SORREL 1

horse sponge *n* : a sponge of ʻhe genus *Hippiospongia*

horse stinger *n, dial Eng* : DRAGONFLY

horse sugar *n* : SWEETLEAF

horse syphilis *n* : DOURINE

horsetail \ˈ=,=\ *n* [ME *horse tayle* fr. *horse, hors* + *tayle, tail*] **1** : the tail of a horse **2** : a plant of the genus *Equisetum*

horsetail agaric *or* **horsetail fungus** *n* : SHAGGYMANE

horsetail corn *n* : INDIAN CORN

horsetail family *n* : EQUISETACEAE

horsetail lichen *n* : HORSEHAIR LICHEN

horsetaillike \ˈ=,=,=\ *adj* : resembling a plant of the genus *Equisetum*

horsetail milkweed *n* : WHORLED MILKWEED

horsetail tree *n* : a tree of the genus *Casuarina; esp* : a tree (*C. equisetifolia*) planted in the southern and southwestern U.S. that is used for windbreaks and planting on sand dunes and also as an ornamental

horse thistle *n* [ME *hors thistel*, fr. *hors* + *thistel* thistle] : PRICKLY LETTUCE

horse thyme *n, dial Eng* : WILD BASIL

horse tick *n* **1** : a louse fly attacking horses — compare HIPPOBOSCIDAE **2** : any tick attacking horses

horse trade *n* **1** : a swap of horses usu. accompanied by bargaining and compromise **2** : negotiation accompanied by shrewd bargaining and usu. by reciprocal concessions : practical compromise ⟨a political *horse trade*⟩ ⟨his *horse trades* with foreign governments have been masterpieces of commercial diplomacy —J.D.Ratcliff⟩

horse-trade \ˈ=,=\ *vi* [back-formation fr. *horse trading* & *horse trader*] : to engage in a horse trade

horse trader *n* : one who engages in horse trading

horse trading *n* : the act or practice or an instance of making a horse trade ⟨the . . . foreign ministers had finally gotten down to *horse trading* —*Newsweek*⟩ ⟨lively *horse trading* in . . . smoke-filled back rooms —*N. Y. Herald Tribune*⟩

horse·tree \ˈ=(,)trē, -,tri\ *n, dial Eng* : WHIFFLETREE

horse violet *n* : BIRD'S-FOOT VIOLET

horseweed \ˈ=,=\ *n* **1** : a common No. American weed (*Erigeron canadense*) with linear leaves and small discoid heads of yellowish flowers **2** : HORSE BALM **3** : GREAT RAGWEED **4** : WILD LETTUCE 1b(3)

¹horsewhip \ˈ=,=\ *n* [¹*horse* + *whip*] : a whip for horses

²horsewhip \ˈ"\ *vt* : to flog with a horsewhip

horsewoman \ˈ=,==\ *n, pl* **horsewomen** **1** : a woman horseback rider **2** : a woman skilled in riding horseback or in caring for or managing horses

horsewood \ˈ=,=\ *n* : SEA GRAPE 1b

horse wrangler *n* : a ranch hand who takes care of the saddle horses

hors·ey *also* **horsy** *pronunc at* ¹HORSE + ē *or* i\ *adj* **horsier**; **horsiest** **1** : relating to, resembling, or suggestive of a horse ⟨bounced the boy on his knee in a ~ manner —Wright Morris⟩ ⟨not ~ or masculine, but a woman of whom one could be proud —Kathleen Freeman⟩ **2** : addicted to or having to do with horses or horse racing or characteristic of the manners, dress, or tastes of horsemen ⟨the ~ set⟩ ⟨a ~, flashy, tweedy sort of man —Lewis Mumford⟩

hors·ford·ite \ˈhȯ(r)sfə(r),dīt\ *n* -s [Eben N. *Horsford* †1893 Am. chemist + E *-ite*] : a mineral Cu_5Sb consisting of a massive silver-white copper antimony alloy (sp. gr. 8.8)

hors·i·ly *pronunc at* ¹HORSE + əlē *or* əli\ *adv* : in a horsey manner

hors·i·ness \-sēnəs, -sin-\ *n* -ES : the quality or state of being horsey

horsing *adj* [fr. pres. part. of ²*horse*] *of a mare* : being in heat

horst \ˈhȯ(ə)rst\ *n* -s [G, thicket, eyrie, horst, fr. OHG *hurst* thicket — more at HURST] : a tract or block of the earth's crust separated by faults from adjacent tracts or blocks that have been relatively depressed — compare GRABEN

hort *abbr* horticultural; horticulture

hor·ta·tion \hȯ(r)ˈtāshən\ *n* -s [L *hortation-, hortatio*, fr. *hortatus* (past part. of *hortari* to urge, exhort) + *-ion-, -io* -ion — more at YEARN] : EXHORTATION

hor·ta·tive \ˈhȯ(r)d·əd·iv\ *adj* [LL *hortativus*, fr. L *hortatus* + *-ivus* -ive] : giving exhortation : ADVISORY, EXHORTATIVE — **hor·ta·tive·ly** \-d·əvlē\ *adv*

hor·ta·to·ri·ly \ˌ==ˈtōrəlē\ *adv* : in a hortatory manner

hor·ta·to·ry \-d·ə,tōrē\ *adj* [LL *hortatorius*, fr. L *hortatus* + *-orius* -ory] : giving or characterized by exhortation : EXHORTATORY, HORTATIVE

hor·tense blue \ˈhȯr,ten(t)s-, =ˈ=-\ *n, often cap H* [prob. fr. the name *Hortense*] : PRUSSIAN BLUE 2

hortense violet *n, often cap H* [prob. fr. the name *Hortense*] : a moderate purple that is bluer and duller than heliotrope (sense 4a), bluer, lighter, and stronger than average amethyst, and bluer, stronger, and slightly lighter than manganese violet

hor·ti·cul·tur·al \ˌhȯ(r)d·əˈkəlch(ə)rəl, -)tə|-\ *adj* **1** : relating to horticulture **2** : produced under cultivation (as by breeding) — compare BOTANICAL — **hor·ti·cul·tur·al·ly** \-rəlē, -li\ *adv*

horticultural bean *n* : a shell bean characterized by pods splashed with carmine or red and white and by white or buff-colored seeds marked with red

horticultural variety *n* : a variety of plant that has originated under cultivation as distinct from a botanical variety

hor·ti·cul·ture \ˈhȯ(r)d·ə,kəlchə(r), -)tə,- *also* ,==ˈ=\ *n* [L *hortus* garden + E *-i-* + *culture* — more at YARD] : the cultivation of an orchard, garden, or nursery on a small or large scale : the science and art of growing fruits, vegetables, flowers, or ornamental plants — compare FLORICULTURE, OLERICULTURE, POMOLOGY

hor·ti·cul·tur·ist \ˌ==ˈ=kəlch(ə)rəst\ *n* : a specialist in horticulture

hor·ton·o·lite \hȯ(r)ˈtänᵊl,īt, ˈhȯ(r)tᵊn-\ *n* -s [Silas R. *Horton*, 19th cent. Am. mineralogist + E *-o-* + *-lite*] : a mineral $(Fe,Mg,Mn)_2SiO_4$ of the olivine series consisting of a dark silicate of iron, magnesium, and manganese

hor·to·ri·um \hȯ(r)ˈtōrēəm, -tȯr-\ *n, pl* **hortoriums** \-ēəmz\ *or* **horto·ria** \-ēə\ [NL, fr. L *hortus* + *-orium* -ory] : an institution or museum for the collection, preservation, and study of horticultural specimens

hor·tu·lan \ˈhȯ(r)chələn\ *adj* [L *hortulanus*, fr. *hortulus* small garden (dim. of *hortus* garden) + *-anus* -an] : of or relating to a garden

hortulan plum *n* [NL *hortulana* (specific epithet of *Prunus hortulana*), fr. L, fem. of *hortulanus*] : a wild-goose plum (*Prunus hortulana*)

hor·tus sic·cus \ˌhȯ(r)d·ə(s)ˈsikəs\ *n* [NL, lit., dry garden] : a collection of dried botanical specimens : HERBARIUM

hos *pl of* HO

ho·sack·ia \hōˈsakēə, -ˈza-\ *n, cap* [NL, fr. David *Hosack* †1835 Am. botanist + NL *-ia*] : a large genus of mostly western No. American herbs (family Leguminosae) having pinnate leaves, yellow or red flowers, and linear flat pods

¹ho·san·na \hōˈzanə *sometimes* -zä- *or* -za-\ *n* -s [ME *osanna*, fr. LL, fr. Gk *hōsanna*, fr. Heb *hōshīʿāh nnā* save now, we pray] : an expression of enthusiastic praise : ACCLAMATION ⟨the law was passed with a considerable fanfare of editorial ~*s* —Herbert Asbury⟩ ⟨men with loud ~*s* will confess her greatness —John Milton⟩ — used interjectionally as a cry of acclamation and adoration ⟨*hosanna!* Blessed be he who comes in the name of the Lord —Mk 11: 9 (RSV)⟩

²hosanna \ˈ"\ *vt* -ED/-ING/-S : to acclaim with or as if with shouts of "hosanna" : APPLAUD ⟨the act of him who has been ~*ed* as if he were a savior —Henry Angus⟩

¹hose \ˈhōz\ *n, pl* **hose** *or* **hoses** [ME, fr. OE *hosa* stocking, husk; akin to OS, OHG, & ON *hosa* leg covering, Gk *kystis* bladder, OE *hȳd* hide — more at HIDE] **1** *pl* **hose** **a** (1) : a cloth leg covering that reaches down to the ankle and sometimes covers the foot ⟨footless athletic ~ worn over socks are part of a baseball uniform⟩ (2) : STOCKING, SOCK ⟨a pair of ~⟩ — usu. used in pl. **b** (1) : a close-fitting garment similar to tights that covers the body from the waist to and sometimes including the feet and is usu. attached to a doublet by points ⟨eight times thrust through the doublet, four through the ~ —Shak.⟩ (2) : short breeches often reaching to the knee — see TRUNK HOSE **2** *now dial Brit* : a sheath enclosing an inflorescence (as a spathe or the ensheathing leaves about the developing spike of a cereal grass) **3** *pl sometimes* **hoses** **a** : a flexible tube (as of rubber, plastic, or fabric) for conveying fluids (as air, steam, powdered coal, or water from a faucet or hydrant) **b** : such a tube with nozzle and attachments **c** : the tubing as material **4** : HOSEL

hose 3a

²hose \ˈ"\ *vt* -ED/-ING/-S [ME *hosen*, fr. *hose*, n.] **1** *archaic* : to provide with hose for the legs **2 a** : to spray or water with a hose ⟨~ the garden⟩ **b** : to wash or drench with water from a hose — usu. used with *down* ⟨the bridge . . . had been *hosed* down by the fire department —*N.Y.Times*⟩

hose·bird \ˈhōz,bərd\ *n* [prob. alter. of *whore's brood*] *dial Eng* : RASCAL, RAPSCALLION

hose bridge *or* **hose jumper** *n* : a contrivance that permits traffic to pass over or under lines of fire hose

hose cart *or* **hose wagon** *also* **hose truck** *or* **hose carriage** *n* : a wheeled vehicle for carrying fire hose

hose clip *n* : a device for clamping or supporting a hose

hose cock *or* **hose bib** *n* **1** : SILL COCK **2** : PINCHCOCK

hose company *n* : a company of men who bring and manage hose in fire fighting

hose-in-hose \ˌ==ˈ=\ *n* : a double flower in which one corolla appears to be within another (as in various daturas and primulas)

ho·sel \ˈhōzəl\ *n* -s [¹*hose* + *-el*] : a socket in the head of a golf club into which the shaft is inserted — see GOLF illustration

hose·less \ˈhōzləs\ *adj* : having no hose to wear

hose·man \-mən, -,man\ *n, pl* **hosemen** : one who uses, tends, or repairs hose; *esp* : a fireman who belongs to a hose company

ho·sen \ˈhōzᵊn\ *now dial pl of* HOSE

hose net *n, chiefly Scot* : a fishnet shaped like a stocking

hosepipe \ˈ=,=\ *n* : HOSE 3

ho·sha·na *or* **ho·sha·nah** \hōˈshä(,)nä, -nə\ *n, pl* **hoshanoth** *or* **hosha·not** \-,nōt(h), -ōs\ [Heb *hōshīʿāh nnā*, lit., save now, we pray] **1** : a cry of entreaty in the liturgical litany chanted in the synagogue on Sukkoth esp. during the processional circuits around the altar on Hoshana Rabbah **2** : the prayer chanted on Hoshana Rabbah

hoshana rab·bah *or* **hoshanah rab·bah** *or* **hoshana rab·ba** \-ˈrä(,)bä, -bə\ *n, usu cap H&R* [Aram *hōshaʿnā rabbā*] : the 7th day of the Festival of Sukkoth observed on the 21st day of Tishri with special prayers and ceremonies in the synagogue by Orthodox and Conservative Jews

ho·sier \ˈhōzhə(r)\ *n* -s [ME *hosyere*, fr. *hose* + *-yere* -ier] : one who deals in hosiery

ho·siery \ˈhōzh(ə)rē, -ri, ÷ -z(ə)-\ *n* -ES *often attrib* [*hosier* + *-y*] **1** : HOSE 1a **2** *chiefly Brit* : KNITWEAR

hos·pice \ˈhäspəs\ *n* -s [F, fr. L *hospitium* hospitality, lodging, inn, fr. *hospit-, hospes* host, stranger, guest — more at HOST] **1** : an establishment providing rest or entertainment for travelers; *esp* : one kept by a religious order **2** : a lodging for students, young workers, or the underprivileged often maintained by a religious order — compare HOSTEL

hos·pi·ta·ble \häˈspid·əbəl, ˈhä,spi|, |tə-, *also* ˈhäspə| *sometimes* hōˈs- *or* ˈhō(,)s- *or* həˈspi|\ *adj* [NL *hospitabilis*, fr. L *hospitare* to be a guest, lodge + *-abilis* -able] **1 a** : marked by or given to generous and cordial reception and entertainment of guests or strangers ⟨they are ~ . . . : give a guest everything, and leave him free to do as he likes —Bram Stoker⟩ ⟨this ~, talkative man who was everywhere bustling about, trying to be of service —O.E.Rölvaag⟩ **b** : promising or suggesting generous and cordial welcome and entertainment ⟨wrote off immediately on his return to his inn the most ~ of invitations —W.M.Thackeray⟩ ⟨small incommunicable mysteries . . . chambered in their inner hearts and guarded by their ~ faces —A.T.Quiller-Couch⟩ **c** : offering a pleasant or sustaining environment : not hostile ⟨hard sandstone ridges carry a soil sufficiently ~ for forest growth —*Amer. Guide Series: N.J.*⟩ ⟨the British Isles enjoy a ~ climate, but the British gardener does not have life too easy —Emily Hahn⟩ **2** : marked by ready or willing receptivity (as of new ideas) : favorably disposed esp. to the new or strange ⟨keep the mind open and ~ to new evidence on any side of the question —W.J.Reilly⟩ ⟨freedom to inquire and teach . . . provides a climate more ~ to fresh vision —Sidney Hook⟩ **syn** see SOCIAL

hos·pi·ta·ble·ness *n* -ES *archaic* : the quality or state of being hospitable

hos·pi·ta·bly \-blē, -bli\ *adv* : in a hospitable manner

¹hos·pi·tal \ˈhä|,spi|d·əl, |tᵊl *also* |,spə| *sometimes* ˈhō|\ *n* -s *often attrib* [ME, fr. OF, fr. LL *hospitale*, fr. L, bedroom, fr. neut. of *hospitalis* of a guest, hospitable, fr. *hospit-, hospes* host, stranger, guest + *-alis* -al — more at HOST] **1** *archaic* : HOSPICE 1 ⟨an adjacent ~ founded by the princess . . . for the reception of pilgrims —Horace Walpole⟩ **2** : a charitable institution for the needy, aged, infirm, or young; *specif* : one for the education of the young ⟨received his formal education at Christ's *Hospital* in London⟩ **3 a** : an institution or place where sick or injured persons are given medical or surgical care — usu. used Brit. without an article when the object of a preposition ⟨so badly wounded that he died in ~ —*Manchester Guardian Weekly*⟩ ⟨diagnosed frostbitten toes and removed him immediately to ~ —Alexander Tewnion⟩; compare CLINIC, MEDICAL CENTER, SANATORIUM **b** : a place for the care and treatment of sick or injured animals **4** : a workshop for the repair of any of various small objects ⟨a doll ~⟩ ⟨a fountain-pen ~⟩

²hospital *adj* [L *hospitalis*] *obs* : HOSPITABLE

hospital apprentice *n* : an enlisted man in the U. S. Navy training to be a hospitalman

hospital bed *n* : a bed with a frame in three sections equipped with mechanical spring parts that permit raising the head end, foot end, or middle as required

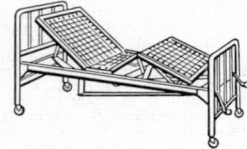

hospital bed

hospital corpsman *n* : a petty officer of the U. S. Navy performing general medical duties, giving first aid, and serving as a technician and assistant to the medical officer

hos·pi·tal·er *or* **hos·pi·tal·ler** *pronunc at* HOSPITAL + ə(r), ⸗ˈ⸗⸗⸗\ *n* -s [ME *hospitalier, hospiteler*, fr. MF *hospitalier*, fr. ML *hospitalarius*, fr. LL *hospitale* hospice + L *-arius* -ary — more at HOSPITAL] **1** *usu cap* **:** a member of a religious military order established in Jerusalem in the 12th century and revived as an honorary society in 1879 by Leo XIII — called also *Knight of Malta, Knight of Rhodes, Knight of St. John of Jerusalem* **2 :** a member of any of numerous religious orders chiefly concerned with the care of the sick or needy **3 :** a chaplain of a London hospital

hospital fever *n* : typhus fever or fever associated with hospital gangrene prevalent in hospitals before the development of modern sanitation

hospital gangrene *n* : gangrene prevalent in crowded hospitals before the development of modern sanitation

hos·pi·tal·ism \-,lizəm\ *n* -s **1 a :** the factors and influences (as of system or custom) that adversely affect the health of hospitalized persons **b :** the effect of such factors on mental or physical health **2 :** the physical and mental effects on infants and children resulting from their living in foundling homes

hos·pi·tal·i·ty \,häspəˈtalədē, -ətē, -i *sometimes* ,hȯs-\ *n* -ES [ME *hospitalite*, fr. MF *hospitalité*, fr L *hospitalitat-, hospitalitas*, fr. *hospitalis* of a guest, hospitable + *-itat-, -itas* -ity — more at HOSPITAL] **1 a :** the cordial and generous reception and entertainment of guests or strangers socially or commercially ⟨built a house, and later a tavern . . . whose ~ was known to thousands —*Amer. Guide Series: Vt.*⟩ ⟨the meaning of country ~ . . . extends far beyond threshold and board —Louise D. Rich⟩ **b :** an instance of hospitality — usu. used in pl. ⟨convivial and domestic *hospitalities* —R.W. Emerson⟩ **2 :** ready receptivity esp. to new ideas and interests ⟨hope to give ~ on my walls to new and promising American talent —Bennett Cerf⟩ ⟨the great tradition in poetry has always offered ungrudging ~ to ideas —J.L.Lowes⟩

hos·pi·tal·iza·tion \,⸗(,)⸗⸗əˈzāshən, -,īˈz-\ *n* -s **1 :** the act or process of being hospitalized ⟨pain persisted constantly through a two-day period, finally necessitating ~ —*Jour. Amer. Med. Assoc.*⟩ **2 :** the period of stay in a hospital ⟨drug treatment shortened the length of ~ —*Today's Health*⟩ ⟨entitled to ~ for two weeks —*Newsweek*⟩

hospitalization insurance *n* : insurance that provides benefits to cover or partly cover hospital expenses — see HOSPITAL SERVICE CONTRACT

hos·pi·tal·ize \ˈ⸗(,)⸗⸗,īz\ *vt* -ED/-ING/-s **:** to place in a hospital as a patient — compare INSTITUTIONALIZE ⟨the child was *hospitalized* at once for diagnosis and treatment —*Jour. Amer. Med. Assoc.*⟩

hospital light *n* : HOPPER FRAME

hos·pi·tal·man \ˈ⸗(,)⸗⸗ mən\ *n, pl* **hospitalmen :** an enlisted man in the U. S. Navy performing general medical duties

hospital service contract *n* : hospitalization insurance that provides for payment of actual hospital charges within specified limits as contrasted with cash benefits

hospital ship *n* : a ship equipped as a hospital; *esp* **:** one constructed or assigned specif. to assist the wounded, sick, and shipwrecked in time of war in accordance with international law

hospital train *n* : a railway train equipped for the transport of sick and wounded military personnel

hos·pi·tious \(ˈ)häˈspishəs\ *adj* [L *hospitium* hospitality, lodging, inn + E *-ous* — more at HOSPICE] *archaic* : HOSPITABLE

hos·pi·ti·um \häˈspishēəm, -idē-\ *n, pl* **hospi·tia** \-ēə\ [L] **1 :** HOSPICE 1 **2** *chiefly Brit* **:** HOSTEL 2a (1)

hos·po·dar \ˈhäspə,där\ *n* -s [Romanian, fr. Ukrainian, fr. *hospod'* lord, master; akin to OSlav *gospodĭ, gospodinŭ* lord, master — more at GOSPODIN] **:** a governor of Moldavia and Walachia under Turkish rule

¹host \ˈhōst\ *n* -s [ME *ost, oost, host, hoost*, fr. OF *ost, host*, fr. LL *hostis*, fr. L, stranger, enemy — more at GUEST] **1 :** a large number of men gathered for war **:** ARMY ⟨the destruction of Pharaoh's ~ in that sea —W.L.Sperry⟩ ⟨walls that must be directly stormed by the ~s of courage —A.E.Stevenson b.1900⟩ **2 a :** ANGELS ⟨a multitude of the heavenly ~ praising God —Lk 2:13 (RSV)⟩ **b :** the sun, moon, and stars ⟨all the ~ of heaven —Deut 4:19 (RSV)⟩ **3 :** a very large number **:** a great quantity **:** MULTITUDE, MYRIAD ⟨a whole ~ of children began to push at the door —Ernest Beaglehole⟩ ⟨hotel with its long lobbies filled with . . . ~s of rocking chairs —Marjory S. Douglas⟩ ⟨writing a ~ of accumulated book reviews —H.J.Laski⟩ ⟨a whole ~ of national monuments, military parks, memorials, and cemeteries —C.L.With⟩

²host \"\ *vi* -ED/-ING/-s **:** to gather in a host **:** assemble usu. for a hostile purpose

³host \"\ *n* -s [ME *oste, hoste* host, guest, fr. OF, fr. L *hospit-, hospes* host, stranger, guest, fr. *hostis* stranger, enemy] **1 a :** INNKEEPER **b :** one who receives or entertains guests or strangers socially or commercially ⟨ourself will mingle with society and play the humble ~ —Shak.⟩ **2 a :** a living animal or plant affording subsistence or lodgment to a parasite — see ALTERNATE HOST, DEFINITIVE HOST, INTERMEDIATE HOST **b :** the larger, stronger, or dominant one of a commensal or symbiotic pair **c** (1) **:** an individual into which a tissue or part is transplanted from another (2) **:** an individual in whom an abnormal growth (as a cancer) is proliferating **3 :** a mineral or rock that is older than other minerals or rocks introduced into it or formed within or adjacent to it

⁴host \"\ *vb* -ED/-ING/-s [ME *osten, hosten*, fr. *oste, hoste*, n.] *vi, obs* **:** LODGE ⟨go bear it to the Centaur, where we ~, and stay there —Shak.⟩ ~ *vt* **1 :** to receive or entertain socially **:** serve as host to ⟨will ~ the cadets during their visit —*Springfield (Mass.) Daily News*⟩ **2 a :** to receive or entertain guests at **:** serve as host at ⟨the garden party he had ~*ed* last spring —*Saturday Rev.*⟩ ⟨~*ed* the shower, at which 70 relatives were present to meet the bride —*Sacramento (Calif.) Bee*⟩ **b :** EMCEE ⟨successfully ~*ed* a series of television programs⟩

⁵host \"\ *n* -s [ME *oste, hoste*, fr. MF *osté, hosté*, back-formation fr. *ostez, hostez*, pl. of *ostel, hostel* — more at HOSTEL] *obs* **:** LODGING — used in the phrase *at host* ⟨lay at ~ . . . in the Centaur —Shak.⟩

⁶host \"\ *n* -s *usu cap* [ME *oste, hoste*, fr. MF *oiste, hoiste*, fr. LL & L; LL *hostia* Eucharist, fr. L, sacrifice] **1 :** the eucharistic wafer or bread before or after consecration **2** *obs* **:** SACRIFICE

hos·ta \ˈhōstə, ˈhäs-\ *n* [NL, after Nicolaus T. *Host* †1834 Austrian botanist] **1** *cap* **:** a genus of Asiatic perennial herbs (family Liliaceae) that have ribbed basal leaves often blotched or bordered with white and scapes of white, blue, or lilac flowers and that are widely cultivated as ornamentals **2** -s **:** any plant of the genus *Hosta*

hos·tage \ˈhästij, -tēj *sometimes* ˈhȯs-\ *n* -s [ME *ostage, hostage*, fr. OF, fr. *oste, hoste* host, guest + *-age* — more at HOST] **1 a** *obs* **:** the state of a person given or kept as a pledge pending the fulfillment of an agreement, demand, or treaty ⟨if he stand in ~ for his safety —Shak.⟩ **b :** a person in such a state ⟨two boys . . . had been held as ~s for seven years —*N.Y. Times*⟩ **c :** a pledge, security, or guarantee usu. of good faith or intentions ⟨you know now your ~s: your uncle's word and my firm faith —Shak.⟩ **2** *archaic* **:** HOSTEL, INN **syn** see PLEDGE

hos·tage·ship \-,ship\ *n* -s **:** the quality or state of a hostage

host·al \ˈhōstᵊl\ *adj* [³*host* + *-al*] **:** relating to hosts ⟨a parasite with wide ~ range⟩

¹hos·tel \ˈhästᵊl\ *n* -s [ME *ostel, hostel*, fr. OF, fr. LL *hospitale* hospice — more at HOSPITAL] **1 :** a public house for entertaining or lodging travelers **:** INN ⟨folks used to ride up the bumpy road . . . to dine at the little ~ —Hodding Carter⟩ **2 a** *chiefly Brit* **:** housing maintained by a public or private organization or institution: (1) **:** DORMITORY 2 (2) **:** a rest home or rehabilitation center for the chronically ill, the aged, or the physically handicapped (3) **:** living quarters for newly arrived immigrants **b :** one of a system of supervised inexpensive lodgings or shelters for use by youth esp. on hiking or bicycling trips — called also *youth hostel* **3** *obs* **:** TOWN HOUSE

²hos·tel \", *dial* -səl\ *vi* -ED/-ING/-s [ME *hostelen*, fr. *hostel*, n.] **1** *dial Eng* **:** LODGE **2 :** to travel usu. by foot or by bicycle staying at hostels overnight ⟨hundreds of outdoor-minded vacationers will ~ alone or in independent groups of two or three this summer —Phil Spelman⟩

hos·tel·er \-stələ(r), *in sense 1* " *or* -slə-\ *n* -s [ME *osteler, hosteler*, fr. OF *ostelier, hostelier*, fr. *ostel, hostel* + *-ier*] **1 :** one that lodges or entertains guests or strangers: **a :** the officer in charge of guests in a religious house **b** *archaic* **:** INNKEEPER **2 a :** one residing in a hostel **b :** one that goes hosteling

hos·tel·ry \ˈhästᵊlrē *sometimes* ˈhäsəl-\ *n* -ES [ME *ostelrie, hostelrie*, fr. MF *ostelerie, hostelerie*, fr. *ostel, hostel* + *-erie* -ery] **:** a place where food and lodging are available to the traveler **:** INN, HOTEL ⟨a large wooden-porched building with mansard roof is a typical ~ of the Civil War period —*Amer. Guide Series: Vt.*⟩

¹host·ess \ˈhōstəs\ *n* -ES [ME *ostesse, hostesse*, fr. OF, fr. *oste, hoste* host, guest + *-esse* -ess — more at HOST] **1 :** a female innkeeper ⟨had a good understanding with the brother of mine ~ —Washington Irving⟩ **2 :** a woman who receives and entertains guests socially ⟨successful party giving amounts to little more than the friendly enthusiasm of the host and ~ —Emily Post⟩ **3 :** one whose job is to serve patrons: as **a :** a woman in charge of a public dining room who seats diners and ensures pleasant and efficient service **b :** a woman who directs social activities at a hotel or resort **c** (1) **:** a woman employed by a railroad or bus line to give personal service to passengers (2) **:** AIR HOSTESS **d :** a woman who acts as social partner in a dance hall or nightclub

²hostess \"\ *vb* -ED/-ING/-ES *vi* **:** to act as hostess ⟨had to arrange for the afternoon she was ~*ing* —W.L.George⟩ ~ *vt* **:** to serve as hostess at ⟨enjoyed ~*ing* the party⟩

hostess cart *n* : DINNER WAGON, TEA CART

hostess gown *n* : a dressy negligee or housecoat worn esp. for informal entertainment at home

hostess house *n* : an establishment at military installations for the lodging and entertainment of visitors

host·ess-ship \ˈhōstə(sh),ship, -təs,sh-\ *n* **:** the position or role of hostess

¹hos·tile \ˈhäl|stᵊl *also* |,stīl *or* |(,)stil *sometimes* ˈhȯ|\ *adj* [MF or L; MF, fr. L *hostilis*, fr. *hostis* stranger, enemy + *-ilis* -ile — more at GUEST] **1 a :** of or relating to an enemy ⟨a ~ army⟩ ⟨~ territory⟩ ⟨turned the guns toward a ~ position⟩ **b :** marked by malevolence and a desire to injure ⟨might commit some ~ act, attempt to strike me or choke me —Jack London⟩ **c :** marked by antagonism or unfriendliness ⟨the instinct of Americans has always been ~ to the alignment of classes in political parties —H.S.Commager⟩ **d :** marked by resistance esp. to new ideas **:** unfavorable esp. to the new or strange ⟨are ~ to the idea of literature for the sake of enjoyment —M.R.Cohen⟩ **e :** offering an unpleasant or forbidding environment **:** not hospitable ⟨searching the ~ glaring desert for gold —*Amer. Guide Series: Ariz.*⟩ ⟨maps of the area indicated the ~ character of the land —C.L. Walker⟩ **2 a :** of or relating to an opposing party in a legal controversy ⟨~ claim⟩ **b :** adverse to the interests of an owner or possessor of property ⟨~ use⟩ ⟨~ title⟩ **c** *of a witness* **:** subject to cross-examination because of evident hostility shown during direct examination

²hostile \"\ *n* -s **:** one that is hostile; *esp* **:** an American Indian unfriendly to whites ⟨ought to have guessed the ~s would try to come in here —Alan LeMay⟩

hostile embargo *n* : a government's embargo on the movement of enemy ships — compare CIVIL EMBARGO

hostile fire *n* : a fire that is not confined in a receptacle specif. made to contain fire — used in fire-insurance contracts; compare FRIENDLY FIRE

hos·tile·ly \-tᵊl(l)ē, -tīll, -til(l)|, |i\ *adv* **:** in a hostile manner

hos·tile·ness \-ᵊlnəs, -īln-, -iln-\ *n* -ES **:** the quality or state of being hostile

hostile possession *n* : ADVERSE POSSESSION

hos·til·i·ty \häˈstiləd.ē, -ətē, -i *sometimes* hȯˈ-\ *n* -ES [MF or LL; MF *hostilité*, fr. LL *hostilitat-, hostilitas*, fr. L *hostilis* + *-itat-, -itas* -ity] **1 a :** a hostile or antagonistic state ⟨the civilized south and the barbarous north stood in perpetual ~ —Kemp Malone⟩ **b** (1) **:** hostile action ⟨the Spanish expedition encountered ~ . . . and was forced to flee —R.W.Murray⟩ (2) **hostilities** *pl* **:** overt acts of warfare **:** WAR ⟨the outbreak of *hostilities*⟩ **2 :** antagonism, opposition, or resistance in thought or principle **:** ANIMOSITY ⟨there was tension, there was ~ and envy in the air —Theodor Reik⟩ ⟨~ to annexation has different grounds in different places —B.K.Sandwell⟩ **syn** see ENMITY

hos·ti·mel·a \,hästəˈmelə\ *n, cap* [NL, fr. *Hostim*, Czechoslovakia, its locality + NL *-ella*] **:** a form genus of fossil plants based on naked sporangia that are now commonly believed to be the fruiting structures of plants of the genus *Asteroxylon*

host·ing \ˈhōstiŋ\ *n* -s [ME, fr. ¹*host* + *-ing*] **1 a :** the mustering of armed men **b :** a hostile incursion or encounter ⟨strange to us it seemed . . . that angel should with angel war, and in fierce ~ meet —John Milton⟩ **2 :** GATHERING ⟨the good people who come out about this time of night to hold their ~ on the hills —O.S.J.Gogarty⟩

hos·tler \ˈ(h)äslə(r) *sometimes* ˈhəs-\ *n* -s [ME *osteler, hosteler, hostler* innkeeper, hostler — more at HOSTELER] **1 a** *also* **os·tler** \ˈäs-\ **:** one who takes care of horses at an inn or stable **:** GROOM **b :** one who is in charge of the horses or mules used in an industry **:** STABLEMAN **2 a :** one who takes charge of a railroad locomotive after a run **:** one who moves and services locomotives in enginehouse or roundhouse territory **b :** one employed in the storage garage of a transportation company to assist with the moving about and servicing of trucks or buses **c :** a worker who cleans, oils, or otherwise services machines (as cranes, dinkeys, boilers) that are in almost constant use

hostler's control *n* : a simplified throttle provided to move the unit of a diesel locomotive not equipped with a regular engineer's control

host·less \ˈhōstləs\ *adj* [³*host* + *-less*] **:** having no host

hos·tling \ˈ(h)äsliŋ *sometimes* ˈhəs-\ *n* -s [perh. alter. of *hosteling*, gerund of ²*hostel*] **:** the act or process of handling a locomotive between runs that includes taking it to the enginehouse and delivering it to the road crew

host·ly \ˈhōstlē\ *adj* [³*host* + *-ly*] **:** of or appropriate to a host ⟨still so young-looking that people did not instinctively lay upon him ~ duties —John Updike⟩

hos·try \ˈhōstrē\ *n* -ES [ME *ostrie, hostrie*, fr. MF *osterie, hosterie*, fr. *oste, hoste* host, guest + *-erie* -ery — more at HOST] *archaic* **:** HOSTELRY

hosts *pl of* HOST, *pres 3d sing of* HOST

¹hot \ˈhät, *usu* -äd.+V\ *adj* **hotter; hottest** [ME *hoot, hot*, fr. OE *hāt*; akin to OFris & OS *hēt* hot, OHG *heiz*, ON *heitr* hot, Goth *heito* fever, Lith *kaĩsti* to get hot] **1 :** having heat in a degree exceeding normal body heat **:** having a relatively high temperature **:** giving or capable of giving a sensation of heat **:** capable of burning, searing, or scalding ⟨~ stove⟩ ⟨~ forehead⟩ **2 a :** ARDENT, FIERY ⟨~ blood of youth⟩ ⟨~ tempers⟩ **:** VEHEMENT ⟨~ words were exchanged⟩ **b :** VIOLENT, RAGING ⟨~ battle⟩ **c :** URGENT, FEVERISH ⟨messengers sent in ~ haste⟩ **d** (1) *of an animal* **:** being in heat (2) **:** LUSTFUL, LECHEROUS **e :** ZEALOUS, EAGER ⟨~ for reform⟩ ⟨~ patriot⟩ ⟨~ baseball fan⟩ ⟨~ fisherman⟩ **f** (1) *of jazz* **:** ecstatic and emotionally exciting and usu. marked by complex rhythms and free contrapuntal improvisations on the melody — often contrasted with *sweet* (2) *of a jazz performer* **:** stimulated and inspired to complete rhythmic and melodic freedom **3 a :** having the sensation of an uncomfortable degree of body heat **:** too warm for comfort ⟨~ and tired⟩ ⟨I'm too ~ in this sweater⟩ **b :** causing discomfort or distress through excessive warmth or humidity ⟨~ climate⟩ ⟨this room is ~ and stuffy⟩ ⟨~ sunshine⟩ **c** (1) **:** naturally or constitutionally possessing heat — used in medieval physiology, natural philosophy, and astrology to name one of the qualities of the four elements (2) *of a sign of the zodiac* **:** having a hot complexion **4 a :** having or retaining the heat of cooking ⟨this pudding is best when served ~⟩ ⟨will you have ~ or iced coffee⟩ **b :** not yet grown cool or stale **:** newly made or received **:** FRESH ⟨news ~ from the press⟩ ⟨following a ~ scent⟩; *also* **:** close to something pursued or sought ⟨~ on the trail of the murderer⟩ ⟨guess again, you're getting *hotter*⟩ **c :** suggestive of heat ⟨~ smell of burning rubber⟩ ⟨~ sound of buzzing flies⟩ or of burning or glowing objects ⟨I like ~ colors . . . hot orange and red and shocking pink —Mitzi Gaynor⟩ **d** (1) *of type* **:** made by the casting of hot metal into a mold (2) **:** using type so made ⟨~ composition⟩ — compare COLD **e :** uncomfortable to an intolerable or dangerous degree **:** UNSAFE ⟨the police were making the town too ~ for him⟩ **5 :** PUNGENT, PEPPERY, BITING ⟨~ sauce⟩ ⟨~ pickles⟩ **6 :** showing energy or activity in an unusual degree: as **a :** of intense and immediate interest ⟨~ news story⟩ ⟨~ scandal⟩ **b :** unusually lucky or successful ⟨~ streak at poker⟩ or favorable ⟨the dice are ~ for me tonight⟩ **c :** temporarily capable of unusual performance (as in a sport) ⟨any one of half a dozen golfers might get ~ and win this tournament⟩ ⟨~ favorite in the race⟩ **d** *of merchandise or securities* **:** readily salable **:** enjoying current popularity ⟨~ items in women's wear⟩ **e** (1) **:** very good — used as a generalized term of approval ⟨a real ~ lawyer⟩ ⟨he's ~ in math⟩ (2) *slang* **:** ABSURD, UNBELIEVABLE ⟨wants to fight the champion? that's a ~ one⟩ **7 :** having or charged with high energy: as **a :** electrically charged; *esp* **:** charged with high voltage **b** *of a cartridge* **:** having a powder load which gives a high muzzle velocity and corresponding high chamber pressure and flat trajectory — used esp. of hand-loaded ammunition **c :** RADIOACTIVE ⟨~ material⟩; *also* **:** dealing with radioactive material ⟨~ laboratory⟩ **d** *of an airplane* **:** FAST; *esp* **:** characterized by a high landing speed **8 a :** stolen or otherwise illegally obtained ⟨~ jewels⟩ ⟨~ bonds⟩; *also* **:** CONTRABAND **b :** wanted by the police **:** fugitive from justice **c** *of a commodity* **:** prohibited by law or agreement from being shipped or handled ⟨~ oil⟩

²hot \"\ *adv* [ME *hoote, hote*, fr. OE *hāte*, fr. *hāt*, adj.] **:** HOTLY ⟨the sun shines ~ —Shak.⟩ ⟨*hot*-glowing coals⟩ ⟨took a club and gave it to him ~ and heavy⟩

³hot \"\ *n* -s [ME *hoot, hot*, fr. *hoot, hot*, adj.] **1** *dial* **:** HEAT **2 :** HOT DOG

⁴hot \"\ *vb* **hotted; hotted; hotting; hots** [¹*hot*] *vi, chiefly Brit* **:** to become warm or heated — usu. used with *up* ⟨fresh air ~s up quickly⟩ ⟨the argument had *hotted* up considerably⟩ ~ *vt, chiefly Brit* **:** WARM, HEAT; *specif* **:** to warm over (food) — usu. used with *up* ⟨there's some stew and dumplings left I can ~ up in a minute —Victoria Lincoln⟩

⁵hot \"\ *n* -s [ME *hott*, fr. OF *hotte, hote*, of Gmc origin; akin to G dial. *hutte, hotte* basket, pannier, MHG *hotte, hotze* cradle — more at HOD] **1** *now dial Eng* **:** a basket for carrying earth or manure **2** *dial Brit* **:** a little heap or pile (as of manure) **3** *obs* **:** a padded sheath for the spur of a gamecock

hot air *n* : empty talk **:** unsubstantiated and often boastful statements ⟨used to talk a lot of *hot air* about medicine —A.J. Cronin⟩ ⟨threats both ways are just *hot air*, big talk and face saving —*Kiplinger Washington Letter*⟩

hot-air engine *n* : an engine using heated air as the working substance

hot-air furnace *n* : a heating unit enclosed in a casing from which warm air is circulated through the building in ducts by gravity convection or by fans

hotbed \ˈ⸗,⸗\ *n* **1 :** a bed of soil enclosed in a low glass frame heated by fermenting manure or by other means and used for forcing or for raising early seedlings — compare COLD FRAME **2 :** a place or environment which favors rapid growth or development ⟨~ of crime⟩ **3 :** a frame or area in a rolling mill on which hot bars or rails are laid to cool

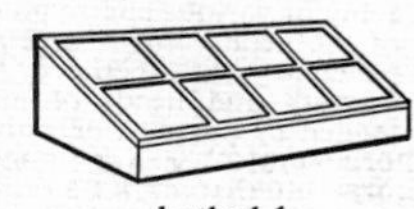
hotbed 1

hot-blast stove *n* : an apparatus used to preheat the blast for an iron blast furnace and consisting of firebrick passages which alternately receive heat from burning gas and then give up this heat to the incoming blast

hotblood \ˈ⸗,⸗\ *n* **:** one that is hotblooded: as **a :** one having strong passions or a quick temper **b :** THOROUGHBRED 1b

hot-blooded \ˈ⸗ˈ⸗⸗\ *adj* **1 :** having hot blood **:** EXCITABLE, HIGH-SPIRITED, ARDENT, PASSIONATE **2 a** *of a horse* **:** having Arab or Thoroughbred ancestors **b** *of a horse and other livestock* **:** of pure or superior breeding — **hot-blood·ed·ness** *n* -ES

hotbox \ˈ⸗,⸗\ *n* **1 :** a journal bearing (as of a railroad car) overheated by friction **2 :** SWEATBOX 2

hot-brain \ˈ⸗,⸗\ *n, archaic* **:** HOTHEAD

hot-brained \ˈ⸗ˈ⸗\ *adj, archaic* **:** HOTHEADED

hot bread *n* : bread, rolls, biscuits, or muffins served still hot from baking — usu. used in pl.

hot-bulb \ˈ⸗ˈ⸗\ *adj* **:** having an ignition system in which the charge is ignited by spraying it into a separate chamber kept above the ignition temperature of the charge by the heat of compression — used of a semidiesel engine

hot buttered rum *n* : a hot drink consisting of rum and water spiced and sweetened and served with a lump of butter floating on the surface

hot cake *n* : GRIDDLE CAKE

hot cap *n* : a paper or plastic cap set over growing plants in early spring for protection from frost

hot-cathode \ˈ⸗ˈ⸗,⸗\ *adj* **:** operated by thermionic emission from a heated cathode ⟨*hot-cathode* tube⟩

hotch \ˈhäch\ *vb* -ED/-ING/-ES [prob. fr. MF *hocher* to shake, fr. OF *hochier*, of Gmc origin; akin to MHG *hotteln, hotzeln* to shake — more at HOD] *vi* **1** *dial Brit* **:** to shake, jog, and wiggle **:** FIDGET **2** *dial Brit* **:** to change position or shift weight to make room **:** HITCH ~ *vt, chiefly Scot* **:** to cause to shake or shift

hot·cha \ˈhä(,)chä, -,chə\ *n* -s [prob. irreg. fr. ¹*hot*] *slang* **:** hot jazz ⟨band began to play the blatant ~ —John Fante⟩

hot chisel *n* : a chisel used in cutting hot metal

hotch·pot \ˈhäch,pät\ *n* [ME *hochepot*, fr. MF, fr. OF, fr. *hochier* to shake + *pot* — more at HOTCH, POTAGE] **1 :** HOTCHPOTCH 1 **2 :** HODGEPODGE 1 **3** [AF *hochepot*, fr. OF, hotchpotch] **:** a throwing into a common lot of property for equality of division which requires that advancements to a child be made up to the estate by contribution or by an accounting **:** COLLATION 5

hotch·potch \-,päch\ *n* -ES [alter. of *hotchpot*] **1 a :** a thick soup of barley, peas, and other vegetables, and often also meat **b :** a stew of meat and vegetables **2** *chiefly Brit* **:** HODGEPODGE 1 **3 :** HOTCHPOT 3

hot cockles *n pl but sing in constr* **:** a game in which one player covers his eyes and tries to guess who strikes him

hot corner *n* : the fielding position of the third baseman in baseball

hot cross bun *n* : a raisin bun marked with a cross made of sugar frosting traditionally served on Good Friday

hot deck *n* : a pile of logs from which logs are hauled to the mill as soon as they are cut and yarded — compare COLD DECK

hot dish *n* : CASSEROLE 3 ⟨had a *hot dish* and salad for lunch⟩

¹hot dog *n* [prob. so called fr. the fancied resemblance of a frankfurter to a dachshund] **:** a cooked frankfurter usu. served in a long split roll and garnished with mustard, onion, or other savory substance

²hot dog *interj* — used to express approval or gratification

hot-draw \ˈ⸗ˈ⸗\ *vt* **:** to draw (as metal or nylon) while hot or with application of heat

¹ho·tel \(ˈ)hōˈtel\ *n* -s [F *hôtel*, fr. OF *ostel, hostel* — more at

HOSTEL] **1** *obs* **:** a city mansion of a person of rank or wealth **2 a :** a house licensed to provide lodging and usu. meals, entertainment, and various personal services for the public **:** INN **b :** a building of many rooms chiefly for overnight accommodation of transients and several floors served by elevators, usu. with a large open street-level lobby containing easy chairs, with a variety of compartments for eating, drinking, dancing, exhibitions, and group meetings (as of salesmen or convention attendants), with shops having both inside and street-side entrances and offering for sale items (as clothes, gifts, candy, theater tickets, travel tickets) of particular interest to a traveler, or providing personal services (as hairdressing, shoe shining), and with telephone booths, writing tables, and washrooms freely available

²hotel \"\ *vt* **hotelled; hotelled; hotelling; hotels :** to lodge at a hotel

³hotel \"\ *usu cap* — a communications code word for the letter *h*

hotel car *n* **:** a railroad car with facilities for preparing and serving food and for sleeping

hô·tel de ville \(,)(h)ō,teldə'vēl\ *n, pl* **hôtels de ville** \-l(z)d-\ [F] **:** a town hall in France and other European countries

ho·tel dieu \-l'dyə(r), -yə̄\ *n, pl* **hotels dieu** \-l(z)'d-\ *cap D* [F *hôtel-Dieu*, fr. OF *ostel Dieu*, fr. *ostel, hostel* hostel, hospice + *Dieu* God, fr. L *deus* — more at HOSTEL, DEITY] **:** a medieval hospital

ho·tel·dom \hō'teldəm\ *n* -s **:** hotels and hotel workers ⟨you can't talk connectedly to anybody except . . . to a minor part of ~ and of officialdom —Laura Z. Hobson⟩

ho·tel·ier \,ōtel'yā\ *n* -s [F *hôtelier*, fr. OF *ostelier, hostelier* — more at HOSTELER] **:** HOTELKEEPER

hotelkeeper \(')⸗'⸗,⸗⸗\ *n* **:** a proprietor or manager of a hotel

ho·tel·less \hō'telləs\ *adj* **:** lacking a hotel ⟨some parts of the country are nearly ~⟩

hotel lock *n* **:** a knob lock that can be operated by a master key

ho·tel·man \(')⸗'⸗mən, -,man\ *n, pl* **hotelmen :** HOTELKEEPER

hotel rack *n* **:** the unsplit rib section of a foresaddle of lamb

hot flash *or* **hot flush** *n* **:** a sudden usu. brief sensation of heat and reddening of the skin accompanying sudden dilation of skin capillaries usu. associated with endocrine imbalance esp. that accompanying menopause

¹hotfoot \'hät,fu̇t, *usu* -u̇d·+V\ *adv* [ME *hot fot*] **:** in haste **:** without delay **:** HASTILY ⟨sent ambassadors ~ to the Turk —Francis Hackett⟩ ⟨drove his vessel ~ for the Boston pier —Mary H. Vorse⟩

²hotfoot \"\ *vi* **:** to go hotfoot **:** HASTEN, HURRY — used with *it* ⟨~*ing* it north . . . with a Texas posse on its heels —W.F. Harris⟩ **~** *vt* **:** to give (someone) a hotfoot **:** ANNOY, GOAD

³hotfoot \"\ *n* -s [¹*hot* + *foot*] **1 :** a practical joke in which a match is surreptitiously inserted in the side of a victim's shoe and lighted **2 a :** a stinging rebuke **:** INSULT, TAUNT ⟨administers one intellectual ~ after another to the Philistine public —Edgar Johnson⟩ **b :** GOAD, SPUR ⟨has given tradition-bound Baltimore a ~ —*Newsweek*⟩

hot-galvanize \'⸗'⸗⸗,⸗\ *vt* **:** to galvanize by dipping in molten zinc

hot-gospeler \'⸗,⸗⸗⸗\ *n* **:** an evangelical preacher **:** REVIVALIST

hothead \'⸗,⸗\ *n* **:** a hotheaded person

hotheaded \'⸗'⸗⸗\ *adj* **1 :** having a hot head (as from drinking) **2 :** FIERY, HASTY, IMPETUOUS — **hot·head·ed·ly** *adv* — **hot·head·ed·ness** *n* -ES

hothearted \'⸗'⸗⸗\ *adj* **:** HOTHEADED

¹hothouse \'⸗,⸗\ *n* [¹*hot* + *house*] **1** *obs* **:** TURKISH BATH **2** *obs* **:** BROTHEL **3 :** a room or building kept heated for drying something (as green pottery) **4 :** a greenhouse maintained at a high temperature for the culture of tender or tropical plants and other plants (as cucumbers and tomatoes) requiring such a temperature **5 :** SWEAT HOUSE 1 **6 :** HOTBED 2 ⟨the prose is a ~ of clichés —*New Yorker*⟩ ⟨the great city is . . . a ~ of decadence and of every perversion —François Bondy⟩

²hothouse \"\ *adj* **1 :** grown in a hothouse **:** artificially cultivated ⟨~ grapes⟩ **2 :** having the qualities of a plant raised in a hothouse **:** lacking normal resistance to cold or adversity **:** SOFT, DELICATE, DECADENT ⟨~ voluptuousness⟩ ⟨her father . . . was a brittle, ~ sort of creature —Frederick Prokosch⟩

hothouse lamb *n* **:** the meat of a lamb born out of the normal lambing season and usu. marketed during the period from January to March

ho·tis test \'hōd·əs-\ *n, usu cap H* [after R. P. *Hotis* †1935 Amer. agricultural marketing specialist] **:** a test for the presence of the common streptococcus of bovine mastitis in milk made by incubating a sample of milk with the aniline dye bromcresol purple, the appearance of yellow patches or coloration being indicative of the presence of the organism

hot lead *n* **:** fired bullets **:** GUNFIRE ⟨settled arguments with *hot lead*⟩

hot logging *n* **:** logging in which the logs are taken from stump directly to stream landing or mill — compare COLD DECK

hot·ly *adv* **:** in a hot or fiery manner **:** ARDENTLY, EAGERLY, PUNGENTLY, VIOLENTLY, HASTILY, LUSTFULLY

hotmelt \'⸗,⸗\ *n* **:** a fast-drying nonvolatile adhesive made of synthetic resins and plasticizers and applied hot in the molten state

hot money *n* **:** money of foreign ownership deposited or invested to avoid depreciation and constituting a threat to national currency and credit by being liable to sudden withdrawal — called also *funk money*

hot·ness *n* -ES **1 :** the quality or state of being hot **:** the sensation of heat **2 :** TEMPERATURE ⟨a thermometer measures the ~ of an object⟩

hot·not \'hät,nät\ *n* -s *usu cap* [Afrik] *Africa* **:** HOTTENTOT

hot oven *n* **:** a baking oven heated to a temperature between 400° and 450° F

hot pack *n* **:** absorbent material (as a blanket or squares of gauze) wrung out in hot water, wrapped around the body or a portion of the body, and covered with dry material to hold in the moist heat ⟨*hot pack* for an infected arm⟩

hot-pack method *n* **:** a method of canning in which food is partly cooked in an open kettle before being put in containers and then sterilized as in the cold-pack method

hot pants *n pl* **:** EAGERNESS, IMPETUOSITY; *esp* **:** impatient sexual desire ⟨still got *hot pants* for her, if you want to call that love —Mary McCarthy⟩

hot papa *n, slang* **:** HOT SUITMAN

hot pepper *n* **1 :** any of various capsicum fruits (as cayenne) that contain significant amounts of capsaicin, are characterized by marked pungency, usu. have rather thin walls, and vary in form from spherical to greatly elongated — compare SWEET PEPPER **2 :** a plant (as a bird pepper or cone pepper) that bears hot peppers

hot plate *n* **1 :** a heated iron plate (as on a cooking range) for cooking or for keeping food warm **2 :** a simple portable gas or electric heater for heating liquids or laboratory materials or for cooking in limited spaces **3 :** a food plate with a hot-water jacket for keeping food warm (as for infants or invalids)

hot plates: electric, *A;* gas, *B*

hot pond *n* **:** a log pond kept open by means of hot water and steam

hot pot *n* **:** a stew of meat and vegetables

hot potato *n* **:** a question or issue that involves unpleasant or dangerous consequences for anyone dealing with it ⟨bingo parties and church raffles have . . . developed into such a *hot potato* that everyone concerned now is seeking some easy solution —*N.Y. Times*⟩

¹hot-press \'⸗,⸗\ *n* **1 :** a calendering machine in which paper or cloth is glossed by being pressed between glazed boards and hot metal plates **2 :** a hydraulic oil press in which the contents are kept hot by steam radiators

²hot-press \'⸗'⸗\ *vt* **1 :** to gloss (paper or cloth) or to express (oil) by combined heat and pressure **2 :** to press (wood or metal) while hot

hot press *n, Brit* **:** a small heated room for drying laundry

hot-presser \'⸗,⸗⸗\ *n* **:** one that operates a hot-press

hot pursuit *n* **:** fresh pursuit esp. across state or territorial lines

hot-quench \'⸗'⸗\ *vt* **:** to quench (a metal) in a hot bath (as of molten salt, lead, or oil)

hot rock *n* **:** a highly skilled or daredevil airplane pilot

hot rod *n* **:** an automobile rebuilt or modified for high speed and fast acceleration

hot rod·der \-¦räda(r)\ *n* **1 :** a hot-rod driver, builder, or enthusiast **2 :** one who drives a car in a showy or reckless manner

hot roll *n, West* **:** BEDROLL

hot-roll \'⸗¦⸗\ *vt* **:** to roll (metal) while hot or with the application of heat — compare COLD-ROLL

hots *pl of* HOT, *pres 3d sing of* HOT

hot saw *n* **:** a power saw for cutting hot metal — distinguished from *cold saw*

hot seat *n* **1** *slang* **:** ELECTRIC CHAIR **2 :** a position of uneasiness or embarrassment or anxiety **:** a position involving oppressive responsibility ⟨on the *hot seat*, directing a half-million dollar gamble —Mark Stroock & Percy Knauth⟩ ⟨kept Iran on a political *hot seat* —*Armed Forces Talk*⟩ **3** *slang* **:** an ejection seat in an airplane

hot-short \'⸗¦⸗\ *adj, of metal* **:** short or brittle when heated beyond a red heat — compare COLD-SHORT, RED-SHORT — **hot-short·ness** *n*

hot shot *n* **:** shot heated to redness in order to set fire to buildings or ships

¹hotshot \'⸗,⸗\ *n* [¹*hot* + *shot*] **1 a :** a fast freight usu. hauling merchandise or perishables in scheduled service **b :** a very fast airplane or vehicle **2** *slang* **:** a skillful, showy, and aggressive person; *esp* **:** one holding a position of importance by exercise of skill, showiness, and aggression **3 a :** a skilled workman **b :** a skilled performer in a sport (as golf, basketball, baseball) that involves shooting or aiming **4 :** FIRE FIGHTER

²hotshot \"\ *adj* **1** *slang* **:** highly skilled, fast-working, or showy; *also* **:** important or successful by exercise of skill, adroitness, or showiness ⟨a ~ surgeon with more business than he can handle⟩ **2** *of a freight carrier* **:** NONSTOP, THROUGH, FAST ⟨a ~ freight train⟩

hot slaw *n* **:** coleslaw prepared with a cooked dressing

hot spot *n* **1 :** a place that is hotter than the surrounding surface: as **a :** a spot in the intake manifold of an internal-combustion engine which is heated by the exhaust gases to aid in the vaporization of the fuel **b :** an overheated spot in the combustion chamber tending to cause preignition **c :** a place in the shell of a furnace hotter than the rest **d :** an uncooled portion of a combustion chamber against which a charge is sprayed for ignition in a semidiesel engine **2 :** a region of high forest-fire frequency **3 a :** an area in a plastered wall containing alkaline salts that cause paper and paints to discolor **b :** an area on a negative or print representing excessive illumination of a part of the subject **c :** an area of excessive illumination (as on a subject or on the easel of an enlarger) in a pictorial reproduction **4 :** a center of night life **:** NIGHTCLUB

hot-spot \'⸗,⸗\ *vt* [*hot spot*] **:** to check a forest fire at hot spots

hot spring *n* **:** THERMAL SPRING; *esp* **:** a spring with water above 98° F

hotspur \'⸗,⸗\ *n* [ME *hatspore*, fr. *hat, hoot, hot* hot + *spore* spur — more at HOT, SPUR] **:** a rash hotheaded impetuous man

hot stove league *n* **:** sports followers (as of baseball) gathering for off-season discussion ⟨first place a baseball fan might look for some good, between-seasons, *hot stove league* reading —J.K.Hutchens⟩

hot stuff *n, slang* **:** something or someone unusually good or extraordinary or formidable ⟨in surf casting . . . the man who can average one hundred yards is *hot stuff* —*Fisherman's Encyc.*⟩

hot stuff man *n* **:** a bakery worker who removes baked goods from pans

hot suit·man \-'sütmən\ *n, pl* **hot suitmen :** a man esp. equipped to rescue the crew of a burning airplane

hot-swage \'⸗¦⸗\ *vt* **:** to swage (metal) while hot

hot·sy-tot·sy \¦hätsē¦tätsē\ *adj* [coined *ab*1926 by Billie De Beck †1942 Am. cartoonist] *slang* **:** comfortably stable or secure **:** PERFECT, OK ⟨had a quarrel, but everything is *hotsy-totsy* now⟩

hott \'hät\ *var of* ⁵HOT

hotted *past of* HOT

hot-tempered \'⸗¦⸗⸗\ *adj* **:** having a quick or violent temper

hot·ten \'hätᵊn\ *vb* -ED/-ING/-S [¹*hot* + *-en*] *vt, dial* **:** HEAT ⟨~ up the soup, ma⟩ **~** *vi, dial* **:** to grow hot **:** become angry or lively ⟨warmed and then ~*ed* to his subject —Adria Langley⟩

hot·ten·tot \'hätᵊn,tät, *usu* -äd·+V\ *n* -s [Afrik *Hottentot, Hotnot*] **1** *usu cap* **a :** a people of southern Africa apparently akin to both the Bushmen and the Bantus and having moderately negroid features, typically very long heads, and prominent buttocks — see GRIQUA, NAMA **b :** a member of such people **2** *usu cap* **:** the Khoisan language of the Hottentot people **3 :** a common So. African marine sparid food fish (*Pachymetopon blochii*)

hottentot apron *n, usu cap H* **:** an excessive development of the labia minora occurring in Hottentot women

hottentot bread *or* **hottentot's bread** *n, usu cap H* **1 :** ELEPHANT'S-FOOT 1 **2 :** the thick edible rootstock of elephant's-foot

hottentot bustle *n, usu cap H* **:** STEATOPYGIA

hottentot fig *or* **hottentot's fig** *n, usu cap H* **:** a low-growing woody southern African perennial (*Carpobrotus edulis*) of the family Aizoaceae that has angular stems, opposite succulent leaves united at the base, and large yellow or purplish rose flowers, that is cultivated as a ground cover, and that sometimes occurs as an escape in the southwestern U.S.

¹hotter *comparative of* HOT

²hot·ter \'hätə(r\ *vi* -ED/-ING/-S [perh. fr. Flem *hotteren* to shake; akin to MHG *hotteln, hotzeln* to shake — more at HOD] **1** *dial Brit* **a :** to shake esp. with rage or laughter **b :** to move shakily **:** JOLT **c :** to crowd together in confusion **2** *dial Brit* **a :** RUMBLE ⟨~*ing* thunder⟩ **b :** to talk incoherently **:** MUTTER, MUMBLE, STAMMER

³hotter \"\ *n* -s **1** *dial Brit* **:** the act or motion of hottering **2** *dial Brit* **:** a swarm or heap of things

hottest *superlative of* HOT

hotting *pres part of* HOT

hot·tish \'häd·ish\ *adj* **:** somewhat hot

hot·to·nia \hä'tōnēə\ *n, cap* [NL, fr. Peter *Hotton* †1709 Dutch botanist + NL *-ia*] **:** a genus of aquatic herbs (family Primulaceae) with submerged crowded leaves and small white or purplish racemose flowers — see FEATHERFOIL

hot top *n* **:** a feedhead for an ingot mold

hot-trod \'⸗,⸗\ *n* **1** *Scot* **:** the pursuit with hounds and horn in old border forays **2** *Scot* **:** the signal for such pursuit

hot up *vi* **1 :** to grow hot, lively, or exciting ⟨the gossip began to *hot up* —*Life*⟩ **2 :** to speed up ⟨the air raids began to *hot up* about the beginning of February —George Orwell⟩ **~** *vt* **1 :** AROUSE, ANNOY ⟨getting him all *hotted up* —Lord Beaverbrook⟩ **2 :** to make livelier or speedier ⟨a protest against . . . the genteel *hotting up* of Shakespearean productions robbed of all poetry —Stephen Spender⟩

hot-walker \'⸗,⸗⸗\ *n* **:** one employed to cool out horses ⟨got odd jobs as a *hot-walker* and exercise boy —*Time*⟩

hot wall *n* **:** a wall provided with heating flues for hastening the growth or ripening of fruit

hot war *n* **:** an armed conflict **:** a shooting war — compare COLD WAR

hot water *n* **:** a dangerous or distressing predicament **:** TROUBLE, DIFFICULTY ⟨primitive people take exception to a camera . . . so that indiscriminate snap shooting has landed more than one explorer in *hot water* —W.W.Howells⟩

hot-water bag *or* **hot-water bottle** *n* **1 :** a stoppered rubber bag or earthenware bottle filled with hot water to provide warmth **2** *Brit* **:** HEATING PAD ⟨electric *hot-water bottles*⟩

hot-water heating *n* **:** central heating by means of hot water circulated through pipes or radiators

hot-water treatment *n* **:** a treatment of plants or plant parts for the eradication of parasites (as loose smut of wheat) involving immersion in water at a temperature above the thermal death point of the parasite but below that of the host

hot-water bag

hot wave *n* **:** a period of relatively high temperatures; *specif* **:** one caused by the southerly winds in front of an advancing cyclone or by the accumulating heat in a stagnant anticyclone — called also *heat wave*

hot well *n* **1 :** HOT SPRING **2 :** a reservoir in a condensing steam-engine or turbine installation for receiving the warm condensed steam drawn from the condenser

hot-wire \'⸗¦⸗\ *adj* **:** operated by the thermal expansion of a wire through which an electric current is passed or by the convective cooling (as by air) of a wire heated by passage through it of an electric current, the expansion or contraction of the wire usu. deflecting a pointer ⟨*hot-wire* ammeter⟩ ⟨*hot-wire* anemometer⟩

hot-work \'⸗¦⸗\ *vt* **:** to roll, forge, press, or shape (metal) while hot

hou·ba·ra \hü'bärə\ *n* -s [Ar *ḥubārā* bustard] **:** a bustard (*Chlamydotis undulata* syn. *Houbara undulata*) of northern Africa or its eastern form (*C. u. macqueenii*) found in Persia, India, and sometimes in England — called also *ruffed bustard*

houdah *var of* HOWDAH

hou·dan \'hü,dan, ü'dä̃\ *n* -s *usu cap* [F, fr. *Houdan*, village in northern France where it was developed] **:** a domestic fowl of a French breed of medium size with a V-shaped leaf comb, mottled black-and-white or pure-white plumage and crest, and five toes

hou·die \'hau̇dī\ *var of* HOWDIE

hou·dry process \'hüdrē-\ *n, usu cap H* [after Eugene *Houdry* *b*1892 Am. engineer] **:** a cracking process for making high-octane gasoline by passing oil vapors through a fixed bed of an aluminum silicate catalyst in the form of pellets

houf \'hau̇f\ *var of* HOWF

¹hough \'hak, 'hōk\ *n* -s [ME *hoch, hough* — more at HOCK] *chiefly Scot* **:** ⁴HOCK

²hough \"\ *vt* -ED/-ING/-S [ME *houghen*, fr. *hough*, n.] *now chiefly Scot* **:** HAMSTRING ⟨thou shalt ~ their horses, and burn their chariots —Josh 11:6 (AV)⟩

hough·er \'häkə(r)\ *n* -s **:** one that hamstrings cattle; *specif* **:** one of a band of lawbreakers in Ireland that hamstrung cattle

hough·ma·gan·dy \,hȯkmə'gandi\ *n* -ES [perh. irreg. fr. ¹*hough* + *canty*] *Scot* **:** FORNICATION

hou·here \hō'herə\ *n* -s [Maori] **1** *NewZeal* **:** RIBBONWOOD 1 **2** *NewZeal* **:** RIBBON TREE

hounce \'hau̇n(t)s\ *n* -s [origin unknown] *dial Eng* **:** an ornament on the collar of a cart horse

¹hound \'hau̇nd\ *n* -s [ME, fr. OE *hund;* akin to OHG *hunt* dog, ON *hundr*, Goth *hunds*, L *canis*, Gk *kyōn*, Skt *śvā*] **1 a :** DOG **b :** a dog of any of various breeds used in the chase that have typically large drooping ears and a deep voice and follow their prey by scent **c** *Brit* **:** FOXHOUND **2 a :** a mean or despicable person ⟨that low-down, sneaking ~⟩ **3 a :** DOGFISH 1 **b** *Newfoundland* **:** OLD-SQUAW **4 :** one of the chasers in the game hare and hounds **5 :** one closely attached to a habit or pursuit **:** ADDICT ⟨autograph ~⟩ ⟨an expert lens ~ —H.H.Miller⟩ — often used in combinations ⟨booze*hound*⟩ ⟨chow*hound*⟩

²hound \"\ *vt* -ED/-ING/-S [ME (Sc dial.) *hounden*, fr. *hound*, n.] **1 a :** to hunt, chase, or track with hounds or as if with hounds **b :** to pursue unrelentingly ⟨was ~*ed* by his creditors⟩ **:** heckle or harass unceasingly ⟨~*ed* from office by the press⟩ **2 :** to set on the chase **:** incite to pursuit ⟨~ a dog at a hare⟩ — often used with *on* ⟨~ on pursuers⟩ **syn** see BAIT

³hound \"\ *n* -s [ME *hune, hownde*, of Scand origin; akin to ON *húnn* cube, knob at the top of a masthead, young of an animal, bear cub — more at CAVE] **1 hounds** *pl* **:** the framing at the masthead of a ship for supporting the heel of the topmast and the upper parts of the lower rigging **2 :** a sidebar connecting the tongue of a wagon with the forecarriage or the reach with the hind carriage in order to give additional rigidity to those parts

hound band *n* **:** an iron band at the mast hounds of a ship for attaching the shrouds

hound color *n* **:** a color pattern typical of hound breeds and consisting of black and tan distributed in clearly defined patches on a white ground

hound dog *n, chiefly South* **:** HOUND

hound·er \'hau̇ndə(r)\ *n* -s **:** one that hounds

houndfish \'⸗,⸗\ *n* [ME, fr. *hound* + *fish*] **1 :** DOGFISH 1 **2 :** NEEDLEFISH

hound·ing \'hau̇ndiŋ\ *n* -s [³*hound* + *-ing*] **:** the portion of a mast between the hounds and deck or of a bowsprit between the cap and gammon iron

hound·ish \'hau̇ndish\ *adj* **:** of, relating to, or having the characteristics of a hound ⟨a mongrel with a vaguely ~ look⟩

houndman \'hau̇n(d)mən\ *n, pl* **houndmen :** a keeper of hounds

hound-marked \'⸗¦⸗\ *adj* **:** marked with hound color

hound music *n* **:** the baying of hounds on a scent

houndsbane \'hau̇n(d)z,⸗\ *n* -s **:** HOREHOUND

houndsberry *n* [ME *houndesberye*, fr. *hound* + *berye* berry — more at BERRY] **1** *obs* **:** BLACK BRYONY **2** *obs* **:** BLACK NIGHTSHADE

houndsfoot \'⸗,⸗\ *n* -s [¹*hound* + *foot;* intended as trans. of G *hundsfott* or D *hondsvot*, lit., dog's vulva] *archaic* **:** a worthless rascal

houndshark \'⸗,⸗\ *n* **:** DOGFISH 1

hound's-tongue \'⸗,⸗\ *n, pl* **hound's-tongues** [ME *hundestunge*, fr. OE, fr. *hund* dog + *tunge* tongue — more at HOUND, TONGUE] **1 :** any of various coarse plants of the genus *Cynoglossum* (esp. *C. officinale*) having tongue-shaped leaves and reddish flowers succeeded by nutlets covered with barbed prickles **2 :** YELLOW CLINTONIA

houndstooth check *or* **hound's-tooth check** \'⸗,⸗-\ *n* **:** a small broken-check pattern; *also* **:** a fabric woven in this pattern

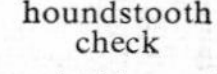

houndstooth check

houndy \'hau̇ndē\ *adj* **:** HOUNDISH

houpe *var of* ⁴HOOP

houp-la *var of* HOOPLA

houppe·lande \'hü,pländ, ⸗'⸗\ *n* -s [F, fr. OF *hoppelande*] **:** a loose belted overgown of the 14th and 15th centuries usu. with long wide sleeves, dagged edges, a fur lining, and full-length skirt often with slits in it

hour \'au̇(ə)r, 'au̇ə, *esp in the South* 'au̇wə(r\ *n* -s [ME *our, hour*, fr. OF *ore, ure, hore, hure, heure*, fr. LL & L; LL *hora* canonical hour, fr. L, season of the year, time of day, part of the day, hour, fr. Gk *hōra* — more at YEAR] **1 hours** *pl* **a :** the times of the day ecclesiastically set for prayer (as matins and vespers) — see CANONICAL HOUR **b :** the prayers appointed for such times ⟨book of ~*s*⟩ **2 a** *obs* **:** the 12th part of the time between sunrise and sunset or between sunset and sunrise and hence of varying duration **b :** the 24th part of a mean solar day **:** 60 minutes of mean solar time **3 a :** the time of day expressed in hours and minutes as indicated by a timepiece ⟨the ~ is half past ten⟩ ⟨what are you doing here at this ~⟩; *specif* **:** the number of full hours elapsed since noon or midnight ⟨the clock has just struck the ~⟩ **b :** the time reckoned from midnight to midnight — used chiefly in the armed services ⟨dinner would come about 1700 ~*s* —*Infantry Jour.*⟩ ⟨a conference at 0900 ~*s*⟩ **4 a :** a fixed, stated, or customary time or period of time ⟨~*s* of business⟩ ⟨during his leisure ~*s*⟩ ⟨cocktail ~⟩ **b :** a particular time ⟨help in his ~ of need⟩ ⟨hottest ~*s* of the day⟩ **c hours** *pl* **:** time of going to bed ⟨late ~*s* ruined his health⟩ ⟨keep early ~*s* out here in the country⟩ **5 :** one twelfth of a natural day or of a natural night as determined by sunrise and sunset and assigned in astrology to the special influence of a planet — called also *inequal hour, planetary hour* **6 a :** 60 minutes of sidereal time **b :** an angular unit of right ascension equal to 15 degrees measured along the equinoctial **7 :** a unit of measure of work equal to the normal amount done in an hour (as a token of presswork) **8 :** a measure of distance estimated by the time normally taken to cover it ⟨the city was two ~*s* away⟩ **9 a :** a class session or period ⟨~ tests, lasting fifty minutes each, are given several times during the semester⟩ **b :** CREDIT HOUR, SEMESTER HOUR ⟨three-*hour* course⟩ — **after hours** *adv* **1 a :** after the close of the regular working day ⟨worked on his invention at home *after hours*⟩ **b :** after classroom hours **2 :** after the legal closing time set for a public place (as a saloon) — **on the hour** *adv* **:** at exactly the full hour ⟨from 8 a.m. to 10 p.m. trains leave every hour *on the hour*⟩

hour·age \'au̇(ə)rij\ *n* -s : aggregate working or traveling time in hours
hour angle *n* : the angle between the celestial meridian of an observer and the hour circle of a celestial object measured westward from the meridian — compare MERIDIAN ANGLE
hour circle *n* **1** : a circle of the celestial sphere passing through the two poles **2** : the circle upon an equatorial telescope mounted perpendicular to the polar axis and graduated in hours and subdivisions of hours of right ascension **3** : a small metal circle attached to the pole of an artificial globe and divided into 24 parts to mark differences of time at different places
1hourglass \'ˌ=ˌ=\ *n* [*hour* + *glass*] **1** : an instrument for measuring time consisting of a glass vessel having two symmetrical compartments from the uppermost of which a quantity of sand, water, or mercury occupies an hour in running through a small aperture into the lower one and an hour returning when the instrument is turned upside down **2** : the space of time measured by an hourglass

hourglass

2hourglass \"\ *adj* : shaped like an hourglass ⟨~ waistline⟩ ⟨~ contraction of the stomach⟩ ⟨~ tumor⟩
hourglass screw *or* **hourglass worm** *n* : HINDLEY'S SCREW
hourglass spider *n* : a black widow or a closely related spider
hourglass stomach *n* : a stomach divided into two communicating cavities by a circular constriction usu. caused by the scar tissue around an ulcer
hour hand *n* : the index showing the hour on a timepiece
hou·ri *or* **hu·ri** \'hu̇rē, 'hu̇rē, 'hau̇rē, ⸗ˈ⸗\ *n* -s [F *houri*, fr. Per *hūrī*, fr. Ar *ḥūrīyah*, sing. of *ḥūr* (in *ḥūr al-'ayn* fair black-eyed women)] **1** : one of the dark-eyed virgins of perfect beauty that in Muslim belief live with the blessed in paradise **2** : a voluptuously beautiful young woman
hour·less \'⸗ləs\ *adj* : being outside of time : TIMELESS
hour line *n* : a dial line for indicating the hour
hour–long \'⸗ˈ⸗\ *adj* : lasting for an hour ⟨*hour-long* radio program⟩
1hour·ly *pronunc at* HOUR + lē *or* lī\ *adv* [ME, fr. *hour* + *-ly* (adv. suffix)] : at or during every hour : FREQUENTLY : CONTINUALLY ⟨strife, which ~ was renewed —John Dryden⟩
2hourly \"\ *adj* [*hour* + *-ly* (adj. suffix)] **1** *obs* : happening within an hour : BRIEF, RECENT **2** : happening or done every hour : occurring hour by hour : renewed hour by hour : FREQUENT, CONTINUAL ⟨~ train service⟩ ⟨in ~ expectation of the rain's stopping⟩ **3** : using an hour as the unit for determining an amount (as for reckoning wages) ⟨engaged and paid on an ~ basis⟩
hourly–rated \ˌ⸗⸗ˈ⸗⸗\ *adj* : receiving a fixed wage of a certain amount per hour — contrasted with *salaried*
hours *pl of* HOUR
hour wheel *n* : the wheel in a timepiece that carries the hour hand
hou·sa·ton·ic \ˌhüsəˈtänik, -üzə-\ *n* -s *usu cap* [fr. the *Housatonic* river, Mass. & Conn.] : STOCKBRIDGE
1house \'hau̇s; *sing. possessive* -au̇səz, -au̇zəz\ *n, pl* **hous·es** \-au̇zəz *chiefly substand* -au̇səz\ *often attrib* [ME *hous*, fr. OE *hūs*; akin to OHG & ON *hūs* house, Goth gud*hūs* temple, and prob. to OE *hȳd* hide — more at HIDE] **1 a** : a structure intended or used for human habitation : a building that serves as one's residence or domicile esp. as contrasted with a place of business : a building containing living quarters for one or a few families — sometimes used at law of a room or other part of such a building; see BUNGALOW, COTTAGE, MANSION; APARTMENT BUILDING, BOARDINGHOUSE, DWELLING HOUSE, LODGING HOUSE, ROOMING HOUSE, TENEMENT HOUSE; compare APARTMENT, HOME, HOMESTEAD, HOTEL, INN, TENEMENT **b** : regular existence in or as if in a house ⟨left home to set up ~ in another town⟩ ⟨children imitating their elders by playing ~⟩ **c** : a place of habitation, rest, or abode ⟨~ of death⟩ ⟨fleshly ~ of the soul⟩ **d** *dial Eng* : the chief living room (as the kitchen) of a farmhouse or cottage **2 a** : something (as a shell, nest, den) that serves an animal for shelter or habitation ⟨muskrat ~⟩ **b** : a building in which something is kept or stored ⟨carriage ~⟩ ⟨reptile ~⟩ ⟨a ~ for hens⟩ **3 a** : MUNDANE HOUSE **b** : a zodiacal sign regarded as the seat of a planet's greatest influence — called also *mansion, planetary house* **c** *obs* : a square on a chessboard **d** : the circular area 12 feet in diameter surrounding the tee within which a curling stone must rest in order to count **4 a** *archaic* : those who dwell in the same house : HOUSEHOLD ⟨himself believed and his whole ~ —Jn 4:53 (AV)⟩ **b** : a family of ancestors, descendants, and kindred : a race of persons from the same stock; *esp* : a noble family ⟨the great ~*s* of England⟩ **5 a** : the residence of a religious community **b** : the members of a religious community **6 a** : a college in a university **b** : a hall or dormitory in a college or school ⟨~ dinner⟩; *also* : the students in a hall or dormitory ⟨~ team⟩ **7 a** : one of the estates of a kingdom or other government assembled in parliament or legislature : a body of men united in a legislative capacity ⟨the *House* of Lords⟩ *also* : a quorum of such a body — see HOUSE OF ASSEMBLY, HOUSE OF COMMONS, HOUSE OF DELEGATES, HOUSE OF REPRESENTATIVES **b** : the building or the chamber in which such a body holds its sessions **8** : a body of men forming a deliberative or consultative assembly esp. of an ecclesiastical or a collegiate character ⟨~ of bishops⟩ ⟨~ of convocation⟩ **9 a** : a business organization : FIRM, PARTNERSHIP ⟨banking ~⟩ ⟨~ of tea importers⟩ ⟨printing ~⟩ ⟨publishing ~⟩ **b** (1) : the operators of a gambling game : the management of a gambling establishment ⟨a percentage of each pot goes to the ~⟩ (2) : a gambling establishment : CASINO **10 a** : HOTEL, RESTAURANT, BARROOM ⟨have a drink on the ~⟩ **b** : BROTHEL **11 a** : a building for dramatic or musical performances : THEATER **b** : an audience esp. in a theater ⟨playing to small ~*s*⟩ ⟨a good ~ at the opening⟩ ⟨I'll concentrate on acting, because I don't have to count the ~ —*Newsweek*⟩ **12** : a structure rising above the deck of a tanker or cargo ship that encloses living quarters or the bridge **13** *archaic Brit* : WORKHOUSE — used with *the* **14** : a clump of trees or shrubs growing on a slight elevation in a Florida prairie **15** *Brit* : any of several lotto or keno games
2house \'hau̇z, *chiefly substand* -au̇s\ *vb* -ED/-ING/-S [ME *housen*, fr. OE *hūsian*, fr. *hūs* house] *vt* **1 a** : to provide with a permanent dwelling place or living quarters ⟨trying to feed and ~ his family⟩ **b** : to lodge or shelter temporarily ⟨guests were *housed* in a separate cottage⟩ : find shelter for **c** : to confine within a house ⟨*housed* with a bad cold⟩ — often used with *up* ⟨*housed* up all day in these four walls⟩ **d** : to store in a house ⟨~ garden tools in a shed⟩ **2 a** : to encase, enclose, or shelter as if by putting in a house ⟨so timorous a soul *housed* in so impressive a body —A.W.Long⟩ **b** : to stow or secure in a safe place ⟨~ the upper spars of a ship⟩ ⟨~ a yacht for the winter⟩ **c** : to cover (a deck) with a roof **3** : to serve as shelter for : CONTAIN ⟨those caves may ~ snakes⟩ ⟨library ~*s* thousands of volumes⟩ ⟨former stately homes now ~ professional and business offices⟩ **4** : to provide (as a play or opera) with a theater **5** : to fit (as machinery or gears) with shrouds or protective walls or housings **6 a** : to cut a housing in (as a timber) **b** : to insert into or put together by means of a housing ~ *vi* **1** : to take shelter : find refuge : LODGE, DWELL, HARBOR ⟨graze where you will, you shall not ~ with me —Shak.⟩ — used often with *up* ⟨~ up in a cave for the winter⟩ **2** *of a planet* : to have position in a mundane house or a mansion
3house \'hau̇s, -au̇z\ *n, pl* **hous·es** \-au̇zəz,-au̇səz\ [ME *houce, house*, fr. MF *houce, housse*, of Gmc origin; akin to MHG *hulst, hulft* covering, OE *heolstor* darkness, cover — more at HOLSTER] : ²HOUSING
4house \'hau̇z, -au̇s\ *vt* -ED/-ING/-S : to cover with or as if with a housing : CAPARISON ⟨a gaily *housed* horse⟩
house agent *n, chiefly Brit* : a real-estate broker or agent
house amish *n, usu cap A* : Amish Mennonites who have no churches, who purposely avoid owning church property, and who worship in the various homes of members on a rotating basis
house ant *n* : any of various ants common in human dwellings — compare PHARAOH ANT
house arrest *n* : confinement often under guard to one's house or quarters or a hospital instead of in a jail or prison
house bill *n* : a bill originating in the U.S. House of Representatives
house board *n* : a display board on the front of a theater
1houseboat \'ˌ=ˌ=\ *n* [¹*house* + *boat*] **1** : a barge fitted up with cabins and designed for use as a dwelling or for leisurely cruising in quiet waters **2** : a yacht having sleeping accommodations for several people
2houseboat \"\ *vi* : to live or cruise in a houseboat

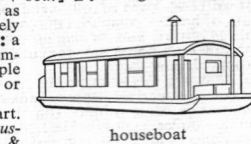

houseboat

housebote \'ˌ=ˌ=\ *n* -s [part. trans. of (assumed) ME *housbote* (whence ML *husbota* & AF *ousbote*), fr. ME *hous* house + *bote* repair, deliverance — more at BOOT] : wood allowed to a tenant for repairing a house — compare ESTOVERS
housebound \'ˌ=ˌ=\ *adj* : confined to the house ⟨bad weather kept us ~ for days⟩ ⟨~ with a severe cold⟩
houseboy \'ˌ=ˌ=\ *n* : HOUSEMAN 1
1house·break \'hau̇s,brāk\ *vi* [back-formation fr. *housebreaker* & *housebreaking*] : to commit housebreaking
2housebreak \"\ *vt* [back-formation fr. *housebroken*] **1** : to train (an animal or a baby) to live in a domestic environment with respect to sanitary habits **2 a** : to teach acceptable social manners to : accustom to indoor living : make tractable or polite **b** : to break the spirit of : TAME, SUBDUE
house·break·er \-kə(r)\ *n* [ME *housbreker*, fr. *hous* house + *breker* breaker] **1** : one that commits housebreaking **2** *chiefly Brit* : one that pulls down old buildings : WRECKER
housebreaking \'ˌ=ˌ=ˌ=\ *n* [¹*house* + *breaking*] **1** : an act of breaking open and entering with a felonious purpose the dwelling house of another by day or night — compare BURGLARY **2** : an act of pulling down old buildings
housebroken \'ˌ=ˌ=ˌ=\ *or* **housebroke** \'ˌ=ˌ=\ *adj* : trained to live in a house : adjusted to indoor conditions ⟨~ dog⟩ ⟨~ plant⟩
housebuilder \'ˌ=ˌ=ˌ=\ *n* : one whose business is to build houses
house–building rat \'ˌ=ˌ==-\ *n* : a large Australian rat (*Leporillus conditor*) that builds a large nest of sticks
houseburn \'ˌ=ˌ=\ *n* : an injury to tobacco leaves in the curing barn resulting from fungus activity caused by excess moisture — compare POLE ROT
house car *n* **1** : an enclosed freight car (as a boxcar, refrigerator car, stockcar) **2** : a railroad car for handling goods to be loaded or unloaded at a freight house
housecarl \'ˌ=ˌ=\ *also* **hus·carl** \'hüs,-\ *n* [OE *hūscarl*, fr. ON *hūskarl*, fr. *hūs* house + *karl* carl — more at HOUSE, CARL] : a member of the small standing army or bodyguard of a Danish or early English king or noble
house cat *n* : CAT 1a
house centipede *n* : a widespread long-legged centipede (*Scutigera coleoptrata*) common in damp sheltered places (as the cellars of buildings) and believed to be valuable as a destroyer of flies, roaches, and other noxious insects
house·clean \'hau̇,sklēn\ *vb* [back-formation fr. *housecleaning*] *vi* **1** : to remove dirt and accumulated rubbish from a house, room, or building : clean a house and its furniture **2** : to get rid of unwanted or useless or obnoxious items or people : clean house ~ *vt* **1** : to set (a house or room) in order by thorough cleaning of surfaces and furnishings **2** : to improve or reform (as an administrative department) by ridding of undesirable people or inefficient practices
housecleaner \'ˌ=ˌ=ˌ=\ *n* [*house* + *cleaner*] : one that housecleans
housecleaning \'ˌ=ˌ=ˌ=\ *n* [*house* + *cleaning*] **1** : the removal of dirt and rubbish from a house esp. after long accumulation ⟨spring ~⟩ **2** : the act of improving or reforming by removal of undesirable, inefficient, or corrupt elements ⟨a thorough ~ which will sweep away the cobwebs of learning and clear our attics of academic lumber —Marjorie Nicolson⟩ ⟨urged that a thorough ~ was needed to rid the business of sharp practices —*Advertising Age*⟩
housecoat \'ˌ=ˌ=\ *n* : an informal garment for wear around the house: as **a** : a woman's one-piece usu. long-skirted garment that has a front closing and is similar in cut to a dressing gown or negligee ⟨wearing . . . an emerald-green taffeta ~ —Edmund Wilson⟩ **b** : a man's lounging coat or jacket usu. of fine material (as silk or velvet) — compare SMOKING JACKET
housecraft \'hau̇s,kräft\ *n, Brit* : HOUSEHOLD ART
house cricket *n* : any of various crickets living in or about dwellings; *esp* : a widely distributed American cricket (*Acheta domesticus*)
house crow *n* : a common crow (*Corvus splendens*) of India familiar as a scavenger and resembling the hooded crow of Europe
housed *past of* HOUSE
house detective *or* **house dick** *n* : one who is employed by a department store, hotel, or place of entertainment to prevent disorderly or improper conduct of patrons
housedoor \'ˌ=ˌ=\ *n* : the front or main door of a house
house drain *n* : the horizontal drain in a basement that receives the waste discharge from stacks and extends a few feet outside the foundation — called also *building drain, collection line*
house dramatist *n* : a writer of plays for a particular theater
housedress \'ˌ=ˌ=\ *n* : a dress with simple lines suitable for work about the house and made usu. of a washable printed fabric
house dust *n* : an airborne respiratory allergen of uncertain origin found about houses and held to be the chief cause of nonseasonal hay fever
house·fast \'hüs,fast\ *adj, chiefly Scot* : HOUSEBOUND
housefather \'ˌ=ˌ=ˌ=\ *n* : the father or male head of any collection of persons living together as a family; *specif* : a man in charge of a dormitory, hall, or hostel for young people or children
house finch *n* : a small redheaded finch (*Carpodacus mexicanus*) closely related to the purple finch and represented by several races in the western U.S. and Mexico including the common familiar house finch (*C. m. frontalis*) that often nests about houses and is a good singer
house flag *n* **1** : a flag with an emblem denoting a commercial house or line to which a merchant ship belongs **2** : the personal flag of a yacht owner
housefly \'ˌ=ˌ=\ *n* **1** : a two-winged fly (*Musca domestica*) with mouthparts adapted for lapping or sipping that is found in all habitable parts of the world, being often a most abundant and familiar insect about human habitations during the warm part of the year and acting as a mechanical agent in transmitting diseases (as typhoid fever) by alighting on infected substances and then on food **2** : any of various flies of similar appearance or habitat (as the lesser housefly or the stable fly)
housefront \'ˌ=ˌ=\ *n* : the facade of a house
house·ful \'hau̇,sfu̇l\ *n* -s : as much or as many as a house will accommodate ⟨~ of guests⟩
house fungus *n* : any of several saprophytic fungi (as *Coniophora cerebella* and *Merulius lacrymans*) developing upon and rotting wood exposed to moisture in houses
housefurnishings \'ˌ=ˌ=ˌ=ˌ=\ *n pl* : furnishings for a house; *esp* : small articles of household equipment (as kitchen utensils)
house girl *n* : HOUSEMAID
house god *n* : HOUSEHOLD GOD
houseguest \'ˌ=ˌ=\ *n* : a guest staying overnight or longer
househeating \'ˌ=ˌ=ˌ=\ *n* **1** : HOUSEWARMING **2** : central heating of a dwelling
1house·hold \'hau̇,sōld, -au̇s,hō-\ *n* [ME *houshold*, fr. *hous* house + *hold*] **1** *obs* **a** : the maintaining of a house : HOUSEKEEPING **b** : household goods and chattels **2** : those who dwell under the same roof and compose a family : a domestic establishment; *specif* : a social unit comprised of those living together in the same dwelling place **3 households** *pl* : ALL-PURPOSE FLOUR
2household \"\ *adj* [ME *houshold*, fr. *houshold*, n.] **1** : of or relating to a household : DOMESTIC ⟨~ tasks⟩ **2** : FAMILIAR : COMMON ⟨~ remedy⟩ ⟨~ legend⟩
household ammonia *n* : dilute ammonia water for household use often containing small amounts of detergents
household art *n* : one of the arts or techniques (as cooking, sewing, baby care) concerned with the maintenance and care of a household — usu. used in pl.
household economics *n pl but usu sing in constr* : HOME ECONOMICS
house·hold·er \-də(r)\ *n* [ME *householder*, fr. *hous* + *holder*] **1** : the master or head of a family : one who occupies a house or separate tenement with his family or alone **2** : FREEHOLDER
house·hold·er·ship \-(r),ship\ *n* : the position or status of a householder
household franchise *n* : the right of voting in parliamentary and other elections in Great Britain restricted before 1918 to householders
household god *n* **1 household gods** *pl* : LARES AND PENATES **2** : a deeply respected or revered person, thing, idea, or custom ⟨the Victorian *household gods* Respectability, Prudery and Humbug squat smugly on their pedestals —*N.Y.Herald Tribune*⟩
house·hold·ing \-diŋ\ *n* [ME *housholding*, fr. *hous* + *holding*, gerund of *holden* to hold — more at HOLD] : the management or occupation of a house or tenement
house·hold·ry \-drē\ *n* -ES : HOUSEHOLDING, DOMESTIC ECONOMY, HOUSEKEEPING
household stuff *n, archaic* : housefurnishings and furniture
household troops *n pl* : troops appointed to attend and guard a sovereign or his residence
household word *n* : a common word or phrase : BYWORD ⟨*penicillin* has become a new *household word* —W.E.Swinton⟩
house·keep \'hau̇,skēp\ *vi* [back-formation fr. *housekeeping* & *housekeeper*] : to keep house : act as housekeeper; *esp* : to prepare meals regularly for oneself and family ⟨a large cafeteria for those who do not wish to ~ —Diana Rice⟩
house·keep·er \-pə(r)\ *n* [ME *howskepare*, fr. *hows, hous* house + *kepare, keper* keeper — more at KEEPER] **1** *archaic* : HOUSEHOLDER **2** *obs* : one who exercises hospitality **3 a a** : woman who is employed on a permanent basis to do the work in a private home either supervised by or taking the place of a housewife ⟨she came as a general domestic but we gave her the status of ~ —Margo Fischer⟩ **b** : a woman who is employed in a hotel or an institution to supervise the cleaning personnel **4** : one in charge of a house : CARETAKER, JANITOR
housekeeping \'ˌ=ˌ=ˌ=\ *n* [*house* + *keeping*] **1** *archaic* : the state of occupying a dwelling house as a householder **2** : the care or management of domestic concerns : the management of a house and home affairs **3** : the physical care and control of industrial or state property to ensure maintenance, proper and full utilization, and disposition
1housel *n* -s [ME, fr. OE *hūsel* sacrifice, Eucharist; akin to Goth *hunsl* sacrifice, and prob. to Av *spənta-* holy, Lith *šventas*] *archaic* : the Eucharist or the act of administering or receiving it
2housel *vt* -ED/-ING/-S [ME *houselen*, fr. OE *hūslian*, fr. *hūsel*, n.] *archaic* : to administer the Eucharist to
houseleek \'ˌ=ˌ=\ *n* [ME *howsleke*, fr. *hows, hous* house + *leke, lek* leek — more at HOUSE, LEEK] : a plant of the genus *Sempervivum*: as **a** : a common European succulent (*S. tectorum*) found on old walls and roofs and having pink flowers and leaves clustered in a basal rosette which produces numerous offsets **b** : a plant (*S. soboliferum*) having the offsets produced high among the leaves of the rosette
house·less \'hau̇sləs\ *adj* [ME *housles*, fr. *hous* + *-les* -less] **1** : destitute of the shelter of a house : SHELTERLESS, HOMELESS ⟨~ wanderer⟩ **2** : destitute of houses ⟨~ desert⟩ — **houseless·ness** *n* -ES
house·let *n* -s \-lət\ : a very small house
houselights \'ˌ=ˌ=\ *n pl* : the lights that illuminate the spaces in a theater occupied by an audience before and after performance on the stage ⟨the ~ went down and the footlights came up —W.L.White⟩ ⟨the ~ darkened and the curtain rose —Thyra S. Winslow⟩
houseline \'ˌ=ˌ=\ *n* [so called fr. the use of small tarred lines to wrap around large ropes] : a light rope made of three strands left-laid and used for seizing
house machine *n* : a mechanical device for laying and forming rope
house magazine *n* : HOUSE ORGAN
house·maid \'hau̇s,mād\ *n* : a female servant employed to do housework
house·maid·ing \-diŋ\ *n* -s : the work of a housemaid
housemaid's knee *n* [so called fr. its frequent occurrence among servant girls who work a great deal on their knees] : a swelling over the knee due to an enlargement of the bursa in the front of the patella
house·man \'hau̇smən\ *n, pl* **housemen** **1** : one hired to perform general work or the heavy duties about a house, hotel, or similar establishment — called also *houseboy* **2** : an attendant in a gambling house who sells and cashes in chips, collects house fees from players, explains rules, or plays games for the house **3 a** : HOUSE DETECTIVE **b** : BOUNCER 3 **4** *chiefly Brit* : ⁴INTERN 1b
house martin *n* : ²MARTIN 1
housemaster \'ˌ=ˌ=ˌ=\ *n* : a master in charge of a house in a boys' boarding school
housemastership \'ˌ=ˌ=ˌ=ˌ=\ *n* : the position of a housemaster
housemate \'ˌ=ˌ=\ *n* : one that lives in the same house with another
housemistress \'ˌ=ˌ=ˌ=\ *n* **1** : a mistress of a house **2** : a woman in charge of a house in a girls' boarding school
house mite *n* : CLOVER MITE
house money *n* : money used or set aside for household expenses
house mosquito *n* : any of various mosquitoes frequenting houses; *esp* : a widespread mosquito (*Culex pipiens*) of Europe and No. America
house moss *n, dial* : rolls of soft dust that commonly collect on floors and under furniture
housemother \'ˌ=ˌ=ˌ=\ *n* : a mother of a family : a woman living at the head of a household or small community; *specif* : a woman acting as hostess, chaperon, and often as housekeeper in a dormitory, hall, or hostel where young people or children reside
house mouse *n* : a mouse that frequents houses; *esp* : a common nearly cosmopolitan usu. gray mouse (*Mus musculus*) that lives and breeds about buildings and is important as a consumer of human food, as a vector of diseases, and as an experimental animal
hous·en \'hau̇zᵊn\ *dial pl of* HOUSE
house of assembly : a legislative body or the lower house of a legislature (as in the American colonies and various British colonies, protectorates, and countries of the Commonwealth)
house of assignation : a house maintained and used for illicit sexual intercourse : BROTHEL
house of cards : CARDHOUSE
house of commons : the lower house of a legislative body in some countries (as Great Britain, Canada)
house of correction : an institution where persons are confined who have committed a minor offense and are considered capable of reformation — compare REFORMATORY
house of delegates : the lower house of the legislature of some states (as Virginia, Maryland)
house of detention **1** : a place where prisoners and occasionally witnesses are detained pending a criminal trial **2** : DETENTION HOME
house officer *n, Brit* : ⁴INTERN 1b
house of god *cap G* [trans. of LL *domus Dei*] : TEMPLE, CHURCH — called also *house of prayer, house of worship*
house of ill fame *or* **house of ill repute** : BROTHEL
house of issue : an investment bank that originates new security offerings for public distribution or joins with other houses in purchase groups that underwrite such offerings
house of life : HOUSE OF THE ASCENDANT
house of mercy **1** : a charitable institution for lodging, relieving, or reclaiming those in distress or disgrace **2** : HOSPITAL
house of office [ME *hous of offyce*] *obs* : a building or room (as a kitchen or pantry) used for domestic purposes; *esp* : PRIVY
house of refuge : a charitable institution for giving shelter and protection to the homeless or destitute
house of representatives : the lower house of the legislature of many countries and states

house of the ascendant [ME *hous of the ascendent*] **:** the first mundane house

house of worship *or* **house of prayer :** HOUSE OF GOD

house organ *n* **1 :** a publication typically in magazine format issued periodically by a business concern to further its interest among employees and sales personnel or among agents and customers **2 :** a publication put out by or for a professional group with relevant matter of special interest

house painter \ˈ=,==\ *n* **:** one whose business or occupation is painting houses

houseparent \ˈ=,==\ *n* **:** one of a married couple in charge of a dormitory, hall, or hostel where children or young people reside **:** HOUSEFATHER, HOUSEMOTHER

house party *n* **:** a gathering and entertainment lasting over one or more nights of a party of guests usu. in a house in the country; *also* **:** the guests in a house

housephone \ˈ=,=\ *n* **:** a telephone that is connected to the switchboard of a building (as a hotel or apartment house) but not directly to the exchange

house physician *n* **:** a physician who is employed by and lives in a hospital — compare ⁴INTERN 1b, RESIDENT

house place *n, dial* **:** ¹HOUSE 1d

houseplant \ˈ=,=\ *n* **:** a plant grown or kept indoors

housepride \ˈ=,=\ *n* **:** pride in one's house or housekeeping

house-proud \ˈ=,=\ *adj* **:** proud of one's house or housekeeping

hous·er \ˈhau̇zə(r)\ *n* -s [²*house* + *-er*] **1 :** one that promotes or administers housing projects **2 :** HOUSEBOAT

house-raising \ˈ=,==\ *n* **:** the joint erection of a house or its framework by a gathering of neighbors

house rat *n* **:** any of several rats (as the black rat) common about dwellings

houseroom \ˈ=,=\ *n* **:** space for accommodation in a house **:** LODGING ⟨getting food, raiment, and ~ for three people ashore —Joseph Conrad⟩

house rule *n* **:** a rule applying to a game only among a certain group or in a certain place (as a gambling house)

houses *pl of* HOUSE, *pres 3d sing of* HOUSE

house seat *n* **:** a seat (as in a theater) reserved by the management for special guests

house sewer *n* **:** a prolongation of a house drain extending from a few feet outside a foundation to a connection with a public sewer in the street or alley — called also *building sewer*

house shrew *n* **:** a common European shrew (*Crocidura russula*) sometimes found in barns and other outbuildings

house slipper *n* **:** a slipper for indoor wear — compare BEDROOM SLIPPER

housesmith \ˈ=,=\ *n* **:** an ironworker who assists in erecting a steel skeleton or other steelwork used in buildings

house snake *n* **1 :** MILK SNAKE **2 :** any of several harmless African colubrid snakes (genus *Boaedon*) that live chiefly on mice and rats

house sparrow *n* **:** a sparrow (*Passer domesticus*) native to most of Europe and parts of Asia that has been intentionally introduced into America, Australia, New Zealand, and elsewhere to destroy insects and caterpillars although it feeds largely upon grain seeds — called also *English sparrow*

house spider *n* **:** any of various spiders (as members of the genus *Tegenaria*) that habitually live in buildings

house staff *n* **:** the resident physicians and surgeons in a hospital

house steward *n* **:** one employed to manage the domestic affairs of a large household or a club

house surgeon *n* **:** a surgeon fully qualified in his specialty and resident in a hospital

house-to-house \ˈ=,=ˈ=\ *adj* **:** made or applying successively to all the residences in an area ⟨a *house-to-house* canvass for signatures⟩

housetop \ˈ=,=\ *n* **:** the roof of a house; *esp* **:** the level surface of a flat roof — **from the housetops** *adv* **:** for all to hear **:** PUBLICLY, OPENLY ⟨shouted *from the housetops* that our defenses were fully adequate —F.D.Roosevelt⟩

house track *n* **:** a railroad track alongside or inside a freight house for loading and unloading cars **:** STATION TRACK

house trailer *n* **:** a trailer that can be used as living quarters

house-train \ˈ=,=\ *vt, chiefly Brit* **:** ²HOUSEBREAK

house trap *n* **:** a trap in the house drain for preventing the entrance of gases from a sewer

house trailer

house·ward \ˈhau̇swə(r)d\ *adv* **:** toward the house **:** HOMEWARD

housewares \ˈ=,=\ *n pl* **:** HOUSEFURNISHINGS

housewarming \ˈ=,==\ *n* **:** a party to celebrate the taking possession of a house or premises

¹**house·wife** \ˈhau̇,swīf *or esp in sense 2* ˈhəzəf *or* ˈhəsəf\ *n, pl* **house·wives** \-īvz,-əfs\ [ME *houswif*, fr. *hous* house + *wif* woman, wife — more at HOUSE, WIFE] **1 :** a married woman in charge of a household; *specif* **:** a married woman who occupies herself with the domestic affairs of her household and who engages in no employment for pay or profit **2 :** a pocket-size container (as a bag or roll of cloth) for carrying small articles (as thread, needles, scissors) — called also *hussy*

²**house·wife** \ˈhau̇,swīf\ *vb* -ED/-ING/-S *vt, archaic* **:** to manage with skill and economy **:** HUSBAND ~ *vi, archaic* **:** ECONOMIZE

house·wife·li·ness \-īflēnəs -lin-\ *n* -ES **:** the quality or state of being housewifely

house·wife·ly \-īflē, -li\ *adj* **:** relating, belonging, or appropriate to a housewife ⟨~ virtues⟩ ⟨~ indignation over high prices⟩ **:** DOMESTIC, THRIFTY

house·wife·ry \ˈhau̇,swīf(ə)rē, -ri, *chiefly Brit* -,swəf-\ *n* -ES [ME *houswiferie*, fr. *houswif* + *-erie* -ery] **:** the business of a housewife **:** HOUSEKEEPING

house·wif·ish \-,swīfish\ *adj* **:** belonging or appropriate to a housewife **:** DOMESTIC, PETTY

housework \ˈ=,=\ *n* **:** the work of housekeeping (as kitchen work, sweeping, scrubbing)

houseworker \ˈ=,==\ *n* **:** one that does general housework for wages **:** HOUSEMAID

housewrecker \ˈ=,==\ *n* **:** WRECKER 1b

house wren *n* **:** a common wren (*Troglodytes aedon*) that nests about houses and walls throughout the U.S. and migrates south in winter

housewright \ˈ=,=\ *n* **:** a builder of wooden houses **:** a house carpenter

housey-housey *or* **housie-housie** \ˌhau̇sēˈhau̇sē\ *n* -s [¹*house* + *-ie* or *-ey* (var. of *-ie*)] *Brit* **:** HOUSE 15

¹**hous·ing** \ˈhau̇ziŋ, -zēŋ\ *n* -s [ME; partly fr. *hous*, n., house + *-ing*; partly fr. gerund of *housen* to house — more at HOUSE] **1 :** SHELTER, LODGING **2 a :** the act of placing under shelter **b :** the act of living in a house **3 :** dwellings provided for numbers of people or for a community ⟨~ for the aged⟩ **4 a :** something that covers or protects (as of boards over a ship's deck) **b :** a case or enclosure esp. for a machine or part, an instrument, a lamp ⟨the differential ~ on an automobile⟩ **c :** a tube or cylindrical sleeve or casing (as an enclosed bearing) in which a shaft revolves **5 :** a portion of a mast that is beneath the deck or of a bowsprit that is inboard **6 a :** the space taken out of a structural member (as a timber) to admit the insertion of part of another — compare MORTISE **b :** a hollowed space (as a niche) for holding a piece of sculpture **7** [perh. fr. D *huizing* (fr. *huis* house + *-ing*) or LG *hūsing*, fr. *hus* house + *-ing*)] **:** HOUSELINE

²**housing** \"\ *n* -s [ME, fr. *house* housing + *-ing* — more at HOUSE] **1 :** an ornamental cover for a horse's saddle **2 housings** *pl* **:** TRAPPINGS, ORNAMENTATION

housing development *n* **:** a group of individual dwellings or of apartment houses commonly of similar design and built and leased under one management — compare COLONY 4c

housing estate *n, Brit* **:** HOUSING DEVELOPMENT

housing project *n* **:** a publicly supported and administered housing development planned usu. for low-income families

hous·ton \ˈ(h)yüstən\ *adj, usu cap* [fr. *Houston, Tex.*] **:** of or from the city of Houston, Texas ⟨a *Houston* shopping center⟩ **:** of the kind or style prevalent in Houston

hous·to·nia \(h)yüˈstōnēə, hü'-,hau̇'-\ *n* [NL, fr. William *Houston* †1733 Scot. botanist + NL *-ia*] **1** *cap* **:** a genus of No. American herbs (family Rubiaceae) with entire leaves and small blue, lilac, or white tubular lobed flowers — see BLUET **2** -s **:** any plant of the genus *Houstonia*

hous·to·ni·an \(h)yüˈstōnēən\ *n* -s *cap* [*Houston*, Tex. + E *-ian*] **:** a native or resident of Houston, Texas

hous·ton's fold *or* **houston's valve** \ˈ(h)yü|stənz-, ˈhü|, ˈhau̇|\ *n, usu cap H* [after John *Houston* †1845 Irish surgeon] **:** any of the valvular folds in the lining of the rectum

hout·ing \ˈhau̇diŋ\ *n* -s [D, fr. MD *houtic*, perh. fr. *hout* wood; akin to OHG *holz* wood — more at HOLT] **:** an anadromous fish (*Coregonus oxyrhynchus*) of the North sea that ascends rivers and estuaries of northwestern Europe to spawn

hou·tou \ˈhü(,)tü\ *n* -s [modif. of Arawak *hotoli*, of imit. origin] **:** a So. American motmot (*Momotus momota*)

hou·va·ri \(h)üvəˈrē\ *n* -s [AmerSp *huvari, hurivari*] **:** a severe thunderstorm with strong land breezes in the West Indies

ho·va \ˈhōvə, ˈhüv\ *n, pl* **hova** *or* **hovas** *usu cap* **1 a :** the dominant native people of central Madagascar **b :** a member of such people — compare MALAGASY **2 :** the language of the Hova people

¹**hove** *past of* HEAVE

²**hove** *vb* -ED/-ING/-S [fr. *hove*, past of *heave*] *vi, archaic* **:** RISE, HEAVE ~ *vt, archaic* **:** to lift or swell up **:** RAISE

³**hove** \ˈhōv\ *dial Eng var of* HALF

⁴**hove** *vi* -ED/-ING/-S [ME *hoven*] *obs* **:** HOVER 1, 4

hoved *dial past of* HEAVE

¹**hov·el** \ˈhəvəl *sometimes* ˈhäv-\ *n* -s [ME] **1** *chiefly dial* **:** an open shed or canopy for sheltering livestock or protecting produce **2 a :** TABERNACLE **b :** a niche like those that replace pinnacles on some Gothic churches and shelter statues **3 a :** a shed or open-roofed shelter for human beings **b :** a poor cottage **:** a small mean house **:** HUT **4 :** a large conical or conoidal brick structure within which a firing kiln is built

²**hovel** \"\ *vt* **hoveled** *or* **hovelled; hoveled** *or* **hovelled; hoveling** *or* **hovelling** \-v(ə)liŋ\ **hovels 1 :** to put in a hovel **:** provide with a roof ⟨~ thee with swine, and rogues forlorn —Shak.⟩ **2 :** to shape (as a chimney) like a hovel or hut

³**hov·el** \ˈhävəl *also* ˈhəv-\ *vb* **hoveled** *or* **hovelled; hoveled** *or* **hovelled; hoveling** *or* **hovelling; hovels** [back-formation fr. *hoveler*] *vt, Brit* **:** to aid (a ship) by pilotage, unloading, or landing passengers ~ *vi, Brit* **:** to aid ships in the capacity of a hoveler

hov·el·er *or* **hov·el·ler** \-v(ə)lə(r\ *also* **huf·fler** \ˈhəflə(r\ *n* -s [origin unknown] **1 :** a usu. unlicensed coast boatman who does odd jobs in assisting ships or goes out to wrecks to land passengers or secure salvage **2 :** a boat that is used by a hoveler

¹**ho·ven** \ˈhōvən\ *archaic & dial past part of* HEAVE

²**hoven** \"\ *adj* [fr. archaic past part. of *heave*] **:** afflicted with bloat

³**hoven** \"\ *n* -s **:** BLOAT 2

ho·ve·nia \hōˈvēnēə\ *n, cap* [NL, fr. David ten *Hove* †1787 Dutch senator + connective *-n-* + NL *-ia*] **:** a genus of Asiatic trees or shrubs (family Rhamnaceae) having alternate serrate leaves, small greenish flowers, and indehiscent fruit

¹**hov·er** \ˈhəvə(r) *also* ˈhäv-\ *vb* **hovered; hovered; hovering** \-v(ə)riŋ\ **hovers** [ME *hoveren*, freq. of *hoven* to hover] *vi* **1 a :** to hang fluttering in the air or on the wing ⟨the hawk ~*ed* searching the ground below⟩ **:** remain floating or suspended about or over a place or object ⟨clouds of smoke ~*ed* over the building⟩ **b** *of an airplane* **:** to maintain altitude without forward motion **2 a :** to hang about **:** move to and fro near a place threateningly, watchfully, uncertainly, irresolutely ⟨doormen annoy me . . . ~*ing* anxiously over people —Evelyn Barkins⟩ ⟨the shark was still ~*ing* about —Francis Birtles⟩ ⟨the thermometer ~*ed* around 90⟩ ⟨the boat ~*ed* outside the three-mile limit⟩ **b :** to be in a state of uncertainty, irresolution, or suspense ⟨when he was hesitating or ~*ing* over a word —David Abercrombie⟩ ⟨~*ing* uncomfortably behind a cigar —Tennessee Williams⟩ ⟨the country ~*ed* on the brink of famine⟩ **3 :** to crouch in hiding **:** COWER ⟨as if a gash had been torn in the web of restraint behind which she forced him to ~ —Marcia Davenport⟩ ⟨the bathtub fell . . . and crushed the woman ~*ing* in the cellar —*Springfield (Mass.) Union*⟩ **4** *dial Brit* **:** WAIT, LINGER ~ *vt* **1** *obs* **:** to flutter (the wings) so as to remain suspended in air **2 :** to brood over ⟨a hen ~*s* her chicks⟩

²**hover** \"\ *n* -s **1 :** the act or state of hovering ⟨the sweep and ~ of the pale birds —Mary H. Vorse⟩ ⟨the smoke from the croft house rises, a ~ of peat-scented blue —Naomi Mitchison⟩ **2 :** a group of trout **3 a** *dial* **:** a shelter (as an overhanging bank or hedge) for an animal or fish **b :** a floating island of vegetation **4 :** a canopy or other device for holding the heat of a brooder near the floor or ground so that it is available to young birds or animals cared for in the brooder

hov·er·er \-vərə(r)\ *n* -s **:** one that hovers

hover fly *n* **:** a syrphus fly or other fly that hovers in air

hover hawk *n* **:** a kestrel (*Falco tinnunculus*)

hovering *adj* **:** SUSPENDED, UNCERTAIN, WAVERING, POISED — **hov·er·ing·ly** *adv*

hovering accent *or* **hovering stress** *n* **:** distribution of energy, pitch, or duration in two adjacent syllables in some utterance of verse when a heavy syllable occurs next to a syllable bearing the metrical ictus so that for perception the stress seems to be divided or diffused nearly equally over both (as *cornfield* in the line "that o'er'/the green'/cornfield/did pass'")

hovering act *n* [fr. gerund of ¹*hover*] **:** an act prohibiting or regulating the roving or hovering of domestic or foreign ships within certain limits; *esp* **:** an act providing for the boarding of foreign ships and inspection of cargo manifests outside the three-mile limit (as within four leagues of the coast) in order to enforce revenue or security laws esp. for protection of the commerce of a coastal nation

hoverplane \ˈ==,=\ *n, Brit* **:** HELICOPTER

hove to *adv (or adj)* [fr. past part. of *heave to*] **:** in a stationary position with head to wind **:** at a standstill ⟨ore freighters *hove to* in the fog —Richard Bissell⟩ ⟨lying *hove to* on the fishing bank⟩

Ho·vis \ˈhōvəs\ *trademark* — used for a wheat flour or bread made from it that includes wheat germ made inactive by heating

¹**how** \(ˈ)hau̇\ *adv* [ME *hou, how*, adv & conj., fr. OE *hū*; akin to OFris *hū, hō* how, OS *hū, hwō*, OHG *hwuo* how, OE *hwā* who — more at WHO] **1 a :** in what manner or way ⟨~ explain behavior so contrary to the principles of good authorship —G.M.Fess⟩ ⟨the continuing problems of . . . ~ to say what we mean —Stuart Chase⟩ ⟨learn ~ to enter a room properly⟩ ⟨tell him ~ to do it⟩ — often used as an intensive ⟨~ they laughed⟩ **b :** by what means or process ⟨at his wit's end regarding ~ to support himself —C.S.Forester⟩ ⟨question of ~ to increase the benefits under the . . . Retirement System —W.J.Kennedy⟩ **c** *obs* **:** SOMEHOW, ANYHOW ⟨by ransom or ~ else —John Milton⟩ **2 a :** to what extent, degree, number, or amount ⟨~ little we know of human motives⟩ ⟨~ far can he be trusted⟩ **b :** by what measure or quantity ⟨concerned with ~ much to eat⟩ ⟨decided ~ deep to cut⟩ ⟨~ hard do you plan to make it⟩ **3 a :** in what state, condition, or plight ⟨~ are things at home⟩ ⟨~ are you⟩ ⟨~ are you off for money⟩ **b :** at what price ⟨~ is the market today⟩ **4 a :** for what reason or excuse ⟨in the face of his own knowledge, ~ can he make such a statement —Weston LaBarre⟩ **:** for what possible or plausible reason ⟨~ could he have said that⟩ — often used with *ever* ⟨~ can I ever leave you⟩ **b :** from what cause **:** WHY ⟨~ did you come to sell your house⟩ **5 a** *archaic* **:** by what name or designation ⟨~ art thou called —Shak.⟩ **b :** with what meaning **:** to what effect ⟨~ are we to interpret such behavior⟩ **6 a :** what in that case **:** what then ⟨~ if, when I am laid into the tomb, I awake before the time —Shak.⟩ ⟨~ if I had denounced you when you forced your way in there —Max Peacock⟩ **b :** WHAT — used to introduce or imply a question ⟨~ about the other one, do you want it too⟩ ⟨~ say you, maiden, will you wed —W.S.Gilbert⟩ or in requests to repeat what has not been understood ⟨~ is that again⟩ **c** *dial* **:** what did you say **7** — used to express surprise or admiration ⟨~ do you like that⟩ ⟨prices are going up, *and how*⟩ — **and how** — used as an intensive — **how about :** what do you say to or think of ⟨*how about* a game of tennis⟩ ⟨would you like to have ⟨*how about* some more pie⟩ or give ⟨*how about* a couple of dollars until payday⟩ or agree to ⟨well, *how about* it, are you coming⟩ — **how come :** how does it happen that **:** WHY ⟨*how come* you're here so early⟩ — **how do you do :** HELLO — used to express a polite greeting or formal salutation face-to-face — **how so :** how is that so **:** what do you mean **:** WHY ⟨it won't work? *how so*⟩

²**how** \"\ *conj* [ME *hou, how*] **1 a** (1) **:** the way or manner in which ⟨it was odd ~ writers never seemed to have anything to do except write —Martha Gellhorn⟩; *also* **:** the state or condition in which (2) **:** to what degree or extent ⟨knows ~ small the town is⟩ (3) **:** of the way or manner in which ⟨be careful ~ you talk⟩ **b :** THAT ⟨told them ~ he had a situation —Charles Dickens⟩ **2 :** in whatever way or manner **:** AS ⟨a reader can shift his attention ~ he likes —William Empson⟩

³**how** \ˈhau̇\ *n* -s [¹*how*] **1 :** the manner or method in which something is done or comes about ⟨most of the film is devoted to the grim ~*s* and not the difficult whys of battle —John McCarten⟩ **2 :** a question concerning manner or method ⟨the eternal whys and ~*s* of small children —Jeanne Massey⟩

⁴**how** \ˈhü\ *n* -s [ME *houwe, how*, fr. OE *hūfe* — more at CYPHELLA] **1** *Scot* **:** COIF, HOOD; *esp* **:** NIGHTCAP **2** *Scot* **:** an infant's caul

⁵**how** \ˈhau̇\ *n* -s [ME, fr. ON *haugr* hill; akin to OHG *houg* hill, ON *hār* high — more at HIGH] *now dial Eng* **:** a low hill **:** MOUND, HILLOCK — used chiefly in place names

⁶**how** \"\ *interj* [ME] **1** *now chiefly dial* — used to attract attention or express greeting ⟨~, now, my masters!⟩ or to urge on (as a sheep dog) ⟨~ sheep!⟩ **2** *chiefly Scot* — used to express pain or grief

⁷**how** \ˈhau̇\ *var of* HOWE

⁸**how** \ˈhau̇\ *interj* [of Siouan origin; akin to Dakota *háo*, Omaha *hau*] — used as a greeting esp. in imitation of American Indian speech

⁹**how** \"\ *usu cap* — a communications code word for the letter *h*

how *abbr* howitzer

how·ard·ite \ˈhau̇ə(r),dīt\ *n* -s [Luke *Howard* †1864 Eng. meteorologist + E *-ite*] **:** a stony meteorite composed essentially of anorthite, olivine, and bronzite

¹**how·be·it** \(ˈ)hau̇ˈbēət\ *adv* [ME *how be it*] **:** be it as it may **:** NEVERTHELESS ⟨~, the whole problem . . . cannot be solved —G.A.Llano⟩

²**howbeit** \"\ *conj* **:** ALTHOUGH ⟨are highly ingenious . . . and pleasantly diverting, ~ in certain passages of somewhat lowbrow content —Ben Crisler⟩

¹**howd** \ˈhau̇d\ *vi* -ED/-ING/-S [origin unknown] *chiefly Scot* **:** to move from side to side or up and down

²**howd** \"\ *n* -s **:** a lurching rocking movement

how·dah *or* **hou·dah** \ˈhau̇də\ *n* -s [Hindi *hauda*, fr. Ar *haudaj*] **:** a seat or covered pavilion on the back of an elephant or camel

how·der \ˈhau̇dər\ *vt* -ED/-ING/-S [freq. of *howd*] *chiefly Scot* **:** to heap or crowd together **:** HUDDLE

how·die *or* **how·dy** \ˈhau̇di\ *n, pl* **howdies** [origin unknown] *chiefly Scot* **:** MIDWIFE

how do \(ˈ)hau̇ˈdü\ *interj* [short for *how do you do*] *dial* — used to express greeting

howdah

how-do-you-do *also* **how-d'ye-do** *or* **how-de-do** \ˌhau̇dəyəˈdü, -dəyēˈdü, ˌhau̇dēˈdü, -au̇dīˈdü, (ˈ)hau̇ˈdü\ *n* [fr. the phrase *how do you do?* or *how d'ye do?*] **:** an embarrassing situation **:** a troublesome fix ⟨this is a pretty *how-do-you-do*⟩

¹**how·dy** \ˈhau̇dē, -di\ *interj* [alter. of *how do*] — used to express greeting

²**howdy** \"\ *vb* -ED/-ING/-ES *vt, dial* **:** to say the words *how do you do* to ~ *vi, dial* **:** to exchange greetings

¹**howe** \ˈhau̇\ *n* -s [ME (northern dial.) *how*, alter. of *holl* — more at HOLL] **1** *chiefly Scot* **:** HOLLOW, DEPRESSION; *esp* **:** VALLEY **2** *Scot* **:** the middle part of a night or of winter

²**howe** \"\ *adj* [ME (northern dial.) *how*, alter. of *holl* — more at HOLL] *Scot* **:** HOLLOW, DEEP

³**howe** \"\ *adv, Scot* **:** in a hollow voice ⟨it spak right ~, my name is Death —Robert Burns⟩

⁴**howe** \ˈhō, ˈhau̇\ *dial Eng var of* HOE

how·ea \ˈhau̇ēə\ *n, cap* [NL, fr. Lord *Howe* island, in the southwestern Pacific] **:** a genus of feather palms having papery spathes and flowers each with 30 to 40 stamens and sunken in pits on the spadix that are succeeded by fruits resembling pecans

ho·wei·tat \(,)hōˌwāˈtat\ *n, pl* **howeitat** *or* **howeitats** *usu cap* **1 a :** a Bedouin people of northern Arabia **2 :** a member of the Howeitat people

¹**howel** \ˈhau̇(ə)l\ *n* -s [prob. fr. LG *hövel* plane, fr. MLG *hövel*; akin to OHG *hubil* hill, OE *hȳf* beehive — more at HIVE] **1 :** a cooper's plane having a convex sole for smoothing the insides of casks and for chamfering, crozing, and chiming **2 :** a rounded cut above and below the croze in a barrel stave

²**howel** \"\ *vt* **howeled** *or* **howelled; howeled** *or* **howelled; howeling** *or* **howelling; howels :** to smooth with a howel

how·ell \ˈhau̇(ə)l\ *n* -s *usu cap* [after E. C. *Howell* †1907 Am. journalist and whist expert] **1 :** HOWELL SYSTEM **2 a :** a duplicate game conducted by the Howell system **b :** a game of duplicate bridge in which match-point scoring is used

howell-jol·ly body \-ʒōˈlē-, -ˈjälē-\ *n, usu cap H&J* [after William H. *Howell* †1945 Am. physiologist and Justin M. J. *Jolly* †1953 Fr. physician] **:** one of the basophilic granules that are probably nuclear fragments, that sometimes occur in red blood cells, and that indicate by their appearance in circulating blood that red cells are leaving the marrow while incompletely mature (as in certain anemias)

howell settlement *n, usu cap H* [after E. C. *Howell*] **:** a method of scoring in the game of hearts whereby after the play of each deal each player puts into a pot for every heart he has taken as many chips as there are other players in the game and withdraws from the pot the number of chips representing the difference between 13 and the number of hearts he has taken

howell system *or* **howell movement** *n, usu cap H* [after E. C. *Howell*] **:** a method of conducting a game of duplicate bridge or whist so that each pair plays one set of boards against each other pair — compare MITCHELL MOVEMENT

howe truss \ˈhau̇-\ *n, usu cap H* [after William *Howe* †1852 Am. inventor] **:** a truss having vertical and diagonal members between the upper and lower horizontal members

Howe truss

¹**how·ev·er** \hau̇ˈ(w)evə(r)\ *conj* [ME, fr. *how* + *ever*] **1 a :** in whatever manner or way ⟨can go ~ he likes⟩ **b :** no matter to what degree or extent ⟨~ much he gives her, she wants more⟩ **2** *archaic* **:** ALTHOUGH ⟨*howe'er* thou art a fiend, a woman's shape doth shield thee —Shak.⟩

²**however** *adv* **1 a :** to whatever degree or extent ⟨has done this for ~ many thousands of years —Emma Hawkridge⟩ ⟨every device, ~ paltry, was resorted to —W.H. Prescott⟩ **b :** in whatever manner or way ⟨shall serve you, sir, truly, ~ else —Shak.⟩ **2 :** in spite of that **:** on the other hand **:** BUT ⟨it still seems possible, ~, that conditions will improve⟩ ⟨I would like to go; ~, I think I'd better not⟩ **3** *archaic* **:** at all events **:** at least **:** in any case **4 :** how in the world ⟨~ did you manage it⟩

¹**howf** *or* **howff** \ˈhau̇f\ *n* -s [D *hof* enclosure, burial ground, garden, resort; akin to OE *hof* enclosure, court, dwelling, temple, OHG, court, garden, landed property, ON, enclosure, roofed temple, OE *hȳf* beehive — more at HIVE] **1** *chiefly Scot* **:** a dwelling place **2** *chiefly Scot* **:** an accustomed haunt or resort; *specif* **:** a favorite tavern

²**howf** *or* **howff** \"\ *vi* -ED/-ING/-S **1** *Scot* **a :** to take up one's abode **:** LODGE **b :** to make frequent visits **2** *Scot* **:** to take shelter

how·go·zit curve \hau̇ˈgōzət-\ *n* [alter. of the phrase *how goes it?*] **:** a running graph of the progress of an airplane flight involving the distance covered, fuel consumed, and time elapsed and enabling the pilot to determine the equitime point

how·ish \ˈhau̇ish\ *adj* [short for *I don't know howish*, fr. the phrase *I don't know how* + *-ish*] *archaic* **:** feeling vaguely ill

how·it·zer \ˈhau̇ətsə(r)\ *n* -s [D *houwitser*, fr. G *haubitze*, fr.

MHG *haufnitz* ballista, fr. Czech *houfnice*] **:** a cannon shorter than a gun of the same caliber employed to fire projectiles at medium muzzle velocities at relatively high angles of elevation at a target (as enemy artillery behind a ridge) which cannot be reached by flat-trajectory weapons

¹howk \ˈhōk\ *dial Brit var of* HAWK

²howk \"\ *vb* -ED/-ING/-S [ME *holken;* akin to MLG *holken* to hollow out; derivatives fr. the root of OE *hol* hollow — more at HOLE] *vt, dial Brit* **:** to hollow out **:** EXCAVATE, DIG — often used with a preposition ⟨lobsters had got at it . . . and ~*ed* pieces out of it —E.F.Benson⟩ ~ *vi, dial Brit* **:** DIG ⟨the dog was ~*ing* in the yard⟩

howk·it \ˈhəukət\ *adj* [fr. Sc past part. of ²*howk*] *Scot* **:** dug up **:** hollowed out

¹howl \ˈhaul, *esp before pause or consonant* -auəl\ *vb* -ED/-ING/-S [ME *houlen;* akin to MD *hūlen* to howl, MHG *hiulen, hiuweln* to howl, OHG *hūwila* owl, Gk *kōkyein* to shriek, wail, lament, Skt *kauti* he cries out] *vi* **1 :** to utter or emit a loud sustained doleful sound or outcry characteristic of dogs and wolves ⟨wolves ~*ing* in the arctic night⟩ ⟨the only sound is a melancholy wind ~*ing* —John Buchan⟩ **2 :** to cry out or exclaim with lack of restraint and prolonged loudness through strong impulse, feeling, or emotion ⟨the scalded men ~*ing* in agony⟩ ⟨the hungry mob ~*ed* about the Senate house, threatening fire and massacre —J.A.Froude⟩ ⟨proctors ~*ing* at the blunder⟩ **3 :** to go on a spree or rampage ⟨this is my night to ~⟩ ~ *vt* **1 :** to utter or announce noisily with unrestrained demonstrative outcry ⟨newsboys ~*ing* the news⟩ **2 :** to affect, effect, or drive by adverse outcry — used esp. with *down* ⟨supporters of the Administration . . . ready to ~ down any suggestion of criticism —*Wall Street Jour.*⟩ **syn** see ROAR

²howl \"\ *n* -S **1 :** a loud protracted mournful rising and falling cry characteristic of a dog or a wolf **2 a :** a prolonged cry of distress **:** WAIL **b :** a yell or outcry of disappointment, rage, or protest **3 :** PROTEST, COMPLAINT ⟨raise a ~ over high taxes⟩ ⟨set up a ~ that he was being cheated⟩ **4 :** something that provokes laughter ⟨his act was a ~⟩ **5 :** a noise produced in an electronic amplifier usu. by undesired regeneration of alternating currents of audio frequency **:** OSCILLATION — called also *squeal*

howl·er \ˈhaulə(r)\ *n* -S **1 :** one that howls; *specif* **:** a professional wailer for the dead **2 :** HOWLER MONKEY **3 :** a glaringly stupid and ridiculous blunder esp. in the use of words ⟨his autobiography is spotted with ~*s* such as his description of the winter of 1938–39 as one of "peaceful preparation for war" —Geoffrey Parsons †1956⟩ **4 :** an electric buzzer **syn** see ERROR

howler monkey *or* **howling monkey** *n* **:** any of various So. and Central American monkeys having a long prehensile tail and a peculiar enlargement of the hyoid and laryngeal apparatus enabling them to make remarkable howling noises and constituting the genus *Alouatta*

howl·et \ˈhaulət, *dial Brit* ˈhül-\ *n* -S [ME *howlat, howlott,* prob. fr. *oule, owle, howle* owl + *-at, -ott* (vars. of *-et*) — more at OWL] **1** *now dial* **:** OWL, OWLET **2** *dial Brit* **:** a noisy dirty person

howling *adj* **1 :** producing, filled with, or marked by howling ⟨~ storm⟩ **2 :** WILD, SAVAGE, DESOLATE ⟨~ wilderness⟩ **3 :** very great **:** EXTREME, PRONOUNCED ⟨~ success⟩ — **howl·ing·ly** *adv*

how·lite \ˈhau̇,līt\ *n* -S [Henry *How* †1879 Canadian mineralogist + E *-lite*] **:** a mineral $Ca_2SiB_5O_9(OH)_5$ consisting of a white nodular or earthy calcium borosilicate

howm \ˈhəu̇m\ *chiefly Scot var of* ¹HOLM

how·rah \ˈhau̇rə\ *adj, usu cap* [fr. *Howrah,* India] **:** of or from the city of Howrah, India **:** of the kind or style prevalent in Howrah

hows *pl of* HOW

how's about [by alter.] *substand* **:** how about

how·ship's lacuna \ˈhau̇,ships-\ *n, usu cap H* [after John *Howship* †1841 Eng. anatomist] **:** a groove or cavity containing osteoclasts in bone that is undergoing absorption

how·so \ˈhau̇(,)sō\ *adv* [ME, fr. *how* + *so*] *archaic* **:** HOWEVER

how·so·ev·er \ˌhau̇sə¦wevə(r), -(,)sō¦ev-\ *adv* [ME, fr. *how* + *so* + *ever*] **1 :** in what manner soever **:** to whatever degree or extent ⟨I am glad he's come, ~ he comes —Shak.⟩ **2** *archaic* **:** HOWEVER

how·som·ev·er \ˌhau̇sə¦mevə(r)\ *adv* [alter. of *howsoever*] *chiefly dial* **:** HOWSOEVER, NEVERTHELESS, HOWEVER

how-to \ˈ=¦tü\ *adj* [fr. *how to* in phrases like *how to make a birdhouse*] **:** giving practical instruction and advice (as on a craft, trade, hobby) ⟨publishing paperbound books, mostly of a *how-to* nature —*Publishers' Weekly*⟩ ⟨the magazine has a regular *how-to* section⟩

hox \ˈhäks\ *vt* -ED/-ING/-ES [ME *hoxen,* fr. *hox* hock sinew, fr. OE *hōhsinu,* fr. *hōh* heel + *sinu, seonu* sinew — more at HOCK, SINEW] **1 :** HAMSTRING **2 :** to pester by following **:** HARASS, ANNOY

¹hoy *or* **hoi** \ˈhȯi\ *interj* [ME] — used in greeting or in calling attention or in driving animals or to express surprise or alarm

²hoy \"\ *n* -S **:** HAIL, SHOUT, CALL ⟨better give that boat a ~⟩

³hoy \"\ *n* -S [ME *hoy, hoye,* fr. MD *hoei*] **1 :** a small usu. sloop-rigged coasting ship formerly used in conveying passengers and goods from place to place or as a tender to larger ships in port **2 :** a heavy barge used for weighty or bulky cargo

¹hoya \ˈhȯi(y)ə\ *n* [NL, after Thomas *Hoy* †1821 Eng. gardener] **1** *cap* **:** a large genus of climbing Australasian shrubs (family Asclepiadaceae) having fleshy leaves and nectariferous flowers with a rotate corolla and a star-shaped crown — see WAX PLANT, HONEY PLANT **2** -S **:** any plant of the genus *Hoya*

²hoya \"\ *n* -S [AmerSp, fr. Sp, large hole, pit, ditch, valley, fr. L *fovea* small pit] **:** a valley or basin high in rugged mountains (as the Andes)

¹hoy·den \ˈhȯidᵊn\ *n* -S [perh. fr. obs. D *heiden* country lout, fr. MD *heidijn, heiden* heathen, one that lives on a heath; akin to OE *hǣthen* heathen — more at HEATHEN] **1** *obs* **:** a rude clownish youth **2 :** a girl or woman of loud, boisterous, or carefree behavior **:** TOMBOY ⟨dancing in public with a troop of country ~*s* —Thomas Hardy⟩

²hoyden \"\ *vi* -ED/-ING/-S **:** to act like a hoyden

³hoyden \"\ *adj, of a girl* **:** RUDE, ILL-BRED, ROISTERING

hoy·den·ish \-ᵊnish\ *adj* **:** LIVELY, TOMBOYISH, UNLADYLIKE ⟨horsey, ~, six feet tall and far from shrinking —Sara H. Hay⟩

hoy·den·ism \-ᵊn,izəm\ *n* -S **:** unladylike or tomboyish behavior

¹hoyle \ˈhȯil, *esp before pause or consonant* -ȯiəl\ *n* -S [origin unknown] **:** a natural object (as a molehill) used as an archery mark at short range

²hoyle \"\ *n* -S *often cap* [after Edmond *Hoyle* †1769 Eng. writer on games] **:** an encyclopedia of card games and usu. other indoor games; *esp* **:** a book of rules accepted as standard or authoritative

hoyle shooting *n* [¹*hoyle*] **:** an archery pastime like roving except that the marks are always at short range

hoy·man \ˈhȯimən\ *n, pl* **hoymen :** one who owns or navigates a hoy

HP *abbr* **1** half pay **2** handmade paper **3** high-pass **4** high power **5** high pressure **6** high priest **7** hire purchase **8** horizontal parallax **9** *often not cap* horsepower **10** house physician **11** House of Parliament

HPH *abbr, often not cap* horsepower-hour

h-pile \ˈ=,=\ *n, cap H* **:** a steel pile having an H-shaped cross section

HPO *abbr* highway post office

h pole *n, cap H* **:** a telegraph pole built up of two parallel poles braced together

hps *abbr* harpsichord

HQ *abbr* **1** headquarters **2** *often not cap* [L *hoc quaere*] look for this; see this

hr *abbr* hour

HR *abbr* **1** high resistance **2** high run **3** home rule **4** home run **5** House of Representatives

hrd *abbr* hard

hr factor \(ˈ)āˈchär-\ *n, usu cap H* **:** an agglutinogen present in Rh-negative blood and apparently reciprocally related to the Rh factor

HRH *abbr* Her Royal Highness; His Royal Highness

HRIP *abbr* [L *hic requiescit in pace*] here rests in peace

hrt *abbr* heart

hrtwd *abbr* heartwood

HS *abbr* **1** hemstitched **2** [L *hic sepultus; hic situs*] here is buried **3** high school **4** high speed **5** *often not cap* [L *hoc sensu*] in this sense **6** honorary secretary **7** house surgeon

h's *or* **hs** *pl of* H

h-scope \ˈ=,=\ *n, usu cap H* **:** a radarscope on which signals appear as two dots joined by a line whose slope indicates the angle of elevation — compare B-SCOPE

hse *abbr* house

HSE *abbr* [L *hic sepultus est; hic situs est*] here is buried

h section *n, cap H* **:** a rolled structural metal section with an H-shaped cross section and wide flanges

hsg *abbr* housing

HSH *abbr* Her Serene Highness; His Serene Highness

h-shaped \ˈ=,=\ *adj, cap H* **:** having the shape of a capital H

hsia \shēˈä\ *n, usu cap H* [Chin (Pek) *hsia⁴*] **1 :** the first dynasty of China said to have been founded by the legendary emperor Yu **2** -S **:** the people of the Hsia dynasty

hsi-fan \ˈshēˈfän\ *n, pl* **hsi-fan** *usu cap H&F* [Chin (Pek) *hsi¹ fan¹* fr. *hsi¹* west, western + *fan¹* foreign, barbarous] **:** any of several east Tibetan peoples on the western border of China

hsin \ˈshin\ *n* -S [Chin (Pek) *hsin⁴*] *Confucianism* **:** the cardinal virtue faithfulness or veracity

hsiung-nu \shēˈu̇ŋˈnü\ *n, pl* **hsiung-nu** *usu cap H&N* [Chin (Pek) *hsiung¹ nu²,* fr. *hsiung¹* cruel, fierce + *nu²* slave, servant] **:** an ancient horse-using people related to or identical with the Huns, including the Jung and Ti peoples of Chinese history, and recorded in Chinese annals as being a powerful nation and in the 3d century B.C. occupying all the country between the Caspian sea and the Great Wall and dominating much of Mongolia

HSM *abbr* Her Serene Majesty; His Serene Majesty

h-stretcher \ˈ=,==\ *n, cap H* **:** a common leg brace for furniture consisting of two stretchers from front to back joined by a central crossbar

H-stretcher

ht *abbr* **1** heat **2** height

HT *abbr* **1** half time **2** herd test **3** high-tension **4** high tide **5** *often not cap* [L *hoc tempore*] at this time **6** *often not cap* [L *hoc titulo*] under this title

HTA *abbr* heavier than air

htg *abbr* heating

HTH *abbr* high-test hypochlorite

hu \ˈhü\ *n, pl* **hu** *or* **hus** *usu cap* [Chin (Pek) *hu²,* lit., dewlap of an ox] **:** an ancient Tatar people of northwest China related to the Hsiung-Nu

hua \ˈhyüə\ *n, cap* [NL] **:** a genus of freshwater snails of eastern Asia (family Thiaridae) including important intermediate hosts of the Chinese liver fluke and the human lung fluke

huabi *usu cap, var of* HUAVE

hua·ca \ˈwäkə\ *or* **gua·ca** \ˈgw-\ *n* -S [Sp *guaca, huaca,* fr. Quechua *wáka*] **:** an ancient Peruvian sacred object: **a :** GOD, SPIRIT **b :** any object (as a mountain, animal, shrine, or artifact) inhabited by a god or spirit **:** FETISH — compare MANITOU, NAGUAL, ZEMI **c :** a pre-Columbian ruin (as a tomb or burial mound)

hua·co \-(,)kō\ *n* -S [Sp *guaco, huaco,* fr. Quechua *wáko, wáku,* fr. *wáka*] **:** a pre-Columbian relic of Peru (as an object discovered in a tomb)

hua·ji·llo \wäˈhē(,)(y)ō\ *also* **hua·ji·lla** \-ē(y)ə\ *n* -S [MexSp *guajillo, huajillo, guajilla, huajilla,* dim. of *guaje* gourd, fr. Nahuatl *huaxin*] **:** either of two honey plants from Texas and adjacent Mexico: **a :** a spiny shrub (*Pithecolobium brevifolium*) **b :** a sweet-scented shrub (*Acacia berlandieri*)

hualapai *or* **hualpai** *usu cap, var of* WALAPAI

hualpi *usu cap, var of* WALPI

hua·mu·chil \wäˈmü,chēl\ *or* **gua·mu·chil** \gw-\ *also* **cua·mu·chil** \kw-\ *n* -S [MexSp *guamúchil, huamúchil, cuamúchil* — more at CAMACHILE] **:** CAMACHILE

huanaco *var of* GUANACO

huan·ca·pam·pa \,wäŋkəˈpämpə\ *n, pl* **huancapampa** *or* **huancapampas** *usu cap* [Sp, fr. *Huancapampa* (now *Huancabamba*), region of Peru] **:** CHINCHAISUYU

hua·nu·co coca \ˈwänə,kō-\ *n, usu cap H* [AmerSp (Peru) *huánuco,* prob. fr. *Huánuco,* town and department in Peru] **:** COCA 2a

hua·pan·go \wäˈpäŋ(,)gō\ *n* -S [MexSp, a festival celebrated in the state of Veracruz, dance typical of this festival, *huapango,* fr. *Huapango,* town in Veracruz, Mexico] **:** a fast and complicated Mexican couple dance that is usu. performed on a wooden platform to accentuate the rhythmic beating of heels and toes

hua·ra·che \wəˈräche\ *also* **gua·ra·che** \"\ *or* **hua·ra·cho** \-(,)chō\ *n* -S [MexSp *guarache, huarache*] **:** a low-heeled sandal; *esp* **:** a sling-backed sandal having an upper made of interwoven leather thongs

huarache

hua·ri \ˈwä(,)rē\ *n, pl* **huari** *or* **huaris** *usu cap* [Pg, of AmerInd origin] **1 a :** an Indian people of western Mato Grosso, Brazil **b :** a member of such people **2 :** the language of the Huari people

hua·ri·zo \wäˈrē(,)zō, -ē(,)sō\ *n* -S [AmerSp] **:** the offspring of a male llama and a female alpaca

huar·pe \ˈwär(,)pā\ *n, pl* **huarpe** *or* **huarpes** *usu cap* [Sp, of AmerInd origin] **1 a :** a group of Indian peoples of western Argentina including the Allentiac of the San Juan province **b :** a member of such peoples **2 :** a language family consisting of the languages spoken by the Huarpe peoples — **huar·pe·an** \-,pēən\ *adj or n, usu cap*

huasima *var of* GUACIMO

huas·tec *or* **hua·x·tec** \ˈwä,stek\ *also* **huas·teca** \wäˈstākə, -tekə\ *or* **huas·te·co** \-(,)kō\ *n, pl* **huastec** *or* **huastecs** *or* **huaxtec** *or* **huaxtecs** *usu cap* [Sp *guasteco, guaxteco, huasteco, huaxteco,* of AmerInd origin] **1 a :** an Indian people of the states of San Luis Potosi, Veracruz, and Tamaulipas, Mexico **b :** a member of such people **2 :** the Mayan language of the Huastec people — **huas·tecan** \(ˈ)wä¦stākən, -tek-\ *adj, usu cap*

hua·ve \ˈwävē\ *or* **hua·bi** \", -äbē\ *n, pl* **huave** *or* **huaves** *or* **huabi** *or* **huabis** *usu cap* [Sp, of AmerInd origin] **1 a :** an Indian people of the region between the lagoons and the Gulf of Tehuantepec, Oaxaca, Mexico **b :** a member of such people **2 :** the language of the Huave people that is without proven affinities — **hua·ve·an** \-vēən\ *adj, usu cap*

huayule *var of* GUAYULE

¹hub \ˈhəb\ *n* -S [prob. alter. of ²*hob*] **1 a :** the usu. cylindrical central part of a wheel **:** NAVE — compare AXLE BOX **b :** the central part of a propeller or motor-driven fan to which the blades are attached ⟨raising the propeller ~ above water so that we could get the prop off —K.M.Dodson⟩ **2 a :** a chief center of activity **:** FOCAL POINT ⟨heart, ~, and pivot of this new Virginia Metropolis is the Pentagon —A.W.Atwood⟩ ⟨Indianapolis . . . became the ~ of a rail center with lines running in all directions —R.H.Brown⟩ ⟨this fact must serve as the ~ of the analysis —*Political Science Quarterly*⟩ ⟨the ~ of every hemoglobin molecule is one atom of iron —D.C. Peattie⟩ ⟨Boston Statehouse is the ~ of the solar system —O.W.Holmes †1894⟩; *specif* **:** a center of circulation in architectural planning ⟨the dwelling has a novel ~ floor plan, permitting easy access between rooms —*N.Y. Herald Tribune*⟩ **b :** a durable marker placed at an important point of a survey for use (as in triangulation) **3 a :** a steel punch from which a working die for a coin or medal is made and which in modern processes bears the design as cut by a reducing machine copying the engraver's model **b :** ²HOB 4a(4) **c :** MASTER TAP **d** (1) **:** a boss that resembles the hub of a wheel (2) **:** BARREL 3d **e :** a piece in a lock that is turned by the knob spindle passing through it and that moves the bolt **4 :** a ridge on the backbone of a book (as a leather-bound book) formed by a sewing cord or a strip of cardboard **:** ¹BAND 5b(1) **5 :** a connection or point of confluence: as **a** (1) **:** a short coupling used to join pipes in plumbing (2) *also* **hubb :** BELL 5i **b :** a hole on the panelboard of a piece of electrical equipment into which a wire is plugged **:** electrical contact **c :** the enlarged base by which a hollow needle (as for a hypodermic) may be attached to a syringe or other device **syn** see CENTER

²hub \"\ *vt* **hubbed; hubbed; hubbing; hubs :** ³HOB 2b

³hub \"\ *adj, usu cap* [fr. *the Hub,* nickname for Boston, Mass.] *chiefly NewEng* **:** of or relating to the city of Boston, Mass. ⟨*Hub* officials⟩

hu·ba·bo \(h)üˈbä(,)bō\ *n, pl* **hubabo** *or* **hubabos** *usu cap* [Sp, of AmerInd origin] **1 :** an Indian people of the northern part of the Dominican Republic **2 :** a member of the Hubabo people

hu·bam clover \ˈhyü,bam-\ *also* **hubam** *n* -S *often cap H* [Harold DeMott *Hughes* b1882 Am. agronomist, its discoverer + *Alabama,* state in the U.S., source of the seed for the experimental plot in which it was discovered] **:** an annual variety (*Melilotus alba annua*) of sweet clover

hub-and-spigot joint \ˌ==ˈ==-\ *n* **:** BELL-AND-SPIGOT JOINT

hubba-hubba \ˌhəbəˈhəbə\ *interj* [origin unknown] — used to express approval, excitement, or enthusiasm

hub·bard squash \ˈhəbə(r)d-\ *also* **hubbard** *n* -S *usu cap H* [prob. fr. the name *Hubbard*] **:** any of various winter squashes having the fruit generally ovoid and pointed at the end away from the stem, the skin smooth to strongly warted, and ranging in color from dark green to orange

hub·bell·ite \ˈhəbə,līt\ *n* -S [fr. *Hubbellite,* a trademark] **:** an oxychloride cement that contains finely powdered copper, is fungicidal and germicidal, possesses high tensile strength and adhesive properties, and is resistant to abrasion

hub·ber \ˈhəbə(r)\ *n* -S [¹*hub* + *-er*] **:** one that sinks hobs into steel for die stamping

hub·bite \ˈhə,bīt\ *n* -S *usu cap* [the *Hub,* nickname for Boston + E *-ite*] **:** BOSTONIAN

hub·ble \ˈhəbəl\ *n* -S [prob. short for *hubbleshew*] *dial Brit* **:** HUBBUB, UPROAR

hubble-bubble \ˈhəbəl¦bəbəl\ *n* -S [redupl. of *bubble*] **1 :** WATER PIPE 2; *esp* **:** a rudimentary water pipe sometimes consisting merely of a bowl mounted on a coconut in which there is a hole that serves as a mouthpiece — compare HOOKAH, NARGILEH **2 :** a burble of sound or flurry of activity **:** COMMOTION ⟨for hours a merry but rather tedious *hubble-bubble,* suggesting liquor, was heard ascending from the cabin skylight —R.A.W.Hughes⟩ ⟨the *hubble-bubble* of spring-cleaning —*Manchester Guardian Weekly*⟩

hub·ble·shew *or* **hub·ble·show** \ˈhəbəl,shō, -shü\ *n* -S [perh. fr. obs. Flem *hobbel-sjobbel, hobbel-sobbel* in an uproar, confusedly] *chiefly Scot* **:** UPROAR, TUMULT, COMMOTION

hub·bly \ˈhəb(ə)lē\ *adj* [alter. of *hobbly*] **:** having an uneven surface **:** ROUGH ⟨a ~ road⟩ ⟨a ~ sea⟩

hub·bub \ˈhə,bəb\ *n* -S [prob. of Celt origin; akin to ScGael *ub ub, ubub,* an interj. of contempt] **1 :** a noisy confusion of sound **:** DIN, UPROAR ⟨a ~ of cocks crowing and children shouting —Alan Moorehead⟩ ⟨~ of an orchestra tuning up⟩ **2 :** a state of tumultuous confusion or excitement **:** TURMOIL ⟨swarmed onto the field in a wild ~ after winning the game⟩ ⟨the animated excitement and ~ that gives the . . . institution its friendly vitality —Aline B. Saarinen⟩ ⟨it behoves culture to . . . save the individual in the midst of this industrial ~ —J.C. Powys⟩ **3 :** an Indian game resembling dice played with bones and a tray — used by New England settlers **syn** see DIN

hub·bu·boo *or* **hub·ba·boo** \ˌhəbəˈbü\ *n* -S [prob. of Celt origin like *hubbub*] **:** HUBBUB 1, 2

hub·by \ˈhəbē, -bi\ *n* -ES [by alter.] **:** HUSBAND — not often in formal use

hubcap \ˈ=,=\ *n* **:** a removable metal cap screwed or clamped over the end of an axle; *esp* **:** such a cap used on the wheel of a motor vehicle

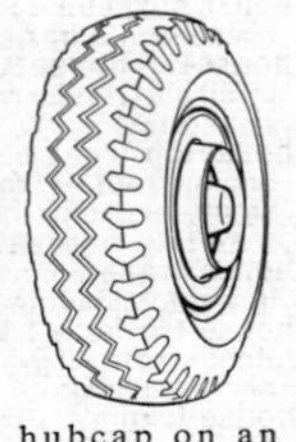

hubcap on an automobile wheel

hu·bris \ˈh(y)übrəs\ *also* **hy·bris** \ˈhīb-\ *n* -ES [Gk *hybris* — more at OUT] **:** overweening pride or self-confidence **:** ARROGANCE ⟨the very best critics of the past have made so many blunders . . . that our own critics today should be careful to avoid ~ —*Times Lit. Supp.*⟩ — contrasted with *sophrosyne*

hu·bris·tic \hyüˈbristik\ *adj* [Gk *hybristikos,* fr. *hybristēs* violent, wanton, insolent man (fr. *hybris*) + *-ikos* -ic] **:** INSOLENT, VAIN, ARROGANT — **hu·bris·ti·cal·ly** \-tək(ə)lē\ *adv*

hubs *pl of* HUB, *pres 3d sing of* HUB

hu·chen \ˈhükən, -k̲-\ *also* **huch** \-k,-k̲\ *n* -S [G] **:** a large elongate predacious game fish (*Hucho hucho*) of the Danube that resembles the Atlantic salmon but may attain a weight of 130 pounds

huch·nom \ˈhüchnəm\ *n, pl* **huchnom** *or* **huchnoms** *usu cap* [Yuki] **1 a :** an Indian people of the Eel river valley in northwestern California **b :** a member of such people **2 :** the Yuki dialect of the Huchnom people

hu·cho \ˈh(y)ü(,)kō\ *n* [NL, fr. G *huchen, huch*] **1** *cap* **:** a European genus of large riverine fishes (family Salmonidae) that are closely related to the salmons and trouts of the genus *Salmo* from which they are distinguished esp. by the absence of teeth along the median line of the hyoid bone **2** -S **:** any fish of the genus *Hucho*; *esp* **:** HUCHEN

¹huck \ˈhək\ *vi* -ED/-ING/-S [ME *hukken,* prob. back-formation fr. *hukster, hokster* huckster — more at HUCKSTER] *now dial Eng* **:** HIGGLE, BARGAIN

²huck \"\ *n* -S [ME *hokebone* — more at HUCKLE] *chiefly dial* **:** HIP, HAUNCH

³huck \"\ *n* -S [by shortening] **:** HUCKABACK

⁴huck \"\ *n* -S [by alter.] *dial* **:** HUSK

huck·a·back \ˈhəkə,bak, -,bək\ *n* [origin unknown] **1 :** a textured weave in which yarns are floated on a plain ground to form small allover patterns **2 :** an absorbent durable cotton, linen, or cotton and linen fabric with a huckaback weave used chiefly for towels

huck·le \ˈhəkəl\ *n* -S [akin to ME *hokebone* hip, haunch, and perh. to ON *hūka* to squat — more at HAWKER] **:** HIP, HAUNCH

huckleback \ˈ==,=\ *n* **:** HUMPBACK

¹huck·le·ber·ry \ˈhəkəl- — *see* BERRY\ *n* [perh. alter. of *hurtleberry*] **1 a :** an edible dark-blue to black berry with 10 hard bony nutlets that is typically smaller and more acid than a blueberry **b :** any of several No. American shrubs of the genus *Gaylussacia* (esp. *G. baccata*) whose fruit is a huckleberry — see BOX HUCKLEBERRY **2 :** BLUEBERRY 1: as **a :** a dark-fruited as distinguished from a blue-fruited blueberry **b :** WHORTLEBERRY 1 **c :** a stiff evergreen shrub (*Vaccinium ovatum*) with edible garnet to black berries and glossy foliage much used as greenery in floral arrangements and decorations

²huckleberry \"\ *vi* **:** to pick or look for huckleberries ⟨go ~*ing*⟩

huckleberry family *n* **:** ERICACEAE

huckleberry oak *n* **:** a low, spreading, often prostrate shrub (*Quercus vaccinifolia*) of southwestern U.S. with slender branches and green leaves that resemble those of the huckleberry

hucklebone \ˈ==,=\ *n* **1 :** HIPBONE, HOOK 5c(2) **2 :** TALUS **3** *archaic* **:** KNUCKLEBONE 2

¹huck·ster \ˈhəkstə(r)\ *n* -S [ME *hukster, hokster,* fr. MD *hokester, hoekster,* fr. *hoken, hoeken* to peddle, bear on the back, squat + *-ster* — more at HAWKER] **1 :** one that sells goods along the street or from door to door **:** HAWKER, PEDDLER **2 a** *archaic* **:** one that buys to resell at a profit **:** MIDDLEMAN **b :** one that acts primarily from mercenary motives **3 a :** one that produces advertising material for commercial clients **:** ADMAN ⟨home is not the plastic chromium dream . . . the ~*s* promised to them —R.W.Kenny⟩; *specif* **:** one that prepares or delivers commercials for radio or television ⟨~*s* speak only to sponsors; and sponsors don't speak at all, they read sales charts —Walter Goodman⟩ ⟨a syrupy-voiced ~ proclaiming the virtues of Dinkelspiel's Deodorant —Bennett Cerf⟩ **b :** one that employs persuasive showmanship to make a sale or attain an objective ⟨the most adroit ~ of $1000 trinkets in our time —Maurice Zolotow⟩ ⟨minds taught to respond without reflection to the slogans of our political ~*s* —*New Republic*⟩

²huckster \"\ *vb* **huckstered; huckstered; huckstering** \-t(ə)riŋ\ **hucksters** *vi* **:** HAGGLE ⟨~ over prices on the black market⟩ ~ *vt* **1 :** to deal in or bargain over **:** retail for profit ⟨~ fresh eggs⟩ ⟨~ real estate⟩ ⟨~ his services⟩ **2 :** to promote by showmanship ⟨a store where cheap stuff is ballyhooed and ~*ed* into seeming richness —C.W.Drepperd⟩

huck·ster·er \-t(ə)rə(r)\ *n* -s *archaic* **:** HUCKSTER

huckstering *n* -s [fr. gerund of ²*huckster*] **:** the activities or occupation of a huckster

huck·ster·ism \-tə,rizəm\ *n* -s **:** persuasive showmanship in advertising or selling **:** COMMERCIALISM 2 ⟨sponsoring the Metropolitan Opera broadcasts . . . without the faintest trace of bad taste or ~ —Howard Taubman⟩ ⟨the unashamed ~ practiced by our present government —R.L.Riggs⟩

hud \'həd\ *n* -s [ME *hudde*] *dial Eng* **:** a husk or hull esp. of a berry

hud·ders·field \'hədə(r)z,fēld\ *adj, usu cap* [fr. *Huddersfield*, England] **:** of or from the county borough of Huddersfield, England **:** of the kind or style prevalent in Huddersfield

¹hud·dle \'həd°l\ *vb* **huddled; huddled; huddling** \-d(°)liŋ\ **huddles** [prob. fr. or akin to ME *hoderen* to huddle together, wrap up; prob. akin to ME *hiden* to hide — more at HIDE] *vt* **1** *Brit* **:** to throw together or complete carelessly or hurriedly ⟨things happened as in a badly directed moving picture, all *huddled*, all hurried —Donn Byrne⟩ — often followed by a directional adverb ⟨the solemnities had to be *huddled* through at express speed —*Manchester Examiner*⟩ ⟨weakness . . . to ~ up his stories rather than to wind them off to an orderly conclusion —George Saintsbury⟩ **2 :** to conceal from view **:** cover up ⟨political deaths are *huddled* and secret —*Time & Tide*⟩ **3 a :** to mass together **:** CROWD ⟨give me your tired, your poor, your *huddled* masses yearning to breathe free —Emma Lazarus⟩ ⟨ours is a nation in which military and civilian targets are *huddled* together —D. H. McLachlan⟩ ⟨all over the country people are *huddled* round their radios —F.L.Allen⟩ **b :** to draw (oneself) together **:** CROUCH ⟨the men *huddled* themselves low against the wind —A.J.Cronin⟩ ⟨he was *huddled* in his cot, trying to keep warm —Gertrude Atherton⟩ **4** *dial chiefly Eng* **:** HUG, EMBRACE **5 a** *archaic* **:** to herd into or out of a place in a disorderly mass ⟨we were *huddled* out like a flock of sheep, by a file of soldiers —Frederick Marryat⟩ **b :** to pull on unceremoniously or wrap oneself closely in (clothes) ⟨she *huddled* her purple woolen coat round her —Rumer Godden⟩ — often used with *on* ⟨I *huddled* on my clothes —A.T.Quiller-Couch⟩ ~ *vi* **1 a :** to gather in a group **:** press close together **:** ASSEMBLE, BUNCH ⟨passengers . . . ~ like sheep at entrance gates —Bennett Cerf⟩ ⟨an opera chorus ~*s* round a few haughty soloists —G.B. Shaw⟩ ⟨little printers' cafés . . . ~ near the thundering presses —Francis Aldor⟩ **b :** to curl up **:** CROUCH ⟨*huddled* in the lee of a rock, trying to get a little protection from the wind —H.D. Quillin⟩ ⟨a long gray cat *huddled* watchfully in the window —Katherine A. Porter⟩ — often used with *up* ⟨*huddled* up, closed his eyes, and went quite . . . peacefully to sleep —James Hilton⟩ **c :** to dress oneself hurriedly or wrap something around oneself ⟨hip-length coat, with a big collar to ~ —Lois Long⟩ **2** *obs* **:** to act in a precipitate manner ⟨fools ~ on, and always are in haste —Nicholas Rowe⟩ **3 a :** to hold a consultation **:** CONFER ⟨worried financiers *huddled* to discuss the possible effects of the blow on California's economy —*Newsweek*⟩ ⟨the gang . . . ~*s* around a table in a small upstairs room —John Mason Brown⟩; *specif* **:** to gather behind the scrimmage line in a football game and agree on team strategy **b :** to pause for thought in a bridge game

²huddle \"\ *n* -s **1 a :** a close-packed group **:** JUMBLE, BUNCH ⟨~*s* of cows and sheep⟩ ⟨the ugly ~ of weather-beaten shacks and wharves where the fishermen kept their tackle —L.C. Douglas⟩ ⟨~ of meaningless words —Edith Sitwell⟩ ⟨the four harpooners, the cooper, and myself were sitting in a ~ in the steerage —H.A.Chippendale⟩ **b :** a shapeless mass **:** LUMP ⟨a ~ of black against the starlight —Marjory S. Douglas⟩ **2 :** CONFUSION, DISARRAY, MUDDLE ⟨equally free from the dullness of slow or the hurry and ~ of quick time —Earl of Chesterfield⟩ **3 a :** MEETING, DISCUSSION, CONFERENCE ⟨spent some eight hours in a ~ with a dozen laymen and priests —M.E.Bennett⟩ ⟨secret ~*s* were held by five leading Republicans —*Newsweek*⟩ ⟨a ~ of social scientists put the finishing touches on a massive study of American life —F.L.Allen⟩ — often used in the phrase *go into a huddle* ⟨at the end of the bout the judges go into a ~ to determine the winner⟩ ⟨she went into a series of ~*s* with cheese experts —Harry Thompson⟩ ⟨go into a ~ with yourself about it —Mary D. Gillies⟩ **b :** a strategy conference of football players behind the line of scrimmage **c :** a long pause for thought by a bridge player before he bids or plays ⟨went into a ~ before making his first discard —Oswald Jacoby⟩

hud·dler \'həd(°)lə(r)\ *n* -s **:** one that huddles

huddling *adj* **:** in a huddle or hurry **:** JUMBLED, RUSHING ⟨horsemen charged the ~ crowd⟩ ⟨the ~ and tumultuous brook —Sir Walter Scott⟩ — **hud·dling·ly** *adv*

hud·dup \(,)hə'dəp, -dap; hə'rəp, hə̄'rəp\ *v imper* [perh. alter. of *get up*] — used as a command to horses or oxen to go ahead or go faster

¹hu·di·bras·tic \¦hyüdə¦brastik\ *adj, usu cap* [*Hudibras*, mock-heroic satirical poem in octosyllabic couplets by Samuel Butler †1680 Eng. poet + E *-tic* (as in *fantastic*)] **1 :** written in humorous octosyllabic couplets **2 :** smartly and sportively burlesque **:** MOCK-HEROIC — **hu·di·bras·ti·cal·ly** \-tək(ə)lē\ *adv, usu cap*

²hudibrastic \"\ *n* -s **:** an octosyllabic couplet used in humorous verse

hud·son bay pine \'hədsən,bā-\ *n, usu cap H&B* [fr. *Hudson bay* or *Hudson's bay*, inland sea in northern Canada] **:** JACK PINE 1

hudson bay sable *n, usu cap H&B* **:** AMERICAN SABLE

hud·so·nia \,həd'sōnēə\ *n* [NL, fr. William *Hudson* †1793 Eng. botanist + NL *-ia*] **1** *cap* **:** a genus of low heathlike No. American herbs (family Cistaceae) with hoary or villous foliage and usu. bright yellow flowers **2 :** any plant of the genus *Hudsonia*

hud·so·ni·an \¦həd¦sōnēən\ *adj, usu cap* [*Hudson* (bay) + E *-ian*] **1 :** of or relating to Hudson bay **2** *of*, relating to, or being a subdivision of the biogeographic Boreal zone extending across No. America from Labrador to Alaska, being bounded to the south and in certain high mountain regions by the isotherm indicating a mean temperature of 57.2° Fahrenheit during the 6 hottest weeks of the year, and marking the northern extent of the coniferous forest belt

hudsonian chickadee *n, usu cap H* **:** CHICKADEE

hudsonian curlew *n, usu cap H* **:** the No. American variety (*Numenius phaeopus hudsonicus*) of the whimbrel

hudsonian godwit *n, usu cap H* **:** an American godwit (*Limosa haemastica*) with a long slightly upturned bill and underparts that are finely black barred during the spring

hudson's bay blanket *n, usu cap H&B* **:** a heavy woolen blanket with one or more broad stripes usu. black on a red ground or varicolored on a white ground at each end to indicate its weight

¹hue \'hyü\ *n* -s [ME *hewe* appearance, shape, kind, color, fr. OE *hīw, hēow*; akin to ON *hȳ* fine hair, down, Goth *hiwi* form, appearance, OE *hār* hoary — more at HOAR] **1 :** SHAPE, COMPLEXION, ASPECT ⟨a ghost town in modern ~ —*Springfield (Mass.) Union*⟩ ⟨songs . . . of a sad and somber ~ —William Black⟩ ⟨political parties of every ~ —Louis Wasserman⟩ **2 a :** COLOR 1; *esp* **:** gradation of color ⟨the work of an inspired painter can reveal to us the ~*s* and shades of twilight —Colin Clark⟩ **b :** the attribute of colors that permits them to be classed as red, yellow, green, blue, or an intermediate between any contiguous pair of these — used in psychology; see COLOR 1b **c :** hue in the Munsell color system — used in psychophysics; see the Color Charts explanation at COLOR **syn** see COLOR

²hue \"\ *vb* -ED/-ING/-S [ME *hewen* to form, fashion, color, fr. OE *hīwian*, fr. *hīw*, n.] *vt* **:** TINGE ⟨*hued* their sight with rainbow beauty —Peggy Bennett⟩ ~ *vi* **:** to take on color **:** become colored ⟨in highlights it *hued* to dull silver gray —William Beebe⟩

³hue \"\ *vb* -ED/-ING/-S [ME *huwen*, fr. OF *huer* to shout, hoot, fr. *hu*, interj. used esp. to apprise of danger] *vi, now dial* **:** to make outcry **:** SHOUT ~ *vt, obs* **:** to shout at **:** drive with shouts

⁴hue \"\ *n* -s [ME *hew, hu*, fr. OF *hue*, outcry, noise, fr *huer*] **:** SHOUT, OUTCRY

hue and cry *n* [⁴*hue*] **1 a :** a loud outcry used in the pursuit of felons and joined and taken up by all who heard it in the pursuit **b :** the pursuit of a felon or a written proclamation for the capture of a felon or the finding of stolen goods **2 a :** clamor of pursuit or protest ⟨had visions of sheriffs . . . posses and *hue and cry* —Esther Forbes⟩ ⟨conservative politicians joined in the *hue and cry* against the school and its doctrines —Hunter Mead⟩ **3 :** HUBBUB ⟨the unloading . . . was being conducted with a *hue and cry*, with raucous bangs and crashes —Jean Stafford⟩

hueb·ner·ite \'hēbnə,rīt, 'hyüb-\ *n* -s [G *hübnerit*, fr. Adolf *Hübner*, 19th cent. Ger. foundry superintendent + G *-it* -ite] **:** a mineral $MnWO_4$ consisting of manganese tungstate, having a brownish red to nearly black color, occurring in columnar or foliated masses, and being isomorphous with wolframite

hue circle *or* **hue circuit** *also* **hue cycle** *n* **:** COLOR CIRCLE

hued \'hyüd\ *adj* [ME *hewed* formed, fashioned, colored, fr. OE *gehīwod, hīwod*, past part. of *gehīwian, hīwian* to hue — more at HUE] **:** COLORED — usu. used in combination ⟨green-*hued*⟩ ⟨rich, many-*hued* prose —Ray Corsini⟩

hue·ful \'hyüfəl\ *adj* **:** having hue and saturation **:** CHROMATIC

hue·huetl \(')wā¦(h)wā'l\ *n* -s [MexSp, fr. Nahuatl] **:** an ancient vertically cylindrical Mexican Indian drum usu. hollowed from a tree trunk and fitted with a skin head

hue·less \'hyüləs\ *adj* [ME *heweles* shapeless, colorless, fr. OE *hīwlēas*, fr. *hīw* appearance, shape, kind, color + *-lēas* -less — more at HUE] **1 :** COLORLESS **2 :** having no hue **:** GRAY — **hue·less·ness** *n* -ES

huemul *var of* GUEMAL

huer·ta \'wer(,)tä\ *n* -s [Sp, large vegetable garden or orchard, fr. *huerto* small vegetable garden or orchard, fr. L *hortus* garden — more at YARD] **:** a piece of highly cultivated land (as for an orchard) in Spain

¹huff \'həf\ *vb* -ED/-ING/-S [imit.] *vi* **1 a :** to emit puffs (as of air or steam) **:** BLOW, PANT ⟨he ~*ed* and he puffed and he blew the house down —*Three Little Pigs*⟩ ⟨another tug ~*s* quietly somewhere down below —W.V.Anderson⟩ **b :** to progress with puffing ⟨the first cyclists ~*ed* into sight —*Time*⟩ **2 a :** to speak in a threatening and bombastic manner **:** make empty threats **:** BLUSTER, RANT ⟨faced with new wage demands, management ~*s* about spiraling costs and the dangers of inflation⟩ ⟨children will soon discover that this is only ~*ing* and puffing on your part —H.R.Litchfield & L.H.Dembo⟩ **b** (1) **:** to react indignantly **:** speak resentfully **:** SNAP, STORM ⟨the father ~*s* and puffs and says, "Do you think I'm made of money" —Peter DeVries⟩ (2) **:** to behave indignantly **:** FLOUNCE ⟨resigned in pique and ~*ed* off to London —Janet Flanner⟩ **3** *archaic* **:** to become angry **:** take offense ⟨the woman has ~*ed* and won't trust me —Frederick Marryat⟩ **4** *now dial* **:** to expand in size **:** ENLARGE ⟨the bread ~*s*⟩ **5 :** to remove an opponent's checker from the board for failure to make a possible jump ~ *vt* **1 a :** to blow into **:** INFLATE, PUFF ⟨it ~*s* air steadily . . . through its hollow shaft —*Newsweek*⟩ ⟨their buying ~*ed* low-priced motor shares —*Time*⟩ **b :** to accomplish with puffing ⟨~*ed* himself up and stumped out of the room —Jackson Burgess⟩ **2** *archaic* **:** to treat with contempt **:** BULLY ⟨quarreling with his bread and butter and ~*ing* the waiter —Washington Irving⟩ ⟨the beast in scorn ~*ed* the uplifted club —J.C.Fairbairn⟩ **3 :** to make angry or petulant **:** PROVOKE, ANNOY ⟨this astounding rigidity of custom ~*ed* the king —Francis Hackett⟩ **4 :** to remove (an opponent's checker) from the board for failure to make a possible jump

²huff \"\ *n* -s **1 :** ²PUFF 1a ⟨at the moment of firing he might actually turn his face away from his sights to avoid the ~ from the pan —Odell & Willard Shepard⟩ **2 :** a fit of anger or pique ⟨in an . . . unprecedented display of parliamentary ~, refused to join the traditional procession —Mollie Panter-Downes⟩ — usu. used in the phrase *in a huff* ⟨the dissenting experts will secede in a ~ —Ernst Pulgram⟩ ⟨if you encounter a person who's in a ~ about something, you'd better wait until he cools off —W.J.Reilly⟩ **3** *obs* **a :** an attitude or display of arrogance ⟨quell . . . the ~ of the proud —Randle Cotgrave⟩ **b :** an arrogant or conceited person ⟨this young ~ commanded a sergeant to pay him respect —William Darrell⟩ **4** *dial Eng* **a :** light leavened pastry **b :** HUFF CAP 1 **5 :** an act of huffing in checkers **syn** see OFFENSE

³huff \"\ *adj, dial* **:** HUFFED, OFFENDED

¹huffcap \'=,=\ *n* -s [¹*huff* + *cap*] **1** *obs* **:** strong ale **2** *obs* **:** SWAGGERER, BULLY

²huffcap \"\ *adj* **1** *obs* **:** INTOXICATING **2** *archaic* **:** SWAGGERING ⟨a ~ hero . . . mouthed and strutted out his hour on the stage —A.C.Swinburne⟩

huff·i·ly \'həfəlē, -li\ *adv* **:** in a huffy manner

huff·i·ness \-fēnəs, -fin-\ *n* -ES **:** the quality or state of being huffy

huff·ing·ly *adv, archaic* **:** in an arrogant or sulky manner

huff·ish \'həfish\ *adj* **:** ARROGANT, SULKY **syn** see IRRITABLE

¹huf·fle \'həfəl\ *vi* -ED/-ING/-S [¹*huff* + *-le*] *now dial Eng* **:** to blow in gusts ⟨the winds do ~ queerer tonight than ever afore —Thomas Hardy⟩

²huffle \"\ *n* -s **:** GUST ⟨five haggard pines . . . knuckle together against the ~*s* of wind —Leah B. Drake⟩

huffler *var of* HOVELER

huff-snuff *n* -s [¹*huff* + *snuff*] *obs* **:** SWASHBUCKLER

huffy \'həfē, -fi\ *adj* -ER/-EST [²*huff* + *-y*] **1 :** HAUGHTY, ARROGANT ⟨relapsed into . . . ~ complacency —*Harper's*⟩ **2 a :** roused to indignation **:** IRRITATED, SULKY ⟨stayed ~ a good while —Mark Twain⟩ — usu. used with *get* ⟨now don't get ~ if I offer a frank criticism⟩ **b :** easily offended **:** TOUCHY ⟨not ~ and crabbed like yourself —Augusta Gregory⟩ **syn** see IRRITABLE

¹hug \'həg\ *vb* **hugged; hugged; hugging; hugs** [perh. of Scand origin; akin to ON *hugga* to comfort, soothe; akin to OE *hycgan* to think, consider, understand, OHG *huggen* to think, ON *huga & hyggja*, Goth *hugjan*, and perh. to Gk *kyknos* swan — more at CYGNET] *vt* **1 a :** to press tightly **:** CLUTCH ⟨the grip of her knees *hugging* Saidi's hot, rippling withers —L.C.Douglas⟩; *specif* **:** to clasp within the arms ⟨hurries down the gangplank to ~ his waiting wife⟩ ⟨she sat up in bed and *hugged* her knees —Louis Auchincloss⟩ **b :** to squeeze between the forelegs ⟨discounting the chances of being . . . *hugged* to death in the claws of a 9-foot anteater —George Weller⟩ **2 a** *archaic* **:** to show fondness for ⟨*hugged* the authors as his bosom friends —John Arbuthnot⟩; *specif* **:** to curry favor with ⟨refused to fight, on the ground that his opponent had been guilty of *hugging* attorneys —T.B.Macaulay⟩ **b :** CONGRATULATE, FELICITATE ⟨*hugged* ourselves that we hadn't had to be told —A.N.Whitehead⟩ **c :** to cling to or hold fast **:** CHERISH, KEEP ⟨~ our half belief in ghosts —W.W. Howells⟩ ⟨*hugged* his miseries like a sulky child —John Buchan⟩ ⟨an effort to ~ all credit to himself —Jonathan Daniels⟩ **3 :** to stay close or adhere to ⟨the road ~*s* the river⟩ ⟨this blast . . . helps the normal airflow ~ the contour of the flap —Richard Witkin⟩ ⟨collars either ~ the neck or stand away —*Women's Wear Daily*⟩ ⟨berries ~ the stem⟩ ⟨skaters ~ the bonfire⟩ ⟨a sailboat ~*s* the wind⟩ ⟨the faint aroma . . . *hugged* them like smog —Sally Benson⟩ **4** *dial Eng* **:** to carry with difficulty **:** LUG ~ *vi* **1 :** to press together **:** CROWD ⟨in groups that *hugged* together —Francis Hackett⟩ **2 a :** to embrace or adhere closely ⟨they *hugged* and kissed⟩ ⟨the revolving part is *hugging* closely against one side —Terrell Croft⟩ **b :** to crush a victim by squeezing with the forelegs ⟨'tis a bear's talent not to kick but ~ —Alexander Pope⟩ — **hug one's chains :** to be glad of servitude

²hug \"\ *n* -s **1 :** an affectionate embrace ⟨gave him a motherly ~⟩ **2 :** a crushing or restraining grasp ⟨bitter ~ of mortality —Walt Whitman⟩

¹huge \'hyüj *also* 'yüj\ *adj* -ER/-EST [ME *huge, hoge*, modif. of OF *ahuge, ahoge*] **:** very large or extensive: as **a :** of great size or area **:** GIGANTIC, VAST ⟨the two ships settled . . . to the bottom, each with a ~ hole in her hull —T.E.Cooney⟩ ⟨~ organizations like the American Express Company —Richard Joseph⟩ ⟨a ~ country estate⟩ ⟨~ number of stories —G.B. Saul⟩ **b :** of sizable scale or degree **:** ENORMOUS ⟨the days of the NRA when there was ~ government spending —T.W. Arnold⟩ ⟨~ popular demand for higher education —V.S. Pritchett⟩ ⟨glowered . . . from under his heavy brows with a ~ disgust —G.D.Brown⟩ ⟨turns . . . a dismal failure into a ~ success —Jeanne Massey⟩ **c :** of limitless scope or character **:** UNBOUNDED ⟨his ~ personal talent —Virgil Thomson⟩ ⟨go through rubbish heaps and find rings and scissors and broken noses buried in the ~ past —Virginia Woolf⟩ ⟨~ sense of destiny —Henry Wallace⟩

syn VAST, IMMENSE, ENORMOUS, ELEPHANTINE, MAMMOTH, GIANT, GIGANTIC, GIGANTEAN, COLOSSAL, GARGANTUAN, HERCULEAN, CYCLOPEAN, TITANIC, BROBDINGNAGIAN: HUGE is a rather general term indicating extreme largeness, usu. in size, bulk, or capacity ⟨an enormous volume of heavy, inky vapor, coiling and pouring upward in a *huge* and ebony cumulus cloud —H.G.Wells⟩ ⟨the Texan question and Mexican War made *huge* annexations of Southwestern territory certain —Allan Nevins & H.S.Commager⟩ VAST denotes extreme largeness or broadness, esp. of extent or range ⟨the Great Valley of California, a *vast* elliptical bowl averaging 50 miles in width and more than 400 miles long —*Amer. Guide Series: Calif.*⟩ ⟨consider the *vast* varieties of religions ancient and modern —M.R.Cohen⟩ IMMENSE suggests size far in excess of ordinary measurements or accustomed concepts ⟨an *immense* quill, plucked from a distended albatross' wing —Herman Melville⟩ ⟨found the balloon at an *immense* height indeed, and the earth's convexity had now become strikingly manifest —E.A. Poe⟩ ⟨the *immense* waste of war —D.W.Brogan⟩ ENORMOUS also indicates a size or degree exceeding accustomed bounds or norms ⟨heavy wagons, *enormous* loads, scarcely any less than three tons —*Amer. Guide Series: Calif.*⟩ ⟨the princes of the Renascence lavished upon private luxury and display *enormous* amounts of money —Lewis Mumford⟩ ELEPHANTINE suggests the cumbersome or ponderous largeness of the elephant ⟨similar *elephantine* bones were being displayed . . . as relics of the "giants" mentioned in the Bible —R.W.Murray⟩ ⟨*elephantine* grain elevators —*Amer. Guide Series: N.Y.*⟩ MAMMOTH is similar to ELEPHANTINE ⟨her parties were . . . *mammoth* — she rarely invited fewer than 100 people —*Time*⟩ ⟨a *mammoth* cyclotron —G.F.Whicher⟩ GIANT indicates unusual size or scope ⟨loaded with a typical unit of *giant* industrial equipment, the new car weighs more than a million pounds —*Pa. Railroad Annual Report*⟩ ⟨his *giant* intellect⟩ GIGANTIC and the less common GIGANTEAN are close synonyms of GIANT, perhaps more likely to be used in metaphorical extensions ⟨*gigantic* jewels that a hundred negroes could not carry —G.K.Chesterton⟩ ⟨a justice of the Supreme Court . . . however *gigantic* his learning and his juridic rectitude —H.L.Mencken⟩ COLOSSAL may suggest vast proportion ⟨three sets of *colossal* figures of men and animals . . . the largest man is 167 feet long —*Amer. Guide Series: Calif.*⟩ ⟨the sun blazed down . . . the heat was *colossal* —C.S.Forester⟩ GARGANTUAN suggests the hugeness of Rabelais's Gargantua and is often used in reference to appetites and similar physical matters ⟨*gargantuan* breakfasts . . . pigs' knuckles and sauerkraut, liver and bacon, ham and eggs, beef stew —Edna Ferber⟩ HERCULEAN suggests the superhuman power of the Greek hero Hercules or the superhuman difficulties of his famous labors ⟨a *Herculean* task confronted them. Some 1700 miles of track had to be laid through a wilderness —Allan Nevins and H.S.Commager⟩ CYCLOPEAN suggests the superhuman size and strength of the Cyclops of Greek mythology ⟨of *cyclopean* masonry, consisting of very large blocks of stone —*Scientific American*⟩ TITANIC suggests colossal size and, often, primitive earth-shaking strength ⟨*titanic* water fronds speedily choked both these rivers —H.G. Wells⟩ ⟨it was his *titanic* energy that broke the fetters of medievalism —M.R.Cohen⟩ BROBDINGNAGIAN suggests the hugeness of the inhabitants of the Brobdingnag of *Gulliver's Travels* ⟨a brand-new *Brobdingnagian* hotel —Isaac D'Israeli⟩

²huge \"\ *adv* [ME, fr. *huge, hoge*, adj.] **:** HUGELY ⟨the sky was swelling ~ with the last dusk —John Dos Passos⟩

huge·ly *adv* [ME, fr. *huge, hoge* + *-ly*] **:** in a huge manner **:** EXTREMELY, IMMENSELY ⟨a ~ interesting account —Bernard De Voto⟩ ⟨~ successful work —Roger Shattuck⟩ ⟨children enjoyed themselves ~ in games —Rex Ingamells⟩ ⟨business gained ~ at the expense of government —Herbert Agar⟩

huge·ness *n* -ES [ME *hugenes*, fr. *huge, hoge* huge + *-nes* -ness] **:** the quality or state of being huge **:** IMMENSITY

huge·ous \-jəs\ *adj* [¹*huge* + *-ous*] **:** HUGE — **huge·ous·ly** *adv*

hug·ga·ble \'həgəbəl\ *adj* **:** of a kind that invites hugging **:** CUDDLESOME ⟨a ~ teddy bear⟩

hugged *past of* HUG

hug·ger \'həgə(r)\ *n* -s **:** one that hugs

¹hugger-mugger \'həgə(r),məgə(r), ·=·=·=\ *n* [origin unknown] **1 :** the act or practice of concealment **:** SECRECY ⟨had always had the impression that sex was sin . . . here it was treated without any *hugger-mugger* or snickering —A.W.Long⟩ **2 :** a disorderly jumble **:** CONFUSION, MUMBO JUMBO ⟨engage in the *hugger-mugger* of international politics and moneymaking —H.R.Isaacs⟩ ⟨apart from the effect of all this unwholesome *hugger-mugger* on their minds, there was the greater tragedy that they were being shortchanged educationally —Victor Boesen⟩

²hugger-mugger \"\ *adv* **:** in secrecy or confusion

³hugger-mugger \"\ *adj* **1 :** of a clandestine nature **:** SECRET ⟨an eventual *hugger-mugger* hanging —P.H.Newby⟩ **2 :** of a confused or disorderly nature **:** JUMBLED ⟨readers will be puzzled by what at first appears a completely *hugger-mugger* haphazard arrangement —Ralph Abercrombie⟩

⁴hugger-mugger \"\ *vb* **hugger-muggered; hugger-muggered; hugger-muggering** \-g(ə)riŋ\ **hugger-muggers** *vt* **:** to keep secret **:** hush up ~ *vi* **1 :** to act or confer stealthily **2 :** to muddle around

hugger-muggery \-g(ə)rē, -ri\ *n* -ES **:** HUGGER-MUGGER 1

hugging *adj* **:** tending to hug **:** CLINGING — **hug·ging·ly** *adv*

hug·gle \'həgəl, 'hüg-\ *vt* **huggled; huggled; huggling** \-g(ə)liŋ\ **huggles** [freq. of ¹*hug*] *dial Eng* **:** HUG, CUDDLE

hug-me-tight \'=·=,=\ *n* -s **1 :** a woman's short close-fitting bed jacket or undergarment usu. knitted of wool and sleeveless **2 :** a woman's short wraparound jacket

hug-me-tight 1

hu·go·esque \¦(h)yü(,)gō¦esk\ *adj, usu cap* [Victor *Hugo* †1885 Fr. writer + E *-esque*] **:** of, relating to, or characteristic of Victor Hugo or his works

hu·go·nis \(h)yü'gōnəs\ *n* -ES [NL (specif. epithet of *Rosa hugonis*), after Father *Hugo* — more at FATHER HUGO'S ROSE] **:** FATHER HUGO'S ROSE

hugo rose *n, usu cap H* [after Father *Hugo*] **:** FATHER HUGO'S ROSE

hugs *pres 3d sing of* HUG, *pl of* HUG

hu·gue·not \'hyügə,nät *sometimes* -nōt, + V *usu* -äd· *or* -ōd·; *sometimes* -nō\ *n, pl* **huguenots** \-äts, -ōts, -ō(z)\ *usu cap* [MF, fr. (Geneva dial.) *huguenot* Genevan partisan of an alliance with Fribourg and Bern as a means of preventing annexation by Savoy, alter. (after Besançon *Hugues* †1532 leader of the movement in Geneva to prevent annexation by Savoy) of *eidgnot*, fr. G (Swiss dial.) *eidgnoss* confederate, fr. MHG *eitgenōz*, fr *eit* oath (fr. OHG *eid*) + *genōz* comrade, fr. OHG *ginōz*; akin to OHG *niozzan* to use, enjoy — more at OATH, NEAT] **:** a French Protestant in the 16th and 17th centuries **:** a member of the Reformed or Calvinistic communion — **hu·gue·not·ic** \¦==¦näd·ik, -nōd·, ¦ēk\ *adj, usu cap*

hu·gue·not·ism \'==,nät,izəm, -,nōd, l,tiz-, -,nō,iz-\ *n* -s *usu cap* **:** the doctrines and practices of the French Huguenots

huh *typically a snort or a strong h-sound followed by an m-sound or by the vowel* 'ə *usu nasalized, the last part varying in intonation; often read as* 'hə\ *interj* [origin unknown] — used typically to express surprise, disbelief, or disgust

hüh·ner·ko·bel·ite \¦h(y)ünə(r)¦kōbə,līt\ *n* -s [*Hühnerkobel*, region in Bavaria, Germany, its locality + E *-ite*] **:** a mineral $(Na,Ca)(Fe,Mn)_2(PO_4)_2$ consisting of phosphate of sodium, calcium, iron, and manganese and being isomorphous with varulite

huh·ner test \'h(y)ünə(r)-\ *n, usu cap H* [after Max *Huhner* †1947 Am. surgeon] **:** a test used in sterility studies that involves postcoital examination of aspirated vaginal and intracervical fluid to determine the presence or survival of spermatozoa in these areas

hu·hu \'hü(,)hü\ *n* -s [Maori] **:** a large creamy white roundheaded grub that is the larva of a yellowish brown New Zealand beetle (*Prionoplus reticularis*), bores in dead trees and timber, and was formerly much used as food by the Maori

hui \'hü(,)ē\ *n* -s [Hawaiian] **1** *Hawaii* **a :** PARTNERSHIP, SYNDICATE ⟨efforts by mainland capital to gain control of

Hawaiian Airlines are believed to have been thwarted by a local ~ that has secretly bought close to 70,000 shares —*Honolulu Advertiser*⟩ **b :** CLUB, ASSOCIATION ⟨the ~ is an organization of civic-minded . . . women who cooperate in furthering the interests of the Y.W.C.A. —*Honolulu Star-Bull.*⟩ **2** [Hawaiian & Maori] **:** community gathering **:** ASSEMBLY ⟨when the ~ broke up at 4 p.m. the issue was still in doubt —*New Zealand Jour. of Agric.*⟩

hu·ia \ˈhüyə\ *also* **huia bird** *n* -s [Maori *huia*] **:** a bird (*Neomorpha acutirostris* or *Heteralocha acutirostris*) related to the starlings, confined to a small region in the mountains of New Zealand, and having black white-tipped tail feathers prized by Maori chiefs and worn as insignia of rank

hui·chol \wēˈchōl\ *n, pl* **huichol** \"\ *or* **huicho·les** \-ōlēz, -ō(ˌ)lās\ *usu cap* [Sp, of AmerInd origin] **1 a :** a Nahuatlan people of the mountains between Zacatecas and Nayarit, Mexico **b :** a member of such people **2 :** the language of the Huichol people

huid \ˈhēd, -ˈēe-\ *Scot var of* HOOD

huil \ˈhēl, -ˈēe-\ *Scot var of* HULL

hui·lie \ˈhēli\ *var of* HOOLY

hui·pil \wēˈpēl\ *n, pl* **huipils** \-lz\ *or* **huipi·les** \-(ˌ)lās\ [MexSp, fr. Nahuatl *huipilli*] **:** a straight slipover one-piece garment that is made by folding a rectangle of material end to end, sewing up the straight sides but leaving openings near the folded top for the arms, and cutting a slit or a square in the center of the fold to furnish an opening for the head, is often decorated with embroidery, and is worn as a blouse or dress by women chiefly in Mexico and Central America

hui·pi·lla \wēˈpē(y)ə\ *n* -s [MexSp] **:** PINGUIN

hui·sa·che \wēˈsächē\ *n* -s [MexSp, fr. Nahuatl *huixachi*, fr. *huitztli* thorn + *izachi* abundant] **:** a thorny shrub or small tree (*Acacia farnesiana*) found abundantly in the southern U.S. and throughout tropical regions and having fragrant yellow flowers used in making perfumery — called also CASSIE

huis·co·yol \ˌ¦wēskə¦yōl\ *n* -s [MexSp, fr. Nahuatl *huitzcoyolli*, fr. *huitztli* thorn + *coyolli, coyulli*, a nut-bearing palm] **:** a shrubby Central American palm (*Bactris subglobosa*) that forms impenetrable thickets

huis·quil \ˈwē,skēl\ *or* **guis·quil** \ˈgw-\ *n* -s [AmerSp *huisquil, güisquil*] **:** CHAYOTE

hui·tain \wēˈtān, *F* wʸētaⁿ\ *n, pl* **huitains** \-ānz, -aⁿ(z)\ [MF, fr. *huit* eight (fr. L *octo*) + *-ain*, fr. L *-anus* -an — more at EIGHT] **1 :** OCTASTICH **2 :** OCTAVE 2b

hukama *pl of* HAKIM

huke \ˈhyük\ *n* -s [ME *huyke, huke*, fr. MD *huik*] **1 :** a medieval hooded cloak worn orig. by women but later by both sexes **2 :** a late medieval close-fitting gown for either sex

hu·ki·lau \ˌhükēˌlau\ *n* -s [Hawaiian, fr. *huki* pull + *lau* net] *Hawaii* **:** a seine-fishing party often involving large numbers of people and much revelry

¹hu·la \ˈhülə\ *also* **hula-hula** \ˌ≈≈¦≈≈\ *n* -s [Hawaiian] **1 :** a sinuous mimetic Polynesian dance of conventional form and topical adaptation performed by men and women singly or together and usu. accompanied by chants and rhythmic drumming ⟨the ~ was in essence a magical ritual designed to bring rain and cause fertility —E.S.C.Handy⟩ ⟨a lovely brown maiden performed a ~ in the aisle of the cabin to entertain the passengers —Horace Sutton⟩ **2 :** the music to which a hula is performed ⟨snatches of ~s being sung —Armine von Tempski⟩

²hula \"\ *vi* -ED/-ING/-S **:** to dance a hula

³hula \"\ *n, pl* **hula** *or* **hulas** *usu cap* **1 a :** a people of the Territory of Papua **b :** a member of such people **2 :** the Austronesian language of the Hula people

Hula–Hoop *trademark* — used for a hoop made usu. of plastic or rubber for twirling about the body by movements like those of the hula

hula–hoop \ˈ≈≈,≈\ *vi* [*Hula-Hoop*] **:** to twirl a Hula-Hoop hoop about one's body

hula skirt *n* **:** a grass skirt worn by a hula dancer or an imitation of such a skirt ⟨a young girl, wearing a *hula skirt* of cellophane, came to the car and took their order —Speed Lamkin⟩

hula skirt

hulch *adj* [origin unknown] *obs* **:** HUMPED ⟨a man with a ~ back —Charles Cotton⟩

hule *var of* ULE

hul gul *var of* HULL-GULL

¹hulk \ˈhəlk\ *n* -s [ME *hulke*, fr. OE *hulc*, fr. ML *holcas, hulca*, fr. Gk *holkas* barge, trading vessel, fr. *helkein* to pull, drag, tow — more at SULCUS] **1 :** SHIP; *specif* **:** a heavy ship of clumsy build ⟨the colossal ~ was the Great Eastern, the forerunner of today's ocean liners —James Dugan⟩ **2 :** one that is bulky or unwieldy ⟨faced by a ~ of a man, well over six feet tall and professionally broad-shouldered —William Phillips b. 1878⟩ ⟨towering ~s of two vast apartment houses —Lewis Mumford⟩ ⟨the black ~s of the mountains across the bay —H.T.DeSa⟩ **3** *obs* **:** HULL ⟨her ~ painted over with sparkling vermilion —James Hayward⟩ **4 a :** the body of an old wrecked or dismantled ship unfit for sea service ⟨for a clubhouse the boys used an abandoned ~ they found on the waterfront⟩ **b :** an abandoned wreck or shell ⟨the ~s of British tanks rusting in the fields —J.A.Phillips⟩ ⟨once-glittering halls were left empty ~s —*Foreign Affairs*⟩ ⟨the moribund ~ of the Spanish Empire —J.H.Plumb⟩ **c :** a ship used as a prison ⟨a celebrated lock picker . . . serving time in a prison ~ —Rufus Jarman⟩ — usu. used in pl. ⟨every prisoner sent to the ~s —Kenneth Roberts⟩

²hulk \"\ *vb* -ED/-ING/-S *vi* **1** *dial Eng* **:** to move lazily or ponderously ⟨~s up from his chair by the hearth —Emmett Gowen⟩ **2 :** to appear impressively large or massive **:** BULK, LOOM ⟨the smoking port and Vesuvius ~*ing* beyond —William Sansom⟩ ⟨and it ~*ed* there against the sky —Hugh Fosburgh⟩ ~ *vt* **:** to condemn to or lodge in a hulk

³hulk \"\ *vt* -ED/-ING/-S [alter. of *holk* to hollow out — more at HOWK] *dial* **:** DISEMBOWEL

hulking *adj* [¹*hulk* + *-ing*] **:** of great size or powerful build **:** HUSKY, MASSIVE ⟨a big ~ figure of a man with thick shoulders and no neck worth mentioning —Claudia Cassidy⟩ ⟨three ~ battleships —Norris Houghton⟩

hulky \ˈhəlkē, -ki\ *adj* -ER/-EST [¹*hulk* + *-y*] **:** HULKING

¹hull \ˈhəl\ *n* -s [ME *hul, hull, hole*, fr. OE *hulu*; akin to OHG *helawa* oat chaff, *hala* hull, OE *helan* to conceal — more at HELL] **1 a :** the outer covering of a fruit or seed (as the husk of a grain or nut or the pod of the pea) **b :** the persistent calyx or involucre that subtends some fruits (as the strawberry) **2** *dial Eng* **:** HUT, HOVEL, SHED **3 a** (1) **:** the frame or body of a ship exclusive of masts, yards, sails, and rigging — see SHIP illustration (2) *obs* **:** HULK 4a **b** (1) **:** the portion of a flying boat which furnishes buoyancy when in contact with the water and to which the main supporting surfaces and other parts are attached (2) **:** the main structure of a rigid airship consisting of a covered elongated framework which encloses the gasbags and supports the cars and equipment **c :** the armored body of a vehicle ⟨casting . . . huge steel tank ~s in a single piece —G.H.Johnston⟩ ⟨the ~ of an armored car is . . . of lighter-weight plate —*Principles of Automotive Vehicles*⟩ **4 :** COVERING, CASING: as **a :** the shell of a crustacean ⟨shrimp ~s and heads are used as fertilizer⟩ **b :** a film of water encasing a soil particle **c** (1) **:** an empty ammunition shell case ⟨hot, spent cartridge ~s would be showering all over —Thomas Anderson⟩ (2) **:** CARTRIDGE ⟨won the national crown for the second time with a variety of . . . .22 ~s —Charles Askins b.1907⟩

²hull \"\ *vb* -ED/-ING/-S [ME *holen, hullen*, fr. *hole, hul, hull*, n.] *vt* **1 a :** to remove the husks or shells of **:** SHUCK ⟨~ ears of corn⟩ ⟨~ peas⟩ ⟨~ pecans⟩ ⟨~ oysters⟩ **b :** to remove the outer skin of **:** DECORTICATE ⟨~ kernels of corn⟩ ⟨~ coffee beans⟩ ⟨~ barley⟩ **c :** to remove the calyx of ⟨~ strawberries⟩ **2 :** to pierce or strike the hull of (as a ship) ~ *vi* **1 :** to float or drift with sails furled **:** lie ahull **2** *archaic* **:** IDLE ⟨I am to ~ here a little longer —Shak.⟩

³hull \"\ *adj, usu cap* [fr. *Hull*, England] **:** of or from the county borough of Hull, or Kingston upon Hull, England **:** of the kind or style prevalent in Hull

¹hul·la·ba·loo *also* **hul·la·bal·loo** \ˈhələbə,lü, ˌ≈≈≈¦≈ *sometimes* -lēb- *or* -lib-\ *or* **hel·la·bal·loo** \ˈhel-, ˌhel-\ *n* -s [perh. irreg. fr. *hallo* + Sc *baloo*, interj. used to hush children] **1 :** a babel of noise and confusion **:** HUBBUB ⟨didn't whisper because there was such a ~ down in the cut that nobody could hear him anyhow —J.B.Benefield⟩ **2 :** an excited clamor or controversy **:** UPROAR ⟨this attempt was accompanied by a big propaganda ~ —*Cavalry Jour.*⟩ ⟨a terrific ~ at the Met this season over the merits of these rival supersopranos —Winthrop Sargeant⟩ **syn** see DIN

²hullabaloo \"\ *vb* -ED/-ING/-S *vi* **:** to make a hullabaloo ~ *vt* **:** BALLYHOO 2

hull down *adv* (*or adj*) **1** *of a ship* **a :** at such a distance that only the superstructure is visible ⟨had cleared with a leading wind . . . and was *hull down* long before dark —Raymond McFarland⟩ **b :** with main deck awash ⟨one ship . . . after another went *hull down* into the sucking tide —D.C.Peattie⟩ **2** *of a tank or other armored vehicle* **:** in a place of concealment but in position to observe the enemy and deliver fire ⟨were standing *hull down* behind a hillock and on each of their turrets was a figure staring forward through field glasses —Peter Rainier⟩

hulled barley *n* **:** barley in which the husks adhere to the kernel — called also *Scotch barley*

hulled corn *n* **:** whole grain corn from which the hulls have been removed by soaking or boiling in lye water — see HOMINY

hull·er \ˈhələ(r)\ *n* -s **:** one that hulls: as **a :** a machine that removes the hulls from grain, nuts, or castor beans **b :** a machine that threshes clover and separates the seeds from the hulls **c :** a small hand tool for removing hulls from strawberries

huller c

hul·let \ˈhələt, ˈhu̇l-\ *var of* HOWLET

hull–gull *or* **hul gul** \ˈhəl,gəl\ *n* [origin unknown] **:** a children's game in which one player guesses how many beans or other small objects are in another's handful and gives up or receives beans according as his guess is high, low, or exact

hull insurance *n* **:** insurance protecting the owners against loss caused by damage or destruction of waterborne craft or aircraft

hul·lion \ˈhəlyən\ *var of* HALLION

hull–less *or* **hul·less** \ˈhəlləs\ *adj* **1 :** having no hull **2 a** *of barley* **:** having the kernels free within the husk **b** *of popcorn* **:** having short thick ears and pointed kernels with a white tender seed coat

hul·lo \(ˌ)həˈlō, ˈhə(ˌ)lō, ˈhəˈlō\ *chiefly Brit var of* HELLO

hullock *n* -s [origin unknown] *obs* **:** a small piece of sail kept standing to hold a ship's head to the wind in a storm

hul·loo \(ˌ)həˈlü, ˈhə(ˌ)lü, ˈhəˈlü\ *var of* HALLO

hu·lock \ˈhü-\ *also* **hulock gibbon** *or* **hulock monkey** *n* -s [*hulock* fr. native name in Assam or Burma] **:** HOOLOCK

hul·site \ˈhəl(t),sīt\ *n* -s [Alfred *Hulse* Brooks †1924 Am. scientist + E *-ite*] **:** a mineral $(Fe,Ca,Mg)_4(Fe,Sn)_2B_2O_{10}$(?) consisting of a hydrous iron calcium magnesium tin borate

hul·ver \ˈhəlvə(r)\ *n* -s [ME *hulver, holver*, fr. ON *hulfr* — more at HOLLY] *dial Eng* **:** HOLLY

¹hum \ˈhəm\ *vb* **hummed; hummed; humming; hums** [ME *hummen*; akin to MHG *hummen* to hum, D *hommelen* to hum, *hommel* bumblebee, OHG *humbal*] *vi* **1 a :** to utter a sound like or suggestive of that of the speech sound \m\ prolonged **:** continue voicing a nasal on one pitch or on varying pitches ⟨~ in time to the music⟩; *esp* **:** to utter such a sound to express dissent, approval, surprise, or embarrassment ⟨*hummed* and hawed and finally blurted out his views⟩ **b :** to make the natural noise of an insect (as a bumblebee) in motion ⟨a bee *hummed* by —Zane Grey⟩ ⟨mosquitoes *humming* —R.A.W. Hughes⟩ **c :** to make a low prolonged sound like that of an insect **:** DRONE, BUZZ ⟨the top ~s⟩ ⟨the snoring of his grandfather *hummed* like the coming of wasps —Elizabeth Enright⟩ ⟨a kettle was *humming* on a small gas stove —Ellen Glasgow⟩ ⟨electric power lines ~ —*Lamp*⟩ **d :** to give forth a low murmuring indistinct sound from the blending of many voices ⟨the sound of children's voices with which the house was always *humming* —J.M.Brinnin⟩ **e :** to produce a continuous blend of nonvocal sounds ⟨all night the printing plants *hummed* —Bill Davidson⟩ ⟨shrapnel and bullets *hummed* through the brush —Dave Richardson⟩ ⟨once, this place had *hummed* with noise: the ring of hammer upon anvil, the rasping of the saws that hewed the oak logs —Elizabeth Goudge⟩ **f :** to have an internal humming ⟨my head ~s⟩ **2 :** to be very active as if noisily ⟨steel and other industries are *humming* along at much higher rates of operation —R.M.Blough⟩ ⟨the business started to ~ —Isabelle M. Hoover⟩ ⟨to make the free world ~ with full productive activity —Max Ascoli⟩ ~ *vt* **1 :** to sing with the lips closed and without articulation ⟨~ a tune⟩ **2 :** to affect by humming ⟨*hummed* me to sleep⟩ ⟨~ herself to rest⟩ **:** express by humming ⟨*hummed* his displeasure⟩

²hum \"\ *n* -s [ME, fr. *hummen*, v.] **:** the act of humming or the sound made by humming ⟨a ~ of approbation⟩: as **a :** a low monotonous noise (as of bees in flight or a whirling wheel) **:** DRONE, BUZZ **b :** the confused noise (as of a crowd or machinery) heard at a distance ⟨the ~ of industry⟩ ⟨the high-pitched ~ of swift power belts —*Amer. Guide Series: Ark.*⟩ **c :** the humming of a melody; *also* **:** MELODY **d :** an undesired audio signal in the output of a piece of electronic equipment usu. of low frequency resulting from direct pickup of a power signal or the residual power signal in a power supply

³hum \"\ *n* -s [imit.] **:** an inarticulate nasal sound or murmur (as from embarrassment or hesitation) ⟨after some evasive ~s he gave his answer⟩ — often used interjectionally to express hesitation or doubt, dissent, deliberation, or embarrassment; compare ⁴HEM

⁴hum \"\ *n* -s [short for ¹*humbug*] **:** HUMBUG

⁵hum \"\ *vt* **hummed; hummed; humming; hums** [short for ²*humbug*] **:** HUMBUG

⁶hum \ˈhüm\ *n* -s [Serbo-Croatian, hill] **:** an isolated residual hill or mass of limestone (as in a region of karst topography)

hum *abbr* **1** [NL *humaniora*] the humanities **2** humor; humorous

hu·ma \ˈhümə\ *usu cap, var of* HIMA

¹hu·man \ˈhyümən *also* ˈyü-\ *adj, sometimes* -ER/-EST [ME *humayne, humain*, fr. MF *humain*, fr. L *humanus*, fr. *hum-* (akin to L *homo* man, human being) + *-anus* -an — more at HOMAGE] **1 a :** of or relating to man **:** characteristic of man ⟨~ voices⟩ ⟨vulnerability of the ~ body⟩ **b :** primarily or usu. harbored by, affecting, or attacking man ⟨~ appendicitis⟩ ⟨the common ~ flea⟩ **2 a :** being a man **:** consisting of men ⟨contrived for the destruction of the ~ species —Tobias Smollett⟩ ⟨the ~ race⟩ ⟨some special quality in the ~ beings who have made this particular transition —A.J.Toynbee⟩ **b :** of or relating to the social life or collective relations of mankind ⟨~ progress⟩ ⟨~ history and evolution⟩ ⟨in the course of ~ events —*U.S. Declaration of Independence*⟩ **3 :** characteristic of or relating to man in his essential nature: as **a :** of, relating to, or resembling man or his attributes in distinction from the lower animals ⟨to be ~ is to understand, to evaluate, to choose, to accept responsibility —Lewis Mumford⟩ ⟨the gregarious impulses of ~ beings —J.B.Conant⟩ **b :** of or relating to man as distinguished from the superhuman, from the divine, or from nature **:** belonging to finite intelligence and powers ⟨to err is ~; to forgive, divine —Alexander Pope⟩ ⟨there are no absolutes and man must content himself with being ~ —H.E.Clurman⟩ **c :** susceptible to, representative of, or exemplifying the range of feelings, strengths, or weaknesses of which man is capable ⟨a very ~ world, filled with joy and sorrow, innocence and evil⟩ ⟨for all his stiff outward bearing, he is very ~⟩ ⟨the story of the ascent is a great ~ document⟩ ⟨far too ~ a creature to care much for art —Max Beerbohm⟩ **d :** having to do with, portraying, or arising from the small or large joys, sorrows, passions, struggles, or other interest-provoking experiences or situations of individual persons ⟨~ comedy⟩ ⟨full of the milk of ~ kindness —Shak.⟩ ⟨those *human*-interest yarns —Erle Stanley Gardner⟩ ⟨no business like book retailing for ~ interest —Allan McMahan⟩ ⟨a careful history of the ~ side of the whole case —M.R.Cohen⟩ ⟨nearly all these books contain the same ~ stories about the Queen —*N.Y. Times Book Rev.*⟩ **4 :** symbolized in a representation of the zodiac or in a configuration of the stars by a man (as Aquarius), woman (as Virgo), or child (as Gemini) **5 :** HUMANE ⟨balance her sharp tongue and uncertain moods against her warmly ~ disposition —Havelock Ellis⟩ **6 :** having some of the characteristics of a living person **:** like a human ⟨the nearest of blood to me a d the ~*est* was not a person nor a villager —H.D.Thoreau⟩ ⟨the woods began to open up, and the country looked more ~ —Willa Cather⟩ ⟨the statue is more ~ than the beings at his feet —Clifton Fadiman⟩ ⟨the humbler aspects of our cities are more ~ than the skyscrapers —Walter Pach⟩ **7 :** consisting of members of the family Hominidae **:** HOMINID ⟨the several fossil ~ genera⟩ **8 :** unpredictably fallible or erratic **:** not behaving by known law **:** ENIGMATIC ⟨must always consider the ~ element⟩ ⟨Americans like other human beings are bewilderingly ~ —Max Lerner⟩ ⟨such an inconsistency is very ~ —P.E.More⟩

²human \"\ *n* -s **:** a human being ⟨sprung of ~s that inhabit earth —George Chapman⟩ ⟨incomprehensible to us ~s —William James⟩ ⟨no ~ since Adam —G.W.Cable⟩ ⟨the least developed of all ancestral ~s —A.L.Kroeber⟩ ⟨what has been found true about rats may be applied to ~s —E.E.Slosson⟩ ⟨like most of us lazy and indecisive ~s —T.H.Fielding⟩ ⟨as completely scientific and objective an approach as a ~ is capable of —R.A.Hall b. 1911⟩ ⟨two thousand million ~s —G.H.T.Kimble⟩

human botfly *n* **:** a large fly (*Dermatobia hominis*) of the family Cuterebridae that has brown wings and bluish body, is widely distributed in tropical America, and undergoes its larval development subcutaneously in man and other mammals

hu·mane \(ˈ)hyüˈmān *also* (ˈ)yü-\ *adj, sometimes* -ER/-EST [ME *humayne, humain* — more at HUMAN] **1** *obs* **:** HUMAN **2 :** marked by compassion, sympathy, or consideration for other human beings or animals ⟨a ~ warden⟩ ⟨~ treatment⟩ ⟨a ~ attitude⟩ **3 :** characterized by or tending to broad humanistic culture **:** HUMANISTIC ⟨~ studies⟩

human ecology *n* **:** a branch of sociology that studies the relationship between a human community and its environment; *specif* **:** the study of the spatial and temporal interrelationships between men and their economic, social, and political organization

hu·mane·ly *adv* **:** in a humane manner

hu·mane·ness \-ānnəs\ *n* -ES **:** the quality or state of being humane

human engineering *n* **1 :** management of human beings and affairs esp. in industry with a view to achieving satisfactory adjustment esp. in terms of maximum work efficiency and job satisfaction **2 :** a science drawing upon various other sciences (as physiology, anatomy, physical anthropology, applied psychology) that deals with the design and positioning of machines, instruments, and controls (as in flying) so that they may be used with maximum efficiency by human beings

human equation *n* **:** the factor of human strength or weakness that needs to be considered in predicting the outcome of any social, political, economic, or mechanical process operated by human agency

humaner *comparative of* HUMAN *or of* HUMANE

humane society *n, often cap H&S* **1** *chiefly Brit* **:** a lifesaving society **2 :** a society concerned with the promotion of humane conduct or ideals or having charitable or philanthropic ends ⟨the *Humane Society* is a child-caring agency —A.E.Fink⟩; *specif* **:** a society for the prevention of cruelty to animals

humanest *superlative of* HUMAN *or of* HUMANE

human geography *n* **:** ANTHROPOGEOGRAPHY

hu·man·ics \hyüˈmaniks *also* yü-\ *n pl but sing in constr* **:** a subject that treats of human nature or human affairs

hu·man·i·o·ra \(ˌ)(h)yü,manēˈōrə\ *n pl* [NL *humaniora* (*studia*), lit., more humane studies] **:** humanistic studies **:** HUMANITIES ⟨on the borderland between science and the ~ —*Chronica Botanica*⟩

hu·man·ism \ˈ(h)yümə,nizəm\ *n* -s [¹*human* + *-ism*; in some senses prob. fr. F *humanisme* or G *humanismus*] **1 a :** devotion to the humanities **:** literary culture **b** *often cap* **:** the learning or cultural impulse that is characterized by a revival of classical letters, an individualistic and critical spirit, and a shift of emphasis from religious to secular concerns and that flowered during the Renaissance **2 :** devotion to human welfare **:** interest in or concern for man **:** HUMANITY, HUMANITARIANISM ⟨born in a city tenement, he early acquired the kind of ~ that is humanitarian —Donald Davidson⟩ ⟨wrote that medicine was a social science and urged doctors to participate in the battles of ~ —B.J.Stern⟩ **3 :** a doctrine, set of attitudes, or way of life centered upon human interests or values: as **a :** a philosophy that rejects supernaturalism, regards man as a natural object, and asserts the essential dignity and worth of man and his capacity to achieve self-realization through the use of reason and scientific method — called also *naturalistic humanism, scientific humanism*; compare INSTRUMENTALISM, PRAGMATISM **b** *often cap* **:** a religion subscribing to these beliefs **:** RELIGIOUS HUMANISM **c :** a philosophy advocating the self-fulfillment of man within the framework of Christian principles — called also *Christian humanism*; see INTEGRAL HUMANISM **4 :** NEW HUMANISM

¹hu·man·ist \-nəst\ *n* -s [prob. fr. MF *humaniste*, fr. L *humanus* + MF *-iste* -ist] **1 a :** a person who pursues the study of the humanities ⟨accused by ~s of having an exclusive interest in social sciences —*Publ's Mod. Lang. Assoc. of Amer.*⟩ ⟨called for a greater understanding betweed scientists and ~s —*Science*⟩ **b :** an adherent or practitioner of Renaissance humanism; *specif* **:** a Renaissance scholar devoting himself to the study of classical letters **2 :** a person who is devoted to human welfare **:** one who is marked by a strong interest in or concern for man **:** HUMANITARIAN ⟨a ~, a lover of all sorts of people —*Yale Rev.*⟩ ⟨a ~, who felt deeply about inequality . . . wherever he saw it —Max Lerner⟩ **3 a** *often cap* **:** a person who subscribes to the doctrines of scientific humanism; *specif* **:** a member of a religious society or cult subscribing to such doctrines **b :** a person who subscribes to a form of philosophical humanism **c :** NEW HUMANIST

²humanist \"\ *or* **hu·man·is·tic** \ˌ≈≈¦nistik, -tēk\ *adj* **1 a :** of or relating to Renaissance humanism or humanists ⟨the *humanistic* revival of learning⟩ **b :** of, relating to, or concerned with the humanities **:** CULTURAL ⟨the fact that *humanistic* subjects . . . have a part in the development of the students —*Science*⟩ ⟨Greek . . . the most exacting *humanist* study —Robert Birley⟩ **2 :** of or relating to philosophical or religious humanism in any of its forms ⟨what we need is a *humanistic* religion . . . man-centered and comfortable —R.C. Hartnett⟩ ⟨supernaturalist and *humanist* strategies of motivation —K.D.Burke⟩ ⟨the *humanist* belief in continuous emergent evolution —Wendell Thomas⟩ **3 :** marked by or expressive of devotion to human welfare or strong interest in or concern for man **:** HUMANITARIAN ⟨the liberal approach has been a *humanist* approach —M.W.Straight⟩ ⟨incorporate the socialist idealism of Russia with the *humanist* individualism of America —Cyril Connolly⟩ ⟨respect and *humanistic* regard for all other members of our species —Weston La Barre⟩

hu·man·is·ti·cal·ly \ˌ≈≈¦nistək(ə)lē, -tēk-, -li\ *adv* **:** in a humanistic manner

¹hu·man·i·tar·i·an \(ˌ)hyü,manəˈterēən, (ˌ)yü-, -taar-,-tär-\ *n* -s [*humanity* + *-arian*] **:** a person actively concerned in promoting human welfare and esp. social reform **:** PHILANTHROPIST

²humanitarian \(ˌ)≈¦≈≈¦≈≈\ *adj* **:** of, relating to, or characteristic of humanitarians or humanitarianism **:** zealously concerned for or active in the promotion of human welfare and esp. of social reform **:** PHILANTHROPIC, HUMANE ⟨to use the A-bomb was wrong on ~ grounds —E.M.Zacharias⟩ ⟨a refreshing example of . . . ~ zeal —Benjamin Farrington⟩ ⟨a hard, stern race . . . little responsive to ~ appeal —V.L. Parrington⟩

hu·man·i·tar·i·an·ism \-ēə,nizəm\ *n* -s **:** concern for human welfare esp. as expressed through philanthropic activities and interest in social reforms **:** the practice or display of humanitarian principles ⟨extended their ~ to include the Indian tribes —H.M.Hyman⟩

hu·man·i·ty \hyüˈmanəd·ē, -ətē, -i *also* yü-\ *n* -ES [ME *humanite*, fr. MF *humanité*, fr. L *humanitat-, humanitas*, fr. *humanus* human, humane + *-itat-, -itas* -ity — more at HUMAN] **1 :** the quality or state of being humane **:** kind or generous behavior or disposition **:** COMPASSION, BENEVOLENCE ⟨which she had intended to do with beautiful mercy, a lovely ~ —Elizabeth Taylor⟩ ⟨bespeaking ~ for the enemy in the midst of a bloody struggle —C.G.Bowers⟩ **2 a :** the totality of attributes which distinguish man from other beings **:** the condition of being human : essential human quality or character ⟨very ape-looking, but with many marks of an incipient ~ —J.S.Weiner⟩ ⟨man's ~ consists of his . . . labor power —Hannah Arendt⟩ ⟨seem coldly to deny him a common ~ —Philip Woodruff⟩ ⟨committed to a belief in the ~ of all men and women —Brendan Sexton⟩ **b humanities** *pl* (1) : human attributes or qualities ⟨his work has the ripeness of the 18th century, and its rough *humanities* —Pamela H. Johnson⟩ (2) : things pleasing to human tastes or sensibilities ⟨it has *humanities:* many mirrors, for example, which augment the numbers of the guests —Philip Wylie⟩ **3** [ML *humanitas,* fr. L] **a** *archaic* : the study of classical language and literature **b** *in Scottish universities* : Latin language and literature **c humanities** *pl* : the branches of learning regarded as having primarily a cultural character and usu. including languages, literature, history, mathematics, and philosophy **4 a** : the totality of human beings : the human race : MANKIND ⟨a fierce compassion for the woes of ~ —Maurice Bowra⟩ **b** : PEOPLE, MEN ⟨the packed mass of ~ below would swing . . . with the movement of the ship —C.S.Forester⟩

hu·man·ization \\ˌhyümənə̇ˈzāshən, -ˌnīˈz- *also* ˌyü-\\ *n* -s : the act or process of humanizing : the fact or condition of being humanized ⟨an increasing ~ of the industrial process —E.M.Erikson⟩ ⟨the changes in the carved figures well illustrate the growing ~ of the divine and the saintly —G.C. Sellery⟩

hu·man·ize \\ˈ==ˌnīz\\ *vb* -ED/-ING/-S [F *humaniser,* fr. MF, fr. L *humanus* + MF *-iser* -ize] *vt* **1 a** : to give a human character or aspect to : treat or regard as human : represent in human form ⟨there is no worship here, . . . but nevertheless they ~ the crocodiles —W.W.Howells⟩ **b** : to adapt or make congenial to human nature, sensibilities, or use : make more sympathetic or responsive to human needs or desires ⟨dedicated himself . . . to the *humanizing* of business and finance —George Wolf⟩ **2** : to make humane : make gentle : SOFTEN, REFINE, CIVILIZE ⟨nations have feebly tried to ~ and regulate war —Vera M. Dean⟩ ⟨New England was appointed to guide the nation, to . . . ~ it —Van Wyck Brooks⟩ ~ *vi* **1** : to become humane **2** : to have or spread a civilizing influence ⟨it is the function of women to ~ —M.F.A.Montagu⟩

humankind \\ˈ==ˌ=\\ *n sing but sing or pl in constr* : the human race : MANKIND

humanlike \\ˈ==ˌ=\\ *adj* : like or resembling humans : like or resembling that of humans ⟨salmon . . . live a ~ existence —June Collins⟩ ⟨very ~ gods inhabit a . . . delightful heaven —Edith Hamilton⟩

hu·man·ly *adv* **1 a** : from the viewpoint of man : as concerns the human aspect ⟨lesser known but more ~ and historically interesting phase of his character —*Publ's Mod. Lang. Assoc. of Amer.*⟩ ⟨dramatic action that is at once ingenious, ~ illuminating, and true —Leslie Rees⟩ ⟨operate a successful organization both economically and ~ —*Current Biog.*⟩ **b** : within the range of human capacity ⟨policy that will insure, so far as it is ~ possible to do so, high employment —A.E.Stevenson b.1900⟩ **2** : in a human manner : after the manner of man ⟨what . . . children need most sorely is to be made ~ articulate —George Sampson⟩ ⟨men want more than merely to live . . . they want to live ~ —Ludwig Von Mises⟩

human nature *n* [ME *nature humayne,* fr. MF *nature humaine*] : the nature of man: **a** : the complex of behavioral patterns, attitudes, and ideas which man has acquired socially — called also *cultural nature* ⟨socially conditioned *human nature* . . . the qualities of the personality that make it like other personalities within the same society —A.L.Kroeber⟩ **b** : the complex of fundamental dispositions and traits of man sometimes considered innate ⟨belief that "you can't change *human nature*" —A.A.Van Duym⟩

hu·man·ness \\-mən(n)ə̇s\\ *n* -ES : the quality or state of being human ⟨we miss the humanity, or ~, that would inspire us to love or to hate his people —*New Yorker*⟩ ⟨the public image of you lacks warmth, and depth, and ~ —Stewart Alsop⟩

[1]**hu·man·oid** \\-məˌnȯid\\ *adj* [[1]*human* + *-oid*] : having human characters esp. as opposed to anthropoid

[2]**humanoid** \\"\\ *n* -s : a humanoid being ⟨the ~*s* and the anthropoids part company between a million and two million years ago —J.A.Thomson⟩

human relations *n pl but usu sing in constr* **1** : the social relations between human beings esp. when being investigated **2** : a study of the human problems arising from organizational and interpersonal relations in industry esp. with reference to the employer-employee relationship and the interaction between personal traits, group membership, and productive efficiency **3** : a course, study, or program designed to develop better interpersonal and intergroup adjustments

humans *pl of* HUMAN

hu·mate \\ˈhyüˌmāt\\ *n* -s [*humic* + *-ate*] : a salt or ester of a humic acid

humbird \\ˈ=ˌ=\\ *n* : HUMMINGBIRD

[1]**hum·ble** \\ˈhəmbəl *also* ˈəm-\\ *adj* -ER/-EST [ME *umble, humble,* fr. OF, fr. L *humilis* low, slight, humble, fr. *humus* earth, ground + *-ilis* -ile; akin to Gk *chthōn* earth, *chamai* on the ground, Skt *kṣam* earth, ground] **1 a** : having a low opinion of one's own importance or merits : modest or meek in spirit, manner, or appearance : not proud or haughty ⟨essentially ~ . . . and self-effacing, he achieved the highest formal honors and distinctions —B.K.Malinowski⟩ ⟨to them even the president was ~ —Sinclair Lewis⟩ ⟨a spot where a man feels his own insignificance and may well learn to be ~ —Samuel Butler †1902⟩ **b** : reflecting, expressing, or offered in a humble spirit ⟨my *humblest* apologies for the long wait —T.B. Costain⟩ ⟨beg to submit my ~ notion —Vicki Baum⟩ ⟨hear my ~ cry —Fanny J. Crosby⟩ ⟨loathed his cringing look and ~ smile⟩ **2 a** : ranking low in the social or political scale ⟨a man of ~ origin⟩ ⟨all civil servants, no matter how ~, should be disenfranchised —J.H.Plumb⟩ ⟨a ~ fisherman⟩ **b** : ranking low in some hierarchy or scale : INSIGNIFICANT ⟨in the study of the life of animals, however ~, we are studying . . . our own complex human life —W.E.Swinton⟩ ⟨the ~ weeds of the field⟩ ⟨the giant stellar family of which our sun is a ~ member —George Gamow⟩ **c** : of inferior value or worth : not costly or luxurious : MEAN, BASE, UNPRETENTIOUS ⟨chief clerks have mahogany desks; to the others is relegated the *humbler* walnut —H.J.Laski⟩ ⟨artisans . . . who work by hand with gold, silver, and the *humbler* metals —*New Yorker*⟩ ⟨the ~ fare of any Mexican peon —Green Peyton⟩ : of modest dimensions or proportions ⟨freighters using the same slips as the ~ powerboats of small fishermen —*Amer. Guide Series: Mass.*⟩ ⟨equally ~ were the beginnings of . . . the important State Department of Agriculture —*Amer. Guide Series: N.Y.*⟩ **syn** MEEK, MODEST, LOWLY: HUMBLE suggests absence of vanity and pride, feeling of weakness or lack of worth, self-depreciation, or an abject attitude and demeanor ⟨love hath made her *humble,* and her race doth she forget, and her noble and mighty heart —William Morris⟩ ⟨she prays there as the light goes out, prays with an *humble* heart, and walks home shrinking and silent —W.M.Thackeray⟩ ⟨the cook drew himself up in a smugly *humble* fashion, a deprecating smirk on his face —Jack London⟩ MEEK may suggest patient, subdued, retiring mildness and gentleness, sometimes even a spiritless, cowed submissiveness ⟨the most modest, silent, sheep-faced and *meek* of little men —W.M.Thackeray⟩ ⟨her father, of course, was the lion of the party, but seeing that we were all *meek* and quite willing to be eaten, he roared to us rather than at us —Samuel Butler †1902⟩ MODEST may contrast with *brash* or *self-assertive*; without any implication of abjectness or submissiveness, it may imply unobtrusive lack of boastfulness or conceited or jealous demand for recognition ⟨a simple, *modest,* retiring man —F.D.Roosevelt⟩ ⟨the anthropologist is entirely proper and *modest* in refusing as an anthropologist to make judgments on other cultural beliefs with respect to their epistemological truth —Weston La Barre⟩ LOWLY, close to *humble,* may stress complete lack of worldly pretentiousness ⟨a monk of Lindisfarne, so simple and *lowly* in temper that he traveled on foot —J.R.Green⟩ ⟨you hold aloof from me because you are rich and lofty — and I poor and *lowly* —W.S. Gilbert⟩

[2]**humble** \\"\\ *vt* **humbled; humbled; humbling** \\-b(ə)liŋ\\ **humbles** [ME *humblen,* fr. *humble,* adj.] **1** : to make humble in spirit or manner : bring down the pride or arrogance of ⟨having *humbled* your heart . . . you may find him —Francis Yeats-Brown⟩ ⟨*humbled* himself before the rich and great⟩ **2** : to destroy the power, independence, or prestige of : defeat decisively : DEGRADE, ABASE ⟨the great marshal *humbled* his enemies in a swift, brilliantly conducted campaign⟩ ⟨it was now the turn of the Church to be *humbled*⟩

humble-bee \\ˈhəmbəlˌbē\\ *n* [ME *humbylbee,* fr. *humbyll-* (akin to MD *hommel* bumblebee) + bee — more at HUM, BEE] : BUMBLEBEE

hum·ble·ness *n* -ES [ME *humblenesse,* fr. *humble* + *-nesse* -ness] : the quality or state of being humble : HUMILITY

humble pie *n* [*humbles*] **1 a** : a meat pie formerly made of the inferior parts of a deer and served to the huntsman and other servants **b** : a meat pie made of the humbles of a hog **2** [influenced in meaning by [1]*humble*] : submission, apology, or retraction esp. made under pressure or in humiliating circumstances : HUMILIATION ⟨would it mean such a deal of *humble pie?* —Margery Sharp⟩ — often used in the phrase *eat humble pie* ⟨forced to eat *humble pie* —H.W.Van Loon⟩ ⟨before I'd go and eat *humble pie* to the sergeant . . . he might break my neck —Henry Lapham⟩

humble plant *n* : SENSITIVE PLANT 1

humbler *comparative of* HUMBLE

hum·bles \\ˈhəmbəlz\\ *n pl* [by folk etymology fr. *umbles*] : the heart, liver, kidneys, and other small pieces of a deer or of a hog — compare HUMBLE PIE 1

humblest *superlative of* HUMBLE

humbling *adj* : tending to humble : causing humbleness ⟨a ~ sense of our power —A.E.Stevenson b.1900⟩ — **hum·bling·ly** *adv*

hum·bly \\ˈhəmblē, -li *also* ˈəm-\\ *adv* [ME *umbly, humbly, humblely,* fr. *umble, humble* + *-ly*] : in a humble manner: as **a** : with humility : with a humble aspect or bearing ⟨must say ~ to the haughty dealers —Pearl Buck⟩ **b** : in a humble position or condition ⟨strategically, though ~ placed, he holds the job of official translator —Ralph de Toledano⟩

hum·boldt·ine \\ˈhəmˌbōlˌtēn, -ltᵊn\\ *n* -s [F *humboldtine,* fr. Baron Alexander von *Humboldt* †1859 Ger. naturalist and traveler + F *-ine*] : a mineral $FeC_2O_4.2H_2O$ consisting of ferrous oxalate

hum·boldt·ite \\-lˌtīt\\ *n* -s [in sense 1, fr. Alex. von *Humboldt* + E *-ite;* in sense 2, fr. G *humboldtit,* modif. of F *humboldtine*] **1** : DATOLITE **2** : HUMBOLDTINE

hum·boldt's lily \\ˈhəmˌbōlts-\\ *n, usu cap H* [after Alex. von *Humboldt*] : a Californian bulbous herb (*Lilium humboldtii*) with showy orange-red purple-spotted flowers

[1]**hum·bug** \\ˈhəmˌbəg\\ *n* -s [origin unknown] **1 a** : something designed to deceive and mislead : QUACKERY, HOAX, FRAUD, IMPOSTURE ⟨contrived so many delicious ~*s* to foist on the gullible public —R.L.Taylor⟩ **b** : a person who usu. willfully deceives or misleads others as to his true condition, qualities, or attitudes : one who passes himself off as something that he is not : SHAM, HYPOCRITE, IMPOSTOR ⟨denounced as ~*s* the playwrights who magnify the difficulties of their craft —*Times Lit. Supp.*⟩ ⟨he's no doctor; he's a ~⟩ **c** : an attitude or spirit of pretense and deception or self-deception ⟨in all his ~, in all his malice and hollowness —Mary Lindsay⟩ **d** : something empty of sense or meaning : DRIVEL, NONSENSE ⟨a frightful lot of ~ talked about glasses —L.B.Somerville-Large⟩ ⟨academic ~⟩ **2** *Brit* : a peppermint candy **syn** see IMPOSTURE

[2]**humbug** \\"\\ *vt* : impose on : DECEIVE, CAJOLE, HOAX ⟨*humbugged* me into buying his worthless stock⟩ ⟨*humbugged* by their doctors, pillaged by their tradesmen —G.B.Shaw⟩ ~ *vi* : to play the part of a humbug

hum·bug·gery \\-ˌbəg(ə)rē, -ri\\ *n* -ES : HUMBUG

hum·ding·er \\ˌhəmˈdiŋə(r)\\ *n* -s [prob. alter. of [1]*hummer*] : something extraordinary or of striking excellence ⟨a ~ in the . . . tradition of fantastic humor —Sarah C. Gross⟩ ⟨a sandstorm roared in, a real ~ —Shine Philips⟩

[1]**hum·drum** \\ˈhəmˌdrəm\\ *adj* [irreg. redupl. of [1]*hum*] : having a routine or commonplace character : lacking interest, excitement, or sparkle : MONOTONOUS, WORKADAY, PROSAIC ⟨makes rather ~ use of a good idea —Eric Keown⟩ ⟨the more ~ aspects of military life, like drill, neatness, and organization —Blair Clark⟩ ⟨the ~ problem of making ends meet —*Amer. Guide Series: Mass.*⟩

[2]**humdrum** \\"\\ *n* : the quality or state of being humdrum ⟨the ordinary, average day, with its good human ~ —C.E.Montague⟩ ⟨give him that very experience of the ~ of clerical life —Compton Mackenzie⟩

hum·dud·geon \\ˌhəmˈdəjən\\ *or* **hum·dur·geon** \\-dərjən\\ *n* -s [prob. fr. [4]*hum* + *dudgeon*] **1** *Scot* : a loud complaint or noise ⟨the auld carline went . . . on top of her head, making such a *humdudgeon* —Hugh McCrae⟩ **2** *Scot* : an imaginary illness or pain

[1]**hum·ean** *or* **hum·ian** \\ˈhyümēən\\ *adj, usu cap* [David *Hume* †1776 Scot. philosopher + E *-an* or *-ian*] : of, like, or relating to the philosophical system or methods of the philosopher Hume esp. his philosophical skepticism

[2]**humean** *or* **humian** \\"\\ *n* -s *usu cap* : a follower of the philosophy of Hume

hu·mect \\hyüˈmekt\\ *vb* -ED/-ING/-S [L *humectare, umectare,* fr. *humectus, umectus* moist, fr. *humēre, umēre* to be moist — more at HUMOR] *archaic* : MOISTEN

[1]**hu·mec·tant** \\-ktənt\\ *adj* [L *humectant-, humectans, umectant-, umectans,* pres. part. of *humectare, umectare*] : MOISTENING ⟨~ properties⟩

[2]**humectant** \\"\\ *n* -s : a substance that promotes retention of moisture (as glycerol, various glycols, sorbitol)

hu·mec·tate \\-kˌtāt\\ *vb* -ED/-ING/-S [L *humectatus, umectatus,* past part. of *humectare, umectare*] *archaic* : MOISTEN

hu·mec·ta·tion \\ˌhyüˌmekˈtāshən\\ *n* -s [LL *humectation-, humectatio, umectation-, umectatio,* fr. L *humectatus, umectatus* + *-ion-, -io* -ion] **1** *archaic* : the action or process of moistening **2** *archaic* : the quality or state of being moist

[1]**hu·mer·al** \\ˈhyümərəl\\ *adj* [prob. fr. F *huméral,* fr. MF *humeral,* fr. NL *humerus* + MF *-al*] **1** : of, relating to, or situated in the region of the humerus : BRACHIAL **2** [LL *humeralis, umeralis,* fr. L *humerus, umerus* + *-alis* -al] : of or belonging to the shoulder ⟨the ~ horny plates or any of several scales on the plastron of turtles⟩ **3** : of, relating to, or being any of several body parts that are analogous in structure, function, or location to the humerus or shoulder ⟨the ~ anterior basal angle of an insect's wing⟩ ⟨the ~ anterior corner of the thorax of a two-winged fly⟩

[2]**humeral** \\"\\ *n* -s **1** : a large bone that forms part of the shoulder girdle of certain fishes not homologous with the humerus **2** : a humeral part (as a scale or plate)

humeral veil *n* [trans. of ML *velum humerale*] : an oblong veil or scarf of the same material as the vestments that is worn around the shoulders at high mass by a subdeacon when he holds the paten between the offertory and pater noster and by a priest when he carries the monstrance in a procession or raises it to give the benediction

humero- *comb form* [ISV, fr. NL *humerus*] : humeral and ⟨*humero*dorsal⟩

hu·mer·us \\ˈhyümərəs\\ *n, pl* **humeri** \\-əˌrī\\ [NL, fr. L *humerus, umerus* upper arm, shoulder; akin to ON *āss* mountain ridge, Goth *ams* shoulder, Gk *ōmos,* Toch A *es,* Skt *aṃsa*] **1** : the long bone of the upper arm or forelimb : the longest bone of the upper extremity articulating above by a rounded head with the glenoid fossa, having below a broad articular surface divided by a ridge into a medial pulley-shaped portion and a lateral rounded eminence that articulate with the ulna and radius respectively, and providing various processes and modified surfaces for the attachment of muscles **2** : the shoulder region of an insect; *also* : any of various structures located in this region (as the coxa of a foreleg or the lateral angle of the prothorax)

hu·met \\hyüˈmet\\ *n* -s [origin unknown] : a heraldic bar or a fess couped at its ends

hu·met·ty \\hyüˈmed·ē\\ *also* **hu·met·tée** \\", ˌhyüməˌtā\\ *adj* [*humet* + *-y* or *-ée* (fr. MF *-é,* past part. ending of some verbs) — more at -EE] *heraldry* : couped at the extremities

hum·hum \\ˈhəmˌhəm\\ *n* -s [Ar *ḥammām* bath; fr. its use as toweling] : a coarse cotton cloth formerly imported from India

humian *usu cap, var of* HUMEAN

hu·mic \\ˈhyümik\\ *adj* [prob. fr. F *humique,* fr. NL *humus* + F *-ique* -ic] : relating to or composed at least in part of organic matter : relating to or derived from humus

humic acid *n* : any of various organic acids that are insoluble in alcohol and organic solvents and are obtained from humus

hu·mid \\ˈhyümə̇d *also* ˈyü-\\ *adj* [F or L; MF *humide,* fr. L *humidus, umidus,* fr. *humēre, umēre* to be moist or damp — more at HUMOR] : containing or characterized by perceptible moisture : DAMP, MOIST, VAPOROUS ⟨~ air⟩ ⟨a hot ~ climate⟩ **syn** see WET

hu·mid·i·fi·ca·tion \\(h)yüˌmidəfə̇ˈkāshən\\ *n* -s [fr. *humidify,* after such pairs as E *identify: identification*] : the process of making humid

hu·mid·i·fi·er \\=ˈ=əˌfī(ə)r, -īə\\ *n* -s **1** : a device for supplying or maintaining humidity **2** : a textile or tobacco worker who tends a humidifying system to keep the moisture content of rooms at the desired level

hu·mid·i·fy \\-fī\\ *vt* -ED/-ING/-ES [prob. fr. F *humidifier,* fr. *humide* humid + *-ifier* -ify] : to make humid (as the atmosphere) : MOISTEN

hu·mid·i·stat \\-dəˌstat\\ *n* -s [*humidity* + *-stat*] : an instrument for regulating or maintaining the degree of humidity — called also *hygrostat*

hu·mid·i·ty \\hyüˈmidəd·ē, -ətē, -i *also* yü-\\ *n* -ES [ME *humidite,* fr. MF *humidité,* fr. LL *humiditas, umiditas,* fr. L *humidus, umidus* moist, damp + *-itat-, -itas* -ity — more at HUMID] : a moderate degree of wetness (as of a solid surface or the air) perceptible to the eye or to touch : MOISTURE, DAMPNESS — see ABSOLUTE HUMIDITY, RELATIVE HUMIDITY

hu·mid·ly *adv* : in a humid manner : WETLY ⟨eyes . . . beaming ~ through their dark lashes —*Dublin Bk. of Irish Verse*⟩

hu·mi·dor \\ˈhyüməˌdȯ(ə)r, -ȯ(ə) *also* ˈyü-\\ *n* -s [*humid* + *-or*] : a case or enclosure (as for storing cigars) in which the air is kept properly humidified : *also* : a contrivance (as a tube containing moistened sponges) placed in a case to keep the air moist

hu·mi·fi·ca·tion \\ˌhyüməfə̇ˈkāshən\\ *n* -s [NL *humus* + E *-i-* + *-fication*] : the process of the formation of humus

hu·mi·fied \\ˈhyüməˌfīd\\ *adj* [NL *humus* + E *-ified* (fr. *-ify* + *-ed*)] : converted into humus ⟨~ organic matter⟩

hu·mi·fuse \\-ˌfyüs\\ *adj* [ISV *humi-* (fr. L *humus* earth, ground) + L *fusus,* past part. of *fundere* to pour — more at FOUND] : spread over the surface of the ground : PROCUMBENT ⟨~ plant stems⟩

hu·mil·i·ate \\hyüˈmilēˌāt, *also* yü-, *usu* -ād·+V\\ *vt* -ED/-ING/-S [LL *humiliatus,* past part. of *humiliare,* fr. L *humilis* low, humble — more at HUMBLE] : to reduce to a lower position in one's own eyes or the eyes of others : injure the self-respect of : HUMBLE, MORTIFY ⟨insulted and *humiliated* his darling niece —Hilaire Belloc⟩

humiliating *adj* : lowering one's position or dignity : HUMBLING, MORTIFYING ⟨a ~ peace⟩ — **hu·mil·i·at·ing·ly** *adv*

hu·mil·i·a·tion \\(ˌ)=ˌ=lēˈāshən\\ *n* -s [ME *humiliacioun,* fr. MF *humiliation,* fr. LL *humiliation-, humiliatio,* fr. *humiliatus* + L *-ion-, -io* -ion] **1 a** : the act of humiliating ⟨His incarnation was the ~ of His godhead —R.J.Wilberforce⟩ **b** : the state of being humiliated ⟨what submission, what cringing and fawning, what servility, what abject ~ —Charles Dickens⟩ **2** : an instance of humiliation ⟨watched China undergo one ~ after another —E.P.Snow⟩

hu·mil·i·a·tive \\=ˈ=lēˌād·iv, -lēəd·-\\ *adj* : tending to humiliate : causing humiliation

hu·mil·i·ty \\hyüˈmiləd·ē, -ətē, -i *also* yü-\\ *n* -ES [ME *humilite,* fr. MF *humilité,* fr. L *humilitat-, humilitas,* fr. *humilis* low, humble + *-itat-, -itas* -ity — more at HUMBLE] **1** : the quality or state of being humble in spirit : freedom from pride or arrogance ⟨we all need . . . ~ in the face of what we do not understand —Nicola Chiaromonte⟩ **2** *New Eng* : any of several snipes

hu·min \\ˈhyümə̇n\\ *n* -s [G, fr. NL *humus* + G *-in*] : any of various dark-colored insoluble usu. amorphous substances formed in many reactions: as **a** : a substance obtained from humus (as the residue from treatment with cold alkali) **b** : a pigment formed in the acid hydrolysis of protein containing tryptophan — compare MELANOIDIN

hu·mir·ia \\hyüˈmirēə\\ *n, cap* [NL, modif. of Pg *umirí* umiri — more at UMIRI] : a genus (the type of the family Humiriaceae) of So. American balsam-yielding trees with small cymose flowers

hu·mir·i·a·ce·ae \\=ˌ==ˈāsēˌē\\ *n pl, cap* [NL, fr. *Humiria,* type genus + *-aceae*] : a family of tropical American and African trees or shrubs (order Geraniales) by some treated as a subfamily of the Linaceae but having bilocular anthers and numerous stamens — **hu·mir·i·a·ceous** \\(ˌ)=ˌ==ˌ=shəs\\ *adj*

hum·ism \\ˈhyüˌmizəm\\ *n* -s *usu cap* [David *Hume* + E *-ism* — more at HUMEAN] : the philosophical system or methods of Hume; *esp* : philosophical skepticism according to which it is impossible to demonstrate any necessary connection between occurrences

hu·mit \\ˈhyümə̇t\\ *n* -s [short for *humiture*] : the unit used in expressing humiture ⟨a humiture of 68 ~*s*⟩

hum·ite \\ˈhyüˌmīt\\ *n* -s [Sir Abraham *Hume* †1838 Eng. mineral collector + E *-ite*] : a white, yellow, brown, or red mineral $Mg_7Si_3O_{12}(F_1OH)_2$ consisting of a basic magnesium silicate containing fluorine that is brittle and of vitreous to resinous luster, that is found in the masses ejected from Vesuvius and elsewhere, and is related to chondrodite, norbergite, and olivine (hardness 6.-6.5.; sp. gr. 3.1-3.2)

humite group *n* : a group of isomorphous minerals consisting of olivine, chondrodite, humite, and clinohumite and closely resembling one another in chemical composition, physical properties, and crystallization

hu·mi·ture \\ˈhyüməˌchu̇(ə)r\\ *n* -s [blend of *humidity* and *temperature*] : a combined measurement of temperature and humidity computed in integers by adding the temperature in degrees Fahrenheit to the relative humidity and dividing by two and choosing the next integer if a fraction of ½ is left over ⟨when the temperature is 75° F and the relative humidity is 60 percent the ~ is 68⟩

hum·lie \\ˈhəmli\\ *n* -s [*hummel* + *-ie*] *Scot* : a polled domestic bovine : DODDIE

hum·ma·ble \\ˈhəməbəl\\ *adj* : capable of or lending itself to being hummed ⟨a ~ melody, a catchy tune —John Mason Brown⟩

hummed *past of* HUM

[1]**hum·mel** *also* **hum·ble** \\ˈhəməl\\ *adj* [ME *hommyll;* akin to LG *hummel* polled animal] **1** *Scot* : AWNLESS — used of grain **2** *Scot* : HORNLESS — used of cattle or stags

[2]**hummel** *also* **humble** \\"\\ *vt* **hummeled** *or* **hummelled** *also* **humbled; hummeled** *or* **hummelled** *also* **humbled; hummeling** *or* **hummelling** *also* **humbling** \\-m(ə)liŋ\\ **hummels** *also* **humbles** *chiefly Scot* : to separate (barley or oats) from the awns and tips of hull

[3]**hummel** \\"\\ *n* -s **1** *chiefly Scot* : HUMLIE **2** *chiefly Scot* : a hornless stag

hum·mel·er *or* **hum·mel·ler** \\-m(ə)lə(r)\\ *n* -s : one that hummels

[1]**hum·mer** \\ˈhəmə(r)\\ *n* -s [[1]*hum* + *-er* (n. suffix)] **1** : one that hums; *specif* : HUMMINGBIRD **2** : HUMDINGER ⟨the early pace was certainly a ~ —G.F.T.Ryall⟩ — **on the hummer** **1** *dial* : not in working order **2** *dial* : not well : under the weather

[2]**hum·mer** \\ˈhəmə(r), ˈhu̇m-\\ *vb* [freq. of [1]*hum*] *dial Brit* : MURMUR, MUMBLE

humming *adj* [ME, fr. pres. part. of *hummen* to hum — more at HUM] **1** : DRONING, BUZZING ⟨the ~ sound of telephone wires⟩ **2** : extremely busy : BOOMING, BRISK ⟨the tobacco warehouses . . . are ~ centers of activity —*Amer. Guide Series: N.C.*⟩ — **hum·ming·ly** *adv*

hummingbird \\ˈ==ˌ=\\ *n* : any of numerous nonpasserine birds constituting a family (Trochilidae) that is noted for the small size of most species and the brilliant iridescent plumage of the males which in some forms have remarkable crests, neck tufts, or elongated tail feathers, and being anatomically related to the swifts and like them having narrow wings with long primaries but a slender bill and a very extensile tongue

hummingbird moth *n* : HAWKMOTH

hummingbird sage *n* : CRIMSON SAGE

hummingbird's trumpet *n* : CALIFORNIA FUCHSIA

[1]**hum·mock** \\ˈhəmə̇k\\ *or* **hom·mock** \\ˈhäm-\\ *n* -s [alter. of [3]*hammock*] **1** : a rounded or conical knoll or hillock : a slight rise of ground above a level surface **2** : a ridge or pile of ice (as in an ice field or floe) **3** : HAMMOCK 2

²hummock \"\ *vb* -ED/-ING/-S : to form into hummocks esp. on an ice field

hum·mocky \-kē,-ki\ *adj* : abounding in hummocks : resembling a hummock : UNEVEN ⟨a ~ road⟩ ⟨~ fields⟩ ⟨stopped by ~ ice —T.H.Manning⟩

hum·mum \ˈhə(ˌ)məm\ *also* **hum·mums** \-məmz\ *n, pl* **hummums** *usu cap* [fr. the *Hummums*, a 17th cent. bathhouse in Covent Garden, London, England, fr. Turk *hamam*, fr. Ar *ḥammām* bath] : TURKISH BATH

hum note *n* : the humming tone given by the whole mass of a vibrating bell sounding an octave below its fundamental note — called also *hum tone*

¹**hu·mor** \ˈ(h)yümə(r)\ *n* -S *see -or in Explan Notes* [ME *humour*, fr. MF *humeur*, fr. ML & L; ML *humor* humor of the body, fr. L *humor*, *umor* moisture, fluid; akin to MD *wac* damp, wet, ON *vǫkr* damp, L *humēre*, *umēre* to be moist or damp, *uvidus* damp, moist, Gk *hygros* wet, Skt *ukṣati* he sprinkles, he moistens] **1 a** (1) : a normal functioning fluid or semifluid of the body (as the blood, lymph, or bile) esp. of vertebrates (2) : a secretion that is itself an excitant of activity (as certain hormones) — see NEUROHUMOR **b** (1) *in medieval physiology* : a fluid or juice of an animal or plant; *specif* : one of the four fluids entering into the constitution of the body and determining by their relative proportions a person's health and temperament — see BLACK BILE, BLOOD, PHLEGM, YELLOW BILE (2) : constitutional or habitual disposition, character, or bent : TEMPERAMENT ⟨are you an agreeable person? Have you a pleasant ~? —Alfred Buchanan⟩ ⟨every word they spoke . . . attested to their mutual love, the combining of their ~s —Djuna Barnes⟩ ⟨the women were horrified or admiring, as their ~ moved them —Edith Wharton⟩ (3) : temporary state of mind : TEMPER, MOOD ⟨not in a ~ to hear you further —Thomas Hardy⟩ ⟨in excellent ~⟩ ⟨after the execution . . . the ~ of the court involuntarily changed —Francis Hackett⟩ (4) : a sudden, unpredictable, or unreasoning inclination : CAPRICE, WHIM, FANCY ⟨a very frolicsome and tricky creature . . . full of wild fantastic ~s —W.H.Hudson †1922⟩ ⟨conceived the ~ of impeaching casual passersby . . . and wreaking vengeance on them —Charles Dickens⟩ ⟨victims of nature's cataclysmic ~s, dust storms and drought —Julian Dana⟩ (5) **humors** *pl* : actions revealing the oddities or quirks of human temperament : whimsical or fantastic actions : VAGARIES ⟨the ~s and small details of ordinary life —John Erskine †1951⟩ **c** *obs* : MOISTURE, VAPOR ⟨the ~s of the dank morning —Shak.⟩ **2 a** : that quality in a happening, an action, a situation, or an expression of ideas which appeals to a sense of the ludicrous or absurdly incongruous : comic or amusing quality ⟨the ~ of his plight⟩ ⟨the delightful ~ of a book⟩ **b** : the mental faculty of discovering, expressing, or appreciating ludicrous or absurdly incongruous elements in ideas, situations, happenings, or acts : droll imagination or its expressions ⟨the man is completely without ~⟩ — compare WIT **c** : the act of or effort at being humorous : something (as an action, saying, or writing) that is or is designed to be humorous ⟨his heavy ~ fell completely flat⟩ ⟨never read any ~ above the so-called comics —Ellie Tucker⟩ ⟨a ~ magazine⟩ **syn** see MOOD, WIT — **out of humor** *adv* : in a bad humor : out of sorts

²**humor** \"\ *vt* **humored**; **humored**; **humoring** \-m(ə)riŋ\ **humors** *see -or in Explan Notes* **1** : to comply with the humor of : soothe or content by indulgence or compliance : INDULGE ⟨one must discover and ~ his weaknesses —H.M. Parshley⟩ **2** : to comply with the nature of : adjust matters to the peculiarities or exigencies of : adapt oneself to ⟨yielding to, and ~*ing* the motion of the limbs and twigs —William Bartram⟩ **syn** see INDULGE

hu·mor·al \-mərəl\ *adj* [MF, fr. ML *humoralis*, fr. *humor* + L *-alis* -al — more at HUMOR] : of, relating to, proceeding from, or involving a bodily humor — now often used of endocrine factors as opposed to neural or somatic ⟨~ control of sugar metabolism⟩

hu·mored \ˌ(h)yümə(r)d\ *adj* : having a specified humor — now used only in combination ⟨a good-*humored* child⟩ ⟨a bad-*humored* man⟩ — **hu·mored·ly** *adv*

hu·mor·esque \ˌ(h)yüməˈresk\ *n* -S [G *humoreske*, fr. *humor* (fr. E) + *-eske* -esque] : a musical composition typically whimsical or fanciful in character : CAPRICCIO

hu·mor·ist \ˈ(h)yümərəst\ *n* -S [MF *humoriste*, fr. *humeur* humor + *-iste* -ist] **1** *archaic* : a person subject to humors or whims : one who has some peculiarity or eccentricity of character which he indulges in odd or whimsical ways **2** : a person given to the display or appreciative of humor: as **a** : a person with a strong sense of humor : a facetious person : JOKER, WAG ⟨two local ~s go in . . . to make a goat of the doctor —*Sydney (Australia) Bull.*⟩ **b** : a writer specializing in or noted for the quality of his humor ⟨a great and powerful ~⟩

hu·mor·is·tic \ˌ==ˈristik\ *adj* : HUMOROUS ⟨that book was to be ~ and undoubtedly . . . would have amused many people —Felix Reichmann⟩

hu·mor·less \ˈ(h)yümə(r)ləs\ *adj* **1** : lacking in humor ⟨heavy, ~, slow-moving, methodical —T.H.Fielding⟩ **2** : offered, said, or done in dead seriousness : reflecting the lack of a sense of humor ⟨~ memorizing of 500 dates . . . for a three-hour third-degree oral examination —L. Ruth Middlebrook⟩ ⟨his ~ proposal aroused covert snickers⟩ — **hu·mor·less·ness** *n* -ES

hu·mor·ous \ˈ(h)yüm(ə)rəs\ *adj* [MF *humereux*, fr. *humeur* + *-eux* -ous] **1** *archaic* : subject to or governed by humor or caprice : CAPRICIOUS, WHIMSICAL **2** *obs* : MOIST, HUMID, WATERY **3 a** : full of or characterized by humor : FUNNY, JOCULAR ⟨a ~ poem⟩ ⟨earned part of his way through college by selling ~ drawings —*Current Biog.*⟩ ⟨stories in a ~ vein⟩ **b** : possessing, indicating, or expressive of a sense of humor : given to the display or appreciative of humor ⟨short, rotund, with . . . ~ brown eyes —R.M.Lovett⟩ ⟨a very kindly and rather ~ man —O.W.Holmes †1935⟩ ⟨vented a low ~ laugh —Thomas Hardy⟩ ⟨studied his own life . . . with a shrewd and ~ eye —Harrison Smith⟩ **syn** see WITTY

hu·mor·ous·ly *adv* : in a humorous manner

hu·mor·ous·ness *n* -ES : the quality or state of being humorous

hu·mor·some \-mə(r)səm\ *adj* : full of humors : WHIMSICAL

humour *Brit var of* HUMOR

hu·mous \ˈ(h)yüməs\ *adj* [NL *humus* + E *-ous*] : of or relating to humus : containing a relatively large amount of humus ⟨~ soils⟩

¹**hump** \ˈhəmp\ *n* -S [akin to Fris *hompe* lump, chunk, D *homp* lump, chunk, MLG *hump* bump, ON *aptrhuppr* flank of an animal, Norw dial. *hupp*, *humpp* flank of an animal, L *incumbere* to lie down, Gk *kymbē* drinking cup, bowl, boat, Skt *kumbha* pot, OE *hype* hip — more at HIP] **1** : a rounded protuberance: as **a** : the protuberance formed by a crooked back in human beings **b** : a fleshy protuberance on the back of an animal (as a camel, bison, or whale) **2** *Brit* : a fit of depression or sulking ⟨enough to give anyone the ~ to see him now —Samuel Butler †1902⟩ **3 a** (1) : MOUND, HUMMOCK (2) : a conspicuous bulge or protruding section of coastline ⟨the ~ of Brazil⟩ (3) : a mountain range or mountain that has to be crossed — used chiefly in aeronautics ⟨over the ~ from Chile to Buenos Aires⟩ ⟨the Himalayan ~⟩ **b** : an elevation in a railroad switch yard up one side of which the cars are pushed by an engine and down the other side of which they are switched by gravity to their proper tracks **4 a** : a difficult, trying, or critical phase (as of an undertaking) — often used in the phrase *over the hump* ⟨in the production of machine tools the Soviet Union is over the ~ —P.E.Mosely⟩ **b** : strenuous exertion or effort : GO, HUSTLE — often used in the phrases *on the hump* ⟨my duties keep me pretty much on the ~ —*New Yorker*⟩ and *get a hump on* ⟨nowadays even ministers of the gospel know how to get a ~ on —J.W.Krutch⟩

²**hump** \"\ *vb* -ED/-ING/-S *vt* **1** : to exert (oneself) ⟨last year he had to ~ himself and make over a million —*Fortune*⟩ **2** : to make humpbacked : HUNCH ⟨stood ~*ed* with pain —F.B. Gipson⟩ **3** *chiefly Brit* : to put or carry on the back or shoulder ⟨we ~*ed* our barracks bags, piled in the wet trucks —H.D. Skidmore⟩ ⟨rose at six in the morning to ~ coal . . . to the neighbors' homes —*Books of the Month*⟩; *also* : to carry in any way ⟨helped . . . ~ in the crates of beer —Audrey Barker⟩ **4** : to sort (freight cars) in a classification yard and assemble in trains by means of a hump **5** : to copulate with — usu. considered vulgar ~ *vi* **1 a** : to exert oneself : HUSTLE, HURRY ⟨will have to ~ to get through . . . tomorrow —Richard Bissell⟩ ⟨keeps me ~*ing* even with three assistants —C.E. Lovejoy⟩ ⟨~ along and do your chores —Howard Troyer⟩ **b** : to move swiftly or at top speed : RACE ⟨it's moving southeast and ~*ing* toward the north —*Springfield (Mass.) Daily News*⟩ ⟨really ~*ing* along ahead of that tail wind —Norman Carlisle⟩ **2** : to rise in a hump : form a hump ⟨the . . . highway ~s and dips in a manner which discourages fast driving —*Amer. Guide Series: Conn.*⟩ ⟨~s up to 11,600 feet —A.H. Brown⟩

humpback \ˈ=ˌ=\ *n* **1** : a crooked back : a humped back : KYPHOSIS **2** : a humpbacked person : HUNCHBACK **3 a** *also* **humpback whale** : a whalebone whale of the genus *Megaptera* related to the rorquals but having very long flippers, being black above and white below, attaining large size, but yielding inferior whalebone and oil **b** (1) : HUMPBACK SALMON (2) : the black sea bass (*Centropristes striatus*)

humpbacked \ˈ=ˌ=\ *adj* : having a humped back

humpbacked whitefish *n* : an Alaskan whitefish (*Coregonus nelsoni*)

humpback grunt *n* : YELLOW GRUNT

humpback salmon *also* **humpbacked salmon** *n* : a small salmon (*Oncorhynchus gorbuscha*) which ascends Pacific coast rivers of Asia and of America from California to Alaska

humpback sucker *n* : a large sucker (*Xyrauchen texanus*) of the Colorado basin reputed to attain a weight of 7 pounds

humped \ˈhəm(p)t\ *adj* : having a hump : HUMPBACKED

humped cattle *n* : domestic cattle developed from an Indian species (*Bos indicus*) and characterized by a hump of fat and muscle above the shoulders : Brahman cattle : domestic zebus

¹**humph** *typically a snort or a strong h-sound followed by a contemptuously intoned m-sound or vowel* ˈə *the* ˈə *usu nasalized; often read as* ˈhəm(p)f\ *n* -S [imit. of a grunt] : a sound expressive of doubt or contempt ⟨voiced many a skeptical ~ —*Time*⟩ — often used as an interjection

²**humph** \ˈhəm(p)f\ *vb* -ED/-ING/-S *vi* : to utter a humph ⟨~*ed* and shagged upstairs —Feike Feikema⟩ ~ *vt* : to utter in a tone suggestive of a humph ⟨might as well give one to the Queen of England, ~*ed* a correspondent —Horace Sutton⟩

humping track *n* : a yard track for sorting freight cars by humping

hump·less \ˈhəmpləs\ *adj* : having no hump

hump rider *n* : a yardman who rides and brakes cars in hump yards not equipped with car retarders

humps *pl of* HUMP, *pres 3d sing of* HUMP

hump-shouldered \ˈ=ˈ=\ *adj* : having a humped shoulder ⟨their life preservers making them appear *hump-shouldered* —H.D.Skidmore⟩

hump sore *n* : infestation of the skin of Indian cattle by a filarial worm (*Stephanofilaria assamensis*); *also* : the hide-damaging lesions it causes esp. about the hump and neck

hump speed *n* : the speed of a seaplane during takeoff at which the water resistance reaches a maximum

hump·ty \ˈhəm(p)ti\ *n* -ES [perh. after *Humpty-Dumpty*] *Brit* : a low soft cushioned seat ⟨the dean, curled on a ~, was frankly listening —Dorothy Sayers⟩

hump·ty-dump·ty \ˌhəm(p)tēˈdəm(p)tē, -ti . . . ti\ *n* -ES *often cap H&D* [after *Humpty-Dumpty*, egg-shaped nursery-rhyme character who fell from a wall and broke into bits] : something that once damaged can never be repaired or made operative again ⟨the exchange crisis . . . that brought the *Humpty-Dumpty* of currency stabilization tumbling —*Atlantic*⟩ ⟨people fled into their suddenly *Humpty-Dumpty* world —Robert O'Brien⟩

¹**humpy** \ˈhəmpē, -pi\ *adj* -ER/-EST [¹*hump* + *-y*] : full of humps or bunches : covered with protuberances : HUMPED

²**hum·py** \"\ *n* -ES [native name in Australia] *Austral* : a small, primitive, or ramshackle dwelling : SHANTY, SHACK, HUT

hump yard *n* : a railroad switch yard having a hump

hums *pres 3d sing of* HUM, *pl of* HUM

humstrum \ˈ=ˌ=\ *n* -S [¹*hum* + *strum*] **1** : a crude fiddle; *broadly* : any out-of-tune musical instrument **2** : HURDY-GURDY

hum tone *n* : HUM NOTE

hu·mu·hu·mu·nu·ku·nu·ku·a·pu·aa \ˌhüməˈhüməˌnükəˈnükəˌäpəˈwä,ä\ *n* -S [Hawaiian] : a small Hawaiian trigger-fish

hu·mu·lene \ˈhyümyəˌlēn\ *n* -S [ISV *humul-* (fr. NL *Humulus*) + *-ene*] : a liquid sesquiterpene $C_{15}H_{24}$ in hop oil and clove oil — called also *alpha-caryophyllene*

hu·mu·lone \-ˌlōn\ *or* **hu·mu·lon** \-ˌlän\ *n* -S [ISV *humul-* (fr. NL *Humulus*) + *-one*] : a bitter crystalline antibiotic $C_{21}H_{30}O_5$ obtained from lupulin

hu·mu·lus \-ləs\ *n, cap* [NL, fr. ML, hop (plant), prob. of Gmc origin; akin to OE *hymele* hop, MLG *homele*, ON *humli*] : a genus of herbaceous vines (family Urticaceae) with palmate leaves and pistillate flowers in clusters resembling catkins or cones — see ³HOP

hu·mus \ˈ(h)yüməs\ *n* -ES [NL, fr. L, earth, ground — more at HUMBLE] : a brown or black complex and varying material formed by the partial decomposition of vegetable or animal matter : the organic portion of soil

¹**hun** \ˈhən\ *n* -S [LL *Hunni*, pl.] **1** *cap* : a member of a nomadic Mongolian people who were driven westward from Mongolia about A.D.200 and obtaining control of a large portion of central and eastern Europe under Attila about the middle of the 5th century forced even Rome to pay tribute until their power was terminated by their defeat at Châlons in 451 and the death of Attila in 453 — compare EPHTHALITE **2 a** *often cap* : a person who is wantonly destructive : VANDAL **b** *usu cap* : GERMAN; *esp* : a German soldier in World War I or World War II ⟨the recoiling Hitlerites and *Huns* are redoubling their ruthless cruelties —*Britannica Bk. of the Yr.*⟩ — usu. used disparagingly

²**hun** \"\ *n* -S [by shortening] *usu cap* : HUNGARIAN PARTRIDGE

hun *abbr* hundred

hu·na·nese \ˌhünəˈnēz, -ēs\ *adj, usu cap* [*Hunan*, province in China + E *-ese*] : of or relating to the province of Hunan

²**hunanese** \"\ *n, pl* **hunanese** *cap* : a native or inhabitant of Hunan

¹**hunch** \ˈhənch\ *vb* -ED/-ING/-ES [origin unknown] *vi* **1** : to push, thrust, or move oneself forward ⟨~*ed* along for a short spell of safe steps —T.B.Costain⟩ ⟨heavy shoulders . . . ~*ed* through the open door —S.H.Adams⟩ **2 a** : to assume a bent or crooked posture esp. in sitting : bend one's body into an arch or hump ⟨a technical sergeant ~*es* in a tiny cubicle —*Fortune*⟩ ⟨gripped the wheel, ~*ing* over it —Gregor Felsen⟩ ⟨folded his hands on the table and ~*ed* forward —Hugh MacLennan⟩ **b** : to draw or compress oneself into a ball : curl up ⟨~*ed* up on the rug —Margery Allingham⟩ ⟨beneath the covers, in my curled red ball of darkness —Randall Jarrell⟩ **c** : HUDDLE, SQUAT ⟨we ~*ed* close to the damp earth —H.D.Skidmore⟩ ⟨the home ~*es* on a one-acre point of land —*Springfield (Mass.) Union*⟩ ⟨the mountains ~*ed* around the valley —Helen Rich⟩ **d** : to rise so as to form a hump or arch : REAR ⟨the sea ~*ed* up and hurled itself on the . . . land —H.E.Rieseberg⟩ ⟨his shoulder ~*ed* convulsively —Bernard DeVoto⟩ **3** : FUDGE 2a ~ *vt* **1** : PUSH, JOSTLE, SHOVE ⟨I would ~ my chair . . . closer to my dear and only cronies —Mary Nash⟩ ⟨tugboats . . . ~*ed* their ocean-going charges to the quayside —Newman Bumstead⟩ **2** : to thrust or bend so as to form a hump or arch : CROOK, ARCH ⟨the crow ~*ed* its shoulders, like an old woman seeking comfort in her moldy coat —Edita Morris⟩ ⟨kept his . . . body ~*ed* slightly forward —Tennessee Williams⟩ ⟨if you ~ yourself up . . . it is probably due to self-consciousness or fatigue —*Farmer's Weekly (So. Africa)*⟩ : HUDDLE ⟨~*ed* ourselves into a little group in the corner⟩

²**hunch** \"\ *n* -ES **1** : the act or an instance of hunching : PUSH ⟨give him a good ~ with your foot —Abraham Tucker⟩ **2** [prob. back-formation fr. *hunchbacked*] **a** : a rounded protuberance : HUMP ⟨his back carried a huge ~ —William Scoresby †1857⟩ **b** : a thick piece : LUMP ⟨barter it for a ~ of cake —Flora Thompson⟩ **3** : a strong intuitive feeling ⟨expressed her ~ that the photograph had slid off the desk —*Saturday Rev.*⟩; *esp* : a strong intuitive feeling as to how something (as a course of action) will turn out ⟨on a ~, resolved to establish a rail and shipping terminus here —*Amer. Guide Series: Texas*⟩

hunchback \ˈ=ˌ=\ *n* [back-formation fr. *hunchbacked*] **1** : a back with a hunch or hump : KYPHOSIS **2** : a hunchbacked person

hunchbacked \ˈ=ˌ=\ *adj* [perh. fr. ¹*hunch* + *-backed* (fr. ¹*back* + *-ed*)] : HUMPBACKED

hund \ˈhən(d), -ü-,-ü-\ *dial var of* HOUND

hund *abbr* hundred

hun·der \ˈhən(d)ə(r)\ *or* **hun·dert** \-(d)ə(r)t\ *dial var of* HUNDRED

hun·di *also* **hoon·dee** *or* **hoon·di** \ˈhündē\ *n* -S [Hindi *huṇḍī*] : a negotiable instrument, bill of exchange, or promissory note of India used esp. in the internal finance of trade

¹**hun·dred** \ˈhəndrəd, ÷ -ndə(r)d, *rapid* -nə(r)d, *dial or substand* -nə(r)t\ *n, pl* **hundreds** *or* **hundred** [ME, fr. OE; akin to OFris *hundred*, *hunderd* hundred, OS *hunderod*, ON *hundrath*; all fr. a prehistoric WGmc-NGmc compound whose constituents are akin respectively to OE *hund* hundred and Goth *garathjan* to count; akin to OHG *hunt* hundred, OS & Goth *hund*, L *centum*, Gk *hekaton*, Skt *śatam*; all fr. a prehistoric word derived fr. the root of E *ten* — more at TEN, REASON] **1** : 10 tens : twice 50 : five twenties : five score : the square of ten — see NUMBER table **2 a** : 100 units or objects ⟨a total of a ~⟩ **b** : a group or set of 100 ⟨arranged by ~s⟩ **3 a** : the numerable quantity symbolized by the arabic numerals 100 **b** : the letter C **4** : the number occupying the position three to the left of the decimal point in the Arabic notation (as 9 in the number 2968) — usu. used in pl. **5 a** : any of various British units of quantity for commercial items (as for 120 boards, 120 nails, or 140 pecks or 35 bushels of lime) **b** : HUNDREDWEIGHT **6 a** : a hundred-pound note **b** : a hundred-dollar bill **7 a** : a division of a county orig. English but later established also in certain British possessions and formerly having its own local court **b** : the body of landholders and residents of a hundred **8** : **hundreds** *pl* — used in combination to designate a specified century ⟨the early fifteen-*hundreds*⟩ — **by the hundred** *or* **by the hundreds** : in great numbers ⟨examples can be found *by the hundreds* —H.S. Morrison⟩

²**hundred** \"\ *adj* [ME, fr. OE, fr. *hundred*, n.] : being 100 in number ⟨a ~ years⟩ — usu. preceded by *a*, *an*, or a numeral (as *one*, *four*)

¹**hun·dred·fold** \ˌ==ˈfōld\ *adv* [ME, fr. ²*hundred* + *-fold*] : by 100 times ⟨increased a ~⟩ ⟨increased one ~⟩ — usu. preceded by *a*, *an*, or a numeral (as *one*, *four*)

²**hundredfold** \"\ *adj* [ME, fr. ²*hundred* + *-fold*] : being 100 times as large, as great, or as many as some understood size, degree, or amount : very great — usu. preceded by *a*, *an*, or a numeral (as *one*, *four*)

hundred-legs \ˈ==ˌ=\ *n pl but sing or pl in constr* : CENTIPEDE

¹**hundred-percent** \ˌ===ˈ=\ *adj* **1** : PERFECT, UNALLOYED, GENUINE **2** : THOROUGHGOING, UNQUESTIONABLE ⟨the resources of the *hundred-percent* American —*The Bookman*⟩

²**hundred-percent** \"\ *adv* : without qualification or reservation : ENTIRELY, COMPLETELY ⟨a *hundred-percent* pure wool⟩

hundred-percent·er \"ə(r)\ *n* -S [*hundred-percent (American)* + *-er*] : a thoroughgoing, unqualified, and often blatant nationalist; *esp* : a self-proclaimed opponent of foreign alliances, influences, and interests ⟨the vociferous nationalism of the *hundred-percenters* . . . is always most eloquent when it is about to be most rowdy —Walter Lippmann⟩ ⟨could never be a *hundred-percenter* as long as he did not possess an American birth certificate —*Amer. Mercury*⟩

hundred-percent·ism \-ˌizəm\ *n* -S : the beliefs and practices of a hundred-percenter ⟨laws . . . passed under the stress of antialien phobia and *hundred-percentism* —*Christian Century*⟩

¹**hun·dredth** \ˈhəndrə|dth, ˈhən(d)ə(r)|, |tth\ *adj* [ME *hundreth*, fr. *hundred* + *-th*] **1** : being number 100 in a countable series ⟨the ~ day⟩ — see NUMBER table **2** : being one of a hundred equal parts into which anything is divisible ⟨a ~ share of the money⟩

²**hundredth** \"\ *n, pl* **hundredths** \-dths, -t(h)s\ **1** : number 100 in a countable series **2** : the quotient of a unit divided by 100 : one of 100 equal parts of anything

hundredweight \ˈ=ˌ=\ *n, pl* **hundredweight** *or* **hundredweights** : any of various units of weight ranging from 100 to about 120 pounds: as **a** : a unit equal to 100 pounds — called also *short hundredweight* **b** *Brit* : a unit equal to 112 pounds — called also *long hundredweight*; see MEASURE table **c** : METRIC HUNDREDWEIGHT

hung *past of* HANG

¹**hun·gar·i·an** \ˌhəŋˈga(a)rēən, -ger-,-gär-\ *n* -S *cap* [*Hungary*, country in central Europe + E *-an*] **1 a** : a native or inhabitant of Hungary : MAGYAR **b** : one that is of Hungarian descent **2** : the language of the Magyars : MAGYAR 2

²**hungarian** \ˈ=ˈ===\ *adj, usu cap* **1** : of, relating to, or characteristic of Hungary **2** : of, relating to, or characteristic of the people of Hungary

hungarian balsam *n, usu cap H* : a resin from the Swiss mountain pine

hungarian blue *n, often cap H* : AZURITE BLUE

hungarian brome *or* **hungarian forage grass** *n, usu cap H* : AWNLESS BROMEGRASS

hungarian goulash *n, usu cap H* : GOULASH

hungarian grass *or* **hungarian millet** *n, usu cap H* : FOXTAIL MILLET

hungarian green *n, often cap H* : MALACHITE GREEN 3

hungarian gypsy scale *n, usu cap H* : a musical scale having a whole step between steps 1 and 2, half steps between 2 and 3, 4 and 5, 5 and 6, 7 and 8, and augmented seconds between 3 and 4, and 6 and 7 — compare HARMONIC MINOR SCALE

c d e♭ f♯ g a♭ b c
1 2 3 4 5 6 7 8

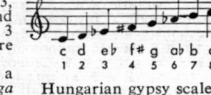

Hungarian gypsy scale

hungarian lilac *n, usu cap H* : a central European shrub (*Syringa josikaea*) having lilac-violet flowers in upright clusters and with the lobes of the corolla nearly upright

hungarian paprika *also* **hungarian pepper** *n, usu cap H* **1** : a paprika produced in Hungary from peppers of slight pungency and distinctive flavor; *esp* : one produced from the fleshy fruit freed from seeds and stalk — see KING'S PAPRIKA **2** : a plant producing peppers suitable for making Hungarian paprika

hungarian partridge *n, usu cap H* : a common European partridge (*Perdix perdix*)

hungarian vetch *or* **hungarian clover** *n, usu cap H* : a European vetch (*Vicia cannonica*) introduced into the Pacific Northwest as a hay, forage, and silage crop esp. on heavy clay soils and having stems and leaves with hair which give the plants a gray color

hun·ga·ry \ˈhəŋgərē, -ri\ *adj, usu cap* [fr. *Hungary*, country in central Europe] : of or from Hungary : of the kind or style prevalent in Hungary : HUNGARIAN

hungary blue *n, often cap H* : COBALT BLUE 2

¹**hun·ger** \ˈhəŋgə(r)\ *n* -S [ME, fr. OE *hungor*; akin to OHG *hungar* hunger, ON *hungr*, Goth *hūhrus* hunger, Gk *kenkei* he is hungry, Skt *kāṅkṣati* he desires, Lith *kanka* pain; basic meaning: burning, hurting] **1 a** : a craving, desire, or urgent need for food **b** : an uneasy sensation occasioned normally by the lack of food and resulting directly from stimulation of the sensory nerves of the stomach by the contraction and churning movement of the empty stomach **c** : a weakened disordered condition brought about by prolonged lack of food ⟨die of ~⟩ **2** : FAMINE ⟨the great ~s and . . . pestilences of the past —*Times Lit. Supp.*⟩ **3** : a strong desire or craving ⟨a ~ for knowledge⟩ ⟨land ~⟩ **4** : a craving for or deterioration from lack of a specified substance ⟨potash ~⟩ — used esp. of plants

²**hunger** \"\ *vb* **hungered**; **hungered**; **hungering** \-g(ə)riŋ\ **hungers** [ME *hungrin*, *hungeren*, fr. OE *hyngran*; akin to OHG *hungaren* to hunger, ON *hungra*, Goth *hungrjan* to hunger, OE *hungor*, n., hunger] *vi* **1** : to feel or be oppressed by hunger ⟨the poor ~, yet are not fed⟩ **2** : to have an eager desire : LONG ⟨the world today ~s for ideals⟩ ~ *vt* : to make hungry : force by hunger ⟨the besiegers ~*ed* the garrison into surrender⟩ **syn** see LONG

hunger flower *n* : a whitlow grass (*Draba incana*) growing in dry soil

hunger grass *n* : SLENDER FOXTAIL

hungering *adj* : having the sensation of hunger ⟨a ~ man⟩ — **hun·ger·ing·ly** *adv*

hun·ger·ly \ˈhəŋgə(r)lē\ *adj, archaic* : having a hungry look

hunger strike *n* **:** the action of one esp. a prisoner who refuses to eat anything or enough to sustain life so as to obtain compliance with his demands

hunger-strike \'==,=\ *vi* [hunger strike] **:** to engage in a hunger strike

hungerweed \'==,=\ *n* **1 :** CORN CROWFOOT **2 :** SLENDER FOXTAIL

hung over *adj* [fr. *hangover*, n., after *hung*, past part. of *hang*, v.] **:** suffering from a hangover ⟨the next morning after the party everybody was *hung over*⟩

hun·gri·ly \'həŋgrəlē, -li\ *adv* [ME, fr. *hungry* + *-ly*] **:** in a hungry manner **:** with avidity **:** LONGINGLY, EAGERLY ⟨looking ~ to the day of cheaper power —Gordon Dean⟩ ⟨I read ~ —Jan Valtin⟩

hun·gri·ness \-grēnəs, -grin-\ *n* -ES **:** the quality or state of being hungry

hun·gry \'həŋgrē, -gri, *chiefly in substand speech* -ŋr-, *dial* 'hȯŋ-\ *adj* -ER/-EST [ME, fr. OE *hungrig*, fr. *hungor* hunger + *-ig* -y — more at HUNGER] **1 a :** feeling hunger **:** feeling distress from lack of food **:** having a keen appetite ⟨the ~ children trooped into the house⟩ **b :** marked by famine or lack of food ⟨gloom reigned in the ~ countryside⟩ ⟨the ~ days of the great famine⟩ ⟨listen, Captain, this town is ~ —John Hersey⟩ **c :** reflecting or indicating hunger or keen appetite ⟨stand at the row of pastries with a ~ look⟩ **2 :** having, reflecting, or characterized by an ardent desire or craving **:** longing eagerly **:** AVID ⟨~ for affection⟩ ⟨with a kind of ~ fervor —Robertson Davies⟩ ⟨~ for jobs and patronage —H.F.Wilkins⟩ — often used in combination ⟨a land-*hungry* people⟩ ⟨the fuel-*hungry* East⟩ ⟨a trade-*hungry* nation⟩ **3 :** not rich or fertile **:** POOR, BARREN ⟨a ~ soil⟩ ⟨~ ore⟩

hungry rice *n* **:** FUNDI

hungryroot \'==,=\ *n* **:** the root of the spikenard (sense 2a)

hung up *adj* [fr. past part. of *hang up*] **:** DELAYED, DETAINED ⟨was *hung up* at the office and missed his train⟩

hunia \'hünēə\ *n* -S [prob. native name in India] **:** a tall long-legged sheep used in southern Asia as a fighting and pack animal

[1]**hunk** \'həŋk\ *n* -S [Flem *hunke*; perh. akin to D *homp* lump, chunk — more at HUMP] **:** a large lump or piece ⟨a ~ of bread⟩ ⟨~s of iron⟩

[2]**hunk** \"\ *also* **hunky** \'həŋkē, -ki\ *adj* [fr. obs. E dial. (New York) *hunk* goal, home (in games), fr. D *honk*, fr. MD *honc* corner, hiding place; akin to WFris *honck*, *honcke* house, hiding place] **1** *slang* **:** ALL RIGHT **:** HUNKY-DORY, OK **2** *slang* **:** EVEN — usu. used with *get* ⟨getting ~ on him —J.B.Benefield⟩ ⟨we'll get ~ with him good —S.F.Eckfeld⟩ ⟨"I'll get ~," I whispered —Harold Robbins⟩

[1]**hun·ker** \'həŋkə(r)\ *vi* **hunkered; hunkered; hunkering** \-k(ə)riŋ\ **hunkers** [perh. of Scand origin; akin to ON *hokra* to crouch, creep, *húka* to squat — more at HAWKER] **:** CROUCH, SQUAT — usu. used with *down* ⟨~*ed* down around the deerskin which they were scraping —Kenneth Roberts⟩ ⟨~*ed* down on his heels —Luke Short⟩

[2]**hunker** \"\ *n* -S [origin unknown] **1** *usu cap* **:** a member of the conservative section of the Democratic party in New York, 1845–1848 **2 :** a conservative in any respect **:** a person opposed to change or innovation ⟨to this day there are ~*s* . . . who object to it —H.L.Mencken⟩

hun·kers \-kə(r)z\ *n pl* [[1]*hunker* + *-s*] **:** HAUNCHES ⟨perched there on his ~ —Gerard Perry⟩

hunks \'həŋks\ *n pl but sing or pl in constr* [origin unknown] **:** a surly ill-natured person **:** a covetous sordid man **:** MISER ⟨some old ~ of a sea captain —Herman Melville⟩ ⟨all the prudence and selfishness of an old ~ —Thomas Gray⟩

hun·ky *also* **hun·kie** \'həŋkē, -ki\ *n, pl* **hunkies** *often cap* [prob. shortening & alter. of *Hungarian* + *-y*, *-ie*] **:** a person of central or east European birth or descent; *esp* **:** an industrial worker of such birth or descent — usu. used disparagingly

hunky-dory \¦həŋkē¦dōrē, -kə¦d-, -ki...ri, -dȯr-\ *adj* [*hunky* (var. of [2]*hunk*) + *-dory* (origin unknown)] **:** quite satisfactory **:** FINE ⟨everything was *hunky-dory*⟩

hun·nic \'hənik, -nēk\ *adj, usu cap* [ML *Hunnicus*, fr. LL *Hunni* Huns + L *-icus* -ic] **:** HUNNISH

hun·nish \-nish,-nēsh\ *adj, usu cap* [*Hun* + *-ish*] **:** of, like, or relating to the Huns **:** BARBAROUS — **hun·nish·ness** *n* -ES *usu cap*

huns *pl of* HUN

[1]**hunt** \'hənt\ *vb* -ED/-ING/-S [ME *hunten*, fr. OE *huntian*; akin to OE *hentan* to attack, seize, OHG *herihunda* battle spoils, ON *henda* to grasp, OSw *hinna* to attain, reach, Goth *frahinthan* to take captive] *vt* **1 a :** to follow or search for (game or prey) for the purpose and with the means of capturing or killing **:** pursue (game or prey) for food or in sport ⟨~ buffalo⟩ ⟨wolves ~ large prey only in packs⟩; *esp* **:** to pursue with weapons and often with trained animals **b :** to use or manage in the search for game ⟨~*s* a pack of dogs⟩ **2 a :** to pursue, follow, or track (a person) esp. with the object of capture — often used with *down* ⟨surviving patriots . . . were ~*ed* down in legal manner and put to death —J.A.Froude⟩ **b :** to try to find, locate, or obtain esp. by sustained or careful search or effort ⟨missing persons are ~*ed* by the police⟩ ⟨he's ~*ing* a job⟩ **c :** to find, uncover, or obtain after diligent search — used with *up*, *out*, or *down* ⟨~*ing* out recondite meanings in poems —Howard M. Jones⟩ ⟨~*ed* up a lot of valuable new evidence⟩ **3 :** to drive or chase esp. by hounding, harrying, or persecuting ⟨members of the colonial council . . . were ~*ed* from their homes —J.T.Adams⟩ **4 :** to traverse or go over in quest of game or quarry ⟨~*s* the swamp for moths —J.D. Hart⟩ ~ *vi* **1 :** to take part in a hunt **:** pursue game **2 :** to attempt to find, uncover, or obtain something esp. by diligent search — used with *for* or *after* ⟨~ for a lost wallet⟩ ⟨~*ing* for a street address⟩ ⟨ideas would not come to me if I went out to ~ for them —Ellen Glasgow⟩ **3 :** to oscillate alternately to each side of a neutral point or to run alternately faster and slower instead of steadily because of insufficient stability controls — used esp. of a device or machine ⟨sudden changes of load frequently cause the governor to ~, i.e., to open too wide, then close too far, and so on —S.H.Mortensen & Sterling Beckwith⟩ ⟨~*ing*, in electrical engineering, is a periodic increase or decrease in the speed of synchronous machinery operating in parallel, such as generators or motors —F.D.Jones⟩ ⟨a magnetic compass . . . must be damped to prevent lengthy oscillation or ~*ing* —Benjamin Dutton⟩ **4** *of a bell* **:** to shift continuously up or down in the order of striking in change ringing **syn** see SEEK

[2]**hunt** \"\ *n* -S [ME *hunte*, fr. *hunten*, v.] **1 :** the act, practice, or an instance of hunting **:** CHASE ⟨the ~ is up; the morn is bright and gray —Shak.⟩ **2 :** an association of huntsmen **:** a number of persons with horses and dogs engaged in hunting or riding to hounds ⟨a gate was being held open . . . and the ~ was streaming through —Adrian Bell⟩ **3 :** an instance of hunting (as in a mechanical device) **4 :** a regular course followed by each bell up or down the striking order in change ringing

hunt·able \'həntəbəl\ *adj* **:** capable of being hunted

hunt and peck *n* **:** a mode of typing in which one looks at the keyboard and uses random fingering ⟨types fast and accurately, by *hunt and peck* —Brendan Gill⟩ — compare TOUCH SYSTEM

huntaway \'==,=\ *adj* [fr. *hunt away*, v.] *NewZeal, of a dog* **:** trained to follow after and drive on a flock of sheep

hunted *adj* **1 :** being the object of a search, pursuit, or persecution ⟨a ~ man⟩ ⟨a ~ minority⟩ **2 :** reflecting or expressing the terror or fears of one who is hunted ⟨the prisoner's face lost its ~, hopeless look —Julian Dana⟩ ⟨a glitter of apprehension in her ~ eyes —Edith Wharton⟩ — **hunt·ed·ly** *adv*

hunt·er \'həntə(r)\ *n* -S [ME, fr. *hunten* + *-er*] **1 a :** a person who hunts game **:** HUNTSMAN **b :** a dog used or trained for hunting **c :** a horse used or adapted for use in hunting; *esp* **:** one exhibiting endurance, speed, and ability to carry weight and trained for facility in cross-country work and jumping **2 :** a person who hunts or searches diligently or systematically for something ⟨~*s* with camera —S.H.Holbrook⟩ ⟨~*s* after the philosopher's stone —M.R.Cohen⟩ — often used in combination ⟨sensation-*hunters*⟩ **3 a :** a large Jamaican cuckoo (*Hyetornis pluvialis*) **b :** HUNTING SPIDER **4 :** a pocket watch having a hunting case **5 :** HUNTER GREEN

hunter green *or* **hunter's green** *n* **:** a variable color averaging a dark yellowish green that is yellower and duller than holly green (sense 1), greener and stronger than deep chrome green, and greener and duller than golf green — called also *elephant green*

hunter-killer \¦==¦==\ *adj* **:** of or relating to a coordinated air-sea operation against enemy submarines ⟨a *hunter-killer* group⟩

hun·ter's canal \'həntə(r)z-\ *n, usu cap H* [after John *Hunter* †1793 Scot. surgeon] **:** an aponeurotic canal in the middle third of the thigh through which the femoral artery passes

hunter's moon *n* **:** the full moon after the harvest moon

hunter's pink *n* **:** any of several vivid or strong reds used for hunting jackets

hunth *abbr* hundred thousand

[1]**hunting** *n* -S [ME, fr. OE *huntung*, fr. *huntian* to hunt + *-ung* -ing] **1 :** the act, practice, or an instance of chasing, taking, or killing game or wild animals **:** CHASE, SHOOTING **2 :** the act, practice, or an instance of trying to find or obtain esp. by diligent search or effort ⟨the bibliographical ~ that lies behind any research work —H.N.Southern⟩ ⟨have had little time for book-*hunting* —H.J.Laski⟩

[2]**hunting** *adj* [fr. pres. part. of [2]*hunt*] **1 :** given to or interested in hunting ⟨a ~ man⟩; *also* **:** PREDACIOUS ⟨a ~ wasp⟩ **2 :** of, relating to, or used or adapted for use in hunting ⟨a ~ saddle⟩

hunting boot *n* **:** a heavy strong boot often extending to the knee and commonly laced from the instep to the top

hunting box *n, chiefly Brit* **:** a hunting lodge

hunting case *n* **:** a watchcase with a hinged cover to protect the crystal from accidents (as on the hunting field)

hunting cat *or* **hunting leopard** *n* **:** CHEETAH

hunting crow *n* **:** any of several tropical Asiatic long-tailed crested birds (genus *Kitta*) that resemble jays and have predominantly pale green, red, or sometimes yellow plumage and red bill and feet

hunting dog *n* **1 :** a dog used in hunting game **2 a :** AFRICAN HUNTING DOG **b :** DHOLE

hun·ting·don elm \'həntiŋdən-\ *n, usu cap H* **:** an erect vigorous hybrid ornamental tree (*Ulmus hollandica vegetata*) with usu. forked stems and pubescent branches

hun·ting·don·shire \-,shi(ə)r, -iə, -,shə(r)\ *or* **hun·ting·don** *adj, usu cap* [fr. *Huntingdonshire* or *Huntingdon* county, England] **:** of or from the county of Huntingdon, England **:** of the kind or style prevalent in Huntingdon

huntingdon willow *n, usu cap H* **:** WHITE WILLOW 1

hunting ground *n* **:** a place or area used for hunting; *specif* **:** a region in which game is hunted ⟨the planting of waterfowl food in the public *hunting grounds* —J.B.Robson⟩ ⟨the *hunting ground* of a peaceful tribe⟩ — compare HAPPY HUNTING GROUND

hunting horn *n* **:** a signal horn used in the chase; *specif* **:** a long conical tube coiled in a large circle and having a large flaring end and a trumpet mouthpiece — compare FRENCH HORN

hunting knife *n* **:** a large stout knife used to skin and cut up and sometimes to dispatch game

hunting knife

hunting seat *n, chiefly Brit* **:** a hunting lodge of some pretensions

hunting shirt *n* **:** a shirt worn for hunting; *esp* **:** a long jacket resembling a shirt and usu. of fringed deerskin worn by frontiersmen

hunting shirt

hunting spider *n* **:** any of several spiders that hunt their prey instead of catching it in a web **:** WOLF SPIDER

hun·ting·ton's chorea \'həntiŋtənz-\ *n, usu cap H* [after George *Huntington* †1916 Am. neurologist] **:** hereditary chorea developing in adult life and ending in dementia

hunting tooth *n* **:** a tooth in the larger of two geared wheels which makes its number of teeth prime to the number in the smaller wheel with the object of equalizing wear

hunting watch *n* **:** HUNTER 4

hunt·ress \'hən·trəs\ *n* -ES [ME *hunteresse*, fr. *hunter* + *-esse* -ess] **:** a female hunter; *specif* **:** one who follows the chase

hunts *pres 3d sing of* HUNT, *pl of* HUNT

hunts·man \'hən(t)smən\ *n, pl* **huntsmen 1 :** HUNTER 1a **2 :** a person who manages a hunt and looks after the hounds esp. in fox hunting

huntsman's-cup \¦==¦=\ *n, pl* **huntsman's-cups :** PITCHER PLANT a

huntsman's-horn \¦==¦=\ *n, pl* **huntsman's-horns :** a pitcher plant (*Sarracenia flava*) of the southern U.S.

hunt's-up \¦hən(t)¦səp\ *n, pl* **hunt's-ups 1 :** a tune played on a hunting horn to call out the hunters; *also* **:** a rousing song or tune **2 :** a pipers' tune used by Christmas wait

hunt table *n* **:** a low table usu. semicircular in shape

hunt the slipper : a circle game in which players attempt to pass a slipper from one to another without being discovered by the player who is it

hun·yak \'hən,yak, 'hün-,'hün-, -yak\ *or* **hun·yock** \-yək\ *also* **hon·yak** \'hän-\ *or* **hon·yock** \-yək\ *n* -S *usu cap* [by alter. (influence of *Polack*)] **:** HUNKY —usu. used disparagingly

hu·on pine \'hyüən-\ *n, usu cap H* [fr. *Huon* river, Tasmania] **:** a large Tasmanian timber tree (*Dacrydium franklinii*) with light yellow aromatic wavy-grained wood used for carving and shipbuilding

[1]**hup** \'həp\ *interj* [origin unknown] **1** — used to urge on a horse **2** — used as a command (1) to a horse to turn to the right or (2) to a dog to down

[2]**hup** \"\ *vb* **hupped; hupped; hupping; hups** *vt, chiefly dial* **:** to turn (a horse) to the right ~ *vi, of a dog* **:** DOWN ⟨promptly *hupped* . . . at a handler's command —*Amer. Field*⟩

hu·pa \'hüpə\ *n, pl* **hupa** *or* **hupas** *usu cap* **1 a :** an Athapaskan people of the Trinity river valley, California **b :** a member of such people **2 :** a language of the Hupa and Chilula peoples

hup·pah *or* **chup·pah** \'ku̇pə, -(,)pä, ku̇'pä\ *n, pl* **hup·poth** *or* **hup·pot** \'ku̇,pōt(h), -ōs, ,='=\ *also* **huppahs** [Heb *ḥuppāh* cover, canopy] **:** a canopy under which bride and groom stand during a Jewish wedding ceremony

hu·ra \'hyu̇rə\ *n, cap* [NL, prob. modif. of Carib *urari* sandbox tree] **:** a genus of tropical American trees (family Euphorbiaceae) having milky juice, monoecious flowers, and capsular fruit

hur·cheon \'hərchən\ *n* -S [ME *hirchoun*, *hurcheoun* — more at URCHIN] **1** *chiefly Scot* **:** HEDGEHOG **2** *chiefly Scot* **:** URCHIN

hurcn *abbr* hurricane

hurd·en \'hərdən\ *var of* HARDEN

hur·dies \'hərdiz\ *n pl* [origin unknown] *dial Brit* **:** BUTTOCKS, RUMP

[1]**hur·dle** \'hərdᵊl, 'həd-,'həid-\ *n* -S [ME *hirdel*, *hurdel*, fr. OE *hyrdel*; akin to OHG *hurd* hurdle, ON *hurth* door, Goth *haurds* door, L *cratis* wickerwork, hurdle, Gk *kartallos* basket, Skt *kṛnatti* he spins, *crtati* he ties, and perh. to L *crassus* thick; basic meaning: to twist] **1 a :** a portable panel of wattled twigs, osiers, or withes and stakes, or sometimes of iron or rails, used for fencing in land or livestock, reinforcing a wall or breastwork, or spanning a bog or ditch **b :** a frame or sled formerly used in England for dragging traitors to a place of execution **c :** an artificial barrier over which men or horses leap in a race **2 :** something that acts as a barrier **:** OBSTACLE ⟨once you have passed the final ~ — an interview with a selection board —E.O.Hauser⟩ ⟨one of the worst ~*s* a staff man faces is the vale of distrust that exists between echelons of command —W.H.Whyte⟩ ⟨a session of the foreign ministers . . . removed the final ~*s* in the way of a peace conference —A.H.Vandenberg †1951⟩ **3 a hurdles** *pl* **:** HURDLE RACE **b :** a jump made after the last approach step and carrying a diver to the end of the board in a running dive

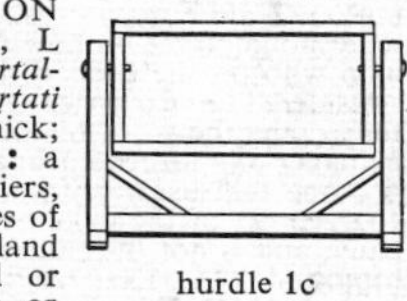
hurdle 1c

[2]**hurdle** \"\ *vb* **hurdled; hurdled; hurdling** \-d(ᵊ)liŋ\ **hurdles** *vt* **1 :** to fence in or reinforce with hurdles **2 :** to leap over (an obstacle) while running **3 :** to get across or past **:** OVERCOME, SURMOUNT ⟨only the boldest pioneers would ~ a pathless wilderness —R.A.Billington⟩ ⟨student performers . . had to ~ a series of competitive auditions —*Collier's*⟩ ⟨engineers . . . wrestle with the multitude of problems to be *hurdled* in the construction of thruway spurs —*N.Y.Times*⟩ ~ *vi* **:** to leap over an obstacle while running; *specif* **:** to run a hurdle race

hurdle gate *n* **:** the crosspiece of a track hurdle that swings up to form a high hurdle or down to form a low hurdle

hur·dler \-d(ᵊ)lə(r)\ *n* -S [[1]*hurdle* + *-er*] **1 :** one that makes hurdles ⟨authoritative minds in postwar Britain are recognizing the value of the . . . thatcher, ~, and kindred craftsmen in the total national economy —Mary E. Jones⟩ **2 :** one that runs in hurdle races ⟨the ~ is actually a sprinter until he reaches the first hurdle —W.H.O'Connor⟩

hurdle race *n* **1 :** a track event in which artificial barriers must be leaped — called also *hurdles*; compare HIGH HURDLES, LOW HURDLES **2 :** a horse race over a flat course equipped with movable hurdles — compare STEEPLECHASE

hurdle racer *n* **:** a horse trained for hurdle racing

hurdlework \'==,=\ *n* **:** work made of hurdles **:** WICKERWORK

hurds \'hərdz\ *n pl* [ME *herdes*, *hurdes* (pl.), fr. OE *heordan* (pl.); akin to OE *-heord* hair of a woman's head, ON *haddr* hair of a woman's head, Gk *keskeon* tow, Russ *kosa* braid] **:** the coarse parts of flax or hemp that adhere to the fiber after it is separated — called also *hards*

hurdy-gurdist \¦hərdē¦gərdəst\ *or* **hurdy-gurdy·ist** \¦==-¦=dēəst\ *n* -S **:** a hurdy-gurdy player

hur·dy-gur·dy \¦hərdē¦gərdē, ¦hədē¦gədē, ¦həidē¦gəidē, -di-¦...di\ *n* -ES [prob. imit.] **1 :** a stringed musical instrument resembling a lute in which the sound is produced by the friction of a rosined wheel turned by a crank against the strings and the pitches are varied by a set of mechanical keys **2 a :** BARREL ORGAN 1 **b :** STREET PIANO **3 :** a crank or windlass used to haul in heavy trawls or lines in deep-sea fishing

hurdy-gurdy 1

hure \'hyu̇(ə)r\ *n* -S [ME, fr. OF, cap, head of a wild animal] **1 :** a close-fitting cap **2** [F, fr. OF] **:** the head of a boar, wolf, or bear

hu·reau·lite \'hyu̇(,)rō,līt, hyə'r-\ *n* -S [F, fr. *Hureaux*, north of Limoges, France + F *-lite*] **:** a mineral $H_2Mn_5(PO_4)_4.4H_2O$ consisting of a hydrous manganese phosphate having a yellowish, orange-red, rose, or grayish color, and occurring in prismatic monoclinic crystals or massive

hur·gi·la \(,)hər'gēlə\ *n* -S [Hindi *hargīlā*, *hargīlā*, lit., bone swallower, fr. *har*, *hār* bone + *gīlā* swallower, fr. Skt *gilati*, *girati* he swallows — more at VORACIOUS] **:** ADJUTANT BIRD

huri *var of* HOURI

hur·kle \'hərkəl\ *vi* -ED/-ING/-S [ME *hurkelen*, *hurklen*; akin to D *hurken* to squat, MLG *hurken*, MHG *hūren*] *now dial Brit* **:** to draw up the limbs and crouch or squat

[1]**hurl** \'hərl *esp before pause or consonant* 'hər·al; 'həl,'həil\ *vb* -ED/-ING/-S [ME *hurlen*, prob. of imit. origin] *vi* **1 a :** to move rapidly or violently **:** RUSH, HURTLE ⟨sent the car ~*ing* over the roads —Sherwood Anderson⟩ ⟨a myriad senseless atoms . . . go ~*ing* forever through the infinite inane —P.E.More⟩ **b :** WHIRL ⟨now I've plenty money I'll make the tavern ~, a bottle of good brandy and on each arm a girl —Carl Sandburg⟩ **2** *chiefly Scot* **:** to wheel or drive in a vehicle esp. with a heavy or clumsy movement ⟨now and then we'll ~ in a coach —Robert Tannahill⟩ **3 a :** to play the game of hurling **b** *baseball* **:** PITCH ~ *vt* **1 a :** to impel with great vigor **:** DRIVE, THRUST ⟨could ~ his great strength into the ax head —Irving Bacheller⟩ ⟨~*ing* its mighty breakers upon the rocky ramparts —*Amer. Guide Series: Mich.*⟩ ⟨the forces that were to be ~*ed* against the Turks —N.T.Gilroy⟩ **b :** to impel (oneself) violently or impetuously ⟨he ~*ed* himself around the corner against the squall . . . with almost drunken violence —Liam O'Flaherty⟩ ⟨the characteristic wholeheartedness with which he continued to ~ himself at life —John Mason Brown⟩ **2 :** to throw down or out with violence ⟨~ the tyrant from his throne⟩ **3 a :** to throw or cast forcefully **:** FLING ⟨for forty-five minutes a battleship and lesser ships ~*ed* salvo after salvo at the field —H.L.Merillat⟩ ⟨a jet of gas . . . ~*s* strings of drill pipe and massive tools upwards —*Irish Digest*⟩ ⟨literally ~*ing* the ring I had given her in my face —Rex Ingamells⟩ **b** *obs* **:** to throw in wrestling **c** *baseball* **:** PITCH ⟨both ~*ed* scoreless ball for five innings —*Los Angeles (Calif.) Examiner*⟩ **4 :** to send or utter with vehemence ⟨~*ed* crisp piercing shrieks at the train —William Beebe⟩ ⟨publishers . . . took a delight in ~*ing* back at the tyro any copy he was venturesome enough to offer —A.W.Long⟩ ⟨he suddenly began to ~ reproaches down on her where she sat a little below him —Josephine Pinckney⟩ **5** *chiefly Scot* **:** to wheel or drive (a vehicle) **:** TRUNDLE **syn** see THROW

[2]**hurl** \"\ *n* -S [ME *hurl*, *hurle* swirl of water, strife, fr. *hurlen*, v.] **1 :** a forceful throw or thrust; *specif* **:** a rushing swirl of water ⟨the halt and ~ of an angry, crashing, tempestuous seaway —C.C.Shaw⟩ **b** *Scot* **:** a downward rush (as of stones on a hill) **2 :** the stick used in the Irish game of hurling

[3]**hurl** \'hərl\ *dial Brit var of* WHIRL

hurl·bar·row \'hərl,barə\ *n* [[1]*hurl* + *barrow*] *chiefly Scot* **:** WHEELBARROW

hurlbat \'==,=\ *n* [ME *hurlebat*, fr. *hurlen* to hurl + *bat*] **1** *obs* **:** either of two ancient Roman weapons: **a :** [3]CESTUS **b :** a short javelin having a thong by which it could be recovered after it was hurled **2 a :** a game resembling hurling and popular in Tudor England **b :** [2]HURL 2

hurlement *n* -S [[1]*hurl* + *-ment*] *obs* **:** TUMULT, CONFUSION

hurl·er \'hərlər; 'hələ(r, 'həil-\ *n* -S **:** one that hurls: as **a :** one that takes part in a game of hurling **b :** a baseball pitcher

hurl·ey *also* **hurly** \-lē\ *n, pl* **hurleys** *also* **hurlies** [[1]*hurl* + *-y*] **1 :** HURLING **2 :** the stick or the ball used in the game of hurling

hur·ley-house \'hərli,hüs\ *n* [*hurley-* (prob. fr. [2]*hurl* + *-y*) + *house*] *Scot* **:** a large dilapidated house

hurling *n* -S [fr. gerund of [1]*hurl*] **1 :** an early form of football popular esp. in Cornwall in which each side tries to throw or carry the ball to its own goal or to get it beyond the parish boundary **2 :** an Irish game resembling field hockey in which teams of 15 players use a broad-bladed stick to catch, balance and run with, or hurl a 9″ to 10″ ball in an effort to score by hurling the ball over or under a crossbar between goalposts

hur·ly \'hərlē\ *n* -ES [prob. short for [1]*hurly-burly*] **:** CONFUSION, UPROAR, TUMULT

[1]**hurly-burly** \¦hərlē¦bərlē, ¦həlē¦bəlē, ¦həilē¦bəilē, -li¦...li\ *n* -ES [prob. alter. & redupl. of *hurling* (gerund of [1]*hurl*)] **1 :** CONFUSION, TURMOIL, TUMULT, UPROAR ⟨through all the *hurly-burly* of the days immediately preceding election —A.D.H. Smith⟩ ⟨men and women relaxing after a hard day in the *hurly-burly* of the garment district —Al Hine⟩ ⟨delighted in the *hurly-burly* of her uninhibited conversation —Ellery Sedgwick⟩ **2 :** an act or instance of tumult **:** MELEE ⟨in the *hurly-burly* the poet is seized by the enemy —Donald Davidson⟩

[2]**hurly-burly** \"\ *adj* **:** TUMULTUOUS, CONFUSED ⟨outrageous clothes and *hurly-burly* antics —G.E.Fox⟩

[3]**hurly-burly** *adv, obs* **:** in a hurly-burly manner

hu·ro \'hyu̇(,)rō\ *n, cap* [NL *Huron-*, *Huro*, fr. Lake *Huron*, lake partly in Michigan and partly in Ontario, Canada] *in some classifications* **:** a genus of sunfishes containing solely the largemouth black bass which is now usu. included in *Micropterus*

[1]**hu·ron** \'hyu̇rən, -yür-, -,rän\ *n, pl* **huron** *or* **hurons** *usu cap* [F, lit., boor, fr. MF, fr. *hure* disheveled head of hair, head of a wild animal] **1 a :** an Iroquoian people orig. of the St. Lawrence valley and Ontario and later of the midwestern U.S. **b :** a member of such people **2 :** the language of the Huron people

[2]**huron** \"\ *n* -S [NL *Huron-*, *Huro*] **:** LARGEMOUTH BLACK BASS

[3]**hu·ron** \ü'rōn, -rȯn\ *n* -S [AmerSp *hurón*, fr. Sp, ferret, fr. ML *furon-*, *furo*, fr. LL, cat, thief, fr. L *fur* thief — more at FURTIVE] **:** a grison (*Grison vittatus*) or related animal of So. America

hu·ro·ni·an \hyü'rōnēən\ *adj, usu cap* [Lake *Huron* (north of which the system was first differentiated)] **:** of or relating to a division of the Proterozoic — see GEOLOGIC TIME table

hur·ple *var of* HIRPLE

[1]**hur·rah** \hə'rō, (')hü¦r-, hu̇'r-, -rä, -rȧ\ *or* **hoo·ray** *also* **hur·ray** \-rā\ *interj* [perh. fr. G *hurra*, prob. fr. MHG *hurrā*, fr.

hurre (imper. of hurren to move quickly, of imit. origin) + ā, interj.] — used to express joy, approbation, or encouragement

2hurrah \"\ or **hoorah** \"\ also **hooray** \-rā\ n -s **1 a :** a display of excitement or acclamation : FANFARE ⟨many institutions were just being founded with the ~ of circuses coming to town —Ernestine Evans⟩ ⟨the everyday business of war as opposed to its ~ and heroism —*New Republic*⟩ **b :** ENTHUSIASM ⟨whose tireless ~ occasionally lifts the . . . book into some sort of magic while he is on the stage —Kappo Phelan⟩ **2 a :** FUSS, CONTROVERSY ⟨raised a big ~ over her reckless extravagance⟩ **b :** RAILLERY ⟨the crew rode them hard, but it was the sort of good-humored ~ that made a kid feel he was one of the bunch —F.B.Gipson⟩ **3 :** SPREE

3hurrah \"\ also **hoorah** \"\ or **hooray** \"\ vb -ED/-ING/-S vi **1 :** to shout hurrah : CHEER **2 :** to behave in a lively or boisterous way : ROMP **3 :** TEASE ~ vt : HARASS, SCOLD

hurrah bush n : FETTERBUSH 1

hurrah's nest \-rōz-,-räz-,-räz-\ also **hoorah's nest** \"\ or **hoo·raw's nest** \"\ n : an untidy heap : MESS ⟨in spite of all efforts, the lockers generally become a *hurrah's nest* . . . a place for everything and nothing in its place —S.S.Rabl⟩; *specif* : a tangle of debris blocking a trail or stream

hurr-bur \'hər,bər\ n -s [prob. redupl. of 1burr] : BURDOCK

hur·ri \'hu̇rē\ also **har·ri** \'härē\ n, pl **hurri** or **hurris** usu cap [Akkadian *hurri*] : HURRIAN

hur·ria \'hərēə\ n pl, cap [NL] : a small genus of East Asian broad-snouted water snakes (family Homalopsidae)

hur·ri·an \'hu̇rēən\ n -s usu cap **1 a :** an ancient non-Semitic people prominent in northern Mesopotamia, Syria, and eastern Asia Minor about 1500 B.C. and regarded by some scholars as identical with the Horites **b :** a member of such people **2 :** the language of the Hurrian people

hur·ri·cane \'hər-|ə,kān, 'hə·r|, |ē,k-, |i,k- also |ēkən or |əkən or |ikən\ n -s often attrib [Sp *huracán*, fr. Taino *hurakán*, fr. *hura* wind, to blow away] **1 a :** a tropical cyclone with winds of 73 miles per hour or greater but rarely exceeding 150 miles per hour, usu. accompanied by rain, thunder, and lightning, and esp. prevalent from August to October in the tropical No. Atlantic and tropical Western Pacific but occas. moving into temperate latitudes — see BEAUFORT SCALE table; compare TYPHOON **b :** something resembling a hurricane esp. in violence : STORM ⟨the noise rose to a ~ —Dorothy C. Fisher⟩ ⟨a rushing ~ of blows struck him as he stood up —Donn Byrne⟩ ⟨the damage done by emotional ~s is not confined to the object of wrath —J.A.O'Brien⟩ **2** *dial* : an area where trees have been blown down by a hurricane or tornado ⟨there was a place about eight miles east of Bloomington which was known for many years as the ~ —J.A.Woodburn⟩ **syn** see WIND

hurricane bird n : FRIGATE BIRD

hurricane deck or **hurricane roof** n : AWNING DECK, PROMENADE DECK

hurricane globe or **hurricane glass** also **hurricane shade** n : a glass chimney placed over a candle to keep it from being blown out by the wind — see HURRICANE LAMP

hurricane lamp n **1** or **hurricane lantern** : an oil lantern having a glass chimney with a perforated metal lid that permits the egress of air but protects the flame from high winds and used usu. on shipboard and to mark outdoor construction projects — called also *tornado lantern* **2 :** a candlestick equipped with a hurricane globe **3 :** an electric lamp equipped with a hurricane globe instead of a shade

hurricane lamp 2

hurricane-proof \'==(,)=|=\ adj : able to withstand a hurricane

hurricano n -ES [modif. of Sp *huracán* hurricane] *obs* **1 :** WATERSPOUT **2 :** HURRICANE

hurried adj [fr. past part. of 1hurry] **1 a :** characterized by speed : FAST ⟨~ rush of a locomotive⟩ **b :** characterized by commotion : TUMULTUOUS ⟨gave ~ life of a city⟩ **2 a :** done or working under pressure ⟨gave ~ last-minute instructions to the crew⟩ ⟨a shorter version for the ~ reader⟩ **b :** done with excessive haste : HASTY ⟨the ~ funeral was a shocking indignity —A.M.Young⟩; *specif* : executed so hastily as to be perfunctory ⟨it is a short book, but never spare or ~ —D.C.DeJong⟩ — **hur·ried·ness** n -ES

hur·ried·ly \'hər-|ədlē, 'hə·r|, |ēd-, -li\ adv : in a hurried manner : QUICKLY, HASTILY

hur·ri·er \|ēə(r)\ n -s : one that hurries or causes to hurry

hur·ri·some \'hərisəm\ adj (or adv) [1hurry + -some] *dial Eng* : HASTY, RUSHED

hur·rite \'hu̇,rīt\ n -s usu cap [*Hurri* + *-ite*] : HURRIAN

hur·rock \'hərək\ n [perh. of Scand origin; akin to ON *hörgr* pile of stones, shrine; akin to OE *hearg* shrine, OHG *harug* sacred grove, shrine, and perh. to OE *heard* hard — more at HARD] *dial Eng* : a heap of stones or rubbish

1hur·ry \'hər·|ē, 'hə·r|, |i\ vb -ED/-ING/-ES [perh. fr. ME *horyen*; prob. of imit. origin like MHG *hurren* to move quickly] vt **1 a :** to carry or cause to go fast : SPEED ⟨an ambulance *hurried* him to the hospital⟩ ⟨the quest to discover whither modern science is ~*ing* us —Howard M. Jones⟩ ⟨fishing for either species don't ~ your lure —L.S.Marceau⟩ **b** *archaic* : to impel to rash or precipitate action ⟨that hard-to-be-governed passion of youth *hurried* me frequently into intrigues with low women —Benjamin Franklin⟩ **2** *dial Eng* : to cause distress to : HARASS ⟨I've been very much *hurried* this morning; for I've just learned of the death of my old friend —A.B.Evans⟩ **3 a :** to impel to greater speed : QUICKEN, PROD ⟨heard the train coming and *hurried* his pace⟩ ⟨used his spurs to ~ the horse⟩ ⟨hates to be *hurried* at mealtime⟩ **b :** to speed up the progress or completion of : EXPEDITE ⟨~ dinner by doing the meat in the pressure cooker⟩ ⟨electronic machines ~ the sorting of data⟩ ⟨cultural exchange can ~ the development of world understanding⟩; *specif* : to perform with undue haste ⟨some of the most perfect passages are *hurried* over as if they were a mistake on the composer's part —Warwick Braithwaite⟩ ~ vi : to move or act with haste : go fast : RUSH ⟨we'll have to ~ if we want to see the curtain go up⟩ ⟨sheep . . . stared at her through the ~*ing* snowflakes —Ellen Glasgow⟩ — often used with an adverb to lend emphasis or indicate direction ⟨~ up or you'll miss the train⟩ ⟨small launches ~*ing* back and forth —Tom Marvel⟩ ⟨a stiff northwest wind was blowing and patches of clouds *hurried* by —H.H.Arnold & I.C.Eaker⟩ ⟨the nation *hurried* forward along the path of . . . consolidation —V.L.Parrington⟩ **syn** see SPEED

2hurry \"\ n -ES **1 a :** DISTURBANCE, TUMULT, COMMOTION ⟨the incessant ~ and trivial activity of daily life . . . seem to prevent, or at least discourage, quiet and intense thinking —C.W.Eliot⟩; **b** *dial Brit* : DISPUTE, RUCTION **2 a** *obs* : disturbance of mind : mental turmoil ⟨there is nothing like hurrying the body, to divert the ~ of the mind —Francis Fuller⟩ **b** *now dial* : a minor illness **3 :** a recurrent agitation of sound ⟨the ~ of water or languor of sand —Michael Sayers⟩ **4 a :** excessive haste : PRECIPITANCE ⟨the blind ~ of the universe —Bertrand Russell⟩ **b :** a state of eagerness or urgency : RUSH ⟨it was going to be a wonderful party and she was in a ~ to get there⟩ ⟨they were all good reporters; but they were all in too big a ~, for fear somebody else would beat them to it —Elmer Davis⟩ **5 :** a tremolo in the strings or a roll on the drum accompanying an exciting situation in dramatic music **syn** see HASTE — **in a hurry** adv : in a short time or at a fast rate : HURRIEDLY, SPEEDILY ⟨they are not translations to be read *in a hurry*; they do not yield their charm easily —T.S. Eliot⟩ ⟨the new grammar can be taught *in a hurry* by a nonlinguist —MacCurdy Burnet⟩

1hurry-burry \'həri'bəri\ n -ES [redupl. (influenced by *hurly-burly*) of 2hurry] *Scot* : HURLY-BURLY

2hurry-burry \"\ adv, *Scot* : in a hurly-burly manner

hurry call n : an emergency summons

hurry-durry adj [redupl. of 2hurry] *obs, of weather* : windy and rainy

hurrying adj [fr. pres. part. of 1hurry] : swiftly moving : HASTENING — **hur·ry·ing·ly** adv

1hurry-scurry or **hurry-skurry** \'hər-|ē|skər-|ē, |hə·r| . . . ə·r|ē, |i| . . . |i\ adv (or adj) [redupl. (prob. influenced by *helter-skelter*) of 2hurry] : in or with disorderly haste : HELTER-SKELTER

2hurry-scurry or **hurry-skurry** \"\ n -ES : a confused rush : TURMOIL

hurry-up \'==|=\ adj [fr. *hurry up*, v.] **1 a :** of an emergency nature : RUSH ⟨*hurry-up* call⟩ ⟨*hurry-up* job⟩ **b :** equipped to respond to an emergency ⟨*hurry-up* wagon⟩ **2 :** speeded up : completed in a hurry : HASTY ⟨*hurry-up* breakfast⟩ ⟨*hurry-up* briefing⟩

hur·sin·ghar \'hərsiŋ'gär\ n -s [Hindi *harsiṅgār, hārsiṅgār, hārsiṅghār*] : an East Indian tree (*Nyctanthes arbortristis*) of the family Oleaceae with flowers that yield a dye used as a substitute for saffron

hurst also **hyrst** \'hərst\ n -s [ME *hurst*, fr. OE *hyrst*; akin to OS & OHG *hurst* thicket, OIr *crann* tree, and perh. to Gk *prinos* holm oak] **1 a :** a grove or wooded knoll — often used in combination in place names ⟨Elm*hurst*⟩ **b** *heraldry* : a clump of trees **2 :** a bank or piece of rising ground; *esp* : a sandbank in a river

1hurt \'hər|t, 'hə̄|, 'hə̇i|, usu |d·+V\ vb **hurt** or *dial* **hurted**; **hurt** or *dial* **hurted**; **hurting**; **hurts** [ME *hurten, hirten* to cause or allow to strike, injure, prob. fr. OF *hurter* to collide with, prob. of Gmc origin; akin to ON *hrūtr* ram (male sheep); akin to ON *hjörtr* hart — more at HART] vt **1 a :** to afflict with bodily pain : INJURE, WOUND ⟨the hot sand ~s my feet⟩ ⟨was badly ~ in the wreck⟩ ⟨got ~ in a bombing raid⟩ **b :** to do physical or material harm to : DAMAGE, IMPAIR ⟨the submarine is ~ by heavy depth charges⟩ ⟨the walkout is not ~*ing* service as much as the strikers hoped⟩ **c :** to do substantial or fundamental harm to : WEAKEN ⟨the story is ~ but not ruined by too many long descriptive passages⟩ **2 a :** to cause pain or anguish to : DISTRESS, OFFEND ⟨disillusions of the mind ~ less than disillusions of the heart —W.L.Sullivan⟩ ⟨was ~ by their lack of confidence in him⟩ ⟨it ~s me to think of all that land wasted —Ellen Glasgow⟩ **b :** to be detrimental to : CHECK, HAMPER ⟨the charges of graft will ~ his chances in the fall election⟩ ⟨a good wife can't help a husband as much as a bad wife can ~ one —W.H.Whyte⟩ ~ vi **1 a :** to feel pain or frustration : ACHE, SUFFER ⟨her hand . . . ~ from lugging the suitcase —John Dos Passos⟩ ⟨knocked a young heifer in the head because he . . . figured she had ~ long enough —Caroline Miller⟩ ⟨atomic-energy programs are ~*ing* from lack of enough scientific help —*Newsweek*⟩ **b** *chiefly Midland* : to be in need : WANT **2 :** to cause damage or distress : do harm ⟨hit the aggressor . . . where it will ~ most —D.H.McLachlan⟩ ⟨essential needs abroad must be met even if it ~s at home —J.S.Carson⟩ ⟨the rain may hold off but it won't ~ to take your umbrella⟩ **syn** see INJURE

2hurt \"\ n -s [ME *hurte, hurt, hirt*, prob. fr. OF *hurte* shock of a collision, stroke, blow, fr. *hurter* to collide with] **1 :** a wounding blow or stroke : cause of injury or damage ⟨the superiority . . . of the United States was a ~ to British prestige —Bernard Brodie⟩ ⟨this tower of granite, weathering the ~s of so many ages —R.W.Emerson⟩ **2 a :** a bodily injury or wound ⟨rattleweed, made into a tincture, is better than arnica for ~s of every sort —Emily Holt⟩ **b :** mental distress or anguish : RESENTMENT, SUFFERING ⟨are apt to be exasperated, and say things in immediate ~ which a little later they realize they do not wholly mean —A.E.Sutherland⟩ ⟨her sympathy eased his ~⟩ **3 :** WRONG, HARM, DISADVANTAGE, DETRIMENT ⟨his soul-stuff, by working on which a sorcerer may do the man himself grievous ~ —J.G.Frazer⟩ ⟨subordinating cosmic to moral considerations, to the ~ of both —M.R.Cohen⟩ **syn** see INJURY

3hurt \"\ adj [ME, fr. past part. of *hurten*, v.] **1 :** injured in body or spirit : WOUNDED, RESENTFUL ⟨ambulances . . . quickly dispose of ~ men and women —J.C.Powys⟩ ⟨an air of ~ innocence⟩ ⟨hoped to avoid ~ feelings over rejection of the plan⟩ **2 :** physically impaired : DAMAGED ⟨~ book sale⟩ ⟨restore ~ land with woods, game cover, and water —Russell Lord⟩

4hurt also **heurt** or **heurte** \'hərt\ n -s [ME *heurte*, prob. fr. *heurter* to collide with, knock, fr. OF *hurter* to collide with; perh. fr. the idea that it represents the mark of a blow] *heraldry* : a roundel azure

hurt·able \'hərd·əbəl\ adj : capable of being hurt

1hur·ter \'hərd·ər\ n -s [ME *hurtur, hurtour* metal reinforcement for the shoulder of an axle, fr. AF *hurteuer*, fr. OF *hurter* to collide with] *archaic* : BUFFER, REINFORCEMENT; *esp* : a bumper that stops the wheels of a gun carriage as the piece is run into battery

2hurt·er \"\ n -s [1hurt + -er] *archaic* : one that injures

hurt·ful \'hərtfəl, 'hə̄t-, 'həit-\ adj : causing injury or suffering : DAMAGING, PAINFUL ⟨regarded as ~ to the profession —H.A. Wagner⟩ ⟨~ to low-income classes —*Dun's Rev.*⟩ ⟨the crippled child hobbling to catch up was a ~ sight⟩ — **hurt·ful·ly** \-fəlē, -li\ adv — **hurt·ful·ness** n -ES

1hurt·ing \'hərd·iŋ\ n -s [ME *hurtinge, hirtinge* injury, hurt, gerund of *hurten, hirten* to cause or allow to strike, injure] *chiefly dial* : PAIN, DISTRESS

2hurting adj [fr. pres. part. of 1hurt] : PAINFUL, DISTRESSING ⟨his breath came in ~ gasps⟩

1hur·tle \'hərd·ᵊl, 'hə̄|, 'həi|, |tᵊl\ vb **hurtled**; **hurtled**; **hurtling** \|d·ᵊliŋ, |t(ᵊ)liŋ\ **hurtles** [ME *hurtlen* to collide, cause or allow to strike, freq. of *hurten* to cause or allow to strike] vi **1** *archaic* : to meet violently : hit with impact : COLLIDE ⟨together *hurtled* both their steeds —Edward Fairfax⟩ **2 :** to progress with the sound or suddenness of violent motion : CLATTER, CRASH ⟨boulders *hurtled* down the cliffs⟩ ⟨the morning gun . . . sent its echoes *hurtling* through the coco palms —G.P.Insh⟩ ⟨stubbed his foot against the doorjamb and *hurtled* into the hall —Liam O'Flaherty⟩ **3 :** to move rapidly : dash headlong : RUSH, SHOOT ⟨you can ~ along at supersonic speeds —Irwin Edman⟩ ⟨somehow he had *hurtled* past the propellers' blades —*Time*⟩ ⟨the country was *hurtling* toward disaster —Sidney Warren⟩ ~ vt **1 :** to propel violently : CATAPULT, FLING ⟨the subway ~s hordes of workers daily into lower Manhattan⟩ ⟨Indians ~ flaming arrows over the stockade wall⟩ ⟨when he ~s himself into a dance —John Mason Brown⟩ **2** *dial Eng* : CROUCH

2hurtle \"\ n -s : an act of hurtling : THROW, COLLISION

hur·tle·ber·ry \'hərd·ᵊl- — see BERRY\ n [ME *hurtilberye*, fr. *hurtil-* (irreg. fr. OE *horte* whortleberry) + *berye* berry] **1** *archaic* : BLUEBERRY 1; *esp* : WHORTLEBERRY 1 **2** *archaic* : HUCKLEBERRY 1

hurt·less \'hərtləs\ adj [ME *hurtles*, fr. *hurte, hurt, hirt* wounding blow + *-les* -less] **1 :** free from harm : UNHURT **2 :** incapable of inflicting injury : HARMLESS — **hurt·less·ly** adv — **hurt·less·ness** n -ES

hurtling adj [fr. pres. part. of 1hurtle] : characterized by rushing violence : SPEEDING, TUMULTUOUS — **hurt·ling·ly** adv

hurts *pres 3d sing of* HURT, *pl of* HURT

hus *pl of* HU

1hus·band \'həzbənd\ n -s [ME *housbonde, husbonde* husbandman, married man, master of a house, fr. OE *hūsbonda* master of a house, fr. ON *hūsbōndi*, fr. *hūs* house + *bōndi* householder, peasant owning his own land — more at HOUSE, BOND] **1** *obs* : HUSBANDMAN 1 **2 a :** a married man ⟨~ and wife should agree on how to budget the family income⟩ **b :** a man who on the basis of his tribal or societal institutions is considered to be married ⟨under the levirate a man was obliged to become the ~ of his brother's widow⟩ **3 a** *archaic* : the manager of another's property : STEWARD **b :** SHIP'S HUSBAND **4 :** one that uses thriftily or saves for future use : HOARDER ⟨barren ~s of the gold —S.V.Benét⟩ ⟨speaks his whole mind gaily, and is not the cautious ~ of a part —W.B.Yeats⟩

2husband \"\ vt -ED/-ING/-S [ME *husbonden*, fr. *housbonde, husbonde*, n.] **1** *archaic* : to plow and grow crops on (land) : CULTIVATE **2 a :** to take care of : utilize to advantage : MANAGE ⟨the ancient Nile is controlled at its source . . . and its waters are to be ~*ed* for the benefit of the farmers —Elizabeth II⟩; *specif* : to equip, supply, and maintain (a ship) **b :** to use sparingly or hold back for future use : CONSERVE, SAVE ⟨~ one's strength or resources⟩ ⟨~ their air strength . . . for the best nights, rather than risk losses from the weather —A.A.Michie⟩ ⟨toys . . . ~*ed* for the benefit of baby —Robert Grant †1940⟩ **3** *archaic* : to marry or find a husband for

hus·band·age \-dij\ n -s : a commission paid to a ship's husband by the owners for managing its affairs

hus·band·er \-d·ə(r)\ n -s : one that husbands

hus·band·land \'həzbən(d)lənd\ n [ME *husbondeland*, fr. *housbonde, husbonde* + *land*] **1 a :** the holding of a manorial tenant **b :** a quantity of arable land equal to two bovates : VIRGATE **2 :** the land occupied and tilled by the tenants of a manor as distinguished from the demesne lands

hus·band·less \'həzbən(d)ləs\ adj : having no husband

hus·band·like \-(d),līk\ adj : HUSBANDLY 1b

1husbandly adv [ME, fr. 1husband + -ly (adv. suffix)] *obs* : in a thrifty manner : ECONOMICALLY

2hus·band·ly \'həzbən(d)lē, -li\ adj [1husband + -ly (adj. suffix)] **1 a** *obs* : of or relating to a farmer or farming **b :** consistent with good farm management practice **2 :** of, relating to, or befitting a husband : MARITAL **3** *obs* : THRIFTY, FRUGAL

hus·band·man \'həzbən(d)mən\ n, pl **husbandmen** [ME *housbondeman*, fr. *housbonde* + *man*] **1 :** one that plows and cultivates land : FARMER ⟨where the menace of erosion has become most manifest . . . both landlords and tenants have become *husbandmen* under grave handicaps —Russell Lord⟩ ⟨the parable of the *husbandmen* in St. Mark's Gospel —Leonardo Olschki⟩ **2** *Brit* : a rural laborer : FARMHAND **3 :** a specialist in a branch of farm husbandry ⟨dairy ~⟩ ⟨poultry ~⟩

hus·band·ry \'həzbəndrē, -ri\ n -ES [ME *housbondrie*, fr. *housbonde* + *-rie* -ry] **1** *obs* : the care of a household : domestic management ⟨I commit into your hands the ~ and manage of my house until my lord's return —Shak.⟩ **2 a :** the judicious use of resources : CONSERVATION, THRIFT ⟨this careful ~ of his remaining powers —W.V.T.Clark⟩ ⟨borrowing dulls the edge of ~ —Shak.⟩ **b :** the control or use of resources : MANAGEMENT ⟨problems of soil conservation and ~ of water resources —*Brit. Book News*⟩ **3 :** the cultivation or production of plants and animals : AGRICULTURE, FARMING ⟨some dealt in corn, others in sheep and wool, others in a mixed ~ —G.M. Trevelyan⟩ ⟨commercial farming has not displaced subsistence ~ —J.M.Mogey⟩ **4** *obs* : the tenantry or husbandland of a manor **5 :** the scientific control and management of a specified branch of farming ⟨more limited experimental work is also being carried out in . . . animal ~ —C.J.Bishop⟩

hus·band·ry·man \'===mən\ n, pl **husbandrymen** : HUSBANDMAN 3

huscarl *var of* HOUSECARL

1hush \'həsh, *when imperative* " or sh *often prolonged*\ vb -ED/-ING/-ES [back-formation fr. 2husht, taken as a past participle] vt **1 :** to repress the agitation or clamor of : LULL, SILENCE, CALM, QUIET ⟨sleep . . . ~*ed* by solemn-sounding waterfalls —John Muir †1914⟩ ⟨his movement ~*ed* the courtroom —B.A.Williams⟩ **2 :** to gloss over or put at rest : MOLLIFY, QUELL ⟨their protests are mild and . . . can be easily ~*ed* —Paul Blanshard⟩ ⟨brings her flowers to ~ his conscience⟩ ⟨his wife . . . serves him quickly and silently, ~*ing* signs of disorder in the children —H.A.Overstreet⟩ — often used with *up* ⟨this contradiction is ~*ed* up —L.A.Fiedler⟩ **3 :** to keep from public knowledge : treat confidentially : SUPPRESS ⟨police attempt to ~ the crime —*Books of the Month*⟩ — usu. used with *up* ⟨the story of her disgrace was ~*ed up* —Edith Sitwell⟩ ⟨trying to ~ it up, but it was plain suicide —Vicki Baum⟩ ~ vi : to become quiet : grow still ⟨the crowd ~*ed*, and she sang —Franc Shor⟩ — used in the imperative to enjoin silence or urge moderation of sound ⟨~, baby, go to sleep⟩ ⟨~, boys, the party's getting noisy⟩

2hush \'həsh\ adj **1 :** devoid of sound : SILENT, STILL ⟨everything was . . . ~ as midnight about the house —Laurence Sterne⟩ **2 :** designed to prevent the dissemination of certain information ⟨~ money⟩ ⟨a ~ policy concerning any faults . . . in the American economy —Jerome Frank⟩ **3** or **hushing** [fr. the use of a prolonged \sh\ sound in hushing (enjoining silence)] : being the sibilants \sh\ and \zh\ — compare HISS

3hush \"\ n -ES **1 a :** silence or freedom from agitation : STILLNESS, CALM ⟨sickroom ~⟩ ⟨cathedral ~ of the deep woods⟩ ⟨a ~ and a solemnity about the proceedings —Hugh Walpole⟩ **b :** a suspension of noise or activity : CESSATION, LULL ⟨after a time there came a profound ~ and out of the stillness a woman's voice rose —Lyle Saxon⟩ **2 :** restriction of information : SECRECY ⟨prompted the policy of ~ in regard to the presence of the disease on their properties —*Australasian*⟩

4hush \'hu̇sh, 'həsh\ vb -ED/-ING/-ES [imit.] vi, *dial Brit* : to gush forth in a rapid stream : RUSH ~ vt, *dial Eng* : to expose (ore) by washing a hillside with water under pressure : FLUSH — **hush·ing** \-shən, -shiŋ\ n -s

5hush \"\ n -ES *dial Brit* : a rushing sound as of wind or water; *specif* : a swell of the sea

hush·a·by or **hush-a-bye** \'həshə,bī\ v imper [1hush + connective -a- + 2bye] : be still and go to sleep — used to soothe a child to sleep

hushed \'həsht\ adj [fr. past part. of 1hush] **1 a :** free of noise or agitation : CALM, STILL ⟨~ silence of the reading room⟩ **b :** marked by suspension of noise or activity : reduced to silence ⟨~ attention of the spectators —L.P.Stryker⟩ ⟨an atmosphere of ~ suspense⟩ **2 :** marked by secrecy or caution : CONFIDENTIAL, DISCREET ⟨~ meeting of political strategists⟩ ⟨counseled his clients in ~ tones⟩ — **hushed·ly** \-shədlē, -shtlē, -li\ adv

hush·ful \'həshfəl\ adj [3hush + -ful] : full of silence : QUIET — **hush·ful·ly** \-fəlē\ adv

1hush-hush \'=|=\ vt [fr. *hush! hush!*, repeated imperative use of 1hush] **1 :** to enjoin to silence ⟨was *hush-hushed* by army censors when he started to report soldier opinion on the issue⟩ **2 :** HUSH vt 3

2hush-hush \"\ adj : marked by secrecy or concealment : kept from public knowledge : SECRET, CONFIDENTIAL ⟨a specific cure for one of the *hush-hush* diseases, gonorrhea —*Science News Letter*⟩ ⟨decreed an end to the . . . *hush-hush* atmosphere that has shielded major presidential policies —Ray Tucker⟩; *specif* : subject to official censorship ⟨military intelligence, cryptography, secret chemical corps projects and other *hush-hush* assignments —Sidney Shalett⟩ ⟨of all air corps planes, this is the most *hush-hush* —D.C.Cooke⟩

3hush-hush \"\ n : a policy or atmosphere of concealment : SECRECY, SUPPRESSION ⟨the *hush-hush* surrounding new car design⟩ ⟨after decades of *hush-hush*, the problem of mental illness is now being openly discussed⟩; *specif* : CENSORSHIP ⟨wartime *hush-hush* concerning plane losses⟩

hush puppy n [1hush + puppy; fr. its occasional use as food for dogs] *chiefly South* : a cornmeal bread shaped into small cakes and fried in deep fat — usu. used in pl.; compare CORN DODGER

1husht \'həsht\ interj [ME *huissht*] *archaic* — used to enjoin silence

2husht \"\ adj [ME *hussht*, fr. *huissht*, interj.] *archaic* : HUSHED

hush tube n : a tube for conducting the inflow beneath the surface of the water in a flush tank to reduce noise

husi *var of* JUSI

1husk \'həsk\ n -s [ME *husk, huske*, prob. modif. of MD *huuskijn, huusken* small house, small cover, fr. *huus* house, cover + *-kijn, -ken* -kin; akin to OE *hūs* house — more at HOUSE] **1 a :** the outer covering of a kernel or seed esp. when dry and membranous : the chaff of grain : HULL, POD; *specif* : CAROB 1b ⟨with the ~s that the swine did eat —Lk 15:16 (AV)⟩ **b :** one of the leaves enveloping an ear of corn : BRACT ⟨corn roasted in the ~*s*⟩ **2 a :** something that resembles a husk : an outer layer or empty framework : SHELL ⟨much of the remote past is conserved in the ~ of convention —Norman Lewis⟩ ⟨the wind . . . blew through that eerie ~ of a room —Edita Morris⟩ **b** *slang* : GUY, FELLOW ⟨you're some ~ —Sinclair Lewis⟩ **c :** a classic drop ornament made of whorls of conventionalized foliage usu. in diminishing series and used esp. in an 18th century style of furniture introduced by Robert Adam **3 a :** the outer skin or shell of an animal ⟨the sea floor is littered with the discarded ~*s* of small crustaceans⟩ **b :** a supporting framework: as (1) : the decorative covering around the holder that supports the socket and bulb of an electric lamp (2) : a frame supporting the arbor of a large circular saw

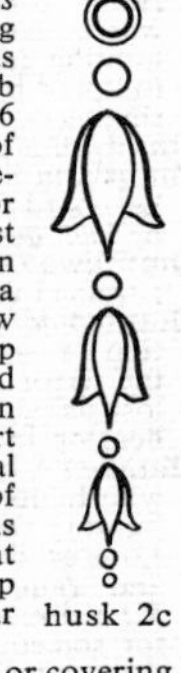

husk 2c

2husk \"\ vt -ED/-ING/-S : to remove the outer skin or covering of : PEEL, STRIP ⟨~ rice⟩ ⟨~ corn⟩ ⟨~ a coconut⟩ ⟨would ~ it of its religious and political bias —S.E.Hyman⟩

3husk \"\ n -s [prob. fr. obs. *husk*, v., to have a dry cough, of imit. origin] **1 :** HOOSE ⟨an outbreak of ~ was observed in a flock of 200 sheep —*Veterinary Bull.*⟩ **2 :** HUSKINESS

4husk \"\ vb -ED/-ING/-S vi : to become husky ⟨tried to keep his voice from ~*ing* with emotion⟩ ~ *vt* : to utter in a husky voice ⟨the sultry singer in the cabaret ~*s* out the latest ballad⟩

¹hus·ka·naw \ˈhəskəˌnȯ\ *or* **hus·ka·naw·ing** \-ōiŋ\ *n* -s [of Algonquian origin; akin to Natick *wuskenoo* he is young] : an initiation rite for youths at puberty practiced by various Indians of Virginia and including fasting and the use of narcotics

²huskanaw \"\ *vt* -ED/-ING/-S : to subject to a huskanaw

husk corn *n* : POD CORN

husked *adj* [¹*husk* + *-ed*] **1** : covered with a husk **2** [fr. past part. of ²*husk*] : stripped or deprived of the husk

husk·ened \ˈhəskənd\ *adj* [prob. irreg. fr. ²*husky* + *-en* + *-ed*] : HUSKY

husk·er \ˈhəskə(r)\ *n* -s : one that husks: as **a** : a participant in a cornhusking **b** : HUSKING GLOVE **c** : HUSKER-SHREDDER

husker–shredder \ˈ=ˌ=ˈ=\ *n* : a power machine that husks corn ears and cuts up the husks and stalks for fodder

husk·i·ly \ˈhəskəlē, -li\ *adv* : in a husky manner

husk·i·ness \-kēnəs, -kin-\ *n* -ES : the quality or state of being husky

husking *n* -s [fr. gerund of ²*husk*] **1** : an act or process of peeling or stripping off an outer layer ⟨the ~ of coffee beans⟩ ⟨corn ready for ~⟩ **2** *also* **husking bee** : a neighborly gathering of farm families to husk corn ⟨~*s*, berry-pickings and winter sleigh rides —Van Wyck Brooks⟩

husking glove *n* : a glove with metal plates and hooks on the palm and palm side of the fingers that is used in husking corn

husking peg *or* **husking pin** *n* : a peg of wood or metal strapped or tied to the hand as an aid in husking corn

husk–tomato *n* : GROUND-CHERRY

¹husky \ˈhəskē, -ki\ *adj* -ER/-EST [¹*husk* + *-y*] **1** : containing or full of husks ⟨the kernels are plump and not very ~ —*Farmers Weekly (So. Africa)*⟩ **2** : of the nature of a husk : MEMBRANOUS, RATTLING, EMPTY ⟨the nut is contained in a ~ shell —S.J.Watson⟩ ⟨his footfalls were ~ in cinders —Richard Llewellyn⟩ ⟨repeated that ~ phrase so often —Willa Cather⟩

²husky \"\ *adj* -ER/-EST [prob. fr. ³*husk* + *-y*] : dry or roughened as with emotion : HOARSE ⟨the voices of the chief women mourners had become worn and ~ —J.A.Lomax⟩ ⟨~ voices bawled at the yokes of steers —Carl Sandburg⟩ ⟨makes all the instruments sound powerful but ~ —Virgil Thomson⟩

³husky \"\ *adj* -ER/-EST [prob. fr. ¹*husk* + *-y*; prob. fr. the toughness and harsh texture of a corn husk] **1** : big and muscular : BURLY, ROBUST ⟨a crew of ~ lumberjacks⟩ **2 a** : of sizable proportions or vigorous potential : LARGE, POWERFUL ⟨a ~ $19 million in the like period last year —Mitchell Gordon⟩ ⟨a big, ~, honestly built . . . power cruiser —*Yankee*⟩ ⟨there still was a ~ United Nations army left in Korea —A.J. Liebling⟩ **b** : having or producing strength : STURDY ⟨a ~ beef stew⟩

⁴husky \"\ *n* -ES : one that is husky or powerful ⟨foremen looked over the *huskies* crowded in these rooms to pick their crews —*Amer. Guide Series: Minn.*⟩ ⟨these four breeds of engines are *huskies* —R.M.Neal⟩

⁵husky \"\ *n* -ES *sometimes cap* [prob. by shortening & alter. fr. *Eskimo*] **1** *dial* : an Eskimo of Labrador and northeastern Canada or his language ⟨a huge whale . . . which the old-time *huskies* had killed with harpoons and lances —D.B.Putnam⟩ — sometimes taken to be offensive **2 a** : a heavy-coated working dog (as an Eskimo dog or malamute) of the New World arctic region used esp. as a sled dog **b** : SIBERIAN HUSKY

hu·so \ˈhyü(ˌ)sō, -ˌzō\ *n* -s [ML, fr. OHG *hūso*; akin to Norw dial. *huse* fish skull, ON *hauss* skull, OE *hȳd* hide, skin; prob. fr. the armored head — more at HIDE] **1** : BELUGA 1 **2** : HUCHEN

huss \ˈhəs\ *n* -ES [alter. of ME *husk, huske*] *dial* : DOGFISH

hus·sar \(ˌ)həˈz|är, |ä(r *sometimes* -ˈs|\ *n* -s [Hung *huszár* hussar, (obs.) highway robber, fr. Serb *husar, gusar* pirate, fr. ML *cursarius* — more at CORSAIR] **1 a** *often cap* : a horseman of the Hungarian light cavalry organized in the 15th century **b** : a member of the light cavalry of various European armies usu. distinguished by a brilliant much-decorated uniform often featuring the dolman and the busby **c** : a member of certain now mechanized European cavalry units **2** : any of several brilliantly colored snappers (family Lutjanidae) — see YELLOW-BANDED HUSSAR

hussar monkey *n* : PATAS

hus·ser·li·an \(ˈ)hu̇ˈsərlēən, -ser-\ *adj, usu cap* [Edmund *Husserl* †1938 Ger. philosopher + E *-ian*] : of or relating to the German philosopher Husserl or his theories ⟨*Husserlian* phenomenology⟩

¹huss·ite \ˈhəˌsīt, ˈhu̇ˌs-\ *n* -s *usu cap* [NL *hussita*, fr. John *Huss* †1415 Bohemian religious reformer + L *-ita* -ite] : a member of the Bohemian religious and nationalist movement originating with John Huss, marked by advocacy of the Wycliffite doctrines of clerical purity and poverty and the supremacy of the Bible and by insistence upon communion in both bread and wine for the laity, and split after the death of Huss into the Calixtin and Taborite parties — compare LOLLARD 2

²hussite \"\ *adj, usu cap* : of, relating to, or characteristic of John Huss or the Hussites

huss·it·ism \-īd-ˌizəm\ *also* **huss·ism** \-ˌsizəm\ *n* -s *usu cap* [*hussitism* fr. ¹*hussite* + *-ism*; *hussism* fr. John *Huss* + E *-ism*] : the beliefs and practices of the Hussites

hus·sy *also* **hus·sey** \ˈhəz|ē, ˈhəs|, |i\ *or* **huz·zy** \ˈhəz|\ *n* -ES [alter. of *housewife*] **1** *obs* : the female head of a house : HOUSEWIFE **2** : a lewd or brazen woman : JADE **3** : a saucy or mischievous girl : MINX **4** *dial* : HOUSEWIFE 2

hus·ting \ˈhəstiŋ, -tēŋ\ *n* -s [ME, fr. OE *hūsting*, fr. ON *hūsthing*, fr. *hūs* house + *thing* assembly — more at HOUSE, THING] **1** : a deliberative assembly or council in early medieval England; *esp* : one called by a king or other leader **2 a** *or* **hustings** *pl but sing in constr* : a court held in London before the lord mayor, recorder, and sheriffs or aldermen **b** **hustings** *pl but sing in constr or* **hustings court** : a local court in some cities in Virginia **3** *or* **hustings** *pl but sing in constr* : the upper end or dais of the guildhall where the London husting sits **4 a** *or* **hustings** *pl but sing in constr* : a raised platform from which candidates for the British Parliament were formerly nominated and from which they addressed their constituency **b** : the place of such a parliamentary election **5** **hustings** *pl but sing or pl in constr* **a** : an election platform : STUMP ⟨the charge . . . is expected to resound from political ~*s* throughout the land —*Foreign Policy Bull.*⟩ **b** : an act or process of electioneering ⟨an election which has generated far more excitement than the usual off-year ~*s* —*Saturday Rev.*⟩ ⟨the rough give-and-take of the ~*s* —*Yale Rev.*⟩

¹hus·tle \ˈhəsəl\ *vb* **hustled**; **hustled**; **hustling** \-s(ə)liŋ\ **hustles** [D *husselen, hutselen* to shake, toss, fr. MD *hutselen*, freq. of *hutsen* to shake; akin to G dial. *hotteln, hotzeln* to shake — more at HOD] *vt* **1** : to shake or jar together in confusion : JOSTLE ⟨~ pennies in a hat⟩ **2 a** : to crowd or push roughly : SHOVE ⟨in the cell into which we were *hustled* were forty or fifty Negroes —R.M.Lovett⟩; *specif* : to jostle with intent to rob ⟨they ~ old gentlemen; the old gentleman glances down, his watch is gone —E.M.Forster⟩ **b** : to convey forcibly or hurriedly ⟨grabbed him by the arm and *hustled* him out the door —John Dos Passos⟩ ⟨~ freight aboard the scow —N.C.McDonald⟩ ⟨allow himself to be *hustled* across the frontier —F.A.Ogg & Harold Zink⟩ **c** : to urge forward precipitately ⟨~ the tourist from one museum to the next⟩ ⟨~ your horse and don't say die —W.S.Gilbert⟩ ⟨trying to ~ history along —N.E.Nelson⟩ **3 a** : to obtain by energetic activity : GATHER, EARN ⟨*hustled* new customers —*Time*⟩ ⟨*hustled* himself a job as a section hand —Pearl Puckett⟩ **b** : to exert pressure on : sell or promote business with : WORK ⟨a waiter has to learn . . . that he must not ~ the customers —Robert Sylvester⟩ ⟨they ~ them for drinks —A.J.Liebling⟩ ⟨played it safe by *hustling* both sides of the street —Nelson Algren⟩ **c** : to deprive of one's possessions by force or fraud : ROB, CHEAT ⟨made the rounds of lovers' lanes . . . *hustling* the occupants of parked cars —C.L.Lamson⟩ ⟨~*s* schoolboys out of their lunch money with phony dice—Nelson Algren⟩; *specif* : to lure into a gambling game ~ *vi* **1** : PUSH, SHOVE, PRESS ⟨curious throngs ~ to the scene of the crime⟩ ⟨someone *hustled* against him in the crowd⟩ **2** : to move or act with vigorous speed : bestir oneself energetically : HURRY ⟨urged her to ~ across the street before the light changed⟩ ⟨ten miles of track a day were laid by *hustling* crews —R.A. Billington⟩ **3 a** : to make strenuous efforts to secure money or business ⟨our quartet was out *hustling* . . . and we knew we stood good to take in a lot of change before the night was over —Louis Armstrong⟩ ⟨diesel boats ~ at the docks —H.G. Nickels⟩ **b** : to solicit for prostitution ⟨there are fewer girls working in houses than there are *hustling* on the streets —Polly Adler⟩ **4** : to obtain money by fraud or deception : SWINDLE; *specif* : to lure a victim into a crooked gambling game

²hustle \"\ *n* -s **1** : an act of jostling or shoving **2 a** : energetic activity ⟨increase of leisure, diminution of ~, are the ends to be sought —Bertrand Russell⟩ ⟨the ~ and bustle in construction of motels —A.L.Himbert⟩ **b** : a hurried motion : MOVE ⟨get a ~ on to stockpile these essential materials —*Congressional Record*⟩ **3** *slang* **a** : an income-producing activity : JOB **b** (1) : an act or instance of fraud : SWINDLE, RACKET (2) : HUSTLER

hustle–bustle \ˌ=ˈ=ˌ=\ *n* : energetic confusion

hustle–cap \ˈ=ˌ=ˌ=\ *n* [¹*hustle* + *cap*] : a game of pitch and toss in which coins are shaken in a cap

hus·tle·ment \ˈhəsəlmənt\ *n* -s [ME *ostelement, hustilment* article of furniture, fr. MF *ostillement, oustillement*, fr. OF *ustillement*, fr. *ustil* article of furniture, tool, utensil, prob. fr. (assumed) VL *usitilia* (pl.) utensils, alter. of L *utensilia* — more at UTENSIL] *now dial* : household goods : FURNITURE, KNICKKNACKS — often used in pl.

hus·tler \ˈhəs(ə)lə(r)\ *n* -s **1 a** : a pickpocket's accomplice **b** : one who obtains money by fraudulent means : petty racketeer; *specif* : a professional gambler **c** : PROSTITUTE **2** : an active, enterprising, sometimes unscrupulous individual : GO-GETTER, LIVE WIRE **3 a** : VENDOR **b** : one that delivers or transports **c** : a pottery worker who carries greenware to the kiln shed or other place of processing **4** *New Zeal* : a tillage implement with tines used to stir the soil

hustling *adj* [fr. pres. part. of ¹*hustle*] **1** : characterized by hustling activity : ENERGETIC **2** : soliciting or productive of illicit gain; *specif* : WHORING

¹hut \ˈhət, *usu* -əd·+V\ *n* -s [MF *hutte* temporary dwelling of simple construction, of Gmc origin; akin to OHG *hutta* temporary dwelling of simple construction; akin to OE *hȳd* hide, skin — more at HIDE] **1 a** : a temporary structure used as living quarters for troops esp. in a theater of operations **b** : a rudimentary structure erected by the army for a special purpose (as a field aid station) **c** : a room or building used as a recreation center for troops in World War I **2 a** : an often small and temporary dwelling of simple construction : COTTAGE, SHACK ⟨sod ~⟩ ⟨the simplest of the primitive dwellings of the colonists were conical ~*s* of branches, rushes, and turf —Fiske Kimball⟩ **b** *Austral* : a house for shearers or other laborers on a ranch **c** : a simple shelter from the elements ⟨bathing ~⟩ ⟨round a winding road you come to a small ~ and a turnstile —Fred Streeter⟩ ⟨small wooden ~*s* inside which fishermen . . . can sit in comparative comfort with a portable stove while waiting for a nibble from far below the frozen surface —James Montagnes⟩; *specif* : overnight cabin ⟨hostel ~*s*⟩ ⟨mountain ~*s*⟩

²hut \"\ *vb* **hutted**; **hutted**; **hutting**; **huts** *vt* : to provide with usu. temporary living quarters : HOUSE, BILLET ⟨were no sooner *hutted* than we were on the march —S.W.Mitchell⟩ ~ *vi* : to become housed or quartered : LODGE ⟨his troops *hutted* among the heights —Washington Irving⟩

¹hutch \ˈhəch\ *n* -ES [ME *hucche, huche*, fr. OF *huche*] **1 a** : a chest or compartment for storage : BIN, LOCKER **b** : a low cupboard with doors usu. surmounted by two open shelves **2 a** : a pen or coop for an animal : CAGE ⟨provided a ~ for them in the garden —T.E.Donne⟩ **b** : a cageful of animals ⟨kept . . . a ~ or two of hare —Joyce Warren⟩ **3 a** : a cramped or flimsy shelter for a man : SHACK, SHANTY **4 a** : a car on low wheels in which coal is drawn and hoisted out of a mine pit **b** (1) : the bottom compartment of an ore-dressing jig (2) : the mineral product that collects there

hutch 1b

²hutch \"\ *vt* -ED/-ING/-ES **1** *archaic* : to put away or store in a hutch : HOARD **2** : to wash (ore) in a box or jig

³hutch *adj* [perh. alter. of *hulch*] *obs* : HUMPED

hutch burn *n* : an inflammation of the skin of rabbits esp. on the hind feet and adjacent parts associated with unclean urine-soiled cages

hutch·e·so·ni·an \ˌhəchəˈsōnēən\ *adj, usu cap* [Francis *Hutcheson* †1746 Scot. philosopher + E *-ian*] : of or relating to the theories of the Scottish philosopher Francis Hutcheson

hutch·et \ˈhəchət\ *n* -s [MF *huchet*, fr. *hucher* to cry out, fr. OF *huchier*, prob. of imit. origin] : a hunter's horn : BUGLE 2

hutch·in·so·ni·an teeth *or* **hutchinsonian incisors** \ˌhəchən-ˈsōnēən-\ *n pl, often cap H* [*hutchinsonian* fr. Sir Jonathan *Hutchinson* + E *-ian*] : HUTCHINSON'S TEETH

hutch·in·son·ite \ˈhəchənsəˌnīt\ *n* -s [Arthur *Hutchinson* †1937 Eng. mineralogist + E *-ite*] : a mineral $(Pb,Tl)_2(Cu,Ag)As_5S_{10}$ consisting of sulfide of lead, copper, and arsenic, with thallium and silver replacing variable amounts of lead and copper, and occurring in small red orthorhombic crystals

hutch·in·son's teeth \ˈhəchənsənz-\ *also* **hutchinson teeth** *n pl but sing or pl in constr, usu cap H* [after Sir Jonathan *Hutchinson* †1913 Eng. surgeon] : peg-shaped teeth having a crescentic notch in the cutting edge and occurring esp. in children with congenital syphilis

hutchinson's triad *n, usu cap H* : a triad of symptoms comprising Hutchinson's teeth, interstitial keratitis, and deafness and occurring in children with congenital syphilis

hutch·ins's goose \ˈhəchənz(əz)-\ *n, usu cap H* [after Thomas *Hutchins* †1790 Eng. attaché of the Hudson's Bay Company] : a variety (*Branta canadensis hutchinsii*) of the Canada goose closely resembling but smaller than the typical form, breeding in arctic America and migrating south through the U.S., but being rare east of the Mississippi

hutch table *n* : a combination table and chest whose top can be tilted back to convert the unit into a chair or settee

hut circle *n* : a ring of stones or earth marking the site of a prehistoric dwelling

hu·tia *also* **ju·tia** \(h)üˈtēə\ *n* -s [Sp *hutía* & AmerSp *jutía*, fr. Taino *hutia*] : any of several large edible hystricomorph rodents that constitute two West Indian genera (*Capromys* and *Geocapromys*) and a related So. American genus (*Procapromys*), are closely related to the coypus, and are now extinct over much of their range

hutkeeper \ˈ=ˌ=\ *n, Austral* : the man in charge of a hut on a ranch

hut·man \ˈhətmən\ *n, pl* **hutmen** : a member of the staff of an overnight hut for hikers

hutmaster \ˈ=ˌ=\ *n* : the manager of an overnight hut for hikers

hut·ment \ˈhətmənt\ *n* -s [²*hut* + *-ment*] **1 a** : a collection of huts : ENCAMPMENT **b** : the act or process of housing people in huts **2** : HUT; *specif* : a prefabricated portable army housing unit usu. made of plywood and accommodating 16 to 20 men

huts *pl of* HUT, *pres 3d sing of* HUT

hutted *adj* [fr. past part. of ²*hut*] : consisting of or supplied with huts ⟨single-story ~ wards —*Lancet*⟩ ⟨a ~ camp⟩

hut·te·ri·an brethren \ˌhəˈtirēən-, hü|, hu̇|\ *n, cap H&B* [*hutterian* fr. Jakob *Hutter* (or *Huter*) †1536 Moravian Anabaptist + E *-ian*] : a Mennonite sect of northwestern U.S. and Canada living in communities and holding property in common

hut·ter·ite *also* **hu·ter·ite** \ˈhə|d·əˌrīt, ˈhü|, ˈhu̇|\ *n* -s *usu cap* : a member of the Hutterian Brethren

hutting *pres part of* HUT

¹hut·to·ni·an \ˌhəˈtōnēən\ *adj, usu cap* [James *Hutton* †1797 Scot. geologist + E *-ian*] : of or relating to the views of the Scottish geologist James Hutton

²huttonian \"\ *n* -s *usu cap* : an adherent of Huttonian theories (as uniformitarianism) of geology — **hut·to·ni·an·ism** \-ēəˌnizəm\ *n* -s *usu cap*

hut·ton·ite \ˈhətᵊnˌīt\ *n* -s [Colin O. *Hutton* b1910 Am. geologist born in New Zealand + E *-ite*] : a mineral $ThSiO_4$ consisting of monoclinic silicate of thorium dimorphous with thorite

hut·ton's vireo \ˈhətᵊnz-\ *n, usu cap H* [prob. fr. the name *Hutton*] : a vireo (*Vireo huttoni*) of western No. America having a dull olive back and dingy white underparts

hut·ton·weed \-ᵊnˌwēd\ *n* [prob. fr. the name *Hutton*] : WILD TEASEL

hu·tu \ˈhü(ˌ)tü\ *n, pl* **hutu** *or* **hutus** *usu cap* : RUNDI

hu·tukh·tu *or* **hu·tuk·tu** \hüˈtu̇k(ˌ)tü\ *n* -s *often cap* [Mongolian *khutukhtu* eminent, fr. *khutuk* eminence] : a Lamaist dignitary believed to be an incarnation of Buddha; *specif* : the spiritual ruler of Mongolia

hut urn *n* : a prehistoric cinerary urn made in the form of a round hut with a conical roof and found esp. in southern Italy

hu·tzul *also* **hu·zul** \hütˈsül\ *n, pl* **hutzul** *or* **hutzuls** *usu cap* **1** : a mountain people of the high Carpathians in Slovakia, Ruthenia, and Poland speaking a Ruthenian dialect **2** : a member of the Hutzul people

hux·le·ian *also* **hux·ley·an** \ˈhəkslēən, ˌ=ˈ=ˌ=\ *adj, usu cap* [Thomas H. *Huxley* †1895 Eng. biologist or Aldous L. *Huxley* b1894 Eng. novelist and critic + E *-an*] : of or relating to the English biologist Thomas H. Huxley or his novelist grandson Aldous Huxley

huy·gens eyepiece \ˈhīgənz-, ˈhȯi|\ *also* **huy·ghe·ni·an eyepiece** \(ˈ)=ˈgēnēən-\ *n, usu cap H* [*huyghenian* irreg. fr. Christian *Huygens* (or *Huyghens*) †1695 Du. physicist + E *-ian*] : a compound eyepiece so designed and placed that its field lens intercepts converging rays from an objective and forms a real image within the eyepiece

huy·gens' principle *also* **huy·ghens' principle** \ˈ=ˌgənz(əz)-\ *n, usu cap H* : a principle in physics: every point of an advancing wave front is a new center of disturbance from which emanate independent wavelets whose envelope constitutes a new wave front at each successive stage of the process

huz \(ˌ)(h)əz, (ˌ)(h)u̇z\ *pron* [by alter.] *dial Brit* : US

huzz \ˈhəz\ *vi* -ED/-ING/-ES [imit.] : BUZZ

¹huz·zah *or* **huz·za** \(ˌ)həˈzä, -zȧ\ *n* -s [origin unknown] : a cheer or shout of applause : HURRAH — often used interjectionally to express joy or approbation

²huzzah *or* **huzza** \"\ *vb* -ED/-ING/-S *vi* : to shout huzzah : HURRAH ~ *vt* : APPLAUD, CHEER

huzzy *var of* HUSSY

HV *abbr* **1** high velocity **2** high voltage

hvy *abbr* heavy

HW *abbr* **1** high water **2** highway **3** hit wicket **4** hot water

hwan \ˈ(h)wän\ *n, pl* **hwan** [Korean] : a former monetary unit of So. Korea established in 1953 and replaced in 1962 by the won

HWL *abbr* high-water line

HWM *abbr* high-water mark

hwy *abbr* highway

hy- *or* **hyo-** *comb form* [NL, fr. Gk *hyo-* upsilon (Υ, υ), fr. *y, hy* upsilon] **1** : connecting with the hyoid arch ⟨*hyo*glossus⟩ **2** : hyoid and ⟨*hyo*thyroid⟩

hy *abbr* **1** heavy **2** henry

hy·a·cinth \ˈhīəˌsin(t)th, -ˌsən-\ *n, pl* **hyacinths** \-n(t)s, -n(t)ths\ [L *hyacinthus*, a precious stone, a flowering plant, fr. Gk *hyakinthos*] **1 a** : a precious stone of the ancients sometimes held to be the sapphire **b** (1) : a transparent red or brownish zircon sometimes used as a gem (2) : a red or brownish essonite used as a gem **2 a** : a plant of the ancients held to be the Turk's-cap lily, iris, larkspur, or gladiolus **b** (1) : a plant of the genus *Hyacinthus; esp* : the common garden hyacinth (*H. orientalis*) widely grown for the beauty and fragrance of its flowers — see ROMAN HYACINTH (2) : any of several other plants of the family Liliaceae — usu. used with preceding qualifier; see SUMMER HYACINTH, WATER HYACINTH **3** : a light violet to moderate purple **4** : PURPLE GALLINULE

hyacinth 2b(1)

hyacinth bacteriosis *n* : a destructive bacterial disease of the hyacinth caused by a bacterium (*Xanthomonas hyacinthi*) that attacks both dry bulbs and growing plants

hyacinth bean *n* : a large twining vine (*Dolichos lablab*) that is native to the Old World tropics, has dark purple racemes of pealike flowers, and is widely grown as an ornamental, less often as a source of fodder, and sometimes for its edible pods and seeds

hyacinth blue *n* : a deep purplish blue that is slightly bluer than mazarine blue, redder and paler than average sapphire (sense 2a), and redder, lighter, and stronger than cyanine blue (sense 1b)

hy·a·cin·thi·an \ˌhīəˈsin(t)thēən\ *adj* : HYACINTHINE

hy·a·cin·thine \ˌhīəˈsin(t)thən, -nˌthīn\ *adj* [L *hyacinthinus*, fr. Gk *hyakinthinos*, fr. *hyakinthos* hyacinth, fr. *-inos* -ine] **1** : having any one of the four colors hyacinth, hyacinth blue, hyacinth violet, or hyacinth red **2 a** : of, relating to, or resembling the hyacinth ⟨his ~ locks descend in wavy curls —Alexander Pope⟩ **b** : adorned or decorated with hyacinths ⟨with ~ chaplet crowned —Francis Fawkes⟩

hyacinth red *n* : a grayish reddish orange that is slightly lighter than Etruscan red and yellower and darker than Persian melon

hyacinth squill *n* : an ornamental bulbous Mediterranean plant (*Scilla hyacinthoides*) with lilac-purple flowers

hy·a·cin·thus \ˌhīəˈsin(t)thəs\ *n, cap* [NL, fr. L, a flowering plant] : a genus of Old World bulbous and scapose herbs (family Liliaceae) having flowers in terminal mostly compact racemes and a bell-shaped corolla with a prominent tube and short limb — see HYACINTH

hyacinth violet *n* : a deep purple that is bluer and slightly darker than petunia violet, redder than pontiff, bluer, lighter, and stronger than imperial purple (sense 2), and bluer and paler than dahlia purple (sense 2)

¹hy·ae·na \hīˈēnə\ *var of* HYENA

²hyaena \"\ *n, cap* [NL, fr. L, hyena — more at HYENA] : the type genus of the family Hyaenidae

hy·ae·nan·che \ˌhīəˈnaŋkē\ *n, cap* [NL, fr. L *hyaena* hyena + NL *-anche* (fr. Gk *anchein* to strangle); fr. the use of the fruit in poisoning hyenas — more at HYENA, ANGER] : a genus of trees (family Euphorbiaceae) of southern Africa with coriaceous whorled leaves, cymose staminate flowers, and solitary pistillate flowers

hy·ae·narc·tos \-ˈnärkˌtäs\ *n, cap* [NL, fr. L *hyaena* hyena + Gk *arktos* bear — more at ARCTIC] : a genus of large Old World Pliocene and Pleistocene bears

hy·ae·nid \hīˈēnəd, -ˈen-\ *n* [NL *Hyaenidae*] : one of the Hyaenidae

hy·aeni·dae \hīˈēnəˌdē, -ˈen-\ *n pl, cap* [NL, fr. *Hyaena*, type genus + *-idae*] : a family of carnivorous mammals comprising the hyenas and usu. the aardwolf

hy·aeno·don \hīˈēnəˌdän, -ˈen-\ *n* [NL *Hyaenodont-, Hyaenodon*, fr. *Hyaena* + *-odont-, -odon* -odon] **1** *cap* : the type genus of Hyaenodontidae comprising extinct carnivorous mammals from Eocene, Oligocene, and possibly Miocene deposits of Eurasia, Africa, and No. America **2** -s : a mammal of the genus *Hyaenodon*

¹hy·aeno·dont \-ˌänt\ *adj* [NL *Hyaenodontidae*] : of or relating to the Hyaenodontidae

²hyaenodont \"\ *n* -s [NL *Hyaenodontidae*] : an animal of the family Hyaenodontidae

hy·aeno·don·ti·dae \(ˌ)hīˌēnəˈdäntəˌdē, -ˌen-\ *n pl, cap* [NL, fr. *Hyaenodont-, Hyaenodon*, type genus + *-idae*] : a family of typically rather slender long-skulled, more or less digitigrade clawed extinct carnivores of the suborder Creodonta varying from a few inches in length to the size of some of the recent large cats (as the leopard)

hy·aeno·don·toid \(ˌ)=ˌ=ˈdänˌtȯid\ *adj* [NL *Hyaenodontidae* + E *-oid*] : of, relating to, or resembling the Hyaenodontidae

hyal- *or* **hyalo-** *comb form* [LL, glass, fr. Gk, fr. *hyalos* transparent stone, glass] **1** : glass : glassy ⟨*hyal*escent⟩ ⟨*hyalo*crystalline⟩ **2** : transparent or translucent substance ⟨*hyalo*gen⟩

hy·a·les·cence \ˌhīəˈlesᵊn(t)s\ *n* -s [*hyal-* + *-escence*] : the quality or state of being hyalescent

hy·a·les·cent \ˌ;==ˈlesᵊnt\ *adj* [*hyal-* + *-escent*] : becoming or appearing hyaline

¹**hy·a·line** \ˈhīələn, -əˌlīn\ *adj* [LL *hyalinus*, fr. Gk *hyalinos*, fr. *hyalos* transparent stone, glass + *-inos* -ine] **1** : of, resembling, or consisting of glass ⟨a glimpse of bay below, a rock-set ~ circlet —Sybille Bedford⟩ **2 a** *biol* : transparent or nearly so ⟨a ~ membrane⟩ **b** *mineralogy* (1) : GLASSY (2) : lacking crystallinity : AMORPHOUS

²**hy·a·line** \", *in sense 2* -əˌlēn *or* -ələn\ *n* -s **1** : something transparent (as the smooth sea or the clear atmosphere) ⟨the morning is as clear as diamond or as ~ —Sacheverell Sitwell⟩ **2** *or* **hy·a·lin** \-ələn\ [prob. ISV *hyal-* + *-ine* or *-in*] **a** : a nitrogenous substance closely related to chitin that forms the main constituent of the walls of hydatid cysts and yields a sugar on decomposition **b** : any of several similar translucent substances collecting around cells, capable of being stained by eosin, and yielding a carbohydrate as a cleavage product

hyaline cartilage *n* [¹*hyaline*] : translucent bluish white cartilage that has the cartilage cells embedded in an apparently homogeneous matrix, is the commonest type of cartilage present in joints and in respiratory passages, and forms most of the fetal skeleton

hyaline cast *n* [¹*hyaline*] : a renal cast characterized by homogeneity of structure

hyaline degeneration *n* [¹*hyaline*] : tissue degeneration chiefly of connective tissues in which structural elements of affected cells are replaced by homogeneous translucent material that stains intensely with acid dyes

hy·a·lin·iza·tion \ˌhīələnəˈzāshən\ *n* -s : the process of becoming hyalinized or the state of being hyaline

hy·a·lin·ize \ˈhīələˌnīz\ *vi* -ED/-ING/-S [¹*hyaline* + *-ize*] : to become hyaline; *esp* : to undergo hyaline degeneration

hy·al·i·no·crystalline \hīˌal(ə)ˌnō+\ *adj* [ISV ¹*hyaline* + *-o-* + *crystalline*; orig. formed as G *hyalinokristallin*] *of rock* : having a texture partly glassy and partly crystalline

hy·a·li·no·sis \ˌhīələˈnōsəs\ *n, pl* **hyalino·ses** \-ōˌsēz\ [NL, fr. LL *hyalinus* hyaline + NL *-osis*] **1** : HYALINE DEGENERATION **2** : a condition characterized by hyaline degeneration

hy·a·lite \ˈhīəˌlīt\ *n* -s [G *hyalit*, fr. Gk *hyalos* transparent stone, glass + G *-it* -ite] : a colorless opal that is sometimes clear as glass and sometimes translucent or whitish and that occurs as globules or crusts lining cavities or cracks in rocks

hy·a·lithe \ˈhīəˌlith, -ˌlīth\ *n* -s [prob. modif. (influenced by E *-lith*) of F *hyalite* hyalithe, hyalite, fr. G *hyalit* hyalite] : an opaque glass that resembles porcelain and is sometimes used as a gemstone

hyalo- — see HYAL-

hy·a·lo·basalt \ˌhīˈə(ˌ)lō+\ *n* [ISV *hyal-* + *basalt*; orig. formed in G] : BASALT GLASS

hy·a·lo·crystalline \"+\ *adj* [*hyal-* + *crystalline*] : HYALINOCRYSTALLINE

hy·al·o·gen \hīˈaləjən, -ˌjen\ *n* -s [ISV *hyal-* + *-gen*; prob. orig. formed in G] : any of several insoluble substances related to mucoids that are found in many animal structures (as hydatid cysts or sponges) and that yield hyalines on hydrolysis

hy·a·loid \ˈhīəˌlȯid\ *adj* [Gk *hyaloeidēs*, fr. *hyalos* glass + *-eidēs* -oid] *anat* : GLASSY, TRANSPARENT

hyaloid membrane *n* : a very delicate membrane enclosing the vitreous humor of the eye

hy·al·o·mere \hīˈaləˌmi(ə)r\ *n* -s [*hyal-* + *-mere*] : the pale nonrefractile portion of a blood platelet — compare CHROMOMERE

hy·a·lom·ma \ˌhīəˈlämə\ *n, cap* [NL, fr. *hyal-* + *-omma*] : an Old World genus of ticks that attack wild and domestic mammals and sometimes man, produce severe lesions by their bites, and often serve as vectors of viral and protozoal diseases

hy·a·lo·mucoid \ˌhīˈə(ˌ)lō+\ *n* [*hyal-* + *mucoid*] : a mucoprotein in the vitreous humor

hy·a·lo·ne·ma \ˌhīəlōˈnēmə\ *n, cap* [NL, fr. *hyal-* + *-nema*] : a genus of hyalosponges having a long stem composed of very long slender transparent siliceous fibers twisted together like the strands of a cord

hy·al·o·phane \hīˈaləˌfān\ *n* -s [G *hyalophan*, fr. *hyal-* + *-phan* -phane] : a mineral $BaAl_2Si_2O_8$ consisting of a monoclinic feldspar isomorphous with and resembling adularia

hy·a·lo·pi·lit·ic \ˌhīˈə(ˌ)lōˌpīˈlid·ik\ *adj* [ISV *hyalopilit-* (fr. G *hyalopilitisch* hyalopilitic, fr. *hyal-* + Gk *pilos* felt + G *-it* -ite + *-isch* -ish, fr. OHG *-isc*) + *-ic* — more at PILE (hair)] : composed of or characterized by innumerable slender microlites embedded in glass ⟨~ structure is frequently found in basic lavas⟩

hy·alo·plasm \hīˈaləˌplazəm, ˈhīəlō,-\ *n* -s [prob. fr. G *hyaloplasma*, fr. *hyal-* + *-plasma* -plasm] : the clear apparently homogeneous ground substance of cytoplasm that is essentially the continuous phase of a multiple-phase colloidal system

hy·a·lo·plas·ma \ˌhīəlōˈplazmə\ *n* [prob. fr. G] : HYALOPLASM

hy·a·lo·sid·er·ite \ˌhīəlōˈsidəˌrīt\ *n* [G *hyalosiderit*, fr. *hyal-* + Gk *sidēros* iron + G *-it* -ite] : an olivine containing much iron

hy·alo·sponge \hīˈalōˌspənj, ˈhīəl-\ *n* [NL *Hyalospongiae*] : one of the Hyalospongiae

hy·a·lo·spon·gea \ˌhīəlōˈspənjēə, -pän-\ [NL, fr. *hyal-* + *-spongea* (irreg. fr. L *spongia* sponge) — more at SPONGE] *syn of* HYALOSPONGIAE

hy·a·lo·spon·gia \"\ [NL, fr. *hyal-* + *-spongia*] *syn of* HYALOSPONGIAE

hy·a·lo·spon·gi·ae \-ēˌē\ *n pl, cap* [NL, fr. *hyal-* + *-spongiae*] : a class of Porifera comprising sponges with 6-rayed siliceous spicules, no surface epithelium, and the choanocytes restricted to finger-shaped chambers — see GLASS SPONGE

hy·a·lo·te·kite \ˌhīəlōˈtēˌkīt\ *n* -s [Sw *hyalotekit*, fr. *hyal-* + Gk *tēkein* to melt + Sw *-it* -ite; fr. the fact that it fuses to a clear glass — more at THAW] : a mineral approximately $(Pb,Ca,Ba)_4BSi_6O_{17}(OH,F)$ consisting of a borosilicate and fluoride of lead, barium, and calcium found in crystalline masses

hy·al·uro·nate \ˌhīəˈlürəˌnāt\ *n* -s [ISV *hyaluronic* + *-ate*] : a salt or ester of hyaluronic acid

hy·al·uron·ic acid \ˌhīəlüˌränik-\ *n* [*hyaluronic* ISV *hyal-* + *-uronic*] : a viscous mucopolysaccharide acid that occurs chiefly in connective tissue or their derivatives — compare MUCOITINSULFURIC ACID

hy·al·uron·i·dase \ˌ===ˈränəˌdās, -āz\ *n* -s [ISV *hyaluronid-* (fr. *hyaluronic acid*) + *-ase*] : an enzyme that splits hyaluronic acid and thus lowers the viscosity of the acid and facilitates the spreading of fluids through tissues either advantageously (as in the absorption of drugs) or disadvantageously (as in the dissemination of infection), that occurs in many normal tissues, in malignant growths, in invasive bacteria, and in certain venoms but is usu. prepared from mammalian testes, and that is used esp. to aid in the dispersion of fluids (as local anesthetics) injected subcutaneously for therapeutic purposes — called also *spreading factor*

hyb *abbr* hybrid

hy·blae·an \(ˈ)hīˈblēən\ *adj, usu cap* [L *hyblae*us of Hybla (fr. Gk *hyblaios*, fr. *Hybla*, ancient town in Sicily famous for the excellence of its honey) + E *-an*] : MELLIFLUOUS, HONEYED ⟨golden and *Hyblaean* eloquence —A.C.Swinburne⟩

¹**hyb·o·dont** \ˈhibəˌdänt\ *adj* [NL *Hybodont-, Hybodus*] : of or relating to the genus *Hybodus* or family Hybodontidae

²**hybodont** \"\ *n* -s [NL *Hybodont-, Hybodus*] : a hybodont shark

hyb·o·dus \-ədəs\ *n, cap* [NL *Hybodont-, Hybodus*, fr. Gk *hybos* hump + NL *-odont, -odus*] : a large genus (the type of the family Hybodontidae) of extinct sharks existing from the Trias to the Lower Cretaceous that are usu. included among the Squaloidea but are sometimes placed with related extinct forms in a separate suborder of the order Pleurotremata

hy·bo·sis \hīˈbōsəs, hə̇ˈ-\ *n, pl* **hybo·ses** \-ōˌsēz\ *also* **hybosises** [NL, fr. Gk *hybos* hump + NL *-osis*] : a virus disease of cotton in which the leaves are reduced and distorted

¹**hy·brid** \ˈhībrə̇d\, *substand* -ˌbred\ *n* -s [L *hybrida* animal whose parents belong to different varieties or to different species, person whose parents belong to different ethnic groups, prob. of non-IE origin; akin to the source of L *imbr-, imber* offspring of a tame sheep and a wild sheep] **1** : an offspring of two animals or plants of different races, breeds, varieties, species, or genera; *specif* : an individual produced by union of gametes from parents of different genotype — compare CROSSBREED, MENDEL'S LAW, MULE **2** : a person or group produced by the blending of two diverse cultures or traditions ⟨the cultural ~ occupies a marginal position between two cultures⟩ ⟨every civilized group . . . has been a ~ —H.J.Muller⟩ **3 a** : one that is heterogeneous in origin or composition : COMPOSITE ⟨most of the tools are original designs or ~s evolved from established forms —Victor Boesen⟩ ⟨the vice-president is a ~ in the government, being both an executive and legislative officer —Arthur Krock⟩ **b** : LOANBLEND

²**hybrid** \"\ *adj* **1 a** : marked by heterogeneity in origin, composition, or appearance : COMPOSITE ⟨difficulties with normal English are . . . its ~ vocabulary and the irregularities of English spelling —G.A.Miller⟩ **b** : being a linguistic hybrid ⟨a ~ term⟩ **2** : of, relating to, or resulting from the union of gametes from parents of different genotype ⟨the high percentage of intermarriage, however, has made the population . . racially ~ —*Current Biog.*⟩ **3** : having characteristics resulting from the blending of two diverse cultures or traditions ⟨a remarkable ~ culture in which Norse and Irish elements are inextricably combined —F.M.Stenton⟩

hy·bri·da \ˈhībrədə\ *n, pl* **hybri·dae** \-rəˌdē\ [NL, fr. L] : an interspecific hybrid

hybrid clover *n* : ALSIKE CLOVER

hybrid coil *n* : a transformer having three windings two of which are in series to facilitate maintenance of voltage balance to ground

hybrid corn *n* **1** : a corn resulting from crossbreeding; *specif* : the grain of Indian corn developed by hybridizing two or more inbred strains **2** : the plant that is grown from the grain of hybrid corn and that conforms to a standard of desirable characteristics including increased size, yield, or disease resistance but whose own grain produces an inferior progeny

hy·brid·ism \ˈhībrə̇ˌdizəm\ *n* -s [ISV *hybrid* + *-ism*] **1** : HYBRIDITY **2** : the fusion of diverse cultures or traditions ⟨the ~ of Puerto Rico combines both No. American and Spanish culture⟩

hy·brid·ist \-də̇st\ *n* -s [*hybrid* + *-ist*] : HYBRIDIZER

hy·brid·i·ty \hīˈbridəd·ē, -ətē, -i\ *n* -ES [ISV *hybrid* + *-ity*] : the quality or state of being hybrid

hy·brid·iz·able \ˈhībrə̇ˌdīzəbəl, ˌ==ˈ===\ *adj* **1** : capable of producing a hybrid by crossing with another species or form **2** : reproducible by hybridization

hy·brid·iza·tion \ˌhībrə̇də̇ˈzāshən, -ˌdīˈz-\ *n* -s : the act or process of hybridizing or the state of being hybridized

hy·brid·ize \ˈhībrə̇ˌdīz\ *vb* -ED/-ING/-S [*hybrid* + *-ize*] *vt* : to cause to produce hybrids : CROSS, INTERBREED ⟨laid out ranches . . . where they could fatten and ~ their stock —R.A.Billington⟩ ~ *vi* : to produce hybrids ⟨the possibility . . . that Homo sapiens and Neanderthal were *hybridizing* in northwest India or central Asia prior to the third interglacial —J.E.Weckler⟩

hy·brid·iz·er \-zə(r)\ *n* -s : one that hybridizes ⟨is a noted botanist and ~ of native iris —*Wild Flower*⟩

hy·brid·ous \ˈhībrə̇dəs\ *adj* : HYBRID

hybrid perpetual *or* **hybrid perpetual rose** *n* : any of certain cultivated bush roses derived chiefly from the bourbon and characterized by vigorous hardy growth, a tendency to recurrent blooming, and good-sized often fragrant flowers borne singly or in groups of two to five — see HYBRID TEA

hybrid polyantha *n* : FLORIBUNDA

hybrid rock *n* : a rock formed by the mixing of two magmas or by the assimilation of the intruded by the intruding rock

hybrids *pl of* HYBRID

hybrid swarm *n* : a variable local population at the junction of the range of two interfertile species or subspecies resulting from extensive interbreeding and hybridization

hybrid tea *or* **hybrid tea rose** *n* : any of numerous cultivated bush roses derived chiefly from crosses of tea roses and hybrid perpetuals and characterized by intermediate hardiness and vigor, strongly recurrent bloom, and long pointed buds followed by large usu. scentless flowers borne singly or in groups of two to five

hybrid vigor *n* : unusual vigor associated with hybridity : HETEROSIS

hybris *var of* HUBRIS

hyd *abbr* **1** hydraulic; hydraulics **2** hydrographic; hydrography **3** hydrostatic; hydrostatics

hy·dan·to·ic acid \ˌhīˌdanˌtōik-\ *n* [*hydantoic* ISV *hydrogen* + *allantoic*] : a white crystalline acid $NH_2CONHCH_2COOH$ obtained esp. by boiling hydantoin with alkalies

hy·dan·to·in \hīˈdantəwə̇n\ *n* -s [ISV *hydrogen* + *allantoin*; prob. orig. formed in G] **1** : a crystalline weakly acidic compound $C_3H_4N_2O_2$ that is a di-oxo derivative of imidazole with a sweetish taste, that is found in beet juice and made synthetically (as by the action of hydriodic acid on allantoin), and that is used in organic synthesis **2** : a derivative of the hydantoin compound (as diphenylhydantoin)

hy·dan·to·in·ate \-əˌnāt\ *n* -s [*hydantoin* + *-ate*] : a salt of hydantoin or one of its derivatives

hydat- *or* **hydato-** *comb form* [prob. fr. NL, fr. Gk, fr. *hydat-*, *hydōr* — more at WATER] : water ⟨*Hydat*ina⟩ ⟨*hydato*genesis⟩

hy·da·thode \ˈhīdəˌthōd\ *n* -s [ISV *hydat-* + *-hode* (fr. Gk *hodos* way, road); prob. orig. formed in G — more at CEDE] : an epidermal structure in higher plants functioning in the exudation of water; *specif* : an opening in the epidermis resembling a stoma below which is a chamber usu. filled or bordered by thin-walled loosely arranged cells — called also *water pore, water stoma*; see GUTTATION, WATER GLAND

hy·da·tid \ˈhīdəd·ə̇d, -ˌīdətə̇d\ *n* [prob. fr. (assumed) NL *hydatid-, hydatis*, fr. Gk, watery vesicle, fr. *hydat-, hydōr* water] **1** *also* **hydatid cyst** : a larval tapeworm typically comprising a fluid-filled sac from the inner walls of which develop daughter cysts and scolices but occas. forming an uncircumscribed proliferating spongy mass that actively invades and metastasizes in the host's tissues — see ECHINOCOCCUS; compare COENURUS, CYSTICERCOID, CYSTICERCUS **2 a** : an abnormal cyst or cystic structure; *esp* : HYDATIDIFORM MOLE **b** : HYDATID DISEASE

hydatid disease *n* : a form of echinococcosis caused by the development of hydatids of a tapeworm (*Echinococcus granulosus*) in the tissues esp. of the liver or lungs of man and certain animals

hy·da·tid·i·form \ˌhīdəˈtidəˌfȯrm\ *also* **hy·dat·i·form** \(ˈ)hīˈdad·əˌfȯrm\ *adj* [*hydatidiform* prob. alter. (influenced by *hydatid*) of *hydatiform*; *hydatiform* ISV *hydat-* (fr. *hydatid*) + *-iform*; prob. orig. formed as F *hydatiforme*] : resembling a hydatid : CYSTIC

hydatidiform mole *n* : a mass in the uterus consisting of enlarged edematous degenerated placental villi growing in clusters resembling grapes and usu. associated with death of the fetus

hy·da·tid·o·cele \ˌhīdəˈtidəˌsēl\ *n* -s [NL, prob. fr. (assumed) NL *hydatid-, hydatis* + NL *-o-* + *-cele*] : a tumorous condition of the scrotum caused by local infestation with echinococcus larvae

hydatid of mor·ga·gni \-mȯ(r)ˈgänyē\ *usu cap M* [after Giovanni B. *Morgagni* †1771 Ital. physician] **1** : a small stalked or pedunculated body found between the testicle and the head of the epididymis in the male or attached to the fimbriae of the fallopian tube or the broad ligament in the female and considered to be a remnant of the duct of the pronephros or of the upper end of the müllerian duct **2** : a small unstalked or sessile body found in the same situation in the male only and considered to be a remnant of the müllerian duct

hy·da·tid·osis \ˌhīdəˌtiˈdōsə̇s\ *n, pl* **hydatid·oses** \-ōˌsēz\ [NL, prob. fr. (assumed) NL *hydatid-, hydatis* + NL *-osis*] : ECHINOCOCCOSIS; *specif* : HYDATID DISEASE

hy·dat·i·na \hīˈdatˈnə\ *n, cap* [NL, fr. *hydat-* + *-ina*] : a genus of stout-bodied naked rotifers (order Monogononta)

hy·da·to·genesis \ˌhīdə(ˌ)tō + \ *n* [*hydat-* + *genesis*] **1** : the crystallization of minerals in certain rocks by the water present in a magma; *esp* : the process of depositing minerals in veins from aqueous solutions **2** : the crystallization of salt or gypsum from normal aqueous solutions

hy·da·to·genetic \"+\ *adj* [fr. *hydatogenesis*, after E *genesis*: *genetic*] : HYDATOGENIC

hy·da·to·gen·ic \ˌhīdətōˈjenik\ *or* **hy·da·tog·e·nous** \ˌhīdəˈtäjənəs\ *adj* [G *hydatogen* hydatogenic (fr. *hydat-* + *-gen* -genic, -genous, fr. Gk *-genēs* born) + E *-ic* or *-ous* — more at -GEN] **1** : crystallized from or deposited by aqueous solutions **2** : of or relating to hydatogenesis

hy·da·to·mor·phic \ˌhīdətōˈmȯrfik\ *adj* [G *hydatomorphose* crystallization from aqueous solutions (fr. *hydat-* + *-morphose* -morphosis) + E *-ic*] : of, relating to, or produced by crystallization from aqueous solutions — **hy·da·to·mor·phism** \ˌ===ˈmȯrˌfizəm\ *n* -s

hy·da·to·pneumatolytic \ˌhīdə(ˌ)tō +\ *or* **hy·da·to·pneumatic** \"+\ *adj* [*hydatopneumatolytic* fr. *hydat-* + *pneumatolytic*; *hydatopneumatic* fr. *hydat-* + *pneumatic*] *of ore deposits* : formed by the joint agency of water and vapor

hy·der·a·bad \ˈhīd(ə)rəˌbad, -ˌbäd, ˌ=(=)=ˈ=\ *adj, usu cap* **1** [fr. *Hyderabad*, city in south central India] : of or from the city of Hyderabad, India : of the kind or style prevalent in Hyderabad **2** [fr. *Hyderabad*, city in southwest Pakistan] : of or from the city of Hyderabad, Pakistan : of the kind or style prevalent in Hyderabad

hyd·na·ce·ae \hidˈnāsēˌē\ *n pl, cap* [NL, fr. *Hydnum*, type genus + *-aceae*] : a family of fungi (order Agaricales) that are distinguished by a hymenium spread out over teeth, spines, or warty emergences or a fleshy, woody, or leathery fruiting body and that include several which cause rot in timbers and a few which are edible

hyd·no·car·pic acid \ˌhidnəˌkärpik-\ *n* [*hydnocarpic*, ISV *hydnocarp-* (fr. NL *Hydnocarpus*) + *-ic*] : a low-melting unsaturated acid $C_5H_7(CH_2)_{10}COOH$ occurring as the glyceride in chaulmoogra oil and hydnocarpus oil; 11-(2-cyclopentenyl)-undecanoic acid

hyd·no·car·pus \ˌ==ˈkärpəs\ *n* [NL, fr. *hydno-* (fr. Gk *hydnon* truffle) + *-carpus*] **1** *cap* : a genus of Indo-Malayan trees (family Flacourtiaceae) with alternate leaves, small dioecious racemose flowers, and capsular fruits — compare CHAULMOOGRA **2** -ES : any tree of the genus *Hydnocarpus*

hydnocarpus oil \ˌ==ˈ==-\ *n* : a fatty oil obtained from seeds of trees of the genus *Hydnocarpus* (esp. *H. wightiana*) — compare CHAULMOOGRA OIL

hyd·noid \ˈhidˌnȯid\ *adj* [NL *Hydnum* + E *-oid*] : of, relating to, or characteristic of the genus *Hydnum*

hyd·no·ra \hidˈnōrə, ˈhidnərə\ *n, cap* [NL, irreg. fr. Gk *hydnon* truffle] : a genus (the type of the family Hydnoraceae) of African root parasites having soft spines on the inner surface of the perianth lobes resembling those of the hymenium of a fungus of the genus *Hydnum*

hyd·no·ra·ce·ae \ˌhidnəˈrāsēˌē\ *n pl, cap* [NL, fr. *Hydnora*, type genus + *-aceae*] : a family of African and Argentinian highly modified flowering plants (order Aristolochiales) that are parasitic on the roots of other plants and consist of a branched subterranean system of leafless rhizoid shoots from which large succulent solitary flowers are sent up to the surface of the ground — compare RAFFLESIACEAE — **hyd·no·ra·ceous** \ˌ==ˈrāshəs\ *adj*

hyd·num \ˈhidnəm\ *n, cap* [NL, fr. Gk *hydnon* truffle] : the type genus of the family Hydnaceae

hydr- *or* **hydro-** *comb form* [alter. (influenced by L *hydr-*, *hydro-*) of ME *ydr-, ydro-*, fr. OF *ydr-* & MF *ydro-*, fr. L *hydr-, hydro-*, fr. Gk, fr. *hydōr* — more at WATER] **1 a** : water ⟨*hydro*gel⟩ ⟨*hydro*electricity⟩ **b** : hydraulic ⟨*hydro*press⟩ **2** : water-loving organism — chiefly in generic names ⟨*Hydrac*arina⟩ ⟨*Hydro*dictyon⟩ **3 a** : hydrogen : containing hydrogen ⟨*hydr*iodic acid⟩ ⟨*hydro*borate⟩ **b** *now usu hydro-* : combined with hydrogen — esp. in names of organic compounds ⟨*hydro*quinidine⟩ **c** : combined with water by hydration ⟨*hydr*acrylic acid⟩ or by hydrolysis ⟨*hydro*cellulose⟩ **4** : characterized by an accumulation of fluid in a (specified) bodily part ⟨*hydro*nephrosis⟩ **5 a** : combined with water — in names of minerals ⟨*hydro*hetaerolite⟩ **b** : characterized by addition of water or its constituents — in names of varieties of minerals ⟨*hydro*mica⟩ **6** [NL, fr. *Hydra* (genus of polyps)] : hydroid ⟨*hydro*medusa⟩ ⟨*hydro*rhiza⟩

hy·dra \ˈhīdrə\ *n* [alter. (influenced by L *Hydra*) of earlier *idre* complicated evil thing, fr. ME *Ydre, Ydra* Hydra (mythical many-headed serpent slain by Hercules that grew two heads in place of each one that was cut off unless the wound was cauterized), fr. MF & L; MF *Ydre* Hydra, fr. L *Hydra*, fr. Gk; akin to Gk *hydros* water snake — more at OTTER] **1** -s : a many-sided problem or obstacle that presents new difficulties each time one aspect of it is solved or overcome **2** [NL, fr. L *Hydra* (mythical serpent)] **a** -s : any of a number of small freshwater hydrozoan polyps constituting *Hydra* and related genera, usu. living attached to sticks, leaves, or other submerged objects, and consisting of a simple tube with a mouth at one extremity surrounded by a circle of tentacles with which to capture food, the young developing either from eggs or as buds that become detached from the side of the parent after differentiating **b** *cap* : a common genus of hydras

hy·dra·car·i·an \ˌhīdrəˈka(a)rēən\ *n* -s [ISV *Hydracar-* (fr. NL *Hydracarina*) + *-ian*] : one of the Hydrachnellae

hy·drac·a·ri·na \hīˌdrakəˈrīnə, -ˈrēnə\ [NL, fr. *hydr-* + *Acarina*] *syn of* HYDRACHNELLAE

hy·drac·a·rine \(ˈ)hīˈdrakəˌrīn, -ˌrēn, -ˌrə̇n\ *adj* [NL *Hydracarina*] : of or relating to the Hydrachnellae

hy·drach·nel·lae \ˌhīˌdrakˈne(ˌ)lē\ *n pl, cap* [NL, fr. *Hydrachna* + *-ellae* (pl. of *-ella*)] : a superfamily or higher group of Acarina comprising freshwater and marine mites that are usu. rather large and often bright red, that have two pairs of eyes, tarsi usu. with two claws and without an empodium, and chelicerae with a sickle-shaped movable digit, and that with few exceptions breathe by means of a well-developed tracheal system — see HALACARIDAE, HYDRACHNIDAE

hy·drach·nid \hīˈdraknə̇d\ *n* -s [NL *Hydrachnidae*] : one of the Hydrachnidae : WATER MITE

hy·drach·ni·dae \-nəˌdē\ *n pl, cap* [NL, fr. *Hydrachna*, type genus (fr. *hydr-* + Gk *achna, achnē* foam, chaff) + *-idae* — more at EAR] *in some classifications* : a large family of water mites (group Hydrachnellae) that includes all the common free-living mites of fresh water and a few parasites of the gills of mollusks and that is now usu. broken up into numerous separate families

hy·drach·noi·dea \ˌhīˌdrakˈnȯidēə\ [NL, fr. *Hydrachna* + *-oidea*] *syn of* HYDRACHNELLAE

hy·dra·coral \ˈhīdrə+\ *n* [perh. irreg. fr. NL *Hydrocorallinae*] : HYDROCORAL

hy·drac·ry·late \hīˈdrakrəˌlāt, ˌhīdrəˈkriˌl-\ *n* -s [ISV *hydracrylic* + *-ate*] : a salt or ester of hydracrylic acid

hy·dracryl·ic acid \ˌhīdrəˌkrilik-\ *n* [*hydracrylic* ISV *hydr-* + *acrylic*] : a syrupy acid $HOCH_2CH_2COOH$ that is isomeric with lactic acid and decomposes easily on heating into acrylic acid

hy·drac·ry·lo·ni·trile \hīˌdrakrə(ˌ)lōˈnī·trəl, -ˌtrēl, -ˌīl\ *n* [*hydr-* + *acrylonitrile*] : ETHYLENE CYANOHYDRIN

hy·drac·tin·ia \ˌhīˌdrakˈtinēə\ *n, cap* [NL, fr. *hydr-* + *Actinia*] : a genus of marine hydroids that have separate and distinctive polyps for nutritive, reproductive, and defensive functions borne on a dense encrusting coenosarc and that are commonly associated with shells containing hermit crabs — **hy·drac·tin·i·an** \ˌ==ˈtinēən\ *adj or n*

hydraemia *var of* HYDREMIA

hy·dra·gogue *also* **hydragog** \ˈhīdrəˌgäg\ *n* -s [obs. *hydragogue*, adj., causing a watery discharge from the bowels, fr. LL *hydragogus*, fr. Gk *hydragōgos*, fr. *hydr-* + *agōgos* leading, drawing forth — more at -AGOGUE] : a cathartic that causes copious watery discharges from the bowels

hydra-headed \ˌ==ˈ==\ *adj* [*Hydra*, mythical many-headed serpent + *headed* — more at HYDRA] : having many centers or branches ⟨a *hydra-headed* organization⟩ ⟨passive but *hydra-headed* resistance —Edward Crankshaw⟩

hy·dral·a·zine \hīˈdraləˌzēn, -ˌzə̇n\ *n* -s [prob. fr. *hydr-* + *phthalazine*] : a crystalline base $C_8H_5N_2NHNH_2$ used in the treatment of hypertension; 1-hydrazino-phthalazine

Hydra–Matic \ˌhīdrəˌmad·ik\ *trademark* — used for an automobile transmission having a fluid coupling and automatic gear-shifting controls

hy·dram·ni·os \hīˈdramnēˌäs\ *also* **hy·dram·ni·on** \-ˌän\ *n*

[NL, fr. *hydr-* + *amnios* or *amnion*] **:** excessive accumulation of the amniotic fluid

hy·dran·gea \hī'drānjə *sometimes* -ran- *or* -raan-, *chiefly in substand speech* ˌhīdə'r-\ *n* [NL, fr. *hydr-* + *-angea* (fr. Gk *angeion* vessel); prob. fr. the shape of the seed capsule — more at ANGI-] **1** *cap* **:** a large genus of widely distributed shrubs and one woody vine (family Saxifragaceae) with opposite leaves and corymbose clusters of usu. showy flowers — compare HYDRANGEACEAE **2** -s **:** a plant of the genus *Hydrangea* having ample white or tinted flower clusters in which all or most of the flowers are sterile: as **a :** a shrub (*H. macrophylla*) commonly grown in greenhouses **b :** a hardy fall-blooming shrub (*H. paniculata* or its variety *H. paniculata grandiflora*) **3 :** the dried rhizome and roots of the wild hydrangea (*Hydrangea arborescens*) formerly used in pharmacy as a diuretic

hydrangea blue *n* **:** a pale purplish blue that is deeper and slightly redder than starlight blue and bluer and deeper than haze blue, moonstone blue, or Ontario violet

hy·dran·ge·a·ce·ae \(ˌ)hīˌdrānjē'āsēˌē, -ran-,-raan-\ *n pl, cap* [NL, fr. *Hydrangea*, type genus + *-aceae*] *in some classifications* **:** a family of shrubs and trees (order Rosales) that are now usu. included in Saxifragaceae

hydrangea family *n* **:** SAXIFRAGACEAE

hydrangea pink *n* **:** a moderate pink that is yellower and less strong than arbutus pink, yellower and paler than blossom pink, and paler than chalk pink — called also *aurore*

hydrangea red *n* **:** a grayish red that is bluer and duller than Pompeian red or bois de rose, yellower and less strong than blush rose, and yellower and duller than appleblossom

hy·drant \'hīdrənt\ *n* -s [*hydr-* + *-ant* (n. suffix)] **1 :** a discharge pipe with a valve and spout at which water may be drawn from the mains of waterworks — called also *fireplug* **2 :** FAUCET

hydrant

hy·dranth \'hīˌdran(t)th\ *n* -s [ISV *hydr-* + *-anth* (fr. Gk *anthos* flower) — more at ANTHOLOGY] **:** one of the nutritive zooids of a hydroid colony, each having a mouth, digestive cavity, and tentacles

hy·drarch \'hīˌdrärk\ *adj* [*hydr-* + *-arch* (adj. comb. form)] **:** originating in water — used of an ecological succession; compare HYDROSERE, MESARCH, XERARCH

hy·drar·gil·lite \hī'drärjəˌlīt\ *n* [*hydr-* + *argillite*] **1** *obs* **:** WAVELLITE **2 :** GIBBSITE

hy·drar·gyr·ia \ˌhī(ˌ)drär'jirēə\ *also* **hy·drar·gy·ri·a·sis** \hīˌdrärjə'rīəsəs\ *n, pl* **hydrargyrias** *also* **hydrargyriasises** [NL, fr. *hydrargyrum* + *-ia* or *-iasis*] **:** MERCURIALISM

hy·drar·gy·rism \hī'drärjəˌrizəm\ *n* -s [ISV *hydrargyr-* (fr. NL *hydrargyrum*) + *-ism*] **:** MERCURIALISM

hy·drar·gy·rum \-ˌrəm\ *n* -s [NL, alter. of L *hydrargyrus*, fr. Gk *hydrargyros*, fr. *hydr-* + *argyros* silver — more at ARGENT] **:** MERCURY — symbol *Hg*

hy·drar·thro·sis \ˌhī(ˌ)drär'thrōsəs\ *n, pl* **hydrarthro·ses** \-ōˌsēz\ [NL, fr. *hydr-* + *arthr-* + *-osis*] **:** a watery effusion into a joint cavity

hydras *pl of* HYDRA

hy·drase \'hīˌdrās, -āz\ *n* -s [*hydr-* + *-ase*] **:** an enzyme that promotes addition of water to its substrate or removal of water therefrom

hy·dras·tine \hī'drasˌtēn, -stən\ *also* **hy·dras·tin** \-stən\ *n* -s [ISV *hydrast-* (fr. NL *Hydrastis*) + *-ine* or *-in*] **:** a bitter crystalline alkaloid $C_{21}H_{21}NO_6$ derived from isoquinoline that is an active constituent of hydrastis and berberis preparations and is the parent compound of narcotine

hy·dras·ti·nine \hī'drastəˌnēn, -nən\ *n* -s [ISV *hydrastine* + *-ine*; prob. orig. formed as G *hydrastinin*] **:** a crystalline base $C_{11}H_{13}NO_3$ formed by the oxidation of hydrastine and useful in controlling uterine hemorrhage; 5-(methylamino-ethyl)-piperonal

hy·dras·tis \hī'drastəs\ *n* [NL, prob. irreg. fr. *hydr-*] **1** *cap* **:** a genus of herbs (family Ranunculaceae) having palmately lobed leaves and small greenish apetalous flowers — see GOLDENSEAL **2** -ES **:** the dried rhizome and roots of the goldenseal (*Hydrastis canadensis*) formerly used in pharmacy as a bitter tonic

[1]**hy·drate** \'hīˌdrāt, -drət, *usu* -d·+V\ *n* -s [ISV *hydr-* + *-ate* (n. suffix)] **:** a product of hydration: as **a :** a compound or complex ion formed by the union of water with some other substance and represented as actually containing water **:** a solvate containing molecules of water — compare WATER OF CRYSTALLIZATION, WATER OF HYDRATION ⟨Glauber's salt is a ~⟩ ⟨the aluminum ion forms a ~ $[Al(H_2O)_6]^{+++}$⟩ **b :** a compound containing hydroxyl ⟨camphene ~ $C_{10}H_{17}OH$⟩ **:** HYDROXIDE ⟨calcium ~⟩ — used chiefly commercially

[2]**hy·drate** \-ˌdrāt\ *vb* -ED/-ING/-S [ISV *hydr-* + *-ate* (v. suffix)] *vt* **1 :** to cause to take up or combine with water or with hydrogen and hydroxyl in the proportion in which they form water (as by chemical reaction or by adsorption) **:** subject to hydration — compare AQUATE **2 :** to maintain or restore the normal proportion of fluid in the body of esp. by oral or intravenous administration **3 :** to subject (paper pulp) to prolonged beating esp. in making glassine and greaseproof papers in order to increase moisture resistance ~ *vi* **:** to take up or combine with water or with hydrogen and hydroxyl **:** undergo hydration

hydrated *adj* [fr. past part. of [2]*hydrate*] **1 :** containing combined water (as in a hydrate) **:** HYDROUS **2** *of paper pulp* **:** subjected to prolonged beating to make moisture-resistant paper

hydrated alumina *n* **:** ALUMINUM HYDROXIDE

hydrated lime *n* **:** a dry white powder consisting essentially of calcium hydroxide obtained by treating lime with water — called also *slaked lime*

hy·dra·tion \hī'drāshən\ *n* -s [[2]*hydrate* + *-ion*] **1 :** the act or process of combining with water: as **a :** the introduction of additional fluid into the body ⟨~ sometimes helps to reduce the concentration of toxic substances in the tissues⟩ **b :** a chemical reaction in which water takes part with the formation of only one product ⟨~ of ethylene to ethyl alcohol⟩; *esp* **:** a reaction in which water takes part in the form of intact molecules ⟨~ of sodium sulfate to the decahydrate⟩ — compare HYDROLYSIS, SOLVATION **c :** the addition of water to a calcium aluminate powder to produce cement **2 :** the quality or state of being hydrated: as **a :** the condition of having adequate fluid in the body tissues **b :** a physical change in paper fibers due to adsorption and imbibition of water caused by prolonged beating

hy·dra·tor \'hīˌdrād·ə(r)\ *n* -s [[2]*hydrate* + *-or*] **:** one that hydrates

hy·dra·trop·ic acid \ˌhīdrəˌträpik-\ *n* [*hydratropic* ISV *hydr-* + *atropic* being an alpha-phenyl-acrylic acid $CH_2{:}C(C_6H_5)COOH$ obtainable by the decomposition of atropine (ISV *atrop-* — fr. *atropine* — + *-ic*)] **:** a colorless liquid acid $C_6H_5CH(CH_3)COOH$ obtained by reduction of alpha-phenyl-acrylic acid; α-phenyl-propionic acid

hydra–tuba \'==(')==\ *n* [*hydra* (polyp) + *tuba* (horn); fr. the similarity in shape to a trumpet] **:** SCYPHISTOMA

hy·drau·cone \'hīdrōˌkōn\ *n* [*hydraulic* + *cone*] **:** a draft tube symmetrical with the axis of a water turbine and enlarging in diameter at the lower end where the water impinges upon a horizontal slab as it enters the tailrace

hydrauli *pl of* HYDRAULUS

[1]**hy·drau·lic** \hī'drōlik, -lēk *also* -räl-\ *n* -s [L *hydraulicus*, adj.] **:** a hydraulic machine or device ⟨brakes are four-wheel ~s —*Motor Life*⟩; *specif* **:** HYDRAULIC ORGAN

[2]**hy·drau·lic** \(')=¦==\ *adj* [L *hydraulicus* being a hydraulic organ, fr. Gk *hydraulikos*, fr. *hydraulis* hydraulic organ (fr. *hydr-* + *-aulis*, fr. *aulos* reed instrument like an oboe) + *-ikos* -ic — more at ALVEOLUS] **1 :** operated, moved, or effected by means of water **2 a :** of or relating to hydraulics ⟨~ engineer⟩ **b :** of or relating to water or other liquid in motion ⟨~ erosion . . . of shore reef fronts —*Scientific Monthly*⟩ **3 :** operated by the resistance offered or the pressure transmitted when a quantity of water, oil, or other liquid is forced through a comparatively small orifice or through a tube — used of a mechanism ⟨~ buffer⟩ ⟨~ brake⟩ ⟨~ equipment⟩ ⟨~ system⟩; *also* **:** relating to a device operated in this way ⟨~ pressure⟩ ⟨~ action⟩ **4 :** hardening or setting under water ⟨~ cement⟩ ⟨~ lime⟩ — **hy·drau·li·cal·ly** \-lək(ə)lē, -lēk-, -li\ *adv*

[3]**hydraulic** \=ˈ==\ *vt* **hydraulicked; hydraulicked; hydraulicking; hydraulics :** to subject to the action of a powerful stream or jet of water or excavate in this manner **:** SLUICE

hydraulic brake *n* **:** a brake (as for a motor vehicle) in which the braking force is applied through a mechanism operated like a small hydraulic press

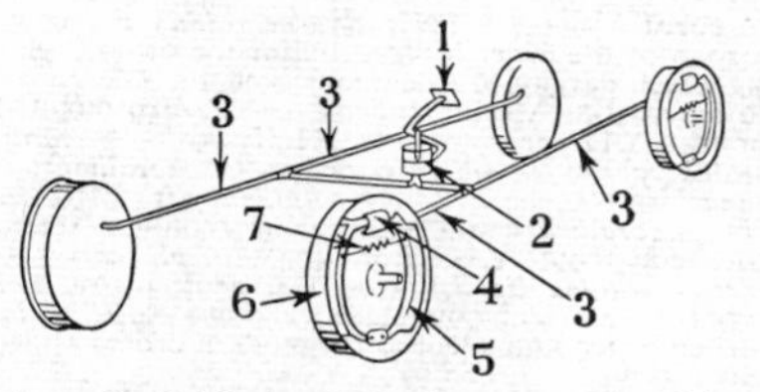

four-wheeled hydraulic brake system: *1* pedal; *2* master cylinder containing piston; *3, 3, 3, 3,* lines to each wheel; *4* wheel cylinder containing opposed pistons; *5* shoe; *6* drum; *7* return spring

hydraulic cement *n* **:** a cement that is capable of hardening under water — see PORTLAND CEMENT, POZZOLANA

hydraulic classification *n* **:** the sorting of small particles (as of ground ore) by allowing them to settle against rising currents of fresh water of different velocities

hydraulic coupling *n* **:** FLUID COUPLING

hydraulic dredge *n* **:** a floating dredge using a centrifugal pump to draw mud or saturated sand (as from a river channel) and discharge it elsewhere

hydraulic elevator *n* **:** an elevator operated by the weight or pressure of water — see HYDRAULIC PLUNGER ELEVATOR, HYDRAULIC ROPE-GEARED ELEVATOR

hydraulic engineering *n* **:** a branch of civil engineering that deals with the use and control of flowing water (as for power or in placer mining)

hydraulic–fill dam *n* **:** a dam constructed by washing earthy materials into place

hydraulic fluid *n* **:** a fluid usu. of low viscosity (as oil or glycerol but seldom water) used in a hydraulically operated mechanism ⟨*hydraulic fluid* in a brake cylinder⟩

hydraulic gradient *or* **hydraulic grade line** *n* **:** a line joining the points of highest elevation of water in a series of vertical open pipes rising from a pipeline in which water flows under pressure

hy·drau·lic·i·ty \ˌhī(ˌ)drō'lisəd·ē\ *n* -ES [ISV [2]*hydraulic* + *-ity*] **:** the capacity which hydraulic cements or their ingredients have for hardening under water

hydraulic jack *n* **:** a jack designed on the principle of the hydraulic press

hydraulic jump *n* **:** a sudden usu. turbulent rise of water flowing rapidly in an open channel where it encounters an obstruction or change in the channel slope

hy·drau·lick·er \hī'drōlikə(r)\ *n* -s [[1]*hydraulic* + *-er*] **:** one that operates a hydraulic mechanism; *specif* **:** a worker who shapes hats in a hydraulic press

hydraulic lift *n* **:** HYDRAULIC ELEVATOR; *esp* **:** one used for lifting motor vehicles (as for servicing in a garage)

hydraulic lime *n* **:** a hydraulic cementitious product made by burning hydraulic limestone

hydraulic limestone *n* **:** a limestone containing silica and alumina and yielding a lime that will harden under water

hydraulic mean depth *n* **:** HYDRAULIC RADIUS

hydraulic mining *n* **:** mining by the action of powerful jets of water — compare PLACER MINING

hydraulic oil *n* **:** an oil used as a hydraulic fluid

hy·drau·li·con \hī'drōləˌkän\ *n* -s [Gk *hydraulikon organon*] **:** HYDRAULUS

hydraulic organ *n* [trans. of Gk *hydraulikon organon*, fr. *hydraulikon* (neut. of *hydraulikos* being a hydraulic organ) + *organon* organ — more at HYDRAULIC] **:** HYDRAULUS

hydraulic packing *n* **:** packing made of a material that is highly resistant to the action of water esp. under high pressure

hydraulic plunger elevator *n* **:** a hydraulic elevator having a steel-tube plunger several feet longer than the travel of the car encased in a cylinder sunk into the ground and actuated by water pressure assisted by a counterweight and controlled by valves operated from the car, the water being forced out as the car descends

hydraulic press *n* **:** a machine in which great force with slow motion is communicated to a large plunger by means of liquid forced into the cylinder in which it moves by a piston pump of small diameter to which the power is applied — called also *Bramah press, hydrostatic press*

hydraulic radius *n* **:** the ratio of the cross-sectional area of a channel or pipe in which a fluid is flowing to the wetted perimeter of the conduit

hydraulic ram *n* **1 :** a pump that forces running water to a higher level by utilizing the kinetic energy of flow, only a small portion of the water being so lifted by the velocity head of a much larger portion when the latter is suddenly checked by the closing of a valve **2 :** the larger output piston of a hydraulic press or similar machine

hydraulic ram: *1* original flow, *2* output pipe, *3* air chamber, *4* check valve

hydraulic rope-geared elevator \-'=,=-\ *n* **:** a hydraulic elevator in which one end of a system of ropes and sheaves is attached to the elevator car and the other end to a piston operating in a cylinder

hy·drau·lics \hī'drōliks, -lēks *also* -räl-\ *n pl but usu sing in constr* **:** a branch of science that deals with practical applications (as the transmission of energy or the effects of flow) of water or other liquid in motion

hydraulic sprayer *n* **:** a machine for the large-scale application of insecticides or fungicides to crops in the form of a spray — compare MIST BLOWER

hy·drau·lus \hī'drōləs\ *n, pl* **hydrauli** *or* **hydrauluses** [L, fr. Gk *hydraulos* hydraulic organ, fr. *hydr-* + *aulos* reed instrument like an oboe — more at ALVEOLUS] **:** an ancient Roman pipe organ using water pressure as a means of compressing the air

hydraz- *or* **hydrazo-** *comb form* [ISV, fr. *hydrazine*] **1 :** related to hydrazine ⟨*hydrazide*⟩ **2** *usu hydrazo-* **:** containing the bivalent radical –NHNH– derived from hydrazine by removal of one hydrogen atom from each nitrogen atom — esp. in names of compounds in which the radical is united to two hydrocarbon radicals ⟨*hydrazo*toluene⟩

hy·dra·zide \'hīdrəˌzīd, -zəd\ *n* -s [ISV *hydraz-* + *-ide*] **:** any of a class of chemical compounds $RCONHNH_2$ resulting from the replacement by an acid radical of hydrogen in hydrazine or in one of its derivatives ⟨acetic ~⟩ — compare PHENYLHYDRAZIDE

hy·draz·i·dine \hī'drazəˌdēn, -dən\ *n* -s [ISV *hydrazine* + *-idin*] **:** an organic base of the general formula $RC({=}NH)NHNH_2$ or $RC({=}NNH_2)NH_2$ formed by the action of hydrazine on an imido ester — compare AMIDINE

hy·dra·zine \'hīdrəˌzēn, -zən\ *n* -s [ISV *hydr-* + *az-* + *-ine*; orig. formed as G *hydrazin*] **:** a colorless fuming corrosive strongly reducing liquid compound NH_2NH_2 that is a weaker base than ammonia, that is usu. made by dehydration of hydrazine hydrate, and that is used chiefly as a component of fuels for rocket and jet engines and in making salts (as the sulfate) and organic derivatives; *also* **:** an organic base (as phenylhydrazine) derived from this compound

hydrazine hydrate *n* **:** a colorless liquid base $N_2H_4.H_2O$ made usu. by reaction of sodium hypochlorite and ammonia or urea and used for the same purposes as hydrazine

hy·dra·zin·i·um \ˌhīdrə'zinēəm\ *n* -s [ISV *hydrazine* + *-ium*] **:** either of two cations derived from hydrazine; *esp* **:** the univalent cation $NH_2NH_3^+$ ⟨~ chloride NH_2NH_3Cl or hydrazine hydrochloride $NH_2NH_2.HCl$⟩

hydrazino- *comb form* [ISV, fr. *hydrazine*] **:** containing the univalent radical NH_2NH– derived from hydrazine by removal of one hydrogen atom ⟨1-*hydrazino*phthalazine⟩

hy·dra·zo·ate \ˌhīdrə'zōˌāt\ *n* -s [*hydrazoic* + *-ate*] **:** a salt of hydrazoic acid **:** AZIDE

hy·draz·o·benzene \hī'drazō, ¦hīdrəzō+\ *n* [ISV *hydraz-* + *benzene*] **:** a crystalline compound $C_6H_5NHNHC_6H_5$ obtained by alkaline reduction of nitrobenzene or azobenzene and capable of being converted into aniline by reduction, into azobenzene by oxidation, and into benzidine by rearrangement in the presence of hydrochloric acid

hy·dra·zo·ic acid \ˌhīdrə¦zōik-\ *n* [*hydrazoic* fr. *hydr-* + *az-* + *-ic*] **:** a colorless volatile poisonous explosive liquid HN_3 when pure that has an unbearable odor, is made usu. by reaction of nitrous oxide with fused sodium amide or of hydrazine hydrate with ethyl nitrite in alkaline alcoholic solution, and yields explosive salts of heavy metals (as lead azide) — called also *azoimide*

hy·dra·zone \'hīdrəˌzōn\ *n* -s [ISV *hydraz-* + ket*one*; orig. formed as G *hydrazon*] **:** any of a class of compounds containing the grouping $>C{=}NNHR$ formed by the action of hydrazine or a substituted hydrazine (as phenylhydrazine) on a compound containing the carbonyl group (as an aldehyde or ketone) ⟨acetone ~ $(CH_3)_2C{:}NNH_2$⟩ — see OSAZONE; compare AZINE 2

hy·dra·zo·ni·um \ˌhīdrə'zōnēəm\ *n* -s [ISV *hydraz-* + *-onium*] **:** HYDRAZINIUM

hy·dre·mia *also* **hy·drae·mia** \hī'drēmēə\ *n* -s [NL, fr. *hydr-* + *-emia*] **:** an abnormally watery state of the blood — **hy·dre·mic** *also* **hy·drae·mic** \(')hī¦drēmik\ *adj*

hy·dren·ceph·a·lus \ˌhī(ˌ)dren'sefələs\ *also* **hy·dren·ceph·a·ly** \-lē\ *n* -ES [*hydrencephalus* fr. NL, fr. *hydr-* + *-encephalus*; *hydrencephaly* ISV *hydr-* + *-encephaly*] **:** HYDROCEPHALUS

hy·dria \'hīdrēə\ *n, pl* **hydri·ae** \-ēˌē\ [L, fr. Gk, fr. *hydōr* water — more at WATER] **:** an ancient Greek or Roman water jar characterized by horizontal side handles and a vertical back handle and in the earlier form an angular and abrupt shoulder — compare KALPIS

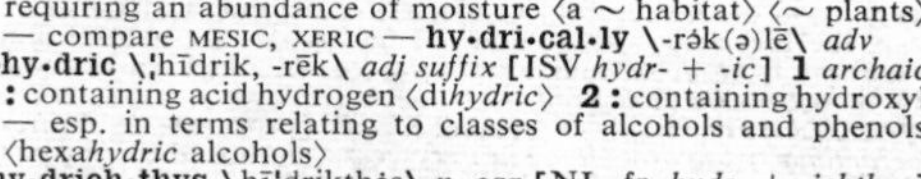

hydriae

[1]**hy·dric** \'hīdrik\ *adj* [ISV *hydr-* + *-ic*] **:** relating to or containing hydrogen

[2]**hydric** \"\ *adj* [*hydr-* + *-ic*] **:** characterized by, relating to, or requiring an abundance of moisture ⟨a ~ habitat⟩ ⟨~ plants⟩ — compare MESIC, XERIC — **hy·dri·cal·ly** \-rək(ə)lē\ *adv*

-hy·dric \¦hīdrik, -rēk\ *adj suffix* [ISV *hydr-* + *-ic*] **1** *archaic* **:** containing acid hydrogen ⟨di*hydric*⟩ **2 :** containing hydroxyl — esp. in terms relating to classes of alcohols and phenols ⟨hexa*hydric* alcohols⟩

hy·drich·thys \hī'drikthəs\ *n, cap* [NL, fr. *hydr-* + *-ichthys*] **:** a genus of colonial hydrozoans parasitic on the skin and tissues of fish

hy·dri·dae \'hīdrəˌdē\ [NL, fr. *hydr-* + *-idae*] *syn of* HYDROPHIDAE

hy·dride \'hīˌdrīd, -drəd\ *n* -s [ISV *hydr-* + *-ide*] **1** *archaic* **:** HYDROXIDE **2 :** a binary of hydrogen usu. with a more electropositive element or radical

hy·dri·do·borate \¦hīdrədō+\ *n* [short for *tetrahydridoborate*] **:** BOROHYDRIDE

hy·dri·form \'hīdrəˌfōrm\ *adj* [prob. fr. (assumed) NL *hydriformis*, fr. NL *Hydra* + *-iformis* -iform] **:** resembling a polyp of the genus *Hydra*

-hy·drin \'hīdrən\ *n comb form* -s [ISV *hydr-* + *-in*] **:** chemical compound containing halogen or cyanogen in place of alcoholic hydroxyl esp. of only part of the hydroxyl ⟨iodo*hydrin*⟩

hy·drin·dene \hī'drinˌdēn\ *n* [ISV *hydr-* + *indene*] **:** INDAN

hy·dri·od·ic acid \¦hīdrē¦ädik-\ *n* [*hydriodic* ISV *hydr-* + *iodic*] **:** a strong liquid acid HI that resembles hydrochloric acid chemically but in addition is a strong reducing agent and that is formed by solution of hydrogen iodide in water

hy·dri·o·dide \hī'drīəˌdīd, -dəd\ *n* [ISV *hydriodic* + *-ide*] **:** a compound of hydriodic acid ⟨pyridine ~⟩ — distinguished from *iodide*; compare HYDROCHLORIDE

hy·dri·on \'hīdrēˌän\ *n* [*hydr-* + *ion*] **:** HYDROGEN ION

hy·dri·o·taph·ia \ˌhīdrēō'tafēə\ *n* -s [NL, fr. *hydrio-* (fr. Gk *hydria* water jar, cinerary urn) + *-taphia* (fr. Gk *taphē* burial); akin to Gk *thaptein* to bury — more at HYDRIA, EPITAPH] **:** URN BURIAL

hydri·ote \'hidrēˌōt, 'hīd-\ *n, usu cap* [*Hydra*, Greek island in the Aegean sea + E *-i-* + *-ote*] **:** a native or inhabitant of the Greek island of Hydra

[1]**hy·dro** \'hī(ˌ)drō\ *n* -s **1** [short for [1]*hydropathic*] *Brit* **a :** a hotel that caters to people taking a water cure **b :** an establishment that furnishes water cures **:** SPA **2** [short for *hydroelectric*] **a** *chiefly Canada* **:** hydroelectric power **b :** a hydroelectric power plant

[2]**hydro** \"\ *adj* [by shortening] **:** HYDROELECTRIC ⟨~ power⟩

[3]**hydro** \"\ *adj* [*hydr-*] **:** HYDROGEN **:** combined with hydrogen ⟨~ derivatives⟩

hydro- \ *in pronunciations below* ¦==¦hī(ˌ)drō *or* -ˌdrə\ — see HYDR-

hy·droa \hī'drōə\ *n* -s [F, prob. alter. (influenced by F *hydr-*, fr. L) of Gk *hidrōa* (pl.) prickly heat, fr. *hidrōs* sweat — more at SWEAT] **:** an itching usu. vesicular eruption of the skin; *esp* **:** one induced by exposure to light

hy·dro·ab·i·et·yl alcohol \¦== *at* HYDRO- + ə'bīəˌtēl- *or* 'abēə¦l\ *n* [*hydroabietyl* fr. *hydr-* + *abiet-* (fr. *abietic acid*) + *-yl*] **:** a soft viscous resinous substance obtained by hydrogenation of the methyl ester of rosin and used esp. as a plasticizer

hy·dro–airplane \¦hī(ˌ)drō+\ *n* **:** SEAPLANE

hy·dro·alcoholic \"+\ *adj* [*hydr-* + *alcohol* + *-ic*] **:** of or relating to water and alcohol ⟨~ solutions⟩

hy·dro·aromatic \"+\ *adj* [ISV *hydr-* + *aromatic*] **:** derived from the aromatic compounds by adding hydrogen to the ring **:** ALICYCLIC ⟨cyclohexane is a ~ compound formed by hydrogenating benzene⟩

hy·dro·atmospheric \"+\ *adj* [*hydr-* + *atmosphere* + *-ic*] **:** of or relating to both water and air

hy·dro·basaluminite \"+\ *n* [*hydr-* + *basaluminite*] **:** a mineral $Al_4(SO_4)(OH)_{10}.36H_2O$ consisting of hydrous sulfate and hydroxide of aluminum

hy·dro·bat·i·dae \ˌ==+'bad·əˌdē,\ *n pl, cap* [NL, fr. *Hydrobates*, type genus (fr. *hydr-* + *-bates*) + *-idae*] **:** a family of birds consisting of the storm petrels

hy·dro·benzoin \¦== *at* HYDRO- + \ *n* [ISV *hydr-* + *benzoin*; orig. formed in G] **:** a crystalline compound $(C_6H_5CHOH)_2$ formed by action of sodium amalgam on benzaldehyde and yielding benzoin on oxidation

hy·dro·biological \"+\ *adj* [*hydrobiology* + *-ical*] **:** of or relating to hydrobiology

hy·dro·biology \"+\ *n* [ISV *hydr-* + *biology*; prob. orig. formed as G *hydrobiologie*] **:** the biology of bodies or units of water; *esp* **:** LIMNOLOGY

hy·dro·bomb \'==+ˌ\ *n* [*hydr-* + *bomb*] **:** an aerial torpedo propelled by a rocket engine after entering the water

hy·dro·boracite \ˌ==+'-\ *n* [obs. G *hydroboracit* (now *hydroborazit*), fr. G *hydr-* + ML *borac-*, *borax* borax + G *-it* -ite] **:** a mineral $CaMgB_6O_{11}.6H_2O$ consisting of a white hydrous calcium magnesium borate and occurring in fibrous and foliated masses

hy·dro·borate \"+'-\ *n* [short for *tetrahydroborate*] **:** BOROHYDRIDE

hy·dro·bromic acid \¦== *at* HYDRO- + . . . -\ *n* [*hydrobromic* ISV *hydr-* + *bromic*] **:** a strong liquid acid HBr that is formed by solution of hydrogen bromide in water, that resembles hydrochloric acid chemically but in addition is a weak reducing agent, and that is used chiefly in making bromides and as a catalyst

hy·dro·bromide \ˌ==+'-\ *n* [ISV *hydrobromic* + *-ide*] **:** a compound of hydrobromic acid — distinguished from *bromide* ⟨pyridine ~ $C_5H_5N.HBr$⟩; compare HYDROCHLORIDE

hy·dro·cal·u·mite \"+ˈkalyə,mīt\ *n* [*hydr-* + *c-* (fr. *calcium*) + *alum-* (fr. *aluminum*) + *-ite*] **:** a colorless to light green mineral $Ca_2Al(OH)_7.3H_2O$ consisting of hydrous hydroxide of calcium and aluminum

hy·dro·carbon \¦==+\ *at* HYDRO- +\ *n* [*hydr-* + *carbon*] **:** any of a large class of organic compounds containing only carbon and hydrogen, comprising paraffins, olefins, members of the acetylene series, alicyclic hydrocarbons (as cyclic terpenes and steroid hydrocarbons), and aromatic hydrocarbons (as benzene, naphthalene, biphenyl), and occurring in many cases in petroleum, natural gas, coal, and bitumens — **hy·dro·car·bonaceous** \"+\ *adj*

hy·dro·carbonate \"+\ *n* [ISV *hydr-* + *carbonate*] **:** BICARBONATE

hydrocarbon cement *n* **:** a cement containing bitumen

hy·dro·carbonic \"+\ *or* **hy·dro·carbonous** \"+\ *adj* **:** of, relating to, or of the nature of a hydrocarbon

hydrocarbon oil *n* **:** any of various oily liquids consisting chiefly or wholly of mixtures of hydrocarbons (as petroleum or many of its products) — compare MINERAL OIL

hy·dro·car·y·a·ce·ae \,==+,karēˈāsē,ē\ *n pl, cap* [NL, fr. *hydr-* + *cary-* + *-aceae*] *in some classifications* **:** a family coextensive with the Trapaceae — **hy·dro·car·y·a·ceous** \¦==,==¦āshəs\ *adj*

hy·dro·cauline \¦== *at* HYDRO- +¦kȯ,līn, -,lən\ *adj* [*hydrocaulus* + *-ine*] **:** resembling a hydrocaulus

hy·dro·cau·lus \,==+ˈkȯləs\ *n, pl* **hydrocau·li** \-ȯ,lī\ [NL, fr. *hydr-* + Gk *kaulos* stem — more at HOLE] **:** the simple or branched stem of a hydroid

hy·dro·cele \ˈ==+,sēl\ *n* -S [L, fr. Gk *hydrokēlē*, fr. *hydr-* + *kēlē* tumor — more at -CELE] **:** an accumulation of serous fluid in a sacculated cavity esp. the scrotum

hy·dro·cellulose \¦== *at* HYDRO- +\ *n* [ISV *hydr-* + *cellulose*; prob. orig. formed in F] **:** a substance obtained as a gelatinous mass or a fine powder by the partial hydrolysis of cellulose usu. by means of acids

¹hy·dro·ce·phal·ic \¦==+səˈfalik\ *adj* [*hydrocephalus* + *-ic*] **:** relating to, characterized by, or exhibiting hydrocephalus

²hydrocephalic \"\ *n* -S **:** one that is afflicted with hydrocephalus

hy·dro·ceph·a·loid \"+¦sefə,lȯid\ *adj* [*hydrocephalus* + *-oid*] **:** resembling hydrocephalus

hy·dro·ceph·a·lous \-,ləs\ *adj* [*hydrocephalus* + *-ous*] **:** having hydrocephalus

hy·dro·ceph·a·lus \,==+ˈsefələs\ *also* **hy·dro·ceph·a·ly** \-lē\ *n* -ES [*hydrocephalus* fr. LL, hydrocephalus, hydrocephalous, fr. Gk *hydrokephalos* characterized by hydrocephalus, fr. *hydr-* + *-kephalos* -cephalous; *hydrocephaly* prob. fr. F *hydrocéphalie*, fr. *hydrocéphale* hydrocephalous (fr. LL *hydrocephalus*) + *-ie* -y] **1 :** an abnormal increase in the amount of cerebrospinal fluid within the cranial cavity, with expansion of the cerebral ventricles, enlargement of the skull esp. the forehead, and atrophy of the brain **2 :** a condition resulting from or an individual affected with such an increase in the cerebrospinal fluid

hy·dro·ce·ram·ic \¦==+səˈramik\ *adj* [prob. fr. F *hydrocéramique*, fr. *hydrocérame* pottery vessel employed for cooling liquid by evaporation of what exudes (fr. *hydr-* + Gk *keramos* pottery, jar) + *-ique* -ic] **:** made of clay that remains porous after firing — used of pottery vessels employed for cooling liquid by evaporation of what exudes; compare GOGLET

hy·dro·ce·rus·site \,==+səˈrə,sīt\ *n* [Sw *hydrocerussit*, fr. *hydr-* + *cerussit* cerussite, fr. G *zerussit*] **:** a mineral $Pb_3(OH)_2(CO_3)_2$ consisting of a basic lead carbonate that crystallizes in thin colorless hexagonal plates

hy·dro·char·i·da·ce·ae \,==+,karəˈdāsē,ē\ [NL, irreg fr. *Hydrocharis* + *-aceae*] *syn of* HYDROCHARITACEAE

hy·dro·char·i·da·ceous \¦==,==¦dāshəs\ *adj* [NL *Hydrocharidaceae* + E *-ous*] **:** HYDROCHARITACEOUS

hy·droch·a·ris \hīˈdräkərəs\ *n, cap* [NL, fr. *hydr-* + Gk *charit-, charis* grace, beauty; akin to Gk *chairein* to rejoice — more at YEARN] **:** a small genus (the type of the family Hydrocharitaceae) of Old World aquatic herbs with petioled floating leaves — see FROGBIT

hy·dro·char·i·ta·ce·ae \,== *at* HYDRO- +,karəˈtāsē,ē\ *n pl, cap* [NL, fr. *Hydrocharit-, Hydrocharis*, type genus + *-aceae*] **:** a family of very simple widely distributed nearly stemless aquatic herbs (order Naiadales) with a 6-parted perianth and somewhat fleshy fruit — see ELODEA, VALLISNERIACEAE — **hy·dro·char·i·ta·ceous** \¦==,==¦tāshəs\ *adj*

hydrochinone *or* **hydrochinon** *var of* HYDROQUINONE

hy·dro·chloric acid \¦== *at* HYDRO- + . . . -\ *n* [*hydrochloric* ISV *hydr-* + *chloric*] **:** a strong corrosive irritating liquid acid HCl that is formed by solution of hydrogen chloride in water and is normally present in dilute form in gastric juice, that is usu. made by the action of sulfuric acid on salt, and that is widely used in industry (as for pickling metals) and in the laboratory — called also *muriatic acid*

hy·dro·chloride \,==+ˈ-\ *n* [ISV *hydrochloric* + *-ide*] **:** a compound of hydrochloric acid — used esp. with the names of organic bases for convenience in naming salts; distinguished from *chloride* ⟨pyridine ~, $C_5H_5N.HCl$ is the same as pyridinium chloride, C_5H_6NCl⟩

hy·dro·chlorinate \¦== *at* HYDRO- +\ *vt* [*hydr-* + *chlorinate*] **:** to treat or combine with hydrochloric acid or hydrogen chloride ⟨~ rubber⟩ — **hy·dro·chlorination** \"+\ *n*

hy·dro·choe·rus \,==+ˈkirəs, -ˈkēr-\ *n, cap* [NL, fr. *hydr-* + *-choerus*] **:** a genus consisting of the capybara

hy·dro·choleresis \¦== *at* HYDRO- +\ *n* [NL, fr. *hydr-* + *choleresis*] **:** increased production of watery liver bile without necessarily increased secretion of bile solids — compare CHOLERESIS

¹hy·dro·choleretic \"+\ *adj* [fr. *hydrocholeresis*, after such pairs as E *diuresis: diuretic*] **:** of, relating to, or characterized by hydrocholeresis

²hydrocholeretic \"\ *n* **:** an agent that produces hydrocholeresis

hy·dro·chore \ˈ==+,kō(ə)r\ *n* -S [*hydr-* + *-chore*] **:** a plant that depends primarily on water for the distribution of its seeds or spores — compare ANEMOCHORE

hy·dro·cho·ry \-ōrē\ *n* -ES [*hydrochore* + *-y*] **:** dissemination of seeds or plants by water

hy·dro·cinchonine \¦== *at* HYDRO- +\ *n* [ISV *hydr-* + *cinchonine*] **:** CINCHOTINE

hy·dro·cin·na·mal·de·hyde \,==+,sinəˈmaldə,hīd\ *n* [*hydrocinnamic* + *aldehyde*] **:** an oily liquid compound $C_6H_5CH_2CH_2CHO$ that has a floral odor, occurs in species of cinnamon, and is used in perfumes

hy·dro·cinnamic acid \¦== *at* HYDRO- + . . . -\ *n* [*hydrocinnamic* ISV *hydr-* + *cinnamic*] **:** a white crystalline acid $C_6H_5CH_2CH_2COOH$ obtained from cinnamic acid by hydrogenation; β-phenyl-propionic acid

hy·dro·cla·di·um \,==+ˈklādēəm\ *n, pl* **hydrocla·dia** \-ēə\ [NL, fr. *hydr-* + Gk *kladion* twig, dim. of *klados* branch — more at GLADIATOR] **:** one of the small branchlets bearing the hydrothecae in a colony of plumularian hydroids

hy·dro·clas·tic \¦== *at* HYDRO- +¦klastik\ *adj* [*hydr-* + *-clastic*] **:** clastic through the agency of water — used of fragmental rocks deposited by the agency of water; compare PYROCLASTIC

hy·dro·cleis \ˈ==+,klīs *or* -,klās\ *n, cap* [NL, fr. *hydr-* + Gk *kleis* key — more at CLOSE] **:** a small genus of Brazilian aquatic herbs (family Butomaceae) with broad leaves and solitary showy yellow flowers — see WATER POPPY

hy·dro·cleys \"\ *syn of* HYDROCLEIS

hy·dro·climate \¦== *at* HYDRO- +\ *n* [*hydr-* + *climate*] **:** the varied physical factors (as temperature, pH, density, turbidity) and often associated chemical factors (as concentration of certain ions) that characterize a particular aquatic habitat

hy·dro·codimer \"+\ *n* [*hydr-* + *codimer*] **:** hydrogenated codimer containing octanes

hy·dro·coele *or* **hy·dro·coel** \ˈ==+,sēl\ *n* -S [*hydr-* + *-coele*] **:** the water-vascular system of an echinoderm or the pouch or cavity in the embryo from which it develops

hy·dro·colloid \¦== *at* HYDRO- +\ *n* [*hydr-* + *colloid*] **:** any of several substances that yield gels with water (as alginic acid salts, agar, carrageenin, and related polysaccharide gums) and that are used esp. as protective colloids and as impression materials in dentistry — **hy·dro·colloidal** \"+\ *adj*

hy·dro·col process \ˈhīdrə,kōl-\ *n, usu cap H* [prob irreg. fr. *hydr-* (hydrogen)] **:** a modified Fischer-Tropsch process for producing chiefly high-octane gasoline from natural gas

hy·dro·cooler \ˈ== *at* HYDRO- + ,-\ *n* **:** an apparatus used in hydrocooling

hy·dro·cooling \"+,-\ *n* **:** the process of removing heat from freshly harvested fruits and vegetables by bathing them in ice water

hy·dro·coral \¦==+\ *n* [NL *Hydrocorallia*] **:** a compound hydrozoan of the order Milleporina or the order Stylasterina having a well-developed calcareous skeleton

hy·dro·co·ral·lia \,==+kəˈralēə\ *or* **hy·dro·cor·al·li·nae** \-,kȯrəˈlī,nē\ [*Hydrocorallia* fr. NL, fr. *hydr-* + *-corallia* (fr. L *corallia*, pl. of *corallium* coral, fr. Gk *korallion*); *Hydrocorallinae* fr. NL, fr. *hydr-* + *-corallinae* (fr. LL *corallinae*, fem. pl. of *corallinus* coral red)] *syn of* HYDROCORALLINA

hy·dro·cor·al·li·na \,==+,kȯrəˈlīnə\ *n pl, cap* [NL, fr. *hydr-* + *-corallina* (fr. LL *corallina*, neut. pl. of *corallinus* coral red) — more at CORALLINE] *in some classifications* **:** a hydrozoan order equivalent to the modern orders Milleporina and Stylasterina

¹hy·dro·cor·al·line \¦== *at* HYDRO- + ¦kȯrə,līn, -,lən\ *adj* [NL *Hydrocorallina*] **:** of or relating to the Hydrocorallina

²hydrocoralline \"\ *n* -S [NL *Hydrocorallina*] **:** a hydrozoan of the order Hydrocorallina **:** MILLEPORE, STYLASTER

hy·dro·cortisone \"+\ *n* [*hydr-* + *cortisone*] **:** a crystalline hormone $C_{21}H_{30}O_5$ occurring in the adrenal cortex and also prepared synthetically that is a dihydro derivative of cortisone and is used similarly; 17-hydroxycorticosterone — called also *cortisol*

hy·dro·cotarnine \"+\ *n* [ISV *hydr-* + *cotarnine*; prob. orig. formed as G *hydrokotarnin*] **:** a crystalline alkaloid $C_{12}H_{15}NO_3$ obtained from opium and also formed by the reduction of cotarnine

hy·dro·cot·y·le \,==+ˈkädᵊlē\ *n, cap* [NL, fr. *hydr-* + Gk *kotylē* cup; prob. fr. the watery habitat and the cuplike shape of the leaves — more at KETTLE] **:** a genus of low creeping widely distributed herbs (family Umbelliferae) with crenate peltate leaves and umbellate flowers — see MARSH PENNYWORT

hy·dro·cracking \ˈ==+,-\ *n* **:** the cracking of hydrocarbons in the presence of hydrogen

hy·droc·te·na \hīˈdräktənə\ *n, cap* [NL, fr. *hydr-* + *-ctena* (fr. Gk *kten-, kteis* comb) — more at PECTINATE] **:** a genus of trachyline medusae resembling ctenophores

hy·dro·cyanic acid \¦== *at* HYDRO- + . . . -\ *n* [*hydrocyanic* ISV *hydr-* + *cyanic*] **:** a very weak poisonous liquid acid HCN or HNC that is formed by solution of hydrogen cyanide in water, is readily made by the action of an acid on a cyanide, and is used chiefly in fumigating against insects, rats, and mice and in organic synthesis — called also *prussic acid*

hy·dro·cyanide \,==+ˈ-\ *n* [ISV *hydrocyanic* + *-ide*] **:** a compound of hydrocyanic acid — distinguished from *cyanide*; compare HYDROCHLORIDE

hy·dro·cycle \ˈ==+,-\ *n* [*hydr-* + *cycle*] **:** a cycle for riding on water

hy·dro·cyclist \"+,-\ *n* [*hydrocycle* + *-ist*] **:** one that rides a hydrocycle

hy·droc·y·on \hīˈdräsē,än\ *n, cap* [NL, fr. *hydr-* + Gk *kyōn* dog — more at HOUND] **:** a genus of large African carnivorous freshwater fishes of the family Characidae — compare TIGER FISH

hy·dro·dam·a·lis \,== *at* HYDRO- + ˈdaməlǝs\ *n, cap* [NL, fr. *hydr-* + Gk *damalis* heifer; akin to Gk *damalēs* young bull — more at DAMA] **:** a genus of aquatic mammals that includes only the Steller's sea cow and is now usu. placed in the family Dugongidae but was formerly made type of a separate family

hy·dro·dic·ty·on \-ˈdiktē,än\ *n, cap* [NL, fr. *hydr-* + Gk *diktyon* net, fr. *dikein* to throw — more at DISH] **:** a genus (the type of the family Hydrodictyaceae) of unicellular freshwater green algae of the order Chlorococcales that associate in colonies of cylindrical multinucleate cells joined by their ends into pentagonal meshes which are linked in a continuous elongate saccular network often reaching a length of 20 centimeters

hy·dro·dynamic \¦== *at* HYDRO- +\ *also* **hy·dro·dynamical** \"+\ *adj* [*hydrodynamic* fr. NL *hydrodynamicus*, fr. *hydr-* + *dynamicus* of or relating to power, fr. Gk *dynamikos* powerful; *hydrodynamical* fr. NL *hydrodynamicus* + E *-al* — more at DYNAMIC] **:** of or relating to hydrodynamics — **hy·dro·dy·namically** \"+\ *adv*

hy·dro·dy·nam·ics \,==+dīˈnamiks\ *n pl but usu sing in constr* [NL *hydrodynamica*, fr. neut. pl. of *hydrodynamicus* hydrodynamic] **:** a branch of hydromechanics that deals with the motion of fluids and the forces acting on solid bodies immersed in fluids and in motion relative to them — compare HYDROSTATICS

hy·dro·electric \¦== *at* HYDRO-+\ *adj* [ISV *hydr-* + *electric*] **:** of, relating to, or employed in the production of electricity by waterpower

hy·dro·electricity \"+\ *n* [*hydr-* + *electricity*] **:** electricity produced by water power

hy·dro·ex·tract \,==+ikˈstrakt, -ek-\ *vt* [back-formation fr. *hydroextractor*] **:** to treat with a hydroextractor — **hy·dro·ex·trac·tion** \-akshən\ *n*

hy·dro·extractor \¦== *at* HYDRO-+\ *n* [*hydr-* + *extractor*] **:** a usu. centrifugal machine for extracting water (as from yarn or cloth)

hy·dro·ferrocyanic acid \"+ . . . -\ *n* [*hydroferrocyanic* ISV *hydr-* + *ferrocyanic* (as in *ferrocyanic acid*)] **:** FERROCYANIC ACID

hy·dro·fin·ing \ˈ==+,fīniŋ\ *n* [*hydr-* + *-fining* (fr. *refining*)] **:** a process for improving the quality of gasoline and other petroleum products by treating with hydrogen in the presence of a catalyst at a temperature below that at which decomposition takes place — compare HYDROFORMING

hy·dro·flap \ˈ==+,-\ *n* [*hydr-* + *flap*] **:** an adjustable planing surface on a fuselage or seaplane hull used to provide a pitching moment to counteract the tendency of an aircraft to dive on its first contact with the water

hy·dro·fluoric acid \¦== *at* HYDRO- + . . .-\ *n* [*hydrofluoric* ISV *hydr-* + *fluoric*; prob. orig. formed as F *hydrofluorique*] **:** a weak poisonous liquid acid HF that is formed by solution of hydrogen fluoride in water, that resembles hydrochloric acid chemically but attacks silica and silicates (as glass or porcelain) forming gaseous silicon tetrafluoride and must therefore be handled and stored in equipment of steel, lead, rubber, wax, or other nonsilicate materials, and that is used chiefly in making other fluorine compounds, in polishing and etching glass, and in pickling metals

hy·dro·flu·or·ide \,==ˈ-\ *n* [ISV *hydrofluoric* + *-ide*] **:** a compound of hydrofluoric acid — distinguished from *fluoride*; compare HYDROCHLORIDE

hy·dro·fluosilicic acid \¦== *at* HYDRO-+ . . .-\ *n* [*hydrofluosilicic* ISV *hydr-* + *fluosilicic*] **:** FLUOSILICIC ACID

hy·dro·foil \ˈ==+,-\ *n* [*hydr-* + *foil*] **1 :** a flat or curved plane surface designed to obtain reaction upon its surfaces from the water through which it moves ⟨ships of all sizes may be effectively stabilized against rolling . . . by the use of controlled ~*s* —F.D.Braddon⟩ — compare AIRFOIL, HYDROPLANE **2 :** an underwater plate or fin attached by struts to a seaplane (where it is retractable) or to a speedboat for lifting the hull clear of the water as speed is increased

hy·dro·form·ate \,==+ˈfȯr,māt\ *n* [*hydroforming* + *-ate*] **:** a product obtained by hydroforming

hy·dro·form·er \ˈ==+,fȯrmər\ *n* [*hydroforming* + *-er*] **:** the unit in a petroleum refinery in which hydroforming is carried out

hy·dro·form·ing \-miŋ\ *n* -S [*hydr-* + *-forming* (fr. *reforming*)] **:** a process for producing high-octane gasoline or aromatic hydrocarbons (as toluene, xylenes) by dehydrogenation and aromatization of petroleum naphthas usu. containing a high ratio of naphthenes in a stream of added hydrogen and in the presence of a catalyst at elevated temperature

hy·dro·for·myl·a·tion \,==+,fȯ(r)məˈlāshən\ *n* -S [*hydr-* + *formyl* + *-ation*] **:** the addition of a hydrogen atom and a formyl group to the molecule of a compound containing a double bond by reaction with hydrogen and carbon monoxide, the chief product being one or more aldehydes — compare OXO PROCESS

hy·dro·fuge \ˈ==+,fyüj\ *adj* [ISV *hydr-* + *-fuge*; prob. orig. formed in F] **:** shedding water — used of the pubescent coating of many aquatic insects

hy·dro·garnet \¦== *at* HYDRO- +\ *n* [*hydr-* + *garnet*] **:** one of a group of minerals of the general formula $A''_3B'''_2(SiO_4)_{3-x}(OH)_{4x}$ that are isomorphous with various garnets — compare HIBSCHITE

hy·dro·gel \ˈ==+,jel\ *n* [*hydr-* + *-gel* (fr. *gelatin*)] *chem* **:** a gel in which the liquid is water

hy·dro·gen \ˈhīdrəjən, -rēj-\ *n* -S [F *hydrogène*, fr. *hydr-* (water) + *-gène* -gen; fr. the fact that water is generated by its combustion] **:** a nonmetallic univalent element that is the simplest and lightest of the elements, that is normally a colorless odorless highly flammable diatomic gas, that occurs in the free state only sparsely on the earth and in its atmosphere though abundantly in the sun, many stars, and nebulae, and in combination as a constituent of innumerable compounds from many of which it can be readily prepared (as from water by electrolysis, from natural gas or other hydrocarbons by reaction with steam or by pyrolysis, from acids by reaction with active metals), and that is used chiefly in synthesis (as of ammonia and methanol), in reducing or hydrogenating a variety of compounds (as in hardening oils to fats), as a mixture with oxygen or as atomic hydrogen in producing very high temperatures (as in welding), as liquid hydrogen for rocket fuel and in producing very low temperatures, and in filling balloons — symbol *H*; see DEUTERIUM, ELEMENT table, ORTHO-HYDROGEN, PARA-HYDROGEN, SYNTHESIS GAS, TRITIUM

hydrogen arsenide *n* **:** ARSINE

hy·dro·gen·ase \-jə,nās, hīˈdräjə,-\ *n* -S [ISV *hydrogen* + *-ase*] *biochem* **:** an enzyme that promotes the formation and utilization of gaseous hydrogen and occurs esp. in bacteria

hy·dro·gen·ate \-āt, *usu* -ād+V\ *vt* -ED/-ING/-S [*hydrogen* + *-ate*] **1 :** to combine with hydrogen ⟨~ a vegetable oil to a fat⟩ **2 :** to treat with or expose to hydrogen ⟨~ rosin⟩ — compare HARDEN *vt* 1a — **hy·dro·gen·a·tor** \-ād·ə(r)\ *n* -S

hy·dro·gen·a·tion \,hīdrəjəˈnāshən, hī,dräjəˈ-\ *n* -S [ISV *hydrogen* + *-ation*] **:** the process of hydrogenating: as **a :** the addition of hydrogen to the molecule of an unsaturated organic compound usu. in the presence of a catalyst (as nickel) and often at elevated temperature and pressure ⟨~ of benzene to cyclohexane⟩ **b :** a decomposition (as of hydrocarbons) at high temperature and pressure with addition of hydrogen to the molecules formed **:** HYDROGENOLYSIS ⟨~ of coal to gasoline and oils⟩ — called also *destructive hydrogenation*

hydrogen bomb \ˈ===-\ *n* **:** a bomb whose violent explosive power is due to the sudden release of atomic energy resulting from the union of light nuclei (as of hydrogen atoms) at very high temperature and pressure to form helium nuclei — called also *fusion bomb*

hydrogen bond *n* **:** a linkage through hydrogen of two electronegative atoms esp. fluorine, oxygen, or nitrogen with one side of the linkage usu. being a conventional covalent bond (as the –O–H bond in water H–O–H or alcohol R–O–H) and the other side being primarily electrostatic in character ⟨the stable hydrogen fluoride ion HF_2^- or $[F^-H^+F^-]^-$ is held together by a *hydrogen bond*⟩ — see ASSOCIATION 7

hydrogen bromide *n* **:** a colorless irritating gas HBr that fumes in moist air and yields hydrobromic acid when dissolved in water and that is formed as a by-product in the bromination of organic compounds but is usu. made by the direct union of hydrogen and bromine vapor or by the reaction of bromine, red phosphorus, and water

hydrogen chloride *n* **:** a colorless pungent nonflammable poisonous gas HCl that fumes strongly in moist air and yields hydrochloric acid when dissolved in water and that is obtained primarily as a by-product of the chlorination of organic compounds or by burning hydrogen in chlorine

hydrogen cyanide *n* **:** a very poisonous mobile volatile liquid or gas HCN or HNC that has an odor of bitter almonds, that occurs in many plants usu. combined as glycosides (as amygdalin) and also in coke-oven gas, that can be synthesized from ammonia and carbon monoxide or from ammonia, oxygen or air, and natural gas, and that yields hydrocyanic acid when dissolved in water

hydrogen dioxide *n* **:** HYDROGEN PEROXIDE

hydrogen electrode *n* **:** an electrode composed typically of platinum black on platinum over which a stream of hydrogen is bubbled and that under specified conditions serves as the standard electrode with an assigned potential of zero to which all other electrode potentials are referred for purposes of comparison

hydrogen fluoride *n* **:** a colorless mobile fuming corrosive poisonous liquid or gas HF or $(HF)n$ that yields hydrofluoric acid when dissolved in water, is made usu. by the action of sulfuric acid on fluorite, and is used chiefly in the manufacture of fluorine and fluorides and as a catalyst esp. in the alkylation of branched-chain paraffins with olefins to produce superior motor fuels — called also *anhydrous hydrofluoric acid*

¹hy·dro·gen·ic \¦== *at* HYDRO- +¦jenik\ *adj* [*hydr-* + *-genic*] **1 :** formed by the agency of water ⟨dinosaur footprints in ~ rock⟩ **2 :** developed under the dominant influence of water (as in a cold humid region) ⟨~ soil⟩

²hydrogenic \"\ *adj* [ISV *hydrogen* + *-ic*] **:** resembling hydrogen in nuclear composition

hy·dro·gen·ide \ˈhīdrəjə,nīd, hīˈdräjə,-\ *n* -S [*hydrogen* + *-ide*] **:** HYDRIDE

hydrogen iodide *n* **:** a heavy colorless gas HI that fumes in moist air and yields hydriodic acid when dissolved in water and that is usu. made by the direct catalytic union of hydrogen and iodine vapor or by the reaction of iodine, red phosphorus, and water

hydrogen ion *n* **1 :** the cation H^+ of acids consisting of a hydrogen atom whose electron has been transferred to the anion of the acid and existing in aqueous solution as a hydronium ion **:** PROTON **2 :** HYDRONIUM

hydrogen-ion concentration *n* **:** the concentration of hydrogen ions in a solution expressed usu. in moles per liter or in pH units and used as a measure of the acidity of the solution ⟨indicator dyes for narrow ranges of *hydrogen-ion concentration*⟩

hy·dro·ge·ni·um \,hīdrəˈjēnēəm\ *n* -S [NL, fr. E *hydrogen* + NL *-ium*] **:** HYDROGEN

hy·dro·gen·ize \ˈhīˈdräjə,nīz, ˈhīdrəjə,-\ *vt* -ED/-ING\-S **:** HYDROGENATE

hy·dro·gen·ol·y·sis \,hīdrəjəˈnäləsəs\ *n* [*hydrogen* + *-o-* + *-lysis*] **:** a chemical reaction analogous to hydrolysis in which hydrogen plays a role similar to that of water **:** destructive hydrogenation ⟨~ of hydrazine to ammonia⟩

hy·dro·gen·om·o·nas \,hīdrəjəˈnäməˌnas\ *n, cap* [NL, fr. ISV *hydrogen* + NL *-o-* + *-monas*] **:** a genus of short rod-shaped soil bacteria (family Methanomonadaceae) that are facultative autotrophs capable of oxidizing hydrogen to form water and using carbon dioxide as a source of carbon for growth

hy·drog·e·nous \(ˈ)hī¦dräjənəs\ *adj* **:** of, relating to, or containing hydrogen

hydrogen oxide *n* **:** WATER

hydrogen peroxide *n* **:** a colorless syrupy explosive corrosive compound H_2O_2 that has a bitter metallic taste and causes blisters on the skin, that is prepared in aqueous solutions in various ways (as by the electrolysis of sulfuric acid and hydrolysis of the persulfuric acid formed, by the action of acid on barium peroxide, or by the autoxidation of anthraquinone derivatives) and can be concentrated usu. by distillation, and that is used chiefly in dilute form as a bleach and antiseptic and in more concentrated forms as an oxidizing agent and propellant (as for rockets)

hydrogen selenide *n* **:** a colorless flammable poisonous gas H_2Se that has a disagreeable odor, resembles hydrogen sulfide, and is usu. formed by the action of acids on selenides

hydrogen sulfide *n* **:** a colorless flammable very poisonous gas H_2S that has a disagreeable odor suggestive of rotten eggs and is slightly soluble in water to give a weakly acidic solution, that is formed by putrefaction esp. of animal matter, that is found also in many mineral waters, in most volcanic gases, and in most natural gas and petroleum deposits and is formed in many industrial processes (as coking of coal) usu. as an objectionable impurity, that is recovered as a by-product from many of these sources or is prepared by the action of an acid on a metallic sulfide or by synthesis from hydrogen and sulfur vapor, and that is used chiefly in making elemental sulfur, sulfuric acid, and other sulfur compounds and in analysis as a precipitant for metallic ions

hy·dro·geology \ˌ≈≈ at HYDRO- +\ *n* [F *hydrogéologie*, fr. *hydr-* + *géologie* geology] **1** : a branch of geology concerned with the occurrence and utilization of surface and ground water and with the functions of water in modifying the earth esp. by erosion and deposition **2** : the phenomena with which hydrogeology deals

hy·dro·glider \ˈ≈≈+ˌ-\ *n* : a glider equipped with floats

hy·drog·no·sy \hīˈdrägnəsē\ *n* -ES [ISV *hydr-* + *-gnosy*] : the history and description of the waters of the earth

hy·dro·graph \ˈ≈≈ at HYDRO- +ˌgraf\ *n* [*hydr-* + *-graph*] **1** : a mechanism for recording on a chart the changing level of water (as in a well, reservoir, stream) **2** : a chart produced by this mechanism

hy·drog·ra·pher \hīˈdrägrəfə(r)\ *n* -S [*hydrography* + *-er*] : a specialist in hydrography

hy·dro·graph·ic \ˌ≈≈ at HYDRO- +ˈgrafik\ *also* **hy·dro·graph·i·cal** \-fəkəl\ *adj* [*hydrographic* fr. F *hydrographique*, fr. MF, fr. *hydr-* + *-graphique* -graphic (fr. LL *-graphicus*); *hydrographical* fr. MF *hydrographique* + E *-al*] : of or relating to hydrography — **hy·dro·graph·i·cal·ly** \-fək(ə)lē\ *adv*

hydrographic basin *n* : the drainage area of a stream

hydrographic surveying *n* : surveying of coastlines, bays, harbors, and of the ocean bed

hy·drog·ra·phy \hīˈdrägrəfē\ *n* -ES [MF *hydrographie*, fr. *hydr-* + *-graphie* -graphy (fr. L *-graphia*)] **1** : the description and study of seas, lakes, rivers, and other waters: as **a** : the measurement of flow and investigation of the behavior of streams esp. with reference to the control or utilization of their waters **b** : the measurement of tides and currents esp. as an aid in navigation **c** : the surveying, sounding, and charting of bodies of water **2** : bodies of water or a representation of them on a map

hy·dro·grossularite \ˌ≈≈ at HYDRO- +\ *n* [*hydr-* + *grossularite*] : a mineral $Ca_3Al_2(SiO_4)_{3-x}(OH)_{4x}$, consisting of silicate of calcium and aluminum in which silicon is partly replaced by hydrogen with *x* near ½ : one of the hydrogarnets intermediate between grossularite (*x*=0) and hibschite (*x*=1)

hy·dro·halide \ˈ"+\ *n* [*hydr-* + *halide*] : a compound (as a hydrochloride) with one of the halogen acids : a hydrogen halide

hy·dro·halite \ˈ"+\ *n* [G *hydrohalit*, fr. *hydr-* + *halit* halite, fr. NL *halites*] : a mineral $NaCl.2H_2O$ consisting of a hydrated chloride of sodium formed only from salty water below the freezing temperature of pure water

hy·dro·hetaerolite \ˈ"+\ *n* [*hydr-* + *hetaerolite*] : a mineral of uncertain composition approximately $Zn_2Mn_4O_8.H_2O$ consisting of a hydrous oxide of zinc and manganese

hy·dro–hotel \ˈhī(ˌ)drō+\ *n* [ˈ*hydro* + *hotel*] *Brit* : HYDRO 1a

¹hy·droid \ˈhīˌdrȯid\ *also* **hy·droidean** \(ˈ)hīˌdrȯidēən\ *adj* [*hydroid* fr. NL *Hydroida*; *hydroidean* fr. NL *Hydroidea* + E *-an* (adj. suffix)] : of or relating to the Hydroida or Hydrozoa : resembling a polyp of the genus *Hydra*

²hydroid \"\ *also* **hydroidean** \"\ *n* -S [*hydroid* fr. NL *Hydroida*; *hydroidean* fr. NL *Hydroidea* + E *-an* (n. suffix)] **1** : one of the Hydroida : HYDROZOAN **2** : the polyp form of a hydrozoan as distinguished from the medusa form — see HYDROMEDUSA

¹hy·droi·da \hīˈdrȯidə\ *n pl, cap* [NL, fr. *Hydra*, included genus + *-oida*] : an order of Hydrozoa comprising forms alternating a well-developed asexual polyp generation with a generation of free medusae or of abortive medusoid reproductive structures on the polyps — *see* LEPTOMEDUSAE

²hydroida \"\ [NL, fr. *Hydra*, included genus + *-oida*] *syn of* HYDROZOA

hydroid coral *n* : HYDROCORAL

hy·droi·dea \hīˈdrȯidēə\ [NL, fr. *Hydra* + *-oidea*] *syn of* HYDROIDA

hy·droi·des \hīˈdrȯi(ˌ)dēz\ *n, cap* [NL, prob. fr. *Hydra* (genus of polyps) + *-oides* (fr. L *-oides* -oid)] : a genus of tube-dwelling marine polychaete worms frequently present in the fouling of ship bottoms

hydroid polyp *n* : HYDROPOLYP

hy·dro·kinetic \ˈ"+\ *adj* [*hydr-* + *kinetic*] : of or relating to the motions of fluids or the forces which produce or affect such motions — opposed to *hydrostatic*

hy·dro·kinetics \ˈ"+\ *n pl but usu sing in constr* [*hydr-* + *kinetics*] : a branch of kinetics that deals with liquids — compare HYDRAULICS

hy·drol \ˈhīˌdrȯl, -rōl\ *n* -S [*hydr-* + *-ol*] **1 a** : the simple water molecule H_2O **b** : a polymer $(H_2O)_n$ of this molecule **2** : a secondary alcohol (as benzhydrol) esp. of the aromatic series **3** [prob. irreg. fr. *hydr-*] *also* **hydrol syrup** : a light brown syrupy mother liquor from the manufacture of dextrose used in the fermentation industries

hy·dro·lase \ˈhīdrəˌlās\ *n* -S [ISV *hydrol* (fr. E) + *-ase*] : a hydrolytic enzyme (as an esterase)

hy·drol·a·try \hīˈdrälə·trē\ *n* -ES [*hydr-* + *-latry*] : the worship of water

hy·dro·lea \hīˈdrōlēə\ *n, cap* [NL, fr. *hydr-* + L *olea* olive; fr. the watery habitat and the resemblance of the leaves to those of the olive — more at OLEA] : a genus of blue-flowered perennial herbs (family Hydrophyllaceae) of warm regions having entire leaves and flowers with two distinct styles and bilocular ovaries and capsules

hy·dro·lith \ˈ≈≈ at HYDRO- +ˌlith\ *n* -S [ISV *hydr-* + *-lith*; prob. orig. formed as F *hydrolithe*] : CALCIUM HYDRIDE

hy·dro·log·ic \ˌhīdrəˈläjik\ *or* **hy·dro·log·i·cal** \-jəkəl\ *adj* [*hydrologic* ISV *hydrology* + *-ic*; *hydrological* fr. NL *hydrologia* hydrology + E *-ical*] : of or relating to hydrology — **hy·dro·log·i·cal·ly** \-jək(ə)lē\ *adv*

hydrologic cycle *n* : a complex sequence of conditions through which water naturally passes from water vapor in the atmosphere through precipitation upon land or water surfaces and ultimately back into the atmosphere as a result of evaporation and transpiration

hy·drol·o·gist \hīˈdrälə̇jə̇st\ *n* -S [*hydrology* + *-ist*] : a specialist in hydrology

hy·drol·o·gy \-jē\ *n* -ES [NL *hydrologia*, fr. L *hydr-* + *-logia* -logy] **1** : a science dealing with the properties, distribution, and circulation of water; *specif* : the study of water on the surface of the land, in the soil and underlying rocks, and in the atmosphere, particularly with respect to evaporation and precipitation **2** : the physical factors studied by hydrologists (as precipitation, stream flow, snow melt, groundwater storage, and evaporation) ⟨the ~ of Mexico⟩

hy·dro·lube \ˈ≈≈ at HYDRO- +ˌ-\ *n* [*hydr-* + *lube*] : any of various nonflammable hydraulic fluids having a water-glycol base

hy·dro·lymph \ˈ"+ˌ-\ *n* [*hydr-* + *lymph*] : a watery circulatory fluid that substitutes for blood or hemolymph in some of the lower invertebrates (as jellyfishes)

hy·drol·y·sate \hīˈdräləˌsāt\ *also* **hy·drol·y·zate** \-ˌzāt\ *n* -S [*hydrolysis* or *hydrolyze* + *-ate*] : a product of hydrolysis

hy·drol·y·sis \hīˈdräləsə̇s\ *n* [ISV *hydr-* + *-lysis*] : a chemical reaction of water in which a bond in the reactant other than water is split and hydrogen and hydroxyl are added with the formation usu. of two or more new compounds, some types of hydration however often being included ⟨~ of a salt to an acid and a base⟩ ⟨~ of an ester to an acid and an alcohol⟩ — compare SAPONIFICATION, SOLVOLYSIS

hy·dro·lyte \ˈ≈≈ at HYDRO- +ˌlīt\ *n* -S [*hydr-* + *-lyte*] : a substance subjected to hydrolysis

hy·dro·lyt·ic \ˌ≈≈+ˈlid·ik\ *adj* [ISV *hydr-* + *-lytic*] : of, relating to, or causing hydrolysis

hy·dro·lyz·able \ˈhīdrəˌlīzəbəl\ *adj* [ISV *hydrolyze* + *-able*] : capable of hydrolyzing or of being hydrolyzed ⟨compounds containing ~ groups⟩

hy·dro·lyze *also* **hy·dro·lyse** \ˈhīdrəˌlīz\ *vb* -ED/-ING/-S [ISV, fr. *hydrolysis*, after such pairs as E *analysis*: *analyze*] *vt* : to subject to hydrolysis ~ *vi* : to undergo hydrolysis

hy·dro·lyz·er \-zə(r)\ *n* -S : a piece of equipment in which hydrolysis is carried out ⟨starch ~s⟩

hy·dro·magnesite \ˌ≈≈ at HYDRO- +\ *n* [G *hydromagnesit*, fr. *hydr-* + *magnesit* magnesite, fr. F *magnésite*] : a mineral $Mg_4(OH)_2(CO_3)_3.3H_2O$ consisting of a basic magnesium carbonate occurring in the form of small white crystals or chalky crusts

hy·dro·man·cer \ˈhīdrəˌman(t)sə(r)\ *n* -S [alter. (influenced by *hydromancy*) of ME *idromauncer*, fr. *ydromancye* hydromancy + *-er*] : one that engages in hydromancy

hy·dro·man·cy \-sē, -si\ *n* -ES [alter. (influenced by L *hydromantia*) of ME *ydromancye*, fr. MF *ydromancie*, fr. L *hydromantia*, fr. (assumed) Gk *hydromanteia*, fr. Gk *hydr-* + *manteia* divination — more at -MANCY] : divination by water or other liquid (as by visions seen therein or the ebb and flow of tides)

hy·dro·mechanics \ˌ≈≈ at HYDRO- +\ *n pl but usu sing in constr* [ISV *hydr-* + *mechanics*] : a branch of mechanics that deals with the equilibrium and motion of fluids and of solid bodies immersed in them

hy·dro·medusa \ˈ"+\ *n, pl* **hydromedusae** [NL, fr. *hydr-* + *medusa*] : a medusa that is produced as a bud from a hydroid (as of the orders Anthomedusae and Leptomedusae) and that constitutes the sexual generation of this hydroid and produces new asexual polyps from eggs and sperm

hy·dro·medusae \ˈ"+\ *n pl, cap* [NL, fr. *hydr-* + *medusae* (pl. of *medusa*)] : a formerly recognized subclass of Hydrozoa nearly coextensive with Hydrozoa as now restricted

¹hy·dro·medusan \ˈ"+\ *or* **hy·dro·medusoid** \ˈ"+\ *adj* [NL *hydromedusa* or *Hydromedusae* + E *-an* (adj. suffix) or *-oid*] : of or relating to a hydromedusa or the Hydromedusae

²hydromedusan \"\ *n* -S [NL *Hydromedusae* + E *-an* (n. suffix)] : one of the Hydromedusae

³hydromedusan \"\ *n* -S [NL *hydromedusa* + E *-an* (n. suffix)] : HYDROMEDUSA

hy·dro·mel \ˈhīdrəˌmel\ *n* -S [alter. (influenced by LL *hydromel*) of ME *ydromel*, fr. MF & LL; MF *ydromel*, fr. LL *hydromel*, fr. L *hydromeli*, fr. Gk, fr. *hydr-* + *meli* honey — more at MELLIFLUOUS] **1** : a liquor consisting of honey diluted in water which upon fermentation becomes mead **2** *pharmacy* : a laxative containing honey and water

hy·dro·meningitis \ˌ≈≈ at HYDRO- +\ *n* [NL, fr. *hydr-* + *meningitis*] : meningitis with serous effusion

hy·dro·metallurgical \ˈ"+\ *adj* [*hydrometallurgy* + *-ical*] : of or relating to hydrometallurgy — **hy·dro·metallurgically** \ˈ"+\ *adv*

hy·dro·metallurgy \ˈ"+\ *n* [ISV *hydr-* + *metallurgy*] : treatment of ores by wet processes (as leaching and accompanying operations)

hy·dro·metamorphism \ˈ"+\ *n* [*hydr-* + *metamorphism*] : the alteration of rock by the addition, subtraction, or exchange of material brought or carried in solution by water and without the influence of high temperature or pressure — compare DYNAMOMETAMORPHISM

hy·dro·meteor \ˈ"+\ *n* [ISV *hydr-* + *meteor*] : a product of the condensation of atmospheric water vapor (as fog, rain, hail)

hy·dro·meteorological \ˈ"+\ *adj* [*hydrometeorology* + *-ical*] : of or relating to hydrometeorology

hy·dro·meteorology \ˈ"+\ *n* [*hydr-* + *meteorology*] : a branch of meteorology having to do with water in the atmosphere esp. as precipitation

hy·drom·e·ter \hīˈdrämə̇d·ə(r)\ *n* [*hydr-* + *-meter*] : an instrument for measuring the specific gravity of a liquid commonly consisting of a thin glass or metal tube graduated to indicate either specific gravities or percentages of solution constituents and weighted so that it floats upright — compare ALCOHOLOMETER, NICHOLSON'S HYDROMETER

hy·dro·me·tra \ˌ≈≈ at HYDRO- +ˈmē·trə\ *n* -S [NL, fr. *hydr-* + *-metra*] : an accumulation of watery fluid in the uterus

hy·dro·met·ric \ˌhīdrəˈme·trik\ *or* **hy·dro·met·ri·cal** \-rə̇kəl\ *adj* [*hydrometric* ISV *hydrometr-* (fr. NL *hydrometria* hydrometry) + *-ic*; *hydrometrical* fr. NL *hydrometria* + E *-ical*] : of or relating to hydrometry

hy·drom·e·trid \hīˈdräm·ə·trə̇d\ *adj* [NL *Hydrometridae*] : of or relating to the Hydrometridae

hy·dro·met·ri·dae \ˌ≈≈ at HYDRO- +ˈme·trəˌdē\ *n pl, cap* [NL, fr. *Hydrometra*, type genus (fr. *hydr-* + *-metra*, fr. Gk *metrein* to measure, traverse, fr. *metron* measure) + *-idae* — more at MEASURE] : a family of small slender long-legged semiaquatic bugs closely related to the water striders

hy·drom·e·try \hīˈdräm·ə·trē\ *n* -ES [NL *hydrometria*, fr. *hydr-* + *-metria* -metry] : the measurement of specific gravity esp. of a liquid

hy·dro·mica \ˌ≈≈ at HYDRO- +\ *n* [*hydr-* + *mica*] : any of several varieties of muscovite that are less elastic and more unctuous than mica and have a pearly luster and some of which contain more water and less potash than ordinary muscovite — **hy·dro·micaceous** \ˈ"+\ *adj*

hy·dro·morphic \ˌ≈≈+ˈmȯrfik\ *adj* [*hydr-* + *-morphic*] : of or relating to an intrazonal soil (as the waterlogged soil of a bog area) characterized by an excess of moisture — compare CALOMORPHIC, HALOMORPHIC

hy·dro·mys \ˈ≈≈+ˌmis\ *n, cap* [NL, fr. *hydr-* + *-mys*] : a genus of myomorph rodents comprising the Australian beaver rats

hy·dro·negative \ˌ≈≈ at HYDRO- +\ *adj* [*hydr-* + *negative*] : characterized by negative hydrotaxis or hydrotropism

hy·dro·ne·phro·sis \ˌ≈≈+nəˈfrōsə̇s\ *n* [NL, fr. *hydr-* + *nephrosis*] : cystic distension of the kidney caused by the accumulation of urine in the kidney pelvis as a result of obstruction to outflow and accompanied by atrophy of the kidney structure and cyst formation

hy·dro·ne·phrot·ic \ˌ≈≈≈ˈfräd·ik\ *adj* [fr. NL *hydronephrosis*, after such pairs as NL *hypnosis*: E *hypnotic*] : affected with hydronephrosis

hy·dro·nitrogen \ˌ≈≈ at HYDRO- +\ *n* [*hydr-* + *nitrogen*] : a compound of hydrogen and nitrogen (as ammonia, hydrazine, hydrazoic acid)

hy·dro·ni·um \hīˈdrōnēəm\ *n* -S [ISV *hydr-* + *-onium*] : a hydrated hydrogen ion; *esp* : OXONIUM — used chiefly in inorganic chemistry ⟨~ perchlorate $[H_3O]^+[ClO_4]^-$⟩; called also *hydrogen ion*

hy·dron·y·my \hīˈdränəmē\ *n* -ES [ISV *hydr-* + *-onymy*] : names of bodies of water

¹hy·dro·path·ic \ˌhīdrəˈpathik, -thēk\ *adj* [ISV *hydropathy* + *-ic*] : of or relating to hydropathy or to an establishment where it is obtainable ⟨advocating and using a ~ system for the cure of fevers —*Amer. Guide Series: Vt.*⟩ — **hy·dro·path·i·cal·ly** \-thə̇k(ə)lē, -thēk-, -li\ *adv*

²hydropathic \"\ *n* -S *Brit* : a water-cure resort or establishment

hy·drop·a·thy \hīˈdräpəthē, -thi\ *n* -ES [ISV *hydr-* + *-pathy*; prob. orig. formed as G *hydropathie*] : a method of treating disease by copious and frequent use of water both externally and internally — compare HYDROTHERAPY

hy·dro·pericardium \ˌ≈≈ at HYDRO- +\ *n* [NL, fr. *hydr-* + *pericardium*] : an excess of watery fluid in the pericardial cavity

hy·dro·period \ˈ"+\ *n* : the period during which a soil area is waterlogged ⟨upland swamps with a 5-month ~⟩

hy·dro·peritoneum \ˈ"+\ *n* [NL, fr. *hydr-* + *peritoneum*] : ASCITES

hy·dro·peroxide \ˈ"+\ *n* [ISV *hydr-* + *peroxide*] : a compound of an element or radical with the univalent group —OOH ⟨sodium ~ NaOOH⟩

hy·dro·phane \ˈ≈≈+ˌfān\ *n* -S [*hydr-* + *-phane*] : a semitranslucent variety of opal that becomes translucent or transparent on immersion in water

hy·droph·a·nous \hīˈdräfənəs\ *adj* [*hydrophane* + *-ous*] : made transparent by immersion in water

hy·droph·i·dae \hīˈdräfəˌdē\ *n pl, cap* [NL, fr. *Hydrophis*, type genus + *-idae*] : a family of aquatic snakes that comprises the sea snakes and was formerly considered to constitute a subfamily of the family Colubridae

hy·dro·phi·idae \ˌhīdrəˈfīəˌdē\ [NL, fr. *Hydrophis* + *-idae*] *syn of* HYDROPHIDAE

hy·dro·phil \ˈhīdrəˌfil\ *n* -S [obs. *hydrophil*, adj., hydrophytic, fr. NL *hydrophilus* water-loving] : HYDROPHYTE

hy·dro·phil·ic \ˌ≈≈ˈfilik\ *also* **hy·dro·phile** \ˈ≈≈ˌfīl\ *adj* [*hydrophilic* fr. NL *hydrophilus* water-loving + E *-ic*; *hydrophile* fr. NL *hydrophilus*] : of, relating to, or having a strong affinity for water ⟨~ colloids swell in water and are relatively stable⟩ : readily wet by water ⟨cotton is a ~ fiber⟩ — opposed to *hydrophobic*; compare HYGROSCOPIC, LIPOPHILIC, LYOPHILIC, ORGANOPHILIC

hydrophilic ointment *n, pharmacy* : an ointment base easily removable with water

hy·droph·i·lid \hīˈdräfələ̇d\ *adj* [NL *Hydrophilidae*] : of or relating to the Hydrophilidae

hy·dro·phil·i·dae \ˌhīdrəˈfiləˌdē\ *n pl, cap* [NL fr. *Hydrophilus*, type genus (fr. *hydr-* + *-philus*) + *-idae*] : a large family of diving beetles that are mostly of scavenging or predaceous habits and of elliptical form and black color and that live chiefly in quiet pools and carry with them a film of air for respiration

hy·droph·i·lism \hīˈdräfəˌlizəm\ *n* -S [*hydrophilous* + *-ism*] : HYDROPHILY

hy·droph·i·lite \hīˈdräfəˌlīt\ *n* -S [G *hydrophilit*, fr. *hydr-* + Gk *philos* loving + G *-it* -ite; fr. the fact that it is very hygroscopic] : a mineral $CaCl_2$ of very rare occurrence consisting of native calcium chloride

hy·droph·i·lous \hīˈdräfələs\ *adj* [NL *hydrophilus* water-loving, fr. *hydr-* + *-philus* -philous, fr. Gk *philos* loving — more at -PHILOUS] **1** : pollinated by the agency of water **2** : HYDROPHYTIC

hy·droph·i·ly \-lē\ *n* -ES [*hydrophilous* + *-y*] : the quality or state of being hydrophilous

hy·dro·phis \ˈhīdrəfə̇s\ *n, cap* [NL, fr. *hydr-* + *-ophis*] : the type genus of the family Hydrophidae comprising sea snakes of the western and southern Pacific ocean

hy·dro·phobe \ˈhīdrəˌfōb\ *n* -S [LL *hydrophobus* one that has hydrophobia, fr. *hydrophobus*, adj., having hydrophobia, fr. Gk *hydrophobos*, fr. *hydr-* + *-phobos* -phobous] : one that is averse to or sheds water

hy·dro·pho·bia \ˌ≈≈ˈfōbēə\ *n* [LL, fr. Gk, fr. *hydr-* + *-phobia*] **1** : a morbid dread of water **2** : RABIES

hydrophobia skunk *also* **hydrophobia cat** *n, Southwest* : LITTLE SPOTTED SKUNK

hy·dro·pho·bic \ˌ≈≈ˈfōbik *also* -ˈfäb-\ *adj* [LL *hydrophobicus* characterized by hydrophobia, fr. Gk *hydrophobikos*, fr. *hydrophobia* + *-ikos* -ic] **1** : of, relating to, or suffering from hydrophobia **2** : resistant to or avoiding wetting ⟨most insects have ~ cuticle⟩ **3** *also* **hydrophobe** [*hydrophobe* fr. LL *hydrophobus* having hydrophobia, fr. Gk *hydrophobos*] **a** : of, relating to, or having a lack of affinity for water ⟨~ colloids are relatively unstable⟩ **b** : not readily wet by water ⟨nylon is a ~ fiber⟩ — opposed to *hydrophilic*; compare LIPOPHILIC, LYOPHOBIC — **hy·dro·pho·bic·i·ty** \ˌhīdrəfōˈbisəd·ē\ *n* -ES

hydrophobous *adj* [LL *hydrophobus* having hydrophobia] *obs* : HYDROPHOBIC

hy·dro·phone \ˈ≈≈ at HYDRO- +ˌfōn\ *n* [*hydr-* + *-phone*] : an electroacoustic transducer for listening to sound transmitted through water ⟨detection of submarines by ~⟩ ⟨underwater seismic surveying by ~⟩

hy·dro·phore \ˈ"+ˌfō(ə)r\ *n* -S [*hydr-* + *-phore*] : an instrument for obtaining specimens of water (as in a river, lake, or ocean) from any desired depth

hy·dro·pho·ria \ˌ≈≈+ˈfōrēə, -ˈfȯr-\ *n* -S [Gk, fr. *hydr-* + *-phoria* act of carrying — more at -PHORIA] : an act of carrying water; *specif* : a scene on a Greek water jar showing women carrying water from a fountain

hy·dro·phyl·la·ce·ae \ˌ≈≈+fəˈlāsēˌē\ *n pl, cap* [NL, fr. *Hydrophyllum*, type genus + *-aceae*] : a family of chiefly No. American herbs or undershrubs (order Polemoniales) having a cymose often helicoid inflorescence and usu. numerous ovules in each cell of a capsular fruit — see HYDROPHYLLUM, PHACELIA — **hy·dro·phyl·la·ceous** \ˌ≈≈≈ˈlāshəs\ *adj*

hy·dro·phyl·li·um \ˌ≈≈+ˈfilēəm\ *n, pl* **hydrophyl·lia** \-ēə\ [NL, fr. *hydr-* + *-phyllium* (fr. Gk *phyllion* small leaf, dim. of *phyllon* leaf) — more at BLOW (to blossom)] : one of the leaflike organs regarded as greatly modified zooids that cover other zooids of many siphonophores

hy·dro·phyl·lum \ˌ≈≈+ˈfiləm\ *n, cap* [NL, fr. *hydr-* + *-phyllum*] : a genus of No. American herbs (family Hydrophyllaceae) having lobed or pinnate deeply and sharply toothed leaves and bell-shaped cymose flowers

hy·dro·phyte \ˈ≈≈+ˌfīt\ *n* -S [ISV *hydr-* + *-phyte*] : a plant growing in water: **a** : a vascular plant growing wholly or partly in water; *esp* : a perennial aquatic plant having its overwintering buds under water — compare HELOPHYTE **b** : a plant requiring an abundance of water for growth and growing in water or in soil too waterlogged for most other plants to survive — compare MESOPHYTE, XEROPHYTE — **hy·dro·phyt·ic** \ˌ≈≈ˈfid·ik\ *adj*

hy·droph·y·ton \hīˈdräfəˌtän\ *n, pl* **hydrophy·ta** \-fəd·ə\ [NL, fr. *hydr-* + Gk *phyton* plant — more at PHYT-] : a common support connecting the zooids of a hydroid colony usu. including a hydrorhiza and a hydrocaulus — **hy·droph·y·tous** \-fəd·əs\ *adj*

hy·drop·ic \hīˈdräpik\ *also* **hy·drop·i·cal** \-pə̇kəl\ *adj* [*hydropic* alter. (influenced by L *hydropicus*) of ME *ydropike*, *idropik*, fr. MF *ydropique*, fr. L *hydropicus*, fr. Gk *hydrōpikos*, fr. *hydrōp-*, *hydrōps* hydrops + *-ikos* -ic; *hydropical* fr. L *hydropicus* + E *-al*] **1** : of, relating to, or exhibiting hydrops; *esp* : EDEMATOUS **2** : characterized by swelling and imbibition of fluid — used of a type of cellular degeneration — **hy·drop·i·cal·ly** \-pə̇k(ə)lē\ *adv*

¹hy·dro·plane \ˌ≈≈ at HYDRO- +ˌ-\ *n* [*hydr-* + *plane*] **1** : a hydrofoil or any surface (as of an airplane pontoon) having a similar shape and tendency **2 a** : a speedboat equipped with hydrofoils or having a stepped bottom that provides more than one lifting surface so that the hull is raised wholly or partially out of the water as the boat attains forward speed **b** : DIVING PLANE **3** : SEAPLANE — not used technically

²hydroplane \"\ *vi* **1** : to skim over the water with the hull either clear of the surface or barely immersed **2** : to drive or ride in a hydroplane

hy·dro·planula \ˌ≈≈+\ *n* [NL, fr. *hydr-* + *planula*] : a larval stage of a coelenterate intermediate between the planula and actinula stages

hy·dro·pneumatic \ˈ"+\ *adj* [ISV *hydr-* + *pneumatic*] : of, relating to, or operating by means of both water and air or other gas ⟨a ~ elevator⟩

hy·dro·pneumothorax \ˈ"+\ *n* [NL, fr. *hydr-* + *pneumothorax*] : the presence of gas and serous fluid in the pleural cavity

hy·dro·polyp \ˈ"+\ *n* [ISV *hydr-* + *polyp*] **1** : a polyp of a hydrozoan **2** : HYDRULA 2

hy·dro·pon·ic \ˌhīdrəˈpänik\ *adj* [fr. *hydroponics*, after such pairs as E *geoponics*: *geoponic*] : of or relating to hydroponics — **hy·dro·pon·i·cal·ly** \-nə̇k(ə)lē\ *adv*

hy·dro·pon·i·cist \ˌ≈≈ˈpänəsə̇st\ *n* -S : a specialist in hydroponics

hy·dro·pon·ics \ˌ≈≈ˈpäniks\ *n pl but usu sing in constr* [*hydr-* + *-ponics* (as in *geoponics*)] : the growing of plants in nutrient solutions with or without sand, gravel, or other inert medium to provide mechanical support

hy·dro·positive \ˌ≈≈ at HYDRO- +\ *adj* [*hydr-* + *positive*] *biol* : characterized by positive hydrotaxis or hydrotropism

hy·drop·o·tes \hīˈdräpəˌtēz\ *n, cap* [NL, fr. Gk *hydropotēs* water drinker, fr. *hydr-* + *potēs* drinker; akin to Gk *pinein* to drink — more at POTABLE] : a genus of deer consisting of a small Chinese species (*H. inermis*) having no antlers

hydropower \ˈ≈≈+\ *n* [²*hydro* + *power*] : hydroelectric power

hy·dro·press \ˈ≈≈ at HYDRO- +ˌ-\ *n* : HYDRAULIC PRESS

hy·drops \ˈhīˌdräps\ *also* **hy·drop·sy** \-psē, -si\ *n* -ES [*hydrops* fr. L, fr. Gk *hydrōps*; *hydropsy* alter. (influenced by L *hydropisis*) of earlier *idropesie*, fr. ME *ydropesie*, fr. OF *idropisie*, fr. L *hydropisis*, modif. of Gk *hydrōps* — more at DROPSY] **1** : EDEMA **2** : distention of a hollow organ with fluid ⟨~ of the gall bladder⟩ **3** *or* **hydrops fetalis** : congenital erythroblastosis

hy·dro·quinine \ˌ≈≈ at HYDRO- +\ *n* [ISV *hydr-* + *quinine*] : a bitter crystalline antipyretic alkaloid $C_{20}H_{26}N_2O_2$ found with quinine in cinchona bark and usu. present in commercial quinine; dihydro-quinine

hy·dro·quinone \ˈ"+\ *also* **hy·dro·chinone** \ˈ"+\ *or* **hy·dro·chi·non** \ˌ≈≈+ˈkīˌnän\ *n* [ISV *hydr-* + *quinone*; orig. formed as G *hydrochinon*] : a white crystalline strongly reducing phenol $C_6H_4(OH)_2$ occurring naturally in the form of the glucoside arbutin, made usu. by reduction of quinone, and used chiefly as a photographic developer, as an antioxidant esp. for fats and oils, and as a stabilizer and inhibitor (as in the polymerization of vinyl compounds); *para*-dihydroxy-benzene — see QUINHYDRONE

hy·dro·rhi·za \ˌ≈≈+ˈrīzə\ *n, pl* **hydrorhi·zae** \-ī(ˌ)zē\ [NL, fr. *hydr-* + *-rhiza*] : a rootstock or decumbent stem by which a hydroid is attached to other objects — **hy·dro·rhi·zal** \¦==¦rīzəl\ *adj*

hy·dro·rrhea \,==+'rēə\ *n* -s [NL, fr. *hydr-* + *-rrhea*] : a profuse watery discharge (as from the nose)

hy·dro·rubber \¦== *at* HYDRO- +\ *n* [*hydr-* + *rubber*] *chem* : a substance $(C_5H_{10})_x$ obtained as an elastic or tough inelastic mass by catalytic hydrogenation of rubber

hydros *pl of* HYDRO

hy·dro·salpinx \"+\ *n* [NL, fr. *hydr-* + *salpinx*] : abnormal distension of one or both fallopian tubes with fluid usu. due to inflammation

hy·dro·scope \'==+,skōp\ *n* [ISV *hydr-* + *-scope*; prob. orig. formed as It *idroscopio*] : a device for enabling a person to see an object at a considerable distance below the surface of water by means of a series of mirrors enclosed in a steel tube — compare WATER GLASS — **hy·dro·scop·ic** \¦==¦skäpik\ *also* **hy·dro·scop·i·cal** \-pəkəl\ *adj*

hy·dro·separator \¦== *at* HYDRO- +\ *n* [*hydr-* + *separator*] : a settling tank (as for an industrial process) in which solids in suspension are separated from the suspending liquid

hy·dro·sere \'==+,-\ *n* : an ecological sere originating in an aquatic habitat

hy·dro·silicate \¦== *at* HYDRO- +\ *n* [ISV *hydr-* + *silicate*] : a hydrous silicate

hy·dro·ski \'==+,-\ *n* : a sometimes retractable hydrofoil attached below the fuselage of a seaplane to accelerate take-offs and simplify landings

hy·dro·sol \"+,sōl, -,säl\ *n* [*hydr-* + *-sol* (fr. *solution*)] *chem* : a sol in which the liquid is water

hy·dro·some \"+,sōm\ *also* **hy·dro·so·ma** \,==+'sōmə\ *n* -s [NL *hydrosoma*, fr. *hydr-* + *-soma*] : the entire colony of a compound hydrozoan : HYDROID

hy·dro·sphere \'==+,-\ *n* [ISV *hydr-* + *sphere*] **1** : the aqueous vapor of the entire atmosphere **2** : the aqueous envelope of the earth including oceans, lakes, streams, and underground waters and the aqueous vapor in the atmosphere

hy·dro·spire \"+,-\ *n* [*hydr-* + *spire* (coil)] : a flattened calcareous pouch or tube on either side of the middle line of the inner surface of the ambulacra of a blastoid, located within the cavity of the calyx, opening on the exterior by a small aperture, and presumed to form part of the respiratory system — **hy·dro·spi·ric** \¦==¦spīrik\ *adj*

hy·dro·stat·ic \¦==+¦stad·|ik, -at|, |ēk\ *also* **hy·dro·stat·i·cal** \-|ǝkǝl, |ēk-\ *adj* [*hydrostatic* prob. fr. NL *hydrostaticus*, fr. *hydr-* + *staticus* static; *hydrostatical* prob. fr. NL *hydrostaticus* + E *-al* — more at STATIC] : of or relating to liquids at rest or to the pressures they exert or transmit — opposed to *hydrokinetic* — **hy·dro·stat·i·cal·ly** \|ǝk(ǝ)lē, |ēk-, -li\ *adv*

hydrostatic arch *n* : an arch designed to bear at each point a pressure proportional to the depth below a datum line

hydrostatic balance *n* : a balance for weighing a substance in water to ascertain its specific gravity

hydrostatic bed *n* : WATER BED

hydrostatic head *n* : a measure of pressure at a given point in a liquid in terms of the vertical height of a column of the liquid which would produce the same pressure

hydrostatic press *n* : HYDRAULIC PRESS

hydrostatic pressure *n* : pressure exerted by or existing within a liquid at rest with respect to adjacent bodies

hy·dro·stat·ics \¦== *at* HYDRO- + 'stad·iks\ *n pl but usu sing in constr* [prob. fr. NL *hydrostatica*, fr. neut. pl. of *hydrostaticus* hydrostatic] : a branch of physics that deals with the characteristics of liquids at rest and esp. with the pressure in a liquid or exerted by a liquid on an immersed body — compare HYDRODYNAMICS

hy·dro·stome \'==+,stōm\ *n* -s [*hydr-* + *-stome*] : the mouth of a hydroid

hy·dro·sulfide \¦== *at* HYDRO- +\ *n* [ISV *hydr-* + *sulfide*] : a compound derived from hydrogen sulfide by the replacement of half its hydrogen by an element or radical ⟨potassium ~ KSH⟩ — compare MERCAPTAN

hy·dro·sul·fite \,==+'səl,fīt\ *n* [ISV *hydrosulfurous* + *-ite*] : a salt of hydrosulfurous acid; *esp* : SODIUM HYDROSULFITE — not used scientifically; called also *dithionite, hyposulfite*

hy·dro·sulfureted \¦== *at* HYDRO- +\ *or* **hy·dro·sulfuretted** \"+\ *adj* [*hydr-* + *sulfureted, sulfuretted*, past part. of *sulfuret*] : combined or impregnated with hydrogen sulfide

hy·dro·sulfuric acid \" + . . . -\ *n* [*hydrosulfuric* ISV *hydr-* + *sulfuric*] : HYDROGEN SULFIDE

hy·dro·sulfurous acid \" + . . . -\ *n* [*hydrosulfurous* ISV *hydr-* + *sulfurous*] : an unstable acid $H_2S_2O_4$ known only in aqueous solution formed by reducing sulfurous acid or in the form of salts — not used scientifically; called also *dithionous acid, hyposulfurous acid*

hy·dro·tac·tic \¦==+¦taktik\ *adj* [fr. NL *hydrotaxis*, after such pairs as NL *chemotaxis*: E *chemotactic*] : of or relating to hydrotaxis

hy·dro·tal·cite \,==+'tal,sīt\ *n* -s [G *hydrotalkit*, fr. *hydr-* + *talk* talc (prob. fr. MF *talc*) + G *-it* -ite] : a pearly-white mineral $Mg_6Al_2(OH)_{16}(CO_3).4H_2O$ consisting of hydrous aluminum and magnesium hydroxide and carbonate

hy·dro·taxis \¦==*at* HYDRO- +\ *n* [NL, fr. *hydr-* + *-taxis*] : a taxis in which moisture is the directive factor

hy·dro·the·ca \,==+'thēkə\ *n* [NL, fr. *hydr-* + L *theca* sheath, case — more at TICK] : a cup-shaped extension of the perisarc in hydroids of the group Leptomedusae that surrounds and protects the hydranths when they are contracted — **hy·dro·the·cal** \¦==¦thēkəl\ *adj*

hy·dro·therapeutic \¦== *at* HYDRO- +\ *or* **hy·dro·thera·peutical** \"+\ *adj* [*hydr-* + *therapeutic, therapeutical*] : of, relating to, or involving the methods of hydrotherapy

hy·dro·therapeutics \"+\ *n pl but usu sing in constr* [*hydr-* + *therapeutics*] : HYDROTHERAPY

hy·dro·therapist \"+\ *n* [*hydrotherapy* + *-ist*] : a specialist in hydrotherapy

hy·dro·therapy \"+\ *n* [ISV *hydr-* + *therapy*] : the treatment of disease or disability by the external application of water ⟨~ by cold compresses to reduce fever⟩ ⟨~ of crippled limbs in a whirlpool bath⟩

hy·dro·thermal \"+\ *adj* [ISV *hydr-* + *thermal*; orig. formed in G] : of or relating to hot water — used esp. of the formation or metamorphism of minerals by the action of hot solutions rising up through the earth's crust from a cooling magma

hy·dro·tho·rax \,==+'thōr,aks, -'thȯ(ə)r,-\ *n* [NL, fr. *hydr-* + L *thorax*] : an excess of serous fluid in the pleural cavity; *esp* : an effusion resulting from a failing circulation (as in heart disease or from lung infection)

hy·dro·trop·ic \¦==+¦träpik\ *adj* [ISV *hydr-* + *-tropic*] **1** : exhibiting or characterized by hydrotropism **2** *chem* : relating to or causing hydrotropy ⟨~ solvents⟩ — **hy·dro·trop·i·cal·ly** \-pək(ə)lē\ *adv*

hy·drot·ro·pism \hī'drä·trə,pizəm\ *n* [ISV *hydr-* + *-tropism*] : a tropism (as in many plant roots) in which water or water vapor constitutes the orienting factor

hy·drot·ro·py \-rəpē\ *n* -ES [ISV *hydr-* + *-tropy*] *chem* : solubilization of a sparingly soluble substance in water brought about by an added agent

hy·dro·tungstite \¦== *at* HYDRO- +\ *n* [*hydr-* + *tungstite*] : a mineral $H_2WO_4.H_2O$ consisting of hydrous tungstic acid

hy·dro·turbine \'==+'-\ *n* : a hydraulic turbine

hy·dro·type \'==+,tīp\ *n* [ISV *hydr-* + *type*] : a positive printing process in photography that uses a gelatin-coated plate containing dichromate on which appears after the plate has been exposed to light under a positive and then soaked in a dye solution a positive image of dye that is transferred to a sheet of paper coated with soft gelatin

hy·dro·ureter \¦== *at* HYDRO-+\ *n* [NL, fr. *hydr-* + *ureter*] : abnormal distension of the ureter with urine

hy·drous \'hīdrəs\ *adj* [*hydr-* + *-ous*] : containing water : WATERY; *specif* : HYDRATED

hydrous wool fat *n* : LANOLIN a

hy·dro·vane \'== *at* HYDRO-+,vān\ *n* [*hydr-* + *vane*] **1** : HYDROFOIL **2** : DIVING PLANE

hy·drox·am·ic acid \,hī,dräk¦samik-\ *n* [*hydroxamic* ISV *hydroxy-* + *am-* (fr. *amide*) + *-ic*] : any of a class of weak acids (as RCONHOH) that are acylated derivatives of hydroxylamine

hy·drox·ide \hī'dräk,sīd\ *n* [ISV *hydr-* + *oxide*] **1** : a compound of hydroxyl with an element or radical — used esp. of bases containing a metal (as lithium hydroxide LiOH) or a quaternary ammonium radical (as tetramethylammonium hydroxide $(CH_3)_4NOH$) **2** : any of various hydrated oxides (as aluminum hydroxide) regarded as containing hydroxyl

hydroxide ion *or* **hydroxyl ion** *n* : the anion OH^- of basic hydroxides

hydroximino- *comb form* [*hydroxy-* + *imin-*] : isonitroso-

hydroxo- *comb form* [*hydroxyl* + *-o-*] : containing hydroxyl as a coordinated group ⟨potassium *hydroxo*stannate $K_2Sn(OH)_6$⟩ ⟨*hydroxo*cobalamin⟩ — compare HYDROXY-

hy·drox·o·ni·um \,hī,dräk'sōnēəm\ *n* -s [*hydroxy-* + *-onium*] : HYDRONIUM

hy·droxy \(')hī¦dräksē\ *adj* [*hydroxy-*] : relating to or containing hydroxyl ⟨~ molecule⟩ — compare -HYDRIC 2, HYDROXY-

hydroxy- *or* **hydrox-** *comb form* [ISV, fr. *hydroxyl*, fr. E] : hydroxyl : containing hydroxyl esp. in place of hydrogen — in names of chemical compounds or radicals ⟨*hydroxy*alkyl⟩ ⟨*hydroxa*mic acids⟩ — compare HYDROXO-

hy·droxy·acetic acid \(¦)hī¦dräksē+ . . .-\ *n* : GLYCOLIC ACID

hydroxy acid *n* : an acid (as lactic acid, tartaric acid, salicylic acid) having one or more hydroxyl groups in the molecule in addition to that present in the acid group itself

hydroxy amine *n* : AMINO ALCOHOL

hydroxyamino- *or* **hydroxamino-** *comb form* [*hydroxy-* + *amin-*] : containing the univalent radical –NHOH of hydroxylamine

hy·droxy·benzoic acid \(¦)hī¦dräksē+ . . .-\ *n* [*hydroxybenzoic* ISV *hydroxy-* + *benzoic*] : any of three crystalline monohydroxy derivatives HOC_6H_4COOH of benzoic acid: as **a** : the colorless para-substituted acid used in making several of its esters that are effective preservatives — called also *para-hydroxybenzoic acid, p-hydroxybenzoic acid* **b** : SALICYLIC ACID

hy·droxy·butyric acid \"+ . . .-\ *n* : a hydroxy derivative $C_3H_6(OH)COOH$ of butyric acid; *esp* : the beta derivative $CH_3CHOHCH_2COOH$ found in the blood and urine esp. in conditions of impaired metabolism — see KETONE BODY

hy·droxy·citronellal \"+\ *n* : a liquid hydroxy aldehyde $(CH_3)_2C(OH)(CH_2)_3CH(CH_3)CH_2CHO$ obtained by hydration of citronellal and used in perfumery to impart an odor of lily of the valley

hy·droxy·corticosterone \"+\ *n* : a hydroxy derivative of corticosterone; *esp* : HYDROCORTISONE

hy·droxy·de·oxy·corticosterone \'hī,dräksē'dē,äksē +\ *or* **hy·droxy·des·oxy·corticosterone** \-'de,zäksē, -'de,sä-+\ *n* [*hydroxy-* + *deoxy-* or *desoxy-* + *corticosterone*] : a crystalline steroid hormone $C_{21}H_{30}O_4$ occurring in the adrenal cortex

hy·droxy·ethyl \(¦)hī¦dräksē+\ *n* : a hydroxy derivative of ethyl; *esp* : the beta or 2-derivative $HOCH_2CH_2$–

hy·droxy·eth·yl·a·tion \(,)hī,dräksē,ethə'lāshən\ *n* -s [*hydroxyethyl* + *-ation*] : the introduction of a hydroxyethyl group into a compound usu. by reaction with ethylene oxide

hydroxy ketone *n* : a hydroxy derivative of a ketone

hy·drox·yl \hī'dräksəl\ *n* -s [*hydr-* + *ox-* + *-yl*] : the univalent group or radical OH consisting of one atom of hydrogen and one of oxygen that is characteristic esp. of hydroxides, oxygen acids, alcohols, glycols, phenols, and hemiacetals

hy·drox·yl·amine \hī¦dräksələ¦mēn; ,hī,dräk'siləmēn, -,mən\ *n* [ISV *hydroxyl* (fr. E) + *amine*] : a colorless low-melting crystalline unstable compound NH_2OH that is a weaker base than ammonia and forms stable crystalline salts with acids, that is made by reaction of its salts with alkali, and that is used chiefly as a reducing agent and as an intermediate — see OXIME

hy·drox·yl·ammonium \(¦)hī¦dräksəl+\ *n* [ISV *hydroxyl* (fr. E) + *ammonium*] : the univalent cation $HONH_3^+$ derived from hydroxylamine and present in its salts which are obtainable by hydrolysis of a primary nitroparaffin (as nitromethane) with water and a strong acid ⟨~ chloride $HONH_3Cl$ or hydroxylamine hydrochloride $NH_2OH.HCl$⟩

hy·drox·yl·apatite \"+\ *or* **hy·droxy·apatite** \(¦)hī¦dräksē+\ *n* [*hydroxylapatite* fr. G *hydroxylapatit*, fr. *hydroxyl* (fr. E) + *apatit* apatite; *hydroxyapatite* fr. *hydroxy-* + *apatite*] : apatite containing hydroxyl: as **a** : apatite in which hydroxyl predominates over fluorine, chlorine, and carbonate **b** : calcium phosphate hydroxide $Ca_5(OH)(PO_4)_3$ — see CALCIUM PHOSPHATE 1b(2)

hy·drox·yl·ate \hī'dräksə,lāt\ *vt* -ED/-ING/-S [*hydroxyl* + *-ate*] : to introduce hydroxyl into (a compound or radical) usu. by replacement of hydrogen — **hy·drox·yl·ation** \hī,dräksə'lāshən\ *n* -s

hydroxyl–herderite \=¦=¦==¦=\ *n* [*hydroxyl* + *herderite*] : a mineral $CaBe(PO_4)(OH)$ consisting of phosphate and hydroxide of calcium and beryllium and being isomorphous with herderite

hy·drox·yl·ic \¦hī,dräk¦silik\ *adj* [ISV *hydroxyl* (fr. E) + *-ic*] : of or relating to hydroxyl

hy·droxy·methyl \(¦)hī¦dräksē+\ *n* : the univalent radical $HOCH_2$– derived from methanol by removal of one hydrogen atom attached to carbon — called also *methylol*

hy·droxy·meth·yl·ation \(,)hī,dräksē,methə'lāshən\ *n* -s [*hydroxymethyl* + *-ation*] : the introduction of a hydroxymethyl group into a compound

hy·droxy·naphthoic acid \(¦)hī¦dräksē+ . . .-\ *n* : any of several crystalline acids $C_{10}H_6(OH)COOH$ derived from the naphthols: as **a** : a yellow acid derived from beta-naphthol and used as an intermediate for azo dyes and pigments — called also *beta-hydroxynaphthoic acid, 3-hydroxy-2-naphthoic acid*; see DYE table I (under *Developer 8*), NAPHTHOL AS **b** : a white to reddish acid derived from alpha-naphthol and used as an analytical reagent — called also *1-hydroxy-2-naphthoic acid*

hy·droxy·proline \"+\ *n* : a crystalline amino acid HOC_4H_7NCOOH obtained in the levorotatory L-form esp. by hydrolysis of gelatin or collagen — called also *4-hydroxyproline*

hy·droxy·quinoline \"+\ *n* : any of seven hydroxy derivatives of quinoline; *esp* : OXINE

hy·droxy·tryptamine \"+\ *n* -s [ISV *hydroxy-* + *tryptamine*] : SEROTONIN

hy·drox·y·zine \hī'dräksə,zēn\ *n* -s [*hydroxy-* + piperazine] : a tranquilizer and antihistamine $C_{21}H_{27}ClN_2O_2$ that is an ether alcohol derived from piperazine

hy·dro·zinc·ite \,hīdrō'ziŋ,kīt\ *n* [G *hydrozinkit*, fr. *hydr-* + *zink* zinc + *-it* -ite] : a mineral $Zn_5(OH)_6(CO_3)_2$ consisting of a basic zinc carbonate occurring as white, grayish, or yellowish masses or crusts (sp. gr. 3.58–3.8)

hy·dro·zoa \,hīdrə'zōə\ *n pl, cap* [NL, fr. *hydr-* (hydroid) + *-zoa*] : a class of coelenterates that includes various simple and compound polyps and jellyfishes having no stomodaeum or gastric tentacles and differing widely in appearance, structure, and habits, some being attached polyps which have no free-swimming stage, others being always free-swimming and the majority having an alternation of a free-swimming sexual generation with an attached asexual generation — see HYDROIDA, MILLEPORINA, SIPHONOPHORA, STYLASTERINA, TRACHYLINA

[1]**hydrozoan** \¦==¦zōən\ *or* **hydrozoal** \-ōəl\ *adj* [NL *Hydrozoa* + E *-an* (adj. suffix) or *-al* (adj. suffix)] : of or relating to the Hydrozoa

[2]**hydrozoan** \"\ *n* -s [NL *Hydrozoa* + E *-an* (n. suffix)] : one of the Hydrozoa

hy·dro·zo·on \¦==¦zō,än\ *n, pl* **hydro·zoa** \-ōə\ *or* **hydrozoons** [NL, fr. *hydr-* + *-zoon*] : HYDROZOAN

hy·dru·la \'hīdrələ\ *n* -s [NL, dim. of *hydra* (hydrozoan polyp)] **1** : a hypothetical primitive polyp of simple type **2** : a developmental phase of many coelenterates (as hydroids) in which they have the form of a simple polyp

hy·dru·ra·ce·ae \,hī,drü'rāsē,ē\ *n pl, cap* [NL, fr. *Hydrurus*, type genus + *-aceae*] : a family of algae (order Chrysocapsales) that includes the genus *Hydrurus* and related forms when these are considered to be algae rather than protozoans

hy·drur·ga \hī'drürgə\ *n, cap* [NL, irreg. fr. *hydr-*] : a genus of mammals (family Phocidae) comprising the leopard seal

hy·dru·rus \hī'drürəs\ *n, cap* [NL, fr. *hydr-* + *-urus*] : a genus of colonial plantlike flagellates (order Chrysomonadina) occurring as sticky foul-smelling branched feathery greenish brown tufts in cold flowing water — see HYDRURACEAE

hydt *abbr* hydrant

hy·e·na *or* **hy·ae·na** \hī'ēnə\ *n* -s [L *hyaena*, fr. Gk *hyaina*, fr. *hys* hog — more at SOW] **1** : any of several large strong nocturnal carnivorous Old World mammals constituting the family Hyaenidae, having a long thick neck, large head, powerful jaws, rough coat, and four-toed feet with nonretractile claws, and feeding largely on carrion — compare CAVE HYENA **2** *Austral* : TASMANIAN WOLF

striped hyena

hyena dog *n* : AFRICAN HUNTING DOG

hy·e·nia \hī'ēnēə\ *n, cap* [NL, fr. *Hyen*, locality near Nord Fjord, western Norway, near which the fossils on which the genus is based were discovered + NL *-ia*] : a genus of small Devonian fossil plants (order Hyeniales) having horizontal rhizomes bearing aerial shoots with small bifurcated leaves in whorls and pendulous terminal sporangia

hy·e·ni·a·les \(,)hī,ēnē'ā(,)lēz\ *n pl, cap* [NL, fr. *Hyenia* + *-ales*] : an order of Devonian sphenopsid plants known only in the fossil state — see CALAMOPHYTON, HYENIA

hy·enic *or* **hy·aenic** \(')hī¦ēnik, -¦en-\ *adj* [*hyena, hyaena* + *-ic*] : of, relating to, or like a hyena

hy·e·ni·form \(')hī¦ēnə,fȯrm\ *adj* [*hyena* + *-iform*] : HYENOID

hy·e·noid \hī'ē,nȯid\ *adj* [*hyena* + *-oid*] : resembling a hyena

hyenoid dog *n* : any of several No. American Miocene and Pliocene carnivorous mammals constituting *Borophagus* and related genera of the family Canidae and being intermediate in character between the true dogs and the hyenas

hyet- *or* **hyeto-** *comb form* [Gk, fr. *hyetos*; akin to Gk *hyei* it is raining — more at SUCK] : rain ⟨*hyet*al⟩ ⟨*hyeto*meter⟩ ⟨*hyeto*graphy⟩

hy·e·tal \'hīəd·ᵊl\ *adj* : of or relating to rain, rainfall, or rainy regions

hy·et·o·graph \hī'ed·ə,graf, -rȧf\ *n* [ISV *hyet-* + *-graph*] **1** : a chart showing average annual rainfall **2** : HYETOMETROGRAPH

hy·et·o·graph·ic \(,)hī¦ed·ə¦grafik\ *also* **hy·et·o·graph·i·cal** \-fəkəl\ *adj* [*hyetography* + *-ic, -ical*] : of or relating to hyetography — **hy·et·o·graph·i·cal·ly** \-fək(ə)lē\ *adv*

hy·e·tog·ra·phy \,hīə'tägrəfē\ *n* -ES [ISV *hyet-* + *-graphy*] : scientific description of the geographical distribution of rain

hy·et·o·log·i·cal \(,)hī¦ed·ᵊl¦äjəkəl\ *adj* [*hyet-* + *-logy* + *-ical*] : of or relating to hyetology

hy·e·tol·o·gy \,hīə'täləjē\ *n* -ES [*hyet-* + *-logy*] : a branch of meteorology that deals with precipitation (as of rain and snow)

hy·e·tom·e·ter \-ämǝd·ǝ(r)\ *n* [*hyet-* + *-meter*] : RAIN GAGE

hy·e·to·met·ro·graph \,hīətō'me·trə,graf, -rȧf\ *n* [*hyet-* + *metr-* (measure) + *-graph*] : a self-registering rain gage

hyg *abbr* hygiene

hy·ge·ian \(')hī¦jēən\ *adj* [*Hygeia*, ancient Greek goddess of health (fr. L *Hygea*, fr. Gk *Hygieia*, fr. *hygieia* health, fr. *hygiēs* sound, healthy) + E *-an*] **1** *usu cap* : of or relating to Hygeia, the ancient Greek goddess of health **2** : of or relating to health or to medical practice

hy·ge·ist \'hījēəst\ *n* -s [Gk *hygei*a health (alter. of *hygieia*) + E *-ist*] : HYGIENIST

hy·giene \'hī,jēn *sometimes* =¦=\ *n* -s [F *hygiène* & NL *hygiena*, *hygieina*, fr. Gk *hygieinē*, fem. of *hygieinos* healthful, relating to health, fr. *hygiēs* sound, healthy, fr. a prehistoric compound whose first and second constituents respectively are akin to OIr *so-* good, well, OSlav *sŭdravŭ* healthy, Av *hugod*, well, Skt *su* and to Lith *gyvas* living — more at QUICK] **1** : the science which deals with the establishment and maintenance of health in the individual and the group ⟨took a course in municipal ~⟩ **2** : conditions or practices conducive to health ⟨infant mortality was very high because of bad ~ and the lack of nourishing foods —P.E.James⟩

hy·gien·ic \¦hījē¦enik, (')hī¦jen-, -nēk *also* (')hī¦jēn-\ *also* **hy·gien·i·cal** \-nəkəl, -nēk-\ *adj* [prob. fr. F *hygiénique*, fr. *hygiène* hygiene + *-ique* -ic, -ical] : of, relating to, or conducive to health or to hygiene **syn** see HEALTHFUL

hy·gien·i·cal·ly \-nək(ə)lē, -nēk-, -li\ *adv* : in a hygienic manner

hy·gien·ics \,hījē'eniks, hī'jen- -nēks *also* hī'jēn-\ *n pl but sing in constr* : HYGIENE 1

hy·gien·ist \(')hī¦jēnəst, (')hī¦jen-, *also* ¦hījē¦en- *or* 'hījən-\ *n* -s [ISV *hygiene* + *-ist*] : a specialist in hygiene; *esp* : one skilled in a specified branch of hygiene ⟨dental ~⟩ ⟨mental ~⟩

hygr- *also* **hygro-** *comb form* [Gk, fr. *hygros* moist, wet — more at HUMOR] **1** : humidity : moisture : moist ⟨*hygr*ic⟩ ⟨*hygro*stat⟩ ⟨*hygro*phobia⟩ ⟨*hygro*phyte⟩ **2** : moisture and : of or relating to moisture and ⟨*hygro*thermal⟩

hy·gric \'hīgrik\ *adj* [ISV *hygr-* + *-ic*] : of, relating to, or containing moisture

hy·grine \'hī,grēn, -grən\ *n* -s [ISV *hygr-* + *-ine*; orig. formed as G *hygrin*] : a colorless liquid ketonic alkaloid $C_8H_{15}NO$ derived from pyrrolidine and obtained from coca leaves

hy·gro·deik \'hīgrə,dīk\ *n* -s [*hygr-* + *-deik* (fr. Gk *deiknynai* to show) — more at DICTION] : a hygrometer having wet-bulb and dry-bulb thermometers and an adjustable index for determining relative humidity

hy·gro·expansivity \¦hī(,)grō+\ *n* : expansivity due to moisture or humidity

hy·gro·graph \'hīgrə,graf, -rȧf\ *n* [ISV *hygr-* + *-graph*] : an instrument for recording automatically variations in the humidity of the atmosphere

hy·grol·o·gy \hī'gräləjē\ *n* -ES [ISV *hygr-* + *-logy*] : a branch of physics that deals with the phenomena of humidity

hy·gro·ma \hī'grōmə\ *n, pl* **hygromas** \-məz\ *or* **hygro·ma·ta** \-məd·ə\ [NL, fr. *hygr-* + *-oma*] **1** : a cystic tumor of lymphatic origin **2** : a cyst esp. of the knee of cattle caused by injury or infection

hy·grom·e·ter \hī'grämǝd·ǝ(r)\ *n* [prob. fr. F *hygromètre*, fr. *hygr-* + *-mètre* -meter] : any of several instruments for measuring the humidity of the atmosphere — see DEW-POINT HYGROMETER, HAIR HYGROMETER, PSYCHROMETER

hy·gro·met·ric \¦hīgrə¦me·trik\ *also* **hy·gro·met·ri·cal** \-rəkəl\ *adj* [prob. fr. F *hygrométrique*, fr. *hygrométrie* hygrometry + *-ique* -ic, -ical] **1** : of or relating to hygrometry or to humidity **2** : HYGROSCOPIC — **hy·gro·met·ri·cal·ly** \-rək(ə)lē\ *adv*

hygrometric water *n* : water in a mineral that can be released by raising its temperature to 110° C

hy·grom·e·try \hī'grämə·trē\ *n* -ES [F *hygrométrie*, fr. *hygr-* + *-métrie* -metry] : a branch of physics that deals with the measurement of humidity esp. of the atmosphere

hy·groph·i·la \hī'gräfələ\ *n* [NL, fr. *hygr-* + *-phila*] **1** *cap* : a genus of aquatic herbaceous or woody plants (family Acanthaceae) having leaves resembling those of the willow **2** -s : any plant of the genus *Hygrophila*

hy·gro·phile \'hīgrə,fīl\ *or* **hy·gro·phil·ic** \¦==¦filik\ *adj* [*hygrophile* fr. F, fr. *hygr-* + *-phile*; *hygrophilic* prob. fr. F *hygrophile* + E *-ic*] : HYGROPHILOUS

hy·groph·i·lous \(')hī¦gräfələs\ *adj* [prob. fr. F *hygrophile* + E *-ous*] : living or growing in moist places

hy·gro·phyte \'hīgrə,fīt\ *n* -s [ISV *hygr-* + *-phyte*] **1** : a plant living under conditions of plentiful moisture **2** : HYDROPHYTE — **hy·gro·phyt·ic** \¦==¦fid·ik\ *adj*

hy·gro·scope \'hīgrə,skōp\ *n* [*hygr-* + *-scope*] : an instrument that shows changes in humidity (as of the atmosphere) — compare HYGROMETER

hy·gro·scop·ic \¦==¦skäpik\ *adj* [*hygroscope* + *-ic*] **1 a** : readily taking up and retaining moisture ⟨glycerol is ~⟩ ⟨~ soils⟩ ⟨common salt is slightly ~⟩ — compare DELIQUESCENT, HYDROPHILIC **b** : taken up and retained under certain conditions of humidity and temperature — used of moisture ⟨~ water is not removed from clay by drying at 110° C⟩ **2 a** *bot* : sensitive to moisture ⟨~ tissues⟩ ⟨~ organs⟩ **b** : induced by moisture ⟨turgor movements are ~⟩ — **hy·gro·scop·i·cal·ly**

\-pȯk(ə)lē\ *adv* — **hy·gro·sco·pic·i·ty** \ˌhīgrəˌskō'pisəd·ē\ *n* -ES

hygroscopic cell *n* : BULLIFORM CELL

hygroscopic coefficient *n* : the percentage of water that is absorbed and held in equilibrium by a soil in a saturated atmosphere

hygroscopic moisture *or* **hygroscopic water** *n* : moisture held firmly as a film on soil particles and not responding to capillary action

hy·gro·stat \'hīgrəˌstat\ *n* -S [*hygr-* + *-stat*] : HUMIDISTAT

hy·gro·thermal \ˌhīgrə+\ *adj* [*hygr-* + *thermal*] : of or relating to a combination of moisture and heat

hy·gro·ther·mo·graph \ˌhīgrə'thərməˌgraf\ *n* [*hygr-* + *therm-* + *-graph*] : an instrument that records both humidity and temperature on the same chart

hying *pres part of* HIE

hyk·sos \'hikˌsōs, -sŭs, -sȯs, -səs\ *adj, usu cap* [Gk *Hyksōs*, dynasty ruling Egypt, fr. Egypt *ḥq3 h3swt* ruler of the countries of the nomads] : of or relating to a Semite dynasty ruling Egypt from about 1650 to 1580 B.C. and known as the Shepherd kings

hyl- *or* **hylo-** *comb form* [Gk, wood, matter, fr. *hylē* wood, forest, material, matter] **1** : matter : material ⟨*hylomorphism*⟩ ⟨*hylomorphous*⟩ **2** : wood ⟨*hylophagous*⟩ : forest ⟨*Hylocichla*⟩

hy·la \'hīlə\ *n* [NL, fr. Gk *hylē* wood, forest] **1** *cap* : a large genus (the type of the family Hylidae) of arciferous amphibians comprising the typical toads that have swollen terminal phalanges resembling claws and forming adhesive pads adapted to an arboreal habitat **2** -S : any amphibian of the genus *Hyla; broadly* : TREE TOAD

hy·lam \(')hī'läm\ *n, pl* **hylam** *or* **hylams** *usu cap* **1 a** : a people of southeastern China derived from intermarriage between the Chinese and the Li tribesmen of the island of Hainan **b** : a member of such people **2** : the language of the Hylam people

hy·le \'hī(ˌ)lē\ *n* -S [LL, matter, fr. Gk *hylē* wood, matter; perh. akin to OE *syll* sill — more at SILL] *philos* : whatever receives form or determination from outside itself : MATTER; *esp* : CHAOS 2

hy·le·an \(')hī'lēən\ *adj* [prob. fr. G *Hyläa*, region of tropical rain forest in the basin of the Amazon river in So. America (fr. Gk *Hylaia*, forested region on what is now the Dnieper river in the Ukraine, fr. *hylaia*, fem. of *hylaios* of the forest, wild, fr. *hylē* wood, forest) + E *-an*] : covered with forest : WOODED

hy·leg \'hīˌleg\ *n* -S [modif. of Per *hailāj* material body] : the astrological position of the planets at the time of birth

hy·le·gi·a·cal \ˌhīlə'jīəkəl\ *adj* [irreg. fr. *hyleg*] : of or relating to a hyleg

hy·le·mya \ˌhīlə'mīə\ *n, cap* [NL, fr. Gk *hylē* wood, forest + *mya, myia* fly — more at MIDGE] : a genus of two-winged flies (family Anthomyiidae) including numerous species having larvae that are maggots (as the onion maggot) boring in economically important plants

hy·lic \'hīlik\ *adj* [LL *hylicus*, fr. Gk *hylikos*, fr. *hylē* wood, matter + *-ikos* -ic] **1** : of or relating to matter : MATERIAL, CORPOREAL ⟨~ wants⟩ **2** : of or relating to the lowest of the three Gnostic divisions of mankind — compare ²PSYCHIC 3, ²PNEUMATIC 1

hy·lid \'hīləd\ *n* -S [NL *Hylidae*] : a tree toad of the family Hylidae

hy·li·dae \'hīləˌdē\ *n pl, cap* [NL, fr. *Hyla*, type genus + *-idae*] : a large family of predominantly arboreal rather slender-bodied frogs with elongated hind limbs, rounded adhesive disks on the digits, and the thumbs not enlarged in the male — see TREE TOAD

hy·lob·a·tes \hī'läbəˌtēz\ *n, cap* [NL, fr. *hyl-* + *-bates*] : a genus of primates comprising the typical gibbons that with the siamang and extinct related forms make up a subfamily of Pongidae or in some classifications a separate family

hy·lo·cereus \ˌhīlō+\ *n, cap* [NL, fr. *hyl-* + *Cereus*] : a genus of climbing sometimes epiphytic tropical American cacti with angular stems and mostly white very showy fragrant flowers — see NIGHT-BLOOMING CEREUS

hy·lo·cich·la \ˌhīlō'siklə\ *n, cap* [NL, fr. *hyl-* + Gk *kichlē* thrush; akin to Gk *chelidōn* swallow — more at CELANDINE] : a genus of thrushes containing the wood thrush, hermit thrush, veery, and other American species

hy·lo·co·mi·um \-'kōmēəm\ *n, cap* [NL, fr. *hyl-* + Gk *komē* hair + NL *-ium*] : a small genus of mostly feathery mosses of the family Hypnaceae

hy·lo·des \hī'lō(ˌ)dēz\ [NL, fr. *Hyla* + *-odes*] *syn of* ELEUTHERODACTYLUS

hy·loid \'hīˌlȯid\ *adj* [NL *Hyla* + E *-oid*] : resembling or belonging to the family Hylidae

hy·lo·mor·phic *also* **hy·le·mor·phic** \ˌhīlə'mȯrfik\ *adj* [*hylomorphism, hylemorphism* + *-ic*] : of, relating to, or based on hylomorphism

hy·lo·mor·phism *also* **hy·le·mor·phism** \ˌ==ˈmȯ(r)ˌfizəm\ *n* -S [*hylomorphism* fr. *hyl-* + *morph-* + *-ism; hylemorphism* alter. (influenced by Gk *hylē* matter) of *hylomorphism*] *Aristotelianism* : a doctrine that corporeal beings consist of a combination of Aristotelian forms and primordial matter

hy·lo·mor·phous \ˌ==ˈmȯrfəs\ *adj* [*hyl-* + *-morphous*] : having a material form

hy·lo·mys \'hīləˌmis\ [NL, fr. *hyl-* + *-mys*] *syn of* ECHINOSOREX

hy·loph·a·gous \(')hī'läfəgəs\ *adj* [*hyl-* + *-phagous*] *zool* : eating wood ⟨~ insects⟩

hy·lo·theism \ˌhīlō+\ *n* [*hyl-* + *theism*] : a doctrine equating God with matter — compare MATERIALISM

hy·lo·the·ist \"+\ *n* [*hyl-* + *-theist*] : an advocate of hylotheism — **hy·lo·the·is·tic** \"+\ *adj*

hy·lot·o·mous \(')hī'läd·əməs\ *adj* [Gk *hylotomos*, fr. *hyl-* + *tomos* cutting, sharp, fr. *temnein* to cut — more at TOME] *zool* : cutting wood ⟨~ insects⟩

hy·lo·zo·ic \ˌhīlə'zōik\ *adj* [*hyl-* + *zo-* + *-ic*] : of or relating to hylozoism

hy·lo·zo·ism \ˌ==ˈzōˌizəm\ *n* -S [*hyl-* + *zo-* + *-ism*] : a doctrine that all matter is animated — used esp. of the theories of early Greek philosophers

hy·lo·zo·ist \ˌhīlə'zōəst\ *n* -S [*hyl-* + *zo-* + *-ist*] : an advocate of hylozoism

hy·lo·zo·is·tic \ˌhīləzō'istik\ *adj* [*hyl-* + *zo-* + *-istic*] : of, relating to, or having the characteristics of hylozoism or the hylozoists

¹hy·men \'hīmən\ *n* -S [L, fr. Gk *hymēn* wedding song, fr. *Hymēn* Hymen, god of marriage (lit., a wedding cry); perh. akin to Gk *hymnos* hymn, song of praise] **1** *archaic* : MARRIAGE **2** *archaic* : a wedding song

²hymen \"\ *n* -S [LL, fr. Gk *hymēn* membrane, caul; prob. akin to Skt *syūman* band, thong, L *suere* to sew — more at SEW] : a fold of mucous membrane partly closing the orifice of the vagina — called also *maidenhead*

hymen- *or* **hymeno-** *comb form* [NL, fr. Gk, fr. *hymen-*, *hymēn* membrane, caul] : hymen : membrane ⟨*hymenotomy*⟩ ⟨*Hymenoptera*⟩

hy·me·naea \ˌhēmə'nēə\ *n, cap* [NL, prob. fr. L *hymenaeus* wedding song, marriage] : a genus of tropical American timber trees (family Leguminosae) having large white or purplish flowers in panicles and pinnate leaves consisting of a single pair of large thick glossy leaflets — see COURBARIL

hy·me·na·ic meter \ˌ==ˈnāik-\ *n* [LL *hymenaicum metrum*] : a dactylic dimeter — symbol -◡◡|-◡◡

hy·men·al \'hīmənᵊl\ *adj* [²*hymen* + *-al*] : of, relating to, or affecting the hymen

¹hy·me·ne·al \ˌhīmə'nēəl\ *adj* [L *hymenaeus* marriage, wedding song (fr. Gk *hymenaios*, fr. *Hymen-*, *Hymēn* Hymen) + E *-al*] : of or relating to marriage : NUPTIAL — **hy·me·ne·al·ly** \-ēəlē, -li\ *adv*

²hymeneal \"\ *n* -S **1 hymeneals** *pl, archaic* : NUPTIALS **2** *archaic* : a wedding hymn

hymenean *n* -S [L *hymenaeus* wedding, wedding song + E *-an*] *obs* : ¹HYMEN

hy·me·ni·al \(')hī'mēnēəl\ *adj* [NL *hymenium* + E *-al*] : of or relating to the hymenium

hymenial layer *n* : HYMENIUM

hy·me·nif·er·ous \ˌhīmə'nif(ə)rəs\ *adj* [NL *hymenium* + E *-ferous*] : having a hymenium

hy·me·ni·um \hī'mēnēəm\ *n, pl* **hyme·nia** \-nēə\ *or* **hymeniums** [NL, fr. *hymen-* + *-ium*] : a spore-bearing layer in fungi or their fruiting bodies (as apothecia or the sporophores of agarics) consisting of a group of asci or basidia often interspersed with paraphyses, setae, and other sterile structures

hy·me·no·cal·lis \ˌhīmənō'kaləs\ *n, cap* [NL, fr. *hymen-* + *-callis* (fr. Gk *kallos* beauty); fr. the delicate texture of the perianth — more at CALLI-] : a genus of tropical and subtropical American bulbous plants (family Amaryllidaceae) with linear basal leaves and umbels of usu. white or pink but sometimes yellow tubular flowers — compare PERUVIAN DAFFODIL

hy·me·no·chae·te \-'kēd·(ˌ)ē\ *n, cap* [NL fr. *hymen-* + Gk *chaitē* long flowing hair — more at CHAETA] : a genus of fungi (family Thelephoraceae) having a corky or leathery sporophore and a hymenium which appears downy because of the many simple cystidia projecting from it — see BROWN ROOT DISEASE

hy·me·no·gas·tra·ce·ae \-(ˌ)nōˌga'strāsēˌē\ *n pl, cap* [NL, fr. *Hymenogastr-*, *Hymenogaster*, type genus (fr. *hymen-* + *-gaster*) + *-aceae*] : a family of basidiomycetous fungi of the order Hymenogastrales forming subterranean irregularly globose sporophores — see FALSE TRUFFLE, RHIZOPOGON

hy·me·no·gas·tra·les \-ā(ˌ)lēz\ *n pl, cap* [NL, fr. *Hymenogastr-*, *Hymenogaster*, genus of fungi + *-ales*] : an order of gasteromycetous fungi (subclass Homobasidiomycetes) having a distinct basidiocarp with a usu. fleshy or waxy gleba which remains closed at least until after the basidia have discharged the basidiospores

hy·men·oid \'hīməˌnȯid\ *adj* [Gk *hymenoeidēs*, fr. *hymeno-* hymen- + *-eidēs* -oid] : MEMBRANOUS

hy·me·no·lep·i·did \ˌhīmənō'lepəˌdid\ *adj* [NL *Hymenolepididae*, family of tapeworms, fr. *Hymenolepid-*, *Hymenolepis*, type genus + *-idae*] : of or relating to the genus *Hymenolepis* or family Hymenolepididae

hy·me·nol·e·pis \ˌ==ˈnäləpəs\ *n, cap* [NL, fr. *hymen-* + *-lepis*] : a genus of small taenioid tapeworms (type of the family Hymenolepididae) including numerous comparatively innocuous parasites (as the dwarf tapeworm of man) of birds and mammals that usu. require insect intermediate hosts but may be able in some cases (as the dwarf tapeworm) to complete the life cycle in a single host by means of a hexacanth which hatches in the intestine, invades a villus, and there develops into a cysticercoid which ultimately escapes and develops into an adult tapeworm in the lumen of the intestine

hy·me·no·lichenes \ˌhīmənō+\ *n pl, cap* [NL, fr. *hymen-* + *Lichenes*] : a subgroup of Lichenes comprising lichens in which the fungal component is a hymenomycete and being coextensive with the group Basidiolichenes

hy·me·no·my·cete \-ˌmīˌsēt, -ˌmī'sēt\ *n* -S [NL *Hymenomycetes*] **1** : a fungus of the order Agaricales **2** : a fungus having a fruiting body with a definite hymenium

hy·me·no·my·ce·tes \-ˌmī'sēd·(ˌ)ēz\ *n pl, cap* [NL, fr. *hymen-* + *-mycetes*] *in some classifications* : a subclass of Basidiomycetes coextensive with the order Agaricales

hy·me·no·my·ce·tous \-sēd·əs\ *adj* [*hymen-* + *-mycetous*] : of, relating to, or being a hymenomycete : being a hymenium

hy·meno·phore \hī'menəˌfō(ə)r, 'hīmənō,-\ *also* **hy·me·noph·o·rum** \ˌhīmə'näfərəm\ *n, pl* **hymenophores** \-ˌfō(ə)rz\ *also* **hymenopho·ra** \-äf(ə)rə\ [NL *hymenophorum*, fr. *hymeno-* (irreg. fr. *hymenium*) + *-phorum*] **1** : the hymenium-bearing portion of the sporophore in fungi **2** : SPOROPHORE

hy·me·no·phyl·la·ce·ae \ˌhīmə(ˌ)nōfə'lāsēˌē\ *n pl, cap* [NL, fr. *Hymenophyllum*, type genus + *-aceae*] : a family of ferns having delicate fronds with sessile sporangia on a receptacle resembling a bristle and surrounded by a cup-shaped, tubular, or 2-valved involucre — **hy·me·no·phyl·la·ceous** \ˌ==(ˌ)==ˈlāshəs\ *adj*

hy·me·no·phyl·li·tes \ˌ==(ˌ)fə'līd·(ˌ)ēz\ *n pl, cap* [NL, fr. *Hymenophyllum*, genus of ferns + *-ites* -ite] : a genus of fossil ferns of the Carboniferous and perhaps of more recent age bearing a superficial resemblance to the existing genus *Hymenophyllum*

hy·me·no·phyl·lum \ˌ===ˈfiləm\ *n, cap* [NL, fr. *hymen-* + *-phyllum*] : a genus (the type of the family Hymenophyllaceae) of tropical hygrophytic and usu. epiphytic ferns distinguished from *Trichomanes* by having the valves of the involucre bearing the sporangia separate

hy·me·nop·ter \ˌhīmə'näptə(r)\ *n* -S [NL *Hymenoptera*] : HYMENOPTERON

hy·me·nop·tera \-'näptərə\ *n pl, cap* [NL, fr. Gk, neut. pl. of *hymenopteros* membrane-winged, fr. *hymeno-* (fr. *hymen-*, *hymēn* membrane, caul) + *-pteros* -pterous — more at HYMEN] : an extensive order of highly specialized insects that include the bees, wasps, ants, ichneumons, sawflies, gall wasps, and related forms, that often associate in large colonies with complex social organization, that have usu. four membranous wings typically with a thickened dark spot near the anterior edge of the forewings, the abdomen generally borne on a slender pedicel, and in the female complex ovipositors at the posterior end of the body which may be modified into sawing, boring, or piercing organs or in one group converted into a sting, and that undergo complete metamorphosis, the larva being usu. a footless grub — **hy·me·nop·ter·ous** \ˌ==ˈ==t(ə)rəs\ *adj*

hy·me·nop·ter·ist \ˌ==ˈ=tərəst\ *or* **hy·me·nop·ter·ol·o·gist** \ˌ===ˈräləjəst\ *n* -S : a specialist in the Hymenoptera

hy·me·nop·ter·ol·o·gy \ˌ===ˈräləjē\ *n* -ES [ISV *hymenoptero-* (fr. NL *Hymenoptera*) + *-logy*; prob. orig. formed as F *hyménoptérologie*] : a branch of entomology concerned with Hymenoptera

hy·me·nop·ter·on \ˌ==ˈ=təˌrän, -ˌrən\ *also* **hy·me·nop·ter·an** \-tərən\ *n, pl* **hymenop·tera** \-tərə\ [*hymenopteron* fr. NL *Hymenopteron*, sing. of *Hymenoptera; hymenopteran* fr. NL *Hymenoptera* + E *-an*] : one of the Hymenoptera

hy·men·ot·o·my \ˌhīmə'näd·əmē\ *n* -ES [ISV *hymen-* + *-tomy*; prob. orig. formed as F *hyménotomie*] : surgical incision of the hymen

hymens *pl of* HYMEN

hy·met·ti·an \(')hī'med·ēən\ *also* **hy·met·tic** \-d·ik\ *adj, usu cap* [L *Hymettius* (fr. *Hymettus*, mountain near Athens, Greece fr. Gk *Hymēttos*) + E *-an* or *-ic*] : of or relating to Mount Hymettus ⟨*Hymettian* marble⟩ ⟨*Hymettian* honey⟩

¹hymn \'him\ *n* -S *often attrib* [ME *ymne, hympne*, partly fr. OE *ymen, hymen*, fr. L *hymnus* and partly fr. MF *himpne*, fr. ML *hympnus*, fr. L *hymnus* and partly fr. OF *ymne*, fr. ML *ymnus*, fr. L *hymnus*; L *hymnus* fr. Gk *hymnos* song of praise] **1 a** : a song of praise to God ⟨grows into the chorus . . . with its triumphal ~: Lift up your heads, O ye gates —J.P.Larsen⟩ **b** : a metrical composition adapted for singing in a religious service ⟨collection of ~s, carols, anthems, gospel songs —*Saturday Rev.*⟩ **2** : a song of praise or joy ⟨in jolly ~s they praise the god of wine —John Dryden⟩ **3** : something resembling a hymn esp. in expressing praise : PAEAN ⟨this prose ~ of contentment in simple and external things —Douglas Bush⟩ ⟨the plot of this ~ to American domesticity —Jack Weeks⟩ ⟨painted a ~ to the wonder of light —Lewis Mumford⟩

²hymn \"\ *vb* **hymned; hymned; hymning** \'himiŋ *sometimes* -mniŋ\ **hymns** *vt* : to sing the praises of : EXTOL ⟨still ~s his love of the earth and proclaims his faith in the race that inhabits it —B.R.Redman⟩; *specif* : to worship in song ~ *vi* : SING ⟨the lark ~s on high⟩; *specif* : to sing a hymn ⟨the choir ~s softly in the chancel⟩

¹hym·nal \'himnəl\ *n* -S [ME *hymnale*, fr. ML *hymnale, hymnare*, fr. L *hymnus* hymn + *-ale* (neut. of *-alis* -al) or *-are* (neut. of *-aris* -ar)] : a collection of church hymns : HYMNBOOK

²hymnal \"\ *adj* [L *hymnus* hymn + E *-al*] : of or relating to a hymn ⟨a ~ rite⟩

hym·na·ry \'himnərē\ *also* **hym·nar·i·um** \him'na(a)rēəm\ *n, pl* **hymnaries** \-nərēz\ *also* **hymnar·ia** \-na(a)rēə\ [ML *hymnarium*, fr. L *hymnus* hymn + *-arium* -ary] : ¹HYMNAL

hymn board *also* **hymn tablet** *n* : a usu. wooden tablet that holds removable numerals and is hung on a wall or pillar of a church to inform the congregation of the numbers of the hymns and responsive readings for a service of worship

HYMNS
29
132
SEL84
PSALM
23

hymn board

hymnbook \'=,=\ *n* : ¹HYMNAL

hymner \'himə(r), -mnə-\ *n* -S : one that sings hymns

hym·nic \'himnik\ *adj* : of, relating to, or having the characteristics of a hymn ⟨~ praise⟩ ⟨~ prose⟩

hym·nist \-nəst\ *n* -S : a writer of hymns

hymn·less \'himləs\ *adj* : lacking a hymn

hymnlike \'=,=\ *adj* : resembling or suggesting a hymn

hym·no·dist \'himnədəst\ *n* -S [LL *hymnodia* hymnody + E *-ist*] : HYMNIST

hym·no·dy \-dē\ *n* -ES [LL *hymnodia*, fr. Gk *hymnōidia*, fr. *hymnōidein* to sing a hymn or song of praise (fr. *hymnos* hymn, song of praise + *aeidein* to sing) + *-ia* -y — more at ODE] **1** : the singing of hymns **2** : the writing of hymns ⟨a pioneer in Byzantine ~, whose compositions were to come into extensive use —K.S.Latourette⟩ **3 a** : a study of hymns and their composition ⟨an authority on ~⟩ **b** : a body of hymns of a specified kind or period ⟨~ of the early church⟩

hym·nog·ra·pher \him'nägrəfə(r)\ *n* -S [Gk *hymnographos* (fr. *hymnos* hymn + *-graphos* -graph) + E *-er*] **1** : a writer on hymnography **2** : HYMNIST

hym·nog·ra·phy \-fē\ *n* -ES [*hymnographer* + *-y*] **1** : an exposition and bibliography of hymns **2** : HYMNODY

hym·no·log·ic \ˌhimnə'läjik\ *or* **hym·no·log·i·cal** \-jəkəl\ *adj* : of or relating to hymnology — **hym·no·log·i·cal·ly** \-jək(ə)lē\ *adv*

hym·nol·o·gist \him'näləjəst\ *n* -S : HYMNIST

hym·nol·o·gy \-jē\ *n* -ES [Gk *hymnologia* singing of hymns, fr. *hymnos* song of praise, hymn + *-logia* -logy] : HYMNODY

hymns *pl of* HYMN, *pres 3d sing of* HYMN

hyne \'hīn\ *adv* [ME, prob. alter. of ME (northern dial.) *hethen*, fr. ON *hethan* hence; akin to OE *heonan* hence — more at HENCE] *now dial Eng* : HENCE

hy·no·bi·i·dae \ˌhīnō'bīəˌdē\ *n pl, cap* [NL, fr. *Hynobius*, type genus (fr. *hyno-* — perh. fr. Gk *hynis* plowshare — + NL *-bius*) + *-idae*] : a small family of primitive Asiatic salamanders (suborder Cryptobranchoidea) sometimes included in the Ambystomidae from which they can be distinguished by more adult skull characters, smaller size, and short saccular egg pouches

¹hyo- — see HY-

²hyo- *comb form* [L&Gk; L, fr. Gk, fr. *hys* swine — more at SOW (swine)] : derived from or related to swine ⟨*hyo*deoxycholic⟩

hyo·branchial \ˌhīō+\ *adj* [*hy-* + *branchial*] : of, relating to, or joining the hyoid and branchial arches

hyo·bran·chi·um \ˌhīō'braŋkēəm\ *n, pl* **hyobran·chia** \-ēə\ [NL, fr. *hy-* + *-branchium* (fr. Gk *branchion* gill) — more at BRANCHIA] : a typically somewhat Y-shaped bone that serves to support the tongue and tongue muscles in a snake and is considered to result from fusion of the hyoid and remnants of the branchial arches

hyo·deoxycholic acid *or* **hyo·desoxycholic acid** \ˌhī(ˌ)ō+ . . . -\ *n* [ISV ²*hyo-* + *deoxy-* or *desoxy-* + *cholic*] : a crystalline bile acid $C_{23}H_{37}(OH)_2COOH$ found in the bile of the pig and wild boar; 3,6-dihydroxy-cholanic acid

hy·o·don \'hīəˌdän\ [NL, fr. *hy-* + *-odon*] *syn of* HIODON

hyo·epiglottic *also* **hyo·epiglottidean** \ˌhī(ˌ)ō+\ *adj* [*hy-* + *epiglottic* or *epiglottidean*] : connecting the hyoid bone and epiglottis

hyo·glossal \ˌhīō+\ *adj* [*hy-* + *glossal*] **1** : of or relating to the tongue and hyoid arch **2** [NL *hyoglossus* + E *-al*] : of or relating to the hyoglossus

hyo·glos·sus \ˌ==ˈgläsəs, -lȯs-\ *n, pl* **hyoglos·si** \-ˌsī\ [NL, fr. *hy-* + *-glossus* (fr. Gk *glōssa* tongue) — more at GLOSS] : a flat muscle on each side of the tongue connecting it with the body and greater cornu of the hyoid

hy·oid \'hīˌȯid\ *also* **hy·oi·dal** \(')hī'ȯidᵊl\ *or* **hy·oi·de·an** \-dēən\ *adj* [*hyoid* fr. NL *hyoides* hyoid bone; *hyoidal* fr. *hyoid* + *-al; hyoidean* fr. NL *hyoides* + E *-an*] **1** : of, relating to, or being the hyoid bone **2** : of, relating to, or being the second postoral visceral arch from which the hyoid bone of the higher vertebrates is in part formed

hyoid bone *also* **hyoid** *n* -S [NL *hyoides*, fr. Gk *hyoeidēs*, adj., shaped like the letter upsilon (Υ, υ), being the hyoid bone, fr. *hyo-* (fr. *y, hy* upsilon) + *-eidēs* -oid] : a bone or complex of bones situated at the base of the tongue and developed from the second and third visceral arches, supporting the tongue and its muscles, and being in man a U-shaped structure placed horizontally with the convexity forward, two large cornua directed backward, and two lesser cornua directed upward and backward

hy·ol·i·thes \hī'äləˌthēz\ *n, cap* [NL, prob. fr. *hy-* + *-lithes* (fr. Gk *lithos* stone)] : a genus of Paleozoic swimming pteropod mollusks esp. common in the Cambrian — **hy·ol·i·thid** \-ˌthəd\ *adj or n*

hyo·mandibula \ˌhī(ˌ)ō+\ *n* -S [NL, fr. *hy-* + LL *mandibula*] **1** : the hyomandibular arch **2** : a bone or cartilage derived from the hyomandibular arch

¹hyo·mandibular \"+\ *adj* [*hy-* + *mandibular*] : of or derived from the hyoid arch and mandible; *specif* : being or relating to the dorsal segment of the hyoid arch

²hyomandibular \"\ *n* -S : a bone or cartilage derived from the dorsal hyoid arch, being part of the articulating mechanism of the lower jaw in fishes, and forming the columella or stapes of the ear of higher vertebrates

hyo·mental \ˌhīō+\ *adj* [*hy-* + *mental* (of the chin)] : of or relating to the hyoid bone and chin

hyo·plastron \"+\ *n, pl* **hyoplastra** [*hy-* + *plastron*] : the second lateral bony plate in the plastron of most turtles — called also *hyosternum*

hyo·scapular \"+\ *adj* [*hy-* + *scapular*] : of or relating to the hyoid bone and scapula

hy·o·scine \'hīəˌsēn, -ˌsən\ *n* -S [ISV *hyosc-* (fr. NL *Hyoscyamus*, genus that produces it) + *-ine*; orig. formed as G *hyoscin*] : SCOPOLAMINE; *esp* : the levorotatory form of scopolamine

hy·o·scy·a·mine \ˌhīə'sīəˌmēn, -ˌmən\ *n* -S [G *hyoscyamin*, fr. NL *Hyoscyamus* (genus that produces it) + G *-in* -ine] : a poisonous crystalline alkaloid $C_{17}H_{23}NO_3$ known in three optically isomeric forms : the ester of tropine and tropic acid; *esp* : the levorotatory form of this alkaloid that readily yields the racemic form atropine (as by treatment with alkali), that occurs in henbane, belladonna, and various other plants of the family Solanaceae (as species of *Datura*), and that is more active than atropine in most pharmacological effects and is used similarly (as in sedation and in relieving spasms)

hy·o·scy·a·mus \-məs\ *n* [NL, fr. L, henbane, fr. Gk *hyoskyamos*, lit., swine's bean, fr. *hyos* (gen. of *hys* swine) + *kyamos* bean — more at SOW (swine)] **1** *cap* : a genus of poisonous Eurasian herbs (family Solanaceae) having simple leaves, somewhat irregular flowers, and circumscissile capsular fruit — see HENBANE **2** -ES : the dried leaves of the henbane containing the alkaloids hyoscyamine and scopolamine and used as an antispasmodic and sedative

hyo·sternal \ˌhīō+\ *adj* [*hy-* + *sternal*] **1** : of or relating to the hyoid bone and sternum **2** [NL *hyosternum* + E *-al*] : of or relating to the hyosternum

hyo·sternum \"+\ *n, pl* **hyosterna** [NL, fr. *hy-* + *sternum*] : HYOPLASTRON

hyo·strongylus \"+\ *n, cap* [NL, fr. ²*hyo-* + *Strongylus* (genus of parasitic nematode worms)] : a genus of nematode worms (family Trichostrongylidae) including the common small red stomach worm (*H. rubidus*) of swine

hy·o·sty·lic \ˌhīō'stīlik\ *adj* [*hy-* + *-stylic*] : having the jaws connected with the cranium by the hyomandibular (a large majority of fishes are ~) — **hyo·sty·ly** \'==ˌlē\ *n* -ES

hy·o·there \'hīōˌthi(ə)r\ *n* -S [NL *Hyotherium*] : a member of the genus *Hyotherium*

hy·o·the·ri·um \ˌhīō'thirēəm\ *n, cap* [NL, fr. ²*hyo-* + *-therium*] : a genus of swine of the Miocene and lower Pliocene on the direct ancestral line of the modern wild boar and domestic swine

hyo·thyreoid \ˌhīō+\ *adj* [*hy-* + *thyreoid*] : THYROHYOID

hyo·thyroid \"+\ *adj* [*hy-* + *thyroid*] : THYROHYOID

hyp *n* -S [by shortening] *obs* : HYPOCHONDRIA

hyp- — see HYPO-

hyp *abbr* hypothesis; hypothetical

hyp·abyssal \¦hip+\ *adj* [ISV *hypo-* + *abyssal;* orig. formed as G *hypabyssisch*] **:** of or relating to a fine-grained igneous rock intermediate in texture between the plutonites and extrusive rocks and usu. formed at a moderate distance below the surface

hyp·acu·sic \¦hipə¦kyüsik, -kü-\ *or* **hyp·acou·sic** \-kü-\ *adj* [NL *hypacusia,* *hypacousia* defective hearing (fr. *hypo-* + *-acusia, -acousia*) + E *-ic*] **:** slightly deaf — used esp. of partial deafness associated with lessened irritability of the auditory nerve

hy·pae·thral \hī'pēthrəl, hə'-\ *adj* [L *hypaethrus* in the open air, uncovered (fr. Gk *hypaithros,* fr. *hypo-* + *-aithros* — fr. *aithēr* ether, heaven, air) + E *-al* — more at ETHER] **1** *of an ancient temple* **:** having a roofless central space — opposed to *cleithral* **2 :** open to the sky **3 :** OUTDOOR

hyp·algesia \¦hip, ¦hīp+\ *also* **hyp·al·gia** \hi'palj(ē)ə, hī'-\ *n* [NL, fr. *hypo-* + *algesia* or *-algia*] **:** diminished sensitivity to pain

hyp·al·lac·tic \¦hipə¦laktik, ¦hīp-\ *adj* [Gk *hypallaktikos,* fr. (assumed) Gk *hypallaktos* (verbal of Gk *hypallassein* to interchange, exchange) + Gk *-icos* -ic] **:** of, relating to, or of the nature of hypallage

hy·pal·la·ge \hi'palə(,)jē, hī'-\ *n* -s [LL, fr. Gk *hypallagē,* lit., interchange, fr. *hypallassein* to interchange, fr. *hypo-* + *allassein* to change (fr. *allos* other) — more at ELSE] **:** interchange in syntactic relationship between two terms (as in "you are lost to joy" for "joy is lost to you")

hy·pan·dri·um \hi'pandrēəm, hī'-\ *n, pl* **hypan·dria** \-ēə\ [NL, fr. *hypo-* + *andr-* + *-ium*] **:** a plate or modified area underlying the genitalia of a male insect; *esp* **:** the fused coxites of the ninth abdominal segment when these form a ventral covering plate for the genitalia

hy·pan·thi·al \(')hi¦pan(t)thēəl, (')hī¦-\ *adj* **:** of, relating to, or of the nature of a hypanthium

hy·pan·thi·um \=ˈ=thēəm\ *n, pl* **hypan·thia** \-ēə\ [NL, fr. *hypo-* + *anth-* + *-ium*] **:** an enlargement of the usu. cup-shaped receptacle bearing on its rim the stamens, petals, and sepals of a flower and often enlarging and surrounding the fruits (as in the rose hip) — called also *calyx tube*

hy·pan·trum \hi'pan·trəm, hī'-\ *n, pl* **hypan·tra** \-rə\ [NL, fr. *hypo-* + LL *antrum* cavity in the body — more at ANTRUM] **:** a notch on the neural arch at the anterior ends of the vertebrae of various reptiles that articulates with the hyposphene — compare ZYGANTRUM

hy·pa·pan·te \,ēpə,pän'dē\ *n* -s *cap* [LL or LGk; LL *hypapante,* fr. LGk *hypapantē,* lit., meeting, fr. Gk *hypapantan* to meet, fr. *hypo-* + *apantan* to meet — more at APANTESIS] **:** a feast celebrated by the Eastern Orthodox Church on February 2 commemorating primarily the presentation of Jesus and his meeting Simeon and Anna in the temple and secondarily the purification of the Virgin Mary — compare CANDLEMAS

hyp·apophysis \¦hip, ¦hīp+\ *n, pl* **hypapophyses** [NL, fr. *hypo-* + *apophysis*] **:** a ventral process or element of a vertebra: as **a :** a hemal spine **b :** HYPOCENTRUM

hy·par·chic \(')hi¦pärkik, (')hī¦-\ *adj* [*hypo-* + *-archic* (as in *autarchic*)] **:** affected by adjacent genes — used of genes in mosaic tissues that do not manifest their effect if epistatic genes are present in adjacent tissues: compare AUTARCHIC

hyp·arterial \¦hip, ¦hīp+\ *adj* [*hypo-* + *arterial*] **:** situated below an artery — used of branches of the bronchi given off below the pulmonary artery; compare EPARTERIAL

hy·pas·pist \hi'paspəst\ *n* -s [Gk *hypaspistēs,* fr. *hypaspizein* to serve as shield bearer, fr. *hypo-* + *aspis* shield + *-izein* -ize — more at ASPID-] **:** SHIELD BEARER; *esp* **:** a Macedonian shield bearer

hyp·automorphic \¦hip, ¦hīp+\ *adj* [*hypo-* + *automorphic*] **1 :** HYPIDIOMORPHIC **2 :** SUBHEDRAL

hyp·axial \(')hip, (')hīp+\ *also* **hyp·axonic** \(¦)hip, (¦)hīp+\ *adj* [*hypaxial* fr. *hypo-* + *axial;* *hypaxonic* fr. *hypo-* + Gk *axon-, axōn* axle, axis + E *-ic* — more at AXIS] **:** beneath the axis of the vertebral column

hype \'hīp\ *n* -s [short for *hypodermic*] **1** *slang* **:** HYPODERMIC **2** *slang* **:** a narcotics addict

hy·per \'hīpə(r)\ *vi* -ED/-ING/-S [origin unknown] *chiefly NewEng* **:** BUSTLE, HURRY ⟨must ~ about —J.R.Lowell⟩

hyper- *prefix* [alter. (influenced by L *hyper-*) of ME *iper-,* fr. LL *hyper-,* fr. L, fr. Gk, fr. *hyper* — more at OVER] **1 :** over **:** above **:** beyond **:** SUPER- ⟨*hyper*barbarous⟩ ⟨*hyper*emphasis⟩ **2 :** overmuch **:** excessively **:** EXTRA- ⟨*hyper*critical⟩ ⟨*hyper*sensitive⟩ **3 a :** excessive in extent or quality ⟨*hyper*esthesia⟩ ⟨*hyper*emesis⟩ **b :** located above ⟨*hyper*apophysis⟩ **4** *in ancient Greek music* **a :** being the upper octave in a disdiapason ⟨*hyper*lydian⟩ **b** *of an interval* **:** measured upward ⟨*hyper*diapason⟩

hy·pera \'hīpərə\ *n, cap* [NL, fr. Gk *hypera* upper rope, brace (of a ship), fr. *hyper* above, over] **:** a large genus of small often mottled or hairy weevils whose legless larvae feed destructively on numerous crop plants (as legumes) and have ventral ridges that function as legs — compare ALFALFA WEEVIL, CLOVER LEAF WEEVIL

hy·per·acid \¦hīpə(r)+\ *adj* [*hyper-* + *acid*] **:** excessively acid **:** containing more than the normal amount of acid ⟨a ~ secretion⟩ — **hy·per·acidity** \"+\ *n* -ES

hy·per·active \"+\ *adj* [*hyper-* + *active*] **:** excessively or pathologically active

hy·per·adre·no·cor·ti·cism \,==,drēnō'kȯ(r)d·ə,sizəm, -,dren-\ *n* -s [*hyper-* + *adrenocortical* + *-ism*] **1 :** the presence of excess adrenocortical products in the body **2 :** the syndrome resulting from hyperadrenocorticism that is often a complication of medication with adrenal hormones, fractions, or stimulants

hyperaemia *var of* HYPEREMIA

hyperaesthesia *var of* HYPERESTHESIA

hy·per·algesia \¦hīpə(r)+\ *n* [NL, fr. *hyper-* + *algesia*] **:** increased sensitivity to pain or enhanced intensity of pain sensation — **hy·per·algesic** \"+\ *adj*

hy·per·apophysis \"+\ *n, pl* **hyperapophyses** [NL, fr. *hyper-* + *apophysis*] **:** a process on the dorsal side of a vertebra that projects laterally and backward

hy·per·azotemia \"+\ *n* [NL, fr. *hyper-* + *azotemia*] **:** the presence of abnormal amounts of nitrogenous substances in the blood

hy·per·bar·ic \¦hīpə(r)¦barik\ *adj* [*hyper-* + Gk *baros* weight + E *-ic* — more at GRIEVE] **:** having a specific gravity greater than that of cerebrospinal fluid — used of solutions for spinal anesthesia; opposed to *hypobaric*

hy·per·ba·ton \hī'pərbə,tän\ *n, pl* **hyperbatons** \-nz\ *or* **hyperba·ta** \-bəd·ə\ [L, fr. Gk, fr. neut. of *hyperbatos* transposed, inverted, fr. *hyperbainein* to step over, scale, fr. *hyper-* + *bainein* to step, walk — more at COME] **:** a transposition or inversion of idiomatic word order (as "echoed the hills" for "the hills echoed")

hy·per·bilirubinemia \¦hīpə(r)+\ *n* [NL, fr. *hyper-* + *bilirubinemia*] **:** BILIRUBINEMIA

hy·per·bo·la \hī'pərbələ, -pəb-,-pəib-\ *n, pl* **hyperbolas** \-ləz\ *or* **hyperbo·lae** \-,lē, -,lī\ [NL, fr. Gk *hyperbolē* hyperbola, excess] **:** a plane curve generated by a point so moving that its distance from a fixed point divided by its distance from a fixed line is a positive constant greater than 1 **:** a curve formed by a section of a right circular cone when the cutting plane makes a greater angle with the base than the cone's side makes

hyperbola

hy·per·bo·le \-(,)lē\ *n* -s [L, fr. Gk *hyperbolē* hyperbole, excess, extravagance, fr. *hyperballein* to exceed, fr. *hyper-* + *ballein* to throw — more at DEVIL] **:** extravagant exaggeration that represents something as much greater or less, better or worse, or more intense than it really is or that depicts the impossible as actual (as "mile-high ice-cream cones") — opposed to *litotes*

¹hy·per·bol·ic \¦hīpə(r)¦bälik, -lēk\ *also* **hy·per·bol·i·cal** \-lėkəl, -lēk-\ *adj* [*hyperbolic* fr. LL *hyperbolicus,* fr. Gk *hyperbolikos* excessive, fr. *hyperbolē* hyperbole, excess + *-ikos* -ic; *hyperbolical,* alter. (influenced by L *hyper-*) of ME *iperbolicalle,* fr. LL *hyperbolicus* + ME *-alle, -al* -al] **:** of, characterized by, or given to hyperbole ⟨a ~ style⟩ — **hy·per·bol·i·cal·ly** \-lėk(ə)lē, -lēk-, -li\ *adv*

²hyperbolic \"\ *also* **hyperbolical** \"\ *adj* [*hyperbolic* fr. NL *hyperbola* + E *-ic;* *hyperbolical* fr. Gk *hyperbolē* hyperbola, excess + E *-ical*] **:** of, relating to, or analogous to a hyperbola

hyperbolic cosecant *n* **:** the hyperbolic function that is analogous to the cosecant and defined by the equation $\operatorname{csch} x = \dfrac{1}{\sinh x}$ — abbr. *csch*

hyperbolic cosine *n* **:** the hyperbolic function that is analogous to the cosine and defined by the equation $\cosh x = \dfrac{e^x + e^{-x}}{2}$ — abbr. *cosh*

hyperbolic cotangent *n* **:** the hyperbolic function that is analogous to the cotangent and defined by the equation $\coth x = \dfrac{\cosh x}{\sinh x}$ — abbr. *coth*

hyperbolic function *n* **:** any of a set of six functions analogous to the trigonometric functions but related to the hyperbola in a way similar to that in which trigonometric functions are related to a circle

hyperbolic geometry *n* **:** geometry that adopts all of Euclid's axioms except the parallel axiom, this being replaced by the axiom that through any point in a plane there pass more lines than one that do not intersect a given line in the plane

hyperbolic navigation *n* **:** a system of radio navigation (as loran) in which the time difference between receipt of signals from two stations of known position determines a line of position in the form of a hyperbola

hyperbolic paraboloid *n* **:** a saddle-shaped quadric surface whose sections by planes parallel to one coordinate plane are hyperbolas while those sections by planes parallel to the other two are parabolas if proper orientation of the coordinate axes is assumed

hyperbolic secant *n* **:** the hyperbolic function that is analogous to the secant and defined by the equation $\operatorname{sech} x = \dfrac{1}{\cosh x}$ — abbr. *sech*

hyperbolic sine *n* **:** the hyperbolic function that is analogous to the sine and defined by the equation $\sinh x = \dfrac{e^x - e^{-x}}{2}$ — abbr. *sinh*

hyperbolic tangent *n* **:** the hyperbolic function that is analogous to the tangent and defined by the equation $\tanh x = \dfrac{\sinh x}{\cosh x}$ — abbr. *tanh*

hy·per·bo·lism \hī'pərbə,lizəm, -pəb-, -pəib-\ *n* -s [*hyperbole* + *-ism*] **:** HYPERBOLE

hy·per·bo·list \-,ləst\ *n* -s **:** a user of hyperbole ⟨humorists and ~s —John Hersey⟩

hy·per·bo·lize \-,līz\ *vb* -ED/-ING/-S *vi* **:** to indulge in hyperbole ~ *vt* **:** to exaggerate to a hyperbolic degree ⟨~ the esthetic modes of the moment —*Times Lit. Supp.*⟩

hy·per·bo·loid \-,lȯid\ *n* -s [NL *hyperbola* + E *-oid*] **:** a quadric surface whose sections by planes parallel to one coordinate plane are ellipses while those sections by planes parallel to the other two are hyperbolas if proper orientation of the coordinate axes is assumed — **hy·per·bo·loi·dal** \=¦==¦lȯid³l\ *adj*

hyperboloid of revolution : the surface generated by a hyperbola rotating about one of its axes

hy·per·bo·re·al \¦hīpə(r)¦bōrēəl, -bȯr-\ *adj* [L *Hyperborei* + E *-al*] *archaic* **:** HYPERBOREAN

¹hy·per·bo·re·an \-ēən, -,bə¦rē-\ *adj* [L *Hyperborei,* ancient legendary people living in the far north (fr. Gk *Hyperboreoi, Hyperboreioi,* fr. *hyper-* + *boreioi,* masc. pl. of *boreios* northern, of the north wind, fr. *Boreas* north, northwind) + E *-an* — more at BOREAS] **1 :** of, relating to, or inhabiting an extreme northern region **:** FRIGID, FROZEN ⟨drags us out of our ~ gloom into the South —John Davenport⟩ **2 :** of or relating to any of the arctic peoples of Asia or No. America

²hyperborean \"\ *n* -s *often cap* **1 :** a member of an arctic people (as the Chukchi and Koryak of northeastern Asia and the Eskimo of No. America) **2 :** one who lives in a cool northern climate ⟨we are *Hyperboreans* — we know well enough how far off we live —W.A.Kaufmann⟩

hy·per·brachycephal \¦hīpə(r)+\ *n* [*hyper-* + *brachycephal*] **:** a hyperbrachycephalic person

hy·per·brachycephalic \"+\ *adj* [*hyper-* + *brachycephalic*] **:** having a very round or broad head with a cephalic index of over 85

hy·per·brachycephaly \"+\ *n* **:** the quality or state of being hyperbrachycephalic

hy·per·brachycranial *or* **hy·per·brachycranic** \"+\ *adj* [*hyper-* + *brachycranial* or *brachycranic*] **:** having a very round or broad skull with a cranial index of 85 to 90

hy·per·brachycrany \"+\ *n* [ISV *hyper-* + *brachycrany*] **:** the quality or state of being hyperbrachycranial

hy·per·brachyskelic \"+\ *adj* [*hyper-* + *brachyskelic*] **:** having the length of the legs less than three-fourths that of the trunk with a skelic index below 75

hy·per·cal·ce·mia *also* **hy·per·cal·cae·mia** \,hīpə(r),kal'sēmēə\ *n* [NL, fr. *hyper-* + *calcemia, calcaemia* calcium in the blood (fr. *calc-* + *-emia, -aemia*)] **:** an excess of calcium in the blood — **hy·per·cal·ce·mic** \¦==¦sēmik\ *adj*

hy·per·cap·nia \,hīpə(r)'kapnēə\ *n* [NL, fr. *hyper-* + *-capnia*] **:** the presence of excessive amounts of carbon dioxide in the blood — **hy·per·cap·nic** \¦==¦nik\ *adj*

hy·per·catalectic \¦==+\ *adj* [LL *hypercatalecticus,* fr. *hypercatalectus* (fr. Gk *hyperkatalēktos,* fr. *hyper-* + *katalēktos* catalectic) + *-icus* -ic — more at CATALECTIC] **:** of, relating to, or exhibiting hypercatalexis

hy·per·catalexis \"+\ *n* [NL, fr. *hyper-* + *catalexis*] **:** occurrence of an additional syllable at the end of a line of verse after the line is metrically complete; *esp* **:** occurrence of a syllable after the last complete dipody in verse measured by dipodies

hy·per·cathexis \"+\ *n* [NL, fr. *hyper-* + *cathexis*] **:** excessive concentration of desire upon a particular object

hy·per·ce·men·to·sis \,hīpə(r),sē,men'tōsəs\ *n, pl* **hypercemento·ses** \-ō,sēz\ [NL, fr. *hyper-* + *cementum* + *-osis*] **:** excessive formation of cementum at the root of a tooth

hy·per·chamaerrhine \¦hīpə(r)+\ *adj* [ISV *hyper-* + *chamaerrhine;* orig. formed as G *hyperchamärrhin*] **:** having a very short broad nose with a nasal index of 58 or above

hy·per·chamaerrhiny \"+\ *n* [ISV *hyper-* + *chamaerrhiny*] **:** the quality or state of being hyperchamaerrhine

hy·per·chlor·hy·dria \¦==,klōr'hīdrēə\ *n* -s [NL, fr. *hyper-* + *-chlorhydria* hydrochloric acid in the gastric juice (fr. *chlor-* + *hydr-* + *-ia*)] **:** the presence of a greater than typical proportion of hydrochloric acid in gastric juice that occurs in many normal individuals but is esp. characteristic of various pathologic states (as ulceration) — compare ACHLORHYDRIA, HYPOCHLORHYDRIA

hy·per·cholesterolemia *or* **hy·per·cholesteremia** \¦==+\ *also* **hy·per·cho·les·ter·in·emia** \"+kə,lestərə'nēmēə\ *n* [NL, fr. *hyper-* + *cholesterolemia,* or *cholesteremia,* or *-cholesterinemia,* (fr. E *cholesterin* + NL *-emia*)] **:** the presence of excess cholesterol in the blood — **hy·per·cho·les·ter·e·mic** \-tə¦rēmik\ *adj*

hy·per·chro·ma·tism \¦=='krōmə,tizəm\ *n* -s [*hyper-* + *chromatin* + *-ism*] **:** the development of excess chromatin or of excessive nuclear staining esp. as a part of a pathologic process

hy·per·chromatosis \¦hīpə(r)+\ *n* [NL, fr. *hyper-* + *chromatosis*] **1 :** HYPERCHROMIA 2 **2 :** HYPERCHROMATISM

hy·per·chro·mia \,=='krōmēə\ *n* -s [NL, fr. *hyper-* + *-chromia*] **1 :** excessive pigmentation (as of the skin) **2 :** a state of the red blood cells marked by increase in the hemoglobin content — **hy·per·chro·mic** \¦==¦mik\ *adj*

hyperchromic anemia *n* **:** any of various anemias (as pernicious anemia) that are characterized by abnormally high color index, increase of hemoglobin in individual red blood cells, and marked reduction in the number of red blood cells and alteration and irregularity in their form and that are associated with deficiency or unavailability of an antianemic factor — compare HYPOCHROMIC ANEMIA

hy·per·conjugation \¦==+\ *n* [*hyper-* + *conjugation*] **:** resonance in an organic chemical structure that involves as part of the resonance hybrid the separation of a proton from a methyl or other alkyl group situated next to an electron-deficient unit (as a double bond or carbonium ion), the electrons released by the proton tending to move toward the electron-deficient function with resultant stabilization of the entire structure (as in a trisubstituted propylene $H{-}CH_2CR{=}CR_2 \longleftrightarrow H^+ \; CH_2{=}CR{-}CR_2^-$) — called also *no-bond resonance*

hy·per·conscious \"+\ *adj* [*hyper-* + *conscious*] **:** excessively aware **:** acutely conscious ⟨~ of strain or falsity —Elizabeth Bowen⟩ ⟨a politically ~ country —J.E.Burchard⟩

¹hy·per·coracoid \"+\ *n* [*hyper-* + *coracoid*] **:** a hypercoracoid bone

²hypercoracoid \"\ *adj* **:** of, relating to, or being the upper of two bones at the base of the pectoral fin of teleost fishes sometimes regarded as homologous with the scapula of the higher vertebrates

hy·per·correct \"+\ *adj* [*hyper-* + *correct*] **1 :** excessively proper **:** FINICKY ⟨fastidious and ~ to the point of prissiness⟩ **2 :** of, characterized by, or constituting hypercorrection

hy·per·correction \"+\ *n* **:** an alteration of a speech habit on the basis of a false analogy (as when *between you and I* is used by one who is substituting *it is I* for *it is me* or when \'fiŋə(r)\ is used for *finger* by one who is attempting to rid himself of pronunciations like \'siŋgə(r)\ for *singer*)

hy·per·critic \"+\ *n* [*hyper-* + Gk *kritikē* criticism — more at CRITIC] **1** *obs* **:** HYPERCRITICISM **2** [NL *hypercriticus,* n. or adj., fr. *hyper-* + L *criticus,* n. or adj., critic — more at CRITIC] **:** a carping or unduly censorious critic

hy·per·critical \"+\ *also* **hy·per·critic** \"+\ *adj* [*hypercritical* fr. NL *hypercriticus* + E *-al;* *hypercritic* fr. NL *hypercriticus*] **:** meticulously or excessively critical esp. of small and trivial matters **:** overnice in judgment **:** CAPTIOUS, FAULTFINDING ⟨only the critical or ~ grammarian . . . discovers anything wrong in it —Otto Jespersen⟩ ⟨constant ~ belittling of the efforts of others —Harold Rosen & H.E.Kiene⟩ **syn** see CRITICAL

hy·per·critically \"+\ *adv* **:** in a hypercritical manner **:** CAPTIOUSLY, CARPINGLY

hy·per·criticism \"+\ *n* [*hyper-* + *criticism*] **:** captious or carping criticism

hy·per·criticize \"+\ *vt* **:** to criticize excessively ~ *vi* **:** to be hypercritical

hy·per·cry·algesia \,hīpə(r),krī+\ *n* -s [NL, fr. *hyper-* + *cry-* + *algesia*] **:** excessive pain due to cold

hy·per·di·a·lect·ism \,hīpə(r)'dīə,lek,tizəm\ *n* -s [*hyper-* + *dialect* + *-ism*] **:** an attempted dialectical form or pronunciation that overreaches dialectical authenticity — compare HYPERURBANISM

hy·per·dimensional \¦==+\ *adj* [*hyper-* + *dimensional*] **:** of or relating to space of more than three dimensions — **hy·per·dimensionality** \"+\ *n* -ES

hy·per·dolichocephal \"+\ *n* [*hyper-* + *dolichocephal*] **:** a hyperdolichocephalic person

hy·per·dolichocephalic \"+\ *adj* [*hyper-* + *dolichocephalic*] **:** having a very long narrow head with a cephalic index of less than 70

hy·per·dolichocephaly \"+\ *n* **:** the quality or state of being hyperdolichocephalic

hy·per·dolichocranial \"+\ *adj* [ISV *hyper-* + *dolichocranial*] **:** having a very long narrow skull with a cranial index of 65 to 70

hy·per·dolichocrany \"+\ *n* [ISV *hyper-* + *dolichocrany*] **:** the quality or state of being hyperdolichocranial

hy·per·dulia \"+\ *n* [ML, fr. L *hyper-* + ML *dulia*] *Roman Catholicism* **:** veneration of the Virgin Mary as the holiest of creatures — compare LATRIA

hypered *past of* HYPER

hy·per·emesis \¦hīpə(r)+\ *n* [NL, fr. *hyper-* + Gk *emesis* vomiting — more at EMESIS] **:** excessive vomiting

hyperemesis grav·i·dar·um \-,gravə'da(a)rəm\ *n* [NL, lit., excessive vomiting in pregnant women] **:** excessive vomiting during pregnancy

hy·per·e·mia *or* **hy·per·ae·mia** \,hīpə'rēmēə\ *n* -s [NL, fr. *hyper-* + *-emia, -aemia*] **:** excess of blood in a body part (as from active dilation of blood vessels or from obstruction of blood flow) — **hy·per·e·mic** \¦==¦rēmik\ *adj*

hy·per·endemic \¦hīpə(r)+\ *adj* [*hyper-* + *endemic*] **1 :** exhibiting a high and continued incidence — used chiefly of human diseases ⟨~ malaria⟩ **2 :** marked by hyperendemic disease — used of geographic areas ⟨a ~ focus of plague⟩ — **hy·per·endemicity** \"+\ *n* -ES

hy·per·er·gic \¦hīpə¦rərjik\ *adj* **:** having a degree of sensitivity toward an allergen greater than that typical of age group and community — compare NORMERGIC

hy·per·er·gy \'==,əjē\ *n* [ISV *hyper-* + allergy; prob. orig. formed as G *hyperergie*] **:** the quality or state of being hyperergic

hy·per·essence \¦hīpə(r)+\ *n* [*hyper-* + *essence*] **:** a concentrated essence (as of flowers)

hy·per·es·the·sia *or* **hyperaesthesia** \,hīpərəs'thēzhə\ *n* [NL, fr. *hyper-* + *-esthesia, -aesthesia* (as in *anesthesia, anaesthesia*)] **1 :** excessive or pathological sensitivity of the skin or of a particular sense **2 :** heightened perceptiveness of or response to the environment

hy·per·esthetic \¦==+\ *adj* **:** of, relating to, or affected with hyperesthesia

hy·per·es·trin·ism \,hīpə'(r)estrə,nizəm\ *n* -s [*hyper-* + *estrin* + *-ism*] **:** a condition marked by the presence of excess estrins in the body and often accompanied by functional uterine bleeding — compare HYPERESTROGENISM

hy·per·es·tro·gen·ism \-trajə,nizəm\ *n* -s [*hyper-* + *estrogen* + *-ism*] **:** a condition marked by the presence of excess estrogens in the body

hy·per·euryene \¦hīpə(r)+\ *adj* [*hyper-* + *euryene*] **:** having a very high wide forehead with an upper facial index of less than 45

hy·per·euryeny \"+\ *n* **:** the quality or state of being hypereuryene

hy·per·euryprosopic \"+\ *adj* [G *hypereuryprosop* hypereuryprosopic (fr. *hyper-* + *euryprosop* euryprosopic) + E *-ic*] **:** having a very short broad face with a facial index below 80

hy·per·euryprosopy \"+\ *n* [ISV *hyper-* + *euryprosopy;* prob. orig. formed as G *hypereuryprosopie*] **:** the quality or state of being hypereuryprosopic

hy·per·eutectic \"+\ *adj* [*hyper-* + *eutectic*] **:** containing the minor component in an amount in excess of that contained in the eutectic mixture

hy·per·eutectoid \"+\ *adj* [*hyper-* + *eutectoid*] **1 :** containing the minor component in an amount in excess of that contained in the eutectoid **2** *of steel* **:** containing more than 0.80 percent carbon

hy·per·fo·cal distance \¦hīpə(r)¦fōkəl-\ *n* [ISV *hyper-* + *focal*] **:** the nearest distance upon which a photographic lens may be focused to produce satisfactory definition at infinity

hy·per·form \'hīpə(r),-\ *n* [*hyper-* + *form*] **:** a speech form resulting from hypercorrection

hy·per·ga·mous \(')hī¦pərgəməs\ *adj* **:** of, relating to, or constituting hypergamy

hy·per·ga·my \='==mē\ *n* -ES [*hyper-* + *-gamy*] **:** marriage into an equal or higher caste or social group — used of Hindu laws forbidding women to marry men of inferior caste

hy·per·geometric *also* **hy·per·geometrical** \¦hīpə(r)+\ *adj* [*hyper-* + *geometric* or *geometrical*] **:** involving, related to, or analogous to operations or series that transcend ordinary geometrical operations or series

hy·per·glob·u·lin·emia \,==,gläbyəlė'nēmēə\ *n* -s [NL, fr. *hyper-* + ISV *globulin* + NL *-emia*] **:** the presence of excess globulins in the blood

hy·per·glu·ce·mia \¦hīpə(r),glü¦sēmēə\ *n* -s [NL fr. *hyper-* + *gluc-* + *-emia*] **:** HYPERGLYCEMIA

hy·per·glycemia \¦==+\ *n* [NL, fr. *hyper-* + *glycemia*] **:** excess of sugar in the blood — compare HYPERINSULINISM — **hy·per·glycemic** \"+\ *adj*

hyperglycemic-glycogenolytic factor *n* **:** GLUCAGON

hy·per·gol \'hīpə(r),gȯl, -gōl\ *n* -s [G, fr. *hyp-* (fr. *hyper-*) + *erg-* + *-ol* (fr. L *oleum* oil) — more at OIL] **:** a hypergolic fluid propellant

hy·per·golic \¦==¦gōlik, -gäl-,-gōl-\ *adj* [*hypergol* + *-ic*] **:** self=

igniting upon contact of components without a spark or other external aid — used esp. of a fluid rocket propellant

hy·per·hep·a·rin·emia \,+hepərə'nēmēə\ *n* -s [NL, fr. *hyper-* + ISV *heparin* + NL *-emia*] **:** the presence of excess heparin in the blood (as from ionizing radiation) usu. resulting in hemorrhage — **hy·per·hep·a·rin·emic** \⸗⸗;⸗⸗;⸗mik\ *adj*

hy·per·hidrosis \⸗⸗+\ *also* **hy·per·idro·sis** \+ə̇'drōsə̇s, -ī,d-\ *n* [NL, fr. *hyper-* + *hidrosis* or *-idrosis*] **:** generalized or localized excessive sweating — opposed to *hypohidrosis*

hy·per·i·ca·ce·ae \hī,perə'kāsē,ē\ *n pl, cap* [NL, fr. *Hypericum*, type genus + *-aceae*] *in some classifications* **:** a family of dicotyledonous plants of warm and temperate regions that are distinguished by opposite resinous-dotted leaves, regular flowers with numerous fascicled stamens, and a 3- to 5⸗loculed ovary and that are often included among the Guttiferae

hy·per·i·ca·les \-ā(,)lēz\ *n pl, cap* [NL, fr. *Hypericum* + *-ales*] *syn of* PARIETALES

hy·per·i·cin \hī'perəsə̇n\ *n* -s [ISV *hyperic-* (fr. NL *Hypericum*, genus that produces it) + *-in*] **:** a violet crystalline pigment $C_{30}H_{16}O_8$ from St.-John's-wort that has a red fluorescence and causes hypericism

hy·per·i·cism \-,sizəm\ *n* -s [NL *Hypericum*, genus that causes it + E *-ism*] **:** a severe dermatitis of domestic herbivorous animals due to photosensitivity resulting from eating St.-John's-wort — compare FAGOPYRISM

hy·per·i·cum \-rə̇kəm\ *n, cap* [NL, fr. L *hypericum, hypericon* a plant, St.-John's-wort, ground pine, fr. Gk *hyperikon, hypereikos*, a plant, St.-John's-wort, prob. fr. *hypo-* + *ereikē* heath, heather — more at BRIER] **:** a large and widely distributed genus of herbs or shrubs (family Guttiferae) that are characterized chiefly by their pentamerous and often showy yellow flowers

hy·per·immune \'hīpə(r)+\ *adj* [*hyper-* + *immune*] **:** exhibiting an unusual degree of immunization ⟨~ swine⟩: **a** *of a serum* **:** containing exceptional quantities of antibody **b** *of an antibody* **:** having the characteristics of a blocking antibody

hy·per·immunization \"+\ *n* **:** the quality or state of being hyperimmunized

hy·per·immunize \"+\ *vt* [*hyper-* + *immunize*] **:** to induce a high level of immunity or of circulating antibodies in (as by a long course of injections of antigen, repeated increasing doses of antigen, or the use of adjuvants along with the antigen)

hy·per·in \'hīpərə̇n\ *n* -s [*hyper-* (fr. NL *Hypericum*, genus that produces it) + *-in*] **:** a glycoside $C_{21}H_{20}O_{12}$ found in various plants (as St.-John's-wort and apples); quercetin 3⸗galactoside

hy·per·infection \'hīpə(r)+\ *n* [*hyper-* + *infection*] **:** repeated reinfection with larvae produced by parasitic worms already in the body due to the ability of various parasites to complete the life cycle within a single host — compare AUTOINFECTION

hypering *pres part of* HYPER

hy·per·in·su·lin·ism \⸗⸗'⸗(⸗)⸗,izəm\ *n* -s [ISV *hyper-* + *insulin* + *-ism*] **:** the presence of excess insulin in the body resulting in hypoglycemia and often accompanied by weakness, susceptibility to fatigue, tremor, sweating, and other evidences of debility

hy·per·irritability \'hīpə(r)+\ *n* [*hyper-* + *irritability*] **:** excessive irritability **:** abnormally great or uninhibited response to stimuli

hy·per·irritable \"+\ *adj* [*hyper-* + *irritable*] **:** marked by hyperirritability

hy·per·keratinization \"+\ *n* [*hyper-* + *keratinization*] **:** HYPERKERATOSIS

hy·per·keratosis \"+\ *n, pl* **hyperkeratoses** [NL, fr. *hyper-* + *keratosis*] **1 :** hypertrophy of the corneous layer of the skin **2 a :** any of various conditions marked by hyperkeratosis **b :** a disease of cattle marked by thickening and wrinkling of the hide and formation of papillary outgrowths on the buccal mucous membranes, often accompanied by watery discharge from eyes and nose, diarrhea, loss of condition, and abortion of pregnant animals, and now believed to result from ingestion of the chlorinated naphthalene of various lubricating oils — called also *X-disease, XX-disease*

hy·per·keratotic \"+\ *adj* [*hyper-* + *keratotic*] **:** of, relating to, or marked by hyperkeratosis

hy·per·kinesia *also* **hy·per·kinesis** \"+\ *n, pl* **hyperkinesias** *also* **hyperkinesises** [NL, fr. *hyper-* + *-kinesia* or *-kinesis*] **:** abnormally increased and usu. purposeless and uncontrollable muscular movement

hy·per·kinetic \"+\ *adj* [*hyper-* + *kinetic*] **:** of, relating to, or marked by hyperkinesia

hy·per·leptene \"+\ *adj* [*hyper-* + *leptene*] **:** having a very high narrow forehead with an upper facial index of 60 or over

hy·per·lepteny \"+\ *n* [*hyper-* + *lepteny*] **:** the quality or state of being hyperleptene

hy·per·leptoprosopic \"+\ *adj* [G *hyperleptoprosop* hyperleptoprosopic (fr. *hyper-* + *leptoprosop*) + E *-ic*] **:** having a very long narrow face with a facial index of 93 and over on the living and of 95 and over on the skull

hy·per·leptoprosopy \"+\ *n* [ISV *hyper-* + *leptoprosopy*; orig. formed as G *hyperleptoprosopie*] **:** the quality or state of being hyperleptoprosopic

hy·per·leptorrhine \'hīpə(r)+\ *adj* [*hyper-* + *leptorrhine*] **:** having a very long narrow nose with a nasal index of 40 to 55

hy·per·leptorrhiny \"+\ *n* [*hyper-* + *leptorrhiny*] **:** the quality or state of being hyperleptorrhine

hy·per·leptosome \"+\ *adj* [*hyper-* + *leptosome*] **:** very tall and slender

hy·per·lipemia \"+\ *n* [NL, fr. *hyper-* + *lipemia*] **:** the presence of excess fat or lipids in the blood — **hy·per·lipemic** \"+\ *adj*

hy·per·makroskelic \"+\ *adj* [*hyper-* + *makroskelic*] **:** having extremely long legs in proportion to the trunk with a skelic index of 100 or over

hy·per·mas·tig·i·da \,hīpə(r),ma'stijədə\ [NL, fr. *hyper-* + *mastig-* + *-ida*] *syn of* HYPERMASTIGINA

hy·per·mas·tig·i·na \-jənə\ *n pl, cap* [NL, fr. *hyper-* + *mastig-* + *-ina*] **:** an order (subclass Zoomastigina) of complex cellulose-producing flagellates that have numerous flagella and are symbiotic in the intestine of termites and other wood⸗consuming insects

¹hy·per·mastigote \'hīpə(r)+\ *adj* [*hyper-* + *mastigote*] **:** of or relating to the Hypermastigina

²hypermastigote \"\ *n* -s **:** a flagellate of the order Hypermastigina

hy·per·mature \"+\ *adj* [*hyper-* + *mature*] **:** having passed the stage of full development or differentiation ⟨a ~ cataract⟩

hy·per·metabolism \"+\ *n* [*hyper-* + *metabolism*] **:** metabolism at an increased or excessive rate

hy·per·metamorphic \"+\ *adj* [*hyper-* + *metamorphic*] **:** exhibiting or involving hypermetamorphosis

hy·per·metamorphosis \"+\ *n* [NL, fr. *hyper-* + *metamorphosis*] **:** a method of development in an insect (as the blister beetle) in which the larva passes through numerous instars each markedly different from the rest in structure

hy·per·me·ter \hī'pərməd·ə(r)\ *n* [LL *hypermeter, hypermetrus* hypercatalectic, fr. Gk *hypermetros* beyond measure, beyond the meter, fr. *hyper-* + *-metros* (akin to *metron* measure, meter) — more at MEASURE] **1 :** a hypercatalectic verse **2 :** a period comprising more than two or three cola — called also *hypermetron*

hy·per·metric *or* **hy·per·metrical** \'hīpə(r)+\ *adj* [Gk *hypermetros* beyond measure, beyond the meter + E *-ic* or *-ical*] **:** exceeding the normal measure; *specif* **:** having a redundant syllable ⟨a poem with numerous ~ lines⟩

hy·per·me·tron \hī'pərmə,trän\ *n* -s [NL, fr. Gk, neut. of *hypermetros* beyond the meter, beyond measure] **:** HYPERMETER 2

hy·per·met·rope \,hīpə(r)'me,trōp\ *n* -s [ISV *hypermetr-* (fr. Gk *hypermetros*) + *-ope*] **:** HYPEROPE

hy·per·me·tro·pia \-,mə·'trōpēə\ *n* -s [NL, fr. Gk *hypermetros* + NL *-opia*] **:** HYPEROPIA — **hy·per·me·tropic** \-⸗'träpik, -rōp-\ *adj* — **hy·per·me·tropi·cal** \-pə̇kəl\ *adj* — **hy·per·met·ro·py** \,⸗⸗'me·trəpē\ *n* -ES

hy·per·me·try \hī'pərmə·trē\ *n* -ES [*hyper-* + *-metry*] **:** the addition of one or more syllables beyond the required measure at the end of a line or other metrical unit

hy·perm·ne·sia \,hī(,)pərm'nēzh(ē)ə\ *n* -s [NL, fr. *hyper-* + *-mnesia*] **:** abnormally vivid or complete memory or the reawakening of impressions long seemingly forgotten (as at a moment of extreme danger) — **hy·perm·ne·sic** \-ēzik, -ēsik\ *adj*

hy·per·morph \'hīpər,mȯrf\ *n* -s [*hyper-* + *-morph*] **1 :** a long-limbed and long-headed person **:** ECTOMORPH — opposed to *hypomorph* **2 :** a mutant gene having a similar but greater effect than the corresponding wild-type gene — compare HYPOMORPH — **hy·per·mor·phic** \⸗;⸗'mȯrfik\ *adj* — **hy·per·mor·phism** \-,fizəm\ *n* -s

hy·per·mor·pho·sis \,⸗⸗'mȯrfəsə̇s *sometimes* -,mȯr'fōsə̇s\ *n* [NL, fr. *hyper-* + *-morphosis*] **:** excessive growth of some member of a body

hy·per·motility \'hīpə(r)+\ *n* [ISV *hyper-* + *motility*] **:** abnormal or excessive movement; *specif* **:** excessive motility of all or part of the gastrointestinal tract — compare HYPOMOTILITY

hy·per·myotonia \"+\ *n* [NL, fr. *hyper-* + *myotonia*] **:** muscular hypertonicity

hy·per·ne·phro·ma \,⸗⸗nə̇'frōmə, -ne'-\ *n, pl* **hypernephromas** \-ōməz\ *or* **hypernephroma·ta** \-məd·ə\ [NL, fr. Gk *hyper-* + *nephr-* + *-oma*] **:** a tumor of the kidney resembling the adrenal cortex in its histological structure

hy·per·nic \⸗;⸗nik\ *n* -s [*hyper-* + *Nicaragua*, country of Central America] **1 :** any of several tropical American dyewoods (as various brazilwoods or logwood) **2 :** a dye or an extract used in dyeing that is obtained from a hypernic

hy·pero·ar·tia \,hīpərō'ärsh(ē)ə, -ärd·ēə\ *n pl, cap* [NL, fr. Gk *hyperōia* palate (fr. fem. of *hyperōios* upper, fr. *hyper* over, above) + NL *-artia* (fr. Gk *artios* complete, perfect); akin to Gk *arti* just, exactly, *arariskein* to fit — more at OVER, ARM] **:** an order of cyclostomi consisting of the lampreys as distinguished from the hagfishes — compare HYPEROTRETA

¹hy·pero·ar·tian \⸗⸗⸗'ärsh(ē)ən, -ärd·ēən\ *adj* [NL *Hyperoartia* + E *-an*] **:** of or relating to the Hyperoartia

²hyperoartian \"\ *n* -s **:** one of the Hyperoartia

hy·pero·ar·tii \,⸗⸗⸗'ärshē,ī, -ärd·ē,ī\ [NL, fr. Gk *hyperōia* palate + NL *-artii* (fr. Gk *artios* complete, perfect)] *syn of* HYPEROARTIA

hy·per·on \'hīpə,rän\ *n* -s [prob. fr. *hyper-* + *-on*] **:** an elementary particle that obeys Fermi-Dirac statistics but differs from nucleons in one or more intrinsic quantum properties

hy·per·on·to·morph \'hīpə'räntə,mȯrf\ *n* -s [*hyper-* + *ont-* + *-morph*] **:** an ectomorphic body type or individual — opposed to *meso-ontomorph*

hy·pero·odon \,hīpə'rōə,dän\ *n, cap* [NL, fr. Gk *hyperōios* upper + NL *-odon*] **:** a genus of beaked whales distinguished esp. by prominent crests on the maxillary bones

hy·per·ope \'hīpə,rōp\ *n* -s [*hyper-* + *-ope*] **:** one affected with hyperopia

hy·per·opia \,⸗⸗'rōpēə\ *n* -s [NL, fr. *hyper-* + *-opia*] **:** a condition in which visual images come to a focus behind the retina of the eye because of defects in the refractive media of the eye or because of abnormal shortness of the eyeball — called also *farsightedness* — **hy·per·opic** \⸗⸗;rōpik, -räp-\ *adj*

hy·per·orthognathous \'hīpə(r)+\ *adj* [*hyper-* + *orthognathous*] **:** having a very flat facial profile with a facial angle of 93 degrees or above

hy·per·os·mia \,hīpə'räzmēə\ *n* -s [NL, fr. *hyper-* + *-osmia* (as in *anosmia*)] **:** extreme acuteness of the sense of smell — **hy·per·os·mic** \⸗⸗;⸗mik\ *adj*

hy·per·os·to·sis \,hīpə,rä'stōsə̇s\ *n, pl* **hyperosto·ses** \-ō,sēz\ [NL, fr. *hyper-* + *-ostosis*] **1 :** excessive formation of bone tissue esp. in the skull **2 a :** the condition resulting from hyperostosis **b :** one of the bony outgrowths produced by hyperostosis

hy·per·os·tot·ic \⸗⸗;⸗'städ·ik\ *adj* [fr. NL *hyperostosis*, after such pairs as NL *exostosis*: E *exostotic*] **:** of, relating to, or affected with hyperostosis

hy·per·o·tre·ta \,hīpərō'trēd·ə\ *n pl, cap* [NL, fr. Gk *hyperōia* palate (fr. fem. of *hyperōios* upper) + NL *-treta* (fr. Gk *trētos* perforated, fr. *tetrainein* to perforate, pierce) — more at THROW] **:** an order of Cyclostomi including the hagfishes as distinguished from the lampreys — compare HYPEROARTIA

¹hy·per·o·tre·tan \⸗⸗⸗'trēt°n\ *or* **hy·per·o·tre·tous** \-ēd·əs\ *adj* [NL *Hyperotreta* + E *-an* or *-ous*] **:** of or relating to the Hyperotreta

²hyperotretan \"\ *n* -s **:** one of the Hyperotreta

hy·per·o·tre·ti \,⸗⸗⸗'trēd·,ī\ [NL, fr. Gk *hyperōia* palate + NL *-treti* (fr. Gk *trētos* perforated)] *syn of* HYPEROTRETA

hy·per·oxide \'hīpə(r)+\ *n* [ISV *hyper-* + *oxide*] **:** a compound containing a relatively large proportion of oxygen; *esp* **:** SUPEROXIDE

hy·per·panchromatic \"+\ *adj* [*hyper-* + *panchromatic*] **:** sensitive to blue and green and highly sensitive to red — used of a photographic film or plate

hy·per·parasite \"+\ *n* [*hyper-* + *parasite*] **:** a parasite that is parasitic upon another parasite **:** a secondary parasite — used esp. of fungi and of hymenopterous insects that attack the primary parasites of other insects — **hy·per·parasitic** \"+\ *adj*

hy·per·parasitism \"+\ *n* [*hyper-* + *parasitism*] **1 :** the quality or state of being hyperparasitic **2 :** parasitism involving excessive numbers of parasites

hy·per·parasitize \"+\ *vt* **:** to live on or in as a hyperparasite

hy·per·par·a·thy·roid·ism \,⸗⸗;⸗⸗'⸗,⸗+,izəm\ *n* [ISV *hyper-* + *parathyroid* + *-ism*] **:** the presence of excess parathyroid hormone in the body resulting in disturbance of calcium metabolism with increase in serum calcium and decrease in inorganic phosphorus, loss of calcium from bone, and renal damage with frequent kidney-stone formation

hy·per·path·ia \-'pathēə\ *n* -s [NL, fr. *hyper-* + *-pathia*] **1 :** disagreeable or painful sensation in response to a normally innocuous stimulus (as touch) **2 :** a condition in which the sensations of hyperpathia occur — **hy·per·path·ic** \⸗⸗;path-ik\ *adj*

hy·per·peristalsis \⸗⸗+\ *n* [NL, fr. *hyper-* + *peristalsis*] **:** excessive or excessively vigorous peristalsis — compare HYPERMOTILITY

hy·per·pha·gia \,⸗⸗'fāj(ē)ə\ *n* -s [NL, fr. *hyper-* + *-phagia*] **:** abnormally increased desire for food frequently resulting from injury to the hypothalamus — compare POLYPHAGIA

hy·per·pha·lan·gism \-fə'lan,jizəm, -fā'-\ *n* -s [ISV *hyper-* + *phalang-* (fr. NL *phalang-, phalanx*) + *-ism*] **:** the presence of supernumerary phalanges in fingers or toes

hy·per·pharyngeal \⸗⸗+\ *adj* [*hyper-* + *pharyngeal*] **:** EPIPHARYNGEAL 2

hy·per·physical \"+\ *adj* [*hyper-* + *physical*] **1 :** being beyond or more than the physical **2 :** independent of the physical or not being within its confines — **hy·per·physically** \"+\ *adv*

hy·per·pi·e·sia \,⸗⸗,pī'ēzh(ē)ə\ *also* **hy·per·pi·e·sis** \-,pī-'ēsə̇s, -'pīəsə̇s\ *n, pl* **hyperpiesias** *also* **hyperpieses** [*hyperpiesia*, NL, fr. *hyper-* + *-piesia* (fr. Gk *piesis* pressure — fr. *piezein* to press — + NL *-ia*); *hyperpiesis*, NL, fr. *hyper-* + Gk *piesis*] **:** HYPERTENSION; *esp* **:** ESSENTIAL HYPERTENSION

¹hy·per·pi·et·ic \⸗⸗,pī'ed·ik\ *adj* [fr. NL *hyperpiesia*, after such pairs as NL *anesthesia*: E *anesthetic*] **:** marked by hyperpiesia

²hyperpietic \"\ *n* -s **:** a person having hyperpiesia

hy·per·pi·tu·i·ta·rism \-pə'tüəta,rizəm, -pə'tyü-\ *n* -s [ISV *hyper-* + *pituitar-* (fr. *pituitary*) + *-ism*] **1 :** excessive activity of the pituitary body esp. in the production of growth⸗regulating hormones — compare HYPOPITUITARISM **2 :** a growth abnormality dependent on hyperpituitarism (as acromegaly and various gigantisms)

hy·per·pituitary \⸗⸗+\ *adj* [*hyper-* + *pituitary*] **:** marked by hyperpituitarism ⟨giant ferns, banana leaves, creepers, and ~ trees —Michael Rosene⟩

hy·per·plane \⸗⸗+\ *n* [*hyper-* + *plane*] **:** a figure in hyperspace corresponding to a plane in ordinary space

hy·per·pla·sia \,⸗⸗'plāzh(ē)ə\ *n* -s [NL, fr. *hyper-* + *-plasia*] **:** an abnormal or unusual increase in the elements composing a part (as of the cells of a tissue) — compare HYPERTROPHY, HYPOPLASIA — **hy·per·plas·tic** \⸗⸗;plastik\ *adj*

hy·per·platycnemic \⸗⸗+\ *adj* [*hyper-* + *platycnemic*] *of a shinbone* **:** much flattened laterally with a platycnemic index of less than 55

hy·per·platymeric \"+\ *adj* [*hyper-* + *platymeric*] *of a thighbone* **:** much flattened laterally with a platymeric index of less than 75

¹hy·per·ploid \'hīpə(r),plȯid\ *adj* [ISV *hyper-* + *-ploid*] **:** having or being a chromosome number slightly greater than an exact multiple of the monoploid number

²hyperploid \"\ *n* -s **:** a hyperploid organism

hy·per·ploidy \-dē\ *n* -ES [ISV *hyperploid* + *-y*] **:** the quality or state of being hyperploid

hy·per·pnea *also* **hy·per·pnoea** \,hīpər'nēə, -,pərp'nēə\ *n* -s [NL, fr. *hyper-* + *-pnea* or *-pnoea*] **:** abnormally rapid or deep breathing **:** HYPERVENTILATION — compare DYSPNEA, EUPNEA — **hy·per·pne·ic** \⸗⸗;(,)⸗;nēik\ *adj*

hy·per·predator \'hīpə(r)+\ *n* [*hyper-* + *predator*] **:** a predator that preys chiefly on another predatory animal

hy·per·prognathous \"+\ *adj* [*hyper-* + *prognathous*] **:** having exceedingly prominent jaws with a facial profile angle below 70 degrees

hy·per·pro·sex·ia \,⸗⸗prə'seksēə\ *n* -s [NL, fr. *hyper-* + Gk *prosexis* attention (fr. *prosechein* to pay attention to, fr. *pros* toward + *echein* to hold) + NL *-ia* — more at PROS-, SCHEME] **:** excessive fixity of attention on a stimulus object

hy·per·pro·throm·bin·emia *or* **hy·per·pro·throm·bin·ae·mia** \-,prō,thrämbə'nēmēə\ *n* -s [NL, fr. *hyper-* + ISV *prothrombin* + NL *-emia* or *-aemia*] **:** excess of prothrombin in the blood

hy·per·pyretic \⸗⸗+\ *adj* [ISV *hyper-* + *pyretic*] **:** of, relating to, or affected with hyperpyrexia

hy·per·pyrexia \"+\ *n* [NL, fr. *hyper-* + *pyrexia*] **:** exceptionally high fever either in comparison to the fever usu. accompanying a particular disease or absolutely (as in heat stroke)

hy·per·re·flex·ia \,hīpə(r)rə̇'fleksēə\ *n* -s [NL, fr. *hyper-* + E *reflex* + NL *-ia*] **:** overactivity of physiological reflexes

hy·per·resonance \'hīpə(r)+\ *n* [*hyper-* + *resonance*] **:** an exaggerated chest resonance heard in various abnormal pulmonary conditions — **hy·per·resonant** \"+\ *adj*

hypers *pres 3d sing of* HYPER

hy·per·secretion \"+\ *n* [ISV *hyper-* + *secretion*] **:** excessive production of a bodily secretion — **hy·per·secretory** \"+\ *adj*

hy·per·sensibility \"+\ *n* [ISV *hyper-* + *sensibility*] **:** HYPERESTHESIA

hy·per·sensitive \"+\ *adj* [*hyper-* + *sensitive*] **1 :** excessively sensitive ⟨extracultivated, ~, delicate manhood —*Saturday Rev.*⟩ **2 a :** abnormally susceptible to an antigen, drug, or other agent — compare ALLERGY 2, ANAPHYLAXIS **b :** reacting violently to attack by a parasite so that sudden death of invaded tissues provides a barrier against further invasion **3 :** of or relating to a photographic emulsion whose speed and sensitivity are increased before the image-forming exposure (as by treatment with ammonia or by exposure to heat or light) — **hy·per·sensitiveness** \"+\ *n* — **hy·per·sensitivity** \"+\ *n*

hy·per·sensitization \"+\ *n* **:** an act or process of hypersensitizing

hy·per·sensitize \"+\ *vt* [*hypersensitive* + *-ize*] **:** to make hypersensitive

hy·per·solid \"+\ *n* [*hyper-* + *solid*] **:** a figure (as a hypersphere) in hyperspace that corresponds to a solid in ordinary three-dimensional space

hy·per·som·nia \,hīpə(r)'sämnēə\ *n* -s [NL, fr. *hyper-* + *-somnia* (as in L *insomnia*)] **1 :** sleep of excessive depth or duration **2 :** the condition of sleeping for excessive periods at intervals with intervening periods of normal duration of sleeping and waking — compare NARCOLEPSY, SOMNOLENCE

hy·per·sonic \⸗⸗+\ *adj* [ISV *hyper-* + *sonic*] **1 :** of, relating to, or being speed five times or more that of sound in air — compare SONIC **2 :** moving, capable of moving, or utilizing air currents that move at hypersonic speed ⟨~ wind tunnel⟩

hy·per·sorp·tion \⸗⸗'sȯrpshən\ *n* [*hyper-* + *adsorption*] **:** the selective adsorption of various hydrocarbons from gaseous mixtures on activated carbon (as propane from natural gas or ethylene from gases produced in the refining of petroleum)

hy·per·space \⸗⸗+\ *n* [ISV *hyper-* + *space*] **1 :** space of more than three dimensions **2 :** space other than ordinary euclidean space

hy·per·spatial \⸗⸗+\ *adj* [*hyper-* + *spatial*] **:** of or relating to hyperspace

hy·per·sphere \'⸗⸗+,-\ *n* [*hyper-* + *sphere*] **:** a sphere that is the analogue in hyperspace of the sphere in ordinary space

hy·per·splenic \⸗⸗+\ *adj* **:** marked by hypersplenism

hy·per·splenism \⸗⸗'splē,nizəm, -le,n-\ *n* -s [ISV *hyper-* + *splen-* + *-ism*] **:** a condition marked by excessive destruction of one or more kinds of blood cells in the spleen

hy·per·stereoscopic \⸗⸗+\ *adj* [*hyper-* + *stereoscopic*] **:** having an enhanced three-dimensional appearance due to an abnormally large separation between the binocular points of view (as with some prism binoculars or in stereoscopic photographs) — **hy·per·stereoscopy** \"+\ *n*

hy·per·sthene \'hīpə(r),sthēn\ *n* -s [F *hypersthène*, fr. *hyper-* + Gk *sthenos* strength — more at ASTHEN-] **:** a mineral $(Mg,Fe)SiO_3$ consisting of an orthorhombic grayish or greenish black or dark brown pyroxene that is a silicate of magnesium and iron isomorphous with enstatite and often has a bronze luster on the cleavage surface — **hy·per·sthenic** \⸗⸗;sthenik, -thēn-\ *adj*

hy·per·sthe·nite \,⸗⸗'sthē,nīt\ *n* -s [G *hypersthenit*, fr. *hypersthen* hypersthene (fr. F *hypersthène*) + *-it* -ite] **1 :** a rock composed of hypersthene and labradorite **2 :** pyroxenite composed essentially of hypersthene

hy·per·sthen·iza·tion \-,sthēnə'zāshən, -,nī'z-\ *n* -s **:** development of hypersthene by metamorphic processes

hy·per·strophic \⸗⸗'sträfik *also* -rōf-\ *adj* [*hyper-* + Gk *strophos* twisted band, cord + E *-ic* — more at STROPHE] **:** characterized by a coiling of the shell to the left combined with an asymmetric arrangement of the organs like that of an individual of the same or related species with a shell coiled to the right

hy·per·surface \"+\ *n* [*hyper-* + *surface*] **:** a surface that is the analogue in hyperspace of a surface in three-dimensional space

hy·per·susceptibility \"+\ *n* [*hyper-* + *susceptibility*] **:** the quality or state of being hypersensitive

hy·per·susceptible \"+\ *adj* [*hyper-* + *susceptible*] **:** HYPERSENSITIVE

hy·per·tel·ic \'hīpə(r);telik\ *adj* **:** of, relating to, or exhibiting hypertely

hy·per·tely \hī'pərd·ᵊlē; 'hīpər,telē, ,⸗⸗'⸗⸗\ *n* -ES [ISV *hyper-* + *tel-* (end) + *-y*] **:** an extreme degree of imitative coloration or ornamentation not explainable on the ground of utility

hy·per·tense \'hīpə(r)+\ *adj* [*hyper-* + *tense*] **:** excessively tense ⟨a furiously ambitious young ~ instructor —Christopher Morley⟩

hy·per·ten·sin \,⸗⸗'ten(t)sə̇n\ *n* -s [ISV *hypertension* + *-in*] **:** any of several vasoconstrictor pressor polypeptides formed by partial hydrolysis of hypertensinogen — called also *angiotonin*

hy·per·ten·sin·ase \-sə̇,nās, -āz\ *n* -s [ISV *hypertensin* + *-ase*] **:** an enzyme found esp. in the kidney and intestine that inactivates hypertensin

hy·per·ten·sin·o·gen \-,ten'sinəjə̇n, -,jen\ *n* -s [ISV *hypertensino-* (fr. *hypertensin*) + *-gen*] **:** a globulin of blood plasma and serum that is produced by the liver and when acted on by renin forms hypertensin

hy·per·tension \⸗⸗+\ *n* [ISV *hyper-* + *tension*] **1 :** abnormally high arterial blood pressure: **a :** such blood pressure occurring without apparent or determinable prior organic changes in the tissues possibly because of hereditary tendency, emotional tensions, faulty nutrition, or hormonal influence **b :** such blood pressure with demonstrable organic changes (as in nephritis, diabetes, and hyperthyroidism) **2 :** a systemic condition resulting from hypertension that is either symptomless or is accompanied by nervousness, dizziness, or headache ⟨a morass of ~ and domestic misery —C.J.Rolo⟩

¹hy·per·ten·sive \-'ten(t)siv, -sēv *also* -səv\ *adj* [ISV *hypertension* + *-ive*] **:** marked by a rise in blood pressure **:** suffering or caused by hypertension

²hypertensive \"\ *n* -s **:** an individual affected with hypertension

Hy·per·therm \'⸗⸗,thərm\ *trademark* — used for an apparatus

using hot humid air to produce artificial fever for remedial
purposes

hy·per·ther·mia \ˌ==ˈthərmēə\ n -s [NL, fr. hyper- + therm-
+ -ia] : hyperpyrexia esp. when induced artificially for therapeutic purposes — **hy·per·ther·mic** \ˌ==ˈthərmik\ adj

hy·per·thyroid \ˌ==+\ adj [ISV hyper- + thyroid] : of,
relating to, or having hyperthyroidism

hy·per·thyroidism \"+\ n [ISV hyper- + thyroid + -ism]
1 : excessive functional activity of the thyroid gland 2 : the
abnormal condition resulting from hyperthyroidism marked
by increased metabolic rate, enlargement of the thyroid gland,
rapid heart rate, high blood pressure, and various secondary
symptoms — see EXOPHTHALMIC GOITER, GOITER

hy·per·thy·ro·sis \ˌ==ˌthīˈrōsəs\ also **hy·per·thy·re·o·sis**
\-ˌthīrēˈōsəs\ n, pl **hyperthyro·ses** also **hyperthyreo·ses**
\-ōˌsēz\ [NL, fr. hyper- + thyr- or thyreo- + -osis] : HYPER-
THYROIDISM

hy·per·to·nia \ˌ==ˈtōnēə\ or **hy·per·tony** \ˈ==ˌtōnē, hī-
ˈpərtᵊnē\ n, pl **hypertonias** or **hypertonies** [NL hyper-
tonia, fr. hyper- + -tonia -tony] : HYPERTONICITY

hy·per·tonic \ˌhīpə(r)+\ adj [ISV hyper- + tonic] 1 of
living tissue : having excessive tone 2 of a fluid : having a
higher osmotic pressure than a fluid under comparison or
used as a standard — compare ISOTONIC

hy·per·tonicity \"+\ n : the quality or state of being hypertonic

hy·per·tonus \"+\ n [NL, fr. hyper- + tonus] : HYPER-
TONICITY

hy·per·trichosis \"+\ n, pl **hypertrichoses** [NL, fr. hyper-
+ Gk trichōsis growth of hair (fr. trich- + -ōsis -osis)] : excessive growth of hair

hy·per·trophic \hīˈpər·trə(ˌ)fik; ˌhīpərˈträfik, -rōf-\ or **hy-
per·tro·phous** \(ˈ)hīˌpər·trəfəs\ adj [hyper- + -trophic or
-trophous] : of or relating to hypertrophy : affected with or
tending to hypertrophy

hypertrophic arthritis n : DEGENERATIVE ARTHRITIS

hy·per·tro·phied \(ˈ)hīˌpər·trəfēd\ adj : marked by hyper-
trophy : excessively or abnormally developed : OVERGROWN
⟨~ tonsils⟩ ⟨a ~ carnival —Janet Flanner⟩ ⟨~ capitalists
—G.B.Shaw⟩

[1]**hy·per·tro·phy** \=ˈ==fē\ n [prob. fr. NL hypertrophia, fr.
hyper- + -trophia -trophy] 1 : overgrowth or excessive
development of an organ or part (as that resulting from
unusually steady or severe use or in compensation for an
organic deficiency); specif : increase in bulk without increase
in the number of constituent elements that is produced by
thickening of the muscle fibers ⟨cardiac ~⟩ — compare
HYPERPLASIA, HYPOTROPHY 2 : exaggerated growth in size
or complexity : excessive enlargement ⟨economic concentration increasing at a parallel rate with business ~ —Paul
Johnson⟩ ⟨a certain ~ in the contrapuntal writing making for
very complicated listening —K.H.Wörner⟩

[2]**hypertrophy** \"\ vb -ED/-ING/-ES vt : to affect with hypertrophy ~ vi : to increase or grow in size beyond the normal
⟨a healthy kidney hypertrophies when the other fails⟩ ⟨ortho-
doxies ~ as inspiration declines⟩

hy·per·urbanism \ˌhīpər+\ n -s [hyper- + urban + -ism]
: a form, pronunciation, or usage that overreaches correctness
in an effort to avoid provincial speech

hy·per·uricemia \ˌhīpə(r)+\ n -s [NL, fr hyper- + uric- +
-emia] : excess uric acid in the blood (as in gout)

hy·per·ventilation \"+\ n [ISV hyper- + ventilation]
: excessive ventilation; specif : excessive rate and depth of
respiration leading to abnormal loss of carbon dioxide from
the blood

hy·per·vi·ta·min·osis \ˌ==ˌvīd·aməˈnōsəs\ n, pl **hypervita-
mino·ses** \-ōˌsēz\ [NL, fr hyper- + ISV vitamin + NL
-osis] : an abnormal state resulting from excessive intake of
one or more vitamins esp. over a long period of time

hy·per·vol·emia \ˌhīpə(r)väˈlēmēə\ n -s [NL, fr. hyper- +
vol- (fr. E volume) + -emia] : an excessive volume of blood in
the body

hyp·es·the·sia \ˌhipəsˈthēzh(ē)ə, ˌhīp-, -ˌpes-\ n [NL, fr.
hypo- + -esthesia (as in anesthesia)] : impaired or lessened
tactile sensibility

hy·pha \ˈhīfə\ n, pl **hy·phae** \-ī(ˌ)ē\ [NL, fr. Gk hyphē
web; akin to Gk hyphos web — more at WEAVE] 1 : one of
the individual threads that make up the mycelium of a fungus,
increase by apical growth, and are coenocytic in the Phycomycetes but transversely septate in the Ascomycetes and
Basidiomycetes 2 : a simple or branched filamentous outgrowth from the cortex or other inner tissues of various large
seaweeds esp. of the order Fucales

hy·phae·ne \hīˈfēnē\ n, cap [NL, fr. Gk hyphainein to weave
— more at WEAVE] : a genus of tropical African fan palms
having branching trunks, dioecious flowers, and one-seeded
fruits with thick rinds — see DOOM PALM

hy·phaer·e·sis \hīˈferəsəs, esp Brit -ˈfi(ə)r-\ n, pl **hyphaere-
ses** \-əˌsēz\ [Gk hyphairesis, fr. hyphairein to take from
under, subtract, fr. hypo- + hairein to take — more at HERESY]
: the omission of a sound, letter, or syllable from the body of a
word — compare SYNCOPE 2a

hy·phal \ˈhīfəl\ adj [NL hypha + E [1]-al] : of, relating to, or
constituting a hypha

hyphal body n : an irregularly shaped often thickened fragment formed (as in members of the genus Entomophthora) by
segmentation of a hypha and sometimes multiplying by fission
or budding

hy·phan·tria \hīˈfan·trēə\ n, cap [NL, fr. Gk, female weaver,
fem. of hyphantēs weaver, fr. hyphainein to weave] : a genus
of arctiid moths including some No. American species having
hairy social larvae that are serious pests of trees — see
FALL WEBWORM

[1]**hy·phen** \ˈhīfən\ n -s [LL & Gk; LL, a diacritical mark (-)
used to indicate that two words are to be read as a compound,
fr. Gk, fr. hyph' hen under one, fr. hypo under + hen (neut. of
heis one) — more at UP, SAME] 1 : the punctuation mark -
used to divide or to compound words or word elements:
a : a mark used for division esp. at the end of a line terminating with a syllable of a word that is completed in the next line,
between letters or syllables repeated to give the effect of stuttering, sobbing, or halting expression (as in s-s-sorry), or
between the letters of a word spelled out letter by letter (as in
p-r-o-b-a-t-i-o-n-a-r-y) b : a mark used for compounding
esp. in a compound containing a prepositional phrase (as in
mother-in-law), in a compound adjective (as in first-rate), in
a compound whose first element is self (as in self-pity), in a
compound whose second element is capitalized (as in pro=
British), in a compound containing reduplication (as in bang=
bang), in a spelled-out compound numeral (as in twenty-five),
in a compound whose meaning differs from that of an otherwise identical word (as in re-formation), in a compound containing a vowel otherwise confusingly doubled (as in co-opt),
or in a compound containing the same letter three successive
times (as in bell-less) 2 : something resembling a hyphen ⟨the
lady whose odd smile is the merest ~ —Karl Shapiro⟩

[2]**hyphen** \"\ vt **hyphened**; **hyphened**; **hyphening** \-f(ə)niŋ\
hyphens : to connect (as two words or the parts of a word)
with a hyphen : mark with a hyphen

[1]**hy·phen·ate** \ˈhīfəˌnāt, usu -ād·+V\ vt -ED/-ING/-S [[1]hyphen
+ -ate] : HYPHEN — **hy·phen·ation** \ˌhīfəˈnāshən\ n -s

[2]**hy·phen·ate** \-ˌnə|t, ˌnā|, usu |d·+V\ n -s [back-formation
fr. hyphenated (adj.)] : a hyphenated person; specif : a
resident or citizen of the U.S. whose recent foreign national
origin divides or is believed to divide his patriotic loyalties
⟨the effect of war hysteria upon a household of so-called ~s
—N.Y. Times⟩ ⟨denounced ~s and called for national
preparedness —Current History⟩

hyphenated adj [fr. past part. of [1]hyphenate; fr. the use of
hyphenated words (as German-American, Irish-American)
to designate foreign-born citizens of the U.S.] : of, relating
to, or constituting a person or unit of mixed or diverse composition or origin ⟨~ Canadians —N.Y. Herald⟩ ⟨~ activity
as both commercial florists and horticultural journalists
—Richard Thruelsen⟩

hy·phen·ic \(ˈ)hīˌfenik\ adj : of or relating to hyphens

hy·phen·ism \ˈhīfəˌnizəm\ n -s [[1]hyphen + -ism; fr. the use
of hyphenated words (as German-American, Irish-American)
to designate foreign-born citizens of the U.S.] : the quality or
state of being a hyphenate : the conduct that marks or is
ascribed to hyphenates ⟨~ in the United States is almost extinct —E.A.Mowrer⟩

hy·phen·iza·tion \ˌhīfənəˈzāshən, -ˌnīˈz-\ n -s : the joining of
syllables or words with hyphens

hy·phen·ize \ˈhīfəˌnīz\ vt -ED/-ING/-S : HYPHEN

hy·phes·so·bry·con \hīˌfesəˈbrīˌkän\ n, cap [NL, fr. hy-
phesso- (fr. Gk hyphēssōn of lesser stature, fr. hypo- + hēssōn
inferior, less) + Brycon, genus of fishes (fr. Gk brykein to
eat greedily, bite, devour)] : a genus of small brilliantly
colored So. American characin fishes including several that are
often kept in the tropical aquarium

hypho- comb form [NL, fr. Gk hyphē, hyphos web — more at
WEAVE] : web : tissue ⟨hyphodrome⟩

hy·pho·chyt·ri·a·les \ˌhīfōˌki·trēˈā(ˌ)lēz\ n pl, cap [NL, fr.
Hyphochytrium genus of fungi (fr. hypho- + Gk chytrion small
pot, cup, dim. of chytris small pot, dim. of chytra earthen pot)
+ -ales — more at CHYTRA] : a small order of lower fungi (subclass Oomycetes) that in general resemble members of the order
Chytridiales but have anteriorly uniflagellate zoospores

hy·pho·mi·cro·bi·a·les \-ā(ˌ)lēz\ n pl, cap [NL, fr. Hyphomicrobium + -ales] : a small order of solitary or colonial
chiefly free-living and aquatic sometimes stalked bacteria that
reproduce by budding or by budding and longitudinal fission

hy·pho·mi·cro·bi·a·ce·ae \ˌhī(ˌ)fō(ˌ)mīˌkrōbēˈāsēˌē\ n pl,
cap [NL, fr. Hyphomicrobium, type genus (fr. hypho- + microbium) + -aceae] : a small family of heterotrophic soil or water
bacteria (order Hyphomicrobiales) that often have the individual cells linked by fine filaments

hy·pho·my·ce·ta·les \ˌhī(ˌ)fōˌmīsəˈtā(ˌ)lēz\ [NL, fr. hypho-
+ mycet- + -ales] syn of MONILIALES

hy·pho·my·cete \ˌhīfōˈmīˌsēt, ˌ==ˌ=ˌ=\ n -s [NL Hyphomycetes]
: a fungus of the subclass Hyphomycetes

hy·pho·my·ce·tes \ˌhīfōˌmīˈsēd·ēz\ n pl, cap [NL, fr. hypho-
+ -mycetes] in some classifications : a subclass of fungi
coextensive with the order Moniliales or including both the
Moniliales and the Mycelia Sterilia — **hy·pho·my·ce·tic**
\ˌ==ˌ=ˌsēd·ik\ adj — **hy·pho·my·ce·tous** \-d·əs\ adj

hy·pho·my·co·sis \ˌhīfōˌmīˈkōsəs\ n [NL, fr. Hyphomycetes
+ -osis] 1 : infection with a hyphomycete 2 : BURSATI 1

hy·pho·po·di·ate \ˌhīfəˌpōdēət, -ēˌāt\ adj [NL hyphopodium
+ E -ate] : having a hyphopodium

hy·pho·po·di·um \ˌ==ˈpōdēəm\ n, pl **hyphopo·dia** \-ēə\
[NL, fr. hypho- + -podium] : a short 1-celled or 2-celled often
lobed outgrowth from the mycelium of various ectoparasitic
fungi that serves to attach the fungus to the host (as in the
sooty molds)

hy·pid·i·o·mor·phic \hīˌpidēōˌmȯrfik\ adj [ISV hypo- +
idiomorphic] : partly idiomorphic — used of a rock only
some of whose constituents have a distinct crystalline form
— **hy·pid·i·o·mor·phi·cal·ly** \-fək(ə)lē\ adv

hypn- or **hypno-** comb form [F hypn-, fr. LL, fr. Gk, fr. hypnos
— more at SOMNOLENT] 1 : sleep ⟨hypnagogic⟩ 2 : hypnotism ⟨hypnogenesis⟩

hyp·na·ce·ae \hipˈnāsēˌē\ n pl, cap [NL, fr. Hypnum, type
genus + -aceae] : a family of mosses (order Hypnobryales)
that usu. grow in dense mats and have asymmetrical capsules
— see HYPNUM — **hyp·na·ceous** \(ˈ)hipˌnāshəs\ adj

hyp·na·gog·ic or **hyp·no·gog·ic** \ˌhipnəˌgäjik\ adj [hyp-
nagogic fr. F hypnagogique, fr. hypn- + -agogique (fr. Gk
-agōgikos as in paidagōgikos pedagogic); hypnogogic, alter. of
hypnagogic] : of, relating to, or associated with the drowsiness
preceding sleep ⟨~ hallucinations⟩ — opposed to hypnopompic

hyp·nea \ˈhipnēə\ n, cap [NL, fr. Hypnum, genus of mosses]
: a genus (the type of the family Hypneaceae) comprising
red algae of the order Gigartinales that have a thallus of
terete fleshy branches with the tips curving inward like tendrils
and that include one (H. musciformis) which is occas. used
as a source of agar

hyp·no·analysis \ˌhipnō+\ n [NL, fr. hypnosis + psycho-
analysis] : psychoanalytic psychotherapy that uses hypnosis
to facilitate transference by helping to dissolve resistance,
assimilate interpretation, and recover repressed memories
— compare HYPNOTHERAPY

hyp·no·bryales \"+\ n pl, cap [NL, fr. hypno- (fr. Hypnum,
genus of mosses) + Bryales] : an order of Musci comprising
mosses with a pleurocarpous sporophyte and a capsule usu.
inclined at the end of a long seta and with an entire endostome

hyp·no·cyst \ˈhipnəˌsist\ n [hypn- + -cyst] 1 : HYPNOSPORE
2 : an encysted form by which various protozoans resist
adverse conditions (as cold or drought)

hyp·no·gen·e·sis \ˌhipnōˈjenəsəs\ n [NL, fr. hypn- + L gen-
esis] : the production of a hypnotic state

hyp·no·ge·net·ic \ˌhipnōjəˌned·ik\ adj [hypn- + -genetic]
1 : inducing a hypnotic state 2 : inducing sleep — **hyp-
no·ge·net·i·cal·ly** \-d·ək(ə)lē\ adv

hyp·nog·e·nous \(ˈ)hipˌnäjənəs\ adj [hypn- + -genous]
: HYPNOGENETIC

[1]**hyp·noid** \ˈhipˌnȯid\ adj [NL Hypnum + E -oid] : of,
relating to, or resembling mosses of the genus Hypnum or
related forms

[2]**hypnoid** \"\ or **hyp·noi·dal** \(ˈ)hipˌnȯidᵊl\ adj [hypnoid fr.
NL hypnosis + E -oid; hypnoidal fr. hypnoid + -al] : of,
relating to, or resembling sleep or hypnosis

hyp·nol·o·gy \hipˈnäləjē\ n -ES [hypn- + -logy] : the scientific
study of sleep and hypnotic phenomena

hyp·none \ˈhipˌnōn\ n -s [ISV hypn- + -one; orig. formed
in F] : ACETOPHENONE

hyp·no·pho·bia \ˌhipnəˈfōbēə\ or **hyp·no·pho·by** \ˈ==ˌ=bē\
n, pl **hypnophobias** or **hypnophobies** [NL hypnophobia,
fr. hypn- + phobia] : morbid fear of sleep — **hy·pno·pho·bic**
\ˌ==ˌfōbik also -ˌfäb-\ adj

hyp·no·pom·pic \ˌhipnəˌpämpik\ adj [hypn- + pomp- (fr.
Gk pompē act of sending, escort, procession) + -ic — more
at POMP] : dispelling sleep : of, relating to, or associated with
the semiconsciousness preceding waking ⟨~ dreams⟩ — opposed to hypnagogic

hyp·no·sis \hipˈnōsəs\ n, pl **hypno·ses** \-ōˌsēz\ [NL, fr.
hypn- + -osis] 1 : a state that resembles normal sleep but
differs in being induced by the suggestions and operations of
the hypnotizer with whom the hypnotized subject remains in
rapport and responsive to his suggestions which may induce
anesthesia, blindness, hallucinations, and paralysis while
suggestions of curative value may also be accepted — compare POSTHYPNOTIC 2 : any of various conditions that
resemble sleep — compare CATAPLEXY 3 : HYPNOTISM 1

hyp·no·sperm \ˈhipnə+ˌ-\ n [hypn- + sperm] : HYPNOSPORE

hyp·no·sporangium \ˌhipnō+\ n [NL, blend of E hypnospore and NL sporangium] : a sporangium containing hyp-
nospores

hyp·no·spore \ˈhipnə+ˌ-\ n [hypn- + spore] : a very thick=
walled asexual resting spore (as of various green algae) —
hyp·no·spo·ric \ˌ==ˌspōrik, -pȯr-\ adj

hyp·no·therapeutic \ˌhipnō+\ adj [fr. hypnotherapy, after E
therapy: therapeutic] : of, relating to, or promoting hypnotherapy

hyp·no·therapy \"+\ n [hypn- + therapy] 1 : the treatment
of disease by hypnotism 2 : psychotherapy that facilitates
suggestion, reeducation, or analysis by means of hypnosis
— compare HYPNOANALYSIS

[1]**hyp·not·ic** \(ˈ)hipˌnäd·|ik, -ät|, |ēk\ adj [F or LL; F hyp-
notique, fr. MF, fr. LL hypnoticus, fr. Gk hypnōtikos inclined
to sleep, putting to sleep, soporific, fr. (assumed) Gk hypnōtos
(verbal of Gk hypnoun to put to sleep, sleep, fr. hypnos sleep)
+ Gk -ikos -ic — more at SOMNOLENT] 1 : tending to produce
sleep : SOPORIFIC 2 [short for neurohypnotic] : of or relating
to hypnosis or hypnotism : being under, susceptible to, or
tending to induce hypnosis ⟨his noble brow and ~ stare
—Julian Maclaren-Ross⟩ ⟨the mother's ~ will —Leslie Rees⟩
⟨~ suspension of all his faculties —Mary Austin⟩

[2]**hypnotic** \"\ n -s 1 : a drug or other agent that produces
or tends to produce sleep : SOPORIFIC 2 : one that is or is
capable of being hypnotized

hyp·not·i·cal·ly \|ək(ə)lē, |ēk-, -li\ adv : in a hypnotic manner
⟨~ interesting from beginning to end —Harper's⟩ : by means
of hypnotism ⟨a fictitious meal ~ suggested —P.S.deQ.Cabot⟩

hyp·no·tism \ˈhipnəˌtizəm\ n -s [short for neurohypnotism]
1 : the study of or the act or practice of inducing hypnosis —
compare MESMERISM 2 : HYPNOSIS 1

hyp·no·tist \ˈhipnətəst, -əd·əst\ n -s : one that practices
hypnotism

hyp·no·tiz·abil·i·ty \ˌhipnəˌtīzəˈbilid·ē\ n : susceptibility
to hypnotism

hyp·no·tiz·able \ˈhipnəˌtīzəbəl, ˌ==ˈ===\ adj : that can be
hypnotized

hyp·no·tize or **hyp·no·tise** \ˈhipnəˌtīz\ vb -ED/-ING/-S [hyp-
notism + -ize or -ise] vt 1 : to induce hypnosis in 2 : to
deaden (judgment or resistance) by or as if by hypnotic suggestion ⟨gave a passion to his oratory which hypnotized
criticism —J.H.Plumb⟩ ~ vi : to practice hypnosis : use
hypnotic art or suggestion

hyp·no·toxin \ˌhipnə+\ n [ISV hypn- + toxin] : a hypothetical hormonal product of brain tissue that is held to induce
sleep

hyp·num \ˈhipnəm\ n [NL, fr. LGk hypnon, a lichen] 1 cap
: the type genus of the family Hypnaceae comprising mosses
with the leaves arranged in three rows — see PLUME MOSS
2 -s : any moss of the genus Hypnum

[1]**hy·po** \ˈhī(ˌ)pō\ n -s [by shortening] : HYPOCHONDRIA
⟨nor is his spirit drooping with the ~s —Amer. Mercury⟩

[2]**hypo** \"\ n -s [short for hyposulfite] : sodium thiosulfate
used as a fixing agent in photography

[3]**hypo** \"\ n -s [short for hypodermic] 1 : HYPODERMIC
SYRINGE 2 : HYPODERMIC INJECTION 3 : STIMULUS ⟨a sure
~ for car sales —Hartford (Conn.) Times⟩

[4]**hypo** \"\ vt -ED/-ING/-S 1 : to administer a hypodermic in-
jection to ⟨purged the calf with laxative, ~ed it with penicillin
—Time⟩ 2 : to stimulate as if with a hypodermic injection
: EXCITE, ACCELERATE ⟨tried to ~ her interest —Saturday
Rev.⟩ ⟨giant giveaways to ~ their sales figures —Bennett
Cerf⟩ ⟨prefer their parties ~ed occasionally with a new face
or figure —Maureen Daly⟩

hypo- \in pronunciations below ˌ=== ˌhī(ˌ)pō or -ˌpə\ or **hyp-**
prefix [alter. (influenced by LL hypo-, hyp-) of ME ypo-,
fr. OF, fr. LL hypo-, hyp-, fr. Gk, fr. hypo — more at UP]
1 : under : beneath : down ⟨hypoblast⟩ ⟨hypodermic⟩
2 : less than normal or normally ⟨hypocalcemia⟩ ⟨hypo-
chromia⟩ ⟨hypochlorhydric⟩ ⟨hyposensitive⟩ 3 : in a lower
state of oxidation : in a low usu. the lowest position in a series
of compounds ⟨hypovanadous⟩ ⟨hypoxanthine⟩ 4 a in ancient
Greek music (1) : being the lower octave in a disdiapason
⟨hypolydian⟩ (2) of an interval : measured downward ⟨hypo-
diapason⟩ b in medieval music : being in a plagal mode
⟨hypodorian⟩

hy·po·adre·nia \ˌ== at HYPO- + əˈdrēnēə\ also **hy·po·adre-
nal·ism** \-nəˌlizəm\ n -s [hypoadrenia fr. NL, fr. hypo- +
adren- + -ia; hypoadrenalism fr. hypo- + adrenal + -ism]
: decreased activity of the adrenal glands; specif : adrenocortical insufficiency

hy·po·aeolian mode \ˌ==+. . .-\ n [LL hypoaeolius hypo-
aeolian (fr. — assumed — Gk hypoaiolios, fr. Gk hypo- +
aiolios Aeolian, fr. Aiolis Aeolis, ancient country in Asia
Minor) + E -an] : a plagal ecclesiastical mode consisting of a
tetrachord and an upper conjunct pentachord represented on
the white keys of the piano by an ascending diatonic scale from
E to E — see MODE illustration

hy·po·aesthesia \"+\ chiefly Brit var of HYPESTHESIA

hy·po·al·bu·min·emia \ˌ==+(ˌ)alˌbyüməˈnēmēə\ n -s [NL,
fr. hypo- + albumin- + -emia] : hypoproteinemia marked by
reduction in serum albumins

hy·po·allergenic \ˌ==+\ adj [hypo- + allergenic] : having
a relatively low capacity to induce hypersensitivity

hypo-alum toning process n [[2]hypo + alum] : a method of
altering a developed silver photographic image to a sepia
color by means of a warm solution containing essentially
hypo and alum

hy·po·bar·ic \ˌ==+ˌbarik\ adj [hypo- + Gk baros weight +
E -ic — more at GRIEVE] : having a specific gravity less than
that of cerebrospinal fluid — used of solutions for spinal
anesthesia; opposed to hyperbaric

hy·po·basal \"+\ adj [ISV hypo- + basal] bot : situated
posterior to the basal wall ⟨the ~ lower segment of a developing embryo⟩ — compare EPIBASAL

hy·po·basidium \"+\ n [NL, fr. hypo- + basidium] : a
special cell constituting the base of the basidium in various
fungi of the orders Auriculariales and Tremellales in which
haploid nuclei fuse and from which the epibasidium arises

hy·po·batholithic \"+\ adj [hypo- + batholithic] : of,
relating to, or constituting ore deposits that occur in deeply
eroded batholiths

hy·po·benthos \"+\ n [NL, fr. hypo- + benthos] : the
fauna of the deep sea

hy·po·blast \ˈ==+ˌblast\ n [hypo- + -blast] : the endoderm
of an embryo

hy·po·blas·tic \ˌ==ˌblastik\ adj : of, relating to, or derived
from hypoblast : ENDODERMAL

[1]**hy·po·branchial** \ˌ==+\ adj [hypo- + branchial] 1 : situated below the gills : of or relating to the ventral wall of the
pharynx; specif : of or relating to the endostyle 2 : of,
relating to, or being the segment of a branchial arch between
the basibranchial and the ceratobranchial

[2]**hypobranchial** \"\ n -s : a hypobranchial bone or cartilage

hy·po·bro·mite \ˌ==+ˈbrōˌmīt\ n -s [ISV hypobrom- (fr.
hypobromous acid) + -ite] : a salt or ester of hypobromous
acid

hy·po·bro·mous acid \ˌ==ˌbrōməs. . .-\ n [ISV hypo- +
bromine + -ous] : an unstable acid HBrO that resembles
hypochlorous acid and is obtained in solution by reaction of
bromine water with silver nitrate or in the form of unstable
salts by reaction of bromine with alkaline solutions

hy·po·bu·lia \ˌ==+ˈbyülēə\ n -s [NL, fr. hypo- + -bulia]
: lowered ability to make decisions or to act — **hy·po·bu·lic**
\ˌ==ˌ=lik\ adj

hy·po·cal·ce·mia also **hy·po·cal·cae·mia** \ˌ==+ˌkalˈsēmēə\
n -s [NL, fr. hypo- + calcemia, calcaemia calcium in the
blood (fr. calc- + -emia, -aemia)] : a deficiency of calcium
in the blood — **hy·po·cal·ce·mic** also **hy·po·cal·cae·mic**
\ˌ==ˌ=ˌ=mik\ adj

hy·po·cap·nia \ˌ==+ˈkapnēə\ n -s [NL, fr. hypo- + -capnia]
: deficiency of carbon dioxide in the blood

hy·po·carp \ˈ==+ˌkärp\ or **hy·po·car·pi·um** \ˌ==+ˈkärpēəm\
n, pl **hypocarps** \-ps\ or **hypocar·pia** \-ēə\ [NL hypo-
carpium, fr. hypo- + -carpium -carp] : an enlarged sometimes
edible peduncle beneath some fruits (as the cashew apple)

hy·po·caust \ˈ==+ˌkȯst\ n -s [L hypocaustum, hypocauston,
fr. Gk hypokauston, fr. neut. of hypokaustos heated by a
hypocaust, fr. (assumed) Gk hypokaustos, verbal of Gk hypo-
kaiein to light (a fire) under, fr. hypo- + kaiein to burn —
more at CAUSTIC] : a central heating system of an ancient
Roman dwelling, public bath, or other building consisting of
an underground furnace or fire chamber and a series of tile
flues for distribution of the heat

hy·po·cellular \ˌ== at HYPO-+\ adj [hypo- + cellular] : containing less than the normal number of cells ⟨~ bone marrow
in chronic lead poisoning⟩

hy·po·center \"+\ n [hypo- + center] : the point on the
earth's surface directly below the center of a nuclear bomb
explosion

hy·po·centrum \"+\ n, pl **hypocentra** [NL, fr. hypo- +
centrum] : a ventral part of the body of a vertebra that is usu.
wedge-shaped or horseshoe-shaped, consists of the fused
lower arcualia of the anterior of the two arches from which
each vertebra is formed, and is characteristic of some fishes,
stegocephalians, and primitive reptiles — called also intercentrum

hy·po·ceph·a·lus \ˌ==+ˈsefələs\ n, pl **hypocepha·li** \-fəˌlī\
[NL, fr. hypo- + -cephalus (fr. Gk kephalē head) — more at
CEPHALIC] : a circular sheet of papyrus containing extracts
from the 162d chapter of the Book of the Dead stiffened with
plastered linen and placed as an amulet under the head of an
ancient Egyptian mummy in the coffin

hy·po·chae·ris \"+ˈkirəs\ n, cap [NL, alter. of L hypo-
choeris, a plant, fr. Gk hypochoiris succory plant, fr. hypo- +
-choiris (fr. choiros young pig, pig) — more at CHAEROPUS]
: a large widely distributed genus of milky-juiced herbs (family
Compositae) that have basal leaves and scapose yellow flower
heads and include some (as the cat's-ear) that are cosmopolitan weeds of open lands

hy·po·chil \ˈ==+ˌkil\ or **hy·po·chil·i·um** \ˌ==+ˈkilēəm\ n -s
[NL hypochilium, fr. hypo- + Gk cheilos lip + NL -ium —
more at GILL] : the lower part of the labellum in orchids

hy·po·chil·o·morph \ˌ==+ˈkīlə,mȯrf\ *adj* [NL *Hypochilomorphae*] **:** of or relating to the Hypochilomorphae

hy·po·chil·o·mor·phae \ˌ==ˌ==ˈmȯr(ˌ)fē\ *n pl, cap* [NL, fr. *hypo-* + *chil-* + *-morphae*] **:** a suborder of Araneida comprising arachnomorph spiders with two pairs of book lungs

hy·po·chloremia \ˈ== *at* HYPO- +\ *n* [NL, fr. *hypo-* + *chloremia*] **:** abnormal decrease of chlorides in the blood — **hy·po·chlor·e·mic** \"+ˌklōrˈēmik\ *adj*

hy·po·chlor·hy·dria \ˌ==+ˌklōrˈhīdrēə\ *n* -s [NL, fr. *hypo-* + *chlorhydria* hydrochloric acid in the gastric juice (fr. *chlor-* + *hydr-* + *-ia*)] **:** deficiency of hydrochloric acid in the gastric juice — compare HYPERCHLORHYDRIA — **hy·po·chlor·hy·dric** \ˈ==ˌ=ˈdrik\ *adj*

hy·po·chlorite \ˈ== *at* HYPO- +\ *n* [ISV *hypochlor-* (fr. *hypochlorous acid*) + *-ite*] **:** a salt or ester of hypochlorous acid: as **a :** SODIUM HYPOCHLORITE **b :** CALCIUM HYPOCHLORITE

hy·po·chlorous acid \ˈ==+...\ *n* [ISV *hypo-* + *chlorous*; orig. formed as F *hypochloreux*] **:** an unstable strongly oxidizing but weak acid HClO that is obtained in solution along with hydrochloric acid by reaction of chlorine with water or in the form of salts by reaction of chlorine with alkaline solutions and that is used chiefly in the form of salts as an oxidizing agent, bleaching agent, disinfectant, and chlorinating agent

hy·poch·na·ce·ae \ˌhī(ˌ)päkˈnāsēˌē\ *n pl, cap* [NL, fr. *Hypochnus* + *-aceae*] *syn of* THELEPHORACEAE

hy·poch·nus \hīˈpäknəs\ [NL, fr. *hypo-* + Gk *chnoos, chnous* dust, fine down; akin to Gk *chnauein* to gnaw, nibble, OE *gnagan* to gnaw — more at GNAW] *syn of* TOMENTELLA

hy·po·choeris \ˌ== *at* HYPO- +ˈkirəs\ [NL, fr. L, a plant — more at HYPOCHAERIS] *syn of* HYPOCHAERIS

hy·po·chon·der *or* **hy·po·chon·dre** \"+ˈkändə(r)\ *n* -s [LL *hypochondria*, pl., abdomen] *archaic* **:** HYPOCHONDRIUM

hy·po·chon·dria \ˌhīpəˈkändrēə, -pōˈ- *sometimes* ˌhip-\ *n* -s [NL, fr. LL, pl., abdomen, belly (formerly supposed to be the seat of hypochondria), fr. Gk, fr. *hypochondria*, neut. pl. of *hypochondrios* under the cartilage of the breastbone, fr. *hypo-* + *-chondrios* (fr. *chondros* cartilage, cartilage of the breastbone, granule, grain) — more at GRIND] **:** extreme depression of mind or spirits often centered on imaginary physical ailments ⟨her ~, her insecurity, her staunch integrity, and loneliness —Bosley Crowther⟩ ⟨the present philosophical and political ~ about moral skepticism —Charles Frankel⟩; *specif* **:** HYPOCHONDRIASIS

¹hy·po·chon·dri·ac \ˌ==ˈ=drē,ak\ *adj* [F *hypochondriaque*, adj. & n., fr. MF, fr. Gk *hypochondriakos*, adj., of the abdomen, fr. *hypochondrion*, sing., *hypochondria*, pl., abdomen + *-akos* (adj. suffix)] **1** *also* **hy·po·chon·dri·al** \-ēəl\ **a :** situated below the costal cartilages **b :** of, relating to, or being the two regions of the abdomen lying on either side of the epigastric region and above the lumbar regions — see ABDOMINAL REGION illustration **2** *or* **hy·po·chon·dri·a·cal** \ˌhīpə\kənˈdrīəkəl, -pō\, \ˌkän- *sometimes* ˌhip-\ **:** affected, characterized, or produced by hypochondria

²hypochondriac \"\ *n* -s [F *hypochondriaque*] **:** one affected by hypochondria or hypochondriasis ⟨a ~ . . . lives in a world of sick imagination —J.W.Krutch⟩ ⟨some miserable ~ whose interests are bounded by his own ailments —Bertrand Russell⟩

hy·po·chon·dri·a·sis \ˌhīpəkənˈdrīəsəs\ *n, pl* **hypochondria·ses** \-ə,sēz\ [NL, fr. *hypochondria* + *-iasis*] **:** hypochondria of pathological proportions **:** morbid concern about one's health esp. when accompanied by delusions of physical disease

hy·po·chon·dri·ast \ˌhīpəˈkändrē,ast\ *n* -s [NL *hypochondria* + E *-ast* (as in *enthusiast*)] **:** HYPOCHONDRIAC

hy·po·chon·dri·um \-ēəm\ *n, pl* **hypochon·dria** \-ēə\ [NL, fr. Gk *hypochondrion* abdomen, belly, fr. neut. sing. of *hypochondrios*] **:** either hypochondriac region of the body

hy·po·chordal \ˈ== *at* HYPO- +\ *adj* [*hypo-* + *chordal*] **:** ventral to the spinal cord

hy·po·chro·mia \ˌ==+ˈkrōmēə\ *n* [NL, fr. *hypo-* + *-chromia*] **1 :** deficiency of color or pigmentation **2 :** deficiency of hemoglobin in the red blood cells (as in nutritional anemia)

hy·po·chro·mic \ˈ==ˈ=mik\ *adj* [NL *hypochromia* + E *-ic*] **:** exhibiting hypochromia

hypochromic anemia *n* **:** any of various anemias that are characterized by abnormally low blood color index, deficiency of hemoglobin, and usu. microcytic red blood cells and are associated with lack of available iron, whether by reason of excessive loss (as in hemorrhage), inadequate intake, or faulty assimilation — compare HYPERCHROMIC ANEMIA

hy·po·clei·di·an \ˈ==+ˈklīdēən\ *adj* [NL *hypocleidium* + E *-an*] **:** of or relating to a hypocleidium

hy·po·clei·di·um \ˌ==ˈ==əm\ *n, pl* **hypoclei·dia** \-ēə\ [NL, fr. *hypo-* + Gk *kleidion* small key, dim. of *kleid-, kleis* key, hook, clavicle — more at CLEID-] **:** a median process on the wishbone of many birds often connected with the sternum by a ligament or ossified with it

hy·po·condylar \ˈ== *at* HYPO- +\ *adj* [*hypo-* + *condylar*] **:** located under or below a condyle

hy·po·cone \ˈ==+,-\ *n* [*hypo-* + *cone*] **:** the principal rear inner cusp of a mammalian upper molar

hy·po·con·id \ˌ==+ˈkänəd\ *n* -s [*hypo-* + ²*con-* + *-id*] **:** the principal rear outer cusp of a mammalian lower molar

¹hy·po·coracoid \ˈ== *at* HYPO- +\ *n* [*hypo-* + *coracoid*] **:** a hypocoracoid bone

²hypocoracoid \"\ *adj* **:** of, relating to, or being the lower of two bones at the base of the pectoral fin attached behind the clavicle and sometimes regarded as homologous with the coracoid of the higher vertebrates

hypoco·rism \hīˈpäkə,rizəm, həˈ-; ˌhīpəˈkōr,izəm, ˌhip-\ *n* -s [LL *hypocorisma* diminutive (n.), fr. Gk *hypokorisma* endearing name, fr. *hypokorizesthai* to call by endearing names, fr. *hypo-* + *korizesthai* to caress (fr. *koros* boy, *korē* girl) — more at CRESCENT] **1 :** a pet name or term of endearment **2 :** the formation or use of pet names ⟨~ is the frequent practice of fond parents⟩ **3 :** BABY TALK 1b ⟨~ is hardly in keeping with human dignity —A.W.Read⟩

¹hy·po·co·ris·tic \ˌhīpəkəˈristik, ˌhip-; hīˌpäk-, hiˌ-\ *adj* [Gk *hypokoristikos* diminutive, fr. (assumed) Gk *hypokoristos* (verbal of Gk *hypokorizesthai*) + Gk *-ikos* -ic] **1 :** of, relating to, or used as a pet name or form of baby talk **2 :** forming a hypocoristic word — used of a suffix, abbreviation, or other modification

²hypocoristic \"\ *n* **:** a hypocoristic term

hy·po·cot·yl \ˈ== *at* HYPO- +,kädˑᵊl, ˌ==ˈ==\ *n* -s [ISV *hypo-* + *-cotyl*] **:** the part of the axis of a plant embryo or seedling below the cotyledon — compare EPICOTYL, RADICLE

hypocotyl arch *n* **:** the part of the stem that is normally below the cotyledons but in various seedlings (as of the bean) grows at a differential rate and curves so as to be the first structure to appear above the ground

hy·po·cotyledonary \"+\ *adj* [*hypocotyledonary*, ISV *hypo-* + *cotyledonary*] **:** located below the cotyledons

hy·po·cre·a·ce·ae \ˌ==+krēˈāsē,ē\ *n pl, cap* [NL, fr. *Hypocrea*, type genus (fr. *hypo-* + Gk *kreas* flesh) + *-aceae* — more at RAW] **:** a family of fungi that have brightly colored fleshy or membranous ascocarps, include parasites of economic plants, and are usu. included in Hypocreales but sometimes placed in Sphaeriales and then held to include the Nectriaceae

hy·po·cre·a·les \-ˈā(ˌ)lēz\ *n pl, cap* [NL, fr. *Hypocrea*, genus of fungi + *-ales*] **:** an order of fungi (subclass Euascomycetes) closely related to and probably derived from the Sphaeriales — see HYPOCREACEAE

hyp·o·crise *or* **hyp·o·crize** \ˈhipə,krīz\ *vi* -ED/-ING/-S [F *hypocriser*, fr. OF *ypocrisie* hypocrisy] **:** to act hypocritically

hy·poc·ri·sy \həˈpäkrəsē, -si *sometimes* hīˈ-\ *n* -ES [ME *ipocrisie*, fr. OF *ypocrisie*, fr. LL *hypocrisis*, fr. Gk *hypokrisis* act of playing a part on the stage, hypocrisy, outward show, fr. *hypokrinesthai* to answer, play a part on the stage, act, pretend, fr. *hypo-* + *krinesthai* to dispute, *krinein* to decide, judge — more at CERTAIN] **1 :** the act or practice of pretending to be what one is not or to have principles or beliefs that one does not have ⟨the passing stranger who took such a vitriolic joy in exposing their pretensions and their ~ —Van Wyck Brooks⟩; *esp* **:** the false assumption of an appearance of virtue or religion ⟨may admit that our conventional morality often serves as a cover for ~ and selfishness —Lucius Garvin⟩ **2 :** an act or instance of hypocrisy ⟨the little *hypocrisies* which are so frequently the rule rather than the exception in human contacts —Erle Stanley Gardner⟩

hy·poc·ri·tal \həˈpäkrədˑᵊl, ˌhipəˈkridˑᵊl\ *adj* **:** HYPOCRITICAL

¹hyp·o·crite \ˈhipə,krit, *usu* -id.+V\ *n* -s [ME *ipocrite*, *ypocrite*, fr. OF *ypocrite*, fr. LL *hypocrita*, fr. Gk *hypokritēs* actor on the stage, pretender, hypocrite, fr. *hypokrinesthai*] **:** one who pretends to be what he is not or to have principles or beliefs that he does not have; *esp* **:** one who falsely assumes an appearance of virtue or religion ⟨I dare swear he is no ~, but prays from his heart —Shak.⟩

²hypocrite \"\ *adj* [ME *ypocrite*, fr. *ypocrite, ipocrite*, n.] **:** HYPOCRITICAL ⟨our ~ century —Wyndham Lewis⟩

hypocrite plant *n* **:** MEXICAN FIRE PLANT 1

hyp·o·crit·i·cal \ˌhipəˈkridˑəkəl, -itˑ, ˌēk-\ *or* **hyp·o·crit·ic** \ˌ\ik, ˌēk\ *adj* [ˈ*hypocrite* + *-ical* or *-ic*] **:** of or relating to a hypocrite or hypocrisy **:** DISSEMBLING, FALSE, SPECIOUS ⟨a ~ gesture of modesty and virtue —Robert Graves⟩ — **hyp·o·crit·i·cal·ly** \ˌək(ə)lē, ˌēk-, -lī\ *adv*

hy·po·crystalline \ˈ== *at* HYPO- +\ *adj* [ISV *hypo-* + *crystalline*] **:** HEMICRYSTALLINE

hy·po·cu·pre·mia *or* **hy·po·cu·prae·mia** \ˌ==+,k(y)üˈprēmēə\ *also* **hy·po·cu·pro·sis** \-ˈrōsəs\ *n, pl* **hypocupremias** *or* **hypocupraemias** *also* **hypocuproses** [NL, fr. *hypo-* + *cupr-* + *-emia* or *-aemia* or *-osis*] **1 :** a deficiency in blood copper esp. of a domestic animal **2 :** a diseased condition resulting from a blood-copper deficiency — **hy·po·cu·pre·mic** \ˈ==ˌ=ˈprēmik\ *adj*

hy·po·cycloid \ˈ== *at* HYPO- +\ *n* [*hypo-* + *cycloid*] **:** a curve traced by a point on the circumference of a circle rolling internally on another circle — compare EPICYCLOID

hypocycloid *H* traced by point *P* on circle *R* rolling within fixed circle *F*

hy·po·derm \ˈ==+,dərm\ *n* [NL *hypoderma* (tissue)] **1 a :** HYPODERMIS 2b **b :** HYPOBLAST **2 :** HYPODERMIS 1

¹hy·po·der·ma \ˌ==+ˈdərmə, -ˈdəmə, -ˈdəimə\ *n* [NL, fr. *hypo-* + Gk *derma* skin, fr. *derein* to skin — more at TEAR] **1** *cap* **:** a cosmopolitan genus (the type of the family Hypodermatidae) of two-winged flies that have larvae parasitic in the tissues of vertebrates **2** -s **:** an insect or maggot of the genus *Hypoderma*

²hypoderma \"\ *n* [NL, fr. *hypo-* + Gk *derma* skin] **1 :** HYPODERMIS 2b **2 :** HYPODERMIS 1

hy·po·der·mal \ˈ==ˈ=məl\ *adj* [NL *hypoderma* + E *-al*] **:** of or relating to a hypodermis ⟨~ tissues⟩ **:** lying beneath an outer skin or epidermis ⟨~ glands⟩

hy·po·dermatic \ˈ==(ˌ)dərˈmad·ik\ *adj* [*hypo-* + *dermatic* dermal (fr. Gk *dermatikos*, fr. *dermat-* + *-ikos* -ic)] **:** HYPODERMIC — **hy·po·der·mat·i·cal·ly** \-d·ək(ə)lē\ *adv*

¹hy·po·der·mic \ˌhīpəˈdərmik, -ˈdəm-, -ˈdəim-, -mēk\ *adj* [ISV *hypo-* + *dermic*] **1 :** of or relating to the parts beneath the skin **2 a :** adapted for use in injecting medication or drugs beneath the skin **b :** administered by injection beneath the skin **3 :** resembling a hypodermic injection in effect **:** ROUSING, STIMULATING ⟨one of the most ~ personalities he had ever known —Robert Rice⟩

²hypodermic \"\ *n* -s **1 :** HYPODERMIC INJECTION **2 :** HYPODERMIC SYRINGE

hy·po·der·mi·cal·ly \-mək(ə)lē, -mēk-, -lī\ *adv* **:** in a hypodermic location or manner; *specif* **:** by means of a hypodermic

hypodermic injection *n* **:** an injection made into the subcutaneous tissues

hypodermic medication *n* **:** application of medicaments by injection under the skin

hypodermic needle *n* **1 :** NEEDLE 1c(2) **2 :** a hypodermic syringe complete with needle

hypodermic syringe *n* **:** a small syringe used with a hollow needle for injection of material into or beneath the skin

hypodermic syringe

hypodermic tablet *n* **:** a water-soluble tablet that contains a specified amount of medication and is intended for hypodermic administration

hy·po·der·mis \ˌ==ˈ=məs\ *n* [NL, fr. *hypo-* + *-dermis*] **1 :** the tissue immediately beneath the epidermis of a plant esp. when lignified, suberized, or otherwise modified to serve as a supporting and protecting layer **2 a :** HYPOBLAST **b :** the cellular layer that underlies and secretes the chitinous cuticle of arthropods and some other invertebrates

hy·po·der·moc·ly·sis \ˌ==(ˌ)dərˈmäkləsəs\ *n, pl* **hypodermocly·ses** \-lə,sēz\ [NL, fr. *hypo-* + *derm-* + *clysis*] **:** subcutaneous injection of fluids (as saline or glucose solution)

hy·po·der·mo·sis \-ˈmōsəs\ *n* -ES [NL, fr. *hypo-* + *derm-* + *-osis*] **:** infestation with warbles

hy·po·der·mous \ˈ==ˈdərməs\ *adj* [NL *hypodermis* + E *-ous*] **:** HYPODERMAL

hy·po·dochmius \ˈ== *at* HYPO- +\ *n* [NL, fr. *hypo-* + L *dochmius*] **:** a metrical line of three trochees the last of which lacks a final unstressed syllable

hy·po·dorian mode \ˌ==+...\ *n* [LL *hypodorius* hypodorian (fr. Gk *hypodōrios*, fr. *hypo-* + *Dōrios* Dorian) + E *-an*; *hypodorian mode*, trans. of Gk *hypodōria harmonia* — more at DORIAN] **1 :** a Greek mode consisting of two disjunct tetrachords represented on the white keys of the piano by a descending diatonic scale from A to A — see GREEK MODE illustration **2 :** a plagal ecclesiastical mode consisting of a tetrachord and an upper conjunct pentachord represented on the white keys of the piano by an ascending diatonic scale from A to A — see MODE illustration

hy·po·dy·namia \ˌ==+,dīˈnamēə, -,dəˈ-, -nām-\ *n* -s [NL, fr. *hypo-* + *-dynamia*] **:** decrease in strength or power

hy·po·dynamic \ˈ== *at* HYPO- +\ *adj* [*hypo-* + *dynamic*] **:** marked by or exhibiting hypodynamia

hypoed *past of* HYPO

hy·po·er·gic \ˈ==+ˌərjik\ *adj* **:** having a degree of sensitivity toward an allergen less than that typical of age group and community — compare NORMERGIC

hy·po·ergy \ˈ==,ərjē\ *n* -ES [ISV *hypo-* + all*ergy*] **:** the quality or state of being hypoergic

hy·po·eutectic \ˈ==+\ *adj* [*hypo-* + *eutectic*] **:** containing the minor component in an amount less than in the eutectic mixture

hy·po·eutectoid \"+\ *adj* [*hypo-* + *eutectoid*] **1 :** containing the minor component in an amount less than that contained in the eutectoid **2** *of steel* **:** containing less than 0.80 percent carbon

hy·po·fer·re·mia *also* **hy·po·fer·rae·mia** \ˌ==+,feˈrēmēə\ *n* -s [NL, fr. *hypo-* + L *ferrum* iron + NL *-emia* or *-aemia* — more at FARRIER] **1 :** deficiency in blood iron esp of a domestic animal **2 :** a diseased condition resulting from a blood iron deficiency

hy·po·function \ˈ== *at* HYPO-+\ *n* [*hypo-* + *function*] **:** decreased or insufficient function esp. of an endocrine gland

hypogaeum *var of* HYPOGEUM

hy·pog·a·my \hīˈpägəmē, həˈ-\ *n* -ES [*hypo-* + *-gamy*] **:** marriage into a lower caste, class, or social group

hy·po·gas·tric \ˈ== *at* HYPO- + ˌgastrik\ *adj* [F *hypogastrique*, fr. MF, fr. *hypogastre* hypogastrium (fr. Gk *hypogastrion*) + *-ique* -ic] **:** of or relating to the lower median region of the abdomen — see ABDOMINAL REGION illustration

hypogastric artery *n* **:** ILIAC ARTERY 3

hypogastric plexus *n* **:** the sympathetic nerve plexus that supplies the pelvic viscera, lies in front of the promontory of the sacrum, and extends down into two lateral portions

hypogastric vein *n* **:** a vein that accompanies the hypogastric artery, drains the pelvis and the gluteal and perineal regions, and unites with the external iliac vein to form the common iliac vein

hy·po·gas·tri·um \ˌ==+ˈgastrēəm\ *n, pl* **hypogas·tria** \-ēə\ [NL, fr. Gk *hypogastrion*, fr. *hypo-* + *gastr-* + *-ion* -ium] **:** the hypogastric region

hy·po·ge·al \ˌ==+ˈjēəl\ *or* **hy·po·ge·ous** \-əs\ *also* **hy·po·ge·an** *or* **hy·po·gae·an** \-ən\ *or* **hy·po·ge·ic** \-ēik\ *adj* [LL *hypogeus* subterranean (fr. Gk *hypogeios, hypogaios*) + E *-al* or *-ous* or *-an* or *-ic*] **1 a** *of a plant or plant part* **:** growing below the surface of the ground; *esp, of a cotyledon* **:** remaining below the ground while the epicotyl elongates **b** *of plant germination* **:** producing hypogeal cotyledons **2 :** living below the surface of the ground — used esp. of an insect; distinguished from *aerial* and *epigeal* **3** *geol* **:** occurring below the surface or within the interior of the earth ⟨~ forces⟩ — **hy·po·ge·al·ly** \-əlē\ *adv*

hy·po·gee \ˈ==+ˌjē\ *n* -s [F or L; F *hypogée*, fr. MF, fr. L *hypogeum*] **:** HYPOGEUM

hyp·o·gene \"+ˌjēn\ *adj* [*hypo-* + *-gene* (as in *epigene*)] **1 :** formed, crystallized, or lying at depths below the earth's surface **:** PLUTONIC — used of various rocks; opposed to *epigene* **2 :** formed by generally ascending solutions — used of ore deposits; opposed to *supergene*

hy·po·gen·e·sis \ˈ== *at* HYPO-+ˈjenəsəs\ *n* [NL, fr. *hypo-* + L *genesis*] **1 :** direct development without alternation of generations **2 :** underdevelopment esp. of an organ or function

hy·po·ge·net·ic \"+jəˈned·ik\ *adj* **:** of, relating to, or exhibiting hypogenesis

hy·po·gen·ic \"+ˈjenik\ *adj* [*hypogene* + *-ic*] **:** of, relating to, or constituting hypogene action or crystallization ⟨a district under the influence of ~ activities reaches a condition of seismic strain —*Encyclopedia Britannica*⟩

hy·po·gen·i·tal·ism \ˌ==+ˈjenəd·ᵊl,izəm\ *n* -s [ISV *hypo-* + *genital* + *-ism*] **:** subnormal development of genital organs **:** genital infantilism

hy·pog·e·nous \(ˈ)hīˈpäjənəs, həˈp-\ *adj* [ISV *hypo-* + *-genous*] **1 :** growing on the lower side (as of a leaf) — used esp. of a fungus **2 :** HYPOGENIC

hy·po·ge·um *or* **hy·po·gae·um** \ˌ== *at* HYPO- + ˈjēəm\ *n, pl* **hypo·gea** *or* **hypo·gaea** \-ēə\ [L, fr. Gk *hypogeion, hypogaion*, fr. neut. of *hypogeios, hypogaios* subterranean, fr. *hypo-* + *gē, gaia* earth, ground] **1 a :** the subterranean part of an ancient building **:** CELLAR **b :** the underground service galleries of an ancient amphitheater **2 :** an ancient underground burial chamber or series of such rooms **:** CATACOMB

hy·po·glos·sal \ˈ==+ˈgläsəl, -lȯs-\ *adj* [NL *hypoglossus* + E *-al*] **:** of, relating to, or constituting the hypoglossal nerve ⟨~ fissure⟩

hypoglossal nerve *also* **hypoglossal** *n* -s **:** either of the 12th and final pair of cranial nerves being a motor nerve arising usu. from three roots in the medulla oblongata and supplying muscles of the tongue and hyoid apparatus in higher vertebrates but being absent in lower forms

hy·po·glos·sus \ˌ==ˈ=səs\ *n, pl* **hypoglos·si** \-ä,sī, -ȯ,sī\ [NL, fr. *hypo-* + *-glossus* (fr. Gk *glōssa* tongue) — more at GLOSS] **:** HYPOGLOSSAL NERVE

hy·po·glot·tis \ˌ==+ˈgläd·əs\ *n* [Gk *hypoglōttis*, fr. *hypo-* + *glōtta, glōssa* tongue] **1 :** the underpart of the tongue **2 :** a sclerite adjoining the labium of various beetles

hy·po·glu·ce·mia *also* **hy·po·glu·cae·mia** \ˌ==+,glüˈsēmēə\ *n* -s [NL, fr. *hypo-* + *gluc-* + *-emia* or *-aemia*] **:** HYPOGLYCEMIA

hy·po·glycemia \ˈ==+\ *n* [NL, fr. *hypo-* + *glycemia*] **:** abnormal decrease of sugar in the blood — see HYPERINSULINISM — **hy·po·glycemic** \"+\ *adj*

hy·pog·na·thous \(ˈ)hīˈpägnəthəs\ *adj* [*hypo-* + *-gnathous*] **1 :** having the lower jaw longer than the upper **2 :** having the mouthparts ventrally directed — used esp. of certain insects with biting mouthparts directed downward and often somewhat backward; compare PROGNATHOUS

hy·po·gonadal \ˈ== *at* HYPO-+\ *adj* **1 :** suffering from or marked by hypogonadism **2 :** marked by or exhibiting deficient development of secondary sexual characteristics

hy·po·gonad·ism \ˌ==+ˈgō,na,dizəm *or* ˈgä,n-\ *n* -s [ISV *hypo-* + *gonad* + *-ism*] **1 :** functional incompetence of the gonads esp. in the male with subnormal or impaired production of both hormonal and reproductive elements **2 :** an abnormal state involving gonadal incompetence **:** EUNUCHOIDISM

hy·pog·y·nous \(ˈ)hīˈpäjənəs\ *adj* [*hypo-* + *-gynous*] **1 :** inserted upon the receptacle or axis below the gynoecium and free from it — used of sepals, petals, and stamens; compare EPIGYNOUS **2** *of a flower* **:** having sepals, petals, or stamens inserted as hypogynous parts— **hy·pog·y·ny** \ˈ==ˌnē\ *n* -ES

hy·po·hal·ite \ˈ== *at* HYPO- + ˈha,līt\ *n* [*hypohalous* acid + *-ite*] **:** a salt or ester of a hypohalous acid

hy·po·hal·ous acid \ˈ==ˈhaləs-\ *n* [*hypo-* + *hal-* + *-ous*] **:** an acid HXO derived from the halogens and including hypochlorous acid, hypobromous acid, and hypoiodous acid

hy·po·hidrosis \ˈ==+\ *n* [NL, fr. *hypo-* + *hidrosis*] **:** abnormally diminished sweating — opposed to *hyperhidrosis*

hy·po·hip·pine \ˌ==+ˈhi,pīn, -ˌpən\ *n* -s [ISV *Hypohippus* + E *-ine* (fr. *-ine*, adj. suffix)] **:** an animal or fossil of the genus *Hypohippus*

hy·po·hip·pus \-ˌpəs\ *n, cap* [NL, fr. *hypo-* + *-hippus*] **:** a genus of extinct long-necked long-bodied short-limbed horses showing adaptations for life in forests and known from remains found in the Miocene of America and the Pliocene of China

hy·po·hy·al \ˈ==+ˈhīəl\ *adj* [*hypo-* + *hyoid* + *-al*] **:** of, relating to, or constituting one or two small elements of each side of the hyoid arch of most fishes between the ceratohyal and the median basihyal

hy·po·hyaline \"+\ *adj* [*hypo-* + *hyaline*] **:** partly glassy — used of rocks

hy·poid \ˈhī,pȯid\ *adj* [short for *hyperboloidal*] **:** utilizing, used for, or relating to hypoid gears ⟨~ rear axle⟩ ⟨~ grease⟩

hypoid gear *also* **hypoid** *n* -s **:** one of a pair of bevel gears that are used esp. in automotive transmissions, are designed so that the axis of the pinion does not intersect the axis of the gear, and have the teeth on the pinion cut spirally and the teeth on the gear cut nonradially

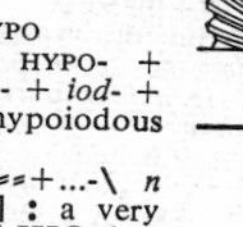
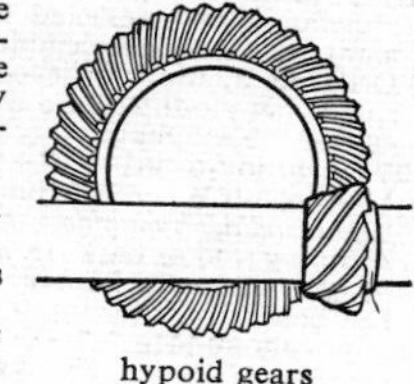
hypoid gears

hypoing *pres part of* HYPO

hy·po·io·dite \ˌ== *at* HYPO- + ˈīə,dīt\ *n* -s [ISV *hypo-* + *iod-* + *-ite*] **:** a salt or ester of hypoiodous acid

hy·po·iodous acid \ˈ==+...\ *n* [ISV *hypo-* + *iodous*] **:** a very unstable very weak acid HIO that resembles hypochlorous acid and is obtained in solution by treating mercury oxide (sense b) with iodine in water or in the form of unstable salts in solution by reaction of iodine with alkali

hy·po·ionian mode \"+...\ *n* [*hypo-* + L *ionius* Ionian + E *-an* — more at IONIAN] **:** a plagal ecclesiastical mode consisting of a tetrachord and an upper conjunct pentachord represented on the white keys of the piano by an ascending diatonic scale from G to G — see MODE illustration

hy·po·ischium \"+\ *n* [NL, fr. *hypo-* + *ischium*] **:** a small median bony rod passing backward from the ischial symphysis and supporting the ventral wall of the cloaca in most lizards

hy·po·ka·le·mia \ˌ==+,kāˈlēmēə\ *n* -s [NL, fr. *hypo-* + *kalium* + *-emia*] **:** a deficiency of potassium in the blood —**hy·po·ka·le·mic** \ˈ==ˌ=ˈmik\ *adj*

hy·po·limnetic \ˈ== *at* HYPO- +\ *or* **hy·po·lim·ni·al** \"+ˈlimnēəl\ *adj* [NL *hypolimnion* + E *-etic* or *-ial*] **:** of or relating to a hypolimnion

hy·po·lim·ni·on \-ˈlimnē,än, -ēən\ *n, pl* **hypolim·nia** \-ēə\ [NL, fr. *hypo-* + Gk *limnion* small lake, dim. of *limnē* lake, sea] **:** the part of a lake below the thermocline made up of water that is stagnant and of essentially uniform temperature except during the period of overturn — compare EPILIMNION

hy·po·lithic \ˈ==+\ *adj* [*hypo-* + Gk *lithos* stone + E *-ic*] *of plants* **:** growing beneath rocks

hy·po·locrian mode \"+...\ *n* [*hypo-* + *locrian*] **:** a plagal ecclesiastical mode consisting of a tetrachord and an upper conjunct pentachord represented on the white keys of the piano by an ascending diatonic scale from F to F but rarely used because its tetrachord and pentachord comprise respectively the forbidden augmented fourth and diminished fifth — see MODE illustration

hy·po·lydian mode \"+...\ *n* [LL *hypolydius* hypolydian (fr. Gk *hypolydios*, fr. *hypo-* + *lydios* Lydian) + E *-an*; *hypolydian mode*, trans. of Gk *hypolydios tonos*] **1 :** a Greek mode consisting of two disjunct tetrachords represented on the white keys of the piano by a descending diatonic scale from F to F — see GREEK MODE illustration **2 :** a plagal ecclesiastical mode consisting of a tetrachord and an upper conjunct pentachord represented on the white keys of the piano by an ascending diatonic scale from C to C — see MODE illustration

hy·po·mag·ne·se·mia \ˌ⁼⁼+ˌmagnəˈsēmēə\ *n* -S [NL, fr. *hypo-* + *magnesium* + *-emia*] **:** deficiency of magnesium in the blood constituting a prime factor in grass tetany or milk fever in cattle — **hy·po·mag·ne·se·mic** \ˌ⁼⁼ˌ⁼⁼ˈsēmik\ *adj*

hy·po·ma·nia \ˌ⁼⁼+ˈmānēə\ *n* [NL, fr. *hypo-* + LL *mania*] **:** a mild mania — **hy·po·man·ic** \ˌ⁼⁼ˈmanik\ *adj*

hy·po·menorrhea \ˌ⁼⁼ *at* HYPO- +\ *n* [NL, fr. *hypo-* + *menorrhea*] **:** decreased menstrual flow

hy·po·metabolism \ˈ"+\ *n* [*hypo-* + *metabolism*] **:** a state (as in myxedema or hypothyroidism) marked by an abnormally low metabolic rate

hy·po·mixolydian mode \ˈ"+...-\ *n* [*hypo-* + *mixolydian (mode)*] **:** a plagal ecclesiastical mode consisting of a tetrachord and an upper conjunct pentachord represented on the white keys of the piano by an ascending diatonic scale from D to D — see MODE illustration

hy·po·moch·li·on \ˌ⁼⁼+ˈmäklēˌän\ *n* -S [L, fr. Gk, fr. *hypo-* + *mochlion* small lever, dim. of *mochlos* lever; akin to Gk *mogos* exertion, labor — more at MOGI-] *archaic* **:** FULCRUM

hy·po·morph \ˈ⁼⁼+ˌmȯrf\ *n* -S [*hypo-* + *-morph*] **1 :** a short-limbed and round-headed person **:** ENDOMORPH — opposed to *hypermorph* **2 :** a mutant gene having a similar but weaker effect than the corresponding wild-type gene — compare HYPERMORPH — **hy·po·mor·phic** \ˌ⁼⁼ˈmȯrfik\ *adj*

hy·po·mor·pho·sis \ˌ⁼⁼+ˈmȯ(r)fəsəs *sometimes* -ˌmȯ(r)ˈfōs-\ *n* [NL, fr. *hypo-* + *-morphosis*] **1 :** DEDIFFERENTIATION 1 **2 :** inhibition of differentiation (as in an embryo)

hy·po·motility \ˌ⁼⁼ *at* HYPO- +\ *n* [ISV *hypo-* + *motility*] **:** abnormal deficiency of movement; *specif* **:** decreased motility of the stomach or intestine — compare HYPERMOTILITY

hy·po·nas·tic \ˈ"+ˈnastik\ *adj* [ISV *hyponasty* + *-ic*] **:** of, relating to, or caused by hyponasty — **hy·po·nas·ti·cal·ly** \-tək(ə)lē\ *adv*

hy·po·nas·ty \ˈ⁼⁼ˌnastē\ *n* -ES [ISV *hypo-* + *-nasty*; orig. formed as G *hyponastie*] **:** a nastic movement in which a plant part is bent inward and upward

hy·po·na·tre·mia \ˌ⁼⁼+nəˈtrēmēə\ *n* -S [NL, fr. *hypo-* + *natrium* + *-emia*] **:** deficiency of sodium in the blood

hy·po·nitrite \ˌ⁼⁼ *at* HYPO- +\ *n* [ISV *hyponitr-* (fr. *hyponitrous acid*) + *-ite*] **:** a salt or ester of hyponitrous acid

hy·po·nitrous acid \ˈ"+ . . .-\ *n* [*hypo-* + *nitrous (acid)*] **:** an explosive crystalline weak acid $H_2N_2O_2$ or HON=NOH obtained usu. in the form of its salts by oxidation of hydroxylamine or by reduction of nitrites

hy·po·nome \ˈ⁼⁼+ˌnōm\ *n* -S [Gk *hyponomē* underground passage, *hyponomos* underground passage, water pipe, conduit, fr. *hyponemesthai* to undermine, fr. *hypo-* + *nemesthai* to inhabit, spread over, be situated upon, middle of *nemein* to distribute, pasture — more at NIMBLE] **:** the swimming funnel of a cephalopod — **hy·po·nom·ic** \ˌ⁼⁼ˈnämik\ *adj*

hy·po·nutrition \ˌ⁼⁼+\ *n* [*hypo-* + *nutrition*] **:** UNDERNUTRITION

hy·po·nych·i·al \ˌ⁼⁼+ˈnikēəl\ *adj* [NL *hyponychium* + E *-al*] **1 :** of or relating to the hyponychium **2 :** located under a nail

hy·po·nych·i·um \ˌ⁼⁼ˈ⁼⁼əm\ *n* -S [NL, fr. *hypo-* + *-onychium*] **1 :** the thickened layer of epidermis beneath the free end of a nail **2 :** MATRIX 1c

hy·po·nym \ˈ⁼⁼+ˌnim\ *n* -S [*hypo-* + *-onym*] **:** NOMEN NUDUM; *specif* **:** a generic name not based on a recognizable species — **hy·po·nym·ic** \ˌ⁼⁼ˈnimik\ *adj* — **hy·pon·y·mous** \(ˈ)hīˈpänəməs, hə̇ˈp-\ *adj*

hy·po–on·to·morph \ˌ⁼⁼+ˈäntōˌmȯrf\ *n* -S [*hypo-* + *ont-* + *-morph*] **:** an endomorphic individual

hy·po·ovar·i·an·ism \ˌ⁼⁼+ōˈva(a)rēəˌnizəm\ *n* -S [*hypo-* + *ovarian* + *-ism*] **:** a condition marked by a deficiency of ovarian function **:** female hypogonadism — compare INFANTILISM

hy·po·parathyroid \ˌ⁼⁼ *at* HYPO- +\ *adj* [prob. back-formation from *hypoparathyroidism*] **:** of or affected by hypoparathyroidism

hy·po·par·a·thy·roid·ism \ˌ⁼⁼+ˌparəˈthīˌrȯiˌdizəm\ *n* -S [ISV *hypo-* + *parathyroid* + *-ism*] **:** deficiency of parathyroid hormone in the body; *also* **:** the resultant abnormal state marked by low serum calcium and a tendency to chronic tetany

hy·po·par·ia \ˌ⁼⁼+ˈpa(a)rēə\ *n pl, cap* [NL, fr. *hypo-* + *-paria* (fr. Gk *pareia* cheek)] **:** an order of trilobites with marginal facial suture and small pygidium known from the Lower Ordovician through the Cambrian — **hy·po·par·i·an** \ˌ⁼⁼ˈ⁼⁼ən\ *adj or n*

hy·po·pha·lan·gism \ˌ⁼⁼+fəˈlanˌjizəm\ *n* -S [*hypo-* + *phalange* + *-ism*] **:** a condition in which the number of phalanges of fingers or toes is less than normal

hy·poph·a·mine \hīˈpäfəˌmēn, -ˌmən\ *n* [NL *hypophysis* + E *amine*] **:** either of two hormones obtained from the posterior lobe of the pituitary gland: **a :** OXYTOCIN **b :** VASOPRESSIN

¹hy·po·pharyngeal \ˌ⁼⁼ *at* HYPO- +\ *adj* [*hypo-* + *pharyngeal*] **1 :** located below or in the lower part of the pharynx **2** [fr. NL *hypopharynx*, after NL *pharynx*: E *pharyngeal*] **:** of or relating to the hypopharynx **3 :** of or relating to a bone behind the last functional gill arch in teleost fishes that represents the ceratobranchial of the fifth branchial arch

²hypopharyngeal \ˈ"\ *n* **:** a hypopharyngeal element esp. of bone

hy·po·pharynx \ˈ"+\ *n* [NL, fr. *hypo-* + *pharynx*] **1 :** an appendage or thickened fold on the floor of the mouth of many insects that resembles a tongue, is very conspicuous in Orthoptera, and is believed to be sensory in function although sometimes modified into a piercing organ **2 :** the pharyngeal end of the esophagus

hy·po·phloe·o·dal \ˈ"+ˈflēədᵊl\ *or* **hy·po·phloe·od·ic** \ˈ"+flēˈädik\ *or* **hy·po·phloe·ous** \ˈ"+ˈflēəs\ *adj* [*hypophloeodal*, *hypophloeodic* fr. *hypo-* + Gk *phloiōdēs* resembling rind or bark (fr. *phloios* bark + *-ōdēs* -ode) + E *-al* or *-ic*; *hypophloeous* fr. *hypo-* + Gk *phloios* + E *-ous*] **:** living just beneath the bark ⟨~ lichens⟩

hy·po·phosphate \ˈ"+\ *n* [ISV *hypophosph-* (fr. *hypophosphoric acid*) + *-ate*] **:** a salt or ester of hypophosphoric acid

hy·po·phos·pha·te·mia \ˌ⁼⁼+ˌfäsfəˈtēmēə\ *n* -S [NL, fr. *hypo-* + ISV *phosphate* + NL *-emia*] **:** deficiency of phosphates in the blood that is due to inadequate intake, excessive excretion, or defective absorption and that results in bone defects and other disturbances

hy·po·phosphite \ˌ⁼⁼+\ *n* [*hypophosphorous (acid)* + *-ite*] **:** a salt of hypophosphorous acid

hy·po·phosphoric acid \ˈ" + . . . -\ *n* [ISV *hypo-* + *phosphoric*] **:** an unstable tetrabasic acid $H_4P_2O_6$ usu. obtained in the form of its salts (as by oxidation of red phosphorus in alkaline solution)

hy·po·phosphorous acid \ˈ" + . . . -\ *n* [F *hypophosphoreux*, fr. *hypo-* + *phosphoreux* phosphorous] **:** a low-melting deliquescent crystalline strong monobasic acid H_3PO_2 usu. obtained by acidifying one of its salts and used as a reducing agent

hy·po·phre·nia \ˌ⁼⁼+ˈfrēnēə\ *or* **hy·po·phre·no·sis** \ˈ"+frəˈnōsəs\ *n, pl* **hypophrenias** \-əz\ *or* **hypophreno·ses** \-ōˌsēz\ [NL, fr. *hypo-* + *-phrenia* or *-phrenosis* (fr. Gk *phren-*, *phrēn* mind, heart + NL *-osis*)] **:** MENTAL DEFICIENCY — **hy·po·phren·ic** \ˌ⁼⁼ˈfrenik *also* -rēn-\ *adj*

hy·po·phrygian mode \ˌ⁼⁼ + . . . -\ *n* [*hypophrygian* (fr. LL *hypophrygius* hypophrygian — fr. Gk *hypophrygios*, fr. *hypo-* + *phrygios* Phrygian, fr. *Phrygia*, ancient country in west central Asia Minor — + E *-an*) + *mode*; trans. of Gk *hypophrygia harmonia*] **1 :** a Greek mode consisting of two disjunct tetrachords represented on the white keys of the piano by a descending diatonic scale from G to G — see GREEK MODE illustration **2 :** a plagal ecclesiastical mode consisting of a tetrachord and an upper conjunct pentachord represented on the white keys of the piano by an ascending diatonic scale from B to B — see MODE illustration

hy·poph·y·ge \hīˈpäfə(ˌ)jē, hə̇ˈp-\ *n* -S [NL, fr. Gk *hypophygē* refuge, recess, fr. *hypo-* + *phygē* flight, fr. *pheugein* to flee — more at FUGITIVE] **:** a hollow curvature esp. under a Doric capital in some Greek buildings — compare APOPHYGE

hy·po·phyl·lous \ˌ⁼⁼ *at* HYPO- +ˈfiləs\ *adj* [*hypo-* + *-phyllous*] **:** located on the under side of a leaf — compare EPIGENOUS

hy·poph·y·se·al \(ˌ)hīˌpäfəˈsēəl, -ˈzē- *also* ˌhīpəˈfizēəl\ *also* **hy·po·phys·i·al** \ˌhīpəˈfizēəl\ *adj* [*hypophyseal*, alter. of *hypophysial*; *hypophysial* fr. NL *hypophysis* + E *-al*] **:** of or relating to the hypophysis

hy·poph·y·sec·to·mize \(ˌ)hīˌpäfəˈsektəˌmīz\ *vt* -ED/-ING/-S **:** to remove the pituitary body from ⟨*hypophysectomized* animals⟩

hy·poph·y·sec·to·my \-təmē\ *n* -ES [ISV *hypophys-* (fr. NL *hypophysis*) + *-ectomy*] **:** surgical removal of the pituitary body

hy·poph·y·sis \hīˈpäfəsə̇s\ *n, pl* **hypophyses** \-əˌsēz\ [NL, outgrowth, pituitary body (esp. in *hypophysis cerebri*, lit., outgrowth of the brain), fr. Gk, outgrowth, attachment underneath, process of a bone, fr. *hypophyein* to grow up below, fr. *hypo-* + *phyein* to grow, produce, bring forth — more at BE] **1** *also* **hypophysis ce·re·bri** \-səˈrēˌbrī, -ˈserə,-\ **:** PITUITARY BODY **2 a :** a cell or cells in a seed plant resulting from the transverse division of the next adjoining suspensor cell and giving rise to the tip of the root **b :** APOPHYSIS 2

hypopi *pl of* HYPOPUS

hy·po·pi·al \(ˈ)hīˈpōpēəl, hə̇ˈp-\ *adj* [NL *hypopus* + E *-ial*] **:** of, relating to, or consisting of a hypopus

hy·po·pi·tu·i·ta·rism \ˌ⁼⁼ *at* HYPO- + pə̇ˈtüətəˌrizəm, -pəˈtyü-\ *n* -S [ISV *hypo-* + *pituitar-* (fr. *pituitary*) + *-ism*] **:** deficient activity of the pituitary body esp. in the production of growth-regulating hormones or of those fractions (as the gonadotrophic or thyrotrophic hormones) that regulate the secretory activity of other endocrine organs — compare HYPERPITUITARISM

hy·po·pituitary \ˌ⁼⁼+\ *adj* [*hypo-* + *pituitary*] **:** of or relating to pituitary deficiency

hy·pop·i·tys \hīˈpäpəd·əs, hə̇ˈ-\ *n, cap* [NL, fr. *hypo-* + Gk *pitys* pine — more at PINE (tree)] *in some classifications* **:** a genus of plants comprising the pinesaps and including leafless saprophytic herbs with erect stems and racemose flowers that are commonly placed in the genus *Monotropa*

hy·po·plankton \ˌ⁼⁼ *at* HYPO- +\ *n* [*hypo-* + *plankton*] **:** the plankton inhabiting the greatest depths esp. immediately over the bottom but sometimes throughout the whole abyssal zone — **hy·po·planktonic** \ˈ"+\ *adj*

hy·po·pla·sia \ˌ⁼⁼+ˈplāzh(ē)ə\ *n* -S [NL, fr. *hypo-* + *-plasia*] **:** a condition of arrested development in which an organ or part remains below the normal size or in an immature state — compare HYPERPLASIA

hy·po·plas·tic \ˌ⁼⁼ˈplastik\ *adj* [*hypo-* + *plastic*] **:** of, relating to, or marked by hypoplasia

hypoplastic anemia *n* **:** APLASTIC ANEMIA

hy·po·plastral \ˌ⁼⁼+\ *adj* **:** of or relating to the hypoplastron

hy·po·plastron \ˈ"+\ *n* [*hypo-* + *plastron*] **:** either of the third lateral pair of bony plates in the plastron of most turtles

hy·po·ploid \ˈ⁼⁼+ˌplȯid\ *adj* [*hypo-* + *-ploid*] **:** having a chromosome number a little smaller than an exact multiple of the monoploid number

hy·po·pneus·tic \ˌ⁼⁼+ˈn(y)üstik, ˌhīˌpäpˈ-\ *adj* [*hypo-* + *-pneustic*] **:** having some of the respiratory spiracles lacking or nonfunctional — used chiefly of larval insects

hy·po·po·tas·se·mia \ˌ⁼⁼+pəˌtaˈsēmēə\ *n* -S [NL, fr. *hypo-* + *potassium* + *-emia*] **:** HYPOKALEMIA — **hy·po·po·tas·se·mic** \ˌ⁼⁼⁼ˌ⁼ˈsēmik\ *adj*

hy·po·pro·sex·ia \ˌ⁼⁼+prəˈseksēə\ *n* -S [NL, fr. *hypo-* + Gk *prosexis* attention (fr. *prosechein* to pay attention to, fr. *pros* toward + *echein* to hold) + NL *-ia*] *psychol* **:** defective fixity of attention on a stimulus object

hy·po·pro·tein·emia \ˈ"+ˌprōˌtēˈnēmēə, ˌprōd·ēəˈn-\ *n* -S [NL, fr. *hypo-* + ISV *protein* + NL *-emia*] **:** abnormal decrease of protein in the blood — **hy·po·pro·te·in·e·mic** \ˌ⁼⁼⁼⁼⁼ˈnēmik\ *adj*

hy·po·pro·throm·bin·e·mia \ˌ⁼⁼+(ˌ)prōˌthrämbəˈnēmēə\ *n* -S [NL, fr. *hypo-* + ISV *prothrombin* + NL *-emia*] **:** deficiency of prothrombin in the blood usu. due to vitamin K deficiency or liver disease (esp. obstructive jaundice) and resulting in delayed clotting of blood or spontaneous bleeding (as from the nose or into the skin) — **hy·po·pro·throm·bin·e·mic** \ˌ⁼⁼(ˌ)⁼ˌ⁼⁼⁼ˈnēmik\ *adj*

hy·pop·ter·on \hīˈpäptəˌrän, hə̇ˈ-\ *n, pl* **hypop·tera** \-ərə\ [NL, fr. *hypo-* + Gk *pteron* feather, wing — more at FEATHER] **:** the tuft of feathers of a bird's wing comprising the axillars

hy·pop·ti·lum \hīˈpäptələm, hə̇ˈ-\ *n, pl* **hypopti·la** \-lə\ [NL, fr. *hypo-* + Gk *ptilon* wing, feather, down; akin to Gk *petesthai* to fly — more at FEATHER] **:** AFTERSHAFT

hyp·o·pus \ˈhipəpəs\ *n, pl* **hypo·pi** \-ˌpī\ [NL, fr. Gk *hypopous* furnished with feet, fr. *hypo-* + *pous* foot — more at FOOT] **:** a nonfeeding migratory larva of some mites that is passively distributed by an animal to which it has attached itself

hy·po·pyg·i·al \ˌ⁼⁼ *at* HYPO- + ˈpijēəl\ *adj* [NL *hypopygium* + E *-al*] **:** of or relating to a hypopygium

hy·po·pyg·i·um \ˌ⁼⁼+ˈpijēəm\ *also* **hy·po·py·gid·i·um** \ˈ"+pəˈjidēəm\ *n, pl* **hypopyg·ia** *also* **hypopygid·ia** \-ēə\ [NL, fr. *hypo-* + *-pygium* (fr. *pyg-* + *-ium*) or *-pygidium* (fr. Gk *pygidion* small rump) — more at PYGIDIUM] **:** a modified 9th abdominal segment of many insects with which the copulatory apparatus is associated; *esp* **:** such a modified segment together with the copulatory apparatus of a dipterous insect

hy·po·py·on \hīˈpōpēˌän, hə̇ˈ-\ *n* -S [NL, fr. Gk, ulcer, fr. *hypopyon*, neut. of *hypopyos* suppurative, fr. *hypo-* + *pyon* pus — more at FOUL] **:** a collection of pus in the anterior chamber of the eye

hyp·or·che·ma \ˌhīpə(r)ˈkēmə\ *or* **hyp·or·cheme** \ˈ⁼⁼⁼(r)ˌkēm\ *n, pl* **hyporchema·ta** \-məd·ə\ *or* **hyporchemes** [Gk *hyporchēma*, fr. *hyporcheisthai* to dance to music, fr. *hypo-* + *orcheisthai* to dance — more at ORCHESTRA] **:** an ancient Greek choral song and dance usu. in honor of Apollo or Dionysus — **hy·por·che·mat·ic** \ˌ⁼⁼⁼kēˈmad·ik\ *adj*

hy·po·rhined \ˌ⁼⁼ *at* HYPO- + ˌrīnd\ *adj* [*hypo-* + *rhin-* + *-ed*] **:** having small nostrils

hy·po·ri·bo·fla·vin·o·sis \ˌ⁼⁼+ˌrībəˌflāvəˈnōsə̇s *also* -rib- *or* -lav-\ *n, pl* **hyporiboflavino·ses** \-ōˌsēz\ [NL, fr. *hypo-* + ISV *riboflavin* + NL *-osis*] **:** ARIBOFLAVINOSIS

hy·por·rhyth·mic \ˌ⁼⁼+ˈrithmik *sometimes* -ithm-\ *adj* [Gk *hyporrhythmos* hyporrhythmic (fr. *hypo-* + *rhythmos* measure, rhythm) + E *-ic* — more at RHYTHM] *in Greek and Latin prosody* **:** deficient as to rhythm — used of a hexameter in which the end of a word coincides with the end of each foot and which accordingly has no true caesura

hypos *pl of* HYPO, *pres 3d sing of* HYPO

hy·po·scleral \ˈ"+\ *adj* [*hypo-* + *scleral*] **:** located beneath the sclera of the eye

hy·po·scope \ˈ⁼⁼+ˌskōp\ *n* [*hypo-* + *-scope*] **:** a military periscope designed for use as a hand instrument or for attachment to a rifle

hy·po·secretion \ˌ⁼⁼ *at* HYPO- +\ *n* [*hypo-* + *secretion*] **:** production of a body secretion at an abnormally slow rate or in abnormally small quantities

hy·po·sensitive \ˈ"+\ *adj* [*hypo-* + *sensitive*] **:** exhibiting or marked by deficient response to stimulation — **hy·po·sensitivity** \ˈ"+\ *n*

hy·po·sensitization \ˈ"+\ *n* [*hypo-* + *sensitization*] **:** the state or process of being hyposensitized

hy·po·sensitize \ˈ"+\ *vt* [*hypo-* + *sensitize*] **:** to reduce the sensitivity of (an individual) esp. to an allergen **:** DESENSITIZE

hy·po·spa·dia \ˌ⁼⁼ˈspādēə\ *or* **hy·po·spa·dy** \ˈ⁼⁼ˌspādē\ *n, pl* **hypospadias** *or* **hypospadies** [NL *hypospadia*, fr. Gk *hypospadias* man with hypospadias] **:** HYPOSPADIAS

hy·po·spa·di·ac \ˌ⁼⁼ˈspādēˌak\ *adj* [Gk *hypospadias* man with hypospadias + E *-ac* (as in *elegiac*)] **:** of or affected with hypospadias

hy·po·spa·di·as \ˌ⁼⁼ˈspādēəs\ *n* -ES [NL, fr. Gk, man with hypospadias, fr. *hypo-* + *-spadias* (prob. fr. *spadōn* eunuch, fr. *span* to tear, pluck off, pull, draw) — more at SPAN] **:** an abnormality of the penis in which the urethra opens on the under surface

hy·po·sphene \ˈ⁼⁼+ˌsfēn\ *n* [*hypo-* + Gk *sphēn* wedge] **:** a median wedge-shaped posterior process on the neural arch of the vertebrae of certain extinct reptiles — compare HYPANTRUM

hypospray \ˈ⁼(ˌ)⁼ˌ⁼\ *n* [³*hypo* + *spray*] **:** a device with a spring and plunger for administering a medicated solution by forcing it in extremely fine jets through the unbroken skin

hy·po·stase \ˈ⁼⁼ *at* HYPO-+ˌstās\ *n* -S [NL *hypostasis*] **:** a disk of lignified tissue formed at the base of the ovule in certain orders of plants

hy·pos·ta·sis \hīˈpästəsə̇s\ *n, pl* **hyposta·ses** \-əˌsēz\ [LL, substance, sediment, fr. Gk, support, sediment, foundation, substance, fr. *hyphistasthai* to support, stand under, fr. *hypo-* + *histasthai* to stand, middle of *histanai* to cause to stand — more at STAND] **1 a :** something that settles at the bottom of a fluid **:** SEDIMENT, DEPOSIT **b :** the settling of blood in the dependent parts of an organ or body **2 a** *in the original Nicene use* **:** the essence or substance of the triune Godhead — called also *ousia* **b** *in later use* (1) one of the persons of the Godhead or Trinity (2) **:** the individual as subject or substance **c :** the whole personality of Christ as distinguished from his human and divine natures **3** *obs* **:** basis of support **:** FOUNDATION **4** *philos* **a** *Plotinism* **:** any of the three aspects or essential principles constituting the Godhead: (1) **:** the transcendent one (2) **:** NOUS, SPIRIT (3) **:** LOGOS, WORLD SOUL **b** *Thomism* **:** the substance or rational nature of an individual or person; *also* **:** PERSON, INDIVIDUAL **c :** substance as an ontological entity or category **:** a self-subsistent reality or mode of being **d :** a hypothetical or conceptual entity **:** a reified abstraction **:** HYPOSTATIZATION ⟨as far as the Buddhist ~ of the law is concerned, we should search in vain for a Christian equivalent —Joachim Wach⟩ ⟨for legal purposes a right is only the ~ of a prophecy —Alfred Lief⟩ **5** [NL, fr. LL] **:** failure of a gene to produce its usual effect when coupled with another gene that is epistatic toward it **6** [NL, fr. LL] **:** HYPOSTASE **7 a :** the mention of a word, grammatical form, or word group (as *in*, *un-*, *in the dark*) as a linguistic element **b :** a linguistic element so referred to — called also *citation form*, *quotation noun*

hy·pos·ta·size \hīˈpästəˌsīz\ *vt* -ED/-ING/-S [LL *hypostasis* + E *-ize*] **:** HYPOSTATIZE

hy·po·stat·ic \ˌ⁼⁼ *at* HYPO-+ˈstad·ik\ *adj* [Gk *hypostatikos*, fr. *hypostatos* substantially existing (verbal of *hyphistasthai* to support, stand under) + *-ikos* -ic] **1** *or* **hy·po·stat·i·cal** \-d·ə̇kəl\ **:** of or relating to substance **:** ELEMENTAL **2** *or* **hypostatical** [F *hypostatique*, fr. MF, fr. ML *hypostaticus*, fr. Gk *hypostatikos*] **:** of or relating to theological hypostasis **3** [fr. NL *hypostasis*, after NL *-stasis*: E *-static*] **a** *of a gene* **:** exhibiting hypostasis in the presence of a corresponding epistatic gene **b** *of a hereditary character* **:** suppressed by epistasis **:** appearing recessive to another character due to mediation by a hypostatic gene **4** [fr. LL *hypostasis*, after such pairs as E *emphasis*: *emphatic*] **:** depending on or due to hypostasis ⟨~ congestion⟩ ⟨~ pneumonia⟩ — **hy·po·stat·i·cal·ly** \-d·ə̇k(ə)lē\ *adv*

hypostatic union *n* [part trans. of F *union hypostatique*, fr. MF] **:** union in one hypostasis; *esp* **:** the union of the divine and human natures of Christ in one hypostasis

hy·pos·ta·ti·za·tion \hīˌpästəd·əˈzāshən\ *n* -S **1 :** an act or instance of hypostatizing **:** REIFICATION ⟨realism is built on the fallacy of ~, the supposition that an abstract term must somehow have a denotation —T.T.Lafferty⟩ **2 :** something that is hypostatized

hy·pos·ta·tize *or* **hy·pos·ta·tise** \hīˈpästəˌtīz\ *vt* -ED/-ING/-S [Gk *hypostatos* substantially existing + E *-ize* or *-ise*] **:** to transform (a make into or regard as a hypostasis: **a :** to transform (a conceptual entity) into or construe as a self-subsistent substance ⟨we are told that the conception of God, or the Sacred, or the Mana, or the Totem, is nothing but *hypostatized* society itself —P.A.Sorokin⟩ **b :** to assume as concrete **:** REIFY ⟨our ingrained habit of *hypostatizing* impressions, of seeing things and not sense-data —Susanne K. Langer⟩

hy·po·sthenia \ˌ⁼⁼ *at* HYPO-+\ *n* [NL, fr. *hypo-* + Gk *sthenos* strength + NL *-ia* — more at STHENIC] **:** lack of strength **:** bodily weakness — **hy·po·sthenic** \ˈ"+\ *adj*

hy·pos·the·nu·ria \hīˌpästhəˈn(y)u̇rēə\ *n* -S [NL, fr. *hypo-* + Gk *sthenos* strength + NL *-uria*] **:** the secretion of urine of low specific gravity due to inability of the kidney to concentrate the urine normally — **hy·po·sthe·nu·ric** \ˌ⁼⁼ˌ⁼ˈn(y)u̇rik\ *adj*

hy·pos·to·ma \hīˈpästəmə, hə̇ˈ-\ *n, pl* **hypostomas** \-məz\ *or* **hy·po·sto·ma·ta** \ˌ⁼⁼ *at* HYPO-+ˈstōməd·ə\ [NL, fr. *hypo-* + *-stoma*] **:** HYPOSTOME

hy·po·sto·ma·ta \ˌ⁼⁼ *at* HYPO-+ˈstōməd·ə\ [NL, fr. *hypo-* + *-stomata*] *syn of* HYPOSTOMIDES

hy·po·sto·mat·ic \ˌ⁼⁼+ˌstōˈmad·ik\ *adj* [*hypo-* + *stomatic*] *of a leaf* **:** having stomata only on the underside

hy·po·stom·a·tous \ˈ"+ˈstäməd·əs, -tōm-\ *adj* [*hypo-* + *-stomatous*] **1** *of a fish* **:** having the mouth on the lower side **2 :** HYPOSTOMATIC

¹hy·po·stome \ˈ⁼⁼+ˌstōm\ *n* -S [ISV *hypo-* + *-stome*] **:** any of several structures associated with the mouth: as **a :** the labrum of a trilobite or crustacean **b :** the manubrium of a hydrozoan **c :** an organ like a rod that arises at the base of the beak in various mites and in ticks

²hypostome \ˈ"\ *n* -S [NL *Hypostoma*, genus of fishes, fr. *hypo-* + *-stoma*] **:** a fish of the order Hypostomides

hy·po·stom·i·des \ˌ⁼⁼+ˈstäməˌdēz\ *n pl, cap* [NL, fr. *Hypostoma*, genus of fishes] **:** an order or suborder of teleost fishes coextensive with the family Pegasidae

hy·pos·to·mous \(ˈ)hīˈpästəməs, hə̇ˈp-\ *adj* [*hypo-* + *-stomous*] **:** HYPOSTOMATOUS

hy·po·stroma \ˌ⁼⁼ *at* HYPO- +\ *n* [NL, fr. *hypo-* + *stroma*] **:** a compact mass of hyphae below the true stroma and beneath the host epidermis of a fungus — **hy·po·stromal** \ˈ"+\ *adj*

¹hy·po·style \ˈ⁼⁼+ˌstīl\ *adj* [Gk *hypostylos* resting upon pillars, fr. *hypo-* + *stylos* pillar] **:** having the roof resting upon rows of columns **:** constructed by means of columns ⟨~ halls of antiquity⟩

²hypostyle \ˈ"\ *n* [¹*hypostyle*] **:** a hypostyle hall

³hypostyle \ˈ"\ *n* [*hypo-* + *style* (cusp)] **:** a small cusp between the hypocone and metacone of a molar tooth

hy·po·stypsis \ˌ⁼⁼ *at* HYPO-+\ *n* [NL, fr. *hypo-* + *stypsis*] **:** mild or moderate astringency

hy·po·styptic \ˈ"+\ *adj* [*hypo-* + *styptic*] **:** mildly or moderately styptic

hy·po·sulfite \ˈ"+\ *n* [*hyposulf-* (fr. *hyposulfurous acid*) + *-ite*] **1 :** THIOSULFATE — used chiefly in photography **2 :** HYDROSULFITE

hy·po·sulfurous acid \ˈ"+. . .-\ *n* [ISV *hypo-* + *sulfurous (acid)*] **1** *archaic* **:** THIOSULFURIC ACID **2 :** HYDROSULFUROUS ACID

hy·po·syllogistic \ˈ"+\ *adj* [*hypo-* + *syllogistic*] **:** having syllogistic value or purpose without the form

hy·po·synergia \ˈ"+\ *n* [NL, fr. *hypo-* + *synergia*] **:** imperfect coordination

hy·po·tac·tic \ˈ"+ˈtaktik\ *adj* [Gk *hypotaktikos*, fr. (assumed) Gk *hypotaktos* (verbal of Gk *hypotassein* to arrange under) + Gk *-ikos* -ic] **:** of, relating to, or exhibiting hypotaxis

hy·po·tarsus \ˈ"+\ *n* [NL, fr. *hypo-* + *tarsus*] **:** CALCANEUM 2

hy·po·tax·is \ˌ⁼⁼+ˈtaksə̇s\ *n* [Gk, subjection, submission, fr. *hypotassein* to arrange under, subject, put after, fr. *hypo-* + *tassein* to arrange — more at TACTICS] **:** syntactic subordination (as by a conjunction) — opposed to *parataxis*

hy·po·tension \ˌ⁼⁼ *at* HYPO-+\ *n* [ISV *hypo-* + *tension*] **:** abnormally low tension esp. of blood vessels — called also *low blood pressure*

¹hy·po·tensive \ˈ"+\ *adj* [ISV *hypotension* + *-ive*] **1 :** characterized by or due to hypotension **2 :** causing low blood pressure or a lowering of blood pressure ⟨~ anesthesia⟩ ⟨~ drugs⟩

²hypotensive \ˈ"\ *n* -S **:** a person with hypotension

hy·pot·e·nuse \hīˈpätᵊnˌ(y)üs *also* -üz\ *also* **hy·poth·e·nuse** \-äthəˌn(y)-\ *n* -S [L *hypotenusa*, fr. Gk *hypoteinousa*, fr. fem. of *hypoteinōn*, pres. part. of *hypoteinein* to subtend, fr. *hypo-* + *teinein* to stretch] **:** the side of a right-angled triangle that is opposite the right angle

hy·po·thalamic \ˌ⁼⁼ *at* HYPO-+\ *adj* [*hypo-* + *thalamic*] **1 :** located below the thalamus **2** [NL *hypothalamus* + E *-ic*] **:** of, relating to, or involving the hypothalamus

hypothalamico- *or* **hypothalamo-** *comb form* [*hypothalamico-* fr. *hypothalamic* + *-o-*; *hypothalamo-* fr. NL *hypothalamus*] **:** hypothalamic and ⟨*hypothalamico*hypophyseal⟩ ⟨*hypothalamo*cortical⟩

hy·po·thalamus \¦⸗⸗+\ *n* [NL, fr. *hypo-* + *thalamus*] **:** a basal part of the diencephalon that lies beneath the thalamus on each side, forms the floor of the third ventricle, and is usu. considered to include vital autonomic regulatory centers and sometimes the posterior pituitary lobe

hy·po·thallus \"+\ *n* [NL, fr. *hypo-* + *thallus*] **1 :** a marginal outgrowth of hyphae from the thallus in crustose lichens **2 :** a residue like a film that remains after the formation of sporangia in slime molds of the class Myxomycetes

hy·poth·ec \hə'päthik, hī'-\ *n* -S [F&LL; F *hypothèque*, fr. MF, fr. LL *hypotheca*, fr. Gk *hypothēkē* deposit, pledge, mortgage, fr. *hypotithenai* to deposit as a pledge, put under, propose — more at HYPOTHESIS] **1** *Roman & civil law* **:** an obligation, right, or security given by contract or by operation of law to a creditor over property of the debtor without transfer of possession or title to the creditor — compare PIGNUS, PLEDGE **2** *Scot* **:** AFFAIR, CONCERN

hy·po·theca \¦⸗⸗ *at* HYPO- +\ *n* [NL, fr. *hypo-* + *-theca*] **:** the inner or bottom half or valve of the diatom frustule — compare EPITHECA — **hy·po·thecal** \"+\ *adj*

hy·poth·e·cary \hə'päthə,kerē, hī'-\ *adj* [LL *hypothecarius*, fr. *hypotheca* hypothec + L *-arius* -ary] **:** of, relating to, or created or secured by a hypothec ⟨~ right⟩

¹hy·poth·e·cate \hə'päthə,kāt, hī'-, *usu* -ād·+V\ *vt* -ED/-ING/-S [ML *hypothecatus*, past part. of *hypothecare* to pledge, fr. LL *hypotheca* pledge, hypothec] **:** to subject to a hypothec **:** to pledge without delivery of title or possession; *specif* **:** to pledge (a ship) by a bottomry bond

²hy·poth·e·cate \hī'-\ *vb* -ED/-ING/-S [Gk *hypothēkē* suggestion, counsel, pledge, mortgage + E *-ate*] **:** HYPOTHESIZE

hy·poth·e·ca·tion \hə,päthə'kāshən, (,)hī,-\ *n* -S [ML *hypothecation-, hypothecatio*, fr. *hypothecatus* (past part.) + L *-ion-, -io* -ion] **1** *Roman, civil, & maritime law* **:** the act or contract by which property (as real property) is hypothecated **2** *Roman, civil, & maritime law* **:** the right or power of a creditor or claimant over property owned by his debtor or another who has pledged it for the debt to cause the property to be sold to satisfy his claim if payment is defaulted

hypothecation certificate *n* **:** a certificate attached to a bill of exchange empowering the holder to dispose of merchandise if payment or acceptance is refused — called also *letter of hypothecation*

hy·poth·e·ca·tor \⸗'⸗⸗,kād·ə(r)\ *n* [¹*hypothecate* + *-or*] **:** one that hypothecates

hy·poth·e·ca·tory \⸗'⸗⸗,kə,tōrē\ *adj* [¹*hypothecate* + *-ory*] **:** HYPOTHECARY

hy·po·thecium \¦⸗⸗ *at* HYPO- +\ *n* [NL, fr. *hypo-* + *thecium*] **:** a layer of dense hyphal tissue just below the hymenium of lichens and fungi — compare EPITHECIUM

¹hy·pothe·nar \hī'päthə,när, ¦,nər, ¦hīpə¦thē|\ *n* [NL, fr. Gk, hypothenar of the hand, fr. *hypo-* + *thenar*] **:** the hypothenar eminence

²hypothenar \(')⸗¦⸗⸗⸗\ *also* **hy·pothe·nal** \-thənᵊl,-thēn-\ *adj* **:** of, relating to, or constituting the prominent part of the palm of the hand above the base of the little finger or a corresponding part in the forefoot of an animal

hypothenuse *var of* HYPOTENUSE

hy·po·the·ria \,⸗⸗ *at* HYPO- + 'thirēə\ *n pl, cap* [NL, fr. *hypo-* + *-theria*] **:** a hypothetical order including the as yet undiscovered ancestors of the mammals

hy·po·thermal \¦⸗⸗+\ *adj* [*hypo-* + *thermal*] **:** of or relating to a hydrothermal metalliferous ore vein deposited at high temperature — compare EPITHERMAL, MESOTHERMAL

hy·po·ther·mia \,⸗⸗+'thərmēə\ *n* -S [NL, fr. *hypo-* + *-thermia*] **:** subnormal temperature of the body often induced artificially to facilitate cardiac surgery — compare REFRIGERATION

hy·poth·e·sis \hī'päthəsəs\ *n, pl* **hypothe·ses** \-ə,sēz\ [L, fr. Gk, fr. *hypotithenai* to suppose, propose, put under, fr. *hypo-* + *tithenai* to place, put — more at DO] **1 :** a proposition tentatively assumed in order to draw out its logical or empirical consequences and so test its accord with facts that are known or may be determined ⟨it appears, then, to be a condition of the most genuinely scientific ~ that it be . . . of such a nature as to be either proved or disproved by comparison with observed facts —J.S.Mill⟩ ⟨most of the great unifying conceptions of modern science are working *hypotheses* —Bernard Bosanquet⟩ **2 a :** an assumption or concession made for the sake of argument **b :** an interpretation of a practical situation or condition taken as the ground for action **3 :** the antecedent clause in a conditional statement **4 :** a hypothetical relation **:** the conditioning of one thing by another

hy·poth·e·size \-ə,sīz\ *vb* -ED/-ING/-S *vi* **:** to make a hypothesis ~ *vt* **:** to adopt as a hypothesis **:** ASSUME ⟨we can ~ any value as truth . . . but there are varying probabilities for each hypothesis we make —Lester Guest⟩

¹hy·po·thet·i·cal \¦hīpə¦thed·ə̇kəl, -et|, |ēk-\ *also* **hy·po·thet·ic** \|ik, |ēk\ *adj* [*hypothetical* fr. LL *hypotheticus* (fr. Gk *hypothetikos*) + E *-al*; *hypothetic* fr. F *hypothétique*, fr. LL *hypotheticus*] **1 :** involving logical hypothesis **:** ASSUMED, CONDITIONAL — distinguished from *categorical* **2 :** of or depending on supposition **:** CONJECTURAL — contrasted with *actual* — **hy·po·thet·i·cal·ly** \|ək(ə)lē, |ēk-, -li\ *adv*

²hypothetical \"\ *n* -S **:** a hypothetical statement or proposition **:** IMPLICATION 2b

hypothetical imperative *n* [trans. of G *hypothetischer imperativ*] **:** an imperative of conduct that springs from expediency or practical necessity rather than from moral law — contrasted with *categorical imperative*

hypothetical question *n* **:** a question based on hypothetical facts concerning which a witness in court is asked for an opinion

hypothetical syllogism *n* [trans. of LL *hypotheticus syllogismus*] **1 :** a syllogism consisting wholly of hypothetical propositions — called also *pure hypothetical syllogism* **2 :** a syllogism consisting partly of hypothetical propositions — called also *mixed hypothetical syllogism;* compare MODUS PONENS, MODUS TOLLENS

hy·po·thet·i·co-deductive \|ə̇kō-\ *adj* [*hypothetic* + *-o-*] **:** of or relating to scientific method in which hypotheses suggested by the facts of observation are proposed and consequences deduced from them so as to test the hypotheses and evaluate the consequences **:** AXIOMATIC

hypothetico-disjunctive *adj* **:** of, relating to, or constituting a logical proposition that combines hypothesis and disjunction

hy·po·thyroid \¦⸗⸗ *at* HYPO- +\ *adj* [*hypo-* + *thyroid*] **:** of, relating to, or affected by hypothyroidism

hy·po·thyroidism \"+\ *n* -S [ISV *hypo-* + *thyroid* + *-ism*] **:** deficient activity of the thyroid gland; *also* **:** a resultant abnormal state marked by lowered metabolic rate and general loss of vigor — compare CRETINISM, MYXEDEMA

hy·po·to·nia \,⸗⸗+'tōnēə\ *or* **hy·pot·o·ny** \hī'pät°nē, hə'-\ *n, pl* **hypotonias** *or* **hypotonies** [NL *hypotonia*, fr. *hypo-* + *-tonia*] **:** HYPOTONICITY

hy·po·tonic \¦⸗⸗ *at* HYPO- +\ *adj* [ISV *hypo-* + *tonic*] **1** *of living tissue* **:** having less than the normal tone **2** *of a fluid* **:** having a lower osmotic pressure than a fluid under comparison or used as a standard — compare ISOTONIC

hy·po·tonicity \"+\ *n* **:** the quality or state of being hypotonic

hy·po·tonus \"+\ *n* -ES [NL, fr. *hypo-* + *tonus*] **:** HYPOTONICITY

hy·po·tra·che·li·um \,⸗⸗+trə'kēlēəm\ *n* [L, fr. Gk *hypotrachēlion*, fr. *hypo-* + *trachēlos* neck] **:** GORGERIN

hy·po·trem·a·ta \"+'tremədə, -rēm-\ *n pl, cap* [NL, fr. *hypo-* + *-tremata*] **:** an order of Chondrichthyes comprising the rays — compare PLEUROTREMATA

hy·po·trich \'⸗⸗+,trik\ *n* -S [NL *Hypotricha*] **:** one of the Hypotricha

hy·pot·ri·cha \hī'pä·trəkə\ *n pl, cap* [NL, fr. *hypo-* + *-tricha*] **:** a suborder of Spirotricha comprising ciliates that have cilia only on the ventral surface and usu. fused to cirri and that often have tactile bristles on the dorsum — compare EUPLOTES, OXYTRICHA, STYLONYCHIA — **hy·pot·ri·chous** \(')⸗¦⸗⸗kəs\ *adj*

hy·po·trich·ia \,⸗⸗ *at* HYPO- + 'trikēə\ *n* -S [NL, fr. *hypo-* + *-trichia*] **:** HYPOTRICHOSIS

hy·po·trich·i·da \-kədə\ [NL, fr. *hypo-* + *trich-* + *-ida*] *syn of* HYPOTRICHA

hy·po·tri·cho·sis \,⸗⸗+trə'kōsəs\ *n* [NL, fr. *hypo-* + Gk *trichōsis* growth of hair (fr. *trich-* + *-ōsis* -osis)] **:** congenital deficiency of hair — **hy·po·tri·chot·ic** \¦⸗⸗⸗¦käd·ik\ *adj*

hy·po·trochanteric \¦⸗⸗ *at* HYPO- +\ *adj* [*hypo-* + *trochanteric*] **:** situated beneath a trochanter

hy·po·trochoid \"+\ *n* [*hypo-* + *trochoid*] **:** a plane curve traced by a point on the radius or extended radius but not on the circumference of a circle rolling on the inside of a fixed circle — compare EPITROCHOID — **hy·po·trochoidal** \"+\ *adj*

hy·pot·ro·phy \hī'pä·trəfē, hə'-\ *n* [ISV *hypo-* + *-trophy*] **1 :** subnormal growth — compare HYPERTROPHY **2 :** greater growth of the lower than of the upper side of horizontal or ascending branches or roots — opposed to *epitrophy*

hy·po·tympanic \¦⸗⸗ *at* HYPO- +\ *adj* [in sense 1, fr. *hypo-* + *tympanic;* in sense 2, fr. NL *hypotympanum* + E *-ic*] **1 :** located below the tympanum **2 :** of or relating to the hypotympanum

hy·po·tympanum \"+\ *n* [NL, fr. *hypo-* + *tympanum*] **:** the lower part of the middle ear — compare EPITYMPANUM

hy·po·type \'⸗⸗+,-\ *n* [*hypo-* + *type*] **:** a specimen of a species not of the original type series but known by published description, figure, or listing

hy·po·typic \¦⸗⸗+\ *or* **hy·po·typical** \"+\ *adj* [in sense 1, fr. *hypo-* + *typic* or *typical;* in sense 2, fr. *hypotype* + *-ic* or *-ical*] **1 :** imperfectly typical **2 :** of or relating to a hypotype

hy·po·ty·po·sis \,⸗⸗+,tī'pōsəs\ *n, pl* **hypotypo·ses** \-ō,sēz\ [Gk *hypotypōsis*, fr. *hypotypoun* to sketch, outline, fr. *hypo-* + *typoun* to stamp, form (fr. *typos* impression, cast)] **:** vivid picturesque description

hy·po·valve \'⸗⸗+,-\ *n* [*hypo-* + *valve*] **1 :** one half of the shell of a dinoflagellate **2 :** the hypotheca of a diatom

hy·po·vanadate \¦⸗⸗+\ *n* [ISV *hypo-* + *vanadate*] **:** a salt (as potassium hypovanadate $K_2V_4O_9$) containing tetravalent vanadium in the anion — called also *vanadite*

hy·po·vi·ta·min·osis \,⸗⸗+,vīd·əmə'nōsəs\ *n* -ES [NL, fr. *hypo-* + ISV *vitamin* + NL *-osis*] **:** AVITAMINOSIS

hy·po·vi·ta·min·ot·ic \¦⸗⸗¦⸗⸗⸗¦näd·ik\ *adj* **:** AVITAMINOTIC

hy·po·vo·le·mia \,⸗⸗+,vä'lēmēə\ *n* -S [NL, fr. *hypo-* + *vol-* (fr. E *volume*) + *-emia*] **:** decrease in the volume of the circulating blood — **hy·po·vo·le·mic** \¦⸗⸗,⸗¦lēmik\ *adj*

hy·po·xanthine \¦⸗⸗+\ *n* [ISV *hypo-* + *xanthine*] **:** a purine base $C_5H_4N_4O$ found in plant and animal tissues, formed by hydrolysis of adenine and inosinic acid, and yielding xanthine on oxidation; 6-hydroxy-purine

hy·pox·e·mia \,hī,päk'sēmēə\ *n* -S [NL, fr. *hypo-* + ¹*ox-* + *-emia*] **:** deficient oxygenation of the blood

hy·pox·ia \hī'päksēə\ *n* -S [NL, fr. *hypo-* + ¹*ox-* + *-ia*] **:** a deficiency of oxygen reaching the tissues of the body whether due to environmental deficiency or impaired respiratory and circulatory organs — **hy·pox·ic** \(')⸗¦⸗sik\ *adj*

hy·pox·is \hī'päksəs, hə'-\ *n, cap* [NL, irreg. fr. *hypo-* + Gk *oxys* sharp — more at OXY-] **:** a genus of small scapose herbs (family Amaryllidaceae) having numerous hairy linear leaves from a corm or short rootstock and umbellate yellow flowers with 6-parted perianth — see STAR GRASS 1

hy·pox·y·lon \hī'päksə,län\ *n, cap* [NL, fr. *hypo-* + *-xylon*] **:** a genus of fungi (family Xylariaceae) having effuse to hemispherical stromata and including a species (*H. pruinatum*) that causes a canker of poplars — compare XYLARIA

hy·po·zeug·ma \,⸗⸗ *at* HYPO- + 'zügmə\ *n* [LL, fr. *hypo-* + L *zeugma*] **:** the joining of several subjects with a single verb

hy·po·zeux·is \"+'züksəs\ *n* -ES [LL, fr. LGk, fr. Gk *hypozeugnynai* to subjugate, yoke under, fr. *hypo-* + *zeugnynai* to yoke — more at YOKE] **:** the use in a parallel construction of successive clauses each complete with subject and verb

hy·po·zoic \¦⸗⸗+¦zōik\ *adj* [ISV *hypo-* + *-zoic*] **:** lying under the fossiliferous systems

hypped \'hipt\ *archaic var of* HIPPED

hyp·pish \'hipish\ *adj* [*hyp* + *-ish*] **:** affected with hypochondria **:** BLUE, DEPRESSED, MELANCHOLIC

hyps *pl of* HYP

hyps- *or* **hypsi-** *or* **hypso-** *comb form* [in sense 1, fr. Gk, fr. *hypsos;* in sense 2, fr. Gk, fr. *hypsi;* Gk *hypsos* & Gk *hypsi* akin to Gk *hypo* under — more at UP] **1 :** height ⟨*hypso*graphy⟩ **2 :** on high **:** aloft ⟨*hypsi*cephalic⟩ ⟨*hyps*odont⟩

hyp·si·brachycephalic \¦hipsə̇, -sē+\ *adj* [*hyps-* + *brachycephalic*] **:** having a high broad head

hyp·si·brachycephalism \"+\ *n* [*hyps-* + *brachycephalism*] **:** the quality or state of being hypsibrachycephalic

hyp·si·brachycephaly \"+\ *n* [*hypsibrachycephalic* + *-y*] **:** HYPSIBRACHYCEPHALISM

hyp·si·ceph·al \,hipsə'sefəl\ *n* -S [ISV *hyps-* + *-cephal* (as in *dolichocephal*)] **:** a person having a high forehead

hyp·si·ce·phal·ic \¦hipsəsə¦falik\ *also* **hyp·si·ceph·a·lous** \¦hipsə¦sefələs\ *adj* [*hyps-* + *-cephalic* or *-cephalous*] **:** having a high forehead with a length-height index of 62.6 or higher — compare HYPSICRANIC

hyp·si·conch \'hipsə,käŋk, -änch\ *adj* [*hyps-* + *-conch* (fr. L *concha* conch, shell) — more at CONCH] *anthropol* **:** having high orbits with an orbital index of 89 or over — **hyp·si·con·chy** \-äŋkē, -änchē\ *n* -ES

hyp·si·cra·ni·al \¦hipsə¦krānēəl\ *or* **hyp·si·cra·nic** \-nik\ *adj* [G *hypsikran* hypsicranial (fr. *hyps-* + Gk *kranion* cranium) + E *-ial* or *-ic* — more at CRANIUM] **:** having a high skull with a length-height index of 75 or over — **hyp·si·cra·ny** \'⸗⸗,krānē\ *n* -ES

hyp·si·dolichocephalic \¦hipsə̇, -sē+\ *adj* [*hyps-* + *dolichocephalic*] **:** having a head that is high and narrow or high and long or high, long, and narrow

hyp·si·dolichocephalism \"+\ *n* [*hyps-* + *dolichocephalism*] **:** the quality or state of being hypsidolichocephalic

hyp·si·dolichocephaly \"+\ *n* [*hyps-* + *dolichocephaly*] **:** HYPSIDOLICHOCEPHALISM

hyp·si·dont \'hipsə,dänt\ *adj* [*hyps-* + *-dont* (fr. *-odont*)] **:** HYPSODONT

hyp·sil·i·form \(')hip¦silə,fȯrm\ *adj* [*hypsil-* (fr. MGk *hy psilon* upsilon) + *-iform*] **:** HYPSILOID

hyp·si·loid \'hipsə,lȯid\ *adj* [MGk *hypsiloeidēs*, fr. *hy psilon* upsilon, lit., simple y + *-oeidēs* -oid] *anat* **:** resembling a Greek capital letter upsilon in form

hyp·si·loph·o·don \,hipsə'läfə,dän\ *n, cap* [NL, fr. Gk *hypsilophos* high-crested (fr. *hyps-* + *lophos* crest) + NL *-odon*] **:** a genus (the type of the family Hypsilophodontidae) of small primitive ornithopod dinosaurs of the Wealden of the Isle of Wight

hyp·si·loph·o·dont \¦⸗⸗¦⸗⸗,dänt\ *adj* [NL *Hypsilophodontidae*, family of dinosaurs, fr. *Hypsilophodont-, Hypsilophodon*, type genus + *-idae*] **:** of or relating to the genus *Hypsilophodon* or family Hypsilophodontidae

hyp·si·prym·no·don \,hipsə'primnə,dän\ *n, cap* [NL, fr. *hyps-* + Gk *prymnos* endmost, hindmost + NL *-odon*] **:** a genus of marsupial mammals comprising the musk kangaroos

hyp·sis·tar·i·an \¦hipsə¦sta(a)rēən\ *n* -S *usu cap* [LGk *Hypsistarioi*, pl., fr. *hypsistarioi*, pl. of *hypsistarios* worshiping the highest (fr. Gk *hypsistos* highest, fr. *hypsi* on high) + E *-an*] **:** a member of a sect of the 4th to the 9th century in Asia Minor combining heathen, Jewish, and Christian tenets

hyp·si·stenocephalic \¦hipsə̇, -sē+\ *adj* [*hyps-* + *stenocephalic*] **:** having an extremely high narrow head

hyp·si·sten·o·ceph·a·lism \,⸗⸗+,stenə'sefə,lizəm\ *n* [*hypsistenocephalic* + *-ism*] **:** the quality or state of being hypsistenocephalic

hyp·si·stenocephaly \¦⸗⸗+\ *n* [*hyps-* + *stenocephaly*] **:** HYPSISTENOCEPHALISM

hypso- — see HYPS-

hyp·so·chrome \'hipsə,krōm\ *n* [ISV *hyps-* + *-chrome*] **:** an atom or group that when introduced into a compound causes a visible lightening of color (as from green toward yellow) — contrasted with *bathochrome* — **hyp·so·chro·mic** \¦⸗⸗¦krōmik\ *adj*

hyp·so·dont \'hipsə,dänt\ *adj* [*hyps-* + *-odont*] **1** *of teeth* **:** having high or deep crowns and short roots (as the molar teeth of a horse) — compare BRACHYDONT **2 :** having hypsodont teeth

hyp·so·dont·ism \-n,tizəm\ *n* -S [*hypsodont* + *-ism*] **:** the quality or state of being hypsodont

hyp·so·donty \-ntē\ *n* -ES [*hypsodont* + *-y*] **:** HYPSODONTISM

hyp·sog·ra·phy \hip'sägrəfē\ *n* -ES [ISV *hyps-* + *-graphy*] **1 :** a branch of geography that deals with the measurement and mapping of the varying elevations of the earth's surface with reference to sea level **2 :** topographic relief or the devices (as color shadings) by which it is indicated on maps

hyp·so·isotherm \¦hip(,)sō+\ *n* [*hyps-* + *isotherm;* trans. of G *höhenisotherme*] **:** an isotherm that is drawn on a vertical section of the atmosphere and sometimes also of the ground to show the distribution of temperature in the vertical

hyp·som·e·ter \hip'sämǝd·ə(r)\ *n* [ISV *hyps-* + *-meter*] **1 :** an apparatus for estimating elevations in mountainous regions from the boiling points of liquids **2 :** any of various instruments used to determine the height of trees by triangulation

hyp·so·met·ric \¦hipsə¦me·trik\ *or* **hyp·so·met·ri·cal** \-rə̇kəl\ *adj* **:** of or relating to hypsometry

hyp·som·e·try \hip'sämə·trē\ *n* -ES [Gk *hypsos* height + E *-metry*] **:** the science of measuring heights (as with reference to sea level)

hyp·so·phyll \'hipsə,fil\ *n* -S [NL *hypsophyllum* trans. of G *hochblatt*, lit., high leaf), fr. *hyps-* + *-phyllum* -phyll] **:** a floral leaf beneath the sporophylls **:** BRACT, SCALE LEAF — **hyp·so·phyl·lar** \¦⸗⸗¦filə(r)\ *or* **hyp·so·phyl·lary** \-lərē\ *or* **hyp·so·phyl·lous** \-ləs\ *adj*

¹hy·pu·ral \(')hī¦pyu̇rəl\ *adj* [*hypo-* + *ur-* (tail) + *-al*] **:** of, relating to, or constituting the bony structure chiefly formed of the expanded and more or less fused hemal spines of the last few vertebrae that supports the caudal fin rays in most teleost fishes

²hypural \"\ *n* -S **:** a hypural bone

hy·ra·ce·um \hī'rāsēəm\ *n* -S [NL, fr. *hyrac-, hyrax* + *-eum* (as in *castoreum*)] **:** a southern African product somewhat like castoreum said to be excreted by the hyrax and formerly much used as a folk remedy and as a fixative for perfumes

hy·rach·y·us \hī'rakēəs\ *n, cap* [NL, fr. *Hyrac-, Hyrax*, genus of ungulates + *-hyus* (fr. Gk *hy-, hys* hog, swine) — more at SOW (female hog)] **:** a genus (the type of the family Hyrachyidae) of primitive perissodactyl ungulates related to the rhinoceroses and common in the No. American Eocene

¹hy·rac·id \(')hī¦rasə̇d\ *adj* [NL *Hyracidae*] **:** of or relating to the Procaviidae

²hyracid \"\ *n* -S **:** a member of the family Procaviidae **:** CONEY

hy·rac·i·dae \hī'rasə,dē\ [NL, fr. *Hyrac-, Hyrax* + *-idae*] *syn of* PROCAVIIDAE

hy·rac·i·form \(')⸗¦⸗⸗,fȯrm\ *adj* [NL *hyrac-, hyrax* + E *-iform*] **:** resembling a hyrax

hy·ra·ci·na \,hīrə'sīnə\ [NL, fr. *Hyrac-, Hyrax* + *-ina*] *syn of* HYRACOIDEA

hy·rac·o·don \hī'rakə,dän\ *n, cap* [NL, fr. *Hyrac-, Hyrax* + *-odon*] **:** a genus (the type of the family Hyracodontidae) of Eocene and Oligocene perissodactyls related to the rhinoceroses but hornless and of light agile build with all feet three-toed

¹hy·rac·o·dont \(')⸗¦⸗⸗,dänt\ *adj* [NL *Hyracodont-, Hyracodon*] **:** of or relating to the genus *Hyracodon* or family Hyracodontidae

²hyracodont \"\ *n* -S **:** a mammal of the genus *Hyracodon* or family Hyracodontidae

hy·ra·coid \'hīrə,kȯid\ *n* -S [NL *Hyracoidea*] **:** one of the Hyracoidea

hy·ra·coi·dea \,⸗⸗'kȯidēə\ *n pl, cap* [NL, fr. *Hyrac-, Hyrax* + *-oidea*] **:** an order of Old World ungulate mammals that is now restricted to Africa and southwestern Asia and that comprises various extinct animals and the surviving hyraxes which find their nearest living relatives in the elephants and sirenians but in many respects resemble rabbits

hy·ra·co·there \'hīrəkō,thir\ *n* -S [NL *Hyracotherium*] **:** an animal or fossil of the genus *Hyracotherium*

hy·ra·co·the·ri·um \,⸗⸗⸗'thirēəm\ *n, cap* [NL *Hyrac-, Hyrax* + *-o-* + *-therium*] **:** a genus of lower Eocene perissodactylous mammals about the size of a fox having four-toed forelimbs and three-toed hind limbs and regarded as among the earliest ancestors of the modern horse — see EQUIDAE illustration

¹hy·rax \'hī,raks\ [NL, fr. Gk, mouse, shrewmouse; akin to L *susurrus* hum, murmur — more at SWARM] *syn of* PROCAVIA

²hyrax \"\ *n, pl* **hyraxes** \-ksəz\ *also* **hyra·ces** \-īrə,sēz\ [NL, fr. ¹*Hyrax*] **:** any of certain small mammals that constitute the order Hyracoidea and are characterized by thickset body with short legs and ears and rudimentary tail, feet with soft pads and broad nails, and teeth of which the molars resemble those of the rhinoceros and the incisors those of rodents — called also *coney*

³hyrax \"\ *n* -ES [origin unknown] **:** a microscopic mounting medium of high refractive index that consists of a naphthalene derivative dissolved in benzene or xylol, is used esp. for mounting semiopaque structures (as diatom frustules), and tends to darken but not crystallize with age

hyr·ca·ni·an \¦hər¦kānēən\ *also* **hyr·can** \'hərkən\ *adj, usu cap* [*hyrcanian* fr. L *Hyrcanius* Hyrcanian (fr. *Hyrcania*, ancient country or province of Asia) + E *-an; hyrcan* fr. L *Hyrcanus* Hyrcanian, fr. Gk *Hyrkanos*, n., Hyrcanian, inhabitant of Hyrcania] **:** of or relating to the ancient land of Hyrcania southeast of the Caspian sea

hyrst *var of* HURST

hy·son \'hīs°n\ *n* -S [Chin (Peking) *hsi¹ ch'un¹*, lit., flourishing spring] **:** a Chinese green tea made from thinly rolled and twisted leaves

hyson skin *n* **:** the light and inferior leaves separated from hyson by a winnowing machine

hy spy \'hī-\ *n* [prob. fr. *hi, spy!* (call used by the hiders in the game as a signal to the searchers to start looking for them), fr. *hi* + *spy*, n.] **:** HIDE-AND-SEEK

hys·sop \'hisəp\ *n* -S [ME *ysop*, partly fr. OE *ysopan* and partly fr. OF *ysope;* OE & OF, fr. L *hysopum, hyssopum, hyssopus*, fr. Gk *hyssōpon, hyssōpos*, of Sem origin; akin to Heb *ēzōbh* hyssop, Assyr-Bab *zūpu*, Syriac *zōfā*] **1 a :** a plant used in bunches for purificatory sprinkling rites by the ancient Hebrews **b :** a European mint (*Hyssopus officinalis*) that has highly aromatic and pungent leaves and is often cultivated in gardens as a remedy for bruises **2 a** [prob. fr. ML *hyssopus* (also, the plant), fr. L] **:** ASPERGILLUM **b :** the holy water sprinkled in the asperges

hyssop loosestrife *n* **:** GRASS POLY

hyssop oil *n* **:** an essential oil obtained from hyssop and used chiefly in liqueurs

hyssop skullcap *n* **:** a perennial herb (*Scutellaria integrifolia*) of the eastern U.S. with showy blue flowers

hys·so·pus \'hisəpəs, hə'sōp-\ *n, cap* [NL, fr. L, hyssop] **:** a Eurasian genus of perennial herbs or subshrubs (family Labiatae) having floral whorls in bracted spikes — see HYSSOP 1

hyssop violet *n* **:** a grayish purple that is redder and stronger than telegraph blue, bluer and deeper than mauve gray, and bluer, lighter, and stronger than average rose mauve

hys·taz·a·rin \hə'stazərə̇n\ *n* -S [ISV *hyst-* (fr. Gk *hysteros* latter, later) + *alizarin;* orig. formed in G] **:** a yellow crystalline compound $C_{14}H_6O_2(OH)_2$ produced along with its isomer alizarin by condensation of phthalic anhydride and pyrocatechol; 2,3-dihydroxy-anthraquinone

hyster- *or* **hystero-** *comb form* [F or L; F *hystér-*, fr. MF, fr. L *hyster-*, fr. Gk, fr. *hystera* womb] **1 :** womb ⟨*hyster*ectomy⟩ ⟨*hystero*myoma⟩ **2** [NL, fr. *hysteria*] **a :** hysteria ⟨*hystero*genic⟩ **b :** hysteria and ⟨*hystero*neurasthenia⟩

hys·ter·ec·to·mize \,histə'rektə,mīz\ *vt* -ED/-ING/-S **:** to remove the uterus of by surgery

hys·ter·ec·to·my \-,mē\ *n* -ES [ISV *hyster-* + *-ectomy*] **:** surgical removal of the uterus

hys·ter·e·sis \,histə'rēsə̇s\ *n, pl* **hystere·ses** \-ē,sēz\ [NL, fr. Gk *hysterēsis* shortcoming, deficiency, need, fr. *hysterein* to come late, be behind (fr. *hysteros* later, latter) + *-ēsis* -esis] **1 a :** the lagging of a physical effect on a body behind its cause (as behind changed forces and conditions) ⟨there is a good deal of ~, that is, a time lag between the cooling and the setting to be expected of the jelly —J.W.McBain⟩ ⟨all manometers must be tested for ~ as well as for sensitivity and natural frequency —H.D.Green⟩ **b :** a lagging of elongation behind tensile stress and of contraction behind release from stress in an elastic solid due to internal friction **c :** a lagging of magnetization and hence of magnetic induction behind magnetic intensity and of demagnetization behind reduction of intensity in a ferromagnetic substance (as iron) **d :** a lagging of electric polarization behind electric intensity and of depolarization behind reduction of intensity in a dielectric **2 a :** the influence of the previous history or treatment of a body on its subsequent response to a given force or changed condition ⟨the influence of the previous treatment of a gel upon its behavior is known as ~ —B.S.Meyer & D.B.Anderson⟩ ⟨a study has been made of the phenomenon of rennet ~, in which the time of coagulation of heated milk is progressively greater with increase in the time interval between heating and addition of rennet —J.S.Fruton⟩ **b :** the changed response of a body that results from this influence ⟨the permeability depends on the past history (magnetically speaking) of the iron, a phenomenon known as ~ —F.W.Sears⟩ **3 :** HYSTERESIS LOSS

hysteresis coefficient *n* **:** the constant in a formula for hysteresis loss that is characteristic of the substance under test

hysteresis loop *n* **:** a cycle of alternating changes involving elastic, magnetic, or dielectric hysteresis; *also* **:** the loop-shaped graph representing such a cycle

hysteresis loss *n* **:** loss of energy in the form of heat due to hysteresis (as in an alternating-current core)

hysteresis motor *n* **:** a synchronous motor that utilizes the hysteresis effect in a solid rotor of permanent-magnet material to achieve synchronism and that is used esp. in sound recording and reproducing machines

hys·ter·et·ic \¦histə¦red·|ik, -et|, |ēk\ *adj* [fr. NL *hysteresis,* after such pairs as NL *exegesis:* E *exegetic*] **:** of, relating to, or marked by hysteresis — **hys·ter·et·i·cal·ly** \|ək(ə)lē, |ēk-, -li\ *adv*

hys·te·ria \hə'sterēə, -tir-\ *n* -s [NL, fr. E *hyster*ic + NL *-ia*] **1 a :** a psychoneurosis that is marked by emotional excitability involving disturbances of the psychic, sensory, vasomotor, and visceral functions **b :** a similar disease of domesticated animals; *specif* **:** CANINE HYSTERIA **2 :** conduct or an outbreak of conduct exhibiting unmanageable fear or emotional excess in individuals or groups ⟨could not fail to destroy his system, never very strong and pitched to ~ from the first —H.M. Ledig-Rowohlt⟩ ⟨weeping generously . . . and wildly giggling, in a ~ which she could not control —Arnold Bennett⟩ ⟨swept up into the systematized ~ of the war —Scott Fitzgerald⟩ ⟨the ghost dance was the religious expression of a social ~ —W.W. Howells⟩ **syn** see MANIA

hys·te·ri·a·ce·ae \hə,stirē'āsē,ē\ *n pl, cap* [NL, fr. *Hysterium,* type genus (fr. Gk *hystera* womb + NL *-ium*) + *-aceae*] **:** a family of ascomycetous fungi (order Hysteriales) that is often considered to be derived from the family Sphaeriaceae from which it is distinguished chiefly by the form and method of opening of the ascomata of its members

hys·te·ri·a·gen·ic \hə¦sterēə¦jenik, -tir-\ *adj* [NL *hysteria* + E *-genic*] **:** HYSTEROGENIC

hys·te·ri·a·les \hə,stirē'ā(,)lēz\ *n pl, cap* [NL, fr. *Hysterium,* genus of fungi + *-ales*] **:** an order of fungi of the subclass Euascomycetes that is characterized by elongated ascomata opening by a longitudinal slit and includes various fungi which cause leaf cast of conifers — see HYSTERIACEAE

1**hys·ter·ic** \hə'sterik, (')hi¦s-, -rēk\ *adj* [L *hystericus* of the womb] **:** HYSTERICAL ⟨raved and ran hither and thither in ~ insanity —W.M.Thackeray⟩

2**hysteric** \"\ *n* -s **1 :** one subject to or suffering from hysteria **2 :** an overemotional or unstable person ⟨Bohemia, which has always been (along with better things) the refuge of fakers, self-deceivers, and ~*s* —C.J.Rolo⟩ ⟨a charlatan, a lucky ~, and a lying demagogue —John Gunther⟩

hys·ter·i·cal \hə'sterəkəl, (')hi¦s-, -rēk-\ *adj* [L *hysteric*us hysterical (fr. Gk *hysterikos,* fr. *hystera* womb + *-ikos* -ic) + E *-al;* fr. its being orig. applied to women thought to be suffering from disturbances of the womb] **1 :** of, relating to, or marked by hysteria ⟨during ~ conditions various functions of the human body are disordered —Morris Fishbein⟩ — compare PSYCHOGENIC **2 :** exhibiting unrestrained emotionalism ⟨had absorbed all the serenity of America, and left none for his restless, rickety, ~ countrymen —R.W.Emerson⟩ — **hys·ter·i·cal·ly** \-rək(ə)lē, -rēk-, -li\ *adv*

hys·ter·icky \-rəkē\ *adj* **:** HYSTERICAL ⟨up I went with all the courage I could muster, but a sort of ~ feeling —W.G. Hammond⟩

hys·ter·ics \hə'steriks, -rēks\ *n pl but usu sing in constr, also* **hys·ter·ic** \-k\ **:** a fit of uncontrollable laughter or crying **:** HYSTERIA ⟨she'll go all to pieces and start bawling and having ~ —Erle Stanley Gardner⟩

1**hys·ter·i·form** \hə'sterə,fȯrm\ *adj* [ISV *hyster-* + *-iform*] **:** resembling hysteria

2**hysteriform** \"\ *adj* [NL *Hysterium,* genus of fungi + E *-form*] **:** HYSTERIOID

hys·te·ri·oid \hə'stirē,ȯid\ *adj* [NL *Hysterium,* genus of fungi + E *-oid* — more at HYSTERIACEAE] **:** BOAT-SHAPED ⟨the ~ apothecia of fungi of the order Hysteriales⟩

hystero- — see HYSTER-

hys·tero·crystalline \¦histə(,)rō+\ *n* -s [ISV *hystero-* (fr. Gk *hysteros* latter, later) + *crystalline;* orig. formed as G *hysterokrystallin*] **:** a secondary crystallization in igneous rock

hys·tero–epilepsy \"+\ *n* [ISV *hyster-* + *epilepsy*] **:** a hysteria characterized by motor convulsions resembling those of epilepsy — **hys·tero–epileptic** \"+\ *adj*

hys·ter·o·gen·ic \¦histərō¦jenik\ *adj* [*hyster-* + *-genic*] **:** inducing hysteria

hys·ter·o·gram \'histərō,gram\ *n* [*hyster-* + *-gram*] **:** a roentgenogram made by hysterography

hys·ter·o·graph \-raf,-råf\ *n* [*hyster-* + *-graph*] **:** HYSTEROGRAM — **hys·ter·o·graph·ic** \¦=≠≠¦grafik\ *adj*

hys·ter·og·ra·phy \,histə'rägrəfē\ *n* -ES [*hyster-* + *-graphy*] **:** examination of the uterus by roentgenography after the injection of an opaque medium

hys·ter·oid \'histə,rȯid\ *also* **hys·ter·oi·dal** \¦=≠¦rȯidᵊl\ *adj* [*hysteroid,* ISV *hyster-* + *-oid; hysteroidal* fr. *hysteroid* + *-al*] **:** resembling hysteria

hys·ter·ol·o·gy \,histə'räləjē\ *n* -ES [LL *hysterologia,* fr. LGk, fr. Gk *hysteros* latter, later + *-logia* -logy] *archaic* **:** HYSTERON PROTERON

hys·ter·o·mor·phous \¦histərō¦mȯrfəs\ *adj* [Gk *hysteros* later, latter + E *-morphous*] **:** of, relating to, or constituting mineral deposits formed on the earth's surface by mechanical or chemical concentration

hys·ter·on pro·ter·on \'histə,rän'prōd·ə,rän\ *n* [LL, fr. Gk, lit., later earlier, the latter earlier] **1 :** a figure of speech consisting of reversal of a natural or rational order (as in "then came the thunder and the lightning") **2 :** a logical fallacy consisting in assuming as a premise something that follows from what is to be proved

hys·tero–oophorectomy \¦histə(,)rō+\ *n* [*hyster-* + *oophor-* + *-ectomy*] **:** surgical removal of the uterus and ovaries

hys·ter·o·pexy \'histərō,peksē\ *n* -ES [ISV *hyster-* + *-pexy*] **:** surgical fixation of a displaced uterus

hys·ter·o·phyte \'histərō,fīt\ *n* -s [NL *hysterophytum,* fr. *hyster-* + *-phytum* -phyte] **:** HETEROPHYTE

hys·ter·or·rha·phy \,histə'rärəfē\ *n* -ES [ISV *hyster-* + *-rrhaphy*] **1 :** a suturing of an incised or ruptured uterus **2 :** HYSTEROPEXY

hys·ter·or·rhex·is \,histərō'reksəs\ *n, pl* **hysterorrhex·es** \-k,sēz\ [NL, fr. *hyster-* + *-rrhexis*] **:** rupture of the uterus

hys·ter·o·sal·pin·gog·raphy \,histərō,sal,piŋ'gägrəfē\ *n* -ES [ISV *hyster-* + *salping-* + *-graphy*] **:** examination of the uterus and fallopian tubes by roentgenography after injection of an opaque medium

hys·tero–salpingo–oophorectomy \¦histə(,)rō+\ *n* [*hyster-* + *salping-* + *oophorectomy*] **:** surgical removal of uterus, oviducts, and ovaries

hys·ter·o·scope \'histərō,skōp\ *n* [ISV *hyster-* + *-scope*] **:** an instrument used in inspection of the uterus — **hys·ter·o·scop·ic** \¦=≠≠¦skäpik\ *adj* — **hys·ter·os·co·py** \,histə'räskəpē\ *n* -ES

hys·ter·o·sto·mat·o·my \,histərō,stō'mad·əmē\ *n* -ES [F *hystérostomatomie,* fr. *hystér-* hyster- + *stoma-* + *-tomie* -tomy] **:** surgical incision of the uterine cervix

hys·ter·o·tely \'histərō,telē\ *n* -ES [Gk *hysteros* latter, later + *telos* end, completion, maturity + E *-y* — more at WHEEL] **:** relatively retarded differentiation of a structure or organ so that it shows a form usu. associated with a stage of development earlier than that shown by the individual plant or animal as a whole — compare PROTHETELY

hys·ter·o·the·ci·um \,histərō'thēs(h)ēəm\ *n* [NL, fr. *hyster-* + *-thecium*] **:** a narrow elongated ascocarp opening at maturity by a narrow lengthwise slit

hys·ter·ot·o·my \,histə'räd·əmē\ *n* -ES [NL *hysterotomia,* fr. *hyster-* + *-tomia* -tomy] **:** surgical incision of the uterus **:** CESAREAN, HYSTEROSTOMATOMY

hys·tric·i·dae \hə'strisə,dē\ *n pl, cap* [NL, fr. *Hystric-, Hystrix,* type genus + *-idae*] **:** a family of Old World hystricomorph rodents comprising the terrestrial porcupines that was formerly extended to include the New World arboreal porcupines — compare ERETHIZONTIDAE

1**hys·tri·coid** \'histrə,kȯid\ *adj* [NL *Hystricoidea*] **:** of or relating to the Hystricoidea

2**hystricoid** \"\ *n* -s **:** a rodent of the superfamily Hystricoidea

hys·tri·coi·dea \,=≠'kȯidēə\ *n pl, cap* [NL, fr. *Hystric-, Hystrix* + *-oidea*] **1** *in some classifications* **:** a major division of hystricomorph rodents equivalent to the Hystricidae **2** *in some classifications* **:** HYSTRICOMORPHA

1**hys·tri·co·morph** \'histrəkō,mȯrf\ *adj* [NL *Hystricomorpha*] **:** of or relating to the Hystricomorpha

2**hystricomorph** \"\ *n* -s **:** a rodent of the suborder Hystricomorpha

hys·tri·co·mor·pha \,=≠≠'mȯrfə\ *n pl, cap* [NL, fr. *Hystric-, Hystrix* + *-morpha*] **:** a suborder of Rodentia comprising forms distinguished by a zygomatic arch in which the jugal bone forms the center block and including porcupines, guinea pigs, chinchillas, and many others — **hys·tri·co·mor·phic** \¦=≠≠¦mȯrfik\ *or* **hys·tri·co·mor·phous** \-fəs\ *adj*

1**hys·trix** \'histriks\ *n, cap* [NL, fr. L, porcupine, fr. Gk] **:** a genus of terrestrial porcupines that is the type of the family Hystricidae

2**hystrix** \"\ *n, cap* [NL] **:** a genus of perennial grasses (family Gramineae) of No. America, Asia, and New Zealand having loosely flowered spikes with spikelets becoming widely divergent — see BOTTLE BRUSH GRASS

hyte \'həit\ *adj* [origin unknown] *Scot* **:** stark raving mad

hy·ther·graph \'hīthə(r),graf, -råf\ *also* **hy·ther·o·graph** \-ərō,-\ *n* [*hyther-* or *hythero-* (fr. Gk *hydōr* water + *thermē* heat) + *-graph*] **:** a climograph that records temperature and rainfall

Hz *abbr* hertz

hzy *abbr* hazy

[1]i \ˈī\ n, pl **i's** or **is** \ˈīz\ often cap, often attrib **1 a** : the ninth letter of the English alphabet **b** : an instance of this letter printed, written, or otherwise represented **c** : a speech counterpart of orthographic i (as long i in side, short i in sit, or i in French élite) **2** : ONE — see NUMBER table **3** : a printer's type, a stamp, or some other instrument for reproducing the letter i **4** : someone or something arbitrarily or conveniently designated i esp. as the ninth in order or class **5** : something having the shape of the capital letter I **6** : a unit vector parallel to the x-axis

[2]i \(ˌ)ī, ə, often ä or ȧ when unemphatic esp in contracted forms as "I'm" & "I'll"\ pron, cap [ME ich, i, fr. OE ic; akin to OHG ih I, ON ek, Goth ik, L ego, Gk egō, egōn, Skt aham] **1** : the one who is speaking or writing ⟨I shall not want —Ps 23:1 (AV)⟩ — used as a nominative pronoun of the first person singular by one speaking or writing to refer to himself as the doer of an action ⟨I will not hurt you⟩ ⟨whither thou goest, I will go —Ruth 1:16 (AV)⟩ or the subject of a predicated condition ⟨I don't feel very well today⟩ or sometimes in the predicate after forms of be ⟨it will not be I —D.D.Eisenhower⟩ ⟨it is I —Mk 6:50 (AV)⟩ or in comparisons after than or as when the first term in the comparison is the subject of a verb ⟨you can do it just as well as I⟩ ⟨he writes much better than I⟩ ⟨thou art stronger than I —Jer 20:7 (AV)⟩ or in some absolute or elliptical constructions esp. when not used with a prepositional phrase or an adjective or a participle ⟨who, I? You're foolish to say that anyone would do it⟩ or after but in a compound subject ⟨no one but I could have known —H.G.Wells⟩ — see ME, MINE, MY; compare WE **2 a** now chiefly substand : ME — used in a compound object ⟨belongs to my mother and I⟩ ⟨between you and I⟩ ⟨he saw my brother and I⟩ **b** now dial Eng : ME — used emphatically as object of a verb ⟨give poor I another chance⟩ or preposition ⟨give the ball to I⟩ ⟨my father hath no child but I —Shak.⟩ **3** : the one who acts as authorized spokesman of a social or military system (as an army) ⟨I order you to report for duty⟩ ⟨I arrest you in the name of the law⟩

[3]i \ˈī\ n, pl **i's** or **is** cap **1** : someone possessing and aware of possessing a distinct and personal individuality : SELF, EGO ⟨there is but one I —Mary B. Eddy⟩ ⟨society has been atomized down to its elemental particles each of which is an I —W.P.Webb⟩; also : the quality or state of possessing such individuality ⟨the crowd is like a community in that it can be any size, the difference being that the We precedes the I —Howard Griffin⟩ **2** : an excessively egotistic person : one that uses the first person pronoun excessively ⟨just a big I⟩ **3** : a dichotomous part of one's self ⟨the other I⟩

[4]i or **i'** \i\ now chiefly dial var of IN

[5]i obs var of AYE

[6]i abbr, often cap **1** [L id] that **2** [L imperator; imperatrix] emperor; empress **3** imperial **4** incendiary **5** incomplete **6** independent **7** indicated; indicative **8** industrial **9** infantry **10** infield **11** inhibitory **12** initial **13** inner **14** inside **15** inspector **16** instantaneous **17** institute; institution **18** instrumental **19** intelligence **20** interceptor **21** interest **22** international **23** intransitive **24** Iraqi **25** iron **26** island; isle **27** Israeli

[7]i symbol, cap **1** iodine **2** candlepower **3** electric current **4** moment of inertia **5** imaginary unit

[1]i- comb form [inactive] : inactive (sense c) ⟨i-inositol⟩ — usu. joined to second element with a hyphen

[2]i- comb form [by shortening] : is- 2b ⟨i-butyl⟩ — usu. joined to second element with a hyphen

-i- [ME, fr. OF, fr. L, thematic vowel of most nouns and adjectives in combination] — used as a connective vowel to join two elements of usu. Latin origin, being either identical with ⟨auriform⟩ or representative of ⟨Herbivora⟩ an original Latin stem vowel or simply inserted ⟨cantilever⟩; compare -O-

[1]-ia \ēə, yə, iə\ n suffix [NL, fr. L & Gk, suffix forming feminine abstract nouns] **1** -s : pathological condition ⟨pneumonia⟩ ⟨hysteria⟩ ⟨diphtheria⟩ **2** : genus consisting of (specified plants or animals) ⟨Wistaria⟩ ⟨Osmia⟩

[2]-ia \"\ n pl suffix [NL, fr. L (neut. pl. of -ius, adj. ending) & Gk, neut. pl. of -ios, adj. ending] **1** : taxonomic division (as class, order) consisting of (specified plants or animals) ⟨Cryptogamia⟩ ⟨Mammalia⟩ **2** : things belonging to or derived from or relating to (something specified) ⟨Marylandia⟩ ⟨tabloidia⟩

[3]-ia pl of -IUM

IA abbr **1** incorporated accountant **2** infected area **3** often not cap [L inter alia] among other things **4** international angstrom

IAA abbr indoleacetic acid

IAC abbr **1** industry advisory committee **2** interview-after-combat

-ial \ēəl, yəl, iəl, əl\ adj suffix [ME, fr. MF -iel, -ial, fr. L -ialis, fr. -i- + -alis -al] : [1]-AL ⟨gerundial⟩

iamb \ˈī,am, -,aa(ə)m also -mb\ n, pl **iambs** \-mz\ [L iambus, fr. Gk iambos] **1** : a metrical foot of two syllables unstressed and stressed respectively (as in above, invent, and Tennyson's 4-foot line "he watches from his mountain walls") or short and long respectively (as in classical prosody) : a disyllabic rising cadence — symbol ⏑– ; compare TROCHEE **2** : verses written in iambs

iam·bel·e·gus \ˌī,amˈbeləgəs\ n -ES [LL, fr. Gk iambelegos, fr. iambos + elegos song of mourning or lamentation, prob. of non-IE origin] : a verse used in classical prosody consisting of an iambic dimeter and half an elegiac pentameter

[1]iam·bic \īˈambik, -bēk\ n -S [L iambicus, adj.] **1** : IAMB **2** : a piece of usu. satiric verse written in iambs (as that developed by the Ionian Greeks in the period succeeding the epic) : a lampoon written in iambs

[2]iambic \(ˈ)=ˈ==\ adj [L iambicus, fr. Gk iambikos, fr. iambos + -ikos -ic] : relating to or consisting of iambs or iambics ⟨~ verse⟩ — **iam·bi·cal·ly** \-bək(ə)lē, -bēk-, -li\ adv

iam·bist \=ˈ=bəst, ˈ=,=-\ n -S [Gk iambistēs, fr. iambizein to write iambs, fr. iambos + -izein -ize] : one who writes iambic verse

iam·bog·ra·pher \ˌī,amˈbägrəfə(r)\ n -S [MGk iambographos writer of iambs (fr. Gk iambos + -graphos, fr. graphein to write) + E -er — more at CARVE] : IAMBIST; esp : one given to or noted for writing iambic lampoons

iam·bus \īˈambəs\ n, pl **iambus·es** \-bəsəz\ also **iam·bi** \-,bī\ [L, fr. Gk iambos] : IAMB

-ian \ēən, yən, iən, ən\ — see -AN

-iana — see -ANA

I and E abbr information and education

I and P abbr indexed and paged

I and R abbr **1** initiative and referendum **2** intelligence and reconnaissance

I and S abbr **1** inspection and security **2** inspection and survey

[1]ian·thi·na \ēˈan(t)thənə, īˈ-\ [NL, by alter.] syn of JANTHINA

[2]ianthina \"\ n -S : JANTHINA 2

ian·thine \ēˈan(t)thən, (ˈ)ī,a-\ adj [L ianthinus — more at JANTHINA] : having a violet color

ian·thin·i·dae \ˌī,anˈthinə,dē\ [NL, fr. Ianthina, type genus + -idae] syn of JANTHINIDAE

ian·thi·nite \ēˈan(t)thə,nīt, īˈ-\ n -S [G ianthinit, fr. L ianthinus + G -it -ite] : a mineral $2UO_2.7H_2O$ consisting of a hydrous uranium dioxide and occurring as violet orthorhombic crystals

[1]iao \(ˈ)ēˈau̇\ n -S [Samoan] : WATTLEBIRD 1a

[2]iao \"\ n -S [native name in Hawaii] : a small silversides often used as bait in fishing

ia·pyg·ian \ˌīəˈpij(ē)ən\ n -S usu cap [Iapygia, ancient region in southeastern Italy (fr. L, fr. Gk) + E -an] **1** : a member of one of several peoples anciently inhabiting the peninsula of Apulia in southeastern Italy **2** : the language of the Iapygians

[2]iapygian \ˌ==ˈ=(=)ə\ adj, usu cap : of or relating to the Iapygians

ia·pyg·i·dae \ˌīəˈpijə,dē\ [NL, fr. Iapyg-, Iapyx, type genus (alter. of Japyg-, Japyx) + -idae] syn of JAPYGIDAE

iarovize var of JAROVIZE

IAS abbr indicated airspeed

-ias pl of -IA

ia·si \ˈyäsh(ē)\ or **ias·sy** \ˈyäsē\ adj, usu cap [fr. Iasi (Jassy), Romania] : of or from the city of Iasi, Romania : of the kind or style prevalent in Iasi

-i·a·sis \ˈīəsəs\ n suffix, pl **-i·a·ses** \-,sēz\ [NL, fr. L, fr. Gk, -sis, suffix of action, fr. verbs in -ian, -iazein (fr. nouns in -ia -y) + -sis] : morbid state or condition : disease having characteristics of (something specified) ⟨satyriasis⟩ : disease produced by (something specified) ⟨ancylostomiasis⟩ ⟨habronemiasis⟩

ias·us \ēˈasəs, īˈ-\ [NL, fr. Iasus, Iassus, ancient city of Asia Minor] syn of JASUS

iat·mul \ˈyät,mül\ n, pl **iatmul** or **iatmuls** usu cap **1** : a Papuan people of the Sepik district, Territory of New Guinea **2** : a member of the Iatmul people

iat·ric \(ˈ)īˈa·trik, -rēk\ also **iat·ri·cal** \-rəkəl, -rēk-\ adj [Gk iatrikos, fr. iatros healer, physician (fr. iasthai to heal) + -ikos -ic, -ical; perh. akin to L ira anger — more at IRE] **1** : of or relating to a physician or medical treatment : MEDICAL ⟨outstanding ~ ability⟩ **2** : MEDICINAL, HEALING, CURATIVE ⟨an extract with a remarkable ~ quality⟩

-i·at·ric \ēˈa·trik, -rēk\ also **-i·at·ri·cal** \-rəkəl, -rēk-\ adj comb form [-iatric fr. NL -iatria -iatry + E -ic; -iatrical fr. -iatric + -al] : of or relating to medical treatment : of or relating to healing ⟨hydriatric⟩ ⟨psychiatric⟩

-i·at·rics \-ks\ n pl comb form usu sing in constr [-iatric + -s] : medical treatment : healing ⟨gyniatrics⟩ ⟨pediatrics⟩

-iatrist \ˈīə·trəst, ēˈa·trəst\ n comb form -S [-iatry + -ist] : physician : healer ⟨psychiatrist⟩ ⟨podiatrist⟩

iatro- comb form [NL, fr. Gk, fr. iatros physician] **1** : physician : medicine : healing ⟨iatrology⟩ ⟨iatrogenic⟩ **2** : physician and ⟨iatrochemist⟩ : medicine or healing and ⟨iatrophysics⟩ ⟨iatro-astrological⟩

iat·ro·chemical \īˈa·trō, ēˈ-+\ adj [iatro- + chemical] : of or relating to iatrochemistry : [1]CHEMICAL 1b

iat·ro·chemist \"+\ n [iatro- + chemist] : one believing in or practicing iatrochemistry

iat·ro·chemistry \"+\ n [iatro- + chemistry] : chemistry combined with medicine — used of the chemistry of the period about 1525–1660 dominated by the teachings of Paracelsus; compare IATROPHYSICS

iat·ro·gen·ic \"+ˈjenik\ adj [iatro- + -genic] : induced by a physician — used chiefly of imagined ailments induced in a patient by autosuggestion based on a physician's words or actions during examination — **iat·ro·ge·nic·i·ty** \=,==jəˈnisəd·ē\ n -ES

iat·ro·mathematics \īˈa·trō, ēˈ-+\ n pl but usu sing in constr [NL iatromathematica, fr. iatro- + L mathematica mathematics, astrology; after Gk iatromathēmatikos one that practices medicine in conjunction with astrology — more at MATHEMATICS] : IATROPHYSICS

iat·ro·physicist \"+\ n, archaic : one who specializes in iatrophysics

iat·ro·physics \"+\ n pl but usu sing in constr [ISV iatro- + physics] : physics combined with medicine — used of a school of medicine of the 17th century that explained disease and the activities of the body in terms of physics rather than of chemistry; compare IATROCHEMISTRY

-i·atry \ˈīə·trē, ēˈa·t-, -ri\ n comb form -ES [F -iatrie, fr. NL -iatria, fr. Gk iatreia art or action of healing, fr. iatros physician + -eia -y — more at IATRIC] : medical treatment : healing ⟨podiatry⟩ ⟨gyniatry⟩ ⟨psychiatry⟩

IAZ abbr inner artillery zone

ib abbr [L ibidem] in the same place

IB abbr **1** in bond **2** inbound **3** incendiary bomb **4** intelligence branch **5** invoice book

iba \ˈēbə\ n -S [Tag] : a medium-sized Philippine tree (Cicca acida) sometimes cultivated for its edible roundish greenish white fruit

IBA abbr indolebutyric acid

ibad \ˈē,bäd\ n, pl **ibad** or **ibads** usu cap **1** : an Arab people in Hira between the Euphrates and the Arabian desert **2** : a member of the Ibad people

iba·dan \ēˈbädᵊn, -bad-\ adj, usu cap [fr. Ibadan, Nigeria] : of or from the city of Ibadan, Nigeria : of the kind or style prevalent in Ibadan

iba·dhi \əˈbädē\ n, pl **ibadhi** or **ibadhis** usu cap [after ʿAbdallah ibn-Ibāḍ] : [1]IBADITE

[1]iba·dite also **aba·dite** \əˈbä,dīt\ n -S usu cap [ʿAbdallah ibn-Ibāḍ (Abāḍ), 7th cent. Arab religious leader + E -ite] : a member of an austere Muslim sect found chiefly in the northern part of Africa

[2]ibadite \"\ n -S usu cap [Ibad + -ite] : IBAD

iba·loi \ˌēbəˈlȯi\ n, pl **ibaloi** or **ibalois** usu cap : NABALOI

iban \(ˈ)ēˈbän\ n, pl **iban** or **ibans** usu cap [Iban] **1 a** : a Dayak people of Sarawak, Borneo — called also Sea Dayak **b** : a member of such people **2** : the Austronesian language of the Iban people

iba·nag \ˌēbəˈnäg\ n, pl **ibanag** or **ibanags** usu cap **1 a** : a people of northern Luzon inhabiting chiefly the Cagayan valley **b** : a member of such people **2** : the Austronesian language of the Ibanag people

i bar n, cap I : a rolled iron or steel bar of I section used in construction work

i beam n, cap I : a rolled iron or steel beam or a cast steel beam of I section; also : a built-up beam of I section used esp. in structural ironwork (as in steel-framed buildings) — called also I girder

[1]ibe·ri·an \īˈbirēən\ n -S cap [Iberia, ancient region of the Caucasus approximately equivalent to modern Georgia (fr. L Iberia, Hiberia, fr. Gk Ibēria) + E -an] : a member of one or more peoples anciently inhabiting the Caucasus in Asia between the Black and Caspian seas in the approximate region of the Soviet republic of Georgia and prob. being the ancestors of the Kartvelians

[2]iberian \(ˈ)=ˈ===\ adj, usu cap : of, relating to, or characteristic of Asiatic Iberia, its inhabitants, or their language : GEORGIAN

[3]iberian \=ˈ===\ n -S cap [Iberia, peninsula in southwestern Europe that contains Spain and Portugal (fr. L Iberia, Hiberia, fr. Gk Ibēria) + E -an] **1 a** : a member of one or more Caucasoid peoples anciently inhabiting the peninsula comprising Spain and Portugal and the Basque region about the Pyrenees, prob. being related in origin to the Mauretanians and other peoples of the northern part of Africa and early known to the Greeks and later conquered by the Romans, being short and dark and dolichocephalic, and being prob. the builders of the neolithic stone structures (as cairns, dolmens) found esp. in Spain and in the northern part of Africa and in France and Great Britain **b** : a native or inhabitant of Spain or Portugal or the Basque region about the Pyrenees **2** : one or more of the languages natively spoken by the ancient Iberians

[4]iberian \(ˈ)=ˈ===\ adj, usu cap : of, relating to, or characteristic of the Iberian peninsula, its inhabitants, or their language ⟨tragedy and death are indeed recurrent themes in Iberian art —George Woodcock⟩

iberian tortoise or **iberian turtle** n, usu cap I : a common tortoise (Clemmys leprosa syn. Testudo ibera) of southwestern Europe and northern Africa

ibe·ric \(ˈ)īˈbirik, -ber-\ adj, usu cap [L Ibericus, Hibericus, fr. Iberia, Hiberia Iberia + -icus -ic] : IBERIAN

ibe·ris \īˈbirəs\ n, cap [NL, fr. L, peppergrass, fr. Gk ibēris, perh. fr. Ibēria (in Europe)] : a genus of Old World mostly glabrous plants (family Cruciferae) having entire or pinnatifid sometimes fleshy leaves and flowers with two long and two short petals succeeded by a broad ovate pod, the herbaceous members being often cultivated for their flat-topped clusters of white or purplish flowers — see CANDYTUFT

ibe·rite \ˈībə,rīt, ˈibi,r-\ n -S [Sw or G iberit, fr. Iberia (in Europe), its locality + Sw or G -it -ite] : an alteration product of cordierite

ibero- comb form, usu cap [L Iberus, Hiberus] : Iberian : Iberian and ⟨Ibero-American⟩

ibero-romance \īˈbirō+\ n, cap I&R [Ibero- + Romance] **1** : the Romance language of the Iberian peninsula prior to the emergence of Spanish, Portuguese, and Catalan as national languages **2** : a language group of the Romance division consisting of Spanish, Portuguese, and Catalan

ibex \ˈī,beks\ n [L] **1** pl **ibex** or **ibex·es a** : one of several wild goats living chiefly in high mountain areas (as the Alps) of the Old World and having large recurved horns transversely ridged in front **b** : a wild goat (Capra aegagrus) now found in Asia Minor and supposed to be the progenitor of the domestic goat **c** (1) : MOUNTAIN GOAT (2) : MOUNTAIN SHEEP **2** cap [NL, fr. L] in some classifications : a genus that comprises the ibex and that is often considered a subgenus of Capra

IBI abbr invoice book, inwards

ibi·bio \ˌibəˈbē(,)ō\ n, pl **ibibio** or **ibibios** usu cap **1 a** : a people of southeastern Nigeria **b** : a member of such people **2** : the language of the Ibibio people, belonging to the Central branch of the Niger-Congo language family

ibid \ˈibəd\ abbr [L ibidem] in the same place

ibi·dem \ˈibə,dem, -dəm; əˈbīdəm, əˈbēd-, -,dem\ adv [L] : in the same place — usu. abbreviated and used (as in a footnote) to avoid repetition of source data (as author, title) in a reference immediately preceding; abbr. ibid., ib.

ibid·i·dae \īˈbidə,dē\ [NL, fr. Ibid-, Ibis, genus of birds (fr. L ibid-, ibis) + -idae] syn of THRESKIORNITHIDAE

ibid·i·um \īˈbidēəm\ [NL, fr. L ibid-, ibis ibis + NL -ium; fr. the shape of the anthers] syn of SPIRANTHES

-ibility — see -ABILITY

ibis \ˈībəs sometimes ˈēb-\ n, pl **ibis** or **ibis·es** [L ibid-, ibis, fr. Gk ibis, fr. Egypt hby] : any of several wading birds related to the herons and constituting the family Threskiornithidae that inhabit warm regions in both hemispheres and feed on aquatic and amphibious animals and are distinguished by a long slender downwardly curved bill resembling a curlew's bill

ibisbill \ˈ==,=\ n : a bluish gray bird (Ibidorhyncha struthersii) of central Asia having a long downcurved red bill and resembling a lapwing

-ible — see -ABLE

IBM abbr or n -S : an intercontinental ballistic missile

ibo \ˈē(,)bō\ or **ig·bo** \ˈig,bō\ n, pl **ibo** or **ibos** or **igbo** or **igbos** usu cap **1 a** : a Negro people of the country about the lower Niger **b** : a member of such people **2** : a Kwa language of the Igbo people used as a language of trade and education in a large area of southern Nigeria

IBO abbr invoice book, outwards

ibo·ga·ine \əˈbōgə,ēn\ n -S [ISV iboga (fr. NL, specific epithet of Tabernanthe iboga, fr. a native name in central Africa) + -ine] : a crystalline alkaloid $C_{20}H_{26}N_2O$ obtained from the roots, bark, and leaves of a plant (Tabernanthe iboga) of equatorial Africa

ibo·li·um privet \īˈbōlēəm-\ or **ibo·ta privet** \īˈbōd·ə-\ n [ibolium, NL (specific epithet of Ligustrum ibolium), irreg. fr. Jap ibota wax tree + L oleum oil — more at OIL] : a privet (Ligustrum ibolium) produced by hybridizing two privets (L. obtusifolium and L. ovalifolium) that has pubescent branches and midribs of the under surfaces of the leaves and a glabrous calyx

ib·sen·ian \(ˈ)ibˈsēnēən, (ˈ)ip'-, -sen-\ adj, usu cap [Henrik Ibsen †1906 Norw. poet and dramatist + E -ian] : of, relating to, or having the characteristics of the playwright Ibsen or his plays

ib·sen·ism \ˈibsə,nizəm, ˈips-\ n -S usu cap [Henrik Ibsen + E -ism] **1** : dramatic invention or construction characteristic of Ibsen whose plays attack conventional hypocrisies **2** : adherence to or championship of Ibsen's plays and ideas

[1]ib·sen·ite \-,nīt\ n -S usu cap [Henrik Ibsen + E -ite] **1** : an admirer or devotee of Ibsen **2** : a dramatist who imitates Ibsen's manner or technique

[2]ibsenite \"\ adj, usu cap : IBSENIAN

[1]-ic \ik, ēk; ,ik in a few words that have a heavy stress on a syllable preceding the penult, as "politic"\ adj suffix [ME -ik, -ic, fr. OF & L; OF -ique, fr. L -icus — more at -Y] **1** : having the character or form of : being ⟨panoramic⟩ ⟨rhombic⟩ ⟨Samoyedic⟩ : consisting of ⟨runic⟩ **2 a** : of or relating to ⟨aldermanic⟩ ⟨daturic⟩ ⟨Koranic⟩ **b** : related to, derived from, or containing ⟨alcoholic⟩ — esp. in names of acids and related compounds ⟨boric⟩ ⟨cinammic⟩ ⟨oleic⟩ **3** : in the manner of : like that of : characteristic of ⟨Byronic⟩ ⟨quixotic⟩ ⟨Puritanic⟩ **4** : associated or dealing with ⟨Vedic⟩ : utilizing ⟨electronic⟩ ⟨atomic⟩ **5** : characterized by : exhibiting ⟨nostalgic⟩ : affected with ⟨allergic⟩ ⟨paraplegic⟩ **6** : caused by ⟨amoebic⟩ **7** : tending to produce ⟨analgesic⟩ **8** : having the highest valence of a (specified) element or a valence relatively higher than in compounds or ions named with an adjective ending in -ous ⟨ferric iron⟩ ⟨sulfuric acid⟩ — compare [1]-ATE 2

[2]-ic \"\ n suffix -S [ME -ik, -ic, fr. OF & L; OF -ique, fr. L -icus (-ic adj. suffix)] : one having the character or nature of : one belonging to or associated with : one exhibiting or affected by ⟨glyconic⟩ : one that produces ⟨ecbolic⟩

IC abbr **1** immediate constituent **2** often not cap in charge **3** index correction **4** information center **5** information circular **6** inspected and condemned **7** interior communications **8** internal combustion **9** internal connection

ica \ˈēkə\ n, pl **ica** or **icas** usu cap [Sp, of AmerInd origin] **1 a** : a Chibchan people of northern Colombia **b** : a member of such people **2** : the language of the Ica people

icac·i·na·ce·ae \i,kasəˈnāsē,ē\ n pl, cap [NL, fr. Icacina, type genus (fr. ISV icaco + NL -ina) + -aceae] : a family of tropical chiefly woody plants of the order Sapindales with alternate leaves, panicled flowers, and drupaceous fruit — **icac·i·na·ceous** \=,==ˈnāshəs\ adj

icaco \iˈka,kō, iˈkä,-\ or **icaco plum** also **hi·caco** \(h)i-\ n -S [Sp icaco, hicaco, fr. Arawak] : COCO PLUM

-i·cal \ə̇kəl, ēk-\ adj suffix [ME, fr. LL -icalis (as in clericalis clerical, grammaticalis grammatical, radicalis radical) — more at CLERICAL, GRAMMATICAL, RADICAL] : -IC ⟨cosmical⟩ ⟨fantastical⟩ — sometimes differing from -ic in that adjectives formed with -ical have a wider or more transferred semantic range than corresponding adjectives in -ic ⟨economical: economic⟩ ⟨prophetical: prophetic⟩

[1]icar·i·an \īˈka(a)rēən, (ˈ)iˌk-\ adj, usu cap [L Icarius of Icarus (fr. Gk Ikarios, fr. Ikaros Icarus, Greek mythological character who flew so high on man-made wings that the sun melted them and sent him to destruction) + E -an] : of, relating to, or characteristic of Icarus: **a** : soaring too high for safety ⟨Icarian flight⟩ **b** : inadequate for or incapable of bringing about an ambitious project ⟨Icarian methods⟩

[2]icarian \"\ adj, usu cap [F Icarien, fr. Icarie, communistic utopia in Voyage en Icarie (1842), novel by Étienne Cabet †1857 Fr. political radical (fr. Icarie Icaria, island in the Aegean sea) + F -en -an] : of, relating to, or constituting a communistic settlement established in the U.S. during the latter half of the 19th century by a group of French immigrants ⟨the last Icarian utopia . . . fizzled out in 1895 —Time⟩

[3]icarian \"\ n -S usu cap [F Icarien, fr. Icarien, adj.] : a member of an Icarian community

ICAS abbr intermittent commercial and amateur service

ICBM abbr or n -S : an intercontinental ballistic missile ⟨the ~ era —Clay Blair⟩

[1]ice \ˈīs\ n -S often attrib [ME is, fr. OE īs; akin to OFris, OS, & OHG īs ice, ON īss, Av isu- icy, aēxa- cold, and perh. to Russ ineĭ frost, Lith ynis] **1 a** : water reduced to the solid state by cooling and when pure constituting a nearly colorless brittle substance that in freezing expands about one eleventh in volume, that has a specific gravity of 0.9166 as compared with 1.0 for water at 4°C, that under normal atmospheric pressure is formed at and has a melting point of 0°C or 32°F, that occurs in the common form as hexagonal crystals, and that in large masses is classed as a rock — compare BLUE ICE, FROST, SNOW; HEAT OF FUSION **b** : the layer of frozen water covering a surface (as of a road, rink, or body of water) ⟨broke through the ~⟩ : the surface of a sheet of ice ⟨slipped on the ~⟩ ⟨skated down the ~⟩ ⟨an ~ carnival⟩ **2** : the quality or state of being emotionally cold (as from formality, reserve, embarrassment, or hostility) ⟨perceptibly chilled by the ~ in his voice⟩ ⟨thawed a little of the ~ that bound his lady's heart —Robert Murphy⟩ — compare BREAK THE ICE **3** : a substance resembling ice in appearance or solid form ⟨these hydrogen ~s might well be retained in meteoritic particles —P.M.Millman⟩; specif : ICING **4 a** : a sweet frozen food containing a fruit juice or other flavoring and usu. served as a dessert or refreshment; specif : one containing no milk or cream (as a fruit ice or water ice) **b** Brit : a serving of ice cream; specif : ICE-CREAM CONE **5** slang : DIAMONDS ⟨fenced the ~ for the gang⟩; broadly : JEWELRY

6 *slang* **:** protection money paid by an operator of illicit business ⟨a $20,000,000-a-year bookmaking syndicate that paid out $1,000,000 in ~ to the police —*N.Y. Times*⟩ **7 :** allowance made in directing a curling stone for its deviation from a straight course ⟨make the shot . . . by using the ~ and weight suggested by his skip —Ken Watson⟩ — **on ice** *adv* **1 a :** with every likelihood of being won ⟨with their lead they had the game *on ice*⟩ **b :** with every likelihood of being fulfilled — used of a contract in a card game **2 :** in reserve ⟨put the project *on ice* until funds were sent⟩ ⟨kept the invention *on ice* for 10 years⟩ **3** *slang* **:** in safekeeping ⟨put you *on ice* quietly till they've had time to settle up their affairs —Dorothy Sayers⟩; *specif* **:** in jail or prison ⟨*on ice* pending his appearance in court —*Front Page Detective*⟩ — **on thin ice :** in a situation involving great risk ⟨in opposing mob passions he was *on thin ice*⟩

²**ice** \"\ *vb* -ED/-ING/-S [ME *isen*, fr. *is*, n.] *vt* **1 a :** to coat with or convert into ice ⟨sleet *iced* the turnpike⟩ ⟨weather that *iced* his breath⟩ **b :** to chill esp. by surface contact with ice ⟨~ the champagne before serving⟩ ⟨an *iced* melon⟩ ⟨a frown that *iced* his enthusiasm⟩ **c :** to load or supply with ice ⟨a portable cooler *iced* with cubes from the refrigerator⟩ ⟨stations for *icing* refrigerator cars containing perishables⟩ **2 :** to cover with or as if with icing ⟨~ a cake⟩ ⟨houses *iced* over with multicolored stuccoes —Norman Lewis⟩ **3 :** to put in a secure place or state or in reserve **:** put on ice ⟨sank a free throw . . . to ~ the victory —*Spokane Spokesman-Rev.*⟩ ⟨has frozen all major route applications . . would probably ~ a merger too —*Time*⟩ ~ *vi* **1 :** to become ice cold **:** FREEZE ⟨the two bottles were *icing* in a bucket —Lionel Trilling⟩ **2 a :** to become covered with ice ⟨at the first sign of snow or *icing*, equipment is deployed along the turnpike —*Roads & Streets*⟩ — often used with *up* ⟨the airplane propeller and wings may ~ up⟩ **b :** to have ice form inside — usu. used with *up* ⟨the airplane carburetor *iced up*⟩

-ice \əs\ *n suffix* -s [ME *-ice*, *-ise*, fr. OF, fr. L *-itius* (masc.), *-itia* (fem.), *-itium* (neut.), suffixes forming adjectives and nouns; akin to Gk *-sios*, Skt *-tya*] **:** act ⟨service⟩ **:** quality ⟨justice⟩ **:** condition ⟨cowardice⟩

ice age *n* **1 :** a time of widespread glaciation **2** *usu cap I&A* **:** the Pleistocene glacial epoch

ice anchor *n* **:** a small anchor usu. having one fluke and used for mooring a boat to ice

ice apron *n* **:** a wedge-shaped structure for protecting a bridge pier from floating ice

ice ax *n* **:** a mountain-climbing tool that has a pick and adze at one end of a shaft and a spike or a ferrule at the other end and that is used esp. for cutting steps, belaying, and glissading

ice bag *n* **:** a waterproof bag designed to hold cracked ice and used for local application of cold to the body — see ICE CAP, ICE COLLAR

ice bag

ice banner *n* **:** SNOW BANNER

ice barrier *n* **:** the outer margin of the antarctic ice sheet

ice bear *n* **:** POLAR BEAR

ice belt *n* **:** ICE FOOT 1

ice·berg \ˈīs,bərg, -bə̄g,-bəig\ *n* [prob. part trans. of Dan or Norw *isberg*, fr. *is* ice + *berg* mountain, fr. ON, rock — more at BARROW] **1 a** *archaic* **:** GLACIER **b :** a large mass of land ice broken from a glacier at the edge of a body of water that when afloat has only a small part above the surface and that in the ocean floats with subsurface currents often to great distances — called also *berg*; compare GROWLER, ICE ISLAND **2 :** an emotionally cold person **3 :** something of which only a fraction is observed or explicit ⟨the seven-eighths of the ~ of personality that is submerged and never seen —W.E.Allen⟩

iceberg lettuce *also* **iceberg** *n* **:** any of various crisp freely blanching head lettuces

ice bird *n* **1 :** any of several sea birds that frequent ice floes: as **a :** DOVEKIE 2 **b :** PRION **2 :** an Indian goatsucker (*Caprimulgus asiaticus*)

iceblink \ˈ=,=\ *n* **1 :** a yellowish or whitish glare in the sky over an ice field (as in polar regions) — called also *ice sky*; compare SNOWBLINK, WATER SKY **2 :** a cliff of ice on a coast (as of Greenland)

ice bloom *n* **:** a brownish purple color imparted to ice in some regions by the growth of desmids of the genus *Ancyclonema*

ice-blue \ˈ=ˈ=\ *adj* **:** very pale greenish blue like the color seen in a cake of clear ice

iceboat \ˈ=,=\ *n* **1 :** a vehicle similar to a boat that has runners, is propelled on ice by sails or sometimes a propeller or jet propulsion, and is used chiefly for sport; *esp* **:** one having a center timber or long slender hull rigged fore-and-aft with a mainsail and sometimes also a jib and resting on a pivoted steering runner at the stern or bow and two other runners outrigged at each end of a running plank **2 :** ICEBREAKER

iceboat 1

iceboating \ˈ=,==\ *n* **:** the sport of sailing in iceboats

ice·bone \ˈīs,=\ *n* [prob. trans. of D *ijsbeen* (fr. MD *isebeen*, *ijsbeen*) or LG *isbeen*, fr. MLG *isbēn*; both prob. by folk etymology fr. L *ischium* + MD *been* bone or MLG *bēn* — more at ISCHIUM] **:** AITCHBONE

icebound \ˈ=ˈ=\ *adj* **1 :** surrounded with ice so as to be incapable of advancing ⟨an ~ ship⟩ **2 :** surrounded or obstructed with ice so as to hinder access **:** iced in ⟨an ~ coast⟩ **3 :** constricted by inhibitions or taboos ⟨sweet young things whose ~ virtue excited them to . . . sighing and languishing whenever a man was about —Max Peacock⟩

icebox \ˈ=,=\ *n* **:** an insulated cabinet or box having a compartment for ice and used for refrigeration (as of food); *broadly* **:** REFRIGERATOR ⟨an electric ~⟩

icebreaker \ˈ=,==\ *n* **1 :** an ice apron or other structure that protects a bridge pier from floating ice **2 :** a ship designed or equipped (as with a reinforced bow) to make and maintain a channel through the ice **3 :** the right whale of the arctic **4 :** something that breaks the ice on a project or social occasion ⟨pictures of girls . . . intended as an ~ between us and the French officers —Nathaniel Benchley⟩; *specif* **:** MIXER 1c

ice candle *n*, *dial* **:** ICICLE

ice cap *n* **1 :** an ice bag shaped to be fitted to the head **2 :** a cover of perennial ice and snow (as in the polar regions or on a mountain peak above the snow line); *specif* **:** a glacier forming on an extensive area of relatively level land (as a plateau, or a large part of a continent) and flowing outward from its center ⟨the endless polar *ice cap* was running between eight and eighty feet thick —W.R.Anderson⟩

ice car *n* **:** a railway car that is specially insulated for transporting ice

ice cave *n* **1 :** a cave so protected from the summer heat that ice remains in it throughout all or most of the year **2 :** a cave or tunnel in ice; *esp* **:** one formed in a glacier by meltwater streams

ice cellar *n* **:** an underground room where foods and drinks are kept cool by ice

ice chest *n* **:** ICEBOX

ice chisel *n* **:** a long-handled chisel for cutting holes in ice (as for fishing) or splitting blocks of ice

ice-cold \ˈ=ˈ=\ *adj* **:** extremely cold or impassive ⟨plunged into the *ice-cold* water⟩ ⟨planning all his battles . . . with an *ice-cold* brain —Brian Horrocks⟩

ice collar *n* **:** an ice bag shaped to fit around the neck

ice color *n* [so called fr. its being treated with a diazo solution in the presence of ice] **:** AZOIC DYE

icecraft \ˈ=,=\ *n* **:** skill in traveling on an ice surface or through waters containing floating ice

ice cream \(ˈ)=ˈ=, ˈ=,=\ *n* **1 :** a frozen food containing cream or butter fat, flavoring, sweetening, and usu. eggs; *specif* **:** such a food made smooth by stirring during freezing — distinguished from *mousse* and *parfait* **2 :** a serving of ice cream

ice-cream *adj* [*ice cream*] **:** of a color similar to that of vanilla ice cream — usu. used of clothing ⟨a gentleman in a blue serge coat and *ice-cream* pants —Conrad Richter⟩

ice-cream cone *n* **:** a crisp conical wafer usu. about five inches long holding ice cream

ice-cream cone

ice-cream fork *n* **:** a fork of medium size that has a bowl-shaped or blade-shaped end terminating usu. in three short tines and is used for eating ice cream or sherbets

ice-cream freezer *n* **:** a hand or power operated machine for freezing and stirring ice cream; *specif* **:** a can rotated by a crank within a tub of ice and salt so that the ice-cream mixture in it is stirred by a dasher

ice-cream soda *n* **:** a sweet food drink of soda water, flavored syrup, and ice cream

ice crusher *n* **:** a device for crushing ice; *specif* **:** a kitchen grinder having a hopper, a crank, blades, and a cup and used for crushing ice cubes

ice crystal *n* **:** ICE NEEDLE

ice cube *n* **:** a small block of artificial ice formed in a mold or cut from a larger block and commonly used for icing drinks

iced *adj* **:** containing cracked ice or ice cubes ⟨~ coffee⟩

iced firn *n* **:** a mixture of ice and firn

ice dike *n* **:** a formation of secondary ice in a glacier along a crevice

iced-tea spoon *n* **:** a teaspoon with a very long handle

ice duck *n* **:** any of various ducks found in icy seas; *esp* **:** OLDSQUAW 1

icefall \ˈ=,=\ *n* **1 :** a frozen waterfall or similar mass of ice **2 :** a falling of ice (as from an iceberg or glacier) **3 :** the mass of jumbled and usu. jagged blocks of ice into which a glacier may break when it moves down a steep declivity

ice feathers *n pl* **:** ¹RIME 2

ice field *n* **1 :** an extensive sheet of sea ice larger than an ice floe **2 :** a large body of glacial ice **:** ICE CAP

icefish \ˈ=,=\ *n* **:** any of several small, shining, more or less translucent fishes: as **a :** a fish of the family Salangidae **b :** CAPELIN **c :** a common No. American smelt (*Osmerus mordax*)

ice fishing *n* **:** fishing through a hole in the ice

ice floe *n* **:** a flat free mass of floating sea ice of usu. visible extent larger than a pan and smaller than an ice field; *broadly* **:** a large floating fragment of sheet ice

ice flower *n* **:** FROST FLOWER 2

ice fog *n* **:** a fog composed of ice particles

ice foot *n* **1 :** a wall or belt of ice frozen to the shore in arctic regions having a base at or below the low-water mark and formed as a result of the rise and fall of the tides, freezing spray, or stranded ice **2 :** the ice at the front of a glacier

ice fork *n* **:** a fork or serrated chisel for splitting or chopping up ice

ice fox *n* **:** ARCTIC FOX

ice-free \ˈ=ˈ=\ *adj* **:** free from ice; *esp* **:** not frozen over in winter ⟨an *ice-free* port⟩

ice front *n* **:** the lower or outer margin of a glacier

ice gland *n* **:** a roughly cylindrical and more or less vertical column of ice in névé

ice green *n* **:** a variable color averaging a very light bluish green that is lighter, stronger, and slightly bluer than spray

ice gull *n* **:** any of several northern gulls; *esp* **:** IVORY GULL

ice hockey *n* **:** a goal game played on an ice rink by two teams of six players on skates whose object is to direct a puck into the opponents' goal with a hockey stick

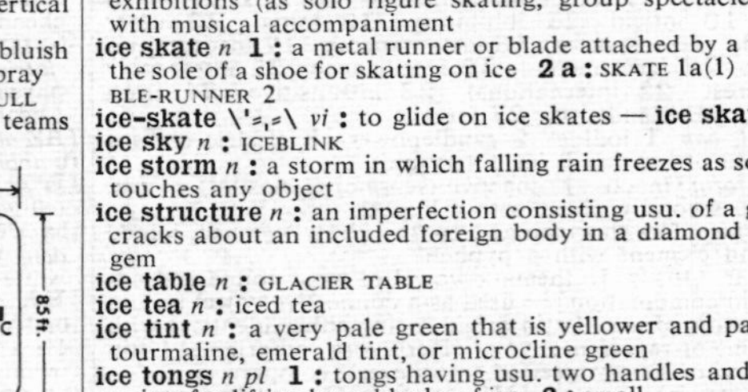
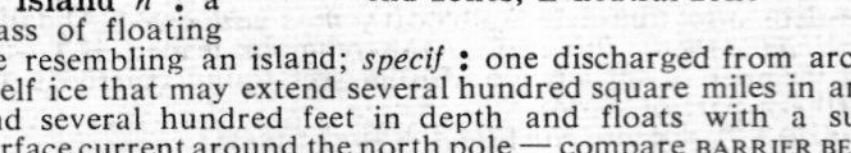

ice hockey rink: *A,A,* penalty shot lines; *B,B,* goal creases; *C,C,* goal cages; *D,D,* end zones; *E* neutral zone

icehouse \ˈ=,=\ *n* **:** a building for storing ice

ice in *vt* **:** to cause to be icebound ⟨a port that is *iced in* during the winter⟩

ice island *n* **:** a mass of floating ice resembling an island; *specif* **:** one discharged from arctic shelf ice that may extend several hundred square miles in area and several hundred feet in depth and floats with a subsurface current around the north pole — compare BARRIER BERG

ice-laid \ˈ=ˈ=\ *adj* **:** deposited by ice ⟨an *ice-laid* boulder till⟩

ice lance *n* **:** an ice tester used by the Eskimo for determining the thickness and therefore the safety of ice

ice·land \ˈīslənd, -,sland, -laa(ə)nd\ *adj*, *usu cap* [fr. *Iceland*, island between the No. Atlantic and the Arctic oceans, fr. ME *Island*, fr. ON *Ísland*, fr. *īss* ice + *land* — more at ICE, LAND] **:** of or from Iceland **:** of the kind or style prevalent in Iceland **:** ICELANDIC

iceland dog *or* **iceland cur** *n*, *usu cap I* **:** a breed of small shaggy-haired dogs supposed to have originated in Iceland and kept in England as pets during the 16th and 17th centuries

ice·land·er \ˈīsləndə(r), -,slən-, -,slaan-\ *n* -s *cap* [Dan *Islænder*, fr. *Island* Iceland + *-er*] **:** a native or inhabitant of Iceland

iceland gull *n*, *usu cap I* **:** a large white-winged gull (*Larus leucopterus*) that is similar to but smaller than the glaucous gull and that breeds in the arctic regions and migrates south to northern France and the northern U.S.

¹**ice·lan·dic** \(ˈ)ī¦slandik, -laan-\ *adj*, *usu cap* [*Iceland* + E *-ic*] **1 a :** of, relating to, or characteristic of Iceland **b :** of, relating to, or characteristic of the Icelanders **2 :** of, relating to, or characteristic of the Icelandic language

²**icelandic** \"\ *n* -s *cap* **:** a Scandinavian language of the Icelandic people — compare OLD ICELANDIC, OLD NORSE; see INDO-EUROPEAN LANGUAGES table

iceland moss *also* **iceland lichen** *n*, *usu cap I* **:** a lichen (*Cetraria islandica*) with branched flattened partly erect thallus that grows in mountainous and arctic regions and is used (as in Scandinavia) as a medicine or as food for humans and livestock and as a source of glycerol

iceland pony *n*, *usu cap I* **:** a short stocky hardy usu. chestnut-colored pony developed in Iceland by interbreeding ponies of European origin

iceland poppy *n*, *usu cap I* **1 :** either of two nearly stemless perennial poppies that tend to grow in a firm close turf: **a :** a subarctic poppy (*Papaver nudicaule*) of both hemispheres that is hairy and somewhat glaucous with pinnately lobed or cleft petioled leaves and fragrant typically yellow and white flowers borne on slender wiry scapes **b :** a similar Old World alpine poppy (*Papaver alpinum*) with white and yellow or often pink or orange flowers and glabrous foliage **2 :** any of various cultivated poppies that are prob. derived from one or the other of the wild Iceland poppies, are commonly grown as biennials or short-lived perennials, and have small or medium-sized single or double flowers chiefly of pastel color — compare SHIRLEY POPPY

iceland sea grass *n*, *usu cap I* **1 :** a sea lettuce (*Ulva latissima*) **2 :** any of various green algae of the genus *Enteromorpha*

iceland spar *also* **iceland crystal** *n*, *usu cap I* **:** a transparent calcite the best of which is obtained in Iceland, which easily cleaves into rhombohedrons, and which is used for polariscope prisms because of its strong double refraction

ice·less \ˈīsləs\ *adj* **:** having or using no ice

icelike \ˈ=,=\ *adj* **:** resembling ice

ice line *n* **:** the graph on a phase diagram of the state of equilibrium between ice and water

ice machine *n* **:** a machine for making ice artificially

ice·man \ˈī,sman, -maa(ə)n *also* -,smən\ *n*, *pl* **icemen 1 :** a man who is skilled in traveling upon ice (as among glaciers) **2 :** one who retails or delivers ice **:** an ice dealer **3 :** one who prepares and cares for an ice rink

ice·man·ship \ˈīsmən,ship\ *n* **:** ICECRAFT

ice milk *n* **:** a frozen food that is soft in texture and is made of skim milk **:** frozen custard

ice needle *n* **:** one of a number of slender ice particles that float in the air in clear cold weather — called also *ice crystal*

ice·ni \īˈsē,nī\ *n pl*, *usu cap* [L] **:** an ancient British people that under its queen Boadicea revolted against the Romans in A.D. 61 — **ice·ni·an** \(ˈ)ī¦sēnēən\ *or* **icenic** \-nik, (ˈ)ī¦sen-\ *adj*, *usu cap*

ice pack *n* **1 :** an expanse of pack ice **2 :** crushed ice placed in a suitable container (as an ice bag) or folded in a towel and applied to the body

ice paper *n* **:** a paper coated with an adhesive containing a salt that crystallizes when the coating dries and gives a frosted appearance

ice partridge *n* **:** IVORY GULL

ice petrel *n* **:** an antarctic shearwater (*Adamastor cinereus*)

ice pick *n* **:** a hand tool with a needlelike spike for chipping ice

ice pick

ice pillar *n* **:** a pedestal of glacial ice covered with a stone or debris that has given protection from solar heat and caused the ice to melt less rapidly than that around it

ice pilot *or* **ice master** *n* **:** a pilot trained in navigating amid ice

ice pink *n* **:** a European alpine dwarf herb (*Dianthus glacialis*) with bright red flowers

¹**ice plant** *n* **:** an Old World annual herb (*Mesembryanthemum crystallinum*) that is widely naturalized in warm regions and that has fleshy foliage covered with glistening papillate dots or vesicles; *broadly* **:** FIG MARIGOLD

²**ice plant** *n* **:** a plant where artificial ice is manufactured

ice plow *n* **:** a grooving device resembling a plow that is used in cutting ice (as on a river or pond) into cakes

ice point *n* **:** the temperature at which ice is in equilibrium with air-saturated water at standard atmospheric pressure and which is commonly used as a fixed point in calibrating thermometers and is represented by 0° C or 32° F

icequake \ˈ=,=\ *n* **:** the concussion attending the breaking up of masses of ice

ic·er \ˈīsə(r)\ *n* -s **:** one that ices: as **a :** a worker who covers food (as fresh produce or cases of milk) with ice before shipment **b :** a worker who mixes icing or ices baked goods

ice raft *n* **:** ICE FLOE

ice-raft \ˈ=,=\ *vt* [*ice raft*] **:** to transport on or in an iceberg or other floating ice ⟨a granitic boulder . . . might have reached its present location by *ice-rafting* —*Jour. of Geol.*⟩ ⟨*ice-rafted* sediment⟩

ice river *or* **ice stream** *n* **:** a valley glacier

iceroot \ˈ=,=\ *n* **:** GOLDENSEAL 1

ices *pl of* ICE, *pres 3d sing of* ICE

-ices *pl of* -ICE

ice shed *n* **:** a glacial divide from which ice moves in opposite directions

ice sheet *n* **:** a glacial ice cover **:** ICE CAP ⟨the *ice sheets* on some Greenland promontories⟩; *esp* **:** one (as a continental glacier) spreading outward over a large land area and concealing all or most surface features ⟨the great *ice sheets* covering much of Europe during the ice age⟩

ice shelf *n* **:** SHELF ICE

ice·shock·le \ˈī,shäkəl\ *dial Brit var of* ICICLE

ice show *n* **:** an ice-skating entertainment consisting of various exhibitions (as solo figure skating, group spectacles) often with musical accompaniment

ice skate *n* **1 :** a metal runner or blade attached by a frame to the sole of a shoe for skating on ice **2 a :** SKATE 1a(1) **b :** DOUBLE-RUNNER 2

ice-skate \ˈ=,=\ *vi* **:** to glide on ice skates — **ice skater** *n*

ice sky *n* **:** ICEBLINK

ice storm *n* **:** a storm in which falling rain freezes as soon as it touches any object

ice structure *n* **:** an imperfection consisting usu. of a group of cracks about an included foreign body in a diamond or other gem

ice table *n* **:** GLACIER TABLE

ice tea *n* **:** iced tea

ice tint *n* **:** a very pale green that is yellower and paler than tourmaline, emerald tint, or microcline green

ice tongs *n pl* **1 :** tongs having usu. two handles and hooked points for lifting large blocks of ice **2 :** small tongs often with claw-shaped ends for handling ice in an ice tub

ice tongs 1

ice tub *n* **:** a container (as of silver or glass) shaped like a tub or bowl to hold ice ready for use

ice water *n* **:** chilled or iced water esp. for drinking

ice well *n* **:** a cold storage pit containing a solid cake of ice built up during freezing weather

ice whale *n* **:** the right whale of the arctic

ice yacht *n* **:** ICEBOAT

icg *abbr* icing

¹**ich** \(ˈ)ich, ˌ(ə)ch\ *pron* [ME — more at I] *archaic & dial Brit* **:** I

²**ich** *also* **ick** \ˈik\ *n* -s [by shortening & modif. fr. NL *ichthyophthirius* or *ichthyophthiriasis*] **:** a severe dermatitis of freshwater fish that results from invasion of the skin by a ciliated protozoan (*Ichthyophthirius multifiliis*) and is esp. destructive in the aquarium and hatchery — called also *ichthyophthiriasis*, *ichthyophthirius*

ich *abbr* ichthyology

ich·a·bod \ˈikə,bäd\ *interj*, *usu cap* [Heb *ī-khābhōdh* inglorious] — used to express regret for departed glory ⟨a refreshingly cheerful note in the thundering chorus whose burden is "*Ichabod*" —G.W.Johnson⟩

ich-laut \ˈik,laủt\ *n* -s *sometimes cap I* [G, fr. *ich* I + *laut* sound] **:** the voiceless palatal fricative sound represented by the *ch* of German *ich* that is phonemically often allophonic with the ach-laut

ichn- *or* **ichno-** *comb form* [Gk, fr. *ichnos*] **:** footprint **:** track ⟨*ichnology*⟩

ich·neu·mia \ikˈn(y)ümēə\ *n*, *cap* [NL, fr. L *ichneumon* + NL *-ia*] **:** a genus of African carnivorous mammals (family Viverridae) containing the white-tailed mongooses

ich·neu·mon \-mən\ *n* -s [L, fr. Gk *ichneumōn*, mongoose, small wasp, lit., tracker, fr. *ichneuein* to track, fr. *ichnos* track, footstep; the mongoose so called fr. the ancient belief that it hunted out the eggs of the crocodile; the wasp so called fr. its hunting of spiders] **1 :** MONGOOSE; *esp* **:** the No. African mongoose (*Herpestes ichneumon*) that was highly regarded in ancient times for being supposed to devour crocodiles' eggs **2 :** ICHNEUMON FLY

ich·neu·mo·nes \-mə,nēz\ *n pl*, *cap* [NL, fr. L, pl. of *ichneumon*] **:** ICHNEUMONOIDEA

ichneumon fly *n* **:** any of a large superfamily (Ichneumonoidea) of hymenopterous insects that have many-jointed antennae, fore wings with a usu. triangular stigma, petiolate abdomen, and in the female a commonly long sheathed ovipositor for use on other insect larvae (as caterpillars) which the larval ichneumon fly burrows in and feeds on and ultimately kills thereby constituting an important natural check on many destructive insects

¹**ich·neu·mo·nid** \(ˈ)=¦=mənə̇d\ *adj* [NL *Ichneumonidae*] **:** of or relating to the Ichneumonidae

²**ichneumonid** \"\ *n* -s **:** an insect of the family Ichneumonidae

ich·neu·mon·i·dae \,==ˈnänə,dē\ *n pl*, *cap* [NL, fr. *Ichneumon*, type genus (fr. L) + *-idae*] **:** a family including the typical ichneumon flies that have no costal cell and two recurrent veins in the fore wing

ich·neu·mo·noi·dea \(,)=,=məˈnȯidēə\ *n pl*, *cap* [NL, fr. *Ichneumon*, genus of ichneumon flies + *-oidea*] **:** a superfamily of Hymenoptera consisting of the ichneumon flies

ich·nite \ˈik,nīt\ *n* -s [*ichn-* + *-ite*] **:** a fossil footprint

ich·no·graph·ic \¦iknə¦grafik\ *or* **ich·no·graph·i·cal** \-fə̇kəl\ *adj* **:** of or having the form of an ichnography

ich·nog·ra·phy \ikˈnägrəfē\ *n* -ES [L *ichnographia*, fr. Gk, fr. *ichno-* ichn- + *-graphia* -graphy] **:** a horizontal section (as of a building) showing true dimensions according to a geometric scale **:** GROUND PLAN, MAP

ich·no·lite \ˈiknə,līt\ *n* -s [*ichn-* + *-lite*] **:** a fossil footprint

ich·nol·o·gy \ikˈnäləjē\ *n* -ES [*ichn-* + *-logy*] **:** the study of fossil footprints

icho \ˈē(,)chō\ *n* -s [Jap *ichō*] **:** GINKGO

ichor \ˈī,kō(ə)r, -ō(ə), -,kə(r)\ *n* -s [LL & Gk; LL, sanies, fr. Gk *ichōr* fluid in the veins of the gods, sanies, prob. of non-IE origin] **1** *Greek mythol* **:** an ethereal fluid taking the place of blood in the veins of the gods **2 :** a thin watery or blood-tinged discharge (as from an ulcer) — compare SANIES **3 :** a concentrated magma rich in mineralizers

ichor·ous \'īkərəs\ *adj* **:** of, resembling, or characterized by ichor **:** THIN, WATERY, SEROUS, SANIOUS

ichs *pl of* ICH

ich·tham·mol \ik'tha,mōl, 'iktha,-, -mōl\ *n* -s [ISV *ichthyo*sulfonate + *ammonium* + *-ol*] **:** a brownish black viscous liquid prepared from a distillate of bituminous schists by sulfonation followed by neutralization with ammonia and used as an antiseptic and emollient

ich·thus \'ikthəs\ *also* **ich·thys** \-thəs\ *n* -ES [Gk *ichthys* fish; akin to Arm *jukn* fish, Lith *žuvis*, OPruss *suckis*] **:** a representation of a fish used in ancient times as a pagan fertility talisman or amulet or as a Christian symbol for the Greek word *ichthys* interpreted as an acrostic in which the Greek letters are the initials of the words *Iēsous Christos theou hyios sōtēr* meaning Jesus Christ Son of God Savior

ichthy- *or* **ichthyo-** *comb form* [L, fr. Gk, fr. *ichthys*] **:** fish ⟨*ichthy*ic⟩ ⟨*ichthyo*logy⟩

ich·thy·ic \'ikthē(,)ik, (')ik¦thīik\ *adj* [*ichthy-* + *-ic*] **:** of or relating to fishes or having the form of a fish

ich·thy·ism \'ikthē,izəm\ *or* **ich·thy·is·mus** \,==='izməs\ *n*, *pl* **ichthyisms** *or* **ichthyismuses** [NL *ichthyismus*, fr. *ichthy-* + *-ismus* -ism] **:** poisoning from fish — compare ICHTHYOSARCOTOXISM

ich·thy·ob·del·la \,==,äb'delə\ *n*, *cap* [NL, fr. *ichthy-* + *-bdella*] **:** a genus (the type of the family Ichthyobdellidae) of elongated freshwater and marine leeches (order Rhynchobdellida) parasitic on fishes and other vertebrates

¹ich·thy·ob·del·lid \,==,=¦deləd\ *adj* [NL *Ichthyobdellidae* family of leeches, fr. *Ichthyobdella*, type genus + *-idae*] **:** of or relating to the genus *Ichthyobdella* or family Ichthyobdellidae

²ichthyobdellid \"\ *n* -s **:** a leech of the genus *Ichthyobdella* or family Ichthyobdellidae

ich·thyo·ceph·a·li \,ikthēō'sefə,lī\ [NL, fr. *ichthy-* + *-cephali*] *syn of* SYNBRANCHOIDEA

ich·thy·o·col *or* **ich·thy·o·coll** \'ikthēə,käl\ *or* **ich·thy·o·col·la** \,==='kälə\ *n* -s [L *ichthyocolla*, fr. Gk *ichthyokolla*, fr. *ichthy-* + *kolla* glue — more at PROTOCOL] **:** ISINGLASS 1

ich·thy·o·dea \,=='ōdēə\ *n pl*, *cap* [NL, fr. *ichthy-* + *-odea*] *in some former classifications* **:** a suborder of Amphibia comprising forms having the gills or gill clefts usu. persistent (as the siren, the congo snake, and members of the genera *Proteus* and *Necturus*) — compare MUTABILIA — **ich·thy·o·di·an** \¦==¦ōdēən\ *adj*

ich·thy·o·dont \'ikthēə,dänt\ *n* -s [*ichthy-* + *-odont*] **:** a fossil fish tooth

ich·thyo·dor·u·lite \,==ō'dȯr(y)ə,līt\ *also* **ich·thyo·dor·y·lite** \-rə,-\ *n* -s [*ichthy-* + *dory-* or *doru-* (alter. of *dory-*) + *-lite*] **:** a fossil fin spine, dermal spine, or tubercle of a fish or ichthyoid vertebrate

ich·thy·fauna \¦===+\ *also* **ich·thy·fauna** \¦ikthē+\ *n* [NL, fr. *ichthy-* + *fauna*] **:** the fish life of a region

¹ich·thy·oid \'ikthē,ȯid\ *adj* [Gk *ichthyoeidēs*, fr. *ichthy-* + *-oeidēs* -oid] **:** resembling a fish — **ich·thy·oi·dal** \¦==¦ȯidᵊl\ *adj*

²ichthyoid \"\ *n* -s **:** an animal that resembles a fish; *specif* **:** one of the Ichthyopsida

ichthyoid blood cell *n* **:** MEGALOBLAST

Ich·thy·ol \'ikthē,ōl, -,ōl\ *trademark* — used for ichthammol

ich·thy·o·lite \'ikthēə,līt\ *n* -s [F *ichtyolithe*, fr. *ichtyichthy-* + *-lithe* -lite] **:** a fossil fish or fragment of a fish — **ich·thy·o·lit·ic** \¦===¦lid·ik\ *adj*

ich·thy·o·log·i·cal \¦==¦läjəkəl\ *adj* **1 :** of or relating to ichthyology **2 :** PISCINE — **ich·thy·o·log·i·cal·ly** \-jək(ə)lē\ *adv*

ich·thy·ol·o·gist \,=='äləjəst\ *n* -s **:** a specialist in ichthyology

ich·thy·ol·o·gy \-jē\ *n* -ES [*ichthy-* + *-logy*] **1 :** a branch of zoology that deals with fishes **2 :** a treatise on fishes

ich·thyo·mor·pha \,ikthēə'mȯrfə\ [NL, fr. *ichthy-* + *-morpha*] *syn of* CAUDATA

ich·thyo·mor·phic \¦===¦=fik\ *also* **ich·thyo·mor·phous** \-fəs\ *adj* [*ichthy-* + *-morphic, -morphous*] **:** having the shape or some other feature of a fish ⟨~ idols⟩

ich·thy·oph·a·gi \,ikthē'äfə,jī\ *n pl* [L, pl., fr. Gk *ichthyophagoi*, pl. of *ichthyophagos* fish-eating, fr. *ichthyophagein* to eat fish, fr. *ichthy-* + *phagein* to eat — more at BAKSHEESH] **:** a people (as in ancient times on the African coast of the Red sea) living largely on sea food **:** fish eaters

ich·thy·oph·a·gist \-jəst\ *n* -s **:** one that eats or subsists on fish

ich·thy·oph·a·gous \¦==¦=gəs\ *adj* [Gk *ichthyophagos*] **:** eating or subsisting on fish **:** PISCIVOROUS

ich·thy·oph·thi·ri·a·sis \,ikthē,äftha'rīəsəs\ *n* [NL, fr. *Ichthyophthirius* + *-iasis*] **:** ICH

ich·thy·oph·thir·i·us \,ikthēäf'thirēəs\ *n* [NL, fr. *ichthy-* + *-phthirius* (fr. *Phthirius*)] **1** *cap* **:** a genus of oval holotrichous ciliates comprising a single species (*I. multifiliis*) that are parasitic in the skin of various freshwater fishes where they encyst and multiply causing a severe and sometimes fatal inflammation **2** -ES **:** ICH

¹ich·thy·op·sid \¦==¦äpsəd\ *adj* [NL *Ichthyopsida*] **:** of or relating to the Ichthyopsida

²ichthyopsid \"\ *n* -s **:** a vertebrate of the group Ichthyopsida

ich·thy·op·si·da \,=='=sədə\ *n pl*, *cap* [NL, fr. *ichthy-* + Gk *opsis* appearance + NL *-ida* — more at OPTIC] *in some esp former classifications* **:** a group of vertebrates comprising the agnathous vertebrates, fishes, and amphibians — compare MAMMALIA, SAUROPSIDA — **ich·thy·op·si·dan** \¦==¦=sədən, -dᵊn\ *adj or n*

¹ich·thy·op·te·ryg·ia \,==,=tə'rijēə\ *n pl*, *cap* [NL, fr. *ichthy-* + Gk *pterygia*, pl. of *pterygion* fin] *in some classifications* **:** a subclass of fossil aquatic reptiles occurring from the late Carboniferous through the Jurassic and including the small freshwater Mesosauria and the extremely ichthyoid Ichthyosauria

²ichthyopterygia \"\ [NL, fr. *ichthy-* + Gk *pterygia*] *syn of* ICHTHYOSAURIA

ich·thy·op·te·ryg·i·um \-jēəm\ *n*, *pl* **ichthyopterygia** \-jēə\ [NL, fr. *ichthy-* + Gk *pterygion* small wing, fin, dim. of *pteryg-*, *pteryx* wing — more at PTERYG-] **:** the vertebrate limb when having the form of a fin whether as a definitive organ or in the course of individual or evolutionary development; *esp* **:** any of the paired fins that are the typical limbs of fishes — compare CHIROPTERYGIUM

ich·thy·or·nis \,=='ȯrnəs\ *n*, *cap* [NL, fr. *ichthy-* + *-ornis*] **:** the type genus of Ichthyornithidae comprising extinct birds of the Upper Cretaceous that have biconcave vertebrae, articulated quadrate bones, sharp conical teeth set in sockets, well-developed wings, and a keeled sternum and that are similar in size and probably in habits to a tern

ich·thy·or·ni·thes \,=='ȯrnə,thēz, -,ȯr'nī(,)thēz\ *n pl*, *cap* [NL, fr. pl. of *Ichthyornis*] *in some classifications* **:** a superorder of extinct birds coextensive with the order Ichthyornithiformes

ich·thy·or·nith·i·dae \-,ȯr'nithə,dē\ *n pl*, *cap* [NL, fr. *Ichthyornith-*, *Ichthyornis*, type genus + *-idae*] **:** a family of extinct birds (order Ichthyornithiformes) from the Upper Cretaceous of No. America that comprises the genus *Ichthyornis* and in some classifications *Apatornis* and possibly one other genus

ich·thy·or·nithi·for·mes \-,ȯrnəthə'fȯr,mēz, -,ȯr,nith-\ *n pl*, *cap* [NL, fr. *Ichthyornith-*, *Ichthyornis* + *-iformes*] **:** an order of extinct toothed birds (superorder Odontognathae) coextensive with the family Ichthyornithidae in its broadest scope

ich·thyo·sar·co·tox·ism \,ikthēō,särkə'täk,sizəm\ *n* -s [*ichthy-* + *sarc-* + *tox-* + *-ism*] **:** poisoning from eating the flesh of poisonous fishes — compare ICHTHYISM

ich·thyo·saur \'===,sȯ(ə)r\ *n* -s [NL *Ichthyosaurus*] **:** a reptile of the order Ichthyosauria

ich·thyo·sau·ria \,==='sȯrēə\ *n pl*, *cap* [NL, fr. *ichthy-* + *-sauria*] **:** an order of Mesozoic marine reptiles most abundant in the Lias having an ichthyoid body, elongated snout, short neck, dorsal and caudal fins, limbs modified into paddles by the flattening of the bones, multiplication of the phalanges and addition of from one to four digits, eyes very large and protected by a ring of bony sclerotic plates, and numerous conical teeth set in grooves and adapted for catching fish — **ich·thyo·sau·ri·an** \¦===¦=rēən\ *adj or n* — **ich·thyo·sau·roid** \-,rȯid\ *adj*

¹ich·thyo·sau·rid \¦===¦=rəd\ *adj* [NL *Ichthyosauridae*] **:** of or relating to the Ichthyosauridae

²ichthyosaurid \"\ *n* -s **:** a reptile of the family Ichthyosauridae

ich·thyo·sau·ri·dae \,===='=rə,dē\ *n pl*, *cap* [NL, fr. *Ichthyosaurus*, type genus + *-idae*] **:** a family of ichthyosaurs widely distributed in Jurassic and Cretaceous rocks of both hemispheres — see ICHTHYOSAURUS

ich·thyo·sau·rus \-rəs\ *n* [NL, fr. *ichthy-* + *-saurus*] **1** *cap* **:** the type genus of Ichthyosauridae comprising highly variable Jurassic ichthyosaurs and orig. including most of the later ichthyosaurs most of which are now placed in other genera **2** -ES **:** any reptile of the genus *Ichthyosaurus*

ich·thy·o·si·form \¦==¦ōsə,fȯrm\ *adj* [NL *ichthyosis* + E *-iform*] **:** resembling ichthyosis or that of ichthyosis

ich·thy·o·sis \,=='ōsəs\ *n*, *pl* **ichthyo·ses** \-ō,sēz\ [NL, fr. *ichthy-* + *-osis*] **:** a congenital disease usu. of hereditary origin characterized by skin that is rough, thick, and scaly and resembles that of a fish — called also *fishskin disease*

ich·thy·ot·ic \¦==¦äd·ik\ *adj* **:** of or relating to ichthyosis

ich·thy·ot·o·mi \,=='äd·ə,mī\ *n pl*, *cap* [NL, fr. *ichthy-* + *-tomi* (fr. Gk *temnein* to cut) — more at TOME] **:** a subclass or order of Chondrichthyes comprising chiefly Carboniferous and early Permian sharks having a slender and elongated body with diphycercal tail and archipterygial fins — compare PLEURACANTHUS — **ich·thy·ot·o·mous** \¦==¦äd·əməs\ *adj*

ich·thyo·tox·ism \,==_ō'täk,sizəm\ *n* -s [*ichthy-* + *tox-* + *-ism*] **:** ICHTHYISM

ichthys *var of* ICHTHUS

-ich·thys \'ikthəs\ *n comb form* [NL, fr. Gk *ichthys* — more at ICHTHUS] **:** fish — in generic names chiefly in ichthyology ⟨*Dinichthys*⟩ ⟨*Nemichthys*⟩

ichu \'ē(,)chü\ *or* **ichu grass** *or* **hi·chu** \'(h)ē-\ *n* -s [Quechua *ichu*] **:** a valuable grass (*Stipa ichu*) of the upper Andes that is used as forage and for thatching

-i·cian \'ishən\ *n suffix* -s [ME *-icien*, *-ician*, fr. OF *-icien*, fr. L *-ica* (as in *rhetorica* rhetoric) + OF *-ien* -ian — more at RHETORIC] **:** a specialist or practitioner in a (specified) field ⟨beaut*ician*⟩ ⟨techn*ician*⟩

ic·i·ca \ə'sēkə\ *n* -s [Pg, fr. Tupi] **1 :** a tropical American timber tree of the genus *Protium* **2 :** any of several Brazilian gum-producing trees; *esp* **:** BALATA

ic·i·cle \'ī,sikəl, -,sək-, -,sēk-\ *n* -s [ME *isikel*, fr. *is* ice + *ikel* icicle, fr. OE *gicel*; akin to OHG *ihilla* icicle, ON *jǫkull* icicle, glacier, *jaki* piece of ice, MIr *aig* ice, W *iâ*] **1 :** a pendent usu. conical mass of ice formed by the freezing of dripping water **2 :** an emotionally unresponsive person **3 :** a long hanging Christmas tree ornament (as a thin strip of lead foil) **4 :** a metal projection forming on the upper inside of a pipe joint during welding

icier *comparative of* ICY

iciest *superlative of* ICY

ic·i·ly \'īsəlē, -li\ *adv* **:** in an icy manner ⟨an ~ unenthusiastic audience of . . . bankers —Mollie Panter-Downes⟩

ic·i·ness \'īsēnəs, -sin-\ *n* -ES **:** the quality or state of being icy ⟨her voice carried . . . a quality of ~ —Louis Bromfield⟩

¹ic·ing \'īsiŋ, -sēŋ\ *n* -s [fr. gerund of *²ice*] **:** a sweet coating for baked goods usu. made from sugar and butter combined with water, milk, or egg white, flavored, often colored, and often cooked — called also *frosting*

²icing *n* -s [fr. the phrase *icing the puck*] **:** the act or an instance of an ice-hockey player's shooting the puck from within his own defensive zone through the neutral zone and beyond the opponents' goal line

icing station *n* **:** railway facilities for icing refrigerator cars

icing sugar *n*, *chiefly Brit* **:** CONFECTIONERS' SUGAR

ick *var of* ICH

ick·er \'ikər\ *n* -s [fr. (assumed) ME (Sc dial.), fr. OE *eher*, var. of *ēar* — more at EAR] *Scot* **:** a head of grain

ick·i·ness \'ikēnəs\ *n* -ES **:** the quality or state of being icky

ick·le \'ikəl\ *n* -s [ME *ikel* — more at ICICLE] *dial Eng* **:** ICICLE

icky \'ikē\ *adj* -ER/-EST [perh. baby-talk alter. of *sticky*] **1 :** STICKY ⟨cooing baby talk at him in an ~ way —Kathleen O'Malley⟩ — often used as a generalized expression of disapproval **2 :** lacking sophistication **:** not hep ⟨music you want to dance to — not wild and not ~ —Ralph Flanagan⟩

icon \'ī,kän *sometimes* -,kən\ *n* -s [L, fr. Gk *eikōn*, fr. *eikenai* to resemble; perh. akin to Lith *paveikslas* example, *įvykti* to occur, come about] **1 :** a usu. pictorial representation **:** IMAGE **2** [LGk *eikōn*, fr. Gk] **a** *also* **ikon** *or* **ei·kon** \"\ **:** a sacred image venerated in churches and homes of Eastern Christianity depicting Christ, the Virgin Mary, a saint, or some other religious subject in the conventional manner of Byzantine art and typically painted on a small wooden panel often with a repoussé metal cover but also enameled on metal or made of mosaic **b :** an object of uncritical devotion **:** IDOL; *esp* **:** a traditional belief or ideal ⟨the ridiculous drudgery of the Ph.D. and the devotion of university administration to the ~ of that degree —*Times Lit. Supp.*⟩ **3** *in philosophy of language and semiotic* **:** a sign (as a straight line on a map) that signifies by virtue of sharing a property with what it represents (as a straight road) — contrasted with *index* and *symbol* ⟨a photograph, a star chart, a model, a chemical diagram are ~s, while the word 'photograph', the names of the stars and of chemical elements are symbols —C.W.Morris⟩

icon- *or* **icono-** *also* **eikon-** *or* **eikono-** *or* **ikon-** *or* **ikono-** *comb form* [Gk *eikon-*, *eikono-*, fr. *eikon-*, *eikōn*] **:** image ⟨*icon*ism⟩ ⟨*icono*mania⟩ ⟨*icono*metry⟩

icon *abbr* iconography

¹ico·ni·an \(')ī¦kōnēən\ *adj*, *usu cap* [*Iconium* (now Konya, Turkey), ancient city of Asia Minor (fr. L) + E *-an*] **:** of or relating to Iconium

²iconian \"\ *n* -s *cap* **:** a native or inhabitant of Iconium

icon·ic \(')ī¦känik\ *adj* [L *iconicus*, fr. Gk *eikonikos*, fr. *eikon-*, *eikōn* image + *-ikos* -ic — more at ICON] **1 :** of, relating to, or having the character of an icon ⟨~ veneration⟩ ⟨~ theories⟩ ⟨~ signs or conventional signs⟩ **2 :** resembling an icon — **icon·i·cal·ly** \-nək(ə)lē\ *adv* — **ico·nic·i·ty** \,īkə'nisəd·ē\ *n* -ES

icon·o·clasm \ī'känə,klazəm\ *n* -s [fr. *iconoclast*, after such pairs as E *baptist: baptism*] **:** the doctrine, practice, or attitude of an iconoclast **:** image breaking

icon·o·clast \-,klast, -aa(ə)st,-aist\ *n* -s [ML *iconoclastes*, fr. MGk *eikonoklastēs*, lit., image destroyer, fr. Gk *eikono-* icon- + MGk *-klastēs* -clast] **1 a :** one who destroys religious images or opposes their veneration **b** *usu cap* **:** one of a religious party in the Eastern Empire in the 8th and 9th centuries that opposed the use of icons **2 :** one who attacks established beliefs, ideals, customs, or institutions ⟨the blundering cruelty of the tough-minded ~ —Lucius Garvin⟩

icon·o·clas·tic \(,)ī¦känə¦klastik, -laas-,-lais-, -tēk\ *adj* **1 :** of or relating to iconoclasm or iconoclasts ⟨~ outbursts associated with the Reformation⟩ ⟨the Byzantine ~ controversy⟩ **2 :** being or befitting an iconoclast **:** marked by or having the character of iconoclasm ⟨an ~ critic of the monarchy⟩ ⟨an ~ article opposing the prevailing educational philosophy⟩ **3 :** tending to produce iconoclasm or overthrow what is established ⟨the ~ influence of modern science⟩ — **icon·o·clas·ti·cal·ly** \-tək(ə)lē, -tēk-, -li\ *adv*

icon·o·dule \ī'känə,d(y)ül\ *n* -s [*icon-* + Gk *doulos* slave] **:** one who venerates icons and defends their devotional use

icon·o·du·list \-,=,d(y)üləst, (,)=¦=='==\ *n* -s [*iconoduly* + *-ist*] **:** ICONODULE

icon·o·du·ly \¦==,=lē\ *n* -ES [*icon-* + ML *dulia* veneration — more at DULIA] **:** the veneration of images

ico·nog·ra·pher \,īkə'nägrəfə(r)\ *n* -s [*iconography* + *-er*] **:** a maker or designer of figures or drawings esp. of a conventional or mechanical type

icon·o·graph·ic \(,)ī¦kanə¦grafik\ *or* **icon·o·graph·i·cal** \-fəkəl\ *adj* **1 :** of or relating to iconography ⟨experimenting in ~ forms⟩ ⟨~ studies⟩ ⟨analyze . . . his use of *iconographical* types, for the art of the Middle Ages and the Renaissance is rich in symbolism —K.M.Setton⟩ **2 :** representing something by pictures or diagrams ⟨cartographic and ~ items illustrative of colonial history⟩ — **icon·o·graph·i·cal·ly** \-fək(ə)lē\ *adv*

ico·nog·ra·phy \,īkə'nägrəfē\ *n* -ES [Gk *eikonographia* sketch, description, fr. *eikonographein* to describe (fr. *eikon-* icon- + *graphein* to draw, write) + *-ia* -y — more at CARVE] **1 a :** illustration of a subject by pictures or other visual representations ⟨figures . . . to be placed alongside the work of such masters of crustacean ~ —*Nature*⟩ **b :** pictures and other visual representations illustrating or relating to a subject ⟨a discovery adding another portrait to the ~ of Columbus⟩; *specif* **:** art representing religious or legendary subjects by conventional images and symbols ⟨sculptures . . . of the highest importance for the history of both Indian art and Buddhist ~ —V.A.Smith⟩ **c** (1) **:** the imagery selected to convey the meaning of a work of art or the identity of its figures and setting and comprising figures or objects or features often fixed (as in medieval religious art) by convention **:** a set of symbolic forms ⟨the guitar, the wine glass, the playing cards together form an ~ suggestive of pleasant, carefree moments —Aline B. Saarinen⟩ (2) **:** the set of conventions or principles governing such imagery ⟨the types of the Muses in art . . . must wait until the Roman period before their ~ and their roles are definitively codified —J.J.Seznec⟩ **2 :** ICONOLOGY **3 :** a book, list, or other record featuring or dealing with iconography

ico·nol·a·ter \-'nälad·ə(r)\ *n* -s [*icon-* + *-later*] **:** a worshiper of images or icons

ico·nol·a·try \-lə·trē\ *n* -ES [Gk *eikono-* icon- + *-latry*] **:** IMAGE WORSHIP

icono·log·i·cal \(¦)ī¦kän°l¦äjəkəl, ¦īkən-\ *adj* **:** of, relating to, or constituting iconology ⟨~ elaboration of abstract painting⟩

ico·nol·o·gist \,īkə'näləjəst\ *n* -s **:** a specialist in iconology

ico·nol·o·gy \-jē\ *n* -ES [F *iconologie*, fr. *icono-* icon- + *-logie* -logy] **:** the description, history, or analysis of symbolic art (as in the medieval church) or of artistic symbolism **:** the study of icons or iconography

icono·mat·ic *or* **ikono·mat·ic** \(¦)ī¦känə¦mad·ik, ¦īkən-\ *adj* [*icon-* + *onomat-*, *onoma* name + E *-ic* — more at NAME] **:** of or relating to a form of writing believed to be intermediate between picture writing and phonetic writing in which pictures or signs stand not for objects themselves but for their names considered as phonetic elements only — **icono·mat·i·cal·ly** \-d·ək(ə)lē\ *adv*

icono·mat·i·cism \(,)ī,känə'mad·ə,sizəm, ,īkən-\ *n* -s **:** iconomatic writing

icon·o·ma·tog·ra·phy *also* **ikon·o·ma·tog·ra·phy** \(,)ī-,känəmə'tägrəfē\ *n* -ES [*iconomatic*, *ikonomatic* + *-o-* + *-graphy*] **:** iconomatic writing

ico·nom·e·ter \,īkə'nämad·ə(r)\ *n* [ISV *icon-* + *-meter*] **1 :** an instrument for determining the distance of an object of known size or the size of an object at known distance by measuring the image of it produced by a lens of known focal length **2 a :** an instrument that determines the proper objective to be used in taking a picture of given size from a given standpoint and that consists of a diopter and an open rectangular frame sliding on a graduated rod **b :** a direct viewfinder having a metal frame

icono·met·ric \(¦)ī¦känə¦me·trik, ¦īkən-\ *adj* **:** of, relating to, or ascertained by iconometry

ico·nom·e·try \,īkə'nämə·trē\ *n* -ES [ISV *icon-* + *-metry*] **:** the art of estimating the distance or size of an object by the use of an iconometer

icon·o·scope \ī'känə,skōp\ *n* [fr. *Iconoscope*, a trademark] **:** a camera tube containing an electron gun and a photo-emissive mosaic screen each cell of which produces a charge proportional to the varying light intensity of the optical image focused on the screen by the camera lenses, these charges being transformed as the beam of electrons from the gun scans the screen into voltages that are subsequently amplified and transmitted as television picture signals — called also *ike*

ico·nos·ta·sis \,īkə'nästəsəs\ *also* **ico·no·stas** \ē¦kȯnə¦stäs\ *n*, *pl* **ico·nostases** \,īkə'nästə,sēz, ē¦kȯnə¦stäsəz\ [*iconostasis* modif. of MGk *eikonostasi*, *eikonostasion*, fr. LGk *eikonostasion* shrine, fr. *eikono-* icon- + *-stasion* (fr. Gk *histanai* to stand); *iconostas* fr. Russ *ikonostas*, fr. MGk *eikonostasi*, *eikonostasion* — more at STAND] **:** a screen or partition with doors and tiers of icons that separates the bema from the nave in Eastern churches

icons *pl of* ICON

icosa- *also* **icosi-** *or* **icos-** *comb form* [Gk *eikosa-*, *eikosi-*, *eikos-*, fr. *eikosi* — more at VICENARY] **:** twenty ⟨*icosa*hedron⟩

icosa·he·dral \(¦)ī¦kōsə¦hēdrəl, -käs- *sometimes chiefly Brit* -hed-\ *adj* **:** of or having the form of an icosahedron

icosa·he·dron \-drən *sometimes* -,drän\ *n* -s [Gk *eikosaedron*, fr. *eikosa-* icosa- + *-edron* -hedron] **1 :** a polyhedron having 20 faces **2 :** an imaginary polyhedron in the Laban system of dance notation representing the 20 principal movement directions of a dancer in its center

regular icosahedron

icosa·se·mic \-¦sēmik\ *adj* [*icosa-* + *-semic*] *in ancient prosody* **:** having or equal to 20 morae

icosa·sphere \=¦==+,-\ *n* [*icosa-* + *sphere*] **:** a spherical tank for volatile liquids built of twenty steel plates corresponding to the faces of a regular icosahedron

icosi·tetrahedron \ī¦kōsə, -käsə +\ *n* [*icosi-* + *tetrahedron*] **:** an isometric crystal form with 24 faces; *specif* **:** TRAPEZOHEDRON

icos·te·idae \,ī,kä'stēə,dē\ *n pl*, *cap* [NL, fr. *Icosteus*, type genus + *-idae*] **:** a family of deepwater fishes (order Malacichthyes) comprising the ragfishes and having a soft skeleton and skin loose and naked or with small prickles or scales

icos·te·us \ī'kästēəs\ *n*, *cap* [NL, fr. Gk *eikein* to yield, give way + NL *-osteus* — more at WEAK] **:** the type genus of the family Icosteidae comprising various typical ragfishes of the Pacific ocean

ico·type \'īkə,tīp\ *n* [Gk *eikōs* like (part. of *eikenai* to resemble) + E *type* — more at ICON] **:** a typical specimen of a species accurately identified but not serving as the basis for a published description

-ics \(,)iks, ,ēks\ *n pl suffix but sing or pl in constr* [*-ic* (as in arithmetic) + *-s*; after Gk pl. nouns ending in *-ika*, as *mathēmatika* mathematics] **1** *usu sing in constr* **:** study **:** knowledge **:** skill **:** practice ⟨opt*ics*⟩ ⟨linguist*ics*⟩ ⟨pediatr*ics*⟩ ⟨homilet*ics*⟩ **2** *usu sing in constr* **:** systematic formulation **:** treatise ⟨econom*ics*⟩ ⟨polit*ics*⟩ **3** *usu pl in constr* **:** characteristic actions or activities ⟨hero*ics*⟩ ⟨hyster*ics*⟩ ⟨gymnast*ics*⟩ **4** *usu pl in constr* **:** characteristic qualities, operations, or phenomena ⟨acoust*ics*⟩ ⟨mechan*ics*⟩ ⟨phonet*ics*⟩

ICSH *abbr* interstitial-cell-stimulating hormone

ic·tal \'iktᵊl\ *adj*, *med* **:** of, relating to, or caused by ictus

ic·ta·lu·rus \,iktə'lürəs, -təl'yü-\ *n*, *cap* [NL, irreg. fr. *ichthy-* + Gk *ailouros* cat] **:** a genus of large catfishes (family Ameiuridae) of the fresh waters of No. America

icter- *or* **ictero-** [MF or L *icter-*, fr. Gk *ikter-*, fr. *ikteros*] *comb form* **1 :** jaundice ⟨*ictero*gen⟩ ⟨*ictero*hemorrhagic⟩ ⟨*icter*oid⟩ **2 :** jaundice and ⟨*ictero*anemia⟩

ic·ter·ic \(')ik¦terik\ *adj* [MF or L; MF *icterique*, fr. L *ictericus*, fr. Gk *ikterikos*, fr. *ikteros* jaundice + *-ikos* -ic; akin to Gk *iktinos* kite, *iktis* yellow-breasted marten] **:** of, relating to, or affected with jaundice

icteric index *var of* ICTERUS INDEX

ic·ter·i·dae \ik'terə,dē\ *n pl*, *cap* [NL, fr. *Icterus*, type genus + *-idae*] **:** a large family of American oscine birds comprising the orioles, the American blackbirds, the bobolinks, and the meadowlarks and having nine primaries, a sharp conical bill, and no rictal bristles

ic·ter·ine \'iktə,rīn, -,rən\ *adj* [NL *Icterus* + E *-ine*] **:** resembling or relating to the family Icteridae

icterine warbler *n* **:** a small greenish warbler (*Hippolais icterina*) common in central Europe

ic·ter·i·tious \¦iktə¦rishəs\ *or* **ic·ter·i·tous** \(')=¦terəd·əs\ *adj* [*icterus* + *-itious* or *-itous*] **:** of a jaundiced color **:** YELLOW

ic·tero·anemia \¦iktə(,)rō+\ *n* [NL, fr. *icter-* + *anemia*] **:** a disease characterized by jaundice, anemia, and marked destruction of red blood cells and seen esp. in swine

ic·ter·o·gen·ic \¦iktərō¦jenik, (¦)ik¦terə¦j-\ *also* **ic·ter·og·e·nous** \¦iktə¦räjənəs\ *adj* [*icter-* + *-genic*, *-genous*] **:** causing or tending to cause jaundice

ic·tero·hematuria \¦iktə(,)rō+\ *n* -s [NL, fr. *icter-* + *hematuria*] **:** an infectious disease of sheep that is marked by jaundice and caused by a parasitic protozoan (*Babesia ovis*) which destroys red blood cells — compare TEXAS FEVER

ic·ter·oid \'iktə,rȯid\ *adj* [ISV *icter-* + *-oid*] **:** resembling jaundice **:** of a yellow tint like that produced by jaundice

ic·ter·us \'iktərəs\ *n* [NL, fr. Gk *ikteros* jaundice, a yellow bird] **1** -ES **:** JAUNDICE **2** *cap* **:** the type genus of the family Icteridae comprising the American orioles

icterus gravis \-'gravə̇s, -räv-,-rāv-\ *n* [NL, lit., severe jaundice] **1 :** a condition marked by severe jaundice; *specif* **:** ERYTHROBLASTOSIS **2** *or* **icterus ne·o·na·to·rum** \-,nēənə'tōrəm\ **:** a common fatal disease of newborn mules related to erythroblastosis fetalis in the human and due to sensitization of the horse dam to blood elements derived from the ass sire

icterus index *or* **icteric index** *n* **:** a figure representing the amount of bilirubin in the blood as determined by comparing the color of a sample of test serum with a set of color standards ⟨an *icterus index* of 15 or above indicates active jaundice⟩

ic·tic \'iktik\ *adj* **:** of or relating to an ictus

ic·tid·o·saur \ik'tidə,sȯ(ə)r\ *n* -S [NL *Ictidosauria*] **:** a reptile of the Ictidosauria

ic·tido·sau·ria \(,)ik,tidə'sȯrēə, ,iktədō's-\ *n pl, cap* [NL, fr. Gk *iktid-, iktis* yellow-breasted marten + NL *-o-* + *-sauria*] **:** an order of Reptilia comprising a number of imperfectly known Upper Triassic forms intermediate in character between the therapsids and the most primitive true mammals — compare MICROCONODON

ic·ti·o·bus \ik'tīəbəs\ *n, cap* [NL, irreg. fr. *ichthy-* + Gk *bous* ox, cow (also, a kind of fish) — more at COW] **:** a common genus of buffalo fishes

ic·to·gen·ic \¦iktə¦jenik\ *adj* [*ictus* + *-o-* + *-genic*] *med* **:** giving rise to ictus

ic·to·nyx \'iktə,niks\ *n, cap* [NL, fr. Gk *iktis* yellow-breasted marten + NL *-onyx*] **:** a genus of African mustelid mammals comprising the zorils

ic·tus \'iktəs\ *n* -ES [L, fr. *ictus*, past part. of *icere* to strike; akin to Gk *aichmē* lance, *iktea* wounded, Lith *iẽšmas* spit, OPruss *aysmis* and perh. to ON *eigin* newly-sprouted seed, MLG *īne* awn] **1 a** (1) **:** recurring stress or beat in a rhythmic usu. metrical series of sounds **:** metrical accent (2) **:** the place of the stress or beat in a metrical foot — compare ARSIS, THESIS **b :** ACCENT 6b **2 a :** a beat or pulsation esp. of the heart **b :** a sudden attack or seizure esp. of apoplexy **:** STROKE

ICW *abbr* interrupted continuous waves

icy \'īsē, -si\ *adj* **icier; iciest;** [¹*ice* + *-y*] **1 a :** covered with, abounding in, or consisting of ice ⟨skidded on the ~ street⟩ ⟨exploring the ~ polar wastes⟩ ⟨the ~ cliffs at the glacier's edge⟩ **b :** intensely cold ⟨~ weather⟩ ⟨an ~ room⟩ **2 :** characterized by coldness (as of manner, influence) **:** CHILLING, FRIGID, COLD ⟨got an ~ stare from the stranger⟩ **3 :** sure to be fulfilled — used of a contract in a card game

¹id \'id\ *n* -S [G, short for *idioplasma* idioplasm — more at IDIOPLASM] **:** a hypothetical structural unit of living matter resulting from the successive aggregation of biophores and determinants

²id \"\ *n* -S [NL, fr. L, it; trans. of G *es*] **:** the primitive undifferentiated part of the psychic apparatus that reacts blindly on a pleasure-pain level, is the seat of psychic energy, and is the ultimate source of higher psychic components (as ego and superego)

³id \"\ *n* -S *often attrib* [¹*-id*] **:** a skin rash that is secondary to a primary infection elsewhere and is considered to be an allergic reaction of the skin to the circulating antigen ⟨a syphilitic ~⟩

¹-id \əd, (,)id\ *n suffix* -S [in sense 1, fr. L *-ides*, masc. patronymic suffix, fr. Gk *-idēs*; in sense 2, fr. It *-ide*, fr. L *-id-, -is*, fem. patronymic suffix, fr. Gk; in sense 3, fr. F *-ide*, fr. L *-id-, -is*, fem. patronymic suffix] **1 a :** one belonging to a (specified) natural group or line of descent ⟨Melanes*id*⟩ ⟨Austral*id*⟩ **b :** one belonging to a (specified) dynastic line ⟨Fatim*id*⟩ **2 a :** meteor associated with or radiating from a (specified) constellation or comet ⟨Perse*id*⟩ ⟨Biel*id*⟩ **b :** variable star of a (specified) source or type ⟨Cephe*id*⟩ **3** *also* **-ide** \,īd, ,əd, (,)id\ **:** skin rash caused by (something specified) ⟨bacter*id*⟩ ⟨syphil*id*⟩

²-id \"\ *adj suffix* **:** of, relating to, or characteristic of a (specified) natural group or line of descent ⟨pre-Mongol*id* artifacts⟩

³-id \"\ — see -IDE

⁴-id \"\ *n suffix* -S [prob. fr. L *-id-, -is*, formative element of some nouns, fr. Gk] **1 :** structural element of a lower molar or premolar ⟨protocon*id*⟩ **2 :** structure, body, or particle of a (specified) kind ⟨chromat*id*⟩

id *abbr* **1** [L *idem*] the same **2** island

ID *abbr* **1** identification **2** inside diameter; internal diameter **3** inside dimensions **4** intelligence department **5** intradermal

-i·da \ədə\ *n pl suffix* [NL (neut. pl. in form), fr. L- *ides*, patronymic suffix] **:** animals that are or have the form of — in names of higher taxa (as orders and classes) ⟨Scorpion*ida*⟩ ⟨Acar*ida*⟩ ⟨Bero*ida*⟩ — **-i·dan** \ədən, əd°n\ *n or adj suffix*

-i·dae \ə,dē\ *n pl suffix* [NL, fr. L (pl. of *-ides*, masc. patronymic suffix), fr. Gk *-idai*, pl. of *-idēs*, masc. patronymic suffix] **:** members of the family of — in patronymic group names ⟨Alcmaeon*idae*⟩ ⟨Homer*idae*⟩ ⟨Seleuc*idae*⟩; in names of families of animals substituted for the last syllable of the genitive case of the name of the type genus ⟨Aphid*idae* from *Aphis*⟩ ⟨Equ*idae* from *Equus*⟩

¹idae·an *or* **ide·an** \(')ī¦dēən\ *adj, usu cap* [L *idaeus* Idaean (fr. Gk *idaios*, fr. *Idē* Mt. Ida in Crete) + E *-an*] **1 :** of, relating to, or dwelling on Mt. Ida in Crete **2 :** of, relating to, or characteristic of the ancient Greek goddess Rhea with whom Mt. Ida was associated

²idaean \"\ *adj, usu cap* [L *idaeus* Idaean (fr. Gk *idaios*, fr. *Idē* Mt. Ida in Asia Minor) + E *-an*] **1 :** of, relating to, or dwelling on Mt. Ida in Asia Minor **2 :** of, relating to, or characteristic of the ancient Greek goddess Cybele with whom Mt. Ida was associated

idae·in *also* **ide·in** \ī'dēən\ *n* -S [ISV *idae-, ide-* (fr. NL *vitis-idaea* — specific epithet of the mountain cranberry *Vaccinium vitis-idaea minus* —, fr. L *vitis* vine + *idaea*, fem. of *idaeus*) + *-in*] **:** an anthocyanin pigment obtained in the form of the greenish brown crystalline chloride $C_{21}H_{21}ClO_{11}$ from the skin of red apples and from cranberries and similar fruit; a galactoside of cyanidin

¹ida·ho \'īdə,hō\ *adj, usu cap* [*Idaho*, state in the northwestern U.S., prob. of AmerInd origin] **:** of or from the state of Idaho **:** of the kind or style prevalent in Idaho **:** IDAHOAN

²idaho \"\ *n, pl* **idahoes** *also* **idahos** *usu cap* **:** an elongated potato rich in starch and suitable for baking that is grown esp. in Idaho

¹ida·ho·an \¦īdə¦hōən\ *adj, usu cap* [*Idaho* + E *-an*] **:** of, relating to, or characteristic of Idaho or Idahoans

²idahoan \"\ *n* -S *cap* **:** a native or resident of Idaho

idaho fescue *n, usu cap I* **:** a tall meadow grass (*Festuca idahoensis*) of central and western No. America with smooth filiform leaves, an open inflorescence, and awns about half as long as the lemmas

idaho white pine *n, usu cap I* **1 :** WESTERN WHITE PINE 1 **2 :** the wood of western white pine

ida·lian \(')ī¦dālēən, lyən\ *adj, usu cap* [*Idalium*, ancient town in Cyprus + E *-an*] **:** of or relating to the ancient town Idalium that was a center of the worship of Aphrodite

idant \'id°nt, 'ī¦, ¦,dant\ *n* -S [ISV ¹*id* + *-ant*; orig. formed in G] **:** a hypothetical structural unit arising from an aggregation of ids and forming a basic element of the germ plasm in the Weismannian theory of heredity

id·dings·ite \'idiŋ,zīt\ *n* -S [Joseph P. *Iddings* †1920 Am. geologist + E *-ite*] **:** a mineral consisting of a silicate of calcium, magnesium, and iron of doubtful composition and forming pseudomorphs after olivine

¹ide \'īd\ *n* -S [back-formation fr. *ides*] **:** one of the ides

²ide \"\ *n* -S [Sw *id* — more at EDIFY] **:** a European freshwater cyprinid food fish (*Idus idus*) — see ORFE

¹-ide \,īd, ,əd, (,)id\ *also* **-id** \əd, (,)id\ *n suffix* -S [G & F; G *-id*, fr. F *-ide* (as in *oxide*) — more at OXIDE] **1 :** binary chemical compound or compound regarded as binary — added to contracted name of the nonmetallic or more electronegative element ⟨iron ox*ide*⟩ ⟨hydrogen sulf*ide*⟩ or radical ⟨am*ide*⟩ ⟨ethox*ide*⟩ **2 a :** chemical compound derived from or related to another (usu. specified) compound ⟨anhydr*ide*⟩ ⟨glycol*ide*⟩ ⟨phthal*ide*⟩ **b :** acetal derivative of a sugar — in names of glycosides replacing final *-e* of the name of the sugar ⟨arabinos*ide*⟩ ⟨cerebros*ide*⟩ — compare -OSIDE **3 :** one of a class of organic esp. naturally occurring compounds ⟨lip*ide*⟩ ⟨phosphat*ide*⟩ ⟨pept*ide*⟩ ⟨sacchar*ide*⟩ **4 :** chemical element of a series of metallic elements of increasing atomic numbers ⟨actin*ide*⟩ ⟨lanthan*ide*⟩

²-ide — see -ID

idea \(')ī¦dēə, (')ī¦diə; *chiefly in southern US* 'ī,dē(ə) *or* 'ī,di(ə); *dial or archaic* (')ī¦dē; *in NewEng extremely frequent with intrusive* r —(')ī¦dēər *or* (')ī¦di(ə)r\ *n* -S [L, fr. Gk, *idein* to see — more at WIT] **1 a :** a presentation of sense, concept, or representation: as (1) *Platonism* **:** an archetype or subsistent form **:** a transcendent universal (2) *Aristotelianism* **:** the form-giving cause **:** FORM (3) *Lockeanism* **:** an immediate object or a compound of immediate objects of sensation or reflection — see COMPLEX IDEA, SIMPLE IDEA (4) *Berkeleianism* **:** an impression of sense or imagination; *esp* **:** PERCEPT (5) *Humism* **:** a representation or construct of memory and association as distinguished from direct impression of sense (6) *Kantianism* **:** a transcendent but nonempirical concept of reason **:** NOUMENON (7) *Hegelianism* **:** the highest category **:** the complete and final product of reason; *also* **:** its realization or embodiment — compare ABSOLUTE **b :** an object of a concept **2 a :** a conception or standard of any perfection **:** IDEAL **b :** a preliminary plan **:** CONCEPTION, DESIGN; *usu* **:** a plan or purpose of action **:** PROJECT ⟨his ~ of going in for law⟩ ⟨a new ~ for decorating the house⟩ **3** *archaic* **:** a visible representation of a conception (as an abstract perfection) or of a design **:** a replica of a pattern or archetype **:** a realized ideal **4 a** *obs* **:** an image or picture recalled by memory **b :** an indefinite or fanciful conception or notion **:** a figment of the imagination **:** FANCY, SUPPOSITION, OPINION ⟨that is a mere ~ of yours⟩ ⟨a head full of absurd ~*s*⟩ ⟨I've an ~ we'll win⟩ **5 :** an object of the mind existing in apprehension, conception, or thought **:** NOTION, THOUGHT, IMPRESSION ⟨a clear ~ of his responsibility⟩ **6 :** a product of reflection or mental concentration **:** a formulated thought or opinion ⟨~*s* on a subject⟩ ⟨clearly defined ~*s*⟩ **7 :** whatever is known, believed, or supposed regarding any object ⟨the child's ~ of air⟩ **8 :** the central or key meaning or the chief end of a particular action or situation ⟨get the ~⟩ — see BIG IDEA **9 :** a musical figure or theme **10** *Christian Science* **:** an image in Mind

syn IDEA, CONCEPT, CONCEPTION, THOUGHT, NOTION, IMPRESSION: IDEA may apply to an image or formulation of something seen or known, of something imagined and visualized, of something vaguely assumed, guessed at, or sensed ⟨practically every American boy who is not tied to his mother's apron strings is going to encounter other boys whose *ideas* of fighting are very different from his own —Margaret Mead⟩ ⟨success with the steamboat inspired Colonel John Stevens to work on the *idea* of a steam railroad —*Amer. Guide Series: N.J.*⟩ ⟨an earlier paper has reviewed the development during the Middle Ages of the *idea* that the Kingdom of France had natural frontiers which it was her right, even her duty, to attain —N.J. G.Pounds⟩ CONCEPT may indicate a fairly definite mental formulation determined by consideration of instances, although the word readily admits of suggesting foundations differing with individuals ⟨thus the popular *concept* of what news was came more and more to be formed upon what news was printed —F.L.Mott⟩ ⟨if his *concept* of the national security he has sworn to defend impels him to dispatch troops into foreign regions and in situations that may involve the United States in war, the sole responsibility is his —Arthur Krock⟩ ⟨the emerging of a fresh *concept* of architecture needed to produce new forms and revitalize tradition —*Amer. Guide Series: Mich.*⟩ CONCEPTION, often interchangeable with CONCEPT, may stress the idea of the mental action of imagining and formulating rather than the notion of its result ⟨the *conception*, building, and profitable sale of the New York, Chicago & St. Louis Railway, commonly known as the Nickel Plate, was in great measure due to him —K.F.Geiser⟩ ⟨the Malays have a whole system of tabooed and substituted words, based as usual on the *conception* of all Nature as animate and sensitive —J.G. Frazer⟩ THOUGHT is a general term but is likely to imply the result of ratiocination, of thinking, reasoning, or meditating, rather than fancying or imagining ⟨the next 10 years Abbot devoted to the final elaboration of his *thought* in abstruse technical form in *The Syllogistic Philosophy* —F.A.Christie⟩ ⟨Adams' first *thought* was that Palmerston wished a quarrel; his second, that it might be connected with a desire for mediation —W.C.Ford⟩ ⟨there are insights which are spoiled by *thought* —Lewis Leary b.1906⟩ NOTION may suggest a vague half-formed idea not resolved by much thought and analysis ⟨the *notion* that primitive languages lack the power of abstraction —A.A.Hill⟩ ⟨the *notion* that history shows a continual progress and especially a progress in the liberation of the individual is amply refuted by many examples —M.R.Cohen⟩ ⟨the British have some queer and quaint *notions* about Americans — some almost as peculiar as our preconceived ideas about them —Richard Joseph⟩ IMPRESSION applies to a first notion frankly lacking in analysis, consideration, and thought ⟨when he steps out on the street his first *impression* is of broad radiating avenues —*Amer. Guide Series: Minn.*⟩ ⟨the additional real difficulty of eliminating all possibility of adding subjective *impressions* to objective findings —W.C.Allee⟩

-id·ea \'idēə\ *n pl suffix* [NL (neut. pl. in form), fr. Gk *-ideus*, n. suffix with quasi-patronymic value] **:** animals that are or have the form of — in names of higher taxa ⟨Car*idea*⟩ ⟨Phoron*idea*⟩

ideaed *also* **idea'd** *pronunc at* IDEA + d\ *adj* **:** having a specified kind of idea or a specified number of ideas ⟨a one-*ideaed* man⟩ ⟨eager bright-*ideaed* students⟩ **:** characterized by ideas ⟨alert ~ men are priceless treasures⟩

idea·is·tic \(¦)ī¦dēə¦istik, ¦ī¦dē¦i-\ *adj* **:** relating to, concerned with, or based on ideas esp. as abstract or symbolic matters of mind

¹ide·al \(')ī¦dē(ə)l, -diəl\ *adj* [F or LL; F *idéal*, fr. LL *idealis*, fr. L *idea* + *-alis* -al] **1 a :** existing as a mere mental image **:** existing in fancy or imagination only **:** IMAGINARY, HYPOTHETICAL ⟨confusing ~ and concrete things⟩; *broadly* **:** lacking practicality **:** VISIONARY ⟨a purely ~ concept of society⟩ **b :** relating to or constituting mental images, ideas, or conceptions **:** IDEATIONAL, CONCEPTUAL ⟨life and death appeared to me ~ bounds —Mary W. Shelley⟩ **c :** embodying or symbolizing an idea **2 :** of or relating to an ideal or to perfection of kind **:** existing as a perfect exemplar **:** embodying or symbolizing an ideal ⟨~ beauty⟩ ⟨an ~ moral character⟩ **3 :** existing as a patterning or archetypal idea; *usu* **:** of or relating to Platonic ideas **4 :** of or relating to philosophical idealism

²ideal \"\ *n* -S [F or G; F *idéal*, fr. G *ideal*, fr. *ideal-* (as in *idealform* ideal form), fr. LL *idealis*, adj.] **1 a :** a conception of something in its highest perfection ⟨a perfect circle is an ~ impossible to construct⟩ **b :** a standard of perfection, beauty, or excellence believed to be capable of realization or attainment ⟨the ~*s* of our civilization⟩ **2 :** one regarded as exemplifying an ideal and often taken as a model for imitation ⟨considered the older man his ~⟩ **3 :** an ultimate object or aim of endeavor **:** GOAL ⟨their ~ was a quiet unhurried life⟩ **4 :** a subset of a ring that contains as an element the sum or difference of any two elements and the product of any element with an element of the ring ⟨the integers ending in 0 are an ~ in the ring of all integers⟩ **syn** see MODEL

ideal engine *n* **:** a heat engine operating on a reversible cycle (as a Carnot cycle)

idea·less *pronunc at* IDEA + ləs\ *adj* **:** lacking an idea or ideas

ideal gas *n* **:** a gas in which there is no attraction between the molecules; *usu* **:** a gas conforming exactly to the ideal-gas law

ideal-gas law *n* **:** GAS LAW c

ide·al·ism \(')ī¦dē(ə),lizəm, -diə,l- *sometimes* 'ī,dēə,- *or* 'ī,diə-\ *n* -S [prob. fr. G or F; G *idealismus*, fr. F *idéalisme*, fr. *idéal* + *-isme* -ism] **1 :** a theory that affirms that mind or the spiritual and ideal is of central importance in reality: as **a :** a theory that regards reality as essentially spiritual or the embodiment of mind or reason esp. by asserting either that the ideal element in reality is dominant (as in Platonism) or that the intrinsic nature and essence of reality is consciousness or reason (as in Hegelianism) — called also *metaphysical idealism* **b :** a theory that identifies reality with perceptibility or denies the possibility of knowing anything except psychical reality and proceeds from the affirmation that the mental life alone is knowable to a dogmatic dualism (as in Cartesianism and Lockeanism) which in metaphysics results in realism, to a subjective idealism in metaphysics (as in Berkeleianism), or to solipsism or skepticism (as in Humism) — called also *epistemological idealism*; see ABSOLUTE IDEALISM, MONISTIC IDEALISM, OBJECTIVE IDEALISM, PERSONAL IDEALISM, PLURALISTIC IDEALISM, SUBJECTIVE IDEALISM, TRANSCENDENTAL IDEALISM **2 a :** the practice of forming ideals or living under their influence **:** tendency to idealize **b :** something that is idealized **:** an ideal representation or experience **3 :** literary or artistic theory or practice that values ideal or subjective types or aspects of beauty more than formal or sensible qualities or that affirms the preeminent value of imagination as compared with faithful copying of nature — opposed to *realism*

¹ide·al·ist \-ləst\ *n* -S [¹*ideal* + *-ist*] **1 a :** an adherent of a philosophical theory of idealism **b :** an artist or author who advocates or practices idealism in art or writing **2 :** one whose conduct is influenced or guided by ideals; *usu* **:** one that places ideals before practical considerations **:** VISIONARY, DREAMER

²idealist \"\ *adj* **:** IDEALISTIC

ide·al·is·tic \(¦)ī¦dē(ə)¦listik, (¦)ī¦diə¦l-, -tēk *sometimes* ¦ī,dēə¦l- *or* ¦ī,diə¦l-\ *adj* **1 :** of, relating to, or advocated by idealists or idealism ⟨~ theories⟩ **2 :** exhibiting, practicing, or characterized by idealism ⟨an ~ man⟩ ⟨an ~ view of life⟩ — **ide·al·is·ti·cal·ly** \-tək(ə)lē, -tēk-, -li\ *adv*

ide·al·i·ty \,īdē'alədˌə, -di'a-, -ətē, -i\ *n* -ES [¹*ideal* + *-ity*] **1 a :** the quality or state of being ideal **b :** existence only in idea **2 :** something imaginary or idealized **:** an unreal or unrealistic thing or concept **3 :** the poetic or creative faculty — used orig. in phrenology

ide·al·iza·tion \(,)ī,dē(ə)lə'zāshən, -diəl-, -,lī'z- *sometimes* ,ī,deə(,)l- *or* ,īdiə(,)l-\ *n* -S **1 a :** an act or the process of idealizing **b :** a product of idealizing **2 :** the employment of idealistic methods

ide·al·ize \(')ī¦dē(ə),līz, -diə,l- *sometimes* 'ī,dēə,l- *or* 'ī,diə,l-\ *vb* -ED/-ING/-S *see -ize in Explan Notes* [prob. fr. G *idealisieren*, fr. *ideal* + *-isieren* -ize] *vt* **1 :** to make ideal **:** give an ideal form or value to **:** attribute ideal characteristics and excellences to ⟨tended to ~ her friends⟩ **2 :** to treat (an artistic subject) idealistically ~ *vi* **1 :** to form ideals **2 :** to work idealistically — **ide·al·iz·er** \-zə(r)\ *n* -S

ideal·less *pronunc at* IDEAL + ləs\ *adj* **:** lacking ideals **:** basing conduct and judgments on the everyday realities of life; *broadly* **:** MATERIALISTIC

ide·al·ly *pronunc at* IDEAL + (l)ē *or* (l)i\ *adv* **1 :** in idea or imagination **:** by means of ideas **:** MENTALLY **2 :** in relation to or in the manner of an exemplar, archetype, or pattern **3 a :** conformably to or in respect to an ideal **:** PERFECTLY **b :** for best results or greatest enjoyment, efficiency, or value ⟨~ each meal should be planned in relation both to activity and to other meals of the day⟩ **c :** in accordance with an ideal or typical standard **:** CLASSICALLY

ide·al·ness *n* -ES **:** the quality or state of being ideal ⟨~ of his prose⟩ ⟨the ~ of such aspirations⟩

idealogue *var of* IDEOLOGUE

idealogy *var of* IDEOLOGY

ideal point *n* **:** a point at infinity that in projective geometry is the assumed intersection of any two parallel lines

ideal realism *n* **:** any of various philosophical theories combining idealistic and realistic elements; *specif* **:** a theory combining idealistic epistemology with realistic metaphysics — called also *real idealism*

ideals *pl of* IDEAL

ideal solution *n* **:** a solution in which the interaction between molecules of the components does not differ from the interactions between the molecules of each component; *usu* **:** a solution that conforms exactly to Raoult's law — compare ACTIVITY 6b, ACTIVITY COEFFICIENT, FUGACITY 2b

ideal truth *n* **:** NORMATIVE TRUTH

ideal type *n* **:** an abstraction of features from empirical reality and their embodiment into a unified conceptual scheme of hypothetical validity ⟨sees the *ideal type* of monogamy in Christian marriage —Rodney Needham⟩ ⟨analysis of social situations by the use of *ideal types*⟩

ideal utilitarianism *n* **:** UTILITARIANISM 1b

idea man *n* **:** a person with an unusual capacity for visualizing and formulating new techniques, approaches, products

ideamonger *pronunc at* IDEA +,-\ *n* **:** one that deals in ideas **:** IDEA MAN

i·de·an *usu cap, var of* IDAEAN

idea·pho·ria \(,)ī,dēə'fōrēə, ,ī,deə-\ *n* -S [NL, fr. L *idea* + NL *-phoria*] **:** capacity for creative thought or imagination

ideas *pl of* IDEA

ideas of reference : a delusion that accompanies certain abnormal mental states in which remarks overheard and people seen seem to be concerned with and usu. inimical to oneself

¹ide·ate \'īdē,āt, ī'd-\ *vb* -ED/-ING/-S [*idea* + *-ate*] *vt* **:** to form in idea **:** CONCEIVE, PRECONCEIVE, PREFIGURE; *usu* **:** to have ideas, thoughts, or impressions of **:** remember, imagine, or think of when not in the actual presence of ~ *vi* **1 :** to form an idea **2 :** to invent by working through ideas

²ide·ate \'īdē,āt, ī'dēət\ *n* -S [NL *ideatum*] **:** IDEATUM

ide·a·tion \,īdē'āshən\ *n* -S **:** the capacity of the mind to form or entertain ideas; *broadly* **:** the process of entertaining and relating ideas

ide·a·tion·al \¦≈≈¦āshən°l, -āshnəl\ *adj* **:** of, relating to, or produced by ideation; *broadly* **:** consisting of or referring to ideas or thoughts of objects not immediately present to the senses — compare IDEALISTIC, PERCEPTUAL — **ide·a·tion·al·ly** \-n°l|ē, -nəl|ē, |ī\ *adv*

ide·a·tive \ī'dēəd.iv, 'īdē,ād.-\ *adj* [¹*ideate* + *-ive*] **:** IDEATIONAL

ide·atum \,īdē'ād.əm\ *n, pl* **ide·ata** \-d.ə\ [NL, fr. L *idea* + *-atum*, neut. of *-atus* -ate — more at IDEA] *philos* **:** the actual existence supposed to correspond with an idea

idée fixe \(,)ē,dā'fēks\ *n, pl* **idées fixes** \-ks(əz)\ [F] **:** FIXED IDEA

idée-force \-'fō(ə)rs\ *n, pl* **idées-forces** \-rs(əz)\ [F, fr. *idée* idea + *force*] **:** an idea considered as a real factor in the behavior of an individual or social group and thus in the course of events

idein *var of* IDAEIN

ide·ist \(')ī¦dēəst, 'ī,dēə-\ *n* -S [*idea* + *-ist*] **:** an adherent of an idealistic philosophy; *specif* **:** an advocate of epistemological idealism

idem *with reference to a person* 'ī,dem *or* 'ē,dem, *with reference to a thing* 'ī,dem *or* 'i,dem, *the masculine Latin form having a long i & the neuter form a short i*\ *pron* [L, same — more at IDENTITY] **:** something previously mentioned **:** SAME — used chiefly in bibliographies to avoid repetition of author's name and title when a reference to an item immediately follows another to the same item ⟨~ page 30⟩; abbr. *id.*

idem so·nans \¦ī,dem'sō,nanz, ¦i,dem'sō,nän(t)s\ [L] **:** having the same sound — used of a rule in law that the occurrence in a document of a spelling of a material word that is wrong but has the sound of the word intended (as *Lawrance* for *Lawrence* or *Kean* for *Keen*) does not vitiate the instrument

-i·dene \ə,dēn\ *n suffix* -S [ISV *-ide* + *-ene*] **:** radical having two valence bonds at the point of attachment ⟨ethyl*idene* $CH_3CH<$⟩ ⟨eth*idene*⟩ — compare -YLIDENE

¹ident \ī'dent\ *n* -S [by shortening] **:** IDENTIFICATION

²ident \"\ *vb* -ED/-ING/-S [by shortening] **:** IDENTIFY

iden·ta·code \ī'dentə,kōd, ə'd-\ *n* [*identi*fication + connective *-a-* + *code*] **:** a means of identification of a pedigreed animal consisting of a tattoo mark that is recorded on both pedigree and certificate of ownership

iden·tic \(')ī¦dentik, ə'd-\ *adj* [prob. fr. ML *identicus*] **:** IDENTICAL ⟨recognition of ~ themes in the apparently incongruous —R.P.Blackmur⟩: as **a :** constituting an action or expression in which two or more governments follow precisely the same course or employ an identical form — compare JOINT 2a(3) **b :** constituting an action or expression in which a government follows precisely the same course or employs identical forms with reference to each of two or more other governments **syn** see SAME

iden·ti·cal \-tə̇kəl, -tēk-\ *adj* [prob. fr. ML *identicus* (fr. LL *identitas* identity + L *-icus* -ic) + E *-al*] **1 :** expressing or effecting identity — used chiefly of propositions in logic and of equations and operations in mathematics **2 :** being the same **:** having complete identity ⟨the ~ place where we stopped before⟩ — often used with *same* or *very* for emphasis ⟨the same ~ money⟩ ⟨the very ~ house⟩ **3 a :** showing exact likeness **:** characterized by such entire agreement in qualities and attributes that identity may be assumed — often used with *with* and sometimes with *to* ⟨a replica that is ~ with the original⟩ **b :** very similar : having such close resemblance and such minor difference as to be essentially the same : appearing or seeming exactly alike ⟨saw the ~ dress on sale for three dollars⟩ ⟨the two plants were ~⟩ — often used with *with* or *to* ⟨his examination paper was ~ to his brother's⟩ ⟨political issues are seldom ~ with religious⟩ **4 :** having the same cause or origin ⟨~ infections⟩ **syn** see LIKE, SAME

identical equation *n* **:** an equation that is satisfied for all values of the literal symbols

iden·ti·cal·i·ty \(ˌ)īˌdentəˈkalədē, əˌden-, -lətē, -i\ *n* -ES **:** IDENTICALNESS

iden·ti·cal·ly \-ˈdentək(ə)lē, -tēk-, -li\ *adv* **:** in an identical manner : with complete identity ⟨shoes ~ alike⟩; *specif* **:** for all values of the mathematical symbols involved

iden·ti·cal·ness \-kəlnəs\ *n* -ES **:** the quality or state of being identical

identical points *n pl* **:** points on the retinas of the two eyes that occupy corresponding positions in respect to the retinal centers

identical proposition *n* **:** a proposition in logic whose subject and predicate are identical in meaning and whose affirmation is therefore superfluous ⟨"nothing inconceivable can be conceived" is an *identical proposition*⟩

identical rhyme *n* **:** RIME RICHE

identical twin *n* **:** either member of a pair of twins produced from a single zygote

iden·ti·fi·a·bil·i·ty \(ˌ)īˌdentəˌfīəˈbilədē, əˌd-, -lətē, -i\ *n* **:** the quality or state of being identifiable

iden·ti·fi·a·ble \ˌ=ˈ==ˌəbəl, (ˌ)=ˌ==ˈ=əbəl\ *adj* **:** subject to identification : capable of being identified — **iden·ti·fi·a·bly** \-blē, -bli\ *adv*

iden·ti·fi·ca·tion \(ˌ)=ˌ==fəˈkāshən\ *n* -S *often attrib* [prob. fr. F, fr. *identité* identity + *-fication* — more at IDENTITY] **1 a :** an act or the action of identifying or the state of being identified **b :** a means of identifying : evidence of identity ⟨experienced travelers always carry some ~⟩ ⟨a driver's license is sufficient ~⟩ **2 a :** a mental mechanism wherein the individual gains gratification, emotional support, or relief from anxiety by attributing to himself consciously or unconsciously the characteristics of another person or group **b :** orientation of the self in regard to something (as a familial or ethnic group, class, nation, ideology) with a resulting feeling of close emotional association ⟨the immigrant's ~ with his new country⟩ **3 :** CONDENSATION 5

identification bracelet *n* **:** a bracelet with a narrow plaque for the owner's name

identification tag *n* **:** either of two metal tags worn suspended around the neck by a member of the armed forces and stamped with his name, serial number, and other information

identification bracelet

iden·ti·fi·ca·to·ry \īˈdentəfəkəˌtōrē, əˈd-, ˌīˌdenˈtif-, *chiefly Brit* =ˌidentifiˈkāt(ə)ri *or* -ā·tri\ *adj* [*identification* + *-ory*] **:** concerned with or serving for identification ⟨~ thinking⟩ ⟨~ traits⟩

iden·ti·fi·er \īˈdentəˌfī(ə)r, əˈd-, -fīə\ *n* -S **:** one that identifies

iden·ti·fy \-ˌfī\ *vb* -ED/-ING/-ES [prob. fr. F *identifier*, fr. *identité* identity + *-fier* -fy — more at IDENTITY] *vt* **1 a :** to cause to be or become identical : regard as identical ⟨*identified* their own interests with those of the rulers⟩ **b :** to link in an inseparable fashion : make correlative with something ⟨may not rationally ~ itself with any one church⟩ **c :** to conceive as united in spirit, principle, outlook, or interest ⟨*identified* himself with the middle classes⟩; *broadly* **:** to associate or join (as oneself) with some interest (as a business or political party) **2 a :** to establish the identity of ⟨soon *identified* the child⟩ : show or prove the sameness of (as with something known, stated, or possessed) ⟨tried to ~ the stolen property as his own⟩ ⟨could not immediately ~ the quotation⟩ **b :** to determine the taxonomic position of (a biological specimen) ⟨*identified* it as a member of the genus *Salix* but could not determine the species⟩ ~ *vi* **:** to be or become the same : associate in such a way as to have unity (as of interests, purpose, effect) ⟨our tastes do not always ~⟩ ⟨people long in association tend to ~ with one another⟩ : practice identification ⟨to ~ is to share the interests and acts of another person until identification results —C.R.Adams⟩

identifying pronoun *n* **:** a pronoun referring to something as identical with what has been mentioned ⟨*same* is an *identifying pronoun*⟩

iden·tism \-nˌtizəm\ *n* -S [*identity* + *-ism*] **:** IDENTITY PHILOSOPHY

iden·ti·ty \īˈden(t)ədē, əˈden-, -ətē, -i\ *n* -ES [MF *identité*, fr. LL *identitat-, identitas*, irreg. fr. L *idem* same (fr. *is* he) + *-itat-, -itas* -ity — more at ITERATE] **1 a :** sameness of essential or generic character in different examples or instances : the limit approached by increasing similarity ⟨the ~ of the red in the rug with the red of a brick⟩ **b :** sameness in all that constitutes the objective reality of a thing : SELFSAMENESS, ONENESS : sameness of that which is distinguishable only in some accidental fashion (as being designated by different names, or the object of different perceptions, or different in time and place) ⟨the ~ of Scott with the author of Waverley⟩ ⟨the sense of ~ arising in shared experience⟩ **c :** an instance of such sameness **2 :** unity and persistence of personality : unity or individual comprehensiveness of a life or character ⟨lost consciousness of his own ~⟩ **3 :** the condition of being the same with something described, claimed, or asserted or of possessing a character claimed ⟨establish the ~ of stolen goods⟩ **4** *archaic* **:** individual or real existence **5** *Schellingian philos* **:** reality at its deepest level at which subject and object are one **6 a :** IDENTICAL PROPOSITION **b :** IDENTICAL EQUATION **7** *Austral* **:** CHARACTER 8a **8** *or* **identity element :** an operator that leaves unchanged an element on which it operates ⟨since if zero is added to any integer, the sum is the same integer, zero is an additive ~⟩

identity card *n* **:** a usu. official card bearing identifying data about the individual to whom it pertains

identity philosophy *n* **:** a monistic philosophical theory (as the philosophy of Schelling) that rejects any ultimate bifurcation into spirit and nature or subject and object and finds fundamental unity in the Absolute

identity principle *n* **:** LAW OF IDENTITY

ideo- *comb form* [F *idéo-*, fr. Gk *idea* — more at IDEA] **:** idea ⟨*ideo*crat⟩ ⟨*ideo*genetic⟩ ⟨*ideo*logy⟩

ide·oc·ra·cy \ˌīdēˈäkrəsē, ˌid-\ *n* -ES [*ideo-* + *-cracy*] **:** government or social management based on abstract ideas

ideo·ge·net·ic \ˈīdē(ˌ)ōjəˈned·ik, ˈid-\ *adj* [*ideo-* + *-genetic*] **:** originating ideas

ideo·gram \ˈīdēəˌgram, ˈid-, -raa(ə)m *sometimes* īˈdēə- *or* īˈdiə-\ *n* [*ideo-* + *-gram*] **1 a :** a picture, a conventionalized picture, or a symbol that symbolizes a thing or an idea but not a particular word or phrase for it **b :** a picture, a conventionalized picture, or a symbol that symbolizes a thing or an idea but not a particular word or phrase for it and that if pictorial symbolizes not the object pictured but some thing or idea that the object pictured is supposed to suggest or emblematize — distinguished from *pictogram* **2 :** a symbol or group of symbols that as used in the writing of a particular language represents usu. a particular morpheme, word, or phrase but without providing separate phonetic representation of the individual phonemes or syllables composing the morpheme, word, or phrase : LOGOGRAM a; *specif* **:** a symbol or group of symbols used for convenience in writing an alphabetic language and directly representing a word or phrase or in some instances an idea expressible by any of two or more different words or phrases (as in English *3* read as *three*, + read as *plus*, & read as *and*, $ read as *dollar* or *dollars*, *1960* read as *one thousand nine hundred and sixty* or *nineteen hundred and sixty* or *nineteen sixty*) **3 :** a composite character in Chinese writing made by combining two or more other characters for words of related meaning

ideo·gram·ic *or* **ideo·gram·mic** \ˌ===ˈgramik, =ˈ==-\ *adj* **:** of, relating to, or characterized by the use of ideograms

ideo·gram·mat·ic \-ˌgrəˈmad·ik, -at|, ēk\ *adj* [*ideogram* + *-atic* (as in *epigrammatic*)] **1 :** being an ideogram **2 :** IDEOGRAMIC

ideo·graph \ˈ===ˌgraf, =ˈ==-, -raa(ə)f, -raif, -rȧf\ *n* [*ideo-* + *-graph*] **:** IDEOGRAM

ideo·graph·ic \ˌ===ˈgrafik, =ˌ==-, -fēk\ *adj* [*ideo-* + *-graphic*] **1 :** consisting of or characterized by the use of ideograms ⟨an ~ script⟩ ⟨the ~ stage in the development of writing⟩ **2 :** being an ideogram ⟨an ~ sign⟩ **3 :** of or relating to an ideogram ⟨these characters had sometimes an ~, and sometimes a phonetic value —David Diringer⟩ — **ideo·graph·i·cal·ly** \-fək(ə)lē, -fēk-, -li\ *adv*

ide·og·ra·phy \ˌīdēˈägrəfē, id-, -fi\ *n* -ES [*ideo-* + *-graphy*] **1 :** the use of ideograms **2 :** the representation of ideas by graphic symbols

ideo·log·i·cal \ˌīdēəˈläjəkəl, ˌid-, -jēk- *sometimes* ˌēd-\ *or* **ideo·log·ic** \-jik, -jēk\ *also* **idea·log·i·cal** \-dēəˈl|-\ *adj* **1 :** of, relating to, or based on ideology ⟨~ conflict⟩ **2 :** relating to or concerned with ideas ⟨an ~ application of a theory⟩ **3 :** symbolically suggestive of an idea or mood ⟨~ drama⟩ — **ideo·log·i·cal·ly** \-jək(ə)lē, -jēk-, -li\ *adv*

ide·ol·o·gist \ˌīdēˈäləjəst, ˌid- *sometimes* ˌēd-\ *n* -S [F *idéologiste*, fr. *idéologie* + *-iste* -ist] **1 a :** a specialist in the science of ideas : a student of the origin and nature of ideas **b :** an advocate or adherent of a particular system or doctrine of ideology **2 :** IDEOLOGUE 1

ide·ol·o·gize \-ˌjīz\ *vt* -ED/-ING/-S [*ideology* + *-ize*] **1 :** to interpret or formulate ideologically ⟨the dogged tendency of our time to ~ all things into grayness —Lionel Trilling⟩ **2 :** to cause (as an individual or a social institution) to accept or conform to a particular ideology ⟨planners who attempt to alter and ~ the fundamental character of our culture⟩

ideo·logue *also* **idea·logue** \ˈīdēəˌlȯg, ˈid-, īˈdē- *also* -läg\ *n* -S [F *idéologue*, back-formation fr. *idéologie*] **1 :** THEORIST, DREAMER, VISIONARY **2 :** IDEOLOGIST 1b

ide·ol·o·gy \ˌīdēˈäləjē, ˌid-, -ji *sometimes* ˌēd-\ *also* **ide·al·o·gy** \ˈ", -ēˈal-\ *n* -ES [F *idéologie*, fr. *idéo-* ideo- + *-logie* -logy] **1 a :** a branch of knowledge concerned with the origin and nature of ideas **b :** a theory in philosophy advocated by Destutt de Tracy (1754–1836): ideas originate from sensation **2 :** visionary speculation : idle theorizing; *often* **:** an impractical theory or system of theories **3 a :** a systematic scheme or coordinated body of ideas or concepts esp. about human life or culture **b :** a manner or the content of thinking characteristic of an individual, group, or culture ⟨bourgeois ~⟩ ⟨medical, legal, and other professional *ideologies*⟩ ⟨kept his ~ inviolate⟩ **c (1) :** the integrated assertions, theories, and aims that constitute a sociopolitical program ⟨a national ~ that was not static but altered with altering circumstances⟩ **(2) :** an extremist sociopolitical program or philosophy constructed wholly or in part on factitious or hypothetical ideational bases

ideo·motor \ˈīdēə, ˈid- +-\ *adj* [ISV *ideo-* + *motor*] **1** *of movement or action* **:** resulting from the impingement of ideas on the system : not reflex **2 :** of, relating to, or concerned with ideomotor activity ⟨~ theory⟩ ⟨~ suggestions⟩

ideo·pho·bia \ˌ===ˈfōbēə\ *n* [NL, fr. *ideo-* + *-phobia*] **:** fear or distrust of ideas or of reason

ideo·plas·tic \ˌ==ōˈplastik\ *adj* [ISV *ideo-* + *-plastic*; orig. formed as F *idéoplastique*] **1 :** modified by mental activity ⟨~ factors in digestion⟩ **2** *of an art form* **:** rendered symbolic or conventional through the mental remodeling of natural subjects — **ideo·plas·tic·i·ty** \-ˌplaˈstisəd·ē\ *n*

ideo·type \ˈ===+ˌ-\ *n* [*ideo-* + *type*] **:** a specimen collected from other than the type locality but identified as belonging to a particular taxon by the author of that taxon

ides \ˈīdz\ *n pl but sing or pl in constr* [MF, fr. L *idus*, prob. of non-IE origin] **:** the 15th day of March, May, July, or October or the 13th day of any other month in the ancient Roman calendar; *broadly* **:** this day and the seven days preceding it counting backward toward the nones — compare CALENDS

-ides *pl of* -IDE

ide·sia \īˈdēzh(ē)ə\ *n* [NL, fr. Evert I. *Ides*, 17th cent. German-born Dutch statesman and traveler in the service of Russia + NL *-ia*] **1** *cap* **:** a monotypic genus (family Flacourtiaceae) comprising a single Asiatic tree (*I. polycarpa*) that has a broad spreading head, large alternate long-petioled cordate leaves, and large terminal panicles of apetalous flowers followed by fleshy orange red berries and that is widely grown as an ornamental where the climate is relatively mild **2** -S **:** any plant of the genus *Idesia*

id·gah \ˈid(ˌ)gä\ *n* -S [Per *ʿīdgāh*, fr. *ʿīd* feast (fr. Ar) + Per *-gāh* place, fr. MPer *gās*, fr. OPer *gāthu-*; akin to Av *gātav-* place, Skt *gātu* going, way, course] **:** a place set apart for public prayers on the two chief Muslim feasts

-idia *pl of* -IDIUM

idi·acan·thus \ˌidēəˈkan(t)thəs\ *n, cap* [NL, fr. Gk *idios* + NL *-acanthus*] **:** a genus (the type of the family Idiacanthidae) of black deep-sea stomiatoid fishes that include a number of typical dragonfish

id·i·asm \ˈidēˌazəm\ *n* -S [Gk *idiasmos* peculiarity, fr. *idiazein* to be peculiar, fr. *idios* one's own, private, peculiar — more at IDIOT] **:** an individual mannerism (as in literary style)

id·ic \ˈidik\ *adj* [¹*id* + *-ic*] **:** relating to or consisting of ids ⟨~ constituents of germ plasm⟩

idig·bo \əˈdig,bō, ˈēdig,bō\ *n* -S [native name in Africa] **1 :** an African tree (*Terminalia worensis*) valued for its light yellow wood **2 :** the wood of the idigbo

-i·din \ədən, əd°n\ *or* **-i·dine** \əˌdēn, ədən, əd°n\ *n suffix* -S [ISV ¹*-ide* + *-in, -ine*] **:** chemical compound related in origin or structure to another compound: as **a** *usu -idin* **:** aglycon of a glycoside ⟨pelargon*idin* from pelargonin⟩ **b** *usu -idine* **:** completely hydrogenated form of a cyclic base ⟨pyrrol*idine* from pyrrole⟩ ⟨thiazol*idine* from thiazole⟩ **c** *usu -idine* **:** base obtained otherwise than by hydrogenation ⟨tolu*idine* or tol*idine* from toluene⟩ ⟨guan*idine* from guanine⟩

idio- *comb form* [Gk, fr. *idios* — more at IDIOT] **1 :** one's own : personal : separate : distinct ⟨*idio*type⟩ ⟨*idio*syncrasy⟩ **2 :** self-produced : arising within ⟨*idio*lysin⟩ ⟨*idio*reflex⟩ ⟨*idio*pathic⟩ ⟨*idio*ventricular rhythm⟩

id·io·adaptation \ˌidē(ˌ)ō+\ *n* [*idio-* + *adaptation*] **:** evolutionary modification involving progressive specialization that results in more perfect adaptation of an organism to a particular environment with corresponding loss of adaptability to new or changing environment

id·io·an·drospo·rous \ˌidē(ˌ)ōˌandrəˈspōrəs, -ˈan|drəˈspər-\ *adj* [*idio-* + *androspore* + *-ous*] *of an alga* **:** bearing androspores and oogonia on separate filaments — compare GYNANDROSPOROUS

id·io·biology \ˌidē(ˌ)ō+\ *n* [ISV *idio-* + *biology*; orig. formed as G *idiobiologie*] **:** a branch of biology concerned with the study of organisms as individuals

id·io·blap·sis \ˌidēōˈblapsəs\ *n* -ES [NL, fr. *idio-* + Gk *blapsis* damage, fr. *blaptein* to damage] **:** a hypothetical familial allergy presumably manifested in alteration of pulse rate following the ingestion of an allergenic food

id·io·blap·tic \ˌ===ˈ=tik\ *adj* [*idio-* + Gk *blaptikos* hurtful, fr. *blaptein* + *-ikos* -ic] **:** of or relating to idioblapsis

id·io·blast \ˈidēəˌblast\ *n* [ISV *idio-* + *-blast*; orig. formed in G] **1 a :** an isolated plant cell (as a sclereid) that differs markedly in form, contents, or wall structure from neighboring cells **b :** a hypothetical structural unit of a living cell — compare BIOPHORE **2 :** a crystal in a metamorphic rock that is bounded by its own faces, looks like a phenocryst, but is of later growth — **id·io·blas·tic** \ˌidēəˈblastik\ *adj*

id·io·chromatic \ˌidē(ˌ)ō+\ *adj* [ISV *idio-* + *chromatic*] **:** colored inherently and characteristically : having a distinctive and constant coloration ⟨copper sulfate is an ~ substance⟩ — used esp. of minerals; compare ALLOCHROMATIC 1

id·io·chromatin \"+\ *n* [ISV *idio-* + *chromatin*] **:** the part of the chromatin of a cell that is thought to transmit genes and function in reproduction — compare TROPHOCHROMATIN

id·io·chromosome \"+\ *n* [ISV *idio-* + *chromosome*] **:** SEX CHROMOSOME

id·i·oc·ra·sy \ˌidēˈäkrəsē\ *n* -ES [LGk *idiokrasia*, prob. MS var. of Gk *idiosynkrasia* idiosyncrasy — more at IDIOSYNCRASY] **:** peculiarity of constitution : IDIOSYNCRASY

id·i·o·crat·ic \ˌidēəˈkrad·ik\ *or* **id·i·o·crat·i·cal** \d·əkəl\ *also* |ək\ *adj* [fr. *idiocrasy*, after such pairs as E *apostasy: apostatic, apostatical*] **:** IDIOSYNCRATIC — **id·i·o·crat·i·cal·ly** \-d·ək(ə)lē\ *adv*

id·i·o·cy \ˈidēəsē, -si\ *n* -ES [fr. *idiot*, after such pairs as E *accurate: accuracy*] **1 :** extreme mental deficiency commonly due to incomplete or abnormal development of the brain and usu. congenital or due to arrest of development following disease or injury in early childhood **2 a :** something notably stupid or foolish ⟨the usual bureaucratic *idiocies* —W.M. Hitzig⟩ **b :** something so light, frothy, and trivial that it is usu. considered silly ⟨amused by his amiable *idiocies*⟩

id·io·cy·cloph·a·nous \ˌidē(ˌ)ōˌsīˈkläfənəs\ *adj* [ISV *idio-* + *cycl-* + *phan-* (fr. Gk *phainein* to show) + *-ous* — more at FANCY] **:** IDIOPHANOUS

id·io·genesis \ˌidēō+\ *n* [NL, fr. *idio-* + *genesis*] **:** spontaneous origin (as of disease)

id·io·genetic \"+\ *adj* [*idio-* + *-genetic*] **:** originating spontaneously ⟨an apparently ~ disorder⟩

id·io·glos·sia \ˌidēōˈgläsēə, -lȯs-\ *n* -S [NL, fr. *idio-* + *-glossia*] **:** a condition in which the affected person pronounces his words so badly as to seem to speak a language of his own

id·io·gram \ˈidēəˌgram\ *n* [ISV *idio-* + *-gram*] **:** a diagrammatic representation of a chromosome complement or karyotype

id·io·graph \-ˌgraf, -rȧf\ *n* [LGk *idiographon* autograph, fr. neut. of Gk *idiographos* specially written, in the author's handwriting, fr. *idio-* + *-graphos* (fr. *graphein* to write) — more at CARVE] **:** a mark or signature peculiar to an individual

id·io·graph·ic \ˌ===ˈgrafik\ *adj* [ISV *idio-* + *-graphic*; orig. formed as G *idiographisch*] **:** relating to, involving, or dealing with the concrete, individual, or unique ⟨considering history an ~ discipline⟩ — contrasted with *nomothetic*

id·io·kinetic \ˌidē(ˌ)ō+\ *adj* [*idio-* + *kinetic*] *of movement* **:** induced by activity of the pyramidal tracts of the brain

id·io·lalia \ˌidēōˈlālēə, -lal-\ *n* -S [NL, fr. *idio-* + *-lalia*] **:** IDIOGLOSSIA

id·i·o·lect \ˈidēəˌlekt\ *n* -S [*idio-* + *-lect* (as in *dialect*)] **:** the language or speech pattern of one individual at a particular period of his life

id·i·om \ˈidēəm\ *n* -S [MF & LL; MF *idiome*, fr. LL *idioma*, fr. Gk *idiōma* peculiarity, peculiarity of style, idiom, fr. *idiousthai* to appropriate, fr. *idios* one's own, private, peculiar — more at IDIOT] **1 a :** the language proper or peculiar to a people or to a district, community, or class : TONGUE, DIALECT **b :** the syntactical, grammatical, or structural form peculiar to a language : the genius, habit, or cast of a language **2 :** an expression established in the usage of a language that is peculiar to itself either in grammatical construction (as *no, it wasn't me*) or in having a meaning that cannot be derived as a whole from the conjoined meanings of its elements (as *Monday week* for "the Monday a week after next Monday"; *many a* for "many taken distributively"; *had better* for "might better"; *how are you?* for "what is the state of your health or feelings?") **3 :** a style or form of artistic expression (as in painting, writing, composing) that is characteristic esp. of an individual, a period or movement, or a medium or instrument ⟨an interesting orchestral ~⟩ ⟨surrealist ~⟩ ⟨imagination has its specific hereditary ~s —George Santayana⟩ **syn** see LANGUAGE

id·i·om·at·ic \ˌidēəˈmad·|ik, -at|, |ēk\ *also* **id·i·om·at·i·cal** \|əkəl, |ēk-\ *adj* [LGk *idiōmatikos* peculiar, characteristic, fr. Gk *idiōmat-, idiōma* + *-ikos* -ic, -ical] **1 :** of, relating to, or conforming to idiom ⟨~ fluency in speech and writing⟩ ⟨a highly ~ concerto⟩ ⟨~ English⟩ **2 :** peculiar to a particular group or individual : INDIVIDUAL ⟨one person acting in his ~ purposeful fashion to evoke a response from another —John Dewey⟩ ⟨grows to value the physical sex life per se rather than as a symbol of ~ relationships —F.S.Chapin⟩ ⟨how vigorous and ~ was the native life —John Buchan⟩ — **id·i·o·mat·i·cal·ly** \|ək(ə)lē, |ēk-, -li\ *adv* — **id·i·o·mat·ic·ness** \|iknəs, |ēk-\ *n* -ES

id·i·om·e·ter \ˌidēˈämədˌə(r)\ *n* [*idio-* + *-meter*] **:** an instrument for ascertaining the personal equation of an astronomical observer

idiom neutral *n, usu cap I&N* **:** an artificial language partially derived from Volapük and having a vocabulary consistently selected on the basis of the maximum internationality of the roots

id·i·om·og·ra·phy \ˌidēəˈmägrəfē\ *n* -ES [F *idiomographie*, fr. *idiome* idiom + *-o-* + *-graphie* -graphy — more at IDIOM] **:** the description of idiom

id·i·om·ol·o·gy \-ˈmäləjē\ *n* -ES [*idiom* + *-o-* + *-logy*] **:** the study of idiom

id·io·morph \ˈidēəˌmȯrf\ *n* -S [*idio-* + *-morph*] **:** a pattern of repeated letters in cryptography ⟨the ~ PXLXAP fits the probable word STATES⟩ — compare ISOMORPH c

id·io·mor·phic \ˌ===ˈmȯrfik\ *adj* [Gk *idiomorphos* + E *-ic*] **1 :** having the proper form or shape : AUTOMORPHIC — used of minerals the growth of whose crystals in a rock has not been interfered with; contrasted with *allotriomorphic* **2 :** of, relating to, or being an idiomorph — **id·io·mor·phi·cal·ly** \-fək(ə)lē\ *adv*

id·io·mor·phism \ˌ===ˈ=ˌfizəm\ *n* -S [*idiomorphic* + *-ism*] **:** the condition of being idiomorphic (sense 1)

id·io·mor·phous \ˌ===ˈ=fəs\ *adj* [Gk *idiomorphos* having a form of its own, fr. *idio-* + *-morphos* -morphous] **:** IDIOMORPHIC 1

id·io·muscular \ˌidē(ˌ)ō+\ *adj* [ISV *idio-* + *muscular*] **:** relating to muscular tissue exclusively; *esp* **:** originating in muscle ⟨~ contraction⟩

-idion — see -IDIUM

id·i·o·path·ic \ˌidēəˈpathik\ *adj* **1 :** peculiar to the individual : INNATE ⟨~ sensitivity⟩ **2 :** arising spontaneously or from an obscure or unknown cause : PRIMARY ⟨~ epilepsy⟩ — **id·i·o·path·i·cal·ly** \-thək(ə)lē\ *adv*

id·i·op·a·thy \ˌidēˈäpəthē\ *n* -ES [Gk *idiopatheia*, fr. *idio-* + *-patheia* -pathy] **:** an idiopathic anomaly or disease

id·i·oph·a·nous \ˌidēˈäfənəs\ *adj* [*idio-* + *phan-* (fr. Gk *phainein* to show) + *-ous* — more at FANCY] *of a crystal* **:** exhibiting interference figures without the aid of a polariscope

id·io·phone \ˈidēəˌfōn\ *n* [G *idiophon*, fr. *idio-* + *-phon* -phone] **:** a musical instrument (as a bell, gong, rattle) the source of whose sound is the vibration of its elastic constituent material unmodified by any special tension (as in a drum) — **id·io·phon·ic** \ˌ==ˈfänik\ *adj*

id·io·plasm \ˈidēəˌplazəm\ *n* [ISV *idio-* + *-plasm*; orig. formed as G *idioplasma*] **:** the part of protoplasm held to function specif. in transmission of hereditary properties and commonly equated with chromatin — opposed to *trophoplasm* — **id·io·plas·mat·ic** \ˌ===ˌplazˈmad·ik\ *or* **id·io·plas·mic** \-zmik\ *adj*

id·io·retinal \ˌidē(ˌ)ō+\ *adj* [*idio-* + *retinal*] **:** peculiar to the retina; *specif* **:** originating subjectively in the retina ⟨~ light⟩

id·i·or·rhythmic \ˌidēə+\ *adj* [LGk *idiorrhythmos* (fr. Gk *idio-* + *rhythmos* measured motion, measure, proportion) + E *-ic* — more at RHYTHM] *Eastern Church* **:** SELF-REGULATING — used of (1) monks that live separately, hold property, work individually in supporting themselves, and though members of a monastery supervised by an elected council are not under direct daily supervision or (2) of monasteries so organized

id·i·or·rhyth·mism \ˌ===ˈrithˌmizəm\ *n* -S **:** a system of monastic self-regulation in the Eastern Church — compare IDIORRHYTHMIC

id·i·o·se·pi·idae \ˌidē(ˌ)ōsəˈpīəˌdē\ *n pl, cap* [NL, fr. *Idiosepion* or *Idiosepius*, type genus (fr. *idio-* + Gk *sēpion* cuttlefish bone) + *-idae* — more at SEPIA] **:** a family of squids that includes a single tiny squid (*Idiosepius pygmaeus* or *Idiosepion pygmaeum*) of the Indian ocean which lacks an internal shell and is considerably less than an inch in length

id·io·some \ˈidēəˌsōm\ *n* -S [*idio-* + *-some*] **:** any of several specialized cellular organelles: as **a :** IDIOBLAST 1b **b :** ACROSOME **c :** an area of modified cytoplasm surrounding a centrosome **d :** SEX CHROMOSOME

id·i·o·syn·cra·sy *also* **id·i·o·syn·cra·cy** \ˌidēəˈsiŋkrəsē, -dēō-, -sink-, -rəsi\ *n* [Gk *idiosynkrasia*, fr. *idio-* + *-synkrasia* (fr. *synkrasis* action of commingling or blending — fr. *synkerannynai* to commingle, blend, fr. *syn-* + *kerannynai* to mingle, mix — + *-ia* -y) — more at CRATER] **1 :** characteristic peculiarity of habit or structure **2 a :** a peculiarity of physical or mental constitution or temperament : a characteristic distinguishing an individual; *broadly* **:** ECCENTRICITY **b :** individual hypersensitiveness (as to a drug or food) ⟨anemia accompanying the use of a sulfa drug is usually considered to be due to ~⟩

¹id·i·o·syn·crat·ic \ˌidēə¦sin¦krad·|ik, -dē(ˌ)ō¦s-, -siŋ¦-, -at|, |ēk\ *adj* [fr. *idiosyncrasy*, after such pairs as E *apostasy: apostatic*] **1 :** peculiar to the individual ⟨an ~ gesture⟩ **:** of, relating to, or resulting from idiosyncrasy ⟨~ response to a drug⟩ ⟨~ disease⟩ **2 :** marked by idiosyncrasy **:** ECCENTRIC ⟨is so ~ in his literary judgments that it is impossible to think of him as a sound critic —*Saturday Rev.*⟩ — **id·i·o·syn·crat·i·cal·ly** \|ə̇k(ə)lē, |ēk-, -li\ *adv*

²idiosyncratic \"\ *n* -s **:** one that is idiosyncratic

¹id·i·ot \ˈidēə|t, *chiefly dial* ˈijə| *or* ˈējə|; *usu* |d.+V\ *n* -s [ME, fr. MF *idiote*, fr. L *idiota*, fr. Gk *idiōtēs* person in a private station, person without professional knowledge, ignorant person, common man, fr. *idios* one's own, private, peculiar; akin to L *sed, se* without, *sui* of oneself — more at SUICIDE] **1** *obs* **:** an ignorant or unschooled person **:** a simple unlearned person **:** CLOWN 1 **2 :** a person afflicted with idiocy; *specif* **:** a feebleminded person that has a mental age not exceeding two years and accordingly requires complete custodial care **3 a :** a silly simple person **:** SIMPLETON, BLOCKHEAD ⟨he means well but he is such an ~⟩ **b :** a person who fails to exhibit normal or usual sense, discrimination, or judgment esp. at a particular time or in respect to a particular subject ⟨I don't know why I was such an ~⟩ ⟨a perfect ~ about budgeting⟩ **c :** a professional fool **:** JESTER **4** [Gk *idiōtēs*] *obs* **:** a person in private station or one not schooled in a trade or profession **:** LAYMAN **syn** see FOOL

²idiot \"\ *adj* [ME, fr. *idiot* (n.)] **1 :** IDIOTIC **2 :** fit for, typical of, or suitable to idiots **:** being such as an idiot might be expected to have, engage in, display ⟨~ terror⟩ ⟨those ~ hats⟩ ⟨such ~ war⟩

idiot board *n* **:** a device (as a projection of a script) used to prompt a television speaker and placed out of range of the camera

id·i·ot·cy \ˈidēətsē, -si\ *n* -ES [¹*idiot* + *-cy*] **1 :** IDIOCY 1 **2 :** something worthy of an idiot **:** utter folly

id·i·ot·ic \ˌidē¦äd·|ik, -ät|, |ēk\ *adj* [LL *idioticus* unskilled, rude, simple, fr. Gk *idiōtikos* private, unprofessional, ordinary, fr. *idiōtēs* + *-ikos* -ic] **1 :** relating to or like an idiot **2 :** characterized by idiocy **:** FOOLISH, SENSELESS

id·i·ot·i·cal \|ə̇kəl, |ēk-\ *adj* [LL *idioticus* + E *-al*] **1** *obs* **:** lacking education **:** IGNORANT, UNSCHOOLED **2 :** IDIOTIC 2

id·i·ot·i·cal·ly \|ə̇k(ə)lē, |ēk-, -li\ *adv* **1 :** like an idiot **:** in an idiot or idiotic way ⟨behaved ~⟩ **2 :** ABSURDLY, RIDICULOUSLY ⟨~ cheap⟩

id·i·ot·i·cal·ness \-kəlnə̇s\ *n* -ES **:** extreme stupidity or foolishness

id·i·ot·ism \ˈidēəd·ˌizəm, -ēə,ti-\ *n* -s [in sense 1, fr. MF *idiotisme*, fr. L *idiotismus* common or vulgar manner of speaking, fr. Gk *idiōtismos* way of a common man, manner of speech of a common man, fr. *idiōtēs* common man + *-ismos* -ism; in sense 2, fr. ¹*idiot* + *-ism* — more at IDIOT] **1 a** *obs* **:** IDIOM 1 **b :** IDIOM 2 **2** *archaic* **:** IDIOCY

id·i·ot·ize \-əd·ˌīz, -əˌtīz\ *vt* -ED/-ING/-S [¹*idiot* + *-ize*] **:** to make a fool of **:** cause to become or behave like an idiot

id·i·ot·ry \-ətrē, -ri\ *n* -ES [¹*idiot* + *-ry*] *chiefly Scots law* **:** IDIOCY

idiot savant *pronunc at* IDIOT + *pronunc at* SAVANT, *or* ē,dyō'sa'vä͞n\ *n, pl* **idiots savants** \-n(t)s, -ä͞n(z)\ [F, lit., skilled idiot] **:** a person that is in general mentally defective but that displays unusual aptitude or brilliance in some special field

idiot's delight *n* **:** any of various solitaire card games

idiot sheet *also* **idiot card** *n* **:** a large card bearing usu. hand-lettered words or phrases for prompting a speaker or actor during a telecast — compare IDIOT BOARD

id·i·o·zome \ˈidēəˌzōm\ *n* -s [ISV *idio-* + Gk *zōma* girdle — more at ZONE] **:** ACROSOME

id·i·tol \ˈidəˌtōl, -tȯl\ *n* -s [ISV *idose* + *-itol*] **:** a sweet crystalline hexahydroxy alcohol $C_6H_{14}O_6C_6H_8(OH)_6$ obtained by a reduction of idose or sorbose

-id·i·um \ˈidēəm\ *also* **-id·i·on** \-ēˌän, -ēən\ *n suffix, pl* **-idi·ums** \-ēəmz\ *or* **-id·ia** \-ēə\ *also* **idions** [NL, fr. Gk *-idion*, dim. suffix] **:** small one **:** lesser one ⟨anther*idium*⟩ ⟨chrom*idium*⟩

¹idle \ˈīdᵊl\ *adj* **idler** \-d(ᵊ)lə(r)\ **idlest** \-d(ᵊ)lə̇st\ [ME *idel* (also, empty, void), fr. OE *īdel*; akin to OFris *īdel* empty, worthless, vain, OS *īdal*, OHG *ītal*] **1 a :** lacking worth or basis **:** leading to nothing **:** GROUNDLESS, USELESS ⟨~ theorizing⟩ ⟨an ~ rumor⟩ ⟨it would be ~ to argue further⟩ **b :** having no particular reason for existing or occurring **:** light, casual, and superficial ⟨~ chatter⟩ ⟨took an ~ glance about⟩ ⟨asked out of ~ curiosity⟩ **2 a :** not occupied or employed: as (1) *of a person* **:** having no employment or business **:** UNEMPLOYED ⟨closed factories and ~ workmen⟩ (2) *of a period of time* **:** marked by want of activity esp. of a useful or constructive nature **:** WASTED ⟨passed his ~ days in sloth⟩ ⟨that ~ hour just before dusk⟩ (3) *of a thing* **:** not turned to normal or appropriate use ⟨~ tenements⟩ **:** not called into active service ⟨~ capital⟩ **b** (1) **:** given to rest or ease **:** seeking to avoid labor or employment **:** TRIFLING, LAZY, SLOTHFUL ⟨a careless ~ worker⟩ ⟨~ boys playing in the streets⟩ (2) **:** having no regular occupation or evident lawful means of support ⟨answer to the charge of being an ~ person⟩ (3) **:** IDLING ⟨an engine running at fast ~ speed⟩ **3** *now dial Eng* **a :** LIGHTHEADED, FOOLISH **b :** MISCHIEVOUS **syn** see INACTIVE, VAIN

²idle \"\ *vb* **idled; idled; idling** \-d(ᵊ)liŋ\ **idles** *vi* **1 :** to lose or spend time in idleness ⟨*idling* in the garden⟩; *esp* **:** to move idly ⟨*idled* along the stream bank⟩ **2 :** to run disconnected or unloaded so that power is not used for external or useful work — used esp. of a motor, engine, pulley wheel ~ *vt* **1 :** to spend (as time) in idleness — often used with *away* ⟨*idling* away a pleasant summer day⟩ **2 :** to make or leave idle ⟨cutbacks in orders that *idled* thousands of workers⟩ ⟨the common cold ~*s* more people than any other disease⟩ **3 :** to cause to idle ⟨~ a motor⟩

³idle \"\ *n* -s [²*idle*] **:** an act or instance or the state of idling ⟨an engine running at ~⟩

idleby *n* -s [¹*idle* + *-by* (as in the name *Crosby*)] *obs* **:** IDLER

idleheaded \ˌ=ˌ=¦=\ *adj* **1 :** FOOLISH, STUPID, SILLY **2** *obs* **:** out of one's head **:** DELIRIOUS, CRAZY

idle·hood \ˈīdᵊlˌhu̇d\ *n, archaic* **:** IDLENESS

idle·man \-ˌmən\ *n, pl* **idlemen** *archaic* **:** a man of substance who does not need to work for a living

idle·ness *n* -ES [ME *idelnesse* (also, vanity) fr. OE *īdelnes*, fr. *īdel* + *-nes* -ness] **:** the quality or state of being idle (as through lack of worth, occupation, employment, industry) ⟨the ~ of our search⟩ ⟨increasing ~ in the auto industry⟩ ⟨a person of unbelievable ~⟩; *also* **:** an instance of such idleness ⟨our yesterday's ~ forgotten⟩

idler \ˈīd(ᵊ)lə(r)\ *n* -s **1 :** one that idles or is unoccupied **:** one that spends his time in inaction **:** a lazy person **2 a :** IDLER GEAR **b :** IDLER PULLEY **c :** IDLER WHEEL **3 :** a member of a ship's crew that has constant day duties and keeps no night watch **4 :** an empty railroad car placed between two cars that support a load; *also* **:** an empty flatcar placed at either end of a loaded flatcar to take the overhang but not the weight of a projecting load **5 :** a member of a fish-dressing gang who washes gutted fish or a wharf laborer who carries fish and supplies to the cleaners and removes scrap

idler gear *n* **1 :** a gear placed between a driving and a driven gear to transfer motion without change of direction or gear ratio **2 :** a gear for support or guidance instead of power transmission

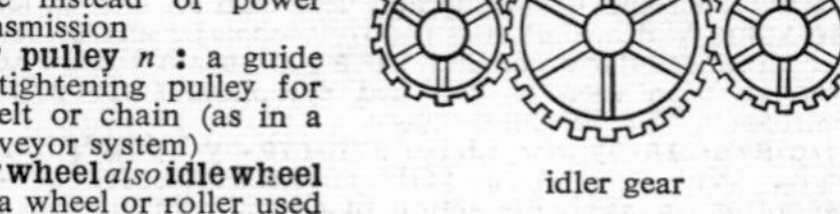

idler gear

idler pulley *n* **:** a guide or tightening pulley for a belt or chain (as in a conveyor system)

idler wheel *also* **idle wheel** *n* **:** a wheel or roller used to transfer motion or to guide or support something: as **a :** IDLER GEAR **b :** IDLER PULLEY **c :** a rubber-surfaced roller in a sound-recording or sound-reproducing mechanism for transferring power by frictional means (as from the motor shaft to the turntable rim in a phonograph)

idleset \ˈ=ˌ=\ *n* [¹*idle* + *set* (setting)] *chiefly Scot* **:** IDLENESS

idlesse \ˈīdlə̇s\ *n* -s [¹*idle* + ME *-esse* -ess] **:** IDLENESS

idling *n* -s **:** the act of one that idles

idly \ˈīd(ᵊ)lē, -li\ *adv* [ME *idilly*, fr. OE *īdellīce*, fr. *īdel* idle + *-līce* -ly — more at IDLE] **:** in an idle manner: as **a :** INEFFECTUALLY, VAINLY **b :** LAZILY, INDOLENTLY; *broadly* **:** without especial interest or effort **:** CASUALLY **c** *obs* **:** FOOLISHLY, INCOHERENTLY

ido \ˈē(ˌ)dō\ *n* -s *cap* [Esperanto, offspring, fr. Gk *-idēs*, patronymic suffix] **:** an international artificial language produced by modification of Esperanto

ido- — see ID-

ido·crase \ˈīdōˌkrās, ˈid-, -āz\ *n* -s [F, fr. Gk *eidos* form, shape + *krasis* mixture fr. *kerannynai* to mix — more at IDYLL, CRATER] **:** a mineral $Ca_{10}(Mg,Fe)_2Al_4Si_9O_{34}(OH)_4$ that is a complex silicate of calcium, magnesium, iron, and aluminum — called also *vesuvianite*

idol \ˈīdᵊl\ *n* -s *often attrib* [ME *idel, idol*, fr. OF *idele, idle, idole*, fr. LL *idolum*, fr. Gk *eidōlon* phantom, image, image of a god; akin to Gk *eidos* shape, form — more at WISE] **1 a :** an image of a divinity **:** a representation or symbol of a deity or any other being or thing made or used as an object of worship; *broadly* **:** a false god **:** a heathen deity **b :** an image (as of a saint) used in Christian worship **2 a :** an appearance, aspect, or likeness of something ⟨sense perception is explained, after the manner of Democritus, by ~*s* or images or thin filmlike forms, which emanate from the objects around us —Frank Thilly⟩ **b** *obs* **:** EFFIGY, STATUE **c** *obs* **:** PRETENDER, IMPOSTOR **3 :** a form or appearance visible but without substance **:** an incorporeal image or phantom **4 :** something or someone on which the affections are strongly and often excessively set **:** an object of passionate devotion **:** a person or thing greatly loved or adored **5 :** a false notion or conception **:** FALLACY, IDOLUM 2

idol·a·ter \īˈdälǝd·ə(r), -ətə- *sometimes* ə̇ˈdä-\ *n* -s [alter. (influenced by MF *idolatre*) of ME *idolatrer, idolatrour*, fr. MF *idolatre* fr. LL *idololatres*, fr. Gk *eidōlolatrēs*, fr. *eidōlon* idol + *-latrēs* -later) + ME *-er* or *-our* -or — more at IDOL] **1 :** a worshiper of idols **:** one that pays divine honors to an image, statue, or natural object as a representation of deity **2 :** a person that devotes intense or excessive and often blind affection, adoration, or admiration to an object not normally or usu. a subject of worship ⟨no indiscriminating ~ of Great Britain —B.J.Hendrick⟩

idol·a·tress \-lətrə̇s\ *n* -ES **:** a female idolater

idol·a·tric \(ˈ)ī¦dälə·(ˌ)trik, ¦īdə¦la·tr-\ *also* **ido·lat·ri·cal** \ˌīdə¦la·trə̇kəl\ *adj* [ML *idolatricus*, fr. LL *idolatria* idolatry + L *-icus* -ic, -ical] **:** IDOLATROUS

idol·a·trize \īˈdäləˌtrīz *sometimes* ə̇ˈd-\ *vb* -ED/-ING/-S [*idolatry* + *-ize*] *vi* **:** to worship idols **:** pay idolatrous worship ~ *vt* **:** to make an idol of **:** IDOLIZE — **idol·a·triz·er** \-zə(r)\ *n* -s

idol·a·trous \(ˈ)ī¦dälə·trəs *sometimes* ə̇ˈd-\ *adj* **:** of or relating to idolatry: as **a :** being or resembling idolatry ⟨~ veneration for antiquity⟩ **b :** given to or practicing idolatry ⟨an ~ worshiper⟩ — **idol·a·trous·ly** *adv* — **idol·a·trous·ness** *n* -ES

idol·a·try \-ə·trē, -ri\ *n* -ES [ME *idolatrie*, fr. OF, fr. ML *idolatria*, alter. of LL *idololatria*, fr. Gk *eidōlolatreia*, fr. *eidōlon* + *latreia* -latry] **1 a :** the worship of a physical object as a god; *esp* **:** such worship of a made image **b :** the giving of absolute religious devotion and ultimate trust to something that is not God **2 :** immoderate attachment or devotion to or veneration for something **:** respect or love that approaches that due a divine power **3** *obs* **:** an object of idolatry

idol·ism \ˈīdᵊlˌizəm\ *n* -s **1 a :** the worship of idols **b :** IDOLIZATION **2 :** IDOLUM 2

idol·ist \-ə̇st\ *n* -s *archaic* **:** IDOLATER 1

idol·i·za·tion \ˌīdᵊlə̇ˈzāshən, -ˌlīˈz-\ *n* -s **:** the act of idolizing or state of being idolized ⟨the ~ to which they were subjected⟩

idol·ize \ˈīdᵊlˌīz\ *vb* -ED/-ING/-S *see -ize in Explan Notes vt* **:** to make an idol of **:** worship idolatrously; *broadly* **:** to love to excess **:** reverence to adoration ⟨~ gold⟩ ⟨boys at just the right age for *idolizing* military or sports heroes⟩ ~ *vi* **:** to practice idolatry — **idol·iz·er** \-zə(r)\ *n* -s

idolo- *also* **eidolo-** *comb form* [LL & Gk; LL *idolo-*, fr. Gk *eidōlo-*, fr. *eidōlon* — more at idol] **:** idol **:** image ⟨*idolo*cracy⟩ ⟨*idolo*mania⟩ ⟨*idolo*clastic⟩

idololatry *n* -ES [LL *idololatria* — more at IDOLATRY] *obs* **:** IDOLATRY

idol shepherd *n* **:** a counterfeit or worthless shepherd ⟨woe to the *idol shepherd* that leaveth the flock —Zech 11:17 (AV)⟩ — compare SHEPHERD 2

idols of the cave [trans. of NL *idola specus*] **:** idola due to individual peculiarities or prejudices — compare IDOLUM 2

idols of the forum *or* **idols of the market** [trans. of NL *idola fori*] **:** idola due to human factors (as language) — compare IDOLUM 2

idols of the theater [trans. of NL *idola theatri*] **:** idola due to traditional doctrines and methods — compare IDOLUM 2

idols of the tribe [trans. of NL *idola tribus*] **:** idola due to human nature itself or to the tribe or race of man (as anthropomorphic projections) — compare IDOLUM 2

ido·lum \īˈdōləm\ *n, pl* **ido·la** \-lə\ [in sense 1, fr. L & Gk; L, phantom, image, fr. Gk *eidōlon* phantom, image, idol; in sense 2, NL, fr. LL, idol, fr. Gk *eidōlon* — more at IDOL] **1 :** EIDOLON **2 :** a form of false thinking **:** FALLACY, IDOL 5; *specif* **:** one of the four varieties of fallacy distinguished by Francis Bacon in his *Novum Organum* (1620) — compare IDOLS OF THE CAVE, IDOLS OF THE FORUM, IDOLS OF THE THEATER, IDOLS OF THE TRIBE

-i·done \əˌdōn\ *n suffix* -s [ISV ¹*-ide* + *-one*] **:** oxo derivative of a compound whose name ends in *-idine* ⟨pyrrol*idone*⟩

ido·ne·i·ty \ˌīdə̇ˈnēəd·ē\ *n* -ES [ML *idoneitas*, fr. L *idoneus* + *-itas* -ity] *archaic* **:** the quality or state of being idoneous **:** SUITABILITY, FITNESS

ido·ne·ous \(ˈ)ī¦dōnēəs\ *adj* [L *idoneus*] *archaic* **:** FIT, APPROPRIATE, SUITABLE, PROPER

idos *pl of* IDO

idose \ˈīˌdōs, ˈiˌd- *also* -ōz\ *n* -s [ISV *id-* (fr. ISV *idonic* — *acid* — $C_6H_{12}O_7$, fr. L *idem* same + ISV *gulonic*) + *-ose* — more at IDENTITY] **:** a sugar $C_6H_{12}O_6$ epimeric with gulose and obtainable along with gulose by synthesis from xylose

ido·tea \īˈdōd·ēə\ [NL, irreg. fr. Gk *Eidothea*, a sea goddess] *syn of* IDOTHEA

idothea \īˈdōthēə, -däth-\ *n, cap* [NL, alter. of *Idotea*] **:** a large and widely distributed genus (the type of the family Idotheidae) of small marine cursorial isopods

i doubt it \ˈ=ˌ=\ *n, cap first I* **:** a card game in which each player tries to be first to empty his hand by laying down a number of cards and calling them the rank it is his turn to play (as two, ten, ace), discarding them if no one says "I doubt it" or if his claim is proved correct, but having to take up all discards on the table if it is shown that the included cards not called for

IDR *abbr* infantry drill regulations

id·ri·a·lite \ˈidrēəˌlīt\ *n* -s [F *idrialite*, fr. *Idria* (Idrija), Yugoslavia + F *-lite*] **:** a mineral prob. $C_{43}H_{32}O$ occurring as a crystalline hydrocarbon and melting at 205° C

-i·dro·sis \ə̇ˈdrōsə̇s\ *n comb form, pl* **-idro·ses** \-ōˌsēz\ [NL, fr. Gk *-idrōsis*, fr. *hidrōsis* act of sweating, fr. *hidroun* to sweat (fr. *hidrōs* sweat) + *-sis* — more at SWEAT] **:** a specified form of sweating ⟨chrom*idrosis*⟩ ⟨brom*idrosis*⟩ ⟨hyper*idrosis*⟩

ids *pl of* ID

-ids *pl of* -ID

¹id·u·mae·an *or* **id·u·me·an** \ˌidyə¦mēən, ¦iјə-, ¦idə¦-\ *n* -s *usu cap* [*Idumaea* or *Idumea*, ancient region south of the Dead sea in Palestine (fr. L *Idumaea*, fr. Gk *Idoumaia*) + E *-an*] **:** EDOMITE

²idumaean \"\ *adj, usu cap* **:** of or relating to the Edomites **:** EDOMITIC

idun·it \(ˈ)ī¦dənə̇t\ *n* -s [alter. of *I done it*] **:** an autobiographical or confessional account usu. of a sensational character

idyll *or* **idyl** \ˈīdᵊl, *chiefly Brit* ˈid-\ *n* -s [L *idyllion, idyllium*, fr. Gk *eidyllion*, dim. of *eidos* shape, form, literary form; akin to Gk *idein* to see — more at WIT] **1 a :** a short descriptive poem usu. dealing with pastoral or rural life **:** ECLOGUE **b :** a simple descriptive work either in poetry or prose that deals with rustic life or pastoral scenes or suggests a mood of peace and contentment **c :** a narrative poem (as Tennyson's *Idylls of the King*) treating more or less fully an epic, romantic, or tragic theme **2 a :** a lighthearted carefree episode or one of such pastoral charm and simplicity as to be a fit subject for a poetic idyll **b :** a romantic or amorous interlude **3 :** a pastoral or romantic musical composition

idyl·lic \(ˈ)ī¦dilik, -lēk *sometimes* ə̇ˈd-\ *adj* **1 :** of, relating to, or being an idyll **2 :** pleasing or picturesque in its natural simplicity ⟨romantic memories of a lost cause threw an ~ haze over earlier times —V.L.Parrington⟩ — **idyl·li·cal·ly** \-lə̇k(ə)lē, -lēk-, -li\ *adv*

idyll·ist \ˈīdᵊlə̇st, *chiefly Brit* ˈid-\ *n* -s **:** a composer of idylls **:** an idyllic writer

idyl·li·um \īˈdilēəm, ə̇ˈd-\ *also* **idyl·li·on** \-ēˌän, -ēən\ *n, pl* **idyl·lia** \-ēə\ [L — more at IDYLL] *archaic* **:** IDYLL

ie \ˈē(ˌ)ā\ *or* **ieie** \ˈē(ˌ)āˈē(ˌ)ā\ *n* -s [Hawaiian] **1 :** a Pacific Islands screw pine (*Freycinetia arborea*) having prop roots which yield a fiber **2 :** a mat or basket made of the fiber of the ie

-ie *also* **-y** *or* **-ey** \ē, i\ *n suffix, pl* **-ies** *or* **-eys** [ME (Sc) *-ie*] **1 a :** little one **:** dear little one ⟨bird*ie*⟩ ⟨boot*ie*⟩ ⟨Jean*ie*⟩ **b** — in names of articles of feminine apparel ⟨night*ie*⟩ ⟨pant*ie*⟩ **2 :** one belonging to **:** one having to do with ⟨book*ie*⟩ ⟨deck*ie*⟩ ⟨hack*ie*⟩ ⟨town*ie*⟩ **3 :** one of (such) a kind or quality ⟨bigg*ie*⟩ ⟨cut*ie*⟩ ⟨smart*ie*⟩ ⟨tough*ie*⟩ ⟨dark*ey*⟩

ie \ˌthad·ˈiz, -aˈtiz; (ˈ)īˈē\ *abbr* [L *id est*] that is

IE *abbr or n* -s **:** industrial engineer

IE *abbr* **1** Indo-European **2** initial equipment **3** inside edge

¹-ier — see ²-ER

²-ier \ˈi(ə)r, ¦iə\ *n suffix* -s [MF — more at -EER] **:** person belonging to, connected with, or engaged in ⟨cash*ier*⟩ ⟨gondol*ier*⟩

ier·oe \ˌēəˈrōi\ *n* -s [ScGael *iarogh*] *Scot* **:** a great-grandchild

¹if \(ˌ)if, əf, f, *chiefly dial* (¦)ef\ *conj* [ME *yif, if*, fr. OE *gif*; akin to OFris *jef, ef* if, OS *ef* if, whether, OHG *ibu, oba* if, whether, Goth *ibai* whether, and perh. to L *is* he, that — more at ITERATE] **1 a :** in the event that **:** in case ⟨~ the train is on time, we'll meet him⟩ ⟨the news ~ false will prove distressing⟩ **b :** allowing, conceding, or granting that ⟨~ he actually did commit the crime⟩ **c :** SUPPOSING ⟨~ the money were right here on the table, you couldn't count it⟩ **d :** so long as **:** on condition that ⟨~ any part of the plan succeeds, you will get the credit⟩ ⟨~ you can keep your head when all about are losing theirs —Rudyard Kipling⟩ **2 :** WHETHER ⟨not knowing ~ the candidate had the necessary qualifications⟩ ⟨asked ~ the mail had come⟩ ⟨doubts ~ two and two make four —Matthew Prior⟩ **3** — used to introduce an exclamation expressing a wish ⟨~ it would only rain⟩ **4 :** even though **:** although perhaps ⟨an interesting ~ untenable argument⟩ ⟨~ we are broke, still we got our money's worth⟩ — **if anything** *adv* **:** on the contrary even **:** perhaps even **:** possibly even ⟨despite reports, conditions had *if anything* worsened⟩ ⟨*if anything* you ought to apologize⟩

²if \ˈif\ *n* -s **1 :** CONDITION ⟨an argument with too many ~*s* in it⟩ **:** STIPULATION ⟨a contract weakened by ~*s*⟩ **2 :** SUPPOSITION ⟨a theory full of ~*s*⟩

IF *abbr* **1** in full **2** *often not cap* intermediate frequency **3** *often not cap* [L *ipse fecit*] he did it himself

ifa·fa lily \ə̇ˈfäfə-\ *n, usu cap I* [*ifafa* fr. native name in southern Africa] **:** a bulbous scapose southern African herb (*Cyrtanthus mackenii*) of the family Amaryllidaceae used as an ornamental and having linear leaves and drooping waxy whitish or yellowish flowers in a terminal umbel

if-bet \ˈ=ˌ=\ *n* **:** a bet placed with a bookmaker whereby a bettor has money on a horse in a subsequent race provided his horse in an earlier race wins

if-clause \ˈ=ˌ=\ *n* **:** a conditional clause — compare THEN-CLAUSE

ife \ˈēfə\ *n* -s [Pg, fr. native name in Angola] **:** a tropical African bowstring hemp (*Sansevieria cylindrica*) the cylindrical leaves of which yield a strong cordage fiber

-if·er·ous \ˈif(ə)rəs\ *adj comb form* [ME, fr. L *-ifer* (fr. *-i-* + *-fer*) & MF *-ifere* (fr. L *-ifer*) + ME *-ous* — more at -FER] **:** -FEROUS

IFF *abbr or n* -s [abbr. of *identification, friend or foe*] **:** the electronic equipment or the system used to identify approaching craft as friendly or hostile ⟨was identified by his *IFF*⟩

if·fen \ˈifən\ *conj* [by alter.] *dial* **:** IF

if·fy \ˈifē, -fi\ *adj, sometimes* -ER/-EST [¹*if* + *-y*] **:** abounding in contingencies or unknown qualities or conditions **:** PROVISORY ⟨an ~ question⟩ ⟨some very ~ political steps —*New Republic*⟩

ifil *var of* IPIL

if money \ˈ=ˌ==\ *n, pl* **if moneys** *or* **if monies :** money from earnings on one race automatically applied to a subsequent race when an if-bet is placed

-i·form \əˌfȯrm, -ō(ə)m\ *adj comb form* [MF & L; MF *-iforme*, fr. L *-iformis*, fr. *-i-* + *-formis* -form] **:** -FORM

i formation *n, cap I* **:** an offensive football formation in which the quarterback, left and right halfbacks, and fullback line up behind the center and perpendicular to the line

-i·for·mes \əˈfȯrˌmēz, -ō(ə)-,\ *n pl comb form* [NL, fr. L, masc. & fem. pl. of *-iformis* -iform] **:** ones having (such a) form — in taxonomic names of animals ⟨Anser*iformes*⟩

IFR *abbr* instrument flight rules

ifrit \ˈiˌfrēt, əˈf-\ *n* -s [Ar *'ifrīt* — more at AFREET] **:** AFREET

ifs *pl of* IF

if-then \ˈ=ˌ=\ *adj* **:** CONDITIONAL, HYPOTHETICAL ⟨an *if-then* proposition⟩

ifu·gao \ˌēfü¦gau̇\ *n, pl* **ifugao** *or* **ifugaos** *usu cap* [Sp, fr. a native name in the Philippines] **1 a :** a people inhabiting northern Luzon, Philippines **b :** a member of such people **2 :** the Austronesian language of the Ifugao people

-i·fy \əˌfī\ *vb suffix* -ED/-ING/-ES [ME *-ifien*, fr. OF *-ifier*, fr. L *-ificare*, fr. *-i-* + *-ficare* -fy] **:** -FY

IG *abbr* **1** inspector general **2** intendant-general

ig·a·la \ēˈgälə\ *also* **iga·ra** \-ärə\ *n, pl* **igala** *or* **igalas** *also* **igara** *or* **igaras** *usu cap* **1 :** a Yoruba-speaking people on the Niger at its confluence with the Benue in Nigeria **2 :** a member of the Igala people

ig·bira *or* **ig·ba·ra** \ˈigbərə\ *n, pl* **igbira** *or* **igbiras** *or* **igbara** *or* **igbaras** *usu cap* **1 :** a Negro people of the Benue river region **2 :** a member of the Igbira people

igbo *usu cap, var of* IBO

ig·dyr \igˈdi(ə)r\ *n, pl* **igdyr** *or* **igdyrs** *usu cap* **1 :** a nomadic Turkoman people in Turkmenistan by the Caspian sea **2 :** a member of the Igdyr people

-ig·er·ous \ˈij(ə)rəs\ *adj comb form* [L *-iger* (fr. *-i-* + *-ger* -gerous) + E *-ous*] **:** -GEROUS

igi·gi \ēˈjējē\ *n pl* [Assyr-Bab, fr. Sumerian] **:** a group of heavenly spirits under the god Anu in Babylonian religion

i girder *n, cap I* **:** I BEAM

ig·loo *also* **ig·lu** \ˈi(ˌ)glü\ *n* -s [Eskimo *iglu, igdlu* house] **1 a :** an Eskimo house usu. made of sod, wood, or stone when permanent or of snow blocks in the shape of a dome when built for temporary purposes **b :** a building shaped like a dome: as (1) **:** a magazine for storing munitions (2) **:** a hut for housing poultry **2 :** a cavity in the snow shaped like a dome and made by a seal over its breathing hole in the ice

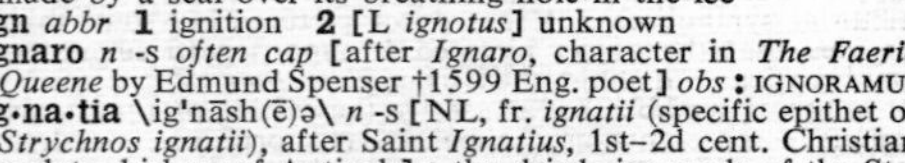

igloo 1a

ign *abbr* **1** ignition **2** [L *ignotus*] unknown

ignaro *n* -s *often cap* [after *Ignaro*, character in *The Faerie Queene* by Edmund Spenser †1599 Eng. poet] *obs* **:** IGNORAMUS

ig·na·tia \igˈnāsh(ē)ə\ *n* -s [NL, fr. *ignatii* (specific epithet of *Strychnos ignatii*), after Saint *Ignatius*, 1st–2d cent. Christian prelate, bishop of Antioch] **:** the dried ripe seeds of the St.-Ignatius's-bean used like nux vomica

¹ig·na·tian \(ˈ)ig¦nāsh(ē)ən\ *adj, usu cap* **1** [St. *Ignatius* of Loyola (Íñigo de Oñez y Loyola) †1556 Span. soldier & ecclesiastic + E *-an*] **a :** of or relating to St. Ignatius of Loyola **b :** of or relating to the Society of Jesus founded by St. Ignatius of Loyola **2** [St. *Ignatius*, bishop of Antioch + E *-an*] **:** of, relating to, or characteristic of St. Ignatius, bishop of Antioch

²ignatian \"\ *n* -s *usu cap* **1 :** a follower of St. Ignatius, bishop of Antioch **2 :** a follower of St. Ignatius of Loyola

ig·na·tius bean \igˈnāsh(ē)əs-\ *n, usu cap I* **:** SAINT-IGNATIUS'S-BEAN

ig·ne·ous \ˈignēəs\ *adj* [L *igneus*, fr. *ignis* fire; akin to Skt *agni* fire, Lith *ugnis*, OSlav *ogni*] **1 :** of, relating to, resembling, or suggestive of fire **:** containing fire **:** FIERY ⟨an ~ desert atmosphere⟩ **2 :** relating to, resulting from, or suggestive of the intrusion or extrusion of magma or the activity of volcanoes

igneous fusion *n* **:** fusion by heat alone unassisted by solution in the water of crystallization

igneous rock *n* **:** rock formed by solidification of a molten magma — compare PLUTONIC ROCK, VOLCANIC ROCK

ig·ne·ri \ig'nerē\ *or* **ine·ri** \ə'-\ *n, pl* **igneri** *or* **igneris** *or* **ineri** *or* **ineris** *usu cap* [F, fr. Carib] **1 a :** an aboriginal Arawakan people of the Lesser Antilles **b :** a member of such people **2 :** the language of the Igneri people

ig·nes·cent \(')ig¦nes³nt\ *adj* [L *ignescent-, ignescens,* pres. part. of *ignescere* to catch fire, fr. *ignis* fire] **1 :** capable of emitting sparks ⟨~ stone⟩ **2 :** INFLAMMATORY, VOLATILE ⟨an ~ personality⟩

igni- *comb form* [L, fr. *ignis* — more at IGNEOUS] **:** fire **:** burning ⟨*igniferous*⟩ ⟨*ignipuncture*⟩

ig·nis fat·u·us \¦ignəs'fachəwəs\ *n, pl* **ig·nes fat·ui** \-,nēz-'fachə,wī\ [ML, lit., foolish fire] **1 :** a light that sometimes appears in the night usu. over marshy ground and that is often attributable to the combustion of marsh gas — called also *jack-o'-lantern, will-o'-the wisp* **2 :** a deceptive or false goal **:** a misleading ideal ⟨the *ignis fatuus* of a world without wars⟩

ig·nit·abil·i·ty *also* **ig·nit·ibil·i·ty** \(,)ig,nīd-ə'bilәd-ē\ *n* -ES **:** the quality or state of being ignitable ⟨the ~ of coal⟩

ig·nit·able *also* **ig·nit·ible** \(')ig¦nīd-əbəl\ *adj* **:** capable of being ignited

¹ignite *adj* [L *ignitus*] *obs* **:** intensely hot **:** FIERY, ARDENT

²ig·nite \ig'nīt, *usu* -īd-+V\ *vb* -ED/-ING/-S [L *ignitus,* past part. of *ignire* to ignite, fr. *ignis* fire] *vt* **1 :** to subject to fire or intense heat; *specif* **:** to render luminous by heat **2 a :** to set aflame ⟨~ paper⟩; *also* **:** KINDLE ⟨~ a fire⟩ **b :** to cause (a fuel mixture) to burn ⟨a rocket . . . ~*ed* by remote control —Milton Bracker⟩ **3 :** to heat up **:** EXCITE, INFLAME ⟨oppression that *ignited* the hatred of the people⟩ ~ *vi* **1 :** to catch fire **:** begin to burn ⟨slowly the fire *ignited*⟩ **2 :** to begin to glow **:** become luminescent

ig·nit·er *or* **ig·ni·tor** \-īd-ə(r)\ *n* -S **:** one that ignites: as **a :** a charge usu. of black gunpowder used to facilitate the ignition of a propelling charge and sometimes of a bursting charge **b :** a device for igniting fuel mixture (as in an internal-combustion engine, a jet engine, or a rocket engine) **c :** a separately energized electrode used for restriking the arc in an ignitron

ig·ni·tion \ig'nishən\ *n* -S **1 :** the act or action of igniting: as **a** (1) **:** subjection to the action of fire or intense heat **:** setting fire **:** KINDLING (2) **:** an analytical procedure of heating an inorganic substance with free access to air — compare INCINERATION **b :** the setting fire to a single point of the charge in the explosion of a charge of powder for ballistic purposes **2 :** the process or means of igniting a fuel mixture (as in an internal-combustion engine, a rocket engine, or an oil-burning furnace)

ignition charge *n* **:** a small charge usu. of black powder used to facilitate the ignition of the main charge

ignition temperature *or* **ignition point** *n* **:** the lowest temperature at which a combustible substance when heated (as in a bath of molten metal) takes fire in air and continues to burn — called also *autogenous ignition temperature;* compare FIRE POINT

ignition tube *n* **:** a heavy-walled test tube of hard glass for examining the behavior of heated substances

ig·ni·tron \ig'nī,trän\ *n* -S [*igni-* + *-tron*] **:** a mercury-containing half-wave-rectifier tube in which the arc is restruck at the beginning of each cycle by a special electrode separately energized by an auxiliary circuit

ig·no·bil·i·ty \,ignō'bilәd-ē\ *n* [L *ignobilitas,* fr. *ignobilis* + *-itas* -ity] **:** the quality or state of being ignoble

ig·no·ble \(')ig¦nōbəl\ *adj* [L *ignobilis,* fr. *i-* (fr. *in-* ¹in-) + *gnobilis, nobilis* noble — more at NOBLE] **1 :** of low birth or common origin **:** PLEBEIAN ⟨an ~ mob⟩ **2 :** displaying, motivated by, or characterized by baseness or meanness **:** DESPICABLE ⟨~ laws⟩ ⟨~ purposes⟩

ignoble hawk *n* **:** a short-winged hawk that rakes for its prey **:** ACCIPITER — used chiefly in the technical language of falconry

ig·no·ble·ness *n* **:** IGNOBILITY

ig·no·bly \-blē,-bli\ *adv* **:** in an ignoble manner

ig·no·min·i·ous \¦ignə¦minēəs\ *adj* [MF or L; MF *ignominieux,* fr. L *ignominiosus,* fr. *ignominia* + *-osus* -ous] **1 :** marked by, full of, or characterized by disgrace or shame **:** DISHONORABLE ⟨an ~ fate⟩ ⟨an ~ peace treaty⟩ **2 :** deserving of shame or infamy **:** DESPICABLE ⟨~ language⟩ **3 :** HUMILIATING, DEGRADING ⟨~ labor⟩

ig·no·min·i·ous·ly *adv* **:** in an ignominious manner

ig·no·min·i·ous·ness *n* -ES **:** the quality or state of being ignominious

ig·nomi·ny \'ignə,minē, -mini *also* -,mən- *or* əg'nämən-\ *n* -ES [MF or L; MF *ignominie,* fr. L *ignominia,* fr. *ig-* (as in *ignorare* to be ignorant of, ignore) + *nomin-, nomen* name + *-ia* -y — more at IGNORE, NAME] **1 :** deep personal disgrace ⟨the ~ of prison⟩ **2 :** disgraceful or dishonorable conduct, quality, or action ⟨~ of abandoning his comrades⟩ **syn** see DISHONOR

ig·no·my \'ignəmē\ *n* -ES [modif. of MF *ignominie* or L *ignominia*] *archaic* **:** IGNOMINY

ig·nor·able \(')ig¦nōrəbəl, -nȯr-\ *adj* **:** capable of being ignored

ig·no·ra·mus \,ignə'rāməs *sometimes* -ram-\ *n* -ES [NL, fr. L, we do not know, 1st pl. pres. indic. of *ignorare* to be ignorant of — more at IGNORE] **1 :** an endorsement formerly written on a bill of indictment by a grand jury when it considered the evidence insufficient to warrant the finding of a true bill; *also* **:** a bill returned with such an endorsement **2** [after *Ignoramus,* an ignorant lawyer in *Ignoramus* (1615), play by George Ruggle †1622, Eng. playwright] **:** an utterly ignorant person **:** DUNCE

ignoramus waltz *n* **:** an easy two-step waltz

ig·no·rance \'ignərən(t)s\ *n* -S [ME *ignoraunce,* fr. OF *ignorance,* fr. L *ignorantia,* fr. *ignorant-, ignorans* + *-ia* -y] **:** the quality or state of being ignorant ⟨~ of facts⟩

ig·no·rant \-nt\ *adj* [ME *ignoraunt,* fr. MF *ignorant,* fr. L *ignorant-, ignorans,* pres. part. of *ignorare* to be ignorant of, ignore — more at IGNORE] **1 a :** destitute of knowledge **:** UNINSTRUCTED, UNLEARNED ⟨an ~ society⟩ **b :** resulting from or exhibiting lack of perception, knowledge, or intelligence ⟨~ errors⟩ ⟨~ public spokesmen⟩ **2 a :** UNAWARE, UNINFORMED ⟨frauds palmed off on an ~ public⟩ — often used with *of* or *in* ⟨~ of the true significance of the news⟩ **b :** INNOCENT, GUILELESS ⟨~ hope⟩ **3 a :** UNCIVILIZED, BACKWARD, UNENLIGHTENED ⟨~ absolutism⟩ **b :** PRIMITIVE, CRUDE ⟨~ devices⟩ **syn** ILLITERATE, UNLETTERED, UNEDUCATED, UNTAUGHT, UNTUTORED, UNLEARNED, NESCIENT: IGNORANT indicates a lack of knowledge, either in general or of a particular point ⟨a population of uncivilized peasants, *ignorant,* illiterate, superstitious, cruel, and land hungry —G.B.Shaw⟩ ⟨the disputants on both sides were *ignorant* of the matter they were disputing about —Havelock Ellis⟩ ILLITERATE is now most commonly used in reference to inability to read and write or to gross unfamiliarity with the written language and the world of learning ⟨*illiterate* in the sense that they could not read or write, or . . . functionally *illiterate* in the sense that they were unable to understand what they read —I.L.Kandel⟩ ⟨as near *illiterate* as one can be who can read and write, her grammar and spelling being equally uncertain —H.S.Canby⟩ UNLETTERED stresses the fact of unfamiliarity with reading and writing or with written learning, often without any implication of condemnation ⟨even written in English, a paper like this would answer every purpose; for the *unlettered* natives, standing in great awe of the document, would not dare to molest us —Herman Melville⟩ ⟨*unlettered* provincials who knew their nets, or trades, or farms, but could hardly be expected to follow the Emperor's physician in his theories of Greek science —J.R. Perkins⟩ UNEDUCATED and UNTAUGHT simply indicate lack of formal schooling; the latter is sometimes used to describe natural spontaneity ⟨*untaught* graces⟩ UNTUTORED is sometimes used to refer to the unschooled condition of primitives ⟨the poor Indian, whose *untutored* mind —Alexander Pope⟩ ⟨taught so many flat lies that their false knowledge is more dangerous than the *untutored* natural wit of savages —G.B. Shaw⟩ UNLEARNED may suggest lack of much learning or ignorance of advanced subjects ⟨such generosity becomes, in effect, a cruel sentimentality, when it crowds the profession with thousands of unwanted persons, most of them relatively unskilled and *unlearned* —Robert Evett⟩ NESCIENT may apply to a deep, determined, or invincible ignorance of what is outside one's immediate ken ⟨most men are not intended to be any wiser than their cocks and bulls — duly scientific of their yard and pasture, peacefully *nescient* of all beyond —John Ruskin⟩

ig·no·rant·ism \-nt-,izəm, -n-,ti-\ *n* -S [F *ignorantisme,* fr. *ignorant* + *-isme* -ism] **:** OBSCURANTISM ⟨fascism . . . founding its educational policy on basic ~ —D.F.Fleming⟩

ig·no·rant·ly *adv* [ME *ignorauntly,* fr. *ignoraunt* + *-ly*] **:** in an ignorant manner

ig·no·rant·ness *n* -ES **:** the quality or state of being ignorant

ig·no·ra·tio elen·chi \,ignə'rād-ē,ōə'leŋ,kē\ *n* [L, lit., ignorance of proof; trans. of Gk *elenchou agnoia*] **:** a fallacy in logic of supposing that the point at issue is proved or disproved by an argument which proves or disproves something not at issue; *also* **:** an argument based on such a fallacy

ig·no·ra·tion \,ignə'rāshən\ *n* -S [L *ignoration-, ignoratio,* fr. *ignoratus* (past part. of *ignorare*) + *-ion-, -io* -ion] **1 :** complete or utter ignorance ⟨the ~ of the true relation of each organism to its environment —A.N.Whitehead⟩ **2** [*ignore* + *-ation*] **:** an act or action of ignoring ⟨changed from complete ~ of my presence to an almost pathetic agreement with every word I said —H.J.Laski⟩

ig·nore \ig'nō(ə)r, -'nȯ(ə)r, -ōə, -ō(ə)\ *vt* -ED/-ING/-S [F *ignorer,* fr. L *ignorare,* fr. *ignarus* ignorant, unknown, fr. *i-* (fr. *in-* ¹in-) + *gnarus* knowing, known; akin to L *gnoscere, noscere* to know — more at KNOW] **1** *archaic* **:** to be ignorant of **2 :** to refuse to take notice of ⟨~ a friendly gesture⟩ **:** shut the eyes to ⟨~ public abuses⟩ **:** disregard willfully ⟨~ evidence⟩ **3 :** to reject or throw out (a bill of indictment) as false or ungrounded — compare IGNORAMUS 1 **syn** see NEGLECT

ig·nor·er \ig'nōrə(r), -nȯr-\ *n* -S **:** one that ignores

ignote *adj* [L *ignotus,* fr. *i-* (fr. *in-* ¹in-) + *gnotus, notus* known, past part. of *gnoscere, noscere* to know] *obs* **:** UNKNOWN

ig·o·rot \,ēgə'rōt, ¦==,=\ *n, pl* **igorot** *or* **igorots** *usu cap* **1 a :** any of several related peoples inhabiting the mountains of northwestern Luzon, Philippines: (1) **:** a people inhabiting the Mountain Province south of Kalinga (2) **:** KANKANAI (3) **:** NABALOI (4) **:** BONTOK **b :** a member of any of these peoples **2 :** any of the Austronesian languages of the Igorot peoples

IGS *abbr* imperial general staff

igua·na \ə'gwänə, ē'-\ *n* [Sp, fr. Arawak *iwana*] **1 a** *also* **gua·na** \'gwänə\ -S **:** any of a number of large herbivorous tropical American lizards (family Iguanidae) being typically dark-colored with a serrated dorsal crest and a gular pouch, attaining a length of several feet, and serving as an important article of human food in their native habitat **b** *cap* [NL, fr. Sp] **:** the type genus of Iguanidae **2** *also* **gua·na** \'gwänə\ *or* **gua·no** \-ä(,)nō\ -S **:** any of various large lizards: as **a :** LACE LIZARD **b :** TUATARA

¹igua·nid \ə'gwänəd, ē'-\ *adj* [NL *Iguanidae*] **:** of or relating to the Iguanidae

²iguanid \"\ *n* -S **:** a lizard of the family Iguanidae

igua·ni·dae \-nə,dē\ *n pl, cap* [NL, fr. *Iguana,* type genus + *-idae*] **:** a large family of chiefly New World lizards including the iguanas and many of the small inoffensive lizards (as the pine lizard and horned toads) of the U. S. and being distinguished from the related Agamidae by possession of pleurodont dentition

igua·no·don \-,dän\ *n, cap* [NL, fr. Sp *iguana* + NL *-odon*] **:** a genus of large herbivorous ornithischian dinosaurs (type of a family Iguanodontidae) from the early Cretaceous of Belgium and England having the head compressed, the jaws probably provided with a horny covering in front like that of a turtle but with numerous spatulate serrated teeth farther back, and the forelimbs comparatively small and provided with large three-toed hind limbs used chiefly in walking and a large heavy tail which doubtless assisted in standing upright — **igua·no·dont** \-nt\ *adj or n*

igua·no·don·toi·dea \=,==,dän·'tȯidēə\ *or* **igua·no·don·tia** \=,==·'dänch(e)ə\ [NL, fr. *Iguanodont-, Iguanodon* + *-oidea* or *-ia*] *syn of* ORNITHOPODA

¹igua·noid \ə'gwä,nȯid, ē'-\ *adj* [*iguana* + *-oid*] **:** of or relating to the iguanids or the iguanas

²iguanoid \"\ *n* -S **1 :** a lizard like an iguana **2 :** a lizard of the family Iguanidae

igua·pe \ē'gwä(,)pā\ *n* -S [fr. *Iguape,* fishing port and river in Brazil] **:** CANDLENUT 1

IGY *abbr* international geophysical year

IH *abbr, often not cap* inside height

i–head \'=¦=\ *adj, cap I* **:** having valves in the cylinder head ⟨an *I-head* gasoline engine⟩

¹ihi \'ē(,)hē\ *n* -S [Maori *hihi*] **:** STITCHBIRD

²ihi \"\ *n* -S [Maori *ihe*] **:** either of two important New Zealand food fishes (order Synentognathi): **a :** a halfbeak (*Hemiramphus intermedius*) **b :** a skipper (*Scombresox forsteri*)

ih·lat \ē'lät\ *n, pl* **ihlat** *or* **ihlats** *usu cap* **1 :** an orig. nomadic Sunnite people of Persia **2 :** a member of the Ihlat people

ih·le·ite \'ēlə,īt, -lē,-\ *n* -S [G *ihleit,* fr. M. *Ihle,* 19th cent. Bohemian superintendent of mines + G *-it* -ite] **:** COPIAPITE

IHP *abbr, often not cap* indicated horsepower

ih·ram \ē'räm\ *n* -S [Ar *iḥrām*] **1 :** a state of consecration assumed by Muslims on pilgrimage to Mecca **2 :** the ceremonially plain clothing worn by Muslims on pilgrimage

IHS *or* **IHC** *or* **JHS** *or* **YHS** *symbol* [LL IHS, IHC, fr. Gk IHC, ΙΗΣ (the capitalized forms of the Greek letters iota, eta, and sigma), short for *Iēsous* Jesus] — used as a Christian symbol and monogram for *Jesus*

IHVH *var of* YHWH

II *abbr* **1** indorsement irregular **2** inventory and inspection

i iron *n, cap 1st I* **:** I BAR

ii·wi \ē'ēwē\ *n* -S [Hawaiian *'i'iwi*] **:** an Hawaiian honeycreeper (*Vestiaria coccinea*) with chiefly bright vermilion plumage formerly used in making feather cloaks

ijo \'ē(,)jō\ *also* **ijaw** \-jȯ\ *n, pl* **ijo** *or* **ijos** *also* **ijaw** *or* **ijaws** *usu cap* **1 a :** a Negro people of the Niger delta **b :** a member of such people **2 :** the language of the Ijo people **3 :** a branch of the Niger-Congo language family containing only the Ijo language

ijo·lite \'ē(y)ə,līt, 'iyə,-\ *n* -S [*Ijo,* river and village in Finland + E *-lite*] **:** a granular igneous rock consisting chiefly of nephelite and augite typically with calcite, apatite, and titanite accessories

ik·a·ry \'ikərē\ *n* -ES [Russ *ikra*] *archaic* **:** CAVIAR

ikat \'ē,kät\ *n* -S [Malay, tying-up, fastening, binding (as yarns prior to dyeing)] **1 :** a technique of fabric decoration common in Malaya, Indonesia, and Latin America in which warp and sometimes also weft yarns are tied-and-dyed before weaving **2 :** a fabric of tied-and-dyed design **:** CHINÉ

ike \'īk\ *n* -S [by alter. and shortening] **:** ICONOSCOPE

ikh·wan \ik'wän\ *n pl, usu cap* [Ar *ikhwān,* lit. brethren] **:** Muslim brethren united by the ties of common membership in the Wahhabi sect of central Arabia

ikmo *var of* ITMO

ikon *var of* ICON

ikon- *or* **ikono-** — see ICON-

il *abbr* illustrated; illustration; illustrator

IL *abbr* **1** including loading **2** inside left **3** *often not cap* inside length **4** interline

il- — see IN-

-il \əl, ᵊl, (,)il\ *also* **-ile** \", ¦ēl, ¦īl\ *n suffix* -S [G *-il* & F *-ile,* prob. fr. F *-ile* & L *-ilis* -ile, adj. suffix] **:** substance related to (something specified) ⟨benzil⟩

ila \'ēlə\ *n, pl* **ila** *or* **ilas** *usu cap* **1 a :** a Bantu-speaking people of northern Rhodesia **b :** a member of such people **2 :** a Bantu language of the Ila people

ila·ma \ə'lämə\ *n* -S [MexSp, fr. Nahuatl *ilamatzapotl,* fr. *ilamatl* old woman + *tzapotl* sapodilla; fr. the fancied resemblance of the fruit to an old woman's head] **1 :** a tropical American tree (*Annona diversifolia*) grown in the southern U.S. that has a whitish fruit with pinkish tinge **2 :** the fruit of the ilama

ilang–ilang *or* **ylang–ylang** \'ē,läŋ'ē,läŋ\ *n* -S [Tag] **1 :** a tree (*Canangium odoratum*) of the Malay archipelago, the Philippines, and adjacent areas that has very fragrant greenish yellow flowers **2 :** a perfume distilled from the flowers of the ilang-ilang tree

ilang–ilang oil *n* **:** a yellowish essential oil that has a fine floral odor, is obtained chiefly in the Philippines and on Réunion Island from the flowers of the ilang-ilang tree, and is used in perfumes, cosmetics, and soaps — compare CANANGA OIL

ila·va \ə'lävə\ *or* **ila·van** \-vən\ *n* -S *usu cap* [Tamil & Malayalam *iravan*] **1 :** a large caste of cultivators in southern India **2 :** a member of the Ilava caste

ile- *also* **ileo-** *comb form* [NL *ileum*] **1 :** ileum ⟨*ileostomy*⟩ **2 :** ileal and ⟨*ileocecal*⟩

¹-ile \əl, ᵊl, ,īl, (,)il\ *adj suffix* [ME, fr. MF, fr. L *-ilis*] **:** of, relating to, suited for, or capable of ⟨contract*ile*⟩ ⟨expans*ile*⟩

²-ile \"\ *n suffix* -S [prob. fr. *-ile* (as in *quartile,* n. — quartile aspect — and *sextile,* n.)] **:** segment of a (specified) size in a frequency distribution ⟨cent*ile*⟩ ⟨dec*ile*⟩

³-ile — see -IL

il·e·al \'ilēəl\ *also* **il·e·ac** \-ē,ak\ *adj* [*ile-* + *-al* or *-ac*] **:** of, relating to, or involving the ileum

il·e·i·tis \,ilē'īd-əs\ *n, pl* **il·e·it·i·des** \-'id-ə,dēz\ [NL, fr. *ile-* + *-itis*] **:** inflammation of the ileum — see REGIONAL ILEITIS

il·eo·cecal \¦ilē(,)ō+\ *adj* [*ile-* + *cecal*] **:** of, related to, or involving both ileum and cecum ⟨the ~ region⟩

ileocecal valve *n* **:** the valve formed by two folds of mucous membrane at the opening of the ileum into the large intestine

il·eo·colic artery \"+. . .-\ *n* [*ile-* + *colic*] **:** a branch of the superior mesenteric supplying the terminal part of the ileum and the beginning of the colon

ileocolic valve *n* **1 :** ILEOCECAL VALVE **2 :** a circular valvular ridge between small intestine and colon in animals (as amphibians) that lack a cecum

ileon *n* -S [ME, modif. of L *ile, ilium, ileum* groin] *obs* **:** ILEUM

il·e·os·to·my \,ilē'ästəmē\ *n* -ES [ISV *ile-* + *-stomy*] **1 :** an operation to create an artificial anus by making an opening from the ileum through the abdominal wall **2 :** the orifice made by ileostomy

ileostomy bag *n* **:** a container designed to receive feces discharged through an ileostomy

iles·ite \'īl,zīt\ *n* -S [M.W.*Iles* †1890 Am. mineralogist + E *-ite*] **:** a mineral $(Mn,Zn,Fe)SO_4.4H_2O$ consisting of a green hydrous manganese zinc iron sulfate

il·e·um \'ilēəm\ *n, pl* **il·ea** \-ēə\ [NL, fr. L *ile, ilium, ileum* groin, viscera; prob. akin to Gk *ilia* female genitals, *ilion* female pubes, and perh. to Pol *jelito* intestine, sausage, Russ *liton'ya* third stomach of ruminants] **:** the last division of the small intestine constituting the part between the jejunum and large intestine, in man forming the last three fifths of the part of the small intestine beyond the end of the duodenum, and being smaller and thinner-walled than the jejunum with fewer circular folds but more numerous Peyer's patches

il·e·us \'ilēəs\ *n* -ES [L, fr. Gk *eileos, ileos,* from *eilein, illein* to roll] **:** obstruction of the bowel; *specif* **:** a condition that is commonly marked by painful distended abdomen, vomiting of dark or fecal matter, toxemia, and dehydration and that results when the intestinal contents back up because peristalsis fails although the lumen is not occluded — called also *paralytic ileus*

ilex \'ī,leks\ *n* [ME, fr. L, prob. of non-IE origin like Gk (Macedonian dial.) *ilax* holm oak] **1** -ES **:** HOLM OAK **2** [NL, fr. L] **a** *cap* **:** a large genus of widely distributed trees and shrubs (family Aquifoliaceae) having small flowers and berries — see HOLLY **b** -ES **:** any plant of this genus

il·ford \'ilfə(r)d\ *adj, usu cap* [fr. *Ilford,* Eng.] **:** of or from the municipal borough of Ilford, England **:** of the kind or style prevalent in Ilford

ilia *pl of* ILIUM

il·i·ac \'ilē,ak\ *adj* [NL *ilium* + E *-ac* (fr. L *-acus,* adj. suffix, fr. Gk *-akos*)] **1** *archaic* **:** ILEAL **2 :** of or relating to the ilium **:** located in the region of the ilium ⟨~ bone⟩ ⟨~ graft⟩ — see ABDOMINAL REGION illustration

iliac artery *n* **1 :** either of the large arteries supplying blood to the lower trunk and hind limbs and arising by bifurcation of the aorta which in man occurs at the level of the fourth lumbar vertebra to form one vessel for each side of the body — called also *common iliac artery* **2 :** the outer branch of either iliac artery that passes beneath Poupart's ligament to become the femoral artery — called also *external iliac artery* **3 :** the inner branch of either common iliac artery that soon breaks into several branches and supplies blood chiefly to the pelvic and gluteal areas — called also *hypogastric artery, internal iliac artery*

iliac crest *n* **:** the thick curved upper border of the ilium

iliac fascia *n* **:** an aponeurotic layer lining the back part of the abdominal cavity and covering the psoas and iliacus muscles

iliac fossa *n* **:** the inner concavity of the ilium

iliac index *n* **:** the anthropometric ratio of the distance between the iliac spines and that between the topmost margin of the crest of the ilium and the lower margin of the acetabulum multiplied by 100

ili·a·cus \ə'līəkəs\ *n, pl* **ilia·ci** \-īə,sī\ [NL, fr. *ilium*] **:** a muscle that flexes the thigh or bends the pelvis and lumbar region forward, has its origin from the iliac fossa, iliac crest, the base of the sacrum, and adjoining parts, and is inserted into the outer side of the tendon of the psoas major, the capsule of the hip joint, and the lesser trochanter of the femur

iliac vein *n* **:** any of three veins on each side of the body corresponding to and accompanying the iliac arteries

il·i·ad \'ilēəd *also* -ē,ad\ *n* -S *often cap* [fr. the *Iliad,* ancient Greek epic poem dealing with the siege of Troy and attributed to Homer, fr. L *Iliad-, Ilias,* fr. Gk *Iliad-, Ilias,* lit., of Ilium, fr. *Ilion* Troy] **1 :** a long narrative; *esp* **:** an epic in the Homeric tradition ⟨the farmer has inspired no ringing saga or ~ —*Scribner's*⟩ **2 a :** a series of martial exploits regarded as suitable for epic commemoration ⟨who leaving his glad school days . . . joined England's bitter *Iliad* —Margaret Wilson⟩ **b :** a series of miseries or disasters ⟨opens another *Iliad* of woes to Europe —Edmund Burke⟩

il·i·ad·ic \¦ilē¦adik\ *adj* **1** *usu cap* **:** of or relating to the *Iliad* of Homer **2** *often cap* **:** of, relating to, or being an iliad ⟨*iliadic* adventures during wartime⟩

ili·a·hi \,ēlē'ähē\ *n* -S [Hawaiian] **:** an Hawaiian sandalwood tree (*Santalum freycinetianum*) yielding an aromatic wood

il·i·al \'ilēəl\ *adj* [NL *ilium* + E *-al*] **:** ILIAC

¹il·i·an \'ilēən\ *adj, usu cap* [*Ilium* (Troy), ancient city in northwestern Asia Minor + E *-an*] **:** of or relating to ancient Troy

²ilian \"\ *n* -S *cap* **:** an inhabitant of ancient Troy

ili·au \,ēlē'aù\ *n* -S [Hawaiian, lit., hidebound] **:** a destructive disease of young sugarcane endemic in Hawaii caused by a fungus (*Gnomonia iliau*) and characterized by binding of the leaf bases tightly about the stem

ili·ca·ce·ae \,īlə'kāsē,ē\ [NL, fr. *Ilic-, Ilex,* type genus + *-aceae*] *syn of* AQUIFOLIACEAE

ili·ma \ə'lēmə\ *n* -S [Hawaiian *'ilima*] **:** a small shrub of the genus *Sida* (esp. *S. fallax*) commonly bearing tiny yellow or orange flowers that are often used in Hawaiian leis

ilio- *comb form* [NL *ilium*] **:** iliac and ⟨*iliocostal*⟩ ⟨*iliopelvic*⟩

il·i·o·cos·ta·lis \,ilēō,kä'stāləs, -tál-, -täl-\ *n* -ES [NL, fr. *ilio-* + LL *costalis* rib, fr. L *costa* rib + *-alis* (fr. *-alis* -al, adj. suffix)] **:** the lateral division of the sacrospinalis muscle that helps to keep the trunk erect and consists of a part from the ilium to the lower ribs which draws the trunk to the same side or depresses the ribs, a part from the lower to the upper ribs which draws the trunk to the same side and approximates the ribs, and a part from the ribs to the cervical transverse processes which draws the neck to the same side and elevates the ribs — called also respectively *iliocostalis lumborum, iliocostalis dorsi, iliocostalis cervicis*

il·io·femoral ligament \¦ilē(,)ō+. . .-\ *n* [ISV *ilio-* + *femoral*] **:** a ligament that extends from the anterior inferior spine of the ilium to the intertrochanteric line of the femur and divides below into two branches

il·io·hypogastric nerve \"+. . .-\ *n* [ISV *ilio-* + *hypogastric*] **:** a branch of the first lumbar nerve distributed to the iliohypogastric regions

ilioinguinal nerve \"+. . .-\ *n* [*ilio-* + *inguinal*] **:** a branch of the first lumbar nerve distributed to the ilioinguinal regions

il·io·lumbar artery \"+...-\ *n* [*ilio-* + *lumbar*] : a branch of the posterior trunk of the iliac artery (sense 3)

iliolumbar ligament *n* : a ligament connecting the transverse process of the last lumbar vertebra with the iliac crest

il·io·pectineal eminence \"+...-\ *n* [*ilio-* + *pectineal*] : an eminence indicating the junction of the ilium and the pubis

iliopectineal line *n* : a line or ridge on the inner surface of the innominate bone marking the border between the true and false pelvis

il·io·psoas \ˌilēō'sōəs, -ē'äpsəwəs\ *n* [NL, fr. *ilio-* + *psoas*] : a muscle consisting of the iliacus and psoas major muscles

il·io·pso·at·ic \¦ilē(ˌ)ōsō¦ad·ik, -ē¦äpsə¦wa-\ *adj* : of or relating to the iliopsoas

il·io·tibial band \¦ilē(ˌ)ō+...-\ *n* [*ilio-* + *tibial*] : a downward continuation of the fascia lata that resembles a tendon and is inserted into the lateral tuberosity of the tibia

il·i·um \'ilēəm\ *n, pl* **il·ia** \-ēə\ [NL, fr. L *ilium, ileum, ile* groin, viscera — more at ILEUM] **1** : the dorsal and upper one of the three bones composing either lateral half of the pelvis being in man broad and expanded above and narrower below where it joins with the ischium and pubis to form part of the acetabulum **2** *archaic* : ILEUM

[1]**ilk** \'ilk, 'iu̇k\ *pron* [ME *ilk, ilke*, fr. OE *ilca* same, fr. a prehistoric compound whose constituents are akin respectively to Goth *is* he and OE *gelīc* like — more at ITERATE, LIKE] *now chiefly Scot* : SAME — used with preceding *that* esp. in the names of landed families ⟨Grant of that ~ means Grant of Grant⟩

[2]**ilk** \"\ *n* -s : FAMILY, SORT, KIND — often used disparagingly ⟨determinists, materialists, agnostics, behaviorists and their ~ —John Dewey⟩ **syn** see TYPE

[3]**ilk** \"\ *adj* [ME, adj. & pron., fr. OE *ylc, ǣlc* — more at EACH] *chiefly Scot* : EACH, EVERY

[4]**ilk** \"\ *pron* [ME] *chiefly Scot* : EACH

il·ka \'ilkə\ *adj* [ME *ilka, ilkan*, fr. *ilk* each + *a, an* (indef. art.)] *chiefly Scot* : EACH, EVERY ⟨and ~ bird sang o' its luve —Robert Burns⟩

ilka day *n, Scot* : WEEKDAY

[1]**ill** \'il\ *adj* **worse** \'wərs, -ə̄s, -əis\ *also sometimes and in sense 2c often* **ill·er** \'ilə(r)\ *or substand* **wors·er** \'wərsə(r), -ə̄s-,-əis-\ **worst** \'wərst, -ə̄st, -əist\ *also sometimes and in sense 2c often* **ill·est** \'iləst\ [ME *ill, ille*, fr. ON *illr*] **1 a** *now chiefly Scot* : immoral or vicious or corrupt or otherwise morally reprehensible **b** : resulting from or accompanied by or evidencing an evil, malicious, or malevolent intention ⟨~ deeds that wrecked their lives⟩ **c** : that imputes evil to or implies evil in something referred to : that ascribes evil to or assumes evil in something referred to ⟨an ~ opinion of everything they did⟩ ⟨attaching an ~ significance to what was said⟩ ⟨in ~ repute⟩ **2 a** : that causes or is accompanied by pain or discomfort or inconvenience or that is otherwise disagreeable ⟨died an ~ death⟩ ⟨the ~ smells of a fish market⟩ ⟨had an ~ taste⟩ **b** : that causes or tends to result in harm : HURTFUL, INJURIOUS, PERNICIOUS ⟨its ~ effects were felt for many generations —Gilbert Highet⟩ ⟨a decision that can have only ~ results⟩ ⟨did them an ~ service⟩ **c** (1) : affected with some ailment : INDISPOSED : not being in good health : AILING, UNWELL, SICK ⟨is ~ with a fever⟩ ⟨incurably ~ with cancer —*Time*⟩ : UNSOUND, FAILING ⟨suffers from chronically ~ health⟩ : UPSET, DISORDERED ⟨emotionally ~⟩ ⟨mentally ~⟩ (2) : affected by nausea often to the point of vomiting : NAUSEATED, SICK ⟨thought she would be ~ after the ride on the roller coaster⟩ **3 a** : that is not suited to circumstances or that is not to one's advantage : UNPROPITIOUS, UNTOWARD, UNLUCKY ⟨its leaders were choosing an ~ moment for a revolution —J.A.Froude⟩ : not promising well : INAUSPICIOUS ⟨an ~ omen⟩ : marked by unfavorable events : contrary to one's hopes and expectations ⟨had a discouraging run of ~ luck⟩ **b** : that involves difficulties with regard to the accomplishment of an objective : HARD, TROUBLESOME ⟨beauty is intangible, vague, ~ to be defined —M.F.Tupper⟩ : so difficult as to make effort useless : POINTLESS ⟨it is ~ prophesying; but one has hope of a regeneration of our literature —*Yale Rev.*⟩ **4 a** : that is not up to an accepted standard of worth or ability : notably imperfect or unsatisfactory : quite faulty : INFERIOR, DEFECTIVE ⟨a period of ~ management⟩ ⟨an ~ specimen of humanity⟩ **b** : that is not up to an accepted standard of propriety : UNPOLISHED, CRUDE, BOORISH ⟨~ manners⟩ ⟨~ behavior⟩ **c** *archaic* : notably unskillful or inexpert or inefficient : MALADROIT ⟨I am ~ at describing female apparel —Charles Lamb⟩ **5 a** : UNFRIENDLY, HOSTILE ⟨~ feeling that culminated in bloody feuds⟩ **b** : HARSH, CRUEL ⟨~ treatment of minorities⟩ **c** *now chiefly dial* (1) *of an animal* : dangerously fierce : FEROCIOUS, SAVAGE (2) *of a person* : cantankerous and irritable : CROSS, SURLY, GRUMPY **syn** see BAD

[2]**ill** \"\ *adv* **worse** \"\ **worst** \"\ [ME *ille*, fr. ON *illa*, fr. *illr*, adj.] **1 a** : with displeasure or offense ⟨the remark was ~ received⟩ **b** : in an unfriendly or harsh or malevolent manner ⟨were ~ treated during their stay⟩ **c** : in such a way as to reflect unfavorable estimation of something referred to or to cast aspersion or blame on something referred to ⟨spoke very ~ of them⟩ ⟨however ~ he might think of that general —John Buchan⟩ **2** : in a reprehensible manner ⟨an *ill*-spent youth⟩ **3** *now dial Eng* : to a grave extent : SERIOUSLY ⟨was ~ hurt⟩ **4 a** : not to any real extent : not really : HARDLY, SCARCELY : by the narrowest margin or none at all ⟨can ~ afford further expense⟩ ⟨they were soon ~ content —A.M. Young⟩ **b** : only with great trouble or difficulty ⟨except in matters of doctrine Pilgrim and Puritan consorted ~ together —V.L.Parrington⟩ **5 a** : UNADVANTAGEOUSLY, UNPROPITIOUSLY, UNLUCKILY ⟨warned them that it would go ~ with them if they insisted⟩ ⟨the whole affair turned out ~⟩ **b** : in a faulty or inefficient or otherwise defective manner : IMPERFECTLY, INEFFECTIVELY ⟨the economic irresponsibility of prison life left me ~ equipped to live up to my good intentions —Frank O'Leary⟩ ⟨has been bad propaganda, ~ calculated to achieve its objects —G.E.G.Catlin⟩ — often used in combination ⟨*ill*-smelling⟩ esp. with adjectives in *-ed* ⟨*ill*-prepared⟩

[3]**ill** \"\ *n* -s [ME, fr. *ill, ille* (adj.)] **1 a** (1) : the reverse of good : EVIL ⟨not knowing whether the outcome would be for good or for ~⟩ ⟨if ~ should befall her —E.T.Thurston⟩ (2) *archaic* : the reverse of virtue : WICKEDNESS **b** *archaic* : the reverse of a good act : a wicked deed **2 a** *archaic* : CALAMITY, DISASTER **b** : MISFORTUNE, DISTRESS ⟨a morbid fear of some future ~⟩ **c** (1) : AILMENT, SICKNESS ⟨measles and other *~s* of childhood⟩ (2) : something that bothers or disturbs or afflicts ⟨once again society is asking the papers to remedy a social ~ by suppressing the facts —Herbert Brucker⟩ : DIFFICULTY, TROUBLE, DISORDER ⟨political and economic *~s*⟩ **3** : something (as an opinion, a remark) that reflects unfavorable estimation or casts aspersion or blame ⟨spoke no ~ of them⟩ **syn** see EVIL

ill *abbr* **1** illuminated; illumination **2** illustrated; illustration; illustrator **3** [L *illustrissimus*] most illustrious

-il·la \'ilə\ *n suffix, pl* **-illae** *or* **-illas** [NL, alter. of L *-ella*] : -ELLA ⟨Spong*illa*⟩

illaborate *adj* [L *illaboratus*, fr. *in-* [1]in- + *laboratus*, past part. of *laborare* to labor — more at LABOR] *obs* : carelessly done : ROUGH

ill-advised \¦==¦=\ *adj* : not well counseled : IMPRUDENT, RASH: **a** : acting without wise and sufficient counsel or deliberation ⟨would be *ill-advised* to accept the offer⟩ **b** : following upon or resulting from or showing a lack of wise and sufficient counsel or deliberation ⟨*ill-advised* efforts⟩ ⟨tactics that were *ill-advised*⟩ ⟨*ill-advised* laws⟩ — **ill-advisedly** \¦==¦===\ *adv*

il·lae·nus \ə'lēnəs\ *n, cap* [NL, fr. Gk *illaenein* to squint] : a genus of Ordovician and Silurian trilobites

ill-affected \¦==¦==\ *adj* **1** *archaic* : not well disposed : alienated in disposition **2** *obs* : not healthy : AILING, DISEASED

il·la·nun \ēl'yä(ˌ)nün\ *n, pl* **illanun** *or* **illanuns** *usu cap* [Maranao *Ilanun*, fr. *i-* from + *lanaw* lake + *-n* suffix denoting a people or language] **1** : the Maranao people of northern Borneo and of the southwest coastal area of the island of Mindanao in the Philippines **2** : a member of the Illanun people

[1]**il·lapse** \ə'laps\ *n* -s [L *illapsus* infusion, influx, fr. *illapsus*, past part. of *illabi* to fall into, flow into, fr. *in-* [2]in- + *labi* to fall, slide — more at SLEEP] : INFLUX, ACCESSION ⟨the ~ of the Spirit at Pentecost —B.J.Kidd⟩

[2]**illapse** \"\ *vi* -ED/-ING/-S [L *illapsus*, past part.] *archaic* : FLOW, GLIDE, SLIP

il·laq·ue·ate \ə'lakwēˌāt\ *vt* -ED/-ING/-S [L *illaqueatus*, past part. of *illaqueare* to trick, enmesh, ensnare, fr. *in-* [2]in- + *laqueare* to ensnare, fr. *laqueus* noose, snare — more at DELIGHT] *archaic* : SNARE

ill at ease *adj* : not feeling easy : UNCOMFORTABLE, ANXIOUS ⟨back of all our lives is the somber setting of a world *ill at ease* and beset by perils —Agnes Repplier⟩ ⟨and wandered around rather *ill at ease* among swirls and eddies of people I didn't know —Scott Fitzgerald⟩

il·la·tion \ə'lāshən\ *n* -s [LL *illation-, illatio*, fr. L, action of bringing in, fr. *illatus* (suppletive past part. of *inferre* to bring in, infer, fr. *in-* [2]in- + *latus*, suppletive past part. of *ferre* to carry) + *-ion-, -io* -ion — more at TOLERATE, BEAR] **1** : the action of inferring : INFERENCE **2** : something inferred

[1]**il·la·tive** \'iləd·iv, ə'lād·iv\ *n* -s [L *illativum* conclusion, fr. neut. of *illativus*] **1 a** : a word (as *therefore*) or phrase (as *as a consequence*) expressing the formation of or introducing an inference **b** : ILLATION 2 **2** [L *illatus* + E *-ive*] **a** : a grammatical case used in some languages (as Hungarian) that expresses a relationship of motion into or direction toward **b** : a word having the inflection of this case

[2]**illative** \"\ *adj* [LL *illativus*, fr. L *illatus* + *-ivus* -ive] **1 a** : expressing the formation of or introducing an inference ⟨an ~ conjunction⟩ **b** : having the nature of, dependent on the use of, or arrived at by inference ⟨an ~ conclusion⟩ ⟨~ reasoning⟩ ⟨the ~ relation between what is asserted in two or more propositions —M.R.Cohen⟩ **c** : of or relating to inference : marked by the use of or by ability in drawing an inference ⟨the ~ faculty of the human mind⟩ **2** [L *illatus* + E *-ive*] : of, relating to, or having the nature of an illative ⟨an ~ case ending⟩ — **il·la·tive·ly** \-d·əvlē\ *adv*

il·laudable \(')i(l), ə +\ *adj* [L *illaudabilis*, fr. *in-* [1]in- + *laudabilis* laudable — more at LAUDABLE] : deserving no praise or commendation ⟨an ~ way of acting⟩ — **il·laudably** \"+\ *adv*

il·la·war·ra ash \¦ilə¦wärə-\ *n, usu cap I* [fr. *Illawarra* district, New South Wales, Australia] : an Australian timber tree (*Elaeocarpus cyaneus*) with racemose flowers and blue globular fruit

illawarra mountain pine *n, usu cap I* : an Australian cypress pine (*Callitris cupressiformis*)

ill-being \'=¦==\ *n* : the condition of being unprosperous or otherwise below a desirable standard of living — opposed to *well-being*

ill blood *n* : BAD BLOOD

ill-boding \'=¦==\ *adj* : boding evil : INAUSPICIOUS

ill-bred \'=¦=\ *adj* **1** : showing (as by rudeness, boorishness) the results of poor upbringing : lacking good manners : IMPOLITE, UNCIVIL, RUDE, LOUTISH ⟨*ill-bred* remarks⟩ ⟨*ill-bred* behavior⟩ **2** : inferior (as in physical characteristics) by reason of being the offspring of mismatched parents ⟨an *ill-bred* animal⟩

ill-come \'il(ˌ)kəm\ *adj* : UNWELCOME ⟨wondered what this *ill-come* visitor might be seeking —Rafael Sabatini⟩

ill-conditioned \¦==¦==\ *adj* : having a bad temper or mean disposition : SURLY, IRRITABLE ⟨three hours after shaving he developed a dark smear about the lips which made him look . . . treacherous and *ill-conditioned* —John Wain⟩ ⟨some *ill-conditioned*, growling fellow —Charles Dickens⟩

ill-contrived \¦==¦=\ *adj, chiefly Scot* : ILL-CONDITIONED

ill convenience *n, archaic* : INCONVENIENCE

ill convenient *adj, archaic* : INCONVENIENT

ill-deed·ie \'=¦dēdi\ *adj* [ME *ille-dedy*, fr. *ille ded* ill deed + *-y*] *Scot* : given to evil deeds or to making trouble

ill-disposed \¦==¦=\ *adj* : not well disposed : UNSYMPATHETIC : alienated in disposition

ill-doer \'=¦==\ *n* : one that does evil

ill-doing \'=¦==\ *n* : the action of perpetrating evil : the action of doing or furthering wrong

ill ease *n* : UNEASINESS

il·lec·e·bra·ce·ae \əˌlesə'brāsēˌē\ [NL, fr. *Illecebrum*, type genus (fr. L *illecebra* attraction, fr. *illicere* to entice, fr. *in-* [2]in- + *-licere*, fr. *lacere* to entice) + *-aceae* — more at DELIGHT] *syn of* CORRIGIOLACEAE

il·legal \(')i(l), ə+\ *adj* [F or ML; F *illégal*, fr. ML *illegalis*, fr. L *in-* [1]in- + *legalis* legal — more at LEGAL] : contrary to or violating a law or rule or regulation or something else (as an established custom) having the force of law : UNLAWFUL, ILLICIT ⟨the ~ use of taxpayers' money⟩ ⟨~ trade restrictions⟩ ⟨an ~ trial⟩ ⟨an ~ pitching technique in baseball⟩ ⟨an ~ chess move⟩ — compare NONLEGAL — **il·legally** \"+\ *adv*

illegal abortion *n* : abortion artificially induced for reasons other than medical

il·legality \¦i(l)+\ *n* [F or ML; F *illégalité*, fr. ML *illegalitat-, illegalitas*, fr. *illegalis* + L *-itat-, -itas* -ity] **1** : the quality or state of being illegal ⟨the ~ of the contract was evident⟩ **2** : an illegal action or procedure ⟨the right to resist ~⟩

il·legalization \(¦)i(l), ə+\ *n* : the action of illegalizing ⟨~ of gambling, drinking, and prostitution did not destroy the demand —H.D.Lasswell⟩

il·legalize \(')i(l), ə+\ *vt, see -ize in Explan Notes* : to make or declare illegal ⟨*~s* excessive or discriminatory initiation fees —*Newsweek*⟩

il·legibility \(¦)i(l), ə+\ *n* : the quality or state of being illegible

il·legible \(')i(l), ə+\ *adj* [[1]*in-* + *legible*] **1** : incapable of being read or deciphered : not legible ⟨injured his right hand in football, making his handwriting almost ~ —E.S.Bates⟩ ⟨no way of knowing by his ~ face whether he told the truth or not —Jean Stafford⟩ **2** : not readable because of language or content ⟨a mediaeval jargon that is now but little less ~ than Coptic —J.B.Cabell⟩ — **il·legibly** \"+\ *adv*

il·legitimacy \¦i(l)+\ *n* **1** : the quality or state of being illegitimate **2** : BASTARDY 2

[1]**il·legitimate** \"+\ *adj* [[1]*in-* + *legitimate*] **1 a** : not recognized by law as lawful offspring : BASTARD; *usu* : born of parents not married to each other **b** : conceived in fornication or adultery **2** : not rightly deduced or inferred : ILLOGICAL ⟨an ~ inference⟩ ⟨an ~ supposition⟩ **3** : departing in some way from the regular or expected : IRREGULAR, ERRATIC ⟨~ unions between broken chromosomes —*Encyc. Britannica*⟩ ⟨~ pollination⟩ **4 a** : contrary to or violating a law or regulation : ILLEGAL : not sanctioned by law : UNWARRANTED ⟨an ~ seizure of power⟩ ⟨an ~ government⟩ **b** : not authorized by good usage : not widely accepted : not reputable ⟨an ~ phrase⟩ **c** *of a taxon* : published either validly or invalidly but not according with the rules of the relevant international code — **il·legitimately** \"+\ *adv*

[2]**il·legitimate** \"+\ *vt* : to make or declare or prove to be illegitimate : BASTARDIZE ⟨testimony that would certainly ~ her older son⟩

[3]**illegitimate** *like* [1]ILLEGITIMATE\ *n* -s : a person that is in some way illegitimate or that is regarded as illegitimate; *esp* : BASTARD

il·legitimation \¦i(l)+\ *n* **1** : the action of illegitimating **2** *obs* : the state of being illegitimate : ILLEGITIMACY

il·legitimatize \"+\ *vt* : ILLEGITIMATE

il·le·ism \'ilēˌizəm\ *n* -s [L *ille* he, that one, that + E *-ism* — more at LARIAT] : excessive use of the pronoun *he* esp. in reference to oneself

il·le·ist \-ˌəst\ *n* -s [L *ille* + E *-ist*] : one who makes excessive use of the pronoun *he* esp. in reference to himself

iller *comparative of* ILL

illest *superlative of* ILL

ill fame *n* [ME] : bad repute; *esp* : reputation for immorality or vice ⟨a house of *ill fame*⟩ — **ill-famed** \'=¦=\ *adj*

illfare \'=ˌ=\ *n* : the condition of faring badly or of not being well off ⟨no regard for the ~ of the workers —W.J.H.Sprott⟩ — opposed to *welfare*

ill-fared \'=¦=\ *adj* : that has fared badly : UNSUCCESSFUL, INAUSPICIOUS ⟨it is surely going too far to assume that the *ill-fared* arrangement was wholeheartedly supported —G.A. Craig⟩

ill-faring \'=¦==\ *adj* : faring badly

ill-fated \'=¦==\ *adj* **1** : having or destined to an evil fate : UNFORTUNATE, HAPLESS ⟨an *ill-fated* army⟩ ⟨an *ill-fated* ship⟩ ⟨started out on the *ill-fated* expedition⟩ **2** : that causes or marks the beginning of misfortune or bad luck ⟨an *ill-fated* suggestion⟩ ⟨met them in an *ill-fated* hour⟩ **syn** see UNLUCKY

ill-favored \'=¦==\ *adj* **1** : unattractive or disagreeable in physical appearance : unpleasant to look at ⟨an *ill-favored* old man⟩ ⟨her *ill-favored* features⟩; *esp* : having an unattractive or ugly face **2** : that gives offense or arouses resentment : OBJECTIONABLE ⟨an *ill-favored* word that no one likes⟩ ⟨*ill-favored* behavior⟩ **syn** see UGLY

ill-given \'=¦==\ *adj, chiefly Scot* : ILL-DISPOSED

ill-gotten \'=¦==\ *also* **ill-got** \'=¦=\ *adj* : obtained dishonestly or otherwise unlawfully or unjustly ⟨*ill-gotten* wealth⟩ ⟨*ill-gotten* gains⟩

illguide \'=¦=\ *vt, Scot* : to treat or handle badly : MISMANAGE

ill humor *n* : a disagreeable mood marked by surliness and irritability : CROSSNESS ⟨was in an *ill humor* and sulked⟩ — **ill-humored** \'=¦==\ *adj* — **ill-hu·mored·ly** \'=¦===\ *adv*

[1]**il·liberal** \(')i(l), ə+\ *adj* [MF or L; MF, fr. L *illiberalis* unworthy of a freeman, ignoble, stingy, fr. *in-* [1]in- + *liberalis* worthy of a freeman, noble, generous — more at LIBERAL] : not liberal: as **a** *archaic* (1) : lacking a liberal education : UNSCHOOLED (2) : lacking culture and refinement : marked by rude manners or behavior : COARSE, VULGAR **b** : requiring or emphasizing physical dexterity rather than intellectual ability : not belonging to or having the qualities of the liberal arts ⟨trades and other ~ occupations⟩ ⟨an ~ education⟩ **c** *archaic* : not generous : STINGY **d** (1) : not broad-minded : having a constricted narrow viewpoint or outlook so as often to be small-minded or pettily prejudiced or bigoted : INTOLERANT ⟨the ~ or fanatically intolerant spirit which war psychology always engenders —M.R.Cohen⟩ ⟨~ thinking⟩ (2) : opposed to liberalism ⟨~ tendencies⟩ — **il·liberally** \"-+\ *adv*

[2]**illiberal** \"+\ *n* : one that is illiberal; *esp* : one that is opposed to liberalism

il·liberalism \"+\ *n* : opposition to liberalism

il·liberality \(¦)i(l), ə+\ *n* [MF or L; MF *illiberalité*, fr. L *illiberalitat-, illiberalitas* conduct unworthy of a freeman, ignobility, stinginess, fr. *illiberalis* + *-itat-, -itas* -ity] : the quality or state of being illiberal

il·liberalize \(')i(l), ə+\ *vt* : to make illiberal

il·licit \(')i(l), ə+\ *adj* [L *illicitus*, fr. *in-* [1]in- + *licitus* lawful — more at LICIT] : not permitted : not allowed : UNLAWFUL ⟨~ trade⟩ — **il·lic·it·ly** \"+\ *adv*

illicit process *n* : a fallacy of distribution in which a term is distributed in a conclusion that has not been distributed in the premises

il·lici·um \ə'lis(h)ēəm, -likē-\ *n* [NL, fr. L, allurement] **1** *cap* : a small genus of evergreen trees (family Magnoliaceae) with aromatic persistent leaves and nodding yellow or purplish flowers — see CHINESE ANISE, STAR ANISE **2** *pl* **il·licia** \-ēə\ *or* **illiciums** : the first spine of the dorsal fin of a pediculate fish migrated to the upper lip and transformed into a complex tentacle that serves as a lure to attract other fish within range of the capacious jaws

illighten *vt* [by alter. (influence of [2]*in-*)] *obs* : ENLIGHTEN

il·limitability \(¦)i(l), ə+\ *n* : the quality or state of being illimitable

[1]**il·limitable** \(')i(l), ə+\ *adj* [[1]*in-* + *limitable*] : incapable of being limited or bounded : MEASURELESS ⟨the ~ reaches of space and time⟩ — **il·limitableness** \"+\ *n* — **il·limit·ably** \"+\ *adv*

[2]**illimitable** \"\ *n* -s : something illimitable ⟨the *~s* that are the past and the future⟩

illimitate *adj* [LL *illimitatus*, fr. L *in-* [1]in- + *limitatus*, past part. of *limitare* to limit — more at LIMIT] *obs* : UNLIMITED

il·limitation \(¦)i(l), ə+\ *n* [[1]*in-* + *limitation*] : the quality or state of being unlimited : freedom from limitation

il·limited \(')i(l), ə+\ *adj* [[1]*in-* + *limited*] *archaic* : free from limitation or restraint : UNBOUNDED ⟨in a fullhearted evensong of joy ~ —Thomas Hardy⟩ — **il·limitedly** \"+\ *adv, archaic* — **il·limitedness** \"+\ *n, archaic*

il·lin·i·um \ə'linēəm\ *n* -s [NL, fr. *Illinois* + NL *-ium*] : chemical element 61 — a name now superseded by *promethium*

il·li·noi·an \¦ilə¦nȯi(y)ən\ *adj, usu cap* [*Illinois* (state) + E *-an*] : belonging to the third glacial stage during the glacial epoch in No. America

[1]**il·li·nois** \¦ilə¦nȯi *sometimes* ¦el- *or esp in southern Illinois & in the southern US* -ȯiz\ *n, pl* **illinois** \-ȯi(z)\ *usu cap* [F, of Algonquian origin; akin to Miami *alänia* man, Shawnee *hilenawe*] **1 a** : a confederacy of Indian peoples of Illinois and Iowa and Wisconsin **b** : a member of such peoples **2** : an Algonquian language of the Illinois and Miami peoples

[2]**illinois** \"\ *adj, usu cap* [*Illinois*, state in the north central U.S., fr. [1]*illinois*] : of or from the state of Illinois : of the kind or style prevalent in Illinois : ILLINOISAN

[1]**il·li·nois·an** \¦==¦nȯi(y)ən, -ȯizᵊn\ *also* **il·li·nois·ian** \-ȯizhən, -zēən\ *or* **il·li·noi·an** \-ȯi(y)ən\ *adj, usu cap* [*Illinois* + E *-an, -ian*] **1** : of, relating to, or characteristic of the state of Illinois **2** : of, relating to, or characteristic of the people of Illinois

[2]**illinoisan** \"\ *also* **illinoisian** \"\ *or* **illinoian** \"\ *n* -s *cap* : a native or resident of Illinois

illinois gooseberry *n, usu cap I* : MISSOURI GOOSEBERRY

illinois nut *n, usu cap I* : PECAN

[1]**il·li·pe** \'ilə(ˌ)pē\ [NL, fr. Malayalam *ilippa* — more at ILLUPI] *syn of* MADHUCA

[2]**illipe** *or* **illipi** *var of* ILLUPI

illipe butter *n* : any of various vegetable fats: as **a** : MOWRAH BUTTER **b** *or* **illipe tallow** : BORNEO TALLOW — used esp. in the chocolate industry

il·liquid \(')i(l), ə+\ *adj* [[1]*in-* + *liquid*] **1** : not being cash or readily convertible into cash ⟨~ holdings⟩ **2** : deficient in liquid assets ⟨an ~ bank⟩ — **il·liquidity** \¦i(l)+\ *n*

il·lite \'iˌlīt\ *n* -s [*Ill*inois (state) + E *-ite*] **1** : a group of minerals found in clays and having essentially the crystal structure of muscovite **2** : one of the minerals of the illite group; *esp* : the mineral having the composition of muscovite or of a hydrated muscovite but giving a line-poor X-ray powder pattern — **il·lit·ic** \(')i¦lid·ik, -līd·-\ *adj*

il·literacy \(')i(l), ə+\ *n* **1** : the quality or state of being illiterate; *esp* : inability to read or write **2** : a mistake or crudity (as in reading, writing, or speaking) made by or typical of one who is illiterate

[1]**il·literate** \"+\ *adj* [L *illiteratus*, fr. *in-* [1]in- + *litteratus* lettered, learned — more at LITERATE] **1** : having little or no education : UNLETTERED, IGNORANT; *esp* : unable to read or write ⟨a largely ~ population⟩ **2 a** : showing or marked by a lack of familiarity with language and literature : deficient in literary background : UNCULTURED ⟨an ~ speaker⟩ ⟨an ~ magazine⟩ ⟨an ~ style of writing⟩ **b** : violating generally accepted usage patterns of speaking or writing in such a way as to indicate ignorance or lack of culture ⟨~ words and phrases⟩ ⟨~ pronunciations⟩ **3** : showing or marked by a lack of acquaintance with the fundamentals or background of a particular field of knowledge ⟨musically ~⟩ ⟨politically ~⟩ **syn** see IGNORANT

[2]**illiterate** \"+\ *n* : an illiterate person; *esp* : a person unable to read or write

il·literately \"+\ *adv* : in an illiterate manner

il·literateness \"+\ *n* -ES : ILLITERACY

ill-judged \'=¦=\ *adj* : UNWISE, INJUDICIOUS ⟨ponderous and *ill-judged* irony —E.M.Forster⟩

ill-judging \'=¦==\ *adj* **1** *archaic* : judging faultily or uncritically **2** *archaic* : judging hostilely or malevolently

ill-kempt \'=¦kem(p)t\ *adj* [[2]*ill* + *-kempt* (as in *unkempt*)] : UNKEMPT ⟨untidy and *ill-kempt*, he looked perfectly at home —W.S.Maugham⟩

ill-looked \'=¦lu̇kt\ *adj, archaic* : not pleasant in appearance

ill-looking \'=¦==\ *adj* : not pleasant in appearance

ill-mannered \'=¦==\ *adj* : marked by bad manners : UNCIVIL ⟨an *ill-mannered* guest⟩ **syn** see RUDE

illmo *abbr* [It *illustrissimo*] most illustrious

ill-natured \'=¦==\ *adj* **1** : having or showing a malevolent or spiteful disposition ⟨*ill-natured* people say . . . that his hair . . . is a wig —W.M.Thackeray⟩ **2** : having or showing a bad temper or peevish disposition : CROSS, SURLY ⟨is pretty *ill-natured* until he's had his coffee⟩ — **ill-natured·ly** \"lē, -li\ *adv*

ill·ness \'ilnəs\ *n* -ES **1** *obs* **a :** WICKEDNESS, DEPRAVITY **b :** DISAGREEABLENESS, UNPLEASANTNESS **2 :** an unhealthy condition of the body or mind **:** MALADY ⟨a severe ~⟩

il·local \(')i(l), ə+\ *adj* [LL *illocalis*, fr. L *in-* ¹in- + LL *localis* local — more at LOCAL] **:** not confined to a particular place ⟨the doctrine that God is ~⟩ — **il·locality** \ˌi(l)+\ *n*

ill off *adv (or adj)* **:** BADLY OFF ⟨were not so *ill off* by the modest standards of that day —G.M.Trevelyan⟩

il·logic \(')i(l), ə+\ *n* [¹*in-* + *logic*] **:** the quality or state of being illogical **:** lack of logic ⟨an argument that was full of ~⟩

il·logical \"+\ *adj* [¹*in-* + *logical*] **1 :** not observing the principles of logic **:** reasoning unsoundly through ignorance or negligence of logic ⟨the speaker seemed most ~ as he developed his argument⟩ **2 :** contrary to or devoid of logic ⟨this policy was extremely ~ —Aidan Mulloy⟩ ⟨~ resentment against a group of his friends —W. F. de Morgan⟩ — **il·logically** \"+\ *adv* — **il·logicalness** \"+\ *n*

il·logicality \(ˌ)i(l), ə+\ *n* **1 :** ILLOGIC ⟨the scientist rebels against the ~ of such reasoning —J.M.Grant⟩ **2 :** an instance of illogic **:** a piece of illogic ⟨the book is full of *illogicalities*⟩

ill-omened \'=ˈ=\ *adj* **:** having or marked by bad omens **:** INAUSPICIOUS, UNLUCKY ⟨it was to be an *ill-omened* day for them⟩

il·loricate *or* **il·loricated** \(')i(l), ə+\ *adj* [¹*in-* + *loricate, loricated*] **:** having no lorica ⟨~ rotifers⟩

ills *pl of* ILL

ill-seen \'=ˈ=\ *adj, archaic* **:** not well regarded or thought of

ill-set \'=ˈ=\ *adj* **1 :** not well set **:** poorly set or placed **2** *chiefly Scot* **:** SPITEFUL

ill-sorted \'=ˈ==\ *adj* **1 :** not well matched **:** badly suited ⟨an *ill-sorted* couple⟩ **2** *Scot* **:** DISPLEASED

ill-starred \'=ˈ=\ *adj* **:** ILL-FATED ⟨an *ill-starred* romance⟩ ⟨the holiday was *ill-starred* from the outset —Bennett Cerf⟩ **syn** see UNLUCKY

ill-tempered \'=ˈ==\ *adj* **:** having a bad temper **:** SURLY, IRRITABLE ⟨*ill-tempered* and tyrannical to his sister —Catherine M. Brown⟩ — **ill-temperedly** *adv* — **ill-temperedness** *n* -ES

illth \'ilth *also* -ltth\ *n* -S [¹*ill* + *-th* (as in *wealth*)] **1 :** the condition of being economically unprosperous or miserable ⟨the glaring disparity between the state's natural wealth and its human ~ —*Christian Century*⟩ **2 :** something that produces or is symptomatic of illth ⟨much of the goods on our shelves is wealth rather than ~ —*Nation*⟩

ill-treat \'=ˈ=\ *vt* **:** to treat cruelly or improperly **:** MALTREAT ⟨they do not *ill-treat* the butlers —C.G.Harper⟩ — **ill-treatment** \'=ˈ==\ *n*

il·lu·ci·date \ə'lüsə,dāt *also* əl'yü-\ *vt* -ED/-ING/-S [²*in-* + L *lucidus* clear + E *-ate* — more at LUCID] *archaic* **:** ELUCIDATE

il·lude \ə'lüd *also* əl'yüd\ *vt* -ED/-ING/-S [ME *illuden*, fr. MF or ML; MF *illuder*, fr. ML *illudere*, fr. L, to mock or jeer at — more at ILLUSION] **1 a :** DELUDE, DECEIVE ⟨in order to ~ him regarding the paternity of the child —R.F.Hawkins⟩ **b :** to subject to an illusion ⟨at the cinema I am . . . completely *illuded* —J.E.Agate⟩ **2** [L *illudere*] *obs* **:** MOCK, DERIDE **3** *archaic* **:** to escape from **:** ELUDE ⟨glad to ~ the burdens of the day —George Crabbe †1832⟩

il·luk \'iləк, -,lük\ *or* **illuk grass** *n* -S [prob. native name in Malaya] **:** COGON

il·lume \ə'lüm *also* əl'yüm\ *vt* -ED/-ING/-S [short for *illumine*] **1** *archaic* **a :** to make bright with or as if with light **:** light up ⟨the beams yet filter through, *illuming* the wide spaces beneath —W.H.Hudson †1922⟩ **b :** ENLIGHTEN ⟨calculated . . . to ~ the minds of all classes of mankind —George Borrow⟩ **2** *obs* **:** IGNITE, KINDLE

il·lu·mi·na·bil·i·ty \=ˌ===ˈbiləd·ē, -ətē, -i\ *n* **:** the capability of being illuminated

il·lu·mi·na·ble \-mənəbəl\ *adj* [LL *illuminabilis*, fr. L *illuminare* to illuminate + *-abilis* -able — more at ILLUMINATE] **:** capable of being illuminated

il·lu·mi·na·graph·ic \=ˌ===ˈgrafik\ *adj* [*illumination* + *-graphic*] *of a camera* **:** designed for photographing the image formed by a convex mirror for recording the sources and intensities of light affecting a specific area

il·lu·mi·nance \=ˈ==nən(t)s\ *n* -S [*illuminate* + *-ance*] **:** ILLUMINATION 2

¹il·lu·mi·nant \-nənt\ *n* -S [L *illuminant-, illuminans*, pres. part. of *illuminare*] **:** something that illuminates; *esp* **:** something (as gas, petroleum, an electric lamp) that gives physical light

²illuminant \"\ *adj* [L *illuminant-, illuminans*] **:** that illuminates **:** ILLUMINATING, ENLIGHTENING

¹il·lu·mi·nate \-nət, *usu* -nəd·+V\ *adj* [ME, fr. L *illuminatus*, past part.] **1** *archaic* **:** made bright with light ⟨leaves ~ with autumnal hues —H.W.Longfellow⟩ **2** *archaic* **:** being or claiming to be intellectually or culturally or spiritually enlightened to a superior extent

²il·lu·mi·nate \ə'lümə,nāt *also* əl'yü-; *usu* -ād·+V\ *vt* [L *illuminatus*, past part. of *illuminare*, fr. *in-* ²in + *luminare* to light up, fr. L *lumin-*, *lumen* light — more at LUMINARY] **1 a** (1) **:** to give physical light to **:** supply with light **:** light up ⟨*illuminated* a picture that hung on the wall —G.B.Shaw⟩ **:** make bright with light **:** bathe in light ⟨destroyers ~ the little boats with their searchlights —H.W.Baldwin⟩ (2) **:** to light up artificially with usu. brilliant lights or decorative lighting effects ⟨the city was *illuminated* in celebration of the victory⟩ ⟨the fountains are beautifully *illuminated* at night⟩ (3) **:** to make luminous or shining ⟨the beautiful smile that slowly ~*s* her face —Vernon Jarratt⟩ **b :** to give spiritual or intellectual light to **:** enlighten spiritually or intellectually ⟨bought a couple of books for the train to Edinburgh, but I can't say I was greatly *illuminated* —H.J.Laski⟩ **c** *archaic* **:** to set alight **:** KINDLE ⟨the butler . . . *illuminated* the antique Gothic chandelier —W.M.Thackeray⟩ **2 :** to make clear **:** clear up **:** remove obscurity from **:** ELUCIDATE ⟨worked out and *illuminated* broad principles of constitutional interpretation —W.P.M.Kennedy⟩ ⟨historical insight clarifies and *illuminates* the critical activity of a period —C.I.Glicksberg⟩ **3 :** to make illustrious or glorious ⟨brilliant achievements that ~ that era⟩ **:** make resplendent ⟨splendid tapestries and paintings *illuminated* the walls⟩ **4 :** to decorate (as a letter or part of a page) with gold or silver or brilliant colors or with often elaborate designs or miniature pictures ⟨beautiful *illuminated* manuscripts of the middle ages⟩

³il·lu·mi·nate \-,nət, *usu* -nəd·+V\ *n* -S [NL *illuminati*, pl.] *archaic* **:** a person possessing or claiming to possess unusual enlightenment

il·lu·mi·na·ti \=ˌ==ˈnäld·(,)ē, -ˈnä|, |(,)t|, |i *also* -ˈnā,tī\ *n pl* [It & NL; It, fr. NL, fr. L, masc. pl. of *illuminatus*, past part. of *illuminare*] **1** *usu cap* **a :** ALUMBRADOS **b :** members of an 18th century German secret society professing deistic and republican principles **2 :** persons who are or who claim to be unusually enlightened ⟨make the enjoyment of poetry primarily an affair of the ~ —J.L.Lowes⟩

illuminating *adj* **:** that illuminates; *esp* **:** highly informative ⟨an ~ lecture⟩ ⟨an ~ remark⟩ ⟨an ~ illustration⟩ — **il·lu·mi·nat·ing·ly** *adv*

illuminating engineer *n* **:** an engineer specializing in illuminating engineering

illuminating engineering *n* **:** a branch of engineering that deals with planning the lighting systems of new buildings and outdoor areas (as streets, parking lots) and the study and correction of old lighting installations

illuminating gas *n* **:** a gas (as coal gas or carbureted water gas) used for lighting

illuminating projectile *n* **:** a projectile that bursts by the action of a time fuze so as to eject a pyrotechnic element that is usu. held suspended by a parachute after ejection and that lights up terrain — compare STAR SHELL

il·lu·mi·na·tion \ə,lümə'nāshən *also* əl,yü-\ *n* -S [ME *illuminacioun*, fr. MF or LL; MF *illumination*, fr. LL *illumination-, illuminatio*, fr. L *illuminatus* (past part. of *illuminare* to illuminate) + *-ion-*, *-io* -ion — more at ILLUMINATE] **1 :** the action of illuminating or condition of being illuminated: as **a :** spiritual or cultural or intellectual enlightenment ⟨claimed she had received divine ~⟩ ⟨found great ~ in the lecture⟩ **b** (1) **:** a giving of physical light or the state of being lighted up ⟨the brilliant ~ of the room⟩ (2) **:** decorative lighting or lighting effects ⟨~ of the city in celebration of the victory⟩ **c :** decoration (as of an initial letter, a text) by the art of illuminating ⟨was much interested in the ~ of manuscripts⟩ **2 :** the luminous flux per unit area on an intercepting surface at any given point — called also *illuminance* **3 :** one of the decorative features used in the art of illuminating or in decorative lighting ⟨marveled at the intricate designs and other ~*s* of the manuscript⟩ ⟨the city was resplendent in its many ~*s*⟩

il·lu·mi·na·tism \=ˈ==_nə,tizəm\ *n* -S [NL *illuminati* + E *-ism*] **:** ILLUMINISM

il·lu·mi·na·tist \=ˌ==ˈnäld·əst, -ˌnä|, |tə- *also* -ˌnā|· =ˈ== nətə-\ *n* -S [NL *illuminati* + E *-ist*] **:** ILLUMINIST

il·lu·mi·na·tive \=ˈ==,nād·|iv, -_nə|, |t|, |ēv *also* |əv\ *adj* **:** of, relating to, or producing illumination ⟨had arrived at what is called the ~ stage of mysticism⟩ **:** ILLUMINATING ⟨had an ~ talk with the scientist⟩

il·lu·mi·na·to \=ˌ==ˈnäld·(,)ō, -ˈnä|, |(,)tō\ *sing of* ILLUMINATI

il·lu·mi·na·tor \=ˈ==,nād·ə(r), -ātə-\ *also* =ˌ==ˈnā,tō(ə)r *or* -ō(ə)\ *n* -S [LL, fr. L *illuminatus* (past part. of *illuminare* to illuminate) + *-or*] **:** one that illuminates: as **a :** one that enlightens intellectually or culturally or spiritually **b :** a device that gives physical light or that is used to direct light to a specific area or that is used to concentrate or reflect light **c :** one that practices the art of illuminating esp. manuscripts

il·lu·mine \=ˈ=mən\ *vt* -ED/-ING/-S [ME *illuminen*, fr. MF or L; MF *illuminer*, fr. L *illuminare* — more at ILLUMINATE] **:** ILLUMINATE

il·lu·min·er \-mənə(r)\ *n* -S [alter. of ME *illuminour*, fr. *illuminen* + *-our* -or] **:** ILLUMINATOR

il·lu·mi·nism \-mə,nizəm\ *n* -S [NL *illuminati* + E *-ism*] **1 :** belief in or claim to a personal intellectual or cultural or spiritual superiority not accessible to mankind in general **2** *usu cap* **:** beliefs or claims viewed as forming the doctrine or principles of the Illuminati

il·lu·mi·nist \-,nəst\ *n* -S *often attrib* [NL *illuminati* + E *-ist*] **1 :** one that professes illuminism **2** *usu cap* **:** one of the Illuminati

il·lu·mi·nom·e·ter \=ˌ==ˈnäməd·ə(r)\ *n* [*illumination* + *-o-* + *-meter*] **:** a photometer for measuring illumination usu. by the brightness of an illuminated surface

il·lu·pi \'ilə,pī, -(,)pē\ *also* **il·li·pe** \-(,)pē\ *or* **il·li·pi** *or* **il·lu·pie** \-,pī, -(,)pē\ *n* -S [Tamil *iluppai* & Malayalam *ilippa*] **:** an important East Indian tree (*Madhuca malabrorum*) whose leaves and juice and bark are used medicinally and whose nuts yield oil and whose very sweet flowers are eaten dried or cooked with other foods — compare MAHUA

illus *abbr* illustrated; illustration; illustrator

ill-usage \'=ˈ==\ *n* **:** harsh, unkind, or abusive treatment **:** MALTREATMENT ⟨my wits sharpened by hunger and *ill-usage* —W.J.Locke⟩

ill-use \'=ˈ=\ *vt* **:** MALTREAT, ABUSE ⟨those who he thought had stolen his ideas or otherwise *ill-used* him —*William & Mary Quarterly*⟩

il·lu·sion \ə'lüzhən *also* əl'yü-\ *n* -S [ME *illusioun*, fr. MF *illusion*, fr. LL *illusion-, illusio*, fr. L, action of mocking, jeering, fr. *illusus* (past part. of *illudere* to mock or jeer at, fr. *in-* ²in- + *ludere* to play, mock, jeer) + *ion-*, *-io* -ion — more at LUDICROUS] **1 a** *obs* **:** the action of deceiving or attempting to deceive **b** (1) **:** the state or fact of being intellectually deceived or deluded or misled by others or by oneself either intentionally or unintentionally in such a way as to have false impressions or ideas marked by the attribution of more to something or less to something than is actually the case **:** MISAPPREHENSION, MISCONCEPTION, DELUSION, FANCY ⟨the happy ~*s* of youth⟩ (2) **:** an instance of such deception or delusion ⟨a dreamy life that was filled with one ~ after another⟩ **2 a** (1) **:** a misleading image presented to the vision **:** false show; *specif* **:** APPARITION ⟨these were all an ~ and a phantasma, a thing that appeared, but did not really exist —F.W.Robertson⟩ (2) **:** something that deceives or deludes or misleads intellectually in such a way as to produce false impressions or ideas that exaggerate or minimize reality or that attribute existence to what does not exist or nonexistence to what does exist ⟨most modern great men are mere ~*s* sprung out of a national hunger for greatness —Sherwood Anderson⟩ **b** (1) **:** perception of something objectively existing in such a way as to cause or permit misinterpretation of its actual nature either because of the ambiguous qualities of the thing perceived or because of the personal characteristics of the one perceiving or because of both factors ⟨heat rays shimmering on the road produced the ~ of pools of water⟩ ⟨the horizontal lines cause an optical ~, making the object appear in a different position from what it really is in —Richard Jefferies⟩ (2) **:** HALLUCINATION 1a (3) **:** a pattern capable of reversible perspective **3 :** a fine plain transparent bobbinet or tulle usu. of silk and used for veils, trimmings, dresses

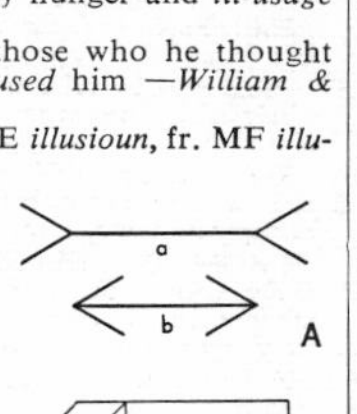

optical illusions: figure *A:* *a* is actually equal to *b;* figure *B:* either side *a* or side *b* may appear nearer the observer; figure *C:* *o* may be regarded as either the near or the far corner of the block

il·lu·sion·al \-zhənᵊl,-zhnəl\ *adj* **:** ILLUSIONARY

il·lu·sion·ary \-zhə,nerē, -ri\ *adj* **:** of, relating to, marked by, or producing illusion ⟨~ stage effects⟩

il·lu·sioned \-zhənd\ *adj* **:** having illusions ⟨~ lovers⟩

il·lu·sion·ism \-zhə,nizəm\ *n* -S **1 :** a theory or doctrine affirming that the phenomenal world is wholly or nearly wholly illusory **2 :** the use of or propensity for the use of often extreme illusionary effects esp. in art and decoration (as in the use of a technique in painting whereby an object represented appears nearer an observer than the surface on which it is painted)

il·lu·sion·ist \-_nəst\ *n* -S *often attrib* **1 :** an adherent of the theory or doctrine of illusionism **2 :** one that produces illusionary effects: as **a :** a painter or sculptor or architect whose work is marked by illusionism **b :** a ventriloquist or sleight-of-hand performer or magician

il·lu·sion·is·tic \=ˌ==ˈnistik\ *adj* **:** of, relating to, or marked by illusionism ⟨~ devices have been abundant in sculpture —P.A.Sorokin⟩

il·lu·sion·less \=ˈ=zhənləs\ *adj* **:** free from illusion ⟨the cold neon light of a modern novelist's ~ imagination —*N.Y. Herald Tribune Bk. Rev.*⟩

il·lu·sive \=ˈ=s|iv, |ēv *also* -z| *or* |əv\ *adj* [*illusion* + *-ive*] **:** ILLUSORY — **il·lu·sive·ly** \|əvlē, -li\ *adv* — **il·lu·sive·ness** \|ivnəs, |ēv- *also* |əv-\ *n* -ES

il·lu·so·ri·ly \ə'lüs(ə)rəlē, -üz(-, -li *also* əl'yü-\ *adv* **:** in an illusory manner

il·lu·so·ri·ness \-rēnəs, -rin-\ *n* -ES **:** the quality or state of being illusory

il·lu·so·ry \-rē,-ri\ *adj* [LL *illusorius* mocking, deceptive, fr. L *illusus* (past part. of *illudere* to mock or jeer at) + *-orius* -ory — more at ILLUSION] **:** of, relating to, or marked by illusion **:** based on or producing illusion **:** DECEPTIVE, UNREAL ⟨a tense period of ~ peace⟩ ⟨filled with ~ hopes⟩ **syn** see APPARENT

illusory appointment *n* **:** an appointment of a nominal or disproportionately small share of property to one of a class (as to one among several brothers) regarded as void in courts of equity because fraudulently defeating the intent of the original donor (as a deceased father) of the power of appointment

il·lus·trat·able \'ilə,strād·əbəl, -ātəb- *also* ə'lə,s-\ *adj* **:** capable of being illustrated

¹il·lus·trate \'ilə,strāt *also* ə'lə,s-; *usu* -ād·+V\ *vb* -ED/-ING/-S [L *illustratus*, past part. of *illustrare*, fr. *in-* ²in + *lustrare* to purify, make bright, fr. *lustrum* — more at LUSTRUM] *vt* **1** *obs* **a :** to enlighten intellectually or culturally or spiritually **b :** to give physical light to **:** light up **2 a** *archaic* **:** to make illustrious **:** confer honor or distinction on **b** *obs* (1) **:** to make luminous or bright (2) **:** ADORN **3 a :** to make clear **:** remove obscurity from **:** make intelligible **:** CLARIFY, ELUCIDATE ⟨*illustrated* the new theory by careful references to what was already known⟩ **b** (1) **:** to make clear by giving examples or instances ⟨used many examples to ~ his lecture on what had been accomplished⟩ (2) **:** to make clear by reason of being an example or instance **:** serve as an example or instance of ⟨a national hero who embodies and ~*s* the nation's passionate love of freedom⟩ **c** (1) **:** to make clear or more helpful or attractive by furnishing or combining with apt visual features (as photographs, charts, slides) or other sensory aids (as recordings of music, speech) ⟨the author has *illustrated* the book with some excellent pictures⟩ ⟨*illustrated* the lecture on the history of art with a couple of short films and some color slides⟩ ⟨discussed some aspects of jazz and *illustrated* the talk with tape recordings⟩ (2) **:** to make clear or more helpful or attractive by reason of being an apt visual feature or other sensory aid ⟨a wealth of photographs ~ the book⟩ **d :** to provide with visual features (as photographs) or other sensory aids (as recordings) ⟨the book is very well *illustrated*⟩ ⟨a beautifully *illustrated* magazine⟩ **4 :** to show to advantage **:** set in a clear light **:** clearly exhibit **:** DEMONSTRATE ⟨the gaiety we too often associate with levity of character is, as the French ~ it, a necessity of mental health —W.C.Brownell⟩ ⟨honoring and *illustrating* the supreme worth of freedom —Agnes Repplier⟩ ⟨a situation that ~*s* the need for tolerance⟩ **~** *vi* **:** to make something clear by furnishing an example or instance ⟨the speaker hesitated and then said he would endeavor to ~⟩

²illustrate *adj* [L *illustratus*] **1** *obs* **:** RESPLENDENT **2** *obs* **:** ILLUSTRIOUS

illustrated *n* -S *chiefly Brit* **:** a newspaper or magazine or other periodical marked by the inclusion of much pictorial material

il·lus·tra·tion \,ilə'strāshən *sometimes* ə,lə's-\ *n* -S [ME *illustracione*, fr. MF *illustration*, fr. L *illustration-, illustratio*, fr. *illustratus* + *-ion-*, *-io* -ion] **1 a :** the action of illustrating or condition of being illustrated **b** *obs* (1) **:** intellectual or cultural or spiritual enlightenment (2) **:** physical illumination **c** *archaic* **:** the action of making or condition of being made illustrious or honored or distinguished ⟨admirably translated by himself in ~ of Shelley —T.L.Peacock⟩ **2 :** something that serves to illustrate: as **a :** an example or instance that helps make something clear ⟨gave an ~ of what he meant⟩ **b :** a picture or drawing or diagram or some other sensory aid that helps make something (as a book, a lecture) clear or more helpful or attractive **syn** see INSTANCE

il·lus·tra·tion·al \ˌ==ˈstrāshənᵊl, -shnəl *sometimes* əˌləˈs-\ *adj* **:** of, relating to, or having the character of illustration **:** serving to illustrate **:** ILLUSTRATIVE ⟨~ technique⟩ ⟨a fine ~ drawing⟩

il·lus·tra·tive \ə'ləstrəld·|iv, |t| *sometimes* ə'lə,strā| *or* 'ilə,strā| *or* |ēv *or* |əv\ *adj* **:** that illustrates **:** serving to illustrate ⟨plenty of ~ material is to be found in the book⟩ ⟨an ~ anecdote⟩ ⟨a remark that was ~ of his attitude toward life⟩ — **il·lus·tra·tive·ly** \|əvlē, |ēv-, -li\ *adv*

il·lus·tra·tor \'ilə,strād·ə(r), -ātə- *also* ə'lə,s-\ *n* -S [LL, fr. *illustratus* (past part. of *illustrare* to illustrate) + *-or* — more at ILLUSTRATE] **:** one that illustrates; *specif* **:** an artist that makes illustrations (as for books, magazines, advertising copy)

il·lus·tra·to·ry \ə'ləstrə,tōrē, -tòr-, -ri\ *n* -ES **:** ILLUSTRATIVE

il·lus·tri·ous \ə'ləstrēəs\ *adj* [L *illustris* (prob. back-formation fr. *illustrare* to illustrate) + E *-ous* — more at ILLUSTRATE] **1 :** notably or brilliantly outstanding because of dignity (as of birth, rank, position) or because of achievements or actions or because of qualities possessed **:** very distinguished **:** greatly respected **:** EMINENT, FAMOUS ⟨a man who comes of an ~ family⟩ ⟨the ~ heroes of antiquity⟩ ⟨~ accomplishments⟩ **2** *obs* **a :** shining brightly with light **b :** clearly evident — **il·lus·tri·ous·ly** *adv* — **il·lus·tri·ous·ness** *n* -ES

il·lu·vi·al \(')i(l)ˈlüvēəl, -vyəl *also* (')iˈlyü-\ *adj* [²*in-* + *-luvial* (as in *alluvial*)] **:** of, relating to, or marked by illuviation or illuviated materials or areas ⟨~ soil⟩

il·lu·vi·ate \iˈlüvē,āt *also* ilˈyü-\ *vi* -ED/-ING/-S [²*in-* + *-luviate* (as in *alluviate*)] **:** to undergo illuviation

il·lu·vi·a·tion \(,)i,=ˈāshən\ *n* -S [²*in-* + *-luviation* (as in *alluviation*)] **:** accumulation of dissolved or suspended soil materials in one area or horizon as a result of eluviation from another

il·lu·vi·um \=ˈ=vēəm\ *n, pl* **illuviums** \-ēəmz\ *or* **illu·via** \-ēə\ [NL, fr. ²*in-* + *-luvium* (as in *alluvium*)] **:** material leached from one soil horizon and deposited in another — compare ALLUVIUM, COLLUVIUM

ill will *n* [ME, part trans. of ON *illvili*, fr. *illr* ill + *vili* will — more at ILL] **:** unfriendly feeling **:** ANIMOSITY, HOSTILITY ⟨a growing *ill will* between the two countries⟩ ⟨bore them no *ill will*⟩ **syn** see MALICE

ill-willer \'=ˈ==\ *n, archaic* **:** one that has an unfriendly disposition toward something specified ⟨an *ill-willer* to the human race —Thomas Hood †1845⟩

ill-will·ie \'=ˈwili\ *adj* [ME (Sc dial.), fr. *ill will* + *-ie*] *chiefly Scot* **:** having an unfriendly disposition

ill-wish \'=ˈ=\ *vt* **1** *dial Eng* **:** to wish evil or ill to **2** *dial Brit* **:** to put an evil spell on **:** BEWITCH, HEX

il·ly \'il(l)ē, -)i\ *adv* [¹*ill* + *-ly*] **:** BADLY, ILL ⟨never were two beings more ~ assorted —Washington Irving⟩ ⟨his ~ concealed pride —Della Lutes⟩

¹il·lyr·i·an \ə'lirēən\ *adj, usu cap* [*Illyria*, ancient country on the eastern shore of the Adriatic sea (fr. L, fr. Gk) + E *-an*] **1 a :** of, relating to, or characteristic of ancient Illyria **b :** of, relating to, or characteristic of the Illyrians **2 :** of, relating to, or characteristic of the Illyrian languages

²illyrian \"\ *n* -S *cap* **1 :** a native or inhabitant of ancient Illyria **2 a :** the Indo-European languages of the Illyrians poorly attested and hence not certainly classified — see INDO-EUROPEAN LANGUAGES table **b** *obs* **:** SERBOCROATIAN

il·lyr·ic \-rik\ *adj, usu cap* [L *illyricus*, fr. Gk *illyrikos*, fr. *Illyria* + Gk *-ikos* -ic] **:** ILLYRIAN

il·men·ite \'ilmə,nīt\ *n* -S [G *ilmenit*, fr. *Ilmen* range, Ural Mts., U.S.S.R. + G *-it* -ite] **:** a usu. massive iron-black mineral $FeTiO_3$ of submetallic luster that is an important ore of titanium and is a compound of iron and titanium and oxygen and may sometimes occur in rhombohedral crystals with very close crystal-structural relations to hematite

il·meno·rutile \ˌilmə(,)nō+\ *n* [G *ilmenorutil*, fr. *Ilmen* range + G *-o-* + *rutil* rutile] **:** black rutile containing niobium

ilmo *abbr* [It *illustrissimo*] most illustrious

ILO *abbr. often not cap* in lieu of

ilo·ca·no *or* **ilo·ka·no** \,ēlō'kä(,)nō\ *n, pl* **ilocano** *or* **ilocanos** *or* **ilokano** *or* **ilokanos** *usu cap* [Sp *ilocano*, fr. *iloko* (native name in the Philippines) + Sp *-ano* -an] **1 a :** a major people inhabiting northern Luzon in the Philippines **b :** a member of such people **2 :** the Austronesian language of the Ilocano people

ilo·ilo \ˌēlōˈē(,)lō\ *adj, usu cap* [fr. *Iloilo*, Philippines] **:** of or from the city of Iloilo in the Philippines **:** of the kind or style prevalent in Iloilo

ilo·ko \ē'lō(,)kō\ *n, pl* **iloko** *or* **ilokos** *usu cap* [native name in the Philippines] **:** ILOCANO

i lon·ga \'ī'lȯngə\ *n* [L, long i] **:** a taller variety of the letter *i* used occas. in writing Latin in classical times to indicate the sound \ē\ as contrasted with \i\

ilon·got \(,)ē,lȯŋ'gōt\ *n, pl* **ilongot** *or* **ilongots** *usu cap* [native name in the Philippines] **1 a :** a people inhabiting northern Luzon in the Philippines **b :** a member of such people **2 :** the Austronesian language of the Ilongot people

ilot \'īlət\ *var of* ISLOT

il più forte \ēl'pyü+\ *adj (or adv)* [It] **:** very loud **:** as loud as possible — used as a direction in music

il più piano \"+\ *adj (or adv)* [It] **:** very soft **:** as soft as possible — used as a direction in music

ILS *abbr* instrument landing system

il·se·mann·ite \'il(t)səmə,nīt, 'ilzə-\ *n* -S [G *ilsemannit*, fr. J. C. *Ilsemann* †1822 Ger. mining commissioner + G *-it* -ite] **:** a mineral $Mo_3O_8.nH_2O$(?) consisting of black, blue-black, or blue earthy massive hydrous oxide or perhaps sulfate of molybdenum

il·va·ite \'ilvə,īt\ *n* -S [G *ilvait*, fr. *Ilva* (Elba), Ital. island in the Mediterranean + G *-it* -ite] **:** a silicate $CaFe_3Si_2O_8(OH)$ of iron and calcium and sometimes manganese related to epidote and occurring in black prismatic crystals and columnar masses (hardness 5.5–6, sp. gr. 4.0)

il·y·san·thes \,ilə'san(t)(,)thēz\ *n, cap* [NL, fr. Gk *ilys* mud + NL *-anthes*] **:** a genus of low herbs (family Scrophulariaceae) with opposite leaves and small solitary usu. purplish flowers — see FALSE HEDGE HYSSOP

il·y·si·idae \ˌilə'sīəˌdē\ [NL, fr. *Ilysia*, genus of burrowing snakes (fr. Gk *ilys* mud + NL *-ia*) + *-idae*; akin to OSlav *ilŭ* mud] + *-idae*] *syn of* ANILIIDAE
im- — see IN
im *abbr* immature
IM *abbr* **1** imperial measure **2** inner marker **3** intramuscular
¹im·age \'imij, -mēj\ *n* -s [ME, fr. OF, short for *imagene*, fr. L *imagin-, imago*; akin to L *imitari* to imitate] **1 :** a reproduction of a person or thing: as **a :** STATUE **b** (1) **:** DEVICE, EMBLEM (2) **:** a figure used as a talisman or amulet esp. in conjurations (as by sorcerers in casting spells) **c** (1) **:** PICTURE, PORTRAIT (2) **:** a sculptured or fabricated object of symbolic value **:** IDOL; *specif* **:** a holy picture (as an ikon) **2 :** a thing actually or seemingly reproducing another: as **a** (1) **:** the optical counterpart of an object produced by a lens, mirror, or other optical system and being the geometric figure made up of the foci corresponding to the points of the object — see REAL IMAGE, VIRTUAL IMAGE (2) **:** an analogous phenomenon in some field other than optics ⟨an acoustic ~⟩ ⟨an electric ~⟩ **b :** any likeness of an object produced on a photographic material **3 :** exact likeness **:** SEMBLANCE **4 a :** a tangible or visible representation **:** INCARNATION ⟨a civil servant who is the ~ of conscientiousness⟩ **b** *archaic* **:** an illusory appearance **:** APPARITION **5 a** (1) **:** a mental picture **:** IMPRESSION ⟨a soldier haunted by ~*s* of battle⟩ ⟨~*s*, as contrasted with sensations, are the responses during a narrative —Bertrand Russell⟩ (2) **:** a mental conception held in common by members of a group and being symbolic of a basic attitude and orientation toward something (as a person, class, racial type, political philosophy, or nationality) ⟨the Frenchman's ~ of America⟩ **b :** the memory of a perception in psychology that is modified by subsequent experience and that contains both intellectual and emotional elements elicited by intrapsychic and extrapsychic stimuli; *also* **:** the representation of a stimulus object on a receptor mechanism **c :** IDEA, CONCEPT ⟨conflicting ~*s* of good and evil⟩ **6 :** a markedly vivid, effective, or graphic representation or description ⟨the set for the play being the ~ of a New England village⟩ **7 a :** something concrete or abstract introduced (as in a poem or speech) to represent something else which it strikingly resembles or suggests (as the use of *sleep* for *death*) — compare EMBLEM, SYMBOL **b :** a figure of speech (as a metaphor or simile) **:** TROPE **8 :** a person who is strikingly like another person in appearance, manner, or thought ⟨a son who is the ~ of his father⟩
²image \"\, *chiefly in pres part* -mәj\ *vt* -ED/-ING/-S **1 :** to describe or portray in language esp. in an effective or vivid manner **2 :** to call up a mental picture of **:** IMAGINE ⟨we no longer ~ the native landscape in the terms beloved of Rossetti and Tennyson —Vincent Buckley⟩ **3 a :** REFLECT, MIRROR ⟨a face *imaged* in a mirror⟩ **b :** to make appear (as in desired form) **:** PROJECT ⟨film *imaged* on a screen⟩ **4 a :** to create a representation of **:** DEPICT, PORTRAY ⟨a national hero *imaged* in bronze on a village green⟩ **b** (1) **:** to create or produce a suggestion of **:** ADUMBRATE ⟨a symphony *imaging* the beauty of nature⟩ (2) **:** to represent symbolically **:** stand as a symbol of ⟨acres of headstones *imaging* the losses of war⟩
image dissector *n* **:** a camera tube resembling the iconoscope and having the electronic image focused electromagnetically through an aperture and voltages that are subsequently amplified and transmitted as television-picture signals being produced by electron multiplication
im·age·less \-lәs\ *adj* **:** characterized by absence of mental images ⟨an ~ thought⟩
image orthicon *n* **:** a camera tube that is similar to the iconoscope or the orthicon and uses secondary emission and electron multiplication to produce the voltages that are subsequently amplified and transmitted as television-picture signals
im·ag·er \'imijә(r), -mēj-\ *n* -s **:** one that images **:** a vivid describer or portrayer
im·ag·ery \-j(ә)rē, -ri\ *n* -ES [ME *imagerie*, fr. MF, fr. *image* + *-erie* -ery] **1 :** the product of image makers (as a statue, emblem, or idol) **:** IMAGES; *also* **:** the art of making images **2** *obs* **:** IMAGE WORSHIP **3 :** ornate or heightened description or figures of speech; *specif* **:** the often peculiarly individual concrete or figurative diction used by a writer in those portions of his texts where he wishes to produce a particular effect (as a special emotional appeal or a train of intellectual associations) ⟨Shakespeare's ~⟩ **4 :** mental images; *esp* **:** the products of imagination ⟨psychotic ~⟩
images *pl of* IMAGE, *pres 3d sing of* IMAGE
image slicer *n* **:** an attachment for a stellar spectrograph comprised of a system of very small mirrors that direct strips of light from various portions of the star-image disk so that they pass through the narrow slit of the spectrograph thereby increasing the intensity of the star's spectrum several times
image space *n* **:** a space in connection with an optical system each of whose points is an image of a corresponding point in the object space
image tube *n* **:** CAMERA TUBE
image worship *n* **:** the worship of images as the special residence of a divine spirit or supernatural power **:** IDOLATRY
imag·in·able \ә'maj(ә)nәbәl\ *adj* [ME, fr. LL *imaginabilis*, fr. L *imaginari* to imagine + *-abilis* -able — more at IMAGINE] **:** capable of being imagined **:** CONCEIVABLE ⟨the biggest lies ~⟩ ⟨any ~ situation⟩ — **imag·in·able·ness** \-nәs\ *n* -ES — **imag·in·ably** \-blē, -bli\ *adv*
imagi·nal \ә'majәnᵊl, *in sense 4* -māgәn- *or* -mägәn- *or* -māgәn- *or* -majәn- *or* -majәn-\ *adj* [*imagine* + *-al*] **1 :** of or relating to imagination ⟨~ objects⟩ **2** [LL *imaginalis*, fr. L *imagin-, imago* image + *-alis* -al — more at IMAGE] **:** of or relating to an image ⟨the idea of weeping can be translated into its ~ equivalent, as rain —K.D.Burke⟩ **3** [NL *imagin-, imago* + E *-al*] **:** relating to mental images **4** [NL *imagin-, imago* + E *-al*] **:** of or relating to the insect imago
imaginal disk *also* **imaginal bud** *n* **:** one of the clusters of undifferentiated cells in the larvae and pupae of some insects from which the wings, legs, and other organs of the adult are formed
imaginal type *n* **:** a tendency of an individual to have images arising predominantly from one or another sense (as from vision, hearing, or taste)
imaginant *n* -s [L *imaginant-, imaginans*, pres. part. of *imaginari* to imagine — more at IMAGINE] *obs* **:** IMAGINER
imag·i·nar·i·ly \ә'majә'nerәlē, -li, ˌiˌ==ˈ===\ *adv* **:** in an imaginary manner
imag·i·nar·i·ness \ә'==ˌnerēnәs, -rin-\ *n* -ES **:** the quality or state of being imaginary
¹imag·i·nary \ә'majәˌnerē, -ri\ *adj* [ME, fr. L *imaginarius*, fr. *imaginari* to imagine + *-arius* -ary] **1 a :** having no real existence **:** existing only in imagination or fancy **:** UNREAL, FANCIED, FICTITIOUS, HYPOTHETICAL ⟨to guard the cattle against their real and their ~ foes, the wolves and the witches —J.G. Frazer⟩ **b :** formed, characterized, or ascribed outside the evidence of reality **:** shaped, endowed, or attributed imaginatively or arbitrarily ⟨the statue of John Harvard . . . is an ~ likeness; no portrait of Harvard is known to exist —*Amer. Guide Series: Mass.*⟩ **2** *obs* **:** of the nature of or suggesting an image **3** *obs* **:** IMAGINATIVE **4 :** containing or related to the imaginary unit
syn FANCIFUL, VISIONARY, FANTASTIC, CHIMERICAL, QUIXOTIC: IMAGINARY stresses lack of reality; it indicates an existence, formation, or ascription by imagination, not fact ⟨those nervous persons who may be terrified by *imaginary* dangers are often courageous in the face of real danger —Havelock Ellis⟩ In relation to things, FANCIFUL indicates formation or conditioning by free, unrestrained fancy or imagination; in relation to people, it indicates a tendency to give free rein to the imagination ⟨*fanciful* tale of his own exploits tells how he was carried, wounded, down the mountainside in a big buckskin bag tied to the back of a wrinkled squaw —*Amer. Guide Series: Calif.*⟩ ⟨one may perhaps without being too *fanciful* see in his art something of the magic of the Celt —Irving Babbitt⟩ VISIONARY applies to a person given to seeing visions or to the ideas and notions from visions rather than real facts and hence impractical, wild, and impossible of fulfillment or fruition ⟨planning, as his *visionary* father might have done, to go to Brazil to pick up a fortune —Carl Van Doren⟩ ⟨unless, therefore, our philosophic vision receives technical development . . . it may rightly be condemned as unsubstantial and *visionary* —M.R.Cohen⟩ FANTASTIC and its variant FANTASTICAL heighten the notion of extravagant fancy far transcending the usual, ordinary, or real ⟨one of those eoan errors to which we are subject before the clear commonplace of daylight orders and moderates our tenebrous and *fantastical* imaginations —Rose Macaulay⟩ ⟨a *fantastic* world inhabited by monsters of iron and steel —Louis Bromfield⟩ ⟨two heroes may mangle each other in every impossible and *fantastic* way, beyond the bounds of the faintest shadow of verisimilitude —H.O.Taylor⟩ CHIMERICAL suggests the wild, utterly unreal, and extravagantly imaginary characteristics of creations of classical mythology ⟨the defeat was more complete, more humiliating . . . the hopes of revival more *chimerical* —*Times Lit. Supp.*⟩ ⟨as *chimerical* as a specter —Bernard Smith⟩ QUIXOTIC describes completely unrealistic and impractical devotion to romantic or chivalric ideals ⟨was *quixotic*, and would not permit a secret service and spies —G.K.Chesterton⟩ ⟨among the last *quixotic* acts of his life was an attempt to set up a Greek academy for aspiring authors —Alfred Kreymborg⟩ ⟨be so *quixotic* as to stand upon principles at the risk of losing the business —R.M.Cunningham⟩
²imaginary \"\ *n* -ES **1** *obs* **:** a figment of imagination **2 :** a complex number (as $2+3i$) whose imaginary part is not zero
imaginary number *n* **:** IMAGINARY 2
imaginary part *n* **:** the part of a complex number (as "3i" in $2+3i$) that has the imaginary unit as a factor
imaginary unit *n* **:** the positive square root of minus 1 **:** $+\sqrt{-1}$ — symbol *i*
imag·i·na·tion \ә,majә'nāshәn\ *n* -s [ME *imaginacioun*, fr. MF *imagination*, fr. L *imagination-, imaginatio*, fr. *imaginatus* (past part. of *imaginari* to imagine) + *-ion-, -io* -ion — more at IMAGINE] **1 :** an act or process of forming a conscious idea or mental image of something never before wholly perceived in reality by the imaginer (as through a synthesis of remembered elements of previous sensory experiences or ideas as modified by unconscious mechanisms of defense); *also* **:** the ability or gift of forming such conscious ideas or mental images esp. for the purposes of artistic or intellectual creation ⟨our simple apprehension of corporeal objects, if present, is sense; if absent, is ~ —Joseph Glanvill⟩ **2 a :** creative ability **:** GENIUS ⟨the great ~*s* of literature⟩ **b :** ability to confront and deal with a problem **:** RESOURCEFULNESS ⟨the attempt shows suggestions of the ~ that the situation demands⟩ **3** *obs* **:** a plotting or scheming esp. of evil **:** PLOT ⟨all their vengeance and all their ~*s* against me —Lam 3:60 (AV)⟩ **4 a :** a mental image, conception, or notion formed by the action of imagination **b :** a creation of the mind; *esp* **:** an idealized or poetic creation ⟨the gory ~*s* of folk poetry⟩ **c :** fanciful or empty assumption ⟨idle ~*s*⟩ **5 :** popular or traditional belief **:** usual or accepted conception ⟨the Magna Charta . . . has operated in the meaning given it in ~ rather than by its literal contents —John Dewey⟩
syn FANCY, FANTASY, PHANTASY: IMAGINATION, freer of derogatory connotations than the other terms, is the most comprehensive, applying to the power of creating, in the mind or in an outward form as in a literary work, images of things once known but absent, of things never seen or never seen in their entirety, of things actually nonexistent, of things created new from diverse old elements, or of things perfected or idealized; it may carry the implication of mere tricky concoction, as of things unreal or odd, but is more frequently nearer the other extreme in suggesting the genuine artist's gift of perceiving more deeply or essentially and creating the interestingly and the significantly new and vital ⟨all youth lives much in reverie; thereby the stronger minds anticipate and rehearse themselves for life in a thousand *imaginations* —H.G.Wells⟩ ⟨*imagination* being little else than another name for illusion —Samuel Butler⟩ ⟨the *imagination* is able to manipulate nature as by creating three legs and five arms but it is not able to create a totally new nature —Wallace Stevens⟩ ⟨the production of vivid images, usually visual images . . . is the commonest and the least interesting thing which is referred to by *imagination* —I.A.Richards⟩ ⟨a product of fancy rather than imagination — if one accepts fancy as decorative and *imagination* as creative —Pamela L. Travers⟩ ⟨*imagination*, in his opinion, gets at relationships that are true at the deepest level of experience —F.A.Pottle⟩ ⟨*imagination* is something akin to what it was in Wordsworth, a means of deepest insight and sympathy —Roy Pascal⟩ ⟨it is only through *imagination* that men become aware of what the world might be —Bertrand Russell⟩ FANCY now usu. suggests the power to conceive and give expression to images of things removed from reality, usu. of things purely, sometimes frivolously though often delightfully, imaginary, often contrasting with IMAGINATION in suggesting a more superficial often factitious power of inventing the novel or unreal by recombining existing elements as opposed to the imagination's gift of grasping a deeper, more organic reality ⟨like all weak men of a vivid *fancy*, he was constantly framing dramas of which he was the towering lord —G.D.Brown⟩ ⟨the associative faculty performs, to a varying extent in individual cases, constantly shifting arrangements and rearrangements of the data of observation, thought, feeling . . . which Coleridge distinguishes from imagination by the word *fancy* —George Whalley⟩ ⟨in a creative artist the imagination functions . . . in three ways. It is partly mere *fancy*, which moves happily into make-believe —K.P.Kempton⟩ FANTASY or PHANTASY suggests the power of unrestrained, often extravagant or delusive, fancy, stressing the unreal more than *fancy*; PHANTASY is used more frequently than FANTASY in the technical sense of image-making power in general ⟨hard to say where the actuality ends and the *fantasy* begins in these sketches of life —B.C.L.Keelan⟩ ⟨fairy stories and *fantasy* are phenomenally popular —Lavinia R. Davis⟩ ⟨an appealing *fantasy*, though its appeal does not lie in what is fantastic about it. It lies in what is realistic and homely —*Time*⟩ ⟨a *fantasy* . . . may be distinguished from the representation of something that actually exists, but it is not opposed to "reality" and not an "escape" from reality. Thus, the idea of a rational society, or the image of a good house to be built, or the story of something that never happened, is a fantasy —Lionel Trilling⟩ ⟨this mechanical man or robot idea has been decidedly overdone in the writings of *fantasy* —C.C. Furnas⟩ ⟨a mixture . . . of comic *phantasy*, improbable adventure and rainbow colors —G.E.Fox⟩ ⟨a novelist is a person who has a highly developed gift of *phantasy* —Bernard De Voto⟩ ⟨its invention is based on the extinction of a wish *phantasy* belonging to the period of puberty —D.F.Tait⟩
imag·i·na·tion·al \-shәnᵊl, -shnәl\ *adj* **:** of, relating to, involving, caused by, or suggestive of the imagination
imag·i·na·tive \ә'maj(ә)nәd·|iv, -jәˌnā|, |t|, |ēv *also* |әv\ *adj* [ME, fr. MF *imaginatif*, fr. *imagination* + *-if* -ive] **1 :** of or relating to the imagination: as **a :** created, inspired, guided, or drawn from the imagination and not from known facts or sources ⟨an ~ biography⟩ **b :** tending to provoke, excite, or enliven the imagination ⟨a few ~ comments⟩ **c** (1) **:** able to handle new or difficult problems **:** RESOURCEFUL ⟨a young and ~ general⟩ (2) **:** imbued with or showing an ability to draw conclusions, suggest hypotheses, make comparisons, or create systems ⟨an ~ interpretation of a poem⟩ ⟨an ~ critic⟩ ⟨~ research⟩ (3) **:** full of freshness, originality, or vividness ⟨~ patterns⟩ **d :** devoid of truth **:** FALSE ⟨the report of his death was wholly ~⟩ **2 :** of or relating to images; *esp* **:** showing a distinctive or fine command of artistic images ⟨~ diction⟩
imag·i·na·tive·ly \|ävlē, -li\ *adv* **:** in an imaginative manner ⟨a play produced ~⟩ ⟨an ~ planned garden⟩
imag·i·na·tive·ness \|ivnәs, |ēv- *also* |әv-\ *n* -ES **:** the quality or state of being imaginative
imag·i·na·tor \ә'majәˌnād·ә(r)\ *n* -s [L *imaginatus* (past part. of *imaginari*) + E *-or*] **:** one that imagines; *esp* **:** a person who creates (as an artistic or intellectual work)
imag·ine \ә'majәn *sometimes* -maaj-; *when "I" precedes or when imperative & sentence-initial often* 'm-\ *vb* **imagined; imagined; imagining** \-j(ә)niŋ\ **imagines** [ME *imaginen*, fr. MF *imaginer*, fr. L *imaginari*, fr. *imagin-, imago* image — more at IMAGE] *vt* **1 :** to form an idea of **:** create a mental image of ⟨~ accidents at every turn⟩ **2 :** to create by or as if by the imagination **:** FABRICATE ⟨*imagining* stories to fool the public⟩ **3 :** THINK, SUPPOSE, GUESS ⟨I ~ it will rain⟩ ~ *vi* **1** *obs* **:** PONDER, MEDITATE **2 :** to use the imagination; *specif* **:** to form images or conceptions **3 :** SUPPOSE, THINK
syn see THINK
imag·in·er \-j(ә)nә(r)\ *n* -s [ME, fr. *imaginen* + *-er*] **:** one that imagines
imaging *pres part of* IMAGE
im·ag·ism \'imiˌjizәm, -mē,-, -mә,-\ *n* -s **:** a movement in poetry (as in America and England before World War I) advocating concrete language and figures of speech, modern subject matter, freedom in the use of meter, and avoidance of romantic or mystic themes — compare SYMBOLISM
¹im·ag·ist \-jәst\ *n* -s [*¹image* + *-ist*] **:** one that follows the precepts of imagism
²im·ag·ist \"\ *or* **im·ag·is·tic** \ˌ==ˈjistik, -tēk\ *adj* **:** of or relating to imagism — **im·ag·is·ti·cal·ly** \-tәk(ә)lē, -tēk-, -li\ *adv*
ima·go \ә'mā(ˌ)gō, -mä-, -mā(-\ *n, pl* **imagoes** *or* **imag·i·nes** \-māgәˌnēz; -mägәˌnēz, -māg-, -ˌnās; -majәˌnēz, -maj-\ [NL, fr. L, image — more at IMAGE] **1 :** an insect in its final adult sexually mature usu. winged state — compare LARVA, NYMPH, PUPA **2 :** a conception of the parent that is retained in the unconscious, elaborated by infantile phantasies, and bound with the affect pertaining to the infantile period; *also* **:** an idealized mental image of any person including the self
imam \ә'mäm, (')ē'-, -mam\ *n* -s [Ar *imām*] **1 :** the prayer leader of a mosque **2 :** the caliph who is the spiritual and secular head of Islam **3 :** one of the twelve divinely inspired leaders of the Shi'a appointed to guide men; *also* **:** one of their earthly representatives descended from Muhammad and appointed head of the Muslim community **4 :** one of the founders of the four orthodox schools of Muslim jurisprudence; *also* **:** any authoritative Muslim scholar who founds a school of interpretation or is followed as an authority in theology and law **5 :** any of various sovereign princes that claim descent from Muhammad and that exercise spiritual and temporal leadership over a Muslim region
imam·ate \-ˌāt\ *n* -s *often cap* **1 :** the office of an imam **2 :** the region or country ruled over by an imam ⟨the ~ of Yemen⟩
imami \-ē\ *n* -s [Ar *imāmī*, fr. *imām*] *usu cap* **:** TWELVER
iman·to·phyl·lum \(ˌ)iˌmantә'filәm\ [NL, irreg. fr. Gk *himanto-* (fr. *himant-, himas* thong) + NL *-phyllum*] *syn of* CLIVIA
ima·ret \ә'märәt\ *n* -s [Turk, fr. Ar *'imārah* building] **:** an inn or hospice in Turkey
ima·ri ware \ә'märē-\ *n, usu cap I* [fr. *Imari*, Japan, where it is made] **:** a Hizen porcelain characteristically decorated in red, green, and blue with a design of bamboo and cherry blossoms or hedges of brushwood growing out of stylized rocks
im·balance \(')im+\ *n* [*¹in-* + *balance*] **:** absence of balance: as **a** (1) **:** loss of parallel relation between the optical axes of the eyes caused by faulty action of the extrinsic muscles and often resulting in diplopia (2) **:** absence of biological equilibrium (as in a gland) **b :** lack of balance between segments of a nation's economy (as between debit and credit in international payments or between costs and prices) **c :** a disproportion between the number of males and females in a population
imbarn *vt* -ED/-ING/-S [*²in-* + *barn* (n.)] *obs* **:** to gather into or store in a barn **:** GARNER
im·base \әm+\ *var of* EMBASE
im·bat \(')im'bät\ *n* -s [Turk] **:** a cooling etesian wind in the Levant (as in Cyprus)
im·ba·uba \ˌimbә'übә\ *also* **im·ba·ubao** \-üˌbaú\ *n* -s [Pg *ambaúba, imbaúba, umbaúba*, fr. Tupi *ambauba, umbauba*] **:** TRUMPETWOOD
im·be \(')im'bā\ *n* -s [Pg *imbé*, fr. Tupi] **1 :** a cordage fiber derived from the stems of an epiphytic Brazilian plant (*Philodendron imbe*) **2 :** the plant that yields imbe fiber
¹im·be·cile \'imbәsәl *also* -(ˌ)sil *or* -ˌsīl, *chiefly Brit* -ˌsēl\ *adj* [MF *imbecille*, fr. L *imbecillus* weak, weak-minded, fr. *in-* ¹in- + *-becillus* (perh. fr. *bacillus, bacillum* small staff) — more at BACILLUS] **1** *archaic* **:** WEAK, FEEBLE **2** [F *imbécile*, fr. L *imbecillus*] **a :** of, relating to, or befitting an imbecile **b :** markedly inane, idiotic, foolish, or stupid — used as a generalized term of contempt
²imbecile \"\ *n* -s [F *imbécile*, fr. *imbécile*, adj] **1 :** one marked by mental deficiency: as **a :** one who has a less-than-normal average intelligence and intellectual capacity that is usu. above that of an idiot but below that of a moron **b :** a feebleminded person who has a mental age of approximately three to seven years and who requires special care and supervision in the performance of routine daily tasks of self-care (as feeding and clothing himself) **2 :** FOOL, IDIOT — used as a generalized term of contempt **syn** see FOOL
im·be·cile·ly \-әl(l)|ē, -il(l)|, -īll|, -ēll|, |i\ *adv* **:** in an imbecile manner
im·be·cil·ic \ˌimbә'silik, -ilēk\ *adj* **:** characteristic or suggestive of an imbecile ⟨an ~ grin⟩ ⟨~ conclusions⟩
im·be·cil·i·ty \ˌimbә'silәd·ē, -lәtē, -i\ *n* -ES [MF *imbecillité*, fr. L *imbecillitat-, imbecillitas* weakness, weak-mindedness, fr. *imbecillus* + *-itat-, -itas* -ity] **1 a :** the quality or state of being weak **b :** INCAPACITY, INABILITY ⟨~ of judgment⟩ **2** [F *imbécillité*, fr. L *imbecillitat-, imbecillitas*] **:** the quality or state of being mentally weak — compare MENTAL DEFICIENCY **3 a :** complete nonsense **:** utter foolishness ⟨the ~ of trying to live without food⟩; *also* **:** FUTILITY **b :** something that is foolish or nonsensical
imbed *var of* EMBED
imbellious *also* **imbellic** *adj* [L *imbellis* (fr. *in-* ¹in- + *-bellis*, fr. *bellum* war) + E *-ous* or *-ic* — more at BELLICOSE] *obs* **:** not warlike
im·bibe \әm'bīb\ *vb* -ED/-ING/-S [in sense 1, fr. ME *enbiben*, fr. MF *embiber*, fr. L *imbibere* to drink in, conceive, fr. *in-* ²in- + *bibere* to drink; in other senses, fr. L *imbibere* — more at POTABLE] *vt* **1** *archaic* **:** to cause to absorb liquid **:** SOAK **2 a :** to receive into the mind and retain **:** ASSIMILATE ⟨~ moral principles⟩ **b :** to assimilate (as gas, light, or heat) or take into solution **3 a :** to consume by drinking ⟨~*s* vast quantities of strong coffee⟩ **b :** to drink in **:** ABSORB ⟨plants can ~ as much nourishment through their leaves as via their roots —F.J.Taylor⟩ ⟨a sponge *imbibing* moisture⟩ ~ *vi* **1 :** DRINK 2 **2 a :** to take in or up liquid **b :** to absorb or assimilate moisture, gas, light, or heat
im·bib·er \-ībә(r)\ *n* -s **:** one that imbibes
im·bi·bi·tion \ˌimbә'bishәn, -mˌbī'bi-\ *n* -s [in sense 1, fr. ME *imbybycyon*, fr. MF *imbibition*, fr. L *imbibitus* (past part. of *imbibere*) + MF *-ion*; in other senses, fr. L *imbibitus* + E *-ion*] **1** *obs* **a :** saturation with or solution in liquid **b :** mixture of solid and liquid by such imbibition **2 :** the act or action of imbibing: as **a :** the taking up and sorption of fluid by a colloidal system resulting in swelling and offering a possible explanation of certain biological phenomena (as the retention of water by desert plants) — compare OSMOSIS 1, SYNERESIS 2 **b :** IMBIBITION PROCESS
im·bi·bi·tion·al \ˌ=(ˌ)=ˈbishәnᵊl, -shnәl\ *adj* **:** of, relating to, or characterized by imbibition
imbibition process *n* **:** a process by which a photographic print is produced by absorption of a water-soluble dye by a relief image or a differentially absorbing image in gelatin or a similar medium or in which a previously formed dye image is transferred by absorption from one layer into another layer
im·bi·rus·sú \ˌimbәrә'sü, -rü'sü\ *n* -s [Pg *embiruçú, embirussú*, fr. Tupi *embirussú, imbirussú*, fr. *embira, imbira* embira + *-ussú* big] **:** a timber tree of So. and Central America that is an undetermined species of the genus *Bombax* and that bears pods yielding a brownish fiber similar to kapok
imbitter *var of* EMBITTER
imbosom *var of* EMBOSOM
imbound *var of* EMBOUND
imbrace *obs var of* EMBRACE
imbreviate *vt* -ED/-ING/-S [ML *imbreviatus*, past part. of *imbreviare*, fr. L *in-* ²in- + ML *brevis, breve* brief — more at BRIEF (n.)] *obs* **:** to write or enter in the form of a brief **:** ENROLL, REGISTER
im·brex \'imˌbreks, -ˌbriks\ *n, pl* **imbri·ces** \-ˌbrәˌsēz, -ә,kās\ [L] **1 :** a curved roof tile used esp. by the ancient Romans **:** PANTILE **2** [NL, fr. L] **:** one of the scales or subdivisions of imbricated ornament
¹im·bri·cate \'imbrәkәt, -rēk-, -rәˌkāt, *usu* |d·+V\ *adj* [LL *imbricatus*, past part. of *imbricare* to cover with imbrices, fr. L *imbric-, imbrex* (fr. *imbr-, imber* rain) + *-atus* -ate; akin to

Gk *ombros* rain, Skt *abhra* cloud, Arm *amb*, and perh. to L *nebula* mist, vapor, cloud — more at NEBULA] **1 :** lying lapped over each other in regular order in the manner of tiles or shingles on a roof — used esp. of bud scales, involucral bracts, fish scales **2 :** overlapping at the margins — used esp. of leaves in the bud — **im·bri·cate·ly** *adv*

²im·bri·cate \-rə,kāt, *usu* -ād.+V\ *vb* -ED/-ING/-S [LL *imbricatus*, past part.] *vt* : to cause (as tiles or layers of tissue in closing a wound) to overlap ~ *vi* : OVERLAP

imbricated snout beetle *n* : a small light-colored weevil (*Epicaerus imbricatus*) destructive to many vegetables and fruits

imbricated texture *n* : a texture in certain minerals (as tridymite) resembling overlapping plates

im·bri·ca·tion \,imbrə'kāshən\ *n* -s **1 :** an overlapping esp. of tiles or shingles or of successive layers of tissue in the closure of a wound **2 :** a decoration or pattern showing imbrication

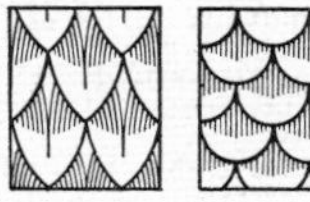
imbrication 1

im·bro·glio \əm'brōl(,)yō, -rōl-\ *or* **em·bro·glio** \", em-\ *n* -s [It *imbroglio*, fr. *imbrogliare* to entangle, confuse, embroil, fr. OIt, fr. MF *embrouiller* — more at EMBROIL] **1 :** a confused mass : CONGLOMERATION ⟨an ~ of papers and books⟩ **2 a :** an intricate or complicated situation (as in a drama or novel) **b :** an acutely painful or embarrassing misunderstanding ⟨an ~ between foreign ministers⟩ **c :** a violently confused or bitterly complicated altercation : EMBROILMENT ⟨an ~ over misuses of public funds⟩ **3 :** a musical passage designed to effect confusion by sharply contrasting the rhythm and meter (as between the voice parts in an opera)

im·brue \əm'brü\ *or* **em·brue** \", em-\ *vt* -ED/-ING/-S [ME *enbrewen*, *embrowen*, prob. fr. MF *abrevrer*, *abreuver*, *embevrer* to soak, drench, fr. (assumed) VL *abbiberare*, fr. L *ad-* + (assumed) VL *biberare* to give to drink, fr. L *bibere* to drink — more at POTABLE] : DRENCH ⟨a nation *imbrued* with the blood of executed men⟩

imbrued *adj* : stained with blood

im·brute \əm+\ *also* **em·brute** \əm, em+\ *vb* -ED/-ING/-S [²*in-* or ¹*en-* + *brute* (n.)] *vi* : to sink to the level of a brute : become bestial ~ *vt* : to degrade to the level of a brute : BRUTALIZE

im·bue \əm'byü\ *also* **em·bue** \", em-\ *vt* -ED/-ING/-S [L *imbuere* to dye, wet, moisten, prob. fr. *in-* ²in- + *-buere* (of unknown origin)] **1 :** to tinge or dye deeply ⟨a landscape deeply *imbued* with shadow⟩ **2 :** to cause to become penetrated : IMPREGNATE, PERMEATE ⟨a statesman *imbued* with a deep sense of national pride⟩ **syn** see INFUSE

im·bu·ia *or* **em·bu·ia** *also* **im·bu·ya** \əm'büyə\ *n* -s [Pg] **1 :** any of several Brazilian timber trees of the genera *Nectandra* and *Phoebe* (family Lauraceae) **2 :** the light to dark brown lustrous durable often strikingly figured wood of the imbuias that is readily polished and much used for fine cabinetwork — called also *Brazilian walnut*

im·er·i·na \,imə'rēnə\ *n, pl* **imerina** *or* **imerinas** *usu cap* : HOVA

im·er·i·nite \,imə'rē,nīt\ *n* -s [F *imerinite*, fr. *Imerina*, province of Madagascar, its locality + F *-ite*] : a monoclinic amphibole $Na_2(Mg,Fe)_6Si_8O_{22}(O,OH)_2$ that is related to richterite and occurs in colorless to blue acicular crystals : a basic silicate of sodium, iron, and magnesium

im·er·i·tian \,imə'rishən\ *also* **im·er·e·tian** \-rēsh-\ *n* -s *cap* [*Imeritia* or *Imeretia*, district of Georgian S.S.R. in the southern Caucasus + E *-an*] **1 :** a Georgian-speaking people of Imeritia **2 :** a member of the Imeritian people

im·hoff tank \'im,hȯf-, -hōf-\ *n, usu cap I* [after Karl *Imhoff* b1876 Ger. engineer] : a tank for sewage clarification consisting of an upper or sedimentation chamber with sloping floor leading to slots through which the solids settle to the lower sludge-digestion chamber

imid- *or* **imido-** *comb form* [ISV, fr. *imide*] **1** *now usu* **imido-** : containing the bivalent group =NH characteristic of imides united to or in one or two radicals of acid character ⟨*imido*carbonic acid $HN{=}C(OH)_2$⟩ ⟨*imido*disulfuric acid $HN(SO_2OH)_2$⟩ ⟨*imid*ate⟩ — distinguished from *imin-* **2 :** IMIN- — now less used than formerly

imidaz- *or* **imidazo-** *comb form* [ISV, fr. *imidazole*] : imidazole ⟨7-*imidazo* [4.5-*d*] pyrimidine⟩

im·id·azole \,imə'da,zōl, -,da'z-\ *n* [ISV *imid-* + *azole*] **1 :** a white crystalline heterocyclic base $C_3H_4N_2$ made by the action of ammonia and formaldehyde on glyoxal and isomeric with pyrazole; 1,3-diazole — called also *glyoxaline*; compare STRUCTURAL FORMULA **2 :** any of a large class of derivatives of imidazole including histidine and histamine

H
HC5 1 N 2CH
HC4 3N

imidazole 1

im·id·az·o·line \,imə'dazə,lēn\ *n* -s [*imidazole* + *-ine*] : any of three dihydro derivatives $C_3H_6N_2$ of imidazole; *also* : a derivative of these — called also *glyoxalidine*

im·id·az·o·lyl \-zə,lil\ *n* -s [ISV *imidazole* + *-yl*] : any of four univalent radicals $C_3H_3N_2$ derived from imidazole by removal of one hydrogen atom

im·ide \'i,mīd, -,məd\ *n* -s [ISV, alter. of *amide*] **1 :** any of a class of compounds derived from ammonia by replacement of two hydrogen atoms by a metal ⟨calcium ~ CaNH⟩ ⟨lithium ~ Li_2NH⟩ — called also *metallic imide* **2 :** any of a class of compounds derived from ammonia by replacement of two hydrogen atoms by one bivalent acid radical or by two univalent acid radicals; *esp* : a cyclic compound (as phthalimide, saccharin) containing a bivalent acyl radical — called also *acid imide*; compare AMIDE — **imid·ic** \(')i'midik\ *adj*

imidic acid *n* [ISV *imide* + *-ic*] : any of various acids characterized by the presence of the imido group; *esp* : one of a class of organic acids containing a carboxyl group in which the carbonyl oxygen atom is replaced by an imido group and having the general formula RC(=NH)OH but known only in the form of derivatives (as esters or acid chlorides)

im·i·do \'imə,dō\ *adj* [*imid-*] **1 :** relating to or containing the group =NH or a substituted group =NR united to one or two radicals of acid character — distinguished from *imino* **2 :** IMINO

imido ester *n* : an ester of an imidic acid

imid·o·gen \ə'midəjən, -,jen\ *n* -s [F *imidogène*, fr. *imid-* + *-gène* -gen] : a bivalent radical =NH derived from ammonia esp. as detected in the free state — compare IMIDO, IMINO

imin- *or* **imino-** *comb form* [ISV, fr. *imine*] : containing the bivalent group =NH characteristic of imines united to or in a nonacid bivalent radical ⟨*imino*porphyrins⟩ — distinguished from *imid-*

im·in·az·ole \,imə'na,zōl, -,na'z-\ *n* [*imin-* + *azole*] IMIDAZOLE

im·ine \'i,mēn, -,mən\ *n* -s [ISV, alter. of *amine*] : any of a class of compounds (as ethylenimine) derived from ammonia by replacement of two hydrogen atoms by a bivalent hydrocarbon radical or other nonacid organic radical — distinguished from *amine*

im·i·no \'imə,nō\ *adj* [*imin-*] : relating to or containing the group =NH or a substituted group =NR united to a radical other than an acid radical — distinguished from *imido*

imino ether *n* : IMIDO ESTER

imit *abbr* imitation; imitative

im·i·ta·bil·i·ty \,iməd·ə'bilәd·ē, -mətə-, -lətē, -i\ *n* **1 :** the quality or state of being imitable **2 :** the power of exhibiting Platonic imitation

im·i·ta·ble \-əbəl\ *adj* [MF, fr. L *imitabilis*, fr. *imitari* + *-abilis* -able] **1 :** capable of being imitated or copied ⟨the music is curiously devoid of those analyzable — and ~ — features —Winthrop Sargeant⟩ **2 :** worthy of imitation — **im·i·ta·ble·ness** *n* -ES

im·i·tan·cy \'iməd·ənsē, -mətə-, -si\ *n* -ES [*imitate* + *-ancy*] : tendency to imitation : IMITATIVENESS

im·i·tant \-nt\ *n* -s [L *imitant-*, *imitans*, pres. part. of *imitari*] : something that imitates : a counterfeit or substitute article or product

im·i·tate \'imə,tāt, *usu* -ād.+V\ *vt* -ED/-ING/-S [L *imitatus*, past part. of *imitari* — more at IMAGE] **1 :** to follow as a pattern, model, or example : copy or strive to copy (as in acts, manners, conduct) : assume the form or likeness of ⟨drama that ~s life⟩ **2 :** to produce a likeness of (as in form, character, color, qualities, conduct, manners) : REPRODUCE, COPY **3 :** to be or appear like : resemble in external appearance ⟨paper finished to ~ leather⟩ **4 a :** MIMIC, MOCK ⟨~ another's intonations⟩ ⟨*imitating* his father's halting walk⟩ **b :** to exhibit or assume mimicry of : MIMIC 4 ⟨chameleons *imitating* their background⟩ ⟨the viceroy butterfly is said to ~ the monarch⟩ **5** *dial Eng* : ATTEMPT, ENDEAVOR — usu. followed by an infinitive ⟨that colt will ~ to throw you, give him a chance⟩ **syn** see COPY

im·i·tat·ee \,imə,tād·'ē, -ā'tē\ *n* -s [*imitate* + *-ee*] : one that is imitated

im·i·ta·tion \,imə'tāshən, *attrib* ¦==¦==\ *n* -s *often attrib* [L *imitation-*, *imitatio*, fr. *imitatus* + *-ion-*, *-io* -ion] **1 :** an act or instance of imitating : an assumption of or mimicking of the form of something that serves or is regarded as a model ⟨~ is the sincerest form of flattery⟩ ⟨the ~ of leaves by certain butterflies is unbelievably perfect⟩ ⟨a style developed in ~ of classic models⟩ **2 :** something that is made or produced as a copy : an artificial likeness : COUNTERFEIT ⟨risible ~s of his schoolfellows⟩ ⟨a convincing ~ of colonial architecture⟩ **3 a :** a literary work or composition designed to reproduce the style or manner of another author **b :** a free translation or an adaptation or parody esp. when involving transformation of cultural, social, or temporal situation **4 :** the repetition in a voice part of the melodic theme, phrase, or motive previously found in another part **5 a** *in Platonism* : the process through which a sensible object is informed by or participates in a subsistent idea or transcendent archetype — compare PARTICIPATION **b** *in Aristotelianism* (1) : the artistic simulation of anything as it is actually (2) : its representation as it is ideally or as it ought to be **6 a :** the execution of an act supposedly as a direct response to the perception of another person performing the act **b :** the assumption of the modes of behavior observed in other individuals

im·i·ta·tion·al \,imə'tāshənᵊl, -shnəl\ *adj* : relating to, marked by, or employed in imitation ⟨~ propensities⟩

imitation art paper *n* : a paper that is heavily filled with clay and given a high finish on the calenders

imitation brick *n* : brick made of material other than clay or shale but having the same appearance

imitation leather *n* : a material (as a coated fabric, rubber or plastic composition, or paper) made and finished to resemble genuine leather

im·i·ta·tive \'imə,tād·iv, -məd·əl, |t|, |ēv *also* |əv\ *adj* [LL *imitativus*, fr. L *imitatus* + *-ivus* -ive] **1 a :** marked by imitation : exhibiting some of the qualities of or formed after a model, pattern, or original ⟨acting is an ~ art⟩ **b :** ONOMATOPOEIC ⟨~ words intended to reproduce or represent a natural sound⟩ **c :** exhibiting mimicry **2 :** inclined to imitate : given to imitation ⟨man is an ~ being⟩ **3 :** imitating something superior : COUNTERFEIT — **im·i·ta·tive·ly** \|əvlē, |li\ *adv* — **im·i·ta·tive·ness** \|ivnəs, |ēv- *also* |əv-\ *n* -ES

imitative magic *n* : magic based on the assumption that a desired result (as rain, the death of an enemy) can be brought about or assured by mimicking it — called also *homeopathic magic*; compare SYMPATHETIC MAGIC

im·i·ta·tor \'imə,tād·ə(r), -ātə-\ *n* -s [L, fr. *imitatus* (past part. of *imitari* to imitate) + *-or* — more at IMAGE] : one that imitates : one that gives or produces imitations

im·i·ta·tress \'imə'tā·trəs\ *also* **im·i·ta·trix** \-riks\ *n, pl* **imitatress·es** \-rəsəz\ *also* **imitatri·ces** \,=='tā·trə,sēz, -,tə'trī(,)sēz\ *or* **imitatrix·es** \'=='tā·triksəz\ : a female imitator

im·mac·u·la·cy \ə'makyələsē, -si\ *n* -ES : the quality or state of being immaculate

im·mac·u·late \-lət, *usu* -ləd.+V\ *adj* [ME *immaculat*, fr. L *immaculatus*, fr. *in-* ¹in- + *maculatus*, past part. of *maculare* to spot, stain — more at MACULATE] **1 :** having no stain or blemish : SPOTLESS, UNDEFILED, PURE ⟨an ~ heart⟩ **2 :** containing no flaw, fault, or error ⟨an ~ book⟩ **3 a :** lacking any spot, soil, or smirch : spotlessly clean ⟨his linen was ~⟩ **b** *biol* : having no colored spots or marks — **im·mac·u·late·ly** *adv* — **im·mac·u·late·ness** *n* -ES

immaculate conception *n* [trans. of ML *immaculata conceptio*] **1** *usu cap I & C* : a conception in which the offspring is immediately and constantly preserved free from original sin by divine grace — used of the conception of the Virgin Mary in the womb of Saint Anne and made an article of faith of the Roman Catholic Church by Pius IX; distinguished from *virgin birth* **2 :** conception not preceded by sexual intercourse; *broadly* : production of something without evident source or origin ⟨the naturalist must insist that reason is not of *immaculate conception* —H.J.Muller⟩

im·malleable \(')i(m), ə+\ *adj* [¹*in-* + *malleable*] : lacking malleability : UNYIELDING, RIGID

im·manacle \ə+\ *vt* [²*in-* + *manacle* (n.)] *archaic* : MANACLE, FETTER

im·mane \(')i¦mān, ə'm-\ *adj* [L *immanis*, fr. *in-* ¹in- + *manis*, *manus* good — more at MATURE] **1** *archaic* : vast in size or extent : HUGE **2** *archaic* : extremely cruel : INHUMAN

im·ma·nence \'imənən(t)s\ *n* -s **1 :** the state or quality of being indwelling or inward or of not going beyond a particular domain : INHERENCE: as **a :** the condition of being in the mind or experientially given **b** *in Kantianism* : the condition of being within the limits of possible experience — contrasted with *transcendence* **2 :** the indwelling presence of God in the world

im·ma·nen·cy \-nənsē, -si\ *n* -ES **1 :** IMMANENCE **2 :** the doctrine of immanence; *esp* : the principle that God is immanent in the world — distinguished from *transcendence*

im·ma·nent \-nənt\ *adj* [LL *immanent-*, *immanens*, pres. part. of *immanēre* to remain in place, inhabit, fr. *in-* ²in- + L *manēre* to remain — more at MANSION] **1 a :** remaining or operating within the subject considered : INDWELLING, INHERENT, INTRINSIC ⟨considering both ~ and external factors in social evolution⟩ ⟨in many cults . . . objects of cult are the temporary abodes of spirits; when the spirits are ~ the objects receive ceremonial treatment —*Notes & Queries on Anthropology*⟩ **b** *of a mental event* : confined to consciousness or to the mind : SUBJECTIVE ⟨a cognition is an ~ act of mind —William Hamilton †1856⟩ — contrasted with *transcendent* **2 :** being or characterizing the relation of the world to mind according to various philosophies — **im·ma·nent·ly** *adv*

im·ma·nen·tal \¦imə¦nentᵊl\ *adj* : relating to the doctrine of immanence : affirming and emphasizing the indwelling presence of God in the world ⟨an ~ religion⟩

immanent cause *n, Spinozism* : a cause originating and evolving within an entity ⟨God is the *immanent cause* of all things rather than the transient cause —*transl*⟩ — contrasted with *transient cause*

im·ma·nent·ism \'imənənt·,izəm, -nən·,ti-\ *n* -s **1 :** an epistemological theory according to which the relation of the world to the mind of an individual is one of immanence **2 :** any of several theories according to which the relation of God, mind, or spirit to the world including individuals is one of immanence ⟨the high ~ or near pantheism of Emerson and of the whole transcendentalist school owed not a little to oriental thought —C.S.Braden⟩

im·ma·nent·ist \-nəntəst, -,nen-\ *n* -s : an advocate of immanentism

im·ma·nen·tis·tic \¦imənən·¦tistik\ *or* **im·ma·nent·ist** \'imənəntəst, -,nen-\ *adj* : relating to or characteristic of immanentism

im·ma·nent·iza·tion \,imənəntə'zāshən, -,nentə'z-, -,nənt-ī'z-\ *n* -s : the process of rendering immanent

im·manifest \(')i(m), ə+\ *adj* [¹*in-* + *manifest*] : not manifest

immanity *n* -ES [L *immanitas*, fr. *immanis* immane + *-itas* -ity — more at IMMANE] *obs* : MONSTROSITY

im·mantle \ə+\ *vt* [²*in-* + *mantle* (n.)] : to cover or encircle with or as if with a mantle

im·marble *var of* EMMARBLE

im·mar·ces·ci·ble *or* **im·mar·ces·si·ble** \¦i(m),mär¦sesəbəl\ *adj* [LL *immarcescibilis*, fr. L *in-* ¹in- + LL *marcescibilis* withering, fr. L *marcescere* to wither, fade away + *-ibilis* -ible — more at MARCESCENT] : IMPERISHABLE, INDESTRUCTIBLE — **im·mar·ces·ci·bly** *or* **im·mar·ces·si·bly** \-blē\ *adv*

im·marginate \(')i(m), ə+\ *adj* [¹*in-* + *marginate*] : lacking a definite margin

immask *vt* [²*in-* + *mask* (n.)] *obs* : to cover with or as if with a mask : DISGUISE

im·material \¦i(m)+\ *adj* [ME *immateriel*, fr. MF, fr. LL *immaterialis*, fr. L *in-* ¹in- + LL *materialis* material — more at MATERIAL] **1 :** not consisting of matter : INCORPOREAL, SPIRITUAL, DISEMBODIED ⟨in making mind purely ~ . . . the body ceases to be living —John Dewey⟩ ⟨ghosts and other ~ entities⟩ **2** *obs* : having little body or substance : FLIMSY **3 a :** of no substantial consequence : UNIMPORTANT ⟨wholly ~ whether he stays or not⟩ ⟨the exact form of government appears ~ —Aidan Mulloy⟩ **b :** not material or essential to a legal matter or case — **im·materially** \"+\ *adv* — **im·materialness** \"+\ *n*

im·materialism \"+\ *n* **1 :** immaterial state or being **2 :** a philosophical theory that views external bodies as being of the essence of mind; *specif* : BERKELEIANISM

im·materialist \"+\ *n* : an advocate of philosophical immaterialism

im·materiality \"+\ *n* : the quality or state of being immaterial; *also* : something immaterial

im·materialize \"+\ *vt* : to render immaterial or incorporeal

im·ma·te·ri·als \-lz\ *n pl* : immaterial or incorporeal things

im·matriculate \,i+\ *vt* [ML *immatriculatus*, past part. of *immatriculare* to join, fr. L *in-* ²in- + ML *matricula* — more at MATRICULA] *archaic* : MATRICULATE, ENROLL

im·matriculation \,i+\ *n* [prob. fr. G *immatrikulation*, fr. ML *immatriculatus* + G *-ion*] : an act, state, or process of being enrolled (as in an official register) ⟨lands on which a native title can be shown are put through a process of ~; a tax is then levied —F.M.Keesing⟩

¹im·mature \¦i(m)+\ *adj* [L *immaturus*, fr. *in-* ¹in- + *maturus* mature — more at MATURE] **1** *archaic* : PREMATURE, UNTIMELY **2 a :** lacking complete growth, differentiation, or development ⟨poor thin ~ soils⟩ ⟨~ animals⟩ : UNRIPE ⟨~ fruit⟩ **b** (1) : having capacities or potentialities for attaining but not yet having attained a definitive form or state ⟨~ talents⟩ ⟨a vigorous but ~ school of art⟩ : CRUDE, UNFINISHED (2) *of a topographic feature* : predictably due to undergo further changes : not having attained maturity — used esp. of valleys and drainages while most of the area is well above base-level **c :** exhibiting less than a normal or expected degree of maturity ⟨emotionally ~ adults⟩ ⟨the alcoholic is an ~, maladjusted individual —W.L.Wilkins⟩ — **im·maturely** \"+\ *adv* — **im·matureness** \"+\ *n*

²im·mature \"+\ *n* -s : an immature individual; *esp* : a young bird that has molted the juvenal plumage but has not yet acquired complete adult plumage

im·matured \"+\ *adj* [¹*in-* + *matured*, past part. of *mature*] : IMMATURE

im·maturity \"+\ *n* [L *immaturitas*, fr. *immaturus* + *-itas* -ity] **1 :** the state or quality of being immature ⟨emotional and cultural ~⟩ ⟨the ~ of such coarse mineral soils⟩ **2 :** something immature ⟨childish *immaturities*⟩ ⟨always within his *immaturities* is the saving grace of his willingness . . . to accept responsibility —*Times Lit. Supp.*⟩

im·measurability \(')i(m)+\ *n* : the quality or state of being immeasurable

im·measurable \(')i(m)+\ *adj* [ME *ynmesurable*, fr. *yn-* ¹in- + *mesurable* measurable — more at MEASURABLE] : incapable of being measured : IMMENSURABLE; *broadly* : indefinitely extensive : ILLIMITABLE — **im·measurableness** \"+\ *n* — **im·measurably** \"+\ *adv*

im·measured \"+\ *adj* [¹*in-* + *measured*] : IMMEASURABLE, VAST

im·mechanical \¦i(m)+\ *adj* [¹*in-* + *mechanical*] *archaic* : not mechanical : UNTECHNICAL

im·me·di·a·cy \ə'mēdēəsē, -si, *chiefly Brit* -mējəs- *or* -mēdyəs-\ *n* **1 :** the quality or state of being immediate; *usu* : freedom from or absence of an intervening medium : direct presence : DIRECTNESS, CONTIGUITY ⟨the ~ of personal experience —*London Calling*⟩ ⟨television has on occasion furnished a startling ~ . . . to news reports —F.L.Mott⟩ — opposed to *mediacy* **2 :** something that is immediate ⟨the ~ of our need⟩ — usu. used in pl. ⟨the *immediacies* of life⟩ **3 :** the state or relation under feudal law of being immediate lord or vassal **4 a :** the direct content of consciousness or consciousness itself as distinguished from what consciousness represents or mediates a knowledge of **b :** direct awareness or presentations of sense as contrasted with what is added by memory and association or thought **c :** the quality of something that is self-evident or intuited as contrasted with something that is arrived at by thought or reason

im·me·di·ate \ə'mēdēə|t, *usu* |d.+V; *chiefly Brit* -mējə| *or* -mēdyə|\ *adj* [LL *immediatus*, fr. L *in-* ¹in- + *mediatus* mediate — more at MEDIATE] **1 a :** acting or being without the intervention of another object, cause, or agency : DIRECT, PROXIMATE ⟨the ~ cause of death⟩ **b :** of or relating to psychic immediacy : being or occurring without reference to other states or factors : INTUITIVE ⟨~ knowledge⟩ **2** *of relations between persons* **a :** having no individual intervening : being next in line or relation : not secondary or remote ⟨the ~ parties to the quarrel⟩ ⟨only the ~ family was present⟩ ⟨you are most ~ to our throne —Shak.⟩ **b :** standing in or being the relation of vassal and lord when the one holds directly of the other **3 a :** occurring, acting, or accomplished without loss of time : made or done at once : INSTANT ⟨an ~ need for help⟩ ⟨~ expenses⟩ ⟨agreed to an ~ marriage⟩ **b** *of time* : near to or related to the present ⟨sometime in the ~ past⟩ ⟨the ~ future is uncertain⟩ **4 :** characterized by contiguity : existing without intervening space or substance ⟨bring the chemicals into ~ contact very cautiously⟩; *broadly* : being near at hand : not far apart or distant ⟨hid the money in the ~ neighborhood⟩

immediate annuity *n* : an annuity which is purchased with a single premium and on which the initial payment is made to the annuitant within the first year

immediate constituent *n* : any of the two or three meaningful parts directly forming a larger expression

immediate inference *n* **1 :** an inference drawn from a single premise **2 :** the operation of drawing an inference from a single premise

¹im·me·di·ate·ly *pronunc at* IMMEDIATE +lē *or* li; *or* ÷-mēdət-\ *adv* [ME *immediatly*, fr. LL *immediatus* + ME *-ly*] **1 :** without intermediary : in direct connection or relation : CLOSELY ⟨~ contiguous⟩ ⟨~ away from the shore⟩ **2 :** without interval of time : without delay : STRAIGHTWAY ⟨~ after the meeting⟩ ⟨come home ~⟩

²immediately \"\ *conj* : as soon as ⟨~ his intentions are understood, he may leave⟩

im·me·di·ate·ness *pronunc at* IMMEDIATE +nəs\ *n* -ES : the quality or state of being immediate : IMMEDIACY ⟨the ~ of their relationship⟩

im·me·di·a·tism \-ə,tizəm\ *n* -s **1 :** IMMEDIATENESS **2 :** a policy or practice of gaining a desired end by immediate action; *specif* : a policy advocating the immediate abolition of slavery **3 :** an epistemological theory that views the object of perception as directly knowable

im·me·di·a·tist \-əd·əst, -ətə-\ *n* -s : one that advocates or believes in immediatism

im·medicable \(')i(m)+\ *adj* [L *immedicabilis*, fr. *in-* ¹in- + *medicabilis* medicable — more at MEDICABLE] : being such as cannot be healed or remedied : INCURABLE ⟨this ~ evil⟩ — **im·medicably** \"+\ *adv*

im·mel·mann \'imәlmən, -l,män\ *vi* -ED/-ING/-S *often cap* [*Immelmann (turn)*] : to execute an Immelmann turn

immelmann turn *also* **immelmann** *n, usu cap I* [after Max *Immelmann* †1916 Ger. aviator] : a maneuver in which an airplane is first made to complete half of a loop and is then rolled half of a complete turn — called also *reverse turn*

im·melodious \¦i(m)+\ *adj* [¹*in-* + *melodious*] : not melodious

im·memorable \(')i(m)+\ *adj* [L *immemorabilis*, fr. *in-* ¹in- + *memorabilis* memorable — more at MEMORABLE] **1 :** not memorable **2 :** IMMEMORIAL — **im·memorably** \"+\ *adv*

im·memorial \¦i(m)+\ *adj* [prob. fr. F *immémorial*, fr. MF *immemorial*, fr. *in-* ¹in- + *memorial* — more at MEMORIAL] : extending beyond the reach of memory, record, or tradition : indefinitely ancient ⟨existing from time ~⟩ ⟨a chapel of ~ age —Andrew Lang⟩ ⟨~ elms —Alfred Tennyson⟩ — **im·memorially** \"\ *adv*

1im·mense \ə'men(t)s\ *adj, sometimes* -ER/-EST [MF, fr. L *immensus* immeasurable, boundless, vast, fr. *in-* 1in- + *mensus*, past part. of *metiri* to measure — more at MEASURE] **1 :** marked by greatness in size, amount, number, degree, force, significance; *often* **:** transcending usual procedures of measuring and estimating ‹the Los Angeles Aqueduct . . . like an ~ snake along the base of the mountains —*Amer. Guide Series: Calif.*› ‹thousands of lakes and ponds afford congenial haunts for ~ numbers of water birds —*Amer. Guide Series: Minn.*› ‹the ~ relief of the armistice —Mary Austin› **2 :** supremely good **:** EXCELLENT, FINE ‹the reading has been ~ . . . started on the *Odyssey* and read six books with uncritical joy —H.J.Laski› **syn** see HUGE

2immense \"\ *n* -S **:** immense space, extent, or number **:** IMMENSITY ‹the dark ~ of air —Alfred Tennyson›

im·mense·ly *adv* **:** to an immense degree **:** VERY, EXCEEDINGLY

im·mense·ness *n* -ES **:** the quality or state of being immense **:** IMMENSITY

im·men·si·ty \-n(t)səd-ē, -ətē, -i\ *n* -ES [ME *immensitee*, fr. MF or L; MF *immensité*, fr. L *immensitat-, immensitas*, fr. *immensus* + *-itat-, -itas* -ity] **1 a :** immeasurable or boundless size, quantity, or degree **:** vastness in extent or bulk **:** unlimited extension ‹the starry ~ of the heavens› **b :** greatness of scope ‹the ~ of this concept› ‹undertook a task of grave ~› **2 :** something that is immense **:** vast or infinite being, existence, or space ‹the gigantic temples of Egypt, those massive *immensities* of granite —Edith Hamilton› ‹the mountain reared its white ~ before us›

im·mensurability \(ˌ)i(m)+\ *n* [ML *immensurabilitas*, fr. LL *immensurabilis* + L *-itas* -ity] **:** the quality or state of being immensurable

im·mensurable \(ˈ)i(m)+\ *adj* [LL *immensurabilis*, fr. L *in-* 1in- + LL *mensurabilis* measurable — more at MEASURABLE] **:** not capable of being measured; *esp* **:** vastly large — **im·mensurableness** \"+\ *n* -ES

im·mensurate \(ˈ)i(m)ˈmen(t)s(ə)rət, -mench(ə)-\ *adj* [LL *immensuratus*, fr. L *in-* 1in- + LL *mensuratus*, past part. of *mensurare* to measure — more at MENSURABLE] **:** UNMEASURED, UNLIMITED

im·merd \i'mərd\ *vt* -ED/-ING/-S [2in- + L *merda* dung; akin to Gk *smordoun* to copulate, OSlav *smrŭděti* to stink, and prob. to L *mordēre* to bite — more at SMART] *archaic* **:** to cover with ordure

im·merge \(ˈ)i(m)ˈmərj\ *vb* [L *immergere* — more at IMMERSE] *vt, archaic* **:** to plunge (something) into, under, or within a fluid or other medium **:** IMMERSE ~ *vi* **1 a** *obs* **:** to plunge into a fluid **b :** to plunge into or immerse oneself in something ‹no need to ~ further into this topic› **2** *obs, of a celestial body* **:** to disappear by passing behind some obscuring agent (as a horizon or another celestial body)

im·mer·gence \-jən(t)s\ *n* **:** act of immerging

immerit *n* [1in- + *merit*] *obs* **:** lack of worth **:** DEMERIT

immerited *adj* [1in- + *merited*] *obs* **:** UNDESERVED

im·mer·sal \ə'mərsəl, -məs-, -məis-\ *n* -S [*immerse* + *-al*] **:** the state of being immersed ‹his complete ~ in affairs of state›

im·merse \ə'mərs, -məs, -məis\ *vb* -ED/-ING/-S [L *immersus*, past part. of *immergere*, fr. *in-* 2in- + *mergere* to dip, merge — more at MERGE] *vt* **1 a** (1) **:** to plunge or dip into a liquid ‹~ the cut beans in boiling water to blanch› ‹test the temperature before *immersing* yourself in the pool› (2) **:** to baptize by immersion **b :** to enclose in something **:** EMBED, INCLUDE, SINK, BURY ‹fossils *immersed* in sandstone› ‹the lower half of the cuttings should be *immersed* in moist sand› **2 :** to engross the attention of **:** engage deeply **:** ABSORB ‹~s himself completely in his work› ‹has been *immersed* almost all his life in the business of the law —M.R.Cohen› ~ *vi* **:** to become absorbed **:** PLUNGE, SINK **syn** see DIP

immersed *adj* **:** submerged in or as if in a fluid: as **a :** completely engrossed **b** (1) *of a bodily structure* **:** completely embedded in or sunk below the surface of another part or organ (2) *of the capsule of a moss* **:** covered by the perichaetium **c** *of a plant* **:** growing wholly under water

immersed wedge *n* **:** the wedge-shaped portion of a ship that becomes immersed when the ship rolls

im·mers·ible \-səbəl\ *adj* **:** capable of being immersed

im·mer·sion \-mər|zhən, -mə̄|, -məi|, |sh-\ *n* -S [LL *immersion-, immersio*, fr. L *immersus* + *-ion-, -io* -ion] **:** an act of immersing or a state of being immersed: as **a** (1) **:** a sinking or plunging usu. into or within a fluid **:** DIPPING ‹the sense of chill that follows ~ of the hand in a volatile liquid› (2) **:** submersion in water for the purpose of Christian baptism **:** baptism by complete submersion of the person in water — compare AFFUSION, ASPERSION **b :** disappearance of a celestial body either by passing behind another (as in the occultation of a star by the moon) or by passing into its shadow (as in the eclipse of a satellite) — compare EMERSION **c :** SIMPLE IMMERSION

im·mer·sion·al \-zhənᵊl, -zhnəl, -sh-\ *adj* **:** of, relating to, or occurring through immersion ‹~ baptism›

immersion cup *n* **:** a cup used for examining a gem immersed in a liquid of high refractive index

immersion foot *n* **:** a painful condition of the feet marked by inflammation and stabbing pain and followed by discoloration, swelling, ulcers, and numbness due to prolonged exposure to moist cold usu. without actual freezing — compare TRENCH FOOT

immersion heater *n* **:** a usu. electric unit for heating a liquid by immersion

im·mer·sion·ism \-zhəˌnizəm, -sh-\ *n* -S **:** a doctrine that immersion is essential to Christian baptism **:** the practice of baptism by immersion

im·mer·sion·ist \-nəst\ *n* -S **:** one that advocates or practices immersionism

immersion lens *or* **immersion objective** *n* **:** an objective of short focal distance designed to work with a drop of liquid (as oil or water) between front lens and cover glass

immersion liquid *n* **:** a liquid of known refractive index used by gemmologists to reduce refraction of light at the surfaces of a gem and facilitate examination of the interior

immersion heater

immesh *var of* ENMESH

im·methodical *also* **im·methodic** \ˌi(m)+\ *adj* [1in- + *methodical, methodic*] **:** lacking method or order **:** not methodical ‹a careless ~ program› — **im·methodically** \"+\ *adv*

im·metrical \(ˈ)i(m)+\ *adj* [1in- + *metrical*] **:** lacking meter **:** UNMETRICAL ‹a harsh ~ line of verse› — **im·metrically** \"+\ *adv*

im·meu·bles \ēmœbl(ᵊ), -b(lə)\ *n pl* [F, pl. of *immeuble* piece of fixed property, fr. MF, fr. *immeuble* immovable (in *biens immeubles* immovable property), fr. OF *immoble*, fr. L *immobilis* — more at IMMOBILE] **:** a class of property under French law that consists essentially of immovables — compare MEUBLES

im·mie \'imē\ *n* -S [*imm-* (fr. *imitation agate*) + *-ie*] **:** MARBLE 2a; *esp* **:** a glass marble streaked with colors

1im·mi·grant \'iməgrənt, -mēg- *sometimes* -ˌgrant *or* -ˌgraa(ə)nt\ *n* -S [L *immigrant-, immigrans*, pres. part. of *immigrare*] **:** one that immigrates: **a :** a person that comes to a country for the purpose of permanent residence — compare EMIGRANT **b :** a plant or animal that appears and becomes established in an area in which it was previously unknown

2immigrant \"\ *adj* **:** of, relating to, or composed of immigrants ‹an ~ fauna› ‹department concerned with ~ affairs› **:** IMMIGRATING ‹~ birds›

im·mi·grate \'iməˌgrāt\ *vb* [L *immigratus*, past part. of *immigrare* to remove, go in, fr. *in-* 2in- + *migrare* to migrate — more at MIGRATE] *vi* **:** to come to dwell or settle **:** to enter and usu. become established ‹white blood cells ~ to the site of the injury›; *esp* **:** to come into a country of which one is not a native for the purpose of permanent residence ~ *vt* **:** to bring in or send as immigrants

im·mi·gra·tion \ˌimə'grāshən\ *n* -S *often attrib* **1 :** an act or instance of immigrating; *specif* **:** a going into a country for the purpose of permanent residence **2 :** a party of immigrants; *broadly* **:** the number of immigrants arriving during a given period

im·mi·gra·tion·al \ˌimə¦grāshənᵊl, -shnəl\ *adj* **:** relating to or concerned with immigration

immigration pressure *n* **:** the effect on the makeup of a natural population of recurrent immigrations of individuals capable of interbreeding with the original stock

im·mi·gra·to·ry \'iməgrəˌtōrē, -mēg-, -ōr-, -ri\ *adj* **:** of, relating to, or constituting immigration ‹~ movements of populations›

immind *vt* [2in- + *mind* (n.)] *obs* **:** REMIND

im·mi·nence \'imənən(t)s\ *n* -S [L *imminentia*, fr. *imminent-, imminens* + *-ia* -y] **1** *also* **im·mi·nen·cy** \-nənsē, -si\ -ES **:** the quality or state of being imminent **2 :** something that is imminent; *usu* **:** impending evil or danger

im·mi·nent \-nənt\ *adj* [L *imminent-, imminens*, pres. part. of *imminēre* to project, threaten, fr. *in-* 2in- + *-minēre* (akin to L *mont-, mons* mountain) — more at MOUNT] **1 :** ready to take place **:** near at hand **:** IMPENDING ‹our ~ departure›; *usu* **:** hanging threateningly over one's head **:** menacingly near ‹in ~ jeopardy› ‹this ~ danger› **2 :** IMMANENT — **im·mi·nent·ly** *adv* — **im·mi·nent·ness** *n* -ES

im·min·gle \i+\ *vb* [2in- + *mingle*] **:** BLEND, INTERMINGLE

im·mi·nu·tion \ˌimə'n(y)üshən\ *n* -S [L *imminution-, imminutio*, fr. *imminutus* (past part. of *imminuere* to lessen, fr. *in-* 2in- + *minuere* to lessen) + *-ion-, -io* -ion — more at MINOR] *archaic* **:** DIMINUTION

im·miscibility \(ˌ)i(m)+\ *n* **:** inability to mix or become homogeneous

im·miscible \(ˈ)i(m)+\ *adj* [1in- + *miscible*] **:** incapable of mixing or being mixed **:** unable to blend or attain homogeneity ‹makes separate polyphonic lines more ~ by writing them sometimes in different keys —Joseph Kerman› — used esp. of liquids ‹~ solvents›; compare INCOMPATIBLE — **im·miscibly** \"+\ *adv*

im·mis·er·i·za·tion \iˌmizərə'zāshən, -ˌrī'z-\ *n* -S [2in- + *miserable* + *-ization*; intended as trans. of G *verelendung*] **:** act of making or state of becoming miserable; *esp* **:** IMPOVERISHMENT ‹the ~ of the proletariat›

im·mis·sion \(ˈ)i¦mishən\ *n* [L *immission-, immissio*, fr. *immissus* past part. of *immittere* to send in (fr. *in-* 2in- + *mittere* to send) + *-ion-, -io* -ion — more at SMITE] **1 a** *archaic* **:** an act of sending or letting in **:** INJECTION, ADMISSION, INTRODUCTION **b** *obs* **:** something introduced **2 :** COMMIXTURE 2

im·mit \i'mit\ *vt* **immitted; immitted; immitting; immits** [L *immittere*] *archaic* **:** to send or let in **:** INJECT, ADMIT, INTRODUCE

im·mitigable \(ˈ)i(m)+\ *adj* [LL *immitigabilis*, fr. L *in-* 1in- + *mitigare* to mitigate + *-abilis* -able — more at MITIGATE] **:** not capable of being mitigated, softened, lessened, or appeased (such ~ evil) — **im·mitigableness** \"+\ *n* -ES — **im·mitigably** \"+\ *adv*

im·mix \i'miks\ *vt* [back-formation fr. *immixed* mixed in, fr. ME *immixte*, fr. L *immixtus*, past part. of *immiscēre* to mix in, fr. *in-* 2in- + *miscēre* to mix — more at MIX] **:** to mix intimately **:** mix in or up **:** COMMINGLE

im·mix·able \(ˈ)i(m)¦miksəbəl\ *adj* [1in- + *mixable*] **:** IMMISCIBLE

im·mixture \i+\ *n* [L *immixtus* + E *-ure*] **:** the act of immixing **:** the quality or state of being immixed **:** an intimate mixture

im·mobile \(ˈ)i(m), ə+\ *adj* [ME *in-mobill*, fr. L *immobilis*, fr. *in-* 1in- + *mobilis* movable — more at MOBILE] **:** incapable of being moved **:** IMMOVABLE, FIXED, STABLE; *broadly* **:** UNMOVING, MOTIONLESS

im·mo·bi·lism \ə'mōbəˌlizəm\ *n* -S [F *immobilisme*, fr. *immobile* (fr. L *immobilis*) + *-isme* -ism] **:** a governmental policy characterized by compromise and moderation often to the point of ignoring basic issues and stagnation of progressive trends

im·mo·bi·list \-ləst\ *n* -S **:** one who advocates immobilism

im·mobility \ˌi(m)+\ *n* [MF *immobilité*, fr. LL *immobilitat-, immobilitas*, fr. L *immobilis* + *-itat-, -itas* -ity] **:** the quality or state of being immobile **:** FIXEDNESS; *broadly* **:** MOTIONLESSNESS

im·mobilization \(ˌ)i(m), ə+\ *n* [F *immobilisation*, fr. *immobiliser* + *-ation*] **:** the act of immobilizing or state of being immobilized: as **a** (1) **:** quiet rest in bed for a prolonged period used in the treatment of disease (as tuberculosis) (2) **:** fixation (as by a plaster cast) of a body part usu. to promote healing in normal structural relation **b :** loss of evolutionary plasticity due to existence in a relatively constant environment resulting in elimination of mutations and variability

im·mobilize \(ˈ)i(m), ə+\ *vt, see -ize in Explan Notes* [F *immobiliser*, fr. *immobile* + *-iser* -ize] **:** to make immobile **:** fix in place or position **:** render incapable of movement: as **a :** to interfere with or prevent freedom of movement or effective use of (as military forces or equipment) ‹our planes were *immobilized* by bad weather› ‹the enemy was *immobilized* by lack of transport› **b :** to fix (as a body part) so as to reduce or eliminate motion usu. by means of a cast or splint, by strapping, or by strict bed rest ‹*immobilizing* a fractured bone by a cast and continuous traction› ‹~ an injury› ‹the patient was *immobilized* for three months› **c** (1) **:** to withhold (specie) from circulation to serve as security for other money (2) **:** to convert (circulating capital) into fixed capital

im·mo·bi·liz·er \"ə(r)\ *n* **:** one that immobilizes

im·moderacy \(ˈ)i(m), ə+\ *n* -ES **:** IMMODERATENESS

im·moderate \"+\ *adj* [ME *immoderat*, fr. L *immoderatus*, fr. *in-* 1in- + *moderatus*, past part. of *moderare* to moderate — more at MODERATE] **1 :** lacking in moderation **:** exceeding just, usual, or suitable bounds **:** EXTRAVAGANT, UNREASONABLE ‹~ demands› ‹an ~ speed› ‹~ appetites› ‹an ~ theorist› **2** *obs* **a :** characterized by excess **:** INTEMPERATE **b :** having no limits **:** BOUNDLESS **syn** see EXCESSIVE

im·moderately \"+\ *adv* [ME, fr. *immoderat* + *-ly*] **:** without moderation **:** to an immoderate degree

im·moderateness \"+\ *n* **:** the quality or state of being immoderate

im·moderation \(ˌ)i(m), ə+\ *n* [MF *immoderacion*, fr. L *immoderation-, immoderatio*, fr. *in-* 1in- + *moderation-, moderatio* moderation — more at MODERATION] **:** lack of moderation

im·modest \(ˈ)i(m), ə\ *adj* [L *immodestus*, fr. *in-* 1in- + *modestus* modest — more at MODEST] **:** lacking or deficient in modesty: as **a :** failing in the reserve or restraint that decorum or custom requires ‹brash ~ boasting› ‹the ~ claims of the billboards› **b :** deficient in sexual modesty **:** not conforming to the sexual mores of a particular time or place **:** BRAZEN, INDECENT ‹a thoroughly ~ costume› ‹~ conduct› — **im·modestly** \"+\ *adv*

im·modesty \"+\ *n* [L *immodestia*, fr. *immodestus* + *-ia* -y] **1 :** lack of modesty, delicacy, or decent reserve **:** FORWARDNESS, BOLDNESS **2 :** lack of decency **:** IMPROPRIETY, UNCHASTITY

im·modulated \"+\ *adj* [1in- + *modulated*] **:** lacking modulation

im·mo·late \'iməˌlāt, *usu* -ād·+V\ *vt* -ED/-ING/-S [L *immolatus*, past part. of *immolare*, fr. *in-* 2in- + *mola* spelt grits; fr. the ancient custom of sprinkling victims with sacrificial salted meal; akin to *molere* to grind — more at MILL] **1 :** to offer in sacrifice (as to a deity); *esp* **:** to kill as a sacrificial victim **2 :** to sacrifice or abnegate (as oneself) usu. in the interests of some cause or objective ‹the end to which she has *immolated* all her affections —T.L.Peacock› ‹*immolating* himself for his family's sake› **3 :** KILL, DESTROY ‹the millions *immolated* in war› ‹a party of [African] hunting dogs would assuredly chase and ~ any single domestic canine —James Stevenson-Hamilton›

im·mo·la·tion \ˌimə'lāshən\ *n* -S [L *immolation-, immolatio*, fr. *immolatus* + *-ion-, -io* -ion] **1 :** the act of immolating or state of being immolated **2 :** something that is immolated

im·mo·la·tor \'iməˌlād·ə(r), -ātə-\ *n* -S [L, fr. *immolatus* + *-or*] **:** one that immolates

im·mo·ment \i+\ *or* **im·momentous** \ˌi(m)+\ *adj* [1in- + *moment* (n.) *or momentous*] **:** TRIFLING, UNIMPORTANT

im·moral \(ˈ)i(m), ə+\ *adj* [1in- + *moral*] **:** not moral **:** inconsistent with purity or good morals **:** contrary to conscience or moral law **:** WICKED, LICENTIOUS ‹an ~ man› ‹such ~ acts›; *broadly* **:** opposed to, critical of, or in conflict with generally or traditionally held moral principles ‹refusal to acknowledge the boundaries set by convention is the source of frequent denunciations of art as ~ —John Dewey› — compare UNMORAL

im·moralism \"+\ *n* [G *immoralismus*, fr. *immoral* (fr. F or E) + *-ismus* -ism] **:** an ethical viewpoint (as that of Nietzsche) that would institute a new scale of values in opposition to the traditional

im·moralist \"+\ *n* **1 :** an advocate or practicer of immorality **2 :** an advocate of immoralism

im·morality \ˌi(m)+\ *n* [1in- + *morality*] **1 :** the quality or state of being immoral **:** VICE, WICKEDNESS; *esp* **:** UNCHASTITY **2 :** an immoral act or practice

im·moralize \(ˈ)i(m), ə+\ *vt* **:** to make immoral **:** DEMORALIZE

im·morally \"+\ *adv* **:** in an immoral manner **:** with immorality

im·mor·ta·bil·i·ty \(ˌ)i(m)ˌmȯ(r)d·ə'biləd·ē, əˌm-\ *n* **:** the quality or state of being capable of attaining or fit for immortality

im·mor·ta·ble \(ˈ)i(m)ˈmȯ(r)d·əbəl, ə'm-\ *adj* [*immortal* + *-able*] **:** capable of attaining immortality

1im·mortal \(ˈ)i(m), ə+\ *adj* [ME, fr. L *immortalis*, fr. *in-* 1in- + *mortalis* mortal — more at MORTAL] **1 :** not mortal **:** exempt from liability to die ‹the ~ gods› **2 :** connected with or relating to immortality ‹I have ~ longings in me —Shak.› **3 :** destined to persist through the ages **:** exempt from oblivion **:** IMPERISHABLE, ABIDING ‹those ~ words› ‹his fame ~›

2immortal \"\ *n* **1 a :** an immortal being **:** one exempt from death **b immortals** *pl, often cap* **:** the gods of the Greek and Roman pantheon **2 a immortals** *pl, often cap* **:** a body of troops immortal in some way: as (1) **:** the royal bodyguard of ancient Persia whose number was always kept full (2) **:** troops famous for gallant behavior in war (3) **:** troops that never see war **b :** a person (as an author) whose fame is lasting **c** *usu cap* **:** any of the 40 members of the Académie française **3 a** *in Confucianism* **:** an ideal human being of antiquity **b** *in Taoism* **:** one that has reached a divine state that is the highest to which man can attain **c :** a Chinese saint **4** *also* **immortal hand :** a stud-poker hand that is sure to win

im·mortalism \"+\ *n* **:** a doctrine of or belief in the soul's immortality

im·mortalist \"+\ *n* **:** one that affirms a belief in immortalism

im·mor·tal·i·ty \ˌi(m)ˌmȯ(r)¦taləd·ē, -lətē, -i *sometimes* ēˌmȯ(r)- *or* ˌimə(r)-\ *n* [ME *immortalite*, fr. MF *immortalité*, fr. L *immortalitat-, immortalitas*, fr. *immortalis* + *-itat-, -itas* -ity] **:** the quality or state of being immortal: as **a :** exemption from death or annihilation **:** unending existence **:** everlasting life ‹the ~ of the soul› ‹human ~› **b :** exemption from oblivion **:** lasting fame ‹the ~ of these stirring words› ‹his deeds have earned him ~ in the hearts of men›

im·mor·tal·iz·able \i(m)'mȯ(r)d·ᵊlˌīzəbəl, ə'm-, -)tᵊl-, (ˌ)ē-\ *adj* **:** capable of being immortalized

im·mor·tal·iza·tion \-ə'zāshən, -ˌī'z-\ *n* -S [F *immortalisation*, fr. *immortaliser* to immortalize + *-ation*] **:** the act or process of making immortal; *also* **:** the state of being made immortal

im·mor·tal·ize \-ˌīz\ *vt* -ED/-ING/-S *see -ize in Explan Notes* [MF *immortaliser*, fr. *immortal* (fr. L *immortalis*) + *-iser* -ize — more at IMMORTAL] **:** to make immortal: **a :** to cause to live or exist forever **:** endow with everlasting life **b :** to exempt from oblivion **:** perpetuate in fame

im·mor·tal·iz·er \"ə(r)\ *n* -S **:** one that immortalizes something; *esp* **:** a writer who preserves in his work something of the present for posterity

im·mortally \(ˈ)i(m), ə+\ *adv* **1 :** ETERNALLY, EVERLASTINGLY, FOREVER, PERPETUALLY **2 :** to a superhuman or excessive degree **:** INFINITELY

im·mor·telle \ˌiˌmȯ(r)¦tel, ēˌ-\ *n* -S [F, fr. fem. of *immortel* immortal, fr. L *immortalis* — more at IMMORTAL] **1 :** EVERLASTING 3 **2** *or* **immortelle tree :** any of various coral trees; *esp* **:** a large red-flowered tree (*Erythrina micropteryx*) widely used in tropical America as an ornamental and as a shade tree in cacao plantations

im·mortification \(ˌ)i(m)+\ *n* [F, fr. MF, fr. ML *immortificatus* disciplined, fr. L *in-* 2in- + LL *mortificatus*, past part. of *mortificare* to mortify — more at MORTIFY] *archaic* **:** a lack of discipline (as of bodily appetites and desires)

im·motile \(ˈ)i(m), ə+\ *adj* [1in- + *motile*] **:** lacking motility **:** incapable of movement — **im·motility** \ˌi(m)\ *n*

im·motive \(ˈ)i(m)+\ *adj* [1in- + *motive*] **:** UNMOVING, IMMOVABLE

im·movability \(ˌ)i(m), ə+\ *n* **:** the quality or state of being immovable

1im·movable *also* **im·moveable** \(ˈ)i(m), ə+\ *adj* [ME *immovable*, fr. 1in- + *movable*] **1 :** incapable of being moved **:** firmly fixed **:** FAST ‹the ~ hills›; *broadly* **:** not moving or not intended to be moved **:** STATIONARY **2 a :** STEADFAST, UNALTERABLE, UNYIELDING ‹an ~ purpose› **b :** not capable of being moved in feeling or sympathies **:** UNIMPRESSIBLE, IMPASSIVE ‹a stern ~ man› **3 :** not liable to be removed **:** permanent in place or tenure **:** FIXED ‹an ~ estate› — **im·movableness** \"+\ *n*

2immovable *also* **immoveable** \"\ *n* **1 :** one that cannot be moved **2 immovables** *pl, Roman & civil law* **a :** lands, houses thereon, and all things adhering or belonging there by nature (as trees, minerals) or by act of man (as planted crops, fertilizer) — compare ACCESSION 2c **b :** all personal property permanently attached to immovable property that cannot be removed without injury to the latter — see FIXTURE 2c **c :** all personal property placed on immovable property by the owner for its service, improvement, or exploitation **d :** an interest or estate in immovable property **3** *Scots law* **:** heritable property as opposed to movable property

immovable feast *n* **:** an ecclesiastical feast that always occurs on the same day of the year

immovable fixture *n* **:** FIXTURE 2c(1)

im·movably \(ˈ)i(m), ə+\ *adv* [ME, fr. *immovable* + *-ly*] **:** so as to be incapable of movement or of being moved ‹hills brooding ~ over the town›

im·mund \ə'mənd\ *adj* [L *immundus*, fr. *in-* 1in- + *mundus* clean — more at MOTHER (dregs)] **:** UNCLEAN, FILTHY — **im·mun·di·ty** \-dəd·ē\ *n* -ES

1im·mune \ə'myün\ *adj* [L *immunis* exempt from public service, exempt, fr. *in-* 1in- + *-munis* (fr. *munia* services, obligations) — more at MEAN (common)] **1 a :** FREE, EXEMPT ‹~ from further taxation› ‹a book is a tool . . . and should be as ~, almost, from decoration as a crowbar or a cartridge —Holbrook Jackson› **b :** PROTECTED, GUARDED — usu. used with *from* or *against* ‹~ from political pressures by reason of his office› ‹a full life is ~ against boredom› **2** [F *immun*, fr. L *immunis*] **:** not susceptible or responsive — usu. used with *to* ‹~ to all pleas› ‹the Soviet Union has not been ~ to the pressures of coexistence —L.S.Feuer› ‹a streptococcus ~ to antibiotics›; *esp* **:** having a high degree of natural or acquired resistance to a disease ‹~ to diphtheria› **3 a :** having or producing antibodies to a corresponding antigen or hapten ‹an ~ serum› **b :** produced in response to the presence of a corresponding antigen ‹~ agglutinins› **4** *of cotton yarn* **:** treated so as to repel the usual dyes for cotton

2immune \"\ *n* -S **:** an immune individual

immune body *n* **:** ANTIBODY

im·muned \-nd\ *adj* [*immune* + *-ed*] **:** IMMUNIZED — used chiefly of domestic animals

immune globulin *or* **immune serum globulin** *n* **:** globulin from the blood of a person or animal immune to a particular disease

immune serum *n* **:** ANTISERUM

im·mun·ist \ə'myünəst, 'imyən-\ *n* -S [F *immuniste*, fr. *immun* + *-iste* -ist] **:** one that enjoys an immunity (as from service or payment of some due)

im·mu·ni·ty \ə'myünəd·ē, -ətē, -i\ *n* -ES [L *immunitas*, fr. *immunis* + *-itas* -ity] **1 a :** freedom or exemption from a charge, duty, obligation, office, tax, imposition, penalty, or service esp. as granted by law to a person or class of persons **b :** a freedom granted to a special category of persons from the normal burdens and duties arising out of a legal relationship with other persons ⟨legislative ~⟩ ⟨judicial ~⟩ **2** *obs* **:** unrestrained license or an instance of it **3 a :** lack of susceptibility (as to a natural hazard) ⟨this alloy has complete ~ to rust⟩ ⟨no one has assured ~ from error⟩ **b :** freedom from or security against something noxious or injurious ⟨the long ~ of America from outside threats or dangers —D.W. Brogan⟩ **4** [F *immunité*, fr. *immun* + *-ité* -ity] **:** a condition of being able or the capacity to resist a particular disease esp. through preventing development of a pathogenic microorganism or by counteracting the effects of its products — see ACTIVE IMMUNITY, ACQUIRED IMMUNITY, NATURAL IMMUNITY, PASSIVE IMMUNITY

im·mu·ni·za·tion \ˌimyənə'zāshən, ˌnī'z- *also* ə̇ˌmyü\ *n* -s **:** the creation of immunity usu. against a particular disease ⟨~ against smallpox⟩; *esp* **:** treatment of an organism for the purpose of making it immune to subsequent attack by a particular pathogen

im·mu·nize \'imyəˌnīz\ *vt* -ED/-ING/-s *see -ize in Explan Notes* [G *immunisieren*, fr. *immun* immune (fr. F) + *-isieren* -ize — more at IMMUNE] **:** to make immune ⟨the best known examples . . . are in semiarid regions, a circumstance that has *immunized* the scarps from attack by vigorous consequent rivers —C.A.Cotton⟩; *esp* **:** to cause to produce antibodies against an antigen or hapten

immuno- *comb form* [ISV, fr. *immune*] **:** immune and **:** immunity ⟨*immuno*compatible⟩ ⟨*immuno*diagnosis⟩ ⟨*immuno*-body⟩

im·mu·no·biologic *also* **immunobiological** \ˌimyə(ˌ)nō, ə̇ˌmyü(ˌ)nō+\ *adj* [*immuno-* + *biologic, biological*] **:** of or relating to the physiological reactions characteristic of the immune state ⟨~ anomalies in leprosy —*Biol. Abstracts*⟩ — **im·mu·no·biology** \"+\ *n*

im·mu·no·chemical \"+\ *adj* [*immuno-* + *chemical*] **:** of or relating to immunochemistry — **im·mu·no·chemically** \"+\ *adv*

im·mu·no·chemist \"+\ *n* [*immuno-* + *chemist*] **:** a specialist in immunochemistry

im·mu·no·chemistry \"+\ *n* [ISV *immuno-* + *chemistry*] **:** a branch of chemistry that deals with substances (as antibodies, antigens, or haptens) and reactions (as concerned in the phenomena of immunity-antibody production)

im·mu·no·gen \ə̇'myünəjən, -ˌjen\ *n* -s [fr. *Immunogen*, a trademark] **:** an antigen that is prepared by extracting fresh living organisms and is usu. highly specific in antigenic action and low in protein of the organism

im·mu·no·genesis \ˌimyə(ˌ)nō, ə̇ˌmyü(ˌ)nō+\ *n* [NL, fr. *immuno-* + *genesis*] **:** immunity production

im·mu·no·genetic *also* **immunogenetical** \"+\ *adj* [*immuno-* + *genetic, genetical*] **:** of or relating to immunogenetics

im·mu·no·genetics \"+\ *n pl but sing or pl in constr* [*immuno-* + *genetics*] **1 :** a branch of immunology that deals with the interrelation of immunity to disease and genetic makeup **2 :** a study of biological interrelationships by serological means

im·mu·no·gen·ic \"+ˈjenik\ *adj* [*immuno-* + *-genic*] **:** producing immunity — compare ANTIGENIC — **im·mu·no·gen·i·cal·ly** \-nə̇k(ə)lē\ *adv* — **im·mu·no·ge·nic·i·ty** \-jə'nisəd·ē\ *n* -ES

im·mu·no·log·ic \"+ˈläjik\ *also* **im·mu·no·log·i·cal** \-jə̇kəl\ *adj* **:** of or relating to immunology — **im·mu·no·log·i·cal·ly** \-jə̇k(ə)lē\ *adv*

im·mu·nol·o·gist \ˌimyə'näləjə̇st\ *n* -s **:** a specialist in immunology

im·mu·nol·o·gy \-jē\ *n* -ES [ISV *immuno-* + *-logy*] **1 :** a science that deals with the phenomena and causes of immunity **2 :** a treatise on immunology

im·mu·no·therapy \ˌimyə(ˌ)nō, ə̇ˌmyü(ˌ)nō+\ *n* [ISV *immuno-* + *therapy*] **:** treatment of or prophylaxis against disease that is based on the production of antibodies and induction of immunity and that chiefly employs antigens or antigenic preparations (as antisera, toxoids, vaccines)

im·mu·no·transfusion \"+\ *n* [ISV *immuno-* + *transfusion*] **:** transfusion of blood from a donor in whom there has been stimulated the production of antibodies for an infectious agent affecting the recipient

im·mu·ra·tion \ˌimyə'rāshən\ *n* -s **:** act of immuring or state of being immured

im·mure \ə̇'myù(ə)r, -ùə\ *vt* -ED/-ING/-S [ML *immurare*, fr. L *in-* ²in- + *murus* wall — more at MURAL] **1** *obs* **:** to enclose or fortify with a wall **2 a :** to enclose within or as if within walls ⟨*immured* in an isolated outpost⟩ ⟨scientists who — themselves in special research⟩ **b :** to shut up **:** IMPRISON, INCARCERATE ⟨a fairy princess *immured* in a tower⟩ **3 :** to build into a wall ⟨an ancient altar half-*immured*⟩; *esp* **:** to punish by entombing within a wall or between walls ⟨a nun who broke her vow might be *immured*⟩ ⟨*immuring* these heretics⟩

im·mure·ment \-ü(ə)rmənt, -ùəm-\ *n* -s **:** the quality or state of being immured ⟨the ~ within colleges of the artist, the poet in residence —Marcus Cunliffe⟩

im·musical \(ˈ)i(m), ə+\ *adj* [¹*in-* + *musical*] **:** INHARMONIOUS, UNMUSICAL, DISCORDANT — **im·musically** \"+\ *adv*

im·mutability \(ˌ)i(m), ə+\ *n* [L *immutabilitas*, fr. *immutabilis* immutable + *-itas* -ity] **:** the quality or state of being immutable

im·mutable \(ˈ)i(m), ə+\ *adj* [ME, fr. L *immutabilis*, fr. *in-* ¹in + *mutabilis* mutable — more at MUTABLE] **:** not capable or susceptible of change **:** UNCHANGEABLE, UNCHANGING, INVARIABLE, UNALTERABLE ⟨~ laws⟩ — **im·mutableness** \"+\ *n* — **im·mutably** \"+\ *adv*

immutation *n* [L *immutation-*, *immutatio*, fr. *immutatus* (past part. of *immutare* to change, alter, fr. *in-* ²in- + *mutare* to change) + *-ion-*, *-io* -ion — more at MUTABLE] *obs* **:** CHANGE, ALTERATION, MUTATION

immy *abbr* immediately

imo·chagh *also* **imo·shagh** \ˌēmōˈshäg\ *n* -s *usu cap* **:** a member of the southern branch of the Tuareg people

imo·hagh \ˌēmōˈhäg\ *n* -s *usu cap* **:** a member of the northern branch of the Tuareg people

imo·ni·um \(ˈ)iˈmōnēəm, (ˈ)ī,m-\ *n* -s [*imine* + *ammonium*] **:** ammonium in which a bivalent radical is a substituent

imou pine \'ē,mü-\ *n* [prob. native name in New Zealand] *NewZeal* **:** RIMU

¹**imp** \'imp\ *n* -s [ME *impe*, fr. OE *impa*, fr. *impian* — more at ²IMP] **1 a** *obs* **:** SHOOT, BUD, SLIP; *also* **:** GRAFT **b** *archaic* **:** OFFSPRING, PROGENY, CHILD, SCION **2 a** *archaic* **:** an evil or malicious child **b :** a small demon, devil, or wicked spirit ⟨~s released from a sorcerer's bottle —William Peden⟩ **c :** a mischievous child **:** URCHIN ⟨as disagreeable a young ~ as you'd ask to see —G.B.Shaw⟩

²**imp** \"\ *vt* -ED/-ING/-S [ME *impen*, fr. OE *impian*; akin to OHG *impfōn* to graft; both fr. a prehistoric OHG-OE word derived fr. (assumed) VL *imputare* (whence OF *enter* to graft), fr. L *in-* ²in- + *putare* to cut, prune — more at PAVE] **1** *archaic* **:** to graft into or on **:** IMPLANT **2 a :** to graft or repair (a wing, tail, or feather) with a feather to improve a falcon's flying capacity **b** *archaic* **:** to fasten wings on or to **:** equip with wings **c** *archaic* **:** eke out **:** REPAIR, INCREASE, STRENGTHEN, EQUIP

imp *abbr* **1** imperative **2** [L *imperator; imperatrix*] emperor; empress **3** imperfect **4** imperial **5** implement **6** import; imported; importer **7** important **8** impression **9** imprimatur **10** [L *imprimis*] in the first place **11** imprint **12** improved; improvement

¹**im·pact** \(ˌ)imˈpakt\ *vb* -ED/-ING/-S [L *impactus*, past part. of *impingere* to strike or push at or against — more at IMPINGE] *vt* **1 a :** to fix firmly by or as if by packing or wedging ⟨a substance ~*ed* in the upper intestine⟩ ⟨the mule lay . . . ~*ed* in the loam —Ben Johnson⟩ **b :** to press together or mix into a clotted, wedged, or tightly bound mass ⟨goblets of clay and drops of sweat ~*ed* into a hot mulch —*Time*⟩ ⟨puns that can ~ the scabrous with the sublime in a word —Eleanor Clark⟩ **c :** to press down and wedge or force in or under ⟨the golden nuggets of wisdom being ~*ed* in tons of verbosity —Dwight MacDonald⟩ **d :** to fill up **:** CROWD, CONGEST ⟨~s the area with military and defense workers and their families —Tait Trussell⟩ **2 a :** to have an impact upon **:** make contact with **:** impinge upon ⟨the images ~*ing* the human retina —T.H. Benton b. 1889⟩ **b :** to drive or transmit with a forceful impact ⟨the critic who . . . is supposed to ~ his messianic visions of jazz perfection to musicians struggling at his feet —*Saturday Rev.*⟩ ~ *vi* **:** to have an impact ⟨the world did not ~ upon me until I got to the post office —Christopher Morley⟩ **:** impinge or make contact esp. forcefully ⟨image the ~*ing* ball splashing into the loose mass of surface balls —R.A.Bagnold⟩ ⟨how will total war ~ on such a poet —*Times Lit. Supp.*⟩

²**im·pact** \'imˌpakt\ *n* -s **1 a :** the act of impinging or striking (as of one body against another or of a stream squarely against a fixed or moving surface) **b :** a forceful contact, collision, or onset **:** the degree or concentration of force in a collision **:** the impetus communicated in or as if in a collision ⟨felt the terrific ~ of the blow⟩ ⟨air rendered incandescent by the vehemence of the ~s of the electrons against its molecules —K.K.Darrow⟩ **2 :** the force of impression of one thing on another: **a :** the notable ability to arouse and hold attention and interest **:** the power of impressing ⟨a way of securing a maximum of dramatic ~ on the reader —W.M.Frohock⟩ **b :** a concentrated force producing change **:** an esp. forceful effect checking or forcing change **:** an impelling or compelling effect ⟨the ~ of modern science and technology upon society as a whole —Harrison Brown⟩ ⟨the ~ of terror⟩ ⟨loses the ~ of the basic story in a maze of philosophies —Whitney Betts⟩; *also* **:** the degree of such force ⟨American youth in the early 1930s felt spiritually paralyzed by the ~ of confusing events —J.W.Chase⟩

syn BRUNT, COLLISION, CLASH, SHOCK, BUMP, JOLT, JAR, IMPINGEMENT, PERCUSSION, CONCUSSION: IMPACT now commonly suggests the driving impetus or momentum in or as if in a collision or the dynamic force in impressing or compelling change ⟨the aunt's home shook at the *impact* and the windows were smashed —Norman Cousins⟩ ⟨the *impact* of world war on the lives of countless millions —R.H.Jackson⟩ BRUNT now indicates the major part of the force of an onset, collision, jar, stress, or strain ⟨a number of the leaders had . . . fled from the persecution, leaving the little people to bear its *brunt* —Maurice Samuel⟩ ⟨the national financial panic was felt throughout the state, but it was Duluth that bore the *brunt* of the disaster . . . it was rendered almost totally bankrupt —*Amer. Guide Series: Minn.*⟩ COLLISION implies a forceful running together of more or less complex things through accident and with resulting harm, or a sharp opposition or conflict ⟨the *collision* between two ships in a fog⟩ ⟨the buyers and sellers of capital could do almost as they pleased with it, no matter how much damage a *collision* between them might bring about —F.L.Allen⟩ CLASH suggests a noisy, metallic striking together, a sharp skirmish or brawl, or a sharp direct variance, opposition, or contrast ⟨roll of cannon and *clash* of arms —Alfred Tennyson⟩ ⟨fishermen from the Michigan mainland . . . violently opposed further settlement by the Mormons. *Clashes* occurred at several places —*Amer. Guide Series: Mich.*⟩ ⟨a *clash* or conflict between his demands and the strict limitations upon the supply⟩ SHOCK may refer to a very forcible onslaught or violent collision literally or figuratively ⟨the *shock* of the cavalry charge⟩ ⟨the discoveries of physical science came as a *shock* to the general mind of Europe —Laurence Binyon⟩ ⟨the *shock* of physical dislocation effected a very considerable modification of old attitudes —John Dewey⟩ BUMP indicates a sudden thudding blow, esp. one checking forward progress with some force ⟨a *bump* on the head⟩ ⟨the springs were broken by the bad *bump* during the detour⟩ JOLT refers to an abrupt violent blow or movement tending to shake, agitate, or unsettle, or, figuratively, to a shock or major surprise ⟨newly picked fruit being bruised by the *jolts* of shipment⟩ ⟨we have no offensive naval policy . . . I fear there will be some horrible *jolts* in the future —F.D. Roosevelt⟩ JAR usu. refers to some wrenching dislodgment or break in continuity ⟨the bottles were cracked by the *jars* they underwent in shipment⟩; it may refer to an agitation or shaking up ⟨the fall gave him a *jar*⟩ IMPINGEMENT now is less likely to indicate violent collision than lighter overlaying or more subtle infringement or penetration ⟨each little *impingement* of sound struck on her consciousness —Adria Langley⟩ PERCUSSION, more common in technical than in general language, may suggest a sharp, purposive tapping or knocking ⟨musical instruments that sound by *percussion*, as the drum⟩ CONCUSSION, which may mean a blow or collision, is now more likely to suggest the shattering effects, including noise, of a collision or explosion, or the stunning, weakening effect of a heavy blow ⟨from the shelter survivors heard the *concussions* of the bombing raid⟩ ⟨suffered a *concussion* in the collision⟩

impact bomb *n* **:** a bomb that detonates on striking an object

impacted *adj* **1 :** driven together (as the broken ends of a fractured bone) **2 a :** wedged into a passage (as a fetus in the birth canal, a calculus in a duct, a foreign body in the larynx) **b** *of a tooth* **:** wedged between the jawbone and another tooth ⟨~ and unerupted normal teeth are excised —K.H. Thoma⟩

impacted crop *n* **:** crop-bound of poultry

impact extrusion *n* **:** a process in which metal is forced by a quick blow to flow around a punch; *also* **:** the product so formed

im·pact·ful \'ˌ=ˌfəl, ˌ='=-\ *adj* **:** having a forceful impact **:** producing a marked impression ⟨some of the most ~ heroines of current films —Martha Wolfenstein & Nathan Leites⟩

im·pac·tion \imˈpakshən\ *n* -s [LL *impaction-*, *impactio*, fr. L *impactus* + *-ion-*, *-io* -ion] **:** the act of becoming or the state of being impacted; *specif* **:** lodgment or an instance of lodgment of something (as a tooth or feces or calculi) in a body passage or cavity ⟨fecal ~⟩ ⟨~ of the rumen⟩

im·pact·ite \'imˌpakˌtīt\ *n* -s [²*impact* + *-ite*] **:** a glassy object produced by fusion of rock or meteoritic fragments by the heat developed from the impact of a meteorite on the earth's surface

im·pac·tive \(ˈ)imˈpaktiv\ *adj* **1 :** having an impact or marked effect ⟨the ~ wonder that is in natural things —R.L.Cook⟩ ⟨the ~ scrutiny of strange faces —Scott Fitzgerald⟩ **2 :** resulting from impact ⟨~ shocks —G.L.Riddell⟩

im·pac·tor *or* **im·pact·er** \-tə(r)\ *n* -s **:** a machine (as a steam hammer or a pile driver) or part that operates by striking blows

impact parameter *n* **:** the perpendicular distance from the center of the force field to the initial path of the particle deflected by the field in nuclear scattering

impact pressure *n* **:** DYNAMIC PRESSURE

impact strength *n* **:** the resistance of a material (as metal or ceramic ware) to fracture by a blow, expressed in terms of the amount of energy absorbed before fracture

impact test *n* **:** a test for determining the impact strength of a material ⟨the *impact test* of the pottery was made with a dropping metal ball⟩

impact tube *n* **:** a Pitot tube having its orifice headed directly into an oncoming stream of fluid

impact wrench *n* **:** an electrically or pneumatically operated wrench that gives a rapid succession of sudden torques

impaint *vt* [²*in-* + *paint* (n.)] *obs* **:** PAINT, DEPICT

¹**im·pair** \imˈpa(a)(ə)r, -pe|, |ə\ *vb* -ED/-ING/-S [ME *empeiren*, *empairen*, *impairen*, fr. MF *empeirer*, *emperer*, *empirer*, fr. OF *empeirier*, *empirier*, fr. (assumed) VL *impejorare*, fr. L *in-* ²in- + LL *pejorare* to make worse — more at PEJORATIVE] *vt* **:** to make worse **:** diminish in quantity, value, excellence, or strength **:** do harm to **:** DAMAGE, LESSEN ⟨the output of produce was ~*ed* by the cold weather⟩ ⟨~ their health by wild living⟩ ⟨had to teach so many pupils it ~*ed* his own musical career⟩ ⟨his pleasure was ~*ed* by worry about money⟩ ~ *vi*, *obs* **:** DETERIORATE **syn** see INJURE

²**impair** \"\ *n* -s *archaic* **:** IMPAIRMENT, DETERIORATION, INJURY

³**im·pair** \'imˌpa(ə)r, -pe|, |ə\ *n* -s [F, fr. *impair* odd, fr. L *impar* — more at IMPAR] **:** the odd numbers in roulette when a bet is made on them ⟨made a large bet on ~⟩

im·pair·able \imˈpa(a)rəbəl, -per-\ *adj* **:** capable of being impaired

impaired life *or* **impaired risk** *n* **:** a person whose physical condition according to insurance ratings is below that required for life insurance at standard rates

im·pair·er \-rə(r)\ *n* -s **:** one that impairs ⟨lack of confidence is often an ~ of efficiency⟩

im·pair·ment \-a(a)(ə)rmənt, -e|, |əm-\ *n* -s [ME *empeirment*, fr. MF *empeirement*, fr. OF, fr. *empeirier*, to impair + *-ment* — more at IMPAIR] **:** the act of impairing or the state of being impaired **:** INJURY ⟨physical and mental diseases and ~s of man —*Current Biog.*⟩ **:** DETERIORATION ⟨any ~ . . . of his bodily vigor through sickness or age —J.G.Frazer⟩ **:** LESSENING ⟨an ~ of the pain⟩

im·pala *also* **im·pal·la** \imˈpalə, -ˈpälə\ *n, pl* **impalas** *or* **impala** *also* **impallas** *or* **impalla** [Zulu] **:** a large African antelope (*Aepyceros melampus*) of a brownish bay color, white below, with a black crescentic stripe on the haunch, the male being distinguished by slender annulated lyrate horns

impala lily *n* **:** a succulent-stemmed shrub (*Adenium multiflorum*) of the family Apocynaceae of southern Africa with showy pink and white flowers borne after the leaves fall

im·palatable \(ˈ)im+\ *adj* [¹*in-* + *palatable*] **:** UNPALATABLE

im·pale \əmˈpāl, *esp before pause or consonant* -āəl\ *also* **em·pale** \əm,em-\ *vt* [MF & ML; MF *empaler*, fr. ML *impalare*, fr. L *in-* ²in- + *palus* stake, pole — more at POLE] **1** *archaic* **a :** to enclose with poles, stakes, or a palisade **b :** to hem in **:** ENCLOSE, SURROUND, CONFINE, ENCIRCLE **2 a :** to pierce or pierce through with a pole or with something pointed; *esp* **:** torture or kill by fixing on a sharp stake **b :** to fix in a position by piercing or piercing through with something pointed or to cause to be so fixed ⟨the head . . . *impaled* upon the bowsprit of his sloop —Nike Anderson⟩ ⟨having some man rush at you so that he *impaled* his chest upon the ice pick —Erle Stanley Gardner⟩ ⟨a butterfly *impaled* by a pin —Louis Bromfield⟩ **c :** to fix in a position as if by piercing or piercing through in such a manner **:** fix in a position of defeat or helplessness or one from which there is no escape or retreat ⟨*impaled* itself on a dilemma —S.W.Chapman⟩ ⟨a question on which . . . he had always been insecurely *impaled* —Marcia Davenport⟩ ⟨*impaled* his victim neatly with his logic —V.L.Parrington⟩ **d :** to deflate by telling logic or biting wit **3 :** to join or conjoin in heraldry by impalement

im·pale·ment \-mənt\ *n* -s [MF *empalement*, fr. *empaler* + *-ment*] **1 :** the act of impaling or the state of being impaled: as **a** (1) *archaic* **:** ENCLOSING, ENCIRCLING, CONFINING (2) **:** the union of two or more coats of arms side by side on a heraldic shield divided palewise **b :** a piercing or piercing through with a pale, spike, or other pointed thing (as for fixing in a position or by an accidental fall) **c** (1) **:** a placing or a being placed in an inescapable and awkward position (as of defeat or helplessness) (2) **:** a deflating or a being deflated by telling logic or biting wit **2 :** an enclosing fence or palisade

im·palpability \(ˌ)im+\ *n* **:** the quality or state of being impalpable

¹**im·palpable** \(ˈ)im+\ *adj* [¹*in-* + *palpable*] **1 a :** incapable of being felt by the touch ⟨an ~ pulse⟩ **:** not palpable **:** INTANGIBLE ⟨as ~ as a dream —Nathaniel Hawthorne⟩ ⟨the ~ aura of power that emanated from him —Osbert Sitwell⟩ **b :** extremely fine so that no grains or grit can be felt ⟨an ~ cloud⟩ ⟨an ~ powder⟩ ⟨the ~ mud —*Encyc. Britannica*⟩ **2 :** not readily apprehended by the mind ⟨an ~ beauty of style⟩ — **im·palpably** \"+\ *adv*

²**impalpable** \"\ *n* -s **:** something impalpable ⟨an intellectual, dealing eternally in ~s⟩

im·panate \imˈpanə̇t, 'impəˌnāt\ *or* **im·pa·nat·ed** \'impəˌnād·ə̇d\ *adj* [*impanate* fr. ML *impanatus*, fr. L *in-* ²in- + L *panis* bread + *-atus* -ate; *impanated* fr. ML *impanatus* + E *-ed* — more at FOOD] **:** embodied in bread in impanation

im·pa·na·tion \ˌimpə'nāshən\ *n* -s [ML *impanation-*, *impanatio*, fr. *impanatus* impanate + L *-ion-*, *-io* -ion] **1 :** the inclusion of the body of Christ in the eucharistic bread in a hypostatic union without change in either substance — compare INVINATION **2 :** the Christian theological doctrine affirming the real presence of Christ in the Eucharist by impanation and invination — compare CONSUBSTANTIATION, TRANSUBSTANTIATION

im·pa·na·tor \'impəˌnād·ə(r)\ *n* -s [ML, fr. *impanatus* + L *-or*] **:** one holding the doctrine of impanation

im·panel \əm+\ *also* **em·panel** \əm, em+\ *vt* [²*in-* or ¹*en-* + *panel* (n.)] **:** to enter in or on a panel **:** enroll (as a list of jurors) in a court of justice

im·papy·rat·ed \ˌimpə'pīˌrād·ə̇d, imˈpapəˌr-\ *adj* [²*in-* + *papyrus* + *-ate* + *-ed*] **:** recorded on or as if on papyrus

im·par \'imˌpär\ *adj* [NL, fr. L, unequal, uneven, fr. *in-* ¹in- + *par* equal — more at PAIR] *anat* **:** UNPAIRED, AZYGOUS

im·paradise \əm+\ *or* **em·paradise** \əm,em+\ *vt* [²*in-* or ¹*en-* + *paradise* (n.)] **1 a :** to put in paradise ⟨an *imparadised* saint⟩ **b :** to make supremely happy **:** transport with delight or joy ⟨*imparadised* in her lover's arms⟩ **2 :** to convert into a paradise

imparalleled *adj* [¹*in-* + *paralleled*] *obs* **:** UNPARALLELED

im·paripinnate \(ˌ)im+\ *adj* [NL *imparipinnatus*, fr. L *impar* + NL *-i-* + *pinnatus* pinnate — more at PINNATE] **:** ODD-PINNATE

im·parisyllabic \(ˌ)im+\ *adj* [*impar* + E *-i-* + *-syllabic*] **:** not having the same number of syllables in all declensional cases ⟨the Latin words *lapis*, *lapidis* and *mens*, *mentis* are ~⟩

im·parity \(ˈ)im+\ *n* [LL *imparitas*, fr. L *impar* + *-itas* -ity] **:** difference esp. of degree, rank, excellence, number **:** INEQUALITY, DISPARITY

impark *vt* [ME *imparken*, fr. AF *emparker*, fr. OF *en-* ¹en- + *park*, *parc* — more at PARK] **1** *obs* **a :** to enclose or confine in a park **b :** ENCLOSE **2** *obs* **:** to enclose (as woods) for a park

im·parl \əmˈpär(ə)l\ *or* **em·parl** \əm,em-\ *vi* -ED/-ING/-S [ME *enparlen*, fr. MF *emparler*, fr. *en-* ¹en- + *parler* to speak — more at PARLEY] **:** to have an imparlance **:** confer esp. regarding settlement of a dispute

im·par·lance \-lən(t)s\ *n* [AF *emparlance*, fr. MF *emparler* + *-ance*] **1** *obs* **:** mutual discourse **:** CONFERENCE, DISCUSSION **2 a :** time formerly given to a party before pleading in a lawsuit for making an amicable settlement **b :** the delay or continuance of a suit **c :** a petition or leave for such a delay

im·part \əmˈpär|t, -pȧ|, *usu* |d.+V\ *vb* [MF&L; MF *impartir*, fr. L *impartire*, *impertire*, fr. *in-* ²in- + *partire* to divide, part — more at PART] *vt* **1 :** to give or grant (what one has or of what one has) or give rise to (in another) by contact, association, or influence ⟨~*ed* his fortune to the needy⟩ ⟨his manner of speaking ~*ed* authority to a mediocre plan⟩ ⟨the chief hope of ~*ing* a new direction and purpose to the lives of prisoners —*Times Lit. Supp.*⟩ **:** COMMUNICATE, TRANSMIT ⟨his very position ~*ed* a political significance to whatever he did⟩ ⟨their elegance was ~*ed* to the passengers . . . who were forced to sit ramrod straight —*Fortnight*⟩ ⟨a sudden motion ~*ed* to the air —*Encyc. Americana*⟩ ⟨the musician ~*ed* a lyric quality to the piece⟩ ⟨~ knowledge to students⟩ **2 :** to communicate the knowledge of **:** DISCLOSE ⟨told to ~ what he knew to the police⟩; *esp* **:** to give utterance to **:** reveal in writing or speaking ⟨~*ed* her plans to him in their talk⟩ ⟨~*ed* the events in a letter⟩ ~ *vi* **:** GIVE, BESTOW ⟨the aspect of receiving, and the aspect of ~*ing* —S.W.Rowland & Brian Magee⟩

im·par·ta·tion \ˌimˌpärˈtāshən, -pȧ't-\ *n* -s **:** the act of imparting or the state of being imparted

im·partial \(ˈ)im, əm+\ *adj* [¹*in-* + *partial*] **:** not partial; *esp* **:** not favoring one more than another **:** treating all alike **:** UNBIASED, EQUITABLE ⟨in any criminal trial . . . the jury may be ~ but it is never neutral —M.C.Bernays⟩ ⟨law shall be uniform and ~ —B.N.Cardozo⟩ **syn** see FAIR

impartial chairman *n* **:** an arbitrator, referee, or umpire jointly employed by union and management to interpret or to resolve differences arising out of the terms of a labor agreement

im·partiality \(ˌ)im, əm+\ *n* **:** the quality or state of being impartial **:** freedom from bias or favoritism **:** DISINTERESTEDNESS, FAIRNESS ⟨the ~ of the scientific spirit —John Dewey⟩ ⟨with wonderful ~, the play admits shenanigans and sentiment —*Time*⟩

im·partially \(ˈ)im, əm+\ *adv* **:** in an impartial manner **:** without bias or special favor ⟨smiled at them both ~ —T.B. Costain⟩

im·par·tial·ness *n* -ES **:** the quality or state of being impartial

im·partibility \(ˌ)im+\ *n* **:** the quality or state of being impartible

im·partible \(ˈ)im+\ *adj* [LL *impartibilis*, fr. L *in-* ¹in- + *partibilis* partible — more at PARTIBLE] **:** not partible **:** not subject to partition ⟨decided that the office should be held jointly by his two sisters, an absurd decision which ignored the historic principle that great offices of state are ~ —G.H. White⟩ ⟨an ~ inheritance⟩ — **im·partibly** \"+\ *adv*

im·participable \ˌim+\ *adj* [ˡin- + *participable*] **:** not participable **:** incapable of being shared ⟨an ~ office⟩

im·par·tite \(ˈ)im¦pär,tīt\ *adj* [LL *impartitus*, fr. L *in-* ˡin- + *partitus*, past part. of *partire* to divide — more at PART] **:** UNDIVIDED

im·part·ment \imˈpärtmənt\ *n* -s **:** the act of imparting or something that is imparted **:** COMMUNICATION, TRANSMISSION

im·passability \(ˌ)im+\ *n* **:** the quality or state of being impassable ⟨stopped by the complete ~ of the road⟩

im·passable \(ˈ)im+\ *adj* [ˡin- + *passable*] **:** incapable of being passed: as **a :** incapable of being traveled, traveled through, or crossed ⟨an ~ road⟩ ⟨an ~ jungle⟩ ⟨an ~ river⟩ **b :** incapable of being put into circulation ⟨counterfeit bills so crude they were ~⟩ **c :** INSURMOUNTABLE ⟨an ~ obstacle to discussion⟩ — **im·passableness** \"+\ *n* — **im·passably** \"+\ *adv*

im·passe \ˈim,pas, -paa(ə)s, -pais, -pȧs *also* imˈp- *or* ˈam,p- *or* amˈp-\ *n* -s [F, fr. *in-* ˡin- + *-passe* (fr. *passer* to pass — more at PASS)] **1 :** an impassable road or way **:** BLIND ALLEY, CUL-DE-SAC **2 a :** a predicament affording no obvious escape ⟨placed himself in an impossible ~ by at one and the same time attacking the heads of the party and recognizing its supreme authority —*Times Lit. Supp.*⟩ **b :** DEADLOCK ⟨negotiations between the two parties had reached an ~ since neither side would compromise in any way⟩

im·passibility \(ˌ)im, əm+\ *n* -ES [ME *impassibilite*, fr. MF or LL; MF *impassibilité*, fr. LL *impassibilitat-, impassibilitas*, fr. *impassibilis* + *-itat-, -itas* -ity] **:** the quality or state of being impassible ⟨the ~ or aloofness she showed sometimes toward me —Mary McCarthy⟩

im·passible \əm, (ˈ)im+\ *adj* [ME, fr. MF or LL; MF, fr. LL *impassibilis*, fr. L *in-* ˡin- + *passibilis* passible — more at PASSIBLE] **1 a :** incapable of suffering or of experiencing pain ⟨the Godhead is ~, for where there is perfection and unity, there can be no suffering —Aldous Huxley⟩ **b :** incapable of being harmed **:** inaccessible to injury ⟨as ~ as a ghost —Walker Percy⟩ **2 :** incapable of feeling **:** IMPASSIVE, UNFEELING, COLD ⟨the murderer stood ~ gazing down at his victim⟩ — **im·pas·si·bly** \-əblē, -li\ *adv*

im·pas·sion \əmˈpashən, -paash-,-paish-\ *vt* **impassioned; impassioned; impassioning** \-sh(ə)niŋ\ **impassions** [prob. fr. It *impassionare*, fr. *in-* ²in- (fr. L) + *passione* passion, fr. LL *passion-, passio* — more at PASSION] **:** to move or affect strongly **:** arouse the feelings or passions of ⟨dampens the ardor of the most ~ed newcomer —*Amer. Guide Series: Tenn.*⟩ ⟨the ideal of an elected emperor that ~ed the revolutionaries —Norbert Mühlen⟩ **:** fill with passion or mark by evidence of strong feeling ⟨public speaking is more ~ed than private speaking —A.T. Weaver⟩

ˡim·pas·sion·ate \-sh(ə)nət, *usu* -əd.+V\ *adj* [It *impassionato*, past part. of *impassionare*] **:** IMPASSIONED — **im·pas·sion·ate·ly** *adv*

²im·pas·sion·ate \-shə,nāt, *usu* -ād.+V\ *vt, archaic* **:** IMPASSION

³im·passionate \(ˈ)im+\ *adj* [ˡin- + *passionate*] *archaic* **:** without passion or feeling **:** DISPASSIONATE

im·pas·sioned \əmˈpashənd, -paash-,-paish-\ *adj* **:** actuated or characterized by or filled with passion or zeal **:** showing great warmth of feeling **:** ARDENT ⟨an ~ oration⟩ ⟨the expression of ~ love of ideal beauty —Richard Garnett †1906⟩

syn PASSIONATE, ARDENT, FERVENT, FERVID, PERFERVID: IMPASSIONED indicates intense, strong, and fiery feeling demanding expression ⟨much would I have given to have understood some of his *impassioned* bursts; when he tossed his arms overhead, stamped, scowled, and glared, till he looked like the very Angel of Vengeance —Herman Melville⟩ ⟨as his *impassioned* language did its work the multitude rose into fury —J.A.Froude⟩ PASSIONATE applies to vehemence or violence of emotion sometimes extinguishing rationality ⟨he heard for the first time mamma's *passionate* appeal to him never to let Judy forget mamma —Rudyard Kipling⟩ ⟨may profess Socialism or Communism in *passionate* harangues from one end of the country to the other, and even suffer martyrdom for it —G.B. Shaw⟩ ⟨it had not been condemned in the court of human reason, but lynched outside of it by the *passionate* and uncompromisingly ruthless war spirit, common to Communists and Fascists —M.R.Cohen⟩ ARDENT is almost always complimentary and may apply to the fiery or warm expression of lasting intense zeal and militancy ⟨an *ardent* Jeffersonian, vigorously partisan in the pulpit —H.E.Starr⟩ ⟨a man of violent temper, strong prejudices and an *ardent* Tory had left Virginia because of the unpopularity he had stirred up there against himself —*Amer. Guide Series: Md.*⟩ FERVENT may connote a depth and intensity of glowing feeling, often sustained and steady ⟨a strong and popular preacher, *fervent*, sometimes fiery, inclined to speak everywhere as though addressing a congregation —J.A.Faulkner⟩ ⟨a *fervent* loyalty such as soldiers feel for a general who leads them in some cause dear to all —Rebecca West⟩ FERVID may apply to a warmly or even feverishly expressed emotion, often spontaneous and always intense ⟨because his *fervid* manner of lovemaking offended her English phlegm —Arnold Bennett⟩ ⟨the most *fervid* and momentous oratory of Revolutionary days —*Amer. Guide Series: Mass.*⟩ PERFERVID may suggest extreme emotional excitement, sometimes overwrought or factitious ⟨in his *perfervid* flag-waving moments —S.H.Adams⟩

im·pas·sioned·ly \-n(ə)dlē, -li\ *adv* **:** in an impassioned manner

im·pas·sioned·ness \-n(d)nəs\ *n* -ES **:** the quality or state of being impassioned ⟨the ~ of his plea for mercy⟩

im·passive \əm, (ˈ)im+\ *adj* [ˡin- + *passive*] **1 :** devoid of passion, feeling, or receptivity to impression: **a** *archaic* **:** unsusceptible to pain, suffering, injury, or harm **:** INVULNERABLE **b :** unsusceptible to physical feeling **:** INSENSIBLE, INANIMATE ⟨a dial cut in ~ stone —Virginia Woolf⟩ **c :** unsusceptible to or destitute of emotion **:** UNIMPRESSIONABLE ⟨the violet pallor of death ... enveloped her in an ~ remoteness —Ellen Glasgow⟩ ⟨a large dull ~ man⟩ **2 :** giving no sign of feeling or emotion **:** EXPRESSIONLESS ⟨beneath a reserved and ~ surface, a highly nervous and sensitive person —Havelock Ellis⟩ ⟨a cold ~ stare —Charles Dickens⟩ **3 :** not moving in any way **:** MOTIONLESS ⟨we can load up a piece of amber ... with the greatest possible excess of negative charge, and still it remains absolutely ~ in the presence of a magnet —K.K.Darrow⟩

syn STOIC, APATHETIC, PHLEGMATIC, STOLID: IMPASSIVE applies to one who shows no passion, emotion, sensation, or noticeable interest in situations in which such a reaction might be expected ⟨the veil of *impassive* reserve with which I concealed the whole of my intimate personal life —Havelock Ellis⟩ ⟨I watched the man's face while Nelson was relating the story, but he remained *impassive*, showing neither interest in nor concern for our plight —C.B.Nordhoff & J.N.Hall⟩ STOIC may suggest an indifference to pain or pleasure, perhaps through a conscious schooling of oneself in fortitude ⟨it sums up not only the cataclysm of a world, but also the *stoic* and indomitable temper that endures it —J.L.Lowes⟩ ⟨a *stoic* atmosphere of fortitude in adversity —Orville Prescott⟩ APATHETIC may describe a puzzling, remiss, or blameworthy indifference or a preoccupation with something else that precludes normal interest and reactions ⟨enforcement of the liquor laws was lax, and sentiment was *apathetic* to the evils of excessive drinking —C.A.Dinsmore⟩ ⟨the row of stolid, dull, vacant plowboys, ungainly in build, uncomely in face, lifeless, *apathetic* —Samuel Butler †1902⟩ PHLEGMATIC describes a temperament or disposition not given to ready emotional reaction or similar response ⟨the religious mysticism that lurked in the heart of primitive Puritanism found no response in his *phlegmatic* soul —V.L.Parrington⟩ STOLID implies an accustomed heavy or cloddish obtuse imperceptive and incurious lack of interest, emotion, or other response ⟨an agricultural parish, peopled by *stolid* Saxon rustics, in whom the temperature of religious zeal was little, if at all, above absolute zero —Aldous Huxley⟩ ⟨watched for an expression of hatred, or pity, or horror, on the faces of the multitude. No emotion whatsoever was displayed —nothing but *stolid* indifference —V.G.Heiser⟩

im·passively \"+\ *adv* **:** in an impassive manner ⟨submitted ~ to arrest —*Time*⟩

im·passiveness \"+\ *n* **:** IMPASSIVITY

im·passivity \ˌim+\ *n* **:** the quality or state of being impassive **:** a lack or absence of feeling or expression ⟨behind her ~ lay passionate growing anxiety —Marcia Davenport⟩ ⟨his majestic ~ contrasting with the overt astonishment with which a row of savagely ugly attendant chiefs grinned —G.B.Shaw⟩

im·paste \imˈpāst\ *vt* [It *impastare*, fr. *in-* ²in- (fr. L) + *pasta* dough, paste, fr. LL — more at PASTE] **1 :** to make into a paste **2 :** to decorate by impasto

im·pas·to \imˈpa(,)stō, -pä-,-paa-,-pȧ-\ *n* -s *often attrib* [It, fr. *impastare*] **:** the thick application of a pigment to a canvas or panel in painting ⟨~ tempera —Ralph Mayer⟩ ⟨~ effects —*Yankee*⟩; *also* **:** the body of pigment so applied ⟨paint laid on in so thick an ~ that it appears almost in bas-relief —R.M. Coates⟩

im·pa·ter·nate \ˌimpə¦tərnət\ *adj* [ˡin- + *paternal* + *-ate*] **:** fatherless as a result of parthenogenetic development

im·patience \(ˈ)im, əm+\ *n* [ME *impacience*, fr. OF & L; OF *impacience, impatience*, fr. L *impatientia*, fr. *impatient-, impatiens* + *-ia* -y] **:** the quality or state of being impatient: as **a :** restlessness or chafing of spirit (as under irritation, delay, or opposition) ⟨~ of restraint⟩ **b :** manifest disapproval or intolerance ⟨~ of delay or incompetence⟩ **:** manifest unwillingness to be tolerant ⟨~ with red tape and outworn procedure —R.M.Dawson⟩ **c :** restless or eager desire or longing ⟨~ to get his mark completed on time⟩

im·patiency \"+\ *n* [L *impatientia*] *archaic* **:** IMPATIENCE

im·pa·tiens \əmˈpāshənz, -shē,enz, -shən(t)s\ *n* [NL, fr. L, adj., impatient; fr. the fact that the ripe pods burst open and scatter their seeds when slight pressure is applied] **1** *cap* **:** a large genus of widely distributed annual plants (family Balsaminaceae) with watery juice, irregular spurred or saccate flowers, and dehiscent capsules — see BALSAM 4, JEWELWEED **2** *or* **impatience**, *pl* **impatiens** *or* **impatiences :** any plant of the genus *Impatiens*

ˡim·patient \(ˈ)im, əm+\ *adj* [ME *impacient*, fr. MF *impacient, impatient*, fr. L *impatient-, impatiens*, fr. *in-* ˡin- + *patient-, patiens* patient — more at PATIENT] **1 a :** not patient **:** restless or short of temper esp. under irritation, delay, or opposition **:** FRETFUL ⟨an ~ mood⟩ ⟨an ~ disposition⟩ ⟨the temper of the youth of his country is violent, ~, and revolutionary —Louis Fischer⟩ **b :** not bearing with composure **:** INTOLERANT ⟨~ of poverty or delay⟩ ⟨~ of this prolonged parting from their pets —F.D.Smith & Barbara Wilcox⟩ ⟨~ of preaching without practice —A.J.Russell⟩ **:** showing quickly an unwillingness to be unconcerned or tolerant (as with something one dislikes or disapproves of) ⟨~ with anything like dishonesty —W.L.Frierson⟩ **2 :** prompted by or giving evidence of impatience ⟨an ~ speech⟩ ⟨~ restlessness⟩ ⟨an ~ honesty —S.H.Adams⟩ **3 a :** restlessly or eagerly desirous **:** ANXIOUS ⟨~ to see his sweetheart⟩ ⟨quite ~ for the concert evening —Jane Austen⟩ ⟨~ to know what did occur —E.K. Brown⟩ ⟨~ for home —E.A.Weeks⟩ **b :** marked by intolerance of delay ⟨an ~ wait⟩ ⟨~ hours⟩ **4** *obs* **:** UNENDURABLE — **im·patiently** \"+\ *adv* — **im·patientness** \"+\ *n*

²impatient \"\ *n* **:** one that is impatient

impatronize *vt* [MF *impatroniser*, fr. *in-* ²in- + *patron* patron, master + *-iser* -ize — more at PATRON] *obs* **:** to give or take possession of

im·pavid \(ˈ)im+\ *adj* [L *impavidus*, fr. *in-* ˡin- + *pavidus* fearful — more at PAVID] *archaic* **:** FEARLESS — **im·pavidly** \"+\ *adv*

im·pawn \im+\ *vt* [²in- + *pawn* (n.)] *archaic* **:** to put in pawn

im·pay·able \aⁿpāyäbl(ᵊ), -b(lə)\ *adj* [F, fr. MF, incapable of being paid, fr. *in-* ˡin- + *payable* — more at PAYABLE] **:** PRICELESS, INVALUABLE

ˡim·peach \əmˈpēch\ *vt* -ED/-ING/-ES [ME *empechen*, fr. MF *empecher*, fr. OF *empeechier*, fr. LL *impedicare* to entangle, fetter, fr. L *in-* ²in- + *pedica* fetter, fr. *ped-, pes* foot — more at FOOT] **1** *obs* **:** HINDER, PREVENT, IMPEDE **2 a :** to bring an accusation (as of wrongdoing or impropriety) against **:** charge with a crime or misdemeanor; *specif* **:** to charge (a public official) before a competent tribunal with misbehavior in office **:** arraign or cite for official misconduct ⟨~ the president⟩ ⟨~ a circuit-court judge⟩ **b :** to inform against or give incriminating evidence against **:** accuse or aid in accusing **:** peach on **c :** to challenge, impugn, or charge as having some fault esp. as biased, venal, not credible, or invalid ⟨the testimony of the 1850 federal census ... ~es the accuracy of his memory —Dixon Wecter⟩ ⟨in a state of mind to ~ the justice of the republic —Charles Dickens⟩ ⟨~ the testimony of a witness⟩ **3 :** to convict of impropriety, misdemeanor, misconduct in office, or bias, venality, or invalidity; *also* **:** to cause (an official) to be removed from office because of such a conviction **syn** see ACCUSE

²impeach *n, obs* **:** IMPEACHMENT

im·peach·able \-chəbəl\ *adj* **1 :** capable of being impeached **:** chargeable with misconduct, inadequacy, or other fault which might lead to being impeached **2 :** capable of being used as the charge in an impeachment ⟨an ~ offense⟩

im·peach·ment \-chmənt\ *n* -s [ME *empechement*, fr. MF, fr. *empecher* + *-ment*] **:** the act or result of impeaching: **a** *obs* **:** HINDRANCE, OBSTRUCTION, IMPEDIMENT **b** *obs* **:** INJURY, HARM, DAMAGE **c :** a calling into question or discrediting (as the purity of one's motives or one's honesty) ⟨the ~ of his character⟩ ⟨the ~ of the witness's testimony⟩ **d :** a calling to account for some high crime or offense before a competent tribunal **:** ARRAIGNMENT; *esp* **:** the arraignment (as of a public official) for misconduct while in office **e** (1) **:** conviction of bias, venality, invalidity, or other fault (2) **:** conviction of misconduct and usu. removal from office — **without impeachment of waste** *of a tenant* **:** exempt from suit for waste committed — used in a real estate lease

im·pearl \əm+\ *or* **em·pearl** \əm,em+\ *vt* [prob. fr. MF *emperler*, fr. *en-* ˡen- + *perle* pearl — more at PEARL] **:** to form into pearls or into the likeness of pearls; *also* **:** to form of or adorn with or as if with pearls

im·pec·ca·bil·i·ty \(,)im,pekəˈbiləd-ē, əm-, -lətē, -i\ *n* **:** the quality or state of being impeccable ⟨have never pretended to ~ —George Meredith⟩

im·pec·ca·ble \(ˈ)im¦pekəbəl, əmˈp-\ *adj* [L *impeccabilis*, fr. *in-* ˡin- + *peccare* to sin + *-abilis* -able — more at PECCANT] **1 :** not capable of sinning or liable to sin **:** exempt from the possibility of wrongdoing ⟨no soul is absolutely ~ —F.W. Robertson⟩ **2 :** free from fault or blame **:** FLAWLESS, IRREPROACHABLE ⟨women of ~ character and honorable life —Herbert Mitgang⟩ ⟨this masterly record ... written with ~ discretion and understanding —John Hayward b.1905⟩ ⟨an ~ figure in trim dinner jacket and starched shirt —Truman Capote⟩ — **im·pec·ca·ble·ness** \-bəlnəs\ *n* -ES — **im·pec·ca·bly** \-blē,bli\ *adv*

im·pec·can·cy \-kənsē, -si\ *n* [LL *impeccantia*, fr. L *in-* ˡin- + LL *peccantia* sinfulness — more at PECCANCY] **:** the quality or state of being impeccant **:** SINLESSNESS

im·pec·cant \-nt\ *adj* [ˡin- + *peccant*] **:** free from error or fault **:** SINLESS

im·pectinate \(ˈ)im+\ *adj* [ˡin- + *pectinate*] **:** not pectinate

im·pecuniary \ˌim+\ *adj* [ˡin- + *pecuniary*] *archaic* **:** IMPECUNIOUS

im·pe·cu·nios·i·ty \,impə,kyünēˈäsəd-ē, -pē,-, -nˈyü-, -sətē, -i\ *n* -ES **:** IMPECUNIOUSNESS

im·pe·cu·nious \¦impə¦kyünyəs, -pē¦-, -nēəs\ *adj* [ˡin- + obs. E *pecunious* rich, fr. ME *pecunyous*, fr. L *pecuniosus*, fr. *pecunia* money + *-osus* -ose — more at FEE] **:** having very little or no money usu. habitually **:** INDIGENT, PENNILESS ⟨this eager ~ young man who has fared so richly in his poverty —Edith Wharton⟩ **syn** see POOR

im·pe·cu·nious·ly *adv* **:** in an impecunious manner ⟨an ~ situated family⟩ ⟨plodding his way ~ through life⟩

im·pe·cu·nious·ness *n* -ES **:** the quality or state of being impecunious **:** INDIGENCE, POVERTY

im·pe·cu·ni·ty \,impəˈkyünəd-ē, -pēˈ-, -nətē, -i\ *n* -ES [*impecunious* + *-ty*] **:** IMPECUNIOUSNESS

imped *past of* IMP

im·ped·ance \əmˈpēdᵊn(t)s\ *n* -s [*impede* + *-ance*] **1 a :** the apparent opposition in an electrical circuit to the flow of an alternating current that is analogous to the actual electrical resistance to a direct current and that is the ratio of effective electromotive force to the effective current **b :** the resistance to passage of a substance (as water or water vapor) through a film **2 :** the ratio of the pressure to the volume displacement at a given surface in a sound-transmitting medium

impedance bond *n* **:** an iron-core coil of low resistance and relatively high reactance used on electrified railroads to provide a continuous path around insulated joints for the return propulsion current and to confine the alternating-current signaling energy to its own track circuit

impedance bridge *n* **:** BRIDGE

im·pede \əmˈpēd\ *vt* -ED/-ING/-S [L *impedire*, fr. *in-* ²in- + *-pedire* (fr. *ped-, pes* foot) — more at FOOT] **:** to interfere with or get in the way of the progress of ⟨storms *impeded* the vessels —*Amer. Guide Series: N.C.*⟩ ⟨are further *impeded* in our work by financial stringency —C.A.Robinson⟩ **:** hold up **:** BLOCK ⟨the departure was *impeded* by heavy rain⟩ ⟨his progress was *impeded* by sickness and poverty⟩ **:** detract from ⟨no heavy weight of fable *impedes* the reader's enjoyment —Elizabeth Janeway⟩ **syn** see HINDER

im·pe·di·ent impediment \əmˈpēdēənt-\ *n* [*impedient* fr. L *impedient-*, impediens, pres. part. of *impedire*] **:** a bar to marriage that is an obstacle to the marriage if known but that does not make the marriage void after it has been solemnized — called also *hindering impediment*

im·ped·i·ment \əmˈpedəmənt\ *n* -s [L *impedimentum*, fr. *impedire* + *-mentum* -ment] **1 a :** the act or state of being impeded **:** OBSTRUCTION ⟨trying to determine where the ~s of growth lay in the life cycle⟩ **b :** something that impedes **:** HINDRANCE, BLOCK ⟨some ~ lay between him and advancement⟩ ⟨the destruction of all ~s to love —C.D.Lewis⟩ ⟨strove to get ahead despite all ~s in his path⟩; *esp* **:** an organic obstruction to speech ⟨some small ~ slowed his conversation⟩ **2 impediments** *pl, archaic* **:** IMPEDIMENTA **3 a :** a bar to the formation of a contract arising out of the lack of capacity of one of the parties (as from minority or want of sufficient mental capacity) **b :** a bar or hindrance (as lack of sufficient age, lack of genuine consent) to a lawful marriage sometimes resulting in complete nullity of marriage without any decree or declaration or in the marriage being voidable by the injured party — see ABSOLUTE IMPEDIMENT, DIRIMENT IMPEDIMENT, IMPEDIENT IMPEDIMENT, PROHIBITIVE IMPEDIMENT, RELATIVE IMPEDIMENT **syn** see OBSTACLE

im·ped·i·men·ta \əm,pedəˈmentə, ,im-\ *n pl* [L, pl. of *impedimentum* impediment] **:** things that impede or hinder progress or movement; *esp* **:** baggage, equipment, or supplies ⟨the photographer left all his ~ in the hall⟩ ⟨the supply trains dropped the ~ at convenient stopping places on the army's route⟩ ⟨clubs, bag, cart, umbrella, spiked shoes and all the other ~ of the golfer⟩

im·ped·i·men·tal \(ˌ)im¦pedə¦mentᵊl, əm¦-\ *adj, archaic* **:** being an impediment **:** HINDERING, OBSTRUCTIVE

im·ped·i·tive \(ˈ)imˈpedəd-iv, əmˈp-\ *adj* [F *impéditif*, fr. MF *impeditif*, fr. L *impeditus* (past part. of *impedire* to impede) + MF *-if* -ive — more at IMPEDE] **:** tending to impede **:** hindering or being a hindrance **:** OBSTRUCTIVE

im·pe·dor \əmˈpēdə(r)\ *n* -s [*impede* + *-or*] **:** an electric-circuit element that introduces impedance

im·pel \əmˈpel\ *vt* **impelled; impelled; impelling; impels** [L *impellere*, fr. *in-* ²in- + *pellere* to drive — more at FELT] **1 a :** to urge or drive by force or constraint ⟨*impelled* out of England ... by religious dissension —Evelyn Wrench⟩ **:** exert strong moral pressure on or affect with marked moral compulsion in a particular direction ⟨*impelled* to resist oppressive laws⟩ ⟨felt *impelled* to tolerate what he intensely disliked⟩ ⟨continued to write, *impelled* by profit instead of vision and recollection —*Saturday Rev.*⟩ **b :** to create or generate by force or constraint ⟨land hunger *impelled* the deceit, trickery, bribery which whites practiced upon the red man —H.M. Hyman⟩ ⟨his symphonies and symphonic poems are *impelled* by picturesque Celtic folklore —Norman Demuth⟩ **2 :** to impart motion to **:** give a physical impulse to **:** PROPEL ⟨*impelling* a wheelbarrow along the street —Nathaniel Hawthorne⟩ **syn** see MOVE

ˡim·pel·lent \(ˌ)im¦pelənt, əmˈp-\ *adj* [L *impellent-, impellens*, pres. part. of *impellere*] **:** IMPELLING

²impellent \"\ *n* -s **:** something that impels

im·pel·ler *also* **im·pel·lor** \əmˈpelə(r)\ *n* -s **1 :** one that impels **2 :** ROTOR 1a, 1b; *also* **:** a blade of a rotor — see JET ENGINE illustration

impelling *adj* **:** markedly effective **:** FORCEFUL ⟨an ~ personality⟩ ⟨an ~ skill as a teller of tales⟩ — **im·pel·ling·ly** *adv*

im·pend \əmˈpend\ *vi* -ED/-ING/-S [L *impendēre*, fr. *in-* ²in- + *pendēre* to hang — more at PENDANT] **1** *archaic* **:** to hang suspended (as over one's head) ⟨a profuse crop of hair ~*ing* over the top of his face —Thomas Hardy⟩ **:** jut out and seem to hang suspended ⟨the crags ... now begin to ~ terribly over your way —Thomas Gray⟩ **2 a :** to threaten from near at hand or as in the immediate future **:** MENACE ⟨trouble ~*ed* over the entire enterprise⟩ **b :** to be imminent **:** give promise of occurring in the immediate future ⟨went indoors because rain ~*ed*⟩ **:** be about to occur ⟨the most critical contests ~ —Cabell Phillips⟩

impendence *or* **impendency** *n, pl* **impendences** *or* **impendencies** *obs* **:** the quality or state of being impending

im·pend·ent \-dənt\ *adj* [L *impendent-, impendens*, pres. part. of *impendēre*] **:** IMPENDING

impending *adj* **:** that is about to occur **:** IMMINENT ⟨an ~ crisis⟩ ⟨an ~ storm⟩ ⟨~ danger⟩

im·penetrability \(ˌ)im, əm+\ *n* **1 :** the quality or state of being impenetrable **2 :** the property of matter from which two portions of matter cannot occupy the same space at the same time

im·penetrable \(ˈ)im, əm+\ *adj* [ME *impenetrabel*, fr. MF *impenetrable*, fr. L *impenetrabilis*, fr. *in-* ˡin- + *penetrabilis* penetrable — more at PENETRABLE] **1 a :** incapable of being penetrated or pierced **:** not admitting the passage of other bodies **:** not to be entered **:** IMPERVIOUS ⟨an ~ shield⟩ ⟨an ~ forest⟩ ⟨an ~ barrier⟩ **b :** inaccessible to knowledge, reason, sympathy **:** not to be moved by logic or other method of persuasion **:** UNIMPRESSIBLE ⟨an ~ heart⟩ ⟨an ~ stupidity⟩ **c :** incapable of being dealt with in a way that brings a usu. warm, cordial, or unguarded response ⟨an ~ reserve⟩ ⟨an ~ gloom⟩ **2 :** incapable of being comprehended **:** INSCRUTABLE, UNFATHOMABLE ⟨an ~ mystery⟩ ⟨a child speaking in an ~ language of its own⟩ **3 :** having the property of impenetrability ⟨~ matter⟩ — **im·penetrableness** \"+\ *n* — **im·penetrably** \"+\ *adv*

im·penetrate \əm+\ *vt* [²in- + *penetrate*] **:** to penetrate thoroughly ⟨power to isolate and ~ Poland and the Balkan States —John Gunther⟩ **syn** see PERMEATE

im·penetration \(ˌ)im, əm+\ *n* **:** the act of impenetrating or the state of being impenetrated

im·penitence *also* **im·penitency** \(ˈ)im, əm+\ *n* [LL *impaenitentia*, fr. *impaenitent-, impaenitens* + L *-ia* -y] **:** the quality or state of being impenitent **:** failure or refusal to repent

ˡim·penitent \"+\ *adj* [LL *impaenitent-, impaenitens*, fr. L *in-* ˡin- + *paenitent-, paenitens* penitent — more at PENITENT] **:** not penitent **:** not repenting of sin **:** not contrite — **im·penitently** \"+\ *adv* — **im·penitentness** \"+\ *n* -ES

²impenitent \"\ *n* **:** one that is impenitent

imper *abbr* imperative

im·pe·ra·ta \,impəˈrād-ə\ *n, cap* [NL, after Ferrante *Imperato* †1625 It. apothecary] **:** a genus of tropical grasses having slender erect culms and a narrow panicle with spikelets surrounded by long silky hairs — see COGON

ˡim·per·ate \ˈimpə,rāt\ *vt* -ED/-ING/-S [L *imperatus*, past part. of *imperare* to command — more at EMPEROR] **:** COMMAND, GOVERN — **im·per·a·tion** \,impəˈrāshən\ *n* -s

²imperate *adj* [L *imperatus*] *obs, of an act* **:** COMMANDED — contrasted with *elicit*

im·per·a·ti·val \(ˌ)im¦perə¦tīvəl, əm-\ *adj* **:** of or relating to the grammatical imperative **:** expressing an imperative meaning **:** having an imperative function — **im·per·a·ti·val·ly** \-vəlē\ *adv*

ˡim·per·a·tive \əmˈperəd-|iv, -rət|\ *adj* [LL *imperativus*, fr. L *imperatus* (past part. of *imperare* to command) + *-ivus* -ive — more at EMPEROR] **1 a :** of, relating to, or being the grammatical mood that expresses the will to influence the behavior of another (as in a command, entreaty, or exhortation) — compare INDICATIVE **b :** expressive of or being a command, entreaty, or exhortation ⟨an ~ rule of conduct⟩ ⟨an ~ tone of voice⟩ **:** commanding often imperiously ⟨an ~ manner⟩ ⟨~ persons rush about giving orders⟩ ⟨"you must let me speak," said the woman, in an ~ voice —A. Conan Doyle⟩ **c** : restraining, controlling, and directing ⟨the democratic instinct is in France too ~ —W.C.Brownell⟩ **2** : not to be avoided or evaded : URGENT, OBLIGATORY, BINDING, COMPULSORY ⟨an ~ duty⟩ ⟨an ~ engagement⟩ **syn** see MASTERFUL, PRESSING

²imperative \"\ *n* -s **1** : the imperative mood or a verb form or verbal phrase expressing it ⟨an ~ of the verb⟩ **2** : COMMAND, ORDER ⟨a sheep dog emits ~s to his flock hardly distinguishable from those that the shepherd employs toward him —Bertrand Russell⟩; *also* : RULE, GUIDE ⟨lived by certain simple ~s⟩ **3 a** : an obligatory act or duty ⟨the social ~s of our time —M.J.Rosenberg⟩ ⟨it is an ~ that we try again before giving up⟩ **b** : an imperative judgment, proposition, or statement — see CATEGORICAL IMPERATIVE, HYPOTHETICAL IMPERATIVE **c** : NECESSITY, NEED ⟨the terrible ~ of reaching the springs —D.L.Morgan⟩ ⟨the sheer ~ of survival —*New Republic*⟩ **d** : an unavoidable fact compelling or insistently calling for action ⟨the ~s of physical battle —*N.Y. Herald Tribune Bk. Rev.*⟩ ⟨economic ~s⟩ **e** : a quality or aspect that gives authority or obligatoriness or that demands action ⟨the ~ of law is not simply the ~ of grammatical form —Glenn Negley⟩ ⟨by the conscious direction of the people quite apart from the ~ of events —T.K.Finletter⟩

im·per·a·tive·ly \|ə̇vlē, -li\ *adv* : in an imperative manner

im·per·a·tive·ness \|ivnə̇s\ *n* -ES : the quality or state of being imperative

im·pe·ra·tor \ˌimpəˈrädˌər, ˌ==ˈrāˌtȯ(ə)r\ *n* -s [L — more at EMPEROR] : supreme leader esp. of the ancient Romans : COMMANDER, EMPEROR — **im·per·a·to·ri·al** \(ˌ)imˌperəˈtōrēəl\ *adj*

imperatorious *adj* [L *imperatorius*, fr. *imperator* + *-orius* -ory] *obs* : IMPERATORIAL

im·per·a·tor·ship \ˌimpəˈräd·ər,ship\ *n* : the position of imperator

im·perceivable \ˌim+\ *adj* [¹*in-* + *perceivable*] *archaic* : IMPERCEPTIBLE

im·perceptibility \ˌim+\ *n* : the quality or state of being imperceptible

¹im·perceptible \ˌim+\ *adj* [MF, fr. ML *imperceptibilis*, fr. L *in-* ¹in- + LL *perceptibilis* perceptible — more at PERCEPTIBLE] : not perceptible: **a** : not capable of being perceived by a sense or of affecting a sense ⟨color is ~ to the touch⟩ ⟨made an almost ~ gesture of assent⟩ **b** : not capable of being perceived or discriminated mentally ⟨the difference between the two propositions was ~ to him⟩ **c** : extremely slight, gradual, or subtle ⟨saw him grow up by ~ gradations⟩ — **im·perceptibleness** \"+\ *n* -ES — **im·perceptibly** \"+\ *adv*

²imperceptible \"\ *n* -s : something that is imperceptible

im·perception \ˌim+\ *n* [¹*in-* + *perception*] : a lack of perception

im·perceptive \"+\ *adj* [¹*in-* + *perceptive*] : not perceptive : UNPERCEIVING : lacking perception ⟨~ persons have been intolerably bored by masterpieces —*N.Y.Herald Tribune*⟩ ⟨stupid and ~ of even the grossest differences between foods⟩ — **im·perceptiveness** \"+\ *n* — **im·perceptivity** \"+\ *n*

im·percipience \ˌim+\ *n* : the quality or state of being unperceptive : lack of perception

im·percipient \"+\ *adj* [¹*in-* + *percipient*] : UNPERCEPTIVE ⟨agitated by the strangely ~ criticisms of his work —Hesketh Pearson⟩

im·per·ence \ˈimpərən(t)s\ *n* -s [by alter.] *substand Brit* : IMPUDENCE

imperf *abbr* **1** imperfect **2** imperforate

¹im·perfect \(ˈ)im, əm+\ *adj* [alter. (influenced by L *imperfectus*) of ME *imperfit, imparfit*, fr. MF *imparfait*, fr. L *imperfectus*, fr. *in-* ¹in- + *perfectus* perfect — more at PERFECT] **1 a** : falling short of perfection : not perfect (as in form, development, or function) : not complete in parts or attributes : not satisfying the standard or ideal : DEFECTIVE, INADEQUATE, INCOMPLETE ⟨had only an ~ understanding of his task⟩ ⟨in the ~ light of the moon —Anthony Trollope⟩ ⟨what an ~ husband he had always been —H.G.Wells⟩ ⟨~ mortals⟩ ⟨drainage of the region is ~ —*Jour. of Geol.*⟩ **b** : DICLINOUS **2** : of, relating to, or being a verb tense used to designate a continuing state or an incomplete action esp. in the past **3 a** *in medieval church music* (1) : twofold rather than threefold in time value — used of notation; compare PERFECT (2) : having a duple rather than triple rhythm — used of a rhythmic mode **b** : DIMINISHED 2 **4** : not enforceable at law : lacking some essential element required by law : depending for fulfillment upon moral rather than legal duty ⟨an ~ obligation⟩ : enforceable only under certain conditions : DEFEASIBLE ⟨an ~ mortgage⟩ ⟨an ~ grant avoidable by the government⟩ — **im·perfectly** \"+\ *adv* — **im·perfectness** \"+\ *n* -ES

²imperfect *vt*, *obs* : to make imperfect

³im·perfect \(ˈ)im, əm+\ *n* : an imperfect tense; *also* : the verb form expressing it

imperfect cadence *n* **1** : an authentic or plagal cadence in which the third or the fifth of the final chord appears in the soprano part or in which one or both of the cadential chords are inverted — compare PERFECT CADENCE; see CADENCE illustration **2** : HALF CADENCE

imperfect competition *n* : competition among sellers of inhomogeneous products in which the sellers are sufficiently few in number so that each exerts an influence upon the market : limited competition

imperfect diphthong *n* : PARTIAL DIPHTHONG

im·perfected \(ˌ)im, əm+\ *adj* [¹*in-* + *perfected*] : not perfected : IMPERFECT — **im·perfectedly** \"+\ *adv*

imperfect flower *n* : a diclinous flower

imperfect fungus *n* : a fungus of which only the conidial stage is known : one of the Fungi Imperfecti

im·perfectibility \(ˌ)im, əm+\ *n* [¹*in-* + *perfectibility*] : the quality or state of being imperfectible

im·perfectible \(ˌ)im, əm+\ *adj* [¹*in-* + *perfectible*] : incapable of being made perfect

im·perfection \ˌim+\ *n* [ME *imperfeccioun*, fr. MF or LL; MF *imperfection* fr. LL *imperfection-, imperfectio*, fr. L *perfectus* + *-ion-, -io* -ion — more at IMPERFECT] **1 a** : the quality or state of being imperfect : lack of perfection : INCOMPLETENESS ⟨dissatisfied with the ~ of man⟩ ⟨saw the ~ of the dress⟩ **b** : the quality or aspect in which something is incomplete : DEFICIENCY, FAULT, BLEMISH ⟨tried to cover up the ~s in the cloth⟩ **2** *in medieval church music* **a** : duple time **b** : the occasional division of a triple measure into two equal parts **3 a** : a sheet that is rejected because of faulty printing; *also* : a replacement for such a sheet **b** : a printed or folded book section or a complete gathered or sewed but unbound book that has been rejected for any reason **4** : a piece of type cast to fill a deficiency in a type font

¹im·perfective \(ˌ)im, əm+\ *adj* [¹*in-* + *perfective*] *of a verb form or aspect* : expressing action as incomplete or without reference to completion : expressing action as continuing : expressing action as reiterated : DURATIVE — opposed to *perfective* — **im·perfectivity** \"+\ *n*

²imperfective \"\ *n* : the imperfective aspect or form of a verb

imperfect number *n* : a number (as 15) that is not equal to the sum of its divisors — compare PERFECT NUMBER; see ABUNDANT NUMBER, DEFICIENT NUMBER

imperfect stage *n* : any of various conidial or asexual stages in the life history of a fungus

imperfect usufruct *n* : the right of usufruct allowed in a thing consumed in the using — called also *quasi usufruct*

im·perforata \(ˌ)im, əm+\ *n pl, cap* [NL, fr. ¹*in-* + *Perforata*] *in some classifications* : a division of the Foraminifera having imperforate shells

¹im·perforate \(ˈ)im, əm+\ *adj* [¹*in-* + *perforate*] **1** : not perforated : having no opening or aperture; *specif* : lacking the normal opening ⟨an ~ anus⟩ **2** *of a stamp or a sheet of stamps* : lacking perforations or rouletting **3** : having the umbilicus obliterated by the later whorls — used of various spiral shells

²imperforate \"\ *n* -s : an imperforate stamp

im·perforated \(ˈ)im, əm+\ *adj* [¹*in-* + *perforated*] : IMPERFORATE

im·perforation \(ˌ)im, əm+\ *n* [F, fr. *in-* ¹in- + *perforation* — more at PERFORATION] : the quality or state of being without perforation

¹im·pe·ri·al \(ˈ)imˈpirēəl, əmˈp-, -pēr-\ *adj* [ME *emperial, imperial*, fr. MF, fr. LL *imperialis*, fr. L *imperium* command, supreme authority, empire + *-alis* -al — more at EMPIRE] **1 a** : of or relating to an empire or an emperor esp. of a particular or implicit empire ⟨the national poet of the empire, in whom ~ patriotism found its highest expression —James Bryce⟩ ⟨~ Caesar⟩ ⟨his view was ~ rather than provincial —Carl Bridenbaugh⟩ **b** : of, relating to, or befitting supreme authority or one that exercises it : of the rank of or suitable to an emperor or supreme ruler : ROYAL, SOVEREIGN **c** : of or relating to a state as governing or being supreme over colonies, dependencies, or many subdivisions; *specif, usu cap* : of or relating to Britain as such a state ⟨make an essential contribution . . . to New Zealand and *Imperial* history —*Notes & Queries*⟩ ⟨British *Imperial* communications —*Brit. Book News*⟩ **d** : HAUGHTY, REGAL, COMMANDING, IMPERIOUS ⟨stood there, tall, broad, ~ —Donn Byrne⟩ ⟨the rigid, ~ hyacinth —Rebecca West⟩ ⟨humoring us with her fatigued ~ smiles —Arnold Bennett⟩ **2 a** : of superior or unusual size or excellence ⟨a rich man living on an ~ diet⟩ ⟨grow from the little old town of the nineties to the ~ city that stands there now —W.A.White⟩ ⟨a homicidal mania on an ~ scale —Ellery Sedgwick⟩ **b** : of fancy quality — used as a designation for various commercial products **c** : SELF-AGGRANDIZING, GRANDIOSE ⟨thoughts that were partly dreams . . . ~, childish dreams —Audrey L. Barker⟩ **3** *of a measure or weight* : being the British legal standard : belonging to the official British series of weights and measures ⟨the ~ gallon⟩ — **im·pe·ri·al·ly** \-ēəlē, -li\ *adv* — **im·pe·ri·al·ness** \-ēəlnə̇s\ *n* -ES

²imperial \"\ *n* -s **1** : a medieval silk and gold fabric of oriental origin **2** *usu cap* [Russ, prob. fr. Pol *imperjal*, a kind of coin, fr. ML *imperialis*, a medieval coin, fr. LL *imperialis*, adj., imperial] : an adherent of the Holy Roman emperor or a soldier of his troops : IMPERIALIST **3** : a person of imperial rank : EMPEROR, EMPRESS **4** : a size of paper usu. 23 x 31, 22½ x 29, or 22 x 30 inches **5** : a game similar to piquet but having a trump; *also* : any of several scoring combinations in the game **6 a** : a luggage case for the top of a coach **b** : the top, roof, or second-story compartment of a coach or carriage, esp. a diligence **7** : a gold coin of imperial Russia worth 10 rubles when first issued in 1745 and 15 rubles from 1897–1917 **8** [F *impériale*, fr. fem. of *impérial* imperial, fr. LL *imperialis*; fr. the beard worn as a young man by Napoleon III †1873 emperor of France] : a pointed beard growing below the lower lip **9** : something of unusual size or excellence **10** : a dark reddish purple that is lighter and stronger than average plum (sense 6a), bluer and stronger than violet carmine or average grape wine, and bluer and deeper than royal purple (sense 1) — called also *Cotinga purple*

imperial 8

imperial blue *n* : a deep blue that is greener and deeper than Yale blue, greener, lighter, and stronger than royal (sense 8b), and greener and stronger than Napoleon blue

imperial bushel *n* : BUSHEL 1b

imperial city *n* **1** : a city (as Rome) that is the seat of empire **2** : a city that is an immediate vassal of the emperor of the Holy Roman Empire

imperial crown *n, often cap I, sometimes cap C* **1** : a crown emblematic of independent sovereignty: as **a** : the crown in the royal regalia of England that is used for the crowning in the coronation ceremony, that consists of a circlet of gold heightened with four crosses formée alternately with four fleurs-de-lis and has two arches rising from the crosses and surmounted by a mound and a cross formée, and that is ornamented with precious stones — called also *St. Edward's crown* **b** : the crown of an emperor or of an empire **2** : a conventionalized representation of an imperial crown; *esp* : a figure of a crown in the style of the imperial crown of England often used as an emblem of the sovereignty of the British monarch or as a heraldic bearing **3** : IMPERIAL STATE CROWN

imperial crown of state *often cap I&C&S* : IMPERIAL STATE CROWN

imperial dome *or* **imperial roof** *n* : a pointed dome or roof the vertical section of which is an ogee

imperial eagle *n* : an eagle (*Aquila heliaca*) of southern Europe and Asia the adult of which is dark brown with white shoulder patches — called also *king eagle*

imperial gallon *n* : GALLON 1b

imperial green *n* **1** : PARIS GREEN 2b **2** : EMERALD GREEN

im·pe·ri·al·ism \ə̇mˈpirēə,lizəm, -pēr-\ *n* -s **1 a** : the power or the government of an emperor : imperial authority : an imperial system ⟨the ~ of Caesar⟩ ⟨educational ~ —*Current Biog.*⟩ **b** : an imperial quality ⟨with dramatic ~ and disarming gentility . . . the epitome of mysterious womanhood —Louise Mace⟩ **2 a** : the policy, practice, or advocacy of seeking or the acquiescing in the extension of the control or empire of a nation by the acquirement of new territory or dependencies esp. when lying outside the nation's natural boundaries, by the extension of its rule over other races of mankind (as where commerce demands the protection of the flag), or by the closer union of more or less independent parts (as for war, copyright, or internal commerce) **b** : any extension of power or authority or an advocacy of such extension ⟨union ~ —S.H.Slichter⟩ ⟨cultural ~⟩

¹im·pe·ri·al·ist \-lə̇st\ *n* -s [¹*imperial* + *-ist*] **1** : one that adheres to an emperor or to his party; *esp* : one loyal to the Holy Roman Empire **2** : one who favors or practices imperialism

²imperialist \"\ *or* **im·pe·ri·al·is·tic** \(ˌ)imˌ===ˈlistik, əm-, -tēk\ *adj* : of, relating to, practicing, or favoring imperialism ⟨the great faiths . . . are *imperialistic*, going out to bring into the fold others than those people among whom they grew up —W.W.Howells⟩ ⟨an ~ war⟩ ⟨*imperialistic* in seeking to convert almost the whole of political science to his own interests —David Easton⟩ ⟨autocratic control and *imperialistic* expansion —Sigmund Neumann⟩ ⟨*imperialistic* policies of aggression among the weaker races —Lewis Mumford⟩ — **im·pe·ri·al·is·ti·cal·ly** \-tə̇k(ə)lē, -tēk-, -li\ *adv*

im·pe·ri·al·iza·tion \=,===lə̇ˈzāshən, -,līˈz-\ *n* -s : the act of imperializing or the state of being imperialized

im·pe·ri·al·ize \=ˈ==ə,līz\ *vt* -ED/-ING/-s : to make imperial : invest with an imperial quality or character : bring to the form of an empire

imperial jade *n, usu cap I* : ³JADE 1a

imperially crowned *adj, of a heraldic bearing* : crowned with an imperial crown

imperial mammoth *also* **imperial elephant** *n* : the largest known mammoth (*Archidiskidon imperator*) of the American Pleistocene reaching a height of 14 feet

imperial moth *n* : a large American saturniid moth (*Eacles imperialis*) marked with yellow, lilac, or purplish brown whose rough hairy larva feeds esp. on maple, sumach, and pine trees

imperial pigeon *n* : any of various very large Asiatic and Australasian pigeons that constitute a distinct subfamily of Columbidae — compare NUTMEG PIGEON

imperial preference *n* : the preferential lowering of tariff rates accorded in the British Commonwealth to its members

imperial purple *n* **1** : a grayish violet **2** *of textiles* : a deep purple that is redder and duller than hyacinth violet or petunia violet and redder and less strong than dahlia purple (sense 2)

imperial red *also* **imperial scarlet** *n* : vermilion or a color resembling it

imperials *pl of* IMPERIAL

imperial state crown *n, usu cap I&S&C* : an English royal crown worn on various state occasions that is more richly jeweled than the imperial crown but lighter in weight and usu. remade for successive sovereigns — called also *state crown*

imperial stone *n* : a light olive brown that is deeper than drab or sponge and deeper and slightly redder than average mustard tan

imperial tea *n* : a high-grade Chinese green tea made usu. from older leaves

imperial woodpecker *n* : a woodpecker (*Campephilus imperialis*) of northern Mexico that has black plumage with white markings on the wings and neck, a red crest in the male, and a white bill and that is the largest woodpecker known, the male being about two feet in length

imperial yellow *n* : YELLOW OCHER

im·peril \ə̇m+\ *vt* **imperiled** *or* **imperilled**; **imperiled** *or* **imperilled**; **imperiling** *or* **imperilling**; **imperils** [²*in-* + *peril* (n.)] : to bring into peril : expose to danger of imminent harm or loss : endanger or threaten danger to ⟨a jungle of aggressive power politics which ~s . . . the healing of the wounds of war —Mark Starr⟩ ⟨people whose investments were ~*ed* —G.W.Johnson⟩ ⟨stray mines . . . began to turn up off the Pacific coast, ~*ing* commercial shipping —Alan Hynd⟩ **syn** see VENTURE

im·per·il·ment \-mənt\ *n* -s : the act of imperiling or the state of being imperiled ⟨cut down on the convoy escort to the ~ of shipping everywhere⟩

im·pe·ri·ous \(ˈ)imˈpirēəs, əmˈp-, -pēr-\ *adj* [L *imperiosus*, fr. *imperium* command, supreme authority, empire + *-osus* -ous — more at EMPIRE] **1 a** *obs* : IMPERIAL 1a, 1b **b** : COMMANDING, DOMINANT, LORDLY ⟨sweeps through her social duties with ~ kindness —Margaret Landon⟩ **c** *obs* : MAJESTIC, STATELY **2** : ARROGANT, OVERBEARING, DOMINEERING **3** : IMPERATIVE, URGENT, COMPELLING ⟨at the mercy of the most ~ of instincts, of passions, and of intoxications —Arthur Symons⟩ ⟨so ~ became the commercial demand —Lewis Mumford⟩ **syn** see MASTERFUL

im·pe·ri·ous·ly *adv* : in an imperious manner ⟨drew him ~ apart from the others —George Meredith⟩ ⟨clung to authority as ~ as a king who refuses to abdicate —Ellen Glasgow⟩

im·pe·ri·ous·ness *n* -ES : the quality or state of being imperious

im·perishability \(ˌ)im, əm+\ *n* : the quality or state of being imperishable

¹im·perishable \(ˈ)im, əm+\ *adj* [¹*in-* + *perishable*] : not perishable : not subject to decay : enduring permanently : INDESTRUCTIBLE ⟨an ~ monument⟩ ⟨~ fame⟩ ⟨peace is not ~ —M.W.Straight⟩ ⟨an ~ memory⟩ — **im·perishableness** \"+\ *n* — **im·perishably** \"+\ *adv*

²imperishable \"\ *n* : something imperishable ⟨a classic to take its place among the ~s⟩

im·pe·ri·um \ə̇mˈpirēəm, -per-, -pēr-\ *n* -s [L, command, supreme authority, empire — more at EMPIRE] **1 a** (1) : supreme power or absolute dominion esp. over a large area ⟨surrender the showy shadow of ~ to secure the solid substance of colonial loyalty and cooperation —Oliver Benson⟩ (2) : regulatory powers or control ⟨had relinquished all ~ . . . over the land in question —*U.S. Code*⟩ ⟨existing governments had exhausted their ~ —Walter Lippmann⟩ **b** : an area over which such power or dominion is exercised : TERRITORY, EMPIRE ⟨the portentous ~ of the cartels —R.M.MacIver⟩ **2 a** : the right to command : the right of jurisdiction which includes the right to employ the force of the state to enforce the laws : executive power : SOVEREIGNTY **b** *Roman law* : the power to hear and determine cases and to give judgments — compare DOMINIUM, JURISDICTION

imperium in im·pe·rio \-,inəmˈpirē,ō, -per-,-pēr-\ *n* [NL] : a government, power, or sovereignty within a government, power, or sovereignty

im·permanence *or* **im·permanency** \(ˈ)im+\ *n* [¹*in-* + *permanence, permanency*] : the quality or state of being impermanent ⟨the ~ . . . of all the dear world of beauty —C.E.Montague⟩ ⟨the sense of the ~ of things, the transitoriness of life —Laurence Binyon⟩ ⟨the foolishness of love and the *impermanency* of all human relationships —Lafcadio Hearn⟩

im·permanent \"+\ *adj* [¹*in-* + *permanent*] : not permanent : not lasting : TRANSIENT ⟨politics is an ~ factor of life —James Thurber⟩ : UNSTABLE ⟨broken homes, ~ family life —Bingham Dai⟩ : soon destroyed ⟨~ log and palm cottages raised on stilts above the bayous —*Amer. Guide Series: La.*⟩ — **im·permanently** \"+\ *adv*

im·permeability \(ˌ)im, əm+\ *n* : the quality or state of being impermeable

im·per·me·a·bi·li·za·tion \(,)im,pərmēə,biləˈzāshən; -bələˈz-, -bə,līˈz-\ *n* -s [F *imperméabilisation*, fr. *imperméabiliser* + *-ation*] : the act of impermeabilizing something

im·per·me·a·bi·lize \=ˈ===bə,līz\ *vt* -ED/-ING/-s [F *imperméabiliser*, fr. LL *impermeabilis* + F *-iser* -ize] : to make impermeable esp. to liquids

im·permeable \(ˈ)im, əm+\ *adj* [LL *impermeabilis*, fr. L *in-* ¹in- + LL *permeabilis* permeable — more at PERMEABLE] : not permeable : not permitting passage (as of a fluid) through its substance : IMPASSABLE, IMPERVIOUS ⟨an ~ stone⟩ ⟨a coat ~ to rain⟩ ⟨an ~ layer of scum⟩ — **im·permeableness** \"+\ *n* — **im·permeably** \"+\ *adv*

im·permissibility \ˌim+\ *n* : the quality or state of being impermissible

im·permissible \"+\ *adj* [¹*in-* + *permissible*] : not permissible ⟨his secret and legally ~ objective —B.N.Meltzer⟩ ⟨has taken ~ liberties —J.D.Clarkson⟩ — **im·permissibly** \"+\ *adv*

impers *abbr* impersonal

im·personable \(ˈ)im, əm+\ *adj* [¹*in-* + *personable*] : not personable : UNATTRACTIVE

¹im·personal \"+\ *adj* [LL *impersonalis*, fr. L *in-* ¹in- + LL *personalis* personal — more at PERSONAL] **1 a** (1) *of a verb* : not predicated of a personal or determinate subject : denoting the action of an unspecified agent and hence used with no expressed subject (as *methinks*) or with a merely formal subject (as *is raining* in *it is raining*) (2) : consisting of either an indefinite pronoun and an impersonal verb (as *it is raining* or French *on dit*) or the expletive *there* and such a verb (as *there is* in *there is fog ahead*) **b** *of a pronoun* : INDEFINITE **c** *of a proposition* : having an indeterminate subject **2 a** (1) : having no personal reference or connection : not referring or belonging to any particular person ⟨when I say that a belief is ~ I mean that those desires which enter into its causation are universal human desires, and not such as are peculiar to the person in question —Bertrand Russell⟩ ⟨the brightly ~ sunshine —K.M.Dodson⟩ ⟨an ~ coat of arms⟩ (2) : not engaging the human personality or person ⟨the machine as compared with the hand tool is an ~ agency —John Dewey⟩ **b** : not representing or existing as a person : not having personality ⟨nature becomes an ~ slave —W.H.Auden⟩ **c** : not primarily affecting or involving the emotions of the person who has it ⟨an ~ interest in law⟩ ⟨the ~ attitude of a doctor⟩ — **im·personally** \"+\ *adv*

²impersonal \"\ *n* : something impersonal; *specif* : an impersonal verb

im·personalism \(ˈ)im, əm+\ *n* **1** : IMPERSONALITY ⟨the ~ of research in the sciences⟩ ⟨the trend toward ~ in office relations⟩ **2** : the policy of being impersonal in relations with other persons or of maintaining impersonal relations among a group

im·personality \(ˌ)im, əm+\ *n* [¹*impersonal* + *-ity*] **1** : the lack or absence of a personal or human character ⟨the ~ of natural law⟩ **2** : the quality or state of not involving personal feelings or the emotions or of being unemotional and disinterested ⟨marveled at the ~ of the thinking of so passionate a man⟩ ⟨the emotional detachment and ~ required of a good playwright —Leslie Rees⟩ ⟨so much ~, so much coldness and emphasis on technique —Manny Farber⟩ **3 a** : the quality or state of not involving, not being activated by, or not tracing to a personal agent ⟨the ~ of the popular ballad⟩ ⟨the ~ of the machine⟩ **b** : a quality or state marked by an absence or suppression of human expression or a minimizing of the significance of personality ⟨the ~ of society⟩ ⟨the ~ of the world money market⟩ **c** : the quality of not bearing on only a single or a particular person ⟨the ~, the universality of his remarks⟩ **4** : something impersonal ⟨forced to deal with *impersonalities* such as the state or the law⟩

im·personalization \(ˌ)im, əm+\ *n* : the act of impersonalizing or the state of being impersonalized ⟨the growing ~ of higher civilizations —A.L.Kroeber⟩

im·personalize \(ˈ)im, əm+\ *vt* [¹*impersonal* + *-ize*] : to make impersonal ⟨one cannot ~ entirely a cosmic human drama like that war —W.A.White⟩

¹im·per·son·ate \ə̇mˈpərsᵊn,āt, -pə̄s-, -pəis-, *usu* -ād.+V\ *vt* [²*in-* + *person* + *-ate* (v. suffix)] **1 a** *obs* : to give or ascribe the qualities of a person to : PERSONIFY **b** *archaic* : TYPIFY, EXEMPLIFY **2** : to assume the character of : pretend to be in actuality or personality, appearance, or behavior : PERSONATE ⟨caught trying to ~ an officer⟩ ⟨do not have the correct intonation for the character they are trying to ~ —Samuel Selden⟩ ⟨the dancers *impersonated* animals⟩ **3 a** : to give personal expression to ⟨an actor who could ~ any emotion⟩

b : to give expression to the person of ⟨music to ~ the hero of the opera⟩

²**im·per·son·ate** \-sᵊnət, *usu* -əd.+V\ *adj* [²*in-* + *person* + *-ate* (adj. suffix)] : invested with personality ⟨in the dictator all the forces of evil found an ~ expression⟩

im·per·son·a·tion \əm,=ˈ=ˈāshən, ˌim-\ *n* : the act of impersonating or the state of being impersonated ⟨arrested for his ~ of an army major⟩ ⟨a man noted for his ~ of women⟩ ⟨the musical ~ of the hero himself —Eric Blom⟩

im·per·son·a·tor \=ˈ==ˌād·ə(r), -ātə-\ *n* : one that impersonates; *esp* : an entertainer who impersonates an individual, a type of person, an animal, or an inanimate object

im·personification \ˌim+\ *n* [²*in-* + *personification*] : EMBODIMENT

im·personify \"+\ *vt* [²*in-* + *personify*] *archaic* : to give a personal form or expression to : PERSONIFY

im·pertinence *also* **impertinency** \im+, əm+, *or in senses* 1a & 2a ˈim+ˌ-\ *n* [*impertinence* fr. F, fr. ML *impertinentia*, fr. LL *impertinent-*, *impertinens* + L *-ia* -y; *impertinency* fr. F *impertinence* + E *-y*] **1** : the quality or state of being impertinent: as **a** : lack of relevance or appropriateness : IRRELEVANCE, UNFITNESS **b** : lack of due respect for others in conduct : INCIVILITY, INSOLENCE ⟨the ~, the brashness had gone forever —Katharine F. Gerould⟩ **2** : something impertinent or an instance of impertinence: **a** : an irrelevant thing or matter ⟨at the climax of high tragedy all scenic adjuncts become an ~ —W.B.Adams⟩ **b** : an impertinent or uncivil act or person ⟨irritated by the man's social faults and ~s⟩ ⟨unwilling to scold the young ~ that was his son⟩

¹**im·pertinent** \(ˈ)im, əm+\ *adj* [ME, fr. MF, fr. LL *impertinent-*, *impertinens*, fr. L *in-* ¹*in-* + *pertinent-*, *pertinens*, pres. part. of *pertinēre* to reach out, extend, pertain — more at PERTAIN] **1 a** : not pertinent : not significantly belonging or related to the matter in hand : IRRELEVANT, INAPPLICABLE ⟨should rigidly exclude courses of study ~ to their central purposes —H.W.Sams⟩ **b** *obs* : not suitable or congruous : INAPPROPRIATE **c** *archaic* : FRIVOLOUS, FOOLISH **2** : not restrained within the due or proper bounds esp. of propriety or good breeding in words or actions : guilty of or prone to rudeness or incivility ⟨a child taught not to make ~ remarks to his elders⟩ ⟨approach complete strangers, ask them a battery of ~ questions —S.L.Payne⟩

syn IMPERTINENT, OFFICIOUS, MEDDLESOME, INTRUSIVE, OBTRUSIVE: IMPERTINENT implies a concerning of oneself offensively with what is another's business ⟨all that had occurred to make my former interference in his affairs absurd and *impertinent* —Jane Austen⟩ ⟨we were secure from all *impertinent* interference in our concerns —Herman Melville⟩ ⟨something so extremely *impertinent* in entering upon a man's premises, and using them without paying —William Cowper⟩ OFFICIOUS implies an offering of unwelcome or offensive services, attentions, or assistance ⟨cannot walk home from office, but some *officious* friend offers his unwelcome courtesies to accompany me —Charles Lamb⟩ ⟨had no desire to call in a detective for fear the man might become an *officious* nuisance⟩ MEDDLESOME stresses an annoying and usu. prying interference in others' business ⟨turns with scorn upon the Abolitionists and their *meddlesome* interference with the beneficent ways of Providence —V.L.Parrington⟩ ⟨a vain, *meddlesome* vagabond, and must needs pry into a secret which certainly did not concern him —Charles Kingsley⟩ INTRUSIVE applies to one who has or something that reveals a disposition to be unduly curious about another's business ⟨made an inconspicuous fourth in their small world, always at hand yet never *intrusive* —B.A.Williams⟩ ⟨to protect oneself by silence from well-meaning but *intrusive* friends⟩ OBTRUSIVE is like INTRUSIVE but usu. stresses more objectionable actions than a disposition, suggesting an undue, improper, or offensive conspicuousness of interference ⟨she knelt and watched, quietly, without expressing any *obtrusive* concern for his safety —Floyd Dell⟩ ⟨the *obtrusive* attentions of sycophants and henchmen⟩

²**impertinent** \"\ *n* : an impertinent person : one that is presumptuous, meddlesome, or insolent

im·per·ti·nent·ly *adv* [ME, fr. *impertinent* + *-ly*] : in an impertinent manner ⟨prying ~ into my affairs⟩

im·per·ti·nent·ness *n* -ES : IMPERTINENCE

im·per·turb·abil·i·ty \ˌimpər,tərbəˈbiləd·ē\ *n* : the quality or state of being imperturbable ⟨no excitement or depression ever disturbed his extraordinary ~⟩

im·per·turb·able \-ˈtərbəbəl\ *adj* [ME, fr. LL *imperturbabilis*, fr. L *in-* ¹*in-* + *perturbare* to perturb + *-abilis* -able — more at PERTURB] : marked by extreme calm, impassivity, assurance, and steadiness : unlikely to be disconcerted, agitated, or alarmed ⟨hitherto ~, he now showed signs of alarm⟩ ⟨an ~ self-possession —Albert Dasnoy⟩ **syn** see COOL

im·per·turb·able·ness *n* -ES : IMPERTURBABILITY ⟨a certain calm indifference, a certain ~ —J.C.Powys⟩

im·per·turb·ably \-blē\ *adv* : in an imperturbable manner ⟨stalked ~ about the streets . . . or stood impassively in doorways —Green Peyton⟩

im·perturbation \(ˌ)im+\ *n* [LL *imperturbation-*, *imperturbatio*, fr. L *in-* ¹*in-* + *perturbation-*, *perturbatio* perturbation — more at PERTURBATION] : freedom from agitation : CALMNESS, QUIETUDE

im·perturbed \ˌim+\ *adj* [¹*in-* + *perturbed*] : not perturbed : CALM

im·per·vi·a·ble \(ˈ)imˌpərvēəbəl\ *adj* [alter. (influenced by *impermeable*) of *impervious*] : IMPERVIOUS, IMPERMEABLE

im·pervious \(ˈ)im+\ *adj* [L *impervius*, fr. *in-* ¹*in-* + *pervius* pervious — more at PERVIOUS] **1 a** : not allowing entrance or passage through : IMPENETRABLE ⟨waterproofed so that the coat was ~ to rain⟩ ⟨a steel ~ to bullets⟩ **b** : not capable of being damaged or harmed ⟨a carpet material ~ to most rough treatment⟩ **2** : not capable of being affected or disturbed ⟨a man ~ to criticism⟩ ⟨looked at her, ~ to her tears —Jean Stafford⟩ : not open ⟨~ to arguments or facts⟩ — **im·perviously** \"+\ *adv* — **im·perviousness** \"+\ *n*

im·pest \əmˈpest\ *archaic var of* EMPEST

impester *vt* [MF *empestrer* — more at PESTER] *obs* : ENTANGLE, EMBARRASS

im·pe·tig·i·nized \ˌimpəˈtijə,nīzd\ *adj* [L *impetigin-*, *impetigo* + E *-ize* + *-ed*] : secondarily covered with crusts — used of skin diseases or lesions ⟨~ dermatitis⟩

im·pe·tig·i·nous \-ˌnəs\ *adj* [LL *impetiginosus*, fr. L *impetigin-*, *impetigo* + *-osus* -ous] : of, relating to, or like impetigo — **im·pe·tig·i·nous·ly** *adv*

im·pe·ti·go \ˌimpəˈtī(ˌ)gō, -tī(-\ *n* -S [L, fr. *impetere* to attack — more at IMPETUS] : an acute contagious skin disease characterized by the formation of vesicles, pustules, and yellowish crusts and caused by staphylococci or streptococci transmitted by contact between persons or between healthy and infected skin

im·pe·trate \ˈimpə,trāt\ *vt* -ED/-ING/-S [L *impetratus*, past part. of *impetrare*, fr. *in-* ²*in-* + *-petrare* (fr. *patrare* to accomplish) — more at PERPETRATE] **1** : to obtain by request or entreaty : PROCURE **2** : to ask for : ENTREAT

im·pe·tra·tion \ˌimpəˈtrāshən\ *n* -S [L *impetration-*, *impetratio*, fr. *impetratus* + *-ion-*, *-io* -ion] **1** : the act of impetrating : petition or a procuring by petition **2** *Old Eng law* : the act of obtaining from Rome by solicitation a benefice which belonged to the disposal of the king or other lay patron of the realm

im·pe·tra·tive \ˈimpə,trād·iv\ *adj* [LL *impetrativus*, fr. L *impetratus* + *-ivus* -ive] : of, relating to, or being impetration : consisting of, getting, or tending to get by entreaty

im·pe·tra·to·ry \ˈimpə·trə,tōrē\ *adj* [L *impetratus* + E *-ory*] *archaic* : IMPETRATIVE

im·pet·u·os·i·ty \(ˌ)im,pechəˈwäsəd·ē, əm-, -sətē, -i\ *n* -ES [MF *impetuosité*, fr. OF, fr. LL *impetuosus* + OF *-ité* -ity] **1** : the quality or state of being impetuous ⟨the ~ of his proposal —Louis Auchincloss⟩ **2** : an impetuous action or impulse ⟨a man driven by *impetuosities* and whims⟩

im·pet·u·o·so \(ˌ)im,pechəˈwō(ˌ)sō, -)zō\ *adj* (*or adv*) [It, fr. LL *impetuosus*] : IMPETUOUS — used as a direction in music

im·pet·u·ous \(ˈ)imˈpechəwəs, əmˈp-\ *adj* [ME, fr. MF *impetueux*, fr. LL *impetuosus*, fr. L *impetus* + *-osus* -ous] **1** : marked by force and violence of movement or action : FURIOUS ⟨an ~ wind⟩ ⟨with ~ speed⟩ ⟨match his more ~ neighbors working furiously at their hobbies —G.B.Shaw⟩ **2** : impulsively vehement in feeling ⟨of a very warm and ~ nature, responded to their affection with quite a tropical ardor —W.M.Thackeray⟩ : hastily or rashly energetic or passionate ⟨~ in his habits . . . lost his temper and punched another officer in the nose —J.G.Cozzens⟩ ⟨restless, energetic, ~, temperamental, and at times a little irascible —A.W.Long⟩ **syn** see PRECIPITATE

im·pet·u·ous·ly *adv* : in an impetuous manner ⟨a stream rushing ~ over rocks⟩

im·pet·u·ous·ness *n* -ES [ME *impetuousnes*, fr. *impetuous* + *-nes* -ness] : the quality or state of being impetuous

im·pe·tus \ˈimpəd·əs, -pətəs\ *n* -ES [L, attack, assault, impetus, fr. *impetere* to attack, fr. *in-* ²*in-* + *petere* to go to or toward, rush at, attack, seek — more at FEATHER] **1 a** (1) : a driving or impelling force ⟨trying to discover the ~ behind all this activity⟩ : IMPULSE ⟨an intermittent force, each ~ being of only the shortest duration⟩ (2) : INCENTIVE, STIMULUS ⟨felt no ~ to do well in school⟩ **b** : stimulation or encouragement resulting in increased activity ⟨gave a good deal of ~ to the musical activity of the city⟩ **2** : the property possessed by a moving body in virtue of its mass and its motion — used of bodies moving suddenly or violently to indicate the origin and intensity of the motion rather than the quantity or effectiveness

im·pey·an pheasant \ˈimpēən-\ *n* [Sir Elijah *Impey* †1809 Eng. jurist, and Lady *Impey* †1818 his wife, who introduced the bird into England + E *-an*] : a monal (*Lophophorus impejanus*) ranging from Afghanistan to Assam

impf *abbr* imperfect

im·phee \ˈim(p)fē\ *n* -S [Zulu *imfe*] : any of several African sorghums

im·pi \ˈimpē\ *n* -S [Zulu] : a body of Kaffir warriors or other southern African native armed men

im·picture \əm+\ *vt* [²*in-* + *picture* (n.)] *archaic* : to represent as if in a picture : PORTRAY

im·piety \(ˈ)im, əm+\ *n* [MF *impieté*, fr. L *impietat-*, *impietas*, fr. *impius* impious + *-tat-*, *-tas* -ty — more at IMPIOUS] **1 a** : the quality or state of being impious : lack of piety : IRREVERENCE, UNGODLINESS ⟨~, in denying the gods recognized by the state —J.S.Mill⟩ **b** : UNDUTIFULNESS ⟨guilty of filial ~ in showing no respect for his father's advice⟩ **2** : an impious act ⟨his sins turned into his *impieties* —William Empson⟩

im·pig·no·rate \əmˈpignə,rāt\ *vt* [LL or ML *impignoratus*, *impigneratus*, past part. of *impignorare*, *impignerare*, fr. L *in-* ²*in-* + *pignorare*, *pignerare* to pledge — more at PIGNORATE] : PLEDGE, PAWN, MORTGAGE — **im·pig·no·ra·tion** \=,==ˈrāshən\ *n*

imp·ing \ˈimpiŋ\ *n* -S [ME, fr. gerund of *impen* to graft — more at IMP] : the process in falconry of mending a broken pinion by inserting one end of a specially prepared needle into the stub of the feather and the other into the shaft of the original feather or a replacement feather

im·pinge \əmˈpinj\ *vb* -ED/-ING/-S [L *impingere* to strike or push at or against, fr. *in-* ²*in-* + *-pingere* (fr. *pangere* to fasten, drive in) — more at PACT] *vi* **1** : to strike or dash esp. with a sharp collision : come into sharp contact — usu. used with *on*, *upon*, or *against* ⟨when an elastic ball ~s on another —K.K.Darrow⟩ ⟨I heard the rain ~ upon the earth —James Joyce⟩ ⟨the creak of oarlocks *impinged* on his ear⟩ ⟨something ~s violently on your senses —Peggy Durdin⟩ ⟨a strong light *impinging* on the eyes and causing a sudden pain⟩ **2** : to come into a relationship as if impinging : make an impression : touch closely or bear directly — usu. used with *on* or *upon* ⟨waiting for the germ of a new idea to ~ upon my mind —Phyllis Bentley⟩ ⟨the objects that *impinged* upon his imagination with the greatest impact —*Times Lit. Supp.*⟩ ⟨in that line of reasoning we ~ upon an abstruse metaphysical problem⟩ ⟨political forces that ~ on everyone's daily life⟩ **3** : ENCROACH, INFRINGE — usu. used with *on* ⟨*impinging* on other people's rights⟩ ⟨not that I want to ~ on any man's recreation —Ezra Pound⟩ ~ *vt* : to cause (as a gas or a flame) to strike ⟨*impinging* live steam on the printed surface —*Chem. & Engineering News*⟩

im·pinge·ment \-mənt\ *n* -S : the act of impinging or the state of being impinged upon: as **a** : a sharp collision : a striking or dashing against **b** : INFLUENCE, EFFECT, ENCROACHMENT, INFRINGEMENT ⟨the ~ of American power upon Asiatic life without adequate comprehension of the vast complexities of Asiatic politics —Reinhold Niebuhr⟩ ⟨the ~ of Russia's security aims upon interests of Britain or the U. S. —Allan Taylor⟩ **syn** see IMPACT

impingement black *n* : CHANNEL BLACK

im·pin·gent \-jənt\ *adj* [L *impingent-*, *impingens*, pres. part. of *impingere*] : IMPINGING ⟨ecological factors ~ upon the production and use of foods —Theodore Stern⟩

im·ping·er \-jə(r)\ *n* -S : an instrument for collecting samples of dust or other suspended particles esp. in air by impinging a stream of the suspension on a surface or in a liquid (as water)

impinguate *vt* -ED/-ING/-S [LL *impinguatus*, past part. of *impinguare*, fr. L *in-* ²*in-* + *pinguis* fat — more at PINGUID] *obs* : FATTEN

im·pi·ous \ˈimpēəs, (ˈ)imˈpīəs\ *adj* [L *impius*, fr. *in-* ¹*in-* + *pius* pious — more at PIOUS] : not pious : IRREVERENT: **a** : lacking reverence for God, a deity, or for what is sacred : PROFANE, IRRELIGIOUS ⟨an ~ life⟩ **b** : lacking in proper respect (as for parents or for something usu. held in general respect) ⟨an ~ son⟩ ⟨an ~ flouting of experience —Donagh MacDonagh⟩ ⟨any alteration in the ceremonies that surrounded Thanksgiving would have been considered ~ and heartbreaking by my mother —John Cheever⟩

syn PROFANE, BLASPHEMOUS, SACRILEGIOUS: IMPIOUS usu. implies extreme disrespect for a divinity or his attributes and manifestations ⟨the *impious* challenge of power divine —William Cowper⟩ ⟨who is there more *impious* than a backsliding priest? —John Steinbeck⟩ PROFANE in this sense may suggest not only the disrespect involved in IMPIOUS but also desecration, intentional or not, of something to be held inviolate ⟨hitherto no liberal statesman has been so audacious as to "imagine the king's death" and lay *profane* hands on the divine right of nations to seek their own advantage at the cost of the rest by such means as the rule of reason shall decide to be permissible —Thorstein Veblen⟩ ⟨I collected bones from charnel houses; and disturbed, with *profane* fingers, the tremendous secrets of the human frame —Mary W. Shelley⟩ BLASPHEMOUS may apply to strong and intentional impiety or profanation fervently expressed or performed or to the harboring and abetting of ideas calculated to lower the awesome dignity of a deity ⟨*blasphemous* conversation⟩ ⟨it is *blasphemous* because it attributes to God purposes which we would not respect even in an earthly parent —J.A.Pike⟩ SACRILEGIOUS commonly may describe any flagrant depredation, disrespect, or contempt ⟨*sacrilegious* in his scandalous burlesques of the gods⟩ All of these words lend themselves to broad and inexact uses.

im·pi·ous·ly *adv* : in an impious manner

im·pi·ous·ness *n* : IMPIETY

imp·ish \ˈimpish, -pēsh\ *adj* : of, relating to, or befitting an imp; *esp* : MISCHIEVOUS ⟨the spectacle is weird and grotesque, and suggests something ~ and uncanny —John Burroughs⟩ ⟨took ~ delight in pestering his parents⟩ ⟨the child's ~ face⟩ — **imp·ish·ly** *adv* — **imp·ish·ness** *n* -ES

im·pit·e·ous \(ˈ)imˈpid·ēəs\ *adj* [¹*in-* + *piteous*] : PITILESS, CRUEL

impl *abbr* **1** imperial **2** implement

im·placa·bil·i·ty \(ˌ)im,plakəˈbiləd·ē, əm-, -lətē, -i *also* -plāk-\ *n* [LL *implacabilitas*, fr. L *implacabilis* + *-itas* -ity] : the quality or state of being implacable ⟨the ~ of his resentments —Jane Austen⟩ ⟨the ~ of a Greek tragedy —Arthur Schlesinger b. 1917⟩

im·placa·ble \(ˈ)imˈplakəbəl, əmˈp- *also* -plāk-\ *adj* [MF or L; MF, fr. L *implacabilis*, fr. *in-* ¹*in-* + *placabilis* placable — more at PLACABLE] **1 a** : not placable : not capable of being appeased or pacified : INEXORABLE ⟨an ~ enemy⟩ ⟨an ~ resentment⟩ ⟨single-minded and ~, even unmerciful, in his servitude to the law —M.S.Mayer⟩ **b** : incapable of being significantly changed or modified : following a due unalterable course ⟨the ~ lives of plants —Clifford Gessler⟩ ⟨the ~ logic of his career⟩ ⟨the measured, arranged, ~ movement of the universe —A.J.Cronin⟩ **2** : incapable of being relieved or mitigated ⟨an ~ disease⟩ ⟨the horns of an ~ dilemma —J.C. Powys⟩ ⟨his ~ interest in love —William McFee⟩ ⟨watched that ~ blaze of space as far as the mountainous horizon —D.C.Peattie⟩ — **im·placa·ble·ness** \-bəlnəs\ *n* — **im·placa·bly** \-blē, -bli\ *adv*

im·place·ment \əmˈplāsmənt\ *n* [modif. (influenced by ²*in-*) of F *emplacement* — more at EMPLACEMENT] : EMPLACEMENT

im·placentalia \(ˌ)im+\ *n pl*, *cap* [NL, fr. ¹*in-* + *Placentalia*] *in former classifications* : the monotremes and marsupials regarded as a systematic unit characterized by the absence or rudimentary development of a placenta

¹**im·plant** \əm+\ *also* **em·plant** \əm,em+\ *vt* [²*in-* or ¹*en-* + *plant*] **1 a** : to fix or set securely or deeply ⟨a ruby ~*ed* in a gold ring⟩ **b** : to set or fix as permanent in the consciousness, the psyche, or habit patterns : INSTILL, INCULCATE ⟨~ good habits in children⟩ ⟨~ in a person the idea that the end of the world is near⟩ ⟨such a taste . . . simply cannot be ~*ed* —H.L.Mencken⟩ **2** *archaic* : PLANT **3 a** : to insert in a living site for growth, formation of an organic union, or absorption **b** : to insert an implant in ⟨100 patients have been ~*ed* with nylon ribbons without complications —U.K.Henschke⟩

syn IMPLANT, INCULCATE, INSTILL can mean, in common, to introduce into the mind. IMPLANT implies teaching and stresses a fixing firmly in the mind of what is taught or advocated ⟨the duty of Congress to see that educational institutions *implant* only sound ideas in the minds of students —Elmer Davis⟩ ⟨the teacher, the parent, or the friend can often do much to *implant* this conviction —C.W.Eliot⟩ ⟨in me especially, she *implanted* a respect for pioneering tradition —Rex Ingamells⟩ ⟨sea voyagers . . . may remain to *implant* their knowledge and practices in the new territory —C.D. Forde⟩ INCULCATE lays stress on repeated persistent efforts to impress on or fix in the mind ⟨it is no part of the duty of a university to *inculcate* any particular philosophy of life —Walter Moberly⟩ ⟨a means of *inculcating* in the conscripts intense patriotism and religious devotion to the state —Chitoshi Yanaga⟩ ⟨the seriousness *inculcated* in men by two cataclysmic world wars —S.P.Lamprecht⟩ INSTILL implies a gradual usu. gentle method of imparting knowledge usu. over a long period of time ⟨the principles which had been *instilled* in her soul from the time she began to speak —Ruth Park⟩ ⟨schools must plan to *instill* not only knowledge, but more of permanent refined interests; not only scholarship, but more of character and social purpose —A.C.Ellis⟩ ⟨a profound sense of public duty will be *instilled* into boys and girls of the governing class as soon as they are able to understand such an idea —Bertrand Russell⟩

²**im·plant** \ˈim+,-\ *n* : something implanted esp. in tissue (as a graft, a small container of radioactive material for treatment of cancer, or a pellet containing hormones to be gradually absorbed)

im·plan·ta·tion \ˌim,planˈtāshən, -laan-,-län-\ *n* **1** : the act or process of implanting or the state of being implanted: as **a** : the placement of the root of a tooth in an artificially prepared socket in the jawbone **b** *in placental mammals* : the process of attachment of the embryo to the maternal uterine wall **c** : experimental addition of tissue or other material to an intact embryo **d** : medical treatment by the insertion of an implant **2** : the spontaneous passage of cells esp. of tumors to a new site with subsequent growth — compare METASTASIS

im·plastic \(ˈ)im+\ *adj* [¹*in-* + *plastic*] : not plastic : not readily molded : STIFF — **im·plasticity** \ˌim+\ *n*

im·plausibility \(ˌ)im, əm+\ *n* **1** : the quality or state of being implausible ⟨put on his guard by the ~ of the man's explanation⟩ **2** : something implausible

im·plausible \(ˈ)im, əm+\ *adj* [¹*in-* + *plausible*] : not plausible : having a quality that provokes disbelief ⟨experienced a number of ~ adventures⟩ ⟨gave the teacher an ~ explanation of his absence from school⟩ — **im·plausibleness** \"+\ *n* — **im·plausibly** \"+\ *adv*

im·pleach \əm+\ *vt* [²*in-* + *pleach*] : PLEACH, INTERWEAVE

im·plead \əmˈplēd\ *vb* [ME *empleden*, *impleden*, fr. MF *empleider*, *emplaider*, fr. OF *empleidier*, *emplaidier*, fr. *en-* ¹*en-* + *pleidier*, *plaidier* to plead — more at PLEAD] *vt* **1 a** : to institute and prosecute a suit against in a court : sue or prosecute at law ⟨the government, as a general rule, claims an exemption from being sued in its own courts . . . will not permit itself to be ~*ed* therein —H.M.Hart⟩ **b** *archaic* : ACCUSE, IMPEACH **2** *archaic* : PLEAD **3** : to include or incorporate as part of or party to a legal suit or action ⟨modern procedure permits a defendant to ~ . . . a third person —Herbert Peterfreund⟩ ⟨the bond . . . was ~*ed* as a part of the motion for judgment —*Southeastern Reporter*⟩ ~ *vi*, *archaic* : PLEAD

im·plead·able \-dəbəl\ *adj*, *archaic* : capable of being sued or prosecuted at law

im·plead·er \-də(r)\ *n* **1** : one that impleads **2** : INTERPLEADER

im·pledge \əm+\ *vt* [²*in-* + *pledge* (n.)] *archaic* : PLEDGE

¹**im·ple·ment** \ˈimpləmənt\ *n* -S [ME, fr. LL *implementum* action of filling up, fr. L *implēre* to fill up, finish (fr. *in-* ²*in-* + *plēre* to fill) + *-mentum* -ment — more at FULL] **1 a** : an article (as of apparel or furniture) serving to equip ⟨the ~s of religious worship⟩ **b** : a tool or utensil forming part of equipment for work ⟨a farm ~⟩ ⟨an ~ of war⟩ ⟨the ~s of his trade⟩ ⟨useful ~s such as axes, chisels, gouges, arrowheads, pestles and mortars, and ornamented pipes —*Amer. Guide Series: R.I.*⟩ ⟨the need for an ~ to help roll the heavy logs —*McGill News*⟩ **c** : one that serves as an instrument or tool ⟨judges striving to be efficient ~s of justice⟩ ⟨the most stringent ~ that could be employed . . . would be withdrawal of safe conduct for Swedish ships plying the Atlantic —*Newsweek*⟩ **2** *Scots law* : FULFILLMENT, PERFORMANCE

syn IMPLEMENT, TOOL, INSTRUMENT, APPLIANCE, UTENSIL apply in common to any device usu. relatively simple for performing a mechanical or manual operation. IMPLEMENT applies to anything, usu. a contrivance, necessary to effect an end or perform a task ⟨spades and other gardener's *implements*⟩ ⟨swords, guns, and *implements* of war⟩ ⟨propaganda as an *implement* of cold war⟩ ⟨the quill pen was an early *implement* of communication⟩ TOOL suggests an implement adapted to facilitate a given work, esp. the work of a craftsman or artisan ⟨carpenter's *tools*⟩ ⟨a pipe wrench and other plumber's *tools*⟩ ⟨a new research *tool*, in the form of a bibliography of all the literature on the arctic put out in the last 75 years —*Science*⟩ ⟨reference *tools* like the dictionary and the encyclopedia —*English Language Arts*⟩ ⟨the breeder uses three basic *tools* to bring about the genetic improvement of animals . . . selection, inbreeding, and crossing —*Science in Farming*⟩ INSTRUMENT suggests delicate construction or precision work as in dentistry, surgery, or surveying and may extend beyond mechanical or manual operation as in instruments for recording temperatures or rates of speed or musical instruments or in any more or less precise device for achieving any end ⟨the laboratory *instruments* necessary to careful scientific research⟩ ⟨an oscilloscope and other radio-testing *instruments*⟩ ⟨language is the essential *instrument* for the acquirement and communication of ideas —L.J.Shehan⟩ ⟨in a day when novels were considered *instruments* of Satan —*Amer. Guide Series: N.Y.*⟩ APPLIANCE is used usu. for a device which effects work but which is moved by some power other than or in addition to guidance or control by hand ⟨washing machines, vacuum cleaners, and other household *appliances*⟩ ⟨*appliance* means current-consuming equipment, fixed or portable; for example, heating, cooking, and small motor-operated equipment —*Nat'l Electric Safety Code*⟩ ⟨the clutch cleats for the sheet lines, reefing gears, and many other *appliances* used with the enormous sails —E.J.Schoettle⟩ UTENSIL suggests something useful in accomplishing work, esp. domestic work or work similar to it, and usu. manageable by hand ⟨pipe, pipe cleaners, and other smoking *utensils*⟩ ⟨a rolling pin, a fork, a frying pan and an oven are the *utensils* with which she makes her pie —Gilbert Ryle⟩ ⟨kitchen *utensils*⟩ ⟨fingers were the only eating *utensils* —H.A.Chippendale⟩

²**im·ple·ment** \-ˌment, -mənt — *see* ²-MENT\ *vt* -ED/-ING/-S **1 a** : to carry out : ACCOMPLISH, FULFILL ⟨wondering how he might best ~ his purpose⟩ ⟨continued to clamor for action to ~ the promise —*N.Y.Times*⟩ ⟨a committee to ~ the plans so well formulated⟩; *esp* : to give practical effect to and ensure of actual fulfillment by concrete measures ⟨failure to carry out and ~ the will of the majority —Clement Attlee⟩ ⟨an

agency created to ~ the recommendation of the committee⟩ ⟨programs to ~ our foreign policy⟩ **b :** to provide instruments or means of practical expression for ⟨survey the problem as a whole and ~ the joint interest in an expanding economy —George Soule⟩ **2 :** SUPPLEMENT **syn** see ENFORCE

im·ple·men·tal \¦==¦mentᵊl\ *adj* **:** of, relating to, or being an implement or relating to or providing implementation

im·ple·men·ta·ry \-ntərē, -n·trē, -ri\ *adj* **:** providing implementation ⟨~ legislation⟩

im·ple·men·ta·tion \,==,mən·'tāshən, -(,)men-·\ *n* -s **:** the act of implementing or the state of being implemented

im·ple·ment·er *or* **im·ple·men·tor** \'==,mentə(r)\ *n* -s **:** one that implements

im·ple·men·tif·er·ous \¦==(,)=·¦tif(ə)rəs\ *adj* **:** bearing or containing implements ⟨~ strata at an archaeological site⟩

im·ple·tion \əm'plēshən\ *n* -s [LL *impletion-, impletio,* fr. L *impletus* (past part. of *implēre* to fill up) + *-ion-, -io* -ion — more at IMPLEMENT] *archaic* **:** the act of filling or the state of being full

im·pli·able \(,)im¦plīəbəl, əm'p-\ *adj* [¹*in-* + *pliable*] **:** not pliable **:** INFLEXIBLE

im·pli·cant \'impləkənt, -lēk-\ *n* -s [L *implicant-, implicans,* pres. part. of *implicare*] **:** something that implies (as a proposition)

¹im·pli·cate \-kə̇|t, -,kā|, *usu* |d.+V\ *adj* [L *implicatus*] **1** *obs* **:** INTERTWINED, ENTANGLED, INVOLVED **2 :** IMPLIED, IMPLICIT ⟨content to let this accusation remain ~ in her questions —Osbert Sitwell⟩

²im·pli·cate \-,kāt, *usu* -ād·+V\ *vt* [L *implicatus,* past part. of *implicare* to infold, involve, implicate, engage — more at EMPLOY] **1** *archaic* **:** to fold or twist together **:** INTERWEAVE, ENTWINE ⟨the meeting boughs and *implicated* leaves —P.B. Shelley⟩ **2 :** to involve as a consequence, corollary, or natural inference **:** IMPLY **3 a :** to bring into intimate or incriminating connection **:** involve deeply or unfavorably ⟨evidence *implicating* many high officials in the conspiracy⟩ ⟨an innocent person *implicated* by circumstances in a crime⟩ ⟨all men, even the most virtuous and wise, are *implicated* in historic evil —Reinhold Niebuhr⟩ **b :** to involve in the nature or operation of something **:** connect intimately **:** require or entail as a natural or necessary cause, concomitant, or consequence ⟨local diseases often ~ a general derangement of the system⟩ ⟨each element in life forms part of a cultural mesh: one part *implicates* . . . the other —Lewis Mumford⟩ **syn** see INCLUDE

³im·pli·cate *same as adj*\ *n* -s [¹*implicate*] **:** something (as a proposition) implied or involved ⟨made ethics independent of theology and theology a series of ~*s* from the moral life —E.E. Aubrey⟩

im·pli·ca·tion \,==¦kāshən\ *n* -s [ME *implicacioun,* fr. L *implication-, implicatio,* fr. *implicatus,* + *-ion-, -io* -ion] **1 :** the act of implicating or the state of being implicated **a** *archaic* **:** a twisting together **:** ENTWINEMENT, INTERWEAVING **b :** close connection, relationship, or involvement (as from long association, logical inevitability, intimate accompaniment) ⟨in the arts, in literature, and in science . . . all these activities were freeing themselves from their religious ~*s* —Stringfellow Barr⟩ ⟨looked upon railroad operation purely in its engineering ~*s* —O.S.Nock⟩; *esp* **:** an incriminating involvement ⟨suspected of ~ in a number of robberies⟩ **2 a :** the act of implying or the state of being implied ⟨no concept that by ~ views a functional bureaucracy as the ruling class can be tolerated —K.A.Wittfogel⟩ ⟨speak of their own language with at least an ~ of disparagement —George Sampson⟩ ⟨whether in words or by ~ —O.W.Holmes †1935⟩ **b :** one of several formal logical relationships or a statement containing propositions in such a relationship: (1) **:** a logical relationship of the form symbolically rendered "if *p* then *q*" in which *p* and *q* are propositions and in which *p* is false or *q* is true or both; *also* **:** a statement in this form — called also *material implication* (2) **:** a logical relationship of the form symbolically rendered "if *p* then strictly *q*" in which *q* is deducible from *p; also* **:** a statement in this form — called also *logical implication, strict implication* **c :** the symbol used to indicate one of these two formal relationships and rendered "if . . . then" or the logical operation implicit in one of them **3 :** something implied ⟨two propositions with a clear ~⟩ **:** INFERENCE ⟨was aware of the ~ to be found in his remarks⟩ **:** SUGGESTION, CONNOTATION ⟨tea is very important in British life, and a spectacular rise in its price does have political ~*s* —Michael Davie⟩ ⟨a book is a bulwark against the ~ of lack of culture —Allan McMahan⟩

im·pli·ca·tion·al \¦==¦kāshənᵊl\ *adj* **:** IMPLICATIVE — **im·pli·ca·tion·al·ly** \-ᵊlē, -əl, |i\ *adv*

im·plica·tive \'impl·ə,kād·iv, im'plikəd·-\ *adj* **:** of, relating to, or being implication or an implication **:** involving implication ⟨an ~ statement⟩ ⟨an ~ function⟩; *also* **:** tending to implicate — **im·plica·tive·ly** \-d·əvlē\ *adv* — **im·plica·tive·ness** \-d·ivnə̇s\ *n* -ES

im·plica·to·ry \'impləkə,tōrē, im'plik-, *chiefly Brit* ¦implə¦kātəri *or* -ā·tri\ *adj* **:** IMPLICATIVE

im·plic·it \(')im¦plisə̇t, əm'p-, *usu* -əd·+V\ *adj* [L *implicitus,* past part. of *implicare* to infold, involve, implicate, engage — more at EMPLOY] **1** *obs* **:** tangled or twisted together **:** INTERWOVEN **2 a** (1) **:** tacitly involved in something else **:** capable of being understood from something else though unexpressed **:** capable of being inferred **:** IMPLIED — compare EXPLICIT ⟨draws no social conclusions of his own, but they are ~ —Robert Lasch⟩ ⟨the artistic standards of our time are . . . ~ rather than codified —Michael Kitson⟩ (2) **:** involved in the nature or essence of something though not revealed, expressed, or developed **:** POTENTIAL ⟨the oak is ~ in the acorn⟩ ⟨a sculptor may see different figures ~ in a block of stone —John Dewey⟩ ⟨the drama ~ in an idea becomes explicit when it is shown as a point of view which a person holds and upon which he acts —F.J.Hoffman⟩ **b** (1) **:** not appearing overtly **:** confined in the organism ⟨~ behavior⟩ ⟨~ speech⟩ (2) *of a culture* **:** capable of being derived only as an implication from behavior **:** not apparent or overt to the people it characterizes **:** tacit and underlying **3 a :** lacking doubt or reserve **:** UNQUESTIONING, WHOLEHEARTED ⟨~ obedience⟩ ⟨an ~ trust⟩ **b** *obs* **:** UNQUALIFIED, ABSOLUTE ⟨~ ignorance —Francis Bacon⟩ **4** *archaic* **:** marked by an implicit faith, credulity, or obedience — **im·plic·it·ly** *adv* — **im·plic·it·ness** *n* -ES

implicit definition *n* **:** CONTEXTUAL DEFINITION

implicit function *n* **:** a mathematical function defined by means of a relation that is not solved for the function in terms of the independent variable or variables — opposed to *explicit function*

im·plic·i·ty \əm'plisəd·ē\ *n* -ES [prob. fr. F *implicité,* fr. *implicite* implicit (fr. L *implicitus*) + *-té* -ty] **:** the quality or state of being implicit ⟨the strangeness of a man's life and the ~ with which he accepts it —Albert Camus⟩

implied *past of* IMPLY

implied authority *or* **implied agency** *n* **:** authority that is not proved expressly but by inferences and reasonable deductions and that arises out of the language and course of conduct of the principal toward his agent and the agency

implied contract *n* **1 :** a contract inferred to have been entered into by the parties to it from their conduct or from a special relationship existing between them **2 :** QUASI CONTRACT

im·plied·ly \əm'plī(ə̇)dlē\ *adv* [ME, fr. *implied* (past part. of *implien* to imply) + *-ly* — more at IMPLY] **:** by implication ⟨uncataloged situations will arise and, not being specifically prohibited, will be taken as ~ permitted —W.E.Jackson b. 1919⟩

implied malice *n* **:** malice proved indirectly from all the attendant circumstances when it is impossible to prove the actual state of mind as evincing it — called also *constructive malice;* distinguished from *malice in fact*

implied power *n* **:** a power that is reasonably necessary and appropriate to carry out the purposes of a power expressly granted — usu. used in pl.

implied trust *n* **1 :** a trust created by operation of law for reasons based on considerations of morality, justice, conscience, and fair dealing, or to prevent unjust enrichment **2 :** a trust found by judicial construction to have been intended by the settlor notwithstanding the intent was not clearly manifested in express terms

implied warranty *n* **:** a warranty raised in the operation of law though not expressly made and arising out of a particular transaction for reasons of public policy (as, that a ship chartered is seaworthy, that food sold to people is fit for human consumption, that goods sold are merchantable)

im·plode \əm'plōd\ *vi* -ED/-ING/-S [²*in-* + *-plode* (as in *explode*)] **:** to burst inward ⟨when a vacuum tube breaks it ~*s*⟩

im·plo·ra·tion \,implə'rāshən -lō'r-, -lȯ'r-\ *n* -s [MF or L; MF, fr. L *imploration-, imploratio,* fr. *imploratus* (past part. of *implorare* to implore) + *-ion-, -io* -ion] **:** earnest supplication **:** IMPLORING

im·plore \əm'plō(ə)r, -ȯ(ə)r, -ōə, -ȯ(ə)\ *vb* -ED/-ING/-S [MF or L; MF *implorer,* fr. L *implorare,* fr. *in-* ²in- + *plorare* to cry out, wail, lament, prob. of imit. origin] *vt* **1 :** to call upon in supplication **:** urgently petition **:** BESEECH ⟨*implored* his Maker for help out of his trouble⟩ ⟨but don't, I ~ you, let the metropolis monopolize your attention or your time —Richard Joseph⟩ **2 :** to call for or pray for earnestly or in supplication ⟨~ someone else's help in a crisis⟩ ⟨~ another chance to prove his innocence⟩ ⟨asked in a voice that *implored* a favorable answer —Aldous Huxley⟩ ~ *vi* **:** ENTREAT, PRAY ⟨wished he would stop begging and *imploring*⟩ **syn** see BEG

im·plor·ing·ly *adv* **:** in the manner of one that implores **:** BESEECHINGLY

im·plor·ing·ness *n* -ES **:** the quality or state of one that implores

im·plo·sion \əm'plōzhən\ *n* -s [²*in-* + *-plosion* (as in *explosion*)] **1 :** the action of imploding — contrasted with *explosion* **2 a :** APPLOSION **b :** the inrush of air in forming a suction stop

¹im·plo·sive \-ōs|iv, |ēv *also* -ōz| *or* |əv\ *adj* [²*in-* + *-plosive* (as in *explosive*)] **:** of, relating to, or being an implosion **:** formed or uttered with implosion — **im·plo·sive·ly** \|əvlē, -li\ *adv*

²implosive \"\ *n* -s **:** an implosive consonant **:** SUCTION STOP

im·ploy \əm'plȯi\ *archaic var of* EMPLOY

im·plume \əm+\ *or* **em·plume** \əm,em+\ *vt* [²*in-* or ¹*en-* + *plume* (n.)] **:** to furnish with or as if with plumes

im·plumed \(')im, əm+\ *adj* [¹*in-* + *plumed*] *archaic* **:** having no feathers

implunge *vb* [²*in-* + *plunge*] *obs* **:** PLUNGE

im·plu·vi·um \(')im¦plüvēəm, əm'p-\ *n, pl* **implu·via** \-ēə\ [L, fr. *in-* ²in- + *-pluvium* (fr. *pluere* to rain) — more at FLOW] **:** a cistern or tank in the atrium or peristyle of a house of ancient Rome to receive the water falling through the compluvium

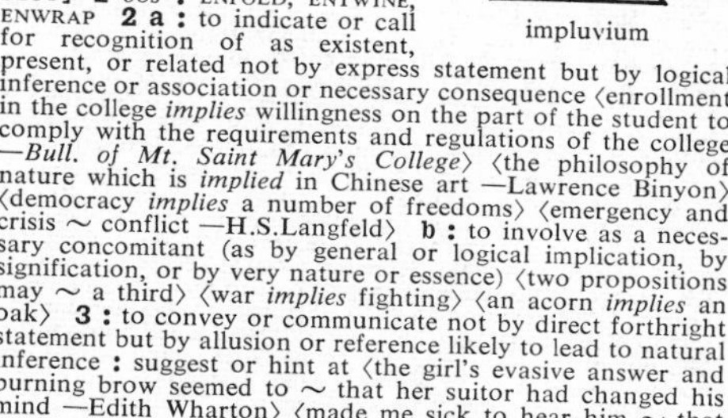

impluvium

im·ply \əm'plī\ *vt* **implied; implied; implying; implies** [ME *emplien, implien,* fr. MF *emplier,* fr. L *implicare* to infold, involve, implicate, engage — more at EMPLOY] **1** *obs* **:** ENFOLD, ENTWINE, ENWRAP **2 a :** to indicate or call for recognition of as existent, present, or related not by express statement but by logical inference or association or necessary consequence ⟨enrollment in the college *implies* willingness on the part of the student to comply with the requirements and regulations of the college —*Bull. of Mt. Saint Mary's College*⟩ ⟨the philosophy of nature which is *implied* in Chinese art —Lawrence Binyon⟩ ⟨democracy *implies* a number of freedoms⟩ ⟨emergency and crisis ~ conflict —H.S.Langfeld⟩ **b :** to involve as a necessary concomitant (as by general or logical implication, by signification, or by very nature or essence) ⟨two propositions may ~ a third⟩ ⟨war *implies* fighting⟩ ⟨an acorn *implies* an oak⟩ **3 :** to convey or communicate not by direct forthright statement but by allusion or reference likely to lead to natural inference **:** suggest or hint at ⟨the girl's evasive answer and burning brow seemed to ~ that her suitor had changed his mind —Edith Wharton⟩ ⟨made me sick to hear him ~ that somebody would make a report against him —Joseph Conrad⟩ ⟨the tone of the book was *implied* by shrewd advertisements —J.D.Hart⟩ **syn** see INCLUDE, SUGGEST

im·pocket \əm+\ *vt* [²*in-* + *pocket* (n.)] *archaic* **:** to keep or put in a pocket

im·po·fo \əm'pō(,)fō\ *n* -s [Zulu *im-pofu*] **:** ELAND

impolder *var of* EMPOLDER

im·policy \əm+\ *n* [¹*in-* + *policy*] **:** the quality or state of being impolitic **:** unsuitableness to the end in view **:** INEXPEDIENCY; *also* **:** an impolitic act

impolished *adj* [¹*in-* + *polished*] *obs* **:** not polished

im·polite \¦im+\ *adj* [L *impolitus* unpolished, unrefined, fr. *in-* ¹in- + *politus* polished, refined — more at POLITE] **:** not polite: **a** *obs* **:** lacking culture, cultivation, polish **b :** lacking in politeness, in etiquette, or in consideration of others **syn** see RUDE

im·po·lite·ly *adv* **:** in an impolite manner **:** RUDELY ⟨~ turning his back on her⟩

im·po·lite·ness *n* **:** the quality or state of being impolite **:** RUDENESS; *also* **:** an impolite act or remark

im·politic \(')im, əm+\ *also* **im·political** \¦im+\ *adj* [¹*in-* + *politic, political*] **:** not politic **:** contrary to or lacking in policy **:** UNWISE, INEXPEDIENT ⟨unjust and ~ discriminations between racial and other classes of citizens —E.P.Hutchinson⟩ ⟨would be manifestly ~ to start a brawl —Max Peacock⟩ — **im·politically** \¦im+\ *adv* — **im·politicalness** \"+\ *n* -ES — **im·politicly** \(')im, əm+\ *adv* — **im·politicness** \"+\ *n* -ES

im·pon·der·a·bil·ia \(,)im,pändərə'bilēə, əm-, -lyə\ *n pl* [NL, fr. neut. pl. of ML *imponderabilis*] **:** IMPONDERABLES ⟨it ignores these ~ without which life is no life, history no history, and a people no people —*Amer. Quarterly*⟩

im·ponderability \(,)im, əm+\ *n* **:** the quality or state of being imponderable

¹im·ponderable \(')im, əm+\ *adj* [ML *imponderabilis,* fr. L *in-* ¹in- + LL *ponderabilis* ponderable — more at PONDERABLE] **:** not ponderable **:** incapable of being weighed, measured, or evaluated with exactness ⟨supposed that there was an ~ electrical fluid which pervaded all space —S.F.Mason⟩ ⟨such ~ human factors as one's aesthetic sensitivity —Hunter Mead⟩ — **im·ponderableness** \"+\ *n* -ES — **im·ponderably** \"+\ *adv*

²imponderable \"\ *n* **:** an imponderable thing, element, or agency ⟨spiritual ~*s*⟩ ⟨that huge ~ which enters the courtroom: public opinion —Catherine Bowen⟩ ⟨the overriding importance of ~*s* in determining human conduct —John Russell b. 1872⟩

im·ponderous \(')im, əm+\ *adj* [¹*in-* + *ponderous*] **:** having no weight or insignificant weight **:** very light

impone *vt* -ED/-ING/-S [L *imponere* to put upon, impose, fr. *in-* ²in- + *ponere* to put, place — more at POSITION] *obs* **:** STAKE, WAGER

im·po·nent \əm'pōnənt, 'im,p-\ *n* -s [L *imponent-, imponens,* pres. part. of *imponere*] **:** one that imposes

imporous *adj* [¹*in-* + *porous*] *obs* **:** not porous

¹im·port \(')im¦pō(ə)r|t, əm'p-, -ȯ(ə)r|, -ōə|, -ȯ(ə)|, *usu* |d.+V\ *vb* -ED/-ING/-S [ME *importen,* fr. L *importare* to bring or carry into, introduce, cause, fr. *in-* ²in- + *portare* to carry — more at PORT] *vt* **1 a :** to bear or convey as purport, meaning, information, or portent **:** MEAN, SIGNIFY ⟨his words ~*ed* that some change in plans had to be made⟩ ⟨the verse then would ~ that the riders have let their freedom . . . get out of hand —Warren Carrier⟩ **b** *archaic* **:** EXPRESS, STATE **c :** to involve as a consequence or inevitable concomitant **:** IMPLY ⟨honor ~*s* justice⟩ **2 :** to bring from a foreign or external source **:** introduce from without ⟨food ~*ed* into the city from surrounding farms⟩ ⟨another murder case . . . distinguished by the local animosities sought to be ~*ed* into the trial —H.W. H.Knott⟩ ⟨~*ed* some college boys for the dance⟩; *esp* **:** to bring (as wares or merchandise) into a place or country from another country ⟨a business that ~*ed* toys from Japan⟩ ⟨~*ed* wheat during the grain shortage⟩ ⟨Icelanders . . . ~*ed* the literature of the Continent, translating it into their own tongue —Charlton Laird⟩ ⟨Canada also ~*s* a great many leading scientists —*Report: (Canadian) Royal Commission on Nat'l Development*⟩ — opposed to *export* **3** [MF *importer,* fr. OIt *importare,* fr. L] *archaic* **:** to be of importance or consequence to **:** have to do with **:** have a bearing on **:** CONCERN ~ *vi* [MF *importer*] **:** to be of moment or consequence **:** MATTER ⟨it ~*s* little that we are early or late⟩ **syn** see MEAN

²im·port \'im,p-\ *n* -s **1 :** something contained as signification or intention **:** PURPORT, MEANING ⟨trying vainly to fathom the ~ of the speaker's words⟩ ⟨a gesture whose ~ he knew immediately⟩ **2 :** WEIGHT, CONSEQUENCE, SIGNIFICANCE ⟨less concerned about the literary value of his books than about their social ~⟩ ⟨a man of great ~⟩ **3 :** something (as an article of merchandise) brought in from an outside source (as a foreign country) ⟨the car was a British ~ —Frances G. Patton⟩ ⟨chief ~*s* were machinery and vehicles, raw wool and cotton —*Americana Annual*⟩ **4 :** IMPORTATION ⟨a proclamation allowing the ~ of an additional 51 million pounds of peanuts —*Time*⟩ **syn** see IMPORTANCE

¹importable *adj* [ME, fr. MF, fr. LL *importabilis,* fr. L *in-* ¹in- + *portare* to carry, bear + *-abilis* -able — more at PORT] *obs* **:** UNENDURABLE, INTOLERABLE

²im·port·able \(')im¦pōr|d·əbəl, əm'p-, -pȯ(r)|, -pōə|, |tə-\ *adj* [¹*import* + *-able*] **:** capable of being imported ⟨an ~ article of merchandise⟩

im·por·tance \əm'pȯr|tᵊn(t)s, -ȯ(ə)|, *chiefly in NewEng & the South* |d·ən- *or* |tən-\ *n* -s [MF, fr. OIt *importanza,* fr. *importante*] **1 a :** the quality or state of being important **:** WEIGHT, SIGNIFICANCE ⟨an event of ~ in the history of the country⟩ ⟨a natural resource of great ~ to industry⟩ **b :** an important aspect or bearing ⟨this feat has several ~*s* —*Time*⟩ **2** *obs* **:** IMPORT, MEANING, SIGNIFICATION **3** *obs* **:** IMPORTUNITY, SOLICITATION **4** *obs* **:** a matter of importance

syn CONSEQUENCE, SIGNIFICANCE, IMPORT, MOMENT, WEIGHT: IMPORTANCE, the most general of these nouns, signifies a quality or state that is of value or influence, often with the implication that this is in someone's opinion ⟨issues which, whilst not the major significance, have some *importance* —*Current History*⟩ ⟨the *importance* of taking a wide, strategic view has prevailed —A.P.Ryan⟩ ⟨her sense of *importance* will help her —H.M.Parshley⟩ ⟨a position of some *importance* in industry⟩ ⟨clusters of huge inverted pleats that add *importance* to the skirt —Lois Long⟩ When used interchangeably with IMPORTANCE, CONSEQUENCE often applies to social rank, public position, or reputation but more generally implies an importance by reason of effects, results, or interrelationships ⟨a man of some *consequence*⟩ ⟨a subscription library in every town of *consequence* in the country —*Amer. Guide Series: Pa.*⟩ ⟨the newspapers have been demanding these things for years, and nothing of any real and lasting *consequence* ever seems to happen —Herman Kogan⟩ SIGNIFICANCE can be used interchangeably with IMPORTANCE or CONSEQUENCE, although in meaning basically *that which is signified* (*to anyone*) it usu. stresses strongly the mere fact of having value or worth and sometimes the relativity of that value or worth ⟨a person of some *significance*⟩ ⟨here, in 1864, occurred a battle of some strategic *significance* —*Amer. Guide Series: Ark.*⟩ ⟨a temper tantrum once in a while should be overlooked for it has little *significance* —H.R.Litchfield & L.H.Dembo⟩ ⟨such trivia take on *significance* only if the reader is able to catch the subtle hints of impending disaster —Leland Miles⟩ ⟨a generation of boys and girls who understand the social *significance* of the family —*Current Biog.*⟩ IMPORT usu. stresses, even more than SIGNIFICANCE, the relativity of the value or worth, bringing out the idea of a significance bearing upon or in relation to person or thing specified or strongly implied ⟨the Contemporary Theater, concentrating on plays of sociological *import* —*Amer. Guide Series: Mich.*⟩ ⟨when we allow our mind to dwell upon such considerations as these, the entire *import* of the illustration changes —John Dewey⟩ ⟨the differences between one variety of man and another, points of negligible *import* in medicine —A.L.Kroeber⟩ ⟨other measures of international *import* upon which he voted —*Current Biog.*⟩ MOMENT, very like SIGNIFICANCE or IMPORT though less frequent in oral communication, usu. suggests worthiness of consideration, often stressing the conspicuousness or self-evidence of the significance or worthiness ⟨some excerpts describe matters of greater *moment* than do others —*Times Lit. Supp.*⟩ ⟨the questions before the Department of State were many and of grave *moment* —W.C.Ford⟩ ⟨the material inequalities of our worldly life will be found to be of no *moment* in the hereafter —P.G.Waris⟩ WEIGHT tends to stress largeness of possible consequence or import as of something that must be taken into account or whose presence does or may seriously alter an outcome ⟨men who take the lead, and whose opinions and wishes have great *weight* with the others —J.G.Frazer⟩ ⟨the author's expertness in the field lends *weight* to his conclusions —H.M.Hyman⟩ ⟨a gap between their appreciation of a man's value at any moment and his real *weight* —Hilaire Belloc⟩ ⟨diplomatic questions remained, but they had no such *weight* as those of the wartime —W.C.Ford⟩

im·por·tan·cy \-nsē,-nsi\ *n* -ES *archaic* **:** IMPORTANCE

im·por·tant \-nt\ *adj* [MF, fr. OIt *importante* (verbal of *importare* to be important), fr. L *important-, importans,* pres. part. of *importare* to bring or carry in, convey, cause — more at IMPORT] **1 a :** marked by or possessing weight or consequence **:** valuable in content or relationship **:** SIGNIFICANT ⟨an ~ day in one's life⟩ ⟨an ~ consideration⟩ ⟨a country producing petroleum in ~ quantities⟩ **b :** significant or large in amount or size ⟨spent ~ money on a small gem for his wife⟩ ⟨an ~ part of the architect's time was devoted to department-store design —*Current Biog.*⟩ **2 a :** giving evidence of or seeming to relate to something of consequence ⟨holding the attorney's letter in his hand, and with so solemn and ~ an air that his wife . . . thought the worst was about to befall —W.M.Thackeray⟩ ⟨took long ~ strides in the direction of the courthouse⟩ **b :** giving evidence of a feeling of personal importance **:** marked by self-complacency, ostentation, or pompousness ⟨an ~ manner⟩ **3** *obs* **:** IMPORTUNATE, URGENT — **im·por·tant·ly** *adv* — **im·por·tant·ness** *n* -ES

im·por·ta·tion \,im,pōr'tāshən, -pȯ(r)'-, -pōə'- *also* -,pə(r)'-\ *n* -s [¹*import* + *-ation*] **1 :** the act or practice of bringing in (as merchandise) from an outside or foreign source ⟨the ~ of goods from Holland⟩ ⟨the ~ of foreign labor⟩ **2 :** IMPORT 3 ⟨the car was an ~ from Italy⟩

import credit *n* **:** a credit which is opened by an importer with a bank in his own country and upon which the exporter he deals with may draw bills of exchange — compare EXPORT CREDIT

imported *past of* IMPORT

imported cabbageworm *n* **:** the larva of the common white cabbage butterfly that is a serious pest of cabbage and related plants

imported currantworm *n* **:** a larval sawfly (*Nematus ribesii*) that is native to Europe but now widespread in No. America and that is very destructive to the foliage of currants, gooseberries, and related plants

im·por·tee \¦im,pōr¦tē, -,pər-\ *n* -s [¹*import* + *-ee*] **:** one that has been imported ⟨~*s* brought in to harvest the cherry crop⟩

im·port·er *pronunc at* ¹IMPORT + ə(r)\ *n* **:** one that imports; *esp* **:** one whose business is the importation and sale of goods from a foreign country

importing *pres part of* IMPORT

imports *pres 3d sing of* IMPORT, *pl of* IMPORT

im·por·tu·na·cy \əm'pȯrchənəsē; ,impər'tün-, -r·'tyün-\ *n* -ES **:** IMPORTUNATENESS

im·por·tu·nate \əm'pȯrchənə̇t; ¦impər¦tünə̇t, -r·¦tyü-\ *adj* [prob. fr. ¹*importune* + *-ate*] **1 :** BURDENSOME, TROUBLESOME **2 :** troublesomely urgent **:** unreasonably solicitous **:** overly persistent in request or demand ⟨an ~ petitioner⟩ ⟨an ~ curiosity⟩ ⟨~ requests for assistance⟩ **syn** see PRESSING

im·por·tu·nate·ly *adv* **:** in an importunate manner

im·por·tu·nate·ness *n* -ES **:** the quality or state of being importunate

¹im·por·tune \¦impər¦tün, -,pȯr-, -r·¦tyün; əm'pȯrchən, -(,)chün\ *adj* [ME, fr. MF & L; MF *importun,* fr. L *importunus* unfit, troublesome, rude, fr. *in-* ¹in- + *-portunus* (as in *opportunus* fit, convenient) — more at OPPORTUNE] **:** IMPORTUNATE — **im·por·tune·ly** *adv*

²importune \"\ *vb* -ED/-ING/-S [MF or ML; MF *importuner,* fr. ML *importunare,* fr. L *importunus*] *vt* **1 a :** to press or urge with frequent or unreasonable requests or troublesome persistence ⟨were being *importuned* to try their luck with the play —Claudia Cassidy⟩ ⟨*importuned* many businessmen to come to Washington —John McDonald⟩ **b** *archaic* **:** to request or beg for urgently **2 a :** ANNOY, WORRY, TROUBLE **b :** to make immoral or lewd advances toward ⟨arrested for *importuning* a male person in the park⟩ ~ *vi* **1 :** to beg, urge, or solicit persistently or troublesomely **2 :** to make immoral or lewd advances toward another ⟨fined for *importuning* in a public convenience —T.A.Cullen⟩ **syn** see BEG

im·por·tun·er \-nər\ *n* -s **:** one that importunes

im·por·tu·ni·ty \,impər'tünəd·ē, -,pȯr-, -r·'tyü-\ *n* -ES [ME *importunite*, fr. MF *importunité*, fr. L *importunitat-, importunitas*, fr. *importunus* + *-itat-, -itas* -ity] **:** the quality or state of being importunate **:** pressing or pertinacious solicitation **:** troublesome pertinacity

im·pose \əm'pōz\ *vb* -ED/-ING/-S [MF *imposer*, modif. (influenced by *poser* to put, place) of L *imponere* to put upon, impose, deceive, cheat, fr. *in-* ²in- + *ponere* to put, place — more at POSE, POSITION] *vt* **1** *obs* **:** CHARGE, IMPUTE **2 :** to give or bestow (as a name or title) authoritatively or officially **3 a** *obs* **:** to cause to be burdened **:** SUBJECT — used with *to* **b** (1) **:** to make, frame, or apply (as a charge, tax, obligation, rule, penalty) as compulsory, obligatory, or enforcible ⟨~ a duty on a city official⟩ ⟨the obligations *imposed* by international law —*Encyc. Americana*⟩ **:** LEVY ⟨~ a tax on all unmarried men⟩ **:** INFLICT ⟨~ punishment upon a traitor⟩ ⟨flying ~*s* a heavy nervous strain on the individual —H.G. Armstrong⟩ **:** force one to submit to or come into accord with — usu. used with *on* or *upon* ⟨moved the newspapers to ~ a uniformity upon the written language —Oscar Handlin⟩ ⟨~ their dictates on the smaller nations —Vera M. Dean⟩ ⟨~ restraints upon the children⟩ (2) **:** to establish forcibly ⟨he *imposed* himself as leader⟩ ⟨~ law and order on a primitive people⟩ ⟨*imposed* a uniform organization over the whole of Lowland Britain —L.D.Stamp⟩ (3) **:** to make to prevail as a basic pattern, order, or quality ⟨neoclassic styles were *imposed* on the landscape —*Amer. Guide Series: Ariz.*⟩ **c** *archaic* **:** to lay (as a charge) upon a person **d :** to bring into being **:** CREATE, GENERATE ⟨the dangers and irritations *imposed* by many railroad grade crossings —*Amer. Guide Series: Minn.*⟩ **4 a** *obs* **:** to lay (the hands) on in an ecclesiastical rite (as blessing or confirmation) **b** *archaic* **:** SET, PLACE, PUT, DEPOSIT **c** (1) **:** to arrange (type or plated pages) on an imposing stone preparatory to locking up in a chase; *sometimes* **:** to arrange and lock up (pages) (2) **:** to arrange (the component parts of a nonletterpress printing surface) in a similar manner **5 a :** to force into the company or upon the attention of another ⟨~ oneself upon others⟩ **b :** to inflict by deception or fraud **:** pass off ⟨~ fake documents upon a gullible public⟩ ⟨so long as imaginary events are not *imposed* upon the reader as historical evidence —J.L. Clifford⟩ ~ *vi* **:** to take usu. unwarranted advantage of something ⟨I was not formally invited to my friend's party and I would not wish to ~ by going uninvited⟩ **syn** see DICTATE — **impose on** *or* **impose upon 1 a :** to force oneself esp. obnoxiously on (others) **b** *obs* **:** to encroach or infringe on **:** INFRINGE **2 :** to take unwarranted advantage of **:** exploit a personal relationship with ⟨got a reputation for *imposing on* friends for their time and money⟩ **:** ABUSE ⟨did not wish to *impose upon* what privileges he had⟩ **3 :** to practice deception on **:** DECEIVE, DEFRAUD, CHEAT ⟨an attempt to *impose on* the good-natured tolerance of the public —Roger Fry⟩ ⟨succeed in deceiving, and *imposing upon*, others —George Meredith⟩

imposed load *n* **:** the part of the total load sustained by a structure or member thereof that is applied to it after erection — compare DEAD LOAD

im·pos·er \-zə(r)\ *n* **:** one that imposes; *esp* **:** STONEMAN 1

imposing *adj* **1** *archaic* **:** insistent and exacting **2** *archaic* **:** DECEPTIVE, TREACHEROUS **3 :** impressive because of size, scope, bearing, dignity, or grandeur **:** COMMANDING ⟨an ~ building⟩ ⟨an ~ appearance⟩ **syn** see GRAND

im·pos·ing·ly *adv* **:** in an imposing manner; *esp* **:** IMPRESSIVELY

im·pos·ing·ness *n* -ES **:** the quality or state of being imposing

imposing stone *or* **imposing table** *or* **imposing surface** *n* **:** a slab of stone or metal on which matter to be printed is imposed

im·po·si·tion \,impə'zishən\ *n* [ME *imposicioun*, fr. MF & LL; MF *imposition*, fr. LL *imposition-, impositio*, fr. L *impositus* (past part. of *imponere*) + *-ion-, -io* -ion] **1 :** the act of imposing: as **a :** the laying on of the hands as a religious ceremony (as in ordination or confirmation) **b :** a putting, placing, or laying on ⟨the ~ of color on the clear wood⟩ ⟨the ~ of a second layer on the first⟩ **c :** an applying by compelling means ⟨the ~ of rigid censorship⟩ ⟨the ~ of a foreign form on a domestic product⟩ **d :** a levying or assessment (as of a tax or a fine) ⟨the ~ of extra charges for extra services⟩ ⟨the ~ of a high tariff⟩ **e :** the arranging on an imposing stone of matter to be printed **2 :** something imposed: as **a :** LEVY, TAX ⟨an ~ of 5000 francs on a coat⟩ **b** *obs* **:** COMMAND, CHARGE **c :** an excessive, unwarranted, or uncalled-for requirement or burden ⟨severe ~*s* on her children —John Dollard⟩ **d :** an exercise imposed as punishment on a student (as at an English public school) **3 :** the act of imposing upon another or the condition of being imposed upon **:** DECEPTION ⟨know that their tricks are ~*s* —W.W.Howells⟩ **4 :** the order of arrangement of imposed pages or other matter ⟨the standard ~*s* are simple multiples of 16 pages —*Plan for a Good Book*⟩

im·pos·i·tor \əm'päzəd·ə(r), -z(ə)tə(r)\ *n* -S [*impose* + *-itor* (as in *compositor*)] **:** STONEMAN 1

im·possibilism \(')im, əm+\ *n* [L *impossibilis* + E *-ism*] **1 :** a political purpose or plan felt to be impossible of achievement **2 :** the advocacy of an impossible purpose or plan

¹im·possibilist \"+\ *n* [L *impossibilis* + E *-ist*] **:** an advocate of impossibilism

²impossibilist \"\ *adj* **:** of or relating to impossibilism

im·possibility \(,)im, əm+\ *n* [ME *impossibilite*, fr. MF & LL; MF *impossibilité*, fr. LL *impossibilitat-, impossibilitas*, fr. L *impossibilis* + *-itat-, -itas* -ity] **1 :** the quality or state of being impossible: as **a :** IMPRACTICABILITY ⟨never deterred by the seeming ~ of any task⟩ **b :** incapability of being dealt with by reasonable or acceptable means ⟨his cool cheek, his frightful temper, his sheer ~ —James Cameron⟩ ⟨the ~ of the political setup for an honest man⟩ **2** *obs* **:** INABILITY **3 :** something impossible of attainment ⟨a child who always goes after *impossibilities*⟩

¹im·possible \(')im, əm+\ *adj* [ME, fr. MF & L; MF, fr. L *impossibilis*, fr. *in-* ¹in- + *possibilis* possible — more at POSSIBLE] **1 a :** incapable of being or of occurring **:** not within the realm of the possible **:** contrary to the nature of reality ⟨an ~ motion⟩ ⟨an ~ creature⟩ **b** (1) **:** felt to be incapable of being done, attained, or fulfilled **:** felt to be utterly impracticable ⟨a land ~ of conquest⟩ (2) **:** extremely and almost insuperably difficult under the circumstances **:** having little likelihood of accomplishment or completion ⟨spent his time indefatigably doing ~ tasks for the committee⟩ **c** *of a statement* **:** SELF-CONTRADICTORY **2 a :** out of the question **:** UNACCEPTABLE ⟨~ coloring in a picture⟩ ⟨an ~ political candidate⟩ **:** extremely undesirable ⟨relieving ~ and unfair economic conditions —F.D.Roosevelt⟩ ⟨his claret was ~ —Elinor Wylie⟩ **:** marked by very undesirable qualities ⟨his wife is simply ~ . . . uses perfumery, and has an awful voice —Margaret Deland⟩ **b :** difficult or extremely awkward to deal with or so markedly odd as to be unpleasant or objectionable ⟨a positive genius for collecting ~ people —Ngaio Marsh⟩ ⟨an almost ~ man to have for an enemy —Bruce Catton⟩ — **im·possibleness** \"+\ *n*

²impossible \"\ *n* [ME, fr. *impossible*, adj.] **:** something impossible **:** IMPOSSIBILITY

im·possibly \"+\ *adv* **1 :** in an impossible manner or to an impossible degree ⟨an ~ idealistic young man⟩ **2 :** to a degree that causes hardship or prevents a remedy ⟨food and clothing are ~ expensive⟩ ⟨~ far away from all sources of supply —June Platt⟩

¹im·post \'im,pōst\ *n* [MF, fr. ML *impositum*, fr. neut. of L *impositus*, past part. of *imponere* to put upon, impose — more at IMPOSE] **1 :** something imposed or levied **:** TAX, TRIBUTE, DUTY **2 :** the weight carried by a horse in a handicap race

²impost \"\ *vt* **:** to classify (imports) in order to fix import duties

³impost \"\ *n* [F *imposte*, fr. MF, fr. OIt *imposta*, fr. fem. of *imposto* (past part. of *imporre* to put upon, impose), fr. L *impositus*] **:** a block, capital, or molding (as of a pillar, pier, or wall) from which an arch springs — see ARCH illustration

imposteous *adj, obs* **:** IMPOSTROUS

im·pos·tor *or* **im·pos·ter** \əm'pästə(r)\ *n* -S [MF & LL; MF *imposteur*, fr. LL *impostor*, fr. L *impostus, impositus* (past part. of *imponere* to put upon, impose, deceive, cheat) + *-or* — more at IMPOSE] **:** one that practices imposture **:** one that assumes an identity, character, or title not his own for the purpose of deception **:** PRETENDER, FRAUD, HUMBUG

im·pos·trous \(')im¦pästrəs, əm'p-\ *adj* **:** of, relating to, or being an imposture **:** DECEITFUL, FRAUDULENT

impostumate *or* **imposthumate** *vb* -ED/-ING/-S [¹*impostume*, *imposthume* + *-ate*] *vt, obs* **:** to affect with an impostume **:** to cause to have an impostume ~ *vi, obs* **:** to form an impostume

¹im·pos·tume \əm'päs(,)chüm, -s(,)t(y)üm, -stəm\ *or* **im·pos·thume** \", -s(,)thüm, -s·thəm\ *n* -S [ME *emposteme*, *empostyme*, *imposteme*, fr. MF *apostume*, *empostume*, fr. L *apostema* — more at APOSTEME] **1** *archaic* **:** ABSCESS, CYST **2** *archaic* **:** an instance or source of moral corruption

²impostume *vb* [ME *empostemen*, fr. *emposteme*, n.] *obs* **:** IMPOSTUMATE

¹im·pos·ture \əm'päschə(r)\ *n* [LL *impostura*, fr. L *impostus*, *impositus* (past part. of *imponere* to put upon, impose, deceive, cheat) + *-ura* -ure — more at IMPOSE] **1 :** the act or practice of imposing on or deceiving someone by means of an assumed character or name **:** the act or conduct of an impostor ⟨careful not to detect cases of malingering . . . and thus placed a premium on ~ —G.E.Fussell⟩ **2 :** an instance of imposture ⟨admitted under oath that the whole defense of insanity was an ~ and a sham —B.N.Cardozo⟩

syn CHEAT, FRAUD, DECEIT, DECEPTION, COUNTERFEIT, SHAM, FAKE, HUMBUG, SIMULACRUM: IMPOSTURE applies to any situation in which a spurious object or action is passed off as genuine and bona fide ⟨its values . . . are an *imposture:* pretending to honor and distinction it accepts all that is vulgar and base —Edmund Wilson⟩ CHEAT applies to any abuse of credence and faith by misleading or trickery and also to delusion induced by the victim's credulousness ⟨though the counts allowed the *cheat* for fact . . . and let the tale o' the feigned birth pass for true —Robert Browning⟩ ⟨the *cheat* which still leads us to work and live for appearances —R.W.Emerson⟩ FRAUD is likely to indicate a calculated perversion of the truth; applied to a person it may be less condemnatory and suggest pretence and hypocrisy ⟨many persons persisted in believing that his supposed suicide was but another *fraud* —Justin M'Carthy⟩ ⟨the pious *fraud* who freely indulges in the sins against which he eloquently preaches —Oliver LaFarge⟩ DECEIT indicates anything that deceives or misleads, usu. purposefully, and is strongly condemnatory ⟨Indians were . . . treacherous according to the white man's standards, since they held that the basest trickery or *deceit* was not dishonorable if directed against a foe —*Amer. Guide Series: R.I.*⟩ DECEPTION is often interchangeable with DECEIT but is used without condemnation in reference to sleights and feints and to innocent or natural characteristics likely to mislead ⟨practice gross *deception* on the public with all the earnestness of a moral "crusade" —K.S.Davis⟩ ⟨a fast backfield trained in *deception*⟩ COUNTERFEIT refers to a close imitation or copy of a thing, usu. one made or circulated for dishonest gain ⟨this bill's a *counterfeit*⟩; in reference to persons or ideas or qualities it suggests spurious although close imitation without culpable intent to deceive ⟨not really a married woman and a housemistress but only a kind of *counterfeit* —Arnold Bennett⟩ SHAM is severe in censuring what fraudulently imitates or purports to be a genuine reality ⟨perhaps her devotion to Marcellus was a *sham* and her real intention was that Agrippa should be goaded into putting him out of the way —Robert Graves⟩ ⟨if people would only build on facts, not on *shams* —Ellen Glasgow⟩ FAKE refers to something factitious or assumed with plausible closeness to the original, genuine, or true; it may or may not condemn, depending on culpable intent to deceive ⟨Gaston B. Means's volume, *The Strange Death of President Harding*, . . . bears every imprint of being a thoroughgoing *fake* —S.H.Adams⟩ ⟨he pretends everything is what it is not, he is a *fake* —Katherine A. Porter⟩ HUMBUG indicates elaborate pretense, esp. so flagrant that it approaches transparency ⟨you're a *humbug*, sir . . . I will speak plainer, if you wish it. An imposter, sir —Charles Dickens⟩ ⟨these liars warn't no kings nor dukes, at all, but just low-down *humbugs* and frauds —Mark Twain⟩ SIMULACRUM indicates an image or imitation but usu. lacks the suggestion that it is made to defraud; it may indicate an image utterly wanting in essential substance or reality ⟨nothing but a coat and a wig and a mask smiling below it — nothing but a great *simulacrum* —W.M.Thackeray⟩ ⟨something whose essence was not there at all, a stiff lifeless *simulacrum* —J.C. Powys⟩

²imposture *vi, obs* **:** to practice imposture ~ *vt* **1** *obs* **:** to show to be an imposture **2** *obs* **:** DECEIVE

im·pos·tur·ing \-chəriŋ\ *n* **:** IMPOSTURE 2 ⟨think . . . these concealments and ~*s* can be exaggerated —John Cheever⟩

im·pos·tur·ous \(')im¦päschərəs, əm'p-\ *adj* **:** IMPOSTROUS

im·potable \(')im+\ *adj* [LL *impotabilis*, fr. L *in-* ¹in- + LL *potabilis* potable — more at POTABLE] **:** not suited for drinking **:** UNDRINKABLE

im·po·tence \'impəd·ən(t)s, |tən- *also* |t³n- *sometimes except in sense b* (')im¦pō| *or* əm'pō|\ *also* **im·po·ten·cy** \-nsē,-nsi\ *n, pl* **impotenc·es** *also* **impoten·cies** [ME *impotence*, *impotencie*, fr. MF & ML; MF *impotence*, fr. ML *impotentia*, fr. L, lack of self-control, fr. *impotent-, impotens* + *-ia* -y] **1 :** the quality or state of being impotent: as **a :** lack of strength **:** WEAKNESS, FEEBLENESS ⟨the very ~ of the government, the impossibility of doing anything —Upton Sinclair⟩ **:** HELPLESSNESS ⟨reduce them to intellectual ~ —H.J.Laski⟩ ⟨a small force . . . reduced to ~ a fortress that had been expected to withstand attack for at least 2 weeks —*Military Rev.*⟩ **b** (1) **:** a physical or psychological abnormal state usu. of a male characterized by inability to copulate — compare STERILITY (2) **:** STERILITY — not used technically **2** [L *impotentia*] *obs* **:** lack of self-restraint or self-control

¹im·po·tent \-nt\ *adj* [ME, fr. MF & L; MF, fr. L *impotent-, impotens*, fr. *in-* ¹in- + *potent-, potens* potent — more at POTENT] **1 a :** not potent **:** lacking in power, strength, or vigor **:** deficient in capacity **:** WEAK, POWERLESS ⟨he liked to be bad and see them all ~ to correct him —Stuart Cloete⟩ ⟨its ~ ruling classes —Edward Shils⟩ ⟨a relatively ~ preparation of penicillin⟩ ⟨a lame and ~, and a trite, conclusion —Howard M. Jones⟩ **b :** unable to copulate **:** wanting in procreative power; *broadly* **:** STERILE — usu. used of males **2** [L *impotent-, impotens*] *obs* **:** incapable of self-restraint **:** UNGOVERNABLE, VIOLENT **syn** see STERILE

²impotent \"\ *n* **:** one that is impotent

im·po·tent·ly *adv* **:** in an impotent manner **:** FEEBLY, WEAKLY, HELPLESSLY

im·po·tent·ness *n* **:** IMPOTENCE

¹im·pound \əm'paund\ *vt* -ED/-ING/-S [²*in-* + *pound* (enclosure)] **1 a :** to shut up in or as if in a pound **:** CONFINE, ENCLOSE ⟨to catch and ~ stray dogs⟩ ⟨explosive release of the breath which had been ~*ed* in the mouth cavity —A.L. Kroeber⟩ **b :** to seize and hold in the custody of the law ⟨~ stray cattle⟩ ⟨~ the files of a court⟩ ⟨all slave ships that put into Bahama ports were ~*ed* and their cargoes freed —Marjory S. Douglas⟩ **c :** to take possession of **:** APPROPRIATE **2 :** to collect (water) for irrigation, hydroelectric use, flood control, or similar purpose **:** confine and store (water) in an impound

²im·pound \'im,p-\ *n* **:** a reservoir for impounding

im·pound·able \(')im¦paundəbəl, əm'p-\ *adj* **:** capable of or liable to impoundment

im·pound·ment \əm'paun(d)mənt\ *also* **im·pound·age** \-ndij\ *n* -S **1 :** the act of impounding or the state of being impounded **2 :** a body of water formed by impounding (as by a dam) **:** *also* **:** the quantity of water in such a body

im·pov·er·ish \əm'päv(ə)rish, -rēsh, *esp in pres part* -rəsh\ *vt* -ED/-ING/-ES [ME *enpoverisen*, fr. MF *empovriss-*, stem of *empovrir*, fr. *en-* ¹en- + *povre* poor — more at POOR] **1 :** to make poor **:** reduce to poverty or indigence ⟨a family ~*ed* by misfortune and sickness⟩ ⟨a foolish effort to ~ life by robbing men of sustaining vision —M.R.Cohen⟩ ⟨the provinces were ~*ed* of their scientific talent —S.F.Mason⟩ **2 :** to exhaust the strength, richness, or fertility of **:** make sterile ⟨worked the land year after year until it was ~*ed*⟩ **syn** see DEPLETE

impoverished *adj, of a fauna or flora* **:** represented by few species or individuals **:** SCANTY

im·pov·er·ish·ment \-mənt\ *n* -S [AF *empoverissement*, fr. MF *empovriss-* + *-ment*] **:** the act of impoverishing or the state of being impoverished ⟨soil ~⟩ ⟨spiritual ~⟩

impower *obs var of* EMPOWER

impr *abbr* improved; improvement

im·practicability \(,)im, əm+\ *n* **1 :** the quality or state of being impracticable **2 :** something impracticable

im·practicable \(')im, əm+\ *adj* [¹*in-* + *practicable*] **1 a :** not practicable **:** incapable of being performed or accomplished by the means employed or at command **:** INFEASIBLE ⟨economically ~ to maintain an air force which will provide absolute security —*Nat'l Aviation Policy*⟩ ⟨regretted that his appointment as chaplain . . . was at present ~ —Rose Macaulay⟩ **b :** incapable of being passed, scaled, or conveniently negotiated ⟨an ~ road⟩ ⟨an ~ cliff⟩ **2** *archaic* **:** UNMANAGEABLE, INTRACTABLE **3 :** IMPRACTICAL, UNWISE, IMPRUDENT ⟨the tear is apt to go clear across the sail, making it ~ for you to continue —H.A.Calahan⟩ **:** lacking common sense in practical matters ⟨given him up for many years as ~ and hopeless —George Meredith⟩ — **im·practicableness** \"+\ *n* — **im·practicably** \"+\ *adv*

im·practical \(')im, əm+\ *adj* [¹*in-* + *practical*] **:** not practical: as **a** (1) **:** not wise to put into or keep in practice or effect **:** not pleasing to common sense or prudence ⟨slavery, we have been taught, was economically ~ —Carol L. Thompson⟩ (2) **:** IDEALISTIC ⟨an ~ pipe dream —James Laughlin⟩ **:** THEORETICAL ⟨an anchorite living austerely and owning little, but rich in ~ and priceless honor —W.L.Sullivan⟩ **b :** incapable of dealing sensibly or prudently with practical esp. economic matters ⟨a totally ~ man who would have starved but for his wife's common sense⟩ **c :** IMPRACTICABLE **:** incapable of being put into use or effect or of being accomplished or done successfully or without extreme trouble, hardship, or expense ⟨all of the aircraft-engine mufflers . . . have been found ~ —H.G.Armstrong⟩ ⟨feels that any . . . plan might prove so expensive — and so ~ — that he does not intend to try a new one —*Time*⟩ ⟨a totally ~ scheme for making a quick million⟩ ⟨led him to write music that is vocally ~ —A.T.Davison⟩ — **im·practicality** \(,)im, əm+\ *n* — **im·practicalness** \(')im, əm+\ *n*

im·pre·cate \'imprə,kāt, -rē,-, *usu* -ād·+V\ *vb* -ED/-ING/-S [L *imprecatus*, past part. of *imprecari*, fr. *in-* ²in- + *precari* to ask, entreat, pray — more at PRAY] *vt* **1 a** *archaic* **:** to call down by prayer **:** INVOKE **b :** to invoke evil upon **:** CURSE ⟨*imprecated* the weather when the ink froze in his fountain pen —Stanley Snaith⟩ **2** *archaic* **:** to beg or pray for ~ *vi* **1** *obs* **:** to invoke evil **2 :** to utter imprecations **:** CURSE

im·pre·cat·ing·ly \'==,===, ,=='===\ *adv* **:** in the manner of one cursing **:** with curses

im·pre·ca·tion \,=='kāshən\ *n* -S [L *imprecation-, imprecatio*, fr. *imprecatus* + *-ion-, -io* -ion] **1 :** the act of imprecating esp. by invoking evil **:** CURSING **2 a :** PLEA, SUPPLICATION ⟨the ~*s* to the Lord for forgiveness —W.A.White⟩ **b :** CURSE, MALEDICTION ⟨uttered ~*s* under his breath⟩

im·preca·to·ry \'imprəkə,tōrē, 'imprek-, əm'prek-, -tȯr-, -ri, *chiefly Brit* ¦impri¦kātəri *or* -ā·tri\ *adj* **:** of, relating to, or being imprecation **:** invoking evil **:** CURSING

im·precise \¦im+\ *adj* [¹*in-* + *precise*] **:** not precise: as **a :** not exact ⟨~ astronomical observation⟩ **b :** vague or indefinite in nature, form, or outline ⟨~ dawn changes to photographic clearness —Han Suyin⟩ ⟨made him a rather ~ offer⟩ — **im·precisely** \"+\ *adv* — **im·preciseness** \"+\ *n*

im·precision \¦im+\ *n* [¹*in-* + *precision*] **:** the quality or state of being imprecise **:** lack of precision ⟨it is the indefiniteness, the ~ of the process that is baffling —Herbert Read⟩ ⟨an ~ of language⟩ **:** INACCURACY ⟨trying to mark as accurately as possible with tools calibrated with great ~⟩

im·predicable \(')im, əm+\ *adj* [¹*in-* + *predicable*] **:** not predicable

im·preg \'im,preg\ *n* -S [*impregnated* (*wood*)] **:** wood impregnated with a resin so that face checking is reduced and compressional strength and hardness, electrical resistance, and resistance to moisture, acid, and decay are increased

im·pregn \im'prēn\ *vt* -ED/-ING/-S [LL *impraegnare* — more at IMPREGNATE] *archaic* **:** IMPREGNATE

im·preg·na·bil·i·ty \(¦)im,pregnə'biləd·ē, əm-, -lətē, -i\ *n* -ES **:** the quality or state of being impregnable

¹im·preg·na·ble \(')im¦pregnəbəl, əm'p-\ *adj* [alter. (influenced by *impregnate*) of earlier *impreignable*, alter. (influenced by such words as *reign, deign*, with silent *g*) of earlier *imprenable*, fr. ME, fr. MF, fr. *in-* ¹in- + *prenable* capable of being captured, fr. *pren-* (stem of *prendre* to take, capture, fr. L *prehendere* to grasp, seize) + *-able* — more at GET] **1 :** incapable of being taken by assault **:** able to resist attack **:** UNCONQUERABLE, UNASSAILABLE ⟨an ~ fortress⟩ ⟨~ virtue⟩; *also* **:** incapable of being broken into or escaped from ⟨an ~ cell⟩ **2 :** being beyond criticism or question **:** not subject to higher authority ⟨an ~ social position⟩ ⟨of ~ financial standing⟩ ⟨an ~ reputation for honesty⟩ — **im·pregnableness** \"+\ *n* -ES — **im·pregnably** \"+\ *adv*

²im·preg·na·ble \əm'pregnəbəl\ *adj* [²*impregnate* + *-able*] **:** capable of being impregnated (as an egg)

¹im·preg·nant \əm'pregnənt\ *adj* [LL *impraegnant-, impraegnans*, pres. part. of *impraegnare*] **1** *obs* **:** IMPREGNATED, SATURATED, PERMEATED, IMBUED **2** *archaic* **:** IMPREGNATING

²impregnant \"\ *n* -S **:** an agent (as an oil, plastic, insecticide, resin) used to penetrate another substance (as cloth, paper, plaster, concrete, pulp, wood)

¹im·preg·nate \əm'pregnət, *usu* -nəd·+V\ *adj* [LL *impraegnatus*, past part.] **:** IMPREGNATED

²im·preg·nate \əm'preg,nāt, 'im,p-, *usu* -ād·+V\ *vt* -ED/-ING/-S [LL *impraegnatus*, past part. of *impraegnare*, fr. L *in-* ²in- + *praegnas* pregnant — more at PREGNANT] **1 a** (1) **:** to make pregnant **:** cause to conceive **:** get with child or young (2) **:** to introduce sperm cells into **:** INSEMINATE **b :** to infuse an active principle into **:** make fruitful or fertile **:** FERTILIZE, IMBUE **2 a :** to cause to be filled, imbued, mixed, furnished, or saturated (as with particles of another substance) ⟨~ wood with creosote⟩ ⟨gauze *impregnated* with medicament⟩ ⟨a cake strongly *impregnated* with brandy⟩ ⟨the chamber . . . *impregnated* with the odor of furniture paste —Arnold Bennett⟩ **b** (1) **:** to mix with **:** INTERPENETRATE ⟨quicksilver ore ~*s* sandstone in California —A.M.Bateman⟩ (2) **:** to have a marked permeating or coloring effect upon ⟨a very notable poem *impregnated* with the pessimism of a time —R.M.Lovett⟩ ⟨criticism . . . richly *impregnated* with history —C.W.Shumaker⟩ **c :** to force by impregnation ⟨plastics *impregnated* into cloth —Jack DeMent⟩ **3 :** to influence markedly **:** INDOCTRINATE ⟨*impregnated* with socialistic ideas⟩ **syn** see PERMEATE

im·preg·na·tion \,im,preg'nāshən\ *n* -S [F or L; F *imprégnation*, fr. MF *impregnation*, fr. ML *impraegnation-, impraegnatio*, fr. LL *impraegnatus* + L *-ion-, -io* -ion] **1 :** the act of impregnating or the state of being impregnated: as **a :** a causing to conceive **:** FECUNDATION, FERTILIZATION **b :** INFUSION, SATURATION **c :** INDOCTRINATION **2 :** something with which something else is impregnated **:** as **a :** a mineral concentration consisting of small scattered grains in a rock matrix **b :** IMPREGNANT

im·preg·na·tor \əm'preg,nād·ə(r), 'im,p-, -ātə-\ *n* -S [ML *impraegnator*, fr. LL *impraegnatus* + L *-or*] **:** one that impregnates: as **a :** an operator of a machine that impregnates (as a fabric with a chemical compound) **b :** an instrument used for artificial insemination

impresa *n* -S [It, undertaking, chivalric deed, heraldic device, motto, fr. fem. of *impreso*, past part. of *imprendere* to undertake, fr. (assumed) VL *imprehendere* — more at EMPRISE] **1** *obs* **:** DEVICE, EMBLEM **2** *obs* **a :** a sentence usu. accompanying an impresa **b :** MOTTO, PROVERB, MAXIM

im·pre·sar·i·al \¦imprə¦särēəl, -sa(a)r-,-ser-,-sår-\ *adj* **:** of or belonging to an impresario

im·pre·sar·io \,=='=rē,ō\ *n* -S *see sense 1* [It, manager, impresario, fr. *impresa* + *-ario* -ary (fr. L *-arius*)] **1** *pl also* **im·pre·sa·ri** \-,rē\ **:** the projector, manager, or conductor of an opera or concert company **2 :** one who puts on or sponsors an entertainment (as a concert, television show, art exhibition, or sports contest) **3 :** MANAGER, PRODUCER, DIRECTOR ⟨a former beerhall ~ —Upton Sinclair⟩ ⟨an egregious ~ of letters, who kept a squad of writers churning out copy marketed under his signature —C.J.Rolo⟩ ⟨the ~ of the best intelligent conversation to be heard in his time —*Times Lit. Supp.*⟩

im·prescribable \ˌim+\ *adj* [¹*in-* + *prescribe* + *-able*] **:** IMPRESCRIPTIBLE

im·prescriptibility \ˌim+\ *n* **:** the quality or state of being imprescriptible

im·prescriptible \ˌim+\ *adj* [MF; fr. *in-* ¹in- + *prescriptible* — more at PRESCRIPTIBLE] **:** not subject to prescription **:** INALIENABLE ⟨the ~ rights of man⟩; *also* **:** ABSOLUTE — **im·prescriptibly** \"+\ *adv*

imprese *n* -S [MF, fr. OIt *impresa* — more at IMPRESA] *obs* **:** IMPRESA

¹**im·press** \əmˈpres\ *vb* [ME *impressen*, fr. L *impressus*, past part. of *imprimere*, fr. *in-* ²in- + *-primere* (fr. *premere* to press) — more at PRESS] *vt* **1 a :** to apply with pressure so as to press or imprint ⟨~ a signet ring on wax⟩ ⟨the fingerprint file . . . in which all 10 fingers are ~*ed* on the card —*FBI Bull.*⟩ **b :** to produce (as a mark or image) by pressure ⟨a perfect spiral ~*ed* on such a cylinder —S.F. Mason⟩ **:** IMPRINT ⟨~ one's name on a metal strip by machine⟩ ⟨~ an odd design on the wood⟩ **c :** to press, stamp, or print in or upon ⟨~*ed* the wax with his seal⟩ **:** mark by or as if by pressure ⟨~ his children with the right attitudes⟩ **2 a :** to produce or imprint an esp. vivid impression of (as on the mind or memory) ⟨~ an idea on the mind⟩ ⟨the general custom for boys to be whipped on certain days to ~ things on their memories —T.B.Costain⟩ ⟨beliefs which have been ~*ed* upon us in our childhood —Frank Thilby⟩ **:** cause to have a strong effect (as of compulsion) ⟨~*ing* his will upon others by sheer force of character —V.L.Parrington⟩ **b :** to produce an impression on **:** affect esp. forcibly or deeply ⟨~ a friend with the sincerity of one's intentions⟩ ⟨~ one favorably⟩ **:** arouse strong feeling (as concern, admiration, dislike) in ⟨the altered manner of his son ~*ed* him strangely —George Meredith⟩ ⟨the bigness of it awed them, the resources ~*ed* them —Joseph Baily⟩ **c :** to mark with an imposed quality or characteristic ⟨~ the poem with the cynicism of his outlook⟩ **3 a** *obs* **:** PRINT ⟨~ the Bible⟩ **b :** to print (a stamp) directly on (a postcard, envelope) ⟨~*ed* with a 2 cent stamp⟩ **4 a :** EXERT ⟨~ a force upon a sail⟩ **b :** to transfer or transmit (as a movement) by communication ⟨~ a motion upon a ball⟩ **c :** to apply (an electromotive force or voltage) to a circuit from an outside source (as a generator) ~ *vi* **:** to produce an impression **:** arouse the strong interest or admiration of another ⟨did not wish to make friends at parties but only to ~ with his sense of personal destiny⟩ ⟨a small child acting up before company in an effort to ~⟩ **syn** see AFFECT

²**im·press** \ˈim,p- *sometimes* əmˈp-\ *n* **1 :** the act of impressing or stamping ⟨sealing by the old-time process of ~ —L.F.Middlebrook⟩ **2 a :** a mark made by pressure that produces indentation or embossment **:** IMPRINT ⟨noting the ~ of wheels in lava —Richard Llewellyn⟩ ⟨a matrix in fairly durable metal to receive the ~ of the punch —G.C.Sellery⟩ **b :** an image or figure of something formed by or as if by pressure; *esp* **:** SEAL ⟨the most beautiful seal cuttings are shown on the ~*es* of the old Salem documents —L.F.Middlebrook⟩ **c :** a product of pressure or influence **3 :** a characteristic mark of distinction **:** STAMP ⟨the picture bore the ~ of the artist⟩ **:** distinctive quality ⟨his soft mind had . . . taken an ~ from the society which surrounded him —T.B.Macaulay⟩ ⟨the ~ of a fresh and vital intelligence is stamped unmistakably upon all that is best in his work —Lytton Strachey⟩ **4** *archaic* **:** IMPRESA **5 :** IMPRESSION ⟨his work has made a decided ~ upon our time —W.R.Benét⟩ **:** EFFECT ⟨words are but symbols and, like all symbols, have a varying ~ —Philip Wittenberg⟩ ⟨made his strongest ~ upon the country by his . . . two speeches —G.H.Haynes⟩ ⟨left an enduring ~ on my life, although our relations were always impersonal —A.J. Liebling⟩

³**im·press** \əmˈp-\ *vt* [²*in-* + *press* (take by force)] **1 :** to levy or take by force for public service; *esp* **:** to take or force by impressment (as into naval service) ⟨in searching for British sailors upon our ships, she ~*ed* our own —Owen Wister⟩ **2 a :** to enlist or procure the services or aid of by forcible argument or persuasion ⟨all able-bodied survivors were ~*ed* for the task of finding and caring for the injured —*Amer. Guide Series: Texas*⟩ **b :** to force or forcibly persuade ⟨~*ed* him into a white coat for the Christmas festivities —Nancy Hale⟩

⁴**im·press** \ˈim,p-, əmˈp-\ *n* **:** IMPRESSMENT

⁵**impress** *n* [alter. of ²*imprest*] *obs* **:** pay in advance

⁶**im·press** \əmˈpres\ *vt* [alter. of ¹*imprest*] *archaic* **:** to make an advance payment of (money)

⁷**im·press** \ˈim,p-, əmˈp-\ *n* [alter. of *imprese*] **:** EMBLEM, DEVICE ⟨their shields broken, their ~*es* defaced —Edmund Burke⟩

im·press·able \əmˈpresəbəl\ *adj* **:** capable of being impressed

im·pressed \əmˈprest\ *adj* [ME, fr. past part. of *impressen*] **1 :** deeply or markedly affected by impression **2 a :** lying below the general surface as if stamped into it ⟨~ dots⟩ **b :** having markings lying below the surface ⟨an ~ skin⟩ — **im·pressed·ly** \-sədlē, -stlē, -li\ *adv*

impressed species *n* **:** SENSIBLE SPECIES

impressed stamp *n* **:** a stamp (as for postage or revenue) printed directly on a cover, document, or other paper bearing it — compare EMBOSSED STAMP

impressed watermark *n* **:** an imitation watermark made by pressing rubber letters or a design on the paper web before drying

im·press·ibil·i·ty \(,)im,presəˈbilədē, əm-, -lətē, -i\ *n* -ES **:** the quality or state of being impressible

im·press·ible \əmˈpresəbəl\ *adj* [¹*impress* + *-ible*] **:** capable of being impressed **:** SUSCEPTIBLE, SENSITIVE — **im·press·ible·ness** \-bəlnəs\ *n* -ES — **im·press·i·bly** \-blē, -bli\ *adv*

im·pres·sion \əmˈpreshən\ *n* -S [ME *impressioun*, fr. MF *impression*, fr. L *impression-*, *impressio*, fr. *impressus* (past part of *imprimere* to impress) + *-ion-*, *-io* -ion — more at IMPRESS] **1 :** the act or process of impressing: as **a** (1) **:** an affecting by stamping, bearing upon, pressing, pressing into, or otherwise exerting a physical force that marks, grooves, embosses, or prints in some way ⟨the worker held the metal firm during the ~ by the die⟩ ⟨a firm ~ of the seal on the wax⟩ (2) *archaic* **:** the printing process **b :** a communicating or giving of a mold, style, trait, or character by an external force or influence ⟨a parent concerned with the ~ of good traits on the mind and personality of his children⟩ **2 :** the effect or product of an impression: as **a** (1) **:** an indentation, stamp, embossment, form, or figure resulting from physical contact usu. with pressure ⟨the strokes became wedge-shaped ~*s* which gave cuneiform its name —Peter Lawrence⟩ ⟨a banking system whose principal features would be a circulation of notes bearing a common ~ —*Encyc. Americana*⟩ ⟨a well-printed book has a sharp, clean ~ —Joseph Blumenthal⟩ (2) *obs* **:** a telling mark or trace (3) **:** a negative imprint in plastic material of the surfaces of the teeth and adjacent portions of the jaw from which a positive likeness may be produced in dentistry (4) **:** METER IMPRESSION **b :** an esp. marked influence or effect on feeling, sense, or mind ⟨the bad dream made a terrible ~ on the child⟩ ⟨the ~ of the ocean was vivid in his mind⟩ ⟨made a favorable ~ on the audience⟩ ⟨the more emotion the reading arouses, the deeper the ~ on the learner —W.F.Mackey⟩ ⟨square chimneys thrusting upward add to the ~ of weight —*Amer. Guide Series: Ark.*⟩ **c** (1) **:** a characteristic trait or feature resulting from influence ⟨the ~ produced by an environment on a person's habits⟩ (2) **:** an effect of alteration or improvement ⟨the fur traders . . . made little permanent ~ on the wilderness —R.A.Billington⟩ ⟨a candle or lamp struggled feebly from a window but made no ~ on the darkness —S.H.Holbrook⟩ **d :** a telling image impressed on the senses or the mind ⟨looking over the steep hills, the first ~ is of an immense void like the sea —Richard Jefferies⟩ ⟨drank in all the new ~*s* eagerly —Havelock Ellis⟩ **3 :** a piece of wax, metal, or other substance on which a seal has been impressed **4** *archaic* **a :** CHARGE, ATTACK **b :** strong effect **:** IMPACT, SHOCK **5** *obs* **:** an atmospheric condition or phenomenon **6 a :** the amount of pressure with which an inked printing surface deposits its ink on the paper in the printing process ⟨each form should be made ready with as light an ~ as practicable —John Southward⟩ **b :** one instance of the meeting of a printing surface and the material being printed ⟨plates badly worn after a million ~*s*⟩; *also* **:** a single print or copy so made **c :** all the copies of a book or other publication printed in one continuous operation from a single makeready ⟨first published in 1939 and now available in a third ~ —*Times Lit. Supp.*⟩ — called also *printing;* compare EDITION **7 :** a usu. indistinct or imprecise notion, remembrance, belief, or opinion ⟨an ~ of familiarity with a face⟩ ⟨the mistaken ~ that they were out of enemy territory⟩ ⟨cold, and mysterious, and ghostly — that is my first and lasting ~ of Mycenae —Mary Chubb⟩ **8 a :** the first coat of color in painting **b :** a coat of paint for ornament or preservation **9 :** an imitation or representation of salient features in an artistic or theatrical medium (as a ballet, painting, or theatrical monologue) ⟨the novel was an ~ of the battle from the point of view of the common soldier⟩; *esp* **:** an imitation in caricature of a noted personality as a form of theatrical entertainment ⟨the comedian gave several ~*s* of famous movie and television stars⟩ **syn** see IDEA

im·pres·sion·abil·i·ty \əm,presh(ə)nəˈbilədē, -lətē, -i\ *n* **:** the quality or state of being impressionable **:** susceptibility to impressions ⟨that flabby ~ which is dignified under the name of creative temperament —John O'Hara⟩

im·pres·sion·able \əmˈpresh(ə)nəbəl\ *adj* [F *impressionnable*, fr. *impression* + *-able*] **:** capable of being easily impressed: **a :** easily influenced or affected ⟨the ~ years of a child's life⟩ ⟨an ~ heart⟩ **b :** capable of being molded or printed on ⟨an ~ plastic material⟩ ⟨paper that was very ~⟩ — **im·pres·sion·able·ness** \-bəlnəs\ *n* -ES — **im·pres·sion·a·bly** \-blē, -bli\ *adv*

im·pres·sion·al \-shənᵊl, -shnəl\ *adj* **:** of, relating to, or being impressions — **im·pres·sion·al·ly** \-ᵊlē, -əlē\ *adv*

im·pres·sion·ary \-shə,nerē\ *adj* **:** IMPRESSIONISTIC

impression cylinder *n* **:** the cylinder of a rotary printing press that carries the paper and impresses it by counterrotation against the inked printing surface on the plate cylinder; *also* **:** the cylinder of a cylinder press

im·pres·sion·ism \əmˈpreshə,nizəm\ *n* -S [F *impressionnisme*, fr. *impression* + *-isme* -ism] **1 a** *often cap* **:** a theory or practice in painting esp. among French painters of about 1870 of depicting the natural appearances of objects by means of dabs or strokes of primary unmixed colors in order to simulate actual reflected light, the subject matter being generally outdoor scenes painted directly — often contrasted with *expressionism;* compare LUMINISM, NEO-IMPRESSIONISM, PLEIN AIR, POSTIMPRESSIONISM **b :** a rough modeling or texturing of a surface in sculpture to produce a shimmering or scintillating effect **2 a :** the depiction of scene, emotion, or character (as in literature) by the use of detail that is sometimes brief and essential but often of great intricacy and elaborateness and that is intended to achieve a vividness, colorfulness, or effectiveness more by evoking subjective and sensory impressions (as of mood and atmosphere) than by re-creating or representing an objective reality **b :** a style of musical composition designed to create vague impressions and moods through rich and varied harmonies and timbres — often contrasted with *expressionism* **c :** the creation of the impression of a scene or its mood or atmosphere in a drama by the use of undramatic dialogue or nonobjective or symbolic scenery **d :** the creating of a general impression in a movie by the use of a series of shots that have no immediate logical or narrative connection **3 a** (1) **:** a practice in esp. literary criticism of presenting and elaborating one's subjective reactions to a work of art (2) **:** a critical theory that advocates or defends such a practice as the only valid one in criticism **b :** a vague and subjective response (as to a work of art) ⟨her attack is almost always human, rather critical, highly personal, degenerating occasionally into vague ~ —Mark Schorer⟩

im·pres·sion·ist \-sh(ə)nəst\ *n* -S [F *impressionniste*, fr. *impression* + *-iste* -ist] **:** an adherent or follower of impressionism; *specif, usu cap* **:** a member of a group of artists in France who exhibited together between 1874 and 1886 and many of whom practiced impressionism in their painting

im·pres·sion·is·tic \(ˌ)im¦preshəˈnistik, əm-, -tēk\ *or* **im·pres·sion·ist** \əmˈpresh(ə)nəst\ *adj* **:** of, belonging to, or being impressionism; *specif, usu cap* **:** of or belonging to the French Impressionists — **im·pres·sion·is·ti·cal·ly** \(ˌ)im¦preshə¦nistək(ə)lē, əm-, -tēk-, -li\ *adv*

impressions *pl of* IMPRESSION

im·pres·sive \əmˈpresiv, ˈim,p-, -sēv *also* -səv\ *adj* [¹*impress* + *-ive*] **1** *obs* **:** IMPRESSIBLE **2 :** making or tending to make a marked impression (as because of size, eminence, dignity of bearing, or achievement) **:** having the power to impress **:** notably exciting attention or feeling or arousing awe or admiration ⟨the Grand Canyon of the Colorado, one of the world's most ~ natural wonders —*Amer. Guide Series: Ariz.*⟩ ⟨an ~ speech⟩ ⟨an ~ list of titles to a man's name⟩ ⟨a very ~ play⟩ ⟨the country is ~ for the immensity of the barren reaches and the vast horizons —*Amer. Guide Series: Oregon*⟩ **syn** see MOVING

im·pres·sive·ly \-səvlē, -li\ *adv* **:** in an impressive manner ⟨a garrulous young man with ~ complete information on all strata of shipboard life —T.O.Heggen⟩

im·pres·sive·ness \-sivnəs, -sēv- *also* -səv-\ *n* -ES **:** the quality or state of being impressive ⟨the man's ~ was due to his enormous size and thunderous voice⟩

im·press·ment \əmˈpresmənt\ *n* -S [³*impress* + *-ment*] **:** the act of seizing for public use or of impressing into public service ⟨the ~ of sailors⟩ ⟨opposed such measures as the conscription of state officials and ~ of private property —Hallie Farmer⟩

im·pres·sure \-eshə(r)\ *n* [¹*impress* + *-ure*] **1** *archaic* **:** the act of pressing or impressing **2** *archaic* **a :** an impressed mark **b :** a mental or sensory impression

¹**im·prest** \əmˈprest\ *vt* -ED/-ING/-S [prob. fr. It *imprestare*, fr. *in-* ²in- (fr. L) + *prestare* to lend, fr. L *praestare* to stand before, go surety for, furnish, present — more at PREST] **1** *archaic* **:** to make an advance or loan of (money) **2** *obs* **a :** to make an advance of money to **b :** to draw (as money) by way of advance

²**im·prest** \ˈim,p-\ *n* -S **:** a loan or advance of money: **a :** pay advanced to a soldier or sailor **b :** money advanced from government funds to enable a person to discharge his duties

³**imprest** \"\ *adj* **:** advanced or lent esp. as an imprest

⁴**imprest** *n* -S [prob. alter. (influenced by ²*imprest*) of ⁴*impress*] *obs* **:** IMPRESSMENT

⁵**imprest** *vt* -ED/-ING/-S [prob. alter. (influenced by ¹*imprest*) of ³*impress*] *obs* **:** to impress into army or naval service

imprest accountant *n, Eng law* **:** a person to whom an advance of public money is legally made

imprest fund *n* **:** a sum kept on hand, periodically replenished, and used for small expenditures

im·pri·ma·tur \,imprəˈmä¦d·ə(r), ¦tə- *also* -mā¦\ *n* -S [NL, let it be printed, 3d sing. pres. subj. passive of *imprimere* to print, fr. L, to impress — more at IMPRESS] **1 a :** a license to print or publish (as a book or paper) **b :** approval of that which is published under the circumstances that censorship of the press exists **c :** IMPRINT b(1) **2 a :** SANCTION, APPROVAL ⟨gives its ~ to the shameless attack —Eugene Lyons⟩ **b :** a sign or mark of approval ⟨puts the ~ of approval on the morals and decency of wholesale, universal betting —T.E. Dewey⟩

im·pri·ma·tu·ra \(ˌ)im,prēməˈtu̇rə\ *or* **im·prim·a·ture** \imˈprimə,chu̇(ə)r\ *n* -S [modif. of It *imprimitura*, fr. *imprimito* (past part. of *imprimere* to impress, print, stamp, mark, fr. L, to impress) + *-ura* -ure — more at IMPRESS] **:** a thin preliminary glaze applied to the ground in painting

imprime *vt* [prob. fr. ²*in-* + *prime* (first)] *obs* **:** to separate (as a deer) from the herd

imprimery *n* -ES [F *imprimerie*, fr. MF, fr. *imprimer* to print (fr. NL *imprimare*) + *-erie* -ery — more at IMPRIMATUR] *obs* **:** a printing office

im·pri·mis \imˈprīməs, -rēm-\ *adv* [ME *inprimis*, fr. L *in primis* among the first (things)] **:** in the first place — used to introduce a list of items or considerations

¹**im·print** \əmˈprint\ *vt* [ME *emprenten*, *imprenten*, fr. MF *empreinter*, fr. OF, fr. *empreinte* imprint (n.)] **1 a :** to mark by pressure (as a figure on an object or as the object itself with the figure) **:** IMPRESS ⟨a machine to ~ code numbers on metal merchandise⟩ **b** *archaic* **:** PRINT **c :** to add an imprint to ⟨~*ed* statement enclosures⟩ ⟨~ a missing letter⟩ **2 :** to fix indelibly or permanently (as on the memory) ⟨~*ing* her features, her look, her smile, her voice, upon his memory —Edith Sitwell⟩ **3 :** to stamp the characteristics of ⟨~*ing* his own personality on his productions —E.Bentley⟩ **4 :** to establish a response in by imprinting ⟨ducklings of five species were ~*ed* on human beings as their parent-companions at hatching —Margaret M. Nice⟩

²**im·print** \ˈim,p-\ *n* [modif. (influenced by ²*in-*) of MF *empreinte*, fr. OF, fr. fem. of *empreint*, past part. of *empreindre* to imprint, impress, fr. L *imprimere* to impress, imprint — more at IMPRESS] **:** something imprinted or printed: as **a :** a mark (as a figure or symbol) made by pressure ⟨the footstep left its ~ in the mud⟩ ⟨bore the ~ of a circle and dot in the center —Zane Grey⟩ ⟨an ~ of the town seal on each bond —*Springfield (Mass.) Union*⟩ **b** (1) **:** a publisher's name often with address and date of publication usu. placed in a book at the foot of a title page (2) **:** a printer's name or identifying device usu. placed in a book on the copyright page (3) **:** a dealer's or retailer's name and address printed on matter (as a blotter, catalog, or promotional piece) put out by a wholesaler or supplier (4) **:** a correction (as of a letter that shows imperfectly in a run of printed sheets) struck in by running the printed sheets through the press a second time (5) **:** the name of the manufacturer of a stamp printed in the margin of a sheet or of a single stamp **c :** an indelible distinguishing effect or influence ⟨the teacher left her ~ on several generations of students⟩ ⟨the raw western settlements . . . so strongly marked by the ~ of the industrial process —Sinclair Lewis⟩ ⟨their work bears a sort of regional ~ —Malcolm Cowley⟩

imprinted stamp *n* **:** a postage or revenue stamp printed directly on the piece of paper on which it is to be used as distinguished from an adhesive stamp

imprinting *n* **:** a speedy and usu. stable learning pattern appearing early in the life of a member of a social species and involving recognition of identification characters for its own kind or for a surrogate ⟨the young of many precocial birds establish family relations by ~ that involves attraction to the first moving object seen⟩

im·pris·on \əmˈprizᵊn\ *vt* **imprisoned; imprisoned; im·prisoning** \-z(ᵊ)niŋ\ **imprisons** [ME *enprisonen*, *imprisonen*, fr. OF *emprisoner*, fr. *en-* ¹en- + *prison* — more at PRISON] **1 :** to put in prison **:** confine in a jail **2 :** to limit, restrain, or confine as if by imprisoning ⟨have ~*ed* its turbulent water between granite walls —Arnold Bennett⟩ ⟨~*s* him with her possessiveness —*Newsweek*⟩ ⟨deftly and with one arm only, he ~*ed* her —Susan Ertz⟩ ⟨~*ed* little sausages in pastry and baked them —Robertson Davies⟩

im·pris·on·able \-z(ᵊ)nəbəl\ *adj* **1 :** capable of being imprisoned **2 :** legally entailing imprisonment as a penalty ⟨an ~ offense⟩

im·pris·on·ment \-zᵊnmənt\ *n* -S [ME *enprisonement*, *inprisonment*, fr. MF *emprisonnement*, fr. OF, fr. *emprisoner* + *-ment*] **1 :** the act of imprisoning or the state of being imprisoned **:** CONFINEMENT, RESTRAINT **2 :** constraint of a person either by force or by such other coercion as restrains him within limits against his will

im·probability \(ˌ)im, əm+\ *n* **1 :** the quality or state of being improbable **2 :** something improbable

im·probable \(ˈ)im, əm+\ *adj* [MF or L; MF, fr. L *improbabilis*, fr. *in-* ¹in- + *probabilis* probable — more at PROBABLE] **:** not probable **:** unlikely to be true or to occur **:** not easily believable ⟨an ~ story⟩ ⟨an ~ event⟩ ⟨characters unreal, dialogue artificial, plots highly ~ —C.J.Rolo⟩ — **im·probably** \"+\ *adv*

im·pro·ba·tion \,imprōˈbāshən\ *n* [MF, fr. L *improbation-*, *improbatio* disapprobation, fr. *improbatus* (past part. of *improbare* to disapprove, fr. *in-* ¹in- + *probare* to examine, approve, prove) + *-ion-*, *-io* -ion — more at PROVE] **1** *archaic* **:** DISAPPROVAL **2** [L *improbation-*, *improbatio*] *Scots law* **:** an act by which falsehood and forgery are proved **:** an action brought for the purpose of having some instrument declared false or forged

im·probative *also* **im·probatory** \əm+\ *adj* **:** of or belonging to improbation

im·probity \(ˈ)im, əm+\ *n* [MF or L; MF *improbité*, fr. L *improbitat-*, *improbitas*, fr. *improbus* bad, dishonest (fr. *in-* ¹in- + *probus* good, honest) + *-itat-*, *-itas* -ity — more at PROVE] **:** lack of probity **:** lack of integrity or rectitude **:** DISHONESTY

im·proficiency \ˌim+\ *n* [¹*in-* + *proficiency*] *archaic* **:** lack of proficiency

im·profitable \(ˈ)im, əm+\ *adj* [ME, fr. MF, fr. *in-* ¹in- + *profitable* — more at PROFITABLE] **:** UNPROFITABLE

im·progressive \ˌim+\ *adj* [¹*in-* + *progressive*] *archaic* **:** UNPROGRESSIVE — **im·progressively** \"+\ *adv, archaic* — **im·progressiveness** \"+\ *n, archaic*

¹**im·promp·tu** \əmˈpräm(p)(ˌ)t(y)ü, -(ˌ)chü\ *adv* [F, fr. L *in promptu* in readiness, at hand] **:** without previous study, preparation, or consideration **:** on the spur of the moment **:** EXTEMPORANEOUSLY ⟨being able to speak ~ and at length on any given subject —Bryan MacMahon⟩ ⟨any cry of contrition that ever came ~ from a human being —C.E.Montague⟩

²**impromptu** \"\ *n* -S [F, fr. *impromptu*, adv.] **1 :** something made or done impromptu **:** an extemporaneous composition, address, or remark ⟨the witty ~ must not smack of the midnight oil —Cecil Lavery⟩ **2 a :** a piece of music composed or played impromptu **b :** a musical composition suggesting improvisation

³**impromptu** \"\ *adj* [F, fr. *impromptu*, adv.] **1 :** made, done, or formed on or as if on the spur of the moment **:** IMPROVISED, MAKESHIFT ⟨postponements or changes of plan were always ~ —Marcia Davenport⟩ ⟨delegates . . . formed for an ~ parade through the aisle —C.E.Egan⟩ ⟨an ~ bench was made of a long board placed on two chairs and covered with quilts —B.A.Botkin⟩ **2 :** composed or uttered without previous study, preparation, or consideration **:** EXTEMPORANEOUS, UNREHEARSED ⟨an ~ addition to his prepared text —Foster Hailey⟩ ⟨a short ~ speech⟩

⁴**impromptu** \"\ *vb* -ED/-ING/-S [¹*impromptu*] **:** EXTEMPORIZE, IMPROVISE

im·proper \(ˈ)im, əm+\ *adj* [MF *impropre*, fr. L *improprius*, fr. *in-* ²in- + *proprius* own, proper — more at PROPER] **:** not proper: as **a :** not accordant with fact, truth, or right procedure **:** INCORRECT, INACCURATE ⟨arrived at an ~ conclusion from the premises⟩ ⟨charges of bribery, falsification of records, acceptance of ~ fees —*Current Biog.*⟩ **b :** not regularly or normally formed or not properly so called ⟨~ fractions⟩ **c :** not suited to the circumstances, design, or end ⟨an ~ medicine⟩ ⟨wore an ~ dress to the tea⟩ **d :** not in accord with propriety, modesty, good taste, or good manners **:** INDECOROUS ⟨most ~ to intrude a dog into the houses of the people they were calling on —Joseph Conrad⟩ ⟨highly ~ to dress ship at any time with college banners —C.D.Lane⟩ **:** INDECENT ⟨guilty of using ~ language⟩ ⟨wearing a scandalously ~ dress⟩ — **im·properly** \"+\ *adv* — **im·properness** \"+\ *n*

improper diphthong *n* **1 :** a vowel digraph **2 :** PARTIAL DIPHTHONG **3 :** an alpha, eta, or omega with an iota subscript

improper fraction *n* **:** a fraction in which the numerator is greater than or equal to the denominator or is of higher or equal degree

improper integral *n* **:** a definite integral whose region of integration includes a point at which the integrand is undefined or tends to infinity or whose region of integration does not have all limits finite

improportion *n, obs* **:** DISPROPORTION — **improportionate** *adj, obs*

improportionable *adj* [¹*in-* + *proportionable*] *obs* **:** DISPROPORTIONATE

¹**im·pro·pri·ate** \əmˈprōprē,āt\ *vt* -ED/-ING/-S [ML or NL *impropriatus*, past part. of *impropriare*, fr. L *in-* ²in- + *proprius* own + NL *-are* to appropriate — more at APPROPRIATE] **1** *obs* **:** APPROPRIATE **2 a :** to take over (a benefice or ecclesiastical property) and make one's own ⟨the town which had *impropriated*

the revenues of the church —T.D.Atkinson⟩ **b :** to transfer (monastic property) to lay control or ownership — distinguished from *appropriate*

[2]im·pro·pri·ate \-ˌət\ *adj* [NL or ML *impropriatus*] **:** IMPROPRIATED **:** lay as distinguished from clerical

im·pro·pri·a·tion \(ˌ)imˌprōprēˈāshən, əm-\ *n* -s **1 :** the act of impropriating or state of being impropriate **2 :** something impropriated **:** APPROPRIATION

im·pro·pri·a·tor \əmˈprōprēˌād·ə(r)\ *n* -s **:** one to or by whom something is impropriated

im·propriety \ˌim+\ *n* [F or LL; F *impropriété*, fr. LL *improprietat-, improprietas*, fr. L *improprius* improper + *-tat-, -tas* -ty — more at IMPROPER] **1 :** the quality or state of being improper ⟨shocked by the ~ of the young man's action⟩ ⟨guilty of ~ of speech and indecency of dress⟩ ⟨saw no ~ in giving preferment to personal friends and relatives —W.E. Stevens⟩ **2 :** something improper **:** an unsuitable or improper act or remark ⟨puns and jokes and pungent *improprieties* —*Times Lit. Supp.*⟩; *specif* **:** an unacceptable use of a word or of language

im·prosperous \(ˈ)imˌəm+\ *adj* [[1]*in-* + *prosperous*] *archaic* **:** not prosperous **:** POOR, UNSUCCESSFUL

im·prov·abil·i·ty \(ˌ)imˌprüvəˈbiləd·ē, əm-, -lətē, -i\ *n* **:** the quality or state of being improvable **:** capability of improving or of being improved

im·prov·able \əmˈprüvəbəl\ *adj* [[2]*improve* + *-able*] **1** *archaic* **:** capable of being profited from or turned to good account **2 :** capable of improving or of being improved **:** susceptible of improvement — **im·prov·able·ness** \-bəlnəs\ *n* — **im·prov·a·bly** \-blē,-bli\ *adv*

[1]im·prove \əmˈprüv\ *vt* [ME *improven*, fr. MF *improver*, fr. L *improbare* to disapprove, blame, reject — more at IMPROBATION] **1 a** *obs* **:** to show to be wrong **:** CONFUTE **b** *Scots law* **:** to prove false or forged **:** DISPROVE, INVALIDATE **2** *obs* **:** REPROVE, CENSURE

[2]improve \"\ *vb* [alter. (influenced by *approve*) of earlier *emprou, emprow*, fr. AF *emprouer* to invest profitably, to cultivate profitably, fr. OF *en-* [1]en- + *prou* profit — more at PROW] *vt* **1 a :** to make greater in amount or degree **:** INCREASE, AUGMENT, ENLARGE, INTENSIFY ⟨*improved* the chance that the committee could reach agreement⟩ **b** *obs* **:** to raise the price of **c** *obs* **:** to make (an evil) worse **2 a :** to enhance in value or quality **:** make more profitable, excellent, or desirable ⟨~ the appearance of a display⟩ ⟨~ one's health by exercise⟩ ⟨exhibited an *improved* optical viewfinder —*Americana Annual*⟩ **b** *archaic* **:** to speak on in order to make more generally profitable or turn to better spiritual account **c :** to increase the value of (land or property) by bringing under cultivation, reclaiming for agriculture or stock raising, erecting buildings or other structures, laying out streets, or installing utilities (as sewers) ⟨*improved* farmland⟩ **d** *Scots law* **:** to grant (a lease) for a long term to encourage a tenant in good husbandry **e :** to grade and drain (a road) and apply surfacing material (as gravel, crushed rock, or oil) other than pavement **3** *archaic* **a :** to avail oneself of **:** EMPLOY, USE **b :** OCCUPY **4 a :** to turn to profit or to good account **:** employ to good purpose **:** use to advantage ⟨~ an opportunity to make friends⟩ ⟨~ one's time by studying⟩ **b** *archaic* **:** to cause (money or capital) to yield a profit by investment **5 a :** to turn or convert by improving ⟨~ a nag into a racehorse⟩ **b :** to spend, remove, or dissipate by improvements ⟨a tribe *improved* out of existence⟩ ~ *vi* **1 a :** INCREASE, AUGMENT ⟨the price of cotton is *improving*⟩ ⟨the demand for more commodities *improved*⟩ **b :** to rise in value **:** enhance in price ⟨stocks are *improving*⟩ **2 :** to advance or make progress in what is desirable **:** grow better ⟨the invalid's health *improved* daily⟩

syn IMPROVE, BETTER, AMELIORATE, and HELP mean to correct, make more acceptable, or bring nearer to a higher standard of goodness in part or in some degree. IMPROVE and BETTER are general and interchangeable and are often used of things that are orig. bad or unacceptable ⟨famed for his quick wit and his ability to *improve* a script during a performance —G.S. Perry⟩ ⟨increase his powers of field observation and notation while he *improves* his knowledge of the area —J.F.Hart & Eugene Mather⟩ ⟨*bettering* the general conditions of tenant farmers —*Current Biog.*⟩ ⟨has invariably *bettered* the tunes and often transformed a doggerel text into excellent poetry —*Amer. Guide Series: Tenn.*⟩ AMELIORATE is applied chiefly to things that are unacceptable, esp. conditions difficult to endure or causing suffering, and implies partial relief or alterations that make the conditions more tolerable ⟨*ameliorate* the lot of thousands of victimized human beings —Arnold Bennett⟩ ⟨abolish feudalism or *ameliorate* its vices —W.O. Douglas⟩ ⟨his care in *ameliorating* personality conflicts —Harold Koontz & Cyril O'Donnell⟩ HELP implies a bettering that still leaves room for improvement ⟨*help* farmers meet the fertilizer shortage⟩ ⟨exercises to *help* overcome a speech defect⟩

— **improve on** *or* **improve upon :** to improve or make useful additions or amendments to ⟨an inventor who *improved on* the carburetor system of the automobile⟩ ⟨remembered all the backwoods stories his customers told him — and doubtlessly *improved on* them a little —G.S.Perry⟩

improved cylinder *n* **:** a gun barrel with a choke

improved wood *n* **:** wood that has been strengthened by the filling in or closing of the voids in the cellular structure and by compression under heat

im·prove·ment \-vmənt\ *n* -s [alter. of ME *emprowment* profitable investment, profitable cultivation of land, fr. AF *emprouement*, fr. *emprouer* + OF *-ment*] **1 :** the act or process of improving: as **a :** profitable employment or use ⟨the ~ of one's time in reading⟩ **b :** BETTERMENT ⟨went to college not for a degree but for professional ~⟩ **:** AMELIORATION ⟨the ~ of the patient's state of health⟩ **c :** the enhancement or augmentation of value or quality **:** an increasing of profitableness, excellence, or desirability ⟨an ~ of farm stock⟩ ⟨an ~ of the property by building several outbuildings and a new barn⟩ ⟨an ~ in living standards⟩ **2 a :** the state of being improved; *esp* **:** enhanced value or excellence ⟨saw a great ~ in the man's health and frame of mind⟩ ⟨pleased by the ~ of the transportation system⟩ **b :** an instance of such improvement **:** something that improves in this way: as (1) **:** a permanent addition to or betterment of real property that enhances its capital value and that involves the expenditure of labor or money and is designed to make the property more useful or valuable as distinguished from ordinary repairs — see BENEFICIAL IMPROVEMENT, NECESSARY IMPROVEMENT, VOLUNTARY IMPROVEMENT (2) **:** an alteration or addition to an existing subject of invention or discovery that does not destroy its identity or essential character but accomplishes greater efficiency or economy **:** a modification improving and making more valuable an existing discovery or invention

improvement factor *n* **:** an annual increase in compensation that enables workers to share in the benefits from increased productivity — usu. used in labor negotiations

improvements and betterments insurance *n* **:** insurance for the benefit of a tenant covering improvements made by the tenant to property which he occupies under lease

im·prov·er \əmˈprüvə(r)\ *n* **:** one that improves: as **a** *chiefly Brit* (1) **:** an employee who accepts instruction or the opportunity to work in place of wages (2) **:** a worker who has completed an apprenticeship but is not yet qualified as a full-fledged member of a trade or occupation **b :** a device for giving shape to a dress; *esp* **:** BUSTLE **c :** an agent added to improve a substance ⟨potassium bromate is used as a flour ~⟩

im·providence \(ˈ)imˌəm+\ *n* [MF or LL; MF, fr. LL *improvidentia*, fr. *improvident-, improvidens* + L *-ia* -y] **:** the quality or state of being improvident ⟨unemployment compensation and pensions against ~ in old age —C.O.Gregory⟩

im·provident \(ˈ)im, əm+\ *adj* [LL *improvident-, improvidens*, fr. L *in-* [1]in- + *provident-, providens* provident — more at PROVIDENT] **:** not provident **:** lacking foresight or forethought **:** not foreseeing or providing for the future **:** NEGLIGENT, THRIFTLESS ⟨~ throughout his brilliant career . . . in later years became penniless —*Amer. Guide Series: Md.*⟩ ⟨I'm ~: I live in the moment when I'm happy —Edith Wharton⟩ — **im·providently** \"+\ *adv*

im·providentially \(ˌ)im, əm+\ *adv* **:** IMPROVIDENTLY

improving *adj* [fr. pres. part. of [2]*improve*] **:** morally or intellectually uplifting or designed to be so often to the detriment of any intrinsic excellence ⟨urged his children to read only ~ literature⟩ — **im·prov·ing·ly** *adv*

im·provi·sate \əmˈprävəˌzāt *sometimes* ˈimprəvəˌz- *or* əmˈprävəˌsāt\ *vb* -ED/-ING/-S [back-formation fr. *improvisation*] **:** IMPROVISE

im·provi·sa·tion \(ˌ)imˌprävəˈzāshən, əm- *also* ˌimprəvəˈz- *sometimes* (ˌ)=ˌprävəˈsā- *or* ˌimprəˌvīˈzā- *or* (ˌ)=ˌprōvəˈzā- *or* -ōvəˈsā-\ *n* -s [F, fr. *improviser* + *-ation*] **1 :** the act of improvising or the quality or state of being improvised: as **a** (1) **:** extemporaneous composition (as of music or poetry) (2) **:** the extemporaneousness of such composition **b** (1) **:** a course pursued in accordance with no previously devised plan, policy, or consideration ⟨his conduct at the time was merely an ~⟩ ⟨the policy of a democracy thus becomes an eternal ~ —H.L.Mencken⟩ ⟨the flight into the East was not an ~, a sudden, last-minute, desperate measure —A.R. Williams⟩ (2) **:** the extemporaneous quality of such a course ⟨the ~ of the country's relation with foreign powers⟩ **2 :** something improvised or designed to seem improvised **:** IMPROMPTU — **im·provi·sa·tion·al** \-āshənᵊl,-āshnəl\ *adj*

im·provi·sa·tor *pronunc at* IMPROVISATE + ə(r)\ *n* -s [F or It; F *improvisateur*, fr. It *improvvisatore*, fr. *improvvisato* (past part. of *improvvisare*) + *-ore* -or] **:** IMPROVISER, IMPROVISATORE ⟨he has been a great ~, and that his improvisation is not without merit is proved by his spectacular career —O.D. Tolischus⟩

im·prov·i·sa·to·re \əmˌprävəzəˈtōrē\ *n, pl* **improvisato·ri** \"\ *or* **improvisatores** \-ēz\ [It *improvvisatore*] **:** IMPROVISER; *esp* **:** one who composes and recites verse extempore

im·prov·i·sa·to·ri·al \əmˌprävəzəˈtōrēəl\ *adj* **:** of or relating to improvisation — **im·prov·i·sa·to·ri·al·ly** \-ēəlē\ *adv*

im·provi·sa·to·ry \əmˈprävəzəˌtōrē, ˌimprəˈvīz-, *chiefly Brit* ˌimprəˌvīzātəri *or* -ā·tri\ *adj* **:** IMPROVISATORIAL

im·prov·i·sa·tri·ce \əmˌprävəzəˈtrēchē\ *n, pl* **improvisa·tri·ci** \"\ *or* **improvisatrices** \-chēz\ [It *improvvisatrice*, fr. *improvvisatore*] **:** a female improvisatore

im·pro·vise \ˈimprəˌvīz *also* ˌ==ˈ=\ *vb* -ED/-ING/-S [F *improviser*, fr. It *improvvisare*, fr. *improvviso* unprovided, sudden, extempore, fr. L *improvisus* unforeseen, unexpected, fr. *in-* [1]in- + *provisus* foreseen — more at PROVISO] *vt* **1 :** to compose, recite, or sing esp. in verse or to play on an instrument or act extemporaneously ⟨his cast, who ~ dialogue, gags, and situations as they go along —*Current Biog.*⟩ **2 a :** to bring about, arrange, or make on the spur of the moment or without preparation ⟨the cook . . . hastily *improvised* a supper —Willa Cather⟩ ⟨housed in *improvised* temporary quarters —*Report: (Canadian) Royal Commission on Nat'l Development*⟩ ⟨had to ~ policy always —James Cameron⟩ **b :** to construct or fabricate out of what is conveniently at hand ⟨an *improvised* laboratory —*Current Biog.*⟩ ⟨fish . . . with *improvised* hooks and lines —*Amer. Guide Series: N.Y. City*⟩ ~ *vi* **:** to improvise something esp. in verse or music **:** EXTEMPORIZE

im·pro·vis·er *or* **im·pro·vi·sor** \-zə(r)\ *n* -s **:** one that improvises

[1]im·provision \ˌim+\ *n* [[1]*in-* + *provision*] **:** lack of forethought **:** IMPROVIDENCE

[2]im·pro·vi·sion \ˌimprəˈvizhən\ *n* [*improvise* + *-ion*] **:** IMPROVISATION

im·pro·vi·so \ˌimprəˈvē(ˌ)zō\ *adv* (*or adj*) [It *improvviso* — more at IMPROVISE] **:** EXTEMPORE

im·prudence \(ˈ)im, əm+\ *n* [MF or L; MF, fr. L *imprudentia*, fr. *imprudent-, imprudens* + *-ia* -y] **1 :** the quality or state of being imprudent **:** lack of caution, circumspection, or due regard to consequences **2 :** an imprudent act

im·prudency \"+\ *n* -ES [L *imprudentia*] *archaic* **:** IMPRUDENCE

im·prudent \(ˈ)im, əm+\ *adj* [ME, fr. L *imprudent-, imprudens*, fr. *in-* [1]in- + *prudent-, prudens* prudent — more at PRUDENT] **:** not prudent **:** lacking discretion **:** INJUDICIOUS ⟨very ~ in her parent to encourage her . . . in such idolatry and silly romantic ideas —W.M.Thackeray⟩ ⟨the deep ulcer on my leg . . . renders it ~ to take passage at this time —C.B. Nordhoff & J.N.Hall⟩ ⟨would be ~ for a noneconomist to talk about the details of economic policy —A.M.Schlesinger b.1917⟩ — **im·prudently** \"+\ *adv* — **im·prudentness** \"+\ *n* -ES

imps *pl of* IMP, *pres 3d sing of* IMP

imp·son·ite \ˈim(p)səˌnīt\ *n* -s [*Impson* valley, Oklahoma + E *-ite*] **:** a mineral consisting of an asphalt much like albertite but almost insoluble in turpentine

impt *abbr* important

imptr *abbr* importer

im·puberty \(ˈ)im, əm+\ *n* [ML *impubertas*, fr. L *in-* [1]in- + *pubertas* puberty — more at PUBERTY] **:** the quality or state of not having reached puberty

im·pubic \"+\ *adj* [L *impubes* (fr. *in-* [1]in- + *pubes* adult) + E *-ic* — more at PUBES] **:** not arrived at puberty **:** IMMATURE ⟨toiled in the fields with her ~ children —Thomas Beer⟩

im·pu·dence \ˈimpyədən(t)s *also* -dᵊn-\ *also* **im·pu·den·cy** \-nsē,-si\ *n, pl* **impudences** *also* **impudencies** [*impudence* fr. ME, fr. L *impudentia*, fr. *impudent-, impudens* impudent + *-ia* -y; *impudency* fr. L *impudentia*] **1 :** the quality or state of being impudent: as **a** *obs* **:** SHAMELESSNESS, INDECENCY **b :** an attitude marked by disrespect or insolence **:** cocky self-assurance **c** *archaic* **:** cool self-possession or self-reliance **2 :** an impudent remark or act ⟨the mother would not endure her son's ~s⟩

im·pu·dent \-nt\ *adj* [ME, fr. L *impudent-, impudens*, fr. *in-* [1]in- + *pudent-, pudens*, pres. part. of *pudēre* to feel shame — more at PUDIC] **1** *obs* **:** lacking modesty **2 :** marked by contemptuous or cocky boldness or disregard of others ⟨an arrogant and ~ boy given to insulting strangers⟩ **:** INSOLENT ⟨stood there . . . in an ~ swaggering posture —Helen T. Lowe⟩ **:** FORWARD, DISRESPECTFUL ⟨entertainingly ~ stories —Gerald Bullett⟩ **:** bold and brazen ⟨one of the most ~ miscarriages of justice⟩ **syn** see SHAMELESS

im·pu·dent·ly *adv* **:** in an impudent manner

im·pu·dent·ness *n* -ES **:** IMPUDENCE

im·pu·dic·i·ty \ˌimpyəˈdisəd·ē, -yüˈ-\ *n* [MF *impudicité*, fr. L *impudicus* immodest, shameless (fr. *in-* [1]in- + *pudicus* bashful, modest, chaste) + MF *-ité* -ity — more at PUDIC] **:** IMMODESTY, SHAMELESSNESS

im·pugn \əmˈpyün\ *vt* -ED/-ING/-S [ME *impugnen, impungnen*, fr. MF *impugner*, fr. L *impugnare*, fr. *in-* [2]in- + *pugnare* to fight — more at PUGNACIOUS] **1** *obs* **a :** to assail physically **:** FIGHT **b :** OPPOSE, RESIST **2 :** to assail by words or arguments **:** call into question **:** make insinuations against **:** GAINSAY ⟨~ one's honesty⟩ ⟨~ one's claim to property⟩ ⟨frequent recourse to sword or pistol, whenever honor was ~*ed* —*Amer. Guide Series: La.*⟩ **syn** see DENY

im·pugn·able \-nəbəl\ *adj* **:** capable of being impugned **:** subject to question

im·pugna·tion *n* -s [ME *impugnacioun, impungnacioun*, fr. MF or L; MF *impugnation*, fr. L *impugnation-, impugnatio*, fr. *impugnatus* (past part. of *impugnare* to impugn) + *-ion-, -io* -ion] **1** \ˌimˌpəgˈnāshən\ *obs* **:** ATTACK, OPPOSITION **2** \ˌimˌpyüˈn-\ *archaic* **:** IMPUGNMENT

im·pugn·ment \əmˈpyünmənt\ *n* -s **:** the act of bringing into question or gainsaying or the state of being brought into question or gainsaid

im·puissance \(ˌ)im, əm+\ *n* [MF, fr. *in-* [1]in- + *puissance* — more at PUISSANCE] **:** POWERLESSNESS, WEAKNESS

im·puissant \"+\ *adj* [F, fr. MF, fr. *in-* [1]in- + *puissant* — more at PUISSANT] **:** POWERLESS, FEEBLE

[1]im·pulse \ˈimˌpəls *also* -lts\ *n* [L *impulsus*, fr. *impulsus*, past part. of *impellere* to impel — more at IMPEL] **1 a :** the act of driving onward with sudden force **:** IMPULSION, THRUST, DRIVE, PUSH **b :** the effect of an impelling force **:** motion produced by a sudden or momentary force **:** IMPETUS ⟨the ~ of the pumping by the heart is carried down so that a finger applied to the artery anywhere near the surface permits a counting of the pulse rate —Morris Fishbein⟩ **c :** a wave of excitation transmitted through certain tissues and esp. nerve fibers and muscles that results in physiological activity or inhibition **d :** an electrical or mechanical action or force usu. of brief duration ⟨the ~*s* received by the radio set are . . . unimaginably small —A.C.Morrison⟩; *specif* **:** such an action or force actuating an operation (as in a computer) ⟨can be started either by hand or by an air ~ —*Swiss Industry & Trade*⟩ **2 a :** a force so communicated as to produce motion suddenly or immediately ⟨an ~ of the wind⟩: (1) **:** the motive force given by the escape wheel in the driving train of a timepiece to the pendulum or balance (2) **:** the muscular effort initiating a rhythmic dance movement (3) **:** a short directed motion ⟨written with one ~ of the pen —J.R.Gregg⟩ **b :** INCENTIVE ⟨under the ~ of transportation profits —*Amer. Guide Series: Mich.*⟩ **c :** an inspiration or motivation esp. giving a usu. new form or tendency ⟨those who give the religious life a new ~ need disciples to organize the impulse before it runs to seed —Hallam Tennyson⟩ ⟨his more successful stories derive from the same kind of ~ as his poetry —F.R.Leavis⟩ ⟨he received from America fresh artistic ~*s* —Anatole Chujoy⟩ **3 a :** a sudden spontaneous inclination or an incitement of the mind or spirit arising either directly from feeling or from some outer influence and prompting some usu. unpremeditated action ⟨constitutionally inclined to resist ~ and to take long views —George Santayana⟩ ⟨some uncontrollable ~ . . . may have driven the defendant to the commission of the murderous act —B.N.Cardozo⟩ ⟨act on ~⟩; *also* **:** the force actuated by such a motive or propensity ⟨a man who is driven chiefly by ~⟩ ⟨~*s* of greed —Bertrand Russell⟩ **b :** a propensity or natural tendency usu. other than rational ⟨a man of good ~*s*⟩ ⟨the sexual ~⟩ ⟨the fundamental ~ of self-expression —Havelock Ellis⟩ ⟨the systematizing ~, the restless passion for order of the Greeks —John Buchan⟩ ⟨never approaches a new task save with the ~ to postpone it —H.A.Overstreet⟩ **4 a :** the product of the average value of a force and the time during which it acts being a quantity equal to the change in momentum produced by the force if the body acted on is free **b :** PULSE 4a **syn** see MOTIVE

[2]im·pulse \", əmˈp-\ *vt* [L *impulsus*, past part.] **1 :** to give an impulse to **2 :** to initiate an impulse in (a counter of a computer)

impulse buying *n* **:** the buying of merchandise on impulse rather than from premeditation

impulse charge *n* **:** an explosive used to provide an initial impetus (as to a torpedo)

impulse excitation *n* **:** a method of producing damped alternating current in which the duration of the impressed voltage is short compared with the duration of the current produced — compare QUENCHED GAP

impulse face *n* **:** the lifting plane of one of the club teeth of the escape wheel in a lever-escapement watch or the surface of the pallet stone which is engaged thereby

impulse goods *n* **:** merchandise (as inexpensive or luxury items) likely to be bought on impulse or without significant forethought as opposed to staple or essential goods

impulse movement *n* **:** a clock movement (as of a turret clock) in which the hands are driven by means of energy received by its pendulum in the form of electromagnetic impulses

impulse pallet *n* **:** a pallet stone in a roller of a chronometer balance that receives the driving impulse of the teeth of the escape wheel

impulse pin *n* **:** ROLLER JEWEL

impulse turbine *n* **:** a turbine in which the rotor is driven by fluid jets impinging directly against the blades — compare REACTION TURBINE

im·pul·sion \əmˈpəlshən\ *n* -s [ME, fr. MF or L; MF, fr. L *impulsion-, impulsio*, fr. *impulsus* (past part. of *impellere* to impel) + *-ion-, -io* -ion — more at IMPEL] **1 a :** the act of impelling or the state of being impelled **:** the sudden or momentary action of a body in motion impinging on another body **b :** the impelling force or impulse **c :** an onward tendency derived from an impulsion **:** IMPETUS; *specif* **:** a marked or vigorous forward drive of a horse in a gait **2 a :** an influence acting usu. unexpectedly or temporarily on the mind or will and urging to action; *also* **:** an action provoked by such an influence **b :** drive to motor activity or creative effort **c :** IMPULSE 2c **3 :** COMPULSION 2

im·pul·sive \(ˈ)imˈpəls|iv, əmˈp-, |ēv *also* -l(t)s| *or* |əv\ *adj* [prob. fr. MF *impulsif*, fr. *impulsion* + *-if* -ive] **1 :** having the power of or actually driving or impelling ⟨an ~ force⟩ ⟨an ~ influence⟩ **2 a :** actuated by or esp. prone to act on impulse ⟨a houseful of ~ children⟩ ⟨the ~ buying of luxury items⟩ ⟨~, capricious and touchy —D.C.Buchanan⟩ ⟨men's thoughtless or ~ acts —M.R.Cohen⟩ **b :** COMPULSIVE 3 **3 :** acting momentarily ⟨a motor giving the mechanism ~ thrusts⟩ **syn** see SPONTANEOUS

im·pul·sive·ly \|əvlē, -li\ *adv* **:** in an impulsive manner ⟨so happy she flung her arms ~ around his neck and kissed him⟩

im·pul·sive·ness \|ivnəs, |ēv- *also* |əv-\ *n* -ES **:** the quality or state of being impulsive ⟨the ~ with which he took up attractive theories —H.E.Scudder⟩

im·pul·siv·i·ty \ˌimˌpəlˈsivəd·ē, -vətē, -i *also* -ltˈs-\ *n* -ES **:** IMPULSIVENESS

impulsor *n* -s [L, fr. *impulsus* (past part.) + *-or*] *obs* **:** one that impels

im·punctate \(ˈ)im, əm+\ *adj* [[1]*in-* + *punctate*] **:** lacking pores ⟨an ~ brachiopod shell⟩ or impressed punctate markings ⟨a beetle with elytra ~⟩

impunely *adv* [obs. E *impune* unpunished (fr. L *impunis*) + *-ly*] *obs* **:** with impunity

im·pu·ni·bly \(ˈ)imˈpyünəblē, əmˈp-\ *adv* [L *impunis* + E *-ible* + *-ly*] *archaic* **:** with impunity

im·pu·ni·ty \əmˈpyünəd·ē, -nətē, -i\ *n* -ES [MF or L; MF *impunité*, fr. L *impunitat-, impunitas*, fr. *impunis* unpunished (back-formation fr. *impune*, adv., without punishment, fr. *in-* [1]in- + *-pune*, irreg. fr. *poena* punishment, pain) + *-itat-, -itas* -ity — more at PAIN] **:** exemption or freedom from punishment, harm, or loss ⟨trespassing with ~⟩ ⟨many individuals can with apparent ~ remain essentially infants forever, intellectually —Weston La Barre⟩

[1]im·pure \(ˈ)im, əm+\ *adj* [F & L; F, fr. L *impurus*, fr. *in-* [1]in- + *purus* pure — more at PURE] **1 :** not pure: as **a :** UNCHASTE, LEWD, OBSCENE ⟨~ language⟩ ⟨given to ~ ideas⟩ **b :** containing something unclean **:** DIRTY, FOUL, FILTHY, UNWHOLESOME ⟨~ water⟩ ⟨~ air⟩ **c :** unclean for ceremonial or religious purposes or not purified or hallowed by rites **:** DEFILED, UNHOLY, UNHALLOWED **d :** not accurate **:** not idiomatic ⟨~ Latin⟩ **:** marked by an intermixture of foreign elements ⟨an ~ dialect⟩ or by substandard, incongruous, or objectionable locutions ⟨an ~ style⟩ **e :** mixed or impregnated with an extraneous esp. inferior substance **:** ADULTERATED, UNRECTIFIED ⟨an ~ chemical⟩ ⟨~ food⟩ ⟨an ~ diamond⟩ **f** *of art or decoration* **:** MIXED, BASTARD ⟨an ~ style of ornamentation⟩ **g :** designed to serve a purpose chiefly other than artistic — used of art or an art form (as a poem or painting) ⟨there is ~ poetry, social and political poetry —Jacob Isaacs⟩ **2 :** HETEROZYGOUS — **im·purely** \"+\ *adv* — **im·pureness** \"+\ *n*

[2]impure *vt, obs* **:** to make impure

im·pu·ri·fy \əmˈpyu̇rəˌfī\ *vt* [[1]*impure* + *-ify*] **:** to make impure **:** ADULTERATE ⟨a source that is being continually *impurified* by alien additions —Walter de la Mare⟩

im·puritan \(ˈ)im, əm+\ *n* [[1]*in-* + *puritan*] **:** one who is not a puritan or who is opposed to puritanism

im·purity \(ˈ)im, əm+\ *n* [ME *impurite*, fr. L *impuritas* fr. *impurus* + *-itas* -ity] **1 :** the quality or state of being impure **2 :** something impure (as foul matter or obscene language) or something that makes impure (as a foreign ingredient)

impurple *obs var of* EMPURPLE

imput *var of* INPUT

im·put·abil·i·ty \(ˌ)imˌpyüd·əˈbiləd·ē, əm-, -ütəˈ-, -lətē, -i\ *n* **:** the quality or state of being imputable

im·put·able \əmˈpyüd·əbəl, -ütə-\ *adj* [F or ML; F, fr. MF, fr. ML *imputabilis*, fr. L *imputare* to impute + *-abilis* -able — more at IMPUTE] **1 :** capable of being imputed **:** ASCRIBABLE, ATTRIBUTABLE, REFERABLE ⟨insofar as he was only acting as an agent the oversight was not ~ to him⟩ ⟨an occasional blurring of outline . . . is ~ to the music rather than the words —*Times Lit. Supp.*⟩ **2** *archaic* **:** capable of being accused or blamed **:** CULPABLE — **im·put·able·ness** \-bəlnəs\ *n* -ES — **im·put·a·bly** \-blē,-bli\ *adv*

im·pu·ta·tion \ˌimpyəˈtāshən\ *n* -s [MF or LL; MF, fr. LL *imputation-, imputatio*, fr. L *imputatus* (past part. of *imputare* to impute) + *-ion-, -io* -ion] **1 :** the act of imputing: as **a :** ATTRIBUTION, ASCRIPTION ⟨the ~ of emotions, attitudes, and purposes as an explanation of overt behavior —Ernest Nagel⟩ **b :** ACCUSATION ⟨if . . . told that we are wrong we resent the ~ —J.H.Robinson †1936⟩ **:** INSINUATION ⟨resented the

~ that he had any direct responsibility for what she wrote —Millicent Bell⟩ **c :** the theological attribution of sin or righteousness to one on account of another's sin or righteousness **2 :** something imputed **3 :** the determining of the significance usu. to final profit of an element or factor or of each element or factor in a total industrial or merchandising process

im·pu·ta·tion·al \ˌimpyəˈtāshənᵊl, -shnəl\ *adj* **:** of or relating to imputation

im·pu·ta·tive \əm'pyüd·əd·|iv, -ütət|\ *adj* [LL *imputativus,* fr. L *imputatus* + *-ivus* -ive] **:** transferred by imputation ⟨the ~ sin of Adam⟩ — **im·pu·ta·tive·ly** \|əvlē, -li\ *adv* — **im·pu·ta·tive·ness** \|ivnəs\ *n* -ES

im·pute \əm'pyüt, *usu* -üd·+V\ *vt* -ED/-ING/-S [ME *inputen,* fr. L *imputare,* fr. *in-* [2]in- + *putare* to consider, think — more at PAVE] **1 a :** to attribute accusingly **:** lay the responsibility or blame for sometimes falsely or unjustly ⟨accused him of her own fault, in *imputing* to him the wreck of her project —George Meredith⟩ **b :** to credit or ascribe to a person or a cause ⟨*imputing* to me better qualities than I possess⟩ ⟨our vices as well as our virtues have been *imputed* to bodily derangement —B.N.Cardozo⟩ ⟨*imputing* his visit to a wish of hearing that she was better —Jane Austen⟩ often falsely, accusingly, or unjustly ⟨soon began to believe in the opulence *imputed* to me —L.P.Smith⟩ ⟨*imputing* to him a guilt of which he was innocent —Edith Sitwell⟩ ⟨how dare you . . . ~ such monstrous intentions to me —G.B.Shaw⟩ **c :** to make a legal imposition of (as a charge against someone) **d :** to credit by transferal (a virtue or the benefit of a good work) to the account of someone other than the initiating agent **2** *obs* **:** RECKON, CONSIDER, REGARD **3 :** IMPART, GIVE ⟨with his hand he ~*s* life to clay —Samuel Alexander⟩ **4** *obs* **:** to charge someone with a wrongdoing or crime **syn** see ASCRIBE

imputed *adj* **:** being the value in terms of money or hypothetical income receivable from something one has or owns that would yield real income if one wished (as a house one owns and uses but might rent) ⟨~ rent⟩ ⟨~ income)

im·put·ed·ly *adv* **:** by imputation

imputed value *n* **:** the value of a thing determined from its utility rather than by adding the cost of its constituent elements

im·putrescibility \ˌim+\ *n* **:** the quality or state of being imputrescible

im·putrescible \ˌim+\ *adj* [LL *imputrescibilis,* fr. L *in-* [1]in- + LL *putrescibilis* putrescible — more at PUTRESCIBLE] **:** not subject to putrescence **:** not capable of putrefaction

impv *abbr* imperative

impx *abbr* [L *imperatrix*] empress

[1]in \(ˌ)in, ən; *usu* ᵊn *after* t, d, s, *or* z *as in "split in two", often* ᵊm *after* p *or* b *as in "up in front", often* ᵊŋ *after* k *or* g *as in "sick in bed", often* n *before* ə *as in "he's in a hurry"*\ *prep* [ME, fr. OE; akin to OHG *in,* prep., in, ON *ī,* Goth *in,* L *in,* Gk *en,* OPruss *en,* Russ *v, vo, vn-*] **1 a** (1) — used as a function word to indicate location or position in space or in some materially bounded object ⟨put the key ~ the lock⟩ ⟨travel ~ Italy⟩ ⟨play ~ the street⟩ ⟨wounded ~ the leg⟩ ⟨read ~ bed⟩ ⟨look up a quotation ~ a book⟩ (2) *chiefly Brit* **:** ON ⟨squatting down ~ his heels —R.M.Daw⟩ ⟨tramcars which run ~ tracks—*Manual of Firemanship* (*Gt. Brit.*)⟩ ⟨best dwelling house ~ the island —Padraic Fallon⟩ (3) **:** INTO ⟨broke ~ pieces⟩ ⟨called ~ council on many occasions —*U.S.Investor*⟩ ⟨threw it ~ the fire⟩ ⟨wouldn't let her ~ the house —*Springfield* (*Mass.*) *Daily News*⟩ **b** (1) — used as a function word to indicate position or location in something immaterial or intangible ⟨saw him ~ my dreams⟩ ⟨the position of the artist ~ society⟩ or the fact of belonging to a group or association ⟨you're ~ the army now⟩ ⟨are you ~ the orchestra⟩ (2) — used as a function word to indicate activity, occupation, or purpose ⟨advanced ~ hot pursuit⟩ ⟨~ search of lost treasure⟩ ⟨~ honor of this event⟩ ⟨what is all this ~ aid of . . . —*Sydney* (*Australia*) *Bull.*⟩ (3) — used as a function word to indicate a position or relationship of authority or responsibility ⟨~ charge of the company's affairs⟩ ⟨~ command of the garrison⟩ (4) **:** in the course of ⟨~ cooling this material hardens⟩ ⟨drowned ~ crossing the river⟩ (5) — used as a function word to indicate close connection by way of implication or active participation ⟨~ the plot⟩ ⟨~ an amateur play⟩ (6) — used as a function word to indicate engagement in a business identified with a particular commodity ⟨he's ~ oil, he's ~ rice —Ethel Merman⟩ ⟨her mother's family were . . . ~ butter —Mary Manning⟩ ⟨was ~ buttons but had started to expand into novelties —Mary Barrett⟩ **c** (1) — used as a function word to indicate a material, mental, or moral situation or condition ⟨a house ~ ruins⟩ ⟨a boy ~ love⟩ ⟨he's ~ luck⟩ ⟨~ great pain⟩ ⟨up to his waist ~ water⟩ or an environing condition ⟨the city lay ~ darkness⟩ ⟨basking ~ sunshine⟩ (2) — used as a function word to indicate something that envelops or covers ⟨a book bound ~ buckram⟩ ⟨covered ~ mud —Nevil Shute⟩ ⟨covered ~ . . . cotton plaid —*Spiegel's Catalog*⟩ (3) — used as a function word to indicate a cultivated or natural plant cover ⟨valley bottom is ~ grass —P.E. James⟩ ⟨75 percent of all the cropped land is ~ cereals —Samuel Van Valkenburg & Ellsworth Huntington⟩ ⟨most of the surface is ~ woods or brush —L.E.Klimm⟩ (4) — used as a function word to indicate something that is being worn ⟨a tall man ~ a bowler hat —Christopher Isherwood⟩ ⟨racing the horse ~ blinders⟩; often used to indicate a salient characteristic of what is being worn ⟨a lady ~ black⟩ **d** — used as a function word with an accompanying concrete word to indicate a physiological condition or process (as pregnancy or the condition of producing or yielding) ⟨~ lamb⟩ ⟨a cow ~ milk⟩ **e** (1) — used as a function word with an accompanying concrete word to indicate affluence or easy financial circumstances ⟨the Madrileño ~ the money loves to make a splash —E.D.Hauser⟩ ⟨I am generally ~ cash —Lord Byron⟩ (2) — used as a function word to indicate possession or display of some trait or attribute ⟨a gentleman ~ a gray goatee —Al Hine⟩ ⟨the sheep are ~ wool⟩ ⟨the corn's ~ silk and tassel —G.S.Perry⟩ ⟨~ figure slim —W.H.Hudson †1922⟩ **f :** under the influence of (an alcoholic drink) ⟨when ~ liquor, he would scutter up a tree like a squirrel —S.H.Adams⟩ ⟨~ drink⟩ ⟨~ one's cups⟩ **2 a** (1) **:** within the limits of a space of time expressed or implied ⟨early ~ April⟩ ⟨come ~ time⟩ ⟨~ the days of my childhood⟩ ⟨~ a few minutes he was there⟩ (2) **:** during the course of **:** DURING ⟨~ his long journeys throughout the country —Darcy Ribeiro⟩ ⟨~ all that time I never saw him⟩ (3) **:** during the space of **:** at any time during **:** FOR ⟨the coldest day ~ twenty years⟩ ⟨have not seen him ~ months⟩ **b :** AT ⟨united ~ this time of peril⟩ ⟨vested in the governor acting ~ his discretion —*Achievement in the Gold Coast*⟩ **c** — used as a function word to indicate a proportion or rate ⟨the mix was one ~ twenty —F.W.Crofts⟩ **3 a** (1) — used as a function word to indicate means or instrumentality ⟨scribbled and scratched over . . . ~ pencil or nail —William Faulkner⟩ ⟨caught his coat ~ the gate latch —L.Y.Erskine⟩ ⟨treated ~ moist heat —F.D.Smith & Barbara Wilcox⟩ (2) **:** by virtue of **:** on account of **:** for the reason that ⟨it is also complex, ~ being an integral part of a rich and many-sided mind —E.R.Bentley⟩ ⟨resemble the . . . Uplands ~ the fact that generally they provide an environment unfriendly to human occupancy —Samuel Van Valkenburg & Ellsworth Huntington⟩ — often used in the phrase *in that* ⟨a fallacious argument ~ that it is based on false premises⟩ (3) — used as a function word to indicate material or constituents ⟨a memorial ~ Vermont granite —Bernard De Voto⟩ ⟨tell the court . . . ~ what her cargo consisted —F.W.Crofts⟩ ⟨an artist ~ oils⟩ (4) — used as a function word to indicate degree, extent, or measure ⟨flock to his exhibitions ~ thousands —Herbert Read⟩ ⟨~ the main, we are in agreement⟩ ⟨not discouraged ~ the least⟩ (5) — used as a function word to indicate a class of objects ⟨something ~ a vacuum cleaner —John Steinbeck⟩ ⟨the latest thing ~ cars⟩ **b** — used as a function word to indicate manner, form, or arrangement ⟨buying a pig ~ installments —Dodie Smith⟩ ⟨told ~ confidence⟩ ⟨written ~ French⟩ ⟨carry all your funds ~ traveler's checks —Richard Joseph⟩ **c :** with reference to **:** as concerns ⟨wonder if actors of other countries are as happy ~ their audiences as we are —Phyllis Robbins⟩ ⟨care must be exercised ~ the amount of tannic acid used —C.M.Whittaker & C.C. Wilcock⟩ ⟨~ fall color they have few peers —Laurence Lowry⟩ ⟨Greek ~ language, culture, and religion —Franc Shor⟩ ⟨six feet ~ height⟩ ⟨a library rich ~ manuscripts⟩ ⟨~ the matter of your account⟩ **4 a** — used as a function word to indicate consideration of a thing strictly limited to its own essence, nature, or merits, apart from its relations to others ⟨~ itself, the matter has no importance⟩ ⟨nothing is beautiful ~ itself⟩; compare THING-IN-ITSELF **b** — used as a function word to indicate the specific object, sphere, or aspect to which a qualification is restricted ⟨~ him you have a fine leader⟩ ⟨much remains to be done ~ this field⟩ ⟨a very worthy gentleman, ~ truth⟩ ⟨that we expect ~ persons of your station —W.S. Gilbert⟩ ⟨my trust is ~ the Lord⟩ ⟨believe ~ his good faith⟩ ⟨rich ~ hope —Shak.⟩ **c** (1) **:** WITHIN — used of an inherent quality, attribute, or significance ⟨has no pity ~ him⟩ ⟨there is nothing ~ that story⟩ (2) **:** within the capacity or powers of ⟨if I . . . had anything like that ~ me, it would have made itself felt before now —Hamilton Basso⟩ **d :** in spiritual union with ⟨love one's brothers ~ Christ⟩ **e :** within the grant of **:** in the power or control of ⟨the scholarship is ~ the trustees of the fund⟩ **5 :** in the key of ⟨~ F⟩ — **not in it** *slang* **:** not in the same class **:** hopelessly outclassed ⟨simply is *not in it* as far as skill and brains are concerned⟩

[2]in \ˈin\ *adv* [ME, fr. OE *in, inn;* akin to OHG *in,* adv., in, ON & Goth *inn,* OE *in,* prep.] **1 a** (1) **:** to or toward the inside esp. of a house or other building **:** into a certain space **:** INSIDE ⟨the door is locked, I can't get ~⟩ ⟨opened the window and climbed ~⟩ ⟨broke ~ and made the arrest⟩ (2) **:** in a particular direction **:** to or toward some destination ⟨drove 20 miles ~ and walked the rest of the way⟩ ⟨flew ~ on the first plane⟩ ⟨it was shank's mare from there ~ —Shelby Foote⟩ (3) **:** into a position of proximity **:** so as to be near some point **:** NEAR ⟨trackless trolleys able to swing ~ to the curb —*Springfield* (*Mass.*) *Union*⟩ ⟨the enemy closed ~⟩ **:** at close quarters ⟨advised the infielders to play ~⟩ (4) **:** so as to envelop gradually with something intangible or nebulous ⟨darkness closed ~⟩ ⟨the fog moved ~⟩ **b :** into the midst or into the surface of something so as to form a part ⟨put ~ some sugar⟩ ⟨mix ~ the flour⟩ ⟨paint ~ another figure⟩ — often used in combination ⟨built-*in* stabilizers⟩ **c** (1) **:** to its place ⟨fit a piece ~⟩ (2) **:** so as to conform, agree, or submit **:** into line ⟨fell ~ with our plans⟩ ⟨will he fit ~⟩ **d** (1) **:** to or into a particular place ⟨get your orders ~ early⟩ ⟨called us ~ for a conference⟩ (2) **:** to one's house ⟨had some friends ~ for dinner⟩ ⟨had a girl ~ to serve⟩ **2 a** (1) **:** within a particular place; *esp* **:** within the customary place of residence, practice, or business ⟨is your mother ~⟩ ⟨the doctor will be ~ at 2⟩ (2) **:** in a place that is the goal of a journey or course **:** at one's destination or terminus ⟨the whole whaling fleet was ~ —H.A.Chippendale⟩ ⟨wild riders of the High Plains, ~ from the ranches —*Amer. Guide Series: Texas*⟩ ⟨is the train ~⟩ ⟨two runs ~ last inning⟩ (3) **:** in place or position ⟨is the key ~⟩ ⟨had to climb a ladder because the stairs were not yet ~ —*Current Biog.*⟩ ⟨the footings are already ~ —*Building Estimating & Contracting*⟩ **b** (1) **:** on the interior or inner side **:** WITHIN ⟨shut a person ~⟩ (2) **:** so as to confine or surround ⟨snowed ~⟩ ⟨fence cattle ~⟩ (3) **:** in jail or prison ⟨what offense is he ~ for⟩ (4) *of a ship's sails* **:** in a furled or stowed condition **c** (1) **:** in the position of a participant, accomplice, insider, or observer — usu. used with *on* ⟨it's exciting to be ~ on that —May Sarton⟩ ⟨was ~ on the scheme —E.S.Morgan⟩ ⟨let some members of the diplomatic corps ~ on the government's intention —Sydney Gruson⟩ ⟨bankers who are ~ on current . . . thinking —*Wall Street Jour.*⟩ ⟨time his visit so that he might sit ~ on the Civil War —*Theatre Arts*⟩ (2) **:** in or into participation in a pot by betting as required by the rules ⟨come ~ for three chips⟩ ⟨count me ~⟩ ⟨stay ~ the pot⟩ **d** (1) **:** in office or power ⟨the Tories were ~ again —John Strachey⟩; *also* **:** in the position of having won an election ⟨~ by a landslide⟩ (2) **:** with legal privilege or title **:** in possession — used of a holding, possession, or seisin ⟨~ by descent⟩ (3) **:** in someone's good graces **:** on good terms — usu. used with *with* ⟨~ with the courthouse gang —D.D.McKean⟩ ⟨~ strong with the white folks —Ralph Ellison⟩ (4) **:** in a specified relation as regards favor, esteem, or terms of association ⟨~ bad with the boss⟩ (5) **:** in a position of assured or definitive success ⟨by the end of the performance I was ~ —Emmett Kelly⟩ ⟨why, you're ~, fellow —*Amateur Athlete*⟩; *also* **:** in vogue or style ⟨jewelry is ~ this year —G.A.Wagner⟩ **e** (1) *chiefly Brit* **:** in or into a burning or lighted condition ⟨blow ~ a fire⟩ ⟨the streetlights . . . were ~ —E.M.Lustgarten⟩ (2) **:** in season ⟨strawberries are ~⟩ **:** in cultivation ⟨had some two hundred acres ~ —Eve Langley⟩ **:** in condition to be harvested **:** in mature condition ⟨when cotton is ~ their devotion to the crop alters them completely —*Amer. Guide Series: Ark.*⟩ (3) **:** at bat (as in cricket) ⟨the last man ~⟩ (4) *of an oil well* **:** in or into production ⟨the well has come ~⟩ (5) **:** in effect ⟨rationing by points is over and rationing by the purse is ~ —*Economist*⟩ **f** (1) **:** in one's possession or control **:** at one's disposal **:** at hand ⟨the evidence is not all ~ —W.C.Allee⟩ ⟨the answers aren't ~ —Roscoe Drummond⟩ (2) **:** in a completed or terminated state ⟨when our own crops were ~ —A.W.Barkley⟩ ⟨after harvests are ~⟩ (3) **:** in evidence **:** on hand ⟨October was ~, mild and languorous —Maurice Hewlett⟩ (4) **:** in a specified service or employment ⟨had ~ enough time as mate —H.A.Chippendale⟩ ⟨put ~ a lot of time on that job⟩ **3 :** to the end **:** INDEFINITELY — used as an intensive with *on* ⟨every feeding time from there on ~ —Land Kaderli⟩ — **in for :** certain to experience something, pleasant or unpleasant ⟨*in for* a whale of one hour's entertainment —Goodman Ace⟩ ⟨*in for* a storm⟩ — **in for it 1 :** committed to a course **2 :** certain to suffer punishment or other unpleasant experience ⟨sees us as ineluctably *in for it* —J.W.Krutch⟩ ⟨will be *in for it* if he doesn't get home on time⟩

[3]in \"\ *vt* **inned; inned; inning; ins** [ME *innen,* fr. OE *innian* to include, go in, fr. *in, inn,* adv.] *now dial chiefly Eng* **:** ENCLOSE, RECLAIM; *also* **:** HARVEST

[4]in \"\ *adj* [[2]*in*] **1 a :** that is located inside or within ⟨the ~ part⟩ **b :** that is in position, connection, operation, or power ⟨the ~ party⟩ **c :** having its inning ⟨the ~ team⟩ **2 :** that is directed inward **:** proceeding or bound toward the interior or inner side **:** INCOMING ⟨the ~ train⟩

[5]in \"\ *n* -s [[2]*in*] **1 :** one who is in office or power or on the inside ⟨wanted to be an ~ —W.A.White⟩ — usu. used in pl. ⟨a matter of ~*s* versus outs —L.K.Caldwell⟩ **2 :** INFLUENCE, PULL ⟨enjoyed some sort of ~ with the commandant —Henriette Roosenburg⟩ ⟨must have an ~ someplace —W.R. Burnett⟩ **3 :** a ball hit in bounds in tennis or squash

[1]in- *or* **il-** *or* **im-** *or* **ir-** *prefix* [ME, fr. MF, OF, & L; ME *in-* fr. OF, fr. L; ME *il-* fr. MF, fr. L, fr. *in-;* ME *im-* fr. OF, fr. L, fr. *in-;* ME *ir-* fr. OF, fr. L, fr. *in-;* akin to OE *un-* — more at UN-] **:** not **:** NON-, UN- — usu. *il-* before *l* ⟨*il*logical⟩ and *im-* before *b, m,* or *p* ⟨*im*balance⟩ ⟨*im*moral⟩ ⟨*im*provident⟩ and *ir-* before *r* ⟨*ir*reducible⟩ and *in-* before other sounds ⟨*in*active⟩ ⟨*in*apt⟩ ⟨*in*conclusive⟩

[2]in- *or* **il-** *or* **im-** *or* **ir-** *prefix* [ME, fr. OF, MF, & L; ME *in-* fr. OF *in-, en-,* fr. L *in-,* fr. *in* in, into; ME *il-* fr. MF, fr. L, fr. *in;* ME *im-* fr. MF *im-, em-,* fr. L *im-,* fr. *in;* ME *ir-* fr. L, fr. *in* — more at [1]IN] **1 :** in **:** within **:** inward **:** into **:** toward **:** on ⟨*im*plode⟩ ⟨*ir*radicate⟩ **2 :** [1]EN- ⟨*il*lucidate⟩ ⟨*im*barn⟩ ⟨*im*marble⟩ ⟨*im*panel⟩ ⟨*im*peril⟩ ⟨*in*spirit⟩ — in both senses usu. *il-* before *l, im-* before *b, m,* or *p, ir-* before *r,* and *in-* before other sounds

[3]in- *or* **ino-** *comb form* [NL *in-,* fr. Gk, tendon, fr. *in-, is;* prob. akin to L *viēre* to plait — more at WITHY] **:** fiber **:** fibrous tissue ⟨*in*itis⟩ ⟨*ino*gen⟩

-in \ən, ᵊn, ˌin\ *n suffix* -s [F *-ine,* fr. L *-ina* (with long *ī*), fem. of *-inus* (with long *ī*) of or belonging to — more at -INE] **1 a :** neutral chemical compound or compound not distinctly basic or acidic ⟨picrotox*in*⟩ ⟨hematoporphyr*in*⟩ — esp. in names of glycerides ⟨acet*in*⟩ ⟨stear*in*⟩, glycosides ⟨amygdal*in*⟩ ⟨quercitr*in*⟩, proteins ⟨gelat*in*⟩ ⟨insul*in*⟩, and 6-membered heterocyclic compounds ⟨diox*in*⟩; usu. distinguished from *-ine* **b :** enzyme ⟨emuls*in*⟩ ⟨myros*in*⟩ — compare -ASE **c :** antibiotic ⟨penicill*in*⟩ ⟨streptomyc*in*⟩ **2 :** [2]-INE 2a, 2b — not used systematically **3 :** pharmaceutical product ⟨niac*in*⟩ ⟨aspir*in*⟩

in *abbr* **1** inch **2** inlet

In *symbol* indium

INA *abbr* international normal atmosphere

[1]-i·na \'īnə, 'ēnə\ *n suffix, pl* **-ina** [NL, fr. L, fem. sing. and neut. pl. of *-inus* (with long *ī*) [1]-ine] **:** one or ones related to, resembling, or characterized by — in taxonomic names in biology ⟨Acar*ina*⟩ ⟨Clathr*ina*⟩ ⟨Fistul*ina*⟩

[2]-i·na \'ēnə *sometimes* 'īnə\ *also* **-ine** \ˌēn *sometimes* ˌīn\ *n suffix* -s [prob. fr. It *-ina* (dim. suffix), fr. L *-ina* (with long *ī*), fem. of *-inus* (with long *ī*) [1]-ine] **1 :** musical instrument ⟨concert*ina*⟩ ⟨seraph*ine*⟩ **2 :** musical device ⟨aeol*ine*⟩

in·ability \ˌin+\ *n* [ME *inabilite,* fr. MF *inhabilité,* fr. *in-* [1]in- + *habilité* ability — more at ABILITY] **:** the quality or state of being unable **:** lack of ability **:** lack of sufficient power, strength, resources, or capacity ⟨plead an ~ in mathematics —John Dollard⟩

in ab·sen·tia \ˌinab'sench(ē)ə, ˌinəb-, -sentēə\ *adv* [L] **:** in absence (as of the accused person or of a person receiving a degree) ⟨awarded a degree *in absentia*⟩ ⟨condemned *in absentia*⟩

in·absorbability \ˌin+\ *n* **:** the quality or state of being inabsorbable

in·absorbable \"+\ *adj* [[1]*in-* + *absorbable*] **:** not capable of being absorbed

in ab·strac·to \ˌinəbz'trak(ˌ)tō, -b'st-\ *adv* [L, in the abstract] **:** in or from an abstract point of view **:** in the abstract ⟨the question could not be settled *in abstracto* —Yuen-li Liang⟩ ⟨discovering the problem purely theoretically, *in abstracto* —*Mathematical Biophysics*⟩

in·acceptable \ˌin+\ *adj* ['*in-* + *acceptable*] **:** not acceptable

in·accessibility \ˌin+\ *n* [prob. fr. MF *inaccessibilité,* fr. *inaccessible* + *-ité* -ity] **:** the quality or state of being inaccessible

in·accessible \ˌin+\ *adj* [MF or LL; MF, fr. LL *inaccessibilis,* fr. L *in-* [1]in- + LL *accessibilis* accessible — more at ACCESSIBLE] **1 :** not accessible: as **a :** not capable of being reached, entered, or approached ⟨~ except by heavy two-wheeled carts —C.L.Jones⟩ **b :** not capable of being obtained ⟨a rare work, today almost ~⟩ **c :** not easy to form friendly or close relations with **:** not susceptible to advances or influence **:** UNAPPROACHABLE ⟨peculiarly ~ to such questioning —Christine Weston⟩ ⟨a cold ~ figure⟩ **d :** difficult or impossible to comprehend or enter into **:** ABSTRUSE, ESOTERIC ⟨poetry . . . ~ to contemporary criticism —Frederick Morgan⟩ ⟨the novel . . . seems to me among the most ~ —C.J.Rolo⟩ **2 :** reflecting or evidencing inaccessibility ⟨a look which was austere, ~ —Ellen Glasgow⟩ ⟨an air of ~ respectability —John Buchan⟩ — **inaccessibleness** \"+\ *n* — **in·accessibly** \"+\ *adv*

in·accuracy \(ˈ)in, ən+\ *n* [[1]*in-* + *accuracy*] **1 :** the condition of being inaccurate ⟨avoiding muddle and ~ —W.H. Dowdeswell⟩ **2 :** an instance of being inaccurate **:** MISTAKE, ERROR ⟨when all his *inaccuracies* . . . have been acknowledged —D.C.Peattie & Eleanor R. Dobson⟩

in·accurate \(ˈ)in, ən+\ *adj* [[1]*in-* + *accurate*] **:** not accurate: as **a :** containing a mistake or error **:** INCORRECT, ERRONEOUS ⟨an ~ account⟩ **b :** not functioning with accuracy or precision **:** FAULTY, DEFECTIVE ⟨the limbs are useless and sense organs are ~ —Abram Kardiner⟩ ⟨this thermometer is ~⟩ — **in·accurately** \"+\ *adv* — **in·accurateness** \"+\ *n*

in·action \(ˈ)in, ən+\ *n* [[1]*in-* + *action*] **:** lack of action or activity **:** abstention from labor **:** IDLENESS, LETHARGY ⟨impatience with hypocrisy and ~ —Lillian Smith⟩

in·activate \(ˈ)in, ən+\ *vt* [*inactive* + *-ate*] **:** to make inactive: as **a** (1) **:** to destroy certain biological activities of ⟨~ the complement of normal serum by heat⟩ — compare REACTIVATE (2) **:** to cause (as an infective agent) to lose disease-producing capacity ⟨~ bacteria⟩ **b :** to remove (a unit) from the active list of a military service without disbanding — **in·activation** \(ˌ)in, ən+\ *n*

in·active \(ˈ)in, ən+\ *adj* [[1]*in-* + *active*] **:** not active: as **a** (1) **:** marked by deliberate or enforced absence of activity or effort **:** SEDENTARY ⟨forced by illness to lead an ~ life⟩ (2) **:** not given to action or effort **:** not diligent, energetic, or industrious **:** INDOLENT, SLUGGISH ⟨dreamy and ~ by nature⟩ ⟨a very ~ police chief⟩ ⟨the rentier class, an ~ class in the economy —L.R.Klein⟩ **b** (1) **:** being unused or out of use **:** lying idle **:** not functioning ⟨an ~ mine⟩ ⟨an ~ machine⟩ (2) **:** relating to or consisting of officers and enlisted personnel of the armed forces who are not performing or available for military duties ⟨~ list⟩ ⟨~ reserve⟩ ⟨~ status⟩ (3) **:** being a commodity for which there is relatively little demand or in which relatively little trading occurs ⟨active, ~ and obsolete sterling patterns —*Christian Science Monitor*⟩ ⟨~ stocks⟩ (4) *of a disease* **:** not progressing or fulminating **:** QUIESCENT **c** (1) **:** chemically inert **:** UNREACTIVE ⟨~ charcoal⟩ (2) **:** not exhibiting any action on polarized light **:** optically neutral — used of stereoisomeric forms of various substances ⟨~ fructose⟩ ⟨~ camphor⟩; compare MES- 4b, RACEMIC

syn IDLE, INERT, PASSIVE, SUPINE: INACTIVE applies to anyone or anything not in action or not usu. in action (as in operation or use) or at work ⟨*inactive* machines⟩ ⟨an *inactive* child⟩ ⟨an *inactive* charge account⟩ IDLE applies chiefly to persons without occupation at the moment but usu. without occupation as a general or habitual thing, or to their powers, organs, or implements ⟨give work to an *idle* laborer⟩ ⟨an *idle* lathe⟩ ⟨an *idle* mind⟩ ⟨an *idle* pen⟩ INERT implies lack of power in a thing to set it in motion or by itself to produce a given effect, or suggests in a person a general indisposition to activity ⟨aimless accumulation of precise knowledge, *inert* and unutilized —A.N. Whitehead⟩ ⟨this amorphous spreading of responsibility will result in a sort of *inert,* ponderous bureaucracy —Stanley Walker⟩ ⟨would lie for hours on a chaise longue, so *inert* that the folds of chiffon which dripped from her body to the floor hung as steady as if they were stone —Rebecca West⟩ ⟨the greatest menace to freedom is an *inert* people —L.D.Brandeis⟩ PASSIVE implies immobility or a lack of positive reaction when acted upon by an external force or agent, often implying a submissiveness consisting of failure to be provoked to resistance or of a planned avoidance of any action that will give aid to the dominating force or agent ⟨some of those hours were spent in intensive cerebration, some in *passive* listening to lectures —H.M.Wriston⟩ ⟨*passive* obedience to authority⟩ ⟨*passive* resistance to oppression⟩ SUPINE implies abject inertia or passivity, often from indolence ⟨he is *supine;* he accepts his mother's truculence on his behalf with an indolence of temper which distinguishes him in this, as in all matters —Edward Hyams⟩ ⟨political and religious dissension . . . had split a weary and *supine* people into a dozen factions —P.J. Searles⟩

in·actively \"+\ *adv* **:** in an inactive manner

inactiveness \"+\ *n* **:** the quality or state of being inactive

in·activity \ˌin+\ *n* **:** the quality or state of being inactive **:** IDLENESS, SLUGGISHNESS

in·adaptability \ˌin+\ *n* **:** the quality or state of being inadaptable

in·adaptable \ˌin+\ *adj* [[1]*in-* + *adaptable*] **:** incapable of adaptation **:** belonging to a fixed type

in·adaptive \ˌin+\ *adj* [[1]*in-* + *adaptive*] **:** not adaptive

in·adequacy \(ˈ)in, ən+\ *n* [fr. *inadequate,* after *adequate: adequacy*] **:** the quality or state of being inadequate **:** INSUFFICIENCY ⟨~ of unemployment benefits —*Collier's Yr. Bk.*⟩

in·adequate \(ˈ)in, ən+\ *adj* [[1]*in-* + *adequate*] **:** not adequate **:** INSUFFICIENT, DEFICIENT ⟨~ equipment⟩ ⟨~ leadership⟩ *specif* **:** lacking the capacity for psychological maturity ⟨the ~ individual⟩ **:** unable to make adequate social adjustment ⟨an offender coming from an ~ family⟩ ⟨~ parents⟩ — **in·adequately** \"+\ *adv* — **in·adequateness** \"+\ *n* -ES

in·admissibility *also* **in·admissability** \ˌin+\ *n* **:** the quality or state of being inadmissible

in·admissible *also* **in·admissable** \ˌin+\ *adj* [[1]*in-* + *admissible*] **:** not proper to be allowed or received **:** not admissible ⟨~ behavior⟩ — **in·admissibly** \"+\ *adv*

in-a-door bed \'⸗⸗,⸗-\ *also* **in-a-door** *n* [fr. *In-a-Dor-Bed,* a trademark] **:** MURPHY BED

[1]in·adu·nate \ˌinəˈd(y)ünət, (ˈ)iˌnajən-\ *adj* [[1]*in-* + L *adunatus,* past part. of *adunare* to unite, fr. *ad-* + *unus* one — more at ONE] **:** not united; *specif* **:** having the arms completely free from the calyx — used of a crinoid

[2]inadunate \"\ *n* -s **:** an inadunate crinoid

in·ad·ver·tence \ˌinəd'vərtᵊn(t)s, ˌiˌnad-, -vət-, -vəit-\ *n* [ML *inadvertentia,* fr. L *in-* [1]in- + *advertent-, advertens* (pres. part. of *advertere* to advert) + *-ia* -y — more at ADVERT] **1 :** the fact or action of being inadvertent; lack of care or attentiveness **:** INATTENTION ⟨mistakes proceed from ~⟩ **2 :** an effect of inattention **:** a result of carelessness **:** an oversight, mistake, or fault from negligence ⟨annoying misprints and ~s —Tor Ulving⟩

in·ad·ver·ten·cy \-tᵊnsē, -si\ *n* [ML *inadvertentia*] **:** INADVERTENCE ⟨wars sometimes start through . . . sheer ~ —*Reporter*⟩

in·ad·ver·tent \¦=(,)=¦=ᵊnt\ *adj* [back-formation fr. *inadvertence, inadvertency*] **1 :** not turning the mind to a matter **:** HEEDLESS, NEGLIGENT, INATTENTIVE ⟨an ~ remark⟩ **2 :** UNINTENTIONAL ⟨~ violations of trade laws —*Current Biog.*⟩ — **in·ad·ver·tent·ly** *adv*

in·advisability \¦in+\ *n* **:** the quality or state of being inadvisable

in·advisable \¦in+\ *adj* [¹*in-* + *advisable*] **:** not advisable **:** INEXPEDIENT

-i·nae \ī(,)nē\ *n pl suffix* [NL, fr. L, fem. pl. of *-inus* -ine] **:** members of the subfamily of — in recent classifications substituted for the last syllable of the genitive case of the name of the type genus in all names of zoological subfamilies ⟨*Felinae*⟩ ⟨Meliponinae⟩

in·aesthetic \¦in+\ *adj* [¹*in-* + *aesthetic*] **1 :** violating aesthetic canons or requirements **:** deficient in tastefulness or beauty **:** offensive from lack of beauty ⟨peered through those ~ spectacles —Maurice Cranston⟩ **2 :** lacking aesthetic sensibility ⟨~ and quite unintellectual —A.L.Rowse⟩

in·agglutinability \¦in+\ *n* **:** the quality or state of being inagglutinable

in·agglutinable \"+\ *adj* [¹*in-* + *agglutinable*] **:** not subject to agglutination **:** not agglutinable

in·a·ja \,ina'zhä\ *n* -s [Pg *inajá*, fr. Tupi] **:** a tall pinnate-leaved Brazilian palm (*Maximiliana regia*) with immense prickle-tipped spathes used for baskets, tubs, and other containers

in·alienability \(¦)in, ən+\ *n* **:** the quality or state of being inalienable

in·alienable \(')in, ən+\ *adj* [prob. fr. F *inaliénable*, fr. *in-* ¹in- + *aliénable* alienable — more at ALIENABLE] **:** incapable of being alienated, surrendered, or transferred ⟨~ human rights⟩ — compare INDEFEASIBLE — **in·alienableness** \"+\ *n* -ES — **in·alienably** \"+\ *adv*

in all *adv* **:** all told **:** ALTOGETHER ⟨some 70 ships *in all*⟩ ⟨*in all* we drove more than 40,000 miles⟩

in alt *adv (or adj)* **:** in the octave beginning with the second G above middle C ⟨ranging up to E *in alt*⟩ — see PITCH illustration

in·alterability \(¦)in, ən+\ *n* **:** the quality or state of being inalterable

in·alterable \(')in, ən+\ *adj* [¹*in-* + *alterable*, fr. F *altérable*, fr. *altérer* to alter + *-able* -able] **:** not alterable **:** UNALTERABLE — **in·alterably** \"+\ *adv*

in altissimo *adv (or adj)* [It, lit., in the highest] **:** in the octave beginning with the third G above middle C — see PITCH illustration

in·amissible \¦in+\ *adj* [F or LL; F, fr. LL *inamissibilis*, fr. L *in-* ¹in- + LL *amissibilis* amissible — more at AMISSIBLE] **:** incapable of being lost

in·am·o·ra·ta \(,)i,namə'räd·ə, ə,n-\ *n* -s [It *innamorata*, fr. fem. of *innamorato*, past part. of *innamorare* to inspire with love, fr. *in-* ²in- + *amore* love, fr. L *amor* — more at AMOROUS] **:** a woman with whom one is in love or has intimate relations; *specif* **:** MISTRESS

in·am·o·ra·to \-äd·(,)ō\ *n* -s [It *innamorato*, fr. past part. of *innamorare*] **:** a male lover

in-and-in \¦=¦=\ *adv (or adj)* **:** in repeated generations of the same or closely related stock ⟨families . . . of one blood through mating or marrying *in-and-in* —F.H.Giddings⟩ ⟨this freak of color in range-bred horses is the result of *in-and-in* breeding —Andy Adams⟩

¹**in and out** *adv* **1 :** alternately in and out ⟨he's been *in and out* all day⟩ **2 :** to the last detail **:** EXHAUSTIVELY, THOROUGHLY ⟨understands his business *in and out*⟩ ⟨knew each other *in and out* —Virginia Woolf⟩

²**in and out** *n* **:** an obstacle found in fox hunting and steeplechasing consisting of two fences in close proximity but impossible to clear in the same jump

in-and-out \¦=¦=\ *adj* [¹*in and out*] **:** now good and now bad in performance ⟨an *in-and-out* showing —*Williams Alumni Rev.*⟩

in-and-out bolt *n* **:** a bolt running through from outside to inside of a ship's framing

in-and-out bond *n* **:** a masonry bond formed by headers and stretchers alternating vertically esp. at a corner

in-and-out plating *or* **in-and-out system** *n* **:** a system of construction for steel ships in which each alternate strake of plating laps over the edge of each adjoining strake

¹**inane** \(')i¦nān, ə'nān\ *adj, sometimes* -ER/-EST [L *inanis*] **1 :** EMPTY, INSUBSTANTIAL ⟨azure of *inanest* space —Walter de la Mare⟩ **2 :** lacking significance, meaning or profundity **:** SHALLOW, VACANT, FATUOUS, SILLY ⟨made some ~ remark on the weather —Joseph Conrad⟩; *also* **:** reflecting or indicating such condition ⟨an ~ face⟩ **syn** see INSIPID

²**inane** \"\ *n* -s **:** something that is empty **:** the emptiness of space ⟨a voyage into the limitless ~ —V.G.Childe⟩

inane·ly *adv* **:** in an inane manner

inan·ga \'ē,näŋgä\ *n, pl* **inangas** *or* **inanga** [Maori] **:** any of several freshwater fishes (family Galaxiidae) of New Zealand and Tasmania

¹**in·animate** \(')in, ən+\ *adj* [LL *inanimatus*, fr. L *in-* ¹in- + *animatus*, past part. of *animare* to quicken, enliven, endow with breath or soul — more at ANIMATE] **1 a :** not animate **:** not endowed with life or spirit ⟨the inorganic world is ~⟩ **:** not endowed with consciousness or animal life ⟨trees are ~⟩ **b :** deprived of consciousness or of life ⟨an ~ body⟩ **c** *of a grammatical gender* **:** referring typically to dead things or things considered as dead — opposed to *animate* **2 :** not animated or lively **:** DULL, SPIRITLESS ⟨her ~ movement when on the stage —W.B.Yeats⟩ — **in·animately** \"+\ *adv* — **in·animateness** \"+\ *n*

²**inanimate** *vt* [LL *inanimatus*, past part. of *inanimare*, fr. L *in-* ²in- + *animare*] *obs* **:** ANIMATE

in·a·ni·tion \,inə'nishən\ *n* -s [ME *in-anisioun*, fr. ML *inanition-, inanitio*, fr. *inanitus* (past part. of *inanire* to make empty, fr. *inanis* empty, inane) + L *-ion-, -io* -ion] **:** the condition or result of being empty: **a :** the exhausted condition which results from a complete lack of food and water **:** MARASMUS **b :** absence or loss of social, moral, or intellectual vitality or vigor **:** LETHARGY ⟨an old society protects itself from ~ by expanding —Lovell Thompson⟩

inan·i·ty \ə'nanəd·ē, -ətē, -i\ *n* -ES [F or L; F *inanité*, fr. L *inanitat-, inanitas*, fr. *inanis* inane + *-itat-, -itas* -ity] **1 :** the quality or state of being inane: as **a :** the condition of lacking all substance or content **:** EMPTINESS, HOLLOWNESS ⟨the present situation in the North is political ~ —J.V.Kelleher⟩ **b :** vapid, pointless, or fatuous character **:** lack of profundity **:** meaningless quality **:** SHALLOWNESS ⟨the ~ and dullness of most conversations —Hunter Mead⟩ ⟨a master who has suffered . . . from the ~ of his interpreters —A.E.Wier⟩ **2 :** something that is foolish, trivial, or pointless ⟨fulsome *inanities* —Walker Evans⟩ ⟨the statement was a downright ~⟩

in an·tis \ə'nantəs\ *adv* [L, in antae] **:** between two antas ⟨a Greek Doric entrance *in antis* —Nikolaus Pevsner⟩

in·apparent \¦in+\ *adj* [¹*in-* + *apparent*] **:** not apparent; *specif* **:** not apparent clinically — used of subclinical infections

in·appeasable \¦in+\ *adj* [¹*in-* + *appeasable*] **:** UNAPPEASABLE

in·appetence \(')in, ən+\ *n* [¹*in-* + *appetence*] **:** lack of appetite ⟨complained of ~ and slight nausea —*Jour. Amer. Med. Assoc.*⟩ — **in·appetent** \"+\ *adj*

in·applicability \(¦)in, ən+\ *n* **:** the condition of being inapplicable

in·applicable \"+\ *adj* [¹*in-* + *applicable*] **:** not applicable **:** incapable of being applied **:** not adapted **:** not suitable — **in·applicableness** \"+\ *n* -ES — **in·applicably** \"+\ *adv*

in·apposite \(')in, ən+\ *adj* [¹*in-* + *apposite*] **:** not apposite **:** not pertinent ⟨so ~, so incongruous as to sound extremely bizarre —*Times Lit. Supp.*⟩ — **in·appositely** \"+\ *adv* — **in·appositeness** \"+\ *n*

in·appreciable \¦in+\ *adj* [prob. fr. F *inappréciable*, fr. MF *inappreciable*, fr. *in-* ¹in- + *appreciable* — more at APPRECIABLE] **1** *archaic* **:** INVALUABLE **2 :** not appreciable **:** too small to be perceived ⟨became ~ at 615° C. —E.B.Shaud⟩ — **in·appreciably** \"+\ *adv*

in·appreciation \¦in+\ *n* [¹*in-* + *appreciation*] **:** lack of appreciation ⟨~ of his most vital criticism —F.R.Leavis⟩

in·appreciative \¦in+\ *adj* [¹*in-* + *appreciative*] **:** not appreciative — **in·appreciatively** \"+\ *adv* — **in·appreciativeness** \"+\ *n* -ES

in·approachable \¦in+\ *adj* [¹*in-* + *approachable*] **:** not approachable **:** INACCESSIBLE

in·appropriate \¦in+\ *adj* [¹*in-* + *appropriate*] **:** not appropriate **:** UNBECOMING, UNSUITABLE ⟨noise seems ~ in a place of sadness —Franz Boas⟩ — **in·appropriately** \"+\ *adv* — **in·appropriateness** \"+\ *n*

in·apt \(')in, ən+\ *adj* [¹*in-* + *apt*] **:** not apt: **a :** not suitable or appropriate ⟨a very ~ analogy⟩ **b :** not qualified or skilled **:** INEPT, INADEQUATE ⟨unstable, queer, ~ individuals —*Psychological Abstracts*⟩ — **in·apt·ly** *adv* — **in·apt·ness** *n* -ES

in·aptitude \(')in, ən+\ *n* [¹*in-* + *aptitude*] **:** lack of aptitude

¹**in·arch** \ən+\ *vt* [²*in* + *arch*] **:** to form an approach graft of or with ⟨successfully ~*ed* water sprouts to bridge rabbit damage on the apple trees⟩

²**in·arch** \'in+,-\ *n* -ES **:** APPROACH GRAFT; *also* **:** the plant resulting from a successful approach graft

in·arguable \(')in, ən+\ *adj* [¹*in-* + *arguable*] **:** not arguable — **in·arguably** \"+\ *adv*

In·articulata \¦in+\ *n pl, cap* [NL, fr. neut. pl. of *inarticulatus*] **:** a class of Brachiopoda comprising forms with unhinged usu. chitinophosphatic valves without teeth or sockets and including the orders Atremata and Neotremata

in·articulate \¦in+\ *adj* [LL *inarticulatus*, fr. L *in-* ¹in- + *articulatus*, past part. of *articulare* to utter distinctly — more at ARTICULATE] **1 a** *of a sound* **:** uttered or formed without the definite articulations which produce intelligible speech ⟨gave a little ~ grunt —Edith Wharton⟩ **:** indistinctly articulated or pronounced ⟨speech so ~ it resembled a growl⟩ **b** (1) **:** incapable of speech esp. under stress of emotion **:** MUTE ⟨almost ~ with excitement —Kenneth Roberts⟩ ⟨almost pathologically shy, he at times became totally ~ —C.B. Forcey⟩ (2) **:** intense or compelling to the point of preventing speech **:** not accompanied or attended by speech **:** incapable of being expressed by speech ⟨dazed with ~ pain —Edith Wharton⟩ ⟨~ misery⟩ (3) **:** not voiced or expressed **:** UNSPOKEN ⟨~ judicial notions of rightfulness or wrongfulness of motive —C.O.Gregory⟩ ⟨their ~ major premises —*Times Lit. Supp.*⟩ ⟨expressed the ~ feelings of many scientists —Harrison Brown⟩ **c** (1) **:** unable to speak coherently, forcefully, or purposefully ⟨remained stupidly ~, saying something noncommittal —Victoria Sackville-West⟩ ⟨~ as most of their class, they could do no more than utter bald phrases —Ruth Park⟩ (2) **:** having an incoherent or disjointed character ⟨the stumbling, almost ~, speech of the boy —G.W.Russell⟩ **d :** incapable of giving clear and effective expression to one's feelings, ideas, or aspirations in any way ⟨the vast majority of the natives are politically ~ —A.F.Macdonald⟩ **2** [NL *inarticulatus*, fr. ¹*in-* + *articulatus* jointed — more at ARTICULATA] **a :** not jointed **:** having no distinct body segments ⟨an ~ worm⟩ **b :** lacking a hinge — used esp. of certain brachiopod shells **c** [NL *Inarticulata*] **:** of, resembling, or relating to the Inarticulata **syn** see DUMB

in·articulately \"+\ *adv* **:** in an inarticulate manner

in·articulateness \"+\ *n* -ES **:** the quality or state of being inarticulate

in ar·ti·cu·lo mor·tis \,i,när'tikyə,lō'mórd·əs\ *adv (or adj)* [L] **:** at the point of death ⟨the king appeared to be *in articulo mortis* —M.A.S.Hume⟩

in·artificial \(¦)in, ən+\ *adj* [L *inartificialis*, fr. *in-* ¹in- + *artificialis* artificial — more at ARTIFICIAL] **1** *archaic* **:** not characterized by art or skill **:** CLUMSY, INARTISTIC **2 :** not characterized by affectation **:** ARTLESS, UNAFFECTED, PLAIN — **in·artificially** \"+\ *adv*

in·artistic \¦in+\ *adj* [¹*in-* + *artistic*] **:** not artistic **:** not conforming to the principles of art **:** lacking in taste or appreciation for art — **in·artistically** \"+\ *adv*

-inas *pl of* -INA

in·as·much as \¦inəz¦məchəz\ *conj* [ME *in as muche as*] **1 :** in the degree that **:** insofar as ⟨everything else that is desired is desired *inasmuch as* it leads to pleasure —*Times Lit. Supp.*⟩ **2 :** in view of the fact that **:** for the reason that **:** SINCE, BECAUSE ⟨should not be used for the relief of pain *inasmuch as* its analgesic value is slight —D.W.Maurer & V.H. Vogel⟩

in·attention \¦in+\ *n* [¹*in-* + *attention*] **:** failure to pay attention **:** DISREGARD

in·attentive \¦in+\ *adj* [¹*in-* + *attentive*] **:** not attentive **:** HEEDLESS, NEGLIGENT ⟨an ~ student⟩ — **in·attentively** \"+\ *adv* — **in·attentiveness** \"+\ *n*

in·audibility \(¦)in, ən+\ *n* **:** the quality or state of being inaudible

in·audible \(')in, ən+\ *adj* [LL *inaudibilis*, fr. L *in-* ¹in- + LL *audibilis* audible — more at AUDIBLE] **:** not audible **:** incapable of being heard ⟨his voice was hushed, almost ~ —E. K.Gann⟩ — **in·audibleness** \"+\ *n* -ES — **in·audibly** \"+\ *adv*

¹**in·au·gu·ral** \ə'nógyərəl, ÷ -g(ə)rəl\ *adj* [L *inaugurare* + E *-al*] **1 :** relating to or performed or pronounced at a formal induction or investiture ⟨new recruits . . . are given an ~ address by their chief superintendent —*Times Lit. Supp.*⟩ ⟨the president's ~ address⟩ **:** held in connection with such an investiture ⟨an ~ ball⟩ — opposed to *exaugural* **2 :** marking the commencement **:** being the first in a projected series ⟨an ~ meeting of a new historical society⟩ ⟨the ~ performance of a dramatic group⟩ ⟨the ~ run of the new luxury train —*Americas*⟩ ⟨the new association's ~ venture —W.F.Brown b. 1903⟩

²**inaugural** \"\ *n* -s **1 :** an inaugural address **2 :** the process or ceremony of inaugurating or of being inaugurated ⟨the president's ~ was held inside due to inclement weather⟩ ⟨will continue in that capacity until after the ~ —*N.Y. Times*⟩

in·au·gu·rate \ə'nógyə,rāt, ÷ -gə,r-, *usu* -ād·+V\ *vt* [L *inauguratus*, past part. of *inaugurare* to practice augury, to inaugurate, fr. *in-* ²in- + *augurare* to prophesy, augur; fr. the ceremonies connected with the telling of auguries — more at AUGUR] **1 :** to introduce or induct into an office with suitable ceremonies or solemnities **:** invest with power or authority in a formal manner **:** INSTALL ⟨~ a president⟩ **2 :** to begin, introduce, or mark a start or opening of: **a :** to dedicate, consecrate, or observe the opening or beginning of formally, auspiciously, and publicly ⟨a temple *inaugurated* by the emperor⟩ ⟨national assemblies and military expeditions were *inaugurated* by public prayers —G.L.Dickinson⟩ **b :** to start, commence, or institute sometimes publicly, ceremoniously, or formally with the prospect of continuing as a public service or beneficial agency or force ⟨passenger and freight service on the river was *inaugurated* in 1832 —*Amer. Guide Series: Maine*⟩ ⟨various conservation projects in the state have been *inaugurated* —*Amer. Guide Series: Del.*⟩ ⟨compulsory school attendance was not *inaugurated* . . . until 1919 —*Amer. Guide Series: Fla.*⟩ ⟨*inaugurated* the study of Greek —H.O. Taylor⟩ **c :** to begin or bring about the beginning of ⟨turning from the hero to the common man, we *inaugurated* the era of realism —J.W.Krutch⟩ ⟨until the Civil War *inaugurated* a new chapter in Kansas-Missouri relations —W.H.Stephenson⟩ **syn** see BEGIN

in·au·gu·ra·tion \ə,=='rāshən\ *n* -s [L *inauguration-, inauguratio*, fr. *inauguratus* + *-ion-, -io* -ion] **:** the act or an instance of inaugurating: as **a :** investiture by appropriate ceremonies ⟨knighted by the king of Scotland on his ~ —L. G.Pine⟩ **b :** formal initiation, opening, or introduction ⟨~ of a new museum⟩ ⟨~ of a conference on educational problems⟩ **c :** beginning of the operation, use, or practice of something **:** START, INSTITUTION ⟨~ of a giant calculating machine . . . was announced —*Current Biog.*⟩ ⟨decided to postpone the ~ of fluoridation —J.M.Burns⟩ ⟨~ of scientific systems of tillage —Samuel Van Valkenburg & Ellsworth Huntington⟩

inauguration day *n, usu cap I & D* **:** a day set for the inauguration of the president of the U. S. now the January 20 but before 1934 the March 4 following the presidential election

in·au·gu·ra·tor \ə'==,rād·ə(r), -ātə-\ *n* -s **:** a person who inaugurates

in·auspicious \¦in+\ *adj* [¹*in-* + *auspicious*] **:** not auspicious **:** ILL-OMENED, UNLUCKY, UNPROPITIOUS ⟨you come at a singularly ~ moment —Rafael Sabatini⟩ **syn** see OMINOUS

in·auspiciously \¦in+\ *adv* **:** in an inauspicious manner

in·authentic \¦in+\ *adj* [¹*in-* + *authentic*] **:** not authentic — **in·authenticity** \(¦)in, ən+\ *n*

in·balance \(')in+\ *n* [¹*in-* + *balance*] **:** IMBALANCE ⟨physiological ~ in hyperthyroidism⟩

inbd *abbr* inboard

in·bearing \'=,==\ *adj* [²*in* + *bearing*] *chiefly Scot* **:** OFFICIOUS

¹**in between** *adv* [²*in* + *between* (adv.)] **:** BETWEEN ⟨*in between* are the groves of banana trees —Henry Swanzy⟩

²**in between** *prep* [²*in* + *between* (prep.)] **:** BETWEEN ⟨came *in between* us⟩ ⟨*in between* the houses⟩

¹**in-between** \¦=¦==\ *n* -s [¹*in between*] **:** INTERMEDIATE, INTERMEDIARY ⟨no *in-betweens*, no compromises —Richard Watts⟩ ⟨for the novice, the expert, or the *in-between* —Johannes Mattern⟩

²**in-between** \"\ *adj* [¹*in between*] **:** INTERMEDIATE ⟨his *in-between* stand on civil rights —*Newsweek*⟩ ⟨planning to carry *in-between* styles into spring —*N.Y. Times*⟩ ⟨this *in-between* status of the gibbon —Weston La Barre⟩

inblowing \'=,==\ *adj* [⁴*in* + *blowing* (after *blow in*, v.)] **:** blowing inward or centripetally ⟨~ winds⟩

¹**inboard** \¦=¦=\ *adv* [¹*in* + *board*] **1 :** inside the line of a ship's bulwarks or hull **:** toward the center line of a ship — contrasted with *outboard* **2 :** from without inward **:** toward the inside ⟨pull the throttle ~ —Clay Blair⟩ **3 :** in a position closer or closest to the longitudinal axis of an aircraft ⟨flaps located ~ on a wing⟩

²**inboard** \"\ *adj* **:** located, moving, or being inboard ⟨~ engine⟩ ⟨~ section of a wing⟩

inbond \'=,=\ *adj* [⁴*in* + *bond* (connection)] **:** laid across a wall **:** having bricks or stones laid as headers — opposed to *outbond*

inborn \'=¦=\ *adj* [²*in* + *born*] **1 :** born in or with one **:** implanted by nature **:** NATURAL ⟨man's ~ desire to fly —H.G. Armstrong⟩ ⟨the ~ conservatism of man⟩ **2 :** INHERITED, HEREDITARY ⟨the tendency toward schizophrenia was ~ —*N.Y. Times*⟩ **syn** see INNATE

inbound \'=¦=\ *adj* [²*in* + *bound*] **1 :** inward bound ⟨an ~ ship⟩ ⟨~ baggage⟩ — contrasted with *outbound* **2 :** relating to inward or inbound traffic ⟨~ station⟩

inbounds line \'=,=\ *n* [fr. the phrase *in bounds*] **:** either of the broken lines running at right angles to the yard lines and dividing the field of play of a football field into three equal parts — see FOOTBALL illustration

inbreak \'=,=\ *n* [⁴*in* + *break* (after *break in*, v.)] **:** a breaking in **:** INROAD, INVASION, INCURSION

inbreathe \'=¦=\ *vt* [²*in* + *breathe*] **:** to breathe (something) in **:** INHALE

¹**inbred** \'=¦=\ *adj* [²*in* + *bred*] **1 :** bred within ⟨~ worth⟩ ⟨there was in him an ~ goodness —J.A.Froude⟩ **2 :** subjected to or produced by inbreeding **syn** see INNATE

²**inbred** \'=,=\ *n* -s **:** an individual resulting from the mating of closely related parents **:** a product of inbreeding

in·breed \'=¦=\ *vb* [²*in* + *breed*] *vt* **1** *archaic* **:** PRODUCE, GENERATE ⟨~ and cherish in a great people the seeds of virtue —John Milton⟩ **2 :** to subject to inbreeding — compare CROSSBREED, OUTBREED ~ *vi, of closely related individuals* **:** to breed together

inbreeding \'=,==\ *n* [fr. gerund of *inbreed*] **1 :** the interbreeding of closely related individuals occurring naturally (as in a closed population), as a result of social or religious custom (as in some royal families), or as a deliberately chosen system of breeding (as of cattle or poultry) and serving esp. to preserve and fix desirable characters of and to eliminate unfavorable characters from a suitably selected stock but tending to effect an unwanted decline (as in size, vigor, or fertility) through the fixation of undesirable and often recessive characters when the initial stock is in any way defective — distinguished from *outbreeding*; compare LINEBREEDING **2 a :** confinement to a narrow range of intellectual and cultural resources issuing chiefly from a limited field of specialization ⟨the ~ of ideas —Joseph Pelej⟩ ⟨the ~ of continental philosophy —Max Rieser⟩ ⟨must avoid nationalist ~ —Mark Starr⟩ **b :** employment in an institution or locality of an excessive number of people who received their training there ⟨academic ~ is marked —Dallas Finn⟩

inbring \'=¦=\ *vt* [ME *inbringen*, fr. OE *inbringan* (prob. trans. of L *inferre* to bring in), fr. *in, inn* in (adv.) + *bringan* to bring — more at INFER, BRING] **:** to bring in; *esp* **:** to bring into court or to confiscate by legal process in Scots law

inbuilt \'=¦=\ *adj* [²*in* + *built*] **:** BUILT-IN ⟨the machine has no ~ knowledge of prime numbers —D.R.Hartree⟩

¹**in·bye** *also* **in·by** \'in¦bī\ *adv* [²*in* + *bye* (var. of *by*), *by*, adv.] *chiefly Scot* **:** in an inward direction **:** INSIDE, WITHIN; *specif* **:** toward the workings of a mine

²**inbye** *also* **inby** \"\ *adj, chiefly Scot* **:** situated close by esp. near to the house ⟨the ~ land⟩

³**inbye** *also* **inby** \"\ *n, pl* **inbyes** *Scot* **:** land situated close by ⟨80 acres of ~⟩

inc *abbr* **1** [L *incisus*] engraved **2** inclosure **3** included; including; inclusive **4** income; incoming **5** incorporated; incorporation **6** increase **7** incumbent

¹**in·ca** \'iŋkə\ *n, pl* **incas** *also* **inca** *usu cap* [Sp, fr. Quechua *inka* king, prince, male of royal blood] **1 a :** a ruler of the Incaic Empire prior to the Spanish conquest **b :** a member of this empire's royal house; *broadly* **:** a person of high rank or exalted position under this empire **2 a :** a small Quechuan people of the valley of Cuzco in Peru that established hegemony over surrounding peoples to form the Incaic Empire from about 1100 until the Spanish conquest in 1531–35 **b :** any of the constituent Quechuan peoples of the Incaic Empire **3 :** a member of an Inca people

²**inca** \"\ *adj, usu cap* **:** INCAIC

In·ca·bloc \-,bläk\ *trademark* — used for a shock-resistant balance jewel mounting and balance staff design in watches

inca bone *n, usu cap I* **:** the interparietal when developed as a separate bone in the skull (as frequently found in Peruvian mummies)

inca dove *n, usu cap I* **:** a small dove (*Scardafella inca*) found from Arizona to Central America

in·ca·ic \(')iŋ¦kāik, (')in¦-\ *adj, usu cap* [Sp *incaico*, fr. *inca* + *-ico* -ic (fr. L *-icus*)] **:** of or relating to the Incas or their empire

in·calculability \(¦)in, ən+\ *n* **:** the quality or state of being incalculable ⟨her alleged ~ turns out to be unscrupulousness which defies all morals —J.C.Blankenagel⟩

in·calculable \(')in, ən+\ *adj* [¹*in-* + *calculable*] **:** not capable of being calculated **:** UNPREDICTABLE ⟨the influence of environment on character is ~ and far-reaching —S.P.B.Mais⟩: as **a :** being beyond calculation **:** very great ⟨during the last few thousands of years, ~ quantities of hortatory literature have been produced —Aldous Huxley⟩ **b :** not foreseeable or foreseen ⟨justified in the most ~ way —Havelock Ellis⟩ **:** UNCERTAIN ⟨an ~ temper⟩ — **in·calculableness** \"+\ *n* -ES — **in·calculably** \"+\ *adv*

in·ca·les·cence \,inkə'lesᵊn(t)s, ,iŋk-\ *n* -s [L *incalescere* + E *-ence*] **:** incalescent state **:** a growing warm or ardent

in·ca·les·cent \¦==¦lesᵊnt\ *adj* [L *incalescent-, incalescens*, pres. part. of *incalescere* to become warm, fr. *in-* ²in- + *calescere* to become warm, incho. of *calēre* to be warm — more at LEE] **:** growing warm **:** increasing in ardor

in-calf \¦=¦=\ *adj* [¹*in* + *calf*] *of a cow, chiefly Brit* **:** PREGNANT

in·calculate \¦in+\ *adj* [¹*in-* + *calliculate*] **:** having no calyculus ⟨~ corals⟩

inca magic flower *n, usu cap I* **:** CANTUTA

incamp *obs var of* ENCAMP

¹**in·can** \'iŋkən\ *adj, usu cap* [¹*Inca* + *-an*] **:** INCAIC

²**incan** \"\ *n* -s *usu cap* **1 :** an inhabitant or subject of the Incaic Empire **2 :** QUECHUA 3a

in·can·desce \,inkən'des, -,kan-, -,kaan-\ *vb* -ED/-ING/-S [L *incandescere*] *vi* **:** to be or become incandescent ~ *vt* **:** to cause to become incandescent

in·can·des·cence \,=(,)=¦desᵊn(t)s\ *n* -s [prob. fr. F, fr. *incandescent*] **:** the quality or state of being incandescent ⟨a single white flame, an ~ of the passion of avarice —Van Wyck Brooks⟩; *usu* **:** the glowing of a body due to its high temperature **:** emission by a hot body of radiation that renders it visible

in·can·des·cent \¦=(,)=¦desᵊnt\ *adj* [prob. fr. F, fr. L *incandescent-, incandescens*, pres. part of *incandescere* to become white, to become hot, fr. *in-* ²in- + *candescere* to become white, to become hot, incho. of *candēre* to shine, be white — more at CANDID] **1 a :** white, glowing, or luminous with intense heat ⟨~ carbon⟩ **b :** strikingly bright, radiant, or clear ⟨all those flowers ~ — the lilies, the roses, and clumps of white flowers and bushes of burning green —Virginia Woolf⟩ **c :** BRILLIANT, LAMBENT, LUCID ⟨set thoughts aglowing in ~ language —Antonio Iglesias⟩ ⟨~ wit⟩ ⟨one of his ~ masterpieces, the Symphony No. 99 —B.H.Haggin⟩ **d :** GLOWING, HOT, ARDENT ⟨a . . . youth ~ with martial ardor —*Times Lit. Supp.*⟩ **2 :** of, relating to, or being light produced by incandescence **:** producing light by incandescence ⟨the most common artificial light source is the ~ bulb —*This Is Glass*⟩ — compare INCANDESCENT LAMP, MANTLE 7a **syn** see BRIGHT

incandescent lamp *also* **incandescent** *n* -s **:** an electric lamp consisting essentially of a glass or quartz bulb evacuated or filled with an inert gas in which a filament commonly of tungsten gives off light when it is heated to incandescence by an electric current

incandescent lamp: *1* base, *2* lead-in wire, *3* filament, *4* bulb

incandescent light *n* **:** light from a source of incandescence

in·can·des·cent·ly *adv* **:** in an incandescent manner **:** with incandescence

incandescent mantle *n* **:** MANTLE 7a

in·ca·ne·stra·to \,ēŋ,kānə'sträd·(,)ō\ *n* -s [It *incanestrato, incannestrato,* fr. past part. of *incanestrare, incannestrare* to put into a basket, fr. *in-* (fr. L *in-* ²in-) + *canestro, cannestro* basket, fr. L *canistrum;* fr. its being poured into baskets and sold in this form — more at CANISTER] **:** a sharp white Sicilian cheese that is made of cow's milk often together with goat's milk, seasoned with salt and various spices, and used chiefly grated as a seasoning or garnish

in·ca·nous \ən'kānəs\ *adj* [L *incanus,* back-formation fr. *incanescere* to become white, fr. *in-* ²in- + *canescere* to become white, incho. of *canēre* to be gray, white — more at CANESCENT] **:** hoary with white pubescence

in·cant \ən'kant, -aa(ə)nt\ *vt* [L *incantare*] **1 :** ENCHANT, CHARM **2 :** to utter by way of incantation ⟨~*ing* garbled ritual to cast a spell⟩

in·can·ta·tion \,in,kan'tāshən, -kaan-\ *n* -s [ME *incantacioun,* fr. MF *incantation,* fr. LL *incantation-, incantatio,* fr. L *incantatus* (past part. of *incantare* to enchant) + *-ion-, -io* -ion — more at ENCHANT] **1 a :** a use of spells or verbal charms spoken or sung as a part of a ritual of magic **b :** a ceremonial chanting or reciting of incantations (as for curing disease) **c :** a use of words to obscure rather than illuminate **:** OBFUSCATION ⟨their habit of hypnotizing and magnetizing a subject by the ~*s* of repetitive argument —V.S.Pritchett⟩ **2 a :** a formula of words chanted or recited in a magic ritual for their special virtues or particular effects **b :** words used in the manner of a formula without conscious concern as to their aptness or relevance to a particular situation ⟨the ~*s* of the propagandists⟩ **c :** an expression (as of music or poetry) designed to move rather than amuse or convince ⟨uses repetition as it is used in spell and litany, as an ~ to heighten emotion, and perhaps to bypass reason —*Times Lit. Supp.*⟩ **3 :** MAGIC, SORCERY, ENCHANTMENT — **in·can·ta·tion·al** \¦==¦tāshən°l, -shnəl\ *adj*

in·can·ta·to·ry \ən'kantə,tōrē\ *adj* [L *incantatus* + E *-ory*] **:** constituting, employing, dealing with, or suitable for use in incantation ⟨mystic words with ~ power⟩ ⟨an ~ vocal style⟩

in·capability \(¦)in, ən+\ *n* **:** the quality or state of being incapable

¹**in·capable** \(')in, ən+\ *adj* [MF, fr. *in-* ¹in- + *capable* — more at CAPABLE] **1 :** lacking capacity, ability, or qualification for the purpose or end in view: as **a** *obs* **:** not able (as because of smallness) to take in, contain, hold, or keep **b** *obs* **:** not able to receive or endure **:** INTOLERANT **c** *archaic* **:** not being in a state to receive so as to be affected or moved or so as to be sensible **:** not receptive **:** not susceptible **d :** not in a state or of a kind to admit **:** not able to admit **:** INSUSCEPTIBLE — now used only with *of* **e :** not able or fit for the doing or performance **:** INCOMPETENT ⟨an ~ helper⟩ ⟨~ of understanding the matter⟩ ⟨~ of doing the work⟩ **2 a :** lacking legal qualification or power esp. because of some fundamental legal disqualification **b :** lacking the personal ability, power, or understanding required in some legal matter; *esp* **:** suffering from such a degree of mental or physical weakness as to require supervision of one's affairs by a court (as through a conservator) — compare INCOMPETENT, INSANE **c :** legally incompetent from any cause — not used technically — **in·capableness** \"+\ *n* -ES

²**incapable** \"\ *n* -s **:** one that is incapable or inefficient; *esp* **:** a person (as an imbecile or a simpleton) that is so by reason of defective mentality

in·capably \"+\ *adv* **:** in an incapable manner **:** without competence or capability; *esp* **:** to a degree that renders incapable ⟨~ drunk⟩

in·capacious \¦in+\ *adj* [LL *incapac-, incapax* (fr. L *in-* ¹in- + *capac-, capax* capacious) + E *-ious* — more at CAPACIOUS] **1** *obs* **:** having little or insufficient size or capacity **:** CRAMPED, NARROW, STRAIT **2** *archaic* **:** mentally weak **:** lacking perception, insight, or understanding

in·ca·pac·i·tate \,inkə'pasə,tāt, -paas-, *usu* -ād·+V\ *vt* [*incapacity* + *-ate*] **1 :** to deprive of capacity or natural power **:** render incapable or unfit **:** DISABLE, DISQUALIFY ⟨age *incapacitated* him for war⟩ **2 :** to deprive of legal requisites or qualification **:** make legally incapable or ineligible ⟨in some states the appointment of a guardian ~*s* the ward from carrying on his business or from marriage⟩

in·ca·pac·i·ta·tion \¦==,==¦tāshən\ *n* **:** the act of incapacitating or state of being incapacitated **:** INCAPACITY

in·capacity \¦in+\ *n* [F *incapacité,* fr. MF, fr. *in-* ¹in- + *capacité* capacity — more at CAPACITY] **:** the quality or state of being incapable **:** INABILITY, INCAPABILITY; *esp* **:** lack of physical or intellectual power or of natural or legal qualification

in ca·pi·te \(')in'käpə,tā\ *adj* [L, in chief] *of a feudal tenant* **:** holding immediately of one's lord; *esp* **:** holding directly of the crown

¹**incapsulate** *var of* ENCAPSULATE

²**in·cap·su·late** \ən'kapsələt, -,lāt\ *adj* [²*in-* + *capsule* + *-ate* (adj. suffix)] **:** ENCAPSULATED

¹**in·car·cer·ate** \ən'kärs(ə)rət, -kās-, *usu* -əd·+V\ *adj* [L *incarceratus*] **:** IMPRISONED

²**in·car·cer·ate** \-sə,rāt, *usu* -ād·+V\ *vt* -ED/-ING/-S [L *incarceratus,* past part. of *incarcerare,* fr. *in-* ²in- + *carcer* prison] **1 :** to put in prison **:** IMPRISON **2 :** to shut up or away **:** CONFINE, ENCLOSE ⟨*incarcerated* in his own sensibility —J.P. Bishop⟩

incarcerated *adj, of a hernia* **:** IMPRISONED, CONFINED; *esp* **:** constricted but not strangulated

in·car·cer·a·tion \(,)in,==¦rāshən, ən-\ *n* -s [LL *incarceration-, incarceratio,* fr. L *incarceratus* + *-ion-, -io* -ion] **1 :** a confining or state of being confined **:** IMPRISONMENT **2 :** abnormal retention or confinement of a body part; *specif* **:** a constriction of the neck of a hernial sac so that the hernial contents become irreducible

in·car·cer·a·tor \='==,rād·ə(r), -ātə-\ *n* -s **:** one that incarcerates

in·car·di·nate \ən'kärd°n,āt\ *vt* -ED/-ING/-S [LL *incardinatus,* past part. of *incardinare* to ordain as chief priest, fr. L *in-* ²in- + LL *cardinalis,* adj., principal — more at CARDINAL] **1 :** to adopt canonically or to receive formally (a cleric from another diocese) **2 :** to elevate to the cardinalate

in·car·di·na·tion \(,)in,=d°n'āshən, ən,-\ *n* -s [LL *incardination-, incardinatio* appointment of a priest, fr. *incardinatus* + L *-ion-, -io* -ion] **:** the act of incardinating a cleric within the enrolled clergy of a diocese

in·car·mined \ən'kärmənd, -kām-, -,mīnd *also* -,mēnd\ *adj* [²*in-* + *carmine* + *-ed*] **:** RED, REDDENED

in·carn \ən'kärn\ *vb* -ED/-ING/-S [ME *incarnen,* fr. MF *incarner,* fr. LL *incarnare* to make flesh, make fleshy, incarnate — more at INCARNATE] *vt, archaic* **:** to cause to heal **:** cover with flesh ~ *vi, archaic* **:** to cause healing **:** become healed **:** heal over

¹**in·car·na·dine** \ən'kärnə,dīn, -,dən, -,dēn\ *adj* [MF *incarnadin,* fr. OIt *incarnadino, incarnatino,* fr. *incarnato* flesh-colored (fr. LL *incarnatus,* past part.) + *-ino* -ine (fr. L *inus*)] **1 :** of the color flesh or flesh pink **2 :** of a color of red hue

²**incarnadine** *also* **en·car·na·dine** \ən'-,en'-\ *vt* -ED/-ING/-S **:** to make incarnadine **:** REDDEN; *esp* **:** to dye flesh-colored, pink, red, or crimson

³**incarnadine** \"\ *n* -s **:** an incarnadine color

¹**in·car·nate** \(')in¦kärnə̇t, ən'k-, -kān-, -,nā|, *usu* |d·+V\ *adj* [ME *incarnat,* fr. LL *incarnatus,* past part. of *incarnare*] **1 a :** invested with flesh or bodily nature and form, esp. with human nature and form ⟨a monarch . . . regarded as a god ~ —D.L.Oliver⟩ ⟨an ~ spirit⟩ **b :** that is the very type or essence of ⟨purity ~⟩ ⟨that remote valley was peace ~⟩ ⟨confusion ~⟩; *broadly* **:** UTTER, UNSPEAKABLE ⟨a fiend ~⟩ **c :** made manifest or comprehensible **:** EMBODIED ⟨in the . . . United Nations there is now ~ the hope of people everywhere that this world may become one in spirit as it is in fact —H.L.Stimson⟩ **2 :** INCARNADINE — used chiefly of floral colors ⟨~ clover⟩

²**in·car·nate** \ən'kär,nāt, 'in,k-, -kā,n-, *usu* -ād·+V\ *vb* -ED/-ING/-S [LL *incarnatus,* past part. of *incarnare* to make flesh, make fleshy, incarnate, fr. L *in-* ²in- + *carn-, caro* flesh — more at CARNAL] *vt* **1 :** to make incarnate: as **a :** to give bodily form and substance to ⟨*incarnating* the devil as a serpent⟩ ⟨most peoples have some tradition of spiritual powers that ~ themselves as man⟩ **b :** to give a concrete or actual form to **:** embody in reality or in a more definite ideal form **:** ACTUALIZE ⟨~ a political theory in institutions⟩ ⟨*incarnating* ideals by helping others⟩ **c :** to constitute an embodiment or type of ⟨an international organization that ~*s* all our hopes for lasting peace⟩ ⟨in this man the spirit of the times is *incarnated*⟩ **2** *obs* **:** INCARN ~ *vi, obs* **:** INCARN

in·car·na·tion \,in,kär'nāshən, -kā'n-\ *n* -s [ME *incarnacioun,* fr. OF *incarnation,* fr. LL *incarnation-, incarnatio,* fr. *incarnatus* + L *-ion-, -io* -ion] **1 :** a clothing or state of being clothed with flesh **:** a taking on of or being manifested in a fleshly body **2 :** an incarnated being or idea: as **a** (1) **:** the embodiment of a deity or spirit in some form of earthly existence (as a person, an animal, or a plant) (2) *usu cap* **:** the union of divinity with humanity in Jesus Christ **b :** a concrete or actual form incorporating or exemplifying a principle, ideal, or other quality or concept **:** EMBODIMENT ⟨this busy grimy port, the very ~ of commerce and industry⟩; *esp* **:** a person showing a trait or typical character to a marked degree ⟨the very ~ of deceit⟩ **3** *archaic* **:** a rosy or red color **:** FLESH 6, CARNATION **4** *archaic* **:** a process or product of healing **5 :** a period of incarnation **:** time passed in a particular bodily form or state ⟨each ~ leading to a higher⟩ ⟨the old building had passed through several ~*s* as church, workshop, stable, and finally tearoom⟩

in·car·na·tion·al \¦=,=¦nāshən°l, -shnəl\ *adj* **:** of, relating to, or emphasizing incarnation or a doctrine of incarnation ⟨an ~ religion⟩

in·car·na·tion·ist \,=,='nāsh(ə)nə̇st\ *n* -s **:** one that believes in the union of divinity with humanity in the person of Jesus Christ

in·car·vil·lea \,in,kär'vilēə\ *n* [NL, after Pierre d'*Incarville* †1757 Fr. Jesuit missionary] **1** *cap* **:** a genus of Asiatic herbs (family Bignoniaceae) with racemose trumpet-shaped flowers **2** -s **:** any plant of the genus *Incarvillea*

incas *pl of* INCA

incase *var of* ENCASE

incast \'=,=\ *n* [⁴*in* + *cast* (after *cast in,* v.)] *dial Eng* **:** something added for good measure

incautelous *adj* [¹*in-* + *cautelous*] *obs* **:** INCAUTIOUS

in·caution \(')in, ən-\ *n* [¹*in-* + *caution*] **:** lack of caution **:** CARELESSNESS, HEEDLESSNESS

in·cautious \"+\ *adj* [¹*in-* + *cautious*] **:** lacking in caution **:** INJUDICIOUS, HEEDLESS, CARELESS, RASH ⟨an ~ step⟩ ⟨~ talk⟩ ⟨an ~ reader⟩ — **in·cautiously** \"+\ *adv* — **in·cautiousness** \"+\ *n*

in·ca·va·tion \,inkə'vāshən\ *n* -s [L *incavatus* (past part. of *incavare* to hollow out, fr. *in-* ²in- + *cavare* to hollow out, fr. *cavus* hollow) + *-ion-, -io* -ion — more at CAVE] **:** a hollow thing or place

incave *obs var of* ENCAVE

in·ca·vo \ēŋ'kä(,)vō, ən'kā(-\ *n* -s [It, lit., cavity, hollow, fr. *incavare* to make hollow, fr. L] **:** the part of an intaglio that is incised

ince *abbr* insurance

in·celebrity \¦in+\ *n* [¹*in-* + *celebrity*] **:** lack of celebrity

in·cend \ən'send\ *vt* -ED/-ING/-S [L *incendere* to kindle, set on fire — more at INCENSE] *archaic* **:** INFLAME, EXCITE

in·cen·di·a·rism \ən'sendēə,rizəm\ *n* -s **1 :** a deliberate and unjustifiable setting of fire to property — compare ARSON, PYROMANIA **2 :** incendiary behavior ⟨party ~⟩

in·cen·di·a·rist \-,rəst\ *n* -s **:** INCENDIARY 1

¹**in·cen·di·ary** \-dē,erē, -ri\ *n* -ES [L *incendiarius,* adj. & n., fr. *incendium* conflagration (fr. *incendere* to kindle, set afire) + *-arius* -ary — more at INCENSE] **1 a :** a person who deliberately sets fire to a building or other property **b :** an incendiary agent (as a bomb) **2 :** a person who excites or inflames factions and promotes quarrels or sedition **:** AGITATOR, EXCITER **3** *obs* **:** an exciting or causative factor esp. of something bad or unpleasant

²**incendiary** \"\ *adj* [L *incendiarius*] **1 :** of, relating to, or involving a deliberate burning of property ⟨~ fires⟩ ⟨an ~ crime⟩ **2 a :** tending to excite or inflame factions, sedition, or quarrels **:** INFLAMMATORY, SEDITIOUS ⟨an ~ speech⟩ ⟨~ literature⟩ **b :** sexually stimulating ⟨an ~ blonde⟩ **3 a :** igniting combustible materials spontaneously ⟨an ~ agent⟩ **b :** relating to, being, or involving the use of an explosive missile containing chemicals that ignite on bursting ⟨~ grenade⟩ ⟨~ warfare⟩ — see INCENDIARY BOMB

incendiary bomb *n* **:** a bomb that contains an incendiary agent (as jellied gasoline) and is designed to kindle fires at its objective — called also *fire bomb*

in·cen·di·um \ən'sendēəm\ *n, pl* **incen·dia** \-ēə\ [ML, fr. L, conflagration] *Roman law & Roman Dutch law* **:** a crime corresponding to but of wider scope than arson in the English common law

in·cen·sa·tion \,in,sen'sāshən, ,in(t)sən'-\ *n* -s [LL *incensatus* (past part. of *incensare*) + E *-ion*] **:** the action of censing

¹**in·cense** \'in,sen(t)s *sometimes* -,sən-\ *n* -s [ME *encens, incense,* fr. OF *encens,* fr. LL *incensum* incense, fr. L, neut. of *incensus,* past part. of *incendere* to kindle, set on fire, irritate, fr. *in-* ²in- + *-cendere* to burn (akin to L *candēre* to shine, be glowing hot, be white) — more at CANDID] **1 :** material (as gums or woods) used to produce a fragrant odor when burned **2 :** the perfume or the smoke exhaled from spices and gums when burned in celebrating religious rites or as an offering to a deity; *broadly* **:** a pleasing scent or fragrance **3 :** pleasing attention **:** HOMAGE, FLATTERY **syn** see FRAGRANCE

²**in·cense** \" *sometimes* ən'sen-\ *vb* -ED/-ING/-S [ME *encensen, incensen,* fr. MF *encenser,* fr. LL *incensare,* fr. *incensum*] *vt* **1 a :** to apply or offer incense to **:** burn incense before **b :** to burn or offer as an incense offering **2 a :** to perfume with or as if with incense **:** SCENT **b** *archaic* **:** FLATTER ~ *vi* **:** to burn or offer incense

³**in·cense** \(')in¦sen(t)s, ən's-\ *vt* -ED/-ING/-S [ME *encensen,* fr. MF *incenser,* fr. L *incensus,* past part. of *incendere* to kindle, set on fire, irritate — more at ¹INCENSE] **1** *obs* **a :** to set fire to **:** KINDLE **b :** to consume with fire **:** BURN **2 a** *archaic* **:** to excite (a passion or an emotion) into activity **:** cause to become aroused **b** *obs* **:** to inflame (a person) with a passion or emotion **c :** to cause to be extremely angry **:** arouse the wrath or indignation of ⟨such careless waste *incensed* her⟩ **3** *obs* **:** to urge to some course or action

⁴**incense** *var of* INSENSE

incense burner *n* **:** one that burns incense; *specif* **:** a vessel (as a stationary vase) for holding burning incense — compare CENSER

incense cedar *n* **:** any of various trees of the genus *Libocedrus; esp* **:** a tall tree (*L. decurrens*) of the No. American Pacific coast with a light soft straight-grained wood that is highly resistant to moisture, foliage suggesting that of a cypress, and cinnamon red bark — called also *pencil cedar, red cedar, white cedar*

incensed *adj* [fr. past part. of ³*incense*] **1 :** ANGERED, ENRAGED, INDIGNANT **2** *of a heraldic figure* **:** represented as enraged usu. by means of fire issuing from mouth and eyes

incense juniper *n* **:** a European juniper (*Juniperus thurifera*) with paired awl-shaped leaves whitened on the upper surface and fragrant wood that is sometimes burned as incense

in·cense·less \'=(,)=ləs\ *adj* **:** employing no incense ⟨~ churches⟩

in·cense·ment \ən'sen(t)smənt\ *n* -s **:** the state of being incensed **:** intense anger or indignation

incense shrub *n* **:** INDIAN CURRANT 2

incense tree *n* **:** any of various chiefly tropical trees (as members of the genera *Commiphora, Boswellia,* and *Protium*) that produce fragrant gums or resins

incense wood *n* **:** the fragrant wood of either of two tropical American trees (*Protium heptaphyllum* and *P. guianense*)

in·cen·so·ry \'in,sen(t)s(ə)rē, ən's-; 'insən,sōrē\ *n* -ES [ML *incensorium,* fr. neut. of LL *incensorius* having burning power, fr. L *incensus* (past part. of *incendere* to kindle) + *-orius* -ory — more at INCENSE] **:** CENSER, THURIBLE

incenter \'=,==\ *n* [⁴*in* + *center*] **:** the center of a circle inscribed in a triangle or of a sphere inscribed in a tetrahedron

¹**in·cen·tive** \ən'sentiv, -tēv *also* -t·əv\ *n* -s [ME, fr. LL *incentivum,* fr. neut. of L *incentivus*] **:** something that incites or has a tendency to incite to determination or action **:** something (as fear or hope of reward) that constitutes a motive or spur **:** INDUCEMENT ⟨money is still a major ~ in most occupations⟩ ⟨his father's promise of a bicycle was a real ~ to harder study⟩ **syn** see MOTIVE

²**in·cen·tive** \(')in¦s-, ən's-\ *adj* [LL *incentivus,* fr. L, setting the tune, fr. *incentus* (past part. of *incinere* to set the tune, fr. *in-* ²in- + *-cinere,* fr. *canere* to sing) + *-ivus* -ive — more at CHANT] **1 a :** serving to encourage, rouse, or move to action **:** STIMULATIVE **:** motivative in a particular direction or course ⟨increasing needs are often ~ to invention⟩ ⟨this charming book is ~ to further study⟩ **b** (1) **:** designed to enhance or improve production esp. in industry ⟨~ pay⟩ ⟨disadvantages of an ~ system⟩ (2) **:** concerned with, based on, or employing incentive measures or techniques in business or industry ⟨~ management⟩ ⟨long-term ~ experience⟩ ⟨~ studies⟩ **2** *obs* **:** serving to set on fire **:** KINDLING — **in·cen·tive·ly** \-tə̇vlē, -li\ *adv*

incentive wage *n* **:** a wage based on the number of units produced by a factory pieceworker — compare BONUS SYSTEM

¹**in·cept** \ən'sept\ *vb* -ED/-ING/-S [L *inceptus,* past part. of *incipere* — more at INCEPTION] *vt* **1** *archaic* **:** BEGIN, COMMENCE, UNDERTAKE **2** [influenced in meaning by L *capere* to take] **:** to take in: as **a :** INGEST ⟨phagocytes ~*ing* foreign particles⟩ **b :** to receive as a member ~ *vi* **:** to obtain an advanced degree and therewith the right to teach or practice a learned profession — now used only at Cambridge University

²**in·cept** \'in,sept\ *n* -s **:** ANLAGE

in·cep·tion \ən'sepshən\ *n* -s [L *inception-, inceptio,* fr. *inceptus* (past part. of *incipere* to begin, fr. *in-* ²in- + *-cipere,* fr. *capere* to take) + *-ion-, -io* -ion — more at HEAVE] **1 :** an act, process, or instance of beginning (as of an institution, organization, or concept) **:** COMMENCEMENT, INITIATION **2 :** an act of incepting: as **a :** a public lecture in which the candidate for a master's degree in a medieval university demonstrated his learning and competence to teach **b :** INGESTION **syn** see ORIGIN

¹**in·cep·tive** \-tiv\ *n* -s [LL *inceptivus,* adj.] **:** INCHOATIVE

²**in·cep·tive** \(')in¦s-, ən's-\ *adj* [LL *inceptivus,* fr. L *inceptus* (past part. of *incipere* to begin) + *-ivus* -ive — more at INCEPTION] **1 a :** BEGINNING **b :** relating to a beginning **2 :** INCHOATIVE 2 — **in·cep·tive·ly** \-tə̇vlē\ *adv*

in·cep·tor \ən'septə(r), 'in,s-\ *n* -s [ME, fr. L, beginner, fr. *inceptus* + *-or*] **1** *Brit* **:** one that incepts at a university **2 :** one that begins or introduces

in·cer·tae se·dis \iŋ¦ker,tī'sādə̇s, in,sərd·ē'sēdə̇s\ *adv* [L, of uncertain place] **:** in an uncertain position **:** without assurance of relationship — used of taxa ⟨the Acanthocephala have often been placed *incertae sedis* among the Nemathelminthes⟩

incertain *adj* [MF, fr. *in-* ¹in- + *certain*] *obs* **:** UNCERTAIN — **incertainly** *adv, obs* — **incertainty** *n, obs*

in·certitude \(')in, ən+\ *n* [MF, fr. LL *incertitudo,* fr. L *in-* ¹in- + LL *certitudo* certitude — more at CERTITUDE] **:** UNCERTAINTY: **a :** absence of assurance or confidence **:** DOUBT, INDECISION **b :** uncertain or insecure condition

in·ces·san·cy \ən'ses°nsē, -nsi\ *n* -ES **:** the quality or state of being incessant

in·ces·sant \(')in¦ses°nt, ən's-\ *adj* [ME *incessaunt,* fr. LL *incessant-, incessans,* fr. L *in-* ¹in- + *cessant-, cessans,* pres. part. of *cessare* to delay — more at CEASE] **1 :** continuing or following without interruption **:** UNCEASING ⟨~ rains⟩ ⟨this ~ chatter⟩ **2** *obs* **:** EVERLASTING **syn** see CONTINUAL

in·ces·sant·ly *adv* [ME *incessauntly,* fr. *incessaunt* + *-ly*] **1 :** in an unceasing manner or course **:** without intermission or relief **:** CONTINUALLY ⟨the question ran ~ through his mind —Arnold Bennett⟩ ⟨poor and uncomfortable persons toiling ~ to create riches —G.B.Shaw⟩ **2** *archaic* **:** at once **:** IMMEDIATELY

in·ces·sant·ness *n* -ES **:** the quality or state of being incessant

in·ces·sion \ən'seshən\ *n* [LL *incession-, incessio* pace, gait, fr. L *incessus* (past part. of *incedere* to go along, move forward, fr. *in-* ²in- + *cedere* to go, proceed) + *-ion-, -io* -ion — more at CEDE] *archaic* **:** movement onward or forward

in·cest \'in,sest\ *n* -s [ME, fr. L *incestus* unchastity, incest (fr. *incestus* impure, unchaste, fr. *in-* ¹in- + *-cestus,* fr. *castus* pure, chaste) & *incestum,* fr. neut. of *incestus* — more at CASTE] **1 :** sexual intercourse or interbreeding between closely related individuals esp. when they are related or regarded as related (as by reason of affinity or membership in a tribal kinship, group, or clan) within degrees wherein marriage is prohibited by law or custom — compare ENDOGAMY, EXOGAMY, INBREEDING **2 :** the statutory crime of cohabitation, marriage, or sexual intercourse without marriage of parties related to each other within the degrees of consanguinity or often of affinity within which marriage is prohibited by law

in·ces·tu·ous \(')in¦ses(h)chəwəs, ən's-, -)chəs\ *adj* [LL *incestuosus,* fr. L *incestus* incest + *-osus* -ous] **1 a :** constituting or involving incest ⟨an ~ relation⟩ ⟨~ unions⟩ **b :** of, relating to, or guilty of incest ⟨these ~ beasts⟩ **c :** begotten by incest ⟨~ offspring⟩ **2 :** INGROWN, DERIVATIVE, IMITATIVE — **in·ces·tu·ous·ly** *adv* — **in·ces·tu·ous·ness** *n* -ES

¹**inch** \'inch\ *n* -ES *often attrib* [ME *inch, inche,* fr. OE *ince, ynce,* fr. L *uncia* twelfth part, ounce, inch — more at OUNCE] **1 :** a unit of length equal to 1/36 yard or formerly to the length of 3 grains of barley placed end to end ⟨a 6-*inch* rule⟩ ⟨a width of six ~*es*⟩— see MEASURE table **2 :** a small amount, distance, or degree (as of time or space) **:** a narrow margin or little bit ⟨escaped death by an ~⟩ ⟨couldn't see an ~ before them in the storm⟩ **3 inches** *pl* **:** STATURE, HEIGHT ⟨wore raised heels to make the most of his ~*es*⟩ ⟨a man of his ~*es* would be noticeable in any crowd⟩ **4 a :** a fall (as of rain or snow) sufficient to cover a surface or to fill a gage to the depth of one inch ⟨two ~*es* of rain⟩ **b :** a degree of atmospheric or other pressure sufficient to balance the weight of a column of mercury or other specified liquid one inch high in a barometer or manometer ⟨an atmospheric pressure of 30 ~*es*⟩ **c :** WATER-INCH **d** *chiefly Midland* **:** one twelfth of the light period of a day ⟨worked a full 12 ~*es* getting in the hay⟩ **e :** COLUMN INCH — **by inches** *also* **inch by inch** *adv* **:** very gradually or slowly — **by inch of candle :** by auction in which bidding is open only while a small piece of candle burns — **every inch** *adv* **:** to the utmost degree **:** ENTIRELY ⟨looks *every inch* a winner⟩ — **within an inch of :** almost to the point of **:** nearly to **:** very near ⟨broke down when we were *within an inch of* our destination⟩ ⟨came *within an inch of* death⟩

²**inch** \"\ *vb* -ED/-ING/-ES *vi* **:** to advance or retire by small degrees ⟨~*ed* back from the lip of the crevasse⟩; *broadly* **:** to move slowly or in little increments ⟨~*ing* along the slippery ridge⟩ ⟨Canada and the U.S. are ~*ing* back to the unity of action achieved 10 years ago —M.W.Straight⟩ ⟨prices are ~*ing* down⟩ ~ *vt* **1 :** to cause to advance or retire by small degrees ⟨~*ed* himself nearer⟩; *broadly* **:** to cause to move slowly or in little increments ⟨~*ing* their feet slowly over the ice⟩ ⟨~*ing* not only the U.S. but the United Nations forward into a war that did not have to be fought —H.L.Ickes⟩ **2** *obs* **:** to give sparingly **:** deal out in small amounts

³**inch** \"\ *n* -ES [ME *inch, ynche,* fr. ScGael *innis;* akin to OIr *inis* island, W *ynys,* Bret *enez*] **1** *now dial* **:** ISLAND — often used in the names of small islands off the coast of Scotland ⟨*Inchcolm*⟩ ⟨*Inchkeith*⟩ **2** *now dial* **:** low grassy ground by a river

inch *abbr* inchoative

inchant *obs var of* ENCHANT

incharitable *adj* [ME, fr. ¹*in-* + *charitable*] *obs* **:** UNCHARITABLE

incharity *n* [¹*in-* + *charity*] *obs* **:** lack of charity

inchase *archaic var of* ENCHASE

inched \ˈincht\ *adj* [¹*inch* + *-ed*] **:** having or measuring a specified number of inches ⟨a 4-*inched* hook⟩

inch·er \ˈinchə(r)\ *n* -s [¹*inch* + *-er*] **:** something having a dimension of a specified number of inches; *specif* **:** a gun having a bore of a specified number of inches — usu. used in combination with a numeral ⟨heard the 14-*inchers* firing on the coast⟩

in chief *adj* **1 :** heading a staff **:** LEADING — often used in combination ⟨editor-*in-chief*⟩ **2 :** PRIMARY, BASIC, INITIAL ⟨evidence *in chief*⟩ ⟨a fabric dutiable on its *in chief* value of wool⟩

inch·ling \ˈinchliŋ\ *n* -s [¹*inch* + *-ling*] **:** a small being of a kind likely to grow larger ⟨drive in a netful of ~*s*⟩

inch·ma·ree clause \ˈinchmə,rē-\ *n, usu cap I* [after *Inchmaree*, Brit. steamer; fr. its formulation as a result of the sinking of the Inchmaree in Liverpool harbor March, 1884] **:** a clause in a marine insurance policy on the hull of a ship that assuming the owners and managers of the ship have exercised due diligence makes the underwriter liable for loss or damage to hull or machinery arising from the negligence of the master, charterers, mariners, engineers or pilots from explosions, bursting of boilers, breakage of shafts, or any latent defect in hull and machinery, from contact with aircraft or land conveyances, or from any accident at docking facilities (as when loading or unloading or entering a dry dock)

inch·meal \ˈ=¦mē(ə)l\ *adv* [¹*inch* + *-meal* (as in *piecemeal*)] **:** little by little **:** GRADUALLY — often used with *by*

¹**in·cho·ate** \(ˈ)in¦kōət, ən'kō-, 'inkə,wāt\ *adj* [L *inchoatus, incohatus*, past part. of *inchoare, incohare* to begin (lit., to hitch up), fr. *in-* ²in- + *cohum* strap fastening a plow beam to the yoke; perh. akin to Bret *morgo* hame, W *mynci* hame, OE *haga* hedge — more at HEDGE] **:** being recently begun or undertaken **:** INCIPIENT **:** being partly but not fully in existence or operation **:** INCOMPLETE: as **a :** imperfectly formed or formulated **:** DISORDERED, INCOHERENT, UNORGANIZED ⟨the general plan is ~ and incoherent, and the particular treatments disconnected —Hilary Corke⟩ ⟨the solar system . . . far out from the hub of this great wheel of stars and ~ dust and gas —L.C. Eiseley⟩ ⟨vague consumer longings and ~ needs —J.S.Gambs⟩ **b** *of a legal right or instrument or interest* **:** not yet perfected **:** not yet made certain or specific **:** not yet vested **:** INCIPIENT, EXPECTANT, POTENTIAL, CONTINGENT, IMPERFECTED ⟨an ~ right of dower⟩ ⟨an ~ equity⟩ ⟨an instrument that the law requires to be recorded is an ~ instrument until it is recorded —Besse May Miller⟩ — **in·cho·ate·ly** *adv* — **in·cho·ate·ness** *n* -ES

²**in·cho·ate** \'inkə,wāt, ən'kō,āt\ *vb* -ED/-ING/-S [L *inchoatus, incohatus*, past part. of *inchoare, incohare*] *vt, archaic* **:** to cause to begin ~ *vi, archaic* **:** to make a beginning **:** START

in·cho·a·tion \,inkə'wāshən\ *n* -s [LL *inchoation-, inchoatio, incohation-, incohatio*, fr. L *inchoatus, incohatus* + *-ion-, -io* -ion] **:** an act of beginning **:** COMMENCEMENT, INCEPTION

¹**in·cho·a·tive** \(ˈ)in¦kōəd·iv, ən'k-\ *n* -s [LL *inchoativum, incohativum*, fr. neut. of *inchoativus, incohativus*] **:** an inchoative verb

²**inchoative** \"\ *adj* [LL *inchoativus, incohativus*, fr. L *inchoatus, incohatus* + *-ivus* -ive] **1 :** INITIAL, FORMATIVE ⟨~ stages⟩ **2 :** denoting the beginning of an action, state, or occurrence — used of certain verbs (as *begin, set out, get, awake*) or of certain verb forms (as *tremesco* "I fall to trembling" and some other Latin verbs in *-sco*) — **in·cho·a·tive·ly** \-d·əvlē\ *adv*

in·chon \(ˈ)in¦chän\ *adj, usu cap* [fr. *Inchon*, Korea] **:** of or from the city of Inchon, Korea **:** of the kind or style prevalent in Inchon

inch-ounce *n* **1 :** a unit of work equal to the work done in raising one ounce against the force of gravity through a distance of one inch **2 :** a unit of moment equal to the moment of a force of one ounce acting at a distance of one inch from a center of moments

inch plant *n* **:** a wandering Jew (*Tradescantia fluminensis*) that is often grown as a house plant

inch-pound \ˈ=¦=\ *n* **:** one twelfth of a foot-pound

inch-ton \ˈ=¦=\ *n* **:** a unit of energy or work that is equal to the work done in raising one ton against the force of gravity the height of one inch

¹**inchworm** \ˈ=,=\ *n* [¹*inch* + *worm*] **:** LOOPER 1

²**inchworm** \"\ *vb* **:** CRAWL

in·cide \ən'sīd\ *vb* -ED/-ING/-S [L *incidere* — more at INCISE] *vi* **1** *archaic* **:** CUT, INCISE **2** *obs* **:** to cause loosening or resolution ~ *vt* **1** *archaic* **:** to cut into (as a lesion or tissue) **2** *archaic* **:** to cause loosening or resolution of (as phlegm)

in·ci·dence \'in(t)sədən(t)s *also* -d³n- *or* -,den-\ *n* -s [ME, fr. MF, fr. LL *incidentia*, fr. L *incident-, incidens* + *-ia* -y] **1** *now chiefly dial* **:** INCIDENT **2 a :** an act or the fact or manner of falling upon or affecting **:** OCCURRENCE ⟨diseases of domestic ~ —*Science*⟩ ⟨control of both the ~ of expense and the meeting of expense must lie primarily in the hands of management⟩ **b :** rate, range, or amount of occurrence or influence ⟨a rising ~ of poverty⟩; *sometimes* **:** the rate of occurrence of new cases of a particular disease in a population being studied — compare PREVALENCE **3 :** the falling of a tax upon a person who is unable to shift it onto someone else and who therefore bears the money burden of the tax ⟨the ultimate ~ of most corporation taxes is on the consumer⟩ — compare DIRECT TAX **4 a :** the arrival of something (as a projectile or a ray of light) at a surface **b :** ANGLE OF INCIDENCE 2

incidence wire *n* **:** STAGGER WIRE

incidency *obs var of* INCIDENCE

¹**in·ci·dent** \-nt\ *n* -s [ME, fr. MF, fr. ML *incident-, incidens*, fr. L, pres. part. of *incidere* to fall into, fall on, meet up with, occur, happen, fr. *in-* ²in- + *-cidere* (fr. *cadere* to fall) — more at CHANCE] **1 a :** an occurrence of an action or situation felt as a separate unit of experience **:** an occurrence or sometimes a situation or thing taking place as part of a larger continuum but unimportant or nonessential **:** HAPPENING ⟨conflict is an inevitable ~ in any active system of cooperation —Lewis Mumford⟩ **b :** an accompanying minor occurrence or condition **:** CONCOMITANT ⟨Madison's view . . . that taxation is a necessary ~ anyway to the exercise of any power —C.P.Curtis⟩ **c :** an occurrence noticeably varying a set or accustomed course or routine **:** an uncommon happening ⟨to remain at variance with his wife seemed to him a considerable ~ —Joseph Conrad⟩ **d :** an occurrence calling forth a sequel **:** a motivating event or situation **:** FACTOR ⟨the ~ of that conflict was slavery, but it was not its true cause —*Congressional Record*⟩ **e :** a happening or related group of happenings subordinate to a main narrative plot ⟨the melodrama and the romance . . . must be made up of swift successions of startling ~ —E.G.Sutcliffe⟩ **f :** a frequent, accustomed, or routine occurrence unworthy of note or comment ⟨a quite ordinary ~ of daily life —Arnold Bennett⟩ **2 a :** a contretemps, fracas, disturbance, or other action likely to lead to grave consequences esp. in matters diplomatic ⟨repeated minor ~*s* led finally to the danger of open combat at the boundary —*Amer. Guide Series: Maine*⟩ **b :** a military situation marked by fighting without formally declared war ⟨the Korea ~⟩ **c** *chiefly Brit* **:** a bomb explosion or other sudden violent disturbance ⟨air-raid wardens checking on ~*s*⟩ **3 a :** something dependent upon, appertaining or subordinate to, or accompanying something else of greater or principal importance ⟨an alimony agreement may be an ~ of a divorce proceeding⟩ **b :** something arising or resulting from something else of greater or principal importance ⟨a power to employ a broker may be an ~ of an express power to sell real estate⟩ **syn** see OCCURRENCE

²**incident** \"\ *adj* [ME, fr. L *incident-, incidens*, pres. part.] **1 a :** occurring or likely to occur esp. as a minor consequence or accompaniment ⟨confusion ~ to a quick change⟩ **:** associated or naturally related or attaching ⟨the privileges ~ to increased rank⟩ **b** *obs* **:** PERTINENT, APPOSITE, LIABLE, SUBJECT **2** *archaic* **:** occurring accidentally and without essential relationship **:** INCIDENTAL **3** *law* **:** dependent on or appertaining to another thing **:** directly and immediately relating to or involved in something else though not an essential part of it **4 a :** falling or striking on something — used esp. of light rays on a plane **b :** acting from without **:** EXTERNAL ⟨attacks by ~ forces⟩ **syn** see LIABLE

¹**in·ci·den·tal** \¦==¦dent³l\ *adj* [¹*incident* + *-al*; prob. influenced in meaning by ML *incidenter* incidentally, adv., fr. L *incident-, incidens*] **1 :** subordinate, nonessential, or attendant in position or significance: as **a :** occurring merely by chance or without intention or calculation **:** occurring as a minor concomitant ⟨allowing a few dollars extra for ~ expenses⟩ ⟨the ~ gain which such a policy may win —J.A.Hobson⟩ ⟨man may be an ~ host of the sheep liver fluke⟩ **b :** being likely to ensue as a chance or minor consequence — usu. used with *to* ⟨labor problems ~ to rapidly expanding factories —*Amer. Guide Series: Mass.*⟩ **c :** lacking effect, force, or consequence **:** not receiving much consideration or calculation ⟨a cool, purely ~, and passive contempt —Herman Melville⟩ **d :** presented purposefully but as though without consideration or intention; *often* **:** DIGRESSIVE ⟨an ~ allusion, purposely thrown out, to the day of the week —Charles Dickens⟩ **2 :** met or encountered casually or by accident **:** CHANCE ⟨~ traveling companions⟩ ⟨an ~ shipboard acquaintance⟩ **syn** see ACCIDENTAL

²**incidental** \"\ *n* -s **1 :** something that is incidental **:** a subordinate or incidental item ⟨no such ~ as personal sensibilities can be allowed to interfere with the overall plan of the survey⟩ **2 incidentals** *pl* **:** minor items (as of expense) that are not particularized ⟨a bill for tuition and ~*s*⟩

in·ci·den·tal·ist \,==ˈdent³ləst\ *n* -s **:** one that is more concerned with the minutiae of incident than with broad overall views or concepts

in·ci·den·tal·ly \¦==¦dentlē, -t³lē, -li\ *adv* **1 :** by chance **:** as a matter of minor import **:** CASUALLY ⟨in this discussion grave questions were ~ brought up⟩ **2 :** by way of interjection or digression **:** in passing **:** PARENTHETICALLY ⟨touching ~ on the waterpower values⟩ ⟨another leading industry, ~, has quadrupled its business in five years⟩

incidental music *n* **:** descriptive music played or to be played during the action of a play to heighten a situation or project a mood (as of a battle, a storm, a death scene) or to relate directly to stage action (as a song or a dance); *broadly* **:** any music related to a play (as an overture or entr'acte) — compare BACKGROUND MUSIC

in·ci·den·tal·ness \,==ˈdent³lnəs\ *n* -ES **:** the quality or state of being incidental **:** CONCOMITANCE

in·ci·dent·less \'in(t)sədəntləs, -d³n-, -,den-\ *adj* **:** free from incident **:** UNEVENTFUL

in·ci·dent·ly \'in(t)sədəntlē, -d³n-, -li, ¦==¦dent- — *in sense 2 always the last*\ *adv* **1 :** so as to be incident **2 :** INCIDENTALLY

inciding *pres part of* INCIDE

in·ci·en·so \,in(t)sē'en(t)(,)sō\ *n* -s [AmerSp, fr. Sp, incense, fr. L *incensum* — more at INCENSE] **:** a shrubby encelia (*Encelia farinosa*) of rocky desert uplands of the southwestern U. S. and adjacent Mexico that has grayish green to almost white tomentose foliage and showy cymes of yellow flowers and that produces a resin that has been used as incense, in folk medicine, and in varnish

in·cin·er·ate \ən'sinə,rāt, *usu* -ād.+V\ *vb* -ED/-ING/-S [ML *incineratus*, past part. of *incinerare*, fr. L *in-* ²in- + *ciner-, cinis* ashes; akin to Gk *konis, konia* ashes, dust; basic meaning: to rub, scratch, tickle] *vt* **:** to cause to burn to ashes **:** consume by or as if by fire ⟨*incinerating* the trash⟩ ~ *vi* **:** to be or become completely burned ⟨paper and dry leaves ~ easily⟩

in·cin·er·a·tion \(,)in,sinə'rāshən, ən,-\ *n* -s [ML *incineration-, incineratio*, fr. L *incineratus* (past part. of *incinerare* to incinerate) + *-ion-, -io* -ion] **:** the act of incinerating or the state of being incinerated **:** CREMATION; *esp* **:** an analytical procedure of heating an organic substance with free access to air until only its ash remains — compare IGNITION

in·cin·er·a·tor \=ˈ==,rād·ə(r), -ātə-\ *n* -s **:** one that incinerates; *esp* **:** a furnace or a container for incinerating waste materials

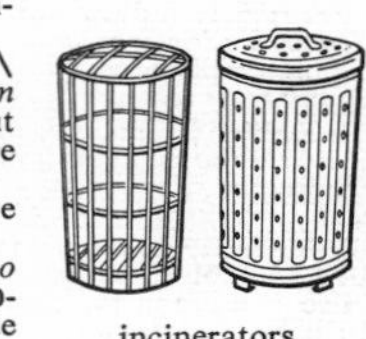
incinerators

¹**in·cip·i·a·tive** \ən'sipē,ād·iv, -ēəd-·\ *adj* [*incipient* + *-ative*] *of a verb form or aspect* **:** expressing action about to begin or just beginning — compare HABITUATIVE

²**incipiative** \"\ *n* -s **:** an incipiative form of a verb

in·cip·i·en·cy \ən'sipēənsē, -si\ *also* **in·cip·i·ence** \-ēən(t)s\ *n, pl* **incipiencies** *also* **incipiences :** the state or fact of being incipient **:** BEGINNING, COMMENCEMENT

in·cip·i·ent \(ˈ)in¦sipēənt, ən's-\ *adj* [L *incipient-, incipiens*, pres. part. of *incipere* to begin, fr. *in-* ²in- + *-cipere* (fr. *capere* to take) — more at HEAVE] **:** beginning to be or become apparent **:** COMMENCING, INITIAL ⟨the ~ stage of a fever⟩ ⟨~ light of day⟩ ⟨~ civil disorders⟩ — **in·cip·i·ent·ly** *adv*

incipient species *n* **:** a natural population that is more or less interfertile with another related population but is inhibited from interbreeding in nature by some specific barrier — compare ECOSPECIES

incipient wilting *n* **:** partial and temporary loss of turgor in a plant that occurs in the presence of adequate soil moisture and is associated with excessive water loss through transpiration

in·ci·pit \'in(t)səpət, 'iŋkə-, *esp in senses b & c* 'inchə-\ *n* -s [L, it begins, 3d pers. sing. pres. indic. of *incipere*] **:** BEGINNING: as **a :** the introductory words or part of a medieval manuscript or early printed book ⟨reproducing two ~*s* with superb miniatures —Raphael Levy⟩ — compare EXPLICIT **b :** the opening words of the text in a Gregorian chant or psalm tone sung usu. by the cantor **c :** the word given at the beginning of the tenor in a cantus-firmus motet that serves as a reference to the tenor's origin in the liturgy

in·circumscription \¦in+\ *n* [LL *incircumscription-, incircumscriptio*, fr. *incircumscriptus* not circumscribed (fr. L *in-* ¹in- + *circumscriptus*, past part. of *circumscribere* to circumscribe) + L *-ion-, -io* -ion — more at CIRCUMSCRIBE] *archaic* **:** the quality or state of being free from bounds or limits

incircumspect *adj* [LL *incircumspectus*, fr. L *in-* ¹in- + *circumspectus*, past part. of *circumspicere* to look around, be cautious — more at CIRCUMSPECT] *obs* **:** IMPRUDENT, INDISCREET — **incircumspection** *n, obs* — **incircumspectly** *adv, obs*

incis *abbr* [L *incisus*] engraved

in·ci·sal \(ˈ)in¦sīzəl\ *adj* [L *incisus* + E *-al*] **:** CUTTING ⟨the ~ edge of a tooth⟩

in·cise \(ˈ)in¦sīz, -īs\ *vb* -ED/-ING/-S [MF or L; MF *inciser*, fr. L *incisus*, past part. of *incidere*, fr. *in-* ²in- + *-cidere* (fr. *caedere* to cut) — more at CONCISE] *vi, obs* **:** to make an incision ~ *vt* **1 :** to cut into **:** make an incision in ⟨*incised* the swollen tissue⟩ **2 a :** to carve figures, letters, or devices into **:** ENGRAVE ⟨~ a tablet with an inscription⟩ **b :** to produce (as letters, figures, or devices) by carving into a surface ⟨~ an inscription on a monument⟩ **3 a :** to produce (a narrow steep-walled valley) by downward erosion ⟨caused the streams to ~ their valleys —C.O.Dunbar⟩ **b :** to lower (itself) by eroding a deeper channel ⟨the streams then *incised* themselves to the new baselevel —C.O.Dunbar⟩ **c :** to intersect as a deep narrow cut ⟨more than twenty different submarine canyon systems ~ the continental border —J.C.Crowell⟩

incised *adj* **1 a :** CUT-IN, CARVED, ENGRAVED ⟨~ ornamentation⟩; *esp* **:** decorated with incised figures ⟨~ pottery⟩ **b** *of a cut or wound* **:** made with or as if with a sharp knife or scalpel **:** clean and well defined **2 :** having a margin that is deeply and sharply and more or less irregularly notched ⟨an ~ leaf⟩

incised meander *n* **:** the curve of a winding river with steep slopes on both sides rising to a former floodplain and usu. interpreted as due to rejuvenation of a meandering stream but prob. also formed by a combination of vertical and lateral erosion in a single cycle of valley development — compare ENTRENCHED MEANDER

in·ci·si·form \in'sīzə,fȯrm, -īsə-\ *adj* [*incisor* + *-iform*] **:** having the form of or resembling a typical incisor tooth **:** shaped for cutting

in·ci·sion \ən'sizhən\ *n* -s [ME *inscicioun*, fr. MF & L; MF *incision*, fr. L *incision-, incisio*, fr. *incisus* + *-ion-, -io* -ion] **1 a :** a separation of parts made or such as might be made by a cutting or pointed instrument (as a notch in the margin of a leaf or of an insect's wing) **b :** CLEFT, CUT, GASH; *specif* **:** an incised wound made by a surgeon into the tissues or an organ (as in reaching a site of injury or establishing drainage) ⟨an abdominal ~⟩ **2 :** an act or action of incising (as into a substance) ⟨a Pliocene uplift which caused valley ~ —A.M. Bateman⟩ ⟨the surgeon's skillful ~ of the tissues⟩ **3 :** the quality or state of being incisive (as in comprehension or action) **:** ACUTENESS, PENETRATION

in·ci·sive \(ˈ)in¦sīs|iv, ən'sī-, |ēv *also* |əv *sometimes* -īz|\ *adj* [ML *incisivus*, fr. L *incisus* + *-ivus* -ive] **1 :** having a cutting edge or piercing point **:** facilitating cutting or piercing ⟨as sharp and ~ as the stroke of a fang —T.B.Costain⟩ **2 :** marked by sharpness and penetration esp. in keen clear unmistakable resolution of matter at issue or in pointed decisive effectiveness of presentation ⟨the clear, ~ genius which could state in a flash the exact point at issue —A.N.Whitehead⟩ ⟨the . . . ~ irony . . . serves to put the literary crackpots in their proper place —S.C.Chew⟩ **3 :** of, relating to, or situated near the incisors

syn CLEAR-CUT, CRISP, TRENCHANT, CUTTING, BITING: INCISIVE indicates a keen penetration and sharp presentation that is effective or decisive ⟨Bismarck's will had not that *incisive*, rapier quality, that quality of highly tempered steel — flexible, unbreakable, of mortal effect, decisive, a sword — which had Richelieu's —Hilaire Belloc⟩ CLEAR-CUT indicates either unmistakably clear and lucid outlining, analysis, or presentation, or finite certainty defying disbelief or question ⟨this *clear-cut* and consistent political creed is set forth throughout with the lucidity and brevity that makes a first-class popular orator —*Times Lit. Supp.*⟩ ⟨the current decision . . . was neither *clear-cut* nor definite . . . it appeared to be an attempted compromise —*N.Y. Times*⟩ CRISP in this series has a variety of suggestions: keenness, freshness, clarity, animation, terseness, vigor, sureness, effectiveness ⟨a languorous work . . . with occasional interludes of *crisp* brilliance —Anthony West⟩ ⟨*crisp* epigrams —George Santayana⟩ TRENCHANT suggests sharp penetrating acuteness often in criticism or detraction and may suggest sarcastic asperity ⟨a *trenchant* critic of the rising capitalism, delighting in exposing the fallacies of the new economics and in pricking the bladders of political reputations —V.L.Parrington⟩ CUTTING and BITING apply to sharp sarcasm, ridicule, or detraction; the former may suggest a tendency to wound by penetrating acuteness, the latter a mordant, implacable harshness ⟨the *cutting* sarcasm . . . the cruel epigrams and occasional harsh witticisms —Jack London⟩ ⟨domineering and censorious of any that stood in his way, with a *biting* wit, although he mellowed somewhat as he grew older —T.D.Bacon⟩

incisive bone *n* **:** PREMAXILLA

incisive foramen *n* **:** a pit or in some animals two pits just behind the incisor teeth transmitting the nasopalatine nerves and the greater palatine artery

incisive fossa *n* **:** a depression on the front of the maxillary bone above the incisor teeth

in·ci·sive·ly \|əvlē, -li\ *adv* **:** in an incisive manner: as **a :** CUTTINGLY ⟨outspokenly and ~ critical —W.A.Taylor⟩ **b :** with exactitude and precision ⟨high-court judges of long experience cannot ~ say how many laws are still in force —Mark Priestley⟩ ⟨enabled him to prove ~ that the concept of a Jewish race was erroneous —W.D.Wallis⟩

in·ci·sive·ness \|ivnəs, |ēv- *also* |əv-\ *n* -ES **:** the quality or state of being incisive; *esp* **:** concise precision of utterance or action

in·ci·sor \ən'sīzə(r), 'in,s- *sometimes* -īsə-\ *n* -s *often attrib* [NL, fr. LL, one that cuts, fr. L *incisus* + *-or*] **:** a tooth adapted for cutting; *esp* **:** one of the cutting teeth in mammals arising from the premaxillary bone of the upper jaw in front of the canines when canines are present or one of the corresponding teeth of the lower jaw — see DENTITION illustration

in·ci·su·ra \,in,sī'zhu̇rə, ,in(t)sə'zh-\ *or* **in·ci·sure** \ən'sīzhə(r)\ *n, pl* **incisu·rae** \-u̇,rē\ *or* **incisures** [L *incisura*, fr. *incisus* + *-ura* -ure] **:** a notch, cleft, or fissure esp. of a body part or organ — **in·ci·sural** \¦in,sī¦zhu̇rəl, ¦in(t)sə¦zh-; (ˈ)in'sīzhərəl\ *adj*

¹**in·cit·ant** \ən'sīt³nt\ *adj* [L *incitant-, incitans*, pres. part. of *incitare* to incite] **:** INCITING, CAUSATIVE, STIMULATING ⟨~ of infection⟩ ⟨an ~ factor⟩

²**incitant** \"\ *n* -s **:** an inciting agent; *esp* **:** a factor (as an infective agent) that is the essential causative agent of a particular disease ⟨where the fungal ~ is present mildew is likely to damage foliage in cold wet weather⟩

in·ci·ta·tion \,in,sī'tāshən, ,in(t)sə'-\ *n* -s [MF, fr. L *incitation-, incitatio*, fr. *incitatus* (past part. of *incitare* to incite) + *-ion-, -io* -ion] **1 :** an act of inciting **:** STIMULATION **2 :** something that incites to action **:** INCITEMENT, INCENTIVE ⟨provocative statements that were an open ~ to violence⟩

in·cite \ən'sīt, *usu* -īd.+V\ *vt* -ED/-ING/-S [MF *inciter*, fr. L *incitare*, fr. *in-* ²in- + *citare* to put in movement, summon — more at CITE] **1 :** to move to a course of action **:** stir up **:** spur on **:** urge on ⟨*inciting* the people to rebel⟩ ⟨*incited* to further effects by his mother's enthusiasm⟩ **2 :** to bring into being **:** induce to exist or occur ⟨such behavior is likely to ~ retaliation⟩ ⟨organisms that readily *incited* antibody formation⟩

syn INSTIGATE, FOMENT, ABET: INCITE may indicate both an initiating, a calling into being or action, and also a degree of prompting, furthering, encouraging, or nurturing of activity ⟨his projects for *inciting* war between the two countries⟩ ⟨posters scattered by the thousands throughout the eastern states and Europe to *incite* immigration —*Amer. Guide Series: Minn.*⟩ ⟨their tutors had *incited* them to dig deeply in the older sources of learning⟩ ⟨did I see a young lady in want of a partner, gallantry would *incite* me to offer myself as her devoted knight —T.L.Peacock⟩ INSTIGATE implies initiating or encouraging others to initiate actions or feelings, often questionable actions initiated with dubious intention ⟨pogroms *instigated* or connived at by the government as a safety valve for popular discontent —W.R.Inge⟩ ⟨a comparative study, *instigated* by the director of the investigation, which classifies a series of nonliterate cultures⟩ FOMENT indicates persistent inciting, esp. of something thought of as seething or boiling ⟨radicals *fomenting* a rebellion⟩ ⟨race theories are indeed not only a modern invention to explain such group conflicts, but also a means for *fomenting* them —M.R.Cohen⟩ ABET is likely to indicate seconding, encouraging, or aiding some action already begun, esp. a questionable activity ⟨aiding and *abetting* a friend in obtaining money under false pretenses⟩ ⟨the general, *abetted* by the excited aide-de-camp, made a fatal error⟩ ⟨the will to achieve perfection, though not so rare as it sounds, is all too rarely *abetted* by leisure —Harry Levin⟩

in·cite·ment \-ītmənt\ *n* -s **1 :** the act of inciting or the state of being incited ⟨through emotional ~ of each other . . . they discover paths they need to know —Kathleen Sproul⟩ **2 :** something that incites **:** INCENTIVE ⟨an ~ to further progress⟩

in·cit·er \-īd·ə(r), -ītə-\ *n* -s **:** one that incites

in·cit·ing·ly *adv* **:** so as to incite **:** in an inciting manner

in·ci·tive \(ˈ)in¦sīd·iv, ən's-\ *adj* **:** tending to incite **:** expressive of incitement

in·ci·to·ry \-d·ərē\ *adj* **:** serving to excite **:** STIMULATORY

incity \(ˈ)=¦==, ˈ=,==\ *adj* [fr. the phrase *in city*] **:** lying wholly within or serving the area within a city ⟨~ and suburban bus lines⟩ ⟨the ~ edition of the paper⟩

in·civic \(ˈ)=+\ *adj* [¹*in-* + *civic*] **:** lacking civic responsibility

in·civil \"+\ *adj* [MF, fr. LL *incivilis*, fr. L *in-* ¹in- + *civilis* civil — more at CIVIL] **:** not civil **:** RUDE, BARBAROUS

in·civility \¦in+\ *n* [MF *incivilité*, fr. LL *incivilitat-, incivilitas*, fr. *incivilis* + L *-itat-, -itas* -ity] **1** *obs* **:** INCIVILIZATION **2 :** the quality or state of being uncivil **:** ill-bred behavior **:** DISCOURTESY, RUDENESS ⟨it is gross ~ to refuse to answer when spoken to⟩ ⟨never before met with such ~⟩ **3 :** a rude or ill-bred act ⟨tired of his constant *incivilities*⟩

in·civilization \(¦)in+\ *n* [¹*in-* + *civilization*] **:** the state of being uncivilized

in·civism \(ˈ)in+\ *n* [F *incivisme*, fr. *in-* ¹in- + *civisme* civism — more at CIVISM] **:** lack of civic-mindedness or of patriotism

incl *abbr* **1** inclosure **2** included; including; inclusive

inclasp *var of* ENCLASP

incld *abbr* included

incle *var of* INKLE

in-clearing \ˈ=,==\ *n* [⁴*in*] *Brit* **:** the checks received for payment by a bank during the process of clearing

in·clem·en·cy \(ˈ)in, ən+\ *n* [L *inclementia*, fr. *inclement-, inclemens* + *-ia* -y] **:** the quality or state of being inclement: as **a :** severity of weather **:** STORMINESS ⟨the ~ of the exposed slope⟩ **b :** harshness or cruelty of action or disposition ⟨an honest man but with great ~ of spirit⟩

in·clem·ent \(ˈ)in¦klemənt, ən'k- *sometimes* 'inkləmənt\ *adj* [L *inclement-, inclemens,* fr. *in-* ¹in- + *clement-, clemens* clement — more at CLEMENT] : lacking clemency: as **a** *of the elements or weather* : physically severe : HARSH, ROUGH, STORMY ⟨~ weather⟩; *also* : marked by such weather ⟨an ~ day⟩ **b** : severe in temper or action : UNMERCIFUL, RIGOROUS ⟨the harsh sentence of an ~ judge⟩ — **in·clem·ent·ly** *adv* — **in·clem·ent·ness** *n* -ES

in·clin·able \ən'klīnəbəl\ *adj* [ME, fr. MF *enclinable, inclinable,* fr. *encliner, incliner* to incline + *-able* — more at INCLINE] **1 a** : having an inclination toward something : DISPOSED ⟨had formerly been very ~ to dissipation⟩ **b** : disposed to favor or think well of : FAVORABLE ⟨~ to our pleas⟩ **2** : having a tendency : tending to or toward ⟨somewhat ~ to corpulence⟩ ⟨a heavy soil but ~ to bake and dry out⟩ **3** : capable of being inclined ⟨an ~ punch press⟩

in·cli·na·tion \ˌinklə'nāshən, ˌiŋk-\ *n* -S [ME *inclinacioun,* fr. MF *inclination,* fr. L *inclination-, inclinatio,* fr. *inclinatus* (past part. of *inclinare*) + *-ion-, -io* -ion] **1** : an act or the action of bending or inclining: as **a** : a bending forward of the head or body (as in respect, greeting, or acknowledgment) : BOW, NOD ⟨acknowledged his greeting with a slight ~⟩ **b** : a tilting of something **2 a** *obs* : natural disposition : NATURE, CHARACTER **b** *obs* : a turning of the mind in a particular direction : ATTENTION **c** : a particular disposition of mind or character : PROPENSITY, BENT ⟨a man of fixed ~s⟩; *usu* : favorable disposition esp. toward a particular thing, activity, or end : LIKING, DESIRE ⟨a strong ~ toward study⟩ ⟨an ~ to make the best of things⟩ **3 a** : direction or trend out of the true vertical or horizontal ⟨the ~ of a column⟩ ⟨the roadbed had considerable ~⟩ **b** : amount of deviation from the vertical or horizontal : degree or rate of slope or slant : GRADE ⟨an ~ of 20 degrees⟩ **c** : an inclined surface : SLOPE, INCLINE ⟨worked their way down the steep ~⟩ **d** (1) : the angle determined by two lines or planes ⟨the ~ of two rays of light⟩ (2) *in plane analytic geometry* : the angle made by a line with the x-axis measured counterclockwise from the positive direction of that axis **4 a** : a tendency to a particular aspect, state, character, or action ⟨men judge by the complexion of the sky the state and ~ of the day —Shak.⟩ ⟨some ~ to snow⟩ ⟨the clutch had an ~ to slip⟩ **b** : something to which one is inclined : an object of habit or favor : LIKING **5** : DIP 3b **6** : ENCLISIS — **in·cli·na·tion·al** \¦==¦nāshənᵊl, -shnəl\ *adj*

inclination of an orbit : the angle between the plane of the orbit and the plane of the ecliptic

in·cli·na·tor \'==ˌnād·ə(r)\ *n* -S [*inclination* + *-or*] : a stand with rockers for inclining a carboy to the required angle for pouring

in·cli·na·to·ry \ən'klīnəˌtōrē\ *adj* [L *inclinatus* + E *-ory*] : tending to incline or capable of inclining ⟨the ~ power of a dowsing rod⟩

¹**in·cline** \ən'klīn\ *vb* -ED/-ING/-S [ME *inclinen, enclinen,* fr. MF *encliner, incliner,* fr. L *inclinare,* fr. *in-* ²in- + *clinare* to bend — more at LEAN] *vi* **1** : to bend the head or body forward : BOW ⟨*inclining* toward the speaker to hear more clearly⟩ **2** : to lean, tend, or become drawn esp. toward an opinion or course of conduct : favor an opinion, a course of conduct, or a person ⟨~ as we grow older more and more to traditional ways⟩ ⟨his heart *inclined* to the child⟩ **3** : to deviate from a line, direction, or course : LEAN ⟨converging lines ~ toward each other⟩; *specif* : to deviate from the vertical or horizontal ⟨the shaft ~s almost 30 degrees⟩ ⟨snow-laden birches *inclining* over the road⟩ **4** *of a military formation* : to march or move obliquely to the front so as to gain ground on the flank as well as forward ~ *vt* **1** : to cause to stoop or bow : BEND ⟨*inclining* her head in greeting⟩ **2** : to orient in the direction of : impart a trend toward, liking for, or interest in : influence in favor of something (as a course, interest, view) ⟨increasing knowledge ~s one to further study⟩ ⟨tried to ~ him to help⟩ **3** : to cause to deviate physically esp. from the horizontal or vertical : arrange in a slanting position : give a bend, slope, or slant to ⟨rays of light are *inclined* in passing through a medium of high refractive index⟩ ⟨*inclining* the rake against the fence⟩ **4** : to heel (a ship) experimentally to determine stability or center of gravity — **incline one's ear** : to listen with favor : hear and approve

²**in·cline** \'inˌklīn, ən'k-\ *n* -S : an ascending or descending inclined plane : GRADE, GRADIENT, SLOPE: as **a** : an inclined mine shaft or inclined portion of an otherwise vertical shaft — compare ADIT **b** (1) : a railway track and supporting structure on a grade extending from an adjustable apron or bridge at a transfer slip (2) : a railway built on a slope on which cars are raised and lowered by means of a mechanically operated cable

in·clined \ən'klīnd *or esp in sense 2* 'inˌk-\ *adj* [ME *enclined, inclined,* fr. past part. of *enclinen, inclinen*] **1** : having inclination, disposition, or tendency : well disposed **2 a** : having a leaning or slope usu. from the vertical or horizontal ⟨an ~ roadway⟩ ⟨an ~ stem⟩ **b** : making an angle with a line or plane

inclined plane *n* **1** : a plane surface that makes an oblique angle with the plane of the horizon : a sloping plane **2** : an inclined track on which trains or boats are raised or lowered from one level to another

incline man *n* : DILLYMAN

in·clin·er \ən'klīnə(r), 'inˌk-\ *n* -S : one that inclines

¹**inclining** *n* -S [ME *enclining, inclining,* fr. gerund of *enclinen, inclinen*] **1** : INCLINATION, DISPOSITION **2** *archaic* : those who incline toward (as a person or a cause) : PARTY, FOLLOWING

²**in·clin·ing** \ən'klīniŋ, 'inˌk-, -nēŋ\ *adj* [fr. pres. part. of ¹incline] : LEANING, BENT: as **a** *of a plant part* : bent out of a perpendicular position ⟨an ~ stem⟩ **b** : ENCLITIC 1

in·cli·nom·e·ter \ˌinklə'nämәd·ə(r), -klī'n-\ *n* [²*incline* + *-o-* + *-meter*] **1** : an apparatus for determining the direction of the earth's magnetic field with reference to the plane of the horizon — see DIP CIRCLE, EARTH INDUCTOR **2** : a machinist's clinometer **3 a** : an instrument for indicating the inclination to the horizontal of an esp. longitudinal axis of a ship or an airplane; *broadly* : any of various instruments for indicating inclination (as of the base of an oil well) **b** : an instrument giving the attitude of an airplane with reference to true gravity — called also *absolute inclinometer*

in·clip \ən+\ *vt* [²*in* + *clip*] *archaic* : CLASP, ENCLOSE

incln *abbr* inclusion

incloister *obs var of* ENCLOISTER

inclose *var of* ENCLOSE

in·clud·able *or* **in·clud·ible** \ən'klüdəbəl\ *adj* : capable of being included : proper or suitable for inclusion

in·clude \ən'klüd\ *vt* -ED/-ING/-S [ME *includen, encluden,* fr. L *includere,* fr. *in-* ²in- + *-cludere* (fr. *claudere* to close) — more at CLOSE] **1** : to shut up : CONFINE, ENCLOSE, BOUND ⟨the nutshell ~s the kernel⟩ ⟨that divine spark *included* in every human being⟩ **2 a** : to place, list, or rate as a part or component of a whole or of a larger group, class, or aggregate ⟨*included* a sum for tips in his estimate of expenses⟩ **b** : to take in, enfold, or comprise as a discrete or subordinate part or item of a larger aggregate, group, or principle ⟨in search of a formula which should cover everything . . . even if it *included* more than I wished —T.S.Eliot⟩ **3** *obs* : to bring to an end : TERMINATE

syn SUBSUME, EMBRACE, COMPREHEND, IMPLY, INVOLVE, IMPLICATE: INCLUDE and SUBSUME agree in indicating the enclosure or containment by a larger class or whole of a smaller class or specific item or part. INCLUDE, the more common term, may call more attention to the single item or smaller class by stressing the fact of its existence or the fact of its not having been overlooked ⟨it would not be argued today that the power to regulate does not *include* the power to prohibit —O.W. Holmes †1935⟩ ⟨numerous pretty things, or things supposed to be pretty . . . *including* such absurdities as paper knives with fretwork handles —Herbert Spencer⟩ SUBSUME, orig. a technical term in logic and still an erudite term, may call more attention to the larger class or more comprehensive principle, may stress the fact of its existence ⟨free verse . . . is a larger rhythmic movement which *subsumes* other rhythms —J.L. Lowes⟩ ⟨I suggest that in every beautiful building its uses, its representative elements, are indeed *subsumed* into the form —Samuel Alexander⟩ EMBRACE may sometimes suggest marked effort at enclosing; it may be used with that which is vast or is quite varied n designation or classification ⟨Virginia . . . *embraced* in its possessions the present states of West Virginia, Kentucky, Ohio, Illinois, Indiana, Michigan, and Wisconsin —C.G.Bowers⟩ ⟨freedom of speech . . . *embraces* all discussion which enriches human life and helps it to be more wisely led —Zechariah Chafee⟩ COMPREHEND may suggest a noteworthy range or scope in which something is enclosed or held ⟨to find universal law, to *comprehend* all experience in a closed system —W.R.Inge⟩ ⟨to *comprehend* in a single view polities of the most varied and discrepant character —G.L. Dickinson⟩ IMPLY, INVOLVE, and IMPLICATE indicate somewhat similar relationships. IMPLY suggests drawing attention by inference to a certain existence or relationship, not by direct statement ⟨ordinarily imitation is enough to *imply* that the matter imitated is important at least to the sale of the goods —O.W.Holmes †1935⟩ It is applicable to what is logically inferential but not absolutely certain ⟨it would be argued that culture *implies* a certain freedom from parochialism —Bertrand Russell⟩ INVOLVE, on the other hand, may apply to more certain relationship and connection since it may postulate a necessary effect or consequence ⟨in every genuine metaphysical debate some practical issue, however conjectural or remote, is *involved* —William James⟩ ⟨faith *involves* an act of the will —W.R.Inge⟩ IMPLICATE postulates through one actuality or existence the fact of another but fails to suggest an effect or consequence ⟨purpose *implicates* in the most organic way an individual self —John Dewey⟩ ⟨colors are sumptuous and rich just because a total organic resonance is deeply *implicated* in them —John Dewey⟩ ⟨a catalyzing agent has been compared to a parson, who marries others without participating in the event himself. He is *implicated,* but not *involved* —L.K.Anspacher⟩

in·clud·ed \ən'klüdəd, 'inˌk-\ *adj* : ENCLOSED, CONFINED, EMBRACED ⟨an ~ angle⟩: as **a** : not projecting beyond the mouth of the corolla — used of a stamen and pistil; opposed to *exserted* **b** *of a lower jaw* : overlapped by the upper jaw — **in·clud·ed·ness** *n* -ES

included phloem *n* : phloem tissue lying within the secondary xylem (as in the wood of some dicotyledons)

included sapwood *n* : masses or streaks of tissue in heartwood that have the appearance and characteristics of sapwood

in·clud·er \ən'klüdə(r)\ *n* -S : one that includes

in·clud·ing \ən'klüdiŋ, 'inˌk-, -dēŋ\ *adj* : serving to enclose or cover ⟨an ~ membrane⟩

in·cluse \'inˌklüs, ən'k-, -üz\ *n* -S [ME, fr. L *inclusus,* fr. past part. of *includere* to enclose, include — more at INCLUDE] : a recluse who is voluntarily immured (as in a cave, hut, or isolated cell)

in·clu·sion \ən'klüzhən\ *n* -S [L *inclusion-, inclusio,* fr. *inclusus* + *-ion-, -io* -ion] **1** : the act of including or the state of being included ⟨the ~ of domestic . . . reforms in the social program of the government —H.C.Atyeo⟩ **2** : something that is included: as **a** : a gaseous, liquid, or solid and usu. minute foreign body enclosed in the mass of a mineral **b** : a passive product of cell activity (as a starch grain) visible within the protoplasm **c** : solid and usu. minute foreign particles (as of slag) enclosed in a solid metal **3** : a relation between two classes that obtains when all members of the first are also members of the second — contrasted with *membership*

inclusion body *n* : a rounded or oval intracellular body that consists of elementary bodies in a matrix, is characteristic of certain virus diseases, and is believed to represent a stage in the multiplication of the virus

inclusion disease *n* : a virus disease of infants marked by the presence of inclusion bodies in the nucleus and cytoplasm of cells in the organs most affected (as lungs, liver, brain)

in·clu·sive \ən'klüs¦iv, 'inˌk-, ¦ēv *also* -üz¦ *or* ¦əv\ *adj* [ML *inclusivus,* fr. L *inclusus* + *-ivus* -ive] **1** : ENCLOSING, ENCOMPASSING ⟨~ walls⟩: as **a** : broad in orientation or scope ⟨the concept of history adopted . . . is modern and ~ —C.V.Woodward⟩ ⟨dance is not as ~ an art as literature —George Balanchine⟩ **b** : covering or intended to cover all items, costs, or services ⟨an ~ fee⟩ **c** *of a Protestant Christian church* : extending fellowship to Protestant Christians without regard to rigidly sectarian barriers **d** *in grammar* : referring to the speaker and another or some others including the hearer **2** : comprehending the stated limits or extremes ⟨from Monday to Friday ~⟩ — opposed to *exclusive* — **in·clu·sive·ly** \¦əvlē, -li\ *adv* — **in·clu·sive·ness** \¦ivnəs, ¦ēv- *also* ¦əv-\ *n* -ES

inclusive of *prep* : containing as an integral part ⟨the whole cost *inclusive of* materials⟩

in·coagulable \¦in+\ *adj* [¹*in-* + *coagulable*] : incapable of coagulating

in·coercible \"+\ *adj* [¹*in-* + *coercible*] **1** : incapable of being controlled, checked, or confined ⟨the ~ power of the ballot⟩ **2 a** : not reducible to a liquid by pressure — compare PERMANENT GAS **b** *archaic* : incapable of being confined in or excluded from vessels — used of a so-called imponderable fluid (as heat, light, electricity)

in·cog \'inˌkäg, ən'k-\ *adv or adj or n* [by shortening] : INCOGNITO

in·cog·i·ta·bil·i·ty \(ˌ)inˌkäjəd·ə¦bilәd·ē, ən,==¦==\ *n* : the quality or state of being incogitable

in·cogitable \(ˈ)in, ən+\ *adj* [L *incogitabilis* unthinking, unthinkable, fr. *in-* ¹in- + *cogitabilis* cogitable — more at COGITABLE] : impossible to accept or believe : UNTHINKABLE, INCONCEIVABLE

incogitancy *n* -ES [L *incogitantia,* fr. *incogitant-, incogitans* + *-ia* -y] *obs* : lack of thought or of the power of thinking : THOUGHTLESSNESS

in·cog·i·tant \(ˈ)in¦käjəd·ənt, ən'k-\ *adj* [L *incogitant-, incogitans,* fr. *in-* ¹in- + *cogitant-, cogitans,* pres. part. of *cogitare* to cogitate — more at COGITATE] **1** : failing in due consideration of proper or relevant factors : inattentive and heedless : THOUGHTLESS, INCONSIDERATE **2** : INCOGITATIVE

in·cogitative \(ˈ)in, ən+\ *adj* [¹*in-* + *cogitative*] : lacking the ability to think

¹**in·cog·ni·ta** \÷ˌinˌkäg'nēd·ə, ÷-ētə *also* ən'kägnəd·ə *or* -nətə\ *adv (or adj)* [It, fem. of *incognito*] : INCOGNITO — used only of a woman

²**incognita** \"\ *n* -S [It, fr. *incognita,* adj.] : a woman in disguise; *esp* : one concealing her real quality or state under some unobtrusive appearance

¹**in·cog·ni·to** \÷ˌinˌkäg'nēd·(ˌ)ō, ÷-ē(ˌ)tō *also* ən'kägnəˌtō\ *adv (or adj)* [It, fr. L *incognitus* unknown, fr. *in-* ¹in- + *cognitus,* past part. of *cognoscere* to know — more at COGNITION] **1** : with one's identity concealed or assumed to be concealed; *esp* : in a capacity other than one's official capacity or under a name or title not calling for special recognition — used esp. of a personage of note ⟨the baron turned out to be a king ~⟩ **2** : without recognition : UNKNOWN, UNIDENTIFIED ⟨the Neanderthal skull from Gibraltar, which had lain ~ since its discovery —Jacquetta and Christopher Hawkes⟩

²**incognito** \"\ *n* -S [It, fr. *incognito,* adj.] **1** : one who is appearing or living incognito **2** : the state or disguise of an incognito or incognita **3** : the character assumed by an incognito or incognita

in·cognizable \(ˈ)in, ən+\ *adj* [¹*in-* + *cognizable*] : incapable of being recognized, known, or distinguished

in·cognizance \(ˈ)in, ən+\ *n* : lack of awareness, recognition, or knowledge

in·cognizant \"+\ *adj* [¹*in-* + *cognizant*] : lacking awareness or consciousness — used with *of* ⟨not ~ of the impression he was creating⟩

in·cog·nos·ci·bil·i·ty \ˌinˌkägˌnäsə'bilәd·ē\ *n* -ES : the quality or state of being incognoscible

in·cognoscible \(ˈ)in, ən+\ *adj* [LL *incognoscibilis,* fr. L *in-* ¹in- + LL *cognoscibilis* cognoscible — more at COGNOSCIBLE] : INCOGNIZABLE

in·coherence *or* **in·coherency** \¦in+\ *n* [¹*in-* + *coherence, coherency*] **1** : the quality or state of being incoherent : as **a** : lack of cohesion or adherence **b** : lack of continuity or relevance : INCONGRUITY, INCONSISTENCY **2** : something that is incoherent ⟨tearful *incoherencies*⟩

in·coherent \¦in+\ *adj* [¹*in-* + *coherent*] : lacking coherence: as **a** : lacking physical coherence or adhesiveness : consisting of discrete elements : LOOSE ⟨a dangerous slope covered with ~ shale⟩ **b** : lacking orderly continuity or relevance : INCONGRUOUS, INCONSISTENT ⟨a turgid ~ presentation⟩ **c** : lacking clarity or intelligibility usu. by reason of some emotional stress ⟨a voice ~ with rage⟩ ⟨a man ~ from sorrow⟩ **d** : lacking normal coordination : clumsy and fumbling ⟨a halting ~ gait⟩ **e** : occurring in mixed series or differing from normal patterns of language — used in cryptology of a key or an alphabet — **in·coherently** \"+\ *adv* — **in·coherentness** \"+\ *n* -ES

in·cohering \"+\ *adj* [¹*in-* + *cohering,* pres. part. of *cohere*] : lacking physical coherence

in·cohesion \¦in+\ *n* [¹*in-* + *cohesion*] : INCOHERENCE; *esp* : lack of orderly effective interaction between human groups ⟨difficulties resulting from the ~ of the desert nomads⟩

in·cohesive \¦in+\ *adj* [¹*in-* + *cohesive*] **1** : INCOHERENT : lacking integration **2** : tending to disrupt ⟨certain ~ social forces⟩

in·coincidence \¦in+\ *n* [¹*in-* + *coincidence*] : failure to conform or agree

in·coincident \"+\ *adj* [¹*in-* + *coincident*] : not coinciding

in·combustible \¦in+\ *adj or n* [ME, prob. fr. MF, fr. *in-* ¹in- + *combustible* — more at COMBUSTIBLE] : NONCOMBUSTIBLE — not used technically

¹**in·come** \'inˌkəm, *chiefly attrib also* 'inˌk- *sometimes* 'iŋˌk-\ *n* -S *often attrib* [ME, entry, arrival, fr. *in* + *come, cume* action of coming (after *comen in* to come in) — more at DOWNCOME, COME] **1** *archaic* : an act or an instance of coming in : ENTRANCE, ADVENT, INFLUX **2** *dial Brit* **a** : a place of entry **b** : INCOMER **3** : something that comes in as an increment or addition usu. by chance **4 a** : a gain or recurrent benefit that is usu. measured in money and for a given period of time, derives from capital, labor, or a combination of both, includes gains from transactions in capital assets, but excludes unrealized advances in value : commercial revenue or receipts of any kind except receipts or returns of capital — see EARNED INCOME, GROSS INCOME, NET INCOME, UNEARNED INCOME; compare PROFIT, WAGE **b** : the value of goods and services received by an individual in a given period of time — compare WEALTH

²**income** \"\ *n* -S [⁴*in* + *come* (as in *oncome*)] *dial Brit* : TUMOR, ABSCESS

income account *n* **1** : an account in which items of income or revenue are recorded **2** *or* **income statement** : a financial statement of a business showing the details of revenues, costs, expenses, losses, and profits for a given period grouped under appropriate headings — called also *profit and loss statement*

income basis *n* : a basis of reckoning income (as from investments, profits) according to the percentage that the interest or revenue bears to the actual cost with no allowance being made for the fact that payment at maturity is to be at par ⟨a bond yielding 3-percent interest on its par value and bought at 60 is on an *income basis* of 5 percent⟩

income bond *n* : a bond that is entitled to receive interest only if earned and declared by the board of directors in accordance with its indenture provisions

in·come·less \-ləs\ *adj* : having no income

incomer \'inˌkəmə(r)\ *n* : one that comes in: as **a** *dia chiefly Brit* : one that comes from another place : IMMIGRANT, STRANGER; *esp* : a new tenant **b** : a game bird or a trapshooting target that comes toward the shooter

income splitting *n* : an assigning of income for purposes of taxation in equal shares to two or more persons (as husband and wife) irrespective of which one actually received the income

income tax *n* **1** : a tax on the net income of an individual or business concern (as a corporation) **2 a** : a tax on gross income often levied as a payroll tax by a city **b** : a tax on gross operating revenue (as of a public utility)

¹**in·com·ing** \'inˌkəmiŋ, -mēŋ\ *n* [ME, fr. *in-* + *coming* (after *comen in* to come in)] **1** : the act of coming in : ARRIVAL ⟨all these ~s and outgoings disturbed our daily routine⟩ **2** : money or other gains received : REVENUE, INCOME — usu. used in pl.

²**incoming** \"\ *adj* [²*in* + *coming* (after *come in,* v.)] : coming in: as **a** : taking or coming to occupy a place, position, or status formerly held by another ⟨his ~ tenant⟩ ⟨see what the ~ Congress will do⟩ **b** : arriving at a usual, proper, or normal destination ⟨~ waves⟩ : ACCRUING ⟨~ orders⟩ **c** : STARTING, BEGINNING, ENTERING ⟨high hopes for the ~ year⟩ ⟨all ~ freshmen⟩

in·commensurability \¦in+\ *n* [prob. fr. MF *incommensurableté,* fr. ML *incommensurabilitat-, incommensurabilitas,* fr. LL *incommensurabilis* + L *-itat-, -itas* -ity] : the quality or state of being incommensurable ⟨a genuine ~ between the individual and the universal —M.R.Cohen⟩

¹**in·commensurable** \¦in+\ *adj* [prob. fr. MF, fr. LL *incommensurabilis,* fr. L *in-* ¹in- + LL *commensurabilis* commensurable — more at COMMENSURABLE] : not commensurable : having no common measure ⟨quantities are ~ when no third quantity can be found that is an aliquot part of each⟩; *broadly* : lacking a common basis of comparison in respect to a quality (as value, size, excellence) normally subject to comparison — **in·com·men·su·ra·bly** \-əblē, -li\ *adv*

²**incommensurable** \"\ *n* -S : something that is incommensurable; *esp* : any of two or more quantities having no common measure

in·commensurate \¦in+\ *adj* [¹*in-* + *commensurate*] : not commensurate: as **a** : INCOMMENSURABLE **b** : INADEQUATE ⟨means ~ to our wants⟩ ⟨~ attention⟩

in com·mer·cio \ˌinkə'marshēˌō\ *adj* [L, lit., inside of commerce] *Roman & civil law* : subject to private ownership — opposed to *extra commercium*

in·com·mis·ci·ble \ˌinkə¦misəbəl\ *adj* [LL *incommiscibilis,* fr. L *in-* ¹in- + LL *commiscibilis* able to be mixed together, fr. L *commiscēre* to mix together + *-ibilis* -ible — more at COMMIX] : IMMISCIBLE

incommodate *vt* -ED/-ING/-S [L *incommodatus,* past part. of *incommodare*] *obs* : INCOMMODE

in·commodation \(ˌ)in, ən+\ *n* : DISCOMFORT, INCONVENIENCE, ANNOYANCE

¹**in·com·mode** \ˌinkə¦mōd\ *vt* -ED/-ING/-S [MF *incommoder,* fr. L *incommodare,* fr. *incommodus* inconvenient, disagreeable, fr. *in-* ¹in- + *commodus* convenient — more at COMMODE] **1 a** : to give inconvenience or distress to : put out : DISCOMMODE ⟨such delays often *incommoded* passengers⟩ **b** : DISTURB, MOLEST ⟨should any player of the fielding side ~ the striker by any noise or motion —*Laws of Cricket*⟩ **2** *archaic* : IMPEDE, HANDICAP, OBSTRUCT

²**incommode** *adj* [F, fr. L *incommodus*] *obs* : INCONVENIENT

in·commodious \¦in+\ *adj* [¹*in-* + *commodious*] : tending to inconvenience: as **a** *archaic* : UNPLEASANT, DISAGREEABLE **b** *archaic* : UNCOMFORTABLE, HAMPERING **c** *obs* : HARMFUL, DAMAGING **d** *obs* : UNSUITABLE, IMPROPER **e** : offering inadequate accommodation : unpleasantly small and cramped ⟨an ~ little hall bedroom⟩ — **in·com·mo·di·ous·ly** *adv* — **in·com·mo·di·ous·ness** *n* -ES

in·commodity \¦in+\ *n* [ME *incommodite,* fr. MF *incommodité,* fr. L *incommoditat-, incommoditas,* fr. *incommodus* + *-itat-, -itas* -ity] **1** *obs* : the quality or state of being incommodious **2** : something that causes inconvenience, annoyance, or discomfort — usu. used in pl. ⟨an inconvenient, ill-balanced house . . . its unsuitability as a public building is intensified by such *incommodities* —Claud Phillimore⟩

in·communicability \"+\ *n* : the quality or state of being incommunicable

in·communicable \"+\ *adj* [MF or LL; MF, fr. LL *incommunicabilis,* fr. L *in-* ¹in- + LL *communicabilis* communicable — more at COMMUNICABLE] **1** : incapable of being communicated: as **a** : not subject to sharing or division ⟨the ~ authority of the crown⟩ **b** : impossible to recount or utter : INEFFABLE ⟨an ~ vision⟩ ⟨into the unspeakable and ~ prison of this earth —Thomas Wolfe⟩ **2** : unwilling or unable to communicate : TACITURN, RESERVED, WITHDRAWN ⟨a troubled man, ~ and abstracted⟩ **3** : lacking means of communication ⟨his nature is ~ — he resembles neither dog nor man —Pamela L. Travers⟩ — **in·com·mu·ni·ca·ble·ness** \-nəs\ *n* -ES — **in·communicably** \¦in+\ *adv*

in·com·mu·ni·ca·do *or* **in·co·mu·ni·ca·do** \ˌinkəˌmyünə'kä(ˌ)dō, -kā(-\ *adv (or adj)* [Sp *incomunicado,* fr. past part. of *incomunicar* to deprive of communication, fr. *in-* ¹in- (fr. L) + *comunicar* to communicate, fr. L *communicare* to share,

impart, partake — more at COMMUNICATE] **:** without means of communication ⟨it had sometimes brought good luck for people to be politically ~ —A.N.Whitehead⟩; *esp* **:** in solitary confinement ⟨held ~ for 10 days⟩
in·communicated *or* **in·communicating** \ˌin+\ *adj* [¹*in-* + *communicated* or *communicating*] *archaic* **:** lacking communication
in·communicative \"+\ *adj* [¹*in-* + *communicative*] **:** UNCOMMUNICATIVE 2
in·com·mut·abil·i·ty \ˌinkə,myüd·əˈbiləd·ē\ *n* -ES [LL *incommutabilitas*, fr. L *incommutabilis* + *-itas* -ity] **:** the quality or state of being incommutable
in·commutable \ˌin+\ *adj* [ME, fr. L *incommutabilis*, fr. *in-* ¹in- + *commutabilis* commutable — more at COMMUTABLE] **:** not commutable: **a :** not subject or liable to alteration **:** UNCHANGEABLE **b :** not able to substitute one for another **:** UNEXCHANGEABLE ⟨these ~ skills⟩ **:** not interchangeable ⟨when two sounds are ~ their phonetic difference prevents their being classed under one phoneme —C.E.Bazell⟩ — **in·com·mut·a·bly** \-blē,-bli\ *adv*
in·compact \(ˈ)in, ən+\ *adj* [¹*in-* + *compact*] **:** loosely ordered or organized **:** lacking coherence or firm integration
in·comparability \(ˈ)in, ən+\ *n* **:** the quality or state of being incomparable
in·comparable \(ˈ)in, ən+\ *adj* [ME, fr. MF, fr. L *incomparabilis*, fr. *in-* ¹in- + *comparabilis* comparable — more at COMPARABLE] **1 :** of such quality as to be beyond comparison **:** having no equal **:** eminent beyond comparison **:** MATCHLESS, PEERLESS, TRANSCENDENT ⟨this ~ scholar⟩ ⟨a heavenly, an ~ week of rest and pleasure⟩ **2 :** not suitable for comparison **:** lacking such common bases or points of reference as make comparison useful, informative, or valid — usu. used with *with* or *to* ⟨this report is ~ with the earlier reports because of the use of different breakdowns of data⟩
in·com·pa·ra·ble·ness *n* -ES **:** INCOMPARABILITY
in·comparably \(ˈ)in, ən+\ *adv* [ME, fr. *incomparable* + *-ly*] **:** to an incomparable degree **:** beyond comparison **:** EXCEPTIONALLY
incompass *obs var of* ENCOMPASS
in·compassionate \ˌin+\ *adj* [¹*in-* + *compassionate*] **:** lacking compassion — **in·compassionately** \"+\ *adv*
in·compatibility \ˌin+\ *n* [F *incompatibilité*, fr. MF, fr. *incompatible*] **1 :** the quality or state of being incompatible **:** inability to function or exist in the presence of something else: as **a :** inability to exist in peaceful harmony; *esp* **:** lack of adjustment in marriage **b :** a relation between dignities or public offices such that proper and faithful performance of the duties and exercise of the powers of one is inconsistent with such performance and exercise in another on the part of the same individual **c** (1) **:** lack of interfertility between two plants following pollination (as from characteristics of the pollen) (2) **:** inability of stock and scion to unite successfully in a graft **d :** the exclusion in igneous rock crystallization under conditions of equilibrium of one member of a pair of minerals by the presence of the other member **2 incompatibilities** *pl* **:** mutually antagonistic things or qualities **:** INCOMPATIBLES ⟨the inherent *incompatibilities* of dog and cat⟩
¹**in·compatible** \"+\ *adj* [MF & ML; MF, fr. ML *incompatibilis*, fr. L *in-* ¹in- + ML *compatibilis* compatible — more at COMPATIBLE] **1 :** incapable of being held by one person at one time — used of offices, dignities, or benefices that would make mutually conflicting demands on a holder **2 a :** incapable of appearing or of being thought together or of entering into the same system, theory, or practice ⟨~ ideas⟩ **:** incapable of harmonious combination **:** INCONGRUOUS ⟨~ colors⟩ **:** incapable of harmonious association or of acting in accord **:** DISAGREEING ⟨~ persons⟩ **b** (1) *of drugs or medicaments* **:** unsuitable for use together because of chemical interaction or antagonistic physiological effects — compare SYNERGISTIC (2) *of blood or serum* **:** unsuitable for use in a particular transfusion because of the presence of agglutinins against the recipient's red blood cells **c** *in logic* (1) *of two propositions* **:** not both true — compare STROKE 14 (2) *of terms* **:** not consistently predicable of the same subject — compare ALTERNATIVE DENIAL **d** *of mathematical equations* **:** incapable of being satisfied by the same set of values for the unknowns **e :** incapable of blending into a stable homogeneous mixture — used esp. of solids or solutions ⟨ester gum is ~ with cellulose acetate when formulated into a lacquer —*Glossary of Industrial Coating Terms*⟩ — compare IMMISCIBLE **3** *obs* **:** INTOLERANT — **in·com·pat·i·ble·ness** \-nəs\ *n* -ES — **in·compatibly** \ˌin+\ *adv*
²**incompatible** *n* -S **:** one that is incompatible — usu. used in pl.
in·compensated \(ˈ)in+\ *adj* [¹*in-* + past part. of *compensate*] **:** lacking compensation; *esp* **:** lacking physiological compensation
in·compensation \(ˈ)in, ən+\ *n* [¹*in-* + *compensation*] **:** lack of physiological compensation ⟨cardiac ~⟩ — **in·compensatory** \ˌin+\ *adj*
in·competence \(ˈ)in, ən+\ *n* [F *incompétence*, fr. MF, fr. *in-* ¹in- + *compétence* — more at COMPETENCE] **:** the state or fact of being incompetent: as **a :** lack of physical, intellectual, or moral ability **:** INSUFFICIENCY, INADEQUACY ⟨his ~ was absolute⟩ **b :** lack of legal qualification or fitness ⟨the ~ of an intoxicated man to drive an automobile⟩ **c :** the inability of an organ to perform its function adequately ⟨aortic ~ may lead to enlargement of the heart⟩
in·competency \"+\ *n* [MF *incompétence* + E *-y*] **1 a :** the quality of being incompetent ⟨the ~ typical of idiots⟩ **b incompetencies** *pl* **:** incompetent acts or behavior ⟨the *incompetencies* of such immature executives⟩ **2 :** INCOMPETENCE **3 :** the absence of jurisdiction of a court or judge to determine a civil law case
¹**in·competent** \"+\ *adj* [MF, *incompétent*, fr. *in-* ¹in- + *compétent* — more at COMPETENT] **1 a :** lacking the qualities (as maturity, capacity, initiative, intelligence) necessary to effective independent action **b** (1) **:** lacking specific qualifications to perform a legal function or duty or exercise a legal right — often used without implication of any kind with respect to personal fitness; distinguished from *incapable* ⟨a wife is usually considered ~ to testify against her husband in a criminal case⟩ (2) **:** not acceptable in court because obtained from a legally incompetent source ⟨~ testimony⟩ ⟨~ evidence⟩ **:** INADMISSIBLE **c :** exhibiting or characterized by organic incompetence ⟨an ~ mitral valve⟩ **d :** inadequate to or unsuitable for a particular purpose expressed or implied ⟨certain genotypes are phenotypically ~⟩ ⟨an ~ system of government⟩ ⟨pipes ~ to carry a full head of steam⟩ **2 :** being or forming strata and rock structures that have not the rigidity or strength to transmit particular stresses but that crush or flow under them — **in·competently** \"+\ *adv*
²**incompetent** \"\ *n* -S **:** one that is incompetent: as **a :** a person incapable of managing his affairs because of mental deficiency or immaturity ⟨children and idiots are ~*s* in the eyes of the law⟩ **b :** one incapable of doing properly what is required (as in a particular position) ⟨~*s* in public office⟩
incompetible *adj* [¹*in-* + *competible*] *obs* **:** UNSUITABLE
in·com·plet·abil·i·ty \ˌinkəm,plēd·əˈbiləd·ē\ *n* -ES **:** the quality or state of being incompletable
in·com·plet·able \ˌinkəmˈplēd·əbəl\ *adj* [¹*in-* + *completable* capable of being completed, fr. *complete* + *-able*] **:** impossible to finish or bring to completion — **in·com·plet·able·ness** *n* -ES
in·complete \ˌin+\ *adj* [ME *incompleet*, fr. LL *incompletus*, fr. *in-* ¹in- + L *completus* complete — more at COMPLETE] **:** lacking a part or parts or not having all parts arranged in final or functional order **:** UNFINISHED, IMPERFECTED: as **a** *of a flower* **:** lacking one or more sets of floral organs — compare COMPLETE, DICLINOUS **b :** SYNCATEGOREMATIC **c** *of a fertilizer* **:** containing two but not all three of the fertilizing agents nitrogen, phosphorus, and potassium **d** *of a football pass* **:** not legally caught
incomplete antibody *n* **:** BLOCKING ANTIBODY
in·completed \ˌin+\ *adj* [¹*in-* + *completed*] **:** INCOMPLETE
in·com·plete·ly *adv* **:** in an incomplete manner or to an incomplete degree **:** not wholly, perfectly, or fully ⟨~ grown crops⟩ ⟨words ~ understood⟩
in·com·plete·ness *n* **:** the quality or state of being incomplete
incomplete pupa *n* **:** PUPA LIBERA

incomplete symbol *n* **:** a sign, word, or expression (as the quotation sign or the word *or*) that systematically contributes to the meaning of expressions in which it occurs but has no independent or separable meaning
in·completion \ˌin+\ *n* [¹*in-* + *completion*] **1 :** lack of completion **2 :** an incomplete pass in football
in·complex \(ˈ)in, ən+\ *adj* [ML *incomplexus*, fr. L *in-* ¹in- + *complexus*, past part. of *complecti* to entwine around, embrace — more at COMPLEX] **:** lacking complexity **:** SIMPLE
incompliable *adj* [¹*in-* + *compliable*] *obs* **:** UNCOMPLIANT
in·compliance *or* **in·compliancy** \ˌin+\ *n* [¹*in-* + *compliance, compliancy*] **:** the quality or state of being incompliant **:** OBSTINACY
in·compliant \"+\ *adj* [¹*in-* + *compliant*] **1 :** lacking compliance **:** not cooperative and yielding **2** *of a material thing* **:** lacking pliability **:** STIFF, RESISTANT — **in·compliantly** \"+\ *adv*
in·complicate \(ˈ)in, ən+\ *adj* [¹*in-* + *complicate*] **:** SIMPLE, UNCOMPLICATED
incomplying *adj* [¹*in-* + pres. part. of *comply*] *obs* **:** free from compliance or yielding
incomposed *adj* [¹*in-* + *composed*] **1** *obs* **:** lacking calmness and composure **:** DISTURBED, DISORDERED **2** *obs* **:** not made up of diverse elements **:** SIMPLE
in·composite \(ˈ)in, ən+\ *adj* [L *incompositus*, fr. *in-* ¹in- + *compositus*, past part. of *componere* to put together — more at COMPOSE] **1 :** lacking separable or distinguishable parts **2** *of a number* **:** PRIME
in·compossibility \ˌin+\ *n* **:** the quality or state of being incompossible
in·compossible \ˌin+\ *adj* [ML *incompossibilis*, fr. L *in-* ¹in- + ML *compossibilis* compossible — more at COMPOSSIBLE] **:** not mutually possible **:** INCONSISTENT, INCOMPATIBLE
in·comprehending \(ˈ)in, ən+\ *adj* [¹*in-* + *comprehending*] **:** lacking comprehension or lacking in comprehension — **in·comprehendingly** \"+\ *adv*
in·comprehensibility \(ˈ)in, ən+\ *n* **:** the quality or state of being incomprehensible
¹**in·comprehensible** \(ˈ)in, ən+\ *adj* [ME, fr. L *incomprehensibilis*, fr. *in-* ¹in- + *comprehensibilis* comprehensible — more at COMPREHENSIBLE] **1** *archaic* **:** having or subject to no limits **:** ILLIMITABLE ⟨an infinite and ~ substance —Richard Hooker⟩ **2 a :** impossible to comprehend **:** lying above or beyond the reach of the human mind ⟨the ~ mysteries of creation⟩ **b :** being beyond the powers of comprehension of a particular mind **:** UNINTELLIGIBLE ⟨an ~ subject to him⟩ **c :** being beyond ordinary comprehension **:** UNFATHOMABLE ⟨~ moods⟩ ⟨a whimsical ~ person⟩ **3** *obs* **:** impossible to catch or hold — **in·com·pre·hen·si·ble·ness** \-nəs\ *n* -ES — **in·comprehensibly** \ˌin+\ *adv*
²**incomprehensible** \"\ *n* -S **:** something incomprehensible
in·comprehension \(ˈ)in, ən+\ *n* [¹*in-* + *comprehension*] **:** lack of comprehension or understanding ⟨their ~ of violence, their terror of social upheaval —A.M.Schlesinger b.1917⟩
in·comprehensive \"+\ *adj* [¹*in-* + *comprehensive*] **1 :** lacking comprehensiveness; *esp* **:** deficient in mental grasp **2** *obs* **:** INCOMPREHENSIBLE — **in·comprehensively** \"+\ *adv*
in·compressibility \ˌin+\ *n* **:** the quality or state of being incompressible
in·compressible \"+\ *adj* [¹*in-* + *compressible*] **:** incapable of being compressed; *broadly* **:** resisting compression — **in·com·press·ible·ness** \-nəs\ *n* -ES — **in·com·press·ibly** \-əblē, -li\ *adv*
incompt *adj* [L *incomptus*, fr. *in-* ¹in- + *comptus*, past part. of *comere* to adorn — more at COMPT] *obs* **:** UNKEMPT, UNPOLISHED
in·computable \ˌin+\ *adj* [¹*in-* + *computable*] **:** greater than can be computed or enumerated **:** very great — **in·com·put·ably** \-əblē, -li\ *adv*
incomunicado *var of* INCOMMUNICADO
in·concealable \ˌin+\ *adj* [¹*in-* + *concealable*] **:** impossible to hide
in·conceivability \ˌin+\ *n* **1 :** the quality or state of being inconceivable **2 :** something inconceivable
in·conceivable \ˌin+\ *adj* [¹*in-* + *conceivable*] **1 :** falling outside the limit of what can be comprehended, accepted as true or real, or tolerated: as **a :** impossible to comprehend in the absence of actual experience or knowledge **:** UNIMAGINABLE ⟨color is ~ to those born blind⟩ **b :** impossible to entertain in the mind **:** UNTHINKABLE ⟨it is ~ that a thing can both be and not be⟩ **c :** impossible to accept as an article of faith **:** INCREDIBLE, UNBELIEVABLE ⟨it is ~ that God should wantonly inflict suffering⟩ **2 :** hard to believe or believe in ⟨it is ~ that such losses should continue⟩ ⟨~ losses of revenue⟩ — **in·conceivableness** \"+\ *n* — **in·conceivably** \"+\ *adv*
inconciliable *adj* [¹*in-* + *conciliable*] *obs* **:** IRRECONCILABLE
in·concinnity \ˌin+\ *n* [L *inconcinnitas*, fr. *in-* ¹in- + *concinnitas* concinnity — more at CONCINNITY] **:** lack of suitability or congruity **:** awkward or unsuitable form or character
in·concinnous \"+\ *adj* [L *inconcinnus*, fr. *in-* ¹in- + *concinnus* concinnous — more at CONCINNITY] *archaic* **:** marked by inconcinnity
inconcludent *adj* [¹*in-* + *concludent*] *obs* **:** INCONCLUSIVE
in·con·clu·si·ble \ˌinkənˈklüzəbəl\ *adj* [¹*in-* + obs. *conclusible*, fr. L *conclusus* (past part. of *concludere* to conclude) + E *-ible* — more at CONCLUDE] **:** impossible to bring to an end ⟨an ~ argument⟩
in·conclusive \ˌin+\ *adj* [¹*in-* + *conclusive*] **:** leading to no conclusion or to no definite result, decision, or end ⟨such ~ arguments⟩ ⟨a long and ~ war⟩ — **in·conclusively** \"+\ *adv* — **in·conclusiveness** \"+\ *n*
inconcoct *or* **inconcocted** *adj* [*inconcoct* fr. ¹*in-* + obs. *concoct* digested, matured, fr. L *concoctus*, past part. of *concoquere* to boil together; *inconcocted* fr. ¹*in-* + *concocted*, past part. of *concoct* — more at CONCOCT] *obs* **:** not matured **:** UNDIGESTED — **inconcoction** *n*, *obs*
in·concrete \(ˈ)in, ən+\ *adj* [LL *inconcretus*, fr. L *in-* ¹in- + *concretus*, past part. of *concrescere* to grow together — more at CONCRETE] **:** vague and diffuse **:** ABSTRACT
in·condensable \ˌin+\ *adj* [¹*in-* + *condensable*] **:** incapable of being condensed
in·con·dite \ənˈkändət, -,dīt\ *adj* [L *inconditus*, fr. *in-* ¹in- + *conditus*, past part. of *condere* to put together, fr. *com-* + *-dere* to put — more at DO] **1 :** badly organized or put together **:** lacking finish or polished form — used chiefly of an utterance ⟨valuable factual information obscured by turgid ~ prose⟩ **2 :** lacking in manners **:** CRUDE, UNPOLISHED
in·conducive \ˌin+\ *adj* [¹*in-* + *conducive*] **:** not conducive **:** having no tendency toward
In·co·nel \ˈiŋkə,nel\ *trademark* — used for an alloy of approximately 80 percent nickel, 14 percent chromium, and 6 percent iron
in·conformable \ˌin+\ *adj* [¹*in-* + *conformable*] **:** failing or unwilling to conform ⟨the rebels were ~ to all compromise⟩ ⟨conduct wholly ~ to our principles⟩ — **in·conformably** \"+\ *adv*
in·conformity \"+\ *n* [¹*in-* + *conformity*] **:** lack of conformity **:** NONCONFORMITY
in·confused \ˌin+\ *adj* [¹*in-* + *confused*] **:** free from confusion **:** having the elements distinct **:** CLEAR-CUT — **in·confusedly** \"+\ *adv*
in·congenerous \"+\ *adj* [¹*in-* + *congenerous*] *archaic* **:** not belonging to the same group or kind
in·congruence \(ˈ)in, ən+\ *n* [LL *incongruentia*, fr. L *incongruent-, incongruens* + *-ia* -y] **:** INCONGRUITY
in·congruent \"+\ *adj* [L *incongruent-, incongruens*, fr. *in-* ¹in- + *congruent-, congruens*, pres. part. of *congruere* to come together, coincide, agree — more at CONGRUOUS] **1 :** lacking congruity **:** INCONGRUOUS, UNSUITABLE **2 :** not corresponding in shape and curvature — used of opposed articular surfaces in joints **3 :** relating to the melting point of a molecular compound at which it decomposes into a new solid phase and a liquid of different composition — compare CONGRUENT 3
in·congruently \"+\ *adv* **:** in an incongruent manner
in·congruity \ˌin+\ *n* [MF or LL; MF *incongruité*, fr. LL *incongruitat-, incongruitas*, fr. *incongruus* + L *-itat-, -itas* -ity] **1 :** the quality or state of being incongruous **:** lack of congruity **:** INCONSISTENCY, INHARMONY, DISAGREEMENT **2 :** something that is incongruous **:** a thing that lacks harmonious or rational relation to its environment ⟨Victorian *incongruities* in a typically mid-20th-century setting⟩

in·congruous \(ˈ)in, ən+\ *adj* [LL *incongruus*, fr. L *in-* ¹in- + *congruus* congruous — more at CONGRUOUS] **:** lacking congruity: as **a :** characterized by lack of harmony, consistency, or compatibility with one another ⟨~ colors⟩ ⟨~ desires⟩ **b :** characterized by disagreement or lack of conformity with something ⟨conduct ~ with avowed principles⟩ **c :** characterized by inconsistency or inharmony of its own parts or qualities ⟨an ~ story⟩ **d :** characterized by lack of propriety or suitableness ⟨~ manners⟩ — **in·congruously** \"+\ *adv* — **in·congruousness** \"+\ *n*
in·conjunct \(ˈ)in, ən+\ *adj* [LL *inconjunctus* unconnected, fr. L *in-* ¹in- + *conjunctus*, past part. of *conjungere* to join together — more at CONJOIN] *archaic, of celestial bodies or zodiacal signs* **:** lacking conjunction
in·connected \ˌin+\ *adj* [¹*in-* + *connected*] **:** DISCONNECTED ⟨halting ~ ideas⟩
in·connection \"+\ *n* [¹*in-* + *connection*] *archaic* **:** DISCONNECTION
in·con·nu \ˌinkəˈn(y)ü, ˈiŋk-; ˈaⁿkəˈnüe\ *n* -S [F, fr. *in-* ¹in- + *connu*, past part. of *connaître* to know, fr. L *cognoscere* — more at COGNITION] **1 :** an unknown person **:** STRANGER **2 :** a large oily soft-fleshed food fish (*Stenodus mackenzii*) related to the whitefish and found in Alaska, northwestern Canada, and adjoining Siberian waters
in·conquerable \(ˈ)in, ən+\ *adj* [¹*in-* + *conquerable*] **:** UNCONQUERABLE
in·conscience \(ˈ)in, ən+\ *n* **:** the quality or state of being inconscient
in·conscient \"+\ *adj* [prob. fr. F, fr. *in-* ¹in- + *conscient*, fr. L *conscient-, consciens*, pres. part. of *conscire* to know, be conscious — more at CONSCIENCE] **1 a :** lacking consciousness **:** MINDLESS ⟨inanimate ~ things —Percy Winner⟩ **b :** lacking full awareness **:** ABSTRACTED ⟨he had passed, ~, full gaze the wide-banded irises —Ezra Pound⟩ **2 :** not involving or based on the action of consciousness ⟨holding creation to be the outcome of ~ natural laws⟩ — **in·consciently** \"+\ *adv*
in·con·scio·na·ble \(ˈ)inˈkänch(ə)nəbəl, ənˈk-\ *adj* [¹*in-* + *conscionable*] **:** UNCONSCIONABLE
in·conscious \(ˈ)in+\ *adj* [LL *inconscius*, fr. L *in-* ¹in- + *conscius* conscious — more at CONSCIOUS] **:** UNCONSCIOUS
in·consecutive \ˌin+\ *adj* [¹*in-* + *consecutive*] **:** lacking in sequence and order ⟨formless ~ essays he produced by grouping . . . a miscellany of scattered reflections —*New Yorker*⟩ **:** not arranged in order of occurrence ⟨the entries in the Chronicle are ~ and some of them must have been written appreciably later than the events which they relate —F.M.Stenton⟩ — **in·consecutively** \"+\ *adv* — **in·con·sec·u·tive·ness** \-ivnəs\ *n*
in·consequence \(ˈ)in, ən+\ *n* [L *inconsequentia*, fr. *in-* ¹in- + *consequentia* consequence — more at CONSEQUENCE] **1 :** the quality or state of being inconsequent: as **a :** lack of just or logical inference or argument **:** ILLOGICALITY **b :** lack of sequence **:** INCONSECUTIVENESS, IRRELEVANCE **2 :** character or mood marked by inconsequence ⟨Sterne propagates his ~, while his suavity and ease of style die with him —J.L.Lowes⟩ ⟨the ~*s* of the Boston mind —Henry Adams⟩
in·consequent \"+\ *adj* [LL *inconsequent-, inconsequens*, fr. L *in-* ¹in- + *consequent-, consequens* consequent — more at CONSEQUENT] **1 a :** lacking logical order or ordered sequence of thought or reasoning ⟨it is unfortunate that such a significant book should be so slipshod and ~ —*Saturday Rev.*⟩ **:** ILLOGICAL, INCONSISTENT ⟨a premise based on ~ reasoning⟩ **b :** following no natural sequence **:** INCONSECUTIVE ⟨the string of ~ statements to which she had treated them —Ngaio Marsh⟩ **2 :** marked or characterized by a lack of logic or relevancy ⟨these ~ fellows who would lower taxes but increase public expenditure⟩ **3 :** of no consequence **:** lacking worth, significance, or importance ⟨the gay, debauched, quite ~ lad was managed like a puppet —Hilaire Belloc⟩ ⟨futile ~ dreams⟩ — **in·consequently** \"+\ *adv*
in·con·se·quen·tia \ˌin,kän(t)səˈkwench(ē)ə\ *n pl* [LL, neut. pl. of *inconsequens*] **:** matters of no grave moment or significance **:** TRIVIA ⟨the ~ of daily life⟩
in·consequential \(ˈ)in, ən+\ *adj* **1 :** not regularly following from the premises; *broadly* **:** IRRELEVANT **2 :** INCONSEQUENT 3 — **in·consequentiality** \"+\ *n* — **in·consequentially** \"+\ *adv*
in·considerable \ˌin+\ *adj* [MF, fr. *in-* ¹in- + *considerable*, fr. ML *considerabilis* — more at CONSIDERABLE] **1** *obs* **:** too great to be considered or reckoned **2 a :** unworthy of consideration **:** TRIVIAL ⟨their duties were ~⟩ ⟨earned and spent a not ~ amount of money⟩ ⟨exercised no ~ influence⟩ **b :** SMALL, PETTY ⟨passed his life in an ~ village⟩ ⟨~ size⟩ **3** *obs* **:** INCONSIDERATE, CARELESS — **in·con·sid·er·a·ble·ness** \-nəs\ *n* -ES — **in·considerably** \ˌin+\ *adv*
in·con·sid·er·a·cy \ˌinkənˈsid(ə)rəsē\ *n* -ES [fr. *inconsiderate*, after such pairs as E *accurate: accuracy*] *archaic* **:** INCONSIDERATENESS
¹**in·considerate** \ˌin+\ *adj* [L *inconsideratus*, fr. *in-* ¹in- + *consideratus*, past part. of *considerare* to consider — more at CONSIDER] **1 :** not adequately considered **:** ILL-ADVISED, RASH, PRECIPITATE ⟨hasty and ~ conclusions⟩ **2 a :** acting or tending to act without due or reasonable deliberation **:** HEEDLESS, THOUGHTLESS, CARELESS ⟨some ~ person repeats like a parrot that if you gave everybody the same amount of money —G.B.Shaw⟩ ⟨that ~, wandering, featherheaded race —L.P.Smith⟩ ⟨exploring the carving with ~ fingers⟩ **b :** failing in regard for the rights or feelings of others **:** indifferent to propriety or courtesy ⟨a gross ~ man⟩ ⟨shockingly ~ behavior⟩ **3** *obs* **:** not held in consideration or esteem — **in·considerately** \"+\ *adv* — **in·con·sid·er·ate·ness** *n* -ES
²**inconsiderate** \"\ *n* -S **:** an inconsiderate person
in·consideration \ˌin+\ *n* [LL *inconsideration-, inconsideratio*, fr. L *inconsideratus* + *-ion-, -io* -ion] **:** the quality or state of being inconsiderate **:** INCONSIDERATENESS
in·considered \ˌin+\ *adj* [¹*in-* + *considered*] **:** INCONSIDERATE 1
in·consistency *also* **in·consistence** \ˌin+\ *n* [¹*in-* + *consistency, consistence*] **1 :** the quality or state of being inconsistent: as **a :** lack of agreement, consonance, harmony, or compatibility **b :** lack of stability, uniformity, or steadiness **2 a :** something that is inconsistent **b :** an instance of inconsistent character or condition
in·consistent \ˌin+\ *adj* [¹*in-* + *consistent*] **1 :** lacking consistency **:** INCOMPATIBLE, INCONGRUOUS, INHARMONIOUS: as **a** *of propositions, ideas, beliefs* **:** so related that both or all cannot be true or containing parts so related ⟨~ statements⟩ **b :** so related to something premised or understood that it cannot be true if what is thus assumed is true ⟨an ~ conclusion⟩ **2** *of a person* **a :** incoherent or illogical in thought or actions **:** believing incompatibles or acting in incongruous ways **b :** logically inconsequent **:** lacking in continuity of belief or purpose; *broadly* **:** INCONSTANT, CHANGEABLE, FICKLE **3** *of aesthetic relations* **:** not handled or developed so as to form a harmonious whole **:** INCONSONANT ⟨~ composition⟩ **4 :** INCONGRUOUS, INCOMPATIBLE, IRRECONCILABLE — used of immaterial qualities ⟨wisdom is not ~ with mirth⟩ **5 :** INCOMPATIBLE 2d — **in·consistently** \"+\ *adv* — **in·con·sist·ent·ness** *n* -ES
in·consolable \ˌin+\ *adj* [L *inconsolabilis*, fr. *in-* ¹in- + *consolabilis* able to be comforted, fr. *consolari* to console + *-abilis* -able — more at CONSOLE] **:** incapable of being consoled **:** grieved beyond comfort **:** utterly disconsolate — **in·con·sol·able·ness** \-nəs\ *n* -ES — **in·con·sol·ably** \-əblē, -li\ *adv*
in·consonance \(ˈ)in+\ *n* **:** lack of consonance or harmony of sound, action, or thought **:** DISAGREEMENT
in·consonant \"+\ *adj* [¹*in-* + *consonant*] **:** not consonant or agreeing **:** INCONSISTENT, DISCORDANT
in·conspicuous \ˌin+\ *adj* [L *inconspicuus*, fr. *in-* ¹in- + *conspicuus* conspicuous — more at CONSPICUOUS] **1** *obs* **:** INVISIBLE **2** *obs* **:** not obvious to the mental eye **:** INDISCERNIBLE, IMPERCEPTIBLE **3 :** not readily noticeable **:** hardly discernible **:** not prominent or striking — **in·conspicuously** \"+\ *adv* — **in·conspicuousness** \"+\ *n*
inconstance *n* [ME *inconstaunce*, fr. MF *inconstance*, fr. L *inconstantia*] *obs* **:** INCONSTANCY
in·constancy \(ˈ)in+\ *n* [L *inconstantia*, fr. *inconstant-*,

inconstans + *-ia* -y] **1 :** the quality or state of being inconstant **:** lack of constancy: as **a :** CHANGEABLENESS, FICKLENESS **b :** lack of uniformity **:** VARIABILITY **c** *obs* **:** INCONSISTENCY **2 :** an instance of changeableness or of variability

[1]**in·constant** \"+\ *adj* [ME, fr. MF, fr. L *inconstant-, inconstans,* fr. *in-* [1]in- + *constant-, constans* constant — more at CONSTANT] **1 :** marked by lack of constancy **:** likely to change frequently often without apparent or cogent reason **:** given to change of character, inclination, purpose, or location ⟨unjust I may have been . . . but never ~ —Jane Austen⟩ **2** *obs* **:** INCONSISTENT

syn FICKLE, CAPRICIOUS, MERCURIAL, UNSTABLE: INCONSTANT suggests a tendency to frequent change, often without good reason ⟨for people seldom knew what they would be, young men especially, they are so amazingly changeable and *inconstant* —Jane Austen⟩; it is often used in reference to persons incapable of steadfastness in love or in reference to changeable climatic and meteorological developments ⟨supposing now . . . this lover of yours was not the sort of man we all take him to be, and that he was to turn out false, or *inconstant* —Anthony Trollope⟩ ⟨places where the soil was fertile but the rainfall uncertain and the rivers shallow and *inconstant* —A.M. Schlesinger b.1888⟩ FICKLE intensifies notions of pointless, even perverse, changeability and incapacity for steadfastness ⟨she is *fickle!* How she turns from one face to another face — and smiles into them all —Edna S. V. Millay⟩ ⟨but bitter experience soon taught him that lordly patrons are *fickle* and their favor not to be relied on —Aldous Huxley⟩ ⟨the next morning was gay with *fickle* sun-showers; it was a harlequin day, a strayed reveler from April —Elinor Wylie⟩ CAPRICIOUS is less derogatory than FICKLE but suggests motivation by caprice, whim, or fancy making for unexpected change ⟨he seemed heartless and *capricious*, as ready to drop you as he had been to take you up —George du Maurier⟩ ⟨the more *capricious* incidence of sexual passion —Lewis Mumford⟩ ⟨the *capricious* severity of a mere despot —J.R.Green⟩ ⟨a *capricious* and malevolent race of savages —Bernard De Voto⟩ MERCURIAL in this sense is likely to suggest changeability in mood, esp. rapid rise from discouragement to mirth or elation, or to suggest a versatility of gifts ⟨Allnutt's *mercurial* spirits could hardly help rising under the influence of Rose's persistent optimism —C.S. Forester⟩ ⟨*mercurial*, euphoric, he could blaze into hectic social events and become a rather too brash and boyish "life and soul of the party" —*Times Lit. Supp.*⟩ UNSTABLE, a less colorful word, indicates an incapacity to remain stable or steady, with many changes and fluctuations ⟨of some meddling, bold fanatic, mind *unstable*, weird, erratic —Sophia A. Jamieson⟩ ⟨the occupation [of mining] in general is an *unstable* one —Lewis Mumford⟩ ⟨the blots of shade and flakes of light upon the countenances of the group changed shape and position endlessly. All was *unstable*, quivering as leaves, evanescent as lightning —Thomas Hardy⟩

[2]**inconstant** \"\ *n* **:** one that is inconstant

in·con·stant·ly *adv* **:** in an inconstant manner **:** without constancy

in·con·stant·ness *n* -ES **:** the quality or state of being inconstant

in·consumable \¦in+\ *adj* [[1]*in-* + *consumable*] **1 :** not capable of being consumed or destroyed (as by fire) **2 :** satisfying human wants without being directly consumed in so doing ⟨machinery is commonly thought of as ~⟩ — **in·con·sum·ably** \-blē, -bli\ *adv*

inconsumptible *adj* [[1]*in-* + *consumptible* capable of being consumed, fr. L *consumptus* (past part. of *consumere* to consume) + E *-ible* — more at CONSUME] *obs* **:** INCONSUMABLE

in-contact \(ˈ)=ˌ=ˌ=\ *n* [fr. the phrase *in contact*] **:** an individual that has lived in close association with another and has thereby been exposed to infection with a disease with which that other is affected

in·con·tam·i·na·ble \¦inkən¦tam(ə)nəbəl\ *adj* [LL *incontaminabilis,* fr. L *in-* [1]in- + LL *contaminabilis* capable of contamination, fr. L *contaminare* to contaminate + *-abilis* -able — more at CONTAMINATE] **:** impossible to contaminate

in·con·tam·i·nate \-mənət\ *adj* [L *incontaminatus,* fr. *in-* [1]in- + *contaminatus,* past part. of *contaminare* to contaminate] **:** free from contamination **:** PURE, UNDEFILED

in·con·test·abil·i·ty \ˌinkən¦testəˈbiləd.ē\ *n* -ES **:** the quality or state of being incontestable

in·con·test·able *or* **in·con·test·ible** \¦inkən¦testəbəl\ *adj* [*incontestable* fr. F, fr. *in-* [1]in- + *contestable* capable of being contested, fr. *contester* to contest + *-able; incontestible,* alter. of *incontestable* — more at CONTEST] **1 :** not subject to being disputed, called in question, or controverted ⟨~ evidence⟩ **:** offering no grounds for doubt **:** INDUBITABLE, UNDOUBTED ⟨an ~ genius⟩ **2 :** being such that payment of claims cannot be disputed by a life insurance company for any cause except nonpayment of premiums or other reason specifically stated in the contract when the contract has been in force for a stipulated period (as one or two years) and when an insurable interest existed at its inception — **in·con·test·able·ness** *n* -ES

incontestable clause *n* **:** a clause in a life insurance policy providing the conditions under which the policy is incontestable

in·con·test·a·bly \-blē, -bli\ *adv* **:** in an incontestable manner or to an incontestable degree or level **:** CERTAINLY, INDUBITABLY

incontested *adj* [[1]*in-* + past part. of *contest*] *obs* **:** UNDISPUTED

in·continence \(ˈ)in, ən+\ *n* [ME, fr. MF or L; MF, fr. L *incontinentia,* fr. *incontinent-, incontinens* + *-ia* -y] **1 :** lack of restraint **:** inability or disinclination to resist desire or impulse; *esp* **:** SALACIOUSNESS, DISSOLUTENESS ⟨fell into a life of sexual and alcoholic ~⟩ **2 :** inability to retain a bodily discharge (as urine) voluntarily

in·continency \"+\ *n* [ME, fr. L *incontinentia*] **1 :** INCONTINENCE **2 :** an act of incontinence; *esp* **:** illicit sexual intercourse — usu. used in pl. ⟨the record of his manifold *incontinencies*⟩

in·continent \"+\ *adj* [ME, fr. MF or L; MF, fr. L *incontinent-, incontinens,* fr. *in-* [1]in- + *continent-, continens* continent — more at CONTINENT] **1 :** marked by incontinence **:** lacking control **:** UNRESTRAINED ⟨the thunderous drumming ~ downpour —Gertrude Diamant⟩; *esp* **:** sexually dissolute ⟨the ~ man's evil appetite —J.E.Hankins⟩ **2 :** unable to retain a bodily discharge (as urine) voluntarily

[1]**in·continently** \"+\ *also* **incontinent** *adv* [*incontinently* fr. MF *incontinent* + E *-ly; incontinent* fr. ME, fr. MF, fr. LL *in continenti*] **1 :** at once **:** without delay **:** IMMEDIATELY ⟨~ turned and fled⟩ **2 :** with unceremonious haste **:** PELL-MELL ⟨fled ~ until I reached a herd's cottage —John Buchan⟩

[2]**incontinently** \"\ *adv* [*incontinent* (adj.) + *-ly*] **:** in an incontinent or unrestrained manner: as **a :** LEWDLY, LOOSELY **b :** without due or reasonable consideration ⟨making the speech he had ~ promised⟩

in·continuous \¦in+\ *adj* [[1]*in-* + *continuous*] **:** not continuous

in·controllable \"+\ *adj* [[1]*in-* + *controllable*] **:** UNCONTROLLABLE

in·controllably \"+\ *adv* **:** UNCONTROLLABLY

in·controvertible \(ˌ)in, ən+\ *adj* [[1]*in-* + *controvertible*] **:** not open to question **:** INDISPUTABLE, CERTAIN ⟨~ evidence⟩ ⟨it seemed ~ that he had deceived his friend⟩ — **in·contro·vertibly** \"+\ *adv*

in con·tu·ma·ci·am \ˌin,kȯntəˈmākē,äm\ *adv* [L, lit., in contumacy] **:** in contempt of or in disobedience to an order or summons of a court — used chiefly in ecclesiastical law of one who has refused to submit to or appear in a court and who is thereupon convicted or condemned in his absence

[1]**in·convenience** \¦in+\ *n* [ME, fr. LL *inconvenientia,* fr. L *inconvenient-, inconveniens* + *-ia* -y] **1 :** the quality or state of being inconvenient: as **a** *obs* **:** INCONGRUITY, UNSUITABLENESS, IMPROPRIETY **b** *obs* **:** HARM, MISCHIEF, MISFORTUNE, TROUBLE; *also* **:** an injury esp. when general or public as distinguished from an injury to one or a few **c :** the quality or state of being unsuited or unadapted to personal needs or comfort **:** DISADVANTAGE, DISCOMFORT ⟨the ~ of his quarters⟩ **2 :** something that is inconvenient **:** something that gives trouble, embarrassment, or uneasiness **:** something that disturbs or impedes **:** DISADVANTAGE, HANDICAP ⟨loss of this extra income was a serious ~⟩ ⟨found the daily trip an ~⟩

[2]**inconvenience** \"\ *vt* **:** to subject to inconvenience **:** INCOMMODE

in·conveniency \¦in+\ *n* [LL *inconvenientia*] **:** INCONVENIENCE

[1]**in·convenient** \"+\ *adj* [ME, fr. MF, fr. L *inconvenient-, inconveniens,* fr. *in-* [1]in + *convenient-, conveniens,* convenient — more at CONVENIENT] **1** *obs* **a :** not agreeing **:** INCONGRUOUS, IRRATIONAL **b :** not suitable **:** UNFIT **c :** morally unbecoming **:** IMPROPER **2 :** not convenient **:** giving trouble, uneasiness, or annoyance **:** DISADVANTAGEOUS, INOPPORTUNE ⟨an ~ house⟩ ⟨a most ~ arrangement⟩ — **in·con·ve·nient·ness** *n* -ES — **in·conveniently** \"+\ *adv*

[2]**inconvenient** *n* -S [ME, fr. *inconvenient,* adj.] *obs* **:** something inconvenient: as **a :** INCONGRUITY, INCONSISTENCY, ABSURDITY **b :** an unbecoming or improper act **c :** INCONVENIENCE

in·conversable \¦in+\ *adj* [[1]*in-* + *conversable*] **:** UNCOMMUNICATIVE, RESERVED

in·conversant \(ˌ)in, ən+\ *adj* [[1]*in-* + *conversant*] **:** lacking experience in or familiarity with

in·convertibility \¦in+\ *n* **:** the quality or state of being inconvertible

in·convertible \"+\ *adj* [prob. fr. LL *inconvertibilis,* fr. L *in-* [1]in- + *convertibilis* changeable — more at CONVERTIBLE] **:** not capable of being changed into or exchanged for something else ⟨the alchemists were unwilling to accept the ~ nature of elemental metals⟩: **a** *of paper money* **:** not exchangeable on demand for specie **b** *of a currency* **:** not exchangeable for a foreign currency — **in·con·vert·ibly** \-əblē, -li\ *adv*

in·convincible \¦in+\ *adj* [prob. fr. LL *inconvincibilis,* fr. L *in-* [1]in- + *convincibilis* able to be convinced, fr. L *convincere* to convince + *-ibilis* -ible — more at CONVINCE] **:** incapable of being convinced

incony *adj* [origin unknown] *obs* **:** PRETTY

in·cooperative \¦in+\ *adj* [[1]*in-* + *cooperative*] **:** lacking in cooperation or in ability or will to cooperate ⟨the patient's family was wholly ~⟩ **:** UNCOOPERATIVE

in·coordinate *also* **in·coordinated** \"+\ *adj* [[1]*in-* + *coordinate, coordinated*] **:** lacking coordination **:** not coordinate

in·coordination \¦in+\ *n* [ISV [1]*in-* + *coordination*] **:** lack of coordination; *esp* **:** lack of coordination of muscular movements resulting from loss of voluntary control and usu. associated with disease — compare ATAXIA

in·coronate *also* **in·coronated** \ən+\ *adj* [*incoronate* fr. ML *incoronatus,* past part. of *incoronare* to crown, fr. L *in-* [2]in- + *coronare* to crown; *incoronated* fr. [2]*in-* + *coronated* — more at CROWN] **:** CROWNED, CORONATED

in·coronation \"+\ *n* [ML *incoronation-, incoronatio,* fr. *incoronatus* + L *-ion-, -io* -ion] **:** CORONATION

in·corporable \ən'kȯ(r)p(ə)rəbəl\ *adj* [L *incorporare* + E *-able*] **:** capable of being incorporated

in·corporal \(ˈ)in, ən+\ *adj* [L *incorporalis,* fr. *in-* [1]in- + *corporalis* corporal — more at CORPORAL] **:** INCORPOREAL

[1]**in·cor·po·rate** \ən'kȯ(r)pə,rāt, *usu* -ād.+V\ *vb* -ED/-ING/-S [ME *incorporaten,* fr. LL *incorporatus,* past part. of *incorporare,* fr. L *in-* [2]in- + *corpor-, corpus* body — more at MIDRIFF] *vt* **1 a :** to unite with or introduce into something already existent usu. so as to form an indistinguishable whole that cannot be restored to the previously separate elements without damage ⟨the complex processes by which food is *incorporated* with living tissues⟩ ⟨the committee recommended that we ~ several new rules into the bylaws⟩ **b :** to admit to membership in a corporation; *esp* **:** to admit (a person) to the rank, status, and privileges of an advanced degree at a British university on the basis of possession of a like degree earned at another institution **2 a :** to combine (ingredients) into one consistent whole **:** unite intimately (as into a new substance or presentation) ⟨*incorporated* his ideas in a monograph on classical philology⟩ **:** blend, combine, or mingle thoroughly to form a homogeneous product ⟨mechanically *incorporating* the materials into a smooth uniform paste⟩ **b :** to bring together in an association; *specif* **:** to form into a corporation recognized by law as an entity and having particular functions, rights, duties, and liabilities **3 :** to give material form to **:** EMBODY ~ *vi* **1 :** to become unified with something into a composite whole ⟨these ideas gradually *incorporated* with existing religious beliefs to form a new philosophy⟩ **2 a** *archaic* **:** to mingle together so as to form a new whole **b :** to form or become a corporation ⟨they will ~ as soon as they have a little more capital⟩

[2]**in·cor·po·rate** \ən'kȯrp(ə)rət, -ō(ə)p-, *usu* -əd.+V\ *adj* [ME *incorporat,* fr. LL *incorporatus,* past part.] **1 :** made one body or united in one body **:** intimately united or blended **:** EMBODIED ⟨the doctrines ~ in scriptural writings⟩ **2 a :** formed into a corporation **:** INCORPORATED ⟨an ~ municipality⟩ **b** *obs, of people* **:** associated as members of a corporation

[3]**in·cor·po·rate** \(ˈ)in¦kȯrp(ə)rət, ən'k-\ *adj* [LL *incorporatus,* fr. L *in-* [1]in- + *corporatus,* past part. of *corporare* to make into a body — more at CORPORATE] *archaic* **:** INCORPOREAL, SPIRITUAL

incorporated *adj* **:** united in one body **:** formed into a corporation **:** made a legal entity

in·cor·po·rat·ed·ness *n* -ES **:** the quality or state of being incorporated **:** INCORPORATION

incorporated territory *n* **:** a portion of the domain of the U.S. that does not constitute and is not a part of any state but that is considered a part of the U.S. proper and is entitled to all the benefits of the Constitution that are not specifically reserved to the states ⟨Arizona, Oklahoma, and New Mexico were all *incorporated territories* before attaining statehood⟩

incorporating *adj* **1 :** serving to incorporate **:** uniting in one body **2** *of language or grammar* **:** POLYSYNTHETIC

incorporating union *n* **:** a union of two or more states into one political whole ⟨the association of the several sovereign states of Germany into the German Empire can be considered an *incorporating union*⟩

in·cor·po·ra·tion \(ˌ)in,kȯ(r)pəˈrāshən, ən-\ *n* [ME *incorporacioun, incorporacioun,* fr. LL *incorporation-, incorporatio,* fr. *incorporatus* (past part. of *incorporare* to incorporate) + L *-ion-, -io* -ion — more at INCORPORATE] **1 :** an act of incorporating or the state of being incorporated: as **a :** a union of something with an existing whole into a new intimate and usu. permanent new whole ⟨~ of plasticizer with a resin⟩ ⟨~ of the conquered territory into the empire⟩ **b :** a union of diverse things into a whole **:** intimate mingling **:** COMBINATION, SYNTHESIS ⟨the ~ of these rough notes into a coherent report⟩ **c :** a creation of a corporation or esp. of a legal corporate entity **d :** INCARNATION, EMBODIMENT **2 a** *obs* **:** a charter of incorporation **b :** an incorporated association or entity **:** CORPORATION **3 :** the process of word and sentence formation characteristic of incorporating languages

incorporation by reference : a doctrine in law: the terms of a contemporaneous or earlier writing, instrument, or document capable of being identified can be made an actual part of another writing, instrument, or document by referring to, identifying, and adopting the former as part of the latter

in·cor·po·ra·tive \ən'kȯ(r)pə,rād.iv, -p(ə)rə|, |t|, |ēv *also* |əv\ *adj* **:** incorporating or tending to incorporate: as **a** *of language* **:** AGGLUTINATIVE, POLYSYNTHETIC **b** *of a state* **:** growing by taking over and incorporating adjacent territories ⟨the Russian Empire was a typical ~ state⟩

in·cor·po·ra·tor \-pə,rād.ə(r), -ātə-\ *n* **:** one that incorporates: as **a :** any of the persons who join as original members in incorporating a company **:** a member at any time of a corporation aggregate **:** a corporator in a corporation having no capital stock **:** a promoter of a corporation named as an original member **b :** a member of one British university who is incorporated in another

in·cor·po·ra·tor·ship \-,ship\ *n* -S **:** membership in a corporation

[1]**in·corporeal** \¦in+,=¦=ˌ=\ *adj* [L *incorporeus* (fr. *in-* [1]in- + *corporeus* of the body) + E *-al* — more at CORPOREAL] **1 :** not corporeal **:** having no material body or form **:** not consisting of matter **:** IMMATERIAL **2 :** of, relating to, or characteristic of beings who lack material substance ⟨~ speed⟩ ⟨that ~ music⟩ **3 :** of, relating to, or constituting a right that has no physical existence but that issues out of corporate property which has a physical existence and that concerns or is annexed to or exercisable in relation to such property (as stocks, bonds, mineral rights, patents) **:** existing only in contemplation of law ⟨an ~ hereditament⟩ — **in·corporeality** \¦in+\ *n* — **incorporeally** \"+,=¦=ˌ=\ *adv*

[2]**incorporeal** \"\ *n* **:** something that is incorporeal **:** an immaterial or spiritual being

incorporeal chattel *n* **:** CHOSE IN ACTION

in·cor·po·re·i·ty \,in,kȯ(r)pəˈrēəd.ē\ *n* [*incorporeal* + *-ity*] **:** the quality or state of being incorporeal **:** IMMATERIALITY; *also* **:** an incorporeal attribute or entity

incorporeous *adj* [L *incorporeus*] *obs* **:** INCORPOREAL 1

in·corpsed \ən'kȯ(r)rpst\ *adj* [[2]*in-* + *corpse* + [1]*-ed*] **:** made one with **:** incorporated into

in·correct \¦in+\ *adj* [ME, fr. MF or L; fr. L *incorrectus,* fr. *in-* [1]in- + *correctus,* past part. of *corrigere* to correct — more at CORRECT] **1** *obs* **:** not corrected or chastened ⟨it shows a will most ~ to heaven —Shak.⟩ **2 :** failing to agree with a copy or model or with established rules **:** INACCURATE, FAULTY ⟨a careless ~ transcription⟩ ⟨an ~ edition⟩ **3 a :** failing to agree with the requirements of duty, morality, or propriety **:** UNBECOMING, IMPROPER ⟨~ behavior⟩ ⟨this neglect was most ~⟩ **b :** not acceptable to the best taste ⟨gray flannels are ~ for tennis⟩ **4 :** failing to coincide with the truth **:** INACCURATE, IMPRECISE ⟨your answers are all ~⟩ **5** *of a word or expression* **:** formed or used in violation of grammatical principles

in·correctly \"+\ *adv* **:** in an incorrect manner

in·correctness \"+\ *n* **:** the quality or state of being incorrect

in·correspondence *or* **in·correspondency** \(ˌ)in+\ *n* [[1]*in-* + *correspondence, correspondency*] **:** lack of correspondence or harmony

in·corrigibility \(ˌ)in, ən+\ *n* **:** the quality or state of being incorrigible

[1]**in·corrigible** \"+\ *adj* [ME, fr. LL *incorrigibilis,* fr. L *in-* [1]in- + *corrigere* to correct + *-ibilis* -ible — more at CORRECT] **:** incapable of being corrected or amended: as **a** (1) **:** bad beyond the possibility of correction or rehabilitation **:** utterly bad or depraved ⟨an ~ criminal⟩ ⟨such ~ conduct⟩ (2) **:** *of a child* **:** persistently bad **:** DELINQUENT ⟨a training school for ~ boys⟩ **b** *archaic* **:** INCURABLE, IRREMEDIABLE **c :** requiring no improvement or alteration **:** being perfect as formed or formulated ⟨his judgment is not infallible or ~ —T.D.Weldon⟩ ⟨~ truth⟩ **d :** UNMANAGEABLE, UNRULY ⟨~ hair⟩ **e** (1) **:** unwilling to change or to give something up ⟨an ~ traveler⟩ ⟨an ~ amateur mechanic⟩ (2) **:** not readily altered **:** STRONG, INTENSE ⟨felt an ~ optimism⟩ ⟨irritating ~ self-assurance⟩

[2]**incorrigible** \"\ *n* -S **:** something incorrigible; *esp* **:** an incorrigible person

in·cor·ri·gi·ble·ness \-nəs\ *n* -ES **:** the quality or state of being incorrigible

in·corrigibly \(ˈ)in, ən+\ *adv* **:** in an incorrigible manner

in·corrodable *also* **in·corrodible** \¦in+\ *adj* [*incorrodable* alter. of *incorrodible; incorrodible* fr. [1]*in-* + *corrodible*] **:** impervious to corrosion

in·corrupt *also* **in·corrupted** \"+\ *adj* [*incorrupt* fr. ME, fr. L *incorruptus,* fr. *in-* [1]in- + *corruptus* past part. of *corrumpere* to corrupt; *incorrupted* fr. [1]*in-* + past part. of *corrupt* — more at CORRUPT] **:** free from corruption: as **a** *obs* **:** not affected with decay **:** not putrefied or rotten **:** SOUND **b :** INCORRUPTIBLE **c :** not defiled or depraved **:** PURE, SOUND, UNTAINTED, UPRIGHT, HONEST **d :** free from error ⟨an ~ edition prepared from the original text⟩ — **in·corruptly** \"+\ *adv* — **in·corruptness** \"+\ *n*

in·corruptibility \¦in+\ *n* [ME *incorrumptibiletee,* fr. LL *incorruptibilitas,* fr. *incorruptibilis* incorruptible + L *-itas* -ity] **:** the quality or state of being incorruptible

[1]**in·corruptible** \"+\ *adj* [ME, fr. MF or LL; MF, fr. LL *incorruptibilis,* fr. L *in-* [1]in- + LL *corruptibilis* corruptible — more at CORRUPTIBLE] **:** incapable of corruption: as **a :** not subject to decay or dissolution ⟨gold is ~ by most chemical agents⟩ **b :** incapable of being bribed or morally corrupted **:** inflexibly just and upright

[2]**incorruptible** \"\ *n* -S **:** something that is not subject to corruption; *esp* **:** something of spiritual nature

in·cor·rupt·ible·ness \-nəs\ *n* **:** INCORRUPTIBILITY

in·cor·rupt·ibly \-əblē, -li\ *adv* **:** in an incorruptible manner

in·corruption \¦in+\ *n* [LL *incorruption-, incorruptio,* fr. L *in-* [1]in- + *corruption-, corruptio* corruption — more at CORRUPTION] **1** *archaic* **:** the quality or state of being free from physical decay **2 :** freedom from corrupt practices **:** UPRIGHTNESS, HONESTY

incounter *obs var of* ENCOUNTER

incourage *obs var of* ENCOURAGE

incr *abbr* increase; increased; increasing

[1]**incrassate** *vb* -ED/-ING/-S [LL *incrassatus,* past part. of *incrassare,* fr. L *in-* [2]in- + *crassare* to thicken, fr. *crassus* thick — more at HURDLE] *obs* **:** THICKEN, INSPISSATE — **incrassation** *n* -S

[2]**in·cras·sate** \ən'kra,sāt\ *also* **in·cras·sat·ed** \-ād.əd\ *adj* [LL *incrassatus*] **1 :** THICKENED **2** *of a plant or animal structure* **:** SWOLLEN, INFLATED ⟨an ~ cell wall⟩

in·creas·able \(ˈ)in¦krēsəbəl, ən'k-\ *adj* **:** capable of being increased ⟨his income was no way ~⟩

[1]**in·crease** \(ˈ)in¦krēs, ən'k-\ *vb* -ED/-ING/-S [ME *encresen, incresen,* fr. MF *encreiss-,* stem of *encreistre, encroistre,* fr. L *increscere,* fr. *in-* [2]in- + *crescere* to grow — more at CRESCENT] *vi* **1 :** to become greater in some respect (as in size, quantity, number, degree, value, intensity, power, authority, reputation, wealth) **:** GROW, ADVANCE, WAX — opposed to *decrease* ⟨his wealth *increased* over the years⟩ ⟨*increasing* in knowledge through study⟩ **2 :** to multiply by the production of young **:** be prolific ⟨the herd ~s yearly⟩ **3** *of a Latin noun or adjective* **:** to have a syllable more in the genitive than in the nominative (as in *rex, regis*) ~ *vt* **1 :** to make greater in some respect (as in bulk, quantity, extent, value, or amount) **:** add to **:** ENHANCE ⟨~ his possessions⟩ **2** *archaic* **:** to cause to be richer, more prosperous, or more powerful **:** ENRICH, PROMOTE **3 :** to add (a stitch) to knitting by knitting twice in the same stitch (as in the front and the back of the stitch)

syn ENLARGE, AUGMENT, MULTIPLY: INCREASE intransitively may carry the idea of progressive growth in numbers, size, amount, quantity or intensity ⟨our population is *increasing*⟩ ⟨prices *increased* on all necessities —*Collier's Yr. Bk.*⟩ ⟨the rice yield to the acre *increased* with improved methods —*Amer. Guide Series: Texas*⟩; transitively this notion is not so prominent ⟨the trustees *increased* salaries⟩ ENLARGE suggests expansion or extension of any sort ⟨to *enlarge* a building⟩ ⟨*enlarging* the farm⟩ ⟨*enlarging* the personnel of the department⟩ ⟨the abundant opportunities which the aesthetic realm provides to *enlarge* our experience —Hunter Mead⟩ ⟨early New England life when strong men enjoyed religion and *enlarged* their minds by profound metaphysical discussion —C.A.Dinsmore⟩ AUGMENT intransitively may suggest further growth, development, or increase of something already grown or developed ⟨the literature of cryptography, both in the form of secret government manuals and openly published books, had *augmented* enormously since 1880 —Fletcher Pratt⟩; transitively it may suggest addition to sufficiency or ampleness ⟨the city police, *augmented* by special deputies, were also called out —*Amer. Guide Series: Tenn.*⟩ ⟨by their weight, which was *augmented* by laying a number of old rails on the top, these slabs have the effect of preventing any tendency for the clay to work up —O.S.Nock⟩ MULTIPLY intransitively may suggest increase by natural generation ⟨in those days the Anglo-American stock, a very fine one, *multiplied* like rabbits —W.R. Inge⟩ ⟨mosquitoes *multiply* rapidly⟩; in all uses it is likely to indicate increasing manifold ⟨skins which would *multiply* Mr. Astor's wealth —Meridel Le Sueur⟩ ⟨those ships had *multiplied* until their very numbers were menacing —Kenneth Roberts⟩

[2]**in·crease** \ˈin,krēs *also* ən'k-\ *n* -S [ME *encres, incres,* fr. *encresen, incresen,* v.] **1 :** act of increasing: as **a :** addition or enlargement in size, extent, quantity, number, intensity, value, substance **:** AUGMENTATION, GROWTH, MULTIPLICATION ⟨an ~ of knowledge⟩ **b** *obs* **:** production of young **:** PROPAGATION **c** *obs* (1) **:** growth in wealth, dignity, or influence **:** ADVANCEMENT (2) **:** the rising of flood or tidal waters **2 :** something that results from or is produced by increasing **:** an addition or increment **:** something that is added to the original stock by augmentation or growth (as progeny, issue, offspring, produce, profit, interest)

increased *adj* **:** subjected to augmentation **:** made or become greater ⟨~ time for study⟩ ⟨the ~ wealth of the nation⟩ — **in·creased·ly** \(ˈ)in¦krēsədlē, ən'k-, -stl-, -li\ *adv*

increaseful *adj, obs* **:** full of increase **:** PRODUCTIVE

in·crease·ment \(ˈ)in¦krēsmənt, ən'k-\ *n* -S [ME *encresement,* fr. *encresen* to increase + *-ment*] *archaic* **:** INCREASE

in·creas·er \-sə(r)\ *n* -s : one that increases: as **a** : an agent that causes something to increase ⟨these ~s of public turmoil⟩ **b** *archaic* : one that promotes or furthers something (as a cause, a group) **c** : a plant or animal that tends to multiply freely ⟨several of the new glads proved to be excellent ~s⟩ **d** : a coupling for joining a pipe to another of larger diameter

increaser d: *1* smaller pipe, *2* increaser, *3* larger pipe

increasing *adj* : becoming progressively greater ⟨to an ~ degree⟩ ⟨settlers came in in ~ numbers⟩

increasing function *n* : a mathematical function whose value algebraically increases as the independent variable algebraically increases over a given range

in·creas·ing·ly *adv* : to an increasing degree : more and more ⟨became ~ apparent⟩ ⟨~ of the opinion —W.H.Camp⟩

in·cre·ate \ˈinkrēˌāt, ənˈkrēət\ *adj* [ME increat, fr. LL *increatus*, fr. L *in-* ¹in- + *creatus*, past part. of *creare* to create — more at CRESCENT] : UNCREATED, SELF-EXISTENT — **in·cre·ate·ly** *adv*

in·creative \(ˈ)in, ən+\ *adj* [¹*in-* + *creative*] : incapable of creating

in·credibility \(ˌ)in, ən+\ *n* **1** : the quality or state of being incredible ⟨the sheer ~ of this situation⟩ **2** : something that is incredible ⟨all these tales and *incredibilities*⟩

in·credible \(ˈ)in, ən+\ *adj* [ME, fr. L *incredibilis*, fr. *in-* ¹in- + *credibilis* credible — more at CREDIBLE] **1 a** : surpassing belief : too extraordinary and improbable to admit of belief ⟨an ~ cost⟩ **b** : hard to believe real or true : UNLIKELY, IMPROBABLE ⟨the children's appetite was ~⟩ **2** *obs* : INCREDULOUS, UNBELIEVING — **in·credibleness** \"+\ *n* — **in·credibly** \"+\ *adv*

in·creditable \"+\ *adj* [¹*in-* + *creditable*] *archaic* : not creditable

in·credulity \ˌin+\ *n* [ME *incredulite*, fr. L *incredulitas*, fr. *incredulus* + *-itas* -ity] : the quality or state of being incredulous : a withholding or refusal of belief : DISBELIEF

in·credulous \(ˈ)in, ən+\ *adj* [L *incredulus*, fr. *in-* ¹in- + *credulus* credulous — more at CREDULOUS] **1** : indisposed to admit or accept what is related as true ⟨~ of such statements⟩ **2** : caused by disbelief or incredulity ⟨an ~ stare⟩ **3** *obs* : not to be believed : INCREDIBLE — **in·credulously** \"+\ *adv* — **in·credulousness** \"+\ *n*

in·creep \ˈ=,=\ *vi* [ME *increpen*, fr. ²*in* + *crepen* to creep — more at CREEP] : to enter bit by bit or by slow degrees : creep in ⟨the ~*ing* frost⟩

in·cremation \ˌin+=ˈ==\ *n* [²*in* + *cremation*] : CREMATION

in·cre·ment \ˈiŋkrəmənt, ˈink-\ *n* -s [ME, fr. L *incrementum*, fr. *increscere* to increase + *-mentum* -ment — more at INCREASE] **1** : an increasing or growth in bulk, quantity, number, or value : ENLARGEMENT, INCREASE **2 a** : something that is gained or added : an added quantity or character **b** : one of a series of regular consecutive additions of like or proportional size or value — compare UNEARNED INCREMENT **c** : one of a series of minute additions : a slight or imperceptible augmentation **3** : increase in volume or value of a forest or its products during a given period **4 a** : a positive or negative change in the value of one or more of a set of variables **b** : an amount of powder packed in a bag that may be added to or removed from the propelling charge of semifixed or separate loading ammunition to permit fire at varying ranges and with varying angles of impact

in·cre·men·tal \ˌ==ˈmentᵊl\ *adj* : of, relating to, constituting, or resulting from increments, increase, or growth

incremental repetition *n* : repetition in each stanza after the first of part of the preceding stanza — used esp. of popular ballads

increment borer *n* : ACCRETION BORER

in·cre·pa·tion \ˌinkrəˈpāshən\ *n* -s [MF or LL; MF, fr. LL *increpation-*, *increpatio*, fr. L *increpatus* (past part. of *increpare* to make a noise, upbraid, fr. *in-* ²in- + *crepare* to crack, creak, break) + *-ion-*, *-io* -ion — more at RAVEN] *archaic* : CHIDING, REBUKE, REPROOF

¹in·crescent \(ˈ)in, ən+\ *n* [L *increscent-*, *increscens*, pres. part.] : an increscent representation of the moon

²increscent \"+\ *adj* [L *increscent-*, *increscens*, pres. part. of *increscere* to increase — more at INCREASE] **1** : becoming greater by gradual augmentation : INCREASING **2** *of the moon* : WAXING; *specif* : having the horns pointing to the dexter side

increscent

in·cre·tion \(ˈ)inˈkrēshən, ən-\ *n* -s [ISV ²*in-* + *secretion*] **1** : internal secretion : secretion into the blood or tissues rather than into a cavity or outlet of the body **2** : a product of internal secretion : AUTACOID, HORMONE — **in·cre·tion·ary** \-shəˌnerē\ *adj*

in·cre·to·ry \(ˈ)inˈkrēd·ərē, ənˈk-\ *adj* [²*in-* + *secretory*] : ENDOCRINE ⟨~ organs⟩

in·crim·i·nate \ənˈkriməˌnāt, *usu* -ād·+V\ *vt* [LL *incriminatus*, past part. of *incriminare*, fr. L *in-* ²in- + *crimin-*, *crimen* crime — more at CRIME] **1 a** : to charge with a crime or fault ⟨he *incriminated* the other boys to the teacher⟩ **b** : to furnish evidence or proof of circumstances tending to show the guilt of ⟨the testimony certainly ~s the brother⟩ ⟨those feathers under the cage are enough to ~ the cat⟩ **c** : to involve (as oneself) in a criminal prosecution or the risk of one ⟨unwilling to testify for fear of *incriminating* himself⟩ **2** : to charge with involvement in or establish as sharing responsibility for some undesirable effect or result ⟨eye gnats have been *incriminated* in some outbreaks of pinkeye⟩ ⟨poor lighting is often *incriminated* in eyestrain⟩ **syn** see ACCUSE

in·crim·i·na·tion \(ˌ)inˌkriməˈnāshən, ənˌk-\ *n* [LL *incrimination-*, *incriminatio*, fr. *incriminatus* + L *-ion-*, *-io* -ion] : the act of incriminating or the state of being incriminated

in·crim·i·na·tor \ˈ=ˈ==ˌnād·ə(r), -ātə-\ *n* : one that incriminates

in·crim·i·na·to·ry \-nəˌtōrē, -tȯrē, -ri\ *adj* : tending to incriminate

incroach *obs var of* ENCROACH

¹incross \ˈ=,=\ *n* [⁴*in* + *cross* (n.)] **1** : an individual produced by crossing inbred lines of the same breed or strain — compare INCROSSBRED **2** : an instance or act of crossing inbred lines of the same breed or strain

²incross \ˈ=,=\ *vt* [²*in* + *cross* (v.)] : to interbreed (inbred lines of a breed or strain)

incrossbred \ˈ=ˈ=,=\ *n* [⁴*in* + *crossbred*] : an individual produced by crossing inbred lines of separate breeds or strains — compare INCROSS

incrossbreed \ˌ=ˈ=,=, ˈ=ˈ=,=\ *vt* [²*in* + *crossbreed*] : to cause (inbred lines of different breeds or strains) to interbreed

in·crotchet \ən+\ *vt* [²*in-* + *crotchet* (n.)] *archaic* : to enclose in brackets

in·croy·a·ble \aⁿkrwäyäbl(ᵊ), -b(lə)\ *n* -s [F, fr. *incroyable*, adj., incredible, fr. MF, fr. *in-* ¹in- + *croyable* credible, fr. *croire* to believe (fr. L *credere*) + *-able*; fr. their extravagant dress and speech — more at CREED] : a French dandy of the late 18th century : DANDY, FOP

incruent *also* **incruental** *or* **incruentous** [*incruent*, *incruentous* fr. L *incruentus*, fr. *in-* ¹in- + *cruentus* bloody; *incruental* fr. L *incruentus* + E *-al*] *adj*, *obs* : UNBLOODY

incrust *var of* ENCRUST

incrustant *var of* ENCRUSTANT

¹in·crus·tate \ənˈkrəˌstāt, ˈin,k\ *vt* -ED/-ING/-S [L *incrustatus*, past part. of *incrustare* — more at ENCRUST] : ENCRUST

²in·crus·tate \ənˈk-\ *adj* [L *incrustatus*] **1** : formed into or like a crust **2** : having a crust

in·crus·ta·tion \ˌinˌkrəˈstāshən\ *or* **en·crus·ta·tion** \ˌen,-\ *n* [L *incrustation-*, *incrustatio*, fr. *incrustatus* + *-ion-*, *-io* -ion] **1** : the act of encrusting or state of being encrusted : formation of a crust **2 a** : a crust or hard coating of something upon or within a body **b** : a growth or accumulation (as of habits, opinions, customs) resembling an encrusting layer **3** : a covering or inlaying (as of marble or mosaic) attached to masonry by cramp irons or cement **4** : something applied as an overlay or inlay ⟨~ of diamonds⟩

in·cu·bate \ˈiŋkyəˌbāt, ˈink-, *usu* -ād·+V\ *vb* -ED/-ING/-S [L *incubatus*, past part. of *incubare* to lie upon, hatch, fr. *in-* ²in- + *cubare* to lie down, lie upon — more at HIP] *vt* **1** : to sit upon (eggs) so as to hatch by the warmth of the body in the manner of most birds : BROOD **2** : to maintain (as eggs, embryos of animals, or bacteria) under prescribed and usu. controlled conditions (as of temperature and moisture) favorable for hatching or development esp. in an incubator **3** : to maintain (a chemically active system) under controlled conditions for the development of a reaction **4** : to cause to develop : give form and substance to ⟨*incubated* the new idea for a while before giving it to his supervisor⟩ ~ *vi* **1** : to sit on eggs : BROOD **2** : to undergo incubation ⟨the cultures must ~ for five more days⟩ **3** : to acquire form and substance : DEVELOP ⟨the plan *incubated* slowly on his nightly walks from work⟩

in·cu·ba·tion \ˌ==ˈbāshən\ *n* -s [L *incubation-*, *incubatio*, fr. *incubatus* + *-ion-*, *-io* -ion] **1** : the act or process of incubating (as eggs, bacteria, or milk) ⟨during the ~ of the culture⟩ **2** : the act or an instance of brooding over something in order to give it form and substance ⟨definitely named the four stages of creative thought as preparation, ~, illumination, and verification —R.S.Woodworth⟩ **3** : the period between the infection of a plant or animal by a pathogen and the manifestation of the disease it causes **4** : a rite among the ancient Greeks and Romans of sleeping on a skin or on the ground in order to enter into communion with the chthonic gods through dreams

in·cu·ba·tion·al \ˌ==ˈbāshənᵊl, -shnəl\ *adj* : of or relating to incubation

incubation period *n* : the period of brooding or incubating required to bring an egg to hatching; *broadly* : the length of incubating required to attain a desired or expected result ⟨many children's diseases have an *incubation period* of less than one week⟩

INCUBATION PERIODS

BIRD	DAYS	BIRD	DAYS
canary	14	ostrich	42
common fowl	21	peafowl	28
duck	28	pheasant	21–24
goose	28–32	pigeon	17–18
guinea fowl	26–28	swan	42
muscovy duck	35–37	turkey	28

in·cu·ba·tist \ˈ==ˌbātəst\ *n* -s *Brit* : a poultry hatcheryman

in·cu·ba·tive \-ād·iv\ *adj* : of or relating to incubation ⟨~ technique⟩ : characteristic of or marked by incubation ⟨~ period⟩

in·cu·ba·tor \-ād·ə(r), -ātə-\ *n* -s : one that incubates: as **a** : an apparatus by which eggs are hatched artificially consisting essentially of an insulated cabinet containing the eggs in trays or drawers, a source of artificial heat and of moisture, and controls to maintain a desired level of heat and moisture **b** : an apparatus for the maintenance of controlled conditions of heat and usu. moisture (as for the cultivation of microorganisms) **c** : an apparatus for housing premature or sick babies in an environment of controlled humidity, oxygen supply, and temperature

incubator bird *n* : MEGAPODE

in·cu·ba·to·ri·um \ˌ==ˌbaˈtōrēəm, (ˌ)inˌkyüba'-t-\ *n*, *pl* **incubato·ria** \-rēə\ *also* **incubatoriums** [NL, fr. L *incubatus* (past part. of *incubare* to lie upon, hatch) + *-orium* -ory — more at INCUBATE] **1** : the ventral brooding pouch of a monotreme **2** : MARSUPIUM 1a(1)

in·cu·ba·to·ry \ˈiŋkyəbəˌtōrē, ˈink-, ˌ==ˈbād·ərē, ənˈkyübə,-tōrē\ *adj* : relating to or serving for incubation

in·cu·bous \ˈiŋkyəbəs, ˈink-\ *adj* [L *incubare* to lie upon + E *-ous* — more at INCUBATE] **1** *of leaves* : being so arranged that the anterior margin of each overlaps the posterior margin of the next younger **2** : having incubous leaves ⟨~ liverworts⟩ — compare SUCCUBOUS

in·cu·bus \-bəs\ *n*, *pl* **incu·bi** \-ˌbī\ *also* **incubuses** [ME, fr. LL, fr. L *incubare* to lie upon, hatch] **1** : an evil spirit believed to lie upon persons in their sleep and esp. to have sexual intercourse with women by night — compare SUCCUBUS **2** : NIGHTMARE 2 **3** : a person or thing that oppresses or burdens like a nightmare ⟨the security council — free for once from the ~ of the veto — was able to act swiftly and decisively —C.P.Romulo⟩

incud- *or* **incudo-** *comb form* [NL *incud-*, *incus*] : incus : incus and ⟨*incud*ectomy⟩ ⟨*incudo*malleal⟩

in·cu·date \ˈi|ŋ|kyəˌdāt, |n|, (ˈ)=ˈkyüdət\ *also* **in·cu·dal** \-dᵊl\ *adj* [*incud-* + *-ate* or *-al*] **1** : of or relating to the incus **2** : having an incus

incudes *pl of* INCUS

in cuerpo *adv* (*or adj*) [modif. of Sp *en cuerpo*, lit., in body] **1** *obs* **a** : in clothing that exposes the shape of the body **b** : in dishabille **2** *obs* : without clothing : in a naked or uncovered state

in·cul·cate \ənˈkəlˌkāt, ˈin(ˌ)kə-, *usu* -ād·+V\ *vt* -ED/-ING/-S [L *inculcatus*, past part. of *inculcare*, lit., to tread on, fr. *in-* ²in- + *-culcare* (fr. *calcare* to tread on, trample, fr. *calc-*, *calx* heel) — more at CALK] **1** : to teach and impress by frequent repetitions or admonitions : urge on or fix in the mind ⟨they *inculcated* these principles at every opportunity⟩ ⟨the current emotional religious revivals *inculcated* an enthusiasm for its strong feelings and vivid scenes —J.D.Hart⟩ — often used with *in* or *into*, sometimes with *upon* ⟨social pressures ~ behavior patterns in the young⟩ ⟨the techniques of plumbing were gradually *inculcated* upon his mind⟩ **2** : to cause (as a person) to become impressed or instilled with something ⟨teachers who fail to ~ students with love of knowledge⟩ ⟨*inculcated* with every virtue⟩ — **in·cul·ca·tive** \ˈin(ˌ)kəlˌkād·iv, ənˈkə-\ *adj* — **in·cul·ca·to·ry** \ənˈkəlkəˌtōrē, ˌin(ˌ)kəlˈkād·ərē\ *adj* **syn** see IMPLANT

in·cul·ca·tion \ˌin(ˌ)kəlˈkāshən\ *n* -s [LL *inculcation-*, *inculcatio*, fr. L *inculcatus* + *-ion-*, *-io* -ion] : an act of inculcating : teaching and impressing by frequent repetitions or admonitions

in·cul·ca·tor \ənˈkəlˌkād·ə(r), ˈin(ˌ)kə-, -ātə-\ *n* -s [LL, fr. L *inculcatus* + *-or*] : one that inculcates

in·culpability \(ˌ)in, ən+\ *n* : the quality or state of being free from blame : INNOCENCE

in·culpable \(ˈ)in, ən+\ *adj* [LL *inculpabilis*, fr. L *in-* ¹in- + *culpabilis* culpable — more at CULPABLE] : free from guilt : BLAMELESS, INNOCENT — **in·culpably** \"+\ *adv*

in·cul·pate \ənˈkəlˌpāt, ˈin(ˌ)kə-, *usu* -ād·+V\ *vt* -ED/-ING/-S [LL *inculpatus*, past part. of *inculpare*, fr. L *in-* ²in- + *culpatus*, past part. of *culpare* to blame — more at CULPABLE] : to impute guilt to : involve or implicate in a charge of misconduct : BLAME, INCRIMINATE ⟨his whole behavior tended to ~ him⟩ ⟨*inculpating* his brother to escape punishment himself⟩ — **in·cul·pa·tion** \ˌin(ˌ)kəlˈpāshən\ *n* -s — **in·cul·pa·tive** \ˈin(ˌ)kəlˌpād·iv; (ˈ)inˈkəlpəd-, ənˈk-\ *adj* — **in·cul·pa·to·ry** \ənˈkəlpəˌtōrē, *chiefly Brit* ˌin(ˌ)kəlˈpātəri, -ā·tri\ *adj*

in·cult \(ˈ)inˈkəlt, ənˈk-\ *adj* [L *incultus*, fr. *in-* ¹in- + *cultus*, past part. of *colere* to cultivate — more at WHEEL] **1** *archaic* : lacking the order that depends on tillage and cultivation **2** : lacking finish or polish : CRUDE, DISORDERED — used esp. of literary style or its products or producers **3** : lacking ease or smoothness of manner : UNCULTURED, RUDE, COARSE ⟨had not been an ~ sort of man in his day —F.M. Ford⟩

in·cul·ti·vate \(ˈ)inˈkəltəˌvāt\ *also* **in·cul·ti·vat·ed** \-ād·əd\ *adj* [*incultivate*, fr. ¹*in-* + ML *cultivatus*, past part. of *cultivare* to cultivate; *incultivated*, fr. ¹*in-* + *cultivated* — more at CULTIVATE] *archaic* : UNCULTIVATED

in·culture \(ˈ)in+\ *n* [¹*in-* + *culture*] *archaic* : lack of culture

in·cum·bence \ənˈkəmbən(t)s\ *archaic var of* INCUMBENCY

in·cum·ben·cy \-bənsē, -si\ *n* -ES **1** : the quality or state of being incumbent: as **a** *archaic* : a condition of bearing upon or overshadowing **b** *archaic* : the quality of being morally incumbent or incumbent as a correlate of something else **c** : the state of occupying a particular position (as a benefice or office) ⟨the mere ~ of the Labour party in the seats of authority —Edward Shils⟩ **2** : something that is incumbent: as **a** *archaic* : a burdening or oppressive weight **b** : a duty, obligation, or responsibility incumbent usu. as a correlate of some position or relationship held ⟨felt it an ~ as his older brother to rebuke him⟩ ⟨these varied *incumbencies* of the father of a family⟩ **3** : the sphere of action or period of office of an incumbent ⟨during an ~ of over 30 years⟩ ⟨six years of senatorial ~ —S.H.Adams⟩

¹in·cum·bent \-bənt\ *n* -s [ME, fr. L *incumbent-*, *incumbens*, pres. part. of *incumbere* to lie down on, give attention to, fr. *in-* ²in- + *-cumbere* to lie down (akin to L *cubare* to lie down) — more at HIP] **1 a** : the holder of an ecclesiastical benefice ⟨an archdiocese of which he was the first ~ —R.P.Casey⟩ **b** : the holder of an office esp. a public or academic office ⟨the hold-over Republican ~s⟩ ⟨the last ~ of the professorship⟩ **2** : one that occupies : OCCUPANT ⟨the previous ~s insisted that the house was haunted⟩ ⟨the modified bloomer . . . [makes] the lower part stay put, no matter how the ~ sprawls —Lois Long⟩

²incumbent \"\ *adj* [L *incumbent-*, *incumbens*] **1 a** : lying or resting on something else esp. so as to exert a downward pressure : bearing down **b** : lying upon or apposed to — used either of cotyledons folded so that the hypocotyl is applied to the back of one of them or of an anther lying against the side of a filament but attached at only one point; compare ACCUMBENT 2 **c** *of a geologic stratum* : SUPERIMPOSED, OVERLYING **d** *of a bird's hind toe* : so placed that its whole length rests on the ground when the bird is standing — opposed to *insistent* **2** *obs* : busily engaged : ASSIDUOUS **3** : falling or imposed as a duty, responsibility, or obligation — usu. used with *on* or *upon* ⟨~ on us to help⟩ ⟨demands ~ upon his position⟩ **4** : having the status of an incumbent ⟨his duties while ~ of the secretaryship⟩; *esp* : occupying a specified office or position at a time expressed or implied ⟨defeated the ~ governor by a large plurality⟩ **5 a** *archaic* : bending over : OVERHANGING **b** *obs* : IMPENDING, THREATENING **c** : bent over so as to rest on or touch an underlying surface ⟨~ hairs on the body of an insect⟩

in·cum·bent·ly *adv* : in the manner of a duty, responsibility, or obligation

in·cum·ber \ənˈkəmbə(r)\ *var of* ENCUMBER

in·cu·na·ble \ənˈkyünəbəl\ *n* -s [F, fr. NL *incunabulum*] : INCUNABULUM

in·cu·nab·u·lar \ˌinkyəˈnabyələ(r)\ *adj* : relating to or typical of incunabula ⟨an ~ form of musical expression⟩

in·cu·nab·u·list \ˌ==ˈ==ləst\ *n* -s : one that makes a special study of incunabula

in·cu·nab·u·lum \-ləm\ *n*, *pl* **incunabu·la** \-lə\ [in sense 1, L *incunabula* swaddling clothes, cradle, origin, birthplace, fr. *in-* ¹in- + *cunae* cradle + *-bulum* (n. suffix); in other senses, fr. NL, back-formation fr. L *incunabula* — more at CEMETERY] **1** *incunabula*, *pl* : earliest stages : BEGINNINGS, INFANCY ⟨the resulting symposium . . . outgrew its *incunabula* —*Times Lit. Supp.*⟩ **2 a** : a book printed before 1501 — called also *cradle book*, *fifteener* **b** : a work of art or of human industry of an early epoch **c** : a record, example, or memento of the early period of an art or human activity ⟨old record catalogs . . . any of the *incunabula* of . . . jazz —Ralph de Toledano⟩ **3** : the cocoon of an insect

in·cur \R ənˈkər, + *vowel* -kər·; -R -kə̄, + *suffixal vowel* -kər· *also* -kə̄r, + *vowel in a following word* -kər· *or* -kə̄ *also* -kə̄r\ *vb* **incurred**; **incurred**; **incurring**; **incurs** [L *incurrere*, lit., to run into, fr. *in-* ²in- + *currere* to run — more at CURRENT] *vt* **1** : to meet or fall in with (as an inconvenience) : become liable or subject to : bring down upon oneself ⟨*incurred* large debts to educate his children⟩ ⟨fully deserving the penalty he *incurred*⟩ **2** *obs* : to render liable or subject to : BRING, ENTAIL ~ *vi* **1** *obs* : to fall as a part or lot, within a scope, or during or at a time **2** *archaic* : to occur as a result : become involved : ACCRUE

in·curability \(ˌ)in, ən+\ *n* : the quality or state of being incurable : INCURABLENESS

¹in·curable \(ˈ)in, ən+\ *adj* [ME, fr. MF or LL; MF, fr. LL *incurabilis*, fr. L *in-* ¹in- + *curabilis* curable — more at CURABLE] **1** : impossible to cure ⟨an ~ disease⟩ **2** : admitting of no remedy or correction ⟨~ optimism⟩ : being a thing specified beyond any possibility of alteration or control ⟨these ~ busybodies⟩

²incurable \"\ *n* -s : a person diseased beyond cure

in·cur·able·ness *n* -ES : the quality or state of being incurable

in·cur·ably \-blē, -bli\ *adv* : in an incurable manner : to an incurable degree ⟨an ~ social nature⟩

in·curiosity \(ˌ)in, ən+\ *n* [prob. fr. F *incuriosité*, fr. LL *incuriositat-*, *incuriositas*, fr. L *incuriosus* + *-itat-*, *-itas* -ity] : the quality or state of being incurious : INCURIOUSNESS

in·curious \(ˈ)in, ən+\ *adj* [L *incuriosus*, fr. *in-* ¹in- + *curiosus* curious — more at CURIOUS] **1** : not curious or inquisitive : having no care or interest : INATTENTIVE, CARELESS ⟨a dull ~ gaze⟩ **2 a** *archaic* : done without care or nicety : HOMELY, COARSE **b** *obs* : not particular, fastidious, or critical **3** *archaic* : devoid of interest : dull and unappealing : not remarkable or attractive of attention **syn** see INDIFFERENT

in·curiously \"+\ *adv* : in an incurious manner : without curiosity or interest

in·cu·ri·ous·ness *n* : the quality or state of being incurious : lack of curiosity or interest

in·cur·ment \ənˈkərmənt, -kə̄m-\ *n* -s : the act of incurring or state of being incurred ⟨prevented the ~ of further debts⟩ ⟨~ of guilt⟩

in·cur·ra·ble \-ˈkərəbəl *also* -ˈkə̄rə-\ *adj* : capable of being incurred

in·cur·rence \-ˈkər·ən(t)s *also* -ˈkə̄rə-\ *n* -s : the act or process of incurring ⟨~ of new responsibilities⟩

in·cur·rent \-nt\ *adj* [L *incurrent-*, *incurrens*, pres. part. of *incurrere* to run into, incur — more at INCUR] : running in: as **a** : occurring within a given time **b** : giving passage to a current that flows inward ⟨the ~ siphon of a bivalve mollusk⟩ ⟨an ~ pore on a sponge⟩ — see CLAM illustration

in·cur·sion \ənˈkər|zhən, -kə̄|, -kəi|, *chiefly Brit* |shən\ *n* -s [ME, invasion, fr. MF or L; MF, fr. L *incursion-*, *incursio*, fr. *incursus* (past part. of *incurrere* to run into, attack, incur) + *-ion-*, *-io* -ion — more at INCUR] **1** : an entering into a territory with hostile intention : a sudden invasion : a predatory or harassing inroad : RAID ⟨partners in the Suez ~ —*Newsweek*⟩ **2 a** : a running, bringing, or entering in or into ⟨~ of water through a weakened seam⟩ ⟨his only ~ into the arts⟩ ⟨the inevitable ~ of new techniques⟩ **b** : such action involving vigorous, forceful, or determined effort ⟨the barrier should have been sufficient to protect the adjoining owner against the ~s, not of all pigs, but of pigs of average vigor and obstinacy —B.N.Cardozo⟩ ⟨a very sudden ~ of "ah" into London speech between 1780 and 1790 —C.H.Grandgent⟩

in·cur·sion·ary \-zhəˌnerē, -sh-, -ri\ *adj* : entering by or engaging in incursion : INVADING ⟨~ clays⟩ ⟨traces of this ~ nomad people⟩

in·cur·sion·ist \-zh(ə)nəst, -sh-\ *n* -s : a maker of an incursion : INVADER

in·cur·sive \(ˈ)inˈkərsiv, ənˈk-\ *adj* [L *incursus* + E *-ive*] : making incursions : INVASIVE, AGGRESSIVE

¹in·cur·var·i·id \ˌinˌkərˈva(a)rēəd\ *adj* [NL *Incurvariidae*] : of or relating to the family Incurvariidae

²incurvariid \"\ *n* -s : a moth of the family Incurvariidae

in·cur·va·ri·idae \ˌinˌkərvəˈrīəˌdē\ *n pl*, *cap* [NL, fr. *Incurvaria*, type genus (fr. L *incurvus* curved in — fr. *in-* ²in- + *curvus* curved — + NL *-aria*) + *-idae*] : a small family of minute inconspicuous moths usu. having larvae that are initially leaf miners and later casebearers

¹in·cur·vate \ˈin(ˌ)kərˌvāt, ənˈk-\ *vb* -ED/-ING/-S [L *incurvatus*, past part. of *incurvare*, fr. *in-* ²in- + *curvare* to curve (fr. *curvus* curved) — more at CROWN] *vt* : to turn from a straight line or course : BEND, CROOK : cause to curve inward — used chiefly as past participle ⟨the gracefully *incurvated* column⟩ ~ *vi*, *obs* : to curve inward : BOW

²in·cur·vate \ˈin(ˌ)kərˌvāt, (ˈ)inˈkərvət\ *adj* [L *incurvatus*] : having an inward curvature : INCURVED

in·curvation \ˌin+\ *n* [L *incurvation-*, *incurvatio*, fr. *incurvatus* + *-ion-*, *-io* -ion] **1** : the act, fact, or process of incurving or state of being incurved : CURVATURE, INCURVATURE **2** *obs* : GENUFLECTION, BOW

in·curvature \(ˈ)in+\ *n* [L *incurvatus* + E *-ure*] : the act, fact, or process of curving inward or state of being curved inward

¹in·curve \(ˈ)in+\ *vb* [L *incurvare*] *vt* : to bend so as to curve

: CURVE, CROOK; *esp* : to bend so that the resulting curve projects inward ~ *vi* : to bend or curve inward ⟨the corners ~ gracefully⟩

2incurve \'=,=\ *n* [4*in* + *curve*] **1** : a curving in ⟨clasped the jewel with a graceful ~ of the hands⟩ **2** : something that curves in ⟨the ~ at the head of the bay⟩; *esp* : DROP 2a(3)

in·cus \'iŋkəs, -,küs\ *n, pl* **in·cu·des** \iŋ'k(y)ü(,)dēz\ [NL, fr. L, anvil, fr. *incudere* to incuse, stamp, strike] **1 a** : the middle of a chain of three small bones in the ear of mammals — called also *anvil;* see EAR illustration **b** : the median Y-shaped structure in the mastax of a rotifer upon which the mallei work **2** : an anvil-shaped top of a thundercloud

1in·cuse \(')in¦kyüz, -üs\ *adj* [L *incusus*, past part. of *incudere* to incuse, stamp, fr. *in-* 2in- + *cudere* to beat, stamp — more at HEW] : formed by stamping or punching in — used chiefly of old coins or features of their design

2incuse \"\ *n* -s : an incuse space, design, or lettering on a coin

3in·cuse \-üz\ *vt* -ED/-ING/-S [L *incusus*] : to punch or stamp in (as lettering or a design on a coin) : impress by striking

in·cuse·ly *adv* : in the form of an incuse or an incuse square

incuse square *n* : a sunken square on various ancient Greek coins with or without a raised design inside it

in cus·to·dia le·gis \¦in,kü'stōdēə'lāgəs\ *adv* [L] : in the custody of the law

1ind- *or* **indo-** *comb form, usu cap* [Gk, India, of or connected with India, fr. *indos* of or connected with India, fr. *Indos* India (subcontinent in southern Asia), Indus (river in the northwestern part of the Indian subcontinent) — more at INDIA] **1** : India or the East Indies ⟨*Indo*phile⟩ : of or connected with India or the East Indies ⟨*ind*aconitine⟩ ⟨*Indo*-Briton⟩ ⟨*Indo*-African⟩ **2** : of or connected with the Indus river ⟨*Indo*-Gangetic⟩ **3** : Indo-European ⟨*Indo*-Hittite⟩

2ind- *or* **indi-** *or* **indo-** *comb form* [ISV, fr. L *indicum* — more at INDIGO] **1** : indigo ⟨*ind*ole⟩ ⟨*indi*rubin⟩ ⟨*indo*phenin⟩ **2** : resembling indigo (as in color) ⟨*ind*amine⟩ ⟨*indo*phenol⟩

ind *abbr* **1** independence; independent **2** index; indexed **3** indicated; indicative; indicator **4** indigo **5** indirect **6** induction **7** industrial; industry

in·da·ba \in'däbə\ *n* -s [Zulu *in-daba* matter, affair] **1** *southern Africa* : a conference esp. among representatives of native tribes : PARLEY, TALK **2** *Brit* : a gathering for camping or conference

in·da·con·i·tine \,ində'känə,tēn, -,tən\ *n* [1*ind-* + *aconitine*] : a crystalline alkaloid $C_{34}H_{47}NO_{10}$ found in an herb (*Aconitum chasmanthum*) native to India

in·da·gate \'ində,gāt\ *vt* -ED/-ING/-S [L *indagatus*, past part. of *indagare*, fr. *indagin-*, *indago* examination, investigation, act of enclosing or surrounding, fr. OL *indu* in, within + L *agere* to drive — more at INDIGENOUS, AGENT] *archaic* : to search into : INVESTIGATE — **in·da·ga·tion** \,=='gāshən\ *n* -s *archaic* — **in·da·ga·tor** \'==,gād·ə(r)\ *n* -s *archaic*

In·da·lone \'ində,lōn\ *trademark* — used for butopyronoxyl

in dam *adv (or adj), of a domestic animal* : in the fetal state ⟨pigs sold *in dam*⟩

in·da·mine \'ində,mēn, -,mən\ *n* [ISV 2*ind-* + *amine;* orig. formed as G *indamin*] : any of a class of organic bases that are amino-phenyl derivatives of quinone diimine, that in the form of salts are unstable blue and green dyes, and that are used chiefly as intermediates for azine dyes (as safranines); *esp* : the simplest base $NH_2C_6H_4N{=}C_6H_4{=}NH$ that is the parent compound of the class

in·dan \'in,dan\ *also* **in·dane** \-dān\ *n* -s [ISV *ind*ene + *-an* or *-ane*] : an oily cyclic hydrocarbon C_9H_{10} obtained by reducing indene — called also *hydrindene*

indanger *obs var of* ENDANGER

in·dan·throne \ən'dan,thrōn\ *n* -s [obs. E *indanthr*ene indanthrone (ISV 2*ind-* + *-anthrene;* prob. orig. formed as G *indanthren*) + E *-one*] : a blue anthraquinone-azine dye that is the parent compound of several halogenated dyes — see DYE table I (under *Vat Blue 4*)

in·dart \ən+\ *vt* [2*in* + *dart*, v.] *archaic* : to cause (as a dart) to be hurled or thrust into something

in·da·zole \'ində,zōl\ *n* [ISV *ind*ole + *azole;* orig. formed as G *indazol*] **1** : a feebly basic crystalline bicyclic compound $C_7H_6N_2$ made by pyrolysis of *ortho*-hydrazino-cinnamic acid; benzo-pyrazole **2** : a derivative of indazole

indear *obs var of* ENDEAR

in·de·bi·ta·tus assumpsit \ən,debə'tād·əs-\ *n* [NL, lit., being indebted he undertook] : COMMON ASSUMPSIT

inde blue \'ind-\ *n* [ME *inde*, n., indigo blue, fr. OF *inde*, adj., indigo-blue, fr. L *indicum*, n., indigo — more at INDIGO] : INDIGO 3

in·debt \ən'det\ *vt* -ED/-ING/-S [back-formation fr. *indebted*] *archaic* : to place (as oneself) under an obligation (as of returning something borrowed)

in·debt·ed \ən'ded·əd, -etəd\ *adj* [alter. (influenced by 2*in-* and *debt*) of ME *endetted*, modif. (influenced by ME *-ed*, adj. suffix forming past participles) of OF *endeté*, past part. of *endeter* to involve in debt, fr. *en-* 1en- + *dette*, *dete* debt — more at DEBT] **1** : being under the obligation of paying or repaying money : owing money : held to payment or repayment ⟨was heavily ~ to the bank for loans extended to him —A.C.Cole⟩ **2** : owing gratitude (as for a favor received or kind act done) or recognition (as of a useful service) to another ⟨felt deeply ~ to her for having given him a home⟩ ⟨was ~ to the book for most of his information⟩

in·debt·ed·ness *n* -ES **1 a** : the condition of being indebted ⟨should provide for the refinancing of mortgage and other ~ —F.D.Roosevelt⟩ ⟨the ~ was canceled —P.N.Garber⟩ **b** : the extent to which one is indebted ⟨admitted his deep ~ to the accomplishments of those who preceded him⟩ **2** : something (as a sum of money) that is owed ⟨Hawthorne's literary ~*es* are . . . chiefly to English writers —*Publ's Mod. Lang. Assoc. of Amer.*⟩ **syn** see DEBT

in·debt·ment \-'detmənt\ *n* -S *archaic* : INDEBTEDNESS

indecence *n* -S [prob. fr. F *indécence*, fr. L *indecentia*] *obs* : INDECENCY

in·de·cen·cy \ən'dēsᵊnsē, (')in-, -nsi\ *n* [L *indecentia*, fr. *indecent-*, *indecens* indecent + *-ia* -y] **1** : the quality or state of being indecent **2** : something (as a word or an action or a manner of behavior) that is indecent : an offense against decency ⟨innocent and shameless like a child's *indecencies* —W.A.White⟩

in·de·cent \-ᵊnt\ *adj, sometimes* -ER/-EST [MF or L; MF *indécent*, fr. L *indecent-*, *indecens*, fr. *in-* 1in- + *decent-*, *decens* decent] **1** : not decent: as **a** : altogether unbecoming : contrary to what the nature of things or what circumstances would dictate as right or expected or appropriate : hardly suitable : UNSEEMLY ⟨hurried away with ~ haste⟩ **b** : not conforming to generally accepted standards of morality : tending toward or being in fact something generally viewed as morally indelicate or improper or offensive : being or tending to be obscene ⟨an ~ gesture⟩ ⟨~ language⟩ ⟨an ~ costume⟩ **2** *archaic* : unpleasant to look at : UNSIGHTLY, UNCOMELY — **in·de·cent·ly** *adv*

indecent assault *n* : an immoral act or series of acts exclusive of rape or an attempt to commit rape committed by a male against the person of a female without her consent

indecent exposure *n* : intentional exposure of part of one's body (as the genitals) in a place where such exposure is likely to be an offense against the generally accepted standards of decency in a community

in·de·cid·ua \,ində'sijəwə\ *n pl, cap* [NL, fr. 1*in-* + L *decidua*, neut. pl. of *deciduus* deciduous] : NONDECIDUATA

in·de·cid·u·ate \¦==¦==wət\ *adj* [NL *indeciduatus*, fr. 1*in-* + *deciduatus* deciduate] *of a placenta* : having the maternal and fetal elements associated but not fused so that no maternal tissue is carried off in the placenta at parturition

in·de·cid·u·ous \-wəs\ *adj* [1*in-* + *deciduous*] : not deciduous ⟨~ leaves⟩ : EVERGREEN ⟨~ trees⟩

in·de·ci·pher·able \¦ində¦sīf(ə)rəbəl, -dē¦-\ *adj* [1*in-* + *decipherable*] : that cannot be deciphered ⟨an ~ inscription⟩ ⟨making people whose inner life has seemed to us ~ emerge as human and understandable —C.J.Rolo⟩ — **indecipherableness** *n* -ES — **in·de·ci·pher·ably** \-blē, -li\ *adv*

in·de·ci·sion \¦ində¦sizhən, -dē¦-\ *n* [F *indécision*, fr. *indécis* irresolute, undecided (fr. MF *indecis* not yet settled, fr. LL *indecisus*, fr. L *in-* 1in- + *decisus*, past part. of *decidere* to decide, settle) + *-ion*] : a wavering between two or more possible courses of action : VACILLATION, IRRESOLUTION : inability or failure to arrive at a decision ⟨in a constant state of ~⟩ ⟨halted before the door in ~ —James Joyce⟩

in·decisive \¦in+\ *adj* : not decisive: as **a** : not being of such a sort as would definitely settle something or make something final : INCONCLUSIVE ⟨a drawn-out ~ war⟩ **b** : marked by or prone to indecision : WAVERING, VACILLATING, IRRESOLUTE : unable or failing to arrive at a decision ⟨an ~ state of mind⟩ ⟨a timid ~ sort of individual⟩ **c** : not clearly marked out : not definite : INDISTINCT, UNFIXED, VAGUE ⟨~ boundaries between right and wrong⟩ ⟨an outline that was blurred and ~⟩ — **in·de·ci·sive·ly** *adv* — **in·de·ci·sive·ness** *n*

1in·de·clin·able \¦ində¦klīnəbəl, -dē¦-\ *adj* [MF, fr. LL *indeclinabilis*, fr. L *in-* 1in- + LL *declinabilis* capable of being inflected, fr. L *declinare* to inflect grammatically + *-abilis* -able — more at DECLINE] : having no grammatical inflections : used without case endings ⟨some Latin nouns are ~⟩

2indeclinable \"\ *n* -S : an indeclinable word

in·de·com·po·ni·ble \¦in,dēkəm¦pōnəbəl\ *adj* [1*in-* + *decompon-* (fr. L *de* from, down, away + *componere* to compose, put together) + *-ible* — more at DE-, COMPOUND] *archaic* : INDECOMPOSABLE

in·de·com·pos·able \-¦pōzəbəl\ *adj* [1*in-* + *decomposable*] : not capable of being broken up into component parts ⟨a substance that resists analysis and is apparently ~⟩

in·dec·or·ous \ən'dekərəs, (')in¦d- *also* -krəs ¦ində¦kōr-, -dē¦-, -kȯr-\ *adj* [L *indecorus*, fr. *in-* 1in- + *decorus* decorous] : not decorous : not proper : conflicting with accepted standards of propriety or good taste or good breeding ⟨an ~ remark⟩ ⟨~ behavior⟩ — **in·dec·or·ous·ly** *adv* — **in·dec·or·ous·ness** *n*

in·de·co·rum \¦ində¦kōrəm, -dē¦k-, -kȯr-\ *n* [L, neut. of *indecorus* indecorous] **1** : something (as an action) that is indecorous : an offense against decorum ⟨an ~ for which she refused to forgive him⟩ **2** : the quality or state of being indecorous : lack of decorum : IMPROPRIETY ⟨the general ~ of their lives —Lionel Trilling⟩

in·deed \ən'dēd\ *adv* [ME *in dede*, fr. 1*in* + *dede* deed] **1 a** : in very fact : without any question : in truth : TRULY, CERTAINLY, ASSUREDLY, POSITIVELY ⟨was ~ glad to see her⟩ — used as an intensive often postpositively ⟨was glad ~⟩ ⟨was a king ~⟩ ⟨found themselves in real trouble ~⟩ and sometimes to reiterate a remark of another speaker ⟨you may well ask who knows how it will end; who knows, ~⟩; often used as an interjection to express irony or disbelief or surprise **b** : by all means : by any means — used to emphasize a reply or remark made in answer to an actual or implied question ⟨yes ~ I intend to go⟩ ⟨no ~ they aren't away⟩ **c** : REALLY, HONESTLY — used interrogatively to indicate that one seeks confirmation from a speaker that a statement just made by the speaker is really true ⟨~? You would like to go home?⟩ **2** : in reality : so far as the truth of the matter is concerned : in actual fact — used to indicate or emphasize that something stated or about to be stated is true and is at the same time opposed to something stated or implied or about to be stated or implied that is either untrue or merely external or apparent ⟨what seems to be cause for grief is ~ a reason for joy⟩ ⟨they were ~ heroes, though the world failed to recognize them as such⟩ **3** : all things considered : as a matter of fact : so far as that goes — used to confirm or amplify something stated ⟨he likes to have things his own way; ~, he can be quite a tyrant⟩ ⟨she is quite stupid, ~ a simpleton⟩ **4** : ADMITTEDLY, UNDENIABLY ⟨the problems involved are ~ serious ones, but I am convinced they can be solved⟩

in·deedy \-'dēdē, -di\ *adv* [by alter.] : INDEED 1b — not in formal use

indef *abbr* indefinite

in·de·fat·i·ga·bil·i·ty \¦ində,fad·¦əgə¦biləd·ē, -dē,-, -at¦, ¦ēg-, -ətē, -i\ *n* -ES : the quality or state of being indefatigable

in·de·fat·i·ga·ble \¦==¦==gəbəl\ *adj* [MF, fr. L *indefatigabilis*, fr. *in-* 1in- + *defatigare* to fatigue, tire (fr. *de* from, down, away + *fatigare* to tire) + *-abilis* -able — more at FATIGUE] : incapable of being fatigued : that continues or proceeds unremittingly and without becoming wearied : UNTIRING, UNWEARYING ⟨an ~ worker⟩ ⟨has ~ patience⟩ — **in·de·fat·i·ga·ble·ness** *n* -ES — **in·de·fat·i·ga·bly** \-blē, -li\ *adv*

in·de·fea·si·bil·i·ty \¦ində,fēzə¦biləd·ē, -dē,f-, -ətē, -i\ *n* -ES : the quality or state of being indefeasible

in·de·fea·si·ble \¦==¦fēzəbəl\ *adj* [1*in-* + *defeasible*] : not defeasible : not capable of or not liable to being annulled or voided or undone : that cannot be forfeited ⟨an ~ right to freedom⟩ ⟨an ~ claim to the title⟩ — compare INALIENABLE — **in·de·fea·si·bly** \-blē, -li\ *adv*

in·de·fec·ti·bil·i·ty \¦ində,fektə¦biləd·ē, -(,)dē,-, -ətē, -i\ *n* : the quality or state of being indefectible

in·de·fec·ti·ble \¦==¦fektəbəl\ *adj* [1*in-* + *defectible*] **1** : not subject to failure or decay : LASTING : that will not and cannot collapse or be done away with ⟨an ~ friendship⟩ ⟨maintained that the church is ~⟩ **2** : free from and incapable of defects or error : having no shortcomings : free of faults : FLAWLESS ⟨possessed what appeared to be a sort of ~ wisdom⟩ ⟨a spokesman who could hardly be considered ~⟩ — **in·de·fec·ti·bly** \-blē, -li\ *adv*

in·defective \¦in+\ *adj* [1*in-* + *defective*] **1** *archaic* : free from defects : FAULTLESS, FLAWLESS **2** *archaic* : INDEFECTIBLE 1 — **in·de·fec·tive·ly** *adv, archaic*

in·de·fen·si·bil·i·ty \¦ində,fen(t)sə¦biləd·ē, -(,)dē,-, -ətē, -i\ *n* : the quality or state of being indefensible

in·de·fen·si·ble \¦==¦fen(t)səbəl\ *adj* [1*in-* + *defensible*] : not defensible: **a** (1) : incapable of being maintained as right or valid : UNTENABLE ⟨an ~ viewpoint⟩ ⟨an ~ argument⟩ (2) : incapable of being justified or excused : UNJUSTIFIABLE, INEXCUSABLE ⟨~ error⟩ ⟨~ behavior⟩ ⟨an ~ waste of public funds⟩ **b** : incapable of being secured or protected against physical force or attack ⟨a totally ~ city⟩ — **in·de·fen·si·bly** \-blē, -li\ *adv*

indeficiency *n* [*indeficient* + *-cy*] *obs* : the quality or state of being unceasing or unfailing

indeficient *adj* [MF, fr. LL *indeficient-*, *indeficiens*, fr. L *in-* 1in- + *deficient-*, *deficiens*, pres. part. of *deficere* to be lacking — more at DEFICIENT] *obs* : UNCEASING, UNFAILING

in·definability \¦in+\ *n* : the quality or state of being indefinable

1in·definable \¦in+\ *adj* [1*in-* + *definable*] : not definable: **a** : incapable of being precisely or readily described : not easily put into words ⟨an ~ feeling of terror⟩ **b** : incapable of being precisely or readily given a logical analysis ⟨an abstract concept that seems ~⟩ **c** : incapable of being precisely or readily given a semantic analysis ⟨prepositions often have a relationship to words with which they are used that is purely functional and ~⟩ **d** (1) : not clearly recognizable or ascertainable : UNCERTAIN ⟨a bent, dignified peasant of ~ age —Marcia Davenport⟩ (2) : lacking a clear outline or definitely set limits : not precisely or readily located or fixed or marked off : INDETERMINATE, VAGUE ⟨an area with ~ boundaries⟩ ⟨the lights of the December evening bathing his face with little splashes that left his eyes and mouth almost ~ —E.L.Wallant⟩ — **in·de·fin·able·ness** *n* -ES — **in·definably** \"+\ *adv*

2indefinable \"\ *n* -S : something (as a word or concept) that is indefinable

1in·definite \(')in+, ən, (')in+\ *adj* [L *indefinitus*, fr. *in-* 1in- + *definitus*, past part. of *definire* to limit, determine — more at DEFINITE] : not definite: as **a** (1) *of a grammatical modifier* : typically designating an unidentified or not immediately identifiable person or thing ⟨*some* in "some books", *someone's* in "someone's house" are ~ modifiers⟩ ⟨the ~ articles *a* and *an*⟩ (2) *of an adjective form or set of adjective forms* : STRONG 16b (3) *of a verb form or set of verb forms in French* : typically denoting completed occurrence of an action — usu. used in the phrase *past indefinite* ⟨*j'ai dit* "I said" contains a past ~ verb⟩ (4) *of a verb form or set of verb forms in English* : denoting an action as neither completed nor continuing ⟨*saw* in "I saw the show" is the past ~ of *see*⟩ — compare PERFECT 5, PROGRESSIVE 7 **b** : being of a nature that is not or cannot be clearly determined : not precise : VAGUE, OBSCURE, UNCERTAIN, AMBIGUOUS ⟨what he really meant to say remains ~⟩ **c** (1) : having no exact limits : indeterminate in extent or amount : not clearly fixed ⟨sentenced to an ~ prison term⟩ ⟨an area with ~ boundaries⟩ ⟨an ~ number of people⟩ (2) : not narrowly confined or restricted ⟨~ extent⟩ : continuing with no immediate end being fixed : UNLIMITED ⟨planned to spend an ~ period in Europe⟩ **d** *of floral organs* (1) : numerous and not easy to determine by reason of being neither constant in number nor in multiples of the petal number (2) : RACEMOSE — **in·def·i·nite·ly** *adv* — **in·def·i·nite·ness** *n*

2indefinite \"\ *n* : something that is indefinite; *esp* : a word that is grammatically indefinite ⟨*a*, *some*, and other ~*s*⟩

indefinite failure of issue : a failure of issue which determines an estate and for which no time or period is fixed in the devise — called also *general failure of issue*

indefinite integral *n, of a function of a variable* : a function containing an arbitrary additive and having a derivative of a function that is the given function

indefinite proposition *n* : a statement in logic whose subject is a common term with nothing to indicate distribution or nondistribution (as "the Chinese eat rice")

indefinite sentence *n* : INDETERMINATE SENTENCE

indefinite term *n* : an unlimited negative term in logic

in·definitive \¦in+\ *adj* [1*in-* + *definitive*] : not definitive : not clearly fixed : INDETERMINATE — **in·de·fin·i·tive·ly** *adv* — **in·de·fin·i·tive·ness** *n*

in·de·fin·i·tude \,ində'finə,tüd, -dē'-, -ə·,tyüd\ *n* -S [fr. *indefinite*, prob. after E *infinite: infinitude*] : INDEFINITENESS

in·de·flec·ti·ble \¦ində¦flektəbəl\ *adj* [1*in-* + *deflect* + *-ible*] : that cannot be deflected ⟨~ courage⟩ — **in·de·flec·ti·bly** \-blē\ *adv*

in·dehiscence \¦in+\ *n* [fr. *indehiscent*, after E *dehiscent: dehiscence*] : the quality or state of being indehiscent

in·dehiscent \"+\ *adj* [1*in-* + *dehiscent*] : not dehiscent : remaining closed at maturity ⟨~ fruits⟩ — see FRUIT illustration

in·deliberate \¦in+\ *adj* [1*in-* + *deliberate*] : not deliberate : marked by lack of forethought or intention ⟨an ~ remark⟩ — **in·de·lib·er·ate·ly** *adv* — **in·de·lib·er·ate·ness** *n* — **indeliberation** \"+\ *n*

in·del·i·bil·i·ty \(,)in,delə'biləd·ē, -ətē, -i\ *n* -ES : the quality or state of being indelible

in·del·i·ble \ən'deləbəl, (')in¦d-, (')in¦deləbəl\ *adj* [ML *indelibilis*, alter. (influenced by L *-ibilis* -ible) of L *indelebilis*, fr. *in-* 1in- + *delebilis* delible] **1** : that cannot be removed, washed away, or erased ⟨an ~ stain⟩ ⟨an ~ mark⟩ : that cannot be effaced or obliterated : PERMANENT, LASTING ⟨made an ~ impression on his mind⟩ **2** : that makes marks that cannot easily be removed (as by erasing) ⟨an ~ pencil⟩; *specif* : not attacked by strong acids or alkalies and so not easily removed by washing ⟨india ink is ~⟩ ⟨bought some ~ ink⟩ — **in·del·i·bly** \-blē, -li\ *adv*

in·delicacy \ən, (')in+\ *n* [1*in-* + *delicacy*] **1** : the quality or state of being indelicate ⟨~ of speech⟩ ⟨~ of behavior⟩ **2** : something (as a coarse expression) that is indelicate ⟨a rollicking tale full of *indelicacies*⟩

in·delicate \"+\ *adj* [1*in-* + *delicate*] : not delicate: **a** (1) : lacking in or offending against propriety : IMPROPER, RUDE, UNREFINED ⟨~ behavior⟩ (2) : verging on the indecent : COARSE, GROSS ⟨an ~ anecdote⟩ **b** : marked by or showing a lack of feeling for the sensibilities of others : TACTLESS ⟨an ~ allusion to her family's poverty⟩ — **in·del·i·cate·ly** *adv* — **in·del·i·cate·ness** *n*

in·dem·ni·fi·ca·tion \ən,demnəfə'kāshən\ *n* -S [fr. *indemnify*, after such pairs as E *amplify: amplification*] **1 a** : the action of indemnifying ⟨~ of the countries that had suffered the worst damage⟩ **b** : the condition of being indemnified ⟨did not lose hope of ~⟩ **2** : INDEMNITY 2b ⟨paid an enormous ~⟩

in·dem·ni·fi·ca·tor \='===,kād·ə(r)\ *n* -S [fr. *indemnification*, after such pairs as E *creation: creator*] : INDEMNIFIER

in·dem·nif·i·ca·to·ry \¦in,dem¦nifəkə,tōrē\ *adj* [fr. *indemnification*, after such pairs as E *explanation: explanatory*] : of, relating to, or designed for indemnification ⟨~ court action⟩

in·dem·ni·fi·er \ən'demnə,fī(ə)r\ *n* -S : one that indemnifies or that is under obligation to indemnify

in·dem·ni·fy \-,fī\ *vt* -ED/-ING/-ES [L *indemnis* unharmed + E *-fy*] **1 a** : to secure or protect against hurt or loss or damage : give indemnity to ⟨a plan for ~*ing* workers against time lost through illness⟩ **b** : to exempt from incurred penalties or liabilities ⟨was made a partner and *indemnified* against his previously overdrawn accounts⟩ **2** : to make compensation to for incurred hurt or loss or damage ⟨*indemnified* the town for the buildings that had been bombed⟩ **syn** see PAY

in·dem·ni·tee \=¦=nə¦tē\ *n* -S [*indemnity* + *-ee* (person furnished with a specified thing)] : one that is indemnified or that is entitled to be indemnified

in·dem·ni·tor \='=nəd·ə(r), -ətə(r)\ *n* -S [*indemnity* + *-or*] : INDEMNIFIER

in·dem·ni·ty \ən'demnəd·ē, -ətē, -i\ *n* -ES [ME *indempnyte*, fr. MF *indemnité*, fr. L *indemnitat-*, *indemnitas*, fr. *indemnis* unharmed (fr. *in-* 1in- + *damnum* damage, harm) + *-tat-*, *-tas* -ty — more at DAMN] **1 a** : security or protection against hurt or loss or damage ⟨a plan that offered ~ against further financial loss⟩ **b** : exemption from incurred penalties or liabilities ⟨received ~ for his overdrawn accounts⟩ **2 a** : INDEMNIFICATION 1 **b** : something (as a sum of money paid in compensation) that indemnifies ⟨had to pay a large ~⟩

in·dem·ni·za·tion \=,=nə'zāshən\ *n* -S [F *indemnisation*, fr. *indemniser* to indemnify (fr. MF, fr. *indemne* unharmed — fr. L *indemnis* — + *-iser* -ize) + *-ation*] : INDEMNIFICATION

in·demonstrability \¦in+\ *n* : the quality or state of being indemonstrable

in·demonstrable \¦in+\ *adj* [1*in-* + *demonstrable*] : incapable of being demonstrated : not subject to proof ⟨a theory that seems valid but is ~⟩ — **in·demonstrably** \"+\ *adv*

indemy *abbr* indemnity

in·dene \'in,dēn\ *n* -S [ISV *ind*ole + *-ene;* prob. orig. formed as G *inden*] : a liquid readily polymerizable hydrocarbon C_9H_8 obtained from coal tar by distillation or from petroleum by cracking and used chiefly in making resins — compare COUMARONE-INDENE RESIN

indenize *vt* [alter. (influenced by 2*in-*) of *endenize*] *obs* : ENDENIZEN

1in·dent \ən'dent\ *vb* -ED/-ING/-S [ME *indenten*, *endenten*, fr. MF *endenter*, fr. OF, fr. *en-* 1en- + *dent* tooth, fr. L *dent-*, *dens* — more at TOOTH] *vt* **1 a** : to cut or otherwise divide (a sheet of parchment or paper carrying two or more copies esp. of a deed or contract) so that sections having one or more edges with angular projections or a scalloped or curved outline are produced, each section being later fitted if necessary to the section having an exactly tallying edge as proof that the sections are parts of an original authentic document ⟨an ~*ed* deed⟩ **b** : to draw up (as a deed or contract) in two or more exactly corresponding copies ⟨~*ing* the agreement⟩ **2 a** (1) : to cut into or notch the edge of in such a way as to produce a scalloped outline or one with angular projections ⟨an ~*ed* stick⟩ (2) : to cut into (as a board) for the purpose of mortising or dovetailing **b** : to penetrate the edge of in such a way as to produce an outline marked by one or more recesses ⟨the coastline is ~*ed* by the sea into a succession of small bays —Han Suyin⟩ **3 a** *obs* : to come to a formal or express agreement about **b** : INDENTURE ⟨~*ed* servants⟩ **4** : to space in (as a line of a paragraph) from a left-hand margin or sometimes from a right-hand margin ⟨~*ing* the first word of a paragraph⟩ ⟨~*ed* the column of figures one inch from the right-hand margin⟩ **5** : to join together (as two boards) by or as if by mortises or dovetails **6** *chiefly Brit* : to order by an indent ⟨~*ed* guns and ammunition⟩ ⟨~*ing* books⟩ ~ *vi* **1** *obs* : to make a formal or express agreement ⟨thus would I have ecclesiastical and civil historians ~ about the bounds and limits of their subjects —Thomas Fuller⟩ **2** *obs* : to wind in and out : ZIGZAG **3** : to form an indentation ⟨the long line of coast with its series of ~*ing* bays —*Amer. Guide Series: N.J.*⟩ **4** *chiefly Brit* : to make out an indent for something ⟨~*ing* for books⟩ — **indent on** *or* **indent upon 1** *chiefly Brit* : to make an official requisition on ⟨*indented on* the governor for food⟩ **2** *chiefly Brit* : to draw on ⟨*indenting on* reserves to cover the deficit⟩

2in·dent \ən'dent, 'in,dent\ *n* -S **1 a** : INDENTURE 1 **b** : a certificate of indebtedness (as of interest on the public debt) issued by the federal or a state government in the late 18th or early 19th century **2** *chiefly Brit* **a** : an official requisition (as for supplies) **b** : a purchase order for goods esp. when sent from a foreign country **3** : INDENTION

3indent \"\ *vb* -ED/-ING/-S [ME *endenten*, fr. 1*en-* + *denten* to dent — more at DENT] *vt* **1** : to force inward (as by striking or pressing) so as to form a depression (as a dent or hollow) ⟨~*ing* a pattern in a metal surface⟩ **2 :** to form a depression (as a dent or hollow) in the surface of by or as if by striking or pressing ⟨~*ing* the pillow with his head⟩ **:** make an indentation in ⟨wore tight-fitting pince-nez which ~*ed* the sides of his nose in two red grooves —O.S.J.Gogarty⟩ ~ *vi* **:** DENT ⟨this asphalt ~*s* easily⟩

4**indent** \"\ *n* -S **:** INDENTATION ⟨the damp grass was everywhere marked with the ~*s* of his sharp hooves —Llewelyn Powys⟩

in·den·ta·tion \ˌinˌden·'tāshən\ *n* -S [1*indent* + *-ation*] **1 a :** an angular cut (as a notch) or something resembling such a cut in an edge ⟨~*s* along the edge of a leaf⟩ **b :** a usu. deep recess (as in a coastline) ⟨many bays pockmark the coast with ~*s*⟩ **2 :** the action of indenting or condition of being indented **3** [3*indent* + *-ation*] **:** a usu. small surface depression (as a dent or hollow) made by or as if by striking or pressing ⟨noticed that the metal was covered with ~*s*⟩ **4 :** INDENTION 2

in·dent·ed·ly \ən'dentədlē\ *adv* [*indented* (past part. of 3*indent*) + *-ly*] **:** by indentation **:** in intaglio ⟨a design made ~ in the surface of the stone⟩

in·dent·er *or* **in·den·tor** \-'dentə(r)\ *n* -S [partly fr. 1*indent* + *-er* or *-or*, partly fr. 3*indent* + *-er* or *-or*] **:** one that indents: **a** *usu* *indentor* **:** one that orders by an indent (sense 2) **b :** an object (as of diamond, carbide, hard steel) having a pointed or rounded tip that is forcibly pressed against the surface of a metal so as to test for hardness and resistance to indentation

in·den·tion \-'denchən\ *n* -S [1*indent* + *-ion*] **1** *archaic* **:** INDENTATION 1 **2 a :** the action of indenting (as a line of a paragraph) or condition of being indented **b :** the blank space produced by indenting

1**in·den·ture** \ən'denchə(r)\ *n* -S [ME *endenture, indenture*, fr. MF *endenture*, fr. OF, fr. *endenter* to indent (a document) + *-ure* — more at 1INDENT] **1 a** (1) **:** a document (as a deed or contract) or a section of a document that is indented (sense 1a) (2) **:** a document (as a deed or contract) or a copy of a document that is not indented (sense 1a) but that is usu. formal and under seal and executed in two or more copies (3) **:** a contract binding one person to work for another for a given period of time (as an apprentice for a master craftsman or a new immigrant for an established colonist) — usu. used in pl. **b :** a document (as an inventory, voucher) that is not indented (sense 1a) and that may or may not be executed in two or more copies and that is formal or official and authenticated and prepared for purposes of control **2** *obs* **:** a zigzag course (as of one running) **3 :** INDENTATION 1 **4** [3*indent* + *-ure*] **:** INDENTATION 3

2**indenture** \"\ *vt* -ED/-ING/-S **1 :** to bind (as an apprentice) by indentures **2** *archaic* **:** to make an indentation (sense 3) in

indentured labor *n* [*indentured* fr. past part. of 2*indenture*] **:** CONTRACT LABOR 2

in·den·ture·ship \=ˈ==ˌship\ *n* [1*indenture* + *-ship*] **:** the condition of being indentured ⟨completed the three years of his ~⟩

in·dependable \ˈin+\ *adj* [1*in-* + *dependable*] **:** UNDEPENDABLE

in·de·pen·dence \ˌində'pendən(t)s, -dē'-\ *n* [fr. *independent*, after such pairs as E *competent: competence*] **1 :** the quality or state of being independent **:** FREEDOM, LIBERTY ⟨their declaration of ~⟩ ⟨national ~⟩ ⟨political ~⟩ ⟨intellectual ~⟩ ⟨~ from the mother country⟩ ⟨enjoyed ~ of outside control⟩ **2** *archaic* **:** COMPETENCE 2 ⟨had a considerable ~, besides two good livings —Jane Austen⟩ **3 :** a grayish to dark purplish blue that is redder and stronger than flag blue

independence day *n, usu cap I&D* **:** a day set aside for public celebration of an anniversary connected with the beginnings of national independence; *specif* **:** July 4 observed as a legal holiday in the U.S. commemorating the adoption of the Declaration of Independence in 1776

in·de·pen·den·cy \-dənsē, -si\ *n* [*independent* + *-cy*] **1 :** INDEPENDENCE 1 **2** *usu cap* **a :** a religious movement originated in England by Robert Browne (1550?–?1633) who taught that a church consists of a body of believers bound by a covenant to God and each other and that it is independent of any higher ecclesiastical authority **b :** CONGREGATIONALISM 2 **3** *archaic* **:** COMPETENCE 2 **4 :** an independent political state (as a country, a nation)

1**in·de·pen·dent** \ˈ==ˈ=dənt\ *adj* [1*in-* + *dependent*] **1 :** not dependent: as **a** (1) **:** not subject to control by others **:** not subordinate **:** SELF-GOVERNING, AUTONOMOUS, FREE ⟨an ~ nation⟩ ⟨was ~ of outside control⟩ (2) **:** not affiliated with or integrated into a larger controlling unit (as a business unit) ⟨an ~ retail store⟩ (3) **:** originating from outside a given unit (as a business unit) ⟨the corporation hired ~ auditors to check its books⟩ or made by individuals from outside a given unit ⟨an ~ audit⟩ **b** (1) **:** not requiring or relying on something else (as for existence, operation, efficiency) **:** not contingent **:** not conditioned ⟨an ~ conclusion⟩ ⟨~ action⟩ ⟨two effects that are quite ~ of each other⟩ (2) **:** being or acting free of the influence of something else ⟨an ~ witness⟩ ⟨conducting an ~ investigation⟩ (3) **:** not looking to others for one's opinions or for the guidance of one's conduct **:** not biased by others **:** acting or thinking freely or disposed to act or think freely ⟨an ~ mind⟩ ⟨leading an ~ life⟩ ⟨an ~ journal of opinion⟩ (4) **:** not bound by or committed definitively to a political party **:** exercising a totally free political choice ⟨an ~ voter⟩ **c** (1) **:** not requiring or relying on others (as for support, supplies, a livelihood) ⟨was altogether ~ of the praise or condemnation of others⟩ ⟨an ~ source of revenue⟩ ⟨the job made him ~ of his parents⟩ (2) **:** not needing to work for a living **:** having a competence ⟨spent most of his time traveling idly about, having been ~ for years⟩ (3) **:** that is enough to free from the necessity of working for a living **:** making up a competence ⟨a gentleman of ~ means⟩ **d** (1) **:** refusing to look to others for help **:** disliking or refusing to accept assistance or to be under obligation to others ⟨too ~ to accept charity⟩ (2) **:** showing a desire for or love of freedom and absence of constraint **:** marked by impatience with or annoyance at restriction ⟨a bold and ~ manner of acting⟩ ⟨had an ~ air about her⟩ **2** *usu cap* **:** of, relating to, or holding the doctrines of the Independents ⟨an *Independent* church⟩ **3 a :** MAIN 6 ⟨an ~ clause⟩ **b :** ISOLATIVE — used of sound change **c :** that is neither derivable from nor incompatible with another statement ⟨an ~ proposition in logic⟩ **syn** see FREE

2**independent** \"\ *n* **1** *usu cap* **:** an adherent of Independency **2 :** one that is independent ⟨free-lance artists and other ~*s*⟩ ⟨large corporations and the smaller ~*s*⟩; *esp* **:** one that is not bound by or definitively committed to a political party ⟨one third of the voters classify themselves as ~*s* —E.S.Griffith⟩

independent audit *n* **:** an audit made by usu. professional auditors who are wholly independent of the company where the audit is being made — contrasted with *internal audit*

independent baptist *n, usu cap I&B* **:** a member of a pacifist Baptist sect organized in 1927

independent chuck *n* **:** a chuck for holding work by means of four jaws that may be moved separately

independent component *n* **:** a component in a physical-chemical system that may be varied without fixing the condition of the system

independent contractor *n* **:** one that contracts to do work or perform a service for another and that retains total and free control over the means or methods used in doing the work or performing the service

independent chuck

in·de·pen·dent·ly *adv* **:** in an independent manner **:** without dependence on another **:** FREELY ⟨living ~⟩ ⟨thinking and acting ~⟩

independently of *prep* **:** without regard to **:** apart from **:** aside from **:** irrespective of ⟨*independently of* what you may think, I have my own convictions⟩ ⟨it aims rather at persuading the people, *independently of* what the state may or may not want —M.R.Masani⟩

independent of *prep* **:** independently of ⟨*independent of* how others felt, they were sure they were right⟩ ⟨obligation . . . to obey a law, *independent of* those resources which the law provides for its own enforcement —R.P.Ward⟩

independent variable *n* **:** a mathematical variable not dependent on other variables

independing *adj* [1*in-* + *depending* (pres. part. of *depend*)] *obs* **:** INDEPENDENT

in·deprivable \ˈin+\ *adj* [1*in-* + *deprivable*] *archaic* **:** INALIENABLE

in·der·bo·rite \ˌindər'bōˌrīt, -bȯˌ-\ *n* -S [Russ *inderborit*, fr. Lake *Inder*, Kazakhstan, U.S.S.R., its locality + Russ *bor-* + *-it* -ite] **:** a mineral $CaMgB_6O_{11}.11H_2O$ consisting of a hydrous borate of calcium and magnesium

in·der·ite \'indəˌrīt\ *n* -S [Russ *inderit*, fr. Lake *Inder*, Kazakhstan, U.S.S.R., its locality + Russ *-it* -ite] **:** a mineral $Mg_2B_6O_{11}.15H_2O$ consisting of a hydrous borate of magnesium

in·describability \ˈin+\ *n* **1 :** the quality or state of being indescribable **2 :** something indescribable

1**in·describable** \"+\ *adj* [1*in-* + *describable*] **:** that cannot be described: **a :** that cannot be described with precision **:** too vague or indefinite or intangible or complex to be described ⟨a strange ~ feeling —J.C.Powys⟩ **b :** that is beyond description **:** that surpasses description **:** too extreme or too much beyond experience to be adequately described ⟨filled with ~ joy⟩ ⟨scenes of ~ horror⟩ — **in·de·scrib·able·ness** *n* -ES — **in·describably** \"+\ *adv*

2**indescribable** \"\ *n* -S **1 :** something indescribable ⟨a box full of curious trinkets and other ~*s*⟩ **2 indescribables** *pl, archaic slang* **:** TROUSERS

indesert *n* [1*in-* + 3*desert*] *obs* **:** the quality or state of being undeserving **:** lack of merit

1**in·designate** \ən, (ˈ)in+\ *adj* [1*in-* + L *designatus*, past part. of *designare* to point out, designate] **:** not quantified ⟨an ~ proposition in logic⟩

2**indesignate** \"\ *n* -S **:** an indesignate term or proposition in logic

indesinent *adj* [LL *indesinent-, indesinens*, fr. L *in-* 1in- + *desinent-, desinens*, pres. part. of *desinere* to leave off, cease — more at DESINENT] *obs* **:** UNCEASING

in·destructibility \ˈin+\ *n* **:** the quality or state of being indestructible ⟨the ~ of matter⟩

in·de·struc·ti·ble \ˈindəˈstrəktəbəl, -dēˈ-\ *adj* [prob. fr. LL *indestructibilis*, fr. L *in-* 1in- + *destructus* (past part. of *destruere* to tear down, destroy) + *-ibilis* -ible — more at DESTROY] **:** not destructible **:** incapable of being destroyed ⟨any belief more ~ than the belief in the ultimate triumph of justice —Robert Lynd⟩ — **in·de·struc·ti·ble·ness** *n* -ES — **in·de·struc·ti·bly** \-blē, -li\ *adv*

in·detectable \ˈin+\ *adj* [1*in-* + *detectable*] **:** not detectable

in·determinable \ˈin+\ *adj* [1*in-* + *determinable*] **:** not determinable: **a** *obs* **:** not subject to limitation **b :** incapable of being definitely decided or settled ⟨would have raised a host of delicate and ~ questions —Leslie Stephen⟩ **c :** incapable of being definitely fixed ⟨handed out free shoes and clothes to ~ thousands —Dwight Macdonald⟩ or ascertained ⟨a questionable and ~ relationship —Jacob Viner⟩ — **in·de·ter·min·able·ness** *n* — **in·determinably** \"+\ *adv*

in·determinacy \ˈin+\ *n* [*indeterminate* + *-cy*] **:** INDETERMINATION

indeterminacy principle *n* **:** UNCERTAINTY PRINCIPLE

in·determinate \ˈin+\ *adj* [ME *indeterminat*, fr. LL *indeterminatus*, fr. L *in-* 1in- + *determinatus*, past part. of *determinare* to limit, determine — more at DETERMINE] **:** not determinate **:** not definitely determined **:** not clearly established **:** not fixed **:** not settled **:** INDEFINITE, UNCERTAIN, VAGUE, INDISTINCT: as **a** (1) **:** not precisely fixed in extent or size or number or nature ⟨a material used in an ~ number of varieties⟩ ⟨a huge container of ~ volume⟩ ⟨an insect of ~ sex⟩ (2) **:** lacking precision of meaning **:** semantically vague or unfixed ⟨an ~ and obscure phrase⟩ **b :** not fixed beforehand **:** not known in advance ⟨their future remains ~⟩ ⟨when the rebellion will occur is ~⟩ **c :** not leading to a definite end or result ⟨an ~ debate⟩ **:** remaining doubtful and unclear ⟨an ~ point of law⟩ **d** (1) **:** not limited as to the number of possible solutions ⟨an ~ problem in mathematics⟩ (2) *of a number* **:** not limited to one fixed value or to a series of fixed values — opposed to *determinate* **e :** not predetermined by some external force **:** not constrained **:** acting freely **:** SPONTANEOUS ⟨maintaining that moral choice is ~⟩ **f** (1) **:** having a capacity for indefinite elongation **:** not exhibiting determinate growth ⟨~ plants⟩ ⟨an ~ stem⟩; *esp* **:** RACEMOSE ⟨an ~ inflorescence⟩ (2) **:** having no critical photoperiod **g :** phonetically neutral ⟨an ~ vowel⟩ — **in·de·ter·mi·nate·ly** *adv* — **in·de·ter·mi·nate·ness** *n*

indeterminate cleavage *n* **:** cleavage in which all the early cleavage cells possess the potencies of the entire zygote — compare DETERMINATE CLEAVAGE

indeterminate equation *n* **:** an equation in which the unknown quantities admit of an infinite number of values or sets of values

indeterminate form *n* **:** any of the seven undefined expressions

$$\frac{0}{0},\ \frac{\infty}{\infty},\ 0 \cdot \infty,\ \infty - \infty,\ 0^0,\ \infty^0,\ \text{and } 1^\infty$$

that a mathematical function may assume by formal substitution

indeterminate growth *n* **:** growth in which a plant axis is not limited by development of a terminal flower bud or other reproductive structure and so continues to elongate indefinitely (as in racemose inflorescence) — compare DETERMINATE GROWTH

indeterminate sentence *n* **:** a punitive sentence that fixes the term or amount of punishment only within certain limits and leaves the exact term or amount of punishment to be determined by administrative authorities

in·determination \ˈin+\ *n* [*indeterminate* + *-ion*] **:** the quality or state of being indeterminate

in·determined \ˈin+\ *adj* [1*in-* + *determined* (past part. of *determine*)] *archaic* **:** INDETERMINATE

in·determinism \ˈin+\ *n* [1*in-* + *determinism*] **1 :** a theory that the will is free and that deliberate choice and the action following such choice are not completely or not at all determined by or predictable from antecedent causes — compare DETERMINISM **2 :** the quality or state of being indeterminate; *esp* **:** UNPREDICTABILITY

in·determinist \"+\ *n* [fr. *indeterminism*, after such pairs as E *determinism: determinist*] **:** one that holds the theory of indeterminism

in·deterministic \"+\ *adj* **:** of or relating to indeterminism ⟨a mere ~ account of the moral life —Alexander Darroch⟩

in·devotion \ˈin+\ *n* [1*in-* + *devotion*] *archaic* **:** lack of devotion

in·devout \ˈin+\ *adj* [ME *indevout* (trans. of LL *indevotus*), fr. 1*in-* + *devout*] **:** not devout — **in·de·vout·ly** *adv*

1**in·dex** \'inˌdeks\ *n, pl* **indexes** \-ksəz\ *or* **in·di·ces** \-ˌdəˌsēz\ *see sense 8* [L *indic-, index*, fr. *indicare* to point out, indicate — more at INDICATE] **1 :** INDEX FINGER 1, FOREFINGER **2 :** ALIDADE c **3 a :** a usu. alphabetical list that includes all or nearly all items (as topics, names of people and places) considered of special pertinence and fully or partially covered or merely mentioned in a printed or written work (as a book, catalog, or dissertation), that gives with each item the place (as by page number) where it may be found in the work, and that is usu. put at or near the end of the work **b** (1) **:** CARD INDEX (2) **:** STEP INDEX (3) **:** TAB INDEX (4) **:** THUMB INDEX **c :** a computer-processed usu. alphabetical list esp. of bibliographical information; *esp* **:** a bibliographical analysis of groups of publications that is usu. published periodically ⟨*Index* Medicus⟩ **4 :** something that serves as a pointer or indicator: as **a :** a pointer (as of metal, plastic, wood) that moves along a graduated scale (as of a weighing machine) or that remains fixed while the scale moves past its tip **b :** one of the hands on a timepiece **c :** the gnomon of a sundial **5** *obs* **:** DIRECT 1 **6 a :** something (as a manner of speaking or acting, a distinctive physical feature) in another person or thing that leads an observer to surmise a particular fact or draw a particular conclusion **:** SIGN, TOKEN, INDICATION ⟨her fatuous laugh is an ~ of her pygmy intelligence⟩ ⟨the fertility of the land is an ~ of the country's wealth⟩ **b :** a sign whose specific character is causally dependent on the object to which it refers but independent of an interpretant ⟨a bullet hole in a fence is an ~ that a shot has been fired⟩ — contrasted with *icon* and *symbol* **7 a :** a list of restricted or prohibited or otherwise proscribed material ⟨an ~ of forbidden books⟩ **b** *usu cap* **:** INDEX LIBRORUM PROHIBITORUM **8** *pl usu indices* **:** a number or symbol or expression written to the left or right of and above or below or otherwise associated with another number or symbol or expression to indicate use or position in an arrangement or expansion or to indicate a mathematical operation to be performed ⟨the *indices* 2 and 3 used to locate the element a_{23} in the second row and third column of a determinant⟩ ⟨3 is the ~ in the expression $\sqrt[3]{5}$ to specify a cube root of 5⟩ **9** *or* **index mark :** a character ☞ used to direct particular attention (as to a note or paragraph) and as the seventh in series of the reference marks — called also *fist, hand* **10 a :** a ratio or other number derived from a series of observations and used as an indicator or measure (as of a condition, property, or phenomenon) ⟨a discrepancy ~ based on the differences between the students' predicted and attained honor-point ratios —*Educational & Psychological Measurement*⟩ ⟨the ~ of variation . . . is obtained by considering the positive differences between every pair of incomes in the group and averaging these differences —*Economica*⟩ ⟨an ~ is a measurable aspect of society which indicates the extent to which certain more complex aspects are present —Mabel Elliott & Francis Merrill⟩; *specif* **:** INDEX NUMBER ⟨the ~ of industrial production increased from 113.2 in December 1950 to 122.0 by November 1951 (1946 = 100) —*Americana Annual*⟩ — see CONSUMER PRICE INDEX, DOW-JONES INDEX; INDEX OF REFRACTION **b :** the ratio of one dimension of a thing (as an anatomical structure) to another dimension — see CEPHALIC INDEX **11 :** a miniature indication of denomination and value often printed on the corners of playing cards to make it unnecessary to view the full face of each card

index 11

2**index** \"\ *vb* -ED/-ING/-ES *vt* **1 a :** to provide (as a book) with an index ⟨the book will be ~*ed* in its next edition so as to make it more useful⟩ **b :** to list (as the contents of a book) in an index ⟨all persons and places mentioned are carefully ~*ed*⟩ **2 a :** to serve as an index of ⟨wrinkles ~ advancing age⟩ **b :** to point to **:** INDICATE ⟨a compass needle that ~*es* true north⟩ **3 :** to move (a machine or a piece of work held in a machine tool) so that a specific operation (as the cutting of gear teeth) will be repeated at definite intervals of space **4 :** to determine the fertility or yielding ability or disease resistance or some other character of (a plant or seed) by planting and testing a sample in advance of release for general use — used esp. of potatoes ⟨~*ing* potato eyes⟩ ⟨~*ing* a potato of each hill⟩ ~ *vi* **:** to index something

index bar *n* **:** the movable arm of a sextant

index center *n* **:** one of a pair of machine-tool centers or jaws provided with means of rotating a piece of work by predetermined equal amounts (as in cutting gear teeth)

index crank *n* **:** the crank of an index head whose turning a specified amount transmits through gearing a definite angular movement to the index-head spindle

in·dex·er \-sə(r)\ *n* -S **1 :** one that makes an index or works at indexing **2 a :** one who operates a machine for cutting index indentations into pages (as of reference books) **b :** one who prepares material (as reference books) for a machine that cuts index indentations or who prepares material for the insertion of index tabs

index ex·pur·ga·to·ri·us \-ikˌspərgə'tōrēəs, -ek-, -ȯr-\ *n, pl* **indices expurgato·rii** \-rēˌī, -rēˌē\ [NL, expurgatory index] **1** *sometimes cap I&E* **:** a list of proscribed material (as books) **2** *usu cap I&E* **:** a list of books once separately published and now included in the Index Librorum Prohibitorum that gives titles of works forbidden by church authority to Roman Catholics pending revision or deletion of some sections

index finger *n* **1 :** the digit next to the thumb **:** FOREFINGER **2 :** INDEX 9

index forest *n* **:** a forest that in density, volume, and increment reaches the highest average in a given locality

index fossil *n* **:** a fossil that is usu. of narrow time range and wide spatial distribution and that is used in the identification of related geologic formations (as in locating new petroleum reserves)

index finger 1

index glass *n* **:** the mirror on the index bar of a sextant or similar instrument

index hand *n* **:** a pointer or hand for indicating something (as a reading on a dial) **:** INDICATOR

index head *or* **indexing head** *n* **:** a headstock attachable to the table of a milling machine, planer, or shaper on which work may be mounted by a chuck or centers for indexing

in·dex·i·cal \ən'deksəkəl, (ˈ)inˈd-,\ *adj* [1*index* + *-ical*] **:** of, relating to, or resembling an index ⟨~ errors⟩ ⟨~ lists⟩

in·dex·i·cal·ly \-sək(ə)lē\ *adv* [1*index* + *-ical* + *-ly*] **:** by way of an index **:** in the manner of an index ⟨what is ~ referred to —C.W.Morris⟩

in·dex·less \'inˌdeksləs\ *adj* **:** having no index ⟨an ~ book⟩

index li·bro·rum pro·hib·i·to·rum \-lī'brōrəmprōˌhibə'tōrəm, -ȯr-\ *n, pl* **indices librorum prohibitorum** [NL, index of prohibited books] **1** *sometimes cap I&L&P* **:** a list of proscribed books **2** *usu cap I&L&P* **:** a list of books condemned in whole or in part as dangerous to faith or morals by church authority and forbidden to Roman Catholics — compare INDEX EXPURGATORIUS

index liquid *n* **:** a liquid of known refractive index used (as in crystallography) in the determination of the refractive index of powdered substances with a microscope

index map *n* **:** a map that shows (as by enclosing a small area in a rectangle on a large map) the location of one or more small areas in relation to a larger area and that typically points up special features in the small areas about which information is desired

index mark *n* **:** INDEX 9

index number *n* **:** a number used to indicate change in magnitude (as of cost, price, or volume of production) as compared with the magnitude at some specified time usu. taken as 100 ⟨if the cost of an item in 1930 was one and one half as much as its cost in 1913, its *index number*, relative to 1913, was 150⟩ ⟨relative *index numbers* representing changes in price level of the particular type of asset being considered would be used for the purpose of converting fixed assets to current dollar values —*Accountants Digest*⟩ — used esp. in statistics

index of refraction : the ratio of the velocity of light or other radiation in the first of two media to its velocity in the second as it passes from one into the other, the first medium being usu. taken to be a vacuum — called also *refractive index*

index percent *n* **:** the increase in value of a tree or of a forest due to the combined volume, quality, and price increments and expressed as an annual percent of its present value

index plane *also* **index horizon** *n* **:** a surface (as the top of a sedimentary bed) used in working out geological structure

index plate *n* **:** a graduated circular plate or one with circular rows of holes differently spaced that is used in machines (as for graduating circles or cutting gear teeth)

index re·rum \-'rērəm\ *n, pl* **indices rerum** [NL, index of things] **:** an index of topics covered (as in a book)

index species *n* **:** a plant or animal species so highly adapted to a particular kind of environment that its presence is sufficient indication that a habitat under investigation belongs to the kind to which the species is adapted

index table *n* **:** a horizontal index head

in·dexterity \ˈin+\ *n* [1*in-* + *dexterity*] **:** lack of dexterity

index ver·bo·rum \-(ˌ)vər'bōrəm, -bȯr-\ *n, pl* **indices verborum** [NL, index of words] **:** an index of words or terms (as those discussed in a book)

indi- — see IND-

1**in·dia** \'indēə *chiefly Brit* -dyə\ *adj, usu cap* [fr. *India*, republic and subcontinent (including the Republic of India and Pakistan) in southern Asia, fr. L *India*, subcontinent in southern Asia, fr. Gk, fr. *Indos* India (subcontinent in southern Asia), Indus (river in the northwestern part of the Indian subcontinent), fr. OPer *Hindu* India; akin to Skt *sindhu* river, Indus, region of the Indus] **1 :** of or from the subcontinent of India **:** of the kind or style prevalent in the subcontinent of India **:** INDIAN **2 :** of or from the Republic of India **:** of the kind or style prevalent in the Republic of India

²india \"\ *usu cap* — a communications code word for the letter *i*

india buff *n, often cap I* **:** a light yellowish brown that is redder, lighter, and stronger than khaki, yellower than walnut brown, and yellower and paler than cinnamon

india drugget *n, usu cap I* **:** DRUGGET 3

india gum *usu cap I, var of* INDIAN GUM

india ink *n, often cap 1st I* [so called fr. a belief that it was made in India] **1 :** a black pigment (as specially prepared lampblack mixed with a glutinous binder and sometimes perfume) in the form of sticks or cakes and used in drawing and lettering **2 :** a fluid ink consisting usu. of a fine suspension of india-ink pigment in a liquid medium (as water containing a gum) — called also *China ink, Chinese ink*

india malacca *n, usu cap I* **:** any of several rattan palms of the genus *Calamus* used for making walking sticks

in·dia·man \-mən\ *n, pl* **indiamen** *usu cap* **:** a merchant ship formerly used in trade with India; *esp* **:** a large sailing ship used in this trade

¹in·di·an \'indēən *chiefly Brit* -dyən, *in sense 2 chiefly dial* 'injən *or sometimes* 'in(,)din\ *n* -s *cap* [prob. fr. (assumed) ML *Indianus*, fr. ML *indianus*, adj.] **1 a :** a native or inhabitant of the subcontinent of India or of the East Indies — compare PAKISTANI **b :** one of the native languages of the subcontinent of India or of the East Indies **2 a** [so called fr. the belief on the part of Columbus that the lands discovered by him in 1492 and later were part of Asia] **:** AMERICAN INDIAN **b :** one of the native languages of American Indians

²indian \"\ *adj, usu cap* [prob. fr. ML *indianus*, fr. L *India*, subcontinent in southern Asia + *-anus* -an (adj. suffix)] **1 a** (1) **:** of, relating to, or characteristic of the subcontinent of India or the East Indies (2) **:** of, relating to, or characteristic of one of the peoples of the subcontinent of India or the East Indies **b :** of, relating to, or characteristic of one of the native languages of the subcontinent of India or the East Indies **c** (1) **:** ORIENTAL 4 (2) **:** of, relating to, or constituting the subregion of the biogeographical region that includes Ceylon and the subcontinent of India north to the Himalayas and west to the Persian gulf or sometimes these areas excepting Ceylon and the adjacent part of the subcontinent of India **2 a** [after ¹*indian* 2a] **:** of, relating to, or characteristic of the American Indians **b :** of, relating to, or characteristic of one of the native languages of American Indians **3 :** of, relating to, or characteristic of the West Indies

¹in·di·ana \,indē'anə\ *adj, usu cap* [fr. *Indiana*, state in the north central U. S., fr. NL *indiana*, fem. of *indianus*, adj., Indian (sense 2a), fr. ML, Indian (sense 1a)] **:** of or from the state of Indiana ⟨*Indiana* writers⟩ **:** of the kind or style prevalent in Indiana **:** INDIANAN

²indiana \"\ *n, often cap* [fr. *Indiana*, state in the north central U. S.] **:** a vivid purplish red that is redder, lighter, and stronger than rubellite and bluer and deeper than malmaison rose

indiana ballot *n, usu cap I* [so called fr. its adoption by Indiana in 1889] **:** an Australian ballot upon which the names of candidates are placed in separate columns according to their party affiliations with the party name and sometimes emblem at the top of each column — called also *party-column ballot;* compare MASSACHUSETTS BALLOT, OFFICE-BLOCK BALLOT

indian agent *n, usu cap I* **:** an official representative of the U. S. federal government to American Indian tribes esp. on reservations

in·di·an·a·ite \,indē'anə,īt\ *n* -s [*Indiana*, state in the north central U. S., its locality + E *-ite*] **:** a variety of halloysite

indiana limestone *n, usu cap I* [so called fr. its quarrying site in southern Indiana] **:** a usu. gray or buff oolitic Mississippian limestone of the lower Carboniferous that is uniform and easily worked and widely used for building

indian almond *n, usu cap I* [²*indian* 1] **:** MALABAR ALMOND

¹in·di·an·an \;indē;anən\ *or* **in·di·an·i·an** \-;anēən, -nyən\ *adj, usu cap* [*Indiana* + E *-an*, *-ian* (adj. suffix)] **1 :** of, relating to, or characteristic of the state of Indiana **2 :** of, relating to, or characteristic of the people of Indiana

²indianan \"\ *or* **indianian** \"\ *n* -s *cap* [*Indiana* + E *-an*, *-ian* (n. suffix)] **:** a native or resident of Indiana

indian antelope *n, usu cap I* [²*indian* 1] **:** BLACK BUCK 1

in·di·an·ap·o·lis \;indēə;nap(ə)ləs *sometimes* -di;-\ *adj, usu cap* **:** of or from Indianapolis, the capital of Indiana ⟨an *Indianapolis* lawyer⟩ **:** of the kind or style prevalent in Indianapolis

in·di·an·a·pol·i·tan \,indē,anə'pälət°n\ *n* -s *cap* [fr. *Indianapolis*, after such pairs as E *metropolis: metropolitan*] **:** a native or resident of Indianapolis, Indiana

indian apple *n, usu cap I* [²*indian* 2] **:** MAYAPPLE

indian arrow *n, usu cap I* [²*indian* 2] **:** ²WAHOO a

indian arrowroot *n, usu cap I* [²*indian* 2] **1 a :** a tropical American arrowroot (*Maranta arundinacea*) **b :** starch from this arrowroot — called also *West Indian arrowroot* **2** [²*indian* 1] **a :** a stemless perennial herb (*Tacca leontopetaloides*) widely cultivated in the tropics for its starchy tuberous rootstock **b :** starch from this plant — called also *East Indian arrowroot*

indian arrowwood *n, usu cap I* [²*indian* 2] **1 :** FLOWERING DOGWOOD **2 :** ²WAHOO a

indian azalea *n, usu cap I* [²*indian* 1] **1 a :** a somewhat bristly evergreen Japanese azalea (*Rhododendron indicum*) with paired or solitary bright red or rosy red flowers containing 5 stamens **b :** a hairy or bristly evergreen Chinese azalea (*Rhododendron simsii*) with large clustered rosy red to dark red flowers containing 10 stamens **2 :** any of numerous usu. tender cultivated azaleas that have single or double flowers in many colors and color combinations and that have been developed by selection from and hybridization of the Chinese Indian azalea and other evergreen azaleas

indian balm *n, usu cap I* [²*indian* 2] **:** PURPLE TRILLIUM

indian barberry *n, usu cap I* [²*indian* 1] **:** any of several deciduous barberries of southern Asia including some (as *Berberis aristata*) that are occas. cultivated — see DYER'S BARBERRY

indian bark *n, usu cap I* [²*indian* 2] **:** EVERGREEN MAGNOLIA

indian bean *n, usu cap I* **1 a :** a No. American catalpa (*Catalpa bignonioides*) with flat pods resembling beans **b :** a pod of this catalpa **2 :** the fruit of the groundnut **3 :** HYACINTH BEAN

indian beech *n, usu cap I* **:** an Asiatic tree (*Pongamia glabra*) of the family Leguminosae that has glossy pinnate leaves and racemose creamy-white scented flowers and that is used as a shade tree and as the source of an oil used for illumination

indian beet *n, usu cap I* [²*indian* 2] **:** WILD LUPINE

indian berry *n, usu cap I* [²*indian* 1] **:** COCCULUS INDICUS

indian birch *n, usu cap I* **:** a Himalayan tree (*Betula utilis*) with bark resembling that of the common paper birch

indian bison *n, usu cap I* [²*indian* 1] **:** GAUR

indian bitters *n, usu cap I* **:** an American magnolia (*Magnolia fraseri*) having a bitter bark formerly used as a tonic

indian blanket *n, usu cap I* **1 :** a blanket made by American Indians or made in imitation of Indian designs — compare NAVAHO BLANKET **2 :** an annual herb (*Gaillardia pulchella*) of the central U. S. that has showy yellow flower heads marked with scarlet or purple in the center

indian block *n, usu cap I* **:** a close-quarter block used in lacrosse in which the stick is directed across the opponent's stick

indian blue *n, usu cap I* [²*indian* 1] **:** INDIGO 3

indian blue pine *n, usu cap I* [²*indian* 1] **:** BHOTAN PINE

indian boys and girls *n pl, usu cap I* [²*indian* 2] **:** DUTCHMAN'S-BREECHES

indian bread *n, usu cap I* [²*indian* 2] **1 :** CORN BREAD **2 :** TUCKAHOE 2

indian breadroot *n, usu cap I* [²*indian* 2] **:** BREADROOT 1

indian bridle *n, usu cap I* [²*indian* 2] **:** a rope bridle in which the cord passes from the animal's mouth through a loop about its throat

indian brown *n, usu cap I* [prob. fr. ²*indian* 1] **:** OLD ENGLISH BROWN

indian buffalo *n, usu cap I* **:** an upland buffalo of eastern Asia kept for draft and milk production esp. in areas where the true water buffalo does not thrive

indian bullfrog *n, usu cap I* **:** a large loud-voiced frog (*Rana tigrina*) of India and Malaysia

indian butter *n, usu cap I* **:** butter derived from the Himalayan butter tree — called also *phulwa butter*

indian cane *n, usu cap I* [²*indian* 1] **1 :** INDIAN SHOT **2 :** the stem of the turmeric **3 :** BAMBOO

indian cedar *n, usu cap I* [²*indian* 1] **1 :** DEODAR **2** [²*indian* 2] **:** HOP HORNBEAM **3** [²*indian* 2] **:** SPANISH CEDAR **4 :** TOON

indian cherry *n, usu cap I* [²*indian* 2] **1 :** YELLOW BUCKTHORN **2 :** JUNEBERRY

indian chickweed *n, usu cap I* [²*indian* 2] **:** CARPETWEED

indian chief *n, usu cap I* [²*indian* 2] **:** SHOOTING STAR 2

indian cigar tree *n, usu cap I* [²*indian* 2] **:** INDIAN BEAN 1

indian civet *n, usu cap I* [²*indian* 1] **:** ZIBET

indian clover *n, usu cap I* [²*indian* 2] **:** a plant of the genus *Trifolium* (esp. *T. dichotomum*)

indian club *n, usu cap I* [²*indian* 1] **:** a fairly heavy club (as of wood or metal) shaped like a large bottle or tenpin and swung about usu. with one in each hand to strengthen the muscles of the arms

Indian club

indian cobra *n, usu cap I* **:** a very venomous cobra (*Naja naja*) that is found esp. about settled areas and dwellings in southern and eastern Asia and eastward to the Philippines, that is yellowish to dark brown usu. with spectacle-shaped black and white markings on the expansible hood, and that sometimes reaches a length of 6 feet — called also *spectacled cobra*

indian cockle *n, usu cap I* [²*indian* 1] **:** COCCULUS INDICUS

indian cork tree *n, usu cap I* **:** an East Indian timber tree (*Millingtonia hortensis*) of the family Bignoniaceae that yields an inferior cork and is used for decoration

indian corn *n, usu cap I* [²*indian* 2] **1 :** a tall cereal grass (*Zea mays*) bearing kernels on typically large ears and long cultivated in America **2 a :** the ripened ears of Indian corn **b :** the kernels of Indian corn widely used as food for human beings and livestock

indian couch grass *n, usu cap I* [²*indian* 1] **:** BERMUDA GRASS

indian creeper *n, usu cap I* [²*indian* 2] **:** TRUMPET CREEPER

indian cucumber *or* **indian cucumber root** *n, usu cap I* **:** a small American herb (*Medeola virginiana*) of the lily family with a white succulent rootstock and with leaves in two whorls of which the upper whorl subtends an umbel of small greenish yellow flowers

indian cup *n, usu cap I* [²*indian* 2] **1 :** a plant of the genus *Sarracenia; esp* **:** PITCHER PLANT a **2 :** CUP PLANT

indian currant *n, usu cap I* **1 a :** a No. American shrub (*Symphoricarpos orbiculatus*) **b :** the red fruit of this shrub resembling a berry **2 :** a shrub (*Ribes glutinosum*) of the Pacific coast of No. America with showy racemose red flowers and black fragrant fruit

indian devil *n, usu cap I* [²*indian* 2] **:** WOLVERINE 1a

indian doctor *n, usu cap I* [²*indian* 2] **1 :** MEDICINE MAN **2 :** a white man professing himself a medical practitioner and resorting chiefly to the use of medicinal herbs

indian dye *n, usu cap I* [²*indian* 2] **:** GOLDENSEAL

indian ebony *n, usu cap I* [²*indian* 1] **:** a tree of the genus *Diospyros; esp* **:** a green ebony (*Diospyros melanoxylon*)

indian elm *n, usu cap I* [²*indian* 2] **:** SLIPPERY ELM 1

indian fiber *n, usu cap I* [²*indian* 2] **:** PIASSAVA 1

indian fig *n, usu cap I* [²*indian* 1] **1 :** BANYAN **2** [²*indian* 2] **a :** any of several plants of the genus *Opuntia:* as (1) **:** a tropical American prickly pear (*Opuntia fidus-indica*) (2) **:** an eastern No. American prickly pear (*Opuntia compressa*) **b :** the edible acid fruit of one of these plants

¹indian file *n, usu cap I* [²*indian* 2; fr. the Indian practice of going through woods in single file] **:** SINGLE FILE ⟨along this road the inhabitants slowly moved in *Indian file* —*Newsweek*⟩

²indian file *adv, usu cap I* **:** in single file ⟨where two people have to walk *Indian file* —Elizabeth Montizambert⟩

indian fire *n, usu cap I* [²*indian* 1] **:** BENGAL LIGHT 1

indianfish \'==,=\ *n* [²*indian* 2] **1 :** an angelfish (*Pomacanthus paru*) of the western Atlantic from Florida to Brazil **2 :** WARMOUTH

indian fog *n, usu cap I* [²*indian* 2] **:** DWARF HOUSELEEK

indian frankincense *n, usu cap I* [²*indian* 1] **:** FRANKINCENSE 1

indian game *n, usu cap I&G* [²*indian* 1; fr. its having been produced by crossing English game fowl with Indian and Sumatran game fowl] **:** CORNISH 2

indian gift *n, usu cap I* **:** something given by an Indian giver

indian giver *n, usu cap I* [²*indian* 2] **:** one who gives something to another and then takes it back or expects an equivalent in return

indian giving *n, usu cap I* **:** the type of giving typical of an Indian giver

indian gooseberry *n, usu cap I* [²*indian* 1] **:** EMBLIC

indian gram *n, usu cap I* [²*indian* 1] **:** CHICK-PEA

indian grass *n, usu cap I* [²*indian* 2] **:** WOOD GRASS 1

indian gravelroot *n, usu cap I* [²*indian* 2] **:** JOE-PYE WEED

indian gum *also* **india gum** *n, usu cap I* [²*indian* 1 *or india* + *gum*] **1 :** GHATTI GUM **2 :** STERCULIA GUM; *esp* **:** the common karaya gum of India

indian harvest *n, usu cap I* [²*indian* 2] *obs* **:** a harvest of Indian corn

indian hawthorn *n, usu cap I* [²*indian* 1] **:** an ornamental evergreen shrub (*Raphiolepis indica*) with sharp-serrate leaves and racemes of pink-tinged white flowers

indian hemp *n, usu cap I* [²*indian* 2] **1 :** a No. American dogbane (*Apocynum cannabinum*) that yields a tough fiber formerly used in cordage; *broadly* **:** DOGBANE 1 — compare RHEUMATISM WEED **2** [²*indian* 1] **:** HEMP 1 **3** [²*indian* 1] **:** an Indian mallow (*Abutilon theophrasti*) **4** [²*indian* 1] **:** SUNN **5 :** SWAMP MILKWEED

indian–hemp resin *n, usu cap I* [*indian hemp* (sense 2) + *resin*] **:** CHARAS

indian hen *n, usu cap I* [²*indian* 2] **1 :** AMERICAN BITTERN **2 :** PILEATED WOODPECKER

indian hippo *n, usu cap I* [²*indian* 2 + *hippo* (perh. alter. of ¹*hypo*)] **1 :** INDIAN PHYSIC 1 **2 :** the rhizome and roots of Indian hippo used as a mild emetic

indianian *usu cap, var of* INDIANAN

indian ink *n, usu cap I* [²*indian* 1; fr. a belief that it was made in India] *Brit* **:** INDIA INK

indian ipecac *n, usu cap I* [²*indian* 1] **1 a :** an Asiatic vine (*Tylophora asthmatica*) resembling milkweed **b :** the root of this vine **2** [²*indian* 2] **:** INDIAN PHYSIC **3** [²*indian* 2] **:** IPECAC 1

in·di·an·ism \'indēə,nizəm, -dyə,n-\ *n* -s *usu cap* **1 :** the qualities or culture distinctive or felt to be distinctive of Indians, esp. of American Indians **2 a :** action or policy directed toward furthering the interests and culture of Indians, esp. of American Indians **b :** specialized interest in or emulation or glorification of the arts and crafts and other achievements of Indians, esp. of American Indians **3 :** a word or phrase distinctive or felt to be distinctive of the speech of Indians, esp. of American Indians

in·di·an·ist \-,nəst\ *n* -s *usu cap* **:** a specialist in or advocate of Indianism

in·di·an·iza·tion \,indēənə'zāshən\ *n* -s *usu cap* **:** the act or process of indianizing or the state of being indianized

in·di·an·ize \'indēə,nīz\ *vt* -ED/-ING/-s *see -ize in Explan Notes, often cap* [²*indian* 1&2 + *-ize*] **1 :** to make Indian (as in manner of behavior or in culture or appearance) **:** cause to have Indian characteristics **:** adapt to Indian conditions or practices ⟨contact with Indians gradually *indianized* some of the settlers⟩ **2 :** to cause (as the staff of a government agency) to be made up largely or wholly of Indians

indian jacana *n, usu cap I* [²*indian* 1] **:** PHEASANT-TAILED JACANA

indian jalap *n, usu cap I* [²*indian* 1] **:** TURPETH 1

indian jujube *n, usu cap I* [²*indian* 1] **1 :** a shrub or small tree (*Ziziphus mauritiana*) of southeastern Asia cultivated in the southeastern U.S. **2 :** the globose dark red fruit of the Indian jujube

indian kale *n, usu cap I* [²*indian* 2] **:** any of several large-leaved arums (family Araceae) with edible farinaceous rootstocks: as **a :** TARO **b :** YAUTIA

indian laburnum *n, usu cap I* [²*indian* 1] **:** DRUMSTICK TREE

indian lacquer *n, usu cap I* **:** a natural black varnish obtained in Ceylon and the subcontinent of India as an exudation from the marking nut or a related tree (*Holigarna longifolia*)

indian ladder *n, usu cap I* [²*indian* 2] **:** a ladder made of or as if of a small tree so trimmed that several inches of each branch are left as a support for the foot

indian lake *n, usu cap I* [prob. fr. ²*indian* 1] **1 :** a red lake prepared from lac dye and formerly used by painters **2** *often cap I* **:** a dark to deep purplish red that is bluer and slightly lighter than magenta (sense 2c)

indian lamb *n, usu cap I* [²*indian* 1] **:** the pelt of the young of an Indian sheep of Persian type usu. white with a looser curl to the hair than Persian lamb and usu. dyed gray before use

indian laurel *also* **indian laurelwood** *n, usu cap I* **1 :** an Asiatic tree (*Persea indica*) that produces canary wood **2 :** any of various trees of the genus *Terminalia* (esp. *T. alata* and *T. tomentosa*)

indian lettuce *n, usu cap I* [²*indian* 2] **1 :** ROUND-LEAVED WINTERGREEN **2 :** AMERICAN COLUMBO **3 :** a succulent herb (*Montia perfoliata*) of the Pacific coast of No. America; *broadly* **:** a plant of the genus *Montia* (as blinks)

indian licorice *n, usu cap I* **:** an East Indian twining herb (*Abrus precatorius*) with pinnate leaves and axillary clusters of small purple flowers and a root that is used as a substitute for licorice — see JEQUIRITY

indian lilac *n, usu cap I* [²*indian* 1] **1 :** CHINABERRY 2 **2 :** CRAPE MYRTLE

indian lotus *n, usu cap I* **:** an aquatic plant (*Nelumbo nucifera*) native to eastern Asia and widely cultivated for its foliage and large pink flowers — compare LOTUS 3

indian madder *n, usu cap I* **1 :** an East Indian plant (*Rubia cordifolia*) used for dyeing in the Orient — called also *munjeet* **2 :** CHAY

indian mahogany *n, usu cap I* [²*indian* 1] **1 :** TOON **2 a :** ROHUN **b :** the wood of rohun

indian maize *n, usu cap I* [²*indian* 2] **:** INDIAN CORN

indian mallow *n, usu cap I* [²*indian* 1] **1 :** any of several abutilons; *esp* **:** a tall annual herb (*Abutilon theophrasti*) that has velvety cordate leaves and yellow flowers, yields a long strong fiber for which it is sometimes cultivated, and is native to India but widely naturalized as an escape in warm and temperate regions — called also *velvetleaf* **2** [²*indian* 2] **:** a tropical American weed (*Sida spinosa*) with pale yellow or orange flowers that has been introduced into the U.S. and is found esp. in the southern U.S.

indian maple *n, usu cap I* **:** a Himalayan maple (*Acer caesium*) with large palmate leaves

indian meal *n, usu cap I* [²*indian* 2] **:** CORNMEAL

indian meal moth *n, usu cap I* [*indian meal* + *moth*] **:** a small variably marked pyralid moth (*Plodia interpunctella*) having an equally variably colored larva that feeds on cereal products and other dried foods and by its extensive webbing destroys more than it consumes

indian melon *n, usu cap I* [²*indian* 2] **:** BARREL CACTUS

indian millet *n, usu cap I* [²*indian* 1] **1 :** DURRA **2 :** PEARL MILLET 1 **3** [²*indian* 2] **:** SILKGRASS 2

indian moccasin *n, usu cap I* [²*indian* 2] **:** STEMLESS LADY'S-SLIPPER

indian mound *n, usu cap I* [²*indian* 2] **:** one of the mounds of the Mound Builders

indian mulberry *n, usu cap I* **1 :** an East Indian shrub or small tree (*Morinda citrifolia*) with axillary heads of flowers and pulpy fruit **2 a :** WHITE MULBERRY **b :** a related mulberry (*Morus indica*)

indian mustard *n, usu cap I* **:** an Asiatic mustard (*Brassica juncea*) that has pods growing at an angle with their stems and that is used as a potherb and is widely naturalized as a weed — called also *leaf mustard*

indian nut *n, usu cap I* [²*indian* 1] **1 :** BETEL NUT **2** [²*indian* 2] **:** PINE NUT 2

indian oak *n, usu cap I* [²*indian* 1] **1 :** TEAK **2 :** any of several oaks (esp. *Quercus dilatata*) of India

indian ocher *n, usu cap I* [²*indian* 1] **:** INDIAN RED 1a

indian orange *n, often cap I* [prob. fr. ²*indian* 1] **:** a vivid reddish orange that is paler than international orange and redder and darker than golden poppy or chrome orange

indian ox *n, usu cap I* [²*indian* 1] **:** ZEBU

indian paint *n, usu cap I* [²*indian* 2] **1 :** BLOODROOT 1 **2 :** STRAWBERRY BLITE **3 :** HOARY PUCCOON

indian paintbrush *n, usu cap I* [²*indian* 2] **1 :** any of various American plants of the genus *Castilleja; esp* **:** a widely distributed annual or biennial (*C. coccinea*) of the eastern U.S. that usu. has bright scarlet floral bracts — called also *painted cup* **2 :** ORANGE HAWKWEED

indian paint fungus *n, usu cap I* [²*indian* 2] **:** a tooth fungus (*Echinodontium tinctorum*) that causes heartrot in fir or spruce or western hemlock

indian pangolin *n, usu cap I* [²*indian* 1] **:** a scaly anteater (*Manis crassicaudata* syn. *Phatages crassicaudata*) with heavily scaled tail and feet and small ears

indian pea *n, usu cap I* [²*indian* 1] **1 :** PIGEON PEA **2 :** GRASS PEA

indian peacock *or* **indian peafowl** *n, usu cap I* [²*indian* 1] **:** the common domesticated peafowl (*Pavo cristatus*) which is native to India and Siam and in which the wings of the male are largely barred in black and buff — compare JAPANNED PEACOCK

indian pear *n, usu cap I* [²*indian* 2] **:** JUNEBERRY

indian physic *n, usu cap I* **1 :** either of two American herbs (*Gillenia trifoliata* and *G. stipulata*) with emetic roots **2 :** INDIAN BITTERS **3 :** INDIAN HEMP 1

indian pine *n, usu cap I* [²*indian* 2] **:** LOBLOLLY PINE 1

indian pink *n* [²*indian* 1] **1** *usu cap I* **a :** CHINA PINK **b** *or* **indian pinkroot** [²*indian* 2] **:** PINKROOT a **c** [²*indian* 2] *West Indies* **:** CYPRESS VINE **d** [²*indian* 2] **:** GAYWINGS **e** [²*indian* 2] **:** INDIAN PAINTBRUSH 1 **f** [²*indian* 2] **:** any of several wild pinks of the genera *Silene* and *Lychnis* **g** [²*indian* 2] **:** CARDINAL FLOWER **2** *often cap I* **:** a light reddish brown that is redder, lighter, and stronger than copper tan or monkey skin and redder and duller than peach tan

indian pipe *n, usu cap I* [²*indian* 2; perh. fr. the use of its pithy stems by American Indians for the stems of tobacco pipes] **:** a leafless saprophytic herb (*Monotropa uniflora*) native to Asia and the U.S. that is waxy white and turns black in drying and has a solitary nodding flower that becomes erect in fruit; *broadly* **:** SWEET PINESAP

indian–pipe family *n, usu cap I* **:** PYROLACEAE

indian pitcher *n, usu cap I* [²*indian* 2] **:** PITCHER PLANT a

indian plantain *n, usu cap I* **:** any of various plants of the genus *Cacalia* that have leaves resembling those of plantains

indian plum *n, usu cap I* [²*indian* 1] **1 a :** any of several tropical trees of the genus *Flacourtia* (esp. *F. indica*) — compare GOVERNOR'S PLUM **b :** the edible rather acid plum-shaped fruit of one of these trees **2** [²*indian* 2] **:** OSOBERRY

indian plume *n, usu cap I* [²*indian* 2] **:** BUTTERFLY WEED 1

indian–plum family *n, usu cap I* **:** FLACOURTIACEAE

indian poke *n, usu cap I* **:** AMERICAN HELLEBORE 1

indian pony *n, usu cap I* **1 :** an unimproved typically small hardy vigorous not esp. graceful horse of western No. America descended from stock introduced by Spaniards and redomesticated by Indians that is valuable as a utility range horse and for crossbreeding — compare MUSTANG, QUARTER HORSE **2 :** ¹PINTO

indian posy *n, usu cap I* **1 :** any of several American everlastings (as *Anaphalis margaritacea* and *Gnaphalium obtusifolium*) **2 :** BUTTERFLY WEED 1

indian potato *n, usu cap I* **:** any of several American plants with edible tuberous roots: as **a :** GROUNDNUT 2a **b :** GIANT SUNFLOWER **c :** BREADROOT 1 **d :** a yamp (*Carum gairdneri*)

indian puccoon *n, usu cap I* [²*indian* 2] **:** HOARY PUCCOON

indian pudding *n, usu cap I* [²*indian* 2] **:** a pudding usu. made of cornmeal, milk, sugar, butter, molasses, and spices and baked and served as a dessert

indian purple *n, often cap I* [prob. fr. ²*indian* 1] **:** a dark purplish red that is paler and slightly redder than pansy purple, redder and paler than raisin, bluer and paler than Bokhara, and redder and less strong than Schoenfeld's purple

indian python *n, usu cap I* **:** a very large python (*Python molurus*) of southeastern Asia that is mottled with dark blotches on an olive to pinkish tan ground

indian red *n* [²*indian* 1] **1** *usu cap I* **a :** a yellowish red ferruginous earth containing hematite and used as a pigment — called also *Persian red* **b :** any of various light red to purplish brown iron oxide pigments made by calcining iron salts (as copperas) **2** *often cap I* **a :** a strong reddish brown that is redder and slightly darker than Venetian red — called also *Japanese red, Prussian red* **b :** a moderate reddish brown — called also *Chinese red, Majolica earth, Persian earth, Persian red, scarlet ocher, Spanish brown*

indian redroot *n, usu cap I* [2*indian* 2] **:** REDROOT

indian redwood *n, usu cap I* [2*indian* 1] **1 :** INDIAN MAHOGANY **2 :** SAPPANWOOD

indian reed *n, usu cap I* [2*indian* 1] **1 :** INDIAN SHOT **2** [2*indian* 2] **:** a tall American grass (*Cinna arundinacea*) resembling reed **3** [2*indian* 2] **:** WOOD GRASS 1

indian rhubarb *n, usu cap I* [2*indian* 1] **1 :** HIMALAYAN RHUBARB **2** [2*indian* 2] **:** a stout herb (*Peltiphyllum peltatum*) of the family Saxifragaceae of the Pacific coast of No. America with leaves that have edible petioles

indian rice *n, usu cap I* [2*indian* 2] **:** WILD RICE 1a

indian ricegrass *n, usu cap I* [2*indian* 2] **:** SILK GRASS 2

indian robin *n, usu cap I* **:** any of various songbirds of India resembling or related to the English robin

indian root *n, usu cap I* [2*indian* 2] **1 :** INDIAN PHYSIC **2 :** SPIKENARD 2a

indian rosewood *n, usu cap I* [2*indian* 1] **1 :** BLACKWOOD b **2 :** SISSOO

indian runner *n, usu cap I&R* [2*indian* 1; fr. a belief that it originated in India] **:** a breed of small upright domestic ducks noted for their egg production and known in fawn and white or pure white or penciled varieties

indians *pl of* INDIAN

indian saffron *n, usu cap I* [2*indian* 1] **1 :** SAFFLOWER 1 **2 :** ZEDOARY

indian sage *n, usu cap I* [2*indian* 2] **:** BONESET 1

indian sago palm *n, usu cap I* [2*indian* 1] **:** JAGGERY PALM

indian salad *n, usu cap I* **:** a waterleaf (*Hydrophyllum virginianum*) of the eastern U.S. with divided leaves and cymose bell-shaped flowers that are white or violet

indian sandalwood *n, usu cap I* [2*indian* 1] **:** SANDALWOOD 1a

indian sanicle *n, usu cap I* [2*indian* 2] **:** WHITE SNAKEROOT

indian sarsaparilla *n, usu cap I* **1 :** an East Indian shrub (*Hemidesmus indicus*) of the family Asclepiadaceae **2 :** the root of Indian sarsaparilla used as a substitute for sarsaparilla

indian's-dream \ˈ===ˌ=\ *n, pl* **indian's-dreams** *usu cap I* [*indian's* (gen. of 1*indian* 2)] **1 :** CLIFF BRAKE **2 :** OREGON CLIFF BRAKE

indian senna *n, usu cap I* [2*indian* 1] **:** TINNEVELLY SENNA

indian shamrock *n, usu cap I* [2*indian* 2] **:** PURPLE TRILLIUM

indian shoe *n, usu cap I* [2*indian* 2] **1 :** STEMLESS LADY'S-SLIPPER **2 :** YELLOW LADY'S-SLIPPER

indian shot *n, usu cap I* [2*indian* 1] **:** a plant of the genus *Canna* (esp. *C. indica*) that has hard black seeds about the size of buckshot

indian sign *n, usu cap I* [prob. fr. 2*indian* 2] **1 :** a magic spell for immobilizing or making powerless an opponent or rival ⟨have put the *Indian sign* on that team and beaten them nearly every game⟩ or for subjecting another to one's full control or slightest whims or desires ⟨she's put the *Indian sign* on every bachelor in town⟩ — usu. used with *the* **2 :** HEX, JINX ⟨thought the cow had got the *Indian sign* when it wouldn't give any more milk⟩

indian slipper *n, usu cap I* [2*indian* 2] **:** STEMLESS LADY'S-SLIPPER

indian soap *or* **indian soap-plant** *n, usu cap I* [2*indian* 2] **:** SOAPBERRY TREE 1

indian squill *n, usu cap I* [2*indian* 1] **:** squill from an herb of the genus *Urginea* (esp. *Urginea indica*) that is the official source of the drug in Great Britain

indian strawberry *n, usu cap I* [prob. fr. 2*indian* 1] **1 :** a low East Indian herb (*Duchesnea indica*) naturalized in eastern No. America and resembling the true strawberry but having yellow flowers and tasteless involucrate fruit **2** [prob. fr. 2*indian* 2] **:** STRAWBERRY BLITE

indian summer *n, usu cap I* [2*indian* 2] **1 :** a period of warm or mild weather late in autumn or in early winter usu. characterized by a clear or cloudless sky and by a hazy or smoky appearance of the atmosphere esp. near the horizon **2 :** a period of tranquillity or happiness or prosperity or other generally favorable conditions occurring for the first time or more usu. anew toward the latter part or end of something ⟨if the nineteen-twenties constituted a sort of *Indian summer* of the old order —F.L.Allen⟩ ⟨life in the *Indian summer* of Czarist Russia —John Davenport⟩ ⟨an *Indian summer* of wartime literature —*Blackwood's*⟩ ⟨the *Indian summer* of her widowhood —Dixon Wecter⟩

indian tan *n, often cap I* [2*indian* 2] **:** AZTEC 3

indian tapir *n, usu cap I* **:** a tapir (*Tapirus indicus*) that is blackish with a broad white area on the body and that is found in Sumatra and the Malay peninsula

indian tea *n, usu cap I* [2*indian* 2] **1 :** a yaupon (*Ilex vomitoria*) **2 :** NEW JERSEY TEA **3 :** LABRADOR TEA a

indian teakettle *n, usu cap I* [2*indian* 2] **:** PITCHER PLANT

indian thistle *n, usu cap I* [2*indian* 2] **:** WILD TEASEL

indian tobacco *n, usu cap I* [2*indian* 2] **1 :** an American wild lobelia (*Lobelia inflata*) with small blue flowers and inflated capsules formerly used as an antispasmodic **2** [prob. fr. 2*indian* 1] **:** HEMP **3 :** a wild tobacco (*Nicotiana rustica*) **4 :** a plant of the genus *Antennaria*; *esp* **:** a common cat's-foot (*A. plantaginifolia*) of eastern No. America

indian turmeric *n, usu cap I* [2*indian* 2] **:** GOLDENSEAL

indian turnip *n, usu cap I* [2*indian* 2] **1 a :** JACK-IN-THE-PULPIT 1 **b :** the acrid root of the jack-in-the-pulpit **2 :** BREADROOT

indian warrior *n, usu cap I* [2*indian* 2; fr. its brilliant red crest] **:** a lousewort (esp. *Pedicularis densiflora* and *P. bracteosa*) of the western U.S.

indian wayfaring tree *n, usu cap I* **:** a Himalayan shrub (*Viburnum cotinifolium*) with roundish leaves and showy flowers

indian wheat *n, usu cap I* [2*indian* 2] **1 :** INDIAN CORN **2** [prob. fr. 2*indian* 1] **:** TARTARIAN BUCKWHEAT **3 :** any of several plants of the genus *Plantago* (esp. *P. fastigiata*)

indian whort *n, usu cap I* [2*indian* 2] **:** BEARBERRY 1

indian wick·a·pe \-ˈwikəpē\ *n, usu cap I* [2*indian* 2] **:** LEATHERWOOD

indian wickup *or* **indian wicopy** *n, usu cap I* [2*indian* 2] **:** FIREWEED b

indian wild dog *n, usu cap I* [2*indian* 1] **:** DHOLE

indian wolf *n, usu cap I* **:** a light-colored wolf (*Canis pallipes*) that is widely distributed in desert and upland areas from the northern part of the subcontinent of India westward to northern Arabia and Iran and that is often considered to constitute a small Asiatic race of the common wolf of Europe

indian-wrestle \ˈ===ˌ==\ *vb, usu cap I* [back-formation fr. *indian wrestling*] **:** to engage in Indian wrestling

indian wrestling *n, usu cap I* [2*indian* 2] **1 :** wrestling in which two wrestlers lie side by side on their backs in reversed position locking their near arms and raising and locking the corresponding legs and attempt to force each other's leg down and turn the other wrestler on his face **2 a :** wrestling in which two wrestlers stand face to face gripping usu. their right hands and setting the outsides of the corresponding feet tightly against each other and attempt to force each other off balance **b :** wrestling in which two wrestlers sit face to face gripping usu. their right hands, setting corresponding elbows firmly on a surface (as the top of a table), and holding the length of the arm from the elbow to the hand tightly against each other and attempt to force each other's arm down

indian yellow *n* [2*indian* 1] **1** *usu cap I* **:** a yellow coloring matter: as **a :** a pigment made from the evaporated urine of cows fed on mango leaves — called also *piuri* **b :** COBALT YELLOW 1 **c :** a brilliant yellow pigment made from Naphthol Yellow S and used in coatings for paper and in distemper colors **2** *often cap I* **:** a moderate to strong orange yellow that is slightly lighter than Dutch orange — called also *purree, snowshoe*

india oilstone *n, usu cap I* **1 :** a manufactured abrasive material **2 :** a grinding wheel or whetstone or similar tool made of India oilstone

india paper *n, usu cap I* [so called fr. a belief that it originally came fr. India] **1** *also* **india proof paper :** a smooth thin delicate but not glossy paper esp. suitable for taking full-bodied impressions (as proofs of engravings, woodcuts) **2 a :** a smooth thin tough opaque printing paper — called also *Bible paper*

india print *n, usu cap I* **:** a plain lightweight cotton cloth that usu. has hand-blocked Indian designs in rich colors on a natural ground and is used esp. for bedspreads, drapes, or skirts

india red *n, often cap I* **:** a deep reddish brown — called also *Arabian red, red robin*

india rubber *n, often cap I* **1 :** RUBBER 2a **2 a :** RUBBER 3a **b :** RUBBER 1b(3)

india-rubber tree *or* **india-rubber plant** *also* **india-rubber fig** *n, often cap I* **:** a rubber plant (*Ficus elastica*)

india-rubber vine *n, often cap I* **:** a woody vine (*Cryptostegia grandiflora*) sometimes cultivated as a source of rubber

india tan *n, often cap I* **:** RUSSIAN CALF

india tint *n, usu cap I* **:** a light shade of buff often used in coated paper and ordinary book paper

india wheat *n, usu cap I* **:** TARTARIAN BUCKWHEAT

1**in·dic** \ˈindik\ *adj, usu cap* [L *indicus*, fr. Gk *indikos*, fr. *Indos* India (subcontinent in southern Asia), Indus (river in the northwestern part of the Indian subcontinent) + *-ikos* -ic — more at INDIA] **1 :** of or relating to the subcontinent of India **:** INDIAN **2 :** of, relating to, or constituting Indic

2**indic** \"\ *n, cap* **:** a branch of the Indo-European language family containing Sanskrit, Pali, the Prakrits, and related modern languages of India, Pakistan, and Ceylon (as Hindi, Urdu, Sinhalese) — see INDO-EUROPEAN LANGUAGES table

3**indic** \"\ *adj* [*indium* + *-ic*] **:** of or relating to indium

indic *abbr* indicated; indicative; indicator

in·di·can \ˈindəˌkan\ *n* -s [L *indicum* indigo + E *-an*] **1 :** a colorless crystalline glucoside $C_{14}H_{17}NO_6$ occurring esp. in indigo plants and in woad and yielding indoxyl and glucose on hydrolysis — see INDIGO 1a **2 :** the sulfuric acid ester $C_8H_6NOSO_3H$ of indoxyl or the crystalline potassium salt of this ester occurring in urine and other animal fluids as a derivative of the indole formed in the alimentary canal and yielding indigo on oxidation

in·di·cant \-dəkənt\ *n* -s [obs. *indicant*, adj., serving to indicate, fr. L *indicant-, indicans*, pres. part. of *indicare* to indicate] **:** something that serves to indicate ⟨a paragraph printed with a directional arrow before it as an ~⟩

in·di·cat·able \ˈindəˌkād·əbəl, -dē¦-, -ātə-, ˌ==ˈ===\ *adj* **:** capable of being indicated

in·di·cate \ˈindəˌkāt, -dē-, *usu* -ād·+V\ *vt* -ED/-ING/-S [L *indicatus*, past part. of *indicare*, fr. *in-* 2in- + *dicare* to proclaim, dedicate — more at DICTION] **:** to point out or point to or toward with more or less exactness **:** show or make known with a fair degree of certainty: as **a** (1) **:** to show the probable presence or existence or nature or course of **:** give fair evidence of **:** be a fairly certain sign or symptom of **:** reveal in a fairly clear way ⟨their laughter *indicated* their happiness⟩ ⟨his reply *indicated* total disagreement⟩ ⟨*indicated* his impatience by shrugging⟩ ⟨an anecdote that ~*s* the kind of people they were⟩ ⟨a fever that ~*s* severe illness⟩ (2) **:** to demonstrate or suggest the probable necessity or advisability of ⟨conflicting findings ~ further neurological research —*Collier's Yr. Bk.*⟩ ⟨increased luggage space is *indicated* for the family car —R.F.Loewy⟩ ⟨radical surgery is *indicated* in advanced cancer⟩ (3) **:** to show the general outlines of in advance **:** sketch beforehand **:** PRESAGE ⟨his enthusiasm ~*s* a bright future for him⟩ **b :** to act as a more or less exact index of **:** show or suggest the probable extent or degree of ⟨their records must ~ ability to do successful academic work —*Bull. of Bates Coll.*⟩ ⟨their popularity is *indicated* by the warm welcome they receive everywhere⟩ **c :** to state or express in a brief or cursory way **:** state or express without going into great detail **:** SUGGEST, INTIMATE, HINT ⟨the commission also *indicated* it might take action —*Wall Street Jour.*⟩ ⟨*indicated* a willingness to negotiate —*World*⟩ ⟨the general outlines of it can be *indicated* —R.L.Duffus⟩ **d :** to show the general position or direction of ⟨a map ~*s* where the ship was sunk⟩ **:** direct attention to with more or less preciseness (as by pointing with the finger or making a gesture) ⟨*indicated* the tray of sandwiches —Kay Boyle⟩ **:** point at ⟨the hands of the clock *indicated* noon⟩

syn INDICATE, BETOKEN, ATTEST, BESPEAK, ARGUE, PROVE can mean, in common, to give evidence of, or serve as a ground for, a valid or reasonable inference or an action validated by the inference. INDICATE signifies to serve as a sign or symptom pointing to (the inference or action), stressing only a general, usu. unspecified, connection between subject and object ⟨to assume that Ginger's invitation *indicated* something serious —Clarissa F. Cushman⟩ ⟨the results thus obtained are believed to be the first to *indicate* a possible magnetic effect directly attributable to a solar eclipse —H.D. Harradon⟩ ⟨the results of the physical examination *indicated* some sort of antibiotic medication⟩ BETOKEN stresses the idea of visible or otherwise perceivable evidence or portent ⟨the air with which she looked at the heathmen *betokened* a certain unconcern at their presence —Thomas Hardy⟩ ⟨towering business buildings, great warehouses, and numerous factories *betoken* its importance —*Amer. Guide Series: N.C.*⟩ ATTEST usu. implies the more or less indisputable nature of the evidence ⟨Washington's strong, natural love of children, nowhere *attested* better than in his expense accounts —J.C. Fitzpatrick⟩ ⟨the skill with which they executed these tasks *attested* to their considerable executive talents —R.A.Billington⟩ ⟨the fighting had been hard and continuous, that was *attested* by all the senses —Ambrose Bierce⟩ BESPEAK is interchangeable with *indicate* though it stresses possibly a little more the role of the subject as evidence or token ⟨a freshness and an originality that *bespeak* the intellectual vigor and intuition that he possessed —D.G.Mandelbaum⟩ ⟨a glint of pride in her eyes that *bespoke* her new dignity —Mary Lasswell⟩ ARGUE usu. stresses a reasonable or logical connection between subject and object ⟨his evasion, of course, was the height of insolence, but it *argued* unlimited resource and nerve —Rudyard Kipling⟩ ⟨a becoming deference *argues* deficiency in self-respect —A.N.Whitehead⟩ ⟨what a mistake to say that complexity *argues* culture —Norman Douglas⟩ PROVE is to demonstrate or make manifest the truth of (a conclusion), suggesting the inferential validity of the relationship between subject and object ⟨to become a writer was, however, in Thoreau's mind; his verses *prove* it, his journal proves it —H.S.Canby⟩ ⟨to them, faith is a belief in something which cannot be *proven* and understood rationally —Erich Fromm⟩ ⟨many studies have *proved* that the failure of an employee is seldom due to his lack of ability —W.J.Reilly⟩

indicated airspeed *n* **:** the airspeed of an airplane as indicated on an airspeed indicator **:** the airspeed in an atmosphere of standard sea-level density that would give rise to a dynamic pressure equal to that encountered

indicated altitude *n* **:** the height above sea level as read on an altimeter

indicated horsepower *n* **:** the power developed in the cylinders of an engine as calculated from the average pressure of the working fluid, the piston area, the stroke, and the number of working strokes per minute

in·di·ca·tion \ˌindəˈkāshən, -dē'-\ *n* -s [MF, fr. ML *indication-, indicatio* action of pointing out, fr. L, valuation, price, fr. *indicatus* (past part. of *indicare* to indicate) + *-ion-, -io* -ion] **1 :** the action of indicating **2 a :** something (as a signal, sign, suggestion) that serves to indicate ⟨refusal to accept the gift was an ~ of her displeasure⟩ ⟨gave no ~ that he heard me⟩ ⟨an ~ of what they could expect⟩; *specif* **:** a symptom or particular circumstance that indicates the advisability or necessity of (as a specific medical treatment or procedure) ⟨postpartum hemorrhage is the chief ~ for the use of ergot preparations and derivatives —C.H.Thienes⟩ **b :** something that is indicated as advisable or necessary ⟨in case of collapse the immediate ~ is artificial respiration —*Jour. Amer. Med. Assoc.*⟩ **3 :** the degree indicated in a specific instance or at a specific time on a graduated physical instrument (as a thermometer) **:** READING **4 :** suggestion (as by the use of conventionalized techniques or symbols) of architectural features (as in a drawing) rather than detailed representation of such features ⟨cross-hatching is used as an ~ of brick⟩

1**in·dic·a·tive** \ənˈdikəd·iv, -kətiv\ *adj* [MF *indicatif*, fr. LL *indicativus*, fr. L *indicatus* (past part. of *indicare* to indicate) + *-ivus* -ive] **1 :** of, relating to, or constituting a verb form or set of verb forms that represents an attitude toward or concern with a denoted act or state as an objective fact **:** of, relating to, or constituting a verb form or set of verb forms used invariably in simple declarative sentences and in questions that can be answered by simple declarative sentences and often also in a great variety of other situations ⟨the ~ mood⟩ ⟨*is writing* in "is he writing now" is an ~ verb form⟩ — compare IMPERATIVE, SUBJUNCTIVE **2 :** that indicates **:** that points out more or less exactly **:** that reveals fairly clearly or suggests or intimates ⟨the situation was ~ of the fear, bordering on panic, which had seized the people —F.D.Roosevelt⟩ — **in·dic·a·tive·ly** *adv*

2**indicative** *n* -s **:** the indicative mood of a language ⟨*writes* is in the ~⟩ **:** a form in the indicative mood ⟨*writes* is an ~⟩

in·di·ca·tor \ˈindəˌkād·ə(r), -dē,k-, -ātə-\ *n* [LL, fr. L *indicatus* (past part. of *indicare* to indicate) + *-or*] **1** -s **:** one that indicates: as **a :** an index hand (as on a dial) **:** POINTER **b** (1) **:** a pressure gauge (2) **:** an instrument for automatically making a diagram that indicates the pressure in and volume of the working fluid of an engine throughout the cycle so that the horsepower and other characteristics may be deduced **c :** a speed counter for an engine **d :** a registering dial (as on a dial telegraph) **e :** ANNUNCIATOR 2a **2** -s **a :** a substance (as a dye) used to show visually usu. by its capacity for color change the condition of a solution with respect to the presence of free acid or alkali or some other substance (as in detecting the end point of a titration) ⟨litmus and phenolphthalein are acid-base ~*s*⟩ ⟨oxidation-reduction ~*s*⟩ **b :** TRACER ⟨radioactive ~*s*⟩ **3 a** *cap* [NL, fr. LL] **:** the type genus of the family Indicatoridae — see HONEY GUIDE **b** -s **:** any bird of the genus *Indicator* **:** HONEY GUIDE **4** -s [so called fr. a belief that its occurrence indicates that there is ginseng nearby] **:** VIRGINIA GRAPE FERN **5** -s **:** an organism or a kind of organism (as a species) or an ecological community that is so strictly associated with particular environmental conditions that its presence is indicative of the existence of these conditions in a particular environment **6** -s **:** a narrow pyritiferous seam the intersections of which with auriferous quartz veins are usu. accompanied by an ore shoot in the vein **7** -s **:** a deciphering instruction accompanying a message: as **a :** a code or cipher designation of the key **b :** INTERRUPTER b

indicator card *or* **indicator diagram** *n* **:** the diagram made by an indicator (sense 1b(2))

in·di·ca·tor·i·dae \ˌindəkəˈtōrəˌdē\ *n pl, cap* [NL, fr. *Indicator*, type genus + *-idae*] **:** a family of birds (order Piciformes) that comprises the honey guides and is sometimes considered a subfamily of Capitonidae

indicator telegraph *n* **:** NEEDLE TELEGRAPH

in·dic·a·to·ry \ənˈdikəˌtōrē, *chiefly Brit* ˈindiˌkātəri *or* -ā·tri\ *adj* [LL *indicatorius*, fr. L *indicatus* (past part. of *indicare*) + *-orius* -ory] **:** INDICATIVE 2

in·dica·trix \ˌindəˈkāˌtriks, ənˈdikə·(ˌ)t-\ *n* -ES [NL, fem. of LL *indicator* — more at -TRIX] **:** an ellipsoid whose axes are proportional to the principal refractive indices of a crystal and from which various optical properties of the crystal may be deduced

in·di·ca·vit \ˌindəˈkāvət\ *n* -s [L, he has indicated, 3d pers. sing. perf. indic. act. of *indicare* to indicate — more at INDICATE] **:** a writ of prohibition from a common-law court commanding the removal to that court of a case pending in an ecclesiastical court and prohibiting the ecclesiastical court from exercising any further jurisdiction

indices *pl of* INDEX

in·di·cia \ənˈdish(ē)ə\ *n, pl* **indicia** *or* **indicias** [L, pl. of *indicium* sign, mark, fr. *indicare* to point out, indicate] **1 a :** a distinctive mark that indicates or that is felt to indicate the nature or quality or existence or reality of something **:** INDICATION, SIGN, TOKEN, CRITERION ⟨he had in fact all the ~ of divinity —Wallace Stevens⟩ ⟨many ~ of truth —J.E.Davies⟩ ⟨the real ~ of civilization —H.J.Laski⟩ ⟨press opinion and other ~ of public sentiment —H.H.Sprout⟩ **b :** a significant or apparently significant fact or piece of evidence connected with or deduced from a set of circumstances and giving rise to conjectures having some probability of accord with the truth ⟨studied her belongings carefully but could discover no ~ as to what had become of her⟩ **2 a** (1) **:** a postal marking (as on bulk mail or business reply envelopes) often imprinted on mail or on labels to be affixed to mail and used in place of postage stamps to indicate prepayment of postage (as by use of a postage meter or by receipt of a special permit) (2) **:** a postal marking or verbal statement often imprinted on mail or on labels to be affixed to mail and used to indicate the class or type of a piece of mail or to give directives (as with regard to the proper place for an address) or some other information (as that a piece of mail may be opened for inspection by a postmaster) **b :** an identifying marking or verbal statement used to single out one thing from another ⟨each object had a tag carrying its ~⟩ or to serve as directional guides ⟨each card in the file has ~ that show the location of each book on the shelf⟩

in·di·cial \(ˈ)inˈdishəl, ənˈd-\ *adj* [*indicia* + *-al*] **1 :** of, relating to, or having the nature of an indication **:** INDICATIVE ⟨a remark ~ of their pride⟩ **2** [L *indic-, index* index finger, index + E *-ial*] **a :** of, relating to, or having the nature of an index ⟨an ~ glossary⟩ **b :** of or relating to the index finger — **in·di·cial·ly** \-shəlē\ *adv*

in·di·ci·ble \-isəbəl\ *adj* [MF, fr. LL *indicibilis*, fr. L *in-* 1in- + *dicere* to say + *-ibilis* -ible — more at DICTION] **:** UNSPEAKABLE, INEXPRESSIBLE

in·di·ci·um \ənˈdishēəm\ *n, pl* **indicia** *or* **indiciums** [L, sign, mark] **:** INDICIA 1

indico *obs var of* INDIGO

in·dic·o·lite \ənˈdikəˌlīt\ *n* -s [F, fr. *indico-* (fr. L *indicum* indigo) + *-lite* — more at INDIGO] **:** an indigo-blue variety of tourmaline

1**in·dict** \ənˈdīt, *usu* -īd·+V\ *vt* -ED/-ING/-S [alter. (influenced by ML *indictare* to indict, fr. AF *enditer*) of earlier *indite, endite*, fr. ME *inditen, enditen*, fr. AF *enditer*, fr. OF, to write down, compose — more at INDITE] **1 :** to charge with some wrong or fault or inadequacy usu. formally and after carefully weighing the matter and as if summoning for trial **:** bring a charge against **:** formally accuse; *esp* **:** to attack by accusation and condemn ⟨I ~ those citizens whose easy consciences condone such wrongdoings —F.D.Roosevelt⟩ **2 :** to charge with a crime by the finding or presentment of a jury (as a grand jury) in due form of law ⟨was ~*ed* for murder⟩ ⟨were ~*ed* with conspiracy to defraud⟩ **syn** see ACCUSE

2**indict** *vt* -ED/-ING/-S [MF *indicter*, fr. *indict* decreed, fr. L *indictus*, past part. of *indicere*, fr. *in-* 2in- + *dicere* to say — more at DICTION] *obs* **:** PROCLAIM, DECREE

in·dict·able \-əbəl\ *adj* [1*indict* + *-able*] **1 :** subject to being indicted **:** liable to indictment ⟨~ as he might be for bad taste —Oscar Cargill⟩ **2 :** that makes one liable to indictment ⟨an ~ offense⟩ — **in·dict·ably** \-blē, -bli\ *adv*

in·dict·ee \(ˌ)inˌdīd·ˈē, ən-, ˌ=ˈ=(ˌ)=\ *n* -s [alter. (influenced by 1*indict*) of *enditee*, fr. *endite* (earlier form of 1*indict*) + *-ee*] **:** one that is indicted

in·dic·tion \ənˈdikshən\ *n* -s [ME *indiccioun*, fr. LL *indiction-, indictio*, fr. L, proclamation, fr. *indictus* (past part. of *indicere* to proclaim) + *-ion-, -io* -ion] **1 a :** a 15-year cycle used as a chronological unit in several ancient and medieval systems — see ROMAN INDICTION **b** (1) **:** the edict of a Roman emperor establishing the valuation for assessing a property tax at the beginning of each 15-year cycle (2) **:** the tax or subsidy levied by this edict **2** [L *indiction-, indictio*] *archaic* **:** PROCLAMATION — **in·dic·tion·al** \-shənᵊl, -shnəl\ *adj*

in·dict·ment \ənˈdītmənt\ *n* -s [alter. (influenced by ML *indictare* to indict, fr. AF *enditer*) of earlier *indytement, enditement*, fr. ME *inditement, enditement*, fr. AF *enditement*, fr. *enditer* to indict + OF *-ment* — more at INDICT] **1 a :** the action of indicting; *specif* **:** the legal process by which a bill of indictment is preferred to and presented by a jury (as a grand jury) **b :** the state of being indicted **2 :** a formal written statement framed by the prosecuting authority of a state and found by a jury (as a grand jury) charging a person with an offense — compare BILL OF INDICTMENT **3** *Scots law* **:** a process of bringing a person to trial for a crime at the instance of the lord advocate

in·dict·or *or* **in·dict·er** \ənˈdīd·ə(r), -ītə-\ *n* -s [*indictor* alter. (influenced by ML *indictare* to indict) of earlier *endightour*, fr. ME *enditour*, fr. AF, fr. *enditer* to indict + OF *-our* -or; *indicter* alter. (influenced by ML *indictare* to indict) of earlier *inditer*, fr. ME *inditer, enditer*, alter. (influenced by ME *-er*) of *enditour*] **:** one that indicts

in·die \ˈindē\ *n* -s [by shortening & alter. fr. *independent*] *slang* **:** something (as a motion-picture company, a radio or television station) that is independent

1in·dienne \ˌandēˌen\ *n* -s [F, fr. fem. of *indien* Indian, fr. ML *indianus* — more at INDIAN] **:** a light cotton fabric with designs painted or printed in imitation of designs used orig. in subcontinental India

2indienne \"\ *adj, often cap* [F, fem. of *indien* Indian] **:** seasoned (as with curry) in East Indian style ⟨rice ~⟩

in·dif·er·ous \(ˈ)inˌdif(ə)rəs\ *adj* [*indi*um + *-ferous*] **:** containing indium

in·dif·fer·ence \ənˈdifərn(t)s, -f(ə)rən-, *-R sometimes* -fən-\ *n* [MF, fr. L *indifferentia* lack of difference, fr. *indifferent-, indifferens* indifferent + *-ia* -y] **1 a :** the quality or state of being indifferent ⟨an age of ~ to religion⟩ **b :** a manifestation or instance of this quality ⟨was much distressed by his ~ toward her⟩ **2 a** *archaic* **:** lack of difference or distinction between two or more things ⟨journeys discover to us the ~ of places —R.W.Emerson⟩ **b :** absence of compulsion to or toward one thing or another ⟨maintaining the freedom of the will and its ~⟩

indifference curve *n* **:** a curve used in economics to indicate all possible comparative quantities of goods or services equally demanded by or of equal use to a consumer

in·dif·fer·en·cy \-nsē\ *n* [L *indifferentia*] *archaic* **:** INDIFFERENCE

1in·dif·fer·ent \(ˈ)inˌdifərnt, ənˈd-, -f(ə)rənt, *-R sometimes* -fənt\ *adj* [ME, fr. MF or L; MF, that is looked upon as not mattering one way or another, fr. L *indifferent-, indifferens* neither good nor bad, unconcerned, fr. *in-* 1in- + *different-, differens*, pres. part. of *differre* to carry apart, be different — more at DIFFERENT] **1 :** marked by impartiality **:** UNBIASED, UNPREJUDICED ⟨an ~ judge in a trial⟩ ⟨the jurors remained ~⟩ ⟨a remarkably ~ critic⟩ **2 a** (1) **:** that is looked upon as not mattering one way or another **:** that is regarded as being of no significant importance or value **:** that is viewed with neutrality ⟨what others think is altogether ~ to him⟩ (2) **:** that actually does not matter one way or the other **:** that actually lacks significant importance or value **:** that is of little consequence **:** that is unimportant or immaterial ⟨whether you choose to do it or not is a matter that is quite ~⟩ **b :** that has nothing that calls for sanction or condemnation in either observance or neglect **:** that may be done or not done or observed or not observed with no importance or value one way or the other ⟨ceremonies that are considered essential in some religious sects and ~ in others⟩ ⟨revived an ~ custom⟩ **3 a** (1) **:** marked by no special liking for or dislike of something ⟨she always seemed ~ to the arrival of visitors⟩ (2) **:** marked by no special preference for one thing over another **:** not inclined to one thing more than another ⟨was ~ to their acceptance or rejection of her invitation⟩ ⟨were ~ about which book you would decide to give them⟩ **b :** marked by a total or nearly total lack of interest in or concern about something **:** dully unconcerned or unfeeling **:** UNMOVED, LISTLESS, APATHETIC ⟨was ~ to suffering and poverty⟩ ⟨remained ~ to her pleas⟩ ⟨seemed unaffected and quite ~ in the presence of beauty⟩ **4 :** neither excessive nor defective (as in size, extent, intensity) **:** MODERATE, AVERAGE ⟨had a couple of hills of ~ height to climb⟩ ⟨the wind was blowing with a negligible ~ strength⟩ ⟨inherited an ~ fortune⟩ **5 a** (1) **:** neither good nor bad **:** deserving neither praise nor censure **:** PASSABLE, MEDIOCRE, UNIMPRESSIVE ⟨does ~ work at the office⟩ ⟨turned in an ~ performance of the role⟩ (2) **:** that has a morally neutral nature **:** that is neither right nor wrong ⟨many human acts are viewed as ~⟩ **b :** not very good **:** rather bad **:** fairly poor **:** INFERIOR ⟨with an ~ voice like hers she shouldn't even attempt singing⟩ ⟨has ~ qualifications for the job⟩ **6** *now chiefly dial* **:** marked by poor general health **:** SICKLY **7 :** characterized by lack of active quality **:** NEUTRAL ⟨an ~ chemical⟩ ⟨the ~ part of a magnet⟩ **8 a :** UNDIFFERENTIATED ⟨~ tissues of the human body⟩ **b :** capable of development in more than one direction ⟨~ blastema cells⟩; *esp* **:** not yet embryologically determined

syn UNCONCERNED, INCURIOUS, ALOOF, DETACHED, UNINTERESTED, DISINTERESTED: INDIFFERENT, often interchangeable with others of this group, may imply uninterested neutrality of attitude or marked lack of feeling, inclination, preference, or prejudice ⟨a soldier rigidly bound by his oath to the state and *indifferent* to the political ends to which his services might be put —Gordon Harrison⟩ ⟨nature had no sympathy with our hopes and fears, and was completely *indifferent* to our fate —L.P.Smith⟩ ⟨to be *indifferent* to any circumstances — to be quite thoughtless as to drafts and chills, careless of heat —Richard Jefferies⟩ UNCONCERNED suggests personal lack of interest, feeling, or being moved or worried or otherwise affected, perhaps arising from insensitiveness, selfishness, or stoicism ⟨how could one, knowing the warmth and beauty of living bodies, of all the glory and tenderness the world might show, go plodding *unconcerned* through life; go plodding unconcerned yoked to a life and a companionship unvarying, savorless, and without hope of gusto —James Boyd⟩ INCURIOUS may suggest lack of normal curiosity or of intellectual capacity for interest ⟨indifferent to technique, abnormally *incurious*, in fact, of all the means of the literary art —Van Wyck Brooks⟩ ⟨the faintly pained, heavy, *incurious* unamazement of cattle —R.P.Warren⟩ ALOOF applies to a show of indifference arising from great temperamental reserve, a cold, forbidding character, or a sense of superiority or disdain ⟨with a glassily *aloof* expression as though afraid he might be subjected to some unwelcome, impertinent advance by strangers —Claud Cockburn⟩ ⟨always quite *aloof* from the ordinary social life of the town —Arnold Bennett⟩ DETACHED may indicate a calm objective lack of feeling coming from absence of prejudice or selfishness ⟨Iceland, which cool island remained a little *detached* about the war —Rose Macaulay⟩ ⟨looking at him with a peculiarly *detached* and interested air —Sherwood Anderson⟩ ⟨from the cool and *detached* point of view she had attained, life appeared to her to be essentially comic —Ellen Glasgow⟩ UNINTERESTED simply indicates the fact of lack of interest ⟨*uninterested* in the election⟩ DISINTERESTED is often used with this general meaning despite efforts to restrict its application to objectivity, freedom from personal interests, especially financial, and impartiality ⟨teaching the letters of the alphabet to her wiggling and supremely *disinterested* little daughter —C.L.Sulzberger⟩ ⟨the *disinterested* advice of a parting friend, who can possibly have no personal motive to bias his counsels —J.C.Fitzpatrick⟩

2indifferent \"\ *n* -s **1 a :** one that is indifferent (as in religion or politics) **b :** a morally indifferent act **2 :** a plant or a kind of plant (as a species) that has relatively unspecialized requirements and may occur more or less by chance in a variety of habitats or ecological communities — compare INDICATOR 5

3indifferent \"\ *adv, archaic* **:** INDIFFERENTLY

in·dif·fer·ent·ism \-nt·ˌizəm, -n·ˌti-\ *n* -s [F *indifférentisme*, fr. *indifférent* that is looked upon as not mattering one way or another (fr. MF *indifferent*) + *-isme* -ism] **1 a :** INDIFFERENCE; *esp* **:** a consciously nurtured spirit or attitude or philosophy of indifference (as toward religion) **b :** the principle or conviction that differences in religious beliefs are essentially unimportant **:** ADIAPHORISM; *specif* **:** the principle or conviction that one religion is as good as another **2 :** IDENTITY PHILOSOPHY

in·dif·fer·ent·ist \-ntəst\ *n* -s [F *indifférentiste*, fr. *indifférent* + *-iste* -ist] **:** one that is marked by or adheres to indifferentism

in·dif·fer·ent·ly *adv* **:** in an indifferent manner

in·di·gen \ˈindəjən, -ˌjen\ *also* **in·di·gene** \-ˌjēn\ *n* -s [L *indigena*] **1** *usu indigene* **:** NATIVE 8a **2 :** a biological species that is known from both wild and cultivated forms — compare CULTIGEN

in·di·gence \ˈindəjən(t)s, -dēj-\ *n* -s [ME, fr. MF, fr. L *indigentia*, fr. *indigent-, indigens* + *-ia* -y] **1** *archaic* **:** DEFICIENCY **2 :** poverty that is usu. not severe or total **:** NEEDINESS

in·di·gen·cy \-jənsē, -si\ *n* -ES [L *indigentia*] **:** INDIGENCE

in·dig·e·nist \ənˈdijənəst\ *n* -s [Sp *indigenista*, fr. *indígena* native (fr. L *indigena*) + *-ista* -ist (fr. L)] **:** an advocate of Indianism esp. in Latin America

in·dig·e·ni·za·tion \=ˌ==nəˈzāshən, -ˌnīˈz-\ *n* -s **:** the action or process of indigenizing

in·dig·e·nize \=ˈ==ˌnīz\ *vt* -ED/-ING/-S [*indigen*ous + *-ize*] **1 :** to cause to have indigenous characteristics **:** adapt to indigenous conditions or practices ⟨an excellent way of *indigenizing* what would otherwise remain a foreign system —F.M.Keesing⟩ **2 :** to cause to be made up chiefly of an indigenous personnel ⟨*indigenizing* the teaching staff of a school⟩

in·dig·e·nous \ənˈdijənəs\ *adj* [LL *indigenus*, fr. L *indigena*, n., native, fr. OL *indu, endo* in, within (akin to Gk *endina* entrails, Hitt *anda* within, into) + L *-gena* (akin to L *gignere* to beget); OL *indu, endo* and its cognates all fr. a prehistoric IE or Indo-Hittite compound whose first constituent is represented by L *in* and whose second constituent is akin to L *de* from, down, away — more at IN, DE-, KIN] **:** NATIVE: **a** (1) **:** not introduced directly or indirectly according to historical record or scientific analysis into a particular land or region or environment from the outside ⟨Indians were the ~ inhabitants of America⟩ ⟨species of plants that are ~ to that country⟩ (2) **:** originating or developing or produced naturally in a particular land or region or environment ⟨an interesting example of ~ architecture⟩ ⟨a people with a rich ~ culture⟩ (3) **:** of, relating to, or designed for natives ⟨the establishment of ~ schools⟩ **b :** INBORN, INNATE, INHERENT ⟨a type of behavior that is ~ to human beings⟩ **syn** see NATIVE

in·dig·e·nous·ly *adv* **:** in an indigenous manner

1in·di·gent \ˈindəjənt, -dēj-\ *adj* [ME, fr. MF, fr. L *indigent-, indigens*, pres. part. of *indigēre* to need, lack, fr. OL *indu, endo* in + *egēre* to need, be needy, lack; akin to OHG *ekrōdi* thin, weak, ON *ekla* scarcity] **1 :** being in a condition of indigence **:** being poor usu. without being destitute **:** IMPOVERISHED, NEEDY ⟨helping the ~ by means of medical insurance⟩ **2 a** *archaic* **:** DEFICIENT **b** *archaic* **:** totally lacking in something specified ⟨tangible parts ~ of moisture —Francis Bacon⟩ **c** *obs* **:** being in need of something specified ⟨naturally ~ of protection —Richard Steele⟩ **syn** see POOR

2indigent \"\ *n* -s **:** one that is indigent

in·di·gest \ˌindəˈjest, -ˌdīˈ-, ənˈdīˌj-\ *adj* [ME, immature, fr. L *indigestus* confused, not arranged, fr. *in-* 1in- + *digestus*, past part. of *digerere* to digest] **1** *archaic* **:** not carefully thought out or arranged **2** *archaic* **:** FORMLESS

in·digested \ˌin+(ˌ)=ˈ==\ *adj* [1*in-* + *digested*, past part. of *digest*] **1** *archaic* **a :** not carefully thought out or arranged **b :** FORMLESS **2** *archaic* **:** not having undergone digestion

in·digestibility \ˌin+\ *n* **:** the quality of being indigestible

1in·digestible \"+\ *adj* [LL *indigestibilis*, fr. L *in-* 1in- + LL *digestibilis* digestible] **:** that cannot be digested or that is not easily digested: **a :** not capable of being assimilated as food or not easily or comfortably assimilated as food ⟨green bananas are ~⟩ **b** (1) **:** not capable of being assimilated by the mind or not easily or comfortably assimilated by the mind **:** incomprehensible or nearly incomprehensible ⟨an ~ mass of facts⟩ (2) **:** that is repugnant to the mind or sensibilities **:** intellectually or aesthetically unendurable or nearly unendurable ⟨a book full of ~ pedantry⟩ ⟨clashing colors that make the painting quite ~⟩ — **in·di·gest·ibly** \-blē,-bli\ *adv*

2indigestible \"\ *n* -s **:** something indigestible

in·di·ges·tion \ˌindəˈjes(h)chən, -ˌdīˈ-\ *n* [ME *indygestyon*, fr. MF *indigestion*, fr. LL *indigestion-, indigestio*, fr. L *in-* 1in- + *digestion-, digestio* digestion — more at DIGESTION] **1 :** inability to digest something or difficulty in digesting something: **a :** inability to assimilate or difficulty in assimilating food **:** incomplete or imperfect assimilation of food **:** DYSPEPSIA ⟨troubled with chronic ~⟩ **b :** inability to assimilate or difficulty in assimilating something other than food **:** incomplete or imperfect assimilation of something other than food ⟨the uniform impression created everywhere . . . was staleness on the part of the teachers, ~ on the part of the students —Benjamin Fine⟩ **2 :** a case or attack of indigestion ⟨spoke of various ~*s* she had suffered —Booth Tarkington⟩ ⟨a comment that I would get an ~ from so much mental nourishment —Rafael Sabatini⟩

in·digestive \ˌin+\ *adj* [1*in-* + *digestive*] **:** DYSPEPTIC ⟨an ~ single woman —Charles Dickens⟩

indigitate *vb* -ED/-ING/-S [ML *indigitatus*, past part. of *indigitare* (influenced in meaning by L *digitus* finger), fr. L *indigitare, indigetare* to invoke (a deity), fr. *indiget-, indiges* native deity, fr. OL *indu, endo* in, within + *-iget-, -iges* (perh. fr. L *agere* to drive, lead, act) — more at INDIGENOUS, AGENT, TOE] *obs* **:** INDICATE

in·dign \(ˈ)inˌdīn, ənˈd-\ *adj* [ME *indigne*, fr. MF, fr. L *indignus*] **1** *archaic* **:** UNWORTHY, UNDESERVING **2** *obs* **a :** UNBECOMING, DISGRACEFUL **b :** not merited **:** UNDESERVED

in·dig·nance \ənˈdignən(t)s\ *n* -s *archaic* [fr. *indignant*, after such pairs as E *abundant: abundance*] **:** INDIGNATION

in·dig·nan·cy \-gnənsē, -si\ *n* -ES [*indignant* + *-cy*] *archaic* **:** INDIGNATION

in·dig·nant \ənˈdignənt\ *adj* [L *indignant-, indignans*, pres. part. of *indignari* to be indignant, be offended, fr. *indignus* unworthy, fr. *in-* 1in- + *dignus* worthy — more at DECENT] **1 :** filled with or marked by indignation ⟨grew suddenly quite ~ about the matter —James Hilton⟩ ⟨~ at the injustice —W. M.Thackeray⟩ ⟨were ~ over their mistreatment⟩ ⟨felt quite ~ with them⟩ **2 :** arising from or prompted by or indicative of indignation ⟨wrote an ~ letter⟩ ⟨looked at her with an ~ frown⟩ **syn** see ANGRY

in·dig·nant·ly *adv* **:** with indignation **:** in a manner indicative of indignation ⟨~ denied the accusation⟩

in·dig·na·tion \ˌin(ˌ)digˈnāshən, -ˌdēg-\ *n* -s [ME *indignacioun*, fr. MF & L; MF *indignation*, fr. L *indignation-, indignatio*, fr. *indignatus* (past part. of *indignari* to be indignant) + *-ion-, -io* -ion] **:** typically intense deep-felt resentment or anger aroused by annoyance at or displeasure with or scorn over something that actually is or is felt to be unjust or unworthy or mean ⟨aroused public ~⟩ ⟨~ at the injustice⟩ ⟨~ over the wrong they had suffered⟩ ⟨could feel only ~ with his children⟩ ⟨~ against the ill-treatment of human beings —Leslie Rees⟩ **syn** see ANGER

indignation meeting *n* **:** a meeting held for the purpose of expressing and discussing grievances ⟨the new law was objectionable to nearly everyone and there were numerous *indignation meetings*⟩

indignify *vt* [1*in-* + *dignify*] *obs* **:** DISHONOR

indignities to the person : misconduct (as habitual incivility or ridicule or neglect) by a spouse constituting grounds for divorce in some states that makes the life of an offended spouse intolerable and burdensome, subverts the family relationship, and evidences the settled hatred of the offending spouse

in·dig·ni·ty \ənˈdignəd·ē, -ətē, -i\ *n* [L *indignitat-, indignitas*, fr. *indignus* unworthy + *-itat-, -itas* -ity] **1** *obs* **:** lack or loss of dignity or honor **2 a :** something that offends against one's personal dignity or self-respect **:** something humiliating or injurious to one's self-esteem **:** INSULT, OUTRAGE ⟨forced to suffer one ~ after another⟩ **b :** treatment that offends against or is humiliating or injurious to one's personal dignity or self-respect ⟨treated them with ~⟩ **3** *obs* **:** INDIGNATION **syn** see AFFRONT

1in·di·go \ˈindəˌgō, -dēˌ-\ *n, pl* **indigos** *or* **indigoes** [It *indaco* & It dial. (northern) *indigo, endego*, fr. L *indicum*, fr. Gk *indikon*, fr. neut. of *indikos* Indic — more at INDIC] **1 a :** a blue vat dye that was obtained orig. from plants (as indigo plants or woad) by hydrolysis of the indican present and oxidation by air of the resulting indoxyl and that unless specially purified contained other substances (as indirubin) besides the principal coloring matter — called also *natural indigo* **b** *or* **indigo blue :** the principal coloring matter $C_{16}H_{10}N_2O_2$ of natural indigo that is synthesized as a blue crystalline powder with a coppery luster usu. by oxidation of synthetic indoxyl with air in the presence of alkali and that is used chiefly as a vat dye for cotton and wool — called also *indigotin, synthetic indigo;* see DYE table I (under *Vat Blue 1*); compare INDIGO WHITE, STRUCTURAL FORMULA **c :** any of several blue vat dyes derived from or closely related to indigo **2 a :** INDIGO PLANT **b :** any of various plants resembling the indigo plant **3** *or* **indigo blue :** a variable color averaging a dark grayish blue that is redder and deeper than night blue — called also *inde blue, Indian blue*

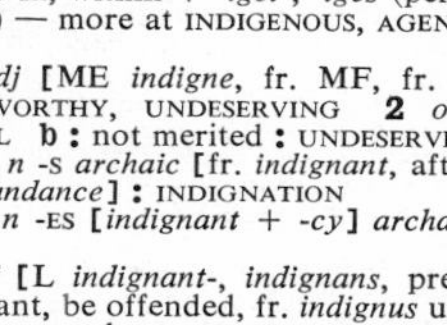

indigo 1b

2indigo \"\ *or* **indigo–blue** \ˌ==(ˌ)=ˌ=\ *adj* **:** being of the color indigo

indigo bird *n* **:** INDIGO BUNTING

indigo blue B *or* **indigo blue R** *n, usu cap I & B* **:** a vat dye — see DYE table I (under *Vat Blue 35*)

indigo broom *n* **:** a wild indigo (*Baptisia tinctoria*) having bright yellow flowers and trifoliolate leaves with cuneate leaflets

indigo brown *n* **:** a brown substance found in crude natural indigo

indigo bunting *n* **:** a common small finch (*Passerina cyanea*) of the eastern U. S. marked by indigo-blue coloration in the male

indigobush \ˈ==(ˌ)=ˌ=\ *n* **1 :** FALSE INDIGO 1 **2 :** SMOKE TREE 2 **3 :** MOCK LOCUST

indigo carmine *n* **1 :** a soluble blue dye that is the sodium salt of indigodisulfonic acid and is used chiefly as a biological stain and food color but is no longer used to any extent as a textile dye — called also *Indigotine IA* **2 :** a strong greenish blue that is bluer and duller than grotto, greener and duller than cobalt blue, and greener and darker than average cerulean blue (sense 1a) — called also *chemic blue, duck blue*

indigo copper *n* **:** COVELLITE

in·di·go·disulfonic acid \ˌ==(ˌ)=+ . . . -\ *n* [*indigodisulfonic* ISV *indigo* + *disulfonic*] **:** a water-soluble disulfonic acid $C_{16}H_8N_2O_2(SO_3H)_2$ obtained by treating indigo with concentrated sulfuric acid — called also *indigo extract, 5,5′=indigotindisulfonic acid*

indigo extract *n* **1 :** INDIGODISULFONIC ACID **2 :** INDIGO CARMINE

in·di·gof·era \ˌindəˈgäf(ə)rə\ *n, cap* [NL, fr. ISV *indigo* + NL *-fera* (fr. L, fem. of *-fer*, adj. comb. form) — more at -FER] **:** a genus of tropical herbs and shrubs (family Leguminosae) having odd-pinnate leaves and flowers with keel petals laterally spurred — see INDIGO PLANT

in·di·gof·er·ous \ˌ==ˈgäf(ə)rəs\ *adj* [1*indigo* + *-ferous*] **:** yielding indigo

in·di·goid \ˈ==ˌgȯid\ *adj* [ISV 1*indigo* + *-oid*] **:** related to or resembling indigo esp. in chemical structure and dyeing properties ⟨the ~ character of a blue pigment⟩

indigoid dye *or* **indigoid vat dye** *also* **indigoid** *n* -s **:** any of a class of vat dyes characterized by the same chromophore as indigo (sense 1b) — compare THIOINDIGOID DYE

in·dig·o·lite \ənˈdigəˌlīt\ *n* -s [by alter. (influenced by 1*indigo*)] **:** INDICOLITE

indigo plant *n* **1 :** a plant that yields indigo: as **a :** any of several plants of the genus *Indigofera* (as *I. tinctoria* of Africa and India, *I. anil* of So. America, *I. auriculata* of Arabia and Egypt) **b :** an East Indian woody vine (*Marsdenia tinctoria*) that yields rank indigo **c :** an Asiatic herb (*Polygonum tinctorium*) **2 a :** an Australian plant (as the Darling pea) of the genus *Swainsona* **b :** BOX BRIER

indigos *pl of* INDIGO

indigo snake *n* **:** a large blue-black colubrid snake (*Drymarchon corais couperi*) of the southern U. S. sometimes reaching a length of almost eight feet — called also *gopher snake*

in·di·go·sol \ˈ==ˌ=ˌsäl\ *n* -s [fr. *Indigosol*, a trademark] **:** any of various solubilized vat dyes (as that derived from indigo white)

indigo thorn *n* **:** SMOKE TREE 2

in·di·got·ic \ˌindəˌgäd·ik\ *adj* [ISV 1*indigo* + connective *-t-* + *-ic*] **:** of, relating to, or being of the color of indigo

in·digo·tin \ənˈdigətən, -gəd·ən,-gətᵊn, ˌindəˌgōtᵊn\ *n* -s [ISV 1*indigo* + connective *-t-* + *-in*] **1 :** INDIGO 1b **2** *or* **indigotine IA** \"+ˌīˈā\ *usu cap* **:** INDIGO CARMINE — see DYE table I (under *Acid Blue 74*)

indigotindisulfonic acid \"+ . . . -\ *n* [*indigotindisulfonic* fr. *indigotin* + *disulfonic*] **:** INDIGODISULFONIC ACID

indigo weed *n* **:** INDIGO BROOM

indigo white *n, sometimes cap I & W* **:** a pale yellow crystalline compound $C_{16}H_{12}N_2O_2$ obtained by reduction of indigo and easily changed back to it by oxidation — called also *leucoindigo;* see DYE table I (under *Vat Blue 1*)

indiligent *adj* [L *indiligent-, indiligens*, fr. *in-* 1in- + *diligent-, diligens*, pres. part. of *diligere* to esteem highly, love — more at DILIGENT] **1** *obs* **:** INATTENTIVE, HEEDLESS **2** *obs* **:** LAZY, IDLE

in·direct \ˌin+\ *adj* [ME, fr. ML *indirectus*, fr. L *in-* 1in- + *directus* direct] **:** not direct: as **a** (1) **:** deviating from a direct line or course **:** not proceeding straight from one point to another **:** proceeding obliquely or circuitously **:** ROUNDABOUT ⟨following an ~ route across the continent⟩ (2) **:** not going straight to the point **:** not proceeding to an intended end by the most direct course or method ⟨making ~ but perfectly legitimate inquiries into his prospects —Mary Austin⟩ **b :** not straightforward and open **:** tending to mislead **:** DECEITFUL, DISHONEST ⟨seemed to me to be an untrustworthy ~ individual⟩ **c :** not directly aimed at or achieved ⟨doubtless they had some not clearly recognized ~ purpose in mind⟩ **:** not resulting directly from an action or cause ⟨there will be many ~ consequences of their stupidity⟩ **d** (1) **:** stating what a real or supposed original speaker said without directly quoting the actual words and marked by changes that conform the statement grammatically to the words of the one making the statement ⟨the words *he could come* in the sentence "he said that he could come" are an ~ quotation⟩ ⟨~ discourse⟩ ⟨an example of an ~ question is *how she was* in the statement "he asked her how she was"⟩ (2) *of the object of a verb* **:** being the secondary goal of an action ⟨*borrower* in "I gave the borrower the book" is an ~ object⟩ (3) *of a passive verb or verb form* (a) **:** having a subject that becomes an indirect object when the verb is made active (as *he* in the statement "he was given a book by them" becomes *him* in "they gave him a book") ⟨*was given* in "he was given a book" is an ~ passive⟩ (b) **:** constituting a passive verb phrase made up of a verb and prepositional adverb of such a kind that when the verb phrase is made active the prepositional adverb is necessarily retained as a preposition having an object that is the word that had been used as subject of the passive verb phrase ⟨the passive verb phrase *was shot at* in the statement "the fugitive was shot at by the police" is an ~ passive that is made active in the statement "the police shot at the fugitive"⟩ **e :** HETEROXENOUS — **in·directly** \"+\ *adv* — **in·directness** \"+\ *n*

indirect contempt *n* **:** CONSTRUCTIVE CONTEMPT

indirect cost *also* **indirect charge** *n* **:** a cost that is not identifiable with a specific product, function, or activity — contrasted with *direct cost*

indirect development *n* **:** biologic development accompanied by a metamorphosis

indirect evidence *n* **:** evidence that establishes immediately collateral facts from which the main fact may be inferred **:** CIRCUMSTANTIAL EVIDENCE

indirect exchange *n* **1 :** exchange (as of checks, drafts) between three or more places **2 :** exchange in which rates give the value of the unit of home currency in terms of foreign currencies — compare FIXED EXCHANGE

indirect fire *n* **:** gunfire by indirect aiming at a target not visible from the gun

indirect initiative *n* **:** the legislative initiative where a proposed measure is considered by the legislature and goes to the people by referendum if the legislature rejects it — distinguished from *direct initiative*

in·di·rec·tion \ˌindəˈrekshən *also* -ˌdīˈ-\ *n* [*indirect* + *-ion*] **1 a :** lack of straightforwardness and openness **:** DECEITFULNESS, DISHONESTY ⟨unable to tolerate their double-dealing and ~⟩ **b :** something (as an act, a statement) marked by lack of straightforwardness or by deceitfulness ⟨hated diplomatic ~*s* —*Rev. of Reviews*⟩ **2 a** (1) **:** indirect action or movement or procedure **:** a roundabout course or means or method ⟨free from moralizing even by ~ —Lavinia R. Davis⟩ ⟨usurp the executive power by ~ —R.W.Ginnane⟩ (2) **:** an action or procedure or method marked by suggestion and free of direct obvious expression ⟨creative experiments in ~ —Louis Untermeyer⟩ **b :** lack of clear-cut action or movement toward a definite objective **:** lack of direction **:** aimless wandering about ⟨a piece of writing ruined by its ~⟩ ⟨a bizarre and pathetic ~ —St. Clair McKelway⟩ ⟨a querulous old woman who seemed to be always in a dither of ~⟩ **c :** something (as an act, a statement, a method) marked by indirection ⟨a suave and elegant little comedy of ~*s* —*Time*⟩

indirect labor *n* **1 :** labor (as clerks, repair men, maintenance men) applied indirectly to a product in the manufacturing process so that the cost is not computable in, identifiable with, or chargeable directly to the specific product — compare DIRECT LABOR **2 :** the wages paid to workers who are classed as indirect labor

indirect laying *n* **:** the laying of an artillery piece with the line of sighting indirectly upon a target not visible from the gun

indirect lighting *n* **:** lighting in which the source of light is concealed and the light emitted is diffusely reflected (as by the ceiling or a wall panel)

indirect material *n* **:** material (as tools, cleaning supplies, lubricating oil) used in manufacturing processes which does not become an integral part of the product and the cost of which is not identifiable with or directly chargeable to it — compare DIRECT MATERIAL

indirect method of difference : a method of scientific induction devised by J. S. Mill according to which if two or more instances in which a phenomenon occurs have only a single circumstance in common and two or more instances in which it does not occur have nothing in common except the absence of the circumstance, the circumstance in which the two sets of instances differ is the effect, cause, or necessary part of the cause of the phenomenon

indirect process *n* **:** a process involving production of pig iron from which metal is then made — compare DIRECT PROCESS

indirect reduction *n* **1 :** the process of reducing a syllogistic argument to the first figure by taking the contradictory of the conclusion as a premise and getting the contradictory of one premise as the new conclusion — contrasted with *direct reduction* **2** *also* **indirect proof :** a reductio ad absurdum

indirect rein *n* **:** the use of a rein that can be pressed against a horse's neck on the side opposite the direction in which it is required to move — compare DIRECT REIN

indirect selling *n* **:** a selling through middlemen

indirect syllogism *n* **:** a syllogism that results from another by indirect reduction

indirect tax *n* **:** a tax exacted indirectly from a person other than the one on whom the ultimate burden of the tax is expected to fall ⟨excise and customs duties are generally included under *indirect taxes*⟩

indirect vision *n* **:** vision resulting from rays of light falling upon peripheral parts of the retina

in·di·ru·bin \ˌində'rübən\ *n* -S [²*ind-* + *rub-* (fr. L *ruber* red) + *-in* — more at RED] **:** a dark red crystalline compound $C_{16}H_{10}N_2O_2$ isomeric with indigo (sense 1b) found in natural indigo but usu. made by reaction of indoxyl with isatin

in·dis·cern·ibil·i·ty \ˌində,s|ərnə'biləd-ē, |ən-, |əin-, -lətē, -i *also* -,z|\ *n* -ES **:** the quality or state of being indiscernible

¹**in·dis·cern·ible** \¦in+\ *adj* [¹*in-* + *discernible*] **:** incapable of being discerned: **a :** not visible or perceptible ⟨his features were ~ —G.B.Shaw⟩ **b :** incapable of being recognized as distinct ⟨thought that good was ~ from evil⟩ — **in·dis·cern·ible·ness** \"+\ *n* — **in·dis·cern·ibly** \"+\ *adv*

²**indiscernible** \"\ *n* -S **:** something indiscernible; *specif* **:** something that cannot be recognized as distinct

in·dis·cerp·ible \¦in+\ *adj* [¹*in-* + *discerpible*] *archaic* **:** INDISCERPTIBLE

in·dis·cerp·ti·bil·i·ty \ˌində,sərptə'biləd-ē, -də,zər-\ *n* -ES **:** the quality or state of being indiscerptible

in·dis·cerp·ti·ble \¦in+\ *adj* [¹*in-* + *discerptible*] **:** not discerptible **:** not subject to being separated into parts ⟨simple and ~ entities —James Ward⟩

in·dis·ci·plin·able \(¦)in, ən+\ *adj* [¹*in-* + *disciplinable*] **:** not subject to or capable of being disciplined ⟨full of ~ energy⟩

in·dis·ci·pline \(')in, ən+\ *n* [¹*in* + *discipline*] **:** lack of discipline ⟨coping with ~ and laxity —Cecil Sprigge⟩

in·dis·ci·plined \"+\ *adj* [¹*in-* + *disciplined* (past part. of *discipline*)] **:** UNDISCIPLINED ⟨~ imagination —Joseph Conrad⟩

in·dis·cov·er·able \¦in+\ *adj* [¹*in-* + *discoverable*] **:** UNDISCOVERABLE

in·dis·creet \"+\ *adj* [ME *indiscrete*, fr. MF & LL; MF *indiscret*, fr. LL *indiscretus*, fr. L, indistinguishable, not separated, fr. *in-* ¹in- + *discretus*, past part. of *discernere* to separate, distinguish between — more at DISCERN] **1 :** not discreet: as **a :** IMPRUDENT, INJUDICIOUS, UNTACTFUL, INCONSIDERATE ⟨an ~ question⟩ ⟨~ behavior⟩ **b :** not carefully restrained **:** UNWARY, INCAUTIOUS ⟨an ~ display of interest⟩ **2** *Scot* **:** UNCIVIL, IMPOLITE — **in·dis·creet·ly** \"+\ *adv* — **in·dis·creet·ness** \"+\ *n*

in·dis·crete \"+\ *adj* [L *indiscretus*] **:** not discrete **:** not separated into distinct parts ⟨an ~ mass of material⟩

in·dis·cre·tion \ˌində'skreshən *sometimes* ÷ -rēsh-\ *n* [ME *indiscrecioun*, fr. MF *indiscretion*, fr. LL *indiscretion-, indiscretio*, fr. *indiscretus* indiscreet + L *-ion-, -io* -ion] **1 :** lack of discretion: as **a :** IMPRUDENCE, INJUDICIOUSNESS, UNTACTFULNESS, INCONSIDERATENESS ⟨warned him against ~ in his conversation⟩ **b :** lack of careful restraint **:** UNWARINESS, INCAUTION ⟨spoke calmly to her and without ~⟩ **2 :** something (as an act, procedure, remark) marked by lack of discretion ⟨had destroyed his political career by an ~ —Gamaliel Bradford⟩; *specif* **:** an act at variance with the accepted morality of a society ⟨careful not to mention the ~*s* of her earlier life⟩ **3** *Scot* **:** INCIVILITY, IMPOLITENESS

in·dis·crim·i·nate \¦in+\ *adj* [¹*in-* + *discriminate*] **1 a (1) :** not marked by discrimination **:** not marked by careful distinction **:** not evidencing discernment ⟨~ reading habits⟩ ⟨~ viewing of television programs⟩ ⟨launched ~ destruction⟩ **(2) :** HAPHAZARD, RANDOM, HIT-AND-MISS, SWEEPING ⟨~ application of a law⟩ ⟨~ censure⟩ **(3) :** UNRESTRAINED, PROMISCUOUS ⟨~ sexual intercourse⟩ **b (1) :** not separated into distinct parts **:** JUMBLED, CONFUSED ⟨the babble of the crowd was an ~ mixture of several languages⟩ **(2) :** MOTLEY, HETEROGENEOUS ⟨a book filled with an ~ assortment of pictures⟩ **2 :** not exercising discrimination or discernment **:** not making careful distinctions **:** not carefully choosing **:** UNDISCRIMINATING ⟨a hospitable but not ~ host —Sarah G. Bowerman⟩ — **in·dis·crim·i·nate·ly** \"+\ *adv* — **in·dis·crim·i·nate·ness** \"+\ *n*

in·dis·crim·i·nat·ing \"+\ *adj* [¹*in-* + *discriminating*] **:** UNDISCRIMINATING — **in·dis·crim·i·nat·ing·ly** \"+\ *adv*

in·dis·crim·i·na·tion \¦in+\ *n* [¹*in-* + *discrimination*] **1 :** an act or instance of not discriminating or discerning ⟨greater ~*s* than were possibly his —Marguerite Young⟩ **2 :** the quality of not discriminating or the condition of not being discriminated **:** lack of discrimination ⟨show habitual ~ in the choice of their friends⟩ ⟨the various parts of the book are marked by ~⟩

in·dis·crim·i·na·tive \¦in+\ *adj* [¹*in-* + *discriminative*] **:** UNDISCRIMINATING — **in·dis·crim·i·na·tive·ly** \"+\ *adv*

in·dis·crim·i·na·to·ry \"+\ *adj* [¹*in-* + *discriminatory*] **:** not discriminatory

in·dis·cuss·ible \"+\ *adj* [¹*in-* + *discussible*] **:** not capable of being discussed ⟨the problem has now become ~⟩

in·dis·pens·abil·i·ty \ˌində,spen(t)sə'biləd-ē, -lətē, -i\ *n* **:** the quality or state of being indispensable

¹**in·dis·pens·able** \¦in+\ *also* **in·dis·pens·ible** \"\ *adj* [¹*in-* + *dispensable*] **1 :** that cannot be set aside or neglected or disregarded ⟨his ~ duty to help them⟩ ⟨an ~ obligation⟩ **2 :** that cannot be dispensed with **:** that is absolutely necessary or requisite or essential **:** that cannot be done without ⟨their assistance was ~⟩ ⟨an ~ book in this field⟩ ⟨was an ~ worker⟩ ⟨freedom to read is one of the ~ conditions of a democratic society —W.S.Dix⟩ **syn** see NEEDFUL

²**indispensable** \"\ *n* -S **1 :** something indispensable ⟨need clothing and food and other ~*s*⟩ **2 indispensables** *pl*, *archaic* **:** TROUSERS

in·dis·pens·able·ness \¦in+\ *n* **:** INDISPENSABILITY

in·dis·pens·ably \ˌində'spen(t)səblē, -li\ *adv* **:** without the possibility of being dispensed with **:** to an absolutely necessary extent ⟨help that is ~ required⟩

in·dis·pose \¦ində'spōz\ *vt* [prob. back-formation fr. *indisposed*] **1 a :** to put out of the proper condition for something **:** make unfit ⟨not to get one's sleep . . . ~*s* one more or less for the day —Edward FitzGerald⟩ **b :** to cause to be disinclined **:** make averse ⟨felt the science of mathematics to ~ the mind to religious belief —J.H.Newman⟩ **2** *archaic* **:** to cause to be in poor physical health **3** *archaic* **:** to cause to be hostile **:** make unfriendly

in·dis·posed \-zd\ *adj* [ME, not prepared for, unfitted, malevolently inclined, fr. ¹*in-* + *disposed*] **1 :** being usu. temporarily in poor physical health; *esp* **:** somewhat unwell usu. temporarily ⟨refused to see him because, she said, she felt ~⟩ **2 :** not being in the proper disposition for something **:** AVERSE ⟨you know how ~ tenant farmers are to doing their share of work —Ellen Glasgow⟩ **3** *archaic* **:** having an unsympathetic or unfriendly or hostile attitude toward something **syn** see DISINCLINED

in·dis·posed·ness \ˌində'spōzədnəs, -z(d)n-\ *n* -ES **:** INDISPOSITION

in·dis·po·si·tion \(¦)in, ən+\ *n* [ME *indisposicioun* unfitness, prob. fr. *indisposed* unfitted, after ME *disposed: disposicioun*] **:** the condition of being indisposed: **a (1) :** DISINCLINATION ⟨a certain ~ to face reality⟩ **(2)** *archaic* **:** lack of sympathy **:** UNFRIENDLINESS, HOSTILITY **b :** a usu. temporary condition of poor health; *esp* **:** a usu. temporary condition of being somewhat unwell ⟨has fully recovered from her recent ~⟩

in·dis·put·abil·i·ty \(¦)in, ən+\ *n* **:** the quality or state of being indisputable

in·dis·put·able \(¦)in, ən+\ *adj* [LL *indisputabilis*, fr. L *in-* ¹in- + *disputabilis* disputable] **1 :** that cannot be disputed or called into question **:** that is beyond argument **:** UNQUESTIONABLE, INCONTESTABLE, UNDENIABLE, INDUBITABLE ⟨gave ~ proof that he had been there⟩ ⟨these are facts that are clearly ~⟩ **2 :** truly existing **:** existing beyond the possibility of doubt or denial **:** REAL, ACTUAL ⟨the first ~ author I ever met —W.T.Scott⟩ ⟨secured against aggression by ~ law —Sir Winston Churchill⟩ — **in·dis·put·able·ness** \"+\ *n* — **in·dis·put·ably** \"+\ *adv*

in·dis·put·ed \¦in+\ *adj* [¹*in-* + *disputed*, past part. of *dispute*] *archaic* **:** UNDISPUTED

in·dis·so·cia·ble \"+\ *adj* [¹*in-* + *dissociable*] **:** that cannot be dissociated ⟨a problem that parallels the other one and is ~ from it⟩ — **in·dis·so·cia·bly** \-blē, -bli\ *adv*

in·dis·sol·u·bil·i·ty \(¦)in, ən+\ *n* **:** the quality or state of being indissoluble ⟨maintaining the ~ of marriage⟩

in·dis·sol·u·ble \"+\ *adj* [¹*in-* + *dissoluble*] **:** not dissoluble: as **a :** incapable of being annulled or undone or broken **:** perpetually binding or obligatory **:** perpetually lasting **:** PERMANENT ⟨an ~ contract⟩ ⟨bound by ~ vows⟩ **b (1) :** incapable of being dissolved into separate elements or particles **:** incapable of being decomposed or disintegrated ⟨a hard ~ mass of material⟩ **(2) :** incapable of being dissolved in a liquid **:** INSOLUBLE ⟨a substance that is ~ in water⟩ **(3)** *archaic* **:** incapable of being melted or liquefied **:** INFUSIBLE — **in·dis·sol·u·ble·ness** \-nəs\ *n* -ES — **in·dis·sol·u·bly** \-blē, -bli\ *adv*

in·dis·solv·able \¦in+\ *adj* [¹*in-* + *dissolvable*] *archaic* **:** INDISSOLUBLE

in·dis·tinct \"+\ *adj* [L *indistinctus*, fr. *in-* ¹in- + *distinctus* distinct] **1 :** not distinct: as **a :** not sharply outlined or separable **:** BLURRED, CONFUSED ⟨buildings that were ~ in the fog⟩ **b :** FAINT, DIM ⟨far away he saw the ~ light of a lantern⟩ **c :** not clearly perceived **:** not clearly recognizable or understandable **:** UNCERTAIN ⟨a peculiar ~ thumping sound⟩ ⟨could hear the ~ murmur of the crowd outside her window⟩ **2** *archaic* **:** UNDISCRIMINATING — **in·dis·tinct·ly** \"+\ *adv* — **in·dis·tinct·ness** \"+\ *n*

in·dis·tinc·tion \¦in+\ *n* [¹*in-* + *distinction*] **1** *archaic* **:** failure to make distinctions **2 :** absence of identifying or individualizing qualities **:** INDISTINGUISHABLENESS ⟨the leaves' shadows had a curious grayness and ~ —P.D.Boles⟩

in·dis·tinc·tive \"+\ *adj* [¹*in-* + *distinctive*] **1 :** UNDISCRIMINATING **2 :** marked by a lack of individualizing qualities ⟨an ~ group of weather-beaten shacks —Fred Beck⟩ — **in·distinctively** \"+\ *adv* — **in·dis·tinc·tive·ness** \"+\ *n*

in·dis·tin·guish·abil·i·ty \¦in+\ *n* **:** the quality or state of being indistinguishable

in·dis·tin·guish·able \"+\ *adj* [¹*in-* + *distinguishable*] **:** not distinguishable: as **a :** lacking clearly distinguishable parts or a clearly distinguishable outline **:** indeterminate in shape or structure ⟨an ~ mass of material⟩ ⟨~ forms seen in the mist⟩ **b :** not capable of being clearly perceived **:** not clearly recognizable or understandable **:** not discernible ⟨the two specimens are actually different from each other, but the differences are almost ~⟩ **c (1) :** not capable of being discriminated **:** lacking identifying or individualizing qualities ⟨a colorless person quite ~ from the colorless mass of humanity⟩ **(2) :** not capable of being analyzed into clearly separate and distinct parts ⟨an ~ blend of happiness and sorrow⟩ — **in·dis·tin·guish·able·ness** \"+\ *n* — **in·dis·tin·guish·ably** \"+\ *adv*

in·dis·tin·guished \"+\ *adj* [¹*in-* + *distinguished*] **:** UNDISTINGUISHED

in·dis·trib·ut·able \"+\ *adj* [¹*in-* + *distributable*] **:** not capable of being distributed

in·dis·tur·bance \"+\ *n* [¹*in-* + *disturbance*] *archaic* **:** freedom from disturbance **:** TRANQUILLITY

¹**in·dite** \ən'dīt, *usu* -īd·+V\ *vb* -ED/-ING/-S [ME *enditen*, fr. OF *enditer* to write down, compose, tell, make known, fr. (assumed) VL *indictare* to make known, proclaim, fr. L *indictus*, past part. of *indicere* to proclaim, fr. *in-* ²in- + *dicere* to say — more at DICTION] *vt* **1 a :** to make up or compose (as a poem or story) ⟨~ four lines of verse⟩ ⟨~ an epistle⟩ **b :** to give literary or formal expression to **c :** to put down in writing ⟨~ a message to a friend⟩ **2** *obs* **:** to dictate or prescribe esp. the exact verbal form for (something to be repeated or copied) **3** *obs* **:** INVITE ~ *vi* **:** COMPOSE, WRITE — **in·dit·er** \-īd·ə(r), -ītə-\ *n* -S

²**indite** \"\ *archaic var of* ¹INDICT

in·dite·ment \-mənt\ *n* -S **:** the act of inditing or the process of being indited **:** COMPOSITION

in·di·um \'indēəm\ *n* -S [NL, fr. ISV ²*ind-* + NL *-ium*; fr. the two indigo-blue lines in its spectrum] **:** a soft malleable easily fusible silvery white metallic element that is resistant to tarnishing and resembles aluminum and gallium in being chiefly trivalent, that occurs in very small quantities in sphalerite and other ores, and that is used chiefly as a plating for lead-coated silver bearings for airplanes — symbol *In*; see ELEMENT table

in·di·vert·ible \¦in+\ *adj* [¹*in-* + *divert* + *-ible*] **:** not to be diverted or turned aside — **in·di·vert·ibly** \-blē, -bli\ *adv*

individable *adj* [¹*in-* + *dividable*] *obs* **:** INDIVISIBLE

individua *pl of* INDIVIDUUM

¹**in·di·vid·u·al** \¦ində¦vij(ə)wəl, -jəl\ *adj* [ME *indyvyduall*, fr. ML *individualis* indivisible, individual, fr. L *individuus* indivisible (fr. *in-* ¹in- + *dividuus* divided, divisible, fr. *dividere* to divide) + *-alis* -al — more at DIVIDE] **1** *obs* **a :** not divisible **:** of one essence or nature **b :** not to be parted **:** INSEPARABLE **2 a :** of, belonging to, arising from, or possessed or used by an individual ⟨~ traits⟩ ⟨~ possessions⟩ ⟨the secular, modern . . . belief in ~ human rights —A.J.Toynbee⟩ ⟨~ self-reliance⟩ ⟨no private adventures, no purely ~ experiences —J.W.Krutch⟩ **b :** being an individual **:** marked by a distinctness and a complexity within a unity that characterizes organized things, concepts, organic beings, and persons **c :** intended for one person ⟨served the pudding in ~ portions⟩ **:** designed to accommodate enough for one person ⟨a small ~ baking dish⟩ **:** applying to one person ⟨an ~ policy in life insurance⟩ **3 :** existing as a separate and distinct entity **:** SINGLE, SINGULAR, PARTICULAR ⟨dolls, with movable legs and arms, glass eyes, and ~ teeth —Green Peyton⟩ ⟨a bookseller . . . handling ~ copies of net books —James Britton⟩ ⟨consists of 96 island units (comprising some 2,141 ~ islands and coral atolls) —*Americana Annual*⟩ **4** *archaic* **:** SELFSAME, IDENTICAL **5 a :** having marked individuality **:** being peculiar, striking, or uncommon enough in character to be easily identified or distinguished ⟨an ~ style of writing⟩ ⟨the odor from the dump was so putrid in so ~ a way that it was quite impossible to describe —Jean Stafford⟩ **b :** serving to distinguish or identify **c :** DISTINCTIVE, PECULIAR ⟨a threshold of susceptibility which is ~ to each system —G.W.Gray b. 1886⟩ **syn** see CHARACTERISTIC, SPECIAL

²**individual** \"\ *n* -S **1 :** a single or particular being or thing or group of beings or things: as **a :** a particular being or thing as distinguished from a class, species, or collection ⟨the primary subject matter of literature is precisely all that science leaves out: the ~, the particular, the concrete —H.J.Muller⟩ **(1) :** a single human being as contrasted with a social group or institution ⟨the rights of the ~⟩ ⟨countries in distress, like ~*s* in ill health, are inclined to be quarrelsome —Samuel Van Valkenburg & Ellsworth Huntington⟩ **(2) :** a single organism as distinguished from a group **b :** a particular person ⟨a rather odd ~⟩ ⟨attempting to capture rather than kill their enemies, in order that the supply of ~*s* for human sacrifice might be augmented —R.W.Murray⟩ **c :** the product of a single fertilization — called also *genetic individual* **d :** all the vegetative progeny of an organism exhibiting alternation of generations — called also *genetic individual;* compare CLONE **e :** a single chemical substance — compare MIXTURE 2a **2 :** an indivisible entity or a totality which cannot be separated into parts without altering the character or significance of these parts **3** *archaic* **:** SELF, PERSONALITY **4** *logic* **a :** something that cannot have instances **:** PARTICULAR **b :** something referred to by a proper name; *specif* **:** something referred to by a name or variable of the lowest logical type in a formalized language or calculus **5 :** a tournament in contract bridge in which each player changes partners after each round so that one person rather than a pair or team may be determined as winner

individual bond *n* **:** a fidelity bond specifying a single person as principal — compare BLANKET BOND

in·di·vid·u·al·ism \ˌində'vij(ə)wə,lizəm, -jə,l-\ *n* -S [F *individualisme*, fr. ML *individualis* individual + F *-isme* -ism] **1 a (1) :** the ethical doctrine or principle that the interests of the individual himself are or ought to be paramount in determination of conduct **:** ethical egoism; *also* **:** conduct guided by the principle **(2) :** the conception that all values, rights, and duties originate in individuals and that the community or social whole has no value or ethical significance not derived from its constituent individuals **b (1) :** the doctrine which holds that the chief end of society is the promotion of individual welfare and the chief end of moral law is the development of individual character; *also* **:** conduct or practice guided by such a doctrine **(2) :** a theory or policy having primary regard for individual rights and esp. maintaining the political and economic independence of the individual or maintaining the independence of individual initiative, action, and interests (as in industrial organization or in government); *also* **:** conduct or practice guided by such a theory or policy — compare COLLECTIVISM, PATERNALISM, SOCIALISM **c :** any vigorous and independent striving toward an individual goal or any markedly independent assertion of individual opinions esp. without regard for others or in defiance of an institution or larger authority **2 a :** INDIVIDUALITY ⟨the ~ of the backwoodsman —Theodore Roosevelt⟩ **b :** an individual peculiarity **:** IDIOSYNCRASY **3 :** the philosophical doctrine that reality is constituted of individual entities (as the monads of Leibniz) **4 :** an association of two nutritionally interdependent organisms which produces a distinct individual unlike either of the components in form and conditions of life (as in lichens)

in·di·vid·u·al·ist \-ˌləst\ *n* -S [F *individualiste*, fr. ML *individualis* + F *-iste* -ist] **1 :** one that pursues a markedly independent course in thought or action **:** one that speaks or acts with marked individuality ⟨he is apt to be an ~ who has never mastered the important arts of political cooperation and teamwork —R.E.Fitch⟩ ⟨an ~, independent to excess, in conflict with . . . society —H.S.Canby⟩ ⟨a race of ~*s* acknowledging no authority save that of their flintlocks —Deneys Reitz⟩ **2 :** one that advocates or practices individualism ⟨the ~ . . . was soon transformed into a collectivist —Alexander Brady⟩

in·di·vid·u·al·is·tic \¦=·=¦(=)=¦listik, -tēk\ *or* **individualist** *adj* **:** of, belonging to, or being individualism or an individualist: as **a :** favoring or allowing individualism ⟨the ~ polity of churches congregationally organized enables any single company of Christians to call and to ordain their own minister —W.L.Sperry⟩ **b :** consisting of individualism ⟨Spinoza's ethics is ~ in the sense that its fundamental motive is the desire for individual perfection or happiness —Frank Thilly⟩ ⟨~ theory . . . that the state, being a necessary evil, should be strictly limited to the preservation of order and the protection of the rights of the individual —W.S.Sayre⟩ **c :** arising from individualism in theory or practice ⟨transferring the democratic tradition from ~ to collectivist economic foundations —Paul Woodring⟩ **d :** characterized by marked individuality ⟨erratic and strongly ~ personalities —*Book-of-the-Month Club News*⟩ ⟨peculiarly ~ interior paintings —*Time*⟩ — **in·di·vid·u·al·is·ti·cal·ly** \¦=·=¦(=)=¦listək(ə)lē, -tēk-, -li\ *adv*

in·di·vid·u·al·i·ty \ˌ=·=,vijə'waləd-ē, -lətē, -i\ *n* -ES **1 a :** the total character peculiar to and distinguishing an individual from others **:** the complex of characteristics serving to individualize or set off a person or a thing from others **:** distinctive character ⟨believed that one was born with a particular biochemical ~ just as one was born with a certain physical and psychological personality —*Lancet*⟩ ⟨only slowly does the child become aware of his ~⟩; *esp* **:** a markedly individual or distinctive quality ⟨though he had no great . . . originality, there was a delicate ~ in his gracious and homely pictures —Havelock Ellis⟩ **b :** an individual or individualizing quality ⟨managed to give the borrowed product a distinctive national ~ —A.L.Kroeber⟩ ⟨white wines, which have considerable ~ —*N.Y. Times*⟩ ⟨they were strikingly alike in gifts and tastes, but each had marked ~ of character —H.E.Starr⟩ ⟨the ~ or, better, the personality of each instrument of the orchestra —Nicolas Nabokov⟩ **c :** PERSONALITY ⟨quietened her by sheer force of ~ —Arnold Bennett⟩ ⟨not only is the author unknown, but in the pure ballad there is no trace of his ~ —*Encyc. Americana*⟩ **2** *archaic* **:** INDIVISIBILITY, INSEPARABILITY **3 a :** an individual characteristic ⟨the effort . . . of getting the *individualities* of a fresh group of people into one's head, is becoming every year harder for me —A.C.Benson⟩ **b :** an individual thing; *esp* **:** an individual person **4 :** the quality or state of existing as an individual or of constituting an individual **:** separate or distinct existence ⟨the great artist can transcend his own ~ —Harold Nicolson⟩ **5 :** the tendency to pursue one's course with marked independence or self-reliance **:** INDIVIDUALISM ⟨distinguished by a strong streak of ~ and independence, the counterpart probably of the same pioneer spirit which originally marked the commerce and industry of the New World —W.T. & Barbara Fitts⟩ **syn** see DISPOSITION

in·di·vid·u·al·iza·tion \-,vij(ə)wələ'zāshən, -jəl-, -,lī'z-\ *n* -S **1 :** the act of individualizing or the state of being individualized **2 :** a program of correctional or penal treatment for a delinquent or adult offender which is coordinated with expert information regarding his personal history and rehabilitative needs

in·di·vid·u·al·ize \-'vij(ə)wə,līz, -jə,l-\ *vt* -ED/-ING/-S [¹*individual* + *-ize*] **1 a :** to make individual in character **:** invest with individuality ⟨the trace of huskiness in her voice . . . proved to be an asset, helping to ~ her screen personality —*Current Biog.*⟩ ⟨the city is further *individualized* by the many university buildings —*Amer. Guide Series: Mich.*⟩ ⟨the population . . . inevitably becomes depersonalized on the one hand, *individualized* on the other —A.L.Kroeber⟩ **b :** to treat or notice individually **:** PARTICULARIZE, SPECIFY **c :** DISTINGUISH ⟨the sounds were *individualized* by sharpness of tone, incisiveness of utterance —William Beebe⟩ **2 :** to put into the hands or management of an individual ⟨more and more of our savings are institutionalized rather than *individualized* —R.R.Nathan⟩ **3 :** to adjust or adapt (as a treatment or justice) to the needs or the special circumstances of an individual — **in·di·vid·u·al·iz·er** \-līzə(r)\ *n* -S

individual key *n* **:** CHANGE KEY

individual liberty *n* **:** the liberty of those persons who are free from external restraint in the exercise of those rights which are considered to be outside the province of a government to control — compare CIVIL LIBERTY, POLITICAL LIBERTY

in·di·vid·u·al·ly \-'vijəlē, -j(ə)wəlē, -li\ *adv* **:** in an individual manner: as **a** *obs* **:** INDIVISIBLY, INSEPARABLY **b** *obs* **:** in respect to individual identity **c :** one by one, SINGLY, SEPARATELY ⟨the students went in ~ to consult about their programs⟩ ⟨~ constructed houses⟩ **d :** with markedly individual qualities or characteristics ⟨each of the artists paints ~⟩ **e :** as an individual **:** PERSONALLY ⟨whatever action the state takes will affect me ~⟩

individual medley *n* **:** a swimming race in which each competitor swims one third of the total course with the backstroke, one third with the breaststroke, and one third freestyle

individual psychology *n* [trans. of G *individualpsychologie*] **:** a modification of psychoanalysis developed by the Austrian psychologist Alfred Adler emphasizing feelings of inferiority and a will to power as the primary motivating forces in human behavior

individual variable *n, logic* **:** a variable which may be replaced by a name or a description of an individual

[1]**in·di·vid·u·ate** \\ˌində'vij(ə)wə̇\|t, -jəˌwā\|, *usu* \|d·+V\\ *adj* [ML *individuatus*, past part. of *individuare* to individuate] **1 :** UNDIVIDED, INSEPARABLE **2** *obs* **:** INDIVIDUALIZED

[2]**in·di·vid·u·ate** \\-jəˌwāt, *usu* -ād·+V\\ *vt* -ED/-ING/-S [ML *individuatus*, past part. of *individuare*, fr. L *individuus* indivisible — more at INDIVIDUAL] **1 :** to give individuality to **:** distinguish from others of the same species ⟨the characters that . . . ~ him from all other writers —George Saintsbury⟩ **2 :** to form into a distinct entity **:** give individual form to ⟨symbolism of language which ~*s* a man's private memories —D.G.Mitchell⟩

in·di·vid·u·a·tion \\-ˌvijə'wāshən\\ *n* -S [ML *individuation-*, *individuatio*, fr. *individuatus* (past part. of *individuare*) + L *-ion-*, *-io* -ion] **:** the act or process of individuating or the state of being individuated: as **a** (1) **:** the development of the individual from the universal or the determination of the individual in the general ⟨in scholastic philosophy the principle of ~ was variously held to be matter, form, and particularity of the subject in time and space⟩ (2) **:** the process by which individuals in society become differentiated from one another, come to occupy different statuses and roles, and tend to lose group or class identity (3) **:** regional differentiation along a primary embryonic axis **:** field formation — contrasted with *evocation;* compare INDUCTOR **b :** existence as a person or individual **:** INDIVIDUALITY

individuity *n* -ES [LL *individuitat-*, *individuitas*, fr. L *individuus* indivisible + *-itat-*, *-itas* -ity] **1** *obs* **:** INDIVISIBILITY **2** [ML *individuitat-*, *individuitas*, fr. LL, indivisibility] *obs* **:** INDIVIDUALITY

in·di·vid·u·um \\ˌində'vijəwəm\\ *n, pl* **individ·ua** \\-wə\\ *or* **individuums** [LL, fr. L, indivisible entity, atom, fr. neut. of *individuus* indivisible] **1 :** an individual instance or an individual being as distinguished from a group of similar instances or beings **2** [L] **:** an indivisible entity; *specif* **:** ATOM 1a

in·divisibility \\ˌ¦in+\\ *n* **:** the quality or state of being indivisible

[1]**in·divisible** \\"+\\ *adj* [ME *indyvysible*, fr. LL *indivisibilis*, fr. L *in-* [1]in- + LL *divisibilis* divisible] **:** not divisible **:** not separable into parts ⟨the ~ responsibility of school and college in matters of general education —A.W.Griswold⟩ ⟨one nation, ~ —Francis Bellamy⟩ ⟨reality is one and ~ —C.D.Lewis⟩ — **in·divisibleness** \\"+\\ *n* — **in·di·vis·i·bly** \\-blē,-bli\\ *adv*

[2]**indivisible** \\ˌ¦in+\\ *n* -S **:** something indivisible; *specif* **:** a mathematical quantity that is assumed to admit of no further division

in·division \\"+\\ *n* [ML *indivision-*, *indivisio*, fr. L *in-* [1]in- + *division-*, *divisio-* division] **:** the state of being undivided **:** ONENESS

indm *abbr* indemnity

in·do \\'in(ˌ)dō\\ *n* -S *usu cap* [D, short for *Indo-Europeaan*, fr. *ind-* [1]ind- + *Europeaan* European, fr. L *europaeus* European (adj.) + D *-aan* -an (n. suffix) — more at EUROPEAN] **:** a native or inhabitant of Indonesia who has a Western education and is of mixed European usu. Dutch and Indonesian descent

indo- — see IND-

in·do-african \\ˌ¦in(ˌ)dō+\\ *adj, usu cap I&A* **:** of, relating to, or constituting a terrestrial biogeographic realm that includes intertropical Asia and intertropical Africa

[1]**indo-aryan** \\"+\\ *adj, usu cap I&A* **1 :** of, relating to, or characteristic of Indo-Aryans **2 :** of, relating to, or characteristic of one of the Aryan languages of India

[2]**indo-aryan** \\"\\ *n, cap I&A* **1 :** a member of one of the peoples of India of Aryan speech and physique characterized by tall stature, dolichocephaly, fair complexion with dark hair and eyes, plentiful beard, and narrow and prominent nose — compare INDIAN 1a **2 :** one of the early Indo-European invaders of Persia, Afghanistan, and India **3 :** the Indo-European languages of India and Pakistan as a group

in·do-briton \\ˌ¦in(ˌ)dō+\\ *n, cap I&B* **:** a person born in India of mixed Indian and British descent

indo-burmese \\"+\\ *adj, usu cap I&B* **:** BURMO-CHINESE

[1]**in·do-chinese** \\"+\\ *adj, usu cap I&C* [*Indochina*, region in southeastern Asia + E *-ese*] **1 a :** of, relating to, or characteristic of Indochina — usu. used of the countries Cambodia, Laos, and Vietnam comprised in the former French Indochina but sometimes of the region comprising all the countries of southeastern Asia: Burma, Malaya, Thailand, Cambodia, Laos, and Vietnam **b :** of, relating to, or characteristic of the Indo-Chinese esp. of Cambodia, Laos, and Vietnam **2** [[1]*ind-* + *chinese*] **:** of, relating to, characteristic of, or constituting the Tibeto-Burman, Thai, Chinese, and various neighboring languages **3** [[1]*ind-* + *chinese*] **:** BURMO-CHINESE

[2]**indo-chinese** \\"\\ *n, cap I&C* **1 :** a native or inhabitant of Indochina — usu. used of the people of the countries Cambodia, Laos, and Vietnam comprised in the former French Indochina but sometimes of the peoples of southeastern Asia including also those of Burma, Malaya, and Thailand **2 :** an assumed family of languages comprehending Tibeto-Burman, Thai, Chinese, and various neighboring groups

indocibility *n* **:** the quality or state of being indocible

indocible *adj* [LL *indocibilis*, fr. L *in-* [1]in- + LL *docibilis* docible] **:** UNTEACHABLE

in·docile \\(')in, ən+\\ *adj* [MF, fr. L *indocilis*, fr. *in-* [1]in- + *docilis* docile] **:** unwilling or indisposed to be taught, trained, or disciplined **:** not easily instructed or controlled **:** UNRULY ⟨a large, ~, irresponsible, domineering man —G.P.Elliott⟩

in·docility \\ˌ¦in+\\ *n* [*indocile* + *-ity*] **:** the quality or state of being indocile **:** UNTEACHABLENESS, INTRACTABLENESS

in·doc·tri·nate \\ə̇n'däktrə̇ˌnāt, *usu* -ād·+V\\ *vt* -ED/-ING/-S [prob. fr. *indoctrine* + *-ate*, v. suffix] **1 a :** to give instructions esp. in fundamentals or rudiments **:** TEACH ⟨the function of *indoctrinating* youth was given to and accepted by . . . the family and the priesthood —L.O.Garber & W.B.Castetter⟩ ⟨the recruits were *indoctrinated* for a month and then sent to specialist schools⟩ **b :** to imbue or make markedly familiar (as with a skill) ⟨*indoctrinated* themselves with the teamwork of attack —Ira Wolfert⟩ **2 :** to cause to be impressed and usu. ultimately imbued (as with a usu. partisan or sectarian opinion, point of view, or principle) ⟨had to be *indoctrinated* with the will to win —J.P.Baxter b.1893⟩ ⟨*indoctrinating* young people with alien ideologies⟩ **:** cause to be drilled or otherwise trained (as in a sectarian doctrine) and usu. persuaded ⟨~ the immigrants in a new way of life⟩ — **in·doc·tri·na·tor** \\-ād·ə(r), -atə-\\ *n* -S

in·doc·tri·na·tion \\(ˌ)inˌdäktrə̇'nāshən, ənˌd-\\ *n* -S [*indoctrinate* + *-ion*] **1 :** the act or process of indoctrinating or the state of being indoctrinated ⟨the proper and adequate ~ of a newly received prisoner is one of the most important points of the rehabilitation program —W.H.Maglin⟩ ⟨evidence of attempts at subversive ~ or disloyal teaching —B.F.Wright⟩ ⟨~ can be smuggled in . . . in the name of democratic education —F.C.Neft⟩ **2 :** something with or in which one is indoctrinated ⟨freedom of minds, the maxims of logic and experimental proof, of intellectual honesty, of tolerance and persuasion . . . constitute a body of ~ to which no objection can consistently be raised —R.B.Perry⟩ — **in·doc·tri·na·tion·al** \\(¦)=¦==¦nāshənᵊl, -shnəl\\ *adj*

indoctrine *vt* -ED/-ING/-S [alter. (influenced by E [2]*in-*) of ME *endoctrinen*, fr. MF *endoctriner*, fr. OF, fr. *en-* [1]en- + *doctrine* (n.)] *archaic* **:** INDOCTRINATE

in·doc·tri·ni·za·tion \\ə̇nˌdäktrə̇nə̇'zāshən, -ˌnī'z-\\ *n* -S **:** INDOCTRINATION

in·doc·tri·nize \\ə̇n'däktrə̇ˌnīz\\ *vt* -ED/-ING/-S [*indoctrinate* + *-ize*] **:** INDOCTRINATE

[1]**in·do-dravidian** \\ˌ¦in(ˌ)dō+\\ *adj, usu cap I&D* **:** of, relating to, or characteristic of Indo-Dravidians

[2]**indo-dravidian** \\"\\ *n, cap I&D* **:** a member of a composite people resulting from intermixture between the native Dravidians of India and the Aryan invaders but having some elements of the Munda-speaking racial group

[1]**indo-european** \\ˌ¦in(ˌ)dō+\\ *adj, usu cap I&E* [Gk *ind-*, *indo-* India, of or connected with India + E *european* — more at IND-] **:** of, relating to, characteristic of, or constituting the Indo-European languages

[2]**indo-european** \\"\\ *n, cap I&E* **1 a :** the Indo-European languages **b :** the unrecorded prehistoric language from which the Indo-European languages are descended **2 a :** a speaker of Indo-European (sense 1b) **b :** a member of a people whose original tongue is one of the Indo-European languages **3 :** one who is a native or inhabitant of a country of southeastern Asia and esp. Indochina and who is of European or part-European origin or descent **:** EURASIAN

indo-euro·pe·an·ist \\¦=(ˌ)=ˌ=='==ə̇st\\ *n* -S *cap I&E* **:** a specialist in Indo-European linguistics

indo-european languages *n pl, usu cap I&E* **:** a family of languages comprising those spoken in most of Europe and in the parts of the world colonized by Europeans since 1500 and also in Persia, the subcontinent of India, and some other parts of Asia

INDO-EUROPEAN LANGUAGES

BRANCH	GROUP	LANGUAGES AND MAJOR DIALECTS[1]			PROVENIENCE
		ANCIENT	MEDIEVAL	MODERN	
GERMANIC	East		*Gothic*		eastern Europe
	North		*Old Norse*	Icelandic Faeroese Norwegian Swedish Danish	Iceland Faeroe islands Norway Sweden Denmark
	West		*Old High German* *Middle High German*	German	Germany, Switzerland, Austria
				Yiddish	Germany, eastern Europe
			Old Saxon *Middle Low German*		Northern Germany
			Middle Dutch	Dutch Afrikaans	Netherlands So. Africa
			Middle Flemish *Old Frisian*	Flemish Frisian	Belgium Netherlands, Germany
			Old English *Middle English*	English	England
CELTIC	Continental	*Gaulish*			Gaul
	Brythonic		*Old Welsh* *Middle Welsh*	Welsh	Wales
			Old Cornish *Middle Breton*	*Cornish* Breton	Cornwall Brittany
	Goidelic		*Old Irish* *Middle Irish*	Irish Gaelic	Ireland
				Scottish Gaelic *Manx*	Scotland Isle of Man
ITALIC	Osco-Umbrian	*Oscan* *Umbrian* *Sabellian*			ancient Italy
	Latinian or Romance[2]	*Venetic* *Lanuvian* *Faliscan* *Praenestine* Latin			ancient Italy
				Portuguese Spanish Judeo-Spanish	Portugal Spain Mediterranean lands
			Old Provençal	Catalan Provençal	Spain (Catalonia) southern France
			Old French *Middle French*	French	France, Belgium, Switzerland
				Haitian Creole Italian Rhaeto-Romanic Sardinian *Dalmatian* Romanian	Haiti Italy, Switzerland Switzerland, Italy Sardinia Adriatic coast Romania, Balkans
Poorly preserved and of uncertain affinities within Indo-European, "Thraco-Phrygian", "Illyrian", etc.		*Ligurian* *Messapian* *Illyrian* *Thracian* *Phrygian*			ancient Italy ancient Italy Balkans Balkans Asia Minor
Albanian				Albanian	Albania, southern Italy
Greek		Greek ("Ancient Greek")	Greek ("Byzantine Greek", "Middle Greek")	Greek ("Modern Greek", "New Greek")	Greece, the eastern Mediterranean
Baltic			*Old Prussian*	Lithuanian Latvian	East Prussia Lithuania Latvia
SLAVIC	South		Old Church Slavonic	Slovene Serbo-Croatian (Serbian, Croatian) Macedonian Bulgarian	Yugoslavia Yugoslavia Macedonia Bulgaria
	West		*Old Czech*	Czech Slovak Polish Kashubian Wendish *Polabian*	Czechoslovakia Czechoslovakia Poland Poland Germany Germany
	East		*Old Russian*	Russian Ukrainian Belorussian	Russia Ukraine White Russia
Armenian			Armenian ("Old Armenian")	Armenian ("Modern Armenian")	Asia Minor, Caucasus
IRANIAN	West	*Old Persian*			ancient Persia
			Pahlavi Persian ("Classical Persian")	Persian ("Modern Persian")	Persia (Iran)
				Kurdish Baluchi Tajiki	Persia, Iraq, Turkey West Pakistan central Asia
	East	Avestan			ancient Persia
			Sogdian *Khotanese*		central Asia central Asia
				Pashto Ossetic	Afghanistan, West Pakistan Caucasus
INDIC	Dard			Shina Khowar Kafiri	upper Indus valley
				Kashmiri	Kashmir
	Sanskritic	Sanskrit Pali *Prakrits*	*Prakrits*		India
				Lahnda Sindhi Panjabi Rajasthani Gujarati Marathi Konkani Oriya Bengali Assamese Bihari Hindi Urdu Nepali Sinhalese Romany	western Punjab Sind Panjab Rajasthan Gujarat western India western India Orissa Bengal Assam Bihar northern India Pakistan, India Nepal Ceylon uncertain
Tocharian			*Tocharian A* *Tocharian B*		central Asia
The following is sometimes considered as another branch of Indo-European, and sometimes as coordinate with Indo-European, the two together constituting Indo-Hittite					
Anatolian		*Hittite* *Luwian* *Palaic* *Hieroglyphic Hittite* *Lydian* *Lycian*			ancient Asia Minor

[1]Italics denote dead languages. Listing of a language only in the ancient or medieval column but in roman type indicates that it survives only in some special use, as in literary composition or liturgy

[2]Romance is normally applied only to medieval and modern languages; Latinian is normally applied only to ancient languages

in·do·gae·an *or* **in·do·ge·an** \ˌindōˈjēən\ *adj, usu cap* [NL *Indogaea*, Oriental biogeographic realm or region (fr. ¹*ind-* + *-gaea*) + E *-an*] : ORIENTAL

indo–gangetic \ˌin(ˌ)dō+\ *adj, usu cap I&G* : of or relating to the area drained by the Indus and Ganges rivers esp. the lowland plain south of the Himalayas

in·dogen·ide \ˈindəjəˌnīd; ənˈdäjə,n-, -nəd\ *n* -s [ISV *indogen* bivalent nitrogen-containing radical C_8H_5NO (ISV ²*ind-* + *-gen*) + *-ide*] : a compound that is an alkylidene substitution product of indoxyl formed by reaction of indoxyl with an aldehyde or ketone

¹**in·do–germanic** \ˌin(ˌ)dō+\ *adj, usu cap I&G* [trans. of G *indogermanisch*] : INDO-EUROPEAN

²**indo–germanic** \"\ *n, cap I&G* : INDO-EUROPEAN 1

in·do–hittite \ˌin(ˌ)dō+\ *n, cap I&H, often attrib* [¹*ind-* + *hittite*] **1** : a language family comprehending Indo-European and Anatolian — see INDO-EUROPEAN LANGUAGES table **2 a** : a hypothetical parent language of Indo-European and Anatolian

¹**indo–iranian** \"+\ *adj, usu cap both Is* : of, relating to, characteristic of, or constituting a subfamily of the Indo-European languages that consists of the Indic and the Iranian branches

²**indo–iranian** \"\ *n, cap both Is* **1 a** : the Indo-Iranian languages **b** : the unrecorded prehistoric language from which the Indo-Iranian languages are descended **2 a** : a speaker of Indo-Iranian (sense 1b) **b** : a member of a people whose original tongue is one of the Indo-Iranian languages

indol- *or* **indolo-** *comb form* [ISV, fr. *indole*] **1** : indole ⟨*indoloid*⟩ **2** : containing an indole ring fused on one side to one side of another ring ⟨*indolo*quinoline⟩

in·dole \ˈinˌdōl\ *n* -s [ISV ²*ind-* + *-ole*; orig. formed as G *indol*] **1** : a crystalline compound C_8H_7N that is found esp. in jasmine oil, civet, and coal tar and along with skatole in the intestines and feces as a decomposition product of proteins containing tryptophan, that may be formed by reductive distillation of indigo with zinc, and that in spite of its unpleasant odor when concentrated is used as a trace component of floral perfumes (as jasmine, gardenia, or lilac) — compare STRUCTURAL FORMULA **2** : a derivative of indole

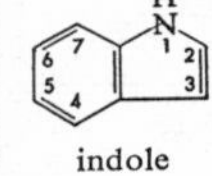

indole

indoleacetic acid \ˌ=ˌ==ˈ==-\ *n* [*indoleacetic* fr. *indole* + *acetic*] : a crystalline plant hormone $(C_8H_6N)CH_2COOH$ present in urine, made synthetically, and used to promote growth and rooting of plants — called also *beta-indolylacetic acid, 3-indoleacetic acid, heteroauxin*; see AUXIN

indolebutyric acid \ˌ=ˌ=ˈ==-\ *n* [*indolebutyric* fr. *indole* + *butyric*] : a crystalline acid $(C_8H_6N)CH_2CH_2CH_2COOH$ similar to indoleacetic acid in its effects on plants

in·do·lence \ˈindələn(t)s\ *n* -s [F, fr. L *indolentia* freedom from pain, fr. *in-* ¹in- + *dolentia* pain, fr. *dolent-, dolens* (pres. part. of *dolēre* to feel pain, grieve) + *-ia* -y — more at CONDOLE] **1** *or* **indolency** -ES *obs* **a** : insensibility or indifference to pain **b** : freedom from pain or a tranquillity of mind marked by neither pain nor pleasure : apathetic ease **2** *med* **a** : a condition of causing little or no pain ⟨deceptive ~ of the tumor⟩ **b** : a condition of growing or progressing slowly **c** : slowness in healing **3** : laziness or inactivity arising from a love of ease or aversion to work : indisposition to labor : SLOTH ⟨the hot moist air of the tropics spreads a feeling of lethargy and ~ over everything that moves —G.H.Reed b.1887⟩ ⟨~, tardiness or even downright opposition to improvements —*Farmer's Weekly (So. Africa)*⟩ ⟨literary ~, mere unwillingness to take the necessary pains —Brand Blanshard⟩

¹**in·do·lent** \-nt\ *adj* [LL *indolent-, indolens* insensitive to pain, fr. L *in-* ¹in- + *dolent-, dolens* (pres. part. of *dolēre*)] **1** *med* **a** : causing little or no pain ⟨an ~ tumor⟩ **b** (1) : growing or progressing slowly ⟨leprosy is an ~ infectious disease⟩ (2) : slow to heal ⟨an ~ ulcer⟩ **2 a** : constantly indulging in ease : chronically averse to labor and exertion ⟨a goad for an ~ writer —Van Wyck Brooks⟩ ⟨old and fat and ~ —A.E.Stevenson b.1900⟩ **b** : conducing to or encouraging laziness or avoidance of exertion ⟨the ~ heat of the afternoon⟩ **c** : giving evidence of or exhibiting indolence ⟨an ~ sigh —Willard Robertson⟩ ⟨an ~ amiability⟩ **syn** see LAZY

²**indolent** \"\ *n* -s : one that is indolent ⟨thousands of scoundrelly ~s lived there despising any honest toil —P.I.Wellman⟩

in·do·lent·ly *adv* : in an indolent manner

in·do·line \ˈindəˌlēn, -lən\ *n* -s [ISV *indol-* + *-ine*; prob. orig. formed as G *indolin*] : a liquid base C_8H_9N that is a stronger base than indole and is obtained from indole by reduction; 2,3-dihydro-indole

in·do·log·i·cal \ˌindəˈläjəkəl\ *adj, often cap* : of or relating to Indology

in·dol·o·gist \ənˈdäləjəst\ *n* -s *often cap* : a specialist in Indology

in·dol·o·gy \-jē\ *n* -ES *usu cap* [¹*ind-* + *-logy*] : the study of India and its people (as through its languages, literature, history, philosophy, customs, antiquities)

in·do·lyl \ˈindəˌlil, -lēl\ *n* -s [ISV *indol-* + *-yl*] : the univalent radical C_8H_6N derived from indole by removal of one hydrogen atom

indolylacetic acid \ˌ==ˌ=ˈ==-\ *n* [*indolylacetic* fr. *indolyl* + *acetic*] : INDOLEACETIC ACID

in·do–malay \ˌin(ˌ)dō+\ *adj, usu cap I&M* : INDO-MALAYAN 1

¹**indo–malayan** \"+\ *adj, usu cap I&M* **1** : of or relating to the insular and mainland areas of southeastern Asia **2** : of or relating to the Malayan biogeographic subdivision : MALAYAN

²**indo–malayan** \"\ *n, cap I&M* : a member of one of the major ethnic groups that embrace the inhabitants of mainland and insular southeastern Asia including the island chains from Indonesia through the Ryukyus

in·dom·i·ta·bil·i·ty \(ˌ)inˌdämədəˈbilədē, ən-, -mətə-, -lətē, -i\ *n* -ES : the quality or state of being indomitable

in·dom·i·ta·ble \ənˈdämədəbəl, -mətə-\ *adj* [LL *indomitabilis*, fr. L *in-* ¹in- + *domitare* to tame + *-abilis* -able — more at DAUNT] : incapable of being subdued : INTRACTABLE ⟨~ courage⟩ ⟨an ~ will⟩ — **in·dom·i·ta·ble·ness** \-nəs\ *n* -ES — **in·dom·i·ta·bly** \-blē, -bli\ *adv*

in·do·ne·sia \ˌindəˈnēzh|ə *also* -ēsh| *or* -ēzē\ *adj, usu cap* [fr. *Indonesia*, country (also called the Republic of Indonesia) and archipelago (also called the Malay Archipelago or Malaysia) off the southeast coast of Asia] : of or from Indonesia : of the kind or style prevalent in Indonesia : INDONESIAN

¹**in·do·ne·sian** \|ən\ *n* -s *cap* [*Indonesia* + E *-an* (n. suffix)] **1** : MALAYSIAN 1 **2** : PROTO-MALAY **3 a** : a native or inhabitant of the Republic of Indonesia **b** : the Malay dialect that is the national language of the Republic of Indonesia

²**indonesian** \"\ *adj, usu cap* [*Indonesia* + E *-an* (adj. suffix)] **1** : of or relating to the Republic of Indonesia, the Malay archipelago, or Indonesians **2** : of, relating to, or constituting the subfamily of Austronesian languages spoken chiefly in the Malay peninsula and archipelago

in·door \ˈin,=, ənˈ=\ *adj* [alter. (influenced by E ¹*in*) of obs. E *within-door*, adj., fr. the phrase *within door* in a building] : of or relating to the interior of a building ⟨an ~ scene⟩ ⟨an ~ swimming pool⟩: as **a** : of or relating to something done inside a building ⟨an ~ job⟩ ⟨an ~ sport⟩ **b** : designed for use indoors ⟨an ~ dress⟩ ⟨an ~ flag⟩ **c** : living inside an institution ⟨~ paupers⟩ : given within an institution ⟨~ relief⟩ **d** : inclined to stay indoors ⟨Americans have become an ~ people —J.M.Fitch⟩

indoor baseball *n* : softball played indoors

in·doors \(ˈ)inˈ=, ənˈ=\ *adv* [alter. (influenced by E ¹*in*) of *withindoors*] **1** : in a building ⟨worked ~ all afternoon⟩ ⟨stayed ~ during the storm⟩ **2** : into a building ⟨went ~ as soon as it began to rain⟩

in·do–pacific \ˌin(ˌ)dō+\ *adj, usu cap I&P* : of or relating to the Indo-Malayan areas of the Pacific ocean ⟨an *Indo-Pacific* fish⟩ ⟨*Indo-Pacific* coral reefs⟩

in·do·phe·nin \ˌindəˈfēnən, ənˈdäfənən\ *n* [ISV ²*ind-* + *phene* + *-in*; fr. a belief that it was a derivative of benzene; orig. formed in G] : a blue crystalline compound $C_{24}H_{14}N_2O_2S_2$ formed by reaction of thiophene with isatin and sulfuric acid and used as a color test for the presence of thiophene in technical benzene

in·do·phenol \ˌindō+\ *n* [ISV ²*ind-* + *phenol*; prob. orig. formed in G] : any of a class of blue or green dyes derived from quinone imines and used chiefly as intermediates for sulfur dyes and as dyes formed in color photography; *esp* : the simplest phenol $HOC_6H_4N{=}C_6H_4{=}O$

in·do·planorbis \ˌin(ˌ)dō+\ *n, cap* [NL, fr. ¹*ind-* + *Planorbis*] : an Asiatic genus of freshwater snails (family Planorbidae) of veterinary importance as an intermediate host of the bovine blood fluke and other trematode worms

in·dore \(ˈ)inˈdō(ə)r, ənˈd-\ *adj, usu cap* [fr. *Indore*, city in central India] : of or from the city of Indore, India : of the kind or style prevalent in Indore

in·do red MV-6632 \ˈin(ˌ)dō-\ *n, usu cap I&R* [perh. fr. ²*ind-*] : an organic pigment — see DYE table I (under *Pigment Red 87*)

indorse *var of* ENDORSE

indos *pl of* INDO

indow *obs var of* ENDOW

in·dox·yl \ənˈdäksəl, ˈin,d-\ *n* -s [ISV ²*ind-* + hydr*oxyl*; prob. orig. formed in G] : a yellow crystalline phenolic compound $(C_8H_6N)OH$ that has a strong fecal odor, that occurs combined in plants and animals but is usu. made from phenylglycine by heating with sodamide, and that on oxidation yields indigo; 3-hydroxy-indole — see INDICAN

in·draft \ˈin,=\ *n* [⁴*in* + *draft*] **1** *obs* : an opening into land from the sea : INLET **2 a** : a drawing or pulling in : an inward attraction **b** : an inward flow or current (as of air or water)

in·drape \ənˈ=\ *vt* [²*in-* + *drape*] *archaic* : to make into cloth : WEAVE

¹**indrawing** \ˈ=ˌ==\ *n* [ME *indrawinge*, fr. *in* + *drawinge*, gerund of *drawen* to draw (after ME *drawen in*, v., to draw in)] : the act of drawing in or inward ⟨a sharp ~ of her breath —W.G.Hardy⟩

²**indrawing** \"\ *adj* [²*in* + *drawing*, pres. part. of *draw* (after *draw in*, v.)] : drawing in or inward

indrawn \ˈ=ˌ=\ *adj* [²*in* + *drawn*, past part. of *draw* (after *draw in*, v.)] **1** : drawn in ⟨an ~ breath⟩ **2** : tending to reserve, taciturnity, or egocentricity ⟨an aloof, aristocratic, ~ man —W.S.White⟩ ⟨seen as selfish, ~ —*Times Lit. Supp.*⟩

indre *abbr* indenture

indrench *vt* [²*in-* + *drench*] *obs* : DRENCH, DROWN

in·dri \ˈindrē\ *n* [F, fr. Malagasy *indry* look!; prob. fr. an erroneous belief by the French naturalist Pierre Sonnerat (†1814), who observed the animal in its native habitat about 1780, that the natives were uttering its name when in fact they were only calling attention to its presence] **1** -s : the largest of the lemurs of Madagascar (*Indris brevicaudatus*) about two feet long with a rudimentary tail and brightly marked in black and white **2** [NL, fr. F] *cap* : a genus containing the indri and being the type of the family Indridae

¹**in·drid** \-drəd\ *adj* [NL *Indridae*] : of or relating to the indris

²**indrid** \"\ *n* -s [NL *Indridae*] : INDRI

in·dri·dae \-drəˌdē\ *n pl, cap* [NL, fr. *Indri*, type genus + *-idae*] : a family of lemurs comprising the indri, avahi, sifaka, and various related extinct forms

indsl *abbr* industrial

in·dubious \(ˈ)in, ən+\ *adj* [perh. fr. L *indubius*, fr. *in-* ¹in- + *dubius* dubious] *archaic* : INDUBITABLE, CERTAIN

in·du·bi·ta·bil·i·ty \(ˌ)inˌd(y)übədəˈbilədē, ən-, -bətə-, -lətē, -i\ *n* -ES : the quality or state of being unquestionable : CERTAINTY ⟨the English empiricists tended to lean on the ~ of the facts given —S.C.Pepper⟩

¹**in·du·bi·ta·ble** \ˈ=ˈ===bəl\ *adj* [F or L; F, fr. L *indubitabilis*, fr. *in-* ¹in- + *dubitabilis* dubitable] : not dubitable : not open to question or doubt : too evident to be doubted : UNQUESTIONABLE ⟨there is a core of ~ knowledge in education, but most of the teacher's task consists in imparting methods for understanding what is still unknown —Zechariah Chafee⟩ — **in·du·bi·ta·ble·ness** *n* -ES

²**indubitable** \"\ *n* -s : something that is indubitable

in·du·bi·ta·bly \-blē, -bli\ *adv* : without any doubt : UNQUESTIONABLY ⟨it is ~ true that the civilization of the West . . . has been evolving for centuries —G.C.Sellery⟩

in·duce \ənˈd(y)üs\ *vt* -ED/-ING/-s [ME *enducen, inducen*, fr. L *inducere*, fr. *in-* ²in- + *ducere* to lead — more at TOW] **1 a** : to move and lead (as by persuasion or influence) ⟨powers of persuasion that would have *induced* the atheist to religion⟩ : prevail upon : INFLUENCE, PERSUADE ⟨was unable to ~ his customers to try the product⟩ ⟨condition which had *induced* many persons to emigrate from the old country —John Dewey⟩ **b** : to inspire, call forth, or bring about by influence or stimulation ⟨the gift had been solicited or *induced* by the plaintiff —R.N.Wilkin⟩ ⟨the menace of *induced* immigration —H.M.Diamond⟩ **2** *archaic* **a** : to bring in (as a practice, condition, custom) : INTRODUCE **b** : ADDUCE **3 a** : to bring on or bring about : EFFECT, CAUSE ⟨anesthesia *induced* by drugs⟩ ⟨prices that will cover the costs and ~ the production —*Defense Against Recession*⟩ ⟨an antivitamin . . . was shown to ~ gross malformation in the young —*Americana Annual*⟩ ⟨believed the Christianity . . . *induced* kindliness in men —H.J.Laski⟩: as (1) *embryol* : to cause the formation of ⟨the optic cup *induces* lens in the adjacent ectoderm⟩ (2) : to produce (as an electric current, an electric charge, or magnetic polarity) by induction (3) *psychol* : to arouse by indirect stimulation ⟨~ a contrast color⟩ **b** : AROUSE ⟨music *induces* in us concepts that are vague —H.A.Overstreet⟩ ⟨*induced* a nostalgia for New England in persons who never saw the place —Mark Van Doren⟩ **4** : to conclude or infer from particulars or by induction — contrasted with *deduce* **5** *obs* : to draw on : OVERSPREAD

syn PERSUADE, PREVAIL: INDUCE may indicate overcoming indifference, hesitation, or opposition, usu. by offering for consideration persuasive advantages or gains that bring about a desired decision ⟨well-meaning but misguided professors and teachers felt they were fulfilling their vocations by *inducing* brilliant boys and girls to flee the drudgery of the country and enter the elite professions —*Irish Digest*⟩ ⟨Burt, aided by his father and friends, *induced* Congress to aid his state in building such a canal —C.W.Mitman⟩ PERSUADE may suggest a winning over by an appeal, entreaty, or expostulation addressed as much to feelings as to reason ⟨*persuade* management to recognize collective bargaining —*Current Biog.*⟩ ⟨deputed by the firm of lawyers to *persuade* her to resume her married life —Anthony Powell⟩ PREVAIL may be used in situations in which strong opposition or reluctance is overcome by sustained argument and entreaty ⟨a group of citizens of all parties had *prevailed* on him to enter the race —*Current Biog.*⟩ ⟨I will go now and try to *prevail* on my mother to let me stay with you —G.B.Shaw⟩ ⟨*prevailed* upon the men in the sloop to sail up the river again, to rescue any survivors —Marjory S. Douglas⟩

induced development *n* [*induced* fr. past part. of *induce*] : EPIGENESIS 1

induced draft *n* : a draft produced by a suction steam jet or fan on the stack side of a furnace

induced drag *n* : the portion of the wing drag induced by or resulting from the generation of the lift

induced investment *n* : investment in inventories and equipment which is derived from and varies with changes in final output — distinguished from *autonomous investment*

induced radioactivity *n* : ARTIFICIAL RADIOACTIVITY

induced reaction *n* : a chemical reaction that proceeds more rapidly than it ordinarily would because of the influence of a second and faster reaction in the same system

in·duce·ment \-mənt\ *n* -s **1 a** : the act or process of inducing ⟨put into effect a system of ~ to encourage workers to turn out more work⟩ **b** : a quality or state which induces (as to action) or lures or entices ⟨the ~ of philosophy was that it freed one from a sense of enslavement to circumstance⟩ **2 a** : something that induces : a motive or consideration that leads one to action ⟨reward is an ~ to effort⟩ ⟨offer larger ~s to students to do good work⟩ **b** *in Roman, Scots, and civil law* : the consideration, reason, or motive for entering into a contract or the benefit or advantage furnished in a contractual bargain **3 a** *obs* : INTRODUCTION, PREFACE **b** : matter presented by way of introduction or background to explain the principal allegations of a legal cause, plea, or defense — distinguished from *surplusage* **4** : COLLOQUIUM 2 **syn** see MOTIVE

in·duc·er \-sə(r)\ *n* -s : one that induces; *specif* : the part of a centrifugal blower or compressor that feeds air into the axial region of the impeller

in·du·ci·ae \ənˈd(y)üshēˌē\ *n pl* [L *induciae, indutiae* truce, pause] **1** : a delay allowed for the performance of a legal obligation: as **a** *in Roman, civil, English, or Scots law* (1) *or* **induciae le·ga·les** \-ləˈgā(ˌ)lēz\ : time granted to a party to appear in answer to a summons or citation (2) : time granted for the preparation of a case for trial **b** *in old maritime law* : a period of 20 days after the safe arrival of a vessel under bottomry allowed for the sale of the cargo and the payment of the creditor's claim **2** *in international law* : a truce or cessation of hostilities : ARMISTICE

in·duc·ible \ənˈd(y)üsəbəl\ *adj* : capable of being induced

inducing *pres part of* INDUCE

in·du·cive \-siv\ *adj, archaic* : tending to induce

in·duct \ənˈdəkt\ *vt* -ED/-ING/-s [ME *inducten*, fr. ML *inductus*, past part. of *inducere*, fr. L, to lead in, introduce, induce — more at INDUCE] **1 a** : to put in formal possession of a benefice or living ⟨has taken orders and been ~*ed* to a small country living —Nathaniel Hawthorne⟩ **b** : to put in office with appropriate ceremonies : INSTALL ⟨was ~*ed* as president of the college⟩ **c** : to admit as a member ⟨~ three men into a scholastic society⟩ **d** : to introduce or initiate esp. into something secret or demanding special knowledge ⟨~*ing* neophytes into the mysteries of a cult⟩ ⟨important that teachers be properly ~*ed* into the profession⟩ ⟨~ a youngster into the use of his language —Stuart Chase⟩ **e** (1) : to enroll for training or service under a selective-service act (2) : to bring into federal service as part of the National Guard of the U.S. **2** : LEAD, CONDUCT ⟨swung the leaves of the door at just the right angle that ~*ed* you to the café —Mary Austin⟩

in·duc·tance \-ən(t)s\ *n* -s [*induct* + *-ance*] **1** : a property of an electric circuit by which an electromotive force is induced in it by a variation of current either (1) in the circuit itself or (2) in a neighboring circuit, which is expressed in henrys and is dependent upon the size, shape, and relative positions of the circuits and upon the proximity of magnetic materials, and which in electrical theory plays a role analogous to that of inertia in mechanics — called also respectively (1) *self-inductance* and (2) *mutual inductance* **2** : a circuit or a device possessing inductance

inductance coil *n* : REACTOR 3

in·duct·ee \(ˌ)inˌdəkˈtē, ən,-, =ˈ=ˌ=\ *n* -s : a person brought up for induction esp. into one of the armed forces or one who is to be or has been so inducted

in·ductile \(ˈ)in, ən+\ *adj* [¹*in-* + *ductile*] : not ductile : INFLEXIBLE, UNYIELDING

in·duc·tion \ənˈdəkshən\ *n* -s [ME *induccioun*, fr. AF or ML; AF *induccion*, fr. ML *induction-, inductio*, fr. *inductus* (past part. of *inducere* to induct) + L *-ion-, -io* -ion] **1** : the act or process of inducting, the state of being inducted, or an instance or product of induction: as **a** (1) : a formal or symbolic and ceremonial bringing into or introducing to actual possession (as of an office) ⟨my ~ into the presidency —F.D.Roosevelt⟩ (2) *Eng. eccl. law* : the ceremony of giving the actual possession of an ecclesiastical living or its temporalities to a clergyman already presented and instituted **b** : an initial experience : an exposure that introduces one to something previously mysterious or unknown : INITIATION ⟨six weeks of hard physical effort was his ~ into the arts of war⟩ ⟨this grade of exercise supplies easy ~ to the technique for learners —J.M. Mitchell⟩ **c** : an official usu. formal and ceremonial admittance (as to membership in a club) ⟨awaiting his acceptance by and ~ into the secret order⟩ **d** : the formality by which a civilian is inducted into military service under the provisions of a draft law **2** [ME *induccioun*, fr. MF or L; MF *induction* reasoning from a part to a whole, fr. L *induction-, inductio* (trans. of Gk *epagōgē*), fr. *inductus* (past part. of *inducere* to lead in, introduce, induce) + *-ion-, -io* -ion] **a** : an instance of reasoning from a part to a whole, from particulars to generals, or from the individual to the universal : a conclusion arrived at by reasoning from a part to a whole, from particulars to generals, or from the individual to the universal : INFERENCE **2 b** (1) : reasoning from a part to a whole, from particulars to generals, or from the individual to the universal — compare BACONIAN INDUCTION, ENUMERATIVE INDUCTION, EPAGOGE (2) : a process of mathematical demonstration in which the general validity of a law is inferred from its observed validity in particular cases by proving that if the law holds in a certain case it must hold in the next and therefore in succeeding cases **3** [L *induction-, inductio* action of introducing, fr. *inductus* (past part. of *inducere* to lead in, introduce, induce) + *-ion-, -io* -ion] **a** : a preface, prologue, or introductory scene esp. of an early English play **b** *obs* : something that leads into something else **c** *obs* : an initial step or action **4** [L *induction-, inductio* action of introducing] : the act or process of introducing, the state of being introduced, or an instance or product of introducing: as **a** : the act of bringing forward or adducing (as facts or particulars) **b** : the act of causing, initiating, or bringing on or about esp. at an early time or to a preliminary degree ⟨~ of labor⟩; *specif* : the establishment of an initial state of anesthesia often with an agent other than that used subsequently to maintain the anesthetic state **c** : the production of an electric charge, magnetism, or electromotive force in an object (as an electric conductor, a magnetizable body, an electric circuit) by the proximity without contact of a similarly energized body or by the variation of a magnetic flux — see ELECTROMAGNETIC INDUCTION, ELECTROSTATIC INDUCTION, MAGNETIC INDUCTION, MUTUAL INDUCTION, SELF-INDUCTION **d** : arousal by indirect stimulation (as contrast colors from parts of the retina adjacent to a directly stimulated area) **e** : the inspiration of the fuel-air charge from the carburetor into the combustion chamber of an internal-combustion engine **f** : the sum of the processes by which the fate of embryonic cells is determined and morphogenetic differentiation brought about

induction accelerator *n* : BETATRON

induction coil *n* : an apparatus for obtaining intermittent high voltage often used to produce spark discharges and consisting of a primary coil through which the direct current flows, a mechanical or electrical interrupter, and a secondary coil of a larger number of turns in which the high voltage is induced

induction compass *n* : a compass the indications of which depend on the current generated in a coil revolving in the earth's magnetic field

induction furnace *n* : an electric furnace heated by a current which is caused to flow through the charge by electromagnetic induction — compare ARC FURNACE

induction–harden \=ˈ==ˌ==\ *vt* : to harden (a ferrous alloy) by heating above the transformation temperature by means of electromagnetic induction and then cooling as rapidly as necessary

induction heating *n* : a process of heating by means of an electric current that is caused to flow through the material to be heated or through its container (as a crucible) by electromagnetic induction — compare DIELECTRIC HEATING

induction machine *n* **1** : an electric machine operating by electrostatic induction **2** : an alternating-current machine (as an induction motor or induction generator) in which primary and secondary windings rotate with respect to each other and in which energy is transferred from one circuit to the other circuit by electromagnetic induction

induction motor *n* : any of several alternating-current motors in which the torque is produced by the reaction between a varying or rotating magnetic field that is generated in stationary field magnets and the current that is induced in the coils or circuits of the rotor

induction period *n* **1** : the time that elapses between the immersion of an exposed photographic emulsion in a developer and the appearance of the photographed image **2** : a period at the beginning of some chemical reactions during which little or no action takes place (as in the oxidation of fats by air because of the presence of antioxidants)

inductions *pl of* INDUCTION

in·duc·tive \(ˈ)inˈdəktiv, ənˈd-, -tēv *also* -təv\ *adj* [in sense 1, fr. ML *inductivus*, fr. L *inductus* (past part. of *inducere* to induce) + *-ivus* -ive; in other senses, fr. *induction*, after such pairs as E *deduction*: *deductive* — more at INDUCE] **1** : leading on : drawing on : INDUCING, TEMPTING ⟨~ to the sin of Eve —John Milton⟩ **2** : of or relating to logical induction ⟨the ~ method⟩ ⟨~ reasoning⟩ : employing the methods of induction ⟨~ science⟩ **3 a** : of, relating to, or produced or operated by electrical induction **b** : of, relating to, or having inductance esp. mutual inductance **4** : INTRODUCTORY, PREFATORY **5** : involving the action of an inductor ⟨~ effect of chordamesoderm) : tending to produce induction ⟨~ reactions in the embryo⟩ — **in·duc·tive·ly** \-tәvlē, -li\ *adv* — **in·duc·tive·ness** \-tivnәs, -tēv- *also* -tәv-\ *n* -ES

inductive coupler *n* : a mutual inductor used in radio apparatus to provide coupling between two circuits

inductive coupling *n* : electrical coupling in which the influence is that of mutual induction usu. between two coils close together or wound on a common core

inductive inference *n* : INDUCTION 2b(1)

inductive logic *n* : a branch of logic that deals with induction; *esp* : the logic or theory of the methods and reasonings of empirical science

inductive reactance *n* : the part of the reactance of an alternating-current circuit that is due to inductance

in·duc·tiv·ism \әn'dәktә,vizәm\ *n* -S : a policy or the practice of using an inductive method or of stressing induction in one's methods

in·duc·tiv·ist \-,vәst\ *n* -S : one that is characterized by or advocates inductivism

in·duc·tom·e·ter \,in,dәk'tämәd·ә(r)\ *n* [*induction* + *-o-* + *-meter*] : a variocoupler calibrated in units of inductance

in·duc·tor \әn'dәktә(r)\ *n* -S [partly fr. *induct* + *-or;* partly prob. fr. *induction*, after such pairs as E *conduction: conductor*] **1** : one that inducts; *esp* : a person who inducts another into an office or benefice **2 a** : an inductance coil or reactor **b** : a mass of iron used in certain magnetic train-control devices **3** : a substance that increases the rate of a chemical reaction and that is used up during the reaction — distinguished from *catalyst* **4** : a substance capable under certain circumstances of inducing a specific type of development in embryonic or other undifferentiated tissue ⟨chordamesoderm acts on embryonic ectoderm as an ~ of neural tissue⟩ — compare COMPETENCE 5

inductor compass *n* : INDUCTION COMPASS

inductor generator *n* : a generator that induces voltage in a fixed armature by rotation of a rotor magnetized by current through a fixed field coil

in·duc·to·ri·um \,in,dәk'tōrēәm\ *n* -S [NL, fr. *induct-* (fr. ISV *induction*) + *-orium*] : a battery-operated apparatus containing induction coils used for producing a continuous pulsing electric current or a single pulse of current (as for physiological or pharmacological experiments)

in·duc·to·ther·my \әn'dәktә,thәrmē\ *n* -ES [blend of *Inductotherm* (a trademark) and E *-thermy*] : fever therapy by means of an electromagnetic induction field with the body or a part of it acting as a resistance

inducts *pres 3d sing of* INDUCT

indue *var of* ENDUE

in·dulge \әn'dәlj\ *vb* -ED/-ING/-S [L *indulgēre* to grant as a favor, be courteous, be kind, fr. *in-* ²in- + *-dulgēre* (prob. akin to OE *tulge* firmly, well, OS *tulgo* very, Goth *tulgus* firm, steadfast, Gk *dolichos* long, Skt *dīrgha*); basic meaning: long, enduring] *vt* **1** *archaic* : to grant as a favor : BESTOW in concession or in compliance with a wish or request — usu. used in the passive ⟨a privilege seldom *indulged* to ordinary men⟩ **2 a** : to give free rein to ⟨*indulging* idle conjectures as to what might be the news —Rafael Sabatini⟩ ⟨likes to ~ a taste for the difficult —*Current Biog.*⟩ ⟨an excellent place to ~ a normal curiosity about clocks and watches —Ellwood Kirby⟩ : take unrestrained pleasure in : yield to : GRATIFY ⟨~ a taste for exotic dishes⟩ **b** : to allow (oneself) unrestrained pleasure (as in the gratification of a normally restrained habit or desire) or unrestrained freedom (as in the expression of a normally restrained feeling) ⟨*indulged* himself in the delights of leisure⟩ ⟨~ oneself in eating and drinking⟩ ⟨*indulging* herself in histrionics⟩ **3 a** : to yield to the desire of or be forbearing in respect to out of favor or kindness under circumstances where one would not usually yield : gratify by unusual compliance : allow to proceed or act free from the restraints one would ordinarily impose : HUMOR ⟨~ a convalescing child in whatever he wishes to eat⟩ ⟨*indulged* her husband until he would not lift a finger around the house⟩ : favor in a way that pampers or treats with undue liberality ⟨a time when schoolboys were less *indulged* with pocket money than they seem to be nowadays —Archibald Marshall⟩ **b** : to grant an indulgence to or on ~ *vi* : to indulge in something ⟨offered him a drink but he protested that he did not ~⟩ — **indulge in 1** : to gratify one's taste or desire for ⟨prone to *indulge in* too many evenings of pleasure⟩ ⟨*indulging in* candy and ice cream⟩ ⟨*indulging in* the bad habit of swearing⟩ **2** : to give free rein to ⟨*indulge in* heated argument and violent language⟩ **3** : to engage in ⟨all birds *indulge in* some seasonal movement —W.H.Dowdeswell⟩ ⟨*indulging in* the curious hobby of raising tropical fish —*Times Lit. Supp.*⟩ : UNDERTAKE ⟨those who *indulge in* high-altitude flights and suffer from a mild degree of oxygen want —H.G.Armstrong⟩

syn INDULGE, PAMPER, HUMOR, SPOIL, BABY, and MOLLYCODDLE can mean, in common, to treat a person or his desires or feelings with unusual or special usu. undue favor or attention. INDULGE with a personal object implies extreme compliance and often weakness in gratifying another's wishes or desires which have little claim to fulfillment ⟨I wanted to *indulge* him in all his particular food fancies and very soon the air in the apartment became almost visible with the reek of garlic sausage, smoked kippers and cheeses of strong character —Virginia D. Dawson & Betty D. Wilson⟩ ⟨grandmamma is always wanting to see them, for she humors and *indulges* them to such a degree, and gives them so much trash and sweet things, that they are sure to come back sick —Jane Austen⟩ PAMPER implies inordinate gratification of an appetite or taste esp. for luxuries or for what is softening in its physical or moral effects ⟨he preserved without an effort the supremacy of character and mind over the flesh he neither starved nor *pampered* —G.L.Dickinson⟩ ⟨no country can afford to *pamper* snobbery —G.B.Shaw⟩ ⟨*pamper* a child with rich foods and constant solicitude⟩ HUMOR implies an unusual attention to or a voluntary yielding to what are regarded as another's whims or caprices, often suggesting a purposeful sometimes patronizing accommodation to another's moods ⟨*humoring* a pet fawn which had a predilection for soap and cigarette butts —Ray Corsini⟩ ⟨the tone of your voice, when you speak, is too gentle, as if you were *humoring* the vagaries of a blind man's mind —Ben Hecht⟩ ⟨*humor* a customer for the sake of making a sale⟩ SPOIL implies a foolish or excessive indulging or pampering and throws strong stress upon its injurious effects upon the character or disposition ⟨the new queen played with and *spoiled* the little stepdaughter —Edith Sitwell⟩ ⟨he had been a noisy boastful youth and had been *spoiled* by his father —Sherwood Anderson⟩ BABY implies excessive attentions, as to one unable to care for himself and needing the assistance of a mother or nurse; when applied to one presumably capable, it carries the idea of treating with excessive usu. foolish care or carefulness ⟨if he thinks I'm going to spend my days catering to his whims, *babying* him and watching over him like a child, he's mistaken —Helen S. Rush & Mary Sherkanowski⟩ ⟨your old records will last longer with this new device to *baby* them —*Coronet*⟩ MOLLYCODDLE is the strongest of this group in implying inordinate attention and suggesting a ridiculously undue care for another's health or physical comfort or for the relieving of the strain or hardship he presumably, usu. fictitiously, suffers or may suffer ⟨a mother who *mollycoddles* her children by constantly dosing them, keeping them in when it's at all cold or damp and away from other children for fear of germs⟩ ⟨protests against the policy of *mollycoddling* prisoners —J.F.Steiner & R.M.Brown⟩

indulged *past of* INDULGE

¹in·dul·gence \-jәn(t)s\ *also* **in·dul·gen·cy** \-nsē, -nsi\ *n, pl* **indulgences** *also* **indulgencies** [*indulgence* in sense 1 fr. ME, fr. MF, fr. ML *indulgentia*, fr. L, quality or state of being indulgent, kindness, complaisance, fr. *indulgent-, indulgens* indulgent + *-ia* -y; *indulgence* in sense 2a fr. ME, fr. L *indulgentia*; *indulgence* in other senses fr. L *indulgentia*; *indulgency* in sense 1 fr. ML *indulgentia*; *indulgency* in other senses fr. L *indulgentia*] **1** : remission of the temporal punishment including canonical penances and esp. purgatorial atonement that according to Roman Catholicism is due by divine justice for sins whose eternal punishment has been remitted and whose guilt has been pardoned by the reception of the sacrament of penance **2** : the act of indulging or the state of being indulgent: as **a** : a special often excessive leniency (as toward a sick child) : HUMORING ⟨had learned to treat his moody child with ~⟩ : any treatment marked by forbearance ⟨a crotchety old man who expected more ~ than he deserved⟩ **b** : FONDNESS, LIKING ⟨his ~ for the government of England —H.J. Laski⟩ **c** : benign tolerance ⟨mocking elegance that has little respect but much ~ for the foibles of man —Claudia Cassidy⟩ **3 a** : an indulgent act : a favor granted or an instance of forbearance ⟨sorry she allowed the children all the ~s she had in the past⟩ **b** (1) *sometimes cap* : a grant or offer of certain religious liberties as special favors made by Charles II and James II to Protestant dissenters and Roman Catholics (2) : the permission given during the same reigns to Scotch Presbyterian ministers to hold services **c** : an extension of time for payment or performance granted as a favor — compare MORATORIUM **4** : the act of indulging in something or the thing indulged in ⟨a commendable degree of ~ in outdoor sports⟩ ⟨excessive ~ in daydreaming⟩ ⟨acquired that habit of romantic reading which was to be a lifetime ~ —H.S.Canby⟩ ⟨his trips abroad were almost the only ~s he had ever allowed himself⟩ ⟨had to be content with the weekly ~ of an ice-cream soda⟩ : gratification of a kind usu. forbidden or frowned on or to a degree usu. considered excessive; *esp* : SELF-GRATIFICATION, SELF-INDULGENCE

²indulgence \"\ *vt* -ED/-ING/-S *Roman Catholicism* : to attach an indulgence to (as an act or an object's use) ⟨*indulgenced* prayers⟩

in·dul·gent \-nt\ *adj* [L *indulgent-, indulgens*, pres. part. of *indulgēre* to indulge] : indulging, prone to indulge, or characterized by indulgence ⟨a smile of ~ pity such as one might grant to a mistaken child —Jane Addams⟩ : benignly tolerant : FORBEARING : markedly permissive ⟨indictments and civil pleadings are viewed with ~ eyes —B.N.Cardozo⟩ ⟨more appreciative of his success, more ~ of his shortcomings —Nathaniel Hawthorne⟩ **syn** see FORBEARING

in·dul·gent·ly *adv* : in an indulgent manner ⟨very often the young girl who goes wrong is dishonored, whereas the misconduct of the wife is viewed ~ —H.M.Parshley⟩

in·dulg·er \-jә(r)\ *n* -S : one that indulges

indulges *pres 3d sing of* INDULGE

indulging *pres part of* INDULGE

in·du·line \'ind(y)ә,lēn, -lәn\ *n* -S *usu cap* [ISV *ind-* + *-ule* + *-ine*] : any of a class of blue or violet dyes related to the safranines: as **a** : a reddish to greenish blue dye derived from phenosafranine and made by heating amino-azobenzene and aniline in the presence of hydrochloric acid — called also *Induline Spirit Soluble;* see DYE table I (under *Solvent Blue 7*) **b** : a water-soluble acid dye made by sulfonating the free base obtained by treating Induline Spirit Soluble with alkali — see DYE table I (under *Acid Blue 20*)

in·dult \'in,dәlt, әn'd-\ *n* -S [ME (Sc), fr. ML *indultum*, fr. LL, grant, privilege, fr. L, neut. of *indultus*, past part. of *indulgēre* to grant as a favor — more at INDULGE] : a special privilege granted by ecclesiastical authority for a definite or indefinite period of time; *specif*, **indults** *pl* : general faculties granted in the Roman Catholic Church by the pope to bishops and others to act in cases not otherwise permitted

in·dul·to \әn'dül(,)tō\ *n* -S [Sp, license, exemption, fr. ML *indultum* indult] *archaic* : INDULT

in·du·ment \'ind(y)әmәnt\ *n* -S [L *indumentum* garment, fr. *induere* to put on, don (fr. *ind-* — fr. OL *indu, endo* in — + *-uere* — as in *exuere* to take off) + *-mentum* -ment — more at INDIGENOUS, EXUVIAE] **1** *archaic* : CLOTHING, GARMENT, INVESTITURE **2** [NL *indumentum*, fr. L] : INDUMENTUM

in·du·men·tum \,==='mentәm\ *n, pl* **indumen·ta** \-tә\ *or* **indumentums** [NL, fr. L] **1** : the entire feathery covering of a bird **2** : a dense woolly pubescence (as on a leaf or an insect)

in·du·na \әn'dünә\ *n* -S [Zulu *in-duna* government officer] : a headman or councilor of an African people esp. the Zulus

in·duplicate \әn +\ *adj* [prob. fr. (assumed) NL *induplicatus*, fr. L *in-* ²in- + *duplicatus* bent, doubled up, doubled, past part. of *duplicare* to double — more at DUPLICATE] **1** : having the edges bent abruptly toward the axis — used of the parts of the calyx or corolla in a bud **2** : having the edges rolled inward and then arranged about the axis without overlapping — used of leaves in a bud

indurance *obs var of* ENDURANCE

¹in·du·rate \'ind(y)әrәt, әn'd(y)ür-\ *adj* [ME *indurat*, fr. L *induratus*, past part. of *indurare*] : physically or morally hardened ⟨this man whom enemies describe as cold-blooded and ~ to public opinion —M.L.Bach⟩

²in·du·rate \'ind(y)ә,rāt, *usu* -ād·+V\ *vb* -ED/-ING/-S [L *induratus*, past part. of *indurare*, fr. *in-* ²in- + *durare* to harden, fr. *durus* hard — more at DURE] *vt* **1** : to make unfeeling, stubborn, or obdurate ⟨the instability of many religionists . . . ~s secular men in their impiety —Isaac Taylor⟩ **2** : to make hardy : INURE ⟨had been *indurated* to want, exposure and toil —A.W.Tourgee⟩ **3** : to make hard: as **a** : to make into a compact hard rock mass by the action of heat, pressure, or cementation ⟨conglomerates are the *indurated* equivalents of gravel —F.J.Pettijohn⟩ **b** : to increase the fibrous elements of : make sclerosed ⟨*indurated* tissue⟩ **4** : to establish firmly : make deep-rooted : CONFIRM ⟨the *indurated* goat habit . . . every family keeps a goat —Ellery Sedgwick⟩ ~ *vi* **1** : to grow hard : HARDEN **2** : to become established or deep rooted

in·du·ra·tion \,ind(y)ә'rāshәn\ *n* -S [ME *induracion*, fr. MF *induration*, fr. LL *induration-, induratio*, fr. L *induratus* + *-ion-, -io* -ion] **1** : the act or process of growing hard or the state of having grown hard: as **a** : hardness or inflexibility of character, manner, or feeling : OBSTINACY, OBDURATENESS, CALLOUSNESS **b** : the act of becoming inured (as to drudgery) ⟨~ to hackwork —*Saturday Rev.*⟩ **c** : the process by which a rock or rock material is indurated **d** : an increase in the fibrous elements in tissue commonly associated with inflammation and marked by loss of elasticity and pliability : SCLEROSIS **2** : a hardened mass or formation

in·du·ra·tive \'ind(y)ә,rād·iv, әn'd(y)ürәd·-\ *adj* : of, relating to, or producing induration

in·du·rite \'ind(y)ә,rīt\ *n* -S [²*indurate* + *-ite*] : a smokeless powder made by treating guncotton with nitrobenzene

indus *abbr* industrial; industry

in·du·sial \әn'd(y)üzēәl, -zh(ē)әl\ *adj* [*indusium* + *-al*] : of, relating to, or being an indusium

in·du·si·um \-z(h)ēәm\ *n, pl* **indu·sia** \-zēә, -zh(ē)ә\ [NL, fr. L, woman's undergarment, tunic, perh. fr. *induere* to put on — more at INDUMENT] **1 a** : an outgrowth of the leaf which covers or invests the sori in many ferns **b** : a cuplike fringe of collecting hairs surrounding the stigma in the Goodeniaceae **c** : the annulus in some fungi esp. when skirtlike (as in members of the genus *Dictyophora*) **2** : a membrane serving as a covering; *esp* : AMNION

¹in·dus·tri·al \әn'dәstrēәl\ *adj* [partly fr. MF, produced by systematic labor, fr. *industrie* employment involving skill (fr. L *industria* diligence) + *-al;* partly fr. F *industriel* of or belonging to industry (esp. manufacturing), fr. *industrie* industry (fr. L *industria* diligence) + *-el* -al, fr. L *-alis* — more at INDUSTRY] **1** : of or belonging to industry: as **a** : being in or part of industry ⟨~ work⟩ ⟨an ~ employment⟩ **b** : being or constituting an industry ⟨an ~ enterprise⟩ **c** : characterized by highly developed industries or being chiefly dependent economically upon industry ⟨an ~ nation⟩ **d** : engaged in industry or in industries esp. at manual labor ⟨the ~ classes⟩ **e** : derived from human industry rather than from natural advantages only or from profit only ⟨~ wealth⟩ ⟨an ~ crop⟩ **f** : belonging to or aiding those engaged in industry ⟨~ wages⟩ ⟨~ safety⟩ ⟨~ training⟩ **g** : produced by an organized industry ⟨~ products⟩ **h** : used or designed or developed for use in industry ⟨~ fabrics⟩ ⟨an ~ diamond⟩ ⟨wrapping, building, and other ~ papers⟩ **2** : belonging to industrial life or accident and health insurance

²industrial \"\ *n* -S **1 a** : one that is employed in a manufacturing industry or service **b** : a company engaged in industrial production or service **2 industrials** *pl* : stocks or bonds of industrial companies **3** : something industrial (as an industrial diamond) as opposed to something else that is of the same class of things but used or designed for use for a nonindustrial purpose

industrial accession *n, Roman, civil, & Scots law* : accession brought about by human industry as opposed to some natural process

industrial accident *n* : an accident occurring during the course of employment

industrial accident and health insurance *n* : accident and health insurance usu. written in small amounts and subject to frequent premium payments and covering persons exposed to the hazard of occupational injury

industrial alcohol *n* : alcohol for industrial use; *usu* : ethyl alcohol either mixed only with water or denatured — see DENATURED ALCOHOL

industrial art *n* : a subject taught in elementary and secondary schools that aims at developing a manual skill, a familiarity with tools and machines, or an acquaintance with industrial processes and design

industrial bank *n* : a financial institution deriving funds from the sale of investment certificates and from deposits made by individual savers and investing such funds in personal loans often secured by a comaker note or chattel mortgage

industrial carrier *n* : a means of transportation owned, controlled, or operated by one or more industries as a private, exclusive, or common carrier

industrial center *n* : a Salvationist institution that provides work (as the salvaging of waste materials) and an opportunity for rehabilitation for homeless or handicapped men

industrial chemistry *n* : chemistry in its industrial applications esp. to processes in manufacturing and the arts and to commercial production of chemicals

industrial democracy *n* : the determination of a company's policies affecting the welfare of its workers by joint action of management and worker representatives

industrial design *n* : design concerned with the appearance of three-dimensional machine-made products; *also* : the study of the principles of such design

industrial designer *n* : one that works at industrial design

industrial disease *n* : OCCUPATIONAL DISEASE

industrial engineer *n* : a specialist in industrial engineering

industrial engineering *n* : the application of engineering principles and training and the techniques of scientific management to the maintenance of a high level of productivity at optimum cost in industrial enterprises (as by analytical study, improvement, and installation of methods and systems, operating procedures, quantity and quality measurements and controls, safety measures, and personnel administration)

industrial geography *n* : a branch of geography that deals with the location of industries, the geographic factors that influence their location and development, the raw materials used in them, and the distribution of their finished products

industrial hygiene *n* : a science devoted to the protection and improvement of the health and well-being of workers in their vocational environment

industrial insurance *n* **1 a** : INDUSTRIAL LIFE INSURANCE **b** : INDUSTRIAL ACCIDENT AND HEALTH INSURANCE **2** : WORKMEN'S COMPENSATION INSURANCE

in·dus·tri·al·ism \-ēә,lizәm\ *n* -S [F *industrialisme*, fr. *industrial-* (fr. *industriel* industrial) + *-isme* -ism — more at INDUSTRIAL] : social organization in which industries and esp. large-scale industries are dominant — compare CAPITALISM, COMMERCIALISM, MILITARISM

¹in·dus·tri·al·ist \-lәst\ *n* -S [F *industrialiste* advocate of industrialism, fr. *industrial-* (fr. *industriel*) + *-iste* -ist] : one owning or engaged in the management of an esp. large-scale industry; *esp* : MANUFACTURER

²industrialist \"\ *adj* [F *industrialiste*, fr. *industrialiste*, n.] : of, relating to, or characterized by industrialism

in·dus·tri·al·iza·tion \=,===lә'zāshәn, -,lī'z-\ *n* -S : the act or process of industrializing or the state of being industrialized

in·dus·tri·al·ize \='===,līz\ *vb* -ED/-ING/-S — *see -ize in Explan Notes* [F *industrialiser*, fr. *industrial-* (fr. *industriel*) + *-iser* -ize] *vt* : to make industrial : convert to industrialism ~ *vi* : to become industrial : become converted to industrialism ⟨country has been steadily *industrializing* —Eric Goldman⟩

industrial life insurance *n* : life insurance which is written upon individual lives in small amounts and for which the premiums are collected weekly or monthly by agents

in·dus·tri·al·ly \-ēәlē, -li\ *adv* : in or by means of industry

in·dus·tri·al·ness \-ēәlnәs\ *n* -ES : the quality or state of being industrial

industrial park *n* : an area that is at a distance from the center of a city and that is designed (as by homogeneous architecture) esp. for a community of industries and businesses

industrial property *n* : intangible property rights (as ownership of a trademark or patent) connected with agriculture, commerce, and industry

industrial psychology *n* : the application of the findings and methods of experimental, clinical, and social psychology to industrial problems (as personnel selection and training) — compare PSYCHOTECHNOLOGY

industrial railroad *n* : a short railroad feeder owned or controlled and operated by an industrial concern — called also *tap line*

industrial relations *n pl* : the dealings or relationships of a usu. large business or industrial enterprise with its own workers, with labor in general, with governmental agencies, or with the public or the relationships between industries or large businesses

industrial revolution *n* [prob. trans. of F *révolution industrielle*] **1** : an economic revolution (as in England beginning in 1760) characterized by a marked acceleration in the output of industrial goods correlative with the introduction of power-driven machinery into industry and consequent decline of handwork and domestic production **2** : a marked general alteration in industrial or production methods in the direction of machine production and away from manual labor or personal control

industrial school *n* : a school specializing in the teaching of the industrial arts; *specif* : a public institution of this kind for juvenile delinquents

industrial sociology *n* : sociological analysis directed at institutions and social relationships within and largely controlled or affected by industry

industrial store *n* : COMPANY STORE

industrial union *n* : a labor union that admits to membership workmen in an industry irrespective of their occupation or craft — called also *vertical union*

in·dus·tri·ous \әn'dәstrēәs\ *adj* [MF *industrieux*, fr. L *industriosus* diligent, fr. *industria* diligence + *-osus* -ose] **1** *obs* : SKILLFUL, CLEVER, INGENIOUS **2** : perseveringly active : ZEALOUS ⟨~ in seeking out and questioning new arrivals —Gilbert Armitage⟩ **3** : characterized by industry: as **a** : marked by steady dependable energetic work : not lazy : DILIGENT ⟨an ~ worker⟩ ⟨an ~ group of campaigners⟩ **b** : constantly, regularly, or habitually occupied : BUSY ⟨an ~ housewife whose tasks seemed never-ending⟩ **c** : conducive to purposeful work or enterprise ⟨an ~ home environment⟩ **4** *obs* : characterized by design or purpose : INTENTIONAL **syn** see BUSY

in·dus·tri·ous·ly *adv* : in an industrious manner

in·dus·tri·ous·ness *n* -ES : the quality or state of being industrious ⟨a prosperity credited largely to the ~ of the people⟩

in·dus·try \'in(,)dәstrē, -ri *sometimes* әn'd-\ *n* -ES [ME *industrie*, fr. MF, skill, employment involving skill, fr. L *industria* diligence, fr. *industrius* diligent, fr. OL *indostruus*, fr. *indu, endo* in, within + *-struus* (akin to L *struere* to arrange, build) — more at INDIGENOUS, STRUCTURE] **1** *obs* **a** : SKILL, CLEVERNESS **b** : a use or application of skill or cleverness **2 a** : diligence in an employment or pursuit : steady attention to business ⟨all his long years of service gone . . . all his ~ and diligence thrown away —James Joyce⟩ ⟨sewing with no great amount of ~ on pieces of white material —Lillian Hellman⟩ **b** : habitual or constant work or effort ⟨a man of fine mental powers . . . unceasing ~, and simple charm —C.B.Fisher⟩ ⟨he had immense ~ but he didn't know how to think —Archibald Marshall⟩ **3 a** : systematic labor esp. for the creation of value ⟨had left the country . . . to live by his own ~ in England —Charles Dickens⟩ **b** : a department or branch of a craft, art, business, or manufacture : a division of productive or profit-making labor; *esp* : one that employs a large personnel and capital esp. in manufacturing ⟨put his money into an ~ that sold its goods on an international scale⟩ ⟨all the large *industries* in the city⟩ **c** : a group of productive or profit-making enterprises or organizations that have a similar technological structure of production and that produce or supply technically substitutable goods, services, or sources of income ⟨the automobile ~⟩ ⟨the air transport ~⟩ ⟨the poultry ~⟩ ⟨the smuggling of gold, liquor, and other contraband has become a secondary ~ —James Reach⟩ ⟨the tourist ~⟩ **d :** manufacturing activity as a whole ⟨conditions that were auspicious for the nation's ~⟩ ⟨an energetic promoter of New England ~ —*Current Biog.*⟩ **4 a :** a well-developed technique of a people esp. as evidenced in archaeological discoveries **b :** an assemblage of prehistoric implements giving clear evidence that they were used by one group of men

in·dwell \(ˈ)in, ən+\ *vb* [ME *indwellen* to inhabit, fr. ²*in* + *dwellen* to dwell] *vi* **:** to exist as an inner activating spirit, force, or principle ⟨a creative power ~*ing* in the world —Lawrence Binyon⟩ ⟨a divinity ~*ing* in nature —V.L. Parrington⟩ **~** *vt* **:** to exist within or inhabit as an activating spirit, force, or principle ⟨a life of God ~*s* the universe —J.H.Randall⟩ ⟨endowed with or *indwelt* by some supernatural power —E.A.Nida⟩

in·dwell·er \"ə(r)\ *n* [ME, fr. *indwellen* + *-er*] **1 a :** INHABITANT **b :** SOJOURNER **2 :** an inner spirit, force, or principle

indwelling *adj* **1 :** existing or residing as an inner activating spirit, force, or principle ⟨an ~ divinity —B.B.Cohen⟩ ⟨an ~ goodness⟩ **2 :** left for a period of time within an organ or passage to maintain drainage, prevent obstruction, or provide a route for administration of food or drugs — used of a catheter or similar tube

in·dyl \ˈindᵊl, -ˌdil\ *n* -s [by shortening] **:** INDOLYL

¹-ine \ˌīn, ən, (ˌ)in, ˌēn\ *adj suffix* [ME *-ine, -in*, fr. MF *-in* & L *-inus* (with long ī), *-inus* (with short ĭ); MF *-in* partly fr. L *-inus* (with long ī) of or belonging to; MF *-in* partly fr. L *-inus* (with short ĭ) made of, of or belonging to, fr. Gk *-inos* — more at -EN] **1 :** of, belonging to, or relating to ⟨estuar*ine*⟩ **2 :** made of **:** like ⟨opal*ine*⟩

²-ine \ˌēn, ən\ *n suffix* -s [ME *-ine, -in*, fr. MF & L; MF *-ine*, fr. L *-ina* (with long ī), fem. of *-inus* (with long ī) of or belonging to] **1 :** ¹-ITE 4 ⟨hatchett*ine*⟩ **2 :** chemical substance: as **a :** chemical element — in names of the halogens ⟨asta*tine*⟩ ⟨chlor*ine*⟩ **b (1) :** basic carbon compound — in names of alkaloids ⟨quin*ine*⟩ or other organic nitrogenous bases ⟨anil*ine*⟩ ⟨guanid*ine*⟩ including six-membered ring compounds ⟨pyrid*ine*⟩ and intermediate hydrogenated forms of cyclic compounds ⟨pyrrol*ine*⟩ ⟨thiazol*ine*⟩ — usu. distinguished from *-in* (2) **:** carbon compound containing a basic group — in names of amino acids ⟨glyc*ine*⟩ ⟨cyst*ine*⟩ **c :** mixture of chemical compounds — esp. in commercial names (as of mixtures of hydrocarbons) ⟨gasol*ine*⟩ ⟨keros*ine*⟩ **d :** -YNE **e :** hydride ⟨ars*ine*⟩ **3 :** -IN 1a — not used systematically **4 :** commercial product or material ⟨glass*ine*⟩

³-ine — see ²-INA

⁴-ine \ˌēn\ *n suffix* -s [ME *-ina, -ine, -in* (in feminine given names), fr. OE *-ina* (in feminine given names), fr. L *-ina* (with long ī, in feminine names such as *Agrippina*), fr. fem. of *-inus* (with long ī) of or belonging to] **:** female person ⟨chor*ine*⟩ ⟨dud*ine*⟩

-in·e·ae \ˈinēˌē\ *n pl suffix* [NL, fr. L, fem. pl. of *-ineus* (as in *gramineus* gramineous)] **:** plants including those of (such) a genus ⟨Abiet*ineae*⟩ **:** plants characterized by (such) a feature ⟨Dinocaps*ineae*⟩ — in names of botanical suborders

in·earth \ən+\ *vt* [²*in-* + *earth* (n.)] *archaic* **:** BURY, INTER

¹in·ebri·ant \əˈnēbrēənt\ *n* -s [L *inebriant-, inebrians*, pres. part. of *inebriare* to make drunk] **:** INTOXICANT

²inebriant \"\ *adj* [L *inebriant-, inebrians*, pres. part. of *inebriare*] **:** INTOXICATING

¹in·ebri·ate \-brēˌāt, *usu* -ād+V\ *vt* -ED/-ING/-S [L *inebriatus*, past part. of *inebriare*, fr. *in-* ²in- + *ebriare* to intoxicate, fr. *ebrius* drunk — more at SOBER] **1 :** to make drunk **:** INTOXICATE **2 :** to disorder the senses of **:** exhilarate as if by liquor **:** deprive of sense and judgment ⟨*inebriated* by his own verbosity —N.A.Jones⟩

²in·ebri·ate \-brēə̇t, -ēˌāt, *usu* |d+V\ *adj* [L *inebriatus*] **1 :** INTOXICATED, DRUNK **2 :** addicted to drinking to excess

³inebriate \"\ *n* -s **:** one who is drunk or intoxicated; *esp* **:** an habitual drunkard ⟨an asylum for ~*s*⟩

inebriated *adj* **:** exhilarated or confused by or as if by alcohol **:** TIPSY, INTOXICATED ⟨drinking steadily . . . getting neither more nor less ~ —Herman Melville⟩ ⟨~ with the exuberance of his own verbosity —Benjamin Disraeli⟩ **syn** see DRUNK

in·ebri·a·tion \əˌnēbrēˈāshən\ *n* -s [LL *inebriation-, inebriatio*, fr. *inebriatus* + *-ion-, -io* -ion] **1 :** the action of inebriating or the condition of being inebriated **2 :** habitual intoxication **:** DRUNKENNESS

in·ebri·ety \ˌinəˈbrīəd·ē, -ītē, |i\ *n* [prob. blend of *inebriation* and *ebriety*] **:** INEBRIATION, INTOXICATION ⟨the only opportunities for ~ were the visits to town —P.A. Rollins⟩ **:** DRUNKENNESS ⟨public facilities for dealing with ~ —Robert Straus & R.G.McCarthy⟩

in·ebri·ous \əˈnēbrēəs\ *adj* [perh. blend of *inebriation* and obs. E *ebrious* addicted to drink, drunk, fr. L *ebrius* drunk] **1** *obs* **:** INEBRIATING **2 :** INEBRIATED, INTOXICATED **3 :** addicted to drink

ined *abbr* [L *ineditus*] unpublished

in·edible \(ˈ)in, ən+\ *adj* [¹*in-* + *edible*] **:** not edible **:** not fit for food

in·ed·i·ta \(ˈ)iˈnedəd·ə, -ətə\ *n pl* [NL, fr. L, neut. pl. of *ineditus* not made known, fr. *in-* ¹in- + *editus*, past part. of *edere* to proclaim, publish — more at EDITION] **:** unpublished literary material

in·edited \(ˈ)in, ən+\ *adj* [NL *ineditus* + E *-ed*] **:** UNPUBLISHED ⟨~ document⟩ ⟨~ letters⟩

in·educabilia \(ˌ)in, ən+\ *n pl, cap* [NL, fr. ¹*in-* + *Educabilia*] *in former classifications* **:** a superorder of placental mammals including the bats, rodents, edentates, and insectivores in which the brain is less developed than in the Educabilia

in·educability \"+\ *n* **:** the quality or state of being ineducable

in·educable \(ˈ)in, ən+\ *adj* [¹*in-* + *educable*] **:** incapable of being educated; *esp* **:** mentally retarded or psychologically disturbed so as to be unable to benefit from education provided for the normal majority

in·education \(ˌ)in, ən+\ *n* [¹*in-* + *education*] **:** lack of education

in·ef·fa·bil·i·ty \(ˌ)iˌnefəˈbiləd·ē, əˌn-, -lətē, -i\ *n* -ES **:** the quality or state of being ineffable

¹in·effable \(ˈ)in, ən+\ *adj* [ME, fr. MF, fr. L *ineffabilis*, fr. *in-* ¹in- + *effabilis* effable — more at EFFABLE] **1 :** incapable of being expressed in words **:** UNUTTERABLE, INDESCRIBABLE ⟨~ joy⟩ ⟨~ torture⟩ **:** UNSPEAKABLE ⟨~ disgust⟩ ⟨~ bungler⟩ **2 :** not to be uttered **:** TABOO ⟨the ~ name of Jehovah⟩ — **in·ef·fa·ble·ness** \-nə̇s\ *n* -ES — **in·ef·fa·bly** \-blē, -bli\ *adv*

²ineffable \"\ *n* -s **:** something that is ineffable

in·ef·face·abil·i·ty \ˌinə̇ˌfāsəˈbiləd·ē\ *n* -ES **:** the quality or state of being ineffaceable **:** INDELIBILITY

in·effaceable \ˌin+\ *adj* [prob. fr. F *ineffaçable*, fr. MF, fr. *in-* ¹in- + *effaçable* effaceable (fr. *effacer* to efface + *-able*) — more at EFFACE] **:** not effaceable **:** INDELIBLE, INERADICABLE — **in·ef·face·ably** \-blē, -bli\ *adv*

¹in·effective \ˌin+\ *adj* [¹*in-* + *effective*] **1 :** not producing or incapable of producing an intended effect ⟨~ remedy⟩ **2 :** not capable of performing the required work or duties **:** INCAPABLE ⟨~ figurehead⟩ ⟨~ troops⟩ **3 :** lacking in aesthetic merit ⟨~ design⟩ — **in·effectively** \"+\ *adv* — **in·effectiveness** \"+\ *n*

²ineffective \"\ *n* **:** an ineffective person or thing **:** one unfit for service (as in an army)

¹in·effectual \ˌin+\ *adj* [ME, fr. ¹*in-* + *effectual*] **:** not effectual **:** not producing the proper or usual effect **:** INEFFECTIVE, FUTILE, UNAVAILING ⟨~ attempt⟩ ⟨~ expedient⟩ ⟨~ protests⟩ — **in·effectually** \"+\ *adv* — **in·effectualness** \"+\ *n*

²ineffectual \"\ *n* -s **:** INEFFECTIVE ⟨a program of training for the ~*s* —Eugene Davidoff⟩

in·effectuality \ˌin+\ *n* **:** the quality or state of being ineffectual

in·efficacious \(ˌ)in, ən+\ *adj* [¹*in-* + *efficacious*] **:** not efficacious **:** lacking the power to produce a desired effect **:** INADEQUATE — **in·efficaciously** \"+\ *adv* — **in·efficaciousness** \"+\ *n*

in·efficacity \"+\ *n* [¹*in-* + *efficacity*] **:** INEFFICACY

in·efficacy \(ˈ)in, ən+\ *n* [LL *inefficacia*, fr. L *inefficac-, inefficax* inefficacious (fr. *in-* ¹in- + *efficac-, efficax* efficacious) + *-ia* -y — more at EFFICACIOUS] **:** lack of power to produce a desired or the proper effect **:** INEFFECTUALNESS ⟨~ of laws in preventing crime⟩

in·efficiency \ˌin+\ *n* [¹*in-* + *efficiency*] **:** the quality, state, or fact of being inefficient **:** lack of power or energy sufficient for a desired effect **:** INCAPACITY ⟨the ugliness and ~ of legal prose —Malcolm Muggeridge⟩ ⟨operations . . . common to all printing processes have hidden in them great *inefficiencies* and enormous waste —P.R.Russell⟩

¹in·efficient \"+\ *adj* [¹*in-* + *efficient*] **:** not efficient: **a :** not producing the effect intended or desired **:** INEFFICACIOUS, INSUFFICIENT ⟨~ measures⟩ **b :** wasteful of time or energy in performing work ⟨statistics show that retailing . . . is ~ —*Wall Street Jour.*⟩ **c :** incapable of or indisposed to the effective performance of duties ⟨~ workman⟩ — **in·efficiently** \"+\ *adv*

²inefficient \"\ *n* -s **:** an inefficient person

in·egalitarian \ˌin+\ *adj* [¹*in-* + *egalitarian*] **:** marked by disparity in economic and social standing ⟨assumed that society would be aristocratic and ~ . . . that there would be a sufficiently large class of persons with independent incomes —Christopher Hollis⟩

in·elaborate \ˌin+\ *adj* [¹*in-* + *elaborate*] **:** not elaborate **:** SIMPLE

in·elastic \"+\ *adj* [¹*in-* + *elastic*] **1 :** not elastic **:** slow to react or respond to changing conditions ⟨~ price structure⟩ ⟨~ demand for a commodity⟩ **2 :** INFLEXIBLE, RIGID, UNYIELDING — **in·elasticity** \"+\ *n*

inelastic collision *n, physics* **:** a collision in which part of the kinetic energy of the colliding particles changes into another kind of energy (as radiation)

inelastic scattering *n, physics* **:** scattering of material particles due to collisions in which the total kinetic energy of the colliding particles increases or decreases

in·elegance \(ˈ)in, ən+\ *n* **:** the quality or state of being inelegant **:** lack of elegance **:** lack of refinement, beauty, or polish (as in language, manners)

in·elegancy \"+\ *n* **1** *archaic* **:** INELEGANCE **2 :** something that is inelegant ⟨*inelegancies* of prose style⟩

in·elegant \"+\ *adj* [MF *inelegant*, fr. L *inelegant-, inelegans*, fr. *in-* ¹in- + *elegant-, elegans* elegant — more at ELEGANT] **:** not elegant **:** deficient in beauty, polish, refinement, grace, or ornament **:** lacking in something that correct taste requires — **in·elegantly** \"+\ *adv*

in·eligibility \(ˌ)in, ən+\ *n* **:** the condition or fact of being ineligible

¹in·eligible \(ˈ)in, ən+\ *adj* [F *inéligible*, fr. *in-* ¹in- + *éligible* — more at ELIGIBLE] **1 :** not eligible **:** not qualified to be chosen for an office **:** not worthy to be chosen or preferred ⟨~ for marriage⟩ ⟨~ for the football team⟩ **2 :** not expedient or desirable ⟨shawls will be brought by injudicious mothers at precisely the most ~ moments —W.L.Alden⟩

²ineligible \"\ *n* **:** one that is ineligible

ineligible paper *n* **:** notes and bills that do not meet the requirements for discount or rediscount by the Federal Reserve banks

in·eliminable \ˌin+\ *adj* [¹*in-* + *eliminable*] **:** incapable of being eliminated or excluded

in·eloquent \(ˈ)in, ən+\ *adj* [¹*in-* + *eloquent*] **:** not eloquent **:** lacking in eloquence — **in·eloquently** \"+\ *adv*

in·eluc·ta·bil·i·ty \ˌinə̇ˌləktəˈbiləd·ē\ *n* -ES **:** the quality or state of being ineluctable ⟨~ of fate⟩

in·eluc·ta·ble \ˌinə̇ˈləktəbəl\ *adj* [L *ineluctabilis*, fr. *in-* ¹in- + *eluctari* to struggle out + *-abilis* -able — more at ELUCTATION] **:** not to be avoided, changed, or resisted **:** INESCAPABLE, INEVITABLE ⟨~ facts of human existence⟩ ⟨~ conclusions of logical deduction⟩ — **in·eluc·ta·bly** \-blē, -bli\ *adv*

in·elud·ible \ˌinə̇ˈlüdəbəl\ *adj* [¹*in-* + *elude* + *-ible*] **:** INESCAPABLE — **in·elud·ibly** \-blē, -bli\ *adv*

in·enar·ra·ble \ˌinēˈnarəbəl\ *adj* [ME, fr. MF *inenarrable*, fr. L *inenarrabilis*, fr. *in-* ¹in- + *enarrabilis* capable of being explained, fr. *enarrare* to explain in detail + *-abilis* -able — more at ENARRATION] **:** incapable of being narrated **:** INDESCRIBABLE, INEFFABLE ⟨~ mystery of artistic creation —N.E.Nelson⟩

in·ept \(ˈ)iˈnept, əˈn-\ *adj* [F *inepte*, fr. L *ineptus*, fr. *in-* ¹in- + *aptus* apt — more at APT] **1** *archaic* **:** not apt or fit — often used with *to* or *for* **2 :** not apt for the occasion **:** likely to fail in its purpose **:** out of place **:** INAPPROPRIATE ⟨an ~ and highly artificial comparison —Donald Wayne⟩ ⟨the square is one of those anomalous, shabby-ornate, ~, and pitifully pretentious places —Thomas Wolfe⟩ **3 :** lacking sense or reason **:** FOOLISH, PREPOSTEROUS ⟨it is ~, absurd, downright silly, to argue that in a world torn by . . . convulsions . . . literature can hide away in a hothouse —J.T.Farrell⟩ **4 a :** lacking in skill or aptitude for a particular role or task ⟨an ~ farmer . . . too easily distracted by contemplation —H.V.Gregory⟩ ⟨often a little ~, clumsy about the practical things of life —Rumer Godden⟩ **b :** generally incompetent **:** INADEQUATE, BUNGLING ⟨they found many English officers blundering . . . the brave but ~ Braddock would have done well to take . . . Washington's advice —Allan Nevins & H.S.Commager⟩ **5** *Scots law* **:** NULL, VOID **syn** see AWKWARD

in·ep·ti·tude \əˈneptəˌtüd, -ptə·ˌtyüd\ *n* -s [L *ineptitudo*, fr. *ineptus* inept + *-i-* + *-tudo* -tude] **1 :** UNFITNESS, UNSUITABLENESS ⟨~ of a comparison⟩ ⟨~ that ought to have kept him out of business —Van Wyck Brooks⟩ **2 :** a foolish action or utterance **:** ABSURDITY

in·ept·ly \-ptlē, -li\ *adv* **:** in an inept manner

in·ept·ness \-p(t)nə̇s\ *n* -ES **:** the quality or state of being inept

in·equable \(ˈ)in, ən+\ *adj* [L *inaequabilis*, fr. *in-* ¹in- + *aequabilis* equable — more at EQUABLE] **:** not evenly distributed **:** not uniform **:** UNFAIR

in·equal \"+\ *adj* [ME, fr. L *inaequalis*, fr. *in-* ¹in- + *aequalis* equal, fr. *aequus* even, equal] **1** *archaic* **:** UNEQUAL **2 :** uneven in quality ⟨library of several ~ books —Holbrook Jackson⟩

inequal hour *n* [ME] **:** HOUR 5

in·equalitarian \ˌin+\ *adj* [fr. *inequality* + *-arian* (as in *equalitarian*)] **:** INEGALITARIAN ⟨privileged and leisured class, the product of a thoroughly ~ order of society —Walter Moberly⟩

in·equality \"+\ *n* [MF *inequalité*, fr. L *inaequalitat-, inaequalitas*, fr. *inaequalis* + *-itat-, -itas* -ity] **1 :** the quality of being unequal or uneven **:** lack of equality: as **a :** UNEVENNESS ⟨hampered by the ~ of the ground⟩ **b :** social disparity ⟨combination of democracy with ~ —H.S.Commager⟩ **c :** disparity of distribution ⟨~ of income⟩ or opportunity ⟨educational ~⟩ **d :** VARIABLENESS, CHANGEABLENESS ⟨~ of temperament⟩ ⟨~ of the climate⟩ **2 :** an instance of being unequal (as in position, proportion, evenness, regularity) ⟨*inequalities* of a surface⟩ **3 :** an irregularity or a deviation in the motion of a planet or satellite; *also* **:** the amount of such deviation **4 :** a statement of inequality between two quantities usu. with a sign of inequality (as <or> or ≠ signifying respectively *is less than, is greater than, is not equal to*) between them ⟨$2<3$, $4>1$, and $a \neq b$ are *inequalities*⟩ **5 :** difference in height of successive high or low tides due chiefly to the moon's declination — called also *diurnal inequality*

in·equigranular \(ˌ)in, ən+\ *adj* [¹*in-* + *equigranular*] **:** having or characterized by crystals of different sizes ⟨a rock of ~ texture⟩

in·equilateral \"+\ *adj* [¹*in-* + *equilateral*] **1 :** having the two ends unequal ⟨~ bivalve mollusk⟩ **2 :** having the convolutions of the shell wound obliquely around an axis

in·equitable \(ˈ)in, ən+\ *adj* [¹*in-* + *equitable*] **:** not equitable **:** not just **:** contrary to principles of equity **:** UNFAIR ⟨~ taxation⟩ ⟨~ division of an estate among the heirs⟩ — **in·equitableness** \"+\ *n* — **in·equitably** \"+\ *adv*

in·equity \"+\ *n* [¹*in-* + *equity*] **1 :** lack of equity **:** INJUSTICE, UNFAIRNESS **2 :** an instance of injustice or unfairness ⟨adequate authority to correct maladjustments and *inequities* in wage rates —H.S.Truman⟩

in·equivalve \"+\ *also* **in·equi·valved** \-lvd\ *adj* [¹*in-* + *equi-* + *valve* or *valved* (fr. *valve* + *-ed*)] *of a bivalve mollusk or its shell* **:** having the valves unequal in size and form

in·eradicable \ˌin+\ *adj* [¹*in-* + *eradicate* + *-able*] **:** incapable of being eradicated ⟨~ superstitions⟩ — **in·eradicableness** \"+\ *n* -ES — **in·eradicably** \"+\ *adv*

in·erasable \"+\ *adj* [¹*in-* + *erase* + *-able*] **:** incapable of being erased — **in·eras·able·ness** \-nə̇s\ *n* -ES — **in·erasably** \-blē, -bli\ *adv*

in·er·get·ic \ˌin(ˌ)ərˈjed·ik\ *also* **in·er·get·i·cal** \-d·ə̇kəl\ *adj* [¹*in-* + *energetic*] *archaic* **:** lacking energy

ineri *usu cap, var of* IGNERI

in·er·mia \əˈnərmēə\ [NL, fr. L, neut. pl. of *inermis* unarmed, defenseless, fr. *in-* ¹in- + *-ermis* (fr. *arma* arms) — more at ARM] *syn of* SIPUNCULOIDEA

in·er·mi·cap·si·fer \əˌnərməˈkapsəfər\ *n, cap* [NL, fr. L *inermis* + *capsi-* (fr. L *capsa* chest, case) + *-fer* — more at CASE] **:** a genus of tapeworms (family Anoplocephalidae) parasitic in African and Central American rodents and occas. in man

in·errability \(ˌ)in, ən+\ *n* **:** INFALLIBILITY

in·errable \(ˈ)in, ən+\ *adj* [L *inerrabilis*, fr. *in-* ¹in- + *errabilis* errable, fr. *errare* to err + *-abilis* -able — more at ERR] **:** incapable of erring **:** UNERRING **syn** see INFALLIBLE

in·errancy \"+\ *n* **:** exemption from error **:** INFALLIBILITY ⟨doctrine of the ~ of scripture writings —*Interpreter's Bible*⟩

in·errant \"+\ *adj* [L *inerrant-, inerrans* inerrant, fr. *in-* ¹in- + *errant-, errans*, pres. part. of *errare* to err — more at ERR] **1** *obs* **:** INERRATIC **2 :** free from error or mistake **:** UNERRING **syn** see INFALLIBLE

in·errantly \"+\ *adv* **:** INFALLIBLY, UNERRINGLY

in·erratic \ˌin+\ *adj* [¹*in-* + *erratic*] **:** not erratic or wandering **:** following a set course **:** FIXED ⟨~ star⟩

inerring *adj* [¹*in-* + *erring*] *obs* **:** UNERRING

¹in·ert \(ˈ)iˈnərt, əˈn-, -nə̄, -nəi|, *usu* |d·+V\ *adj* [L *inert-, iners* unskilled, idle, motionless, fr. *in-* ¹in- + *art-, ars* skill, art — more at ARM] **1 :** not having the power to move itself ⟨the Newtonian world which was composed of units, or atoms, that were material, ~, and all alike —S.F.Mason⟩ ⟨~ ammunition⟩ **2 :** not having or manifesting active properties **:** not affecting other substances when in contact with them **:** chemically unreactive **:** powerless for an expected or desired biological effect ⟨~ drug⟩ **:** NEUTRAL **3 :** very slow to move or act **:** LIFELESS, SLUGGISH, INDOLENT ⟨~ bureaucrats⟩ ⟨~ contemplation of television programs⟩ ⟨politically ~ citizenry⟩ **4** *of a paint pigment* **:** possessing little or no hiding power when ground in oil **syn** see INACTIVE

²inert \"\ *n* -s **:** an inert person, constituent, or material: as **a :** a noncombustible gas (as nitrogen or carbon dioxide) present in a gaseous fuel **b :** EXTENDER 1a (1)

in·ert·ance \|tᵊn(t)s\ *n* -s **:** ACOUSTIC INERTANCE

inert gas *n* **1 :** a gas (as nitrogen or carbon dioxide) that is normally chemically inactive esp. in not burning or supporting combustion **2 a :** one of the group of gases comprising helium, neon, argon, krypton, xenon, and sometimes radon **b :** a member of the helium group — called also *noble gas, rare gas*

in·er·tia \əˈnərshə, -nə̄sh-, -nəish- *also* -shēə\ *n, pl* **iner·tias** \-əz\ *also* **iner·ti·ae** \-shēˌē\ [NL, fr. L, lack of skill, idleness, laziness, fr. *inert-, iners* + *-ia* -y] **1 a :** a property of matter by which it remains at rest or in uniform motion in the same straight line unless acted upon by some external force, any change in the motion being measured by the acceleration of the center of mass ⟨~ carried the train past the station⟩ **b :** an analogous property of other physical quantities (as electricity) ⟨electromagnetic ~⟩ **2 :** indisposition to motion, exertion, or action **:** INERTNESS ⟨the Soviets had to overcome the deep-rooted conservatism and ~ of the peasants —A.R. Williams⟩ **:** resistance to change ⟨social ~, the tendency of animals to continue repeating the same action in the same place —W.C.Allee⟩ **3 :** lack of activity **:** SLUGGISHNESS — used esp. of the uterus in labor when its contractions are weak or irregular **4 :** the period of exposure before there is a detectable effect upon a photographic emulsion

in·er·tial \-sh(ē)əl\ *adj* [NL *inertia* + E *-al*] **:** of, relating to, or of the nature of inertia ⟨~ resistance to change of direction⟩

inertial force *n* **:** a force opposite in direction to an accelerating force acting on a body and equal to the product of the accelerating force and the mass of the body

inertial guidance *or* **inertial navigation** *n* **:** guidance (as of a missile or aircraft) by means of self-contained automatically controlling devices that respond to inertial forces

inertial mass *n* **:** mass as determined by impact experiments in accordance with the law that the masses of bodies are inversely proportional to the velocities which a given force will impart to them in a given time

inertial system *n* **:** a frame of reference with respect to which Newton's laws of motion are valid

inertia starter *n* **:** an internal-combustion engine starter that utilizes the energy of a spinning flywheel set in motion by means of a hand crank or electric motor

in·er·tion \-shən\ *n* -s [¹*inert* + *-ion* (as in *exertion*)] *archaic* **:** INERTNESS, QUIETUDE

in·ert·ly *adv* **:** in an inert manner **:** PASSIVELY, LIFELESSLY

in·ert·ness *n* -ES **:** the quality or state of being inert **:** lack of activity **:** PASSIVITY ⟨chemical ~ makes glass a good food container⟩

in·erudite \(ˈ)in, ən+\ *adj* [L *ineruditus*, fr. *in-* ¹in- + *eruditus* learned, skilled, experienced — more at ERUDITE] **:** not erudite **:** IGNORANT

-ines *pl of* -INE

in·escapable \ˌin+\ *adj* [¹*in-* + *escape* + *-able*] **:** incapable of being avoided, ignored, or denied ⟨the ~ mark of his genius —F.R.Leavis⟩ **:** UNAVOIDABLE **:** necessarily present or to be reckoned with **:** following of strict logical necessity or moral compulsion **:** INEVITABLE ⟨~ that a man must owe economic obligations to his wife and to his children —Weston La Barre⟩ ⟨continuity in design appears to be ~ —J.E.Gloag⟩ — **in·es·cap·able·ness** \-nə̇s\ *n* -ES — **in·es·cap·ably** \-blē, -bli\ *adv*

in·esculent \(ˈ)in, ən+\ *adj* [¹*in-* + *esculent*] **:** not esculent **:** INEDIBLE

in·escutcheon *also* **in·escucheon** \ˌin+\ *n* [⁴*in* + *escutcheon, escucheon*] **:** a small escutcheon borne within a shield

inescutcheon

ines·ite \ˈīnəˌsīt, ˈin-, -ˌzīt\ *n* -s [G *inesit*, fr. Gk *ines* (pl. of *is* sinew, tendon) + G *-it* -ite — more at WITHY] **:** a mineral $Ca_2Mn_7Si_{10}O_{28}(OH)_2.5H_2O$ consisting of a pale red hydrous manganese calcium silicate, in small prismatic crystals or massive (hardness 6, sp. gr. 3.03)

in es·se \ˌinˈesē\ *adv (or adj)* [ML] **:** in actual existence — contrasted with *in posse*

in·essential \ˌin+\ *adj* [¹*in-* + *essential*] **1 :** having no essence or being **2 :** not essential **:** UNESSENTIAL, NONESSENTIAL

²inessential \"\ *n* **:** something that is not essential **:** UNESSENTIAL

in·essentiality \ˌin+\ *n* **:** the quality or state of being inessential

¹in·es·sive \əˈnesiv\ *adj* [L *inesse* to be in (fr. *in-* ²in- + *esse* to be) + E *-ive* — more at IS] *of a grammatical case* **:** denoting position or location within

²inessive \"\ *n* **:** the inessive case of a substantive

in·es·ti·ma·bil·i·ty \(ˌ)iˌnestəməˈbiləd·ē\ *n* -ES **:** INESTIMABLENESS

in·estimable \(ˈ)in, ən+\ *adj* [ME, fr. MF, fr. L *inaestimabilis*, fr. *in-* ¹in- + *aestimabilis* estimable — more at ESTIMABLE] **1 :** incapable of being estimated or computed ⟨~ errors⟩ **2 :** too valuable or excellent to be measured or appreciated **:** above all price ⟨has performed an ~ service for his country⟩ — **in·estimable·ness** \"+\ *n* — **in·es·ti·ma·bly** \-blē, -bli\ *adv*

in·euphonious \ˌin+\ *adj* [¹*in-* + *euphonious*] **:** not euphonious **:** harsh in sound

in·evaporable \"+\ *adj* [¹*in-* + *evaporable*] **:** incapable of being reduced in volume by evaporation

in·eva·si·ble \ˌinə̇ˈvāzəbəl, -āsə-\ *adj* [¹*in-* + L *evasus* (past part. of *evadere* to evade) + E *-ible* — more at EVADE] **:** INEVITABLE

in·evidence \(ˈ)in, ən+\ *n* **1** *obs* **:** lack of evidence or manifestation **2 :** the state or fact of being inevident

in·evident \"+\ *adj* [LL *inevident-, inevidens*, fr. L *in-* ¹in-

+ *evident-, evidens* evident — more at EVIDENT] **:** not evident **:** not clear or obvious

in·ev·i·ta·bil·i·ty \(,)i,nevəd·ə'bilәd·ē, ə,n-, -v(ə)tə'-, -lətē, -i\ *n* -ES **:** the quality or state of being inevitable ⟨habits . . . seem to have all of the ~ that belongs to the movement of the fixed stars —John Dewey⟩ ⟨less inclined to accept the ~ of servitude —Ray Lewis & Angus Maude⟩

¹in·ev·i·ta·ble \ə'nevəd·əbəl, -v(ə)təb-\ *adj* [ME, fr. L *inevitabilis*, fr. *in-* ¹in- + *evitabilis* evitable — more at EVITABLE] **1 :** incapable of being avoided or evaded ⟨~ result⟩ ⟨~ day of reckoning⟩ **:** being or seeming to be in the natural order of things or foreordained ⟨~ phrase⟩ ⟨landscape, as an ~ expression of the Romantic spirit —F.J.Mather⟩ ⟨once we admit . . . that war is natural and ~ —Vera M. Dean⟩ **2 :** certain to occur or to confront one ⟨allowing for the ~ delays of such a journey⟩ ⟨the ~ gas stations at every crossroad⟩ ⟨over the pine mantel . . . were the ~ antlers —Gertrude Atherton⟩ — **in·ev·i·ta·ble·ness** \-nəs\ *n* -ES — **in·ev·i·ta·bly** \-blē, -bli\ *adv*

²inevitable \"\ *n* -S **:** something that is inevitable ⟨should the symptoms of aging be studied as the natural ~*s* of a cyclic process —Louis Berman⟩

inevitable accident *n, law* **:** an accident that could not have been foreseen or prevented by the due care and diligence of any human being involved in it **:** an accident caused by forces beyond the power of any human being involved to foresee or overcome by the exercise of ordinary prudence — compare ACT OF GOD

in·exact \¦in+\ *adj* [F, fr. *in-* ¹in- + *exact* — more at EXACT] **1 :** not exact **:** not precisely correct or true **:** INACCURATE ⟨~ translation⟩ **2 :** not rigorous and careful ⟨~ reasoner⟩ — **in·exactly** \"+\ *adv* — **in·exactness** \"+\ *n*

in·exactitude \"+\ *n* [F, fr. *in-* ¹in- + *exactitude* — more at EXACTITUDE] **1 :** lack of exactitude or precision **:** the quality of being inexact or inaccurate **2 :** an instance of inexactness

in ex·cel·sis \,inək'selsəs, ,i(,)nek-, -ks'kel-, -ks'chel-, -k'shel-\ *adv* [L] **:** in the highest degree **:** SUPERLATIVELY ⟨he had *in excelsis* what some people term . . . the legal mind —*Blackwood's*⟩

in·excitability \¦in+\ *n* **:** calmness of temper

in·excitable \"+\ *adj* [¹*in-* + *excitable*] **1 :** not readily excited or aroused **2** *of a nerve* **:** not subject to excitation **:** not responsive to stimulation

in·excusability \"+\ *n* -ES **1 :** the quality of being inexcusable **2 :** something that is inexcusable

in·excusable \"+\ *adj* [L *inexcusabilis*, fr. *in-* ¹in- + *excusabilis* excusable — more at EXCUSABLE] **:** not excusable **:** being without excuse or justification ⟨~ carelessness⟩ — **in·excusableness** \"+\ *n* — **in·excusably** \"+\ *adv*

in·executable \(¦)in, ən+\ *adj* [¹*in-* + *executable*] **:** impossible of execution or performance **:** IMPRACTICABLE

in·execution \"+\ *n* [prob. fr. F *inexécution*, fr. MF *inexecution*, fr. *in-* ¹in- + *execution* — more at EXECUTION] **:** failure to carry out (as an order) or enforce (as a law) **:** NONPERFORMANCE

in·exertion \¦in+\ *n* [¹*in-* + *exertion*] **:** lack of exertion or effort **:** INDOLENCE, LAZINESS

in·exhausted \"+\ *adj* [¹*in-* + *exhausted*] *archaic* **:** that is not exhausted

in·exhaustibility \"+\ *n* **:** the quality or state of being inexhaustible **:** UNFAILINGNESS

in·exhaustible \"+\ *adj* [¹*in-* + *exhaust* + *-ible*] **:** not exhaustible: as **a :** incapable of being used up **:** UNFAILING ⟨~ supplies of coal⟩ ⟨an ~ spring⟩ **b :** incapable of being wearied or worn out ⟨~ fertility of invention⟩ ⟨~ patience⟩ — **in·ex·haust·ible·ness** \-nəs\ *n* -ES — **in·ex·haust·ibly** \-blē, -bli\ *adv*

in·exhaustive \¦in+\ *adj* [¹*in-* + *exhaustive*] **1** *archaic* **:** INEXHAUSTIBLE **2 :** not exhaustive — **in·exhaustively** \"+\ *adv*

in·exhaustless \"+\ *adj* [¹*in-* + *exhaustless*] *archaic* **:** EXHAUSTLESS

in·exigible \(')in, ən+\ *adj* [¹*in-* + *exigible*] **:** not exigible

in·exist \¦in+\ *vi* [²*in-* + *exist*] *archaic* **:** to exist in something else **:** INHERE

¹in·existence \"+\ *n* [¹*in-* + *existence*] **:** NONEXISTENCE

²inexistence \"\ *n* [²*in-* + *existence*] *archaic* **:** INHERENCE

¹in·existent \¦in+\ *adj* [LL *inexsistent-, inexistent-, inexsistens, inexistens*, fr. L *in-* ²in- + *exisistent-, existent-, exsistens, existens*, pres. part. of *exsistere, existere* to exist — more at EXIST] *archaic* **:** INHERENT

²inexistent \"\ *adj* [LL *inexistent-, inexsistent-, inexistens, inexsistens*, fr. L *in-* ¹in- + *existent-, exsistent-, existens, exsistens*] **:** not having being **:** NONEXISTENT

in·ex·o·ra·bil·i·ty \(,)i,neks(ə)rə'bilәd·ē, ə,n-, -lətē, -i *also* -negz(- *sometimes* ,inig,zōr- *or* ,i(,)neg,zōr- *or* ¦zōr-\ *n* -ES [L *inexorabilitas*, fr. *inexorabilis* + *-itas* -ity] **:** the quality of being inexorable ⟨moral world of humans does not behave with the same rigor and ~ as the physical world —Weston La Barre⟩

in·ex·o·ra·ble \(')i¦neks(ə)rəbəl, ə'n- *also* -negz(- *sometimes* ,inig¦zōr- *or* ¦i(,)neg¦zōr- *or* -¦zōr-\ *adj* [L *inexorabilis*, fr. *in-* ¹in- + *exorabilis* exorable, fr. *exorare* to prevail upon, persuade (fr. *ex-* ¹ex- + *orare* to speak, plead, pray) + *-abilis* -able — more at ORATION] **:** not to be persuaded or moved by entreaty or prayer **:** UNYIELDING, INFLEXIBLE, RELENTLESS ⟨~ doom⟩ ⟨~ logic⟩ ⟨~ necessity⟩ ⟨~ opponent⟩ — **in·ex·o·ra·ble·ness** \-nəs\ *n* -ES — **in·ex·o·ra·bly** \-blē, -bli\ *adv*

in·expansible \¦in+\ *adj* [¹*in-* + *expansible*] **:** not expansible

in·expectancy \"+\ *n* [¹*in-* + *expectancy*] **:** lack of expectancy ⟨it isn't surfeit alone but ~ which makes entertainment so feeble —J.M.Barzun⟩

in·expectant \"+\ *adj* [¹*in-* + *expectant*] **:** lacking expectation ⟨small ~ audience⟩

in·expediency *or* **in·expedience** \"+\ *n* [¹*in-* + *expediency, expedience*] **:** the quality or fact of being inexpedient

in·expedient \"+\ *adj* [¹*in-* + *expedient*] **1 :** not expedient **:** not likely to achieve a purpose or bring success **:** INADVISABLE, UNPROFITABLE ⟨to rely on a deterrent that will bring the maximum of suffering to all mankind is immoral as well as ~ —Denis Healey⟩ **2 :** INCONVENIENT ⟨it was occasionally ~ to carry about measuring chains —Rudyard Kipling⟩ — **in·expediently** \"+\ *adv*

in·expensive \"+\ *adj* [¹*in-* + *expensive*] **:** not expensive **:** reasonable in price **:** CHEAP — **in·expensively** \"+\ *adv* — **in·expensiveness** \"+\ *n*

in·experience \"+\ *n* [MF, fr. LL *inexperientia*, fr. L *in-* ¹in- + *experientia* experience — more at EXPERIENCE] **:** lack of practical experience **:** lack of knowledge of the ways of the world or of a particular kind of work or activity

in·experienced \"+\ *adj* **:** lacking practical experience **:** UNTRAINED, UNTRIED, GREEN

¹in·expert \(¦)in, ən+\ *adj* [ME *inexperte*, fr. MF *inexpert*, fr. L *inexpertus*, fr. *in-* ¹in- + *expertus*, past part. of *experiri* to try — more at EXPERIENCE] **1 :** INEXPERIENCED **2 :** not expert **:** not skilled or dexterous — **in·expertly** \"+\ *adv* — **in·expertness** \"+\ *n*

²in·expert \"\ *n* **:** an inexpert person **:** NOVICE

in·expiable \(¦)in, ən+\ *adj* [L *inexpiabilis*, fr. *in-* ¹in- + *expiare* to expiate + *-abilis* -able — more at EXPIATE] **1 :** not capable of being expiated or atoned for **:** UNFORGIVABLE ⟨~ offense⟩ **2** *obs* **:** IMPLACABLE, UNAPPEASABLE — **in·ex·pi·a·ble·ness** \-nəs\ *n* -ES — **in·ex·pi·a·bly** \-blē, -bli\ *adv*

in·expiate \"+\ *adj* [LL *inexpiatus*, fr. L *in-* ¹in- + *expiatus*, past part. of *expiare*] **1 :** not expiated **2** *obs* **:** not appeased

in·explainable \¦in+\ *adj* [¹*in-* + *explainable*] **:** INEXPLICABLE

in·explicability \(¦)in, ən+\ *n* -ES **:** the quality of being inexplicable

in·explicable \"+\ *adj* [MF, fr. L *inexplicabilis*, fr. *in-* ¹in- + *explicabilis* explicable — more at EXPLICABLE] **1** *obs* **:** incapable of being unfolded or unraveled **:** INEXTRICABLE **2 :** not explicable **:** incapable of being explained, interpreted, or accounted for ⟨~ action⟩ ⟨~ mystery⟩ — **in·ex·plica·ble·ness** \-nəs\ *n* -ES — **in·ex·plica·bly** \-blē, -bli\ *adv*

in·explicit \¦in+ (,)=¦==\ *adj* [¹*in-* + *explicit*] **:** not explicit — **in·ex·plic·it·ly** *adv* — **in·ex·plic·it·ness** *n*

in·explosive \¦in+\ *adj* [¹*in-* + *explosive*] **:** not liable to explode

in·exportable \(¦)in, ən+\ *adj* [¹*in-* + *exportable*] **:** not capable of being exported **:** not suitable for export

in·expressibility \¦in+\ *n* -ES **:** the quality of being inexpressible

in·expressible \"+\ *adj* [¹*in-* + *expressible*] **:** not capable of being expressed **:** INDESCRIBABLE, INEFFABLE ⟨~ delight⟩ **:** UNUTTERABLE, UNSPEAKABLE ⟨~ villainy⟩ — **in·ex·press·ible·ness** \-nəs\ *n* -ES — **in·ex·press·ibly** \-blē, -bli\ *adv*

in·ex·press·ibles \,==ˈ==bəlz\ *n pl, archaic* **:** TROUSERS

in·expressive \¦in+\ *adj* [¹*in-* + *expressive*] **1** *obs* **:** INEXPRESSIBLE **2 :** lacking expression **:** not expressive **:** DULL, WOODEN ⟨~ face⟩ **3 :** lacking meaning ⟨~ music⟩ ⟨~ gestures⟩ — **in·expressively** \"+\ *adv* — **in·expressiveness** \"+\ *n*

in·ex·pugna·bil·i·ty \,inik,spyüna'bilәd·ē, ,i(,)nek-,-,spəgnə-\ *n* -ES **:** IMPREGNABILITY

in·expugnable \¦in+\ *adj* [MF, fr. L *inexpugnabilis*, fr. *in-* ¹in- + *expugnabilis* expugnable — more at EXPUGNABLE] **1 :** incapable of being taken by assault or subdued by force **:** IMPREGNABLE ⟨his position though strong was not ~ —G.B. Sansom⟩ **2 :** incapable of being overthrown or driven out ⟨most common and ~ error of criticism —Meyer Schapiro⟩ **:** STABLE, FIXED ⟨~ hatred⟩ — **in·ex·pugna·ble·ness** \-nəs\ *n* -ES — **in·ex·pugna·bly** \-blē, -bli\ *adv*

in·ex·pung·ibil·i·ty \¦=(,)=,==ˈbilәd·ē\ *n* -ES **:** the quality or state of being inexpungible **:** INERADICABLENESS, INDELIBILITY ⟨~ of popular myths⟩

in·ex·pung·ible *also* **in·ex·punge·able** \¦inik¦spənjəbəl, ¦i(,)nek-\ *adj* [¹*in-* + *expunge* + *-ible, -able*] **:** incapable of being obliterated or got rid of ⟨~ scent of a bottle of perfume he had . . . broken —Louis Auchincloss⟩

in·extended \¦in+\ *adj* [¹*in-* + *extended*] **:** lacking extension **:** not occupying space

in·extensibility \"+\ *n* [¹*in-* + *extensibility*] **:** incapability of being drawn out or stretched ⟨~ of a rope⟩

in·extensible \"+\ *adj* [¹*in-* + *extensible*] **:** not extensible **:** incapable of being stretched

in·extensile \"+\ *adj* [¹*in-* + *extensile*] **:** not extensible

in·extension \"+\ *n* [¹*in-* + *extension*] **:** lack of extension

in·extensional \"+\ *adj* **:** marked by or relating to absence of stretching out

inextensional deformation *n* **:** a bending of a surface that preserves unchanged the length of each line element and the measure of curvature at every point

in·extensive \¦in+\ *adj* [¹*in-* + *extensive*] **:** not extensive

in ex·ten·so \,inik'sten(t)(,)sō, ,i(,)nek-\ *adv* [L] **:** at length rather than in summary ⟨the details of all the observations will be reported *in extenso* elsewhere —*Science*⟩

in·exterminable \¦in+\ *adj* [LL *inexterminabilis*, fr. L *in-* ¹in- + LL *exterminabilis* capable of being exterminated, exterminable, fr. L *exterminare* to exterminate + *-abilis* -able — more at EXTERMINATE] **1** *obs* **:** INTERMINABLE **2 :** incapable of extermination

in·extinct \"+(,)=¦=\ *adj* [L *inexstinctus, inextinctus*, fr. *in-* ¹in- + *exstinctus, extinctus*, past part. of *exstinguere, extinguere* to extinguish — more at EXTINGUISH] **:** UNEXTINGUISHED

in·extinguishable \¦in+\ *adj* [¹*in-* + *extinguishable*] **:** not extinguishable ⟨~ flame⟩ **:** UNQUENCHABLE, IRREPRESSIBLE ⟨~ hope⟩ ⟨~ laughter⟩ — **in·extinguishably** \"+\ *adv*

in·ex·tir·pa·ble \(¦)i¦nekstərpəbəl, ə'n-; ¦i(,)nek¦s-\ *adj* [F or L; F, fr. L *inexstirpabilis, inextirpabilis*, fr. *in-* ¹in- + *exstirpare, extirpare* to extirpate + *-abilis* -able — more at EXTIRPATE] **:** not capable of being extirpated **:** INERADICABLE — **in·ex·tir·pa·ble·ness** \-nəs\ *n* -ES

in ex·tre·mis \,inik'strāməs, ,i(,)nek-, -rēm-\ *adv* [L] **:** in extreme circumstances **:** in desperate case; *esp* **:** at the point of death

in·extricability \(¦)in, ən+\ *n* -ES **:** the quality or state of being inextricable ⟨~ of form and content —Peter Viereck⟩

in·extricable \"+\ *adj* [MF or L; MF, fr. L *inextricabilis*, fr. *in-* ¹in- + *extricabilis* extricable — more at EXTRICABLE] **1 :** not permitting extrication **:** forming a maze or tangle from which it is impossible to get free **2 a :** incapable of being disentangled or untied ⟨~ knot⟩ ⟨~ unity⟩ **b :** UNSOLVABLE ⟨~ confusion⟩ **3 :** INTRICATE, INVOLVED **:** highly elaborated ⟨~ design⟩ — **in·ex·trica·ble·ness** \-nəs\ *n* -ES — **in·ex·trica·bly** \-blē, -bli\ *adv*

inf *abbr* **1** infantry **2** inferior **3** infield; infielder **4** infinitive **5** infinity **6** infirmary **7** information **8** infra **9** infused; infusion

inface \'=,=\ *n* [⁴*in* + *face*] **:** the steeper of the two slopes of a cuesta

in fa·cie cu·ri·ae \-'fāshē,ē'kyürē,ē\ *adv* [ML] **:** before or in the presence of the court

infall \'=,=\ *n* [⁴*in* + *fall*] **1 :** INCURSION ⟨~ of pirates⟩ **2 :** INLET, CONFLUENCE, JUNCTION **3 :** a falling into or on ⟨~ of meteorites⟩ ⟨~ of a cavern roof⟩

in·fallibilism \(')in+\ *n* **1 :** support of or adherence to the dogma of papal infallibility **2 :** a belief that scientific laws are not subject to change — opposed to *fallibilism*

in·fallibilist \"+\ *n* **1 :** one who believes in infallibility; *esp* **:** a supporter of the dogma of papal infallibility **2 :** one who believes that scientific laws are not subject to change

in·fallibility \(¦)in+\ *n* [ML *infallibilitas*, fr. *infallibilis* infallible + L *-itas* -ity] **:** the quality or state of being infallible

in·fallible \(')in, ən+\ *adj* [ML *infallibilis*, fr. L *in-* ¹in- + LL *fallibilis* fallible — more at FALLIBLE] **1 :** not fallible **:** incapable of error **:** UNERRING ⟨~ marksman⟩ ⟨~ ear for pitch in music⟩ ⟨~ memory⟩ **2 :** not liable to mislead, deceive, or disappoint **:** SURE, CERTAIN, INDUBITABLE ⟨~ remedy⟩ ⟨his accent is an almost ~ index of his family background and education —Richard Joseph⟩ ⟨~ scheme for making money⟩ **3 :** incapable of error in defining doctrines touching faith or morals

syn INERRABLE, INERRANT, UNERRING: INFALLIBLE describes that which is exempt from possibility of error or mistake or that which has been errorless ⟨no mathematician is *infallible;* he may make mistakes —A.S.Eddington⟩ ⟨believed in an *infallible* Bible —W.W.Sweet⟩ INERRABLE and INERRANT are erudite synonyms for INFALLIBLE sometimes used in its stead to escape connotations arising from the discussion of papal infallibility; the latter may imply that whatever is described has not so far erred ⟨the Church was ubiquitous, omniscient, theoretically *inerrant* and omnicompetent —G.G.Coulton⟩ ⟨at the moment we lack, in all English-speaking countries, the *inerrant* literary sense which gave us the Prayer Book Collects, often quite as beautiful in translation as in the original Latin —W.L.Sperry⟩ UNERRING may imply freedom from error coupled with sureness, reliability, and exactness ⟨an *unerring* marksman⟩ ⟨a man's language is an *unerring* index of his nature —Laurence Binyon⟩ ⟨the *unerring* scent of the hounds in pursuit —George Meredith⟩

in·fal·li·ble·ness *n* **:** INFALLIBILITY

in·fallibly \"+\ *adj* **:** without fail **:** SURELY, CERTAINLY ⟨must make the proper use of his opportunities or he will ~ perish —A.C.McGiffert⟩

in·fam·a·tory \ən'famə,tōrē, -tȯr-\ *adj* [ML *infamatorius*, fr. L *infamatus* (past part. of *infamare*) + *-orius* -ory] *archaic* **:** DEFAMATORY

in·fame \ən'fām\ *vt* -ED/-ING/-S [ME *enfamen*, fr. MF *enfamer, infamer*, fr. L *infamare*, fr. *infamis*] *archaic* **:** DEFAME

in·fa·mize \'infə,mīz\ *vt* -ED/-ING/-S [*infamous* + *-ize*] *archaic* **:** to make infamous **:** DEFAME

in·fa·mous \'infəməs\ *adj* [ME *infamis, infamous*, fr. L *infamis*, fr. *in-* ¹in- + *-famis* (fr. *fama* fame) — more at FAME] **1 :** having a reputation of the worst kind **:** notorious as being of vicious, contemptible, or criminal character **:** DETESTABLE, ABHORRENT ⟨one of the most ~ spies and bullies of all time —*Time*⟩ ⟨~ outlaw⟩ ⟨~ traitor⟩ ⟨~ dog has got every vice except hypocrisy —W.M.Thackeray⟩ **2 :** causing or bringing infamy **:** deserving hatred or detestation ⟨~ conduct⟩ ⟨~ vices⟩ ⟨~ treatment of prisoners⟩ ⟨men to whom totalitarianism is ~ —Jerome Frank⟩ ⟨most ~ of quack nostrums —*Time*⟩ **3 :** having a bad name as being associated with something disgraceful or detestable ⟨the street outside Newgate had not obtained one ~ notoriety that has since attached to it —Charles Dickens⟩ **4 :** convicted of an offense judged infamous ⟨~ person⟩ **syn** see VICIOUS

infamous crime *n* **:** a crime judged infamous because it constitutes treason or a felony, because it involves moral turpitude of a nature that creates a strong presumption that the one guilty is unworthy of belief in a court of law, or because it subjects the one guilty to infamy ⟨no person shall be held to answer for a capital or otherwise *infamous crime*, unless on a presentment or indictment of a grand jury, except in cases arising in the land or naval forces, or in the militia, when in actual service in time of war or public danger —*U.S.Constitution*⟩

infamous crime against nature : SODOMY

in·fa·mous·ly *adv* **:** in an infamous manner **:** in a manner deserving infamy ⟨how ~ he treats his wife —George Meredith⟩ **:** ATROCIOUSLY ⟨just as the work was nearly completed, being ~ done, it fell down again —L.H.Chambers⟩

in·fa·my \'infəmē, -mi\ *n* -ES [ME *infamye*, fr. MF *infamie*, fr. L *infamia*, fr. *infamis* + *-ia* -y] **1 a :** a lasting, widespread, and deep-rooted evil reputation brought about by something criminal, shocking, or brutal **:** the highest degree of dishonor ⟨a series of treacherous murders added to his ~⟩ **b :** an indication of such notoriety **:** strong condemnatory utterance **2 a :** an extreme and publicly known criminal, shocking, or brutal act ⟨an ~ greater than any mutiny⟩ **b :** the state or condition of being rightly and widely known for such an act ⟨his name will live in ~ for this night's work⟩ **3 :** the public disgrace or loss of character and honor or loss of civil or political rights incurred by a person convicted of an infamous crime **syn** see DISHONOR

in·fan·cy \'infənsē, -si\ *n* -ES [ME, fr. L *infantia*, fr. *infant-, infans* infant + *-ia* -y] **1 :** the state or period of being an infant **:** the first part of life **:** early childhood — called also *babyhood* **2 :** the beginning or early period of existence ⟨mechanical engineering was then in its ~ —O.S.Nock⟩ ⟨~ of a city⟩ **3 :** the legal status of an infant or one under age or under the age of twenty-one years **:** NONAGE, MINORITY **4 :** the initial or very early stage (as of a river) in a cycle of erosion

infang *n* -S [by shortening] *obs* **:** INFANGTHIEF

in·fang·thief \'infaŋ,thēf\ *n* [ME *infangenthef, infangthef*, fr. OE *infangenetheōf, infangentheōf*, fr. *in, inn* in + *fangen* (past part. of *fōn* to seize, capture) + *theōf* thief — more at IN, PACT, THIEF] **:** a medieval franchise of exercising jurisdiction over a thief caught within the limits to which the franchise was attached **:** the right of the lord of a manor to judge a thief taken within the seigniory of such lord — distinguished from *outfangthief*

in·fans \'in,fanz\ *n, pl* **infan·tes** \ən'fan,tēz\ [L] *civil law* **:** a child under seven years of age **:** a child not having the ability to speak

¹in·fant \'infənt\ *n* -S [ME *enfaunt, infaunt*, fr. MF *enfant*, fr. L *infant-, infans*, fr. *infant-, infans*, adj., incapable of speech, young, fr. *in-* ¹in- + *fant-, fans*, pres. part. of *fari* to speak — more at BAN] **1 a :** a child in the first year of life **:** BABY **b :** a child several years of age **2 a :** a person who is not of full age **:** MINOR **b** *common law* **:** a person under the age of 21 — see AGE 3 **3** *Brit* **:** a pupil in an infant school

²infant \"\ *adj* **1 :** of, relating to, exemplifying, or being in infancy or young childhood ⟨~ king⟩ ⟨~ martyr⟩ **2 :** being in an early stage of development **:** not matured or fully developed ⟨~ fruit⟩ ⟨~ navy⟩; *esp* **:** needing protection and care ⟨~ animals⟩ ⟨our ~ steel industry⟩

¹in·fan·ta \ən'fantə\ *n* -S [Sp & Pg, fem. of *infante*] **1 :** a daughter of the king and queen of Spain or Portugal **2 :** the wife of an infante

²infanta \"\ *adj, of a fashion in dress* **:** derived from Velasquez's portraits of 17th century Spanish princesses and usu. having wide skirts with side extensions

in·fan·te \ən'fan,tā\ *n* -S [Sp & Pg, lit., infant, fr. L *infant-, infans*] **:** a son of the king and queen of Spain or Portugal who is not the eldest — compare PRINCIPE

in·fant·hood \'infənt,hu̇d\ *n* **:** INFANCY

in·fan·ti·ci·dal \ən¦fantə¦sīdᵊl\ *adj* **:** relating to the killing of infants

¹in·fanticide \ən'fantə,sīd\ *n* -S [LL *infanticidium*, fr. L *infant-, infans* infant + *-i-* + *-cidium* -cide (killing) — more at INFANT] **1 :** a killing of a newly or recently born child **2 :** a practice of killing infants — compare ABORTION 1, FETICIDE

²infanticide \"\ *n* -S [LL *infanticida*, fr. L *infant-, infans* + *-i-* + *-cida* -cide (killer)] **:** one that kills an infant

in·fan·tile \'infən,tīl *also* -n·tәl *sometimes* -n,tēl *or* -n·(,)til\ *adj* [prob. fr. F, fr. L *infantilis*, fr. *infant-, infans* infant + *-ilis* -ile] **1 :** of or relating to infants or infancy ⟨~ disease⟩ ⟨~ state⟩ **2 :** suitable to an infant **:** characteristic of an infant **:** very immature **:** CHILDISH ⟨~ level of entertainment⟩ ⟨~ tantrum⟩ **3 :** affected with infantilism **4** *of topography* **:** being in a very early stage of development presumably following an uplift or equivalent change with respect to base level ⟨~ stream⟩ ⟨~ mountain range⟩

infantile myxedema *n* **:** CRETINISM

infantile paralysis *n* **:** POLIOMYELITIS

infantile sexuality *n* **:** needs and strivings in early childhood for libidinal gratification **:** pregenital eroticism

in·fan·til·ism \'infəntə,lizəm *sometimes* ən'fantᵊl,i-\ *n* -S [ISV *infantile* + *-ism*] **1 :** a condition of being abnormally childlike **:** a retention of childish physical, mental, or emotional qualities in adult life; *esp* **:** failure to attain sexual maturity **2 :** an act or expression characteristic of lack of maturity **:** PUERILITY ⟨~*s* of thought⟩ ⟨the ~ of selfishness —Agnes E. Meyer⟩

in·fan·ti·lis·tic \¦infəntə¦listik\ *adj* **:** abnormally immature **:** showing infantile behavior

in·fan·til·i·ty \,infən'tiləd·ē\ *n* -ES [ML *infantilitas*, fr. L *infantilis* infantile + *-itas-* -ity] **:** the quality or state of being infantile **:** CHILDISHNESS

in·fan·tine \'infən,tīn, -tēn\ *adj* [F *infantin*, fr. MF, alter. (influenced by L *infant-, infans* infant) of *enfantin*, fr. OF, fr. *enfant* infant + *-in* -ine — more at INFANT] **:** INFANTILE ⟨~ wailing⟩ **:** CHILDISH

infant mortality *n* **:** the rate of deaths occurring in the first year of life

in·fan·try \'infəntrē, -ri\ *n* -ES [MF & OIt; MF *infanterie*, fr. OIt *infanteria*, fr. *infante* infant, boy, footman, foot soldier (fr. L *infant-, infans* infant) + *-eria* -ry — more at INFANT] **1 a :** soldiers trained, armed, and equipped to fight on foot **b :** a branch of an army composed of such soldiers **c :** an infantry regiment ⟨the 8th *Infantry*⟩ **d :** MOONLIGHT BLUE **2** [influenced in meaning by ¹*infant*] **:** a body of children

in·fan·try·man \-mən\ *n, pl* **infantrymen :** an infantry soldier **:** FOOT SOLDIER

infant's breath \'==ˌ=\ *n* **1 :** WILD MADDER 2a **2 :** MONEYWORT

infant school *n, Brit* **:** PRESCHOOL, KINDERGARTEN

in·farct \'in,färkt, ən'f-\ *n* -S [L *infarctus*, past part. of *infarcire, infercire* to stuff, stuff full, fr. *in-* ²in- + *farcire* to stuff, fill — more at FARCE] **:** an area of coagulation necrosis in a tissue (as of the heart) resulting from obstruction of the local circulation by a thrombus or embolus

in·farct·ed \ən'färktəd\ *adj* **:** affected with infarction ⟨~ kidney⟩

in·farc·tion \-kshən\ *n* -S **:** the producing of an infarct

in·fare \'in,fa(a)ər, -fe(ə)r\ *n* [ME *infer, infair* entrance, infare, fr. OE *infær* entrance, fr. *in, inn* in + *fær* way, journey, fr. *faran* to go, travel — more at IN, FARE] *chiefly dial* **:** a feast and reception for a newly married couple usu. at the home of the groom's family a day or two after the wedding

infatigable *adj* [L *infatigabilis*, fr. *in-* ¹in- + *fatigare* to fatigue + *-abilis* -able] *obs* **:** INDEFATIGABLE

¹in·fat·u·ate \ən'fachəwət\ *adj* [ME, fr. L *infatuatus*, past part.] **:** marked by infatuation **:** INFATUATED ⟨knowing the inwardness of that grand, ~ gabble —R.P.Warren⟩

²in·fat·u·ate \-chə,wāt, *usu* -ād.+V\ *vt* -ED/-ING/-S [L *infatuatus*, past part. of *infatuare*, fr. *in-* ²in- + *fatuus* foolish, fatuous — more at FATUOUS] **1** *obs* **:** to turn (as counsel) into foolishness or show to be foolish **:** FRUSTRATE **2 :** to make foolish **:** affect with folly **:** weaken the intellectual powers of or deprive of sound judgment ⟨the toys that ~ men —R.W. Emerson⟩ **3 :** to inspire with a foolish and extravagant love or desire ⟨you have *infatuated* this boy to such an extent that he would agree with you in anything —W.J.Locke⟩

³in·fat·u·ate \-wət\ *n* -S [¹*infatuate*] **:** an infatuated person

in·fat·u·at·ed \ən'fachə,wād·əd\ *adj* **:** possessed with or marked by a strong attachment or foolish or unreasoning love or desire ⟨a man absolutely ~ and delivered over to certain

destruction —F.R.Leavis⟩ ⟨how ~ she was with her lover, and how regardless of what anyone could say to her on the subject —Anthony Trollope⟩
in·fat·u·at·ed·ly *adv* : in an infatuated manner
in·fat·u·a·tion \ən,fachə'wāshən\ *n* -s [LL *infatuation-, infatuatio*, fr. L *infatuatus* + *-ion-, -io* -ion] **1** : the act of infatuating or state of being infatuated : strong and unreasoning attachment esp. to something unworthy of attachment ⟨an ~ with the rare that is the mark of a limited understanding —D.C.Peattie⟩ ⟨a sentimentalizing and transitory ~ for India —Paul Potts⟩ ⟨American ~ with big cars and big engines —Eugene Jaderquist⟩ ⟨the victim of a ridiculous ~ —John Morrison⟩ **2** : something that infatuates : the object of an unreasoning or foolish attachment ⟨the heady ~ of speed —Ray Hare⟩ ⟨if they would turn aside from their cinquecento ~ —Norman Douglas⟩
in·fat·u·a·tor \-ˈ==,wād·ə(r)\ *n* -s : one that infatuates
in·faust \ən'fau̇st, -'fȯst\ *adj* [F or L; F *infauste*, fr. L *infaustus*, fr. *in-* ¹in- + *faustus* lucky; akin to L *favēre* to be favorable — more at FAVOR] : not favorable : UNLUCKY, UNPROPITIOUS
in·feasibility \(¦)in+\ *n* : IMPRACTICABILITY
in·feasible \(')in+\ *adj* [¹in- + *feasible*] : not feasible : IMPRACTICABLE — **in·fea·si·ble·ness** *n*
¹**infect** *adj* [ME, fr. MF or L; MF, fr. L *infectus*, past part. of *inficere*] *obs* : INFECTED
²**in·fect** \ən'fekt\ *vb* -ED/-ING/-S [ME *infecten*, fr. L *infectus*, past part. of *inficere* to stain, dye, taint, infect, fr. *in-* ²in- + *-ficere* (fr. *facere* to do, make) — more at DO] *vt* **1** : to taint with decaying matter : contaminate with a disease-producing substance, germs, or bacteria ⟨~ a lancet⟩ **2 a** : to communicate a pathogen or a disease to (an individual or organ) ⟨clouds of mosquitoes ~*ed* the unprotected troops with malaria parasites⟩ ⟨condemned liver ~*ed* with flukes⟩ **b** *of a pathogenic organism* : to invade (an individual or organ) usu. by penetration — often used only of the actual penetration of the pathogen as distinguished from its subsequent growth in the host ⟨the polio virus probably usually ~*s* man through the nasal mucous membrane⟩; compare INFECTION 2 **3** : to communicate or affect as if by some subtle contact: as **a** : to taint by communication of something noxious or pernicious ⟨he is deeply upset and manages to ~ her with a sense of guilt —*London Calling*⟩ ⟨intellectuals . . . become agents of discontent who ~ rich and poor, high and low —Irving Howe⟩ **b** : to work upon or seize upon so as to induce sympathy, belief, or support ⟨~*ed* everyone with his zeal for nature —Van Wyck Brooks⟩ ⟨an exuberance that tends to ~ the whole enterprise —E.J.Kahn⟩ **4** *obs* : DYE, STAIN **5** [by alter.] : INFEST ⟨fish ~*ed* with parasites⟩ **6** : to subject (a whole cargo of an owner) to forfeiture because a part is contraband **7** : to induce a change in quality in (the sound of a neighboring syllable) ~ *vi* : to become infected ⟨didn't pay any attention to it because I never ~ —Ernest Hemingway⟩
¹**in·fect·ant** \ən'fektənt\ *adj* [²*infect* + *-ant*] : producing infection : INFECTING ⟨~ power⟩
²**infectant** *n* -s : an agent of infection (as a bacterium or virus)
infected *adj* **1** : having undergone infection ⟨~ wound⟩ **2** : CONTAMINATED ⟨obliged to go into ~ rooms —Jane Austen⟩ — **in·fect·ed·ness** *n* -ES
in·fect·ibil·i·ty \ən,fektə'bilәd·ē\ *n* -ES : susceptibility to infection
in·fect·ible \ən'fektəbəl\ *adj* [*infect* + *-ible*] : capable of being infected
in·fec·tion \ən'fekshən\ *n* -s [ME *infeccioun*, fr. MF & LL; MF *infection*, fr. LL *infection-, infectio*, fr. L *infectus* + *-ion-, -io* -ion] **1** : the act or result of affecting or infecting injuriously: **a** : contamination or pollution of matter (as air or water) **b** : corruption of character, morals, faith, loyalty ⟨focal point of moral and political ~⟩ **2** : an act or process of infecting ⟨syphilis ~ is chiefly venereal⟩; *also* : the establishment of a pathogen in its host after invasion **3** : the state produced by the establishment of an infective agent in or on a suitable host ⟨hampered by an ~ in his foot⟩ : a contagious or infectious disease ⟨among the more serious ~*s* of childhood are scarlet fever and meningitis⟩ **4** : an infective agent (as a fungus, bacterium, or virus) : material contaminated with an infective agent and capable of causing disease **5** : the communication of emotions or qualities through example or contact ⟨from such people . . . goes forth the ~ of goodwill —W.F.Hambly⟩ ⟨always open to the ~ of the holiday mood —Mary Austin⟩ **6** : the subjecting of an entire cargo to forfeiture because of the contraband nature of part of it **7** : the influence on a speech sound of a vowel sound next following or preceding **8** : the acquisition of inductive power by embryonic cells through diffusion from adjacent organizer
infection–exhaustion psychosis *n* : any one of a group of mental disorders characterized esp. by delirium and mental confusion and occurring in connection with infections, fevers, and exhausted states
infection hypha *or* **infection thread** *n* : the hypha of a parasitic fungus that penetrates the host and establishes an infection
infection period *also* **infection stage** *n* : the period from the first evident manifestation of an infectious disease to the final host reaction — used chiefly in plant pathology
in·fec·tious \ən'fekshəs\ *adj* [*infection* + *-ous*] **1 a** : capable of causing infection : INFECTIVE ⟨a carrier remains ~ without himself showing signs of disease⟩ ⟨viruses and other ~ agents⟩ **b** : communicable by infection ⟨an ~ disease⟩ — compare CONTAGIOUS **2** : CORRUPTING, CONTAMINATING, VITIATING, DEMORALIZING ⟨fear is exceedingly ~ : children catch it from their elders —Bertrand Russell⟩ ⟨they say cowardice is ~ —R.L.Stevenson⟩ **3** : capable of being easily diffused or spread : readily communicated : CATCHING, SYMPATHETIC ⟨his own delight in his great theme is ~ —Ernest Newman⟩ ⟨~ excitement⟩ ⟨~ good humor⟩ **4** *obs* : INFECTED **5** *of contraband goods* : having the effect of subjecting the entire cargo to forfeiture — **in·fec·tious·ly** *adv* — **in·fec·tious·ness** *n* -ES
infectious abortion *n* : CONTAGIOUS ABORTION
infectious anemia *n* : a serious often fatal virus disease of horses and mules marked by intermittent fever, depression, weakness, jaundice, and mucosal hemorrhages and frequently by anemia — called also *swamp fever*
infectious bronchitis *n* **1** : a virus disease of chickens marked by inflammation of the bronchial tubes and abundant secretion of mucus interfering with respiration and causing gasping and choking that is often fatal in young birds and in adults seriously interferes with egg production — compare INFECTIOUS LARYNGOTRACHEITIS **2** : any of various infective diseases of the bronchial tubes (as in horses or cows)
infectious bulbar paralysis *n* : PSEUDORABIES
infectious chlorosis *n* : a general chlorosis or a variegation due to a virus that can be transmitted from chlorotic to normal green plants by budding, grafting, or insect vectors
infectious disease *n* : a disease caused by the entrance into and growth and multiplication in the body of bacteria, protozoans, fungi, or analogous organisms (as filterable viruses) — compare CONTAGIOUS DISEASE
infectious ectromelia *n* : MOUSEPOX
infectious equine encephalomyelitis *n* : ENCEPHALOMYELITIS
infectious hepatitis *n* **1** : an acute virus inflammation of the liver characterized by jaundice, fever, nausea, vomiting, and abdominal discomfort — called also *catarrhal jaundice, homologous serum hepatitis, serum hepatitis* **2** : WEIL'S DISEASE **3** : BLACKHEAD 3
infectious jaundice *n* **1** : INFECTIOUS HEPATITIS 1 **2** : WEIL'S DISEASE
infectious laryngotracheitis *n* : a severe highly contagious and often fatal virus disease of chickens affecting chiefly adult birds and taking the form of an inflammation of the trachea and larynx often marked by local necrosis and hemorrhage and by the formation of purulent or cheesy exudate interfering with breathing — compare INFECTIOUS BRONCHITIS, NEWCASTLE DISEASE
infectious mastitis *n* : BOVINE MASTITIS
infectious mononucleosis *n* : an acute infectious disease of unknown cause characterized by fever, malaise and prostration, swelling of lymph glands, and lymphocytosis and seen chiefly in children and young adults — called also *glandular fever, lymphadenosis*
infectious necrotic hepatitis *n* : BLACK DISEASE
infectious sinusitis *n* : a virus disease of turkeys marked by inflammation of the lining of the infraorbital sinuses resulting in great distention of the sinuses and by exudate that interferes with vision and indirectly with nutrition
infectious vaginitis *n* : EPIVAGINITIS
in·fec·tive \ən'fektiv\ *adj* [ME, fr. ML *infectivus*, fr. L *infectus* (past part. of *inficere* to stain, dye, taint, infect) + *-ivus* -ive — more at INFECT] **1** : producing infection : able to produce infection : INFECTING **2** : affecting others : INFECTIOUS — **in·fec·tive·ness** *n* -ES
in·fec·tiv·i·ty \,in,fek'tivəd·ē\ *n* -ES : the quality of being infective : the ability to produce infection; *specif* : a tendency to spread rapidly from host to host — distinguished from *virulence*
in·fec·tor \ən'fektə(r)\ *n* -s : one that infects
infects *pres 3d sing of* INFECT
in·fec·tum \ən'fektəm\ *n* -s [NL, fr. L, neut. of *infectus* undone, unfinished, fr. *in-* ¹in- + *-fectus* (fr. *factus*, past part. of *facere* to do, make) — more at DO] : an aspectual category of tenses in Latin which includes all that indicate that action or state is in progress in contrast with those tenses which indicate that action or state is completed — compare PERFECTUM
infectuous *adj* [ME, fr. L *infectus* + ME *-ous*] *obs* : INFECTIOUS
in·fecund \(')in+\ *adj* [ME *infecounde*, fr. L *infecundus*, fr. *in-* ¹in- + *fecundus* fruitful — more at FEMININE] : not fecund : UNFRUITFUL
in·fecundity \¦in+\ *n* [L *infecunditas*, fr. *infecundus* + *-itas* -ity] : lack of fecundity
infeeble *obs var of* ENFEEBLE
¹**infeed** \'=,=\ *n* [⁴*in* + *feed* (n.)] **1 a** : a feed for infeeding a tool or wheel **b** : a mechanism for feeding material into a machine ⟨bottles go into the ~ of washing machine —*Manila Times*⟩ **2** : the process of infeeding
²**infeed** \"\ *vt* [²*in* + *feed* (v.)] : to feed (a tool or wheel) into work (as on a lathe) in a direction normal to that of the axis about which the work revolves
in·feft \in'feft\ *vt* **infeft** *also* **infefted**; **infeft** *also* **infefted**; **infefting; infefts** [ME (Sc dial.) *infeften*, alter. of *enfeffen* to enfeoff — more at ENFEOFF] *Scots law* : to invest with or give symbolical possession of inheritable property — **infeftment** *n* -s
in·felicific \(¦)in+\ *adj* [¹*in-* + *felicific*] : not productive of happiness : productive of unhappiness
in·felicitous \¦in+\ *adj* [¹*in-* + *felicitous*] : not felicitous: **a** : UNFORTUNATE ⟨~ remark⟩ **b** : not appropriate in application : AWKWARD ⟨~ phrase⟩ **c** : DEFECTIVE, IMPERFECT ⟨~ typesetting due to illegible copy⟩ — **in·fe·lic·i·tous·ly** *adv* — **in·fe·lic·i·tous·ness** *n*
in·felicity \¦in+\ *n* [ME *infelicite*, fr. L *infelicitas*, fr. *infelic-, infelix* unfortunate, unhappy (fr. *in-* ¹in- + *felic-, felix* fruitful, happy) + *-itas* -ity — more at FEMININE] **1** : the quality or state of being infelicitous: **a** : UNHAPPINESS, WRETCHEDNESS, MISFORTUNE ⟨confusion and ~ of her emotions —Elinor Wylie⟩ **b** : lack of suitableness or appropriateness **2** : something (as an act or word) that is infelicitous ⟨examined for *infelicities* before printing —E.P.Cheyney⟩
infelt \'=,=\ *adj* [²*in* + *felt*] *archaic* : felt inwardly : HEARTFELT
in·feminine \(')in+\ *adj* [¹*in-* + *feminine*] : UNFEMININE
infeodation *var of* INFEUDATION
infeoff *obs var of* ENFEOFF
in·fer \R ən'fər, + *vowel* -fər·; -R -fə̄, + *suffixal vowel* -fər· *also* -fər, + *vowel in a following word* -fər· *or* -fə̄ *also* -fər\ *vb* **inferred; inferred; inferring; infers** [MF or L; MF *inferer*, fr. L *inferre* to carry or bring into, attack, enter, introduce, cause, deduce, fr. *in* ²in- + *ferre* to carry, bring — more at BEAR] *vt* **1** *obs* **a** : to bring about : PROCURE **b** : to bring upon : INFLICT **c** : CONFER, BESTOW **2** : to derive by reasoning or implication : conclude from facts or premises ⟨we see smoke and ~ fire —L.A.White⟩ : accept or derive as a consequence, conclusion, or probability ⟨task of physical science is to ~ knowledge of external objects from a set of signals passing along our nerves —A.S.Eddington⟩ ⟨the child ~*s* the existence of an environment which is not part of itself —James Jeans⟩ — compare IMPLY **3** : GUESS, SURMISE ⟨given some utterance, a person may ~ from it all sorts of things which neither the utterance nor the utterer implied —I.A. Richards⟩ ⟨as may be *inferred* from the picture, travel through this type of forest was comparatively easy —C.B.Hitchcock⟩ **4 a** : to lead to as a conclusion or consequence : involve as a normal outcome of thought ⟨democracy ~*s* such loving comradeship —Oscar Cargill⟩ **b** : to point out : INDICATE ⟨this doth ~ the zeal I had to see him —Shak.⟩ — compare IMPLY **5** : to give reason to draw an inference concerning : HINT ⟨did not take part in the debate except to ask a question *inferring* that the constitution must be changed —*Manchester Guardian Weekly*⟩ ⟨complain of the American accent, *inferring* that American culture is unworthy of notice —W.C.Greet⟩ **6** *obs* : to bring in : INTRODUCE ~ *vi* : to draw inferences ⟨men have been thinking for ages . . . have observed, *inferred*, and reasoned in all sorts of ways and to all kinds of results —John Dewey⟩
syn DEDUCE, CONCLUDE, JUDGE, GATHER: INFER indicates arriving at an opinion or coming to accept a probability on the basis of available evidence, which may be slight ⟨the population of Gloucester may readily be *inferred* from the number of houses which King found in the returns of hearth money —T.B.Macaulay⟩ ⟨your letter has just arrived and allows me to *infer* that you are as well as ever —O.W. Holmes †1935⟩ ⟨most of the material in this book was spoken before it was printed, as may perhaps be *inferred* from the style —Elmer Davis⟩ DEDUCE adds to INFER implications of ordered logical thought processes used in the study of logic to draw a specific inference from a general principle, in popular use to infer a truth from analysis of evidence ⟨for the apprehension of new elements requires a sensitive perception and familiarity with new details and cannot be *deduced* from established principles —M.R.Cohen⟩ ⟨a register at the head of the stairs on a wooden shelf. The last entry was in pencil, three weeks previous as to date, and had been written by someone with a very unsteady hand. I *deduced* from this that the management was not overparticular —Raymond Chandler⟩ CONCLUDE may indicate attaining to a fact, truth, or belief after ordered consideration following through with necessary consequences of evidence weighed or facts observed ⟨do not *conclude* that all state activities will be state monopolies —G.B.Shaw⟩ ⟨*concluded* that all of the senses were of equal value in obtaining knowledge of the world, and that with one sense alone "the understanding has as many faculties as with the five joined together" —S.F. Mason⟩ JUDGE stresses careful, critical examination of evidence in attempting to arrive at a wise or fit conclusion ⟨there is a unifying as well as a discriminating phase of judgment — technically known as synthesis in distinction from analysis. This unifying phase, even more than the analytic, is a function of the creative response of the individual who *judges* —John Dewey⟩ ⟨the lawfulness or unlawfulness of taking part in deeds of violence must be *judged* on the merits of each particular case —W.R.Inge⟩ GATHER implies conclusion by reflection, but not pondering on impressions formed from cumulative evidence ⟨piecing together classical tradition and references in Egyptian and Hebrew records, we *gather* that for some three centuries onwards from 1600 B.C. Phoenicia was a dependency of the Pharaohs —Edward Clodd⟩ ⟨that I myself believe there may be more than one kind of good poetry might, I think, have been *gathered* from that paragraph of mine which Professor Grierson then quotes —F.R.Leavis⟩
in·fer·able *also* **in·fer·ible** *or* **in·fer·ri·ble** \-'fərəbəl *also* 'inf(ə)rə- *or* ən'fə̄rə-\ *adj* : capable of being inferred ⟨portion most used by travelers . . . for reasons ~ from the map —R.H.Brown⟩ — **in·fer·ably** \-blē\ *adv*
in·fer·ence \'inf(ə)rən(t)s *also* -fərn-\ *n* -s [ML *inferentia*, fr. L *inferent-, inferens* (pres. part. of *inferre*) + *-ia* -y] **1** : the act or process of inferring : the act of passing from one or more propositions, statements, or judgments considered as true to another the truth of which is believed to follow from that of the former ⟨this reasoning . . . is . . . stronger than some modern ~*s* of science —Henry Adams⟩ ⟨~*s* are made, but implications are discovered⟩ — see IMMEDIATE INFERENCE, MEDIATE INFERENCE; compare DEDUCTION 1, INDUCTION 2b, TRANSFORMATION RULE **2** : something that is inferred : DEDUCTION 2; *esp* : a proposition or conclusion arrived at by inferring ⟨the following ~*s* may be fairly drawn from these facts⟩ **3** : the premises and conclusion that represent a process of inferring or that form the determinants of a belief ⟨the conviction that action should be based not on shadowy ~ . . . but on solid fact —C.W.Eliot⟩
in·fer·en·tial \¦infə¦renchəl\ *adj* [ML *inferentia* + E *-al*] **1** : relating to, involving, or resembling inference ⟨~ judgment⟩ ⟨~ procedure⟩ **2** : deduced or deducible by inference ⟨~ evidence of his departure⟩
in·fer·en·tial·ly \-chəlē, -li\ *adv* : by way of inference : through inference ⟨answers to these questions are only ~ contained in this latest biography —Bosley Crowther⟩
¹**in·fe·rior** \ən'firēə(r), -'fēr-, (')in¦f-\ *adj* [ME, fr. L, comp. of *inferus* low, situated beneath — more at UNDER] **1** : situated lower down or nearer what is regarded as the bottom or base : LOWER, NETHER ⟨~ latitudes⟩ ⟨~ rock strata⟩ **2 a** : of lower degree or rank ⟨was a member of an ~ caste⟩ ⟨a major is ~ to a colonel⟩ **b** : of low degree or rank ⟨~ classes of society⟩ **3 a** : of less importance, value, or merit : of poorer quality ⟨the child . . . considers himself ~ to the adult figures —G.S.Blum⟩ ⟨declined to an ~ position among the world powers⟩ ⟨~ chess move⟩ ⟨easily beat his ~ opponent⟩ **b** *of a railroad train* : required to yield right of way in the absence of specific orders **c** : of poor quality : MEDIOCRE : SECOND-RATE ⟨furniture of ~ workmanship⟩ ⟨~ pupil⟩ ⟨~ violinist⟩ **4 a** *of a part of the upright body* : situated below another and esp. another similar part — compare SUPERIOR 6a ⟨~ vena cava⟩ ⟨~ meatus of the nose⟩ ⟨~ rectus muscle of the eye⟩ **b** *of a part of the quadrupedal body* (1) : situated in a more posterior position (2) : situated more ventrad than another and esp. another similar part : VENTRAL **5** *of a part of a plant* **a** : situated below another organ: (1) *of a calyx* : free from the ovary (2) *of an ovary* : adnate to the calyx or other floral envelope **b** : ABAXIAL **c** : situated low on the stipe **6** : SUBSCRIPT ⟨~ letter⟩ ⟨~ number⟩ — used usu. postpositionally ⟨for "H_2O" read "H, 2 ~, O"⟩; contrasted with *superior*
²**inferior** \"\ *n* -s **1** : a person or thing inferior to another (as in worth, status, or importance) ⟨disdainful of his social ~*s*⟩ **2** : a subscript character (as in printing)
inferior alveolar artery *n* : a branch of the internal maxillary artery that is distributed to the mucous membrane of the mouth and through the mandibular canal to the teeth of the lower jaw
inferior alveolar canal *n* : MANDIBULAR CANAL
inferior alveolar nerve *n* : a branch of the mandibular division of the fifth cranial nerve that passes into the mandibular canal to the teeth of the lower jaw
inferior alveolar vein *n* : the vein accompanying the inferior alveolar artery
inferior colliculus *n* : either member of the posterior and lower pair of quadrigeminate bodies together constituting one of the lower coordinating centers for hearing
inferior conjunction *n* : a conjunction in which a lesser or secondary celestial body passes nearer the observer than the primary body around which it revolves ⟨*inferior conjunction* of Venus to the sun⟩ — see CONFIGURATION illustration
inferior court *n* : a court having limited and specified rather than general jurisdiction — compare SUPERIOR COURT
inferior good *n* : a commodity the consumption of which decreases as its price declines or as the income of consumers rises because of the increased income available to buy preferred though more expensive commodities
in·fe·ri·or·i·ty \(,)in,firē'ȯrəd·ē, -fēr-, -'är-, -ətē, -i\ *n* -ES [MF or ML; MF *inferiorité*, fr. ML *inferioritat-, inferioritas*, fr. L *inferior* + *-itat-, -itas* -ity — more at INFERIOR] **1** : the state of being inferior : a lower state or condition ⟨making you feel her superiority, your ~; how poor she was; how rich you were —Virginia Woolf⟩ **2** : sense of being inferior ⟨adolescence's indecisive shames and *inferiorities* —Ruth Park⟩
inferiority complex *n* [prob. trans. of G *minderwertigkeitskomplex*] : an acute sense of personal inferiority resulting either in timidity or through overcompensation in exaggerated aggressiveness; *broadly* : sense of being inferior or at a disadvantage : lack of assurance
inferior laryngeal *n* : a branch of the vagus nerve that supplies most of the muscles of the larynx
in·fe·ri·or·ly *adv* **1** : in an inferior manner or to an inferior degree **2** : in a lower position
inferior maxillary nerve *n* : MANDIBULAR NERVE
inferior oblique *n* : OBLIQUE 2b(2)
inferior olive *n* : a large gray nucleus that forms a lateral eminence on the medulla oblongata and has connections with the thalamus, cerebellum, and spinal cord
inferior planet *n* : a planet whose orbit lies within that of the earth
inferior tide *n* : the tide corresponding to the moon's transit of the lower meridian
inferior valve *n* : the valve by which certain bivalve mollusks become attached to an object or surface
¹**in·fer·nal** \ən'fərnᵊl, -'fə̄n-, -'fəin-\ *adj* [ME, fr. OF, fr. LL *infernalis*, fr. *infernus* hell (fr. L *infernus* lower, lying beneath, of the lower regions) + L *-alis* -al; akin to L *inferus* low, situated beneath — more at UNDER] **1** : relating or belonging to a nether world of the dead and of earth deities : CHTHONIC — compare HADES **2 a** : relating to or inhabiting hell ⟨~ fires⟩ ⟨~ spirit⟩ **b** : resembling or suitable to hell or the character of its inhabitants : HELLISH, DIABOLICAL, FIENDISH ⟨~ scheme⟩ ⟨~ wickedness⟩ **3** : DAMNABLE, DAMNED ⟨~ nuisance⟩ ⟨~ gadget⟩ ⟨~ racket⟩ — **in·fer·nal·ly** \-ᵊlē, -ᵊli\ *adv*
²**infernal** \"\ *n* -s **1** *archaic* : an infernal person or thing — usu. used in pl. **2 infernals** *pl, obs* : the infernal regions : HELL
infernal blue *n* : SCOTCH BLUE
infernal machine *n* : a machine or apparatus maliciously designed to explode and destroy life or property : a concealed or disguised bomb
in·fer·no \ən'fər(,)nō, -'fə̄(,)-, -'fəi(,)-\ *n* -s [It, hell (esp. as the title of one of the books of the *Divina Commedia*, long allegorical & philosophical poem by Dante Alighieri †1321 Ital. poet), fr. LL *infernus* — more at INFERNAL] **1** : a place or a state of torment and suffering ⟨the ~ of the passions —Edmund Wilson⟩ ⟨~ of war⟩ ⟨~ of seething misery and poverty —G.B.Shaw⟩ **2** : a place that resembles or suggests hell in being dark, noisy, chaotic, lawless ⟨the factory seemed an ~ of dirt and noise⟩ ⟨plunge into the ~ of the engine room —Joseph Whitehill⟩ **3** : intense heat ⟨roaring ~ of the blast furnace⟩ : CONFLAGRATION ⟨girders melted in the ~⟩
infero- *comb form* [L *inferus* low, situated beneath — more at UNDER] **1** : on the underside ⟨*infero*branchiate⟩ **2** : below and ⟨*infero*lateral⟩
in·fe·ro·branchiate \¦infə(,)rō+\ *adj* [*infero-* + *branchiate*] : having the gills on the sides under the mantle margin ⟨~ mollusk⟩
inferred *past of* INFER
in·fer·rer \ən'fər·ə(r) *also* -'fə̄rə(r\ *n* -s : one that infers
inferrible *var of* INFERABLE
inferring *pres part of* INFER
infers *pres 3d sing of* INFER
in·fertile \(')in, ən+\ *adj* [MF, fr. LL *infertilis*, fr. L *in-* ¹in- + *fertilis* fertile — more at FERTILE] : not fertile or productive : BARREN ⟨~ egg⟩ ⟨~ soil⟩ **syn** see STERILE
in·fertility \,in+\ *n* [F *infertilité*, fr. LL *infertilitat-, infertilitas*, fr. *infertilis* infertile + *-itat-, -itas* -ity] : the quality or state of being infertile : BARRENNESS, STERILITY
in·fest \ən'fest\ *vt* -ED/-ING/-S [MF *infester*, fr. L *infestare*, fr. *infestus* hostile — more at DARE] **1** *archaic* : to attack or harass persistently : WORRY, ANNOY **2 a** : to visit persistently or in large numbers : OVERRUN, HAUNT ⟨street ~*ed* with children⟩ ⟨lawn ~*ed* with weeds⟩ ⟨~*ed* with ghosts and poltergeists⟩ **b** : to live in or on as a parasite — used esp. of metazoan parasites of animals ⟨the flea that ~*s* cats⟩ ⟨horses ~*ed* with worms⟩
in·fes·tant \-tənt\ *n* -s : one that infests: as **a** : a visible parasite **b** : any of the smaller organisms (as clothes moth,

flour beetle, vinegar eel) that attack fabrics or processed foods or liquids

in·fes·ta·tion \ˌin(ˌ)feˈstāshən\ *n* -s [MF, fr. LL *infestation-, infestatio*, fr. *infestatus* (past part. of *infestare* to infest) + *-ion-, -io* -ion] **1** : the act of infesting ⟨protecting grain against ~⟩ : PLAGUE, ANNOYANCE **2** : something that infests : SWARM ⟨~ of grasshoppers⟩ **3** : the state of being infested esp. with metazoan parasites in or on an animal or plant body

¹infester *vt* [²*in-* + *fester* (v.)] *obs* : to cause to fester

²in·fest·er \ənˈfestə(r)\ *n* -s [*infest* + *-er*] : one that infests

in·fes·tious \ənˈfes(h)chəs\ *adj* [*infest* + *-ious* (as in *infectious*)] : INFESTING ⟨to certain ~ bipeds any graft is legitimate —H.L.Ickes⟩

¹in·fes·tive \ənˈfestiv\ *adj* [*infest* + *-ive*] : likely to infest : TROUBLESOME ⟨~ weeds⟩

²in·festive \(ˈ)in+\ *adj* [¹*in-* + L *festivus* festive — more at FESTIVE] : not festive : MIRTHLESS

in·festivity \ˌin+\ *n* [¹*in-* + *festivity*] : lack of festivity : MIRTHLESSNESS, DULLNESS

in·fest·ment \ənˈfestmənt\ *n* -s *archaic* : INFESTATION

infestuous *adj* [*infest* + *-uous* (as in *infectuous*)] *obs* : MISCHIEVOUS, HARMFUL

in·feu·da·tion *also* **in·feo·da·tion** \ˌinfyüˈdāshən\ *n* -s [ME *infeodacioun*, fr. ML *infeudation-, infeudatio, infeodation-, infeodatio*, fr. *infeudatus, infeodatus* (past part. of *infeudare, infeodare* to enfeoff, fr. *in-* ²in- + *feudum, feodum* feoff) + L *-ion-, -io* -ion — more at FEUD] **1** : ENFEOFFMENT **2** : a granting of tithes to laymen

in·fib·u·late \ənˈfibyəˌlāt\ *vt* -ED/-ING/-S [L *infibulatus*, past part. of *infibulare* to infibulate, practice infibulation upon, fr. *in-* ²in- + *fibulare* to pin, buckle together, fr. *fibula* — more at FIBULA] : to fasten with or as if with a buckle or clasp

in·fib·u·la·tion \(ˌ)inˌfibyəˈlāshən\ *n* -s [L *infibulatus* + E *-ion*] : an act or practice of fastening by ring, clasp, or stitches the labia majora in girls and the prepuce in boys in order to prevent sexual intercourse

in·fi·cete \ˌinfəˈsēt\ *adj* [L *inficetus, infacetus*, fr. *in-* ¹in- + *facetus* courteous, elegant, witty, facetious] : not witty : HEAVY-FOOTED

¹in·fi·del \ˈinfədᵊl, -əˌdel\ *n* -s [MF *infidele*, adj. & n., fr. LL *infidelis*, fr. L, untrustworthy, unfaithful, fr. *in-* ¹in- + *fidelis* faithful — more at FEAL] **1** : one that is not a Christian or opposes Christianity **2 a** : an unbeliever in respect to a particular religion **b** : one that acknowledges no religious belief — distinguished from *heretic* **3** : one that does not believe (as in something specified or understood) : SKEPTIC, DISBELIEVER

²infidel \"\ *adj* [MF *infidele*] **1 a** : not holding the faith of a given religion; *esp* : non-Christian ⟨the ~ nations⟩ ⟨an ~ Saracen⟩ **b** : opposing or traitorous to Christianity ⟨~ writers⟩ ⟨an ~ sect⟩ **2** : relating to or characteristic of unbelief or unbelievers ⟨~ tract⟩

in·fi·del·ic \ˌinfəˈdelik\ *or* **in·fi·del·i·cal** \-ləkəl\ *adj* : INFIDEL 2

in·fi·del·i·ty \ˌinfəˈdeləd·ē, -ətē, -i *sometimes* -ˌfīˈ-\ *n* [MF *infidelité*, fr. LL & L; LL *infidelitat-, infidelitas* disbelief in Christianity, heathenism, fr. L, unfaithfulness, fr. *infidelis* + *-itat-, -itas* -ity] **1** : lack of faith or belief in a religion : state or character of being infidel **2** *archaic* : SKEPTICISM, INCREDULITY **3 a** : breach of trust : unfaithfulness to a charge or a moral obligation : DISLOYALTY, PERFIDY **b** : marital unfaithfulness or an instance of it ⟨made no secret of his many *infidelities*⟩ **4** : failure to reproduce (as a text or a model) exactly; *also* : an instance of such failure ⟨numerous *infidelities* in the translation⟩ ⟨~ in size also made printing from . . . plastic plates a hazard —*Graphic Arts Rev.*⟩

infield \ˈ=ˌ=\ *n* [⁴*in* + *field*] **1 a** : a field near a farmhouse **b** : land regularly manured and used year after year for the same crop (as hay or fruit) **2 a** (1) : the area of a cricket field relatively near the wickets (2) : a fieldsman stationed there — contrasted with *outfield* **b** (1) : the area of a baseball or softball field enclosed by the three bases and home plate : DIAMOND (2) : the defensive positions comprising first base, second base, shortstop, and third base ⟨a strong ~⟩ — contrasted with *outfield* **3** : the area enclosed by a racetrack or running track

in·field·er \-də(r)\ *n* **1** : a fielder stationed in the infield in cricket **2** : a baseball player who covers a position in the infield

infield fly *n* : a fair fly ball other than a line drive or an attempted bunt that can be handled by an infielder and that is declared an automatic out if it occurs at a time when there are less than two outs and when runners are occupying first and second or first, second, and third bases

in·fields·man \-l(d)zmən\ *n* : INFIELDER 1

in fi·eri \(ˈ)inˈfēərē\ *adj* [ML] **1** : being in process of accomplishment : PENDING **2** : beginning to have existence : not yet completely formed

infighter \ˈ=ˌ==\ *n* [⁴*in* + *fighter*] : one that practices or is skilled at infighting ⟨able political ~⟩

infighting \ˈ=ˌ==\ *n* -s [⁴*in* + *fighting*] **1 a** : fighting or boxing at close range ⟨his bowie . . . was the unexcelled weapon for ~ —*Amer. Guide Series: Ark.*⟩ **b** : fighting (as between rivals) that is not openly acknowledged or conducted **2** : fighting without rules : rough-and-tumble fighting

infill \ˈ=ˌ=\ *vt* [²*in-* + *fill*] : to fill in ⟨fractures . . . broadened by ice growth within them . . . and then ~*ed* from above as the ice melted —*Jour. of Geol.*⟩

infilling \ˈ=ˌ==\ *n* : material used (as in building) to fill in space between structural members ⟨steel skeleton with an ~ of brickwork⟩

infilter \=ˈ==\ *vi* [²*in* + *filter*] : to filter or sift in

¹in·fil·trate \ənˈfilˌtrāt *also* ˈin(ˌ)fil- *sometimes* -fəl-, *usu* -ād·+V\ *vb* [²*in-* + *filtrate*] *vt* **1** : to cause something, (as a liquid) to enter by penetrating the pores of ⟨~ tissue with a local anesthetic⟩ **2** : to pass into or through (a substance) by filtering or permeating **3** : to advance (troops) by sending single men or small groups through gaps or weak points in the enemy line **4** : to enter or become established in (as an organization) gradually or unobtrusively and in large numbers ⟨parties which labor leaders accused of being . . . infiltrated by extreme nationalists —Clifton Daniel⟩ ~ *vi* **1** : to enter, permeate, or pass through a substance by filtering ⟨many Hebrew idioms have *infiltrated*, in translated forms, into various Jewish dialects —William Chomsky⟩ **2** *of troops* : to advance or to enter a hostile area by proceeding singly or in small dispersed groups ⟨tend rather to ~ to supply lines and rear installations —*Cavalry Jour.*⟩

²infiltrate \"\ *n* : something that infiltrates; *specif* : a substance that passes into the bodily tissues and forms an abnormal accumulation

in·fil·tra·tion \ˌin(ˌ)filˈtrāshən *sometimes* -ˌfəl-\ *n* **1** : the act or process of infiltrating ⟨~ of water through a gravel bed⟩ ⟨~ of air into a building⟩ **2** : something that infiltrates ⟨fatty ~⟩ ⟨anesthetic drug ~⟩ **3** : a gradual penetration by scattered units ⟨socialist ~ into a labor union⟩ ⟨~ of settlers into new territory⟩

infiltration anesthesia *n* : anesthesia of an operative site accomplished by injection of anesthetics under the skin

infiltration capacity *n* : the rate at which a soil can absorb water

infiltration vein *n* : a vein formed in country rock by interstitial deposition from percolating waters — compare IMPREGNATION 2a

in·fil·tra·tive \ˈinfəlˌtrād·iv, ənˈfiltrəd-\ *adj* : relating to or characterized by infiltration

in·fil·tra·tor \ənˈfilˌtrād·ə(r), ˈinfəl-\ *n* -s : one that infiltrates ⟨if the first human agents that come into contact with a given culture . . . are traders, then economic values are the first ~s —P.A.Sorokin⟩

in·fil·tree \ˌinfəlˈtrē, ənˌfilˈtrē\ *n* -s [¹*infiltrate* + *-ee*] : one who has entered another country or territory in a manner resembling military infiltration ⟨American policy to provide temporary food and housing to all ~s —Samuel Lubell⟩

in·fil·trom·e·ter \ˌin(ˌ)filˈträməd·ə(r)\ *n* -s [*infiltration* + *-o-* + *-meter*] : an apparatus for measuring the rate at which a soil can absorb water

in·fi·ma species \ˈinfəmə-\ *n* [L] : the lowest species in a classification or logical division — compare TREE OF PORPHYRY

infin *abbr* infinitive

¹in·fi·nite \ˈinfənə̇t *sometimes* -fəˌnīt *sometimes as opposed to "finite"* (ˈ)inˈfīˌnīt *or* ənˈfīˌnīt; *usu* |d.+V\ *adj* [ME *infinit*, fr. MF or L; MF *infinit*, fr. L *infinitus*, fr. *in-* ¹in- + *finitus* limited, finite — more at FINITE] **1** : being without limits of any kind : subject to no limitation or external determination ⟨philosophy compels faith in real personality, finite and relative in man, ~ and absolute in nature —F.A.Christie⟩ **2 a** : having no end : extending indefinitely ⟨speculate and wonder as to the structure of the universe, whether it is bounded or ~ —W.V.Houston⟩ ⟨~ duration⟩ **b** : having innumerable parts : capable of endless division or distinction within itself ⟨electrophones capable of ~ gradations of pitch —Robert Domington⟩ **3** : having no limit in power, capacity, knowledge, or excellence : immeasurably or inconceivably great : BOUNDLESS ⟨~ mercy⟩ ⟨~ wisdom⟩ ⟨~ patience⟩ ⟨~ discretion⟩ **4 a** : indefinitely large or extensive : indefinite in number : IMMEASURABLE **b** : VAST, IMMENSE **c** : ENDLESS, INEXHAUSTIBLE ⟨~ ingenuity of man —Mary Webb⟩ **5** *pre-Socratic philosophy* : constituting the matrix or an ingredient of formed and determined reality **6** *of a verb form* : having neither person, number, nor mood **7 a** : not finite : extending or lying beyond any preassigned value however large ⟨the number of positive numbers is ~⟩ **b** : extending to infinity ⟨~ plane surface⟩ ⟨~ branch of a curve⟩ **c** : having the same power as a proper subset of itself : capable of being put into a one-to-one correspondence with a subset of itself — used of a mathematical aggregate — **in·fi·nite·ly** *adv* — **in·fi·nite·ness** *n*

²infinite \"\ *n* : something that is infinite **a** : boundless space or duration : INFINITY **b** : an incalculable or very great number ⟨an ~ of possibilities⟩ **c** : an infinite quantity or magnitude

infinite canon *n* : CIRCULAR CANON 1

infinite integral *n* : an improper integral having one or both of its limits infinite

infinite proposition *n* : a logical proposition that has an indefinite negative predicate

infinite regress *n* : an endless chain of reasoning leading backward by interpolating a third entity between any two entities — compare THIRD MAN

infinite series *n* : an endless succession of terms or of factors proceeding according to some mathematical law

¹in·fin·i·tes·i·mal \ˌinˌfinəˈtesəməl, -tezə- *sometimes* -sm- *or* -zm-\ *n* -s [NL *infinitesimus* infinite in rank (fr. L *infinitus* infinite + *-esimus*, ordinal suffix + E *-al* — more at INFINITE] **1** : a function that can be made arbitrarily close to zero **2** : an infinitesimal quantity

²infinitesimal \ˌ;=ˌ==ˈ=(=)=\ *adj* **1** : capable of being made arbitrarily close to zero **2** : immeasurably or incalculably small : very minute — **in·fin·i·tes·i·mal·ly** \-səməlē, -zəmə-ˌli *sometimes* -sməl- *or* -zməl- *or* -səml- *or* -zəml-\ *adv* — **in·fin·i·tes·i·mal·ness** \-səməlnə̇s, -zəm- *sometimes* -sm- *or* -zm-\ *n* -ES

infinitesimal calculus *n* : either differential calculus or integral calculus

in·fin·i·tes·i·mal·ism \ˌ;=ˌ==ˈ=(=)məˌlizəm\ *n* -s : a doctrine that the more a drug is diluted the more potent it becomes

in·fin·i·tes·i·mal·i·ty \-ˌtesəˈmaləd·ē\ *n* -ES : the quality or state of being infinitesimal

infinite term *n* : an indefinite term in a logical proposition

in·fin·i·ti·val \(ˌ)inˌfinəˈtīvəl, ənˌ-\ *adj* : relating to the infinitive — **in·fin·i·ti·val·ly** \-əlē\ *adv*

¹in·fin·i·tive \ənˈfinəd·iv, -ətiv\ *adj* [LL *infinitivus*, fr. L *infinitus* infinite + *-ivus* -ive — more at INFINITE] : formed with the infinitive ⟨~ phrase⟩ — **in·fin·i·tive·ly** \-əvlē, -li\ *adv*

²infinitive \"\ *n* -s : an infinite verb form normally identical in English with the first person singular that performs certain functions of a noun and at the same time displays certain characteristics (as association with objects and adverbial modifiers) of a verb and is used with *to* (as "*to err* is human"; "I asked him *to go*") except with auxiliary and certain other verbs (as "he *can see*"; "let me *go*"; "no one saw him *leave*")

in·fin·i·tize \ənˈfinəˌtīz\ *vt* -ED/-ING/-S [¹*infinite* + *-ize*] : to make infinite : make free of finite limitations ⟨man's anxious effort to deny his finitude and to ~ himself by the perverse use of his freedom in pride —Will Herberg⟩

in·fin·i·tude \ənˈfinəˌtüd, -əˌtyüd\ *n* [prob. fr. F, fr. MF, fr. *infinit* infinite] **1** : the quality or state of being infinite : INFINITENESS **2** : something that is infinite; *esp* : a real as distinct from an ideal or theoretical infinity ⟨~ of outer space⟩ ⟨~ of time⟩ **3** : an infinite number : an innumerable quantity

in·fin·i·ty \ənˈfinəd·ē, -ətē, -i\ *n* -ES [ME *infinite*, fr. MF *infinité*, fr. L *infinitat-, infinitas*, fr. *infinitus* infinite + *-itas* -ity] **1 a** : the quality of being infinite **b** : that which is infinite : unlimited extent of time, space, or quantity : BOUNDLESSNESS ⟨there cannot be more *infinities* than one; for one of them would limit the other —Walter Raleigh⟩ **2** : unlimited capacity, energy, excellence, or knowledge ⟨~ of God's power⟩ **3** : an indefinitely great number or amount ⟨~ of stars⟩ **4 a** : a nonexistent limit of a function that can be made to become and remain numerically larger than any preassigned value — symbol ∞ **b** : a nonexistent part of a magnitude that lies beyond any part whose distance from a given reference position is finite — symbol ∞ **c** : a transfinite number **5** : a distance so great that the rays of light from a point source at that distance may be regarded as parallel

¹in·firm \(ˈ)inˈfərm, ənˈf-, -fə̄m,-fəim\ *adj* [ME *infirme*, fr. L *infirmus, infirmis*, fr. *in-* ¹in- + *firmus* strong, firm — more at FIRM] **1** : not strong or sound physically : of poor or deteriorated vitality esp. as a result of age : FEEBLE ⟨~ body⟩ ⟨support of the poor, the insane, and the ~ —Calvin Coolidge⟩ **2** : weak of mind, will, or character : FRAIL, IRRESOLUTE, VACILLATING ⟨~ judgment⟩ ⟨~ of purpose: give me the daggers —Shak.⟩ **3** : not solid or stable : INSECURE, PRECARIOUS ⟨rendered this agreeable assumption . . . permanently ~ —Berton Roueché⟩ **syn** see WEAK

²in·firm \ənˈf-\ *vt* -ED/-ING/-S [ME *infirmen*, fr. L *infirmare*, fr. *infirmus* infirm] **1** *obs* : to make infirm : deprive of strength : WEAKEN **2 a** : to make doubtful or challenge the validity of **b** : INVALIDATE ⟨either to confirm or to ~ allegations of fact⟩ — **in·firm·able** \-məbəl\ *adj*

in·fir·ma·rer \ənˈfərmərər\ *n* -s [ME, prob. fr. ML *infirmaria, infirmarium* + ME *-er*] : INFIRMARIAN

in·fir·ma·ress \-mərə̇s\ *n* -ES : a female infirmarian

in·fir·mar·i·an \ˌinfə(r)ˈma(a)rēən\ *n* -s : a person having charge of an infirmary (as in a monastic institution)

in·fir·ma·ry \ənˈfərm(ə)rē, -fə̄m-, -fəim-, -ri\ *n* -ES [ML *infirmarium, infirmaria*, fr. L *infirmus* infirm + *-arium, -aria* -ary] : a hospital or place where the infirm or sick are lodged for treatment; *esp* : a building or part of a building for the sick or injured members of an institution ⟨convent ~⟩

in·fir·ma·tion \ˌinfə(r)ˈmāshən\ *n* -s [L *infirmation-, infirmatio*, fr. *infirmatus* (past part. of *infirmare* to infirm) + *-ion-, -io* -ion] : the process of infirming or making invalid — opposed to *confirmation*

in·fir·mi·ty \ənˈfərməd·ē, -fə̄m-, -fəim-, -ətē, -i\ *n* -ES [ME *infirmite*, fr. L *infirmitas*, fr. *infirmus* infirm + *-itas* -ity — more at INFIRM] **1** : the quality or state of being infirm : FEEBLENESS, FRAILTY **2 a** : an unsound, unhealthy, or debilitated state : DISEASE, MALADY ⟨~ of body⟩ ⟨~ of mind⟩ **b** : a defect of personality or weakness of the will : FAILING, FOIBLE ⟨a friend should bear his friend's *infirmities* —Shak.⟩ ⟨fame . . . that last ~ of noble mind —John Milton⟩

in·firm·ly *adv* : in an infirm manner : FEEBLY, INSECURELY

in·firm·ness *n* : the quality or state of being infirm

¹in·fix \ˈ(ˈ)inˈfiks, ənˈ-\ *vt* [L *infixus*, past part. of *infigere* to drive in, fasten in, fr. *in-* ²in- + *figere* to fasten, pierce — more at DIKE] **1** : to fasten or fix by piercing or thrusting in ⟨and deep within her heart ~*ed* the wound —John Dryden⟩ **2** : INSTILL, INCULCATE, IMPRESS ⟨~ an idea in a pupil's mind⟩ **3** : to insert (a sound or letter) as an infix **syn** see IMPLANT

²in·fix \ˈinˌfiks\ *n* -ES : a derivational or inflectional affix appearing in the body of a word or base rather than at its beginning or end (as Sanskrit *-n-* in *vindami* "I know" as contrasted with *vid* "to know"; English *stand* as contrasted with *stood*) ⟨~*es* are sometimes inserted in the Hebrew word in order to lend it a different shade of meaning —William Chomsky⟩ — compare PREFIX

in·fix·a·tion \ˌin(ˌ)fikˈsāshən\ *also* **in·fix·ion** \ənˈfikshən\ *n* -s **1** : the process of infixing **2** : the state of being infixed

infl *abbr* **1** inflammable **2** inflorescence **3** influence; influenced

in·flame \ənˈflām\ *also* **en·flame** \en-\ *vb* [ME *enflamen, inflamen*, fr. MF *enflamer, enflammer*, fr. L *inflammare*, fr. *in-* ²in- + *flammare* to flame, fr. *flamma* flame — more at FLAME] *vt* **1** : to set on fire : cause to burn, flame, or glow : KINDLE **2** : to excite (as passion or appetite) to an excessive or unnatural action or heat : INTENSIFY, ROUSE ⟨*inflamed* mob of religious partisans —Robert Trumbull⟩ **3 a** : to provoke to anger or rage : EXASPERATE, IRRITATE, INCENSE, ENRAGE **b** : to cause to redden or grow hot from anger or excitement ⟨had been so careful to irritate and then to ~ him —Ngaio Marsh⟩ ⟨face *inflamed* with passion⟩ **4** : to cause inflammation in (bodily tissue) : produce abnormal heat in or swelling of ⟨~ the eyes⟩ ~ *vi* **1** : to burst into flame **2** : to become excited or angered **3** : to become affected with inflammation

inflamed *adj* [fr. past part. of *inflame*] *heraldry* : represented as burning or as adorned with tongues of flame

in·flam·er \-mə(r)\ *n* : one that inflames

in·flam·ing·ly *adv* : in an inflaming manner

in·flam·ma·bil·i·ty \(ˌ)inˌflaməˈbiləd·ē, ən-, -ətē, -i\ *n* : the quality or state of being inflammable : tendency to ignite readily

¹in·flam·ma·ble \ənˈflaməbəl\ *adj* [F or ML; F, fr. ML *inflammabilis*, fr. L *inflammare* to inflame + *-abilis* -able] **1** : capable of being easily set on fire and burning violently : FLAMMABLE **2** : easily inflamed, excited, or angered : IRASCIBLE ⟨~ temper⟩ — **in·flam·ma·ble·ness** *n* -ES — **in·flam·ma·bly** \-blē, -li\ *adv*

²inflammable \"\ *n* : an inflammable substance : FLAMMABLE

inflammable air *n*, *archaic* : HYDROGEN

inflammable cinnabar *n* : IDRIALITE

in·flam·ma·tion \ˌinfləˈmāshən\ *n* [L *inflammation-, inflammatio*, fr. *inflammatus* (past part. of *inflammare* to inflame) + *-ion-, -io* -ion — more at INFLAME] **1** : the act of inflaming or the state of being inflamed ⟨impossible to distinguish an ~ from an explosion by the amount of violence produced —*Gaseous Fuels*⟩ ⟨~ of nationalism precipitated the next great war —Hans Kohn⟩ **2** : a local response to cellular injury (as by infection or trauma) characterized by capillary dilatation, leukocytic infiltration, heat, and commonly pain and serving as a primary mechanism for control of noxious agents and elimination of damaged tissue

in·flam·ma·tive \ənˈflaməd·iv\ *adj* [L *inflammatus* + E *-ive*] : INFLAMMATORY

in·flam·ma·to·ri·ly \(ˌ)inˌflaməˈtōrəlē, ən-, -tȯr-, -li\ *adv* : in an inflammatory manner : so as to inflame

in·flam·ma·to·ry \ənˈflaməˌtōrē, -tȯr-, -ri\ *adj* [L *inflammatus* + E *-ory*] **1** : tending to inflame or excite the senses **2** : tending to excite anger, animosity, disorder, or tumult : SEDITIOUS ⟨~ speech⟩ **3** : of, relating to, or marked by inflammation ⟨an ~ response⟩ ⟨an ~ process⟩

¹in·flat·able \ənˈflād·əbəl\ *adj* [²*inflate* + *-able*] : capable of being inflated

²inflatable \"\ *n* -s : a toy or plaything capable of being inflated

¹in·flate \ənˈflāt, *usu* -ād·+V\ *adj* [ME *inflat*, fr. L *inflatus*, past part.] *archaic* : INFLATED

²inflate \"\ *vb* -ED/-ING/-S [L *inflatus*, past part. of *inflare*, fr. *in-* ²in- + *flare* to blow — more at BLOW] *vt* **1** : to swell or distend with air or gas ⟨~ a balloon⟩ — opposed to *deflate* **2** : to puff up : ELATE ⟨~ one with pride⟩ **3** : to expand or increase abnormally or improperly : extend imprudently; *esp* : to increase (the volume of money and credit) so that a general rise in the price level occurs ⟨deliberately *inflating* the currency⟩ ~ *vi* : to undergo inflation : fill with or as if with air : DISTEND **syn** see EXPAND

inflated *adj* **1** : distended with air or gas **2** : TURGID, BOMBASTIC, POMPOUS ⟨~ style⟩ : EXAGGERATED ⟨~ statements are made without anyone being able to check them —G.A. Craig⟩ **3** : expanded abnormally or unjustifiably in volume ⟨~ currency⟩ or level ⟨~ prices⟩ **4** : hollow and distended ⟨~ stem⟩ ⟨~ capsule⟩ : open and swelled out or enlarged ⟨~ perianth⟩ : BLADDERY

syn INFLATED, FLATULENT, TUMID, and TURGID all mean filled with something insubstantial, as air or gas, or something that causes usu. abnormal swelling or distention. INFLATED implies a blowing up to the point of tautness of surface or empty distention ⟨an *inflated* balloon⟩ or, figuratively, a stretching, expanding, heightening, or puffing up by artificial or empty means ⟨*inflated* rhetoric⟩ ⟨an *inflated* speech⟩ ⟨an *inflated* opinion of oneself⟩ FLATULENT, applying chiefly to persons affected by excessive distention by gas of the stomach or bowels, can be extended to apply to anything that is empty or lacking substance but that gives the transparent impression of fullness or substantiality ⟨enthusiasts who read into him all sorts of *flatulent* bombast —H.L.Mencken⟩ ⟨he was an over-ornate speaker; at his worst he was a purveyor of *flatulent* claptrap —S.H.Adams⟩ TUMID stresses noticeable esp. morbid or abnormal enlargement as by swelling or bloating or, figuratively, an empty but marked pretentiousness ⟨his face looked damp, pale under the tan, and slightly *tumid* —J. G.Cozzens⟩ ⟨the genuine scientist would never employ *tumid* phrases or half-baked simplifications —J.E.Gloag⟩ TURGID is similar to TUMID without suggesting morbidity but often adds the idea of disorder or esp. emotional unrestraint as in the use of bombast, rant, or rhapsody ⟨the book is so *turgid*, so repetitive, so full of nearly meaningless tables —Geoffrey Gorer⟩ ⟨much too much of it dwells on the *turgid* adventures of a man who marries the less attractive of a pair of sisters and indulges a yen for the other —Henry Hewes⟩ ⟨the contrast between the vivid dialogue and the *turgid* narrative passages —David Greene⟩ ⟨a *turgid* speech praising the political boss⟩

in·flat·ed·ly *adv* : in an inflated manner

in·flat·ed·ness *n* -ES : the quality or state of being inflated : POMPOSITY, TURGIDITY

in·fla·tion \ənˈflāshən\ *n* -s [ME *inflacioun*, fr. L *inflation-, inflatio*, fr. *inflatus* + *-ion-, -io* -ion] **1** : an act of inflating or a state of being inflated: as **a** : DISTENTION **b** : empty pretentiousness : POMPOSITY ⟨~ either of language or imagination —Cyril Connolly⟩ **2** : an increase in the volume of money and credit relative to available goods resulting in a substantial and continuing rise in the general price level — contrasted with *deflation*

in·fla·tion·ary \-shəˌnerē, -ri\ *adj* : of, relating to, or productive of inflation ⟨~ signs⟩ ⟨~ policies⟩

inflationary gap *n* : an excess of total disposable income over the value of the available supply of goods at a specified price level sufficient to cause an inflation of prices — compare DEFLATIONARY GAP

inflationary spiral *n* : a continuous rise in prices that is sustained by the tendency of wage increases and cost increases to react on each other

in·fla·tion·ism \-ˌnizəm\ *n* -s : the advocacy of economic inflation

in·fla·tion·ist \-sh(ə)nə̇st\ *n* -s *often attrib* : one who favors economic inflation

in·fla·tor *or* **in·flat·er** \ənˈflād·ə(r), -ātə-\ *n* -s : one that inflates; *esp* : a hand air pump ⟨tire ~⟩

in·fla·tus \ənˈflād·əs\ *n* -ES [L, fr. *inflatus*, past part. of *inflare* to inflate — more at INFLATE] : AFFLATUS, INSPIRATION

in·flect \ənˈflekt\ *vt* -ED/-ING/-S [ME *inflecten*, fr. L *inflectere*, fr. *in-* ²in- + *flectere* to bend, turn] **1** : to turn from a direct line or course : BEND, CURVE ⟨in him . . . snobbery reappeared . . . as the refusal of reality unless it was highly ~*ed* —V.S. Pritchett⟩ ⟨profound feeling for music has ~*ed* all his major works —Irving Kolodin⟩ **2** : to give inflection to (a word) : vary (a word) by inflection : DECLINE ⟨~ a noun⟩ : CONJUGATE ⟨~ a verb⟩ **3** : to change or vary the pitch of (as the voice or an utterance) : MODULATE **4** : to bend (part of a plant) inward toward the main axis of the part or body ~ *vi* : to become modified by inflection ⟨languages in which adjectives ~ like nouns⟩

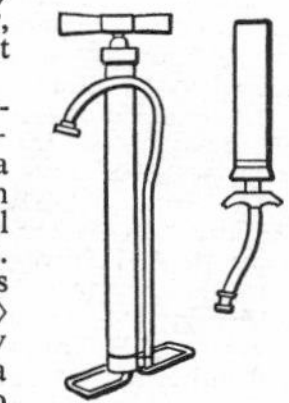

inflators

inflected *adj* **1 :** subjected to or characterized by inflection ⟨~ words⟩ ⟨an ~ language⟩ **2 :** INFLEXED 2 — **in·flect·ed·ness** *n* -ES

in·flect·ible \-təbəl\ *adj* **:** capable of being inflected

in·flec·tion \ən'flekshən\ *n* -s [LL *inflection-, inflectio,* L *inflexion-, inflexio,* fr. *inflectus, inflexus* (past part. of *inflectere* to inflect) + *-ion-, -io* -ion — more at INFLECT] **1 :** the act or result of curving or bending ⟨excel in movements and ~*s* of the hands —Sacheverell Sitwell⟩ **:** BEND, CURVE ⟨enclosed by ~*s* of the river —Anthony Powell⟩ **2 :** change or variation of pitch or loudness **:** modulation of the voice in speaking or singing ⟨questions end on a rising ~⟩ ⟨~*s* of humor, irony, and sentiment which are obvious to a native speaker —Geoffrey Bullough⟩ **3 a :** a modification in pitch or dynamics in a musical line **b :** a change from the monotone in liturgical chanting **4 a :** the variation or change of form that words undergo to mark distinctions of case, gender, number, tense, person, mood, voice, comparison **b :** a form, suffix, or element involved in such variation **c :** ACCIDENCE **5 a :** change of curvature from concave to convex or conversely **b** *or* **inflection point :** the point where such a change takes place

in·flec·tion·al \-shən³l, -shnəl\ *adj* **1 :** of, relating to, or characterized by inflection ⟨*-ed* in *played* is an ~ suffix⟩ — distinguished from *derivational* **2** *of a language* **:** characterized by the expression of grammatical relations by means of formal modification through internal change (as in *sing, sang, sung*) or fusional affixation of modifying elements (as in *walk, walked, walking, walks*) — distinguished from *agglutinative* and *isolating* — **in·flec·tion·al·ly** \-ᵊl|ē, -əl|ē, li\ *adv*

in·flec·tion·less \-shənləs\ *adj* **:** having no inflections

in·flec·tive \ən'flektiv, -tēv\ *adj* **1 :** capable of, relating to, or tending to inflection **:** DEFLECTING **2 :** INFLECTIONAL ⟨~ language⟩

in·flexed \(')in¦flekst, ən'f-\ *adj* [L *inflexus* (past part. of *inflectere* to inflect) + E *-ed* — more at INFLECT] **1 :** TURNED, BENT **2 :** bent or turned abruptly inward or downward or toward the axis ⟨~ petals of a flower⟩ ⟨~ tentacles⟩

in·flexibility \(¦)in, ən+\ *n* **:** the quality or state of being inflexible **:** UNYIELDINGNESS

in·flexible \(')in, ən+\ *adj* [ME, fr. L *inflexibilis,* fr. *in-* ¹in- + *flexibilis* flexible — more at FLEXIBLE] **1 :** not capable of being bent **:** RIGID **2 :** firm in will or purpose **:** UNYIELDING, INEXORABLE ⟨a man of upright and ~ temper —Joseph Addison⟩ ⟨~ purpose⟩ **3 :** incapable of change **:** UNALTERABLE, IMMUTABLE ⟨arbitrary and ~ rulings of bureaucracy —Edward Shils⟩ **syn** see STIFF

in·flex·i·ble·ness *n* **:** INFLEXIBILITY

in·flexibly \(')in, ən+\ *adv* **:** RIGIDLY, UNALTERABLY, STUBBORNLY, INEXORABLY

in·flex·ion \ən'flekshən\ *chiefly Brit var of* INFLECTION

in·flex·ive \ən'fleksiv\ *adj* [L *inflexus* (past part. of *inflectere* to inflect) + E *-ive*] *chiefly Brit* **:** INFLECTIVE

in·flict \ən'flikt\ *vt* -ED/-ING/-S [L *inflictus,* past part. of *infligere,* fr. *in-* ²in- + *fligere* to strike — more at PROFLIGATE] **1 :** to lay (a blow) on **:** cause (something damaging or painful) to be endured **:** IMPOSE ⟨threaten punishments you do not mean to —Bertrand Russell⟩ ⟨nor cruel and unusual punishments ~*ed* —*U. S. Constitution*⟩ ⟨~ defeat⟩ ⟨~ a beating⟩ **2 :** AFFLICT ⟨miners are still out, and industry . . . is ~*ed* with a kind of creeping paralysis —H.J.Laski⟩

in·flict·able \-təbəl\ *adj* **:** capable of being inflicted ⟨the largest ~ fine for this offense⟩

in·flict·er *or* **in·flic·tor** \-tə(r)\ *n* -s **:** one that inflicts ⟨death with his comrade, the ~ of wounds, roamed the darkened streets —Sean O'Casey⟩

in·flic·tion \ən'flikshən\ *n* -s [MF or LL; MF, fr. LL *infliction-, inflictio,* fr. L *inflictus* + *-ion-, -io* -ion] **1 :** the act of inflicting ⟨if the reader will bear one further ~ of statistics and formal description —Ernest Barker⟩ ⟨~ of damage by an economic association —C.A.Cooke⟩ **2 :** something inflicted ⟨I do not call these people visitors at all . . . they are ~*s* —F.A. Swinnerton⟩

in·flic·tive \-ktiv\ *adj* **:** causing infliction **:** acting as an infliction ⟨*The Raven* . . . delighted the ~ instincts of thousands of reciters for so long —*Times Lit. Supp.*⟩

in·flood \ən+\ *vb* [²*in-* + *flood*] *vi* **:** to flow in ~ *vt* **:** to overwhelm by flowing in upon ⟨unexpectedly in a gust of wind the scent of a plowed field . . . we are caught up, ~*ed* and informed —Alan Devoe⟩

in·florescence \,in+\ *n* [NL *inflorescentia,* fr. LL *infloresc-*

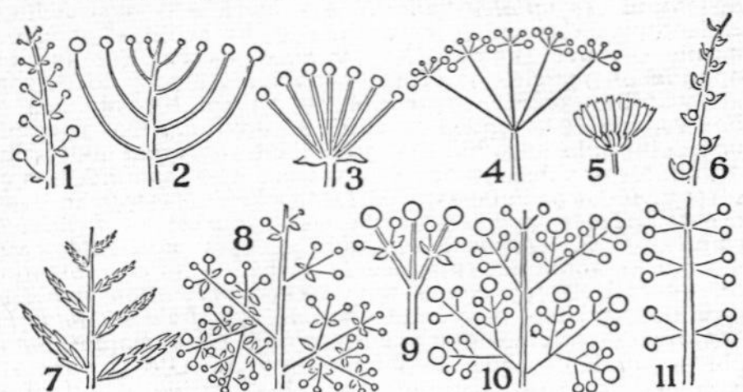

types of inflorescence diagrammatically illustrated: *1* raceme, *2* corymb, *3* umbel, *4* compound umbel, *5* capitulum, *6* spike, *7* compound spike, *8* panicle, *9* cyme, *10* thyrse, *11* verticillaster

cent-, inflorescens (pres. part. of *inflorescere* to begin to bloom, fr. *in-* ²in- + *florescere* to begin to bloom) + *-ia* -y — more at FLORESCENCE] **1 a** (1) **:** the mode of development and arrangement of flowers on an axis (2) **:** a floral axis with its appendages **:** a flower cluster or sometimes a solitary flower **b :** a cluster of reproductive organs on a moss usu. subtended by a bract ⟨many mosses have separate male ~*s*⟩ **2 :** the budding and unfolding of blossoms **:** FLOWERING

in·florescent \¦in+\ *adj* [LL *inflorescent-, inflorescens,* pres. part.] **:** BLOSSOMING, FLOWERING

¹**in·flow** \(')=¦=\ *vi* [²*in-* + *flow*] **1 :** to flow in **2** *obs, of a celestial body* **:** INFLUENCE

²**inflow** \'=,=\ *n* **1 :** the act of inflowing **2 :** something that flows in **:** INFLUX ⟨~ of air⟩ ⟨~ of water⟩ ⟨~ of bank deposits⟩ ⟨~ of imports⟩

¹**in·flu·ence** \'in,flüən(t)s *sometimes* ən'f-\ *n* -s [ME, fr. MF, fr. ML *influentia,* fr. L *influent-, influens,* pres. part. of *influere* to flow in, fr. *in-* ²in- + *fluere* to flow + *-ia* -y — more at FLUID] **1 a :** an ethereal fluid thought to flow from the stars and to affect the actions of men **b :** a supposed emanation of occult power from stars **c** *obs* **:** character or temperament due to such power **2 :** the exercise of a power like the supposed power of the stars **:** an emanation of spiritual or moral force **3** *obs* **:** INFLOW, INFLUX **4 a :** the act, process, or power of producing an effect without apparent exertion of tangible force or direct exercise of command and often without deliberate effort or intent ⟨primitive men thinking that almost everything is significant and can exert ~ of some sort —William James⟩ **b :** corrupt interference with or manipulation of authority for personal gain ⟨~ may have had something to do with getting government money for the hotels —Marcus Duffield⟩ ⟨charges of corruption and ~ peddling —*Christian Science Monitor*⟩ **c :** the exertion of force at a distance ⟨tides are caused by the ~ of the moon and sun⟩ **5 :** the power or capacity of causing an effect in indirect or intangible ways **:** DOMINANCE, SWAY, ASCENDANCY ⟨under the ~ of liquor⟩ ⟨you don't necessarily measure the ~ of a religion by the number of churches it puts up —Green Peyton⟩ ⟨the intoxicating ~ of the mountain air —W.S.Gilbert⟩ **6 :** a person or thing that exerts influence ⟨open water affected by continental ~*s* —R.E.Coker⟩ ⟨Scotch-Irish, who still constitute the dominant ~, began to flow into the settlement —*Amer. Guide Series: Pa.*⟩ **7 :** INDUCTION 4c

syn AUTHORITY, PRESTIGE, WEIGHT, CREDIT: INFLUENCE refers to power exerted over others, often through high position, strength of intellect, force of character, or degree of accomplishment, sometimes exercised unconsciously and felt insensibly, sometimes consciously or calculatedly brought to bear ⟨as provost of the Swedish clergymen he exercised a quickening *influence* over all the Swedish congregations —G. H.Genzmer⟩ ⟨swept aside by the *influence* of the special interests bent on maintaining price levels against deflation —T. W.Arnold⟩ AUTHORITY signifies power resident in a person to command belief, acceptance, or allegiance, often through learning or wisdom ⟨Aristotle's *authority* was so great, and the homocentric system which he had espoused became so enmeshed in literature, that his system had its followers throughout the Middle Ages —G.C.Sellery⟩ ⟨the personal *authority* [of Augustus] which, far more than any legal or constitutional device, was the true secret of his later power —John Buchan⟩ ⟨to face a good orchestra with inward and outward *authority* and assurance —J.N.Burk⟩ PRESTIGE refers to the force of conspicuous excellence or of continued repute as superior, with resultant ability to command deference ⟨the almost magical *prestige* that had belonged to the original humanists —Aldous Huxley⟩ ⟨Napoleon insisted on a strict etiquette. He was right. It was only by keeping up the fiction of grandeur that he could maintain his *prestige* —André Maurois⟩ WEIGHT applies to power over or influence over others, often measurable and undeniable, and sometimes decisive ⟨Mrs. Hawthorne's authoritative air was beginning to have some *weight* with him —Archibald Marshall⟩ ⟨men who take the lead, and whose opinions and wishes have great *weight* with the others —J.G.Frazer⟩ CREDIT applies to ability to influence arising from merit or favorable reputation ⟨his position was distinctly stronger and once more he had shown his ability to handle a delicate situation to the *credit* of his government and himself —W.C.Ford⟩ ⟨the film was a success, with much of the *credit* going to the newcomer —*Current Biog.*⟩
— **under the influence :** in an intoxicated condition ⟨charged with driving *under the influence*⟩

²**influence** \"\ *vb* -ED/-ING/-S *vt* **1 :** to affect or alter the conduct, thought, or character of by indirect or intangible means **:** SWAY ⟨pilots . . . by listening to passengers who have *influenced* better judgment —*Skyways*⟩ ⟨economic and political factors that ~ decisions by managers of European zones —R.S.Thoman⟩ **2 :** to have an effect on the condition or development of **:** determine partially **:** MODIFY ⟨output was strongly *influenced* by the feelings of the worker about the job —Stuart Chase⟩ ⟨outdoor living has *influenced* the design . . . of furniture —N.C.Brown⟩ **3** *obs* **:** INDUCE, INFUSE ~ *vi, archaic* **:** to exert influence **syn** see AFFECT

in·flu·ence·abil·i·ty \,in,flüənsə'biləd·ē *sometimes* ən,f-\ *n* -ES **:** liability to influence

in·flu·ence·able \'=,==səbəl *sometimes* =ˈ==-\ *adj* [¹*influence* + *-able*] **:** liable to be influenced **:** readily subject to influence

influence fuse *n* **:** PROXIMITY FUSE

influence line *n, often cap I* **1 :** LINE OF INFLUENCE **2 :** a graph showing the variation of the longitudinal stress, shear, bending moment, or other effect upon a structural member due to a moving load as a function of the position of that load

influence machine *n* **:** INDUCTION MACHINE

in·flu·enc·er \-sə(r)\ *n* -s **:** one that influences

in·flu·en·cive \'in,flüənsiv\ *adj, archaic* **:** INFLUENTIAL

¹**in·flu·ent** \'in,flüənt\ *adj* [ME, fr. L *influent-, influens,* pres. part. of *influere* to flow in — more at INFLUENCE] **1 :** flowing in; *esp* **:** contributing water to the zone of saturation and thereby sustaining or raising the water table ⟨~ seepage⟩ **2** *archaic* **:** exercising influence ⟨beneath the ~ heavens —Elizabeth B. Browning⟩

²**influent** \"\ *n* -s **1 :** a tributary stream **:** AFFLUENT; *also* **:** a stream or part of a stream that contributes water to the zone of saturation underground **2 a :** an animal or rarely a plant that has an important effect on the balance and stability of an ecological community ⟨rabbits and prairie dogs are important ~*s* in some rangelands⟩ **b :** a determining factor in the ecological balance of a human community ⟨location of home in relation to job is an ~ in city growth⟩

in·flu·en·tial \¦in,flü¦enchəl\ *adj* [ML *influentia* influence + E *-al* — more at INFLUENCE] **1 :** exerting or possessing influence **:** POTENT, EFFECTIVE ⟨as ~ as any newspaper in the country —Morley Callaghan⟩ **2 :** having authority or ascendancy **:** IMPORTANT ⟨exert ~ leadership for peace —D.D. Eisenhower⟩ **3** *obs* **:** of the nature of or relating to occult influence — **in·flu·en·tial·ly** \-ch(ə)lē, -li\ *adv*

in·flu·en·za \,in,flü'enzə\ *n* -s [It, influence, epidemic, influenza, fr. ML *influentia* influence; fr. the fact that epidemics were formerly attributed to the influence of the stars — more at INFLUENCE] **1 :** an acute highly contagious infectious virus disease that occurs in endemic, epidemic, or pandemic forms, is characterized by sudden onset, fever, prostration, severe aches and pains, and progressive inflammation of the respiratory mucous membrane, and is frequently complicated by secondary infections (as pneumonia); *broadly* **:** a human respiratory infection of undetermined cause **2 :** any of numerous febrile usu. virus diseases (as shipping fever of horses, swine influenza, infectious laryngotracheitis of poultry) marked by respiratory symptoms, inflammation of mucous membranes, and varying degrees of systemic involvement **3 :** a respiratory disease of dogs and cats that is perhaps identical with human influenza

influenza vaccine *n* **:** a vaccine against influenza; *specif* **:** a mixture of strains of formaldehyde-inactivated influenza virus from chick embryo culture

in·flux \'in,fləks\ *n* [LL *influxus,* fr. L *influxus,* past part. of *influere* to flow in — more at INFLUENCE] **1** *obs* **:** INFLUENCE **2 :** a flowing in **:** INFLOW ⟨~ of light⟩ ⟨~ of air⟩ **3 :** a continuous coming esp. of individuals in large numbers ⟨the city expected an ~ of holiday visitors⟩ **4 :** the mouth or debouchment of a river

in·flux·ion \ən'fləkshən, 'in,f-\ *n* [LL *influxion-, influxio,* fr. L *influxus* (past part.) + *-ion-, -io* -ion] **:** INFLUX ⟨continual ~*s* of new blood —John Galsworthy⟩

in·fo \'in(,)fō\ *abbr or n* -s information

in·fold \ən'fōld\ *vb* [ME *ynfoldyn, fr. yn-, in-* ²in- + *foldeyn, folden* to fold — more at FOLD] *vt* **:** ENFOLD ~ *vi* **:** to fold inward or toward one another ⟨the neural crests ~ and fuse⟩ ⟨an ~*ed* leaf margin⟩ ⟨~*ing* of the hindgut walls⟩

¹**in·form** \ən'fȯ(ə)rm, -ȯ(ə)m\ *vb* [ME *enfourmen, informen,* fr. MF *enformer, enfourmer,* fr. L *informare,* fr. *in-* ²in- + *formare* to form — more at FORM] *vt* **1** *obs* **a :** to give material form to **:** mold or shape physically **b :** to set in order **:** ARRANGE **2 a :** to give character or essence to ⟨to what extent can the practice of science ~, render more significant the objects of common sense —Gail Kennedy⟩ ⟨a piety . . . quietly ~*ing* the outlook of men in politics as elsewhere —W.L. Miller⟩ **b :** to be the formative principle of ⟨eternal objects ~ actual occasions with hierarchic patterns —A.N.Whitehead⟩ ⟨everything that is made from without and by dead rules, and does not spring from within through some spirit ~*ing* it —Oscar Wilde⟩ **c :** to permeate or impregnate so as to become the characteristic quality of **:** ANIMATE, INSPIRE, INFUSE ⟨these poems are ~*ed* with sincerity —Richard Eberhart⟩ ⟨sentimental, Protestant ethos that has always ~*ed* his writing —L.A.Fiedler⟩ **3** *obs* **:** to form (the mind) in respect to character, disposition, or ability **:** TRAIN, DISCIPLINE, INSTRUCT **4** *obs* **:** GUIDE, DIRECT ⟨if old respect hither hath ~*ed* your younger feet —John Milton⟩ **5** *obs* **:** to make known **:** give instruction in (as a doctrine) **6 :** to communicate knowledge to **:** make acquainted **:** TELL, ADVISE, ENLIGHTEN ⟨accused shall enjoy the right . . . to be ~*ed* of the nature and cause of the accusation —*U.S.Constitution*⟩ ⟨obligation as a citizen is to ~ himself . . . regarding the controversial issues —Clifford Houston⟩ ⟨program of ~*ing* the rest of the world about our way of life —H.H.Davis⟩ ~ *vi* **1 :** to give information **:** impart knowledge ⟨in theory news ~*s* while advertising sells —*Banking*⟩ **2 :** to give information or intelligence to a civil authority **:** lay information **:** act as a common informer ⟨I shall not ~ upon you —Oscar Wilde⟩

syn ACQUAINT, APPRISE, ADVISE, NOTIFY, ADVERTISE: These verbs signify to make aware or cognizant (of something). INFORM implies the imparting of knowledge, esp. of facts or events necessary to the understanding of a pertinent matter ⟨to *inform* the students there would be no classes on Saturday⟩ ⟨kept the staff *informed* of Chinese public opinion concerning the American military action there —*Current Biog.*⟩ ACQUAINT usu. lays stress upon less centrally significant matter than INFORM does or suggests a process of introducing to or familiarizing with rather than informing of ⟨these writings were of the nature of travel books, and served . . . to *acquaint* the world with a new country —*Amer. Guide Series: Minn.*⟩ ⟨*acquainting* students with political practices —F.A.Ogg & Harold Zink⟩ To APPRISE someone of something is to communicate something usu. of interest or importance to him ⟨this church, so I was then *apprised,* was founded by St. James the Less —T.G.Henderson⟩ ⟨Tristram's cutting the hazel and writing upon it with his knife in order to *apprise* the queen of his presence —Grace Frank⟩ ⟨to touch him on the sleeve and *apprise* him that I was there —Mary Austin⟩ To ADVISE someone of something is to inform him of something that may make a significant difference to him in an action, policy, or plan; it often suggests a forewarning or counseling ⟨consulted the wine card and *advised* me that the wine I had chosen had no special merit —R.M.Lovett⟩ ⟨I *advised* him strongly of the danger of switching professions without acquiring new professional qualifications —R.G.G.Price⟩ To NOTIFY is to send a notice or make a usu. formal communication generally about something requiring or worthy of attention ⟨the court clerk *notified* the witnesses when to appear⟩ ⟨*notify* a man of his acceptance in a club⟩ To ADVERTISE, rare in current use in this sense, is to inform or notify by way of warning ⟨the translators, good Protestants, were careful to *advertise* the reader that what they offered was Le Clerc's Moreri —*Times Lit. Supp.*⟩

²**inform** *adj* [MF *informe,* fr. L *informis,* fr. *in-* ¹in- + *forma* form — more at FORM] **1** *obs* **:** lacking regular form **:** SHAPELESS, DEFORMED **2** *obs* **:** lacking created form **:** UNFORMED

in·formal \(')in, ən+\ *adj* [¹*in-* + *formal*] **1 :** not formal **:** conducted or carried out without formal, regularly prescribed, or ceremonious procedure **:** UNOFFICIAL ⟨~ hearing⟩ ⟨~ discussion⟩ ⟨~ contract⟩ ⟨~ inquiries⟩ ⟨~ gathering of friends⟩ **2 :** characteristic of or appropriate to ordinary, casual, or familiar use ⟨~ English⟩ ⟨genial, ~ manner⟩ ⟨~ essay⟩ **3** *obs* **:** DERANGED, MAD ⟨poor ~ women are no more but instruments —Shak.⟩ **4** *of a design* **:** having an asymmetrical composition or arrangement made from unequal shapes and distances ⟨~ balance in a stage set⟩

in·formality \¦in+\ *n* [¹*in-* + *formality*] **1 :** the quality or state of being informal **:** lack of regular, prescribed, or customary form ⟨wayside camps, where the ~ of hardships loosened tongues —Mabel R. Gillis⟩ ⟨everyday speech in all its ~ and ease —R.A.Hall b. 1911⟩ **2 :** an informal act or proceeding ⟨the wedding ceremony was enlivened by several unexpected *informalities*⟩

in·for·ma·lize \ən'fȯ(r)mə,līz\ *vt* [*informal* + *-ize*] **:** to make informal or less formal ⟨college education of the future must . . . be greatly simplified and *informalized* —*Nation*⟩

in·formally \(')in, ən+\ *adv* **:** in an informal manner **:** without ceremony or formality ⟨addressed the gathering ~⟩ ⟨~ dressed in flannels and jacket⟩ **:** UNOFFICIALLY ⟨fast train . . . began to be called, more or less ~, the Cannonball —A.F. Harlow⟩

informal planning *n* **:** architectural planning in which dominant axes and strong visual climaxes are avoided in favor of freer circulation patterns and more subtle dramatic effects

in·for·mant \ən'fȯrmənt, -ȯ(ə)m-\ *n* -s [L *informant-, informans,* pres. part. of *informare* to inform — more at INFORM] **:** one that informs **:** one who gives information: as **a :** INFORMER **b :** one who supplies cultural or linguistic data in response to interrogation by an investigator ⟨findings . . . based on . . . statements of ~*s* from among both the educated and the uneducated —B.B.Ashcom⟩ ⟨analysis of great civilizations by the use of living ~*s* —Gregory Bateson⟩

in for·ma pau·pe·ris \-,fȯrmə'pȯpərəs, -'paup-\ *adj* (*or adv*) [L, in the form of a pauper] **:** as a poor man **:** relieved of fees and costs in a legal action because of inability to pay ⟨permission was granted to file an appeal *in forma pauperis*⟩

in·for·ma·tion \,infə(r)'māshən\ *n* -s *often attrib* [ME *informacioun,* fr. *enfourmen, informen* to inform + *-acioun* -ation — more at INFORM] **1 a** *obs* **:** an endowing with form **b** *obs* **:** the act of animating or inspiring **c** *obs* **:** TRAINING, DISCIPLINE, INSTRUCTION **d :** the communication or reception of knowledge or intelligence ⟨the function of a public library is ~⟩ ⟨we enclose a price list for your ~⟩ **2 :** something received or obtained through informing: as **a :** knowledge communicated by others or obtained from investigation, study, or instruction **b :** knowledge of a particular event or situation **:** INTELLIGENCE, NEWS, ADVICES ⟨latest ~ from the battle front⟩ ⟨securing ~ about conditions in the upper atmosphere⟩ ⟨~ bureau⟩ **c :** facts or figures ready for communication or use as distinguished from those incorporated in a formally organized branch of knowledge **:** DATA ⟨reliable source of ~⟩ **d :** a signal (as one of the digits in dialing a telephone number) purposely impressed upon the input of a communication system or a calculating machine **3 :** the act of informing against a person or party **4 a :** a formal accusation of a crime made by a prosecuting officer on information brought to his attention as distinguished from an indictment presented by a grand jury **:** COMPLAINT **b :** a pleading by an attorney general or other public officer setting forth a civil case or relief in which some public right of the state is asserted **c :** the document containing the depositions of the witnesses against one accused of crime **5 :** the process by which the form of an object of knowledge is impressed upon the apprehending mind so as to bring about the state of knowing **6 :** a logical quantity belonging to propositions and arguments as well as terms and comprising the sum of the synthetical propositions in which the term, proposition, or argument taken enters as subject or predicate, antecedent or consequent — see QUANTITY 5c **7 :** a numerical quantity that measures the uncertainty in the outcome of an experiment to be performed ⟨when an event occurs whose probability was *p*, the event is said to communicate an amount of ~ log (1/*p*) —W.F.Brown b. 1904⟩ ⟨the amount of ~ is defined, in the simplest cases, to be measured by the logarithm of the number of available choices —C.E. Shannon & Warren Weaver⟩ **syn** see KNOWLEDGE

in·for·ma·tion·al \¦==¦māshən³l, -shnəl\ *adj* **:** relating to or giving information **:** INFORMING ⟨~ service of a library⟩

information girl *n* **1 :** a telephone operator who gives information from the central office switchboard **2 :** a clerk at an information desk

information theory *n* **:** a theory that utilizes statistical techniques in dealing with the effect of encoding on the efficiency of processes of signal transmission and of communication between men (as in telecommunication or the printed word) or between men and machines or between machines and machines (as in computing machines)

in·form·a·tive \ən'fȯ(r)məd·iv, -ətiv\ *adj* [¹*inform* + *-ative*] **1** *obs* **:** having power to inform, animate, or vivify **2 :** imparting knowledge **:** INSTRUCTIVE ⟨~ lecture⟩ ⟨~ brochure⟩ **3 :** INFORMATORY — **in·form·a·tive·ly** \-əvlē, -li\ *adv* — **in·form·a·tive·ness** \-ivnəs\ *n*

in·form·ato·ry \-mə,tōrē, -tȯr-, -ri\ *adj* [*information* + *-ory*] **:** INFORMING, INSTRUCTIVE ⟨a witty and ~ book⟩; *specif* **:** devised or intended to convey information ⟨~ bid in contract bridge⟩

informatory double *n* **:** a double made in bridge to convey information to one's partner and to invite a bid from him — called also *takeout double*

informed *adj* [fr. past part. of ¹*inform*] **1 :** having information ⟨an ~ citizenry⟩ ⟨a well-*informed* man⟩ **:** based on possession of information ⟨~ estimate of next year's tax receipts⟩ **2 :** EDUCATED, INTELLIGENT, CULTIVATED ⟨~ taste⟩ ⟨~ opinion⟩ ⟨transition . . . from blind habit to ~ works of art —Ernest Nagel⟩

in·form·er \ən'fȯrmər, -ȯ(ə)mə(r)\ *n* [ME *enformer,* fr. *enfourmen* to inform + *-er* — more at INFORM] **1** *obs* **:** one that informs, animates, or inspires ⟨nature, ~ of the poet's art —Alexander Pope⟩ **2 :** one that informs or imparts knowledge or news **3 :** one that informs against another: **a :** one that informs a magistrate of a violation of law **:** one that lays an information; *esp* **:** one that makes a practice of informing against others for violations of penal laws particularly when the informer may receive as a reward a share of the money penalty imposed — called also *common informer;* compare QUI TAM **b :** one secretly in the service of the police or of a diplomatic agency (as an embassy) that supplies information ⟨a nest of spies and ~*s*⟩

informidable *adj* [¹*in-* + *formidable*] *obs* : not formidable ⟨foe not ~ —John Milton⟩
informing *adj* [fr. pres. part. of ¹*inform*] **1** : ANIMATING, INSPIRING ⟨the concrete and the external are . . . the medium through which the ~ spirit is expressed —J.L.Lowes⟩ **2** : INFORMATIVE, INSTRUCTIVE
in·form·ing·ly *adv* : INFORMATIVELY, INSTRUCTIVELY
informs *pres 3d sing of* INFORM
in fo·ro \-ˈfō(ˌ)rō\ *adv* [L, in the forum] : before the court : within the jurisdiction
in foro con·sci·en·ti·ae \-ˌkänchēˈenchēˌē\ *adv* [L, in the forum of conscience] : privately or morally rather than legally ⟨an extrajudicial oath is binding only *in foro conscientiae*⟩
in·for·tu·nate \ənˈfȯ(r)chənət\ *adj* [ME *infortunat*, fr. L *infortunatus*, fr. *in-* ¹in- + *fortunatus* fortunate — more at FORTUNATE] **1** *obs* : UNFORTUNATE **2** : causing or presaging misfortune : UNPROPITIOUS
in·for·tune \(ˈ)inˈfȯrchən, ənˈ-\ *n* [ME, fr. MF, fr. L *infortunium*, fr. *in-* ¹in- + *-fortunium* (fr. *fortuna* fortune) — more at FORTUNE] : one of the malevolent planets (Saturn, Mars, or sometimes Mercury) in an unfavorable aspect
infortunity *n* -ES [MF *infortunité*, fr. L *infortunitat-, infortunitas*, fr. *in-* ¹in- + *fortuna* fortune + *-itat-, -itas* -ity] *obs* : MISFORTUNE
infos *pl of* INFO
in·fra \ˈinfrə, -n(ˌ)frä, -n(ˌ)frȧ\ *adv* [L] **1** : UNDER, BELOW **2** : LATER
infra- *prefix* [L *infra* below, underneath — more at UNDER] **1 a** : below : lower in status than — esp. in adjectives formed from adjectives ⟨*infra*human⟩ **b** : after : later than ⟨*infra*lapsarian⟩ **2** : within — esp. in adjectives formed from adjectives ⟨*infra*territorial⟩ **3** : below in a scale or series — esp. in adjectives formed from adjectives ⟨*infra*red⟩ **4** : below or beneath (a designated part of the anatomy) — esp. in adjectives formed from adjectives ⟨*infra*costal⟩
in·fra·angelic \ˌinfrə+\ *adj* [*infra-* + *angelic*] : less than angelic : HUMAN
in·fra·basal \"+\ *adj* [*infra-* + *basal*] *zool* : lying below a basal structure ⟨~ skeletal plate of a crinoid⟩
in·fra·branchial \"+\ *adj* [*infra-* + *branchial*] : lying below the gills — used esp. of the ventral part of the pallial chamber in the lamellibranchs
in·fra·central \"+\ *adj* [*infra-* + *central*] *anat* : lying below the centrum
in·fra·class \ˈinfrə+,-\ *n* [*infra-* + *class*] : a subdivision of a subclass that is more or less exactly equivalent to a superorder
in·fra·clavicle \ˌinfrə+\ *n* [*infra-* + *clavicle*] : a bony element in the shoulder girdle lying below the cleithrum in some ganoid and crossopterygian fishes and supposed to be the true homologue of the clavicle of higher animals
in·fra·clavicular \"+\ *adj* [*infra-* + *clavicular*] : relating or belonging to the infraclavicle
in·fra·cos·ta·lis \ˌinfrəˌkäˈstaləs, -täl-, -täl-\ *n, pl* **infra·costa·les** \-a(ˌ)lēz, -ā(ˌ)lēz, -ä(ˌ)lās\ [NL, fr. *infra-* + L *costa* rib + *-alis* -al — more at COAST] : SUBCOSTALIS
in·fract \ənˈfrakt\ *vt* -ED/-ING/-S [L *infractus*, past part. of *infringere* to break, break off, destroy — more at INFRINGE] : BREAK, INFRINGE, VIOLATE ⟨~ the Constitution⟩
in·fract·ible \-təbəl\ *adj* [LL *infractus* unbroken (fr. L *in-* ¹in- + *fractus*, past part. of *frangere* to break) + E *-ible* — more at BREAK] : INVIOLABLE ⟨a thorough and ~ eight hours devoted to his work in Wall Street —Scott Fitzgerald⟩
in·frac·tion \ənˈfrakshən\ *n* -S [L *infraction-, infractio*, fr. *infractus* (past part. of *infringere*) + *-ion-, -io* -ion] **1** : the act of breaking or violating : BREACH, VIOLATION, INFRINGEMENT ⟨~ of a treaty⟩ ⟨minor ~s of the rules⟩ ⟨~ of code⟩ ⟨~ of discipline⟩ **2** : an incomplete fracture without displacement of the bone **syn** see BREACH
in·frac·tor \-ktə(r)\ *n* -S [prob. fr. MF *infracteur*, fr. LL *infractor*, fr. L *infractus* (past part. of *infringere*) + *-or*] : one that infracts or infringes : VIOLATOR, BREAKER
in·fra dig \ˌinfrəˈdig\ *adj* [modif. of L *infra dignitatem* beneath dignity] : being beneath one's dignity : UNDIGNIFIED ⟨it was clear . . . that off-season cruising was rather *infra dig* —Richard Gordon⟩ ⟨considered helping with the dishes to be *infra dig*⟩
in·fra·foliar \ˌinfrə+\ *adj* [*infra-* + *foliar*] : situated below the leaves ⟨~ flower clusters⟩
in·fra·glacial \"+\ *adj* [*infra-* + *glacial*] : SUBGLACIAL
in·fra·glenoid \"+\ *adj* [*infra-* + *glenoid*] : situated below the glenoid cavity of the scapula
infraglenoid tubercle *n* : a tubercle on the scapula for the attachment of the long head of the triceps muscle
in·fra·gular \"+\ *adj* [*infra-* + *gular*] : SUBESOPHAGEAL
in·fra·human \"+\ *adj* [*infra-* + *human*] : less or lower than human ⟨~ attributes⟩; *specif* : ANTHROPOID — compare SUPERHUMAN
¹in·fra·labial \"+\ *adj* [*infra-* + *labial*] : lying below the lip : SUBLABIAL
²infralabial \"\ *n* : a scale or plate bordering the lower jaw on either side of the mental of various reptiles
¹in·fra·lap·sar·i·an \ˌinfrəˌlapˈserēən, -sa(a)r-\ *n* -S [*infra-* + L *lapsus* lapse, fall + E *-arian* — more at LAPSE] : one that adheres to the doctrine of infralapsarianism — compare SUPRALAPSARIAN
²infralapsarian \ˌ≈≈ˌ≈ˈ≈≈≈\ *adj* : of or relating to the doctrine of infralapsarianism
in·fra·lap·sar·i·an·ism \ˌ≈≈ˌ≈ˈ≈≈ə,nizəm\ *n* -S : the doctrine that God foresaw and permitted the fall of man and that after the fall he then decreed election as a means of saving some of the human race — compare SUPRALAPSARIANISM
in·fra·linear \ˌinfrə+\ *adj* [*infra-* + *linear*] : placed below the line of writing : SUBLINEAR ⟨an ~ system of vocalization for Hebrew⟩
in·fra·littoral \"+\ *adj* [*infra-* + *littoral*] : situated to seaward of the region of littoral deposits ⟨~ zone⟩
¹in·fra·marginal \"+\ *adj* [*infra-* + *marginal*] **1** : situated below a margin : SUBMARGINAL ⟨~ convolution of the brain⟩ **2** : situated below the marginal cell of an insect's wing
²inframarginal \"\ *n* : an inframarginal element
in·fra·natant \"+\ *adj* [*infra-* + *natant*] : lying below a supernatant body ⟨unfiltered ~ solution from a growing culture —*Science*⟩
in·fra·neritic \"+\ *adj* [*infra-* + *neritic*] : lying at a depth greater than 120 feet below the ocean surface ⟨~ environment of sedimentation⟩ — opposed to *epineritic*
in·frangibility \(ˌ)in, ən+\ *n* : INVIOLABILITY ⟨the ~ of the given word is the first rule of politics —H.D.Scott⟩
in·fran·gi·ble \(ˈ)inˌfranjəbəl, ənˈf-, -raan-\ *adj* [MF, fr. LL *infrangibilis*, fr. L *in-* ¹in- + *frangere* to break + *-ibilis* -ible — more at BREAK] **1** : not capable of being broken ⟨~ resolution of character⟩ or separated into parts ⟨~ series⟩ **2** : not to be infringed or violated ⟨~ law⟩ — **in·fran·gi·ble·ness** *n* — **in·fran·gi·bly** \-blē, -bli\ *adv*
in·fra·orbital \ˌinfrə+\ *adj* [*infra-* + *orbital*] : situated beneath the orbit ⟨~ bone⟩
in·fra·pose \ˌinfrəˈpōz\ *vt* [*infra-* + *-pose* (as in *superpose*)] : to place under or beneath — **in·fra·position** \ˌinfrə+\ *n*
in fra prae·si·dia \ˌinfrəprēˈzidēə\ *adv* [L, under the protection] *of captured property* : in safe custody : completely under control
¹in·fra·red \ˌinfrəˈred, -ˈfrä-, -ˈfrȧ- *sometimes* ˌinfəˈr- *by r-dissimilation*\ *adj* [*infra-* + *red*] **1** : lying outside the visible spectrum at its red end — used of thermal radiation of wavelengths longer than those of visible light **2** : relating to, producing, or employing infrared radiation ⟨~ therapy⟩ ⟨~ photography⟩ **3** : sensitive to infrared radiation and capable of photographing in darkness or through haze ⟨~ film⟩
²infrared \"\ *n* : infrared radiation
infrared lamp *n* : a high-power incandescent lamp operating at a lower filament temperature than a lamp used for illumination and yielding a large percentage of infrared radiation that is useful for heating purposes
in·fra·roentgen ray \"+...-\ *n* [*infra-* + *roentgen*] : GRENZ RAY
in·fra·scap·u·la·ris \ˌinfrəˌskapyəˈla(a)rəs\ *n, pl* **infra·scapula·res** \-a(a)(ˌ)rēz\ [NL, fr. *infra-* + *scapula* + *-aris* -ar] : the teres minor
In·fra·si·zer \ˈinfrəˌsīzə(r)\ *trademark* — used for an apparatus for determining the degree of fineness to which a material (as a mineral or rock) has been ground
in·fra·social \ˌinfrə+\ *adj* [*infra-* + *social*] *of insects* : lacking social organization : SOLITARY
in·fra·sonic \"+\ *adj* [*infra-* + *sonic*] **1** : having a frequency lower than about 16 cycles per second and therefore below the audibility range of the human ear and producing only a fluttering sensation with no sense of pitch — compare SONIC, SUPERSONIC **2** : utilizing or produced by infrasonic waves or vibrations
in·fra·specific \"+\ *adj* [*infra-* + *specific*] : included within a species ⟨~ categories⟩
in·fra·spinal \"+\ *adj* [*infra-* + *spinal*] : INFRASPINOUS
in·fra·spi·na·tus \ˌinfrə(ˌ)spīˈnādəs\ *n, pl* **infraspinati** [NL, fr. *infra-* + L *spina* spine + *-atus* -ate — more at SPINE] : a muscle that occupies the chief part of the infraspinous fossa of the scapula and is inserted into the greater tuberosity of the humerus
in·fra·spinous \ˌinfrə+\ *adj* [*infra-* + *spinous*] : lying below a spine; *esp* : lying below the spine of the scapula
infraspinous fossa *n* : the part of the dorsal surface of the scapula below the spine of the scapula
in·fra·structure \ˈinfrə+,-\ *n* [*infra-* + *structure*] : the underlying foundation or basic framework (as of an organization or a system) : SUBSTRUCTURE; *esp* : the permanent installations required for military purposes
in·fra·temporal \ˌinfrə+\ *adj* [*infra-* + *temporal*] : situated below the temple or temporal bone — used esp. of the lower or more lateral of the two divisions of the temporal fossae of various reptiles
infratemporal fossa *n* : a fossa in man and some other vertebrates bounded above by the plane of zygomatic arch, laterally by the ramus of the mandible, and medially by the pterygoid plate, and lodging the masseter and pterygoid muscles and the mandibular nerve
in frau·dem le·gis \-ˈfrȯdəm ˈlējəs\ *adv* [L] : in circumvention of the rules of law
in·frequency \(ˈ)in, ən+\ *or* **in·frequence** \"+\ *n* [L *infrequentia*, fr. *infrequent-, infrequens* infrequent + *-ia* -y] **1** *obs* : the quality or state of not being frequented : SOLITUDE, ISOLATION **2** : the state of rarely occurring : UNCOMMONNESS, RARENESS ⟨comparative ~ of typhoid fever⟩
in·frequent \"+\ *adj* [L *infrequent-, infrequens*, fr. *in-* ¹in- + *frequent-, frequens* frequent — more at FREQUENT] **1** *obs* : UNFREQUENTED **2** : seldom happening or occurring : RARE, UNCOMMON ⟨far from being ~, the crystalline state is almost universal among solids —K.K.Darrow⟩ **3** : placed or occurring at considerable distances or intervals : OCCASIONAL, SPARSE ⟨~ openings in a wall⟩ — **in·fre·quent·ly** *adv*
in·frig·i·date \ənˈfrijəˌdāt\ *vt* -ED/-ING/-S [LL *infrigidatus*, past part. of *infrigidare*, fr. L *in-* ²in- + LL *frigidare* to make cold, fr. L *frigidus* cold — more at FRIGID] : to make cold : CHILL
in·fringe \ənˈfrinj\ *vb* -ED/-ING/-S [L *infringere* to break, break off, weaken, destroy, fr. *in-* ²in- + *-fringere* (fr. *frangere* to break) — more at BREAK] *vt* **1** *obs* **a** : to break down : DESTROY **b** : DEFEAT, FRUSTRATE **c** : CONFUTE, REFUTE **d** : IMPAIR, WEAKEN **2** : to commit a breach of ⟨~ the peace⟩ : neglect to fulfill or obey : VIOLATE, TRANSGRESS ⟨~ a treaty⟩ ⟨~ an edict⟩ ⟨~ a contract⟩ ⟨~ a patent⟩ ⟨~ a copyright⟩ ⟨both these limits of gradient and curve must be *infringed* to reach the plateau —James Bird⟩ ⟨the statute . . . would ~ fundamental principles —O.W.Holmes †1935⟩ ~ *vi* : ENCROACH, TRESPASS — used with *on* or *upon* ⟨where the siesta is no catnap and a ten-o'clock dinner practically ~s on tea time —Claudia Cassidy⟩ **syn** see TRESPASS
in·fringe·ment \-jmənt\ *n* -S **1** : the act of infringing : BREACH, VIOLATION, NONFULFILLMENT ⟨~ of a treaty⟩ ⟨~ of the constitution⟩ **2** : an encroachment or trespass on a right or privilege : TRESPASS: **a** : the unlawful manufacture, use, or sale of a patented or copyrighted article, such as constitutes a tort in law **b** : the unlawful use of a trademark or trade name **syn** see BREACH
in·fring·er \-jə(r)\ *n* -S : one that infringes ⟨~ of a patent⟩
in·fruc·tes·cence \ˌinˌfrəkˈtesən(t)s\ *n* [F, fr. *in-* ²in- + L *fructus* fruit + F *-escence* (as in *inflorescence*) — more at FRUIT] : the fruiting stage of an inflorescence
in·fructuous \(ˈ)in, ən+\ *adj* [L *infructuosus*, fr. *in-* ¹in- + *fructuosus* fruitful — more at FRUCTUOUS] **1** : UNFRUITFUL **2** : FRUITLESS, UNPROFITABLE — **in·fruc·tu·ous·ly** *adv*
in·fu·la \ˈinfyələ\ *n, pl* **infu·lae** \-əˌlē\ [L; perh. akin to L *redimire* to tie, wreathe, *geminus* twin — more at GEMINATE] **1** : a fillet of red and white wool worn in ancient Rome as a token of religious consecration or inviolability **2** [ML, fr. L] **a** : one of two lappets that hang from the back of a bishop's miter **b** : a chasuble used principally in France and England from the 11th to the 16th century

infulae

in·fu·mate \ˈinfyəˌmāt, ənˈfyümət\ *or* **in·fu·mat·ed** \-ˌmādəd\ *adj* [*infumate* fr. L *infumatus*, past part. of *infumare* to dry by smoking, fr. *in-* ²in- + *fumare* to smoke, fr. *fumus* smoke; *infumated* fr. L *infumatus* + E *-ed* — more at FUME] : clouded with blackish color ⟨~ insect wing⟩
in·fu·ma·tion \ˌinfyəˈmāshən\ *n* -S [L *infumatus* + E *-ion*] : the act or process of drying in smoke
in·fun·dib·u·lar \ˌin(ˌ)fənˈdibyələ(r)\ *adj* [NL *infundibulum* + E *-ar*] **1** : resembling a funnel **2 a** : of or relating to an infundibulum **b** : INFUNDIBULATE
in·fun·dib·u·la·ta \ˌ≈(ˌ)≈ˌdibyəˈläd·ə, -ˈlād·ə\ [NL, fr. *infundibulum* + *-ata*] *syn of* GYMNOLAEMATA
in·fun·dib·u·late \ˌ≈(ˌ)≈ˈdibyəˌlāt, -ˌlət\ *adj* [NL *infundibulum* + E *-ate*] **1** : having an infundibulum **2** : INFUNDIBULIFORM
in·fun·dib·u·li·form \-yələˌfȯrm\ *adj* [NL *infundibulum* + *-iform*] : having the form of a funnel or cone ⟨~ corolla⟩
in·fun·dib·u·lum \ˌ≈(ˌ)≈ˈdibyələm\ *n, pl* **infundibu·la** \-lə\ [NL, fr. L, funnel, fr. *infundere* to pour in — more at INFUSE] : any of various conical or dilated organs or parts: as **a** : the hollow conical process of gray matter that is borne on the tuber cinereum and constitutes the stalk of the neurohypophysis by which the pituitary body is continuous with the brain **b** : any of the small spaces having walls beset with air sacs in which the bronchial tubes terminate in the lungs **c** : the enlarged process of the right ventricle from which the pulmonary artery arises **d** : the passage by which the anterior ethmoid cells and the frontal sinuses communicate with the nose **e** : the calyx of a kidney **f** : the abdominal opening of a fallopian tube **g** : a central cavity in the Ctenophora into which the gastric sac leads
¹in·fu·ri·ate \ənˈfyu̇rēˌāt, *usu* -ād·+V\ *vt* -ED/-ING/-S [ML *infuriatus*, past part. of *infuriare*, fr. L *in-* ²in- + *furiare* to madden, fr. *furia* fury — more at FURY] : to make furious : ENRAGE, MADDEN ⟨his book will . . . ~, enlighten, and rejoice different types of readers —D.W.Brogan⟩
²in·fu·ri·ate \", -ēət\ *adj* [ML *infuriatus*, past part.] : furiously angry : INFURIATED ⟨the hunchback weak, but ~, buffeting, biting, and whimpering —Arthur Morrison⟩ — **in·fu·ri·ate·ly** *adv*
in·fu·ri·at·ing·ly *adv* : to a maddening degree ⟨his sorely tried and ~ trying wife —Charles Lee⟩ : so as to infuriate ⟨~ unfair⟩
in·fu·ri·a·tion \ənˌfyu̇rēˈāshən\ *n* -S : the act of infuriating or state of being infuriated
in·fus·cate \ənˈfəˌskāt, -ˌskət\ *or* **in·fus·cat·ed** \-ˌskād·əd\ *adj* [*infuscate* fr. L *infuscatus*, past part. of *infuscare* to obscure, fr. *in-* ²in- + *fuscare* to darken, fr. *fuscus* dark brown, blackish; *infuscated* fr. L *infuscatus* + E *-ed* — more at DUSK] : OBSCURED ⟨~ minds⟩; *specif* : darkened with a brownish tinge ⟨~ wing of an insect⟩ — **in·fus·ca·tion** \ˌin(ˌ)fəˈskāshən\ *n* -S
in·fuse \ənˈfyüz\ *vb* -ED/-ING/-S [ME *infusen*, *enfusen*, fr. MF & L; MF *infuser*, fr. L *infusus*, past part. of *infundere* to pour in, fr. *in-* ²in- + *fundere* to pour — more at FOUND] *vt* **1** *obs* : to pour (a liquid) into something **2 a** : to instill or inculcate a principle or quality in ⟨attributes the fine spirit of the whole project to the self-respect with which men had been *infused* —Dixon Wecter⟩ **b** : INTRODUCE, INSINUATE, SUGGEST ⟨~ an idea⟩ ⟨~ a belief⟩ ⟨*infused* an aviation curriculum into some forty university departments —Phil Gustafson⟩ **3** : INSPIRE, IMBUE, ANIMATE, FILL ⟨brought together the main ideas . . . and *infused* them with the conception that the universe was the product of a historical development —S.F. Mason⟩ ⟨*infused* only with her passion for her child —Ethel Wilson⟩ **4** : to steep in water or other fluid without boiling for the purpose of extracting useful qualities : DRENCH ⟨~ tea leaves⟩ ~ *vi* : to undergo the process of infusion ⟨letting the tea stand a few minutes to ~ —Flora Thompson⟩
syn SUFFUSE, IMBUE, INGRAIN, INOCULATE, LEAVEN: INFUSE implies the introducing into one thing of a second that gives life, vigor, or new significance ⟨*infusing* life into an inanimate body —Mary W. Shelley⟩ ⟨the extraordinary force which Lawrence's imagination *infused* into his prose —*Times Lit. Supp.*⟩ ⟨whose work is for the most part *infused* with the spirit of scientific materialism —L.A.White⟩ ⟨it *infused* into them the feeling that they were not at the mercy of blind economic forces —A.R.Williams⟩ SUFFUSE implies the spreading over or through one thing of a second that gives the first thing an unusual color, aspect, texture, or quality ⟨I felt a large, healthy blush *suffuse* my features —L.P.Smith⟩ ⟨the western sky was *suffused* with the transparent yellow-green of August evenings —Ellen Glasgow⟩ ⟨an exalted feeling of martyrdom well earned *suffused* the exiles —E.J.Simmons⟩ ⟨the novel was *suffused* with a feeling for water and air, with sunlight hot and shifting —Leo Gurko⟩ IMBUE implies the introduction into a person or thing of something that completely permeates ⟨*imbued* so strongly with a sense of duty and obedience —Hanama Tasaki⟩ ⟨*imbued* with a dynamic faith —*Amer. Guide Series: Minn.*⟩ ⟨*imbue* the army with a national spirit —Hajo Holborn⟩ ⟨the mind becomes *imbued* with the scientific method —J.B.Conant⟩ INGRAIN implies a pervading of something with an irremovable dye or something suggesting such a dye ⟨morality *ingrained* in the national character —J.A.Froude⟩ ⟨the principle of serfdom was *ingrained* in medieval society —G.G.Coulton⟩ ⟨her instinctive humility and good manners were too deeply *ingrained* —Helen Howe⟩ ⟨this idea of equality was *ingrained* in the New York cabdriver —D.F.Karaka⟩ INOCULATE, in this extended sense, implies an imbuing of a person with something resembling a disease germ, often suggesting a surreptitious means ⟨those who believe that the great mass of the people are unreasoning beasts that must be controlled by *inoculating* them with myths or fictions —M.R. Cohen⟩ ⟨the democratic leveling had helped to *inoculate* the public with the idea of free schools disassociated from charity —*Amer. Guide Series: Va.*⟩ ⟨third-rate southerners *inoculated* with all the worst traits of the Yankee sharper —H.L.Mencken⟩ LEAVEN implies a transforming of something by introducing into it something else which enlivens, elevates, tempers, or markedly alters the total quality, usu. for the better ⟨*leaven* the dense mass of facts and events with the elastic force of reason —J.H.Newman⟩ ⟨there was need of idealism to *leaven* the materialistic realism of the times —V.L.Parrington⟩ ⟨knowledge . . . must be *leavened* with magnanimity before it becomes wisdom —A.E.Stevenson b. 1900⟩
in·fus·er \-zə(r)\ *n* -S : one that infuses; *esp* : a device for infusing tea leaves
in·fusibility \ˌin+\ *n* : the quality or state of being infusible
in·fusible \(ˈ)in, ən+\ *adj* [¹*in-* + *fusible*] : not fusible : incapable or very difficult of fusion; *specif, of a mineral* : having a melting point higher than the temperature (about 1500°C) of the ordinary blowpipe flame — **in·fu·si·ble·ness** *n* -ES
infusible white precipitate *n* : AMMONIATED MERCURY
in·fusion \ənˈfyüzhən\ *n* -S [ME, fr. MF & L; MF, fr. L *infusion-, infusio*, fr. *infusus* (past part. of *infundere* to pour in) + *-ion-, -io* -ion — more at INFUSE] **1 a** : the act or process of infusing ⟨an ~ of ordinary men and women would lessen the alleged remoteness of the higher civil servants from the life of the people —Ray Lewis & Angus Maude⟩ **b** : something that is infused ⟨horses of this type carry some ~ of . . . Thoroughbred blood —C.F.Rooks⟩ **2 a** : the introducing of a solution (as of glucose or salt) into a vein; *also* : the solution so used **b** (1) : the steeping or soaking usu. in water of a substance (as a plant drug) in order to extract its virtues (2) : the liquid extract obtained by this process **3** : a watery suspension of decaying organic material ⟨culturing soil amoebas in lettuce ~⟩
in·fu·sion·ism \-zhəˌnizəm\ *n* -S : the doctrine that the soul is preexistent to the body and is infused into it at conception or birth — compare CREATIONISM, TRADUCIANISM
in·fu·sion·ist \-nəst\ *n* : one who adheres to the doctrine of infusionism
infusion process *n* : a mashing process in which the whole mash is kept at about 70°C — compare DECOCTION PROCESS
in·fu·sive \ənˈfyüsiv, -üziv\ *adj* : INSPIRING, INFLUENCING ⟨the ~ force of Spring on man —James Thomson †1748⟩
in·fu·so·ria \ˌinfyəˈzȯrēə, -ˈs|, -ȯr-\ *n pl* [NL, fr. neut. pl. of *infusorius*, fr. L *infusus* (past part. of *infundere* to pour in) + *-orius* -ory] **1** *cap* : a group of minute organisms typically found in infusions of decaying organic matter: **a** *in early classifications* : a heterogeneous group comprising various plant and animal organisms (as bacteria, algae, fungi, protozoans, and small metazoans) **b** *in later classifications* : a heterogeneous group of animals comprising protozoans and small metazoans **c** *in early modern classifications* : a major division of Protozoa comprising protozoans with differentiated locomotor organelles and including the ciliates **d** *in some recent classifications* : a class of Protozoa coextensive with the subphylum Ciliophora **2** *often cap* : microscopic animal life — not used technically
in·fu·so·ri·al \ˌ≈≈ˈ≈≈əl\ *adj* [NL *Infusoria* + E *-al*] : relating to, containing, or having Infusoria
infusorial earth *n* : KIESELGUHR
¹in·fu·so·ri·an \-ēən\ *adj* [NL *Infusoria* + E *-an*] : INFUSORIAL
²infusorian \"\ *n* -S : one of the Infusoria
¹in·fu·so·ri·form \ˌ≈≈ˈ≈≈ˌfȯrm\ *adj* [NL *Infusoria* + E *-form*] : resembling an infusorian
²infusoriform \"\ *or* **infusoriform larva** *n* -S : the minute ciliated infective larva of the Dicyemida
in·fu·so·ri·gen \ˌ≈≈ˈ≈rəjən, -rəˌjen\ *also* **in·fu·so·ri·gene** \-rəˌjēn\ *n* -S [²*infusoriform* + *-gen, -gene*] : a reduced individual of certain mesozoans that is formed within the rhombogen and that gives rise to the infusoriform larva
in·fu·so·ri·oid \ˌ≈≈ˈ≈rēˌȯid\ *adj* [NL *Infusoria* + E *-oid*] : like an infusorian
in·fu·so·ri·um \ˌ≈≈ˈ≈rēəm\ *n, pl* **infuso·ria** \-ēə\ [NL, back-formation fr. *Infusoria*] : INFUSORIAN
in·fu·so·ry \ənˈfyüzərē, -üsə-\ *n* -ES [NL *Infusoria*] *archaic* : INFUSORIAN — usu. used in pl.
ing \ˈiŋ\ *n* -S [ME *enge, ynge*, of Scand origin; akin to ON *eng, engi* meadow, Norw & Dan *eng*; akin to MLG *enge* meadowland, OS & OHG *angar* meadow, pasture, OE *anga* hook — more at ANGLE] *dial Eng* : a low-lying pasture or meadow
¹-ing \iŋ, ēŋ, ən, ēn *after any sound; after* t (*but usu not when* f, k, p, *or* s *precedes*) & *after* d (*but usu not when* l *or* n *precedes*), ᵊn; *after* k (*but usu not when* s *precedes*) *or* g, *sometimes* ᵊŋ; *after* p, b, *or* v (*the* v *assimilating to* b), *sometimes* ᵊm *as in* ˈräbᵊm *for "robbing" or* ˈmübᵊm *for "moving"; in rapid speech, often* ŋ *or* n *after* ē, ā, ī, *or* ȯi *as in* ˈsāŋ *or* ˈsān *for "saying"; in NewEng often with intrusive* r *preceding when* ȯ *is the last sound in the infinitive form as in* ˈdrȯriŋ *or* ˈdrȯrin *for "drawing"; some have* ŋ *as their only consonant in this suffix & regard any other consonant as inelegant or substandard; some use consonants other than* ŋ *chiefly in informal speech; some use consonants other than* ŋ *for all styles of speech & of these some regard* ŋ *as artificial; for economy of space,* ŋ *is usu the only consonant shown for the suffix* -ing *in entries in this dictionary*\ *vb suffix or adj suffix* [ME *-inge, -ing*, alter. (influenced by *-inge* ³-ing) of *-inde, -ende*, fr. OE *-ende*, fr. *-e-* (vowel historically belonging to the verb stem) + *-nde*, pres. part. suffix — more at -ANT] — used to form the present participle ⟨*going*⟩ ⟨*sailing*⟩ and sometimes to form an adjective resembling a present participle but not derived from a verb ⟨*hulking*⟩ ⟨*swashbuckling*⟩; regularly accompanied by omission of final postconsonantal *e* of the base word ⟨*hoping*⟩ ⟨*loving*⟩, change of final *ie* of the base word to *y* ⟨*tying*⟩, or doubling of the final consonant of the base word immediately after a short stressed vowel ⟨*hopping*⟩ ⟨*planning*⟩

²-ing \"\ *n suffix* -s [ME, fr. OE *-ing, -ung* one of a (specified) kind, one belonging to, one descended from; akin to OHG *-ing* one of a (specified) kind, one belonging to, one descended from, ON *-ingr, -ungr,* Goth *-ings* one of a (specified) kind] **:** one of a (specified) kind ⟨sweet*ing*⟩ ⟨wild*ing*⟩

³-ing \"\ *n suffix* -s [ME *-inge, -ing* (in early ME a suffix forming nouns from verbs, in later ME becoming also a gerundial suffix), fr. OE *-ung, -ing,* suffix forming nouns from verbs; akin to OHG *-unga, -ung,* suffix forming nouns from verbs, ON *-ing,* suffix forming nouns from verbs, *-ung,* suffix forming nouns from nouns] **1 :** action or process ⟨becom*ing*⟩ ⟨draw*ing*⟩ ⟨runn*ing*⟩ ⟨sleep*ing*⟩ ⟨wash*ing*⟩ **:** instance of an action or process ⟨a bless*ing*⟩ ⟨a meet*ing*⟩ ⟨my com*ings* and go*ings*⟩ — in nouns formed from any fully inflected verb and functioning either as gerunds capable of being modified by an adverb and capable of having an object if the base verb is transitive ⟨after casually read*ing* the letter twice⟩ or as ordinary nouns ⟨after two casual read*ings* of the letter⟩ **2 :** something connected with an action or process: **a :** product, accompaniment, or result of an action or process ⟨an engrav*ing*⟩ ⟨a paint*ing*⟩ — in nouns formed from verbs; often in plural ⟨earn*ings*⟩ ⟨leav*ings*⟩ ⟨shav*ings*⟩ **b :** something used in an action or process ⟨a bed cover*ing*⟩ ⟨the lin*ing* of a coat⟩ — in nouns, esp. collectives ⟨carpet*ing*⟩ ⟨hous*ing*⟩ ⟨rigg*ing*⟩ ⟨shipp*ing*⟩, formed from verbs **3 :** action or process connected with (a specified thing) ⟨blackberry*ing*⟩ ⟨capital*ing*⟩ — in nouns formed from nouns **4 :** something connected with, consisting of, or used in making (a specified thing) ⟨sack*ing*⟩ ⟨scaffold*ing*⟩ ⟨shirt*ing*⟩ — in nouns, esp. collectives, formed from nouns **5 :** something related to (a specified concept) ⟨off*ing*⟩ — in nouns formed from parts of speech other than verbs and nouns; regularly accompanied by omission of final postconsonantal *e* of the base word, change of final *ie* of the base word to *y,* or doubling of the final consonant of the base word immediately after a short stressed vowel

in·ga *in sense 1* ˈiŋgə, *in senses 2 & 3* iŋˈgä *or* ˈiŋgə\ *n* [NL, fr. Pg *ingá* huamuchil, fr. Tupi *ingá, engá*] **1** *cap* **:** a genus of tropical shrubs and trees (family Leguminosae) having white or red flowers and large pods that contain an edible pulp and yielding an inferior timber of little durability — see GUAMA **2** -s **:** any plant of the genus *Inga* **3** [Pg *ingá*] -s **:** CAMACHILE

in·gae·vo·nes \ˌinjəˈvō(ˌ)nēz\ *n pl, usu cap* [L] **:** a group of Teutonic peoples inhabiting the northern coast of Europe in ancient times

in·gae·von·ic \ˌ═ˌ═ˈvänik, -ˈvōn-\ *adj, often cap* **:** of or relating to the Ingaevones

in·ga·lik \ˈiŋgəˌlik\ *n, pl* **ingalik** *or* **ingaliks** *usu cap* **1 a :** an Athapaskan people of the lower Yukon and Kuskokwim river valleys of Alaska **b :** a member of such people **2 :** the language of the Ingalik people

¹in·gate \ˈinˌgāt\ *n* [ME, fr. *in* + *gate* way, street — more at GATE] **1** *dial Eng* **:** ENTRANCE **2** *obs* **a :** a thing that enters **:** IMPORT **b :** import duty

²ingate \"\ *n* [⁴*in* + *gate* (channel in a mold)] **:** a gate through which the metal is poured into a foundry mold

ingather \ˈ═ˌ═\ *vb* [²*in* + *gather*] *vt* **:** to gather in; *esp* **:** HARVEST ~ *vi* **:** to gather together **:** ASSEMBLE

ingatherer \ˈ═ˌ═══\ *n* **:** one that gathers in **:** HARVESTER

ingathering \ˈ═ˌ═(═)═\ *n* [⁴*in* + *gathering*] **1 :** the act of gathering **:** COLLECTION, HARVEST ⟨~ of lenten boxes⟩ ⟨members of the needlework guild turn in their finished garments at the annual ~⟩ **2 :** ASSEMBLY ⟨revivalist ~⟩

ing·ber·lach \ˈiŋbərlək\ *n* -s [Yiddish, pl. of *ingberl* piece of ginger candy, dim. of *ingber* ginger, fr. MHG *ingeber, ingewer,* fr. OF *gingebre* — more at GINGER] **:** a candy made chiefly of ginger and honey

in·geminate \ən+\ *vt* [L *ingeminatus,* past part. of *ingeminare,* fr. *in-* ²in- + *geminare* to geminate — more at GEMINATE] **:** REDOUBLE, REITERATE **syn** see REPEAT

in·gemination \(ˌ)in, ən+\ *n* **:** REPETITION, DUPLICATION

ingender *obs var of* ENGENDER

in·gen·er·a·ble \ənˈjen(ə)rəbəl\ *adj* [ME, fr. LL *ingenerabilis,* fr. L *in-* ¹in- + *generabilis* generable — more at GENERABLE] **:** incapable of being engendered or produced **:** ORIGINAL — **in·gen·er·a·bly** \-blē\ *adv*

¹in·gen·er·ate \ənˈjenəˌrāt\ *vt* [L *ingeneratus,* past part. of *ingenerare,* fr. *in-* ²in- + *generare* to beget, create — more at GENERATE] **:** to bring about the generation of **:** BEGET, CAUSE

²in·gen·er·ate \-en(ə)rət\ *adj* [L *ingeneratus*] **1 :** INBORN, INNATE **2** *obs* **:** GENERATED, PRODUCED — **in·gen·er·ate·ly** *adv*

³in·generate \(ˈ)inˈjen(ə)rət, ənˈj-\ *adj* [LL *ingeneratus,* fr. L *in-* ¹in- + *generatus,* past part. of *generare*] **:** not generated ⟨God is ~⟩

ingenies *pl of* INGENY

in·ge·nios·i·ty \(ˌ)inˌjēnēˈäsəd·ē, ənˌj-, -jēnˈyä-\ *n* -ES [F *ingéniosité,* fr. *ingénieux* ingenious + *-ité* -ity] **:** INGENUITY, SKILL, CLEVERNESS

in·ge·nious \ənˈjēnyəs *sometimes* -nēəs\ *adj* [MF *ingenieux,* fr. L *ingeniosus,* fr. *ingenium* natural capacity, natural disposition + *-osus* -ous — more at ENGINE] **1** *obs* **:** showing or calling for intelligence **:** marked by mental power ⟨~ studies —Shak.⟩ **2 :** marked by especial aptitude at clever discovering, inventing, or contriving ⟨the invention of the knitting frame by another ~ English clergyman —Lewis Mumford⟩ **3 :** marked by originality, resourcefulness, and cleverness in conception or execution ⟨the iron safe built into the wall . . . made by an ~ locksmith —Thomas Hardy⟩ **4** [by alter. (influence of L *ingenuus* ingenuous)] *obs* **:** INGENUOUS **syn** see CLEVER

in·ge·nious·ly *adv* **:** in an ingenious manner

in·ge·nious·ness *n* -ES **:** INGENUITY

in·genital \ən+\ *adj* [L *ingenitus* inborn (fr. *in-* ²in- + *genitus,* past part. of *gignere* to beget, bring forth) + E *-al* — more at KIN] **:** INNATE, INHERENT

¹in·ge·nue \ˈanjəˌnü, ˈaⁿzhə-, ÷ˈäⁿzhə-, ÷ˈänjə-, ˌ══ˈ═\ *n* -s [F *ingénue,* fr. fem. of *ingénu* ingenuous, fr. L *ingenuus*] **1 a :** an ingenuous unsophisticated girl or young woman **:** a girl just entering society **:** DEBUTANTE ⟨suitable dress for an ~⟩; *esp* **:** a stage part representing a character that is youthful, innocent, appealing, sweet, sympathetic ⟨musical comedy ~⟩ — compare SOUBRETTE **b :** a naive or inexperienced person ⟨this is no time to have a political ~ as secretary of state —H.L.Ickes⟩ **2 :** a pale to grayish yellow green that is greener and less strong than water green

²ingenue \"\ *adj* **:** of, related, or appropriate to an ingenue ⟨artless ~ air about her⟩ ⟨~ party dress⟩

in·ge·nu·i·ty \ˌinjəˈn(y)üəd·ē, -ətē, -i\ *n* -ES [L *ingenuitas* ingenuousness, fr. *ingenuus* ingenuous + *-itas* -ity; in sense 2 & 3, influenced in meaning by *ingenious*] **1** *obs* **:** INGENUOUSNESS, CANDOR **2 a** *obs* **:** GENIUS, TALENT **b :** the power or quality of ready invention **:** skill or cleverness in devising or combining ⟨infinite ~ of man . . . in finding new methods of torture for his fellows —Mary Webb⟩ **c :** cleverness or aptness of design or contrivance ⟨despite the ~ of this etymological contention, the origin of the name is still disputed —*Amer. Guide Series: Minn.*⟩ ⟨all the perverted ~ of propaganda —Dean Acheson⟩ **3 :** an ingenious device or contrivance ⟨sophistication in the *ingenuities* of language —T.S.Eliot⟩ ⟨explore our stateroom, and scan eagerly the *ingenuities* by which we are to be surrounded for the journey —Frank A. Swinnerton⟩

in·gen·u·ous \ənˈjenyəwəs\ *adj* [L *ingenuus,* fr. *in-* ²in- + *-genuus* (akin to L *gignere* to beget, bring forth) — more at KIN] **1 :** FREEBORN ⟨~ Roman subjects⟩ **2** *obs* **:** of a superior character **:** NOBLE, HONORABLE ⟨symptoms of an ~ mind rather unfrequent in this age of brass —William Cowper⟩ **3 :** marked by lack of reserve, dissimulation, or guile: **a :** showing innocent or childlike simplicity, straightforwardness, frankness ⟨the Earl of Kildare's ~ explanation that he would not have burned a church if he had not thought the bishop was in it —Douglas Bush⟩ **b :** marked by lack of subtle analysis or consideration **:** SIMPLE, UNWARY, UNAWARE, OPEN ⟨a new invention (the telephone) in which it would seem ~ to believe too soon —Edith Wharton⟩ ⟨at times he was astoundingly ~, and then his dodges would not deceive the dullest —Arnold Bennett⟩ **4** [by alter. (influence of L *ingeniosus* ingenious)] *obs* **:** INGENIOUS **syn** see NATURAL

in·gen·u·ous·ly *adv* **:** in an ingenuous manner

in·gen·u·ous·ness *n* -ES **:** the quality of being ingenuous **:** absence of guile, reserve, or disguise **:** CANDOR, SIMPLICITY ⟨his airs of importance were comical in their ~ —Arnold Bennett⟩

ingeny *n* -ES [L *ingenium* natural character, natural disposition — more at ENGINE] *obs* **:** INTELLIGENCE, GENIUS, INGENUITY

inger \ˈiŋ(g)ə(r)\ *n* -s *cap* **:** INGRIAN

in·ger·ence \ˈinjərən(t)s, aⁿzhäˈräⁿs\ *n, pl* **ing·er·ences** \-rən(t)səz, -ˈräⁿs\ [F *ingérence,* fr. *ingérer* to intrude (fr. L *ingerere*) + *-ence*] **:** INTERFERENCE, INTRUSION ⟨~ in the domestic affairs of a neighboring country⟩

inger·man \ˈiŋ(g)ə(r)mən\ *n* -s *cap* **:** INGRIAN

in·gest \ənˈjest\ *vt* -ED/-ING/-S [L *ingestus,* past part. of *ingerere* to carry in, press upon, fr. *in-* ²in- + *gerere* to bear, wage, cherish — more at CAST] **1 :** to take in for digestion (as into the stomach) **2 :** to take in **:** SWALLOW, ABSORB ⟨for a country of forty-seven million, *~ing* twelve million visitors . . . is a big swallow —Robert Shaplen⟩ ⟨trying to ~ the ideas of philosophers⟩ **syn** see EAT

in·ges·ta \ənˈjestə\ *n pl* [NL, fr. L, neut. pl. of *ingestus*] **:** food and other materials taken into the body by way of the digestive tract — compare EGESTA

in·ges·tant \-tənt\ *n* -s **:** something taken into the body by ingestion; *esp* **:** an allergen so taken

in·gest·ible \-təbəl\ *adj* **:** capable of being ingested

in·ges·tion \-jes(h)chən\ *n* -s [LL *ingestion-, ingestio* action of pouring in, fr. L *ingestus* + *-ion-, -io* -ion] **1 :** the taking of material (as food) into the digestive system **2 :** the taking of air, gas, or liquid into an engine

in·ges·tive \-stiv\ *adj* **:** of or relating to ingestion

in·gine \ənˈjīn\ *n* -s [L *ingenium* natural character, natural disposition — more at ENGINE] *Scot* **:** GENIUS, INGENUITY

ingiver \ˈ═ˌ══\ *n* [⁴*in* + *giver*] *Brit* **:** HANDER-IN

ingiving \ˈ═ˌ══\ *n* [⁴*in* + *giving* (after *give in,* v.)] **:** the act of handing in thread to a loom

¹ingle \ˈiŋ(g)əl\ *n* -s [ScGael *aingeal* light, fire] **1 :** FLAME, BLAZE **2 :** FIREPLACE **3 :** CORNER, ANGLE ⟨cabin . . . with its one large room and small *~s,* or sleeping closets —H.C. Forman⟩

²ingle *n* -s [origin unknown] *obs* **:** CATAMITE

³ingle *vt* -ED/-ING/-S **1** *obs* **:** FONDLE, CARESS **2** *obs* **:** CAJOLE, WHEEDLE

ingle cheek *n* [¹*ingle*] *chiefly Scot* **:** FIRESIDE

inglenook \ˈ═ˌ═\ *n* [¹*ingle* + *nook*] **1 :** CHIMNEY CORNER **2 :** a high-backed wooden settle placed close to a fireplace

ingle recess *n* [¹*ingle*] **:** a recessed seating area at a fireplace **:** INGLENOOK

ingleside \ˈ═ˌ═\ *n* [¹*ingle* + *side*] **:** FIRESIDE

ingliding \ˈ═ˌ══\ *adj* [⁴*in* + *gliding* (after *glide in,* v.)] *of a diphthong or triphthong* **:** CENTERING — compare OUTGLIDING

inglenooks 2

in·glorious \(ˈ)in, ən+\ *adj* [L *inglorius,* fr. *in-* ¹in- + *-glorius* (fr. *gloria* glory) — more at GLORY] **1 :** not glorious **:** not bringing honor or glory **:** not accompanied with fame or honor ⟨some mute ~ Milton here may rest —Thomas Gray⟩ **2 :** SHAMEFUL, IGNOMINIOUS ⟨~ defeat⟩ — **in·gloriously** \"+\ *adv* — **in·gloriousness** \"+\ *n*

in·glu·vi·al \ənˈglüvēəl\ *adj* [*ingluvies* + *-al*] **:** of or relating to a crop ⟨~ membrane⟩ ⟨crop-milk is an ~ secretion⟩

in·glu·vi·es \-vēˌēz\ *n, pl* **ingluvies** [L, fr. *in-* ²in- + *-gluvies* (akin to *gluttire* to swallow) — more at GLUTTON] **:** the crop of a bird or insect

in·glu·vi·itis \(ˌ)inˌglüvēˈīd·əs, ən-\ *or* **in·glu·vi·tis** \ˌinˌglüˈvīd·əs\ *n* -ES [NL, fr. L *ingluvies* + NL *-itis*] **:** catarrhal inflammation of the crop in fowls

in-goal \ˈ═ˌ═\ *n* [⁴*in*] **:** either of the two areas of a rugby field bounded by the goal line, the dead-ball line, and the touch-in-goal lines — see RUGBY illustration

¹ingoing \ˈ═ˌ══, ═ˈ══\ *n* [ME, fr. *in* + *going*] **1 :** the act of going in **:** ENTRANCE **2** *Brit* **:** a sum paid when taking over a business

²ingoing \ˈ═ˌ══\ *adj* [²*in* + *going*] **1 :** going in ⟨~ tide⟩ **:** ENTERING ⟨~ administration⟩ **2 :** PENETRATING, THOROUGH ⟨~ mind⟩

in·golds·by car \ˈiŋgəl(d)zbē-\ *n* [fr. *Ingoldsby,* a trademark] **:** a dump car used to transport certain ores and concentrates

in·got \ˈiŋgət *also* -ˌgät; *usu* |d·+V\ *n* -s [ME, prob. modif. (resulting from incorrect division of MF *lingot* as *l'ingot,* understood as containing *l',* the contr. of *le,* def. art., the, fr. L *ille* that one, that) of MF *lingot* mass of metal cast into a convenient shape — more at LINGOT, LARIAT] **1 :** a mold in which metal is cast **2 :** a mass of metal cast into a convenient shape for storage or transportation and to be later remelted for casting or finished (as by rolling or forging) — compare PIG

ingot iron *n* **:** iron containing usu. less than 0.05 percent carbon and similarly small proportions of manganese and other impurities

in-grade \ˈ═ˌ═, ═ˈ═\ *adj* [fr. the phrase *in grade*] **:** occurring within a specified labor grade or rate range or occupational classification ⟨*in-grade* wage increase⟩

ingraft *var of* ENGRAFT

¹in·grain \ənˈgrān, ˈinˌ═\ *vt* -ED/-ING/-S [²*in-* + *grain* (n.)] **1** *obs* **:** ENGRAIN 1 **2 :** to work into the natural texture or mental or moral constitution **:** infix deeply **:** SATURATE, IMBUE **syn** see INFUSE

²in·grain \ˈ═ˌ═\ *adj* [fr. the phrase (dyed) *in grain*] **1** *obs* **:** dyed with kermes **2 a :** made of fiber (as wool) that is dyed before being spun into yarn **b :** made of yarn that is dyed before being knitted ⟨~ hose⟩ **3 :** of or relating to the formation of a dye or color by chemical reaction on the fiber **4 :** thoroughly worked in **:** INNATE, NATIVE ⟨~ stubbornness of character⟩

³ingrain \"\ *n* -s **1 :** an article made with ingrain yarns; *specif* **:** INGRAIN CARPET **2 :** innate quality or character

ingrain carpet *n* **:** a reversible carpet made of ingrain wool and having a similar design with the colors reversed appearing on each side

ingrain dye *or* **ingrain color** *n* **:** a dye or color formed on the fiber; *esp* **:** AZOIC DYE — see DYE table I

ingrained \ˈ═ˌ═, ═ˈ═\ *adj* [fr. past part. of ¹*ingrain*] **:** worked into the grain or fiber **:** forming a part of the essence or inmost being **:** DEEP-SEATED ⟨~ prejudice⟩ — **in·grained·ly** \-ān(ə)dlē, -li\ *adv* — **in·grained·ness** \-ānədnəs, -ān(d)nəs\ *n*

ingrandize *var of* ENGRANDIZE

¹in·grate \ˈinˌgrāt *sometimes* ənˈg-, *usu* -ād·+V\ *adj* [ME *ingrat,* fr. L *ingratus,* fr. *in-* ¹in- + *gratus* pleasing, grateful — more at GRACE] **1 a** *obs* **:** DISAGREEABLE, UNPLEASANT, UNCONGENIAL **b** *obs* **:** UNFRIENDLY **2** *archaic* **:** showing ingratitude **:** UNGRATEFUL — **in·grate·ly** *adv*

²ingrate \"\ *n* -s **:** an ungrateful person

ingrateful *adj* [¹*in-* + *grateful*] *obs* **:** not grateful

in·gra·ti·ate \ənˈgrāshēˌāt, *usu* -ād·+V\ *vt* -ED/-ING/-S [²*in-* + L *gratia* favor, grace + E *-ate* — more at GRACE] **:** to commend to favor **:** find favor or favorable acceptance for **:** make agreeable to someone ⟨show that Newman's imagery . . . helps to ~ the view that education is a good thing in itself —Geoffrey Tillotson⟩ — usu. used with *with* ⟨where, he flattered himself, his manners would ~ him with the housewives of the district —James Joyce⟩ ⟨with what unwearying politeness he kept on trying to ~ himself with all —R.L. Stevenson⟩

ingratiating *adj* **1 :** capable of winning favor **:** PLEASING ⟨~ smile⟩ ⟨we are prone to respond to art works . . . in terms of their ~ effect —H.E.Clurman⟩ **2 :** intended or adopted in order to gain favor **:** pleasantly persuasive **:** FLATTERING ⟨her manner is quiet and ~ and a little too agreeable —Gordon Bottomley⟩ ⟨~ manner . . . one does not think compatible with deep spiritual experience —W.B.Yeats⟩ ⟨some of his superiors were even younger than he, but it's possible that they were also more ~ and discreet —L.M.Hughes⟩

in·gra·ti·at·ing·ly *adv* **:** in an ingratiating manner **:** PLEASINGLY, FLATTERINGLY

in·gra·ti·a·tion \-ˌgrāshēˈāshən\ *n* -s **1 :** the act of ingratiating **:** process of getting oneself in favor ⟨practice the various arts of ~⟩ **2 :** something that ingratiates ⟨American art . . . had no native conviction with which to resist this wealth of ~ —C.D.Maginnis⟩

in·gra·tia·to·ry \-ˈgrāsh(ē)əˌtōrē\ *adj* **:** tending to ingratiate **:** INGRATIATING

in·gratitude \(ˈ)in, ən+\ *n* [ME, fr. MF, fr. ML *ingratitudo,* fr. L *in-* ¹in- + LL *gratitudo* gratitude — more at GRATITUDE] **:** lack of gratitude **:** forgetfulness of or poor return for kindness received **:** UNGRATEFULNESS ⟨blow, thou winter wind! thou art not so unkind as man's ~ —Shak.⟩

in·gra·ves·cence \ˌingrəˈvesᵊn(t)s\ *n* -s **:** the state of becoming progressively severe ⟨persistence and ~ of behavior disorders in spite of improved circumstances —Norman Cameron⟩

in·gra·ves·cent \ˌ═ˌ═ˈvesᵊnt\ *adj* [L *ingravescent-, ingravescens,* pres. part. of *ingravescere* to become heavier, to become worse, fr. *in-* ²in- + *gravescere* to become heavy, fr. *gravis* heavy, severe — more at GRIEVE] **:** gradually increasing in severity ⟨~ disease⟩ ⟨~ abnormality of function⟩

in·grav·i·date \ənˈgravəˌdāt\ *vt* -ED/-ING/-S [LL *ingravidatus,* past part. of *ingravidare,* fr. L *in-* ²in- + LL *gravidare* to make pregnant, fr. L *gravidus* pregnant — more at GRAVID] *archaic* **:** IMPREGNATE

in·gre·di·ence \ənˈgrēdēən(t)s\ *n* -s [in sense 1, alter. of *ingredients,* pl. of ¹*ingredient;* in sense 2, fr. L *ingredi* + E *-ence*] **1 a** *archaic* **:** an ingredient or a mixture of ingredients ⟨later, the gold lost its purity and contained up to ⅓ other *~s* —H.M.F.Schulman and H.W.Holzer⟩ **b :** the fact of entering as an ingredient ⟨this complete ~ in an occasion, so as to yield . . . fusion of individual essence with other eternal objects —A.N.Whitehead⟩ **2** *obs* **:** ENTRANCE, INGRESS

¹in·gre·di·ent \-nt\ *n* -s [ME, fr. L *ingredient-, ingrediens,* pres. part. of *ingredi* to go into, enter, fr. *in-* ²in- + *-gredi* (fr. *gradi* to step, go) — more at GRADE] **1 :** something that enters into a compound or is a component part of any combination or mixture **:** CONSTITUENT ⟨formula which will have just about the same *~s* as mother's milk —Morris Fishbein⟩ ⟨fashionable books that one must read, because they are *~s* of the talk of the day —T.L.Peacock⟩ ⟨understanding is one of the most important *~s* of a successful marriage —Grace Nagel⟩ **2** *obs* **:** something that moves into or penetrates **syn** see ELEMENT

²ingredient \"\ *adj* [L *ingredient-, ingrediens,* pres. part.] **1** *obs* **:** entering in **:** PENETRATING **2 :** present as or forming an ingredient **:** COMPONENT ⟨can be used as an ~ product in breads, pies, cakes —*Shareholder*⟩ ⟨when a sequence of words has not yet congealed into phrase, while we can ask whether he knows how to use the ~ words —Gilbert Ryle⟩

in gre·mio \(ˈ)inˈgrēmēˌō, -rēm-\ *adv* [L, in the bosom, in the lap] **:** in abeyance

¹in·gress \ˈinˌgres\ *n* -ES [ME *ingresse,* fr. L *ingressus,* fr. *ingressus,* past part. of *ingredi* to go into, enter — more at INGREDIENT] **1 :** the act of entering **:** ENTRANCE ⟨~ of air into the lungs⟩ ⟨~ of immigrants⟩ ⟨~ of summer tourists⟩ **2 :** the power or liberty of entrance or access ⟨~ visa⟩ **:** means of entering ⟨gate providing ~ to the meadow⟩ **3 :** a point in an astrological direction where a significator transits the place of any other planet, the ascendant, or midheaven **4 :** an entrance of the moon into the shadow of the earth in an eclipse or of an inferior planet upon the sun's disk in transit or of a satellite or its shadow on a planet **:** the sun's entrance (as into a sign)

²in·gress \(ˈ)inˈgres, ənˈg-\ *vi* -ED/-ING/-ES [L *ingressus,* past part.] **1 :** to go in **:** ENTER **2 :** to mark an ingress — said of an astrological significator

in·gres·sion \ənˈgreshən\ *n* -s [ME, fr. L *ingression-, ingressio,* fr. *ingressus* (past part.) + *-ion-, -io* -ion] **1 :** the action of entering **:** ENTRANCE **2 :** the process whereby potentialities or eternal objects enter into or become complex actual occasions or events ⟨the ~ of an object into an event is the way the character of the event shapes itself in virtue of the being of the object —A.N.Whitehead⟩ **3 :** inward migration in gastrulation of large yolk-laden macromeres formed by holoblastic but markedly unequal cleavage

¹in·gres·sive \(ˈ)inˈgresiv, ənˈg-\ *adj* [L *ingressus* (past part.) + E *-ive*] **:** of or relating to ingress **:** ENTERING; *specif* **:** INCHOATIVE ⟨~ aspect⟩ — **in·gres·sive·ness** *n* -ES

²ingressive \"\ *n* -s **:** an ingressive verb

ingri·an \ˈiŋ(g)rēən\ *n* -s *cap* [*Ingria,* district of early Russia on the eastern end of the Gulf of Finland + E *-an*] **:** a member of a western division of the Finns native to the old Baltic province in which St. Petersburg was built — called also *Inger, Ingerman*

ingross *obs var of* ENGROSS

ingroup \ˈ═ˌ═\ *n, often attrib* [⁴*in* + *group*] **:** a social group possessing a sense of solidarity or community of interests as opposed to other social groups — compare OUTGROUP

ingrowing \ˈ═ˌ══\ *adj* [²*in* + *growing* (after *grow in,* v.)] **:** growing or tending inwards ⟨~ emotions⟩ **:** developing within confining limits ⟨~ toenail⟩ ⟨French playwriting was ~ and was becoming provincial —Sheldon Cheney⟩

ingrown \ˈ═ˌ═\ *adj* [²*in* + *grown*] **1 :** grown in **:** ENCLOSED; *esp, of a hair or nail* **:** having the free tip or edge embedded in the flesh **2 :** having the direction of growth or activity or interest inward rather than outward **:** WITHDRAWN, CONTRACTED ⟨the contrast between an outgoing, cultural, vibrant, liberal-aristocratic Athens and an ~, inbred, militaristic, oligarchic Sparta —Norman Cousins⟩ **3** *of a stream* **:** having enlarged the original course by undercutting the banks of the outer curves — **in·grown·ness** \-nnəs\ *n* -ES

ingrown meander *n* **:** an incised meander (as of a river) with a steep undercut slope on one side and a gentle slip-off slope on the other side

ingrowth \ˈ═ˌ═\ *n* [⁴*in* + *growth*] **:** a growth or development inward ⟨~ of cells⟩; *also* **:** something that grows inward

-ings *pl of* -ING

in·guen \ˈiŋgwən, -ˌgwen\ *n, pl* **ingui·na** \-ˌgwənə\ [L] **:** GROIN

inguin- *or* **inguino-** *comb form* [NL, fr. L *inguin-, inguen*] **:** inguinal ⟨*inguin*odynia⟩ **:** inguinal and ⟨*inguino*scrotal⟩

¹in·gui·nal \-gwənᵊl\ *adj* [L *inguinalis,* fr. *inguin-, inguen* groin + *-alis* -al — more at ADEN-] **1 :** of, relating to, or in the region of the groin **2 :** of or relating to either of the lowest lateral regions of the abdomen — compare ABDOMINAL REGION

²inguinal \"\ *n* -s **:** one of the plates on the posterior surface of the bridge of a turtle

inguinal canal *n* **:** a passage about one and one half inches long that lies parallel to and a half inch above Poupart's ligament: as **a :** a passage in the male through which the testis descends into the scrotum and in which lies the spermatic cord **b :** a passage in the female accommodating the round ligament

inguinal gland *n* **:** any of the superficial lymphatic glands of the groin made up of two more or less distinct groups of which one is disposed along Poupart's ligament and the other about the saphenous opening

inguinal ligament *n* **:** POUPART'S LIGAMENT

inguinal ring *n* **:** ABDOMINAL RING

ingulph *obs var of* ENGULF

in·gurgitate \ən+\ *vb* -ED/-ING/-S [L *ingurgitatus,* past part. of *ingurgitare,* fr. *in-* ²in- + *gurgit-, gurges* whirlpool, abyss — more at VORACIOUS] *vt* **1 :** to swallow, devour, or drink greedily or in large quantity **:** GUZZLE ⟨produces cocktails . . . and *~s* them absentmindedly without reflection —Aldous Huxley⟩ **2** *obs* **:** to overload by eating or drinking **:** CRAM ~ *vi* **:** GUZZLE, GORMANDIZE, SWILL

in·gurgitation \(ˌ)in, ən+\ *n* [LL *ingurgitation-, ingurgitatio,* fr. L *ingurgitatus* + *-ion-, -io* -ion] **:** the act of devouring or swallowing ⟨basically Puritan foundations were undermined by the ~ of German transcendentalism —Oskar Seidlin⟩

in·gush \ˈinˌgüsh, ═ˈ═\ *n, pl* **ingush** *or* **ingushes** *usu cap* **1 :** a Muhammadan people living north of the Caucasian mountains and related to the Chechen **2 :** a member of the Ingush people

in·habile \(ˈ)in+\ *adj* [F, fr. L *inhabilis,* fr. *in-* ¹in- + *habilis* easily managed, apt, skillful — more at ABLE] *archaic* **:** not fit or qualified

in·hab·it \ən'habət, *usu* -əd.+V\ *vb* -ED/-ING/-S [ME *enhabiten, inhabiten,* fr. MF & L; MF *enhabiter,* fr. L *inhabitare,* fr. *in-* ²in- + *habitare* to dwell — more at HABIT] *vt* **1 :** to occupy as a place of settled residence or habitat **:** live or dwell in ⟨~*ed* by a rich fauna and flora —W.H.Dowdeswell⟩ ⟨~*ed* a small apartment —Alfred Hayes⟩ **2 a :** to be at home in (a particular sphere of activity or thought) **:** OCCUPY ⟨endlessly varied characters who ~ the world of medicine —*N.Y.Times*⟩ ⟨the intellectual world we ~ —Cyril Connolly⟩ **b :** to occupy, be present in, or be resided in in any manner or form ⟨the human beings who ~ this tale —Al Newman⟩ ⟨the individual is ~*ed* by multiple wills, persons, or spirits —Weston La Barre⟩ ⟨a sculptural quality that ~*s* many of his most successful prints —Vincent Garofalo⟩ ~ *vi, archaic* **:** to have residence in a place **:** DWELL, LIVE

in·hab·it·abil·i·ty \ən,habəd·ə'biləd·ē, -bət·ə-, -lətē, -i\ *n* **:** the condition of being inhabitable

¹**inhabitable** *adj* [ME, fr. MF, fr. L *inhabitabilis,* fr. *in-* ¹in- + *habitabilis* habitable — more at HABITABLE] *obs* **:** not habitable; *also* **:** UNINHABITED

²**in·hab·it·able** \ən'habəd·əbəl, -bət·ə-\ *adj* [LL *inhabitabilis,* fr. L *inhabitare* + *-abilis* -able] **:** capable of being inhabited **:** HABITABLE

in·hab·i·tance \-bəd·ən(t)s, -bətən- *also* -bət³n-\ *n* -S [*inhabit* + *-ance*] **:** RESIDENCE ⟨grateful for his almost solitary ~ of the city —William Saroyan⟩

in·hab·i·tan·cy \-nsē,-nsi\ *n* **1 :** the act of inhabiting or the state of being inhabited **:** the state, rights, or privileges of one who is an inhabitant **:** RESIDENCE, OCCUPANCY **2 :** the site of the principal office or place of business of a corporation or association; *sometimes* **:** a fixed place of abode

¹**in·hab·i·tant** \-nt\ *n* [ME *inhabitaunt,* fr. AF *enhabitant,* fr. MF (pres. part. of *enhabiter*), fr. L *inhabitant-, inhabitans,* pres. part. of *inhabitare* to inhabit] **1 :** a person who dwells or resides permanently in a place as distinguished from a transient lodger or visitor ⟨an ~ of a house⟩ ⟨an ~ of a state⟩ — compare CITIZEN, DOMICILE, RESIDENT **2 :** one that makes its habitat or is commonly found in a place ⟨with respect to its insect ~*s* —*Am Guide Series: N.H.*⟩ ⟨a normal ~ of the intestines of both man and animals —*Farmer's Weekly (So. Africa)*⟩

²**inhabitant** \"\ *adj* [L *inhabitant-, inhabitans,* pres. part.] *archaic* **:** RESIDENT, DWELLING

inhabitate *vt* -ED/-ING/-S [L *inhabitatus,* past part.] *obs* **:** INHABIT

in·hab·i·ta·tion \ən,habə'tāshən\ *n* [ME *inhabitacioun,* fr. LL *inhabitation-, inhabitatio,* fr. L *inhabitatus* (past part. of *inhabitare* to inhabit) + *-ion-, -io* -ion — more at INHABIT] **:** the act or an instance of inhabiting **:** the state of being inhabited ⟨space flight and space ~ —J.N.Leonard⟩

inhabited *adj* **:** having inhabitants ⟨an ~ area⟩

in·hab·it·er \ən'habəd·ə(r), -ət·ə-\ *n* -S [ME *enhabiter, inhabiter,* fr. *enhabiten, inhabiten* to inhabit + *-er* — more at INHABIT] *archaic* **:** one that inhabits

inhabiting *n* -S [ME *enhabiting, inhabiting,* fr. gerund of *enhabiten, inhabiten*] *archaic* **:** a dwelling place

in·hab·i·tive·ness \-bəd·ivnəs, -bət·iv-\ *n* -ES [*inhabit* + *-ive* + *-ness*] **:** a propensity to remain permanently in the same place or residence ⟨you know my (what the phrenologists call) ~ —J.R.Lowell⟩

in·hab·i·tress \-bə·trəs\ *n* -ES [*inhabiter* + *-ess*] *archaic* **:** a female inhabitant

¹**in·hal·ant** \(')in¦hālənt, ən'h-\ *n* -S [¹*inhale* + *-ant* (n. suffix)] **:** something (as an allergen, an anesthetic vapor, or a medicated nasal spray) that is inhaled

²**inhalant** \"\ *also* **in·hal·ent** \"\ *adj* [¹*inhale* + *-ant* or *-ent* (adj. suffixes)] **1 :** used for inhaling or constituting an inhalant ⟨~ allergens⟩ **2 :** INCURRENT ⟨~ pores⟩

in·ha·la·tion \,in(h)ə'lāshən\ *n* -S *often attrib* [¹*inhale* + *-ation*] **:** the act or an instance of inhaling; *specif* **:** the action of drawing air into the lungs by means of a complex of essentially reflex actions that involve changes in the diaphragm and in muscles of the abdomen and thorax which cause enlargement of the chest cavity and lungs resulting in production of relatively negative pressure within the lungs so that air flows in until the pressure is restored to equality with that of the atmosphere

in·ha·la·tion·al \¦==¦lāshən³l,-shnəl\ *adj* **:** by or involving inhalation ⟨~ therapy⟩

in·ha·la·tor \'==,lād·ə(r), -ātə-\ *n* -S [¹*inhale* + *-ator*] **:** a device designed to provide a suitable mixture of oxygen and carbon dioxide for inhalation and used esp. in conjunction with manual artificial respiration

¹**in·hale** \ən'hāl, *chiefly before pause or consonant* -āəl\ *vb* -ED/-ING/-S [²*in-* + *-hale* (as in *exhale*)] *vt* **1 :** to draw in by breathing ⟨~ air⟩ **2 :** to consume or swallow esp. eagerly or greedily ⟨*inhaled* about four meals at once —Ring Lardner⟩ ⟨*inhaling* it from their cupped fingers until their cheeks bulged —R.D.Bowen⟩ ⟨*inhaled* a strong love decoction —Abram Kardiner⟩ ~ *vi* **:** to breathe in **:** inhale air, gas, smoke, or other vapor — opposed to *exhale*

²**in·hale** \", 'in,=\ *n* -S **:** the act or an instance of inhaling ⟨kept taking deep ~*s* —J.W.Ellison b. 1891⟩

in·hal·er \ən'hālə(r)\ *n* -S **1 :** one that inhales **2 :** a device by means of which vapors, volatilized remedies, medicinal dusts, or anesthetics can be inhaled — compare INHALATOR **3 :** SNIFTER ⟨pouring a liberal amount of brandy into an ~ —Caroline Slade⟩

in·harmonic \¦in+\ *adj* [¹*in-* + *harmonic*] **:** not harmonic **:** DISCORDANT

inharmonic theory *n* **:** a postulate in phonetics: the reinforcing vibrations produced in the superglottic cavities in vowel articulation need not be multiples of the fundamental vocal-cord note — compare FORMANT, HARMONIC THEORY

in·harmonious \¦in+\ *adj* [¹*in-* + *harmonious*] **1 :** UNMUSICAL, DISCORDANT ⟨~ sounds⟩ **2 :** being not in harmony **:** CONFLICTING, JARRING, UNCONGENIAL ⟨~ surroundings⟩ — **in·harmoniously** \"+\ *adv* — **in·harmoniousness** \"+\ *n*

in·harmony \(')in, ən+\ *n* [¹*in-* + *harmony*] **:** lack of harmony **:** DISCORD

inhaul \'=,=\ *n* [⁴*in* + *haul* (after *haul in,* v.)] **:** a rope used to draw in a ship's sail (as a spanker on its gaff)

in·haust \ən'hȯst\ *vt* -ED/-ING/-S [²*in-* + *-haust* (as in *exhaust*)] **:** INHALE, IMBIBE ⟨~*ing* mint juleps —Virginius Dabney⟩

in·hell \ən+\ *vt* [²*in-* + *hell*] *archaic* **:** to put or fix in hell

in·here \ən'hi(ə)r, -iə\ *vi* -ED/-ING/-S [L *inhaerēre,* fr. *in-* ²in- + *haerēre* to stick, adhere — more at HESITATE] **:** to be inherent **:** be a fixed element or attribute **:** BELONG ⟨thought all virtue *inhered* in the farmer —H.S.Commager⟩ ⟨the excellence *inhering* in the democratic faith —V.L.Parrington⟩

in·her·ence \ən'hirən(t)s, -her-,-hēr-\ *n* -S [ML *inhaerentia,* fr. L *inhaerent-, inhaerens* + *-ia* -y] **1 :** the quality, state, or fact of inhering or of being inherent **:** permanent existence as an attribute ⟨the ~ of multiple meanings and allusions in the particulars of a literary work —B.T.Spencer⟩ **2 :** the relation of a quality to a substance or subject ⟨~ rather than existence is said of accidents —James Albertson⟩

in·her·en·cy \-nsē, -nsi\ *n* -ES [ML *inhaerentia*] **1 :** INHERENCE **2 :** an inherent character or attribute ⟨culture classifications with purely taxonomic *inherencies* —W.W.Taylor⟩

in·her·ent \-nt\ *adj* [L *inhaerent-, inhaerens,* pres. part. of *inhaerēre*] **:** structural or involved in the constitution or essential character of something **:** belonging by nature or settled habit **:** INTRINSIC, ESSENTIAL ⟨~ rights⟩ ⟨shortcomings ~ in our approach —David Cherin⟩ ⟨an ~ laziness⟩ — **in·her·ent·ly** *adv*

in·her·it \ən'herət, *usu* -əd.+V\ *vb* -ED/-ING/-S [ME *enheriten* to make heir, inherit (influenced in meaning by MF *heriter* & L *hereditare* to inherit), fr. MF *enheriter* to make heir, fr. LL *inhereditare,* fr. L *in-* ²in- + LL *hereditare* to inherit — more at HERITAGE] *vt* **1 :** to come into possession of **:** POSSESS, RECEIVE ⟨power . . . which he ~*s* from the Creator himself —Eric Linklater⟩ **2 a :** to take by descent from an ancestor **:** take by inheritance **:** receive as a right or title descendible by law from an ancestor at his decease **b :** to be heir to **:** SUCCEED ⟨a son ~*s* his father⟩ **3 a :** to receive by genetic transmission **:** derive or acquire from ancestors ⟨~ a strong constitution⟩ **b :** to have in turn or receive as if from an ancestor ⟨much of the girl's clothing had been ~*ed* from the more fortunate children —Grace Metalious⟩ ⟨~*ed* from antiquity two rather contradictory views of the organic world —S.F.Mason⟩ ~ *vi* **:** to take or hold a possession, property, estate, or rights by inheritance

in·her·it·abil·i·ty \-,herəd·ə'biləd·ē,-rətə-, -lətē, -i\ *n* **:** the quality of being inheritable or descendible to heirs

in·her·it·able \-'herəd·əbəl, -rətə-\ *adj* [ME *enheritable,* fr. AF, fr. MF *enheriter* + *-able*] **1 a :** capable of being inherited **:** TRANSMISSIBLE, DESCENDIBLE ⟨an ~ title⟩ **b** (1) **:** capable of taking by inheritance (2) **:** entitled to as a birthright **2 :** capable of being transmitted from parent to child ⟨~ qualities⟩ — **in·her·it·able·ness** \-nəs\ *n* -ES — **in·her·it·ably** \-blē,-bli\ *adv*

in·her·i·tage \-'herəd·ij\ *n* [*inherit* + *-age*] *archaic* **:** INHERITANCE

in·her·i·tance \ən'herəd·ən(t)s, -rətən-,-rət³n-\ *n* -S [ME *enheritaunce,* fr. AF *enheritance,* fr. MF *enheriter* + *-ance*] **1 a :** the act of inheriting property: as (1) **:** the acquisition of real or personal property as heir to another **:** the perpetual or continuing right which a person and his heirs have to an estate or property (2) *common, feudal, & Scots law* **:** the acquisition of an ancestor's real estate upon his death by the heir under the Statute of Descent as distinguished from the successsion to his personal property by the next of kin under the Statute of Distribution (3) *Roman & Civil law* **:** the succession upon the death of an owner either by testament or by operation of law by the heir to all the estate, rights, and liabilities of the decedent, the liabilities being restricted to the value of the estate when the heir was given the benefit of inventory **b :** the reception or acquisition of genetic characters or qualities by transmission from parent to offspring **c :** the acquisition of a material or immaterial possession, condition, or trait by transmission from the past or from past generations ⟨resented his children's ~ of slavery from their mothers —Anne K. Gregorie⟩ ⟨hard-won freedoms that are ours by just ~⟩ **2 :** something that is or may be inherited: as **a** (1) **:** something that is derived by an heir from an ancestor or other person or that may be transmitted to an heir by a person (2) *common, feudal, & Scots law* **:** an estate of inheritance (as a fee simple or a fee tail) **b :** the sum total of genetic characters or qualities transmitted from parent to offspring ⟨on the maternal side his ~ was a happy one⟩ **c :** something material or immaterial that is derived or acquired from the past or from past generations ⟨the random brutality that is the ~ of centuries of blackness —Irving Howe⟩; *esp* **:** a permanent or valuable possession that is a common heritage or that is received from God or nature ⟨our great ~ of water and land —A.E.Stevenson b.1900⟩ ⟨their most precious ~, that thin layer of topsoil —K.D. White⟩ ⟨books are the major channel by which the intellectual ~ is handed down —*New Republic*⟩ **3** *obs* **:** right of possession **:** POSSESSION, OWNERSHIP

inheritance tax *n* **1 :** an excise tax levied upon the privilege of receiving property as heir or next of kin under the law governing intestate succession, measured by the value of the interest each successor receives, and usu. increased in rate as kinship with the deceased becomes more remote — compare LEGACY TAX **2 :** ESTATE TAX

inherited *adj* **:** constituting something received by inheritance ⟨~ characteristics⟩ ⟨shackled by a mass of ~ conventions —J.L.Lowes⟩ ⟨a city which follows an ~ type of industry —Samuel Van Valkenburg & Ellsworth Huntington⟩ **syn** see INNATE

in·her·i·tor \ən'herəd·ə(r), -rətə-\ *n* [ME *enheritour, enheriter,* fr. *enheriten* to inherit + *-our* -or or *-er* — more at INHERIT] **:** one that inherits **:** HEIR ⟨~*s* of an ancient culture⟩

in·her·i·tress \-rə·trəs\ *also* **in·her·i·trix** \-rə·(,)triks\ *n* -ES [*inheritress* fr. *inheritor* + *-ess; inheritrix* fr. *inheritor,* after such pairs as E *mediator: mediatrix*] **:** a female inheritor

inherits *pres 3d sing of* INHERIT

in·he·sion \ən'hēzhən\ *n* -S [L *inhaesus* (past part. of *inhaerēre* to inhere) + E *-ion* — more at INHERE] **:** the condition of being inherent in something **:** INHERENCE

in·hib·it \ən'hibət, *usu* -bəd.+V\ *vb* -ED/-ING/-S [ME *inhibiten,* fr. L *inhibitus,* past part. of *inhibēre,* fr. *in-* ²in- + *-hibēre* (fr. *habēre* to have, hold) — more at HABIT] *vt* **1 :** to prohibit from doing something **:** FORBID, INTERDICT ⟨~*s* the legislature from levying an income tax —*Britannica Bk. of the Yr.*⟩ **2 a** (1) **:** to repress, restrain, or discourage from free or spontaneous activity esp. through the operation of inner psychological impediments or conflicts or of social and cultural controls ⟨~*ed* from bold speculation by his personal loyalties and interests —V.L.Parrington⟩ ⟨a people long ~*ed* by the prevailing taboos —R.S.Ellery⟩ (2) **:** to operate against the full development or activity of **:** check, restrain, or diminish the force, intensity, or vitality of ⟨~*ed* the creative process at its sources —Harry Sylvester⟩ ⟨the heavy tax load that ~*s* investment in capital goods —*Time*⟩ **b** (1) **:** to reduce or suppress the activity of ⟨many of the iron or copper enzymes are ~*ed* by cyanides —Felix Haurowitz⟩ ⟨lubricating oil ~*ed* against rust, corrosion, and oxidation⟩ (2) **:** to retard or prevent the formation of ⟨~ rust⟩ (3) **:** to retard, interfere with, or prevent (a chemical process or reaction) ⟨~ oxidation⟩ ~ *vi* **:** to cause inhibition ⟨something that entraps and ~*s* —John Portz⟩ **syn** see FORBID, RESTRAIN

in·hib·it·able \-əbəl\ *adj* **:** capable of being inhibited

inhibited *adj* **:** being repressed, discouraged, reduced, or retarded: as **a :** characterized by, displaying, or reflecting inhibition ⟨a shy and ~ boy —Alan Harrington⟩ ⟨~ respectability —H.C.Webster⟩ **b :** having its activity reduced or suppressed ⟨~ oils⟩

inhibiting *adj* **:** tending to inhibit or causing inhibition ⟨an overly strict or ~ discipline —H.V.Gregory⟩

in·hi·bi·tion \,inə'bishən, ,inhə'-, ,in(,)(h)i'-\ *n* -S [ME *inhibicioun,* fr. MF *inhibition,* fr. L *inhibition-, inhibitio,* fr. *inhibitus* + *-ion-, -io* -ion] **:** the act or an instance of inhibiting or the state of being inhibited: as **a :** the act or an instance of formally forbidding or barring something from being done **:** PROHIBITION ⟨plain ~*s* to the exercise of that power in a particular way —John Marshall⟩; *also* **:** something that formally forbids or debars **:** IMPEDIMENT ⟨the constitutional ~ of his alien birth —F.L.Paxson⟩ **b** (1) **:** a writ from a higher court (as an ecclesiastical court) staying an inferior judge from further proceedings (2) *Eng eccl law* **:** a command of an ecclesiastical authority (as a bishop) to a minister not to perform ministerial duties (3) *Scots law* **:** a personal order prohibiting a party from contracting debts to the prejudice of the rights of others in his heritable property or realty; *also* **:** an order procured by a husband prohibiting the giving of credit to his wife **c** (1) **:** a stopping or checking of a bodily action **:** a restraining of the function of an organ or an agent (as a digestive fluid or enzyme) ⟨~ of the heartbeat by stimulation of the vagus nerve⟩ ⟨~ of plantar reflexes⟩ (2) **:** interference with or retardation or prevention of a chemical process or activity ⟨~ of a catalyst⟩ ⟨~ of rust⟩ **d** (1) **:** a desirable restraint or check upon the free or spontaneous instincts or impulses of an individual effected through the operation of the human will guided or directed by the social and cultural forces of the environment ⟨the self-control so developed is called ~ —C.W.Russell⟩ ⟨creating ~*s*, socializing the child, obviously should be one of the goals of a training school —Erwin Schepses⟩ (2) **:** a neurotic restraint upon a normal or beneficial impulse or activity caused by psychological inner conflicts or by sociocultural forces of the environment ⟨other outspoken neurotic manifestations are general ~*s* such as inability to think, to concentrate —Muriel Ivimey⟩ ⟨~*s*, phobias, compulsions, and other neurotic patterns —*Psychological Abstracts*⟩ (3) **:** repression of or restraint upon an urge, impulse, or activity of any kind ⟨locked in Puritan ~*s* —H.S.Canby⟩ ⟨obstacles and ~*s* to rural reading —C.M.Wieting⟩ ⟨throwing all her moral teachings and ~*s* overboard —Ruth Park⟩ ⟨laughed without ~ —Jean Stafford⟩

in·hib·i·tive \ən'hibəd·iv, -bətiv\ *adj* **:** INHIBITORY

in·hib·i·tor *or* **in·hib·it·er** \-bəd·ə(r), -bətə-\ *n* -S **:** one that inhibits: as **a** (1) **:** a substance for reducing corrosion or rust formation (as in an antifreeze) (2) **:** a substance for delaying gum formation (as in gasoline) (3) **:** ANTIOXIDANT **b :** a substance that interferes with a chemical process or reaction ⟨polymerization ~*s*⟩ **:** NEGATIVE CATALYST **c :** a substance that reduces the activity of another substance (as an enzyme) — compare ANTIMETABOLITE **d :** a gene that checks the normal effect of another nonallelic gene when both are present

in·hib·i·to·ry \-bə,tōrē, -tȯr-, -ri\ *adj* [ML *inhibitorius,* fr. L *inhibitus* (past part. of *inhibēre* to inhibit) + *-orius* -ory — more at INHIBIT] **:** of, relating to, or producing inhibition **:** tending or serving to inhibit **:** PROHIBITORY ⟨~ nervous action⟩ ⟨the ~ action of fluorides —*Americana Annual*⟩

inholding \'=,==\ *n* [⁴*in* + *holding*] **:** privately owned land inside the boundary of a national park

in home *n* **:** INSIDE HOME

in·homogeneity \(¦)in, ən+\ *n* [¹*in-* + *homogeneity*] **1 :** lack of homogeneity **:** the condition of not being homogeneous ⟨the degree of microscopic ~ in an alloy⟩ **2 :** a part that is not homogeneous with the larger homogeneous mass in which it is incorporated

in·homogeneous \"+\ *adj* [¹*in-* + *homogeneous*] **:** not homogeneous **:** lacking homogeneity — **in·homogeneously** \"+\ *adv*

inhoop *vt* [²*in-* + *hoop* (n.)] *obs* **:** to enclose in a hoop

in·hospitable \(¦)in, ən+\ *adj* [¹*in-* + *hospitable*] **1 a :** not hospitable **:** not disposed to show hospitality ⟨an ~ person⟩ **b :** reflecting or evidencing inhospitality **:** UNFRIENDLY ⟨gave me a brief, ~ look —Louis Auchincloss⟩ **2 :** providing no shelter or sustenance **:** BARREN, DESERT ⟨~ mountain areas⟩ — **in·hospitableness** \"+\ *n* -ES — **in·hospitably** \"+\ *adv*

inhospital *adj* [prob. fr. MF, fr. L *inhospitalis,* fr. *in-* ¹in- + *hospitalis* hospitable — more at HOSPITAL] *obs* **:** INHOSPITABLE

in·hospitality \(¦)in, ən+\ *n* [prob. fr. MF *inhospitalité,* fr. L *inhospitalitat-, inhospitalitas,* fr. *inhospitalis* + *-itat-, -itas* -ity] **:** the quality or state of being inhospitable **:** a cold or unfriendly reception or treatment of a guest or visitor

in·human \(')in, ən+\ *adj* [MF & L; MF *inhumain,* fr. L *inhumanus,* fr. *in-* ¹in- + *humanus* human — more at HUMAN] **1 a :** lacking the qualities of mercy, pity, kindness, or tenderness **:** CRUEL, BARBAROUS, SAVAGE ⟨an ~ tyrant⟩ ⟨what ~ rogues there are in the world —A. Conan Doyle⟩ **b :** lacking warmth or geniality **:** COLD, IMPERSONAL, MECHANICAL ⟨his usual quiet, almost ~ courtesy —F. Tennyson Jesse⟩ **c :** not worthy of or conforming to the needs of human beings ⟨living in conditions that are ~ —*Collier's Yr. Bk.*⟩ ⟨has the world's most ~ subways —*Time*⟩ ⟨one large block which would tend to be ~ and monotonous —*Architect & Building News*⟩ **2 a :** belonging to, resembling, or suggesting a nonhuman species or class of beings ⟨there is something a little ~ about them —Lewis Mumford⟩ ⟨a momentary glimpse . . . of something I didn't understand: something dark and ~ —Kenneth Roberts⟩ **b :** SUPERHUMAN ⟨models of ~ perfection —H.B. Parkes⟩ **syn** see FIERCE

in·humane \(¦)in, ən+\ *adj* [MF *inhumain* & L *inhumanus*] **:** not humane **:** INHUMAN 1 — **in·humanely** \"+\ *adv*

in·humanity \¦in+\ *n* [MF *inhumanité,* fr. L *inhumanitat-, inhumanitas,* fr. *inhumanus* + *-itat-, -itas* -ity] **1 :** the quality or state of being cruel or barbarous **:** CRUELTY ⟨abhorrence of its sickening ~ —G.B.Shaw⟩; *also* **:** a cruel or barbarous act **2 :** absence of warmth or geniality **:** IMPERSONALITY ⟨a professional ~ toward their job —Nicholas Monsarrat⟩

in·hu·man·ly *adv* **:** in an inhuman manner

in·hu·man·ness \-n(n)əs\ *n* **:** the quality or state of being inhuman

in·hu·ma·tion \,inhyü'māshən\ *n* -S [F *inhumation,* fr. *inhumer* to inhume (fr. L *inhumare*) + *-ation*] **:** BURIAL, INTERMENT

in·hume \ən'hyüm\ *vt* -ED/-ING/-S [prob. fr. F *inhumer,* fr. L *inhumare,* fr. *in-* ²in- + *humus* earth — more at HUMBLE] **:** to deposit in the earth **:** BURY, INTER

-i·ni \ə,nī, ¹ē,nī, 'ē(,)nē, 'ēni, 'ī,nī\ *n pl suffix* [NL, fr. L, masc. pl. of *-inus* -ine] **:** animals that are or have the form of — in names of higher taxa esp. of tribes and orders ⟨Ana*canthini*⟩

in·i·ac \¹inē,ak\ *also* **in·i·al** \-ēəl\ *adj* [NL *inion* + E *-ac* (as in *iliac*) or *-al*] **:** relating to the inion

in·im·i·ca·ble \ə'niməkəbəl\ *adj* [L *inimicus* + E *-able* (as in *amicable*)] **:** INIMICAL, HOSTILE ⟨~ to the public peace or safety —*U.S. Code*⟩

in·im·i·cal \ə'niməkəl, -mēk-\ *adj* [LL *inimicalis,* fr. L *inimicus* enemy + *-alis* -al — more at ENEMY] **1 a :** having the disposition or temper of an enemy **:** viewing with disfavor **:** HOSTILE ⟨mutually ~ blocs —*Wall Street Jour.*⟩ ⟨~ to that heresy —George Meredith⟩ **b :** reflecting or indicating hostility **:** UNFRIENDLY ⟨a voice apparently cold and ~ —Arnold Bennett⟩ ⟨under the ~ gaze of his father —Marguerite Steen⟩ **2 :** prejudicial in tendency, influence, or effects **:** HARMFUL, ADVERSE ⟨~ to the interests of the consumer —*Current Biog.*⟩ ⟨~ to the best interests of the company —L.M.Hughes⟩ **syn** see ADVERSE

in·im·i·cal·ly \-mək(ə)lē, -mēk-, -li\ *adv* **:** in an inimical manner

in·im·i·cal·ness \-kəlnəs\ *n* -ES **:** the quality or state of being inimical

in·im·i·ci·tious \ə¦nimə¦sishəs\ *adj* [L *inimicitia* hostility (fr. *inimicus* enemy + *-tia,* suffix used to form abstract nouns) + E *-ous*] *archaic* **:** INIMICAL

inimicous *adj* [L *inimicus,* fr. *inimicus,* n., enemy] *obs* **:** INIMICAL

in·im·i·ta·bil·i·ty \(¦)i,nimad·ə'biləd·ē, ə,n-, -mətə-, -lətē, -i\ *n* **:** the quality or state of being inimitable **:** INIMITABLENESS

in·im·i·ta·ble \(')i¦niməd·əbəl, ə'n-, -mətə-\ *adj* [MF or L; MF, fr. L *inimitabilis,* fr. *in-* ¹in- + *imitabilis* imitable — more at IMITABLE] **:** not capable of being imitated **:** being beyond imitation **:** MATCHLESS ⟨an ~ style⟩ **:** not worthy of imitation — **in·im·i·ta·ble·ness** \-nəs\ *n* — **in·im·i·ta·bly** \-blē, -bli\ *adv*

in in·vi·tum \,inən'wē,tüm, -'vīd·əm\ *adv* [L, against an unwilling person] **:** against a person's will or consent **:** by force of law irrespective of assent

in·i·o·mi \,inē'ō,mī\ *n pl, cap* [NL, fr. *inion* + *-omi* (fr. Gk *ōmos* shoulder) — more at HUMERUS] **:** an order of mostly deep-sea teleost fishes lacking fin spines and air bladder and usu. having a dorsal adipose fin and including the lantern fishes, the lizard fishes, and related forms — **in·i·o·mous** \¦==¦ōməs\ *adj*

in·i·on \'inē,än, -ēən\ *n* -S [NL, fr. Gk, back of the head, dim. of *in-, is* sinew, tendon — more at WITHY] **:** the external occipital protuberance of the skull — see CRANIOMETRY illustration

in·iq·ui·tous \ə'nikwəd·əs, -wətəs\ *adj* [*iniquity* + *-ous*] **:** characterized by iniquity **:** UNJUST, WICKED ⟨~ deeds⟩ **syn** see VICIOUS

in·iq·ui·tous·ly *adv* **:** in an iniquitous manner

in·iq·ui·tous·ness *n* -ES **:** the quality or state of being iniquitous

in·iq·ui·ty \ə'nikwəd·ē, -wətē, -i\ *n* -ES [ME *iniquite,* fr. MF *iniquité,* fr. L *iniquitat-, iniquitas,* fr. *iniquus* uneven, unjust (fr. *in-* ¹in- + *-iquus,* fr. *aequus* level, equal) + *-itat-, -itas* -ity] **1 :** absence of or deviation from just dealing **:** gross injustice **:** WICKEDNESS ⟨the ~ of bribery⟩ **2 :** an iniquitous act or thing **:** SIN ⟨whose *iniquities* are forgiven —Ps 31:1 (DV)⟩ **3** *Scots law* **:** INEQUITY, INJUSTICE — used of a decision contrary to law

iniquous *adj* [L *iniquus*] *obs* **:** INIQUITOUS

in·irritability \(¦)in, ən+\ *n* **:** the quality or state of not being irritable

in·irritable \"+\ *adj* [¹*in-* + *irritable*] **:** not irritable

in·isle \ən+\ *archaic var of* ENISLE

¹**ini·tial** \ə'nishəl\ *adj* [MF & L; MF, fr. L *initialis,* fr. *initium* beginning (fr. *initus* — past part. of *inire* to go into, begin, fr. *in-* ²in- + *ire* to go — + *-ium,* suffix used to form abstract nouns) + *-alis* -al — more at ISSUE] **1 :** of or relating to the beginning **:** marking the commencement **:** INCIPIENT, FIRST ⟨~ symptoms of a disease⟩ ⟨this ~ series of outbreaks —Thomas Cadett⟩ **2 :** placed or standing at the beginning ⟨the ~ word of a verse⟩ **3 :** of that form regularly employed only at the beginning of a word — used of a letter in an alphabet that has two or more positional forms

²**initial** \"\ *n* -S **1 a** (1) **:** the first letter of a proper name (2) **initials** *pl* **:** the initial letters of an individual's name and surname; *also* **:** the initial letters of the name of an organization, state, or other entity (as U.S.A. for "United States of America" or C.I.O. for "Congress of Industrial Organizations") or of any group of words ⟨the ~*s* "PE" (meaning

"Previous Experience") —*U.S. Code*⟩ **b** (1) **:** a form of an alphabetical letter that regularly is used only at the beginning of a word (2) **:** a large letter beginning a text or a division or paragraph usu. capital and extending over two or more text lines and sometimes ornate and in more than one color **2 :** ANLAGE, PRECURSOR; *specif* **:** a meristematic cell

³initial \"\ *vt* **initialed** *or* **initialled; initialed** *or* **initialled; initialing** *or* **initialling** \-sh(ə)liŋ\ **initials** [²*initial*] **1 :** to affix an initial to ⟨~ a memorandum⟩ **:** to mark (as a handkerchief) with an initial **2 :** to authenticate and approve (as the draft of an international agreement) in a preliminary manner by the affixing of the initials of an authorized representative

initial condition *n* **:** any of a set of starting-point values belonging to or imposed upon the variables in an equation that has one or more arbitrary constants

ini·tial·er \-sh(ə)lə(r)\ *n* -s **:** a person who initials ⟨the ~s of a memorandum⟩

initial letter *n* **:** INITIAL 1b

initial line *n* **:** a ray that is rotated about the vertex to make an angle

ini·tial·ly \-sh(ə)lē, -li\ *adv* [¹*initial* + -*ly*] **:** in the first place **:** at the beginning

initial reserve *n* **:** the terminal reserve for a life-insurance policy as of the close of the preceding year plus the net premium for the current year

initial rhyme *n* **1 :** ALLITERATION **2 :** BEGINNING RHYME

initial series *n, cap I&S* **:** a Maya carved or written dating usu. at the start of a text including the date according to the long count and the date according to the positions reached in the 260-day and 365-day periods

initial side *n* **:** the stationary straight line that contains the point about which another straight line is revolved in forming a trigonometric figure

initial stress *n* **:** stress existing in a structure or mass not subjected to the action of external forces except gravity

¹ini·ti·ate \ə'nishē,āt *sometimes* -isē-; *usu* -ād·+V\ *vt* -ED/-ING/-S [L *initiatus*, past part. of *initiare*, fr. *initium* beginning — more at INITIAL] **1 a :** to begin or set going **:** make a beginning of **:** perform or facilitate the first actions, steps, or stages of **:** establish as an institution, custom, or trend ⟨~ a change in fashions⟩ ⟨*initiated* a new road-building program⟩ ⟨~ progressive education⟩ ⟨special powers which actively ~ and actively promote progress —W.H.Mallock⟩ ⟨~ a chain reaction⟩ **b :** to bring about the initial formation of **:** ORIGINATE ⟨polymerization chains so *initiated* —Otto Reinmuth⟩ **c :** to mark the beginning of ⟨the wholesale confiscation of property which *initiated* the Nazi regime —R.H.Jackson⟩ **2 :** to begin the instruction of in some field **:** lead to knowledge of elements or rudiments **:** foster the first steps or beginning progress of **:** aid in becoming familiar or knowing ⟨*initiated* into this tradition by his residence in Italy —Irving Babbitt⟩ ⟨felt that he was finally *initiated* —D.H.Lawrence⟩ **3 :** to receive or induct into membership of a society, club, or group, or into a certain status by or as if by special rites or formalities ⟨*initiated* into a social fraternity⟩ ⟨the club will ~ new members Tuesday⟩ **syn** see BEGIN

²ini·tiate \-sh(ē)ə|t, -shē,ā| *sometimes* -sē-; *usu* |d·+V\ *adj* [L *initiatus*] **1 :** initiated or properly admitted (as to an office, secret society, or secret learning) **2** *obs* **:** relating to an initiate ⟨my strange and self-abuse is the ~ fear —*Shak.*⟩

³initiate \"\ *n* -s **1 a :** a person who is undergoing an initiation (as into a secret order) ⟨the relationship between ~s and initiated —*Notes & Queries on Anthropology*⟩ **b :** one who has passed such an initiation or has been properly admitted (as to a fraternal organization) **2 a :** a person who is instructed or adept in some esoteric learning or mode of expression ⟨abstruse and erudite papers intelligible only to the ~ —H.C. Dent⟩ **b :** one who has been previously exposed to some experience **:** one who is at home in some area of experience or activity ⟨the ~ knows that dinner is nearing an end when the rice and tea appear —V.G.Heiser⟩

ini·ti·a·tion \ə,nishē'āshən *sometimes* -isē-\ *n* -s **1 a :** the act or an instance of formally initiating (as into an office, sect, or society) **:** the process of being formally initiated ⟨the practice of anointing with oil . . . became attached to the ~ of a king —*Brit. Book News*⟩ ⟨~ is regarded as a great occasion —A.A.Trouwborst⟩ **b** (1) **:** the rites, ceremonies, ordeals, or instructions with which one is made a member of a sect or society or is invested with a particular function or status ⟨the college fraternity has a scheme of ruthless mock ~s —C.W.Ferguson⟩ (2) **:** the ceremonies and ordeals with which a youth is formally invested with adult status in a primitive community ⟨attended some of the girls' ~, and took part in many functions of native life —Margaret C. Hubbard⟩ **c** (1) **:** the process or an instance of being initiated into some experience or sphere of activity **:** INTRODUCTION ⟨while still in high school, the youth received his ~ into his lifework —*Current Biog.*⟩ ⟨part of the child's ~ into the life of man —George Sampson⟩ ⟨his ~ to venal love is sordid —Henri Peyre⟩ ⟨had already had her ~ into court . . . and is now on probation —Beatrice Griffith⟩ (2) **:** the condition of being initiated or an initiate **:** KNOWLEDGEABLENESS ⟨clear to a reader of any degree of ~ —J.W.Beach⟩ ⟨that dullness which perhaps was due simply to lack of ~ —George Santayana⟩ **2 :** the act, process, or an instance of beginning, setting on foot, or originating **:** the condition of being begun **:** ORIGINATION, BEGINNING ⟨~ of a program to produce and test a vaccine —*Americana Annual*⟩ ⟨does not give them much power of ~ —R.H.Rovere⟩ ⟨the ~ of a leaf⟩

¹ini·tia·tive \ə'nishə|d·iv, |tiv *sometimes* -shē,ā| *or* -shēə| *or* -shiv *or* -shtēv\ *adj* [*initiate* + -*ive*] **:** of or relating to initiation **:** serving to initiate **:** INTRODUCTORY, PRELIMINARY

²initiative \"\ *n* -s **1 :** an introductory step or movement **:** an act designed to originate or set on foot (as a process or train of events) ⟨a new Russian ~ must now be anticipated —Frank Gorrell⟩ — often used in the phrase *on one's own initiative* ⟨don't blame me, he acted on his own ~⟩ **2 :** energy or aptitude displayed in initiation esp. of action that pioneers in some field **:** self-reliant enterprise ⟨a man of great ~⟩ ⟨unable to control the product of his ~, science —Norman Kelman⟩ **3 a :** the right or power to introduce a new measure or course of action ⟨the ~ in respect to revenue bills is in the House of Representatives⟩ **b :** a procedure or device which enables a specified number of voters by petition to propose a law and secure its submission to the electorate for approval — compare DIRECT INITIATIVE, INDIRECT INITIATIVE, REFERENDUM

ini·ti·a·tor \ə'nishē,ād·ə(r), -ātə- *sometimes* -isē-\ *n* -s [LL, fr. L *initiatus* (past part. of *initiare* to initiate) + -*or* — more at INITIATE] **:** one that initiates: as **a :** a person who originates or sets on foot some process or movement ⟨a great ~ in art⟩ **b :** DETONATOR c **c :** a substance that initiates a reaction ⟨benzoyl peroxide is used as an ~ in polymerization⟩ — compare CATALYST 1

ini·tia·to·ry \ə'nish(ē)ə,tōrē, -tòr-, -ri *sometimes* -isēə-\ *adj* [*initiate* + -*ory*] **1 :** constituting an introduction or beginning **:** INTRODUCTORY, OPENING, FIRST ⟨abolished as soon as its ~ horrors were known —J.L.Motley⟩ **2 :** tending or serving to initiate **:** introducing by instruction or by the use and application of symbols or ceremonies **:** ELEMENTARY, RUDIMENTARY ⟨~ rites⟩

inj *abbr* inject; injection

in·ject \ən'jekt\ *vt* -ED/-ING/-S [L *injectus*, past part. of *inicere*, *injicere*, fr. *in-* ²in- + -*icere*, -*jicere* (fr. *jacere* to throw) — more at JET] **1 a :** to throw, drive, or force in ⟨~ cold water into a condenser⟩ **b** (1) **:** to force a fluid into (a vessel, cavity, or tissue of man, animal, or plant) for preserving, hardening, or coloring structures (2) **:** to introduce (as by injection or gravity flow) a fluid into (a living body) esp. for the purpose of restoring fluid balance, treating nutritional deficiencies or disease, or relieving pain; *also* **:** to treat (an individual) with injections **c :** INTRUDE **2 :** to introduce as an element or factor in or into some situation or subject ⟨able to ~ both color and humor into this rather formidable subject —C.B.Palmer b. 1910⟩ ⟨~*ed* a disruptive element into the situation —Oscar Handlin⟩ ⟨the twists of raw emotion which she ~*s* into her portrayal —Roger Manvell⟩

in·ject·able \-təbəl\ *adj* **:** capable of being injected

injected *adj* **1 :** forced in or introduced esp. in the form of a fluid **2 :** CONGESTED 1

in·jec·tion \ən'jekshən\ *n* -s [MF or L; MF, fr. L *injection-*, *injectio*, fr. *injectus* + -*ion-*, -*io* -ion] **1 a** (1) **:** the act or an instance of injecting a drug or other substance into the body (2) **:** a solution of a drug, nutrient, or other substance injected (as by catheter or needle) into the tissues, a vein, or a body cavity (3) **:** a solution or suspension of a drug intended for administration under or through the skin or mucous membranes by means of a hypodermic syringe (4) **:** an act or process of injecting vessels or tissues; *also* **:** a specimen prepared by injection — compare CORROSION (5) **:** the state of being injected **:** CONGESTION **b :** the intrusion of molten magma between rocks **c :** the introduction under pressure of one substance (as fuel oil, combustion air, or water spray) into a working space (as a diesel cylinder, a gas-turbine combustor, or a steam desuperheater) **2 :** the act or an instance of introducing some element or factor into a situation or subject ⟨~ into news reports of the editor's political prejudices —Martin Gardner⟩

injection gneiss *n* **:** MIGMATITE

injection molding *n* **:** a method of forming articles of plastic or rubber by heating the molding material until it is able to flow and injecting it into a mold

injection well *n* **:** a well into which gas, air, or water is pumped in order to increase the yield of adjacent wells

in·jec·tor \ən'jektə(r)\ *n* -s **:** one that injects; *specif* **:** a jet pump for injecting feedwater into a boiler or fuel into a combustion chamber

injoint *vt* [²*in-* + *joint* (n.)] *obs* **:** JOIN

in·ju·cun·di·ty \,injü'kəndəd·ē\ *n* -s [L *injucunditas*, fr. *injucundus* unpleasant, fr. *in-* ¹in- + *jucundus* pleasant — more at JOCUND] *archaic* **:** UNPLEASANTNESS

in·judicial \¦in+\ *adj* [¹*in-* + *judicial*] **:** INJUDICIOUS — **in·judicially** \"+\ *adv*

in·judicious \"+\ *adj* [¹*in-* + *judicious*] **1 :** not judicious **:** lacking in sound judgment **:** INDISCREET ⟨brought by ~ mothers at precisely the most ineligible moments —W.L. Alden⟩ **2 :** not according to sound judgment or discretion **:** UNWISE ⟨an ~ measure⟩ — **in·judiciously** \"+\ *adv* — **in·judiciousness** \"+\ *n*

in·jun \'injən\ *n* -s *cap, often attrib* [alter. of ¹*indian*] **:** AMERICAN INDIAN ⟨he'd tell tales — of *Injuns*, or folks he'd known, or things that was plumb impossible to of happened anywheres —Helen Eustis⟩

in·junct \ən'jəŋ(k)t\ *vt* -ED/-ING/-S [*back-formation* fr. *injunction*] **:** to restrain by injunction

in·junc·tion \ən'jəŋ(k)shən\ *n* -s [MF & LL; MF *injonction*, fr. LL *injunction-*, *injunctio*, fr. L *injunctus* (past part. of *injungere* to enjoin) + -*ion-*, -*io* -ion — more at ENJOIN] **1 :** the act or an instance of enjoining **:** an earnest admonition **:** ORDER, PROHIBITION ⟨the Hindu religion has no ~s against birth control —Mildred Gilman⟩ ⟨laid an ~ of secrecy on me⟩ ⟨delivered stern ~s —Gilbert Millstein⟩ ⟨his father's dying ~s⟩ **2 :** an equitable writ granted by a court of equity whereby one is required to do or to refrain from doing a specified act — compare INTERDICT

¹in·junc·tive \-ŋ(k)tiv\ *adj* [L *injunctus* + E -*ive*] **1 a :** constituting an order, prohibition, or admonition **:** ENJOINING ⟨this ~ maxim —C.H.Hamburg⟩ **b :** constituting a mood or set of verb forms usu. with imperative, optative, or subjunctive meaning **2 :** of or relating to a legal injunction ⟨~ relief was not available to the state —*New Republic*⟩ ⟨an ~ order⟩

²injunctive \"\ *n* -s **:** the injunctive grammatical mood or a verbal form expressing it

in·jur·ant \'inj(ə)rənt\ *n* -s [*injure* + -*ant*] **:** an injurious agent or substance ⟨some poison gases are lung ~s⟩

in ju·re \(')in'jùrē, -'yü-\ *adv* [L] **:** in right, law, or justice **:** in court

in·jure \'injə(r)\ *vt* **injured; injured; injuring** \-j(ə)riŋ\ **injures** [back-formation fr. ¹*injury*] **1 a :** to do an injustice to **:** WRONG, OFFEND ⟨the *injured* husband sued for divorce⟩ **b :** to harm, impair, or tarnish the standing of (as a reputation or other intangible quality or asset) ⟨~ his authority —H.J. Laski⟩ ⟨~ your prospects —Thomas Hardy⟩ **c :** to give pain to (the sensibilities or feelings) ⟨~ a man's pride⟩ **2 a :** to inflict bodily hurt on ⟨*injured* by a falling brick⟩ **b :** to impair the soundness of ⟨~ your health⟩ **c :** to inflict material damage or loss on ⟨many houses were *injured* by the storm⟩ ⟨this tax will ~ all business⟩

syn HARM, HURT, DAMAGE, IMPAIR, MAR, SPOIL: INJURE implies the doing of an injustice to, or a wronging of, someone, esp. intentionally; it implies also an inflicting upon someone of anything detrimental to looks, health, comfort, success ⟨*injure* a man's reputation by slander⟩ ⟨*injure* a shoulder in a football game⟩ ⟨*injure* a friendship by resentment⟩ HARM stresses the inflicting of pain, suffering, or loss ⟨*harm* a dog by overfeeding it⟩ ⟨bitterness among the elders must not be permitted to *harm* or wound the innocent children of either race —Beverly Smith⟩ ⟨*harm* one's country by careless talk in wartime⟩ HURT implies the inflicting of a wound upon something (as the body, the feelings, or the commonwealth) capable of sustaining an injury ⟨seriously *hurt* in a landing under shore fire⟩ ⟨*hurt* a man's pride by belittling his accomplishments⟩ ⟨*hurt* the state by publicizing its rare and petty political feuds⟩ DAMAGE implies injury resulting in loss of value, completeness, efficiency, function ⟨furniture *damaged* by careless handling by movers⟩ ⟨an eye *damaged* by strain under bad light⟩ ⟨*damage* a motor by overheating it⟩ IMPAIR suggests a making less complete or efficient as by deterioration or diminution ⟨her excitement *impaired* her power of listening —Willa Cather⟩ ⟨beauty *impaired* by age⟩ ⟨labor with the hands or at the desk distorts or *impairs* the body —G.L.Dickinson⟩ ⟨individual rights should not be *impaired* without good reason⟩ MAR implies an injury that makes less perfect ⟨a case of smallpox which *marred* his face for life —*Time*⟩ ⟨his intellect, which was amazingly spotty, *marred* by great gaps —Norman Mailer⟩ ⟨a life of drudgery disfigures the body and *mars* and enervates the soul —G.L. Dickinson⟩ SPOIL in this connection suggests not only impairment or marring but usu. destruction or ruin ⟨they had the long Carroll upper lip that *spoiled* their looks a bit —Mary Deasy⟩ ⟨few streams and lakes which were clear and un*spoiled* by the works of man—Alexander MacDonald⟩ ⟨a great novel *spoiled* by hasty (and lazy) composition—H.J.Laski⟩

in ju·re ces·sio \-¦jùrē'ses(h)ē,ō, -¦yùre'kesē,ō\ *n* [L, lit., surrender in law] **:** a procedure in Roman law whereby a defendant formally admits or concedes before the praetor the justice of the plaintiff's claim to specific property and the praetor then adjudges it to belong to the plaintiff

injured *adj* **1 a :** WRONGED, OFFENDED ⟨clearing the reputation of the ~ youth —J.A.Froude⟩ ⟨an air of ~ innocence⟩ ⟨~ vanity⟩ **b :** reflecting or indicating a sense of injury ⟨talking in an ~ way —William Black⟩ ⟨gave her a suspicious, ~ expression —Willa Cather⟩ ⟨relapsed into ~ gloom —Athene Seyler⟩ **2 :** physically damaged or hurt ⟨held up his ~ finger⟩ — **in·jured·ly** *adv*

in·jur·er \-jərə(r), -j(ə)rə\ *n* -s **:** one that injures

in·ju·ria \ən'jùrēə, -'yü-\ *n, pl* **injuri·ae** \-jùrē,ē, -yùrē,ī\ [L, injury] **:** invasion of another's rights **:** actionable wrong **:** INJUSTICE

injuria abs·que dam·no \-¦abz(,)kwē'dam(,)nō, -¦äps(,)kwā'däm(,)nō\ [L, injury without damage] — used in reference to the rule that a wrong that causes no damage will not sustain an action; compare DAMNUM ABSQUE INJURIA

in·ju·ri·ous \ən'jùrēəs\ *adj* [ME, fr. MF *injurieux*, fr. L *injuriosus*, fr. *injuria* + -*osus* -ous] **1 :** inflicting or tending to inflict injury **:** HURTFUL, HARMFUL, DETRIMENTAL ⟨inaccurate news stories ~ of national dignity —*Quill*⟩ ⟨routine detection of ~ defects —*Steel*⟩ ⟨~ to health⟩ **2 :** ABUSIVE, OFFENSIVE, DEFAMATORY ⟨speak not ~ words —George Washington⟩ — **in·ju·ri·ous·ly** *adv* — **in·ju·ri·ous·ness** *n* -ES

¹in·ju·ry \'inj(ə)rē, -ri\ *n* -ES [ME *injurie*, fr. L *injuria*, fr. *injurus*, *injurius* injurious, unjust, wrong (fr. *in-* ¹in- + -*jurus*, -*jurius*, fr. *jur-*, *jus* right, law) + -*ia* -y — more at JUST] **1 a :** an act that damages, harms, or hurts **:** an unjust or undeserved infliction of suffering or harm **:** WRONG ⟨take it as a personal ~ —W.R.Inge⟩ ⟨his tone was one of mingled admiration and ~ —R.H.Davis⟩ ⟨adding insult to ~⟩ **b :** a violation of another's rights for which the law allows an action to recover damages or specific property or both **:** an actionable wrong — distinguished from *harm;* compare TORT **c** *obs* **:** offensive or defamatory speech **:** INSULT **2 :** hurt, damage, or loss sustained ⟨with consequent ~ to morale and efficiency —Adam Yarmolinsky⟩ ⟨*injuries* to health⟩ ⟨without ~ to the concrete —J.R.Dalzell⟩ ⟨suffered severe *injuries* in the accident⟩

syn INJURY, HURT, DAMAGE, HARM, and MISCHIEF mean in common the act or result of inflicting on a person or thing something that causes loss, pain, distress, or impairment. INJURY is the most comprehensive, applying to an act or result involving an impairment or destruction of right, health, freedom, soundness, or loss of something of value ⟨sustain a leg *injury* in a fall⟩ ⟨mental or emotional upset is just as truly an *injury* to the body as a bone fracture, a burn, or a bacterial infection —G.W.Gray b. 1886⟩ ⟨the fundamental skepticism . . . inflicts the most serious *injury* on both science and religion —W.R.Inge⟩ ⟨such change is . . . a great *injury* to the child's independence and freedom from responsibility —Abram Kardiner⟩ HURT applies chiefly to physical injury but in any application it stresses pain or suffering whether injury is involved or not ⟨a would-be fighter . . . that gross, brutal frame was still capable of doing a great deal of *hurt* —Hamilton Basso⟩ ⟨wrongfully withholding from him something which is his due . . . inflicting on him a positive *hurt*, either in the form of direct suffering, or of the privation of some good which he had reasonable ground, either of a physical or of a social kind, for counting upon —J.S.Mill⟩ ⟨leaving forever to the aggressor the choice of time and place and means to cause greatest *hurt* to us at least cost to himself —D.D.Eisenhower⟩ ⟨the dentist's drill may cause quite a *hurt* though it does no injury⟩ DAMAGE applies to injury involving loss, as of property, value, or usefulness ⟨the collision inflicted great *damage* on the car⟩ ⟨realize the immense *damage* his action has done to the good name of America —H.J.Laski⟩ ⟨enough *damage* to a watch so that it no longer keeps accurate time⟩ HARM applies to any evil that injures or may injure ⟨the men were terrified of Yusuf's cruelty, and wanted to retreat out of *harm's* way —C.S. Forester⟩ ⟨a well-founded apprehension of bodily *harm* is sufficient to justify the taking of life —H.W.H.Knott⟩ ⟨a scandal may prove of great *harm* to a man's political career⟩ MISCHIEF is used to avoid the suggestion or image of particular harm or injury, designating generally any misdoing or injury, esp. irresponsible, and stressing the role of an agent, usu. personal ⟨the nearest policeman, who most likely won't turn up until the worst of the *mischief* is done —G.B.Shaw⟩ ⟨he was most violent; if Captain Downing had not been there to restrain him, I vow he'd have done me a *mischief* —Max Peacock⟩ ⟨a fence was defective, and the pigs straying did *mischief* to a trolley car —B.N.Cardozo⟩

²injury *vt* -ED/-ING/-ES [ME *injurien*, fr. MF *injurier*, fr. L *injuriari*, fr. *injuria*] *obs* **:** INJURE

injust *adj* [ME *injuste*, fr. MF *injuste*, fr. L *injustus*] *obs* **:** UNJUST

in·justice \(')in, ən+\ *n* [ME, fr. MF, fr. L *injustitia*, fr. *injustus* unjust (fr. *in-* ¹in- + *justus* just) + -*ia* -y — more at JUST] **1 :** absence of justice **:** violation of right or of the rights of another **:** INIQUITY, UNFAIRNESS ⟨flamed out against ~ —John Galsworthy⟩ **2 :** an unjust act or deed **:** WRONG ⟨the ~s that angered him were never genuine —Norman Mailer⟩

¹ink \'iŋk\ *n* -s *often attrib* [ME *enke*, *inke*, fr. OF *enke*, *enque*, fr. LL *encaustum* ink (orig. the purplish ink used by the late Roman emperors to sign their edicts), fr. neut. of L *encaustus* burned in, painted in encaustic, fr. Gk *enkaustos* — more at ENCAUSTIC] **1 a :** a fluid or viscous material of various colors but commonly black or blue-black that is composed essentially of a pigment or dye in a suitable vehicle and is used for writing and printing — see INDELIBLE INK, PRINTING INK, WRITING INK **b :** a similar solid preparation (as india ink) **2 :** the black protective secretion of a cephalopod

²ink \"\ *vt* -ED/-ING/-S **1 :** to cover or smear with ink **:** apply ink to or touch up with ink **2 a :** to go over in ink — usu. used with *in* or *over* **b :** to obliterate with ink — usu. used with *out* ⟨~*ed* out many lines⟩ **c :** to write or draw in ink ⟨~*ed* their crosses to documents they had not the skill to read —G.M.Trevelyan⟩ ⟨pointed out the neatly ~*ed* entry on the bill —Irwin Shaw⟩ **3 a :** to affix one's signature to ⟨the baseball player was offered a raise and readily ~*ed* his contract⟩ **b :** to sign to a contract ⟨~*ed* the players with little difficulty⟩

ink ball *also* **inking ball** *n* **:** a ball-shaped inking pad formerly used by printers

inkberry \'iŋk — *see* BERRY\ *n* **1 :** a holly (*Ilex glabra*) of eastern No. America with evergreen oblong leathery leaves and small black berries — called also *gallberry* **2 :** BOX BRIER **3 :** POKEWEED **4 :** the fruit of an inkberry

ink black *n* **:** the color of dried blue-black ink **:** a dark grayish blue to bluish black — called also *inky black*

inkblot \'ₛ,ₛ\ *n* **1 :** a blot of ink **2 :** any of several plates showing blots of ink for use in psychological testing

inkblot test *n* **:** RORSCHACH TEST

inkbush \'ₛ,ₛ\ *n* **:** INKWEED 1

ink cap *n* **:** INKY CAP

ink disease *n* **1 :** a destructive disease of the chestnut in Europe that is caused by a fungus (*Phytophthora cambivora*) and that produces dark cankers and a black exudate on the trunk — called also *black canker* **2 :** a destructive disease of walnuts caused by a fungus (*Phytophthora citrophthora*)

ink·er \'iŋkə(r)\ *n* -s **:** one that inks: as **a :** INKWRITER **b :** a worker who applies ink or stain to goods (as shoe parts or cloth); *specif* **:** a worker who touches up imperfectly dyed cloth or hosiery

inkfish \'ₛ,ₛ\ *n* **:** CUTTLEFISH, SQUID

ink fountain *n* **:** the mechanism in a printing press that contains the ink and releases it to the rollers

¹ink·horn \'iŋk,hò(ə)rn, 'iŋ,kòrn\ *n* [ME *enkehorn*, *inkehorn*, fr. *enke*, *inke* ink + *horn* horn] **:** a small portable bottle of horn or other material for holding ink

²inkhorn \"\ *adj* **:** affectedly learned or pedantic ⟨~ terms and crude Latinisms —J.W.H.Atkins⟩

in·kie *or* **in·ky** \'iŋkē, -ki\ *n, pl* **inkies** [by shortening & alter.] *slang* **:** INCANDESCENT LAMP

inkier *comparative of* INKY

inkiest *superlative of* INKY

ink·i·ness \'iŋkēnəs, -kin-\ *n* -ES **:** the quality or state of being inky

ink knife *n* **:** a spatula for mixing printing ink

¹in·kle *also* **in·cle** \'iŋkəl\ *vt* -ED/-ING/-S [back-formation fr. *inkling*] *chiefly dial Eng* **:** to have an inkling of ⟨began to ~ what a silly combat weapon it is —E.V.Westrate⟩

²inkle *also* **incle** \"\ *n* -s [origin unknown] **:** a colored linen tape or braid woven on a very narrow loom and used for trimming; *also* **:** the thread used

ink·less \'iŋkləs\ *adj* [¹*ink* + -*less*] **:** devoid of ink

in·kling \'iŋkliŋ, -lēŋ, *esp in sense 1* -lən\ *n* -s [ME *yngkiling*, prob. fr. gerund of *inclen* to hint at, indicate; akin to OE *inca* suspicion, doubt, quarrel, OFris *jink* angry, ON *ekki* pain, Lith *ingis* sluggard, OSlav *jędza* illness] **1** *dial chiefly Eng* **a :** a faintly perceptible sound **:** UNDERTONE ⟨could not hear an ~ of his breathing —Elizabeth Enright⟩ **b :** RUMOR **2 a :** a faint or slight suggestion **:** HINT, INTIMATION ⟨there was no path — no ~ even of a track —*New Yorker*⟩ ⟨give only a dim ~ of its native intelligence —H.J.Morgenthau⟩ **b :** a slight knowledge or vague notion ⟨had not the faintest ~ of what it was all about —H.W.Carter⟩ ⟨got his first ~s as to the roles of natural selection —E.H.Colbert⟩

ink·man \'iŋk,man, -,mən\ *n, pl* **inkmen :** a worker who blends inks, powders, or pastes to obtain printing inks of desired colors

ink mushroom *n* **:** INKY CAP

ink plant *n* **1 :** a plant of the genus *Coriaria:* as **a :** a plant (*C. thymifolia*) of tropical America and New Zealand the fruits of which yield a red dye used as ink in Ecuador **b :** a European plant (*C. myrtifolia*) the leaves of which yield a black dye **2 :** POKEWEED

inkpot \'ₛ,ₛ\ *n* **:** a container for ink

ink print *n* **:** matter printed from inked type as distinguished from embossed matter for reading by the blind

in·kra \iŋ'krä, in'k-\ *n, pl* **inkra** *or* **inkras** *usu cap* **:** GA

inks *pl of* INK, *pres 3d sing of* INK

ink sac *n* **:** an organ in most cephalopods (as the squid) secreting an inky fluid that can be ejected from a duct opening into the terminal part of the rectum

inkshed \'ₛ,ₛ\ *n* -s [¹*ink* + -*shed* (as in *bloodshed*)] *archaic* **:** profuse use or unnecessary waste of ink in writing ⟨to spare mine own pains and prevent ~ —Andrew Marvell⟩

inkslinger \ˈ=,==\ *n* **1 :** WRITER, SCRIBBLER **2 :** a timekeeper in a logging camp

ink spot *n* **:** a plant disease characterized by black blemishes; *specif* **:** a disease of the aspen caused by fungi of the genus *Sclerotinia*

inkstand \ˈ=,=\ *n* **:** a small vessel for holding ink into which a pen can be dipped **:** INKWELL; *also* **:** a stand with fittings for holding ink and pens

inkstandish \ˈ=,=(,)=\ *n* [¹*ink* + *standish*] *archaic* **:** INKSTAND ⟨desired me to hand him the paper and ~ —Frederick Marryat⟩

inkweed \ˈ=,=\ *n* **1 :** any of several western No. American shrubby plants of the genus *Suaeda* used by the Indians for dyeing — called also *inkbush* **2 :** POKEWEED

inkwell \ˈ=,=\ *n* **:** a container for writing ink

inkwood \ˈ=,=\ *n* **:** a small tree (*Exothea paniculata*) of the family Sapindaceae of Florida and the West Indies having dark-colored wood and purple fruits

inkwriter \ˈ=,==\ *n* **:** a telegraph receiver in which the message is recorded in ink (as in dots and dashes)

inkwell

¹**inky** \ˈiŋkē, -ki\ *adj* -ER/-EST **:** consisting of, using, or resembling ink ⟨the ~ blackness of the ocean —F.G.Kay⟩ **:** soiled with or as if with ink **:** BLACK ⟨~ collars and dirty fingernails —Angela Thirkell⟩

²**inky** *var of* INKIE

inky black *n* **:** INK BLACK

inky cap *n* **:** a mushroom of the genus *Coprinus* (esp. *C. atramentarius*) having a pileus that melts into an inky fluid after the spores have matured

inlaid \(ˈ)=ˈ=\ *adj* [fr. past part. of ¹*inlay*] **:** set into a surface so as to form a decorative design or decorated with a design so formed; *specif* **:** CHAMPLEVÉ

inlaid binding *n* **:** MOSAIC BINDING

in·laik \ˈin,lāk, -lak\ *n* -S [ME (Sc), alter. of ME (Sc) *inlake*, fr. ME *in* + *lake*, *lak*, *lac* lack] *Scot* **:** LACK, DEFICIENCY

in-lamb \=ˈ=\ *adj, of ewes* **:** PREGNANT

¹**in·land** \ˈin,land, -ˌlənd, -,laa(ə)nd\ *n* -S [ME, fr. OE, fr. *in* + *land* — more at LAND] **1** *Old Eng & feudal law* **:** the demesne land of the lord of a manor **2 :** the interior part of a country or the part remote from the centers of population ⟨the far ~ of Australia —T.C.Roughley⟩

²**inland** \"\ *adj* **1** *chiefly Brit* **:** confined to a country or state **:** not foreign **:** DOMESTIC, INTERNAL ⟨the consolidated foreign and ~ debt —*Statesman's Yr. Bk.*⟩ ⟨~ revenue⟩ **2 a :** of or relating to the inlands or interior parts of a country **:** lying in the interior **:** INTERIOR ⟨any college town, however ~ and ivory-towered —Nell G. Ahern⟩ **b :** being within the land **:** not bordering on the sea ⟨maritime and ~ provinces⟩ **3 :** limited to the inland or interior or to inland routes ⟨~ transportation⟩ ⟨~ commerce⟩

³**inland** \"\ *adv* **:** into or toward the interior **:** away from the frontier **:** away from the coast ⟨live ~⟩

inland bill *n* **:** a bill of exchange that is or on its face purports to be both drawn and payable within the jurisdiction (as country or state) where it is presented — compare FOREIGN BILL

in·land·er \-də(r)\ *n* -S [¹*inland* + *-er*] **:** one that lives inland

inland marine insurance *n* **:** insurance against loss of or damage to property transported in domestic commerce, instruments of transport and communication, and personal property — compare FLOATER 8, MARINE INSURANCE, OCEAN MARINE INSURANCE

inland water *n* **1 :** any of the waters (as lakes, canals, rivers, watercourses, inlets, and bays) within the territory of a state as contrasted with the open seas or marginal waters bordering another state subject to various sovereign rights of the bordering state — usu. used in pl. **2 :** water of the interior that does not border upon marginal or high seas or is above the rise and fall of the tides — usu. used in pl.; compare MARGINAL SEA, TERRITORIAL SEA, TERRITORIAL WATER

inland waterway *n* **1 :** a navigable river, canal, or sound **2 :** a system of navigable inland bodies of water — usu. used in pl.

in·large \ən+\ *archaic var of* ENLARGE

in·laut \ˈin,laut\ *n, pl* **inlau·te** \-au̇d·ə\ *also* **inlauts** [G, fr. *in* (fr. OHG) + *laut* sound, fr. MHG *lūt*; akin to OE *hlūd* loud — more at IN, LOUD] **:** a medial sound or position in a word or syllable — compare ANLAUT, AUSLAUT

in·law \(ˈ)inˈlȯ, ənˈlȯ\ *vt* -ED/-ING/-S [ME *inlawen*, fr. OE *inlagian*, fr. *in* ²in + *-lagian* (fr. *lagu* law) — more at LAW] *Old Eng law* **:** to clear of outlawry or attainder **:** place under the protection of the law

in-law \ˈin,lȯ\ *n, pl* **in-laws** [back-formation fr. *mother-in-law*, etc.] **:** a relative by marriage — usu. used in pl. ⟨how to get along with parents and *in-laws* —Emily H. Mudd⟩

¹**in·lay** \(ˈ)inˈlā, ənˈlā\ *vt* **inlaid; inlaid; inlaying; inlays** [²*in* + *lay*] **1 a** (1) **:** to set into the body of a surface or ground material ⟨~ arabesques⟩ (2) **:** to pattern or adorn (a surface or ground) by the insertion of other material ⟨~ a panel with contrasting wood⟩ **:** adorn by inlaying ⟨~ wood with mother-of-pearl⟩ (3) **:** to ornament (a leather book cover) by fitting leather or other material into cut-in areas (4) **:** to ornament (a book cover) by affixing printed paper or other decorative material into depressed areas **b** (1) **:** to insert (as a color plate) into a heavier or stouter sheet serving as a mat, frame, or support (2) **:** to provide (a book) with inlaid illustrations **c :** to reinforce (silver-plated ware) at points of wear with an additional coating of silver or piece of silver embedded before electroplating **2 :** to burnish, beat, or fuse (as wire) into an incised cavity in metal, wood, stone, or other material

²**in·lay** \ˈin,lā\ *n* -S **1 :** the process or art of inlaying **2 a :** material inlaid or prepared for inlaying; *also* **:** the ornament or pattern formed by inlaying **b** (1) **:** a tooth filling of metal or porcelain shaped to fit a cavity and then cemented into place (2) **:** a piece of tissue (as bone) laid into the site of missing tissue to bridge a defect **3 a :** an allowance (as an extra-wide seam) for clothing alteration **b :** a set-in section on a garment usu. decorative or contrasting

¹**in·lay·er** \(ˈ)inˈlāər, ənˈl-, -le(ə)r\ *n* -S [¹*inlay* + *-er*] **:** one that inlays

²**in·lay·er** \ˈin,l-\ *n* [⁴*in* + *layer*] **:** an inner layer or sheathing

inlay graft *n* **:** a plant graft made by inserting, fastening, and sealing an accurately cut scion in a V-shaped notch in the end of a truncated stock

inlaying *n* -S **1 :** INLAY 1,2a **2 :** the burnishing, beating, or fusing of material (as wire) in an incised cavity in metal, wood, stone, or other material

inleakage \ˈ=,==\ *n* [⁴*in* + *leakage*] **:** the quantity that leaks in ⟨an actual ~ of 20,150 cubic feet per hour —*Lumber and its Utilization*⟩

¹**in·let** \ˈin,le|t, -,lə|, *usu* |d.+V\ *n* -S *often attrib* [⁴*in* + *let*, n. (after *let in*, v.)] **1 :** the act or an instance of letting in **2 a** (1) **:** a bay or recess in the shore of a sea, lake, or river (2) **:** a waterway into a sea, lake, or river **:** CREEK (3) **:** a narrow strip of water running into the land or between islands; *specif* **:** a passage through a barrier island or barrier reef leading to a bay or lagoon ⟨Barnegat *Inlet*⟩ **b :** a place of entrance **:** an opening by which entrance is made **:** ORIFICE ⟨oil ~s⟩ ⟨air ~⟩ ⟨~ and outlet valves⟩ **3 :** something that is let in or inlaid **:** an inserted material **4 :** the upper opening of the cavity of the true pelvis bounded by the brim

²**in·let** \ˈin,let, *usu* -ed·+V\ *vt* **inlet; inlet; inletting; inlets** [²*in* + *let* (v.)] **:** to let in **:** INSERT, INLAY ⟨~ the trigger mechanism down into the stock —*Amer. Rifleman*⟩

in·li·er \ˈin,lī(ə)r\ *n* [⁴*in* + *-lier* (as in *outlier*)] **1 :** a mass of rock whose outcrop is wholly surrounded by rock of younger age **2 :** a distinct area or formation that is completely surrounded by another ⟨~s of an older, wilder landscape surrounded by improvement —H.C.Darby⟩; *also* **:** ENCLAVE ⟨abolish the numerous outliers and ~s of territory —R.E. Dickinson⟩

in-line engine \ənˈlīn, ˈin,l-\ *n* **:** an internal-combustion engine in which the cylinders are arranged in one or more straight lines — compare RADIAL ENGINE

in·list \ənˈlist\ *archaic var of* ENLIST

in lo·co pa·ren·tis \ən,lō(,)kōpəˈrentəs\ *adv* [L] **:** in the place of a parent ⟨parents or persons standing *in loco parentis* —*U.S.House Bill*⟩

in-lot \ˈ=,=\ *n* [⁴*in* + *lot*] **1 :** a lot of land within a larger plot **:** INTERIOR LOT ⟨in a retail district, the corner is more desirable than the *in-lots* —H.E.Hoagland⟩ **2 :** a homestead lot on a townsite granted or sold to an early settler in No. America

in·ly \ˈinlē, -li\ *adv* [ME *inliche, inly*, fr. OE *inlīce*, fr. *inlīc*, adj., inward, interior, fr. *in, inn* in + *-līc* -ly — more at IN] **1 :** INWARDLY, WITHIN ⟨~ excited about her —Vance Palmer⟩ **2 :** INTIMATELY, THOROUGHLY ⟨~ know all wisdom —John Masefield⟩

¹**inlying** \ˈ=,==\ *n* -S [⁴*in* + *lying*, gerund of *lie* (after *lie in*, v.)] *chiefly Scot* **:** CONFINEMENT

²**inlying** \"\ *adj* [²*in* + *lying*, pres. part. of *lie*] **:** placed or situated inside or in the interior

inmarriage \ˈ=,==\ *n* [⁴*in* + *marriage*] **:** marriage within one's own family, race, or other grouping **:** ENDOGAMY — contrasted with *outmarriage*

inmarry \ˈ=,==\ *vi* [²*in* + *marry*] **:** to marry within one's own family, race, profession, or other grouping

¹**in·mate** \ˈin,māt, *usu* -ād·+V\ *n* [⁴*in* + *mate*] **1 a** *obs* **:** LODGER, TENANT **b** *archaic* **:** one who lives in the same house or apartment with another ⟨inquired whether he was a pleasant ~ and a kind neighbor —Harriet Martineau⟩ **2 :** one of a family, community, or other group occupying a single dwelling, home, or other place of residence ⟨rush the enemy settlement when all its ~s are asleep —C.D.Forde⟩ ⟨lifted the door of a pen, stirred up its ~s with his hand —Adrian Bell⟩ ⟨entered the house and seized all its ~s⟩; *esp* **:** a person confined or kept in an institution (as an asylum, prison, or poorhouse)

²**inmate** \"\ *adj, archaic* **:** living in the house of another **:** dwelling with another

inmeats \ˈ=,=\ *n pl* [⁴*in* + *meats*] *dial Eng* **:** the inner parts of an animal that are used for food

in me·di·as res \ən,mādēˌäsˈrās, -med-\ *adv* [L, lit., into the midst of things] **:** in or into the heart or substance of a matter; *esp* **:** in or into the middle of a narrative or plot without the formality of an introduction or other preliminary ⟨plunges the reader . . . *in medias res* —J.W.Aldridge⟩

in me·mo·ri·am \,inməˈmōrēəm, -ˈmȯr-, -ē,am, -ē,aa(ə)m, -ē,äm\ *adv* [L] **:** in memory of — used esp. in epitaphs and inscriptions and on floral pieces for the dead

inmesh *var of* ENMESH

in-migrant \ˈ=,==\ *n* [⁴*in* + *migrant*] **:** a person who in-migrates

in-migrate \(ˌ)in+\ *vi* [²*in* + *migrate*] **:** to come to live in a community esp. for work in an expanding industry and often as part of a large-scale movement of workers — compare OUT-MIGRATE — **in-migration** \ˌin+\ *n*

in·most \ˈin,mōst *also chiefly Brit* -ˌməst\ *adj* [ME *inmast, inmost*, alter. (influenced by *mast, most* most) of *innest*, fr. OE *innemest*, superl. of *inne*, adv., in, inside, within, fr. *in, inn*, adv., in — more at IN] **:** deepest within **:** farthest from the surface or external part **:** INNERMOST ⟨one's ~ self —J.B.Noss⟩

¹**inn** \ˈin\ *n* -S *often attrib* [ME *inn, in*, fr. OE *inn* (akin to ON *inni* dwelling, refuge, inn), fr. *inn, in*, adv. — more at IN] **1 a :** a public house for the lodging of travelers for compensation and until capacity is reached **:** HOTEL, HOSTELRY **b :** a place of public entertainment that does not provide lodging **:** TAVERN **2 :** a residence or hostel for students — formerly used of such a residence at a British university and of various houses connected with the study and admission to the practice of law in London — compare INN OF CHANCERY, INN OF COURT

²**inn** \"\ *vi* -ED/-ING/-S [ME *innen, innien*, fr. OE *innian*, fr. *inn*, n.] **:** to lodge, stop, or put up at an inn

inn *abbr* inning

in·nards \ˈinə(r)dz\ *n pl* [alter. of *inwards*] **1 :** the internal organs of a man or animal ⟨treating their ~ at state expense —Mollie Panter-Downes⟩; *esp* **:** VISCERA ⟨his ~ were rumbling⟩ **2 :** the internal parts or interior of something ⟨churned up from the earth's ~ —*Time*⟩ ⟨the insidious ~ of the women's magazines —Hugh Mulligan⟩; *esp* **:** the internal parts of a structure or mechanism ⟨the iron ~ of a great four-faced clock —*New Yorker*⟩

in·nate \(ˈ)iˈnāt, əˈn- *sometimes* (ˈ)inˈn-; *usu* -ād·+V\ *adj* [ME *innat*, fr. L *innatus*, past part. of *innasci* to be born, be a native, be naturally suitable, fr. *in-* ²in- + *nasci* to be born — more at NATION] **1 a :** existing in or belonging to some person or other living organism from birth **:** NATIVE, NATURAL ⟨~ vigor⟩ **b :** belonging to the essential nature of something **:** INHERENT ⟨the ~ defect in a plan⟩ **c :** originating in, derived from, or inherent in the mind or the constitution of the intellect rather than derived from experience ⟨~ ideas of God, immortality, right and wrong⟩ — compare A PRIORI, INTUITIVE **2** *obs* **:** formed internally **:** hidden within **:** INTERNAL **3 a :** attached to the apex of the support of a plant (as an anther to the tip of a filament) — compare ADNATE 2 **b :** ENDOGENOUS **c :** immersed or embedded in (as the fruiting bodies in the thallus of a fungus)

syn INBORN, INBRED, CONGENITAL, HEREDITARY, INHERITED: INNATE applies to qualities or characteristics belonging to something as part of its inner essential nature. INNATE designates that which is part of lasting essential character, sometimes present or potential at birth ⟨simple ideas should be kept simple, and their *innate* strength should not be undermined by the use of big words and by periphrases —E.S.McCartney⟩ ⟨because of her ability to sense the *innate* talent of young and untried actors —*Amer. Guide Series: Mich.*⟩ ⟨this stubbornness has been explained as being *innate* in the Germans, as a natural racial cussedness —R.C.Wood⟩ INBORN may describe a natural native distinctive characteristic so deep-seated as to have been born in one, often present at birth ⟨there was in him a rush of *inborn* vitality like an Alpine torrent —Agnes Repplier⟩ ⟨the psychopathic personality is held to be an *inborn* (though not hereditary) deficit and is of the nature of a functional alteration —*Yr. Bk. of Neurology, Psychiatry & Neurosurgery*⟩ INBRED describes that which becomes deeply ingrained into one's nature by early environmental influences without being part of one's nature at birth ⟨those *inbred* sentiments which are . . . the true supporters of all liberal and manly morals —Edmund Burke⟩ ⟨a methodical man, an *inbred* Yankee —W.A.White⟩ CONGENITAL applies to a characteristic present at the birth of a person or inception of a thing or notion, whatever the provenience of that characteristic ⟨the newborn child's chances of survival and healthy development depend in part on his *congenital* equipment —*Times Lit. Supp.*⟩ ⟨yet art for art's sake suffers from a *congenital* disease; it professes to create substance out of form, which is physically impossible —George Santayana⟩ HEREDITARY and INHERITED describe characteristics and conditions not only present at birth but definitely coming from heredity, that is, brought about by transmission from parents and ancestors ⟨an *hereditary* propensity to kill men and eat them. True, he came from a race of cannibals —Herman Melville⟩ ⟨most of us, of course, held fast to the Republican party, for political beliefs were *hereditary*, transmissible in the male line —Ben Riker⟩ ⟨a tendency in the past to confuse *congenital* with *inherited*. It is a commonplace now that conditions present at birth are not necessarily inherited in the biological sense of the word, to quote only congenital syphilis as an example. It is also generally known that many inherited conditions first manifest themselves long after birth —Hans Grüneberg⟩

innated *adj* [L *innatus* + E *-ed*] *obs* **:** INNATE

in·nate·ly *adv* **:** in an innate manner

in·nate·ness *n* -ES **:** the quality or state of being innate

in·nat·ism \əˈnād,izəm\ *n* -S [*innate* + *-ism*] **:** a belief in innate ideas

in·na·tive \(ˈ)i(n)ˈnād·iv\ *adj* [L *innatus* + E *-ive*] **:** INNATE, NATURAL ⟨some ~ weakness . . . in him who condescends to victory —J.R.Lowell⟩

in·navigable \(ˈ)i(n), ə+\ *adj* [L *innavigabilis*, fr. *in-* ¹in- + *navigabilis* navigable — more at NAVIGABLE] **:** not navigable

inned *past of* IN *or of* INN

¹**in·ner** \ˈinə(r)\ *adj* [ME *inner, inre*, fr. OE *innera, innra*, compar. of *inne* in — more at INMOST] **1 a :** situated farther in ⟨an ~ chamber⟩ ⟨the ~ bark⟩ **b :** near to a center esp. of influence ⟨the ~ circles of the administration⟩ **c :** INTRAMOLECULAR — used esp. of compounds ⟨~ esters⟩ **2 :** of or relating to the mind or spirit or its phenomena ⟨the ~ life of man⟩

syn INWARD, INSIDE, INTERIOR, INTERNAL, INTESTINE, INTESTINAL are often interchangeable. INNER may apply to something far within or near a center; consequently it may apply to something deeply intimate or inaccessible ⟨an *inner* room⟩ ⟨no wish to write anything but a spiritual biography, and outer events only interest me here insofar as they affected my *inner* life —Havelock Ellis⟩ ⟨he had not chosen his course. It had sprung from a necessity of his nature, an *inner* logic that he scarcely questioned —Van Wyck Brooks⟩ INWARD is close in suggestion to INNER; it may apply to direction within ⟨an *inward* curve⟩ ⟨the little houses splashed in the thousands across the countryside sheltered the men turning *inward* in the quest for peace of mind —Oscar Handlin⟩ ⟨that *inward* eye which is the bliss of solitude —William Wordsworth⟩ INSIDE, used often of space relationships, may suggest the restricted, secret, or confidential not shared by those outside ⟨an *inside* room⟩ ⟨*inside* work⟩ ⟨speculating on *inside* information⟩ ⟨even the bare outline was sufficient to gratify the public's craving for the abnormal and the spectacular. But the *inside* story of the catastrophe surpassed even the wildest flights of public fancy —W.H.Wright⟩ INTERIOR may contrast with *exterior* and stress the fact of being within ⟨*interior* decorating⟩ ⟨not to be found in institutionalism, nor in the Scriptures, but in the *interior* life and spirit of man —W.R.Inge⟩ ⟨frightened by an *interior* quietness and by the thought that she had for once in her life stopped thinking —Elizabeth Bowen⟩ INTERNAL, contrasted with *external*, may apply to inner activity, force, development, or effect ⟨interested more in *internal* affairs than foreign⟩ ⟨the slavery which would be imposed upon her by her external enemies and her *internal* traitors —F.D.Roosevelt⟩ ⟨a more general process of *internal* migration that involved both regional shifts and a drift to the cities —Oscar Handlin⟩ INTESTINE and, more rarely, INTESTINAL are occas. used as synonyms for *civil* and *domestic*, in contrast to *foreign*, to describe wars and disturbances ⟨the common people fused, not without considerable *intestine* struggle, to form an Etrusco-Latin blend —R.A.Hall b.1911⟩

²**inner** \"\ *n* -S **:** a forward line player in various team sports (as soccer and field hockey) stationed between the left or right wing and the center forward

inner anhydride *n* **:** an anhydride formed by elimination of water from a single molecule

inner bar *n, Eng law* **:** the queen's or king's counsel who are permitted to plead within the bar of the court — compare OUTER BAR

inner barrister *n, Eng law* **:** a barrister ranking lowest among the barristers belonging to an Inn of Court

inner bottom *n* **:** the plating in a ship that is laid over the frames and longitudinals and that with the shell plating forms a double bottom — called also *tank top*

inner cell mass *n* **:** the portion of the blastodermic vesicle of a primate embryo that is destined to become the embryo proper

inner closure *n* **:** the inner of the two ends of the chamber formed by a stop articulation ⟨the bottom of the lungs, the glottis, or the tongue and velum may be the *inner closure*⟩ — compare OUTER CLOSURE

inner-directed \ˌ==(,)=ˌ==\ *adj* **:** directed in thought and action by one's own scale of values as opposed to external norms **:** NONCONFORMIST ⟨the American is undergoing a basic change from *inner-directed* to other-directed —H.S.Commager⟩

inner-direction \ˌ==(,)=ˌ==\ *n* **:** a sense of direction based on one's own scale of values or standards as opposed to external norms

inner ear *n* **:** the essential part of the vertebrate ear consisting typically of a bony labyrinth in the temporal bone enclosing a fluid-filled membranous labyrinth innervated by the auditory nerve and made up of a vestibular apparatus and three semicircular canals primarily concerned with the labyrinthine sense and a cochlea which is the seat of the actual sound receptor

inner endodermis *n* **:** the endodermal layer separating the stele from the pith (as in a stem where two endodermal layers are present)

inner form *n* **:** a form that prints the side of a sheet on which the second page appears — contrasted with *outer form*; compare SHEET IMPOSITION

inner jib *n* **:** a jib immediately forward of the forestaysail on a ship where several jibs are carried — see SAIL illustration

inner keel *n* [³*keel*] **:** KEELSON

inner light *n, cap I&L* **:** the divine presence in the soul of every man held in Quaker doctrine to give spiritual enlightenment, moral guidance, and religious assurance to all who seek such through faith — called also *Christ Within, Light Within*

¹**in·ner·ly** \ˈinə(r)lē, -li\ *adv* [ME, fr. *inner* + *-ly* (adv. suffix)] **:** INWARDLY, INLY ⟨a world that was ~ divided —Dorothy Thompson⟩

²**innerly** \"\ *adj* [ME, fr. *inner* + *-ly* (adj. suffix)] **1** *Scot* **:** INWARD, INLYING **2 :** pleasantly familiar and sociable

inner man *n* **1 :** the spiritual or intellectual part of man **2 :** STOMACH ⟨the *inner man* will consume the largest part of your bankroll —T.H.Fielding⟩

inner mission *n* [trans. of G *innere mission*] **:** a movement originating in the 19th century within the Evangelical Church of Germany that sought partly through sisterhoods and lay brotherhoods to serve neglected and unfortunate members of society and that founded Christian lodging houses, Sunday schools, orphanages, and hospitals

innermore \ˈ=ˌ=ˈ=\ *adj* [ME, fr. ¹*inner* + *more*] *now dial Eng* **:** located farther within **:** INNER

in·ner·most \ˈ==,mōst *also chiefly Brit* -ˌməst\ *adj* [ME, fr. *inner* + *-most*] **:** farthest inward **:** INMOST ⟨it is his ~ being that is judged —D.C.Hodges⟩ ⟨the ~ part of the nation —F.D.Roosevelt⟩ — **inner·most·ly** *adv*

²**innermost** \"\ *n* **:** the inmost part **:** inmost being

in·ner·ness *n* -ES **:** the quality or state of being inner **:** inner character ⟨its superior moral sense and its more intense ~ —W.K.Ferguson⟩

inner part *or* **inner voice** *n* **:** a line or part intermediate between the highest and lowest (as the alto or tenor in four-part vocal music)

inner phase *n* **:** DISPERSED PHASE

inner planet *n* **:** one of the four principal planets whose orbits are innermost in the solar system ⟨Mercury, Venus, Earth, and Mars are the *inner planets*⟩

inner post *n* **:** a timber on the forward side of the sternpost to receive the hooding ends of the planking and in square-stern ships to support the transoms

inner product *n* **:** SCALAR PRODUCT

inner proscenium *n* **:** an inner frame (as a wooden framework) built esp. for a stage production to mask lighting equipment or narrow the stage opening or by means of special shape to give a desired design-quality to the production

inner quantum number *n* **:** a vector quantum number denoting the total angular momentum of an atom exclusive of nuclear spin — symbol *J* or *j*

inner salt *n* **:** a salt formed by reaction within the molecule of a compound having both acid and basic properties — compare DIPOLAR ION

inner sanctum *n* **:** SANCTUM

innersole \ˈ==ˌ=\ *n* **:** INSOLE

inner speech *n* **:** use of words or word images in thinking without audible or visible speaking

innerspring \ˈ==,=\ *adj* **:** having coil springs inside a padded casing ⟨~ mattress⟩ ⟨~ cushion⟩

inner table *n* **:** either half of a backgammon board as determined by the players but usu. the half nearer the source of light

inner tube *n* **:** an airtight tube of rubber placed inside the casing of a pneumatic tire to hold air under pressure

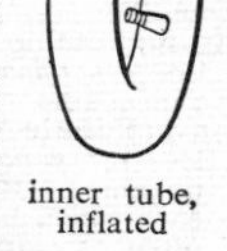

inner tube, inflated

in·ner·vate \iˈnər,vāt ˈi(,)nər-\ *vt* -ED/-ING/-S [²*in-* + *nerve* + *-ate*] **1 :** to supply with nerves **2 :** to arouse or stimulate (a nerve or an organ) to activity

in·ner·va·tion \,i(,)nərˈvāshən\ *n* [²*in-* + *nerve* + *-ation*] **1 :** the act, process, or an instance of innervating **:** the state of being innervated; *specif* **:** the nervous excitation necessary for the maintenance of the life and functions of the various organs **2 :** the distribution of nerves to or in a part **:** the nerve supply (as of a part or organ) — **in·ner·va·tion·al** \ˌ=(,)=ˈvāshənᵊl, -shnəl\ *adj*

in·nerve \i+\ *vt* -ED/-ING/-S [²*in-* + *nerve* (n.)] **:** to give nervous energy or power to : give increased energy, force, or courage to : INVIGORATE, STIMULATE

in·ness \'innəs\ *n* -ES [2*in* + *-ness*] : inner nature : INWARDNESS

innholder \'≈,≈≈\ *n* [ME *inhalder*, fr. *in*, *inn* inn + *halder*, *holder* holder — more at INN, HOLDER] : INNKEEPER

1inn·ing \'iniŋ, -nēŋ\ *pres part of* INN

2in·ning \"\ *n* -s [in sense 1, fr. gerund of 3*in;* in sense 2, fr. 2*in* + *-ing*] **1 a :** the act of taking in, gathering, or enclosing; *specif* **:** the act of reclaiming land esp. from the sea or a marsh **b innings** *pl* **:** reclaimed lands **2 a innings** *pl but sing or pl in constr* **:** a division of a cricket match in which one side continues batting until ten players are retired or the side declares; *also* **:** the time a player stays as a batsman until he is out, until ten teammates are out, or until his side declares **b :** a team's turn at bat in baseball ending with the third out; *also* **:** a division consisting of a turn at bat for each team **c :** a division of a contest in other sports (as a turn at serving in badminton, two throws by one player or two throws by each contestant in horseshoes, or a player's turn in croquet) **d :** a chance or turn for action or accomplishment (as to display one's prowess, caliber, or ability) ⟨the factual . . . romance has had its ~ —Parker Tyler⟩ ⟨the young conductor who is currently having his ~*s* —Douglas Watt⟩ ⟨the opposition party now had its ~*s*⟩ ⟨keep silent in order to give the adversary his ~ —Edmond Taylor⟩

innkeeper \'≈,≈≈\ *n* **:** the landlord of an inn

inn·less \'inləs\ *adj* **:** being without an inn

in·no·cence \'inəsən(t)s\ *n* -s [ME, fr. MF, fr. L *innocentia*, fr. *innocent-*, *innocens* innocent + *-ia* -y] **1 a** (1) **:** freedom from guilt or sin esp. through being unacquainted with evil **:** purity of heart **:** BLAMELESSNESS ⟨postulates a state of primitive ~⟩ (2) **:** CHASTITY ⟨supposed to have not yet lost her ~ —T.B.Macaulay⟩ (3) **:** the state of being not chargeable for or guilty of a particular crime or offense **b** (1) **:** freedom from guile or cunning **:** ARTLESSNESS, SIMPLICITY ⟨the ~ of childhood⟩ (2) **:** lack of understanding or penetration **:** SILLINESS, NAÏVETÉ ⟨the ~ . . . to propose remaking the world and human nature —L.O.Coxe⟩ (3) **:** lack of knowledge **:** IGNORANCE ⟨written in entire ~ of the Italian language —E.R.Bentley⟩ ⟨full of a chuckling mirth at the ~ of our detractors —Warwick Braithwaite⟩ ⟨~ of the craft of writing —J.W.Aldridge⟩ **2 :** one that is innocent; *esp* **:** an innocent person **3 a :** BLUET 1c(1) **b :** either of two plants: (1) **:** a small herb (*Collinsia verna*) of the central U.S. (2) **:** a Californian herb (*C. bicolor*)

in·no·cen·cy \-sənsē, -nsi\ *n* -ES [ME *innocencie*, fr. L *innocentia*] **:** INNOCENCE; *also* **:** an innocent action, quality, or thing ⟨associated in my mind with milk and rice and similar *innocencies* of childhood —Elinor Wylie⟩

1in·no·cent \-sənt\ *n* -s [ME, fr. MF] **1 :** an innocent one: as **a :** a person free from or unacquainted with sin; *esp* **:** a young child **b** *obs* **:** a person guiltless of a crime charged **c :** a naïve, artless, or unsophisticated person ⟨an ~ and a novice in the ways of the world —Fred Whishaw⟩ **d :** a person who lacks the requisite experience, training, or knowledge **:** TENDERFOOT ⟨lending a wrench to some ~ who forgot to bring his own —W.L.Worden⟩ **2** [F, short for *herbe de Saint Innocent* Saint Innocent's herb] **:** BLUET 1c(1) — usu. used in pl.

2innocent \"\ *adj, sometimes* -ER/-EST [ME, fr. MF, adj. & n., fr. L *innocent- innocens*, fr. *in-* 1in- + *nocent-*, *nocens* bad, wicked, fr. pres. part. of *nocēre* to harm, hurt — more at NOXIOUS] **1 a** (1) **:** free from guilt or sin esp. through lack of knowledge of evil **:** BLAMELESS, PURE, UNTAINTED ⟨an ~ child⟩ (2) **:** being without evil influence or effect **:** not arising from evil intention ⟨~ deception⟩ ⟨~ sport⟩ ⟨searching for a hidden motive in even the most ~ conversation —Leonard Wibberley⟩ (3) **:** reflecting or indicating freedom from guilt or sin **:** CANDID ⟨a child's trusting ~ eye⟩ ⟨turned on me her ~ gaze⟩ **b** (1) **:** free from legal guilt or fault ⟨a person ~ of a particular crime⟩ ⟨an ~ agent⟩ **:** free from an illegality **:** being without knowledge of circumstances giving notice of a defect in title or of rights existing in third persons ⟨an ~ holder or purchaser for value⟩ **:** being without intention of evading or circumventing the law (2) **:** having a lawful character **:** PERMITTED ⟨a wholly ~ transaction⟩; *specif* **:** not being contraband ⟨an ~ trade⟩ (3) **:** lacking or devoid of something **:** DESTITUTE ⟨~ of any linguistic training —A.F.Hubbell⟩ ⟨her face ~ of cosmetics —Marcia Davenport⟩ ⟨glass still ~ of water and soap —William Faulkner⟩ **2 a** (1) **:** lacking or reflecting lack of sophistication, guile, or self-consciousness **:** ARTLESS, INGENUOUS, NAÏVE ⟨a disappointing figure to ~ persons who seek his acquaintance —C.E.Montague⟩ ⟨~ vanity⟩ ⟨what an ~ notion —F.L.Allen⟩ ⟨not ~ . . . but academic and a little self-conscious —Philip Toynbee⟩ (2) **:** foolishly ignorant or trusting **:** subject to being duped **:** SIMPLEMINDED ⟨when it comes to a trade, he is not as ~ as he looks⟩ **b** (1) **:** not adept in or conversant with something **:** IGNORANT ⟨almost entirely ~ of Latin —C.L.Wrenn⟩ ⟨the curious but ~ explorer will find himself hopelessly lost —B.R.Redman⟩ (2) **:** UNSUSPECTING, UNAWARE ⟨perfectly ~ of the confusion he had created —B.R.Haydon⟩ **3 :** lacking capacity to injure **:** INNOCUOUS, HARMLESS ⟨unarmed hands or feet are relatively ~ —Lewis Mumford⟩ ⟨fine ~ weather —John Muir †1914⟩; *specif* **:** BENIGN 3c ⟨an ~ heart murmur —*Lancet*⟩ — **in·no·cent·ly** *adv* — **in·no·cent·ness** *n* -ES

innocent converter *n* **:** a person who in good faith believes himself entitled to take and possess a chattel that in fact belongs to another but is nevertheless liable for conversion of the chattel

innocent conveyance *n, early English & American law* **:** a conveyance of a greater estate than the grantor has that does not produce a forfeiture of an estate in reversion or in remainder

innocent misrepresentation *n* **:** a representation in good faith reasonably believed true by the one making it but in fact untrue

innocent party *n* **:** one who has no notice of a fact tainting a litigated transaction with illegality **:** one not responsible or to blame for a situation which is the basis for relief in court

innocent passage *n* **:** the right of a foreign ship in grave distress or when overcome by a force majeure to anchor in or stop at a port within the territorial waters of another state without being subject to the general jurisdiction of the latter

innocents' day *n, usu cap I&D* **:** HOLY INNOCENTS' DAY

in·no·cu·i·ty \,i,nä'kyüəd·ē\ *n* -ES [prob. fr. F *innocuité*, fr. L *innocuus* + F *-ité* -ity] **:** the quality or state of being innocuous; *also* **:** something that is innocuous ⟨conversation will lag and digress politely to *innocuities* —*Plain Talk*⟩

in·noc·u·ous \(')i¦näkyəwəs, ə'n-\ *adj* [L *innocuus*, fr. *in-* 1in- + *-nocuus* (fr. *nocēre* to harm, hurt) — more at NOXIOUS] **1 :** producing no ill effect **:** working no injury **:** HARMLESS ⟨preliminary tests have proved it to be ~ —*Jour. of Chem. Education*⟩ **2 a :** not likely to arouse animus or give offense **:** INOFFENSIVE ⟨confined himself to ~ generalities⟩ **b :** not likely to arouse strong feelings **:** lacking the capacity to excite ⟨elaborate concealment of ~ regions —P.M.Gregory⟩ or move **:** PALLID, INSIPID, INSIGNIFICANT ⟨a pleasant but ~ suite —Arthur Berger⟩ — **in·noc·u·ous·ly** *adv* — **in·noc·u·ous·ness** *n* -ES

inn of chancery *usu cap I&C* **1 :** a house or group of buildings in London formerly used by law students for residence and study but now occupied chiefly by attorneys and solicitors — usu. used with *inn* in pl. **2 :** a society occupying an Inn of Chancery — usu. used with *inn* in pl.

inn of court *usu cap I&C* **1 :** one of four sets of buildings in London belonging to four societies of students and practicers of the law ⟨Inner Temple, Middle Temple, Lincoln's Inn, and Gray's Inn are the *Inns of Court*⟩ **2 :** one of four societies which alone admit to practice at the English bar — usu. used with *inn* in pl.

in·nominable \(')i, ə+\ *adj* [ME, fr. L *innominabilis*, fr. *in-* 1in- + *nominare* to name + *-abilis* -able — more at NOMINATE] **:** incapable of being named

in·nominate \(')i¦nämənət, ə'nä-\ *adj* [LL *innominatus*, fr. L *in-* 1in- + *nominatus*, past part. of *nominare*] **1 a :** having no name **:** UNNAMED ⟨there were no fields, as in England, each called by an ancient name; the slender tributaries were often ~ —John Buchan⟩ **b :** having an unknown or unrevealed name **:** ANONYMOUS ⟨progress . . . made by the accumulated activities of large groups of ~ people —*Times Lit. Supp.*⟩ **2** *Roman & civil law* **a :** of, relating to, or being any of certain classes of contracts that are real but have no special name **b :** of, relating to, or being a commutative contract in any of several categories

innominate artery *n* [trans. of NL *arteria innominata*] **:** a large artery arising from the arch of the aorta and dividing into the right common carotid and the right subclavian arteries

innominate bone *n* [trans. of NL *os innominatum*] **:** the large flaring bone that makes a lateral half of the pelvis in mammals and is composed of the ilium, ischium, and pubis which are consolidated into one bone in the adult — called also *hipbone*

innominate vein *n* [trans. of NL *vena innominata*] **:** a large vein on each side of the lower part of the neck formed by the union of the internal jugular and subclavian veins and in man uniting to form the superior vena cava

in·nom·i·ne \(')in'nämə,nā, -,nē, -'nōmə,nā\ *n* -s [L *in nomine* (in *in nomine Jesu* in the name of Jesus, the opening words of an introit for which such compositions were orig. written)] **:** an English polyphonic composition of the 16th and 17th centuries written for an instrumental ensemble (as for viols and keyboard) and using as a cantus firmus a fragment of plainsong from the antiphon for Trinity Sunday

in·no·vant \'inəvənt, 'inōv-\ *adj* [L *innovant-*, *innovans*, pres. part. of *innovare*] **:** having innovations (sense 3)

in·no·vate \'inə,vāt, 'inōv-, *usu* -ād·+V\ *vb* -ED/-ING/-S [L *innovatus*, past part. of *innovare*, fr. *in-* 2in- + *novare* renew, modify, fr. *novus* new — more at NEW] *vt* **1 :** to introduce as or as if new ⟨~ a design⟩ **2** *archaic* **:** to make innovations in **:** CHANGE ~ *vi* **:** to introduce novelties **:** make changes ⟨he is not to ~ at pleasure —B.N.Cardozo⟩

in·no·va·tion \,≈≈'vāshən\ *n* -s [prob. fr. MF, fr. LL *innovation-*, *innovatio*, fr. L *innovatus* + *-ion-*, *-io* -ion] **1 :** the act or an instance of innovating **:** the introduction of something new ⟨~ as the driving force in practical economic advance —*Times Lit. Supp.*⟩ **2 :** something that deviates from established doctrine or practice **:** something that differs from existing forms **:** CHANGE, NOVELTY ⟨the technical ~*s* of the agrarian revolution —S.F.Mason⟩ ⟨another ~ is a new straight mile course —*London Calling*⟩ ⟨his most important ~ . . . was the introduction of the seminary method of instruction for advanced students —C.F.Smith⟩ **3 a :** a shoot that arises at or near the apex of the stem of a moss plant usu. after the reproductive organs have completed their development **b :** the formation of such a shoot **4** *Scots law* **:** an exchange of one obligation for another, the obligor and obligee remaining the same

in·no·va·tion·al \¦≈≈¦vāshənᵊl, -shnəl\ *adj* **:** of or relating to innovation **:** tending to innovate ⟨a mind so ~ —John Mason Brown⟩

in·no·va·tive \'≈≈,vād·iv\ *adj* **:** characterized by, tending to, or introducing innovations ⟨~ behavior⟩

in·no·va·tor \-,vād·ə(r), -ātə-\ *n* -s [prob. fr. MF *innovateur*, fr. LL *innovator*, fr. L *innovatus* + *-or*] **:** one that innovates ⟨a theological ~⟩ ⟨~ of a new technique⟩

in·no·va·to·ry \-_və,tōrē, -,vād·ərē\ *adj* **:** INNOVATIVE

in·noxious \(')i(n), ə+\ *adj* [L *innoxius*, fr. *in-* 1in- + *noxius* harmful — more at NOXIOUS] **:** INNOCUOUS ⟨an ~ substance⟩ — **in·noxiously** \"+\ *adv* — **in·noxiousness** \"+\ *n*

inns *pl of* INN, *pres 3d sing of* INN

inns·bruck \'inz,brůk, 'in(t)s,b-\ *adj, usu cap* [fr. *Innsbruck*, Austria] **:** of or from the city of Innsbruck, Austria **:** of the kind or style prevalent in Innsbruck

in nu·ce \(')in'nü(,)kā\ *adv* [L, in a nut] **:** in a nutshell ⟨the opening act contains the tragedy *in nuce* —Karl Polanyi⟩

1in·nu·en·do \,inyə'wen(,)dō\ *adv* [L, by hinting, abl. of *innuendum*, gerund of *innuere* to hint, intimate, fr. *in-* 2in- + *nuere* to nod — more at NUMEN] **:** in other words **:** NAMELY — formerly used in legal documents to introduce matter explanatory of the text

2innuendo *also* **inuendo** \"\ *n, pl* **innuendos** *or* **innuendoes** **1 :** veiled, oblique, or covert allusion to something not directly named **:** HINT, INSINUATION ⟨glossy fantasy, stylishness, naughty ~ —*Time*⟩ ⟨a talk punctuated with ~*s* on both sides —J.T.Farrell⟩; *esp* **:** veiled or equivocal allusion reflecting upon the character, ability, or other trait of the person referred to ⟨try to undermine him by ~ —*Kiplinger Washington Letter*⟩ ⟨how difficult it is to set up a proper defense against ~ —M.S.Watson⟩ ⟨anonymous accusations, rumors, ~*s* —Nathan Schachner⟩ **2 :** a parenthetical explanation of the text of a legal document; *esp* **:** an interpretation in a pleading of expressions alleged to be injurious or libelous

3innuendo *also* **inuendo** \"\ *vb* -ED/-ING/-S [2*innuendo*] *vi* **:** to make innuendo ~ *vt* **:** to give effect to by innuendo

in·nu·it *also* **in·u·it** \'inyəwət, 'i,nyüət\ *n, pl* **innuit** *or* **innuits** *also* **inuit** *or* **inuits** *usu cap* [Esk, men, people, Eskimo people, pl. of *innuk*, *inuk* person, man, Eskimo] **1 a** (1) **:** the Eskimo people of America as distinguished from the Eskimo people of Asia — compare YUIT (2) **:** the arctic Eskimo as distinguished from the Aleuts **b :** a member of the Innuit people **2 :** the language of the Innuit people

in·nu·mer·a·bil·i·ty \ə,n(y)üm(ə)rə'biləd·ē\ *n* -ES [L *innumerabilitas*, fr. *innumerabilis* + *-itas* -ity] **:** innumerable quality ⟨without any sense of the ~ of the human race —Thornton Wilder⟩

in·nu·mer·a·ble \ə'n(y)üm(ə)rəbəl\ *adj* [ME, fr. L *innumerabilis*, fr. *in-* 1in- + *numerabilis* numerable — more at NUMERABLE] **1 :** too many to be numbered or counted **:** indefinitely numerous **:** NUMBERLESS ⟨~ coral reefs and islets —*Americana Annual*⟩ **2 :** characterized by vast or countless number ⟨an ~ throng of people⟩ — **in·nu·mer·a·ble·ness** \-nəs\ *n* -ES — **in·nu·mer·a·bly** \-blē,-bli\ *adv*

in·numerous \(')i(n), ə+\ *adj* [L *innumerus*, fr. *in-* 1in- + *numerus* number — more at NIMBLE] **:** NUMBERLESS, INNUMERABLE

in·nutrition \¦i(n)+\ *n* [1*in-* + *nutrition*] **:** lack of nutrition **:** failure of nourishment

in·nutritious \"+\ *adj* [1*in-* + *nutritious*] **:** not nutritious ⟨harsh and ~ fare —*Experiment Station Record*⟩

innyard \'≈,≈\ *n* **:** the yard of an inn

ino- — see 3IN-

inobedience *n* [ME, fr. OF & LL; OF, fr. LL *inoboedientia*, fr. *inoboedient-*, *inoboediens* + L *-ia* -y] *obs* **:** DISOBEDIENCE

inobedient *adj* [ME, fr. MF & LL; MF, fr. LL *inoboedient-*, *inoboediens*, fr. L *in-* 1in- + *oboedient-*, *oboediens* obedient — more at OBEDIENT] *obs* **:** DISOBEDIENT

in·obnoxious \¦in+\ *adj* [1*in-* + *obnoxious*] **:** INOFFENSIVE

inobservable *adj* [L *inobservabilis*, fr. *in-* 1in- + *observabilis* observable — more at OBSERVABLE] *obs* **:** incapable of being observed

in·observance \¦in+\ *or* **in·observancy** \"+\ *n* [F & L; F *inobservance*, fr. L *inobservantia*, fr. *in-* 1in- + *observantia* observance — more at OBSERVANCE] **1 :** lack of attention **:** HEEDLESSNESS **2 :** failure to observe **:** NONOBSERVANCE

in·observant \¦in+\ *adj* [LL *inobservant-*, *inobservans*, fr. L *in-* 1in- + *observant-*, *observans* observant — more at OBSERVANT] **:** UNOBSERVANT

in·obtrusive \¦in+\ *adj* [1*in-* + *obtrusive*] **:** UNOBTRUSIVE ⟨tried hard to be ~ —L.S.Feuer⟩

in·obvious \(')in+\ *adj* [1*in-* + *obvious*] **:** not obvious

in·occupation \¦in+\ *n* [1*in-* + *occupation*] **:** lack of occupation

ino·cer·a·mus \,inō'serəməs, ,īn-\ *n, cap* [NL, fr. 3*in-* + Gk *keramos* potter's clay, pottery] **:** a genus of large filibranchiate bivalve mollusks (suborder Mytilacea) esp. characteristic of the Cretaceous

in·oc·u·la·ble \ə'näkyələbəl\ *adj* [*inoculate* + *-able*] **:** susceptible to inoculation **:** not immune; *also* **:** transmissible by inoculation

in·oc·u·lant \-lənt\ *n* -s [*inoculate* + *-ant*] **:** INOCULUM

in·ocular \(')in, ən+\ *adj* [2*in-* + *ocular*] **:** inserted in a notch in the corner of the eye ⟨~ antennae⟩

in·oc·u·late \ə'näkyə,lāt, *usu* -ād·+V\ *vb* -ED/-ING/-S [ME *inoculaten*, fr. L *inoculare*, fr. *in-* 2in- + *oculus* eye, bud — more at EYE] *vt* **1 a** *archaic* **:** to insert a bud into or graft (as a tree) by budding **b :** to treat (seeds) with bacteria esp. for the promotion of nitrogen fixation (as in root nodules on legumes) **2 a** (1) **:** to communicate a disease to (an organism) by inserting its causative agent into the body ⟨12 mice *inoculated* with anthrax⟩ (2) **:** to introduce microorganisms or viruses onto or into (an organism or substrate) ⟨~ the culture with one loopful of spore suspension⟩ ⟨*inoculated* a rat with bacteria⟩ (3) **:** to introduce (as microorganisms or immune sera) into or onto a culture medium ⟨~ the spirochetes into blood agar⟩ **b :** SEED 1d **3 :** to introduce something into the mind of **:** IMBUE ⟨*inoculated* them with their own ideas of revolution —Raymond Schuessler⟩ ⟨~ the few who influence the many —*Current Biog.*⟩ ~ *vi* **1** *obs* **:** to graft by inserting buds **2 :** to introduce microorganisms, vaccines, or sera by inoculation **syn** see INFUSE

in·oc·u·la·tion \≈,≈≈'lāshən\ *n* -s [L *inoculation-*, *inoculatio*, fr. *inoculatus* + *-ion-*, *-io* -ion] **:** the act, process, or an instance of inoculating: as **a** (1) **:** the introduction of a microorganism into a suitable medium for its growth ⟨~ of mosaic virus into stocks by aphids⟩; *specif* **:** the communication of an infective agent (as smallpox virus) to a healthy individual to induce a mild case of disease under optimum conditions and establish lasting immunity (2) **:** the introduction of a serum or vaccine into a living body to establish immunity to a disease ⟨travelers in the tropics should have typhoid ~*s*⟩ **b :** the introduction of organisms into soil, seed, or water to promote nitrogen fixation or control insect pests or for other purposes **c :** the introduction of a substance into a metallic melt for the purpose of providing additional centers for crystallization **d :** the act or process of imbuing or familiarizing **:** the fact or an instance of being so imbued or familiarized ⟨getting a weekly or monthly ~ in ways of living and of thinking that were middle-class —F.L.Allen⟩ ⟨~ with alien attitudes and tastes⟩

in·oc·u·la·tive \≈'≈≈,lād·iv\ *adj* **:** of, relating to, or characterized by inoculation

in·oc·u·la·tor \-d·ə(r)\ *n* -s [L, one that engrafts, fr. *inoculatus* + *-or*] **:** one that inoculates

in·oc·u·lum \ə'näkyələm\ *n, pl* **inocu·la** \-lə\ *or* **inoculums** [NL, fr. L *inoculare*] **:** material (as spores, bacteria, or contaminated fluids) used in or suitable for use in inoculating or inoculation

ino·des \ə'nō(,)dēz, ī'-\ *n, cap* [NL, fr. Gk *inōdēs* fibrous, fr. *in-* 3in- + *-ōdēs* -ode] *in some classifications* **:** a genus of fan palms comprising various arborescent palmettos of the southern U.S., the West Indies, and Mexico that are now usu. included in the genus *Sabal*

inodiate *vt* -ED/-ING/-S [LL *inodiatus*, past part. of *inodiare* — more at ANNOY] *obs* **:** to make odious or hateful

in·odorous \(')in, ən+\ *adj* [L *inodorus*, fr. *in-* 1in- + *odorus* odorous — more at ODOROUS] **:** emitting no smell **:** SCENTLESS, ODORLESS

in–off \'≈,≈\ *n* [fr. the phrase *in off* (*the red ball* or *the white ball*)] **:** a losing hazard in English billiards

in·offensive \¦in+\ *adj* [1*in-* + *offensive*] **1 :** causing no harm or injury **:** UNOFFENDING ⟨an ~ animal⟩ **2 a :** giving no offense or provocation **:** causing no disturbance **:** not quarrelsome **:** PEACEABLE ⟨a quiet, ~ man —Herman Melville⟩ **b :** giving no offense to the senses **:** not objectionable ⟨a refreshing, ~ . . . stimulant —*Americas*⟩ — **in·of·fen·sive·ly** *adv* — **in·of·fen·sive·ness** *n*

in·official \¦in+\ *adj* [1*in-* + *official*] **:** UNOFFICIAL

in·officious \¦in+\ *adj* [L *inofficiosus*, fr. *in-* 1in- + *officiosus* dutiful — more at OFFICIOUS] **1** *obs* **:** indifferent to obligation or duty **2 :** regardless of or contrary to natural duty

inofficious testament *or* **inofficious will** *n* **:** a will made in violation of natural duty and affection and without just legal cause and depriving children and parents and sometimes others of their legitim of the testator's estate

ino·gen \'inəjən, 'īn-, -,jen\ *n* -s [G, fr. *ino-* 3in- + *-gen*] **:** a hypothetical substance supposed to be continually decomposed and reproduced in the muscles and to serve as an oxygen reserve

in·op·er·a·bil·i·ty \¦i,näp(ə)rə¦biləd·ē\ *n* **:** the quality or state of being inoperable

in·operable \(')in, ən+\ *adj* [prob. fr. F *inopérable*, fr. *in-* 1in- + *opérable* operable — more at OPERABLE] **1 :** not suitable for surgical operation ⟨an advanced and ~ cancer⟩ ⟨a developing cataract still ~⟩ **2 :** not operable

in·operative \(')in, ən+\ *adj* [1*in-* + *operative*] **:** not operative or not in operation **:** not active **:** producing no effect ⟨the law has become ~⟩ ⟨the quarry has been ~ for some time —L.N.Yedlin⟩ — **inoperativeness** *n*

in·opercular \¦in+\ *adj* [1*in-* + *opercular*] **:** INOPERCULATE

1in·operculate \¦in+\ *adj* [1*in-* + *operculate*] **:** having no operculum ⟨~ gastropod shells⟩ ⟨~ mosses⟩

2inoperculate \"\ *n* **:** an inoperculate animal or shell

in·opportune \(¦)in, ən+\ *adj* [L *inopportunus*, fr. *in-* 1in- + *opportunus* opportune — more at OPPORTUNE] **:** not opportune **:** UNSEASONABLE, INCONVENIENT ⟨arrive at the most ~ hours —D.R.Murphy⟩ — **in·op·por·tune·ly** \-ünlē\ *adv* — **in·op·por·tune·ness** \-ünnəs\ *n*

in·orb \ən+\ *vt* [2*in-* + *orb* (n.)] **:** ENSPHERE, ENCIRCLE

in·or·di·na·cy \ə'nȯ(r)dᵊnəsē\ *n* -ES [*inordinate* + *-cy*] *archaic* **:** the quality, state, or an instance of being inordinate **:** EXCESSIVENESS

in·or·di·nance \-ᵊnən(t)s\ *also* **in·or·di·nan·cy** \-ᵊnənsē\ *n, pl* **inordinances** *also* **inordinancies** **:** the quality, state, or an instance of being inordinate

in·ordinary \(')in, ən+\ *adj* [1*in-* + *ordinary*] **:** not ordinary **:** EXTRAORDINARY

in·or·di·nate \ə'nȯ(r)dᵊnət, *usu* -əd·+V\ *adj* [ME *inordinat*, fr. L *inordinatus*, fr. *in-* 1in- + *ordinatus*, past part. of *ordinare* to order, arrange — more at ORDAIN] **1 :** lacking order **:** not regulated **:** DISORDERLY **2 :** exceeding in amount, quantity, force, intensity, or scope the ordinary, reasonable, or prescribed limits **:** EXTRAORDINARY ⟨his ~ desire for approval —Van Wyck Brooks⟩ ⟨~ joviality can atone for an entire lack of ideas —Oscar Wilde⟩ ⟨a book of ~ length⟩ ⟨burns an ~ quantity of gasoline —H.W.Baldwin⟩ **syn** see EXCESSIVE

in·or·di·nate·ly *adv* [ME *inordinatly*, fr. *inordinat* + *-ly*] **:** in an inordinate manner **:** to an excessive or unreasonable degree **:** EXTRAORDINARILY ⟨~ ambitious⟩ ⟨the symphony is ~ long⟩ ⟨~ fond of grasshoppers —C.H.Grandgent⟩

in·or·di·nate·ness *n* -ES **:** the quality or state of being inordinate **:** lack of moderation **:** EXCESS

in·or·di·na·tion \ə,nȯ(r)dᵊn'āshən\ *n* -s [LL *inordination-*, *inordinatio*, fr. L *inordinatus* + *-ion-*, *-io* -ion] *archaic* **:** INORDINATENESS

1in·organic \¦in+(,)≈¦≈≈\ *adj* [1*in-* + *organic*] **1 a** (1) **:** being or composed of matter other than plant or animal **:** MINERAL ⟨the ~ world⟩ (2) **:** forming or belonging to the inanimate world **b :** being, containing, or relating to a chemical substance or substances not usu. classed as organic ⟨hydrochloric, sulfuric, nitric, and chlorosulfonic acids are called ~ acids —R.E.Kirk⟩ ⟨~ fertilizers⟩ **c :** being in the form of such a substance ⟨~ selenium as in sodium selenite⟩ **2 :** not arising from a process of natural or inevitable growth **:** ARTIFICIAL ⟨an ~ and unnatural lingo never spoken by man —Kenneth Rexroth⟩ **:** lacking organic structure, character, or vitality ⟨dull ~ things, without individuality or prestige —John Buchan⟩ **3** *of a sound or letter* **:** lacking an etymological justification — **in·organically** \"+\ *adv*

2inorganic \"\ *n* **:** an inorganic substance

inorganical *adj* [1*in-* + *organical*] *obs* **:** INORGANIC

inorganic chemistry *n* **:** a branch of chemistry that deals with chemical elements and their compounds excluding hydrocarbons and their derivatives but usu. or often including carbides and other relatively simple carbon compounds esp. some carbon-oxygen and carbon-sulfur compounds (as the oxides of carbon, metallic carbonates, and carbon disulfide) and some carbon-nitrogen compounds (as hydrogen cyanide and metallic cyanides) — compare ORGANIC CHEMISTRY

in·organization \¦in+\ *n* [1*in-* + *organization*] **:** lack of organization

in·organized \(')in, ən+\ *adj* [1*in-* + *organized*] **:** lacking organization

in·ornate \¦in+(,)≈¦≈\ *adj* [L *inornatus*, fr. *in-* 1in- + *ornatus* adorned — more at ORNATE] **:** lacking adornment **:** UNADORNED ⟨the scrupulously ~ clergyman than which nothing could be less liable to suspicion —E.A.Poe⟩

in·osculate \ən+\ *vb* -ED/-ING/-S [2*in-* + *osculate*] **:** to unite by apposition or contact **:** unite or join so as to become or make as if one **:** BLEND ⟨efforts to ~ past and present —R.M.Wendlinger⟩

in·osculation \ən+\ *n* [²*in-* + *osculation*] **:** the act, process, or an instance of inosculating; *specif* **:** ANASTOMOSIS
ino·silicate \ˌinō, ˈīnō+\ *n* [*ino-* + *silicate*] **:** a class of polymeric silicates in which the silicon-oxygen tetrahedral groups share half of their oxygen atoms so as to form straight chains of indefinite length; *also* **:** a member of this class — called also *metasilicate;* compare CYCLOSILICATE, NESOSILICATE, PHYLLOSILICATE, SOROSILICATE, TECTOSILICATE
ino·sine \ˈinəˌsēn, ˈīn-, -ˌsən\ *n* -s [ISV *inos-* (fr. Gk *inos*, gen. of *is* sinew, tendon) + *-ine* — more at WITHY] **:** a crystalline nucleoside $C_{10}H_{12}N_4O_5$ formed by partial hydrolysis of inosinic acid or by deamination of adenosine and yielding hypoxanthine and ribose on hydrolysis
ino·sin·ic acid \ˌ==ˈsinik-\ *n* [part trans. of G *inosinsäure*, fr. *inosin* inosine + *säure* acid] **:** an amorphous nucleotide $C_{10}H_{13}N_4O_8P$ that is found in muscle and is formed by deamination of adenylic acid and that yields hypoxanthine, ribose, and phosphoric acid on hydrolysis
ino·si·tol \əˈnōsəˌtōl, ī-, -ˌtōl\ *n* -s [ISV *inosite* inositol (fr. Gk *inos* + ISV *-ite*) + *-ol*] **:** any of nine crystalline stereoisomeric cyclic hexahydroxy alcohols $C_6H_6(OH)_6$; cyclohexane-hexol: as **a :** an optically inactive alcohol that is a component of the vitamin B complex and a lipotropic agent, that occurs widely in plants usu. combined in the form of phytic acid, in microorganisms, and in higher animals and man esp. in vital organs and tissues (as the heart and brain) and often combined in the form of phosphatides, that is obtained chiefly from corn steepwater, and that is used in medicine — called also *i-inositol, meso-inositol, myoinositol* **b :** a sweet dextrorotatory alcohol occurring esp. in the form of its methyl ether pinitol — called also *dextro-inositol* **c :** a sweet levorotatory alcohol occurring esp. in the form of its methyl ether quebrachitol — called also *levo-inositol* **d :** SCYLLITOL
ino·trop·ic \ˌinəˈträpik, ˌīn-\ *adj* [ISV ³*in-* + *-tropic*] **:** influencing muscular contractility — **inot·ro·pism** \əˈnä·trəˌpizəm, ī'-\ *n* -s
in ovo \iˈnō(ˌ)vō\ *adv* [L] **:** in the egg **:** in embryo
in·oxidizable \(ˈ)in+\ *adj* [¹*in-* + *oxidizable*] **:** not capable of being oxidized
in·paint \ən+\ *vt* [²*in* + *paint*] **:** to repair or restore (a painting) by repainting obliterated areas
in pais \-ˈpā\ *adv* [*pais* fr. MF *pais, pays* country — more at PAYSAGE] **:** in the country as distinguished from in court
in pa·ri causa \-ˈpärē-\ *adv* [LL, in a like case] **:** in a case where all parties stand equal in right according to law
in pari de·lic·to \-dəˈlik(ˌ)tō\ *adv* [L, in a like offense] **:** in equal fault or wrong — used of parties in a legal case
in pari ma·te·ria \-məˈtirēə\ *adv* [LL, in a like matter] **:** on the same subject or matter **:** in a similar case ⟨there is virtually nothing of known date *in pari materia* with which it can be compared —*Times Lit. Supp.*⟩
in par·ti·bus in·fi·de·li·um \(ˌ)inˈpärd·əbəˌsinfəˈdālēəm\ *also* **in partibus** *adv* [ML, lit., in the regions of infidels] **:** in ideologically hostile or unsympathetic surroundings ⟨made himself missionary *in partibus infidelium* for American philosophic naturalism —J.H.Randall⟩
in par·vo \-ˈpär(ˌ)vō\ *adv* [L] **:** in little **:** in miniature ⟨the reflection, *in parvo*, of the defects of the larger whole —Sonya Forthal⟩
inpatient \ˈ=ˌ==\ *n* [⁴*in* + *patient*] **:** a patient in a hospital or infirmary who receives lodging and food as well as treatment — distinguished from *outpatient*
in pa·tri·mo·nio \-ˌpa·trəˈmōnē,ō\ *adv* [L, lit., within inheritance] **:** IN COMMERCIO
inpayment \ˈ=ˌ==\ *n* [⁴*in* + *payment*] **1 :** the act or an instance of paying in **2 :** a payment to — contrasted with *outpayment*
in pec·to·re \-ˈpektərē\ *adv* [L, lit., in the breast] **:** in secret ⟨must hold their names *in pectore* —Thomas Barbour⟩
in per·pe·tu·um \-pə(r)ˈpechəwəm\ *adv* [L] **:** in perpetuity **:** FOREVER ⟨left certain royalties to the home *in perpetuum* —Joseph Wechsberg⟩
in per·so·nam \-pə(r)ˈsōˌnam\ *adv* (*or adj*) [L, against a person] **:** against a particular person for the purpose of imposing upon him a personal liability, debt, or obligation to do or not to do a designated act ⟨proceedings and judgments are *in personam* where the court or tribunal has jurisdiction over the defendant and power to enforce obedience against him personally⟩ — compare IN REM
in pet·to \-ˈped·(ˌ)ō\ *adv* (*or adj*) [It, lit., in breast; prob. trans. of L *in pectore*] **1 :** in private **:** SECRETLY — used esp. of a cardinal appointed by the pope but not named in consistory **2** [influenced in meaning by E *petty*] **:** in miniature **:** on a small scale ⟨an epic *in petto* —*Saturday Rev.*⟩
inphase \ˈ=ˌ=\ *adj* [fr. the phrase *in phase*] **:** being of the same electrical phase
inphase component *n* **:** the active component of an alternating current in a reactive circuit
in–pig \ˈ=ˌ=\ *adj* [fr. the phrase *in pig*] *of a sow* **:** PREGNANT
in–plant \ˈ=ˌ=\ *adj* [fr. the phrase *in plant*] **:** carried on, occurring within, or restricted to the confines of a manufacturing establishment or factory ⟨*in-plant* training programs⟩ ⟨the *in-plant* medical director⟩
in·polygon \ˈin+ˌ-\ *n* [⁴*in* + *polygon*] **:** an inscribed polygon
in·polyhedron \ˈ"+ˌ-\ *n* [⁴*in* + *polyhedron*] **:** an inscribed polyhedron
in pos·se \-ˈpäsē\ *adv* (*or adj*) [ML] **:** in possibility or capacity **:** not in actuality ⟨contains within itself, *in posse*, implicitly, ideally, the entire logico-dialectical process —Frank Thilly⟩ **:** POTENTIALLY — contrasted with *in esse*

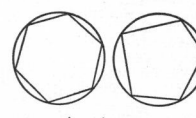

inpolygons

¹inpour \ˈ=ˌ=\ *n* [⁴*in* + *pour* (after *pour in*, v.)] **:** a pouring in **:** INRUSH ⟨the ~ of tumultuous Irish immigrants —Helen Sullivan⟩
²in·pour \(ˈ)=ˈ=\ *vb* **:** to pour in ⟨goods and money *inpoured* —J.J.Mallon⟩
inpouring \ˈ=ˌ==\ *n* -s [⁴*in* + *pouring* (after *pour in*, v.)] **:** INPOUR ⟨viewed the ~ of bedraggled foreigners with alarm —A.D.Graeff⟩
in–print \ˈ=ˌ=\ *n* [fr. the phrase *in print*] **:** a title that is in print
in–process \ən+\ *adj* [fr. the phrase *in process*] **:** being worked on in manufacture in distinction from raw materials and from finished products
in pro·pria per·so·na \ənˈprōprēəpə(r)ˈsōnə\ *adv* [L] **:** in one's own person **:** without the assistance of an attorney **:** PERSONALLY
in·put \ˈinˌpu̇t, *usu* -ùd·+V\ *also* **im·put** \ˈim,-\ *n* [*input* fr. ⁴*in* + *put* (after *put in*, v.); *imput* alter. of *input*] **1 :** something that is put in: as **a** *chiefly Scot* **:** a contribution of money **b :** an amount put in ⟨increase the ~ of fertilizer⟩ **c** (1) **:** power or energy put into a machine or system for storage (as into a storage battery) or for conversion in kind (as into a mechanically driven electric generator or a radio receiver) or conversion of characteristics (as into a transformer or electronic amplifier) usu. with the intent of sizable recovery in the form of output (2) *on an electrical device* **:** the terminal for the input **d :** a component of production (as land, labor, or materials) ⟨~*s* such as seed, twine, ginning fees, and containers —D.G. Johnson⟩ **e :** data or similar information fed into a computer or accounting machine **2 :** the act, process, or an instance of putting in ⟨requires a continuous ~ of energy both for maintenance and for propagation —G.A.Bartholomew & J.B. Birdsell⟩
input well *n* **:** INJECTION WELL
in querpo *var of* IN CUERPO
in·quest \ˈinˌkwest\ *n* [ME *enquest, inquest*, fr. OF *enqueste*, fr. fem. of (assumed) *enquest*, fr. (assumed) VL *inquaestus*, past part. of *inquaerere* to inquire — more at INQUIRE] **1 a :** a judicial or official inquiry or examination esp. before a jury ⟨a coroner's ~⟩ ⟨an ~ to fix damages⟩ **b :** a body of men esp. a jury assembled to hold such an inquiry **c :** the finding of the jury upon such inquiry or the document recording it **2 :** INQUIRY, INVESTIGATION ⟨a two-year ~ into the conduct of the executive —W.E.Binkley⟩ **syn** see INQUIRY
inquest of office : an inquiry made by authority or direction of the proper officer into matters (as escheat of lands) affecting the rights and interests of the crown or of the state
in·quiet \ən+\ *vt* [ME *inquieten*, fr. MF *inquieter*, fr. L *inquietare*, fr. *inquietus* restless, unquiet, fr. *in-* ¹in- + *quietus* quiet — more at QUIET] *archaic* **:** to disturb the peace of **:** DISQUIET
in·qui·e·ta·tion \(ˌ)inˌkwīəˈtāshən\ *n* -s [ME, fr. MF, fr. L *inquietation-, inquietatio*, fr. *inquietatus* (past part. of *inquietare*) + *-ion-, -io* -ion] *archaic* **:** DISTURBANCE
in·quietude \(ˈ)in, ən+\ *n* [ME, fr. MF or LL; MF, fr. LL *inquietudo*, fr. L *inquietus* (fr. *in-* ¹in- + *quietus* quiet) + *-tudo* -tude — more at QUIET] **1 :** disturbed state **:** UNEASINESS, RESTLESSNESS, DISQUIETUDE ⟨the dreadful ~ that comes before a surgical operation —Arnold Bennett⟩ **2 :** a disquieting or anxious thought ⟨occupied by a thousand ~*s* —Sir Walter Scott⟩
¹in·qui·line \ˈinkwəˌlīn, ˈiŋk-, -ˌlən\ *n* -s [L *inquilinus* tenant, lodger, fr. *in-* ²in- + *-quilinus* (fr. the stem of *colere* to cultivate, dwell) — more at WHEEL] **:** an animal that lives habitually in the nest or abode of some other species (as the burrowing owl in prairie dog colonies or any of several beetles and flies that live with social insects) — **in·qui·lin·ism** \-ˌlə,nizəm\ *n* -s — **in·qui·lin·i·ty** \ˌ==ˈlinəd·ē\ *n* -ES — **in·qui·li·nous** \ˌ==ˈlīnəs\ *adj*
²inquiline \ˈ"\ *adj* **:** having the character of an inquiline
in·qui·li·no \ˌēŋkēˈlē(ˌ)nō\ *n* -s [AmerSp, fr. Sp, tenant, lodger, fr. L *inquilinus*] **:** a worker on a Chilean landed estate who is usu. given the use of a small plot of land, implements, seed, and a small wage in return for his labor
in·qui·nate \ˈinkwəˌnāt\ *vt* -ED/-ING/-S [L *inquinatus*, past part. of *inquinare*, fr. *in-* ²in- + *-quinare* (akin to L *caenum* filth, ordure) — more at OBSCENE] **:** DEFILE, CORRUPT — **in·qui·na·tion** \ˌ==ˈnāshən\ *n* -s
in·quir·able \ənˈkwīrəbəl\ *adj* [ME *enquirable*, fr. *enquiren* + *-able*] *archaic* **:** capable of being inquired into **:** subject or liable to inquiry
in·quire *also* **en·quire** \ənˈkwī(ə)r, -īə\ *vb* -ED/-ING/-S [ME *enquiren, inqueren, inquiren*, alter. (influenced by L *inquirere* to inquire) of *enqueren*, fr. OF *enquerre*, fr. (assumed) VL *inquaerere*, alter. (influenced by L *quaerere* to seek, ask) of L *inquirere*, fr. *in-* ²in- + *-quirere* (fr. *quaerere*)] *vt* **1 :** to ask about or ask **:** seek to know by asking or questioning ⟨some kindred spirit shall ~ thy fate —Thomas Gray⟩ ⟨*inquired* the way to the station⟩ ⟨*inquired* what the weather was likely to be⟩ **2 a :** to search or search into **:** INVESTIGATE, EXAMINE ⟨failed to ~ the limits of what can be said —Allen Tate⟩ **b** *archaic* **:** to search or ask for — often used with *out* **c** *obs* **:** INTERROGATE, QUESTION ~ *vi* **1 :** to put a question **:** seek for truth or information by questioning **:** ASK ⟨*inquired* about the horses —*Amer. Guide Series: La.*⟩ **2 :** to make investigation or inquiry **:** engage in study or scrutiny — often used with *into* ⟨their right to ~ into the activities of the teachers⟩ ⟨~ briefly into the effect that comes from the combination of phrases —E.K.Brown⟩ **syn** see ASK — **inquire after :** to ask about the health or well-being of ⟨the parents of the boys he played with always *inquired after* his father and mother —Scott Fitzgerald⟩
in·qui·ren·do \ˌinkwəˈren(ˌ)dō\ *n* -s [L, by inquiring, ablative of *inquirendum*, gerund of *inquirere* to inquire] **:** an inquiry or an authority to conduct an inquiry
in·quir·er \ənˈkwīrə(r)\ *n* -s **:** one that inquires **:** QUESTIONER
inquiring *adj* **1 :** given to inquiry **:** INVESTIGATIVE ⟨an ~ mind⟩ **2 :** appearing to inquire **:** INQUISITIVE ⟨rolled ~ eyes toward my father —Kenneth Roberts⟩ ⟨~ looks⟩ — **in·quir·ing·ly** *adv*
in·quiry *also* **en·quiry** \ˈinˌkwī(ə)rē, ənˈkwī, ˈinkwə|, -ri *sometimes* iŋkwə| *or* ˈinˌkwi|\ *n* -ES [alter. of ME *enquery*, fr. *enqueren* + *-y*] **1 :** the act or an instance of seeking truth, information, or knowledge about something **:** examination into facts or principles **:** RESEARCH, INVESTIGATION ⟨complete freedom of ~⟩ ⟨the scientific method of ~ —C.W.Eliot⟩ ⟨that most modern of *inquiries*, the study of the cosmic rays —K.K.Darrow⟩ ⟨an ~ into the nature of truth⟩; *specif* **:** a formal or official investigation of a matter of public interest by a body (as a legislative committee) with power to compel testimony ⟨witnesses convicted of contempt of congressional *inquiries* —*Current Biog.*⟩ **2 :** the act or an instance of asking for information **:** a request for information **:** QUERY, QUESTION ⟨upon ~, I learned that he was out⟩ ⟨the information desk receives many *inquiries*⟩ ⟨would not answer my ~⟩
syn INQUISITION, INVESTIGATION, INQUEST, PROBE, RESEARCH: INQUIRY is a general term applicable to any quest for truth, knowledge, or information ⟨make *inquiries* about a prospective employee⟩ ⟨they made *inquiries*, and learned that Wild Bill was then in the Mint saloon —S.H.Holbrook⟩ ⟨a letter of *inquiry* to the authorities⟩ ⟨the True, which is the goal of all scientific and all philosophical *inquiry* —W.R.Inge⟩ INQUISITION suggests a sustained search, thorough and often unrelenting, for hidden facts; it may apply to merciless unremitting volleys of questions ⟨an *inquisition* into the bankruptcy proceedings⟩ ⟨the investigating committee subjecting him to a long *inquisition*⟩ INVESTIGATION may apply to a sustained and systematic inquiry, esp. of some specific proceeding ⟨an auditor *investigation* of the reported shortages⟩ ⟨the conduct of men in important areas may often be very legitimately subject to properly conducted Congressional *investigation* —Norman Thomas⟩ ⟨by their bullying tactics, by their having turned needed *investigations* into regrettable *inquisitions* —John Mason Brown⟩ INQUEST, once in more general use as a close synonym for INQUIRY, now usu. applies to an investigation, often by a coroner and his jury, into a cause of death or to a similar investigation into something disastrous or troubling ⟨it turned out on a final *inquest* that the learned lecturer had translated his piece into English —H.J.Laski⟩ ⟨it was decided at the *inquest* that the deceased had committed suicide⟩ ⟨an *inquest* on the fall of Singapore and the sinking of H.M.S. *Repulse* and H.M.S. *Prince of Wales* —*New Yorker*⟩ PROBE, in this sense, may apply to any deep, painstaking inquiry to discover something wrong or improper ⟨a *probe* resulting in the disbarring of several attorneys⟩ ⟨a *probe* into improper tax refunds⟩ RESEARCH applies to careful, prolonged study, esp. to uncover new knowledge ⟨*research* has shown and practice has established the futility of the charge that it was a usurpation when this Court undertook to declare an Act of Congress unconstitutional —O.W.Holmes †1935⟩ ⟨the *researches* . . . in the 17th century into the theory of probabilities greatly advanced the accuracy of calculations —*Encyc. Americana*⟩
inquiry agent *n, Brit* **:** a private detective
in·quis·ite \ənˈkwizət\ *vb* -ED/-ING/-S [L *inquisitus*, past part. of *inquirere* to inquire — more at INQUIRE] **1 :** to subject to inquisition; inquire into **:** INVESTIGATE, QUESTION ⟨people can stand only a small amount of *inquisiting* —G.P.Wilson⟩ **2** *obs* **:** INQUISITION
¹in·qui·si·tion \ˌinkwəˈzishən\ *n* -s [ME *inquisicioun*, fr. MF *inquisition*, fr. L *inquisition-, inquisitio*, fr. *inquisitus* (past part. of *inquirere* to inquire) + *-ion-, -io* -ion] **1 :** the act or an instance of inquiring **:** INQUIRY, SEARCH, EXAMINATION, INVESTIGATION ⟨nominated himself for this delicate ~ —S.H. Adams⟩ ⟨proposed a brief ~ into the politics of the place —John Buchan⟩ **2 :** a judicial or official inquiry or examination usu. before a jury (as for ascertaining taxable property or for fixing the guilt of nuisances); *also* **:** the finding of such a jury or the document on which it is recorded **3** [ML *inquisition-, inquisitio*, fr. L] **a** *usu cap* **:** a Roman Catholic ecclesiastical tribunal esp. of medieval times and the early modern period having as its primary objective the discovery, punishment, and prevention of heresy; *specif* **:** an ecclesiastical tribunal set up in Spain under state control in 1478–80 with the object of proceeding against lapsed converts from Judaism, crypto-Jews, and other apostates that was marked by the extreme severity of its proceedings **b :** an official inquiry or investigation conducted with little or no regard for individual rights or characterized by undue harshness, bias, or hostility on the examiner's part ⟨his ~*s* were backed by the authority of the United States government —Elmer Davis⟩ ⟨the whole notion of loyalty ~*s* is a natural characteristic of the police state —*New Republic*⟩ **c :** a severe or searching questioning **:** the ordeal of such a questioning **:** GRILLING ⟨pushed toward the edge by the ~*s* of the psychiatrists —*Time*⟩ ⟨mumbled my way . . . through these ~*s* —Adrian Bell⟩ **syn** see INQUIRY
²inquisition \ˈ"\ *vb* -ED/-ING/-S *vi* **:** to make inquisition or inquiry ~ *vt* **:** to subject to inquisitional examination
in·qui·si·tion·al \ˌ==ˈzishənᵊl, -shnəl\ *adj* **:** relating to, characteristic of, or resembling an inquisition ⟨the ~ system that seeks a confession, by physical or moral torture —Janet Flanner⟩ ⟨an ~ tribunal⟩
¹in·quis·i·tive \ənˈkwizəd·|iv, -ət|\ *adj* [ME *inquisitif*, fr. MF, fr. LL *inquisitivus*, fr. L *inquisitus* + *-ivus* -ive] **1 :** given to examination, investigation, or research ⟨be curious, attentive, ~ as to everything —Earl of Chesterfield⟩ **2 a :** disposed to ask questions out of curiosity ⟨if somebody saw a citizen climbing a street sign they might get ~ —Bant Singer⟩; *esp* **:** inordinately or improperly curious about the affairs of another **:** PRYING ⟨I mustn't be ~ and ask questions —W.F.de Morgan⟩ ⟨she was a bit ~, as girls are —Dorothy Sayers⟩ **b :** reflecting or indicating curiosity esp. about the affairs of another ⟨his ~ face beamed with mischief —Dorothy Sayers⟩ ⟨with bright, ~ eyes —Claudia Cassidy⟩ **syn** see CURIOUS
²inquisitive \ˈ"\ *n* -s **:** an inquisitive person ⟨visible to such ~*s* as myself —William Sansom⟩
in·quis·i·tive·ly \|əvlē, -li\ *adv* **:** in an inquisitive manner
in·quis·i·tive·ness \|ivnəs\ *n* -ES **:** the quality or state of being inquisitive
in·quis·i·tor \ənˈkwizəd·ə(r), -ətə-\ *n* -s [MF & L; MF *inquisiteur*, fr. L *inquisitor*, fr. *inquisitus* + *-or*] **1 a :** INQUIRER, INVESTIGATOR, QUESTIONER ⟨I am come as an ~ . . . to ask you certain questions —Max Peacock⟩ **b :** a person (as a coroner or sheriff) whose official duty it is to examine and inquire **2** [ML, fr. L] **a :** a member or officer of an Inquisition **b :** a person who conducts an official inquiry or investigation with little or no regard for individual rights or with undue harshness, bias, or severity ⟨bare his entire life and personality to official ~*s* under pain of dismissal —E.A. Mowrer⟩
in·quis·i·to·ri·al \(ˌ)inˌkwizəˈtōrēəl, -ˈtȯr-\ *adj* **1 a :** of or relating to an ecclesiastical inquisitor **:** having the functions of such an inquisitor ⟨with royal and ~ authorities on the watch for him —G.C.Boyce⟩ **b :** like or typical of an ecclesiastical inquisitor **:** heedless of or flouting individual rights in seeking information or enforcing conformity **:** marked by extreme harshness or cruelty ⟨a practical police force with true ~ talents —Waldo Frank⟩ ⟨beyond discovery by the most ~ and powerful methods —J.M.Keynes⟩ **c :** offensively searching or importunate in inquiry **:** PRYING ⟨felt the press ~ to the point of antagonism —*N.Y. Times*⟩ ⟨questioned them in his ~ way —Carleton Beals⟩ **2 :** constituting or relating to a system of criminal procedure in which the judge also acts as prosecutor or in which the proceedings are secretly conducted and the accused must answer questions **3 :** relating to or having the authority to conduct official investigations ⟨the ~ power of the Senate is . . . of the highest importance —Lindsay Rogers⟩ ⟨an ~ agency⟩ — contrasted with *accusatorial* — **in·quis·i·to·ri·al·ly** \-əlē, -li\ *adv* — **in·quis·i·to·ri·al·ness** *n* -ES
in·quis·i·tory \ənˈkwizəˌtōrē\ *adj* [ML *inquisitorius*, fr. *inquisitor*] **:** INQUISITORIAL, SEARCHING ⟨held to a high, persistent, ~ note —Scott Fitzgerald⟩
inquisitous *adj* [L *inquisitus*, past part.] *obs* **:** INQUISITIVE
in·quis·i·tress \-zəˌtrəs\ *n* -ES [*inquisitor* + *-ess*] **:** a female inquisitor
inradius \ˈ=ˌ===\ *n* [⁴*in* + *radius*] **:** a radius of an inscribed circle or sphere — opposed to *exradius*
¹in re \-ˈrā, -ˈrē\ *or* **in re·bus** \-ˈrābəs, -ˈrēb-\ *adv* [*in re* fr. L, in the thing; *in rebus* fr. L, in the things] **:** in the thing or individual **:** in something existing outside the mind **:** in reality ⟨traits or relations of the properties *in re* —Alan Gewirth⟩ — compare REALISM
²in re *prep* [L] **:** in the matter of **:** CONCERNING, RE — often used in the title or name of a law case where the proceeding is in rem or quasi in rem and not in personam or in an ex parte proceeding (as a matter involving a probate or bankrupt estate, a guardianship, an application for laying out a public highway)
in rem \-ˈrem\ *adv* (*or adj*) [L, against a thing] **:** against a thing (as a right, status, property) ⟨proceedings and judgments are *in rem* when they adjudicate a right or a status or a title to property within the jurisdiction of a court or tribunal without having power over the person of the parties affected thereby and without power to compel personal obedience of the parties affected⟩ — compare IN PERSONAM, QUASI IN REM
in req *abbr* information requested
in re·rum na·tu·ra \-ˈrārəmnəˈtu̇rə, -ˈrēr-\ *adv* [L] **:** in the nature of things in the world of nature as distinguished from the world of human beings **:** in the realm of material things ⟨they do not signify anything *in rerum natura* —R.F.McRae⟩
¹inring \ˈ=ˌ=\ *n* [⁴*in* + *ring*] **:** INWICK
²in·ring \ən+\ *vi* **:** INWICK
¹inroad \ˈ=ˌ=\ *n* [⁴*in* + *road*] **1 :** a sudden hostile incursion or forcible entrance **:** RAID, FORAY ⟨protecting their crops of barley from the ~*s* of sparrows —J.G.Frazer⟩ ⟨their new homes would be reserved to them against future ~*s* by whites —P.W.Gates⟩ **2 :** an advance or penetration esp. at the expense of something or someone **:** a serious encroachment ⟨another sharp ~ on the principle of free speech —*Civil Liberties*⟩ ⟨the ~*s* of the conformist spirit on American literary life —C.J.Rolo⟩ ⟨make ~*s* on the domestic markets of their local competitors —Patrick McMahon⟩ ⟨synthetic materials made deep ~*s* into the use of leather —J.F.W. Anderson⟩
²in·road \ən+\ *vb* -ED/-ING/-S *vt* **:** to make an inroad into ~ *vi* **:** to make inroads
in·roll \ənˈrōl\ *archaic var of* ENROLL
inrooted \ˈ=ˌ==\ *adj* [²*in* + *rooted*] **:** deeply rooted ⟨the ~ American philosophy of competition —William Best⟩
inrun \ˈ=ˌ=\ *n* [⁴*in* + *run*] **:** an inclined trestle down which a ski jumper moves prior to the takeoff
in·rup·tion \ənˈrəpshən\ *n* -s [by alter.] **:** IRRUPTION
inrush \ˈ=ˌ=\ *n* [⁴*in* + *rush* (after *rush in*, v.)] **:** the action or an instance of rushing or pouring in **:** INFLUX ⟨an ~ of cool maritime air —*Farmer's Weekly (So. Africa)*⟩
inrushing \ˈ=ˌ==\ *adj* [⁴*in* + *rushing* (after *rush in*, v.)] **:** rushing in ⟨the ~ immigrant masses —D.W.Brogan⟩
ins *pl of* IN, *pres 3d sing of* IN
-ins *pl of* -IN
ins *abbr* **1** inscribed **2** inside **3** inspected; inspector **4** insular **5** insulated; insulation **6** insurance
in·salivate \ən+\ *vt* [²*in-* + *salivate*] **:** to mix (food) with saliva by mastication — **in·salivation** \ˈ"+\ *n*
in·salubrious \ˌin+\ *adj* [L *insalubris*, fr. *in-* ¹in- + *salubris* healthful + E *-ous* — more at SALUBRIOUS] **:** tending to impair health **:** UNWHOLESOME, NOXIOUS ⟨an ~ environment⟩
in·salubrity \ˌin+\ *n* [F *insalubrité*, fr. MF, fr. *insalubre* insalubrious (fr. L *insalubris*) + *-ité* -ity] **:** unhealthfulness or unwholesomeness esp. of climate
in·salutary \(ˈ)in, ən+\ *adj* [LL *insalutaris*, fr. L *in-* ¹in- + *salutaris* salutary] **:** not healthful or wholesome ⟨a thoroughly ~ outlook on life⟩
in·san·able \(ˈ)inˈsanəbəl, ənˈs-\ *adj* [L *insanabilis*, fr. *in-* ¹in- + *sanabilis* curable — more at SANABLE] **:** INCURABLE, IRREMEDIABLE
ins and outs *n pl* **1 :** physical twists and turns or windings and uncertainties (as of a road) ⟨knows all the *ins and outs* of the short way to the camp⟩ **2 :** characteristic peculiarities or technicalities ⟨had to learn the *ins and outs* of the new plane⟩ **:** RAMIFICATIONS ⟨the *ins and outs* of a mathematical theory⟩
in·sane \(ˈ)inˈsān, ənˈs-\ *adj, sometimes* -ER/-EST [L *insanus*, fr. *in-* ¹in- + *sanus* sane] **1 a** *obs, of the mind* **:** UNSOUND, DISORDERED **b** *of a person* **:** exhibiting unsoundness or disorder of mind **:** affected with insanity **:** MAD; *esp* **:** disordered in mind to such a degree as to be unable to function safely and competently in ordinary human relations — compare PSYCHOTIC **2** *obs* **:** causing insanity **3 :** used by, typical of, or for insane persons ⟨an ~ hospital⟩ ⟨~ ravings⟩ **4 :** utterly foolish or ridiculous **:** lacking any logical or practical basis **:** wildly visionary ⟨a perfectly ~ idea⟩ ⟨such ~ extravagance⟩ ⟨the *insanest* thing you ever saw⟩ — **in·sane·ness** \-ānnəs\ *n*
in·sane·ly *adv* **:** in an insane manner ⟨behaved ~⟩ **:** to an

insane degree : beyond the bounds of reason ⟨~ jealous⟩ : ABSURDLY, RIDICULOUSLY ⟨~ extravagant⟩
insane root *n* **1** : a root believed in medieval times to cause madness in those eating it and usu. identified with either henbane or hemlock **2** : HENBANE 1a
in·san·i·tar·i·ness \(ˈ)in¦sanə,terēnəs, ən's-, -rin-\ *n* -ES : the quality or state of being insanitary
in·sanitary \(ˈ)in, ən+\ *adj* [¹*in-* + *sanitary*] : deficient in sanitation : unclean to such a degree as to be injurious to health : CONTAMINATED, FILTHY, UNHEALTHY ⟨working in ~ surroundings⟩ ⟨~ storage of food⟩
in·sanitation \(¦)in, ən+\ *n* [¹*in-* + *sanitation*] : lack of sanitation : careless or dangerous hygienic conditions
in·san·i·ty \ən'sanəd·ē, -ətē, -i\ *n* [L *insanitas*, fr. *insanus* insane + *-itas* -ity] **1 a** : the state of being insane : unsoundness or derangement of the mind usu. occurring as a specific disorder (as schizophrenia or dementia praecox) and usu. excluding such states as mental deficiency, the psychoneuroses, and various character disorders **b** : a mental disorder ⟨dementia praecox is one of the commoner *insanities*⟩ **2** : such unsoundness of mind or lack of understanding as prevents one from having the mental capacity required by law to enter into a particular relationship, status, or transaction or as excuses one from criminal or civil responsibility **3 a** : extreme folly or unreasonableness ⟨the ~ of war⟩ **b** : something utterly foolish or unreasonable ⟨the *insanities* of daily life⟩
syn LUNACY, PSYCHOSIS, MANIA, DEMENTIA: INSANITY, more commonly used in law than in medicine, applies to any mental disorder of such severity as to render the person unfit to manage his own affairs or to enjoy his liberty because of the unreliability of his behavior that makes him a danger to himself and to others. LUNACY, a term legally interchangeable with insanity, popularly implies periodic mental disorder or alternating madness and lucidity. PSYCHOSIS is the technical psychiatric term for any far-reaching and prolonged behavior disorder (as dementia praecox or manic-depressive psychosis). MANIA is a phase of a mental disorder (as manic-depressive psychosis) marked by a mood of sustained and exaggerated elation, emotional expansiveness, overtalkativeness, excessive physical activity, or delusions of greatness, that characterizes any of several psychoses. DEMENTIA is the technical psychiatric term that denotes mental deterioration that is psychogenic in origin (as dementia praecox) or that results from disease that damages the brain substance (as neurosyphilis or arteriosclerosis)
in·sa·tia·bil·i·ty \(¦)in,sāshə'bilədē, ən,⸗⸗'⸗⸗⸗, -lətē, -i *sometimes* -shēə-\ *n* [prob. fr. F or LL; F *insatiabilité*, fr. MF, fr. LL *insatiabilitas*, fr. L *insatiabilis* insatiable + *-itas* -ity] : the quality or state of being insatiable
in·sa·tia·ble \(ˈ)in¦sāshəbəl, ən's-, *sometimes* -shēə-\ *adj* [ME *insaciable, insessiabyll*, fr. MF or L; MF *insaciable*, fr. OF, fr. L *insatiabilis*, fr. *in-* ¹in- + *satiare* to satisfy + *-abilis* -able — more at SATIATE] : incapable of being satisfied or appeased ⟨an ~ desire for knowledge⟩ — **in·sa·tia·ble·ness** *n* -ES
in·sa·tia·bly \-blē,-bli\ *adv* : in an insatiable way : without being satisfied ⟨clawing ~ at the framework of tradition⟩ : in an insatiable degree; *broadly* : EXTREMELY, VERY ⟨~ hungry⟩
in·sa·tiate \(ˈ)in¦sāsh(ē)ət, ən's-\ *also* **in·sa·ti·at·ed** \-shē,ād·əd\ *adj* [*insatiate* fr. L *insatiatus*, fr. *in-* ¹in- + *satiatus* satiate, satiated; *insatiated* fr. ¹*in-* + *satiated*] : not satiated : not satisfied : INSATIABLE ⟨~ thirst⟩ ⟨such ~ cruelty⟩ — **in·sa·tiate·ly** *adv* — **in·sa·tiate·ness** *n* -ES
in·satiety \¦in+\ *n* [MF *insacieté, insatieté*, fr. L *insatietas*, fr. *in-* ¹in- + *satietas* satiety — more at SATIETY] : lack of satiety; *esp* : unsatisfied desire ⟨clothes they can never hope to own, changes they cannot afford to keep up with — must set up a tremendous store of ~ in the poor and the modest-income groups —P.M.Gregory⟩
insatisfaction *n* [¹*in-* + *satisfaction*] *obs* : DISSATISFACTION
in·saturation \¦in+\ *n* [¹*in-* + *saturation*] : the quality or state of being unsaturated
insc *abbr* inscribed
in·scape \'inz,kāp, 'in(t)sk-\ *n* [²*in-* + *-scape*] : inward significant character or quality belonging uniquely to objects or events in nature and human experience esp. as perceived by the blended observation and introspection of the poet and in turn embodied in patterns of such specif. poetic elements as imagery, rhythm, rhyme, assonance, sound symbolism, and allusion : INWARDNESS — compare HAECCEITY
insce *abbr* insurance
in·sce·na·tion \,in,sē'nāshən, ,in(t)sē'-, ,in(t)sə'-\ *n* -S [²*in-* + *scene* + *-ation*; intended as trans. of G *inszenierung*] : MISE EN SCÈNE
in·science \'insh(ē)ən(t)s, 'in(t)sēə-\ *n* [L *inscientia*, fr. *inscient-, insciens* inscient + *-ia*] : lack of knowledge : NESCIENCE
in·scient \-nt\ *adj* [L *inscient-, insciens*, fr. *in-* ¹in- + *scient-, sciens*, pres. part. of *scire* to know — more at SCIENCE] : exhibiting or based on inscience
in·scrib·able \ənz'krībəbəl, ən'sk-\ *adj* : capable of being inscribed
in·scribe \ənz'krīb, ən'sk-\ *vt* [L *inscribere*, fr. *in-* ²in- + *scribere* to write — more at SCRIBE] **1 a** : to write, engrave, print, or otherwise set down (as characters, symbols, words, or a text) esp. so as to form a lasting or public record **b** : to enter the name of esp. on a list : ENROLL **c** : to write (letters or other characters) in a particular format in cryptology; *esp* : to write (letters or other characters of a plaintext message) according to an agreed-upon route in an agreed-upon geometrical pattern preparatory to transcribing in another manner **2 a** : to write, engrave, print, or otherwise mark characters upon esp. so as to create a lasting or public record **b** : to autograph (a copy of a work of which one is the author) — often used with *to* or *for* ⟨~ one's book to an old friend⟩ **c** : to stamp deeply or impress esp. on the memory **3** : to assign or address (as a work of literature) in a style less formal than that of a dedication **4** : to draw (a figure) within a figure so as to touch in as many places as possible ⟨~ a polygon in a circle⟩ **5** *Brit* : to register the name of the holder of (a stock or other security)
inscribed *adj* [fr. past part. of *inscribe*] **1** : having lines or other markings deeply impressed or having the appearance of written letters (as certain insects) **2** *of a holding of stock or other security, Brit* : having the owner's name entered in a list kept by the issuing company or at a bank authorized to keep it and until recently transferable only by personal attendance of the owner or one entitled to act as his attorney **3** : bearing the author's signature often accompanied by an inscription — used in the book trade of a copy of a book ⟨an ~ copy⟩
¹**in·scrib·er** \-bə(r)\ *n* : one that inscribes
²**in·scrib·er** \'inz,krībə(r), 'in,sk-\ *n* [prob. fr. *in-* (fr. *input*) + *-scriber* (fr. *transcriber*)] : a device for transferring data from a punched tape onto a medium (as magnetic wire) for use in an electronic computer — compare OUTSCRIBER
in·script \'inz,kript, 'in,sk-\ *n* [L *inscriptum*, fr. neut. of *inscriptus* (past part.)] : INSCRIPTION
in·scrip·tion \ənz'kripshən, ən'sk-\ *n* [ME *inscripcioun* superscription, heading, fr. L *inscription-, inscriptio* act of writing upon, inscription on a monument, title, fr. *inscriptus* (past part. of *inscribere* to inscribe) + *-ion-, -io* -ion] **1** : something that is inscribed: as **a** : a text inscribed in order to form a lasting or public record (as on a monument, tablet, pillar, wall) **b** : a brief description of the character, contents, authorship, or occasion of a book or other composition placed at its beginning : TITLE, SUPERSCRIPTION, HEADING **c** (1) : a name and often a message prefixed to a work of literature addressing it to someone in a style or manner less formal than that of a dedication (2) : EPIGRAPH 2 **d** : the wording on a coin, medal, seal, stamp, or currency note : LEGEND **2** *archaic* : a tendinous line intersecting a muscle **3 a** : the act or process of inscribing **b** : the writing of characters in a particular format in cryptology; *esp* : the writing of the characters of a plaintext message along an agreed-upon route in an agreed-upon geometrical pattern before copying them off in another order to make a transposition cipher **c** : the entering of a name on or as if on a list : ENROLLMENT **4** *Brit* **a** : the act of inscribing securities **b inscriptions** *pl* : inscribed securities **5** : the part of a medical prescription that contains the names and quantities of the drugs to be compounded

in·scrip·tion·al \-shən°l,-shnəl\ *adj* **1** *archaic* : bearing an inscription **2** : of or relating to an inscription **3** : characteristic of inscriptions ⟨the revival of classical ~ capitals —*Times Lit. Supp.*⟩
in·scrip·tion·less \-shənləs\ *adj* : lacking any inscription ⟨buried beneath an ~ stone⟩
in·scrip·tive \-ptiv\ *adj* [L *inscriptus* (past part. of *inscribere* to inscribe) + E *-ive*] **1** *obs* : INSCRIBED **2** : relating to or constituting an inscription ⟨traced out the ~ lines⟩ — **in·scrip·tive·ly** \-ptəvlē\ *adv*
inscroll *var of* ENSCROLL
in·scrutability \(,)inz,krüd·ə'biləd·ē, ən-, -n,sk-, -ütə-, -lətē, -i\ *n* : the quality or state of being inscrutable
in·scru·ta·ble \ənz'krüd·əbəl, ənz'k-, -n¦sk-, -ütə-\ *adj* [ME, fr. LL *inscrutabilis*, fr. L *in-* ¹in- + LL *scrutabilis* scrutable] **1** : incapable of being investigated and understood ⟨attempting to look into the ~ future⟩ ⟨obeying ancient and ~ laws⟩; *broadly* : not readily comprehensible : MYSTERIOUS ⟨an ~ smile⟩ ⟨many fathers feel that, if they are to maintain their authority, they must be a little distant and ~ —A.C. Benson⟩ **2** : impossible to see or see through physically ⟨an ~ fog⟩ ⟨~ deeps⟩
in·scru·ta·ble·ness *n* -ES : INSCRUTABILITY
in·scru·ta·bly \-blē, -bli\ *adv* : in an inscrutable manner
in·sculp \ənz'kəlp, ən'sk-\ *vt* [ME *insculpen*, fr. L *insculpere*, fr. *in-* ²in- + *sculpere, scalpere* to cut, carve — more at SHELF] *archaic* : ENGRAVE, SCULPTURE
in·sculpture \ənz'k-,ən'sk-\ *n* [prob. fr. obs. F, fr. MF, fr. *in-* ²in- + *sculpture*, fr. L *sculptura* sculpture] : CARVING, INSCRIPTION
in·sculptured \ənz'k-,ən'sk-\ *adj* [²*in-* + *sculptured*] : CUT-IN, SCULPTURED ⟨~ epitaphs⟩ ⟨an ~ border⟩
in·seam \'in,sēm\ *n* [²*in-* + *seam*] : an inner seam: as **a** : the seam from the crotch to the leg bottom of trousers **b** : a seam showing on the inside only used for articles (as gloves) often made with outside seams **c** : a hidden seam in a welt shoe fastening the welt, lining, and shoe upper to the insole
in·seam·er \-mə(r)\ *n* : a worker that sews inseams (as on trouser legs or shoes)
in-season *adj* **1** *of a female mammal* : being in heat **2** : SEASONAL ⟨*in-season* accommodations⟩ ⟨*in-season* fruits⟩
¹**in·sect** \'in,sekt\ *n* -S [L *insectum*, fr. neut. of *insectus*, past part. of *insecare* to cut into, fr. *in-* ²in- + *secare* to cut; trans. of Gk *entomon* — more at SAW, ENTOMOLOGY] **1 a** : any of numerous small invertebrate animals that are more or less obviously segmented and that include members of the class Insecta and others (as spiders, mites, ticks, centipedes, sowbugs) having superficial resemblance to members of Insecta — not used technically **b** [NL *Insecta*] : a member of the class Insecta (as an ant, bee, fly) **2** *now chiefly substand* : any of various small animals (as an earthworm, coral polyp, turtle) **3** : a small, trivial, or contemptible person

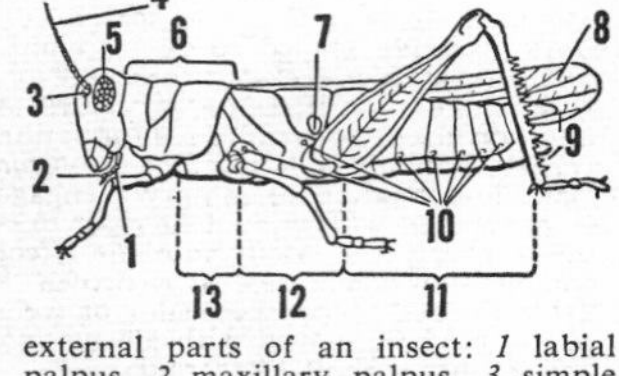

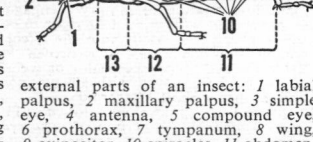

external parts of an insect: *1* labial palpus, *2* maxillary palpus, *3* simple eye, *4* antenna, *5* compound eye, *6* prothorax, *7* tympanum, *8* wing, *9* ovipositor, *10* spiracles, *11* abdomen, *12* metathorax, *13* mesothorax

²**insect** \"\ *adj* **1** : of, relating to, or being insects ⟨~ bites⟩ ⟨~ pests⟩ **2** : used on, for, or against insects ⟨~ pins⟩ ⟨~ powder⟩ ⟨an ~ cabinet⟩ **3** : using or depending on insects ⟨~ feeders⟩ ⟨~ fertilization⟩
in·sec·ta \ən'sektə\ *n pl, cap* [NL, fr. L, pl. of *insectum* insect] **1** *in former classifications* : a large group of segmented animals including (1) many worms and the arthropods, (2) all the arthropods, (3) the true insects, the myriapods, and the arachnids, or (4) the myriapods and the insects **2** : a class of Arthropoda comprising segmented animals that as adults have a well-defined head bearing a single pair of antennae, three pairs of mouthparts, and usu. a pair of compound eyes, a 3-segmented thorax each segment of which bears a pair of legs ventrally with the second and third often bearing also a pair of dorsolateral wings, and an abdomen usu. of 7 to 10 visible segments without true jointed legs but often with the last segments modified or fitted with specialized extensions (as claspers, stings, ovipositors), that breathe air usu. through a ramifying system of tracheae which open externally through spiracles or gills, that exhibit a variety of life cycles often involving complex metamorphosis, and that include the greater part of all living and extinct animals — see PROTURA; compare COLLEMBOLA
¹**in·sec·tan** \(ˈ)in¦sektən, ən's-\ *adj* [NL *Insecta* + E *-an*] : of or relating to the class Insecta
²**insectan** \"\ *adj* [¹*insect* + *-an*] : of or relating to insects
in·sec·tary \'in,sektərē, ən's-, 'in,sek,terē\ *or* **in·sec·tar·i·um** \,⸗,⸗'ta(a)rēəm\ *n, pl* **insectaries** \-ēz\ *or* **in·sec·tar·ia** \-ēə\ [NL *insectarium*, fr. L *insecta* + *-arium* -ary] : a place for the keeping or rearing of living insects
insect bed *n* : a geologic stratum rich in insect remains
in·sect·ed \(ˈ)in¦sektəd, ən's-\ *adj* [L *insectus* (past part. of *insecare* to cut into) + E *-ed*] : cut into : SEGMENTED ⟨the ~ body of a sea anemone⟩
insect flower *n* : PYRETHRUM 2a — usu. used in pl.
insecti- *comb form* [L *insectum*] : insect ⟨*insecti*ferous⟩ ⟨*insecti*fuge⟩
in·sec·ti·ci·dal \ən¦sektə¦sīd°l\ *adj* **1** [*insecti-* + *-cidal*] : destroying or controlling insects **2** [*insecticide* + *-al*] : of or relating to an insecticide — **in·sec·ti·ci·dal·ly** \-°lē\ *adv*
¹**in·sec·ti·cide** \ən'sektə,sīd\ *n* -S [*insecti-* + *-cide* (killing)] : the killing of insects ⟨a carefully controlled mass ~ was going on —*Newsweek*⟩
²**insecticide** \"\ *n* -S [ISV *insecti-* + *-cide* (killer)] : an agent that destroys insects; *broadly* : an agent hostile or repellent to insects — compare LARVICIDE
in·sec·tic·o·lous \¦in,sek¦tikələs\ *adj* [*insecti-* + *-colous*] : dwelling on the bodies of insects ⟨~ mites⟩
in·sec·ti·fuge \ən'sektə,fyüj\ *n* -S [*insecti-* + *-fuge*] : an agent that drives away insects usu. without destroying them : an insect repellent
¹**in·sec·tile** \(ˈ)in¦sekt°l, ən's-, -,tīl, -(,)til\ *adj* [L *insectum* + E *-ile*] : like or being an insect : consisting of insects ⟨an ~ mixture for feeding songbirds⟩
²**insectile** \"\ *adj* [¹*in-* + L *sectilis* divided, cut, sectile — more at SECTILE] : not sectile : incapable of being divided
in·sec·tion \ən'sekshən\ *n* [LL *insection-, insectio* incision, fr. L *insectus* (past part. of *insecare* to cut into) + *-ion-, -io* -ion — more at INSECT] : a notched or segmented part ⟨~s of a leaf margin⟩
in·sec·ti·val \¦in,sek¦tīvəl\ *adj* [¹*insect* + *-ive* + *-al*] : typical of an insect
in·sec·tiv·o·ra \,in,sek'tivərə\ *n pl, cap* [NL, fr. *insecti-* + *-vora*] : an order of mammals comprising the moles, shrews, hedgehogs, and certain related forms that are mostly small, insectivorous, terrestrial or fossorial, and nocturnal — see LIPOTYPHLA, MENOTYPHLA
in·sec·tiv·o·rae \-,rē\ *also* **in·sec·tiv·o·ra** \-,rə\ [NL, fr. *insecti-* + *-vorae* (fr. L, fem. pl. of *-vorus* -vorous) *or* *-vora*] *syn of* MICROCHIROPTERA
in·sec·ti·vore \ən'sektə,vō(ə)r\ *n* -S **1** [NL *Insectivora*] : a mammal of the order Insectivora **2** [F, fr. *insectivore* insectivorous, fr. *insecti-* + *-vore* (fr. L *-vorus* -vorous)] : an insectivorous plant or animal : a carnivore that feeds on insects
in·sec·tiv·o·rous \¦in,sek¦tiv(ə)rəs\ *adj* [L *insectum* insect + E *-ivorous* (as in *carnivorous*)] : feeding on insects : depending on insects as food
insectivorous plant *n* : a plant that captures and digests insects either passively (as the common pitcher plant or the sundew) or by the movement of certain organs (as the Venus's-flytrap) — compare DROSERACEAE, LENTIBULARIACEAE, SARRACENIACEAE
in·sec·tol·o·gy \,in,sek'täləjē\ *n* -ES [F *insectologie*, fr. *insecte* insect (fr. L *insectum*) + *-o-* + *-logie* -logy — more at INSECT] : ENTOMOLOGY
insect orchis *n* : a twayblade of the genus *Listera*
insect powder *n* : a powder for the extermination of insects; *esp* : PYRETHRUM 2a
in·sec·tu·ous \(,)in¦sekch(əw)əs, ən's-\ *adj* [¹*insect* + *-uous* (as in *contemptuous*)] : involving or full of insects : BUGGY
insect wax *n* : a waxlike substance secreted by an insect; *esp* : CHINESE WAX
in·secure \¦in+\ *adj* [ML *insecurus*, fr. L *in-* ¹in- + *securus* secure] : lacking security: **a** : not confident or sure : UNCERTAIN ⟨feeling somewhat ~ of his reception⟩ **b** : not effectually guarded, protected, or sustained : exposed to danger : UNSAFE ⟨an ~ investment⟩ ⟨property was very ~ during the riots⟩ **c** : not tightly fastened : not firmly fixed in position : SHAKY ⟨the hinge is ~⟩ **d** : not highly stable or well-adjusted : lacking likelihood of permanence or success : UNSTABLE, UNSURE ⟨a marriage ~ from the beginning⟩ ⟨his fortune was increasingly ~⟩ — **in·se·cure·ly** *adv* — **in·se·cure·ness** *n*
in·security \¦in+\ *n* [perh. fr. ML *insecuritas* danger, hazard, fr. L *in-* ¹in- + *securus* secure + *-itas* -ity] : the quality or state of being insecure: as **a** : lack of assurance : APPREHENSIVENESS ⟨a feeling of ~⟩ **b** : lack of safety : HAZARD, RISK ⟨the ~ of his capital⟩ **c** : an insecure condition or circumstance ⟨the minor *insecurities* of life⟩ ⟨noticed the ~ of the lock⟩
inseeing \'⸗¦⸗⸗\ *adj* [²*in-* + *seeing*, pres. part. of *see*] **1** : having insight **2** : tending to look inward : subjective or egocentric in orientation
in·sel·berg \'in(t)səl,bərg, 'inzəl-, 'inzəl,berg\ *n, pl* **insel·bergs** \-gz\ *or* **in·sel·ber·ge** \-gə\ [G, fr. *insel* island + *berg* mountain] : an isolated mountain partly buried by the debris derived from and overlapping its slopes
in·sem·i·nate \ən'semə,nāt, *usu* -ād·+V\ *vt* -ED/-ING/-S [L *inseminatus*, past part. of *inseminare*, fr. *in-* ²in- + *seminare* to beget, plant, fr. *semin-, semen* seed — more at SEMEN] **1** : to sow or sow in ⟨~ the minds of the young with practical ideals⟩ **2** : to introduce semen into (the female genital tract) by coitus or by other means **syn** see IMPLANT
in·sem·i·na·tion \(,)in,semə'nāshən, ən-\ *n* -S : the act or process of inseminating — compare ARTIFICIAL INSEMINATION
in·sem·i·na·tor \⸗'⸗⸗,nād·ə(r), -ātə-\ *n* -S : one that practices the technique of artificial insemination esp. of cattle
in·sensate \(ˈ)in¦sen,sā|t, ən's-, -n(t)sə|, *usu* |d·+V\ *adj* [LL *insensatus*, fr. L *in-* ¹in- + LL *sensatus* gifted with sense, intelligent — more at SENSATE] **1** : having no capacity to perceive : INSENTIENT, INANIMATE ⟨the ~ stones⟩ **2** : lacking or marked by lack of sense or understanding ⟨dull ~ rustics⟩ ⟨~ ignorance⟩ : not based on plan or reason : FOOLISH, FATUOUS ⟨this ~ project⟩ **3 a** : lacking awareness, sensibility, or sensitivity : having no conception of or feeling for ⟨~ to beauty⟩ ⟨~ to his privileges and responsibilities⟩ **b** : lacking humane feeling : UNFEELING; *broadly* : CRUEL, HARSH, BRUTAL ⟨~ destruction⟩ ⟨~ hatred⟩ — **in·sen·sate·ly** *adv* — **in·sen·sate·ness** *n* -ES
in·sense \ən'sen(t)s\ *vt* [ME *ensensen*, fr. MF *ensenser*, fr. OF, fr. *en-* ²in- + *sens* sense, fr. L *sensus* — more at SENSE] *dial Brit* : to give (a person) a sense of the importance or significance of something : impress or imbue firmly with a fact or idea : INSTRUCT, INFORM
in·sensibility \(¦)in, ən+\ *n* [LL *insensibilitas*, fr. L *insensibilis* insensible + *-itas* -ity] : the quality or state of being insensible: as **a** : an unconscious or comatose state **b** : lack of physical feeling or sensitivity : an unresponsive or unreactive condition : INSENSITIVITY ⟨marked ~ to cold⟩ ⟨increasing ~ to stimuli⟩ **c** : lack of mental or emotional feeling or response : APATHY ⟨her complete ~ to the honor done her⟩
¹**in·sensible** \(ˈ)in, ən+\ *adj* [ME, fr. MF & L; MF, fr. L *insensibilis*, fr. *in-* ¹in- + *sensibilis* sensible] **1** : incapable or bereft of feeling or sensation: as **a** : not endowed with consciousness : INANIMATE, INSENTIENT ⟨~ earth⟩ **b** : deprived of consciousness : UNCONSCIOUS ⟨to fall ~⟩ **c** : lacking sensory perception : failing to react to stimuli either wholly or to some degree ⟨markedly ~ to pain⟩; *also* : deprived of such perception or ability to react ⟨hands ~ from cold⟩ **2** : incapable of being perceived by the senses or perceptible only with difficulty : IMPERCEPTIBLE; *broadly* : MINUTE, SLIGHT, GRADUAL ⟨~ motion⟩ ⟨~ gradations⟩ **3** *archaic* : lacking sense or intelligence : STUPID, SENSELESS, UNREASONING **4** : devoid or insusceptible of emotion or passion : void of feeling : APATHETIC, INDIFFERENT ⟨~ to fear⟩; *also* : UNAWARE ⟨~ of their danger⟩ **5** : not intelligible : MEANINGLESS — used chiefly in law **6** : devoid of sensibility : lacking delicacy or refinement — **in·sensibleness** \"+\ *n* — **in·sensibly** \"+\ *adv*
²**insensible** \"\ *n* -S : one that is insensible
in·sensitive \(ˈ)in, ən+\ *adj* [¹*in-* + *sensitive*] : not sensitive: as **a** *obs* : INSENTIENT, INANIMATE **b** : lacking feeling : INSENSIBLE **c** : not physically or chemically sensitive **d** : not morally or mentally sensitive : UNIMPRESSIONABLE — **in·sensitively** \"+\ *adv* — **in·sensitiveness** \"+\ *n* or **in·sensitivity** \(¦)in, ən+\ *n*
in·sentience \(ˈ)in, ən+\ *n* [fr. *insentient*, after E *sentient: sentience*] : the quality or state of being insentient
in·sentient \"+\ *adj* [¹*in-* + *sentient*] : not sentient : not having perception or feeling : lacking consciousness or animation
in·separability \(¦)in, ən+\ *n* : the quality or state of being inseparable
¹**in·separable** \(ˈ)in, ən+\ *adj* [ME, fr. L *inseparabilis*, fr. *in-* ¹in- + *separabilis* separable] **1** : not separable : incapable of being separated or disjoined **2** : invariably attached to a word, stem, or root ⟨*un-* is an ~ prefix⟩ — **in·separableness** \"+\ *n* — **in·separably** \"+\ *adv*
²**inseparable** \"\ *n* -S : one that is inseparable from another — usu. used in pl.
in·separate \(ˈ)in, ən+\ *adj* [LL *inseparatus*, fr. L *in-* ¹in- + *separatus* separate] : not separate : UNITED; *usu* : INSEPARABLE — **in·separately** \"+\ *adv*
in·sequent \(ˈ)in, ən+\ *adj* [¹*in-* + *sequent*] *of the course of a stream* : apparently uncontrolled by the associated rock structure
¹**in·sert** \ən'sər|t, -sə̄|, -səi|, *usu* |d·+V\ *vb* -ED/-ING/-S [L *insertus*, past part. of *inserere*, fr. *in-* ²in- + *serere* to join, bind together — more at SERIES] *vt* **1 a** : to set (something) in : put or thrust in : INTRODUCE ⟨~*ing* the scions in hardy stocks⟩ ⟨~ a key noiselessly in a lock⟩ **b** : to put or introduce into the body of : INTERPOLATE ⟨~*ed* a few words of description⟩ **c** : to set in and make fast (as a piece of fabric) ⟨~ a patch in a pair of torn trousers⟩ ⟨~ a decorative medallion in a tooled leather cover⟩; *esp* : to insert by sewing between two cut edges ⟨~*ing* bands of lace on the front of the blouse⟩ **2** : to attach or fix in a particular position in the course of natural growth — used only in past part. ⟨the meristem is ~*ed* between more or less differentiated tissue regions —Katherine Esau⟩ ~ *vi, of a muscle* : to be in attachment to the part to be moved ⟨retraction is accomplished by two fairly thick bands of retractor muscles which ~ on the lophophore and originate in the body wall —Mary Rogick⟩
²**in·sert** \'in,s-\ *n* -S : something that is inserted or is for insertion : INSERTION, INSET: as **a** : written or printed material inserted (as a map or plate between the leaves of a book, a circular within the folds of a newspaper, an instruction sheet in a carton of merchandise) **b** : a removable portion of a die or mold **c** : a part of a casting placed in the mold and becoming integral with the metal cast around it **d** : a piece of cloth set into a garment for decoration, ease, and additional fullness
in·sert·able *or* **in·sert·ible** \ən'sərd·əbəl\ *adj* : capable of being inserted
inserted \(ˈ)⸗¦⸗⸗\ *adj* [fr. past part. of ¹*insert*] : set in : fitted in: as **a** : having the basal part set into another structure ⟨an insect with ~ mouthparts⟩ **b** : attached by natural growth (as a muscle or tendon or the parts of a flower) **c** : not in one piece with the main body and therefore replaceable ⟨an *inserted*-tooth saw⟩ ⟨an ~ valve seat⟩
in·sert·er \ən'sərd·ə(r)\ *n* -S : one that inserts
in·ser·tion \ən'sərshən, -səsh-, -səish-\ *n* -S [LL *insertion-, insertio*, fr. L *insertus* (past part. of *inserere* to insert) + *-ion-, -io* -ion] **1** : the act or process of inserting ⟨the

~ of new ball bearings⟩ **2 :** something that is inserted **:** INSERT: as **a :** the part of a muscle by which it is attached to the part to be moved — distinguished from *origin* **b :** narrow banding (as of lace or embroidery) with finished edges for insertion as ornament between two pieces of fabric **c :** a single appearance of an advertisement (as in a newspaper) **3 :** the mode or place of attachment of an organ or part ⟨the ~ of a muscle⟩ ⟨deep ~ of the petals of a flower⟩ — **in·ser·tion·al** \-shən³l,-shnəl\ *adj*

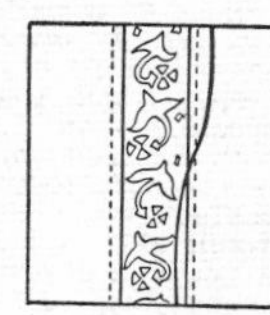
insertion 2b

in·ser·tive \ən'sərd·iv\ *adj* [L *insertivus*, fr. *insertus* (past part.) + -*ivus* -ive] **1** *obs* **:** marked by insertion **:** INSERTED **2 :** tending to insert

in–service \(ˈ)in¦==, ən'==\ *adj* **:** going on or continuing while in service ⟨*in-service* training⟩ ⟨*in-service* care of delicate fabrics⟩

in·serviceable \(ˈ)in, ən+\ *adj* [¹*in-* + *serviceable*] **:** UNSERVICEABLE

in·ser·vi·ent \ən'sərvēənt\ *adj* [L *inservient-, inserviens*, pres. part. of *inservire* to serve, fr. *in-* ²in- + *servire* to serve — more at SERVE] *archaic* **:** serving or subservient to (as an end or purpose) **:** CONDUCIVE

insession *n* -s [LL *insession-, insessio*, lit., act of sitting in, act of sitting down, fr. L *insessus* (past part. of *insidēre* to sit in, sit on, fr. *in-* ²in- + *sedēre* to sit) + *-ion-, -io* -ion — more at SIT] *obs* **:** the act of sitting in a bath; *also* **:** SITZ BATH

in·ses·so·res \,in,se'sōr(,)ēz\ *n pl, cap* [NL, fr. LL, pl. of *insessor* waylayer (lit., one that sits on), fr. L *insessus* (past part.) + *-or*] *in former classifications* **:** an order of birds that have the feet adapted for perching including the Passeres and many others

in·ses·so·ri·al \¦in,se¦sōrēəl\ *adj* **1** [L *insessus* (past part.) + E *-orial*, as in *raptorial*] **:** perching or adapted for perching ⟨~ feet⟩ **2** [NL *Insessores* + E *-ial*] **:** of or relating to the order Insessores

¹inset \'=,=\ *n* [⁴*in* + *set* (n.)] **1 a :** a place where something (as water) flows in **:** CHANNEL **b :** a setting in or inflowing (as of a tide) **2 :** something that is inset: as **a :** INSERT a; *esp* **:** one or more separate leaves inserted in a book usu. before binding **b :** a small but not necessarily small-scale graphic representation (as a map or illustration) set within the compass of a larger one **c :** a piece of cloth set into a garment (as for decoration) ⟨a satin skirt with ~s of ruffled chiffon⟩ **d :** a part or section of a utensil that fits into an outer part ⟨the ~ of a double boiler⟩ **e** [intended as trans. of G *einsprengling*] **:** PHENOCRYST

²inset \", ən'=\ *vt* **inset** *or* **insetted**; **inset** *or* **insetted**; **insetting**; **insets** [²*in-* + *set* (v.)] **1 :** to set in **:** place in as an insert ⟨~ an embroidered panel⟩ **2 :** to provide with an insert ⟨~ a belt with rhinestones⟩

in·set·ter \"+ə(r)\ *n* **:** one that puts in insets (as in a book)

in·severable \(ˈ)in, ən+\ *adj* [¹*in-* + *severable*] **:** incapable of being severed **:** INDIVISIBLE **:** impossible to separate — **in·sev·er·ably** \-blē\ *adv*

in·sheathe *also* **in·sheath** \ən+\ *var of* ENSHEATHE

inshining \(ˈ)in,==, ən'==\ *n* -s [⁴*in* + *shining*, gerund of *shine*] **:** ILLUMINATION ⟨when the soul feels the divine ~ —H.W. Beecher⟩

¹inship *vt* [²*in-* + *ship*] *obs* **:** EMBARK

²inship \(ˈ)in¦=, ən'=\ *adv* [fr. the phrase *in ship*] **:** on shipboard

inshipment \'in,==\ *n* [⁴*in* + *shipment*] **:** IMPORT — usu. used in pl. ⟨~s dropped 4 percent . . . but 8 percent more chicks hatched locally —J.M.Gwin⟩

inshoot \'in,=\ *n* [⁴*in* + *shoot*] **:** a pitched baseball that breaks toward a right-handed batter

¹inshore *vt* [²*in-* + *shore* (n.)] *obs* **:** to put on or bring to shore

²inshore \(ˈ)in¦=, ən'=\ *adj* [fr. the phrase *in shore*] **:** situated or carried on near shore **:** moving toward shore ⟨~ fishing⟩ ⟨an ~ wind⟩

³inshore \"\ *adv* [fr. the phrase *in shore*] **:** to or toward shore **:** near shore ⟨drifted ~ during the night⟩

inshore current *n* **:** an ocean current that flows in or to landward of the zone of breaking waves

in·shrine \ən+\ *archaic var of* ENSHRINE

¹inside \(ˈ)in¦=, ən'=\ *n* [⁴*in* + *side*] **1 :** an inner side or surface: as **a :** the right side of a sword in fencing **b :** the part of a footpath or sidewalk furthest from an adjoining roadway **c :** the concave aspect of a curve **d :** the side of home plate nearer the batter in baseball **2 :** an interior or internal portion or content **:** the part within: as **a :** inward nature, mind, thoughts, or feeling **b :** the inner parts of the body; *usu* **:** VISCERA, ENTRAILS — usu. used in pl. **c :** an inside passenger or seat (as in a stagecoach) **3 :** the middle or principal part of a division of time ⟨the ~ of a week⟩ **4 insides** *pl* **:** the 18 first-quality quires between the outside quires of a ream of writing or drawing paper; *broadly* **:** reams of which all quires or sheets are of first quality — compare OUTSIDE **5 a :** a situation in which information not generally available may be obtained **:** a position of trust and confidence ⟨he was on the ~ in all those deals⟩ ⟨only someone on the ~ could have told⟩ **b** *slang* **:** information not generally available **:** confidential information ⟨has the ~ on what happened at the convention⟩ **6** *or* **inside forward a :** INSIDE LEFT **b :** INSIDE RIGHT

²inside \"\ *adj* **1 a :** of, relating to, or being on the inside ⟨an ~ wall⟩ ⟨~ views⟩ **b :** included or enclosed in something ⟨the ~ furnishings⟩ **c :** used inside ⟨~ clothing⟩ **d :** measured from within usu. so as to include the cavity but not the substance ⟨~ diameter⟩ **2 :** employed or working indoors ⟨kept both an ~ man and a gardener⟩ **3 a :** relating or known to a select group **:** coming from an assuredly informed source ⟨~ information⟩ **b :** placed in an organization as an undercover representative of an actually or potentially antagonistic interest ⟨party ~ men in the unions⟩ **4** *of a union* **:** representing the employees of a single employer **syn** see INNER

³inside \"\ *prep* **1 a :** within the boundaries of **:** in the interior of ⟨waited ~ the church⟩ ⟨pain originating ~ the muscle⟩ **b :** on the inner side of ⟨place the dot ~ the curve⟩ **2 :** before the end of ⟨answered ~ an hour⟩

⁴inside \"\ *adv* **:** on or in the inside **:** INTERNALLY, WITHIN ⟨a house that was spotlessly clean both ~ and outside⟩ ⟨stayed ~ during the storm⟩

inside and out *adv* **:** INSIDE OUT

inside attack *n* **:** a division of a lacrosse team consisting of the inside home, the outside home, and the first attack — compare INSIDE DEFENSE

inside ball *n* **:** baseball play characterized by skillful use of strategy and fine points of technique

inside caliper *n* **:** a caliper for measuring dimensions of a cavity (as the inner diameter of an engine cylinder)

inside clinch *n* **:** a clinch knot in which the seized end of the line is inside the noose — compare OUTSIDE CLINCH

inside defense *n* **:** a division of a lacrosse team consisting of point, cover point, and the first defense — compare INSIDE ATTACK

inside finish *n* **:** the final work in a building necessary for its completion (as the adding of doors, paneled jambs, baseboards) — compare OUTSIDE FINISH

inside form *n* **:** INNER FORM

inside half *n* **:** SCRUM HALF

inside home *n* **:** a lacrosse player whose position is on the right side of the opponent's goal — called also *in home*

inside job *n* **:** an irregular or criminal act perpetrated by or with the connivance of a person occupying a position of trust in respect to the victim of the act ⟨the payroll robbery was an *inside job*⟩; *also* **:** such an act perpetrated by the apparent victim

inside left *n* **:** a forward on a soccer team whose position is between the center forward and the outside left

inside loop *n* **:** ²LOOP 2f

inside lot *n* **:** INTERIOR LOT

insident *adj* [L *insident-, insidens*, pres. part. of *insidēre* to sit in, sit on — more at INSESSION] *obs* **:** residing in **:** INHERENT

inside of *prep* **:** WITHIN **:** in the compass or on the inner side of ⟨*inside of* the city walls⟩ **:** in no more than ⟨back *inside of* an hour⟩

inside out *adv* **1 :** in such a manner that the inner surface becomes the outer ⟨peeled her gloves off *inside out*⟩ **2 :** THOROUGHLY ⟨knows his material *inside out*⟩

inside–out flower *n* **:** any of several western No. American herbs constituting the genus *Epimedium* of the family Berberidaceae and distinguished by sharply reflexed sepals

inside quire *n* **:** a quire of paper lying between the outside quires

in·sid·er \(ˈ)in'sīdə(r), ən-\ *n* -s [¹*inside* + *-er*] **:** a person recognized or accepted as a member of some group, category, or organization: as **a :** a person having access to confidential information because of his position **b :** an officer or a director of a company or a beneficial owner of 10 percent or more of an equity security registered on an exchange ⟨laws regulating the manipulation of a company's securities by ~s⟩

inside right *n* **:** a forward on a soccer team whose position is between the center forward and the outside right

inside straight *n* **:** four cards of a poker hand (as 9,8,6,5) that will make a straight if a card of one particular rank is added

inside stuff *n, slang* **:** confidential information

inside track *n* **1 :** the inner side of a curved racecourse **2 :** a position of advantage in competition ⟨the candidate who had the *inside track*⟩

inside turn *n* **:** a normal aircraft turn in which the top surfaces of the aircraft incline toward the inside of the curve

insidiate *vb* -ED/-ING/-S [L *insidiatus*, past part. of *insidiari*, fr. *insidiae* ambush, fr. *insidēre* to sit in — more at INSESSION] *vt, obs* **:** to plot or scheme against **:** lie in wait for ~ *vi, obs* **:** to lie in ambush **:** PLOT, SCHEME — **insidiation** *n* -s *obs* — **insidiator** *n* -s *obs*

in·sid·i·ous \ən'sidēəs *sometimes* -ijəs\ *adj* [L *insidiosus* insidious, cunning, deceitful, fr. *insidiae* ambush + *-osus* -ous] **1 a :** watching for an opportunity to ensnare ⟨an ~ tempter⟩ **:** lying in wait **:** intended to entrap or trick ⟨an ~ plot⟩ **b :** enticing and deleterious ⟨these ~ drugs⟩ **2 a :** acting by imperceptible degrees **:** having a gradual, cumulative, and usu. hidden effect **:** SUBTLE ⟨~ charm⟩ ⟨the ~ pressures of modern life⟩ ⟨an ~ drink⟩ **b** *of a disease* **:** developing so gradually as to be well established before becoming apparent **syn** see SLY

in·sid·i·ous·ly *adv* **:** in an insidious manner **:** GRADUALLY, SLYLY, SECRETIVELY

in·sid·i·ous·ness *n* -ES **:** the quality or state of being insidious

¹insight \'in,=\ *n* [ME *insight, insiht*, fr. *in* + *sight, siht* sight — more at SIGHT] **1 :** the power or act of seeing into a situation or into oneself **:** DISCERNMENT, PENETRATION, UNDERSTANDING **2 :** the act or fact of apprehending the inner nature of things or of seeing intuitively **:** clear and immediate understanding ⟨an extraordinary ~ into the complexity of women's emotions —*Current Biog.*⟩ **3** *obs* **:** a physical view **:** INSPECTION, LOOK **4 a :** recognition that one is ill esp. in mind (as in many neuroses but usu. not in typical insanities) **b :** comprehension or awareness of the nature of such illness or of the unconscious forces contributing to the emotional conflict involved **5 :** immediate and clear learning that takes place without recourse to overt trial-and-error behavior

²insight \"\ *n* -S [ME *insicht*] *archaic Scot* **:** PERSONAL PROPERTY; *esp* **:** household goods

in·sight·ed \'=,sīd·əd\ *adj* [¹*insight* + *-ed*] **:** endowed with insight

in·sight·ful \'=,sītfəl\ *adj* [¹*insight* + *-ful*] **:** exhibiting or characterized by insight ⟨the chapter . . . is ~ and suggestive of new perspectives —R.C.Angell⟩ — **in·sight·ful·ly** \-fəlē\ *adv*

in·sig·nia \ən'signēə\ *also* **insig·ne** \-(,)nē\ *n, pl* **insignia** *or*

Insignia of the United States Army: *1* General Staff; *2* Adjutant General's Corps; *3* Inspector General; *4* Judge Advocate General's Corps; *5* Quartermaster Corps; *6* Finance Corps; *7* Corps of Engineers; *8* Ordnance Corps; *9* Signal Corps; *10* National Guard Bureau; *11* Military Intelligence Reserve; *12* Infantry; *13* Armor; *14* Artillery; *15* Chemical Corps; *16* Transportation Corps; *17* Dental Corps; *18* Veterinary Corps; *19* Army Security Reserve; *20* Army Nurse Corps; *21* Medical Corps; *22* United States Military Academy; *23* Chaplain, Christian faith; *24* Chaplain, Jewish faith; *25* Medical Service Corps; *26* Aide to a Major General; *27* Warrant Officer; *28* Military Police Corps; *29* Civilian Affairs and Military Government

insignias [*insignia* fr. L, distinctive marks, badges, signs, pl. of *insigne* distinctive mark, badge, sign, fr. neut. of *insignis* marked, distinguished, fr. *in-* ²in- + *signum* mark, sign — more at SIGN] **1 :** a distinguishing mark of authority, office, or honor **:** BADGE, EMBLEM ⟨the *insignia* of royalty⟩ ⟨a collector of *insignias*⟩ **2 :** a typical and characteristic mark or sign by which something is distinguished ⟨the gay *insigne* of the new fighter squadron⟩ ⟨sports letters were originally *insignia* granted for especial competence in a competitive sport⟩

in·significance \¦in+\ *n* [fr. *insignificant*, after E *significant: significance*] **:** the quality or state of being insignificant **:** UNIMPORTANCE ⟨the ~ of the sum involved⟩

in·significancy \"+\ *n* [¹*in-* + *significancy*] **1 :** INSIGNIFICANCE **2 :** an insignificant thing or person

¹in·significant \"+\ *adj* [¹*in-* + *significant*] **:** not significant: as **a :** lacking meaning or import **:** MEANINGLESS ⟨forget this ~ quarrel⟩ **b** *obs* **:** INEFFECTIVE, FUTILE **c :** having no importance **:** UNIMPORTANT ⟨our losses were ~⟩ **d :** lacking weight or position (as from character, social standing, influence) **:** CONTEMPTIBLE ⟨this ~ hanger-on⟩ **e :** of little size or importance **:** SMALL ⟨an ~ town⟩ ⟨hard to believe that this ~ insect could be so deadly⟩ — **in·significantly** \"+\ *adv*

²insignificant \"\ *n* **:** something that is insignificant

insignificative *adj* [¹*in-* + *significative*] *obs* **:** not significative

in·sig·nis pine \ən'signəs-\ *n* [part trans. of NL *Pinus insignis*] *Austral & New Zeal* **:** MONTEREY PINE

in·simplicity \¦in+\ *n* [¹*in-* + *simplicity*] **:** lack of simplicity; *also* **:** a thing lacking in simplicity

in·sincere \"+\ *adj* [L *insincerus*, fr. *in-* ¹in- + *sincerus* sincere] **:** lacking sincerity or genuineness: **a** *of a person* **:** not being or expressing what one appears to be or express **:** HYPOCRITICAL ⟨a charming but thoroughly ~ woman whose words could never be taken at face value⟩ **b :** not based on reality, fact, or an honest appraisal ⟨an ~ denial⟩ ⟨the ~ and pity-seeking sigh of a spoilt animal —Arnold Bennett⟩ — **insincerely** \"+\ *adv*

in·sincerity \"+\ *n* [L *insincerus* insincere + E *-ity*] **1 :** the quality or state of being insincere ⟨the patent ~ of his answer⟩ **2 :** something that is insincere ⟨forgiving her evasions and *insincerities*⟩

in·sin·u·ant \ən'sinyəwənt\ *adj* [L *insinuant-, insinuans*, pres. part. of *insinuare* to insinuate] **:** INSINUATING, INSINUATIVE

in·sin·u·ate \ən'sinyə,wāt, *usu* -ād.+V\ *vb* -ED/-ING/-S [L *insinuatus*, past part. of *insinuare*, fr. *in-* ²in- + *sinuare* to bend, curve, fr. *sinus* curve, fold — more at SINUS] *vt* **1 a :** to introduce (as an idea or point of view) stealthily, slyly, or artfully **:** convey in a subtle, indirect, or covert way **:** instill imperceptibly ⟨cautiously *insinuating* doubts of his guardian's probity into the mind of the boy⟩ ⟨these fears craftily *insinuated* by enemy propaganda⟩ **b :** to impart or communicate with artful indirect wording or oblique reference and without direct or forthright expression **:** HINT, IMPLY ⟨Newman says of a gentleman that . . . he never . . . ~s evil which he dare not say out — Sir A. T. Quiller-Couch⟩ **2** [ML *insinuatus*, past part. of *insinuare*, fr. L] *Roman & civil law* **:** to register or file for registration (as a will or a gift) **3 :** to introduce (as oneself) by stealthy, smooth, or artful means ⟨*insinuating* himself into the confidence of the villagers⟩ ⟨gently the cat *insinuated* himself into the snug corner between the chairs⟩; *broadly* **:** to introduce gradually or without fuss and turmoil ⟨as time went on saner ideas *insinuated* themselves into the minds of the members⟩ **4** *obs* **:** to draw or attract (as the mind) to something or to a course by artful or indirect means **5 :** to push, work, or introduce slowly, carefully, or by a roundabout way ⟨cautiously *insinuating* herself into the crowd⟩ ⟨~ a car through traffic⟩ ~ *vi* **1** *archaic* **:** to enter gently, slowly, or imperceptibly **:** CREEP, WIND, FLOW **2** *archaic* **:** to ingratiate oneself **:** obtain access subtly **syn** see SUGGEST

insinuating *adj* **1 :** tending to gradually cause doubt, distrust, or change of outlook ⟨~ remarks⟩ **2 :** winning favor and confidence by imperceptible degrees ⟨these ~ attentions⟩ **:** INGRATIATING **3** *archaic* **:** entering or penetrating slowly or by a roundabout course — **in·sin·u·at·ing·ly** *adv*

in·sin·u·a·tion \ən,sinyə'wāshən\ *n* -s [L *insinuation-, insinuatio*, fr. *insinuatus* (past part.) + *-ion-, -io* -ion] **1 :** the act or process of insinuating: as **a :** stealthy or indirect hinting or suggestion **b** [MF & LL; MF, fr. LL *insinuation-, insinuatio*, fr. L] *Roman & civil law* (1) **:** the copying of an act or legal transaction (as a gift) in a public record (2) **:** the first production of a will for probate **c :** the gaining of favor, affection, or influence by gentle or artful means **:** INGRATIATION **d** *archaic* **:** slow or indirect entry or penetration **2 :** something that is insinuated: as **a :** an utterance intended to hint at or imply something subtly, slyly, or indirectly; *esp* **:** one intended to convey something derogatory ⟨his ~s about the governor's income⟩ **b** *obs* **:** an ingratiating act or speech

in·sin·u·a·tive \ən'sinyə,wād|iv, -,wə|, |t|, |ēv *also* |əv\ *adj* [L *insinuatus* (past part.) + E *-ive*] **1 :** tending or intended to insinuate **:** INGRATIATING ⟨a timidly ~ look⟩ **2 :** given to, characterized by, or involving insinuation **:** giving hints **:** INSINUATING ⟨an ~ remark⟩ — **in·sin·u·a·tive·ly** \|əvlē, -li\ *adv*

in·sin·u·a·tor \-,wād·ə(r), -ātə-\ *n* -s [LL, warner, fr. L *insinuatus* (past part. of *insinuare* to insinuate) + *-or*] **:** one that insinuates

in·sin·u·a·to·ry \-_wə,tōrē, -tȯrē, -ri\ *adj* [*insinuate* + *-ory*] **:** INSINUATIVE

in·sin·u·en·do \ən,sinyə'wen(,)dō\ *n* -s [blend of *insinuation* and *innuendo*] **:** INSINUATION 2a

¹in·sip·id \ən'sipəd\ *adj* [F & LL; F *insipide*, fr. MF, fr. LL *insipidus*, fr. L *in-* ¹in- + LL *sapidus* well-tasted, savory, wise, prudent — more at SAPID] **1 :** lacking taste or savor to such a degree as to be unpleasing or unappetizing to the palate **:** SAVORLESS, TASTELESS ⟨~ overcooked boiled cabbage⟩ **2 :** lacking in qualities that interest, attract, stimulate, or challenge **:** DULL, UNINTERESTING, STALE, COMMONPLACE ⟨which may give occasion to wit and mirth within that circle, but would seem flat and ~ in any other —Earl of Chesterfield⟩ **3 :** cloyingly sentimental or sweet ⟨manages to be appropriately babyish without becoming ~ —Robert Hatch⟩

syn VAPID, FLAT, JEJUNE, INANE, BANAL, WISHY-WASHY: INSIPID indicates a lack of sufficient taste or savor to please, attract, interest, or stimulate; it applies to that which leaves one uninterested or bored ⟨you have so much animation, which is exactly what Miss Andrews wants; for I must confess there is something amazingly *insipid* about her —Jane Austen⟩ ⟨all former delights of turf, mess, hunting field, and gambling-table; all previous loves and courtships . . . were quite *insipid* when compared with the lawful matrimonial pleasures which of late he had enjoyed —W.M.Thackeray⟩ VAPID, often interchangeable with INSIPID, indicates a want of savor, tang, or sparkle likely to please, or liveliness, force, or spirit likely to interest ⟨Sulpicius had a genius for making the most interesting things seem utterly *vapid* and dead —Robert Graves⟩ ⟨his prose is *vapid* and feeble in the essay, and stilted and artificial in the oration —V.L.Parrington⟩ ⟨the *vapid* and silly chatter of ordinary sociability among men and women —J.C.Powys⟩ FLAT is less precisely suggestive of deficiency than the preceding but as strongly condemnatory in indicating want of stimulation, animation, or interest ⟨a thing of frigid conceits worn bare by iteration; of servile borrowings; of artificial sentiment, *flat* as the lees and dregs of wine —J.L.Lowes⟩ ⟨though his men are *flat* his women characters are done with real insight and intuitive understanding —*Times Lit. Supp.*⟩ JEJUNE suggests a meager scantness of substance, a dearth of anything satisfying, nourishing, or strengthening ⟨mere annalists . . . whose work is as colorless as it is *jejune* —J.R.Green⟩ ⟨registration in the universities dwindled as the instruction they offered became increasingly *jejune* and lifeless —S.E.Morison⟩ INANE suggests a vacant emptiness, an utter want of purport, significance, or cogency ⟨the passive, suggestible, mentally monocellular human being whose vast *inane* face is to be met with in all the Broadways and Main Streets of the world, the end product of picture magazines, bad education, mass entertainment, and a vulpine competitive society —Clifton Fadiman⟩ ⟨Blanche's life, begun with who knows what bright hopes and what dreams, might just as well have never been lived. It all seemed useless and *inane* —W.S.Maugham⟩ BANAL indicates complete absence of the freshness that stimulates; it may stress the unrelieved commonplace ⟨the average man, doomed to some *banal* and sordid drudgery all his life long —H.L.Mencken⟩ ⟨the representation of life [in moving pictures] is hollow, stupid, *banal*, childish —J.T.Farrell⟩ WISHY-WASHY may imply weakness through dilution or vacillation ⟨talent is a *wishy-washy* thing unless it is solidly founded on honest hard work —E.G.Coleman⟩

²insipid \"\ *n* -s *archaic* **:** one that is insipid

in·si·pid·i·ty \,in(t)sə'pidəd·ē, -ətē, -i\ *n* -ES [F *insipidité*, fr. MF, fr. ML *insipiditas*, fr. LL *insipidus* insipid + L *-itas* -ity] **1 :** the quality or state of being insipid **:** VAPIDITY ⟨the ~ of her thoughts⟩ **2 :** something (as a remark or an idea) that is notably insipid ⟨these *insipidities* of expression⟩

in·sip·id·ly *adv* **:** in an insipid manner **:** so as to be insipid ⟨~ expressed thoughts⟩

in·sip·id·ness *n* -ES **:** INSIPIDITY

in·sip·i·ence \ən'sipēən(t)s\ *n* -s [ME, fr. MF, fr. OF, fr. L *insipientia* folly, fr. *insipient-, insipiens* insipient + *-ia* -y] *archaic* **:** the quality or state of being insipient **:** lack of intelligence

in·sip·i·ent \-nt\ *adj* [MF or L; MF, fr. L *insipient-, insipiens*, fr. *in-* ¹in- + *sapient-, sapiens* wise, fr. pres. part. of *sapere* to taste, have taste — more at SAGE] *archaic* **:** lacking wisdom **:** STUPID, FOOLISH

in·sist \ən'sist\ *vb* -ED/-ING/-S [MF or L; MF *insister*, fr. L *insistere* to stand upon, persist, dwell upon, fr. *in-* ²in- + *sistere* to stand, cause to stand, fr. *stare* to stand — more at STAND] *vi* **1** *archaic* **:** to find support **:** STAND, REST — used with *on* or *upon* **2** *archaic* **:** to continue determinedly or urgently (as in a course of action) : PERSEVERE, PERSIST **3 a** : to take a stand and refuse to give way : hold firmly to something ⟨~ed on the accuracy of his account⟩ **b** : to be persistent, urgent, or pressing ⟨~ed on going with them⟩ ~ *vt* : to take a firm stand about : persist in a point of view about — used with a clause as object ⟨~ed that we come in⟩ ⟨the moderate confederation may ~ that the radicals be ejected from the government⟩ ⟨~ he had done right⟩

in·sis·tence *also* **in·sis·tance** \-tən(t)s\ *n* -s [*insist* + *-ence* or *-ance*] **1** : the act or an instance of insisting ⟨his ~ on coming⟩ **2** : the quality or state of being insistent : PERSISTENCE, URGENCY

in·sis·ten·cy \-tənsē, -si\ *n* -ES : INSISTENCE

1in·sis·tent \-tənt\ *adj* [L *insistent-, insistens,* pres. part. of *insistere* to insist, stand upon] **1** *archaic* : standing or resting on something **2 a** : insisting or disposed to insist : PERSISTENT, PERSEVERING ⟨~ demands⟩ **b** : compelling attention : obtrusively conspicuous ⟨working in the ~ heat⟩ ⟨~ pounding of waves⟩ ⟨a bold ~ butte⟩ **3** [F *instant,* pres. part. of *insister* to insist] *of a bird's hind toe* : inserted so far above the base of other toes that only the tip will reach to the ground — opposed to *incumbent* **syn** see PRESSING

2insistent \"\ *n* -s : an insistent person

in·sis·tent·ly *adv* : in an insistent manner

in·sist·er \-tə(r)\ *n* -s : one that insists

in·sist·ing·ly *adv* [fr. *insisting* (pres. part. of *insist*) + *-ly*] : with insistence : INSISTENTLY, URGENTLY

in·sis·tive \ən'sistiv\ *adj* : tending to insist or urge

in·si·tion \in'sishən\ *n* -s [L *insition-, insitio,* fr. *insitus* (past part.) + *-ion-, -io* -ion] **1** *obs* : the act of grafting or a graft **2** : a taking in or adding as if through grafting (as by inoculation)

in·si·ti·tious \¦in(t)sə¦tishəs\ *adj* [L *insiticius,* fr. *insitus,* past part. of *inserere* to engraft, fr. *in-* 2in- + *serere* to plant, sow — more at SOW] : constituting an insertion : INTERPOLATED

in si·tu \(')in'sī(,)tü, -sē(-, -si(-, -)chü\ *adv (or adj)* [L, in position] : in the natural or original position ⟨motion pictures of the heart beating *in situ*⟩ ⟨combines . . . panels with reinforced concrete *in situ* columns —*London Calling*⟩

in·snare \ən+\ *archaic var of* ENSNARE

insoak \'in,=\ *n* [4*in* + *soak* (after *soak in,* v.)] : the taking up of free surface water by unsaturated soil

in·sobriety \¦in+\ *n* [1*in-* + *sobriety*] : lack of sobriety, moderation, or calmness; *esp* : intemperance in drinking

in·sociability \(¦)in, ən+\ *n* : the quality or state of being insociable : lack of sociability

in·sociable \(')in, ən+\ *adj* [L *insociabilis,* fr. *in-* 1in- + *sociabilis* sociable] **1** *obs* : incapable of being combined **2** : not sociable : not companionable : UNSOCIABLE, TACITURN — **in·sociably** \"+\ *adv*

insocial *adj* [LL *insocialis,* fr. L *in-* 1in- + *socialis* social] *obs* : UNSOCIABLE — **insocially** *adv, obs*

insofar \¦==¦=\ *adv* : in such measure : to such extent or degree ⟨pledged himself to follow a party line through thick and thin and ~ abandoned his freedom to think —Sidney Hook⟩

insofar as *conj* : in such measure as : to such extent or degree as ⟨we will succeed only *insofar as* we are prepared to sacrifice secondary objectives⟩

insofar that *conj* : in the measure that : to the extent or degree that ⟨cooperated fully *insofar that* many of their projects were jointly conducted⟩

insol *abbr* insoluble

in·so·late \'in(t)(,)sō,lāt, -,sə,-\ *vt* -ED/-ING/-S [L *insolatus,* past part. of *insolare,* fr. *in-* 2in- + *sol* sun — more at SOLAR] : to place in the sunlight : expose to the sun's rays (as for curing, drying, ripening)

in·so·la·tion \,=(,)='lāshən\ *n* -s [F or L; F, fr. MF, fr. L *insolation-, insolatio,* fr. *insolatus* (past part.) + *-ion-, -io* -ion] **1** : exposure (as of fruits or drugs) to the rays of the sun usu. to induce curing, drying, maturing **2** : SUNSTROKE **3 a** : solar radiation that has been received (as by the earth) **b** : the rate of delivery of all direct solar energy per unit of horizontal surface

insole \'=,=\ *n* [4*in* + *sole*] **1** : an inside sole of a shoe **2** : a loose thin strip (as of leather or felt) placed inside a shoe for warmth or ease

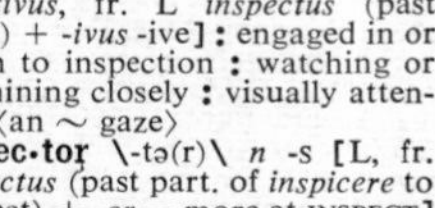
insole 2

in·so·lence \'in(t)s(ə)lən(t)s\ *n* -s [ME, fr. L *insolentia,* fr. *insolent-, insolens* insolent + *-ia* -y] **1** : the quality or state of being insolent : HAUGHTINESS, IMPUDENCE : gross disrespect ⟨~ is often an expression of insecurity⟩ **2** : an instance of insolent conduct or treatment : INSULT ⟨unwilling to put up with her petty ~s⟩

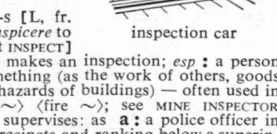

in·so·len·cy \-lənsē, -si\ *n* -ES **1** : INSOLENCE **2** *obs* : a strange or unusual thing or occurrence

1in·so·lent \-lənt\ *adj* [ME, fr. L *insolent-, insolens;* akin to L *insolescere* to grow haughty and prob. to L *solēre* to be accustomed, *sodalis* comrade — more at ETHICAL] **1 a** : haughty and contemptuous or brutal in behavior or language : OVERBEARING ⟨how ~ of late he is become —Shak.⟩ **b** : lacking usual or proper respect for rank or position : presumptuously disrespectful or familiar toward equals or superiors : provokingly free or pert ⟨~ street-corner loafers⟩ ⟨I will not tolerate an ~ child⟩ **2** : proceeding from or characterized by insolence ⟨heard out his ~ speech⟩ **3 a** *obs* : exceeding due bounds : EXCESSIVE, EXTRAVAGANT **b** : of such scope as to give an effect of contemptuous self-assurance ⟨the modern world, with its quick material successes and its ~ belief in the boundless possibilities of progress —Bertrand Russell⟩ ⟨mastered the violin with ~ ease⟩ **4** *obs* : not customary : NOVEL, STRANGE, UNUSUAL **syn** see PROUD

2insolent \"\ *n* -s : one who is insolent

in·so·lent·ly *adv* : in an insolent manner : to an insolent degree

in·so·lent·ness *n* -ES : the quality or state of being insolent

in·solidity \¦in+\ *n* [1*in-* + *solidity*] : lack of solidity : weak flimsy form or quality

in so·li·do \(')in'sälə,dō\ *also* **in so·li·dum** \-dəm\ *adv (or adj)* [L] : for the whole : involving all — used in civil law of a solidary obligation or contract ⟨an *in solido* obligation⟩ ⟨action may be brought against both the insured and the insurer, jointly and *in solido*⟩; compare JOINT AND SEVERAL

in·solubility \(¦)in, ən+\ *n* [LL *insolubilitas,* fr. L *insolubilis* insoluble + *-itas* -ity] : the quality or state of being insoluble: as **a** : INDISSOLUBILITY **b** (1) : INEXPLICABILITY (2) : something inexplicable

in·solubilization \"+\ *n* : the process of insolubilizing

in·solubilize \(')in, ən+\ *vt* [L *insolubilis* + E *-ize*] : to render insoluble

1in·soluble \(')in, ən+\ *adj* [alter. (influenced by L *insolubilis*) of ME *insolible,* fr. L *insolubilis,* fr. *in-* 1in- + *solvere* to free, dissolve + *-bilis* -able — more at SOLVE] : not soluble: as **a** *archaic* : incapable of being loosened : INDISSOLUBLE **b** : having or admitting of no solution or explanation : UNSOLVABLE ⟨an ~ doubt⟩ **c** *obs, of an argument* : UNANSWERABLE, IRREFUTABLE **d** : incapable of being dissolved in a liquid ⟨chalk is ~ in water⟩; *broadly* : soluble only with difficulty or to a slight degree ⟨a very ~ salt, dissolving no more than 1 part in 500,000 of water⟩ — **in·solubleness** \"+\ *n* — **in·solubly** \"+\ *adv*

2insoluble \"\ *n* [alter. (influenced by L *insolubilis,* adj.) of ME *insolible,* fr. *insolible,* adj.] **1** : something (as a problem or difficulty) that cannot be solved **2** : an insoluble substance ⟨the ~s in a tanning extract⟩

in·solvability \(¦)in, ən+\ *n* : the quality or state of being insolvable

in·solvable \(')in, ən+\ *adj* [1*in-* + *solvable*] : INSOLUBLE; *esp* : incapable of being solved ⟨an apparently ~ problem⟩ — **in·solv·ably** \-blē, -bli\ *adv*

in·sol·vence \(')in¦sälvən(t)s, ən's-\ *n* -s *archaic* : INSOLVENCY

in·sol·ven·cy \-vənsē, -si\ *n, often attrib* [prob. fr. ML *insolventia,* fr. L *in-* 1in- + *solvent-, solvens* (pres. part. of *solvere* to pay, free, dissolve) + *-ia* -y] **1** : the fact or state of being insolvent : inability to pay debts **2** : insufficiency (as of an estate) to discharge all enforceable debts

insolvency law *or* **insolvent law** *or* **insolvency statute** *or* **insolvent statute** *n* : a state statute that affords to an insolvent debtor relief from and sometimes full discharge of debts upon his surrender for the benefit of his creditors of all his property not exempt by law and that is suspended when it conflicts with the Federal Bankruptcy Act or covers a field occupied thereby or affects persons or property within the purview of that act

1in·sol·vent \-vənt\ *adj* [1*in-* + L *solvent-, solvens* (pres. part.)] **1 a** : unable or having ceased to pay debts as they fall due in the usual course of business; *specif* : having liabilities in excess of a reasonable market value of assets held — compare BANKRUPT **b** : insufficient to pay all debts charged against it ⟨an ~ estate⟩ **c** : IMPOVERISHED, DEFICIENT ⟨these miserably ~ teachers⟩ ⟨~ beliefs⟩ **2** : relating to or for the relief of insolvents ⟨~ regulations⟩

2insolvent \"\ *n* : an insolvent debtor

in·som·nia \ən'sämnēə\ *n* -s [L, fr. *insomnis* sleepless (fr. *in-* 1in- + *somnus* sleep) + *-ia* — more at SOMNOLENT] : prolonged inability to obtain adequate sleep : abnormal wakefulness : SLEEPLESSNESS

1in·som·ni·ac \-ē,ak\ *n* -s [L *insomnia* + E *-ac* (as in *maniac*)] : a person suffering from insomnia

2insomniac \"\ *adj* **1** : affected with insomnia ⟨an ~ boy⟩ **2 a** : characteristic of or occurring during a period of sleeplessness ⟨~ distress⟩ ⟨these tumbling ~ ideas⟩ **b** : associated with or tending to cause sleeplessness ⟨humid ~ nights⟩ ⟨the ~ flapping of the canvas —S.N.Behrman⟩

in·som·ni·ous \ən'sämnēəs\ *adj* [L *insomniosus,* fr. *insomnia* + *-osus* -ous] : affected with insomnia : SLEEPLESS

in·somnolence *or* **in·somnolency** \(')in, ən+\ *n* [1*in-* + *somnolence* or *somnolency*] : SLEEPLESSNESS, INSOMNIA

insomuch \¦==¦=\ *adv* [ME *in so muche, in so moche* — more at MUCH] : so much : to such a degree : so — usu. used with *that* or *as* ⟨they made no mistakes at all. *Insomuch* that . . . it is impossible to imagine a more successful outcome —Bernard De Voto⟩

insomuch as *conj* : INASMUCH AS ⟨*insomuch as* news reports have irretrievably blackened our motives⟩

in·sonorous \(¦)in, ən+\ *adj* [1*in-* + *sonorous*] : lacking resonance

in·sooth \ən'=\ *adv* [ME *in soth, in soothe* — more at SOOTH (n.)] *archaic* : in truth or reality : TRULY, ACCURATELY, FACTUALLY

in·sorb \ən'sȯ(ə)rb\ *vt* -ED/-ING/-S [2*in-* + L *sorbēre* to suck up — more at ABSORB] : to take in : ABSORB

in·sordid \(')in, ən+\ *adj* [1*in-* + *sordid*] : free from sordidness : GENEROUS

in·sou·ciance \ən'süsēən(t)s, -üshən-, F aⁿsüsyäⁿs\ *n* -s [F, fr. *in-* 1in- + *soucier* to trouble, disturb (fr. L *sollicitare* to disturb, agitate, move) + F *-ance* — more at SOLICIT] : freedom from concern or care : absence of studied attention : an attitude of indifference or unconcern esp. to the impression created (as by one's work, conduct, or comportment) on others ⟨moved on with a sort of elegant ~⟩ ⟨the utter ~ of this financial policy⟩ ⟨the light ~ of these lyrics⟩

in·sou·ciant \-sēənt, -shənt, F -syäⁿ\ *adj* [F, fr. *in-* 1in- + *souciant,* pres. part. of *soucier*] : exhibiting or characterized by insouciance ⟨an ~ manner⟩ ⟨a gay ~ person⟩ — **in·sou·ciant·ly** \-sēəntlē, -shən-, -li\ *adv*

insoul *var of* ENSOUL

insp *abbr* inspector

in·span \(')inz'pan, ənz'p-, -n¦sp-\ *vb* [Afrik, fr. MD *inspannen,* fr. *in* in (adv.) + *spannen* to stretch, span, hitch up — more at SPAN] *vt, chiefly Africa* : to yoke or harness (draft animals) to a vehicle : hitch draft animals to (a vehicle) ~ *vi, chiefly Africa* : to inspan animals or a vehicle ⟨*inspanned* as soon as we had eaten⟩

inspeak *vt* **inspoke** *or archaic* **inspake; inspoken; inspeaking; inspeaks** [2*in-* + *speak;* prob. trans. of G *einsprechen*] : to instill or infuse by or as if by speaking

1inspect *n* -s [L *inspectus,* fr .*inspectus,* past part.] *obs* : INSPECTION

2in·spect \ənz'pekt, ən'sp-\ *vb* -ED/-ING/-S [partly fr. L *inspectus,* past part. of *inspicere,* fr. *in-* 2in- + *-spicere* (fr. *specere* to look), & partly fr. L *inspectare,* fr. *inspectus* — more at SPY] *vt* **1** : to view closely and critically (as in order to ascertain quality or state, detect errors, or otherwise appraise) : examine with care : SCRUTINIZE ⟨let us ~ your motives⟩ ⟨~ed the herd for ticks⟩ **2** : to view and examine officially (as troops or arms) ~ *vi, archaic* : to look carefully : make an examination (as into a situation) : SEARCH **syn** see SCRUTINIZE

in·spect·able \-təbəl\ *adj* : capable of being inspected or publicly observed

in·spect·ing·ly *adv* : so as to inspect : with an effect of inspecting

in·spec·tion \-kshən\ *n* -s [ME *inspeccioun,* fr. MF *inspection,* fr. L *inspection-, inspectio,* fr. *inspectus* (past part.) + *-ion-, -io* -ion] **1** : the act or process of inspecting : a strict or close examination: as **a** (1) : the physical examination of the injured part of a person suing for damages for personal injury (2) : the examination of articles of commerce to determine their fitness for transportation or sale **b** : official examination to determine and report on the condition of military or naval personnel and matériel **c** : visual observation of the body in the course of a medical examination — compare PALPATION **d** : an investigation of an applicant for insurance **e** : an examination or a survey of a community, of premises, or of an installation by an authorized person (as to determine compliance with regulations or susceptibility to fire or other hazards) **2** : INSIGHT, PERCEPTION — obs. except in the philosophy of A. N. Whitehead

in·spec·tion·al \-shən°l, -shnəl\ *adj* **1** : of or relating to inspection : by means of or involving inspection ⟨~ services⟩ **2** : being or designed to be comprehensible immediately and without study or analysis ⟨an ~ comparison of two languages⟩

inspection arms *n* **1** : a position in the manual of the rifle, carbine, and pistol in which the weapon is held with the chamber open for inspection **2** : the command to take this position

inspection car *n* : a small motorized vehicle with flanged wheels for inspecting railroad track and roadway

inspection car

in·spec·tive \-ktiv\ *adj* [LL *inspectivus,* fr. L *inspectus* (past part.) + *-ivus* -ive] : engaged in or given to inspection : watching or examining closely : visually attentive ⟨an ~ gaze⟩

in·spec·tor \-tə(r)\ *n* -s [L, fr. *inspectus* (past part. of *inspicere* to inspect) + *-or* — more at INSPECT] **1** : one that inspects or makes an inspection; *esp* : a person employed to inspect something (as the work of others, goods imported, the state and hazards of buildings) — often used in combination ⟨customs ~⟩ ⟨fire ~⟩; see MINE INSPECTOR **2** : one that oversees or supervises: as **a** : a police officer in charge of a number of precincts and ranking below a superintendent or deputy superintendent **b** : a person appointed to oversee the conduct of an election (as with respect to the provisions of law and propriety)

in·spec·tor·ate \-tərət, *usu* -əd·+V\ *n* -s **1** : the office, position, work, or district of an inspector **2** : a body of inspectors

inspector general *n, pl* **inspectors general** [trans. of F *inspecteur général*] : a person that heads an inspectorate : the supervisor of a body of inspectors or a department or system of inspection (as of an army) ⟨the *inspector general* of agriculture⟩; *also* : an officer of a military corps of inspectors that investigates and reports on organizational matters (as discipline, morale, supply, accounts)

in·spec·to·ri·al \¦inz,pek¦tōrēəl, ən-, -n,sp-\ *or* **in·spec·tor·al** \ənz'pekt(ə)rəl, ən'sp-\ *adj* [*inspector* + *-ial* or *-al*] : of, relating to, or involving inspection, an inspector, or an inspector's duties

in·spec·tor·ship \ənz'pektə(r),ship, ən'sp-\ *n* : the status or position of an inspector ⟨obtained his ~ at 35⟩

in·spec·to·scope \ənz'pektə,skōp, ən'sp-\ *n* [fr. *Inspectoscope,* a trademark] : an x-ray device with fluoroscope designed to detect contraband articles (as on the person or in parcels or baggage)

in·spec·tress \-ktrəs\ *n* -ES [*inspector* + *-ess*] : a female inspector; *esp* : a woman who inspects the work of hotel chambermaids and advises the housekeeper of the need for renovation of rooms and replacement of furniture

in·spec·trix \-ktriks\ *n* -ES [LL, fem. of L *inspector*] : INSPECTRESS

inspersion *n* -s [MF, fr. LL *inspersion-, inspersio,* fr. L *inspersus* (past part. of *inspergere* to sprinkle, fr. *in-* 2in- + *-spergere,* fr. *spargere* to scatter) + *-ion-, -io* -ion — more at SPARK] *obs* : SPRINKLING

in·spex·i·mus \ənz'peksəməs, ən'sp-\ *n* -ES [L, we have inspected] : an English charter or letters patent beginning with the Latin word *inspeximus* in which the grantor confirms and recites a former charter

insphere *var of* ENSPHERE

in·spir·able \ənz'pīrəbəl, ən'sp-\ *adj* [*inspire* + *-able*] **1** : capable of being inspired ⟨while still ~ with a sense of responsibility⟩ **2** : fit for inspiration ⟨barely ~ air⟩

in·spi·rate \'inzpə,rāt *sometimes* -(,)pi,- *or* -,pē,- *or chiefly Brit* -,pī,-; 'in(t)(,)sp-\ *vt* -ED/-ING/-S [L *inspiratus,* past part. of *inspirare* to inspire, breathe into] **1** *archaic* : INSPIRE **2** *phonet* : to articulate during inhalation

in·spi·ra·tion \,=(,)='rāshən\ *n* -s [ME *inspiracioun,* fr. MF or LL; MF *inspiration,* fr. OF, fr. LL *inspiration-, inspiratio,* fr. L *inspiratus* (past part. of *inspirare* to breathe into, inspire) + *-ion-, -io* -ion] **1** : a divine influence or action upon the lives of certain persons that is believed to qualify them to receive and communicate sacred revelation and is interpreted within Christianity as the direct action of the Holy Spirit **2** [MF or LL; MF, fr. LL *inspiration-, inspiratio*] : the act of breathing in; *specif* : the drawing of air into the lungs — opposed to *expiration* **3 a** : the act or power of moving the intellect or emotions : capacity to inspire ⟨the ~ of this lovely scene⟩ **b** : the act of suggesting or influencing opinions or information esp. on a public matter ⟨the ~ of this rumor was traced to a source near the governor⟩ **4 a** : the quality or state of being inspired ⟨an artist whose ~ came from many sources⟩ ⟨found his ~ weakening⟩ **b** : something that is inspired ⟨had a new ~ as he waited⟩ ⟨a scheme that was a pure ~⟩ **5** : someone or something that inspires : an inspiring agent or influence

in·spi·ra·tion·al \¦=,=¦rāshən°l, -shnəl\ *adj* **1** : produced by or moved by inspiration ⟨an ~ speaker⟩ **2** : of or relating to inspiration ⟨the ~ element in Scripture⟩ **3** : communicating inspiration ⟨~ talks⟩ — **in·spi·ra·tion·al·ly** \-°lē, -əl, -li\ *adv*

in·spi·ra·tion·ist \,=(,)='rāsh(ə)nəst\ *n* -s : one who holds a theory of or belief in inspiration esp. of Scripture

in·spira·tive \ənz'pīrəd·iv, ən'sp-; 'inzpə,rād·iv, 'in(t)sp-\ *adj* [L *inspiratus* (past part.) + E *-ive*] : tending to inspire : INSPIRING

in·spi·ra·tor \'inzpə,rād·ə(r), 'in(t)sp-\ *n* -s [LL, fr. L *inspiratus* (past part. of *inspirare* to inspire) + *-or*] **1** : INSPIRER **2** : one that inhales or draws in something: as **a** : INJECTOR **b** : RESPIRATOR

in·spir·a·to·ry \ənz'pīrə,tōrē, ən'sp-, -tȯr-, -ri\ *adj* [L *inspiratus* (past part.) + E *-ory*] : relating to, aiding, used for, or associated with inspiration ⟨~ muscles⟩ ⟨the ~ whoop of whooping cough⟩

in·spire \ənz'pī(ə)r, ən'sp-, -īə\ *vb* -ED/-ING/-S [ME *inspiren, enspiren,* fr. MF & L; MF *inspirer, enspirer,* fr. OF, fr. L *inspirare,* fr. *in-* 2in- + *spirare* to breathe — more at SPIRIT] *vt* **1 a** *archaic* : to breathe or blow into or upon **b** *archaic* : to infuse (as life) by breathing ⟨*inspired* into him an active soul —Wisd Sol 15:11⟩ **c** *obs* : to breathe or blow (as air or vapor) into or upon something **2** : to draw in by breathing : breathe in : INHALE ⟨*inspiring* the crisp fall air⟩ ⟨the baby will ~ the mucus down into its lungs —*Fire Manual (Mass.)*⟩ ⟨be accomplished by increasing the oxygen percentage in the *inspired* air —H.G.Armstrong⟩ — distinguished from *expire* **3 a** : to influence, move, or guide (as to speech or action) through divine or supernatural agency or power ⟨the gods were believed to ~ the oracles⟩ ⟨spoke like a prophet *inspired* from above⟩ **b** : to have an animating, enlivening, or exalting effect upon esp. in a degree or with a result suggestive of the workings of some extraordinary power or influence ⟨had been *inspired* by his mother⟩ ⟨our ability to ~ the plodder —Ellie Tucker⟩ ⟨Milton and Shakespeare ~ the active life of England . . . through exceptional individuals —W.B.Yeats⟩ ⟨books that have *inspired* countless generations⟩ — often used with *with; specif* : to stimulate to creative activity in an art **c** : ENCOURAGE, IMPEL, MOTIVATE — usu. used with *to* ⟨*inspired* them to greater efforts⟩ ⟨a success which *inspired* him to broaden his activities⟩ **d** : AFFECT — usu. used with *with* ⟨experiences that *inspired* him with a yearning for education⟩ ⟨poverty that ~s the beholder with pity and disgust⟩ **4 a** : to communicate or impart (as an utterance) to an agent through divine or supernatural power ⟨spoke in words *inspired* by God⟩ **b** : to infuse or introduce into the mind or communicate to the spirit ⟨a steadfastness that *inspired* confidence in his followers⟩ ⟨conduct that ~s nothing but disgust⟩ : AROUSE, PROVOKE **5 a** : to bring about : OCCASION, PRODUCE ⟨events that *inspired* a new fashion⟩ ⟨studies that *inspired* several inventions⟩ ⟨hoping that improvement in business would ~ a tax cut⟩ ⟨the attacks *inspired* the passing of stringent food and drug regulations —E.S.Turner⟩ **b** : INCITE, FOMENT ⟨communist-*inspired* riots⟩ **6** : to cause to be said or written by influence and without acknowledgment of actual source or authorship ⟨a rumor that had been *inspired* by interested parties⟩ ~ *vi* **1** : to impart inspiration **2** *obs* : BREATHE, BLOW **3** : to draw in breath : inhale air into the lungs ⟨*inspired* deeply from a small bottle he had taken from his pocket —E.C.Bentley⟩

inspired *adj* [ME *enspired,* fr. past part. of *enspiren* to inspire] **1 a** : moved by or as if by a divine or supernatural influence : affected by divine inspiration ⟨~ prophets⟩ **b** : communicated by divine or supernatural inspiration : having divine authority ⟨the ~ books of the Bible⟩ **2** : breathed in : INHALED **3 a** : suggested by someone in power or in a position to know ⟨~ views⟩ **b** : having received or publishing authoritative views or information ⟨an ~ newspaper⟩ **4** : outstanding or brilliant in a way or to a degree suggestive of divine or supernatural inspiration ⟨an ~ mechanic⟩ ⟨an ~ performance of a concerto⟩ ⟨an ~ answer to an awkward question⟩ — **in·spired·ly** \-īrədlē, -ī(ə)rd-\ *adv*

in·spir·er \-īrə(r)\ *n* -s [alter. (influenced by *-er*) of ME *inspirour,* fr. *inspiren* to inspire + *-our* -or] : one that inspires

inspiring *adj* : that inspires or tends to inspire ⟨~ thoughts⟩ ⟨the music was ~⟩ — **in·spir·ing·ly** *adv*

in·spirit \ənz'p-, ən'sp-\ *also* **en·spirit** \", en-\ *vt* -ED/-ING/-S [2*in-* or 1*en-* + *spirit* (n.)] **1** : to infuse spirit into : fill with courage, determination, hope, vigor, or exaltation : ANIMATE, HEARTEN ⟨unconquerable jests have ~ed men's hearts in long periods of disaster —Agnes Repplier⟩ **2** : to cause to be possessed by a spirit **syn** see ENCOURAGE

in·spir·it·er \"ə(r)\ *n* -s : one that inspirits

inspiriting *adj* : tending or able to inspirit ⟨an ~ letter⟩ — **in·spir·it·ing·ly** *adv*

in·spi·rom·e·ter \,inzpə'räməd·ə(r), ,inz,pī'-, ,in(t)(,)sp-\ *n* [*inspire* + *-o-* + *-meter*] : an apparatus for measuring air inspired in breathing

1in·spis·sate \(')inz'pisət, ənz'p-, -i,sāt, 'inzpə,sāt, -n(t)(¦)sp-\ *or* **in·spis·sat·ed** \-ād·əd\ *adj* [*inspissate* fr. LL *inspissatus* (past part.); *inspissated* fr. past part. of 2*inspissate*] : thickened in consistency; *broadly* : made thick, heavy, or intense ⟨shed a flood of *inspissated* darkness on a cloud of confusing uncertainties —G.B.Barbour⟩ ⟨*inspissated* class-consciousness —Vincent Sheean⟩

2in·spis·sate \ənz'pi,sāt, 'inzpə,-, -n(t)(')sp-\ *vb* -ED/-ING/-S [LL *inspissatus,* past part. of *inspissare,* fr. L *in-* 2in- + *spissare* to thicken, fr. *spissus* thick; akin to Gk *aspis* shield — more at ASPID-] *vt* : to bring to a heavier consistency : CONDENSE ⟨*inspissating* the serum in the Petri dishes⟩; *broadly* : to make thick, heavy, or intense ⟨parties of school children and factory girls *inspissating* the gloom of the museum atmosphere —Clive Bell⟩ ~ *vi* : to reach or assume a heavier consistency ⟨sap *inspissating* over a fire⟩ — **in·spis·sa·tor** \-ād·ə(r)\ *n* -s

in·spis·sa·tion \,inzpə'sāshən, -(,)pi'-, ,in(t)(,)sp-\ *n* -s [F or ML; F, fr. MF, fr. ML *inspissation-, inspissatio,* fr. LL *inspissatus* (past part.) + L *-ion-, -io* -ion] : the act or process of inspissating or the state of being inspissated

in spite of *prep* [ME] : without being blocked or prevented by the opposing force of : regardless of the adverse effect of : DESPITE, NOTWITHSTANDING ⟨went *in spite of* the rain⟩ ⟨a handsome man *in spite of* his baldness⟩ ⟨plunged ahead *in spite of* all efforts to stop him⟩

inspoke *past of* INSPEAK

inspoken *past part of* INSPEAK

inst *abbr* **1** installment **2** instant; instantaneous **3** institute; institution **4** instruction; instructor **5** instrument; instrumental

in·stability \¦inztə¦===, ¦in(t)stə-\ *n* [ME *instabilitee*, fr. MF or L; MF *instabilité*, fr. L *instabilitas*, fr. *instabilis* + *-itas* -ity] **:** the quality or state of being unstable: as **a :** lack of physical firmness **:** INSECURITY ⟨the ~ of a building⟩ **b :** lack of determination or uniformity ⟨economic ~⟩ **:** INCONSTANCY ⟨~ of temper⟩ ⟨increasing ~ of cherished institutions⟩; *also* **:** tendency to react violently or explosively ⟨emotional ~⟩ ⟨the extreme ~ of certain chemicals⟩ **c :** an unstable state of the atmosphere that results when the vertical distribution of temperature or moisture is such that an air particle when set in motion will tend to move at increasing speed either upward or downward from its previous position

in·stable \(ˈ)in¦zˈtābəl, -n¦st-\ *adj* [MF or L; MF, fr. L *instabilis*, fr. *in-* ¹in- + *stabilis* firm, stable — more at STABLE] **:** UNSTABLE

in·stall *also* **in·stal** \ənzˈtȯl, ənˈst-\ *vt* **installed; installed; installing; installs** *also* **instals** [MF *installer*, *instaler*, fr. ML *installare*, fr. L *in-* ²in- + ML *stallum*, *stallus* stall, fr. OHG *stal* place, stall — more at STALL] **1 a :** to place in possession of an office or dignity by seating in a stall or official seat **b :** to place in an office, rank, or order **:** INDUCT ⟨~*ed* the new college president⟩ **2 :** to introduce and establish (oneself or another) in an indicated place, condition, or status ⟨~*ing* himself in the big chair before the fire⟩ ⟨~*ed* his sister as secretary⟩ **3 :** to set up for use or service ⟨the electrician ~*ed* the new fixtures⟩ ⟨had gas heating ~*ed*⟩

in·stal·lant \-lənt\ *n* -s [ML *installant-*, *installans*, pres. part of *installare* to install] **:** one that formally installs another to office

in·stal·la·tion \ˌinztəˈlāshən, ˌin(t)stə-\ *n* -s [F or ML; F, fr. MF, fr. ML *installation-*, *installatio*, fr. *installatus* (past part. of *installare*) + L *-ion-*, *-io* -ion] **1 :** an act of installing or the state of being installed: as **a :** the giving possession of an office, rank, or order with the usual rites or ceremonies **b :** ESTABLISHMENT **c :** the setting up or placing in position for service or use **2 a :** something that is installed for use ⟨admired the new plumbing ~⟩ **b installations** *pl* **:** APPOINTMENTS, FURNISHINGS, EQUIPMENT ⟨the ~*s* were of excellent quality and in very good taste⟩ **3 :** land and improvements installed thereon devoted to military purposes ⟨forts, training camps, and other army ~*s*⟩

in·stall·er \ənzˈtȯlə(r), ənˈst-\ *n* -s **:** one that installs ⟨repairmen and ~*s* of new equipment⟩

installing officer *n* **:** a person that supervises or conducts a formal installing of an officer of an organization

¹**in·stall·ment** *or* **in·stal·ment** \-lmənt\ *n* -s [*install* or *instal* + *-ment*] **1 :** an act of installing or the state of being installed **2** *obs* **:** the seat or place in which one is installed

²**installment** *also* **instalment** \"\ *n* -s [alter. of earlier *estallment*, *estalment* arrangement for payment by installments, prob. fr. MF *estaler* to stop, place, fix (fr. OF, fr. *estal* stop, place, position, fr. OHG *stal* place, stall) + E *-ment* — more at STALL] **1 a :** one of the portions into which a sum of money or a debt is divided for payment at set and usu. regular intervals ⟨the balance may be paid in three equal quarterly ~*s*⟩ **b :** a payment that is part of a sum owed ⟨surprised to get even an ~ on the money he had loaned⟩ **2 a :** one of several parts (as of a publication) presented at intervals **:** FASCICLE **b :** one portion of a story published serially (as in a magazine)

³**installment** *also* **instalment** \"\ *adj* **:** of, relating to, based on, or involving periodic payments of a fixed sum or of a predetermined percentage of a total ⟨~ buying⟩ ⟨~ credit⟩ ⟨~ loan⟩ ⟨an ~ account⟩

installment mortgage *n* **:** a mortgage in which the sum loaned is to be repaid in installments over a period of time

installment plan *n* **:** a plan that involves payment by installments

installment sales insurance *n* **:** insurance that covers the seller's interest in merchandise which is sold on installment terms

installment selling *n* **:** the selling of consumer goods on credit under conditional sales contracts that provide for regular periodic payments after an initial down payment

¹**in·stance** \ˈinztən(t)s, ˈin(t)stə-, ˈinsən-\ *n* -s [ME *instaunce*, fr. MF *instance* act of urging, motive, instant, fr. L *instantia* presence, vehemence in speech, urgency, fr. *instant-*, *instans* (pres. part.) + *-ia* -y — more at INSTANT] **1 a** *archaic* **:** urgent or earnest solicitation **:** urgency or exercise of pressure in either petition or action **b :** INSTIGATION, SUGGESTION, REQUEST ⟨work undertaken at the ~ of the householder⟩ **c** *obs* **:** something that urges **:** an impelling cause or motive **2** [ML *instantia*, trans. of Gk *enstasis*] **a** *archaic* **:** a case or example brought forward in disproof or rebuttal of a generalization **:** EXCEPTION **b :** something that is available or is offered as an illustrative case **:** something cited in proof or as an example ⟨an ~ of true heroism⟩ ⟨carefully documenting each ~ of the use of this diphthong⟩ **c** *obs* **:** TOKEN, SIGN, SYMPTOM **d** *obs* **:** DETAIL, CIRCUMSTANCE **3** [F or LL; F, fr. LL *instantia*, fr. L] **a :** the institution and prosecution of a lawsuit **:** a legal proceeding or process **:** SUIT **b (1) :** a demand set forth in a civil law proceeding **(2) :** a specific case referred to as an example **(3) :** a case in an ecclesiastical court that is brought at the request of a party and not upon official request **4 a :** a step, stage, or situation viewed as part of a process or series of events **:** an occasion or period defined by certain events ⟨a well-known writer who prefers, in this ~, to remain anonymous —*Times Lit. Supp.*⟩ ⟨appointments will be made for a three-year period in the first ~⟩ **b :** SUBSTITUTION INSTANCE

syn CASE, ILLUSTRATION, EXAMPLE, SAMPLE, SPECIMEN: INSTANCE and CASE are less specific in meaning and suggestion than the others. The former may be used in reference to any particular person, thing, or situation which may be given to illustrate or explain ⟨the *instance* may be rejected, but the principle abides —B.N.Cardozo⟩ ⟨wanted to work out the problem on a definite *instance* —A.L.Guérard⟩ CASE is now very general in meaning and poor in connotative power; it is used to designate a situation or occurrence showing characteristics to be grouped together and viewed as a configuration or pattern ⟨the *case* of payments made under the head of profits to entrepreneurs, financiers, speculators, and middlemen in various markets —J.A.Hobson⟩ ⟨usually isolated *cases* of deaf and dumb, feebleminded, or otherwise unfortunate children —R.W.Murray⟩ ILLUSTRATION is likely to suggest an instance adduced for the sake of clarifying or demonstrating ⟨the resolution of Washington and his men at Valley Forge is an *illustration* of bravery⟩ EXAMPLE suggests a single item or incident taken as typical or representative ⟨perhaps the best of many American *examples* of the creative artist and thinker . . . in a country and an era dominantly materialistic —H.S.Canby⟩ SAMPLE may indicate a part or a unit of a whole taken more or less at random but still presumed to be typical or representative in showing a general nature, character, or quality ⟨so many happy youths . . . so many divers *samples* from the growth of life's sweet season —William Wordsworth⟩ ⟨the barest *sample* of the riches which the gleaner may gather —B.N.Cardozo⟩ SPECIMEN is close to SAMPLE in its meaning but may suggest scientific or otherwise close analysis ⟨made it my business to examine some *specimens* of the writing —Charles Dickens⟩ SPECIMEN may indicate either the typical or representative example or the merely existent instance ⟨there were a few boomtowns in the Middle West, but the finest *specimens* began to be seen only with the discoveries of gold and silver in the Far West —A.F.Harlow⟩ — **for instance** \fə(r)in- *sometimes* ˈfrin-\ *adv* **:** as an example

²**instance** \"\ *vb* -ED/-ING/-S *vt* **1** *obs* **:** URGE, IMPORTUNE **2 :** to illustrate or demonstrate by an instance ⟨his meaning is well *instanced* in the passage quoted⟩ **3 :** to mention as a case or example **:** CITE ⟨we might ~ the increase in delinquency⟩ ~ *vi* **:** to mention an instance **syn** see MENTION

instance court *n* **:** a branch of a court of admiralty that has jurisdiction over all maritime contracts and torts except prize cases

in·stan·cy \-ənsē, -si\ *n* -ES [L *instantia*] **1 :** URGENCY, INSISTENCE ⟨continued to press his claim with some ~⟩ ⟨the vivid ~ of an involuntary cry —C.E.Montague⟩ **2 :** nearness of approach **:** IMMINENCE ⟨the ~ of peril —*Yale Rev.*⟩ **3 :** immediateness of occurrence or action **:** INSTANTANEOUSNESS ⟨the ~ of their response⟩ ⟨the *instancies* of aviation and television —Mary Madeleva⟩

¹**in·stant** \ˈinztənt, ˈin(t)stə-\ *n* -s [ME, prob. fr. MF, fr. *instant*, adj.] **1 a :** an infinitesimal space of time **:** a point of time ⟨came not an ~ too soon⟩; *esp* **:** a point without temporal duration separating two states each with temporal duration ⟨at the ~ of death⟩ **b :** a point of time present or regarded as present in respect to a particular context **:** MOMENT ⟨the ~ we met⟩ ⟨come here this ~⟩ ⟨the ~ she opened her eyes⟩ **2 :** the present or current month

²**instant** \"\ *adj* [ME, fr. MF or L; MF, fr. L *instant-*, *instans*, fr. pres. part. of *instare* to stand upon, press upon, urge, fr. *in-* ²in- + *stare* to stand — more at STAND] **1 :** INSISTENT, IMPORTUNATE, PRESSING, URGENT ⟨~ in argument⟩ **2 a :** PRESENT, CURRENT ⟨the ~ case being tried⟩ **b :** of or occurring in the present month — abbr. *inst.* ⟨received your letter of the 10th *inst.*⟩; compare PROXIMO, ULTIMO **3 :** closely pressing in respect to time ⟨running an ~ risk of suffocating⟩ **4 :** IMMEDIATE, DIRECT ⟨the ~ dependence of form upon soul —R.W.Emerson⟩ **5 a :** premixed or precooked for easy final preparation ⟨~ cake mix⟩ ⟨~ mashed potatoes⟩ **b :** immediately soluble in water ⟨~ coffee⟩ **syn** see PRESSING

³**instant** \"\ *adv* **:** at once **:** INSTANTLY

in·stan·ta·ne·i·ty \ˌinzˌtantᵊnˈēədē, ənz-, -antəˈnē-, ˌinztəntəˈnē-, -n(ˌ)st-\ *n* -ES [*instantaneous* + *-ity*] **:** the quality or state of being instantaneous

in·stan·ta·neous \¦inztən¦tānēəs, ¦in(t)stə-, -ānyəs\ *adj* [ML *instantaneus*, fr. L *instant-*, *instans* (pres. part.) + *-aneus* (as in *subterraneus* subterranean)] **1 :** done, occurring, or acting without any perceptible duration of time ⟨~ death⟩ ⟨~ heaters⟩ **2 a :** done without any delay being introduced purposely ⟨~ action⟩ **b** *of a sound recording* **:** capable of being used as soon as recorded **3 :** occurring or present at a particular instant ⟨~ value⟩ ⟨~ velocity⟩ ⟨~ voltage⟩ — **in·stan·ta·ne·ous·ly** *adv* — **in·stan·ta·ne·ous·ness** *n* -ES

instantaneous exposure *n* **:** exposure of photographic materials for a short time by an automatic device — compare TIME EXPOSURE

in·stan·ter \ənzˈtantə(r), ənˈsta-\ *adv* [ML, fr. L, earnestly, vehemently, fr. *instant-*, *instans* instant] **:** at once **:** IMMEDIATELY, INSTANTLY

in·stan·tial \(ˈ)inz¦tanchəl, ənzˈt-, -n¦sta-\ *adj* [L *instantia* presence, urgency + E *-al* — more at INSTANCE] **:** of, relating to, constituting, or providing an instance ⟨empirical laws for which there is ~ evidence —Arthur Pap⟩

in·stan·ti·ate \=ˈ=chēˌāt\ *vt* -ED/-ING/-S [L *instantia* presence, urgency + E *-ate*] **:** to represent (an abstraction or universal) by a concrete instance — **in·stan·ti·a·tion** \(ˌ)=ˌ==ˈāshən\ *n* -s

¹**in·stant·ly** *adv* [ME, fr. *instant* (adj.) + *-ly*] **1 :** with urgency or importunity **:** PRESSINGLY **2** *obs* **:** in this or in the most recent moment **:** just now **3 :** without the least delay **:** at once **:** IMMEDIATELY

²**in·stant·ly** \"\ *conj* **:** as soon as **:** IMMEDIATELY, DIRECTLY ⟨recognized her ~ I saw her⟩

in·stant·ness *n* -ES **:** the quality or state of being instant

¹**in·star** \ənzˈt-, ənˈst-\ *also* **en·star** \ən-,en-\ *vt* [²in- or ¹en- + *star* (n.)] **1** *archaic* **:** to place as a star **:** turn into a star **2 :** to adorn or stud with or as if with stars ⟨a coronet *instarred* with precious stones⟩

²**in·star** \ˈinzˌtär, ˈinˌst-, -tä(r\ *n* -s [NL, fr. L, figure, form, perh. alter. of *instare* to approach, to be evenly balanced, stand upon — more at INSTANT] **:** a stage in the life of an insect or other arthropod between two successive molts ⟨some insects may have seven or more ~*s*⟩; *also* **:** an individual in a specified instar ⟨collected several third-*instar* larvae⟩

in·state \ənzˈtāt, -nˈstāt, *usu* -ād.+V\ *also* **en·state** \ən-,en-\ *vt* [²in- or ¹en- + *state* (n.)] **1 :** to set, place, or establish esp. in a rank, office, or status **:** INSTALL ⟨hoped to ~ his sister in her estate⟩ **2** *obs* **a :** INVEST, ENDOW **b :** BESTOW, CONFER

in·state·ment \-mənt\ *n* -s **:** INSTALLATION

in sta·tu nas·cen·di \ən¦stā(ˌ)tünəˈsendē, -¦stal, ¦(ˌ)chü-, -ˌdī; -¦stä(ˌ)tünäˈskendē\ [L, in the state of being born] **:** in the nascent state ⟨produce the aldehyde *in statu nascendi* —C.D.Hurd⟩ **:** in the course of being formed or developed ⟨if . . . isolation can promote the formation of full species, such species must *in statu nascendi* pass through a phase of less than specific distinction —Fridthjof Økland⟩

in statu quo \-ˈkwō\ [L] **:** in the state in which something is or was **:** in the former or same state

in·stau·ra·tion \ˌinˌztȯˈrāshən, ˌinˌst-\ *n* -s [L *instauration-*, *instauratio*, fr. *instauratus* (past part. of *instaurare* to renew, restore) + *-ion-*, *-io* -ion — more at STORE] **1 :** restoration after decay, lapse, or dilapidation **2** *obs* **:** an act of instituting or establishing something

in·stau·ra·tor \ˈ==ˌrād.ə(r)\ *n* -s [LL, fr. L *instauratus* (past part.) + *-or*] **:** one that engages in instauration

in·stead \ənzˈted, ənˈst-, *more often before "of" than in other positions* + -tid\ *adv* [fr. the phrase *instead of*] **1 :** in the place **:** in lieu **:** as a substitute or equivalent ⟨he came ~⟩ **2 :** as an alternative to something expressed or implied **:** in the place of something **:** RATHER ⟨longing ~ for a quiet country life⟩

instead of *prep* [ME *in sted of*] **:** as a substitute for or alternative to ⟨had peanut butter *instead of* jelly⟩ ⟨sent his helper *instead of* coming himself⟩

in·steep \ənzˈtēp, ənˈst-\ *vt* [²in- + *steep*] **:** STEEP, SOAK **:** IMBRUE

in·stel·la·tion \ˌinzˌteˈlāshən, ˌinˌste-\ *n* -s [²in- + L *stella* star + E *-ation* — more at STAR] **1 :** a setting among the stars **2 :** a turning into a star

in·step \ˈinzˌtep, ˈinˌstep\ *n* [perh. fr. ⁴in + *step*] **1 :** the arched middle portion of the human foot next in front of the ankle joint; *esp* **:** the upper surface of this part **2 :** the part of the hind leg of the horse and related animals between the hock and the pastern joint **3 :** the part of a shoe or stocking over the instep **4 :** something (as the slope of a hill) that is felt to resemble the human instep

in·sti·gate \ˈinztəˌgāt, ˈin(t)stə-, *usu* -ād.+V\ *vt* -ED/-ING/-S [L *instigatus*, past part. of *instigare* — more at STICK] **:** to goad or urge forward **:** set on **:** PROVOKE, INCITE ⟨his past experience *instigated* him to boldness⟩ ⟨*instigating* a plot to overthrow the government⟩ **syn** see INCITE

in·sti·gat·ing·ly *adv* **:** in an instigating manner

in·sti·ga·tion \ˌ==ˈgāshən\ *n* -s [ME *instigacioun*, fr. MF or L; MF *instigation*, fr. L *instigation-*, *instigatio*, fr. *instigatus* (past part.) + *-ion-*, *-io* -ion] **1 :** an act of instigating or the state of being instigated **:** INCITEMENT ⟨they agreed at our ~ to confer⟩ ⟨the ~ of the new program⟩ **2 :** something that instigates **:** INCENTIVE ⟨his friends' approval was a real ~ to succeed⟩

in·sti·ga·tive \ˈ==ˌgād.iv\ *adj* [L *instigatus* (past part.) + E *-ive*] **:** tending to instigate

in·sti·ga·tor \ˈ==ˌgād.ə(r), -ātə-\ *n* -s [L, fr. *instigatus* (past part.) + *-or*] **:** one that instigates

in·still *also* **in·stil** \ənzˈtil, ənˈstil\ *vt* **instilled; instilled; instilling; instills** *also* **instils** [MF & L; MF *instiller*, fr. L *instillare*, fr. *in-* ²in- + *stillare* to drip, trickle — more at DISTILL] **1 :** to introduce a drop at a time **:** cause to enter drop by drop ⟨~ a few drops of warm olive oil⟩ **2 :** to impart or introduce gradually **:** cause to be taken in little by little ⟨~*ing* a reverence for honest dealings⟩ ⟨~*ed* the teachings of his own faith⟩ **syn** see IMPLANT

in·stil·la·tion \ˌinztəˈlāshən, ˌin(t)stə-\ *n* -s [MF & L; MF, fr. L *instillation-*, *instillatio*, fr. *instillatus* (past part.) + *-ion-*, *-io* -ion] **1 :** an act of instilling **:** introduction by instilling ⟨repeated ~ of penicillin⟩ **2 :** something that is instilled or designed for instillation ⟨an oily ~⟩ ⟨silver ~ for use in the eyes of the newborn⟩

in·still·er \ənzˈtilə(r), ənˈsti-\ *n* -s **:** one that instills

in·still·ment *also* **in·stil·ment** \-lmənt\ *n* -s **:** INSTILLATION 1

¹**in·stinct** \ˈinz(ˌ)tiŋ(k)t, -ˌtēŋ-, ˈin(ˌ)st-\ *n* -s [ME, fr. L *instinctus*, fr. *instinctus* (past part.)] **1** *obs* **:** INSTIGATION, IMPULSE **2 :** a natural or inherent aptitude, tendency, impulse, or capacity ⟨an ~ for the right word⟩ ⟨his ~ toward success⟩ ⟨the religious ~*s* of primitive peoples⟩ **3 a :** complex and specific response on the part of an organism to environmental stimuli that is largely hereditary and unalterable though the pattern of behavior through which it is expressed may be modified by learning, that does not involve reason, and that has as its goal the removal of a somatic tension or excitation **b :** behavior that is mediated by reactions (as reflex arcs) below the conscious level — usu. not used technically

²**in·stinct** \(ˈ)inz¦tiŋ(k)t, ənzˈt-, -n¦sti-\ *adj* [L *instinctus*, past part. of *instinguere* to instigate, incite; akin to L *instigare* to instigate, incite — more at STICK] **1** *obs* **:** implanted by nature **:** INNATE **2** *obs* **:** impelled by an inner or animating or exciting agency **3 :** profoundly imbued **:** FILLED, CHARGED — usu. used postpositively and with *with* ⟨a spirit ~ with human kindness⟩ ⟨~ with patriotism⟩

³**instinct** *vt* -ED/-ING/-S [L *instinctus* (past part.)] **1** *obs* **:** INSTIGATE, IMPEL **2** *obs* **:** to implant as an animating power

in·stinc·tion \ənzˈtiŋ(k)shən, ənˈst-\ *n* -s [obs. E, instigation, inspiration, fr. MF, fr. LL *instinction-*, *instinctio*, fr. L *instinctus* (past part.) + *-ion-*, *-io* -ion] **1** *obs* **:** INSTINCT **2 :** instinctive behavior

in·stinc·tive \(ˈ)inz¦tiŋ(k)tiv, ənˈst-, -)tēv *also* -)təv\ *adj* [¹*instinct* + *-ive*] **:** of, relating to, or constituting instinct **:** derived from or prompted by instinct **:** determined by natural impulse or propensity **:** UNLEARNED, UNREASONED ⟨an ~ dread of mice⟩ ⟨~ behavior⟩ **syn** see SPONTANEOUS

in·stinc·tive·ly \-təvlē, -li\ *adv* **:** in an instinctive manner **:** as a matter of instinct ⟨reached ~ for some support⟩ ⟨~ proud of their traditions⟩

¹**in·stinc·tiv·ist** \=ˈ=tәvәst, -tēv-\ *n* -s [*instinctive* + *-ist*] **:** one that views society as a manifestation of various instinctive drives; *broadly* **:** one that views human behavior and social adaptation as the resultant of the interplay of various instinctive drives (as for survival) with environmental factors (as group relations)

²**in·stinc·tiv·ist** \(ˈ)=¦===\ *or* **in·stinc·ti·vis·tic** \(¦)=¦=ˌvistik, -tēk\ *adj* **:** based on the predominance of instinct **:** of or relating to instinctivists ⟨~ theories⟩

in·stinc·tu·al \(ˈ)=¦=ch(əw)əl\ *adj* [¹*instinct* + *-ual* (as in *actual*)] **:** of, relating to, or based on instincts ⟨~ behavior⟩ ⟨the ~ society of social insects⟩ — **in·stinc·tu·al·ly** \-)əlē, -li\ *adv*

in·sti·tor \ˈinztəˌtȯ(ə)r, ˈin(t)stə-\ *n* -s [L, fr. *instit-* (perf. stem of *insistere* to occupy a place in, stand upon, persist) + *-or* — more at INSIST] **:** a person (as the manager of a commercial or manufacturing business, a broker, factor, or commission agent) to whom the transaction of some business is committed as agent to such a degree as to bind the principal — used chiefly in Roman and civil law — **in·sti·to·ri·al** \¦==¦tōrēəl\ *adj*

¹**in·sti·tute** \ˈinztəˌtüt, ˈin(t)stə-, -əˌtyüt, *in rapid speech* ˈinzˌt(y)ət *or* ˈin(t)ˌst(y)-; *usu* -üd.+V\ *vt* -ED/-ING/-S [ME *instituten*, fr. L *institutus*, past part. of *instituere*, fr. *in-* ²in- + *-stituere* (fr. *statuere* to stand up, set, place) — more at STATUTE] **1 :** to establish in a particular position or office: as **a :** to invest with spiritual charge of a benefice **:** put (as a pastor) in charge of the care of souls **b :** to appoint as heir under Roman or civil law **2 a :** to originate and get established **:** set up **:** cause to come into existence **:** ORGANIZE ⟨the man that *instituted* these reforms in lexicography⟩ **b :** to set on foot **:** INAUGURATE, INITIATE ⟨*instituting* an investigation of the charges⟩ **3 a** *obs* **:** to ordain or enjoin to be or to be done **b** *archaic* **:** to ground or establish in principles or rudiments **:** INSTRUCT, EDUCATE **syn** see FOUND

²**institute** \"\ *n* -s [L *institutum*, fr. neut. of *institutus* (past part.)] **1** *obs* **:** DESIGN, PLAN, PURPOSE **2** *obs* **:** an act of instituting **3** [MF & L; MF *institut*, fr. L *institutum*] **:** something that is instituted: as **a (1) :** an elementary principle **:** a precept or rule recognized as authoritative **(2) institutes** *pl* **:** a collection of such principles and precepts; *esp* **:** a comprehensive summary of legal principles and decisions — compare DIGEST **b (1) :** an organization for the promotion of some estimable or learned cause or the welfare of some group ⟨an ~ for the blind⟩ ⟨an ~ for psychical research⟩ **(2) :** an association of persons or organizations that collectively constitute a technical or professional authority in a field of work or study ⟨Horological *Institute* of America⟩ ⟨an ~ of architects⟩ **(3)** *chiefly Brit* **:** a school or academy esp. for part-time education of workers ⟨teaching in the village ~⟩ **(4) :** an institution for advanced education esp. in science or technology ⟨spent two years at the textile ~⟩ **(5) :** a brief course of instruction or seminars (as for teachers or poultrymen) on business or professional problems **c :** a building or group of buildings occupied by an institute **4** [L *institutus* (past part.)] **a** *Scots law* **:** the person to whom an estate is first given by destination or testament — compare SUBSTITUTE **b** *civil law* **:** an heir appointed by will under a duty to transfer the property to a person designated in the will

in·sti·tut·er \-üd.ə(r)\ *n* -s **:** INSTITUTOR

in·sti·tu·tion \ˌinztəˈtüshən, ˌin(t)stəˈ-, -təˈtyü-, *in rapid speech* ˌinzˈt(y)ü- *or* ˌin(t)ˈst(y)ü-, *chiefly in substand speech* ˌin(t)səˈ-\ *n* -s [ME *institucioun*, fr. MF & L; MF *institution*, fr. OF, fr. L *institution-*, *institutio* arrangement, custom, instruction, element of instruction, appointment of an heir, fr. *institutus* (past part.) + *-ion-*, *-io* -ion] **1 :** an act or the process of instituting: as **a** [ME *institucioun*, fr. ML *institution-*, *institutio*, fr. L] **:** the investing of a clergyman with the spiritual part of a benefice by which the care of souls is committed to his charge followed in the Church of England by induction **b (1) :** the appointment of an heir **(2) :** the appointment of an institute (sense 4a) **c :** ESTABLISHMENT, FOUNDATION, ENACTMENT ⟨the ~ of this custom dates back to the 15th century⟩ **d** *obs* **:** reduction to order or form **:** REGULATION, ORDERING **e** *obs* **:** INSTRUCTION, EDUCATION **f :** the establishment of a sacrament; *usu* **:** the designation, authorization, or ordination by Christ of various signs or ceremonies as sacraments ⟨the words of ~ form part of the eucharistic rite⟩ **2 :** something that serves to instruct (as a textbook or a system of rules or principles) — now usu. restricted to law; compare INSTITUTE 3a **3 :** something that is instituted: as **a (1) :** a significant and persistent element (as a practice, a relationship, an organization) in the life of a culture that centers on a fundamental human need, activity, or value, occupies an enduring and cardinal position within a society, and is usu. maintained and stabilized through social regulatory agencies ⟨~ of marriage⟩ ⟨the family is a fundamental social ~⟩ **(2) :** a custom that is usu. widely sanctioned or tolerated and that in some degree contributes to group welfare ⟨the old New England ~ of bundling⟩ ⟨the coffee break has become an ~ in many places⟩ **(3) :** something or someone well established in some customary relationship **:** FIXTURE ⟨the old man was an ~ along the waterfront⟩ ⟨father's Sunday breakfast in bed was a family ~⟩ **b :** an established society or corporation **:** an establishment or foundation esp. of a public character ⟨a literary ~⟩ ⟨the Smithsonian *Institution*⟩ ⟨~*s* of higher learning⟩ **c :** a building or the buildings occupied or used by such organization

in·sti·tu·tion·al \¦==¦t(y)üshənᵊl, (ˈ)=¦t(y)ü-, -shnəl\ *adj* **1 :** of, relating to, involving, or constituting an institution ⟨an ~ investor⟩ ⟨~ elements of a political system⟩ ⟨~ care of the blind⟩: as **a :** of or relating to the institution of a sacrament **b** *of advertising* **:** designed to create goodwill and prestige for a company and its products rather than to produce immediate sales of specific products **2 :** provided with or characterized by institutions **:** having or sponsoring institutions esp. of a charitable or educational nature ⟨~ society⟩ — **in·sti·tu·tion·al·ly** \-ᵊlē, -əl|, |li\ *adv*

institutional economics *n pl but sing or pl in constr* **:** a school of economics that emphasizes the importance of nonmarket factors (as social institutions) in influencing economic behavior, economic analysis being subordinated to consideration of sociological factors, history, and institutional development

in·sti·tu·tion·al·ism \ˌ==ˈt(y)üshənᵊlˌizəm, =ˈt(y)ü-, -shnə-, ˌli-\ *n* -s **1 :** adherence to, upholding of, or acceptance of established institutions (as of society or religion) **:** belief in or dependence on that which is sanctified and given authority as an institution ⟨exhibiting an excessive conventionalism and ~ in religion⟩ **2 a :** a policy or theory favoring extended use of public institutions (as for defectives and criminals);

also : such use of public institutions ⟨with declining family solidarity ~ became increasingly important in the care of the sick, the unwanted, the aged⟩ **b** : the characteristics (as regimentation, standardization, and impersonality) that are associated with institutional life ⟨there was no ~ about this happy home⟩ **3 a** : the doctrines and teachings of institutional economics **b** : a theory that regards the establishment and maintenance of institutions (as for education, charity, and social activities) as an essential function of a church

in·sti·tu·tion·al·ist \-ᵊləst, -ələ-\ *n* -s **1** : a writer on or of institutes esp. of the law **2** : an adherent to, teacher of, or believer in any form of institutionalism : a defender of traditional institutions

in·sti·tu·tion·al·iza·tion \-ᵊlə'zāshən, -ᵊl,ī'z-, -ə,līz-, -ələ'z-, -ə,lī'z-\ *n* -s **1** : the quality or state of being or becoming institutionalized ⟨a pleasant custom always has a tendency toward ~⟩ **2** : the action or a result of institutionalizing ⟨the ~ of the insane⟩

in·sti·tu·tion·al·ize \-ᵊl,īz, -ə,līz\ *vt* -ED/-ING/-S *see -ize in Explan Notes* [*institutional* + *-ize*] **1** : to give the character of an institution to : make into or treat like an institution ⟨modern society tends to ~ its burdens⟩; *esp* : to incorporate into a system of organized and often highly formalized belief, practice, or acceptance ⟨the Japanese *institutionalized* suicide⟩ ⟨*institutionalized* graft⟩ **2** : to place in or commit to the care of a specialized institution (as for the insane, alcoholics, epileptics, delinquent youth, or the aged) **3** : to accustom (a person) so firmly to the care and supervised routine of an institution as to make incapable of managing a life outside

in·sti·tu·tion·ary \¦==¦t(y)üshə,nerē, (')=¦t(y)ü-, -shnərē, -ri\ *adj* : of or relating to institution in office ⟨an ~ banquet⟩

in·sti·tu·tion·ize \,==¦t(y)üshə,nīz, =¦t(y)-\ [*institution* + *-ize*] *vt* -ED/-ING/-S : INSTITUTIONALIZE 1

institutions *pl of* INSTITUTION

in·sti·tu·tive \'==,t(y)üd·iv, '=,t(y)-\ *adj* [L *institutus* (past part. of *instituere* to institute) + E *-ive* — more at INSTITUTE] **1** : tending to institute : concerned with or leading to the institution of something ⟨~ factors⟩ ⟨an ~ meeting⟩ **2** *obs* : characterized or formed by institution : CONVENTIONAL

in·sti·tu·tor \-üd·ə(r), -ütə-\ *n* -s [L, fr. *institutus* (past part.) + *-or*] : one that institutes: as **a** : FOUNDER, ORDAINER, ESTABLISHER ⟨the ~ of this pleasant custom⟩ **b** *archaic* : TEACHER, INSTRUCTOR **c** : a Protestant Episcopal bishop or a priest delegated by him who institutes a rector or assistant minister into a parish or church

in·sti·tu·tress \¦==¦t(y)ü·trəs, (')=¦t(y)-\ *also* **in·sti·tu·trix** \-ü·triks\ *n, pl* **institutress·es** \-ü·trəsəz\ *also* **institutrix·es** \-ü·triksəz\ *or* **institutri·ces** \,==¦t(y)ü·trə,sēz, =¦t(y)-; ,==(,)t(y)ü·'trī(,)sēz\ [*institutress* fr. *instituter* + *-ess*; *institutrix* fr. *institutor*, after such pairs as E *director: directrix*] : a female institutor

instl *abbr* installation

instmt *abbr* instrument

instn *abbr* **1** institution **2** instruction

in store *adv (or adj)* : at or from the point where stored with subsequent storage and shipping costs to be paid by the buyer ⟨goods sold *in store*⟩ ⟨payment to be made *in store*⟩ — compare EX STORE, FREE ON BOARD

instore *vt* [ME *instoren*, fr. ML *instaurare*, fr. L, to renew, restore — more at INSTAURATION] *obs* : FURNISH, PROVIDE

instr *abbr* **1** instruction; instructor **2** instrument; instrumental

¹instreaming \'inz,t-, 'in,st-\ *adj* [²*in* + *streaming*, pres. part. of *stream* (after *stream in*, v.)] : streaming in : entering like flowing water

²instreaming \"\ *n* [⁴*in* + *streaming*, gerund of *stream* (after *stream in*, v.)] : the action of entering like a stream of water : a flowing in ⟨the . . . ~ of beauty and truth —Cecil Sprigge⟩

in·strength·en \ənz't-,ən'st-\ *vt* [²*in-* + *strengthen*] : to give an inner strength to : strengthen in body or spirit

instrn *abbr* instruction

instroke \'inz,t-,'in,st-\ *n* [⁴*in* + *stroke*] : an inward stroke; *specif* : a stroke in which the piston in a steam or other engine is moving away from the crankshaft — opposed to *outstroke*

¹instruct *adj* [ME *instructe*, fr. L *instructus* (past part.)] **1** *obs* : INSTRUCTED **2** *obs* : PROVIDED, EQUIPPED

²in·struct \ənz'trəkt, ən'st-\ *vb* -ED/-ING/-S [ME *instructen*, fr. L *instructus*, past part. of *instruere*, fr. *in-* ²in- + *struere* to build, establish — more at STRUCTURE] *vt* **1** : to give special knowledge or information to: as **a** : to train in some special field : give skill or knowledge in some art or field of specialization : educate in respect to a particular subject or area of knowledge ⟨had a tutor to ~ him in English⟩ **b** : to provide with information about something : APPRISE ⟨~*ed* us that the toilets were downstairs⟩ ⟨the senses ~ us of most material dangers⟩ **c** : to impart knowledge systematically to ⟨~*ed* three generations of children in the village school⟩ **2 a** : to furnish with directions based on informed or technical awareness of a problem ⟨the judge ~*ed* the jury⟩ **b** : to give an order or command to esp. authoritatively, formally, and with attention to clearness : DIRECT ⟨~*s* the eleven companions to await on the hill the outcome of the fight —R.M.Lumiansky⟩ **3 a** *archaic* : to put in order : PREPARE **b** : to actuate and establish the controls of (an automatic electronic machine) **4** *Scots law* : to prove or establish on the basis of evidence : PROVE, CONFIRM ~ *vi* : to serve as an instructor ⟨~*ed* in the public schools for many years⟩ **syn** see COMMAND, TEACH

instructed *adj* **1** : EDUCATED, CULTURED ⟨the ~ person is usually tolerant⟩ ⟨planned by an ~ taste⟩ **2 a** : furnished with and restricted in action by specific instructions ⟨sent ~ delegates to the convention⟩ **b** : ordered by informed authority : DIRECTED ⟨an ~ verdict⟩ — **in·struct·ed·ly** *adv* — **in·struct·ed·ness** *n* -ES

in·struct·ible \-ktəbəl\ *adj* [L *instructus* (past part.) + E *-ible*] : capable of being instructed or taught ⟨~ children⟩ ⟨a very ~ subject⟩

in·struc·tion \-kshən\ *n* -s [ME *instruccioun*, fr. MF&LL; MF *instruction*, fr. LL *instruction-*, *instructio*, fr. L, act of constructing, act of arranging, fr. *instructus* (past part. of *instruere* to instruct) + *-ion-*, *-io* -ion — more at INSTRUCT] **1** : something that instructs or is imparted in order to instruct: as **a** : LESSON, PRECEPT ⟨children should profit from the ~*s* of their elders⟩ **b** *obs* : INFORMATION, NEWS, REPORT **c** (1) : something given by way of direction or order — usu. used in pl. ⟨gave the maid ~*s* to wait for the grocer⟩ (2) : information in the form of an outline of procedures : DIRECTIONS — usu. used in pl. ⟨the ~*s* for assembling the model⟩ **2** : the action, practice, or profession of one that instructs : TEACHING ⟨new theories of ~⟩ ⟨engaged in ~ rather than active service⟩ **3** : the quality or state of being instructed ⟨where ~ is more widely diffused —Havelock Ellis⟩

in·struc·tion·al \-shənᵊl, -shnəl\ *adj* **1** : relating to, serving for, or promoting instruction : EDUCATIONAL ⟨~ methods⟩ ⟨used for ~ purposes⟩ ⟨the director of ~ services⟩ **2** : containing or conveying instruction or information ⟨an ~ film⟩

instruction card *n* : JOB SHEET

in·struc·tive \-ktiv, -tēv *also* -təv\ *adj* [prob. fr. MF *instructif*, fr. L *instructus* (past part.) + MF *-if* -ive] : conveying knowledge : serving to instruct or inform ⟨experience furnishes very ~ lessons⟩ ⟨such experiences are ~⟩ — **in·struc·tive·ly** \-tə̇vlē, -lī\ *adv* — **in·struc·tive·ness** \-tivnəs, -tēv- *also* -təv-\ *n* -ES

in·struc·tor \-ktə(r)\ *n* -s [ME *instructour*, fr. MF or ML; MF *instructeur*, fr. ML *instructor*, fr. L, arranger, preparer, fr. *instructus* (past part. of *instruere* to arrange, prepare, instruct) + *-or*] : one that instructs : TEACHER ⟨our older brother was our ~ in woodcraft⟩ ⟨an ~ in the local high school⟩; *specif* : a teacher in a college or university of a rank below any of the various grades of professor ⟨most colleges recognize the following ascending order of ranks: ~, assistant professor, associate professor, professor⟩

in·struc·to·ri·al \¦=,=¦tōrēəl\ *adj* : of or relating to an instructor ⟨miserable ~ salaries⟩ ⟨~ carelessness⟩

in·struc·tor·ship \ənz'trəktə(r),ship, ən'st-\ *n* : the position or status of an instructor ⟨obtained an ~ at the university⟩

in·struc·tress \-ktrəs\ *n* -ES [*instructor* + *-ess*] : a female instructor

¹in·stru·ment \'inztrəmənt, 'in(t)strə-\ *n* -s [ME, fr. L *instrumentum*, fr. *instruere* to construct, equip, arrange, instruct + *-mentum* -ment] **1 a** : a means whereby something is achieved, performed, or furthered ⟨the modern university is the ~ for preserving, enlarging, and disseminating our ever-increasing body of knowledge —Harlan Hatcher⟩ **b** : a person or group made use of by another as a means or aid : DUPE, TOOL ⟨suspecting . . . that I only wished to make an ~ of him —W.H.Hudson †1922⟩ **2** : UTENSIL, IMPLEMENT ⟨surgical ~*s*⟩ ⟨~*s* of torture⟩ **3** : an implement used to produce music esp. as distinguished from the human voice — see PERCUSSION INSTRUMENT, STRINGED INSTRUMENT, WIND INSTRUMENT **4** *obs* : an organ of the body **5 a** : a legal document (as a deed, will, bond, lease, agreement, mortgage, note, power of attorney, ticket on carrier, bill of lading, insurance policy, warrant, writ) evidencing legal rights or duties esp. of one party to another **b** : something capable of being presented as evidence to a court for inspection **c** : an act recorded in writing by a notary : a notarial act **6 a** : a measuring device for determining the present value of a quantity under observation; *broadly* : a device (as for controlling, recording, regulating, computing) that functions on data obtained by such a measuring device **b** : an electrical or mechanical device used in navigating an airplane; *specif* : such a device used as the sole means of navigating when there is limited or no visibility **syn** see IMPLEMENT, MEAN — **on instruments** : by means of airplane instruments ⟨flying *on instruments*⟩

²in·stru·ment \-,ment, -mənt — *see* ²-MENT\ *vt* -ED/-ING/-S **1** : to address a legal instrument (as a petition) to **2** : to prepare or score for one or more musical instruments ⟨~ a sonata for orchestra⟩ : ORCHESTRATE **3** : to equip (as a process, machine, or vehicle) with instruments ⟨the whole factory is well ~*ed* —*Farm Chemicals*⟩ ⟨an ~*ed* satellite⟩

¹in·stru·men·tal \¦==¦mentᵊl\ *adj* [ME, fr. ML *instrumentalis*, fr. L *instrumentum* + *-alis* -al] **1** : serving as a means or intermediary determining or leading to a particular result : being an instrument that functions in the promotion of some end or purpose ⟨this novel was ~ in bringing on open conflict⟩ ⟨an ~ act leading to a reward⟩ **2** : relating to, composed for, or performed on a musical instrument ⟨~ music⟩ ⟨~ ensemble⟩ — compare VOCAL **3** : of, relating to, or done with an instrument ⟨~ design⟩ ⟨~ navigation⟩ **4 a** : of, relating to, or being a case in grammar expressing means or agency ⟨English shows a surviving trace of the ~ case in *the* of "the more the merrier"⟩ **b** : being a suffixal element that denotes means or agency **5** : based on or in accordance with instrumentalism — **in·stru·men·tal·ly** \-ᵊlē,-ᵊlī\ *adv*

²instrumental \"\ *n* -s **1** *obs* : INSTRUMENT, MEANS **2** : the instrumental case or a word in that case **3** : a composition played on or for playing on a musical instrument — compare VOCAL

instrumental goods *n pl* : PRODUCER GOODS

in·stru·men·tal·ism \,==¦mentᵊl,izəm\ *n* -s [¹*instrumental* + *-ism*] : a conception that the significant factor of a thing is its value as an instrument; *specif* : the doctrine that ideas are instruments of action and that their usefulness determines their truth

¹in·stru·men·tal·ist \-ᵊləst\ *n* -s [¹*instrumental* + *-ist*] **1 a** : a player of a musical instrument **b** : a composer of instrumental music **2** : a proponent of instrumentalism

²in·stru·men·tal·ist \¦==¦===\ *adj* : advocating instrumentalism : INSTRUMENTAL

in·stru·men·tal·i·ty \,==mən·'taləd·ē, -,men·-, -lətē, -i\ *n* -ES **1** : the quality or state of being instrumental : a condition of serving as an intermediary ⟨the agreement was reached through the ~ of the governor⟩ **2 a** : something by which an end is achieved : MEANS ⟨precious metals purified through the ~ of heat⟩ ⟨*instrumentalities* of production⟩ ⟨mechanical *instrumentalities*⟩ **b** : something that serves as an intermediary or agent through which one or more functions of a controlling force are carried out : a part, organ, or subsidiary branch esp. of a governing body ⟨the judicial *instrumentalities* of the federal government⟩ ⟨a Chilean government ~ devoted to developing the country's natural resources —*Ethyl News*⟩ **syn** see MEAN

in·stru·men·tal·ize \,==¦mentᵊl,īz\ *vt* -ED/-ING/-S : to render instrumental : DIRECT, ORGANIZE, ADAPT

instrumental theory *n* : INSTRUMENTALISM

in·stru·men·tar·ium \,inztrəmən·'ta(a)rēəm, ,inst-, -,men·-\ *n, pl* **instrumentar·ia** \-ēə\ [NL, prob. fr. ML, case for storing papers, cartulary, fr. L *instrumentum* instrument + *-arium*] : the equipment needed for a particular surgical, medical, or dental procedure; *also* : the professional instruments of a surgeon, physician, or dentist

in·stru·men·ta·ry \¦==¦mentərē, -n·trē\ *adj* : of or relating to a legal instrument ⟨an ~ witness⟩

in·stru·men·tate \'inztrəmən·,tāt, 'in(t)strə-\ *vt* -ED/-ING/-S [¹*instrument* + *-ate* (after *orchestrate*)] : INSTRUMENT 2

in·stru·men·ta·tion \,==='tāshən, -,men·-\ *n* -s [¹*instrument* + *-ation*] **1** : a use of or operation with instruments: as **a** : the use of one or more instruments in treating a patient (as in the passing of a cystoscope) **b** : the application of instruments esp. for observation, measurement, or control (as in a manufacturing process or the operation of a machine or vehicle) **2** : MEANS, AGENCY, INSTRUMENTALITY **3 a** [F, fr. *instrument* (fr. MF, fr. L *instrumentum* instrument) + *-ation*] : the arrangement or composition of music for instruments esp. for a band or orchestra — compare ORCHESTRATION **b** : the act or manner of playing musical instruments **c** : the arrangement and distribution of instruments (as in a band or orchestra) **4 a** : a branch of science concerned with the development, manufacture, and utilization of instruments **b** : instruments or the group of instruments employed for a particular purpose (as the control of a machine or recording the data about the function of a vehicle)

in·stru·men·ta·tor \'==mən·,tād·ə(r)\ *n* -s [*instrumentate* + *-or*] : one that arranges a musical score for performance by a specific group of instruments

instrument board *or* **instrument panel** *n* : a panel on which instruments are mounted; *esp* : DASHBOARD 2

instrument board

instrumented *past of* INSTRUMENT

instrument flight *n* : an airplane flight made on instruments : blind flight

instrument flying *n* : navigation solely according to information given by instruments within an airplane usu. including radio or radar devices : blind flying — contrasted with *contact flying*

instrumenting *pres part of* INSTRUMENT

instrument landing *n* : a landing made with no external visibility and solely by means of instruments within an airplane and by ground radio directive devices : blind landing

instrument landing system *n* : a system for airplane landings in which the pilot is guided by radio beams — abbr. *ILS*; compare GROUND-CONTROLLED APPROACH

in·stru·ment·man \'===,man\ *n, pl* **instrumentmen** : a surveyor who operates a transit, level, or similar instrument

instrument rating *n* : a license or rating given to an airplane pilot authorized to do instrument flying

instruments *pl of* INSTRUMENT, *pres 3d sing of* INSTRUMENT

instrument weather *n* : weather in which the ground is so invisible from the air that instrument flying is required

instyle *vt* [²*in-* + *style*] *obs* : CALL, DENOMINATE

in·suav·i·ty \(')in, ən+\ *n* [L *insuavitas*, fr. *insuavis* unpleasant (fr. *in-* ¹in- + *suavis* pleasant) + *-itas* -ity — more at SWEET] : lack of suavity : BRUSQUENESS

in·sub·jec·tion \¦in+\ *n* [¹*in-* + *subjection*] : lack of subjection : a state of disobedience or opposition to authority (as of government)

in·sub·merg·ible *or* **in·sub·mers·ible** \"+\ *adj* [*insubmergible* fr. ¹*in-* + *submerge* + *-ible*; *insubmersible* prob. fr. F, fr. *in-* ¹in- + L *submersus* (past part. of *submergere* to submerge) + F *-ible*] : incapable of sinking

in·sub·mis·sive \"+\ *adj* [¹*in-* + *submissive*] : unwilling to submit

¹in·sub·or·di·nate \"+\ *adj* [¹*in-* + *subordinate*] : not subordinate: as **a** : unwilling to submit to authority : DISOBEDIENT, MUTINOUS ⟨~ boys⟩ **b** : not holding a lower or inferior position ⟨the bankers of Antwerp placed no limit on their enterprise: economic activity was not subordinate; it had become, from the medieval point of view, ~ —Stringfellow Barr⟩

syn REBELLIOUS, MUTINOUS, SEDITIOUS, FACTIOUS, CONTUMACIOUS: INSUBORDINATE applies to disobedience of orders, infraction of rules, or a generally disaffected attitude toward authority, often in military or other organization similarly constituted ⟨*insubordinate* deckhands confined to the brig⟩ ⟨*insubordinate* native troops feeling that they were being discriminated against⟩ REBELLIOUS may suggest forceful resistance to or insurgence against authority in addition to insubordination and temperamental opposition ⟨*rebellious* mountaineers proposing to set up their own independent republic⟩ ⟨temperamentally *rebellious*, instinctively disliking externally imposed authority —Francis Biddle⟩ MUTINOUS suggests either opposing authority by destroying discipline and order or the forceful overthrow of authority ⟨for more than a year Cortes stayed in the new land, a desolate sandy waste, while the *mutinous* soldiers cursed him —*Amer. Guide Series: Calif.*⟩ ⟨the guards might be overpowered, the palace forced, the king a prisoner in the hands of his *mutinous* subjects —T.B.Macaulay⟩ SEDITIOUS suggests treasonable activities, esp. those designed to weaken or overthrow a government or foster separatist tendencies ⟨*seditious* factionalism went on a rampage and began to wreck our foreign policy —Max Ascoli⟩ ⟨revolutions that were not made in Boston, by Boston gentlemen, were quite certain to be wicked and *seditious* —V.L.Parrington⟩ FACTIOUS suggests an addiction to factions with contentious perversity and irreconcilability threatening central constituted authority ⟨Florence . . . wearing out her soul by *factious* struggles —Margaret Oliphant⟩ ⟨the opposition will be vigilant but not *factious*. We shall not oppose merely for the sake of opposition —Clement Attlee⟩ CONTUMACIOUS indicates persistent, willful, or overt defiance of authority and disobedience, sometimes contemptuous, of authority ⟨a fine was appointed for every failure to obey the bishop's summons; he was empowered to excommunicate *contumacious* persons —F.M.Stenton⟩ ⟨magistrates and populace were incensed at a refusal of customary marks of courtesy and respect for the laws, which in their eyes was purely *contumacious* —W.R.Inge⟩

²insubordinate \"\ *n* : an insubordinate person

in·subordinately \¦in+\ *adv* : in an insubordinate manner : with insubordination

in·subordination \"+\ *n* [prob. fr. F, fr. *in-* ¹in- + *subordination*] : the quality or state of being insubordinate : defiance of authority : MUTINY

in·substantial \"+\ *adj* [prob. fr. F *insubstantiel*, fr. LL *insubstantialis*, fr. *in-* ¹in- + *substantialis* substantial] : not substantial: as **a** : lacking substance or reality : IMAGINARY, APPARITIONAL ⟨an ~ mirage floating near the horizon⟩ **b** : lacking firmness or solidity of structure : FLIMSY, FRAIL ⟨delicate ~ wrists and ankles⟩ — **in·substantiality** \"+\ *n*

in·subvertible \"+\ *adj* [LL *insubvertibilis*, fr. *in-* ¹in- + L *subvertere* to overturn, overthrow + *-ibilis* -ible — more at SUBVERT] : incapable of being overthrown or altered in course or orientation ⟨the ~ physical laws⟩

in·success \"+\ *n* [¹*in-* + *success*] : lack of success : FAILURE

insucken \'=,==\ *adj* [¹*in* + *sucken*] *Scot* : situated in or astricted to a sucken

in·sufferable \(')in, ən+\ *adj* [¹*in-* + *sufferable*] : incapable of being endured ⟨an ~ injury⟩ : intolerable esp. by reason of pompous assurance or assumed superiority ⟨~ self-importance⟩ ⟨a thoroughly ~ child⟩ — **in·sufferableness** \"+\ *n* — **in·sufferably** \"+\ *adv*

in·suf·fi·cience \¦insə¦fishən(t)s\ *n* -s [ME, fr. MF or LL; MF, fr. LL *insufficientia*] : INSUFFICIENCY

in·suf·fi·cien·cy \-shensē, -si\ *n* [LL *insufficientia*, fr. *insufficient-*, *insufficiens* insufficient + *-ia* -y] **1** : the quality or state of being insufficient : lack of sufficiency: as **a** : lack of mental or moral fitness : INABILITY, INCOMPETENCY ⟨the ~ of a man for an office⟩ **b** : lack of adequate supply of something (as force, quality, quantity) : INADEQUACY ⟨~ of provisions⟩ **c** : lack of physical power or capacity : IMPOTENCE; *specif* : inability of an organ or body part to function normally ⟨cardiac ~⟩ ⟨renal ~⟩ **2** : something insufficient ⟨sadly aware of his own neglects and *insufficiencies*⟩

in·suf·fi·cient \-shənt\ *adj* [ME, fr. MF, fr. LL *insufficient-*, *insufficiens*, fr. *in-* ¹in- + L *sufficient-*, *sufficiens* sufficient — more at SUFFICIENT] : not sufficient: as **a** : lacking in strength, power, ability, capacity, or skill : INCOMPETENT, UNFIT ⟨a person ~ to discharge the duties of an office⟩ **b** *obs* : not sufficiently furnished or supplied : deficient or lacking in something **c** : inadequate to some implied or designated need, use, or purpose ⟨provisions ~ in quantity⟩ — **in·suf·fi·cient·ly** *adv*

in·suf·flate \'in(t)sə,flāt, ən'sə-\ *vt* -ED/-ING/-S [LL *insufflatus*, past part. of *insufflare*, fr. L *in-* ²in- + *sufflare* to blow, sufflate — more at SUFFLATE] **1** : to blow or breathe upon or into : subject to insufflation ⟨~ a room with insecticide⟩ **2** : to blow or breathe (something) onto a surface or into a void : practice insufflation of ⟨*insufflated* the metallic powder onto the hot surface⟩ ⟨*insufflated* the drug into the depths of the wound⟩

in·suf·fla·tion \,in(t)sə'flāshən\ *n* -s [MF, fr. LL *insufflation-*, *insufflatio*, fr. *insufflatus* (past part.) + L *-ion-*, *-io* -ion] : an act or the action of breathing or blowing on, into, or in: as **a** : the breathing upon a person or thing in the ritual of various liturgical churches to symbolize (as at baptism) the inspiration of a new spiritual life and the expulsion of evil spirits **b** : the act of blowing (as a gas, powder, or vapor) into a cavity of the body ⟨~ of gas into a fallopian tube to determine its patency⟩

in·suf·fla·tor \'in(t)sə,flād·ə(r), ən'sə-\ *n* -s [*insufflate* + *-or*] : a device for insufflating: as **a** : an injector for forcing air into a furnace **b** : a device used in medical insufflation (as of a drug) **c** : a device for blowing the powder used in developing latent fingerprints (as in criminal investigation)

in·su·la \'in(t)s(y)ələ, 'inshə-\ *n, pl* **insu·lae** \-,lē, 'in(t)sə,lī\ **1** [L, lit., island — more at ISLE] : an ancient Roman building or a group of buildings standing together forming a block or square and usu. constituting an apartment building **2** [NL, fr. L] : ISLAND OF REIL

in·su·lant \'in(t)sələnt *sometimes* 'in(t)syəl- *or* 'inshəl-\ *n* -s [¹*insulate* + *-ant*] : INSULATION

¹in·su·lar \-lə(r)\ *adj* [LL *insularis*, fr. L *insula* island + *-aris* -ar — more at ISLE] **1 a** : of or relating to an island : being or having the characteristics of an island : dwelling or situated on or forming an island **b** *usu cap* (1) : of or relating to Great Britain or to the British isles as distinct from the continent of Europe — compare CONTINENTAL (2) : of, relating to, or characteristic of the Insular hand **2 a** : INSULATED, ISOLATED, DETACHED ⟨an ~ building⟩ **b** *of a plant or animal* : having a restricted or isolated natural range or habitat **3 a** : of or relating to the people of an island **b** : resulting from isolation or characteristic of isolated people **c** : NARROW, CIRCUMSCRIBED, ILLIBERAL, PREJUDICED **4** [NL *insula* + E *-ar*] : of or relating to an island of cells or tissue (as the islets of Langerhans or islands of Reil)

²insular \"\ *n* -s : ISLANDER

insular celtic *n, usu cap I&C* : the Celtic languages excluding Gaulish

insular hand *or* **insular script** *n, usu cap I* : a script characterized by thick initial strokes and heavy shading developed from half uncial under the influence of uncial by Irish scribes about the 5th and 6th centuries A.D. and used in England until the Norman conquest and in Ireland with modifications to the present day

in·su·lar·ism \-lə,rizəm\ *n* -s : the quality or state of being insular and esp. of exhibiting narrowness and rigidity of outlook or mind

in·su·lar·i·ty \,==¦larəd·ē, -ətē, -i *also* -'ler-\ *n* -ES **1** : the quality or state of being an island or consisting of islands ⟨the ~ of Great Britain⟩ **2 a** : condition of dwelling on an island or in isolation **b** : narrowness or illiberality of opinion or custom

in·su·lar·ize \'==,lə,rīz\ *vt* -ED/-ING/-S [¹*insular* + *-ize*] : to form into or represent as an island

in·su·lar·ly *adv* **1** : in an insular manner : NARROWLY, RIGIDLY ⟨an ~ prejudiced mind⟩ **2** : throughout an island ⟨~ distributed Philippine plants⟩

1in·su·lary \'⸗⸗,lerē\ *n* -ES [prob. modif. (influenced by E *-ary*) of F *insulaire*, fr. *insulaire*, adj., insular, fr. LL *insularis*] *archaic* : ISLANDER

2insulary \"\ *adj* [prob. modif. (influenced by E *-ary*) of LL *insularis*] *archaic* : INSULAR

1in·su·late \'in(t)sə,lāt *sometimes* 'in(t)syə- *or* 'inshə-; *usu* -ād·+V\ *vt* -ED/-ING/-S [L *insula* island + E *-ate* — more at ISLE] **1** *archaic* : to form an island of : isolate by surrounding water **2 a** : to separate or shield (a conductor) from conducting bodies by means of nonconductors so as to prevent transfer of electricity, heat, or sound **b** : to place in a detached situation or in a state of isolation : set apart : SEGREGATE, ISOLATE ⟨hysterical symptoms quite commonly serve to ~ the patient —Norman Cameron⟩ ⟨*insulating* man from the natural world⟩ **c** : to remove (as specie or a commodity) from the open market : STERILIZE ⟨a program designed to ~ the government-held surpluses by using them for special purposes⟩; *also* : to stabilize (a market) by such removal

2in·su·late \-,lət, -,lāt\ *adj* [L *insula* island + E *-ate*] : set apart : ISOLATED

insulating *adj* : serving to insulate : functioning as insulation ⟨~ material⟩ ⟨an ~ calm⟩

insulating board *or* **insulation board** *n* : a board with insulating properties; *esp* : a structural or finish material that consists of sheets of lightly compressed vegetable pulp variously finished and is used esp. for its thermal insulating effect resulting from great numbers of minute included air spaces

insulating oil *n* : any of various oily liquids (as a hydrocarbon oil) used as insulators and cooling mediums in transformers, switches, or other electrical equipment

insulating varnish *n* : varnish used to insulate electrical apparatus (as certain coils or glass fittings)

in·su·la·tion \,⸗⸗'lāshən\ *n* -S **1 a** : an act or action of insulating ⟨work on the ~ of the house⟩ **b** : the quality or state of being insulated ⟨his complete ~ in regard to current events⟩ : ISOLATION ⟨~ as a factor in evolution⟩ **2** : something that insulates; *usu* : material that retards the passage of heat, electricity, or sound : nonconducting material that is used in insulating

insulation resistance *n* : the alternating-current resistance between two electrical conductors or two systems of conductors separated by an insulating material

in·su·la·tive \'⸗⸗,lād·|iv, -āt|, |ēv *also* |əv\ *adj* : relating to or constituting insulation ⟨~ value⟩ ⟨an ~ effect⟩

in·su·la·tor \-,lād·ə(r), -ātə-\ *n* -S **1** : one that insulates; *esp* : a worker that applies electrical or thermal insulation **2 a** : a material or body that is a poor conductor of electricity, heat, or sound **b** : a body of electrically nonconducting material for keeping charged conductors from contact with each other or from grounding and often also for supporting them

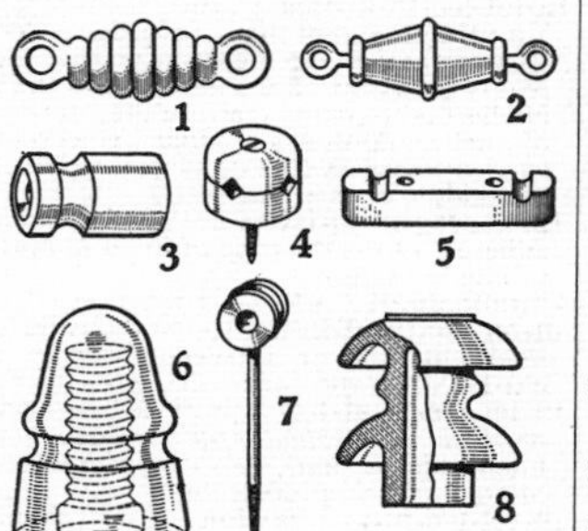

insulators 2b: *1, 2* used with antennas; *3* knob, *4* split-knob, *5* cleat, *6, 8* petticoat, *7* standoff

in·su·lin \'in(t)sələn *sometimes* 'in(t)slən *or* 'in(t)syəl- *or* 'inshə-\ *n* -S [NL *insula* + E *-in*] : a protein pancreatic hormone secreted by the islets of Langerhans that is essential esp. for the metabolism of carbohydrates, that is obtained commercially in crystalline form usu. from beef or pork pancreas, and that is used in the treatment and control of diabetes mellitus

in·su·lin·ase \-lə,nās, -āz\ *n* -S [*insulin* + *-ase*] : an enzyme found esp. in liver that inactivates insulin

in·su·lin·ize \-,nīz\ *vt* -ED/-ING/-S : to treat with insulin

insulin shock *n* : hypoglycemia associated with the presence of excessive insulin in the system and characterized by progressive development of coma

insulin shock therapy *n* : the treatment of mental disorder (as schizophrenia) by insulin in doses sufficient to produce deep coma — compare INSULIN SHOCK

in·sulse \ən'səl(t)s\ *adj* [L *insulsus*, lit., unsalted, fr. *in-* 1in- + *-sulsus* (fr. *salsus*, past part. of *salere* to salt, fr. *sal* salt) — more at SALT] *archaic* : TASTELESS, FLAT, STUPID — **in·sul·si·ty** \-)səd·ē\ *n* -ES

1in·sult \ən'səlt\ *vb* -ED/-ING/-S [MF or L; MF *insulter*, fr. L *insultare*, lit., to spring upon, leap, fr. *in-* 2in- + *-sultare* (fr. *saltare* to leap) — more at SALTANT] *vi* **1** *archaic* : to behave with pride or insolence : display arrogance or contempt : exult or boast usu. insolently or contemptuously : TRIUMPH, VAUNT **2** *obs* : to make an attack or assault ~ *vt* **1 a** : to treat with insolence, indignity, or contempt by word or action : affront wantonly ⟨his impertinences ~*ed* his sister's guests⟩ **b** : to make little of : affect offensively or depreciatively ⟨~*ed* the traditions of the sea by ordering "right" and "left" to be substituted . . . for "starboard" and "port" —Bruce Bliven b.1889⟩ ⟨editorial slovenliness that ~*s* the reader's mind⟩ **2** *obs* : to make an attack on : ASSAULT, ASSAIL; *esp* : to make a sudden military attack on without the usual preliminaries or formalities **syn** see OFFEND

2in·sult \'in,səlt\ *n* -S [MF or LL; MF *insult*, *insulte*, fr. LL *insultus*, prob. fr. L *in-* 2in- + *-sultus* (fr. *saltus* leap) (prob. influenced by L *insultare* to insult, spring upon); akin to L *salire* to leap — more at SALLY] **1** *archaic* : an act of attacking : ONSET, ATTACK **2** : a gross indignity offered to another either by word or act : an act or speech of insolence or contempt ⟨his words were a studied ~⟩ ⟨such an offer was an ~ to our intelligence⟩ **3** : damage or an instance of injury to the body or one of its parts ⟨repeated acute vascular ~*s*⟩ ⟨any ~ to the constitution of a patient suffering from active tuberculosis —*Jour. Amer. Med. Assoc.*⟩; *also* : an agent that produces such an insult ⟨a thermal ~⟩ ⟨damage resulting from malnutritional ~*s*⟩ **syn** see AFFRONT

in·sult·abil·i·ty \(,)in,səltə'biləd·ē, ən-, -lətē, -i\ *n* -ES : capacity for being or readiness to be insulted

in·sult·able \ən'səltəbəl\ *adj* : capable of being insulted; *esp* : easily insulted : OVERSENSITIVE

in·sul·ta·tion \,in,səl'tāshən\ *n* -S [MF, fr. L *insultation-*, *insultatio*, fr. *insultatus* (past part. of *insultare* to insult) + *-ion-*, *-io* -ion] **1** *archaic* : an act of insulting : contemptuous or insolent treatment : scornful exultation **2** *obs* : ATTACK, ONSET

insulted *adj* [fr. past part. of 1*insult*] *chiefly dial* : affected with irritation or distaste : OFFENDED, ANNOYED

in·sult·er \ən'səltə(r)\ *n* -S : one that insults

insulting *adj* : containing, characterized by, or constituting insult ⟨~ language⟩ ⟨the ~ agent in a pathologic process⟩ — **in·sult·ing·ly** *adv* — **in·sult·ing·ness** *n* -ES

insultproof \¦⸗,⸗¦⸗\ *adj* : not susceptible to insult

in sunder *adv* (*or adj*) [ME, fr. OE *onsundran*, *onsundrum* — more at ASUNDER] *archaic* : ASUNDER ⟨breaketh the bow and cutteth the spear *in sunder* —Ps 46:9 (AV)⟩

in·superability \(¦)in, ən+\ *n* : the quality or state of being insuperable

in·superable \(')in, ən+\ *adj* [ME, fr. MF & L; MF, fr. L *insuperabilis*, fr. *in-* 1in- + *superabilis* superable — more at SUPERABLE] : incapable of being surmounted: as **a** : incapable of being vanquished : INVINCIBLE ⟨these ~ heroes who dared the northern seas⟩ **b** : impossible to overcome ⟨~ difficulties⟩ **c** : incapable of being passed over : IMPASSABLE ⟨an ~ barrier⟩ **d** : UNSURPASSABLE — **in·su·per·a·ble·ness** \-nəs\ *n* — **in·su·per·a·bly** \-blē, -bli\ *adv*

in·supportability \¦in+\ *n* : INSUPPORTABLENESS

in·supportable \"+\ *adj* [MF or LL; MF, fr. LL *insupportabilis*, fr. L *in-* 1in- + *supportare* to carry, convey + *-abilis* -able — more at SUPPORT] : impossible to support: as **a** : incapable of being borne : UNENDURABLE ⟨~ burdens⟩ ⟨an ~ pain⟩ **b** : incapable of being sustained : UNJUSTIFIABLE ⟨~ charges⟩ **c** *obs* : IRRESISTIBLE — **in·supportably** \"+\ *adv*

in·supportableness \"+\ *n* -ES : the quality or state of being insupportable

in·supposable \"+\ *adj* [1*in-* + *supposable*] : impossible to suppose : UNBELIEVABLE

in·suppressible \"+\ *adj* [1*in-* + *suppress* + *-ible*] : impossible to suppress — **in·suppressibly** \"+\ *adv*

in·suppressive \"+\ *adj* [1*in-* + *suppress* + *-ive*] : INSUPPRESSIBLE

in·sur·abil·i·ty \ən,shu̇rə'biləd·ē, -lətē, -i\ *n* -ES : the quality or state of being insurable

in·sur·able \ən'shu̇rəbəl\ *adj* [*insure* + *-able*] : capable of being or proper to be insured against loss, damage, death ⟨~ property⟩ : affording a sufficient ground for insurance

insurable interest *n* : an interest (as based on a blood tie or likelihood of financial injury) that is judged to give an insurance applicant a legal right to enforce the insurance contract against the objection that it is a wagering contract contrary to public policy

insurable value *n* : the value of property stated in an insurance contract indicating the limit of indemnity that will be paid at the time of loss

in·sur·ance \ən'shu̇r(ə)n(t)s, *chiefly in southern U.S.* 'in,⸗(⸗)\ *n* -S *often attrib* [*insure* + *-ance*] **1 a** : the action or process of insuring or the state of being insured usu. against loss or damage by a contingent event (as death, fire, accident, or sickness) **b** : means of insuring against loss or risks ⟨provide ~ against floods⟩ **2 a** : the business of insuring persons or property; *specif* : a device for the elimination or reduction of an economic risk common to all members of a large group and employing a system of equitable contributions out of which losses are paid **b** : coverage by contract whereby for a stipulated consideration one party undertakes to indemnify or guarantee another against loss by a specified contingency or peril **c** : the principles and practices of the business of insuring — see ACCIDENT INSURANCE, AUTOMOBILE INSURANCE, BUSINESS INTERRUPTION INSURANCE, CASUALTY INSURANCE, DISABILITY INSURANCE, FIRE INSURANCE, GROUP INSURANCE, HEALTH INSURANCE, LIABILITY INSURANCE, LIFE INSURANCE, MARINE INSURANCE, SOCIAL INSURANCE, UNEMPLOYMENT INSURANCE, WORKMEN'S COMPENSATION INSURANCE; compare ANNUITY, CORPORATE SURETYSHIP, INSURABLE INTEREST, LOSS, MUTUAL, POLICY, PREMIUM, RATE, REINSURANCE, REPRESENTATION, RESERVE, RISK TONTINE, WARRANTY **3 a** : the premium paid for insuring something **b** : the sum for which something is insured

insurance adjuster *n* : a person employed by insurer or insured to determine the loss under an insurance policy

insurance agent *n* : an agent of an insurer authorized to negotiate contracts of insurance

insurance broker *n* : a broker who usu. acts as the agent of the insured in making contracts of insurance but sometimes as the agent of the insurer for some purposes (as payment of the premium) and of the insured for all other purposes

insurance certificate *n* **1** : a certificate issued by an insurer to a shipper as evidence that a shipment of merchandise is covered under a marine policy **2** : CERTIFICATE 5

insurance reserve *n* : the part of the reserve of an insurance company to be absorbed from the initial reserve in any year in payment of losses — compare INVESTMENT RESERVE

insurance trust *n* : an agreement providing for the receipt and distribution of life insurance proceeds by a trustee

in·sur·ant \ən'shu̇r(ə)nt\ *n* -S [*insure* + *-ant*] : a person who takes out a policy of insurance; *also* : one on whose life a policy of life insurance is taken out

in·sure \ən'shu̇(ə)r, -u̇ə\ *vb* -ED/-ING/-S [ME *insuren*, prob. alter. (influenced by *in-* 2in-) of *assuren* to assure — more at ASSURE] *vt* **1** *obs* : to declare to with confidence : ASSURE : promise solemnly **2** : to assure against a loss by a contingent event on certain stipulated conditions or at a given rate or premium : give, take, or procure an insurance on or for : enter into or carry a contract of insurance on — used of either the person who pays the insurance premiums or the society, corporation, or underwriter that undertakes the risk as subject and of the thing to which the risk attaches (as life or property) or the sum secured as object **3** : ENSURE 3 ~ *vi* : to contract to give insurance : UNDERWRITE; *also* : to procure or effect insurance **syn** see ENSURE

insured *n* -S [fr. *insured*, past part. of *insure*] : a person whose life, physical well-being, or property is the subject of insurance : the owner of a policy of insurance : POLICYHOLDER

insured plan *n* : a pension or retirement plan under which contributions are used to purchase life insurance or annuities as a means of funding the benefits promised

in·sur·er \ən'shu̇rə(r)\ *n* -S [*insure* + *-er*] **1** : one that makes certain or secure : one that guarantees ⟨these ~*s* of peace⟩ **2** : one that contracts to indemnify another by way of insurance : an insurance company or underwriter **3** *archaic* : INSURED

1in·surge \ən+\ *vb* [L *insurgere*, fr. *in-* 1in- + *surgere* to rise — more at SURGE] *vi* : to become insurgent : behave insurgently ~ *vt* : to make insurgent

2insurge \'in+,-\ *n* [4*in* + *surge*] : a surging in

in·sur·gence \ən'sərjən(t)s, -sə̄j-,-səij-\ *n* -S [prob. fr. F, fr. *insurgent*, n. (fr. E) + *-ence*] : an act or the action of being insurgent : UPRISING, INSURRECTION ⟨the recurrent ~ of the lower house⟩

in·sur·gen·cy \-jənsē, -si\ *n* -ES [1*insurg*ent + *-ency*] **1** : the quality or state of being insurgent; *specif* : a condition of revolt against a recognized government that does not reach the proportions of an organized revolutionary government and is not recognized as belligerency **2** : INSURGENCE

1in·sur·gent \-nt\ *n* -S [L *insurgent-*, *insurgens*, pres. part. of *insurgere* to rise up, insurge] **1** : a person who rises in revolt against civil authority or an established government : REBEL; *esp* : a rebel not recognized as a belligerent — compare RIOT, TREASON **2** : one that acts contrary to the policies and decisions of his political party

2in·sur·gent \"\ *adj* **1** : rising in opposition to civil or political authority or against an established government : INSUBORDINATE, REBELLIOUS **2** : surging in ⟨the quick ~ sea⟩ — **in·sur·gent·ly** *adv*

in·sur·ges·cence \,in(t)(,)sər'jesᵊn(t)s\ *n* -S [1*insurge* + *-escence*] : tendency to make insurrection

insuring clause *n* : a clause in an insurance policy that sets out the risk assumed by the insurer or defines the scope of the coverage afforded

in·surmountable \¦in+\ *adj* [1*in-* + *surmountable*] : incapable of being surmounted, passed over, or overcome : INSUPERABLE ⟨~ disadvantages⟩ — **in·surmountableness** \"+\ *n* -ES — **in·surmountably** \"+\ *adv*

in·sur·rect \¦in(t)sə¦rekt\ *vi* [back-formation fr. *insurrection*] : to make or engage in insurrection

in·sur·rec·tion \,in(t)sə'rekshən\ *n* -S [ME *insurrecioun*, fr. MF *insurrection*, fr. LL *insurrection-*, *insurrectio*, fr. L *insurrectus* (past part. of *insurgere* to rise against, insurge) + *-ion-*, *-io* -ion — more at INSURGE] **1** : an act or instance of revolting against civil or political authority or against an established government **2** : an act or instance of rising up physically **syn** see REBELLION

in·sur·rec·tion·al·ly \-ᵊl|ē, -əl|, |i\ *adv* : in respect to insurrection : from an insurrectionary point of view

1in·sur·rec·tion·ary \-shə,nerē, -ri\ *also* **in·sur·rec·tion·al** \¦⸗⸗¦rekshənᵊl, -shnəl\ *adj* [*insurrection* + *-ary* or *-al*] : of, relating to, or constituting insurrection : given to or tending to induce insurrection : REBELLIOUS ⟨~ activity⟩ ⟨~ movements⟩

2insurrectionary \"\ *n* -ES : a participant in insurrection : INSURGENT

in·sur·rec·tion·ist \,⸗⸗'reksh(ə)nəst\ *n* -S : a favorer of or participant in insurrection : INSURGENT

in·sur·rec·tion·ize \-shə,nīz\ *vt* -ED/-ING/-S : to cause (as a people) to be insurgent : make insurrection in (a country)

in·sur·rec·to \,in(t)sə'rek(,)tō\ *n* -S [Sp, fr. L *insurrectus* (past part.)] : INSURRECTIONARY, INSURGENT, REBEL

in·susceptibility \¦in+\ *n* : the quality or state of being insusceptible : lack of susceptibility

in·susceptible \"+\ *adj* [1*in-* + *susceptible*] : not susceptible : incapable of being moved, affected, or impressed ⟨~ of pity⟩ ⟨~ to disease⟩ ⟨~ animals⟩ — **in·susceptibly** \"+\ *adv*

inswarming \'⸗,⸗⸗\ *adj* [2*in* + *swarming*, pres. part. of *swarm* (after *swarm in*, v.)] : entering in or like a swarm

insweeping \'⸗,⸗⸗\ *adj* [2*in* + *sweeping*, pres. part. of *sweep* (after *sweep in*, v.)] : moving sweepingly in

inswinger \'⸗,⸗⸗\ *n* [2*in* + *swing* (v.) + *-er*] : a bowled cricket ball that swerves in the air from off to leg — compare OUTSWINGER

int *abbr* **1** intelligence **2** intercept **3** interest **4** interim **5** interior **6** interjection **7** interleaved **8** intermediate **9** internal **10** international **11** interpreter **12** interval **13** interview **14** intransitive

in·tabulation \ən·+\ *n* [2*in-* + *tabulation*] : TABLATURE 1a

in·tact \ən·'takt\ *adj* [ME *intacte*, fr. L *intactus*, fr. *in-* 1in- + *tactus*, past part. of *tangere* to touch — more at TANGENT] **1** : untouched esp. by anything that harms or diminishes : left complete or entire : UNINJURED ⟨obtain your uncle's estate ~ —Kenneth Roberts⟩ ⟨houses largely ~ after some 3500 years —Jacquetta & Christopher Hawkes⟩ ⟨the memory of that night remained ~ —Elinor Wylie⟩ **2** *of a living body or its parts* : physically and functionally complete : having no relevant component removed or destroyed: **a** : physically virginal **b** : sexually competent : UNCASTRATED — used chiefly of a domestic animal — **in·tact·ness** \-k(t)nəs\ *n* -ES

in·ta·gliat·ed \ən·'ta|l,yād·əd, -tä|, |glē,ā-\ *adj* [It *intagliato* (past part. of *intagliare*) + E *-ed*] : engraved in or as if in intaglio

1in·ta·glio \ən·'ta|l(,)yō, -tä|, |glē,ō\ *n* -S *often attrib* [It, fr. *intagliare* to engrave, carve, cut, fr. ML *intaleare*, fr. L *in-* 2in- + LL *taliare* to cut — more at TAILOR] **1 a** : an engraving or incised figure in stone or other hard material; *specif* : a figure or design depressed below the surface of the material with the normal elevations of the design hollowed out so that an impression from the design yields an image in relief **b** : the art or process of executing intaglios **c** : a process or method of printing from a face in which the ink-carrying part is sunk that produces raised printing (as in die stamping) or plane printing (as in gravure) — compare LETTERPRESS, PLANOGRAPHY, STENCIL **2** : something carved in intaglio or stamped so as to resemble an intaglio carving; *esp* : a carved gem with the figures or designs carved into a generally flat surface — compare CAMEO **3** : a countersunk die for producing a figure in relief

2intaglio \"\ *vt* -ED/-ING/-ES : to cut or represent in intaglio

intaglio ri·le·va·to \-,rēlə'vä(,)tō\ *or* **intaglio ri·lie·vo** \-rē'lē(,)vō, -rēl'yā(-, -ye(-\ *n* [It, fr. *intaglio* + *rilevato* raised or *rilievo* relief] : SUNK RELIEF

intagliotype *n* [1*intaglio* + *type*] : a process for producing from a design drawn on a coated metal plate an intaglio plate for printing; *also* : a print from such a plate

intake \'⸗,⸗\ *n*, *often attrib* [4*in* + *take* (after *take in*, v.)] **1** *dial chiefly Brit* : a portion of land taken in or enclosed from a moor, common, or road : ENCLOSURE : hillside pasture or land reclaimed (as from the sea) **2 a** : an opening through which air, water, steam, or other fluid enters an enclosure ⟨the fuel-mixture ~ of an engine cylinder⟩ ⟨the ~ of an aqueduct⟩ — see JET ENGINE illustration **b** : a main passageway for air in a coal mine **3 a** : the act, process, or an instance of taking in ⟨~ . . . of various life-sustaining material —H.A.Overstreet⟩ ⟨stop the ~ of new clerks —Christopher Strachey⟩ ⟨an ~ of breath⟩ ⟨after the first quick ~ of surprise —Ethel Wilson⟩ ⟨the rate of ~ is an important index —W.F. Mackey⟩; *specif* : initial procedures (as interviews) conducted by a social worker, juvenile-court officer, or clinician in considering a client for treatment or service ⟨the role of the ~ worker⟩ ⟨an ~ official⟩ **b** (1) : the amount taken in ⟨an adequate ~ of food⟩ ⟨strictly limited my ~ during the day —*Sydney (Australia) Bull.*⟩ (2) : energy taken in : INPUT (3) : the persons taken into a group or organization ⟨half the total ~ were the sons of plebeians —J.W.Saunders⟩ (4) *chiefly Brit* : a person taken into a military service : RECRUIT ⟨just arrived with a new ~ —Derek Stanford⟩ **4** *Scot* **a** : SWINDLE **b** : SWINDLER

intake stroke *n* : the stroke in the cycle of an internal-combustion engine during which the fuel mixture is drawn in before compression

int al *abbr* [L *inter alia*] among other things; [L *inter alios*] among other persons

in·tangibility \(¦)in·, ən·+\ *n* **1** : the quality or state of being intangible ⟨there is a certain ~ about this problem⟩ **2** : something that is intangible : an intangible element ⟨fond of the pretty *intangibilities* of romance —Hugh Miller b. 1891⟩

1in·tangible \(')in·, ən·+\ *adj* [F or ML; F, fr. MF, fr. ML *intangibilis*, fr. L *in-* 1in- + LL *tangibilis* tangible — more at TANGIBLE] **1** : incapable of being touched or perceived by touch : not tangible : IMPALPABLE, IMPERCEPTIBLE ⟨that more subtle and ~ thing, the soul —John Buchan⟩ ⟨the ~ constituent of energy —James Jeans⟩ **2** : incapable of being defined or determined with certainty or precision : VAGUE, ELUSIVE ⟨with an ~ feeling of impending disaster —Guy Fowler⟩ ⟨this menace from the North was ~ and evasive —John Buchan⟩ — **in·tangibleness** \"+\ *n* — **in·tangibly** \"+\ *adv*

2intangible \"\ *n* : something intangible; *specif* : an asset (as goodwill or a patent right) that is not corporeal

intangible assets *n pl* : INTANGIBLES

intangible property *n* : property having no physical substance apparent to the senses : incorporeal property (as choses in action) often evidenced by documents (as stocks, bonds, notes, judgments, franchises) having no intrinsic value or by rights of action, easements, goodwill, trade secrets

in·tar·sia \ən·'tärsēə\ *n* -S [G, prob. modif. (influenced by It *tarsia*) of It *intarsio*, fr. *intarsiare* to inlay, fr. *in-* 2in- + *tarsiare* to inlay, fr. *tarsia* intarsia, fr. Ar *tarṣī*ʻ] **1** : a mosaic usu. of small pieces of wood which are inserted and glued into hollows of a wooden support that was popular in 15th century Italy for decoration featuring esp. scrolls, arabesques, architectural scenes, and flowers **2** : the art or process of making such work — **in·tar·si·ate** \-ē,āt, -ēət\ *adj*

in·tar·si·a·tu·ra \ən·,tärsēə'tu̇rə\ *n*, *pl* **intarsiatu·re** \-(,)rā\ [It, fr. *intarsiato* (past part. of *intarsiare*) + *-ura* -ure (fr. L)] : INTARSIA

in·tar·sio \-sē,ō\ *n*, *pl* **intar·si** \-(,)sē\ [It] : INTARSIA

in·tar·sist \-,səst\ *n* -S [*intars*ia + *-ist*] : a person who works in intarsia

intcl *abbr* intercoastal

in·te·ger \'intəjə(r), -tēj-\ *n* -S [L, adj., untouched, entire — more at ENTIRE] **1** : any of the natural numbers (as 1, 2, 3, 4, 5), the negatives of these numbers, or 0 **2** : a complete entity ⟨governmental policy is an ~ —Dean Acheson⟩ ⟨they become a whole, an ~, of people who have the same aspirations and hopes —William Faulkner⟩ **syn** see NUMBER

in·te·gra·bil·i·ty \,intəgrə'biləd·ē, -lətē, -i\ *n* -ES : the fact or character of being integrable

in·te·gra·ble \'intəgrəbəl\ *adj* [3*integr*ate + *-able*] : capable of being integrated ⟨a differential equation that is ~⟩ ⟨an ~ function⟩

1in·te·gral \'intəgrəl, 'integ- *also* in·'tegrəl *or* in·'tēgrəl *or* ÷'in·trəgəl *or* ÷'in·trēgəl\ *adj* [ME, fr. ML *integralis*, fr. L *integr-*, *integer* untouched, entire + *-alis* -al] **1 a** : of, relating to, or serving to form a whole : essential to completeness : organically joined or linked : CONSTITUENT, INHERENT ⟨science has become an ~ part of his cultural environment —C.I.Glicksberg⟩ ⟨an ~ part of the empire⟩ ⟨in great dramas character is always . . . somehow ~ with plot —T.S.Eliot⟩ ⟨political and economic power are ~ one to the other —*Commonweal*⟩ **b** (1) : of, being, or relating to a mathematical integer (2) : relating to or concerned with mathematical integrals or integration **c** : formed as a unit with another part (as the main part) — often used with *with*; used esp. of a part of a tool or mechanism ⟨the pin is ~ with the pump body —H.F.Blanchard & Ralph Ritchen⟩ ⟨heat transfer through tubes with ~ spiral fins —*Transactions of Amer. Society of Mech. Engineers*⟩ ⟨the steam chest may be an ~ part of the turbine casing or may be bolted to it —B.G.A.Skrotzki & W.A.Vopat⟩ **2** : composed of constituent parts making a whole : COMPOSITE, INTEGRATED ⟨a hospital, a medical school, and a laboratory of science all in one ~ group —V.G.Heiser⟩ **3** : having nothing omitted or taken away : lacking nothing that belongs to it : COMPLETE,

ENTIRE, PERFECT ⟨if vocations are declining, it is because ~ Catholic living is declining —J.H.Wilson⟩ — **in·te·gral·ly** \-əlē,-əli\ *adv*

²integral *n* -s **1 :** an entire thing **:** TOTALITY, WHOLE **2** *obs* **:** an integral part **:** CONSTITUENT, COMPONENT **3 :** the result of a mathematical integration either of a function or of an equation

integral calculus *n* [prob. part trans. of NL *calculus integralis*] **:** a branch of mathematics that deals chiefly with the methods of finding indefinite integrals of functions and the evaluation of definite integrals, calculation (as of lengths of curves, areas, volumes, moments of inertia) by definite integration, mean values of functions, and the solution of certain simple types of differential equations

integral cover *n* **:** SELF-COVER

integral equation *n* **:** an equation in which the dependent variable is included at least once under a definite integral sign

integral humanism *n* **:** a Christian humanism based on Thomistic principles and advocated esp. by Jacques Maritain

in·te·gral·i·ty \,intə'graləd·ē\ *n* -ES **:** integral quality or state

integral rational function *n* **:** POLYNOMIAL

integral tripack *n* **:** a photographic film or plate consisting of three superposed emulsions each sensitive to a different primary color and coated on a single support — called also *monopack;* compare BIPACK

in·te·grand \'intə,grand, ,==\'=\ *n* -s [L *integrandus*, gerundive of *integrare* to integrate] **:** a mathematical expression to be integrated **:** the function under the integral sign

¹in·te·grant \'intəgrənt, -tēg-\ *adj* [F or L; F *intégrant*, fr. MF, fr. L *integrant-, integrans*, pres. part. of *integrare* to integrate] **:** INTEGRAL ⟨all these are ~ parts of the republic —Edmund Burke⟩

²integrant \"\ *n* -s **:** an integral part **:** COMPONENT **syn** see ELEMENT

in·te·graph \-,graf, -råf\ *n* [ISV, blend of *integrate* and *-graph*] **:** an instrument that draws mechanically the graph of an antiderivative of a given mathematical function

¹in·te·grate \-,grət, -,grāt\ *adj* [ME *integrat*, fr. L *integratus* (past part.)] **:** INTEGRATED ⟨we may consider logic . . . as an ~ whole —William Hamilton †1856⟩

²integrate \"\ *n* -s **:** something that is integrated **:** a complete, organically unified, or perfect entity usu. resulting from a combination of elements **:** WHOLE ⟨an ~ of images which portray the person at his future best —C.K.Kluckhohn & H.A. Murray⟩ ⟨the cell, the molecule are not aggregates but ~*s* —H.J.Muller⟩

³in·te·grate \'intə,grāt, *usu* -ād·+V\ *vb* -ED/-ING/-S [L *integratus*, past part. of *integrare*, fr. *integr-, integer* untouched, entire — more at ENTIRE] *vt* **1** *obs* **:** to make complete **:** CONSTITUTE ⟨the particular doctrines which ~ Christianity —William Chillingworth⟩ **2 :** to form into a more complete, harmonious, or coordinated entity often by the addition or arrangement of parts or elements ⟨that conquest rounded and *integrated* the glorious empire —Thomas De Quincey⟩ ⟨if man is to ~ himself, he must discover his springs of action —P.W.Bridgman⟩ **3 :** to combine to form a more complete, harmonious, or coordinated entity: **a :** to unite (as a part or element) with something else ⟨a system of free enterprise carefully *integrated* with teamwork —J.C.Penney⟩ ⟨he who ~*s* this knowledge with the pattern of culture —David Daiches⟩ **b :** to combine together (as units or elements) ⟨~ the seventeen . . . reports into a few policy statements —E.C.Banfield⟩ ⟨this course . . . is designed to assist him to ~ all of his college experiences —A.C.Eurich⟩ ⟨a customs union that . . . would ~ the economies of the two countries —*Current Biog.*⟩ **c** (1) **:** to incorporate (as an individual or group) into a larger unit or group ⟨~ the West German divisions into the Atlantic defense system —*New Statesman & Nation*⟩ ⟨the South of that era was never *integrated* into the nation —H.W.Odum⟩ ⟨~ hundreds of thousands of Puerto Rican . . . workers into the organized labor movement —*N.Y. Times*⟩ (2) **:** to end the segregation of and bring into common and equal membership in society or an organization ⟨attempt to ~ Negroes into the church in a cautious gradual manner —*Jour. of Social Issues*⟩ ⟨moves . . . to ~ Indian children in the public school systems —*Indian Affairs*⟩ **4 :** DESEGREGATE ⟨a well-staffed state agency managed . . . to ~ forty formerly segregated school districts —Douglass Cater⟩ **5 :** to indicate the whole of **:** give the sum or total of **6 :** to find the integral of (as a function or equation) ~ *vi* **:** to become integrated ⟨some of the white parishioners . . . were willing to go along with the decision to ~ —*Jour. of Social Issues*⟩ ⟨the show begins to ~ again —Alfred Bester⟩ **syn** see UNIFY

integrated *adj* **1 :** characterized by integration: **a :** composed of separate parts united together to form a more complete, harmonious, or coordinated entity ⟨her tightly plotted, admirably ~ novel —John Barkham⟩ ⟨an ~ series of twenty-six dams —*Lamp*⟩ **b :** combining elements usu. taught in separate academic courses or departments ⟨to establish the behavior sciences on an ~ footing —J.W.Bennett⟩ ⟨~ courses⟩ **c :** having in common and equal membership individuals or groups differing in some group characteristic (as race) ⟨Negro units were broken up and reassigned in ~ groups —*New Republic*⟩ ⟨an ~ school⟩ **d :** characterized by psychological integration ⟨an ~ personality⟩ **e :** characterized by close cooperation or partial unity of constituent units ⟨a more closely ~ economic and political system —D.D.Eisenhower⟩ ⟨an ~ Europe⟩ ⟨an ~ military staff⟩ **f** (1) **:** operating economically as a single coordinated physically interconnected unit or system usu. confined to a specific region ⟨an ~ public utility system⟩ (2) **:** characterized by possession of sources of supply and continuous control of production and often distribution from raw materials to diversified finished products ⟨an ~ company . . . occupies a favored position as compared with a competitor which is at the mercy of the market —*Financial World*⟩ **g** *of the bar* **:** characterized by the compulsory membership of all lawyers practicing in a specific area (as a state) ⟨the states having an ~ bar have codes of professional ethics enforceable upon all members —*Jour. of the Amer. Judicature Society*⟩ **h :** characterized by social solidarity, coherency of form and function, and moral or psychological unity among members ⟨its culture is . . . more stable and better ~ —A.L.Kroeber⟩ **2 :** incorporated into a group or organization on the basis of common and equal membership despite differing characteristics (as race) ⟨most Indians are ~ with the other residents —W.R.Moore⟩ ⟨Negroes . . . have long been ~ in the police department —Gladwin Hill⟩

integrated logging *n* **:** a system of logging planned to remove in one cutting all usable timber and to separate the primary products and distribute them to industries where they will bring the highest returns

integrating factor *n* **:** a factor that renders immediately integrable a differential equation multiplied by it

integrating sphere *n* **:** a spherical shell used to determine total luminous flux by means of photometric measurement of a spot of light through an aperture in the shell whose white interior produces thorough diffusion of light from a source placed at its center

integrating wattmeter *n* **:** WATT-HOUR METER

in·te·gra·tion \,intə'grāshən\ *n* -s [L *integration-, integratio* act of renewing, act of restoring, fr. *integratus* (past part. of *integrare* to renew, integrate) + *-ion-, -io* -ion — more at INTEGRATE] **1 :** the act, process, or an instance of integrating **:** the condition of being formed into a whole by the addition or combination of parts or elements **2 a :** a combination and coordination of separate and diverse elements or units into a more complete or harmonious whole ⟨the automobile is an ~ of a multitude of machine parts —C.C.Furnas⟩ ⟨large-scale ~ of efforts —Oscar Handlin⟩ **b :** a unification and mutual adjustment of diverse groups or elements into a relatively coordinated and harmonious society or culture with a consistent body of normative standards ⟨most urban communities possess some degree of ~ around primary group norms —Kimball Young⟩ ⟨the total ~ of any given culture about its technology —David Bidney⟩ **c :** the organization of teaching matter to interrelate or unify subjects usu. taught in separate academic courses or departments ⟨through ~ it is possible to teach science, health, and safety as part of the regular program —E.J.Goebel⟩ **d :** an arrangement usu. on a hierarchical basis of functions or units of an organization to promote coordination and responsibility ⟨the need for administrative ~ at the county level —C.F.Snider⟩ ⟨an ~ of units previously scattered . . . in departments or otherwise —F.A.Ogg & P.O.Ray⟩ **e :** an incorporation into society or an organization (as a public school) on the basis of common and equal membership of individuals differing in some group characteristic (as race) ⟨ordered ~ of all white and Negro troops in the armed forces —*New Republic*⟩ ⟨the native Polynesian group that strongly objects to ~ with Europeans —*N.Y. Times*⟩ ⟨a positive ~ of the African into the South African community —Margaret Ballinger⟩ **f** (1) **:** the coordination and correlation of the total processes of perception, interpretation, and reaction ensuring a normal effective life ⟨failure of association and failure of ~ take place among neurotic individuals —R.M.Dorcus & G.W. Shaffer⟩ (2) **:** a harmonious coordination of the behavior and personality of an individual with his environment ⟨she attempts to enter the world of her fellow teenagers, and after many mistakes she achieves such ~ —Eleanor Scott⟩ **g :** the establishment of close cooperation among or some degree of unification of distinct entities (as countries or groups of countries) esp. in a specific area (as trade or defense) ⟨West European ~ is the first condition for the survival of every country concerned —William Petersen⟩ ⟨the . . . proposal for the economic ~ of Europe into one single market —*Current Biog.*⟩ **h :** the unified control of a number of successive or similar economic esp. industrial processes formerly carried on independently ⟨~ may result in important cost reductions⟩ **3 :** the operation of finding a function of which the integrand is the derivative of a function or of solving a differential equation **4 :** the sum of the processes by which the developing parts of an organism are formed into a functional and structural whole ⟨at the molecular level of ~ many studies are needed —*Science*⟩

integration by parts : a method of integration by means of the reduction formula $\int udv = uv - \int vdu$

in·te·gra·tion·ist \-sh(ə)nəst\ *n* -s **:** a person that believes in, advocates, or practices integration ⟨opposition to the ~*s* came from many groups in the small southern town⟩

in·te·gra·tive \'==,grād·|iv, -āt|, |ēv *also* |əv\ *adj* [³*integrate* + *-ive*] **1 :** tending to integrate ⟨the ~ action of the nervous system —J.R.Newman⟩ **2 :** favoring or implementing integration ⟨the widespread ~ trend of modern science —Weston La Barre⟩ ⟨anthropology's ~ tools —Abraham Edel⟩

in·te·gra·tor \-ād·ə(r), -ātə-\ *n* -s [LL, renewer, restorer, fr. L *integratus* (past part.) + *-or*] **:** one that integrates ⟨religion has been the supreme ~ of intellectual and emotional experience —H.N.Fairchild⟩; *specif* **:** a device (as a planimeter or pedometer) that totalizes by mechanical, electromechanical, electronic, or other physical means a multiplicity of variable quantities in a manner comparable to that in which mathematical solutions are arrived at by means of differential equations or integral calculus

integri- *comb form* [L, fr. *integr-, integer* — more at ENTIRE] **:** whole **:** entire ⟨*integri*folious⟩ ⟨*integri*palliate⟩

in·teg·ri·ty \ən'tegrəd·ē, -rətē, -i\ *n* -ES [ME *integrite*, fr. MF & L; MF *intégrité*, fr. L *integritat-, integritas*, fr. *integr-, integer* untouched, entire + *-itat-, -itas* -ity] **1 a :** an unimpaired or unmarred condition **:** entire correspondence with an original condition **:** SOUNDNESS ⟨personality function depends greatly upon the ~ of brain function —*Diagnostic & Statistical Manual*⟩ ⟨maintenance of the ship's watertight ~ —*Manual of Seamanship*⟩ ⟨designed to assure structural ~ of the aircraft —*Index to Current Tech. Publications*⟩ ⟨the ~ of the national currency is not dependent on its convertibility —*Current Biog.*⟩ **b :** an uncompromising adherence to a code of moral, artistic, or other values **:** utter sincerity, honesty, and candor **:** avoidance of deception, expediency, artificiality, or shallowness of any kind ⟨an example of great physical vigor, business ~, and thrift —*Current Biog.*⟩ ⟨a writer of ~ has a duty toward his opinions —C.L.Carmer⟩ ⟨a serious reflection on the intellectual ~ of the accusers —C.R.Davenport⟩ ⟨his ~ told him that this would be at variance with the dramatic truth of his opera —Robert Lawrence⟩ ⟨the ~, the clean drive, and the unforced power that distinguishes the good primitive novel —Frederic Morton⟩ **2 :** the quality or state of being complete or undivided **:** material, spiritual, or aesthetic wholeness **:** organic unity **:** ENTIRENESS, COMPLETENESS ⟨the emphasis is always on the ~ and the uniqueness of the finished poem —David Daiches⟩ ⟨has a feeling for the ~ of each separate person —Malcolm Cowley⟩ ⟨seen in its ~ . . . it is a crumbling tower of waste —Charles Dickens⟩ ⟨guarantee the ~ of the British Empire forever —Upton Sinclair⟩ ⟨aesthetic experience is experience in its ~ —John Dewey⟩

in·teg·u·ment \ən'tegyəmənt\ *n* -s [L *integumentum*, fr. *integere* to cover (fr. *in-* ²in- + *tegere* to cover) + *-mentum* -ment — more at THATCH] **1 :** something that covers or encloses **:** COVERING, ENVELOPE ⟨still encased in a dry brittle ~ that had once been leather —A.B.Chandler⟩ ⟨almost any ~ of a book before the age of cloth, is attractive —R.W.Chapman⟩ **2 :** an external coating or investment: as **a :** one of the usu. two envelopes that enclose the nucellus of an ovule, that are often fused, and that sometimes with other parts form the seed coat **b :** an enveloping layer, membrane, or structure (as the skin of a fish or the exoskeleton of an insect)

in·teg·u·men·tal \=;==;'mentᵊl\ *or* **in·teg·u·men·ta·ry** \-ntərē, -n·trē\ *adj* **:** of or relating to the integument; *esp* **:** CUTANEOUS

in·tel·lect \'intᵊl,ekt\ *n* -s [ME, fr. MF or L; MF, fr. L *intellectus*, fr. *intellectus*, past part. of *intellegere, intelligere* to perceive, understand — more at INTELLIGENT] **1 a :** the power or faculty of knowing as distinguished from the power to feel and to will **b** *Aristotelianism* (1) **:** passive reason (2) **:** active reason **c** *Scholasticism* **:** the faculty of penetrating appearances and getting at the substance through abstraction from and elimination of the individual **d** *Thomism* (1) **:** the receptive faculty of cognition that makes apprehensible the phantasms or intelligible forms — called also *passive intellect, possible intellect, potential intellect* (2) **:** the aspect of the soul that is immortal and constitutes the active power of thought operating upon the phantasms or intelligible forms — called also *active intellect, agent intellect* **e :** UNDERSTANDING, REASON **2 a :** a person given to reflective thought or reasoning **:** a person of notable intellect **:** BRAIN ⟨the outstanding ~ of the whole convention —*Hispanic Amer. Hist. Rev.*⟩ **b :** the totality of intellectual persons ⟨the ~ of the country recognized his superiority⟩ **3 intellects** *pl, now chiefly dial* **:** WITS, FACULTIES ⟨she wishes I had more ~*s* —Eden Phillpotts⟩ **syn** see MIND

in·tel·lec·tion \,intᵊl'ekshən\ *n* -s [ME *intelleccioun* intellect, understanding, fr. L *intellection-, intellectio* synecdoche, lit., understanding, fr. *intellectus* (past part.) + *-ion-, -io* -ion] **1 :** exercise of the intellect **:** REASONING, COGNITION, APPREHENSION ⟨one of the most sublime acts of ~ of all time —*New Yorker*⟩ **2 :** a specific act of the intellect **:** NOTION, THOUGHT, IDEA ⟨mazy ~*s* —Alan Devoe⟩

in·tel·lec·tive \'==;'=tiv\ *adj* [MF or LL; MF *intellectif*, fr. LL *intellectivus*, fr. L *intellectus* (past part.) + *-ivus* -ive] **1 :** relating to, based on, or possessed by the intellect **:** INTELLECTUAL ⟨those more ~ artificial features which find their expression in refined syntax and style —M.A.Pei⟩ **2 :** having intellectual power **:** INTELLIGENT, RATIONAL, COGNITIVE ⟨awareness of a spiritual ~ soul —Beatrice H. Zedler⟩ — **in·tel·lec·tive·ly** \-tə̇vlē\ *adv*

¹in·tel·lec·tu·al \,intᵊl'ekch(əw)əl, -ksh-\ *adj* [ME, fr. MF & L; MF *intellectuel*, fr. L *intellectualis*, fr. *intellectus* intellect + *-alis* -al] **1 a :** of, belonging to, or relating to the intellect or its use **:** REFLECTIVE, REASONING ⟨satire is an ~ weapon —Herbert Read⟩ ⟨~ powers⟩ ⟨enabling them to function on the ~ plane —Bruce Bliven b.1889⟩ ⟨began his ~ career as a mathematician —F.S.C.Northrop⟩ — contrasted with *animal* **b :** having its source in or being preeminently guided by the intellect as distinguished from emotion or experience **:** RATIONAL ⟨has a tremendous ~ sympathy for oppressed people —Green Peyton⟩ ⟨think of such playwrights as coldly ~ —E.R.Bentley⟩ ⟨in no sense an ~ or metaphysical painter —Herbert Read⟩ ⟨the most subtle and ~ edifice ever made by man —Weston La Barre⟩ ⟨disseminated the severe and ~ Florentine style —*Nat'l Gallery of Art*⟩ **c :** calling the intellect into play **:** requiring use of the intellect ⟨as abstruse and ~ as a chess problem⟩ ⟨there should be a distinction . . . between manual or copying work and ~ work —K.C.Wheare⟩ **2** *obs* **:** apprehensible by the intellect alone **:** IMMATERIAL, SPIRITUAL, IDEAL **3 a** *archaic* **:** endowed with the power to know and reason **:** INTELLIGENT **b** (1) **:** devoted to matters of the mind and esp. to the arts and letters **:** given to study, reflection, and speculation esp. concerning large or abstract issues ⟨sort of the ~ type, but most of the gang are real people —W.H. Whyte⟩ ⟨maintain a person can be ~ and not be intelligent —Jean Stafford⟩ (2) **:** engaged in activity requiring preeminently the use of the intellect **:** engaged in mental as distinguished from manual labor; *esp* **:** engaged in creative literary, artistic, or scientific labor ⟨~ workers should be able to deduct from their income tax the amounts which they must spend for books, documents, research work, and materials in general —*Report: (Canadian) Royal Commission on Nat'l Development*⟩ (3) **:** reflecting, indicating, or suggesting devotion to matters of the mind **:** indicating or associated with a studious reflective temper or large mental endowment ⟨had a high ~ forehead —Edmund Wilson⟩ **syn** see MENTAL

²intellectual \"\ *n* -s **1** *obs* **:** INTELLECT, UNDERSTANDING **2 intellectuals** *pl, archaic* **:** intellectual powers or faculties **3 a :** a person of superior intelligence **:** a brainy person ⟨an uneducated ~ who had directed his great powers to accumulation and exploitation —S.H.Adams⟩ ⟨an ~ is a person endowed with unusual mental capacity —*Saturday Rev.*⟩ **b** (1) **:** a person devoted to matters of the mind and esp. to the arts and letters **:** one given to study, reflection, and speculation esp. concerning large, profound, or abstract issues ⟨afraid to be an ~ — if you wanted to go to art galleries, you were immediately suspect —P.E.Deutschman⟩ ⟨a friendly manner, a quiet voice, and the face of an ~ —William Ridsdale⟩ (2) **:** a person claiming to belong to an intellectual elite or caste, given to empty theorizing or cerebration, and often inept in the solution of practical problems **:** EGGHEAD ⟨don't go for the ~ who knows nothing but $2 words —J.P.Whitcomb⟩ ⟨that dreary and narrow creature an ~ —*Manchester Guardian Weekly*⟩ ⟨~ is an ugly word . . . it implies consummate snobbery —Russell Kirk⟩ **c :** a person engaged in activity requiring preeminently the use of the intellect **:** one engaged in mental as distinguished from manual labor ⟨~*s* . . . are functioning groups of society, like any of the professionals, such as lawyers, doctors, engineers, professors —F.G.Wilson⟩

intellectual history *n* **:** a branch of history that deals with the rise and evolution of ideas **:** history of ideas

in·tel·lec·tu·al·ism \,intᵊl'ekch(əw)ə,lizəm, -ksh-\ *n* -s **1 a :** the viewpoint that knowledge is derived from pure reason **:** RATIONALISM **b :** the doctrine that the ultimate principle of reality is reason **2 a :** devotion to the exercise of intellect or intellectual pursuits ⟨restore the true ~; that is to say, a love of intellectual things —August Heckscher⟩ **b :** such devotion carried to excess ⟨the unnatural ~ which society inflicts upon the middle class —Ian Watt⟩

¹in·tel·lec·tu·al·ist \-,ləst\ *n* -s [¹*intellectual* + *-ist*] **1 :** an adherent of the doctrine of intellectualism **2 :** a person given to intellectualism

²intellectualist \"\ *adj* **:** INTELLECTUALISTIC

in·tel·lec·tu·al·is·tic \,==;=(=)=;listik, -tēk\ *adj* **:** relating to intellectualism or intellectualists — **in·tel·lec·tu·al·is·ti·cal·ly** \-tə̇k(ə)lē, -tēk-, -li\ *adv*

in·tel·lec·tu·al·i·ty \,intᵊl,ekchə'waləd·ē, -ksh-, -lətē, -i\ *n* -ES [LL *intellectualitat-, intellectualitas*, fr. L *intellectualis* intellectual + *-itat-, -itas* -ity] **:** intellectual power **:** the quality or state of being intellectual

in·tel·lec·tu·al·i·za·tion \,intᵊl,ekchə(wə)lə'zāshən, -ksh-, -,lī'z-\ *n* -s **:** the act, process, or an instance of intellectualizing ⟨opposed to any ~ of art —Herbert Read⟩

in·tel·lec·tu·al·ize \,==;=(=)=,līz\ *vb* -ED/-ING/-S *see -ize in Explan Notes* [¹*intellectual* + *-ize*] *vt* **1 :** to give intellectual or rational form or content to **:** treat or analyze intellectually ⟨tendency to ~ . . . problems —*Current Biog.*⟩ ⟨~*s* traditional forms like the sonnet and madrigal —Douglas Bush⟩ **2 :** to avoid (conscious recognition of the emotional basis of an act or feeling) by substituting a superficially plausible explanation ⟨conflicts that are *intellectualized* —L.E.Hinsie⟩ ~ *vi* **:** to engage in intellectual discussion **:** REASON, PHILOSOPHIZE ⟨sat . . . and simply *intellectualized* —Johnny George⟩

in·tel·lec·tu·al·ly \,intᵊl'ekch(əw)əlē, -ksh-, -kshlē, -li\ *adv* **:** in an intellectual manner

in·tel·lec·tu·al·ness \,intᵊl'ekch(əw)əlnə̇s, -ksh-\ *n* -ES **:** the quality or state of being intellectual

intellectual virtue *n, Aristotelianism* **:** a virtue (as wisdom) concerned with the apprehension of rational principles

¹in·tel·li·gence \ən'teləjən(t)s\ *n* -s *often attrib* [ME, fr. MF, fr. OF, fr. L *intelligentia, intellegentia*, fr. *intelligent-, intelligens* (pres. part.) + *-ia* -y — more at INTELLIGENT] **1 a** (1) **:** the faculty of understanding **:** capacity to know or apprehend **:** INTELLECT, REASON ⟨~, which emerged during the revolutionary cycles of matter as the highest form yet achieved —Hermann Reith⟩ ⟨conceived of history as the expression of a divine ~⟩ (2) *Christian Science* **:** the basic eternal quality of divine Mind **b :** the available ability as measured by intelligence tests or by other social criteria to use one's existing knowledge to meet new situations and to solve new problems, to learn, to foresee problems, to use symbols or relationships, to create new relationships, to think abstractly **:** ability to perceive one's environment, to deal with it symbolically, to deal with it effectively, to adjust to it, to work toward a goal **:** the degree of one's alertness, awareness, or acuity **:** ability to use with awareness the mechanism of reasoning whether conceived as a unified intellectual factor or as the aggregate of many intellectual factors or abilities, as intuitive or as analytic, as organismic, biological, physiological, psychological, or social in origin and nature **c :** mental acuteness **:** SAGACITY, SHREWDNESS ⟨did all he was asked to do with ~ and great good humor⟩ **2 a :** an intelligent being; *esp* **:** an incorporeal spirit **:** ANGEL ⟨hierarchies of angelic ~*s* —S.F.Mason⟩ **b :** a person of some intellectual capacity ⟨all those ~*s* we have agreed to call great —*Times Lit. Supp.*⟩ ⟨the greatest all-round ~ writing in England —P.S.O'Hegarty⟩ **3 a :** the act of understanding **:** COMPREHENSION, KNOWLEDGE ⟨faith is necessary to the ~ of the Christian mysteries —*Encyc. Americana*⟩ **b** (1) **:** information communicated **:** NEWS, NOTICE, ADVICE ⟨more weight is laid upon ~ than on editorials —Horace Greeley⟩ ⟨the joyful ~ that there is hope —Georgina Grahame⟩ ⟨from the engine-room voice tube came ~ of more importance —M.S.Boylan⟩ (2) **:** interchange of information **:** COMMUNICATION ⟨accused of maintaining ~ with the enemy⟩ (3) *obs* **:** a piece of information — usu. used in pl. (4) *archaic* **:** common understanding or mutual relations **:** ACQUAINTANCE, INTERCOURSE (5) **:** evaluated information concerning an enemy or possible enemy or a possible theater of operations and the conclusions drawn therefrom; *also* **:** the section, agency, or persons engaged in obtaining such information **:** SECRET SERVICE ⟨investigated me and told me I was qualified for Navy ~ —T.F.Murphy⟩ ⟨an ~ bureau⟩ ⟨available to American and allied ~ organizations —L.W.Doob⟩ **syn** see MIND

²intelligence *vt* -ED/-ING/-S *obs* **:** to bring tidings of (something) or to (someone)

in·tel·li·genced \-jən(t)st\ *adj* [¹*intelligence* + *-ed*] **1 :** having mental power **:** INTELLIGENT **2 :** having information **:** INFORMED

intelligence office *n* **:** an agency where servants (as domestic help) may be hired ⟨you would know the best real estate and *intelligence offices* —Emily Post⟩

intelligence officer *n* **:** a staff officer who gathers, evaluates, interprets, and disseminates intelligence and attempts to thwart enemy attempts to gather such information

intelligence quotient *n* **:** a number held to express the relative intelligence of a person determined by dividing his mental age by his chronological age with chronological years above 14 or sometimes 16 disregarded and then multiplying by 100 to eliminate decimals —abbr. *IQ, I.Q.*

in·tel·li·genc·er \-jənsə(r), -,jen(t)s-, =,==='jen-\ *n* -s [¹*intelligence* + *-er*] **:** one that conveys intelligence or news: as **a :** a secret agent **:** SPY **b :** a bringer of news **:** REPORTER ⟨made this wearied ~ sit up and listen —Virgil Thomson⟩ **c :** newspaper — usu. used as the names of newspapers

intelligence test *n* **:** any of various tests consisting of standardized questions and tasks designed to determine the mental age of the person examined or his relative capacity to absorb information and solve problems : a test designed to measure capacity to learn apart from actual achievement — compare ACHIEVEMENT TEST, APTITUDE TEST

in·tel·li·gen·cy \-jənsē, -si\ *n* -ES [L *intelligentia* — more at INTELLIGENCE] *archaic* : INTELLIGENCE

1in·tel·li·gent \-nt\ *adj* [L *intelligent-*, *intelligens*, pres. part. of *intelligere*, *intellegere* to perceive, understand, fr. *inter-* + *legere* to choose, select, gather — more at LEGEND] **1 a :** possessing intelligence or intellect : having the power of reflection or reason ⟨assumes the existence of other worlds peopled by ~ beings⟩ **b :** guided or directed by intelligence or intellect : RATIONAL ⟨in the other kind of behavior, often called ~, the animal is able to benefit from its past experience —*New Biology*⟩ **2 a :** having or indicating a high or satisfactory degree of intelligence and mental capacity or powers of perception, consideration, and correct decision : not stupid or foolish ⟨Puritanism presupposed an ~ clergy capable of interpreting Scripture —*Amer. Guide Series: Mass.*⟩ ⟨though she could not read, both her face and conversation were ~ —Willa Cather⟩ **b :** well adapted to its purpose : being the product of intelligence of a high order : revealing or reflecting good judgment or sound and comprehensive thought : WISE, SKILLFUL ⟨an ~ decision⟩ ⟨~ propaganda⟩ ⟨an ~ essay⟩ **3 a :** marked by quick active perception and understanding ⟨an ~ person, looking out of his eyes and hearkening in his ears —R.L.Stevenson⟩ **b** *archaic* : showing or having some special knowledge, skill, or aptitude

syn KNOWING, BRILLIANT, SMART, BRIGHT, QUICK-WITTED, CLEVER, ALERT: INTELLIGENT, limited in connotational range, indicates mental capacity and power, often to a high degree, enabling one to perceive, learn, consider, and judge ⟨what should a mature and *intelligent* nation do in such a crisis? . . . we ought to keep our heads . . . be alert to really serious dangers —Elmer Davis⟩ ⟨it is fairly easy for any *intelligent* mother to know when the baby is hungry —Morris Fishbein⟩ KNOWING may indicate ability to know or possession of special knowledge; it often applies to intimations of special information or sophistication ⟨the *knowing* collectors of records —*Saturday Rev.*⟩ ⟨the two young officers exchanged *knowing* glances —W.M.Thackeray⟩ BRILLIANT indicates uncommon, quick, shining mental keenness, capacity, achievement against difficulty ⟨a shrewd sensible man, only not *brilliant* —George Meredith⟩ ⟨first revealed with bitter and *brilliant* incisiveness the cynical desperation of early postwar adolescents —*Amer. Guide Series: Minn.*⟩ SMART suggests quickness in perceiving, in cannily calculating, or in successful resourcefulness ⟨he was top of the class, and the master said he was the *smartest* lad in the school —D.H.Lawrence⟩ ⟨for hundreds of years the *smartest* businessmen in the world have been coming in to the City of London —D.W.Brogan⟩ SMART may indicate facetious pertness ⟨*smart* retorts are also cherished, especially by the young —L.J.Davidson⟩ BRIGHT indicates a lively alert quickness in learning and understanding ⟨the teachers all knew he was *bright* as brass . . . he took every last one of the prizes —Ellen Glasgow⟩ ⟨foreordained that any *bright* person ought to have seen it coming —*Harper's*⟩ QUICK-WITTED indicates quickness in arising to an occasion, in perceiving and coping with problems or dangers ⟨a *quick-witted* debater hard to entangle or confuse⟩ ⟨making their way through enemy territory under the *quick-witted* leadership of the captain⟩ CLEVER may suggest quick, apt facility at improvising, finding expedients, contriving to cope with problems ⟨*clever* boys and girls like to test their minds on difficulties —Bertrand Russell⟩ ⟨he was a *clever* lawyer . . . and had the jury eating out of his hand —Dorothy Sayers⟩ ALERT indicates a wide-awake care about and concern with any emergent development that might have been unnoticed ⟨*alert* and wary, making off at the first alarm —James Stevenson-Hamilton⟩ ⟨*alert* to this need, Congress authorized five military highways —*Amer. Guide Series: Mich.*⟩ **syn** see in addition MENTAL

2intelligent \"\ *n* -S **1** *obs* : a person who conveys information : SPY **2 :** an intelligent being

in·tel·li·gen·tial \ən-¦telə¦jenchəl\ *adj* : of, like, relating to, or having intelligence : exercising or implying understanding ⟨the existential and the ~ elements —Heinrich Zimmer⟩

in·tel·li·gent·ly *adv* : in an intelligent manner ⟨delivered an ~ reasoned summation⟩

in·tel·li·gen·tsia *also* **in·tel·li·gen·tzia** \(,)in-,telə'jentsēə, ən-,tel- *also* -'jench(ē)ə *or* -'gentsēə\ *n* -S [Russ *intelligentsiya*, fr. L *intelligentia* intelligence — more at INTELLIGENCE] **1 a :** a class of well-educated articulate persons constituting a distinct, recognized, and self-conscious social stratum within a nation and claiming or assuming for itself the guiding role of an intellectual, social, or political vanguard ⟨the basic function of the Encyclopedists and of all later ~*s* . . . includes both the iconoclastic and the pedagogic, the destructive and the constructive element —Arthur Koestler⟩ ⟨an inferior helot people without any national consciousness, without any ~ —O.D.Tolischus⟩ ⟨it has a restless, unstable, rebellious, and brilliant ~ —R.H.Markham⟩ **b :** a class of persons devoted to matters of the mind and esp. to the arts and letters : a class of persons given to study, reflection, and speculation esp. concerning large, profound, or abstract issues ⟨a café where the local ~ gathered⟩ ⟨a trifling comedy scorned by the ~⟩ **2 :** a class of persons engaged in activity requiring preeminently the use of the intellect : a class of persons engaged in mental as distinguished from manual labor ⟨best opinion in this country accords to professional men and women the status of ~ —M.L.Cooke⟩

in·tel·li·gi·bil·i·ty \(,)=,==jə'bilәd-ē, -lətē, -i\ *n* -ES **1 :** the quality or state of being intelligible : CLARITY, UNDERSTANDABILITY ⟨the immediate ~ of the prose —Richard Eberhart⟩ **2 :** something that is intelligible

1in·tel·li·gi·ble \ən-'teləjəbəl\ *adj* [ME, fr. L *intelligibilis*, fr. *intelligere* to perceive, understand + *-ibilis* -able — more at INTELLIGENT] **1** *obs* : INTELLIGENT **2 :** capable of being understood or comprehended ⟨an ~ description⟩ ⟨~ pronunciation⟩ **3 a :** apprehensible by the intellect only : purely conceptual ⟨the classical conception, according to which thinking is the inspection of ~ objects —Norman Malcolm⟩ **b :** relating to something that is beyond perception : SUPERSENSIBLE, SUPRASENSUOUS ⟨made the ~ world . . . the starting point of their speculations —Frank Thilly⟩ — **in·tel·li·gi·ble·ness** \-nəs\ *n* -ES — **in·tel·li·gi·bly** \-blē,-bli\ *adv*

2intelligible \"\ *n* -S : an object of the intellect ⟨the intellect's natural capacity for the intuition of ~*s* —L.J.Thro⟩

intelligible species *n*, *Thomism* : an object as apprehended through an act of intellectual cognition — contrasted with *sensible species*

in·tem·er·ate \ən-'temə,rāt, -rət\ *adj* [L *intemeratus*, fr. *in-* 1in- + *temeratus*, past part. of *temerare* to violate, defile, fr. *temere* rashly, by chance — more at TEMERITY] : INVIOLATE, PURE, UNDEFILED

in·temperance \(')in, ən+\ *n* [ME *intemperaunce*, fr. L *intemperantia*, fr. *intemperant-*, *intemperans* intemperate (fr. *in-* 1in- + *temperant-*, *temperans* temperate, fr. pres. part. of *temperare* to temper, regulate) + *-ia* -y — more at TEMPER] **1 :** inclemency or severity esp. of weather **2 a :** excess or lack of moderation in an action ⟨much ~ of statement in the current condemnation of our education —F.N.Robinson⟩ and esp. in satisfying an appetite or passion; *specif* : habitual or excessive drinking of intoxicants **b :** an intemperate act ⟨these daily ~*s* were disquieting, because men can't talk themselves into permanent rages —*New World*⟩

intemperancy *n* -ES [L *intemperantia*] *obs* : INTEMPERANCE

in·temperate \(')in, ən+\ *adj* [ME *intemperat*, fr. L *intemperatus*, fr. *in-* 1in- + *temperatus* temperate — more at TEMPERATE] : not temperate: as **a :** immoderate in satisfying an appetite or passion; *specif* : given to excessive use of intoxicating liquors ⟨an ~ drinker⟩ **b :** lacking temperance or moderation : EXCESSIVE, INORDINATE, IMMODERATE, VIOLENT ⟨~ language⟩ ⟨~ zeal⟩ ⟨~ attacks⟩ **c :** not mild : EXTREME, INCLEMENT, SEVERE ⟨~ weather⟩ ⟨an ~ zone⟩ — **in·tem·per·ate·ly** *adv* — **in·tem·per·ate·ness** *n*

in·temperature \ən+\ *n* [1*in-* + *temperature*] *n*, *archaic* : distempered state : INTEMPERANCE ⟨this season, the ~ of which may last till the middle of May —Tobias Smollett⟩

in·tem·pes·tive \¦in(,)tem¦pestiv\ *adj* [L *intempestivus*, fr. *in-* 1in- + *tempestivus* tempestive] : UNTIMELY, INOPPORTUNE

in tempo *adv* (*or adj*) [It] : in time : a tempo — used as a direction in music

in·tem·po·ral \(')in-¦temp(ə)rəl, ən-'t-\ *adj* [1*in-* + *temporal*] : transcending temporal relations : TIMELESS ⟨a cruelly abstract and ~ truth —Claude Vigée⟩ — **in·tem·po·ral·ly** \-rəlē\ *adv*

in·tend \ən-'tend\ *vb* -ED/-ING/-S [alter. (influenced by L *in-* 2in-) of ME *entenden*, fr. OF *entendre*, fr. LL *intendere*, fr. L, to intend, attend, stretch out, extend, fr. *in-* 2in- + *tendere* to stretch, stretch out — more at TEND] *vt* **1 a** *archaic* : to understand or construe in a certain manner : APPREHEND, INTERPRET **b** (1) : SIGNIFY, MEAN ⟨what was ~*ed* by that remark⟩ ⟨by teleology is ~*ed* the purposefulness of nature⟩ (2) : to have in mind : have reference to : refer to ⟨this tavern I think must have been the one ~*ed* . . . in his novel —*Notes & Queries*⟩ **2 a** [ME *intenden*, *entenden*, fr. MF *entendre*, fr. L *intendere*] (1) : to have in mind as a design or purpose : PLAN ⟨~*s* to do all in his power⟩ ⟨~ not to retrace the march of occupation in detail —Russell Lord⟩ (2) : to have in mind as an object to be gained or achieved ⟨~*s* that general opulence to which it gives occasion —Adam Smith⟩ ⟨~*ed* the advantage of a great number of people —H.E. Scudder⟩ ⟨~*s* only his own advancement⟩ **b :** to design for or destine to a specified purpose or future ⟨the engravings are not ~*ed* for sale —Mary Zimmer⟩ ⟨~*ed* him to be the next president⟩ **3** *archaic* : to proceed on (one's course or way) **4** [ME *intenden*, *entenden*, fr. L *intendere*] *archaic* **a :** to direct the mind on : attend to : take care of ⟨~*s* his brother's will —George Chapman⟩ **b :** to direct (the eyes) toward something **5** *obs* : ASSERT, MAINTAIN : PRETEND **6** *archaic* : to stretch out or forth : make tense : EXTEND, STRETCH ~ *vi* **1** [ME *entenden*, fr. MF *entendre*] : to have an aim or end in mind ⟨none of our first plans . . . could be carried out as we ~*ed* —R.L.Stevenson⟩ **2** *archaic* **a** [ME *intenden*, *entenden*, fr. L *intendere*] : to direct one's course or way : PROCEED **b :** to start or set out : intend to go or set out

syn INTEND, MEAN, DESIGN, PROPOSE, and PURPOSE can mean to have in mind as an end, aim, or function. INTEND implies that the mind is directed to some definite accomplishment or end, often with determination ⟨*intended* 24 books, sketched 14, but left only four —Gilbert Highet⟩ ⟨did not *intend* annexation of Italian land —Hilaire Belloc⟩ or that, in the mind, one conceives a thing as in a particular occupation or function, serving a given purpose, or carrying a particular meaning ⟨the volume was *intended* for reading in the public schools —Agnes Repplier⟩ ⟨was *intended* for the church —L.O. Howard⟩ ⟨the five- and six-year courses are *intended* for pupils likely to proceed to the university —H.C.Dent⟩ ⟨the meaning of the phrase was not what the writers *intended*⟩ MEAN can come close to the sense of INTEND though it carries a weaker implication of determination, often indicating little more than volition or decision ⟨*mean* to pay back a debt⟩ ⟨put something to a use for which it was not *meant*⟩ ⟨*mean* to go to the movies tonight⟩ DESIGN usu. stresses forethought in arriving at an intention, often implying contriving or scheming ⟨*designs* a companion volume in which she will carry further her discussion —Marjorie Nicolson⟩ ⟨plans we had *designed* to put into effect immediately⟩ ⟨putting a machine to uses for which it was not *designed*⟩ ⟨have no protection against *designing* and dishonest people⟩ PROPOSE implies a clear setting forth, in the mind or before others, of one's intention, connoting clear definition or open avowal ⟨*proposed* to live as if the golden age had come again —Van Wyck Brooks⟩ ⟨*proposes* to give a summary of titles at the end of the work —H.O.Taylor⟩ ⟨*proposed* to carry out the preposterous plan —*Lamp*⟩ ⟨the plan turned out better than he had *proposed* at the committee meeting⟩ PURPOSE differs little from PROPOSE except in implying a stronger determination or clearer intent ⟨*purpose* staying there about a month —Mary W. Shelley⟩ ⟨*purpose* to arrange a typical program in this chapter —W.F.Brown b.1903⟩ ⟨*purpose* to write a history of England —T.B.Macaulay⟩

in·tend·ance \ən-'tendən(t)s\ *n* -S [F, fr. MF, fr. *intendant* + *-ance*] **1 :** the care, control, or management of an office, department, or other public business : SUPERINTENDENCE **2 :** an administrative department esp. of an army; *specif* : an army supply service in some countries (as France)

in·tend·an·cy *also* **in·tend·en·cy** \-dənsē, -si\ *n* -ES [*intendancy* prob. fr. F *intendance* + E *-y*; *intendency* prob. fr. MF *intendance* + E *-ency*] **1 :** the office, function, or employment of an intendant; *also* : a body of intendants **2** *usu* *intendency* [Sp *intendencia*, fr. *intendente*] : a district under an intendant

in·tend·ant \ən-'tendənt\ *n* -S [F, fr. MF, fr. L *intendent-*, *intendens-*, pres. part. of *intendere* to intend, attend — more at INTEND] : a person who has the charge, direction, or management of some public business: as **a :** an administrator of a French province under the centralized system introduced by Richelieu **b :** an administrative officer next to the governor in Canada under French rule **c :** an official in charge of the colonial treasury sometimes having the governorship of the province in various Spanish and Portuguese colonies **d :** a chief administrative official (as governor of a district or mayor of a city) esp. in some Spanish-American countries

1intended *adj* [fr. past part. of *intend*] **1 a :** PROPOSED ⟨the first volume of an ~ series⟩; *specif* : BETROTHED, AFFIANCED ⟨his ~ bride⟩ **b :** INTENTIONAL ⟨an ~ insult⟩ **2** *obs* : EXTENDED, STRAINED — **in·tend·ed·ly** *adv* — **in·tend·ed·ness** *n* -ES

2intended *n* -S : an affianced person : BETROTHED ⟨went to the residence of his ~ —D.D.Martin⟩

in·tend·ence \ən-'tendən(t)s\ *n* -S [*intend* + *-ence*] : ATTENDANCE, ATTENTION

in·ten·den·cia \,in(,)ten'den(t)sēə\ *n* -S [Sp, fr. *intendente*] : the house, office, or administrative area of an intendant in a country of Spanish or Portuguese speech

in·ten·den·te \-'dentē\ *n* -S [Sp, fr. F *intendant*] : an intendant in a country of Spanish or Portuguese speech

in·tend·er \ən-'tendə(r)\ *n* -S : a person who intends

intendiment *n* -S [ML *intendimentum* meaning, interpretation, hidden purpose, fr. L *intendere* to intend, attend + *-mentum* -ment — more at INTEND] *obs* : INTENTION; *also* : ATTENTION

intending *adj* : PROSPECTIVE, ASPIRING ⟨the ~ solicitor has a long and expensive training —T.G.Lund⟩ ⟨~ students⟩

in·tend·ment \ən-'ten(d)mənt\ *n* -S [alter. (influenced by E *intend*) of ME *entendement*, fr. MF, fr. OF, fr. *entendre* to intend + *-ment* — more at INTEND] **1 :** INTENTION, DESIGN, PURPOSE ⟨voted for it . . . because its ~*s* were good —A.J. Beveridge⟩ **2 a :** MEANING, SIGNIFICANCE ⟨acquired further ~ as later men discerned a broader symbolism in them —H.O. Taylor⟩ **b :** the true meaning, understanding, or intention of a law or other legal instrument — compare COMMON INTENDMENT

intends *pres 3d sing of* INTEND

in·ten·er·ate \ən-'tenə,rāt\ *vt* -ED/-ING/-S [2*in-* + L *tener* soft, tender + E *-ate* — more at TENDER] : to make tender or sensitive : SOFTEN ⟨contrives to ~ the granite —R.W.Emerson⟩ — **in·ten·er·a·tion** \ən-,tenə'rāshən\ *n* -S

intens *abbr* intensive

in·ten·sate \ən-'ten,sāt\ *vt* -ED/-ING/-S [*intense* + *-ate*] : INTENSIFY

in·tense \ən-'ten(t)s\ *adj*, *sometimes* -ER/-EST [ME, fr. MF, fr. L *intensus* stretched, tight, intense, fr. *intensus*, past part. of *intendere* to stretch out, intend] **1 a :** existing in a strained or extreme degree : revealed in the height of its distinctive character ⟨an ~ light⟩ ⟨an expression of ~ anxiety —T.B. Costain⟩ ⟨~ cold⟩ **b** *of color* : very deep ⟨dyed an ~ blue⟩ **c :** having or showing its characteristic trait in extreme degree ⟨an ~ sun shone down⟩ ⟨the moon, ~ and white as the snow —Eudora Welty⟩ ⟨~ bright frosty stars —John Masefield⟩ **d :** extremely marked or pronounced : INTENSIVE ⟨rock alteration is ~, leaving few minerals or rocks in their original condition —*Univ. of Ariz. Record*⟩ ⟨a neurodermatitis with ~ itching and burning of the skin —H.G.Armstrong⟩ **e :** very large : CONSIDERABLE ⟨giving off ~ amounts of radiation —Arthur Charlesby⟩ **2 :** strained or straining in or as if in an extreme effort : done or performed with great zeal, energy, or eagerness : highly concentrated ⟨~ study⟩ ⟨a pursuit of learning *intenser* perhaps than any before or since —Ellery Sedgwick⟩ ⟨listened with ~ attention⟩ **3 a** *obs* : INTENT, BENT, RESOLVED — used with *upon* or *about* **b** (1) : feeling deeply esp. by nature or temperament : exhibiting or reflecting strong feeling or earnestness of purpose ⟨my only love, you are so ~ —Edna S. V. Millay⟩ ⟨so ~ in his moral convictions —G.G.Coulton⟩ ⟨~ in everything he does —*Current Biog.*⟩ ⟨an ~ expression on his face⟩ (2) : charged with artistic emotion or intellectual excitement : possessing the quality of artistic tension ⟨his style is ~, eloquent, personal to himself —H.O.Taylor⟩ ⟨painted his most mature and ~ work —*Americas*⟩ (3) : deeply felt ⟨a man of ~ convictions⟩ — **in·tense·ly** *adv* — **in·tense·ness** *n*

in·ten·si·fi·ca·tion \ən-,ten(t)səfə'kāshən\ *n* -S : the act, process, or an instance of intensifying ⟨an ~ of a process that has already been long at work —Barbara Ward⟩

in·ten·si·fi·er \ən-'ten(t)sə,fī(ə)r\ *n* -S : one that intensifies: as **a :** a device (as a two-part cylinder with rigidly connected pistons of different diameters) for stepping up fluid pressure **b :** a photographic intensifying reagent **c :** a gene that enhances the normal effect of another nonallelic gene when both are present **d :** INTENSIVE ⟨words . . . which have been used emotively as ~*s* —William Empson⟩

in·ten·si·fy \-,fī\ *vb* -ED/-ING/-S [*intense* + *-ify*] *vt* **1 :** to make intense or more intensive : STRENGTHEN, INCREASE, DEEPEN ⟨are ~*ing* our sales effort —*Wall Street Jour.*⟩ ⟨~ farming on a wide scale —*Farmer's Weekly (So. Africa)*⟩ **2 a :** to increase the density and contrast of (an image on a photographic film or plate) by treating with any of various reagents that act either by producing an additional deposit or by rendering the original deposit more opaque **b :** to make more acute : SHARPEN ⟨~ still more the resultant problems of health and nutrition —R.W.Steel⟩ ~ *vi* : to become intense or more intense: as **a :** to grow stronger : INCREASE, DEEPEN ⟨within her own narrowed sphere her sympathies seemed to ~ —*McGill News*⟩ **b :** to grow sharper or more acute ⟨the drought has *intensified* and spread —K.S.Davis⟩ ⟨rivalry among the three departments . . . is ~*ing* —*Newsweek*⟩

syn AGGRAVATE, HEIGHTEN, ENHANCE: INTENSIFY indicates a deepening or strengthening until very noticeable or unusually deep or strong ⟨in the lustrous air all colors were *intensified* —Mary Webb⟩ ⟨the depression of the early thirties *intensified* his dissatisfaction with the capitalist system —Granville Hicks⟩ AGGRAVATE, often used in connection with the unpleasant or evil, applies to an increase in seriousness and demand for attention ⟨the external symptoms of decline have served to *aggravate* long existing internal tensions —J.G. Colton⟩ ⟨the din of its two small rooms *aggravated* by the peripheral racket that came from the kitchen —Jean Stafford⟩ HEIGHTEN may suggest a lifting above the ordinary or accustomed ⟨a painter discards many trivial points of exactness, in order to *heighten* the truthfulness of a few fundamentals —C.E.Montague⟩ ⟨a dramatic incident may *heighten* the popular indignation that leads toward war —Dexter Perkins⟩ ENHANCE suggests a lifting or strengthening above normal, esp. in attractiveness, desirability, or value ⟨the charm of this wild land is *enhanced* by the presence of deer and the famous forest ponies —S.P.B.Mais⟩ ⟨a blue serge suit freshly pressed which *enhanced* the impression he gave of neatness and cleanliness —Henry Miller⟩ ⟨the political prestige of the C.I.O. was *enhanced* by the election —*Collier's Yr. Bk.*⟩

intensifying screen *n* : a fluorescent screen placed usu. on each side of an X-ray photographic film so as to augment the direct effect of the X rays between two such screens

in·ten·sion \ən-'tenchən\ *n* -S [L *intension-*, *intensio*, fr. *intensus* (past part. of *intendere* to stretch forth) + *-ion-*, *-io* -ion — more at INTEND] **1** *archaic* : an act of straining, stretching, or bending : TENSION **2 a :** degree or marked degree (as of a quality) : INTENSITY **b :** increase of power or energy : INTENSIFICATION **c :** strong or energetic exercise (as of the mind) : INTENTNESS, DETERMINATION **3 :** CONNOTATION 3 ⟨the ~ of "*triangle*" implies or includes that of "plane figure"⟩ — contrasted with *extension*

in·ten·sion·al \-chənᵊl, -chnəl\ *adj* : of, relating to, or marked by intension; *specif* : CONNOTATIVE ⟨literature works by ~ means . . . by the manipulation of the informative and affective connotations of words —S.I.Hayakawa⟩ — **in·ten·sion·al·ly** \-ᵊlē, -əlē, -i\ *adv*

in·ten·si·tom·e·ter \ən-,ten(t)sə'tämədə(r)\ *n* [*intensito-* (fr. *intensity*) + *-meter*] : an instrument for measuring the intensity of X rays

in·ten·si·ty \ən-'ten(t)səd-ē, -ətē, -i\ *n* -ES [*intense* + *-ity*] **1 :** the quality or state of being intense: as **a :** extreme or very high degree : extreme strength, force, or energy ⟨the ~ of the sun's rays⟩ ⟨the ~ and accuracy of this fire —S.L.A.Marshall⟩ ⟨strikingly signalizes the ~ of the hope —Bernard De Voto⟩ ⟨rains of unparalleled ~ —W.E.Swinton⟩ **b :** extreme depth of feeling : passionate quality : extreme sensibility ⟨her ~, which would leave no emotion on a normal plane —D.H. Lawrence⟩ ⟨the most striking feature . . . is the ~ of his nature —R.A.Hall b.1911⟩ ⟨instinctively kept to ~, knowing that without passion no art can live —Louise Bogan⟩ **c :** the quality of aesthetic or intellectual emotion or excitement : compactness of artistic statement or expression : artistic tension ⟨lacks the ~ and the profundity that the greatest poetry has —R.A.Hall b.1911⟩ ⟨with ~ the poem may survive anything — even archaic language —J.P.Bishop⟩ ⟨compressed into poetic ~ . . . instead of sprawling forth sloppy, formless, and diffuse —Peter Viereck⟩ ⟨a painting of dramatic ~⟩ ⟨impress their poetry with density and ~, cutting out irrelevancies and long-windedness —Mary M. Colum⟩ **d :** depth of conviction ⟨his voice was hoarse with the ~ of his belief —Irwin Shaw⟩ **e :** strenuousness of effort or application : ENERGY ⟨the campaign was waged with great ~ by both parties⟩ **2 :** the degree or amount of a quality or condition: as **a :** the relative loudness or softness of a tone or a tonal effect **b :** the energy with which air is propelled through the vocal tract in articulating : LOUDNESS **c :** a specified measure of the effect of certain physical agencies expressed as the magnitude of force or energy per unit (as of surface, charge, or mass) — see ELECTRIC INTENSITY, GRAVITATIONAL INTENSITY, LUMINOUS INTENSITY, MAGNETIC INTENSITY, RADIANT INTENSITY, SOUND INTENSITY; compare LUMINOUS-FLUX DENSITY, RADIANT-FLUX DENSITY **d :** SATURATION 4a **e :** a measure of the magnitude of an earthquake **f :** intensive quality : INTENSIVENESS ⟨carried on agriculture with varying degrees of ~ —A.C.Parker⟩ **g :** the vivacity or strength of a sensation ⟨his shame reached a high degree of ~⟩ **h :** cultural vigor esp. of a primitive people as expressed in quantity of cultural content and complexity and interrelations of cultural patterns ⟨a contrast in the . . . ~ of cultural systems —E.H. Spicer⟩ **3 :** an instance of intense quality, condition, or experience ⟨the *intensities*, the moments of feeling and depths of experience that constitute the fundamental part of living —Leon Edel⟩

intensity modulation *n* : modulation in which the brightness of the light displayed on a cathode-ray tube varies with the intensity of the signal

intensity of light : LUMINOUS-FLUX DENSITY

intensity of magnetization : MAGNETIZATION

intensity of radiation : RADIANT-FLUX DENSITY

1in·ten·sive \(')in-¦ten(t)siv, ən-'t-, -sēv *also* -səv\ *adj* [prob. fr. MF *intensif*, fr. ML *intensivus*, fr. L *intensus* intense, stretched + *-ivus* -ive — more at INTENSE] **1** *obs* : INTENSE, VEHEMENT **2 :** of, relating to, or marked by intensity or intensification: as **a :** highly concentrated : ZEALOUS, EAGER, EXHAUSTIVE ⟨~ study⟩ ⟨~ effort⟩ **b :** INTENSIFYING; *esp* : tending to give force or emphasis ⟨an ~ adverb, as *dreadfully* in "it was *dreadfully* cold"⟩ **c** (1) : constituting or relating to a method of cultivation of land designed to increase the productivity of a given area by the expenditure of more capital and labor upon it — opposed to *extensive* (2) : constituting or relating to the method of conducting an industry so as to increase its returns by perfecting its methods and appliances rather than by enlarging its scale **d :** relating to intension **e :** involving the use of large doses or substances having great therapeutic activity **f :** presenting a large and concentrated amount of material to be studied intensely ⟨~ course⟩ ⟨~ training⟩ ⟨~ program⟩ — **in·ten·sive·ly** \-səvlē, -li\ *adv* — **in·ten·sive·ness** \-sivnəs, -sēv- *also* -səv-\ *n* -ES

²intensive \"\ *n* -s **:** an intensive linguistic element (as a word, particle, or prefix)
intensive pronoun *n* **1 :** a pronoun that emphasizes a preceding noun or another pronoun (as *itself* in "borrowing is itself a bad habit") **2 :** a personal pronoun compounded with *-self* and used in apposition with a noun or pronoun or as pronominal adjunct (as *itself* in "the cat looked innocence itself" or *himself* in "he made it himself")
intensive proposition *n* **:** a proposition stating a relation of intension between concepts or one whose meaning is to be understood in intension
¹in·tent \ən·ˈtent\ *n* -s [alter. (influenced by L *in-* ²in-) of ME *entent, entente;* ME *entent,* fr. OF, fr. LL *intentus* aim, purpose, intent, fr. L, act of stretching out, fr. *intentus,* past part. of *intendere* to stretch out, intend; ME *entente,* fr. OF, fr. L *intentus* (past part.) — more at INTEND] **1 a** (1) **:** the act, fact, or an instance of intending **:** PURPOSE, DESIGN ⟨suspect him of hostile ~ —S.M.Crothers⟩ ⟨came with ~ to kill⟩ (2) **:** the design or purpose to commit any wrongful or criminal act that is the natural and probable consequence of other voluntary acts or conduct (3) **:** the state of mind or mental attitude with which an act is done **:** VOLITION **b :** an end or object proposed **:** AIM ⟨used his leisure time to good ~⟩ **2 a :** MEANING, PURPORT, IMPORT, SIGNIFICANCE ⟨paraphrase in speech the ~ of the communication —Edward Sapir⟩; *specif* **:** INTENDMENT 2b **b :** the connotation of a term **syn** see INTENTION — **to all intents and purposes** *also* **to all intents** *or* **to all intent and purpose :** in all applications or senses **:** PRACTICALLY, REALLY, VIRTUALLY ⟨the process is *to all intents and purposes* identical with that practiced today —A.C.Morrison⟩
²intent \"\ *adj* [L *intentus,* fr. past part. of *intendere* to stretch forth] **1 :** directed with strained or eager attention **:** CONCENTRATED, EARNEST, INTENSE ⟨a gaze so ~ that the girl flushed a little —P.B.Kyne⟩ ⟨his face was ~ as he examined each picture —Lyle Saxon⟩ **2 a** (1) **:** having the mind or attention closely or fixedly directed on something **:** PREOCCUPIED, ENGROSSED ⟨the two men, ~ on their figures, did not notice —Sherwood Anderson⟩ ⟨still too ~ upon his own thoughts —W.M.Thackeray⟩ ⟨so ~ on this fantastic . . . narrative that she had hardly stirred —Walter de la Mare⟩ (2) **:** reflecting or evidencing strained or concentrated attention or preoccupation ⟨her forehead was painfully anxious and ~ as she gave this evidence —Charles Dickens⟩ **b :** having the mind or will concentrated on some end or purpose **:** DETERMINED, RESOLVED, BENT ⟨a selfish interest ~ upon privilege for itself —H.J.Laski⟩ ⟨~ upon making his way in the corporation —Lee Rogow⟩ ⟨~ that we should have a week of climbing —E.A.Weeks⟩
in·ten·tion \ən·ˈtenchən\ *n* -s [ME *entencioun, intencioun,* fr. MF & L; MF *entention, intention,* fr. OF, fr. L *intention-, intentio,* lit., act of stretching out, fr. *intentus* (past part.) + *-ion-, -io* -ion] **1 a** (1) **:** an act of intending **:** RESOLVE ⟨announced its ~ to divide its Indian Empire into two dominions —*Current Biog.*⟩ ⟨certainly had no ~ of doing so —Rose Macaulay⟩ (2) **intentions** *pl* **:** purpose with respect to marriage ⟨inquired concerning the young man's ~s toward his daughter⟩ (3) **:** a written or printed statement of intention ⟨filed his ~ to run for mayor⟩ **b** (1) **:** the will to administer a sacrament in the form and spirit prescribed by the Roman Catholic Church (2) **:** the will to apply the benefits of a mass or prayers to a particular person or purpose; *also* **:** the person or purpose contemplated **c** (1) *Roman law* **:** the part of a formula in which the plaintiff's claims and the defendant's defenses are stated (2) *old English law* **:** a declaration in a real action **2 :** an intended object **:** AIM, END ⟨complete and final victory was his ~⟩ ⟨his ~ (the intended significance of the poem) . . . and what he actually contrives as a poet to do, conflict —F.R.Leavis⟩ **3 :** the import or meaning of something **:** something that is conveyed or intended to be conveyed to the understanding **:** SIGNIFICANCE ⟨shook his head with a double ~ —James Joyce⟩ **4 a** *archaic* (1) **:** strenuous mental application **:** close attention (2) **:** the act or an instance of straining or tensing (as the eye) **b :** a concept or notion; *esp* **:** a concept considered as the product of attention directed to an object of knowledge — see FIRST INTENTION, SECOND INTENTION **5 :** a process or manner of healing of incised wounds — see FIRST INTENTION, SECOND INTENTION
syn INTENT, PURPOSE, DESIGN, AIM, END, OBJECT, OBJECTIVE, GOAL: INTENTION simply indicates what one proposes to do or accomplish ⟨the main *intention* of the poem has been to make dramatically visible the conflict —Allen Tate⟩ ⟨it was Buchanan's *intention* that his administration should be chiefly characterized by a vigorous foreign policy —C.R.Fish⟩ INTENT may imply more deliberate and clear formulation ⟨to tell a lie, also, with *intent* to deceive was a serious offense —Havelock Ellis⟩ ⟨the clear *intent* of the Taft-Hartley law's provision on secondary boycotts —*Wall Street Jour.*⟩ PURPOSE can apply to what one proposes with resolution and determination ⟨the missionary was here for a *purpose,* and he pressed his point —Willa Cather⟩ ⟨writing her excellent period stories for girls, Elizabeth Howard has a well-defined *purpose* in view —*Current Biog.*⟩ DESIGN may suggest careful ordering, calculating, or scheming ⟨that sense of inherent *design* that characterizes the English or the Russian novel —J.A.Michener⟩ ⟨the TVA is substituting order and *design* for haphazard, unplanned, and unintegrated development —*Amer. Guide Series: Tenn.*⟩ ⟨to keep this strategic peninsula out of the hands of any power which might harbor aggressive *designs* —C.A. Fisher⟩ AIM may imply clear and definite singleness of purpose or intention ⟨the theoretical understanding of the world, which is the *aim* of philosophy —Bertrand Russell⟩ ⟨the next *aim* of the company was to secure the St. Louis and Missouri river trade —Grace L. Nute⟩ END stresses intended effect and may subordinate or contrast with notions of means ⟨the final *end* of government is not to exert restraint but to do good —Rufus Choate⟩ ⟨He knows us and our true *end* is to know Him —J.A.Pike⟩ OBJECT is closely synonymous with END but may be used for more individually determined desires or intentions to accomplish ⟨my *object* all sublime I shall achieve in time — to let the punishment fit the crime —W.S.Gilbert⟩ ⟨the *object* of this society is to elevate the architectural profession as such —*Amer. Institute of Architects*⟩ OBJECTIVE may be used in relation to that which is quite concrete and tangible and immediately attainable ⟨getting the child to want to write is the new-style teacher's first *objective* —John Haverstick⟩ ⟨to fight wars of limited *objective* and to make moderate and reasonable peace settlements —W.H.Chamberlin⟩ GOAL may indicate that which is attained by struggle and endurance of hardship ⟨the achievement of understanding, which is man's highest *goal* —Ida C. Merriam⟩ ⟨could not help thinking that this was my *goal,* that I had been brought to this spot with a purpose, that in this wild and solitary retreat some tremendous adventure was about to befall me —W.H.Hudson †1922⟩
in·ten·tion·al \-chənᵊl, -chnəl\ *adj* [ML *intentionalis,* fr. L *intention-, intentio* intention, attention + *-alis* -al] **1 :** relating to intention or design **:** having an intention ⟨deeply ~ in its message —Fanny Butcher⟩ **2 :** done by intention or design **:** INTENDED, DESIGNED ⟨~ damage⟩ **3 a :** of, relating to, or based on intention (sense 4b) or particular conception of intention ⟨a simple categorical statement (for example, "Parsifal sought the Holy Grail") is ~ if it uses a substantival expression (in this instance, "the Holy Grail") without implying either that there is or there isn't anything to which the expression truly applies —R.M.Chisholm⟩ **b :** referring or pointing beyond itself ⟨the ~ structure of consciousness —Hannah Arendt⟩ **syn** see VOLUNTARY
intentional fallacy *n* **:** the fallacy that the value or meaning of a work of art (as a poem) may be judged or defined in terms of the artist's intention
in·ten·tion·al·ism \-ᵊlˌizəm, -əˌli-\ *n* -s [ISV *intentional* + *-ism*] **:** ACT PSYCHOLOGY
in·ten·tion·al·i·ty \ən·ˌtenchəˈnaləd·ē\ *n* -ES [ML *intentionalitat-, intentionalitas,* fr. *intentionalis* intentional + L *-itat-, -itas* -ity] **:** the quality or state of being intentional; *specif* **:** the characteristic of being conscious of intending an object ⟨three forms of ~ or objective reference, idea, judgment, and desire —Vivian J. McGill⟩
in·ten·tion·al·ly \ən·ˈtenchənᵊlē, -chnəlē, -i\ *adv* **:** in an intentional manner **:** with intention **:** PURPOSELY ⟨~ vague and misleading language⟩
intentional object *n* **:** something whether actually existing or not that the mind thinks about **:** a referent of consciousness — compare PHENOMENOLOGY
intentional pass *n* **:** the act or an instance of deliberately walking a batter in baseball
intentional species *n* **:** mental images or forms produced by sensation and cognition — compare SPECIES
in·ten·tioned \ən·ˈtenchənd\ *adj* **:** having intentions of a specified kind ⟨seriously ~ radio work —Leslie Rees⟩ — often used in combination ⟨justify a well-*intentioned* lie —Lucius Garvin⟩
in·ten·tion·less \ən·ˈtenchənləs\ *adj* **:** being without intention
intentions *pl of* INTENTION
intention tremor *n* **:** a slow tremor of the extremities that increases on attempted voluntary movement and is observed in certain diseases (as multiple sclerosis) of the nervous system
in·ten·tive \ən·ˈtentiv\ *adj* [alter. (influenced by L *in-* ²in-) of ME *ententif,* fr. OF, fr. LL *intentivus* intensive, fr. L *intentus* (past part. of *intendere* to intend, attend) + *-ivus* -ive — more at INTEND] **:** ATTENTIVE, INTENT — **in·ten·tive·ly** \-əvlē\ *adv* — **in·ten·tive·ness** \-ivnəs\ *n* -ES
in·tent·ly *adv* **:** in an intent manner
in·tent·ness *n* -ES **:** the quality or state of being intent
intents *pl of* INTENT
in·ter *R* ən·ˈtər, + *vowel* -tər·; *-R* -tə̄, + *suffixal vowel* -tər· *also* -tə̄r, + *vowel in a following word* -tər· *or* -tə̄ *also* -tə̄r\ *vt* **interred; interred; interring; inters** [alter. (influenced by L *in-* ²in-) of ME *enteren,* fr. MF *enterrer,* fr. OF, fr. (assumed) VL *interrare,* fr. L *in-* ²in- + L *terra* earth — more at TERRACE] **1 :** to deposit (a dead body) in the earth or in a grave or tomb **:** BURY, INHUME ⟨the good is oft *interred* with their bones —Shak.⟩ **2** *obs* **:** to enclose the dead body of **3** *obs* **:** to put in the ground **:** cover with earth
inter- *prefix* [ME *inter-, entre-, enter-;* ME *inter-,* fr. MF & L; MF, fr. L, fr. *inter;* ME *entre-,* fr. OF, fr. L *inter-;* ME *enter-,* fr. MF & L; MF *entre-,* fr. OF, fr. L *inter-;* akin to OHG *untar* between, among, ON *ithrar,* pl., intestines, OIr *etar, eter* between, among, Gk *enteron* intestine, Skt *antar* between, within, in, and OE *in* — more at IN] **1 :** between, among, in the midst ⟨*inter*mediate⟩ ⟨*inter*polar⟩ ⟨*inter*space⟩ **2 :** mutual, reciprocal ⟨*inter*marry⟩ ⟨*inter*mesh⟩ ⟨*inter*relation⟩ ⟨*inter*twine⟩ **3 :** between or among the parts of ⟨*inter*costal⟩ ⟨*inter*dental⟩ **4 :** carried on between ⟨*inter*collegiate⟩ ⟨*inter*communication⟩ ⟨*inter*national⟩ **5 :** occurring between **:** intervening ⟨*inter*glacial⟩ ⟨*inter*tidal⟩ **6 :** shared by or derived from two or more ⟨*inter*departmental⟩ ⟨*inter*faith⟩ **7 :** between the limits of **:** within ⟨*inter*tropical⟩
inter *abbr* **1** intermediate **2** interrogative
in·ter·academic \ˌintə(r)+\ *adj* [*inter-* + *academic*] **:** among or between or common to schools, colleges, or universities ⟨~ exchanges⟩ ⟨~ courtesies⟩
in·ter·acinous \"+\ *also* **in·ter·acinar** \"+\ *adj* [*interacinous* fr. *inter-* + *acinous; interacinar* fr. *interacinous* + *-ar*] **:** situated between or among the acini of a gland
¹in·ter·act \ˈintəˌ(r)akt\ *n* [*inter-* + *act;* intended as trans. of F *entr'acte*] **:** ENTR'ACTE ⟨a mask proper was closely associated with an early Tudor play as an afterpiece rather than as an ~ —E.K.Chambers⟩
²in·ter·act \ˌ==ˈ=\ *vi* [*inter-* + *act*] **:** to act upon each other **:** have reciprocal effect or influence ⟨required many generations of ~*ing* human beings to make such discoveries and inventions —P.A.Sorokin⟩
in·ter·ac·tant \-ktənt\ *n* -s [²*interact* + *-ant*] **:** one that interacts; *specif* **:** one of two or more substances taking part in a chemical reaction **:** REACTANT
in·ter·ac·tion \ˌintəˈ(r)akshən\ *n* **1 :** mutual or reciprocal action or influence ⟨~ of the heart and lungs⟩ ⟨~ of an individual with his social environment⟩ ⟨~ admits causal action between physical events, between mental events, and also between mental and physical events —Vivian J. McGill⟩ **2 :** a measure of how much the effect of one statistical variable upon another is determined by the values of one or more other variables
in·ter·ac·tion·al \-shənᵊl, -shnəl\ *adj* **:** of or relating to interaction or to a theory of interaction ⟨~ ecology⟩ — **interactionally** *adv*
in·ter·ac·tion·ism \-shəˌnizəm\ *n* -s **1 :** a theory that mind and body are distinct and interact causally upon one another — compare DOUBLE-ASPECT THEORY, PSYCHOPHYSICAL PARALLELISM **2 :** a theory that derives social processes (conflict, competition, cooperation) from human interaction
in·ter·ac·tion·ist \-ˌnəst\ *n* **:** a proponent of interactionism
in·ter·active \ˌintə(r)+\ *adj* [*inter-* + *active*] **1 :** mutually or reciprocally active **2 :** INTERACTIONAL
in·ter·activity \"+\ *n* **:** the fact or process of interacting
in·ter·adaptation \"+\ *n* [*inter-* + *adaptation*] **:** mutual adaptation
¹in·ter·agency \"+\ *n* [*inter-* + *agency*] **:** the action or function of an intermediary
²interagency \"\ *adj* [*inter-* + *agency* (n.)] **:** involving two or more public or government agencies ⟨~ dispute⟩ ⟨~ committee⟩
in·ter·agent \"+\ *n* [*inter-* + *agent*] **:** an intermediate agent **:** INTERMEDIARY
in·ter alia \ˌintəˈ(r)ālēə, -lyə\ *adv* [L] **:** among other things ⟨the commission recommended, *inter alia,* that:⟩ ⟨rate of progress will depend upon, *inter alia,* the number of . . . engineers available —L.L.Goodman⟩
inter ali·os \-lēˌōs\ *adv* [L] **:** among other persons
in·ter·allied \ˌintə(r)+\ *also* **in·ter·ally** \"+\ *adj* [*inter-* + *allied* (adj.) *or ally* (n.)] **:** involving or relating to all or a number of allies ⟨British policy on both German reparations and *Interallied* debts —*Atlantic*⟩ ⟨~ agreement⟩
in·ter·ambulacral \"+\ *adj* [*inter-* + *ambulacral*] **:** situated between ambulacra
in·ter·ambulacrum \"+\ *n* [NL, fr. *inter-* + *ambulacrum*] **:** one of the areas between two ambulacra in an echinoderm
in·ter-american \"+\ *adj, usu cap A* **:** involving or concerning some or all of the nations of No. and So. America ⟨~ affairs⟩ ⟨~ treaties⟩
in·ter·am·ni·an \ˌintəˈ(r)amnēən\ *adj* [LL *interamnus* interamnian (fr. L *inter-* + *amnis* river) + E *-ian*] **:** situated between or enclosed by rivers
in·ter·animate \ˌintə(r)+\ *vt* [*inter-* + *animate*] **:** to animate mutually ⟨love with one another so ~s two souls —John Donne⟩
in·ter·animation \"+\ *n* **:** mutual animation
in·ter·articular \"+\ *adj* [*inter-* + *articular*] **:** situated between articulating surfaces ⟨~ cartilage⟩
in·ter·association \"+\ *n* [*inter-* + *association*] **:** mutual association **:** INTERRELATION ⟨~ of sense perceptions⟩
in·ter·astral \"+\ *adj* [*inter-* + *astral*] **:** situated or occurring between or among stars
in·ter·atomic \"+\ *adj* [*inter-* + *atomic*] **:** situated or acting between atoms ⟨~ forces⟩
in·ter·atrial \"+\ *adj* [*inter-* + *atrial*] **:** situated between the atria of the heart ⟨~ septum⟩
in·ter·aural \"+\ *adj* [*inter-* + *aural*] **:** situated between or connecting the ears ⟨~ plane⟩
in·ter·availability \"+\ *n* [*inter-* + *availability*] *Brit* **:** availability mutually extended throughout a specified system or grouping
in·ter·axial \"+\ *also* **in·ter·axal** \"+\ *adj* [NL *interaxis* + *-ial or -al*] **:** lying between the axes ⟨~ space in an architectural plan⟩
in·ter·axillary \"+\ *adj* [*inter-* + *axillary*] **:** situated within or between the axils of leaves
in·ter·axis \"+\ *n* [NL, fr. L *inter-* + *axis*] **:** the space between two axes (as of a building plan)
in·ter·balance \"+\ *vt* [*inter-* + *balance*] **:** to balance mutually or reciprocally **:** achieve mutual balance among ⟨intricate *interbalancing* of lead, glass, and stone —M.W.Baldwin⟩
in·ter·banded \"+\ *adj* [*inter-* + *banded*] **:** deposited in alternating layers of different materials ⟨~ quartz and galena⟩
in·ter·bank \"+\ *adj* [*inter-* + *bank* (n.)] **:** involving two or more banks ⟨~ deposits⟩ ⟨~ relations⟩
¹in·ter·bed \"+\ *vb* [*inter-* + *bed*] **:** INTERSTRATIFY
²in·ter·bed \ˈintə(r)ˌbed\ *n* **:** a typically thin layer of one kind of sedimentary material between layers of another kind
in·ter·behavior \"+\ *n* [*inter-* + *behavior*] **:** interaction between two or more individuals **:** social behavior — **in·ter·behavioral** *adj*
in·ter·bel·la \ˌintə(r)ˈbelə\ *or* **interbel·lum** \-ləm\ *adj* [NL, fr. L *inter* between, among + *bella* (pl. of *bellum* war) or *bellum* — more at INTER-, BELLICOSE] **:** extending or occurring between wars ⟨~ period⟩ ⟨*interbellum* generation of writers⟩
in·ter·blend \ˌintə(r)+\ *vb* [*inter-* + *blend*] **:** to blend together **:** INTERMINGLE, COMMINGLE
in·ter·bonding \"+\ *n* [*inter-* + *bonding,* gerund of *bond*] **:** a bonding together ⟨~ of concrete and rock⟩
in·ter·borough \"+\ *adj* [*inter-* + *borough*] **:** relating to, situated in, or operating between two or more boroughs ⟨~ subway system⟩
in·ter·bourse \"+\ *adj* [*inter-* + *bourse* (n.)] **:** issued simultaneously in different countries ⟨~ securities⟩
in·ter·brain \ˈintə(r)+ˌ-\ *n* [*inter-* + *brain*] **:** DIENCEPHALON
in·ter·branch \ˌintə(r)+\ *adj* [*inter-* + *branch* (n.)] **:** occurring between branches ⟨~ rivalry in the armed forces⟩
in·ter·breed \"+\ *vb* [*inter-* + *breed*] *vi* **:** to breed together: as **a :** CROSSBREED **b :** to breed within a closed population **:** INBREED ~ *vt* **:** to cause (individuals or groups) to breed together
in·ter·ca·lary \ən·ˈtərkəˌlerē, -tə̄k-, -təik-, -ri, ˌintə(r)ˈkal(ə)r-\ *adj* [L *intercalarius,* fr. *intercalare* to intercalate + *-arius* -ary; influenced also by L *intercalaris* intercalary, fr. *intercalare* + *-aris* -ar] **1 a** *of a day or month* **:** inserted in a calendar by intercalation **:** INTERCALATED **b** *of a year* **:** containing an intercalary period **2 :** inserted or introduced between the usual or original elements or components **:** INTERPOLATED ⟨~ matter in a text⟩ ⟨~ tissue in a plant⟩ ⟨~ line in a poem⟩
intercalary meristem *n* **:** a meristem developing between regions of mature or permanent tissue (as at the base of the grass leaf) — compare APICAL MERISTEM, LATERAL MERISTEM
in·ter·ca·late \ən·ˈtərkəˌlāt, -tə̄k-, -təik-, *usu* -ād·+V\ *vt* -ED/-ING/-S [L *intercalatus,* past part. of *intercalare,* fr. *inter-* + *calare* to call, summon — more at LOW] **1 :** to insert (as a day or month) in a calendar by intercalation **2 :** to insert between or among existing elements **:** INTERPOLATE ⟨~ a vowel into a cluster of consonants⟩ ⟨stories *intercalated* into a narrative⟩ **3 :** to insert (as a sheet of lava) between layers or beds of other rock **:** INTERSTRATIFY — usu. used in the past part.
in·ter·ca·la·tion \=,==ˈlāshən\ *n* -s [MF or L; MF, fr. L *intercalation-, intercalatio,* fr. *intercalatus* (past part.) + *-ion-, -io* -ion] **1 a :** the insertion of one or more days at regular intervals in a calendar in order to bring it into accord with the solar year **b :** a period so inserted **2 a :** the insertion or introduction of something among other existing or original things **b :** something that is so inserted ⟨the poet was reluctant to vary the metrical arrangement of the poem to accommodate an ~ —A.K.Moore⟩ **3 :** the introduction or existence of a bed or layer between other layers or of a particular fossil horizon between fossil zones of different character; *also* **:** an intercalated bed or lenticular deposit ⟨a few lenses of volcanic ash are present as ~s⟩
in·tercameral \ˌintə(r)+\ *adj* **:** occurring between two chambers of a legislature ⟨~ deadlock⟩
in·ter·capillary \"+\ *adj* [*inter-* + *capillary*] **:** situated between capillaries
¹in·ter·cardinal \"+\ *n* [*inter-* + *cardinal*] **:** an intercardinal point of the compass ⟨~s are four points from the cardinals and eight points from one another —H.A.Calahan⟩
²intercardinal \"\ *adj* **:** lying midway between the cardinal points ⟨~ points of the compass⟩
in·ter·carotid body \"+...-\ *n* [*inter-* + *carotid*] **:** CAROTID BODY
in·ter·carpal \"+\ *adj* [*inter-* + *carpal*] **:** situated between carpal bones
in·ter·cartilaginous ossification \"+...-\ *n* [*inter-* + *cartilaginous*] **:** ENDOCHONDRAL OSSIFICATION
in·ter·caste \"+\ *adj* [*inter-* + *caste* (n.)] **:** existing between or involving two or more castes ⟨~ education⟩ ⟨~ mobility⟩
in·ter·catenated \"+\ *adj* [*inter-* + *catenated,* past part. of *catenate*] **:** chained or linked together ⟨~ ideas⟩
in·ter·cavernous \"+\ *adj* [*inter-* + *cavernous*] **:** situated between and connecting the cavernous sinuses behind and in front of the pituitary body ⟨~ sinus⟩
in·ter·cede \ˌintə(r)ˈsēd\ *vi* [L *intercedere,* fr. *inter-* + *cedere* to move, go — more at CEDE] **1** *obs* **a :** to get in the way **:** INTERVENE **b :** to come or lie esp. in time or space **2 :** to act between parties with a view to reconciling differences **:** to beg or plead in behalf of another **:** MEDIATE ⟨the Western powers would not ~ in behalf of the people —N.S.Timasheff⟩ ⟨she it was who *interceded* for the old woman with her uncle —Hilaire Belloc⟩
in·ter·ced·er \-də(r)\ *n* **:** one that intercedes
in·ter·cellular \ˌintə(r)+\ *adj* [*inter-* + *cellular*] **:** lying between cells ⟨~ space in plant tissue⟩ ⟨~ canals in lumber⟩
intercellular substance *n* **:** MIDDLE LAMELLA
in·ter·cen·sal \"+ˈsen(t)səl\ *adj* [*inter-* + *census* + *-al*] **:** occurring between censuses ⟨~ study⟩ ⟨~ figures⟩
in·ter·central \"+\ *adj* [*inter-* + *central*] **1 :** lying or extending between centers ⟨~ nerve fibers⟩ **2** [NL *intercentrum* + E *-al*] **:** of or relating to an intercentrum
in·ter·centrum \"+\ *n* [NL, fr. *inter-* + *centrum*] **1 :** an element of the vertebral column alternating with the true centra of the vertebrae in several different classes of vertebrates **2 :** HYPOCENTRUM **3 :** one of the ossified intervertebral disks characteristic of certain mammals
¹in·ter·cept \ˌintə(r)ˈsept\ *vt* -ED/-ING/-S [L *interceptus,* past part. of *intercipere,* fr. *inter-* + *-cipere* (fr. *capere* to take, seize) — more at HEAVE] **1 :** to take, seize, or stop by the way or before arrival at the destined place **:** stop or interrupt the progress or course of ⟨~ a letter⟩ ⟨telegram will ~ him at Paris⟩ ⟨~ a forward pass⟩ ⟨~ an attacking bomber⟩ **2** *obs* **:** to stop or prevent from doing something **:** HINDER ⟨who ~s me in my expedition —Shak.⟩ **3** *obs* **:** to interrupt communication or connection with ⟨while storms vindictive ~ the shore —Alexander Pope⟩ **4 :** to include (part of a curve, surface, or solid) between two points, curves, or surfaces ⟨the part of a circumference ~*ed* between two radii⟩
²in·ter·cept \ˈ==,=\ *n* -s **1 :** a part intercepted; *specif* **:** the part of a coordinate axis included between the origin and the point where a graph crosses the axis **2 :** an interception of a ball passed or thrown by an opponent (as in lacrosse) **3 :** a picked-up code or message (as one sent by radio)
in·ter·cept·er \ˌ==ˈseptə(r)\ *n* -s **:** INTERCEPTOR
in·ter·cep·tion \-pshən\ *n* -s [MF or L; MF, fr. L *interception-, interceptio,* fr. *interceptus* (past part.) + *-ion-, -io* -ion] **1 :** the act of intercepting or state of being intercepted ⟨~ of vital information to and from enemy agents —*All Hands*⟩ ⟨rushing skyward like a fighter going up on an ~ —Terrence Horsley⟩ **2 :** an intercepted segment **:** INTERCEPT
in·ter·cep·tive \ˌ==ˈseptiv\ *adj* [¹*intercept* + *-ive*] **:** tending to intercept
in·ter·cep·tor \ˌ==ˈ=tə(r)\ *n* -s [L, fr. *interceptus* (past part.) + *-or*] **:** one that intercepts: as **a :** a device for preventing the entrance of solid matter, grease, or other material into a drain subject to clogging **b :** a light high-speed fast-climbing fighter plane designed for defense against raiding bombers
in·ter·cerebral \ˌintə(r)+\ *adj* [*inter-* + *cerebral*] **:** situated between the cerebral hemispheres
in·ter·ces·sion \ˌintə(r)ˈseshən\ *n* -s [MF or L; MF, fr. L *intercession-, intercessio* intervention, act of becoming surety, interposition of a veto, fr. *intercessus* (past part. of *intercedere* to intervene, become surety) + *-ion-, -io* -ion — more at INTERCEDE] **1 a :** the act of interceding **:** interposition between parties at variance with a view to reconciliation **:** MEDIATION **b :** prayer, petition, or entreaty in favor of another **2** *Roman & civil law* **:** assumption of liability for the debt of another either by substitution or by the addition of a new debtor or surety — compare ADPROMISSION, CUMULATIVE INTERCESSION, EXPROMISSION, FIDEJUSSION
in·ter·ces·sion·al \ˌ==ˈseshənᵊl, -shnəl\ *adj* **:** relating to or characterized by intercession or entreaty
in·ter·ces·sive \ˌ==ˈsesiv\ *adj* [L *intercessus* (past part.) + E *-ive*] **:** INTERCESSORY
in·ter·ces·sor \ˌ==ˈsesə(r)\ *n* -s [ME *intercessour,* fr. MF & L; MF *intercesseur,* fr. L *intercessor,* fr. *intercessus* (past part.) + *-or*] **1 :** one who intercedes **:** MEDIATOR **2 :** a bishop who

during a vacancy of the see administers the bishopric till a successor is installed

in·ter·ces·so·ri·al \ˌintə(r)sə¦sōrēəl, -sȯr-\ *adj* **:** of or belonging to an intercessor

in·ter·ces·so·ry \ˌintə(r)¦ses(ə)rē, -ri\ *adj* [ML *intercessorius*, fr. L *intercessus* (past part. of *intercedere* to intercede) + *-orius* -ory — more at INTERCEDE] **:** relating to or marked by intercession ⟨~ prayer⟩

interchain *vt* [*inter-* + *chain*] *obs* **:** to link together

[1]**in·ter·change** \ˌintə(r)¦chānj\ *vb* [alter. (influenced by L *inter-*) of ME *entrechaungen*, fr. MF *entrechangier*, fr. OF, fr. *entre-* inter- + *changier* to change — more at CHANGE] *vt* **1 :** to put each of (two things) in the place of the other ⟨~ two tires⟩ **2 :** to give and take mutually ⟨~ blows⟩ ⟨~ ideas⟩ ⟨~ goods⟩ **3** *archaic* **:** to cause to follow alternately **:** ALTERNATE, VARY ~ *vi* **:** to change places mutually **:** take part in an exchange ⟨vowels on each side of the triangle tend to ~ in accordance with certain specific rules —William Chomsky⟩

[2]**in·ter·change** \'==,=\ *n* [alter. (influenced by L *inter-*) of earlier *enterchange*, *enterchaunge*, fr. MF *entrechange*, fr. *entrechangier*, v.] **1 :** an act of changing each for the other or one for another **:** EXCHANGE ⟨~ of currency between nations⟩ ⟨~ of clothing⟩ ⟨~ of segments between chromosomes⟩ **2 :** an act of mutually giving and receiving ⟨~ of gifts⟩ ⟨~ of notes⟩ **3** *archaic* **:** alternate succession **:** ALTERNATION ⟨sweet ~ of hill and valley —John Milton⟩ **4 a :** a process of moving cars among railroads to provide uninterrupted movement by rail without unloading and reloading **b :** an act of transferring passengers or freight from one carrier to another **5 :** a junction of two or more highways by a system of separate levels that permit traffic to pass from one to another without the crossing at grade of traffic streams — compare CLOVERLEAF, GRADE SEPARATION

interchange 5

in·ter·change·abil·i·ty \ˌintə(r),chānjə'biləd·ē, -ətē, -i\ *n* **:** the quality or state of being interchangeable ⟨standardization and ~ of parts has taken place in a series of small steps —A.D.H.Kaplan⟩ ⟨~ of mass and energy, which has become an essential principle in physics —Bertrand Russell⟩

in·ter·change·able \¦==¦chānjəbəl\ *adj* [alter. (influenced by L *inter-*) of ME *entrechaungeable*, *entrechaungable*, fr. MF *entrechangeable*, *entrechangable*, fr. OF, fr. *entrechangier* (v.) + *-able*] **1 :** capable of being interchanged **2** *obs* **:** MUTUAL, RECIPROCAL **3 :** following each other in alternate succession **:** ALTERNATING **4** *obs* **:** CHANGEABLE, VARIABLE **5 :** permitting mutual substitution without loss of function or suitability ⟨same instrument, known in English by the ~ terms virginal and spinet —A.E.Wier⟩ ⟨each car is like every other . . . and parts are so completely standardized that they are ~ —A.M. Sievers⟩ ⟨standard kit consists of . . . four ~ cutting blades —*Steel*⟩ **6 :** capable of being exchanged or bartered ⟨~ bond⟩ — **in·ter·change·able·ness** *n* — **in·ter·change·ably** \-blē, -li\ *adv*

interchangeable manufacturing *n* **:** the making of the parts of machines with such tolerances that any of the parts will properly function in any of the machines

interchangement *n* [alter. (influenced by L *inter-*) of earlier *enterchangement*, fr. F *entrechangement*, fr. MF, fr. OF, fr. *entrechangier* to interchange + *-ment* — more at INTERCHANGE] *obs* **:** reciprocal exchange ⟨contract . . . strengthened by ~ of your rings —Shak.⟩

interchange point *n* **:** a location at which freight in transit is transferred from one carrier to another

in·ter·chang·er \ˌ=='chānjə(r)\ *n* **:** one that interchanges; *esp* **:** HEAT EXCHANGER

interchange track *n* **:** a track for transfer of freight cars moving in interchange

in·ter·chapter \'intə(r)+,-\ *n* [*inter-* + *chapter*] **:** an intervening or inserted chapter

in·ter·chromomere \¦intə(r)+\ *n* [*inter-* + *²chromomere*] **:** a nongenic area of a chromonema thought to alternate with the genic chromomeres

in·ter·church \"+\ *adj* [*inter-* + *church* (n.)] **:** common to or shared by many or all churches **:** emphasizing cooperation and joint action between religious denominations **:** INTERDENOMINATIONAL ⟨~ movement⟩ ⟨~ aid⟩

intercision *n* -s [L *intercision-*, *intercisio*, fr. *intercisus* (past part. of *intercidere* to cut apart, fr. *inter-* + *-cidere* — fr. *caedere* to cut, strike, beat) + *-ion-*, *-io* -ion — more at CONCISE] **1** *obs* **:** a cutting off, through, or asunder **:** INTERRUPTION, INTERSECTION **2** *obs* **:** a falling off **:** FAILING

in·ter·citizenship \¦intə(r)+\ *n* [*inter-* + *citizenship*] **:** citizenship or the right to civic privileges in different bodies politic at the same time ⟨~ in different states of the U.S.⟩

in·ter·city \"+\ *adj* [*inter-* + *city* (n.)] **:** extending or operating between cities ⟨~ bus⟩ ⟨~ broadcasting network⟩

in·ter·civic \"+\ *adj* [*inter-* + *civic*] **:** existing or taking place between or among fellow citizens

in·ter·class \"+\ *adj* [*inter-* + *class* (n.)] **:** relating to or involving more than one class ⟨~ religious movement⟩ ⟨~ marriage⟩

in·ter·clavicle \"+\ *n* [*inter-* + *clavicle*] **:** a ventral median membrane bone in front of the sternum and between the clavicles in certain vertebrates (as the monotremes and most reptiles)

in·ter·clavicular \"+\ *adj* [*inter-* + *clavicular*] **1 :** situated between the clavicles **2** [fr. *interclavicle*, after E *clavicle: clavicular*] **:** of or relating to the interclavicle

in·ter·club \"+\ *adj* [*inter-* + *club* (n.)] **:** involving or relating to more than one club ⟨~ yacht race⟩

interclude *vt* -ED/-ING/-S [L *intercludere*, fr. *inter-* + *-cludere* (fr. *claudere* to close) — more at CLOSE] *obs* **:** to shut off, out, or up **:** INTERCEPT, CONFINE

in·ter·coastal \"+\ *adj* [*inter-* + *coastal*] **:** extending or operating between sea coasts ⟨~ steamers running between Atlantic and Pacific ports⟩ ⟨~ railroad traffic⟩

in·ter·coccygeal \"+\ *adj* [*inter-* + *coccygeal*] **:** lying between the segments of the coccyx

in·ter·college \"+\ *adj* [*inter-* + *college* (n.)] **:** INTERCOLLEGIATE

in·ter·collegiate \"+\ *adj* [*inter-* + *collegiate*] **:** characterized by participation or cooperation of two or more colleges or universities **:** belonging to related colleges ⟨~ athletic competition⟩ — compare EXTRAMURAL

in·ter·col·line \¦intə(r)¦kälən, -ä,līn\ *adj* [*inter-* + L *collis* hill + E *-ine* — more at HILL] **:** situated between hills

in·ter·colonial \¦intə(r)+\ *adj* [*inter-* + *colonial*] **:** existing between or among colonies **:** relating to the intercourse or mutual relations of colonies ⟨~ trade⟩ — **in·ter·colonially** \"+\ *adv*

in·ter·column \"+\ *n* [L *intercolumnium*, fr. *inter-* + *columna* column — more at COLUMN] **:** the space between two columns

in·ter·columnar \"+\ *also* **in·ter·columnal** \"+\ *adj* [*inter-* + L *columna* column + E *-ar* or *-al*] **:** existing between pillars ⟨~ space⟩

in·ter·co·lum·ni·a·tion \ˌintə(r)kəˌləmnē'āshən\ *also* **in·ter·col·um·na·tion** \ˌintə(r)ˌkäləm'nā-\ *n* [L *intercolumnium* intercolumn + E *-ation*] **1 a :** the clear space between the columns of a series **b :** the distance between the centers of a series of columns measured at the bottom of the shaft **2 :** the system of spacing the columns of a colonnade measured in terms of the base diameter of the shafts — see ARAEOSTYLE, ARAEOSYSTYLE, DIASTYLE, EUSTYLE, PYCNOSTYLE, SYSTYLE

intercolumniation 2 *a* pycnostyle, *b* systyle, *c* eustyle, *d* diastyle, *e* araeostyle

in·ter·com \'intə,käm\ *n* -s [by shortening] **:** INTERCOMMUNICATION SYSTEM

in·ter·com·mon \ˌintə(r)'kämən\ *vi* -ED/-ING/-S [ME *intercomounen*, *entercomenen*, fr. AF *entrecomuner*, fr. OF *entre-* inter- + *comuner* to put in common, share — more at COMMUNE] **1** *obs* **:** to have dealings or association **2** *obs* **:** to share with others **:** participate mutually **3 :** to enjoy a right of pasture together

in·ter·com·mon·age \-nij\ *n* **:** the practice or right of intercommoning

in·ter·communal \¦intə(r)+\ *adj* [*inter-* + *communal*] **:** existing between communities

in·ter·com·mune \ˌintə(r)kə'myün\ *vb* [alter. (influenced by L *inter-*) of ME *entrecomunen*, *entrecommunen*, fr. AF *entrecomuner*, *entrecommuner*] *vi* **:** to have mutual communion or intercourse by conversation ~ *vt*, *obs* **:** to deprive of intercourse with other men **:** OUTLAW

in·ter·communicability \¦intə(r)+\ *n* **:** the quality of being mutually communicable ⟨~ of human and bovine disease⟩

in·ter·communicable \"+\ *adj* [fr. *intercommunicate*, after E *communicate: communicable*] **:** capable of being mutually communicated

in·ter·communicate \"+\ *vi* [prob. fr. *inter-* + *communicate*] **1 :** to communicate mutually **:** give and receive information **:** hold conversation **2 :** to afford passage from one to another ⟨*intercommunicating* rooms⟩

in·ter·communication \"+\ *n* [prob. fr. *inter-* + *communication*] **:** mutual communication ⟨~ telephone⟩ ⟨unhampered ~ among the scientists of the world⟩

intercommunication system *n* **:** a two-way communication system with microphone and loudspeaker at each station for communicating within a limited area (as between offices in the same building or between operating stations on an airplane)

in·ter·communicator \"+\ *n* **:** an instrument for intercommunication

in·ter·communion \"+\ *n* [*inter-* + *communion*] **:** open communion between churches or denominations based on official recognition of other bodies and ratified usu. by an agreement between cooperating parties

[1]**in·ter·community** \"+\ *n* [*inter-* + *community*] **:** the quality of being common to two or more **:** participation in common ⟨~ of measurements is achieved by the metric system⟩

[2]**in·ter·community** \"\ *adj* [*inter-* + *community* (n.)] **:** existing between two or more communities ⟨~ rivalry⟩

in·ter·company \"+\ *adj* [*inter-* + *company* (n.)] **:** existing between two or more companies ⟨~ agreements⟩

in·ter·comparable \"+\ *adj* [*inter-* + *comparable*] **:** capable of being compared

in·ter·compare \"+\ *vt* [*inter-* + *compare*] **:** to compare (as members of a specified group or their qualities) with one another ⟨to return to the open clusters . . . we can . . . ~ their total luminosities . . . compare them also with the open clusters in our own system —Harlow Shapley⟩

in·ter·comparison \"+\ *n* [*inter-* + *comparison*] **:** reciprocal or mutual comparison

in·ter·condenser \"+\ *n* [*inter-* + *condenser*] **:** one of the intermediate stages in a multistage steam-engine condenser

in·ter·confessional \"+\ *adj* [*inter-* + *confessional*] **:** involving, supported by, or common to groups (as Anglicans and Eastern Orthodox) having different confessions of faith

in·ter·con·nect \¦intə(r)kə¦nekt\ *vt* [*inter-* + *connect*] **:** to connect mutually or with one another ⟨~*ed* generating stations⟩

in·ter·con·nect·ed·ness \-tədnəs\ *n* **:** the quality or state of being interconnected **:** INTERRELATEDNESS ⟨the ~ of the interests of all nations has become so great —H.J.Morgenthau⟩

in·ter·connection \¦intə(r)+\ *n* [*inter-* + *connection*] **:** connection between two or more **:** mutual connection ⟨~ of members of an electric power system⟩ ⟨basis of rational belief lies in the ~ of judgments each independently formed —J.H.Muirhead⟩

in·ter·consonantal \"+\ *or* **in·ter·consonantic** \"+\ *adj* [*inter-* + *consonantal*, *consonantic*] **:** immediately preceded and immediately followed by a consonant

in·ter·continental \"+\ *adj* [*inter-* + *continental*] **1 :** existing or extending between or among continents ⟨~ flight⟩ **:** subsisting or carried on between continents ⟨~ war⟩ **2 :** capable of traveling between continents ⟨~ missile⟩ ⟨~ bomber⟩

in·ter·conversion \"+\ *n* [*inter-* + *conversion*] **:** conversion into one another **:** mutual conversion ⟨~ of chemical compounds⟩

in·ter·convert \"+\ *vt* [*inter-* + *convert*] **:** to change each into the other **:** INTERCHANGE ⟨ordinary and extraordinary rays were ~*ed* when the crystals were placed at right angles —S.F.Mason⟩

in·ter·convertibility \"+\ *n* **:** the quality of being interconvertible ⟨~ of currencies⟩

in·ter·convertible \"+\ *adj* [*inter-* + *convertible*] **:** convertible the one into the other **:** INTERCHANGEABLE ⟨matter and energy are ~⟩ — **in·ter·con·vert·ibly** \-blē, -li\ *adv*

in·ter·cool \¦intə(r)¦kül\ *vt* [back-formation fr. *intercooler*] **:** to cool (a fluid) in an intercooler

in·ter·cool·er \-lə(r)\ *n* [*inter-* + *cooler*] **:** a device for cooling a fluid (as air) between successive heat-generating processes (as in a multistage air compressor)

in·ter·corporate \¦intə(r)+\ *adj* [*inter-* + *corporate*] **:** existing between, involving, or belonging to two or more corporations ⟨~ council⟩ ⟨~ control of stock⟩

in·ter·correlate \"+\ *vt* [*inter-* + *correlate*] **:** to correlate (members of a group) with each other

in·ter·correlation \"+\ *n* [*inter-* + *correlation*] **:** correlation between members of a group; *esp* **:** one of the correlations existing among independent statistical variables excluding the dependent variable criterion

in·ter·cosmic \"+\ *adj* [*inter-* + *cosmic*] **:** situated between or among the planets or stars ⟨~ dust⟩ — **in·ter·cosmically** \"+\ *adv*

[1]**in·ter·cos·tal** \"+¦käst°l\ *adj* [NL *intercostalis*, fr. L *inter-* + *costa* rib + *-alis* -al — more at COAST] **1 a :** situated between the ribs **b :** of, relating to, or produced by the intercostal muscles **2 :** situated between the veins or nerves of a leaf **3 :** lying or fitted between the continuous members of a ship's frame ⟨~ plate⟩ ⟨~ keelson⟩ ⟨~ angle iron⟩ — see SHIP illustration — **in·ter·cos·tal·ly** \-°lē, -°li\ *adv*

[2]**intercostal** \"\ *n* **:** an intercostal part or structure

intercostal artery *n* **:** any of the arteries supplying or lying in the intercostal spaces and being mostly branches of the aorta

intercostal muscle *n* **:** any of the short muscles that extend between the ribs filling in most of the intervals between them and serving to move the ribs in respiration

intercostal nerve *n* **:** one of the anterior divisions of the thoracic nerves that lie in the intercostal spaces

intercostal vein *n* **:** one of the veins of the intercostal spaces

in·ter·cos·to·brachial nerve \¦intə(r)¦kästō+ . . . -\ *n* [*intercostal* + *-o-* + *brachial*] **:** the lateral cutaneous branch of the second intercostal nerve that crosses the axilla and supplies the skin of the inner and back part of the upper half of the arm

in·ter·country \¦intə(r)+\ *adj* [*inter-* + *country* (n.)] **:** INTERNATIONAL

in·ter·course \'intər,kō(ə)rs, -kȯ(ə)rs, -tə,kōəs, -tə,kȯ(ə)s\ *n* [ME *intercurse*, prob. modif. (influenced by L *inter-*) of MF *entrecours*, fr. OF, fr. ML *intercursus*, fr. L, intervention, act of running between, fr. *intercursus*, past part. of *intercurrere* to run between, fr. *inter-* + *currere* to run — more at CURRENT] **1 :** dealings or connection (as in common affairs, civilities, or business) between persons, organizations, or nations **:** COMMUNICATION ⟨diffidence . . . renders me inapt for social ~ —Havelock Ellis⟩ ⟨as trade ~ increases between nations —J.A. Hobson⟩ ⟨welcomes extraclass ~ with students and encourages them to think critically —G.H.White⟩ **2 :** exchange or interchange esp. of thought and feeling **:** COMMUNION ⟨sweet ~ of looks and smiles —John Milton⟩ ⟨believed he had direct ~ with the Deity —Ruth Gruber⟩ **3 :** COPULATION, COITUS — used chiefly of humans **4** *obs* **a :** alternate succession **:** ALTERNATION **b :** INTERVENTION, INTERPOSITION **c :** INTERCOMMUNICATION, INTERCONNECTION

in·ter·cranial \¦intə(r)+\ *adj* [*inter-* + *cranial*] **:** situated or occurring within the cranium

in·ter·create \"+\ *vt* [*inter-* + *create*] **:** to create jointly with another

in·ter·creedal \"+\ *adj* [*inter-* + *creedal*] **:** INTERDENOMINATIONAL

in·ter·cres·cence \ˌintə(r)'kresᵊn(t)s\ *n* -s [*inter-* + *-crescence* (as in *excrescence*)] **:** a growing together of tissues

[1]**in·ter·crop** \¦intə(r)+\ *vb* [*inter-* + *crop*] *vt* **1 :** to grow a crop in between (another) ⟨*intercropped* their tree fruit . . . with market garden crops —*Biol. Abstracts*⟩ **2 :** to use (ground) for a catch crop ~ *vi* **:** to grow two or more crops simultaneously (as in alternate rows) in the same ground

[2]**in·ter·crop** \'intə(r)+,-\ *n* **:** CATCH CROP ⟨sweet clover ~⟩

[1]**in·ter·cross** \¦intə(r)+\ *vb* [*inter-* + *cross*] *vi* **1 :** to cross each other ⟨various shapes and colors . . . ~*ing* without confusion —Earl of Shaftesbury †1713⟩ **2 :** CROSS 5 ~ *vt* **1 :** to place across each other ⟨framed of iron bars ~*ed*, which formed . . . an immense cage —S.T.Coleridge⟩ **2 :** CROSS 9

[2]**in·ter·cross** \'intə(r)+,-\ *n* **:** an instance or a product of crossbreeding

in·ter·crystalline \¦intə(r)+\ *adj* [*inter-* + *crystalline*] **:** occurring between crystals ⟨~ crack in a metal⟩ — compare TRANSCRYSTALLINE

in·ter·crystallization \"+\ *n* [*inter-* + *crystallization*] **:** the process of intercrystallizing

in·ter·crystallize \"+\ *vi* [*inter-* + *crystallize*] **:** to crystallize together at the same time with resulting mutual inclusion so that each component retains through the mass its own crystallographic identity including crystallographic and optical orientation; *sometimes* **:** to form a solid solution — used of two or more associated minerals

in·ter·cultural \"+\ *adj* [*inter-* + *cultural*] **1 :** cultivated between the rows of some other crop **2 :** occurring during the growing period ⟨~ tillage⟩ ⟨~ hoeing⟩ **3 :** existing between or relating to two or more cultures ⟨~ contact⟩ ⟨~ tension⟩ ⟨~ education⟩

in·ter·culture \'intə(r)+,-\ *n* [*inter-* + *culture*] **:** INTERCROPPING

in·ter·current \¦intə(r)+\ *adj* [L *intercurrent-*, *intercurrens*, pres. part. of *intercurrere* to run between — more at INTERCOURSE] **1 :** running between or among **2 a** *obs* **:** coming in between or among **:** lying between **b :** INTERVENING **3 :** occurring in the midst of a process **:** INTERRUPTING ⟨~ sense impressions during a dream⟩ **4 :** occurring in and modifying the course of another disease ⟨~ infection⟩ — **in·ter·cur·rent·ly** *adv*

[1]**in·ter·cut** \"+\ *vb* [*inter-* + *cut*] *vt* **1 :** to insert a contrasting camera shot into (a take) by cutting ⟨*intercutting* panoramic long shots with closeups of action and expression —*Time*⟩ **2 :** to insert (a contrasting camera shot) into a take by cutting ⟨rapidly ~ news shots and animated maps —*New Republic*⟩ ~ *vi* **:** to alternate contrasting camera shots of the same scene or of different scenes by cutting ⟨*intercutting* for dramatic suspense —Budd Schulberg⟩

[2]**in·ter·cut** \'intə(r)+,-\ *n* **:** an intercut camera shot or film sequence ⟨cartoon sequences to be used as ~s when the camera fades out on the principals —T.M.Pryor⟩

in·ter·denominational \¦intə(r)+\ *adj* [*inter-* + *denominational*] **:** occurring between or among or common to different denominations ⟨~ cooperation between Methodists and Presbyterians⟩

in·ter·denominationalism \"+\ *n* **:** the principle of fostering intercommunion and cooperative activities among different religious denominations

in·ter·dental \"+\ *adj* [*inter-* + *dental*] **1 :** situated or placed between the teeth **2 :** formed with the tip of the tongue protruded between the upper and lower front teeth ⟨~ consonants⟩ — **in·ter·dentally** \"+\ *adv*

in·ter·den·tal·i·ty \ˌintə(r)(ˌ)den'taləd·ē\ *n* [ISV *interdental* + *-ity*] **:** interdental articulation**: a :** substitution of the interdental sounds \th\ and \t͟h\ for \s\ and \z\ respectively **:** LISP **b :** interdental articulation of other alveolars or dentals (as \t\, \d\, \n\, \l\)

in·ter·dentil \ˌintə(r)+\ *n* [*inter-* + *dentil*] **:** the space between two dentils

in·ter·departmental \"+\ *adj* [*inter-* + *departmental*] **:** existing, exchanged, or carried on between departments; *esp* **:** characterized by participation or cooperation of two or more departments of an educational institution ⟨~ major⟩ — **in·ter·departmentally** \"+\ *adv*

in·ter·depend \"+\ *vi* [*inter-* + *depend*] **:** to depend upon one another

in·ter·dependence \"+\ *n* [*inter-* + *dependence*] **:** mutual dependence ⟨~ of members of a family⟩ ⟨~ of statistical variables⟩

in·ter·dependency \"+\ *n* [*inter-* + *dependency*] **:** INTERDEPENDENCE

in·ter·dependent \"+\ *adj* [*inter-* + *dependent*] **:** mutually dependent — **in·ter·de·pend·ent·ly** *adv*

in·ter·determination \"+\ *n* [*inter-* + *determination*] **:** cause and effect operating among several factors **:** multiple causation

in·ter·determined \"+\ *adj* [*inter-* + *determined*, past part. of *determine*] **:** mutually determined

in·ter·dialect \"+\ *or* **in·ter·dialectal** \"+\ *adj* [*interdialect* fr. *inter-* + *dialect* (n.); *interdialectal* fr. *inter-* + *dialectal*] **:** existing or occurring between dialects ⟨~ loans⟩ ⟨~ influences⟩

[1]**in·ter·dict** \'intə(r),dikt *sometimes* -dīt *or* + V -dīd-\ *n* -s [alter. (influenced by L *interdictum*) of ME *entredit*, fr. OF, fr. L *interdictum* prohibition, interdict of a praetor, fr. neut. of *interdictus*, past part. of *interdicere* to interpose, forbid, interdict, fr. *inter* between, among + *dicere* to say — more at INTER-, DICTION] **1 :** an ecclesiastical censure of the Roman Catholic Church barring a person or the people of a region from the sacraments, religious services, and Christian burial **2 :** a prohibitory decree **:** PROHIBITION **3 a** *Roman civil law* (1) **:** an administrative order of the praetor for prevention of encroachments on or wrongs concerning sacred or public property or breaches of the peace (2) **:** an order issued as a remedy in certain cases (as of disputed possession) forbidding certain things to be done **b :** an order in systems founded on Roman civil law corresponding to the injunction of the English law **c** *civil & Scots law* **:** one incompetent to manage his affairs by reason of mental weakness, facility, or insanity **:** one under curatorship as an incompetent **:** an interdicted person **:** one under voluntary or judicial interdiction

[2]**in·ter·dict** \¦==¦=\ *vt* -ED/-ING/-S [alter. (influenced by L *interdictum*, n., and *interdictus*, past part.) of ME *entrediten*, prob. fr. OF *entredit*, past part. of *entredire*, fr. L *interdicere*] **1 :** to lay under or prohibit by an interdict ⟨~*ed* under heavy penalties the use of the Book of Common Prayer —T.B. Macaulay⟩ **2 :** PROHIBIT, DEBAR ⟨~ trade with a foreign nation⟩ **3 :** to destroy, cut, or damage by ground or aerial firepower (enemy lines of reinforcement, supply, or communication) in order to stop or hamper enemy movement and to destroy or limit enemy effectiveness **syn** see FORBID

[3]**in·ter·dict** \¦==¦=\ *adj* [ME *interdicte*, fr. L *interdictus*, past part.] *archaic* **:** INTERDICTED

in·ter·dic·tion \ˌintə(r)'dikshən\ *n* [ME (Scot. dial.) *interdiccioun*, fr. L *interdiction-*, *interdictio*, fr. *interdictus* (past part.) + *-ion-*, *-io* -ion] **1 :** the act of interdicting or state of being interdicted **:** INTERDICT, TABOO ⟨in primitive society . . . the same ~ is very frequently laid on the names of common objects —J.G.Frazer⟩ ⟨so little did he comprehend the rigid ~s of Montreal society —Walter O'Meara⟩ **2** *civil & Scots law* **:** a voluntary or judicial restraint placed upon a person suffering from mental weakness with respect to acts which may affect his estate **3 :** artillery fire or air attack directed on a route or area to deny its use to the enemy ⟨~ bombing⟩ ⟨~ of an airstrip⟩

in·ter·dic·tive \¦==¦diktiv\ *adj* [²*interdict* + *-ive*] **:** INTERDICTORY

in·ter·dic·tor \,==ˈdiktə(r)\ *n* -s [LL, fr. L *interdictus* (past part.) + *-or*] **1 :** one that interdicts **2** *Scots law* **:** a person whose consent is made necessary by a bond of voluntary interdiction to certain acts of the person executing the bond

in·ter·dic·tory \¦==¦dikt(ə)rē, -ri\ *adj* [LL *interdictorius*, fr. L *interdictus* (past part. of *interdicere* to interdict) + *-orius* -ory] **:** having the power or effect of interdicting **:** relating or belonging to interdiction **:** PROHIBITORY ⟨~ decree⟩ ⟨coastal road was still under heavy ~ fire —R.E.Lawless⟩

in·ter·dic·tum \,==ˈdiktəm\ *n*, *pl* **interdic·ta** \-tə\ [L] **:** INTERDICT, INJUNCTION

in·ter·dig·i·tate \,intə(r)ˈdijə,tāt\ *vb* -ED/-ING/-S [*inter-* + L *digitus* finger + *-ate* — more at TOE] *vi* **:** to interlock like the fingers of folded hands **:** INTERFINGER ⟨forests ~ with the grasslands⟩ **~** *vt* **:** INTERSTRATIFY ⟨fluvial and marine sediments form an *interdigitated* succession —Daniel Wirtz & Henning Illies⟩

in·ter·dig·i·ta·tion \,==,==ˈtāshən\ *n* **:** the act of interlocking or the condition of being interlocked or interpenetrated ⟨produce, by ~, alternate strips of warm and cold water —*Encyc. Britannica*⟩

in·ter·dine \¦intə(r)+\ *vi* [*inter-* + *dine*] **:** to join in a common meal ⟨subdivided into subcastes which do not intermarry or ~ —D.G.Mandelbaum⟩

in·ter·disciplinary \"+\ *adj* [*inter-* + *disciplinary*] **:** characterized by participation or cooperation of two or more disciplines or fields of study ⟨an ~ conference⟩ **:** drawing on or contributing to two or more disciplines ⟨~ approach to anthropology⟩

in·ter·district \"+\ *adj* [*inter-* + *district* (n.)] **:** existing between districts ⟨~ athletic contests⟩

in·ter·dome \ˈintə(r)+,-\ *n* [*inter-* + *dome*] **:** an open space between the inner and outer shells of a dome or cupola

in·ter·dotting \"+,-\ *n* -s [*inter-* + *dotting*, gerund of *dot*] **:** dots applied to an area (as of an engraving) for producing a light shading

in·ter·epimeral \¦intə(r)+\ *adj* [*inter-* + *epimeral*] **:** situated between adjacent epimera

¹interess *n* -ES [ME *interesse*] *obs* **:** RIGHT, CONCERN, INTEREST

²interess *vt* -ED/-ING/-ES **1** *obs* **:** INTEREST; *esp* **:** to admit to a right or privilege **2** [MF *interesser*, fr. L *interesse* to be between, differ, concern] *obs* **:** to affect injuriously **:** INJURE

in·ter·es·se \,intəˈresē\ *n* -s [ML] **1 :** a legal interest in property **2 :** interest upon money

in·ter·es·see \¦intərə¦sē\ *n* -s [²*interess* + *-ee*] **:** a party in interest

interesse ter·mi·ni \-ˈtərmə,nī\ *n* [ML, lit., interest of term or end] **:** the right of entry legally conferred by the demise of a leasehold estate before entry is made

¹in·ter·est \ˈin·trəst *also* ˈintərəst *or* ˈintə,rest *or* ˈinˈtərst *sometimes* ˈin·,trest\ *n* -s [ME, prob. alter. of earlier *interesse*, fr. AF & ML; AF *interesse*, fr. ML, legal interest, compensation, interest on money, fr. L, to concern, be of importance, fr. *inter-* + *esse* to be; influenced by MF *interest* damage, loss, compensation for damage, fr. OF, damage, loss, fr. L, it concerns, is of importance, 3d pers. sing. pres. indic. of *interesse* — more at IS] **1 a :** right, title, or legal share in something ⟨what exactly is your ~ in this affair⟩ **:** participation in advantage, profit, and responsibility ⟨half ~ in a hardware business⟩ ⟨offered to buy out his ~ in the company⟩ **:** STAKE, CLAIM **b :** something in which one has a share of ownership or control **:** BUSINESS ⟨has ~*s* all over the world⟩ **c** *obs* **:** a share in producing a total effect or result **2 a :** the state of being concerned or affected esp. with respect to advantage or well-being **:** GOOD, BENEFIT, PROFIT ⟨engaged a lawyer to look after his ~*s*⟩ ⟨acting always in his own ~⟩ ⟨each faction made concessions in the common ~⟩ ⟨speed laws passed in the ~ of safety⟩; *specif* **:** SELF-INTEREST ⟨sacrifice of personal ~ by men who believed in the job they were doing —T.W.Arnold⟩ ⟨distinguish fact from fiction . . . ~ from impartiality —Elmer Davis⟩ **b :** something that is the object of desire ⟨natural ~ in seeing his children well educated⟩ **3 a :** the price paid for borrowing money generally expressed as a percentage of the amount borrowed paid in one year ⟨~ on a loan⟩ ⟨~ on a bond⟩ — see COMPOUND INTEREST, SIMPLE INTEREST **b :** the money so paid ⟨~ on certain indebtedness is deductible from taxable income⟩ **c :** the share received by capital from the product of industry as distinguished from rent and profit and wages — see PURE INTEREST **4 :** an excess over and above an exact equivalent ⟨returned the insults with ~⟩ **5 :** the power of influencing ⟨~ with the boss⟩ **6 a :** the persons effectively controlling an enterprise or dominating a field of activity ⟨landed ~⟩ ⟨iron ~⟩ ⟨banking ~⟩ ⟨Protestant ~⟩ **b interests** *pl* **:** the dominating group of owners in a field of business, industry, or finance considered locally, regionally, nationally, or internationally; *sometimes* **:** BIG BUSINESS **7 a :** a feeling that accompanies or causes special attention to some object **:** CURIOSITY, CONCERN ⟨took a lively ~ in the divorce proceedings in court⟩ ⟨lifelong ~ in sports⟩ ⟨~ in arctic exploration⟩ ⟨~ in child welfare⟩ **b :** readiness to attend to and be stirred by a certain class of objects ⟨testing the aptitudes, ~*s*, emotions of the patient⟩ **c :** something that causes or arouses curiosity or concern ⟨campaign of great intrinsic ~ to military students⟩ ⟨question of great philosophic ~⟩ **8 a** *obs* **:** INJURY **b** *obs* **:** compensation for injury **:** DAMAGES

²interest \"\ *vt* -ED/-ING/-S **1 :** to cause to share or participate ⟨this holding company through which the public is ~*ed* in the Emperor mine —*Sydney (Australia) Bull.*⟩ **2 :** to involve the interest or welfare of **:** AFFECT, CONCERN — used with *in* ⟨~*ed* herself exuberantly in the progress of the political campaign —Robert Grant †1940⟩ ⟨thanked those who had ~*ed* themselves in his behalf⟩ **3 :** to cause or induce to have a share or interest **:** persuade to participate or engage ⟨city authorities began to ~ themselves in the parking problem⟩ ⟨~ a banker in a loan⟩ ⟨can I ~ you in a game of bridge⟩ **4 :** to engage or attract the attention of **:** arouse interest in ⟨would find some picture that ~*ed* him, in an old magazine —Floyd Dell⟩ ⟨offer a market that ought to ~ any businessman —Andrew Boyd⟩

interested *adj* [fr. past part. of ²*interest*] **1 :** having the attention engaged **:** having curiosity or sympathy aroused ⟨~ listeners⟩ ⟨a nice widowed doctor up there who is ~ in her —Hamilton Basso⟩ **2 :** having a share or concern in some affair or project **:** liable to be affected or prejudiced **:** CONCERNED, INVOLVED ⟨in addition to the lender and borrower, the state considers itself an ~ party to these operations —*U.S.Investor*⟩; *esp* **:** having self-interest **:** not disinterested ⟨generosity proceeding from ~ motives⟩ ⟨~ witness⟩ — **in·ter·est·ed·ly** *adv* — **in·ter·est·ed·ness** *n* -ES

in·ter·esterification \¦intə(r)+\ *n* [*inter-* + *esterification*] **:** TRANSESTERIFICATION

interest group *n* **:** a group of persons having a common identifying interest that often provides a basis for action

interesting *adj* [fr. pres. part. of ²*interest*] **1** *obs* **:** of concern **:** IMPORTANT **2 :** engaging the attention **:** capable of arousing interest, curiosity, or emotion ⟨~ news⟩ ⟨~ personality⟩

syn ENGROSSING, ABSORBING, INTRIGUING: INTERESTING may imply a power to provoke attentive interest to an unspecified degree through some such quality as curiosity, sympathy, desire to understand, enthusiasm, or vicarious identification ⟨seemed to me to be increasingly *interesting*; she was acquiring new subtleties, complexities, and comprehensions —Rose Macaulay⟩ ⟨the effect of the moonlight on Netta's face was *interesting*. It was even complicated. It emphasized a certain haggardness, a certain battered, woebegone pitifulness in her —J.C.Powys⟩ ENGROSSING may suggest power to divert attention from other matters and to hold it by challenge, stimulation, provocation ⟨an *engrossing* account of his research problems⟩ ⟨an *engrossing* mystery drama⟩ ⟨the fight with the hooked trout is only one phase of the sport, albeit a very *engrossing* one —Alexander MacDonald⟩ ABSORBING may imply power to hold interest and attention utterly, the person concerned being oblivious to all else ⟨but Maugham's skill as a storyteller is so impelling that one must follow through this *absorbing* tale to its end —R.A.Cordell⟩ ⟨when a woman takes up some *absorbing* pursuit, and finds it and its associations more interesting than her husband's company and conversation and friends —G.B.Shaw⟩ INTRIGUING usu. applies to what attracts attention, esp. by arousing curiosity, puzzling one, archly fascinating, or challenging ingenuity ⟨these *intriguing* beginnings stimulated a great research effort —A.G. N.Flew⟩ ⟨her eyes had a definite slant from some Oriental ancestor, and, with her flaxen hair, gave her face an *intriguing* prettiness —Winifred Bambrick⟩

— in an interesting condition *of a woman* **:** PREGNANT

in·ter·est·ing·ly *adv* **:** in an interesting manner ⟨when he ceases to be just ~ neurotic and . . . gets locked up —*Time*⟩

in·ter·est·ing·ness *n* -ES **:** the quality or state of being interesting ⟨others who felt the essential ~ of his writings —*Times Lit. Supp.*⟩

interest lottery *n* **:** a lottery that issues bonds for borrowed money at less than the normal rate of interest and gives chances for prizes as the consideration for the low interest

interest policy *n* **:** an insurance policy which requires insurable interest in the property covered only at the time of loss and not at the inception of the policy

interests *pl of* INTEREST, *pres 3d sing of* INTEREST

in·ter·estuarine \¦intə(r)+\ *adj* [*inter-* + *estuarine*] **:** lying between two estuaries

¹in·ter·face \ˈintə(r)+,-\ *n* [*inter-* + *face*] **1 :** a plane or other surface forming a common boundary of two bodies or spaces ⟨passage of ~*s* of the diametrically opposed air masses —*Yr. Bk. of General Medicine*⟩ ⟨the ~ between two separate types of oil flowing along a pipeline —*Canadian Banker*⟩ ⟨heat transfer at an air-earth ~ —J.E.Vehrencamp⟩ **2 :** the boundary between two phases in a heterogeneous physical-chemical system ⟨the boundary between . . . two phases is designated as an ~, although the term *surface* is often used with a general meaning which includes all types of interfaces —W.D.Harkins⟩ — compare SURFACE 1

²in·ter·face \¦intə(r)+\ *vt* [*inter-* + *face*] **:** to make (a garment) with an interfacing

in·ter·facial \"+\ *adj* [*inter-* + *face* + *-ial*] **1 :** included between two plane surfaces or faces ⟨an ~ angle⟩ **2** [*interface* + *-ial*] **:** relating to or situated at an interface ⟨~ layer⟩ ⟨~ strength of felt⟩

interfacial tension *n* **:** surface tension at the interface between two liquids

in·ter·facing \ˈintə(r)+,-\ *n* [*inter-* + *facing*] **:** a firm cloth shaped and sewn between the facing and outside of a garment for stiffening and shape retention and used esp. in revers, collars, cuffs

in·ter·factional \¦intə(r)+\ *adj* [*inter-* + *factional*] **:** existing between factions ⟨~ disputes⟩

in·ter·faith \"+\ *adj* [*inter-* + *faith* (n.)] **:** occurring between or among people or organizations of different religious faiths or creeds ⟨~ marriage⟩ ⟨~ conference⟩

in·ter·family \"+\ *adj* [*inter-* + *family* (n.)] **:** occurring or existing between families ⟨~ marriage⟩ ⟨~ grafting of plants⟩

in·ter·fascicular \"+\ *adj* [*inter-* + *fascicular*] **:** situated between fascicles ⟨~ tissue⟩

interfascicular cambium *n* **:** cambium located between vascular bundles — compare FASCICULAR CAMBIUM

in·ter·felted \"+\ *adj* [*inter-* + *felted*] **:** pressed closely together ⟨~ fibers⟩ ⟨~ layers of rock⟩

in·ter·fenestral \"+\ *adj* [*inter-* + *fenestral*] **:** situated between windows ⟨~ panel⟩

in·ter·fenestration \,intə(r)+\ *n* [*inter-* + L *fenestratus* (past part. of *fenestrare* to provide with openings or windows) + E *-ion* — more at FENESTRATED] **1 :** width of pier between two windows **2 :** arrangement of windows with relation to the distance between them from axis to axis or from opening to opening

in·ter·fe·rant \,intə(r)ˈfirənt, -fēr-\ *n* -s [*interfere* + *-ant*] **:** the holder of or an applicant for a patent that conflicts with a patent granted earlier

in·ter·fere *R* ¦intə(r)¦fi(ə)r, *-R* -tə¦fiə *or* +V -i(ə)r\ *vi* -ED/-ING/-S [alter. (influenced by L *inter-*) of MF *(s')entreferir* to strike each other, fr. OF, fr. *entre-* inter- + *ferir* to strike, fr. L *ferire* — more at BORE (pierce)] **1 :** to strike one foot against the opposite foot or ankle in walking or running — used esp. of horses **2 :** to come in collision **:** to be in opposition **:** to run at cross-purposes **:** CLASH ⟨*interfering* claims⟩ — used with *with* ⟨carbon dioxide ~*s* with the liberation of oxygen to the tissues —H.G.Armstrong⟩ **3 :** to enter into or take a part in the concerns of others **:** INTERMEDDLE, INTERPOSE, INTERVENE **4** *obs* **:** to run into another or each other **:** INTERSECT **5 :** to act reciprocally so as to augment, diminish, or otherwise affect one another — used of waves **6 :** to claim substantially the same invention and thus question the priority of invention between the claimants — distinguished from *infringe* **7** *of a football player* **a :** to run ahead of the ballcarrier and provide allowed blocking protection for him **b :** to hinder illegally an attempt of a player to receive a pass or make a fair catch of a punt **syn** see MEDDLE

in·ter·fer·ence \,==ˈfirən(t)s, -fēr-\ *n* -s [*interfere* + *-ence*] **1 :** the act or process of interfering **:** a brushing or kicking of feet or ankles in walking or running **2 :** the act of meddling in or hampering an activity or process ⟨~ in the affairs of another nation⟩ **:** OBSTRUCTION, INHIBITION ⟨cause of our present economic troubles is laid to political ~ with the beneficent workings of private competitive effort for gain —John Dewey⟩ **3 :** the mutual effect on meeting of two wave trains of the same type so that such wave trains of light produce lines, bands, or fringes either alternately light and dark or variously colored and such wave trains of sound produce silence, increased intensity, or beats — compare FRINGE 2e, INTERFERENCE COLORS, INTERFERENCE FIGURE, INTERFERENCE PATTERN, INTERFERENCE SPECTRUM **4 a :** incorrect meshing of gear teeth resulting in contact along other than the proper lines of action **b :** contact so close as to produce deformation and stress **5 :** an instance of interfering with a patent; *also* **:** the proceeding for determining the question of priority involved **6 a :** the act of illegally hampering an opponent (as in football) **b :** the act of protecting a ballcarrier or a passer by blocking would-be tacklers; *also* **:** a player providing this protection **7 :** the inhibiting of coincident crossing over of genes at loci immediately adjacent to a chiasma **8 a :** confusion of received radio signals due to strays or undesired signals **b :** something that produces such confusion **9 :** the disturbing effect exerted by the learning of an act on the performance of a previously learned act with which it is inconsistent **10 :** prevention of typical growth and development of a virus in a suitable host by the presence of another virus in the same host individual — see INTERFERENCE PHENOMENON

interference colors *n pl* **:** colors produced by the strengthening or the weakening of certain wavelengths of a composite beam of light in consequence of interference

interference figure *n* **:** a figure observed with a conoscope when a section of a doubly refracting crystal is in the path traversed by convergent plane-polarized light (as when a centered black cross is superimposed over a black spot at the center of a series of concentric colored rings)

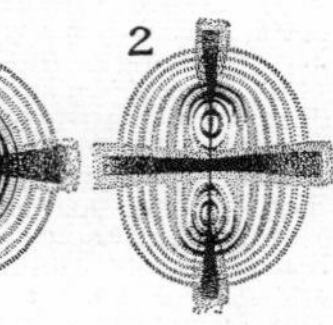

interference figures: *1* produced by a uniaxial crystal; *2* produced by a biaxial crystal when polarizer and analyzer are set at right angles to each other

interference fringe *n* **:** FRINGE 2e

interference pattern *n* **:** an arrangement of fringes or bands (as Newton's rings) due to interference — compare OPTICAL FLAT

interference phenomenon *n* **:** preoccupation of the route of invasion of a pathogenic virus (as by competition for available nutrients) by another virus postulated as the basis of interference — called also *cell-blockade phenomenon*

interference spectrum *n* **:** a spectrum (as in a transparent film) in which the dispersion is due to interference of light

in·ter·fe·ren·tial \¦intə(r)fə¦renchəl\ *adj* [fr. *interference*, after such pairs as E *difference: differential*] **:** of, relating to, or depending on interference (as of light)

in·ter·fer·er *R* ,intə(r)ˈfirər, *-R* -təˈfirə(r\ *n* -s **:** one that interferes

interfering *adj* **:** OBSTRUCTING, MEDDLING ⟨~ old woman⟩ — **in·ter·fer·ing·ly** *adv* — **in·ter·fer·ing·ness** *n* -ES

in·ter·fer·o·gram \,==ˈfirə,gram\ *n* [*interferometer* + *-gram*] **:** a record made by an interferograph

in·ter·fer·o·graph \-raf, -rȧf\ *n* [ISV *interferometer* + *-graph*] **:** an apparatus for making photographic records of optical interference phenomena (as patterns of interference fringes)

in·ter·fer·om·e·ter \,==fəˈrämədə(r)\ *n* [ISV *interfero-* (fr. *interfere*) + *-meter*] **:** an instrument for precise determinations of wavelength, spectral fine structure, indices of refraction, and very small linear displacements through the separation of light by means of a system of mirrors and glass plates into two parts that travel unequal optical paths and when reunited consequently interfere with each other — see ACOUSTIC INTERFEROMETER — **in·ter·fer·o·met·ric** \,==¦firə¦me·trik\ *adj* — **in·ter·fer·o·met·ri·cal·ly** \-rək(ə)lē\ *adv* — **in·ter·fer·om·e·try** \,==fəˈrämə·trē\ *n* -ES

in·ter·fertile \¦intə(r)+\ *adj* [*inter-* + *fertile*] **:** capable of interbreeding — **in·ter·fertility** \,intə(r)+\ *n*

in·ter·fibrillar \"+\ *adj* [*inter-* + *fibrillar*] **:** situated between fibrils

in·ter·filamentary \¦intə(r)+\ *adj* [*inter-* + *filamentary*] **:** existing between filaments

in·ter·file \"+\ *vt* [*inter-* + *file*] **:** to file among ⟨~ cards in a catalog⟩

in·ter·finger \,intə(r)+\ *vi* [*inter-* + *finger*] *of rocks* **:** to intergrade through a series of interlocking or overlapping wedge-shaped layers **:** INTERPENETRATE, INTERDIGITATE

in·ter·firm \¦intə(r)+\ *adj* [*inter-* + *firm* (n.)] **:** INTERCOMPANY

¹in·ter·flow \"+\ *vi* [*inter-* + *flow*] **1 :** to flow between **2 :** to pass into one another **:** INTERMINGLE

²in·ter·flow \ˈintə(r)+,-\ *n* **:** a flowing into one another **:** INTERMINGLING

in·ter·flu·ence \¦intə(r)¦flüən(t)s, ənˈtərfləwən(t)s\ *n* -s [fr. *interfluent*, after such pairs as E *confluent: confluence*] **:** INTERFLOW

in·ter·flu·ent \-nt\ *adj* [L *interfluent-, interfluens*, pres. part. of *interfluere* to flow between, fr. *inter-* + *fluere* to flow — more at FLUID] **:** flowing between or among **:** passing into one another as if by a natural flow **:** INTERMINGLING

in·ter·flu·mi·nal \¦intə(r)¦flümənᵊl\ *adj* [*inter-* + L *flumin-, flumen* river + E *-al* — more at FLUME] **:** INTERFLUVIAL

in·ter·flu·ous \ənˈtərfləwəs\ *adj* [L *interfluus*, fr. *interfluere* to flow between] **:** INTERFLUENT

in·ter·fluve \ˈintə(r),flüv\ *n* -s [*inter-* + L *fluvius* river, stream, fr. *fluere* to flow] **:** the area between adjacent streams flowing in the same direction

in·ter·fluvial \¦intə(r)+\ *adj* [*inter-* + *fluvial*] **:** lying between streams

¹in·ter·fold \"+\ *vt* [*inter-* + *fold*] **:** to fold (paper sheets) together **:** INTERLOCK ⟨~*ing* machine⟩

²interfold \"\ *adj* **:** arranged in interlocking folded sheets ⟨~ paper towels⟩

in·ter·foliar \"+\ *or* **in·ter·foliaceous** \"+\ *adj* [*inter-* + L *folium* leaf + E *-ar* or *-aceous* — more at BLADE] **:** borne between the leaves; *esp* **:** borne between opposite or verticillate leaves ⟨~ stipules in Rubiaceae⟩

in·ter·fo·li·ate \,intə(r)ˈfōlē,āt\ *vt* [*inter-* + L *folium* + E *-ate*] **:** INTERLEAVE

in·ter·fraternity \¦intə(r)+\ *adj* [*inter-* + *fraternity* (n.)] **:** existing or occurring between fraternities ⟨~ dance⟩ ⟨~ council⟩

in·ter·fret \ˈintə(r)+,-\ *n* [*inter-* + *fret* (network)] **:** the interaction between two wind currents of different velocities or directions producing a wave motion of the air often of great amplitude and frequently creating special cloud effects (as mackerel sky or billow clouds)

in·ter·frontal \¦intə(r)+\ *adj* [F, fr. *inter-* + *frontal*] **:** lying between the frontal bones

in·ter·fruitful \"+\ *adj* [*inter-* + *fruitful*] **:** capable of reciprocal cross-pollination ⟨~ strawberry⟩ — **in·ter·fruit·ful·ness** *n*

in·ter·fuel \"+\ *adj* [*inter-* + *fuel* (n.)] **:** existing between fuels ⟨~ competition⟩

in·ter·fuse \,intə(r)ˈfyüz\ *vb* [L *interfusus*, past part. of *interfundere* to pour between, fr. *inter-* + *fundere* to pour — more at FOUND] *vt* **1 :** to combine (one thing and another) as if by scattering or mixing **:** combine intimately as if by fusing or blending **:** INTERMINGLE ⟨curricular designs that would seek to ~ the social sciences and humanities rather than subordinate one to another —Theodore Brameld⟩ **2 :** to pass (one thing or element) into or through others by pouring or spreading **:** INFUSE, DIFFUSE ⟨clustered round the texts, *interfused* with the texts, are all the values discovered in them or added to them by students, critics —Malcolm Cowley⟩ **3 :** to enter widely or deeply into **:** blend with **:** PERVADE, PERMEATE ⟨wit that *interfused* all his writings⟩ **~** *vi* **:** BLEND, FUSE ⟨these patterns, which overlap and ~ —R.B.Heilman⟩

in·ter·fu·sion \-üzhən\ *n* [LL *interfusion-, interfusio* act of flowing between, fr. L *interfusus* (past part.) + *-ion-, -io* -ion] **:** the action or result of interfusing ⟨~ of religion and virtue is not in fact so close as to secure their habitual coexistence —James Martineau⟩ ⟨a national culture is the ~ of many elements⟩ ⟨~ of one color into another⟩

in·ter·galactic \¦intə(r)+\ *adj* [*inter-* + *galactic*] **:** situated or taking place in the vast spaces between galaxies ⟨~ gas⟩

intergatory *n* -ES [by contr.] *obs* **:** INTERROGATORY

in·ter·generic \¦intə(r)+\ *adj* [*inter-* + *generic*] **:** existing or occurring between genera ⟨~ hybridization⟩

in·ter·genic \"+\ *adj* [*inter-* + *genic*] **:** occurring between genes ⟨~ change⟩ ⟨~ interaction⟩

in·ter·ge·no·mal \"+¦jē¦nōməl\ *adj* [*inter-* + *genome* + *-al*] **:** occurring between genomes ⟨~ pairing⟩

¹in·ter·glacial \"+\ *adj* [ISV *inter-* + *glacial*; orig. formed in G] **:** occurring or formed between glacial epochs ⟨~ climate⟩

²interglacial \"\ *n* -s **:** an age or time of comparatively warm or dry climate between times of glaciation

in·ter·globular \"+\ *adj* [*inter-* + *globular*] **:** situated in the peripheral part of the dentine of teeth ⟨the ramifications of the tubules end in ~ spaces⟩

in·ter·glyph \ˈintə(r)+,-\ *n* [*inter-* + *glyph*] **:** the space between glyphs

in·ter·governmental \¦intə(r)+\ *adj* [*inter-* + *governmental*] **:** between or involving participation by two or more governments or levels of government ⟨~ discussions of commodity stabilization arrangements —Henry Brodie⟩ ⟨an ~ committee⟩

in·ter·gradation \"+\ *n* [*inter-* + *gradation*] **1 :** transition through a series of grades, forms, or kinds that vary (as in evolution) only by consecutive and related differences ⟨may merely represent parallel evolution rather than ~ —Charlotte Avers⟩ **2 :** an intermediate or transitional form **:** a member of a continuously varying series — **in·ter·gradational** \"+\ *adj*

¹in·ter·grade \"+\ *vi* [*inter-* + *grade*] **:** to merge gradually one with another through a continuous series of intermediate forms, kinds, or types

²in·ter·grade \ˈintə(r)+,-\ *n* **:** an intermediate or transitional form

in·ter·graft \¦intə(r)+\ *vi* [*inter-* + *graft*] **:** to be reciprocally capable of being grafted **:** to become united by grafting ⟨most plums ~ freely⟩

in·ter·granular \"+\ *adj* [*inter-* + *granular*] **:** lying or occurring between grains or granules ⟨~ spaces in metamorphic rocks⟩ ⟨~ corrosion of a metal⟩

in·ter·grave \"+\ *vt* [*inter-* + *grave*] **:** to grave or carve between **:** engrave in alternate parts

in·ter·grind \"+\ *vt* [*inter-* + *grind*] **:** to grind together with **:** blend in grinding ⟨resin *interground* with cement⟩

in·ter·group \"+\ *adj* [*inter-* + *group* (n.)] **:** existing or occurring between two or more social groups

in·ter·grow \"+\ *vi* [*inter-* + *grow*] **:** to grow among each other **:** grow intermixed **:** exhibit intergrowth

in·ter·grown \"+\ *adj* **:** characterized by intergrowth ⟨~ knot in timber⟩

in·ter·growth \ˈintə(r)+,-\ *n* [*inter-* + *growth*] **1 :** a growing between, among, or together; *also* **:** the product of such growth **2 :** growth by intussusception

¹in·ter·hemal \ˌintə(r)+\ *adj* [*inter-* + *hemal*] **:** lying between the hemal arches or hemal spines

²interhemal \"\ *n* -s **:** one of the slender elongated bones extending into the flesh of fishes between the hemal spines

in·ter·hemispheric \"+\ *adj* [in sense 1, fr. *inter-* + *hemisphere* + *-ic;* in sense 2, fr. *inter-* + *hemispheric*] **1 :** lying between the cerebral hemispheres **2 :** extending or occurring between hemispheres ⟨~ air flights⟩ ⟨~ warfare⟩

in·ter·house \"+\ *adj* [*inter-* + *house* (n.)] **:** taking place between dormitories, sorority houses, or fraternity houses ⟨an ~ track meet⟩

in·ter·human \"+\ *adj* [*inter-* + *human*] **:** existing or occurring between human beings ⟨~ relations⟩ ⟨~ contagion⟩

¹in·ter·im \ˈintərəm *also* -ntəˌrim *sometimes* -nˌtrəm\ *n* -s [L, adv., meanwhile, fr. *inter* between — more at INTER-] **1 :** a time intervening **:** MEANTIME, INTERVAL ⟨~ between phases of the battle⟩ ⟨~ between arrival and departure⟩ **2 :** a provisional decision or arrangement; *specif* **:** a compromise attempting to settle controversies between Catholics and Protestants ⟨Ratisbon *Interim*⟩ **syn** see BREAK

²interim \"\ *adv* [L] **:** in the meantime **:** MEANWHILE ⟨had tasted ~ of the life of the sporting gentleman —Adrian Bell⟩

³interim \"\ *adj* **:** belonging to an interim **:** done, made, or occurring for an interim or meantime **:** TEMPORARY, PROVISIONAL ⟨~ committee⟩ ⟨~ government⟩ ⟨~ lease⟩

interim certificate *n* **:** a temporary or preliminary certificate (as of securities)

interim dividend *n* **:** a preliminary distribution of profits by way of a dividend before determining the full dividend to be paid for the year; *also* **:** a dividend declared and paid between regular dividend dates

interim ethics *n* **:** an interpretation of the ethical teachings of Jesus as principles enunciated for governing the conduct of the disciples during the anticipated brief span of time before the coming of the second advent and the passing of the terrestrial world

in·ter·im·is·tic \ˌintərəˈmistik\ *adj* [¹*interim* + *-istic*] **:** of or relating to an interim **:** falling in or designed for an interim **:** PROVISIONAL

in·ter·imperial \ˌintə(r)+\ *adj* [*inter-* + *imperial*] **:** carried on between or concerning empires or parts of an empire ⟨~ trade⟩

in·ter·industrial \"+\ *or* **in·ter·industry** \"+\ *adj* [*inter-* + *industrial* or *industry* (n.)] **:** existing or occurring between industries ⟨~ transactions⟩ ⟨~ commodity flow⟩ or throughout the parts of an industry ⟨~ wage structure⟩

in·ter·influence \"+\ *vt* [*inter-* + *influence*] **:** to influence reciprocally ⟨dialectic *interinfluencing* —Edward Sapir⟩

in·ter·insular \"+\ *adj* [*inter-* + *insular*] **:** existing or occurring between islands ⟨~ currents⟩

in·ter·insurance \"+\ *n* [*inter-* + *insurance*] **:** RECIPROCAL INSURANCE

in·ter·insurer \"+\ *n* [*inter-* + *insurer*] **:** an underwriter of reciprocal insurance

in·ter·ionic \"+\ *adj* [*inter-* + *ionic*] **:** situated or acting between ions ⟨~ distance⟩ ⟨~ force⟩

¹in·te·ri·or \(ˈ)inˌtirēə(r), ən·ˈt-, -tēr-\ *adj* [MF & L; MF, fr. L, compar. of (assumed) OL *interus* inward, on the inside; akin to L *inter* between, among — more at INTER-] **1 :** being within the limiting surface or boundary ⟨~ communication⟩ **:** INSIDE, INNER — opposed to *exterior* **2 :** remote from the surface, border, or shore **:** situated toward the center of a mass, area, or structure ⟨~ recesses of the castle⟩ **:** INLAND ⟨~ lake⟩ ⟨~ markets⟩ **3 :** belonging to the inner constitution or operation of something or to its private or concealed nature ⟨~ meaning of a poem⟩ **4 :** belonging to mental or spiritual life ⟨~ monologue⟩ **:** not bodily or worldly **syn** see INNER

²interior \"\ *n* -s **1 :** something that is within **:** the internal or inner part of a thing **:** INSIDE ⟨~ of a house⟩ **2 :** the inland part (as of a country, state, kingdom) ⟨deep into the ~ of Australia⟩ **3 :** the inner or spiritual nature **:** inner character **4 :** the internal affairs of a state or nation ⟨Department of the *Interior*⟩ **5 :** a scene or view of the interior of a building ⟨learned to draw ~*s*⟩ **6 :** an indoor setting or scene in a play or motion picture

interior angle *n* **:** an angle formed between two sides within any rectilinear figure (as a polygon) or between either of two parallel lines and the segment of an intersecting line that lies between them

interior angles: a g h, b g h, g h d, g h c

interior ballistics *n pl but usu sing in constr* **:** a branch of ballistics that deals with the combustion of powder in a gun, the pressure developed, and the motion of the projectile along the bore of the gun — compare EXTERIOR BALLISTICS

interior basin *n* **:** a depression from which no stream flows outward to the sea

interior decorating *n* **:** INTERIOR DESIGN

interior decoration *n* **1 :** INTERIOR DESIGN **2 :** the materials and furnishings of the interior of a building

interior decorator *n* **1 :** INTERIOR DESIGNER **2 a :** one who supplies house furnishings **b :** one who paints or wallpapers building interiors **:** DECORATOR

interior design *n* **:** the art or practice of selecting and organizing the surface coverings, draperies, furniture, and furnishings of an architectural interior

interior designer *n* **:** one who specializes in interior design

interior drainage *n* **:** drainage toward the center of an interior basin rather than to the sea

interior guard *n* **:** a guard maintained within a military installation (as for keeping order, protecting property, guarding prisoners)

in·te·ri·or·i·ty \ənˌtirēˈȯrəd·ē, -tēr-, -ˈär-, -ətē, -i\ *n* -ES [prob. fr. F or ML; F *intériorité*, fr. ML *interioritat-, interioritas*, fr. L *interior* + *-itat-, -itas* -ity] **:** the quality or state of being interior, internalized, or private — contrasted with *exteriority*

in·te·ri·or·iza·tion \ənˌtirēərəˈzāshən, -tēr-, -rī-\ *n* -s **:** the act or process of interiorizing ⟨~ of social values⟩ ⟨~ of the ideals of womanhood —Margaret Cormack⟩

in·te·ri·or·ize \ə'=rēəˌrīz\ *vt* -ED/-ING/-S *see -ize in Explan Notes* [¹*interior* + *-ize*] **:** to make interior; *esp* **:** to make a part of one's own inner being or mental structure ⟨explanation may lie in women's having *interiorized* cultural notions of feminine inferiority —Helen M. Hacker⟩

interior lines *n pl* **:** lines of operation of an armed force that is operating from a center against converging forces — compare EXTERIOR LINES

interior live oak *n* **:** an evergreen oak (*Quercus wizlizenii*) of western No. America much resembling the coast live oak but occurring chiefly in the foothills of mountain ranges somewhat removed from the coast and forming an important part of the chaparral

interior lot *n* **:** a lot bounded by a street on only one side — called also *inside lot*

in·te·ri·or·ly *adv* **:** on or toward the inside **:** INWARDLY ⟨laughing ~⟩ ⟨grooved ~⟩

interior monologue *n* **:** a usu. extended representation in monologue of a fictional character's sequence of thought and feeling ⟨constant shuttling between *interior monologue* and direct narrative —Dan Wickenden⟩

in·te·ri·or·ness *n* -ES **:** the quality or state of being interior

interior plain *n* **:** a plain remote from the borders of a continent — contrasted with *coastal plain*

interior planet *n* **:** INFERIOR PLANET

interior slope *n* **:** the slope connecting the interior crest with the banquette tread in a fortification

interior spring *n, Brit* **:** an innerspring mattress

in·ter·island \ˌintə(r)+\ *adj* [*inter-* + *island* (n.)] **:** existing or operating between islands ⟨~ transport⟩

interj *abbr* interjection

in·ter·ja·cen·cy \ˌintə(r)ˈjāsᵊnsē\ *n* -ES **:** the state of being interjacent **:** INTERVENTION

in·ter·ja·cent \ˌ==ˈjāsᵊnt\ *adj* [L *interjacent-, interjacens*, pres. part. of *interjacēre* to lie between, fr. *inter-* + *jacēre* to lie — more at GIST] **:** lying or being between or among others **:** INTERVENING, INTERPOLATED ⟨~ remarks⟩

in·ter·jac·u·late \ˌintə(r)ˈjakyəˌlāt\ *vt* -ED/-ING/-S [*inter-* + *-jaculate* (as in *ejaculate*)] **:** to ejaculate parenthetically

in·ter·jac·u·la·to·ry \ˌ==ˈjakyələˌtōrē, -tȯr-, -rē\ *adj* [*inter-* + *-jaculatory* (as in *ejaculatory*)] **:** thrown in **:** interspersed parenthetically ⟨~ comment⟩

in·ter·ject \ˌintə(r)ˈjekt\ *vb* -ED/-ING/-S [L *interjectus*, past part. of *interjacere, interjicere*, fr. *inter-* + *jacere* to throw — more at JET] *vt* **:** to throw in between or among other things **:** INTERPOSE, INTERPOLATE ⟨~ a statement⟩ ⟨~ a remark⟩ ~ *vi* **1 :** to throw oneself between or among others **:** come between **:** INTERPOSE **2** *obs* **a :** to cross one another **b :** INTERVENE

in·ter·jec·tion \ˌ==ˈjekshən\ *n* -s [ME *interieccioun*, fr. MF & L; MF *interjection*, fr. L *interjection-, interjectio*, fr. *interjectus* (past part.) + *-ion-, -io* -ion] **1 :** the act of interjecting: as **a :** the act of uttering exclamations **:** EXCLAMATION, EJACULATION **b :** the act of putting in between **:** INTERPOSITION ⟨~ of new issues into a debate⟩ ⟨~ of a third party into a quarrel⟩ **2 :** something that is interjected or that interrupts **:** an interposed remark or exclamation ⟨editorial ~*s*⟩ ⟨topical ~*s*⟩ **3 a :** an ejaculatory word (as *Heavens! Wonderful!*) or form of speech (as *Alas! eh? ha ha!*) usu. lacking grammatical connection **b :** a cry or inarticulate utterance (as *ouch! phooey! ugh!*) expressing an emotion

in·ter·jec·tion·al \ˌ==ˈjekshənᵊl, -shnəl\ *adj* **1 :** thrown in between other words **:** PARENTHETICAL ⟨~ remark⟩ **2 :** relating to or of the nature of an interjection **:** consisting of natural and spontaneous exclamations **:** EJACULATORY ⟨~ grunts⟩ — **in·ter·jec·tion·al·ly** \-ᵊlē, -əlē, -i\ *adv*

in·ter·jec·tion·al·ize \ˌ==ˈjekshənᵊlˌīz, -shnəˌlīz\ *vt* -ED/-ING/-S **:** to make or turn into an interjection

in·ter·jec·tion·ary \ˌ==ˈjekshəˌnerē\ *adj* **:** INTERJECTORY, INTERJECTIONAL

interjection point *n* **:** EXCLAMATION POINT

in·ter·jec·tor \ˌ==ˈjektə(r)\ *n* -s **:** one that interjects

in·ter·jec·to·ri·ly \ˌ==ˈjektərəlē\ *adv* **:** in an interjectory manner

in·ter·jec·to·ry \ˌ==ˈjekt(ə)rē, -ri\ *adj* [*interject* + *-ory*] **:** characterized by interjection **:** thrust in between

in·ter·jec·tur·al \ˌ==ˈjekchərəl, -ksh(ə)rəl\ *adj* [L *interjectura* insertion (fr. *interjectus* — past part. — + *-ura* -ure) + E *-al*] **:** INTERJECTIONAL

in·ter·join \ˌintə(r)ˈjȯin\ *vt* [*inter-* + *join*] **:** to join mutually **:** INTERCONNECT

in·ter·junc·tion \ˌintə(r)ˈjəŋkshən\ *n* [L *interjunctus* (past part. of *interjungere* to join together, fr. *inter-* + *jungere* to join, yoke) + E *-ion* — more at YOKE] **:** a joining of two or more things ⟨~ of roads⟩

in·ter·ki·ne·sis \ˌintə(r)kəˈnēsəs, -ˌkī-\ *n* [NL, fr. *inter-* + *-kinesis*] **:** the period between any two mitoses of a nucleus (as between the first and second meiotic divisions)

in·ter·ki·net·ic \ˌ==+ˈned·ik\ *adj* [fr. NL *interkinesis*, after NL *kinesis*: E *kinetic*] **:** belonging or relating to interkinesis ⟨~ period⟩

in·ter·knit \ˌintə(r)+\ *vb* [*inter-* + *knit*] **:** to knit together **:** INTERTWINE, INTERRELATE

in·ter·knot \"+\ *vt* [*inter-* + *knot*] **:** to knot together

¹in·ter·lace \ˌintə(r)ˈlās\ *vb* [alter. (influenced by L *inter-*) of ME *entrelacen*, fr. MF *entrelacer*, fr. OF *entrelacier*, fr. *entre-* inter- + *lacier* to lace — more at LACE] *vt* **1 :** to unite by or as if by lacing together **:** INTERWEAVE ⟨*interlaced* boughs⟩ ⟨*interlaced* fibers⟩ **2 :** to vary or diversify by alternation, interpolation, or intermixture **:** ALTERNATE, INTERSPERSE, MIX ⟨narrative *interlaced* with anecdotes⟩ ~ *vi* **:** to cross one another as if woven together **:** INTERTWINE, INTERLOCK ⟨*interlacing* letters⟩ ⟨*interlacing* circles⟩

²in·ter·lace \ˈ==,=\ *n* **a :** a form of surface decoration consisting of a number of straps or ribbons so interwoven as to produce a symmetrical design **:** INTERLACEMENT **b :** INTERLACED SCANNING

interlaced *adj* [fr. past part. of ¹*interlace*] **:** INTERLINKED, INTERWOVEN, INTERLOCKED

interlaced scanning *n* **:** television scanning in which each frame is scanned in two successive fields each consisting of all the odd or all the even horizontal lines

in·ter·lace·ment \ˌ==ˈlāsmənt\ *n* -s [alter. (influenced by L *inter-*) of earlier *enterlacement*, fr. F *entrelacement*, fr. MF, fr. OF, fr. *entrelacier* (v.) + *-ment*] **:** the process or result of interlacing **:** a pattern of interlacing elements

in·ter·lac·er \ˌ==ˈlāsə(r)\ *n* **1 :** one that laces shoes during manufacture **2 :** one who makes basketry designs in shoe uppers by cutting slits and weaving in leather strips

in·ter·lac·ery \-s(ə)rē\ *n* [¹*interlace* + *-ery*] **:** interlaced bands, lines, or fibers **:** INTERLACEMENT

interlacing *n* [fr. gerund of ¹*interlace*] **:** INTERLACED SCANNING

interlacing arches *n pl* [fr. pres. part. of ¹*interlace*] **:** usu. circular arches so constructed that their archivolts intersect and seem to be interlaced

interlacing arches

in·ter·lacustrine \ˌintə(r)+\ *adj* [*inter-* + *lacustrine*] **:** situated between lakes

in·ter·lamellar \"+\ *adj* [*inter-* + *lamellar*] **:** situated between lamellae

in·ter·lamellation \"+\ *n* [*inter-* + L *lamella* + E *-ation*] **:** a placing in alternate layers

in·ter·laminate \"+\ *vt* [*inter-* + *laminate*] **1 :** to insert between laminae **2 :** to arrange in alternate laminae ⟨*interlaminated* clay and quartz⟩ — **in·ter·lamination** \"+\ *n*

in·ter·language \ˈintə(r)+,-\ *n* [*inter-* + *language*] **:** language or a language for international communication

in·ter·lap \ˌintə(r)ˈlap\ *vi* [*inter-* + *lap*] **:** to lap over one another **:** OVERLAP ⟨flew with our wings *interlapping* —*Newsweek*⟩

in·ter·lard \ˌintə(r)ˈlärd, -lȧd\ *vt* [alter. (influenced by L *inter-*) of earlier *enterlard*, fr. MF *entrelarder*, fr. OF, fr. *entre-* inter- + *larder* to lard — more at LARD] **1** *obs* **:** to alternate with layers or strips of fat **:** insert lard or bacon in **:** LARD **2 :** to insert between **:** MIX, MINGLE; *esp* **:** to introduce something that is foreign or irrelevant into ⟨~ a conversation with oaths⟩ ⟨~ a text with photographs⟩ ⟨English ~*ed* with Spanish terms⟩

¹in·ter·lay \ˈintə(r)+,-\ *vt* [*inter-* + *lay*] **:** to provide (as a mounted printing plate) with an interlay

²interlay \"\ *n* **:** something (as a sheet of tissue) placed between a printing plate and its base to make the plate or certain areas a suitable height for proper impression — compare OVERLAY, UNDERLAY

¹in·ter·layer \ˌintə(r)+\ *vt* [*inter-* + *layer* (n.)] **:** INTERSTRATIFY, INTERBED

²in·ter·layer \ˈ==+,-\ *n* **:** a layer placed between other layers ⟨plastic ~ in safety glass⟩; *specif* **:** INTERBED

¹in·ter·leaf \ˌintə(r)+\ *vt* [*inter-* + *leaf* (n.)] **:** INTERLEAVE

²in·ter·leaf \ˈ==+,-\ *n* **1 :** a usu. blank leaf inserted or fastened between two leaves of a book (as for written notes or for protecting a color plate) **2 :** SLIP SHEET

in·ter·league \ˌintə(r)+\ *adj* [*inter-* + *league* (n.)] **:** existing or occurring between leagues ⟨~ trading of players⟩

in·ter·leave \ˌintə(r)ˈlēv\ *vt* -ED/-ING/-S [*inter-* + *-leave* (back-formation fr. *leaved*, taken as a past participle)] **1 a :** to equip (as a manifold business form) with an interleaf **b :** SLIP-SHEET **2 :** INTERLAMINATE, INTERSTRATIFY

in·ter–lending \ˌintə(r)+\ *adj, Brit* **:** of or relating to interlibrary loan

in·ter·lens \"+\ *adj* [*inter-* + *lens* (n.)] *of a photographic shutter* **:** situated between lens elements

in·ter·library \"+\ *adj* [*inter-* + *library* (n.)] **:** taking place between libraries ⟨~ loan⟩

in·ter·light \"+\ *vt* [*inter-* + *light*] **:** to light intermittently ⟨misery is *interlit* with flashes of pure joyousness —Edmond Taylor⟩

¹in·ter·line \"+\ *vb* [alter. (influenced by L *inter-*) of ME *enterlinen*, fr. ML *interlineare*, fr. L *inter-* + *linea* line — more at LINE] *vt* **1 :** to write or insert between lines already written or printed ⟨*interlined* additions to a manuscript⟩ **:** write or print something between the lines of ⟨~ a page⟩ ⟨~ a book⟩ **2 :** to add an interline to (ruled paper) ~ *vi* **:** to make insertions between written or printed lines

²interline \ˈintə(r)+,-\ *n* **:** a light often broken line ruled between horizontal lines

³in·ter·line \ˌ==+\ *vt* [ME *interlinen*, fr. *inter-* + *linen* to line — more at LINE] **:** to provide (as a garment) with an interlining

⁴in·ter·line \"+\ *adj* [*inter-* + *line* (n.)] **:** relating to, involving, or carried by two or more transportation lines ⟨~ traffic⟩ ⟨~ freight⟩ ⟨~ haul⟩ ⟨~ costs⟩

in·ter·lin·e·al \"+ˈlinēəl\ *adj* [*interlinear* + *-al*] **:** INTERLINEAR — **in·ter·lin·e·al·ly** \-əlē\ *adv*

¹in·ter·linear \"+\ *adj* [ME *interliniare*, fr. ML *interlinearis*, fr. L *inter-* + *linearis* linear — more at LINEAR] **1 :** situated between lines **2 :** inserted between lines already written or printed ⟨~ gloss⟩ ⟨~ corrections⟩ ⟨~ translation⟩ **3 a :** containing insertions between lines ⟨~ manuscript⟩ **b :** written or printed in different languages or texts in alternate lines ⟨~ bible⟩ — **in·ter·lin·e·ar·ly** *adv*

²interlinear \"\ *n* -s **:** a book having interlinear matter; *esp* **:** a school text of a work in a foreign language with interlinear translation

¹in·ter·lin·e·ary \"+ˈlinēˌerē\ *adj* [prob. alter. (influenced by E *-ary*) of ML *interlinearis*] **:** INTERLINEAR

²interlineary \"\ *n* -ES **:** INTERLINEAR ⟨infinite helps of *interlinearies*, breviaries, synopses —John Milton⟩

in·ter·lin·e·ate \ˌintə(r)ˈlinēˌāt\ *vb* -ED/-ING/-S [ML *interlineatus*, past part. of *interlineare* to interline — more at INTERLINE] **:** INTERLINE

in·ter·lin·e·a·tion \ˌ==,==ˈāshən\ *n* [ML *interlineatus* (past part.) + E *-ion*] **1 :** the act of interlining **2 :** something interlined ⟨~*s* in a later hand⟩ ⟨editorial ~*s*⟩ ⟨a printed form with typewritten ~*s* —*N.Y.Times*⟩

in·ter·lin·er \ˌ==ˈlīnə(r)\ *n* **1 :** one that interlines **2 :** INTERLINING ⟨~*s* for arctic and military clothing⟩

in·ter·lin·gua \ˌintə(r)ˈliŋgwə\ *n* -s [It, fr. *inter-* + *lingua* language, tongue, fr. L — more at TONGUE] **1 :** INTERLANGUAGE **2** *usu cap* **:** an artificial interlanguage that is based on the linguistic elements common to English and the chief Romance languages and is promoted by the International Auxiliary Language Association

in·ter·lingual \ˌintə(r)+\ *adj* [*inter-* + *lingual*] **:** of, relating to, or existing between two or more languages ⟨~ alphabet⟩ ⟨~ dictionary⟩ ⟨~ idiom⟩

in·ter·linguistic \"+\ *adj* [*inter-* + *linguistic*] **1 :** INTERLINGUAL ⟨~ influences⟩ **2 :** of or relating to an interlanguage

in·ter·linguistics \"+\ *n pl but sing in constr* [ISV *inter-* + *linguistics*] **:** the study of interlingual similarities and relationships esp. for the purpose of devising an interlanguage

¹in·ter·lin·ing \"+ˈlīniŋ\ *n* [ME, fr. gerund of *interlinen*, *enterlinen* to interline — more at INTERLINE] **:** INTERLINEATION

²in·ter·lining \"+\ *n* [*inter-* + *lining*] **1 :** an inner lining (as of a coat or jacket) consisting of a warm or firm fabric shaped and sewn between the ordinary lining and the outside fabric **2 :** any fabric used for making interlinings

¹in·ter·link \"+\ *vt* [*inter-* + *link*] **:** to link together

²interlink \"\ *n* **:** an intermediate or connecting link

in·ter·linkage \"+\ *n* **1 :** the act of interlinking or state of being interlinked **2 :** a system of links ⟨molecular ~⟩

in·ter·lobate \"+\ *adj* [*inter-* + *lobate*] **:** lying between lobes ⟨~ moraines of a retreating glacier⟩

in·ter·lobular \"+\ *adj* [*inter-* + *lobular*] **:** lying between or connecting lobules ⟨~ connective tissue⟩

in·ter·local \"+\ *or* **in·ter·locality** \"+\ *adj* [*inter-* + *local* (adj.) or *locality* (n.)] **:** existing between localities ⟨~ tax differences⟩ — **in·ter·locally** \"+\ *adv*

in·ter·located \"+\ *adj* [*inter-* + *located*, past part. of *locate*] **:** placed between others **:** INTERPOSED

¹in·ter·lock \"+\ *vb* [*inter-* + *lock*] *vi* **:** to engage or interrelate with one another **:** lock into one another **:** interlace firmly ⟨~*ing* fingers⟩ ⟨bolt ~*s* with its striker⟩ ⟨~*ing* stitches⟩ ~ *vt* **1 :** to lock together **:** unite closely ⟨walls . . . contrived to ~ stone with stone without using an ounce of mortar —John McNulty⟩ **2 :** to connect in such a way that the motion of any part is constrained by another part; *esp* **:** to arrange the connections of (as railroad switches or signals) to ensure successive movement in proper sequence

²in·ter·lock \ˈintə(r)+,-\ *n* **1 :** the fact or state of being interlocked ⟨~ of corporate directorates⟩ **2 :** an arrangement whereby the operation of one part or mechanism automatically brings about or prevents the operation of another ⟨~ on an elevator door⟩ **3 :** a mechanism for or the act of synchronizing a motion-picture camera and sound-recording devices

³in·ter·lock \ˌ==+\ *adj* **:** knitted with interlocking stitches by the use of two alternating sets of needles ⟨~ hosiery⟩

interlocked grain *also* **interlocking grain** *n* **:** a wood grain in which the fibers incline in one direction in a number of annual rings and in a reverse direction in succeeding rings

in·ter·lock·er \"+ˈläkə(r)\ *n* **:** one that interlocks

interlocking director *n* [fr. pres. part. of ¹*interlock*] **:** one who serves as a director of two or more corporations at one time

interlocking directorate *n* **:** a directorate linked with that of another corporation by interlocking directors so that the businesses managed by them are to some degree under one control

in·ter·loculus \ˌintə(r)+\ *n* [NL, fr. *inter-* + *loculus*] **:** a space or part between two loculi

in·ter·lo·cu·tion \ˌintə(r)lōˈkyüshən, -lə'-\ *n* [L *interlocution-, interlocutio*, fr. *interlocutus* (past part. of *interloqui* to speak between, fr. *inter-* + *loqui* to speak) + *-ion-, -io* -ion] **1 :** interchange of speech **:** CONVERSATION **2 :** an interruptive utterance **:** INTERRUPTION, INTERPOLATION, PARENTHESIS **3 a** *obs* **:** responsive reading or recital **b** *obs* **:** a speech in reply **:** RESPONSE **c :** mode of intercommunication **4 a** [LL *interlocution-, interlocutio*, fr. L] **:** the making of an interlocutory legal order or decree; *also* **:** the order or decree **b** *Roman law* **:** a constitution of the emperor in the form of an informal expression of the imperial wish

in·ter·loc·u·tor \ˌintə(r)ˈläkyəd·ə(r), |tə(r)\ *n* -s [L *interlocutus* (past part.) + E *-or*] **1 :** one who takes part in dialogue or conversation **2 :** a man in the middle of the line in a minstrel show who questions the end men and acts as leader **3** [ML *interlocutorium*, fr. neut. of *interlocutorius*, adj.] *Scots law* **:** a judgment or order of a court whether interlocutory or finally determining the issues

¹in·ter·loc·u·to·ry \ˌ==ˈläkyəˌtōrē, -tȯr-, -rē\ *adj* [*interlocution* + *-ory*] **1 :** consisting of or having the nature of dialogue **:** CONVERSATIONAL ⟨~ observations⟩ **2 :** of or belonging to an interruptive speech or question **:** spoken as an interlocution **3** [ME (Scot. dial.), fr. ML *interlocutorius*, fr. LL *interlocutus* (past part. of *interloqui* to pronounce an interlocutory sentence, fr. L, to speak between) + L *-orius* -ory] *law* **:** not final or definitive **:** made or done during the progress of an action **:** INTERMEDIATE, PROVISIONAL ⟨~ decree in a divorce suit⟩ ⟨~ motion⟩

²in·ter·loc·u·to·ry *n* -ES *obs* **:** an interlocutory decree

in·ter·loc·u·tress *or* **in·ter·loc·u·trice** \ˌ==ˈläkyəˌtrəs\ *or* **in·ter·loc·u·trix** \-ˌtriks\ *n, pl* **interlocutresses** \-rəsəz\ *or* **interlocutri·ces** \ˌ==,==ˈtrī(ˌ)sēz\ [*interlocutress* fr. *interlocutor* + *-ess; interlocutrice* fr. F, fem. of *interlocuteur* interlocutor; *interlocutrix* fr. *interlocutor* + *-trix*] **:** a female interlocutor

in·ter·lope \ˌintə(r)ˈlōp\ *vb* -ED/-ING/-S [prob. back-formation fr. *interloper*] *vi* **1 :** to encroach on the rights (as in trade) of others **:** trade without a proper license **2 :** INTRUDE, INTERMEDDLE, INTERFERE ~ *vt, obs* **:** INTERPOLATE

in·ter·lop·er \ˈ==ˌlōpə(r), ˌ=='==\ *n* -s [alter. (influenced by L *inter-*) of earlier *enterloper*, prob. fr. *enter-* inter- + *-loper* (as in *landloper*)] **1 :** one that interlopes **:** an unlawful intruder on a property or sphere of action **2 :** one that interferes or thrusts himself in wrongfully or officiously

in·ter·lot \ˌintə(r)+\ *vt* [*inter-* + *lot*] **:** to pool (as star lots of wool) into large lots for auction

in·ter·lu·ca·tion \ˌintə(r)lüˈkāshən *also* -)lyü'-\ *n* -s [L *interlucation-, interlucatio* act of pruning, act of thinning, fr. *interlucatus* (past part. of *interlucare* to thin, top, fr. *inter-* + *-lucare* — fr. *luc-, lux* light) + *-ion-, -io* -ion — more at LIGHT] **:** the cutting of trees from a stand so that the remaining trees will grow rapidly

in·ter·lu·cent \ˌintə(r)ˈlüsənt *also* -)lˌyü-\ *adj* [L *interlucent-, interlucens*, pres. part. of *interlucēre* to shine, fr. *inter-* + *lucēre* to shine — more at LIGHT] **:** shining or glowing between or in the midst of other things

1in·ter·lude \ˈintə(r),lüd *also* -)l,yüd\ *n* -s [alter. (influenced by L *inter-*) of ME *enterlude*, fr. ML *interludium*, fr. L *inter-* + *ludus* play — more at LUDICROUS] **1 a :** an entertainment of a light or farcical character introduced between the acts of an old mystery or morality play or forming a feature of a festival or fete **b :** one of the farces or comedies derived from these entertainments **2 :** a performance or entertainment between the acts of a play **3 a :** an irrelevant change or happening in a course of events **:** EPISODE ⟨romantic ~⟩ **b :** an intervening or interruptive space of time or such a feature or event **:** INTERVAL ⟨forests with ~s of open meadow⟩ ⟨brief ~ of sanity⟩ ⟨~s of wit and humor in a tragic story⟩ **4 :** a musical composition inserted between the parts of a musical or dramatic entertainment or religious service; *specif* **:** a short organ piece played between verses of a hymn or psalm

2interlude \"\ *vi* -ED/-ING/-s **1 :** to perform an interlude **2 :** to occur as an interlude

in·ter·lu·di·al \ˌ==ˈlüdēəl *also* -)l,yü-\ *adj* **:** of, relating to, or resembling an interlude ⟨~ passage between fugues⟩

in·ter·lu·nar \ˌintə(r)ˈlünə(r) *also* -)lˈyü-\ *also* **in·ter·lu·na·ry** \-nərē\ *adj* [*interlunar* prob. fr. MF *interlunaire*, fr. L *interlunium* interlunation (fr. *inter-* + *luna* moon) + MF *-aire* (fr. L *-aris* -ar); *interlunary* prob. modif. (influenced by E *lunary*) of MF *interlunaire* — more at LUNAR] **:** relating to the interval between old and new moon when the moon is invisible ⟨silent as the moon . . . hid in her vacant ~ cave —John Milton⟩

in·ter·lu·na·tion \ˌintə(r)+\ *n* [prob. fr. *inter-* + *lunation*] **1 :** the interlunar period **2 :** a period of darkness or blankness

in·ter·ly·ing \ˌintə(r)+\ *adj* [*inter-* + *lying*, pres. part. of *lie*] **:** lying in between ⟨~ beds of gravel⟩

in·ter·mandibular \ˌintə(r)+\ *adj* [*inter-* + *mandibular*] **1 :** situated between the mandibles **2 :** INTERRAMAL

in·ter·marine \"+\ *adj* [*inter-* + *marine*] **:** carried on between seas or ships on the sea ⟨~ communication⟩

in·ter·marriage \"+\ *n* [*inter-* + *marriage*] **1 :** marriage between members of different racial, social, or religious groups ⟨~ between Negroes and whites⟩ ⟨~ of invaders and the conquered⟩ ⟨Protestant-Catholic ~⟩ **2 a :** INMARRIAGE, ENDOGAMY **b :** INBREEDING

in·ter·marry \"+\ *vi* [*inter-* + *marry*] **1 a :** to marry each other — used of a couple or of one of the contracting parties ⟨statute legitimatizing children whose parents *intermarried* after their birth —Morris Ploscowe⟩ **b :** to marry within a group ⟨the deaf are likely to ~ —H.J.Baker⟩ **2 :** to become connected by marriage between their members **:** give and take mutually in marriage — used of families, castes, social or religious or ethnic groups or of their members ⟨if a peeress by marriage should afterwards ~ with a commoner —T.E.May⟩

in·ter·maxilla \"+\ *n* [NL, fr. *inter-* + *maxilla*] **:** PREMAXILLA

in·ter·maxillar \"+\ *adj* [*inter-* + *maxillar*] **:** INTERMAXILLARY

1in·ter·maxillary \"+\ *adj* [*inter-* + *maxillary*] **1 :** lying between maxillae; *esp* **:** joining the two maxillary bones ⟨~ suture⟩ **2 :** of or relating to the premaxillae

2intermaxillary \"\ *n* **:** PREMAXILLA

intermean *n* [*inter-* + *mean*] *obs* **:** something intermediate **:** INTERLUDE

in·ter·meddle \ˌintə(r)+\ *vb* [ME *entermedlen*, fr. MF *entremedler, entremeller, entremesler*, fr. OF, fr. *entre-* inter- + *medler, meller, mesler* to mix — more at MEDDLE] *vt* **1** *obs* **:** INTERMINGLE **2** *obs* **:** INTERPOSE ~ *vi* **:** to meddle with the affairs of others **:** meddle officiously **:** INTERFERE ⟨must know and ~ with mysteries —Mary Webb⟩ ⟨any *intermeddling* with slavery in the federal district —S.E.Morison & H.S.Commager⟩ **syn** see MEDDLE

in·ter·meddler \"+\ *n* **1 :** one who intermeddles ⟨out-of-state ~s⟩ **2 a** *obs* **:** INTERMEDIARY **b** *obs* **:** INTERLOPER

in·ter·mede \ˈintə(r),mēd\ *n* -s [F *intermède*, fr. It *intermedio*, fr. LL *intermedium* — more at INTERMEDIUM] **1** *archaic* **:** INTERMEDIUM **2** *or* **in·ter·mède** \aⁿtermed\ **:** INTERMEZZO 1

1intermedia *pl of* INTERMEDIUM

2in·ter·me·dia \ˌintə(r)ˈmēdēə\ *n, pl* **intermedi·ae** \-dē,ē\ [NL, fr. L, fem. of *intermedius* intermediate — more at INTERMEDIATE] **:** either member of the middle pair of tail feathers of a bird

in·ter·me·di·a·cy \ˌintə(r)ˈmēdēəsē, -si, *chiefly Brit* -mējəs- *or* -mēdyəs-\ *n* [fr. *2intermediate*, after E *immediate: immediacy*] **:** INTERMEDIATENESS

in·ter·me·di·al \ˌintə(r)ˈmēdēəl\ *n* [L *intermedius* + E *-al*] **:** INTERMEDIATE

1in·ter·me·di·ary \ˌintə(r)ˈmēdē,erē, -ri, *chiefly Brit* -mējər- *or* -mēdyər-\ *adj* [prob. fr. F *intermédiaire*, fr. L *intermedius* + F *-aire* -ary] **1 :** lying, coming, or done between **:** INTERMEDIATE ⟨~ distribution of perishable products⟩ ⟨importing and other ~ trades⟩ **2 :** acting or capable of acting between others as a mediator ⟨~ agent⟩

2intermediary \"\ *n* -ES [prob. fr. F *intermédiaire*, fr. *intermédiaire*, adj.] **1 :** one that is intermediate: **a :** MEDIATOR, INTERAGENT, GO-BETWEEN ⟨~ between the people and God⟩ **b :** something that serves as a medium or means **:** mediating agency **2 :** an intermediate form, stage, or product

intermediary host *n* **:** INTERMEDIATE HOST

1in·ter·me·di·ate \ˌintə(r)ˈmēdē,āt, *usu* -ād.+V\ *vi* [ML *intermediatus*, past part. of *intermediare*, fr. L *inter-* + LL *mediare* to mediate — more at MEDIATE] **1 :** to come between **:** INTERVENE, INTERPOSE **2 :** to act as intermediate agent **:** MEDIATE

2in·ter·me·di·ate \ˌintə(r)ˈmēdēət, *chiefly Brit* -mējə̇- *or* -mēdyə̇-; *usu* -ə̇d.+V\ *adj* [ML *intermediatus*, fr. L *intermedius* intermediate (fr. *inter-* + *medius* mid, middle) + *-atus* -ate — more at MID] **1 :** lying or being in the middle place or degree **:** between extremes or limits **:** coming or done in between **:** INTERVENING ⟨~ hue⟩ ⟨~ credit⟩ ⟨~ stage of growth⟩ ⟨~ stops on a journey⟩ ⟨~ sizes⟩ **2 a :** of or relating to the period between primary and secondary education usu. comprising the fourth, fifth, and sixth grades **b :** of or relating to the stage between the introductory and advanced stages of a course of study or training ⟨~ French⟩ ⟨~ piano pupil⟩ **c :** taken during the first year after matriculation at a British university other than Oxford or Cambridge ⟨~ examination⟩ ⟨an ~ course⟩ — compare PREVIOUS EXAMINATION, RESPONSION 2b

3intermediate \"\ *n* -s **1 :** something intermediate **:** a term, member, class, or quality between others of a series **2 :** one that acts between others **:** MEDIATOR, INTERMEDIARY **3 :** an intermediate biological type or form **4 :** a chemical compound formed as an intermediate step between the starting material and the final product (as a dye intermediate) **5 a :** a wool-carding machine that comes between the breaker and the finisher **b :** a machine in cotton manufacture placed between the slubbing billy and the roving frame **6 a :** IDLER WHEEL **b :** the second speed in a vehicle having three forward speeds

4intermediate \"\ *prep* **:** in the time intervening between — used in law ⟨waste committed ~ the sale and the period when the right to redeem expired —T.M.Cooley⟩

intermediate carrier *n* **:** a transportation line participating in a through movement which neither originates nor terminates the passengers or freight

intermediate disk *n* **:** KRAUSE'S MEMBRANE

intermediate frequency *n* **:** a relatively low frequency to which a signal is converted before demodulation in heterodyne reception — abbr. *i.f.*

intermediate girl scout *n* **:** a member of the Girl Scouts in the age group ranging approximately from 10 through 13 years old

intermediate goods *n pl* **:** PRODUCER GOODS

intermediate host *n* **1 :** a host which is normally used by a parasite in the course of its life cycle and in which it may multiply asexually but not sexually — compare DEFINITIVE HOST **2 :** RESERVOIR 6a; *sometimes* **:** VECTOR 2

in·ter·me·di·ate·ly *adv* **1 :** in an intermediate position **:** between things or times **2 :** to an intermediate degree ⟨~ hot⟩ **3 :** not immediately **:** INDIRECTLY

in·ter·me·di·ate·ness *n* -ES **:** the quality or state of being intermediate

intermediate school *n* **1 :** JUNIOR HIGH SCHOOL **2 :** a school comprising the fourth, fifth, and sixth grades **3 :** a part of the British school system serving children from 12 to 14 years of age — compare JUNIOR SCHOOL, SENIOR SCHOOL

intermediate stock *n* **:** a stock grafted between the basal stock and the scion (as in a double-worked apple tree)

intermediate tissue *n* **:** CONJUNCTIVE TISSUE

intermediate wheatgrass *n* **:** an Asiatic grass (*Agropyron intermedium*) introduced into the rangelands of western U.S. for pasture and fodder use

intermediate wheel *n* **:** an idler wheel in the driving train or the dial train of a timepiece

in·ter·me·di·a·tion \ˌintə(r),mēdēˈāshən\ *n* [ML *intermediatus* (past part.) + E *-ion*] **:** the act of coming between **:** INTERVENTION, MEDIATION

in·ter·me·di·a·tor \-ˈmēdē,ād.ə(r), -ātə-\ *n* [ML *intermediatus* (past part.) + E *-or*] **:** MEDIATOR

in·ter·mediatory \ˌintə(r)+\ *adj* **:** MEDIATORY

in·ter·me·din \ˌintə(r)ˈmēdᵊn\ *n* -s [ISV *intermed-* (fr. NL *pars intermedia*) + *-in*] **:** a hormone secreted by the pars intermedia or the anterior lobe of the pituitary body that induces expansion of chromatophores in various vertebrates

intermedio- *comb form* [L *intermedius*] **:** intermediate and ⟨*intermedio*lateral⟩

in·ter·me·di·um \ˌintə(r)ˈmēdēəm\ *n, pl* **interme·dia** \-dēə\ *or* **intermediums** [LL, fr. L, neut. of *intermedius* intermediate — more at INTERMEDIATE] **1** *obs* **:** an intermediate space or time **:** INTERVAL **2 :** a musical or dance interlude **3 :** an intervening agent **:** INTERMEDIARY, MEDIUM **4 :** a bone or cartilage situated between the radiale and ulnare in the carpus and between the tibiale and fibulare in the tarsus in many vertebrates

in·ter·me·di·us \ˌ==ˈmēdēəs\ *adj* [NL, fr. L, intermediate] **:** tending to be moderately virulent — used esp. of strains of diphtheria bacilli — compare GRAVIS, MITIS

in·ter·meil \ˌ==ˈmel\ *vb* [ME *entremellen, entermellen*, fr. MF *entremeller* — more at INTERMEDDLE] *archaic* **:** INTERMEDDLE, INTERMINGLE

in·ter·member \ˌintə(r)+\ *vb* -ED/-ING/-s [*inter-* + *member* (n.)] **:** to fit into a uniform or harmonious group ⟨storage cupboard which ~s with the vertical cabinets —Estelle B. Hunter⟩ ⟨filing sections ~*ed* in a stack⟩

in·ter·membral \"+\ *adj* [*inter-* + *membral*] **:** existing between members — **in·ter·membrally** \"+\ *adv*

intermembral index *n, anthrop* **:** the ratio of the length of the whole arm to the length of the whole leg multiplied by 100

in·ter·membranous \"+\ *adj* [*inter-* + *membranous*] **:** situated or occurring between membranes

intermembranous ossification *n* **:** ossification that takes place in connective tissue without prior development of cartilage — compare ENDOCHONDRAL OSSIFICATION

in·ter·meningeal \"+\ *adj* [*inter-* + *meningeal*] **:** situated or occurring between the meninges ⟨~ hemorrhage⟩

in·ter·menstrual \"+\ *adj* [*inter-* + *menstrual*] **:** occurring between the menses ⟨~ pain⟩

in·ter·ment \ənˈtərmənt, -tōm-\ *n* -s [ME *enterment*, fr. MF *enterrement*, fr. OF, fr. *enterrer* to inter + *-ment* — more at INTER] **1 :** the act or ceremony of depositing a dead body in a grave or tomb **:** BURIAL, SEPULTURE, INHUMATION ⟨change from ~ to cremation⟩ **2 :** the act of removing from sight or consideration ⟨decision . . . will result in the ~ of the women's program —Helen Fuller⟩

in·ter·mesenteric \ˌintə(r)+\ *adj* [*inter-* + *mesenteric*] **:** situated between mesenteries

in·ter·mesh \"+\ *vi* [*inter-* + *mesh*] **:** to mesh with one another ⟨~*ing* twin rotors⟩

in·ter·metallic \"+\ *adj* [*inter-* + *metallic*] **:** composed of two or more metals or of a metal and a nonmetal in an alloy

intermetallic compound *n* **:** an alloy having a characteristic crystal structure and usu. a definite composition not necessarily conforming with the normal rules of valence — often distinguished from *solid solution*

in·ter·mewed \"+\ *adj* [*inter-* + *mewed*, past part. of *mew* (to molt); prob. trans. of MF *entremué*] *of a hawk* **:** having molted once in confinement

in·ter·mez·zo \ˌintə(r)ˈmet(,)sō *sometimes* -ed(,)zō\ *n, pl* **intermez·zi** \-sē, -zē\ *or* **intermezzos** [It, fr. LL *intermedium* — more at INTERMEDIUM] **1 :** a short light sometimes burlesque musical or dramatic piece presented between the acts of serious drama or opera **2 a :** a humorous musical play in the 16th and 17th centuries the acts of which alternated with those of the principal work **b :** a movement coming between the major sections of a symphony or other extended work **c :** a short independent instrumental composition **3 :** DIVERSION, EPISODE, AFFAIR, INTERLUDE ⟨pretty lady who created a domestic ~ —*Newsweek*⟩

in·ter·micellar \ˌintə(r)+\ *adj* [*inter-* + *micellar*] **:** situated between micelles ⟨~ cavities⟩

in·ter·migration \"+\ *n* [*inter-* + *migration*] **:** mutual migration **:** migration in both directions ⟨~ of fauna of neighboring continents⟩

in·ter·mi·na·bil·i·ty \ən,tərmənəˈbiləd.ē\ *n* -ES **:** ENDLESSNESS

in·ter·mi·na·ble \ənˈtərmənəbəl, -tōm-, -təim- *also* -mn-\ *adj* [ME, fr. LL *interminabilis*, fr. L *in-* 1in- + *terminare* to terminate + *-abilis* -able — more at TERMINATE] **:** having no termination **:** wearisomely protracted **:** BOUNDLESS, ENDLESS ⟨~ sermons⟩ ⟨~ debates⟩ ⟨~ forest⟩ — **in·ter·mi·na·ble·ness** *n* -ES — **in·ter·mi·na·bly** \-blē, -li\ *adv*

in·ter·mi·nate \-mə,nāt, -nə̇t\ *adj* [L *interminatus*, fr. *in-* 1in- + *terminatus*, past part. of *terminare*] *archaic* **:** having no end or limit

interminated *adj* [1*in-* + *terminated*] *obs* **:** LIMITLESS, BOUNDLESS

in·ter·mingle \ˌintə(r)+\ *vb* [*inter-* + *mingle*] **:** to mingle or mix together ⟨*intermingling* different races⟩ ⟨fat and lean *intermingled*⟩

in·ter·ministerial \"+\ *adj* [*inter-* + *ministerial*] **:** existing between ministries ⟨~ commission⟩

in·ter·mis·sion \ˌintə(r)ˈmishən\ *n* -s [L *intermission-, intermissio*, fr. *intermissus* (past part. of *intermittere* to cease, intermit) + *-ion-, -io* -ion] **1 :** the act of intermitting or state of being intermitted **:** INTERRUPTION, BREAK ⟨~ between acts of a play⟩ **2 :** cessation for a time **:** an intervening period of time **:** INTERVAL ⟨work without ~⟩ **3 :** the space of time between two paroxysms of a disease — distinguished from *remission*

in·ter·mis·sive \ˌ==ˈmisiv\ *adj* [L *intermissus* + E *-ive*] **:** INTERMITTENT

in·ter·mit \ˌintə(r)ˈmit, *usu* -id.+V\ *vb* **intermitted; intermitted; intermitting; intermits** [L *intermittere*, fr. *inter-* + *mittere* to send — more at SMITE] *vt* **1 :** to cause to cease for a time or at intervals **:** DISCONTINUE, INTERRUPT, SUSPEND ⟨pray to the gods to ~ the plague —Shak.⟩ ⟨never *intermitted* the custom of dressing for dinner⟩ **2 :** to cause (as a spark) to come and go at intervals ~ *vi* **:** to cease at intervals **:** to be intermittent ⟨a fever that *intermitted* with great regularity⟩ **syn** see DEFER

in·ter·mit·tence \ˌ==ˈmitᵊn(t)s\ *n* -s **1 :** the quality or state of being intermittent **:** periodic cessation or interruption **:** INTERMITTENCY ⟨~ of the pulse⟩ **2 :** periodic recurrence **:** FITFULNESS ⟨violent ~s of physical passion —Aldous Huxley⟩

in·ter·mit·ten·cy \-sē, -si\ *n* -ES **:** intermittent character or condition **:** INTERMITTENCE ⟨~ of employment and uncertainty of wages⟩

intermittency effect *n* **:** the photographic effect in which intermittent exposures fail to give the same density as a continuous exposure of the same total energy

in·ter·mit·tent \ˌ==ˈmitᵊnt\ *adj* [L *intermittent-, intermittens*, pres. part. of *intermittere* to intermit — more at INTERMIT] **:** coming and going at intervals **:** not continuous **:** ALTERNATING, RECURRENT, PERIODIC ⟨~ fever⟩ ⟨~ rain⟩ ⟨~ publication⟩ ⟨~ stream⟩ ⟨~ spark⟩ — **in·ter·mit·tent·ly** *adv*

intermittent claudication *n* **:** cramping pain and weakness in the legs esp. the calves on walking that disappears after rest and is usu. associated with inadequate blood supply to the muscles (as in thromboangiitis obliterans, vascular spasm, or arteriosclerosis)

intermittent current *n* **:** an electric current that flows and ceases to flow at regular or irregular intervals but is not reversed

intermittent light *n* **:** a signal or beacon light having equal periods of shining and eclipse — compare FLASHLIGHT, OCCULTING LIGHT

intermittent movement *n* **:** the motion produced by a mechanical device that advances a motion-picture film one or more frames at a time with stationary intervening periods; *also* **:** any such mechanical device

intermittent pulse *n* **:** a pulse that occas. skips a cardiac beat

intermittent sterilization *n* **:** sterilization by heating to boiling several times at intervals of about 24 hours in order that any resistant spores may germinate and be destroyed

in·ter·mit·ter *or* **in·ter·mit·tor** \ˌintə(r)ˈmid.ə(r)\ *n* -s **:** one that intermits; *esp* **:** a device for producing intermittent movement

in·ter·mix \ˌintə(r)+\ *vb* [back-formation fr. earlier *intermixt* intermingled, fr. L *intermixtus*, past part. of *intermiscēre* to intermix, fr. *inter-* + *miscēre* to mix — more at MIX] **:** to mix together **:** INTERMINGLE ⟨coal seams ~*ed* with iron ore⟩

in·ter·mixable \"+\ *adj* **:** capable of being mixed or blended together ⟨~ paint colors⟩

in·ter·mixedly \"+\ *adv* **:** in a mixed manner

in·ter·mixture \"+\ *n* [L *intermixtus* + E *-ure* (as in *mixture*)] **1 a :** the act of mixing together or the state of being mixed together **b :** a mass formed by mixture **:** a mass of ingredients mixed ⟨~ of letters and figures in a cryptogram⟩ **2 :** an additional ingredient **:** ADMIXTURE **3 :** MISCEGENATION

in·ter·modulation \"+\ *n* [ISV *inter-* + *modulation*] **:** the production in an electrical device of currents having frequencies equal to the sums and differences of frequencies supplied to the device or of their harmonics; *also* **:** distortion (as of amplified sound) caused by intermodulation

in·ter·molecular \"+\ *adj* [*inter-* + *molecular*] **:** existing or acting between molecules ⟨~ forces⟩ ⟨~ condensation⟩ — **in·ter·mo·lec·u·lar·ly** *adv*

in·ter·mon·tane \ˌintə(r)ˈmän,tān\ *or* **in·ter·mont** \-ˈmänt\ *adj* [*intermontane* fr. *inter-* + L *montanus* of a mountain; *intermont* fr. *inter-* + L *mont-, mons* mountain — more at MOUNTAIN] **:** situated between mountains ⟨~ basin⟩

in·ter·morainic \ˌintə(r)+\ *adj* [*inter-* + *morainic*] **:** situated between moraines ⟨~ depression⟩

in·ter·mountain \"+\ *adj* [*inter-* + *mountain*] **:** INTERMONTANE

in·ter·mundane \"+\ *adj* [*inter-* + *mundane*] **:** existing between worlds ⟨~ space⟩

in·ter·mun·di·al \"+ˈməndēəl\ *or* **in·ter·mun·di·an** \-ēən\ *adj* [L *intermundia* + E *-al* or *-an*] **:** INTERMUNDANE

in·ter·mun·di·um \ˌ==ˈməndēəm\ *n, pl* **intermun·dia** \-ēə\ [NL, back-formation fr. L *intermundia*, pl., spaces between worlds, fr. *inter-* + *-mundia* (fr. *mundus* world) — more at MUNDANE] **:** space between worlds

in·ter·mural \ˌintə(r)+\ *adj* [L *intermuralis*, fr. *inter-* + *muralis* of a wall — more at MURAL] **:** lying between walls — **in·ter·murally** \"+\ *adv*

in·ter·muscular \"+\ *adj* [*inter-* + *muscular*] **:** lying between and separating muscles ⟨~ fat⟩

in·ter·mutual \"+\ *adj* [*inter-* + *mutual*] **:** MUTUAL — **in·ter·mutually** *adv* \"+\

1in·tern *or* **in·terne** \(ˈ)inˈtərn, ənˈt-, -tōn,-təin\ *adj* [MF *interne*, fr. L *internus* — more at INTERNAL] *archaic* **:** INTERNAL

2intern \"\ *vt* -ED/-ING/-s [F *interner*, fr. *interne*, adj.] **1 a :** to confine within prescribed limits esp. during a war ⟨the plane was landed safely and the crew was ~*ed* —T.W.Lawson⟩ **b :** to impound esp. during a war ⟨duty of a neutral to ~ belligerent ships and planes⟩ **2 :** to confine to or as if to a hospital ⟨meddling fools who propose to ~ the dear lady —Norman Douglas⟩

3in·tern \ˈin,t-\ *n* -s **:** a person interned **:** INTERNEE

4intern \"\ *or* **interne** \"\ *n* -s *often attrib* [F *interne*, fr. *interne*, adj.] **1 a :** an advanced student or recent graduate in a professional field (as teaching) who is getting practical experience under the supervision of an experienced worker **b :** one who after completion of an undergraduate medical curriculum serves in residence at a hospital — compare INTERNIST, RESIDENT **2 :** one trained in a profession allied to medicine (as nursing or dentistry) who undergoes a period of practical clinical experience prior to practicing his profession

5intern \"\ *vi* -ED/-ING/-s **:** to act as an intern

1in·ter·nal \(ˈ)inˈtərnᵊl, ənˈt-, -tōn-,-təin-\ *adj* [L *internus* internal (fr. *inter* between) + E *-al* — more at INTER-] **1 a :** existing or situated within the limits or surface of something **:** INWARD, INTERIOR ⟨~ structure⟩ ⟨~ parts of the body⟩ ⟨~ regions of the earth⟩ ⟨~ mechanism of a toy⟩ ⟨~ funds of a business⟩ — opposed to *external* **b :** situated near the inside of the body ⟨~ layer of abdominal muscle⟩ **:** situated on the side toward the median plane of the body ⟨the ~ surface of the lung⟩ **2 :** capable of being applied through the stomach by being swallowed ⟨~ remedy⟩ ⟨~ stimulant⟩ **3 :** relating to the inner being or consciousness **:** belonging to or existing within the mind **:** SUBJECTIVE ⟨~ monologue⟩ **:** PRIVATE ⟨~ opinion⟩ ⟨~ resentment⟩ ⟨~ sensations⟩ **4 :** originating in or dependent on the thing itself **:** belonging to the mutual relations of the parts of a thing **:** INTRINSIC, INHERENT ⟨~ evidence of forgery in a document⟩ ⟨test a theory for ~ consistency⟩ **5 a :** present or performed within an organism ⟨~ senses⟩ ⟨~ speech⟩ **b :** arising within a sense organ ⟨~ stimulus⟩ **6 :** of or relating to the domestic affairs or administrative functions of a country or state ⟨~ commerce⟩ ⟨~ discord⟩ ⟨~ improvement⟩ ⟨~ debt⟩ **syn** see INNER

2internal \"\ *n* -s **1 internals** *pl* **:** the internal organs of the body **:** INNARDS **2 a :** an inner or essential quality or property **b** *obs* **:** spiritual nature **:** SOUL

internal angle *n* **:** INTERIOR ANGLE

internal audit *n* **1 :** a usu. continuous examination and verification of books of account conducted by employees of a business — contrasted with *independent audit* **2 :** a review of systems of internal check and internal control of a business

internal auditory meatus *also* **internal acoustic meatus** *n* **:** a short canal in the petrous portion of the temporal bone through which pass the facial, auditory, and glossopalatine nerves

internal ballistics *n pl but usu sing in constr* **:** INTERIOR BALLISTICS

internal black spot *n* **:** a breakdown of garden beets due to boron deficiency and characterized by hard dark necrotic masses of tissue in the root

internal brown spot *or* **internal brown fleck** *n* **:** a nonparasitic disease of the potato that is of unknown cause and is characterized by brown corky spots scattered throughout the interior of the tuber and sometimes by ring-shaped corky surface lesions — called also *corky ring spot*

internal capsule *n* **:** CAPSULE 1b (1)

internal carotid artery *n* **:** the inner branch of the carotid artery supplying the brain, eyes, and other internal structures of the head

internal check *n* **:** an accounting procedure whereby routine entries for transactions are handled by more than one employee in such a manner that the work of one employee is automatically checked against the work of another for detection of errors and irregularities

internal-combustion engine *n* **:** a heat engine in which the combustion that generates the heat takes place inside the engine proper instead of in a furnace — compare DIESEL ENGINE, GAS ENGINE, GASOLINE ENGINE, GAS TURBINE, JET ENGINE, ROCKET ENGINE, EXTERNAL-COMBUSTION ENGINE

internal control *n* **:** a system or plan of accounting and financial organization within a business comprising all the methods and measures necessary for safeguarding its assets, checking the accuracy of its accounting data or otherwise substantiating its financial statements, and policing previously adopted rules, procedures, and policies as to compliance and effectiveness

internal conversion *n* **:** transformation of nuclear gamma-ray energy into electron-emission energy within the atom itself

internal cork *n* **1 :** a virus disease of sweet potatoes characterized principally by the small brown to black corky spots which develop within the roots becoming prominent after harvest and storage **2 :** CORK 5

internal degree *n* **:** a degree granted by a university to a student who has completed the prescribed course in that university — compare EXTERNAL DEGREE

internal energy *n* **:** the total amount of kinetic and potential energy possessed by the molecules of a body and their ultimate parts owing to their relative positions and their motions inside the body and excluding the energy due to the passage of waves through the body and to vibrations of the body

internal environment *n* **:** the fluid medium in which the cells of the body exist

internal friction *n* **:** frictional interaction between adjacent portions in the interior of a substance due to viscous deformation or flow and resulting in the generation of heat

internal gear *n* **:** a gear having teeth on the inside of its circular rim

in·ter·nal·i·ty \ˌin(ˌ)tərˈnaləd·ē\ *n* -ES **:** the quality or state of being internal **:** INTERIORITY

in·ter·nal·iza·tion \ən-ˌtərnᵊlə̇ˈzāshən\ *n* -S **:** the act of internalizing ⟨man's conscience is an ~ of parental . . . authority —Asher Moore⟩

in·ter·nal·ize \ən-ˈtərnᵊlˌīz\ *vt* -ED/-ING/-S *see -ize in Explan Notes* [¹*internal* + *-ize*] **:** to make internal **:** give subjective character to **:** INTERIORIZE; *specif* **:** to incorporate (as values, patterns of culture, motives, restraints) within the self as conscious or subconscious guiding principles through learning and socialization — compare INTROJECT

internal gear

internal law *n* **:** the law of a state regulating its domestic affairs as opposed to that regulating its foreign affairs

in·ter·nal·ly \(ˈ)in¦tərnᵊlē, ən-ˈt-, -tᵊn-, -təin-, -li\ *adv* **1 :** within the termini, enveloping surface, or boundary of a thing **:** within the body **:** beneath the surface **:** INWARDLY **2 :** MENTALLY **:** SPIRITUALLY **3 :** in or in respect to the inner constitution or affairs of something ⟨a doctrine ~ inconsistent⟩

internally fired boiler *n* **:** a boiler whose furnace is wholly or partly surrounded by water — compare EXTERNALLY FIRED BOILER

internal mammary artery *n* **:** a branch of the subclavian artery of each side that runs down along the anterior wall of the thorax and rests against the costal cartilages

internal mammary vein *n* **:** a vein accompanying the internal mammary artery of each side

internal medicine *n* **:** a branch of medicine that deals with the diagnosis and treatment of nonsurgical diseases

internal navigation *n* **:** navigation on inland waterways

in·ter·nal·ness *n* -ES **:** INTERNALITY

internal oblique *n* **:** a sheet of diagonally arranged abdominal muscle lying between the external oblique and transverse layers on either side of the trunk

internal phase *n* **:** DISPERSED PHASE

internal phloem *n* **:** primary phloem internal to the primary xylem and either in contact with it or in discrete strands

internal porch *n* **:** VESTIBULE, LOBBY, NARTHEX 2

internal pressure *n* **:** pressure inside a portion of matter due to attraction between molecules

internal relation *n* **:** a relation that is involved in or essential to the nature of the thing related ⟨logical equivalence of propositions is an *internal relation* —Arthur Pap⟩ — contrasted with *external relation*

internal respiration *n* **:** the exchange of gases (as oxygen and carbon dioxide) between the cells of the body and the blood by way of the fluid bathing the cells — distinguished from *external respiration*

internal revenue tax *n* **:** EXCISE 1b, 1c, 1d

internal rhyme *n* **:** rhyme between a word within a line and another either at the end of the same line or within another line

internal secretion *n* **:** HORMONE

internal student *n* **:** a student studying in the same university from which he expects to receive a degree — compare EXTERNAL STUDENT

internal thread *n* **:** a screw thread on an inner or concave surface (as of a nut that fits on a bolt)

¹**in·ter·nasal** \¦intə(r)¦+\ *adj* [*inter-* + *nasal*] **:** situated between the nostrils ⟨~ septum⟩ ⟨~ scale⟩

²**internasal** \"\ *n* **:** an internasal part; *esp* **:** any of certain scales lying just behind the nostril in snakes

¹**in·tern·ation** \ˌin,tərˈnāshən\ *n* -S [F, fr. *interner* to intern + *-ation* — more at INTERN] **:** the act of interning or the state of being interned **:** INTERNMENT

²**in·ter·nation** \¦intə(r)+\ *n* [*inter-* + *nation*] **:** a population composed of or representing several nationalities

³**internation** \"\ *adj* [*inter-* + *nation*] **:** existing or occurring between nations ⟨~ rivalry⟩

¹**in·ter·na·tion·al** \R ¦intər¦nashənᵊl, -shnəl, -naash-,-naish-, -R ¦intə¦na- *sometimes* ¦intᵊn¦a-\ *adj* [*inter-* + *national*] **1 :** existing between or among nations or their citizens **:** relating to the intercourse of nations **:** participated in by two or more nations **:** common to or affecting two or more nations ⟨~ trade⟩ ⟨~ labor union⟩ ⟨~ trade association⟩ **2 :** belonging or relating to an organization or association having members in two or more countries ⟨~ congress⟩ ⟨~ movement⟩ **3 a** *of a unit of measurement* **:** fixed by the mutual agreement of authorized representatives of different countries **b** *of an electrical unit* **:** accepted by the International Conference in London in 1908 and used as a legal unit prior to 1950 ⟨~ coulomb⟩ **4 :** of or relating to the International Code

²**international** \"\ *n* **1 :** a person having relations with or obligations to more than one nation (as through citizenship in one and permanent residence in another) **2 :** a participant in an international contest **3 :** INTERNATIONAL STOCK **4 a :** a party, organization, or association that transcends national limits; *specif* **:** an international socialist organization **b :** a craft or industrial union with local affiliates in several countries **5 :** a class of racing sailboats that are 33 feet long, sloop-rigged, and of one design; *also* **:** a boat in this class

international auxiliary language *n* **:** INTERLANGUAGE

international candle *n* **:** CANDLE 4a

international carat *n* **:** CARAT 1b

international code *n, usu cap I&C* **:** a marine code adopted by all the leading nations for holding communication at sea by means of 26 flags each standing for a different letter of the Roman alphabet and an additional triangular code flag or answering pennant which are hoisted in various combinations each of which represents according to the code a different word, phrase, or sentence

international copyright *n* **:** copyright secured by treaty between nations

international crime *n* **:** a crime (as piracy, illicit trade in narcotics, slave trading) in violation of international law

international date line *n* **:** DATE LINE

in·ter·na·tio·nale \ˌ=ˌ=sha'nal, -näl,-nȧl\ *n* -S [F, fr. fem. of *international*, adj., fr. E] **:** INTERNATIONAL 4a ⟨a Communist ~⟩

in·ter·na·tion·al·ism *pronunc at* ¹INTERNATIONAL + ˌizəm\ *n* **1 a :** international character, principles, interests, or outlook **b :** international organization, influence, or common participation ⟨friction between governments is . . . reduced by administrative ~ —C.J.Friedrich⟩ **c :** COSMOPOLITANISM ⟨~ in art⟩ **2 :** the doctrine or belief that world peace may be attained by the friendly association of all nations on a basis of equality and without sacrifice of national character for the securing of international justice and for cooperation in all matters of worldwide interest ⟨the alternatives of outright nationalism and outright ~ —*Fortune*⟩ — compare ISOLATIONISM **3 :** the doctrine or belief of an international political association or party ⟨the ~ of the socialists found any barriers of race or nationality repugnant —Oscar Handlin⟩

¹**in·ter·na·tion·al·ist** \"+ˌəst\ *n* [¹*international* + *-ist*] **1 :** an advocate of internationalism **2 :** a specialist in international law **3 :** a member of a team selected from the country at large to play against the team of another country ⟨tennis ~⟩

²**internationalist** \"\ *or* **in·ter·na·tion·al·is·tic** \¦=¦=(=)=ˈistik, -tēk\ *adj* **:** advocating or influenced by internationalism ⟨~ thought⟩

in·ter·na·tion·al·i·ty \ˌ=ˌ=shəˈnaləd·ē, -lətē, -i\ *n* **:** the quality or state of being international ⟨~ of the use of scientific language —Otto Neurath⟩

in·ter·na·tion·al·iza·tion \ˌ=ˌ=(=)=əˈzāshən, -ˌīˈz-\ *n* **:** an act or process of internationalizing ⟨~ of a waterway⟩

in·ter·na·tion·al·ize \ˌ=ˈ=(=)=ˌīz\ *vt* [¹*international* + *-ize*] **:** to make international in relations, effect, or scope ⟨~ a war⟩ ⟨~ a market⟩; *esp* **:** to place under international control or protection

international language *n* **:** INTERLANGUAGE

international law *n* **:** a body of rules that control or affect the rights of states in their relations with each other and of individuals in their relations to foreign states and with each other when public international factors are involved, that are based in the practice of Great Britain and the U. S. on the customs and usages of civilized nations, treaties, the acts of the executive in international matters, statutes, and judicial decisions esp. including those of international tribunals and in the practice of European continental countries also on the opinions of text writers, and that are generally accepted as binding and enforceable by the participant nations — called also *law of nations*

international legislation *n* **:** the law found in the treaties and international agreements among nations binding the parties thereto but not necessarily being a part of the body of international law binding all nations

in·ter·na·tion·al·ly \¦=¦nashənᵊlē, -shnəlē, -naash-,-naish-, -ᵊli,-əli\ *adv* **:** in an international manner ⟨~ agreed⟩ **:** from an international point of view ⟨~ famous⟩ **:** between different nations or their citizens

international map *n* **:** a map of the world at a scale of one to one million having a uniform set of symbols and conventional signs and printed in modified polyconic projection on sheets each covering an area of 4 degrees latitude by 6 degrees longitude except above the 60th parallel where the longitude covered is 12 degrees on each sheet

international match point *n* **:** a scoring unit used in contract-bridge tournaments played in Europe and based on but not directly proportional to the winning margin of a board

international orange *n* **:** a vivid reddish orange that is redder and much darker than golden poppy and redder, stronger, and much darker than chrome orange

international phonetic alphabet *n, usu cap I, P, & A* **:** IPA

international pitch *n* **1 :** DIAPASON NORMAL **2 :** the tuning standard adopted in 1939 of 440 vibrations per second for A above middle C

international private law *n* **:** CONFLICT OF LAWS

international relations *n pl but sing in constr* **:** a branch of political science concerned with relations between political units of national rank and dealing primarily with foreign policies, the organization and function of governmental agencies concerned with foreign policy, and the factors (as geography and economics) underlying foreign policies

international salute *n* **:** a salute of 21 guns to a national flag

international scientific vocabulary *n, usu cap I&S&V* **:** a part of the vocabulary of the sciences and other specialized studies that consists of words or other linguistic forms current in two or more languages and differing from New Latin in being adapted to the structure of the individual languages in which they appear — abbr. *ISV*

international stock *n* **:** a stock marketable at financial centers outside as well as within the country of issue

international style *n* **1 :** a school of painting showing delicate linearity and decorative treatment of surface popular in Europe during the 14th and early 15th centuries **2 :** functional architectural design employing the latest of building techniques and avoiding traditional or regional influences

international temperature scale *n* **:** a practical temperature scale defining all temperatures above −183° C by specified formulas relating temperatures at one atmosphere pressure to the indications of instruments calibrated at six reproducible fixed points: the boiling point of oxygen (−182.97° C), the ice point (0° C), the steam point (100° C), the boiling point of sulfur (444.6° C), the freezing point of silver (960.8° C), the freezing point of gold (1063° C)

international unit *n* **:** a quantity of a biological (as a vitamin, hormone, antibiotic, antitoxin) or its equivalent based on bioassay that produces a particular biological effect agreed upon internationally

interne *var of* INTERN

in·ter·necine \¦intər¦nē,sēn, -nē,̄ |,sīn, |sᵊn, |sə̇n; ¦intərnə̇-ˈsēn; ən-ˈtərnə,sēn, -nəsə̇n, -nə,sīn\ *adj* [L *internecinus*, fr. *internecare* to destroy, kill (fr. *inter-* + *necare* to kill, fr. *nec-, nex* violent death) + *-inus* -ine — more at NOXIOUS] **1 a :** marked by great slaughter **:** DEADLY ⟨the alternatives only of ~ war or absolute surrender —W.E.Gladstone⟩ **b :** involving or accompanied by mutual slaughter **:** mutually destructive ⟨zealots who stabbed each other in ~ massacre —F.W.Farrar⟩ **2 :** of, relating to, or involving conflict within a group; *broadly* **:** INTERNAL ⟨absorbed in incurable, rancorous ~ feuds —Barbara Ward⟩ ⟨a bitter ~ struggle among artists —Roger Fry⟩

in·ter·ne·cion \ˌ=ˈneshən, -nēsh-\ *n* -S [L *internecion-, internecio*, fr. *internecare* + *-ion-, -io* -ion] **:** mutual destruction **:** MASSACRE

in·ter·ne·cive \¦=¦nesiv, -nēs-; ən-ˈtərnəs-\ *adj* [L *internecivus*, fr. *internecare* + *-ivus* -ive] **:** INTERNECINE

interned *past of* INTERN

in·tern·ee \ˌin,tərˈnē, -tə̄ˈ-, -təiˈ-; ən-ˈ=,=\ *n* -S [²*intern* + *-ee*] **:** a person interned

¹**in·ter·neural** \¦intə(r)+\ *adj* [*inter-* + *neural*] **:** situated between neural arches or neural spines

²**interneural** \"\ *n* -S **:** one of the spiny bones that extend into the flesh of certain fishes between the neural spines and articulate with the rays of the dorsal fins

in·ter·neuron \"+\ *also* **in·ter·neurone** \"+\ *n* [*inter-* + *neuron, neurone*] **:** an internuncial neuron — **in·ter·neuronal** \"+\ *adj*

interning *pres part of* INTERN

in·ter·nist \ən-ˈtərnə̇st, -tᵊn-\ *n* -S [*intern-* (fr. *internal medicine*) + *-ist*] **:** a specialist in internal medicine **:** a specialist in the diagnosis and medical treatment of internal diseases

in·tern·ment \ən-ˈtərnmənt, -tᵊn-,-təin-\ *n* -S [F *internement*, fr. *interner* to intern + *-ment* — more at INTERN] **:** the act of interning or the state of being interned ⟨~ of enemy aliens⟩

in·ter·nodal \¦intə(r)+\ *adj* [*inter-* + *nodal*] **:** lying between nodes ⟨~ stem gall⟩ ⟨~ loop of a vibrating string⟩

in·ter·node \ˈintə(r),nōd\ *n* [L *internodium*, fr. *inter-* + *nodus* knot, joint + *-ium* (n. suffix) — more at NET] **:** an interval or part between two nodes **:** SEGMENT

interns *pres 3d sing of* INTERN, *pl of* INTERN

in·tern·ship *also* **in·terne·ship** \ˈin·,tərn,ship, -tᵊn-,-təin-\ *n* [⁴*intern, interne* + *-ship*] **1 :** the state or position of being an intern **2 a :** a period of service as an intern **b :** the phase of medical training covered during such service **c :** a training period in actual service as an employee in a technical or business establishment **3 :** a grant enabling a student or recent graduate to serve as an intern

in·ter·nuclear \¦intə(r)+\ *adj* [*inter-* + *nuclear*] **:** situated or extending between nuclei ⟨~ distances in molecules⟩

in·ter·nunce \ˈintə(r),nən(t)s\ *n* -S [L *internuntius, internuncius* — more at INTERNUNCIO] *archaic* **:** INTERNUNCIO

¹**in·ter·nun·cial** \¦intə(r)¦nən|(t)sēəl, -nún-, |sh(ē)əl, |ch-\ *adj* [*internuncio* + *-al*] **1 :** of or relating to an internuncio **:** serving as a conveyer of messages **2 :** serving to link sensory and motor neurons — **in·ter·nun·cial·ly** \-əlē\ *adv*

²**internuncial** \"\ *or* **internuncial neuron** *n* -S **:** a nerve fiber intercalated in the path of a reflex arc in the central nervous system and tending to modify the arc and coordinate it with other bodily activities

in·ter·nun·ci·ary \|(t)sē,erē, |shē-, |chē-; |sharē, |chə-\ *adj* [*internuncio* + *-ary*] **:** INTERNUNCIAL 1

in·ter·nun·cio \ˌintə(r)ˈnən|(t)sē,ō, -nún|, |shē,ō, |chē,ō\ *n* [It *internunzio*, fr. L *internuntius, internuncius*, fr. *inter-* + *nuntius, nuncius* messenger] **1 :** a messenger between two parties **:** GO-BETWEEN **2 :** a diplomatic papal representative of lower rank than a nuncio **3 :** a minister formerly representing a government (as the Austrian government) at Constantinople

in·ter·nun·ci·us \-ēəs\ *n, pl* **internun·cii** \-ē,ī, -ē,ē\ [L] **:** INTERNUNCIO

in·ter·nuptial \¦intə(r)+\ *adj* [*inter-* + *nuptial*] **1 :** relating to intermarriage **2 :** intervening between married states

in·ter·objective distance \¦intə(r)+ . . . -\ *n* [*inter-* + *objective*] **:** the distance between the pupils of the two eyes

in·ter·oceanic \"+\ *adj* [*inter-* + *oceanic*] **:** existing or extending between oceans ⟨~ communication⟩

in·ter·o·cep·tive \¦intərō¦septiv\ *adj* [*inter-* (as in *interior*) + *-o-* + *-ceptive* (as in *receptive*)] **:** of, relating to, or functioning as an interoceptor — compare EXTEROCEPTIVE, PROPRIOCEPTIVE

in·ter·o·cep·tor \-ptə(r)\ *n* -S [*inter-* (as in *interior*) + *-o-* + *-ceptor* (as in *receptor*)] **:** a receptor (as in the wall of the alimentary tract) responsive to stimuli originating within the body and esp. in the viscera — compare EXTEROCEPTOR

in·ter·ocular \¦intə(r)+\ *adj* [*inter-* + *ocular*] **:** situated between the eyes

in·ter·o·fec·tive \¦intərō¦fektiv\ *adj* [*inter-* (as in *interior*) + *-o-* + *-fective* (as in *effective*)] **:** of, relating to, dependent on, or constituting the autonomic nervous system — distinguished from *exterofective*

in·ter·office \¦intə(r)+\ *adj* [*inter-* + *office*] **:** existing between the offices of an organization ⟨~ memo⟩

in·ter·operation \"+\ *n* [*inter-* + *operation*] **:** reciprocal operation ⟨~ of factors⟩

in·ter·oper·cle \ˌintərōˈpərkəl\ *n* [NL *interoperculum*] **:** the membrane bone between the preopercle and the branchiostegals of a fish

¹**in·ter·oper·cu·lar** \¦=¦=¦pərkyələ(r)\ *adj* [NL *interoperculum* + E *-ar*] **:** of or relating to an interoperculum

²**interopercular** \"\ *n* -S **:** INTEROPERCLE

in·ter·oper·cu·lum \ˌ=ˌ=ˈ=ləm\ *n* [NL, fr. *inter-* + *operculum*] **:** INTEROPERCLE

in·ter·optic \¦intə(r)+\ *adj* [*inter-* + *optic*] **:** lying between the optic lobes

in·ter·orbital \"+\ *adj* [*inter-* + *orbital*] **:** situated or extending between the orbits of the eyes ⟨~ septum⟩ ⟨~ distance⟩

interorbital breadth *n* **:** the distance between the dacrya

in·ter·osculant \"+\ *adj* [*inter-* + *osculant*] *math* **:** osculating with each other **:** INTERSECTING ⟨~ curves⟩

in·ter·osculate \"+\ *vi* [*inter-* + *osculate*] **:** to osculate with each other **:** INTERMIX ⟨*interosculating* blood vessels⟩ — **in·ter·osculation** \"+\ *n*

in·ter·osseous \"+\ *adj* [*inter-* + *osseous*] **:** situated between bones; *esp* **:** lying between the bones of the leg or forearm ⟨~ membrane⟩ ⟨~ artery of the hand⟩ ⟨~ nerve⟩

in·ter·os·se·us \ˌintəˈ(r)äsēəs\ *n, pl* **interos·sei** \-ē,ī\ [NL, fr. *inter-* + L *osseus*, adj., osseous — more at OSSEOUS] **:** any of various small muscles arising from the metacarpals and metatarsals and inserted into the bases of the first phalanges

in·ter·ownership \¦intə(r)+\ *n* [*inter-* + *ownership*] **:** interlocking ownership

in·ter·page \"+\ *vt* [*inter-* + *page*] **:** to insert or put between pages ⟨*interpaged* translation⟩

in·ter·parental \"+\ *adj* [*inter-* + *parental*] **:** existing between parents ⟨~ tension⟩

¹**in·ter·parietal** \"+\ *adj* [*inter-* + *parietal*] **:** lying between parietal elements; *esp* **:** lying between the parietal bones

²**interparietal** \"\ *n* **:** an interparietal element (as a bone or scale)

interparietal bone *n* **:** a median triangular bone lying at the junction of the parietal and occipital bones and rarely present in man but conspicuous in various lower mammals — see INCA BONE

in·ter·pa·ri·e·ta·le \ˌintə(r)pə,rīəˈtālē\ *n* -S [NL, fr. *inter-* + LL *parietale*, neut. of *parietalis* parietal — more at PARIETAL] **:** an interparietal bone or cartilage

in·ter·parliamentary \¦intə(r)+\ *adj* [*inter-* + *parliamentary*] **:** existing among or involving several national legislatures ⟨~ congress⟩

in·ter·paroxysmal \"+\ *adj* [*inter-* + *paroxysmal*] **:** occurring between paroxysms

in·ter·party \"+\ *adj* [*inter-* + *party*] **:** existing between parties ⟨~ cooperation⟩

in·ter·peduncular \"+\ *adj* [*inter-* + *peduncular*] **:** lying between the peduncles of the brain

interpeduncular ganglion *n* **:** a mass of nerve cells lying between the cerebral peduncles in the median plane just dorsal to the pons

in·ter·pel \ˌintə(r)ˈpel\ *vt* **interpelled; interpelled; interpelling; interpels** [MF *interpeller*, fr. L *interpellare* — more at INTERPELLATE] **1** *obs* **:** INTERRUPT **2** *Scots law* **:** PREVENT, PRECLUDE, INTERCEPT

¹**in·ter·pel·lant** \¦=¦=pelənt\ *adj* [L *interpellant-, interpellans*, pres. part. of *interpellare*] **:** INTERRUPTING

²**interpellant** \"\ *n* -S **:** INTERPELLATOR

in·ter·pel·late \ˌ=ˈpe,lāt, *usu* -ād·+V; ən-ˈtərpə,-, -tᵊp-, -təip-, *usu* -ād·+V\ *vt* -ED/-ING/-S [L *interpellatus*, past part. of *interpellare*, fr. *inter-* + *-pellare* (fr. *pellere* to drive, beat, push) — more at FELT] **1** *obs* **:** INTERRUPT **2 :** to question formally about a governmental policy or decision

in·ter·pel·la·tion \ˌ=ˌ=pəˈlāshən; =ˌ=ˈ=ˈlāshən\ *n* -S [L *interpellation-, interpellatio*, fr. *interpellatus* + *-ion-, -io* -ion] **1** *obs* **:** an act of interposing **:** INTERCESSION **2 :** INTERRUPTION **3 :** the act of formally bringing into question (as in a European legislature) a ministerial policy or action ⟨~ . . . is the particular method by which the deputies exercise their power of controlling and dismissing cabinets —Ernest Barker⟩ **4** *Scots law* **:** INTERCEPTION, PREVENTION

in·ter·pel·la·tor \ˌ=ˈpelˈād·ə(r); =ˈ=ˌ=ˌlād·ə(r)\ *n* -S [L, fr. *interpellatus* + *-or*] **:** one that interpellates

in·ter·pendent \¦intə(r)+\ *adj* [*inter-* + *pendent*] **1** *archaic* **:** hanging between **:** HESITANT **2** *archaic* **:** INTERDEPENDENT

in·ter·penetrable \"+\ *adj* [*inter-* + *penetrable*] **:** capable of being mutually penetrated ⟨portrays good and evil as ~ and relative —K.O.Myrick⟩

in·ter·penetrant \"+\ *adj* [*inter-* + *penetrant*] **:** mutually penetrating ⟨~ crystals⟩

in·ter·penetrate \"+\ *vb* [*inter-* + *penetrate*] *vt* **:** to penetrate between, within, or throughout **:** penetrate thoroughly **:** PERMEATE ⟨Westerners who *interpenetrated* the East in the nineteenth century —Elmer Davis⟩ ~ *vi* **:** to penetrate mutually ⟨the territories of the two peoples ~ a good deal —C.D. Forde⟩ **syn** see PERMEATE

in·ter·penetration \"+\ *n* [*inter-* + *penetration*] **1 :** thorough penetration **:** PERMEATION **2 :** mutual penetration; *esp* **:** the effect in painting of two or more forms crossing and including shapes in common — compare TRANSPARENCY

in·ter·penetrative \"+\ *adj* [*inter-* + *penetrative*] **:** tending to penetrate mutually ⟨for him realism and mysticism are ~ —B.R.Redman⟩ — **in·ter·penetratively** \"+\ *adv*

in·ter·personal \"+\ *adj* [*inter-* + *personal*] **1 :** existing between persons ⟨~ situation in which speech occurs —Z.S. Harris⟩ **2 :** being or relating to or involving personal and social relations out of which develop systems of shared expectations, patterns of emotional relatedness, and modes of social adjustment ⟨disrupted ~ relationships —M.J.Pescor⟩ — **in·ter·personally** \"+\ *adv*

in·ter·petaloid \"+\ *adj* [*inter-* + *petaloid*] **:** lying between ambulacral areas ⟨~ spaces on a sea urchin⟩

in·ter·phalangeal \"+\ *adj* [*inter-* + *phalangeal*] **:** existing between phalanges ⟨~ flexion⟩

in·ter·phase \ˈintə(r)+,-\ *n* [*inter-* + *phase*] **:** INTERKINESIS — **in·ter·phasic** \¦intə(r)+\ *adj*

in·ter·phone \ˈintə(r),fōn\ *n* [fr. *Interphone*, a trademark] **:** a telephone system (as in an airplane, tank, ship, or office building) for intercommunication between points within a small area

in·ter·piece \-,pēs\ *n* [*inter-* + *piece*] **:** INTERLUDE

in·ter·pilaster \ˌintə(r)+\ *n* [*inter-* + *pilaster*] **:** the space between two pilasters

interplace *vt* [*inter-* + *place*] **1** *obs* **:** to place between or among **:** INSERT **2** *obs* **:** to place alternately

in·ter·plait \ˌintə(r)+\ *vt* [*inter-* + *plait*] **:** to plait together

in·ter·plane \"+\ *adj* [in sense 1, fr. *inter-* + *plane* (section of an airplane); in sense 2, fr. *inter-* + *plane* (airplane)] **1 :** situated or extending between the upper and lower wing of an airplane ⟨~ strut⟩ **2 :** existing between airplanes ⟨~ communication⟩

in·ter·planetary \"+\ *adj* [*inter-* + *planetary*] **:** existing, carried on, or operating between planets ⟨the density of hydrogen in ~ and interstellar space —*Science*⟩

¹**in·ter·plant** \"+\ *vt* [*inter-* + *plant* (v.)] **:** to plant (a crop) between plants of another kind **:** set out (young trees) among existing growth

²**in·ter·plant** \ˈ=+,-\ *n* **:** a crop planted between plants of another crop

³**in·ter·plant** \¦=+\ *adj* [*inter-* + *plant* (n.)] **:** existing between manufacturing plants ⟨~ transfer of material⟩

1**in·ter·play** \ˈintə(r)+,-\ *n* [*inter-* + *play*] **:** mutual action or influence **:** reciprocal or contrasting action or effect **:** INTERACTION ⟨bureaucratic controls are imposed upon . . . an ~ of private interests —Irving Howe⟩ ⟨~ of character and circumstance —Hallam Tennyson⟩

2**in·ter·play** \ˌ==+\ *vi* **:** to exert interplay ⟨there enter into imaginative creation three factors which reciprocally ~ —J.L. Lowes⟩

in·ter·plea \ˈintə(r)+,-\ *n* [*inter-* + *plea*] **:** the plea of a defendant disclaiming any interest in the subject matter of a controversy and calling for an interpleader proceeding between the true claimants

in·ter·plead \ˌintə(r)ˈplēd\ *vb* [AF *enterpleder*, fr. *enter-* inter- + *pleder* to plead, fr. OF *plaidier* — more at PLEAD] *vi* **:** to go to trial with each other in order to determine a right on which the action of a third party depends ~ *vt* **:** to bring (two or more claimants) into court in order to compel the litigation of the ownership of a claim ⟨insurance company, not knowing where the payment should go between the three, ~*ed* the claimants —W.H.Atwell⟩

1**in·ter·plead·er** \-də(r)\ *n* [AF *enterpleder*, fr. *enterpleder*, v.] **:** a proceeding devised to enable a person of whom the same debt, duty, or thing is claimed adversely by two or more parties to compel them to litigate the right or title between themselves and thereby to relieve himself from the suits which they might otherwise bring against him

2**interpleader** \"\ *n* [*interplead* + *-er*] **:** one that interpleads

in·ter·plical \ˌintə(r)+\ *adj* [*inter-* + *plical*] **:** lying between folds

1**in·ter·pluvial** \"+\ *adj* [*inter-* + *pluvial*] **:** comparatively dry and occurring between times of greater precipitation ⟨~ age⟩

2**interpluvial** \"\ *n* -s **:** an interpluvial age or time

in·ter·point \ˈintə(r)+,-\ *n* [*inter-* + *point*] **:** the printing of braille on both sides of the paper in such a way that the points of one side fall between points of the other side

in·ter·polar \ˌintə(r)+\ *adj* [*inter-* + *polar*] **:** situated or extending between poles ⟨~ field of a magnet⟩ ⟨~ wire⟩

in·ter·po·late \ənˈtərpə,lāt, -tə̄p-, -təip-, *usu* -ād.+V\ *vb* -ED/-ING/-S [L *interpolatus*, past part. of *interpolare* to give a new appearance to, alter, interpolate, fr. *inter-* + *-polare* (fr. *polire* to polish, furbish) — more at POLISH] *vt* **1 a :** to alter or corrupt (as a text) by inserting new or foreign matter; *esp* **:** to change by inserting matter that is new or foreign to the purpose of the author ⟨was both *interpolated* and misunderstood —*Modern Language Notes*⟩ **b :** to insert (words) into a text ⟨*interpolated* editorial comment⟩ **;** put in (a remark) in a conversation **2 :** to insert between other things or parts **:** INTERCALATE ⟨letter which I here ~ as a good example of his style — Osbert Sitwell⟩ ⟨~ a layer of insulating material between ceiling and floor⟩ **3 :** to estimate values of (a function) between two known values ~ *vi* **:** to make insertions — compare EXTRAPOLATE

in·ter·po·lat·er \-ād·ə(r), -ātə-\ *n* -s **:** one that interpolates

in·ter·po·la·tion \ˌ==ˈlāshən\ *n* -s [L *interpolation-, interpolatio*, fr. *interpolatus* + *-ion-, -io* -ion] **1 :** an act of interpolating or state of being interpolated **:** introduction or insertion of something spurious or foreign **2 :** something that is introduced or inserted **:** INSERTION **3 :** the process of calculating approximate values by interpolating between values already known

in·ter·po·la·tor \=ˈ==,lād·ə(r), -ātə-\ *n* -s [L, fr. *interpolatus* + *-or*] **1 :** INTERPOLATER **2 :** a mechanically rotated clockwork instrument with two cams worked in conjunction with a relay to secure the correct telegraphic retransmission of any given number of consecutively repeated dots or dashes

in·ter·pole \ˈintə(r)+,-\ *n* [*inter-* + *pole*] **:** a supplementary pole placed between the regular poles of a direct-current dynamo or motor in order to regulate commutation — called also *commutating pole*

in·ter·political \ˌintə(r)+\ *adj* [*inter-* + *political*] **:** INTERCITY — used of the Greek city-states

in·ter·polymer \"+\ *n* [*inter-* + *polymer*] **:** COPOLYMER

in·ter·polymerization \"+\ *n* **:** COPOLYMERIZATION

in·ter·polymerize \"+\ *vt* [*interpolymer* + *-ize*] **:** COPOLYMERIZE

in·ter·pone \ˌintə(r)ˈpōn\ *vt* -ED/-ING/-S [L *interponere* — more at INTERPOSE] *archaic* **:** INTERPOSE

in·ter·por·tal \ˌ==+ˈpōrd·ᵊl, -pȯr-\ *adj* [*inter-* + *port* + *-al*] **:** existing between ports of the same country ⟨~ trade⟩

in·ter·pos·al \ˌintə(r)ˈpōzəl\ *n* -s [*interpose* + *-al*] **:** the act of interposing **:** INTERPOSITION, INTERVENTION

in·ter·pose \-ōz\ *vb* [MF *interposer*, modif. (influenced by *poser* to put, place) of L *interponere* (perfect stem *interpos-*), fr. *inter-* + *ponere* to put, place — more at POSE, POSITION] *vt* **1 a :** to place between or in an intermediate position **:** cause to intervene ⟨dense . . . forests ~ an almost impassable barrier —Samuel Van Valkenburg & Ellsworth Huntington⟩ ⟨tending to ~ objects of worship between God and man —W.R.Inge⟩ **b :** to put (oneself) between **:** thrust in **:** INTRUDE ⟨what watchful cares do ~ themselves betwixt your eyes and night? —Shak.⟩ **2 :** to put forth by way of interference or intervention ⟨prevent a decision's being reached by *interposing* a veto⟩ **3 :** to introduce or throw in between the parts of a conversation or argument ⟨interrupted by questions from the class, and listened to whatever we might so ~ —C.I.Lewis⟩ ⟨~ objections⟩ **4 :** to move (a chessman) so as to shield a checked king or a piece that is directly attacked ~ *vi* **1 :** to be or come between ⟨cut through an *interposing* thicket⟩ **2 :** to step in between parties at variance **:** INTERVENE, MEDIATE ⟨listened . . . to their dispute, and at length *interposed* once more on the old man's side —W.H.Hudson †1922⟩ **3 :** to make an interruption or digression ⟨here Adam *interposed* —John Milton⟩

in·ter·pos·er \-zə(r)\ *n* -s **:** one that interposes

in·ter·pos·ing·ly *adv* **:** so as to interpose

in·ter·po·si·tion \ˌintə(r)pəˈzishən\ *n* [ME *interposicioun*, fr. MF *interposition*, fr. L *interposition-, interpositio*, fr. *interpositus* (past part. of *interponere*) + *-ion-, -io* -ion] **1 :** the act of interposing or the state of being interposed **:** a being, placing, or coming between **:** MEDIATION, INTERVENTION ⟨~ of the state between the federal government and the citizen of the state⟩ **2 :** something that is interposed

interposition growth *n* **:** INTRUSIVE GROWTH

interposure *n* -s *obs* **:** INTERPOSITION

interpr *abbr* interpreter

in·ter·pret \ənˈtərprət, ÷-pət, -tə̄p-, -təip-, *usu* -əd.+V\ *vb* -ED/-ING/-S [ME *interpreten*, fr. MF & L; MF *interpreter*, fr. L *interpretari*, fr. *interpret-, interpres* broker, negotiator, expounder, interpreter, fr. *inter-* + *-pret-, -pres* (prob. akin to L *pretium* value, price) — more at PRICE] *vt* **1 :** to explain or tell the meaning of **:** translate into intelligible or familiar language or terms **:** EXPOUND, ELUCIDATE, TRANSLATE ⟨Emmanuel, which being ~*ed* is, God with us —Mt. 1:23 (AV)⟩ ⟨~ dreams⟩ ⟨can only ~ his conduct as caused by fear⟩ **2 :** to understand and appreciate in the light of individual belief, judgment, interest, or circumstance **:** CONSTRUE ⟨~ a law⟩ ⟨~ a contract⟩ ⟨the gift was naturally ~*ed* as a bribe⟩ ⟨~ the signs of a coming storm⟩ **3 :** to apprehend and represent by means of art **:** show by illustrative representation **:** bring (a score or script) to active realization by performance ⟨an actor ~*s* a role⟩ ⟨~ a song⟩ ~ *vi* **:** to act as an interpreter **:** TRANSLATE

in·ter·pret·abil·i·ty \=,=p(r)əd·əˈbiləd·ē, -)ətə-, -lətē, -i\ *n* -ES **:** the quality or state of being interpretable ⟨~ of signs⟩

in·ter·pret·able \=ˈ=p(r)əd·əbəl, -)ətəb-\ *adj* [LL *interpretabilis*, fr. L *interpretari* + *-abilis* -able] **:** capable of being interpreted or explained ⟨~ as a confession of guilt —P.A. Rollins⟩ — **in·ter·pret·able·ness** *n* -ES — **in·ter·pret·ably** \-blē, -bli\ *adv*

interpretament *n* -s [LL *interpretamentum*, fr. L *interpretari* + *-mentum* -ment] *obs* **:** INTERPRETATION

in·ter·pre·tant \=ˈ=p(r)əd·ənt, -)ətə-\ *n* -s [L *interpretant-, interpretans*, pres. part. of *interpretari*] **1 a :** the disposition or readiness of an interpreter to respond to a sign **b :** a sign or set of signs that interprets another sign **c :** the response or reaction to a sign **2 :** INTERPRETER

in·ter·pre·tate \-)ə,tāt\ *vi* -ED/-ING/-S [L *interpretatus*, past part. of *interpretari* to interpret — more at INTERPRET] *archaic* **:** INTERPRET

in·ter·pre·ta·tion \ən,tərprəˈtāshən, ÷-pə-, -tə̄p-, -təip-\ *n* -s [ME *interpretacioun*, fr. MF & L; MF *interpretation*, fr. L *interpretation-, interpretatio*, fr. *interpretatus* + *-ion-, -io* -ion] **1 :** the act or the result of interpreting: as **a :** explanation of what is not immediately plain or explicit ⟨~ of a dream⟩ or unmistakable ⟨~ of a law⟩ ⟨~ of a biblical passage⟩ ⟨~ of an aerial photograph⟩ ⟨~ of symptoms of disease⟩ **b :** translation from one language into another — used of oral translation by interpreters **c :** explanation of actions, events, or statements by pointing out or suggesting inner relationships or motives or by relating particulars to general principles ⟨Marxist ~ of history⟩ ⟨allegorical ~ of a novel⟩ ⟨poetic ~*s* of natural phenomena⟩ **2 :** representation in performance, delivery, or criticism of the thought and mood in a work of art or its producer esp. as penetrated by the personality of the interpreter ⟨~ is a transcendental effort . . . in which the player seeks not to reproduce but to re-create the music the composer wrote —C.M.Smith⟩ ⟨famous for her original ~*s* of several dramatic roles⟩ **3 :** a particular adaptation or application of a method or style or set of principles ⟨the stone house . . . shows a naive and unusual ~ of classical elements —*Amer. Guide Series: Pa.*⟩ ⟨an amusing ~ of the shirt vogue in black cotton —Virginia Pope⟩ **4 :** activity directed toward the enlightenment of the public concerning the significance of the work of a public service or agency; *sometimes* **:** PUBLICITY, PUBLIC RELATIONS ⟨program of ~ developed by a natural-history museum⟩ — **in·ter·pre·ta·tion·al** \=ˌ=ˈtāshənᵊl, -shnəl\ *adj*

interpretation clause *n* **:** a clause inserted in a statute or contract declaring the interpretation that is to be put upon certain words

in·ter·pre·ta·tive \ənˈtərp(r)ə,tād·iv, -tə̄p-, -təip-, |t|, |ēv *also* |əv *sometimes* -)ətə|\ *adj* [*interpret* + *-ative*] **1 :** designed or fitted to interpret **:** EXPLANATORY ⟨~ magazine article⟩ **2 :** according to interpretation ⟨~ distortions in a translation⟩ ⟨~ elasticity of a statute⟩ — **in·ter·pre·ta·tive·ly** \|əvlē, -li\ *adv*

interpretative bigamy *n* **:** BIGAMY 2b

interpretative dance *or* **interpretive dance** *n* **:** a dance depicting a story or a definite emotion rather than following an abstract pattern

in·ter·pret·er \ənˈtərprəd·ə(r), ÷ -pə-, -tə̄p-,-təip-, -ətə-\ *n* -s [alter. (influenced by *-er*) of ME *interpretour*, fr. *interpreten* to interpret + *-our* -or — more at INTERPRET] **1 :** one that interprets, explains, or expounds ⟨early decipherers and ~*s* of hieroglyphic —W.T.Albright⟩ **2 :** one that translates; *esp* **:** a person who translates orally for parties conversing in different tongues **3 :** a machine that prints on punched cards the symbols recorded in them by perforations

in·ter·pret·er·ship \-,ship\ *n* **:** the position of interpreter

in·ter·pre·tive \ənˈtərp(r)əd·|iv, -tə̄p-,-təip-, -)ət|\ *adj* **:** INTERPRETATIVE — **in·ter·pre·tive·ly** \|əvlē, -li\ *adv*

in·ter·pre·tress \-ˈtərp(r)ə·trəs\ *also* **in·ter·pret·ess** \-)əd·əs\ *n* -ES **:** a female interpreter

interprets *pres 3d sing of* INTERPRET

in·ter·provincial \ˌintə(r)+\ *adj* [*inter-* + *provincial*] **:** existing between provinces ⟨~ compact⟩

in·ter·proximal \"+\ *also* **in·ter·proximate** \"+\ *adj* [*inter-* + *proximal* or *proximate*] **:** situated between adjacent parts or surfaces; *esp* **:** situated between adjoining teeth ⟨~ space⟩

in·ter·pulmonary \"+\ *adj* [*inter-* + *pulmonary*] **:** situated between the lungs

in·ter·punct \ˈintə(r),pəŋkt\ *n* -s [L *interpunctus*, past part.] **:** INTERPOINT

in·ter·punc·tion \ˌ==ˈpəŋkshən\ *n* -s [L *interpunction-, interpunctio*, fr. *interpunctus* (past part. of *interpungere* to punctuate, interpoint, fr. *inter-* + *pungere* to prick) + *-ion-, -io* -ion — more at PUNGENT] *n* -s **:** PUNCTUATION; *also* **:** PUNCTUATION MARK

in·ter·punctuate \ˌintə(r)+\ *vt* [*inter-* + *punctuate*] **:** PUNCTUATE — **in·ter·punctuation** \"+\ *n*

in·ter·pupillary \"+\ *adj* [*inter-* + *pupillary*] **:** extending between the pupils of the eyes; *also* **:** extending between the centers of a pair of spectacle lenses ⟨~ distance⟩

in·ter·quartile range \"+ . . . -\ *n* [*inter-* + *quartile*] **:** the range of values of the variable in a statistical distribution that lies between the upper and lower quartiles

in·ter·racial \"+\ *or* **in·ter·race** \"+\ *adj* [*inter-* + *racial* or *race*] **1 :** existing between or involving two or more races or members of different races ⟨~ understanding⟩ ⟨an ~ conference⟩ **2 :** of, relating to, or designed for two or more races or members of different races ⟨~ housing⟩

in·ter·radial \"+\ *adj* [*inter-* + *radial*] **:** of or relating to an interradius — **in·ter·radially** \"+\ *adv*

in·ter·ra·di·um \ˌintə(r)ˈrādēəm\ *n, pl* **interra·dia** \-ēə\ [NL, fr. *inter-* + *-radium* (fr. *radius*)] **1 :** one of the areas between radii **2 :** INTERAMBULACRUM

in·ter·radius \ˌintə(r)+\ *n, pl* **interradii** [NL, fr. *inter-* + *radius*] **:** a radius in a coelenterate halfway between two perradii

in·ter·ramal \"+\ *adj* [*inter-* + *ramal*] **:** situated between rami esp. of the lower jaw

in·ter·ramification \"+\ *n* [*inter-* + *ramification*] **:** the union of branches to form a network

in·ter·react \"+\ *vi* [*inter-* + *react*] **:** to react reciprocally — **in·ter·reaction** \"+\ *n*

interred *past of* INTER

in·ter·reef \"+\ *adj* [*inter-* + *reef* (n.)] **:** situated between reefs ⟨~ sedimentation⟩

in·ter·reflection \"+\ *n* [*inter-* + *reflection*] **:** reciprocal reflection ⟨~ of light between surfaces of a lens⟩

in·ter·regional \"+\ *adj* [*inter-* + *regional*] **:** existing between regions ⟨~ zone⟩

in·ter·reg·nal \"+ˈregnᵊl\ *adj* **:** of or relating to an interregnum

in·ter·reg·num \-nəm\ *n, pl* **interregnums** \-mz\ *or* **in·terreg·na** \-nə\ [L, fr. *inter-* + *regnum* dominion — more at REIGN] **1** *obs* **:** reign or tenure of power during a temporary vacancy of a throne or suspension of the ordinary government **2 a :** the time during which a throne is vacant between the death, abdication, or expulsion of a sovereign and the accession of his successor **b :** a period between two regimes of the same form or of different forms of government **3 :** a period during which the normal functions of government or control are suspended **4 a :** a period of freedom from customary authority **b :** a lapse, break, or pause in a continuous series

1**in·ter·reign** \ˈintə(r),rān\ *n* [MF *interregne*, fr. L *interregnum*] **:** INTERREGNUM

2**in·ter·reign** \ˌintə(r)+\ *vi* [*inter-* + *reign* (v.)] **:** to reign between other reigns

in·ter·relate \"+\ *vb* [*inter-* + *relate*] *vt* **:** to bring into mutual relation ⟨has not yet learned to ~ his characters —*Saturday Rev.*⟩ ~ *vi* **:** to have mutual relationship ⟨the linguistic system ~*s* with the other systems of the culture —:I.L. Smith b.1913⟩

in·ter·related \"+\ *adj* [*inter-* + *related*] **:** having a mutual or reciprocal relation or parallelism **:** CORRELATIVE — **in·ter·re·lat·ed·ly** *adv* — **in·ter·re·lat·ed·ness** *n*

in·ter·relation \"+\ *n* [*inter-* + *relation*] **:** mutual relation **:** INTERRELATEDNESS

in·ter·relationship \"+\ *n* **:** mutual relationship **:** CORRESPONDENCE ⟨~*s* of animal structure and function⟩

in·ter·religious \"+\ *adj* [*inter-* + *religious*] **:** existing between religions ⟨~ goodwill⟩

1**in·ter·renal** \"+\ *adj* [*inter-* + *renal*] **:** lying between the kidneys

2**interrenal** \"\ *n* -s **:** INTERRENAL BODY

interrenal body *or* **interrenal gland** *n* **:** a small body of discrete adrenal cortical tissue lying between the kidneys of certain fishes

in·ter·rer \ənˈtər·ə(r) *also* -tərə(r)\ *n* -s **:** one that inters

in·ter·rex \ˈintə(r),reks\ *n, pl* **interre·ges** \ˌ==ˈrē(,)jēz\ [L, fr. *inter-* + *rex* king — more at ROYAL] **:** one who exercises supreme or kingly power during an interregnum **:** a provisional ruler

interring *pres part of* INTER

in·ter·ro·ga·ble \ənˈterəgəbəl, (ˈ)inˌt-\ *adj* [*interrogate* + *-able*] **:** capable of being interrogated

in·ter·ro·gant \ənˈterəgənt\ *n* -s [L *interrogant-, interrogans*, pres. part. of *interrogare*] **:** INTERROGATOR

in·ter·ro·gate \-rə,gāt, *usu* -ād.+V\ *vb* -ED/-ING/-S [L *interrogatus*, past part. of *interrogare*, fr. *inter-* + *rogare* to ask, request — more at RIGHT] *vt* **1 :** to question typically with formality, command, and thoroughness for full information and circumstantial detail ⟨~ a witness⟩ **2** *obs* **:** to ask questions about **3 :** to examine in detail **:** research into the causes, reasons, nature of ⟨modern potters ~ in their laboratories the glazes used in ancient China —C.E.Montague⟩ ~ *vi* **:** to ask questions of someone **:** conduct an examination ⟨frank I will respond as you ~ —Robert Browning⟩ **syn** see ASK

in·ter·ro·gat·ing·ly *adv* **:** QUESTIONINGLY

in·ter·ro·ga·tion \ən,terəˈgāshən\ *n* -s [ME *interrogacioun*, fr. MF *interrogation*, fr. L *interrogation-, interrogatio*, fr. *interrogatus* + *-ion-, -io* -ion] **1 a :** the act of interrogating **b :** a question put **:** INQUIRY **2 a :** a question regarded as a type of sentence or unit of discourse **b :** a questioning with the force of an emphatic affirmation or denial **3 :** QUESTION MARK — **in·ter·ro·ga·tion·al** \=ˌ==ˈgāshənᵊl, -shnəl\ *adj*

interrogation point *or* **interrogation mark** *n* **:** QUESTION MARK

1**in·ter·rog·a·tive** \ˌintəˈrägəd·iv, -ətiv\ *adj* [LL *interrogativus*, fr. L *interrogatus* + *-ivus* -ive] **1 :** having the form or the force of a question ⟨~ sentence⟩ **:** used in a question ⟨~ pronoun⟩ **:** requiring or seeming to require an answer from the hearer or reader ⟨~ inflection in his voice⟩ **2 :** QUESTIONING, INQUISITIVE ⟨had an ~ nose⟩ — **in·ter·rog·a·tive·ly** \-əvlē, -li\ *adv*

2**interrogative** \"\ *n* -s **1 :** an interrogative utterance **:** QUESTION **2 :** a word (as *who, what, which*) or a particle (as Latin *-ne*) used in asking questions

in·ter·ro·ga·tor \ənˈterə,gād·ə(r), |tə- *sometimes* ˌintəˈrägə|\ *n* -s [LL, fr. L *interrogatus* (past part. of *interrogare* to interrogate) + *-or* — more at INTERROGATE] **1 :** one that interrogates **:** QUESTIONER; *specif* **:** one who interrogates prisoners of war ⟨born a German and . . . served as ~ in the American Army —Virgilia Peterson⟩ **2 :** a radio transmitter and receiver combined for sending out a signal that triggers a transponder and for receiving and displaying the reply

1**in·ter·rog·a·to·ry** \ˌintəˈrägə,tōrē, -tȯr-, -ri\ *n* -ES [ML *interrogatorium*, fr. neut. of LL *interrogatorius*] **1 :** a formal question or inquiry; *esp* **:** a question put in writing and required by law to be answered under direction of a court **2 :** a sign or signal denoting interrogation

2**interrogatory** \ˌ==ˈ==,==\ *adj* [LL *interrogatorius*, fr. L *interrogatus* + *-orius* -ory] **:** containing, expressing, or implying a question **:** INTERROGATIVE ⟨ends most of her remarks with an ~ upward inflection —Dan Wickenden⟩

interrogatory action *n, Roman law* **:** an action in which preliminary issues are tried before litiscontestation

in·ter·ro·gee \ən,terəˈgē\ *n* -s [*interrogate* + *-ee*] **:** someone interrogated

in ter·ro·rem \ˈin,teˈrä,rem\ *adv* (*or adj*) [L, for terror] **:** by way of threat or intimidation ⟨if, after becoming aware of the other party's offense, the injured party could hold it *in terrorem* over his or her head —Edward Jenks⟩

in·ter·rupt \ˌintəˈrəpt\ *vb* -ED/-ING/-S [ME *interrupten*, fr. L *interruptus*, past part. of *interrumpere*, fr. *inter-* + *rumpere* to break — more at REAVE] *vt* **1 :** to stop by breaking in **:** halt, hinder, or interfere with the continuation of (some activity) **:** prevent (one) from proceeding by intrusive or interpolated comment or action ⟨the . . . recovery was ~*ed* by the depression of 1883–85 —F.A.Bradford⟩ ⟨~ a speaker with frequent questions⟩ **2 :** to break or stop the uniformity, continuity, sequence, or course of **:** introduce a difference in ⟨an affair of copious eating and still more copious drinking, ~*ed* by bouts of homemade fun —Aldous Huxley⟩ ⟨the plain narrows and is ~*ed* by broad spurs from the Pennines —L.D.Stamp⟩ **3** *obs* **:** OBSTRUCT, THWART, PREVENT ~ *vi* **:** to break in upon some action or discourse **:** INTERPOLATE; *esp* **:** to break in with questions or remarks while another is speaking ⟨a bad habit of ~*ing*⟩ **syn** see ARREST

interrupted *adj* **1 :** broken in upon **:** DISCONTINUOUS ⟨an ~ stripe⟩ ⟨~ suture⟩ **2 :** not uniform **:** broken in arrangement or symmetry ⟨~ inflorescence⟩ **3 :** consisting of or containing a stop in articulation ⟨\k\ is an ~ consonant⟩ ⟨\dzh\ is an ~ phoneme⟩ **4** *of a map projection* **:** not having continuous outlines **:** split (as along meridians) so as to give better shape and scale for each continent or ocean — **in·ter·rupt·ed·ly** *adv* — **in·ter·rupt·ed·ness** *n* -ES

interrupted cadence *n* **:** DECEPTIVE CADENCE

interrupted continuous waves *n pl* **:** radio waves that are continuous except for periodic interruptions at a materially lower frequency

interrupted current *n* **:** a pulsating electric current produced by opening and closing a continuous-current circuit in a regular manner

interrupted fern *n* **:** an American fern (*Osmunda claytoniana*) with tall erect pinnate fronds and a few pairs of sporogenous pinnae borne at or near the center of the fertile fronds

interrupted key *n, cryptology* **:** an aperiodic keying sequence formed by interrupting a short key at various points and resuming from its beginning each time

interrupted perforation *n* **:** perforation on postage stamps for vending machines or dispensers in which there are unperforated spaces between groups of holes

interrupted screw *n* **:** a screw from which sectors have been removed by longitudinal cuts through the threads so that it can be thrust into a reciprocally machined mating part and locked by only a fraction of a turn

in·ter·rupt·er *also* **in·ter·rup·tor** \ˌintəˈrəptə(r)\ *n* -s **:** one that interrupts: as **a :** a device for periodically and automatically interrupting an electric current **b** *cryptology* **:** a message element or insertion signaling a change of key

in·ter·rupt·ible \ˌ==ˈrəptəbəl\ *adj* **:** capable of being interrupted ⟨~ utility service at reduced rates⟩

in·ter·rup·tion \ˌ==ˈrəpshən\ *n* -s [ME *interrupcioun*, fr. L *interruption-, interruptio*, fr. *interruptus* + *-ion-, -io* -ion] **1 :** an act of interrupting or state of being interrupted **2 :** a breach or break caused by the abrupt intervention of something foreign **3 :** obstruction caused by breaking in upon a course, current, progress, or motion **:** STOP **4 :** temporary cessation **:** INTERMISSION, SUSPENSION **5** *Scots law* **:** an act or proceeding that defeats an adverse title or claim based on prescription by stopping the running of the period of time required for the perfection of the title or claim and starting it running anew **syn** see BREAK

in·ter·rup·tive \ˌ==ˈrəptiv, -tēv *also* -təv\ *also* **in·ter·rup·to·ry** \-tərē\ *adj* [*interrupt* + *-ive* or *-ory*] **:** tending to interrupt — **in·ter·rup·tive·ly** \-təvlē\ *adv*

inters *pres 3d sing of* INTER

1**in·ter·scapular** \ˌintə(r)+\ *adj* [*inter-* + *scapular*] **:** situated between the shoulder blades **:** of or relating to the region between the shoulders ⟨~ feathers⟩

2**interscapular** \"\ *n* **:** an interscapular feather

in·ter·scene \ˈintə(r)+,-\ *n* [*inter-* + *scene*] **:** a scene (as in a motion picture) inserted between portions of the main narrative ⟨the passing of time has been done very adroitly by the use of cartoon ~*s* —W.H.Rudkin⟩

in·ter·scholastic \ˌintə(r)+\ *adj* [*inter-* + *scholastic*] **:** characterized by participation or cooperation of two or more secondary schools ⟨has withdrawn from ~ athletics⟩ — compare EXTRAMURAL

in·ter·school \"+\ *adj* [*inter-* + *school*] **:** existing between schools ⟨won first prize in the ~ debating competition⟩ — opposed to *intraschool*

in·ter se \ˈintə(r)ˈsē\ *adv* (*or adj*) [L] **:** among or between themselves ⟨all species will breed *inter se* —*Farmer's Weekly* (*So. Africa*)⟩ ⟨relations of the several parts of the empire *inter se* are not subject to international law —*Manchester Guardian Weekly*⟩

in·ter·seamed \ˌintə(r)ˈsēmd\ *adj* [by folk etymology fr. MF *entresemer* to intersperse (fr. *entre-* inter- + *semer* to sow, fr. L *seminare*) + E *-ed* — more at DISSEMINATE] *archaic* **:** INTERSPERSED, SOWN ⟨borders of lilies ~ with roses —Robert Greene⟩

1**in·ter·sect** \ˌintə(r)ˈsekt\ *vb* -ED/-ING/-S [L *intersectus*, past part. of *intersecare*, fr. *inter-* + *secare* to cut — more at SAW] *vt* **1 :** to pierce or divide by passing through or across (a line or area) **:** CROSS ⟨any two diameters of a circle ~ each other⟩ ⟨canals ~ the city in every direction —*Encyc. Americana*⟩ **2 :** to determine the position of by triangulation ⟨opportunity was taken to ~ some twenty odd peaks —*Geog. Jour.*⟩

3 : to write (as a shorthand stroke) so as to cut across another or be cut across by another ~ *vi* **1 :** to meet and cross at a point ⟨~*ing* roads⟩ **2 :** to cut into one another so as to share an area in common **:** OVERLAP ⟨where positive law and morals ~ —Herbert Agar⟩

²intersect \ˈ=₌,=\ *n* -S **:** a point or curve of intersection

in·ter·sec·tant \¦==ˈsektənt\ *adj* **:** INTERSECTING

intersecting arcade *n* **:** a Romanesque arcade having interlacing arches

in·ter·sec·tion \,==ˈsekshən, *in sense 3* " *or* ˈ==,==\ *n* -S [L *intersection-, intersectio,* fr. *intersectus* + *-ion-, -io* -ion] **1 :** an act, state, or place of intersecting ⟨understand the ~ of visible with invisible worlds —Stephen Spender⟩ **2 :** the sum total of points of a line, surface, or volume that it has in common with another line, surface, or volume ⟨the ~ of a plane with a spherical surface in a circle⟩ **3 :** a place where two or more highways join or cross; *specif* **:** an area of potential collision between vehicles traveling on different roadways that cross

¹in·ter·sec·tion·al \¦==ˈsekshənᵊl, -shnəl\ *adj* [*intersection* + *-al*] **:** of or relating to an intersection

²in·ter·sec·tion·al \"\ *adj* [*inter-* + *sectional*] **:** existing between sections ⟨~ football game⟩

in·ter·segmental \¦intə(r)+\ *adj* [*inter-* + *segmental*] **:** lying between segments; *specif* **:** lying between the primordial segments of the embryo ⟨~ artery⟩

in·ter·septal \"+\ *adj* [*inter-* + *septal*] **:** situated between septa ⟨~ space⟩

intersert *vt* -ED/-ING/-S [L *intersertus,* past part. of *interserere,* fr. *inter-* + *serere* to join, bind together — more at SERIES] *obs* **:** INTERPOLATE, INSERT — **in·ter·ser·tion** *n* -S *obs*

in·ter·sertal \¦intər¦sərd·ᵊl\ *adj* [G, fr. L *intersertus* + G *-al* (fr. L *-alis* -al)] *of an igneous rock* **:** of an ophitic texture in which the interstitial material is glass or a constituent other than augite

in·ter·service \¦intə(r)+\ *adj* [*inter-* + *service*] **:** occurring between or relating to two or more of the armed services ⟨~ rivalry⟩

in·ter·sesamoid \"+\ *adj* [*inter-* + *sesamoid*] **:** situated between sesamoid bones ⟨~ ligament of a horse's fetlock⟩

in·ter·session \ˈintə(r)+,-\ *n* [*inter-* + *session*] **:** a period between two academic sessions or terms sometimes utilized (as in an adult education program) for brief concentrated courses — **in·ter·sessional** \¦==+\ *adj*

in·ter·set \¦intə(r)+\ *adj* [*inter-* + *set* (past part.)] **1 :** set between or among other things **2 :** set about ⟨hills ~ with white villas⟩

in·ter·sex \ˈintə(r)+,-\ *n* [ISV *inter-* + *sex*] **:** an intersexual individual **:** an intergrade between the sexes

in·ter·sexual \¦intə(r)+\ *adj* [ISV *inter-* + *sexual*] **1 :** existing between sexes ⟨~ hostility⟩ **2 :** intermediate in sexual characters between a typical male and a typical female — **in·ter·sexually** \"+\ *adv*

in·ter·sexuality \"+\ *or* **in·ter·sexualism** \"+\ *n* [ISV *inter-* + *sexuality* or *sexualism*] **:** the quality or state of being intersexual

in·ter·shoot \"+\ *vb* [*inter-* + *shoot*] *vi* **:** to shoot or flash at intervals ⟨hues . . . ~*ing* and to sight lost and recovered —William Wordsworth⟩ ~ *vt* **:** to intermingle with **:** color in streaks ⟨flames ~*ing* the dense smoke⟩

in·ter·social \"+\ *adj* [*inter-* + *social*] **:** relating to the mutual intercourse or relations of persons in society

in·ter·societal \"+\ *adj* [*inter-* + *societal*] **:** existing or occurring between societies ⟨~ comparisons of culture⟩ ⟨~ diffusion⟩

intersole *obs var of* ENTRESOL

in·ter·sow \"+\ *vt* [*inter-* + *sow*] **1 :** to sow, scatter, or sprinkle among other things **:** INTERSPERSE **2 :** to intersperse (a planting) with seed of another crop

¹in·ter·space \ˈintə(r)+,-\ *n* [*inter-* + *space* (n.); trans. of LL *interspatium*] **1 :** intervening space or time **:** INTERVAL: as **a :** a space between printed letters **b :** an air space in a building **c :** the space between two related body parts whether void or filled by another kind of structure ⟨an ~ between dorsal fins⟩ ⟨the skin of the ~ between the 5th and 6th ribs⟩ **2 :** interplanetary or interstellar space

²in·ter·space \¦==+\ *vt* [*inter-* + *space* (v.)] **:** to put an interval between (two things) **:** separate (as the members of a series) by spaces ⟨a line of *interspaced* hyphens⟩ ⟨periods of work *interspaced* by drinking sprees⟩

in·ter·spatial \"+\ *adj* [LL *interspatium* (fr. L *inter-* + *spatium* space) + E *-al* — more at SPACE] **:** of or relating to an interspace — **in·ter·spatially** \"+\ *adv*

in·ter·specific \"+\ *or* **in·ter·species** \"+\ *adj* [*inter-* + *specific* or *species*] **:** existing between species ⟨~ hybrid⟩

in·ter·sper·sal \,intərˈspərsəl\ *n* -S [*intersperse* + *-al*] **:** INTERSPERSION

in·ter·sperse \,intərˈspərs, -təˈspəs, -pəis\ *vt* -ED/-ING/-S [L *interspersus* interspersed, fr. *inter-* + *sparsus,* past part. of *spargere* to strew, scatter — more at SPARK] **1 :** to scatter or set here and there among things **:** insert at intervals ⟨~ pictures in a book⟩ **2 :** to diversify or adorn with things set or scattered at intervals **:** place something at intervals in or among ⟨~ a book with pictures⟩

in·ter·spers·ed·ly \-sədlē\ *adv* **:** in an interspersed or scattered manner

in·ter·sper·sion \,intərˈspərzhən, təˈspə̄l, -pəi| *Brit usu & US sometimes* \shən\ *n* -S **:** the act or fact of interspersing or state of being interspersed: as **a :** the intermingling of kinds of organisms (as species) within an ecological community **b :** the state or degree of intermingling of one kind of organism with others ⟨certain forbs show a high level of ~ in grasslands⟩

in·ter·sphere \¦intə(r)+\ *vi* [*inter-* + *sphere*] **:** to fall or come within the spheres or influences of one another

in·ter·spicular \"+\ *adj* [*inter-* + *spicular*] **:** situated between spicules

in·ter·spinal \"+\ *or* **in·ter·spinous** \"+\ *adj* [*inter-* + *spinal* or *spinous*] **:** lying between spines; *esp* **:** lying between the spines of adjacent vertebrae ⟨~ ligament⟩

in·ter·spi·na·lis \,intə(r),spīˈnāləs, -nāl-, -nal-\ *n, pl* **inter·spina·les** \-a(,)lēz, -ā(,)lēz, -ä,läs\ [NL, fr. *inter-* + LL *spinalis* spinal — more at SPINAL] **:** any of various short muscles connecting the spinous processes of contiguous vertebrae

in·ter·sporal \¦intə(r)+\ *adj* [*inter-* + *sporal*] **:** situated between spores

in·ter·sprinkle \"+\ *vt* [*inter-* + *sprinkle*] **:** INTERSPERSE

in·ter·sta·di·al \,intə(r)ˈstādēəl\ *n* -S [ISV *inter-* + NL *stadium* + ISV *-al*] **:** a substage within a glacial stage marking a temporary retreat of the ice

in·ter·stage \¦intə(r)+\ *adj* [*inter-* + *stage*] **:** placed between the stages ⟨~ steam turbine⟩ ⟨~ radio amplifier⟩

in·ter·state \"+\ *also* **in·ter·statal** \"+\ *adj* [*inter-* + *state* or *statal*] **:** relating to the mutual relations of states **:** existing between or including different states — used esp. of the states of the U.S. and of the states of Australia ⟨~ commerce⟩ ⟨~ highway⟩

interstate extradition *or* **interstate rendition** *n* **:** extradition from one of the states of the U.S. or one of its territories according to procedure authorized by the U.S. Constitution and by acts of Congress

in·ter·stellar \"+\ *adj* [*inter-* + *stellar*] **:** located among the stars of the Milky Way or of other galaxies or passing from one star to another ⟨~ space⟩

interstellar line *n* **:** one of the dark spectral lines of a star or other distant celestial body that is caused by the absorption of atoms and molecules in the intervening interstellar gas and that does not partake of the Doppler shift of the spectral lines produced in the star itself

in·ter·sterile \"+\ *adj* [*inter-* + *sterile*] **:** characterized by sterility in which pollen of either variety will not fertilize the other **:** mutually incapable of fertilizing ⟨~ subspecies of a plant⟩

in·ter·sterility \"+\ *n* [*inter-* + *sterility*] **:** mutual infertility between related groups or individuals

in·ter·sternite \"+\ *n* [*inter-* + *sternite*] **:** an intersegmental plate on the undersurface of the insect abdomen

in·ter·stice \ən·ˈtərstəs, -tə̄s-, -təis-\ *n, pl* **interstic·es** \÷ -stə,sēz, -stəsəz\ [F, fr. LL *interstitium,* fr. L *interstitus* (past part. of *intersistere* to stand still or stop in the middle of something, fr. *inter-* + *sistere* to place, stand) + *-ium* (n. suffix) — more at SOLSTICE] **1 :** a space that intervenes between one thing and another **:** a space between things (as the parts of a body) closely set **:** CRACK, CREVICE, INTERVAL ⟨~*s* of a wall⟩ ⟨the ~*s* of network⟩ **2 a :** an interval of time **b :** the intervals that the canon law requires between the reception of the various degrees of orders in the Roman Catholic Church

in·ter·sticed \-stəst\ *adj* **:** provided with interstices **:** having interstices between **:** situated at intervals ⟨~ fence palings⟩

in·ter·stimulate \¦intə(r)+\ *vt* [*inter-* + *stimulate*] **:** to stimulate reciprocally — **in·ter·stimulation** \"+\ *n*

¹in·ter·sti·tial *also* **in·ter·sti·cial** \¦intə(r)¦stishəl\ *adj* [*interstitial* fr. LL *interstitium* + E *-al; intersticial* alter. (influenced by *interstice*) of *interstitial*] **1 :** relating to or situated in the interstices **2 :** situated within but not restricted to or characteristic of a particular organ or tissue — used chiefly of isolated cells of uncertain origin and function and of the fibrous tissues that bind together cells and tissues **3 :** affecting the interstitial tissues of an organ or part ⟨~ hepatitis⟩ **4 :** relating to, characteristic of, or being a solid structure in which usu. smaller atoms or ions of one or more nonmetals occupy holes between larger metal atoms or ions in a crystal lattice ⟨~ carbides . . . in which the small carbon atoms occupy ~ positions in the crystal lattices of the metals—Therald Moeller⟩ — **in·ter·sti·tial·ly** \-shəlē, -li\ *adv*

²interstitial \"\ *n* -S **:** a plant growing in the interstices of an association

interstitial area *n* **:** a transitional urban area (as between an industrial and residential district) that may be characterized by a degree of cultural isolation and consequent incidence of crime and delinquency

interstitial–cell–stimulating hormone *n* **:** LUTEINIZING HORMONE

in·ter·sti·tium \,==ˈstishēəm\ *n, pl* **intersti·tia** \-ēə\ [LL — more at INTERSTICE] **1** *obs* **:** INTERSTICE **2** [NL, fr. LL] **:** interstitial tissue

in·ter·stock \ˈintə(r)+,-\ *n* **:** INTERMEDIATE STOCK

in·ter·stratification \¦intə(r)+\ *n* [*inter-* + *stratification*] **:** the state of being interstratified

in·ter·stratify \"+\ *vb* [*inter-* + *stratify*] *vt* **:** to insert between other strata **:** arrange in alternate strata ⟨lava flow *interstratified* with sedimentary rock⟩ ~ *vi* **:** to settle in layers between other layers

in·ter·stream \"+\ *adj* [*inter-* + *stream*] **:** situated between streams ⟨~ divide⟩

in·ter·strial \"+\ *adj* [*inter-* + L *stria* + E *-al*] **:** situated between striae

in·ter·subjective \"+\ *adj* [*inter-* + *subjective*] **1 :** connecting or interrelating two consciousnesses or subjectivities ⟨~ communication⟩ **2 :** existing between, accessible to, or capable of being established for two or more subjects **:** OBJECTIVE ⟨~ reality of the physical world⟩ — **in·ter·subjectively** \"+\ *adv* — **in·ter·subjectivity** \"+\ *n*

in·ter·tangle \"+\ *vt* [*inter-* + *tangle*] **:** ENTANGLE, INTERTWINE — **in·ter·tanglement** \"+\ *n* -S

in·ter·tentacular \"+\ *adj* [*inter-* + *tentacular*] **:** situated between tentacles

in·ter·tergal \"+\ *adj* [*inter-* + *tergal*] **:** situated between tergites

in·ter·tergite \"+\ *n* [*inter-* + *tergite*] **:** one of the small plates intercalated between the tergites of some insects

in·ter·terminal switching \"+...-\ *n, pl* **interterminal switchings** [*inter-* + *terminal*] **:** the moving of cars from a point on one railroad line to a point on another when both points are within the switching limits of the same station or industrial switching district — compare INTRATERMINAL SWITCHING

in·ter·territorial \"+\ *adj* [*inter-* + *territorial*] **:** existing or carried on between territories

in·ter·tessellation \"+\ *n* [*inter-* + *tessellation*] **:** intricate or complex interrelation comparable to a mosaic design

in·ter·testamental \"+\ *adj* [*inter-* + *testamental*] **:** of, relating to, or being the period of approximately two centuries between the composition of the last canonical book of the Old Testament and the writing of the books of the New Testament

in·ter·texture \"+\ *n* [*inter-* + *texture*] **1 :** the act of interweaving or state of being interwoven **2 :** something that is interwoven

in·ter·threaded \"+\ *adj* [*inter-* + *threaded,* past part. of *thread*] **:** intercrossed by or as if by interwoven threads

in·ter·tidal \"+\ *adj* [*inter-* + *tidal*] **:** of, relating to, or being the part of the littoral zone that is above low-tide mark ⟨~ faunal elements⟩

¹in·ter·tie \"+\ *vt* [*inter-* + *tie*] **:** to connect or fasten mutually ⟨~ power systems⟩

²in·ter·tie \ˈintə(r)+,-\ *n* **1 :** a horizontal tie other than the sill and plate or other principal ties that secures uprights to one another in a framed work **2 :** the act of intertying

in·ter·till \¦intə(r)+\ *vt* [*inter-* + *till*] **1 :** to cultivate between the rows of (a crop) **2 :** INTERCROP

in·ter·tillage \"+\ *n* [*inter-* + *tillage*] **:** cultivation between rows of a crop

in·ter·tissued \"+\ *adj* [*inter-* + *tissue* + *-ed;* trans. of MF *entretissu*] **:** INTERWOVEN

in·ter·tone \ˈintə(r)+,-\ *n* [*inter-* + *tone*] **:** a tone of intermediate pitch heard when two other tones of slightly different pitches are sounded simultaneously

in·ter·tongue \"+\ *vi* [*inter-* + *tongue*] **:** INTERLOCK ⟨beds of dark limestone . . . ~ with the white limestone —C.O.Dunbar⟩

in·ter·tonic \"+\ *adj* [*inter-* + *tonic*] **:** occurring between stressed syllables (as *-con-* in *uncontested*)

in·ter·trabecular \"+\ *adj* [*inter-* + *trabecular*] **:** situated between trabeculae

in·ter·trade \"+\ *n* [*inter-* + *trade*] **:** reciprocal trade

in·ter·traffic \"+\ *n* [*inter-* + *traffic*] **:** mutual traffic or exchange ⟨legitimate ~ between Russia and the border countries —*Newsweek*⟩ ⟨literary ~ between England and Spain has been sporadic and haphazard —*Times Lit. Supp.*⟩

in·ter·tra·gi·an \¦intə(r)ˈtrājēən\ *adj* [*inter-* + NL *tragus* + E *-ian*] **:** situated between the tragus and antitragus ⟨~ canal⟩

in·ter·transversalis \¦intə(r)+\ *n* [NL, fr. *inter-* + *transversalis*] **:** any of a series of small muscles connecting the transverse processes of contiguous vertebrae and most highly developed in the neck

in·ter·trappean \"+\ *adj* [*inter-* + ⁵*trap* + *-ean*] **:** lying between successive basaltic lava flows

in·ter·tribal \"+\ *adj* [*inter-* + *tribal*] **:** existing or occurring between tribes ⟨~ warfare⟩ **:** common to or shared by several tribes ⟨~ problems⟩

in·ter·trig·i·nous \¦intə(r)¦trijənəs\ *adj* [L *intertriginosus,* fr. *intertrigin-, intertrigo* + *-osus* -ous] **:** exhibiting or affected with intertrigo

in·ter·triglyph \¦intə(r)+\ *n* [*inter-* + *triglyph*] **:** METOPE

in·ter·tri·go \,intə(r)·ˈtrī(,)gō\ *n* -S [L, fr. *inter-* + *-trigo* (fr. *terere* to rub) — more at THROW] **:** inflammation produced by chafing of adjacent areas of skin

in·ter·trochanteric \¦intə(r)+\ *adj* [*inter-* + *trochanteric*] **:** being or lying between trochanters

in·ter·tropical \"+\ *also* **in·ter·tropic** \"+\ *adj* [*inter-* + *tropical, tropic*] **:** situated between or within the tropics **:** relating to regions within the tropics **:** TROPICAL

intertropical front *n* **:** a zone of convergence of trade winds and equatorial winds often marked by heavy rains in tropical regions — compare DOLDRUM 3

in·ter·tropics \"+\ *n pl* **:** the zones between the tropics of Cancer and Capricorn or any region in them

in·ter·trude \,intə(r)·ˈtrüd\ *vt* -ED/-ING/-S [LL *intertrudere,* fr. L *inter-* + *trudere* to thrust, push — more at THREAT] **:** to bring in intrusively **:** INTERPOLATE

in·ter·tubercular \¦intə(r)+\ *adj* [*inter-* + *tubercular*] **:** situated between tubercles

in·ter·tubular \"+\ *adj* [*inter-* + *tubular*] **:** lying between tubules

in·ter·twine \¦intə(r)·¦twīn\ *vb* [*inter-* + *twine*] *vt* **:** to unite by twining one with another **:** ENTANGLE, INTERLACE, INTERTWIST ⟨the sex impulse is closely *intertwined* with the life impulse—Susanne K. Langer⟩ ~ *vi* **:** to twine about one another **:** become mutually entangled or involved ⟨theological concepts are inevitably *intertwining* —Robert Root⟩ — **in·ter·twinement** \-nmənt\ *n* -S

in·ter·twin·ing·ly *adv* **:** in an intertwining manner

¹in·ter·twist \¦intə(r)+\ *vb* [*inter-* + *twist*] *vt* **:** to twist together one with another **:** INTERTWINE ⟨~*ed* roots⟩ ⟨so ~*ed* are our emotions —Roger Fry⟩ ~ *vi* **:** to twist about one another ⟨~*ing* tendrils⟩

²in·ter·twist \ˈ==+,-\ *n* **:** an act or fact of intertwisting **:** the state of being intertwisted **:** TANGLE ⟨peering through an ~ of vines and shrubs⟩

in·ter·university \¦intə(r)+\ *adj* [*inter-* + *university*] **:** existing or carried on between universities ⟨~ research⟩

in·ter·urban \"+\ *adj* [*inter-* + *urban*] **:** going between or connecting cities or towns ⟨~ electric railways⟩ ⟨~ buses⟩

in·ter·val \ˈintə(r)vəl\ *n* -S [ME *intervalle,* fr. MF, fr. L *intervallum* space between ramparts, interval, fr. *inter-* + *vallum* rampart — more at WALL] **1 a :** a space of time between the recurrences of similar conditions or states **:** PAUSE ⟨~ between coughing spells⟩ ⟨~*s* of sanity⟩ ⟨~ of thousands of years between glaciations⟩ **b** *Brit* **:** INTERMISSION **c :** the time between two events or points of time ⟨firing at ~*s* of ten minutes⟩ ⟨~ between a lightning flash and the following thunder⟩ **d :** a portion of the total time cycle of a traffic signal during which the signal indications do not change **2 a :** a space between things **:** empty space between objects ⟨posts set up at regular ~*s* along the road⟩ ⟨buildings placed at wide ~*s*⟩ **b (1) :** the space between elements in military formation in the direction of width — contrasted with *distance* (2) **:** the distance between the foremasts of the guides of adjacent units in a compound naval formation **c :** the relative difference in pitch between two simultaneous or successive notes or tones **3 :** something that breaks or interrupts a uniform series or surface **:** an intervening part ⟨grazing land with brief ~*s* of forest⟩ ⟨the road follows a winding course except for a few straight ~*s*⟩ **4** *chiefly NewEng* **:** BOTTOM 6 **5 a :** the totality of numbers belonging to a given set of real numbers **b :** the totality of such numbers between and either including or excluding one or both of two end numbers of the set **c :** the totality of such numbers greater or less than and either including or excluding one of the numbers of the set **d :** a set of points on a line segment that represents one of these totalities **6 :** a gap between different qualities or states that may be ideally filled with intervening grades ⟨~ between savagery and culture⟩ ⟨~ between landlord and tenant, master and servant, was less —T.B.Macaulay⟩ **syn** see BREAK

in·ter·vale \-,vāl, -,vəl\ *n* [fr. obs. E *intervale* interval, fr. ME *intervalle;* influenced in meaning by *vale*] *chiefly NewEng* **:** BOTTOM 6 ⟨~ land⟩

in·ter·valed \ˈintə(r)vəld\ *adj* [*interval* + *-ed*] **:** having intervals **:** interrupted at intervals **:** placed at intervals ⟨march is being made with platoons ~ at two yards —Peter Bowman⟩

in·ter·val·lic \¦intə(r)¦valik\ *adj* [*interval* + *-ic*] **:** of or relating to an interval ⟨~ relationships of the notes of a melody⟩

in·ter·val·om·e·ter \,intə(r)vəˈlämǝd·ə(r)\ *n* [*interval* + *-o-* + *-meter*] **:** a device that operates a control at regular intervals; *specif* **:** an electrical device that regulates the interval between exposures made with an aerial camera

interval timer *n* **:** TIMER 1a

in·ter·varietal \¦intə(r)+\ *adj* [*inter-* + *varietal*] **:** obtaining between varieties ⟨~ sterility⟩ ⟨~ differences in basal metabolism⟩

in·ter·varsity \"+\ *adj* [*inter-* + *varsity*] *Brit* **:** INTERUNIVERSITY ⟨~ sports⟩

in·ter·vascular \"+\ *adj* [*inter-* + *vascular*] **1 :** lying between or surrounded by blood vessels **2 :** situated within a seed vessel or vascular structure

in·ter·vein \"+\ *vt* [*inter-* + *vein*] **:** to interlace with or as if with veins

in·ter·veinal \"+\ *adj* [*inter-* + *veinal*] **:** situated or occurring between veins

in·ter·vene \¦intə(r)¦vēn\ *vb* -ED/-ING/-S [L *intervenire,* lit., to come between, fr. *inter-* + *venire* to come — more at COME] *vi* **1 :** to enter or appear as an irrelevant or extraneous feature or circumstance ⟨business seldom follows any projected course exactly, because unforeseeable developments . . . ~ —*Fortune*⟩ **2 :** to occur, fall, or come between points of time or events ⟨an instant *intervened* between the flash and the report⟩ ⟨*intervening* years⟩ **3 :** to come in or between by way of hindrance or modification **:** INTERPOSE ⟨~ to settle a quarrel⟩ ⟨death *intervened* soon after⟩ **4 :** to occur or lie between two things ⟨Paris, where the same city lay on both sides of an *intervening* river —*Amer. Guide Series: N. Y. City*⟩ **5 a :** to become a party to an action or other legal proceeding begun by others for the protection of an alleged interest **b :** to interfere usu. by force or threat of force in another nation's domestic affairs in order to protect the lives or property of the nationals of the interfering nation or to further some other purpose deemed vital to its welfare ~ *vt, obs* **:** to come between **:** interfere with

in·ter·ven·er *also* **in·ter·ve·nor** \-nə(r)\ *n* -S **:** one that intervenes

in·ter·ve·nience \,==ˈvēnyən(t)s\ *n* -S **:** the act or fact of intervening **:** INTERVENTION

¹in·ter·ve·nient \¦==¦vēnyənt\ *adj* [L *intervenient-, interveniens,* pres. part. of *intervenire*] **1 :** being or coming in incidentally or extraneously ⟨~ circumstances⟩ **2 :** situated or occurring between different points or events **:** INTERVENING ⟨deep ~ ravines —C.E.Craddock⟩ **3 :** INTERMEDIARY

²intervenient \"\ *n* -S **:** one that intervenes

in·ter·ven·tion \,==ˈvenchən\ *n* -S [LL *intervention-, interventio,* fr. L *interventus* (past part. of *intervenire* to intervene) + *-ion-, -io* -ion] **1 :** the act or fact of intervening **:** INTERPOSITION ⟨~ of divine providence⟩ ⟨surgical ~⟩ **2 :** interference that may affect the interests of others: as **a** *civil law* **:** the act of a person who pays commercial paper for honor — called also *payment by intervention* **b :** the act by which a third person in order to protect his own interest interposes and becomes a party to a legal proceeding pending between other parties **c :** the interference of a country in the affairs of another country for the purpose of compelling it to do or forbear doing certain acts or of maintaining or altering the actual condition of its domestic affairs irrespective of its will — compare MEDIATION — **in·ter·ven·tion·al** \¦==¦venchənᵊl, -chnəl\ *adj*

in·ter·ven·tion·ism \-chə,nizəm\ *n* -S **:** the theory or practice of intervening **:** interference (as by a government) in economic affairs at home or in political affairs of another country — compare ISOLATIONISM, LAISSEZ-FAIRE

in·ter·ven·tion·ist \-nəst\ *n* -S **:** one that intervenes or favors intervention

in·ter·ven·tor \-ˈventə(r)\ *n* -S [L, fr. *interventus* (past part. of *intervenire* to intervene) + *-or* — more at INTERVENE] **1 :** a person designated by a church to reconcile parties and unite them in the choice of officers **2 :** a temporary administrator (as of a province in Central America or So. America) in time of disturbance

¹in·ter·ventral \¦intə(r)+\ *adj* [*inter-* + *ventral*] **:** of or relating to the posterior pair of primitive ventral structural elements of a typical vertebra

²interventral \"\ *n* **:** an interventral cartilage or ossification

in·ter·ventricular foramen \"+. . .-\ *n* [*inter-* + *ventricular*] **:** FORAMEN OF MONRO

interversion *n* -S [LL *interversion-, interversio,* fr. L *interversus* (past part. of *intervertere*) + *-ion-, -io* -ion] *obs* **:** MISAPPROPRIATION, EMBEZZLEMENT

intervert *vt* -ED/-ING/-S [L *intervertere,* lit., to turn aside, fr. *inter-* + *vertere* to turn — more at WORTH] **1** *obs* **:** to turn to a course or use other than the proper one **:** MISUSE; *esp* **:** EMBEZZLE **2** *obs* **:** CHANGE, INVERT

in·ter·vertebral \¦intə(r)+\ *adj* [*inter-* + *vertebral*] **:** situated between vertebrae — **in·ter·vertebrally** \"+\ *adv*

intervertebral disk *n* **:** one of the tough elastic disks that are interposed between the centra of adjoining vertebrae and that consist of an outer fibrous ring enclosing an inner pulpy nucleus

in·ter·vesicular \"+\ *adj* [*inter-* + *vesicular*] **:** lying between vesicles

¹in·ter·view \ˈintə(r),vyü\ *n* [alter. (influenced by *inter-*) of earlier *enterview,* fr. MF *entrevue,* fr. fem. of *entrevu,* past part. of (*s'*)*entrevoir* to see one another, meet, fr. *entre-* inter- + *voir* to see —more at VIEW] **1 a** *obs* **:** a mutual sight or view **b :** a meeting face to face **:** a private conversation; *usu* **:** a formal meeting for consultation : CONFERENCE ⟨candidates for the position were called in for ~s⟩ **c** : a transient or secret meeting (as of lovers) ⟨the stolen ~s of those spring mornings —William Black⟩ **2 a** : a meeting in which a writer or reporter or radio or television commentator obtains information from someone for publication or broadcast **b** : the statement so obtained **c** : a news story reporting or reproducing such a conversation **3** : a scheduled meeting between a teacher and a student for purposes of instruction or counseling

²interview \"\ *vt* : to have an interview with : question or converse with esp. in order to obtain information or ascertain personal qualities ⟨~*ing* job applicants⟩ ⟨~ housewives about their color preferences⟩ ⟨~*ing* witnesses in a criminal investigation⟩ ⟨~*ed* the highest government officials and even strangers on buses —J.M.Mead⟩ ~ *vi* : to carry on an interview ⟨technique of ~*ing*⟩

in·ter·view·ee \ˈ≠≠,vyüˈē\ *n* -s [²*interview* + -*ee*] : one that is interviewed ⟨~s voted 22 percent for giving food to western Europe —*Newsweek*⟩

in·ter·view·er \ˈ≠≠,vyüə(r)\ *n* : one that interviews: *specif* : a clerk who does preliminary interviewing of applicants for employment and arranges interviews with the employing officials

in·ter·villous \ˌintə(r)+\ *adj* [*inter-* + *villous*] : situated between villi

in·ter·visibility \"+\ *n* : the quality or state of being mutually visible

in·ter·visible \"+\ *adj* [*inter-* + *visible*] : mutually visible ⟨~ surveying stations⟩

in·ter·visit \"+\ *vi* [alter. (influenced by *inter-*) of F *entrevisiter*, fr. MF, fr. *entre-* + *visiter* to visit — more at VISIT] : to exchange visits

in·ter·visitation \"+\ *n* [*inter-* + *visitation*] : exchange of visits : mutual visiting ⟨classroom ~s of schoolteachers⟩

in·ter·vital \"+\ *adj* [*inter-* + *vital*] : occurring between two lives

in·ter vi·vos \ˌintə(r)ˈvēˌvōs, -ˈvīˌv-\ *adv* (*or adj*) [L] : between living persons : from one living person to another ⟨transaction *inter vivos*⟩ ⟨*inter vivos* trust⟩ — compare DONATIO MORTIS CAUSA

in·ter·vo·cal·ic \ˌintə(r)(ˌ)vōˈkalik, -lēk\ *also* **in·ter·vocal** \ˈ≠≠ˈvōkəl\ *adj* [*inter-* + *vocalic* or *vocal*] : immediately preceded and immediately followed by a vowel ⟨~ consonant⟩ — **in·ter·vo·cal·i·cal·ly** \ˈ≠≠(ˌ)≠ˈlək(ə)lē, -lēk-, -li\ *adv*

in·ter·vo·lu·tion \ˌintə(r)vōˈlüshən\ *n* [fr. *intervolve*, after such pairs as E *revolve: revolution*] : the state or fact of being intervolved or coiled up

in·ter·volve \ˌintə(r)ˈvälv, -ˈvȯlv\ *vb* -ED/-ING/-S [*inter-* + -*volve* (as in *involve*)] *vt* : to involve or roll up one within another ⟨mazes intricate, eccentric, *intervolved* —John Milton⟩ ~ *vi* : to twist or coil within one another

in·ter·war \ˌintə(r)+\ *adj* [*inter-* + *war* (n.)] : lying between wars ⟨~ years⟩

¹in·ter·weave \"+\ *vb* [*inter-* + *weave*] *vt* **1** : to weave together ⟨*interweaving* a wool warp with a silk weft⟩ **2** : to intermingle or blend together ⟨*interweaving* his own insights . . . with letters and memoirs —Phoebe Adams⟩ ~ *vi* : INTERTWINE, INTERMINGLE

²in·ter·weave \ˈintə(r)+,-\ *n* : the act or result of interweaving ⟨~ of caste and religion . . . is so close that each merges into and is part of the other —Andrew Mellon⟩

in·ter·wed \ˌintə(r)+\ *vi* [*inter-* + *wed*] : INTERMARRY

in·ter·wind \"+\ *vb* [*inter-* + *wind*] : INTERTWINE, INTERVOLVE

in·ter·word \"+\ *adj* [*inter-* + *word* (n.)] : occurring between words ⟨~ juncture⟩

in·ter·work \"+\ *vb* [*inter-* + *work*] *vt* : to work into something else : INTERWEAVE ~ *vi* : to work with or act upon each other : INTERACT

in·ter·world \ˈintə(r)+,-\ *n* [*inter-* + *world*] : a world existing between other worlds ⟨~s of the imagination⟩

in·ter·wo·ven \ˌintə(r)ˈwōvən\ *adj* [fr. past part. of *interweave*] : woven together in texture or construction

in·ter·wo·ven·ness \-n(n)əs\ *n* -ES : the quality or state of being interwoven : close or inseparable connection

in·ter·wreathe \ˌintə(r)+\ *vb* [*inter-* + *wreathe*] : INTERTWINE

in·ter·wrought \"+\ *adj* [*inter-* + *wrought*] : worked into or through one another : complexly associated

in·ter·xylary \"+\ *adj* [*inter-* + *xylem* + -*ary*] : existing among xylem elements

in·ter·zonal \"+\ *or* **in·ter·zone** \"+\ *adj* [*inter-* + *zonal* or *zone*] : occurring or carried on between zones ⟨~ travel⟩ ⟨~ competition⟩

in·ter·zooecial \"+\ *adj* [*inter-* + *zooecial*] : existing between or among zooecia

in·tes·ta·ble \(ˈ)inˈtestəbəl, ənˈt-\ *adj* [LL *intestabilis*, fr. L, execrable, accursed, fr. *in-* ¹in- + *testari* to be a witness, make a will + -*abilis* -able] **1** : not competent to make a will ⟨an ~ minor⟩ ⟨insane and ~⟩ **2** *obs* : incompetent to be a witness

in·tes·ta·cy \ənˈtestəsē, -si\ *n* [¹*intestate* + -*cy*] : the quality or state of being or dying intestate

¹in·tes·tate \ənˈteˌstā\|t, -ˌstə\|, *usu* \|d.+V\ *adj* [ME, fr. L *intestatus*, fr. *in-* ¹in- + *testatus*, past part. of *testari* to be a witness, make a will, fr. *testis* witness — more at TESTAMENT] **1** : having made no valid will ⟨die ~⟩ **2** : not bequeathed or devised : not disposed of by will ⟨an ~ estate⟩ ⟨the administration of ~ property⟩

²intestate \"\ *n* -s : one who dies intestate

in·tes·ti·nal \ənˈtestənᵊl, *in rapid speech* -s(ᵊ)nəl; *sometimes chiefly Brit* ˌinˌteˈstīn-\ *adj* [prob. fr. MF, fr. *intestin* + -*al*] **1 a** : of or relating to the intestine ⟨the ~ tube⟩ ⟨~ ferments⟩ : affecting the intestine ⟨~ catarrh⟩ : taking place in the intestine ⟨~ digestion⟩ **b** : living within the intestine ⟨the ~ flora⟩ ⟨an ~ worm⟩ **2** : suggesting an intestine: as **a** : being internal or subterranean ⟨the rumbling ~ routes of the subways —Molly L. Bar-David⟩ **b** : intricately circuitous or involute ⟨tangled carvings in gluttonous ~ designs —Peggy Bacon⟩ **syn** see INNER

intestinal calculus *or* **intestinal concretion** *n* : DUST BALL

intestinal canal *n* : INTESTINE

intestinal flu *n* : any of various acute usu. transitory gastrointestinal conditions marked by nausea, vomiting, diarrhea, and griping pains

intestinal fortitude *n* : COURAGE, STAMINA, GUTS ⟨the qualities we have discussed — common sense, *intestinal fortitude*, leadership . . . are not the only ones desirable in a second lieutenant —*Infantry Jour.*⟩ ⟨only a man of powerful will and *intestinal fortitude* could have done these things —*Newsweek*⟩

in·tes·ti·nal·ly \-ᵊlē, -əl, \|i\ *adv* : in or upon the intestines

¹in·tes·tine \ənˈtestən, *chiefly dial* -ˌstīn\ *adj* [MF or L; MF *intestin*, fr. L *intestinus*, fr. *intus* within — more at ENT-] **1 a** : of or relating to the internal affairs of a state or country — usu. used of something evil or troublesome ⟨an ~ disorder⟩ ⟨an ~ calamity⟩ ⟨~ war⟩ **b** : of or relating to the internal parts of the body **2** : INWARD ⟨an ~ necessity⟩ **3** *obs* : INTERNAL **syn** see INNER

²intestine \"\ *n* -s [MF *intestin*, fr. L *intestinum*, fr. neut. of *intestinus*] **1** : the tubular portion of the alimentary canal that in the vertebrate lies posterior to the stomach from which it is separated by the pyloric valve and consists typically of a slender but long anterior part made up of duodenum, jejunum, and ileum which function in digestion and assimilation of nutrients and a broader shorter posterior part made up usu. of cecum, colon, and rectum which serve chiefly to extract moisture from the by-products of digestion and evaporate them into feces — often used in pl. ⟨the shot pierced his ~s in several places⟩ — see LARGE INTESTINE, SMALL INTESTINE **2** : the entire alimentary canal esp. when more or less straight and tubular (as in many invertebrates)

in·tes·ti·ni·form \-ˈstənəˌfȯrm\ *adj* [²*intestine* + -*iform*] : like an intestine in form

in·tes·ti·no·intestinal \ənˈtestə(ˌ)nō+\ *adj* [²*intestine* + -*o-* + *intestinal*] : originating in and acting on the intestine ⟨an ~ reflex⟩

in·tes·ti·no·vesical \"+\ *adj* [²*intestine* + -*o-* + *vesical*] : of or relating to the intestine and bladder

in·tex·ine \ˈinˌtekˌsēn, \|in\ *or* **in·tex·tine** \-kˌst\|\ *n* -s [*intexine* fr. G, fr. *int-* (fr. L *intus* within) + *exine*; *intextine* alter. (influenced by *extine*) of *intexine*] : the inner membrane of the exine when this exists in two layers

intg *abbr* interrogate; interrogator

inthrall *or* **inthral** *vt* **inthralled**; **inthralled**; **inthralling**; **inthralls** *or* **inthrals** [by alter. (influenced by ²*in-*)] : ENTHRALL

inthralment *n* -s *archaic* : ENTHRALLMENT

inthronization *n* -s [MF or ML; MF *intronisation*, fr. ML *inthronization-*, *inthronizatio*, fr. LL *inthronizatus* (past part. of *inthronizare* to enthrone, modif. — influenced by L *in-* ²in- — of Gk *enthronizein*) + L -*ion-*, -*io* -ion — more at ENTHRONIZE] : ENTHRONEMENT, ENTHRONIZATION

¹inthrow \ˈ≠,≠\ *n* [⁴*in* + *throw* (after *throw in*, v.)] : the act or process of throwing soil toward the crop by the cultivating gangs of a row-crop cultivator; *also* : the amount of soil thrown

²inthrow \"\ *vt* : RIDGE *vt* 2b

intice *archaic var of* ENTICE

in·ti·chi·u·ma \ˌintēchēˈümə\ *n, pl* **intichiuma** *usu cap* [native name in central Australia] : an Australian magical ceremony having as its object the increase of a clan's totemic species

in·til *or* **in·till** \ənˈtil\ *prep* [ME, fr. ²*in* + *til*, *till* to — more at TILL] *chiefly Scot* : IN, INTO

in·ti·ma \ˈintəmə\ *n, pl* **inti·mae** \-ˌmē, -ˌmī\ *or* **intimas** [NL, fr. L, fem. of *intimus* innermost] **1** : the innermost coat of an organ (as a blood vessel or lymphatic) consisting (as in larger blood vessels) of an endothelial lining backed by a layer of connective tissue and one of elastic tissue **2** : the innermost coat of a trachea of an insect — **in·ti·mal** \-məl\ *adj*

in·ti·ma·cy \ˈintəməsē, -si\ *n* -ES [²*intimate* + -*cy*] **1** : the state of being intimate: as **a** : close association or connection ⟨the furnishings suggested at least some ~ with the outside world —C.L.Jones⟩ ⟨in the city you are more free from unwelcome ~ —M.R.Cohen⟩ **b** : close personal relationship esp. marked by affection or love (as in close friendship) ⟨a long ~ with the governor of the state⟩ ⟨long continued ~ with the fields and meadows about him —*Encyc. Americana*⟩ ⟨a common danger had made of these two enemies friends . . . and now that the danger had passed their ~ was done —Jack McLaren⟩ **c** : a relationship marked by depth of knowledge or broadness of information ⟨his ~ with the history of the middle ages⟩ **d** : complete intermixture, compounding, or interweaving ⟨would call for some effort to disentangle a relationship of things marked by such ~⟩ **2** : the quality or state of being careful and searching in notation of details ⟨an ~ of observation which few scientists can equal —H.S.Canby⟩ **3 a** : a sexual liberty taken ⟨resented the pawing *intimacies* of the man who was driving the car —Erle Stanley Gardner⟩; *specif* : sexual intercourse ⟨denied charges of having an affair with a married woman . . . though she said ~ between them had taken place about 25 times —*New York Enquirer*⟩ or an instance of it ⟨indicates that she had recently experienced an ~ —R.O.Lawson & S.D.Greene⟩ **b** : an objectionable liberty taken with the person ⟨became embarrassingly familiar with the *intimacies* of fame —Green Peyton⟩ **4** : the quality of affecting one in a usu. pleasant intimate personal way ⟨music marked by an ~ of expression⟩ **5** : the state of seeming to be in a close friendly personal relationship — used of inanimate things ⟨the almost cloistered ~ of much of the route —*Amer. Guide Series: Vt.*⟩ **6** : the capacity for establishing oneself quickly in an intimate personal relationship ⟨only one other man possessing this curious ~ with wild things —Edison Marshall⟩

in·ti·ma·do \ˌintəˈmä(ˌ)dō\ *n* -s [prob. alter. (influenced by Sp -*ado*, as in *renegado*) of ³*intimate*] *archaic* : an intimate friend : INTIMATE

¹in·ti·mate \ˈintəˌmāt, *usu* -ād.+V\ *vt* -ED/-ING/-S [LL *intimatus*, past part. of *intimare* to make known, fr. L *intimus* innermost, superl. of (assumed) OL *interus* inward, on the inside — more at INTERIOR] **1** : to give notice of : ANNOUNCE, NOTIFY **2** : to impart or communicate with delicate or indirect wording or covert slight gesture without forthright blunt expression ⟨said that he . . . might not be able to say all that he thought, thus *intimating* to his hearers that they might infer that he meant more —O.W.Holmes †1935⟩ **syn** see SUGGEST

²in·ti·mate \-mət, *usu* -əd.+V\ *adj* [LL *intimatus*, past part. of *intimare* to make known; E *intimate* influenced in meaning by L *intimus* innermost] **1 a** : of or relating to an inner character or essential nature : INNERMOST : characteristic of the genuine core of something ⟨it is in the purposes he entertains . . . that an individual most completely . . . realizes his ~ selfhood —John Dewey⟩ **b** : belonging to or characterizing the inmost true self : indicative of one's deepest nature ⟨his ~ reflections⟩ **2** : marked by a very close physical, mental, or social association, connection, or contact: as **a** : showing complete intermixture, compounding, fusion : thoroughly or closely interconnected, interrelated, interwoven ⟨the ~ relations . . . between economics, politics, and legal principles —V.L.Parrington⟩ ⟨an ~ mixture of rock particles⟩ ⟨an ~ affiliation of house and garden —*Amer. Guide Series: N.Y.*⟩ **b** : showing depth of detailed knowledge and understanding and broadness of information from or as if from long association, near contact, or thorough study and observation ⟨this girl, so ~ with nature —W.H.Hudson †1922⟩ ⟨an ~ knowledge of admiralty law —H.W.H.Knott⟩ **c** : marked by or as if by knowledge of esp. personal details which only an eyewitness or very close confidant might have ⟨of St. Francis and St. Bernard their ~ biographers assure us that . . . they . . . never allowed themselves actual laughter —G.G.Coulton⟩ **d** : marked by or as if by a warmly personal attitude esp. developing through long or close association, by friendliness, unreserved communication, mutual appreciation and interest ⟨pretend that they are in smart society and on ~ terms with people they slander —Oscar Wilde⟩ : manifesting warm personal interest ⟨his voice low, ~, full of meaning —Aurelia Levi⟩ : arousing a warm personal response ⟨a lyrical and ~ painting⟩ **e** : showing or fostering close personal interests and relations rather than those colder and more distant, formal, or routine : suggesting or furthering easy unreserved personal expression, feeling, or relationships through smallness, exclusiveness, limitation, or privacy ⟨an ~ sense of being a member of some mystic brotherhood —W.S.Maugham⟩ ⟨the ~ politics of the eighteenth century were an involved web of human passions —J.H.Plumb⟩ ⟨two plush rooms, one formal, the other cozy and ~ —T.H.Fielding⟩ ⟨an ~ theater that served coffee between its films⟩ ⟨an ~ cocktail lounge⟩; *also* : designed or composed chiefly for presentation to a small group ⟨~ opera⟩ ⟨~ music⟩ **f** : marked by or appropriate to very close personal relationships : marked by or befitting a relationship of love, warm or ardent liking, deep friendship, or mutual cherishing ⟨always ~ relations between a mother and her young child —Edward Westermarck⟩ ⟨their hand grasp was very ~ and mutually comprehending —Arnold Bennett⟩ **g** : of, relating to, or befitting deeply personal (as emotional, familial, or sexual) matters or matters usu. kept private or discreet ⟨to his intensely aristocratic nature this discussion of his ~ family affairs . . . was most abhorrent —A. Conan Doyle⟩ ⟨clean-minded youth horrifies its elders by facing the ~ facts of life —G.A.Bartlett⟩ **h** : engaged in or marked by sexual relations : SEXUAL, MARITAL ⟨ladies were supposed to be without sexual desire . . . in their ~ relations with their husbands they consented graciously —W.E.Woodward⟩ **i** : worn next to the skin ⟨~ underwear⟩ : worn in the home ⟨an ~ negligee⟩ **j** : designed or prepared (as by waterproofing) for immediate contact with something to be wrapped ⟨the efficiency of ~ wraps and carton overwraps in preventing corrosion —*Corrosion & Material Protection*⟩ ⟨aluminum foil laminated to paper finds use as an ~ wrapper for a variety of products —N.A.Cooke⟩ **syn** see FAMILIAR

³intimate \"\ *n* -s : one who associates or has associated intimately (as with a person or place) ⟨writes as one who . . . has been an ~ of the Parisian scene —R.J.Goldwater⟩ : an intimate friend or confidant ⟨counted a banker among his ~*s*⟩ **syn** see FRIEND

in·ti·mate·ly \-mətlē, -li\ *adv* : in an intimate manner ⟨the physical and the economic background of poverty are most ~ related —P.E.James⟩ ⟨a city she knows ~ —*Americas*⟩ ⟨every one of which he could have named ~ had he put his memory to it —Kay Boyle⟩ ⟨the author leads his audience easily and ~ —S.W.Reed⟩

in·ti·mate·ness \-mətnəs\ *n* -ES : INTIMACY

in·ti·mat·er \-ˌmād.ə(r), -ātə-\ *n* -s [¹*intimate* + -*er*] : one that intimates

in·ti·ma·tion \ˌintəˈmāshən\ *n* -s [ME *intimacion*, fr. MF *intimation*, fr. LL *intimation-*, *intimatio*, fr. *intimatus* (past part. of *intimare*) + L -*ion-*, -*io* -ion] **1** : the act of intimating or the state of being intimated: as **a** : ANNOUNCEMENT, NOTIFICATION **b** : an indirect usu. hinted suggestion or notice ⟨~s of immortality —William Wordsworth⟩ ⟨gave only ~ of the fact he was guilty of rudeness⟩ **2** : something intimated ⟨never learned what his ~ was⟩

in·time \aⁿtēm\ *adj* [F, fr. L *intimus* innermost] : INTIMATE

in·tim·i·date \ənˈtiməˌdāt, *usu* -ād.+V\ *vt* -ED/-ING/-S [ML *intimidatus*, past part. of *intimidare*, fr. L *in-* ²in- + *timidus* timid] : to make timid or fearful : inspire or affect with fear : FRIGHTEN ⟨despite his imposing presence and all the grandeur surrounding him, I was not *intimidated* —Polly Adler⟩; *esp* : to compel to action or inaction (as by threats) ⟨charged with *intimidating* public officials to get the government to buy machine guns he was selling —*Time*⟩

syn INTIMIDATE, COW, BULLDOZE, BULLY, BROWBEAT agree in meaning to frighten or coerce by frightening means into submission or obedience. INTIMIDATE suggests a display or application (as of force or learning) so as to cause fear or a sense of inferiority and a consequent submission ⟨most of these officials have been badly *intimidated* by the specter of a summons to appear before a Congressional committee —*New Republic*⟩ ⟨many authors and publishers are not merely *intimidated* by the thought of footnotes; they are positively terrified —G.W. Sherburn⟩ COW implies a reduction to a state where the spirit is broken or all courage lost ⟨*cowed* into cooperation through fear of the gangsters —Michael Blundell⟩ ⟨*cowed* the gang with his detective's star —J.T.Farrell⟩ ⟨a ship's company *cowed* to groveling point —John Masefield⟩ BULLDOZE, in its earliest sense signifying to intimidate or coerce by violence, now often can mean to force into line by an application of great force, not necessarily implying though often involving intimidation ⟨a *bulldozed* people, shaking with the ague of the terrorized —W.L.Sullivan⟩ ⟨the sheer strength of his reputation and the force of his will *bulldozing* them into making loans —F.L. Allen⟩ ⟨the highly reputable gentlemen who were *bulldozed* into taking this responsibility have resigned —Robert Moses⟩ BULLY implies intimidation or attempts to intimidate by swaggering overbearing behavior or by the use of unfair force ⟨a mild, long-suffering woman will permit her husband to *bully* her for years, whereas another woman will react violently to the first beating —Jacob Fried⟩ ⟨inevitable that the older boys should become mischievous louts; they *bullied* and tormented and corrupted the younger boys —H.G.Wells⟩ BROWBEAT implies a cowing by scornful contemptuous treatment, esp. intellectual or moral oppression ⟨were *browbeaten* into the hardest and most menial tasks —F.V.W.Mason⟩ ⟨no wish to *browbeat* the reader into accepting my theory of myself or of anything else —George Santayana⟩ ⟨*browbeat* students by a great display of learning⟩

in·tim·i·da·tion \ənˌtiməˈdāshən\ *n* -s [F, fr. MF, fr. *intimider* (fr. ML *intimidare* to intimidate) + -*ation*] : the act of intimidating or the state of being intimidated ⟨the voters were kept from the polls by ~⟩ ⟨cringed to see the woman's ~ before her husband's cruelty⟩

in·tim·i·da·tor \ənˈtiməˌdād.ə(r), -ātə-\ *n* -s : one that intimidates

in·tim·i·da·to·ry \-ˌdəˌtōrē, *chiefly Brit* ≠ˌ≠≠ˈdātəri *or* -ā·tri\ *adj* [*intimidate* + -*ory*] : tending to intimidate ⟨an ~ array of obstacles —F.S.Mitchell⟩ : designed to intimidate ⟨the similarity, in some species, between ~ and courtship displays —E.A. Armstrong⟩

in·ti·mism \ˈintəˌmizəm\ *n* -s [*intimist* + -*ism*] : a principle or practice among painters (as in early 20th century France) of selecting as subject matter familiar or intimate scenes or occasions from their own everyday life — compare GENRE

¹in·ti·mist \-məst\ *n* -s *often cap* [F *intimiste*, fr. *intime* intimate + -*iste* -ist] : an intimist painter

²intimist \"\ *adj*, *often cap* **1** : of, relating to, or practicing intimism **2** *of fiction* : dealing chiefly with intimate and private esp. psychological experiences ⟨the peculiarly modern feeling of individual helplessness that the war brought into . . . people's consciousness, and it made sense of that emotion as the ~ novel does not as a rule —Anthony West⟩

in·tim·i·ty \ənˈtimədˌē\ *n* -ES [F *intimité*, fr. *intime* intimate + -*ité* -ity] *archaic* : intimate privacy

in·tinc·tion \ənˈtiŋ(k)shən\ *n* -s [LL *intinction-*, *intinctio* immersion, fr. L *intinctus* (past part. of *intingere* to dip in, fr. *in* ²in- + *tingere* to dip, moisten) + -*ion-*, -*io* -ion — more at TINGE] : the administration of the sacrament of Communion by dipping the bread in the wine and giving both together to the communicant

in·tine \ˈinˌtēn, -tīn\ *n* -s [prob. fr. G, fr. L *intus* within, in — more at ENT-] : the inner of the two layers forming the wall of a spore (as a pollen grain) — called also *endosporium*; compare EXINE, PERINIUM

intire *archaic var of* ENTIRE

in·ti·sy \ˈintəsē\ *n* -ES [NL (specific epithet of *Euphorbia intisy*)] : a spurge (*Euphorbia intisy*) from which rubber-yielding latex is obtained in limited quantities

intitle *archaic var of* ENTITLE

intitulate *vt* -ED/-ING/-S [LL *intitulatus*, past part. of *intitulare*, fr. L *in-* ²in- + *titulus* title] *obs* : ENTITLE

in·tit·u·la·tion \ənˌtichəˈlāshən\ *n* -s [MF or ML; MF, fr. ML *intitulation-*, *intitulatio* name, title, fr. LL *intitulatus* (past part. of *intitulare*) + L -*ion-*, -*io* -ion] *archaic* : the act of giving a title to; *also* : the title itself

in·ti·tule \ənˈti(ˌ)chül, -ˌchəl\ *vt* -ED/-ING/-S [MF *intituler*, fr. LL *intitulare*] *Brit* : to give a title or designation to — now used chiefly of a legislative act

intl *abbr* international

intmd *abbr* intermediate

intmt *abbr* intermittent

intn *abbr* intention

in·to \ˈintə, -n·tü, -n-(ˌ)tü, +V *often* -ntəw\ *prep* [ME, fr. OE *intō*, fr. ²*in* + *tō* to] **1 a** — used as a function word primarily denoting motion so directed as to terminate, if continued, when the position denoted by *in* has been reached and usu. after a verb that carries the idea of motion or a word implying or suggesting motion or passage to indicate a place or thing entered or penetrated or enterable or penetrable by or as if by a movement from the outside to an interior part ⟨came ~ the house⟩ ⟨the river ran ~ the sea⟩ ⟨traveled ~ the next state⟩ ⟨a route ~ the wilderness⟩ ⟨imports ~ this country⟩ ⟨the mountains merge ~ the plain⟩ ⟨brought ~ membership in the club⟩ ⟨off we go ~ the wide blue yonder⟩ but sometimes in constructions in which the idea of motion is carried by the very use of *into* in preference to *in* ⟨among the first ~ the field —*N. Y. Herald Tribune*⟩ ⟨they were ~ their clothes and on deck —H.A.Chippendale⟩ ⟨the child was ~ the cookie jar as soon as no one was looking⟩ ⟨stores them away ~ an inner pocket —A.J.Coutts⟩ ⟨baptized ~ the Catholic Church⟩ **b** : in toward ⟨sailed the boat ~ the pier⟩ ⟨the batter leaned ~ the pitch⟩ ⟨it stood close ~ a fine cottonwood grove —Willa Cather⟩ ⟨keeping well ~ the foot or lower slopes of the scarpside —S.G.Joseph⟩ **2** *chiefly Scot* : IN 1a(1) ⟨living ~ his new house⟩ **3 a** — used as a function word indicating a state or condition assumed, brought into being (as by force), or allowed to come about ⟨enter ~ bliss⟩ ⟨drive someone ~ despair⟩ ⟨fall ~ decay⟩ ⟨land brought ~ cultivation⟩ ⟨collapses ~ hysterics and quits —H. F. & Katharine Pringle⟩ **b** — used as a function word that usu. follows words carrying an idea of alteration or suggesting or implying alteration and that indicates a form or condition assumed often with loss of original or essential identity and emergence as something else ⟨came ~ being⟩ ⟨develop ~ a butterfly⟩ ⟨compounds resolved ~ simple substances⟩ ⟨translate a book ~ French⟩ ⟨divide a hospital ~ several wards⟩ ⟨fold a paper ~ four⟩ ⟨the barn was remodeled ~ a garage⟩ ⟨the land was plowed ~ broad ridges and hollows —L.D.Stamp⟩ ⟨the book went ~ edition after edition⟩ ⟨divide the theme ~ a beginning, a middle, and an ending⟩ **4** — used as a function word to indicate something accepted or acquired (as for possession) ⟨talked himself ~ a good job⟩ ⟨came ~ an inheritance⟩ **5 a** (1) *obs* : TO, TOWARD (2) : toward and as far as (something considered central) ⟨go ~

town⟩ ⟨go ~ market⟩ **b** : in the direction of ⟨looking ~ the sun⟩ ⟨looked ~ his plate and said nothing⟩ ⟨turned ~ the wind⟩ **c** : up to : as far as ⟨since then — right ~ today — you and I have enjoyed . . . the economic idea of roaring production —Sylvia F. Porter⟩ **d** : AGAINST 2a ⟨run ~ a wall⟩ ⟨fell ~ a fence⟩ ⟨the mixture is run ~ an endless moving wire screen —*Amer. Guide Series: La.*⟩ **6 a** — used as a function word to indicate the dividend in mathematical division ⟨dividing 3 ~ 6 gives 2⟩ **b** *archaic* : BY : together with — used with *multiply* **7** — used as a function word to indicate a set of circumstances, a function, action, or occupation entered upon or taken on ⟨get ~ trouble⟩ ⟨go ~ business⟩ ⟨force ~ compliance⟩ ⟨might be tortured ~ divulging military information —G.A. Craig⟩ **8 a** — used as a function word indicating something in which a literal or figurative insertion or introduction is made or in which there is inclusion ⟨pushed the hose ~ the pipe⟩ ⟨read a new meaning ~ a sentence⟩ ⟨water enters ~ the composition of the human body⟩ ⟨marry ~ an influential family⟩ ⟨introduced a bill ~ the legislature⟩ ⟨play a song ~ a microphone⟩ ⟨soon got ~ the act⟩ **b** — used as a function word to indicate something penetrated by the sight or insight or by an intellectual process (as investigation, reflection, or analysis) ⟨peer ~ the distance⟩ ⟨look ~ the future⟩ ⟨search ~ his motives⟩ ⟨inquire ~ his activities⟩ ⟨insights ~ religion and poetry⟩ ⟨seek to look . . . ~ the hopes and fears of men and women —F.D.Roosevelt⟩ **c** : so as to impress, dent, or force inward ⟨pressed the marble ~ the palm of his hand⟩ ⟨force the grease ~ the bearings⟩ **d** — used as a function word to indicate something slowed or stopped in its course or impeded by interruption ⟨~ the path of a train⟩ ⟨stepped ~ a punch on the jaw⟩ ⟨butt ~ their conversation⟩ **e** : so as to permeate or fill ⟨gases expanding ~ a vacuum —S.F.Mason⟩ **f** : in direct connection or contact with ⟨I am ~ a heavy fish . . . have already taken a twelve-inch bass on the same plug —Paul Brooks⟩ **9** — used as a function word indicating a period of time or an extent of space of which a portion is used or occupied ⟨sang far ~ the night⟩ ⟨went some distance ~ the next month before paying the bill⟩ ⟨stretched ~ the distance⟩ **10** — used as a function word to indicate something contributed to, paid, received in exchange, or dealt with by handling in some way ⟨all the sugar we had went ~ the cake⟩ ⟨his pay check went ~ the rent⟩ ⟨their spare cash went ~ some new furniture⟩ ⟨all their brain power went ~ solving the problem⟩ **11** : so as to include ⟨the company then expanded ~ bakery machines and specialized sewing machines —*Time*⟩

in·to·cos·trin \ˌintəˈkästrən\ *n* -s [fr. *Intocostrin*, a trademark] : an extract of purified curare

in·toed \ˈinˌtōd\ *adj* [²*in* + *toed*] : having the toes turned inward

in·tolerability \(ˌ)in, ən+\ *n* : the quality or state of being intolerable

¹in·tolerable \(ˈ)in-, ən+\ *adj* [ME, fr. L *intolerabilis*, fr. *in-* ¹in- + *tolerabilis* tolerable] **1** : not tolerable : not capable of being borne or endured : UNBEARABLE ⟨~ pain⟩ ⟨~ anguish⟩ ⟨an ~ burden⟩ ⟨an almost ~ beauty —Bernard DeVoto⟩ **2** *archaic* : not to be withstood : IRRESISTIBLE **3** : EXTREME, EXCESSIVE ⟨sometimes gives way to an ~ degree of sentimentality over some of his women —C.H.Sykes⟩ ⟨scarcely to have made an impression upon the ~ multitude of volumes which everyone is supposed to have read —Arnold Bennett⟩ ⟨an ~ amount of airless inner space —Lewis Mumford⟩ — **in·tolerableness** \"+\ *n* — **in·tolerably** \"+\ *adv*

²intolerable \"\ *adv* : INTOLERABLY

in·tolerance \"+\ *n* [F *intolérance*, fr. L *intolerantia*, fr. *intolerant-*, *intolerans* intolerant + *-ia* -y] **1** : the quality or state of being intolerant: as **a** : the lack of an ability to endure ⟨an ~ of strong light⟩; *specif* : exceptional sensitivity to a drug, food, or other substance ⟨~ to quinine⟩ **b** : ILLIBERALITY, BIGOTRY **2** : an instance of intolerance

in·tolerancy \"+\ *n* [L *intolerantia*] *archaic* : INTOLERANCE

¹in·tolerant \"+\ *adj* [F or L; F *intolérant*, fr. L *intolerant-*, *intolerans*, fr. *in-* ¹in- + *tolerant-*, *tolerans* tolerant] **1** : unable to endure ⟨a plant ~ of direct sunlight⟩ ⟨a constitution ~ of excesses⟩ **2 a** : unwilling to endure ⟨~ of all strangers⟩ **b** : unwilling to tolerate a difference of opinion or feeling esp. in religious matters : refusing to allow others the free enjoyment of their opinions or worship : BIGOTED **c** : unwilling to grant equal social, political, or professional rights; *specif* : unwilling to tolerate social equality with one of another racial group — **in·tol·er·ant·ly** *adv*

²intolerant \"\ *n* -s : an intolerant person

in·tolerating \(ˈ)in-, ən+\ *adj* [¹*in-* + *tolerating*, pres. part. of *tolerate*] *archaic* : INTOLERANT

in·toleration \(ˌ)in-, ən+\ *n* [¹*in-* + *toleration*] : INTOLERANCE

intomb *archaic var of* ENTOMB

in·ton·able \ənˈtōnəbəl\ *adj* : that can be intoned

in·to·na·co \ənˈtänəˌkō, -tōn-\ *n* -s [It, fr. *intonacare* to coat with plaster, fr. (assumed) VL *intunicare*, fr. L *in-* ²in- + *tunica* tunic, coating] : the finishing coat of fine plaster in fresco painting — compare ARRICCIO

in·to·nate \ˈintəˌnāt, -tō-, *usu* -ād·+V\ *vt* -ED/-ING/-S [ML *intonatus*, past part. of *intonare*] **1** : INTONE **2** : to sound esp. with a particular intonation : UTTER

in·to·na·tion \ˌ==ˈnāshən\ *n* -s [ML *intonation-*, *intonatio*, fr. *intonatus* (past part. of *intonare*) + L *-ion-*, *-io* -ion] **1** : the act of intoning: **a** (1) : the act of singing the opening phrase of a plainsong, psalm, or canticle (2) : the act of musically reciting usu. in monotone any part of a liturgy **b** (1) : the act of sounding musical tones (as of a scale) (2) : the singing and playing of music according to the aural perception of the prevailing standard of accuracy in pitch **c** : the act of reciting in a singing voice usu. in a monotone **2** : something intoned; *specif* : the opening tones of a Gregorian chant preceding the reciting note usu. sung by the priest alone **3 a** : the manner of singing, playing, or uttering tones ⟨spoke with a foreign ~⟩ ⟨played the piece with a romantic ~⟩ **b** : pitch phenomena in speech; *esp* : such a phenomenon insofar as it makes a syntactical or emotional distinction (as between a declarative and interrogative statement) — **in·to·na·tion·al** \ˌ==ˈnāshənᵊl, -shnəl\ *adj*

intonation pattern *n* : a unit of speech melody in a language or dialect that contributes to the total meaning of an utterance ⟨one's *intonation pattern* in the utterance of *dead* may reveal one's emotional reaction to an announcement of death⟩ ⟨one *intonation pattern* makes *leave* a command, another makes it a question⟩

in·tone \ənˈtōn\ *vb* -ED/-ING/-S [alter. (influenced by ML *intonare*) of earlier *entone*, fr. ME *entonen*, fr. MF *entoner*, fr. ML *intonare*, fr. L *in-* ²in- + *tonus* tone] *vt* **1 a** : to utter in musical or prolonged tones : recite in singing tones or in a monotone ⟨~ the service⟩ ⟨~ the hours of the night⟩ ⟨*intoning* the marriage ceremony with the regular orthodox allowance for nasal recitative —T.L.Peacock⟩ **b** : to sing (as a song) or play (as a sonata) with special attention to the continuity of sound **2** : to sing usu. as a solo or semichorus (the opening phrase of a plainsong, psalm, or canticle) ~ *vi* : to utter something in singing tones or in monotone (as in chanting) — **in·ton·er** \-ōnə(r)\ *n*

in·to·neme \ənˈtōˌnēm\ *n* -s [*intone* + *-eme*] : INTONATION PATTERN

in·tone·ment \-ōnmənt\ *n* -s : the act of intoning or the state of being intoned ⟨the ~ of the service⟩

intoothed \ˈ=ˌ=\ *adj* [²*in* + *toothed*] : having the teeth turned inward

in·tor·sion *or* **in·tor·tion** \ənˈtȯrshən\ *n* -s [LL *intortion-*, *intortio* action of curling, fr. L *intortus* (past part. of *intorquēre* to twist, fr. *in-* ²in- + *torquēre* to twist) + *-ion-*, *-io* -ion — more at TORTURE] : a winding, bending, or twisting around (as of the stem of a plant); *specif* : inward rotation (as of a body part) about an axis or a fixed point — compare EXTORSION

in·tort·ed \-rdəd\ *adj* [L *intortus* (past part. of *intorquēre*) + E *-ed*] : twisted inward or in and out : TWINED, WREATHED, TANGLED

in to·to \inˈtōd·(ˌ)ō, -tō(ˌ)tō\ *adv* [L, on the whole] : TOTALLY, ENTIRELY, ALTOGETHER ⟨promised to publish the book *in toto*⟩ ⟨accepted the plan *in toto*⟩

intower *vt* [²*in-* + *tower* (n.)] *obs* : to imprison in a tower (as the Tower of London)

intown \ˈ==, =ˈ=\ *adj* [¹*in* + *town*] : being in the built-up part of a town ⟨an ~ section of the city⟩

¹in·tox·i·cant \ənˈtäksəkənt, -sēk-\ *n* [ML *intoxicant-*, *intoxicans*, pres. part. of *intoxicare*] : something that intoxicates : an intoxicating agent; *esp* : an alcoholic drink ⟨felt he should abstain from the use of ~*s*⟩

²intoxicant \"\ *adj* [ML *intoxicant-*, *intoxicans*, pres. part. of *intoxicare*] : INTOXICATING ⟨the drink was warm and ~⟩ ⟨the air comes up from the heights, fine and ~ —Sacheverell Sitwell⟩ — **in·tox·i·cant·ly** *adv*

¹in·tox·i·cate \-kə̇t, -ˌkāt| *usu* |d·+V\ *adj* [ME *intoxicat*, fr. ML *intoxicatus*, past part. of *intoxicare*] **1** *obs* : POISONED **2** *archaic* : excited or exhilarated beyond self-control by alcoholic drinks or to the point of enthusiasm or frenzy (as by pleasure) or stupefied by a narcotic

²in·tox·i·cate \-ˌkāt, *usu* -ād·+V\ *vt* -ED/-ING/-S [ML *intoxicatus*, past part. of *intoxicare*, fr. L *in-* ²in- + *toxicum* poison — more at TOXIC] **1** : POISON **2 a** : to excite or stupefy by alcoholic drinks or a narcotic esp. to the point where physical and mental control is markedly diminished : make drunk : INEBRIATE **b** : to excite to the point of enthusiasm, frenzy, or madness : elate strongly and often excessively ⟨found the idea *intoxicating* and ennobling⟩ ⟨*intoxicated* with dreams of fortune —Van Wyck Brooks⟩ ⟨*intoxicated* by success⟩

intoxicated *adj* **1** : being under the marked influence of an intoxicant : DRUNK, INEBRIATED **2** : emotionally excited, elated, or exhilarated (as by great joy or extreme pleasure) **syn** see DRUNK

in·tox·i·cat·ed·ly \=ˈ==ˌ==, =ˌ=ˈ===\ *adv* : in an intoxicated manner ⟨found herself ~ striving for that careless, exhilarating blitheness —Harriet LaBarre⟩

intoxicating *adj* : producing or fitted to produce intoxication ⟨an ~ beverage⟩ ⟨~ flattery⟩ ⟨~ beauty⟩ — **in·tox·i·cat·ing·ly** \=ˈ===, =ˌ=ˈ==\ *adv*

in·tox·i·ca·tion \=ˌ==ˈkāshən\ *n* -s [ML *intoxication-*, *intoxicatio* poisoning, fr. ML *intoxicatus* + L *-ion-*, *-io* -ion] **1** : poisoning or the abnormal state induced by a chemical agent (as a drug, serum, or toxin) ⟨barbiturate ~ may occur as an intractable dermatitis⟩ ⟨lead ~ is a hazard of some occupations⟩ **2 a** : the quality or state of being drunk : INEBRIATION **b** : a strong excitement of mind or feelings (as from joy or pleasure) : an elation that rises to enthusiasm, frenzy, or madness **3** : the act of intoxicating

in·tox·i·ca·tive \=ˈ==ˌkād·iv\ *adj, archaic* : of, relating to, or tending to cause intoxication

In·tox·im·e·ter \ˌin-ˌtäkˈsimədˑə(r)\ *trademark* — used for a device used to measure the degree of an individual's intoxication by means of chemical tests of the breath

intpr *abbr* interpreter

intr *abbr* **1** intransitive **2** introduced; introducing; introduction; introductory

in·tra- *in pronunciations below*, ˌ== = |in·trə *or* -·(ˌ)trä *or* -·(ˌ)trā\ *prefix* [LL, fr. L *intra* within, fr. (assumed) OL *interus* inward, on the inside — more at INTERIOR] **1 a** : within — esp. in adjectives formed from adjectives ⟨*intra*glacial⟩ ⟨*intra*vaginal⟩ ⟨*intra*cellular⟩ ⟨*intra*-European⟩ ⟨*intra*cosmical⟩ **b** : during — esp. in adjectives formed from adjectives ⟨*intra*natal⟩ ⟨*intra*febrile⟩ ⟨*intra*pyretic⟩ ⟨*intra*vital⟩ **c** : between layers of — esp. in adjectives formed from adjectives ⟨*intra*cutaneous⟩ **d** : underneath — esp. in adjectives formed from adjectives ⟨*intra*dural⟩ **2** : INTRO- ⟨an *intra*muscular injection⟩ ⟨*intra*venation⟩ ⟨*intra*cerebral⟩ **3** : internal ⟨*intra*selection⟩

in·tra–abdominal \ˌ==+\ *adj* [*intra-* + *abdominal*] : being within the abdomen ⟨*intra-abdominal* pressure⟩ or going into the abdomen ⟨an *intra-abdominal* injection⟩ — **in·tra–abdominally** \"+\ *adv*

in·tra–atomic \"+\ *adj* [*intra-* + *atomic*] : existing within an atom ⟨the project which led to man's first practical utilization of *intra-atomic* energy —Julian Huxley⟩

in·tra·bi·on·tic \"+(ˈ)bīˈäntik\ *adj* [prob. irreg. fr. *intra-* + Gk *biount-*, *biōn* living + E *-ic* — more at -BIONT] : existing or occurring within an individual

in·tra·cartilaginous \ˌ==+\ *adj* [*intra-* + *cartilaginous*] *of bone development* : taking place within the substance of cartilage : ENDOCHONDRAL — compare INTRAMEMBRANOUS

in·tra·cav·i·tar·i·ly \"+ˌkavəˈterəlē\ *adv* : in an intracavitary manner

in·tra·cav·i·tary \-ˌterē\ *adj* [*intra-* + *cavity* + *-ary*] : being within or from within a body cavity ⟨~ irradiation of cervical cancer⟩

in·tra·cellular \ˌ==+\ *adj* [ISV *intra-* + *cellular*] : being or occurring within a body cell or within the body cells : ENDOCELLULAR — **in·tra·cellularly** *adv*

in·tra·cerebral \"+\ *adj* [ISV *intra-* + *cerebral*] : going into the cerebrum ⟨~ inoculation⟩ — **in·tra·cerebrally** \"+\ *adv*

in·tra·cervical \"+\ *adj* [ISV *intra-* + *cervical*] : situated within the cervix of the uterus

in·tra·chordal \"+\ *adj* [*intra-* + *chordal*] : being or occurring within a chord (as the notochord)

in·tra·cisternal \"+\ *also* **in·tra·cistern** \"+\ *adj* [*intra-* + *cisternal* or *cistern*] : going into or being or occurring within a cisterna — **in·tra·cis·ter·nal·ly** \"+(ˈ)sisˈtərnᵊlē *or* +səˈ-\ *adv*

in·tra·city \ˌ==+\ *adj* [*intra-* + *city*] : being, occurring, or operating within a particular city ⟨~ buses⟩

in·tra·coastal \"+\ *adj* [*intra-* + *coastal*] : being within and close to the coast or belonging to the inland waters near the coast ⟨an ~ waterway⟩

in·tra·company \"+\ *adj* [*intra-* + *company*] : being or occurring within a company ⟨for the sake of ~ relations —*Current Biog.*⟩

in·tra·continental \"+\ *adj* [*intra-* + *continental*] : being within a particular continent

in·tra·cortical \"+\ *adj* [*intra-* + *cortical*] : being or situated within the cortex

in·tra·cranial \"+\ *adj* [*intra-* + *cranial*] : being or occurring within the cranium ⟨~ pressure⟩ — **in·tra·cra·ni·al·ly** \"+ˈkrānēəlē\ *adv*

intracranial cast *n* : a cast of the brain cavity in a skull

in·tra·crystalline \ˌ==+\ *adj* [*intra-* + *crystalline*] : being or occurring within a crystal ⟨an ~ field⟩

in·tractability \(ˌ)in, ən+\ *n* : the quality or state of being intractable

¹in·tractable \(ˈ)in, ən+\ *adj* [L *intractabilis*, fr. *in-* ¹in- + *tractabilis* tractable] **1** : not easily governed, managed, or directed : not disposed to be taught, disciplined, or tamed : OBSTINATE, REFRACTORY ⟨an ~ temper⟩ ⟨an ~ child⟩ : unwilling to submit ⟨~ to force⟩ **2** : not easily manipulated or wrought ⟨an ~ metal⟩ **3** : not easily relieved or cured ⟨an ~ pain⟩ ⟨an ~ malady⟩ : not responsive (as to a medicine) ⟨~ to remedies⟩ **syn** see UNRULY

²intractable \"\ *n* -s : one that is intractable ⟨most of the group was docile but it did contain ~*s*⟩

in·tractableness \(ˈ)in, ən+\ *n* : the quality or state of being intractable : STUBBORNNESS, REFRACTORINESS

in·tractably \"+\ *adv* : in an intractable way

in·tra·cutaneous *pronunc at* INTRA- +\ *adj* [ISV *intra-* + *cutaneous*] : INTRADERMAL — **in·tra·cutaneously** \"+\ *adv*

intracutaneous test *n* : a test for immunity or hypersensitivity to a particular antigen made by injecting a minute amount of diluted antigen into the skin — compare PATCH TEST, SCRATCH TEST

in·tra·cytoplasmic \ˌ==+\ *adj* [ISV *intra-* + *cytoplasmic*] : lying or occurring in cytoplasm (as of a cell) ⟨~ multiplication of sporozoans⟩

in·tra·da \ənˈträdə\ *n* -s [modif. of It *intrata*, *entrata* entrance, introduction, fr. fem. of *intrato*, *entrato*, past part. of *intrare*, *entrare* to enter, fr. L *intrare* — more at ENTER] : a musical introduction or prelude esp. in 16th and 17th century music : ENTRÉE

in·tra·departmental *pronunc at* INTRA- +\ *adj* [*intra-* + *departmental*] : being or occurring within a department ⟨~ rivalry⟩

in·tra·dermal \"+\ *also* **in·tra·dermic** \"+\ *adj* [*intradermal* fr. *intra-* + *dermal*; *intradermic* ISV *intra-* + *dermic*] : being within the skin ⟨an ~ nevus⟩ : being between the layers of the skin ⟨an ~ injection⟩ — **in·tra·der·mal·ly** \"+ˈdərməlē\ *also* **in·tra·der·mi·cal·ly** \-mək(ə)lē\ *adv*

in·tra·disciplinary \ˌ==+\ *adj* [*intra-* + *disciplinary*] : being or occurring within the scope of a scholarly or academic discipline or between the people active in such a discipline

in·tra·district \"+\ *adj* [*intra-* + *district*] : being or occurring within a district ⟨interdistrict and ~ services —D.H.Nucker⟩

intrado *n* -s [modif. of Sp *entrada* entry, income, fr. fem. of *entrado*, past part. of *entrar* to enter, fr. L *intrare* — more at ENTER] *obs* : INCOME

in·tra·dos \ˈin·trəˌdäs, -ˌdōs, -ˌdō; in·ˈträ|ˌdäs, -rä|, |ˌdəs\ *n*, *pl* **intrados** \-ˌdōz\ *or* **intradoses** \-äsəz, -ōsəz, -əsəz\ [F, fr. L *intra* within + F *dos* back — more at INTRA-, DOSSIER] **1** : the interior curve of an arch; *esp* : the inner curved face of the whole body of voussoirs **2** : the inner surface of a vault — compare EXTRADOS

in·tra·ductal *pronunc at* INTRA- +\ *adj* [*intra-* + *duct* + *-al*] : being or occurring within a duct ⟨~ pressure⟩

in·tra·dural \"+\ *adj* [ISV *intra-* + *dural*] : being or occurring within the dura mater

in·tra–european \"+\ *adj, usu cap E* [*intra-* + *european*] : being or occurring within the boundaries of Europe or between the countries of Europe ⟨*intra-European* political movements⟩

1 intrados 1

in·tra·fascicular \"+\ *adj* [*intra-* + *fascicular*] : being or occurring within a vascular bundle

in·tra·formational \"+\ *adj* [*intra-* + *formational*] : being or occurring within a geologic formation : originating more or less contemporaneously with the enclosing geologic material — see BRECCIOLA

in·tra·genic \"+\ *adj* [*intra-* + *genic*] : being or occurring within a gene ⟨~ changes⟩

in·tra·glacial \"+\ *adj* [*intra-* + *glacial*] : being or occurring within a glacier or a glacial stage

in·tra·granular \"+\ *adj* [*intra-* + *granular*] : being or occurring within a grain ⟨~ microstructures —*Jour. of Geol.*⟩

in·tra·group \"+\ *also* **in·tra·group·al** \"+ˈgrüpəl\ *adj* [*intragroup* fr. *intra-* + *group*; *intragroupal* fr. *intra-* + *group* + *-al*] : being or occurring within a single group ⟨increased ~ hostility —J.B.Carroll⟩

in·tra·hepatic \"+\ *adj* [ISV *intra-* + *hepatic*] : being within or originating in the liver — compare EXTRAHEPATIC

intrail *archaic var of* ENTRAIL

in·tra·imperial *pronunc at* INTRA- +\ *adj* [*intra-* + *imperial*] : being, occurring, or carried on within an empire

in·tra·individual \"+\ *adj* [*intra-* + *individual*] : being or occurring within the individual

in·tra–industry *or* **in·tra·industrial** \"+\ *adj* [*intra-* + *industry* or *industrial*] : being or occurring within an industry or between the independent enterprises of an industry

in·tra·island \"+\ *adj* [*intra-* + *island*] : being within or limited to the confines of an island ⟨~ distances are not great —J.H.S.Billmyer⟩ ⟨~ telephone and courier service —John Hersey⟩

in·trait \ˈinˌtrā, ˈan·-\ *n* [F, fr. *in-* ²in- + *-trait* (as in *extrait* extract, fr. MF, fr. past part. of *extraire* to extract, fr. L *extrahere*) — more at EXTRACT] : one of a class of extracts prepared from plants in which the enzymes are killed before drying

in·tra·lamellar *pronunc at* INTRA- +\ *adj* [*intra-* + *lamellar*] : situated within a lamella — used esp. of the trama in agarics

in·tra·luminal \"+\ *adj* [*intra-* + *luminal*] : being within or arising from within the lumen ⟨~ inflammation of the esophagus⟩

in·tra·marginal \"+\ *adj* [*intra-* + *marginal*] : being, occurring, or operating within a margin

in·tra·matrical \"+\ *adj* [*intra-* + *matrical*] : being or occurring within a matrix — **in·tra·matrically** \"+\ *adv*

in·tra·medullary \"+\ *adj* [ISV *intra-* + *medullary*] : being or lying within a medulla ⟨an ~ tumor of the spinal cord⟩; *esp* : involving use of the marrow space of a bone for support ⟨~ pinning of a fracture of the thigh⟩

in·tra·membranous \"+\ *adj* [*intra-* + *membranous*] *of bone development* : taking place through the ossification of a membrane — compare INTRACARTILAGINOUS

in·tra·mental \"+\ *adj* [*intra-* + *mental*] : INTRAPSYCHIC

in·tra·mercurial *also* **in·tra·mercurian** \"+\ *adj* [*intramercurial* ISV *intra-* + *mercurial*; *intramercurian* fr. *intra-* + *mercurian*] : being within the orbit of the planet Mercury

in·tra·micellar \"+\ *adj* [*intra-* + *micellar*] : being or taking place within a micelle ⟨~ swelling of cellulose by water⟩ — **in·tra·mi·cel·lar·ly** *adv*

in·tra·molecular \ˌ==+\ *adj* [ISV *intra-* + *molecular*] : situated or occurring within the molecule ⟨~ rearrangement⟩ : formed by reaction between different parts of the same molecule — **in·tra·mo·lec·u·lar·ly** *adv*

intramolecular respiration *n* : the production of carbon dioxide and of organic acids by aerobic organisms or tissues while deprived of atmospheric oxygen

intramolecular salt *n* : INNER SALT

in·tra·montane \ˌ==+\ *adj* [ISV *intra-* + *montane*] : being within a mountainous region

in·tra·morainic \"+\ *adj* [*intra-* + *morainic*] : being or occurring within the lobate curve of a moraine

in·tra·mundane \"+\ *adj* [*intra-* + *mundane*] : being or occurring within the material world — opposed to *extramundane*

in·tra·mural \"+\ *adj* [*intra-* + *mural*] **1** : being, occurring, or undertaken within the limits usu. of a state, community, organization, or institution (as an academic institution) ⟨the most extensive ~ investigation undertaken in the history of our government —W.H.Hale⟩ ⟨an ~ squabble within the corporation⟩ ⟨the ~ conflicts of four generations of a prolific family —Harrison Smith⟩ ⟨the college's ~ sports program⟩ ⟨~ competition between the departments of the state university⟩ — opposed to *extramural* **2** : being or occurring within the substance of the walls of an organ ⟨~ infarction⟩ ⟨~ circulation⟩ — **in·tra·murally** \"+\ *adv*

in·tra·muscular \"+\ *adj* [ISV *intra-* + *muscular*] : being within a muscle ⟨~ fat⟩ : going into a muscle ⟨~ injection⟩ — **in·tra·muscularly** \"+\ *adv*

in·tra·nasal \"+\ *adj* [*intra-* + *nasal*] : lying within or going into the nasal structures — **in·tra·nasally** \"+\ *adv*

in·tra·natal \"+\ *adj* [*intra-* + *natal*] : occurring chiefly with reference to the child during the act of birth ⟨~ accident⟩ — compare INTRAPARTUM, NEONATAL

in·tra·national \"+\ *adj* [*intra-* + *national*] : being or occurring within a nation ⟨~ movements of the population⟩

intrance *archaic var of* ²ENTRANCE

in·tra·ne·ous \(ˈ)in·ˈtrānēəs, ən·ˈt-\ *adj* [LL *intraneus*, fr. L *intra* within — more at INTRA-] : being or growing within an area : INTERNAL — opposed to *extraneous*

in·tra·neural *pronunc at* INTRA- +\ *adj* [*intra-* + *neural*] : being or occurring within or going into a nerve or nervous tissue — **in·tra·neurally** \"+\ *adv*

in·tranquil \(ˈ)in·, ən+\ *adj* [¹*in-* + *tranquil*] : not tranquil : DISTURBED, RESTLESS ⟨an ~ sleep⟩ — **in·tranquillity** \ˌin·+\ *n*

in trans *abbr* in transit

intrans *abbr* intransitive

in·transferable \ˌin·, (ˈ)in·, ən+\ *adj* [¹*in-* + *transferable*] : incapable of being transferred

in·transgressible \ˌin·+\ *adj* [¹*in-* + *transgress* + *-ible*] : that cannot or may not be transgressed

in·tran·si·geance \ənˈtran(t)səjən(t)s, -raan- *also* -ra(a)nzəj- *sometimes* ˌin·ˌtra(a)nˈsij(ē)ən(t)s *or* -ˈzi-\ *also* **in·tran·si·gean·cy** \-nsē, -nsi\ *n*, *pl* **intransigeanc·es** *also* **intransigeancies** [*intransigeance* fr. F, fr. *intransigeant*, after F *-ant*: *-ance*; *intransigeancy* fr. ²*intransigeant* + *-cy*] : INTRANSIGENCE ⟨assume attitudes of bohemian ~ toward society —Philip Rahv⟩

¹in·tran·si·geant \-nt\ *n* -s [F (trans. of Sp *intransigente*), fr. *in-* ¹in- + *transigeant*, pres. part. of *transiger* to compromise, fr. L *transigere* to transact] : ¹INTRANSIGENT

²intransigeant \"\ *adj* [F (trans. of Sp *intransigente*), fr. *in-* ¹in- + *transigeant*, pres. part. of *transiger*] : ²INTRANSIGENT — **in·tran·si·geant·ly** *adv*

in·tran·si·gence \ən'tran(t)səjən(t)s, -raan- *also* -ra(a)nzəj-\ *also* **in·tran·si·gen·cy** \-nsē,-nsi\ *n, pl* **intransigenc·es** *also* **intransigencies** [*intransigence* fr. ²*intransigent*, after such pairs as E *abstinent: abstinence; intransigency* fr. ²*intransigent* + *-cy*] **:** the quality or state of being intransigent ⟨his absolute ~ on any question —*Current History*⟩ ⟨~ in the face of harsh realities —R.J.Slavin⟩ ⟨the desire not . . . to prejudice the integration and defense of the West by ~ on issues —*Current History*⟩ ⟨who, by their ~, do most to block the peace —*New Republic*⟩

¹**in·tran·si·gent** \-jənt\ *n* -s [Sp *intransigente*, fr. *in-* ¹in- + *transigente*, pres. part. of *transigir* to compromise, fr. L *transigere* to transact — more at TRANSACT] **:** one that is intransigent

²**intransigent** \"\ *adj* [Sp *intransigente*, fr. *in-* ¹in- + *transigente*, pres. part. of *transigir*] **1 a :** refusing to compromise or budge from an often extreme position taken or held **:** preserving an immovable independence of position or attitude **:** UNCOMPROMISING ⟨an ~ imperialist who opposed with great force . . . every liberal tendency —R.P.Casey⟩ ⟨felt the man was ~ because of his youth and would modify his views as he grew older⟩ **b** *of two or more* **:** IRRECONCILABLE ⟨the ~ parties to the dispute⟩ **2 :** befitting one that is uncompromising ⟨its previous ~ attitude toward modern art —*Americana Annual*⟩ — **in·tran·si·gent·ly** *adv*

in·tran·si·gent·ism \-nt,izəm, -n,ti-\ *n* -s **:** the quality or state of being intransigent or the policy of an intransigent ⟨the militant ~ of the antislavery forces —A.C.Cole⟩

in–transit \'≈,≈≈, ≈'≈≈\ *adj* [fr. the phrase *in transit*] **:** being in transit ⟨worried about *in-transit* passengers to Europe during the storm⟩ **:** of or relating to something in transit ⟨*in-transit* freight rates⟩

in·transitable \(')in, ən+\ *adj* [¹*in-* + *transitable*] **:** not capable of being crossed or passed over ⟨an ~ gorge⟩

¹**in·transitive** \(')in, ən+\ *adj* [LL *intransitivus*, fr. L *in-* ¹in- + LL *transitivus* transitive] **:** not transitive: as **a** *archaic* **:** not transmitted to another **:** not passing beyond particular limits **b** (1) **:** not passing over directly to an object ⟨an ~ action⟩ (2) **:** expressing an action or state as limited to the agent or subject or as ending in itself **:** not taking a direct object — used of a verb form ⟨the verbs in "the bird flies" and "he runs" are ~⟩; compare ¹ABSOLUTE 4d (3) **:** being a construction containing an intransitive verb form **c :** characterizing a logical relationship between the three statements *x*, *y*, and *z* that occurs when *x* is related to *y* as *y* but not *x* is related to *z* — **in·transitively** \"+\ *adv* — **in·transitiveness** \"+\ *n*

²**intransitive** \"\ *n* **:** an intransitive verb form or construction

in·transitivity \(¦)in, ən+\ *n* **:** the quality or state of being intransitive **:** INTRANSITIVENESS

in·tran·si·tiv·ize \(')≈¦≈(≈)≈,īz\ *vt* -ED/-ING/-S **:** to make intransitive — **in·tran·si·tiv·iz·er** \-zə(r)\ *n* -s

in tran·si·tu \(')in'tran(t)sə,tü, -ranzə-\ *adv* [L] **:** during passage from one place to another

in·translatable \(¦)in+\ *adj* [¹*in-* + *translate* + *-able*] **:** not translatable

in·transmissibility \"+\ *n* **:** the quality or state of being intransmissible

in·transmissible \"+\ *adj* [¹*in-* + *transmissible*] **:** not transmissible

in·transmutable \"+\ *adj* [¹*in-* + *transmutable*] **:** not transmutable

in·trant \'intrənt\ *n* -s [L *intrant-*, *intrans*, pres. part. of *intrare* to enter — more at ENTER] *archaic* **:** ENTRANT; *esp* **:** one entering an educational institution or a holy or fraternal order

in·tra·nuclear *pronunc at* INTRA- +\ *adj* [ISV *intra-* + *nuclear*] **:** being or occurring within or going into a nucleus

in·tra·ocular \"+\ *adj* [ISV *intra-* + *ocular*] **:** being or occurring within or going into the eyeball

in·tra·oral \"+\ *adj* [*intra-* + *oral*] **:** being or occurring within the mouth

in·tra·organismal \"+\ *adj* [*intra-* + *organismal*] **:** situated or originating inside an organism ⟨~ conflicts⟩ ⟨interpretation of ~ processes and relationships —L.A.White⟩

in·tra·organizational \"+\ *adj* [*intra-* + *organizational*] **:** being or occurring within an organization

in·tra·parietal \"+\ *adj* [*intra-* + *parietal*] **1 :** INTRAMURAL 2 **2 :** located within the parietal lobe of the cerebrum

in·tra·par·tum \"+¦pärd·əm\ *adj* [NL *intra partum*, lit., during birth, fr. L *intra* during, within + *partum*, accus. of *partus* birth — more at INTRA-, ANTEPARTUM] **:** occurring chiefly with reference to a mother during the act of birth — compare INTRANATAL

in·tra·party \¦≈≈+\ *adj* [*intra-* + *party*] **:** being or occurring within the membership or scope of a usu. political party ⟨~ feuding⟩ ⟨~ organization⟩

in·tra·pelvic \"+\ *adj* [*intra-* + *pelvic*] **:** situated within the pelvis

in·tra·pericardiac \"+\ *adj* [*intra-* + *pericardiac*] **:** situated within or going into the pericardium ⟨~ injections⟩

in·tra·peritoneal \"+\ *adj* [ISV *intra-* + *peritoneal*] **:** being within or going into the peritoneal cavity; *also* **:** going through the peritoneum — **in·tra·peritoneally** \"+\ *adv*

in·tra·petiolar \"+\ *adj* [ISV *intra-* + *petiolar*] **1 :** enclosed by the expanded base of the petiole ⟨~ leaf buds in the plane tree⟩ **2 :** situated between the petiole and the stem ⟨~ stipules in plants of the family Rubiaceae⟩

in·tra·pial \"+\ *adj* [*intra-* + *pial*] **:** being or occurring within the pia mater

in·tra·plant \"+\ *adj* [*intra-* + *plant*] **:** being or occurring within an industrial plant ⟨~ working conditions and policies —*Americana Annual*⟩ ⟨~ disputes⟩

in·tra·psychic *or* **in·tra·psychical** \"+\ *adj* [*intra-* + *psychic* or *psychical*] **:** being or occurring within the psyche, the mind, or the personality ⟨~ conflicts⟩ ⟨~ processes⟩ — **in·tra·psychically** \"+\ *adv*

in·tra·pulmonic \"+\ *adj* [*intra-* + *pulmonic*] **:** occurring within the lungs ⟨~ pressure⟩

in·tra·school \"+\ *adj* [*intra-* + *school*] **:** existing within a school ⟨an ~ athletic program⟩ — opposed to *interschool*

in·tra·selection \"+\ *n* [ISV *intra-* + *selection*] **:** hypothetical competition between structural elements of a tissue or organ resulting in survival of those best suited to a particular function or situation

in·tra·service \"+\ *adj* [*intra-* + *service*] **:** being or occurring within the armed services ⟨~ rivalry⟩ or within a branch of the armed services ⟨~ advancement⟩

in·tra·shop \"+\ *adj* [*intra-* + *shop*] **:** being within or confined to a single shop ⟨~ agencies for collective bargaining⟩

in·tra·species \"+\ *adj* [*intra-* + *species*] **:** INTRASPECIFIC

in·tra·specific \"+\ *adj* [*intra-* + *specific*] **:** being or occurring within a species or involving the members of one species

in·tra·spinal \"+\ *adj* [*intra-* + *spinal*] **:** being within or going into a spine; *esp* **:** going into the spinal canal — **in·tra·spinally** \"+\ *adv*

in·tra·state \"+\ *adj* [*intra-* + *state*] **:** existing within a state ⟨interstate and ~ commerce⟩

in·tra·stelar \"+\ *adj* [*intra-* + *stelar*] **:** being or occurring within a stele

in·tra·stratal \"+\ *adj* [*intra-* + *stratal*] **:** being or occurring within strata ⟨~ solution⟩

in·tra·telluric \"+\ *adj* [*intra-* + *telluric*; trans. of G *intratellurisch*] **1 :** situated, formed, or occurring deep within the earth — used esp. of a mineral of an igneous rock **2 :** of, relating to, or constituting the period or stage of crystallization of igneous rocks prior to eruption

intraterminal switching *n, pl* **intraterminal switchings :** the moving of cars from one place to another on the same railroad line and within the switching limits of one station or industrial switching district — compare INTERTERMINAL SWITCHING

in·tra·thecal \"+\ *adj* [*intra-* + *thecal*] **1 a :** being within a sheath **b :** being or going under the membranes covering the brain or spinal cord ⟨an ~ injection⟩ **2 :** being within the theca esp. of a coral — **in·tra·thecally** \"+\ *adv*

in·tra·thoracic \"+\ *adj* [ISV *intra-* + *thoracic*] **:** being or occurring within the thorax ⟨~ extension of the disease —Cecil Wakeley⟩ ⟨~ pressure⟩

in·tratom·ic \¦in·trə¦tämik\ *adj* [irreg. fr. *intra-* + *atomic*] **:** INTRA-ATOMIC

in·tra·tracheal *pronunc at* INTRA- +\ *adj* [ISV *intra-* + *tracheal*] **:** being or occurring within or going into the trachea

in·tra·tropical \"+\ *adj* [*intra-* + *tropical*] **:** INTERTROPICAL

in·tra·uterine \"+\ *adj* [ISV *intra-* + *uterine*] **:** being or occurring within the uterus; *esp* **:** occurring during the part of development that takes place in the uterus

in·tra·vaginal \"+\ *adj* [ISV *intra-* + *vaginal*] **1 :** situated within a sheath — used esp. of branches in grasses **2 :** being or occurring within or going into the vagina

in·trav·a·sation \(,)in,travə'sāshən\ *n* -s [prob. fr. *intra-* + *-vasation* (as in *extravasation*)] **:** the entrance of foreign matter into a vessel of the body

in·tra·venous *pronunc at* INTRA- +\ *adj* [ISV *intra-* + *venous*] **:** being within or going into or by way of the veins ⟨~ feeding⟩ ⟨an ~ inflammation⟩; *also* **:** used in intravenous procedures ⟨an ~ needle⟩ ⟨an ~ solution⟩ — **in·tra·venously** \"+\ *adv*

in·tra vi·res \¦in·trə¦vī(,)rēz\ *adv* [NL] *law* **:** within the powers — opposed to *ultra vires*

in·tra·vital *pronunc at* INTRA- +\ *adj* [ISV *intra-* + *vital*] **:** INTRAVITAM

in·tra vi·tam \¦in·trə'vī,tam, -trä'wē,täm\ *adv* [NL, during life, fr. L *intra* during, within + *vitam*, accus. of *vita* life — more at INTRA-, VITAL] **:** during life **:** while the subject is alive ⟨the symptoms of fatty liver are . . . not sufficient in most cases to make an accurate diagnosis *intra vitam* —O.V.Brumley⟩

in·tra·vi·tam \¦≈≈¦≈,≈\ *adj* [fr. *intra vitam*, adv.] **1 :** performed upon or occurring in a subject that is alive ⟨an ~ diagnosis⟩ ⟨~ blood clotting⟩ **2** *of a stain* **:** having the property of tinting living cells without killing them

in·tra·vitelline *pronunc at* INTRA- +\ *adj* [*intra-* + *vitelline*] **:** being or occurring within the yolk of an egg

in·tra·vitreous \"+\ *adj* [*intra-* + *vitreous*] **:** being or occurring within the vitreous humor

in·tra·xylary \"+\ *adj* [*intra-* + *xylem* + *-ary*] **:** situated within the xylem

in–tray \'≈,≈\ *n* [⁴*in* + *tray*] **:** a shallow wood or metal basket usu. placed on a desk and used for holding incoming material (as letters) or material still to be dealt with — distinguished from *out-tray*

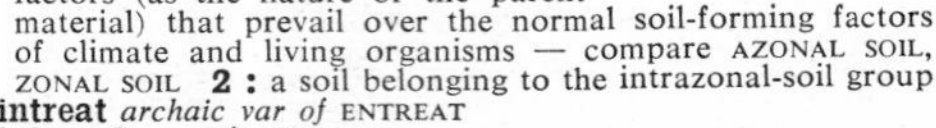

in-tray (top)

in·tra·zonal *pronunc at* INTRA- +\ *adj* [*intra-* + *zonal*] **:** of or belonging to intrazonal soil or an intrazonal soil

intrazonal soil *n* **1 :** a major soil group classified as a category of the highest rank and including soils with more or less well-developed soil characteristics determined by relatively local factors (as the nature of the parent material) that prevail over the normal soil-forming factors of climate and living organisms — compare AZONAL SOIL, ZONAL SOIL **2 :** a soil belonging to the intrazonal-soil group

intreat *archaic var of* ENTREAT

intrench *var of* ENTRENCH

in·trep·id \(')in¦trepəd, ən't-\ *adj* [L *intrepidus*, fr. *in-* ¹in- + *trepidus* alarmed — more at TREPIDATION] **:** characterized by resolute fearlessness in meeting dangers or hardships and enduring them with fortitude ⟨an ~ explorer⟩ ⟨an ~ attitude⟩ **syn** see BRAVE

in·tre·pid·i·ty \,in·trə'pidəd·ē, -tre'-, -idətē, -i\ *n* **:** the quality or state of being intrepid **:** resolute bravery **:** VALOR ⟨a girl of immense ~ and she struggled on gallantly —J.C.Powys⟩

in·trep·id·ly *adv* **:** in an intrepid manner

in·trep·id·ness *n* -ES **:** INTREPIDITY

in·tri·ca·cy \'in·trəkəsē, -trēk-, -si *sometimes* ən'trik- *or* 'in,trik-\ *n* -ES [¹*intricate* + *-cy*] **1 :** the quality or state of being intricate **:** complexity or involution in structure or arrangement (as of parts) ⟨these improvements . . . greatly increase the ~ of the mechanisms —Bryan Morgan⟩ ⟨the ~ of his philosophic notions⟩ **2 :** something intricate; *esp* **:** an intricate part, aspect, or relationship ⟨who know and admire the *intricacies* of bullfighting —Murray Sinclair⟩ ⟨with all its *intricacies* of fibers, muscles, and veins —Mary W. Shelley⟩ ⟨involved in the *intricacies* of his own success at law school —Mary Deasy⟩

¹**in·tri·cate** \-kət, *usu* -kəd·+V\ *adj* [ME (Sc), fr. L *intricatus*, past part. of *intricare* to entangle] **1 :** having many interwinding, intermeshing, or nicely or complexly interrelating parts, phases, patterns, or elements and being consequently perplexing and hard to grasp in detail, follow through, or execute ⟨a mazy dance in imitation of the ~ windings of the labyrinth —J.G.Frazer⟩ ⟨the wheels, cogs, levers, all the ~ parts of the hay-loading machine —Sherwood Anderson⟩ ⟨~ interlaced diamonds —*Amer. Guide Series: Md.*⟩ **2 :** showing an involvement or complexity of various detailed considerations or notions and hence requiring precise analysis **:** difficult to cope with, resolve, analyze, solve ⟨the ~ task of reorganizing the economic system on an equitable basis —J.A.Hobson⟩ ⟨our system of civil courts was very ~, and no explanation could be given of it without a long historical preamble —F.W.Maitland⟩ **syn** see COMPLEX

²**in·tri·cate** \'in·trə,kāt, -trē,-, *usu* -ād·+V\ *vt* -ED/-ING/-S [L *intricatus*, past part. of *intricare* to entangle, fr. *in-* ²in- + *tricae* trifles, impediments, perplexities; perh. akin to L *torquēre* to twist — more at TORTURE] **1 a** *obs* **:** ENTANGLE, ENSNARE **b :** INTERRELATE, INTERLOCK, INTERMESH ⟨so consistently *intricated* that one rests on another and is involved with what was earlier —Marianne Moore⟩ ⟨a career . . . *intricated* with an epoch —Lucien Price⟩ ⟨pseudopodia, reticulated and *intricated* —*Biol. Abstracts*⟩ **2** *archaic* **:** to make intricate **:** COMPLICATE

in·tri·cate·ly *pronunc at* ¹INTRICATE +lē *or* li\ *adv* **:** in an intricate manner ⟨an ~ designed floral pattern⟩ ⟨an ~ abstruse philosophical doctrine⟩

in·tri·cate·ness \"+nəs\ *n* -ES **:** INTRICACY

in·tri·ca·tion \,in·trə'kāshən, -trē'-\ *n* -S [ME *intricacion*, fr. ML *intrication-*, *intricatio*, fr. L *intricatus* + *-ion-*, *-io* -ion] **1** *obs* **:** COMPLICATION, COMPLEXITY **2 :** INTERRELATION, INTERMESHING

in·tri·gant *or* **in·tri·guant** \¦in·trē¦gänt, ¦an·t-\ *n* -S [F *intrigant*, fr. *intrigant*, adj., that intrigues, fr. It *intrigante*, pres. part. of *intrigare* to intrigue] **:** one that intrigues **:** INTRIGUER ⟨talked almost in whispers, like ~s —E.P.O'Donnell⟩

in·tri·gante *or* **in·tri·guante** \"\ *n* -S [F *intrigante*, fem. of *intrigant*] **:** a female intriguer ⟨the most fascinating woman they had ever known, but also . . . an ~ of dark and winding ways —Gertrude Atherton⟩

¹**in·trigue** \ən'trēg *sometimes* 'in,t-\ *vb* -ED/-ING/-S [F *intriguer* to puzzle, intrigue, fr. It *intrigare* to intrigue, fr. L *intricare* to entangle] *vt* **1** *archaic* **:** CHEAT, TRICK **2 :** to get, make, or accomplish by intrigue ⟨~ some bill through the senate —Thornton Wilder⟩ ⟨*intrigued* their way through ballrooms and bedrooms —*Time*⟩ ⟨*intrigued* themselves into office —F.M.Ford⟩ **3** *obs* **:** ENTANGLE, COMPLICATE **4 a :** to arouse the interest, desire, or curiosity of (as by beguiling or baffling) **:** BEGUILE ⟨a tale that ~s the reader⟩ ⟨an *intriguing* smile⟩ ⟨became *intrigued* with sketching children —*Newsweek*⟩ **b :** to engage by intriguing in this way ⟨has become something distinctive enough to ~ our interest —Charlton Laird⟩ ⟨have *intrigued* my attention and tightly gripped my fancy —Paul Ives⟩ **~** *vi* **:** to carry on an intrigue: as **a :** PLOT, SCHEME ⟨*intrigued* and conspired against him to the end —Hilaire Belloc⟩ **b :** to engage in a clandestine or illicit affair or intimacy

²**in·trigue** \'in,trēg, ən't-\ *n* -S [F, crafty scheme, plot, love affair, fr. It *intrigo* crafty scheme, fr. *intrigare* to intrigue] **1** *obs* **:** INTRICACY, COMPLEXITY **2 a :** a covert and involved scheme to accomplish one's end by devious maneuvering and crafty stratagem ⟨the party politicians . . . reverted to their familiar ~s and maneuvers —H.G.Wells⟩ ⟨the ~s and conspiracies of the middle ages —Edmond Taylor⟩ **b :** a tendency toward or the practice of engaging in such schemes ⟨jealousy and ~ and backbiting, producing a poisonous atmosphere of underground competition —Bertrand Russell⟩ ⟨ambitious, unscrupulous, and cruel, a master of ~ —Victor Seroff⟩ **3 :** the plot of a literary or dramatic work esp. marked by an intricacy of design or action or a complex interrelation of events ⟨the play rightly shows greater concern for comic ~ than for human probability —*Time*⟩ **4 :** a clandestine affair or intimacy esp. involving a married woman ⟨that hard-to-be-governed passion of youth hurried me frequently into ~s with low women —Benjamin Franklin⟩ **syn** see PLOT

in·trigu·er \-gə(r)\ *n* -S **:** one that intrigues

intriguing \≈'≈≈ *sometimes* '≈,≈≈\ *adj* **:** engaging the interest to a marked degree ⟨rather an ~ poem —William Strachey⟩ **:** FASCINATING ⟨a subject of ~ intricacy⟩ **:** BEGUILING ⟨a small and ~ young woman⟩ **syn** see INTERESTING

in·trigu·ing·ly *adv* **:** in an intriguing manner

¹**in·trin·sic** \(')in¦trinz|ik, ən't-, -rin(t)s|, |ēk\ *adj* [MF *intrinsèque* inner, internal, fr. LL *intrinsecus*, fr. L, adv., inwardly, inwards, fr. (assumed) L *intrim* (fr. — assumed — OL *interus* inward, on the inside) + L *-secus* (fr. *sequi* to follow) — more at INTERIOR, SUE] **1** *obs* **:** PRIVATE, SECRET **2 a :** belonging to the inmost constitution or essential nature of a thing **:** essential or inherent and not merely apparent, relative, or accidental ⟨form was treated as something ~, as the very essence of the thing in virtue of the metaphysical structure of the universe —John Dewey⟩ ⟨recommend this book for its ~ interest —Daniel George⟩ ⟨~ merit⟩ ⟨a wide gap between ~ feelings and the social expressions of them —H.J.Muller⟩ — opposed to *extrinsic* **b :** originating or due to causes or factors within a body, organ, or part ⟨~ asthma⟩ **c :** being good in itself or irreducible **:** being desirable or desired for its own sake and without regard to anything else ⟨when anyone says that values are merely matters of opinion or subjective liking, he is speaking only of ~ values —L.W.Beck⟩ **d :** REAL, ACTUAL ⟨a fine big bird, he is . . . but there is no ~ beauty about him —Richard Jefferies⟩ **3 :** originating and included wholly within an organ or part — used esp. of certain muscles; opposed to *extrinsic* — **in·trin·si·cal·ly** \|ək(ə)lē, |ēk-, -li\ *adv* — **in·trin·si·cal·ness** \|əkəlnəs, |ēk-\ *n* -ES

²**intrinsic** *n* -S *obs* **:** an intrinsic quality

in·trin·si·cal \|əkəl, |ēk-\ *adj* [alter. (influenced by ¹*intrinsic*) of earlier *intrinsecal*, fr. LL *intrinsecus* + E *-al*] *archaic* **:** INTRINSIC

intrinsic factor *n* **:** a substance produced by normal stomach and intestinal mucosa that facilitates absorption of vitamin B_{12} from the gastrointestinal tract and thereby assists in the development and maturation of red blood cells — compare EXTRINSIC FACTOR

intrinsic fraud *n* **:** fraud (as by the use of forged documents, false claims, perjured testimony) that misleads a court or jury relying upon it in determining issues and induces the court or jury to find for the party perpetrating the fraud — compare EXTRINSIC FRAUD

in·tro \'in·(,)trō\ *n* -S [short for *introduction*] **:** a musical introduction in jazz and popular music

intro- *prefix* [ME, fr. MF, fr. L, fr. *intro*, adv., inwardly, to the inside, fr. (assumed) OL *interus* inward, on the inside — more at INTERIOR] **1 :** in **:** into ⟨*intro*jection⟩ **2 :** inward **:** within ⟨*intro*active⟩ ⟨*intro*flex⟩ ⟨*intro*reception⟩ — opposed to *extro-*

in·tro·cep·tive \¦in·trə¦septiv, -rō¦-\ *adj* [*intro-* + *-ceptive* (as in *receptive*)] **:** capable of receiving within itself

introd *abbr* introduction

in·tro·duce \¦in·trə¦d(y)üs, -rō¦d-, *in rapid speech* ¦in(t)ə(r)¦d-\ *vt* -ED/-ING/-S [ME *introducen* to initiate, instruct, fr. L *introducere* to introduce, fr. *intro-* + *ducere* to lead — more at TOW] **1 a :** to lead, bring, conduct, or usher in esp. for the first time ⟨~ a person into a drawing room⟩ ⟨~ European birds into America⟩ **b :** to cause to take part or be involved by introducing ⟨the fruits of *introducing* party men into municipal affairs —*Sydney (Australia) Bull.*⟩ **2 a :** to bring into play (as in action or thought) ⟨~ abuses into court practices⟩ **:** bring forward in the course of an action or sequence ⟨~ irrelevancies into the discussion⟩ **:** add or contribute (as a new element or feature) ⟨~ new business into a play⟩ ⟨*introduced* amendments to the draft extension bill —*Current Biog.*⟩ ⟨*introduced* a new and mutually beneficial element into crop and livestock husbandry —N.C.Wright⟩ **b :** to bring into practice or use **:** INSTITUTE ⟨~ a new fashion in hats⟩ ⟨the first officer to ~ gunpowder into the French Army —Edmond Taylor⟩ ⟨*introduced* club cars on certain important business expresses —O.S.Nock⟩ ⟨slow to ~ new processes, slow to adopt new inventions —Leo Wolman⟩ **3** *obs* **:** to cause to exist **:** bring into being **4 :** to lead to or make known by a formal act, announcement, or recommendation: as **a :** to cause to be acquainted **:** cause to know each other personally ⟨~ two strangers⟩ **:** make (one person) known to another ⟨~ the boy to her father⟩ **b :** to present formally at court or into society ⟨a party to ~ his daughter to London society⟩ **c :** to present or announce formally or officially or by an official reading ⟨~ a bill to Congress⟩ **d :** to make preliminary explanatory or laudatory remarks about (as a performer or act in a show) ⟨a master of ceremonies . . . to ~ acts on the bill —*Current Biog.*⟩ **e** (1) **:** to bring (as an actor, singer, or literary character) before the public for the first time (as in a play, a concert, or a novel) ⟨a Hollywood extravaganza *introducing* a young Broadway star⟩ ⟨several excellent mysteries *introducing* a French detective —A.C.Ward⟩ (2) **:** to bring (as a commercial product) to the attention of the public (as by an advertising campaign) **5 :** to lead into or preface ⟨*introduces* his study with a detailed description and careful evaluation of the publisher materials used in his report —W.H.Voskuil⟩ **:** START, BEGIN ⟨~ a subject by a long preface⟩ **6 a :** to put or insert into ⟨~ a catheter into a vein⟩ ⟨some 1800 eggs were *introduced* into a tiny drop of sea water —W.C.Allee⟩ **b :** to put (an atom or group of atoms) into a molecule **7 :** to bring to a knowledge of **:** bring into intellectual acquaintanceship with (as by contact, instruction, representation) ⟨~ readers to the poet's works⟩ — **in·tro·duc·er** \-sə(r)\ *n* -S

in·tro·duce·ment \,≈≈'≈mənt\ *n* -S *archaic* **:** INTRODUCTION

in·tro·duc·ible \¦≈≈¦d(y)üsəbəl\ *adj* **:** capable of being introduced **:** fit to be introduced

introduct *vt* -ED/-ING/-S [L *introductus*, past part. of *introducere* to introduce] *obs* **:** INTRODUCE

in·tro·duc·tion \,in·trə'dəkshən, -rō'd-, *in rapid speech* ,in(t)ə(r)'d-\ *n* -S [ME *introduccion* action of introducing, fr. MF *introduction*, fr. L *introduction-*, *introductio*, fr. *introductus* (past part. of *introducere* to introduce) + *-ion-*, *-io* -ion] **1 :** something that introduces: as **a** *obs* (1) **:** a preliminary step **:** PREPARATION (2) **:** initial instruction **:** a first lesson **:** instruction in rudiments **b** (1) **:** a distinguishable part (as of a book or treatise) that provides explanation, information, or comment preparatory or preliminary to the main portion or subject — compare PREFACE, PROEM (2) **:** a formal or elaborate preliminary treatise esp. introductory to other treatises or to a course or field of study ⟨an ~ to metaphysics⟩ ⟨an ~ to European drama⟩ (3) **:** a course or a subject matter preparatory to a particular study; *specif, cap* **:** a branch of the study of the Bible that applies the contributions of literary and historical criticism to textual problems (as of date, authorship, place of origin, structure, sources, and purpose) of the books of Scripture **c :** a form esp. polite and conventional used in the introduction of one person to another **d :** a series of chords or a short movement or passage preparing the listener for the main body of a musical composition **e :** an initial anticipatory, explanatory, or promotional statement or set of remarks (as in introducing a speaker, an entertainment, or a commercial product) **2 :** the act or process of introducing or the state of being introduced: as **a :** a leading, bringing, conducting, or ushering in or the state of being led, brought, conducted, or ushered in esp. for the first time ⟨responsible for the ~ of aliens into the country⟩ ⟨anticipated his ~ into the dining room⟩ **b :** a causing to take part or be involved ⟨the ~ of crooked politicians into city government⟩ **c :** INSTITUTION ⟨the ~ of new manufacturing processes⟩ ⟨the ~ of a newspaper to cover local events⟩ ⟨the ~ of new rules governing behavior⟩ **d :** a making known or acquainted or a being made known or acquainted ⟨the ~ of the two men to each other⟩ **e :** a formal presentation ⟨the ~ of a young girl to society⟩ ⟨the ~ of a bill into Congress⟩ **f :** a preliminary, preparatory, or initial explaining, talking up, or advertising ⟨an ~ to the subject matter in a preface to a book⟩ ⟨the ~ of an act by a master of ceremonies⟩ ⟨the ~ of a new product on a TV commercial⟩ **g :** a putting in **:** INSERTION ⟨the ~ of new matter into the recipe⟩ ⟨the ~ of a catheter into a vein⟩ ⟨the ~ into the stomach and esophagus of material which is opaque in appearance under the X ray —Morris Fishbein⟩ **h :** a bringing into play or adding or contributing in the course of an action or sequence or the state of being brought, added, or contributed in this way ⟨the ~ of a spirit of bitterness into the discussion⟩ ⟨the ~ of rude remarks into his report⟩ **3 :** something introduced ⟨resented all new ~s into his old methods of doing things⟩; *specif* **:** an exotic plant (as a new variety of horticultural derivation) or an animal brought into a region where it is not native

in·tro·duc·tive \¦==¦dəktiv, -tēv *also* -təv\ *adj* [fr. *introduction*, after such pairs as E *induction: inductive*] **:** INTRODUCTORY

in·tro·duc·tor \-tə(r)\ *n* -s [LL, fr. L *introductus* (past part. of *introducere* to introduce) + *-or*] *archaic* **:** INTRODUCER

in·tro·duc·to·ri·ly \-kt(ə)rəlē, -li\ *adv* **:** in an introductory manner

in·tro·duc·to·ri·ness \,==ˈ=t(ə)rēnəs, -rin-\ *n* -ES **:** the quality or state of being introductory

in·tro·duc·to·ry \¦=¦=t(ə)rē, -ri\ *adj* [LL *introductorius*, fr. L *introductus* (past part. of *introducere* to introduce) + *-orius* -ory] **:** being or belonging to an introduction or serving to introduce **:** PRELIMINARY, PREFATORY ⟨an ~ section of a book⟩ ⟨an ~ course in mathematics⟩ ⟨remarks ~ to a main speaker⟩

in·tro·flex \¦in·trə¦fleks, -rō¦-\ *vb* -ED/-ING/-ES [*intro-* + *flex*] **:** to flex inward

in·tro·flex·ion *also* **in·tro·flec·tion** \¦==¦flekshən\ *n* [fr. *introflex*, after E *flex: flection*] **:** inward flexion **:** an act or instance of introflexing

in·tro·fy \ˈ==,fī\ *vt* -ED/-ING/-ES [modif. (influenced by E *-fy*) of L *introferre* to carry in, fr. *intro-* + *ferre* to carry — more at BEAR] **:** to increase the impregnating power of (as sulfur for wood pulp)

in·tro·gres·sion \,==ˈgreshən\ *n* -s [*intro-* + *-gression* (as in *digression*)] **:** the entry or introduction of a gene from one gene complex into another (as in introgressive hybridization)

in·tro·gres·sive \¦==¦gresiv\ *adj* [fr. *introgression*, after such pairs as E *digression: digressive*] **:** of, belonging to, or marked by introgression

introgressive hybridization *n* **:** the spread of genes of one species into the gene complex of another as a result of hybridization between numerically dissimilar populations in which extensive backcrossing prevents formation of a single stable population

in·troit \ˈin,trōət, ˈin,trȯit, ənˈtrōət, ənˈtrȯit *sometimes* ˈin·trəwət\ *n* -s [MF *introite*, fr. ML *introitus*, fr. L, entrance, fr. *introitus*, past part. of *introire* to go into, enter, fr. *intro-* + *ire* to go — more at ISSUE] **1** *often cap* **:** the first part of the proper of the mass in the Roman rite consisting orig. of the processional psalm but now usu. consisting of an antiphon and verse from one of the psalms followed by the Gloria Patri **2 :** a psalm, anthem, or hymn sung or played at the beginning of the communion service esp. in Anglican churches **3 :** a choral response sung at the beginning of a worship service

in·troi·tal \(ˈ)in¦trōəd·ᵊl, ənˈt-, -rȯid- -\ *adj* [*introitus* + *-al*] **:** of or relating to an introitus

in·troi·tus \ənˈtrōəd·əs, -rȯid- -\ *n, pl* **introitus** [NL, fr. L, entrance] **:** the orifice of a body cavity; *esp* **:** the vaginal opening

in·tro·ject \¦in·trə¦jekt, -rō¦-\ *vb* -ED/-ING/-S [back-formation fr. *introjection*] *vt* **1 :** to incorporate or assimilate into oneself subconsciously or unconsciously (attitudes or ideas of others esp. parental figures, or in infantile fancy actual parts or all of another's body) — opposed to *project;* compare INTERNALIZE **2 :** to turn toward oneself (the love felt for another) or against oneself (the hostility felt toward another) ~ *vi* **:** to enter into a situation and play the role either in actuality or in fantasy that the situation suggests or demands

in·tro·jec·tion \,==ˈjekshən\ *n* -s [*intro-* + *-jection* (as in *projection*)] **1 :** a throwing in; *esp* **:** a throwing of oneself into some pursuit or action **2** [ISV *intro-* + *-jection* (as in *projection*); orig. formed as G *introjektion*] **:** a theory that sense perceptions are mental counterparts of the objects perceived **3** [ISV *intro-* + *-jection* (as in *projection*); orig. formed as G *introjektion*] **:** the act or process of introjecting attitudes, ideas, or body parts — opposed to *projection*

in·tro·jec·tive \¦==¦jektiv\ *adj* **:** of, belonging to, marked by, or given to introjection

in·tro·mis·si·ble \¦==¦misəbəl\ *adj* [fr. *intromission*, after such pairs as E *admission: admissible*] **:** capable of intromission

in·tro·mis·sion \,==ˈmishən\ *n* -s [ML *intromission-, intromissio*, fr. *intromissus* (past part. of ML — with reflexive pronoun object — *intromittere*) + L *-ion-, -io* -ion — more at SMITE] **1** *Scots law* **:** an intermeddling with the affairs or effects of another — see LEGAL INTROMISSION, VICIOUS INTROMISSION **2** [F, fr. MF, fr. L *intromissus* (past part. of *intromittere* to send in, let in) + MF *-ion*] **a :** the act of sending, letting, or putting in or the state of being sent, let, or put in **:** INSERTION, ADMISSION; *specif* **:** the introduction of the penis into or its maintenance within the vagina during coitus **b :** the time during which intromission is sustained during coitus

in·tro·mis·sive \¦==¦misiv\ *adj* [fr. *intromission*, after such pairs as E *permission: permissive*] **:** of or belonging to intromission

in·tro·mit \¦==¦mit\ *vb* **intromitted; intromitted; intromitting; intromits** [ME *intromitten*, fr. ML (with reflexive pronoun object) *intromittere* to concern (oneself), meddle, fr. L *intromittere* to send in, let in, fr. *intro-* + *mittere* to send — more at SMITE] *vi*, *Scots law* **:** to interfere or intermeddle esp. with the effects or goods of another — compare INTROMISSION 1 ~ *vt* [L *intromittere* to send in, let in] **:** to send or put in **:** INSERT, INTRODUCE; *also* **:** to allow to pass **:** ADMIT — **in·tro·mit·ter** \-mid·ə(r)\ *n* -s

in·tro·mit·tent \-mitᵊnt\ *adj* [L *intromittent-, intromittens*, pres. part. of *intromittere* to send in, let in] **:** adapted for or functioning in intromission — used of the copulatory organ of an animal

in·tro·punitive \¦in·trō+\ *adj* [*intro-* + *punitive*] **:** tending to blame or to inflict punishment on the self — opposed to *extrapunitive*

in·trorse \ˈin·,trȯrs, ənˈtrō(ə)rs\ *adj* [prob. fr. (assumed) NL *introrsus*, fr. L *introrsus*, adv., inward, contr. of *introversus*, fr. *intro-* + *versus* toward, fr. *versus*, past part. of *vertere* to turn — more at WORTH] **:** facing inward or toward the axis of growth ⟨an ~ anther⟩ **:** having its line of dehiscence toward the gynoecium — compare EXTRORSE — **in·trorse·ly** *adv*

intros *pl of* INTRO

in·tro·spect \¦in·trə¦spekt, -rō¦-\ *vb* -ED/-ING/-S [L *introspectus*, past part. of *introspicere* to look into, fr. *intro-* + *-spicere* (fr. *specere* to look) — more at SPY] *vt* **:** to look within (as one's own mind or psyche) **:** examine (as oneself) with introspection ~ *vi* **:** to engage in or practice introspection — **in·tro·spec·tor** \-ktə(r)\ *n* -s

in·tro·spect·able *or* **in·tro·spect·ible** \-ktəbəl\ *adj* **:** capable of being observed by introspection

in·tro·spec·tion \-kshən\ *n* -s [L *introspectus* + E *-ion*] **:** the examination of one's own thought and feeling **:** a looking into oneself **:** SELF-EXAMINATION; *also* **:** such examination including one's sensory and perceptual experience esp. undertaken under controlled conditions of experiment — opposed to *extrospection* — **in·tro·spec·tion·al** \-shənᵊl, -shnəl\ *adj*

in·tro·spec·tion·ism \-shə,nizəm\ *n* -s **:** a doctrine that psychology must be based essentially on data derived from introspection — compare BEHAVIORISM

¹in·tro·spec·tion·ist \-sh(ə)nəst\ *n* -s **1 :** one esp. given to introspection **2 :** an adherent of introspectionism

²introspectionist \"\ *or* **in·tro·spec·tion·is·tic** \¦==,=shə¦nistik\ *adj* **:** of or relating to introspectionism ⟨a special ~ technique was devised —Ethel Albert⟩

in·tro·spec·tive \¦==¦spektiv,-tēv *also* -təv\ *adj* [*introspect* + *-ive*] **:** of or belonging to introspection **:** employing, marked by, or tending to introspection — opposed to *extrospective* — **in·tro·spec·tive·ly** \-təvlē, -li\ *adv* — **in·tro·spec·tive·ness** \-tivnəs, -tēv- *also* -təv-\ *n* -ES

in·tro·susception \,in·trə, ,in·(,)trō+\ *n* [*intro-* + *susception*] **:** INTUSSUSCEPTION

in·trou·va·ble \aⁿ·trüvȧbl(ᵊ), -b(lə)\ *adj* [F, fr. *in-* ¹in- + *trouvable* capable of being found, fr. MF, fr. *trouver* to find (prob. fr. — assumed — VL *tropare* to compose) + *-able* — more at TROUBADOUR] **:** impossible to find ⟨pamphlets, all now almost ~ —*Times Lit. Supp.*⟩ — **in·trou·va·bly** \ən-ˈtrüvəblē\ *adv*

in·tro·ver·si·ble \¦in·trə¦vərsəbəl, -rō¦-\ *adj* [*introversion* + *-ible*] **:** capable of being introverted

in·tro·ver·sion \¦in·trə¦vər|zhən, --trō¦-, -vȧ|, -vəi| *also* |sh-\ *n* -s [*intro-* + *-version* (as in *diversion*)] **1 :** the act of introverting or the state of being introverted ⟨economic ~ —Peter Schmid⟩ ⟨an ~ and not an expansion —D.S.Savage⟩ **2 a :** the act of directing one's attention toward or getting gratification from one's own thoughts and feelings and other intrapsychic experience ⟨neurotic ~ — too much preoccupation with oneself —*Irish Digest*⟩ — opposed to *extroversion* **b :** the state of being wholly or predominantly concerned with and interested in one's own intrapsychic experience **c :** a habitual tendency toward such introversion

in·tro·ver·sive \|siv *also* |ziv\ *adj* [*introversion* + *-ive*] **:** characterized by or given to introversion: **a :** turned in upon itself **:** drawn in or invaginated **b :** tending to turn one's attention to one's own experience **:** notably marked by psychological introversion — opposed to *extroversive;* contrasted with *extratensive* — **in·tro·ver·sive·ly** \|səvlē, |zə-\ *adv*

¹in·tro·vert \ˈ==,vər|t, -vȧ|, -vəi|, ,==ˈ=, *usu* |d·+V\ *vt* -ED/-ING/-S [*intro-* + *-vert* (as in *divert*)] **1 a :** to turn inward or in upon itself: as (1) **:** to bend inward (2) **:** to turn (as the thoughts) introversively **b :** to direct upon oneself ⟨served the purpose of ~*ing* aggressive intentions —Ernst Simmel⟩ **2 :** to draw in or invaginate (one tubular part or organ) within another **3 :** to produce introversion in **:** make an introvert of **:** cause to be introvert

²in·tro·vert \ˈ==,=\ *n* -s **1 :** something that is or can be introverted (as the eyestalks of certain snails or the retractile proboscis of a sipunculid worm) **2 :** one whose personality is characterized by introversion — opposed to *extrovert*

³introvert \"\ *adj* [²*introvert*] **:** of or belonging to psychological introversion **:** characterized by or tending to introversion ⟨~ tendencies⟩ ⟨~ behavior⟩

introverted *adj* [fr. past part. of ¹*introvert*] **1 :** INTROVERSIVE: **a :** turned in upon itself ⟨the ~ Old Kingdom did not carry on extensive intercourse with foreign lands —J.W.Curtis⟩ **b :** marked by introversion ⟨the ~ young man given to odd moods and uncommunicativeness⟩ — opposed to *extroverted* **2** *of a quatrain* **:** having an enclosed rhyme

in·tro·vert·ish \¦==¦ish\ *adj* [²*introvert* + *-ish*] **:** somewhat introverted

in·tro·ver·tive \¦==¦iv\ *adj* [¹*introvert* + *-ive*] **:** INTROVERSIVE

in·trude \ənˈtrüd\ *vb* -ED/-ING/-S [L *intrudere* to force in, fr. *in-* ²in- + *trudere* to thrust, push — more at THREAT] *vi* **1 :** to thrust oneself in **:** come or go in without invitation, permission, or welcome **:** enter by intrusion **:** ENCROACH, TRESPASS ⟨where none might ~ upon his grief —P.B.Kyne⟩ ⟨manifest no wish to ~ on academic prerogatives —*Saturday Rev.*⟩ ⟨abashed at *intruding* on all these busy people —Jule Mannix⟩ **2** *geol* **:** to enter as if by force ~ *vt* **1 :** to thrust or force in, into, on, or upon esp. without permission, welcome, or fitness ⟨~ political theory into his play⟩ ⟨~ these confidences on you —G.B.Shaw⟩ ⟨didn't want to ~ himself upon her uninvited⟩ ⟨improper to ~ the dog into the houses of other people they were calling on —Joseph Conrad⟩ ⟨the right to ~ its judgment upon questions of policy or morals —O.W.Holmes †1935⟩ **2 :** to settle (a minister) in a parish against the will of the people ⟨ecclesiastical adventurers from the Continent were *intruded* by hundreds into lucrative benefices —T.B.Macaulay⟩ **3** *geol* **:** to cause to enter as if by force

in·trud·er \-də(r)\ *n* -s **:** one that intrudes ⟨the swarming ~s upon the peace of that hill looked like sheep —Kenneth Roberts⟩; *specif* **:** a military aircraft assigned to penetrate alone into enemy territory usu. at night

in·trud·ing·ly *adv* [*intruding* (pres. part. of *intrude*) + *-ly*] **:** in the manner of one that intrudes

in·tru·sion \ənˈtrüzhən\ *n* -s [ME *intrusioun* invasion, usurpation, fr. MF *intrusion* act of intruding, fr. ML *intrusion-, intrusio*, fr. L *intrusus* (past part. of *intrudere* to intrude) + *-ion-, -io* -ion] **:** the act of intruding or the state of being intruded: as **a** (1) **:** the entry of a stranger after a particular estate of freehold is determined before the person who holds it in remainder or reversion has taken possession (2) **:** the act of wrongfully entering upon, seizing, or taking possession of the property of another (as in trespassing upon crown lands or in the usurpation of an office) **b :** a trespassing or encroachment **:** an undesirable or unwelcome bringing in or entering ⟨the fire replenished, and the house shut against ~ —Mary Austin⟩ ⟨that other shattering of illusion which comes by way of the ~ of fact —J.L.Lowes⟩ ⟨resented the man's ~ upon his privacy⟩ **c :** a settlement of a minister in a parish against the wishes of the parishioners **d** (1) **:** the forcible entry of molten rock or magma into or between other rock formations; *also* **:** the body of igneous rock resulting from solidification of the intruded magma (2) **:** the plastic injection of masses of salt into overlying rocks; *also* **:** the intruded salt

¹in·tru·sive \(ˈ)in¦trüs|iv, ənˈt-,ü̇z|, |ēv *also* |əv\ *adj* [*intrusion* + *-ive*] **1 a :** characterized by intrusion or encroachment ⟨an ~ remark⟩ ⟨far too sensitive to be ~ —Mollie Panter-Downes⟩ ⟨an ~ culture⟩ **b :** showing a tendency to intrusion **:** given to habitual intrusion **:** thrusting one's way into a place, group, or activity where one is not welcome or invited ⟨a loud and ~ individual⟩ **2 a :** thrusting or projecting inward ⟨an ~ arm of the sea⟩ **b :** thrust or forced in: as (1) *of a rock* **:** having been forced while in a plastic or liquid state into cavities or cracks or between layers of other rock — contrasted with *extrusive;* compare ¹BOSS 2, ¹DIKE 3c, SILL (2) **:** PLUTONIC **3** *of an organism* **:** having a range that extends into an area in which it or the group it represents would not be expected to be found **4** *of an archaeological object* **:** lying in a stratum that is not the place of original deposit **5** *of a sound or letter* **:** having nothing that corresponds to it in orthography or etymon ⟨~ \t\ in \ˈmints\ for *mince*⟩ ⟨~ *d* in *thunder*⟩ ⟨~ \r\ in the pronunciation \,indēəˈriŋk\ for *India ink*⟩ **syn** see IMPERTINENT

²intrusive \"\ *n* -s **:** something that is intrusive; *specif* **:** intrusive rock or an intrusive rock

intrusive growth *n* **:** differential growth of the wall of a cell resulting in projection of newly formed parts between adjacent cells or into intercellular spaces — compare GLIDING GROWTH, SYMPLASTIC GROWTH

in·tru·sive·ly \|əvlē, -li\ *adv* **:** in an intrusive manner

in·tru·sive·ness \|ivnəs, |ēv- *also* |əv-\ *n* -ES **:** the quality or state of being intrusive ⟨have lost much of my taste for the special ~ of modern journalism, and it is no longer my opinion that it is necessary for the public to know the whole truth about anybody who has had the misfortune to acquire a little celebrity —Wolcott Gibbs⟩

intrust *var of* ENTRUST

in·tu·bate \ˈin·,t(y)ü,bāt, ənˈt-\ *vt* -ED/-ING/-S [²*in-* + *tube* + *-ate*] **:** to treat by intubation **:** perform intubation on

in·tu·ba·tion \,=,=ˈbāshən\ *n* -s [²*in-* + *tube* + *-ation*] **:** the introduction of a tube into a hollow organ (as the trachea or intestine) to keep the latter open or to restore its patency if obstructed

in·tue \ənˈt(y)ü\ *vt* [L *intueri*] *archaic* **:** INTUIT

in·tu·ent \(ˈ)in¦t(y)üənt, ənˈt(y)ü-, ˈintəwənt, ˈin·tyəw-\ *adj* [L *intuent-, intuens*, pres. part. of *intueri*] *archaic* **:** knowing by intuition

in·tu·it \(ˈ)in¦t(y)üət, ənˈt(y)ü-, ˈintəwət, ˈin·tyəw-\ *vb* -ED/-ING/-S [L *intuitus*, past part. of *intueri*] *vt* **:** to know or apprehend directly or by intuition ⟨only through the sensuous can the ideal be ~*ed* —Murray Krieger⟩ ⟨an imaginative artist ~*ing* the motives of men long dead —Howard M. Jones⟩ ~ *vi* **:** to have knowledge directly or by intuition

in·tu·it·able \ənˈt(y)üəd·əbəl\ *adj* **:** knowable through intuition

in·tu·i·tion \,in·(,)t(y)üˈishən, ,intəˈwi-, ,in·tyəˈwi-\ *n* -s [ME *intuycion*, fr. LL *intuition-, intuitio*, fr. L *intuitus* (past part. of *intueri* to look at, contemplate, fr. *in-* ²in- + *tueri* to look at) + *-ion-, -io* -ion — more at TUITION] **1 a** *obs* **:** the act of looking upon, regarding, examining, or inspecting **b** *archaic* **:** the act of contemplating or considering **:** CONTEMPLATION, CONSIDERATION **c** *obs* **:** a view, regard, or consideration of something as an ulterior goal or acquisition **2 a :** the act or process of coming to direct knowledge or certainty without reasoning or inferring **:** immediate cognizance or conviction without rational thought **:** revelation by insight or innate knowledge **:** immediate apprehension or cognition **b :** knowledge, perception, or conviction gained by intuition ⟨trusting . . . to what are called ~s rather than reasoned conclusions —A.C.Benson⟩ **c :** the power or faculty of attaining to direct knowledge or cognition without rational thought and inference **d** *in Bergsonism* **:** a form of knowing that is akin to instinct or a divining empathy and that gives direct insight into reality as it is in itself and absolutely **e :** quick and ready insight ⟨with one of her quick leaps of ~ she had entered into the other's soul —Edith Wharton⟩ **syn** see REASON

in·tu·i·tion·al \¦=(,)=¦(w)ishənᵊl, -shnəl\ *adj* **1 :** of, belonging to, derived from, characterized by, or perceived by intuition **:** INTUITIVE **2 :** of or belonging to intuitionism ⟨an ~ theory⟩ — **in·tu·i·tion·al·ly** \-ᵊl|ē, -əl|, |i\ *adv*

in·tu·i·tion·al·ism \,=(,)=ˈ(w)ishənᵊl,izəm, -shnə,li-\ *n* -s **:** INTUITIONISM

¹in·tu·i·tion·al·ist \-shənᵊləst, -shnəl-\ *n* -s **:** ¹INTUITIONIST

²in·tu·i·tion·al·ist \¦=(,)=¦=-\ *or* **in·tu·i·tion·al·is·tic** \¦==-¦(w)ishənᵊl¦istik, -shnə¦li-\ *adj* **:** ²INTUITIONIST

in·tu·i·tion·ism \,=(,)=ˈ(w)ishə,nizəm\ *n* -s **1 a :** a doctrine that there are self-evident truths intuitively known which form the basis of human knowledge **b :** a doctrine that objects of perception are intuitively known to be real ⟨radical empiricism, naïve realism, and ~ . . . are expressions of an intense longing for reality —Frank Thilly⟩ **2 a :** a doctrine holding that the rightness or wrongness of particular actions or of kinds of actions is immediately intuitable through a special faculty (as the conscience) or that fundamental principles about what is right and wrong can be intuited **b :** a system of ethics that bases its ultimate conceptions on intuitions; *specif* **:** one according to which moral values (as the good) are intuitively apprehended and indefinable or irreducible **3 :** a thesis that mathematics is based upon special intuitions and requires rejection of the law of excluded middle — contrasted with *formalism* and *logicism*

¹in·tu·i·tion·ist \-sh(ə)nəst\ *n* -s **:** an adherent of intuitionism

²in·tu·i·tion·ist \¦=(,)=¦=-\ *or* **in·tu·i·tion·is·tic** \-¦(w)ishə¦nistik\ *adj* **1 :** of, belonging to, or based on intuitionism **2 :** advocated by intuitionists

intuition line *n, usu cap I* **:** LINE OF INTUITION

in·tu·i·tive \ənˈt(y)üəd·iv, -üət|\ *adj* [ML *intuitivus*, fr. L *intuitus* (past part. of *intueri* to look at, contemplate) + *-ivus* -ive] **1 :** knowing or perceiving by intuition **:** capable of knowing by direct insight or cognition ⟨the ~ faculty⟩ ⟨an ~ power⟩ **2 a :** acquired, known, arrived at, or perceived by intuition ⟨an ~ awareness of another's feelings⟩ ⟨an ~ understanding of the parallelogram of forces —S.F. Mason⟩ ⟨an ~ conviction⟩ **:** known immediately or without the use of inference **:** directly apprehended ⟨~ knowledge⟩ ⟨~ truths⟩ — contrasted with *discursive;* compare INNATE **b :** knowable by intuition **c :** made by intuition or private judgment ⟨the ~ estimates of individuals —H.J.Morgenthau⟩ **3 :** possessing or using intuition or gifted with marked insight ⟨an ~ poet⟩ ⟨an ~ mind⟩ ⟨he was not a systematic critic, but was purely ~ —F.A.Swinnerton⟩ **4 :** ²INTUITIONIST — **in·tu·i·tive·ly** \|əvlē, -li\ *adv* — **in·tu·i·tive·ness** \|ivnəs\ *n* -ES

intuitive reason *n* **:** the faculty of apprehending a priori truths or principles — contrasted with *discursive reason;* compare PURE REASON

in·tu·i·tiv·ism \|i,vizəm\ *n* -s **:** INTUITIONISM 2

¹in·tu·i·tiv·ist \-,vəst\ *n* -s **:** ¹INTUITIONIST

²intuitivist \"\ *adj* **:** ²INTUITIONIST

in·tu·mesce \¦in·(,)t(y)ü¦mes\ *vi* -ED/-ING/-S [L *intumescere* to swell, rise, fr. *in-* ²in- + *tumescere* to swell, incho. of *tumēre* to swell — more at THUMB] **:** to enlarge, expand, swell, or bubble up (as from being heated)

in·tu·mes·cence \,==ˈmesᵊn(t)s\ *n* -s [F, fr. L *intumescere* + F *-ence*] **1 a :** an enlarging, swelling, or bubbling up (as under the action of heat) **b :** the state of being swollen **:** marked enlargement **:** INFLATION **2 :** something swollen or enlarged (as a tumor); *specif* **:** an enlargement resembling a knob or pustule and consisting of a group of abnormally enlarged cells appearing on leaves or other plant parts as a result of physiological disturbances

in·tu·mes·cent \¦=(,)=¦məsᵊnt\ *adj* [L *intumescent-, intumescens*, pres. part. of *intumescere*] **1 :** marked by intumescence **:** swelling, enlarging, or bubbling up **2** *of paint* **:** swelling and charring when exposed to flame and forming an insulating fire-retardant barrier between the flame and the coated material

in–turn \ˈ=-,=\ *n* [²*in* + *turn*, after *turn in* v.] **:** a moving curling stone that is rotating clockwise — compare OUT-TURN

inturned \ˈ=-¦=\ *adj* [²*in* + *turned*, past part. of *turn*] **:** turned inward ⟨ladies' hose with an ~ knitted welt —W.E.Shinn⟩ **:** INTROVERTED ⟨were somewhat dour and ~ —Oliver La Farge⟩

in·tus·sus·cept \¦intəsə¦sept\ *vb* -ED/-ING/-S [prob. fr. (assumed) NL *intussusceptus*, past part. of (assumed) NL *intussuscipere*, fr. L *intus* within + *suscipere* to take up — more at ENT-, SUSCEPTIBLE] *vt* **:** to cause to turn inward esp. upon itself or to be received in some other thing or part; *esp* **:** to cause (an intestine) to undergo intussusception ⟨the bowel became ~*ed*⟩ ~ *vi* **:** to undergo intussusception ⟨some 3 ft. of the ileum had ~*ed* through the ileocecal valve into the cecum —*Veterinary Record*⟩

in·tus·sus·cep·tion \,===ˈsepshən\ *n* -s [prob. fr. (assumed) NL *intussusception-, intussusceptio*, prob. fr. (assumed) NL *intussusceptus* + L *-ion-, -io* -ion] **1 :** the reception of one part within another **:** INVAGINATION; *esp* **:** the passing of one portion of the intestine into an adjacent portion producing intestinal obstruction **2 :** the deposition of new particles of formative material among those already embodied in a tissue or structure (as in the growth of living organisms) — usu. distinguished from *accretion* and *apposition*

in·tus·sus·cep·tive \¦===¦septiv\ *adj* **:** of, belonging to, or characterized by intussusception

in·tus·sus·cep·tum \,===ˈseptəm\ *n, pl* **intussuscep·ta** \-tə\ [NL, prob. neut. sing. of (assumed) NL *intussusceptus*] **:** the portion of the intestine that passes into another portion in intussusception

in·tus·sus·cip·i·ens \-səˈsipē,enz, -ēənz\ *n, pl* **intussus·cipien·tes** \-,sipēˈen·(,)tēz\ [NL, prob. fr. pres. part. of (assumed) NL *intussuscipere*] **:** the portion of the intestine that receives the intussusceptum in intussusception

intwine *var of* ENTWINE

intwist *var of* ENTWIST

inuendo *var of* INNUENDO

inug·suk \ˈēnəg,sük\ *adj, usu cap* **:** of or relating to a stage of Eskimo culture in west Greenland (A.D. 1200–1400) resulting from contact between Thule Eskimo and medieval Norse cultures

in·u·la \ˈinyələ\ *n* [NL, fr. L, elecampane, modif. of Gk *helenion* — more at HELENIUM] **1** -s **:** the dried roots and rhizomes of elecampane used as an aromatic stimulant and esp. formerly as a remedy in pulmonary diseases **2** *cap* **:** a genus of Old World perennial herbaceous or rarely shrubby plants (family Compositae) having large yellow radiate heads with anthers caudate at base — see ELECAMPANE **3** -s **:** any plant or root of the genus *Inula*

in·u·lase \ˈinyə,lās, -āz\ *also* **in·u·lin·ase** \-yələ,nās, -āz\ *n* -s [*inulase* ISV *inul-* (fr. *inulin*) + *-ase; inulinase* ISV *inulin* + *-ase*] **:** an enzyme obtained esp. from molds (as *Aspergillus niger*) and capable of converting inulin into levulose but without action on starch

in·u·lin \ˈinyələn\ *n* -s [prob. fr. G *inulin*, fr. NL *Inula* genus of plants (family Compositae) + G *-in*] **:** a tasteless white nondigestible polysaccharide that occurs usu. in place of starch in many composite and other plants esp. in the tubers or roots of Jerusalem artichoke, dahlia, or chicory, that on hydrolysis yields levulose, and that is used as a source of levulose and as a diagnostic agent in a test for kidney function

in·um·brate \ˈinəm,brāt, əˈnə-\ *vt* -ED/-ING/-S [L *inumbratus*, past part. of *inumbrare*, fr. *in-* ²in- + *umbrare* to shade, fr. *umbra* shadow — more at UMBRAGE] **:** to put in shadow **:** SHADE

in·unct \əˈnəŋ(k)t\ *vt* -ED/-ING/-S [L *inunctus*, past part. of *inunguere* — more at ANOINT] **:** ANOINT 1

in·unc·tion \əˈnəŋ(k)shən\ *n* -s [ME, fr. L *inunction-, inunctio*, fr. *inunctus* (past part. of *inunguere*) + *-ion-, -io* -ion] **1 :** an act of applying an oil or ointment : ANOINTING; *specif* : the rubbing of an ointment into the skin for therapeutic purposes **2** : OINTMENT, UNGUENT, INUNCTUM

in·unc·tum \-ŋ(k)təm\ *n* -S [NL, fr. L, neut. of *inunctus*, past part. of *inunguere*] : an ointment for rapid absorption usu. containing lanolin as a base

inund *vt* -ED/-ING/-S [L *inundare*] *obs* : INUNDATE

in·un·da·ble \ə'nəndəbəl, 'i(,)nənd-\ *adj* [*inundate* + *-able*] : exposed to inundation

in·un·dant \-dənt\ *adj* [L *inundant-, inundans*, pres. part. of *inundare*] : FLOODING, INUNDATING

in·un·date \'inən,dāt *sometimes* 'i,nə- *or* ə'nə-; *usu* -ād + V\ *vt* -ED/-ING/-S [L *inundatus*, past part. of *inundare*, fr. *in-* [2]in- + *undare* to rise in waves, fr. *unda* wave — more at WATER] **1 a** : to flood with water : SUBMERGE ⟨rising rivers ~ low-lying farms⟩ ⟨a tidal wave ~*s* the island⟩ **b** : to flood as if with water ⟨red blood *inundated* her face, previously so pale —Thomas Hardy⟩ ⟨I have never felt . . . more *inundated* with frustration —John Mason Brown⟩ **2** : to overwhelm by great numbers or a superfluity of something : SWAMP ⟨was *inundated* by calls, telegrams, and letters —Marya Mannes⟩ ⟨*inundated* the nation with carloads of literature —Estes Kefauver⟩

in·un·da·tion \,i(,)nən'dāshən\ *n* -S [ME *inundacion*, fr. L *inundation-, inundatio*, fr. *inundatus* (past part. of *inundare*) + *-ion-, -io* -ion] **1** : a rising and spreading of water over land not usu. submerged : FLOOD ⟨the threat of ~ by the sea —Lewis Mumford⟩ ⟨his tears were not drops but a little ~ down his cheeks —Glenway Wescott⟩ ⟨fossil shells give evidence of prehistoric ~*s*⟩ **2** : DELUGE, SWARM ⟨an ~ of telegrams⟩ ⟨an ~ of tourists⟩

in·un·da·tor *pronunc at* INUNDATE +ə(r)\ *n* -S : one that inundates

in·un·da·to·ry \ə'nəndə,tōrē, -tȯr-, -ri\ *adj* [*inundate* + *-ory*] : tending to inundate

inu·pik \ə'nüpik\ *n* -S *cap* : an Eskimo-Aleut language of southwestern Alaska

in·urbane \(')in, ən+\ *adj* [L *inurbanus*, fr. *in-* [1]in- + *urbanus* of the city, refined — more at URBAN] : lacking in refinement or courtesy — **in·urbanity** \,in+\ *n*

in·ure \ə'n(y)u̇(ə)r, -u̇ə\ *or* **en·ure** \ə'-, e'-\ *vb* -ED/-ING/-S [*inure* alter. (influenced by [2]*in-*) of *enure*, fr. ME *enuren*, fr. [1]*en-* + *ure*, n., use, custom — more at ACCUSTOM] *vt* **1** : discipline to accept something : HABITUATE ⟨*inured* to the smell of the stable⟩ ⟨a public . . . that is *inured* to certain ways of seeing and thinking —John Dewey⟩ ⟨being stationed at an arctic base ~*s* a man to cold⟩ ~ *vi* : to come into operation : become operative ⟨we are dealing with a relation . . . that might virtually ~ by usage only —W.E.Gladstone⟩ : ACCRUE ⟨the profits ~ to the benefit of hospitals for crippled children —D.A. Reed⟩; *specif* : to become legally effective ⟨when there is such an identity of interest between the taxpayers that a refund to one will ~ to the benefit of the other . . . the unsatisfied liability may be recovered —W.T.Plumb⟩ **syn** see HARDEN

in·ured \-u̇(ə)rd, -u̇əd\ *adj* [fr. past part. of *inure*] : adapted to existing conditions : accustomed to adverse elements : DISCIPLINED, HARDY ⟨our successors . . . may be graver, more ~ and equable men —V.S.Pritchett⟩ ⟨a peasant . . . lean-faced, dark, wind-*inured* —Robert Lynd⟩ — **in·ured·ness** \-u̇rdnəs, -u̇əd-, -u̇rəd-\ *n* -ES

in·ure·ment \-u̇(ə)rmənt, -u̇əm-\ *n* -S : the quality or state of being inured

in·urn \ən+\ *vt* -ED/-ING/-S [[2]*in-* + *urn*, n.] **1** : to enclose in or as if in an urn : ENTOMB ⟨the body was cremated and the ashes ~*ed*⟩ ⟨where . . . storied cenotaphs ~ sweet human hopes —R.W.Emerson⟩ — **in·urn·ment** \-mənt\ *n* -S

inusitate *adj* [L *inusitatus*, fr. *in-* [1]in- + *usitatus* usual, customary, fr. past part. of *usitor* to use often, fr. *usus*, past part. of *uti* to use — more at USE] *obs* : UNFAMILIAR

in·us·tion \ə'nəschən\ *n* -S [LL *inustion-, inustio* branding, fr. L *inustus* (past part. of *inurere* to brand, burn in, fr. *in-* [2]in- + *urere* to burn) + *-ion-, -io* -ion — more at EMBER] *archaic* : CAUTERIZATION

in ute·ro \ə'n(y)üd·ə,rō\ *adv* [L] : in the uterus : before birth ⟨the infection is apparently acquired *in utero* from a mother with a latent disease —*Yr. Bk. of Pediatrics*⟩

in·utile \(')in, ən+\ *adj* [ME, fr. MF, fr. L *inutilis*, fr. *in-* [1]in- + *utilis* useful — more at UTILE] : of no practical value : USELESS, UNUSABLE ⟨being myth it is ~ —Donald Davidson⟩ ⟨the large proportion of ~ tree volume due to decay —*Ecology*⟩ — **in·utility** \,in+\ *n*

in utro·que ju·re \,inyü·,trōkwē'jürē, ,inü·,trō(,)kwā'yü·\ *adv* [NL, lit., in both laws] : in or under both canon and civil law

in·utterable \(')in, ən+\ *adj* [[1]*in-* + *utterable*] *archaic* : UNUTTERABLE

inv *abbr* **1** [L *invenit*] he designed; he devised; he invented **2** invented; invention; inventor **3** inventory **4** investment **5** invitation **6** invoice

in va·cuo \ən'vakyə,wō\ *adv* [NL] **1** : in a vacuum ⟨this residue may be fractionally distilled *in vacuo* —T.P.Hilditch⟩ **2** : without reference to pertinent facts or materials ⟨the theoretical technique has been evolved *in vacuo* —D.L. Bolinger⟩

in·vad·able \ən'vādəbəl\ *adj* : capable of being invaded

in·vade \ən'vād\ *vb* -ED/-ING/-S [ME *invaden*, fr. L *invadere*, fr. *in-* [2]in- + *vadere* to go — more at WADE] *vt* **1 a** : to enter in a hostile manner : overrun with a view to conquest or plunder ⟨soldiers ~ enemy territory⟩ **b** *obs* : to make a personal attack upon : ASSAULT ⟨what madness could provoke a mortal man to ~ a sleeping god —John Dryden⟩ **2** : to encroach, intrude, or trespass upon : INFRINGE ⟨you can obtain legal counsel to determine if any of your rights have been *invaded* —R.O.Case⟩ ⟨when government ~*s* the traditional area of business —A.L.Nickerson⟩ ⟨during his absence his house was *invaded* and plundered —E.D.Dickinson⟩ ⟨resented these queries as *invading* the family privacy —John Dollard⟩ **3** : to penetrate in the manner of an invader: **a** (1) : to grow over or spread into : PERMEATE ⟨the growing city has *invaded* the surrounding countryside —P.E.James⟩ ⟨the imagery of movement . . . *invaded* secular as well as religious literature —R.W.Southern⟩ ⟨doubts ~ his mind⟩ ⟨an odor of onions ~*s* the room⟩ (2) : to affect injuriously and progressively ⟨gangrene ~*s* healthy tissue⟩ ⟨cholera ~*s* the city⟩ (3) : to push into : enter intrusively ⟨the bow-roofed . . . South Ferry Terminal, its upper deck *invaded* by the el structure —*Amer. Guide Series: N.Y.City*⟩; *specif* : to enter in a molten state ⟨compression . . . forces the granitic part of the crust downward to form a solid root and upward to ~ the thick sediments of the mountain-forming belt as molten rock —W.H.Bucher⟩ **b** : to enter or take possession of : PENETRATE, ENGULF ⟨at midmorning, the sun finally ~*s* the very bottom of the gorge —Lester Womack⟩ ⟨two thousand skiers . . . ~ this alpine region —R.S.Monahan⟩ ⟨layfolk . . . *invaded* ecclesiastical offices and revenues —G.G.Coulton⟩; *specif* : to penetrate steadily by taking up residence in (an area occupied by a population of a different class or ethnic composition) **c** : to raid or take by storm ⟨possums ~ the corn patch⟩ ⟨a young and ambitious small-town girl . . . came to New York to ~ the public-relations field —*Publishers' Weekly*⟩ ~ *vi* : to make an invasion **syn** see TRESPASS

in·vad·er \-də(r)\ *n* -S : one that invades

invading *adj* : of, relating to, or being an invader ⟨~ army⟩ ⟨~ tourists⟩ ⟨~ culture⟩ ⟨~ virus⟩

in·vag·i·nate \ən'vajə,nāt, *usu* -ād·+V\ *vb* -ED/-ING/-S [ML *invaginatus*, past part. of *invaginare*, fr. L *in-* [2]in- + *vagina* sheath — more at VAGINA] *vt* **1** : ENCLOSE, SHEATHE ⟨external . . . sex organs of the male, contrasted to the *invaginated* organs of the female —*Yr. Bk. of Neurology, Psychiatry & Neurosurgery*⟩ **2** : to fold in so that an outer becomes an inner surface : INTUSSUSCEPT ⟨~ the sac into the lumen —E.A. Graham⟩ ~ *vi* : to become sheathed or infolded ⟨the sphere of cells then *invaginated* to give a cuplike double-walled gastrula —S.F.Mason⟩

in·vag·i·na·tion \(,)in,vajə'nāshən, ən,v-\ *n* -S **1** : an act or process of invaginating: as **a** : the formation of a gastrula by an infolding of part of the wall of the blastula **b** : intestinal intussusception **2** : an invaginated part

[1]**in·val·id** \(')in'valəd, ən'v-\ *adj* [L *invalidus* not strong, infirm, weak, inadequate, fr. *in-* [1]in- + *validus* strong — more at VALID] **1 a** : being without foundation in fact or truth : INDEFENSIBLE, UNJUSTIFIED ⟨this argument . . . is ~ on two counts —*Monsanto Mag.*⟩ ⟨now that rockets can escape gravity it is ~ to say that what goes up must come down⟩ **b** : lacking in effectiveness : INADEQUATE, WEAK ⟨acceptance of the new method was a tacit admission that the old technique was ~ and inferior⟩ **2** [ML *invalidus*, fr. L] : being without legal force or effect ⟨declared the wills technically ~ because of some legal flaw —Robert Graves⟩

[2]**invalid** \"\ *vt* -ED/-ING/-S *archaic* : INVALIDATE

[3]**in·va·lid** \'invələd, *Brit* ¦invə¦lēd\ *adj* [L & F; F *invalide*, fr. L *invalidus*] **1 a** : suffering from disease or disability : SICKLY, DISABLED ⟨hired a nurse to care for his ~ mother⟩ **b** : of, relating, or suited to one that is sick ⟨~ chair⟩ ⟨the whole family lived on ~ fare, on custards and broths and arrowroot pudding —Jean Stafford⟩ **2** : being in poor condition : WEAKENED, UNSOUND ⟨reminding me that, if my chimney was allowed to stand in that ~ condition, my policy of insurance would be void —Herman Melville⟩

[4]**in·va·lid** \'invələd; *Brit* 'invə,lēd *also* ,invə'lēd\ *n* -S : one that is sickly or disabled ⟨arranged a bed table for the ~ —Eden Phillpotts⟩ ⟨an exaggeration to assume that France is a chronic economic ~ —Paul Johnson⟩; *specif, archaic* : one member of the armed forces who has become unfit for active duty by illness or injury ⟨his garrison at present consists of a few hundreds of ~*s* —Tobias Smollett⟩

[5]**in·va·lid** \'invələd, *esp before a syllable-increasing suffix* -,lid; *Brit* ¦invə¦lēd\ *vb* -ED/-ING/-S *vt* **1** : to make sickly or disabled ⟨because of a bone ailment, has been ~*ed* since childhood —*Sat. Eve. Post*⟩ **2** : to classify as sick or disabled and remove from active duty ⟨of the 185 firemen . . . sixty were ~*ed* home because of smoke poisoning, burns, or exhaustion —Joseph Millard⟩; *specif* : to release from military service because of illness or injury ⟨~*ed* out of the Norfolk Yeomanry with rheumatic fever —*Saturday Rev.*⟩ ⟨received three bullets through the body, and was due to be ~*ed* home —Joyce Cary⟩ ~ *vi, archaic* **1** : to become an invalid ⟨cannot conceal from myself that I am ~*ing* —R.W.Sibthorp⟩ **2** : to become released from active duty because of disability ⟨the conscripts . . . ~ at an inexplicable rate —*Spectator*⟩

in·val·i·date \ən'valə,dāt, *usu* -ād·+V\ *vt* [[1]*invalid* + *-ate*] : to weaken or make valueless : DISCREDIT ⟨how far the facts confirm or ~ this proud claim —Aldous Huxley⟩ ⟨deviation from a rule which does not affect any important rights of the alien should not ~ a deportation hearing —*Harvard Law Rev.*⟩ **syn** see NULLIFY

in·val·i·da·tion \(,)in,valə'dāshən, ən,v-\ *n* : the act or process of invalidating or the state of being invalidated

in·va·lid·ish \'invələdish, -,lid-, *Brit* ¦invə¦lēd-\ *adj* : resembling or characteristic of an invalid

in·va·lid·ism \'invələ,dizəm, *Brit* ¦invə¦lē,d-\ *n* -S : the quality or state of being an invalid : a usu. chronic condition of disability

in·va·lid·i·ty \,invə'lidəd·ē, ,inva'-, -idətē, -i\ *n* [MF or ML; MF *invalidité*, fr. ML *invaliditat-, invaliditas*, fr. *invalidus* void, without legal force + L *-itat-, -itas* -ity] **1** : lack of sound foundation or binding legal force **2** [[3]*invalid* + *-ity*] **a** : incapacity to work because of prolonged illness or disability ⟨insurance for sickness and ~ and for the provision of medical service for the working class —R.V.Sires⟩ **b** : INVALIDISM

in·val·id·ly \(')in¦valədlē, ən'v-, -li\ *adv* : in an invalid manner : ILLEGALLY

in·val·id·ness *n* : the quality or state of being invalid

in·valuable \ən+\ *adj* [[1]*in-* + *value*, v. + *-able*] **1** : of an excellence or worth beyond measure : of incalculable value : PRICELESS ⟨fellow townsmen gave him a standing ovation for his ~ services to the community⟩ ⟨a flair for languages is ~ to the career diplomat⟩ ⟨his firsthand knowledge of the area was ~ to the search party⟩ **2** *archaic* : of no value : WORTHLESS ⟨flattered myself I might not be altogether ~ to your ladyship —George Colman †1836⟩ **syn** see COSTLY

in·valuableness \"+\ *n* : the quality or state of being invaluable

in·valuably \"+\ *adv* : to an invaluable degree : IMMEASURABLY

in·valued \"+\ *adj* [[1]*in-* + *valued* (past part. of *value*, v.)] *archaic* : INVALUABLE ⟨no vulgar price the ~ treasure brought —John Hoole⟩

in·var \'in,vär\ *n* -S [fr. *Invar*, a trademark] : an iron-nickel alloy containing about 36 percent nickel and having a coefficient of linear expansion of approximately 0.000001 inch per inch per degree centigrade at ordinary temperatures

in·variability \(')in, ən+\ *n* : the quality or state of being invariable

[1]**in·variable** \(')in, ən+\ *adj* [prob. fr. F, fr. MF, fr. *in-* [1]in- + *variable*] : CONSISTENT, UNIFORM : showing no deviation : UNCHANGING, UNFAILING ⟨where many words . . . are relatively ~ in meaning from one sentence to another —I.A. Richards⟩ ⟨after dinner . . . retired to the library, according to his ~ habit —Valentine Williams⟩ ⟨was respected for his ~ courtesy and undoubted integrity —H.W.H.Knott⟩ — **in·variableness** \"+\ *n*

[2]**invariable** \"\ *n* : one that remains constant

in·variably \(')in, ən+\ *adv* : without exception or change : ALWAYS, CONSISTENTLY ⟨those most loved . . . are ~ those who have the capacity for believing in others —W.J.Reilly⟩ ⟨the scene . . . was ~ the room in which I lay —Charles Lamb⟩ ⟨a desire to conduct my life ~ —Arnold Bennett⟩

in·variance \"+\ *n* [[1]*invariant* + *-ance*] : invariability under prescribed or implied conditions

[1]**in·variant** \"+\ *n* [[1]*in-* + *variant*] : a constant factor : one that does not change; *specif* : a mathematical expression or magnitude that remains unchanged under prescribed or implied conditions

[2]**invariant** \"\ *adj* [[1]*in-* + *variant*] **1** : CONSTANT, UNCHANGING, UNVARYING, UNIVERSAL ⟨16 subjects were presented, on 4 successive days, with 300 ~ stimuli —*Biol. Abstracts*⟩ ⟨basic human emotions . . . are ~ —H.B.Parkes⟩; *specif* : unaffected by the group of mathematical operations under consideration **2** : having no degree of freedom — used of a physical-chemical system; compare PHASE RULE

invaried *adj* [[1]*in-* + *varied*] *obs* : UNVARIED

in·va·sion \ən'vāzhən\ *n* -S [ME (Sc) *invasioune*, fr. MF *invasion*, fr. LL *invasion-, invasio*, fr. L *invasus* (past part. of *invadere* to invade) + *-ion-, -io* -ion — more at INVADE] **1 a** : a hostile entrance or armed attack on the property or territory of another for conquest or plunder ⟨the ~ of So. Korea resulted in the first police action by United Nations forces⟩ **b** *obs* : an attack on a person : ASSAULT **2** : an inroad of any kind: as **a** : an entry into or establishment in an area not previously occupied ⟨~ of agricultural Lowland Britain by . . . industries from the Highland Margin —L.D. Stamp⟩ ⟨an ~ of catbrier⟩ ⟨~ of sediments by granite —W.H. Bucher⟩ **b** : the introduction or spread of something hurtful or pernicious ⟨~ of locusts⟩; *specif* : the period through which a pathogen multiplies in and is distributed through the body of a host prior to the development of clinically evident disease ⟨vaccine helps to defeat a virus ~ by promoting the production of antibodies in the bloodstream⟩ **c** : a penetration or occupation by an outside force or agency ⟨tourists . . . making their annual ~ of France —James Pope-Hennessy⟩ ⟨insidious ~*s* of experience into the heart —Mark Schorer⟩ ⟨knew I would not disapprove of this ~ of my place by my young cousin —R.H.Davis⟩; *specif* : the penetration and gradual occupation of an area by a population group of different socioeconomic status or racial or cultural origin than its original inhabitants — compare SUCCESSION **d** : VISIT, TOUR ⟨guest ~*s* by famed choreographers —*Time*⟩ ⟨the enterprising candidate made a two-day ~ of nearby tank towns⟩ **3** : ENCROACHMENT, INTRUSION; *specif* : an encroachment upon a right protected by law affording grounds for an action for damages or some other remedy

in·va·sion·ary \-zhə,nerē, -ri\ *adj* : INVASIVE

invasion currency *or* **invasion money** *n* : paper money issued for use by military forces in an invasion

in·va·sive \ən'vāsiv, -āziv\ *adj* [ME (Sc), fr. MF *invasif*, fr. ML *invasivus*, fr. L *invasus* (past part. of *invadere*) + *-ivus* -ive] **1** *obs* : of, relating to, or characterized by military aggression ⟨shall we . . . make compromise, insinuation, parley, and base truce to arms ~ —Shak.⟩ **2** : tending to spread ⟨for years we have been trying to get rid of ~ bulbs —E.H.M.Cox⟩; *specif* : tending to invade healthy tissue ⟨~ cancer cells⟩ — compare PREINVASIVE **3** *archaic* : tending to encroach on or infringe ⟨~ of tribal rights —H.J.S.Maine⟩

in·va·sive·ness *n* -ES : the quality or state of being invasive; *specif* : the tendency of a pathogenic organism to penetrate into and grow within the host away from the original site of inoculation ⟨~ is a major factor in virulence⟩

in·vecked \(')in¦vekt, ən'v-\ *adj* [modif. (influenced by E [1]*-ed*) of L *invectus*, past part. of *invehere* to carry in, bring in] : INVECTED

in·vec·ta et il·la·ta \ən'vektə,ed·ə'läd·ə\ *n pl* [LL, lit., things brought in and things carried in] *Roman & civil & Scots law* : goods of a tenant brought upon the leased premises or goods of others brought there by their consent and for other than temporary use

in·vect·ed \(')in¦vektəd, ən'v-\ *adj* [L *invectus* (past part. of *invehere* to carry in, bring in) + E [1]*-ed*] *heraldry* : edged by convex semicircles or arcs : SCALLOPED — compare ENGRAILED

in·vec·tion \-kshən\ *n* -S [L *invection-, invectio*, fr. *invectus* (past part. of *invehere* to carry in, bring in) + *-ion-, -io* -ion] : an introduction of something from an outside source ⟨an ~ of . . . battle smoke floated among islands of rose-tinted altocumulus —K.M.Dodson⟩

[1]**in·vec·tive** \ən'vektiv, -tēv *also* -təv\ *adj* [ME *invectiff*, fr. MF *invectif*, fr. LL *invectivus*, fr. L *invectus* (past part. of *invehere*) + *-ivus* -ive] : of, relating to, or characterized by insult or abuse : DENUNCIATORY ⟨a sharp corrective message, suitably ~ —Edith G. Blanchard⟩

[2]**invective** \"\ *n* -S **1** : an abusive expression or diatribe : a vehement verbal attack ⟨replied with ~*s* fierce and scurrilous —J.A.Froude⟩ ⟨thundering ~ against sin —Ernest Beaglehole⟩ **2** : critical or insulting language : violent abuse : VITUPERATION ⟨as his anger mounted, ridicule and ~ poured from his mouth searing and burning all that they touched —D.L.Cohn⟩ **syn** see ABUSE

in·vec·tive·ly \-təvlē, -li\ *adv, obs* : in an invective manner ⟨thus most ~ he pierceth through the body of our country, swearing —Shak.⟩

in·veigh \ən'vā\ *vb* -ED/-ING/-S [L *invehi* to sail into, attack, inveigh, pass. infin. of *invehere* to carry in, bring in, fr. *in-* [2]in- + *vehere* to carry — more at WAY] *vi* : to protest bitterly or violently : complain vehemently : RAIL — used with *against* ⟨~ against injustice⟩ ⟨~*s* against the arbitrary character of all such unscientific procedures —G.M.Messing⟩ ~ *vt* : [L *invehere*] *obs* : INVEIGLE

in·veigh·er \-āə(r)\ *n* -S : one that inveighs

in·vei·gle \ən'vāgəl *also* -'vēg- *or* -'vig-\ *vt* **inveigled**; **inveigled**; **inveigling** \-g(ə)liŋ\ **inveigles** [modif. (influenced by E [2]*in-*) of MF *aveugler* to blind, hoodwink, fr. OF *avogler*, fr. *avogle, avugle* blind, fr. ML *ab oculis*, fr. L *ab* from + *oculis*, abl. pl. of *oculus* eye — more at OF, EYE] **1** *obs* : DELUDE, MISLEAD, HOODWINK, BEGUILE ⟨your rhetorical flourishes . . . contributed in an high degree to ~ the jury, and bring that noble lord to the scaffold —Robert Atkyns⟩ **2** : to snare by ingenuity or flattery : ENTICE, CAJOLE ⟨used the most subtle means to ~ the author into the office —Edward Bok⟩ ⟨with patience and diplomacy, she can eventually ~ him into marrying her —Nellie Maher⟩ **3** : to acquire by ingenuity or flattery ⟨over gin and water we *inveigled* from him a pack of well-worn cards —Ernest Beaglehole⟩ **syn** see LURE

in·vei·gle·ment \-gəlmənt\ *n* -S : an act, process, or means of inveigling : ENTICEMENT, LURE

in·vei·gler \-g(ə)lə(r)\ *n* -S : one that inveigles

inveil *var of* ENVEIL

in·vent \ən'vent\ *vt* -ED/-ING/-S [ME *inventen*, fr. L *inventus*, past part. of *invenire*, fr. *in-* [2]in- + *venire* to come — more at COME] **1** : to search out or come upon : FIND, DISCOVER ⟨must ~ beds for them —Frederick Way⟩ ⟨this polymer was ~*ed* in England and is an outgrowth of earlier research —Leonard Maner & Harry Wechsler⟩ **2** : to think up or imagine : concoct mentally : FABRICATE ⟨his fund of knowledge seemed inexhaustible, for what he didn't know he ~*ed* —Alvin Redman⟩ ⟨preparing in his mind the harshest response he could ~ —W.F.Davis⟩ **3** : to create or produce for the first time : be the author of : DEVISE, ORIGINATE ⟨he ~*ed* and secured a patent . . . for a rock-boring machine —B.A.Soule⟩ ⟨if the Semitic letters were not derived from Egypt they must have been ~*ed* by the Phoenicians —Edward Clodd⟩ ⟨~*ed* an ingenious kind of ball game —Margaret Bean⟩ ⟨has ~*ed* plenty of good tunes of his own —Sigmund Spaeth⟩ **4** *obs* : FOUND, ESTABLISH, INSTITUTE, INITIATE ⟨festival days in old time were ~*ed* for recreation —John Northbrooke⟩ **syn** see CONTRIVE

in·vent·able *or* **in·vent·ible** \-təbəl\ *adj* : capable of being invented

inventary *n* -ES [LL *inventarium* — more at INVENTORY] *obs* : INVENTORY

in·ven·tion \ən'venchən\ *n* -S [ME *invencioun*, fr. MF *invention*, fr. L *invention-, inventio*, fr. *inventus* (past part. of *invenire* to find) + *-ion-, -io* -ion] **1** : an act of finding or of finding out : DISCOVERY ⟨~ of the principle of leverage⟩ **2 a** : the power to conceive new ideas and relationships : productive imagination : INVENTIVENESS ⟨old crates and boxes are often more stimulating to a child's ~ than expensive toys⟩ **b** : a faculty for creative selection of theme and imaginative treatment of design or content ⟨the variety and excellence of the classical legacy demonstrate the abundant ~ of the ancient Greeks⟩ ⟨as a teller of tales he had rich ~ and adroit construction —Brander Matthews⟩ **c** : a product of creative imagination or fertile wit ⟨the ~*s*, the devices which serve a novelist best grow . . . out of his necessity —Caroline Gordon⟩ ⟨a cascade of melodic ~ —Harold Sinclair⟩ ⟨those pillars, that stair and varnished roof . . . were among the worst ~*s* of the Gothic revival —W.B.Yeats⟩ **d** : a musical composition or piece imitative in style, usu. short, and usu. written for the piano or other keyboard instrument **3 a** : an act of mental creation or organization : application of knowledge : CONCEPTION, FORMULATION ⟨~ of agreements or compromises —Weston La Barre⟩ ⟨no continuing agency to interpret the party platform after its slapdash ~ every four years —R.L. Strout⟩ ⟨tried a long play of her own ~ —Leslie Rees⟩ **b** : a product of thought or mental synthesis : IDEA, CONCEPT ⟨the idea that the royal family should be a symbol of respectability was an ~ of Queen Victoria —Fritz Stern⟩ ⟨characterized the Supreme Court as the great political ~ of the framers of the Constitution —Felix Frankfurter⟩ ⟨new social ~*s* are made by those who suffer from the current conditions —Ralph Linton⟩; *specif* : a fictitious idea or statement ⟨race theories are . . . a modern ~ to explain such group conflicts —M.R.Cohen⟩ ⟨the whole purpose of the . . . argument being to invalidate the generally accepted romance and prove it an ~ —E.V.Lucas⟩ **4 a** : the creation of something not previously in existence : purposeful experimentation leading to the development of a new device or process : ORIGINATION ⟨necessity is the mother of ~⟩ ⟨machinery of their own ~ —*Amer. Guide Series: Md.*⟩ **b** : an original device or process ⟨writing was a greater ~ than the steam engine —A.N.Whitehead⟩; *specif, U.S. patent law* : a device or process that is not only novel and useful but that reflects creative genius, makes a distinct contribution to and advances science, is recognized by masters of science as such an advance and reveals more than the skill of expert artisans or mechanics in discovering new and useful gadgets or processes of wide commercial application

inventious *adj* [fr. *invention*, after such pairs as E *contention: contentious*] : INVENTIVE

in·ven·tive \ən'ventiv, -tēv *also* -təv\ *adj* [ME *inventif*, fr. MF, fr. *invention*, after such pairs as MF *action: actif* active] **1** : having the capacity for or being a prolific producer of inventions : CREATIVE, INGENIOUS ⟨an ~ writer⟩ ⟨an ~ composer⟩ ⟨the preposition . . . is a tremendously ~ word —R.M. Weaver⟩ **2** : of, relating to, or characterized by invention ⟨the war gives rise to incidents . . . beyond the ~ power of the human imagination —Maya Deren⟩ ⟨exquisite gold work and ~ ceramics —Angélica Mendoza⟩ ⟨a mechanic of an ~ turn of mind —J.Q.Dealey⟩ — **in·ven·tive·ly** \-tivlē, -li\ *adv*

in·ven·tive·ness \-tivnəs, -tēv- *also* -təv-\ *n* -ES : the quality or state of being inventive : INGENUITY, CREATIVITY

in·ven·tor *also* **in·vent·er** \ən'ventə(r)\ *n* -S [*inventor* fr. L, fr. *inventus* (past part. of *invenire*) + *-or*; *inventer* alter. (influenced by E [2]*-er*) of *inventor*] **1** *obs* : one that finds or finds out **:** DISCOVERER ⟨first ~ of the nervous system —John Freind⟩ **2 :** one that conceives by creative imagination ⟨~ of a new ballet⟩ ⟨one must be an ~ to read well —S.P.Sherman⟩ ⟨the next step is to discover what makes a man an ~ rather than a passive culture carrier —Ralph Linton⟩ **3 :** one that creates a new device or process **:** ORIGINATOR ⟨Eli Whitney was the ~ of the cotton gin⟩

in·ven·to·ri·able \ˈinvən·ˌtōrēəbəl, -tȯr-, ˌ==ˈ====\ *adj* **1 :** capable of being inventoried **2 :** includable in an inventory or in its valuation

in·ven·to·ri·al \ˌ==ˈ=rēəl\ *adj* **:** of or relating to an inventory — **in·ven·to·ri·al·ly** \-rēəlē\ *adv*

inventorize *vt* -ED/-ING/-S [MF *inventoriser*, fr. *inventoire* inventory (fr. ML *inventorium*) + *-iser* -ize] *archaic* **:** INVENTORY

¹in·ven·to·ry \ˈinvən·ˌtōrē, -tȯr-, -ri\ *n* -ES *often attrib* [alter. (influenced by ML *inventorium*) of ME *invitory*, modif. of ML *inventorium*, alter. (influenced by L *-orium* -ory) of LL *inventarium*, fr. L *inventus* (past part. of *invenire* to find) + *-arium* -ary] **1 :** an itemized list of current assets: as **a :** a written list or catalog usu. made by a fiduciary under oath of the tangible or intangible property of an individual, organization, or estate describing the items or classes of property so as to be identifiable and usu. placing a valuation thereon **b** (1) **:** a list or schedule of raw materials, supplies, work in process, and finished goods on hand as of a given date (2) **:** a list of merchandise held for sale (3) **:** the aggregate value assigned to an inventory **c :** a survey of natural resources; *specif* **:** an estimate or enumeration of the wildlife (as game animals) of a region **d :** a questionnaire designed to provide an index of individual interests or personality traits **2 :** a detailed study or recapitulation **:** SURVEY, SUMMARY ⟨offered a brief ~ of the chief inventions of the middle ages —Benjamin Farrington⟩ ⟨the replies . . . provide a nearly complete ~ of the ideas which are afloat among the young people —W.J.Cahnman⟩ ⟨Whitman's verses . . . are often more *inventories* than imaginative projections of America —H.S.Canby⟩ **3 a :** the quantity of goods or materials on hand **:** STOCK, SUPPLY ⟨adequate *inventories* of washing machines to meet local demand⟩ ⟨it took quite an ~ of heavy tools . . . to do all this —George Woodbury⟩ **b :** a surplus of goods or materials accumulated against future needs **:** RESERVE ⟨there has piled up a 2000 million dollar ~ of foodstuffs —John Boyd Orr⟩ ⟨industry would purchase for a year in advance what would amount to an ~ of labor —Leland Hazard⟩ **4 :** the act or process of taking an inventory ⟨the annual ~ takes two weeks⟩ ⟨depends on a careful and continuing ~ of the entire staff —J.B.Conant⟩ **5 :** a comprehensive list of personality traits, personal preferences, attitudes, interests, or abilities used to measure subjective judgments and to evaluate individual characteristics and skills

²inventory \"\ *vb* -ED/-ING/-ES *vt* **1 a :** to make an itemized report or record of **:** take stock of **:** CATALOG ⟨~ home troops⟩ ⟨~ waterfowl⟩ ⟨walked in uninvited and *inventoried* the room with one long glance —John Selby⟩; *specif* **:** to count and list the assets of together with their valuation ⟨~ an estate⟩ **b :** to include in a business inventory **2 :** to make a study or recapitulation of **:** SURVEY, SUMMARIZE ⟨a book of criticism that . . . completely *inventoried* the mind of the age —Rebecca West⟩ ~ *vi* **:** to have a value by inventory ⟨his estate *inventories* at close to half a million⟩

inventory control *n* **:** coordination and supervision of the supply, storage, distribution, and recording of materials to maintain quantities adequate for current needs without excessive oversupply or loss

in·ven·tress \ənˈven·trəs\ *n* -ES [*inventor* + *-ess*] **:** a female inventor

in·ven·trix \-en·triks\ *n* -ES [L, fem. of *inventor* — more at -TRIX] **:** INVENTRESS

in·veracity \ˌin+\ *n* [¹*in-* + *veracity*] **1 :** lack of truth **:** FALSENESS ⟨forced to recognize its inadequacy, its palpable ~ —G.J.Becker⟩ **2 :** an intentional falsehood **:** LIE ⟨the bogus anecdotes of his conversation were not, I am convinced, plain *inveracities*, but things which he had imagined —Christopher Hollis⟩

¹in·ver·ness \ˌinvə(r)ˈnes\ *adj* [fr. *Inverness*, burgh and county in Scotland] **1 :** of or from the burgh of Inverness, Scotland **:** of the kind or style prevalent in Inverness **2 :** INVERNESS-SHIRE

²inverness \"\ *n* -ES **:** a loose belted coat having an often detachable shoulder cape with a close-fitting round collar

inverness-shire \ˌinvə(r)ˈnes(h),shi(ə)r, -iə, -,shə(r)\ *or* **inverness** \ˌinvə(r)ˈnes\ *adj, usu cap I* [fr. *Inverness-shire* or *Inverness*, county in Scotland] **:** of or from the county of Inverness, Scotland **:** of the kind or style prevalent in Inverness

inverness

¹in·verse \(ˈ)in¦vərs, ənˈv-, -vəs,-vəis\ *vt* -ED/-ING/-S [L *inversus*, past part. of *invertere*] **:** INVERT, REVERSE

²in·verse \ˈ=,=, =ˈ=\ *adj* [L *inversus*, past part. of *invertere* to invert — more at INVERT] **1** *archaic* **:** being upside down **:** INVERTED ⟨a tower builded on a lake, mocked by its ~ shadow —Thomas Hood †1845⟩ **2 :** opposite in nature or relationship **:** CONTRARY, REVERSED ⟨as high as 70 percent . . . were engaged in repair and conversion work, a condition ~ to prewar operation —*Collier's Yr. Bk.*⟩ ⟨attendance of the students . . . is in ~ ratio to the work in the cornfields —Joaquin Noval⟩ **3 a :** opposite in nature and effect — used of two mathematical operations which when both are performed in succession upon any quantity reproduce that quantity ⟨division is the ~ operation of multiplication⟩ **b** *of a mathematical function* **:** expressing the same relationship as another function but from the opposite viewpoint

³inverse \"\ *n* -S **1 :** something of a contrary nature or quality **:** OPPOSITE, REVERSE ⟨had no luck with his experiment so he tried the ~ of this process and got a positive result⟩; *specif* **:** the opposite color from that of the first card dealt in the winning row in the game of rouge et noir — compare COULEUR 2 **2 :** the result of an inversion; *specif* **:** a proposition which is inferred immediately from another and in which the subject term is the negative of the subject of the given proposition and the predicate term is unchanged ⟨the ~ of "no purposeful effort is entirely wasted" is "some not-purposeful effort is entirely wasted"⟩ — compare CONTRAPOSITION **3 :** an inverse function, operation, or point

inverse cosecant *n* **:** ARC COSECANT

inverse cosine *n* **:** ARC COSINE

inverse cotangent *n* **:** ARC COTANGENT

inverse feedback *n* **:** NEGATIVE FEEDBACK

inverse function *n* **:** either of two mathematical functions such that each is the inverse of the other

in·verse·ly \(ˈ)=ˈ==\ *adv* **:** in an inverse order or manner **:** by inversion

inversely proportional *adj* **:** having their product constant — used of two variable quantities one of which varies directly as the reciprocal of the other

inverse point *n* **:** either of two points on a diametral line of a fixed circle or sphere the product of whose distances from the center equals the square of the radius

inverse proportion *n* **:** the relation between two inversely proportional quantities

inverse ratio *n* **:** the ratio of the reciprocals of two quantities

inverse secant *n* **:** ARC SECANT

inverse sine *n* **:** ARC SINE

inverse spelling *n* **:** REVERSE SPELLING

inverse-square \ˌ=ˈ=\ *adj* [fr. the phrase *inverse square*] **:** according with or relating to the inverse-square law

inverse-square law *n* **:** a statement in physics: the manner in which a physical quantity (as illumination) varies with the distance from the source is inversely as the square of the distance

inverse tangent *n* **:** ARC TANGENT

inverse taper *n, of an airfoil* **:** increase in the chord with distance outboard from the root

inverse-time \ˌ=,=ˈ=\ *adj* [fr. the phrase *inverse time*] **:** done with a purposely delayed action that decreases as the operating force increases — used esp. of electrical relays

inverse trigonometric function *n* **:** the inverse of any of the six trigonometric functions

inverse voltage *n* **:** the voltage moving through a rectifier during the reverse half of the alternating-current cycle

in·ver·sion \ənˈvərzhən, -vō̇, -vəi| *also* |shən\ *n* -S [L *inversion-, inversio*, fr. *inversus* (past part. of *invertere* to invert) + *-ion-, -io* -ion — more at INVERT] **1 :** an act or result of turning inside out or upside down **:** FLEXURE, DOUBLING: as **a :** a folding back of rock strata upon themselves by which their sequence seems reversed **b :** a dislocation of a bodily organ in which it is turned partially or wholly inside out ⟨~ of the uterus⟩ **c :** a condition of being turned inward ⟨~ of the foot⟩ **d :** RETROFLEXION 3 **2 :** a reversal of position, order, or relationship: as **a :** the reverse of an established pattern ⟨the structure of an insect . . . is an almost complete ~ of what prevails in a vertebrate animal —A.D.Imms⟩ ⟨so strange an ~ of the paternal and filial relations as this proposition of his son to pay him a hundred pounds —George Eliot⟩ **b** (1) **:** INVERTED ORDER (2) **:** ANASTROPHE **c :** a change of cadence by the introduction in a metrical series of a foot in which arsis and thesis have positions symmetrically opposed to the positions they have in the normal esp. adjacent feet of the series **:** shift of cadence from rising to falling or from falling to rising — compare SUBSTITUTION **d** (1) *of an interval* **:** a raising of the lower or dropping of the upper tone by an octave (2) *of a triad or seventh chord* **:** a transposition of the root to some voice other than the bass (3) *of a melody* **:** a repetition of a phrase or subject (as of a fugue) with each ascending interval inverted into a corresponding descending interval and vice versa (4) *in double counterpoint* **:** a transposition of an upper and a lower voice part (5) **:** a transferring of a pedal point from the bass to an upper part **e** *logic* **:** the operation of immediate inference which gives an inverse proposition — see ³INVERSE 2 **f** (1) **:** a breaking off of a chromosome section and its subsequent reattachment in reversed position (2) **:** such a chromosome section **3 a :** a change in the order of the terms of a mathematical proportion effected by inverting each ratio **b :** the operation of inverting or forming the inverse either of a magnitude or of an operation **c :** a change from the order in which elements or parcels of objects are arranged naturally or normally **4 :** HOMOSEXUALITY **5 a :** a conversion of a substance showing dextrorotation into one showing levorotation or vice versa ⟨the ~ of sucrose involves hydrolysis of a dextrorotatory material to an equimolar mixture of D-glucose and D-fructose that is levorotatory⟩ **b :** a substitution of one of the groups attached to the asymmetric atom of an optically active organic molecule so that an original clockwise arrangement of atoms or groups becomes counterclockwise **c :** a change of a crystalline substance from one polymorphic form into another **6 :** a conversion of direct current into alternating current **7 :** a reversal of normal atmospheric temperature gradient **:** increase of temperature of the air with increasing altitude

in·ver·sion·ist \-zh(ə)nəst, -sh-\ *n* -S **:** one who habitually writes upside down and backward

inversion point *n* **1 :** TRANSITION POINT **2 :** a point (as on a temperature scale) at which a physical quantity reaches a maximum or minimum or at which it changes algebraic sign

inversion spectrum *n* **:** a microwave absorption spectrum (as of ammonia vapor) attributed in quantum mechanics to quantized changes in molecular structure from one arrangement to another that is the mirror image of the first

in·ver·sive \(ˈ)in¦vərsiv, ənˈv-, -rziv\ *adj* [*inversion* + *-ive*] **:** marked by inversion ⟨~ error⟩ ⟨~ personality⟩

¹in·vert \ənˈvər|t, -vō̇, -vəi|, *usu* |d·+V\ *vb* -ED/-ING/-S [L *invertere*, fr. *in-* ²in- + *vertere* to turn — more at WORTH] *vt* **1 a :** to turn inside out or upside down ⟨the magician ~*s* the bag to show it is empty⟩ ⟨the gardener ~*s* a bell jar over his rose cutting⟩; *specif* **:** to print (a part of a stamp or an overprint) upside down **b :** to turn inward ⟨when a foot is ~*ed* its forepart tends to approach the midline of the body —*Jour. Amer. Med. Assoc.*⟩ **2 :** to reverse in position, order, or relationship ⟨both poems ~ the original affective situation, turning despair into success —Malcolm Brown⟩ ⟨in singing the second half of "Ten Little Indians" you ~ the numbers⟩ ⟨the generality concerning molecular weight may not be ~*ed*, for it is not true that salts with light molecules are invariably salty tasting —F.A.Geldard⟩; *specif* **:** to subject (a melody) to inversion **3 a :** to subject (as sucrose) to inversion **b :** to change (a crystalline compound) from one polymorphous form to another ~ *vi* **:** to undergo inversion ⟨sucrose ~*s*⟩ ⟨the quartz starts to ~ to cristobalite —F.H.Norton⟩

²in·vert \ˈin,v-\ *n* -S **:** one that is characterized by inversion: as **a :** INVERTED ARCH **b :** the lowest point in the internal cross section of an artificial channel **c :** a stamp having an overprint or some portion of its design inverted **d :** HOMOSEXUAL

³invert \"\ *adj* **:** subjected to chemical inversion **:** INVERTED 3 ⟨~ sugar⟩

invert *abbr* invertebrate

in·vert·ase \ənˈvərd·ˌās, ˈin,v-, -āz\ *n* -S [ISV ¹*invert* + *-ase*; prob. orig. formed in F] **:** an enzyme found in many microorganisms and plants and in animal intestines that is capable of effecting the inversion of sucrose and that is usu. prepared from yeast as a white powder — called also *sucrase*

in·ver·te·bra·cy \ənˈvərd·əbrəsē\ *n* -ES [²*invertebrate* + *-cy*] **:** SPINELESSNESS

in·vertebral \(ˈ)in, ən+\ *adj* [¹*in-* + *vertebral*] **:** INVERTEBRATE

in·vertebrata \(ˌ)in, ən+\ *n pl, cap* [NL, fr. neut. pl. of *invertebratus* invertebrate] *in some esp former classifications* **:** a primary division of the animal kingdom including all except the Vertebrata

¹in·vertebrate \(ˈ)in, ən+\ *n* [NL *Invertebrata*] **1 :** an animal having no backbone or internal skeleton ⟨in the lower ~*s* such as coelenterates —W.H.Dowdeswell⟩ **2 :** one that is weak or indecisive ⟨its new dangers are the innocuous and the ~ —Sacheverell Sitwell⟩

²invertebrate \"\ *adj* [NL *invertebratus*, fr. L *in-* ¹in- + NL *vertebratus* vertebrate] **1 :** lacking a spinal column ⟨~ jellyfish⟩ **2 :** lacking in structure or vitality **:** DISORGANIZED, WEAK ⟨his book is completely ~, breaking sharply in the middle into two books —S.E.Hyman⟩ ⟨moves far beyond the often ~ lyricism . . . into a rhetoric that has intellectual iron —Mark Schorer⟩

inverted *adj* **1 a :** turned upside down or inside out ⟨~ rock strata⟩ ⟨~ lumen of the intestine⟩ ⟨the blood rushed to his head as he zoomed across the field in ~ flight⟩ **b :** inverted in relation to the rest of a stamp — used of parts of a stamp or stamp design ⟨~ center⟩ **c** *heraldry* **:** having the tip pointing down — used of a wing ⟨an eagle, wings expanded and ~⟩ **d :** RETROFLEX **2 :** reversed in position, order, or relationship **:** contrary to an established pattern ⟨~ spellings⟩ ⟨~ seasons of the southern hemisphere⟩ ⟨much ~ snobbery in the idealization of the English working class —Roy Lewis & Angus Maude⟩; *specif* **:** based on or characterized by musical inversion ⟨~ melody⟩ **3 :** transformed by inversion **4 :** HOMOSEXUAL — **in·vert·ed·ly** *adv*

inverted arch *n* **:** an arch with the crown downward that is much used in foundations, sewers, and tunnels and is often made of solid concrete

inverted comma *n* **1 a :** a type comma reversed so as to produce an upside-down comma at the top of the printed line **b :** the comma so printed that is commonly used singly or in pairs to mark the beginning of a quotation **2** *chiefly Brit* **:** QUOTATION MARK

inverted engine *n* **:** an engine whose crankshaft is above the cylinders

inverted interval *n* **:** a simple musical interval having its lower tone raised or its upper tone lowered an octave

inverted mordent *n* **:** PRALLTRILLER

inverted order *n* **:** an arrangement of the elements of a sentence (as subject, predicate) that is the reverse of the usual order and is designed to achieve variety or emphasis (as in "among them were the following" "again she called") or to indicate a question (as in "what does he say") — compare ANASTROPHE

inverted passive *n* **:** a passive construction in which the subject of the passive verb corresponds to the indirect object of the verb in an active construction (as in "he was awarded a medal by the club")

inverted perspective *n* **:** REVERSE PERSPECTIVE

inverted pleat *n* **:** a pleat formed by bringing two folded edges toward or to a center point on the outside of the material to form a box pleat on the inside

inverted pleat

inverted-pyramid indention *n* **:** HALF-DIAMOND INDENTION

inverted siphon *n* **:** a pipe for conducting water beneath a depressed place

inverted talon *n* **:** an ogee molding with the convex part at the top

inverted triad *n* **:** a triad with a tone other than the root in the bass

in·ver·tend \ˌin(,)vərˈtend\ *n* -S [L *invertendus*, gerundive of *invertere* to invert — more at INVERT] **:** a proposition upon which the operation of inversion is performed

in·vert·er \ənˈvər|d·ə(r), -vō̇|, -vəi|, |tə(r)\ *n* -S **1 :** one that inverts **2 :** a device for converting direct current into alternating current by mechanical or electronic means

in·vert·ible \|d·əbəl|, |təbəl\ *adj* **1 :** capable of being inverted or subjected to inversion **2 :** admitting of musical inversion

in·vert·in \ənˈvərtᵊn\ *n* -S [ISV ¹*invert* + *-in*] **:** INVERTASE

inverting *pres part of* INVERT

inverting telescope *n* **:** a telescope in which the image is seen or photographed upside down usu. because it has no optical erecting system

in·ver·tor \ənˈvər|d·ə(r), -vō̇, -vəi|, |tə(r)\ *n* -S [NL (influenced in meaning by L *in* and L *vertere* to turn), irreg. fr. L *invertere* to invert + *-or* — more at ¹IN, WORTH] **:** a muscle that turns a part (as the foot) inward

inverts *pres 3d sing of* INVERT

invert soap *n* **:** CATIONIC DETERGENT

invert sugar *n* **:** a mixture of D-glucose and D-fructose that is sweeter than sucrose, that occurs naturally in fruits and honey, that is usu. made commercially from a solution of cane sugar by hydrolysis (as with acid), and that is used chiefly as a difficultly crystallizable syrup in foods and in medicine

¹in·vest \ənˈvest\ *vt* -ED/-ING/-S [ML *investire*, fr. L, to clothe, cover, surround, fr. *in-* ²in- + *vestire* to clothe, fr. *vestis* garment — more at WEAR] **1 a :** to array in the symbols of office or honor **:** install in an office or honor with customary ceremonies ⟨was ~*ed* by Queen Elizabeth . . . in a private ceremony —*Springfield (Mass.) Union*⟩ ⟨was ~*ed* with the George Medal, Britain's highest award for civilian heroism —*Charlottetown (Canada) Guardian*⟩ **b :** to furnish with or make a formal grant (as of power or authority) to **:** establish officially ⟨by the Constitution of the United States, the president is ~*ed* with certain important political powers —John Marshall⟩ **c :** to put in possession or control of someone **:** VEST ⟨provincial life in Tsarist Russia . . . ~*ed* absolute authority in the head of the family —*London Calling*⟩ **2** [L *investire*] **:** to envelop or cover completely **:** SURROUND, COAT ⟨things are ~*ed* with mystery in the degree that their origins and causes are unknown —Edward Clodd⟩ ⟨could ~ a common murder case with the atmosphere of an Aeschylean drama —Van Wyck Brooks⟩; *specif* **:** to place (a pattern) in refractory material in the process of investment casting ⟨bell-form bowl, ~*ed* with a rich turquoise blue glaze —*Parke-Bernet Galleries Catalog*⟩ — see CIRE PERDUE **3** [L *investire*] **a :** CLOTHE, ADORN ⟨brought a light raincoat with which he now ~*ed* his ample person —John Buchan⟩ ⟨went to the pains of ~*ing* the production richly, for sets and costumes are fabulous —Louise Mace⟩ **b** *obs* **:** to put on **:** DON ⟨cannot find one this girdle to ~ —Edmund Spenser⟩ **4** [MF *investir*, fr. OIt *investire*, fr. L, to surround] **:** to surround with troops or ships so as to prevent escape or entry **:** lay siege to ⟨Charleston was never besieged, nor was any serious effort made . . . to ~ it on the land side —O.L.Spaulding⟩ **5 :** to endow with some quality or characteristic **:** INFUSE, ENRICH ⟨talent for ~*ing* the commonplace with significance —Gerald Bullett⟩ ⟨the realist . . . ~*s* contemporary events with values that are eventually established as history —Bernard Smith⟩ ⟨the tone of his . . . voice which he tried to ~ with candor and modesty —Bernard De Voto⟩ ⟨swept off his hat with a gesture that ~*ed* it with plumes —Edna Ferber⟩

²invest \"\ *vb* -ED/-ING/-S [It *investire*, fr. L, to clothe, cover, surround] *vt* **1 a :** to commit (money) for a long period in order to earn a financial return ⟨~*ed* his savings in stocks, bonds, and real estate⟩ **b :** to place (money) with a view to minimizing risk rather than speculating for large gains at greater hazard **2 :** to make use of with particular thought of future benefits or advantages ⟨~*ed* his savings in a year of study —Norman Foerster⟩ ⟨I am avaricious of time and uneasy if I don't ~ it well —O.W.Holmes †1935⟩ ~ *vi* **:** to commit funds for future gain or purchase something of intrinsic value **:** make an investment ⟨anyone who wants to know more before ~*ing* can write the editor —*Monsanto Mag.*⟩ — often used with *in* ⟨decided to ~ in a first edition as a birthday gift for her husband⟩ ⟨the burghers . . . would not ~ in factories —William Petersen⟩

in·vest·able *also* **in·vest·ible** \-təbəl\ *adj* [²*invest* + *-able*, *-ible*] **:** available for investment ⟨~ surplus⟩

investient *adj* [L *investient-, investiens*, pres. part. of *investire*] *obs* **:** SURROUNDING, ENVELOPING

in·ves·ti·ga·ble \ənˈvestəgəbəl, -tēg-\ *adj* [LL *investigabilis*, fr. L *investigare* to investigate + *-abilis* -able] *archaic* **:** INVESTIGATABLE

in·ves·ti·gat·able \ənˈvestə,gād·əbəl, =ˌ=ˈ===\ *adj* **:** capable of being investigated

in·ves·ti·gate \ənˈvestə,gāt, *usu* -ād·+V\ *vb* -ED/-ING/-S [L *investigatus*, past part. of *investigare*, fr. *in-* ²in- + *vestigare* to track, trace; akin to L *vestigium* trace, footprint] *vt* **:** to observe or study closely **:** inquire into systematically **:** EXAMINE, SCRUTINIZE ⟨the whole brilliance of this novel lies in the fullness with which it ~*s* a past —Mark Schorer⟩ ⟨a commission to ~ costs of industrial production —Broadus Mitchell⟩ ⟨synthetic resins *investigated* for possible use in printing inks —H.J.Wolfe⟩ ⟨*investigating* every square cubit of terrain which she might have covered —L.C.Douglas⟩; *specif* **:** to subject to an official probe ⟨~ a crime⟩ ⟨~ marine casualties⟩ ⟨the F.B.I. ~*s* every applicant for federal employment⟩ ~ *vi* **:** to make a systematic examination **:** STUDY; *specif* **:** to conduct an official inquiry ⟨the power of Congress to ~ is an implied power in the Constitution —*New Republic*⟩

investigating *adj* **:** INVESTIGATIVE 2 — **in·ves·ti·gat·ing·ly** \=ˈ==,===, =,=ˈ===\ *adv*

in·ves·ti·ga·tion \ən,vestəˈgāshən\ *n* -S [ME *investigacioun*, fr. MF *investigation*, fr. L *investigation-, investigatio*, fr. *investigatus* (past part. of *investigare*) + *-ion-, -io* -ion] **1 :** the action or process of investigating **:** detailed examination **:** STUDY, RESEARCH ⟨success of the . . . blend in knitwear has led to active ~ of blends with other fibers —*Amer. Fabrics*⟩ ⟨a strong movement to make American universities centers of scholarly work and scientific ~ —J.B.Conant⟩ **2 :** a searching inquiry **:** EXAMINATION, SURVEY ⟨his doctoral thesis was a penetrating ~ of the causes of race conflict⟩ ⟨carried on energetic ~*s* of the medicinal flora of Mexico —*Amer. Guide Series: Mich.*⟩; *specif* **:** an official probe ⟨the first Congressional ~ of loyalty in government —Will Herberg⟩ **syn** see INQUIRY

in·ves·ti·ga·tion·al \=ˌ==ˈgāshənᵊl, -shnəl\ *adj* **:** INVESTIGATIVE 2

in·ves·ti·ga·tive \=ˈ==,gād·|iv, -āt|, |ēv *also* |əv\ *adj* **1 :** characterized by or having a tendency toward investigation ⟨~ scientist⟩ **2 :** of or relating to investigation ⟨~ power⟩ ⟨~ technique⟩

in·ves·ti·ga·tor \-,gād·ə(r), -ātə-\ *n* -S [L, fr. *investigatus* (past part. of *investigare*) + *-or*] **:** one that investigates: as **a :** one that conducts systematic inquiries or experiments **:** STUDENT, RESEARCHER **b :** an insurance claim adjuster or an underwriter **c :** one who is employed to examine the quality of goods or services of a business, its type of personnel, or the condition of its property — called also *spotter* **d :** one who inquires into the history of an applicant for employment to determine his integrity and loyalty **e :** DETECTIVE

in·ves·ti·ga·to·ry \-gə,tōrē, -tȯrē, -ri *chiefly Brit* ≈ˈ≈≈-ˌgātəri *or* -ā·tri\ *adj* [*investigate* + *-ory*] : INVESTIGATIVE

in·ves·ti·tive \ən'vestəd·iv\ *adj* [ML *investitus* (past part. of *investire* to invest) + E *-ive*] : of, relating to, or having the power of vesting a right

in·ves·ti·ture \-tə,chu̇(ə)r, -,chüə, -,chə(r), -tə,tü-, -tə,tyü-\ *n* -s [ME, fr. ML *investitura*, fr. *investitus* (past part. of *investire* to invest) + L *-ura* -ure] **1 a** : the ceremonial conferral of symbols of office or honor ⟨the six newly appointed Master Knights . . . immediately after their ~ with the Cloak and Cross of Malta —*Springfield (Mass.) Catholic Observer*⟩ **b** : an act of ratifying or establishing in office : CONFIRMATION ⟨the ~ of Parliament yesterday was marked by an extreme lack of enthusiasm and applause —Janet Flanner⟩ **c** : LIVERY OF SEIZIN **2** : an act of infusing or enriching **3 a** : an act of clothing or decorating ⟨to dress the sovereign in a linsey-woolsey garb would . . . be a very unsuitable ~ —R.C.Singleton⟩ **b** : something that covers or adorns ⟨the heavy red damask ~ of the four-poster⟩ ⟨regrettable that the drama does not live up to its rich ~ —*Newsweek*⟩ **4** *archaic* : ²INVESTMENT 2 **5** : BLOCKADE, SIEGE ⟨the enemy fleet riding to the ~ of Japan —*This World*⟩

¹in·vest·ment \ən'ves(t)mənt\ *n* -s [¹*invest* + *-ment*] **1 a** *archaic* : VESTMENT **b** : an outer layer of any kind : COATING, ENVELOPE: as (1) : an outward habiliment : GUISE ⟨one man asserts his right to grow a beard . . . as the ~ of his motley —*Times Lit. Supp.*⟩ (2) : an external covering of a cell, part, or organism (3) : a layer of heat-resistant material in which a dental appliance (as a bridge or inlay) is cast or in which it is embedded before soldering (4) : refractory material that forms the mold in investment casting **2** : INVESTITURE 1 ⟨~ with the ring has been an integral part of each coronation —*Literary Digest*⟩ **3** : BLOCKADE, SIEGE ⟨his proposals for an attack on Montreal . . . and a complete ~ of Quebec by land and sea —J.B.Brebner⟩

²investment \"\ *n* -s *often attrib* [²*invest* + *-ment*] **1 a** : an expenditure of money for income or profit or to purchase something of intrinsic value : capital outlay ⟨~ in common stocks⟩ ⟨~ in a diamond brooch⟩ **b** : the sum invested or the property purchased ⟨has a large ~ in a copper mine⟩ ⟨a fine painting is an ~⟩ **2** : the commitment of funds with a view to minimizing risk and safeguarding capital while earning a return — contrasted with *speculation* **3** : the commitment of something other than money to a long-term interest or project ⟨the job calls for the ~ of a great deal of hard thinking and planning —D.F.Cavers⟩

investment bank *n* [²*investment*] : an institution that specializes in buying and selling large blocks of securities (as new issues) and in raising funds for capital expansion — **investment banking** *n*

investment banker *n* **1** : a person employed by an investment bank or engaged in investment banking **2** : INVESTMENT BANK

investment casting *n* [¹*investment*] : casting by the cire perdue process

investment company *or* **investment trust** *n* [²*investment*] : a company that holds securities of other corporations for investment benefits only — compare HOLDING COMPANY

investment counselor *or* **investment adviser** *n* [²*investment*] : an individual or firm that analyzes and makes recommendations on a client's securities for a fee but does not have physical custody of these securities ⟨*investment counselors* or advisers must register under the Investment Advisers Act of 1940 —J.O.Kamm⟩

investment reserve *n* [²*investment*] : the terminal reserve of an insurance company in any year — compare INSURANCE RESERVE

in·ves·tor \ən'vestə(r)\ *n* -s [¹*invest* & ²*invest* + *-or*] : one that invests; *specif* : one that seeks to commit funds for long-term profit with a minimum of risk — contrasted with *speculator*

invests *pres 3d sing of* INVEST

in·ves·ture \ən'ves(h)chə(r)\ *n* -s [¹*invest* + *-ure*] *archaic* : INVESTITURE 1

in·vet·er·a·cy \ən'ved·ərəsē, -vetər-,-ve·tr-, -si\ *n* -ES [¹*inveterate* + *-cy*] *archaic* **1** : prejudiced animosity : HOSTILITY **2** : the quality or state of being obstinate : TENACITY

¹in·vet·er·ate \-rət, *usu* -rəd·+V\ *adj* [L *inveteratus*, past part. of *inveterare* to make old, to age, fr. *in-* ²in- + *veter-*, *vetus* old — more at WETHER] **1** *archaic* : obstinately prejudiced or antagonistic : BIASED, HOSTILE ⟨felt ~ against him —Charles Dickens⟩ **2 a** : CONTINUOUS, RECURRENT, CHRONIC ⟨~ bursitis⟩ **b** : deep-rooted or widely accepted : INGRAINED, ESTABLISHED ⟨~ tendency to naturalize foreign words —George Woodcock⟩ ⟨supported by precedent so ~ that the chance of abandonment is small —B.N.Cardozo⟩ ⟨~ and skillful biographer —Marvin Lowenthal⟩ **c** : stubbornly inflexible : ADAMANT, OBSTINATE ⟨~ prejudice⟩ ⟨his ~ demand for the imposition of a severe discipline —C.I.Glicksberg⟩ **d** : long-lasting : PERSISTENT ⟨the ~ smell of ether in a hospital⟩ **3** *obs* : of an advanced age : ANCIENT ⟨rotten wood . . . taken out of an ~ willow tree —John Evelyn⟩ **4** : fixed by long habit or usage : CONFIRMED, HABITUAL ⟨~ sightseers —Astrid Peters⟩ ⟨an ~ love of alcohol —C.B.Nordhoff & J.N.Hall⟩ ⟨the punishment for ~ idleness was a whipping on the bare back —W.E.Woodward⟩

syn CHRONIC, CONFIRMED, DEEP-ROOTED, DEEP-SEATED: INVETERATE suggests resolute persistence in an idea or attitude making change or moderation impossible or most unlikely ⟨Frenchmen do not crave a master . . . the average Frenchman is probably the world's most *inveterate* individualist —*Christian Century*⟩ ⟨*inveterate* habits of animistic thinking —Lewis Mumford⟩ ⟨the *inveterate* hostility of "creative" writers to criticism —P.E.More⟩ CHRONIC implies long continuation or frequent recurrence of a usu. detrimental condition or trait but lacks the suggestion of determination that may accompany INVETERATE ⟨his *chronic* state of mental restlessness —George Eliot⟩ ⟨envy and rebellion and class resentments are *chronic* moral diseases with us —G.B.Shaw⟩ ⟨the total lack of adequate means of transportation rendered the problem of a grain market a *chronic* difficulty to the frontier farmers —V.L.Parrington⟩ CONFIRMED suggests a pattern that has become fixed by habit or usage ⟨I am a *confirmed* wanderer —Isaac D'Israeli⟩ ⟨a *confirmed* bachelor⟩ ⟨his intense egoism rendered him impatient of all reproof or instruction and . . . he soon became a victim of *confirmed* mannerisms —*Nation*⟩ DEEP-ROOTED and DEEP-SEATED in general refer to qualities so deeply engrained that they have become part of the core of personal character, or to conditions of deep significance and lasting endurance ⟨Lincoln had a *deep-rooted* aversion to slavery⟩ ⟨the *deep-rooted* causes of Indian discontent —*Current History*⟩ ⟨the conviction of Thomas Aquinas, that between true science and true religion there can be no contradiction, is exceedingly *deep-seated* —J.H.Randall⟩ ⟨*deep-seated* sources of cultural antipathy between Asia and the U.S. —M.W.Straight⟩

²in·vet·er·ate \-ved·ə,rāt\ *vt* -ED/-ING/-S [L *inveteratus*, past part. of *inveterare*] *archaic* : to establish firmly : root deeply : CONFIRM

in·vet·er·ate·ly \ved·ərətlē, -vetər-,-ve·tr-, -li\ *adv* : in an inveterate manner : PERSISTENTLY

in·vet·er·ate·ness \-ətnəs\ *n* -ES : the quality or state of being inveterate : PERSISTENCE

in·viability \(ˌ)in, ən+\ *n* : inability to live — used esp. of a genetic constitution that precludes survival ⟨~ of intergeneric hybrids —E.R.Sears⟩

in·viable \(ˈ)in, ən+\ *adj* [ISV ¹*in-* + *viable*] : incapable of surviving

in·vid·i·ous \ən'vidēəs\ *adj* [L *invidiosus*, fr. *invidia* envy + *-osus* -ose — more at ENVY] **1** : detrimental to reputation : DEFAMATORY ⟨the ~ implication of the phrase is . . . against those who pursue self-interest through politics —Felix Frankfurter⟩ **2** : likely to cause discontent or animosity or envy ⟨the four confidential advisers of the crown soon found that their position was embarrassing and ~ —T.B. Macaulay⟩ **3** : full of envious resentment : JEALOUS ⟨his professional abilities as an officer . . . had to stand ~ scrutiny —J.G.Cozzens⟩ **4 a** : of an unpleasant or objectionable nature : HATEFUL, OBNOXIOUS ⟨~ remarks that were sometimes neither kind nor true —John Hurkan⟩ **b** : causing harm or resentment : INJURIOUS ⟨would be ~ to select for special mention a more or less haphazard list of names —*Survey Graphic*⟩ ⟨far from our purpose to institute any ~ comparisons between these two gifted women —Eugene Field⟩ **syn** see HATEFUL

in·vid·i·ous·ly *adv* : in an invidious manner : ODIOUSLY

in·vid·i·ous·ness *n* -ES : the quality or state of being invidious : ODIOUSNESS

in·vigilancy \(ˈ)in+\ *n* -ES [¹*in-* + *vigilancy*] *archaic* : lack of vigilance

in·vig·i·late \ən'vijə,lāt\ *vb* -ED/-ING/-S [L *invigilatus*, past part. of *invigilare*, fr. *in-* ²in- + *vigilare* to watch — more at VIGILANT] *vi* : to keep watch ⟨that invisible power that ~s over all things —Henry More⟩; *specif, Brit* : to proctor an examination ~ *vt* : to make watchful

in·vig·i·la·tion \(ˌ)in,vijə'lāshən, ən,v-\ *n* -s : an act of surveillance; *specif* : the proctoring of an examination

in·vig·i·la·tor \ən'vijə,lād·ə(r)\ *n* -s *Brit* : PROCTOR 2b

in·vig·or *or* **in·vig·our** \ən'vigə(r)\ *vt* [alter. (influenced by E ²*in-*) of earlier *envigor*, fr. ¹*en-* + *vigor*, n.] *archaic* : INVIGORATE

in·vig·o·rate \ən'vigə,rāt, *usu* -ād·+V\ *vt* -ED/-ING/-S [prob. fr. ²*in-* + obs. E *vigorate* to invigorate, fr. L *vigoratus*, past part. of *vigorare*, fr. *vigor* — more at VIGOR] : to give life and energy to : ANIMATE ⟨a lotion to ~ the skin⟩ ⟨that puzzling out of new possibilities which ~s the imagination —H.A.Overstreet⟩ ⟨an industrial center *invigorated* by defense contracts —R.M.Hodesh⟩ **syn** see STRENGTHEN

invigorating *adj* : having an enlivening effect : BRACING, STIMULATING ⟨~ climate⟩ ⟨thought that he would try these ~ berries since he was inclined to fall asleep during his prayers —Charles Cooper⟩ ⟨his writings are tonic and . . . ~ to those who stand in need of inspiration —R.L.Cook⟩ — **in·vig·o·rat·ing·ly** \≈'≈≈,≈≈≈, ≈,≈≈'≈≈≈\ *adv*

in·vig·o·ra·tion \≈,≈≈'rāshən\ *n* -s **1** : the act or process of invigorating ⟨demands for . . . ~ of the Articles were made even before they became effective —Allan Nevins⟩ **2** : the quality or state of being invigorated ⟨the ~ that derives from . . . the cultural atmosphere of a great city —A.A.Houghton⟩

in·vig·o·ra·tor \≈'≈≈,rād·ə(r), -ātə-\ *n* -s : one that invigorates

in·vi·nate \ən'vī,nāt, 'in,v-\ *vt* -ED/-ING/-S [prob. fr. (assumed) NL *invinatus*, past part. of (assumed) NL *invinare*, fr. L *in-* ²in- + *vinum* wine — more at WINE] : to make present by invination

in·vi·na·tion \,in,vī'nāshən\ *n* -s [F, prob. fr. (assumed) NL *invination-*, *invinatio*, fr. (assumed) NL *invinatus* + L *-ion-*, *-io* -ion] : the inclusion of the blood of Christ in the eucharistic wine without change in either substance — compare IMPANATION

in·vin·ci·bil·i·ty \(ˌ)in,vin(t)sə'biləd·ē, ən,v-, -lətē, -i\ *n* -ES : the quality or state of being invincible

¹in·vin·ci·ble \(ˈ)in¦vin(t)səbəl, ən'v-\ *adj* [ME, fr. MF, fr. LL *invincibilis*, fr. L *in-* ¹in- + *vincibilis* conquerable — more at VINCIBLE] **1 a** : incapable of being vanquished or subjugated : impervious to attack or conquest : UNBEATABLE ⟨~ army⟩ ⟨has been ~ in eight-oared Olympic rowing —*Collier's Yr. Bk.*⟩ **b** : impossible to overcome or subdue : ABSOLUTE, UNSWERVING ⟨the ~ obscurity of his origins —Joseph Conrad⟩ ⟨a resolute, yet not ~, skepticism —A.G.N.Flew⟩ ⟨~ respect for authority⟩ ⟨man's ~ conviction that a sublime soul cannot be imprisoned —W.L.Sullivan⟩ **2** : beyond an individual's control and so not involving moral responsibility : UNAVOIDABLE — used esp. of lack of knowledge about theological concepts ⟨~ ignorance⟩ — **in·vin·ci·ble·ness** \-nəs\ *n* -ES — **in·vin·ci·bly** \-blē,-bli\ *adv*

²invincible \"\ *n* -s : one that is invincible

in·violability \(ˌ)in, ən+\ *n* : the quality or state of being inviolable

in·violable \(ˈ)in, ən+\ *adj* [MF or L; MF, fr. L *inviolabilis*, fr. *in-* ¹in- + *violabilis* violable] **1** *obs* : incapable of being broken or destroyed : INDESTRUCTIBLE **2 a** : secure from violation or infringement : INCORRUPTIBLE, SACROSANCT ⟨thinking of conscience as an ~ source of moral certitude —Lucius Garvin⟩ ⟨bound by mores more strict, more rigorous, more ~ than most religious denominations would dare to require —Jessie Bernard⟩ **b** : secure from assault or trespass : UNTOUCHABLE, UNASSAILABLE ⟨the person of the king is ~⟩ ⟨~ frontier⟩ ⟨~ green lawns⟩ — **in·vi·o·la·ble·ness** \-nəs\ *n* — **in·vi·o·la·bly** \-blē, -bli\ *adv*

in·vi·o·la·cy \ən'vīələsē, -si\ *n* -ES [*inviolate* + *-cy*] : the quality or state of being inviolate

in·violate \(ˈ)in¦vīələ̇t, ən'v- *also* -,lāt; *usu* |d·+V\ *also* **in·violated** \-,lād·əd, -ātəd\ *adj* [ME *inviolat*, fr. L *inviolatus*, fr. *in-* ¹in- + *violatus*, past part. of *violare* to violate — more at VIOLATE] **1 a** : free from change or blemish : PURE, UNBROKEN ⟨desired the Italian culture to be ~ and predominant —John Buchan⟩ ⟨cease searching for the perfect shell, the whole ~ form —Anne M. Lindbergh⟩ ⟨while I continue to keep this oath ~ —*Hippocratic Oath*⟩ **b** : free from assault or trespass : UNTOUCHED, INTACT ⟨as he had fallen on the plain, ~ he lay —R.C.Trench⟩ ⟨the . . . first white settlers agreed to keep this ground ~ —*Amer. Guide Series: Conn.*⟩ **2** : INVIOLABLE 2 ⟨they . . . regarded their hunting zones as their own ~ property —L.S.B.Leakey⟩ ⟨the confidences of this Club are ~ —R.H.Davis⟩ — **in·vi·o·late·ly** *adv* — **in·vi·o·late·ness** *n* -ES

invious *adj* [L *invius*, fr. *in-* ¹in- + *via* road — more at VIA] *obs* : lacking roads : TRACKLESS

inviron *obs var of* ENVIRON

in·vir·tu·ate \ən'vərchə,wāt\ *vt* -ED/-ING/-S [²*in-* + *virtue* + *-ate*] *archaic* : to endow with virtue

in·vis·cate \ən'vi,skāt, 'in,v-\ *vt* -ED/-ING/-S [LL *inviscatus*, past part. of *inviscare* to snare as with birdlime, fr. L *in-* ²in- + *viscare* to smear with birdlime, fr. *viscum* mistletoe, birdlime — more at VISCID] : to encase in a sticky substance : make viscid — **in·vis·ca·tion** \,in,vi'skāshən\ *n* -s

in·viscid \(ˈ)in, ən+\ *adj* [¹*in-* + *viscid*] **1** : not having viscosity ⟨~ fluid⟩ **2** : relating to the flow of an inviscid body ⟨~ theory⟩

in·visibility \(ˌ)in, ən+\ *n* [LL *invisibilitat-*, *invisibilitas*, fr. L *invisibilis* invisible + *-itat-*, *-itas* -ity] **1** : the quality or state of being invisible **2** : something that is invisible

¹in·visible \(ˈ)in, ən+\ *adj* [ME, fr. MF, fr. L *invisibilis*, fr. *in-* ¹in- + *visibilis* visible] **1 a** : incapable of being seen through lack of physical substance : not perceptible by vision : INTANGIBLE, UNSEEN ⟨another thriller about an ~ man⟩ ⟨an angel and a high-frequency wave are equally ~ to the mass of mankind —Lewis Mumford⟩; *specif* : not appearing in published financial statements ⟨~ assets and liabilities⟩ **b** : of or relating to service or capital transactions not reflected in statistics of foreign trade ⟨the nation's greatest ~ export, tourism —T.H.Fielding⟩ ⟨a bit of unconscious humor is the listing of movies among ~ imports —George Soule⟩ ⟨Ireland's trade deficit was met by ~ items, including immigrant remittances —Alzada Comstock⟩ **2** : inaccessible to view : out of sight : HIDDEN ⟨~ hinge⟩ ⟨in stormy weather the seaman's compass takes the place of ~ stars⟩ ⟨the world's largest and finest private or public assemblage of French art . . . is now ~ in the attic of the Hermitage —Janet Flanner⟩ **3** : of such small size or unobtrusive quality as to be hardly noticeable : IMPERCEPTIBLE, INCONSPICUOUS ⟨~ hair net⟩ ⟨~ plaid⟩ ⟨the translation is almost ~ —Stuart Preston⟩ — **in·visible·ness** \"+\ *n* — **in·visibly** \"+\ *adv*

²invisible \"\ *n* : one that is invisible ⟨the ~s that lurk in haunted houses⟩ ⟨the present deficit gap . . . must be closed either by greater merchandise exports or larger earnings on ~s —J.B.Cohen⟩

invisible church *n* : CHURCH INVISIBLE

invisible government *n* : a government controlled by a person (as a boss) or an agency (as a pressure group) holding no official position and usu. held to be unknown to the public ⟨the interlocking control thus created was an *invisible government* —F.L.Paxson⟩

invisible green *n* **1** : a very dark green to yellowish green **2** : a dark bluish green that is greener and duller than average teal green and bluer and slightly less strong than duck green

invisible ink *n* : SECRET INK

in·vi·tant \'invətənt, ən'vītᵊnt\ *n* -s [*invite* + *-ant*] *archaic* : INVITER

¹in·vi·ta·tion \,invə'tāshən\ *n* -s [MF or L; MF, fr. L *invitation-*, *invitatio*, fr. *invitatus* (past part. of *invitare* to invite) + *-ion-*, *-io* -ion] **1 a** : the act of inviting : the requesting of a person's company or participation ⟨I took the ~ to dinner as a dismissal from tea —O.S.J.Gogarty⟩ ⟨joined the expedition at the ~ of the government⟩ **b** (1) : a written or verbal request to be present or participate ⟨address wedding ~s⟩ ⟨accept an ~ to membership⟩ (2) : a written or verbal request to do or undertake ⟨an ~ to sing at a benefit concert⟩ ⟨an ~ to assume leadership of a project⟩ (3) *often cap* : a brief exhortation immediately preceding the confession in the communion service of the Anglican and other Protestant churches **c** : SUGGESTION, PROPOSAL ⟨the ~s of a master are scarcely to be distinguished from commands —Edward Gibbon⟩ ⟨he refused my ~ to consider the history of Christian intolerance —H.J.Laski⟩ **2 a** : ATTRACTION, STIMULUS, LURE, INCENTIVE ⟨they were forced to move, even though the Sahara desert was no ~ —Emil Lengyel⟩ ⟨good scholarship . . . presents us with evidence which is an ~ to the critical faculty of the reader —T.S.Eliot⟩ **b** : a precipitating factor : INDUCEMENT, CHALLENGE, PROVOCATION ⟨a hatchet painted red was thrown down in a friendly village as an ~ to join in a war —Clark Wissler⟩ ⟨the laws . . . were an ~ to smuggling —Roger Burlingame⟩ ⟨her sultry look was clearly an ~⟩

²invitation \¦≈≈¦≈≈\ *also* **in·vi·ta·tion·al** \¦≈≈¦tāshənᵊl, -shnəl\ *adj* : prepared or entered in response to a request or challenge ⟨~ article⟩ ⟨~ exhibit⟩; *specif* : limited to invited participants ⟨~ tournament⟩

¹in·vi·ta·to·ry \ən'vīd·ə,tōrē\ *adj* [ME, fr. LL *invitatorius*, fr. L *invitatus* (past part. of *invitare*) + *-orius* -ory] : containing an invitation ⟨a brief ~ note⟩ ⟨~ psalm⟩

²invitatory \"\ *n* -ES [ME, fr. ML *invitatorium*, fr. LL, neut. of *invitatorius*, adj.] : any of various liturgical forms of invitation used in church services ⟨common *invitatories* are the Venite and Psalm 95⟩

¹in·vite \ən'vīt, *usu* -īd·+V\ *vb* -ED/-ING/-S [MF or L; MF *inviter*, fr. L *invitare*, prob. fr. *in-* ²in- + *-vitare* (prob. akin to Gk *hiesthai* to hasten, long for) — more at GAIN] *vt* **1 a** : to offer an incentive or inducement to : ENTICE, TEMPT ⟨the book ~s interest⟩ ⟨writes about the people and places that ~ his pen —*Atlantic*⟩ ⟨rock-strewn streams ~ the fisherman —*Amer. Guide Series: N.J.*⟩ ⟨virgin spaces of America *invited* colonization —Douglas Bush⟩ ⟨I loaf and ~ my soul —Walt Whitman⟩ **b** : to provide opportunity or occasion for : increase the likelihood of : open the way to ⟨to shrink from responsibility is to ~ social and economic insecurity —H.G. Armstrong⟩ ⟨so long as there is starvation and joblessness in the midst of abundance we are *inviting* the deluge —Ruth Benedict⟩ ⟨lurid emotionalism and tear-jerking nostalgia . . . *inviting* sighs and hisses —Leslie Rees⟩ ⟨wandered slowly along . . . in that wholly relaxed state which always seems to ~ small adventures —William Beebe⟩ **2 a** : to request the presence or participation of : solicit the company of : ASK ⟨~ guests to dinner⟩ ⟨~ educators to a conference⟩ ⟨~ a team to a tournament⟩ ⟨open the door and ~ him in⟩; *esp* : to send a formal invitation to ⟨an affair open only to those who had been *invited*⟩ **b** : to request formally ⟨~ him to be chief executive⟩ ⟨*invited* her to give a talk on flower arrangement⟩ ⟨it is not as yet very clear which . . . are *invited* to consider becoming signatories —I.A.Richards⟩ **c** : to urge politely or indicate a receptiveness to : ENCOURAGE, WELCOME ⟨leaned forward . . . and *invited* me to continue in English —Barbara Henderson⟩ ⟨*inviting* him to put his own motives under examination —Lionel Trilling⟩ ⟨~ bids on a contract⟩ ⟨~s oral suggestions from his three clerks —J.P.Frank⟩ ⟨his manner did not ~ approach —H.E.Starr⟩ ~ *vi* : to issue an invitation ⟨he did not ~: he commanded —Max Beerbohm⟩ ⟨the spacious campus . . . ~s to the enjoyment of the out-of-doors —*Catalog of Hollins Coll.*⟩

²in·vite \'in,v-\ *n* -s *now chiefly dial* : INVITATION 1 ⟨you sound like you didn't get no ~ to the dance —Richard Bissell⟩

invited *adj* [fr. past part. of ¹*invite*] : present or done by invitation ⟨~ guests⟩ ⟨read an ~ paper at the meeting⟩

in·vi·tee \¦in,vī¦tē, ən¦vī¦tē\ *n* -s [*invite* + *-ee*] : an invited person : GUEST; *specif* : a person (as a customer) present in a place by the express or implied invitation of the occupier in control of that place under circumstances such as impose a duty on the occupier to use reasonable care to protect the safety of such person — compare LICENSEE, TRESPASSER

in·vite·ment \ən'vītmənt\ *n* -s **1** *obs* : INVITATION 1 ⟨would not stand upon ~, but came of himself —George Chapman⟩ **2** *archaic* : INVITATION 2 ⟨unable to resist the delicious ~ to repose —Charles Lamb⟩

in·vit·er *or* **in·vi·tor** \ən'vīd·ə(r), -ītə-\ *n* -s : one that invites

¹inviting *n* -s [fr. gerund of ¹*invite*] *obs* : INVITATION ⟨he hath sent me an earnest ~ —Shak.⟩

²inviting *adj* [fr. pres. part. of ¹*invite*] **1** : giving an invitation ⟨the ~ ship would haul the Stars and Stripes to the peak —H.A.Chippendale⟩ **2** : of an agreeable nature : pleasing to the senses : ATTRACTIVE, TEMPTING ⟨~ climate⟩ ⟨~ prospect⟩ ⟨~ eye⟩ ⟨beautiful binding, ~ type, fine paper —*N.Y. Times Book Rev.*⟩ — **in·vit·ing·ly** *adv* — **in·vit·ing·ness** *n* -ES

in·vi·tress \ən'vī·trəs\ *n* -ES [*inviter* + *-ess*] *archaic* : a female inviter

in vi·tro \(')in'vē·(,)trō\ *adv* (*or adj*) [NL, lit., in glass] : outside the living body : in a test tube or other artificial environment ⟨*in vitro* cultivation of tissues⟩ — compare IN VIVO

in vi·vo \(')in'vē(,)vō\ *adv* (*or adj*) [NL, lit., in that which is alive] : in the living body of a plant or animal ⟨*in vivo* synthesis of vitamin D⟩ ⟨microorganisms are not ordinarily destroyed *in vivo* by bacteriostatic drugs —*Jour. Amer. Med. Assoc.*⟩ — compare IN VITRO

in·vo·ca·ble \ən'vōkəbəl, 'invək-\ *adj* [irreg. (influenced by L *invocare* to invoke) fr. *invoke* + *-able*] : capable of being invoked

in·vo·cant \-kənt\ *n* -s [L *invocant-*, *invocans*, pres. part. of *invocare* to invoke] : one that invokes

in·vo·cate \'invə,kāt\ *vb* -ED/-ING/-S [L *invocatus*, past part. of *invocare*] *vt*, *archaic* : INVOKE ⟨still will I ~ his name —John Wesley⟩ ~ *vi* : to make a supplication : PRAY ⟨after that hour to daybreak 'tis held an ungodly thing to ~ —Thomas Herbert⟩

in·vo·ca·tion \,invə'kāshən, -vō'-\ *n* -s [ME *invocacioun*, fr. MF *invocation*, fr. L *invocation-*, *invocatio*, fr. *invocatus* (past part. of *invocare* to invoke) + *-ion-*, *-io* -ion] **1 a** : the action or an act of petitioning for help or support : SUPPLICATION, APPEAL ⟨~ to the Muses⟩; *specif*, *often cap* : a prayer of entreaty that is usu. a call for the divine presence and is offered at the beginning of a meeting or service of worship **b** : a summoning up or calling upon for authority or justification ⟨~ of economic reasons . . . to justify postponement of wage increases —Frank Gorrell⟩ ⟨~ of a celebrated piece of advice attributed to Talleyrand —*Times Lit. Supp.*⟩ **2 a** : an act of conjuring ⟨~ of an ancestral spirit⟩ **b** : a formula for conjuring : INCANTATION ⟨~s . . . to bring harm to mother or child —Francis Hackett⟩ **3 a** : a judicial call for papers or evidence from another case — used chiefly in admiralty prize procedure **b** : an act of legal or moral implementation : ENFORCEMENT ⟨~ of treaty provisions⟩ — **in·vo·ca·tion·al** \¦≈≈¦≈shənᵊl, -shnəl\ *adj*

in·voca·tive \ən'väkəd·iv; 'invə,kād·iv, -vō,-\ *adj* [LL *invocativus*, fr. L *invocatus* (past part. of *invocare* to invoke) + *-ivus* -ive] : INVOCATORY

in·vo·ca·tor \'invə,kād·ə(r), -vō,-\ *n* -s [LL *invocator*, fr. L *invocatus* (past part. of *invocare* to invoke) + *-or*] : one that invokes

in·voc·a·to·ry \ən'väkə,tōrē\ *adj* [fr. *invocation*, after such pairs as E *revocation*: *revocatory*] : of, relating to, or characterized by invocation ⟨~ prayer⟩

¹in·voice \'in,vȯis\ *n* -s *often attrib* [modif. of MF *envois*, pl. of *envoi* action of sending, message — more at ENVOY] **1 a** : an itemized statement furnished to a purchaser by a seller and usu. specifying the price of goods or services and the terms of sale : BILL ⟨prices shown on this ~ are net⟩ **b** : a consignment of merchandise ⟨received a large ~ of broomstraw⟩ **c** : a printed form used for detailing charges : BILLHEAD ⟨a picture of the factory appears on the ~⟩ **2** : BILL OF LADING

²invoice \"\ *vb* -ED/-ING/-S *vt* **1 a** : to submit a statement of charges for : BILL ⟨~ desk accessories to the stationery buyer⟩ **b** : to send a consignment of (merchandise) : SHIP ⟨where are the sewing machines *invoiced* me by this steamer —R.H.Davis⟩ **2** : INVENTORY **~** *vi* **1** : to make or render an invoice ⟨please ~ and advise where to pay —*advt*⟩ **2** : to be worth on inventory ⟨his little office would not have *invoiced* more than fifteen hundred dollars —W.A.White⟩

in·voke \ən'vōk\ *vt* -ED/-ING/-S [ME *invoken*, fr. MF *invoquer*, fr. L *invocare*, fr. *in-* ²in- + *vocare* to call, fr. *voc-*, *vox* voice — more at VOICE] **1 a** : to petition for help or support : call upon for assistance ⟨the gods had to be *invoked* to bring rain —T.E.Sanford⟩ ⟨she would ~ the Travelers' Aid Society, and they would assist her in getting a . . . place to live —Donn Byrne⟩ **b** : to appeal to as furnishing authority or motive : propound as a logical basis ⟨racist doctrines are *invoked* for political ends —Ruth Benedict⟩ ⟨~ the balance-of-payments difficulties to justify . . . import prohibitions —*Economist*⟩ ⟨four theories . . . *invoked* by geographers to explain the origin of the areas —S.A.Cain⟩ ⟨imaginary lesions . . . *invoked* to account for conditions which had a merely psychogenic origin —R.S.Ellery⟩ **2 a** : to call forth by incantation : CONJURE 2 ⟨spokesmen for the two tribes *invoked* the spirits of departed . . . chiefs to tell them they were now as one —*Time*⟩ ⟨~ a plague on all their houses —W.L.Sperry⟩ **b** : to use (a respected name) to imply endorsement by the owner ⟨more misquotations probably have been attributed to Jefferson than to any other American, because many politicians who ~ his name have read him not at all —L.B. Wright⟩ **3 a** : to make an earnest request for : SOLICIT ⟨~ the board's help in getting his old job back —Dixon Wecter⟩ ⟨the student of genetics ~s the aid of the physicist and biochemist —J.M.Fogg⟩ **b** : ENTREAT, IMPLORE ⟨~ mercy⟩ ⟨*invoked* their forgiveness⟩ **4 a** : to call for (as papers or other evidence) judicially — used chiefly in admiralty prize procedure **b** : to put into legal effect or call for the observance of : ENFORCE, IMPLEMENT ⟨~ the penalties of the law —Albert Mowbray⟩ ⟨military sanctions may be *invoked* only after economic sanctions have failed —Norman Hill⟩ ⟨*invoked* the veto six times in the dispute —C.D.Fuller⟩ ⟨~ a promise⟩ ⟨unhesitatingly *invoked* the health department's broad powers —Leonard Engel⟩ ⟨because it possesses that right . . . can usually discipline the majority without *invoking* its prerogative —*Foreign Affairs*⟩ **5 a** : to introduce or put into operation : INSTIGATE, EMPLOY ⟨controls alien to . . . peacetime custom will have to be *invoked* —Stacy May⟩ ⟨~ bold visions at a time of unrest —Norman Cousins⟩ ⟨discipline should not be *invoked* . . . without first consulting the union —Earl Brown⟩ ⟨alliteration's artful aid is *invoked* on every page —*Irish Digest*⟩ **b** : to bring about : CAUSE, EXCITE ⟨operations . . . ~ new problems of administration, maintenance and supply —H.H.Arnold & I.C.Eaker⟩ ⟨stabilizing the regime and *invoking* social and patriotic fervor —E.P. Snow⟩

in·vok·er \-kə(r)\ *n* -S : one that invokes

in·volatile \(')in, ən+\ *adj* [¹*in-* + *volatile*] : not vaporizing or capable of being vaporized — **in·volatility** \(ˌ)in, ən+\ *n*

in·vol·u·cel \ən'välyəˌsel\ *n* -S [NL *involucellum*, dim. of *involucrum*] : a secondary involucre (as in each secondary umbel of a compound umbel) — **in·vol·u·cel·late** \(ˌ)inˌvälyəˌselət, ənˌv-\ *or* **in·vol·u·cel·lat·ed** \(ˌ)=ˌ==ˌseˌlād·əd\ *adj*

in·vo·lu·cral \ˌinvəˌlükrəl *also* -vəlˌyü-\ *adj* [prob. fr. (assumed) NL *involucralis*, fr. NL *involucrum* involucre + L *-alis* -al] : of, relating to, or resembling an involucre

in·vo·lu·crate \-krət\ *adj* [prob. fr. (assumed) NL *involucratus*, fr. NL *involucrum* involucre + L *-atus* -ate] : having an involucre

in·vo·lu·cre \'invəˌlükə(r) *also* -vəlˌyü-\ *n* -S [F, fr. NL *involucrum* involucre] : one or more whorls of bracts situated below and close to a flower, flower cluster, or fruit (in a seed plant): as **a** : a rosette of bracts surrounding a composite flower head (as a daisy) and often resembling a true calyx — see CUPULE 1a **b** : a whorl of bracts subtending the inflorescence in many members of the Umbelliferae

in·vo·lu·cred \-kə(r)d\ *adj* [*involucre* + *-ed*] : INVOLUCRATE

in·vo·lu·cri·form \ˌ=ˈ=krəˌfȯrm\ *adj* [prob. fr. (assumed) NL *involucriformis*, fr. NL *involucrum* involucre + L *-iformis* -iform] : having the form or appearance of an involucre

in·vo·lu·crum \ˌ==ˈ=krəm\ *n*, *pl* **involu·cra** \-krə\ [L, fr. *involvere* to wrap, envelop] **1** : a surrounding envelope or sheath ⟨each group has its ~ of space from which it drives any encroaching group —C.S.Coon⟩ **2** [NL, fr. L] : INVOLUCRE **3** [NL, fr. L] : a formation of new bone about a sequestrum (as in osteomyelitis)

in·voluntarily \(ˌ)in, ən+\ *adv* : in an involuntary manner

in·voluntariness \"+\ *n* -ES : the quality or state of being involuntary

in·voluntary \(')in, ən+\ *adj* [LL *involuntarius*, fr. L *in-* ¹in- + *voluntarius* voluntary] **1 a** : springing from accident or impulse rather than conscious exercise of the will : UNINTENTIONAL, SPONTANEOUS ⟨an ~ inheritance from her rich and backward husband —Nigel Dennis⟩ ⟨concentration became at first effortless, then ~, then necessitous —Charles Morgan⟩ **b** : dictated by authority or circumstance : COMPULSORY ⟨~ servitude⟩ ⟨~ unemployment⟩ **c** *of bankruptcy* : declared upon petition of creditors **2** : not subject to control of the will : independent of volition : REFLEX ⟨~ contraction⟩ ⟨~ weeping⟩

involuntary deposit *n*, *law* : an accidental or unintentional transference of property to the possession of another without the assent, negligence, or even knowledge of the owner (as of a boat carried onto land by a storm)

involuntary manslaughter *n* : manslaughter resulting from the failure to perform a legal duty expressly required to safeguard human life, or from the commission of an unlawful act not constituting a felony, or from the commission of a lawful act in a negligent or improper manner — compare HOMICIDE, MURDER, VOLUNTARY MANSLAUGHTER

involuntary muscle *n* : muscle governing reflex functions and not under direct voluntary control : SMOOTH MUSCLE

involuntary trust *n* : CONSTRUCTIVE TRUST

¹**in·vo·lute** \'invəˌlüt *also* -vəlˌyüt; ˌ==ˈ=\ *adj* [L *involutus* involved, intricate, fr. past part. of *involvere* to wrap, envelop] **1 a** (1) : curled spirally (2) : having the whorls closely coiled ⟨~ shell⟩ **b** (1) : curled or curved inward (2) : having the edges rolled over the upper surface toward the midrib ⟨an ~ leaf⟩ — compare CONVOLUTE, REVOLUTE **2** : INVOLUTED 3 ⟨the possible moves . . . not only manifold, but ~ —E.A.Poe⟩ **3** : of or relating to an involute ⟨~ curve⟩ ⟨~ gear cutter⟩ — **in·vo·lute·ly** *adv*

²**involute** \"=\ *n* -S : a curve traced by any point of a perfectly flexible inextensible thread kept taut as it is wound upon or unwound from another curve — compare EVOLUTE

³**involute** \ˈ=ˈ=\ *vi* -ED/-ING/-S **1** : to curl inward : become involute ⟨the leaf margin ~s⟩ **2 a** : to return to a former condition ⟨after pregnancy the uterus ~s⟩ **b** : to clear up : DISAPPEAR ⟨the disease ~s without desquamation —*Annals of N.Y. Academy of Sciences*⟩

involuted \'==ˌ==, ˌ==ˈ==\ *adj* [L *involutus* involved, intricate + E *-ed*] **1** : INVOLUTE 1b ⟨~ soil zone⟩ **2** : that has returned to a normal size or condition ⟨~ uterus⟩ **3** : of an involved or complicated nature : ABSTRUSE, INTRICATE ⟨much ~ wordage . . . obscures the fact that the tax law is an issue —Robert Wallace⟩ ⟨a remarkable man, ~, brilliant, and terribly shy —Charles Neider⟩ — **in·vo·lut·ed·ly** *adv* — **in·vo·lut·ed·ness** *n* -ES

involute *a,p,p,p,p*, traced by any point, *p*, of the thread, *t*, unwinding from curve, *c*

involute tooth *n* : a gear tooth that conforms in contact profile to an involute curve, that engages mating teeth with rolling rather than sliding friction, and that transmits motion with speed practically independent of slight changes in center distance

in·vo·lu·tion \ˌinvəˈlüshən *also* -vəlˈyü-\ *n* -S [ML *involution-*, *involutio* envelopment, fr. L, something enveloped, fr. *involutus* (past part. of *involvere* to wrap, envelop) + *-ion-*, *-io* -ion] **1 a** : the act or an instance of infolding or entangling : INVOLVEMENT ⟨her subsequent Red ~ was probably from idealistic reaction . . . rather than from Marxist conviction —Wilbur Burton⟩ ⟨some ~s of the plot I had quite forgotten —Arnold Bennett⟩; *specif* : an involved grammatical construction usu. characterized by the insertion of clauses between the subject and predicate **b** : the quality or state of being involved : ENVELOPMENT, INTRICACY ⟨whatever the degree of ~ . . . tale within tale —*Modern Language Notes*⟩ ⟨his mind . . . is simple; his syntax lacks ~ —Austin Warren⟩ **2** : the act or process of raising a quantity or symbol to any assigned power or affecting it with an assigned exponent — opposed to *evolution* **3 a** : an inward curvature or penetration ⟨~ of a soil deposit⟩ **b** : the formation of a gastrula by ingrowth of cells formed at the dorsal lip **4** : a shrinking or return to a former size ⟨~ of the uterus after pregnancy⟩ **5** : the regressive alterations of a body or its parts that are characteristic of the aging process; *specif* : presenile decline marked by a decrease of bodily vigor and in women by the menopause **6** : a relation of a higher type of reality to a lower type (as mind to matter) upon which it depends

¹**in·vo·lu·tion·al** \ˌinvəˈlüshənᵊl, -shnəl *also* -vəlˈyü-\ *adj* [*involution* + *-al*] : of or relating to an involutional or to involutional melancholia ⟨~ depression⟩ ⟨~ period⟩

²**involutional** \"\ *n* -S : one that suffers from involutional melancholia

involutional melancholia *or* **involutional psychosis** *n* : an agitated depression occurring at the time of the menopause or climacteric and usu. characterized by somatic and nihilistic delusions

involution form *n* : an irregular or atypical bacterium formed under unfavorable conditions (as in old cultures) and variously considered as a degenerating cell or as a specialized reproductive body

in·volve \ən'välv, |ȯlv *also* |ä(ü)v *or* |ȯv\ *vt* -ED/-ING/-S [ME *involven*, fr. L *involvere* to wrap, envelop, fr. *in-* ²in- + *volvere* to roll — more at VOLUBLE] **1** *archaic* : to enfold or envelop so as to encumber ⟨the number of difficulties in which this question is *involved* —Benjamin Jowett⟩ **2 a** : to draw in as a participant : ENGAGE, EMPLOY ⟨size of operations and . . . numbers of workmen *involved* —G.M.Trevelyan⟩ ⟨an organization . . . heavily *involved* in the nation's defense program —R.J.Cordiner⟩ ⟨kings were constantly *involved* in Continental affairs —G.G.Coulton⟩ ⟨he got *involved* in a lawsuit⟩ **b** : to oblige to become associated (as in an unpleasant situation) : EMBROIL, ENTANGLE, IMPLICATE ⟨led the English . . . to ~ India in the war —D.W.Brogan⟩ ⟨the controversies . . . moved on in all their ugliness to ~ others —John Mason Brown⟩ **c** : to occupy (oneself) absorbingly; *esp* : to commit (oneself) emotionally — usu. used with *in* or *with* ⟨we simply don't see enough of her characters . . . to feel personally *involved* in what they say or feel or do —Dan Wickenden⟩ ⟨she . . . never had the slightest intention of *involving* herself with him —Aurelia Levi⟩ **3 a** *archaic* : to enclose in a covering : WRAP ⟨the embryo is still farther *involved*, in two membranes —Oliver Goldsmith⟩ **b** : to surround as if with a wrapping : ENVELOP, SHROUD ⟨rights and privileges at the root . . . are discovered to be *involved* in doubt —B.N.Cardozo⟩ ⟨*involved* in a howling dancing crowd —Arthur Morrison⟩ **4 a** *archaic* : to wind, coil, or wreathe about : ENTWINE ⟨around me they *involved* a giddy dance —P.B.Shelley⟩ **b** : to relate closely : CONNECT, LINK ⟨the problem is closely *involved* with the management of pastures —Allan Fraser⟩ **5 a** : to have within or as part of itself : CONTAIN, INCLUDE ⟨tragic opera . . . must ~ convincing treatment of an elemental conflict —*Opera News*⟩ ⟨two late-arriving costumes . . . ~ magnificent brocaded coats covering deceptively casual sheaths —Lois Long⟩ ⟨a community program *involving* recreational, cultural, and economic . . . features —*Amer. Guide Series: N.C.*⟩ ⟨this course ~s a discussion of the trial rules of evidence —*Loyola Univ. Bulletin*⟩ **b** : to require as a necessary accompaniment : ENTAIL, IMPLY ⟨building their own roads . . . *involved* the construction of over 200 bridges —Joseph Millard⟩ ⟨diseases . . . which ~ long hospitalization —Cecile Starr⟩ ⟨changing those attitudes *involved* a job of mass education —Stanley Frank⟩ ⟨a mission which ~s much danger —T.B. Costain⟩ ⟨fusion ~s disparate materials . . . arranged so as to work together —*College English*⟩ ⟨insensitiveness ~s a meagerness of imagination in human relations —Albert Dasnoy⟩ **c** : to have an effect on : concern directly : AFFECT ⟨biological processes . . . like breathing and digesting, ~ the whole organism —H.J.Muller⟩ ⟨lacerations that ~ muscles or cause severe hemorrhage —H.G.Armstrong⟩ ⟨the problem . . . ~s their future —Harrison Smith⟩ ⟨work stoppages . . . *involved* more than 100 thousand workers —*Collier's Yr. Bk.*⟩ ⟨is never really three-dimensional, hence his conflicts do not ~ the reader —Frances Keene⟩ **6** : FILL ⟨a fire building so *involved* with heat, smoke and flame that immediate access to the interior is not possible —W.Y.Kimball⟩ ⟨drawings . . . *involved* with color become either water colors or pastels —Carlyle Burrows⟩ **7** : to engross or occupy fully : ABSORB ⟨*involved* in these imaginings she knew nothing of time —Thomas Hardy⟩ **syn** see INCLUDE

involved *adj* **1** *obs* : COVERT, SECRETIVE, UNDERHAND ⟨plain and direct, not crafty and ~ —Francis Bacon⟩ **2** *obs* : INVOLUTE, TWISTED **3 a** : COMPLICATED, INTRICATE ⟨~ poem⟩ ⟨~ sentence⟩ ⟨the music becomes more ~ —Warwick Braithwaite⟩ ⟨cup with sturdy base and ~ handle —W.E.Cox⟩ **b** : CONFUSED, TANGLED ⟨at his death . . . left his affairs dreadfully ~ —Jane Austen⟩ **4** : AFFECTED, IMPLICATED ⟨far . . . from an ~ understanding of normal human emotions —Robert Bingham⟩ ⟨dealing with . . . the most severely ~ patients —R.J.Thomas⟩ ⟨a heavily ~ fire floor —J.J.McCarthy⟩ **syn** see COMPLEX

in·volved·ly \-(l)v(ə)dlē\ *adv* : in an involved manner

in·volved·ness \-(l)vədnəs, -(l)v(d)n-\ *n* -ES : INVOLVEMENT

in·volve·ment \-(l)vmənt\ *n* -S **1** : the act or an instance of involving ⟨his ~ of others was inexcusable⟩ ⟨~ is uncalled for because there are no moral and spiritual values at stake —M.W.Straight⟩ ⟨there would be no drama in such a story . . . no ~ of the spectator's own inevitable deep divisions —R.P. Warren⟩ ⟨any action . . . which might be interpreted as ~ in the big power conflict —G.S.Bhargava⟩ **2** : the state or fact of being involved ⟨the fluid se[illegible]s' ~ in the world —Muriel Rukeyser⟩ ⟨increasing ~ in [illegible]ublic life —Herbert Read⟩ ⟨knowledge of . . . diverse peoples, our ~ with them in practical terms and our commitment to them in terms of brotherhood —J.R.Oppenheimer⟩; *specif* : inclusion in a damaged area ⟨rheumatic fever, with or without heart ~ —*Biol. Abstracts*⟩ ⟨the child's face escaped ~ in the injuries —*Springfield (Mass.) Daily News*⟩ **3** : an involved or entangled condition or situation : COMPLEXITY, CONFUSION ⟨further complaints of obscurity, ~ —John Foster⟩

in·volv·er \-(l)və(r)\ *n* -S : one that involves

invt *abbr* **1** [L *invenit*] he designed; he devised; he invented **2** inventory

in·vulnerability \(ˌ)in, ən+\ *n* : the quality or state of being invulnerable

in·vulnerable \(')in, ən+\ *adj* [L *invulnerabilis*, fr. *in-* ¹in- + *vulnerare* to wound + *-abilis* -able — more at VULNERABLE] **1** : incapable of being wounded, injured, or damaged : immune to or proof against assault ⟨an armadillo curls up to make himself ~⟩ : IMPREGNABLE ⟨gunners rake the beaches from ~ positions in overhanging cliffs⟩ **2** : immune to or proof against attack : INVINCIBLE, UNASSAILABLE ⟨~ dignity⟩ ⟨though he was now a partner, his position wa[illegible] not ~ —Hamilton Basso⟩ — **in·vulnerably** \"+\ *adv*

in·vulnerableness \"+\ *n* : INVULNERABILITY

inwale \'=ˌ=\ *n* [⁴*in* + *wale*] : a finishing strip of wood fastened inside the frame of an open boat and extending along the top strake to reinforce the gunwale — compare CLAMP 3

¹**in·wall** \ən+\ *vt* [alter. (influenced by E ²*in-*) of earlier *enwall*, fr. ¹*en-* + *wall*, n.] : to enclose with or as if with a wall

²**in·wall** \'in+ˌ-\ *n* [⁴*in* + *wall*] : an inner wall (as of a blast furnace)

¹**in·ward** \'inwərd, 'inwəd\ *adj* [ME *inward*, fr. OE *inweard*, *inneweard*, *innanweard*; OE *inweard* akin to MD *inwaert* inward, OHG *inwert*, all fr. a prehistoric WGmc compound whose first constituent is represented by OE *in*, *inn*, adv., in, and whose second constituent is represented by OE *-weard* -ward; OE *inneweard* fr. *inne* within (akin to OHG & ON *inni* within, Goth *inna*, all fr. a prehistoric Gmc word derived from the word represented by OE *in*, *inn*, adv., in) + *-weard* -ward; OE *innanweard* akin to ON *innanverthr* inward, both fr. a prehistoric NGmc-WGmc compound whose first constituent is represented by OE & ON *innan* within, from within, OHG *innan*, *innana* within, Goth *innana* (all fr. a prehistoric Gmc word derived from the word represented by OE *in*, *inn*, adv., in) and whose second constituent is represented by OE *-weard* -ward — more at IN (adv.), -WARD] **1 a** : situated on the inside : INNER, INTERNAL ⟨~ smile⟩ ⟨the whole body moves in response to some ~ rhythm —Ellen Glasgow⟩ **b** : produced from within : MUFFLED ⟨her words were ~ and indistinct —Ann Radcliffe⟩ **2 a** : of or relating to the mind or spirit : MENTAL, SPIRITUAL ⟨~ peace⟩ ⟨the scholar . . . lives an ~ and unmaterial life —P.E.More⟩ ⟨~ struggle of the heroes to find their own truth —Leslie Rees⟩ **b** : of or relating to religious faith : DEVOUT, PIOUS ⟨monks . . . free the soul from corporeality and make it ~ —José Ortega y Gasset⟩ **3 a** : of or relating to close acquaintance : FAMILIAR, INTIMATE ⟨intimate and ~, not outward from the child —R.L.Shayon⟩ ⟨more ~ with the Tudor-Stuart dramatists than any man . . . before or since —T.S.Eliot⟩ **b** *obs* : CONFIDENTIAL, SECRET ⟨what is ~ between us, let it pass —Shak.⟩ **4** *archaic* : of or relating to the homeland : DOMESTIC ⟨the dangers ~ they foresaw would be from the noblemen removed from the Queen's Council —Robert Norton⟩ **5** : directed toward the interior : INGOING ⟨~ slope of radiator grille —*Car Life*⟩ **syn** see INNER

²**inward** \"\ *or* **inwards** \"\ *adv* [ME *inward*, *inwardes*; ME *inward* fr. OE *inweard*, fr. *inweard*, adj.; ME *inwardes* fr. *inward* + *-es* (adverbially functioning gen. sing. ending of nouns) — more at INWARD (adj.), -'S] **1 a** : toward the inside : toward the center or interior ⟨the sides of the hole seemed to slope ~ until they met —Gwyn Thomas⟩ ⟨ships . . . that tried to run either ~ or outward through the blockade —C.S. Forester⟩; *specif* : HOMEWARD ⟨~ bound⟩ **b** *obs* : on the inside : INTERNALLY ⟨the maple seldom ~ sound —Edmund Spenser⟩ **2** : toward the inner being : into the mind or spirit ⟨his rich emotions began to turn ~ —H.S.Canby⟩

³**inward** \", *in sense 2 usu* 'inə(r)d\ *n* -S [ME, fr. OE *inneweard*, fr. *inneweard*, adj. — more at INWARD (adj.)] **1** : an inner being or nature : ESSENCE, SPIRIT ⟨make thine ~ like unto thine outward —John Payne⟩ — usu. used in pl. ⟨Jefferson puts the ~s of the issue in these terms —Archibald MacLeish⟩ **2** *or* **inwards** : an inside or interior part ⟨their forms fled to the dusky ~ of his mysterious box —Ross Lockridge⟩ ⟨saw him . . . glare down into the mysterious ~s of the engine —Wallace Stegner⟩; *specif* : INNARDS ⟨the gastroenterologist manages our nervous ~s —Greer Williams⟩ **3** *obs* : an intimate friend : CONFIDANT ⟨I was an ~ of his —Shak.⟩

⁴**in·ward** \'inˌwȯrd\ *n* [ML *inwarda*, *inguarda*, prob. fr. (assumed) OE *inweard*, fr. OE *in*, *inn*, adv., in + *weard* ward, action of guarding — more at IN (adv.), WARD (n.)] : bodyguard service rendered to a king by his sokemen when he visits their shire

inward dive *n* : a competitive diving category including dives in which the body from a backward standing takeoff position rotates forward around a transverse axis — compare BACK DIVE, FRONT DIVE, REVERSE DIVE, TWIST DIVE

inward light *n*, *usu cap I&L* : INNER LIGHT

in·ward·ly *adv* [ME, fr. OE *inweardlice* heartily, fervently, fr. *inweardlic* internal, fr. *inweard*, adj., inward + *-lic* -ly] **1** : in the innermost being : MENTALLY, SPIRITUALLY ⟨women's self-possession is an outward thing; ~ they flutter —Joseph Conrad⟩ ⟨read, mark, and ~ digest —C.L.Becker⟩ **2** *obs* : in a complete or private manner : FULLY, INTIMATELY ⟨acquainting me with the state of affairs, more ~ than I knew before —John Milton⟩ **3 a** : on the inside : INTERNALLY ⟨he had bled ~ —Daniel Defoe⟩ **b** : to oneself : INAUDIBLY, SECRETLY ⟨I'd have thought she'd ~ either cursed or spat —Kenneth Roberts⟩ **4** : toward the center or interior ⟨see ~ and represent the world of the imagination —Herbert Read⟩

in·ward·ness *n* -ES [¹*inward* + *-ness*] **1** : close acquaintance : FAMILIARITY, INTIMACY ⟨read his way into a certain ~ with Chaucer's idiom —John Speirs⟩ **2** : fundamental nature or meaning : ESSENCE, SIGNIFICANCE ⟨apprehending the real ~ of a plowman —C.D.Lewis⟩ ⟨could not grasp the ~ of the text —H.J.Laski⟩ ⟨far from . . . certain as to the true ~ of her violent dismissal —Joseph Conrad⟩ **3** : internal quality or substance ⟨became aware of the ~ of my body, of the blood moving in darkness —R.P.Warren⟩ **4 a** : preoccupation with one's own affairs or attitudes : INTROSPECTION, SUBJECTIVITY ⟨the sensitiveness of James's characters, their seeming ~ —Morris Roberts⟩ ⟨voluntary withdrawal . . . was to mean thereafter an ~ of corporate life —W.L.Sperry⟩ **b** : preoccupation with ethical or ideological values : SPIRITUALITY ⟨Socrates' ~, integrity, and inquisitiveness —H.R.Finch⟩

inwards *var of* INWARD

in·weave \(')in, ən+\ *or* **en·weave** \ən, (')en+\ *vt* [²*in-* or ¹*en-* + *weave*, v.] **1 a** : to weave in or together **b** : to decorate by weaving : INSERT, INTERLACE **c** : to mend or patch by reweaving **2** : to incorporate as if by weaving ⟨the vitality of experience which is *inwoven* with their thorniness —J.H. Hanford⟩

¹**inwick** \'=ˌ=\ *n* [⁴*in* + *wick*, n. (port in curling)] : a shot in curling in which a player's stone is made to carom off the inner edge of an intervening stone so as to knock away from the tee the stone nearest it — compare OUTWICK

²**inwick** \"\ *vi* : to make an inwick

inwind *var of* ENWIND

inwit \'=ˌ=\ *n* [ME, fr. *in*, prep. & adv. + *wit*, n.] : inward knowledge : CONSCIENCE, UNDERSTANDING ⟨acting from ~ —Ezra Pound⟩ ⟨spills his yarns with humor and delight or with an ~ of sadness —I.L.Salomon⟩

inwith \'=ˌ=\ *adj* (*or adv*) [ME, fr. *in*, prep. & adv. + *with*, prep.] *Scot* : INSIDE, BEN

inworn \'=ˌ=\ *adj* [²*in* + *worn*, past part. of *wear* (after *wear in*, v.)] : INGRAINED

in·wound \(')in, ən+\ *adj* [²*in* + *wound*, past part. of *wind* (after *wind in*, v.)] : INTERTWINED

in·woven \(')in, ən+\ *or* **en·woven** \ən, (')en+\ *adj* [fr. past part. of *inweave*] **1 a** : INTERWOVEN **b** : ENTWINED **2** : closely associated ⟨~ with the heath in his boyhood —Thomas Hardy⟩

inwrap *var of* ENWRAP

inwreathe *var of* ENWREATHE

in·wrought \(')in, ən+\ *or* **en·wrought** \ən, (')en+\ *adj* [*inwrought* fr. ²*in* + *wrought*, past part. of *work* (after *work in*, v.); *enwrought* alter. (influenced by ¹*en-*) of *inwrought*] **1 a** : having a decorative element worked or woven in : ORNAMENTED ⟨bonnet . . . with figures —John Milton⟩ **b** *archaic* : WORKED, EMBROIDERED ⟨by beauty's hand ~ —Erasmus Darwin⟩ **2** : worked in as a constituent : INTERWOVEN ⟨~ with the tale are some of the great secrets of philosophy —Marianne Moore⟩

in·ya·la \ən'yälə\ *n*, *pl* **inyala** [Zulu *inxala*] : NYALA 1

in·yo·ite \'in(ˌ)yōˌīt\ *n* -S [*Inyo* county, California, its locality + E *-ite*] : a mineral $Ca_2B_6O_{11}.13H_2O$ consisting of a hydrous calcium borate occurring in colorless monoclinic crystals (hardness 2, sp. gr. 2)

¹**io** *n* -S [L, interj., fr. Gk *iō*] *obs* : a shout of joy or triumph ⟨rocks, valleys, hills, with splitting ~s ring —John Dryden & Nathaniel Lee⟩ — often used interjectionally

²**io** \'ē(ˌ)ō\ *n* -S [Hawaiian] : a large hawk (*Buteo solitarius*) that is the only indigenous raptorial bird of Hawaii

IO *abbr* **1** information officer **2** in order **3** inspecting order **4** intelligence officer

Io *symbol* ionium

ioa *var of* IWA

iod *var of* YODH

iod- *or* **iodo-** *comb form* [F *iode* iodine] **1** : iodine ⟨*iod*hydrate⟩ ⟨*iodo*form⟩ **2 a** *now usu* **iodo-** : containing iodine in place of hydrogen — in names of organic compounds ⟨*iodo*acetophenone⟩ **b** *now usu* **iodo-** : containing iodine regarded as replacing hydroxyl or oxygen or as coordinated to a central atom — in names of inorganic acids and salts ⟨*iodo*argentate⟩ ⟨*iodo*bismuthate⟩ **c** : containing iodine as iodide sometimes replacing another element or group — in names of minerals and salts occurring as minerals ⟨*iodo*sulfate⟩

iod·amoeba \(ˌ)īˌōd, -ˌäd+\ *n, cap* [NL, fr. *iod-* + *amoeba*] **:** a genus of amoebas commensal in the intestine of man and other mammals and distinguished by uninucleate cysts containing a large glycogen vacuole that stains characteristically with iodine

¹io·date \ˈīəˌdāt\ *n* -s [F, fr. *iode* iodine + *-ate*] **:** a salt of iodic acid

²iodate \"\ *vt* -ED/-ING/-S [*iod-* + *-ate*, v. suffix] **:** to impregnate or treat with iodine — **io·da·tion** \ˌīəˈdāshən\ *n* -s

iodhydrin *var of* IODOHYDRIN

iod·ic \(ˈ)īˌädik\ *adj* [F *iodique*, fr. *iode* iodine + *-ique* -ic] **:** of, relating to, or containing iodine — used esp. of compounds in which this element is pentavalent

iodic acid *n* **:** a crystalline oxidizing solid HIO_3 formed by oxidation of iodine (as with fuming nitric acid)

iodic anhydride *n* **:** IODINE PENTOXIDE

io·dide \ˈīəˌdīd, -ˌdəd\ *n* -s [ISV *iod-* + *-ide*] **:** a binary compound of iodine usu. with a more electropositive element or radical **:** a salt or ester of hydriodic acid ⟨potassium ~⟩ ⟨ethyl ~⟩

iodimetry *var of* IODOMETRY

io·di·nate \ˈīədəˌnāt\ *vt* -ED/-ING/-S [*iodine* + *-ate*, v. suffix] **:** to treat or cause to combine with iodine or a compound of iodine **:** introduce iodine into (as an organic compound)

iodinated casein *n* **:** an iodine-containing preparation that is made from casein, resembles the thyroid hormone in physiological activity, and is used in animal feeds (as to increase milk production of cows)

io·di·na·tion \ˌīədəˈnāshən\ *n* -s **:** the process of iodinating

io·dine *also* **io·din** \ˈīəˌdīn *also* -ˌdən *or* -dᵊn *or* -ˌdēn\ *n* -s [F *iode* iodine (fr. Gk *ioeidēs* purple, violet colored, fr. *ion* violet + *-oeidēs* -oid) + E ²*-ine* or *-in* — more at VIOLET] **:** a nonmetallic univalent and polyvalent element belonging to the halogens that is obtained usu. as heavy shining blackish gray crystals subliming to a violet-colored irritating vapor, that occurs naturally only in combination in small quantities esp. in seawater, rocks, soils, and underground brines and in marine plants and animals, that is essential for the normal functioning of the thyroid gland of all vertebrates, that is usu. extracted from the ashes of seaweeds, from Chile saltpeter, or from oil-well brines, and that is used chiefly in medicine (as in antisepsis and in the treatment of cretinism and goiter), photography, and analysis — symbol *I*; see ELEMENT table

iodine bush *n* **:** a shrub (*Allenrolfia occidentalis*) of the family Chenopodiaceae with fleshy jointed stems, leaves resembling scales, and flowers in crowded spikes that grows in moist saline soils in the southwestern U.S. and is used for winter grazing — called also *burroweed, California greasewood, pickleweed*

iodine number *or* **iodine value** *n* **:** a measure of the unsaturation of a substance (as an oil or fat) expressed as the number of grams of iodine or equivalent halogen absorbed by 100 grams of the substance ⟨*the iodine numbers* of linseed oil, olive oil, and coconut oil are approximately 175–201, 77–91, and 8–9.5 respectively⟩

iodine 131 *n* **:** a heavy radioactive isotope of iodine having the mass number 131 and a half-life of 8 days that is produced in the fission of uranium or by bombardment of tellurium with neutrons and that is used esp. in the form of sodium radioiodide in the diagnosis of thyroid disease and the treatment of goiter — symbol I^{131} or ^{131}I; called also *radioiodine*

iodine pentoxide *n* **:** a white crystalline solid I_2O_5 formed by the oxidation of iodine or the dehydration of iodic acid and used to oxidize carbon monoxide quantitatively to carbon dioxide — called also *iodic anhydride*

iodine weed *n* **:** INKWEED 1

io·din·oph·i·lous \ˌīədəˈnäfələs\ *also* **io·din·o·phil** \ˌīəˈdinəˌfil\ *or* **io·din·o·phile** \-ˌfīl\ *or* **io·din·o·phil·ic** \ˌīəˌdinəˈfilik\ *adj* [*iodinophilous* fr. *iodine* + *-o-* + *-philous; iodinophil, iodinophile* fr. *iodine* + *-o-* + *-phile, -phil; iodinophilic* prob. fr. *iodinophil* + *-ic*] **:** taking up or coloring readily with iodine — used esp. of various starchy cell inclusions

io·dism \ˈīəˌdizəm\ *n* -s [*iod-* + *-ism*; prob. intended as trans. of G *jodkrankheit*] **:** an abnormal local and systemic condition resulting from overdosage with, prolonged use of, or sensitivity to iodine or iodine compounds

io·di·za·tion \ˌīədəˈzāshən, -ˌdīˈz-\ *n* -s **:** the process of iodizing

io·dize \ˈīəˌdīz\ *vt* -ED/-ING/-S [*iod-* + *-ize*] **:** to treat with iodine or an iodide ⟨recommended *iodized* salt as a preventive of thyroid trouble⟩

iodized oil *n* **:** a viscous oily liquid that has an odor like garlic, is made by treating a fatty vegetable oil (as poppy-seed oil) with iodine or hydriodic acid, and is used as a contrast medium in X-ray photography

io·do \īˈō(ˌ)dō, ˈīəˌdō\ *adj* [*iod-*] **:** containing iodine — used esp. of organic compounds; compare IOD- 2

iodo- — see IOD-

iodo·acetate \īˌōdō, īˌädō+\ *n* [ISV *iod-* + *acetate*] **:** a salt or ester of iodoacetic acid

iodo·acetic acid \"+ . . .-\ *n* [*iodoacetic* ISV *iod-* + *acetic*] **:** a crystalline acid CH_2I_2COOH made by reaction of chloroacetic acid and a metallic iodide and used in biochemical research esp. because of its inhibiting effect on many enzymes (as in glycolysis in muscle extracts)

iodo·behenate \īˌōdə, īˌädə+\ *n* [*iod-* + *behenate*] **:** a salt of iodobehenic acid

iodo·behenic acid \"+. . .-\ *n* [*iodobehenic* ISV *iod-* + *behenic* (in *behenic acid*)] **:** a solid mono-iodo derivative $C_{21}H_{42}ICOOH$ of behenic acid made by reaction of erucic acid and hydriodic acid

iodo·benzene \īˌōdə, īˌädə+\ *n* [ISV *iod-* + *benzene*] **:** a colorless liquid C_6H_5I made usu. from benzene by reaction with iodine and nitric acid — called also *phenyl iodide*

iodo·bromide \"+\ *n* **:** BROMOIODIDE

iodo·bromite \"+\ *n* -s [obs. G *iodobromit* (now *jodobromit*), fr. obs. G *iod-* (now *jod-*) + G *bromit* bromyrite, fr. *brom-* + *-it* -ite] **:** a mineral $Ag(Br,Cl,I)$ consisting of chloride, iodide, and bromide of silver that is isomorphous with cerargyrite and bromyrite

iodo·casein \"+\ *n* **:** IODINATED CASEIN

iodo·chloride \"+\ *n* **:** CHLOROIODIDE

iodo·ethane \īˌōdō, īˌädō+\ *n* **:** ETHYL IODIDE

iodo·form \īˈōdəˌfórm, īˈäd-\ *n* -s [ISV *iod-* + *-form* (as in *chloroform*)] **:** a yellow crystalline volatile compound CHI_3 that has a penetrating persistent odor, is made usu. by electrolysis of an alkaline solution of a metallic iodide in alcohol or acetone, and is sometimes used as an antiseptic dressing; tri-iodo-methane

iodo·gor·go·ic acid \īˌōdəˌgórˈgōik, īˌäd-\ *n* [*iodogorgoic* fr. *iod-* + *gorgo-* (fr. *gorgonin*) + *-ic*] **:** DIIODOTYROSINE

iodo·hy·drin \īˌōdəˈhīdrən, īˌäd-\ *also* **iod·hy·drin** \ˌīˌōdˈh-, ˌīˌäd-\ *n* -s [ISV *iod-* + *-hydrin*] **:** any of a class of iodine compounds analogous to the chlorohydrins

iodo·mer·cu·rate \īˌōdəˈmərkyərət, īˌäd-, -ˌrāt\ *also* **iodo·mer·cu·ri·ate** \-(ˌ)mərˈkyůrēət, -ēˌāt\ *n* -s [ISV *iod-* + *mercur-* or *mercuri-* + *-ate*] **:** any of a series of complex salts containing iodine and mercury in the anion

iodo·metric \"+\ *adj* [ISV *iodometry* + *-ic*] **:** of, relating to, or by means of iodometry — **iodo·metrically** \"+\ *adv*

io·dom·e·try \ˌīəˈdämə·trē\ *also* **io·dim·e·try** \-dim-\ *n* -ES [*iodometry* ISV *iod-* + *-metry*; *iodimetry* alter. (influenced by E *-i-*) of *iodometry*] **1 :** the volumetric determination of iodine usu. by titration with a standard solution of sodium thiosulfate using starch as indicator **2 :** a method of quantitative analysis involving the use of a standard solution of iodine or the liberation of iodine from an iodide

io·do·ni·um \ˌīəˈdōnēəm\ *n* -s [ISV *iod-* + *-onium*; orig. formed as G *iodonium*] **:** the univalent cation H_2I^+ derived from hydrogen iodide and known only in disubstituted form

¹iodo·phile \īˈōdəˌfīl, īˈäd-\ *or* **iodo·phil·ic** \ˌ=ˌ=ˈfilik\ *adj* [*iodophile* ISV *iod-* + *-phile*; *iodophilic* fr. *iodophile* + *-ic*] **:** staining in a characteristic manner with iodine — used esp. of starch-containing cells staining blue with iodine

²iodophile \"\ *n* -s **:** an iodophile cell or individual

iodo·phthalein \īˌōdə, īˌädə+\ *n* **:** a symmetrical tetraiodo derivative of phenolphthalein or its soluble blue-violet crystalline disodium salt $C_{19}H_8I_4O(ONa)COONa$ used to render the gall bladder opaque to X rays and to treat typhoid carriers

iodo·protein \"+\ *n* **:** an iodine-containing protein (as iodinated casein) — compare THYROPROTEIN

io·dop·sin \ˌīəˈdäpsən\ *n* -s [*iod-* (fr. Gk *ioeidēs* violet-colored + *ops-* (fr. Gk *opsis* sight) + *-in* — more at IODINE, -OPSIS] **:** a photosensitive violet pigment in the retinal cones of most animals that is similar to rhodopsin but more labile, that is formed from vitamin A_1, and that is important in daylight vision

iodo·pyr·a·cet \īˌōdəˈpirəˌset, īˌäd-\ *n* -s [d*iiodo-pyr*idone-N-*acet*ic acid] **:** a salt $C_8H_{19}I_2N_2O_3$ administered intravenously in aqueous solution as a contrast medium for radiography esp. of the urinary tract; the diethanolamine salt of 3,5-diiodo-4-pyridone-*N*-acetic acid — called also *diodone*

iodoso- *comb form* [ISV *iodos-* (fr. *iodous*) + *-o-*] **:** containing the univalent radical —IO consisting of one atom each of iodine and oxygen, esp. replacing hydrogen ⟨*iodoso*benzoic acid $C_6H_4(IO)COOH$⟩

io·do·so·benzene \ˌīəˈdō(ˌ)sō+\ *n* [ISV *iodoso-* + *benzene*] **:** an amorphous solid compound C_6H_5IO that explodes when heated and is formed by treating iodobenzene with chlorine and then with a caustic alkali

iodous \īˈōdəs, īˈäd-, ˈīəd-\ *adj* [ISV *iod-* + *-ous*] **:** relating to or containing iodine and esp. iodine with a valence of three ⟨~ acid HIO_2⟩

iodoxy- *comb form* [ISV *iod-* + *oxy-*] **:** containing the univalent radical —IO_2 of iodic acid, esp. replacing hydrogen ⟨*iodoxy*benzoic acid $C_6H_4(IO_2)COOH$⟩

io·doxy·benzene \ˌīˌädäksē+\ *n* [*iodoxy-* + *benzene*] **:** a crystalline compound $C_6H_5IO_2$ that explodes when heated and is obtained by disproportionation of iodosobenzene

iod·y·rite \īˈädəˌrīt\ *n* -s [*iod-* + arg*yr-* + *-ite*] **:** a yellowish or greenish hexagonal mineral AgI consisting of native silver iodide usu. occurring in thin plates

io·lite \ˈīəˌlīt\ *n* -s [G *iolith*, fr. *io-* (fr. Gk *ion* violet) + *-lith* -lite, -lith — more at VIOLET] **:** CORDIERITE

IOM *abbr* interoffice minute

io moth \ˈī(ˌ)ō-\ *n* [NL *io* (specific epithet of *Automeris io*), fr. L *Io*, mythical priestess of Argos who was loved by Zeus, fr. Gk *Iō*] **:** a large yellowish American moth (*Automeris io*) having a large ocellate spot on each hind wing and a larva covered with fascicles of spines that sting like nettles

ion \ˈīən *also* ˈīˌän\ *n* -s [Gk, neut. of *iōn*, pres. part. of *ienai* to go — more at ISSUE] **1 :** an atom or group of atoms when combined in a radical or molecule that carries a positive or negative electric charge as a result of having lost or gained one or more electrons and that may exist in solution usu. in combination with molecules of the solvent or out of solution, that may be formed during electrolysis and migrate to the electrode of opposite charge, or that may be formed in a gas and be capable of carrying an electric current through the gas — see ANION, CATION; compare HYDROGEN ION **2 :** a free electron or other charged subatomic particle

-ion *n suffix* -s [ME *-ioun, -ion, -iun*, fr. OF *-ion, -iun*, fr. L *-ion-, -io*] **1 a :** act or process ⟨acidulat*ion*⟩ ⟨rebell*ion*⟩ **b :** result of an act or process ⟨construct*ion*⟩ **2 a :** state or condition ⟨subject*ion*⟩ **b :** thing acted upon or conditioned ⟨ambit*ion*⟩

ion chamber *n* **:** IONIZATION CHAMBER

ion engine *n* **:** a jet engine deriving thrust from a stream of ionized particles

ion exchange *n* **:** a reversible interchange that takes place between ions of like charge and usu. between ions present on an insoluble solid and ions present in a solution surrounding the solid and that may occur naturally or be applied for various purposes — see ANION EXCHANGE, CATION EXCHANGE

ion exchanger *n* **1 :** a solid agent (as a zeolite or a synthetic resin) used in ion exchange — compare ANION EXCHANGER, CATION EXCHANGER **2 :** an apparatus or piece of equipment for effecting ion exchange

ion-exchange resin *n* **:** an insoluble material of high molecular weight that contains either acidic groups for exchanging cations or basic groups for exchanging anions and that may be used in medicine (as for reducing the sodium content of the body or the acidity of the stomach) and in ion exclusion as well as in the usual ion-exchange processes

ion exclusion *n* **:** a process of separating materials in solution by means of an ion-exchange resin that excludes highly ionized particles and takes up slightly ionized particles or particles not ionized

¹Io·ni·an \īˈōnēən\ *n* -s *usu cap* [L *ionius*, adj. + E *-an*, n. suffix] **1 :** a native or inhabitant of Ionia; *esp* **:** one of the Greek people descended from an early group of Hellenic invaders of Greece **2 :** a member of a school of philosophers of ancient Greece consisting chiefly of the Milesians but including also the philosophers Heraclitus and Xenophanes

²ionian \(ˈ)ˌ=ˌ=\ *adj, usu cap* [L *ionius* Ionian (fr. *Ionia*, ancient district including the south central part of the west coast of Asia Minor and several nearby Aegean islands such as Chios and Samos, fr. Gk *Iōnia*, fr. *Iōn*, n., Ionian + *-ia*) + E *-an*, adj. suffix] **1 a :** of, relating to, or characteristic of Ionia **b :** of, relating to, or characteristic of the people of Ionia **2 :** of or relating to the Ionian group of Greek philosophers ⟨resumed the *Ionian* tradition of scientific research —Benjamin Farrington⟩

ionian mode *n, usu cap I* **1 :** the Greek hypophrygian mode **2 :** an authentic ecclesiastical mode consisting of a pentachord and an upper conjunct tetrachord represented on the white keys of the piano by an ascending diatonic scale from C to C — called also *Ionic mode*; see MODE illustration

¹ion·ic \(ˈ)īˌänik, -nēk\ *adj* [L & MF; MF *ionique*, fr. L *ionicus*, fr. Gk *iōnikos*, fr. *Iōnia* Ionia + *-ikos* -ic] **1** *usu cap* **:** IONIAN **2** *usu cap* **:** belonging to or resembling the Ionic order of architecture that is lighter and more graceful than Doric and is characterized esp. by the spiral volutes of its capital — see CAPITAL illustration **3 :** of, relating to, or consisting of ionics

²ionic \"\ *n* -s **1** *cap* **:** a dialect of ancient Greek used in Ionia that was the vehicle of an important body of literature **2** [LL *ionicus*, fr. L *ionicus*, adj.] **a :** a foot of verse that consists either of (1) two long and two short syllables or (2) two short and two long syllables — called also respectively (1) *major ionic* and (2) *minor ionic* **b :** a verse or meter consisting of ionics

³ionic \"\ *adj* [ISV *ion* + *-ic*] **1 :** of, relating to, existing in the form of, or characterized by ions ⟨~ charge⟩ ⟨~ hydrogen⟩ ⟨~ crystals⟩ **2 :** operated by, utilizing, or taking place by means of ions ⟨~ loudspeaker⟩ ⟨~ conduction⟩

Ionic order: Greek, *A*; Roman, *B*

ionic alphabet *n, usu cap I* [¹*ionic*] **:** a variety of the eastern form of the ancient Greek alphabet having 24 letters in its developed form and officially accepted late in the 5th cent. B.C. at Athens from which its use in time extended throughout the Greek-speaking world

ionic bond *n* [³*ionic*] **:** ELECTROVALENT BOND

ionic displacement *n* [¹*ionic*] **:** the occurrence in iambic meter of a pyrrhic foot followed or sometimes preceded by a spondaic foot that together create an ionic cadence (as in the third and fourth feet in Shakespeare's line "when to the sessions of sweet silent thought" óó|óó|oó|óó|oó)

ion·i·cism \īˈänəˌsizəm\ *n* -s *usu cap* [¹*ionic* + *-ism*] **1 :** an Ionic feature; *esp* **:** a characteristic feature of the Ionic dialect — called also *Ionism* **2 :** the quality or state of being Ionic

ion·i·cize \-ˌsīz\ *vt* -ED/-ING/-S *often cap* [¹*ionic* + *-ize*] **:** to make Ionic

ionic mode *n, usu cap I* **:** IONIAN MODE

ionic valence *n* [³*ionic*] **:** ELECTROVALENCE

io·nism \ˈīəˌnizəm\ *n* -s *usu cap* [prob. fr. L *Iones* Ionians (fr. Gk *Iōnes*, pl. of *Iōn* Ionian) + E *-ism*] **:** IONICISM

io·ni·um \īˈōnēəm\ *n* -s [*ion* + *-ium*; so called fr. its ionizing action] **:** a naturally occurring radioactive isotope of thorium having mass 230 — symbol Th^{230} or *Io*; see URANIUM SERIES

ion·iza·tion \ˌīənəˈzāshən, -ˌnīˈz-\ *n* -s [ISV ²*ionize* + *-ation*] **:** the process of ionizing or the state of being ionized — compare DISSOCIATION

ionization chamber *n* **:** a partially evacuated tube provided with electrodes so that its conductivity due to the ionization of the residual gas reveals the presence of ionizing radiation (as X rays or beta rays)

ionization constant *n* **:** a constant that depends upon the equilibrium between the ions and the molecules that are not ionized in a solution or liquid — symbol *K*; called also *dissociation constant*

ionization current *n* **:** an electric current produced in an ionized gas subjected to an electric field

ionization gauge *n* **:** a low-pressure vacuum gauge in which the pressure is indicated by the ionization current between two specified electrodes at a prescribed voltage

ionization potential *n* **:** the potential difference corresponding to the energy in electron volts that is just sufficient to ionize a gas molecule

¹io·nize \ˈīəˌnīz\ *vt* -ED/-ING/-S *often cap* [Gk *iōnizein* to speak Ionic, fr. *Iōn*, n., Ionian + *-izein* -ize] **:** IONICIZE

²ion·ize \"\ *vb* -ED/-ING/-S [ISV *ion* + *-ize*] *vt* **:** to convert wholly or partly into ions ⟨a charged particle . . . ~s the air molecules with which it collides —G.W.Gray b. 1886⟩ ⟨*ionized* calcium⟩ ~ *vi* **:** to become converted wholly or partly into ions ⟨a salt ~s in water⟩

ion·o·gen \īˈänəjən, -ˌjen\ *n* -s [ISV *ion* + *-o-* + *-gen*] **1 :** a compound capable of forming ions **:** ELECTROLYTE 2 **2 :** an atom or group capable of being ionized

ion·o·gen·ic \īˌänəˈjenik\ *adj* [*ion* + *-o-* + *-genic*] **:** capable of ionizing

ion·og·ra·phy \ˌīəˈnägrəfē\ *n* -ES [*ion* + *-o-* + *-graphy*] **:** electrochromatography involving the migration of ions (as on wet filter paper)

Io·none \ˈīəˌnōn\ *trademark* — used for either of two oily liquid isomeric ketones $C_{13}H_{20}O$ that have a strong violet odor, are found esp. in the essential oil of an Australian shrub (*Boronia megastigma*) but are usu. obtained from citral, and are used esp. in perfumes

ion·o·pho·re·sis \īˌänəfəˈrēsəs\ *n, pl* **ionophore·ses** \-ēˌsēz\ [NL, fr. *ion* (fr. E) + *-o-* + *-phoresis*] **:** ELECTROPHORESIS; *esp* **:** the movement of relatively small ions — **ion·o·pho·ret·ic** \īˌänəfəˈred·ik\ *adj*

ion·o·sphere \īˈänə+ˌ-\ *n* [*ion* + *-o-* + *-sphere*] **:** the part of the earth's atmosphere beginning at an altitude of about 25 miles and extending outward 250 miles or more, containing free electrically charged particles by means of which radio waves are transmitted to great distances around the earth, and consisting of several regions within which occur one or more layers that vary in height and ionization with time of day, season, and the solar cycle, the gases in this part of the earth's atmosphere being ionized by ultraviolet rays from the sun and to a lesser extent by charged particles from the sun — see D REGION, E REGION, F REGION — **ion·o·spher·ic** \īˌänəˈsfirik, -fer-\ *adj*

io·not·ro·py \ˌīəˈnä·trəpē\ *n* -ES [*ion* + *-o-* + *-tropy*] **:** TAUTOMERISM

ion·oxalis \ˌīən+\ *n, cap* [NL, fr. Gk *ion* violet + NL *Oxalis*] **:** a genus of chiefly tropical American herbs (family Oxalidaceae)

ions *pl of* ION

-ions *pl of* -ION

ionto- *comb form* [NL, fr. Gk *iont-, iōn*, pres. part. of *ienai* to go — more at ISSUE] **:** ion ⟨*ionto*quantimeter⟩ ⟨*ionto*therapy⟩

ion·to·pho·re·sis \īˌäntəfəˈrēsəs\ *n, pl* **iontophore·ses** \-ēˌsēz\ [NL, fr. *ionto-* + *-phoresis*] **1 :** ELECTROPHORESIS **2 :** the introduction of drugs through intact skin by the transfer of ions effected by means of the application of a direct electric current — **ion·to·pho·ret·ic** \īˌäntəfəˈred·ik\ *adj*

ion trap *n* **:** a device that prevents the formation of a discolored spot on a television screen by diverting the negative ions from the cathode that would cause it

io·ra \īˈōrə, ēˈō-\ *n* -s [origin unknown] **:** any of several small bright-colored Asiatic songbirds that are related to the bulbuls and that constitute a genus (*Aegithina*)

ios *pl of* IO

io·ta \īˈōd·ə, -ōtə, *in sense 1 sometimes* ēˈō-\ *n* -s [L *iota, jota*, fr. Gk *iōta* — more at JOT] **1 :** the ninth and smallest letter of the Greek alphabet — symbol Ι or ι; see ALPHABET table **2 :** an infinitesimal amount **:** a very small degree **:** JOT ⟨of statesmanship he had not an ~ —S.H.Adams⟩ ⟨he had used a lance . . . nicely, to extract the last ~ of pain —F.V.W.Mason⟩

iota adscript *n* **:** the unpronounced iota of a Greek improper diphthong when written on the line after the long vowel — used in standard printing practice only when the long vowel is a capital

io·ta·cism \-ˌsizəm\ *n* -s [LL *iotacismus*, fr. Gk *iōtakismos*, fr. *iōta* iota] **:** excessive use of the letter iota or I or a too frequent repetition of its sound; *specif* **:** the use in modern Greek of the sound of iota (Eng. *ē* in *bē*) in speaking words written with other vowels or diphthongs (as *ē, y, ei, oi*) — compare ITACISM

iota subscript *n* **:** the unpronounced iota of a Greek improper diphthong when written small beneath the preceding long vowel [as ᾳ (*āi*), ῃ (*ēi*), ῳ (*ōi*)]

I O U \ˌī(ˌ)ōˈyü\ *n* -s [fr. the pronunciation of *I owe you*] **:** a paper that has on it the letters IOU and a signature as an acknowledgment of debt, that names a sum of money, and that is sometimes used as the equivalent of a promissory note

-ious *adj suffix* [ME, partly fr. OF *-ious, -ios, -ieus, -ieux*, fr. L *-iosus*, fr. *-i-* (penultimate vowel in nouns such as *religio* religion, *malitia* malice, *species* species, appearance, *spatium* space) + *-osus* -ose, and partly fr. L *-ius* (final portion of the nom. sing. masc. form of adjectives such as *meritorius* that brings in money)] **:** -OUS ⟨edac*ious*⟩

¹Io·wa *also* **Io·way** \ˈīəwə, -ˌwā\ *n, pl* **iowa** *or* **iowas** *usu cap* [Dakota *Ayuhwa*, lit., sleepy ones] **1 a :** a Siouan people of Iowa, Minnesota, and Missouri **b :** a member of such people **2 :** a dialect of the Chiwere language

²io·wa \ˈīəwə, ÷ˈīəˌwā, *by outsiders sometimes* īˈōə\ *adj, usu cap* [*Iowa*, state in the north central U. S., fr. ¹*iowa*] **:** of or from the state of Iowa ⟨an *Iowa* cornfield⟩ **:** of the kind or style prevalent in Iowa **:** IOWAN

iowa crab *or* **iowa crab apple** *n, usu cap I* [²*iowa*] **:** a wild crab apple (*Malus ioensis*) of the western U. S. with fragrant pink flowers — called also *western crab apple*

¹io·wan \ˈīəwən\ *adj, usu cap* [*Iowa*, state in the north central U. S. + E *-an*, adj. suffix] **1 :** of, relating to, or characteristic of the state of Iowa **2 :** of, relating to, or characteristic of the people of Iowa

²iowan \"\ *n* -s *cap* [*Iowa*, state in the north central U. S. + E *-an*, n. suffix] **1 :** a native or resident of Iowa **2 a :** a substage of the Wisconsin glacial stage **b :** the drift of such substage

IP *abbr* **1** ice point **2** India paper **3** initial point **4** innings pitched **5** installment paid **6** intermediate pressure

ipa \ˈēpə\ *n* -s *usu cap* [AmerSp, of AmerInd origin] **1 :** a people of the Vilela group **2 :** a member of the Ipa people

IPA \ˌī(ˌ)pēˈā\ *n* -s [International Phonetic Alphabet] **:** an alphabet designed to represent each human speech sound with a unique symbol

IPA *abbr* **1** including particular average **2** intermediate power amplifier

IPC *n* -s [isopropyl N-phenylcarbamate] **:** a crystalline herbicide $C_6H_5NHCOOCH(CH_3)_2$ that is poisonous to grasses but not to broad-leaved plants; isopropyl carbanilate

IPD *abbr* individual package delivery

ip·e·cac \ˈipəˌkak, ˈipē-\ *or* **ipe·cacua·nha** \ˌ=ˌ=ˌkakyəˈwan(y)ə, ēˌpakəˈkwanyə\ *n* -s [*ipecac* short for *ipecacuanha*, fr. Pg, fr. Tupi *ipekaaguéne*] **1 :** a tropical So. American creeping plant (*Cephaelis ipecacuanha*) with drooping flowers **2 a :** the dried rhizome and roots of ipecac formerly used as a medicine and now valued as the source of emetine — called also *Brazilian ipecac* **b :** the dried roots of any of several plants used like ipecac roots — see BASTARD IPECAC, WHITE IPECAC

INSECTS

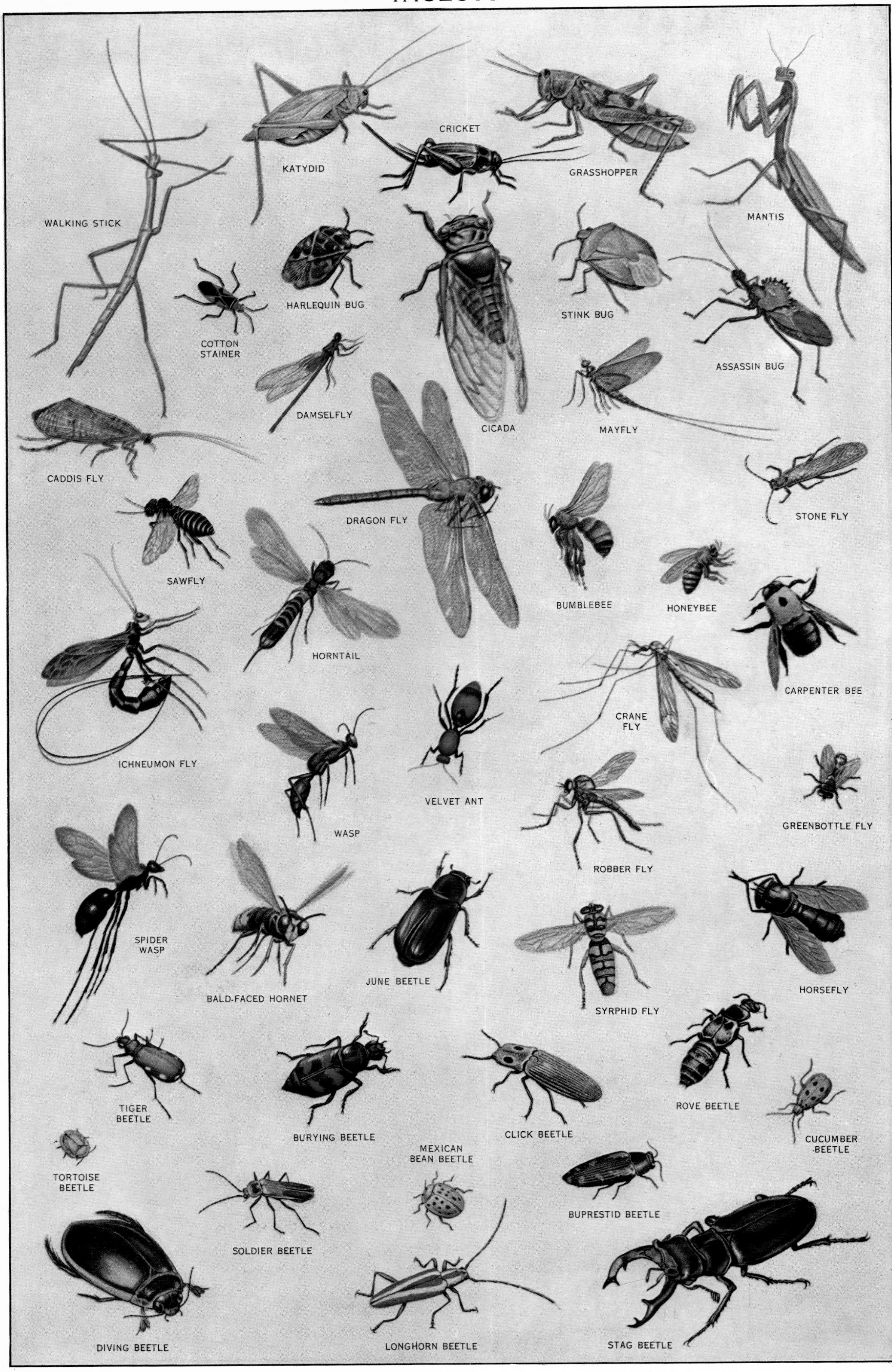

WALKING STICK
KATYDID
CRICKET
GRASSHOPPER
MANTIS
COTTON STAINER
HARLEQUIN BUG
CICADA
STINK BUG
ASSASSIN BUG
DAMSELFLY
MAYFLY
CADDIS FLY
DRAGON FLY
STONE FLY
SAWFLY
BUMBLEBEE
HONEYBEE
HORNTAIL
CARPENTER BEE
ICHNEUMON FLY
CRANE FLY
VELVET ANT
WASP
GREENBOTTLE FLY
ROBBER FLY
SPIDER WASP
BALD-FACED HORNET
JUNE BEETLE
SYRPHID FLY
HORSEFLY
TIGER BEETLE
BURYING BEETLE
CLICK BEETLE
ROVE BEETLE
CUCUMBER BEETLE
TORTOISE BEETLE
MEXICAN BEAN BEETLE
BUPRESTID BEETLE
SOLDIER BEETLE
DIVING BEETLE
LONGHORN BEETLE
STAG BEETLE

ipecac spurge *n* **:** a spurge (*Euphorbia ipecacuanhae*) of the eastern U. S. with a root that is emetic and purgative — called also *American white ipecac*

ip·e·cac·u·a·nhic \¦ipə,kakyə¦wan(y)ik, ¦ipē,-\ *adj* **:** of or relating to ipecac

ipf *abbr* imperfect

iph·i·ge·nia \,ifəjə'nīə\ *n, cap* [NL, fr. L *Iphigenia*, daughter of Agamemnon, fr. Gk *Iphigeneia*] **:** a genus of tropical bivalve mollusks related to *Donax*

IPI *abbr* [L *in partibus infidelium*] in the regions of unbelievers

[1]ip·id \'ipəd\ *adj* [NL *Ipidae*] **:** of or relating to the Scolytidae

[2]ipid \"\ *n* -s [NL *Ipidae*] **:** a member of the Scolytidae

ip·i·dae \'ipə,dē\ [NL, fr. *Ip-*, *Ips*, type genus + *-idae*] *syn of* SCOLYTIDAE

ipil \'ēpəl\ *or* **ifil** \'ēfəl\ *n* -s [Sp *ipil*, fr. Tag] **1 :** a Philippine and Pacific island tree (*Intsia bijuga*) yielding a valuable brown dye and having a very hard and durable dark wood **2 :** the wood of the ipil

ipil-ipil \,ēpə'lēpəl\ *n* -s [Tag *ipil ipil*] **:** a tropical leguminous shrub (*Leucaena glauca*) used esp. in the Philippines as a means of controlling various undesirable grasses in pastures and rangelands

ipin \(')ē¦pin, -pēn\ *adj, usu cap* [fr. *Ipin*, city in south central China] **:** of or from the city of Ipin, China **:** of the kind or style prevalent in Ipin

ip·i·ti \'ipəd·ē\ *n* -s [Xhosa & Zulu *i puti*] **:** BLUE DUIKER

ip·i·u·tak \,ipē'yü,tak\ *adj, usu cap* [*Ipiutak*, locality near Point Hope, northwest Alaska, where remains of the culture were discovered] **:** of or relating to an Eskimo culture in western Alaska of about A.D.100–600 characterized by ivory carvings, finely chipped stone implements resembling Siberian artifacts, and villages of semiunderground earth lodges

IPM *abbr, often not cap* inches per minute

ip·o·moea \,ipə'mēə\ *n* [NL, fr. Gk *ip-*, *ips* worm + NL *-omoea* (fr. Gk *homoios* like); fr. the twining habit of the plants — more at HOME-] **1** *cap* **:** a genus of herbaceous vines (family Convolvulaceae) having showy campanulate or funnelform flowers with capitate stigmas — see MORNING GLORY, SWEET POTATO **2** *also* **ip·o·mea** \"\ -s **:** a plant or flower of the genus *Ipomoea* **3** *usu* **ipomea** -s **:** the dried root of a scammony (*Ipomoea orizabensis*)

IPP *abbr* India paper proofs

ip·pi–ap·pa \,ipē'apə\ *n* -s [by alter.] **:** JIPIJAPA

IPR *abbr, often not cap* inches per revolution

ips \'ips\ [NL *Ip-*, *Ips*, fr. Gk *ip-*, *ips* woodworm] *syn of* SCOLYTUS

IPS *abbr* **1** *often not cap* inches per second **2** iron pipe size

ip·se dix·it \,ipsē'diksət\ *n, pl* **ipse dixits** [L, lit., he himself said it, trans. of Gk (Dor) *autos epha;* fr. the use of this expression by the Pythagoreans in reference to statements made by Pythagoras himself] **:** an assertion made on authority but not proved **:** DICTUM ⟨has had a good many followers ready to accept his *ipse dixit* —D.W.Hering⟩

ip·se·dix·it·ism \-sə̇d·,izəm\ *n* -s **:** dogmatic assertion or assertiveness ⟨denounces all appeals to a moral faculty as sheer ~ —James Martineau⟩

ip·se·ity \ip'sēəd·ē\ *n* -ES *sometimes cap* [L *ipse* self, himself + E *-ity*] **:** individual identity **:** SELFHOOD ⟨those heavenly moments . . . when a sense of the divine ~ invades me—L.P. Smith⟩

ip·si·lateral *also* **ip·se·lateral** \¦ipsē, -sə̇+\ *or* **ip·so·lateral** \-(,)sō+\ *adj* [ISV *ipsi-*, *ipse-*, *ipso-* (fr. L *ipse*) + *lateral*] **:** situated or appearing on or affecting the same side of the body — compare CONTRALATERAL — **ip·si·laterally** \"+\ *adv*

ip·so fac·to \¦ip(,)sō'fak(,)tō\ *adv* [NL] **:** by the fact or act itself **:** as the result of the mere act or fact **:** by the very nature of the case ⟨does one, *ipso facto*, become a censor when he warns against such censorship —H.C.Gardiner⟩ ⟨training in speech . . . is *ipso facto* training in personality —A.T.Weaver⟩

ipso ju·re \-'jůrē, -'yů-\ *adv* [L] **:** by the law itself **:** by operation of law

ips·wich \'ip(,)swich, -,swēch\ *adj, usu cap* [fr. *Ipswich*, county borough of East Suffolk, England] **:** of or from the county borough of Ipswich, England **:** of the kind or style prevalent in Ipswich

ipswich sparrow *n, usu cap I* [fr. *Ipswich*, town in northeastern Massachusetts where it was observed] **:** a sparrow (*Passerculus princeps*) similar to the Savannah sparrow but larger and paler that breeds on Sable island off the coast of Nova Scotia and migrates south along the Atlantic coast to Georgia

IPT *abbr* indexed, paged, and titled

ipu·ri·ná \¦ēpərē¦nä\ *n, pl* **ipuriná** *or* **ipurinás** *usu cap* **1 a :** an Arawakan people of northwestern Brazil **b :** a member of such people **2 :** the language of the Ipuriná people

ipv *abbr* **1** imperative **2** improve

IPW *abbr* interrogation prisoner of war

IQ \(')ī¦kyü\ *abbr or n* -s intelligence quotient

IQ *abbr, often not cap* [L *idem quod*] the same as

IQED *abbr* [L *id quod erat demonstrandum*] that which was to be proved

iqui·to \ē'kēd·(,)ō\ *n, pl* **iquito** *or* **iquitos** *usu cap* [AmerSp] **1 :** a Zaparo people of the upper Amazon **2 :** a member of the Iquito people

ir- — see IN-

IR *abbr* **1** infrared **2** inland revenue; internal revenue **3** intelligence ratio **4** interim report **5** interrogator-responder **6** insoluble residue

Ir *symbol* iridium

ira·cund \'īrə,kənd\ *adj* [L *iracundus*, fr. *ira* anger — more at IRE] *archaic* **:** easily provoked to anger **:** IRASCIBLE

ira·cun·di·ty \,īrə'kəndəd·ē\ *n* -ES *archaic* **:** the quality or state of being iracund **:** ANGER

ira·de \ē'rädē\ *n* -s [Turk, lit., will, wish, fr. Ar *irādah*] **:** a decree of a Muhammadan ruler

i rail *n, cap I* **:** an I-shaped rail

iran \(')i¦ran, -raa(ə)n *sometimes* (')ī¦- *or* (')ē¦-; (')i¦rän, (')ē¦-, -rån\ *adj, usu cap* [fr. *Iran*, country in southwestern Asia] **:** of or from Iran **:** of the kind or style prevalent in Iran **:** IRANIAN, PERSIAN

[1]ira·ni \=ˈ=ē, -i\ *n* -s *cap* [Per *īrānī*, fr. *īrān* Iran] **:** IRANIAN 1

[2]irani \"\ *adj, usu cap* **:** IRANIAN, PERSIAN

[1]ira·ni·an \i'rānēən, *sometimes* -ran- *or* -raan- *or* -rän- *or* (')ī¦rā- *or* (')ī¦ra(a)-\ *adj, usu cap* [*Iran* + E *-ian*] **:** of or relating to Iran or the Iranians or their speech

[2]iranian \"\ *n* -s *cap* **1 :** a native or inhabitant of Iran — see PERSIAN 1 **2 :** a branch of the Indo-European family of languages that includes Avestan, Old Persian, Median, Scythian, Middle Iranian, and Persian — see INDO-EUROPEAN LANGUAGES table

iran·ic \i'ranik, (')ī¦r-\ *adj, usu cap* [*Iran* + E *-ic*] **:** IRANIAN

irano- *comb form, usu cap* [*Iran*] **:** Iranian and ⟨*Irano*-British⟩

[1]irano–afghan \i¦ra(,)nō, -rä-, -rå-, ī¦ra-, ē¦rä-, ē¦rå-+\ *adj, usu cap I&A* [*Irano-* + *Afghan*] **:** of, relating to, or characteristic of the people that constitute the chief element in the population of the upland territory extending from western Iran to northern India

[2]irano–afghan \"\ *n, cap I&A* **:** one of the Irano-Afghan people

iraq *also* **irak** \(')i¦räk, -rak,-råk\ *adj, usu cap* [fr. *Iraq* (*Irak*), country in southwestern Asia] **:** of or from Iraq ⟨*Iraq* oil fields⟩ **:** of the kind or style prevalent in Iraq

[1]iraqi *also* **iraki** \=ˈ=ē, -i\ *n* -s *cap* [Ar *ʻirāqīy*, fr. *ʻIrāq* Iraq] **1 :** a native or resident of Iraq **2 :** the dialect of Modern Arabic spoken in Iraq

[2]iraqi *also* **iraki** \"\ *adj, usu cap* **1 a :** of, relating to, or characteristic of Iraq **b :** of, relating to, or characteristic of the Iraqis **2 :** of, relating to, or characteristic of the Iraqi language

iraq·i·an *also* **irak·i·an** \-ēən\ *n or adj, usu cap* [*Iraq* (*Irak*) + E *-ian*] **:** IRAQI

iras·ci·bil·i·ty \ə̇,rasə'biləd·ē, (,)ī,ras-, -raas-, -lətē, -i\ *n* -ES [F *irascibilité*, fr. MF, fr. *irascible* + *-ité* -ity] **:** the quality or state of being irascible **:** proneness to anger **:** IRASCIBLENESS

iras·ci·ble \ə̇'rasəbəl, (')ī¦r-, -raas-\ *adj* [MF, fr. LL *irascibilis*, fr. L *irasci* to be angry (fr. *ira* anger) + *-ibilis* -ible — more at IRE] **1 :** marked by hot temper and resentful anger **:** having or showing a disposition to be easily incensed ⟨his proud, ~ individualism that went out of its way to pick a quarrel —V. L.Parrington⟩ ⟨became so ~ that within six months he lost his wife and half of his office staff —Herman Wouk⟩ **2 a :** moved by desire for that which is attained only with difficulty or danger **b :** stirred by combative emotions (as anger, pride, courage, fear) — opposed to *concupiscible*

syn CHOLERIC, SPLENETIC, CROSS, TESTY, CRANKY, TOUCHY, TECHY, TETCHY: IRASCIBLE stresses a tendency to fiery anger ⟨the *irascible* but kindhearted deity who indulges in copious curses to ease his feelings —M.R.Cohen⟩ CHOLERIC may convey suggestions of impatience and unreasonableness, in addition to indicating hot temper ⟨that fiery formula which has sprung from the lips of so many *choleric* old gentlemen . . . "I shall write to *The Times*" —Max Beerbohm⟩ SPLENETIC may suggest a strong inclination to quick anger coupled with moroseness, sullenness, malice, vindictiveness, or crusty peevishness ⟨a very queer character, by turns *splenetic* and benevolent —*Times Lit. Supp.*⟩ ⟨that *splenetic* temper, which seems to grudge brightness to the flames of hell —W.S.Landor⟩ CROSS is likely to indicate a snappish grumpy irritability ⟨I am determined I will not be *cross;* it is not a little matter that puts me out of temper —Jane Austen⟩ TESTY may indicate quick anger inspiring sharp acid comment and inspired by relatively trivial irritations ⟨he raged . . . he was ever more autocratic, more *testy* —Sinclair Lewis⟩ ⟨the *testy* major was in fume to find no hunter standing waiting —John Masefield⟩ CRANKY may indicate an irritable temper blended with fretfulness or capriciousness ⟨how *cranky* you are . . . don't be so absurd as . . . to act like a child —Anthony Trollope⟩ ⟨she's going to have a kid, and of course women . . . get *cranky* when they're that way —Sinclair Lewis⟩ TOUCHY, TETCHY, and TECHY, the first now being the most common, indicate an over sensitiveness making for irritability, defensiveness, likelihood of taking offense or being hurt ⟨*techy* and impatient of contradiction, sore with wounded pride —W.H.Hazlitt⟩ ⟨a man who had grown too *touchy* to make judicious decisions —*Time*⟩

iras·ci·ble·ness *n* -ES **:** the quality or state of being irascible

iras·ci·bly \-blē,-bli\ *adv* **:** in an irascible manner

irate \(')ī¦rāt, *usu* -ād·+V\ *adj, sometimes* -ER/-EST [L *iratus*, fr. *ira* anger + *-atus* -ate — more at IRE] **1 :** roused to or given to ire **:** feeling and showing a high degree of anger **:** WRATHFUL, INCENSED ⟨a neighborhood ~ over continued acts of vandalism⟩ ⟨never had enough money to meet his bills, and he was not used to dodging ~ grocers —Sinclair Lewis⟩ ⟨~ against the practice of usury —E.L.Surtz⟩ **2 :** arising from anger ⟨~ words⟩ ⟨an ~ glare⟩ ⟨started to splutter an ~ objection —W.H.Wright⟩ **syn** see ANGRY

irate·ly *adv* **:** in an irate manner **:** ANGRILY

irate·ness *n* -ES **:** the quality or state of being irate

ira·va \i'rävə\ *n, pl* **irava** *or* **iravas** *cap* [native name in India] **1 :** an untouchable Hindu caste of the Malabar coast region of southwest India **2 :** a member of the Irava caste

ira·ya \i'räyə, -rīə\ *n, pl* **iraya** *or* **irayas** *usu cap* [Sp, fr. Iraya, person, human being] **1 a :** a predominantly pagan people inhabiting the mountainous interior of northern Mindoro in the Philippines **b :** a member of such people **2 :** the Austronesian language of the Iraya people

ir·bis \(,)ər'bēs, ir'-\ *n, pl* **irbis** *or* **irbises** [Russ, fr. Mongol *irbis* & Kalmuck *irwṣ*] **:** SNOW LEOPARD

IRBM *abbr or n* -s **:** an intermediate range ballistic missile

IRC *abbr* irregular route carrier

ir drop \(')ī¦är-\ *n, usu cap I&R* [*I*, symbol for effective current in amperes + *R*, symbol for resistance in ohms] **:** the voltage drop due to energy losses in a resistor

[1]ire \'ī(ə)r, 'īə\ *n* -s [ME, fr. OF, fr. L *ira;* akin to OE *ofost* haste, zeal, OS *obast* haste, zeal, ON *eisa* to race forward, Gk *hieros* powerful, supernatural, holy, sacred, *inein*, *inan* to empty out, defecate, *oistros* gadfly, frenzy, Skt *iṣṇāti*, *iṣyati* he sets in motion, swings; basic meaning: moving rapidly] **:** ANGER, WRATH ⟨provocation enough to arouse the ~ of a saint⟩ **syn** see ANGER

[2]ire \"\ *vt* -ED/-ING/-S **:** to provoke to anger **:** arouse ire in ⟨reads a piece in his local newspaper that ~*s* him —Sidney Atkinson⟩ **:** ANGER, IRRITATE

[3]ire \"\ *n* -s [by shortening] *dial* **:** IRON

ire·ful \'ī(ə)rfəl, 'īəf-\ *adj* [ME, fr. *ire* + *-ful*] **1 :** full of ire **:** marked by ire **:** ANGRY, WRATHFUL ⟨an ~ mood⟩ **2 :** given to ire **:** easily angered **:** IRASCIBLE, CHOLERIC ⟨an ill-tempered ~ old man⟩ — **ire·ful·ly** \-fəlē, -li\ *adv* — **ire·ful·ness** *n* -ES

ire·land \'ī(ə)rlənd, 'īəl-\ *adj, usu cap* [fr. *Ireland*, one of the British Isles] **1 :** of or from the island of Ireland **:** of the kind or style prevalent in the island of Ireland **2 :** of or from the republic of Ireland **:** of the kind or style prevalent in the republic of Ireland

ire·land·er \-ləndə(r), -,lan-,-,laan-\ *n* -s *cap* [*Ireland* + E *-er*] **:** a native of Ireland

ireland king of arms *cap I & usu cap K&A* **:** a king of arms for heraldic supervision in Ireland appointed by the king of England and holding an office of which there is record from the reign of Richard II until that of Edward IV — compare ULSTER KING OF ARMS

ire·less \'ī(ə)rlə̇s, 'īəl-\ *adj* **:** being without ire — **ire·less·ly** *adv* — **ire·less·ness** *n* -ES

ire·na \ī'rēnə\ *n, cap* [NL, fr. Gk *eirēnē* peace] **:** a genus of birds (family Aegithinidae) consisting of the fairy bluebirds of India

irene \'ī,rēn, =ˈ=\ *n* -s [ISV *irone* + *-ene*] **:** a liquid hydrocarbon $(CH_3)_4C_{10}H_8$ derived from naphthalene and obtained by reduction and cyclization of irone with hydriodic acid and phosphorus

irenic *or* **ei·renic** \(')ī¦renik, -rēn-\ *also* **ireni·cal** \-nə̇kəl\ *adj* [Gk *eirēnikos*, fr. *eirēnē* peace (prob. of non-IE origin) + *-ikos* -ic, -ical] **:** conducive to or operating toward peace, moderation, harmony, and conciliation and away from contention and partisanship esp. among disputants ⟨~ measures⟩ ⟨~ without being namby-pamby —*Chicago Theol. Seminary Register*⟩ ⟨the viewpoint is ~ and the author seeks to show the best features of each religion and church in turn —N.K. Burger⟩ **syn** see PACIFIC

ireni·cal·ly \-nə̇k(ə)lē\ *adv* **:** in an irenic manner **:** in a way calculated to conciliate or to promote peace

ireni·cism \=ˈ=nə,sizəm\ *n* -s **:** a social temper or condition or a state of public opinion making for peace

irenicon *var of* EIRENICON

irenics \ī'reniks, -rēn-\ *n pl but usu sing in constr, also* **irenic** \-nik\ **:** irenic theology as distinguished from polemic theology **:** theology concerned with securing Christian unity

ire·si·ne \,īrə'sī(,)nē\ *n* [NL, modif. of Gk *eiresiōnē* branch of olive or laurel wound round with wool and hung with fruits; fr. the woolly calyx] **1** *cap* **:** a genus of tropical American opposite-leaved herbs (family Amaranthaceae) having small spicate or paniculate scarious flowers and often colored foliage — see ACHYRANTHES 2 **2** -s **:** any plant of the genus *Iresine*

ir·gun·ist \ir'günə̇st\ *n* -s *usu cap* [NHeb *Irgun* (*Ṣ bai Leumi*), lit., national military organization (fr. *irgun* organization + *ṣbai* military + *leumi* national) + E *-ist*] **:** a member of a militant rightist underground group of Zionists

ir·i·ar·tea \,irē'ärd·ēə\ *n, cap* [NL, after Bernardo de *Iriarte* †1814 Span. diplomat and amateur botanist] **:** a small genus of tall pinnate-leaved chiefly Brazilian palms with smooth trunk and crown of leaves supported by long slender prop roots — see STILT PALM

iri·cism \'īrə,sizəm\ *n* -s *usu cap* [[1]*Irish* + *-cism* (as in *Scotticism*)] **:** IRISHISM

iri·cize \-,sīz\ *vb* -ED/-ING/-S *sometimes cap* [[1]*Irish* + *-cize* (as in *scotticize*)] **:** IRISHIZE

irid \'īrə̇d\ *n* -s [NL *Irid-*, *Iris*] **:** a plant of the family Iridaceae

irid- *or* **irido-** *comb form* [L *irid-*, *iris* — more at IRIS] **1 :** rainbow ⟨*irid*al⟩ ⟨*irid*escent⟩ **2** [NL *irid-*, *iris*] **:** iris of the eye ⟨*irid*ectomy⟩ ⟨*irido*paralysis⟩ **:** iris and ⟨*irido*cyclitis⟩ **3** [*iridescent*] **:** iridescent ⟨*irid*ize⟩ ⟨*irido*cyte⟩ **4** [NL *Irid-*, *Iris*] **:** the genus Iris ⟨*irid*in⟩ **5** [NL *iridium*] **:** iridium **:** iridium and ⟨*irid*osmine⟩

iri·da·ce·ae \,irə'dāsē,ē, ,īr-\ *n pl, cap* [NL, fr. *Irid-*, *Iris*, type genus + *-aceae*] **:** a family of perennial herbs (order Liliales) with usu. only basal ensiform leaves and flowers in racemes or panicles that are subtended individually or in clusters by two spathose bracts and have the perianth petaloid and the ovary inferior

iri·da·ceous \¦==¦dāshəs\ *adj* [NL *Iridaceae* + E *-ous*] **1 :** of or relating to the family Iridaceae or esp. the genus *Iris* **2 :** resembling an iris ⟨silvery blue ~ flowers⟩

iri·dal \'irəd^əl, 'īr-\ *adj* [*irid-* + *-al*] **1 :** of or relating to the rainbow **:** IRIDIAN **2 :** of or relating to the iris of the eye **:** IRIDIC

iri·dec·to·mize \,irə'dektə,mīz, ,īr-\ *vt* -ED/-ING/-S **:** to subject to iridectomy

iri·dec·to·my \-,mē\ *n* -ES [*irid-* + *-ectomy*] **:** the surgical removal of part of the iris of the eye

irides *pl of* IRIS

ir·i·desce \¦irə¦des\ *vi* -ED/-ING/-S [back-formation fr. [1]*iridescent*] **:** to be iridescent

ir·i·des·cence \,irə'desᵊn(t)s\ *n* -s [*irid-* + *-escence*] **1 :** a play of structural colors producing rainbow effects that is exhibited in various bodies as a result of interference in a thin film (as of a soap bubble or mother-of-pearl) or of diffraction of light reflected from a closely ribbed or corrugated surface (as of the plumage of certain birds) and is readily distinguished from the inherent colors of substances by its variation with the angle of incidence of the illumination **2 :** a display or effect suggestive of the play of colors on an iridescent surface in gleaming or glistening or in subtly shifting and changing shades and hues ⟨paled before the ~ of the best of his earlier plays —*Americana Annual*⟩ ⟨a certain ~ of glamor and superiority —Margaret Landon⟩ ⟨no apple tang, no citrous clarity, but the ~ of the papaya, the opaline evanescence of the guava —Waldo Frank⟩ **:** GLITTER, SHEEN, LUSTER, OPALESCENCE

[1]ir·i·des·cent \¦irə¦desᵊnt\ *adj* [*irid-* + *-escent*] **1 :** having iridescence **:** showing colors like those of the rainbow esp. in shifting patterns of hues and shades that vary with a change of light or point of view ⟨a beetle with an ~ back⟩ ⟨as softly ~ as the rays from a jewel —Ellen Glasgow⟩ ⟨smart, lean glass towers with ~ washrooms —Brooks Atkinson⟩ ⟨crunchy, ~, lovely snow —Elaine W. Neal⟩ **:** NACREOUS, OPALESCENT **2 a :** having a gleaming or glittering quality suggestive of the phenomenon of iridescence **:** BRILLIANT, FLASHING ⟨two wickedly witty and ~ novels —*Time*⟩ ⟨a man for whom the map of the present was always ~ with the glories of the past —H.C.Wolfe⟩ ⟨his ~ performance as an art, music, and drama critic —John Mason Brown⟩ **b :** having the constantly shifting fluid character of an iridescence ⟨the life of ~ revery —Edmund Wilson⟩ ⟨that ~ play of meanings —Susanne K. Langer⟩ **3** *of a fabric* **:** CHANGEABLE 4 ⟨curtains of an ~ material, purple in one light, golden brown in another —Howard Moss⟩ ⟨a filmy ~ green carpet —*Amer. Guide Series: Tenn.*⟩

[2]iridescent \"\ *n* -s **:** an iridescent fabric, trimming, or accessory ⟨the green-blue ~*s* are featured in rayon organdy for a party dress —*Women's Wear Daily*⟩

ir·i·des·cent·ly *adv* **:** in an iridescent manner

irid·i·al \ī'ridēəl, ə̇'r-\ *adj* [*irid-* + *-ial*] **:** of or relating to an iris esp. of the eye **:** IRIDIC

irid·i·an \-ēən\ *adj* [*irid-* + *-ian*] **1 :** of or relating to the iris of the eye **:** IRIDIC **2 a :** resembling a rainbow **b :** having the colors of the rainbow **3 :** containing iridium

irid·ic \(')ī¦ridik, ə̇'r-\ *adj* [*irid-* + *-ic*] **1 :** of, relating to, or derived from iridium — used esp. of a compound in which iridium is tetravalent **2 :** of or relating to the iris of the eye ⟨~ grains and a flood of intraocular fluid —*Time*⟩

iri·din \'irədᵊn, 'īr-, -də̇n\ *n* -s [ISV *irid-* + *-in*] **1 :** a crystalline glucoside $C_{24}H_{26}O_{13}$ occurring esp. in orrisroot **2 :** an oleoresin prepared from the common blue flag for use as a purgative and liver stimulant

irid·io–platinum \ī¦ridē(,)ō, ə̇¦r-+\ *n* [*iridio-* (fr. NL *iridium*) + *platinum*] *n* **:** a hard alloy of iridium and platinum

irid·i·um \ī'ridēəm, ə̇'r-\ *n* -s *often attrib* [NL, fr. *irid-* + *-ium;* fr. the colorful appearance of some of its solutions] **:** a silver-white hard brittle very heavy chiefly trivalent and tetravalent metallic element of the platinum group that occurs usu. as a native alloy with platinum or with osmium in iridosmine, is resistant to chemical attack at ordinary temperatures, and is used esp. in hardening platinum for alloys suitable for surgical instruments, electrical and other scientific apparatus, jewelry, and the points of gold pens — symbol *Ir;* see ELEMENT table

iri·di·za·tion \,irədə̇'zāshən, ,īr-, -,dī'z-\ *n* -s **1 :** the action or process of making iridescent **:** IRISATION **2 :** the action or process of exhibiting iridescence **3 :** a semblance of a halo around a light observed by persons affected with glaucoma

iri·dize \'irə,dīz, 'īr-\ *vt* -ED/-ING/-S [*irid-* + *-ize*] **:** to make iridescent

irido- — see IRID-

iri·do·choroiditis \¦irə(,)dō, ¦īr-+\ *n* [NL, fr. *irid-* + *choroiditis*] **:** inflammation of the iris and the choroid

iri·do·cyclitis \"+\ *n* [NL, fr. *irid-* + *cyclitis*] **:** inflammation of the iris and the ciliary body

irid·o·cyte \ī'ridə,sīt, ə̇'r-\ *n* -s [*irid-* + *-cyte*] **:** a cell that occurs esp. in the skin of fishes and reptiles and appears iridescent greenish from included guanine — compare GUANOPHORE

iri·do·do·ne·sis \,irə(,)dōdə'nēsə̇s, ,īr-\ *n, pl* **iridodone·ses** \-ē,sēz\ [NL, fr. *irid-* + Gk *donein* to shake + NL *-sis*] **:** tremulousness of the iris **:** HIPPUS

iri·do·myr·mex \-'mər,meks\ *n, cap* [NL, fr. *irid-* + GK *myrmēx* ant — more at PISMIRE] **:** a genus containing the Argentine ant

irid·o·phore \ī'ridə,fō(ə)r, ə̇'r-\ *n* -s [*irid-* + *-phore*] **:** an iridescent chromatophore — compare IRIDOCYTE

iri·dos·mine \,irə'däz,mēn, ,īr-, -,mə̇n\ *n* -s [G *iridosmin*, fr. *irid-* + NL *osmium* + G *-in* -ine] **:** a mineral consisting of a native iridium osmium alloy usu. containing some rhodium and platinum and found in tin-white or steel-gray grains isomorphous with siserskite

iri·dos·mi·um \-,mēəm\ *n* -s [NL, fr. *irid-* + *osmium*] **:** IRIDOSMINE

irids *pl of* IRID

iring *pres part of* IRE

i ring *n, cap I* **:** a band or hoop secured around the circumference of a metal drum as a reinforcement

[1]iris \'īrə̇s\ *n, pl* **iris·es** \-rə̇sə̇z\ *or* **iri·des** \'irə,dēz, 'īr-\ [ME, fr. L, fr. Gk (basic meaning: rainbow) — more at WIRE] **1 :** a prismatic crystal; *esp* **:** a quartz that is iridescent because of internal cracks **2 a :** RAINBOW **b :** a play of colors resembling a rainbow **:** a circle or arch of rainbow hues **3** [NL, fr. Gk] **a :** the opaque muscular contractile diaphragm that is suspended in the aqueous humor in front of the lens of the eye, is perforated by the pupil and is continuous peripherally with the ciliary body, has a deeply pigmented posterior surface which excludes the entrance of light except through the pupil and a variously colored anterior surface in different individuals which determines the color of the eyes — see EYE illustration **b** (1) **:** IRIS DIAPHRAGM; *esp* **:** one used on a motion-picture camera in fading pictures in or out (2) **:** a masking device having a circular opening of which the diameter can be varied

[2]iris \"\ *n* [NL, fr. L, iris, any of various plants of the family Iridaceae] **1** *cap* **:** the type genus of the family Iridaceae comprising perennial herbaceous plants that develop from rhizomes or bulbs, have linear or sword-shaped mostly basal leaves, erect stalks on which the flowers are borne, and short-lived usu. brightly colored flowers with the three inner perianth segments erect and the three outer spreading or drooping, and include many widely cultivated ornamentals **2** *pl* **irises** *or* **iris** *also* **irides :** any plant or flower of the genus *Iris* — see BEARDED IRIS, BEARDLESS IRIS; DUTCH IRIS, ENGLISH IRIS, GERMAN IRIS, JAPANESE IRIS, SPANISH IRIS **3** *or* **iris blue :** a pale blue to pale purple — called also *endive blue*

[3]iris \"\ *vt* -ED/-ING/-S **1 :** to make iridescent **:** give the form or appearance of a rainbow to ⟨spray ~*ed* above the falls⟩ **2 :** to operate the iris of a motion-picture camera so as to fade (a picture) — used with *in* or *out*

iris·at·ed \'īrə̇,sād·ə̇d\ *adj* **:** IRISED, IRIDESCENT ⟨~ crystal beads⟩

iris·ation \,īrə̇'sāshən\ *n* -s **1 :** the act or process of making iridescent ⟨the ~ of a culture plate by developing bacteria⟩ **2 :** IRIDESCENCE ⟨~*s* in a cloud are evidence that it is composed of water droplets —D.W.Perrie⟩ ⟨in the area of the sun beautiful ~*s* may occur⟩

iris borer *n* **:** a large brown-headed pinkish grub that is the larva of a noctuid moth (*Macronoctua onusta*) and that is destructive to the rhizomes and crowns of various irises

iris diaphragm *n* : an adjustable diaphragm of thin opaque plates that can be turned by a ring so as to change the diameter of a central opening usu. to regulate the aperture of a lens (as in a camera or microscope)

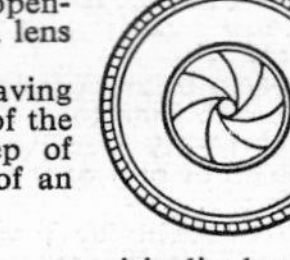
iris diaphragm

irised \ˈīrəst\ *adj* [¹*iris* + *-ed*] **1** : having or characterized by colors like those of the rainbow : IRIDESCENT ⟨the ~ sweep of northern lights⟩ **2** : having an iris of an indicated kind ⟨pale-*irised* eyes⟩
irises *pl of* IRIS, *pres 3d sing of* IRIS
iris family *n* : IRIDACEAE
iris green *n* : MALACHITE GREEN 3
¹irish \ˈīrish, -rēsh\ *adj, usu cap* [ME, fr. (assumed) OE *Īrisc*, fr. OE *Īras* Irishmen (of Celt origin; akin to OIr *Ēriu* Ireland) + *-isc* -ish] **1** : of, relating to, or characteristic of Ireland or its inhabitants : produced in or native or peculiar to Ireland **2 a** : being or belonging to the Celtic speech of Ireland : IRISH-GAELIC **b** *obs* : SCOTTISH-GAELIC
²irish \ˈ"\ *n* -ES *see sense 1a* **1** *cap* **a** *pl in constr* : natives or inhabitants of Ireland or their immediate descendants esp. when of Celtic speech or culture — compare CELT, GAEL **b** *obs* : IRISHMAN, IRISHWOMAN **2** *cap* : the Irish language: **a** : the Irish branch of Goidelic : the Goidelic speech of the Celts in Ireland : IRISH GAELIC — see MIDDLE IRISH, OLD IRISH; INDO-EUROPEAN LANGUAGES table **b** *obs* : SCOTTISH GAELIC **c** : English as spoken by the Irish with more or less dialect change and brogue **3** *usu cap, obs* : an old game resembling backgammon **4** *usu cap* **a** : IRISH LINEN **b** : IRISH WHISKEY **5** *usu cap* : TEMPER, ANGER ⟨don't get your *Irish* up over a little thing like that⟩ **6** *usu cap* : a tap-dance step consisting of a shuffle, hop, and step
irish alphabet *n, usu cap I* : a modified form of the Latin alphabet used by the ancient Britons and still employed in writing and printing Irish — compare INSULAR HAND
irish blight *n, usu cap I* : LATE BLIGHT
irish broom *n, usu cap I* **1** : a low Iberian shrub (*Cytisus patens*) **2** : SCOTCH BROOM
irish bull *n, usu cap I* [⁵*bull*] : an expression containing apparent congruity but actual incongruity of ideas ⟨"it was hereditary in his family to have no children" is a well-known *Irish bull*⟩
irish chippendale *n, usu cap I&C* : ornate carved furniture made prob. in Ireland about the middle of the 18th century and based on Chippendale designs
irish christian brother *n, usu cap I&C&B* : BROTHER OF THE CHRISTIAN SCHOOLS
irish coffee *n, usu cap I* : a mixed drink consisting of hot sugared coffee liberally laced with Irish whiskey and topped with whipped cream
irish confetti *n, usu cap I* [so called fr. the tradition that Irishmen often throw bricks in a fight] : a rock, brick, or fragment of rock or brick
irish crochet *n, usu cap I* : a heavy lace of Irish origin that is hand-crocheted or machine-made with rose or leaf designs on a square mesh ground and is used esp. for insertion, edging, and trimming
irish diamond *n, usu cap I* : CRYSTAL 2
irish dividend *n, usu cap I* : an assessment on stock
irish elk *or* **irish deer** *n, usu cap I* : a large extinct Pleistocene deer (*Megaloceros hibernicus*) remains of which are found esp. under the peat of Ireland and England
irish·er \ˈīrishə(r), -rēsh-\ *n -s cap* : IRISHMAN
irish furze *n, usu cap I* : a columnar compact sparse-flowering shrub (*Ulex europaeus strictus*)
irish gaelic *n, cap I&G* : the Goidelic speech of the Celts of Ireland esp. as used since the end of the medieval period — compare MIDDLE IRISH, OLD IRISH; see INDO-EUROPEAN LANGUAGES table
irish-gaelic \ˌ==ˈ==\ *adj, usu cap I&G* : of, relating to, or characteristic of the Goidelic speech of the Celts of Ireland
irish grazier *n, usu cap I, sometimes cap G* : TAMWORTH
irish green *n, often cap I* : a deep green
irish harp *n, usu cap I* : CLARSACH
irish heath *n, usu cap I* : a low evergreen European shrub (*Daboecia cantabrica*) of the family Ericaceae that has slender leaves dark green above and whitish below and small nodding bell-shaped white or sometimes rosy or purplish flowers borne in erect terminal racemes — called also *St.-Dabeoc's-heath*
irish·ism \ˈīri,shizəm, -rē,-\ *n -s usu cap* **1** : a word, phrase, or mode of expression distinctive of the Irish **2** : IRISH BULL
irish ivy *n, usu cap 1st I* : a European ivy (*Hedera helix hibernica*) that is a variety of English ivy distinguished by larger leaves and fruit
irish·ize \ˈīri,shīz, -rē,-\ *vt* -ED/-ING/-S *often cap* : to make Irish in quality or traits ⟨~ the music⟩
irish juniper *n, usu cap I* : a narrow columnar ornamental juniper (*Juniperus communis hibernica*) that is a horticultural variety of the common juniper
irish linen *n, usu cap I* : a fine lightweight linen fabric made in Ireland and used esp. for clothing
irish lord *n, usu cap I* : any of several sculpins (genus *Hemilepidotus*) of the Bering sea region that are locally important as food fishes
irish·ly *adv, often cap* : in the style or way of the Irish
irish mail *n, usu cap I* : a 3-wheeled or 4-wheeled toy vehicle activated by a hand lever somewhat on the principle of a manually operated railway handcar
irish·man \ˈ==mən\ *n, pl* **irishmen** *cap* [ME, fr. *Irish* + *man*] **1** : a native or inhabitant of Ireland : HIBERNIAN **2** : one that is of Irish descent **3** : TUMATAKURU
irish mile *n, usu cap I* : an old Irish unit of distance equal to 1.273 statute miles

Irish mail

irish moss *n, usu cap I* **1 a** : the dried and bleached plants of two red algae (*Chondrus crispus* and *Gigartina mamillosa*) used as an agent for thickening or emulsifying or as a demulcent (as in cookery or pharmacy) — called also *chondrus* **b** : CARRAGEEN 1 **2** : CYPRESS SPURGE
irish moss extractive *n, usu cap I* : CARRAGEENIN
irish·ness *n -ES usu cap* : the quality or state of being Irish
irish pennant *or* **irish pendant** *n, usu cap I* : a loose untidy object about a ship or naval installation; *esp* : the end of a line left hanging loose or out of place
irish poplin *n, usu cap I* : a fabric with silk warp and worsted filling made orig. in Ireland
irish potato *n, usu cap I* : POTATO 2 a (2)
irish·ry \ˈīrishrē, -rēsh-, -ri\ *n* -ES *usu cap* [ME *Irisherie, Irishrie*, fr. *Irish* + *-erie* -ery or *-rie* -ry] **1** : IRISH 1a **2 a** : Irish quality or character ⟨~ of temperament⟩ **b** : an Irish peculiarity or trait ⟨a deliberate ~⟩
irish setter *n* **1** *usu cap I&S* : a breed of bird dogs that are in general comparable to English setters but have a chestnut-brown or mahogany-red coat **2** *usu cap I, often cap S* : a dog of the Irish Setter breed
irish snipe *n, usu cap I* : an avocet (*Recurvirostra americana*) of No. America
irish stew *n, usu cap I* : a stew having as its principal ingredients meat, potatoes, and onions in a thick gravy
irish strawberry *n, usu cap I, Austral* : STRAWBERRY TREE
irish system *n, usu cap I* : a system of prison management developed for Ireland by Sir Walter Crofton and noted for its mark system and commutation of sentences, classification of prisoners, military discipline, trade and academic training, preparation for free self-control, and release under police supervision
irish terrier *n* **1** *usu cap I&T* : a breed of active medium-sized terriers that originated in Ireland and is characterized by a dense close wiry coat of red, golden red, or reddish wheaten **2** *usu cap I & sometimes cap T* : a dog of the Irish Terrier breed
irish water spaniel *n* **1** *usu cap I&W&S* : a breed of large retrievers developed in Ireland by interbreeding various sporting dogs and the poodle and characterized by a heavy coat of liver-colored curls, a topknot of long curls, and a nearly hairless rattail **2** *usu cap I & sometimes cap W&S* : a dog of the Irish Water Spaniel breed
irish whiskey *n, usu cap I* : whiskey made in Ireland chiefly of barley
irish wolfhound *n, usu cap I & sometimes cap W* : a very large tall hound that in general resembles the deerhound but is much larger and stronger, weighs upward from 90 pounds, and has a shoulder height from 31 inches in the male and 28 inches in the female
irishwoman \ˈ==,==\ *n, pl* **irishwomen** *cap* : a woman born in Ireland or of Irish descent
irishy \ˈīrishē, -rēsh-, -shi\ *adj, often cap* : suggesting or characteristic of the Irish ⟨~ blue eyes⟩
irish yew *n, usu cap I* : a hardy columnar yew (*Taxus baccata stricta*) that has erect branches and dark green foliage and is a horticultural variety of the common Old World yew
iri·sin \ˈīrəsən\ *n* -s [ISV *iris* + *-in*; orig. formed in G] : a polysaccharide $(C_6H_{10}O_5)_x$ occurring esp. in the rhizomes of some irises and like inulin yielding levulose on hydrolysis
irising *pres part of* IRIS
iris mauve *n* : a grayish yellowish pink that is yellower and slightly less strong than cloud pink
irisroot \ˈ==,=\ *n* : ORRISROOT
iris whitefly *n* : a whitefly (*Aleyrodes spiraeoides*) that is sometimes a pest on late potatoes in the northwestern U.S.
iri·tis \īˈrīd·əs\ *n* -ES [NL, irreg. fr. *iris* + *-itis*] : inflammation of the iris of the eye
¹irk \ˈərk, ˈək, ˈəik\ *adj* [ME] *now dial* : weary and disgusted
²irk \ˈ"\ *vb* -ED/-ING/-S [ME *irken*] *vi, now chiefly Scot* : to become tired or wearied esp. to the point of being bored or disgusted or unwilling to do or submit to something ~ *vt* **1** *obs* : to be tired of or disgusted with **2** : to irritate or disgust (as a person) usu. by reason of tiresome or wearying qualities ⟨restrictions that ~*ed* buyers⟩ ⟨it ~*s* me to see such waste⟩ **syn** see ANNOY
³irk \ˈ"\ *n* -s **1** : IRKSOMENESS, TEDIUM ⟨the ~ of a narrow existence⟩ **2** : a cause or source of annoyance or disgust ⟨the main ~ is the wage level⟩
irk·some \-səm\ *adj* [ME *irksom*, fr. *irken* to irk + *-som* -some] **1** *obs* : WEARY, VEXED, DISGUSTED **2** : tending to irk ⟨an ~ task⟩ : IRRITATING, TEDIOUS ⟨such ~ caution⟩ — **irk·some·ly** *adv* — **irk·some·ness** *n* -ES
ir·kutsk \(ˈ)irˈkütsk, ˌəˈr-\ *adj, usu cap* [fr. *Irkutsk*, U.S.S.R.] : of or from the city of Irkutsk, U.S.S.R. : of the kind or style prevalent in Irkutsk
irne *archaic var of* IRON
IRO *abbr* inland revenue officer; internal revenue officer
iro·ha \ˌiˈē(ˌ)rōˈhä, ˌ=ˈ=(ˌ)=\ *also* **iro·fa** \-fä\ *n* -s [Jap, fr. *i* + *ro* + *ha* or *fa*, its first three syllables] : the Japanese kana in its popular order in distinction from the scientific arrangement which is based on that of Sanskrit
iro·ko \əˈrō(ˌ)kō\ *n* -s [Yoruba *ì¹rò³kò¹*] **1** : a very large timber tree (*Chlorophora excelsa*) of tropical western Africa with strong durable streaky lustrous light brown to dark brown wood that is extremely resistant to termite attack and often used as a substitute for teak **2** : the wood of an iroko tree
¹iron \ˈī(ə)rn, ˈīən *sometimes chiefly for the sake of the meter*

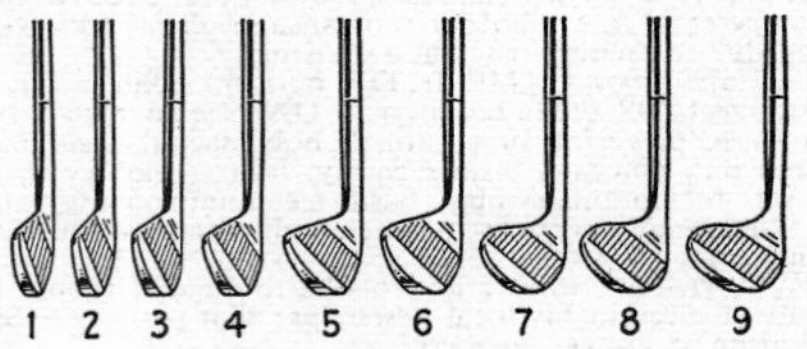
1 2 3 4 5 6 7 8 9

irons 2k: *1* driving iron, *2* midiron, *3* mid-mashie, *4* mashie iron, *5* mashie, *6* mashie niblick, *7* pitcher, *8* pitching niblick, *9* niblick

in a line of poetry ˈīrən\ *n* -s [ME *iren, iron*, fr. OE *īren, īsen, īsern*; akin to OHG *īsan, īsarn* iron, ON *īsarn, jārn*, Goth *eisarn*; all fr. a prehistoric Gmc word prob. of Venetic or Illyrian origin like OIr *īarn* iron, W *haearn*; akin to Venetic *Isaras*, a river; akin to L *ira* anger — more at IRE] **1 a** : a heavy malleable ductile magnetic chiefly bivalent and trivalent metallic element that is silver-white when pure but readily rusts in moist air and is chemically active in other respects (as toward dilute acids), that occurs native in meteorites and combined in most igneous rocks, that is usu. extracted from its ores by smelting with coke and limestone in a blast furnace, that is the most used of metals (as in construction, armaments, tools), and that plays a vital role in biological processes (as in transport of oxygen in the animal body) — symbol *Fe*; see CAST IRON, INGOT IRON, IRON ORE, PIG IRON, STEEL, WROUGHT IRON; ELEMENT table; compare FERRITE **b** : iron in some particular physical or chemical state: as (1) : iron chemically combined ⟨~ in the blood⟩ ⟨a tonic of ~ and wine⟩ (2) : iron that cannot be hardened by quenching (as wrought iron, pig iron) — distinguished from *steel* ⟨the ~ and steel industry⟩ **2** : something (as an instrument, appliance, or tool) made of or commonly, customarily, or orig. made of iron: as **a** (1) : an iron weapon; *esp* : SWORD (2) : armed might : WEAPONRY (3) *slang* : a portable firearm : PISTOL **b** (1) : something (as chains, handcuffs, shackles) used to bind, confine, or restrain — usu. used in pl. ⟨kept the prisoner in ~*s*⟩ (2) *archaic* : BONDS, CAPTIVITY **c** : a branding or cauterizing iron **d irons** *pl, archaic* : dies used in striking coins **e** : HARPOON **f** : a heatable device usu. with a flat metal base of some weight that is used to smooth, finish, or press (as cloth) : FLATIRON **g** : STIRRUP **h** : SOLDERING IRON **i** : an iron weight with a handle sometimes used in curling instead of the customary stone **j** : the cutter in a tool (as a plane) **k** : one of a series of golf clubs numbered 1 through 9 that have heads of iron or occas. other metal laid back at a progressively greater angle so as to give progressively greater height and less distance to the flight of the ball **3** : resemblance to iron in some quality (as strength, inflexibility, hardness, durability) ⟨the ~ of that spirit⟩; *also* : a quality of exhibiting such resemblance ⟨muscles of ~⟩ **4** : a unit of measurement equal to one forty-eighth of an inch used in measuring thickness of a shoe sole ⟨a six-*iron* sole⟩ **5** : MINERAL BROWN **6** : the iron industry or its production esp. as a market factor ⟨~ has remained steady⟩ — **in irons** *or* **into irons 1** *of a sailing vessel while tacking* : having the head to the wind and unable to fill away on either tack : incapable of coming about or filling away **2** : in chains or fetters : in confinement — **iron in the fire 1** : a matter requiring close oversight or attention : ENTERPRISE ⟨was a businessman and had other *irons in the fire* —J.D.Beresford⟩ **2** : a prospective course of action : a project not yet realized ⟨got several *irons in the fire* and I'm hoping to land something before very long —W.S.Maugham⟩
²iron \ˈ"\ *adj* [ME *iren*, fr. OE *īren, īsen, īsern* (akin to OHG *īsarnīn*, adj., iron, Goth *eisarneins*), fr. *īren, īsen, īsern*, n.] **1** : of, relating to, or derived from iron : made of or containing iron ⟨an ~ bar⟩; *broadly* : made of or consisting of steel or other modified iron **2** : resembling iron in appearance or color ⟨a grim ~ sky⟩ **3** : resembling iron in some quality (as hardness, strength, impenetrability, endurance, insensibility): as **a** : having great physical hardness or strength **b** : RUDE, HARD, SEVERE **c** : strong and healthy : ROBUST ⟨an ~ constitution⟩ ⟨~ digestions⟩ **d** : INFLEXIBLE, UNRELENTING ⟨~ determination⟩ **e** : holding or binding fast : not to be broken ⟨the ~ ties of kinship⟩ **f** : metallic in tone : HARSH ⟨an ~ voice⟩ **4** *of a golf shot* : played with an iron
³iron \ˈ"\ *vb* -ED/-ING/-S [ME *irenen*, fr. *iren*, n.] *vt* **1** : to furnish, arm, or cover with iron ⟨~*ed* the new wheel⟩ **2 a** : to shackle with irons : FETTER, HANDCUFF **b** : to attach or make fast with fittings of iron ⟨~ the toolbox to the truck⟩ **3 a** : to smooth with or as if with an instrument of iron; *esp* : to press (as cloth) with a heated flatiron **b** : to remove by ironing — usu. used with an adverb of direction ⟨gently ~*ing* away the wrinkles⟩ **4** : to take (as a fish) with a gaff or harpoon **5** : to thin the walls of (a deep-drawn metal article) by reducing the clearance between punch and die ~ *vi* : to iron clothes ⟨~*ed* all morning⟩
iron age *n, usu cap I&A* : the period of human culture characterized by the smelting of iron and its almost universal use in industry beginning about 1000 B.C. in southern Europe and somewhat earlier in western Asia and Egypt — compare BRONZE AGE, STONE AGE; see HALLSTATT, LA TÈNE
iron alum *n* **1** : an alum containing iron as the trivalent constituent; *esp* : ammonium ferric alum $NH_4Fe(SO_4)_2.12H_2O$ **2** [¹*alum* (aluminum sulfate)] : HALOTRICHITE
ironback \ˈ=(=),=\ *n* : a plate of iron for the back of a fireplace
iron bacteria *n* : any of various bacteria of the order Chlamydobacteriales that act upon iron compounds and produce deposits of ocher and bog ore
ironbark \ˈ=(=),=\ *n* **1** *or* **ironbark tree** : any of several Australian eucalypts (as *Eucalyptus sideroxylon, E. paniculata, E. siderophloia, E. resinifera*) having hard gray bark and useful timber and in some cases yielding eucalyptus gum **2** : the extremely heavy hard strong durable wood of an ironbark which is commonly available in large sizes and is extensively used in heavy construction
ironbark acacia *n* : an Australian timber tree (*Acacia excelsa*) with very hard dark-grained wood
ironbark box *n* [¹*box*] : any of several Australian eucalypts; *esp* : a widely distributed stringybark (*Eucalyptus obliqua*)
iron black *n* : a powder consisting of precipitated antimony which is used in coating various objects to give them the appearance of polished iron or steel
iron blue *n* **1** : STEEL GRAY **2** : any of various strongly colored pigments that range in masstone from reddish blue to jet black and possess good hiding power, that are now usu. made by bringing together solutions of ferrous sulfate, ammonium sulfate, and sodium ferrocyanide and oxidizing the white precipitate formed, that consist of complex compounds regarded as both ferrocyanides and ferricyanides containing positive ions (as ammonium and sodium ions), and that are used chiefly in blueprints, inks, laundry blues, paints and enamels, crayons, and linoleum: as **a** : PRUSSIAN BLUE **b** : TURNBULL'S BLUE
ironbound \ˈ=(=)ˈ=\ *adj* [ME *irenbounden*, fr. *iren* iron + *bounden* bound — more at IRON, BOUND] : bound with or as if with iron: as **a** : HARSH, RUGGED ⟨an ~ coast⟩ **b** : bound with irons : SHACKLED ⟨an ~ prisoner⟩ **c** : RIGID, UNYIELDING, RIGOROUS ⟨~ traditions⟩ ⟨an ~ climate⟩
iron brown *n* : MINERAL BROWN
iron buff *n* : a fast dye composed of hydrated ferric oxide formed on the fiber by the action of an alkali on an iron salt
iron carbide *n* : a binary compound of iron with carbon; *esp* : CEMENTITE
iron carbonate *n* : a carbonate of iron; *esp* : FERROUS CARBONATE
iron carbonyl *n* : a compound formed by reaction of metallic iron with carbon monoxide; *esp* : the flammable unstable poisonous liquid pentacarbonyl $Fe(CO)_5$ used chiefly in making iron powder and pure iron for use as a catalyst
iron cement *n* : a mixture of small cast-iron borings or turnings usu. with ammonium chloride used moist as a cement to make rust joints
iron chink *n* [⁷*chink*; fr. its performance of tasks formerly done by Chinese] : a machine for rapidly cleaning and dressing fish (as salmon) at a cannery
iron chloride *n* : a chloride of iron: as **a** : FERRIC CHLORIDE **b** : FERROUS CHLORIDE
¹ironclad \ˈ=(=)ˈ=\ *adj* [¹*iron* + *clad*] **1** : sheathed in, protected by, or having an exterior of iron — used esp. of naval vessels **2 a** : RIGOROUS, SEVERE, EXACTING ⟨an ~ oath⟩ ⟨~ controls⟩ **b** : INFLEXIBLE, RIGID ⟨an ~ rule⟩ ⟨~ caste distinctions⟩ **c** : vigorously determined : fixed and unshakable ⟨an ~ patriot⟩ ⟨an ~ defense⟩ **3** *of a plant* : highly resistant to unfavorable environmental factors (as cold) ⟨only the most ~ roses thrive so far north⟩ ⟨developed several ~ apricots for the North Central states⟩
²ironclad \ˈ=(=),=\ *n* -s **1** : an armored naval vessel **2** : one (as a knight in armor or a person of precise and rigid morality) that is felt to resemble an armored vessel
iron curtain *n, often cap I&C* [trans. of G *eiserner vorhang* iron fireproof theatrical curtain] **1** : a political, military, and ideological barrier that cuts off and isolates an area (as of Soviet-controlled territory) preventing free communication and contact with differently oriented areas **2 a** : an intangible barrier against communication of information or ideas; *esp* : one that is set up for concealment and bars any opportunity for penetration **b** : a bar to the crossing of a mental or cultural borderline
iron-deficiency anemia *n* **1** : hypochromic anemia in which deficiency of hemoglobin in the individual red blood cells is the characteristic abnormality — see CHLOROSIS **2** : HYPOCHROMIC ANEMIA
irone \ˈī,rōn, =ˈ=\ *n* -s [ISV *iris* + *-one*; orig. formed as G *iron*] : any of several oily liquid isomeric ketones $C_{14}H_{22}O$ or a mixture of some of them that have a strong odor of violet and orrisroot, that occur in orris oil, and that are used in perfumes
ironed *past of* IRON
iron·er \ˈī(ə)rnə(r), ˈīən-\ *n* -s : one that irons: as **a** : a person who presses or shapes something (as clothes, hats, gloves) with a hand or automatic iron or on a heated form **b** : a machine for ironing fabrics : MANGLE
ironfisted \ˈ=(=)ˈ==\ *adj* **1** : STINGY, MEAN, MISERLY **2** : harsh and ruthless ⟨~ methods⟩
iron-free \ˈ=(=)ˈ=\ *adj* : containing no iron
iron front *n* : a cast-iron facade for a building
iron glance *n* [part trans., part modif. of G *eisenglanz*, fr. *eisen* iron + *glanz* brightness] : HEMATITE
iron grass *n* : VERNAL SEDGE
iron gray *n* : a nearly neutral very slightly greenish dark gray — called also *bat*
iron hand *n* : stern or rigorous control
ironhanded \ˈ=(=)ˈ==\ *adj* : having or acting or governing with a strong or heavy hand : INFLEXIBLE, RIGOROUS — **iron·hand·ed·ly** *adv* — **iron·hand·ed·ness** *n* -ES
ironhard \ˈ=(=)ˈ=\ *adj* : having the hardness of iron : very hard or severe ⟨an ~ frost⟩ ⟨an ~ beak⟩
iron hat *n* [ME *iren hat*, fr. *iren* iron + *hat* — more at IRON, HAT] **1 a** : a headpiece of iron or steel used as armor during the middle ages **b** *slang* : DERBY 2a **c** : a metal or plastic safety hat **2** : GOSSAN
ironhead \ˈ=(=),=\ *n* **1 a** : WOOD IBIS 1 **b** : AMERICAN GOLDENEYE **2** : a stupid person
ironheaded \ˈ=(=)ˈ==\ *adj* **1** : furnished or tipped with a head, top, or point of iron **2** : very hardheaded
ironheads \ˈ=(=),=\ *n pl but sing or pl in constr, also* **ironhead** *dial chiefly Eng* : KNAPWEED
ironhearted \ˈ=(=)ˈ==\ *adj* : HARDHEARTED, UNFEELING, CRUEL ⟨an ~ master⟩
iron horse *n* : a locomotive engine
iron hydroxide *n* : a hydroxide of iron: as **a** : FERRIC HYDROXIDE **b** : FERROUS HYDROXIDE
iron·ic \(ˈ)īˈränik, -nēk *sometimes* əˈr-\ *or* **iron·i·cal** \-nəkəl, -nēk-\ *adj* [LL *ironicus*, fr. Gk *eirōnikos* dissembling, fr. *eirōneia* dissimulation + *-ikos* -ic, -ical — more at IRONY] **1** : of or relating to irony : containing, expressing, or constituting irony ⟨an ~ remark⟩ ⟨it was ~ that he should enter then⟩ **2** : addicted to the use of irony : given to irony ⟨a very ~ man⟩ **3** *obs* : DISSEMBLING, PRETENDED **syn** see SARCASTIC
iron·i·cal·ly \-nək(ə)lē, -nēk-, -li\ *adv* : in an ironical manner : with or so as to constitute irony ⟨~ enough the well-planned scheme failed completely⟩ ⟨answered ~⟩
iron·i·cal·ness \-kəlnəs\ *n* -ES : the quality or state of being ironical
ironing *n* -s **1** : the action or process of smoothing or pressing with or as if with a hot flatiron **2** : clothes and linens ironed or to be ironed ⟨found the dampened ~ waiting in a basket⟩ ⟨folded and put away the ~⟩
ironing board *also* **ironing table** *n* : a flat padded cloth-covered surface on which clothes are ironed that was orig. of wood but is now often of ventilated metal, has one end tapered so that gar-

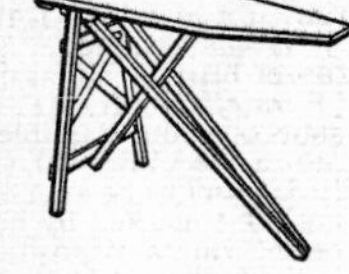
ironing board

ments may be fitted over it, and is usu. equipped with an adjustable support by which it may be held rigid at a convenient working height

iron·ish \ˈī(ə)rnish, ˈīən-, -nēsh\ *adj* **:** resembling or resembling that of iron ⟨an ~ taste⟩

iro·nist \ˈīrənəst\ *n* -s [*irony* + *-ist*] **:** one given to irony **:** a user of irony esp. in the development of a literary work or theme

iro·nize \-ˌnīz\ *vb* -ED/-ING/-S [*ironic* + *-ize*] *vt* **:** to make ironic **:** give an appearance or effect of irony to ⟨*ironizing* her account of the meeting⟩ ~ *vi* **:** to use irony **:** speak or behave ironically ⟨why ~ over such trivia⟩

iron-jawed \ˈ=(=)ˈ=\ *adj* **1 :** having a jaw like or of iron ⟨*iron-jawed* pincers⟩ ⟨an *iron-jawed* boxer⟩ **2 :** rigorously determined ⟨an *iron-jawed* disposition⟩

iron law *n* **:** a law or controlling principle that is incontrovertible and inexorable ⟨*iron laws* of historical necessity⟩

iron law of wages [intended as trans. of G *ehernes lohngesetz*, lit., brazen law of wages] **:** a statement in economics: wages naturally tend to fall to the minimum level necessary for subsistence — called also *brazen law of wages*

iron·less \ˈī(ə)rnləs, ˈīən-\ *adj* **:** having no iron ⟨an ~ culture⟩ **:** free from iron ⟨~ diets⟩

ironlike \ˈ=(=),=\ *adj* **:** resembling iron **:** exhibiting strength or hardness like that of iron ⟨~ determination⟩

iron liquor *n* **:** a black liquid consisting of a solution of crude ferrous acetate $Fe(C_2H_3O_2)_2$ usu. obtained by treating scrap iron with pyroligneous acid and used chiefly as a mordant in dyeing — called also *black liquor*

iron loss *n* **:** the loss of available energy by hysteresis and eddy currents in an electromagnetic apparatus (as a transformer) — compare COPPER LOSS

iron lung *n* **:** a device for artificial respiration in which rhythmic alternations in the air pressure in a chamber surrounding a patient's chest force air into and out of the lungs esp. when the nerves governing the chest muscles fail to function because of poliomyelitis

iron man *in senses 1 & 2* ˈ=(=),man *or* -,maa(ə)n *or* -ˌmən, *in senses 3,4, & 5* ˈ=(=)ˈman *or* -ˈmaa(ə)n\ *n* **1 :** a maker or manufacturer of iron ⟨*iron men* are uncertain about carloadings⟩; *esp* **:** a worker engaged in the manufacture or processing of iron **2 a :** a railroad worker who handles the rails in tracklaying **b :** a cement worker who weighs out ground iron ore and adds it to slurry or dry-ground rock as it goes into the kiln **c :** a worker who makes iron facsimiles of paper shoe-part models for use in cutting cardboard patterns **3 :** a man of unusual physical endurance ⟨took pride in his mastery of the pitching art, in the reputation he bore as the *iron man* —*Collier's*⟩ **4** *slang* **:** DOLLAR; *esp* **:** a silver dollar **5** *slang* **:** a machine or device that does something formerly performed by hand **:** ROBOT

ironmaster \ˈ=(=),==\ *n* **:** one that conducts or manages the founding or manufacture of iron esp. on a large scale

iron mike *n*, *slang* **:** an automatic pilot on a ship or airplane

iron minium *n* **:** BERLIN BROWN

iron mold *n* [[1]*iron* + *mold*, alter. of *mole* (spot)] **:** a spot (as on cloth) due to staining by rusty iron or by ink

iron-mold \ˈ=(=)ˈ=\ *vt* **:** to stain with iron mold

ironmonger \ˈ=(=),==\ *n* [ME *irenmonger*, fr. *iren* iron + *monger* — more at IRON, MONGER] *Brit* **:** a dealer in iron and hardware

ironmongery \ˈ=(=),=(=)=\ *n* -ES **1** *Brit* **:** HARDWARE **2** *Brit* **:** a hardware store or business **3 :** the craft or technical art of a worker in metals **:** SMITHING ⟨a whole new craft of delicate, precise ~ that had to be developed —A.L.Kroeber⟩

iron-monticellite \ˌ=(=),=='=,=\ *n* **:** a silicate $CaFeSiO_4$ of iron and calcium that is isomorphous with monticellite

iron mountain *n* **:** a mountain that contains large or economically important amounts of iron ore

iron·ness \ˈī(ə)rnnəs, ˈīənn-\ *n* -ES **:** the quality or state of being iron ⟨an ~ of constitution⟩ ⟨such ~ of will⟩

iron oak *n* **1 :** any of several American oaks (as the blackjack or the common post oak) having notably hard tough durable wood **2 :** a European Turkey oak

iron ore *n* **:** a native compound of iron (as hematite, limonite, magnetite, siderite, goethite, and the bog and clay iron ores) from which the metal may be profitably extracted

iron-ore cement *n* **:** a German cement in which iron ore is substituted for the clay or shale used in making portland cement

iron out *vt* **1 a :** to make smooth or straight ⟨*ironed out* the curves in the highway⟩ ⟨*ironing* the crumpled paper *out*⟩ **b :** to make uniform ⟨*ironing out* irregularities in the wage scale⟩ **2 :** to make tolerable or harmonious by suppression or modification of extremes (as discordant views or aspirations, technical difficulties, or divergent theories) ⟨conferences will *iron out* any conflicts of interest⟩

iron oxide *n* **:** any of several natural or synthetic oxides or hydrated oxides of iron: as **a :** anhydrous or hydrated ferric oxide varying in color from red, brown, or black to orange or yellow depending in part on the degree of hydration and the purity and used esp. as a pigment — compare OCHER, SIENNA **b :** FERROSOFERRIC OXIDE **c :** FERROUS OXIDE **d :** GOETHITE

iron-oxide red *n* **:** a strong brown to reddish brown — called also *agate*, *Spanish red*, *tarragona*

iron pan *n* **:** a hard soil layer that is cemented with iron oxides and that usu. consists of sand or sand and gravel

iron pentacarbonyl *n* **:** the iron carbonyl $Fe(CO)_5$

iron pot *n* **:** SCOTER

iron putty *n* **:** an acid-resistant putty prepared from ferric oxide and boiled linseed oil

iron pyrites *or* **iron pyrite** *n* **:** PYRITE 2

iron range *n* **:** any of several highly productive iron-ore districts of the U.S. and Canada in the general vicinity of Lake Superior ⟨the Mesabi *iron range*⟩

iron ration *n* **:** an emergency ration

iron red *n* **1 :** a natural or synthetic red pigment (as Indian red or Venetian red) consisting wholly or in part of iron oxide — compare ROUGE 2a **2 :** any of the colors oxide red; *esp* **:** INDIAN RED — compare IRON-OXIDE RED

irons *pl of* IRON, *pres 3d sing of* IRON

iron safe clause *n* **:** a clause in a fire insurance policy covering merchandise that requires inventory records to be kept in a fireproof safe

iron sand *n* **:** sand rich in iron ore (as that of certain New Zealand coastal areas)

iron scale *n* **:** SCALE 4a(1)

iron scrap *n* **1 :** waste pieces or disused articles of wrought iron suitable for reworking **2 :** cast iron or castings suitable only for remelting

ironshod \ˈ=(=)ˈ=\ *adj* **:** shod, cased, or tipped with iron or steel ⟨~ hooves⟩ ⟨an ~ wheel⟩ ⟨~ barge poles⟩

ironshot \ˈ=(=),=\ *adj*, *of a mineral* **:** streaked or speckled with iron or an iron ore

ironside \ˈ=(=),=\ *n* **1 :** a man of great strength or bravery **2 a ironsides** *pl*, *usu cap* **:** any of various bodies of hardy veteran troops **b :** a member of Cromwell's Ironsides cavalry during the English Civil War or of a similar force; *broadly* **:** a hardy veteran puritan soldier **3 ironsides** *pl but sing or pl in constr* **:** an ironclad ship

iron sight *n* **:** a metallic sight for a gun as distinguished from a sight depending on an optical or computing system — compare TELESCOPE SIGHT

iron skull *n*, *slang* **:** a railway boilermaker

ironsmith \ˈ=(=),=\ *n* [ME *iren smyth*, fr. *iren* iron + *smyth*, *smith* smith — more at IRON, SMITH] **1 :** IRONWORKER, BLACKSMITH **2 :** any of several East Indian barbets (as *Megalaima oorti faber*) having notes that resemble the sounds made by a blacksmith

iron spinel *n* **:** HERCYNITE

iron stand *n* **:** a raised and usu. ventilated metal stand on which a hot flatiron may be rested when not in use

ironstone \ˈ=(=),=\ *n* **1 :** a hard sedimentary rock rich in iron; *esp* **:** a siderite in a coal region **2 :** IRONSTONE CHINA

ironstone china *n* **:** a hard white stoneware pottery developed in England during the 18th century as a cheaper substitute for bone china and orig. highly decorated but used most extensively as plain white inexpensive tableware throughout much of the 19th century

iron sulfate *n* **:** a sulfate of iron: as **a :** FERRIC SULFATE **b :** FERROUS SULFATE

iron sulfide *n* **:** any of several compounds of iron and sulfur: as **a :** FERROUS SULFIDE **b :** the disulfide FeS_2 occurring in nature as pyrite and marcasite

iron tree *n* **:** a tree of the genus *Metrosideros* (esp. *M. vera*) with notably hard wood

iron-vane meter *n* **:** MOVING-IRON METER

ironware \ˈ=(=),=\ *n* [ME *irenware*, fr. *iren* iron + *ware* — more at IRON, WARE] **:** articles made of iron; *esp* **:** iron household utensils (as cooking vessels or cutlery)

ironweed \ˈ=(=),=\ *n* **:** any of several chiefly weedy plants: as **a :** KNAPWEED **b :** BLUEWEED 1 **c :** BLUE VERVAIN **d** *chiefly Brit* **:** RAGWEED 2 **e :** any of several American plants of the genus *Vernonia*

ironwood \ˈ=(=),=\ *n* **1 :** any of numerous trees and shrubs (as various ebonies, hornbeams, or acacias) with exceptionally tough or hard wood — compare BASTARD IRONWOOD, BLACK IRONWOOD, WHITE IRONWOOD **2 :** the wood of an ironwood

ironwood wattle *n* **:** IRONBARK ACACIA

ironwork \ˈ=(=),=\ *n* [ME *irenwerk*, fr. *iren* iron + *werk* work — more at IRON, WORK] **1 a :** work in iron **:** beat, smithed, or dressed iron ⟨did all the ~⟩ ⟨a balcony of lacy ~⟩ **b :** the part of something (as a building, a ship, or a wheel) that is made of iron ⟨the ~ of the carriage was forged locally⟩ **c :** iron articles ⟨dealt in ~⟩ **2 ironworks** *pl but sing or pl in constr* **:** a mill or building where iron or steel is smelted or heavy iron or steel products are made

ironworker \ˈ=(=),==\ *n* **:** a worker in iron: as **a :** a person employed at an ironworks **b :** a shopworker who fabricates structural steel parts **c :** one who builds with structural steel or iron

ironworking \ˈ=(=),==\ *n* **:** the process of fashioning things from iron

ironwort \ˈ=(=),=\ *n* [so called fr. the belief that such mints cure sword wounds] **1 :** any of several shrubby or subshrubby mints that constitute the genus *Sideritis*, often have yellow flowers and whitish woolly stem or leaves, and are chiefly native to the eastern Mediterranean region **2 :** HEMP NETTLE

[1]**irony** \ˈī(ə)rnē, ˈīənē, -ni\ *adj* [ME *yrony*, fr. *yron*, *iren* iron + *-y* — more at IRON] **1 :** made or consisting of iron **:** containing or abounding in iron ⟨~ sands⟩ ⟨~ chains⟩ **2 :** resembling iron in some quality (as taste or hardness) ⟨an ~ flavor⟩

[2]**iro·ny** \ˈīrənē, -ni *sometimes* ˈīərn-\ *n* -ES [L *ironia*, fr. Gk *eirōneia*, fr. *eirōn* dissembler (perh. fr. *eirein* to say) + *-eia* -y — more at WORD] **1 a :** feigned ignorance designed to confound or provoke an antagonist **:** DISSIMULATION — compare SOCRATIC IRONY **b :** DRAMATIC IRONY **2 a :** humor, ridicule, or light sarcasm that adopts a mode of speech the intended implication of which is the opposite of the literal sense of the words (as when expressions of praise are used where blame is meant) **b :** this mode of expression as a literary style or form ⟨a gift for ~⟩ **c :** an ironic utterance or expression **3 :** a state of affairs or events that is the reverse of what was or was to be expected **:** a result opposite to and as if in mockery of the appropriate result ⟨the ~ of fate⟩ **syn** see WIT

iron yellow *n* **1 :** any of several permanent synthetic yellow to orange pigments (as Mars yellow) consisting wholly or in part of hydrated iron oxide **2 :** MARS YELLOW 2

[1]**ir·o·quoi·an** \ˌirəˈkwȯi(y)ən, -wäyən\ *adj*, *usu cap* [[2]*Iroquois* + *-an*] **1 :** of, relating to, or characteristic of the language family Iroquoian or one of its members **2 :** of, relating to, or characteristic of the Iroquois

[2]**iroquoian** \"\ *n* -S *cap* **1 :** a language family of eastern No. America including Cayuga, Cherokee, Conestoga, Erie, Huron, Mohawk, Onondaga, Oneida, Seneca, Tuscarora **2 :** a member of any of the peoples constituting the Iroquois

[1]**ir·o·quois** \ˈirəˌkwȯi, -wä *sometimes* -wȯiz\ *adj*, *usu cap* [Fr, adj. & n., fr. Algonquin *Irinakhoiw*, lit., real adders] **1 :** of, relating to, or characteristic of the Iroquois **2 :** of, relating to, or characteristic of the language of the Iroquois

[2]**iroquois** \"\ *n*, *pl* **iroquois** \-ȯi(z), -ä(z)\ *usu cap* [F] **1 a :** an Indian people comprising a confederacy of five peoples that consisted orig. of the Cayuga, Mohawk, Oneida, Onondaga, and Seneca of central New York and later included the Tuscarora and fragments of various other peoples **b :** a member of any of such peoples **2 :** any of the languages of the Iroquois

ir·pex \ˈərˌpeks\ *n*, *cap* [NL, fr. L *irpex*, *hirpex* harrow — more at HEARSE] **:** a genus of tooth fungi (family Hydnaceae) that have shelving or resupinate sporophores and include some forms associated with decay of woody plant tissue

irr *abbr* **1** irredeemable **2** irregular

ir·radiance \ə+\ *n* **1** *obs* **:** emission of rays (as of light) **2 :** something (as intellectual or spiritual illumination) that is emitted like rays of light ⟨informed . . . with so splendid a spiritual ~ —J.P.Bishop⟩ **3 :** radiant flux density on a given surface usu. expressed in watts per square centimeter or square meter

ir·radiancy \"+\ *n* **1 :** the quality or state of being irradiant **2 :** IRRADIANCE 3

ir·radiant \"+\ *adj* [L *irradiant-*, *irradians*, pres. part. of *irradiare*] **:** emitting rays of light **:** serving to or able to illuminate or brighten

[1]**ir·radiate** \"+\ *adj* [L *irradiatus*, past part.] **:** made bright with or as if with light **:** ILLUMINATED ⟨a countenance ~ with love⟩

[2]**ir·radiate** \"+\ *vb* -ED\-ING\-S [L *irradiatus*, past part. of *irradiare*, fr. *in-* [2]in- + *radiare* to radiate — more at RADIATE] *vt* **1 a :** to throw rays of light upon **:** shine upon **:** ILLUMINATE, BRIGHTEN ⟨moonlight *irradiating* the placid water⟩ **b :** to enlighten intellectually or spiritually **:** make clear or brilliant ⟨wisdom *irradiated* his counsel⟩ **c :** to affect or treat by radiant heat or other radiant energy; *specif* **:** to treat by exposure to radiation (as of ultraviolet light or radium) **2 :** to send forth like rays of light **:** RADIATE, SHED, DIFFUSE ⟨*irradiating* strength and comfort⟩ ~ *vi* **1** *archaic* **:** to emit rays **:** SHINE **2** *archaic* **:** to issue in rays

irradiated *adj* **1** *of an heraldic figure or device* **:** represented as surrounded with rays of light **2 :** treated, prepared, or altered by exposure to a specific radiation ⟨~ milk⟩ ⟨~ tissues⟩

ir·ra·di·at·ing·ly \=ˈ==,===, =,=='===\ *adv* **:** so as to irradiate

ir·radiation \(,)i, ə+\ *n* -S [MF, fr. LL *irradiation-*, *irradiatio*, fr. L *irradiatus* + *-ion-*, *-io* -ion] **1 a** *archaic* **:** a giving off of rays of light **b :** the emission of radiant energy (as heat) **c :** an emanation, diffusion, or radiation of something from a common center or point of origin or a result of such activity: as (1) **:** the radiation of a physiologically active agent from a point of origin within the body; *esp* **:** the spread of a nervous impulse beyond the usual conduction path (2) *obs* **:** emission of a supposed influence or immaterial fluid from the eyes (3) **:** apparent enlargement of a light or bright object or surface when displayed against a dark background; *esp* **:** the spreading of light by the grains of a photographic emulsion causing the developed image to be larger and more diffuse at the edges than the optical image — called also *diffusion* **2 a** *archaic* **:** a ray of light **b :** mental or spiritual illumination **3 a :** exposure to rays (as ultraviolet light, X rays, or alpha rays) **b :** application of X rays, radium rays, or other radiation (as for therapeutic purposes) **4 :** IRRADIANCE 3

irradiation sickness *n* **:** RADIATION SICKNESS

ir·radiative \ə+\ *adj* **:** tending to irradiate

ir·radiator \ə+\ *n* -S **:** one that irradiates; *esp* **:** an apparatus for applying radiations (as X rays)

ir·rad·i·ca·ble \(ˈ)iˈradəkəbəl, əˈra-, (ˈ)irˈra-, (ˈ)iəˈra-\ *adj* [ML *irradicabilis*, fr. L *in-* [2]in- + *radicare* to take root + *-abilis* -able — more at RADICATE] **:** impossible to eradicate **:** DEEP-ROOTED — **ir·rad·i·ca·bly** \-blē\ *adv*

ir·rad·i·cate \əˈradəˌkāt\ *vt* -ED/-ING/-S [[2]*in-* + *radicate*] **:** to root deeply

irrationable *adj* [L *irrationabilis*, fr. *in-* [1]in- + *rationabilis* rationable — more at RATIONABLE] **1** *obs* **:** lacking the power of reason **2** *archaic* **:** UNREASONABLE, UNSUITABLE

[1]**ir·rational** \(ˈ)i, ə, (ˈ)ir, (ˈ)iə+\ *adj* [ME *irrationall*, fr. L *irrationalis*, fr. *in-* [1]in- + *rationalis* rational — more at RATIONAL] **:** not rational: as **a** (1) **:** not endowed with reason **:** lacking powers of reasoning or understanding ⟨the lower animals are commonly described as ~⟩ (2) **:** lacking usual or normal mental clarity or coherence ⟨was ~ for several days after the accident⟩ **b :** not governed by or according to reason ⟨~ . . . is a neutral term meaning either what is outside the scope of reason or what has not yet been tested by reason —*Times Lit. Supp.*⟩ **c** *Greek & Latin prosody* (1) *of a syllable* **:** having a quantity other than that required by the meter (2) *of a foot* **:** containing such a syllable (3) *of a meter* **:** containing such feet **d** *of a number* **:** real but not expressible as the quotient of two integers ⟨π and $\sqrt{3}$ are ~ numbers⟩

[2]**irrational** \"+\ *n* -S **1 :** an irrational being **:** a being not acting according to reason **2 :** an irrational quantity or number **:** SURD

ir·rationalism \"+\ *n* **1 :** a viewpoint or system of belief emphasizing the use of intuition, instinct, feeling, or faith rather than a reliance upon reason or holding that the universe is governed by irrational, volitional, or mysterious forces instead of by reason **2 :** the quality or state of being irrational

[1]**ir·rationalist** \"+\ *adj* **:** of, relating to, or advocating irrationalism

[2]**irrationalist** \"\ *n* **:** a proponent of irrationalism

ir·rationalistic \(ˌ)i, ə, (ˌ)ir, (ˌ)iə+\ *adj* **:** not based on reason **:** ILLOGICAL; *sometimes* **:** IRRATIONALIST

ir·rationality \"+\ *n* [ML or NL *irrationalitas*, fr. L *irrationalis* irrational + *-itas* -ity — more at IRRATIONAL] **1 :** the quality or state of being irrational: as **a :** lack of being endowed with reason **b :** lack of accordance with reason **:** UNREASONABLENESS, FOOLISHNESS **2 :** something that is irrational **:** ABSURDITY **3 :** inequality of dispersion of different colors in refraction spectra (as between crown and flint glass)

ir·rationalize \i, ə, ir, iə+\ *vt* **:** to make irrational

ir·rationally \(ˈ)i, ə, (ˈ)ir, (ˈ)iə+\ *adv* **:** so as to be or appear irrational **:** without or beyond the bounds of reason ⟨~ jealous⟩

ir·rationalness \"+\ *n* **:** the quality or state of being irrational

ir·real \"+\ *adj* [[1]*in-* + *real*] **:** not real

ir·reality \ˌi, ˌir, ˌiə+\ *n* [[1]*in-* + *reality*] **:** UNREALITY

ir·realizable \(ˌ)i, ə, (ˌ)ir, (ˌ)iə+\ *adj* [[1]*in-* + *realizable*] **:** UNREALIZABLE, UNATTAINABLE

ir·rebuttable \ˌi, ˌir, ˌiə+\ *adj* [[1]*in-* + *rebut* + *-able*] **:** impossible to rebut **:** not subject to rebuttal ⟨an ~ argument⟩

irrebuttable presumption *n* **:** a presumption that the law does not allow to be rebutted **:** a conclusive presumption

ir·receptive \"+\ *adj* [[1]*in-* + *receptive*] **:** UNRECEPTIVE

ir·reciprocal \"+\ *adj* [[1]*in-* + *reciprocal*] **:** not reciprocal **:** UNILATERAL ⟨~ permeability⟩

ir·reclaimable \"+\ *adj* [[1]*in-* + *reclaim* + *-able*] **:** incapable of being reclaimed ⟨~ swamps⟩; *esp* **:** bad beyond any possibility of redemption ⟨vicious ~ boys⟩ — **ir·reclaimably** \"+\ *adv*

ir·reclaimed \"+\ *adj* [[1]*in-* + *reclaimed*] **:** UNRECLAIMED; *esp* **:** not brought under cultivation ⟨~ wasteland⟩

ir·recognition \(ˌ)i, ə, ˌir, ˌiə+\ *n* [[1]*in* + *recognition*] **:** failure to recognize **:** absence of recognition

ir·recognizable \(ˌ)i, ə, (ˌ)ir, (ˌ)iə+\ *adj* [[1]*in-* + *recognizable*] **:** UNRECOGNIZABLE — **ir·recognizably** \"+\ *adv*

ir·recollection \(ˌ)i, ə, ˌir, ˌiə+\ *n* [[1]*in-* + *recollection*] *archaic* **:** failure to recollect **:** FORGETFULNESS

irrecompensable *adj* [MF, fr. *in-* [1]in- + *recompensable* — more at RECOMPENSABLE] *obs* **:** impossible to requite — **irrecompensably** *adv*, *obs*

ir·reconcilability \(ˌ)i, ə, ˌir, ˌiə+\ *n* **:** the quality or state of being irreconcilable **:** IRRECONCILABLENESS

[1]**ir·reconcilable** \(ˌ)i, ə, (ˌ)ir, (ˌ)iə+\ *adj* [[1]*in-* + *reconcile* + *-able*] **1 :** impossible to bring into friendly accord or understanding **:** hostile beyond the possibility of reconciliation ⟨~ enemies⟩ ⟨~ factions⟩ **2 :** impossible to make consistent or harmonious ⟨these ~ accounts⟩

[2]**irreconcilable** \"\ *n* -S **:** one that is irreconcilable; *esp* **:** a member of a group (as a political party) that vigorously opposes compromise or other collaborative techniques

ir·reconcilableness \"+\ *n* **:** the quality or state of being irreconcilable

ir·reconcilably \"+\ *adv* **:** so as to be irreconcilable **:** beyond the possibility of reaching agreement ⟨~ opposed⟩

irreconcile *vt* [[1]*in-* + *reconcile*] *obs* **:** to put at variance **:** ESTRANGE

ir·reconciliable \(ˌ)i, ə, (ˌ)ir, (ˌ)iə+\ *adj* [MF, fr. LL *irreconciliabilis*, fr. L *in-* [1]in- + *reconciliare* to reconcile + *-abilis* -able — more at RECONCILE] *archaic* **:** IRRECONCILABLE — **ir·reconciliably** \"+\ *adv*, *obs*

ir·reconciliation \(ˌ)i, ə, ˌir, ˌiə+\ *n* [[1]*in-* + *reconciliation*] **:** lack of reconciliation

ir·recoverable \ˌi, ˌir, ˌiə+\ *adj* [[1]*in-* + *recoverable*] **1 :** not capable of being recovered, regained, remedied, or rectified **:** IRREPARABLE ⟨an ~ debt⟩ ⟨suffered an ~ injury⟩ **2** *obs* **:** IRREVOCABLE **3** *archaic* **:** incapable of being restored to health or life — **ir·recoverableness** \"+\ *n*

ir·recoverably \"+\ *adv* **1 :** so as to be irrecoverable **:** beyond any possibility of being recovered, regained, remedied, or rectified ⟨~ lost⟩ ⟨~ ill⟩ ⟨disposed of the evidence finally and ~⟩ **2 :** IRREVOCABLY ⟨determination to commit themselves ~ —J.A.Froude⟩

irrecuperable *adj* [ME, fr. LL *irrecuperabilis*, fr. L *in-* [1]in- + *recuperare* to take back, recover + *-abilis* -able — more at RECOVER] *obs* **:** IRRECOVERABLE — **irrecuperably** *adv*, *obs*

ir·re·cu·sa·ble \ˌirēˈkyüzəbəl\ *adj* [LL *irrecusabilis*, fr. L *in-* [1]in- + LL *recusabilis* capable of being rejected, fr. L *recusare* to reject, refuse + *-abilis* -able — more at RECUSANT] **:** not subject to exception or rejection ⟨an ~ proposition⟩ — **ir·re·cu·sa·bly** \-blē\ *adv*

ir·redeemable \ˌi, ˌir, ˌiə+\ *adj* [[1]*in-* + *redeem* + *-able*] **1 :** not redeemable: as **a** (1) *of mortgaged goods* **:** not recoverable on payment of what is due (2) **:** not terminable by payment of the principal — used of a debt or annuity (3) *of a bond with stated maturity* **:** not callable before maturity **b** *of paper money* **:** not convertible into specie at the pleasure of the holder **:** INCONVERTIBLE **2 a :** admitting of no change or release **:** ABSOLUTE, HOPELESS ⟨~ gloom⟩ **b :** insusceptible of redemption or reform **:** utterly and hopelessly bad **:** IRRECLAIMABLE ⟨~ sinners⟩ — **ir·redeemably** \"+\ *adv*

ir·re·den·ta *or* **ir·ri·den·ta** \ˌirəˈdentə\ *n* -S [It *irredenta* (in *Italia irredenta*, lit., unredeemed Italy — used to refer to Italian-speaking areas not incorporated in Italy), fem. of *irredento* unredeemed, fr. *in-* [1]in- (fr. L) + *redento* redeemed, fr. L *redemptus*, past part. of *redimere* to redeem — more at REDEEM] **:** a region related historically or ethnically to one state but politically subject to another ⟨a frontier ~⟩ ⟨treaty inequities that created needless ~*s*⟩

ir·re·den·tism \-n·ˌtizm\ *n* -S [It. *irredentismo*, the policy of the Italian Irredentists, fr. (*Italia*) *irredenta* + *-ismo* -ism] **:** the principles, policy, or practice of a party or of persons that seek to incorporate within their national boundary territory of which their nation has been deprived or of which the population is ethnically closely related to that of their nation

[1]**ir·re·den·tist** \-ntəst\ *n* -S [It *irredentista* one advocating the incorporation of Italia irredenta into Italy, fr. (*Italia*) *irredenta* + *-ista* -ist] **:** an advocate of irredentism

[2]**irredentist** \ˌ==ˌ==\ *adj* **1 :** of, relating to, or involving irredentists or irredentism ⟨an ~ movement⟩ ⟨~ sentiments⟩ **2 :** living in an irredenta ⟨~ populations⟩ **:** concerning the people of an irredenta ⟨~ problems⟩

ir·reducibility \ˌi, ˌir, ˌiə+\ *n* **:** the quality or state of being irreducible ⟨the ~ of psychological phenomena⟩

ir·reducible \"+\ *adj* [[1]*in-* + *reducible*] **1 :** impossible to bring into a desired state, form, or condition ⟨an ~ hernia⟩ **2 a :** impossible to simplify or make easier or clearer ⟨an ~ formula⟩ ⟨an ~ racial or cultural idiosyncrasy —Abram Kardiner⟩ **b :** impossible to make less or smaller ⟨an ~ minimum⟩ — **ir·reducibly** \"+\ *adv*

irreducible equation *n* **:** a mathematical equation equivalent to one formed by equating an irreducible function to zero

irreducible function *n* **:** an integral rational function of a polynomial that cannot be resolved into integral rational factors of lower degree with coefficients in the same number field

ir·re·duc·ti·ble \ˌi(r)rəˈdəktəbəl, ˌiərə-\ *adj* [[1]*in-* + *reduct* + *-ible*] **:** IRREDUCIBLE

ir·referable \(ˌ)i, ə, (ˌ)ir, (ˌ)iə+\ *adj* [[1]*in-* + *referable*] **:** not referable

ir·reflection also **ir·reflexion** \ˌi, ˌir, ˌiə+\ n [F irréflexion, fr. in- 1in- + réflexion — more at REFLECTION] : lack of mental consideration (as of a project or course of action)

ir·reflective \“+\ adj [1in- + reflective] : not based on reflection : UNTHINKING, HEEDLESS ⟨an ~ delight⟩ — **ir·reflectively** \“+\ adv — **ir·reflectiveness** \“+\ n

ir·reflexive \“+\ adj [1in- + reflexive] **1** : not reflexive **2** of a logical or mathematical relation : never relating a term to itself — **ir·reflexivity** \(ˈ)i, ə, ˌir, ˌiə\ n

ir·reformable \ˌi, ˌir, ˌiə+\ adj [1in- + reformable] **1** : incapable of being reformed : INCORRIGIBLE ⟨an ~ rascal⟩ **2** : not subject to revision or alteration : final or perfect beyond the possibility of improvement ⟨~ dogma⟩ ⟨an ~ judgment⟩

ir·ref·ra·ga·bil·i·ty \(ˌ)i(r)ˌrefrəgəˈbilәd·ē, əˌ-, (ˌ)iəˌ-\ n : the quality or state of being irrefragable

ir·ref·ra·ga·ble \(ˈ)i(r)ˈrefrəgəbəl, əˈ-, (ˈ)iəˈ-\ adj [LL irrefragabilis, fr. L in- 1in- + refragari to resist, oppose (fr. re- + -fragari — as in suffragari to vote for, support) + -abilis -able — more at SUFFRAGE] **1** : impossible to gainsay, deny, or refute ⟨~ arguments⟩ ⟨~ data⟩ ⟨these ~ authorities⟩ **2** : impossible to break or alter : INVIOLABLE, INDESTRUCTIBLE ⟨~ rules⟩ ⟨an ~ cement⟩ — **ir·ref·ra·ga·bly** \-blē\ adv

ir·refrangible \ˌi, ˌir, ˌiə+\ adj [1in- + refrangible] **1** : IRREFRAGABLE 2 **2** : not capable of being refracted — used of visible light and other radiations

ir·refusable \“+\ adj [1in- + refusable] : impossible to refuse

ir·refutability \(ˌ)i, ə, (ˌ)ir, (ˌ)iə+\ n : the quality or state of being irrefutable

ir·refutable \“+\ adj [LL irrefutabilis, fr. L in- 1in- + LL refutabilis refutable — more at REFUTABLE] : impossible to refute : INCONTROVERTIBLE ⟨an ~ argument⟩ — **ir·refutably** \“+\ adv

ir·regardless \ˌi, ˌir, ˌiə+\ adv [prob. blend of irrespective and regardless] nonstand : REGARDLESS

ir·regenerate \“+\ adj [1in- + regenerate] archaic : UNREGENERATE

1**ir·regular** \(ˈ)i, ə, (ˈ)ir, (ˈ)iə+\ adj [ME irreguler, fr. MF, fr. LL irregularis, fr. L in- 1in- + LL regularis regular — more at REGULAR] **1** of a person **a** Roman Catholicism : prevented by an impediment or bar from receiving or exercising clerical orders or offices **b** : behaving without regard to established laws, customs, or moral principles ⟨a wild ~ man in his youth⟩ **c** : not belonging to or not having satisfied the requirements of some particular group or organized body ⟨an ~ physician⟩ **2 a** : failing to accord with what is usual, proper, accepted, or right ⟨~ conduct⟩ : contrary to rule or custom ⟨some of his documents were ~⟩ ⟨although it was ~ we accepted the excuse⟩ **b** of a word or inflection : not conforming to the normal or usual manner of inflection ⟨sell, cast, feed are ~ verbs⟩; specif : STRONG 16a **c** (1) : improper or inadequate because of failure to conform to a prescribed course (2) : of a marriage under Eng or Scots law : celebrated without either proclamation of the banns or publication of intention to marry : CLANDESTINE **d** : not belonging to the regular army organization but raised for a special purpose ⟨~ troops are often used as independent commands to harass the enemy⟩ **3 a** : lacking perfect symmetry of form : not straight, smooth, even, regular ⟨a rough ~ terrain⟩ ⟨a long ~ coastline⟩ ⟨~ teeth⟩ **b** of a flower or its parts : lacking uniformity ⟨an ~ corolla⟩; specif : ZYGOMORPHIC **4 a** : lacking continuity or regularity of occurrence, activity, or function ⟨~ payments⟩ ⟨~ intervals⟩ ⟨an ~ worker⟩ **b** of a physiological function : failing to occur at regular or normal intervals ⟨~ menstruation⟩ ⟨have your bowels been ~⟩ **c** of an individual : failing to defecate at such intervals ⟨was constipated and very ~⟩ **d** of a market : characterized by individual price movements in both directions without establishment of an overall trend ⟨cotton futures were ~⟩

2**irregular** \“\ n -s : one that is irregular: as **a** : a soldier (as a guerrilla or partisan) who is not a member of a regular military force — usu. used in pl. **b irregulars** pl : merchandise that has imperfections or that falls below the manufacturer's usual standard or specifications and is usu. sold unbranded and at a concession in price — compare 2SECOND 4

3**irregular** \“\ adj [NL Irregularia] : EXOCYCLIC

irregular carrier n : a common carrier that operates without regular schedule or over routes not specified in the certificate or permit

irregular deposit n : a deposit of money (as for safekeeping) made with the understanding that an equivalent amount but not necessarily the identical money is to be returned to the depositor

ir·regularia \(ˌ)i, ə, ˌir, ˌiə+\ [NL, fr. LL, neut. pl. of irregularis] syn of EXOCYCLOIDA

ir·regularity \“+\ n [ME irregularite, fr. OF irregularité, fr. ML irregularitat-, irregularitas, fr. LL irregularis irregular + L -itat-, -itas -ity — more at IRREGULAR] **1** : the quality or state of being irregular **2** : something that is irregular; esp : lack of proper and honest conduct (as in respect to a position of trust) — usu. used in pl. ⟨alleged irregularities in the city government⟩ ⟨irregularities in his accounts⟩

ir·regularly \(ˈ)i, ə, (ˈ)ir, (ˈ)iə+\ adv : in an irregular manner : at irregular intervals : so as to be irregular ⟨came to school very ~⟩

irregular ode n : an ode characterized by irregularity of verse and stanzaic structure and by lack of correspondence between parts — called also pseudo-Pindaric ode

irregular peloria n : peloria in which symmetry is attained by increase in number of some part — compare REGULAR PELORIA

irregular variable n : a variable star whose light fluctuations are nonperiodic

1**irregulate** adj [ML irregulatus, fr. L in- 1in- + LL regulatus, past part. of regulare to regulate — more at REGULATE] obs : not regulated

2**irregulate** vt, obs : to make irregular : DISORDER

ir·regulated \(ˈ)i, ə, (ˈ)ir, (ˈ)iə+\ adj [1in- + regulated] : not regulated or controlled ⟨~ moods⟩

ir·relate or **ir·related** \ˌi, ˌir, ˌiə+\ adj [irrelate fr. 1in- + L relatus, suppletive past part. of referre to relate; irrelated fr. 1in- + related — more at RELATE] : not related

ir·relation \“+\ n [1in- + relation] : UNRELATEDNESS

ir·relative \(ˈ)i, ə, (ˈ)ir, (ˈ)iə+\ adj [1in- + relative] : not relative: as **a** : not related or connected : lacking mutual relationship ⟨remote and ~ regions —Douglas Carruthers⟩ **b** : not pertinent or relevant ⟨making ~ statements⟩ — **ir·relatively** \“+\ adv

ir·relevance or **ir·relevancy** \“+\ n, pl **irrelevances** or **irrelevancies** **1** : the quality or state of being irrelevant ⟨the ~ of these remarks⟩ **2** : something irrelevant ⟨a plot full of irrelevancies and digressions⟩

ir·relevant \“+\ adj [1in- + relevant] : not relevant : not applicable or pertinent : FOREIGN, EXTRANEOUS ⟨~ allegations⟩ ⟨~ to the matter in hand⟩

ir·relevantly \“+\ adv : in an irrelevant manner : so as to be irrelevant ⟨spoke idly and ~⟩

ir·relievable \ˌi, ˌir, ˌiə+\ adj [1in- + relieve + -able] : impossible to relieve ⟨~ suffering⟩

ir·religion \“+\ n [MF or L; MF, fr. L irreligion-, irreligio, fr. in- 1in- + religion-, religio religion — more at RELIGION] **1** : the quality or state of being irreligious : lack of religion : IMPIETY **2** obs : a false religion : a perverted form of religion

ir·religionist \“+\ n : a supporter or practicer of irreligion

ir·religiosity \“+\ n [LL irreligiositas, fr. L irreligiosus + -itas -ity] : the quality or state of being irreligious

ir·religious \“+\ adj [L irreligiosus, fr. in- 1in- + religiosus religious — more at RELIGIOUS] **1** : lacking recognized religious emotions, doctrines, or practices : UNGODLY **2** : of or constituting irreligion : PROFANE ⟨~ speech⟩ **3** obs : relating to, believing in, or practicing a false religion — **ir·religiously** \“+\ adv

ir·re·me·able \(ˈ)iˌrēmēəbəl, əˈr-, (ˈ)irˌr-, (ˈ)iəˌr-\ adj [L irremeabilis, fr. in- 1in- + remeare to go back (fr. re- + meare to go) + -abilis -able — more at PERMEATE] **1** : offering no possibility of return ⟨an ~ path⟩ **2** : unable to return to a former place or state : IRREVERSIBLE ⟨an ~ stream⟩ ⟨~ tissue degeneration⟩ — **ir·re·me·ably** \-blē\ adv

ir·remediable \ˌi, ˌir, ˌiə+\ adj [L irremediabilis, fr. in- 1in- + remediabilis remediable — more at REMEDIABLE] : impossible to remedy, correct, redress, alter, cure ⟨an ~ error⟩ ⟨~ defects of character⟩ — **ir·remediableness** \“+\ n — **ir·remediably** \“+\ adv

irremediless adj [1in- + remediless] obs : REMEDILESS

ir·remissible \ˌi, ˌir, ˌiə+\ adj [MF, fr. LL irremissibilis, fr. L in- 1in- + LL remissibilis remissible — more at REMISSIBLE] : not remissible: as **a** : impossible to overlook or forgive : UNPARDONABLE ⟨~ crimes⟩ **b** : impossible to refrain from or escape : OBLIGATORY ⟨~ duties⟩ ⟨an ~ responsibility⟩ — **ir·remissibly** \“+\ adv

ir·remissive \“+\ adj [1in- + remissive] : not remissive

ir·removability \“+\ n : the quality or state of being irremovable

ir·removable \“+\ adj [1in- + removable] : not removable: as **a** : impossible to remove or take away : not displaceable **b** (1) : impossible to remove or dismiss from office or position ⟨an ~ officer⟩ (2) : appointed for or granted for life tenure — used of an incumbent of a benefice who cannot be transferred or dismissed except for a grave crime and by canonical process or to a benefice so held **c** : IMMOVABLE, INFLEXIBLE — **irremovably** adv

ir·repair \“+\ n [1in- + repair] : DISREPAIR

irrepairable adj [1in- + repairable] : not capable of being repaired

ir·reparable \(ˌ)i, ə, (ˌ)ir, (ˌ)iə+\ adj [ME irreperable, fr. MF irreparable, fr. L irreparabilis, fr. in- 1in- + reparabilis reparable — more at REPARABLE] : not reparable : impossible to make good, undo, repair, or remedy : IRRETRIEVABLE ⟨an ~ loss⟩ ⟨~ harm⟩ ⟨~ tissue changes⟩

ir·reparableness \“+\ n -ES : the quality or state of being irreparable

ir·reparably \“+\ adv : in an irreparable manner or to an irreparable degree

ir·re·pa·tri·a·ble \ˌi(r)rēˌpā·trēəbəl ˌiərē-, -rēˌ-\ n -S [1in- + repatriate + -able] : a person who cannot be repatriated usu. for political reasons

ir·repealability \ˌi, ˌir, ˌiə+\ n : the quality or state of being irrepealable

ir·repealable \“+\ adj [1in- + repealable] : not capable of being repealed : impossible to revoke ⟨~ provisions of the statute⟩

ir·repentance \“+\ n [1in- + repentance] : IMPENITENCE

ir·replaceable \“+\ adj [1in- + replaceable] : not replaceable — **ir·replaceableness** \“+\ n -ES — **ir·replaceably** \“+\ adv

ir·repleviable \“+\ adj [1in- + replevin + -able] : not subject to replevin

ir·replevisable \“+\ adj [1in- + replevisable] : IRREPLEVIABLE

ir·reprehensible \(ˌ)i, ə, ˌir, ˌiə+\ adj [ME, fr. LL irreprehensibilis, fr. L in- 1in- + reprehensus (past part. of reprehendere to reprehend) + -ibilis -ible — more at REPREHEND] : not reprehensible : free from blame or reproach ⟨conduct in all respects ~⟩

ir·representable \“+\ adj [1in- + representable] : not representable

ir·repressibility \ˌi, ˌir, ˌiə+\ n -ES : the quality or state of being irrepressible ⟨his constant ~⟩

1**ir·repressible** \“+\ adj [1in- + repress + -able] : impossible to repress, restrain, or control ⟨~ joy⟩ ⟨~ conflict⟩ ⟨an ~ chatterbox⟩

2**irrepressible** \“\ n -S : an irrepressible person

ir·repressibleness \“+\ n -ES : IRREPRESSIBILITY

ir·repressibly \“+\ adv : in an irrepressible manner : so as to be irrepressible ⟨~ gay⟩

ir·repressive \“+\ adj [1in- + repressive] : IRREPRESSIBLE

ir·reproachability \“+\ n : the quality or state of being irreproachable

ir·reproachable \“+\ adj [1in- + reproachable] : not subject to or deserving of reproach : BLAMELESS, FAULTLESS, IMPECCABLE ⟨~ manners⟩ ⟨an ~ character⟩

ir·reproachableness \“+\ n -ES : IRREPROACHABILITY

ir·reproachably \“+\ adv : so as to be beyond reproach : in an irreproachable manner

ir·reproducible \(ˌ)i, ə, ˌir, ˌiə+\ adj [1in- + reproducible] : not reproducible : impossible to duplicate

ir·reprovable \ˌi, ˌir, ˌiə+\ adj [1in- + reprovable] **1** : IRREPROACHABLE **2** obs : INDISPUTABLE

ir·rep·tion \əˈrepshən\ n -S [LL irreption-, irreptio, fr. L irreptus (past part. of irrepere to creep in, fr. in- 2in- + repere to creep) + -ion-, -io -ion — more at REPTILE] : an act or instance of entering by stealth or inadvertence ⟨the ~ of pseudoclassical plurals in technical language⟩

ir·rep·ti·tious \ˌiˌrepˈtishəs\ adj [L irreptus + E -itious] : marked by or resulting from irreption ⟨an ~ error in transliterating⟩ ⟨~ words in a text⟩

ir·resistance \ˌi, ˌir, ˌiə+\ n [1in- + resistance] : lack of resistance : SUBMISSIVENESS

ir·resistibility \“+\ n : the quality or state of being irresistible

1**ir·resistible** or **ir·resistable** \“+\ adj [1in- + resist + -ible, -able] : impossible to successfully resist : superior to opposition ⟨an ~ attraction⟩

2**irresistible** \“\ n -S : an irresistible person or thing

ir·resistibleness \“+\ n : IRRESISTIBILITY

ir·resistibly \“+\ adv : to an irresistible extent or degree : so as to be irresistible

ir·resistless \“+\ adj [blend of irrestible and resistless] archaic : IRRESISTIBLE

ir·resoluble \(ˌ)i, (ˌ)ir, (ˌ)iə, ə+\ adj [L irresolubilis, fr. in- 1in- + resolvere to resolve + -bilis -ble — more at RESOLVE] **1** archaic : incapable of being dissolved or resolved into parts : INSOLUBLE **2** archaic : incapable of being relieved or dispelled **3** : incapable of being solved : impossible to make open, clear, or simple ⟨the question is ~ on the evidence at hand⟩

ir·resolute \(ˈ)i, ə, (ˈ)ir, (ˈ)iə+\ adj [1in- + resolute] **1** obs : not resolved or solved : UNEXPLAINED **2 a** : uncertain how to act or proceed ⟨stood ~ waiting for some inspiration⟩ **b** : lacking strength of purpose or decisiveness of character : weak and vacillating ⟨a kindly man but very ~⟩

ir·resolutely \“+\ adv : in an irresolute manner : so as to be or appear irresolute

ir·resoluteness \“+\ n : the quality or state of being irresolute

ir·resolution \(ˌ)i, ə, ˌir, ˌiə+\ n [prob. fr. MF, fr. in- 1in- + resolution — more at RESOLUTION] **1** obs : the quality or state of not having formed a decided opinion : DOUBT, UNCERTAINTY **2** : lack of resolution : a fluctuation of mind (as in doubt or between hope and fear) : INDECISION, VACILLATION

ir·resolvable \ˌi, ˌir, ˌiə+\ adj [1in- + resolvable] : incapable of being resolved; esp : impossible to separate into component parts

ir·resolved \“+\ adj [1in- + resolved] : not resolved : lacking in certainty, assurance, or decision ⟨a troubled and ~ heart⟩ — **ir·resolvedly** \“+\ adv

ir·respective \“+\ adj [1in- + respective] **1** obs : lacking in respect : DISRESPECTFUL **2** archaic : functioning without or having no regard for persons, conditions, circumstances, or consequences ⟨oversteps in his ~ zeal every decency and every right —S.T.Coleridge⟩

ir·respectively \“+\ adv, obs : in an irrespective manner

irrespective of also **irrespectively of** prep : without respect or regard to : independent or regardless of ⟨values his friends irrespective of what he may hope to gain from them⟩ ⟨this payment is made irrespective of any settlement the court may order⟩

ir·respirable \“+; (ˌ)i, ə, (ˌ)ir, (ˌ)iə+\ adj [F, fr. LL irrespirabilis, fr. L in- 1in + respirare to breathe, respire + -abilis -able — more at RESPIRE] : unfit for breathing ⟨an ~ vapor⟩

ir·responsibility \ˌi, ˌir, ˌiə+\ n : the quality or state of being irresponsible

1**ir·responsible** \“+\ adj [1in- + responsible] : not responsible: as **a** : not required to answer to some higher authority : not liable to be called into question : subject to no oversight or control ⟨shall the planning be done by some ~ dictatorship or by democratic representatives whose acts are subject to discussion and criticism —M.R.Cohen⟩ ⟨the state is ~ and exempt from all ordinary controls⟩ **b** : not based on sound reasoned considerations ⟨~ optimism⟩ ⟨~ dreams⟩; esp : uttered without regard to truth, propriety, or fairness ⟨~ gossip⟩ ⟨these ~ charges⟩ **c** (1) : lacking a proper or adequate sense of responsibility ⟨~ jacks-in-office⟩ (2) : mentally inadequate to bear responsibility in an acceptable or normal manner ⟨the mother . . . was finally declared ~ and of too low intelligence to care for her large brood of children —Eda & Lawrence LeShan⟩ **d** : unprepared or unwilling to meet financial responsibilities ⟨financially ~ drivers⟩

2**irresponsible** \“\ n : one who is irresponsible

ir·responsibleness \“+\ n : IRRESPONSIBILITY

ir·responsibly \“+\ adv : so as to be or appear irresponsible : in an irresponsible degree

ir·responsive \“+\ adj [1in- + responsive] : not responsive: as **a** : not able, ready, or inclined to respond ⟨the patient was ~ to treatment⟩ ⟨~ to control⟩ **b** : IRRESPONSIBLE a — **ir·responsiveness** \“+\ n

ir·restrainable \“+\ adj [1in- + restrain + -able] : UNRESTRAINABLE — **ir·restrainably** \“+\ adv

ir·resultive \“+\ adj [1in- + result + -ive] : lacking result : ABORTIVE

ir·resuscitable \“+\ adj [1in- + resuscitable] : impossible to restore to life or activity — **ir·resuscitably** \“+\ adv

ir·retention \“+\ n [1in- + retention] : failure of retention

ir·retentive \“+\ adj [1in- + retentive] : lacking ability to retain something ⟨a casual ~ mind⟩ — **ir·retentiveness** \“+\ n

ir·reticence \(ˈ)i, ə, (ˈ)ir, (ˈ)iə+\ n [1in- + reticence] : something lacking in reticence ⟨the ~s that are inseparable from military life⟩

ir·retraceable \ˌi, ˌir, ˌiə+\ adj [1in- + retrace + -able] : impossible to retrace

ir·retractile \“+\ adj [1in- + retractile] : not retractile

ir·retrievability \“+\ n : the quality or state of being irretrievable

ir·retrievable \“+\ adj [1in- + retrieve + -able] : not retrievable : impossible to recoup, repair, or overcome ⟨an ~ loss⟩ ⟨~ errors in judgment⟩ ⟨~ ruin⟩

ir·retrievableness \“+\ n -ES : IRRETRIEVABILITY

ir·retrievably \“+\ adv : so as to be irretrievable : to an irretrievable degree or in an irretrievable manner ⟨manuscript ~ lost⟩

ir·rev·e·lant or **ir·rev·a·lent** \(ˈ)i(r)ˌrevələnt, əˈr-, (ˈ)iəˌr-\ adj [by alter.] substand : IRRELEVANT

ir·reverence \(ˈ)i, ə, (ˈ)ir, (ˈ)iə+\ n -S [ME, fr. L irreverentia, fr. irreverent-, irreverens + -ia -y] **1 a** : the quality or state of being irreverent : failure to offer due respect to that which is generally reverenced **b** : an irreverent act or utterance ⟨these pert ~s⟩ **2** : condition of being without reverence : dishonored or neglected state : DISREGARD ⟨treating their elders with complete ~⟩

ir·reverency \“+\ n -ES : IRREVERENCE 1

ir·reverend \“+\ adj [1in- + reverend] **1** : not reverend : not worthy of reverence **2** archaic : IRREVERENT — **ir·reverendly** \“+\ adv

ir·reverent \“+\ adj [L irreverent-, irreverens, fr. in- 1in- + reverent-, reverens reverent — more at REVERENT] : not reverent: as **a** : failing in proper reverence to something entitled to veneration or respect ⟨~ scholars mocking sacred things⟩ **b** : characterized by a lightly pert or exuberant quality or manner ⟨a certain ~ gaiety and ease of manner⟩ — **ir·reverently** \“+\ adv

ir·reverential \(ˌ)i, ə, ˌir, ˌiə+\ adj [1in- + reverential] : lacking in due respect or reverence : IRREVERENT — **ir·reverentially** \“+\ adv

ir·reverentialism \“+\ n -S : the quality or state of being irreverent

ir·reversibility \ˌi, ˌir, ˌiə+\ n : the quality or state of being irreversible

ir·reversible \“+\ adj [1in- + reverse + -ible] : incapable of being reversed: as **a** : impossible to recall, repeal, or annul ⟨an ~ decree⟩ **b** : impossible to turn about, back, or upside down ⟨an ~ cover⟩ ⟨~ cushions⟩ **c** : impossible to make run or take place backward ⟨an ~ engine⟩ ⟨~ chemical syntheses⟩ **d** of a colloid : incapable of undergoing transformation from sol to gel or vice versa **e** : unsymmetrical with respect to constituent elements or terms ⟨an ~ relation⟩ **f** of a pathological process : of such severity that recovery is impossible ⟨~ shock⟩ ⟨~ anoxic damage to the brain⟩ — **ir·reversibly** \“+\ adv

ir·revocability \(ˌ)i, ə, ˌir, ˌiə+\ n : the quality or state of being irrevocable

ir·revocable \(ˌ)i, ə, (ˌ)ir, (ˌ)iə+\ adj [ME, fr. L irrevocabilis, fr. in- 1in- + revocabilis revocable — more at REVOCABLE] : incapable of being recalled or revoked : past recall : UNALTERABLE ⟨an ~ promise⟩ ⟨firm and ~ is my doom —Shak.⟩

ir·revocableness \“+\ n : IRREVOCABILITY

ir·revocably \“+\ adv : so as to be irrevocable : beyond any possibility of change ⟨~ determined⟩

ir·revoluble \“+\ adj [1in- + revoluble] archaic : having no finite period of revolution

irridenta var of IRREDENTA

ir·ri·ga·ble \ˈirəgəbəl, -rēg-\ also **ir·ri·gat·able** \ˈirəˌgād·-əbəl, -ātə-, ˌ==ˈ===\ adj [irrigate + -able] : possible to irrigate : susceptible of or suitable for irrigation ⟨~ land⟩ — **ir·ri·ga·bly** \ˈirəgəblē, -rēg-, -bli\ adv

ir·ri·gate \ˈirəˌgāt, usu -ād·+V\ vb -ED/-ING/-S [L irrigatus, past part. of irrigare, fr. in- 2in- + rigare to water — more at RAIN] vt **1** : WET, MOISTEN ⟨secretions that ~ mucous surfaces⟩: as **a** : to supply (as land or crops) with water by artificial means (as by diverting streams, digging canals, flooding, or spraying) **b** : to apply a continuous stream of liquid to (a part of the body) for a therapeutic purpose **2** : to refresh or make fertile as if by watering ~ vi **1** : to practice irrigation (as of land) **2** slang : to drink intoxicating liquor : IMBIBE

ir·ri·ga·tion \ˌirəˈgāshən\ n -S often attrib [L irrigation-, irrigatio, fr. irrigatus + -ion-, -io -ion] **1** : the action or process of irrigating: as **a** : the artificial watering of land (as by canals, ditches, pipes, or flooding) to supply moisture for plant growth ⟨~ ditches⟩ ⟨growing crops by ~⟩; also : a single watering by such means ⟨the berries will need another ~ if it doesn't rain soon⟩ **b** : application of a continuous stream of liquid to a part of the body for a therapeutic purpose ⟨wound ~⟩ **2** : a refreshing or making fertile as if by watering

ir·ri·ga·tion·al \ˌirəˌgāshənᵊl, -shnəl\ adj : of or relating to irrigation

irrigation efficiency n : the ratio between irrigation water actually utilized by growing crops and water diverted from a source (as a stream) in order to supply such irrigation water

ir·ri·ga·tion·ist \ˌirəˈgāsh(ə)nəst\ n -S : a user or advocate of irrigation esp. in farming

ir·ri·ga·tive \ˈirəˌgād·iv\ adj : IRRIGATIONAL

ir·ri·ga·tor \-ād·ə(r), -ātə-\ n -S : one that irrigates: as **a** : an agriculturist who employs irrigation in the growing of crops **b** : a device, apparatus, or system used to irrigate something (as a wound or a crop) **c** : a worker who supervises agricultural irrigation or irrigating equipment

ir·rig·u·ous \əˈrigyəwəs\ adj [L irriguus, fr. irrigare to irrigate — more at IRRIGATE] **1** archaic : IRRIGATED, MOISTENED; esp : well-watered **2** : serving to irrigate or water ⟨slow ~ streams⟩

ir·ri·sion \əˈrizhən\ n -S [L irrision-, irrisio, fr. irrisus (past part. of irridēre to laugh at, fr. in- 2in- + ridēre to laugh) + -ion-, -io -ion — more at RIDICULOUS] : a laughing at a person or thing : DERISION

1**ir·ri·sor** \əˈrīzər\ [NL, fr. L, mocker, scoffer, fr. irrisus + -or] syn of PHOENICULUS

2**irrisor** \“\ n -S : a bird of the genus Phoeniculus : WOOD HOOPOE

ir·ri·sor·i·dae \ˌirəˈsȯrəˌdē, -ˈzȯ-\ [NL, fr. Irrisor, type genus + -idae] syn of PHOENICULIDAE

ir·riso·ry \-īsərē, -īzə-, -izə-\ adj [LL irrisorius, fr. L irrisus (past part. of irridēre to laugh at) + -orius -ory — more at IRRISION] : given to derision : DERISIVE

ir·ri·ta·bil·i·ty \ˌirəd·əˈbiləd·ē, -rətəˈ-, -lətē, -i\ n -ES [L irritabilitas, fr. irritabilis + -itas -ity] : the quality or state of being irritable: as **a** : quick excitability to annoyance, impatience, or anger : PETULANCE, FRETFULNESS ⟨~ of temper⟩ ⟨showing increasing ~ as he waited⟩ **b** : abnormal excitability of an organ or part of the body (as the stomach or bladder) : heightened responsiveness **c** : the property of protoplasm and of living organisms that permits them to react to environmental changes (as by specific orientation, change of shape, or production or cessation of movement)

ir·ri·ta·ble \ˈirəd·əbəl, -rətə-\ *adj, sometimes* -ER/-EST [L *irritabilis*, fr. *irritare* to irritate + *-abilis* -able — more at IRRITATE] **:** capable of being irritated: as **a :** likely to become impatient, angry, or disturbed **:** easily exasperated ⟨an ~ disposition⟩ ⟨such ~ neurotic people⟩; *broadly* **:** easily excitable **b :** excessively or unduly sensitive to irritants or stimuli **:** exhibiting abnormal irritability ⟨an ~ colon⟩ **c** *of protoplasm or a living organism* **:** responsive to stimuli

syn FRACTIOUS, PEEVISH, SNAPPISH, WASPISH, PETULANT, PETTISH, HUFFY, HUFFISH, FRETFUL, QUERULOUS: IRRITABLE implies ready, impatient excitability whereby one is angered and exasperated easily ⟨a hot day and the clerk in the store was *irritable* . . . had not slept much the night before and he had a headache —Lyle Saxon⟩ FRACTIOUS may suggest a wilful or truculent unruliness or perverse crossness ⟨those who are spoilt and *fractious*, who must have everything their own way —F.A.Swinnerton⟩ ⟨a wary, querulous, grumbling, vain, testy, self-righteous, honorable man, a defiant and *fractious* servant and a high-handed and mistrustful master —Arthur Schlesinger b.1917⟩ PEEVISH may suggest childish irritability about petty matters ⟨*peevish* because he called her and she did not come, and he threw his bowl of tea on the ground like a willful child —Pearl Buck⟩ ⟨*peevish*, and wrathful, often insolent, and quarrelsome —Charles Kingsley⟩ SNAPPISH may apply to an irritability manifesting itself in sharp, tart, sarcastic objections and rejoinders ⟨a little *snappish* at reflecting how many miles he had to post —Samuel Butler †1902⟩ WASPISH may connote testy, resentful, stinging irascibility ⟨a little *waspish* woman who would have been ahead of me snapped out at a man who seemed to be with her —C.S.Lewis⟩ PETULANT may suggest sulky and capricious dissatisfaction and complaint as though resolved to be displeased ⟨in his youth the spoiled child of Boston, in middle life he was *petulant* and irritable, inclined to sulk when his will was crossed —V.L. Parrington⟩ PETTISH may apply to childish, sulky ill humor of or as if of one slighted ⟨she heard Amy's voice in *pettish* exclamation: "Oh, get out, you!" —Arnold Bennett⟩ HUFFY or HUFFISH may suggest a tending to take undue offense or to have one's arrogant pride hurt and to parade one's blustering irritation ⟨rather *huffy*, and somewhat on the high-and-mighty order with him —Harriet B. Stowe⟩ FRETFUL suggests ill-humored continuing irritability and complaining or whining peevishness ⟨his voice was peevish, almost whining, and there were certain overtones in it which recalled the *fretful* complaining voice —W.H.Wright⟩ QUERULOUS stresses the idea of discontented whining complaining, often childishly futile, resentful, and arising from determined inclination to be displeased ⟨the man himself grew old and *querulous* and hysterical with failure and repeated disappointment and chronic poverty —Aldous Huxley⟩

irritable heart *n* **:** CARDIAC NEUROSIS

ir·ri·ta·ble·ness *n* -ES **:** IRRITABILITY

ir·ri·ta·bly \-blē,-bli\ *adv* **:** in an irritable manner **:** with irritability

ir·ri·ta·ment \ˈirəd·əmənt, əˈrid· -\ *n* -S [F, fr. L *irritamentum*, fr. *irritare* to irritate, provoke + *-mentum* -ment] *archaic* **:** INCITEMENT, IRRITANT

¹ir·ri·tan·cy \ˈirəd·ənsē, -ətən-, -si *also* -ətᵊn-\ *n* -ES [¹*irritant* + *-cy*] *Roman, civil, & Scots law* **:** a making or the quality or state of being made null and void **:** INVALIDATION; *also* **:** IRRITANT CLAUSE

²irritancy \ˈ"\ *n* -ES [²*irritant* + *-cy*] **:** the quality or state of being irritating

¹ir·ri·tant \-ənt,-ᵊnt\ *adj* [MF, fr. LL *irritant-, irritans*, pres. part. of *irritare* to invalidate, fr. L *irritus* invalid, fr. *in-* ¹in- + *-ritus* (fr. *ratus* valid, fr. past part. of *reri* to reckon, calculate) — more at REASON] **:** making null and void — compare IRRITANT CLAUSE

²irritant \ˈ"\ *adj* [F, fr. MF, fr. L *irritant-, irritans*, pres. part. of *irritare* to irritate, provoke — more at IRRITATE] **:** IRRITATING; *specif* **:** tending to produce irritation or inflammation

³irritant \ˈ"\ *n* -S **:** something that irritates or excites; *specif* **:** an agent by which irritation is produced ⟨a chemical ~⟩

irritant clause *n* [¹*irritant*] *Scots law* **:** a clause in an instrument providing that if certain specified events shall take place the instrument shall be void

¹ir·ri·tate \ˈirə,tāt, *usu* -ād·+V\ *vb* -ED/-ING/-S [L *irritatus*, past part. of *irritare*, fr. *in-* ²in- + *-ritare* (perh. akin to L *oriri* to rise) — more at RISE] *vt* **1** *obs* **:** to increase the action of **:** heighten excitement in **:** AGGRAVATE **2 :** to excite impatience, anger, or displeasure in **:** PROVOKE, EXASPERATE, ANNOY ⟨*irritated* by the child's insolence⟩ **3 :** to cause (an organ or tissue) to be irritable **:** produce irritation in ⟨harsh soaps may ~ the skin⟩ ⟨avoid *irritating* the sensitive laryngeal reflexes —*Anesthesia Digest*⟩ **4 :** to produce excitation in (as a nerve) **:** STIMULATE **:** cause (as a muscle) to contract ~ *vi* **:** to cause or induce displeasure or irritation ⟨it's the petty things of life that ~ most⟩ ⟨a soothing lotion for burns that is guaranteed not to ~⟩

syn EXASPERATE, NETTLE, ROIL, RILE, PEEVE, AGGRAVATE, PROVOKE: IRRITATE means to arouse angry annoyance or great displeasure evoking feelings ranging from impatience to rage ⟨it *irritated* him that she peered so into everything that was his, searching him out —D.H.Lawrence⟩ ⟨a Mexican carpenter will *irritate* newcomers beyond endurance by taking a three-hour siesta —Green Peyton⟩ EXASPERATE suggests galling vexation or angry annoyance ⟨her unexplained departure had *exasperated* him —Edith Wharton⟩ NETTLE usu. indicates a stinging pique, sometimes a rankling irritation ⟨a touch of light scorn in her tone *nettled* me —W.J.Locke⟩ ROIL and its variant RILE suggest inducing an angry or resentful state of agitated disturbance ⟨her manner of ignoring him. That *roiled* him inexpressibly —C.S.Forester⟩ ⟨with raucous taunting and ribald remarks to *rile* up the proprietor —W.A.White⟩ PEEVE applies to arousing fretful irritation, sometimes petty or querulous ⟨when she ventured to criticize it, even mildly, he was *peeved* —Louis Auchincloss⟩ AGGRAVATE may apply to repeated action or condition that intensifies anger or irritation ⟨he did not sweat and pray over each card as she must, but he did keep an eye out for reneging and demanded a cut now and then just to *aggravate* her —J.F.Powers⟩ PROVOKE may suggest irritation or anger that excites to action ⟨don't think I am trying to *provoke* you or to make fun of what you revere —Ann Bridge⟩ ⟨a Tory resident who *provoked* local animosities and was charged with high treason —*Amer. Guide Series: Conn.*⟩

²irritate \ˈ"\ *vt* [LL *irritatus*, past part. of *irritare* to invalidate — more at IRRITANT] **:** to make null and void **:** DEFEAT

irritated *adj* [fr. past part. of ¹*irritate*] **:** subjected to irritation: as **a :** roused to anger **:** ANNOYED ⟨that tired ~ father⟩ **b :** roughened, reddened, or inflamed by some irritating agent ⟨an ~ skin⟩ ⟨hiding her ~ eyes behind dark glasses⟩ — **ir·ri·tat·ed·ly** \ˈ==,===, ,==ˈ===\ *adv*

irritating *adj* **:** causing displeasure or annoyance **:** PROVOKING — **ir·ri·tat·ing·ly** \ˈ==,===, ,==ˈ===\ *adv*

ir·ri·ta·tion \,irəˈtāshən\ *n* -S [MF, fr. L *irritation-, irritatio*, fr. *irritatus* (past part. of *irritare* to irritate, provoke) + *-ion-, -io* -ion — more at IRRITATE] **1 :** an act of irritating or a state of being irritated: as **a :** excitement to activity **:** STIMULATION **b :** excitement of impatience, anger, or passion **:** ANNOYANCE **c :** IRRITABILITY b **2 :** EXCITATION 3; *esp* **:** the act of exciting a muscle to contraction by artificial stimulation

ir·ri·ta·tive \ˈirə,tād·iv, -ātl, |ēv *also* |əv\ *adj* [¹*irritate* + *-ive*] **1 :** serving to excite **:** IRRITATING ⟨an ~ agent⟩ **2 :** accompanied with or produced by increased action or irritation ⟨an ~ cough⟩

ir·ri·ta·tor \-ād·ə(r), -ātə-\ *n* -S **:** one that irritates

ir·ri·ta·to·motility \,irə,tōt+\ *n* [*irritation* + *-o-* + *motility*] **:** response of plant tissues to external stimuli by means of movements or curvatures

irrogate *vt* -ED/-ING/-S [L *irrogatus*, past part. of *irrogare* to propose against, impose, fr. *in-* ²in- + *rogare* to ask, request — more at RIGHT] *obs Scot* **:** to impose (a penalty) legally — **irrogation** *n* -S *obs*

¹irrorate *vt* -ED/-ING/-S [L *irroratus*, past part. of *irrorare*, fr. *in-* ²in- + *rorare* to moisten, shed moisture, fr. *ror-, ros* dew — more at RORIC] *obs* **:** BEDEW, MOISTEN — **irroration** *n* -S *obs*

²ir·ro·rate \ˈirə,rāt, əˈrōrət\ *also* **ir·ro·rat·ed** \ˈirə,rād·əd\ *adj* [*irrorate* fr. L *irroratus*, past part.; *irrorated* fr. L *irroratus* + E *-ed*] **:** covered with little spots **:** SPECKLED ⟨a tawny butterfly with black-*irrorate* wings⟩

ir·rotational \,i, |ir, |iə+\ *adj* [¹*in-* + *rotational*] **:** not involving rotation **:** free from vortices ⟨~ flow⟩ ⟨an ~ electrostatic field⟩ — **ir·rotationally** \"+\ *adv*

ir·rubrical \(ˈ)i, ə, (ˈ)ir, (ˈ)iə+\ *adj* [¹*in-* + *rubrical*] **:** not rubrical

ir·ru·ma·tion \,irüˈmāshən\ *n* -S [L *irrumation-, irrumatio*, fr. *irrumatus* (past part. of *irrumare* to give suck, extend the penis for fellatio, fr. *in-* ²in- + *-rumare*, fr. *ruma, rumis* breast, teat) + *-ion-, -io* -ion] **:** FELLATIO

ir·rupt \əˈrəpt\ *vb* -ED/-ING/-S [L *irruptus*, past part. of *irrumpere*, lit., to break in, fr. ¹*in-* in + *rumpere* to break — more at RUPTURE] *vi* **1 a :** to enter forceably or suddenly **:** appear without warning **:** INTRUDE ⟨the sea had once ~*ed* into the cavern⟩ ⟨the merchants constituted a very tight caste, rarely ~*ing* into social groups either above or below —G.W. Johnson⟩ **b** *of an animal population* **:** to undergo a sudden upsurge in numbers esp. when natural ecological balances and checks are disturbed **2 :** ERUPT 1c ⟨the crowd ~*ed* in a fervor of patriotism —*Time*⟩ ~ *vt* **:** INTRUDE 3 — opposed to *erupt*

ir·rup·ti·ble \(ˈ)i(r)ˈrəptəbəl, əˈr-, (ˈ)iə|r-\ *adj* **:** UNBREAKABLE

ir·rup·tion \əˈrəpshən\ *n* -S [L *irruption-, irruptio*, fr. *irruptus* + *-ion-, -io* -ion] **:** an act or instance of irrupting: as **a :** a sudden violent or forceable entry **:** a rushing or bursting in ⟨the current ~ of bad manners into everyday life⟩ ⟨an ~ of water through a break in the dike⟩ **b :** a sudden and violent invasion ⟨the ~*s* of the Goths into Italy⟩ **c :** ERUPTION 1 **d :** a sudden sharp increase in the relative numbers of a natural population usu. associated with favorable alteration of the environment

ir·rup·tive \-ptiv\ *adj* **:** irrupting or tending to irrupt ⟨~ forces⟩: as **a :** rushing or bursting in or upon **:** entering forceably or violently ⟨the ~ roar of new engines —J.G. Cozzens⟩ **b** *of an igneous rock* **:** INTRUSIVE **c :** marked by irruption ⟨the ~ stage of rabbit increase⟩ **:** undergoing irruption ⟨the ~ deer herds of the state⟩ — compare CYCLIC — **ir·rup·tive·ly** \-təvlē\ *adv*

IRU *abbr* **1** international radium unit **2** international rat unit

irul \ˈē,rül\ *n* -S [Tamil *irul*] **:** ACLE 1,2

iru·la \ˈirələ\ *n, pl* **irulas** *or* **irula** *usu cap* **:** a primitive Veddoid people inhabiting the Deccan plateau of India and being one of the pre-Dravidian peoples of India

irus·ka \əˈrüskə\ *n* -S [Pawnee, lit., the fire is in me] **:** a dance of a fire-handling sacred male society of the Pawnee Indians that is the precursor of the grass dance

ir·ving·ite \ˈərviŋ,īt\ *n* -S *usu cap* [Edward *Irving* †1834 Scot. clergyman + E *-ite*] **:** a member of the Catholic Apostolic Church — often taken to be offensive

¹is [ME (3d pers. sing. pres. indic. and — northern dial. — 1st & 2d pers. sing. pres. indic. and — northern dial. — 1st & 2d & 3d pers. pl. pres. indic. of *been* — suppletive infinitive — to be), fr. OE (3d pers. sing. pres. indic. of *bēon* — suppletive infinitive — to be); akin to OHG *ist* (3d pers. sing. pres. indic. of *sīn* to be), ON *es, er* (3d pers. sing. pres. indic. of *vesa, vera* — suppletive infinitive — to be), Goth *ist* (3d pers. sing. pres. indic. of *wisan* — suppletive infinitive — to be), L *est* (3d pers. sing. pres. indic. of *esse* to be), Gk *esti* (3d pers. sing. pres. indic. of *einai* to be), Skt *asti* is, he is, Hitt *eszi*] *pres 3d sing of* BE, *dial pres 1st & 2d sing of* BE, *substand pres pl of* BE

²is \ˈiz\ *n* -ES **:** that which is; *specif* **:** that which is factual, empirical, actually the case, or spatiotemporal — contrasted with *ought*

is- *or* **iso-** *comb form* [LL, fr. Gk, fr. *isos* equal] **1 :** equal **:** homogeneous **:** uniform ⟨*isenergic*⟩ ⟨*isacoustic*⟩ ⟨*isocephaly*⟩ ⟨*isotype*⟩ **2** *usu* **iso- a :** isomer of a (specified) compound ⟨*isocyanuric acid* $C_3(NH)_3O_3$⟩ ⟨*isovanillin* $CH_3OC_6H_4(OH)CHO$⟩ **b** (1) **:** of, relating to, or having a branched chain of carbon atoms ⟨*iso*hydrocarbons⟩ ⟨*iso*synthesis⟩ — compare NORMAL 10e (2) **:** having a straight chain of carbon atoms to which one branching methyl group is attached in the position next to one end ⟨*isohexyl* $(CH_3)_2CHCH_2CH_2CH_2$—⟩ **3** *usu* **iso- :** for or from different individuals of the same species ⟨*iso*antigen⟩ ⟨*iso*antibody⟩

is *abbr* island; isle

IS *abbr* **1** interservice **2** interstate

i's *or* **is** *pl of* I

is·a·be·li·ta \,izəbəˈlēd·ə\ *or* **is·a·bel·ite** \-ˈbe,līt\ *n* -S [AmerSp *isabelita*, fr. Sp *Isabelita* (feminine nickname), dim. of *Isabel* (feminine name)] **:** any of various fishes belonging to a genus *Angelichthys* of the family Chaetodontidae; *esp* **:** an angelfish (*A. ciliaris*) colored orange red, sky blue, and golden that is common in the West Indies

is·a·bel·la \,izəˈbelə\ *also* **is·a·bel** \ˈizə,bel\ *n* -S *often cap* [MF *isabelle*, fr. *Isabelle* (feminine name)] **:** a moderate yellowish brown to light olive brown that is lighter and stronger than clay drab or medal bronze

isabella grape \==ˈ==-\ *also* **isabella** *n* -S *usu cap I* [prob. after *Isabella* Gibbs, 19th cent. Am. woman who introduced it into Brooklyn from North Carolina] **:** FOX GRAPE c

isabella moth *n, usu cap I* [NL *isabella* (specific epithet of *Isia isabella*), perh. fr. E *isabella*] **:** a common stout-bodied snuff-colored American arctiid moth (*Isia isabella*) having the hind wings often tinged with orange red

is·a·bel·line \,izəˈbelən, -,līn, -,lēn\ *adj* [*isabella* + *-ine*] **:** of the color Isabella

isabelline bear *n* **:** RED BEAR

is·abnormal \ˈīs *also* |īz+\ *or* **iso·abnormal** \ˈī(,)sō *also* -)zō+\ *n* [*is-* + *abnormal*, adj.] **:** an imaginary line or a line on a chart that connects or marks places on the surface of the earth having equal differences in a given time from the normal temperature of these places or that indicates differences between the calculated and actual temperatures of the different parallels of latitude

is·acoustic \"+\ *adj* [*is-* + *acoustic*] **:** of or relating to equal intensity of sound

is·adelphous \"+\ *adj* [prob. fr. (assumed) NL *isadelphus*, fr. NL *is-* + *-adelphus* -adelphous] **:** having the separate bundles of stamens in a diadelphous flower equal in number

isa·go·ge \ˈīsə,gōjē, ,==ˈ==\ *n* -S [L, fr. Gk *eisagōgē*, fr. *eisagein* to introduce, fr. *eis* into + *agein* to lead; akin to Gk *en* in — more at IN, AGENT] **:** a scholarly introduction to a branch of study or research — **isa·gog·ic** \ˈ==ˈgäjik\ *or* **isa·gog·i·cal** \-jəkəl\ *adj*

isa·gog·ics \,==ˈgäjiks\ *n pl but usu sing in constr, also* **isa·gog·ic** \-ik\ [*isagoge* + *-ics*] **:** introductory studies; *esp* **:** a branch of theology that is preliminary to actual exegesis and deals with the literary and external history of the Bible

isa·ian \īˈzāən, *chiefly Brit* -zīən\ *or* **isa·ian·ic** \ˈ=(,)=ˈanik\ *adj, usu cap* [*isaian* fr. *Isaiah*, 8th cent. B.C. major Hebrew prophet + E *-an*, adj. suffix; *isaianic* fr. *Isaiah* + E *-an*, adj. suffix + *-ic*] **:** of, relating to, or having the characteristics of Isaiah or the book of Isaiah ⟨the *Isaianic* character of this prophesy —Robert Gordis⟩ ⟨the somber and threatening, the almost *Isaian*, utterance —Edmund Wilson⟩

is·allobar \(ˈ)īs *also* (ˈ)īz+\ *n* [ISV *is-* + *all-* + *-bar* (as in *isobar*)] **:** an imaginary line or a line on a chart connecting the places of equal change of atmospheric pressure within a specified time — **is·al·lo·bar·ic** \(ˌ)ī,saləˈbärik, (ˌ)ī,za-, -bar-\ *adj*

is·al·lo·therm \īˈsalə,thərm *also* īˈza-\ *n* [ISV *is-* + *all-* + *-therm*] **:** an imaginary line or a line on a chart connecting the places of equal change of temperature within a specified time

is·an·drous \(ˈ)īˈsandrəs *also* (ˈ)īˈza-\ *adj* [*is-* + *-androus*] **:** having the stamens similar and equal in number to the petals

is·an·e·mone \īˈsanə,mōn, ,īsəˈnemə(,)nē *also* īˈza- *or* ,īzə-\ *n* [ISV *is-* + *-anemone* (irreg. fr. Gk *anemos* wind) — more at ANIMATE] **:** an isogram of wind speed

is·anom·al \,īsəˈnäməl *also* ,īzə-\ *n* -S [ISV *is-* + *-anomal* (fr. LL *anomalus* dissimilar) — more at ANOMALOUS] **:** an imaginary line or a line on a chart connecting places that have the same anomalies esp. of temperature or pressure

is·anomalous \ˈīs *also* |īz+\ *adj* [*isanomal* + *-ous*] **:** relating to an isabnormal or an isanomal

isa·no oil \əˈsä(,)nō-\ *n* [*isano* prob. native name (of the tree *Ongokea klaineana*) in the Congo region of West Africa] **:** an unsaturated fatty oil that is obtained from the kernel of the nuts of a West African tree (*Ongokea klaineana*) of the family Oleaceae, that polymerizes readily, and that is used in coatings

is·an·thous \(ˈ)ī|san(t)thəs *also* -|za-\ *adj* [NL *isanthus*, fr. *is-* + *-anthus* -anthous] **:** having the flowers regular

is·apostolic \(ˌ)īs *also* (ˌ)īz+\ *adj* [LGk *isapostolos* isapostolic (fr. Gk *is-* + *apostolos* apostle) + E *-ic* — more at APOSTLE] **:** equal to or contemporaneous with the apostles — used esp. of bishops consecrated by the apostles

isard *var of* IZARD

isar·ia \īˈsa(a)rēə\ *n, cap* [NL, fr. *is-* + *-aria*] **:** a form genus of imperfect fungi (family Stilbellaceae) that are parasitic on insects and have the conidia borne terminally on slender hyphae that cover the coremiums

isa·rithm \ˈīsə,rithəm, -th- *also* ˈīzə-\ *n* -S [ISV *is-* + *-arithm* (fr. Gk *arithmos* number); orig. formed as G *isarithmus* — more at ARITHMO-] **:** a line drawn on a map or chart to connect points having equal numerical values (as of temperature, elevation, or density of population)

isa·tin \ˈīsətən, -əd·ən\ *n* -S [ISV *isat-* (fr. NL *Isatis*) + *-in*] **:** an orange red crystalline compound $C_8H_5NO_2$ obtained by oxidation of indigo or oxindole or by various syntheses and used as an intermediate for indigoid dyes

isa·tin·ic acid \ˌīsəˈtinik-\ *or* **isat·ic acid** \(ˈ)ī|sad·ik-\ *n* [*isatinic* ISV *isatin* + *-ic*; *isatic* ISV *isatin* + *-ic*] **:** a white solid amino acid $NH_2C_6H_4COCOOH$ obtained by hydrolysis of isatin

-isation — see -IZATION

isa·tis \ˈīsəd·əs\ *n, cap* [NL, fr. L, woad, fr. Gk — more at WOAD] **:** a large genus of herbs (family Cruciferae) having entire leaves, small yellow flowers, and compressed oblong or orbicular pods — see WOAD

isat·o·gen \īˈsad·əjən, -,jen\ *n* -S [ISV *isatin* + *-o-* + *-gen*] **:** a parent compound $C_8H_5NO_2$ isomeric with isatin and known in the form of various colored derivatives that are made by treating an *ortho*-nitro-phenyl-acetylene with sulfuric acid

isa·to·ic anhydride \ˌīsəˈtōik-\ *n* [*isatoic* ISV *isatin* + *-o-* + *-ic*] **:** a high-melting dicarboxylic acid anhydride $C_8H_5NO_3$ made by oxidation of isatin or by reaction of anthranilic acid with phosgene

¹isau·ri·an \īˈsȯrēən\ *n* -S *cap* [*Isauria*, ancient district in south central Asia Minor + E *-an*, n. suffix] **:** a native or inhabitant of Isauria

²isaurian \(ˈ)=ˈ===\ *adj, usu cap* [*Isauria* + E *-an*, adj. suffix] **1 :** of, relating to, or characteristic of Isauria **2 :** of, relating to, or characteristic of the people of Isauria

is·auxesis \ˈīs *also* |īz+\ *n* [NL, fr. *is-* + *auxesis*] **:** ISOGONY — **is·auxetic** \"+\ *adj*

isa·wa \əˈsäwə\ *or* **isa·wi·ya** \,ēsəˈwē(y)ə\ *or* **ais·sa·wa** \īˈsäwə\ *n pl, usu cap* [Ar *ʿIsawīyah*, an order of dervishes] **:** members of a Muslim religious brotherhood founded in Morocco about 1500

is·ba *also* **iz·ba** \əzˈbä\ *n* -S [Russ *izba*, fr. Old Russian *istŭba* bathing room, prob. of Gmc origin; akin to OHG *stuba* heated room — more at STOVE] **:** a Russian log hut

ISC *abbr* interstate commerce

is·car·i·ot·ic \(ˌ)is|karēˈäd·ik, əˈsk-\ *or* **is·car·i·ot·i·cal** \-d·əkəl\ *adj* [Judas *Iscariot*, apostle that betrayed Jesus + E *-ic* or *-ical*] **:** of, relating to, or having the characteristics of Judas Iscariot; *specif* **:** TREACHEROUS

is·che·mia *also* **is·chae·mia** \əˈskēmēə\ *n* -S [NL *ischaemia*, fr. *ischaemus* styptic, stopping blood (fr. Gk *ischaimos*, fr. *ischein* to check, restrain + *haima* blood) + *-ia*; akin to Gk *echein* to have, hold — more at SCHEME, HEM-] **:** localized tissue anemia due to obstruction of the inflow of arterial blood (as by the narrowing of arteries by spasm or disease) ⟨cerebral ~⟩ ⟨renal ~⟩ ⟨myocardial ~⟩ — **is·che·mic** *also* **is·chae·mic** \(ˈ)i|skēmik, əˈs-\ *adj*

ischemic contracture *n* **:** shortening and degeneration of a muscle resulting from deficient blood supply

ischi- *or* **ischio-** *comb form* [L *ischi-*, fr. Gk, fr. *ischion* hip joint] **1 :** ischium ⟨*ischi*algia⟩ ⟨*ischio*podite⟩ **2 :** ischial and ⟨*ischio*caudal⟩ **3 :** resembling a hip joint ⟨*ischio*cerite⟩

is·chi·ad·ic \ˌiskēˈadik\ *adj* [L *ischiadicus* of pain in the hip, fr. Gk *ischiadikos*, fr. *ischiad-, ischias* sciatica (fr. *ischion* hip joint) + *-ikos* -ic] **:** ISCHIAL

is·chi·al \ˈiskēəl\ *adj* [prob. fr. (assumed) NL *ischialis*, fr. L *ischi-* + *-alis* -al] **:** of, relating to, or situated near the ischium

is·chi·at·ic \ˌiskēˈad·ik, -atik\ *adj* [LL *ischiaticus* of pain in the hip, alter. (influenced by adjectives ending in *-aticus* such as LL *dramaticus* dramatic) of L *ischiadicus*] **:** ISCHIAL

is·chio·capsular \ˌiskē(,)ō+\ *adj* [*ischi-* + *capsular*] **:** of, relating to, or being an accessory ligament of the hip joint passing from the ischium below the acetabulum to blend with the capsular ligament

is·chio·cav·er·no·sus \ˌiskē(,)ō,kavə(r)ˈnōsəs\ *n* -ES [NL, fr. *ischi-* + *-cavernosus* belonging to the corpus cavernosum, fr. L *cavernosus* cavernous] **:** a muscle covering the crus of the penis or clitoris

is·chi·oc·er·ite \ˌiskēˈäsə,rīt\ *n* [*ischi-* + Gk *keras* horn, antenna + E *-ite* — more at HORN] **:** a joint of the antenna of a crustacean

is·chi·op·o·dite \-ˈäpə,dīt\ *n* [ISV *ischi-* + *-podite*] **:** the third joint from the base of certain limbs of crustaceans (as the thoracic legs of decapods)

is·chio·rectal \ˌiskē(,)ō+\ *adj* **:** of, relating to, or adjacent to both ischium and rectum

is·chi·um \ˈiskēəm\ *n, pl* **is·chia** \-kēə\ [L, hip joint, fr. Gk *ischion*; perh. akin to Skt *sakthi* thigh] **1 :** the dorsal and posterior of the three principal bones composing either half of the pelvis consisting in man of a thick portion, a large rough eminence on which the body rests when sitting, and a forwardly directed ramus which joins that of the pubis **2 :** ISCHIOPODITE

is·chy·o·dus \əˈskīədəs\ *n, cap* [NL, fr. *ischy-* (fr. Gk *ischys* strength) + *-odus*; akin to Gk *echein* to have, hold — more at SCHEME] **:** a genus of Jurassic and Cretaceous chimaeroid fishes of Europe and New Zealand

is·chy·ro·my·i·dae \ˌiskərōˈmīə,dē\ *n pl, cap* [NL, fr. *Ischyromys*, type genus (fr. Gk *ischyros* strong + *mys* mouse) + *-idae*; akin to Gk *echein* to have, hold — more at MOUSE] **:** a family of primitive extinct sciuromorph rodents widely distributed in the northern hemisphere from the Lower Eocene to the Upper Oligocene, distantly related to the mountain beaver, and distinguished by low-crowned generalized cheek teeth

ise *or* **i'se** \(ˌ)īz\ *usu cap* [contr. of E dial. *I is* I am, fr. E *I* + E dial. *is* — more at IS] *dial* **:** I am

-ise \,īz\ *vb suffix* **:** -IZE — see -IZE in Explan Notes

is·en·trope \ˈīsᵊn,trōp, ˈīzᵊn-\ *also* **is·en·trop·ic** \ˈ==-ˈträpik\ *n* -S [*isentrope* ISV prob. back-formation fr. *isentropic*, adj.; *isentropic*, n. fr. *isentropic*, adj.] **:** an isentropic line or surface (as on a meteorological chart or engineering diagram)

is·en·trop·ic \ˈ==ˈträpik, ,ī,sen·-, ,ī,zen·-\ *adj* [ISV *is-* + *entropy* + *-ic*] **:** having or indicating constant entropy ⟨the ~ chart, a map of the air unaffected by surface heating and cooling, aids in identifying the air from one map to the next —T.M.Longstreth⟩ **:** taking place without change of entropy ⟨if steam could be expanded in a turbine with no friction or other losses, expansion would be ~ —A.G.Christie⟩ — **is·en·trop·i·cal·ly** \-pək(ə)lē\ *adv*

is·ep·ipte·sis \,ī,sepə(p)ˈtēsəs, ,ī,ze-\ *n, pl* **isepipte·ses** \-ē,sēz\ [NL, fr. *is-* + *epi-* + Gk *ptēsis* flight, fr. *petesthai* to fly — more at FEATHER] **:** a line on a map or chart connecting localities reached at one date by different individuals of a species of migratory bird

ises *pl of* IS

is·ethi·o·nate \,ī,səˈthīə,nāt, ,ī,ze-\ *n* [ISV *isethion-* (fr. *isethionic*) + *-ate*] **:** a salt or ester of isethionic acid

is·ethionic acid \(ˌ)īs, (ˌ)īz+ . . . -\ *n* [*isethionic* ISV *is-* + *ethionic*] **:** a crystalline sulfonic acid $HOC_2H_4SO_3H$ obtained by action of sulfur trioxide on alcohol or ether and used in making surface-active agents

is·fa·han \ˈisfə,hän, -han, ,==ˈ=\ *adj, usu cap* [fr. *Isfahan*, city in west central Iran] **:** of or from the city of Isfahan, Iran **:** of the kind or style prevalent in Isfahan

ISG *abbr, often not cap* imperial standard gallon

ish \ˈish\ *n* -ES [ME (Sc) *ische*, fr. ME *ischen, isshen* to come out, go out, fr. MF *issir* — more at ISSUE] **1** *Scots law* **:** right of exit **:** ISSUE, EXIT ⟨~ and entry⟩ **2** *Scots law* **:** time of expiry (as of a lease) **:** EXPIRY, TERMINATION

-ish \ish, ēsh\ *adj suffix* [ME, fr. OE *-isc;* akin to OHG *-isc, -isk* -ish, ON *-skr,* Goth *-isks* -ish, Gk *-iskos,* dim. n. suffix] **1 :** of or belonging to — chiefly in adjectives indicating nationality or ethnic group ⟨Finn*ish*⟩ ⟨Gaul*ish*⟩ ⟨Turk*ish*⟩ **2 a :** characteristic or typical of ⟨boy*ish*⟩ ⟨London*ish*⟩ **:** having the undesirable qualities of ⟨amateur*ish*⟩ ⟨mul*ish*⟩ **b** (1) **:** having a touch or trace of ⟨summer*ish*⟩ **:** somewhat ⟨purpl*ish*⟩ ⟨lat*ish*⟩ (2) **:** having the approximate age of ⟨forty*ish*⟩ (3) **:** being or occurring at the approximate time of — esp. in words formed from numerals indicating an hour of the day or night ⟨five*ish*⟩ ⟨eight*ish*⟩

ish·er·wood system \ˈishə(r),wu̇d-\ *n, usu cap I* [after Benjamin F. *Isherwood* †1915 Am. naval engineer] **:** a technique of ship construction employing large transverse frames widely spaced and light longitudinal members closely spaced — called also *longitudinal framing*

ishi·ha·ra test \ˌishēˈhärə-\ *n, usu cap I* [after Shinobu *Ishihara b*1879 Jap. ophthalmologist who devised it] **:** a widely used test for the detection of color blindness

ishi·ka·wa·ite \ˌishēˈkäwəˌīt\ *n* -s [*Ishikawa* district, north central Honshu, Japan, its locality + E *-ite*] **:** a rare mineral (U, Fe, Y, etc.)(Nb, Ta)O_4 consisting of an oxide of uranium, iron, niobium, tantalum, yttrium, and the rare-earth metals

ish·kash·mi \ishˈkäsh(ˌ)mē\ *n, pl* **ishkashmi** *or* **ishkashmis** *usu cap* **1 :** an Iranian people of the highlands of the southwestern Pamir mountains **2 :** a member of the Ishkashmi people

ish·kyl·dite *or* **ish·kil·dite** \ˈishkəlˌdīt\ *n* -s [Russ *ishkil'dit,* fr. *Ishkyldino,* Middle Volga district, U.S.S.R., its locality + Russ *-it* -ite] **:** a mineral $Mg_{15}Si_{11}O_{27}(OH)_{20}$ consisting of a basic silicate of magnesium

ish·ma·el \ˈishmēəl, -(ˌ)mā-\ *n* -s *usu cap* [after *Ishmael* (AV), *Ismael* (DV), son of Abraham by his concubine Hagar; fr. the statement made concerning him in Gen 16:12 (AV) that "his hand will be against every man, and every man's hand against him"] **:** one at odds with or as if with society **:** OUTCAST, OUTLAW, OUTSIDER ⟨I am an *Ishmael* by instinct —Samuel Butler †1902⟩ ⟨the murder novel, . . . long the *Ishmael* of fiction, shows every sign of rejoining the main fold of literature —Anthony Boucher⟩

ish·ma·el·ite \-ēəˌlīt, -āə-\ *n* -s *usu cap* **1 :** a descendant of Ishmael **2 :** ISHMAEL ⟨individual animals which as *Ishmaelites* lived a solitary life and ranged alone —P.A.Rollins⟩

ish·ma·el·it·ish \ˈ⸗(ˌ)⸗⸗ˌlīd·ish, ⸗(ˌ)⸗⸗ˈ⸗⸗\ *adj, usu cap* **:** of, relating to, or having the characteristics of an Ishmaelite ⟨the wretched, fearful, *Ishmaelitish* condition of every man against his fellowmen —Hastings Lyon⟩

isi·ac \ˈisēˌak, ˈizē-,ˈīsē-\ *or* **isi·a·cal** \əˈsīəkəl, (ˈ)īˈsī-\ *adj, usu cap* [*isiac* fr. L *isiacus,* fr. Gk *isiakos,* fr. *Isis,* orig. Egyptian goddess of motherhood and the family whose cult spread throughout the Mediterranean world in Hellenistic times; *isiacal* fr. L *isiacus* + E *-al*] **:** of or relating to Isis or the cult of Isis

isi·dae \ˈīsəˌdē, ˈizə-\ *n pl, cap* [NL, fr. *Isis,* type genus (fr. Gk, orig. Egyptian goddess of motherhood and the family) + *-idae*] **:** a family of gorgonians having an axis composed of alternating horny and calcareous joints

isid·i·if·er·ous \īˌsidēˈif(ə)rəs\ *or* **isid·i·of·er·ous** \-ēˈäf-\ *adj* [*isidiiferous* fr. *isidium* + *-i-* + *-ferous; isidioferous* fr. *isidium* + *-o-* + *-ferous*] **:** bearing isidia

isid·i·oid \īˈsidēˌȯid\ *adj* [*isidium* + *-oid*] **:** of, relating to, or resembling an isidium

isid·i·ose \-ēˌōs\ *adj* [*isidium* + *-ose*] **:** of or relating to isidia

isid·i·um \īˈsidēəm\ *n, pl* **isid·ia** \-ēə\ [NL, fr. *Isidium,* supposed genus of lichens, irreg. fr. *Isis* genus of gorgonians + Gk *eidos* form; fr. the resemblance of lichens that have isidia to gorgonians — more at IDOL] **:** an outgrowth from the surface of the thallus in certain lichens that resembles a soredium

is·i·do·ri·an *or* **is·i·do·re·an** \ˌizəˈdōrēən\ *adj, usu cap* [*Isidore* of Seville †A.D.636 Span. prelate and scholar + E *-an,* adj. suffix] **:** of, relating to, or characteristic of Isidore of Seville

isi·nai *also* **isi·nay** \ˌēsəˈnī\ *n, pl* **isinai** *or* **isinais** *usu cap* **1 a :** a Christianized people of Nueva Vizcaya, Luzon, Philippines **b :** a member of such people **2 :** the Austronesian language of the Isinai people

isin·glass \ˈīzᵊnˌglas, ˈīziŋˌg-, -zēŋ-, -laa(ə)s, -lais, -läs\ *n* -ES [prob. by folk etymology (influence of E *glass*) fr. obs. D *huizenblas,* fr. MD *huusblase,* fr. *huus* sturgeon + *blase* bladder; akin to OHG *hūso* beluga and to OHG *blāsan* to blow — more at HUSO, BLAST] **1 :** a semitransparent whitish substance consisting of a very pure form of gelatin orig. prepared from the air bladders of sturgeons from the rivers of western Russia but now largely made from those of sturgeons of other areas or of various other fishes and used chiefly as a clarifying agent and in making jellies and glue — called also *fish gelatin, fish glue* **2 :** mica esp. when in thin transparent sheets **3 :** a colloidal extractive substance (as agar) from various algae

is·lam \isˈläm, -izˈläm, -lam, -laa(ə)m, -läm, ˈ⸗,⸗ *also* ˈizləm *or* ˈisləm\ *n* -s *cap* [Ar *islām* submission (to the will of God), fr. *aslama* to surrender] **1 :** the religious faith of Muslims who profess belief in Allah as the sole deity and in Muhammad as the prophet of Allah ⟨*Islam* . . . is the religion of judgment —J.E.Turner⟩ ⟨*Islam* was a fellowship —J.C.Archer⟩ **2 a :** the cultural system or civilization erected in history upon the foundations of Islamic religious faith ⟨for nine centuries the Turks were the principal champions of *Islam* —Emil Lengyel⟩ ⟨the grafting of the spirit of modern nationalism upon the ancient trunk of *Islam* —H.L.Hoskins⟩ **b :** the national political units of the modern world that share the Muslim religion ⟨*Islam* is the principal problem of three hundred million people who might be . . . our friends —Mortimer Graves⟩

is·lam·ic \(ˈ)isˈlämik, (ˈ)izˈl-, -lam-, -läm-, -mēk\ *adj, usu cap* [F *islamique,* fr. *islam* (fr. Ar *islām*) + *-ique* -ic] **:** of, relating to, or characteristic of Islam ⟨*Islamic* traditions⟩ ⟨an *Islamic* republic⟩

is·lam·ics \⸗ˈ⸗miks, -mēks\ *n pl but sing in constr, usu cap* **:** the academic study of Islam

is·lam·ism \⸗ˈ⸗,mizəm, ˈizlə,mi-, ˈislə,-\ *n* -s *usu cap* **:** the faith, doctrine, or cause of Islam

is·lam·ist \-məst\ *n* -s *usu cap* **1 :** an orthodox Muslim **2 :** a student or scholar of Islamics

is·lam·ite \-ˌmīt, *usu* -īd·+V\ *n* -s *usu cap* [F, fr. *islam* + *-ite*] **:** MUSLIM

is·lam·it·ic \ˌizləˈmid·ik, ˌisl-, -it|, ēk\ *adj, usu cap* **:** of, relating to, or characteristic of Islamism **:** MUSLIM

is·lam·iza·tion \ˌizləməˈzāshən, ˌislə-, -mīˈz-, iˌslämə-, iˌslämə-\ *n* -s *usu cap* **:** the act or process of islamizing or being islamized

is·lam·ize \ˈizləˌmīz, ˈislə-, iˈslä,m-, iˈslaˌ-, iˈslä,-\ *vt* -ED/-ING/-S *often cap* **1 :** to make Islamic in quality, traits, or way of thinking or acting; *esp* **:** to convert to Islamism ⟨*Islamizing* the religion of these semibarbarous hordes —P.K. Hitti⟩ **2 :** to bring under the control of Islam

¹is·land \ˈīlənd\ *n* -s *often attrib* [alter. (influenced by E ¹*isle*) of earlier *iland,* fr. ME, fr. OE *īgland;* akin to OFris *eiland* island, ON *eyland;* all fr. a prehistoric NGmc-WGmc compound whose first constituent is represented by OE *īg, īeg* island and whose second constituent is represented by OE *land;* OE *īg, īeg* island akin to OE *ēa* river, OHG *ouwa* land by water, meadow, *aha* river, ON *ey* island, *ā* river, Goth *ahwa* river, L *aqua* water — more at LAND] **1 a :** a tract of land surrounded by water and smaller than a continent **b** *dial* **:** a tract of land cut off on two or more sides by water **:** PENINSULA **2 :** something resembling an island by its isolated, surrounded, or sequestered position: as **a** (1) **:** an elevated piece of land surrounded by swamp or alluvial land ⟨thousands were marooned on ~*s* of high ground —*Time*⟩ (2) **:** a piece of woodland surrounded by flat open country **b :** ISLET 2 c — compare ISLAND OF REIL **c** (1) **:** a small isolated space between lines in a fingerprint (2) **:** a lanceolate interruption in a line on the palm held to be a sign in palmistry ⟨when the line has an ~ in the center . . . it foretells some trouble —Alice D. Jennings⟩ **d** (1) **:** a showcase, counter, or platform standing apart and approachable on all sides ⟨only fast turnover items can be placed on ~*s* —*Printers' Ink*⟩ ⟨double built-in cooking top in an ~ arrangement —*Amer. Builder Catalog Directory*⟩ (2) *or* **island platform :** a platform at a railway station that has tracks on each side of it **e** (1) **:** SAFETY ISLAND (2) **:** SAFETY ZONE **f :** a superstructure (as the forecastle, bridge, or poop) on the deck of an aircraft carrier or other ship **3 :** a group or area isolated from its environment by specific characteristics or conditions: as **a :** an isolated ethnological group ⟨the Hungarian colony . . . is a picturesque racial ~ —*Amer. Guide Series: Mich.*⟩ ⟨there are many cultural ~*s* in the United States —David Riesman⟩ **b :** SPEECH ISLAND

²island \"\ *vt* -ED/-ING/-S **1 :** to make into or as if into an island ⟨a clear brown stream . . . ~*ing* a purple and white rock with an amber pool —John Ruskin⟩ **2 :** to dot with or as if with islands ⟨a fair expanse of level pasture ~*ed* with groves —William Wordsworth⟩ ⟨groups of people ~*ed* upon the dark grass —F.D.Ommanney⟩ **3 :** to place on or as if on an island **:** ISOLATE ⟨the great mystery in whose midst we are ~*ed* —Arthur Symons⟩

island arc *n* **:** an arcuate chain of islands

island carib *n, usu cap I&C* **1 :** an Indian of the Lesser Antilles **2 :** the Arawakan language of the Island Caribs and their modern descendants in British Honduras, Guatemala, and Honduras

island chain *n* **:** a line of islands

island continent *n* **:** an island as large or nearly as large as a continent ⟨the *island continent* of Greenland⟩

is·land·er \ˈīləndə(r)\ *n* -s **:** a native or inhabitant of an island

island-hop \ˈ⸗⸗,⸗\ *vi* **:** to go from island to island ⟨our *island-hopping,* creek-exploring houseboat life —A.W.Baum⟩; *esp* **:** to seize island after island in a military offensive ⟨instead of *island-hopping,* he suggested that we should employ . . . massive strokes —Joseph Driscoll⟩

is·land·ish \ˈīləndish\ *adj* **:** of, relating to, or having the characteristics of an island

is·land·less \-n(d)ləs\ *adj* **:** having no islands **:** lacking islands ⟨a stretch of ~ ocean fully 500 miles across —F.C.Lincoln⟩

is·land·man \-n(d)mən\ *n, pl* **islandmen** *now chiefly Irish* **:** ISLANDER ⟨comparing them with the *islandmen* who walked up and down as cool and fresh-looking as the sea gulls —J.M. Synge⟩

island of langerhans *usu cap L* [after Paul *Langerhans* †1888 — more at ISLET OF LANGERHANS] **:** ISLET OF LANGERHANS

island of reil \-ˈrī(ə)l\ *usu cap R* [after Johann C. *Reil* †1813 Ger. physician born in Holland] **:** the central lobe of the cerebral hemisphere that is situated deeply between the lips of the lateral fissure

island of resistance : a strongpoint in a defensive position that is organized for perimeter military defense and normally is capable of mutual support with other similar positions

is·land·ol·o·gy \ˌīlənˈdäləjē\ *n* -ES **:** a study of islands

island universe *n* **:** a galaxy other than the Milky Way system but not necessarily smaller or less important

is·lay \(ˈ)izˈlī\ *n* -s [AmerSp] **:** a California wild plum (*Prunus ilicifolia*)

¹isle \ˈīl, *esp before pause or consonant* ˈīəl\ *n* -s [ME *isle, ile,* fr. OF, fr. L *insula,* perh. fr. *in* + *-sula* (akin to L *salum* sea, *sal* salt) — more at IN, SALT] **:** ISLAND; *esp* **:** a small island ⟨Australian seas are rich in ~*s* —C.L.Barrett⟩ ⟨this 54-acre ~ is an exclusive residential district —*Amer. Guide Series: Minn.*⟩

²isle \"\ *vt* -ED/-ING/-S **1 :** to make an isle of **2 :** to place on or as if on an isle ⟨the faun is *isled* within the spotted wood —Randall Jarrell⟩

isle·less \ˈī(ə)lləs\ *adj* **:** having no islands

isle·man \ˈī(ə)lmən\ *n, pl* **islemen :** ISLANDER

isle of wight disease \-ˈwīt-\ *usu cap I&W* [*Isle of Wight,* island in the English channel constituting a county of England] **:** a serious European disease of adult honeybees caused by a minute mite (*Acarapis woodi*)

isles·man \ˈī(ə)lzmən\ *n, pl* **islesmen** [*isles* (pl. of ¹*isle*) + *man*] **:** a native or inhabitant of a group of islands (as the Hebrides or Shetland isles)

is·let \ˈīlət, *usu* -əd·+V\ *n* -s [MF *islette,* fr. *isle* + *-ette*] **1 :** a small island **:** ISLE **2 :** something resembling a small island esp. in its isolation or elevation: **a :** ISLAND 2a **b** *chiefly Brit* **:** ISLAND 2c **c :** a small isolated mass of one type of tissue within a different type; *specif* **:** ISLET OF LANGERHANS

is·le·ta \izˈlād·ə\ *n, pl* **isleta** *or* **isletas** *usu cap* [*Isleta,* Indian village and pueblo in central New Mexico occupied by the Isleta people, fr. Sp *isleta* islet, dim. of *isla* island, fr. L *insula*] **1 a :** a Tanoan people of New Mexico **b :** a member of such people **2 :** the language of the Isleta people — compare TIWA

is·let·ed \ˈīləd·əd\ *adj* **:** set like an islet or furnished with islets

islet of lang·er·hans \-ˈläŋə(r),hän(t)s, -hänz\ *usu cap L* [after Paul *Langerhans* †1888 Ger. physician] **:** any of the groups of small slightly granular endocrine cells that form anastomosing trabeculae among the tubules and alveoli of the pancreas and secrete the hormone insulin

is·lot \ˈīlət\ *n* -s [F *ilot,* fr. MF *islot,* dim. of *isle*] *archaic* **:** ISLET

ism \ˈizəm\ *n* -s [*-ism*] **:** a distinctive doctrine, cause, system, or theory — often used disparagingly ⟨against any ~ that isn't Americanism —J.F.O'Neill⟩ ⟨futurism and cubism and all the other ~*s* —J.L.Lowes⟩

-ism \ˌizəm\ *n suffix* -s [ME *-isme,* fr. MF & L; MF *-isme,* partly fr. L *-isma* (fr. Gk), & partly fr. L *-ismus,* fr. Gk *-ismos*] **1 a :** act, practice, or process — esp. in nouns corresponding to verbs in *-ize* ⟨critic*ism*⟩ ⟨hypnot*ism*⟩ ⟨plagiar*ism*⟩ **b :** manner of action or behavior characteristic of a (specified) person or thing ⟨animal*ism*⟩ ⟨Micawber*ism*⟩ **2 a :** state, condition, or property ⟨barbarian*ism*⟩ ⟨polymorph*ism*⟩ **b :** abnormal state or condition resulting from excess of a (specified) thing ⟨alcohol*ism*⟩ ⟨morphin*ism*⟩ **c :** abnormal state or condition characterized by resemblance to a (specified) person or thing ⟨mongol*ism*⟩ **3 a :** doctrine, theory, or cult ⟨Buddh*ism*⟩ ⟨Calvin*ism*⟩ ⟨Platon*ism*⟩ ⟨salvation*ism*⟩ ⟨vegetarian*ism*⟩ **b :** adherence to a system or a class of principles ⟨neutral*ism*⟩ ⟨real*ism*⟩ ⟨social*ism*⟩ ⟨stoic*ism*⟩ **4 :** characteristic or peculiar feature or trait ⟨colloquial*ism*⟩ ⟨latin*ism*⟩ ⟨poetic*ism*⟩

is·ma·el·ism \ˈizmēəˌlizəm, -z(ˌ)mā-\ *n* -s *usu cap* [*Ismael* (DV), *Ishmael* (AV), son of Abraham by his concubine Hagar + E *-ism;* so called fr. a belief that the Arabs are descendants of Ishmael] **:** ISLAMISM

is·ma·ili *or* **is·ma'·i·li** \ˌizmäˈē(ˌ)lē, ˌism-, -məˈē-\ *also* **is·ma·ili·an** \-lēən\ *n* -s *usu cap* [*Ismaili, Isma'ili* fr. Ar *Ismā'īlīy,* fr. *Ismā'īl* †A.D.760 son of the sixth imam Jafar al-Sadiq and in the opinion of the Ismailis his true successor; *Ismailian* fr. Ar *Ismā'īlīy* + E *-an*] **:** one of a Shi'a sect composed of those who recognize the Aga Khan as imam

is·ma·ilism \-ˈēˌlizəm\ *n* -s *usu cap* [*Isma'īl* †A.D.760 + E *-ism*] **:** the Ismaili movement or its doctrines

is·ma·ilite \-ˈēˌlīt\ *n* -s *usu cap* [*Isma'īl* †A.D.760 + E *-ite*] **:** ISMAILI

is·ma·ilit·ic \ˌizmēəˈlid·ik\ *adj, usu cap* **:** of or relating to the Ismailis

is·me·ne \izˈmē(ˌ)nē\ *n* [NL, fr. L *Ismene,* daughter of Oedipus, fr. Gk *Ismēnē*] **1** *cap, in some classifications* **:** a genus of So. American bulbous perennial herbs that have incurved filaments projecting beyond the margin of the floral cup and are usu. included in the genus *Hemerocallis* **2** -s **:** PERUVIAN DAFFODIL

is·nad \iˈsnäd, izˈn-\ *n* -s [Ar *isnād*] **:** the chain of authorities attesting to the historical authenticity of a particular hadith

is·neg \ˈizˌneg, ⸗ˈ⸗\ *n, pl* **isneg** *or* **isnegs** *usu cap* [Apayao] **:** APAYAO

is·ness \ˈiznəs\ *n* -ES [¹*is* + *-ness*] **1 a :** the fact that a thing is ⟨at the very outset there is no ~ to life —*Yale Rev.*⟩ **b :** the quality or state of elemental or factual existence **2 :** the state of things as they are ⟨the economics of the soldier who accepts a rough equation between ~ and oughtness —H.J.Laski⟩ — contrasted with *oughtness*

is·n't \ˈizᵊn(t), *in rapid speech* ˈid|\ [by contr.] **:** is not

iso \ˈī(ˌ)sō\ *adj* [*is-*] **:** ISOMERIC; *esp* **:** having a branched chain ⟨~ acids with branching methyl groups⟩ — compare *is-* 2

iso- *in pronunciations below,* ¦⸗(ˌ)⸗ = ¦ī(ˌ)sō *also* ¦ī(ˌ)zō, ¦⸗⸗ = ¦īsō, ¦īsə *also* ¦īzō, ¦īzə\ — see IS-

iso·abnormal *var of* ISABNORMAL

iso·agglutination \"+\ *n* [ISV *is-* + *agglutination*] **:** agglutination of an agglutinogen of one individual by the serum of another of the same species — **iso·agglutinative** \"+\ *adj*

iso·agglutinin \"+\ *n* [ISV *is-* + *agglutinin*] **:** an agglutinin specific for the cells of another individual of the same species

iso·agglutinogen \"+\ *n* [*isoagglutinin* + *-o-* + *-gen*] **:** a substance capable of provoking formation of or reacting with an isoagglutinin

iso·allele \"+\ *n* **:** a member of a pair of alleles each of which produces such a like result as to be indistinguishable by ordinary means

iso·alloxazine \"+\ *n* **:** a yellow solid $C_{10}H_6N_4O_2$ that differs from alloxazine only in the position of one hydrogen atom attached to nitrogen and that is the parent compound of riboflavin and other flavins

iso·amyl \"+\ *n* [ISV *is-* + *amyl*] **1 :** ISOPENTYL **2 :** AMYL 2a

isoamyl acetate *n* **:** the acetic ester $CH_3COOC_5H_{11}$ of amyl alcohol from fusel oil — called also *amyl acetate, banana oil, pear oil;* not used systematically

isoamyl alcohol *n* **1 :** ISOPENTYL ALCOHOL **2 :** AMYL ALCOHOL 2a

iso·amylene \¦⸗(ˌ)⸗ *at* ISO-+\ *n* [ISV *is-* + *amylene*] **:** a branched-chain amylene; *esp* **:** AMYLENE a

isoamyl nitrite *n* **:** AMYL NITRITE

isoamyl salicylate *n* **:** AMYL SALICYLATE

iso·antibody \¦⸗(ˌ)⸗ *at* ISO- +\ *n* **:** an antibody against an antigen sometimes present in members of a species that is produced by a member of the species lacking that antigen when exposed to it ⟨production of an anti-Rh ~ by an Rh⸗ negative person⟩ — compare RH FACTOR

iso·antigen \"+\ *n* [ISV *is-* + *antigen*] **:** an antigen capable of inducing the production of an isoantibody; *specif* **:** any of several closely similar antigens only one of which may occur in an individual and each of which is capable of inducing the formation of antibodies to any other antigen of its group — **iso·antigenic** \"+\ *adj*

iso·bar \ˈ⸗⸗ *at* ISO- + ˌbär\ *n* [ISV *is-* + *-bar* (fr. Gk *baros* weight) — more at GRIEVE] **1 :** an imaginary line or a line on a map or chart connecting or marking places on the surface of the earth where the height of the barometer reduced to sea level is the same either at a given time or for a certain period **2 a** *also* **iso·bare** \-ˌba(a)(ə)r\ **:** one of two or more atoms having practically the same atomic weights but different atomic numbers and hence different chemical properties ⟨carbon 14 and ordinary nitrogen 14 are ~*s*⟩ **b :** one of two or more nuclides having the same mass numbers but different atomic numbers — **iso·bar·ism** \-ˌbäˌrizəm, -ˌba(a),r-\ *n* -s

iso·barbaloin \¦⸗(ˌ)⸗ *at* ISO- + \ *n* **:** a crystalline compound $C_{20}H_{18}O_9$ isomeric with barbaloin and isolated with it from aloin

iso·bar·ic \¦⸗⸗ *at* ISO- + ¦barik\ *adj* [ISV *isobar* + *-ic*] **1 :** showing equal pressure: as **a :** showing points in the atmosphere having equal barometric pressure ⟨~ lines⟩ **b :** taking place without change of pressure ⟨~ expansion⟩ ⟨~ process⟩ **2 :** of, relating to, or having the relationship of an isobar

iso·barometric \¦⸗(ˌ)⸗+\ *adj* [ISV *is-* + *barometric*] **:** ISOBARIC

iso·base \ˈ⸗⸗ˌbās\ *n* [ISV *is-* + *base*] **:** an imaginary line or a line on a map or chart passing through all points that have been elevated to the same extent since some specified time (as the Glacial epoch)

¹iso·bath \-ˌbath\ *n* [ISV *is-* + *-bath* (fr. Gk *bathos* depth); akin to Gk *bathys* deep — more at BATHY-] **1 :** an imaginary line or a line on a map or chart that connects all points having the same depth below a water surface (as of an ocean, sea, or lake) **2 :** a line similar to an isobath indicating depth below the earth's surface of an aquifer or other geological horizon

²isobath \"\ *or* **iso·bath·ic** \¦⸗⸗¦bathik\ *adj* [*isobath* ISV *is-* + *-bath* (fr. Gk *bathos* depth); *isobathic* fr. ¹*isobath* + *-ic*] **:** having constant depth

iso·bathy·therm \ˌ⸗⸗ˈbathəˌthərm\ *n* [*is-* + *bathy-* + *-therm*] **:** a line connecting points on the earth's surface where a certain temperature is found at the same depth — **iso·bathy·ther·mal** \¦⸗⸗¦⸗⸗¦thərməl\ — **iso·bathy·ther·mic** \-mik\ *adj*

iso·bilateral \¦⸗(ˌ)⸗ *at* ISO- +\ *adj* **:** bilateral with the corresponding opposite parts alike

iso·borneol \¦⸗⸗+\ *n* [ISV *is-* + *borneol*] **:** a volatile crystalline alcohol $C_{10}H_{17}OH$ stereoisomeric with borneol, synthetically obtainable from alpha-pinene or camphene, and yielding camphor on oxidation

iso·bornyl \"+\ *n* [ISV *is-* + *bornyl*] **:** the univalent radical $C_{10}H_{17}$ derived from isoborneol

iso·bront \ˈ⸗⸗ˌbränt\ *also* **iso·bron·ton** \-ˌäntən, ˌ⸗⸗ˈ⸗⸗, ˌ⸗⸗ˈbrän,tän\ *n* [*isobront* ISV *is-* + *-bront* (fr. Gk *brontē* thunder); *isobronton* fr. *is-* + *-bronton* (fr. Gk *brontē* thunder) — more at BRONT-] **:** a line on a chart marking the simultaneous development of a thunderstorm at different points on the earth's surface

iso·bryales \¦⸗⸗+\ *n pl, cap* [NL, fr. *is-* + *Bryales*] **:** a large widely distributed order of Musci comprising mosses that have branched creeping gametophores on which the leaves are so twisted as to appear to be in two rows and usu. pleurocarpous sporophytes with erect capsule and double peristome

iso·butane \"+\ *n* [ISV *is-* + *butane*] **:** a gaseous branched-chain hydrocarbon $(CH_3)_3CH$ usu. accompanying normal butane and used chiefly as an alkylating agent and as a fuel gas; 2-methyl-propane

iso·butene \"+\ *n* [*is-* + *butene*] **:** ISOBUTYLENE — not used systematically

iso·butyl \"+\ *n* [ISV *is-* + *butyl*] **:** the primary alkyl radical $(CH_3)_2CHCH_2$— derived from isobutane

isobutyl alcohol *n* **:** the branched-chain primary butyl alcohol $(CH_3)_2CH_2CH_2OH$ synthetically made usu. from carbon monoxide and hydrogen; 2-methyl-1-propanol

iso·bu·tyl·carbinol \¦⸗⸗ˌ⸗⸗+\ *n* [*isobutyl* + *carbinol*] **:** ISOPENTYL ALCOHOL

iso·butylene \¦⸗⸗ *at* ISO- +\ *n* [ISV *is-* + *butylene*] **:** the branched-chain gaseous butylene $(CH_3)_2C{=}CH_2$ obtainable from isobutane by dehydrogenation and used chiefly in making butyl rubber and gasoline components and in alkylating aromatic hydrocarbons — called also *2-methylpropene*

isobutyr- *or* **isobutyro-** *comb form* [ISV, fr. *isobutyric* (in *isobutyric acid*)] **:** ISOBUTYRIC **:** related to isobutyric acid ⟨*isobutyr*amide⟩ ⟨*isobutyro*nitrile⟩

iso·butyrate \¦⸗⸗ *at* ISO- + \ *n* -s [*isobutyr-* + *-ate*] **:** a salt or ester of isobutyric acid

iso·butyric acid \"+ . . . -\ *n* [*isobutyric* ISV *is-* + *butyric*] **:** a colorless liquid acid $(CH_3)_2CHCOOH$ made by the oxidation of isobutyl alcohol and used chiefly in making esters for use as flavoring materials

iso·butyryl \"+\ *n* [ISV *isobutyr-* + *-yl*] **:** the radical $(CH_3)_2CHCO$— of isobutyric acid

iso·caloric \"+\ *adj* **:** having similar caloric value ⟨~ diets⟩ — **iso·calorically** \"+\ *adv*

iso·candle diagram \ˈ⸗⸗+, . . . -\ *n* [*isocandle* fr. *is-* + *candle*] **:** a system of isocandle lines for various candlepowers of a source of light

isocandle line *n* **:** a line showing in suitable coordinates all directions in space in which a given source of light has a specified candlepower

iso·car·pic \¦⸗⸗¦kärpik\ *also* **iso·car·pous** \-pəs\ *adj* [*isocarpic* fr. *is-* + *-carpic* (fr. ¹*carp-* + *-ic*); *isocarpous* fr. *is-* + *-carpous*] **:** having carpels equaling the perianth divisions in number — compare ANISOCARPIC

iso·cellular \¦⸗⸗+\ *adj* **:** consisting of similar cells

iso·center \ˈ⸗⸗+,-\ *n* [*is-* + *center*] **:** the point on an aerial photograph intersected by the bisector of the angle between the plumb line and the perpendicular to the photograph

iso·ce·phal·ic \¦⸗(ˌ)⸗səˈfalik\ *also* **iso·ceph·a·lous** \¦⸗⸗ˈsefələs\ *adj* [*is-* + *-cephalic* or *-cephalous*] **:** having the heads of the figures in a composition brought to the same level — used esp. of a bas-relief — **iso·ceph·a·ly** \¦⸗⸗ˈsefəlē\ *n* -ES

iso·ce·rau·nic \¦⸗(ˌ)⸗səˈrȯnik\ *or* **iso·ke·rau·nic** \-kə-\ *adj* [*isoceraunic* fr. *is-* + *ceraun-* + *-ic; isokeraunic* fr. *is-* + *keraun-* (fr. Gk *keraunos* thunderbolt) + *-ic* — more at CERAUN-] **:** showing or having equal frequency or severity or simultaneous occurrence of thunderstorms ⟨~ maps⟩

iso·cer·cal \ˌ==ˈsərkəl\ *adj* [*is-* + *-cercal*] **1 :** having symmetrical upper and lower lobes and a gradually tapering vertebral column — used of the tail fin of a fish **2 :** having or relating to an isocercal tail fin — **iso·cer·cy** \ˌ==ˌsərsē, -rkē\ *n* -ES

iso·cheim \ˈ== *at* ISO- +ˌkīm\ *n* -S [prob. modif. (influenced by Gk *cheimōn* winter) of F *isochimène*, fr. *is-* + *-chimène* (fr. Gk *cheimainein* to be stormy, be winter); akin to Gk *cheimōn* winter — more at HIBERNATE] **:** a line joining points on the earth's surface having the same mean winter temperature — compare ISOTHERE

iso·chela \ˌ==+\ *n* [NL, fr. *is-* + *chela*] **:** a chelate spicule having both ends alike

iso·chor \ˈ==ˌkȯ(ə)r\ *also* **iso·chore** \-ˌkō(ə)r\ *n* -S [ISV *is-* + *-chor* (fr. Gk *chōros* place, clear space) — more at CHOR-] **:** a line representing the variation of pressure with temperature when the volume of the substance operated on is constant — **iso·chor·ic** \ˌ==ˈkȯrik, -ˈkōr-\ *adj*

iso·chro·mat \ˌ==ˈkrōˌmat, ˌ==ˈkrōˌm-\ *n* -S [*is-* + *-chromat* (fr. Gk *chrōmat-*, *chrōma* color) — more at CHROMATIC] **:** a graph showing intensity as a function of voltage for a given wavelength of the output from an X-ray source

iso·chromatic \ˌ==+\ *adj* [ISV *is-* + *chromatic*] **1 a :** of or corresponding to constant color ⟨the ~ variation of refractive index with density for a given wavelength⟩ **b :** connecting points of the same color **c :** coincident with a line of equal stress in a photoelastic stress pattern **2 :** ORTHOCHROMATIC **3** *of cells or tissues* **:** having the same color; *specif* **:** staining similarly with like dyes

iso·chromosome \ˌ==+\ *n* **:** a chromosome with identical arms believed to be derived from a telocentric chromosome by fusion of two daughter chromosomes

isoch·ro·nal \(ˈ)īˈsäkrənᵊl\ *adj* [Gk *isochronos* isochronous + E *-al*] **1 :** uniform in time **:** having equal duration **:** recurring at regular intervals **:** ISOCHRONOUS **2** [*isochrone* + *-al*] **:** ISOCHRONIC

iso·chrone \ˈ== *at* ISO- + ˌkrōn\ *n* -S [ISV *is-* + *-chrone* (fr. Gk *chronos* time)] **:** a line on a map or chart connecting points at which an event occurs simultaneously or which represent the same time or time difference (as a line showing the distances that may be reached from a central point in a city in the same length of time)

iso·chron·ic \ˌ==ˈkränik, -rōn-\ *adj* [*isochrone* + *-ic*] **1 :** having isochrones ⟨~ map⟩ **2** [ISV *isochron-* (fr. Gk *isochronos* isochronous) + *-ic*] **:** exhibiting isochronism ⟨a muscle and its nerve must be ~ —Alexis Carrel⟩

isochro·nism \īˈsäkrəˌnizəm; ˌīsəˈkrōˌn- *also* ˌīzəˈkrōˌn-\ *n* -S [F *isochronisme*, fr. Gk *isochronos* isochronous + F *-isme* -ism] **1 a :** the condition or property of having a uniform period of vibration — used of a pendulum or a watch balance **b :** uniformity of rate of operation — used of a timepiece **2 a :** equal duration of units or measures in prosody **b :** emphasis on stable rhythmic units in poetry **3** [*is-* + *chron-* + *-ism*] **:** the condition of having identical chronaxies — used of excitable structures (as motor neurones and muscle fibers)

isoch·ro·nous \(ˈ)īˈsäkrənəs\ *adj* [Gk *isochronos* isochronous (fr. *is-* + *chronos* time) + E *-ous*] **:** equal in duration, interval, or metrical length **:** ISOCHRONAL ⟨the oscillations of a spiral hairspring were ~ —S.F.Mason⟩ ⟨free oscillations of an elastic system were ~ —Adrien Jaquerod⟩ — **isoch·ro·nous·ly** *adv*

isochronous governor *n* **:** a governor that maintains the same speed in the mechanism controlled regardless of the load

iso·citric acid \ˌ== *at* ISO- + . . . -\ *n* **:** a crystalline acid HOOCCH(OH)CH(COOH)CH_2COOH isomeric with citric acid that is found esp. in the leaves of various air plants of the genus *Kalanchoe* and in blackberry juice and is recognized as an intermediate stage in the metabolism of fats and carbohydrates; 2-hydroxy-1,2,3-propane-tricarboxylic acid

iso·cla·site \ˌ==ˈkläˌsīt, īˈsäklə,-, -ˌzīt\ *n* [G *isoklas* isoclasite (fr. *is-* + *-klas* -clase) + E *-ite*] **:** a mineral $Ca_2(PO_4)(OH)$.$2H_2O$ consisting of a basic hydrous calcium phosphate occurring in small white crystals or columnar forms

[1]**iso·cli·nal** \ˌ== *at* ISO- + ˈklīnᵊl\ *adj* [ISV *is-* + *-clinal*] **:** relating to, having, or indicating equality of inclination or dip: as **a** *also* **isoclinic :** being or relating to an isocline **b :** being or relating to an isoclinic line — **iso·cli·nal·ly** \-ᵊlē\ *adv*

[2]**isoclinal** \"\ *n* -S **:** ISOCLINIC LINE

isoclinal fold *n* **:** an isocline or a fold so closely compressed that it approximates an isocline

iso·cline \ˈ==ˌklīn\ *n* -S [*is-* + *-cline*] **:** an anticline or syncline so closely folded that the rock beds of the two sides have the same dip

iso·clin·ic line \ˌ==ˈklinik-\ *also* **isoclinic** *n* [*isoclinic* ISV *is-* + *-clinic*] **:** a line on a map or chart joining points on the earth's surface at which a dip needle has the same inclination to the plumb line — compare ACLINIC LINE

iso·colon \ˌ==+\ *n* [Gk *isokōlon*, fr. neut. of *isokōlos* of equal members, fr. *is-* + *kōlon* limb, member — more at CALK] **1 :** a period consisting of cola of equal length **2 :** the use of equal cola in immediate succession

iso·con·tae *syn of* ISOKONTAE

iso·cortex \ˌ== *at* ISO- +\ *n* [NL, fr. *is-* + L *cortex* bark — more at CORTEX] **:** NEOPALLIUM

iso·corydine \"+\ *n* **:** a crystalline alkaloid $C_{20}H_{23}NO_4$ isomeric with corydine and occurring with it

isoc·ra·cy \īˈsäkrəsē\ *n* -ES [Gk *isokratia*, fr. *isokratēs* having equal power or equal rights (fr. *is-* + *kratos* strength, power) + *-ia* -y — more at HARD] **:** equality of power or rule; *esp* **:** a system of government in which all have equal political power

iso·cryme \ˈ== *at* ISO + ˌkrīm *or* -ˌkrim\ *n* -S [ISV *is-* + Gk *krymos* frost, icy cold — more at CRUST] **:** an imaginary line or a line on a map or chart connecting points having the same mean temperature for a specified coldest time of the year

isocyan- *or* **isocyano-** *comb form* [ISV, fr. *isocyanic* (in *isocyanic acid*)] **:** containing the univalent group —NC isomeric with cyanogen and present in isocyanides ⟨*isocyano*benzene C_6H_5NC⟩

iso·cyanate \ˌ== *at* ISO- +\ *n* -S [ISV *isocyan-* + *-ate*] **:** a compound containing the univalent radical —NCO consisting of an isocyano group united with oxygen **:** a salt or ester of isocyanic acid ⟨phenyl ~ C_6H_5NCO⟩

iso·cyanic acid \ˌ== + . . . -\ *n* [ISV *is-* + *cyanic acid*] **:** cyanic acid regarded as having the formula HNCO and usu. prepared (as by the reaction of phosgene with the salt of a primary amine) in the form of esters of which some are used in making polyurethans and other resins, plastics, foams, and adhesives

iso·cyanide \"+\ *n* [*is-* + *cyanide*] **:** any of a class of compounds that are isomeric with the normal cyanides, that have the structure RNC, and that are in general colorless volatile poisonous liquids of strong offensive odor ⟨phenyl ~ C_6H_5-NC⟩ — called also *carbylamine*

iso·cyanine \"+\ *n* [ISV *is-* + *cyanine*] **:** any of several simple cyanine dyes in whose structure the carbon atom joining the two quinoline or other heterocyclic rings is attached at different positions in the two rings

iso·cyano \"+\ *adj* [*isocyan-*] **:** relating to or containing the group —NC isomeric with cyanogen — used esp. of organic compounds

iso·cyclic \"+\ *adj* [ISV *is-* + *cyclic*] **:** relating to, characterized by, or being a ring composed of atoms of only one element; *esp* **:** CARBOCYCLIC — distinguished from *heterocyclic*

iso·diametric \"+\ *adj* [ISV *is-* + *diametric*] **1 a :** having equal diameters **b :** having dimensions that are equal in all directions ⟨~ parenchyma cells⟩ **2 :** having lateral axes that are equal ⟨~ crystals⟩

iso·di·a·phere \ˌ==ˈdīəˌfi(ə)r\ *n* -S [*is-* + *-diaphere* (fr. Gk *diapherein* to differ, carry across, fr. *dia-* + *pherein* to carry) — more at BEAR] **:** a nuclear species that has the same isotopic number as one or more other nuclear species

iso·dimorphism \ˌ== *at* ISO- +\ *n* [ISV *is-* + *dimorphism*] **:** isomorphism between the two forms of two dimorphous substances (as iron sulfide and cobalt arsenide) in such a way that each form of one is isomorphous with a form of the other — **iso·dimorphous** \"+\ *adj*

iso·dom·ic \ˌ==ˈdämik\ *or* **isod·o·mous** \(ˈ)īˈsädəməs\ *adj* [*isodomon* + *-ic* or *-ous*] **:** of or relating to isodomon

isod·o·mon \īˈsädəˌmän, -ˌmən\ *or* **isod·o·mum** \-məm\ *n* -S [L & Gk; L *isodomum*, fr. Gk *isodomon*, neut. of *isodomos* of equal courses, fr. *is-* + *domos* course of masonry, house — more at TIMBER] **:** masonry having blocks of equal length and thickness laid in courses so that each vertical joint of a course comes over the middle of a block just below

iso·dont \ˈ== *at* ISO- +ˌdänt\ *also* **iso·don·tous** \ˌ==ˈdäntəs\ *adj* [*isodont* ISV *is-* + *-odont*; *isodontous* prob. fr. F *isodonte* isodont + E *-ous*] **1 :** having the teeth all alike **2** *of a snake* **:** having the maxillary teeth of equal length

iso·dose \ˈ==ˌdōs\ *adj* [ISV *is-* + *dose*, n.] **:** of or relating to points or zones in a medium that receive equal doses of radiation ⟨an ~ chart⟩ ⟨the ~ rate lines are in units of roentgens per hour —G.M.Dunning⟩

iso·drin \ˈ==drən\ *n* -S [*is-* + *-drin* (fr. *aldrin*)] **:** a crystalline insecticide $C_{12}H_8Cl_6$ that is a stereoisomer of aldrin and resembles aldrin in properties

iso·durene \ˌ==+\ *n* **:** a liquid aromatic hydrocarbon C_6H_2-$(CH_3)_4$ isomeric with durene; 1,2,3,5-tetramethyl-benzene

iso·dynamic \ˌ=(ˌ)=+\ *adj* [ISV *is-* + *dynamic*] **:** of or relating to equality or uniformity of force

isodynamic line *n* **:** an imaginary line or a line on a map connecting points on the earth's surface at which the horizontal magnetic intensity is the same — called also *isogam*

iso·electric \"+\ *adj* [ISV *is-* + *electric*] **:** having or representing zero difference of electric potential

isoelectric point *n* **:** the point or narrow range on a pH scale at which the concentration of the anionic part of an ampholyte equals that of the cationic part **:** the pH at which the ampholyte will not migrate in an electrical field ⟨the *isoelectric points* of most proteins range from pH values of 4 to 7⟩

iso·electronic \"+\ *adj* [ISV *is-* + *electronic*] **1 :** having the same number of electrons ⟨the fluoride ion, the neon atom, and the sodium ion are ~⟩ — used of atoms or their ions **2 :** having the same number of valency electrons ⟨the carbon dioxide molecule and the cyanate ion are ~⟩ — used of molecules or radicals or ions composed of two or more atoms — **iso·electronically** \"+\ *adv*

iso·eta·les \ˌ=(ˌ)=əˈtā(ˌ)lēz\ *n pl, cap* [NL, fr. *Isoetes* + *-ales*] **:** an order of plants that is assigned to the class Lycopodineae or occas. to the class Filicineae, is known to have existed since the Cenozoic, and comprises *Isoetes* and possibly various extinct genera

iso·etes \īˈsōəˌtēz\ *n* [NL, fr. L, houseleek, fr. Gk, fr. neut. of *isoetēs* equal in years, fr. *is-* + *etos* year — more at WETHER] **1** *cap* **:** a large widely distributed genus (coextensive with the family Isoetaceae) of fern allies comprising the aquatic or marsh-growing quillworts that have a short buried lobed stem from which arises a tuft of quilt-shaped leaves bearing sporangia in their axils — see ISOETALES **2** *pl* **isoetes :** any plant of the genus *Isoetes* **:** QUILLWORT 1

iso·eugenol \ˌ=(ˌ)= *at* ISO- +\ *n* [ISV *is-* + *eugenol*, prob. orig. formed in G] **:** an aromatic liquid phenol CH_3CH=C-$HC_6H_3(OCH_3)$OH found esp. in ilang-ilang oil and nutmeg oil, obtained also from eugenol by isomerization with alkali, and used chiefly in perfumes and in the synthesis of vanillin; 4-propenyl-guaiacol

iso·flavone \"+\ *n* [*is-* + *flavone*] **:** a colorless cyrstalline ketone $C_{15}H_{10}O_2$ that occurs as hydroxy derivatives in many plants often in the form of glycosides (as genistin, prunitrin)

iso·flu·ro·phate \ˌ==ˈflürəˌfāt\ *n* -S [by shortening] **:** DIISOPROPYL FLUOROPHOSPHATE

iso·gam \ˈ==ˌgam\ *n* -S [ISV *is-* + *-gam* (fr. *gamma*)] **:** ISODYNAMIC LINE

iso·gamete \ˌ==+\ *n* [ISV *is-* + *gamete*] **:** a gamete showing no differentiation in form or size or behavior from another gamete with which it is capable of uniting to form a zygote — compare HETEROGAMETE — **iso·gametic** \"+\ *adj*

isog·amous \(ˈ)īˈsägəməs\ *also* **iso·gam·ic** \ˌ== |*at* ISO- + ˈgamik\ *adj* [*isogamous* prob. fr. (assumed) NL *isogamus*, fr. NL *is-* + *-gamus* -gamous; *isogamic* prob. fr. *is-* + *-gamic*] **1** *of sexual reproduction* **:** characterized by fusion of like individuals or gametes — compare ANISOGAMOUS, HETEROGAMOUS, OOGAMOUS **2 :** having isogamous reproduction ⟨the ~ aquatic forms⟩

isog·a·my \īˈsägəmē\ *n* -ES [ISV *is-* + *-gamy*] **:** isogamous reproduction

iso·gen \ˈ== *at* ISO- + jən, ˌjen\ *n* -S [back-formation fr. *isogenous*] **:** an isogenous structure

iso·ge·ne·ic \ˌ==jəˈnēik\ *adj* [by alter. (influenced by *isogeneity*)] **:** ISOGENIC

iso·ge·ne·ity \ˌ==jəˈnēəd·ē\ *n* -ES [*is-* + *-geneity* (irreg. — prob. influenced by *heterogeneity* — fr. *gene*)] **:** the quality or state of being isogenic

iso·gen·er·a·tae \ˌ=(ˌ)=ˌjenəˈrāˌtē, -rā-\ *n pl, cap* [NL, fr. *is-* + L *generatae* (fem. pl. of *generatus*, past part. of *generare* to beget) — more at GENERATE] **:** a class of brown algae including those that have two alternating generations similar in vegetative structure and size — compare HETEROGENERATAE

iso·genesis \ˌ==+\ *n* [NL, fr. *is-* + L *genesis*] **:** similarity of origin or development

iso·genic \ˌ==ˈjenik\ *adj* **:** having the same genic constitution: **a :** HOMOZYGOUS **b :** having all or certain specified genes the same — used of separate individuals

isog·e·nism \īˈsäjəˌnizəm\ *n* -S [*is-* + *gene* + *-ism*] **:** ISOGENEITY

iso·genotypic \ˌ== *at* ISO- +\ *adj* [*is-* + *genotypic*] **:** based on a single genotype — used of two or more generic names

isog·e·nous \(ˈ)īˈsäjənəs\ *adj* [*is-* + *-genous*] **:** having the same origin

iso·geotherm \ˌ== *at* ISO- +\ *n* -S [ISV *is-* + *ge-* + *-therm*] **:** an imaginary line or curved surface beneath the earth's surface through points having the same mean temperature — called also *geoisotherm* — **iso·geothermal** \"+\ *adj* — **iso·geothermic** \"+\ *adj*

iso·gloss \ˈ==ˌgläs, -lȯs\ *n* -ES [ISV *is-* + *-gloss* (fr. Gk *glōssa* language, tongue) — more at GLOSS] **1 :** a boundary line between places or regions that differ in a particular linguistic feature ⟨the ~ separating Low German *maken* "to make" from High German *machen*⟩ ⟨dialect boundaries can be established only by means of ~*es* —Hans Kurath⟩ **2 :** a line on a map representing an isogloss — **iso·gloss·al** \ˌ==ˈ=əl\ *adj*

[1]**iso·gon·ic** \ˌ==+ˈgänik\ *also* **isog·o·nal** \(ˈ)īˈsägənᵊl\ *adj* [ISV *is-* + *gon-* (fr. Gk *gōnia* angle) + *-ic* or *-al* — more at -GON] **:** of, relating to, or having equal angles

[2]**isogonic** \"\ *or* **isogonal** \"\ *n* -S **:** ISOGONIC LINE

[3]**isogonic** \"\ *adj* [*is-* + *gon-* + *-ic*] **:** of, relating to, or marked by isogonism or isogony

isogonic line *n* [[1]*isogonic*] **:** an imaginary line or a line on a map joining points on the earth's surface at which magnetic declination is the same — compare ACLINIC LINE, AGONIC LINE

isog·o·nism \īˈsägəˌnizəm\ *n* -S [*is-* + *gon-* + *-ism*] **:** the quality or state of having similar medusae or gonophores — used of hydroids of different genera

isog·o·ny \-ˌnē\ *n* -ES [*is-* + *-gony*] **:** equivalent relative growth of parts in such a way that relative size differences remain constant — compare HETEROGONY

iso·graft \ˈ== *at* ISO- +ˌ-\ *n* -S [*is-* + *graft*] **:** HOMOGRAFT

iso·gram \ˈ==ˌgram\ *n* -S [*is-* + *-gram*] **:** a line on a map or chart along which there is a constant value (as of temperature, pressure, or rainfall)

iso·graph \-ˌgraf, -râf\ *n* -S [*is-* + *-graph*] **1 :** an instrument consisting of two short straightedges connected by a large circular joint marked with angular degrees that combines the functions of a protractor and a set square **2 :** an electronic calculator for finding both real and imaginary roots of algebraic equations

iso·griv \-ˌgriv\ *n* -S [*is-* + *-griv* (fr. *grivation*)] **:** a line on a map or chart connecting points of equal grivation

isog·y·nous \(ˈ)īˈsäjənəs\ *adj* [ISV *is-* + *-gynous*] **:** ISOCARPIC

iso·gyre \ˈ== *at* ISO- +ˌ-\ *n* [ISV *is-* + *gyre*] **:** the dark shadow in an interference figure representing the locus of all points that correspond to directions of transmission through the crystal plate in which the state of polarization of the incident rays is unchanged by passage through the plate

iso·haline \ˌ==ˈhāˌlēn, -ˈha,-, -ˌlīn\ *or* **iso·hal·sine** \-ˈhalˌsēn, -ˌsīn\ *n* -S [*isohaline* ISV *is-* + *-haline* (fr. Gk *halinos* of salt, fr. *hal-*, *hals* salt + *-inos* -ine); *isohalsine* fr. *is-* + *-halsine* (irreg. fr. Gk *hal-*, *hals* salt) — more at SALT] **:** a line or surface drawn on a map or chart to indicate connecting points of equal salinity in the ocean

iso·hel \ˈ==ˌhel\ *n* -S [*is-* + *-hel* (fr. Gk *hēlios* sun) — more at SOLAR] **:** a line drawn on a map or chart connecting places of equal duration of sunshine

iso·hemagglutination \ˌ==+\ *n* [*is-* + *hemagglutination*] **:** isoagglutination of red blood cells

iso·hemagglutinin \"+\ *n* [*is-* + *hemagglutinin*] **:** a hemagglutinin causing isoagglutination

iso·hemagglutinogen \"+\ *n* -S [*isohemagglutinin* + *-o-* + *-gen*] **:** an antigen inducing the production of or reacting with specific isohemagglutinins

iso·hemolysin \"+\ *n* [ISV *is-* + *hemolysin*] **:** a hemolysin that causes isohemolysis

iso·hemolysis \ˌ==+\ *n* [NL, fr. *is-* + *hemolysis*] **:** the lysis of the red blood cells of one individual of a species by specific antibodies in the serum of another (as in human erythroblastosis fetalis)

iso·hydric \"+\ *adj* [ISV *is-* + *hydr-* + *-ic*] **:** relating to or being solutions of electrolytes having equal concentration of a common ion (as a hydrogen ion) not affecting one another's conductivity on being mixed

iso·hyet \ˌ==+ˈhīət\ *also* **iso·hyetal** \ˌ==+\ *n* -S [*isohyet* ISV *is-* + *-hyet* (fr. Gk *hyetos* rain); *isohyetal* fr. *isohyetal*, adj. — more at HYET-] **:** an isohyetal line on a map or chart

iso·hyetal \ˌ==+\ *adj* [prob. fr. *isohyet* + *-al*] **:** relating to or indicating equal rainfall ⟨~ lines⟩

iso·immunization \ˌ==+\ *n* [ISV *is-* + *immunization*] **:** production by an individual of antibodies against constituents of the tissues of others of his own species (as when transfused with blood from one belonging to a different blood group)

iso·ionic point \ˌ==+...-\ *n* [*isoionic* ISV *is-* + *ionic*] **:** the hydrogen-ion concentration expressed usu. as the pH value at which the ionization of an amphoteric substance as an acid equals the ionization as a base and becomes identical with the isoelectric point in the absence of foreign inorganic ions

isokeraunic *var of* ISOCERAUNIC

iso·kon·tae \ˌ==ˈkänˌtē\ *n pl, cap* [NL, fr. *is-* + *-kontae* (fr. Gk *kontos* punting pole, fr. *kentein* to prick, goad); fr. the equal length of the flagella — more at CENTER] *in some classifications* **:** a class of green algae comprising forms without motile stages or with flagella of equal length and including most of those now usu. placed in Chlorophyceae — compare HETEROKONTAE

iso·la·bil·i·ty \ˌīsəlᵊˈbiləd·ē *also* ˌisə- *sometimes* ˌīzə-\ *n* -ES **:** the quality or state of being isolable

iso·la·ble \ˈ==ləbəl\ *also* **iso·lat·able** \ˈ==ˌlād·əbəl, -ātə-, ˌ==ˈ===\ *adj* [*isolable* fr. [1]*isolate* + *-able*; *isolatable* fr. [1]*isolate* + *-able*] **:** capable of being isolated

iso·lant \ˈ==ˌlənt\ *n* -S [[1]*isolate* + *-ant*] **:** [3]ISOLATE 4, 5

[1]**iso·late** \ˈīsəˌlāt *also* ˈisə- *sometimes* ˈīzə-; *usu* -ād.+V\ *vb* -ED/-ING/-S [back-formation fr. *isolated*] *vt* **1 a** (1) **:** to set apart from others **:** cause to be detached from others and alone **:** place alone **:** make solitary ⟨a tiny village that had been *isolated* from civilization⟩ (2) **:** to cause to be stranded **:** cut off ⟨*isolated* what was left of the fleeing army⟩ **b :** to keep apart or away from others so as to minimize or wholly reduce any effect on others; *specif* **:** to separate (one with a contagious disease) from others not similarly infected ⟨kept very close track of all carriers and *isolated* them whenever they gave positive results —V.G.Heiser⟩ — compare QUARANTINE **c :** to single out **:** PINPOINT ⟨*isolating* the most important sense of a word⟩ **2 :** to separate (as a chemical compound) from all other substances **:** obtain pure or in a free state **3 :** INSULATE 2a ~ *vi* **:** to cause something to be isolated

[2]**iso·late** \-ˌlāt, -lət, -ˌlā|, *usu* |d.+V\ *adj* [prob. fr. [1]*isolate*, after such pairs as *appropriate*, v.: *appropriate*, adj.] **:** ISOLATED

[3]**isolate** \"\ *n* -S **1 :** an isolated factor, function, or process ⟨the smallest human ~ is a culture —J.K.Feibleman⟩ ⟨no one historical epoch and no one cultural ~ can present the permanent features of society —Georgiana Melvin⟩ **2 :** something singled out for observation **:** ABSTRACT 3 ⟨~*s* which could be described . . . as if they completely represented the physical world from which they had been extracted —Lewis Mumford⟩ **3 :** a chemical compound (as geraniol) separated from an essential oil for use in perfumes **4 a :** a spore, single organism, or viable part of an organism that has been isolated (as from diseased tissue, contaminated water, or the air); *often* **:** a pure culture produced from such an isolate **b :** an individual or strain isolated from a natural population (as for the study of a pathogenic fungus or bacterium) **5 :** a relatively homogeneous population separated from related populations by geographic or biologic or social factors or by the intervention of man — compare BIOTYPE, CLONE, ISOLATION 2 **6 :** an individual living in isolation from particular phases of an environment; *esp* **:** an individual socially withdrawn or removed from society through rejection of or incapacity for interpersonal relationships

isolated *adj* [F *isolé* isolated (fr. It *isolato*, fr. *isola* island — fr. L *insula* — + *-ato* -ate) + E *-ate* + *-ed* — more at ISLE] **1 a :** placed alone or apart **:** being alone **:** SOLITARY ⟨could not remain the ~ figure he had been —Sherwood Anderson⟩ **b :** caused to be alone or apart **:** cut off **:** STRANDED ⟨if attacked the ~ pawn can be defended —*New Complete Hoyle*⟩ **2 a :** occurring alone or once **:** UNIQUE ⟨some ~ incident not likely to recur —Dorothy Barclay⟩ **b :** SPORADIC ⟨the reader who has an ~ rather than overall interest —R.S.Browne⟩ ⟨~ instances of ill behavior —Eugene Burr⟩ **3 :** not bonded (as by cement) to an adjacent structure ⟨~ buildings⟩ ⟨an ~ pier⟩ **4 :** separated by more than one single bond in a system of at least two double bonds in a molecule **:** not conjugated ⟨~ double bonds⟩ — **iso·lat·ed·ly** \ˈ==ˌ===, ˌ==ˈ===\ *adv*

isolating *adj* [fr. pres. part. of [1]*isolate*] **:** of, relating to, or being a language in which each word typically expresses a distinct idea and in which variations in parts of speech and syntactical relations are determined almost exclusively by the order in which words are joined and by the use of particles so that a sentence typically consists of a string of formally independent words ⟨an ~ language⟩ ⟨the ~ form of speech of the Sino-Tibetan languages⟩ — distinguished from *agglutinative* and *inflectional*; compare ANALYTIC 4

isolating mechanism *n* **:** something (as a geographical, ecological, physiological, anatomical, or psychological barrier) that limits interbreeding between groups and is thereby a major factor in the differentiation of biologic units (as races or species)

iso·la·tion \ˌ==ˈlāshən\ *n* -S [F, fr. *isoler* to isolate (fr. *isolé* isolated) + *-ation*] **1 :** the action of isolating or condition of being isolated **2 :** a segregation of a group of organisms from related forms in such a manner as to prevent crossing

isolation booth *n* **:** a small soundproof booth used (as in a television studio) as a small studio within a larger studio

iso·la·tion·ism \-shəˌnizəm\ *n* -S **1 a :** a policy directed toward the isolation of a nation from other nations by a deliberate abstention from alliances and other international political and economic relations ⟨American foreign policy was set on a course of ~ —Dorothy B. Goebel⟩ ⟨a peculiarly hopeless kind of new Asian ~ —H.R.Isaacs⟩ **b :** a disposition or tendency to isolate deliberately an individual or group (as a political party) or a field of endeavor (as education or intellectual activity) from outside and esp. foreign relations or influences ⟨uncontrolled ~ would estrange the party from . . . the leaders of friendly cooperative non-Communist parties —H.A.Steiner⟩ ⟨ivory-tower cultural ~ —Leslie Rees⟩ **2 :** an attitude or conviction favoring adherence to a policy of deliberate isolation ⟨~ can never again dominate America —G.W.Chapman⟩ ⟨the hard core of ~ in the United States has been ethnic and emotional —Samuel Lubell⟩ — compare INTERNATIONALISM, INTERVENTIONISM

[1]**iso·la·tion·ist** \ˌ==ˈlāsh(ə)nəst\ *n* -S **:** one that advocates or believes in isolationism ⟨criticism . . . not from ~*s* but from internationalists —*Atlantic*⟩ ⟨anthropological ~*s*⟩

[2]**isolationist** \ˌ==ˈ=(=)=\ *adj* **:** of, characterized by, or favoring isolationism ⟨the orthodox believe that more money can be saved, especially of what now goes to foreign aid, by a more ~ foreign policy —Walter Lippmann⟩ ⟨the country was in an overwhelmingly ~ mood —F.L.Allen⟩ ⟨culturally as well as politically ~ —Christian Gauss⟩

iso·la·tive \ˈ==ˌlād·|iv, -āt|, |ēv *also* |əv\ *adj* **1** *of a sound change* **:** occurring in isolation **:** not dependent on phonetic environment ⟨OE *stǣn* \stān became by ~ change Modern English \stōn*stone*⟩ — compare COMBINATIVE **2 :** ISOLATING

iso·la·tor \-ād·ə(r), -ātə-\ *n* -s : one that isolates; *specif* : a device that absorbs or prevents the transmission of noise or vibration (as of machinery)

iso·lecithal \¦≈(,)≈ *at* ISO-+\ *adj* [ISV *is-* + *lecithal*] : HOMOLECITHAL

iso·lette \¦īsə¦let *also* ¦is-\ *n* -s [fr. *Isolette*, a trademark] : an incubator for premature infants that is designed to provide controlled temperature, humidity, and oxygen supply and to permit feeding and care under aseptic conditions with a minimum of handling

iso·leucine \¦≈≈+\ *n* [ISV *is-* + *leucine*] : a crystalline amino acid $C_2H_5CH(CH_3)CH(NH_2)COOH$ that is isomeric with leucine, that occurs in its dextrorotatory L-form in most dietary proteins but is usu. obtained from the waste from the recovery of sugar from beet molasses, and that like leucine is essential in the nutrition of animals and man; α-amino-β-methyl-valeric acid

iso·line \'≈≈+,līn\ *n* [*is-* + *line*] : ISOGRAM

isol·o·gous \(')ī¦säləgəs\ *adj* [ISV *is-* + *-logous* (as in *homologous*)] : relating to or being any of two or more closely related chemical compounds in a series whose successive members possess a regular difference in composition other than a difference of one carbon and two hydrogen atoms — sometimes distinguished from *homologous*

iso·logue *or* **iso·log** \'≈≈ *at* ISO-+,lȯg *also* ,läg\ *n* -s [ISV, fr. *isologous*, after such pairs as E *analogous: analogue*] : a compound isologous with one or more other compounds

[1]**iso·lo·ma** \,īsə'lōmə\ [NL, fr. *is-* + Gk *lōma* fringe; akin to Gk *eilein* to wind, roll — more at VOLUBLE] *syn of* KOHLERIA

[2]**isoloma** \"\ *n* -s [NL *Isoloma*] : a plant of the genus *Kohleria*

iso·lux \'≈≈ *at* ISO-+,ləks\ *n* -ES [*is-* + L *lux* light — more at LIGHT] : ISOPHOTE

[1]**iso·magnetic** \¦≈(,)≈ *at* ISO-+\ *adj* [ISV *is-* + *magnetic*] : of, relating to, or marked by points of equal magnetic intensity or points of equal value of a component of such intensity ⟨an ~ chart⟩

[2]**isomagnetic** \"\ *n* : a line on a map or chart of the earth's surface connecting points of equal magnetic intensity or points of equal value of a component of such intensity

iso·maltose \¦≈≈+\ *n* [ISV *is-* + *maltose*] : a syrupy disaccharide $C_{12}H_{22}O_{11}$ isomeric with maltose, present in hydrol (sense 3), and obtainable also from dextran by acid hydrolysis, from glucose by reaction with acids, and from gentiobiose octaacetate by rearrangement

iso·mer \'≈≈ *at* ISO-+,mə(r)\ *n* -s [ISV, back-formation fr. *isomeric*; prob. orig. formed in G] **1** : a compound, radical, or ion isomeric with one or more others **2** : a nuclide isomeric with one or more others ⟨a metastable ~⟩ — called also *nuclear isomer*

isom·er·ase \ī'sämə,rās, -āz\ *n* -s [ISV *isomer* + *-ase*] : any of various enzymes that catalyze isomerization (as of glucose phosphate to fructose phosphate) — compare MUTASE 2

iso·mere \'≈≈ *at* ISO-+,mi(ə)r\ *n* -s [*is-* + *-mere*] : a corresponding part or segment

iso·mer·ic \¦≈≈¦merik\ *adj* [ISV *isomer-* (fr. Gk *isomerēs* equally divided, fr. *is-* + *meros* part, share) + *-ic* — more at MERIT] : of, relating to, or exhibiting isomerism ⟨butane and isobutane are ~ compounds⟩ ⟨the thiocyanate and isothiocyanate radicals are ~⟩ — **iso·mer·i·cal·ly** \-rək(ə)lē\ *adv*

isom·er·ide \ī'sämə,rīd\ *n* -s [*isomeric* + *-ide*] : ISOMER 1

isom·er·ism \-,rizəm\ *n* -s [ISV *isomeric* + *-ism*] **1** : the phenomenon exhibited by two or more chemical compounds, radicals, or ions of containing the same numbers of atoms of the same elements in the molecule, radical, or ion and hence having the same molecular formula but differing in the structural arrangement of the atoms and consequently in one or more properties ⟨the ~ of the butyl alcohols⟩ — compare GEOMETRIC ISOMERISM, OPTICAL ISOMERISM, POSITION ISOMERISM, STEREOISOMERISM, TAUTOMERISM **2** : the phenomenon exhibited by two or more nuclides of having the same mass numbers and the same atomic numbers but of differing in energy state and rate of radioactive decay — called also *nuclear isomerism* **3** [prob. fr. *isomerous* + *-ism*] : the condition of having or being made up of corresponding parts or segments; *esp* : the condition (as of a plant having the members of each floral whorl equal in number) of having two or more comparable parts made up of identical numbers of similar segments

isom·er·i·za·tion \ī,sämərə'zāshən, -,rī'z-\ *n* -s [ISV *isomer* + *-ization*] : the process of isomerizing (as of the straight-chain hydrocarbon butane to the branched-chain hydrocarbon isobutane of higher octane number for gasoline)

isom·er·ize \ī'sämə,rīz\ *vb* -ED/-ING/-S [ISV *isomer* + *-ize*] *vi* : to become changed into an isomeric form ~ *vt* : to cause to change into an isomeric form

isom·er·ous \(')ī¦sämərəs\ *adj* [ISV *is-* + *-merous*] : exhibiting isomerism — opposed to *heteromerous*

isom·ery \ī'sämərē\ *n* -ES [ISV *isomeric* + *-y*] : ISOMERISM 1

[1]**iso·metric** \¦≈≈ *at* ISO-+\ *also* **iso·metrical** \"+\ *adj* [*is-* + *metr-* (fr. Gk *metron* measure) + *-ic* or *-ical* — more at MEASURE] : of, relating to, or characterized by equality of measure: as **a** : of, relating to, or having the form of an isometric drawing **b** : EQUIGRANULAR **c** : taking place at constant volume ⟨an ~ change of temperature and pressure⟩ **d** *of muscular contraction* : taking place against resistance, without significant shortening of muscle fibers, and with marked increase in muscle tone — compare ISOTONIC **e** *of a stanza or strophe* : having lines of equal measure — **iso·metrically** \"+\ *adv*

[2]**isometric** \"\ *n* -s : ISOMETRIC LINE

isometric drawing *n* : the representation of an object on a single plane (as a sheet of paper) with the object placed as in isometric projection but disregarding the foreshortening of the edges parallel to the three principal axes of the typical rectangular solid, lines parallel to these axes appearing in their true lengths and producing an appearance of distortion

isometric line *n* **1** : a line (as a contour line) drawn on a map and indicating a true constant value throughout its extent **2** : a line representing changes of pressure or temperature under conditions of constant volume

isometric projection *n* : an axonometric projection in which the three spatial axes of the object are represented as equally inclined to the drawing surface and equal distances along the axes are drawn equal

isometric system *n* : a crystal system characterized by three equal axes at right angles (as in the cube and regular octahedron) — see CRYSTAL SYSTEM illustration

iso·me·tro·pia \¦≈(,)≈ *at* ISO-+mə'trōpēə\ *n* -s [NL, fr. Gk *isometros* of equal measure (fr. *is-* + *metron*) + NL *-opia*] : equality in refraction in the two eyes

cube as seen in isometric projection

iso·morph \'≈≈,mȯrf\ *n* -s [ISV *is-* + *-morph*] : something identical with or similar to something else in form or shape or structure: as **a** : one of two or more substances related by isomorphism **b** : an individual or group exhibiting isomorphism **c** : a cipher text letters ⟨FXEXRF and PZMZTP are ~s⟩

iso·mor·phic \¦≈≈¦mȯrfik\ *adj* [ISV *is-* + *-morphic*] : being of identical or similar form or shape or structure : exhibiting isomorphism; *esp* : having sporophytic and gametophytic generations alike in shape and size ⟨some algae and fungi are ~⟩ — compare HETEROMORPHIC

iso·mor·phism \¦≈≈¦fizəm\ *n* -s [ISV *is-* + *-morphism*; prob. orig. formed as G *isomorphismus*] **1** : the quality or state of being isomorphic: as **a** : similarity in organisms of different ancestry resulting from convergence **b** (1) : similarity of crystalline form and structure between substances of similar compositions (as between sulfates of barium $BaSO_4$ and of strontium $SrSO_4$) — sometimes used only of substances that are so closely similar that they can form a more or less continuous series of solid solutions; compare HETEROMORPHISM 2 (2) : HOMOEOMORPHISM 1 **2** : a hypothetical identity of psychological manifestation and brain process

iso·mor·phous \-,fəs\ *adj* [ISV *is-* + *-morphous*] : ISOMORPHIC; *esp* : isostructural and capable of forming solid solutions together ⟨the ~ components forsterite and fayalite of olivine⟩ ⟨strontium sulfate is ~ with barium sulfate⟩ — used of minerals and other crystalline substances

iso·mor·phy \'≈≈,≈fē\ *n* -ES [ISV *is-* + *-morphy*] : HOMOPLASY

iso·myaria \¦≈≈+\ *n pl, cap* [NL, fr. *is-* + *-myaria*] *in some classifications* : a division of Lamellibranchia comprising bivalve mollusks having two adductor muscles of nearly equal size — compare HETEROMYARIA, MONOMYARIA — **iso·my·ar·i·an** \¦≈(,)≈¦rēən\ *adj*

iso·neph \'≈≈,nef\ *n* -s [ISV *is-* + *-neph* (fr. Gk *nephos* cloud) — more at NEBULA] : a line on a map connecting points that have the same average percentage of cloudiness

iso·ni·a·zid \,≈≈'nīəzəd\ *n* -s [*isonicotinic acid hydrazide*] : a crystalline compound $C_5H_5NCONHNH_2$ used orally or intramuscularly in the treatment of tuberculosis often in conjunction with streptomycin or dihydrostreptomycin and para-aminosalicylic acid; isonicotinic acid hydrazide

iso·nicotinic acid \¦≈≈+...-\ *n* [*isonicotinic* ISV *is-* + *nicotinic*] : a crystalline acid C_5H_4NCOOH made usu. by oxidation of the corresponding picoline or ethyl-pyridine and used chiefly in making isoniazid; 4-pyridine-carboxylic acid

iso·nic·o·ti·no·yl·hydrazine \,≈≈,nikə,tēnəwəl+\ *or* **iso·nicotinyl·hydrazine** \,≈≈,nikə,tēn°l+\ *n* [*isonicotinoylhydrazine* fr. *isonicotin-* (fr. *isonicotinic acid*) + *-o-* + *-yl* + *hydrazine*; *isonicotinylhydrazine* fr. *isonicotin-* (fr. *isonicotinic acid*) + *-yl* + *hydrazine*] : ISONIAZID

iso·nip·e·caine \,≈≈'nipə,kān\ *n* -s [prob. fr. *isonipe-* (fr. *isonipecotic acid* isomer of nipecotic acid, fr. *is-* + *nipecotic acid*) + *-caine*] : meperidine or its hydrochloride

iso·nitrile \¦≈≈+\ *n* [ISV *is-* + *nitrile*] : ISOCYANIDE

iso·ni·tro \¦īsə¦nī-(,)trō\ *adj* [*isonitro-*] : containing the acid bivalent group =NO(OH)

isonitro- *comb form* [*is-* + *nitr-*] : containing the acid bivalent group =NO(OH) related to the nitro group ⟨*isonitro*ethane $CH_3CH=NO(OH)$⟩ — compare ACI-

iso·ni·tro·so \¦īsə,nī-¦trō(,)sō *also* ¦īzə\ *adj* [*isonitroso-*] : containing the bivalent hydroxy-imino group =NOH

isonitroso- *comb form* [ISV *is-* + *nitroso-*] : containing the bivalent hydroxy-imino group =NOH related to the nitroso group and characteristic of oximes ⟨*isonitroso*acetone $CH_3COCH=NOH$⟩

ison·o·my \ī'sänəmē\ *n* -ES [Gk *isonomia*, fr. *isonomos* characterized by equality before the law (fr. *is-* + *nomos* right, law) + *-ia* -y — more at NIMBLE] : equality before the law

iso·nuclear \¦≈≈ *at* ISO-+\ *adj* [*is-* + *nuclear*] : relating to or attached to the same nucleus or ring in the molecule of a chemical compound ⟨an ~ bromo-nitro-naphthalene⟩

iso·octane \¦≈≈+\ *n* [ISV *is-* + *octane*] : an octane of branched-chain structure or a mixture of such octanes: as **a** : the flammable liquid hydrocarbon $(CH_3)_2CH(CH_2)_4CH_3$ in whose molecule there is branching only at one end of the chain; 2-methyl-heptane **b** : a flammable liquid hydrocarbon $(CH_3)_2CHCH_2C(CH_3)_3$ made usu. by hydrogenation of diisobutylene and used esp. as a standard in rating motor fuels by their octane number; 2,2,4-trimethyl-pentane — not used technically **c** : HYDROCODIMER — used chiefly commercially

iso·oc·tyl alcohol \¦≈≈+...-\ *n* [*isooctyl* fr. *is-* + *octyl*] : an octyl alcohol of branched-chain structure or a mixture of such alcohols; *esp* : a mixture of isomeric primary alcohols $C_7H_{15}CH_2OH$ obtained by reaction of heptylenes with carbon monoxide and hydrogen and used esp. in synthesis (as of plasticizers) — not used scientifically

iso·pach \'≈≈,pak\ *n* -s [*is-* + *-pach* (fr. Gk *pachys* thick) — more at PACHY-] : an isogram that connects points of equal thickness of a particular geological stratum formation or group of formations

iso·pach·ous \¦≈≈¦pakəs, (')ī¦säpək-\ *adj* : of, relating to, or having an isopach ⟨~ contours⟩ ⟨an ~ map⟩

iso·pag \'≈≈ *at* ISO-+,pag\ *n* -s [*is-* + *-pag* (fr. Gk *pagos* frost; akin to Gk *pēgnynai* to fasten) — more at PACT] : an equiglacial line on a map or chart that connects the points where ice is present for approximately the same number of days in winter

iso·paraffin \¦≈≈+\ *n* [*is-* + *paraffin*] : a paraffin hydrocarbon of branched-chain structure — **iso·paraffinic** \"+\ *adj*

iso·pec·tic \¦≈≈¦pektik\ *n* -s [*is-* + *pect-* (fr. Gk *pēktos* fixed, frozen, fr. *pēgnynai* to fasten) + *-ic*] : an equiglacial line on a map or chart connecting points where ice begins to form at the beginning of winter

iso·pelletierine \¦≈≈+\ *n* [ISV *is-* + *pelletierine*] : a liquid alkaloid $C_8H_{15}NO$ from the root bark of pomegranate; 2-acetonyl-piperidine

iso·pentane \"+\ *n* [*is-* + *pentane*] : a volatile flammable liquid hydrocarbon $(CH_3)_2CHC_2H_5$ found in petroleum and used in gasoline and as a solvent

iso·pentyl \"+\ *n* [*is-* + *pentyl*] : the pentyl radical $(CH_3)_2CHCH_2CH_2$– derived from isopentane; 3-methyl-butyl — called also *isoamyl*

isopentyl alcohol *n* : a primary pentyl alcohol $(CH_3)_2CHCH_2CH_2OH$ that has a disagreeable odor and pungent taste and is obtained from fusel oil; 3-methyl-1-butanol — called also *isoamyl alcohol, isobutylcarbinol*

iso·perimetric *also* **iso·perimetrical** \"+\ *adj* [Gk *isoperimetros* isoperimetric (fr. *is-* + *perimetros* perimeter) + E *-ic* or *-ical* — more at PERIMETER] **1** : of, relating to, or having equal perimeters — used esp. of geometrical figures **2** : having a constant scale — used of a line on a map

iso·phen·al \¦≈≈¦fēn°l\ *adj* [*isophene* + *-al*] : of, relating to, or having an isophene

iso·phene \'≈≈,fēn\ *also* **iso·phane** \-,fān\ *n* -s [*isophene* fr. *is-* + *-phene* (fr. Gk *phainein* to show); *isophane* ISV *is-* + *-phane* (fr. Gk *phainein* to show) — more at FANCY] **1** : a line on a map or chart connecting places within a region at which a particular biological phenomenon (as the flowering of a given plant) occurs at one time **2** : PHENOCONTOUR

iso·phe·nous \¦≈≈¦fēnəs\ *adj* [*isophene* + *-ous*] : having the same phenotype

iso·phone \'≈≈,fōn\ *n* [ISV *is-* + *-phone*] **1** : a phonetic isogloss (sense 1) **2** : a phonetic feature shared by some but not all of the speakers of a dialect, language, or group of related languages

iso·pho·ria \,≈≈'fōrēə\ *n* -s [NL, fr. *is-* + *-phoria*] : the quality or state of having the visual axes of the two eyes in the same horizontal plane

iso·phorone \¦≈≈+\ *n* [ISV *is-* + *phorone*] : a high-boiling liquid ketone $C_9H_{14}O$ made by condensation of acetone and used as a solvent; 3,5,5-trimethyl-2-cyclohexen-one

iso·phote \'≈≈,fōt\ *also* **iso·phot** \-,fät\ *n* -s [ISV *is-* + *-phote, -phot* (fr. Gk *phōt-, phōs* light) — more at FANCY] : a line or surface on a chart forming the locus of points of equal illumination or light intensity from a given source

iso·pho·tic line \¦≈≈¦fōd·ik-\ *n* [*isophotic* fr. *isophote* + *-ic*] : ISOPHOTE

iso·phthal·ic acid \¦≈≈ *at* ISO-+¦thalik-\ *n* [*isophthalic* ISV *is-* + *phthalic*] : a crystalline diacid $C_6H_4(COOH)_2$ isomeric with phthalic acid made usu. by oxidation of *meta*-xylene and used in making synthetic resins and esters for use as plasticizers; *meta*-benzene-dicarboxylic acid

iso·phyl·lia \,≈≈'filēə\ *n, cap* [NL, fr. *is-* + *phyll-* + *-ia*] : a genus of madrepores comprising the rose corals

iso·phyl·lous \¦≈≈¦filəs\ *adj* [ISV *is-* + *-phyllous*] : having foliage leaves of like form on the same plant or stem — compare ANISOPHYLLOUS

iso·phyl·ly \'≈≈,filē\ *n* -ES [*isophyllous* + *-y*, n. suffix] : the quality or state of being isophyllous

iso·pi·es·tic \¦≈(,)≈,pī¦estik\ *adj* [*is-* + *piest-* (fr. Gk *piestos* compressible, fr. *piezein* to press) + *-ic* — more at PIEZO-] : of, relating to, or marked by equal pressure : ISOBARIC

isoplastic graft \¦≈≈+...-\ *n* [*isoplastic* fr. *is-* + *plastic*] : HOMOGRAFT

iso·pleth \'≈≈,pleth\ *n* -s [ISV *is-* + *-pleth* (fr. Gk *plēthos* quantity, multitude); akin to Gk *plēthein* to be full — more at FULL] **1** : an isogram on a graph showing the occurrence or frequency of a phenomenon as a function of two variables — often used of meteorological elements **2** : a line on a map connecting points at which a given variable has a specified constant value ⟨~s such as isothermal lines or topographic contour lines⟩

iso·pleu·ra \,≈≈'plu̇rə\ [NL, fr. *is-* + *-pleura*] *syn of* AMPHINEURA

iso·ploid \'≈≈,plȯid\ *adj* [*is-* + *-ploid*] : having an even number of genomes in somatic cells

iso·pluvial \¦≈≈+\ *adj* [*is-* + *pluvial*] : of, relating to, or marked by equal rainfall ⟨an ~ line⟩

iso·pod \'≈≈,päd\ *n* -s [NL *Isopoda*] : one of the Isopoda

isop·o·da \ī'säpədə\ *n pl, cap* [NL, fr. *is-* + *-poda*] : a large order of small sessile-eyed malacostracan crustaceans (division Peracarida) that lack a carapace, that have a body usu. depressed with seven free thoracic segments each bearing a pair of similar legs, and that occur in marine, freshwater, or terrestrial habitats or as parasites on invertebrates and fish — compare TANAIDACEA — **isop·o·dan** \(')≈¦≈ədən, -əd°n\ *adj or n* — **isop·o·dous** \-dəs\ *adj*

iso·pod·i·form \¦īsə¦pädə,fȯrm *also* ¦īzə-\ *adj* [NL *isopodiformis*, fr. *Isopoda* + L *-iformis* -iform] : resembling an isopod in form

iso·pogo·nous \¦≈≈ *at* ISO- + pə¦gōnəs, ¦pägən-\ *adj* [NL *isopogonus*, fr. *is-* + *-pogonus* (fr. Gk *pōgōn* beard) — more at -POGON] : having feathers whose two webs are equal

iso·polity \,≈≈+\ *n* -ES [Gk *isopoliteia*, fr. *isopolitēs* having equal or reciprocal political rights (fr. *is-* + *politēs* citizen) + *-ia* -y — more at POLICE] : equality or reciprocity of rights or privileges (as of citizenship) ⟨an agreement between two countries establishing ~ for their citizens⟩

isopoly- *comb form* [ISV *is-* + *poly-*] : containing several groups or ions of the same acid-forming element : POLY- 2b — in names of complex inorganic acids and their salts ⟨*isopoly*-molybdates⟩ — compare HETEROPOLY-

iso·poly acid \¦≈≈¦pälē-\ *n* [*isopoly* ISV *isopoly-*] : any of a large group of complex oxygen-containing acids derived from a single inorganic acid by elimination of water from two or more molecules — distinguished from *heteropoly acid*

iso·por \'≈≈,pō(ə)r\ *n* -s [*is-* + *-por* (fr. Gk *poros* passage, path) — more at FARE] : an imaginary line or a line on a map of the earth's surface connecting points of equal annual change in one of the magnetic elements

iso·por·ic \¦≈≈¦pȯrik\ *adj* : of, relating to, or indicating an isopor

iso·pren·a·line \,≈≈'prenᵊlən, -ᵊl,ēn\ *n* -s [prob. fr. *isopropyl* + *adrenaline*] : ISOPROTERENOL

iso·prene \'≈≈,prēn\ *n* -s [prob. fr. *is-* + *pr-* (fr. *propyl*) + *-ene*] : a flammable liquid diolefin hydrocarbon $CH_2=C(CH_3)CH=CH_2$ obtained usu. by heating rubber or turpentine (sense 2) or in cracking petroleum and used chiefly in making synthetic rubber; 2-methyl-1,3-butadiene — see POLYISOPRENE, TERPENE

[1]**iso·pre·noid** \¦≈≈¦prē,nȯid\ *adj* [*isoprene* + *-oid*] : relating to, containing, or being the branched-chain grouping $(C)_2$-C–C–C of five carbon atoms that is characteristic of isoprene and that recurs in the molecules of many natural compounds (as rubber, terpenes, vitamin A, vitamin E, phytol)

[2]**isoprenoid** \"\ *n* -s : an isoprenoid compound

iso·pro·pa·nol \,≈≈'prōpə,nȯl, -nōl\ *n* -s [*is-* + *propane* + *-ol*] : ISOPROPYL ALCOHOL — not used systematically

iso·pro·pe·nyl \-ōpənᵊl, -,nil\ *n* [ISV *is-* + *propenyl*] : the univalent radical $CH_2=C(CH_3)$– isomeric with propenyl ⟨*isopropenyl*-isopropylidene isomerism . . . is typical of many terpenoids —W.S.Ropp⟩

iso·pro·pox·ide \,≈≈,prō'päk,sīd, -,säd\ *n* -s [prob. fr. *is-* + *propox-* (fr. *propoxyl* + *-ide*] : a binary compound of the radical $(CH_3)_2CHO$– isomeric with propoxyl; *esp* : a base formed from isopropyl alcohol by replacement of the hydroxyl hydrogen with a metal ⟨aluminum ~ $[(CH_3)_2CHO]_3Al$⟩

iso·propyl \¦≈≈+\ *n* [ISV *is-* + *propyl*] : the alkyl radical $(CH_3)_2CH$– isomeric with normal propyl

isopropyl alcohol *n* : a volatile flammable liquid secondary alcohol $(CH_3)_2CHOH$ made usu. by hydration of propylene by means of sulfuric acid and used as a solvent and rubbing alcohol and as a source of acetone by dehydrogenation; 2-propanol

iso·pro·pyl·arterenol \¦≈≈¦≈+\ *n* [*isopropyl* + *arterenol*] : ISOPROTERENOL

iso·pro·pyl·ate \,≈≈'prōpə,lāt\ *n* -s [*isopropyl* + *-ate*] : ISOPROPOXIDE

isopropyl ether *n* : a colorless volatile flammable water-insoluble liquid $[(CH_3)_2CH]_2O$ made from propylene or isopropyl alcohol and used as a solvent

iso·propylidene \¦≈(,)≈+\ *n* [ISV *is-* + *propylidene*] : the bivalent radical $(CH_3)_2C<$ isomeric with propylidene — compare ISOPROPENYL

iso·pro·te·re·nol \,≈≈,prōd·ə'rē,nōl, -nȯl\ *n* -s [short for *isopropylarterenol*] : a crystalline compound $C_{11}H_{17}NO_3$ that is the isopropyl homologue of racemic epinephrine and that is used in the treatment of asthma — called also *isopropylarterenol*

isop·tera \ī'säptərə\ *n pl, cap* [NL, fr. *is-* + *-ptera*] : an order of social insects consisting of the termites — **isop·te·rous** \(')≈¦≈tərəs\ *adj*

iso·pulegol \¦≈≈ *at* ISO- +\ *n* [ISV *is-* + *pulegol*] : a liquid terpenoid alcohol $C_{10}H_{17}OH$ that has an odor like that of menthol and that is obtained as an intermediate in the synthesis of menthol from citronellol

[1]**iso·pyc·nic** \¦≈≈¦piknik\ *also* **iso·pyc·nal** \-nəl\ *adj* [*is-* + *pycn-* + *-ic* or *-al*] : of, relating to, or marked by equal density

[2]**isopycnic** \"\ *or* **isopycnal** \"\ *n* -s : a line or surface on a map connecting points of equal density (as of water, air)

iso·quercitrin \¦≈≈+\ *n* [*is-* + *quercitrin*] : a pale-yellow crystalline glucoside $C_{21}H_{20}O_{12}$ occurring esp. in cotton flowers and maize and yielding quercetin and glucose on hydrolysis

iso·quinoline \"+\ *n* [ISV *is-* + *quinoline*] : a low-melting crystalline or liquid nitrogenous base C_9H_7N that is associated with its isomer quinoline in coal tar and that is the parent structure in many alkaloids (as narcotine, papaverine)

iso·rhythm \'≈≈+,-\ *n* [*is-* + *rhythm*] : a single fixed rhythmic pattern typically long and complex that is reiterated throughout the whole of a sung voice part which is usu. the tenor ⟨~ in late medieval motets⟩ — **iso·rhythmic** \¦≈≈+\ *adj*

iso·safrole \¦≈≈+\ *n* [ISV *is-* + *safrole*] : a liquid acetal $(CH_2O_2)C_6H_3CH=CHCH_3$ that has an odor like that of anise, that is obtained from the essential oils of ilang-ilang and the fruit of Japanese star anise and synthetically from safrole and hot alkali, and that is used chiefly in making piperonal

isos·ce·les \(')ī¦säsə,lēz\ *adj* [LL, fr. Gk *isoskelēs*, fr. *is-* + *skelos* leg — more at CYLINDER] *of a triangle* : having two equal sides — see TRIANGLE illustration

isosceles trapezoid *n* : a trapezoid with its two nonparallel sides equal

iso·sebacic acid \¦≈≈ *at* ISO- + . . . -\ *n* [*isosebacic* fr. *is-* + *sebacic*] : a solid mixture of sebacic acid and two isomeric dicarboxylic acids $C_8H_{16}(COOH)_2$ obtainable by reaction of butadiene with sodium, carbon dioxide, and finally hydrogen and useful esp. for making plasticizers and alkyd resins

[1]**iso·seismal** \"+\ *adj* [*is-* + *seismal*] : of, relating to, or marked by equal intensity of earthquake shock ⟨an ~ line⟩

[2]**isoseismal** \"\ *n* -s : an isoseismal line on a map or chart of the earth's surface connecting points of equal intensity of earthquake shock

iso·seismic \"+\ *adj* [*is-* + *seismic*] : ISOSEISMAL

iso·osmotic \¦īs *also* ¦īz+\ *adj* [ISV *is-* + *osmotic*] : of, relating to, or exhibiting equal osmotic pressure ⟨~ solutions⟩

iso·spon·dyl \¦≈≈+¦spändᵊl\ *n* -s [NL *Isospondyli*] : a fish of the order Isospondyli

iso·spon·dy·li \,≈≈'spändə,lī\ *n pl, cap* [NL, fr. *is-* + *-spondyli*] : a large order of teleost fishes that is the most primitive group of teleosts and that includes about 50 living families (as of the herrings and salmons) whose fishes have soft-rayed fins, an air bladder connected with the alimentary canal by a duct, abdominal pelvic fins, the anterior vertebrae unmodified and similar to the others, and usu. a mesocoracoid or precoracoid arch — **iso·spon·dy·lous** \¦≈≈¦≈dələs\ *adj*

isos·po·ra \ī'säspərə\ *n, cap* [NL, fr. *is-* + *-spora*] : a genus of Coccidia closely related to *Eimeria* and including the only species (*I. hominis*) of coccidium known to be parasitic in man

iso·spore \'≈≈ *at* ISO- +,-\ *n* [ISV *is-* + *spore*] **1** : one of the spores produced by a homosporous organism **2** : a sexual spore exhibiting no sexual dimorphism

iso·spor·ic \¦≈≈¦spōrik\ *adj* [*isospore* + *-ic*] : ISOSPOROUS

iso·spor·ous \¦≈≈¦spōrəs, (')ī¦säspərəs\ *adj* [*is-* + *-sporous*] : of, relating to, or having isospores

iso·spo·ry \'== *at* ISO- + ,spōrē; ī'säspərē\ *n* -ES [ISV *is-* + *-spory*] **:** the quality or state of being isosporous
isos·ta·sist \ī'sästəsəst\ *n* -S **:** a specialist in the study of isostasy
isos·ta·sy *also* **isos·ta·cy** \-təsē\ *n* -ES [*isostasy* ISV *is-* + *-stasy* (fr. Gk *-stasia*); *isostacy* alter. (influenced by E *-cy*) of *isostasy* — more at -STASIA] **1 :** the quality or state of being isostatic **2 :** general equilibrium in the earth's crust maintained by a yielding flow of rock material beneath the surface under gravitative stress and by the approximate equality in mass of each unit column of the earth from the surface to a depth of about 70 miles — compare ISOSTATIC COMPENSATION
iso·static \¦== *at* ISO- +\ *adj* [ISV *is-* + *static;* orig. formed as F *isostatique*] **1 a :** subjected to equal pressure from every side **b :** being in hydrostatic equilibrium **2 :** relating to or characterized by isostasy
isostatic compensation *n* **:** the deficiency of mass in the earth's crust below sea level that exactly balances the mass above sea level
iso·stemo·nous \¦==¦stēmənəs, -stem-\ *adj* [ISV *is-* + *-stemonous*] **:** having stamens equal in number to the perianth divisions
iso·stemo·ny \,=='stēmənē, -stem-\ *n* -ES [ISV *isostemonous* + *-y*] **:** the quality or state of being isostemonous
iso·stere \'==,sti(ə)r\ *also* **iso·ster** \-,ste(ə)r\ *n* -S [*is-* + *-stere, -ster* (fr. Gk *stereos* solid) — more at STARE] **1 :** a line on a map or chart connecting points of equal atmospheric density **2** [prob. back-formation fr. *isosteric*] **:** one of two or more substances related by isosterism
iso·ster·ic \¦==¦sterik\ *adj* [*is-* + *ster-* (fr. Gk *stereos* solid) + *-ic*] **1 :** of, relating to, or exhibiting isosterism **2 :** of, relating to, or marked by equal atmospheric density
isos·ter·ism \ī'sästə,rizəm; '== *at* ISO- + ,sti,rizəm *or* ,ste,r-\ *n* -S [*is-* + *ster-* (fr. Gk *stereos* solid) + *-ism*] **:** the phenomenon of similarity of structure and of resulting similarity of some properties exhibited by two or more molecules or groups or ions containing different atoms though not necessarily the same number of atoms but having the same number of total or valence electrons in the same arrangement (as in carbon monoxide and gaseous nitrogen or in the cyanide and acetylide ions)
iso·structural \¦== *at* ISO- +\ *adj* **:** relating to or having a similar crystal structure in that the atoms correspond in position and function although there may not be close chemical relationship **:** ISOTYPIC 2 — used of minerals and other crystalline substances ⟨calcite and sodium nitrate are ~⟩; compare ISOMORPHOUS
iso·tac \'==,tak\ *n* -S [*is-* + *-tac* (fr. Gk *takēnai* to melt, be dissolved, pass. aor. infin. of *tēkein* to melt, dissolve) — more at THAW] **:** an equiglacial line on a map or chart connecting points where ice melts at the same time in spring
iso·tach \-,tak\ *n* -S [ISV *is-* + *-tach* (fr. Gk *tachys* quick) — more at TACHY-] **:** a line on a map or chart connecting points of equal wind speed
iso·tac·tic \¦==¦taktik\ *adj* [ISV *is-* + *-tactic*] **:** of, relating to, or having a stereochemical regularity of structure in the repeating units of a polymer — compare SYNDYOTACTIC
isote *var of* IZOTE
iso·ther·al \¦== *at* ISO- + ¦thirəl\ *adj* [F *isothère* isothere + E *-al*] **:** of, relating to, or marked by the same mean summer temperature ⟨an ~ line⟩
iso·there \'==,thi(ə)r\ *n* -S [F *isothère*, fr. *is-* + *-thère* (fr. Gk *theros* summer); akin to Gk *thermos* hot] **:** a line on a map or chart of the earth's surface connecting points having the same mean summer temperature
iso·therm \-,thərm\ *n* -S [F *isotherme*, adj., isothermal, fr. *is-* + *-therme* (fr. Gk *thermē* heat, fr. *thermos* hot) — more at WARM] **1 :** a line on a map or chart of the earth's surface connecting points having the same temperature at a given time or the same mean temperature for a given period **2 :** a line on a chart representing changes of volume or pressure under conditions of constant temperature
[1]**iso·ther·mal** \¦==¦thərməl\ *adj* [F *isotherme*, adj. + E *-al*] **1 :** of, relating to, or marked by equality of temperature **2 :** of, relating to, or marked by changes of volume or pressure under conditions of constant temperature
[2]**isothermal** \"\ *n* -S **:** ISOTHERM 1
isothermal curve *n* **:** ISOTHERM 2
isothermal line *n* **:** ISOTHERM 1
isothermal region *n* **:** STRATOSPHERE
iso·ther·mic \-mik\ *adj* [ISV *isotherm* + *-ic*] **:** ISOTHERMAL — **iso·ther·mi·cal·ly** \-mək(ə)lē\ *adv*
iso·ther·mo·bath \,=='thərmə,bath\ *n* -S [*isotherm* + *-o-* + *-bath* (fr. Gk *bathos* depth); akin to Gk *bathys* deep — more at BATHY-] **:** a line on a diagram of a vertical section of the ocean connecting points of equal temperature
isothiocyan- *or* **isothiocyano-** *comb form* [ISV *is-* + *thiocyan-*] **:** containing the univalent radical —NCS isomeric with the thiocyano radical and present in isothiocyanates ⟨*isothiocyano*amines⟩
iso·thio·cyanate \,==,thīō+\ *n* -S [ISV *isothiocyan-* + *-ate*] **:** a compound containing the univalent radical —NCS consisting of an isocyano group united with sulfur **:** a salt or ester of isothiocyanic acid — compare MUSTARD OIL 2
isothiocyanato- *comb form* [*isothiocyanate* + *-o-*] **:** ISOTHIOCYAN- — esp. in names of coordination complexes
iso·thiocyanic acid \¦==¦thīō+ . . .-\ *n* [*isothiocyanic* ISV *is-* + *thiocyanic*] **:** thiocyanic acid regarded as having the formula HNCS and usu. prepared in the form of esters
iso·tone \'==,tōn\ *n* -S [*is-* + *-tone* (prob. fr. Gk *tonos* tension, stretching) — more at TONE] **:** one of two or more nuclides having the same number of neutrons
iso·ton·ic \¦==¦tänik\ *adj* [ISV *is-* + *tonic*] **1 :** of, relating to, or exhibiting equal tension; *specif, of muscular contraction* **:** taking place in the absence of significant resistance with marked shortening of muscle fibers and without great increase in muscle tone — compare ISOMETRIC **2 :** having the same or equal osmotic pressure **:** ISOSMOTIC — used of solutions ⟨an ~ salt solution in which blood cells are counted⟩; compare HYPERTONIC, HYPOTONIC — **iso·ton·i·cal·ly** \-nək(ə)lē\ *adv*
iso·tonicity \,== *at* ISO- +\ *n* [*isotonic* + *-ity*] **:** the quality or state of being isotonic
iso·to·nize \'==,tō,nīz\ *vt* -ED/-ING/-S [*isotonic* + *-ize*] **:** to make isotonic
iso·tope \'==,tōp\ *n* -S [*is-* + *-tope* (fr. Gk *topos* place) — more at TOPIC] **1 a :** one of two or more species of atoms of the same chemical element that have the same atomic number and occupy the same position in the periodic table and that are nearly identical in chemical behavior but differ in atomic mass or mass number and so behave differently in the mass spectrograph, in radioactive transformations, and in physical properties (as diffusibility in the gaseous state) and may be detected and separated by means of these differences ⟨deuterium and tritium are ~*s* of hydrogen⟩; *esp* **:** one such species of atom or a mixture of such species of atoms prepared for use as a tracer or in medicine — usu. indicated for a specific element by the mass number following the name of the element or written superior to the symbol of the element (as carbon 14, C^{14}, or ^{14}C); compare RADIOISOTOPE **b :** the nucleus of such a species of atom **2 :** NUCLIDE
isotope effect *n* **:** the variation of certain characteristics (as density and spectrum) of an element in accordance with the mass of the isotopes involved
iso·topic \¦==¦täpik, -¦tōp-\ *adj* [ISV *isotope* + *-ic*] **:** of, relating to, or having the relationship of an isotope — **iso·topi·cal·ly** \-pək(ə)lē\ *adv*
isotopic number *n* **:** the number of neutrons minus the number of protons in an atomic nucleus
iso·to·py \'==,tōpē, ī'säd·əpē\ *n* -ES [ISV *isotope* + *-y*, n. suffix] **:** the quality or state of being isotopic
isot·ria \ī'sä·trēə\ *n, cap* [NL, fr. *is-* + Gk *tria* three, neut. of *treis* three — more at THREE] **:** a small genus of terrestrial orchids of eastern No. America that are sometimes included in *Pogonia* and that have a nearly terminal whorl of leaves and a usu. solitary greenish yellow flower with long linear sepal — see WHORLED POGONIA
iso·tron \'== *at* ISO- + ·-trän\ *n* -S [prob. fr. *isotope* + *-tron*] **:** an electromagnetic apparatus for separating isotopes introduced as ions from an extended source which group according to their masses under the combined effect of a strong direct field and weak fields that vary at radio frequency
iso·tropic \¦==·¦träpik, -rōp-\ *adj* [ISV *is-* + *-tropic;* orig. formed as F *isotropique*] **1 :** exhibiting properties (as velocity of light transmission, conductivity of heat or electricity, compressibility) with the same values when measured along axes in all directions ⟨an ~ crystal⟩ — compare ANISOTROPIC 1 **2 :** exhibiting equal tendencies to growth in all directions **:** lacking predetermined axes ⟨~ eggs⟩
isot·ro·pism \ī'sä·trə,pizəm\ *n* -S [*isotropic* + *-ism*] **:** ISOTROPY
isot·ro·pous \(')=¦==,pəs\ *adj* [*isotropic* + *-ous*] **:** ISOTROPIC
isot·ro·py \='==pē\ *n* -ES [ISV *isotropic* + *-y*, n. suffix] **:** the quality or state of being isotropic
iso·type \'== *at* ISO- + ,tīp\ *n* [ISV *is-* + *type*] **1 a :** an animal or plant or group common to two or more countries or life regions **b** (1) **:** PARATYPE 1 — usu. used in plant taxonomy (2) **:** a type that is or is considered for technical purposes to be the duplicate of a holotype **2 a :** a conventionalized pictographic symbol (as a drawing or outline or silhouette of a human figure or of a building or of a product) designed to represent (as by repetition or fractionalizing of each symbol or as by scaling each symbol to significantly the same size or to contrasted sizes) a fixed number or quantity of or other unitary fact about the thing symbolized ⟨each ~ of a soldier in that diagram represents an entire army division⟩ or designed to convey other information ⟨public telephones often have a large ~ of a bell over the booths as a directional guide to the booths⟩ and typically used in graphic statistical representations (as diagrams, charts) **b :** a graphic statistical representation (as a chart) that utilizes such isotypes
iso·typ·ic \¦==¦tipik\ *or* **iso·typ·i·cal** \-pəkəl\ *adj* [*isotype* + *-ic* or *-ical*] **1** *usu isotypical* **:** of or relating to an isotype **2 :** relating to or having a chemical formula analogous to and a crystal structure like that of another specified compound **:** ISOSTRUCTURAL — used of minerals and other crystalline substances ⟨some phosphates and silicates are ~⟩
iso·urea \¦=(,)=+\ *n* [NL, fr. *is-* + *urea*] **:** PSEUDOUREA
iso·valerate \¦=(,)=+\ *n* -S [ISV *isovaleric* (in *isovaleric acid*) + *-ate*] **:** a salt or ester of isovaleric acid
iso·valerianic acid \"+ . . . -\ *n* [*isovalerianic* ISV *is-* + *valerianic*] **:** ISOVALERIC ACID
iso·valeric acid \"+ . . . -\ *n* [*isovaleric* ISV *is-* + *valeric*] **:** a liquid acid $(CH_3)_2CHCH_2COOH$ that has a disagreeable odor, that occurs esp. in valerian root in the free state and in some essential oils and marine-animal oils in the form of esters, that is made by oxidation of isopentyl alcohol, and that is used chiefly in making esters for use in flavoring materials; β-methyl-butyric acid
iso·valeryl \"+\ *n* -S [ISV *isovaler-* (in *isovaleric acid*) + *-yl*] **:** the radical $(CH_3)_2CHCH_2CO—$ of isovaleric acid
is·oxazole \(')īs *also* (')īz+\ *n* [ISV *is-* + *oxazole*] **1 :** a liquid heterocyclic compound C_3H_3NO that is isomeric with oxazole, has a penetrating odor like that of pyridine, and is made by the action of hydroxylamine on propiolaldehyde **2 :** a derivative of isoxazole
iso·zooid \¦== *at* ISO- +\ *n* [*is-* + *zooid*] **:** a zooid resembling its parent — opposed to *allozooid*
is·pa·ghul \'ispə,gül, -,gəl\ *n* -S [Per *ispaghōl, aspaghōl*, lit., horse's ear, fr. *asp* horse (fr. MPer) + *ghōl* ear; fr. the shape of the leaf; akin to Skt *aśva* horse — more at EQUINE] **:** an Old World plantain (*Plantago ovata*) with mucilaginous seeds that are used in preparing a beverage
is·pa·han \'ispə,hän, -han, ,=='=\ *n* -S *often cap* [*Ispahan, Isfahan*, city in west central Iran] **:** a handmade Persian rug that is typically deep red or blue or green with floral or animal patterns in antique design and that is usu. long and narrow
i spy \'ī-\ *n, cap I* [prob. alter. (influenced by E *I*, pron.) of *hy spy*] **:** HIDE-AND-SEEK
[1]**is·ra·el** \'iz¦,rēəl *also* 'is¦ *or* ¦(,)rāəl *or* ¦,rāl *or* ÷¦,rəl *sometimes* ¦(,)rā,el *or* ¦(,)rä,el *or* ¦,rī,el *or* ¦(,)ra,el\ *n* -S *cap* [ME, fr. OE, fr. LL, fr. Gk *Israēl*, fr. Heb *Yiśrā'ēl*, lit., let God contend, fr. *sārāh* to fight + *ēl* God] **1 a** (1) **:** the ancient Hebrew people descended from the patriarch Jacob (2) **:** the group of 10 Hebrew tribes anciently inhabiting the northern part of Palestine and constituting a kingdom independent of Judah **b :** the Jewish people of past and present **2 :** a body of individuals (as members of the Jewish or Christian faiths) regarded by itself or others as the actual or spiritual chosen people of God **:** ELECT
[2]**israel** \"\ *adj, usu cap* [*Israel*, independent Jewish state in Palestine, fr. Heb *Yiśrā'ēl*] **:** ISRAELI
[1]**is·rae·li** \iz¦'rālē, -li *sometimes* is¦ *or* ¦=,rē¦ā- *or* ¦=¦,rə¦ā-\ *adj, usu cap* [NHeb *yiśrē'ēlī*, fr. Heb, Israelite, Israelitic, fr. *Yiśrā'ēl*] **:** of or from the republic of Israel **:** of the kind or style prevalent in Israel
[2]**israeli** \"\ *n, pl* **israelis** *also* **israeli** *cap* **:** a native or inhabitant of the republic of Israel
israeli hebrew *n, cap I&H* **:** the Hebrew language in colloquial use in present-day Israel
[1]**is·ra·el·ite** *pronunc at* [1]ISRAEL + ,īt; *usu* -īd·+V\ *n* -S *cap* [ME, fr. LL *Israelita, Israelites*, fr. Gk *Israēlitēs*, fr. *Israēl* Israel + *-itēs* -ite] **1 a** (1) **:** a member of the ancient Hebrew people descended from the patriarch Jacob (2) **:** a member of one of the 10 Hebrew tribes anciently inhabiting the northern part of Palestine — compare SAMARITAN **b :** a member of the Jewish people of past or present **:** JEW **2 :** a member of a body of individuals regarded by itself or others as the actual or spiritual chosen people of God
[2]**israelite** \"\ *also* **is·ra·el·it·ic** \¦=(,)=(=)¦id·ik\ *or* **is·ra·el·it·ish** \-īd·¦ish, -īt¦, ¦ēsh\ *adj, usu cap* [[2]*israelite* fr. [1]*israelite; israelitic* fr. LL *israeliticus*, fr. *Israelita, Israelites* + L *-icus* -ic; *israelitish* fr. [1]*israelite* + *-ish*] **:** of or relating to Israel ⟨*Israelite* conquests in Canaan⟩ ⟨*Israelite* prophets⟩
iss *abbr* issue
is·sa \ē'sä, i'-\ *n, pl* **issas** \-sä(z)\ *or* **issa** *usu cap* **1 :** a Hamitic people of the French territory of the Afars and the Issas **2 :** a member of the Issa people
is·sa·char·ite \'isə,kä,rīt\ *n* -S *usu cap* [*Issachar*, ninth son of Jacob and ancestor of the tribe (fr. LL, fr. Heb *Yissākhār*) + E *-ite*] **:** a member of the Hebrew tribe of Issachar
is·sei \(')ē¦sā\ *n, pl* **issei** *also* **isseis** *often cap* [Jap, lit., first generation, fr. *is* first + *sei* generation] **:** a Japanese immigrant to America and esp. to the U. S. — compare NISEI
is·su·able \'ish(y)əwəbəl, 'i(,)shüəb-, *chiefly Brit* 'isyəwəb- *or* 'i(,)syüəb-\ *adj* **1 :** that is of such a kind as to admit issue being taken or joined ⟨an ~ matter⟩ ⟨~ terms⟩ **2 :** that is authorized for issuing ⟨~ goods⟩ ⟨~ currency⟩ **3 :** that may accrue ⟨~ profits⟩ — **is·su·ably** \-blē,-bli\ *adv*
issuable plea *n* **:** a plea on the merits on which an adverse party may take issue and go to trial
is·su·ance \-əwən(t)s, -üən-\ *n* -S **1 :** ISSUE 9a, 9b **2 :** ISSUE 2a
is·su·ant \-nt\ *adj* **1** *archaic* **:** coming forth from a specified place or source ⟨~ from the eternal throne, came like a cloud of light, the bright response —P.J.Bailey⟩ **2** *heraldry* **a :** depicted or shown as coming forth ⟨a panther with flames ~ from the mouth⟩ **b :** depicted or shown as rising upward (as from the top or bottom line of an ordinary or from another bearing or from the base of an escutcheon) ⟨two sprigs ~⟩ **c** *of an animal figure* **:** rising upward and having only the upper part visible ⟨a lion rampant ~ from a fess⟩
[1]**is·sue** \'i(,)shü, 'ish(,)yü, 'i(,)shu̇, 'ish(,)yu̇, *before a vowel often* -,sh(y)əw; *chiefly in the southern U. S.* -,sh(y)ə *before a consonant or pause or before a vowel in a following word; chiefly Brit* 'i(,)syü *or* 'i(,)syu̇ *or* 'isyəw\ *n* -S [ME, fr. MF, way out, exit, proceeds, fr. OF *eissue, issue*, fr. fem. of *eissu, issu*, past part. of *eissir, issir* to come out, go out, fr. L *exire* to go out, fr. *ex-* [1]ex- + *ire* to go; akin to Goth *iddja* he went, Gk *ienai* to go, Skt *eti* he goes, and prob. to OE *ēode* he went] **1 issues** *pl* **:** proceeds from a source of revenue (as an estate) ⟨rents, profits, and ~*s*⟩ **2 a** (1) **:** the action of going out or coming out or flowing out from something **:** OUTGOING, EGRESS, OUTFLOW ⟨the ~ of water from a broken pipe⟩ ⟨a constant entrance and ~ of visitors⟩ ⟨the river's place of ~⟩ (2) **:** the action of coming forth from or as if from something in which one is immersed **:** EMERGENCE ⟨the ~ of a people from barbarism into a civilized way of life⟩ **b :** the power to go out or come out or flow out from something ⟨potentialities that remain repressed for lack of ~⟩ **3 a :** a means of going out from something **:** EXIT, OUTLET, VENT ⟨a dark labyrinth that had no ~⟩ **b :** a place where something goes out from something **:** place of egress ⟨at the northern ~ of the plaza a beautiful boulevard begins⟩; *specif* **:** the point at which a body of water flows out into another usu. larger body of water ⟨a river whose source and ~ were unknown⟩ **4 :** OFFSPRING, PROGENY ⟨died without ~⟩; *specif* **:** one or more persons descended from a common ancestor **5 a :** final outcome **:** RESULT, CONSEQUENCE ⟨no chance at all of a happy ~ —C.P. Snow⟩ **b** *obs* **:** a final conclusion or decision about something arrived at after consideration **c** *archaic* **:** TERMINATION, END ⟨to hope that his enterprise would have a prosperous ~ —T. B.Macaulay⟩ **6 a :** a point in question of law or fact; *specif* **:** a single material point of law or fact depending in a suit that is affirmed by one side and denied by the other and that is presented for determination at the conclusion of the pleadings **b** (1) **:** a matter that is in dispute between two or more parties or that is to be disputed by the parties **:** a point of debate or controversy ⟨the ~ over which of them was to be leader⟩ ⟨seemed to want to make an ~ of almost everything⟩ (2) **:** a matter not yet finally settled and on the settlement of which something else depends **:** a pregnant unsettled matter **:** vital question ⟨burning ~*s* of the day⟩ ⟨an ~ that could make or wreck careers —T.H.White b. 1915⟩ ⟨to judge of each ~ . . . in the light of fact —Rose Macaulay⟩ **:** PROBLEM ⟨in every genuine metaphysical debate some practical ~, however conjectural and remote, is involved —William James⟩ **:** a controverted subject or topic ⟨the ~ of desegregation⟩ **c :** something entailing alternatives between which to choose or decide **:** something involving judgments or decisions ⟨a situation seen in terms of the ~ it presents —Archibald MacLeish⟩ **d :** the point at which an unsettled matter is ready for a decision **:** the point at which a question is ripe for decision ⟨quickly brought the matter to an ~⟩ **e :** a means of settling a point of debate or controversy; *specif* **:** a test or trial by means of which a question can be settled — used with *put* ⟨the theory was challenged and finally put to the ~⟩ **7 a :** a discharge (as of blood) from the body that is caused by disease or other physical disorder or that is produced artificially ⟨had long suffered from an ~ of blood⟩ **b :** an incision made to produce such a discharge **8 a :** something proceeding or coming forth from a usu. specified source ⟨an ~ of smoke from a chimney⟩; *esp* **:** something proceeding from a usu. specified source by or as if by flowing out or emanating or emerging from it ⟨hallucinations and other ~*s* of a disordered imagination⟩ **b** *obs* **:** something done by a specified agent **:** DEED **9 a** (1) **:** the act of officially putting forth or getting out or printing (as new currency or postage stamps) or making available or distributing (as supplies or material) or giving out or granting (as licenses) or proclaiming or promulgating (as a written order or directive) ⟨eagerly awaiting the next ~ of commemorative stamps⟩ ⟨~ of supplies by the quartermaster⟩ (2) **:** the act of bringing out (as a new book or a revised edition of a book or a new number of a magazine or a fresh printing of a newspaper) for distribution to or sale or circulation among the public **:** PUBLICATION ⟨~ of the enlarged edition is awaited with interest⟩ ⟨the many details involved in each day's ~ of a newspaper⟩ (3) **:** the act of offering securities for sale to investors ⟨a new ~ of government bonds⟩ (4) *chiefly Brit* **:** CIRCULATION 8a, 8c **b :** the condition or fact of being produced or made available by such action ⟨the book's ~ at such a time took everyone by surprise⟩ **c :** the thing (as a bank note or a security or an item of supplies or an individual's license or a copy of a book, magazine, newspaper) or the whole quantity of things (as all the postage stamps put forth with a certain design or the whole extent of supplies given out on a certain date or all the copies of a periodical printed for a specific day or month) produced or made available at one time or on a certain date by such action and usu. distinguished (as in date, design, content, nature) from those produced or made available at some other time ⟨waiting for the next ~ of the magazine⟩ ⟨bought specimens of each new ~ of stamps⟩ **d** *chiefly Brit* **:** CIRCULATION 8b **10 :** the first delivery of a negotiable instrument complete in form (as a bill or note) to a person who takes it as a holder **syn** see EFFECT — **at issue** *adv* **1 :** in a state of controversy **:** at variance **:** at a point where opposing viewpoints are held **:** in disagreement ⟨for years they remained *at issue* with each other⟩ **2** *also* **in issue :** in the process of being critically discussed or questioned **:** under discussion or in question or in dispute ⟨proceeded to inform them of the point *at issue*⟩
[2]**issue** \"\ *vb* -ED/-ING/-S [ME *issuen*, fr. MF *issu*, past part. of *issir* to come out, go out — more at [1]ISSUE] *vi* **1 a :** to go out or come out or flow out ⟨they *issued* out into the street⟩ ⟨a great sigh of relief *issued* from the ancient lungs —T.B.Costain⟩ ⟨the narrow coastal plain into which the Congo ~*s* —Tom Marvel⟩ **b :** to come forth from or as if from something in which one is immersed **:** EMERGE ⟨the external acts which . . . ~ from these precepts —R.W.Southern⟩ **c :** to come to an issue of law or fact in pleading **2 :** ACCRUE ⟨profits *issuing* out of sale of the stock⟩ **3 :** to come forth by way of descent from a specified parent or ancestor **:** become descended **:** be an offspring of a specified parent or ancestor ⟨children that shall ~ from thee —Isa 39:7 (DV)⟩ **4 a :** to proceed or come forth from a usu. specified source ⟨from the dining room *issued* the sound of two voices —Louis Bromfield⟩ ⟨his enmity *issued* from the old man's fear of a possible young rival —C.S.Forester⟩; *esp* **:** to proceed or come forth from a usu. specified source by or as if by flowing out or emanating or emerging from it ⟨blood *issued* from the cut and trickled down his forehead⟩ **b** (1) **:** to be or have a consequence or final outcome **:** RESULT ⟨social unrest *issuing* in several serious conflicts —C.B.Roden⟩ ⟨any unhappiness that we experience ~*s* generally from our circumstances —W.F.Hambly⟩ (2) **:** to be of such a kind or to have such a nature as to have or tend toward a specified end or consequence or outcome **:** turn out to have a certain result **:** end up by being something specified ⟨such a theory of ethics ~*s* in three crucial problems —Iredell Jenkins⟩ ⟨*issuing* in necessary and immutable results —J.H.Newman⟩ **:** EVENTUATE ⟨this change in policy *issued* in a permanent institution —W.R.Inge⟩ **5 a :** to appear or become available through being officially put forth or distributed or granted or proclaimed or promulgated **:** appear through issuance ⟨were astonished at the flood of currency *issuing* each year⟩ **b :** to appear or become available through being brought out for distribution to or sale or circulation among the public **:** appear through publication ⟨no new editions are expected to ~ from that press⟩ **c :** to go forth by authority ⟨there must be an affidavit made showing reasonable grounds before the warrant can ~ —Paul Wilson⟩ ~ *vt* **1 :** to cause to come forth **:** give vent to **:** DISCHARGE, EMIT ⟨a volcano *issuing* smoke and fire⟩ **2** *obs* **:** to bring forth (offspring) **3 a :** to cause to appear or become available by officially putting forth or distributing or granting or proclaiming or promulgating **:** cause to appear through issuance ⟨the government *issued* a new airmail stamp⟩ ⟨*issued* a decree⟩ ⟨*issued* a formal letter to his adherents⟩ ⟨*issued* rifles and rations⟩ **b :** to cause to appear or become available by bringing out for distribution to or sale or circulation among the public **:** PUBLISH ⟨*issued* the book shortly after the author's death⟩ **4 a** *obs* **:** TERMINATE, SETTLE **b** *archaic* **:** to cause to have a specified consequence or final outcome or result **:** cause to end up in something specified **syn** see SPRING
is·sue·less \-üləs, -u̇l-,-əl-\ *adj* [ME *issules*, fr. *issu*, *issue* issue + *-les*, *-lees* -less — more at [1]ISSUE] **:** being without issue: **a :** having no offspring ⟨died ~⟩ **b :** producing no result ⟨an ~ effort⟩ **c :** not maintaining or marked by any stand that would arouse debate or controversy ⟨an ~ piece of writing⟩
issue of fact : FACT IN ISSUE
issue of law : a question involving primarily the application of principles of law as distinguished from an issue involving primarily the determination of facts in a case **:** a question of law rather than of fact — compare FACT IN ISSUE
issue pea *n* **:** a small globular object (as a dried garden pea or a wooden bead) formerly placed in an abscess or ulcer so as to induce or increase a suppurative discharge
is·su·er \-əwə(r), -üə(r), -u̇ə(r)\ *n* -S **:** one that issues something (as securities, currency, books)
ist \'ist\ *n, pl* **ists** \'is(t)s\ *n* -S [[1]*-ist*] **:** one that professes or adheres to or specializes in an ism — usu. used disparagingly
[1]**-ist** \əst *sometimes* ,ist\ *n suffix, pl* **-ists** \-s(t)s\ [ME *-iste*, fr. OF & L; OF *-iste*, fr. L *-ista*, fr. Gk *-istēs*, fr. *-is-* (fr. verb

stems in *-izein -ize*) + *-tēs* (suffix forming agent nouns)] **1 a :** one that does **:** one that performs a (specified) action ⟨cycl*ist*⟩ ⟨balloon*ist*⟩ ⟨duell*ist*⟩ **:** one that makes or produces ⟨novel*ist*⟩ ⟨syllog*ist*⟩ **b :** one that plays a (specified) musical instrument ⟨organ*ist*⟩ ⟨violin*ist*⟩ **c :** one that operates a (specified) mechanical instrument or contrivance ⟨telegraph*ist*⟩ **2 a :** one that practices or studies or specializes in a (specified) art or science or particular field of knowledge or particular skill ⟨geolog*ist*⟩ ⟨mytholog*ist*⟩ ⟨algebra*ist*⟩ ⟨ventriloqu*ist*⟩ **b** (1) **:** one that is usu. professionally occupied with or interested in ⟨fashion*ist*⟩ ⟨color*ist*⟩ (2) **:** one that toys with or dabbles in ⟨controvert*ist*⟩ ⟨speculat*ist*⟩ **3 :** one that professes or adheres to or advocates a (specified) doctrine or theory or system or policy or code of behavior or procedure ⟨de*ist*⟩ ⟨social*ist*⟩ ⟨royal*ist*⟩ ⟨hedon*ist*⟩ ⟨pur*ist*⟩ or that supports the doctrine or theory or system or policy or code of behavior or procedure of a (specified) individual ⟨Calvin*ist*⟩ ⟨Darwin*ist*⟩ ⟨Hitler*ist*⟩ — esp. in nouns corresponding to nouns in *-ism* **4 :** one that is marked by ⟨pessim*ist*⟩ ⟨fatal*ist*⟩ — esp. in nouns corresponding to nouns in *-ism*

²-ist \"\ *adj suffix* **:** of, relating to, or characteristic of (something indicated) ⟨dilettant*ist*⟩

is't \(')ist\ [by contr.] *archaic* **:** is it

is·tan·bul \ˌistə|mˌbül, -ˌstä|, -ˌstal, -ˌstaal, -ˌstä|, |nˌb-, -bül *also* ˌē(ˌ)s-\ *adj, usu cap* [fr. *Istanbul*, city on the European side of the Bosporus in Turkey] **:** of or from the city of Istanbul, Turkey **:** of the kind or style prevalent in Istanbul

¹isth·mi·an \ˈismēən\ *n* -s [L *isthmius*, adj., isthmian (fr. Gk *isthmios*, fr. *isthmos* isthmus) + E *-an*, n. suffix] **1 :** a native or inhabitant of an isthmus **2** *usu cap* **:** a native or inhabitant of the Isthmus of Panama

²isthmian \"\ *adj* [L *isthmius*, adj., isthmian + E *-an*, adj. suffix] **:** of, relating to, or situated in or near an isthmus ⟨an ~ route⟩ ⟨an ~ people⟩: as **a** *often cap* **:** of or relating to the Isthmus of Corinth in Greece or the games anciently held there ⟨the *Isthmian* festival⟩ **b** *often cap* **:** of or relating to the Isthmus of Panama connecting the No. American and So. American continents ⟨the *Isthmian* canal⟩

isth·mi·ate \-mēˌāt\ *adj* [NL *isthmiatus*, fr. *isthmi-* (fr. *isthmus*) + L *-atus* -ate] **:** having an isthmus (sense 2)

isth·mic \-mik\ *adj* [L *isthmicus*, fr. Gk *isthmikos*, fr. *isthmos* isthmus + *-ikos* -ic] **1 :** ISTHMIAN **2** *also* **isth·mal** \-məl\ [*isthmus* + *-ic* or *-al*] **:** of, relating to, or taking place in a bodily isthmus ⟨~ ectopic pregnancy⟩

isth·moid \-ˌmȯid\ *adj* [prob. fr. (assumed) NL *isthmoides*, fr. NL *isthm-* (fr. *isthmus*) + L *-oides* -oid] **:** resembling an isthmus

isth·mus \ˈisməs, *chiefly Brit sometimes* ˈistm-\ *n* -ES [L, fr. Gk *isthmos*; perh. akin to ON *eith* isthmus, Gk *ithma* step, motion, *ienai* to go — more at ISSUE] **1 :** a narrow strip of land running through a body of water and having the water lying at each side and connecting two larger land areas (as two continents or a peninsula and the mainland) **2 :** a contracted part or passage connecting two larger structures or cavities: as **a :** a sharp constriction separating midbrain from hindbrain **b :** the lower portion of the uterine corpus **c :** the fleshy area on the throat of a fish between the gills **d :** a narrow intermediate portion of the pharynx of many nematodes **e :** the constricted connection between the main parts of a desmid

isthmus of the fauces : FAUCES 1

-is·tic \ˈistik, -tēk\ *also* **-is·ti·cal** \-tәkәl, -tēk-\ *adj suffix* [*-istic* fr. MF & L & Gk; MF *-istique*, fr. L *-isticus*, fr. Gk *-istikos*, fr. *-istēs* -ist + *-ikos* -ic; *-istical* fr. MF *-istique* & L *-isticus* & Gk *-istikos* + E *-al*] **:** of, relating to, or characteristic of ⟨panoist*ic*⟩ — often in adjectives corresponding to nouns in *-ism* or nouns in *-ist* ⟨altru*istic*⟩

is·ti·o·phor·i·dae \ˌistēōˈfȯrəˌdē\ *n pl, cap* [NL, fr. *Istiophorus*, type genus + *-idae*] **:** a family of large vigorous marine scombroid fishes comprising important food and sport fishes (as sailfishes, spearfishes, and marlins)

is·ti·oph·o·rus \ˌistēˈäfərəs\ *n, cap* [NL, irreg. fr. Gk *histion* sail + NL *-phorus*; akin to Gk *histanai* to cause to stand — more at STAND] **:** a small but widely distributed genus of fishes comprising the sailfishes (sense 1) and being type of the family Istiophoridae

is·tle *also* **ix·tle** \ˈis(t)lē\ *n* -s [AmerSp *ixtle*, fr. Nahuatl *ichtli*] **:** a fiber obtained from any of various tropical American plants: as **a :** a fiber obtained from the leaves of an epiphytic bromeliad (*Bromelia sylvestris*) **b :** a fiber obtained from any of several Mexican plants of the genus *Agave* (esp. *A. ixtli*) and used esp. for cordage and basketry

¹is·tri·an \ˈistrēən\ *adj, usu cap* [*Istria* + E *-an*, adj. suffix] **1 :** of, relating to, or characteristic of Istria, a peninsula on the northeast coast of the Adriatic sea **2 :** of, relating to, or characteristic of the people of Istria

²istrian \"\ *n* -s *cap* [*Istria* + E *-an*, n. suffix] **:** a native or inhabitant of Istria

ists *pl of* IST

-ists *pl of* -IST

isu·rus \īˈsürəs\ *n, cap* [NL, fr. *is-* + *-urus*] **:** a genus of large voracious sharks that is sometimes made the type of a separate family but usu. included in Lamnidae — see MACKEREL SHARK

ISV *abbr* International Scientific Vocabulary

ISWG *abbr* imperial standard wire gauge

¹it \(ˌ)i|t, ə|, *usu* |d·+V\ *pron* [ME *it, hit*, fr. OE *hit* — more at HE] **1 a :** that one — used as neuter pronoun of the third person singular that is the subject or direct object or indirect object of a verb or the object of a preposition and usu. used in reference to (1) a lifeless thing ⟨took a quick look at the house and noticed ~ was very old⟩ ⟨saw the corpse and walked over to ~⟩ ⟨~ is now no more —E.H.Collis⟩ or (2) a plant ⟨there is a rosebush near the fence and ~ is now blooming⟩ or (3) an insect ⟨felt a fly land on her neck and squirmed as ~ crawled down⟩ or an animal whose sex is unknown or disregarded ⟨saw the horse break away and watched ~ gallop into the canyon⟩ or (4) an infant or child whose sex is unknown or disregarded ⟨if a child were severely beaten every time ~ sneezed —Bertrand Russell⟩ ⟨heard the baby crying and brought ~ some milk⟩ or (5) a group or classification of individuals or things ⟨the football team is in top form and ~ is sure of victory⟩ ⟨buy a bag of apricots . . . plums and grapes for fifteen cents, wash . . . and eat ~ on our way —Claudia Cassidy⟩ or (6) an abstract noun ⟨beauty is everywhere and ~ is a source of joy⟩ or (7) a word viewed as a word ⟨*machine* is a common word and ~ can be applied to a variety of things⟩ or (8) a phrase or clause ⟨"Go ahead," she said, but he didn't hear ~⟩; sometimes used pleonastically together with a noun as subject of a verb esp. in ballad poetry ⟨our love ~ was stronger by far —E.A.Poe⟩ and in substandard speech ⟨the horse ~ ran away⟩; often used with a present participle like the adjective *its* with a gerund in a way that makes distinction between the two constructions impossible except by arbitrary analysis ⟨wet it before applying to the seal, to prevent ~ sticking —H.S. Kingsford⟩ ⟨there was a doubt about ~ being available —Valentine Heywood⟩; see ITS; compare HE, SHE, THEY **b** (1) **:** that male or female one whose identity is unknown or uncertain — used esp. in indirect or direct questions in reference to one that is usu. not directly indicated (as by pointing) or otherwise clearly specified (as by a qualifying clause or phrase) ⟨don't know who ~ is⟩ ⟨the knocking at the door continued and she finally said "who is ~?"⟩ ⟨someone appeared dimly in the fog and ~ spoke like my brother⟩ (2) **:** that male or female one whose identity is known — sometimes used in the speech of children or usu. disparagingly in the speech of others as a subject or object in reference to any person ⟨just look at my daddy and the big car ~ has⟩ ⟨what a little haughty prude ~ is —W.M.Thackeray⟩ ⟨just listen to ~ talk⟩ **c :** YOU — used in speaking to or as if to a baby ⟨did ~ hurt its little knees and chin⟩ — compare HE 4 **d :** ITSELF — used as indirect or direct object of a verb or as object of a preposition ⟨the plane plunged to earth carrying all its occupants with ~⟩ **2 a** — used as an expletive subject of an impersonal verb that expresses a simple condition or an action without direct or implied reference to an agent in statements or questions about (1) the weather ⟨~ is raining⟩ ⟨~ is getting cold⟩ ⟨is ~ a pretty day —Agnes S. Turnbull⟩ or (2) the time ⟨~ is eleven o'clock⟩ ⟨~ is late⟩ or divisions or points of time (as seasons, holidays, generalized parts of day or night) ⟨~'s only a few months until spring —C.W.Morton⟩ ⟨~ will soon be Christmas⟩ ⟨~ is getting on toward evening⟩ ⟨~ will dawn early tomorrow⟩ or (3) physical or mental conditions ⟨~ hurts when I look at a bright light⟩ ⟨~ makes him sad if he thinks about her too much⟩ or (4) an extent of distance or space ⟨~ is five miles to the next town⟩ **b** — used as an expletive subject in other statements or questions having an undefined subject ⟨if ~ hadn't been for you, I don't know what I would have done⟩ ⟨they have what ~ takes⟩ **3 a** (1) — used as an anticipatory subject of a verb whose logical subject is another word or a phrase or a clause ⟨~ is me⟩ ⟨~ is he who is responsible⟩ ⟨~ is the mayor they like⟩ ⟨~ is well you found out in time⟩ ⟨~ is necessary to repeat the whole thing⟩ ⟨~ is said the danger is great⟩ ⟨~ is a wonderful vacation spot, that town⟩ ⟨~ happened that they were away⟩; often used as subject of a periphrasis to shift emphasis from a logical subject to some other part of a statement ⟨~ was in this city that the treaty was signed⟩ (2) — used as an anticipatory object of a verb whose logical object is another word or a phrase or a clause ⟨I take ~ that there was some kind of rift —Hamilton Basso⟩ ⟨he made ~ clear, that answer of his⟩ ⟨found ~ necessary to continue⟩ ⟨made ~ evident that we needed help⟩ **b** *now chiefly dial* — used with the verb *be* where *there* is now used ⟨as so proud, so censorious, that ~ is no living with them —Paul Bayne⟩ ⟨~ was an English lady bright, and she would marry a Scottish knight —Sir Walter Scott⟩ ⟨~'s nobody here but me⟩ **c** — used with many transitive verbs as a direct object with little or no meaning and an almost entirely expletive or reinforcing function ⟨really living ~ up⟩ ⟨decided to rough ~ on his vacation⟩ or with many intransitive verbs as an apparent direct object with the same function ⟨footed ~ back to camp⟩ ⟨the satellites were free to go ~ alone —*Newsweek*⟩ or with some words used as nonce verbs as an apparent direct object with the same function ⟨decided that we would . . . hotel ~ —J.K. Jerome⟩ ⟨a man who likes to chef ~ now and then —Gerald Movius⟩ **4 a** (1) **:** a matter discussed or considered or about to be discussed or considered ⟨remembered she had told him about ~⟩ ⟨~ being agreed then —Walter Goodman⟩ (2) **:** a situation referred to either directly or by implication or about to be referred to either directly or by implication ⟨thought ~ was splendid⟩ ⟨doubted ~ would happen⟩ ⟨~ added up to a strangeness for which nothing in the previous frontier culture was a preparation —Bernard DeVoto⟩ (3) **:** a statement or idea or similar object of attention referred to either directly or by implication or about to be referred to either directly or by implication ⟨if you remember these points ~ will help you⟩ **b :** something read (as a passage in a book, words on a sign) ⟨~ tells in the book about the American Revolution⟩ ⟨~ says in the papers he expects to win the election⟩ ⟨a mile back ~ said to take a right turn⟩ or something looked at (as a traffic signal, a directional arrow) ⟨come on, ~ says to go⟩ **5 :** the general state of affairs or circumstances **:** general situation ⟨~ hasn't gone so well today⟩ ⟨came to that remote place to fish, get away from ~ all —Robert Murphy⟩ ⟨remember me, when ~ is well with you —Gen 40:14 (RSV)⟩ **6 a** (1) **:** something that has been done ⟨do ~ some more⟩ or is being done ⟨quit ~⟩ ⟨cut ~ out⟩ or is to be done ⟨go to ~⟩ ⟨he'll do ~ the right way⟩ ⟨decided to make a long weekend of ~ —Rebecca West⟩ (2) **:** some unpleasant or dreaded eventuality ⟨in for ~ now⟩; *specif* **:** punishment or chastisement or retribution ⟨going to catch ~⟩ ⟨put up with his sneers as long as possible and then let him have ~⟩ **b** (1) **:** all that one can desire or experience ⟨claims he's had ~ and that life is now pretty much a bore⟩ (2) **:** all that one can endure or suffer ⟨had a terrible day and swore he'd really had ~⟩ (3) **:** all that one is going to be allowed to have or do ⟨he's had ~ — I'm not going to put up with that nonsense any longer⟩ **c :** all that is required **:** the total extent of something needed or wanted ⟨when you've finished that job, that's ~ and you can go home⟩ ⟨everyone passes by, shakes hands and that's ~ —D.E.Weinland⟩ **d :** an expenditure of effort in attempting to attain an objective **:** STRUGGLE, CONTEST ⟨stick to ~ and you'll win out⟩ **7 a :** way out of a difficulty **:** answer to a problem **:** SOLUTION ⟨I have ~! This is what we'll do⟩ **8 a :** what is important or essential or tenaciously held to or sought after **:** what counts **:** what matters ⟨haven't got a chance and you should realize ~ is all over now⟩; *specif* **:** LIFE ⟨had stopped breathing and I could see ~ was all over⟩ **b** (1) **:** a crucial moment when much is at stake **:** a crisis on whose outcome much or everything depends ⟨an offensive was about to be launched and headquarters felt that this was ~⟩ (2) **:** a point at which the end of life or the end of everything that matters is imminent ⟨this is ~. From now on no power on earth can save the doomed city —F.V.Drake⟩ **9 a :** a quality or group of qualities requisite or desirable for or evidenced in a particular situation ⟨the legislators had ~ on most of the other delegates in convention maneuvering —Bill Hatch⟩ **b :** something that is expected or desired **:** something suitable or satisfactory ⟨that's ~, you're doing fine⟩ **c** (1) **:** something that perfectly or nearly perfectly meets the requirements of a situation **:** the very thing needed or required **:** just the thing wanted ⟨here's a suggestion for a Christmas gift that is really ~⟩ (2) **:** something that is without equal **:** something peerless ⟨stop acting as though you were ~⟩ ⟨she just seems to think she's ~⟩ (3) **:** something beyond which one cannot go **:** the ultimate **:** PINNACLE, ACME ⟨when it comes to graciousness, she's really ~⟩ **10 :** SEXUAL INTERCOURSE ⟨if I wanted to let you touch me I would . . . can't you see I don't want ~ —Morley Callaghan⟩

²it \"\ *adj* [ME *hit*, fr. *hit* (pron.)] *now chiefly dial* **:** ITS

³it \ˈit, *usu* ˈid·+V\ *n* -s [ˈit] **1 :** the player in a game who performs a key active or passive function (as trying to catch others in a game of tag or to answer questions in a guessing game) essential to the nature of the game **2 :** physical allure esp. when accompanied by personal magnetism and charm **:** SEX APPEAL

-it \ət, əd\ *vb suffix* [ME, alter. of *-ed*] *Scot var of* -ED

it *abbr* item

IT *abbr* **1** immediate transportation **2** immunity test **3** income tax **4** internal thread **5** international tolerance **6** *often not cap* [L *in transitu*] in transit

ita \ˈēd·ə\ *n, pl* **ita** *or* **itas** *usu cap* [Tag] **:** AETA

ita·bi·rite \ˌēd·əˈbiˌrīt\ *n* -s [*Itabira* (now, Presidente Vargas), town in Minas Gerais state, Brazil) + E *-ite*] **:** a quartzite containing micaceous hematite

ita·cism \ˈēd·əˌsizəm\ *n* -s [modif. of Gk *ēta* eta + *-cism* (as in *iotacism*) — more at ETA] **1 :** pronunciation of Greek eta as \ē\ **2 :** IOTACISM

ita·cist \-səst\ *n* -s **:** one that practices or favors itacism — **ita·cis·tic** \ˌ≡≡ˈsistik\ *adj*

it·a·col·u·mite \ˌid·əˈkäl(y)əˌmīt\ *n* -s [*Itacolumi*, mountain in Minas Gerais state, Brazil + E *-ite*] **:** a schistose micaceous quartzite that is flexible when split into thin slabs

it·a·con·ate \ˌid·əˈkäˌnāt\ *n* -s [*itaconic* (acid) + *-ate*] **:** a salt or ester of itaconic acid

it·a·con·ic acid \ˌ≡≡ˈ≡nik-\ *n* [ISV, anagram of *aconitic*] **:** a crystalline dicarboxylic acid $HOOCC(=CH_2)CH_2COOH$ obtained by decomposing aconitic acid or usu. by fermentation of sugars with molds of the genus *Aspergillus* and used as a monomer for both vinyl-type polymers and polyesters; methylene-succinic acid

ital- *or* **italo-** *comb form, usu cap* [*Ital-* fr. L *Italus*; *Italo-* fr. It or L; It, fr. *italo*, fr. L *Italus*] **1 :** Italian ⟨*Ital*american⟩ **2 :** Italian and ⟨*Italo*-Austrian⟩

ital *abbr* italic

¹ital·ian \əˈtalyən, *chiefly dial or substand or disparaging* (ˈ)ī|t-\ *n* -s *cap* [ME, fr. L *Italia* Italy (fr. Gk *Italia*) + ME *-an*] **1 a :** a native or inhabitant of Italy **b :** one that is of Italian descent **2 :** the language of the Italians developed from the Vulgar Latin of ancient times

²italian \"\ *adj, usu cap* **1 a :** of, relating to, or characteristic of Italy **b :** of, relating to, or characteristic of Italians **2 :** of, relating to, or characteristic of the Italian language

¹ital·ian·ate \-ˌnāt\ *vt* -ED/-ING/-S [prob. fr. It *italianato*, adj.] **:** ITALIANIZE

²ital·ian·ate \-nət, -ˌnāt\ *adj, usu cap* [It *italianato*, fr. *italiano* Italian (fr. *Italia* Italy — fr. L — + *-ano* — fr. L *-anus* -an) + *-ato* (fr. L *-atus* -ate)] **1 :** ITALIANIZED ⟨an *Italianate* Englishman⟩ **2 :** having an Italian quality **:** marked by Italian characteristics or influence ⟨*Italianate* architecture⟩

italian bee *n, usu cap I* **:** a honeybee predominantly yellowish in color that resembles the Carniolan bee in habits

italian blue *n, often cap I* **:** a vivid greenish blue

italian chestnut *n, usu cap I* **:** SPANISH CHESTNUT

italian clover *n, usu cap I* **:** CRIMSON CLOVER

italian corn salad *n, usu cap I* **:** a southern European succulent plant (*Valerianella eriocarpa*) used as a salad vegetable

italian cypress *n, usu cap I* **:** a Eurasian tree (*Cupressus sempervirens*) with thin gray bark and erect or ascending branches and dark green leaves resembling scales — called also *Mediterranean cypress*

italian earth *n, often cap I* **1 :** RAW SIENNA **2 :** BURNT SIENNA

italian fennel *n, usu cap I* **:** CAROSELLA

italian green *n* **1** *often cap I* **:** TERRE VERTE **2** *usu cap I&G* **:** a sulfur dye — see DYE table I (under *Sulfur Green 11*)

italian greyhound *n, usu cap I* **:** a toy dog of a breed developed by selective breeding from the standard-sized greyhound

italian hand *n, usu cap I* **1 :** a book hand characterized by roundness and a fine sloping line developed about the 12th century A.D. in Italy from the Roman cursive and revived by calligraphers in the early 15th century and used as the model for the first Italian printers and for modern English handwriting — compare ITALIC **2 :** craftiness or subtlety in the conduct of political, business, or personal affairs — usu. used in the phrase *fine Italian hand*

italian honeysuckle *n, usu cap I* **:** ITALIAN WOODBINE

ital·ian·ism \-yəˌnizəm\ *n* -s *usu cap* [prob. fr. MF *italianisme*, fr. OIt *italiano* Italian + MF *-isme* -ism — more at ITALIANATE] **1 a :** a quality or group of qualities distinctive of Italy or the Italian people **b :** a linguistic feature (as a pronunciation or a word or a phrase or an idiom) borrowed from or suggestive of the Italian language **2 a :** specialized interest in or emulation of Italian qualities or achievements **b :** attachment to or furtherance of Italian policies or ideals

ital·ian·ist \-nəst\ *n* -s *usu cap* **1 :** a specialist in the study of Italy or the Italian people or the Italian language **2 :** one that is attached to or seeks to further Italian policies or ideals

ital·ian·i·ty \əˌtalēˈanəd·ē, -lˈya-\ *n* -ES *usu cap* **:** the quality or state of being Italian (as in character or allegiance)

ital·ian·iza·tion \əˌtalyənəˈzāshən, -ˌnīˈz-\ *n* -s *usu cap* **1 :** the action or process of italianizing or of becoming italianized **2 :** something (as a name or word) that has been italianized

ital·ian·ize \əˈtalyəˌnīz\ *vb* -ED/-ING/-S *often cap, see -ize in Explan Notes* [prob. fr. F *italianiser*, fr. MF, fr. OIt *italiano* Italian + MF *-iser* -ize — more at ITALIANATE] *vi* **:** to act in a fashion regarded as distinctive of Italians; *specif* **:** to follow (as in style or technique) recognized Italian painters ⟨the *italianizing* masters of Antwerp⟩ ~ *vt* **1 :** to make Italian (as in behavior, appearance, culture, style) ⟨foreigners gradually *italianized* by residence in Italy⟩ **:** cause to have Italian characteristics ⟨*italianizing* a style of architecture⟩ **2 :** to change or modify (as a word or expression foreign to Italian) so as to make conform (as in spelling or pronunciation) to characteristics of the Italian language ⟨an *italianized* family name⟩

ital·ian·iz·er \-zə(r)\ *n* -s *often cap* **:** one that italianizes

italian kale *n, usu cap I* **:** SEVEN-TOP TURNIP

italian lake *n, often cap I* **:** YELLOW OCHER 2

ital·ian·ly *adv, usu cap* **:** in an Italian manner

italian millet *n, usu cap I* **:** FOXTAIL MILLET

italian ocher *n, often cap I* **:** RAW SIENNA 2

italian paste *n, usu cap I* **:** ALIMENTARY PASTE

italian pear scale *n, usu cap I* **:** a reddish to purple hard scale (*Epidiaspis piricola*) that is sometimes destructive to various fruit and nut trees in California

italian pink *n, often cap I* **:** DUTCH PINK 2

italian pool *n, usu cap I* **:** pin pool played with four balls

italian poplar *n, usu cap I* **:** LOMBARDY POPLAR

italian roast *n, usu cap I* **:** coffee of an extremely dark roast

italian ryegrass *also* **italian rye** *n, usu cap I* **:** a European grass (*Lolium multiflorum*) much used for hay and in the U.S. also for turf and green-manuring

italians *pl of* ITALIAN

italian sixth *n, usu cap I* **:** an augmented sixth chord consisting of a musical tone with a major third and an augmented sixth above the lowest tone (as A-flat, C, F-sharp)

italian sonnet *n, usu cap I* **:** PETRARCHAN SONNET

italian stone pine *n, usu cap I* **:** STONE PINE 2

italian thistle *n, usu cap I* **:** a hoary thistle (*Carduus pycnocephalus*) native to the Mediterranean region but established as a weed in the southwestern U.S.

italian turnip *or* **italian turnip broccoli** *n, usu cap I* **:** an annual or biennial (*Brassica ruvo*) prob. of European origin but grown elsewhere for its tops and tender flower shoots which are used as greens — called also *broccoli rab*

italian vegetable marrow *n, usu cap I* **:** COCOZELLE

italian vermouth *n, usu cap I* **:** sweet vermouth

italian walnut *n, usu cap I* **:** ENGLISH WALNUT

italian woodbine *n, usu cap I* **:** a Eurasian honeysuckle (*Lonicera caprifolium*) sometimes escaped in America and having the upper leaves connate and the flowers usu. in sessile whorls in the axils

¹ital·ic \əˈtalik, -lēk *also* (ˈ)ī|t-\ *adj* [L *Italicus* Italian, of Italy, fr. Gk *Italikos*, fr. *Italia* Italy + *-ikos* -ic] **1** *usu cap* **a** [NL *Italica*, fr. L, fem. of *Italicus*] **:** COMPOSITE **a** *of handwriting* **:** characterized by a sloping angle suggestive of italics ⟨written in a medieval *Italic* script⟩ — compare GOTHIC 3 **c** (1) **:** of, relating to, or characteristic of ancient Italy (2) **:** of, relating to, or characteristic of the peoples of ancient Italy ⟨vanished *Italic* cultures⟩ **d** (1) **:** of, relating to, or characteristic of a branch of the Indo-European language family that includes Latin and other languages (as Oscan, Umbrian) spoken by the peoples of ancient Italy and that also includes the Romance languages (as Italian, French, Spanish) descended from Latin (2) **:** of, relating to, or characteristic of the ancient languages of the Italic branch of the Indo-European language family as contrasted with the modern Romance languages (3) **:** of, relating to, or characteristic of Osco-Umbrian **2** *sometimes cap* **:** of, relating to, produced in, or characteristic of a style of distinctively printed letters or numbers or other characters that slant upward to the right (as in "*these words are italic*") and that are sometimes distinguished from other faces (as some obliques) having about the same degree of slant by the form of the letter *a* and that are typically used to give emphasis to a word or group of words or to refer to words as words or to indicate words or phrases foreign to the language of a context or to refer to titles of long works ⟨beautifully printed ~ letters⟩ ⟨paragraphs beginning with ~ capitals⟩

²italic \"\ *n* -s **1** *sometimes cap* **a :** an italic character **:** italic type ⟨an ~ is used at the beginning of each subdivision⟩ ⟨introduced ~s as a device for achieving emphasis⟩ ⟨printed in ~⟩ ⟨a font of ~s⟩ **b :** a written letter or number or other character (as in a handwritten or typed manuscript) that is underscored for emphasis or for some other purpose achieved in print by the use of italic type or that is so underscored (as in a handwritten or typed manuscript sent to a printer) to indicate that the matter underscored is to be set in italic type ⟨each ~ is clearly underlined⟩ ⟨writes a delighted "*yes!*" with ~s and a mark of exclamation —R.G.F.Robinson⟩ ⟨after the underscored sentence in the manuscript the author writes "~s mine"⟩ **c** *usu* **italics** *pl but sometimes sing in constr* **:** exaggerated intonation or some similar oral speech device by which one or more words is heavily and usu. affectedly emphasized or otherwise given sharp prominence ⟨was yapping, her silly voice fraught with ~s —Margaret Long⟩ ⟨a woman who has an irritating way of speaking in ~s —W.J. Locke⟩ **2** *cap* **a :** a branch of the Indo-European language family that includes Latin and other languages (as Oscan, Umbrian) spoken by the peoples of ancient Italy and that also includes the Romance languages (as Italian, French, Spanish) descended from Latin — see INDO-EUROPEAN LANGUAGES table **b :** the group of ancient languages of this branch as contrasted with the modern Romance languages **c :** OSCO-UMBRIAN

ital·i·cism \-ləˌsizəm\ *n* -s *usu cap* [¹*italic* + *-ism*] **:** ITALIANISM 1b

ital·i·ci·za·tion \əˌtaləsəˈzāshən, -ˌsīˈ *also* ī,-\ *n* [*italicize* + *-ation*] **:** the use of italics or a single underscore in printing or writing

ital·i·cize \-ˌsīz\ *vb* -ED/-ING/-S *see -ize in Explan Notes* [¹*italic* + *-ize*] *vt* **1 a :** to print in italics ⟨the printer *italicized* the whole passage⟩ **b :** to underscore with a single line for emphasis or for some other purpose achieved in print by the use of italic type or so as to indicate that the matter underscored is to be set in italic type ⟨annoyingly *italicizes* sentence after sentence in her notes⟩ **2 :** ACCENTUATE, EMPHASIZE, STRESS: as **a :** to give sharp prominence to (spoken words) usu. affectedly by the use of some oral speech device esp. exaggerated intonation ⟨she was *italicizing* every other word with that deadly, glittering brightness that a woman puts on —George Orwell⟩ ⟨*italicized* words and even phrases surged about in her conversation —Ngaio Marsh⟩ **b :** to bring out strongly or cause to be highlighted **:** play up ⟨decorative features that ~ the building's perfect symmetry⟩ ⟨his scorn for the orthodox language and logic of the law is *italicized* by such wry remarks —Fred Rodell⟩ ⟨serves especially to ~ the principle —N.F.Adkins⟩ ⟨dramatically *italicizes* the movie's theme —*Newsweek*⟩ **c :** to outline sharply **:** bring into sharp relief ⟨the little carmine smudge of her *italicized* lips —Bruce Marshall⟩ ~ *vi* **:** to use italics ⟨has a habit of *italicizing*⟩

[1]**ital·i·ote** \ə'talē,ōt, -ēət\ *also* **ital·i·ot** \-ēət, -ē,ät\ *n* -s *usu cap* [Gk *Italiōtēs*, fr. *Italia* Italy + *-ōtēs* -ote] **:** a Greek inhabitant of ancient Italy

[2]**italiote** \"\ *adj, usu cap* **:** of or relating to the Italiotes

italo- — see ITAL-

[1]**italo·phile** \ə'talə,fīl, 'id·ᵊlō,f-\ *also* **italo·phil** \-,fil\ *adj, usu cap* [*Ital-* + *-phile* or *-phil*] **:** friendly to or favoring what is Italian ⟨~ policies⟩

[2]**italophile** \"\ *n* -s *usu cap* **:** one that is friendly to or favors what is Italian

it·a·ly \'id·ᵊlē, 'itᵊl-, -li, *in rapid speech* 'itl-\ *adj, usu cap* [fr. *Italy*, country in southern Europe] **:** of or from Italy **:** of the kind or style prevalent in Italy

ita palm *or* **eta palm** \'ēd·ə-\ *n* [of Arawakan origin; akin to Arawak (Guiana) *ité* ita palm, Baniva *itéui*] **:** MIRITI PALM

itas *pl of* ITA

ita·uba \,ēd·ə'übə, ,id-\ *n* -s [Pg *itaúba*, fr. Tupi *itauba*] **1 :** a large South American tree (*Mezilaurus itauba*) of the family Lauraceae that yields a durable russet-brown wood much used in marine and general construction **2 :** the wood of the itauba

[1]**itch** \'ich\ *n* -ES [ME *icche, yicche*, fr. OE *gicce*, fr. *giccan*, v.] **1 a :** a localized or generalized uneasy sensation (as of a crawling, prickling, stinging) in the upper surface of the skin usu. considered to result from mild stimulation of pain receptors and producing a feeling of irritation in the affected area and eliciting an urge to relieve the affected area by scratching **:** ITCHING, PRURITUS ⟨had an ~ and scratched it⟩ **b :** a skin disorder (as a mange) accompanied by such a sensation; *esp* **:** a contagious eruption in man and animals that is marked by this sensation experienced to an intense degree and by surface lesions and that is caused by invasion of the skin by an itch mite (*Sarcoptes scabiei*) that forms minute galleries in the skin and keeps up a constant irritation — usu. used with *the* ⟨has the ~⟩; compare MANGE **2 a** (1) **:** a restless usu. constant often compulsive desire for or hankering after something **:** restless longing **:** uneasy craving ⟨a compelling ~ for money and success —Lee Rogow⟩ ⟨the ~ to travel⟩ ⟨the same restless ~ to be always doing something else —Bertrand Russell⟩ ⟨was uninfected by the ~ of publicity —V.L.Parrington⟩ (2) **:** a restless craving for sensual esp. sexual gratification **:** LUST, PRURIENCE ⟨the ~ of the senses —Bruce Marshall⟩ ⟨with meaty good looks and the gross ~ they often portend —*Time*⟩ ⟨had aroused in him only the vague adolescent ~ of desire which almost any personable woman could satisfy —Aldous Huxley⟩ **b :** a restless usu. constant inclination toward something **:** restless propensity **:** uneasy predisposition or overreadiness ⟨the ~ to justify all conduct on logical grounds —H.J.Muller⟩ ⟨an ~ for activity —Raymond Holden⟩ **3 :** a condition of restless ferment **:** seething agitation **:** STEW ⟨the ~ of aggressive nationalism —Karl Robson⟩ ⟨was in an ~ to be off —Bruce Marshall⟩ ⟨lived in a constant ~ of irritation —Hesketh Pearson⟩

[2]**itch** \"\ *vb* -ED/-ING/-S [ME *ichen, icchen, yicchen*, fr. OE *giccan*; akin to OHG *jucchen* to itch, MD *joken*] *vi* **1 a :** to have a localized or generalized uneasy sensation (as of a crawling, prickling, stinging) in the upper surface of the skin **:** have an itch ⟨seemed to ~ all over⟩ ⟨her arm ~*ed*⟩ **b :** to produce such a sensation ⟨heavy winter underwear that ~*ed*⟩ **2 a :** to have a restless usu. constant often compulsive desire for or hankering after something **:** long restlessly for something **:** crave something uneasily ⟨and ~ to get their hands on a juicy morsel —D.L.Cohn⟩ ⟨were ~*ing* to take immediate action —W.F.Hambly⟩ ⟨~*ed* to see the world⟩ **b :** to have a restless usu. constant inclination toward something **:** have a restless propensity for or uneasy predisposition to something **:** be impatiently eager **:** be overready ⟨killers who ~*ed* to kill again —Hal Burton⟩ **3 :** to be in a restless ferment **:** SEETHE, STEW ⟨~ with one curiosity —Milton Bracker⟩ ⟨~*es* with lechery —J.I.Cope⟩ ~ *vt* **1 :** to cause to have a localized or generalized uneasy sensation (as of a crawling, prickling, stinging) in the upper surface of the skin **:** cause to have an itch ⟨felt it ~ his leg —Joan Williams⟩ ⟨wool socks that ~*ed* his feet⟩ **2 :** IRK, VEX, IRRITATE ⟨had always been amused . . . where the others were ~*ed* —Sinclair Lewis⟩

[3]**itch** \"\ *var of* ECHE

itch·i·ly \'ichəlē, -li\ *adv* **:** in an itchy manner **:** NERVOUSLY, RESTLESSLY ⟨holding it ~, as if it were a snake —*Time*⟩

itch·i·ness \-chēnəs, -chin-\ *n* -ES **:** the quality or state of being itchy

[1]**itching** *adj* [fr. pres. part. of [2]*itch*] **:** that itches: **a :** having, producing, or marked by an uneasy sensation in the skin ⟨bothered with an ~ back⟩ ⟨an ~ skin eruption⟩ **b** (1) **:** having or marked by a restless desire or craving or longing for something ⟨always glad to cater to her ~ public⟩ (2) **:** restlessly or insatiably seeking after what is novel and different ⟨the time is coming when people will not endure sound teaching, but having ~ ears they will accumulate for themselves teachers to suit their own likings—2 Tim 4:3 (RSV)⟩ (3) **:** restlessly or insatiably seeking after acquisitions esp. money **:** AVARICIOUS ⟨had ~ fingers always ready for a bribe⟩ ⟨an ~ palm⟩ **c :** having or marked by a restless inclination toward or predisposition to something **:** impatiently eager ⟨~ anxiety —G.M.Trevelyan⟩ ⟨an ~ impulse —B.A.Williams⟩; *specif* **:** restlessly disposed to travel about and not to remain long in any one place ⟨born . . . with an ~ foot, he started drifting down through the cattle ranges —W.C.Tuttle⟩ ⟨having had ~ feet in his journalistic days, he had at least six different home towns —Volta Torrey⟩ **d :** being in a restless ferment **:** SEETHING, STEWING ⟨~ adolescents⟩

[2]**itching** *n* -S [ME *icchinge, yicching*, fr. gerund of *icchen, yicchen* to itch — more at ITCH] **:** ITCH 1a, 2

itch mite *n* **1 :** any of several minute parasitic mites that burrow into the skin of man and animals and cause itch; *esp* **:** a mite of any of several varieties of a species (*Sarcoptes scabiei*) that causes the itch, is about 1/60 of an inch long, and has a round-ovate body and three-jointed legs and mandibles resembling minute needles **2** *Austral* **:** CHIGGER

itchweed \'=,=\ *n* **:** a white hellebore (*Veratrum album*) of Europe

itchwood \'=,=\ *also* **itchwood tree** *n* **:** a tree (*Semecarpus vitiensis*) of the Pacific islands with an irritant milky juice

itchy \'ichē, -chi\ *adj, usu* -ER/-EST **1 :** ITCHING: as **a :** having, affected by, or resembling an itch or the itch ⟨dirty ~ vagabonds⟩ ⟨an ~ disease⟩ **b :** that causes or tends to cause itching ⟨an ~ sweater⟩ ⟨the thermometer leaped in a day from wind-bitten chill to ~ warmth —Sinclair Lewis⟩ **c** (1) **:** filled with restless desire or longing or craving for something ⟨fresh out of high school and ~ for excitement —*Time*⟩ (2) **:** restlessly craving sensual esp. sexual gratification **:** LUSTING, PRURIENT ⟨~ young profligates⟩ **d :** restlessly or compulsively driven toward action **:** impatiently eager ⟨an ~ reformer —W.L.Sullivan⟩ ⟨when some local rifleman shows evidence of an ~ trigger finger —Horace Sutton⟩ **2 :** nervously restless **:** JUMPY, RESTIVE ⟨gets ~ if you're not around⟩

[1]**-ite** \,īt, *usu* \|īd.+V\ *n suffix* -S [ME, fr. OF & L; OF, fr. L *-ita, -ites*, fr. Gk *-itēs* (n. & adj. suffix)] **1 a :** native **:** inhabitant **:** resident ⟨Gotham*ite*⟩ ⟨Brooklyn*ite*⟩ ⟨New Hampshir*ite*⟩ **:** occupant **:** dweller ⟨flat*ite*⟩ ⟨trailer*ite*⟩ **b :** descendant **:** offspring ⟨Adam*ite*⟩ **c** (1) **:** adherent **:** follower **:** supporter ⟨Jacob*ite*⟩ **:** advocate ⟨Darwin*ite*⟩ **:** devotee ⟨Browning*ite*⟩ (2) **:** member of a (specified) group or organization or movement ⟨Pusey*ite*⟩ **2 a** (1) **:** substance produced through some (specified) process ⟨anabol*ite*⟩ ⟨catabol*ite*⟩ (2) **:** commercially manufactured product ⟨ebon*ite*⟩ ⟨lydd*ite*⟩ ⟨vulcan*ite*⟩ **b :** -ITOL — esp. in commercial names ⟨dulc*ite*⟩ **3** [NL *-ites*, fr. L] **:** fossil ⟨corall*ite*⟩ ⟨filic*ite*⟩ **4 :** mineral ⟨erythr*ite*⟩ **:** rock ⟨chromit*ite*⟩ **5** [F, fr. L *-ita, -ites*] **:** segment or constituent part of a body or of a bodily part ⟨som*ite*⟩ ⟨dendr*ite*⟩

[2]**-ite** \"\ *n suffix* -S [F, alter. of *-ate* (fr. NL *-atum*) — more at -ATE] **:** salt or ester of an acid with a name ending in *-ous* ⟨nitr*ite*⟩ ⟨sulf*ite*⟩

itea \'id·ēə, 'īd-\ *n* [NL, fr. Gk, willow — more at WITHY] **1** *cap* **:** a genus of shrubs (family Saxifragaceae) having racemes of small white flowers with linear petals and a 2-valved capsular fruit — see VIRGINIA WILLOW **2** -S **:** any plant of the genus *Itea*

[1]**item** \'īd·əm, 'ītəm, 'ī,tem\ *adv* [ME, fr. L, fr. *ita* thus, prob. after L *id* it, that: *idem* the same — more at ITERATE] **1 :** and in addition **:** LIKEWISE, ALSO — used to introduce and call special attention to a new fact or particular or statement ⟨a length of chain, ~ a hook —Philip Guedalla⟩ **2 a** — used to introduce and call special attention to an initial statement and to each of the new statements that follow that are viewed as forming a related series with the initial statement **b** — used to introduce and call special attention to a single statement that is not viewed as one of a related series **c** — used (1) to introduce and signalize an initial particular or detail and each of the new particulars or details that follow that are viewed as forming a related group with the initial particular or detail or (2) to introduce and signalize each individual thing (as an article of household goods, an article of apparel, an object in an art collection, a book in a library) belonging to an aggregate of individual things that are being listed one after the other in an enumeration (as an inventory or similar list)

[2]**item** \'īd·əm, 'ītəm\ *n* -S [MF, fr. *item* (adv.), fr. L] **1 a** *obs* **:** an admonition or warning **b** *now dial* **:** HINT, INTIMATION, INKLING **2 a** (1) **:** an individual particular or detail singled out from a group of related particulars or details ⟨support him down to the ~ —*Time*⟩; *esp* **:** a small or tiny detail ⟨a courteous writer will stop short of rubbing into our minds the last ~ of all that he means —C.E.Montague⟩ (2) **:** a detail of information **:** piece of information ⟨gave names and addresses and other relevant ~*s*⟩ (3) **:** an individualizing or distinguishing mark or part or quality or characteristic ⟨an ~ of his customary appearance —Bernard DeVoto⟩ **:** FEATURE ⟨carefully studied each ~ in the landscape⟩ ⟨more than one ~ in the decorative features of the room was highly original⟩ **:** TRAIT ⟨he was pleased by every unlikeness to things American, by every ~ he could hail as characteristic —H.G.Wells⟩ ⟨inherited ~*s* from both ancestral lines, whether hair color or intelligence —Ruth Benedict⟩ **b** (1) **:** an individual thing (as an article of household goods, an article of apparel, an object in an art collection, a book in a library) singled out from an aggregate of individual things (as those being enumerated in a bill or inventory or similar list) ⟨was charged for three ~*s*⟩ ⟨glanced at each ~ in the list⟩ **:** individual object **:** ARTICLE ⟨cherished ~*s* of Americana —Jerome Weidman⟩ (2) **:** something singled out from a specified or implied category of things of the same kind ⟨bread, meat, and other food ~*s*⟩ ⟨an important ~ of international trade⟩ ⟨various ~*s* of clothing⟩ ⟨thousands of ~*s* of mail⟩ (3) **:** a thing of a particular class or kind as contrasted with a related thing of another class or kind ⟨the real ~ in the series —H.J.Laski⟩ (4) **:** something produced by manufacturing or manual labor or in some other way **:** a piece of goods **:** PRODUCT, COMMODITY ⟨a fast-selling ~⟩ ⟨marketing a variety of ~*s*⟩ ⟨where only a very few ~*s* are sold in bulk —A.S.Igleheart⟩ (5) **:** a check or draft or other financial instrument **c** (1) **:** a film or stage presentation or similar production **:** SHOW ⟨a bright new ~ on Broadway⟩ ⟨had seen this ~ brilliantly danced —Winthrop Sargeant⟩ (2) **:** one of the parts of such a production ⟨the main ~ of the show was to be a program of native dances —Ursula G. Bower⟩ **d** *Brit* **:** a selection of instrumental or sung music **:** musical selection **:** piece of music ⟨before even the first ~ is played listeners are relaxed and receptive —Clifford Lawson-Reece⟩ **3 a :** an object of attention or concern or interest to a specified degree ⟨an ~ of great importance⟩ or in a specified field ⟨an essential ~ for every home⟩ or to a specified individual ⟨excellent pictures add to the value of this book as a shipman's ~ —George Horne b. 1902⟩ ⟨an ~ of historical interest to the collector —Edith Diehl⟩ — compare COLLECTOR'S ITEM **b :** one of usu. two or more points of discussion or consideration **:** TOPIC, SUBJECT, MATTER ⟨there was one more ~ he wanted to speak about⟩ ⟨the index of the book listed all ~*s* covered⟩ ⟨added another ~ to the agenda⟩ **4 a** (1) **:** something that forms a contributory or component part or section of something specified ⟨mentioned a separate ~ of income⟩ ⟨obliteration of religion as an ~ of state policy —Hartzell Spence⟩ (2) **:** one of the elements or circumstances or influences that contributes to producing an indicated result **:** FACTOR ⟨a major ~ of school expense⟩ (3) **:** a subdivision of a cultural trait **:** a particular cultural factor or small group of such factors **b :** something usu. written down that forms part of a larger whole: as (1) **:** one of a series of separate listings (as each of the separate details given in a statement of charges for goods ordered or as each of the separate credits or debits detailed in a book of account) **:** ENTRY (2) **:** a brief line (as a remark, observation, comment) or a paragraph or two having a largely self-contained theme or subject and forming a contributory part of a more extensive piece of writing (as a newspaper column, diary, journal) (3) **:** a brief news bulletin or news report **:** a brief piece of news ⟨one ~ of news reached him after another, each more harassing than the one before —C.S.Forester⟩ (4) **:** a piece of writing (as an article, story, poem) usu. relatively short in length that forms a contributory part of a longer work (as an anthology, reference book, periodical) ⟨contributed a couple of ~*s* to the magazine⟩ (5) **:** a subordinate provision **:** CLAUSE ⟨may also veto ~*s* of proposed legislation and accept the parts of which they approve —A.N.Christensen⟩ **c** (1) **:** a unit of measurement (as a question, statement) in a test or scale (as of mental aptitude) (2) **:** a unit of correlated information (as the data indicated on a business punched card) about an individual person or thing **5 a :** something unspecified **:** an indeterminate thing ⟨her shopping bag was loaded with miscellaneous ~*s* she had bought⟩ **b :** something routine in a group of routine things **:** a run-of-the-mill thing ⟨just one more ~ in a busy day⟩ ⟨is an event, not a mere ~ in the year's publishing list —D.W.Brogan⟩

syn ITEM, DETAIL, and PARTICULAR can signify one of the things, either separate and distinct or considered so, that constitute a whole. ITEM applies chiefly to each thing in a list of things or in a group of things that lend themselves to listing ⟨an *item* in a laundry list⟩ ⟨each *item* of income⟩ ⟨an *item* in an inventory⟩ ⟨the first *item* confronting the mason in the building of footings and foundations for a new building is the excavation —J.R.Dalzell⟩ DETAIL in this connection applies to each separate thing which enters into the building, form, or construction of something as a house, a painting, narrative, or operation ⟨*details* of the building's architecture⟩ ⟨the *details* of modern life which pass daily under our eyes —Matthew Arnold⟩ ⟨the *details* of my employment —Mary W. Shelley⟩ ⟨a painter's fine execution of *details*⟩ PARTICULAR in this connection implies a relationship with any whole and stresses that relationship more than ITEM or DETAIL, emphasizing the smallness, singleness, and concreteness of each item or detail in the whole ⟨we know nothing of their language, and only . . . minor *particulars* of their social customs and religion —R.W. Murray⟩ ⟨the real question is what is the world . . . and that can be revealed only by the study of all nature's *particulars* —William James⟩ ⟨things are necessary or probable in kinds or species not simply as *particulars* —John Dewey⟩

[3]**item** \"\ *vt* -ED/-ING/-S **1** *archaic* **:** to figure up **:** COMPUTE, RECKON **2** *archaic* **:** to set down the particular details of **:** make a note or memorandum of

[4]**item** \"\ *usu cap* — a communications code word for the letter *i*

iteming *n* -S [prob. fr. E dial. *iteming* (taken as pres. part.) trifling, fidgeting, fr. [2]*item* + *-ing*] *dial Eng* **:** lack of earnestness **:** FRIVOLITY

item·iza·tion \,īd·əmə'zāshən, ,ītə-, -,mī'z-\ *n* -S **:** the action of itemizing

item·ize \'==,mīz\ *vt* -ED/-ING/-S *see -ize in Explan Notes* [[2]*item* + *-ize*] **1 a** (1) **:** to set down item by item **:** analyze or arrange or present item by item ⟨*itemizing* the cost⟩ ⟨*itemized* all expenses⟩ (2) **:** to specify the separate items of **:** list each item of ⟨*itemized* their contributions to charity⟩ **b :** to make due note of as an item **:** list as an item ⟨must ~ each piece of property —R.B.Gehman⟩ **2 :** to note or state the separate particulars or details of item by item ⟨*itemized* in a glowing eulogy his contribution to science⟩ — **item·iz·er** \-zə(r)\ *n* -S

itemized *adj* **:** arranged or presented with each item listed and detailed ⟨asked for an ~ bill⟩ ⟨an ~ account⟩ **syn** see CIRCUMSTANTIAL

item veto *n* **:** power of an executive (as a governor) to veto separate items of a bill (as an appropriation bill) without vetoing the entire bill

iter \'ī,te(ə)r, 'ī,-\ *n* -S *see sense 2* [L, journey, way, passage, right of way, fr. *ire* to go — more at ISSUE] **1** [ML, fr. L] **:** EYRE **2** *pl* **iti·nera** \ə'tinərə, ī'-\ *or* **iters a :** an ancient Roman road **b** *Roman law* **:** the right to pass over another's land on foot or by horseback — compare ACTUS **3 :** an anatomical passage; *specif* **:** AQUEDUCT OF SYLVIUS

it·er·ance \'id·ərən(t)s, 'itər-\ *n* -S [*iterate* + *-ance* (prob. after *utterance*)] **:** REPETITION, REITERATION, REPETITIOUSNESS, RECURRENCE

it·er·an·cy \-nsē, -nsi\ *n* -ES **:** the quality of being iterant **:** REPETITION, REITERATION, REPETITIOUSNESS, RECURRENCE

it·er·ant \-nt\ *adj* [L *iterant-, iterans*, pres. part. of *iterare*] **:** marked by repetition or reiteration or repetitiousness or recurrence ⟨~ echoes⟩

it·er·ate \-ə,rāt, *usu* -ād.+V\ *vt* -ED/-ING/-S [L *iteratus*, past part. of *iterare* to iterate, fr. *iterum* again, anew; akin to L *is* he, that, *ita* thus, Skt *itara* the other, *iti* thus] **:** REITERATE ⟨*iterated* his complaint⟩ **syn** see REPEAT

iterated integral *n* **:** an integral of a function of several variables that is evaluated by finding the definite integral with respect to one variable and then the definite integral of the result with respect to the second and so continuing until the desired accuracy is achieved

it·er·a·tion \,==+'rāshən\ *n* -S [ME *iteracioun*, fr. L *iteration-, iteratio*, fr. *iteratus* (past part.) + *-ion-, -io* -ion] **:** the action of repeating or reiterating **:** REPETITION, REITERATION ⟨constant ~ of the theme of a world out of joint —R.C.Carpenter⟩

[1]**it·er·a·tive** \'==,rād\|iv, ,rət, \|t\|, \|ēv *also* \|əv\ *adj* [MF *iteratif*, fr. LL *iterativus* frequentative, fr. L *iteratus* (past part.) + *-ivus* -ive] **1 :** marked by or involving repetition or reiteration or repetitiousness or recurrence ⟨~ methods⟩ ⟨~ poetic imagery⟩ **2 :** serving or tending to repeat; *specif, of a verb form or aspect* **:** expressing repetition of an action — compare FREQUENTATIVE, REDUPLICATIVE — **it·er·a·tive·ly** \\|əvlē, -li\ *adv* — **it·er·a·tive·ness** \\|ivnəs, \|ēv- *also* \|əv-\ *n* -ES

[2]**iterative** \"\ *n* -S **:** a word expressing repetition of an action

[1]**-i·tes** \'īd·(,)ēz, 'ī(,)tēz\ *n suffix, pl* **-ites** [NL — more at [1]-ITE] **:** organism or fossil like (a specified group) or from (an indicated place) — chiefly in generic names usu. of fossils ⟨*Agavites*⟩ ⟨*Malayites*⟩

[2]**-ites** *pl of* -ITIS

ith·a·gine \'ithə,jīn\ *n* -S [NL *Ithaginis*] **:** BLOOD PHEASANT

ithag·i·nis \ə'thajənəs\ *n, cap* [NL, irreg. fr. Gk *ithagenēs* legitimate, aboriginal] **:** a genus consisting of the blood pheasants

[1]**ith·er** \'ithə(r)\ *dial Brit var of* OTHER

[2]**ither** \"\ *dial Brit var of* EITHER

ithu·ri·el's spear \ə'th(y)ürēəlz-\ *n, usu cap I* [so called fr. the phrase *Ithuriel with his spear* in *Paradise Lost* (4:810) by John Milton †1674, Eng. poet] **:** GRASSNUT 2

[1]**ithy·phal·lic** \,ithə'falik\ *n* -S [LL *ithyphallicus*, adj.] **1 :** a piece of verse having an ithyphallic meter **2 :** an obscene piece of verse

[2]**ithyphallic** \\|==\|==\ *adj* [LL *ithyphallicus*, fr. Gk *ithyphallikos*, fr. *ithyphallos* phallus + *-ikos* -ic] **1 a :** having a meter typically used in hymns sung at ancient festivals honoring the Greek and Roman god of revelry Bacchus ⟨written in ~ verse⟩; *specif* **:** having the meter of a trochaic dimeter brachycatalectic (—⏑—⏑——) **b** (1) **:** of or relating to festivals anciently celebrated in honor of Bacchus ⟨~ processions⟩ (2) **:** of or relating to the phallus carried in processions held during these festivals **2 a :** having an erect or tumid penis — usu. used of figures in an art representation (as a statue or drawing) ⟨the curious and enigmatical semidisguised human figures are ~ —G.Baldwin Brown⟩ ⟨sketches of ~ bulls⟩ **b** (1) **:** LUSTFUL (2) **:** OBSCENE

ithy·phal·lus \,==+'faləs\ [NL, fr. Gk *ithyphallos* phallus, erect penis, fr. *ithys* straight + *phallos* penis — more at ATHROGENIC, BLOW (move)] *syn of* PHALLUS

-it·ic \,id·\|ik, \|it\|, \|ēk\ *adj suffix* [F *-itique*, fr. MF, fr. L *-iticus*, fr. Gk *-itikos*, fr. *-itis* (n. & adj. suffix) + *-ikos* -ic] **:** of, resembling, or marked by — in adjectives formed from nouns usu. ending in *-ite* ⟨dendr*itic*⟩ and *-itis* ⟨bronch*itic*⟩ and sometimes from other nouns ⟨dactyl*itic*⟩

-itides *pl of* -ITIS

itie \'īd·ē, 'ī,tī\ *n* -S *usu cap* [by alter. and shortening] **:** ITALIAN — usu. used disparagingly

-ities *pl of* -ITY

itinera *pl of* ITER

itin·er·a·cy \ī'tin(ə)rəsē, -si *also* ə't-\ *n* -ES [[2]*itinerate* + *-cy*] **:** ITINERANCY

itin·er·an·cy \-rənsē, -si\ *n* -ES **1 a** (1) **:** the action of itinerating ⟨preached to many people in the course of his ~⟩ (2) **:** the condition of being itinerant ⟨the ~ of a medieval minstrel⟩ **b :** a system (as in the Methodist Church) of rotating ministers who itinerate ⟨features of the episcopacy and the ~ —F.S. Mead⟩ **2 a :** official work or duty that involves traveling about from place to place (as in covering a preaching circuit) ⟨returned to the ~ —J.W.Johnston⟩ **b :** a group of persons (as preachers, judges) having such work or duty ⟨a member of the ~⟩

[1]**itin·er·ant** \-rənt\ *adj* [LL *itinerant-, itinerans*, pres. part. of *itinerari* to journey, fr. L *itiner-, iter* journey — more at ITER] **1 :** that travels about from place to place ⟨an ~ agricultural worker⟩ ⟨an ~ theatrical troupe⟩; *esp* **:** that travels about in covering a circuit ⟨an ~ preacher⟩ **2 :** marked by itinerancy ⟨lived an ~ life⟩ ⟨the ~ ministry⟩ **:** given or done or held in the course of traveling about from place to place ⟨~ discourses⟩ ⟨~ teaching⟩ ⟨~ sketching⟩ ⟨~ tent meetings⟩ — **itin·er·ant·ly** *adv*

[2]**itinerant** \"\ *n* -S **:** one that travels about from place to place; *esp* **:** one that travels about in covering a circuit

itin·er·ar·i·um \(,)ī,tinə'ra(a)rēəm, ə,t-\ *or* **itinerary** *n, pl* **itineraria** *or* **itinerariums** *or* **itineraries** [ML *itinerarium* (also, account of a journey, itinerary), fr. LL] **:** a prayer given in the Roman Catholic breviary that is used for a person who is about to travel

[1]**itin·er·ary** \ī'tinə,rerē, -,reri *also* ə't- *or* -nərē *or* -nəri\ *n* -ES [ME *itinerarie*, fr. LL *itinerarium*, neut. of *itinerarius* of a journey, itinerary] **1 a** (1) **:** a course of travel **:** route of a journey or tour or trip ⟨an ~ that took them through Canada⟩ (2) **:** an official or royal tour or circuit or visitation **:** PROGRESS ⟨when Queen Elizabeth I made one of her periodical *itineraries* of Kent —Richard Church⟩ **b :** a plan or outline of a prospective route to be followed in the course of traveling or touring **:** sketch of the prospective course of a journey or trip ⟨discussed their ~ before leaving⟩ **2 a :** a travel account **:** record of a journey or tour or trip **:** travel diary ⟨wrote the ~ in the course of the expedition⟩ **b :** a guidebook with information designed for travelers or tourists **:** ROADBOOK ⟨a helpful ~⟩ **3** *archaic* **:** ITINERANT

[2]**itinerary** \"\ *adj* [LL *itinerarius*, fr. L *itiner-, iter* journey + *-arius* -ary] **1 :** of or relating to traveling or journeying or touring; *specif* **:** of or relating to routes or roads followed in traveling or journeying or touring ⟨the ~ system developed by the ancient Romans⟩ **2** *archaic* **:** ITINERANT

[1]**itin·er·ate** \ī'tinə,rāt *also* ə't-; *usu* -ād.+V\ *vb* -ED/-ING/-S [LL *itineratus*, past part. of *itinerari* to journey — more at ITINERANT] *vi* **:** to travel about from place to place; *esp* **:** to travel about in covering a circuit ⟨*itinerating* missionaries⟩ ⟨*itinerating* judges⟩ ~ *vt, archaic* **:** to travel through **:** TRAVERSE ⟨~ the country —G.F.Townsend⟩ — **itin·er·a·tion** \(,)ī,tinə'rāshən *also* ə,t-\ *n* -S

[2]**itin·er·ate** \-,rət, -,rāt\ *adj* [LL *itineratus* (past part.)] **:** ITINERANT ⟨~ newspapermen —Turner Catledge⟩

-i·tious \'ishəs\ *adj suffix* [L *-icius, -itius,* adjective suffix added to the base of a noun or past participle] **:** of, relating to, or having the characteristics or properties of (something specified) ⟨excrement*itious*⟩ ⟨cement*itious*⟩

-i·tis \'īd·əs, \|tə̇s *sometimes* 'ē\ *n suffix, pl* **-i·tis·es** \\d·əsə̇z, \|tə̇s-\ *also* **-it·i·des** \'id·ə,dēz, 'itə-\ *sometimes* **-i·tes** \'ī\|d-(,)ēz, \|(,)tēz *sometimes* 'ē\ [NL, fr. L & Gk; L, fr. Gk, n. & adj. suffix] **1 :** disease usu. inflammatory of a (specified) part or organ **:** inflammation of ⟨laryng*itis*⟩ ⟨bronch*itis*⟩ ⟨appendic*itis*⟩ ⟨neur*itis*⟩ **2** *pl usu* **-itises a** (1) **:** malady arising from (something specified) ⟨too-much-money*itis*⟩ ⟨vacation*itis*⟩ (2) **:** affliction with (something specified) **:** forced endurance or suffering of ⟨television*itis*⟩ — chiefly in nonce formations **b** (1) **:** tendency esp. when excessive to or toward (something specified) **:** marked proneness to ⟨accident*itis*⟩ (2) **:** marked fondness for or obsession with (something specified) **:** weakness for **:** infatuation with ⟨adjectiv*itis*⟩ ⟨jazz*itis*⟩ (3) **:** excessive concern for or promotion or advocacy of or reliance on (something specified) ⟨education*itis*⟩ — chiefly in nonce formations **c :** quality or state of being marked to an often excessive degree by certain typical characteristics of (something specified) ⟨big-business*itis*⟩ — chiefly in nonce formations

it·mo \'it(,)mō\ *or* **ik·mo** \'ik(-\ *n* -s [Tag] **:** BETEL

it·neg \'it,neg\ *n, pl* **itneg** *or* **itnegs** *usu cap* [Tinggian] **:** TINGGIAN

-i·tol \ə,tōl, -tȯl, -tōl\ *n suffix* -s [ISV *-it-* (fr. ¹*-ite*) + *-ol*] **:** polyhydroxy alcohol usu. related to a sugar ⟨mann*itol*⟩ ⟨inos*itol*⟩

ito·na·ma \,ēd·ə'nämə\ *n, pl* **itonama** *or* **itonamas** *usu cap* [AmerSp, of AmerInd origin] **1 a :** a people of northeastern Bolivia **b :** a member of such people **2 :** the language of the Itonama people

it·o·nid·idae \,id·ə'nid·ə,dē\ [NL, fr. *Itonida,* genus of gall midges (prob. fr. L, title of the goddess Minerva, irreg. fr. Gk *Itōnid-, Itōnis,* title of the goddess Athena) + *-idae*] *syn of* CECIDOMYIIDAE

¹**its** \(')its, ,əts\ *adj* [¹*it* + *-s* (possessive case ending)] **1 :** of or belonging to it or itself as possessor **:** inherent in it **:** associated or connected with it ⟨going to ~ kennel⟩ ⟨~ weird howl⟩ ⟨did it bump ~ little head⟩ **2 :** of or relating to it or itself as author, doer, giver, or agent **:** effected by it **:** experienced by it as subject **:** that it is capable of ⟨a little child proudly showing the teacher ~ first drawings⟩ ⟨~ remarkable speed⟩ ⟨~ spasmodic reactions⟩ ⟨did ~ very best⟩ **3 :** of or relating to it or itself as object of an action **:** experienced by it as object ⟨this proposal and ~ final enactment into law⟩ ⟨intending ~ betterment⟩ **4 :** that it has to do with or is supposed to possess or to have knowledge of or a share or some special interest in ⟨a dog that knows ~ master⟩ **5 :** that is esp. significant for it **:** that brings it good fortune or prominence — used with *day* or sometimes with other words indicating a division of time ⟨the football team was having ~ day⟩

²**its** \'its\ *pron, sing or pl in constr* **:** its one or its ones — used occas. without a following noun as a pronoun equivalent in meaning to the adjective *its* ⟨women take to a thing, any thing, and go deep enough, and they're ~ —A.S.M.Hutchinson⟩ — compare ³HIS

³**its** \(')its, ,əts\ [by alter.] *substand* **:** ¹IT'S

⁴**its** *pl of* IT

¹**it's** \(')its, ,əts\ [by contr.] **1 :** it is ⟨*it's* good⟩ **2 :** it has ⟨*it's* been a long time⟩

²**it's** \"\ *adj* [by alter.] *now substand* **:** ITS

it·sel \ət'sel\ *dial var of* ITSELF

¹**it·self** \ət+\ *pron* [ME, fr. OE *hit self,* fr. *hit* it + *self* — more at HE] **1 :** that identical one — compare ¹IT 1a; used (1) reflexively as object of a preposition or direct or indirect object of a verb ⟨the dog will have to look out for ~ while its master is gone⟩ ⟨hurt ~ crossing the street⟩ ⟨watched the cat giving ~ a bath⟩; (2) for emphasis in apposition with *it, which, that, this,* or a noun ⟨it is attractive ~⟩ ⟨which ~ is reason enough⟩ ⟨a bookbinding that ~ is valuable⟩ ⟨this ~ was sufficient excuse⟩ ⟨the letter ~ was missing⟩; (3) for emphasis instead of nonreflexive *it* as object of a preposition or direct or indirect object of a verb ⟨its agility is a source of amusement to its master and is a protection for ~⟩; (4) for emphasis instead of *it* or instead of *it itself* as subject of a verb ⟨never used for any purpose other than what ~ was designed for⟩ or as predicate nominative ⟨an animal is generally concerned for just one thing and that is ~⟩ or in comparisons after *than* or *as* ⟨a dog being chased by an animal smaller than ~⟩; (5) in absolute constructions ⟨~ a splendid specimen of classic art, it is sure to be exhibited throughout the world⟩ **2 :** its normal, healthy, or sane condition ⟨the dog seemed quite ill at first but soon came to ~⟩ **:** its normal, healthy, or sane self ⟨fed the little creature milk and it was soon ~⟩ **3 :** YOURSELF — used in speaking to or as if to a baby ⟨did it hurt ~⟩ — compare ¹IT 1c

²**itself** \"\ *adv* **1** *Irish* **:** in very fact **:** INDEED — used as an intensive usu. at the end of a clause ⟨where is he ~ —J.M. Synge⟩ **2** *Irish* **:** ACTUALLY, EVEN — used as an intensive usu. at the end of a clause ⟨though you are hard on your poor mother ~ —Gerald O'Donovan⟩

it·ty-bit·ty \'id·ē'bid·ē\ *or* **it·sy-bit·sy** \'itsē'bitsē\ *adj* [prob. fr. baby talk for *little bit*] **:** extremely small **:** TINY ⟨an *itty-bitty* piece of cake⟩ — not in formal use

it·u·re·an \,ichə'rēən\ *n* -s *usu cap* [L *Ituraeus* Iturean (fr. Gk *Ityraios,* adj., of Iturea, country in ancient Palestine) + E *-an*] **:** a native or inhabitant of Iturea, an Arab kingdom in ancient Palestine south of Damascus

itu·ri·te fiber \,ēd·ə'rēd·ē-\ *n* [origin unknown] **:** the fiber of a So. American herb (*Ischnosiphon obliquus*) of the family Marantaceae

-i·ty \əd·ē, ətē, -i; *when* s, *less often when* r, *precedes, the first vowel is sometimes lost, as in* kə'pastē *for "capacity"*\ *n suffix* -ES [ME *-ite,* fr. OF & L; OF *-ité,* fr. L *-itat-, -itas,* fr. *-i-* (thematic or, rarely, connective vowel) + *-tat-, -tas* -ty] **:** quality **:** state **:** degree ⟨asin*inity*⟩ ⟨theatrical*ity*⟩

it·za \ət'sä\ *n, pl* **itza** *or* **itzas** *usu cap* [Sp *itzá,* of AmerInd origin] **1 a :** a division of the Yucatec people of Petén, Guatemala **b :** a member of such division **2 :** a dialect of Yucatec

IU *abbr* **1** immunizing unit **2** international unit

iu·li·dae \(ī)'yülə,dē\ [NL, fr. *Iulus,* type genus + *-idae*] *syn of* JULIDAE

iu·lus \-ləs\ [NL, alter. of *Julus*] *syn of* JULUS

-ium *n suffix* **1** -s [NL, perh. after such words as L *medium*] **a** (1) **:** chemical element ⟨sod*ium*⟩ ⟨uran*ium*⟩ (2) **:** chemical radical ⟨ammon*ium*⟩ **b :** an ion having a positive charge — in names of complex cations (as those derived from an organic base) ⟨imidazol*ium* $[C_3H_4N_2H]^+$⟩ ⟨pyridin*ium*⟩ ⟨nitrosyl*ium* NO^+⟩ — compare -ONIUM **2** *pl* **-iums** *also* **-ia** [NL, fr. L, fr. Gk *-ion* (n. suffix, often of diminutive force)] **:** small one **:** mass — esp. in biological terms ⟨onch*ium*⟩ ⟨pollin*ium*⟩

ius *var of* JUS

IV *abbr* **1** *often not cap* increased value **2** *often not cap* initial velocity **3** intravenous **4** *often not cap* [L *in verbo; in voce*] under the word **5** *often not cap* invoice value **6** iodine value

iva \'īvə, 'ēvə\ *n* [NL, fr. *iva* (specific epithet of *Ajuga iva*), prob. fr. F *ive* ground pine, fr. MF, fr. OF *yve,* fr. *if* yew, of Celt origin; fr. its similarity in smell; akin to OHG *iwa* yew — more at YEW] **1** *cap* **:** a small genus of American herbs or shrubs (family Ambrosiaceae) with mostly opposite leaves and small greenish flowers and with the staminate and pistillate both in the same head **2** -s **:** any plant of the genus *Iva* — see MARSH ELDER 2

ivan \'īvən *also* ē'vän\ *n* -s *usu cap* [Russ *Ivan,* proper name, John, fr. ORuss *Ioannŭ,* fr. Gk *Iōannēs* — more at JOHN] **:** RUSSIAN; *esp* **:** a Russian soldier

iva·no·vo \ē'vänə,vō, -,vȯ\ *adj, usu cap* [fr. *Ivanovo,* city in U.S.S.R.] **:** of or from the city of Ivanovo, U.S.S.R. **:** of the kind or style prevalent in Ivanovo

iva·tan \,ēvə'tän\ *n, pl* **ivatan** *or* **ivatans** *usu cap* [native name in the Batan Islands] **1 a :** a people inhabiting the Batan islands of the Philippines **b :** a member of such people **2 :** an Austronesian language of the Ivatan people

¹**-ive** \iv, ēv *also* əv\ *adj suffix* [ME *-if, -ive,* fr. MF & L; MF *-if,* fr. L *-ivus;* akin to (assumed) Gk *-eiwos* (whence Gk *-eios* -ive)] **:** that performs or tends toward or serves to accomplish an (indicated) action esp. regularly or lastingly ⟨amus*ive*⟩ ⟨coordinat*ive*⟩

²**-ive** \"\ *n suffix* -s [ME *-if, -ive,* fr. MF & L; MF *-if,* fr. L *-ivus,* fr. *-ivus,* adj. suffix] **:** something that performs or tends toward or serves to accomplish an (indicated) action esp. regularly or lastingly ⟨sedat*ive*⟩ ⟨direct*ive*⟩ ⟨correlat*ive*⟩

ivied \'īvēd, -vid\ *adj* [¹*ivy* + *-ed*] **:** covered with ivy ⟨~ walls⟩ ⟨~ ruins⟩

ivies *pl of* IVY

ivin \'īvən, 'iv-\ *n* -s [alter. of earlier *iven,* fr. ME, fr. OE *ifegn, ifig* — more at IVY] *dial Eng* **:** IVY

ivo·ried \'īv(ə)rēd, -rid\ *adj* **1** *archaic* **:** made of or covered with ivory **2** *archaic* **:** resembling ivory (as in color, smoothness)

ivo·rine \'īvə,rēn, ,=='=\ *n* -s *often attrib* [fr. *Ivorine,* a trademark] **:** a substance resembling ivory in color and texture

¹**ivo·ry** \'īv(ə)rē, -ri\ *n* -ES *see senses 3, 4* [ME *ivor, ivorie,* fr. OF *ivore, ivoire, ivurie,* fr. L *eboreus,* adj., of ivory, fr. *ebor-, ebur* ivory, of Hamitic origin; akin to Egypt *ꜣbw* elephant, ivory] **1 a** (1) **:** the hard creamy-white opaque fine-grained elastic modified dentine that composes the tusks of an elephant (2) **:** the dentine of the tusks of large mammals (as narwhals, walruses) other than elephants (3) **:** the dentine of any tooth **b :** a tusk of an elephant or other large mammal **2 a :** creamy whiteness **b** *or* **ivory yellow** *or* **ivory white** (1) **:** a variable color averaging a pale yellow that is darker, slightly redder, and very slightly less strong than cream, paler and slightly redder than straw, and paler and slightly greener than leghorn (2) *of textiles* **:** a yellowish white that is stronger and slightly redder than milk white and redder and slightly less strong than average shell tint **3** *pl* **ivories** *or* **ivory** *slang* **:** TOOTH ⟨fell down and broke one of his *ivories*⟩ ⟨snarled and showed his ~⟩ **4** *pl* **ivories** *or* **ivory :** something made of ivory or of a substance resembling or suggestive of ivory: as **a** *slang* **:** DIE 1a ⟨rattling the ~⟩ ⟨picked up one of the *ivories*⟩ **b :** a carving in ivory ⟨the museum has a remarkable collection of *ivories*⟩ **c** *slang* **:** a pool or billiard ball ⟨watched them shoot the *ivories* around⟩ **d** *slang* **:** one of the keys of a piano keyboard or of the keyboard of a similar instrument (as an accordion) ⟨tickling the *ivories*⟩

²**ivory** \"\ *adj* [ME *iver,* fr. *iver, ivor,* n.] **1 a :** made of ivory **:** consisting of ivory ⟨an ~ figurine⟩ ⟨a tiny ~ box⟩ **b :** resembling or suggestive of ivory **:** having a finish suggestive of the surface of ivory ⟨a fine-grained wood with a highly polished ~ surface⟩ ⟨~ porcelain⟩; *esp* **:** having a creamy whiteness and smoothness suggestive of ivory ⟨admired her ~ arms and shoulders⟩ **c :** of the color ivory **2 :** IVORY-TOWERED ⟨little men in ~ offices, who . . . fear to carry out their instructions in a liberal and imaginative way —Edward Sackville-West⟩

³**ivory** \"\ *dial var of* IVY

ivory-billed woodpecker \'=(=)=';=-\ *or* **ivorybill** \'=(=)=,=\ *n* **:** a nearly extinct large woodpecker (*Campephilus principalis*) having plumage that is glossy black with white along the neck and wings, a large ivory-white bill, and in the male a large scarlet crest

ivory black *n* **1 :** a fine black pigment prepared by calcining ivory scrap **2 :** a bone black usu. of high quality

ivory board *n* **:** a highly finished paperboard coated on both sides

ivory brown *n* **1 :** a brown pigment made by partially carbonizing ivory **2 :** BONE BROWN 2

ivory coast *adj, usu cap I&C* [fr. *Ivory Coast Republic*] **:** of or relating to the Ivory Coast Republic **:** of the kind or style prevalent in the Ivory Coast Republic

ivory coast·er \-'kōstə(r)\ *n* -s *cap I&C* [*Ivory Coast,* country in West Africa + E *-er*] **:** a native or inhabitant of the Ivory Coast

ivory coral *n* **:** any of several hard and branching madrepores (family Oculinidae) with widely spaced polyps and firm skeleton

ivory-dome \'=(=)=,=\ *n* **:** BONEHEAD

ivory gull *n* **:** a gull (*Pagophila eburnea*) that is circumpolar in distribution and migrates as far south as New Brunswick and England

ivory-leaves *also* **ivory-leaf** \'=(=)=,=\ *n, pl* **ivory-leaves :** WINTERGREEN 2a

ivory nut *n* **1 :** the nutlike seed of a So. American palm (*Phytelephas macrocarpa*) containing a very hard endosperm — see VEGETABLE IVORY **2 :** APPLENUT

ivory palm *or* **ivory-nut palm** *also* **ivory plant** *n* **:** a palm yielding ivory nuts

ivory plum *n* **1 a :** CREEPING SNOWBERRY **b :** the fruit of creeping snowberry **2 :** WINTERGREEN 2a

ivory shell *n* **:** any of several tropical whelks (family Buccinidae) with ivory-white shells spotted and mottled with orange or brown or red

ivory tint *n* **:** a yellowish gray that is greener and duller than sand and greener and paler than natural

ivory tower *n* [trans. of F *tour d'ivoire;* orig. used by C. A. Sainte-Beuve †1869 Fr. poet & critic with reference to Alfred de Vigny †1863 Fr. poet & novelist] **1 a :** a nonrealistic often escapist or visionary attitude marked by usu. studied aloofness from and lack of concern with practical matters or urgent problems **:** a dreamy impractical attitude divorced from reality and often marked by limited vision or narrow-mindedness ⟨her safe *ivory tower* of aloofness from life —Dorothy C. Fisher⟩ **b :** an often complacently blind preoccupation with what is wholly or nearly wholly speculative or theoretical or abstract or esoteric ⟨the *ivory tower* of speculation —J.L.Liebman⟩ **c :** a state of mental withdrawal from and nonparticipation in practical matters and surrounding activity **:** a retreat from concern with or interest in reality and the world outside the self ⟨living in an *ivory tower*⟩ **2 :** something (as a secluded place or environment or a psychological withdrawal into oneself) that affords a means of retreating from reality and practical issues ⟨viewing college as an *ivory tower*⟩ ⟨she entered the *ivory tower* of her deafness and closed the door —Aldous Huxley⟩ ⟨still seek to preserve an *ivory tower* of intellectual sterility —David Worcester⟩

ivory-tower \'=(=)=';=\ *adj* **1 :** marked by failure or refusal to face or cope with reality and practical matters **:** NONREALISTIC, IMPRACTICAL, DREAMY, ESCAPIST ⟨her thinking is *ivory-tower* —J.F.Dinneen⟩ ⟨were this the only result, the work would indeed have been *ivory-tower* —A.A.Twichell⟩ ⟨the *ivory-tower* point of view of certain academicians and librarians —John Farrar⟩ ⟨*ivory-tower* seclusion of the scholar —Sergius Yakobson⟩ **2 :** preoccupied with what is wholly or nearly wholly speculative or theoretical or abstract or esoteric ⟨*ivory-tower* writers and artists⟩

ivory-towered \'=(=)=';=\ *adj* **1 :** divorced from reality and practical matters **:** living in or surrounded by an ivory tower **:** nurturing an ivory-tower outlook or approach **:** cultivating an ivory-tower method of living or acting ⟨*ivory-towered* esthetic antagonists —Bennett Cerf⟩ ⟨an *ivory-towered* recluse⟩ **2 :** far removed from the outside world and everyday activity **:** REMOTE, SOLITARY, ISOLATED ⟨any college town, however inland and *ivory-towered* —Nell G. Ahern⟩ **:** SHELTERED ⟨an *ivory-towered* home —*Newsweek*⟩

ivory-tower·ish \'=(=)='tau̇(ə)rish\ *adj* **:** rather unrealistic or impractical **:** inclined toward aloofness and preoccupation with what is abstract or esoteric ⟨a young man, naïve, scholarly, somewhat *ivory-towerish* —Clifton Fadiman⟩ ⟨fall between the one extreme of being too superficial and the other of becoming esoteric and therefore *ivory-towerish* —R.J.Leach⟩ — **ivory-tower·ish·ness** *n* -ES

ivory-tower·ism \'=(=)='tau̇(ə),rizəm\ *n* -s **:** cultivation of or attachment to an ivory-tower attitude or way of living or acting ⟨an *ivory-towerism* that many young Americans reared in a practical tradition view with mistrust —*Newsweek*⟩ ⟨defend contemporary American criticism from preoccupation with aesthetics and *ivory-towerism* —*Amer. Literature*⟩

ivory-tower·ist \-,rəst\ *or* **ivory-tow·er·ite** \-,rīt\ *n* -s **:** one marked by ivory-towerism ⟨ignore the insipidities of the *ivory-towerites* and try to build a new literature —William Small⟩

ivory tree *n* **:** any of several trees of the family Apocynaceae; *esp* **:** an East Indian tree (*Holarrhena antidysenterica*) with hard white wood and a bark formerly much used as a remedy for diarrhea and dysentery

ivorywood \'=(=)=,=\ *n* **:** an Australian timber tree (*Siphonodon australis*) of the family Celastraceae — called also *native guava*

ivory yellow *or* **ivory white** *n* **:** IVORY 2b

ivray *also* **ivraie** \ēv'rā\ *n* -s [MF *ivraie*] **:** BEARDED DARNEL

iv·ver \'ivə(r)\ *dial var of* EVER

¹**ivy** \'īvē, -vi\ *n* -ES [ME, fr. OE *īfig;* akin to OHG *ebahewi, ebah* ivy, and perh. to L *ibex* (lit., climber), Gk *iphyon,* a plant] **1 a :** a widely cultivated ornamental climbing or prostrate or sometimes shrubby vine (*Hedera helix*) native to Europe and Asia that has evergreen leaves and small yellowish flowers and black berries and that clings to upright surfaces (as of walls, rocks, trees) by means of numerous aerial roots having tiny adhering disks — called also *English ivy* **b** (1) **:** MOUNTAIN LAUREL (2) **:** POISON IVY **2 :** a variable color averaging a dark grayish green that is yellower and duller than Persian green and yellower and paler than hemlock green

ivy

²**ivy** \"\ *adj* **1 :** ACADEMIC 2, 5 ⟨the situation has grown so acute that it is no longer confined to the ~ towers but creeps out into open public discussion —*Music Educators Jour.*⟩ **2 :** IVY LEAGUE ⟨~ college boys⟩

ivy-arum \'=='==\ *n* **:** any of various woody vines constituting the genus *Scindapsus* and often cultivated as ornamentals for their glossy often slotted and variegated foliage; *esp* **:** a much-branched tall climber (*S. aureus*) native to the Solomon islands that has large leathery cordate leaves spotted and lined with golden yellow and that climbs by aerial rootlets arising from the nodes — called also *Ceylon creeper*

ivybells \'==,=\ *n, pl* **ivybells :** a slender creeping European bellflower (*Wahlbergia hederacea*) of the family Campanulaceae that has petioled suborbicular to cordate and sometimes obscurely lobed leaves and small pale blue often nodding flowers and that is widely distributed in damp acid peaty areas throughout western Europe

ivyberry \'==- — *see* BERRY\ *n* **:** WINTERGREEN 2a

ivy bindweed *n* **:** BLACK BINDWEED 1

ivy family *n* **:** ARALIACEAE

ivy geranium *also* **ivy-leaved geranium** \'=='=-\ *n* **:** a commonly cultivated trailing So. African plant (*Pelargonium peltatum*) with peltate to nearly orbicular leaves and usu. rosy carmine flowers

ivy gourd *n* **1 :** a tropical Asiatic vine (*Coccinia cordifolia*) of the family Cucurbitaceae with triangular leaves and large white flowers and scarlet fruit **2 :** the fruit of the ivy gourd

ivy green *n* **:** a variable color averaging a grayish olive green that is yellower and slightly darker and stronger than bronze green and yellower and stronger than privet

ivy league *adj, usu cap I&L* **1 a :** belonging to or characteristic of or derived from one or more of a group of long-established eastern U.S. colleges widely regarded as high in scholastic and social prestige ⟨the manager was young, *Ivy League,* and hoping for an early vice-presidency —Jay Wilson⟩ ⟨leaders with *Ivy League* backgrounds —E.J.Kahn⟩ **b :** belonging to an athletic association made up of teams representing these colleges ⟨a couple of *Ivy League* teams⟩ ⟨likely to become an *Ivy League* champion⟩ **2 :** belonging to or characteristic of the students of Ivy League colleges ⟨the *Ivy League* look⟩ ⟨an *Ivy League* suit⟩

ivy leaguer *n, usu cap I&L* **:** a student at or graduate of an Ivy League college

ivy-leaved speedwell \'=='=-\ *also* **ivy speedwell** *n* **:** a speedwell (*Veronica hederaefolia*) having reniform leaves with two or three small lobes on each side of the base

ivy-leaved toadflax *n* **:** KENILWORTH IVY

ivy owl *n* **:** BARN OWL

ivy scale *n* **:** OLEANDER SCALE

ivy-tod \'==,=\ *n* **:** a growth or clump of ivy

ivy tree *n* **1 :** a small often shrubby New Zealand evergreen tree (*Nothopanax arboreum*) of the family Araliaceae having glossy palmate leaves with 3 to 7 leaflets and large doubly compound umbels of small greenish brown flowers; *broadly* **:** any of several other New Zealand trees or shrubs of the genus *Nothopanax* **2** *dial* **:** MOUNTAIN LAUREL

ivy vine *n* **1 :** a woody vine (*Ampelopsis cordata*) of the central U.S. **2 :** VIRGINIA CREEPER

ivyweed \'==,=\ *n* **:** KENILWORTH IVY

ivywood \'==,=\ *n, dial* **:** MOUNTAIN LAUREL

IW *abbr* **1** inside width **2** isotopic weight

iwa *or* **ioa** \'ēwə\ *n* -s [Hawaiian] **:** FRIGATE BIRD

iwan \'ē,wän\ *n* -s [origin unknown] **:** a large hall or audience chamber often open on one side and found in Parthian architecture

iwis \ē'wis, ÷ī'w-\ *adv* [ME, fr. OE *gewis* certain; akin to OHG *giwisso* certainly, ON *víss* certain, Goth *unwiss* uncertain, unsure, Gk *aistos* unknown, and the prehistoric root of OE *witan* to know — more at Y-, WIT] *archaic* **:** CERTAINLY, INDEED, TRULY

ix·ia \'iksēə\ *n* [NL, fr. Gk *ixos* mistletoe, birdlime + NL *-ia;* akin to L *viscum* mistletoe, birdlime] **1** *cap* **:** a genus of southern African bulbous plants (family Iridaceae) having linear sword-shaped leaves and very showy spikes of mostly pink or purple flowers **2** -s **:** any plant of the genus *Ixia* — called also *corn lily*

ix·i·a·ce·ae \,=='āsē,ē\ [NL, fr. *Ixia,* type genus + *-aceae*] *syn of* IRIDACEAE

ixil \ē'shē(ə)l\ *n, pl* **ixil** \"\ *or* **ixils** \-lz\ *or* **ixi·les** \-shē(,)läs\ *usu cap* **1 a :** an Indian people of central Guatemala **b :** a member of such people **2 :** a Mayan language of the Ixil people

ix·o·des \ik'sō(,)dēz\ *n, cap* [NL, fr. Gk *ixōdēs* like birdlime, sticky, fr. *ixos* birdlime + *-ōdēs* -ode] **:** a widespread genus (the type of the family Ixodidae) of ticks that suck the blood of man and of many domesticated and wild mammals, transmit diseases of cattle and sheep, and sometimes cause paralysis or other severe reactions

ix·o·dic \-sädik, -sōd-\ *adj* [NL *Ixodes* + E *-ic*] **:** IXODID

¹**ix·odid** \-dəd\ *adj* [NL *Ixodidae*] **:** of, relating to, or caused by ticks of the genus *Ixodes*

²**ixodid** \"\ *n* -s **:** a tick of the genus *Ixodes*

ix·od·i·dae \-sädə,dē\ *n pl, cap* [NL, fr. *Ixodes* + *-idae*] **:** a family of ticks distinguished by the presence of a dorsal chitinous shield — see IXODES

ix·o·doid \'iksə,dȯid\ *adj* [NL *Ixodoidea*] **:** of, like, or relating to the Ixodoidea

ix·o·doi·dea \,=='dȯidēə\ *n pl, cap* [NL, fr. *Ixodes,* type genus + *-oidea*] **:** a superfamily of Acarina comprising the ticks — compare ARGASIDAE, IXODIDAE

ix·o·ra \'iksərə\ *n* [NL, irreg. fr. *Ishvara,* Hindu divinity, fr. Skt *īśvara* ruler, lord] **1** *cap* **:** a large genus of tropical shrubs or small trees (family Rubiaceae) that have leathery evergreen leaves and terminal corymbs of showy salver-shaped flowers and are often cultivated as ornamentals in the warm greenhouse **2** -s **:** any plant of the genus *Ixora*

ixtle *var of* ISTLE

iyar *or* **iy·yar** \'ē,yär, -,yər\ *n* -s *usu cap* [Heb] **:** the 8th month of the civil year or the 2d month of the ecclesiastical year in the Jewish calendar — see MONTH table

iynx \'iŋks, 'yiŋ-\ *n* -ES [L, fr. Gk] **:** WRYNECK 1

iyo \'ē(,)(y)ō\ *n* -s [origin unknown] **1 :** African piassava **2 :** a Philippine woody vine (*Tetrastigma harmandii*) of the family Vitaceae having sour but edible fruit

izar \ə'zär\ *n* -s [Hindi *izār,* fr. Ar, veil, covering] **:** a voluminous outer garment of Muslim women that covers the whole body

izard *also* **isard** \ē'zär(d)\ *n, pl* **izard** \"\ *or* **izards** \-r(z), -rdz\ [F, fr. MF, fr. MF dial. (Gascony) *isart*] **:** a chamois found in the Pyrenees

-ization *also* **-isation** \ə'zāshən *also* ,ī'z-\ *n suffix* -s [*-ize* or *-ise* + *-ation*] **:** action or process ⟨desulfur*ization*⟩ ⟨euchromat*ization*⟩ ⟨coni*zation*⟩ **:** state or result ⟨dimer*ization*⟩ ⟨immiser*ization*⟩

izba *var of* ISBA

-ize \,īz *sometimes, as in "baptize",* 'īz\ *vb suffix* -ED/-ING/-S *see -ize in Explan Notes* [ME *-isen,* fr. OF *-iser,* fr. LL *-izare,* fr. Gk *-izein*] **1 a** (1) **:** to cause to be or become or conform to or be like or resemble (something specified) ⟨system*ize*⟩ ⟨american*ize*⟩ ⟨liquid*ize*⟩ **:** cause to be formed into ⟨union*ize*⟩

⟨diphthongize⟩ (2) **:** to subject to action by or treatment of (something specified) ⟨criticize⟩ **:** subject to a (specified) action ⟨plagiarize⟩ (3) **:** to cause to have or appear to have some (specified) quality ⟨rationalize⟩ **:** act upon in such a way as to produce a (specified) result in ⟨brutalize⟩ ⟨commercialize⟩ (4) **:** to impregnate or treat or combine with (something specified) ⟨albuminize⟩ ⟨hydrogenize⟩ (5) **:** to adapt to (something specified) **:** modify by means of ⟨avianize⟩ **b :** to make (a specified thing) of **:** treat like ⟨idolize⟩ ⟨lionize⟩ **c :** to treat in the manner of or according to the method or process of (a specified individual) ⟨bowdlerize⟩ ⟨mesmerize⟩ **2 a :** to become or become like (something specified) ⟨crystallize⟩ **b :** to be productive in or of (something specified) ⟨theorize⟩ **:** engage in or carry on a (specified) activity ⟨botanize⟩ ⟨philosophize⟩ ⟨attitudinize⟩ ⟨concertize⟩ **c :** to follow after someone or something (specified) **:** adopt or spread the manner of activity or the outlook or teaching of someone ⟨calvinize⟩

izhevsk \ˈē,zhe|fsk, |vzk, |vsk, ⸗ˈ⸗; ˈēzhə|\ *adj, usu cap* [fr. *Izhevsk*, city in U.S.S.R.] **:** of or from the city of Izhevsk, U.S.S.R. **:** of the kind or style prevalent in Izhevsk

iz·mir \(ˈ)izˈmi(ə)r\ *adj, usu cap* [fr. *İzmir* (formerly Smyrna), Turkey] **:** of or from the city of Izmir, Turkey **:** of the kind or style prevalent in Izmir

izod test \ˈī,zäd-, ˈīzəd-\ *n, usu cap I* [after E. G. *Izod*, 20th cent. Eng. mechanical engineer] **:** a test of a metal's or plastic's resistance to impact that is made by determining the amount of energy in foot-pounds needed by a swinging hammer to fracture a notched test piece of the material held in a vertical position and supported at its lower end

izo·te *also* **iso·te** \əˈzōd·ē\ *n* -s [MexSp, fr. Nahuatl *iczotl*] **1 :** any of several Mexican plants of the genus *Yucca; esp* **:** SPANISH BAYONET **2 :** the coarse hard fiber of an izote resembling istle

iz·zard \ˈizə(r)d\ *n* -s [alter. of earlier *ezod, ezed*, prob. fr. MF *et zède* and Z — more at ZED] *now chiefly dial* **:** the letter z

iz·zat \ˈizət\ *n* -s [Hindi *ʻizzat*, fr. Ar *ʻizzah* glory] **1 :** personal dignity or respect **:** HONOR ⟨is against my ~ —Rudyard Kipling⟩ **2 :** power to command admiration **:** PRESTIGE ⟨afraid of losing ~⟩

J

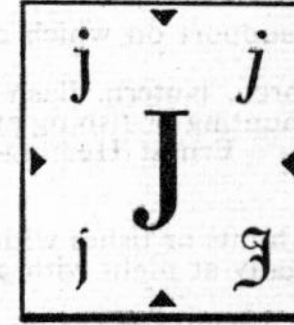

¹j \ˈjā\ *n, pl* **j's** *or* **js** \ˈjāz\ *often cap, often attrib* **1 a :** the 10th letter of the English alphabet **b :** an instance of this letter printed, written, or otherwise represented **c :** a speech counterpart of orthographic *j* (as *j* in *jump, ajar*, German *ja*, Spanish *jefe*) **2 a :** a printer's type, a stamp, or some other instrument for reproducing the letter *j* **b :** ONE — see NUMBER table **c :** a unit vector parallel to the y-axis **3 :** someone or something arbitrarily or conveniently designated *j* esp. as the 10th in order or class **4 :** something having the shape of the letter J

²j *abbr, often cap* **1** jack **2** January **3** join **4** joule **5** journal; journalism **6** [L *judex*] judge **7** July **8** June **9** junior **10** [L *jus*] law **11** justice **12** juvenile

³j *symbol, cap* **1** Yahwistic or Judean — used in biblical criticism to designate Yahwistic material esp. from an ancient epic constituting the earliest and a main source of the Hexateuch ⟨the *J* passages in the creation story⟩ ⟨the *J* text⟩ — compare D, E, P **2** *ital* mechanical equivalent of heat **3** *ital* radiant intensity

JA *abbr* **1** joint account **2** joint agent **3** judge advocate

jaag·siek·te *also* **jaag·ziek·te** *or* **jag·siek·te** *or* **jag·ziek·te** \ˈyäg,sēktə, -,zēk-\ *n* -s [Afrik *jagsiekte*, fr. *jag* hunt + *siekte* sickness] **:** an apparently infectious disease of sheep that is characterized by proliferation of the pulmonary alveolar epithelium and occlusion of the alveoli and terminal bronchioles and that is usu. held to be caused by an unidentified filterable virus

ja·al goat \ˈjāəl, ˈyäəl\ *n* [Heb *yāʻēl* wild goat] **:** an ibex (*Capra nubiana*) of the mountains of Ethiopia, Upper Egypt, and Arabia with long slender horns

¹jab \ˈjab, ˈjaa(ə)b\ *vb* **jabbed**; **jabbed**; **jabbing**; **jabs** [alter. of *job* (to strike)] *vt* **1 a :** to pierce with or as if with something sharp **:** STAB ⟨got *jabbed* in the lower part of his chest, seriously if not fatally —*Westminster Gazette*⟩ **b :** to poke quickly or abruptly **:** THRUST ⟨*jabbing* the poker among the gray ashes —Rebecca Caudill⟩ **2 :** to give a short straight blow to (as a boxing opponent) with the fist ~ *vi* **1 :** to make quick or abrupt thrusts with something sharp ⟨*jabbed* around with my spear, knocking off the stalks of dead mulleins —John Moore⟩ ⟨took up his list of dates and *jabbed* at it with a pencil —Dorothy Sayers⟩ **2 :** to strike a person with a short straight blow ⟨hooking when he should have *jabbed*, . . . his head sometimes a craning target —*Time*⟩

²jab \ˈ"\ *n* -s **:** an act of jabbing **:** a quick or abrupt thrust, stab, or punch; *specif* **:** a short straight punch in boxing delivered with the leading hand

ja·ba·li \,häbəˈlē\ *or* **ja·va·li** \-ävə-\ *n* -ES [AmerSp *jabalí*, fr. Sp, wild boar, fr. Ar *jabalīy*, short for *khinzīr jabalīy*, fr. *khinzīr* pig + *jabal* mountain] **:** PECCARY

ja·ba·li·na \,häbəˈlēnə\ *or* **jave·li·na** \-ävə-\ *n* -s **:** PECCARY

jabalpur *usu cap, var of* JUBBULPORE

jab·a·rite \ˈjabə,rīt\ *n* -s *usu cap* [Ar *jabarīy* (fr. *jabr* power, force) + E *-ite*] **:** a member of an early school of Muslim determinists who denied that man has freedom of choice and affirmed an absolute predestination fashioned by Allah

¹jab·ber \ˈjabə(r)\ *vb* **jabbered**; **jabbered**; **jabbering** \-b(ə)riŋ\ **jabbers** [ME *jaberen*, of imit. origin] *vi* **:** to talk rapidly, indistinctly, or unintelligibly **:** utter gibberish or nonsense **:** CHATTER ⟨~*ing* in incomprehensible tongues —F.L. Allen⟩ ⟨kept ~*ing* away —Edita Morris⟩ ~ *vt* **:** to speak rapidly or indistinctly ⟨~ half a dozen languages —F.L. Lucas⟩

²jabber \ˈ"\ *n* -s **:** an act of jabbering **:** rapid, incoherent, or trivial talk with indistinct utterance **:** GIBBERISH, CHATTER ⟨must we fall into the ~ and babel of discord —Sir Winston Churchill⟩

jab·ber·er \-b(ə)rə(r)\ *n* -s **:** one that jabbers ⟨sweep the ~*s* out of the way of civilization —G.B.Shaw⟩

jabbering *adj* **:** tending to or given to jabber **:** BABBLING ⟨a ~ fool⟩ ⟨was the father of three ~ daughters⟩ — **jab·ber·ing·ly** *adv*

jabbernowl \ˈjäbə(r),nōl, ˈjab-\ *var of* JOBBERNOWL

jab·ber·wocky \ˈjabə(r),wäkē, -ki\ *also* **jab·ber·wock** \-äk\ *n, pl* **jabberwockies** *also* **jabberwocks** *often attrib* [*jabberwocky* fr. *Jabberwocky*, a nonsense poem in *Through the Looking Glass* by Lewis Carroll (Charles L. Dodgson) †1898 Eng. author and mathematician; *jabberwock* fr. *Jabberwock*, the fabulous monster in the poem *Jabberwocky*] **:** meaningless speech, writing, or patter **:** GIBBERISH ⟨bringing the house down with . . . his ~ patter and his energetic clowning —*Life*⟩ ⟨began to babble in ~ —Leo Rosten⟩ ⟨carries on his heated conversations . . . in a sort of *jabberwock* —Arthur Knight⟩

jabbing *adj* [fr. pres. part. of ¹*jab*] **:** THRUSTING, STABBING ⟨a neat, crisp, ~ bitterness —*Horizon*⟩

¹jab·ble \ˈjabəl\ *vb* -ED/-ING/-s [imit.] *vt, Brit* **:** AGITATE, SPLASH ⟨*jabbled* coffee on his saucer —Michael McLaverty⟩ ~ *vi, Brit* **:** to break in small waves **:** RIPPLE

²jabble \ˈ"\ *n* -s **1** *Brit* **:** an agitation on the surface of water **:** SPLASHING, DASHING, RIPPLING **:** CHOPPINESS **2** *Brit* **:** a mental or emotional agitation or turmoil

jabim *usu cap, var of* YABIM

jab·i·ru \,jabəˈrü\ *n* -s [Pg *jabiru, jabirú*, fr. Tupi & Guarani *jaburú, jabirú*] **1 :** a large stork (*Jabiru mycteria*) of tropical America **2 a :** WOOD IBIS 1 **b :** the saddle-billed stork of Africa or a related stork of the genus *Xenorhynchus* of the East Indies and Australia

jab·o·ran·di \,jabəˈrandē\ *n* -s [Pg *jaborandi, jaborandí*, fr. Tupi *yaborandi*] **1 a :** the dried leaves of a So. American rutaceous shrub (*Pilocarpus jaborandi*) that are a source of pilocarpine — called also *Pernambuco jaborandi* **b :** the dried leaves of a closely related shrub (*P. microphyllus*) that are similarly used — called also *Maranham jaborandi* **2 :** the root of a Brazilian plant (*Piper jaborandi*) that is a source of pilocarpine

ja·bot \zhaˈbō, jaˈ-, ˈ⸗(,)⸗\ *n* -s [F, crop, jabot, fr. MF, prob. fr. a dial. word akin to OF *gave* throat, crop] **1 :** a single or tiered fall of lace, cloth, or both attached to the front of a neckband, worn esp. by men in the 18th century, and still worn by some English counsels **2 a :** a ruffle or pleated frill of cloth, lace, or both attached down the center front of a shirt, blouse, or dress bodice **b :** a similar fall of material in drapery

jabot 2a

ja·bot·i·ca·ba \jə,bäd·əˈkäbə\ *n* -s [Pg *jaboticaba, jabuticaba*, fr. Tupi] **1 :** a large shrub or small tree (*Myrciaria cauliflora*) of the family Myrtaceae native to Brazil and the West Indies but introduced into the southern U.S. having flowers and fruit borne all along the trunk and main branches and purplish fruit that resembles grapes in appearance and flavor but has tough thick skin and is borne singly or in small clusters **2 :** the fruit of the jaboticaba

jabs *pres 3d sing of* JAB, *pl of* JAB

ja·ca \ˈjäkə\ *n* -s [Pg — more at JACKFRUIT] **:** JACKFRUIT

ja·cal \həˈkäl\ *n, pl* **jaca·les** \-ä(,)lās\ *also* **jacals** [MexSp, fr. Nahuatl *xacalli*, fr. *xamitl* adobe + *calli* house] **1 :** a crude house or hut in Mexico and southwestern U.S. with a thatched roof and walls made of upright poles or sticks covered and chinked with mud or clay **2 :** the method of construction used in building a jacal

ja·cal·tec \,häkəlˈtāk\ *or* **ja·cal·te·ca** \-kə\ *n, pl* **jacaltec** *or* **jacaltecs** *or* **jacalteca** *or* **jacaltecas** *usu cap* [Sp *jacalteca*, of AmerInd origin] **1 a :** an Indian people of western Guatemala **b :** a member of such people **2 :** a Mayan language of the Jacaltec people

jac·a·mar \ˈjakə,mär\ *n* -s [F, fr. Tupi *jacamá-ciri*] **:** any of many picarian birds of the family Galbulidae inhabiting tropical forests from Mexico to Argentina, being usu. brilliant metallic green or bronze above and rufescent below with a white throat, having a long sharp bill, and feeding on insects which they catch on the wing

jac·a·mar·al·cy·on \,jakə,märˈalsēən\ *n, cap* [NL, fr. F *jacamar* + Gk *alkyōn, halkyōn* kingfisher] **:** a genus of jacamars having only three toes and including a single Brazilian form (*J. tridactyla*)

jac·a·me·ro·pine \,jakəˈmirə,pīn, -,pən\ *adj* [NL *Jacamerops* + E *-ine*] **:** of or relating to the genus *Jacamerops*

jac·a·me·rops \,⸗⸗ˈmē,räps\ *n, cap* [NL, irreg. fr. F *jacamar* + NL *-ops*] **:** a genus of birds comprising the largest of the jacamars which are about 10 inches long

¹jac·a·na \ˈjakənə\ *n* [modif. of Pg *jaçanã*, fr. Tupi & Guarani] **1** -s **:** any of several wading birds that chiefly frequent coastal freshwater marshes and ponds in warm regions, that have long slender legs and very long toes by means of which they run about over floating vegetation, a pointed bill with a frontal shield between the eyes, and usu. a sharp spur at the bend of the wing, and that constitute the nearly tropicopolitan family Jacanidae **2** *cap* [NL, fr. Pg *jaçanã*] **:** the type genus of Jacanidae comprising the New World jacanas

²ja·ca·na \ˈhäkənə\ *n* -s [AmerSp *jácana, ácana, jacana, acana*, prob. fr. Taino] **:** a West Indian timber tree (*Pouteria multiflora*) the hard dark wood of which is valued for furniture

ja·can·i·dae \jəˈkanə,dē\ *n pl, cap* [NL *Jacana*, type genus + *-idae*] **:** a small but widely distributed family of birds (suborder Charadrii) that are related to the plovers and sandpipers and comprise the jacanas

¹jac·a·ran·da \,jakərənˈdä, ,jakəˈrandə\ *n* -s [Pg *jacarandá*, fr. Tupi *yacarandá*] **1 :** any of several Brazilian timber trees (as Brazilian rosewood) with heavy dark wood that resembles rosewood **2 :** the wood of a jacaranda

²jac·a·ran·da \,jakəˈrandə\ *n* [NL & Pg; NL (the genus), fr. Pg (a tree of this genus)] **1** *cap* **:** a genus of pinnate-leaved tropical American trees (family Bignoniaceae) with showy blue flowers in panicles **2** -s **:** a tree of the genus *Jacaranda*

jac·a·re \ˈjakə,rā, ,⸗⸗ˈ⸗\ *n* -s [Pg, fr. Tupi *jacaré, yacaré*] **:** CAIMAN

ja·ca·te \həˈkä,tā\ *n* -s [MexSp] **:** a stout shrub (*Hymenoclea monogyra*) of the family Compositae of the southwestern U.S. and adjacent Mexico, having alternate leaves and heads of greenish flowers and forming dense thickets in sandy arroyos

jacent *adj, obs* [L *jacent-, jacens*, pres. part. of *jacēre* to lie — more at ADJACENT] **:** RECUMBENT, PRONE

j acid *n, usu cap J* **:** a crystalline sulfonic acid $NH_2C_{10}H_5(OH)SO_3H$ made by alkaline fusion of a disulfonic acid of beta-naphthylamine and used as an intermediate esp. for direct azo dyes; 6-amino-1-naphthol-3-sulfonic acid

¹ja·cinth \ˈjāsən(t)th, ˈjas-\ *n* -s [ME *iacinct, iacynth*, fr. OF *jacincte, jacinte, jacinthe*, fr. L *hyacinthus*, a precious stone, a flowering plant — more at HYACINTH] **:** HYACINTH; *sometimes* **:** a gem more nearly pure orange in color than a hyacinth

²jacinth \ˈ"\ *adj* **1 :** being like a jacinth **2 a** *obs* **:** HYACINTHINE **b :** being of the color jacinthe **c :** TAWNY

ja·cinthe \ˈ"\ *n* -s [F *jacinthe*, lit., hyacinth] **:** a moderate orange that is yellower and stronger than honeydew and yellower and slightly lighter than Persian orange

jac·i·ta·ra palm \jasəˈtärə-\ *also* **jacitara** *n* -s [Pg *jacitara*, fr. Tupi] **:** a Brazilian palm of the genus *Desmoncus* the distal pinnae of whose leaves are represented by retrorse hooks that enable the stem to climb — see TIPITI

¹jack \ˈjak\ *n* -s *often attrib* [ME *jacke*, fr. *Jacke*, nickname for *Johan* (John)] **1 a** (1) *cap, obs* **:** a man of the common people; *also* **:** an impertinent or rude fellow ⟨familiar both with peers and *Jacks* —*Brit. Mag.*⟩ (2) *sometimes cap* **:** a human being **:** MAN — used as an intensive in such phrases as *every man jack* ⟨virtually every man ~ —*Time*⟩ or *every jack one* ⟨dead, dead every ~ one of them —W.S.Maugham⟩ (3) *cap, slang* **:** PAL, BUDDY, GUY — usu. used in address ⟨what they get you for, *Jack* —Thurston Scott⟩ ⟨I love it all, *Jack* —Chandler Brossard⟩ **b** (1) *often cap* **:** SAILOR — called also *jack-tar* (2) *sometimes cap* **:** LABORER, SERVANT, ATTENDANT (3) **:** LUMBERJACK (4) *Austral* **:** POLICEMAN **c** (1) **:** a playing card carrying the figure of a servant or soldier and ranking usu. below the queen — called also *knave* (2) [by shortening] **:** JACKPOT 1a(4) (3) **:** a player's bet in a lottery that he can name all five numbers that will be drawn **2 a :** a figure usu. of a man that strikes the time on a bell esp. in a turret clock **b** (1) **:** any of various portable hand-operated machines for lifting heavy weights or otherwise exerting great force by utilizing the principle of the lever, screw, toggle joint, or hydraulic press (2) **:** a clamp commonly of the screw type for holding work firmly in a desired position (as in a machine) (3) **:** a usu. triangular wooden brace fastened to the floor by means of a foot iron and a stage screw and hinged to the back of a wall or other scenic unit in a stage set in order to prop it up from behind **c :** a contrivance for turning a spit **d :** an intermediate upright piece of wood at the inner end of each key in any of several keyboard instruments (as a harpsichord or piano) com-

jack 2e(3)

municating its action to the string by means of a quill, a metal tangent, or a hammer **e** (1) **:** a small white target ball at which bowls are rolled in lawn bowling (2) [prob. short for *jackstone*] **:** a small round stone **:** PEBBLE; *esp* **:** one used in the game of jacks (3) **:** a small six-pointed usu. metal object used in the game of jacks (4) **jacks** *pl but sing in constr* **:** a game played with a set of small objects (as stones, bones, or metal pieces, and often a ball) in which the players toss, catch, and move these objects in a variety of figures requiring coordination of hand and eye (5) [by shortening] **:** JACKKNIFE 2 **f :** a bat to close a masonry course **g** (1) *dial Eng* **:** one fourth of a pint; *also* **:** HALF-PINT (2) [by shortening] **:** APPLEJACK ⟨a side of beef and a gallon of ~ to wash it down —G.A.Chamberlain⟩; *also* **:** BRANDY ⟨the stuff tasted like raisin ~ —Gore Vidal⟩ ⟨an extra supply of prune ~ —*Amer. Guide Series: Pa.*⟩ **h** (1) **:** a lever for depressing the sinkers which push the loops down on the needles in a knitting machine (2) **:** a lever that raises a harness esp. on dobby looms (3) **:** CREEL 3 (4) **:** a machine like a fly frame to handle fine cotton roving **i :** a small flag showing nationality flown by a ship usu. on a jack staff at the bowsprit cap or at the bow but elsewhere in making certain signals **j** (1) **:** a bar of iron athwartships at a topgallant masthead to support a royal mast and spread the royal shrouds (2) **:** LAZY JACK 2 **k :** a pan or frame for the fuel of a torch used in hunting or fishing at night; *also* **:** the torch itself **:** JACKLIGHT 1 **l** (1) **:** a receptacle with one or more connections to electric circuits arranged for convenient plugging in of connections to other circuits (2) **:** a female metallic terminal or junction piece by means of which instruments may be quickly inserted in a line or telephone circuits quickly joined at the central office or exchange **m :** SPHALERITE **n** *slang* **:** MONEY ⟨hadn't that much ~ —Nevil Shute⟩ **3 :** something smaller than the usual or typical of its kind — used in combination ⟨~ rafter⟩ ⟨*jack*shaft⟩ **4 a :** any of several fishes: as (1) **:** PIKE, PICKEREL; *esp* **:** a young or small pike (2) **:** WALLEYED PIKE (3) **:** a fish of the family Carangidae; *esp* **:** a crevalle (*Caranx hippos*) (4) **:** a young male fish ⟨a ~ salmon⟩ **b :** the male of various animals esp. of the domestic ass or donkey **c :** any of several birds: as (1) [by shortening] **:** JACKDAW (2) [by shortening] **:** JACKSNIPE **d :** BONE SPAVIN **e** [by shortening] **:** JACKRABBIT **syn** see FLAG

²jack \"\ *vb* -ED/-ING/-S *vi* **1 :** to hunt or fish at night with a jacklight; *specif* **:** to hunt game esp. deer illegally at night by shining a spotlight that dazzles and holds immobile **2** *slang chiefly Brit* **:** to give up suddenly or readily — used with *up* ~ *vt* **1 :** to hunt or fish at night with a jacklight **:** kill with the aid of a jacklight ⟨a buck that had been ~*ed* on his own land —*N.Y. Herald Tribune*⟩ **2 a :** to move or lift by or as if by means of a jack — usu. used with *up* ⟨~ up an automobile⟩ ⟨~*ed* up my shorts —Harold Robbins⟩ **b :** RAISE, INCREASE ⟨decided to ~ their fees —*Wall Street Jour.*⟩ — usu. used with *up* ⟨stepped in to ~ up . . . the prices he got —F.L. Allen⟩ **c :** to raise the level or quality of **:** BOLSTER — usu. used with *up* ⟨~*ing* up discipline —R.M.Neal⟩ ⟨has ideas about ~*ing* up audiences —*New Yorker*⟩ ⟨this whole business of ~*ing* up the soul —P.G.Wodehouse⟩ **d :** to take to task **:** call to account **:** reprimand or scold sharply — used with *up* ⟨~*ed* up two or three men of the company —R.P.Reeder⟩ **3 :** to pass (boards) up to a piler on top of a lumber pile

³jack \"\ *n* -S [ME *jakke*, fr. MF *jaque, jaques* — more at JACKET] **1 :** a coarse cheap body garment worn for defense during the medieval period; *esp* **:** one made of leather and sometimes lined with metal **2 :** a vessel for holding liquor made orig. of waxed leather and coated on the outside with tar or pitch **:** JUG, TANKARD

⁴jack *var of* JACKFRUIT

⁵jack *var of* JACK CHEESE

jack-a-dan·dy \ˌjakə'dandē\ *n, pl* **jack-a-dandies** [¹*jack* + *a* (of) + *dandy*] **:** a little dandy **:** a little foppish impertinent fellow

¹jack·al \'jakəl *also* -ˌkȯl\ *n* -S *often attrib* [Turk *çakal*, fr. Per *shagāl, shaghāl*, fr. Skt *sṛgāla, śṛgāla*] **1 a :** any of several wild dogs of the Old World, smaller, usu. more yellowish, and less daring than wolves, sometimes hunting in packs at night but more usu. singly or in pairs, and feeding on carrion and small animals (as poultry); *esp* **:** a common wild dog (*Canis aureus*) of southeastern Europe, southern Asia, and northern Africa **b :** the fur or pelt of this animal **2 a :** a person who tends to the routine needs of or performs menial tasks for another **:** DRUDGE **b :** an individual who for mercenary or self-seeking ends serves or collaborates with another esp. in the commission of base or sordid acts ⟨blackmailed by one of his ~*s* —Edmund Wilson⟩ ⟨denounced these ~ tactics —Stringfellow Barr⟩

²jac·kal \hə'käl\ *n* -S [by alter.] **:** JACAL

jack-a'-lantern *var of* JACK-O'-LANTERN

jackal buzzard *n* **:** a southern African hawk (*Buteo rufofuscus*)

jack·a·legs \'jakəˌlegz\ *n pl but sing in constr* [alter. of *jockteleg*] *chiefly Scot* **:** a large clasp knife

jack-a-lent \'jakəˌlent\ *n, pl* **jack-a-lents** *usu cap J&L* [¹*jack* + *a* (of) + *Lent*] **1 :** a small stuffed puppet set up to be pelted as a sport in Lent **2 :** a simple or insignificant fellow **:** PUPPET

jack·a·napes \'jakəˌnāps\ *n* -ES [ME *Jack Napis, Jac Napes*, nickname for William de la Pole †1450 4th earl and 1st duke of Suffolk] **1 :** MONKEY, APE **2 a :** an impertinent or conceited fellow **:** COXCOMB ⟨beribboned ~ —Frank Yerby⟩ **b :** a pert or mischievous child

jack arch *n* [¹*jack* (something smaller)] **:** a flat arch (as a lintel with a keystone)

jack·a·roo \ˌjakə'rü\ *var of* JACKEROO

jack·ass \'jaˌkas, -kaa(ə)s, -kais *also* -kȧs *in New Eng & Brit esp (in Brit at least) in sense 2*\ *n* [¹*jack* + *ass*] **1 a :** a male ass; *also* **:** DONKEY **b** *Austral* **:** KOOKABURRA **2 :** a stupid person **:** FOOL, DOLT ⟨a conceited ~⟩ **3 :** HAWSE BAG

jackass bark *n* **1 :** a 3-masted ship square-rigged on the foremast, setting square topsails and topgallant sails over a fore-and-aft mainsail, and fore-and-aft rigged on the mizzen **2 :** a 4-masted ship square-rigged on the foremast and mainmast and gaff-rigged on the mizzen and jiggermast **3 :** a sailing ship with three or more masts and a combination of gaffsails and square sails in addition to complete square rig on its foremast

jackass bat *n* **:** a large spotted bat (*Euderma maculata*) occurring in the southwestern U. S. and having enormous ears joined across the forehead by a low band

jackass brig *n* **:** a brig-rigged ship not setting a square mainsail and having a fore-topmast and fore-topgallant mast made of one spar

jackass clover *n* **1 :** CALIFORNIA BUR CLOVER **2 :** a rank-scented annual herb (*Wislizenia refracta*) of the family Capparidaceae that has trifoliolate leaves and long-stalked yellow flowers and is found in the western U. S.

jackass deer *n* **1 :** KOB **2 :** MULE DEER

jack·ass·ery \-sərē\ *n* -ES **:** a piece of stupidity or folly **:** DOLTISHNESS ⟨the most preposterous ~ we ever heard of —Hubert Kay⟩

jackass fish *n* **:** a morwong (*Dactylopagrus macropterus*) of Australia, Tasmania, and New Zealand

jackass hare *or* **jackass rabbit** *n* **:** JACK RABBIT

jackass kingfisher *n* **:** KOOKABURRA

jack·ass·ness *n* -ES **:** the quality or state of being a jackass

jackass penguin *n* **:** a penguin (*Spheniscus demersus*) of western So. America and southern Africa whose note suggests the braying of an ass

jackass rig *n* **:** a rig differing in some particular from the type of rig to which it mainly belongs

jack bean *n* **1 :** a bushy semierect annual tropical American plant of the genus *Canavalia*; *esp* **:** a plant (*C. ensiformis*) having long pods with white seeds and grown esp. for forage — compare SWORD BEAN **2 :** the seed of the jack bean

jackbird \'=,=\ *n* **1 :** a passerine bird (*Callaeas cinerea*) of South Island, New Zealand, resembling the starling **2 :** SADDLEBACK 2d

jack block *n* **:** a block fixed aloft for raising and lowering the topgallant and royal yards of a ship

jackboot \'=,=\ *n* **1 :** a heavy military boot esp. of glossy black leather extending well above the knee and having a wide flaring top and worn esp. during the 17th and 18th centuries **2 :** a boot similar in shape to the military jackboot worn esp. by fishermen

jack box *n* **:** a connection box containing one or more jacks into which a piece of electric equipment (as a telephone or loudspeaker) may be plugged

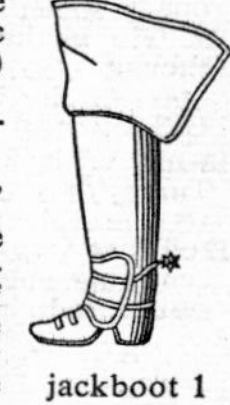
jackboot 1

jackboy \'=,=\ *n, archaic* **:** a boy (as a stableboy) who does menial work

jack-by-the-hedge \'==='=\ *n, usu cap J, dial Eng* **:** GARLIC MUSTARD

jack chain *n* **1 :** a light wire chain whose links are set at right angles to each other resembling a figure eight or having the end of each loop bent round to meet the end of the other loop **2 :** an endless toothed chain for moving logs usu. from the millpond into the sawmill

jack cheese *also* **jack** *n*, -S *often cap J* **:** a semisoft whole-milk cheese with high moisture content

jack crevalle *n* **:** a crevalle (*Caranx hippos*)

jack crow *n* **:** a rare West African bird (*Picathartes gymnocephalus*) resembling a crow and having bluish gray back and wings, white underparts, and a bright yellow and black naked head

jack curlew *n* **1 :** WHIMBREL **2 :** HUDSONIAN CURLEW

jackdaw \'=,=\ *n* [¹*jack* + *daw*] **1 :** a common bird (*Corvus monedula*) of Europe and parts of Asia that is closely related to but smaller than the common crow, is glossy black above and dark gray below with silvery gray markings on head and neck, is a clever mimic capable of learning to imitate the human voice, is gregarious in habits usu. nesting in and about buildings, and is readily tamed **2 :** GRACKLE 2; *esp* **:** BOAT-TAILED GRACKLE

jacked *past of* JACK

jack·een \ja'kēn\ *n* -S [¹*jack* + -*een* (fr. IrGael -*īn*, dim. suffix)] *Irish* **:** an obnoxious self-assertive dude ⟨a jaunty little ~ with a rich brogue —R.B.D.French⟩

jack·er \'jakə(r)\ *n* -S **:** one that jacks: as **a :** a person who hunts or fishes at night with a jacklight **b :** a worker who smooths and toughens leather by rolling it under pressure in a rolling jack **c** (1) **:** a sawmill pondman who guides logs into the jack chain that moves them to the log deck of the mill — called also *jackerman, slipman* (2) **:** JACK CHAIN

¹jack·e·roo \ˌjakə'rü\ *n* -S [alter. of *jackaroo*, fr. ¹*jack* + -*aroo* (as in *kangaroo*)] *Austral* **:** a green hand working as an apprentice on a sheep ranch

²jack·e·roo \"\ *vi* **jackerooed; jackerooed; jackerooing; jackeroos** *Austral* **:** to work as a jackeroo

¹jack·et \'jakət, *usu* -əd·+V\ *n* -S *often attrib* [ME *jaket*, fr. MF *jaquet*, dim. of *jaque, jaques* short jacket, pourpoint, jack, fr. *jacques, jacque* peasant, fr. the name *Jacques* James, Jacob] **1 a** (1) **:** a garment like a coat for the upper body usu. having a front opening, collar, lapels, sleeves, and pockets, made in varying lengths from waist to hip, and worn separately or as part of a suit ⟨cardigan ~⟩ ⟨an embroidered pajama ~⟩ (2) *Midland* **:** a man's vest **b :** something worn or fastened around the body but not for use as clothing: as (1) **:** CORK JACKET (2) **:** STRAITJACKET (3) **:** a casing for the upper part of the body usu. made of plaster and serving a supportive, corrective, or restraining purpose **2 a** (1) **:** the natural covering of an animal (as the skin of a snake or fish) (2) **:** the fur or wool of a mammal sometimes together with the skin ⟨a flock with a fine even ~ of wool⟩ (3) **:** a young seal **b :** the skin of a potato — used chiefly of cooked potatoes in the phrase *in their jackets* **3 :** an outer covering or casing: as **a :** a thermally nonconducting cover or lagging (as for a tank, pipe, or engine cylinder); *also* **:** a covering that encloses an intermediate space through which a temperature-controlling fluid may be circulated (as in water-cooling a gasoline-engine cylinder) **b** (1) **:** a cylindrical hollow forging in a built-up gun that is concentric with and shrunk usu. directly upon the tube, extends from the breech usu. to a little forward of the trunnions, and usu. contains the seat for the breechblock or breech plug (2) **:** the tough cold-worked metal casing which forms the outer shell of a built-up bullet and into which the lead is swaged to form the complete projectile **c** (1) **:** a cloth covering for a machine roller usu. woven or felted in tubular form (2) **:** a felt cover for a couch roll in a papermaking machine **d :** an easily removable form that supports a foundry mold on all four sides during pouring **e** (1) **:** a wrapper or open envelope for a document (as a letter, dispatch, or the case-history file or personal record of a prisoner, serviceman, or agency client) on which are put directions for its disposition and notations as to its contents, dates of being sent and received, or other details (2) **:** an envelope for enclosing registered mail during delivery from one post office to another **f** (1) **:** a detachable protective wrapper for a book typically consisting of a rectangular sheet of paper elaborately printed with descriptive or promotional material, cut flush at head and foot, and folded around the binding with ends tucked between cover board and free endpaper — called also *book jacket, book wrapper, dust cover, dust jacket, dust wrapper, wrapper* (2) **:** the cover of a paperbound book esp. when folded and tucked under at the fore edge (3) **:** the outside leaves for a booklet, pamphlet, or catalog which is to be stitched or wired through the saddle (4) **:** a paper or paperboard sleeve for a phonograph record

²jacket \"\ *vt* -ED/-ING/-S **:** to put a jacket on **:** enclose in or with a jacket ⟨reports which had been ~*ed* —C.R.Cooper⟩

jacket crown *n* **:** an artificial crown that is placed over the remains of a natural tooth

jacketed *adj* **1 :** wearing or having a jacket ⟨~ boys on the road⟩ **2 :** enclosed in or by a jacket ⟨~ bullets⟩

jacketing *n* -S **1 a :** fabric used for jackets **b :** JACKET 3a, 3b **2 :** BEATING ⟨gave him an awful ~⟩

jack·field ware \'jakˌfēld-\ *n, usu cap J* [fr. *Jackfield*, England] **:** pottery made at Jackfield, Shropshire, England, in the 18th century and distinguished esp. by its thick brilliant black glaze applied over a common red clay

jackfish \'=,=\ *n* [¹*jack* + *fish*] **:** JACK 4a (1)

jack fishing *n* **1 :** fishing for jacks (as pike) **2 :** fishing with a jacklight

jack-fool \'='=\ *n, usu cap J* [ME *Jakke fool*] **:** TOMFOOL

jack frost *n, cap J&F* **:** frost or frosty weather personified

jack·fruit \'jakˌfrüt\ *or* **jack** *or* **jak** \'jak\ *or* **jak·fruit** \'jak,-\ *n* -S [*jackfruit, jakfruit* fr. Pg *jaca* jackfruit (fr. Malayalam *cakka*) + E *fruit; jack, jak* fr. Pg *jaca*] **1 :** a large East Indian tree (*Artocarpus heterophyllus*) that is distinguished from the closely related breadfruit by its entire leaves, yields a fine-grained yellow wood, and is widely cultivated in the tropics for its immense fruits which contain an edible but insipid pulp and nutritious seeds that are commonly roasted **2 :** the fruit of the jackfruit **3 :** DURIAN

jackhammer \'=,==\ *n* **1 :** a rock drill of the hammer type usu. held in the hands of the operator **2 :** AIR HAMMER

jack hor·ner pie \'jak'hȯrnə(r)-\ *n, usu cap J&H* [after (*Little*) *Jack Horner*, a nursery-rhyme character depicted as pulling a plum out of a pie] **:** an ornamental pie-shaped container from which favors or toys are extracted often by pulling a ribbon at a party

jack-hunting \'=,==\ *n* **:** hunting with a jacklight

jackies *pl of* JACKY

jack-in-a-bottle \'===,=\ *n, pl* **jacks-in-a-bottle :** LONG-TAILED TIT

jack-in-a-box \'===,=\ *n, pl* **jacks-in-a-box 1 :** a tropical East Indian tree (*Hernandia sonora*) which bears a drupe that rattles in the inflated calyx when dry **2** *Brit* **:** CUCKOOPINT

jacking *n* -S **1 :** a process in spinning for giving extra twist or draft or both to the roving often done on a mule **2 :** the practice or act of hunting or fishing with a jacklight ⟨an effort to stop deer ~ —L.S.Marceau⟩

jack-in-office \'==,==\ *n, pl* **jacks-in-office** *sometimes cap J* **:** an insolent fellow in authority ⟨some little *jack-in-office* of a clerk —O.S.J.Gogarty⟩

jack-in-the-box \'===,=\ *n, pl* **jack-in-the-boxes** *also* **jacks-in-the-box** *sometimes cap J* **1** *obs* **:** SHARPER, CHEAT **2 :** a child's toy consisting of a box out of which a figure springs when the lid is raised **3 :** any of several mechanical contrivances: as **a :** DIFFERENTIAL GEAR **b :** a large wooden screw turning in a nut attached to the cross-piece of a rude press **c :** a lifting jack **:** JACKSCREW **d :** a burglar's tool for opening doors or safes by means of a small but powerful screw **e :** a jim-crow reversing tool **f :** SUN-AND-PLANET MOTION

jack-in-the-green \'===,=\ *n, pl* **jack-in-the-greens** *or* **jacks-in-the-green** *usu cap J&G* **1 :** a man or boy enclosed in a conical framework covered with leaves and boughs to take a prominent part in the May Day games of English chimney sweeps **2 :** an English primrose having sepals resembling leaves

jack-in-the-box 2

jack-in-the-pulpit \'==='=(,)=\ *n, pl* **jack-in-the-pulpits** *or* **jacks-in-the-pulpit 1 :** any of several plants of the genus *Arisaema*; *esp* **:** an American spring-flowering woodland herb (*A. atrorubens*) with sheathing leaves, an upright club-shaped spadix with open overarching green and purple spathe, and fruit consisting of a mass of bright scarlet berries — see GREEN DRAGON 2 **2 :** TURK'S-CAP LILY b **3 :** LOVE-IN-A-MIST 1 **4 :** a figwort (*Scrophularia californica*) of western No. America with dull red flowers **5 :** PRAIRIE WAKE-ROBIN

jack jumper *n* **:** a sled that consists of one thick runner curved much like a barrel stave to which is attached an upright with a seat having grips on either side of its undersurface and that is used on a slope; *also* **:** a person who rides a jack jumper

jack ketch \'jak'kech\ *n, usu cap J&K* [after *Jack* (John) *Ketch* †1686 Eng. executioner] *Brit* **:** a public executioner; *specif* **:** HANGMAN

¹jackknife \'=,=\ *n* [prob. fr. ¹*jack* + *knife*] **1 :** a large strong clasp knife for the pocket **:** a large pocket knife **2 :** a dive executed headfirst either forward or backward in which the diver beginning usu. at the highest point of the dive bends from the waist and touches or clasps his ankles while holding his knees unflexed before straightening out to enter the water

jackknife 1

²jackknife \"\ *vt* **1 :** to cut with a jackknife **2 :** to double up like a jackknife ⟨willing to ~ himself to get in and out —*Springfield (Mass.) Republican*⟩ **3 :** to cause to jackknife ⟨the tractor and trailer were *jackknifed* by the diesel —*Springfield (Mass.) Union*⟩ ~ *vi* **1 :** to double up like a jackknife ⟨~ on the sofa beside the Christmas tree —D.C.Peattie⟩ **2 :** to turn or rise and form an angle of 90 degrees or less with each other — used esp. of a pair of vehicles one of which is attached to and follows the other (as a tractor and its trailer or two railroad cars)

³jackknife \"\ *adj* **:** resembling a jackknife esp. in its manner of opening and closing ⟨a ~ drawbridge⟩ ⟨a ~ door⟩

jackknife clam *n* **:** RAZOR CLAM

jack ladder *n* **1 :** a ship's ladder with wooden rungs and side ropes **2 a :** an inclined plane up which logs are moved from pond to sawmill typically consisting of a V-shaped trough within which an endless chain carries the logs upward **b :** JACK CHAIN

jack lagging *n* **:** rough temporary lagging used in arch centering and brought to the true curve of the intrados to take the weight of the voussoirs

¹jack·leg \'jaˌkleg\ *adj* [¹*jack* + -*leg* (as in *blackleg* "sharper")] **1 a :** characterized by lack of skill or training **:** AMATEUR ⟨simplifies the labors of the ~ editor —D.L.Cohn⟩ ⟨a fair ~ carpenter —Stanley Walker⟩ **b :** characterized by unscrupulousness, dishonesty, or lack of professional standards ⟨two ~ lawyers and a cigar-eating judge —F.B.Gipson⟩ **2 :** designed for use as a temporary expedient **:** MAKESHIFT ⟨rigged up a ~ system of landing lights —W.L.White⟩

²jackleg \"\ *n* **:** one who is jackleg

³jackleg \"\ *n* [*jack*hammer + *leg*] **:** a support on which a jackhammer is mounted while drilling

¹jacklight \'=,=\ *n* [¹*jack* + *light*] **:** a torch, lantern, flashlight, or other artificial light used esp. in hunting or fishing at night ⟨spearing fish in the bay with a ~ —Ernest Hemingway⟩

²jacklight \"\ *vb* **:** JACK

jack·light·er \"+ə(r)\ *n* **:** a person who hunts or fishes with a jacklight; *esp* **:** one who hunts deer illegally at night with a jacklight

jack line *n* [¹*jack* (something smaller)] **1 :** a small rope or line **2 :** a rod or steel cable connecting a central pumping engine with each of two or more oil wells which it powers

jack mackerel *n* **:** either of two fishes of the genus *Trachurus*: **a :** a California market fish (*T. symmetricus*) that is iridescent green or bluish above and silvery below **b :** a closely related Australian fish (*T. novaezelandiae*)

jack·man \'jakmən\ *n, pl* **jackmen 1 :** a textile worker who puts copper printing shells into machines that print cloth **2 :** SCREWMAN **3 :** a repairer of shoes

jack mormon *n, sometimes cap J & usu cap M* **1 :** a non-Mormon living in a Mormon community and sympathetic to or on friendly terms with his neighbors **2 :** a Mormon inactive in the church or not adhering strictly to Mormon tenets **:** a backsliding or nominal Mormon ⟨always paid his tithes — only he had to have his coffee so some called him a *jack Mormon* —*Amer. Guide Series: Ariz.*⟩ ⟨a *Jack Mormon*, which means that . . . he no longer pays tithes or holds with the tenet of total abstinence —A.J.Liebling⟩

jacko *var of* JOCKO

jack oak *n* **1 :** BLACKJACK 5 **2 :** an extremely variable oak (*Quercus ellipsoidalis*) of east central No. America having leaves with sharply pointed lobes and ashy gray turbinate to goblet-shaped acorn cups with persistent dull pubescence

jack-of-all-trades \'=,='=,=\ *n, pl* **jacks-of-all-trades** *sometimes cap J* **:** a person who can do passable work at various trades **:** a handy or versatile individual ⟨was expected to be a *jack-of-all-trades* —Patricia M. Johnson⟩ ⟨every man would be something of a *jack-of-all-trades* —A.L.Kroeber⟩

jack off *vi* **:** MASTURBATE — usu. considered vulgar

jack-o'-lantern *or* **jack-a-lantern** *also* **jack-o'-lanthorn** \'jakə,==\ *or* **jack-with-a-lantern** \'===,=\ *n* **1 a** *obs* **:** a man carrying a lantern **:** a night watchman **b :** IGNIS FATUUS **c :** SAINT ELMO'S FIRE **d :** a lantern made of a pumpkin or other vegetable so prepared as to show in illumination features of a human face **2 :** a large luminescent mushroom (*Clitocybe illudens*)

jack-o'-lantern 1d

jack-over-the-ground \'===,=\ *n, pl* **jacks-over-the-ground :** GROUND IVY 1

jack pike *n* **:** JACK 4a (1)

jack pine *n* **1 :** a slender No. American pine (*Pinus banksiana*) having two stout twisted leaves in each fascicle, one-sided curved cones with spiny-tipped scales, and wood that is used esp. for boxwood and pulpwood **2 :** BRISTLECONE PINE **3 :** LODGEPOLE PINE **4 :** LIMBER PINE

jack-pine sawfly *n* **:** an American sawfly (*Neodiprion pratti banksianae* or *N. banksianae*) having a larva that is a serious defoliator of pine (as jack pine)

jack plane *n* **:** a medium-sized general-purpose bench plane usu. somewhat over a foot in length — see PLANE illustration

jack post *n* **:** either of the posts supporting the crankshaft of a deep-well-boring apparatus

jackpot \'=,=\ *n, often attrib* [¹*jack* (playing card) + *pot*] **1 a** (1) **:** a hand of draw poker in which every player antes in order to increase the gain to the winner and in which no player may open without a pair of jacks or better (2) **:** a game of draw poker in which a pair of jacks or better is required to open — compare ROODLE (3) **jackpots** *pl but sing or pl in constr* **:** draw poker in which every pot is a jackpot (4) **:** an unusually large pot (as in the game of poker) formed by accumulation of stakes from previous play in which no decision was reached **b** (1) **:** a combination on a slot machine which wins for a player a top prize or all the coins in the machine; *also* **:** the sum so won (2) **:** a large fund of money or other impressive reward formed by the accumulation of unwon prizes (as in a quiz contest) ⟨lost TV's biggest ~ so far —*Newsweek*⟩ ⟨the ~ question⟩ (3) : an impressive often unexpected success or reward ⟨lecturing all over the country with an occasional ~ in a friendly town —H.S.Canby⟩ **2 a :** a pool or fund contributed by a number of persons ⟨a ~ which sent the family on their way rejoicing —*Emporia (Kan.) Gazette*⟩ **b :** mail for distant separations for which a postal clerk does not immediately have room in his case and which he masses together in one box or sack for later distribution when space is available **3** *chiefly West* **:** a tight spot : JAM, SCRAPE ⟨apt to get himself and his friends into a ~ —Ross Santee⟩

jack-pudding \ˈ≠,≠\ *n, sometimes cap J* **:** BUFFOON, CLOWN, MERRY-ANDREW

¹jackrabbit \ˈ≠,≠≠\ *n* [¹*jack* (jackass) + *rabbit;* fr. its long ears] **:** any of several large hares (genus *Lepus*) of western No. America having very long ears and long hind legs and living in open country sometimes in such large numbers as to do much injury to forage and crops

²jackrabbit \"\ *vi* -ED/-ING/-S **:** to make a sudden lurch or jump or a fast start ⟨a car ~*ing* down the street —Paul Jones⟩

jack rafter *n* [¹*jack* (something smaller)] **:** a short rafter: **a :** one of the shorter rafters used in a hip or valley roof **b :** a secondary roof timber (as a common rafter resting on purlins); *also* **:** one of the pieces simulating extended rafters under the eaves in some styles of building

jackrod \ˈ≠,≠\ *n* **:** JACKSTAY

jack·roll \ˈja,krōl\ *vt* [back-formation fr. *jackroller*] **:** ROLL 7

jack·roll·er \-lə(r)\ *n* [¹*jack* + *roller*] **:** one who robs a drunken or sleeping person

jack rope *n* **:** a rope fastening the foot of a fore-and-aft sail to a boom

jack rose *n* [fr. *jack rose,* a variety of red rose, alter. of *jacqueminot rose* — more at JACQUEMINOT] **1 :** a vivid red that is bluer and deeper than apple red or scarlet and bluer and stronger than carmine **2** *usu cap J&R* **:** a cocktail consisting of lemon juice, apple brandy, and grenadine shaken in ice and strained before serving

jacks *pl of* JACK, *pres 3d sing of* JACK

jack saddle *n* **:** the saddle of a harness

jack salmon *n* **1 :** WALLEYED PIKE **2** *western No. America* **:** GRILSE; *also* **:** SILVER SALMON

jackscrew \ˈ≠,≠\ *n* **:** a screw-operated jack for lifting or for exerting pressure

jackshaft \ˈ≠,≠\ *n* [¹*jack* (something smaller) + *shaft*] **:** COUNTERSHAFT; *specif* **:** the intermediate driving shaft in an automobile

jack·shay *also* **jack·shea** \ˈjak,shā\ *n* -S [origin unknown] *Austral* **:** a bushman's quart pot used esp. for boiling water

jacks-in-the-box *pl of* JACK-IN-THE-BOX

jacks-in-the-green *pl of* JACK-IN-THE-GREEN

jacks-in-the-pulpit *pl of* JACK-IN-THE-PULPIT

jackscrew

jacksmelt \ˈ≠,≠\ *n* [¹*jack* + *smelt*] **:** a large silversides (*Atherinopsis californiensis*) of the Pacific coast of No. America that sometimes attains a length of 18 inches and is the chief commercial smelt of the California markets

jacksnipe \ˈ≠,≠\ *n, pl* **jacksnipe** *or* **jacksnipes** [¹*jack* + *snipe*] **1 :** a true snipe (*Limnocryptes minima*) of Europe and other parts of the Old World that is smaller and more highly colored than the common snipe **2 a :** PECTORAL SANDPIPER **b :** WILSON'S SNIPE **c :** any of several other snipes

jacks-of-all-trades *pl of* JACK-OF-ALL-TRADES

jack·son \ˈjaksən\ *adj, usu cap* [fr. *Jackson,* Miss.] **:** of or from Jackson, the capital of Mississippi ⟨*Jackson* merchants⟩ **:** of the kind or style prevalent in Jackson

jackson cent *n, usu cap J* [after Andrew *Jackson* †1845 7th U. S. president] **:** HARD-TIMES TOKEN

jackson day *n, usu cap J&D* [after Andrew *Jackson*] **:** the anniversary on January 8 of the successful defense of New Orleans by General Jackson in 1815 which is a legal holiday in Louisiana and generally observed by Democrats throughout the U. S.

jackson haines \-ˈhānz\ *n, usu cap J&H* [after *Jackson Haines* †1875, Amer. figure skater] **:** a figure-skating spin executed on the flat of one skate in which the body gradually assumes a low sitting position with the free leg held in front with knee bent and then gradually straightens to an erect position — called also *sit spin*

jack·so·nia \jakˈsōnēə\ *n, cap* [NL, fr. George *Jackson* 19th cent Brit. botanist + NL *-ia*] **:** a large genus of yellow-flowered Australian shrubs (family Leguminosae) with very variable leaves some of which are like needles and others merely phyllodia

¹jack·so·ni·an \(ˈ)jakˈsōnēən\ *adj, usu cap* [Andrew *Jackson* 7th president of the U. S. (1829–37) + E *-ian*] **:** of or relating to Andrew Jackson, his views or policies, or his era ⟨stunned by the sheer restlessness of *Jacksonian* America —G.W.Pierson⟩; *esp* **:** relating to a body of political ideas commonly associated with Andrew Jackson and vigorously championing the right and ability of the common man to participate in politics and administration and opposing the aristocratic principle of government ⟨*Jacksonian* democracy⟩

²jacksonian \"\ *n* -S *usu cap* **:** a follower of Andrew Jackson **:** an adherent of Jackson's principles or policies

³jacksonian \"\ *adj, often cap* [*Jacksonian* (*epilepsy*)] **:** of or resembling Jacksonian epilepsy

jacksonian epilepsy *n, usu cap J* [John H. *Jackson* †1911 Eng. neurologist + E *-ian*] **:** symptomatic epilepsy produced by injury to the brain (as by trauma or toxic agents) and manifesting symptoms that vary with the part of the brain injured

jack·son·ism \ˈjaksə,nizəm\ *n* -S, *usu cap* [Andrew *Jackson* + E *-ism*] **:** Jacksonian political principles and policies ⟨the sophisticated public, which had had too much of *Jacksonism,* was bored by stories of woodsmen and sailors —Van Wyck Brooks⟩

jack·son·ite \-sə,nīt\ *n* -S *usu cap* [Andrew *Jackson* + E *-ite*] **:** JACKSONIAN

jack·son·ville \ˈjaksən,vil, *esp S* -vəl\ *adj, usu cap* [fr. *Jacksonville,* Fla.] **:** of or from the city of Jacksonville, Fla. ⟨a *Jacksonville* garden⟩ **:** of the kind or style prevalent in Jacksonville

jackson vine *n, usu cap J* [fr. the name *Jackson*] **:** MATRIMONY VINE

jackson white *n, cap J & usu cap W* [prob. after Capt. *Jackson,* Am. slave trader in colonial times] **:** one of a group of people of mixed Negro, Indian, and white ancestry in the Ramapo mountains of New York and New Jersey

jacks-over-the-ground *pl of* JACK-OVER-THE-GROUND

jack spavin *n* **:** BONE SPAVIN

jack spool *n* **:** a large wooden spool on which is wound woolen sliver from a carding machine or woolen yarn for dyeing or warping

jack staff *n* [¹*jack* (flag)] **:** a staff which is fixed on the bowsprit cap or in the bows of a ship and upon which the jack is hoisted

jackstay \ˈ≠,≠\ *n* **1 a :** an iron rod, wooden bar, or wire rope stretching along a yard of a ship to which the sails are fastened **b :** a support of wood, iron, or rope running up and down a mast on which the parrel of a yard travels **c :** a reefing rope stretching along the reef band of a square sail from hole to hole **d :** a fixed bar or rope for hanging esp. clothes bags or for securing awning stops (as around a barbette) **2 :** a longitudinal rigging provided to maintain the correct distance between the heads of various riggings on an airship

jackstock \ˈ≠,≠\ *n* [¹*jack* (ass) + *stock*] **:** male asses

jack·stone \ˈjak,stōn\ *n* [alter. of earlier *chackstone,* alter. of *checkstone,* sing. of *checkstones*] **1 :** JACK 2e (4) — usu. used in pl. **2 :** JACK 2e (3)

jackstraw \ˈ≠,≠\ *n* [¹*jack* + *straw*] **1** *obs* **:** a man without property, worth, or influence **2 a :** one of the pieces used in the game jackstraws **b jackstraws** *pl but sing in constr* **:** a game in which a set of straws or strips (as of bone or wood) are let fall in a heap and each player in turn tries to remove them one at a time with a small instrument and without disturbing the rest of the pile **3** *dial Eng* **:** any of several small European birds using bedstraw in their nests: as **a :** WHITETHROAT **b :** GARDEN WARBLER **c :** BLACKCAP

jack stringer *n* [¹*jack* (something smaller)] **:** a bridge stringer placed outside the main stringers

jack-tar \ˈ≠ˈ≠\ *n, often cap J* **:** JACK 1b(1)

jack timber *n* [¹*jack* (something smaller)] **:** a timber (as a rafter, rib, or studding) that from being intercepted is shorter than the others with which it is used

jack tree *n* [⁴*jack*] **:** JACKFRUIT 1

jack truss *n* [¹*jack* (something smaller)] **:** a minor truss in a hip roof used where the roof has not its full section

jack wax *n* **:** a chewy confection made by pouring boiling maple syrup over snow

jack weight *n, archaic* **:** a weight attached to an endless chain and forming part of a roasting jack

jack-with-a-lantern *var of* JACK-O'-LANTERN

jackwood \ˈ≠,≠\ *n* [⁴*jack* + *wood*] **:** the wood of the jackfruit tree

jacky \ˈjaki\ *n* -ES [¹*jack* (quarter pint) + *-y*] *Brit* **:** GIN ⟨snuff . . . and excellent ~ —W.S.Gilbert⟩

jack yard *n* [¹*jack* (something smaller)] **:** a spar to extend a fore-and-aft topsail beyond the gaff

jacky winter \ˈjakē-\ *n* [fr. *Jacky,* dim. of *Jack*] **:** a small brown flycatcher (*Microeca fascinans*) of Australia

ja·cob \ˈjākəb *sometimes* -əp\ *n* -S *cap* [LL, fr. Gk *Iakōb,* fr. Heb *Ya'ăqōbh,* after *Ya'ăqōbh* (Jacob) in the Bible (Gen. 25:20 ff.), the eponymous ancestor of the Israelites] **:** the ancient Hebrew nation **:** ISRAEL ⟨yet you did not call upon me, O *Jacob;* but you have been weary of me, O Israel —Isa 43:22 (RSV)⟩

¹jaco·be·an \ˌjakəˈbēən *also* ˌjāk- *sometimes* jəˈkōb-\ *adj, usu cap* [NL *jacobaeus* Jacobean (fr. *Jacobus* —James I — †1625 king of England) + E *-an*] **:** of or relating to James I of England, his reign, or his times: as **a :** relating to or representing an early 17th century style of architecture that continued the Elizabethan style with freer use of the classical orders **b :** relating to or exemplifying an early 17th century style in furniture influenced by Renaissance models but somewhat simpler and lighter **c :** of, relating to, or typical of writers or literature of the early 17th century ⟨*Jacobean* drama⟩

²jacobean \"\ *n* -S *usu cap* **:** a Jacobean statesman or writer

³jacobean \"\ *adj, usu cap* [NL *jacobaeus* Jacobean (fr. LL *Jacobus* St. James — in the Bible, Gal 1:19, Jas 1:1, et al. —, fr. Gk *Iakōbos,* fr. Heb *Ya'ăqōbh* Jacob) + E *-an*] **:** of or relating to the New Testament Epistle of James or to its author

jacobean lily *n, often cap J* [³*Jacobean*] **:** a Mexican bulbous herb (*Sprekelia formosissima*) of the family Amaryllidaceae cultivated for its handsome bright red solitary flower — called also *Aztec lily*

ja·co·bi·an \jəˈkōbēən, yə-\ *also* **jacobian determinant** *n* -S *usu cap J* [K. G. J. *Jacobi* †1851 Ger. mathematician + E *-an*] **:** a determinant in which the elements of the first column are the partial derivatives of the first of a set of *n* functions with respect to each of *n* independent variables, those of the second column the partial derivatives of the second function with respect to each independent variable, and so on

jaco·bin \ˈjakəbən *sometimes* ˈjāk- *or* jəˈkōb-\ *n* -S *usu cap* [ME, fr. MF, fr. ML *Jacobinus,* fr. LL *Jacobus* St. James, + L *-inus* -ine; fr. the location of the first Dominican convent in the street of St. James (Rue St.-Jacques) in Paris] **1 :** DOMINICAN **2** [F, fr. *Jacobin* Dominican; fr. the group's having been founded in the Dominican convent in Paris in 1789] **a :** a member of an extremist political group advocating equalitarian democracy and famous for its terrorist policies during the French Revolution of 1789 **b :** a political extremist or radical; *esp* **:** one that advocates the attainment of equalitarian democracy usu. by revolutionary or violent methods ⟨the children of the Boston Federalists grew up under the impression that Democrats, or *Jacobins,* as they were called, were repulsive creatures —C.G.Bowers⟩ **3 a :** a breed of fancy pigeons whose neck feathers are reversed and so form a fluffy hood **b** [F, fr. *Jacobin,* Dominican; fr. the resemblance of the head and neck of such birds to the hood of a Dominican] **:** a tropical American hummingbird of the genus *Florisuga* (esp. *F. mellivora*)

jaco·bin·ia \ˌjakəˈbinēə, ˌjāk-\ *n* [NL, fr. *Jacobina,* Brazil + NL *-ia*] **1** *cap* **:** a genus of tropical American herbs and shrubs (family Acanthaceae) having tubular red or orange bilabiate flowers with two stamens **2** -S **:** any plant of the genus *Jacobinia*

jaco·bin·ic \ˌjakəˈbinik, -nēk *sometimes* ˌjāk-\ *or* **jaco·bin·i·cal** \-nəkəl, -nēk-\ *adj, usu cap* **:** of or relating to the Jacobins or Jacobinism — **jaco·bin·i·cal·ly** \-nək(ə)lē, -nēk-, -li\ *adv, usu cap*

jaco·bin·ism \ˈ≠≠bə,nizəm\ *n* -S *usu cap* [F *jacobinisme,* fr. *jacobin* + *-isme* -ism] **:** the principles and practice of the Jacobins: **a :** the egalitarianism and terrorism of the Jacobins of the French Revolution of 1789 **b :** any violent or revolutionary political extremism ⟨*Jacobinism* . . . means in practice government by a rabble —G.H.Sabine⟩

jaco·bin·ize \-,nīz\ *vt* -ED/-ING/-S *often cap* **:** to make Jacobinic **:** convert to Jacobinism

¹jaco·bite \ˈjakə,bīt *also* ˈjāk-; *usu* -īd-+V\ *n* -S *usu cap* **1** [ME, fr. ML *Jacobita,* fr. *Jacobus* Baradaeus (Jacob Baradai) †578 Syrian monk, founder of the Jacobite Church + L *-ita* -ite] **:** a member of a Syrian monophysite church **2** [ML *Jacobita,* fr. LL *Jacobus* St. James + L *-ita* -ite — more at JACOBIN] **:** DOMINICAN **3** [*Jacobus* (James II) †1701 king of England + E *-ite*] **:** a partisan of James II of England or the Stuarts after the revolution of 1688

²jacobite \"\ *adj, usu cap* **:** of or relating to the Jacobites

jaco·bit·i·cal \ˌ≠≠ˈbid·ə̇kəl, -it-, ˌēk-\ *also* **jaco·bit·ish** \ˈ≠≠,bīd·ish, -īt-, ˌēsh\ *adj, usu cap* [¹*Jacobite* + *-ical* or *-ish*] **:** of or relating to the Stuart pretenders to the English crown or their adherents

jaco·bit·ism \ˈ≠≠,bīd·,izəm\ *n* -S *usu cap* [¹*Jacobite* + *-ism*] **:** the cause and activities of the English Jacobites

ja·cobs·ite \ˈjākəb,zīt *sometimes* -kəp,sīt\ *n* -S [F *jakobsite,* fr. *Jakobsberg,* Sweden, its locality + F *-ite*] **:** a black magnetic isometric mineral $MnFe_2O_4$ consisting of an oxide of manganese and iron and constituting a member of the magnetite series

jacob's ladder *n, usu cap J* [after *Jacob* (Israel), the eponymous ancestor of the twelve tribes of Israel in the Bible, who in a dream saw a ladder extending from earth to heaven (Gen 28:12), fr. LL, fr. Gk *Iakōb,* fr. Heb *Ya'ăqōbh*] **1 a :** a pinnate-leaved European perennial herb (*Polemonium caeruleum*) with bright blue or white flowers —called also *charity, Greek valerian* **b :** any of several related American herbs (as *P. vanbruntiae*) **2 :** CARRION FLOWER 1 **3 :** a marine ladder of rope or chain with wooden or iron rungs **4 :** an elevator consisting typically of an endless chain and buckets used in lifting coal and other materials

jacob's ladder 3

ja·cob·son's cartilage \ˈjākəbs(ə)nz-, -kəps(-\ *or* **jacobson's turbinal** *n, usu cap J* [after Ludvig L. *Jacobson* †1843 Danish surgeon and anatomist] **:** a narrow process of cartilage between the vomer and the cartilage of the nasal septum

jacobson's nerve *n, usu cap J* [after L.L.*Jacobson*] **:** TYMPANIC NERVE 1

jacobson's organ *n, usu cap J* [after L.L.*Jacobson*] **:** a slender horizontal canal in the nasal mucosa that ends in a blind pouch, has an olfactory function, and is rudimentary in adult man but highly developed in most reptiles

jacob's-rod \ˈ≠≠ˈ≠\ *n, pl* **jacob's-rods** *usu cap J* [after *Jacob* in the Bible, who is mentioned as peeling rods of poplar (Gen 30:37)] **:** an asphodel of the genus *Asphodeline*

jacob's staff *n, usu cap J* [after *Jacob* St. James, symbolized in religious art by a pilgrim's staff — more at JACOBIN] **1** *obs* **:** a pilgrim's staff **2 a** *obs* **:** CROSS-STAFF 2 **b** *also* **jacob staff :** a short square rod with a cursor used for measuring heights and distances **c** *also* **jacob staff :** a straight rod or staff pointed and shod with iron at the bottom for insertion in the ground, having a socket joint at the top, and used instead of a tripod for supporting a compass **3** *obs* **:** a staff with a sword or dagger concealed in it

jacob's-staff \ˈ≠≠ˈ≠\ *n, pl* **jacob's-staffs** *usu cap J* [*Jacob's staff* (pilgrim's staff)] **1 :** GREAT MULLEIN **2 :** a plant of the genus *Fouquieria*

ja·co·bus \jəˈkōbəs\ *n* -ES *usu cap J* [after *Jacobus* (King James I) †1625 king of England, during whose reign unites were coined] **:** UNITE

jac·o·net \ˈjakə,net, -,nət, ˌ≠≠ˈnet\ *n* -S [modif. of Urdu *jagannāthī,* fr. *Jagannāth* (Puri), India, where such cloth was first made] **:** a lightweight cotton cloth resembling lawn that is used with or without a semiglaze for clothing and is given a waterproof finish for use in bandages

ja·co·pev·er \ˌyäkəˈpevə(r)\ *n* -S [Afrik *jakopewer,* prob. irreg. fr. *Jacob Evertsen,* 17th cent. Du. sea captain with bulging eyes and red face] **:** any of several large-eyed reddish food fishes of southern Africa; *esp* **:** a common scorpaenid fish (*Sebastichthys capensis*)

ja·cot tool \zhaˈkō, ja-, ˈ≠(,)≠\ *n, usu cap J* [prob. intended as trans. of F *tour Jacot,* lit., Jacot lathe, prob. fr. the name *Jacot*] **:** a small hand lathe in which watch pivots are burnished or polished

jac·quard \ˈja,kärd, jəˈk-, -kȧd\ *n* -S *often cap* [after Joseph M. *Jacquard* †1834 French inventor] **1 a :** a loom apparatus or head for weaving figured fabrics that has a mechanism controlled by a chain of variously perforated cards which cause the warp threads to be lifted in the proper sequence for producing figures **b** *or* **jacquard loom :** a loom having a jacquard **2 :** a fabric of jacquard weave or jacquard-knitted pattern

jacquard board *n, often cap J* **:** a tough and very stiff jute board or pressboard used for making jacquard cards

jacquard knitting *n, often cap J* **:** machine knitting with a jacquard attachment that makes patterns by the use of colored yarns

jacquard weave *n, often cap J* **:** an intricate variegated weave made on a jacquard loom and used for brocade, tapestry, and damask

jacque·mi·not \ˈjakmə,nō\ *n* -S [*Jacqueminot* or *General Jacqueminot,* a variety of red rose, after Viscount Jean François *Jacqueminot* †1865 French general] **:** RASPBERRY RED

jacque·rie \zhäˈkrē\ *n* -S *often cap* [F, fr. *jacquerie,* the 1358 peasant revolt in France, fr. MF, fr. *jacques, jacque* peasant + *-erie* -ery — more at JACKET] **1 :** a peasants' revolt **2 :** the peasant class ⟨stormed and sacked by a famished *Jacquerie* —*Times Lit. Supp.*⟩

jac·tance \ˈjaktən(t)s\ *or* **jac·tan·cy** \-nsē\ *n, pl* **jactances** *or* **jactancies** [MF & L; MF *jactance,* fr. L *jactantia,* fr. *jactant-, jactans* (pres. part. of *jactare* to throw, shake, speak out, boast) + *-ia* -y — more at JET] **:** vainglorious boasting ⟨~, vanity, peculation to the ruin of 20 years' labor —Ezra Pound⟩

jac·ta·tion \jakˈtāshən\ *n* -S [L *jactation-, jactatio,* fr. *jactatus* (past part. of *jactare*) + *-ion, -io* -ion] **1 :** boastful declaration or display ⟨one of his familiar ~s of imperfection —George Saintsbury⟩ **2** [prob. fr. F, fr. L] **:** a throwing or tossing of the body; *specif* **:** JACTITATION

jac·ti·tate \ˈjaktə,tāt\ *vi* -ED/-ING/-S [LL *jactitatus,* past part. of *jactitare,* freq. of L *jactare*] **:** to toss or jerk the body about

jac·ti·ta·tion \ˌ≠≠ˈtāshən\ *n* -S [LL *jactitation-, jactitatio,* fr. *jactitatus* + *-ion-, -io* -ion] **1 a** *archaic* **:** boastful public assertion or ostentation **b :** false boasting or claim or other false assertion made or repeated to the prejudice of another person: as (1) *or* **jactitation of marriage :** false and actionable pretension that one is married to someone (2) **:** SLANDER OF TITLE **2 :** a tossing to and fro or jerking and twitching of the body or its parts **:** excessive restlessness esp. in certain psychiatric disorders

ja·cu \jəˈkü\ *n* -S [Pg *jacu, jacú,* fr. Tupi *jacú*] **:** a So. American guan (esp. *Penelope obscura jacquaçu*)

jacua *var of* JAGUA

jac·u·late \ˈjakyə,lāt\ *vt* -ED/-ING/-S [L *jaculatus,* past part. of *jaculari* — more at EJACULATE] **:** to throw or hurl forward (as a dart)

jac·u·la·tion \ˌ≠≠ˈlāshən\ *n* -S [L *jaculation-, jaculatio,* fr. *jaculatus* + *-ion-, -io* -ion] **:** the act of pitching, throwing, or hurling ⟨hills hurled to and fro with ~ dire —John Milton⟩

ja·cun·da \ˌjäkünˈdä\ *n, pl* **jacunda** *or* **jacundas** *usu cap* [Pg *jacundá,* of AmerInd origin] **1 a :** a Tupian Indian people of northern Brazil **b :** a member of such people **2 :** the language of the Jacunda people

jac·u·tin·ga \ˌjakyəˈtiŋgə\ *n* -S [Pg, fr. Tupi, lit., white jacu] **1 :** a So. American guan (*Pipile jacutinga*) **2** [Pg, fr. *Jacutinga,* village in the state of Rio de Janeiro, Brazil, its locality] **:** a hematitic iron ore that occurs in Brazil and is characterized by thin bedding or lamination

¹jade \ˈjād\ *n* -S [ME] **1 :** a broken-down, vicious, or worthless horse **:** PLUG ⟨strick his armed heels against the panting sides of his poor ~ —Shak.⟩ **2 a :** a low or shrewish woman **:** WENCH, TERMAGANT ⟨the painted ~ into which inevitably she degenerated —Maurice Valency⟩ **b :** a flirtatious girl **:** MINX ⟨a laughing ~ of not ungentle mold —J.G.Saxe⟩

²jade \"\ *vt* -ED/-ING/-S **1 a :** to make a jade of (a horse) **:** wear out by overwork or abuse ⟨when a horse approaches the goal, he does not, unless he is *jaded,* slacken his pace —William Cowper⟩ **b :** to tire by severe or tedious tasks **:** FATIGUE, FAG ⟨constant repetition of often trivial material ~s one's palate —Thomas Heinitz⟩ **2** *obs* **:** to make ridiculous or expose to scorn ⟨do not now fool myself, to let imagination ~ me —Shak.⟩ ~ *vi* **:** to become weary **:** lose heart **:** FLAG ⟨when I feel my Muse beginning to ~, I retire to the solitary fireside of my study — Robert Burns⟩ **syn** see TIRE

³jade \"\ *n* -S [F, fr. obs. Sp (*piedra de la*) *ijada,* lit., loin stone; Sp *ijada* loin, fr. L *ilia,* pl. of *ilium, ileum* groin, viscera; fr. the belief that jade cures renal colic — more at ILEUM] **1 :** a tough compact gemstone that is commonly green but sometimes whitish and takes a high polish: **a :** jade derived from jadeite — called also *imperial jade, true jade* **b :** jade derived from nephrite **2 :** JADE GREEN

jaded *adj* [fr. past part. of ²*jade*] **1 :** fatigued by overwork or abuse **:** WORN OUT, EXHAUSTED ⟨come in plenty ~, looking as thin and gaunt as a gutted snowbird —F.B.Gipson⟩ **2 :** dulled by surfeit or excess **:** SATIATED ⟨might pall on ~ appetites —*Americana Annual*⟩ ⟨all the gilded corruption of a ~ and perverted group of men and women —Pamela Taylor⟩ — **jad·ed·ly** *adv* — **jad·ed·ness** *n* -ES

jade gray *n* **:** a variable color averaging a grayish green that is bluer and duller than average bayberry, bluer, lighter, and stronger than slate green, and yellower and slightly darker than average blue spruce (sense 2a)

jade green *n* **1 :** a variable color averaging a light bluish green that is greener and deeper than robin's-egg blue (sense 2), Eton blue, or turquoise (sense 2b) **2** *of textiles* **:** a variable color averaging a moderate yellowish green that is yellower, lighter, and stronger than tarragon, yellower, lighter, and slightly less strong than malachite green, and yellower and stronger than verdigris

jade·ite \ˈjā,dīt\ *n* -S [F, fr. *jade* + *-ite*] **1 :** a monoclinic mineral $NaAlSi_2O_6$ found chiefly in Burma that consists of a sodium aluminum silicate and when cut constitutes a valuable variety of jade **2 :** a light green that is bluer and deeper than average mint green and bluer and paler than serpentine

jade plant *n* **:** any of various plants of the genus *Crassula* (as *C. argentea* and *C. arborescens*)

jadesheen \ˈ≠,≠\ *n* **:** AMERICAN GREEN

jadestone \ˈ≠,≠\ *n* **:** ³JADE 1

jad·ish \ˈjādish\ *adj* [¹*jade* + *-ish*] **:** having the qualities or characteristics of a jade — **jad·ish·ly** *adv* — **jad·ish·ness** *n* -ES

jady \ˈjādē\ *adj, usu* -ER/-EST [¹*jade* + *-y*] **:** JADISH

jae·ger *also* **ja·ger** \ˈyāgə(r)\ *n* -S [G *jäger,* lit., hunter, fr. OHG *jagāri,* fr. *jagōn* to hunt + *-āri* -er — more at YACHT] **1** *or* **jä·ger** \"\ **:** a German or Austrian rifleman: **a :** one belonging to a military unit composed chiefly of huntsmen using their own weapons **b :** one belonging to a mobile light-infantry unit **2** *or* **jäger a :** HUNTER, HUNTSMAN **b :** an attendant on a person of rank or wealth dressed in hunter's costume **3 :** any of several large and spirited rapacious birds of the family Stercorariidae (as *Stercorarius parasiticus*) that inhabit the northern seas, are usu. blackish brown above and lighter below or chiefly sooty brown or blackish with the bill hooked and cered, are strong flyers, and harass weaker birds until they drop or disgorge their prey — called also *marlinespike;* compare PARASITIC JAEGER, POMARINE JAEGER

1jag \ˈjag, -aa(ə)-, -ai-\ *n* -s [ME *jagge*] **1 a :** one of a series of dangling tabs along the edge of a garment used esp. for ornamentation of medieval apparel **:** DAG **b :** a slashed section or slit of a garment revealing an underlying piece of another color used esp. in Renaissance apparel **2** *now dial* **:** SHRED, RAG, TATTER **3** *now dial Eng* **:** a projecting hair or bristle or a hairy or bristly outgrowth (as the awn of oats) **4 :** a sharp projecting part or protuberance **:** TOOTH, BARB **5** *chiefly Scot* **:** PRICK, STAB, JAB **6 :** a piece of metal screwed on the ramrod of a rifle to hold a rag or tow and used for cleaning the barrel **7 :** JAG BOLT

2jag \"\ *vb* **jagged** \-gd\ **jagged** \"; *see* JAGGED *adj*\ **jagging; jags** [ME *jaggen,* fr. *jagge,* n.] *vt* **1** *now dial* **:** STAB, JAB **2 a :** to slash or pink (a garment) with jags **b :** to cut teeth or other indentations into **c :** to make (an edge) ragged by cutting or notching **:** cut unevenly ⟨his hand shook and *jagged* the leaf⟩ ~ *vi* **1 :** PRICK, THRUST ⟨blackest jealousy *jagging* at their hearts —Llewelyn Powys⟩ **2 :** to move in jerks ⟨a blunt tool not only ~*s* and takes longer to cut but . . . will not cut cleanly —Albert Toft⟩ **:** JOG

3jag \"\ *n* -s [origin unknown] **1 a :** a small or part load ⟨a ~ of hay⟩ **b :** a trip for fetching a jag ⟨on the last ~ before dark⟩ **c** *chiefly dial* **:** PORTION, QUANTITY ⟨give the bay mare a ~ of oats⟩ ⟨people bought ~*s* of things they didn't need⟩ **2 a :** a state or feeling of exhilaration or intoxication esp. when induced by liquor **:** an inebriating load (as of liquor) ⟨had a good ~ on when he left the bar⟩ **:** THRILL ⟨takes the stuff because it gives him a ~⟩ **b :** a period of unrestrained indulgence (as in liquor or an emotion) **:** BENDER, SPREE ⟨went on a weekend ~ to forget his troubles⟩ ⟨addicts on marijuana ~*s*⟩ ⟨enjoying a sentimental ~⟩ **:** SPELL ⟨bringing them to tears . . . and ending in a crying ~ himself —Dixon Wecter⟩ **3** *chiefly Scot* **:** a leather bag or pouch

4jag \"\ *vt, dial* **:** to convey (a load of something) from one place to another **:** CARRY

JAG *abbr* judge advocate general

ja·ga·tai \ˌjagəˈtī\ *n* -s *usu cap* [fr. *Jagatai,* region in central Asia approximately equivalent to Turkistan, fr. *Jagatai* †1242 Mongol ruler who governed it] **1 :** any of various Eastern Turkic languages: as **a :** UIGHUR 2a **b :** UZBEK 2 **2 :** the Eastern Turkic languages collectively

jag bolt *n* [*1jag*] **:** an anchor bolt with a barbed flaring shank which resists retraction when leaded into stone or set in concrete — called also *hacked bolt, rag bolt*

jageer *var of* JAGIR

ja·gel·lo \yäˈge(ˌ)lō\ *or* **ja·giel·lo** \yägˈye-\ *n* -s *usu cap* [after Ladislas II (or V) *Jagello* (Pol *Jagiełło*) †1434 grand duke of Lithuania and king of Poland] **:** a member of a dynasty ruling in Lithuania, Poland, Hungary, and Bohemia during the 14th, 15th, and 16th centuries

ja·gel·lo·ni·an \ˌyägəˈlōnēən\ *or* **ja·giel·lo·ni·an** \-gyəˈ-\ *or* **ja·gel·lon** \ˈyägəˌlōn\ *or* **ja·giel·lon** \-gyəˈ-\ *adj, usu cap* **:** of or relating to the Jagellos

1jager *or* **jäger** *var of* JAEGER

2ja·ger *or* **jae·ger** \ˈyägə(r)\ *n* -s [fr. *Jagers*fontein, town in southwestern Orange Free State, Union of So. Africa, where such diamonds are mined] **:** a high-quality diamond of bluish white grade

jaggar *var of* JUGGER

1jag·ged \ˈjagəd, -aag-, -aig-\ *adj, often* -ER/-EST [ME, fr. *jagge* jag + *-ed*] **1 :** having a sharply uneven edge or surface **:** marked by jags ⟨the ~ skyline of the city⟩ ⟨a ~ coastline with deep coves and rocky points⟩ ⟨a ~ bolt of lightning⟩ ⟨blasted out great ~ chunks of stone⟩ **2 :** having a harsh or rough quality **:** RAGGED ⟨her voice was ~ with excitement —Sinclair Lewis⟩ **:** RUGGED ⟨some of his ideas, once so ~ and uncompromising, have been smoothed by time —Herbert Kupferberg⟩ **3 :** marked by sharply broken or violently varying movement **:** abruptly irregular ⟨harsh, stubborn harmonies, his ~ rhythms —*Time*⟩

2jagged \-gd\ *adj* [*3jag* + *-ed*] *slang* **:** DRUNK

jag·ged chickweed \-gəd-\ *n* **:** a European herb (*Holosteum umbellatum*) naturalized in eastern No. America and having several white flowers in a long-stalked umbel

jag·ged·ly \-gədlē, -li\ *adv* **:** in a jagged manner

jag·ged·ness \-gədnəs\ *n* -ES **:** the quality or state of being jagged

1jag·ger \-gə(r)\ *n* -s [*2jag* + *-er*] **1 :** one that jags; *specif* **:** JAGGING WHEEL **2** *chiefly dial* **:** something sharp or prickly: as **a :** BRAMBLE, THORN **b :** a frayed bit of wire on a worn cable

2jagger \"\ *n* -s [*3jag* + *-er*] *dial Brit* **:** one that carries a jag: as **a :** an itinerant peddler **b :** PACKHORSE

3jagger \"\ *n* -s [D *jager,* lit., hunter, fr. MD, fr. *jagen* to hunt + *-er* — more at YACHT] *archaic* **:** a boat accompanying a fishing fleet to supply and empty the boats

jag·gery *also* **jag·ghery** *or* **jag·ga·ry** \-gərē\ *n* -ES [Hindi *jāgrī;* perh. akin to Skt *śarkarā* gravel, grit, sugar — more at SUGAR] **:** an unrefined brown sugar made esp. from palm sap (as in India)

jaggery palm *n* **:** an East Indian palm (*Caryota urens*) having stout-petioled pinnate leaves with wedge-shaped divisions and being a chief source of jaggery — called also *toddy palm*

jagging *pres part of* JAG

jagging wheel *n* [fr. pres. part. of *2jag*] **:** a wheel with a zigzag or jagged edge for cutting cakes or pastry into ornamental figures

jagging wheel

jag·gy \-gē\ *adj* **jaggier; jaggiest** [*1jag* + *-y*] **1 :** having or abounding in jags **:** JAGGED, NOTCHED, UNEVEN, ROUGH ⟨~ teeth⟩ **2** *chiefly Scot* **:** PRICKLY

ja·gir *also* **ja·ghir** *or* **ja·ghire** *or* **ja·geer** *or* **ja·gheer** \jəˈgi(ə)r\ *n* -s [Per *jāgīr,* fr. *jā* place + *-gīr* keeping, holding (fr. *giriftan* to seize, hold)] **:** a grant of the public revenues of a district in northern India or Pakistan to a person with power to collect and enjoy them and to administer the government in the district; *also* **:** the district so assigned, the revenue from it, or the tenure by which it is held — compare ENAM

ja·gir·dar *also* **ja·ghir·dar** *or* **ja·ghire·dar** *or* **ja·geer·dar** *or* **ja·gheer·dar** \-ˌdär\ *n* -s [Per *jāgīrdār,* fr. *jāgīr* + *-dār* holder — more at BHUMIDAR] **:** the holder of a jagir

ja·gla \ˈjäglə\ *n* -s [of Indic origin; akin to Skt *chāgala* goat] **:** SEROW

jag·less \ˈjagləs, -aag-, -aig-\ *adj* [*3jag* + *-less*] **:** having or producing no jag ⟨a stimulating but ~ beverage⟩

jags *pl of* JAG, *pres 3d sing of* JAG

jagsiekte *or* **jagziekte** *var of* JAAGSIEKTE

jag spike *n* [*1jag*] **:** BOLT

1ja·gua \ˈhägwə\ *also* **ja·cua** \-äkwə\ *n* -s [Sp *jagua,* fr. Taino *ŝawa*] **:** GENIPAP

2ja·gua \", ˈyä-\ *n* -s [modif. of Sp *yagua* — more at YAGUA] **:** INAJA

jag·uar \ˈjag|ˌwär, ˈjaig|, |ˌwå(r *also* -gyə| *sometimes* |ˌwə(r) *or* ÷ -gə|\ *n, pl* **jaguars** *also* **jaguar** [Sp & Pg; Sp *yaguar, jaguar* & Pg *jaguar* fr. Tupi *jaguara* & Guarani *yaguara*] **:** a large powerful cat (*Felis onca*) ranging from Texas to Paraguay but extremely rare in the northern part of its range, having a larger head, heavier body, and shorter thicker legs than the leopard or the cougar, and being of brownish yellow or buff color marked with black spots each of which is surrounded by a somewhat broken ring of smaller ones

jaguar

jag·ua·run·di \ˌjagwəˈrəndē, ˌjaig-, -gyəw-\ *also* **jag·ua·ron·di** \-rän-\ *n* -s [Amer Sp & Pg, fr. Guarani *yaguarundi* & Tupi *jaguarundi*] **:** a slender long-tailed short-legged grayish wildcat (*Felis jaguarondi*) widely distributed from Mexico to Patagonia — see EYRA

ja·güey \häˈgwā\ *n* -s [Amer Sp, fr. Taino] **:** any of several trees of the genus *Ficus; esp* **:** BANYAN

jah \ˈyä, ˈjä, |ä\ *cap, var of* YAH

ja·hi·li·ya \ˌjähəˈlē(y)ə\ *n, cap* [Ar *jāhilīyah*] **:** the pre-Islamic period in Arabia

jahrzeit *often cap, var of* YAHRZEIT

jahve *or* **jahveh** *cap, var of* YAHWEH

jahvism *or* **jahwism** *cap, var of* YAHWISM

jahvist *or* **jahwist** *usu cap, var of* YAHWIST

jahwe *or* **jahweh** *cap, var of* YAHWEH

jai alai \ˈhīˌlī *also* ˌhīəˈlī\ *n, pl* **jai alais** [Sp, fr. Basque, fr. *jai* festival + *alai* merry] **:** a game of Basque origin resembling handball and played (as in Spain and Latin America) on a large walled court by usu. two or four players who use a long curved wicker basket strapped to the right wrist to catch and hurl the ball against the front wall to make it rebound in such a way that the opponent cannot return it before it has bounced more than once — see CESTA, FRONTON, PELOTA

jai alai basket

1jail \ˈjāl, *esp before pause or consonant* -āəl\ *n* -s [ME *jaiole, jaile,* fr. OF *jaiole,* fr. (assumed) VL *caveola,* dim. of L *cavea* cavity, cage — more at CAGE] **1 :** PRISON **2 :** a building for the confinement of persons held in lawful custody (as for minor offenses or some future judicial proceeding) **:** LOCKUP **3 :** confinement in a jail ⟨kept in ~ until he posted bond⟩ ⟨sentenced to ~ for 30 days⟩

2jail \"\ *vt* -ED/-ING/-S **:** to confine in or as if in a jail **:** lock up **:** IMPRISON

jailbait \ˈ=ˌ=\ *n* **1 :** a temptation to commit an offense for which one can be jailed **2** *slang* **:** a girl under the age of consent with whom unlawful sexual intercourse constitutes statutory rape ⟨knocked up some little ~ —Maritta Wolff⟩

jailbird \ˈ=ˌ=\ *n* **:** a person who is or has been confined in jail; *specif* **:** one jailed long or often

jailbreak \ˈ=ˌ=\ *n* **:** a forcible escape from jail

jail delivery *n* **1 :** the clearing of a jail by bringing the prisoners to trial or by having the legality of their commitments reviewed **2 :** the freeing esp. by force of prisoners in a jail

jail·er *or* **jail·or** \ˈjālə(r)\ *n* -s [ME *jailer,* fr. OF *jaiolier,* fr. *jaiole* + *-ier* -er] **1 :** a keeper of a jail or prison **:** GUARD **2 :** one that restricts another's liberty as if by imprisonment

jail fever *n* **:** TYPHUS 1a

jailhouse \ˈ=ˌ=\ *n* **:** JAIL

jail liberties *or* **jail limits** *n pl* **:** a space or district around a jail which is legally considered as part of the prison and within which a prisoner (as a debtor) is allowed to go at large under a bond of security

1jain \ˈjīn, ˈjān\ *also* **jai·na** \-nə\ *or* **jain·ist** \-nəst\ *n* -s *usu cap* [*jain* fr. Hindi, fr. Skt *jaina,* fr. *jina* saint, victorious, fr. *jayati* he conquers; *jaina* fr. Skt; *jainist* fr. Hindi *jain* + E *-ist;* akin to Gk *bia* force] **:** an adherent of Jainism

2jain \"\ *or* **jaina** \"\ *also* **jainist** \"\ *adj, usu cap* **:** of or relating to the Jains or Jainism

jain·ism \-ˌnizəm\ *n* -s *usu cap* **:** a religion of India historically traceable to the jina Vardhamana Mahavira of the 6th century B.C. having scriptures, temples, a cultus, and a monastic class and being characterized by the belief that while gods control the realm of time and matter no being higher than an absolutely perfect human soul is necessary for the creation or moral regulation of the universe, and by the personal ideal of the kevalin worked toward through usu. numerous lives in the pursuit of right knowledge, right faith, and right conduct including ahimsa and in veneration of the jinas often involving images — compare DIGAMBARA, SVETAMBARA

jai·pur \ˈjīˌpu̇(ə)r, =ˈ=\ *adj, usu cap* [fr. *Jaipur,* India] **:** of or from the city of Jaipur, India **:** of the kind or style prevalent in Jaipur

jai·puri \ˈjīpə(ˌ)rē, jīˈpu̇rē\ *n, usu cap* [Hindi *jaipurī* fr. Jaipur, fr. Jaipur, city in India] **:** a dialect of Rajasthani

jaj·man \ˌjəjˈmän\ *n, pl* **jaj·mans** \-nz\ *or* **jaj·ma·ni** \-nē\ [Hindi *jajmān,* fr. Skt *yajamāna,* pres part. of *yajati* he sacrifices; akin to Av *yasna* sacrifice] **:** one of a fixed circle of persons in a Hindu caste system whom a member of an occupational group (as a barber) serves as an exclusive and hereditary right

jajoba *var of* JOJOBA

jak *or* **jakfruit** *var of* JACKFRUIT

jakarta *usu cap, var of* DJAKARTA

1jake \ˈjāk\ *n* -s [fr. *Jake,* nickname for *Jacob*] **:** an uncouth country fellow **:** HICK; *broadly* **:** FELLOW — often used disparagingly

2jake \"\ *adj* [origin unknown] *slang* **:** ALL RIGHT, FINE ⟨it was pretty hot . . . otherwise everything was ~ —Philip Hamburger⟩

3jake \"\ *also* **ja·key** \ˈjākē\ *n, pl* **jakes** *also* **jakeys** [by shortening & alter. fr. *Jamaica (ginger)*] *slang* **:** an alcoholic extract of Jamaica ginger used as a beverage during the prohibition era

jake leg *n* [*3jake*] **:** a paralysis caused by drinking jake or some other strong liquor

jakes \ˈjāks\ *n pl but usu sing in constr* [perh. fr. the F name *Jacques*] **1** *chiefly dial* **:** PRIVY 2 ⟨the fir trees . . . planted to shelter the garden ~ —Llewelyn Powys⟩ **2** *dial Brit* **:** a dirty mess **:** EXCREMENT

ja·khals·bes·sie *also* **jak·kals·bes·sie** *or* **ja·kaals–bes·sie** \ˌjaˌkȯlzˈbesē, -ˌkəl-\ *n* -s [Afrik *jakkalsbessie,* fr. *jakkals* jackal + *bessie* berry] **:** an African ebony (*Diospyros mespiliformis*) with evergreen leaves

jako \ˈja(ˌ)kō\ *n* -s [origin unknown] **:** AFRICAN GRAY

jak tree *n* **:** JACKFRUIT 1

ja·kun \jəˈkün\ *n, pl* **jakun** *or* **jakuns** *usu cap* **1 a :** an aboriginal people of the southern part of the Malay peninsula **b :** a member of such people **2 :** the Mon-Khmer language of the Jakun people

jal·ap \ˈjaləp, ˈjäl-\ *n* -s [F & Sp; F *jalop,* fr. Sp *jalapa,* fr. *Jalapa,* town in Mexico] **1** *also* **ja·la·pa** \jəˈläpə, hə'-\ **a :** the dried purgative tuberous root of a Mexican plant (*Exogonium purga*) or the powdered drug prepared from it that contains the resinous glycosides convolvulin and jalapin and is the official jalap — compare JICAMA **b :** the root or derived drug of related plants constituting an inferior source of the jalap resins **2 :** any of various plants yielding jalap

ja·la·pe·ño \ˌhäləˈpān(ˌ)yō\ *n* -s [MexSp] **:** a Mexican pepper

ja·la·pin \ˈjaləpən, ˈjäl-; jəˈlap-\ *n* -s [*jalap* + *-in*] **:** a cathartic glucosidic constituent of true jalap resin and scammony resin

ja·lee work \ˈjä(ˌ)lē-\ *n* [Hindi *jālī* network, latticework, fr. Skt *jāla* net] **:** carving esp. in marble in the form of a pierced screen **:** LATTICEWORK

ja·leo \həˈlā(ˌ)ō\ *n* -s [Sp, fr. *jalear* to cheer a dancer or singer, fr. *hala,* interj. used to cheer or urge on] **:** a lively Spanish solo dance accompanied by jeering

ja·lopy *also* **jal·lopy** *or* **ja·lop·py** \jəˈläpē, -pi\ *n* -ES [origin unknown] **1** *also* **ja·lop** \-p\ **:** a dilapidated automobile ⟨roaring around in a battered old ~⟩ **2 :** an outdated often mechanically inferior model (as of an airplane)

ja·louse \jəˈlüz\ *vt* -ED/-ING/-S [F *jalouser* to envy, be jealous of, fr. OF, fr. *jalos, jalous, jelous* jealous — more at JEALOUS] **1** *chiefly Scot* **:** SUSPECT, SURMISE ⟨*jaloused* frae your last discourse that ye were perplexed —John Buchan⟩ **2 :** to be jealous of or begrudge jealously ⟨*jaloused* him and planned to do him a harm —Sir Richard Burton⟩

jal·ou·sie \ˈjaləsē, -si *sometimes* ˌ==ˈsē\ *n* -s [F, lit., jealousy, fr. OF *jalousie, jelousie* — more at JEALOUSY] **1 :** a blind or shutter having horizontal slats that are adjustable or fixed at an angle to admit light and air while excluding sun and rain and to permit looking out from behind them without being visible to the outside **2** *or* **jalousie window :** a window made of adjustable glass louvers that control ventilation

jal·ou·sied \"d\ *adj* **:** equipped with jalousies ⟨a ~ porch⟩ **:** having horizontal slats ⟨~ shutters⟩

jal·pa·ite \ˈjalpəˌīt\ *n* -s [G *jalpait,* fr. *Jalpa,* Zacatecas, Mexico, its locality + G *-it* -ite] **:** a mineral consisting of cupriferous argentite

1jam *also* **jamb** \ˈjam, -aa(ə)-\ *vb* **jammed** *also* **jambed; jammed** *also* **jambed; jamming** *also* **jambing; jams** *also* **jambs** [perh. of imit. origin] *vt* **1 a :** to press into a close or tight position **:** wedge in ⟨~*s* the piano between the sides of the doorway⟩ **:** fix tightly ⟨~ his hat on his head⟩ ⟨~ his teeth together to stop their chattering⟩ **:** SQUEEZE ⟨~ 50 people into a bus designed for 30⟩ **b (1) :** to cause (as some movable part of a machine) to become wedged or fixed so as to be unworkable ⟨a misstroke will ~ the typewriter keys⟩ **(2) :** to make (as a machine) unworkable by such jamming ⟨crashed when a loose nut *jammed* the controls⟩ **c :** to impede or block passage of or along **:** OBSTRUCT ⟨could not get through because traffic was completely *jammed* by the crowd⟩ ⟨the communications channels were *jammed* up with priority messages —Ira Wolfert⟩ **d :** to fill or cause to fill closely or to excess **:** PACK ⟨fans ~ the stadium⟩ ⟨newspaper columns were *jammed* with election propaganda⟩ ⟨~*s* authentic details into his stories⟩ **2 :** to push or apply forcibly **:** force violently ⟨*jammed* himself through the porthole⟩ ⟨*jammed* his spurs into the horse's flanks⟩ ⟨~ the bill through a reluctant legislature by party discipline⟩ ⟨*jamming* political opinions down students' throats —Kenneth Roberts⟩; *specif* **:** to apply (the brakes) suddenly with full force — usu. used with *on* ⟨would ~ the brakes on and throw the passengers forward⟩ **3 :** CRUSH, BRUISE ⟨got his right hand severely *jammed* in the door⟩ **4 :** to bring (a boat) close to the wind so that the upper sails are shaking or laid aback ⟨~ the boat into the wind to avoid collision⟩ **5 a :** to cause interference in (radio or radar signals) **:** make unintelligible (as a radio program or broadcast) by intentionally sending out signals or messages in an interfering manner **b :** to make (as a radio or radar apparatus) ineffective by jamming radio or radar signals or by causing reflection of radar waves from a special device ~ *vi* **1 a :** to become blocked, wedged, or fixed **:** stick fast ⟨an odd cartridge may ~ in the gun⟩ ⟨the line *jammed* and the boat hung useless⟩ **b :** to become unworkable through the jamming of a movable part ⟨the overheated machine *jammed*⟩ **2 :** to force one's way esp. into a restricted space **:** mass together tightly **:** CROWD ⟨continued to ~ into the already crowded hall⟩ ⟨the children *jammed* forward to claim their treats⟩ **3 :** to improvise on a musical instrument with a group **:** take part in a jam session ⟨gathered after hours with their instruments and *jammed* all night⟩ **syn** see PRESS

2jam \"\ *n* -s **1 :** something made closely packed, immovable, or unusable by jamming **:** an instance of jamming ⟨lost the pistol match due to a ~ during the rapid fire⟩; *specif* **:** a crowded mass of people or things causing impedance or blockage ⟨a log ~ in the river⟩ ⟨a flood caused by an ice ~⟩ ⟨delayed an hour by a traffic ~⟩ **2 a :** the quality or state of being jammed **:** STOPPAGE, CONGESTION ⟨the ~ of the legislature caused by the piling up of new bills in the final days⟩ **b :** the pressure or congestion of a crowd of people or things **:** CRUSH ⟨escape from the clangor and ~ of the city streets⟩ **3 :** an involved and embarrassing state of affairs **:** DIFFICULTY, MESS, FIX **:** a tight spot ⟨made him late for his date and got him in a ~ with his girl friend⟩ ⟨can get out of its ~ by finding new foreign markets for its products⟩ **4 :** JAM SESSION **syn** see PREDICAMENT

3jam \"\ *adv* **:** COMPLETELY, CLEAR ⟨filled the jar ~ full⟩ ⟨threw the ball ~ across the field⟩

4jam \"\ *n* -s [prob. fr. *1jam*] **1 :** a product made by boiling fruit and sugar to a thick consistency without preserving the shape of the fruit ⟨spread raspberry ~ on a slice of bread⟩ **2** *chiefly Brit* **:** something agreeable or easy ⟨this job isn't all ~; it has its headaches⟩ ⟨the test was ~ for him and he finished first⟩ **3** [so called fr. its scent that resembles that of raspberry jam] **:** a shrubby acacia (*Acacia acuminata*) with elongated slender phyllodes and cylindrical axillary spikes of yellow flowers that is an important browse plant in much of Western Australia

5jam \"\ *vt* **jammed; jammed; jamming; jams 1 :** to spread with jam ⟨munching *jammed* bread⟩ **2 :** to make into jam ⟨fresh, preserved, or *jammed* fruit⟩

6jam \ˈjäm\ *n* -s [Hindi *jām*] **:** the ruler in some northwest Indian states in the region of Cutch, Kathiawar, and the lower Indus

ja·ma *also* **ja·mah** \ˈjämə\ *n* -s [Hindi *jāma,* lit., garment, fr. Per] **:** a long-sleeved cotton coat of at least knee length worn by men in northern India and Pakistan

jamadar *var of* JEMADAR

1ja·mai·ca \jəˈmākə\ *adj, usu cap* [fr. *Jamaica,* island in the West Indies] **:** of or from the island of Jamaica **:** of the kind or style prevalent in Jamaica **:** JAMAICAN

2jamaica \"\ *n* -s *usu cap* [by shortening] **:** JAMAICA RUM

jamaica apple *n, usu cap J* **1 :** CHERIMOYA **2 :** CUSTARD APPLE

jamaica banana *n, usu cap J* **:** the large yellow commercial banana of the Caribbean region

jamaica bayberry *n, usu cap J* **:** BAYBERRY 1a

jamaica bloodwood *n, usu cap J* **:** FALSE LOGWOOD

jamaica buckthorn *n, usu cap J* **:** CHEROKEE ROSE

jamaica bullace plum *n, usu cap J* **:** GENIP 2

jamaica cherry *n, usu cap J* **1 :** a West Indian fig (*Ficus laevigata*) having globose edible fruits the size of a cherry **2 :** CALABUR TREE

jamaica cucumber *n, usu cap J* **:** GHERKIN

jamaica dogwood *n, usu cap J* **:** a West Indian tree (*Piscidia erythrina*) the narcotic root of which is used as a fish poison in Jamaica

jamaica ginger *n, usu cap J* **1 :** a high grade of ginger grown in Jamaica **2 a :** an alcoholic extract of ginger used as a flavoring essence **b :** the powdered root of ginger used as an infusion in medicine (as in colic or diarrhea)

jamaica honeysuckle *n, usu cap J* **:** a West Indian passionflower (*Passiflora laurifolia*) having fragrant flowers, somewhat astringent leaves, and yellow edible fruit — called also *bell apple, sweet cup, water lemon*

jamaica ironwood *n, usu cap J* **:** a small tropical American tree (*Erythroxylon areolatum*) with yellowish white flowers, red drupes, and hard wood

jamaica mignonette *n, usu cap J, West Indies* **:** HENNA

1ja·mai·can \jəˈmākən\ *adj, usu cap* [*Jamaica,* island in the West Indies + E *-an*] **:** of or relating to Jamaica

2jamaican \"\ *n* -s *cap* **:** a native or inhabitant of Jamaica

jamaica pepper *n, usu cap J* **:** ALLSPICE

jamaica plum *n, usu cap J* **:** a hog plum (*Spondias mombin*) of the West Indies

jamaica quassia *n, usu cap J* **1 :** BITTERWOOD 1a **2 :** quassia obtained from bitterwood

jamaica rum *n, usu cap J* **:** a heavy-bodied rum made in Jamaica by slow fermentation using dunder and usu. having a pungent bouquet — see GERMAN RUM

jamaica sarsaparilla *n, usu cap J* **1** [so called fr. its once being shipped from Jamaica] **:** SARSAPARILLA 1 **2 :** an inferior sarsaparilla grown in Jamaica

jamaica seal *n, usu cap J* **:** WEST INDIA SEAL

jamaica senna tree *n, usu cap J* **:** a tropical Old World herb (*Cassia obovata*) commonly naturalized in tropical America and having glaucous foliage and bright yellow flowers

jamaica sorrel *n, usu cap J* **:** ROSELLE

jamaica thistle *n, usu cap J* **:** PRICKLY POPPY

jamaica vervain *n, usu cap J* **:** a cosmopolitan tropical weed (*Stachytarpheta anoides jamaicensis*) with oblong leaves and bright blue flowers in slender spikes

jamaica walnut *n, usu cap J* **:** a small Jamaican tree (*Picrodendron baccatum*) with hard heavy strong dark olive to nearly black very bitter waxy wood and a fruit that is a drupe with thin bitter flesh, woody endocarp, and a rugose seed

ja·man \ˈjämən\ *n* -s [Hindi *jāman, jāmun,* fr. Skt *jambula,* fr. *jambu*] **:** JAVA PLUM

1jamb \ˈjam, -aa(ə)-\ *n* -s [ME *jambe,* fr. MF, lit., leg, fr. LL *gamba, camba* hock (of a horse), leg — more at GAMBOL] **1 :** an upright piece or surface forming the side of an opening (as a doorway, window, fireplace) **2 :** a projecting columnar part (as of a masonry wall) or mass (as of ore) **3 :** LEG, SHANK — used chiefly in heraldry **4** *also* **jambe** \"\ **:** JAMBEAU

2jamb *var of* JAM

jam·ba \'jämbə\ *n* -s [prob. native name in India] : ACLE 1

jam·ba·laya \ˌjəmbə'līə, -lāyə\ *n* -s [LaF, fr. Prov *jambalaia, jabalaia, jambaraia* stew of rice and fowl] **1 :** rice cooked with ham, sausage, chicken, shrimp, or oysters and usu. tomato and seasoned with herbs **2 :** a mixture of diverse elements : POTPOURRI

jamb brick *n* **:** a brick with the corner of one end and side rounded for use on the vertical side of an opening in a brick wall

jam·beau \'jam(ˌ)bō, ='=\ *n, pl* **jam·beaux** \-ō(z)\ [ME, fr. (assumed) AF, fr. OF *jambe* leg — more at JAMB] **:** a piece of medieval plate armor for the leg below the knee : GREAVE — see ARMOR illustration

jam·bee \'jam,bē, ='=\ *n* -s [fr. *Jambi* (Djambi), district and town, Sumatra, Indonesia] *archaic* **:** a walking stick made from East Indian rattans (genus *Calamus*) and popular in the reign of Queen Anne

jam·ber \'jambə(r)\ *n* -s [ME, fr. MF *jambiere*, fr. OF, fr. *jambe* leg] : JAMBEAU

jam·bo \'jam(ˌ)bō\ *or* **jam·bou** *also* **jam·bu** \-)bü\ *n* -s [Hindi *jambū, jambu*, fr. Skt] : ROSE APPLE 1

jam·bok \(')zham¦bäk\ *var of* SJAMBOK

jam·bo·lan \¦jambə¦lan\ *or* **jambolan plum** *also* **jam·bo·la·na** \ˌ==ˈlänə\ *n* [Pg *jambulão*, fr. Hindi *jambūl*] : JAVA PLUM

jam·bone \'jam,bōn\ *n* [origin unknown] **:** a lone euchre hand that is played with the bidder's cards exposed on the table

jam·bool *or* **jam·bul** \ˌjəm'bül\ *n* -s [Hindi *jambūl*, fr. Skt *jambūla*, fr. *jambū, jambu*] **1 :** JAVA PLUM **2 :** a drug obtained from the bark and seeds of Java plum and formerly believed to be of value in treating diabetes

jamborandi *var of* JABORANDI

jam·bo·ree \¦jambə¦rē, ¦jaam-\ *n* -s [origin unknown] **1 :** a euchre hand containing the five highest trumps **2 :** a noisy or unrestrained carousal or frolic : SPREE ⟨got on a ~ last Tuesday and . . . drank repeatedly at every saloon, insulted every person they encountered, brandished pistols and discharged them —D.D.Martin⟩ **3 a :** a large festive gathering (as of a political party or a league of sports teams) often involving a program of variety entertainment or exhibition performances **b :** a national or international camping assembly of boy scouts — compare CAMPOREE **4 :** a long mixed program of entertainment ⟨the summer program also includes Sunday matinees of concerts and fountain play . . . plus four special night ~s featuring fireworks —Janet Flanner⟩

jam·bos \'jam,bäs, -bōs\ *n* [NL, fr. E *jambo*] **1** *cap, in some classifications* **:** a genus of woody plants (family Myrtaceae) with opposite leathery leaves and panicles or corymbs of showy flowers that includes the Java plum, Malay apple, and rose apple which are usu. placed in the genus *Eugenia* **2** *also* **jam·bo·sa** \jam'bōsə\ *pl* **jambos** *also* **jambosas** [*jambosa* fr. NL *Jambosa*, syn. of *Jambos*] : ROSE APPLE 1

jamb peg *n* **:** a device used in faceting gems comprising a piece of wood containing a series of holes in which a dop stick can be fixed at varying angles

jambs *pl of* JAMB, *pres 3d sing of* JAMB

jamb shaft *n* **:** a free or engaged column decorating the jamb of a door opening or window opening (as in medieval architecture) — see ESCONSON

jambstone \'=,=\ *n* **:** a stone set vertically at the edge of a window or door opening so that one of its faces forms a jamb or part of a jamb

jamb stove *n* **:** a stove used in the U. S. in the middle of the 18th century made of five cast-iron plates forming a box and built into a fireplace wall so that the front opens into the fireplace to receive live coals and the back warms an adjoining room

jam cleat *n* [²*jam*] **:** a cleat with a hinged top for belaying with a single turn of rope and without hitches

james *n* -ES [after *James* I †1625 king of England] *slang* : ¹SOVEREIGN 2

diagram of jamb stove: *1* fireplace room, *2* stove room, *3* end plate, *4* side plate, *5* stove leg, *6* stove hole, *7* flue for stove, *8* chimney of fireplace, *9* lintel beam

james·ian *also* **james·ean** \'jāmzēən\ *adj, usu cap* **1** [William *James* †1910 Am. philosopher and psychologist + E *-ian* or *-ean*] **:** of, relating to, or resembling William James or his philosophical or psychological teachings (as pragmatism, radical empiricism) **2** [Henry *James* †1916 Am. writer + E *-ian* or *-ean*] **:** of, relating to, or resembling Henry James or his writings ⟨a *Jamesian* revival⟩ ⟨has written a *Jamesian* novel of psychological tension⟩

james–lange theory \'jāmz'läŋə-\ *n, usu cap J&L* [after William *James* and Carl Georg *Lange* †1900 Dan. physician and psychologist] **:** a theory in psychology: the affective component of emotion follows rather than precedes the attendant physiological changes

jame·son·ite \'jām(p)sə,nīt, -məs-\ *n* -s [Robert *Jameson* †1854 Scot. mineralogist + E *-ite*] **:** a gray orthorhombic mineral $Pb_4FeSb_6S_{14}$ consisting of a lead antimony iron sulfide, having a metallic luster, and occurring in fibrous masses

james's powder *or* **james' powder** \'jāmz(əz)-\ *n, usu cap J* [after Robert *James* †1776 Eng. physician] : ANTIMONIAL POWDER

james·town lily \'jāmz,taůn\ *n, often cap J* [fr. *Jamestown*, Va.] : JIMSONWEED

jamestown weed *often cap J, var of* JIMSONWEED

jammed *past of* JAM

jam·mer \'jamə(r), -aam-\ *n* -s [¹*jam* + *-er*] **:** one that jams: as **a** (1) **:** a vehicular hoist used to load logs by animal or tractor power (2) **:** one that operates such a jammer **b :** a usu. modulated transmitter that emits a signal that is intended to interfere with or make unintelligible radio or radar signals

jamming *pres part of* JAM

jam·my \'jamē, -aam-, -mi\ *adj* -ER/-EST [⁴*jam* + *-y*] **1 :** sticky with jam ⟨fended off the child's ~ hands⟩ **2** *Brit* : DELIGHTFUL, EASY ⟨a way of singing that's just ~⟩

jam nut *n* [²*jam*] : LOCKNUT 1

ja·moke \jə'mōk\ *n* -s [alter. of earlier *jamocha*, blend of *java* and *mocha*] *slang* : COFFEE 1a

jam–pack \'=ˌ=\ *vt* [¹*jam* + *pack*] **:** to fill to overflowing : fill by crowding in as much as possible : pack tightly : CRAM ⟨vacationists *jam-packed* the trains⟩ ⟨*jam-packs* his columns with useful information⟩

jam·pan \'jam,pan\ *n* -s [Beng *jhāpān*] **:** a sedan with two poles used in the hill country of India

jam riveter *n* [²*jam*] **:** a pneumatic riveting hammer designed for use in a restricted space

jam·ro·sade \¦jamrō¦zād\ *n* -s [*jambo* + *rose* + *-ade*] **:** the fruit of the rose apple

jams *pres 3d sing of* JAM, *pl of* JAM

jam session *n* [²*jam*] **:** an impromptu performance by a group of jazz musicians typically for the players' own enjoyment and characterized by group improvisation

jam·shed·pur \'jäm,shed,pů(ə)r\ *adj, usu cap* [fr. *Jamshedpur*, India] **:** of or from the city of Jamshedpur, India **:** of the kind or style prevalent in Jamshedpur

¹**jam–up** \'=,=\ *adj* [prob. fr. *jam up*, v.] **:** very good : FIRST-RATE : BANG-UP ⟨after one course in psychology you turn out to be a whiz-bang, *jam-up* mind reader —J.S.Redding⟩

²**jam–up** \"\ *n* -s [fr. *jam up*, v.] : ²JAM 1

jam weld *n* [²*jam*] : BUTT WELD

jamwood \'=,=\ *n* [⁴*jam* + *wood*] **:** the raspberry-scented wood of the jam used by the aboriginal inhabitants of Australia for spears

JAN *abbr* joint army-navy

ja·nam·bre \hə'näm(ˌ)brā\ *n, pl* **janambre** *or* **janambres** *usu cap* [Sp, of AmerInd origin] **1 a :** an Indian people of northeastern Mexico **b :** a member of such people **2 :** the language of the Janambre people, perhaps Coahuiltecan

jan·a·pa \'janəpə\ *also* **jan·a·pan** \-pən\ *n* -s [Tamil *caṇappu, caṇappai*] : SUNN 2

jan·ders \'jandə(r)z, 'jön-,'jän-,'jaan-,'jän-\ *dial var of* JAUNDICE

J and WO *abbr* jettison and washing overboard

¹**jane** \'jān\ *n* -s *usu cap* [ME, prob. modif. of MF *Genes* Genoa, Italy] **:** a small Genoese coin circulating in England during the 14th and 15th centuries

²**jane** \"\ *n* -s [fr. the name *Jane*] *slang* : GIRL, WOMAN

jane doe \-'dō\ *n, usu cap J&D* [*Jane* + *Doe* (as in *John Doe*)] **:** a female party to legal proceedings whose true name is unknown — called also *Mary Major*; compare JOHN DOE

jane·ite *also* **jan·ite** \'jā,nīt\ *n* -s [*Jane* Austen †1817 Eng. novelist + E *-ite*] **:** an enthusiastic admirer of Jane Austen's writings

janes \'jānz\ *dial var of* JEANS

jan·ga·da \jan'gädə, -aŋ'-\ *n* -s [Pg, fr. Tamil *caṅkaṭam* or Malayalam *caṅṅāṭam*, fr. Skt *saṃghāta* joining of timber, union] **:** a raft made of logs of light wood with a sail, seat, steering oar, and dagger boards and used by fishermen along the northeast coast of Brazil : CATAMARAN

jangada

jangada fiber *n* **:** the bast fiber from the tibourbou

jan·ga·dei·ro \ˌjaŋgə'dā(ˌ)rō\ *n* -s [Pg, fr. *jangada* + *-eiro* -er (fr. L *-arius*)] **:** a Brazilian fisherman who sails a jangada

¹**jan·gle** \'jaŋgəl, 'jaiŋ-\ *vb* **jangled; jangled; jan·gling** \-g(ə)liŋ\ **jangles** [ME *janglen*, fr. OF *jangler*, of Gmc origin; akin to MD *jangelen* to grumble, whine, haggle, *janken* to yelp, whine, squeal, G dial. *jangeln* to talk in a whining manner] *vi* **1** *archaic* **:** to talk idly : BABBLE, CHATTER ⟨some . . . have turned aside unto vain *jangling* —1 Tim 1:6 (AV)⟩ **2 :** to quarrel in words : ALTERCATE, WRANGLE ⟨must ~ till at last we fought —A.E.Housman⟩ **3 :** to sound harshly or discordantly ⟨the alarm clock *jangled* loudly⟩ ~ *vt* **1 :** to utter or sound discordantly or in a babbling or chattering way ⟨the telephone *jangled* a summons⟩ **2 a :** to cause to sound harshly or inharmoniously ⟨~ a bunch of keys⟩ **b :** to excite to tense and discordant irritation ⟨the whimsy that had sometimes *jangled* the nerves of American newsmen —John Lardner⟩

²**jangle** \"\ *n* -s [ME, fr. MF, fr. OF, fr. *jangler*] **1 :** idle talk : CHATTER, BABBLE ⟨his eternal ~ about being the average father of an average American family —Louis Auchincloss⟩ **2 :** noisy altercation : CONTENTION, WRANGLING ⟨she hated . . . a shrill squabble of shrews, a degrading ~ between servant and mistress —Jean Stafford⟩ **3 :** discordant sound : a confused ringing ⟨music that seemed to be a chaotic ~⟩ ⟨the ~ of sleigh bells⟩ : DISCORD ⟨a haven of calm amid the ~ of modern civilization⟩

jan·gler \-g(ə)lə(r)\ *n* -s [ME, fr. *janglen* + *-er*] **:** one that jangles

jan·gly \-g(ə)lē, -li\ *adj, sometimes* -ER/-EST [¹*jangle* + *-y*] **:** marked by jangling ⟨~ costume jewelry⟩ **:** having a jangling quality ⟨the ~ music of the dance hall piano⟩

jani·ceps \'janə,seps 'jān-\ *n* -ES [NL, fr. L *Janus*, a two-faced Roman god + *-ceps* headed, fr. *caput* head — more at JANUARY, HEAD] **:** a double fetal monster joined at thorax and skull and having two equal faces looking in opposite directions

jani·form \-,fȯrm\ *adj* [*Janus* + E *-iform*] **:** having a face on each of two sides ⟨a coin bearing a ~ head⟩

jan·is·sary *or* **jan·i·zary** \'janə,serē, -,ze-, -ri\ *n* -ES [It *gianizzero*, fr. Turk *yeniçeri*, fr. *yeni* new, inexperienced + *çeri* soldier, military force] **1** *often cap* **a :** a soldier of an elite corps of Turkish troops orig. organized in the 14th century as the sultan's guard, drawn chiefly from subject Christian boys seized in tribute, and continuing as the largest and strongest unit of the army until abolished after revolting in 1826 **b :** a Turkish soldier **2 :** a member of a group of loyal or subservient troops, officials, or supporters ⟨a politician with the help of a large following of *janissaries* ready to carry out his personal will⟩ **3 :** a West Indian wrasse (*Clepticus parrae*) that is mostly reddish brown with the caudal region green

janissary music *n, often cap J* **1 a :** music of military bands formed on the Turkish model and featuring shrill fifes and loud oboes and drums, cymbals, triangles, and Turkish crescents **b :** orchestral or other music imitating this music or its qualities — called also *Turkish music* **2 :** BATTERY 12

¹**jan·i·tor** \'janəd·ə(r), -nətə-\ *n* -s [L, fr. *janua* door, fr. *janus* arch, gate; perh. akin to Skt *yāna* road, *yāti* he goes, Lith *joti* to ride, L *ire* to go — more at ISSUE] **1 :** DOORKEEPER **2 :** one that keeps the premises of an apartment, office, or other building clean and free of refuse, tends the heating system, and makes minor repairs

²**janitor** \"\ *vi* **janitored; janitored; janitoring** \-əriŋ, 'janə·triŋ\ **janitors :** to work as a janitor

jan·i·to·ri·al \ˌjanə¦tōrēəl, -tȯr-\ *adj* **:** of or belonging to a janitor : CUSTODIAL ⟨~ duties⟩ ⟨the ~ staff⟩

jan·i·tress \'janə·trəs\ *n* -ES [*janitor* + *-ess*] **:** a female janitor : CHARWOMAN

jan·i·trix \-nə·(ˌ)triks\ *n* -ES [L, fem. of *janitor*] : JANITRESS

jan·ker \'jaŋkər\ *n* -s [origin unknown] *Scot* **:** a long pole on two wheels used esp. for hauling logs

jan·kers \'jaŋkə(r)z\ *n pl but sing in constr* [origin unknown] *Brit* **:** confinement, fatigue duty, or drill imposed as punishment on a member of the armed forces

jan·ko keyboard \'yäŋ(ˌ)kō-\ *n, usu cap J* [after Paul von *Jankó* †1919 Hungarian pianist] **:** a pianoforte keyboard invented in 1882 consisting of six rows of keys with three digitals to each note, those of each row being at whole-step intervals

jan·mash·ta·mi \ˌjən'mäshtə,mē\ *n* -s *usu cap* [Skt *janmāṣṭamī*, fr. *janma* birth (fr. *janati* he begets) + *aṣṭama* eighth, fr. *aṣṭā* eight — more at KIN, EIGHT] **:** a Hindu festival celebrating the birthday of the deified hero Krishna

jann *n* -s [Ar *jānn*] : JINN

jan·ney coupler \'janē-\ *n, usu cap J* [after Eli H. *Janney* †1912 Am. inventor] **:** a device for coupling railroad cars and locomotives invented in the early 1880s and employed in principle in the standard automatic coupler of today

¹**jan·nock** \'janək\ *n* -s [ME *ianock*] *dial Brit* : BANNOCK

²**jannock** \"\ *adj* [origin unknown] *dial Brit* **:** straightforward and fair : UPRIGHT, DECENT ⟨to give a lover a chance of a final scene before leaving him . . . was ~ —F.M.Ford⟩

jan·sen·ism \'jan(t)sə,nizəm\ *n* -s *usu cap* [F *jansénisme*, fr. Cornelis *Jansen* (Cornelius Jansenius) †1638 Dutch theologian + F *-isme* -ism] **1 :** a theological doctrine condemned by the Roman Catholic Church as heretical that flourished esp. in France in the 17th and 18th centuries maintaining among its principal tenets that freedom of the will (as in accepting or resisting grace) is nonexistent and that the redemption of mankind through the death of Jesus Christ was limited to only a part of mankind and that those not so redeemed are by the positive will of God inescapably condemned to hell **2 :** a negative rigoristic moral attitude (as toward sex) associated with adherents of Jansenism : PURITANISM

¹**jan·sen·ist** \-nəst\ *n* -s *usu cap* [F *janséniste*, fr. C. *Jansen* + F *-iste* -ist] **1 :** an adherent of Jansenism **2 :** a member of the Church of Utrecht in Holland originating by schism from the Roman Catholic Church in 1723 and forming part of the Old Catholic Church since 1889

²**jansenist** \"\ *also* **jan·sen·is·tic** \¦==¦nistik\ *adj, usu cap* **:** of, relating to, or characteristic of the Jansenists or Jansenism

jan·thi·na \'jan(t)thənə\ *n* [NL, fr. L *ianthina*, fem. of *ianthinus* violet-blue, fr. Gk *ianthinos*, fr. *ion* violet + *anthos* flower — more at VIOLET, ANTHOLOGY] **1** *cap* **:** the type genus of Janthinidae comprising pelagic snails of warm seas that have a thin spiral purple shell, a large head, and protrusible gills **2** -s **:** any snail of the genus *Janthina*

jan·thin·i·dae \jan'thinə,dē\ *n pl, cap* [NL, fr. *Janthina*, type genus + *-idae*] **:** a family of marine snails (suborder Taenioglossa) comprising the violet snails and floating at the surface by means of a raft of air bubbles enclosed in hardened mucus secreted by the foot — see JANTHINA

janty *also* **jantee** *archaic var of* JAUNTY

jan·u·ary \'janyə,werē, -ri *also* ÷'jen-, *dial* -nə,w-\ *n, pl* **januaries** *or* **januarys** *usu cap* [ME *Januarie*, fr. L *Januarius*, first month of the ancient Roman year, fr. *Janus*, two-faced god or numen of gates and doors and therefore of beginnings (fr. *janus* arch, gate) + *-arius* -ary — more at JANITOR] **:** the first month of the Gregorian calendar — abbr. *Jan.*; see MONTH table

janus–faced \'jānə¦sfāst\ *or* **janus** *adj, usu cap J* [after *Janus*, the god or numen] **1 :** looking in opposite directions ⟨a *Janus-faced* look at the past and future of our national economy⟩ **2 :** having two contrasting aspects ⟨a *Janus-faced* alternation of melodic variations in major and minor throughout the movement⟩ **3 :** TWO-FACED, DECEITFUL

janus green *or* **janus green B** *n, usu cap J* **:** a basic monoazo azine dye made from safranine and dimethylaniline and used chiefly as a biological stain

ja·nus·like \'jānə,slīk\ *adj, usu cap* **:** looking or acting in opposite or contrasting ways ⟨the *Januslike* quality of Soviet foreign policy created confusion . . . among western statesmen —F.C.Barghoorn⟩

jan·war \'janwər\ *usu cap, Scot var of* JANUARY

jap \'jap\ *n* -s *usu cap, often attrib* [by shortening] : JAPANESE — often used disparagingly

¹**ja·pan** \jə'pan, -paa(ə)n *also* (')ja¦p-\ *adj* [fr. *Japan*, country consisting of an island chain in the western Pacific off the eastern coast of Asia] **1** *usu cap* **:** of or from Japan : of the kind or style prevalent in Japan : JAPANESE **2 a :** of, resembling, or characteristic of Japanese lacquered work **b :** coated or treated with japan

²**japan** \"\ *n* -s [fr. *Japan*, whence it orig. came] **1 a :** a varnish yielding a hard brilliant coating on such surfaces as metal or wood **b** *or* **japan drier :** a varnish that contains a large percentage of resins and driers and that is used as a grinding liquid for paste colors or as a liquid drier for paints **c** *or* **japan black :** a quick-drying black varnish consisting usu. of asphaltum, linseed oil, and thinner that is used for coating metal and that is usu. hardened by baking **2 a :** work varnished and figured in the Japanese manner ⟨the likeness of His Majesty . . . was housed in a circular container of its own, of black ~ —John Godley⟩ **b :** Japanese china or silk

³**japan** \"\ *vt* **japanned; japanned; japanning; japans 1 :** to cover with a coat of japan or with some other hard brilliant varnish in the manner of the Japanese : LACQUER **2 :** to give a high gloss to with varnish supplemented by heating; *specif* **:** to give a glossy black to (as leather)

japan allspice *n, usu cap J* **:** a Japanese shrub (*Chimonanthus praecox*) cultivated for its fragrant yellow flowers that blossom before the leaves appear — called also *Japanese allspice*

japan ashberry *n, usu cap J* **:** an Asiatic evergreen shrub (*Mahonia japonica*) with handsome foliage and yellow flowers

japan bittersweet *n, usu cap J* : JAPANESE BITTERSWEET

japan blue *n, often cap J* **:** a dark blue that is redder and duller than Peking blue, redder and deeper than Flemish blue, and stronger and slightly redder than Majolica blue (sense 1)

japan camphor *n, usu cap J* : dextrorotatory camphor

japan cedar *n, usu cap J* : JAPANESE CEDAR

japan clover *n, usu cap J* **:** an annual lespedeza (*Lespedeza striata*) sometimes used as a forage, soil-improving, and pasture crop esp. in the southeastern U.S. — called also *Japanese clover, Jap clover*

¹**jap·a·nese** \ˌjapə¦nēz, -ēs, *in rapid speech attributively sometimes* 'jap,n-\ *adj, usu cap J* [*Japan* + *-ese*] **1 a :** of, relating to, or characteristic of Japan **b :** of, relating to, or characteristic of the Japanese **2 :** of, relating to, or characteristic of the Japanese language

²**japanese** \"\ *n, cap J* **1** *pl* **japanese :** a native or inhabitant of Japan or one of his descendants **2** -s **:** the language of the Japanese

japanese acid clay *or* **japanese acid earth** *n, usu cap J* **:** fuller's earth occurring in Japan — called also *Kambara earth*

japanese allspice *n, usu cap J* : JAPAN ALLSPICE

japanese andromeda *n, usu cap J* **:** a broad-leaved evergreen Asiatic shrub (*Pieris japonica*) with glossy leaves and drooping clusters of whitish flowers that is used as an ornamental — called also *andromeda*

japanese anemone *n, usu cap J* **:** an Asiatic garden plant (*Anemone nupehensis*) having compound leaves and large showy flowers — called also *Japanese windflower*

japanese angelica tree *n, usu cap J* **:** a shrub or small tree (*Aralia elata*) having a much-compounded inflorescence with a short main axis and spreading secondary axes

japanese ape *n, usu cap J* **:** a small brownish ape (*Macaca speciosa*) of Japan that has a naked face and red ischial callosities

japanese apricot *n, usu cap J* **:** a Japanese ornamental tree (*Prunus mume*) with fragrant white flowers and yellow inedible fruits somewhat smaller than those of the common apricot

japanese arborvitae *n, usu cap J* **:** a Japanese evergreen tree (*Thuja standishii*) with reddish brown bark, spreading or somewhat upright branches bearing thick compressed branchlets, and leaves that are bright green above with white triangular markings below and that are of two types, those of the main axes terminating in sharp rigid points and those of the lateral branches ending obtusely

japanese artichoke *n, usu cap J* : CHINESE ARTICHOKE

japanese ash *n, usu cap J* **1 :** an Asiatic tree (*Fraxinus mandschurica*) having light yellowish wood with a grain resembling that of oak **2 :** the wood of Japanese ash used esp. for veneer and joinery — called also *tamo*

japanese aspen *n, usu cap J* **:** a medium-sized Japanese tree (*Populus sieboldii*) with tomentose twigs and thick leaves

japanese azalea *n, usu cap J* **:** any of several ornamental azaleas from Japan and China (esp. *Rhododendron japonica*) — compare KURUME AZALEA

japanese banana *n, usu cap J* **:** an Asiatic banana (*Musa basjoo*) that is cultivated as a foliage plant in Japan

japanese barberry *n, usu cap J* **:** a compact ornamental Japanese shrub (*Berberis thunbergii*) that has simple spines, entire oblong or spatulate leaves, yellowish flowers either solitary or in small umbels, and bright red persistent berries and that is widespread in cultivation esp. for hedges — compare COMMON BARBERRY

japanese barnyard millet *n, usu cap J* : JAPANESE MILLET

japanese bear *n, usu cap J* **:** a small black bear (*Ursus japonicus*) of northern Japan that has a small white breast marking

japanese beauty–berry *n, usu cap J* **:** a Japanese shrub (*Callicarpa japonica*) with long pointed leaves, cymes of pink flowers, and ornamental violet fruit

japanese beech *n, usu cap J* **:** a beech that is native to Japan and is distinguished from the European beech esp. by its soft light yellowish brown wood

japanese beetle *n, usu cap J* **:** a small metallic green and brown scarabaeid beetle (*Popillia japonica*) introduced into America from Japan that as a grub feeds on the roots of grasses and decaying vegetation and as an adult eats foliage and fruits and is a serious pest — see MILKY DISEASE

japanese b encephalitis *n, usu cap J&B* **:** an encephalitis that occurs epidemically in Japan esp. in summer and is caused by an insect-transmitted virus

japanese bitterling *n, usu cap J* **:** any of several small east Asian cyprinid fishes (genus *Acheilognathus*) characterized by development in the female of a very long ovipositor during the breeding season

japanese bittersweet *n, usu cap J* **:** an ornamental Asiatic woody vine (*Celastrus articulata*) that has showy orange-yellow fruit with a persistent scarlet aril — called also *Japan bittersweet*

japanese black pine *n, usu cap J* **:** a large Japanese ornamental tree (*Pinus thunbergii*) having orange-yellow branchlets, leaves three inches or more in length and in bundles of two, and the scales of the cone armed with prickles — called also *black pine*

japanese blue *or* **japanese green** *n, often cap J* **:** a grayish green that is bluer and deeper than slate green and yellower and duller than average blue spruce (sense 2a)

japanese cane *n, usu cap J* **:** a sugarcane that usu. has slender stalks and is widely grown for forage

japanese cedar *n, usu cap J* **:** a large evergreen tree (*Cryptomeria japonica*) grown esp. in Japan and China for its valuable soft wood — called also *Japan cedar*

japanese cherry *n, usu cap J* : JAPANESE FLOWERING CHERRY

japanese chestnut *n, usu cap J* **1** : a Japanese nut tree (*Castanea crenata*) **2** : the fruit of the Japanese chestnut that is larger than the American chestnut but not so sweet

japanese climbing fern *n, usu cap J* : a slender twining fern (*Lygodium japonicum*) with finely divided fronds

japanese clock *n, usu cap J* : a Japanese timepiece indicating six sunrise and six sunset divisions of time whose length varies with the change of seasons

japanese clover *n, usu cap J* : JAPAN CLOVER

japanese cornel *also* **japanese cornel dogwood** *n, usu cap J* : a Japanese dogwood (*Cornus officinalis*) that has scaly bark and is used as an ornamental

[1]**japanese crab** *n, usu cap J* [[1]*crab*] : GIANT CRAB 1

[2]**japanese crab** *or* **japanese crab apple** *n, usu cap J* [[4]*crab*] : SHOWY CRAB APPLE

japanese cypress *n, usu cap J* : any of several Japanese evergreens of the genus *Chamaecyparis; esp* : SUN TREE

japanese deer *n, usu cap J* : a small deer (*Cervus nippon* syn. *C. sika*) of Japan having slightly forked round antlers and a coat that is spotted with white in summer and plain grayish brown in winter — called also *sika*

japanese flood fever *n, usu cap J* : TSUTSUGAMUSHI DISEASE

japanese flowering cherry *n, usu cap J* : any of certain ornamental hybrid cherries developed in Japan chiefly from two species (*Prunus serrulata* and *P. sieboldii*) that bear a profusion of white or pink usu. double and often fragrant flowers followed by small inedible fruit, that have long been admired and revered by the Japanese, and that are now widespread in cultivation in regions of moderate climate — called also *Japanese cherry*

japanese fold *n, usu cap J* : FRENCH FOLD

japanese fowl *n, usu cap J* : one of a Japanese breed of fancy fowls resembling game fowls but having long hackles and tail feathers

japanese gelatin *n, usu cap J* : AGAR 1a

japanese ginger *n, usu cap J* : a commercial ginger root prepared from a Japanese ginger (*Zingiber mioga*) and usu. marketed unscraped and coated with lime

japanese gut *n, usu cap J* : material for fishing leaders made from raw silk fibers bonded with gelatin

japanese hawthorn *n, usu cap J* : an evergreen shrub (*Raphiolepis umbellata*) of China and Japan with glossy dark green leaves and showy white fragrant flowers

japanese hazel *n, usu cap J* : a Japanese shrub (*Corylus sieboldiana*) with edible nuts in a long tubular involucre

japanese hemlock *n, usu cap J* : a Japanese hemlock (*Tsuga diversifolia*) with pubescent branchlets and glossy dark green foliage

japanese herring *n, usu cap J* : a round herring (*Etrumeus micropus*)

japanese holly *n, usu cap J* : a Japanese shrub (*Ilex crenata*) with evergreen, crenate, but not prickly leaves

japanese honeysuckle *n, usu cap J* : an Asiatic twining or trailing honeysuckle (*Lonicera japonica*) that has half-evergreen leaves and fragrant white flowers changing to yellow and that although planted orig. for ornamental purposes has become a troublesome weed in some areas — see HALL'S HONEYSUCKLE

japanese hop *n, usu cap J* : an ornamental climbing vine (*Humulus japonicus*) commonly cultivated for its variegated foliage

japanese horse chestnut *n, usu cap J* : a Japanese tree (*Aesculus turbinata*) sometimes cultivated for its showy, yellowish white, red-spotted flowers

japanese horseradish *n, usu cap J* : WASABI

japanese iris *n, usu cap J* : any of various beardless garden irises that are developed chiefly from two species (*Iris laevigata* and *I. kaempferi*) of eastern Asia and that have ensiform leaves and very large handsome white, blue, reddish purple, or violet flowers with spreading falls and standards

japanese isinglass *n, usu cap J* : AGAR 1a

japanese ivy *n, usu cap J* : BOSTON IVY

japanese kerria *n, usu cap J* : JAPANESE ROSE 1

japanese knot *n, usu cap J* : [3]KNOT c

japanese knotweed *n, usu cap J* : a stout perennial Japanese herb (*Polygonum cuspidatum*) having cordate leaves and panicles of greenish white flowers

japanese lacquer *n, usu cap J* : LACQUER 1b

japanese lacquer tree *n, usu cap J* : JAPANESE VARNISH TREE

japanese lantern *n, usu cap J* : CHINESE LANTERN

japanese lantern plant *n, usu cap J* : CHINESE LANTERN PLANT

japanese larch *n, usu cap J* : a Japanese ornamental tree (*Larix leptolepis*) having leaves with two white bands beneath and each cone scale reflexed at its apex

japanese laurel *n, usu cap J* **1** : an Asiatic dioecious evergreen shrub (*Aucuba japonica*) that has ovate to obtusely acuminate dark green shining leaves often blotched with yellow and that is used as an ornamental — called also *Japan laurel* **2** : JAPANESE RUBBER PLANT

japanese lawn grass *n, usu cap J* : KOREAN LAWN GRASS

japanese leaf *n, usu cap J* : CHINESE EVERGREEN

japanese lilac *n, usu cap J* **1** : a Chinese lilac (*Syringa villosa*) with profuse rose-lilac or whitish late-blooming flowers **2** : JAPANESE TREE LILAC

japanese linden *n, usu cap J* : a Japanese tree (*Tilia japonica*) used as an ornamental

japanese mackerel *n, usu cap J* : a widely distributed mackerel (*Pneumatophorus japonicus*) of the western Pacific — called also *opelu*

japanese maple *n, usu cap J* : a shrub or small tree (*Acer palmatum*) of Japan and Korea that has purple flowers and in most varieties deeply parted green leaves and that is used as an ornamental — called also *full-moon maple*

japanese medlar *n, usu cap J* : LOQUAT

japanese millet *n, usu cap J* : a coarse annual grass with thick appressed purplish inflorescence and awnless spikelets that is considered to be a variety of barnyard grass or a distinct species (*Echinochloa frumentacea*), is cultivated esp. in Japan and southeastern Asia for its edible seeds which resemble millet and for forage, and is an important wildlife food in parts of the U.S. — called also *billion-dollar grass, Japanese barnyard millet, sanwa millet*

japanese mink *n, usu cap J* **1** : an Asiatic weasel (*Mustela sibirica*) **2** *or* **jap mink** : the pale yellowish brown fur of the Japanese mink that is commonly dyed to resemble mink

japanese mint *or* **japanese peppermint** *n, usu cap J* : a Japanese mint (*Mentha arvensis piperascens*) that is a variety of the common mint of Europe

japanese mint oil *or* **japanese peppermint oil** *n, usu cap J* : an essential oil obtained from corn mint and used chiefly as a source of menthol

japanese morning glory *n, usu cap J* : any of certain cultivated morning glories that are derived from an Old World tropical species (*Ipomoea nil*) and are distinguished by a wide color range and by the occurrence of crested, frilled, or double flowers

japanese moss *n, usu cap J* : BABY'S TEARS

japanese mustard *n, usu cap J* : INDIAN MUSTARD

japanese nightingale *n, usu cap J* : an Asiatic hill tit (*Leiothrix lutea*) that is chiefly olivaceous brown with a yellow breast and red bill and feet and that is often kept as a cage bird — called also *Japanese robin*

japanese nutmeg *n, usu cap J* : a Japanese tree (*Torreya nucifera*) with edible seeds

japanese oak *n, usu cap J* : any of several oaks that are native to, grown in, or shipped as timber from Japan: as **a** : an evergreen oak (*Lithocarpus glabra*) closely related to and resembling the tanbark oak of the American Pacific coast **b** : any of several oaks of the genus *Quercus* (esp. *Q. grosseserrata*) with moderately light, fine-grained, even-textured wood

japanese oyster *n, usu cap J* : a large oyster (*Ostrea gigas*) that is native to the coast of Japan and that has been introduced along the Pacific coast of No. America where it is maintained by repeated planting of spat from the natural habitat

japanese pagoda tree *n, usu cap J* : an ornamental Chinese and Japanese tree (*Sophora japonica*) with compound dark green leaves and profuse panicles of yellowish white flowers — called also *Chinese scholartree*

japanese paper *n, usu cap J* : a long-fibered paper made orig. in Japan and often used for printing engravings — called also *Japan paper*

japanese parasol fir *n, usu cap J* : UMBRELLA PINE 1

japanese pear *n, usu cap J* : SAND PEAR 2a

japanese persimmon *n, usu cap J* **1** : an Asiatic persimmon (*Diospyros kaki*) that is prob. native to China but has been developed into numerous horticultural forms esp. in Japan **2** : the fruit of the Japanese persimmon which is usu. larger than native American persimmons

japanese pheasant *n, usu cap J* : a pheasant (*Phasianus colchicus versicolor*)

japanese pine *n, usu cap J* : any of several eastern Asiatic ornamental pines (esp. *Pinus thunbergii* and *P. densiflora*)

japanese pink *n, usu cap J* : a China pink (*Dianthus chinensis heddewigii*) distinguished by dentate or jagged-edged petals

japanese pittosporum *n, usu cap J* : TOBIRA

japanese plum *n, usu cap J* **1** : any of numerous large showy usu. yellow to light red cultivated plums that are sometimes inferior to European plums in flavor **2** : any of numerous plum trees derived from a Chinese tree (*Prunus salicina*) that are somewhat less hardy than most European and American plum trees and produce Japanese plums **3** : LOQUAT

japanese print *n, usu cap J* : a color print executed from wood blocks in water-based inks and developed to a high degree of artistry by the Japanese esp. in the late 18th and early 19th centuries

japanese privet *n, usu cap J* : either of two Asiatic evergreen privets: **a** : an erect shrub or small tree (*Ligustrum lucidum*) of China, Korea, and Japan with glabrous dark green usu. acuminate leaves and flowers in long erect panicles **b** : a somewhat smaller shrub (*L. japonicum*) of Korea and Japan with usu. more obtuse darker green leaves and flowers in looser more lax panicles

japanese quince *n, usu cap J* **1** : LOQUAT **2** : a hardy Chinese shrub (*Chaenomeles lagenaria*) that is distinguished from the common quinces by its scarlet flowers and large stipules and is grown mostly for ornament — called also *Japonica;* compare DWARF JAPANESE QUINCE

japanese radish *n, usu cap J* : DAIKON

japanese raisin tree *n, usu cap J* : a deciduous shrub or small tree (*Hovenia dulcis*) of eastern Asia having a spicy odor, ovate leaves, and reddish edible fruit stalks — called also *honey tree*

japanese red *n, often cap J* : INDIAN RED 2a

japanese red pine *n, usu cap J* : a Japanese ornamental pine (*Pinus densiflora*) that has orange-red bark, yellowish young branches, and minutely serrulate leaves in fascicles of two with the leaf sheaths ending in two long points

japanese river fever *n, usu cap J* : TSUTSUGAMUSHI DISEASE

japanese robin *n, usu cap J* **1** : JAPANESE NIGHTINGALE **2** : a small Japanese bird (*Erithacus akahige*) related to the nightingale

japanese rose *n, usu cap J* **1** : a slender Chinese shrub (*Kerria japonica*) cultivated for its bright yellow often globular flowers — called also *Japan globeflower* **2** : MULTIFLORA ROSE

japanese rubber plant *n, usu cap J* : a succulent shrub (*Crassula argentea*) having very thick shiny green leaves and white or rosy red flowers in close panicles — called also *Japanese laurel*

jap·a·nes·ery \ˌjapəˈnēzərē, -ēsərē\ *n* -ES *sometimes cap* [[1]*Japanese* + *-ery*] : a Japanese ornament : BAUBLE — usu. used in pl. ⟨a shelf full of *japaneseries*⟩

japaneses *pl of* JAPANESE

japanese sago palm *n, usu cap J* : SAGO PALM 2a

japanese sand pear *n, usu cap J* : SAND PEAR 2a

japanese snail *n, usu cap J* : an ovoviviparous freshwater snail (*Viviparus malleatus*) that is native to Japan and is often kept in aquariums where it is a valuable scavenger

japanese snowball *n, usu cap J* **1 a** : a handsome cultivated shrub (*Viburnum plicatum*) with large globose clusters of sterile flowers very similar to those of the guelder rose **b** : the flower cluster of the Japanese snowball **2** *also* **japanese snowbell** : a deciduous shrub or small tree (*Styrax japonica*) having flowers in short glabrous racemes

japanese snowflower *n, usu cap J* : a Japanese shrub (*Deutzia gracilis*) with slender arching branches covered in spring with a profusion of white flowers

japanese spaniel *n, usu cap J* **1** : a toy dog originating in Japan that is bred chiefly as a pet, that differs from the pekingese in its proportions of body and legs, and that is characterized by a silky coat and black and white or red and white coloring **2** : a breed of dogs comprising the Japanese spaniels

japanese spider crab *n, usu cap J* : GIANT CRAB 1

japanese spruce *n, usu cap J* **1** : a Japanese fir (*Abies mariesii*) with densely rusty pubescent twigs **2** : YEDDO SPRUCE

japanese spurge *n, usu cap J* : a low Japanese herb or subshrub (*Pachysandra terminalis*) that has white flowers in terminal spikes and is often used as a ground cover — compare ALLEGHENY SPURGE

japanese star anise *n, usu cap J* : a Japanese evergreen tree (*Illicium anisatum*) with poisonous fruit

japanese storax *n, usu cap J* : JAPANESE SNOWBALL 2

japanese table pine *n, usu cap J* : an umbrella-shaped evergreen shrub (*Pinus densiflora umbraculifera*) grown as an ornamental — called also *Japanese umbrella pine*

japanese tissue *n, usu cap J* : a thin strong lightweight paper orig. handmade in Japan from long native fibers and used for mending tears in book pages and for cleaning lenses

japanese tree lilac *n, usu cap J* : an arborescent lilac (*Syringa amurensis japonica*) of Japan having showy yellowish white flowers — called also *Japanese lilac, Japan tree lilac*

japanese tung oil *or* **japanese wood oil** *n, usu cap J* : a drying oil obtained from a Japanese tung tree (*Aleurites cordata*)

japanese umbrella pine *n, usu cap J* **1** : UMBRELLA PINE 1 **2** : JAPANESE TABLE PINE

japanese varnish tree *n, usu cap J* **1** *or* **japanese sumac** : a Japanese sumac (*Rhus verniciflua*) that resembles the poison sumac and is a source of the natural Japan varnish or Japan lacquer — called also *Japanese lacquer tree* **2** : CHINESE PARASOL TREE

japanese walnut *n, usu cap J* : a valuable Japanese nut tree (*Juglans cordiformis ailanthifolia*) that bears a heart-shaped nut and is used as a walnut stock because of its hardiness — called also *heartnut, Japan walnut*

japanese wax *n, usu cap J* : JAPAN WAX

japanese wax tree *n, usu cap J* : a Japanese sumac (*Rhus succedanea*)

japanese white pine *n, usu cap J* : an evergreen tree (*Pinus parviflora*) used esp. in dwarf form as an ornamental in Japanese gardens

japanese windflower *n, usu cap J* : JAPANESE ANEMONE

japanese wistaria *n, usu cap J* : a Japanese deciduous shrub (*Wisteria floribunda*) that is widely cultivated for ornament and has twining branches and velvety pubescent pods

japanese witch hazel *n, usu cap J* : a Japanese shrub or small tree (*Hamamelis japonica*) that resembles the American witch hazel but bears reddish yellow flowers in midwinter and that is used as an ornamental

japanese wolf *n, usu cap J* : an Asiatic wolf (*Canis hodophylax*)

japanese yellow *n, often cap J* : CHINESE ORANGE 2

japanese yew *n, usu cap J* : a shrubby hardy evergreen (*Taxus cuspidata*) of China and Japan that has lustrous dark green foliage and is cultivated in many horticultural forms

jap·a·nesque \ˌjapəˈnesk, jəˌpaˈ-, ˌjaˌpaˈ-\ *adj, often cap* [*Japan* + *-esque*] : JAPANESY ⟨intensely white and intensely *Japanesque* egrets —William Beebe⟩

jap·a·nesy \ˌjapəˈnēzē, -nēsē\ *adj, usu cap J* [[1]*Japanese* + *-y*] : having or suggesting a Japanese manner or style : resembling what is Japanese ⟨some of the houses had columned verandas and *Japanesy* curved gables —Joseph Wechsberg⟩

japan fox *n, usu cap J* : the pelt of the raccoon dog processed to simulate fox

japan globeflower *n, usu cap J* : JAPANESE ROSE 1

ja·pan·ism \jəˈpaˌnizəm, -paa,- *also* jaˈp-\ *n* -S *usu cap* [*Japan* + *-ism*] **1** : a trait or characteristic distinctive of the Japanese or of their civilization or art ⟨modern trend in fine art toward skeletal frameworks . . . can be traced back to the *Japanism* of the 70s —Edgar Kaufmann⟩ **2** : Japanese nationalism ⟨a rising tide of *Japanism* which was soon to overwhelm foreign missionaries —Hugh Byas⟩

jap·a·ni·za·tion \ˌjapənəˈzāshən, -ˌnīˈz-\ *n* -S *often cap* : the act or process of japanizing

jap·a·nize \ˈ==ˌnīz\ *vt* -ED/-ING/-S *often cap* [*Japan* + *-ize*] **1** : to make Japanese: **a** : to cause to acquire traits or characteristics that are or are believed to be distinctively Japanese **b** : to bring into close conformity with Japanese national customs and institutions : change in behavior and attitude to suit the Japanese way of life **2** : to bring (an area) under the political, cultural, or commercial influence of Japan

japan lacquer *n, usu cap J* : JAPAN 1a

japan laurel *n, usu cap J* : JAPANESE LAUREL

japan leather *n, usu cap J* : JAPANNED LEATHER

japan lily *n, usu cap J* : any of several Japanese lilies (as *Lilium auratum, L. japonicum, L. speciosum*)

japan medlar *or* **japan plum** *n, usu cap J* **1** : LOQUAT **2** : JAPANESE PERSIMMON

japanned *past of* JAPAN

japanned leather *n* [fr. past part. of [3]*japan*] : leather having a smooth shiny usu. black surface obtained by coating with japan — compare PATENT LEATHER

japanned peacock *or* **japanned peafowl** *n* [fr. past part. of [3]*japan;* fr. the lustrous quality of the feathers] : a peafowl which is usu. considered a variety of the Indian peacock and in which the wings of the male are largely deep blue

ja·pan·ner \jəˈpanə(r), -paan- *also* jaˈp-\ *n* -S [*Japan* + *-er*] **1** *usu cap, obs* **a** : JAPANESE 1 **b** : a Japanese ship **2** [[3]*japan* + *-er*] : a worker who applies coatings of enamel or varnish in making japanned leather or other japanned articles

japanners' brown *n* : an iron oxide that contains chiefly ferric oxide and is used as a drier for oils esp. in the patent-leather and oilcloth industries

ja·pan·nery \jəˈpanərē *also* jaˈp-\ *n* -ES [[3]*japan* + *-ery*] : a room or other place where leather is japanned

japanning *n* -S [fr. gerund of [3]*japan*] : the process of varnishing with japan; *also* : the material used

japano- *comb form, usu cap* [*Japan* (the country)] : Japanese ⟨*Japanologist*⟩ ⟨*Japanophile*⟩

ja·pan·o·phile \jəˈpanəˌfīl *also* jaˈp-\ *n* -S *usu cap* [*Japano-* + *-phile*] : one who esp. admires and likes Japan or Japanese ways

japan paper *n, usu cap J* : JAPANESE PAPER

japan quince *n, usu cap J* : JAPANESE QUINCE

japan rose *n, usu cap J* **1 a** : any of several Japanese roses (as *Rosa multiflora* and *R. rugosa*) **b** : CAMELLIA 2 **2** : a moderate yellowish pink to orange

japans *pl of* JAPAN, *pres 3d sing of* JAPAN

japan tea *n, usu cap J* : unfermented Japanese tea of a light color

japan tree lilac *n, usu cap J* : JAPANESE TREE LILAC

japan varnish *n, usu cap J* : the natural varnish obtained from the Japanese varnish tree

japan walnut *n, usu cap J* : JAPANESE WALNUT

japan wax *or* **japan tallow** *n, usu cap J* : a yellowish fat obtained from the berries of sumac (as *Rhus verniciflua*) and used chiefly in polishes and textile finishes

jap clover *n, usu cap J* : JAPAN CLOVER

[1]**jape** \ˈjāp\ *vb* -ED/-ING/-S [ME *japen*, perh. fr. MF *japper* to bark at, nag, of imit. origin] *vi* **1** : to say or do something jokingly or mockingly : play tricks : JEER ⟨wondering why you ~ at him⟩ **2** *now chiefly dial* : to have sexual intercourse ~ *vt* : to make mocking fun of : GIBE, TAUNT ⟨*japed* the actors from the balcony⟩

[2]**jape** \ʺ\ *n* -S [ME *jape*, fr. *japen*] : something designed to arouse amusement or laughter: as **a** : an amusing literary or dramatic production ⟨a merry little ~ that was cribbed from a 1940 movie —*Time*⟩ **b** : JOKE, GIBE ⟨volumes of quips, jests, ~s, boners, sallies, and bright sayings —Lee Rogow⟩ **c** : a trick played in jest : PRACTICAL JOKE ⟨~s and feats of ingenious devilry —Thomas Wood †1950⟩ **syn** see JOKE

jap·er \-pə(r)\ *n* -S [ME, fr. *japen* + *-er*] : one that japes; *esp* : a professional jester

jap·ery \-p(ə)rē\ *n* -ES [ME *japerie*, fr. *japen* + *-erie* -ery] **1** : jesting talk : JOKES ⟨the patterned wheezes and stylized ~ that have stood them in such good stead during nearly two decades of burlesque —Gladwin Hill⟩ **2** : JOKE, JEST ⟨the sort of man who goes in for flippant *japeries* —*Springfield (Mass.) Union*⟩

[1]**ja·phet·ic** \jəˈfed·ik, (ˈ)jāˈf-\ *adj, usu cap* [*Japheth* (Japetus), one of the sons of Noah in the Bible (Gen 5:32 ff.) + E *-ic*] **1** : relating to or derived from Japheth who was a son of Noah — used vaguely as an ethnological epithet for the Caucasians of Europe and some adjacent parts of Asia **2** : of, relating to, or constituting a group of early non-Indo-European languages in Europe and western Asia assumed by some to form one family with the Caucasian languages and including Basque, Etruscan, Minoan, and sometimes Sumerian and Elamite — compare ASIANIC

[2]**japhetic** \ʺ\ *n* -S *cap* **1** : the Japhetic languages **2** : a Japhetic language

jap mink *n, usu cap J* : JAPANESE MINK 2

japonian *n* -S *often cap* [*Japon* (obs. var. of *Japan*) + E *-ian*] *obs* : JAPANESE

ja·pon·ic \jəˈpänik, jaˈp-\ *adj, usu cap* [*Japon* + E *-ic*] : JAPANESE

ja·pon·i·ca \-nəkə\ *n* -S [NL, fr. fem. of *Japonicus* Japanese, fr. *Japonia* Japan + L *-icus* -ic] **1** : CAMELLIA 2 **2** : JAPANESE QUINCE 2 **3** : CRAPE MYRTLE

jap·o·nism \ˈjapəˌnizəm\ *n* -S *usu cap* [F *japonisme*, fr. *Japon* Japan + F *-isme* -ism] : JAPANISM

japs *pl of* JAP

[1]**ja·pyg·id** \jəˈpijəd\ *adj* [NL *Japygidae*] : of or relating to the family Japygidae

[2]**japygid** \ʺ\ *n* -S : an insect of the family Japygidae

ja·pyg·i·dae \-jəˌdē\ *n pl, cap* [NL, fr. *Japyg-, Japyx*, type genus + *-idae*] : a family of soil-inhabiting insects (order Entotrophi) with the anal appendages forcepslike rather than filamentous

ja·pyx \ˈjāpiks\ *n, cap* [NL, prob. after *Japyx*, mythical founder of Japygia, ancient kingdom in southeastern Italy] : the type genus of the family Japygidae

ja·qui·ma \ˈhakəmə\ *n* -S [Sp *jáquima* — more at HACKAMORE] *Southwest* : the headstall of a halter

[1]**jar** \ˈjär, ˈjȧ(r\ *vb* **jarred**; **jarred**; **jarring**; **jars** [prob. of imit. origin] *vi* **1 a** : to make a harsh or discordant sound : GRATE ⟨winced as the iron gate *jarred* against the sidewalk⟩ : RATTLE ⟨an explosion that made the windows ~⟩ **b** : to be out of harmony or in conflict : CLASH — usu. used with *with* ⟨the slapstick tone ~s with the underlying seriousness —Leo Marx⟩; *specif* : BICKER ⟨two of the men had been *jarring* at each other . . . — some old feud —Agnes M. Cleaveland⟩ **c** : to have a harshly disagreeable or disconcerting effect ⟨an unexpected pettiness that ~s⟩ — often used with *on* or *upon* ⟨resounding harmonies that ~ on unaccustomed ears⟩ ⟨savage expressions that ~ upon the sensitivity of some readers⟩ **2** : to shake or vibrate severely (as from a blow) ⟨bolt had *jarred* loose⟩ ⟨the platform ~s as a train rumbles by⟩ ~ *vt* **1** : to cause to jar : affect disagreeably ⟨the din ~s her nerves⟩ : shake up ⟨the boat ride will ~ the patient less⟩ : UNSETTLE ⟨the violent opposition *jarred* his resolve⟩ ⟨soldiering had *jarred* men loose from birthplace and habit as nothing else could have done —Dixon Wecter⟩ **2** : to drill (a well) by repeated percussion **3** : to collect or remove (insects) from a plant by jarring or shaking

[2]**jar** \ʺ\ *n* -S **1 a** : a harsh grating sound ⟨the loose floorboard that was lifted with a slight groaning ~ —Arthur Morrison⟩ **b** : a state or manifestation of discord or conflict : CLASH, DISSENSION ⟨except for a ~ in the case of Hyderabad, this revolution has taken place . . . smoothly and peacefully —*White Paper on Indian States*⟩; *esp* : a petty quarrel ⟨heard the loud harsh words of a family ~⟩ **2 a** : a rough shaking (as from a sharp impact) ⟨lenses should be protected from ~s and jolts —*Kodak Reference Handbook*⟩ **b** : an unsettling blow (as to the mind or feelings) ⟨gave his nerves the ~ needed to break the habit⟩ ⟨gave a ~ to his composure⟩ **c** : a break or conflict in rhythm, flow, movement, or transition typically rough, abrupt, crude, or disconcerting : an unpleasant discontinuity or incongruity ⟨works persistently, swiftly, without ~ —Sinclair Lewis⟩ **3** : a connecting link between a

well-drill cable and the drilling tool so constructed that when the tool sticks the next upward pull causes a sharp jerk tending to dislodge the tool **syn** see IMPACT

³jar \"\ *n* -s [MF *jarre*, fr. OProv *jarra*, fr. Ar *jarrah* earthen water vessel] **1 :** a rigid container having a wide mouth and often no neck and made typically of earthenware or glass ⟨a ~ that had held jam⟩ ⟨a tobacco ~⟩ ⟨an ornamental cold-cream ~⟩ — compare BOTTLE **2 :** JARFUL ⟨buy pickles by the ~⟩ ⟨enough plums to make a dozen ~s of jelly⟩

jar 1

⁴jar \"\ *vt* **jarred; jarred; jarring; jars :** to put in a jar; *specif* **:** to preserve (as fruit) by canning in glass jars

⁵jar \"\ *n* -s [alter. of earlier *char* — more at CHARE] *archaic* **:** TURN — used esp. in the phrase *on the jar* ⟨the door was on the ~ and, gently opening it, I entered —Henry Brooke⟩

ja·ra·be \hə'rä(,)bā\ *n* -s [AmerSp, fr. Sp, syrup, fr. Ar *sharāb* — more at SYRUP] **:** any of several provincial Mexican couple dances (as the hat dance) that have the zapateado as their basic step

ja·ra·gua \¦zharə¦gwä\ *or* **jaragua grass** *n* -s [Pg *jaraguá*, fr. Tupi] **:** a tall forage grass (*Hyparrhenia rufa*) native to Brazil but now used elsewhere for hay and forage

¹ja·ra·na \hə'ränə\ *n* -s [AmerSp] **1 :** a large Central American manbarklak (*Eschweilera jarana*) with hard heavy durable wood used chiefly for heavy construction **2 :** the salmon pink to reddish brown variegated wood of the jarana

²jarana \"\ *n* -s [AmerSp, fr. Sp, fun, merrymaking, trick, deceit, alter. of *harana*, *arana* trick, deceit] **1 :** a couple dance of Yucatan that is performed with waltz and zapateado steps **2 :** a stringed instrument of Mexico resembling a ukulele

ja·ra·ra·ca \,zharə'räkə\ *n* -s [Pg, fr. Tupi *jararaca* & Guarani *yararaca*] **:** any of various So. American pit vipers

ja·ra·ra·cus·su *or* **ja·ra·ra·cu·cu** \,zharə,räkə'sü\ *n* -s [Pg *jararacuçu*, *jararacuçú*, fr. Tupi *jararaca wassu* & Guarani *yararaca wassu*, lit., big jararaca] **:** a venomous pit viper (*Bothrops jararacussu*) of Brazil that is related to the fer-de-lance

jar·a·wa \'jarə,wä\ *n*, *pl* **jarawa** *or* **jarawas** *usu cap* **1 :** an Andamanese people of So. Andaman Island **2 :** a member of the Jarawa people

jarbird \'⸗,⸗\ *n* [²*jar* + *bird*; fr. the noise it makes with its beak on dead branches] **:** a nuthatch (*Sitta caesia*)

jar·bot \'järbət\ *n* -s [origin unknown] **:** dilatation of the esophagus in the horse

jar·di·niere *or* **jar·di·nière** \¦jlärd³n¦i(ə)r, ¦äd-, -d³n¦(y)e(ə)r, -iə,-eə *also* ¦zh|\ *n* -s [F *jardinière*, lit., female gardener, fem. of *jardinier* gardener, fr. OF, fr. *jardin* garden (fr. *jart* garden, of Gmc origin; akin to OHG *gart* enclosure) + *-ier* -er — more at YARD] **1 a :** an ornamental stand for plants or flowers **b :** a large round usu. decorative ceramic flowerpot **2 :** a garnish for meat consisting of several vegetables cubed and cooked separately or together

jardiniere 1b

jar·ed·ite \'ja(a)rə,dīt\ *n* -s *cap* [*Jared*, the eponymous ancestor of the Jaredites according to the *Book of Mormon* (Ether 1:31 ff) + E *-ite*] **:** one of a group of people that according to Mormon belief settled America after the general dispersal accompanying the confusion of tongues at Babel — compare NEPHITE

jarfly \'⸗,⸗\ *n* [²*jar* + *fly*; fr. the harsh whirring noise it produces] **:** CICADA

jar·ful \'⸗,fůl\ *n*, *pl* **jar·fuls** *also* **jars·ful** \'jär,fůlz, 'jä,fůlz, -ärz,fůl, -äz,fůl\ [³*jar* + *-ful*] **:** the quantity held by a jar ⟨mixed several ~s of juice in the bowl⟩

¹jar·gon \'järgən, 'jäg- *also* -,gän\ *n* -s [ME *jargoun*, fr. MF *jargon*, prob. of imit. origin] **1 :** chatter or twitter esp. of a bird or animal **2 a :** confused unintelligible language **:** GIBBERISH; *specif* **:** JARGON APHASIA **b :** a strange, outlandish, or barbarous language or dialect ⟨foreign languages were considered rude ~s⟩ **c :** a hybrid language or dialect arising from a mixture of languages that is typically much simplified in vocabulary and grammar (as pidgin English) and is used for communication between peoples of different speech; *specif*, *usu cap* **:** CHINOOK JARGON — compare LINGUA FRANCA **3 a :** the technical terminology or characteristic idiom of specialists or workers in a particular activity or area of knowledge; *often* **:** a pretentious or unnecessarily obscure and esoteric terminology **b :** a special vocabulary or idiom fashionable in a particular group or clique **4 :** language vague in meaning and full of circumlocutions and long high-sounding words **syn** see DIALECT

²jargon \"\ *vi* -ED/-ING/-s [ME *jargounen*, fr. *jargoun*, n.] **1 :** TWITTER, WARBLE ⟨the birds would begin their early morning ~*ing* —Elizabeth M. Roberts⟩ **2 :** JARGONIZE

jargon aphasia *n* **:** the fluent use of words that bear no relation to the meaning intended

jargon code *n* **:** a full set of code names for use in otherwise plain language communication in order to conceal persons, things, or actions being discussed ⟨in a *jargon code* of Louis XIII, the pope is referred to as "the rose", Rome as "the garden"⟩

jar·gon·ist \'⸗gənəst\ *or* **jar·gon·eer** \¦⸗⸗¦ni(ə)r, -iə\ *n* -s **:** one that is addicted to jargon

jar·gon·is·tic \¦⸗⸗¦nistik, -tēk\ *adj* **:** characterized by the use of jargon **:** phrased in jargon

jar·gon·ize \'⸗⸗,nīz\ *vb* -ED/-ING/-s *vi* **:** to speak or write jargon ~ *vt* **1 :** to express in jargon **2 :** to make into jargon or into a jargon ⟨developed a *jargonized* form of Dutch in communication with native Africans —Leonard Bloomfield⟩

jar·goon \(')jär¦gün, (')jä¦g-\ *or* **jar·gon** \-gän\ *n* -s [F *jargon* — more at ZIRCON] **:** a colorless or pale yellow or smoky zircon

jarhead \'⸗,⸗\ *n* [³*jar* + *head*] *chiefly Midland* **:** MULE; *esp* **:** an army mule

ja·ri·na \zhə'rēnə\ *n* -s [Pg] **:** IVORY NUT 1

ja·risch–herx·hei·mer reaction \'yärish'herks,hīmər-\ *n*, *usu cap J&H* [after Adolf *Jarisch* †1902 Austrian dermatologist & Karl *Herxheimer* †1944 Ger. dermatologist] **:** HERXHEIMER REACTION

jark \'järk\ *n* -s [origin unknown] *archaic* **:** the seal of a counterfeit document

jark·man \-mən\ *n*, *pl* **jarkmen** *archaic* **:** a vagabond counterfeiter of documents (as licenses, passes, certificates)

jarl *R* 'yär(ə)l, *-R* 'yäl\ *n* -s [ON — more at EARL] **:** a Scandinavian noble ranking immediately below the king — used also of the chiefs of Orkney and Shetland; compare EARL

¹jar·less \'järləs, 'jäl-\ *adj* [²*jar* + *-less*] **:** free from jar ⟨a smooth ~ ride⟩

²jarless \"\ *adj* [³*jar* + *-less*] **:** not having or requiring jars ⟨the ~ methods of preserving⟩

jarl·ite \'yär,līt\ *n* -s [C. F. *Jarl*, 20th cent. Danish official in the cryolite industry + E *-ite*] **:** a mineral $NaSr_3Al_3F_{16}$ consisting of an alumino-fluoride of sodium and strontium

jar mill *n* [²*jar*] **:** a small ball mill for pulverizing plastic materials (as paint)

jar·mo·ite \'jär(,)mō,īt\ *n* -s *usu cap* [*Jarmo*, site of a prehistoric town in northeastern Iraq + E *-ite*] **:** a member of a prehistoric people inhabiting the foothills of southern Kurdistan

ja·rool \jə'rül\ *n* -s [Hindi *jarūl*] **:** QUEEN'S CRAPE MYRTLE

ja·ro·site \jə'rō,sīt, 'jarə,s-\ *n* -s [G *jarosit*, fr. Barranco *Jaroso*, Almería, Spain + G *-it* -ite] **:** an ocher-yellow or brown mineral $KFe_3(SO_4)_2(OH)_6$ consisting of basic sulfate of potassium and iron and occurring in minute rhombohedral crystals or in masses — compare AMMONIOJAROSITE, ARGENTOJAROSITE, NATROJAROSITE, PLUMBOJAROSITE

jaro·vi·zation \,yärəvə'zāshən, ,yar-, -,vī'z-\ *n* -s **:** VERNALIZATION

jaro·vize *or* **iaro·vize** *or* **yaro·vize** \'⸗⸗,vīz\ *vt* -ED/-ING/-s [Russ *yarovoe* spring grain (fr. *yara* spring) + E *-ize*; akin to Gk *hōra* season — more at HOUR] **:** VERNALIZE

jar–owl \'⸗,⸗\ *n* [²*jar*; fr. the harsh noise it makes] **:** a European goatsucker

jar·rah \'jarə\ *n* -s [native name in Australia] **1 :** an Australian eucalypt (*Eucalyptus marginata*) with rough bark and ovate leaves **2 :** a red gum (*Eucalyptus rostrata*) **3 :** the wood of jarrah

jarred *past of* JAR

jarring *pres part of* JAR

jar·ring·ly *adv* **:** in a jarring manner ⟨a piano ~ out of tune⟩

jar·ring·ness *n* -ES **:** the quality or state of being jarring

jars *pres 3d sing of* JAR, *pl of* JAR

jar·vey *also* **jar·vie** \'järvē\ *n*, *pl* **jarveys** *also* **jarvies** [fr. *Jarvey*, nickname for *Jarvis*] **1** *chiefly Irish* **:** the driver of a hackney coach or of a jaunting car **2 :** HACKNEY COACH

ja·sey \'jāzē\ *n* -s [prob. alter. of *jersey*] *Brit* **:** a wig made usu. of worsted

jasi·o·ne \,ja|sē'ō(,)nē, ,jä|, |zē-\ *n* [NL, fr. Gk *iasiōnē* bindweed] *cap* **:** a genus of European herbs (family Campanulaceae) having alternate leaves and blue flowers in a solitary involucrate head — see SHEEP'S-BIT

jasm \'jazəm\ *n* -s [origin unknown] **:** zest for accomplishment **:** DRIVE, ENERGY ⟨you must have ~ if you want to amount to anything in this world —*Linotype News*⟩

jas·mi·na·ce·ae \,jazmə'nāsē,ē, -asm-\ [NL, fr. *Jasminum*, type genus + *-aceae*] *syn of* OLEACEAE

jas·mine \'jazmən *sometimes* 'jas- *or* 'jaas-\ *or* **jes·sa·mine** \'jes(ə)mən\ *also* **jas·min** *like* JASMINE\ *n* -s [F *jasmin*, fr. Ar *yāsamīn* (colloq. *yāsmīn*), fr. Per] **1 a** (1) **:** any of numerous usu. limber and often climbing shrubs of temperate and warm regions that constitute the genus *Jasminum* and usu. have extremely fragrant flowers (2) *usu jessamine* **:** a tall-climbing semievergreen Asiatic shrub (*J. officinale*) with slender shoots and fragrant white flowers from which a perfume is extracted **b :** any of numerous other plants having sweet-scented flowers — usu. used with preceding qualifier ⟨cape ~⟩ ⟨red ~⟩ **c** *usu jessamine* **:** YELLOW JESSAMINE 2 **d :** MATRIMONY VINE **2 a :** a perfume having an odor like that of jasmine **b :** a constituent of such a perfume consisting of jasmine oil or a formulated preparation with a similar odor **3 :** a light yellow that is greener, lighter, and stronger than average maize, redder, stronger, and slightly lighter than popcorn, and redder and slightly deeper than chrome lemon — compare BUTTER YELLOW

jasmine

jasmine family *n* **:** OLEACEAE

jasmine mango *or* **jasmine tree** *n* **:** FRANGIPANI

jasmine oil *n* **:** a fragrant essential oil obtained from flowers of a jasmine (as *Jasminum officinale* or *J. grandiflorum*) and used in perfumery

jasmine orange *n* **:** ORANGE JESSAMINE

jasmine tea *n* **:** tea scented by being packed with or fired with jasmine flowers — compare SCENTED TEA

jasminewood \'⸗⸗,⸗\ *n* **1 :** the fragrant wood of a tree (*Ochna mauritiana*) of Mauritius **2 :** the tree that yields jasminewood

jasmine yellow *n* **:** BUTTER YELLOW — compare JASMINE 3

jas·mi·num \'jazmənəm, -asm-\ *n*, *cap* [NL, fr. F *jasmin* jasmine — more at JASMINE] **:** a large genus of tropical chiefly East Indian woody vines or shrubs of the family Oleaceae having mostly pinnate leaves and flowers shaped like salvers

jas·mone \'jaz,mōn, -as,m-\ *n* -s [ISV *jasmine* + *-one*] **:** a liquid ketone $C_{11}H_{16}O$ that is derived from cyclopentene, has an odor like that of jasmine, is found esp. in jasmine oil, and is used in perfumery

jasp \'jasp\ *n* -s [ME *jaspe* — more at JASPER] *archaic* **:** JASPER

jas·pa·chate \'jaspə,kāt\ *or* **jasp·ag·ate** \'jas,pagət\ *n* -s [F & L; F *jaspagate*, fr. L *iaspachates*, fr. Gk *iaspachatēs*, fr. *iaspis* jasper + *achatēs* agate] **:** AGATE JASPER

jas·pé \(')zha¦spā, (')ja-\ *adj* [F, fr. past part. of *jasper* to mottle, fr. *jaspe* jasper] **:** resembling jasper in blending of colors **:** clouded in streaks of contrasting colors; *specif* **:** variegated in weaving by the use of warp yarns of differing shades together with single-color filling yarns

¹jas·per \'jaspə(r), -aas-, -ais- *sometimes* -ās-\ *n* -s [ME *jaspre*, *jaspe*, fr. MF *jaspre*, *jaspe*, fr. L *jaspis*, fr. Gk *iaspis*, of Sem origin; akin to Ar *yashb* jasper, Heb *yāshpheh*] **1 :** an opaque cryptocrystalline quartz of any of several colors (as red, brown, green, yellow) ⟨the wall was built of ~, while the city was pure gold, clear as glass —Rev 21:18 (RSV)⟩; *esp* **:** green chalcedony ⟨one block, pure green as a pistachio nut, there's plenty ~ somewhere in the world —Robert Browning⟩ **2 :** a hard fine-grained ceramic ware containing a high percentage of barium salts and ordinarily stained (as blue or green) with metallic oxides and decorated with sprigged ornamentation **3 :** a blackish green that is bluer than cannon — compare JASPER GREEN

²jasper \"\ *adj* **1 :** relating to or composed of jasper **2 :** PEPPER-AND-SALT

³jasper \"\ *n* -s [fr. the name *Jasper*] **:** FELLOW, GUY ⟨aim to stay sober . . . till I work that ~ over —Ross Santee⟩

jasper bar *n* [¹*jasper*] **:** ¹BAR 8

jas·pered \-pə(r)d\ *adj*, *archaic* **:** of mottled or variegated color **:** SPECKLED

jasper green *n* **:** a moderate green that is yellower and paler than sea green (sense 1a), bluer and paler than myrtle (sense 3a), and bluer, lighter, and stronger than average laurel green (sense 1) — compare JASPER

jas·per·ize \-pə,rīz\ *vt* -ED/-ING/-s **:** to convert into or make to resemble jasper

¹jas·per·oid \-,rȯid\ *adj* [¹*jasper* + *-oid*] **:** resembling jasper

²jasperoid \"\ *n* -s **:** ¹JASPER 1

jasper opal *n* **:** a yellow opal resembling jasper

jasper pink *n* **:** a strong yellowish pink that is redder and darker than salmon pink, redder and deeper than melon, and redder than peach red

jasper red *n* **:** a moderate red that is yellower and paler than cerise, claret (sense 3a), average strawberry (sense 2a), or Turkey red and lighter and stronger than pepper red — called also *old coral*

jasper slip *or* **jasper stone** *n* **:** a slip or stone of reddish quartz that is used in polishing watch parts

jas·per·ware \'⸗⸗,⸗\ *n* **:** JASPER 2

jas·pery \-p(ə)rē, -ri\ *adj* **:** of, resembling, or containing jasper

jas·pid·e·an \(')ja¦spidēən\ *or* **jas·pid·e·ous** \-ēəs\ *adj* [L *jaspid-*, *jaspis* jasper + E *-ean*, *-eous* — more at JASPER] **:** JASPERY

jas·pi·lite *also* **jas·pi·lyte** \'jaspə,līt\ *n* -s [¹*jasper* + *-i-* + *-lite* or *-lyte*] **:** a compact siliceous rock rich in hematite and resembling jasper

jas·pis \'jaspəs\ *n* -ES [ME, fr. L — more at JASPER] **:** JASPER 1

jas·po·nyx \'jaspə(,)niks, -,späniks\ *n* -ES [L *iasponyx*, fr. Gk, fr. *iaspis* jasper + *onyx* — more at ONYX] **:** an onyx part or all of whose layers consist of jasper

jasp·opal \'ja,spōpəl\ *n* [by contr.] **:** JASPER OPAL

jasps *pl of* JASP

jass \'yäs\ *n* -ES [G dial. (Switzerland)] **1 a :** a two-handed game played with a 36-card or 32-card pack in which points are scored by melding certain combinations and by taking scoring cards in tricks **b :** KLABERJASS **2** *or* **jasz** \"\ **:** the jack of trumps as top card in jass or klaberjass

jas·sach·ni \jə'säknē\ *n*, *pl* **jassachni** *or* **jassachnis** *usu cap* **1 :** a Buryat people of southern Transbaikalia in Siberia **2 :** a member of the Jassachni people

¹jas·sid \'jasəd\ *adj* [NL *Jassidae*] **:** of or relating to the Jassidae

²jassid \"\ *n* -s **:** a leafhopper of the family Jassidae; *broadly* **:** LEAFHOPPER

jas·si·dae \'jasə,dē\ *n pl*, *cap* [NL, fr. *Jassus*, type genus (fr. L *Iassus*, *Iasus*, ancient town in southwestern Asia Minor, fr. Gk *Iassos*, *Iasos*) + *-idae*] **:** a family of leafhoppers: **a** *in some classifications* **:** a family coextensive with Cicadellidae **b :** a large cosmopolitan family of small usu. slender leafhoppers that have the ocelli near the margin of the vertex and that include many economically significant pests of cultivated plants some of which (as the beet leafhopper) transmit plant diseases — compare TETTIGELLIDAE

jas·sy \'yäsē\ *adj*, *usu cap* [fr. *Jassy* (*Iaşi*), Romania] **:** IASI

ja·sus \'jāsəs\ *n*, *cap* [NL, fr. L *Iasus*, *Iassus* ancient town] **:** a genus of spiny lobsters including the Cape crawfish

jat \'jät\ *n* -s *usu cap* [Hindi *jāṭ*] **1 :** an Indo-Aryan people of the Punjab and Uttar Pradesh **2 :** a member of the Jat people

ja·ta·co \hə'tä(,)kō\ *n* -s [AmerSp] **:** an amaranth (*Amaranthus caudatus*) sometimes used as a food plant in tropical America

ja·ta·ka \'jädəkə\ *n* -s *usu cap* [Skt *jātaka*, fr. *jāta* born, fr. *janati* he begets — more at KIN] **:** any of some 550 birth stories or narratives of former incarnations of Gautama Buddha collected in Buddhist sacred writings

jat·eo·rhi·za \,jad·ēō'rīzə\ [NL, fr. Gk *iatēr*, *iatēs* physician + NL *-o-* + *-rhiza*] *syn of* JATRORRHIZA

ja·tha \jə'tä\ *n* -s [Panjabi *jathā*] **:** an armed band or organized company esp. of Sikhs

jat·ki \'jätkē\ *n* -s *cap* **:** a dialect of Lahnda

jat·ni \'jätnē\ *n* -s *usu cap* [Hindi *jāṭnī*, fr. *jāṭ*] **:** a female Jat

JATO \'jād·(,)ō, -ā(,)tō\ *abbr*, *often not cap* jet-assisted takeoff

ja·to·ba \,zhad·ə¦bä\ *n* -s [Pg *jatobá*, fr. Tupi] **:** COURBARIL

jato unit *n* **:** a unit for assisting the takeoff of an airplane consisting of one or more rocket engines that are usu. discarded after the fuel has been consumed

jat·ro·pha \'ja·trəfə\ *n*, *cap* [NL, fr. Gk *iatros* physician + *trophē* food, fr. *trephein* to nourish — more at ATROPHY] **:** a widely distributed mainly tropical American genus of herbs, shrubs, and trees (family Euphorbiaceae) usu. having lobed leaves and inconspicuous cymose flowers — see PHYSIC NUT

ja·troph·ic \jə·'träfik\ *adj* [NL *Jatropha* + E *-ic*] **:** of or relating to physic nuts

jat·ror·rhi·za \,ja·trə'rīzə\ *n*, *cap* [NL, fr. *jatro-* (var. of *iatr-*) + *-rhiza*] **:** a genus of woody vines (family Menispermaceae) of eastern Africa and Mauritius having lobed leaves and long loose racemes of flowers — see CALUMBA

jat·ror·rhi·zine \,ja·trə'rī,zēn, -īz³n\ *or* **jat·eo·rhi·zine** \,jad·ēō'r-\ *n* -s [ISV *jatrorrhiz-*, *jateorhiz-* (fr. NL *Jatrorrhiza* or *Jateorhiza*, genus name of *Jatrorrhiza palmata* or *Jateorhiza palmata*) + *-ine*] **:** an alkaloid $C_{20}H_{21}NO_5$ that occurs in calumba and is related in structure to berberine

jaud \'jȯd, 'jäd\ *Scot var of* JADE

jau·die \-di\ *n* -s [alter. of ME *chaudoun*, *chaudern* — more at CHAWDRON] **1** *chiefly Scot* **:** edible entrails; *esp* **:** a pig's stomach **2** *chiefly Scot* **:** a pudding made of jaudie

jaug \'jȯg, 'jäg\ *Scot var of* JAG

jauk \jȯk, 'jäk\ *vi* -ED/-ING/-s [ME (Sc dial.) *jaken*] *Scot* **:** DALLY, DAWDLE

jau·ling·ite \'yaůliŋ,īt\ *n* -s [G *jaulingit*, fr. the *Jauling*, Austria + G *-it*] **:** a fossil resin high in oxygen content

jaun \'jän, -ȯ-, -ȧ-\ *n* -s [Beng *jān*, fr. Skt *yāna* going, vehicle — more at HINAYANA] **:** a small Calcutta palanquin

¹jaunce \'jȯn(t)s, -ä-,-ȧ-\ *vi* -ED/-ING/-s [origin unknown] *archaic* **:** PRANCE ⟨spurgalled and tired by *jauncing* Bolingbroke —Shak.⟩

²jaunce \"\ *n* -s *now dial Eng* **:** a tiring jaunt or journey

jaun·der \'jȯndər, 'jän-\ *vi* -ED/-ING/-s [origin unknown] *Scot* **:** PRATTLE, GABBLE

jaun·ders \'jȯndə(r)z, 'jän-,'jan-,'jaan-,'jän-\ *dial var of* JAUNDICE

¹jaun·dice \'jȯndəs, 'jän-,'jän- *chiefly dial* 'jan- *or* 'jaan- *or* -də(r)z\ *n* -s [ME *jaunis*, *jaundis*, fr. MF *jaunisse*, fr. *jaune* yellow (fr. L *galbinus* yellowish green, fr. *galbus* yellow) + *-isse* -ice] **1 :** yellowish pigmentation of the skin, tissues, and certain body fluids caused by the deposition of bile pigments that follows interference with normal production and discharge of bile (as in certain liver diseases) or excessive breakdown of red blood cells (as after internal hemorrhage or in various hemolytic states) **2 :** a disease or abnormal condition that is characterized by jaundice: as **a :** INFECTIOUS HEPATITIS 1 **b :** LEPTOSPIROSIS **c :** TOXEMIC JAUNDICE **3 :** a state or attitude characterized by satiety, distaste, or hostility ⟨looked at me with some ~ in her eye —Kenneth Roberts⟩ **4 :** GRASSERIE

²jaundice \"\ *vt* -ED/-ING/-s **:** to affect with envy, hostility, or distaste **:** PREJUDICE ⟨my own experience, as a minor poet, may have *jaundiced* my outlook —T.S.Eliot⟩

jaundice berry *n* [so called fr. its use as a remedy for jaundice] **:** the fruit of a barberry (*Berberis vulgaris*)

jaundiced *adj* **1 a :** yellowed by or as if by jaundice ⟨all looks yellow to the ~ eye —Alexander Pope⟩ **b :** YELLOW ⟨barred windows with ~ borders —John Ruskin⟩ **2 :** exhibiting or affected by envy, distaste, or hostility ⟨long ago looked with a ~ eye on the growth of regimentation —Irwin Edman⟩

jaundice root *n* **:** GOLDENSEAL

jaune bril·lant *also* **jaune bril·liant** \¦zhōnbrē¦(y)äⁿ\ *n*, *pl* **jaunes brillants** \-äⁿ(z)\ [F *jaune brillant*, lit., brilliant yellow] **:** any of several yellow pigments used esp. as artists' colors: as **a :** NAPLES YELLOW 1a **b :** cadmium sulfide either alone or in a mixture (as a cadmium yellow)

¹jaunt \'jȯnt, -ä-,-ȧ- *chiefly dial* -a- *or* -aa-\ *vi* -ED/-ING/-s [origin unknown] **1** *archaic* **:** to trudge or trip tediously about ⟨catch my death with ~*ing* up and down —Shak.⟩ **2 :** to make a usu. short journey (as an excursion) for pleasure ⟨~ through orchards and gardens —*Newsweek*⟩

²jaunt \"\ *n* -s **1** *archaic* **:** a difficult or tiring trip or journey ⟨a very long and troublesome ~ —George Washington⟩ **2 :** an excursion undertaken for pleasure ⟨a ~ to the shore or the hills —F.L.Allen⟩

jaun·ti·ly \'jȯnt³l|ē, 'jän-,'jän-, -tȯl, |i, *chiefly dial & archaic* 'jan- *or* 'jaan-\ *adv* **:** in a light or carefree manner **:** AIRILY ⟨~ concluded that life was an affliction —Harry Levin⟩

jaun·ti·ness \-tēnəs, -tin-\ *n* -ES **:** the quality or state of being jaunty **:** SPRIGHTLINESS, UNCONCERN ⟨the synthetic optimism, the false ~ —Bruce Bliven b. 1889⟩

jaunting car *also* **jaunty car** *n*, *Irish* **:** a light horse-drawn two-wheeled open vehicle with seats placed lengthwise either face-to-face or back to back — called also *outside car*, *sidecar*

jaunting car

jaunt·ing·ly *adv* **:** JAUNTILY

¹jaun·ty \-tē,-ti\ *adj* -ER/-EST [alter. of earlier *jentee*, fr. F *gentil* — more at GENTLE] **1** *archaic* **a :** GENTEEL **b :** FASHIONABLE, STYLISH **2 :** nonchalant or sprightly in manner or appearance **:** AIRY, DEBONAIR, PERKY ⟨a ~ straw hat with a garish band —A.M.Schlesinger b. 1917⟩ ⟨a shrewdly ~ optimist —H.E.Clurman⟩ ⟨such writing jars with its ~ banality —C.C.Abbott⟩

²jaun·ty \'jȯnti, 'jän-\ *n* -ES [perh. modif. of F *gendarme* — more at GENDARME] *Brit* **:** the master-at-arms aboard a naval vessel

¹jaup \'jȯp, 'jäp\ *vb* -ED/-ING/-s [prob. of imit. origin] *chiefly Scot* **:** SPLASH, SPATTER

²jaup \"\ *n* -s *chiefly Scot* **:** a splash or spatter esp. of dirty water

¹java \'jävə, 'javə, 'jävə\ *adj*, *usu cap* [fr. *Java*, island in Indonesia] **:** of or from the island of Java **:** of the kind or style prevalent in Java **:** JAVANESE

²java \", *in sense 1 usu* 'javə\ *n* **1** -s *often cap* **:** COFFEE ⟨the boys came down and found me crying into my ~ —John Dos Passos⟩ **2** *usu cap* **a :** a breed of large general-purpose domestic fowls developed in America from oriental stock **b** -s **:** a bird of this breed

java almond *n*, *usu cap J* **1 :** a large East Indian tree (*Canarium commune*) that has large unequally pinnate leaves and white flowers in clustered terminal panicles followed by ovoid drupaceous fruits and that is a source of elemi **2 :** the rich oily seed of the Java almond used as food and as a source of cooking and illuminating oils but having an integument that causes diarrhea

java bean *n*, *usu cap J* **:** a strain or race of the sieva bean grown in southeastern Asia but dangerous as a feed because of the presence of a cyanogenetic glucoside in the seeds

java black rot *or* **java dry rot** *n*, *usu cap J* **:** a storage disease of the sweet potato caused by a fungus (*Diplodia tubericola*) that makes the inside of a root black and brittle

java citronella oil *n*, *usu cap J* **:** CITRONELLA OIL b

java cotton *n*, *usu cap J* **:** KAPOK

java grass *n, usu cap J* **:** a grass (*Polytrias praemorsa*) found in the West Indies and cultivated in Panama and in some parts of the U. S. as a lawn grass
java jute *n, usu cap 1st J* **:** KENAF
javali *var of* JABALI
java man *n, usu cap J* **:** either of two prehistoric men of primitive form (*Pithecanthropus erectus* and *P. robustus*) known chiefly from more or less fragmentary skulls found in Trinil, Java — called also *Trinil man*
¹javan \ˈjävən, ˈjav-, ˈjȧv-\ *adj, usu cap* [*Java*, island in Indonesia + E *-an*] **:** JAVANESE
²javan \"\ *n -s cap* **:** a native or inhabitant of Java
¹java·nese \ˌjavəˈnēz, ˌjäv-, ˌjȧv-, -ēs\ *adj, usu cap* [*Java* + *-nese* (as in *Japanese*)] **1 a :** of, relating to, or characteristic of Java **b :** of, relating to, or characteristic of the Javanese **2 :** of, relating to, or characteristic of the Javanese language
²javanese \"\ *n, pl* **javanese** *usu cap* **1 a :** an Indonesian people inhabiting mainly the island of Java **b :** a member of such people **2 :** an Austronesian language of the Javanese people — compare MADURESE, SUNDANESE
javanese skunk *n, usu cap J* **:** TELEDU
javan ox *n, usu cap J* **:** a domesticated banteng of Java
javan peacock *or* **javan peafowl** *n, usu cap J* **:** a peafowl (*Pavo muticus*) of southeastern Asia in which the plumage is predominantly metallic green with ocellations and markings of blue and coppery yellow — compare INDIAN PEACOCK
javan rhinoceros *n, usu cap J* **:** a small one-horned rhinoceros (*Rhinoceros sondaicus*) of Java, Sumatra, and the Indian region west to Calcutta
javan squirrel *n, usu cap J* **:** JELERANG
javan·thro·pus \jəˈvan(t)thrəpəs; ˌjäˌvanˈthrōpəs, ˌjaˌ-, ˌjȧˌ-\ *n, cap* [NL, fr. *Java* + *-anthropus*] *in some classifications* **:** a genus of Hominidae comprising the Solo man
java pepper *n, usu cap J* **:** a climbing or somewhat arborescent East Indian pepper (*Piper cubeba*) that is sometimes cultivated for its fruits which are the source of cubeb
java plum *n, usu cap J* **:** a large tree (*Eugenia jambolana*) that is found chiefly in the East Indies and Australia and has strongly astringent seeds and bark used as a drug in India
java skull *n, usu cap J* **:** the skull of Java man
java sparrow *n, usu cap J* **:** a weaverbird (*Padda oryzivora*) that is native to Java, has glaucous gray and black upper parts, pinkish underparts, white cheeks, and large pink bill, resembles a finch, and is a common cage bird
java tea *n, usu cap J* **1 a :** the dried leaves of an East Indian mint (*Orthosiphon stamineus*) from which a powerful diuretic is obtained **b :** the mint that bears such leaves **2 :** any of several black teas grown in Java or resembling those grown there
java teak *n, usu cap J* **:** TEAK 1
ja·vé \ˈyä(ˌ)vā, ˈyȧ-, -ve\ *cap, var of* YAHWEH
ja·vel \ˈjavəl\ *n -s* [ME *javel, javell*] *archaic* **:** a vagabond or worthless fellow
ja·vel green \(ˈ)zhaˌ|vel, zhəˈ|\ *n, often cap J* [*javel (water)*] **:** a moderate greenish yellow that is greener and duller than citron yellow and greener and deeper than linden green — called also *eau de Javel green*
¹jav·e·lin \ˈjav(ə)lən\ *n -s* [MF *javeline*, alter. of *javelot*, of Celt origin; akin to W *gaflach* spear, OIr *gabul* forked stick, fork — more at GAFFLE] **1 a :** a light spear cast usu. by hand as a weapon of war or in hunting wild boar and other big game **b** *archaic* **:** a long-shafted combat weapon (as a pike) tipped with metal and used for thrusting **2** *or* **javelin man :** a man armed with a javelin; *esp* **:** a javelin-bearing member of the escort of an English judge **3 a :** a slender shaft of wood not less than 260 centimeters long, tipped with iron or steel, and intended to be thrown for distance as an athletic feat or exercise **b** *or* **javelin throw :** an athletic field event in which a javelin is thrown for distance **4** *or* **javelin formation :** a formation of military airplanes (as bombers) in which the elements fly one behind the other in line though not always at the same altitude
²javelin \"\ *vt* -ED/-ING/-S **1 :** to pierce with or as if with a javelin ⟨lightning ~*s* the hills⟩ **2 :** to throw or hurl like a javelin ⟨pieces of tin and board stuck in the mud where they had been ~*ed* by the heavy explosions —H.D.Skidmore⟩
javelina *var of* JABALINA
javelin bat *n* **:** a large carnivorous spearnose bat (*Phyllostomus hastatus*) of tropical America distinguished by a triangular prolongation of the nose leaf
jav·e·lin·eer \ˌjav(ə)ləˈni(ə)r, -iə\ *n -s* **:** a soldier armed with a javelin
ja·velle water *or* **ja·vel water** \(ˈ)zhaˌ|vel, zhəˈ|\ *n, usu cap J* [*Javel*, former town now included in Paris, France; trans. of F *eau de Javel, eau de Javelle*] **:** either of two aqueous solutions of hypochlorite used as a disinfectant or a bleaching agent and in photography: **a :** a solution of potassium hypochlorite now little used **b :** a solution of sodium hypochlorite
ja·vell·iza·tion \ˌzha,veləˈzāshən\ *n -s* [*Javelle (water)* + *-ization*] **:** chlorination of water with Javelle water
jav·er \ˈjāvə(r)\ *dial var of* JABBER
¹jaw \ˈjȯ\ *n -s* [ME *jow, jowe, jaw, jawe*, prob. fr. MF *joe, joue* cheek] **1 a :** either of two complex cartilaginous or bony structures in most vertebrates that border the mouth, support the soft parts enclosing it, and usu. bear teeth on their oral margin comprising (1) an upper more or less firmly fused with the skull and (2) a lower hinged, movable, and articulated by a pair of condyles with the temporal bone of either side — called also respectively (1) *upper jaw, maxilla*, (2) *lower jaw, mandible* **b :** the bones, muscles, nerves, and other parts constituting the walls of the mouth and serving to open and close it — usu. used in pl. **c :** any of various organs of invertebrates that perform the function (as the biting or masticating of food) of the vertebrate jaws — compare CHELICERA, MANDIBLE 2, MASTAX **2 :** something resembling the jaw of an animal in form or action: as **a :** one of the sides of a narrow opening (as of a gorge) **b :** either of two or more opposing parts (as of a vise, measuring machine, pair of pliers, stone crusher) movable so as to open and close for holding, grasping, clamping, cutting, or crushing something between them — see VISE illustration **c :** a notched or forked part (as a guide allowing vertical play to a railroad-car axle box) adapted for holding an object in place **d** (1) **:** the inner end of a boom or gaff forked or hollowed so as to partly encircle and move freely on the mast (2) **:** projections from a yard at the slings often connected by the parrel **3 a :** a space lying between or as if between open jaws ⟨escaped from out of the ~*s* of the whale⟩ ⟨close the ~ of the shackle with a bolt⟩ **b :** a position or situation in which one is threatened (as with death) ⟨rode into the ~*s* of danger⟩ **4** *slang* **a :** TALK ⟨no time for ~⟩; *esp* **:** impudent or offensive talk **:** SCOLDING ⟨hold your ~ and be off⟩ ⟨don't have to take any of his ~⟩ **b :** a friendly talk **:** CHAT ⟨looked up his friend and had a good long ~⟩ **5 :** the pitch of a helix formed by a strand of a rope ⟨soft-laid, tarred hemp, 3-stranded with rather long ~ —C.W.T.Layton⟩
²jaw \"\ *vb* -ED/-ING/-S *vt* **1 :** to exercise the jaws upon ⟨~*ed* her bubble gum⟩ **2** *slang* **:** to scold at ⟨~*ed* him all evening about the accident⟩ **3** *slang* **:** to talk at tiresomely ⟨~ the customer till his resistance is broken down⟩ ~ *vi* **1 :** to speak abusively or indignantly and at length ⟨left when she began ~*ing* at him⟩ ⟨quit ~*ing* about it⟩ **2 :** to talk at length **:** CHAT, GAB ⟨~*ed* together all day about old times⟩ **syn** see SCOLD
³jaw \"\ *n -s* [origin unknown] *chiefly Scot* **:** WAVE, SPLASH
⁴jaw \"\ *vt* -ED/-ING/-S *chiefly Scot* **:** to throw (liquid) in quantity
ja·wab \jəˈwäb, -wȯb\ *n -s* [Hindi *jawāb*, fr. Ar] **:** a building (as the false mosque of the Taj Mahal) erected to correspond to or balance another
jaw·ba·tion \jȯˈbāshən\ *n -s* [alter. (influenced by ¹*jaw*) of *jobation*] *dial Eng* **:** a long tiresome reproof **:** JAWING
jaw bit *n, chiefly Brit* **:** a bar across the jaws of a pedestal underneath an axle box of a railway car
jawbone \ˈ=ˌ=\ *n* **1 :** JAW 1a; *esp* **:** MANDIBLE **2** *slang* **:** CREDIT, TRUST ⟨got his winter's supplies on ~⟩ ⟨prohibit further ~ at post exchanges —*Newsweek*⟩
jawbreaker \ˈ=ˌ==\ *n* **1 :** a word difficult to pronounce **2 :** a round hard candy made from sugar syrup **3 :** JAW CRUSHER
jawbreaking \ˈ=ˌ==\ *adj* **:** difficult to pronounce ⟨a foreign city with a ~ name⟩ — **jaw·break·ing·ly** *adv*
jaw clutch *n* **1 :** DOG CLUTCH **2** *also* **jaw coupling :** CLAW CLUTCH
jaw crusher *n* **:** a machine for crushing rock or ore between two heavy steel jaws
jawed \ˈjȯd\ *adj* [¹*jaw* + *-ed*] **:** having a specified kind of jaw — usu. used in combination ⟨lean-*jawed*⟩ ⟨lantern-*jawed*⟩
jawfish \ˈ=ˌ=\ *n* **:** a fish of the percoid family Opisthognathidae comprising tropical marine fishes with a single dorsal fin, a single lateral line, and very large mouth
jawfoot \ˈ=ˌ=\ *n* **:** MAXILLIPED
jawhole \ˈ=ˌ=\ *n* [⁴*jaw* + *hole*] *Scot* **:** SEWER, CESSPOOL
jawing *pres part of* JAW
jaw·less \ˈjȯləs\ *adj* **:** having no jaw
jawless fish *n* **:** any of the primitive vertebrates comprising the superclass Agnatha
jawlike \ˈ=ˌ=\ *adj* **:** resembling a jaw or pair of jaws in appearance, function, or action
jawline \ˈ=ˌ=\ *n* **:** the outline of the lower jaw as a facial feature
jaw rope *n* **:** a rope holding the jaws of a gaff to the mast **:** PARREL
jaws *pl of* JAW, *pres 3d sing of* JAW
jaw sealer *n* **:** a machine for sealing flexible package materials by applying pressure with heated bars movable by jaw action
jawsmith \ˈ=ˌ=\ *n* **:** a professional talker **:** DEMAGOGUE
¹jay \ˈjā\ *n -s* [ME, fr. MF *jai*, fr. LL *gaius*, prob. fr. the name *Gaius*] **1 a :** a predominantly fawn-colored Old World bird (*Garrulus glandarius*) with a black-and-white crest and wings marked with black, white, and blue **b :** any of numerous typically brightly colored and frequently largely blue birds that with the common Old World jay constitute a subfamily of the family Corvidae, are distinguished from the related crows by smaller size, more arboreal habits, and frequently by possession of an elongated tail and a definite crest, have roving habits, pugnacious ways, and harsh voices, and are often destructive to the eggs and young of other birds — see BLUE JAY, CANADA JAY **2 a :** an impertinent chatterer **b :** a gaudily or flashily dressed person **:** WANTON, DANDY **c :** a person lacking experience (as in city ways) or polish **:** an unsophisticated, countrified, or gullible person **:** GREENHORN, RUBE **3** *or* **jay blue :** a moderate blue that is greener and duller than average copen, redder and slightly duller than azurite blue, redder and duller than Dresden blue, and redder and paler than bluebird
²jay \"\ *adj* -ER/-EST **:** unsophisticated or countrified in character **:** BACKWARD, UNSKILLED, RUSTIC ⟨~*er* than a real hick⟩
³jay \ˈjā\ *n -s* **:** the letter *j*
jaybird \ˈ=ˌ=\ *n, chiefly Midland* **:** JAY 1, 2 ⟨naked as a ~⟩
jaycee \ˈ=ˈ=\ *n -s usu cap* [³*jay* + *cee* (letter); fr. the initials of *junior chamber*] **:** a member of a junior chamber of commerce
jaygee \ˈ=ˈ=\ *n -s* [³*jay* + *gee* (the letter); fr. the initials of *junior grade*] **:** LIEUTENANT JUNIOR GRADE
¹jayhawk \ˈ=ˌ=\ *n* [¹*jay* + *hawk*] **1 :** JAYHAWKER **2 :** a fictitious bird with a large beak used as an emblem in Kansas
²jayhawk \"\ *vt* -ED/-ING/-S **:** to make a predatory attack on **:** RAID
jay·hawk·er \"ə(r)\ *n* **1 a** *often cap* **:** a member of one of the bands of antislavery guerrillas of the Kansas border in raids on Missouri before and during the Civil War **b :** a member of one of the bands of outlaws engaged in raiding in the West following the Civil War **2** *usu cap* **:** KANSAN — used as a nickname
jaypie \ˈ=ˌ=\ *or* **jaypiet** \ˈ=ˌ==\ *n* [¹*jay* + *pie, piet*] **1 :** a European jay **2** *dial Eng* **:** MISTLE THRUSH
jay teal *n, dial Eng* **:** a European teal (*Nettion crecca*)
jayvee \ˈ=ˈ=\ *n -s* [³*jay* + *vee* (the letter); fr. the initials of *junior varsity*] **1 :** JUNIOR VARSITY **2 :** a member of a junior varsity team — usu. used in pl.
jaywalk \ˈ=ˌ=\ *vi* [¹*jay* + *walk*] **:** to cross a street carelessly or at an unusual or inappropriate place or in a dangerous or illegal direction so as to be endangered by the traffic — **jay·walker** \ˈ=ˌ==\ *n*
jaz·er·ant \ˈjazərənt\ *also* **jaz·er·an** \-n\ *n -s* [ME *jesseraunt*, fr. MF *jaseran, jazerenc*, fr. Ar. *jazāʾirī* Algerian, fr. *al-Jazāʾir* Algiers] **1 :** a coat of armor made of small overlapping metal plates usu. mounted on linen or other lining **2 :** armor of the jazerant type
jaz·y·ges \ˈjazəˌjēz, -ˌgēz\ *n, pl* **jazyges** *usu cap* [L *Jazyges, Iazyges*, fr. Gk *Iazyges*] **1 :** a Sarmatian people orig. occupying the shores of the Black sea **2 :** a member of the Jazyges people
¹jazz \ˈjaz, -aa(ə)-\ *vb* -ED/-ING/-ES [origin unknown] *vt* **1 :** to copulate with — usu. considered vulgar **2 a :** to increase the appeal or excitement of **:** ENLIVEN, POPULARIZE ⟨the newsman who ~*es* a story to sell himself to editor and public —C.K. Streit⟩ — usu. used with *up* ⟨drank bootleg gin to ~ me up —J.D.Hart⟩ **b :** to increase the speed of **:** ACCELERATE ⟨~ the motor⟩ **3 :** to play (music) in the manner of jazz **:** make jazz of ⟨pep up old tunes by ~*ing* them⟩ ~ *vi* **1 :** COPULATE — usu. considered vulgar **2 :** to go seeking pleasure **:** GAD — used with *around* **3 a :** to dance or perform jazz ⟨~*ing* to the music of the band⟩ ⟨a saxophonist who ~*es* at a nightclub⟩ **b :** to dance around in a jazzy manner ⟨chairs and tables . . . ~*ing* crazily to and fro across the cabin —Shevawn Lynam⟩
²jazz \"\ *n* -ES **1 :** COPULATION — usu. considered vulgar **2 a :** American music developed from religious and secular songs (as spirituals, shout songs), blues, ragtime, and other popular music (as brass-band marches) and characterized by improvisation, syncopated rhythms, contrapuntal ensemble playing, special melodic features (as flatted notes, blue notes) peculiar to the individual interpretation of the player, and the introduction of vocal techniques (as portamento) into instrumental performance — see BOP, DIXIELAND; compare SWING **b :** popular dance music influenced by jazz and played (as in the late 1920s) in a loud rhythmic manner **c :** a dance to jazz music with incisive rhythms and often acrobatic and grotesque steps — compare JITTERBUG 1 **3 :** excessively earnest and enthusiastic talk or preoccupation **:** stuffy foolishness **:** HUMBUG ⟨spouted all the scientific ~ at him —Pete Martin⟩
³jazz \"\ *adj* [²*jazz*] **1 :** of, relating to, or having the characteristics of jazz ⟨~ music⟩ ⟨~ fans⟩ **2 :** MOTTLED ⟨the room will be done in ~ colors —Upton Sinclair⟩
jazz ballet *n* **:** a ballet or dance performance in jazz style
jazzbow \ˈ=ˌ=\ *n* **:** a ready-made bow tie
jazz·i·ly \-zəlē, -li\ *adv* **:** in a jazzy manner
jazz·i·ness \-zēnəs, -zin-\ *n* -ES **:** the quality or state of being jazzy
jazz·ist \-zəst\ *n -s* **:** a lover of jazz
jazz·man \-zmən, -zˌman\ *n, pl* **jazzmen :** a performer of jazz
jazzy \-zē, -zi\ *adj* -ER/-EST **1 :** having the character of jazz ⟨loud fast ~ music⟩ **2 :** of an unrestrained, animated, or flashy character ⟨a ~ good-time city⟩ ⟨tuned out the highbrow program for something more ~⟩ ⟨a ~ Hawaiian shirt⟩
JB *abbr* **1** joint board **2** joint bond **3** junction box
j-bar lift \ˈ=ˌ=-\ *or* **j-bar** \ˈ=ˌ=\ *n, cap J* **:** a ski tow consisting of an overhead moving cable carrying a series of suspended bars of J shape on the base of which skiers may half sit and half lean while being pulled uphill
j boat *n, usu cap J* **1 :** a large yacht of the 76-foot rating class **2 :** a small sailboat raced by children
j bolt *n, cap J* **:** a bolt the shape of the letter J with threads usu. only on the longer leg
j-box \ˈ=ˌ=\ *n, cap J* **:** a container having the form of an upright J through which a textile is passed in a wet finishing process (as bleaching)
jc *abbr* junction
JC *abbr* **1** [L *jurisconsultus*] jurisconsult **2** justice clerk **3** juvenile court
JCB *abbr or n -s* [L *juris canonici baccalaureus*] **:** a bachelor of canon law
JCD *abbr or n -s* [L *juris canonici doctor*] **:** a doctor of canon law
JCL *abbr or n -s* [L *juris canonici licentiatus*] **:** a licentiate in canon law
JC of C *abbr* junior chamber of commerce
JCR *abbr* junior common room
JCS *abbr* joint chiefs of staff
jct *or* **jctn** *abbr* junction
jd *abbr* joined
JD *abbr or n -s* **1** [L *juris doctor*] **:** a doctor of law **2** [L *jurum doctor*] **:** a doctor of laws
JD *abbr* **1** Julian day **2** junior deacon **3** junior dean **4** justice department **5** juvenile delinquent
JEA *abbr* joint export agent
jeal·ous \ˈjeləs\ *adj* [ME *jelous, jalous, jelous*, fr. OF *jalos, jalous, jelous*, fr. (assumed) VL *zelosus*, fr. LL *zelus* zeal + L *-osus* -ous — more at ZEAL] **1 a :** intolerant of rivalry or unfaithfulness ⟨shall worship no other god, for the Lord . . . is a ~ God —Exod 34:14 (RSV)⟩ ⟨~ of the slightest interference in household management —Havelock Ellis⟩ **b :** disposed to suspect rivalry or unfaithfulness (as in love) **:** apprehensive of the loss of another's devotion ⟨so ~ she wouldn't let him dance with anyone else⟩ **c :** hostile toward a rival or one believed to enjoy an advantage (as a possession or attainment) **:** ENVIOUS, RESENTFUL ⟨~ because her coat isn't as nice as yours⟩ **2 :** zealous in guarding (as a possession) **:** VIGILANT ⟨his ~ love of privacy and independence —J.W.Beach⟩ **:** SOLICITOUS ⟨students . . . were like sons to him, he was ~ for their welfare —Ellwood Hendrick⟩ **3 :** distrustfully watchful **:** apprehensive of harm or fraud **:** SUSPICIOUS ⟨the ~ caution of New England —Van Wyck Brooks⟩ **syn** see ENVIOUS
jea·louse \jəˈlüz\ *vt* -ED/-ING/-S [modif. (influenced by *jealous*) of F *jalouser* to envy, be jealous of — more at JALOUSE] *archaic* **:** SUSPECT, MISTRUST
jeal·ous·ly \ˈjeləslē, -sli\ *adv* [ME *jelously*, fr. *jelous* jealous + *-ly*] **:** in a jealous manner ⟨a ~ guarded right⟩ ⟨his absorption in a career she ~ hated —Oscar Handlin⟩
jeal·ous·ness *n* -ES [ME *jelousnes*, fr. *jelous* + *-nes* -ness] **:** JEALOUSY
jeal·ou·sy \ˈjeləsē, -si\ *n* -ES [ME *jelousie*, fr. OF *jalosie, jalousie, jelousie*, fr. *jalos, jalous, jelous* jealous + *-ie* -y — more at JEALOUS] **1 a :** a jealous disposition or state of mind **:** a jealous nature, attitude, or feeling ⟨blinded by ~ to the skill of his fellow workers⟩ ⟨felt a natural ~ toward the winner⟩ **:** hostile rivalry ⟨intense local *jealousies* among existing villages —R.A.Billington⟩ **b** *now dial Brit* **:** SUSPICION, MISTRUST **2 :** zealous vigilance ⟨cherish their official political freedom with fierce ~ —Paul Blanshard⟩ **3** [trans. of F *jalousie*] **:** JALOUSIE
jean \ˈjēn *chiefly Brit* ˈjān\ *n -s* [short for *jean fustian*, fr. ME *Jene, Gene* Genoa, Italy (fr. MF *Genes*) + *fustian*] **1** *also* **jeans** *pl but sing in constr* **:** a durable twilled cotton cloth usu. in solid colors or stripes used esp. for sportswear and work clothes — compare DENIM, ⁹DRILL **2 jeans** *pl* **a :** pants usu. made of jean or denim and worn for work or sports — compare BLUE JEANS **b :** TROUSERS ⟨had to dig into his ~*s* to pay for the rest of the albums —*Down Beat*⟩

jeans 2a

jean·pau·lia \jēnˈpȯlēə\ [NL, prob. fr. *Jean Paul* Richter †1825 Ger. author + NL *-ia*] *syn of* BAIERA
jebel *var of* DJEBEL
jeb·u·site \ˈjebyəˌsīt *sometimes* -ˌzīt *or* ˈjēbəˌsīt\ *n -s usu cap* [*Jebus*, ancient city in Palestine (fr. Heb *Yĕbūs*) + E *-ite*] **:** a member of a Canaanite people living in and around the ancient city of Jebus on the site of Jerusalem
jec·o·rin \ˈjekərən\ *n -s* [ISV *jecor-* (fr. L *jecor-, jecur* liver) + *-in*] **:** a complex lipoidal substance $C_{105}H_{186}N_5O_{46}P_3S$ somewhat resembling lecithin, orig. isolated from liver tissue, and occurring in small quantities in blood and in various tissues
jec·o·rize \ˈjekəˌrīz\ *vt* -ED/-ING/-S [L *jecor-, jecur* liver + E *-ize* — more at HEPATIC] **:** to impart to (fats or oils) some of the properties of cod-liver oil (as by irradiation with ultraviolet light)
jed·burgh cast \ˈjedˌbərə-, -ˌb(ə)rə-\ *also* **jed·dart cast** \ˈjedə(r)t-\ *n, usu cap J* [fr. *Jedburgh* or *Jeddart*, town in Roxburgh, Scotland, where in the 17th century a band of marauders was summarily executed] *Scot* **:** a court trial after punishment has been inflicted
jedburgh justice *also* **jeddart justice** *n, usu cap 1st J* **1** *Scot* **:** justice that punishes first and tries afterwards **:** LYNCH LAW **2** *Scot* **:** wholesale punishment or acquittal
jed·ding ax \ˈjediŋ-\ *n* [*jedding* alter. of *jadding*, pres. part. of *jad* to make a long deep hole in a rock, fr. *jad*, such a hole, of unknown origin] **:** a stonecutter's ax with a flat face and a pointed peen
jee *var of* GEE
jeel \ˈjē(ə)l\ *n -s* [ME (Sc dial.) *giell*, fr. MF *gel, giel* frost, jelly, fr. L *gelus, gelu* frost — more at COLD] *Scot* **:** JELLY
¹jeep \ˈjēp\ *n -s* [prob. alter. (influenced by Eugene the *Jeep*, a small fanciful wonder-working animal in the comic strip *Thimble Theatre* by Elzie C. Segar †1938 Am. cartoonist) of *gee pee*, fr. *gee* + *pee* (the letter); fr. the initials *g. p.* of *general purpose*] **1 a** (1) **:** a diminutive multipurpose motor vehicle of 80-inch wheelbase and ¼-ton capacity equipped with four-wheel drive and used by the U. S. Army in World War II — called also *peep* (2) **:** a modified U. S. Army vehicle of this kind having greater horsepower, more comfortable springs, longer wheelbase, increased fuel capacity, and a higher hood **b :** a 1½-ton command car used in the armored divisions of the U. S. Army during World War II **2** *or* **jeep carrier :** ESCORT CARRIER

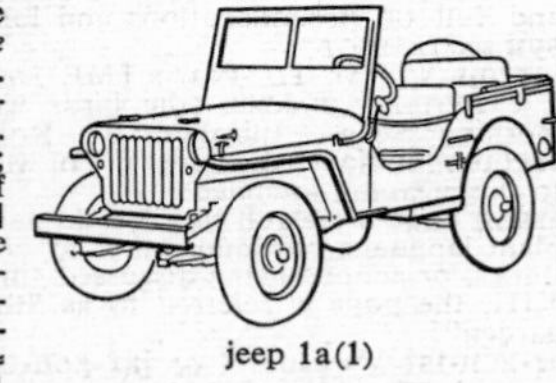

jeep 1a(1)

²jeep \"\ *vb* -ED/-ING/-S *vi* **:** to travel in a jeep ~ *vt* **:** to convey in a jeep
Jeep \"\ *trademark* — used for a civilian automotive vehicle
jeep·able \-pəbəl\ *adj* [¹*jeep* + *-able*] **:** so rough or narrow as to be impassable to motor vehicles except jeeps ⟨a ~ road⟩
jee·pers \ˈjēpə(r)z\ *also* **jeepers cree·pers** \ˈ=ˌ=ˈkrēpə(r)z\ *interj* [*jeepers* euphemism for *Jesus; jeepers creepers* euphemism for *Jesus Christ*] — used as a mild oath
jeep·ney \ˈjēpnē\ *n -s* [fr. *jeep* + *jitney*] **:** a Philippine jitney bus converted from a jeep
¹jeer \ˈji(ə)r, -iə\ *vb* -ED/-ING/-S [origin unknown] *vi* **:** to speak or cry out with derision or mockery **:** show contempt or scorn in often loud or coarse ridicule or sarcasm ⟨the fellows would ~ at him for knowing a girl —Hugh MacLennan⟩ ⟨~*ed* when he struck out⟩ ~ *vt* **:** DERIDE, MOCK, RIDICULE ⟨~*ed* the umpire's decision⟩ ⟨~*ed* his opponent when he tried to speak⟩ **syn** see SCOFF
²jeer \"\ *n -s* **1 :** a jeering remark or sound **:** TAUNT ⟨the tough kid's ~: "If they're good they're probably phony" —*Time*⟩ **2 :** the quality or state of jeering ⟨knew he was angry, though his voice showed nothing but a gentle ~ —Richard Llewellyn⟩
jeer·er \ˈjirə(r)\ *n -s* **:** one that jeers
jeer·ing·ly *adv* **:** in a jeering manner
jeers \ˈji(ə)rz, -iəz\ *n pl* [ME *jeres*] **:** a combination of tackles for hoisting or lowering the lower yards
jeez *also* **geez** \ˈjēz\ *interj* [euphemism for *Jesus*] — used as a mild oath
je·fe \ˈhā(ˌ)fā\ *n -s* [Sp, fr. F *chef* — more at CHIEF] *Southwest* **:** CHIEF, LEADER ⟨labor ~*s* willing to forgive, forget —*Santa Fe New Mexican*⟩
jef·fer·is·ite \ˈjef(ə)rəˌsīt\ *n -s* [William W. *Jefferis* †1906 Am. banker + E *-ite*] **:** a mineral consisting of a vermiculite containing iron, aluminum, and magnesium
jef·fer·son city \ˈjefə(r)sən-\ *adj, usu cap J&C* [fr. *Jefferson City*, Missouri] **:** of or from Jefferson City, the capital of Missouri ⟨*Jefferson City* schools⟩ **:** of the kind or style prevalent in Jefferson City
jefferson da·vis's birthday \-ˈdāvəs(əz)-\ *n, usu cap J&D&B* [after *Jefferson Davis* †1889 president of the Confederate States of America] **:** June 3 observed as a holiday in most of the southern states
jefferson day *n, usu cap J&D* [after Thomas *Jefferson* †1826 Am. president] **:** April 13 observed as a holiday in Alabama, Missouri, and Oklahoma in honor of the birthday of Thomas Jefferson

jef·fer·so·nia \ˌjefə(r)ˈsōnēə, -nyə\ *n, cap* [NL, fr. Thomas *Jefferson* + NL *-ia*] **:** a genus of American and Asiatic herbs (family Berberidaceae) with basal palmately lobed leaves, solitary white flowers, and capsular fruit — see TWINLEAF

¹jef·fer·so·nian \ˌ==ˈsōnēən, -nyən\ *adj, usu cap* [Thomas *Jefferson* + E *-ian*] **:** of, associated with, or favoring Thomas Jefferson or Jeffersonianism ⟨the *Jeffersonian* states' rights school —R.G.McCloskey⟩ ⟨the underlying assumptions of *Jeffersonian* democracy —Gerald Stourzh⟩

²jeffersonian \"\ *n* -s *usu cap* **:** a follower of Thomas Jefferson **:** an adherent of Jeffersonianism ⟨continuity between the Federalists and the *Jeffersonians* — *Times Lit. Supp.*⟩ ⟨modern *Jeffersonians* . . . believe in government intervention in economic life —Reinhold Niebuhr⟩

jef·fer·so·nian·ism \ˌ==ˈsōnēəˌnizəm, -ōnyəˌn-\ *n* -s *usu cap* **:** the political principles and ideas held by Thomas Jefferson or later associated with his name and centering around a belief in states' rights, a strict construction of the federal Constitution, confidence in the political ability of the common man, and an agrarian as opposed to an industrial or commercial economy

jef·fer·son·ite \ˈjefə(r)səˌnīt\ *n* -s [Thomas *Jefferson* + E *-ite*] **:** a mineral $Ca(Mn,Zn,Fe)Si_2O_6$ consisting of a dark green or greenish black pyroxene

jef·frey pine \ˈjefrē-\ *also* **jef·frey's pine** \-ēz-\ *n, usu cap J* [after John *Jeffrey*, 19th cent. Scot. gardener and botanical explorer] **:** a tall symmetrical pine (*Pinus jeffreyi*) of western No. America that has long blue-green needles in groups of three and elongated cones borne on spreading or somewhat pendulous branches and that is sometimes classified as a variety of the ponderosa pine from which it differs chiefly in lighter color of bark and needles

jeffrey pine beetle *n, usu cap J* **:** a bark beetle (*Dendroctonus ponderosae*) destructive to Jeffrey pine in California

jehad *sometimes cap, var of* JIHAD

je·ho·vah \jəˈhōvə\ *n* -s *cap* [NL, intended as a transliteration of Heb *Yahweh*, the vowel points of Heb *'ădhōnāy* my lord being erroneously substituted for those of *Yahweh;* fr. the fact that in some Heb manuscripts the vowel points of *'ădhōnāy* (used as a euphemism for *Yahweh*) were written under the consonants *yhwh* of *Yahweh* to indicate that *'ădhōnāy* was to be substituted in oral reading for *Yahweh*] **:** ²GOD — a Christian transliteration of the tetragrammaton long assumed by many Christians to be the authentic reproduction of the Hebrew sacred name for God but now recognized to be a late hybrid form never used by the Jews; compare YAHWEH

jehovah god *n, cap J&G* **:** a supreme deity recognized and the only deity worshiped by Jehovah's Witnesses

jehovah's witnesses *n pl, cap J & usu cap W* **:** members of a group that witness by distributing literature and by personal evangelism to beliefs in the theocratic rule of God, the sinfulness of organized religions and governments, and an imminent millennium

je·ho·vism \jəˈhōˌvizəm\ *n* -s *cap* **:** YAHWISM

¹je·ho·vist \-ˌvəst\ *n* -s *usu cap* [*Jehovah* + *-ist*] **:** YAHWIST 1

²jehovist \"\ *adj, usu cap* **:** YAHWISTIC 1

je·ho·vis·tic \ˌjēˌhōˈvistik, ˌjēˌhō;v-\ *adj, usu cap* **1 :** of or relating to the religion of Jehovah **2 :** YAHWISTIC

je·hu \ˈjē(ˌ)h(y)ü, ˈjē(ˌ)yü, ˈjā(-\ *n* -s *sometimes cap* [fr. *Jehu* †*ab* 816 B.C. king of Israel who was noted for his furious attacks in a chariot (2 Kings 9:20)] **:** a driver esp. of a cab or coach; *specif* **:** one who drives fast or recklessly ⟨a tattered ~ . . . who took the dune road to Dhaid as though the devil himself were after him —Ralph Hammond-Innes⟩

jeis·tic·corp \ˈjēsti,kȯ(ə)r\ *Scot var of* JUSTACORPS

jejun- *or* **jejuno-** *comb form* [*jejunum*] **1 :** jejunum ⟨*jejunectomy*⟩ **2 :** jejunal and ⟨*jejunoduodenal*⟩

je·ju·nal \jəˈjünᵊl, (ˈ)jēˈjü-\ *adj* [*jejun-* + *-al*] **:** of or relating to the jejunum

je·june \jəˈjün, (ˈ)jēˈjün\ *adj* [L *jejunus*] **1** *obs* **:** lacking food **:** HUNGRY **2 :** inadequate to nourish the body or relieve hunger **:** wanting nutritive value ⟨the ~ diets of the very poor⟩ **3 a :** devoid of interest or significance **:** DULL, FLAT, INANE, VAPID ⟨the lectures . . . seemed ~ and platitudinous —John Buchan⟩ ⟨literary history without evaluative criteria becomes ~ and sterile —C.I.Glicksberg⟩ **b :** giving evidence of lack of experience or information ⟨a singularly brief, all too ~, note on the historical events that occasioned the document —*Times Lit. Supp.*⟩ ⟨not appointed because they are qualified in investment or economics, but their comments on such matters need not be ~ —*Economist*⟩ **c :** IMMATURE, JUVENILE, PUERILE ⟨the ~ behavior of an adolescent boy⟩ ⟨~ remarks on world affairs by one who possessed no relevant knowledge⟩

syn see INSIPID

je·june·ly *adv* **:** in a jejune manner

je·june·ness \-ünnəs\ *n* -ES **:** the quality or state of being jejune

je·ju·ni·ty \jəˈjünəd·ē, jēˈjü-\ *n* -ES [L *jejunitas*, fr. *jejunus* jejune + *-itas* -ity] **:** the quality or state of being jejune

je·ju·nos·to·my \jəˌjüˈnästəmē, (ˌ)jēˌjü-\ *n* -ES [ISV *jejun-* + *-stomy*] **1 :** the surgical formation of an opening through the abdominal wall into the jejunum **2 :** the opening made by jejunostomy

je·ju·num \jəˈjünəm, jēˈ-\ *n, pl* **jeju·na** \-nə\ [L (trans. of Gk *nēstis*, fr. *nēstis* fasting), fr. neut. of *jejunus;* fr. the belief that it is empty after death] **:** the first two fifths of the small intestine beyond the duodenum usu. merging almost imperceptibly with the ileum though somewhat larger, thicker-walled, and more vascular and having more numerous circular folds and fewer Peyer's patches

jekyll–and–hyde \ˌjekələn(d)ˈhīd *also* ˈjēk- *or* ˈjāk-\ *adj, usu cap J&H* [after Dr. *Jekyll* and Mr. *Hyde*, the two sides of the split personality of the chief character in *The Strange Case of Dr. Jekyll and Mr. Hyde* (1886) by Robert Louis Stevenson †1894 Scot. writer] **:** of, relating to, or resembling a person who leads a double life or who has two apparently distinct characters one of which is good and the other evil ⟨the hooded bandit was a *Jekyll-and-Hyde* character —M.D. Portman⟩

jelatong *var of* JELUTONG

jel·er·ang \ˈjeləˌraŋ\ *n* -s [origin unknown] **:** a giant squirrel (*Ratufa bicolor*) of Java and southern Asia

jel·ick \ˈyelik\ *n* -s [Turk *yelek*] **:** the bodice or vest of a Turkish woman's dress

¹jell \ˈjel\ *vb* -ED/-ING/-S [back-formation fr. *jelly*] *vi* **1 :** to reach the consistency of jelly **:** CONGEAL, SET ⟨the grapes ~*ed* readily⟩ **2 :** to achieve distinctness **:** take shape **:** CRYSTALLIZE, SOLIDIFY ⟨romantic interludes that somehow fail to ~ —Hoffman Birney⟩ ⟨both thought and expression require time to ~ —A.T.Weaver⟩ ⟨long after the public's opinion has ~*ed* —J.W.Irwin⟩ ~ *vt* **:** to give distinctness to **:** cause to take form ⟨it was this discovery which did most to ~ his thought after it had been fluid during two decades —Hunter Mead⟩

²jell \"\ *n* -s **:** JELLY

jel·la·ba *or* **djel·la·ba** \jəˈläbə\ *also* **je·lab** \-b\ *n* -s [Ar *jallabah* & *jallāb*, alter. of *jallābīyah*] **:** a full loose garment (as of wool or cotton) with a hood and with sleeves and skirt of varying length orig. worn chiefly in Morocco

jellied gasoline *n* **:** NAPALM

jel·li·fi·ca·tion \ˌjeləfəˈkāshən\ *n* -s **:** the act or process of jellifying or the state of being jellified

jel·li·fy \ˈ==ˌfī\ *vb* -ED/-ING/-ES [¹*jelly* + *-fy*] *vt* **1 :** to make gelatinous **:** JELLY ⟨the red buttery mud is . . . *jellified* —Negley Farson⟩ **2 :** to reduce to slackness or weakness ⟨I turned, all *jellified* at his voice —Eugene Walter⟩ ~ *vi* **:** to become jelly or like jelly ⟨the lazy ear and the ~*ing* mind —*New Republic*⟩

Jell–O \ˈje(ˌ)lō\ *trademark* — used for a gelatin dessert often given the flavor and color of any of various fruits

jelloped *var of* JOLLOPED

¹jel·ly \ˈjelē, -li\ *n* -ES [ME *gelly, gellie*, fr. MF *gelee* frost, jelly, fr. fem. of *gelé* (past part. of *geler* to freeze, congeal), fr. L *gelatus*, past part. of *gelare* to freeze, congeal — more at COLD] **1 :** a semitransparent easily melted food preparation having a soft somewhat elastic consistency due to the presence of gelatin, pectin, or a similar substance: as **a :** ³ASPIC **b :** a dessert made usu. by adding gelatin to fruit juices **c :** a fruit product made by boiling sugar and the juice of fruit containing pectin **2 :** a substance resembling jelly esp. in consistency: as **a :** a transparent elastic gel **b :** a semisolid medicated or cosmetic preparation often having a gum base and usu. intended for local application ⟨ephedrine ~⟩ **c :** a jellylike preparation used in electrocardiography to obtain better conduction of electricity ⟨electrode ~⟩ **3 :** a gelatinous blue-green alga of the genus *Nostoc* found on damp ground esp. after a rain **4 :** JELLYFISH **5 :** a gelatin screen used to color or diffuse light (as of a theater spotlight) **6 :** a moral or emotional state felt to resemble jelly; *esp* **:** a state of fear or irresolution ⟨reduced to quivering ~ at the decisive moment⟩ **7 :** a shapeless structureless mass **:** PULP

²jelly \"\ *vb* -ED/-ING/-ES *vi* **1 :** to become jelly **:** come to the consistency of jelly **:** SET — compare ²GEL **2 :** to make jelly ⟨will be ~*ing* for days —Elizabeth Janeway⟩ ~ *vt* **:** to bring to the consistency of jelly — compare GELATINIZE

³jelly \"\ *adj* [alter. of *jolly*] *Scot* **:** POMPOUS, PROUD

jelly bag *n* **:** a bag typically of cheesecloth or flannel through which the juices for jelly are strained

jelly bean *n* **1 :** a sugar-coated candy bean with a gum or jelly center **2 :** a weak, spineless, or effeminate person ⟨this 50-year-old *jelly bean* —Shelby Foote⟩

jellybread \ˈ==ˌ=\ *n, North* **:** a piece of bread and jelly

jelly doughnut *n* **:** a raised doughnut with jelly filling

jelly end rot *n* **:** a fungous disease of the potato that is caused by fungi of the genera *Fusarium* and *Rhizoctonia* and that produces a soft rot of the stem end of the tubers

jellyfish \ˈ==ˌ=\ *n* **1 a :** any of various usu. marine and free-swimming coelenterates that constitute the sexually reproducing form of hydrozoans and scyphozoans which exhibit alternation of a sexual and an asexual generation and that have a nearly transparent saucer-shaped body with a mouth on the underside which extends by radially situated gastrovascular canals to the margin of the body, extensile marginal tentacles studded with stinging cells, and various sense organs distributed along the margin of the body — called also *sea nettle* **b :** SIPHONOPHORE **c :** CTENOPHORE — not used technically **2 :** a person lacking backbone or firmness ⟨if I should yield to threats . . . I should be a ~ by this time —Elinore M. Herrick⟩

jelly fungus *n* **:** any of various fungi whose appearance or consistency suggests jelly; *specif* **:** any fungus of the order Tremellales

jellyleaf \ˈ==ˌ=\ *n* **:** QUEENSLAND HEMP

jelly lichen *n* **:** a lichen with a gelatinous thallus; *esp* **:** any of numerous lichens having an algal component belonging to the genus *Nostoc*

jellylike \ˈ==ˌ=\ *adj* **:** resembling jelly in appearance or consistency **:** GELATINOUS

jelly of whar·ton \-ˈhwȯrtᵊn *also* -ˈwȯ-\ *usu cap W* [after Thomas *Wharton* †1673 Eng. anatomist] **:** WHARTON'S JELLY

jelly plant *n* **1 :** an Australian edible seaweed (*Eucheuma speciosum*) used in making jelly **2 :** KEI APPLE

jelly powder *n* **:** commercial gelatin mixed with sugar, flavoring, and color for use in making jellied desserts

jelly roll *n* **:** a thin sheet of sponge cake spread with jelly and rolled up while hot

jelly strength *n* **:** the strength of a gel or jelly (as gelatin or glue) expressed often as the weight in grams required to force a plunger into a test sample under specified conditions — called also *gel strength*

jel·u·tong *also* **jel·a·tong** *or* **jel·o·tong** \ˈjeləˌtȯŋ, -täŋ, ˌ==ˈ=\ *n* -s [Malay *jĕlutong*] **1 :** any of several trees constituting a genus (*Dyera*) of the family Apocynaceae **2 :** a glutinous milky juice that is obtained from various jelutongs (esp. *Dyera costulata*), resembles chicle, and is used chiefly in waterproofing, in rubber compounds, and in chewing gum

jem·a·dar \ˈjeməˌdär\ *or* **jam·a·dar** \ˈjəm-\ *n* -s [Hindi *jamā'dar, jam'dar* (influenced in meaning by Per *jamā'at* body of troops), fr. Ar *jam'* collections, assemblage + Per *dār* having] **1 :** an officer in the army of India having a rank corresponding to that of lieutenant in the English army **2 :** any of several police or other officials of the government of India

je·mez \ˈhāməs\ *n, pl* **jemez** *usu cap* [Sp *jemez, jemes*, of AmerInd origin] **1 :** a group of Tanoan Amerindian peoples of New Mexico **2 :** a member of a Jemez people

jem·lah goat \ˈjemlə-\ *n, usu cap J* [*jemlah* prob. native name in the Himalayas] **:** TAHR

¹jem·my \ˈjemi\ *adj* [alter. (influenced by the nickname *Jemmy*) of *jimp* + *-y*] *now dial Eng* **:** SPRUCE, NEAT, SNAPPY

²jemmy \"\ *n* -ES [fr. *Jemmy*, nickname for *James*] **1** *Brit* **:** JIMMY 1 ⟨*jemmies* in action, stealthy footsteps creeping upstairs and down —Rose Macaulay⟩ **2** *Brit* **:** a sheep's head used for food **3** *dial Eng* **:** GREATCOAT

jen \ˈrən\ *n* -s [Chin (Pek) *jen²*] **:** the cardinal Confucian virtue of benevolence to one's fellowmen

je·na glass \ˈyānə-\ *n, usu cap J* [fr. *Jena*, Germany] **:** glass of fine quality esp. suited for chemical and optical ware and other scientific and industrial applications

je ne sais quoi \zhənəˌsāˈkwä\ *n* **:** something that cannot be adequately described or expressed

jen·ne·ri·an \(ˈ)jeˈnirēən\ *adj, usu cap* [Edward *Jenner* †1823 Eng. physician + E *-ian*] **:** of or relating to Edward Jenner or by the method of Jenner ⟨*Jennerian* vaccination⟩

jen·net \ˈjenət\ *n* -s [ME *genett, jennett*, fr. MF *genet*, fr. Catal *ginet, genet* Zenete (member of a Berber people), mounted soldier, a kind of horse, fr. colloq. Ar *zinēti* (Ar *zanātiy*) of the Zenetes, fr. *Zanātah* the Zenete people] **1** *also* **gen·et** \"\ **:** a small Spanish horse **2** [influenced in meaning by ¹*jenny*] **a :** a female donkey **b :** HINNY

jen·nie harp \ˈjenē-, -ni-\ *n* [*jennie* alter. of ¹*jenny*] **:** the female harp seal

jen·ny \ˈjenē, -ni\ *n* -ES [fr. *Jenny*, nickname fr. the name Jane] **1 a :** a female bird or animal — often used in combination ⟨*jenny* wren⟩ **b :** a female donkey **2 :** SPINNING JENNY **3 :** a traveling crane; *esp* **:** a locomotive crane **4 :** JINNY **5** *or* **jen·nie** \"\ **:** a losing hazard in English billiards made at an acute angle to a long side of the table — see LONG JENNY, SHORT JENNY **6** *or* **jennie** -s *usu cap* [so called fr. its having the designation *JN*] **:** a training airplane used in World War I **7 :** a machine for cleaning grease or paint from surfaces by means of a jet of steam

jenny ass *n* **:** JENNET 2a

jenny cutthroat *n, dial Eng* **:** a whitethroat (*Sylvia communis*)

jenny howlet *n, dial Eng* **:** OWL

jenny lind bed \ˈ==ˈlin(d)-\ *n, usu cap J&L* [after *Jenny* (Johanna Maria) *Lind* †1887 Swed. coloratura soprano who successfully toured the U.S. (1850–52)] **:** an American spool bed

jenny wood *n, usu cap J* **:** FREIJO

jenny wren *n* **1 :** WREN **2 :** HERB ROBERT

jen·o·ar \ˈjenəˌwär\ *n* -s [native name in the East Indies] **:** any of several snappers of the Indian ocean; *esp* **:** a snapper (*Lutjanus sebae*) that is a popular food and game fish

jens *pl of* JEN

jeo·fail \ˈjeˌfā(ə)l\ *n* -s [AF *jeo fail, jo faill* I am at fault, I mistake] *archaic* **:** a mistake or oversight in legal pleading or other proceeding or the acknowledgment of such an error

jeop·ard \ˈjepə(r)d\ *vt* -ED/-ING/-S [ME *juparten, jeoparten, jeoparden*, back-formation fr. *jupartie, jeopartie, jeopardie* jeopardy] **:** JEOPARDIZE

jeop·ar·dize \-ˌdīz\ *vt* -ED/-ING/-S [*jeopardy* + *-ize*] **:** to expose to danger (as of imminent loss, defeat, or serious harm) **:** IMPERIL ⟨~ his life⟩ ⟨laws *jeopardizing* freedom of speech⟩ ⟨reforms too long delayed or denied have *jeopardized* peace, undermined democracy and swept away civil and religious liberty —F.D.Roosevelt⟩ **syn** see VENTURE

jeop·ar·dous \-dəs\ *adj* [ME *jupartous, jeopartous*, fr. *jupartie, jeopartie*, + *-ous*] **:** marked by risk or danger **:** PERILOUS, HAZARDOUS ⟨takes such ~ episodes philosophically . . . as occupational liabilities —*Natural History*⟩

¹jeop·ar·dy \-dē, -di\ *n* -ES [ME *jupartie, jeopartie, jeopardie*, fr. AF *juparti, jeu parti*, fr. OF, alternative, poem treating amorous problems in dialogue form, fr. *ju, jeu* game, play (fr. L *jocus* joke, jest, game) + *parti*, past part. of *partir* to divide — more at JOKE, PART] **1** *obs* **:** PROBLEM, DILEMMA; *also, obs* **:** TRICK **2 :** exposure to or imminence of death, loss, or injury **:** DANGER, HAZARD ⟨place a fortune in ~ by gambling⟩ **3 :** the danger that an accused person is subjected to when duly put upon trial for a criminal offense **syn** see DANGER

²jeopardy \"\ *vt* -ED/-ING/-ES **:** JEOPARDIZE, IMPERIL

jeopardy assessment *n* **:** a special assessment under the U.S. income-tax laws levied to collect an alleged deficiency when the taxing officer believes that delay may jeopardize the collection of the claim

je·quir·i·ty \jəˈkwirəd·ē\ *or* **jequirity bean** *n* -ES [Pg *jequiriti, jequiriti*, perh. of Indic origin; akin to Hindi *rattī* ratti — more at RUTTEE] **1 :** the scarlet and black seed of Indian licorice used in India and other tropical regions for beads in rosaries and necklaces and as a standard weight **2 :** INDIAN LICORICE

je·qui·ti·ba \jəˌkēd·əˈbä, zhəˌ-\ *n* -s [Pg *jequitibá*, fr. Tupi] **1 :** a So. American tree (*Cariniana legalis*) that yields a valuable hardwood similar to Colombian mahogany **2 :** the wood of the jequitiba — called also *Brazilian mahogany*

jer·boa \jərˈbōə, jer-\ *n* -s [Ar *yarbū'*] **1 :** any of several social nocturnal jumping rodents (family Dipodidae) inhabiting arid parts of the Old World, having long hind legs, long tail, and often large leaflike ears, and being mostly yellowish brown with white underparts and black-tipped tail **2 :** any of various jumping rodents (as a kangaroo rat or a pouched mouse)

jerboa

jerboa kangaroo *n* **:** any of several brush-tailed rat kangaroos (genus *Bettongia*)

jerboa mouse *n* **:** any of various leaping rodents usu. with elongated hind legs (as the sciuromorph pocket mice and kangaroo rats or the myomorph broad-toothed rat)

jerboa pouched mouse *n* **:** any of several small slender leaping marsupials (genus *Antechinomys*) of the central desert of Australia

jerboa rat *n* **:** any of several relatively large Australian rats (family Muridae) with hind legs adapted to leaping (as members of the genus *Conilurus*)

jer·e·me·jev·ite *also* **er·e·me·yev·ite** \ˌ(y)erəˈmā(y)əˌvīt, |fīt\ *n* -s [F *jérémeiéwite*, fr. Pavel V. Eremeev (*Jeremeiew*) †1899 Russ. mineralogist + F *-ite* -ite] **:** a mineral $AlBO_3$ consisting of aluminum borate in colorless or yellowish hexagonal crystals (hardness 6.5, sp. gr. 3.28)

jer·e·mi·ad \ˌjerəˈmīəd, -īˌad\ *n* -s [F *jérémiade*, fr. *Jérémie* Jeremiah (fr. LL *Jeremias*) + *-ade* -ad] **:** a lamenting and denunciatory complaint **:** a doleful story **:** a dolorous tirade ⟨a ~ against a civilization that values knowledge above wisdom —Lawrence Durrell⟩

jer·e·mi·ah \-īə\ *n* -s *usu cap* [after *Jeremiah* †*ab* 585 B.C. Heb prophet known for his pessimism, fr. LL *Jeremias, Hieremias*, fr. Gk *Hieremias*, fr. Heb *Yirmĕyāh*] **:** a person who complains about the evil, decay, and disaster that he sees about him and who foresees and predicts a calamitous future ⟨*Jeremiahs* lamenting the decline of public morals⟩

jer·e·mi·an·ic \ˌjerəˌmīˈanik\ *also* **jer·e·mi·an** \-ˈmīən\ *adj, usu cap* [*Jeremianic* fr. *Jeremiah* + E *-an* + *-ic; Jeremian* fr. *Jeremiah* + E *-an*] **:** of, relating to, or suggestive of the prophet Jeremiah or the biblical material of Jeremiah ⟨a *Jeremianic* discourse⟩ ⟨a *Jeremianic* tone⟩

je·rez \hāˈrās, -rāth\ *adj, usu cap* [fr. *Jerez*, Spain] **:** of or from the city of Jerez, Spain **:** of the kind or style prevalent in Jerez

jerfalcon *var of* GYRFALCON

jerican *var of* JERRICAN

¹jerk \ˈjərk, -ək, -əik\ *vb* -ED/-ING/-S [prob. alter. of *yerk*] *vt* **1** *obs* **:** to strike with or as if with a whip **2 :** to give a quick and suddenly arrested thrust, push, pull, or twist to ⟨~ a rope⟩ ⟨~ a coat off⟩ ⟨~ out a pistol⟩ **3 :** to throw with a quick motion suddenly arrested ⟨~ money on a table⟩; *specif* **:** to bowl (a cricket ball) illegally (as by bending the arm) **4 :** to utter in an abrupt, snappy, or sharply broken manner ⟨~ out words⟩ **5 :** to prepare and dispense (sodas) ~ *vi* **1 :** to make a sudden spasmodic motion or series of such motions **:** move with a start or starts ⟨fish ~*ing* and tumbling on the deck of a boat⟩ **2 :** to move in short abrupt motions ⟨a cripple ~*ing* along a street⟩ **:** move along with frequent jolts ⟨a train ~*ing* past a station⟩ **3 :** to throw an object with a jerk; *specif* **:** to jerk the ball in bowling in the game of cricket **4** *obs* **:** SNEER

syn SNAP, TWITCH, YANK: JERK indicates sudden, sharp, quick, graceless, forceful movement begun or ended abruptly ⟨thought the train would never start, but at last the whistle blew and the carriages *jerked* forward —G.G.Carter⟩ ⟨*jerked* her head back as if she'd been struck in the face —Dorothy Baker⟩ SNAP may apply to a quite quick action abruptly terminated, as biting or trying to bite sharply or seizing, clutching, snatching, locking, or breaking suddenly ⟨the hounds were fine beasts . . . lank and swift as they bent over the food to *snap* it into their jaws and swallow it quickly —Elizabeth M. Roberts⟩ ⟨the syndicate *snapping* up land as soon as it is for sale⟩ ⟨*snapped* at her because Theophilus did not eat enough —Margaret Deland⟩ TWITCH may indicate quick, sometimes spasmodic, and often light action combining tugging and jerking ⟨shrunken body continued to jerk and quiver, fingers *twitching* at his gray beard —Gerald Beaumont⟩ ⟨one Pan ready to *twitch* the nymph's last garment off —Robert Browning⟩ ⟨put out his hand to *twitch* off a twig as he passed —Willa Cather⟩ YANK indicates quick and heavy tugging and pulling ⟨watches her two-year-old stand passive while another child *yanks* his toy out of his hand —Margaret Mead⟩ ⟨she *yanked* the corset strings viciously —D.B.Chidsey⟩ ⟨by means of long blocks and tackle they set to *yanking* out logs —S.E.White⟩

²jerk \"\ *n* -s *often attrib* **1** *obs* **:** a stroke esp. of a whip **:** LASH **2 :** a single quick motion usu. of short duration and length (as a suddenly arrested pull, thrust, push, or jolt) ⟨get up with a ~⟩ **3 a :** jolting, bouncing, or thrusting motions ⟨a rustic dance full of ~ and rhythm⟩ **b :** tendency to produce spasmodic motions ⟨a car with little ~ and noise⟩ **4 a :** an involuntary spasmodic muscular movement due to reflex action; *esp* **:** one induced by an external stimulus — see KNEE JERK **b jerks** *pl* (1) **:** CHOREA (2) **:** involuntary twitchings due to nervous excitement (as in the dancing mania and sometimes in religious revivals) **5** [prob. fr. *jerk* "masturbator", fr. *jerk (off)*] **:** a stupid, foolish, naïve, or unconventional person ⟨these ~*s* . . . who didn't know anything outside their rank and serial number —J.G.Cozzens⟩ ⟨soapbox orators who . . . vary from philosophers to out-and-out ~*s* —Richard Joseph⟩ **6 :** the pushing of a weight from shoulder height to a position overhead **:** the second phase of the clean and jerk in weight lifting

³jerk \"\ *vt* -ED/-ING/-S [back-formation fr. ³*jerky*] **:** to cut into long slices or strips and dry in the sun ⟨~ beef⟩ — see CHARQUI

jerked *past of* JERK

jerk·er \-kə(r)\ *n* -s **:** one that jerks

jerk·i·ly \-kəlē, -li\ *adv* **:** in a jerky manner ⟨bowed ~, first to the orchestra, then to the audience —*Time*⟩

¹jer·kin \-kən\ *n* -s [origin unknown] **1 :** a close-fitting hip-length jacket made without sleeves or with extended shoulders, being usu. collarless and belted, and cut like the 16th century doublet over which it was orig. worn **2 :** any of various adaptations of the 16th century jerkin often worn now by both men and women

²jerkin \"\ *n* -s [prob. fr. *gerfalcon* + *-kin*] **:** a male gyrfalcon

jerk·i·ness \-kēnəs, -kin-\ *n* -ES **:** the quality or state of being jerky

jerking *pres part of* JERK

jerk·ing·ly *adv* **:** JERKILY

jerkinhead \ˈ==ˌ=\ *n* [prob. alter. (influenced by ¹*jerkin*) of *kirkinhead*] **:** a hipped part of a roof which is hipped only for a part of its height leaving a truncated gable

jerkinhead

jerk line *n* **:** a single rein used orig. in the western U.S. that was fastened to the brake handle and ran through the driver's hand to the bit of the lead animal

jerk off *vb* **:** MASTURBATE — usu. considered vulgar

jerk pump *n* **:** a fuel-injection pump in an oil engine which supplies impulsively an accurately metered charge to the nozzle at the time of the opening of the inlet valve

jerks *pres 3d sing of* JERK

jerkwater \'=,==\ *or* **jerk** *adj* [¹*jerk* + *water;* fr. the fact that rural trains took on water that was carried in buckets from the source of supply] **1 :** insignificant and remote ⟨a ~ town⟩ ⟨a ~ college⟩ **2 :** contemptibly petty, narrow, or trivial **:** PIDDLING ⟨a ~ carnival act⟩ ⟨a ~ politician⟩

¹**jerky** \'jərkē, 'jək-,'-jəik-, -ki\ *adj* -ER/-EST [²*jerk* + -*y*] **1 a :** moving along with or accompanied by fits and starts **:** JOLTING ⟨a ~ vehicle⟩ **b :** characterized by abrupt or awkward transitions ⟨a ~ prose style⟩ **2 a :** INANE, FOOLISH ⟨~ adolescents hanging around drugstores⟩ **b :** contemptibly weak or ineffectual ⟨the ~ policies of an ignorant governor⟩

²**jerky** \"\ *n* -ES **:** a horse-drawn wagon usu. without springs that is used for carrying passengers

³**jer·ky** \"\ *n* -ES [modif. of Sp *charquí* — more at CHARQUI] **:** meat (as beef) that has been jerked

jer·mo·nal \ˌjərməˈnäl\ *n* -S [prob. fr. Hindi *jaṛ* cold + *munāl* pheasant] **:** HIMALAYAN SNOW COCK

jer·o·bo·am \ˌjerəˈbōəm\ *n* -S *sometimes cap* [after *Jeroboam* I †*ab*912 B.C. king of the northern kingdom of Israel referred to as the "mighty man of valor" (1 Kings 11:28—AV)] **1 :** an oversize wine bottle holding about four quarts ⟨a ~ of champagne⟩ **2** *Brit* **:** CHAMBER POT

je·ro·mi·an \jəˈrōmēən\ *adj, usu cap* [St. *Jerome* (Eusebius *Hieronymus*) †420 church father + E -*ian*] **:** of or relating to St. Jerome or his works

jer·ri·can *or* **jerry can** *also* **jeri·can** \ˈjerē,kan\ *n* [²*jerry* + *can*] **:** a 5-gallon fluid container

¹**jer·ry** \ˈjerē, -ri\ *n* -ES [fr. *Jerry,* nickname for the names *Jeremy* & *Jeremiah*] **1** *archaic* **:** the noise that according to custom was made (as by hammering, beating, or rattling) to celebrate the end of someone's term of apprenticeship in the printing trade **2** [by shortening & alter. fr. *jeroboam*] *Brit* **:** CHAMBER POT

²**jerry** \"\ *n* -ES *usu cap* [alter. (influenced by ¹*jerry* and the name *Jerry*) of *German*] *chiefly Brit* **:** GERMAN

³**jerry** \"\ *adj* -ER/-EST [back-formation fr. *jerry-built*] **:** POOR, SLIPSHOD, MAKESHIFT ⟨~ workmanship⟩

jerry-build \'==,=\ *vb* [back-formation fr. *jerry-built*] *vt* **1 :** to build (as a house) flimsily of materials of poor quality **2 :** to put together, contrive, or devise with insufficient care or planning ⟨attempt to *jerry-build* a military pact —Denis Healey⟩ ⟨*jerry-builds* the English language as if it were the English countryside —Cyril Connolly⟩ **~** *vi* **:** to put up a jerry-built structure **:** do building cheaply and with inferior materials

jerry-builder \'==,==\ *n* **:** one that jerry-builds; *esp* **:** a builder who erects cheap buildings of poor materials and unsubstantial construction esp. on speculation for quick sale

jerry-built \'==,=\ *adj* [*jerry* prob. fr. *Jerry,* nickname for *Jeremy* & *Jeremiah*] **1 :** built cheaply and unsubstantially of poor or insufficient materials ⟨*jerry-built* wharves⟩ ⟨buying sagging old houses or *jerry-built* new ones —Vera Connolly⟩ ⟨mean-looking little houses, very *jerry-built* —John Morris⟩ ⟨600 acres of *jerry-built* shacks —Emory Ross⟩ ⟨the thin walls of the *jerry-built* house —Virginia Woolf⟩ **2 :** carelessly or hastily put together **:** constructed without due thought or care **:** unsound in planning or execution **:** FLIMSY; *often* **:** constructed or devised at haphazard ⟨*jerry-built* tax legislation —*N.Y. Times*⟩ ⟨the political empire of Rome became more and more *jerry-built* —Weston La Barre⟩ ⟨the movie is a particularly unsatisfying, *jerry-built* affair —Manny Farber⟩

jerry-come-tumble \'==(,)=ˌ==\ *also* **jerry-go-nimble** \'==-(,)=ˌ==\ *n* -S *usu cap J* **1** *dial Eng* **:** TUMBLER **2** *dial Eng* **:** CIRCUS

jerry man *n* **:** a wasteman in a mine

jerrymander *var of* GERRYMANDER

jer·sey \ˈjərzē, ˈjəz-,ˈjəiz-, -zi, *dial* ˈjärz- *or* ˈjäz-\ *adj, usu cap* [fr. *Jersey,* one of the Channel islands] **:** of or from the island of Jersey, Channel islands **:** of the kind or style prevalent in Jersey

²**jersey** \"\ *n, often attrib* **1** *also* **jersey cloth** -S **a :** a plain weft-knitted fabric in tubular form made of wool, cotton, nylon, rayon, or silk and used for underwear, dresses, sportswear **b :** TRICOT 1 **2** -S **:** any of various close-fitting usu. circular-knitted garments: as **a :** a man's sleeveless cotton undershirt **b :** a pullover with short or long sleeves worn esp. by children, athletes, or sailors **3 a** *usu cap* **:** a breed of rather small short-horned dairy cattle originating on the island of Jersey in the English channel and now widely distributed, being in color predominantly yellowish brown or fawn although sometimes ranging from silvery gray or pale buff to black with occasional white marking, and being noted for the high fat content of their milk **b** -S *often cap* **:** an animal of the Jersey breed

³**jersey** \"\ *adj, usu cap* [fr. (*New*) *Jersey,* the Channel island] **:** NEW JERSEY

¹**jer·sey·an** \-zēən, -ziən\ *n* -S *usu cap* [(*New*) *Jersey* + E -*an*] **:** a native or resident of the state of New Jersey

²**jerseyan** \"\ *adj, usu cap* **:** of, relating to, or characteristic of New Jersey or New Jerseyites

jersey city *adj, usu cap J&C* [fr. *Jersey City,* New Jersey] **:** of or from Jersey City, N.J. ⟨a *Jersey City* physician⟩ **:** of the kind or style prevalent in Jersey City

jersey cream *n, often cap J* [²*Jersey* (cattle)] **:** POLAR BEAR 2

jersey elm *n, usu cap J* [¹*Jersey*] **:** an elm that is a variety (*Ulmus campestris wheatleyi*) of the English elm with erect branches and broader leaves — called also *Guernsey elm*

jersey giant *n* [³*Jersey*] **1** *usu cap J&G* **:** a breed of very large domestic fowls developed in New Jersey by interbreeding large Asiatic fowls with Langshans and being orig. solid black but now having a white variety **2** *usu cap J & often cap G* **:** a bird of the Jersey Giant breed

jer·sey·ite \-zē,īt, -zi,īt\ *n* -S *usu cap* [(*New*) *Jersey* + E -*ite*] **:** a native or resident of the state of New Jersey

jersey justice *n, usu cap 1st J* [³*Jersey;* fr. the supposedly more efficient legal system in New Jersey] **:** speedy and effective justice (as in criminal cases)

jersey lightning *n, usu cap J* [³*Jersey*] *slang* **:** APPLEJACK

jersey·man \'==mən\ *n, pl* **jerseymen** *usu cap* [*Jersey,* the island + *man*] **1 :** a native or resident of the island of Jersey **2 :** NEW JERSEYITE

jersey pine *n, usu cap J* [³*Jersey*] **:** a common open or straggling pine (*Pinus virginiana*) of the eastern U.S. having leaves only an inch or two long

jersey tea *n, usu cap J* [³*Jersey*] **1 :** NEW JERSEY TEA **2 :** WINTERGREEN 2a

jert \ˈjərt\ *chiefly Scot var of* JERK

je·ru·sa·lem \jəˈrüs(ə)ləm *also* -üz| *or* |ə,lem\ *adj, usu cap* [fr. *Jerusalem,* Palestine, fr. LL *Jerusalem, Hierusalem,* fr. Gk *Ierousalēm, Hierousalēm,* fr. Heb *Yĕrūshālaim*] **:** of or from Jerusalem, a city of Palestine now divided between the Republic of Israel of which it is the capital and the Hashimite Kingdom of Jordan **:** of the kind or style prevalent in Jerusalem

jerusalem artichoke *n, usu cap J* [*Jerusalem* by folk etymology fr. It *girasole* — more at GIRASOL] **1 :** a perennial American sunflower (*Helianthus tuberosus*) widely cultivated and often occurring as an escape **2 :** the tuber of Jerusalem artichoke used as a vegetable, as a feed for livestock, and as a source of levulose

jerusalem cherry *n, usu cap J* **:** either of two plants of the genus *Solanum* (*S. pseudo-capsicum* or *S. capsicastrum*) cultivated as ornamental house plants for their bright orange to red berries

jerusalem corn *n, usu cap J* **:** DURRA

jerusalem cricket *n, usu cap J* **:** a burrowing nocturnal insect (*Stenopelmatus fuscus*) of the southwestern U.S. related to the katydids and having a large head and transverse black abdominal stripes — called also *sand cricket*

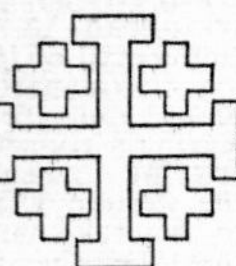
Jerusalem cross

jerusalem cross *n, cap J* **1 :** a cross potent with a small Greek cross in each of the four spaces between the arms **2** [so called fr. the resemblance of the arrangement of the leaves to the shape of the Jerusalem cross] **:** MALTESE CROSS 2

jerusalem haddock *n, usu cap J, West* **:** OPAH

jerusalem oak *n, usu cap J* **1 :** an aromatic oak-leaved goosefoot (*Chenopodium botrys*) **2 :** MEXICAN TEA

jerusalem pea *n, usu cap J* **:** an East Indian perennial bean (*Phaseolus trinervius*) that is closely related to and sometimes considered a variety of the urd bean

jerusalem pine *n, usu cap J* **:** ALEPPO PINE

jerusalem sage *n, usu cap J* **:** any of several plants of the genus *Phlomis* (as *P. fruticosa* or *P. tuberosa*) often cultivated and having dense axillary whorls of purple flowers

jerusalem star *n, usu cap J* **1 :** SALSIFY **2 :** SNOW-IN-SUMMER **3 :** a Eurasian evergreen shrub (*Hypericum calycinum*) with large showy yellow flowers

jerusalem sunday *n, usu cap J&S* **:** MID-LENT SUNDAY

jerusalem tea *n, usu cap J* **:** MEXICAN TEA

jerusalem thorn *n, usu cap J* **1 :** CHRIST'S-THORN **2 :** a large shrub or shrubby tree (*Parkinsonia aculeata*) that is native to tropical America but naturalized in the southern and southwestern U.S., that has pinnate leaves with small deciduous leaflets, sharp spines, and showy racemose yellow flowers, and that is used for hedging and as emergency food for livestock esp. in dry regions — called also *horsebean* **3 :** CATECHU 2

jer·vine \ˈjər,vēn, -ˌvən\ *n* -S [NL *jervina,* fr. Sp *yervina,* perh. fr. *yervo* vetch, chick-pea (fr. L *ervum*) + -*ina* -ine] **:** a crystalline alkaloid $C_{26}H_{39}NO_3$ related in structure to the steroids and found in the rhizomes and roots of white hellebore, American hellebore, and other species of the genus *Veratrum*

jes \ˈjes\ *n* -ES [prob. native name in West Africa] **:** OTTER SHREW

¹**jess** *or* **jesse** \ˈjes\ *n, pl* **jesses** [ME *ges, gesse,* fr. MF *gies, giez,* fr. pl. of *giet, get, jet* throw — more at JET] **:** either of two short straps of leather or other material secured on the legs of a hawk used in falconry and usu. provided with a ring for attaching a swiveled leash

²**jess** \"\ *vt* -ED/-ING/-ES **:** to attach jesses to (a hawk)

jessamine *var of* JASMINE

jes·sa·my \ˈjesəmē, -mi\ *n* -ES [modif. of *jessamine*] **1** *dial Eng* **:** JASMINE **2** [so called fr. the use of perfume] **:** DANDY, FOP

jesses: *1* ring for leash, *2* swivel, *3* ring for jesses, *4* jesses

jes·sant-de-lis *also* **jes·sant-de-lys** \ˌjesᵊn(t)dəˈlē\ *adj* [*jessant* (prob. alter. of *jacent*) + fleur-*de-lis*] **:** having the upper points of a fleur-de-lis arising from the top of the head and the lower points projecting from the mouth — used of a heraldic leopard's face

jes·se *also* **jes·sie** *or* **jes·sy** \ˈjesē, -si\ *n, pl* **jesses** *also* **jessies** [prob. after *Jesse,* father of David in the Bible; fr. "And there shall come forth a rod out of the stem of Jesse" (Isa 11:1—AV)] *chiefly dial* **:** a severe scolding or beating ⟨just as soon as I go home I'll give you ~ —Alice Cary⟩

jessed \ˈjest\ *adj* [¹*jess* + -*ed*] **:** having on jesses

jes·se tree \ˈjesē-, -si-\ *or* **jesse** *n* -S *usu cap J* [after *Jesse,* father of David in the Bible] **:** a genealogical tree in which the lineage of Christ is represented in sculpture and decorative art — called also *tree of Jesse*

jesse window *n, usu cap J* [after *Jesse* in the Bible] **:** a decorative window in which a Jesse tree is a principal subject of the design

jes·sur \ˈjesə(r)\ *n* -S [perh. fr. Beng] **:** RUSSELL'S VIPER

¹**jest** \ˈjest\ *n* -S [ME *geste, jeste,* fr. OF *geste, jeste,* fr. L *gesta* deeds, fr. neut. pl. of *gestus,* past part. of *gerere* to bear, wage, cherish, accomplish — more at CAST] **1 a** *obs* **:** ACT, DEED, EXPLOIT **b :** an act intended to provoke laughter **:** PRANK ⟨began as a ~ and ended as a tragedy⟩ ⟨signs marking the city limits . . . pranksters carry off and plant in remote spots as a ~ —*Amer. Guide Series: Calif.*⟩ **c :** a ludicrous circumstance or incident ⟨a proper ~, and never heard before, that Suffolk should demand a whole fifteenth for costs and charges —Shak.⟩ **2 a :** a jeering remark **:** GIBE, TAUNT ⟨many a foul ribald ~ at the expense of the prisoner —J.L.Motley⟩ **b :** a witty remark **:** clever quip **:** MOT ⟨the kind of wry ~ that had sent the ancient gods into peals of ironic laughter —T.B. Costain⟩ **3 a :** a frivolous mood or manner — usu. used with *in* ⟨done in ~ and not supposed to be taken seriously⟩ ⟨many a true word is spoken in ~⟩ **b :** GAIETY, MERRIMENT ⟨I knew him, Horatio: a fellow of infinite ~, of excellent fancy —Shak.⟩ **4 :** the butt of a joke **:** LAUGHINGSTOCK ⟨to be the standing ~ of all one's acquaintance —R.B.Sheridan⟩ **syn** see FUN, JOKE

²**jest** \"\ *vb* -ED/-ING/-S [ME *gesten* to tell a tale, recite a romance, fr. *geste,* n.] *vi* **1 :** to utter taunts **:** jeer and mock **:** GIBE ⟨mock not nor ~ at anything of importance —George Washington⟩ ⟨~*s* at scars that never felt a wound —Shak.⟩ **2 :** to speak or act without seriousness or in a frivolous manner ⟨you surely ~, interrupted I; I am a foreigner, and you would abuse my ignorance —Oliver Goldsmith⟩ **3 :** to make a witty remark **:** say something amusing **:** QUIP, JOKE ⟨~*ed* with her in a low voice —Anne D. Sedgwick⟩ **4** *obs* **:** to make merry ⟨as gentle and as jocund as to ~ go I to fight —Shak.⟩ **~** *vt* **:** to jeer and mock at **:** make fun of **:** RIDICULE, BANTER ⟨~*ed* his friend over his fondness for horses⟩

jestbook \'=,=\ *n* **:** a book containing jests and jokes — called also *jokebook*

jest·ee \(ˈ)jeˈstē\ *n* -S **:** a person subjected to jesting

jest·er \ˈjestə(r)\ *n* -S [alter. of ME *gestour,* fr. *gesten* + -*our* -or] **1** *archaic* **:** a professional teller of gests ⟨harper's strain and ~'s tale went round in vain —Sir Walter Scott⟩ **2 :** FOOL 2a ⟨a court ~⟩ ⟨the world never has believed its ~*s* even when they knew more than its kings —James Street⟩ **3 :** one given to uttering jests or playing the clown ⟨has played to perfection the role of the world's . . . ~ —*Time*⟩

jest·ing·ly *adv* **:** in a jesting manner

¹**jesu·it** \ˈjezh|əwət *also* -ez| *or* |wət; *usu* -əd· + V\ *n* -S *usu cap* [NL *Jesuita,* fr. LL *Jesus* + L -*ita* -ite] **1 :** a member of a religious society for men founded by St. Ignatius Loyola in 1534 **2 :** one given to intrigue or equivocation **:** a crafty person **:** CASUIST ⟨one fourth of all power is in these ignorant masses, and they are in the hands of the political *Jesuits* of the South —*No. Amer. Rev.*⟩

²**jesuit** \"\ *adj, usu cap* **:** of or relating to the Jesuits or Jesuitism

jesuit berry *n, usu cap J* **:** PARTRIDGEBERRY 1

jesu·it·ed \-(,)wid·əd, -ˌwəd-\ *adj, usu cap, archaic* **:** JESUITIC

jesu·it·ic \ˌ==ˈwid|ik, -ˈ|wit|, |ēk\ *or* **jesu·it·i·cal** \|əkəl, |ēk-\ *adj* **1** *usu cap* **:** of or relating to the Jesuits, Jesuitism, or jesuitry **2** *often cap* **:** having qualities thought to resemble those of a Jesuit — usu. used disparagingly ⟨the low cunning and *Jesuitical* trick with which she deludes her husband —S.T. Coleridge⟩ — **jesu·it·i·cal·ly** \|ək(ə)lē, |ēk-, -li\ *adv, often cap*

jesu·it·ism \'==ˌwəd·,izəm, -wə,ti-\ *n* -S **1** *usu cap* **:** the system, doctrine, or practices of Jesuits **2** *often cap* **:** JESUITRY

jesu·it·ize \-əd·,īz, -ə,tīz\ *vb* -ED/-ING/-S *often cap, vi* **:** to act or teach in the actual or ascribed manner of a Jesuit **~** *vt* **:** to indoctrinate with actual or ascribed Jesuit principles — usu. used disparagingly

jesu·it·ry \-ətrē, -ri\ *n* -ES *often cap* **:** principles or practices ascribed to the Jesuits (as the practice of mental reservation, casuistry, and equivocation) — usu. used disparagingly

jesuits' bark *also* **jesuit bark** *n, usu cap J* [so called fr. the fact that it was brought into Europe from the Jesuit missions in So. America] **:** CINCHONA 3

jesuits' drops *n pl, usu cap J* **:** FRIAR'S BALSAM

jesuits' nut *n, usu cap J* **:** WATER CHESTNUT 1

jesuits' tea *also* **jesuit tea** *n, usu cap J* **1 :** MATÉ **2 :** MEXICAN TEA

jesuit style *n, usu cap J* **:** a baroque style of architecture in ecclesiastical buildings of the 16th and 17th centuries

jesuits' water nut *n, usu cap J* **:** WATER CHESTNUT 1

je·sus bug \ˈjēzəs- *also* -zəz-\ *n, usu cap J* [after *Jesus* Christ; fr. the allusion to his walking on water (Mt 14:25)] **:** WATER STRIDER 1

¹**jet** \ˈjet, *usu* -ed· + V\ *n* -S [ME *get, jet,* fr. MF *jaiet, geet, gest,* fr. L *gagates,* fr. Gk *gagatēs,* fr. *Gagas,* river and ancient town in the district of Lycia in southern Asia Minor] **1 :** a very compact velvet-black mineral of the nature of coal that is often used for jewelry **2 :** JET BLACK

²**jet** \"\ *adj* [ME *get, jet,* n.] **1 :** made of jet **2 :** of the color jet

³**jet** \"\ *vi* **jetted; jetted; jetting; jets** [ME *jetten,* perh. fr. MF *jeter* to throw, but influenced in meaning by L *jactare* to throw, boast] **1** *obs* **:** to walk with a haughty or pompous air **:** STRUT, SWAGGER ⟨how he ~*s* under his advanced plumes —Shak.⟩ ⟨when the stage of the world was hung with black they *jetted* up and down like proud tragedians —Thomas Dekker⟩ **2 a** *archaic* **:** to walk along slowly **:** STROLL **b** *obs* **:** to walk in a sprightly manner **:** CAPER, TRIP **3 :** to move about very quickly **:** DART ⟨hoped to see . . . the wingless squirrel ~ from tree to tree —James Montgomery⟩

⁴**jet** \"\ *n* -S *archaic* **:** an artificial way of walking **:** HITCH, SWAGGER ⟨the genteel trip and the agreeable ~ as they are now practiced at the court of France —Eustace Budgell⟩

⁵**jet** \"\ *vb* **jetted; jetted; jetting; jets** [MF *jeter,* lit., to throw, fr. L *jactare* to throw, shake, speak out, boast, fr. *jactus,* past part. of *jacere* to throw; akin to Gk *hienai* to send, Toch A *ya-* to make, do, Hitt *ijami* I make, I do] *vi* **1 a** *obs* **:** INTRUDE, ENCROACH ⟨insulting tyranny begins to ~ upon the innocent and aweless throne —Shak.⟩ **b :** to project or jut prominently ⟨the rock *jetted* out over the deep canyon⟩ **2 :** to spout forth **:** emit a jet **:** GUSH, SPURT ⟨molten material from the bowels of earth ~*s* up between sedimented water-laid rocks —Russell Lord⟩ ⟨flame and smoke *jetted* from the sides of the five warships —Kenneth Roberts⟩ **~** *vt* **1 :** to make projections on (as a building) **:** cause to project ⟨the second stories of the houses were *jetted,* shadowing the street from the sun⟩ **2** *now dial Eng* **:** to throw (as a ball) with a jerk **3 :** to emit in a stream **:** blow out **:** SPOUT ⟨while I waited . . . the other gun *jetted* smoke —Kenneth Roberts⟩ ⟨*jetted* a powerful stream of water at the burning building⟩ **4 a :** to place (as a pile or caisson) in the ground by means of a jet of water acting at the lower end **b** (1) **:** to bore (as a well) by means of a high-pressure jet of air or water (2) **:** to flush out the drillings from (a well) by means of a jet of water **5 :** to apply an insecticide to (an animal) in small jets under pressure

⁶**jet** \"\ *n* -S [MF, fr. *jeter*] **1 a** (1) **:** a forceful rush of liquid, gas, or vapor through a narrow or restricted opening in spurts or in a continuous flow ⟨trained the powerful ~ of water on the fire⟩ ⟨saw a practical use for these burning ~*s* of gas escaping from the earth's fissures —Gardiner Symonds⟩ (2) **:** a usu. high-speed stream of fluid that is discharged from a nozzle or orifice in a body and that produces reaction forces tending to propel the body in the direction opposite to that of the discharge — see JET PROPULSION **b :** a nozzle for a jet of gas, water, or other fluid ⟨a garden fountain with more than 200 ~*s* —F.J.Taylor⟩ **c :** something issuing in or as if in a jet ⟨sometimes the whole story is a ~ of irony —H.M.Reynolds⟩ ⟨talk poured from her in a brilliant ~ —*Time*⟩ **2** *dial Eng* **:** a large ladle **3 :** a projection at the bottom of a piece of foundry type as it comes from the mold that is planed off in finishing — called also *tail, tang* **4 a :** JET AIRPLANE **b :** JET ENGINE

⁷**jet** \"\ *vi* **jetted; jetted; jetting; jets :** to travel by jet airplane ⟨*jetted* to London to see the show —*Newsweek*⟩

⁸**jet** \"\ *n* -S [prob. alter. of *gist*] **:** the main point **:** GIST ⟨but . . . I don't see the ~ of your scheme —R.B.Sheridan⟩

jet airplane *also* **jet plane** *n* **:** an airplane powered by a jet engine that utilizes the surrounding air in the combustion of fuel or by a rocket-type jet engine that carries its fuel and all the oxygen needed for combustion

jetbead \'=,=\ *n* **:** a shrub (*Rhodotypos scandens*) that has black shining fruit and is used as an ornamental

jet black *n* **:** a very dark black

jet coal *n* **:** CANNEL COAL

je·té \zhəˈtā\ *n* -S [F, fr. past part. of *jeter* to throw, hurl — more at JET] **:** a sharp leap in ballet with an outward thrust of the working leg — see GRAND JETÉ, TOUR JETÉ

jeté en tour·nant \-,äⁿ,türˈnäⁿ\ *n* [F, lit., jeté while turning] **:** TOUR JETÉ

jet engine *also* **jet motor** *n* **:** an engine that produces motion as a result of the rearward discharge of a jet of fluid; *specif* **:** an airplane engine having one or more exhaust nozzles for discharging rearward a continuous jet or intermittent jets usu. of heated air and exhaust gases to produce forward propulsion — see ROCKET 4

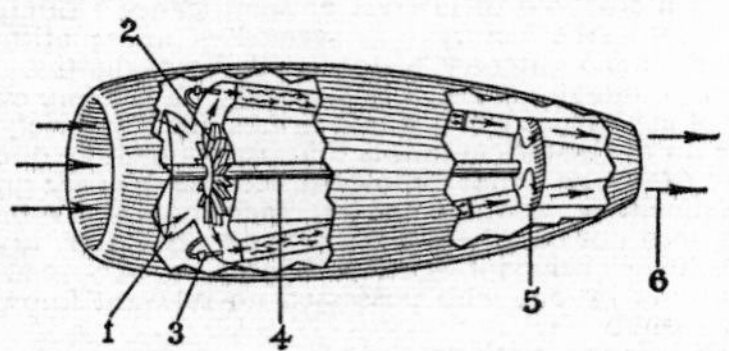

jet engine (simplified cutaway): *1* air intake, *2* impeller or compressor, *3* fuel injection, *4* drive shaft, *5* turbine, *6* exhaust

jeth \ˈjet\ *n* -S *usu cap* [Hindi *Jēṭh,* fr. Skt *Jyaiṣṭha*] **:** a month of the Hindu year — see MONTH table

Jet Liner \'=ˌ==\ *trademark* — used for a jet-propelled airliner

jet·ness *n* -ES [²*jet* + -*ness*] **:** the quality or state of being the color jet black

jeton \ˈjetᵊn, zhəˈtōⁿ\ *or* **jet·ton** \ˈjetᵊn\ *n, pl* **jetons** *or* **jettons** \-tᵊnz, -tōⁿ(z)\ [F *jeton,* fr. MF, fr. *jeter* to throw, cast up (accounts), calculate — more at JET] **:** ¹COUNTER 1a

jet-pile \'=,=\ *n* **:** a pile placed in position by means of a jet of water under high pressure acting at the toe of the pile to form a space for settling of the pile

jetport \'=,=\ *n* **:** an airport designed esp. for jet planes

jet power *n* **:** power derived from jet engines

jet-propelled \ˌ==ˈ=\ *adj* **1 :** propelled by one or more jet engines ⟨*jet-propelled* bomb⟩ ⟨*jet-propelled* airplane⟩ **2 :** suggestive of the speed and force of a jet airplane **:** HIGH-POWERED ⟨a good and successful novelist producing his works at *jet-propelled* speed —Antonia White⟩ ⟨she possesses enthusiasm and restless energy, her songs are *jet-propelled* —*Punch*⟩

jet propulsion *n* **:** propulsion of a body by means of a jet of fluid (as in the motion given to an inflated toy balloon when the compressed air is allowed to escape through the neck or the motion given to a rocket by the rearward discharge of a high-speed stream of hot gases produced by the rocket fuel); *specif* **:** propulsion of an airplane by one or more jet engines

jet pump *n* **:** a pump in which a small jet of steam, air, water, or other fluid in rapid motion lifts or otherwise moves by its impulse a large quantity of the fluid with which it mingles

jets *pl of* JET, *pres 3d sing of* JET

jet·sam \ˈjetsəm\ *n* -S [alter. of ¹*jettison*] **1** *archaic* **:** JETTISON **2 :** the part of a ship, its equipment, or cargo that is cast overboard by the master to lighten the load in time of distress and that sinks or is grounded — distinguished esp. in law from *flotsam* and *lagan* **3 :** FLOTSAM 2

jet·son \ˈjetsən\ *or* **jet·som** \-səm\ *archaic var of* JETTISON

jet stream *n* **:** a long narrow meandering current of high-speed winds near the tropopause blowing from a generally westerly direction and often exceeding a speed of 250 miles per hour

jet·tage \ˈjed·ij\ *n* -S [¹*jetty* + -*age*] **:** dues levied on a ship for the use of a jetty or pier

jet·teau \(,)jeˈtō\ *n* -S [modif. of F *jet d'eau*] **:** a jet of water

¹**jet·ted** \ˈjed·əd\ *adj* [¹*jet* + -*ed*] **:** having ornaments of jet

²**jetted** \"\ *adj* [fr. past part. of ⁵*jet*] *Brit* **:** PIPED, BOUND — used esp. of pockets

¹**jet·ter** \ˈjed·ə(r)\ *n* -S [¹*jet* + -*er*] **:** one that digs jet

²**jetter** \"\ *n* -S [⁵*jet* + -*er*] **:** one (as a geyser) that sends out a jet

jet thrust *n* **:** THRUST 3c(2)

jetting *pres part of* JET

¹**jet·ti·son** \ˈjed·əsən, ˈjet|, |-əzən\ *n* -S [ME *jetteson,* fr. AF *getteson,* fr. OF *getaison, getaisson* action of throwing, fr. L *jactation-, jactatio* — more at JACTATION] **1** *marine insurance* **:** a voluntary sacrifice of cargo of a ship necessitated by immediately impending danger threatening the general interest —

compare GENERAL AVERAGE **2 :** a casting overboard or away (as of an object, a person, an idea) **:** ABANDONMENT ⟨illustrates more forcibly than any election that has yet taken place the ~ of convictions, of honor, of patriotism —*Saturday Rev.*⟩

2jettison \"\ *vt* -ED/-ING/-S **1** *maritime law* **:** to make flotsam and jetsam of ⟨deck loads were so heavy that many carriers had to ~ cargo when they got into a stiff blow —D.H.Clark⟩ **2 :** to cast off as an encumbrance **:** get rid of **:** throw away **:** ABANDON, DISCARD ⟨if a diver does not know how to control his equipment or to ~ it in an emergency . . . he courts disaster —Byron Porterfield⟩ ⟨the obsolete has been calmly ~*ed;* the translation into the contemporary is complete —J.L.Lowes⟩ ⟨an army too soft to ~ its weaklings is on the way out —*Infantry Jour.*⟩ **3 :** to drop (as auxiliary equipment, bombs, cargo, or fuel) from an airplane in flight (as for lightening the load or providing greater safety) ⟨external long-range fuel tanks which can be ~*ed* in combat —Peter Masefield⟩

jet·ti·son·able \-nəbəl\ *adj* **:** designed for being jettisoned or capable of being easily jettisoned from an airplane ⟨~ fuel tanks⟩

jet·to \'je,tō\ *n* -S [It *getto,* fr. *gettare* to throw, fr. L *jactare* — more at JET] **:** JETTEAU

jetton *var of* JETON

jet·tru \'je·(,)trü\ *n* -S *usu cap* **:** a union of seven Turkish peoples of central Asia formed at the end of the 17th or beginning of the 18th century under one khan

1jet·ty \'jed·|ē, -et|, |i\ *n* -ES [ME *getee, jette,* fr. MF *jetee* action of throwing or thrusting, jetty, fr. fem. of *jeté,* past part. of *jeter* to throw — more at JET] **1 a :** a structure (as a pier or mole of wood or stone) extended into a sea, lake, or river to influence the current or tide or to protect a harbor; *also* **:** a protecting frame of a pier **b :** a landing wharf or pier often of framed woodwork **2 :** a part of a building that projects beyond the rest ⟨one of the most common features of New England colonial architecture was the overhanging second story or ~ as it was called —H.S.Morrison⟩ **3 :** a protecting outwork **:** BASTION, BULWARK **4** *dial Eng* **:** a narrow passage or raised footpath **syn** see WHARF

2jetty \"\ *vi* -ED/-ING/-ES **1 :** PROJECT, JUT — used esp. of a part of a building **2 :** to extend like a jetty for a distance into a body of water ⟨the great Municipal Pier which *jetties* out nearly a mile into the lake —*Time*⟩

3jetty \"\ *adj* [¹*jet* + -*y*] **:** having the color jet black ⟨the sky was of a ~ black, and the stars were brilliantly visible —E.A. Poe⟩ ⟨a wine-red lined cowl which she wore demurely over her ~ hair —Herman Wouk⟩

jetware \'=,=\ *n* **:** pottery usu. of red clay covered with a jet-black glaze

jeu \'zhə, |ər(·), |ə̄, *F* |œ̄\ *n, pl* **jeux** \|ə(z), |ərz, |ər(·), |ə̄(z), |œ̄\ [F, fr. L *jocus* joke, jest, game — more at JOKE] **:** GAME

jeu d'es·prit \,=də'sprē\ *n, pl* **jeux d'esprit** [F, lit., play of the mind] **:** a play or piece of writing displaying cleverness or wit ⟨senseless to ignore as a mistaken *jeu d'esprit* the labor that went into those parodies —Hugh Kenner⟩

jeune fille \,zhə(r)n'fē, -ə̄n-, *or as F*\ *n, pl* **jeunes filles** \"\ [F] **:** a young girl

jeune pre·mier \-prəm'yā\ *n, pl* **jeunes premiers** \-ā(z)\ [F] **:** the juvenile lead in a play ⟨bowed low . . . as if he were indeed some real *jeune premier* —H.E.Bates⟩

jeu·nesse do·rée \,zhə(r)¦nesdə'rā, zhə̄;-, -(,)dō'-, -,dō̄'-, *or as F*\ *n* [F, gilded youth] **:** young people of wealth and fashion ⟨one might have taken him for the type of the *jeunesse dorée* of Virginia surrounded with tutors, servants, horses, and dogs —Van Wyck Brooks⟩ ⟨artists are beginning to contest the occupation of that territory with the *jeunesse dorée* —Stuart Preston⟩

1jew \'jü\ *n* -S [ME *Gyu, Jewe, Jew,* fr. OF *gyu, jeu, jué, juef,* fr. L *Judaeus,* adj. & n., fr. Gk *Ioudaios,* fr. Heb *Yĕhūdhī,* fr. *Yĕhūdhāh* Judah, Jewish kingdom in southern Palestine, after *Yĕhūdhāh* Judah, 4th son of Jacob and ancestor of the Judahites] **1** *usu cap* **a :** JUDAHITE **b :** ISRAELITE 1 **2** *cap* **:** a member of the nation existing in Palestine from the 6th century B.C. to the 1st century A.D. within which the elements of Judaism largely developed **3** *cap* **:** a person belonging to the worldwide group constituting a continuation through descent or conversion of the ancient Jewish people and characterized by a sense of community; *esp* **:** one whose religion is Judaism — see ASHKENAZI, SEPHARDI **4** *usu cap* **:** a person believed to drive a hard bargain

2jew \"\ *adj, usu cap* **:** JEWISH — usu. taken to be offensive

3jew \"\ *vt* -ED/-ING/-S *sometimes cap* **:** to cheat by sharp business practice — usu. taken to be offensive

jewbird \'=,=\ *n* [¹*jew* + *bird;* fr. its conspicuous beak] **:** ANI

jewbush \'=,=\ *n* [¹*jew* + *bush;* prob. fr. the shape of the involucres] **:** either of two tropical American low shrubs of the genus *Pedilanthus* (*P. tithymaloides* and *P. padifolius*) possessing powerful emetic and drastic properties

jew crow *n* [prob. so called fr. its prominent curved beak] *dial Eng* **:** CHOUGH

jew down *vt, sometimes cap J* **:** to induce (a seller) by haggling to lower his price **:** get (a price or a sum) reduced by haggling — usu. taken to be offensive

1jew·el \'jüəl, 'jụ̇l *also* |l, *chiefly Brit* |(,)il\ *n* -S *often attrib* [ME *juel, jowel, jewel,* fr. OF *juel, joel, joiel,* dim. of *ju, jo, jeu* game, play — more at JEOPARDY] **1** *archaic* **:** an article with intrinsic value usu. used for adornment ⟨here, wear this ~ for me; 'tis my picture —Shak.⟩ **2 a :** a precious stone; *esp* **:** a stone cut and polished for use as an ornament ⟨they shall fetch thee ~*s* from the deep —Shak.⟩ **b** (1) **:** one that is highly esteemed or prized ⟨had our prince, ~ of children, seen this hour —Shak.⟩ (2) **:** something that resembles a jewel ⟨this lake — a ~ nestling amid mountains —H.J.Laski⟩ ⟨presenting the ~ of truth in a pleasing setting —R.A.Hall b.1911⟩ **3 a :** an ornament of precious metal usu. gold or silver, often set with stones or finished with enamel work and now usu. worn as an accessory of dress or as the badge of an order **b :** an article of costume jewelry **4 a :** a bearing for a pivot in a watch or a delicate instrument (as a compass) made of a crystal or a precious stone (as a ruby or sapphire) or of glass **b :** a lining of brass or other soft metal for a bearing (as on a railroad car) **5 :** an ornamental boss of colored glass

2jewel \"\ *vt* **jeweled** *or* **jewelled; jeweled** *or* **jewelled; jeweling** *or* **jewelling; jewels 1 a :** to adorn with jewels ⟨you are as well ~*ed* as any of them —Ben Jonson⟩ ⟨the kings go by with ~*ed* crowns —John Masefield⟩ **b :** to equip with jewels ⟨company sells more ~*ed* watches than any other in the U.S. —*Time*⟩ ⟨building precision ~*ed* engines by mass-production methods —*Newsweek*⟩ **c :** to trim with jeweling ⟨lacy white wool . . . heavily ~*ed* with iridescent sequins —*Women's Wear Daily*⟩ **2 :** to give beauty or perfection to as if by adorning with jewels ⟨the still swamp water was dark . . . but in open patches it was ~*ed* with reflected stars —Myrtle R. White⟩ ⟨~*ing* all this outer zone of the marsh are the little birds —D.C.Peattie⟩ ⟨a dazzling blaze of ~*ed* words and flashing images —*Times Lit. Supp.*⟩

jewel beetle *n* **:** any of various usu. brightly colored beetles of the family Buprestidae

jewel block *n* **:** a block at the extremity of a yard through which the halyard of a studding sail is rove

jewel box *or* **jewel case** *n* **1 :** a small chest designed to hold jewelry **2 :** something small and exquisite ⟨his house . . . a *jewel box,* quite the most desirable upon the seaside drive —D.C.Peattie⟩

jewel box 1

jewel cloth *n* **:** a usu. gauzy fabric with sparkling metallic bits sprinkled over its surface that is used chiefly for stage costumes and window displays

jew·el·er *or* **jew·el·ler** \-lə(r)\ *n* -S [ME *jueler, joweler,* fr. *juel, jowel* jewel + -*er* — more at JEWEL] **1 a :** an artist who designs and makes jewelry — compare GOLDSMITH **b :** one who repairs jewelry **2 :** one who deals in precious and costume jewelry, precious stones, watches, and usu. silverware, china, and giftwares **3 :** one who specializes in the construction and repair of highly sensitive scientific instruments

jewelers' block insurance *n* **:** all-risk insurance covering jewelers' stocks including property of others in the custody of the insured

jewelers' putty *n* **:** PUTTY POWDER

jewelers' rouge *n* **:** rouge that is of fine quality and fine particle size

jewel fish *n* **:** a small scarlet and olive African cichlid fish (*Hemichromis bimaculatus*) irregularly speckled with emerald green or sapphire that is sometimes kept in a tropical aquarium

jeweling *or* **jewelling** *n* -S **1 :** the act or art of working in or of applying jewels **2 :** the ornamentation of pottery with bosses of glass or glaze **3 :** an arrangement of real or imitation jewels used as a trimming on a dress

jew·el·lery \-lri\ *chiefly Brit var of* JEWELRY

jew·el·ry \-lrē,-lri\ *n* -ES [ME *juelrie, jowelrie,* fr. *juel, jowel* jewel + -*rie* -ry] **1 :** ornamental pieces (as rings, necklaces, bracelets) made of materials that may or may not be precious (gold, silver, glass, plastic) often set with genuine or imitation gems and worn for personal adornment — see COSTUME JEWELRY **2 :** something like jewelry (as in beautifying or adorning) ⟨I wished to see the snow and ice, the divine ~ of winter —John Muir †1914⟩

jewels *pl of* JEWEL, *pres 3d sing of* JEWEL

jewelweed \'=(=),=\ *n* **:** a plant of the genus *Impatiens* **:** BALSAM 4: as **a :** a somewhat glaucous annual herb (*I. capensis*) of No. America that occurs from Newfoundland to Alaska and south to Florida chiefly on wet rather acid soil and has extremely variable but typically crimson-spotted orange open flowers and sometimes minute cleistogamous flowers — called also *celandine* **b :** a glaucous annual herb (*I. pallida*) that occurs on wet and usu. calcareous soil in much of eastern and central No. America and has canary yellow to creamy white flowers sometimes spotted with brownish red — called also *snapweed, touch-me-not*

jewelweed family *n* **:** BALSAMINACEAE

jew·ely *or* **jew·el·ly** *pronunc at* JEWEL + ē *or* i\ *adj* **1 :** having or wearing jewels **2 :** resembling a jewel **:** having the brilliance and sparkle of a jewel ⟨the ~ star of life had descended too far —Thomas De Quincy⟩

jew·ess \'jüəs\ *n* -ES *usu cap* [ME *Jewesse,* fr. *Gyu, Jewe, Jew* Jew + -*esse* -ess — more at JEW] **:** a female Jew

jewfish \'=,=\ *n* **1 :** any of various large groupers usu. dusky green or blackish, thickheaded, and rough-scaled, with a voracious but sluggish disposition: as **a :** GIANT BASS **b :** SPOTTED JEWFISH **c :** BLACK JEWFISH **2 :** any of various other large percoid fishes: as **a :** a western Australian lutjanid (*Glaucosoma hebraicum*) **b :** MULLOWAY

jewing *pres part of* JEW

1jew·ish \'jüish, -üēsh\ *adj, usu cap* **:** of, relating to, or characteristic of a Jew — **jew·ish·ly** *adv, usu cap*

2jewish \"\ *n* -ES *cap* **:** YIDDISH

jewish calendar *n, usu cap J* **:** a lunisolar calendar in use among Jewish peoples which is reckoned from the year 3761 B.C., which received its present form from Hillel II about A.D.360, and in which 19 years constitute a metonic cycle — see MONTH table, YEAR table

jew·ish·ness *n* -ES *usu cap* **:** the quality or state of being Jewish

jewish science *n, cap J&S* **:** a healing cult adapted from Christian Science to persons with a Jewish background

jew·ism \'jü,izəm\ *n* -S *usu cap* **1 :** JUDAISM **2 :** something characteristic of Jews

jew lizard *n, usu cap J* **:** an Australian agamid lizard (*Amphibolurus barbatus*)

jew monkey *n, usu cap J* [prob. so called fr. its beard] **:** any of several sakis and macaques

jew nail *n* **:** CORRUGATED FASTENER

jew plum *n, usu cap J* **:** OTAHEITE APPLE

jew·ry \'jụ̇rē, 'jürē, -ri\ *n* -ES *usu cap* [ME *Gywerie, Jewerie, Jewrie,* fr. OF *juierie, juiverie,* fr. *gyu, jeu, jué, juif* Jew + -*erie* -ery — more at JEW] **1 :** a quarter or district of a city or town inhabited by Jews **:** GHETTO **2** *archaic* **:** the land of Judea ⟨let me have a child . . . to whom Herod of *Jewry* may do homage —Shak.⟩ **3 a :** the part of the population of a country that adheres to Judaism ⟨the titular head of Scotch *Jewry* was both a classical scholar and a Hebraist —Maurice Samuel⟩ **b :** the world Jewish community ⟨the recognition of Israel as the focus of Jewish civilization, the cultural center of the world *Jewry* —*Reconstructionist*⟩

jews *pl of* JEW, *pres 3d sing of* JEW

jew's-ear \'=,=\ *n, pl* **jew's-ears** *usu cap J* [intended as trans. of NL *auricula Judae,* lit., ear of Judas, after *Judas* Iscariot, apostle that betrayed Jesus; fr. its resemblance to a human ear and its frequent growth on elder trees, on one of which Judas reputedly hanged himself] **:** a widely distributed edible fungus (*Auricularia auricula-judae*) growing on decaying wood

jew's harp \'jüz *also* ÷ 'jüs+,-\ *or* **jews' harp** *n, usu cap J* [perh. so called fr. their being purveyed by Jewish peddlers] **1 :** a small lyre-shaped instrument placed between the teeth and played by twanging an elastic metal tongue whose tone is modified by changing the size and shape of the mouth cavity **2** *also* **jews-harp-plant** \'=,=,=\ **:** NODDING TRILLIUM **3 :** the ring of an anchor

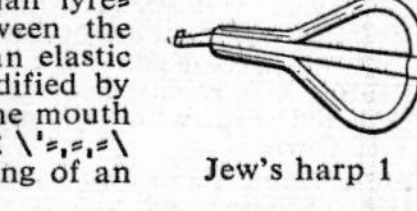

Jew's harp 1

jews' houses *n pl, usu cap J* **:** the remains of ancient tin-smelting furnaces and miners' houses in Cornwall and Devon

jew's mallow *n, usu cap J* **1 :** a stout herb (*Corchorus olitorius*) cultivated in Syria and Egypt as a potherb and in India for its jute fiber **2 :** JUTE 1

jew's-stone \'=,=\ *n, pl* **jew's-stones** *usu cap J* [trans. of ML *lapis Judaicus*] **1 :** a large fossil clavate spine of a sea urchin **2 :** MARCASITE 2

jews'-thorn \'=,=\ *n, usu cap J* [so called fr. the belief that it was used to crown Christ] **:** CHRIST'S-THORN

jew's trump *n, usu cap J* **:** JEW'S HARP 1

jew-tongo \'=¦täŋ(,)gō\ *n, usu cap J&T* [prob. fr. Jew-Tongo, fr. *jew* (fr. E *Jew*) + -*tongo* (as in *ningre-tongo*); perh. fr. the existence among its original speakers of former slaves who had been owned by Portuguese Jews] **:** an English-based creole language of Surinam

jewy \'jüē, -üi\ *adj* -ER/-EST *usu cap* **:** JEWISH — usu. used disparagingly

je·zail \jə'zī(ə)l, -zā(-\ *n* -S [Per *jazā'il*] **:** a long heavy Afghan rifle

jez·e·bel \'jezə,bel *also* -bəl\ *n* -S *often cap* [fr. *Jezebel,* 9th cent. B.C. Phoenician princess and wife of Ahab, king of Israel, known for her wicked conduct (1 Kings 16:31 ff)] **:** an impudent, shameless, or abandoned woman ⟨painted, screaming ~*s* hauled away by the raiding constables —Albert Parry⟩ — **jez·e·bel·ish** \-ish,-ēsh\ *adj, often cap*

jez·ek·ite \'jez(h)ə,kīt\ *n* -S [F *ježekite,* fr. Bohuslav *Ježek* 20th cent. Czech mineralogist + F -*ite*] **:** a mineral $Na_4CaAl_2(PO_4)_2(OH)_2F_2O(?)$ consisting of a basic aluminum calcium sodium fluophosphate occurring in colorless to white monoclinic crystals (hardness 4.5, sp. gr. 2.9)

JG *abbr or n* -S *often not cap* **:** junior grade **:** LIEUTENANT JUNIOR GRADE

jhang·ar \'jəŋə(r)\ *adj, usu cap* [*Jhang,* district in the Punjab where artifacts were found + E -*ar*] **:** of or relating to a culture in the Indus valley of about 2000 B.C. characterized by a crude handmade gray or black pottery having incised geometric ornamentation

jhan·si \'jän(t)sē\ *adj, usu cap* [fr. *Jhansi,* India] **:** of or from the city of Jhansi, India **:** of the kind or style prevalent in Jhansi

jha·ral \'järəl\ *n* -S [Nepali *jhāral*] **:** TAHR

jheel *or* **jhil** \'jē(ə)l\ *n* -S [Hindi *jhīl*] *India* **:** a pool, marsh, or lake esp. remaining from inundation

JHS *var of* IHS

jhu·kar \'jükər, -,kär\ *adj, usu cap* [fr. *Jhukar,* Sind, Pakistan, where artifacts were found] **:** of or relating to a culture of the Indus valley about 2500 B.C. and later, known from settlements built upon those of Harappa, characterized by buildings inferior to Harappa and round crudely decorated seals or seal amulets of pottery

JHVH *or* **JHWH** *var of* YHWH

1jib \'jib\ *n* -S [origin unknown] **1 :** a triangular sail set upon a stay or its own luff and extending from the head of the foremast or foretopmast to the bowsprit or the jibboom — see SAIL illustration **2** *dial Eng* **:** the lower lip or jaw

2jib \"\ *vb* **jibbed; jibbed; jibbing; jibs** *vt* **:** to cause to swing (as a sail or yard) from one side of a sailing vessel to another (as in tacking) ~ *vi* **1 :** to shift across or swing round from one side of a vessel to the other — used of a ship's sail, yard, or boom **2 :** to shift or swing in a way resembling jibbing ⟨the value of dollars, francs, and pounds sterling *jibbing* this way and that —*Time*⟩

3jib \"\ *n* -S [prob. by shortening & alter. fr. *gibbet*] **:** the projecting arm of a crane; *also* **:** a derrick boom

4jib \"\ *also* **gib** \"\ *vi* **jibbed** *also* **gibbed; jibbed** *also* **gibbed; jibbing** *also* **gibbing; jibs** *also* **gibs** [prob. fr. ²*jib*] **1 :** to move restively backward or sidewise **:** refuse to go; *also* **:** to stop short or back out **:** SHY — used of an animal in harness **2 a :** to show hesitation or a tendency to refuse to proceed further or act in a particular way **:** BALK ⟨he *jibbed* on singing because the women were there —Joseph Furphy⟩ ⟨never *jibbed* at the stiffest climb —Roy Saunders⟩ **b :** to show objection **:** balk in opposition ⟨it was only the middle classes at which he *jibbed* for he was genuinely devoted to his servants —Eric Keown⟩ ⟨*jibbed* at all grief which could not be brushed aside —Elizabeth Taylor⟩ **syn** see DEMUR

5jib \"\ *n* -S **:** JIBBER

1jibaro *usu cap, var of* JIVARO

2ji·ba·ro *or* **gi·ba·ro** \'hēbə,rō\ *n* -S [AmerSp *jíbaro, gíbaro,* prob. fr. *jíbaro* Jivaro] **:** a Puerto Rican small farmer, rural worker, or laborer esp. of mountainous regions

jib·ba *or* **djib·bah** *also* **jib·bah** \'jibə\ *n* -S [Egyptian Ar *jibbah,* var. of Ar *jubbah*] **:** a long loose cloth coat usu. with long sleeves worn esp. by Muslims

1jibber *var of* GIBBER

2jib·ber \'jibə(r)\ *n* -S [⁴*jib* + -*er*] **:** one that jibs; *esp* **:** a balky horse

jib·bings \'jibənz, -biŋz\ *n pl* [fr. gerund of Sc *jib* to milk a cow dry (of unknown origin) + -*s*] *Scot* **:** strippings from a cow

jib·boom \(')ji(b)¦büm\ *n* [¹*jib* + *boom*] **:** a spar which serves as an extension of the bowsprit and is sometimes itself extended by a flying jibboom — see SHIP illustration

jib crane *n* [³*jib*] **:** a crane having a jib

jib door \'jib-\ *n* [*jib* of unknown origin] **:** a door made flush with a wall without dressings or moldings and often disguised by continuing the finishings or decorations of the wall across its surface

1jibe *or* **gybe** \'jīb\ *vb* -ED/-ING/-S [perh. modif. (influenced by ¹*jib*) of D *gijben, gijpen*] *vi* **1** *of a fore-and-aft sail or its boom* **:** to shift suddenly and with force from one side to the other when a ship is steered off the wind until the sail fills on the opposite side **2 :** to change the course of a vessel so that the sail jibes — compare TACK 1a ~ *vt* **:** to cause to jibe

2jibe *or* **gybe** \"\ *n* -S **:** the swing of a sail or its boom in jibing or the turn of a sailboat so that its sail jibes

3jibe \"\ *var of* GIBE

4jibe *also* **gibe** \"\ *vi* -ED/-ING/-S [origin unknown] **:** to be in accord ⟨his account of the accident ~*s* pretty well with other accounts⟩ ⟨their inferior status did not ~ with democratic ideals —E.N.Palmer⟩ **syn** see AGREE

jibe-o \'jī(,)bō, jī'bō\ *interj* [¹*jibe* + -*o*] — used by the man at the tiller or wheel of a sailboat in warning that the boat is about to jibe

jib guy *n* [¹*jib*] **:** one of two or more lateral stays running to the head of the jibboom — see SHIP illustration

jibhead \'=,=\ *n* [¹*jib* + *head*] **:** a small iron bar for stretching the head of a jib when the point of the sail has been cut off

jib-headed \'=¦==\ *adj* [¹*jib*] *of a sail* **:** running up to a point at the head like a jib **:** TRIANGULAR — compare GAFF-HEADED

jib-header \'=¦==\ *n* **:** a jib-headed topsail

ji·bi \'jē(,)bē\ *n* -S [origin unknown] **:** a small chiefly yellowish green extinct bird (*Hemignathus obscurus ellisianus*) of Oahu

jib iron *n* [¹*jib*] **:** JIB TRAVELER

jiblet *var of* GIBLET

jib netting *n* [¹*jib*] **:** a triangular safety netting rigged under a jibboom — see SHIP illustration

ji·boa \jə'bōə\ *also* **ji·bo·ya** \-ō(y)ə\ *n* -S [Pg *jibóia,* fr. Tupi] **:** any of several large So. American boas

jib-o-jib \'jibə, jib\ *n* -S [¹*jib* + *o* (of) + *jib*] **:** a small jib set outside of the flying jib

jibs *pl of* JIB, *pres 3d sing of* JIB

jib sheet *n* [¹*jib*] **:** either of two ropes which lead from the clew of a jib to port and starboard respectively and by which the sail is trimmed

jibstay \'=,=\ *n* [¹*jib* + *stay*] **:** a stay on which a jib is set

jib topsail *n* [¹*jib*] **:** a small jib occas. used and set above and outside of all the other jibs

jib traveler *n* [¹*jib*] **:** an iron ring to which the tack of the jib on some cutters is made fast and which travels on the bowsprit

JIC *abbr* **1** joint industrial council **2** joint intelligence committee

ji·ca·ma \'hēkəmə\ *n* -S [MexSp *jícama,* fr. Nahuatl *xicama, xicamatl*] **1 :** a tall-climbing Mexican vine (*Exogonium bracteatum*) with showy flowers and a sweet watery root that is sometimes eaten raw or cooked — compare JALAP **2 :** YAM BEAN **3 :** a small dahlia (*Dahlia coccinea*) with yellow, orange, or scarlet flowers that is sometimes cultivated and is an ancestor of some improved horticultural dahlias

ji·ca·que *or* **xi·ca·que** \hē'kä(,)kā\ *n, pl* **jicaque** *or* **jicaques** *or* **xicaque** *or* **xicaques** *usu cap* [Sp, fr. Nahuatl *xicaque,* lit., ancient person] **1 a :** an Indian people of northern Honduras **b :** a member of such people **2 :** the language of the Jicaque people

ji·ca·que·an \-¸kēən\ *n* -S *usu cap* **:** a language family of the Hokan stock in Honduras comprising only the Jicaque language

ji·ca·ra \'hēkərə\ *n* -S [MexSp *jícara,* fr. Nahuatl *xicalli*] **1 :** CALABASH 2a **2 :** a cup or bowl made from the fruit of a calabash tree

ji·ca·ri·lla \,hēkə'rē(y)ə\ *n, pl* **jicarilla** *or* **jicarillas** *usu cap* [Sp, fr. MexSp, little basket, dim. of *jícara;* fr. the proficiency of the women in basketmaking] **1 a :** an Apache people of the western group ranging through southeastern Colorado, northern New Mexico, and adjacent sections of Kansas, Oklahoma, and Texas **b :** a member of such people **2 :** the language of the Jicarilla people

jiff \'jif\ *n* -S [by shortening] *slang* **:** JIFFY

jif·fle \'jifəl\ *vi* [origin unknown] *dial Eng* **:** to move restlessly **:** FIDGET

jif·fy \'jifē, -fi\ *n* -ES [origin unknown] **:** MOMENT, INSTANT — used chiefly in the phrase *in a jiffy*

1jig \'jig\ *n* -S [prob. fr. MF *giguer* to dance, jig, gambol about, frolic, fr. *gigue* fiddle, of Gmc origin; akin to OHG *gīga* fiddle; akin to ON *geiga* to turn aside — more at GIG] **1 a :** any of several lively springy dances in triple rhythm, popular in 16th and 17th century England and Scotland and still commonly danced in Ireland in a way characterized by intricate and dexterous motions of the feet **b :** music to which a jig may be danced **c :** GIGUE 3 **d :** a rapid usu. jerky up-and-down or to-and-fro motion ⟨the ~ of popcorn in a popper⟩ **2** *obs* **a :** a lively usu. jesting or mocking song **b :** a lively or comic act used at the end of a play or as an interlude **3 :** TRICK, STRATAGEM, GAME — now used chiefly in the phrase *the jig is up* **4 a :** any of several fishing devices (as a spoon hook) that are jerked up and down or drawn through the water — compare SQUID **b :** a device used to maintain mechanically the correct positional relationship between a piece of work and the tool working on it or between parts of work during their assembly **c :** a device in which crushed ore is concentrated or coal is cleaned in water by a rapid reciprocating vertical motion imparted to the substance either by mechanical means or by a pulsating water column **d :** a machine for dyeing piece goods by passing them at full width through the dye liquor by means of rollers **5** *also* **jigg** \"\ **:** NEGRO — often taken to be offensive — **in jig time** *adv* **:** with expeditiousness **:** RAPIDLY ⟨the tire was whipped off and changed *in jig time* —Dillon Ripley⟩

2jig \"\ *vb* **jigged; jigged; jigging; jigs** [prob. fr. MF *giguer*] *vt* **1 :** to dance in the rapid and lively manner of a jig ⟨~ a morris⟩ **2 a :** to give a rapid jerky up-and-down or to-and-fro motion to ⟨*jigged* his feet —Michael McLaverty⟩ ⟨a handful of coins that he rattled by *jigging* his thumb along the table —Saul Bellow⟩ **:** cause to jig ⟨grabbed a girl and started to ~ her around the yard —C.T.Jackson⟩ **b :** to separate (as ore from gangue or coal from slate) by a rapid up-and-down motion usu. in water **3 :** to catch (a fish) with a jig or by jerking a hook into the body **4 :** to drill (as a well) with a spring pole **5 :** to machine, form, or set in place by means of a jig-controlled tool operation ~ *vi* **1 a :** to dance a jig : execute a lively dance or dance step **b :** to move with a jigging motion or with rapid usu. jerky motions up and down or to and fro ⟨*jigged* furiously up and down to limber his leg muscles —A.J.Liebling⟩ **2 :** to fish with a jig ⟨several men in canoes *jigging* for cod —N.C.McDonald⟩ **3 :** to work with the aid of a jig

[3]**jig** \"\ — a communications code word for the letter *j*

jig·a·boo \ˈjigə,bü\ *n* -s [[1]*jig* + *-aboo* (as in *bugaboo*)] : NEGRO — often taken to be offensive

jig-a-jig *or* **jig-a-jog** *var of* JIG-JOG

jig·a·ma·ree \ˈjigəmə,rē, ˌ===ˈ=\ *n* -s [[1]*jig* + *-amaree*, of unknown origin] *slang* : something (as a device or contrivance) felt to be too fanciful, difficult, or small in value to designate accurately

jig-back \ˈ=,=\ *adj* [fr. the phrase *jig back*] : having two carriers that alternately ascend and descend — used of an aerial tramway

jig borer *n* [[1]*jig*] : a precision machine tool resembling a vertical milling machine, equipped with sensitive adjustments for the table and the position of the cutting tool, and used esp. for locating and drilling or boring holes in jigs

[1]**jig·ger** \ˈjigə(r)\ *n* -s [[1] and [2]*jig* + *-er*] **1 :** one that jigs : one that operates a jig: as **a :** one that concentrates ore by jigging — called also *jigman* **b :** one that shakes down the grain into sacks during bagging **c :** the operator of a dyeing jig — called also *jigman, vatman* **2 :** a light tackle usu. consisting of a double and single block and fall : WATCH TACKLE **3 :** [1]JIG 4a **4 a :** a small boat rigged like a yawl **b** *or* **jiggermast** \ˈ==,=\ (1) : a small mast stepped in the stern (as in a yawl or ketch) (2) : the aftermost mast of a four-masted ship **c :** a sail set on a jiggermast **5 a :** a mechanical contrivance esp. operating with a jerky reciprocating motion: as (1) : a machine carrying a revolving mold in which the clay for ceramics is shaped by a profile (2) : a machine for slicking or pebbling leather (3) : a tool for polishing the upper leather or the edge of a boot sole **b :** something (as a contrivance, device, or gewgaw) too complex, tricky, or trivial to designate accurately : GADGET **6 :** a measure used in mixing drinks and holding usu. one and one half ounces **7 :** JIG 4d **8 :** a cooper's drawknife **9 :** a golf iron with a narrow fairly well lofted face used esp. for approach shots **10 :** a part of a commercial fish trap that impounds the fish **11 :** [1]BRIDGE 3e

jigger 6

[2]**jigger** \"\ *vb* **jiggered; jiggered; jiggering** \-g(ə)riŋ\ **jiggers** [freq. of [2]*jig*] *vi, of a fish* : to give repeated tugs on a line ~ *vt* **1 :** to jerk up and down : give a series of tugs on **2 :** to alter or rearrange sometimes by manipulating ⟨~*ed* the records to cover up his theft⟩ **3** [[1]*jigger*] : to shape with a jigger in ceramics

[3]**jigger** \"\ *n* -s [of African origin; akin to Wolof *jiga* insect, Yoruba *jiˈga* jigger] : CHIGGER

jig·gered \ˈjigə(r)d\ *adj* [origin unknown] : DAMNED — used in mild oaths usu. in the phrase *I'll be jiggered*

jigger flea *n* [[3]*jigger*] : CHIGOE

jiggering *n* -s [fr. gerund of [2]*jigger*] : the process of forming ceramic ware by means of a jigger

jigger·man \ˈjigə(r)mən, -,man\ *n, pl* **jiggermen 1 :** one who forms pottery on a jigger **2 :** one who resurfaces and sharpens large grindstones on a stone-dressing lathe

jigger pump *n* [[1]*jigger*] : a pump to force beer into vats

jig·gers \ˈjigə(r)z\ *interj* [origin unknown] — used as a warning esp. that police are coming

jigger saw *n* [by alter.] : JIG SAW

jigger up *vt, slang* : to throw into confusion ⟨won't have the camp arrangements *jiggered up* any more than they are —C.S. Forester⟩ : foul up ⟨the machinery was all *jiggered up*⟩

jiggery-pokery \ˈjigərēˈpōkərē\ *n* -ES [alter. of *joukery-pawkery*] **1** *chiefly Brit* : HUMBUG, NONSENSE **2 :** underhanded dealings, conniving, or manipulations : MONKEY BUSINESS, SKULDUGGERY

jig·get \ˈjigət\ *vi* **jiggeted** *or* **jiggetted; jiggeted** *or* **jiggetted; jiggeting** *or* **jiggetting; jiggets** [[2]*jig* + *-et* (as in *fidget*)] : to move in a jigging or jerky way : JIG

jig·gety \-gəd·ē\ *adj, sometimes* -ER/-EST : JERKY, UNSTEADY

jigging *pres part of* JIG

jig·gish \ˈjigish, -gēsh\ *adj* : resembling or suitable for a jig or lively movement

[1]**jig·gle** \ˈjigəl\ *vb* **jiggled; jiggled; jiggling** \-g(ə)liŋ\ **jiggles** [freq. of [2]*jig*] *vi* : to move with quick little continuous jerks or oscillating motions back and forth or up and down ⟨*jiggling* like a doll on a coiled spring —Raymond Chandler⟩ ~ *vt* : to cause to jiggle ⟨*jiggled* the cup to mix the milk and the coffee —Wirt Williams⟩

[2]**jiggle** \"\ *n* -s **1 :** the motion of one that jiggles **2 :** a brief contrived fluctuation in the price of a stock more limited than a pool operation

jig·gly \ˈjig(ə)lē, -li\ *adj, often* -ER/-EST : tending to jiggle : UNSTEADY, JIGGLING ⟨the short leg of a ~ table —*New Yorker*⟩ : marked by a jiggling motion ⟨a ~ ride in a bus⟩

jig grinder *n* [[2]*jig*] : a precision grinding machine with fine adjustments for work requiring great accuracy (as in the fabrication of jigs and dies)

jiggumbob *n* -s [[2]*jig* + *-umbob* (of unknown origin)] *obs* : a contrivance or trifle felt to be too fanciful, difficult, or trivial to designate accurately

jig·gy \ˈjigē, -gi\ *adj, often* -ER/-EST : suggesting or having the effect of a jig

[1]**jig-jog** \ˈjig,jäg\ *also* **jig-jig** \-,jig\ *or* **jig-a-jog** \ˈjigə,jäg\ *or* **jig-a-jig** \ˈ==,=\ *vi* [[1]*jig* + *jog*] : to move with jigs or jogs : bounce jerkily up and down in proceeding : jolt repeatedly up and down

[2]**jig-jog** *also* **jig-jig** *or* **jig-a-jog** *or* **jig-a-jig** \"\ *n* : the movement of something that jig-jogs

[3]**jig-jog** *also* **jig-jig** *or* **jig-a-jog** *or* **jig-a-jig** \"\ *adv* : in the manner of one that jig-jogs ⟨trotted *jig-jog* down the road⟩

jig-joggy \ˈjig,jägē\ *adj* : jolting or bouncing jerkily up and down : JOGGING

jig·man \ˈjigmən\ *n, pl* **jigmen** [[1]*jig* + *man*] : JIGGER 1a, 1c

jigs *pl of* JIG, *pres 3d sing of* JIG

[1]**jigsaw** \ˈ=,=\ *n* [[1]*jig* + *saw*] **1 a :** a machine saw with a narrow vertically reciprocating blade for cutting curved and irregular lines or ornamental patterns in openwork **b :** SCROLL SAW **2 :** JIGSAW PUZZLE ⟨broken up like a ~ loose in its box —Wright Morris⟩ ⟨as the pieces of the ~ are fitted together —*Economist*⟩

jigsaw 1a

[2]**jigsaw** \"\ *vt* **1 :** to cut or form by or as if by a jigsaw ⟨coat and skirt ~*ed* out of her deceased father's Sunday suit —Francis & Katharine Drake⟩ **2 :** to arrange or place in an intricate or interlocking way in the manner of the parts of a jigsaw puzzle ⟨giant industrial plants ~*ed* together —Cameron Hawley⟩ ⟨the place was full of planes, ~*ed* into every foot of space —Frank Harvey⟩

[3]**jigsaw** \"\ *adj* **1 :** made up of pieces cut by a jigsaw **2 a :** consisting of intricate scrollwork ⟨~ detail around the eaves and windows⟩ ⟨gables decorated with ~ frills —*Amer. Guide Series: Tenn.*⟩ **b :** marked by the use of intricate scrollwork as decoration ⟨ornamental architecture of the ~ period —W.A. White⟩ **c** (1) : suggesting intricate scrollwork ⟨its spectacular ~ pattern of islands and inland waterways —W.R.Moore⟩ ⟨driving through its ~ streets —Kamala Markandaya⟩ ⟨transactions . . . of ~ complexity —*Lamp*⟩ (2) : suggesting a jigsaw puzzle or its separate pieces ⟨the witness may get history across at last in ~ bits —Mitchell Dawson⟩

jigsaw puzzle *n* : a puzzle made by sawing or cutting a picture into small pieces to be fitted together — called also *picture puzzle*

ji·gua \ˈhēgwə\ *n* -s [AmerSp, fr. Carib] : any of several tropical American trees of the genera *Ocotea* and *Nectandra*

jigue *var of* JIQUI

ji·had *also* **je·had** \jəˈhäd, -had\ *n* -s *sometimes cap* [Ar *jihād*] : a holy war waged on behalf of Islam as a religious duty; *broadly* : a bitter strife or crusade undertaken in the spirit of a holy war

ji·kun·gu \jəˈkuŋ(,)gü\ *n* -s [Shambala *zikungu, nkungu*, pl. of *lukungu*] : a tropical African plant (*Telfairia pedata*) of the family Cucurbitaceae cultivated for its edible seeds which also yield an oil

[1]**jill** *often cap, var of* GILL

[2]**jill** \ˈjil\ *n* -s [[1]*jill*] : a female ferret

jill·et \ˈjilət\ *n* -s [[1]*jill* + *-et*] *now Scot* : a vexatiously flirtatious girl : WENCH

[1]**jil·lion** \ˈjilyən\ *n* -s [*j-* + *-illion* (as in *million, billion*)] : an indeterminately large number ⟨any number of spots from one to a ~ —Alfred Bester⟩

[2]**jillion** \"\ *adj* : very great many ⟨climbing those stairs a ~ times a day —Jean Stafford⟩

[1]**jilt** \ˈjilt\ *n* -s [alter. of *jillet*] **1** *obs* : an unchaste woman : WHORE **2 a :** a woman who capriciously casts off one previously accepted as a lover **b :** a man who is capricious and irresponsible in love relations ⟨a young ~ who switched from one woman to another every few months⟩

[2]**jilt** \"\ *vt* -ED/-ING/-S **1 a :** to cast off or reject (as a lover) capriciously or unfeelingly **b :** to sever close relations with **2** *obs* : DECEIVE, CHEAT

jilt·ee \(ˈ)jilˈtē\ *n* -s : one who has been jilted

jilt·er \ˈjiltə(r)\ *n* -s : one that jilts

jim·ber-jawed \ˈjimbə(r)ˈjȯd\ *adj* [prob. alter. of *gimbal* + *jawed*] : having a projecting lower jaw

jimcrack *var of* GIMCRACK

[1]**jim crow** \ˈjimˈkrō\ *n, often cap J&C* [after *Jim Crow*, a stereotype Negro in a song-and-dance act presented by Thomas D. Rice †1860 Am. entertainer that was based on an anonymous song of the early 19th cent. called *Jim Crow*] **1 :** NEGRO — usu. taken to be offensive **2 :** discrimination (as in educational opportunity, social rights, or transportation facilities) against a racial or ethnic group other than white and esp. against the Negro in the southern U.S. by either legal enforcement or traditional sanctions and usu. by restrictive measures designed to prevent intermingling (as of Negroes with whites) on equal terms in public places ⟨the Supreme Court decision outlawing *Jim Crow* in dining cars on interstate trains —*Time*⟩ **3 a :** a machine for bending or straightening rails **b :** a planing machine with a reversing tool that can plane both ways

[2]**jim crow** \ˈ=ˈ=\ *adj, often cap J&C* **1 :** upholding jim crow ⟨gradual relinquishment of *Jim Crow* laws —Raymond Moley⟩ : practicing jim crow ⟨a *jim crow* school⟩ ⟨a *jim crow* town⟩ : marked by jim crow ⟨this *Jim Crow* environment —H.M.Gloster⟩ **2 :** set aside for the use of a racial or ethnic group (as the Negro in the southern U.S.) that is being discriminated against ⟨a *jim crow* railroad car⟩

[3]**jim crow** \"\ *vt, often cap J&C* : to subject to jim crow ⟨the exploited and *jim crowed* life of the Negro —Sidney Finkelstein⟩ ⟨many . . . states *jim crow* the Indians —Oliver La Farge⟩

jim crow·ism \ˈ=ˈ=,izəm\ *n, often cap J&C* : racial segregation

[1]**jim-dandy** \ˈjimˈ==\ *n* [*Jim* (nickname for *James*) + *dandy*] : something fine or wonderful of its kind ⟨the bicycle he got as a gift was a *jim-dandy*⟩

[2]**jim-dandy** \ˈ=ˈ==\ *adj* : fine or wonderful of its kind ⟨had a *jim-dandy* voice⟩ ⟨a *jim-dandy* invention⟩

jim dash \ˈ=,=\ *n* [prob. fr. the name *Jim*] : a short printed dash usu. used to separate the decks of a newspaper headline, individual items under one newspaper heading, or separate stories dealing with one event if they follow each other in the same column

jim fish \ˈ=,=\ *n, usu cap J&F* [*Jim* (nickname for *James*) + *fish*] *SoAfr* : NEGRO — usu. taken to be offensive

jim hill mustard \ˈ=ˈhil-\ *n, usu cap J&H* [after *Jim* (James J.) *Hill* †1916 Am. railroad promoter; fr. the growth of the weed along railroad lines J. Hill promoted] : TUMBLE MUSTARD

jim·i·ny *or* **jim·mi·ny** \ˈjimənē, ˈjēm-, -ni\ *interj* [alter. of *gemini*] — used as a mild oath often in the phrases *by jiminy, jiminy crickets, jiminy Christmas*

jim·jams \ˈjim,jamz, -,jaa(ə)mz\ *n pl* [perh. alter. of *delirium tremens*] *slang* : DELIRIUM TREMENS; *also* : a markedly nervous, overwrought, or depressed condition esp. arising from excess or fear ⟨drink so much coffee I get the ~ —*New Yorker*⟩ ⟨attack the January ~ with love and laughter —*Mademoiselle*⟩

jimmer *var of* GIMMER

jim·mies \ˈjimēz, -miz\ *n pl* [alter. of *jimjams*] **1** *slang* **a :** DELIRIUM TREMENS — used with *the* **b :** extreme nervousness or depression **2 :** a fern poisoning of sheep, cattle, and goats marked by seizures of severe trembling often followed by acute respiratory paralysis and death

[1]**jim·my** \ˈjimē, -mi\ *var of* JEMMY

[2]**jimmy** \"\ *n* -ES [fr. *Jimmy*, nickname for *James*] **1 :** a short crowbar ⟨the window was pried open with a ~⟩ **2 :** a railroad car for coal **3 :** SPOT 7

[3]**jimmy** \"\ *vt* -ED/-ING/-ES : to pry or force open (something fastened) esp. with a jimmy ⟨did he ~ a window or door —T.G.Cooke⟩

jimmyweed \ˈ==,=\ *n* [*jimmies* + *weed*] : RAYLESS GOLDENROD

[1]**jimp** \ˈjimp\ *adj* -ER/-EST [origin unknown] **1** *dial Brit* **a :** slender and trim **b :** neat and spruce **2** *dial Brit* : SCANTY, SKIMPY — **jimp·ly** \-lē\ *adv*

[2]**jimp** \"\ *vt* -ED/-ING/-S *dial Brit* : to cut short : SKIMP

[3]**jimp** \"\ *adv, dial Brit* : BARELY, SCARCELY

jim·son·weed \ˈjim(p)sən,=\ *or* **james·town weed** \ˈjāmz,taun-\ *or* **jimson** *or* **jimp·son·weed** *also* **jimpson** *n* -s *often cap J* [fr. *Jamestown*, Va.] : an intensely poisonous tall coarse annual weed (*Datura stramonium*) of tropical and perhaps Asiatic origin now naturalized in many parts of the world and having rank-smelling foliage and large white or violet trumpet-shaped flowers that are succeeded by globose prickly fruits — called also *apple of Peru*

jimsonweed

jim·swing·er \ˈjim,swiŋə(r)\ *n* [origin unknown] *South & Midland* : a long-tailed coat

ji·na \ˈjinə\ *n* -s *usu cap* [Skt, saint, victorious — more at JAIN] : one who according to Jainism has conquered temporal and material existence through self-discipline and attained a transcendent and eternal state of bliss; *esp* : one venerated as a tirthankara

jin·dy·wor·o·bak \,jindēˈwȯrə,bak\ *n* -s [prob. fr. native name in Australia] : one of a group of strongly nationalistic Australians seeking to promote native ideas and traditions esp. in literature

ji·ne·te \hēˈnād·ē\ *n* -s [MexSp, fr. Sp, Zenete, mounted soldier, horseman, one skilled at horsemanship, fr. colloq. Ar *zinēti* of the Zenetes — more at JENNET] : one who trains young horses to the bridle and saddle

jing \ˈjiŋ\ *interj* [short for [1]*jingo*] — a mild oath usu. used in the phrase *by jing*

jing·bang \ˈjiŋ,baŋ\ *n* -s [origin unknown] *slang* : COMPANY, CROWD — used in the phrase *the whole jingbang*

[1]**jin·gle** \ˈjiŋgəl\ *vb* **jingled; jingled; jingling** \-g(ə)liŋ\ **jingles** [ME *ginglen*, of imit. origin] *vi* **1 :** to make a usu. light sharp continued clinking or varied and mingled tinkling usu. metallic sound ⟨sleigh bells ~⟩ ⟨coins in his pocket *jingled* as he walked⟩ ⟨innumerable pottery bracelets *jingled* up and down upon her arms —Scott Fitzgerald⟩ **2 :** to sound in a way chiefly characterized by continued catchy repetition (as of rhyme, phrase, cadence) — used esp. of verse ~ *vt* : to cause to jingle ⟨*jingled* the coins in his pocket as he talked⟩ ⟨loved to ~ his spurs —Owen Wister⟩ — **jin·gler** \-g(ə)lə(r)\ *n* -s

[2]**jingle** \"\ *n* -s **1 :** a metallic jingling sound ⟨the ~ of the small bells⟩ : a rhythmical cadence ⟨the ~ of the verse as he read it⟩ **2 a :** something that jingles or is designed to jingle ⟨a toy tambourine set about with little ~*s*⟩ **b** (1) : a short verse marked esp. by catchy repetition (as of rhyme, alliterative sounds, cadences) ⟨not so much a poet as a writer of ~*s*⟩ (2) : a short catchy song using such a verse ⟨composing ~*s* for TV advertising⟩ (3) : an incomplete verse used in a contest in which the entrants supply the missing lines **3 :** a two-wheeled covered vehicle used in parts of Ireland and Australia as a public conveyance **4 :** JINGLE SHELL

jingle bell *n* **1 :** a bell mounted on a spring and used to signal the engine room for all speed available **2 a :** CASCABEL **b :** SLEIGH BELL **3 :** a signal bell used on a shop door to announce the entrance of customers

jinglebob \ˈ==,=\ *n* [[1]*jingle* + *bob*] : a cattle marking consisting of an ear slashed so that the halves dangle beside the head; *also* : a steer with such a marking

jin·gled \ˈjiŋgəld\ *adj, slang* : mildly drunk

[1]**jin·gle-jan·gle** \ˈjiŋgəlˈjaŋgəl\ *n* -s [redupl. of [2]*jingle*] : a jingling and jangling sound ⟨the unpleasant ~ of metallic objects in the back of the car truck⟩

[2]**jinglejangle** \"\ *vi* : to make a jinglejangle ⟨~ like goat bells on the Alps —Rose Macaulay⟩

jingle shell *n* : a mollusk of the genus *Anomia* or sometimes of the family Anomiidae having thin flat translucent shell valves that produce noise when dried and shaken together

jingle stick *n* : a usu. toy percussion instrument formed of a stick on which are mounted small metal disks

jin·glet \ˈjiŋglət\ *n* -s [[2]*jingle* + *-et*] : the ball clapper of a sleigh bell

[1]**jingling** *n* [ME *gingling*, fr. gerund of *ginglen* to jingle — more at JINGLE] **1 :** the act or process of producing a jingle **2 :** JINGLE 1

[2]**jingling** *adj* [fr. pres. part. of [1]*jingle*] : making the sound of something that jingles

jingling johnny *n, usu cap 2d J* : PAVILLON CHINOIS

jin·gling·ly *adv* : in a jingling manner

jingling match *n* : an old English game in which blindfolded players try to catch one not blindfolded player who keeps jingling a bell

jin·gly \ˈjiŋ(g)(ə)lē, -li\ *adj, sometimes* -ER/-EST [[2]*jingle* + *-y*] : having a jingling quality : sounding like a jingle ⟨a ~ sound from a vibrating metallic part⟩ ⟨a ~ verse⟩

[1]**jin·go** \ˈjiŋ(,)gō\ *interj* [prob. euphemism for *Jesus*] — used formerly as an exclamation by conjurers when producing something by sleight of hand; now used as a mild oath usu. in the phrase *by jingo*

[2]**jingo** \"\ *n* -ES [fr. *Jingo* supporter of the British belligerent attitude toward Russia in 1878, fr. [1]*jingo*; fr. the fact that the phrase *by jingo* appeared in the refrain of a chauvinistic song sung by the Jingoes] : one characterized by jingoism : a clamorous and belligerent chauvinist ⟨~*es* clamored for war —Ethel Drus⟩

[3]**jingo** \"\ *adj* : of or relating to a jingo : marked by jingoism ⟨a ~ nationalism⟩

jin·go·ish \-ish\ *adj* [[2]*jingo* + *-ish*] : tending to jingoism ⟨a ~ statesman⟩ : marked by jingoism ⟨the ~ remarks of the nationalists⟩

jin·go·ism \-,izəm\ *n* -s [[2]*jingo* + *-ism*] : clamorous chauvinism or arrogant nationalism esp. marked by a belligerent foreign policy ⟨warfare generates ~ —Barbara Ward⟩ ⟨belligerent ~ and narrow isolationism —J.F.Kennedy⟩

[1]**jin·go·ist** \-əst\ *n* -s [[2]*jingo* + *-ist*] : JINGO ⟨the magniloquent parrot cries of the ~ —*Spectator*⟩

[2]**jingoist** \"\ *or* **jin·go·is·tic** \ˈ=(,)=ˈistik\ *adj* : JINGO ⟨a ~ slogan advocating war⟩ ⟨*jingoistic* national pride —*New Republic*⟩ — **jin·go·is·ti·cal·ly** \-tək(ə)lē\ *adv*

jingo ring *n* [[1]*jingo*] *Scot* : a singing game in which children join hands and dance around one in the center

jinjili *var of* GINGELLY

[1]**jink** \ˈjiŋk\ *n* -s [origin unknown] **1 jinks** \ˈjiŋ(k)s\ *pl* : PRANKS, FROLICS ⟨operettas in which the ~*s* of a prewar military aristocracy were reclothed in the fashions of 1932 —Christopher Isherwood⟩ ⟨the ~*s* of a gang of youthful pranksters⟩ **2 :** the act or movement of one that jinks : a dodging away : SLIP

[2]**jink** \"\ *vb* -ED/-ING/-S *vi* **1 a :** to move quickly with sudden turns or changes of direction (as in dancing or dodging) ⟨is constantly flying at fast speed, and is forever ~*ing* all over the sky, twisting, turning, weaving, trying to avoid the flak from below —J.S.Childers⟩ **b :** to run away esp. by agile movements ⟨the bear had ~*ed* sideways and vanished into a cave —Christine Weston⟩ ⟨these little white grouse ~ out over the snowy sidings —Richard Perry⟩ **2** *chiefly Scot* : to play tricks and frolic **3 :** to play for five tricks in spoil five after winning three at the risk of losing if unsuccessful the tricks already taken — used with *it* ~ *vt* **1** *chiefly Scot* : to escape by dodging or ducking **2** *chiefly Scot* : to defeat by cheating or trickery

[3]**jink** \"\ *n* -s [by alter.] *dial Eng* : [3]CHINK

[4]**jink** \"\ *vb* -ED/-ING/-S *dial Eng* : [4]CHINK ⟨a shunt engine groaned, and ~*ed* the buffers of the freight trucks —Robert Westerby⟩

jin·ker \ˈjiŋkə(r)\ *n* -s [alter. of *janker*] **1** *Austral* : a contrivance like a cart having either two or four wheels and used esp. for log and timber carrying **2** *Austral* : a two-wheeled racing sulky

jin·ket \ˈjiŋkət\ *Scot var of* JUNKET

jinks \ˈjiŋ(k)s\ *n pl but sing in constr* [origin unknown] : CHECKERBERRY

jinn \ˈjin\ *also* **jin·ni** *or* **jin·nee** \jəˈnē, ˈjinē\ *or* **djin** *or* **djinn** \ˈjin\ *or* **djin·ni** *n, pl* **jinns** *or* **jinn** [Ar *jinnīy* demon, spirit] **1 :** one of a class of beneficent or malevolent spirits in Islam that inhabit the earth, that are capable of assuming various forms, and that exercise supernatural power **2 :** a supernatural spirit ⟨some ~ of the air made visible for a moment —Osbert Sitwell⟩ ⟨scoffing at the idea of casting out a ~ —Alan Villiers⟩; *esp* : one that takes on human form and serves the one who summons him ⟨magically summoning his private ~ —Hamilton Basso⟩

jin·nah cap \ˈjinə-\ *n, usu cap J* [after Mohammed Ali *Jinnah* †1948 Pakistani statesman] : a hat shaped like a fez but made of real or imitation karakul and worn by Pakistani Muslims

jin·ny \ˈjinē, -ni\ *n* -ES [alter. of *jenny*] : a block carriage on a crane that sustains pulley blocks hung from an eyebar or crossbar — called also *jenny*

jin·rik·i·sha *also* **jin·rik·sha** \(ˌ)jənˈrik(,)shȯ *also* -kə,shȯ\ *n* -s [Jap, fr. *jin* man + *riki* strength, power + *sha* carriage] : a small light two-wheeled usu. passenger vehicle drawn by one man and orig. used in Japan

jinrikisha

[1]**jinx** \ˈjiŋ(k)s\ *n* -ES [prob. alter of *jynx*; fr. the wryneck's being used in witchcraft] : something that unaccountably foredooms or is felt to foredoom to failure or misfortune : something that is felt to bring bad luck; *esp* : an evil spell or intangible force ⟨felt he had finally broken the ~ that kept him from achieving fame⟩

[2]**jinx** \"\ *vt* -ED/-ING/-ES **1 :** to foredoom unaccountably to failure or misfortune : bring bad luck upon ⟨the general belief was that his ghost had ~*ed* the ship —James Dugan⟩ ⟨his race and his color have seemed to ~ his personal life —R.G.Hubler⟩ **2 :** to put a stop or end to : make worthless or pointless ⟨~*ed* my story —F.J.Taylor⟩

ji·pi·ja·pa \,hēpēˈhäpə\ *also* **jippi-jappa** \,hip-\ *n* -s [Sp *jipijapa*, fr. *Jipijapa*, Ecuador] **1 :** a Central and So. American plant (*Carludovica palmata*) resembling a palm — called also *toquilla* **2 :** a hat made from fiber from the young leaves of jipijapa

ji·qui \hēˈkē\ *or* **ji·que** \-kā\ *n* -s [AmerSp *jiquí*] **1 :** SABICU **2 :** a Cuban timber tree (*Malpighia obovata*) with hard wood very resistant to moisture

ji·ra·ja·ra \,hirəˈhärə\ *or* **jirajaras** *usu cap* [Sp, of AmerInd origin] **1 a :** a group of peoples of northwestern Venezuela **b :** a member of any of such peoples **2 :** the language of the Jirajara peoples constituting a language family

jird \ˈji(ə)rd\ *n* -s [Berber *agherda, gherda*] : any of several No. African gerbils constituting a genus (*Meriones*) of the Cricetidae

jir·ga *or* **jir·gah** \ˈjərgə, ˈji(ə)r-\ *n* -s [Pashto, prob. of Mongol origin like Per *jarga* circle of men or beasts] : a council of Afghan tribal leaders

jir·kin·et \'jərkə̇ˌnet\ *n* -s [alter. of *jerkin* + *-et*] *Scot* **:** a jacket or blouse worn by women

jirt \'jərt\ *Scot var of* JERK

jism *or* **gism** \'jizəm\ *n* -s [origin unknown] **:** SEMEN — usu. considered vulgar

jit·ney \'jitnē, -ni\ *n* -s [origin unknown] **1** *slang* **:** NICKEL 2a **2** [so called fr. the original 5 cent fare] **a :** BUS 1; *esp* **:** a small bus designed to carry paying passengers over a regular route according to a flexible schedule **b :** a small electric truck designed for transporting or towing around a train station, air or bus terminal, or a dock

¹jit·ter \'jid·ə(r), -itə-\ *vb* -ED/-ING/-S [origin unknown] *vi* **1 :** to be nervous or act in a nervous way ⟨~*ed* around backstage on the opening night —*Newsweek*⟩; *esp* **:** to experience the jitters ⟨a sense of his awful responsibility without ~*ing* —*Time*⟩ **2 :** to jog or jig continuously **:** make continuous fast repetitive movements ⟨the wash . . . still ~*ed*, stiff and yellowish on the wire line —Raymond Chandler⟩; *also* **:** to progress in short fast repetitive movements ~ *vt* **:** to cause to jitter; *also* **:** cause to move in jittering movements

²jitter \"\ *n* -s **1 :** the state of mind or the movement of one that jitters **2 jitters** *pl but sing or pl in constr* **:** extreme nervousness **:** a sense of panic — often used with *the* ⟨experienced a bad case of the ~*s* before playing the solo⟩ **3 :** irregular random variation in a signal usu. evidenced by variation in the position of a spot on a radar or television screen

¹jitterbug \'ˌ=ˌ=\ *n* [¹*jitter* + ¹*bug*] **1 :** a dance in which couples two-step, balance, and twirl in standardized patterns or with vigorous acrobatics originating in Harlem in the 1920s and persisting in many variants through the periods of lindy, swing, boogie-woogie, and bop — compare JAZZ 2c **2 a :** one who dances the jitterbug **b :** a devotee of jazz music; *esp* **:** one who sways and gestures in time to jazz music

²jitterbug \"\ *vi* **:** to dance the jitterbug

jit·ter·i·ness \-ərēnə̇s, -rin-\ *n* -ES **:** the quality or state of being jittery

jit·tery \-rē,-ri\ *adj* **1 :** suffering from the jitters ⟨our ~ guards began to question everyone at rifle points —F.E. Fox⟩ ⟨he is tense, ~ — a mass of jangled nerves — his fingers tremble as he lights one cigarette after another —S.N.Behrman⟩ **2 :** marked by jittering movements **:** tending to jitter ⟨warblers . . . are small and ~, and stay hidden in the leaves —J.W. Krutch⟩

jiujitsu *or* **jiujutsu** *var of* JUJITSU

ji·va \'jēvə\ *n* -s *sometimes cap* [Skt *jīva*, fr. *jīva* living, alive — more at QUICK] **1** *Hinduism* **a :** the vital energy of life **b :** the individual soul **2** *Jainism* **a :** the individual life monad or separate individual self **b :** the aggregate of all life monads or separate selves **:** LIFE

ji·van·muk·ta \ˌjēvən'mu̇ktə\ *n* -s [Skt *jīvanmukta*, fr. *jīvan-* (fr. *jīvati* he lives) + *mukta* emancipated, set free, fr. *muñcati* he frees, releases; akin to Skt *jīva* living — more at MUCUS] *Hinduism* **:** one who has attained jivanmukti

ji·van·muk·ti \-(ˌ)tē\ *n* -s [Skt *jīvanmukti*, fr. *jīvan-* + *mukti* release, liberation, fr. *muñcati*] *Hinduism* **:** spiritual release or salvation achieved while still alive — compare MOKSHA

ji·va·ran \'hēvərən\ *adj, usu cap* [*Jivaro* + *-an*] **:** JIVAROAN

ji·va·ro \'hēvəˌrō\ *or* **ji·ba·ro** \-ēbə-\ *n, pl* **jivaro** *or* **jivaros** *or* **jibaro** *or* **jibaros** *usu cap* [Sp *jíbaro*, of AmerInd origin] **1 a :** a group of peoples of northwestern Peru and southern Ecuador **b :** a member of any of such peoples **2 :** the language of the Jivaro peoples constituting a language family — **ji·va·ro·an** \ˌ=ˌ=ˈrōən\ *adj, usu cap*

¹jive \'jīv\ *n* -s [origin unknown] **1 a** *slang* **:** glib, deceptive, or foolish talk **b :** the jargon of narcotics addicts or of jazz music and nightclub life **c :** a special jargon of difficult or slang terms ⟨a sort of academic ~ interlarded with lengthy and undigested quotations —Dwight MacDonald⟩ **2 :** hot jazz or the jitterbugging sometimes performed to it

²jive \"\ *vb* -ED/-ING/-S *vi* **1** *slang* **:** to talk jive **:** fool around **:** KID **2 a :** to dance to hot jazz; *esp* **:** JITTERBUG **b :** to play hot jazz ~ *vt* **1** *slang* **:** TEASE, KID **2 :** to play (music) hot ⟨small bands *jiving* in cellar clubs⟩

jiz·ya *also* **jiz·yah** \'jizyə\ *n* -s [Ar *jizyah*] **:** a capitation tax formerly levied on non-Muslims by the Islamic state

JJ *abbr* **1** judges **2** justices

jl *abbr* journal

JMA *abbr* junior military aviator

JMJ *abbr* Jesus, Mary, Joseph

JMT *abbr* job methods training

jn *abbr* **1** join **2** junction

jna·na \jə'nänə\ *n* -s [Skt *jñāna*, fr. *jānāti* he knows — more at KNOW] *Hinduism* **:** KNOWLEDGE

jnana-marga \jəˌnänə'märgə\ *n* -s [Skt *jñānamārga*, fr. *jñāna* + *mārga* road, way] **:** the Hindu approach to salvation by the way of knowledge developed in the Upanishads and the philosophic systems (as Sankhya, Vedanta, Yoga) and involving mental and ascetic self-discipline often in the companionship of a guru — compare KARMA-MARGA

jnana-yoga \-'yōgə\ *n* [Skt *jñānayoga*, fr. *jñāna* + *yoga* — more at YOGA] *Hinduism* **:** spiritual discipline attained by philosophical knowledge

jna·ni \jə'nä(ˌ)nē\ *n* -s [Skt *jñānī*, *fr. jñāna*] **:** a devotee of jnana-marga

jnc *abbr* junction

JND *abbr* just noticeable difference

jnl *abbr* journal

jnlst *abbr* journalist

jnr *abbr* junior

jnt *abbr* joint

¹jo \'jō\ *n* -ES [Sc *jo* joy, alter. of *joy*] *chiefly Scot* **:** SWEETHEART, DEAR — often used in addressing a person ⟨John Anderson, my ~ John —Robert Burns⟩

²jo *var of* JOE

JO *abbr* **1** joint organization **2** junior officer

jo·a·chim·ite \'jōəˌkiˌmīt\ *n* -s *usu cap* [*Joachim* of Floris †*ab* 1202 Ital. mystic + E *-ite*] **:** a follower of Joachim of Floris who divided all time into the three ages of the Father, Son, and Holy Spirit of which the second age lasted from A.D. 1 to 1260 and whose doctrine of a spiritual elite destined to convert the world in the third age influenced the Fraticelli

jo·a·chism \'jōəˌkizəm\ *n* -s *usu cap* [*Joach*im of Floris + E *-ism*] **:** adherence to the doctrines of the Joachimites

joan \'jō(ə)n, jō'an\ *n* -s *usu cap* [fr. the name *Joan*] **:** a country girl

joannes *var of* JOHANNES

joan silverpin \-'=ˌ=ˌ=\ *n, usu cap J* [prob. fr. E dial. *Joan's silver pin* article of beauty in a sordid setting; fr. the fact that this showy flower is often found among weeds] **:** any of several poppies; *esp* **:** OPIUM POPPY

joa·quin·ite \wä'kēˌnīt, wō'-\ *n* -s [fr. *Joaquin* ridge, San Benito co., Calif. + E *-ite*] **:** a mineral consisting of a sodium iron titanium silicate and occurring in honey-yellow orthorhombic crystals

jo·ar \jə'wär\ *var of* JOWAR

¹job \'jäb\ *n* -s [perh. fr. obs. E, lump, fr. ME *jobbe*, perh. alter. of *gobbe* — more at GOB] **1 a :** a piece of work ⟨did odd ~*s* for the neighborhood housewives⟩ ⟨gave up the marriage as a bad ~⟩ ⟨the ~ before her, that of phrasing and rephrasing a fugue —Osbert Sitwell⟩ ⟨the bridge was a bigger and longer ~ than the firm expected⟩ **:** PERFORMANCE, ACHIEVEMENT ⟨the new biography is a superb ~⟩ ⟨too lazy to turn out an honest ~⟩; *specif* **:** a small miscellaneous piece of work undertaken on order at a stated rate ⟨have two offset ~*s* to print up today⟩ ⟨the car needed a brake ~⟩ **b :** a quality, product, or result of work ⟨do a better ~ next time⟩ ⟨a more uniform dye ~ is obtained in skeins —H.R.Mauersberger⟩ **c :** an example of a usu. specified type **:** ITEM ⟨at the truck stop were three tractor-trailer ~*s*⟩ ⟨the blonde ~ sitting at the bar⟩ **2 :** something done for private advantage **:** DEAL; *esp* **:** a collusive piece of business ⟨his appointment as judge was a flagrant ~⟩ ⟨suspected the whole incident was a put-up ~⟩ **3** *chiefly Brit* **:** a state or turn of affairs **:** a piece of luck **:** THING — used with *bad* or *good* ⟨it was a good ~ you didn't hit the old man —E.L.Thomas⟩ **4 :** a criminal enterprise; *specif* **:** ROBBERY ⟨the gang that pulled the bank ~⟩ **5 a :** a regular remunerative employment **:** POSITION, SITUATION ⟨got a part-time ~ as a waiter in a café⟩ ⟨holds a key ~ in the government⟩ **b :** a specific duty, role, or function **:** work customarily performed ⟨the stokers' ~ was to feed coal into the furnaces⟩ ⟨the white blood cells . . . have the ~ of fighting infection —Morris Fishbein⟩ ⟨when more light is needed a stronger bulb will do the ~⟩; *specif* **:** an activity or group of related activities contributing to a larger process ⟨divide the manufacturing process into a number of carefully defined ~*s* assigned to individual workers⟩ **6 :** an undertaking requiring unusual exertion **:** EFFORT ⟨the radio whined so loud that it was a ~ to talk through it —Rose Macaulay⟩ **7 :** the object or material on which work is being done ⟨held the ~ with tongs while he hammered it⟩ **8 :** the actual process of doing a piece of work **:** the activity of a job ⟨learned plumbing on the ~ itself⟩ ⟨get on with the ~ of planning the trip⟩ ⟨stuck to the ~ till the tire was off⟩ **9 :** the area used in carrying on a job (as of construction) ⟨lumber stored in piles on the ~⟩ **10 jobs** *pl* **:** defective or slow-selling goods (as publishers' remainders) sold at reduced prices **11** *slang* **:** a thoroughly damaging piece of work **:** a job of destruction or disablement — usu. used in the phrase *do a job on* ⟨the collision really did a ~ on their car⟩ ⟨did a ~ on his rival in the third game, letting him score only one point⟩ **syn** see TASK — **on the job :** attending to one's work ⟨a mechanical servant that is right *on the job* day and night⟩

²job \"\ *vb* **jobbed**; **jobbed**; **jobbing**; **jobs** *vi* **1 a :** to do odd or occasional pieces of work for hire **:** work by the piece ⟨supported himself by *jobbing* in local orchestras⟩ **b :** to do job work **2 a :** to direct or carry on public business so as to secure private advantage or graft **b :** to seek or give a political favor in return for secret influence or graft ⟨a bit of *jobbing* . . . got a grand jury presentment to make a road which served nobody's interest but his own —Samuel Lover⟩ **3 :** to carry on the business of a middleman **:** trade in wholesale lots ⟨his company ~*s* and doesn't sell to the homeowner⟩ ~ *vt* **1 :** to buy and sell (as stock) or let (as a property) for profit **:** SPECULATE **2 :** to hire or let by the job or for a period of service ⟨~ a carriage for the time he would be in the city⟩ **3 :** to make a job of (a matter of public trust or duty) **:** get, deal with, or effect by jobbery **4 :** to do or cause to be done by separate portions or lots **:** SUBLET ⟨~ the city paving to the lowest bidders⟩ **5 :** to do a job on **:** SWINDLE, TRICK ⟨claimed he had been *jobbed* out of the championship⟩ **:** dispose of (as by political intrigue) ⟨assured his election by *jobbing* his political rival⟩

³job \"\ *adj* **1** *Brit* **:** that is for hire by the job or for a given service or period ⟨~ carriage at 2 guineas a day⟩ ⟨a ~ gardener⟩ **2 a :** used in or suitable for job work ⟨~ type⟩ **b :** engaged in job work ⟨~ printer⟩ ⟨~ shop⟩ **c :** done as job work ⟨~ printing⟩ **3 :** of or relating to a job or to employment ⟨guarantee of ~ security⟩ ⟨gloom in the ~ market⟩

⁴job \"\ *vb* **jobbed**; **jobbed**; **jobbing**; **jobs** [ME *jobben*] *vi*, *chiefly dial* **:** JAB ~ *vt* **1** *chiefly dial* **:** JAB **2** *chiefly Austral* **:** to strike or hit esp. with a heavy blow

⁵job \"\ *n* -s **:** a one-handed stroke used in field hockey by a tackler to push the ball away from an opponent's stick

job analysis *n* **:** determination of the precise characteristics of a job or position through detailed observation and critical examination of the sequential activities, facilities required, conditions of work, and the qualifications needed in a worker usu. as a preparatory step toward a job description

job analyst *n* **:** a specialist in job analysis

jo·ba·tion \jō'bāshən\ *n* -s [*jobe* + *-ation*] *chiefly Brit* **:** a long tedious reproof **:** SCOLDING, LECTURE

job·ber \'jäbə(r)\ *n* -s [²*job* + *-er*] **:** one that jobs: as **a** (1) *chiefly Brit* **:** one that buys livestock from farmers and sells to consumers or other dealers ⟨if the ~ comes you can sell the pig —J.M.Synge⟩ (2) **:** STOCKJOBBER (3) **:** WHOLESALER; *specif* **:** a wholesaler in some trades who operates on a small scale or who sells only to retailers and institutions rather than to other wholesale organizations **b** (1) **:** one that works by the job or on job work (2) **:** one that contracts with lumbermen to do one or more parts of a logging operation (3) **:** JOB PRESS

job·ber·nowl \'jäbə(r)ˌnōl\ *n* -s [prob. alter. of obs. *jobard* blockhead (fr. ME, fr. MF, fr. *Job*, Old Testament patriarch + MF *-ard*) + *nowl*, alter. of *noll*] *Brit* **:**NUMSKULL, NINCOMPOOP

jobber's drill *n* **:** a straight-shank drill somewhat shorter than the taper-shank drill of the same diameter

jobber's reamer *n* **:** a reamer that may be used either in a machine or when provided with a suitable holder as a hand tool

job·bery \'jäb(ə)rē, -ri\ *n* -ES [²*job* + *-ery*] **:** the act or practice of jobbing **:** official corruption **:** political intrigue or graft ⟨all the public posts were filled by ~ —Szyman Askenazy⟩

jobbing *pres part of* JOB

¹job·ble \'jäbəl\ *var of* JABBLE

²jobble *n* -s [¹*job* + *-le*] *dial Eng* **:** a small quantity or load

job card *n* **:** a card in a cost-accounting system on which the detailed costs of an order are accumulated **:** COST SHEET

job case *n* **:** any of a class of typecases carrying with some exceptions both capital and lower-case letters — see CALIFORNIA JOB CASE

job classification *n* **:** the grouping of jobs into classes usu. on the basis of type of work or level of pay

job control *n* **:** union influence over the employment practices of an establishment exercised through contract clauses regulating hiring, promotion, transfer, layoff, and discharge and directed toward union security

job description *n* **:** an orderly record of the essential activities involved in the performance of a task that is abstracted from a job analysis and used in classifying and evaluating jobs and in the selection and placement of employees

jobe \'jōb\ *vt* -ED/-ING/-S [after *Job*, Old Testament patriarch; fr. the scolding tone of his friends' speeches] *archaic* **:** SCOLD, REPROVE, LECTURE

job evaluation *or* **job rating** *n* **:** systematic qualitative appraisal of each job or position in an establishment either through the assignment of points for job characteristics or through comparison of job factors (as mental effort, experience, and responsibility required) for the purpose of determining the relative position of the job in the job hierarchy and for fixing wage rates

jobholder \'=ˌ==\ *n* **:** one that has a regular job; *specif* **:** a government employee

job·less \'jäbləs\ *adj* **1 :** having no employment **2 :** of or benefiting those who are jobless ⟨~ insurance⟩ — **job·less·ness** *n* -ES

jo block \'jō-\ *n, usu cap J* [by contr.] **:** JOHANSSON BLOCK

job lot *n* **1 a :** a miscellaneous collection of goods for sale as a lot usu. to a retailer at a reduced price **b :** a miscellaneous sometimes inferior group ⟨get a *job lot* of deans, dowagers, cabinet ministers, and ambassadors to meet them —W.J.Locke⟩ **2 :** a smaller than normal unit of commodities, goods, or production **3 :** an odd quantity of paper offered for sale at a discount because discontinued or otherwise nonstandard — **in job lots** *adv* **:** in an extensive and often indiscriminate manner **:** WHOLESALE ⟨organizations in elaborate regalia and . . . degrees marketed *in job lots* —C.W.Ferguson⟩

job·mas·ter \'jäbˌmastə(r)\ *n* [¹*job* + *master*] *Brit* **:** the keeper of a livery stable

jo·bo \'hō(ˌ)bō\ *n* -s [Sp, fr. Taino *hobo*] **1** *West Indies & Mexico* **:** HOG PLUM 1 **2** *West Indies & Mexico* **:** GUMBO-LIMBO 1

job of work *chiefly Brit* **:** JOB 1a ⟨an absence which generally occurred when there was a *job of work* to be done —R.H. Sampson⟩

job order *n* **:** the written authority given a worker or shop to perform certain work

job press *n* **:** PLATEN PRESS; *also* **:** a relatively small press — called also *jobber*

job rotation *n* **:** the assigning of an employee to a variety of tasks in turn to provide diversified experience during training or to counteract boredom

jobs *pl of* JOB, *pres 3d sing of* JOB

job's comforter \'jōbz-\ *n, usu cap J* [after *Job*, Old Testament patriarch; fr. the scolding tone of his friends' speeches] **1 :** one that increases (as by tactless or malicious remarks) a person's distress while supposedly comforting him **2 :** FURUNCLE

job sheet *n* **1 :** a page of instruction to aid a worker in performing a task — called also *instruction card* **2 :** JOB CARD

jobsite \'=ˌ=\ *n* [¹*job* + *site*] **:** JOB 9

job specification *n* **:** a specialized job description designed by emphasizing mental and physical qualifications and special skills required in an operative to facilitate selection and placement of employees

job's tears *n pl, usu cap J* [after *Job*, Old Testament patriarch who wept because of his many afflictions (Job 16:16 ff)] **1 :** hard pearly white seeds often sold as beads or strung in necklaces **2** *sing in constr* **:** an Asiatic grass (*Coix lacryma-jobi*) now widely cultivated in the tropics that produces Job's tears in ornamental and edible varieties — called also *tear grass*

job ticket *n* **1 :** an auxiliary printed form that may accompany a job order to a workshop to be used variously for recording worker's time, identifying material, giving brief instructions as to procedure, routing, tools, and destination **2 :** JOB ORDER

job work *n* **:** commercial printing of orders (as for letterheads, circulars, cards, booklets) — compare BOOKWORK

joc *abbr* **1** jocose **2** jocular

JOC *abbr* joint operations center

joch \'yȯk\ *n* -s [G, lit., yoke, fr. OHG *joh* — more at YOKE] **:** COL 1

jo·cism \'jōˌsizəm\ *n* -s *usu cap* [F *jocisme*, fr. Jeunesse Ouvière Chrétienne (lit., Christian Working Youth), a Catholic youth organization + *-isme* -ism] **:** a Roman Catholic movement among young workers directed toward christianizing the ranks of labor and founded in Belgium during the period 1912–1924 by Canon Joseph Cardijn

¹jo·cist \'jōsə̇st\ *n* -s *usu cap* [F *jociste*, fr. Jeunesse Ouvière Chrétienne + *-iste* -ist] **:** a member of the Jocist movement

²jocist \"\ *adj, usu cap* **:** of or relating to Jocism

¹jock \'jäk\ *n* -s *often cap* [fr. *Jock*, Sc & Ir nickname for *John*] **1** *Scot & Irish* **:** a country boy **:** LAD **2 :** a soldier in a Scottish regiment

²jock \"\ *n* -s [short for ¹*jockey*] **1 :** JOCKEY 2a ⟨any one of two dozen top ~*s* will get home with the best horse in a race —Eddie Arcaro⟩ **2 :** DISC JOCKEY

³jock \"\ *var of* JOCKSTRAP

jock·er \'jäkə(r)\ *n* -s [E slang *jock* penis + *-er* — more at JOCKSTRAP] *slang* **:** a male homosexual

¹jock·ey \'jäkē, -ki\ *n, pl* **jockeys** [fr. *Jockey*, chiefly Sc nickname for *John*] **1** *Brit* **:** LADDIE, CHAPPIE, FELLOW ⟨a mischievous ~⟩ ⟨a tough old ~ of a colonel⟩ **2 a :** one who rides or drives a horse; *esp* **:** a professional rider in a horse race **b** *archaic* **:** one who handles or deals in horses **:** HORSE TRADER **c :** a person who operates or manipulates an often specified vehicle or other object **:** DRIVER, OPERATOR ⟨a truck ~⟩ ⟨an elevator ~⟩ ⟨a typewriter ~⟩; *specif* **:** one who parks cars or trucks in a storage garage — compare DISC JOCKEY **3 :** a sometimes padded leather flap on a saddle that covers the point of attachment of the stirrup leather or serves as ornament — see STOCK SADDLE illustration **4 :** HARVARD CRIMSON 1

²jockey \"\ *vb* **jockeyed**; **jockeyed**; **jockeying**; **jockeys** *vt* **1 :** to deal shrewdly or fraudulently with **:** get the better of by craft **:** OUTWIT, TRICK, GULL ⟨dozens of unprincipled hucksters at the resort who ~ the unwary for fair⟩ ⟨the newly established method of party horse trading ~*ed* them out of many deputies —Janet Flanner⟩ **2 a :** to ride (a horse) as a jockey ⟨the winning horse was ~*ed* by his son⟩ **b :** to be the driver, pilot, or operator (a vehicle or other mechanism) ⟨~s a taxi for a living⟩ **3 a :** to maneuver or manipulate (as a person) by adroit or devious means ⟨proposals for public works were ~*ed* through Parliament by a combination of members —E.H. Collis⟩ ⟨trying to ~ you into some sort of trap —Erle Stanley Gardner⟩ **b :** to change the position of esp. by a series of movements **:** MANIPULATE ⟨~*ed* the camera back and forth till he got just the right angle⟩ **:** MANEUVER ⟨~ the furniture around the living room⟩; *specif* **:** to bring by jockeying ⟨~ a car into a parking space⟩ ⟨flew close to ~ the other plane out of formation⟩ ~ *vi* **1 :** to act as a jockey ⟨~*ed* in races till he was too heavy for the horse⟩ **2 :** to maneuver for advantage ⟨~ for position as the horses race the first lap⟩ ⟨watch the racing fleets . . . ~ for the favoring wind —E.A.Weeks⟩ ⟨behind the scenes ~*ing* . . . to determine the Democratic party's candidate for lieutenant governor —*N.Y.Times*⟩

jockey boot *n* **:** TOP BOOT

jockey cap *n* **:** a lightweight cap with a long visor worn esp. by jockeys

jockey club *n* **:** an association of persons interested in horse racing usu. regulating races in a certain district

jockey coat *n, chiefly Scot* **:** GREATCOAT; *esp* **:** one of broadcloth with wide sleeves

jockey pulley *or* **jockey wheel** *n* **:** IDLER PULLEY

jockey cap

jock·ey·ship \'==ˌship\ *n* **:** the art or practice of jockeying

jockey stick *n* **:** a stick fastened to the hame of the near horse and the bit of the off horse for use in driving with a single rein to prevent crowding

jockey weight *n* **:** a weight that rides on the beam of scales or the lever of a testing machine to provide fine adjustment

jock itch *or* **jockey itch** *n* [³*jock* or *jockey (strap)*] **:** ringworm of the crotch **:** TINEA CRURIS

jocko \'jä(ˌ)kō\ *or* **jacko** \'ja(-\ *n* -s [F *jocko*, of African origin; akin to Efik *id³iok¹* chimpanzee] **1 :** CHIMPANZEE **2 :** MONKEY

jocks *pl of* JOCK

jock·strap \'jäkˌstrap\ *also* **jock** *or* **jockey strap** *n* -s [*jockstrap* fr. E slang *jock* penis (short for earlier *jockam*, *jockum*, of unknown origin) + *strap*; *jock* short for *jockstrap*; *jockey strap* alter. of *jockstrap*] **:** a supporter for the genitals worn by men participating in sports or strenuous activities **:** an athletic supporter

jock·te·leg \'jäktəˌleg\ *n* -s [origin unknown] *Scot* **:** a large clasp knife

jo·co \'jō(ˌ)kō\ *adj* [by shortening] *Scot* **:** JOCOSE

jo·cose \(')jō¦kōs\ *adj* [L *jocosus*, fr. *jocus* jest, joke + *-osus* -ose — more at JOKE] **1 :** given to jokes and jesting **:** abounding in jokes ⟨felt the preacher was too ~ for his serious position⟩ **2 :** having the character of or containing a joke **:** sportively humorous ⟨made ~ remarks about things the others didn't consider funny at all⟩ **syn** see WITTY

jo·cose·ly *adv* **:** in a jocose manner **:** JOKINGLY

jo·cose·ness *n* -ES **:** JOCOSITY

jo·cos·i·ty \jō'käsəd·ē, -ətē, -i\ *n* -ES [L *jocosus* + E *-ity*] **1 :** the quality or state of being jocose ⟨talking with loud ~ —Bruce Marshall⟩ **2 :** a jocose act or saying ⟨a book of . . . sly and devastating *jocosities* —*Amer. Mercury*⟩

jo·co·te \hō'kō(ˌ)tā\ *n* -s [AmerSp, fr. Nahuatl *xocotl*] **:** MOMBIN

jocote de mi·co \-dā'mē(ˌ)kō\ *n* [AmerSp, lit., monkey jocote] **:** BARBAS

jo·cu \hō'kü\ *n* -s [AmerSp (Cuba) *jocú*] **:** DOG SNAPPER

joc·u·lar \'jäkyələ(r)\ *adj* [L *jocularis*, fr. *joculus* little jest, little joke, dim. of *jocus* jest, joke + *-aris* -ar — more at JOKE] **1 :** given or disposed to jesting **:** acting in jest **:** overtly jocose ⟨grew ~ and began to tease the others about their fears⟩ **2 :** said or done in joke **:** of, containing, or of the character of a joke **:** PLAYFUL, MERRY ⟨set the table laughing with his ~ remarks⟩ ⟨the more solemn dances were organized by the chiefs . . . the more ~ ones,however, took place without authority —Irving Rouse⟩ **syn** see WITTY

joc·u·lar·i·ty \ˌjäkyə'larəd·ē, -ətē, -i *also* -ler-\ *n* -ES [LL *jocularitas*, fr. L *jocularis* + *-itas* -ity] **1 :** the quality or state of being jocular ⟨a singular display of ~, in which irrelevancy and sheer bad taste are especially conspicuous —N.F.Adkins⟩ **2 :** an instance of being jocular **:** JEST ⟨interspersed . . . were axioms and proverbs and *jocularities* —*New Yorker*⟩

joc·u·lar·ly *adv* **:** in a jocular manner ⟨a subject they had generally avoided or else tried to deal with ~ —Richard Blaker⟩

joc·u·lar·ness *n* -ES **:** JOCULARITY

joc·u·la·tor \'jäkyəˌlād·ə(r)\ *n, pl* **joc·u·la·to·res** \ˌjäkyələ'tō(r)(ˌ)ēz\ *or* **joculators** [ML, fr. L, jester, joker — more at JUGGLER] **:** a wandering entertainer of medieval Europe who for hire practiced the arts of minstrelsy, narration, dancing, juggling, and mime

jo·cum \hō'küm\ *also* **jo·cu·ma** \-mə\ *n* -s [AmerSp *jocuma*, prob. fr. Taino] **:** MASTIC BULLY

joc·und \'jäkənd *sometimes* 'jōk-\ *adj* [ME *jocound*, *jocund*, fr. LL *jocundus*, alter. (influenced by L *jocus* joke) of L *jucundus*, fr. *juvare* to help] **:** feeling, exhibiting, or characteristic of mirth or good cheer **:** CHEERFUL, GAY, LIVELY ⟨singing, dancing, and ~ feasting⟩ ⟨a small and ~ blaze upon the hearth —Elinor Wylie⟩ **syn** see MERRY

jo·cun·di·ty \jō'kəndəd·ē, -ətē, -i\ *n* -ES [LL *jocunditas*, fr. *jocundus* + L *-itas* -ity] **1 :** JOCUNDNESS **2 :** a jocund action or speech **:** PLEASANTRY

joc·und·ly *adv* [ME, fr. *jocund* + *-ly*] **:** in a jocund manner

joc·und·ness *n* -ES [ME *jocundnes*, fr. *jocund* + *-nes* -ness] **:** the quality or state of being jocund

jod *var of* YODH

jo-dart·er *or* **joe dart·er** \'jō'därd·ər\ *n* **:** JIM-DANDY

jodel *var of* YODEL

¹jodh·pur \'jädpə(r), 'jōd-, -,pu̇(ə)r, -ŭə\ *adj, usu cap* [fr. *Jodhpur*, Rajputana, India] **:** of or from the city of Jodhpur, India **:** of the kind or style prevalent in Jodhpur

²jodh·pur \'jädpə(r) *also* ÷ -dfə-\ *n* -S **1** *also* **jodhpur breeches :** pants for horseback riding cut full through the hips, close-fitting from knee to ankle, and usu. having a strap under the foot — usu. used in pl. **2** *or* **jodhpur boot** *also* **jodhpur shoe :** a short riding boot; *esp* **:** an ankle-high boot fastened with a strap that is buckled at the side — compare CHUKKA

jodhpur 2

jo·do \'jō(,)dō\ *n* -S *usu cap* [Jap *jōdo*] **1 :** PURE LAND **2 :** a Japanese Buddhist sect founded 1175 that promises rebirth in the Pure Land to all those who invoke the name of Amida Buddha and live a righteous life

¹joe \'jō\ *var of* ¹JO

²joe *or* **jo** \"\ *n, pl* **joes** [short for *johannes*] **:** a gold dobra worth 12,800 reis

³joe *also* **jo** \"\ *n* -S [prob. alter. of *java*] *slang* **:** COFFEE

⁴joe \"\ *n* -S *often cap* [fr. *Joe*, nickname for *Joseph*] **1** — used informally to address a man whose name the speaker does not know **2** *slang* **:** GUY, FELLOW ⟨he's a good ~⟩ ⟨just an average ~⟩ ⟨a couple of ~s here who don't play a too crippled game of bridge —Al Hine⟩

joe blow *n, usu cap J&B* [*Joe* + *blow* (prob. arbitrarily chosen to rhyme with *Joe*)] *slang* **:** an ordinary man; *specif* **:** one who is self-important

joebush \'=,=\ *n* [*joe* (origin unknown) + *bush*] **:** JOEWOOD

joe college *n, usu cap J&C* [*Joe* + *college*] **:** a college boy; *esp* **:** one devoted to amusement

joe doakes \-'dōks\ *n, pl* **joe doakes** *usu cap J&D* [*Joe* + the name *Doakes*] **1 :** an average man **2 :** SO-AND-SO

joe mil·ler \-'milə(r)\ *n, usu cap J&M* [fr. *Joe Miller's Jest-book* (1739), a collection of jokes by John Mottley †1750 Eng. writer, after *Joe Miller* †1738 Eng. comedian] **1 :** a book of jokes **2 :** JOKE; *esp* **:** a stale joke

joe-pye weed \'jō'pī-\ *n, often cap J&P* [origin unknown] **:** BONESET 1; *esp* **:** either of two tall perennial American herbs (*Eupatorium maculatum* and *E. purpureum*) with stems usu. purplish or blotched with purple, whorled leaves, and terminal clusters of heads of typically purple tubular flowers — see MARSH MILKWEED

joe rocker *n* [origin unknown] **:** GREEN CRAB

joes *pl of* JO

joewood \'=,=\ *n* [*joe* (origin unknown) + *wood*] **:** a West Indian shrub or small tree (*Jacquinia keyensis*) of the family Theophrastaceae with leathery saponaceous leaves and an extremely hard wood — called also *barbasco*

¹jo·ey \'jōē, -ōi,ōi\ *n* -S [native name in Australia] **1** *Austral* **a :** a baby kangaroo ⟨shot a doe with a ~⟩ **b :** a baby animal **c :** a young child **2** *Austral* **:** ODD-JOBMAN

²joey \"\ *n* -S *usu cap* [fr. *Joey*, nickname for *Joseph*] **1** [after *Joseph* Hume †1855 Eng. politician who urged the issue of fourpenny pieces] *Brit* **a :** a fourpenny piece **b :** a threepenny piece **2** [after *Joseph* Grimaldi †1837 Eng. pantomimist and clown] **:** a circus clown

¹jog \'jäg *also* 'jȯg\ *vb* **jogged; jogged; jogging; jogs** [prob. alter. of *shog*] *vt* **1 :** to push or shake by prodding (as with the elbow or hand) **:** JOSTLE, NUDGE; *esp* **:** to push or touch in order to give notice, to excite attention, or to warn ⟨*jogged* the reins and the horses started up⟩ ⟨~ you with my elbow when it's time to go⟩ **2 :** to rouse to alertness or action ⟨tied a string on his finger to ~ his memory⟩ **:** REMIND ⟨~ their customers two or three times a year —Paul Friggens⟩ **3 a :** to cause to jog **:** drive (as a horse) at a jog ⟨an exercise boy . . . ~s the colt around the track —F.A.Wrensch⟩ **b :** to cause (a machine) to operate for an instant ⟨a button permits *jogging* the . . . motor to facilitate positioning tools —*Sweet's Catalog Service*⟩ **4 :** to align the edges of (piled sheets of paper) usu. by winding and knocking on or with a flat surface ~ *vi* **1 :** to move up and down or about with a short often heavy motion ⟨walked away quickly, his white-painted holster *jogging* against his hip —Thomas Williams⟩ **2 :** to run or ride at a slow jogging trot ⟨a substitute *jogged* out to the referee⟩ **3 :** to go at a slow, leisurely, or monotonous pace **:** TRUDGE, PLOD, POKE ⟨a team of oxen *jogged* along . . . drawing a vehicle —O.E.Rölvaag⟩ ⟨prefer to ~ along . . . in stagecoaches instead of whizzing past in a cloud of dust and cinders —Margaret Deland⟩ ⟨under easy sail the fleet *jogged* along before a moderate trade —S.E.Morison⟩ ⟨from then on her life *jogged* peacefully along —C.M.L.Beuf⟩ **4 :** to go one's way **:** JOURNEY ⟨figured I would just ~ back . . . and let you get away —Owen Wister⟩

²jog \"\ *n* -S **1 :** SHAKE, PUSH, JOLT ⟨gave the dispenser a ~ in hopes of jarring the coin loose⟩; *specif* **:** one intended to give notice or awaken attention ⟨gave his sleeping buddy a ~ as the officer approached⟩ ⟨seeing the book there gave his memory a ~⟩ **2 a :** a jogging movement, gait, or trip ⟨getting . . . under weigh for a ~ down to the breakwater and beyond to have a look at the weather —Llewellyn Howland⟩ **b :** a slow pace with marked beats — used of a horse

³jog \"\ *n* -S [prob. alter. of ¹*jag*] **1 :** ¹JAG 4 **2 a :** a short part (as of a line, road, or wall) interrupting the direction of the rest ⟨a window in the ~ facing south⟩ **:** an often right-angled projection, notch, or step ⟨a ~ in the wall enclosing pipes⟩ **b :** the space in the angle of a jog ⟨built shelves in the ~ between chimney and wall⟩ **c :** a brief abrupt change in direction ⟨where the highway makes a ~ around the courthouse square⟩ **3 :** a narrow theatrical flat used in an interior setting (as to form an offset in a wall)

⁴jog \"\ *vi* **jogged; jogged; jogging; jogs :** to form or make a jog ⟨the road ~s to the right over the hill⟩

jog cart *n* [¹*jog*] **:** a training sulky that is narrower and has longer shafts than a racing sulky

jog·ger \-gə(r)\ *n* -S [¹*jog* + *-er*] **:** one that jogs ⟨a memory ~⟩; *specif* **:** LAYBOY

¹jog·gle \'jägəl\ *vb* **joggled; joggled; joggling** \-g(ə)liŋ\ **joggles** [freq. of ¹*jog*] *vt* **:** to shake slightly **:** push suddenly but slightly so as to cause to shake or totter **:** JOSTLE, JOG ⟨skate up to the muskrat house and ~ it —Pete Barrett⟩ ⟨don't want anything . . . that might even ~ your precious status quo —Louis Auchincloss⟩ ~ *vi* **:** to have or go with a shaking or jerking motion **:** shake slightly to and fro or up and down ⟨the faint sounds of rifles *joggling* on backs —Robert De Vries⟩ ⟨when empty, they *joggled* . . . violently on their ironshod wheels —Christopher Rand⟩

²joggle \"\ *n* -S **:** a joggling motion

³joggle \"\ *n* -S [³*jog* + *-le* (dim. suffix)] **1 a :** a notch or tooth in the joining surface of a piece of building material to prevent slipping **b :** a slight step-shaped offset formed into a flat piece of metal (as for providing a flange) **2 :** a dowel for joining two adjacent blocks of masonry **3 :** a joint that is formed by joggles

⁴joggle \"\ *vt* **joggled; joggled; joggling; joggles 1 :** to join by means of a joggle so as to prevent sliding apart **2 :** to offset (sheet metal) at a corner or edge for improved fit

joggle beam *n* [³*joggle*] **:** a built-up beam or flitch beam secured by joggling

joggle piece *n* [³*joggle*] **:** a vertical member in a truss supporting one end of a brace or strut by a shoulder or joggle

joggle plating *n* [³*joggle*] **:** plating construction for steel ships in which one edge or both edges of a plate are joggled over the edge of an adjoining one

joggle post *n* [³*joggle*] **1 :** JOGGLE PIECE **2 :** a post made of timbers joggled together

jog·gler \-g(ə)lə(r)\ *n* -S [⁴*joggle* + *-er*] **:** an operator of a machine for joggling

jogglework \'=,=\ *n* [³*joggle* + *work*] **:** work (as in masonry) done in joggled courses

joggling board *n* [fr. pres. part. of ¹*joggle*] **:** a board suspended between end supports on which one may joggle for play or exercise **:** SPRINGBOARD

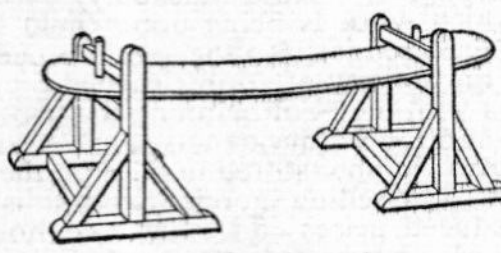

joggling board

jogi *var of* YOGI

jogjakarta *or* **jokyakarta** *usu cap, var of* DJOKJAKARTA

jogs *pl of* JOG, *pres 3d sing of* JOG

jog trot *n* [²*jog* + *trot*] **1 :** a slow regular jolting gait **2 :** a routine habit or method persistently adhered to **:** a slow easygoing way or course of action ⟨the sober *jog trot* of domestic bliss —John Galsworthy⟩

jog-trot \'=,=\ *adj* [*jog trot*] **:** having the character of a jog trot **:** HUMDRUM ⟨the contrast between their violence and our own *jog-trot* existences —Walter de la Mare⟩

jogtrot \"\ *vi* **jogtrotted; jogtrotted; jogtrotting; jogtrots** [*jog trot*] **:** to go at a jog trot ⟨~ all the way home⟩

jo·han·nes *also* **jo·an·nes** \jō'(h)anəs\ *n, pl* **johannes** *also* **joannes** [after *Johannes* or *Joannes* John (or João) V †1750 king of Portugal who first issued such coins and whose name appeared on them] **:** an old Portuguese gold coin first issued in the 18th century and equivalent to 6400 reis — called also *half joe;* compare DOBRA

jo·han·nes·burg \jō'hanəs,bərg, jə'-, -hän-, -nəz,-, -bōg,-bəig *sometimes* yō'-\ *adj, usu cap* [fr. *Johannesburg*, Union of So. Africa] **:** of or from the city of Johannesburg, Union of So. Africa **:** of the kind or style prevalent in Johannesburg

jo·han·nes·burg·er \-gə(r)\ *n* -S *cap* [Afrik, fr. *Johannesburg* + Afrik *-er*] **:** a native or inhabitant of Johannesburg, Union of So. Africa

jo·han·nine \(')jō¦hanən, jō'ha,nīn\ *adj, usu cap* [*Johannes* (John), one of the twelve apostles of Christ + E *-ine*] **:** of, relating to, or having the characteristics of the Apostle John or the New Testament books whose authorship is ascribed to him

jo·han·nite \jō'ha,nīt\ *n* -S [G *johannit*, fr. Archduke *Johann* (John) of Austria †1859 Austrian general, founder of a museum in Graz, Austria + G *-it* -ite] **:** a mineral $Cu(UO_2)_2(SO_4)(OH)_2.6H_2O$ consisting of a green hydrous basic uranyl copper sulfate that occurs in massive form

jo·hann·sen·ite \jō'han(t)sə,nīt\ *n* -S [Albert *Johannsen* †1950 Am. geologist + E *-ite*] **:** a mineral $CaMnSi_2O_6$ consisting of a silicate of calcium and manganese belonging to the pyroxene group

jo·hans·son block \(')jō¦han(t)sən-\ *n, usu cap J* [after C. E. *Johansson*, 20th cent. Swed. engineer] **:** one of a set of gauge blocks ground to an accuracy of one hundred-thousandth of an inch or better — called also *Jo block*

john \'jän\ *n* -S [fr. the name *John*, fr. ME *Johan, Jon, John*, fr. LL *Joannes, Johannes*, fr. Gk *Iōannēs*, fr. Heb *Yōḥānān*] **1 a** *often cap* **:** FELLOW, GUY, CHAP ⟨these Wall Street ~s can be trimmed —Carl Van Vechten⟩ **b** *usu cap* **:** a Chinese man ⟨the melancholy *Johns* with glazed caps and black pigtails —J.H.Beadle⟩ **c** *usu cap, now chiefly Austral* **:** COP, POLICEMAN ⟨a wild-eyed boy rushed in . . . and volunteered to direct the *Johns* to the body —*Sydney (Australia) Bull.*⟩ **2 :** TOILET ⟨have three bathrooms and only two ~s —Mary Manning⟩

john a. grindle *n, usu cap J&A&G* [fr. the name *John* + the initial *A.* (prob. fr. a "of") + *grindle*] **:** BOWFIN

john-a-nokes *or* **john-a-noakes** \,jänə'nōks\ *n, usu cap J&N* [alter. of earlier *John at Noke*, fr. the name *John* + *at Noke*, prob. fr. ME *atten ok* at the oak tree] *archaic* **:** a party to legal proceedings whose true name is unknown ⟨as willing to plead for *John-a-Nokes* as for the first noble of the land —Sir Walter Scott⟩ — compare JOHN-A-STILES

john-apple \'=,=\ *n, usu cap J* [fr. the name *John* + *apple*] *archaic* **:** APPLEJOHN

john-a-stiles *or* **john-a-styles** \,jänə'stī(ə)lz\ *n, usu cap J&S* [alter. of earlier *John at Stile*, fr. the name John + *at Stile*, prob. fr. ME *atte stile* at the stile] *archaic* **:** the second party to legal proceedings when the true names of both parties are unknown — compare JOHN-A-NOKES

john barleycorn *n, usu cap J&B* [fr. the name *John* + *barleycorn*] **:** alcoholic liquor personified

johnboat \'=,=\ *n* [fr. the name *John* + *boat*] **:** a narrow flat-

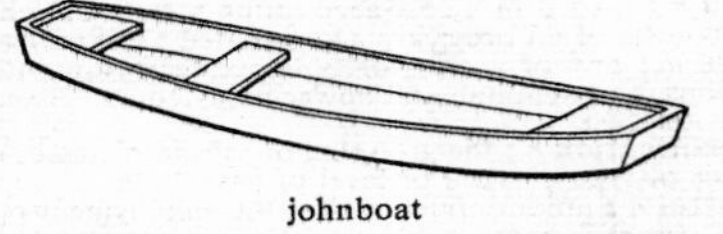

johnboat

bottomed square-ended boat usu. propelled by a pole or paddle and much used on inland rivers and streams ⟨boys on rafts and in ~s —E.W.Smith⟩

john brown *n, usu cap J&B* [fr. the name *John Brown*; prob. trans. of Afrik *Jan Bruin*] **:** a small plump deep-bodied sparid fish (*Gymnocrotaphus curvidens*) of southern Africa that is yellowish to bronzy brown and prized as a sport and food fish

john bull *n, usu cap J&B* [after *John Bull*, a character supposed to typify the English nation in *The History of John Bull*, a satire by John Arbuthnot †1735 Scot. physician and writer] **1 :** the English nation personified **:** the English people ⟨*John Bull* had been weakened by the war —F.A.Magruder⟩ **2 :** a typical or average Englishman ⟨a pipe-smoking *John Bull* astride a bicycle⟩ ⟨he was *John Bull* in a Benedictine robe —Shane Leslie⟩ — **john bull·ish** \-'bu̇lish\ *adj, usu cap J&B* — **john bull·ish·ness** *n, usu cap J&B* — **john bull·ism** \-'bu̇,lizəm\ *n, usu cap J&B*

john chinaman *n, usu cap J&C* [fr. the name *John* + *Chinaman*] **1 :** the Chinese nation personified **:** the Chinese people — usu. taken to be offensive **2 :** a Chinese immigrant; *esp* **:** one living in the U.S. or in Australia — usu. taken to be offensive

john citizen *n, usu cap J&C* [fr. the name *John* + *citizen*] **:** a typical or average citizen **:** JOHN DOE

john crow *n, usu cap J&C* [fr. the name *John* + *crow*] *British West Indies* **:** TURKEY BUZZARD

john doe *n, usu cap J&D* [fr. the name *John Doe*] **1 :** a party to legal proceedings whose true name is unknown; *esp* **:** the first such party when two or more are unknown — compare JOHN STILES, RICHARD MILES, RICHARD ROE **2 :** an anonymous, undistinguished, or average man ⟨brilliant educators and plain *John Does* —K.D.Wells⟩ ⟨the authors of those remarks are now so many *John Does* —Norman Cousins⟩

john dory *n, pl* **john dorys** *usu cap J&D* [fr. the name *John* + *dory* (fish)] **:** a marine fish of the family Zeidae: as **a :** a common European food fish (*Zeus faber*) that is yellow to olive in color and has an oval compressed body, long dorsal spines, and a dark spot on each side **b :** a closely related and possibly identical fish that is sometimes considered a separate species (*Z. capensis*) and is widely distributed in southern seas, being taken often in some quantity off southern Africa, Australia, and New Zealand

john down *n, usu cap J&D* [fr. the name *John* + *down* (feathers)] *Newfoundland* **:** FULMAR 1

joh·ne's bacillus \'yōnəz-\ *n, usu cap J* [after Heinrich A. *Johne* †1910 Ger. bacteriologist] **:** a bacillus (*Mycobacterium paratuberculosis*) that causes Johne's disease

johne's disease *n, usu cap J* [after Heinrich A. *Johne*] **:** a chronic often fatal enteritis of cattle and less commonly of sheep, goats, and horses that is caused by Johne's bacillus and is characterized by persistent diarrhea and gradual emaciation — called also *paratuberculosis*

john-go-to-bed-at-noon \'=,=,=,=,=\ *n, usu cap J* [fr. the name *John*] **:** any of several plants whose flowers close about noon; *esp* **:** GOATSBEARD 1

john han·cock \-'han,käk\ *n, usu cap J&H* [after *John Hancock* †1793 Am. statesman; fr. the size and prominence of his signature on the U.S. Declaration of Independence] **:** an autograph signature ⟨put your *John Hancock* on that line —Sinclair Lewis⟩

john henry *n, usu cap J&H* [fr. the name *John Henry*] **:** an autograph signature ⟨would give anything to scratch his *John Henry* off that . . . sheet of paper —Richard Hallet⟩

joh·nin \'yōnən\ *n* -S [*john-* (fr. *Johne's bacillus*) + *-in*] **:** a sterile solution of the growth products of Johne's bacillus made in the same manner as tuberculin and used to identify Johne's disease by skin tests, conjunctival reactions, or intravenous injection

john law *n, usu cap J&L* [fr. the name *John* + *law*] **:** a law officer **:** POLICEMAN

john ma·rig·gle \-mə'rigəl\ *n, usu cap J&M* [fr. the name *John* + *mariggle*, of unknown origin] **:** TENPOUNDER 1

john·ny *also* **john·nie** \'jänē, -ni\ *n, pl* **johnnies** [fr. *Johnny*, nickname for *John*] **1** *often cap* **a :** JOHN 1a ⟨one of these gilded *johnnies* who used to sell cars on commission —Dorothy Sayers⟩ **b** *now chiefly Austral* **:** JOHN 1c **2 :** JOHN 2 ⟨wash basins, sinks, and, of course, the ~ —S.S.Rabl⟩ **3 :** a short gown with no collar and with an opening in the back for wear by hospital bed patients ⟨the one string at the back of the neck of the ~ was undone —R.M.Keith⟩

johnnycake \'=,=\ *also* **jon·ny cake** \'jänē,-\ *n* [prob. fr. the name *Johnny* + *cake*] **1 a :** a bread made of white or yellow cornmeal mixed with salt and water or milk and either baked thin in a pan or dropped by spoonfuls onto a hot greased griddle **b :** a bread made of cornmeal, water or milk, and leavening with or without shortening and eggs **2** *Austral* **:** a bread either baked as small cakes in hot ashes or fried

johnny collar \'=,=\ *n, often cap J* **:** a small round or pointed dress collar that has a front split and that fits close to the neck

johnny-come-lately *also* **johnnie-come-lately** \'=,=,='=\ *n, pl* **johnny-come-latelies** *or* **johnnies-come-lately** *usu cap J* [fr. the name *Johnny*] **:** a late or recent arrival **:** NEWCOMER ⟨*Johnny-come-latelies* bringing up the rear —*N.Y. Times*⟩ ⟨the *Johnny-come-latelies* climbed the bandwagon —*Chicago Daily News*⟩

johnny cra·paud *or* **johnny cra·peau** \-kra'pō, -'=(,)=\ *n, usu cap J&C* [fr. the name *Johnny* + F *crapaud* toad; fr. the reputation of the French for eating frogs — more at CRAPAUD] **1 :** the French people **2 :** FRENCHMAN

johnny darter *n, usu cap J* [fr. the name *Johnny* + *darter*] **:** a small darter (*Boleosoma nigrum*) found in streams of the central U.S.

johnny house *n* [*johnny* + *house*] *chiefly Midland* **:** an outdoor toilet

johnny jump *n, usu cap 1st J* [fr. the name *Johnny* + *jump*, v.; fr. the rapid growth] **:** SHOOTING STAR

johnny-jump-up \'=,=,=\ *n* -S *usu cap 1st J* [fr. the name *Johnny* + *jump up*, v.; fr. the rapid growth] **1 :** WILD PANSY; *broadly* **:** any of various chiefly small-flowered cultivated pansies **2 :** any of various American violets (as a bird's-foot violet)

johnny-on-the-spot \'=,=,='=\ *n, usu cap J* [fr. the name *Johnny* + the phrase *on the spot*] **:** one who is on hand and ready esp. to perform a service or respond to an emergency ⟨luckily he was *Johnny-on-the-spot* . . . and was given his highly important post —John Dean⟩

johnny raw *n, usu cap J&R* [fr. the name *Johnny* + *raw*] **:** a raw recruit **:** GREENHORN

johnny reb *n, usu cap J&R* [fr. the name *Johnny* + *reb*] **:** a Confederate soldier in the Civil War

johnny rook *n, usu cap J* [fr. the name *Johnny* + *rook*] **:** a hawk (*Phalcoboenus australis*) of the Falkland islands that is related to the caracaras

johnny smokers *n pl but sing or pl in constr, usu cap J* [fr. the name *Johnny* + *smokers;* fr. the appearance of the feathery styles of the fruit] **:** PRAIRIE SMOKE 1

johnny verde \'=,=,vərd\ *n, usu cap J* [fr. the name *Johnny* + Sp *verde* green, fr. L *viridis* — more at VERDANT] **:** SAND BASS 1a

john q. public *also* **john q.** *or* **john q. citizen** *n, usu cap J&Q&P&C* [fr. the name *John* + the initial *Q.* + *public* or *citizen*] **1 :** a member of the public or the community **:** PERSON, CITIZEN ⟨just another *John Q. Citizen* on the road —*Springfield (Mass.) Union*⟩ **2 :** the public or the community personified ⟨Mr. and Mrs. *John Q. Public* suffered no great deprivations —*Domestic Commerce*⟩

johns *pl of* JOHN

john·son bar \'jän(t)sən-\ *n, usu cap J* [fr. the name *Johnson*] **:** the reverse gear lever of a railroad steam locomotive

john·son·ese \¦jän(t)sə¦nēz, -ēs\ *n* -S *usu cap* [Samuel *Johnson* †1784 Eng. lexicographer and writer + E *-ese*] **:** a literary style characterized by balanced phraseology and excessively Latinic diction ⟨fell into the pompous rhythm of the later eighteenth century . . . into *Johnsonese* —Hastings Lyon⟩

johnson grass *n, usu cap J* [after William *Johnston* †1859 Am. farmer] **:** a tall perennial sorghum (*Sorghum halepense*) that spreads by scaly creeping rhizomes, has been widely introduced as a hay and forage grass, and has become naturalized in many warm regions (as the southern U.S.) where it is a serious pest on cultivated land

¹john·so·ni·an \(')jän¦sōnēən\ *adj, usu cap* [Samuel *Johnson* + E *-ian*] **1 :** of, relating to, or characteristic of Samuel Johnson ⟨a thoroughly *Johnsonian* conception of decorum —Donald Davie⟩ **2 :** of, relating to, or resembling the literary style of Samuel Johnson: as **a :** marked by purity, elevation, and grace ⟨the high style is the style that one thinks of as *Johnsonian* —Lillian De La Torre⟩ **b :** marked by balanced phraseology and excessively Latinic diction ⟨in prolix and *Johnsonian* style —Dinah M. Mulock⟩

²johnsonian \"\ *n* -S *usu cap* **:** a student, follower, or imitator of Samuel Johnson or his writings

john·so·ni·ana \jän,sōnē'anə, -'änə, -'ānə *also* -'ānə\ *n pl, usu cap* [Samuel *Johnson* + E *-i-* + *-ana*] **:** collected items by, about, or relating to Samuel Johnson

johnson noise *n, usu cap J* [after John B. *Johnson b*1887 Am. physicist] **:** THERMAL NOISE

john stiles \-'stī(ə)lz\ *n, usu cap J&S* [alter. of *john-a-stiles*] **:** a party to legal proceedings whose true name is unknown; *esp* **:** the third such party when three are unknown — compare JOHN DOE, RICHARD MILES, RICHARD ROE

john·ston's organ \'jän(t)stənz-\ *n, usu cap J* [after Christopher *Johnston* †1891 Am. physician] **:** a sense organ in the second antennal segment of insects that responds to movements of the antennal flagellum and serves as a flight-speed indicator

john·strup·ite \'jän,strə,pīt\ *n* -S [G *johnstrupit*, fr. Frederik *Johnstrup* †1894 Danish mineralogist + G *-it* -ite] **:** a mineral approximately $(Ca,Na)_3(Ce,Ti,Zr)Si_2O_8F$ consisting of a complex silicate of cerium and other metals in prismatic crystals (sp. gr. 3.29)

john's-wort \'=,=\ *n, pl* **john's-worts** *usu cap J* [after St. *John*, one of the twelve apostles of Christ; fr. its having been gathered on the eve of the Feast of St. John (June 24)] **:** SAINT-JOHN'S-WORT

john to·whit \-tü'(h)wit\ *n, usu cap J* [fr. the name *John* + *towhit*, of imit. origin] **:** a West Indian vireo (*Vireo altiloquus*)

john trot *n, usu cap J&T* [fr. the name *John Trot*] **:** a dull man **:** BUMPKIN, BOOR

joie de vi·vre \,zhwädə'vēvr(ᵊ), -vēv(rə)\ *n* [F, lit., joy of living] **:** keen or buoyant enjoyment of life ⟨youthfully innocent *joie de vivre* —John Beaufort⟩

¹join \'jȯin *dial* 'jīn\ *vb* -ED/-ING/-S [ME *joinen*, fr. OF *join-*, *joign-*, stem of *joindre*, fr. L *jungere* — more at YOKE] *vt* **1 a :** to put or bring together and fasten, connect, or relate so as to form a single unit, a whole, or a continuity **:** COMBINE, LINK ⟨~ two blocks of wood with glue⟩ ⟨two moral forces, separate and yet ~*ed*⟩ ⟨~ forces in an effort to stamp out vice⟩ ⟨a bridge ~*ing* the two halves of the city⟩ **b :** to connect (as points) by a line (as a straight line) **c :** ADJOIN ⟨his studio there ~*ed* that of the famous sculptor —J.T.Marshall⟩ **2 :** to put or bring into close contact, association, or relationship **:** ATTACH, UNITE, COUPLE ⟨was later ~*ed* to another battalion⟩ ⟨the agitation of his mind, ~*ed* to the pain of his wound, kept him awake —Francis Parkman⟩ ⟨~*ed* in marriage by a local minister⟩ **3 :** to enter into or engage in (battle) **4 a** (1) **:** to come into the company of : come into local contact or association with ⟨~s his wife and three children around the breakfast table —Stuart Chase⟩ ⟨~ed us for lunch⟩ (2) : to come to ⟨at the next town we ~ another route⟩ **b** : to connect or associate oneself with: (1) : to participate in : enter into ⟨~ed the defense of Paris as commander of naval antiaircraft batteries —*Current Biog.*⟩ (2) : to ally oneself with ⟨~ the government in condemning foreign aggression⟩ (3) : BOARD ⟨~a vehicle⟩; *esp* : to go aboard (a ship) usu. as a member of the personnel ⟨~ed the destroyer as executive officer⟩ (4) : to become a member or associate of ⟨~ a church⟩ ⟨~ a faculty⟩ ⟨ran away from school to ~ a traveling tent show —*Current Biog.*⟩ ~ *vi* **1 a** : to come together so as to be connected or united ⟨English nouns ~ easily to form compounds⟩ **b** : ADJOIN ⟨at this point the two estates ~⟩ **2** : to come into close association or relationship: as **a** : to form or enter into an alliance or league ⟨business interests ~*ed* to maintain the consolidated system —*Amer. Guide Series: Minn.*⟩ — often used with *up* ⟨the three clubs ~*ed* up to improve the town's playground facilities⟩ **b** : to become a member of a group or organization ⟨an ambulance service was organized and I ~*ed* in as a stretcher bearer —Nevil Shute⟩ ⟨he is now a Mason but he did not ~ until last year⟩ ⟨two weeks after he ~*ed* up he was sent into the fighting area and saw immediate action⟩ **c** : to enter into or take part in a collective activity ⟨~ in singing the national anthem⟩ ⟨when there was group dancing . . . they all ~*ed* in together —Cabell Phillips⟩

syn CONJOIN, LINK, CONNECT, RELATE, ASSOCIATE, COMBINE, UNITE all signify a bringing or coming together into a more or less close union. RELATE and ASSOCIATE suggest the loosest and most unspecific of unions; LINK, JOIN, CONJOIN, and CONNECT suggest a closer contact to the point of a physical or moral attachment; COMBINE and UNITE suggest a union to the point of some loss of identity or a complete loss of identity of the separate elements. Of the pair RELATE and ASSOCIATE, ASSOCIATE emphasizes the mere fact of the bringing, coming, or being together of two or more persons or things although it suggests by customary implication some kind of unspecified often intangible but compatible or companionable interaction ⟨*associate* with shady characters⟩ ⟨*associate* the sense of hunger and the search for food⟩ ⟨was *associated* with the hospital from 1889 until 1919 —*Amer. Guide Series: Md.*⟩ ⟨the smooth ultralegato style now often *associated* with English music of the period —E.T.Canby⟩ RELATE can signify a bringing or coming together in any number of ways so that the two or more things have some generally only implied physical, moral, or logical bearing on each other ⟨the wing of a bird and the arm of a man are historically *related*⟩ ⟨an interrogation point which *relates* the title closely to the text —G.W.Johnson⟩ ⟨not the least merit of the book is that it *relates* the history of science to other thought currents —F.L.Baumer⟩ ⟨their ability to *relate* what they observe to what they know or have previously observed —Gertrude H. Hildreth⟩ Although they are used to signify a more specific union, LINK, CONNECT, JOIN, and CONJOIN in their nonphysical application may suggest a bringing or coming together as general and unspecified as that implied by RELATE or ASSOCIATE but tend more, esp. in physical application, to signify a junction of some kind, often an inseparable junction as by a chain or by bonding. CONNECT is the most general of these four and suggests a loose attachment, esp. one that preserves the identity of the elements and the evidence of the connection ⟨*connect* the two ends of the pipe⟩ ⟨*connect* the two houses by a path⟩ ⟨the criminal activity has been *connected* with the names of several prominent men⟩ ⟨a number of articles *connected* with her life —*Amer. Guide Series: R.I.*⟩ LINK suggests a slightly closer coupling esp. in the physical application of the word in which is implied inseparability but of still clearly identifiably separate elements ⟨the bridge *linking* the islands of North Hero and Grand Isle —*Amer. Guide Series: Vt.*⟩ ⟨none of the subjects that *linked* us together could be talked about in a bar —Nevil Shute⟩ ⟨eight Anarchists were condemned to death or life imprisonment in a trial that *linked* them to this Haymarket Riot —J.D.Hart⟩ JOIN usu. suggests strongly the idea of physical or moral contact or junction or the making of a continuity of two or more things ⟨apply glue to the edges to be *joined*⟩ ⟨*join* the ends of the wires with solder⟩ ⟨a common purpose *joined* their efforts⟩ CONJOIN usu. emphasizes both the togetherness of a joining and the separateness of the things joined ⟨three *conjoined* quadrangular beakers with a common cover —*Parke-Bernet Galleries Catalog*⟩ ⟨a scientific realism, based on mechanism, is *conjoined* with an unwavering belief in the world of men . . . as being composed of self-determining organisms —A.N.Whitehead⟩ COMBINE and UNITE usu. emphasize the first a mingling and the second a union or integration in which individual identity is lost in a common aim or in the formation of a new product from the mingling or integration. COMBINE stresses a merging by intermixture ⟨*combine* ingredients in making a cake⟩ ⟨*combines* Georgian Colonial and Classical Revival designs —*Amer. Guide Series: Pa.*⟩ ⟨beauty and melody and graceful motion . . . were *combined* in her —W.H.Hudson †1922⟩ UNITE strongly emphasizes the singleness resulting from the junction of persons or elements ⟨*unite* the separated army divisions⟩ ⟨certain chemical elements *unite* to form gases⟩ ⟨*unite* two people in a common purpose⟩ ⟨*unite* a couple in marriage⟩ ⟨a cooperative community in which manual and intellectual labor might be *united* —Allan MacDonald⟩

— **join hands 1** : to clasp or shake hands in token of agreement or affection **2 a** : to make contact : come together ⟨*joined hands* with forces coming from the east⟩ **b** : to join together in an alliance or corporate enterprise or to a common end ⟨the clergy *joined hands* with the laity in maintaining the inherited verse forms —Kemp Malone⟩ — **join out** *or* **join out the odds** *slang* : to engage in the business of procuring : turn pimp — **join the issue** *or* **join issue 1** : to submit a legal issue jointly for decision **2 a** : to accept, fix on, or clearly define a particular issue as the basis of a controversy or other struggle ⟨*the issue* was clearly *joined* —K.S.Latourette⟩ ⟨the Senator did not endorse unfair play, injustice, and indecency, and thus *join the issue* —W.L.Miller⟩ ⟨the minority report was read and *the issue joined* —Walter Goodman⟩ **b** : to take an opposed or contrary position on some question : take issue ⟨it is with his conclusions that we today would *join issue* —K.H. Hartley⟩

2join \"\ *n* -s **1** : something that joins : a place or line where joining occurs : JOINT ⟨ensure accurately matching ~*s* —W.P. Matthew⟩ ⟨the ~*s* between the veins and the arteries, the capillaries —S.F.Mason⟩ ⟨the ~ of lid and box⟩ **2** : a splice in magnetic recording tape

join·able \-nəbəl\ *adj* : capable of being joined

join·der \'jȯində(r)\ *n* -s [F *joindre* to join — more at JOIN] **1** : act of joining : a putting together : CONJUNCTION ⟨simultaneous production and ~ of these two pieces at the Argentine Embassy —*Blue Bk. on Argentina*⟩ **2 a** : a joining of parties as plaintiffs or defendants in a suit **b** : acceptance of an issue tendered **c** : a joining of causes of action or defense or of parties in an indictment **d** : a joining of two or more parties in a common transaction

joined *past of* JOIN

1join·er \'jȯinə(r) *dial* 'jīn-\ *n* -s [ME *joinour, joiner,* fr. AF *joignour,* fr. OF *joign-, join-* (stem of *joindre* to join) + AF *-our* -or — more at JOIN] **1** : one that joins: as **a** : a person whose occupation is to construct articles by joining pieces of wood : one who does the woodwork (as doors or stairs) necessary for the finishing of buildings — compare CARPENTER **b** : a worker who stitches together the parts of garments **c** : a worker who prepares sheets of glass for grinding and polishing by arranging them on a plaster-covered table **d** : a worker who inserts sections of stained glass into leads preparatory to their placement in windows **e** : a worker who by hand or by machine shapes the edge of the shank sole of shoes at the joint between the shank and heel — called also *jointer* **f** : a worker who fits and joins the parts of interior furnishings of boats and installs the completed units **g** : a worker who puts rubber articles (as baby pants) through a roller-cutter that joins and trims the edges **2** : JOINTER a(1) **3** : a typically gregarious or civic-minded person who joins many organizations : a person temperamentally given to joining many organizations ⟨the young businessman is not markedly a civic ~ —W.H.Whyte⟩ ⟨when it comes to clubs and organizations, she is not a ~ —*Current Biog.*⟩

2joiner \"\ *vi* -ED/-ING/-S : to work as a joiner

joiner work *n* : JOINERY

join·ery \'jȯinərē, -ri\ *n* -ES [1*joiner* + *-y*] **1** : the art or trade of a joiner **2** : work done by a joiner; *also* : things made by a joiner

joining *n* -s [fr. gerund of 1*join*] **1 a** : the act or an instance of joining one thing to another ⟨an easy ~ is always possible —L.A.Leslie⟩ **b** : the condition or fact of being joined together : JUNCTURE ⟨apt to name each separate confluence with its own name, since their later ~*s* are unknown to him —A.A. Hill⟩ **2 a** : the place or manner of being joined together : JOIN, JOINT ⟨the ~ is hardly visible⟩ **b** : something that joins two things together **3** : the practice of joining many organizations ⟨used to be the fashion to decry all forms of American ~ —W.S.Lynch⟩

joins *pres 3d sing of* JOIN, *pl of* JOIN

1joint \'jȯint *dial* 'jīnt\ *n* -s [ME *joint, jointe,* partly fr. OF *jointe* joint of the body, fr. fem. of *joint,* past part. of *joindre* to join; partly fr. MF *joint* joint (place where two parts meet), fr. past part. of *joindre* — more at JOIN] **1 a** (1) : the point of contact between elements of an animal skeleton (as femur and hipbone) whether movable or rigidly fixed together with the parts (as membranes, tendons, ligaments) that surround and support it ⟨the capsule of the shoulder ~⟩ ⟨the antennal ~*s* of a cockroach⟩ (2) : such a structure regarded as a particular type of mechanism ⟨the ball-and-socket ~ of the hip⟩ (3) : NODE 4a ⟨the ~*s* of a stem of grass⟩ **b** : a part or space included between two articulations, knots, or nodes ⟨the first ~ of the arm⟩ ⟨a ~ of cane⟩ **c** : a large piece of meat for roasting **2 a** : a place where two things or parts are joined or united : a union of two or more smooth or even surfaces admitting of a close fitting or junction whether movable or immovable : JUNCTION ⟨a ~ between two pieces of timber⟩ ⟨a ~ in a pipe⟩ **b** : a space between the adjacent surfaces of two bodies (as bricks) joined and held together by means of cement, mortar, or other material ⟨a thin ~⟩ **c** : a fracture or crack in rock not accompanied by dislocation being generally one of many arranged in a systematic pattern, occurring in all firm coherent rocks, and dividing them into blocks **d** : the flexing portion of a cover along either backbone edge of a book; *also* : the groove where the cover hinges — called also *hinge* **e** : the junction of two or more members of a framed structure **f** : a union formed by two abutting rails in a track including the bars, bolts, and other elements necessary to hold the abutting rails together **g** : an area at which two ends, surfaces, or edges are attached (as by adhesive, tape, nails, or staples) **3 a** (1) : a shabby or disreputable place of entertainment or other public house ⟨make a tour of the tough ~*s* —W.S.Maugham⟩ ⟨I wouldn't go there; that place is a ~⟩ (2) : a place (as a nightclub, restaurant, or hotel) open to the public ⟨I'll have you know this is a respectable ~ —William Grampp⟩ ⟨it depended on the social tone of the ~ —Scott Fitzgerald⟩ (3) : PLACE, ESTABLISHMENT, DWELLING ⟨there now are buffaloes all over the ~ —R.M.Yoder⟩ ⟨this is certainly an intellectual ~ —Sinclair Lewis⟩ ⟨come on over to my ~⟩ **b** *slang* : a concession stand at a circus or fair **c** *slang* (1) : a marijuana cigarette (2) : a hypodermic needle; *also* : the needle, dropper, and connection used in taking drugs hypodermically — **out of joint 1 a** *of a bone* : having the head slipped from its socket **b** : being out of adjustment or harmony : being at odds : UNSUITABLE, INCONSISTENT ⟨production costs are now entirely *out of joint* with retail prices —Jack Morpurgo⟩ ⟨impractical, romantic, and wholly *out of joint* with their times —W.P.Webb⟩ **2 a** : being in an unsatisfactory or disordered state : UNPROPITIOUS ⟨the times are *out of joint*⟩ **b** : being out of humor : DISGRUNTLED, DISSATISFIED ⟨find themselves a little *out of joint* with the party arrangements —Sir Winston Churchill⟩ ⟨the Ministry are much *out of joint* —Thomas Gray⟩ ⟨must have been many noses put *out of joint* —Alvin Johnson⟩

joints used in masonry: *1* struck; *2* weathered; *3* flush; *4* raked, *5* tooled, concave; *6* tooled, "V"

2joint \"\ *adj* [ME, fr. MF, fr. past part. of *joindre* — more at JOIN] **1** : JOINED, UNITED, COMBINED ⟨subjected to the ~ influences of culture and climate⟩ **2** : common to two or more: as **a** (1) : involving the united activity of two or more : done or produced by two or more working together ⟨issued a ~ report⟩ ⟨achieved through our ~ efforts⟩ (2) : constituting an activity, operation, or organization in which elements of more than one armed service participate ⟨the *Joint* Chiefs of Staff⟩ (3) : constituting an action or expression in which two or more governments unite as distinguished from an identic action or expression ⟨a ~ intervention⟩ ⟨a ~ note⟩ **b** (1) : shared by or affecting two or more : held or obligating or obligated in common ⟨~ property⟩ ⟨a ~ fine⟩ (2) : united in right, status, interest, power, privilege, duty, or obligation (3) : of or relating to the right of survivorship in property held in joint tenancy or by the entirety as distinguished from that held as tenants in common — compare CORREAL, JOINT AND SEVERAL, SEVERAL, SOLIDARITY **3** : united, joined, or sharing with another (as in a right, obligation, status, or activity) : not solitary in interest or action : holding in common with an associate : acting together ⟨~ heir⟩ ⟨~ creditor⟩ **4** : of or relating to a joint family

3joint \"\ *vb* -ED/-ING/-S [1*joint*] *vt* **1 a** *obs* : JOIN, UNITE, COMBINE ⟨~*ing* their force —Shak.⟩ **b** : to unite by a joint : fit together ⟨~ boards⟩ ⟨her elbows and shoulders are ~*ed* wrong —*Irish Digest*⟩ **c** : to provide with a joint : ARTICULATE **d** : to prepare (as a board) for joining by planing the edge to be joined **e** : to file down (saw teeth) to a correct height **2** : to separate the joints of : divide at the joint : cut up into joints ⟨lamb should present little difficulty if thoroughly ~*ed* beforehand —Noreen Routledge⟩ ~ *vi* **1** : to fit as if by joints : coalesce as joints do ⟨the stones ~ neatly⟩ **2** : to form joints as a stage in growth (as of winter wheat and other small grains)

joint account *n* : a bank or brokerage account owned jointly by two or more persons either of whom may withdraw funds or effect transactions on his signature alone

joint adventure *n* : a partnership or cooperative agreement between two or more persons restricted to a single specific undertaking — called also *joint undertaking;* compare SYNDICATE

joint and several *adj* : constituting or relating to rights which two or more persons entitled thereto may assert either together or separately or to duties and liabilities of two or more persons for which they may be held liable either together or separately (as a note where all makers or any one of them can be held for the full amount) — compare CORREAL, IN SOLIDO, JOINT 2b(3), SEVERAL, SOLIDARITY

joint and survivor annuity *n* : JOINT LIFE AND SURVIVOR ANNUITY

joint annuity *n* : JOINT LIFE ANNUITY

joint assertion *n* : CONJUNCTION 7a

joint author *n* : a person who collaborates with one or more persons in the production of a literary work ⟨*joint authors* of a widely used text⟩

joint bar *n* : a steel member embodying beam strength and stiffness by its structural shape and material and commonly used in pairs to splice rail ends together

joint-bedded \'=¦==\ *adj, of a quarried stone* : bedded in the wall so that its natural bed is set in a joint — compare FACE-BEDDED

joint chair *n* [1*joint*] *Brit* : a chair supporting the ends of abutting rails

joint committee *n* : a committee appointed by both houses of a legislature usu. for the purpose of considering joint action or resolving differences between the houses — compare CONFERENCE 3b

joint contributory *adj* : CONTRIBUTORY

joint convention *n* : a meeting together of both branches of the U.S. Congress or of a state legislature

joint denial *n* : the complex proposition asserting that neither of two propositions is true ⟨the *joint denial* "not *p* and not *q*" is true only if *p* and *q* are false⟩ — compare ALTERNATIVE DENIAL

jointed *adj* [ME, fr. *joint, jointe* joint + *-ed*] : having joints : ARTICULATED ⟨a ~ doll⟩ — often used in combination ⟨loose-jointed⟩ ⟨well-*jointed*⟩

jointed cactus *n* : a cactus of the genus *Opuntia*

jointed charlock *n* : a Eurasian weed (*Raphanus raphanistrum*) closely related to the common radish and having seed pods that are prominently constricted

jointed fern *n* : HORSETAIL 2

joint·ed·ly *adv* : in a jointed manner

joint·ed·ness *n* -ES : the quality or state of being jointed

joint enterprise *n* **1** : JOINT ADVENTURE **2 a** : an undertaking of two or more persons for a common object under circumstances giving each an equal right to control a vehicle or instrumentality and making all chargeable with the negligence of anyone exercising actual control and causing harm to another in actions between the third person and the parties to the enterprise **b** : an undertaking of two or more persons for mutual benefit or pleasure

joint·er \'jȯintə(r)\ *n* -s : one that joints: as **a** (1) : a hand or power planer for smoothing a sawed surface for jointing or mortising (2) : a tool used for filing the points of saw teeth to a uniform height **b** (1) : a bent piece of iron inserted to strengthen joints (2) : a tool for pointing joints (3) : a tool for cutting grooves to indicate joints in freshly laid surfaces of cement **c** : a triangular-shaped edged attachment to a plow beam for covering trash and organic matter in plowing **d** (1) : a worker who joints (as wires, pipes, or scissors blades) (2) : a worker who operates an abrasive saw or wheel for cutting structural stone true for fit in construction (3) : JOINER 1e

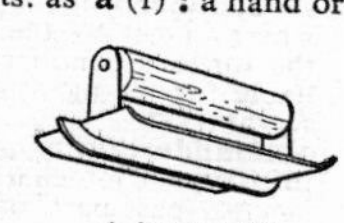
jointer b(3)

jointer gauge *n* : an attachment clamped to one side of a bench plane and made adjustable to secure any desired angle between the edge of a board being planed and its face

jointer plane *n* : a woodworker's plane about 2 feet long used for smoothing long surfaces (as the edges of boards in preparation for joining them)

joint evil *or* **joint ill** *n* : NAVEL ILL

joint facility *n* : railway property that two or more carriers jointly own, maintain, or operate by formal agreement

joint family *or* **joint household** *n* : a consanguineal family unit that includes two or more generations of kindred related through either the paternal or maternal line who maintain a common residence and are subject to common social, economic, and religious regulations

joint fir *n* [1*joint;* fr. the leafless jointed stems] : any of various plants of the family Gnetaceae and esp. of the genera *Gnetum* and *Ephedra* with small scalelike leaves resembling those of some evergreens

joint–fir family *n* : GNETACEAE

joint gap *n* [1*joint*] : the distance in 64ths of an inch between the ends of contiguous rails measured at a point about 5/8 inch below the top of the rail

joint grass *n* [1*joint*] **1** : a coarse creeping grass (*Paspalum distichum*) that roots at the joints and is used as fodder and as a soil binder **2** : HORSETAIL 2 **3** : YELLOW BEDSTRAW

jointing *n* -s [fr. gerund of 3*joint*] **1** : the act or process or an instance of making a joint; *also* : the joint thus produced **2** : the process of filling and finishing the joints in masonry with a special caulking material **3** : a condition or structure in rock characterized by the presence of joints

jointing rule *n* : a long straight rule used by bricklayers for securing straight joints and faces

joint·less \'jȯintləs *dial* 'jīnt-\ *adj* : constituting one piece : having no seam or joint

joint life and survivor annuity *n* : an annuity payable as long as any of two or more designated persons shall live

joint life annuity *n* : an annuity payable only until the death of the first of two or more designated persons

joint life insurance *n* : a policy providing for payment of the proceeds upon the first occurrence of death among the persons insured

joint·ly *adv* [ME, fr. *joint* + *-ly*] **1** : in a joint manner: as **a** : TOGETHER, UNITEDLY ⟨activities carried on ~ with other societies —*Mech. Engineering*⟩ ⟨written ~ with other scientists —*Current Biog.*⟩ ⟨owned ~ by several companies⟩; *specif* : so as to be or become liable to a joint obligation **b** : in joint tenancy or in tenancy by the entirety, or with the right of survivorship **2** : in proportion to the product

joint mouse *n* [1*joint;* fr. the fact that its movement suggests that of a mouse] : a loose fragment (as of cartilage) within a synovial space

joint·ness *n* -ES : the quality or state of being common to two or more persons

joint obligation *n* : an obligation binding each of the obligors to the performance of the entire obligation

joint oil *n* [1*joint*] : SYNOVIA

joint plant *n* [1*joint*] : a wandering Jew (*Tradescantia fluminensis*) with green or green and white striped leaves

joint product *n* **1** : a product of joint effort ⟨view this report as truly a *joint product* —C.E.Osgood & T.A.Sebeok⟩ **2** : one of two or more products of substantial importance derived from the same raw material (as gas and coke from coal) — distinguished from *by-product*

joint rate *n* : a rate from a point on one transport carrier to a point on another line made by agreement and published in a concurrent tariff

joint resolution *n* : a resolution passed by both branches of a legislative body; *esp* : one passed by both houses of the U.S. Congress and having the force of law when signed by the president or passed by a two-thirds majority of both houses over the president's veto ⟨a *joint resolution,* requiring mere congressional majorities, has been resorted to when the treaty-making process . . . broke down —F.A.Ogg & P.O.Ray⟩ — compare BILL 3, CONCURRENT RESOLUTION

joint·ress \'jȯin·trəs\ *n* -ES [obs. E *jointer* man who holds a jointure (fr. *jointure* + *-er*) + *-ess*] : a woman who has a legal jointure

joint ring *n* [1*joint*] *obs* : GEMEL 2

joint runner *n* [1*joint*] : a piece of asbestos rope with clamps placed around a pipe or tile joint to serve as a dam for the retention of poured molten metal later to be caulked in

joint rust *n* [1*joint*] : a disease of grasses caused by the cattail fungus and characterized by the development of fungal stromata esp. about the joints of an affected plant — compare CHOKE 5

joints *pl of* JOINT, *pres 3d sing of* JOINT

joint session *or* **joint meeting** *n* : a session of the two houses of a legislature meeting together and acting as one body

joint shingle *n* [1*joint*] : a short wooden shingle formerly applied by nailing edge to edge instead of overlapping

joint snake *n* [1*joint;* fr. the deep lateral fold on the body] : GLASS SNAKE

joint splice *n* [1*joint*] : a reinforce at a joint intended to hold the parts in their true relation

joint stock *n* : stock or capital held in company : capital held as a common stock or fund

joint–stock bank *n* **1** : a bank organized as a joint-stock association **2** : an English or Australian bank whose capital is subscribed by private persons under statutory law as distinguished from a government bank

joint–stock company *n* **1** : a company or association consisting of a number of individuals organized to conduct a business for gain with a joint stock, the shares owned by any member being transferable without the consent of the rest **2** *also* **joint–stock association** : a form of partnership differing from the ordinary form of partnership by the transferability of shares (as in a corporation), by the fact that the death of a stockholder does not dissolve the company, and by the fact that the managing of the company is limited to persons specially authorized — compare CORPORATION, LIMITED LIABILITY

joint stock land bank *n, usu cap J&S&L&B* : any of several corporations organized to make mortgage loans direct to farmers and to issue bonds similar to farm loan bonds

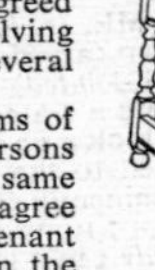

joint stool

joint stool *n* [1*joint*] : a stool formed of parts held together by pegged mortise-and-tenon joints : a stool made by a joiner

joint tariff *n* : a schedule of rates agreed upon by two or more carriers involving charges between points on their several lines

joint tenancy *n* : one of several forms of tenure in which two or more persons hold in concurrent ownership the same estate in realty or personalty and agree that upon the death of one joint tenant the full title to the estate remains in the surviving joint tenants and finally in the last survivor — compare TENANCY BY THE ENTIRETY, TENANCY IN COMMON

joint tenant *n* : one who holds an estate by or in joint tenancy

joint tortfeasor *n* **1** : one of two or more persons acting in concert in the commission of a tort **2 a** : one of two or more persons who may be joined as defendants in the same single cause of action to recover damage for a tort **b** : one of two or more persons jointly and severally fully responsible for all the damage to a third person caused by their concurring though independent tortious acts **c** : one of two tortfeasors where one is by the policy of the law vicariously liable for the tortious conduct of the other (as where the principal is liable for his agent's conduct or the master for that of his servant)

joint undertaking *or* **joint venture** *n* : JOINT ADVENTURE

1**join·ture** \'jȯinchə(r)\ *n* -s [ME, fr. MF, fr. L *junctura*, fr. *junctus* (past part. of *jungere* to join) + *-ura* -ure — more at YOKE] **1 a** : an act of joining : the state of being joined : UNION ⟨the ~ of two odd names in marriage —E.C.Smith⟩ ⟨the battle seemed on its way to ~ —*Time*⟩ **b** : JOINT, JUNCTURE **2 a** *obs* (1) : the joint tenancy of an estate (2) : the estate so held **b** (1) : an estate settled on a wife to be taken by her in lieu of dower (2) : a settlement upon the wife of a freehold estate (as in lands or tenements) for her lifetime at least to take effect upon the decease of the husband and to act as a bar to dower — called also *legal jointure;* compare EQUITABLE DOWER

2**jointure** \"\ *vt* -ED/-ING/-S : to settle a jointure upon

join·tur·ess \-chərə̇s\ *n* -ES [alter. (influenced by 1*jointure*) of *jointress*] : JOINTRESS

joint vein *n* [1*joint*] : a small geological vein occupying a joint

joint vetch *n* [1*joint;* fr. the jointed pod] : a plant of the genus *Aeschynomene*

joint water *n* [1*joint;* trans. of G *gelenkwasser*] : SYNOVIA

jointweed \'=,=\ *n* [1*joint* + *weed*] : a plant of the genus *Polygonella; esp* : an American herb (*P. articulata*) with jointed almost leafless stems and spikelike racemes of small white flowers

joint wire *n* [1*joint*] : hollow wire that is used for joints (as in a watchcase)

jointwood \'=,=\ *n* [1*joint* + *wood*] : an East Indian tree (*Cassia nodosa*) with dense showy racemes of pink or red flowers

joint wood berry *n* : CRANBERRY BUSH 2

jointworm \'=,=\ *n* [1*joint* + *worm*] **1** : the larva of any of several small chalcid flies of the family Eurytomidae and genus *Harmolita* which attack the stems of grain and cause swellings like galls usu. at or just above the first joint **2** [so called fr. its jointed appearance] : BAMBOO WORM

1**joist** \'jȯist *dial* 'jīst\ *n* -s [ME *giste*, *geste*, fr. MF *giste*, fr. (assumed) VL *jacitum*, fr. L *jacēre* to lie + *-itum* (neut. of *-itus*, past participial ending) — more at GIST] **1 a** : any of the small rectangular-sectioned timbers or rolled iron or steel beams ranged parallel from wall to wall in a structure or resting on beams or girders to support the planking, pavement, tiling, or flagging of a floor or the laths or furring strips of a ceiling — see BINDING JOIST, BRIDGING JOIST, CEILING JOIST, TRIMMING JOIST **b** : a similar timber supporting the floor of a bridge or other structure **2** : a stud or scantling about 3 by 4 inches in section

2**joist** \"\ *vt* -ED/-ING/-S : to furnish with joists

joisting *n* -s [1*joist* + *-ing*] : joists esp. when in position supporting a floor

jo·jo·ba \hō'hōbə, hə'-\ *or* **ja·jo·ba** \hə'-\ *n* [MexSp *jojoba*] : a shrub or small tree (*Simmondsia californica*) of the family Buxaceae of southwestern No. America with edible seeds that contain a valuable oil

jo-jotte \jō'jät\ *n* -s [fr. *Jo-Jotte*, a trademark] : a card game based on belotte or klaberjass with some features (as doubling and slam bonuses) of bridge

1**joke** \'jōk\ *n* -s [L *jocus* jest, joke, game; akin to OS *gehan* to say, speak, OHG *gehan*, *jehan* to say, speak, MW *ieith* language, Toch A & B *yask-* to demand, beg, Skt *yācati* he implores; basic meaning: speaking] **1 a** : something said or done to amuse or provoke laughter : something funny or humorous ⟨a tune which can be played backward — a ~ —Edward Sackville-West⟩ ⟨the use of primarily visual ~*s* —*Current Biog.*⟩; *esp* : a brief usu. oral narrative designed to provoke laughter and typically having a climactic humorous twist or denouement ⟨had a great fund of off-color ~*s*⟩ **b** (1) : the spirit of humor or raillery in which something is said or done ⟨knew they were meant in ~ —James Jones⟩ (2) : the humorous or ridiculous element in something ⟨the ~ of it was that the matter was so entirely his own choice —S.E.White⟩ (3) : LAUGHTER, RAILLERY, KIDDING — often used in the phrase *take a joke* ⟨the most valuable thing she taught me was to take a ~ —Polly Adler⟩ **c** : PRACTICAL JOKE ⟨mustn't play ~*s* on poor old ladies⟩ **d** : a person or thing that is the object of laughter or ridicule : LAUGHINGSTOCK ⟨why, he's the ~ of the whole town⟩ ⟨was still . . . a national ~ —Van Wyck Brooks⟩ **2 a** : something lacking substance, genuineness, or quality : something not to be taken seriously : a trivial or trifling matter ⟨palaces and haunts . . . in which the state religion is a ~ —Ray Alan⟩ ⟨consider his skiing a ~ —Harold Callender⟩ — often used in negative construction ⟨it is no ~ . . . to encounter week after week a player of settled reputation —Bernard Darwin⟩ **b** : something presenting no difficulty : something accomplished with ridiculous ease ⟨that exam was a ~⟩

syn JOKE, JEST, JAPE, QUIP, WITTICISM, WISECRACK, CRACK, GAG can mean, in common, a remark, story, or action intended to evoke laughter. JOKE, when applied to a story or remark, suggests something designed to promote good humor, esp. an anecdote with a humorous twist at the end; when applied to an action, it often signifies a practical joke, usu. suggesting a fooling or deceiving of someone at his expense, generally though not necessarily good humored in intent ⟨everyone knows the old *joke*, that "black horses eat more than white horses", a puzzling condition which is finally cleared up by the statement that "there are more black horses" —W.J.Reilly⟩ ⟨issues had become a hopeless muddle and national politics a biennial *joke* —Dixon Wecter⟩ ⟨a child hiding mother's pocketbook as a *joke*⟩ ⟨the whole tale turns out to be a monstrous *joke*, a deception of matchless cruelty —B.R.Redman⟩ JEST, now literary or affected, in an older sense still connotes raillery or sarcasm but generally today suggests humor that is light and sportive, as banter ⟨continually . . . making a *jest* of his ignorance —J.D.Beresford⟩ ⟨won fame by *jests* at the foibles of his time, but . . . his pen was more playful than caustic —S.T.Williams & J.A.Pollard⟩ JAPE, usu. of literary occurrence, orig. signified an amusing anecdote but today is identical with JEST or JOKE ⟨the merry *japes* of fundamentally irresponsible young men —Edmund Fuller⟩ ⟨the *japes* about sex still strike me as being prurient rather than funny —John McCarten⟩ QUIP suggests a quick, neatly turned, witty remark ⟨full of wise saws and homely illustrations, the epigram, the *quip*, the jest —B.N.Cardozo⟩ ⟨many *quips* at the expense of individuals and their villages —Margaret Mead⟩ ⟨enlivened their reviews with *quips* —W.H. Dunham⟩ WITTICISM is a bookish and WISECRACK or CRACK the more general term for a clever or witty, esp. a biting or sarcastic, remark, generally a retort ⟨all the charming *witticisms* of English lecturers —Eric Sevareid⟩ ⟨a vicious *witticism* at the expense of a political opponent⟩ ⟨merely strolls by, makes a goofy *wisecrack* or screwball suggestion —Hugh Humphrey⟩ ⟨though the gravity of the situation forbade their utterance, I was thinking of at least three priceless *cracks* I could make —P.G.Wodehouse⟩ GAG, orig. in this connection and still signifying an interpolated joke or laugh-provoking piece of business, more generally today applies to any remark, story, or piece of business considered funny, esp. one written into a theatrical, movie, radio, or television script, and sometimes has extended its meaning to signify any trick whether funny or not but usu. one considered foolish ⟨*gags* grown venerable in the service of the music halls —*Times Lit. Supp.*⟩ ⟨the *gag* was not meant to be entirely funny —*Newsweek*⟩ ⟨gave a party the other night and pulled a really constructive *gag* . . . had every guest in the place vaccinated against smallpox —*Hollywood Reporter*⟩ ⟨a frivolous person, given to *gags* and foolishness⟩

2**joke** \"\ *vb* -ED/-ING/-S [L *jocari*, fr. *jocus*] *vi* : to make jokes : say or do something as a joke : JEST ⟨*joked* about the possibility of . . . lead poisoning due to bullets —Morris Fishbein⟩ ~ *vt* **1** : to make jokes upon : poke fun at : KID, BANTER ⟨beginning to ~ him a bit about a nice young lady —Ethel Wilson⟩ **2** : to obtain by joking ⟨~ a beggar's penny out of you —Robert Lynd⟩

jokebook \'=,=\ *n* : JESTBOOK

joke·less \'jōklə̇s\ *adj* : lacking jokes

joke·let \-lə̇t\ *n* -s : a little joke

jok·er \'jōkə(r)\ *n* -s **1 a** : a person given to joking : JESTER, HUMORIST, WAG ⟨a ~ with an original turn of mind —*New Yorker*⟩ ⟨one of the town ~*s* put her reluctance to marry down to a hereditary distaste for contracts —Frank O'Connor⟩ **b** : GUY, BLOKE, FELLOW ⟨in walks a ~ very skinny and tall —Garson Kanin⟩ ⟨what a soft bloody job some ~*s* have —David Ballantyne⟩; *sometimes* : an insignificant, obnoxious, or incompetent person : SLOB ⟨a shame to let a ~ like this win —Harold Robbins⟩ ⟨know just what to do with that ~ —Maxwell Griffith⟩ **2 a** : a small object (as a ball or pea) used in playing thimblerig — called also *little joker* **b** (1) : a playing card usu. marked on its face with a picture of a jester and often added to a pack of playing cards as a wild card (as in poker or canasta) or as the highest-ranking card (as in five hundred) (2) : a card designated as wild — see BIG JOKER **c** (1) : a clause that is ambiguous or apparently immaterial inserted in a legislative bill to make it inoperative or uncertain in some respect without arousing opposition at the time of its passage (2) : an unsuspected, misleading, or misunderstood clause, phrase, or word in an agreement, contract, statement, or other document that in effect nullifies or greatly alters its apparent terms or purport (3) : something (as an expedient or stratagem) held in reserve to gain one's end or escape from a difficult situation ⟨retained one ~: they could appeal from a Greek legal decision to Roman law —Jaques-Yves Cousteau⟩ (4) : a fact, factor, or condition unsuspected or not apparent at first that thwarts or nullifies an apparent advantage ⟨depreciation: the ~ in mechanization —Herrele DeGraff & Ladd Haystead⟩ ⟨the ~ . . . is that we have a pretty persistent and devastating way of getting in the way of ourselves —H.A.Overstreet⟩

joker trap *n* : SKEE TRAP

jokes *pl of* JOKE, *pres 3d sing of* JOKE

jokesmith \'=,=\ *n* : a joke writer

joke·ster \'jōkstə(r)\ *n* -S : JOKER

jokey *or* **joky** \'jōkē\ *adj, often* **jokier**; *often* **jokiest** : given to joking : WAGGISH ⟨a ~ old bird —Sinclair Lewis⟩

jok·ing·ly *adv* : in a joking manner

joking relationship *n* : an institutionalized relationship of pronounced familiarity between specified relatives widely found among primitive peoples and involving the exchange of frequently sexually colored banter, jocular insults, and the playing of tricks upon one another — compare AVOIDANCE 5

jo·kul \'yō,ku̇l\ *also* **jö·kul** \'yœ,-\ *n* -s [Icel *jökull* icicle, glacier, fr. ON — more at ICICLE] : an Icelandic mountain covered with ice and snow : an Icelandic snow mountain

jokyakarta *usu cap, var of* DJOKJAKARTA

joll \'jäl\ *vi* -ED/-ING/-S [origin unknown] *dial Eng* : to move or walk clumsily : LURCH

jolley *also* **jollie** *var of* JOLLY

jol·li·er \'jälēə(r)\ *n* -s **1** : a person who jollies, flatters, or banters **2** : a worker who uses a jolly to make pottery hollow ware **3** : a worker who operates a rotary pounding machine for flattening the lower edge of the shoe upper where it folds over the insole and smoothing the bottom for attachment of the outsole

jol·li·fi·ca·tion \,jäləfə'kāshən\ *n* -s [1*jolly* + *-fication*] : FESTIVITY, MERRYMAKING ⟨a pageant and general ~ will begin at noon —*N.Y. Times*⟩

jol·li·fy \'jälə,fī\ *vi* -ED/-ING/-ES [1*jolly* + *-fy*] : to make merry : CAROUSE

jol·li·ly \-lə̇lē, -li\ *adv* [ME *jolifly*, *jolily*, fr. *jolif*, *joly* + *-ly*] : in a jolly manner : CHEERFULLY ⟨passing ~ along the street —Laurence Sterne⟩

jol·li·ness \-lēnə̇s, -lin-\ *n* -ES [ME *jolifnesse*, *jolynesse*, fr. *jolif*, *joly* + *-nesse* -ness] : the quality or state of being jolly ⟨could not wholly eradicate that inherent English ~ —Roy Lewis & Angus Maude⟩

jol·li·ty \'jäləd·ē, -ətē, -i\ *n* -ES [ME *jolifte*, *jolite*, fr. OF *jolivete*, *jolifte*, *jolité*, fr. *jolif*, *joli* + *-té* -ty] **1** : the quality or state of being jolly : GAIETY, MERRIMENT, CHEER ⟨put on a show of bluff ~ —Irwin Shaw⟩ **2** *Brit* : a festive gathering, meeting, or entertainment ⟨the occasion was a ~ of the Bursley Burial Club —Arnold Bennett⟩ **3** *obs* : SPLENDOR, MAGNIFICENCE

jol·loped \'jäləpt\ *or* **jel·loped** \'jel-\ *adj* [obs. E *jollop*, *jellop* dewlap (prob. fr. *joll*, var. of *jowl* + *lap*) + *-ed*] *heraldry* : WATTLED

1**jol·ly** \'jälē, -li\ *adj* -ER/-EST [ME *jolif*, *joli*, fr. OF *jolif*, *joli*, fr. *jol-* (prob. of Scand origin; akin to ON *jōl* Yule, feast) + *-if* -ive — more at YULE] **1 a** (1) : full of high spirits : GAY, JOYOUS ⟨think no more, lad; laugh, be ~ —A.E. Housman⟩ ⟨seems pretty comfortable and ~ —Rachel Henning⟩ (2) : given to conviviality : FESTIVE, JOVIAL ⟨a ~ and carefree companion —R.W.Pickford⟩ ⟨~ sportsmen . . . reserved time enough to frolic —*Amer. Guide Series: Mass.*⟩ **b** : attended or marked by mirth or gaiety : expressing, suggesting, inspiring, or reflecting a mood of gaiety : CHEERFUL, BRIGHT ⟨impressed by his ~ air of success —Arnold Bennett⟩ ⟨the last movement is a ~ rondo —Virgil Thomson⟩ ⟨entirely in the right of it to lead a ~ life —George Eliot⟩ ⟨had a ~ time⟩ ⟨thickets of hawthorn and holly with ~ little streams —S.P.B.Mais⟩ ⟨the countryside has a ~ quality —Rebecca West⟩ **2** *now dial Eng* **a** : gay and attractive in manner and appearance **b** : appearing healthy or in good condition : SLEEK, PLUMP, LARGE **3** : extremely pleasant or agreeable : DELIGHTFUL, SPLENDID, BULLY ⟨~ little open carriages —O.S.Nock⟩ ⟨what a ~ new world it is —T.R. Ybarra⟩ ⟨studying the . . . ~ curve of her cheek —Vera Caspary⟩ ⟨why, that's real ~⟩ **syn** see MERRY

2**jolly** \"\ *adv* : VERY, REMARKABLY ⟨did a lot of things that were ~ foolish —R.H.Newman⟩ ⟨hoped it would be a ~ good lesson to them —Dorothy Sayers⟩ — often used as an intensive ⟨they would kindly do as they were ~ well told —John Stockbridge⟩

3**jolly** \"\ *vb* -ED/-ING/-ES *vi* : to engage in good-natured banter or raillery : CHAFF, KID ⟨*jollied* and joked with sailors in the street —Dixon Wecter⟩ ~ *vt* **1** : to put or seek to put in good humor esp. to gain some end : COAX, WHEEDLE, INDULGE ⟨~*ing* the illiterate populace along towards the new age —Roland Mathias⟩ ⟨*jollied* my mother by joining her on the sofa —Peter De Vries⟩ ⟨do be good . . . and ~ him along —Robertson Davies⟩ ⟨try to pay for their entertainment by ~*ing* us along —S.E.White⟩ **2** : to form or shape with a jolly

4**jolly** \"\ *n* -ES **1** *Brit* : MARINE **2** *chiefly Brit* : a sociable good time : JOLLIFICATION **3** *or* **jol·ley** *also* **jol·lie** \"\ -s : a potter's machine like a jigger used for flatware (as plates or saucers) and hollow ware

jol·ly balance \'jälē-, 'yälē-\ *n, usu cap J* [After Philipp von *Jolly* †1884 Ger. physicist] : a very delicate spring balance used esp. for the determination of densities by the method of weighing in air and in water

jol·ly boat \'jälē-\ *or* **jolly** *n* -ES [origin unknown] : a boat of medium size belonging to a ship and used for general rough or small work

jolly rog·er \-'räjə(r)\ *n, usu cap J&R* [1*jolly* + *Roger* (the name)] : a flag in any of various color combinations bearing one or more emblems of mortality (as a skeleton, a skull and crossbones, or an hourglass) and raised on a pirate ship of the 17th and 18th centuries as a signal that quarter would be given if no resistance were offered but now often believed to have been used by pirates as their ensign; *specif* : a black flag bearing a white skull and crossbones — compare BLACK FLAG

Jolly Roger

jolof *usu cap, var of* WOLOF

1**jolt** \'jōlt\ *vb* -ED/-ING/-S [prob. blend of *joll* (obs. var. of 4*jowl*) and obs. *jot* to bump, prob. of imit. origin] *vt* **1** : to cause to move with a sudden and jerky motion by a push or series of pushes : JOUNCE ⟨the lumbering coach ~*ed* its passengers over the miserable road⟩ ⟨~*ed* about by the car's swift turns⟩ **2 a** : to give a sharp knock to so as to dislodge or move ⟨~ it crosswise and lengthwise with a rawhide hammer —H.F.Blanchard & Ralph Ritchen⟩ **b** : to jar in boxing with a quick or hard blow **3 a** : to administer a psychological shock to : disturb the composure of ⟨crudely ~*ed* out of that mood —Virginia Woolf⟩ ⟨trying to ~ the world into looking at the future —*New Yorker*⟩ **b** : to shake or interfere with roughly, abruptly, and disconcertingly : upset the even tenor or stability of ⟨determination to pursue his own course was ~*ed* badly —F.L. Paxson⟩ ⟨her parents' plans, however, were rudely ~*ed* —Clyde Gilmour⟩ ~ *vi* **1 a** *of a vehicle* : to move with a jolt or a series of jolts ⟨the train ~*ed* to a stop —Nathaniel Benchley⟩ ⟨the wagon ~*ed* up the slope —Ellen Glasgow⟩ **b** : to ride or move on foot with a succession of jolts ⟨on into South Carolina they ~*ed* —Dixon Wecter⟩ ⟨my body ~*s* and jars, for I have not got into the trick of drifting slackly down a hillside —Wynford Vaughn-Thomas⟩ ⟨climbed into the tonga and ~*ed* away —John Masters⟩ **2** *slang* : to take jolts of narcotics; *esp* : to take jolts of heroin ⟨was she still ~*ing* —Wenzell Brown⟩

2**jolt** \"\ *n* -s **1 a** : an abrupt sharp jerky blow or movement knocking or shaking violently and tending to unsettle or dislodge : JOUNCE ⟨well packed for protection against ~*s* in shipment⟩ ⟨received the full ~ from each explosion —L.D. de La Penne & Virgilio Spigai⟩ **b** : a jarring blow in boxing **c** (1) : a sudden feeling of shock, surprise, or disappointment caused by some novel or unexpected event or development : a psychological blow or shock ⟨that a few men have such far-reaching power gave the people quite a ~ —Paul Wooton⟩ ⟨will give an exciting and much-needed ~ to the complacency of those laymen —J.F.Wharton⟩ ⟨this kind of discussion gives a healthy ~ —David Daiches⟩ ⟨the affair dealt quite a ~ to his pride⟩; *also* : an event or development causing such a feeling ⟨his mother's death was quite a ~ to the boy⟩ (2) : a damaging but nonphysical blow : SETBACK, REVERSE ⟨the . . . argument for evolution had received a severe ~ —R.W.Murray⟩ ⟨had a severe financial ~⟩ **2** *slang* : a term in jail **3 a** : a small potent or bracing portion of something : SHOT ⟨a reassuring ~ of fresh air —*Atlantic*⟩ ⟨poured a ~ of brandy —Dorothy Baker⟩ ⟨a new perfume that contains a ~ of gardenia —*New Yorker*⟩ **b** *slang* : a unit of a narcotic (as heroin) for hypodermic injection ⟨a ~ can be had for a nod and a price —J.B.Clayton⟩ **syn** see IMPACT

jolt·er \'jōltə(r)\ *n* -s : one that jolts

jolter-head \'==,=\ *also* **jolt-head** \'=,=\ *n* [*jolter-head* alter. of *jolt-head; jolt-head* prob. fr. 2*jolt* + *head*] **1** *archaic* : a large or heavy head **2** *now dial chiefly Eng* : DUNCE, BOOBY, BLOCKHEAD

jolter-headed \¦==¦==\ *also* **jolt-headed** \'=¦==\ *adj* **1** *archaic* : having a large or heavy head **2** *now dial chiefly Eng* : STUPID, DULL

jolthead porgy \'=,=-\ *also* **jolthead** *n* : a large yellow blue-marked porgy (*Calamus bajonado*) of the tropical western Atlantic

jolt·i·ness \'jōltēnə̇s\ *n* -ES : the quality or state of being jolty

jolting *adj* : tending to jolt : attended by or producing jolts ⟨a ~ ride⟩ ⟨a ~ experience⟩ — **jolt·ing·ly** *adv*

jolt·less \'jōltlə̇s\ *adj* : free from jolts

jolt-wagon \'=,==\ *n, Midland* : a farm wagon

jolty \'jōltē\ *adj* -ER/-EST : causing jolts : tending to jolt ⟨a ~ wagon⟩

1**jo·nah** \'jōnə\ *n* -s *usu cap J* [after *Jonah*, Old Testament prophet who by disobeying God's command caused a storm to endanger the ship he was traveling in (Jon 1:4 ff), fr. Heb *Yōnāh*] : one believed to bring bad luck or misfortune ⟨perhaps I was the *Jonah* — at least I was the thirteenth man —Arthur Langford⟩ ⟨her left foot was her *Jonah;* nothing had ever happened to her right foot —John Hersey⟩

2**jonah** \"\ *vt* -ED/-ING/-S *often cap J* : to bring bad luck to : JINX ⟨ordered the boy on shore again, accusing him of wanting to ~ the whole trip —*Youth's Companion*⟩

jonah crab *n, usu cap J* : a large reddish crab (*Cancer borealis*) of the eastern coast of No. America that is sometimes found along rocky shores but is more common in deep water

jon·a·than \'jänəthən\ *n* -s *usu cap* [fr. the name *Jonathan;* prob. fr. the frequent use of Old Testament given names among the English colonists in America] : AMERICAN; *esp* : NEW ENGLANDER ⟨*Jonathans* are antislavery, but not against foreigners —*Chicago Democrat*⟩ — compare BROTHER JONATHAN

jonathan freckle *n, usu cap J* [fr. *Jonathan*, a variety of apple to which the disease is especially destructive, after *Jonathan* Hasbrouck †1846 Am. jurist] : a nonparasitic storage disease of apples that produces small circular skin-deep discolorations

jonathan spot *n, usu cap J* [fr. *Jonathan*, a variety of apple to which this disease is especially destructive] : a nonparasitic disease of apples that produces circular depressed necrotic areas around the lenticels — called also *spot rot*

jones reductor \'jōnz-\ *n, usu cap J* [after Clemens *Jones*, 19th cent. Am. metallurgist] : a reductor that consists essentially of a long upright tube filled with granular zinc through which a solution to be reduced (as a ferric salt) is poured

jong \'yäŋ\ *n* -s [Afrik, fr. MD *jonge*, fr. *jonc* young; akin to OHG *jung* young — more at YOUNG] *southern Africa* : a young man

jon·glery \'jäŋglərē\ *n* -ES [F *jonglerie*, fr. MF, alter. of OF *joglerie* — more at JUGGLERY] : entertainment provided by a jongleur

jon·gleur \(')zhōⁿ¦glər(·), 'jäŋglər\ *n* -s [F, fr. MF, alter. of OF *jogleour* — more at JUGGLER] **1** : an accompanist for a troubadour in the 12th and 13th centuries **2** : an itinerant medieval minstrel reciting and singing for hire

jonnock *var of* JANNOCK

jonny cake *var of* JOHNNYCAKE

jon·quil \'jä¦nkwəl, ¦ŋk- *sometimes* 'jə¦\ *n* -s [NL & F; NL *junquilia*, fr. F or Sp; F *jonquille*, fr. Sp *junquillo*, dim. of *junco* rush, reed (fr. the appearance of the leaves), fr. L *juncus;* akin to ON *einir* juniper, Sw *en*, L *juniperus* juniper, MIr *aīn* reed] **1 a** : a perennial bulbous herb (*Narcissus jonquilla*) native to southern Europe and northern Africa that has long slender leaves resembling those of a rush and is widely cultivated for its yellow or white fragrant clustered flowers which are smaller than those of typical daffodils and have the corona much shortened — compare NARCISSUS 2 **b** : a narcissus or daffodil with a yellow corona — used chiefly in the florist trade **2 a** : DAFFODIL 2 **b** : a light to moderate yellow that is redder and less strong than amber yellow or apricot yellow and redder and stronger than buff (sense 4a)

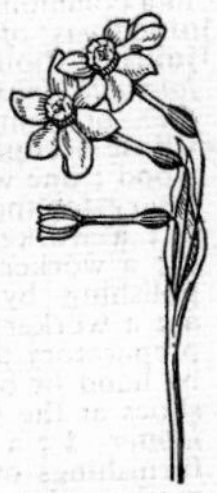

jonquil

jon·so·nian \(')jän¦sōnēən\ *adj, usu cap* [Ben *Jonson* †1637 Eng. dramatist + E *-ian*] : of, relating to, or characteristic of Ben Jonson or his works

jon·ty \'jȯntē, 'jän-, -ti\ *Brit var of* 2JAUNTY

1**jook** *var of* JOUK

²jook \'jük\ *n* -s [Gullah *juke, joog* disorderly — more at JUKE JOINT] *South* **:** JUKE JOINT ⟨a ~ from which she was trying to extricate her husband —Marjorie K. Rawlings⟩
jookerie *or* **jookery** *var of* JOUKERY
jook organ *n, South* **:** JUKEBOX
¹jor·dan \'jȯrdᵊn, 'jȯ(ə)d-\ *n* -s [ME (also, a vessel used by physicians and alchemists), prob. fr. the river *Jordan* in Palestine; perh. fr. medieval pilgrims' bringing water from the Jordan back to England] *dial Brit* **:** CHAMBER POT
²jordan \", *southern US often* 'jərd- *or* 'jōd- *or* 'jəid-\ *adj, usu cap* [fr. *Jordan*, country in southwestern Asia] **:** of or from the Hashemite Kingdom of Jordan **:** of the kind or style prevalent in Jordan **:** JORDANIAN
³jordan \"\ *also* **jordan engine** *or* **jordan refiner** *n* -s *sometimes cap J* [after Joseph *Jordan*, 19th cent. Am. inventor] **:** a machine for refining paper pulp that consists of a stationary hollow cone having projecting knives on its interior surface and fitting over a rapidly rotating adjustable cone having similar knives on its outside surface
⁴jordan \"\ *vt* **jordaned** *also* **jordanned; jordaned** *also* **jordanned; jordaning** *also* **jordanning** \-dᵊniŋ\ **jordans** **:** to refine in a jordan
jordan almond *n, usu cap J* [by folk etymology fr. ME *jardin almande*, fr. MF *jardin* garden + ME *almande* almond — more at JARDINIÈRE, ALMOND] **1 :** an almond imported from Malaga and used extensively in confectionery **2 :** an almond coated with sugar of various colors
jordan chest *n, often cap J* [after Joseph *Jordan*, 19th cent. Am. inventor] **:** a stock chest that holds paper stock ready to be jordaned
jor·dan curve \(')zhō(ə)r¦däⁿ-\ *n, usu cap J* [after Camille *Jordan* †1922 Fr. mathematician] **:** a closed plane curve (as a circle or an ellipse) that does not intersect itself
¹jor·da·ni·an \(')jȯ(r)¦dānēən, -nyən *sometimes* -dan-\ *adj, usu cap* [*Jordan*, country in southwestern Asia + E *-ian*] **1 :** of, relating to, or characteristic of Jordan **2 :** of, relating to, or characteristic of the people of Jordan
²jordanian \"\ *n* -s *cap* **:** a native or inhabitant of Jordan
jor·dan·ite \'jȯ(r)dᵊn,īt\ *n* -s [G *jordanit*, fr. Dr. *Jordan*, 19th cent. Ger. scientist + G *-it* -ite] **:** a mineral $Pb_{14}As_7S_2$(?) consisting of a lead-gray monoclinic lead arsenic sulfide (sp. gr. 6.39)
jor·danon \'jȯ(r)dᵊn,än\ *n* -s [NL, fr. David S. *Jordan* †1931 Am. naturalist + Gk *-on* (neuter n. & adj. suffix)] **:** MICROSPECIES
jordan's law *n, usu cap J* [after David S. *Jordan*] **:** a generalization in evolutionary biology: closely related organisms tend to occupy adjacent rather than identical or distant ranges
jo·ree \jə'rē\ *also* **joree-bird** *n* -s [imit.] *chiefly Midland* **:** CHEWINK
jo·rist \'jōrəst\ *n* -s [Jan David *Joris* (*Jorisz oon*) †1536 Dutch Anabaptist leader + E *-ist*] *usu cap* **:** DAVIDIST 2
jor·na·da \hō(r)'nädə\ *n* -s [Sp, fr. OSp, fr. OProv *jornada*, fr. *jorn* day, fr. LL *diurnum* — more at JOURNEY] *Southwest* **:** an arduous usu. one-day journey across a stretch of desert ⟨almost perished for lack of water on this grim ~ —R.G.Cleland⟩
jo·ro·ba·do \,hōrə'baù\ *n* -s [AmerSp, fr. Sp, humpbacked, fr. *joroba* humpback (fr. OSp *hadruba*, fr. Ar dial. — Spain — *haduba, hudūba*, fr. Ar *hadaba*) + *-ado* -ate (fr. L *-atus*)] **:** either of two moonfishes (*Vomer setipinnis* and *Selene vomer*)
jo·ro·po \hə'rō(,)pō\ *n* -s [AmerSp] **:** the national ballroom dance of Venezuela marked by lilting stamping steps in three-quarter time
jor·ram \'yürəm, 'yȯr-\ *n* -s [ScGael *iorram*] *Scot* **:** a Gaelic boat song
jo·rum \'jōrəm, 'jȯr-\ *n* -s [perh. after *Joram* in the Bible who "brought with him vessels of silver . . . gold, and . . . brass" (2 Sam 8:10—AV)] **1 a :** a large drinking vessel (as a jug or bowl) ⟨the host smiled . . . and shortly afterwards returned with a steaming ~ —Charles Dickens⟩ **b :** the contents of such a vessel ⟨drinking a ~ of hot whiskey and water —J.E.Agate⟩ **2 :** a large quantity ⟨great ~s of ink —Margery Sharp⟩
jo·sef *or* **jo·seph** \'jōzəf\ *or* **jo·sup** \-zəp\ *n* -s [Afrik *josef*, prob. after *Josef* (Joseph), Old Testament patriarch; fr. the brilliant colors of the fish, reminiscent of Joseph's coat of many colors (Gen 37:3 — AV)] **:** an elephant fish (*Callorynchus capensis*) of southern Africa
jo·se·ite \zhə'zā,īt\ *n* -s [G *joseit*, fr. São *José* do Paraiso, Minas Gerais, Brazil + G *-it* -ite] **:** a mineral $Bi_3Te(Se,S)$ consisting of a telluride of bismuth that also contains sulfur and selenium
jo·seph \'jōzəf *also* -ōsəf\ *n* -s [prob. after *Joseph*, Old Testament patriarch; fr. his coat of many colors (Gen 37:3 — AV)] **:** a long cloak; *esp* **:** an 18th century woman's riding coat buttoning down the front
joseph-and-mary \¦==-=¦==\ *n, usu cap J&M* [after *Joseph* and *Mary*, parents of Jesus; fr. the red and blue flowers that suggested representations of the Holy Family in which Joseph was pictured in red and Mary in blue] *dial Eng* **:** LUNGWORT 2a
jo·se·phine \'jōzə,fēn *also* -ōsə-\ *n* -s *often cap* [fr. the name *Josephine*] **:** BLUSH 4a
josephine's-lily *also* **josephine lily** \¦==¦==¦==\ *n, pl* **josephine's-lilies** *also* **josephine lilies** *usu cap J* [after *Joséphine* de Beauharnais †1814 empress of France] **:** a southern African bulbous herb (*Brunsvigia josephinae*) of the family Amaryllidaceae with bright red flowers
jo·se·phin·ite \'jōzəfē,nīt *also* -ōsə-\ *n* -s [*Josephine* co., Oregon + E *-ite*] **:** a natural alloy of iron and nickel occurring in stream gravel — compare AWARUITE
jo·seph·ite \'jōzə,fīt *also* -ōsə-\ *n* -s *usu cap* **1** [*Joseph* of Volokolamsk, 16th cent. leader in the Russian Orthodox Church + E *-ite*] **:** a member of a monastic party rising to prominence in the Russian Orthodox Church in the 16th century, adhering to strict forms of ritualism and asceticism, and believing in a close union between church and state — called also *Possessor* **2** [*Joseph* Smith †1914 Mormon leader + E *-ite*] **:** a member of the Reorganized Church of Jesus Christ of Latter-day Saints
joseph's coat *n, usu cap J* [after *Joseph*, Old Testament patriarch; fr. his coat of many colors (Gen 37:3—AV)] **1 :** a coat of many colors ⟨a country as dappled and patchy as *Joseph's coat* —T.H.Fielding⟩ **2 :** any of certain plants with variegated foliage: as **a :** a tampala with red and green variegated leaves grown as an ornamental **b :** COLEUS 2
¹josh \'jäsh *also* 'jōsh\ *vb* -ED/-ING/-ES [origin unknown] *vt* **:** to make fun of **:** tease good-naturedly **:** joke with ⟨whenever they ~ed her, she could laugh at herself as much as they could laugh at her —Edward Kimbrough⟩ ⟨climbed into our bus and ~ed the women schoolteachers —G.P.Musselman⟩ ~ *vi* **:** to banter lightly **:** JOKE ⟨~ed with the cameramen and was evidently in fine spirits —*N.Y. Times*⟩
²josh \"\ *n* -ES **:** light and good-humored joking **:** JEST, JOKE ⟨thoroughly enjoyed all the chatter and ~⟩
josh·er \-shə(r)\ *n* -s **:** one that joshes ⟨a great little ~ . . . when it comes to kidding —Sinclair Lewis⟩
josh·ua tree \'jäsh(ə)wə-, ÷¦shə,wā- *also* 'jȯ\ *also* **joshua** *n* -s *usu cap J* [prob. after *Joshua*, Old Testament patriarch; fr. the grotesquely extended branches, reminiscent of the outstretched arm of Joshua as he pointed with his spear toward the city of Ai (Josh 8:18—AV)] **:** a branched arborescent yucca (*Yucca brevifolia*) of the southwestern U. S. that has short leaves and clustered greenish white flowers and often grows to a height of 25 feet
jo·si·an·ic \,jō,sī¦anik, -ōzē-\ *adj, usu cap* [*Josiah* †ab608 B.C. king of Judah noted for his reforming spirit + connective -n- + E *-ic*] **:** of or relating to Josiah
jo·sie \'jōzē, -ōsē\ *n* -s [*joseph* + *-ie*] **:** a fitted outer waist formerly worn by women
jos·kin \'jäskən\ *n* -s [perh. fr. the name *Joseph* + *-kin* (as in *bumpkin*)] **:** BUMPKIN
¹joss \'jäs, 'jȯs\ *n* -ES [pidgin English, fr. Pg *deus* god, fr. L — more at DEITY] **:** a Chinese idol or cult image
²joss \'jäs\ *n* -ES [origin unknown] *dial Eng* **:** FOREMAN
³joss \"\ *vi* -ED/-ING/-ES [prob. short for *jostle*] *dial Eng* **:** JOSTLE, CROWD
jos·ser \-sə(r)\ *n* -s [origin unknown] *Brit* **:** FELLOW, CHAP ⟨an absurd old ~ whom her mother made a fool of —G.B.Shaw⟩
joss flower *n* [¹*joss*] **:** CHINESE SACRED LILY
joss house *n* [¹*joss*] **:** a Chinese temple or house of idol worship
joss paper *n* [¹*joss*] **:** gold and silver paper cut to resemble money and burned in front of a joss
joss stick *n* [¹*joss*] **:** a slender stick of incense burned in front of a joss
¹jos·tle \'jäsəl *also* 'jōs-\ *also* **jus·tle** \'jəs-\ *vb* **jostled** *also* **justled; jostled** *also* **justled; jostling** *also* **justling** \-s(ə)liŋ\ **jostles** *also* **justles** [*jostle* alter. of *justle*; *justle* freq. of ¹*joust*, *just*] *vi* **1 a** (1) **:** to come in contact or into collision **:** push and shove ⟨all drift and ~ and barge against one another —J.C.Powys⟩ ⟨wanted to get back to the bright lights . . . to ~ with the crowds —Harold Griffin⟩ (2) **:** to crowd or push or shove another horse in racing ⟨the stewards may disqualify the winner for crossing or *jostling* —Dennis Craig⟩ **b :** to make one's way by pushing and shoving or crowding ⟨men in pearl-buttoned waistcoats and flared trousers *jostling* round the street market —Osbert Lancaster⟩ **c :** to exist in close proximity **:** rub elbows ⟨study of the great groups that have *jostled* and migrated around America —Priscilla Robertson⟩ ⟨survivals of barbaric codes of law *jostled* with varying mixtures of Roman law, local custom, and violence —R.W. Southern⟩ **2 a** *obs* **:** to run atilt in a tournament **:** JOUST **b :** to vie or struggle in gaining an objective **:** CONTEND ⟨tribes began to ~ with one another for room —Daniel Defoe⟩ ⟨a novel good enough to ~ with the others in the great stream —Douglas Stewart⟩ ~ *vt* **1 a** (1) **:** to come in contact or into collision with **:** push and shove against ⟨*jostled* each other in the dance or at the board —W.M. Thackeray⟩ (2) **:** to push or shove against (another horse) in racing **b :** to drive or force by or as if by pushing **:** ELBOW ⟨shrugged his shoulders and *jostled* his way out of the hall —John Buchan⟩ **c :** to stir up **:** AGITATE, DISTURB ⟨a mind *jostled* once more into uncertainty —Owen Wister⟩ **d** *obs* **:** to bring into or as if into contact or collision ⟨the churches . . . clash and ~ supremacies with the civil magistrate —John Milton⟩ **e :** to exist in close proximity with **:** rub elbows with ⟨Europe, where a number of languages ~ each other —D.G. Mandelbaum⟩ ⟨fishing vessels lying close-packed at the moorings, *jostling* each other —Nevil Shute⟩ **2 :** to vie or struggle with in attaining an objective **:** contend with ⟨both men were *jostling* each other for nomination⟩
²jostle \"\ *also* **justle** \"\ *n* -s **1 :** an encounter that jostles ⟨might glide through . . . life among them without a ~ —Thomas Jefferson⟩ **2 a :** the state of being crowded and jostled together ⟨away from the hustle and the ~ that ought to have been congenial to me —Max Beerbohm⟩ **b :** the act of pushing or shoving in horse racing **:** INTERFERENCE ⟨the ~ was wholly caused by the fault of some other horse or jockey —Dan Parker⟩
jos·tle·ment \-lmənt\ *n* -s **:** disturbance by pushing and shoving ⟨bursting in his full-blown way along the pavement, to the ~ of all weaker people —Charles Dickens⟩
jos·tler \-s(ə)lə(r)\ *n* -s **:** one that jostles
josup *var of* JOSEF
¹jot \'jät, *usu* -äd+V\ *n* -s [L *jota* iota, jot, fr. Gk *iōta*, of Sem origin; akin to Heb *yōdh* yodh] **1 :** an instance of iota esp. as the smallest letter of the Greek alphabet — used in translation of the Bible or in allusion to such translation ⟨till heaven and earth pass, one ~ or one tittle shall in no wise pass from the law, till all be fulfilled —Mt 5:18 (AV)⟩ **2 :** the least bit **:** smallest amount **:** IOTA ⟨he who adds a ~ to such knowledge creates new mind —G.B.Shaw⟩
²jot \"\ *vt* **jotted; jotted; jotting; jots :** to write briefly or hurriedly **:** set down in or as if in the form of a note ⟨wake up six times during the night and ~ another name on the pad —G.S.Perry⟩ — usu. used with *down* ⟨*jotted* down a summary of all their private interviews —Peter Quennell⟩
jo·ta \'hōd·ə, -ō(,)tä\ *n* -s [Sp, prob. fr. OSp *sota* dance, fr. *sotar* to dance, fr. L *saltare* — more at SALTANT] **1 :** a Spanish folk dance in ¾ time performed by a man and a woman to intricate castanet and heel rhythms **2 :** the music of the jota
jot·ni·an \'jätnēən\ *adj, usu cap* [ON *jötn-, jötunn* giant + E *-ian*; akin to OE *eoten* giant, MLG *eteninne* giantess, and perh. to OE *etan* to eat — more at EAT] **:** of, relating to, or constituting a division of the Precambrian — see GEOLOGIC TIME table
jot·ter \'jäd·ə(r)\ *n* -s **1 :** one that jots down memoranda ⟨a great ~ of notes —Jack Alexander⟩ **2 :** a memorandum book
jot·ting *n* -s **:** a brief note **:** MEMORANDUM ⟨made rapid ~s on chance bits of paper —Walter Pach⟩
jougs \'jügz\ *n pl but sing in constr, also* **joug** \'jüg\ [alter. of earlier *jogis, jougis*, perh. modif. of MF *joug* yoke, fr. L *jugum* — more at YOKE] **:** an iron collar fastened to a wall or post and used in Scotland as a pillory
jouissance *n* -s [MF, fr. *jouiss-* (stem of *jouir* to enjoy, fr. L *gaudēre* to rejoice) + *-ance* — more at JOY] *obs* **:** USE, ENJOYMENT; *also* **:** JOLLITY
¹jouk \'jük\ *vb* -ED/-ING/-S [origin unknown] *vi* **1** *dial* **a :** DUCK, DODGE **b :** to evade work **2** *dial* **:** FAWN, CRINGE **3** *dial* **:** CHEAT, DECEIVE ~ *vt* **1** *dial* **a :** DUCK, DODGE **b :** to get out of (work) by evasion **2** *dial* **:** CHEAT, DECEIVE
²jouk \"\ *n* -s *chiefly Scot* **:** SWOOP, SWERVE, JERK
jouk·ery \'jükəri\ *n* -ES *chiefly Scot* **:** SWINDLING, TRICKERY
joukerypawkery \¦==¦==¦==\ *n* -ES [*joukery* + *pawkery*] *Scot* **:** JIGGERY-POKERY
joule \'jül, 'jaù(ə)l *sometimes* 'jōl; *the first seems to have been the physicist's own pronunc*\ *n* -s [after James P. *Joule* †1889 Eng. physicist] **1 :** the absolute mks unit of work or energy equal to 10^7 ergs or approximately 0.7375 foot-pounds or 0.2390 gram calorie and taken as standard in U.S. **2 :** a unit of work or energy that is equal to about 1.00017 absolute joules and that was formerly taken as a standard in U.S. — called also *international joule*
joule effect *n, usu cap J* [after J. P. *Joule*] **:** production of heat by mechanical work, an electric current, or change in length due to magnetization — compare MAGNETOSTRICTION
joule heat *also* **joulean heat** \'jülēən-, 'jaùl| *sometimes* 'jōl|\ *n, usu cap J* [after J. P. *Joule*] **:** heat resulting from an electric current through a resistance
joule's cycle *n, usu cap J* [after J. P. *Joule*] **:** BRAYTON CYCLE
joule's equivalent *n, usu cap J* [after J. P. *Joule*] **:** MECHANICAL EQUIVALENT OF HEAT
joule's law *n, usu cap J* [after J. P. *Joule*] **:** either of two statements in physics: (1) the rate at which heat is produced by a steady current in any part of an electric circuit is jointly proportional to the resistance and the square of the current (2) the internal energy of an ideal gas depends only upon its temperature irrespective of volume and pressure — compare JOULE-THOMSON EFFECT
joule-thom·son effect \'=-'täm(p)sən-\ *n, usu cap J&T* [after J. P. *Joule* and Sir William *Thomson* (Lord Kelvin) †1907 Brit. physicist] **:** the change in temperature of a gas on expansion through a porous plug from a high pressure to a lower one under adiabatic conditions, the observation of this change proving among other things that Joule's second law is only approximately true
¹jounce \'jaùn(t)s\ *vb* -ED/-ING/-S [ME *jouncen*] *vi* **1 :** to fall, drop, or bounce so as to shake **2 :** to move or proceed in jounces ⟨the truck *jounced* off across the concrete and the weeds —Josephine Johnson⟩ ⟨*jounced* over a rut —William Attwood⟩ ~ *vt* **:** to cause to jounce
²jounce \"\ *n* -s **:** a shaking fall or bump **:** JOLT
jouncy \-sē\ *adj, usu* -ER/-EST **:** marked by a jouncing motion or effect ⟨innumerable ~ elevator rides —*New Yorker*⟩
jour *abbr* **1** journal; journalism; journalist **2** journey **3** journeyman
¹jour·nal \'jərnᵊl, 'jən-, 'jəin-\ *n* -s [ME, fr. MF, fr. *journal*, adj., daily, fr. L *diurnalis*, fr. *diurnus* of the day, daily (fr. *dies* day + *-urnus*, as in *nocturnus* nocturnal) + *-alis* -al — more at DEITY, NOCTURNAL] **1 a :** a usu. daily record of a journey **b :** a record of current transactions usu. kept daily or regularly: as (1) **:** DAYBOOK 2 (2) **:** a book of original entry in double-entry bookkeeping either for recording transactions of a particular class (as sales or cash transactions) or for recording transactions not cared for in specialized books **c :** an account of usu. day-to-day events written down regularly or as they occur or presented as if written down in this way **d :** a record of experiences, ideas, or reflections kept regularly for private use **e :** a record of transactions kept by a deliberative body or an assembly; *specif* **:** the record of daily proceedings of a legislative body kept by the clerk **f :** LOGBOOK, LOG **2** [F, fr. *journal* (record)] **a :** a daily newspaper **b :** a periodical publication esp. dealing with matters of current interest ⟨the editor of a weekly news ~⟩ — often used of official or semiofficial publications of special groups ⟨the *Journal* of the American Medical Association⟩ **3 :** the part of a rotating shaft, axle, roll, or spindle that turns in a bearing
²journal *adj* [MF — more at ¹JOURNAL] *obs* **:** DIURNAL
³journal *like* ¹JOURNAL\ *vt* -ED/-ING/-S [¹*journal*] **1 :** to support on, provide with, or make into a journal **:** support on a bearing ⟨~ a pulley on a shaft⟩ **2 :** to connect by means of a journal ⟨a connecting rod ~*ed* to one end of a walking beam⟩
jour·nal·ary \-ᵊl,erē\ *adj* **1** *obs* **:** DAILY, DIURNAL **2 :** of or belonging to a journal **:** recorded in or as if in a journal ⟨the ~ form of the novel —A.D.Henderson⟩
journal bearing *n* **:** BEARING 4c
journal box *n* **:** a metal housing to support and protect a journal bearing (as on a railroad-car wheel axle)
jour·nal·ese \,jərnᵊl¦ēz, ,jən-, ,jəin-, -ēs\ *n* -s [¹*journal* + *-ese*] **1 :** a style of writing held to be characteristic of newspapers **2 :** writing marked by simple, informal, and usu. loose sentence structure, the frequent use of clichés, sensationalism in the presentation of material, and superficiality of thought and reasoning
jour·nal·ism \'==,izəm\ *n* -s [F *journalisme*, fr. *journal* (n.) + *-isme* -ism] **1 a :** the collection and editing of material of current interest for presentation through the media of newspapers, magazines, newsreels, radio, or television **b :** the editorial or business management of a newspaper, magazine, or other agency engaged in the collection and dissemination of news **c :** an academic study concerned with the collection and editing of news or the editorial or business management of a news medium **2 :** journalistic writing: **a :** writing designed for publication in a newspaper or popular magazine **b :** writing characterized by a direct presentation of facts or description of events without an attempt at interpretation **c :** writing designed to appeal to current popular taste or current public interest **3 :** newspapers and magazines **4 :** the presentation of events or ideas (as in a painting or play) in a manner regarded as similar to that of journalism
jour·nal·ist \-ᵊəst\ *n* -s [¹*journal* + *-ist*] **1 a :** one engaged in journalism; *esp* **:** one employed to write or edit the subject matter of a news medium **b :** a writer who aims or is felt to aim chiefly at a mass audience or strives for immediate popular appeal in his writings **c :** an enlisted man (as in the U.S. Navy) who performs public information duties **2 :** one who keeps a journal
jour·nal·is·tic \¦==¦istik, -tēk\ *adj* **:** of, relating to, or having the characteristics of journalism or journalists ⟨the brilliant and amusing example of ~ acumen —*N.Y. Times*⟩ ⟨these ~ illustrations . . . had great aesthetic vitality —Lewis Mumford⟩ ⟨resorted to the ~ device of gingering up the actual records —*New Yorker*⟩; *esp* **:** marked by literary qualities appropriate to newspapers and popular magazines — **journal·is·ti·cal·ly** \-tək(ə)lē, -tēk-, -li\ *adv*
jour·nal·ize \'==,īz\ *vb* -ED/-ING/-S *see -ize in Explan Notes* [¹*journal* + *-ize*] *vt* **:** to enter or record in a journal ~ *vi* **1 :** to keep a journal in accounting **2 :** to keep a personal journal **:** write down daily or regularly reflections, observations, or ideas — **jour·nal·iz·er** \-zə(r)\ *n* -s
journal voucher *n* **:** a paper in accounting that authorizes an entry in a journal or a paper that constitutes an authorized entry for direct posting
¹jour·ney \'jərnē, 'jən-, 'jəin-, -ni\ *n* -s [ME *jurne, jorne, journey*, fr. OF *jornee, journee*, fr. *jor, jour* day, fr. LL *diurnum*, fr. neut. of L *diurnus* of the day, daily — more at JOURNAL] **1 a :** travel or passage from one place to another **:** TRIP ⟨a three-day ~⟩ **b** *now chiefly dial* **:** a day's travel; *also* **:** the distance traveled during a day **c** *archaic* **:** a stage of a journey **:** a portion of a trip undertaken at one time **d :** something suggesting travel or passage from one place to another: as (1) **:** the course of one's life from birth to death (2) *obs* **:** the daily course of the sun across the sky (3) **:** an often extended experience that provides new information or knowledge beyond that which one might normally acquire ⟨a ~ into higher mathematics⟩ ⟨a ~ into the customs of another country⟩ ⟨an inviting and pleasant mental ~ for the reader —Frank Mortimer⟩ ⟨his ~ into faith —Florence Bullock⟩ **2 a** *chiefly dial* **:** a day's labor or a fixed amount of work as an equivalent **b :** a weight of metal (as 15 pounds troy of gold or 60 pounds troy of silver) that was the supply for one day's minting of coins by hand in the British mint and that made up into coin constitutes the unit out of which one coin is set aside for the trial of the pyx **c :** a cycle of work done in glass manufacturing in converting a quantity of material into glass or glass products **3** *obs* **a :** FIGHT, BATTLE **b :** a military expedition **:** SIEGE, CAMPAIGN
²journey \"\ *vb* **journeyed; journeyed; journeying; journeys** [ME *jorneyen, journeyen*, fr. MF *journoier*, fr. *journee*] *vi* **:** to go on a journey ⟨spent the summer ~*ing*⟩ **:** go from home to a distant place ⟨packed his belongings and ~*ed* to another country⟩ **:** TRAVEL ⟨~ from place to place in search of treasure⟩ ⟨most of us ~ to work by bus, train, tram —Agnes M. Miall⟩ ~ *vt* **1 :** to travel over or through **:** TRAVERSE ⟨~*ed* many a land —Sir Walter Scott⟩ **2 :** to separate (coins in the British mint) into journeys
journey-bated *adj, obs* **:** worn out with journeying
journeycake \'==,=\ *n* [prob. by folk etymology fr. *johnnycake*] **:** JOHNNYCAKE
jour·ney·man \'==mən\ *n, pl* **journeymen** *often attrib* [ME, fr. *jurne, journey* + *man*] **1 a :** a worker who has learned a handicraft or trade and is qualified to work at it usu. for another by the day — distinguished from *apprentice* and *master* **b :** an experienced usu. competent or reliable workman in any field usu. as distinguished from one that is brilliant or colorful ⟨a good, reliable ~ of the theatre —*Theatre Arts*⟩ ⟨a good ~ trumpeter —*New Yorker*⟩ ⟨~ work, competent but without much distinction —J.G.Villa⟩ ⟨~'s work too slick and trite to prove itself —K.P.Kempton⟩ ⟨*journeymen* rather than first-rate artists —H.E.Clurman⟩ **2** *archaic* **:** one hired to work for another **:** HIRELING **3 :** the first rank earned by members of a Camp Fire Girls Horizon Club — compare ARTISAN
journeys accounts *n pl* **:** the number of days required for travel to a court formerly considered in English law as the fewest within which a new writ could be obtained after the abatement of a previous one
journey weight *n* **:** a journey of coins in the British mint
journeywoman \'==,==\ *n, pl* **journeywomen :** a female journeyman
journeywork \'==,=\ *n* **1 a :** work done by a journeyman esp. by the day **b :** work done for hire **2 :** necessary routine and often servile work **:** HACKWORK
¹joust \'jaùst *sometimes* 'jəst *or* 'jüst\ *or* **just** \'jəst\ *n* -s [ME, fr. OF *joste, juste, jouste*, fr. *joster, juster, jouster*] **1 a :** a combat on horseback between two knights with lances esp. in the lists or an enclosed field; *specif* **:** an often mock combat of this kind as part of a tournament or display **:** TILT **b jousts** *or* **justs** *pl* **:** TOURNAMENT **2 :** an action resembling that of a man or of men jousting esp. in being personal combat or competition ⟨young people in their ~s with ideas —William Van Til⟩ ⟨the producer's Academy Award-winning ~ against anti-Semitism —*Newsweek*⟩ ⟨the ancient ritual of the ~ from boats, striving to knock each other into the water —Paul Engle⟩
²joust \"\ *or* **just** \"\ *vi* -ED/-ING/-S [ME *jousten, justen*, fr. OF *joster, juster, jouster* to gather, unite, joust, fr. (assumed) VL *juxtare*, fr. L *juxta* near, nearby; akin to L *jungere* to join — more at YOKE] **1 :** to fight on horseback as a knight or man-at-arms **2 a :** to engage in combat with lances on horseback **:** engage in a joust **:** TILT ⟨two knights ~*ing* in the lists⟩ **b :** to participate in an action resembling a joust **:** engage in personal combat or competition ⟨cars no longer ~*ing* and jostling at the crossings —R.M.Coates⟩ ⟨passenger-car manufacturers ~ like surly giants over the mighty business of making and selling millions of motorcars —A.W.Baum⟩ — **joust·er** *or* **just·er** \-tə(r)\ *n* -s
jousting *also* **justing** *n* -s [ME, fr. the gerund of ME *justen, jousten*] **:** the action or sport of one that jousts **:** JOUST, TILT
jousting helmet *or* **jousting helm** *n* **:** TILTING HELMET
jou·vence blue \(')zhü¦vä(ⁿ)s-\ *n* [*jouvence* fr. F, youth (in *fontaine de jouvence* fountain of youth), fr. MF, alter. of

jouvente, fr. L *juventa*, fr. *juvenis* young — more at YOUNG] **:** a moderate bluish green to greenish blue that is deeper than gendarme or cyan blue and duller than parrot blue

jouy print \zhəˈwē-, ˈzhwē-\ *n, usu cap J* [*Jouy*-en-Josas, France, its original place of manufacture] **:** TOILE DE JOUY

jo·va \ˈhōvə\ *n, pl* **jova** *or* **jovas** *usu cap* [Sp, of AmerInd origin] **1 :** an important division of the Piman peoples of northeastern Sonora **2 :** a member of the Jova people

jove \ˈjōv\ *interj, usu cap* [fr. *Jove* (Jupiter), ancient Roman god of the sky, fr. L *Jov-, Jupiter* — more at DEITY] — used typically to express surprise or agreement esp. in the phrase *by Jove*

jove's–beard \ˈ=,=\ *n, pl* **jove's–beards** *usu cap J* **:** JUPITER'S-BEARD

jove's–flower \ˈ=,=\ *n, pl* **jove's–flowers** *usu cap J* **:** CLOVE PINK

jove's–fruit \ˈ=,=\ *n, pl* **jove's–fruits** *usu cap J* **1 :** a spicebush (*Benzoin melissaefolium*) of the southern U.S. **2 :** PERSIMMON

jo·vial \ˈjōvēəl, -vyəl\ *adj* [MF & LL; MF, fr. LL *jovialis* of the god Jupiter, fr. *Jov-, Jupiter* Jupiter, ancient Roman god of the sky + L *-alis* -al — more at DEITY] **1 a** *obs* **:** JOVIAN **b :** having the nature, disposition, or aspect that according to astrology is determined by Jupiter as natal or ruling planet **2 :** characterized by or showing marked good humor esp. as exhibited in mirth, hilarity, or conviviality **:** JOYFUL, JOLLY ⟨a ~ portly gentleman⟩ ⟨a ~ grin⟩ **syn** see MERRY

jovialist *n* -s **1** *obs* **:** one born under the planet Jupiter **2** *obs* **:** one having a jovial disposition

jo·vi·al·i·ty \ˌjōvēˈaləd·ē, jōvˈya-, -latē, -i\ *n* -ES **:** the quality or state of being jovial ⟨greeted him with customary ~ —S.E.White⟩ ⟨liked the ~ of the gathering⟩

jo·vial·ize \ˈjōvēə,līz, -vyə-\ *vb* -ED/-ING/-S *vt, archaic* **:** to make jovial ~ *vi, obs* **:** to act in a jovial way

jo·vial·ly \-əlē, -əli\ *adv* **:** in a jovial manner

jo·vial·ness *n* -ES **:** JOVIALITY

jo·vi·an \ˈjōvēən\ *adj, usu cap* [L *Jovius* of Jupiter (fr. *Jov-, Jupiter*) + E *-an*] **1 :** of, relating to, or befitting the chief ancient Roman god Jupiter ⟨*Jovian* thunderbolts⟩ ⟨*Jovian* wrath⟩ ⟨the committee's *Jovian* attitude toward justifying its decisions —Paul Moor⟩ ⟨resolved the trouble by *Jovian* fiat —Agnes de Mille⟩ ⟨a *Jovian* detachment from the pressure of events —H.R.Tolley⟩ **2** [L *Jov-, Jupiter*, the planet Jupiter (fr. *Jov-, Jupiter*, the god Jupiter) + E *-ian*] **:** relating to the planet Jupiter ⟨the *Jovian* satellites⟩

jo·vi·cen·tric \ˌjōvəˈsen·trik\ *also* **jo·vi·cen·tri·cal** \-rəkəl\ *adj, usu cap* [L *Jov-, Jupiter*, the planet Jupiter + E *-i-* + *-centric* or *centrical*] **:** centered upon or revolving around the planet Jupiter **:** appearing as viewed from the center of Jupiter — **jo·vi·cen·tri·cal·ly** \-rək(ə)lē\ *adv*

1jow \ˈjau̇, ˈjō\ *vb* -ED/-ING/-S [alter. of *4jowl*] *vt* **1** *dial Brit* **:** to give a blow to **:** STRIKE **2** *dial Brit* **:** to cause (a bell) to ring or toll ~ *vi, dial Brit, of a bell* **:** TOLL, RING

2jow \"\ *n* -s *chiefly Scot* **:** STROKE, KNOCK, TOLL ⟨and every ~ the dead bell gave cried woe to Barbara Allen —*Barbara Allen*⟩

jo·war \jəˈwär\ *n* -s [Hindi *joār, jawār*; akin to Skt *yava* barley] *India* **:** DURRA

1jow·er \ˈjau̇(ə)r\ *vi* -ED/-ING/-S [perh. of imit. origin] *chiefly dial* **:** QUARREL, WRANGLE

2jower \"\ *n* -s *dial* **:** QUARREL, SPAT

1jowl \ˈjau̇(ə)l *also* ˈjōl *sometimes* ˈjȯl\ *n* -s [alter. (prob. influenced by *1jaw*) of ME *chavel, chauel, chawl*, fr. OE *ceafl*; akin to MHG *kivel, kiver* jaw, OS *kaflos*, pl., jaws, ON *kjaptr* jaw, OIr *gop* beak, mouth, Av *zafar-, zafan-* mouth] **1 a :** JAW; *esp* **:** MANDIBLE **b :** one of the lateral halves of the mandible **2 a :** CHEEK 1 **b :** the boneless cheek meat of a hog ⟨a dinner of boiled ~ and black-eyed peas⟩ — see PORK illustration

2jowl \"\ *n* -s [alter. (prob. influenced by *1jaw*) of ME *cholle*, prob. fr. OE *ceole* throat — more at GLUTTON] **1 a :** the pendulous part of a double chin **b :** the flesh hanging under the jaw of a fat pig **c :** the dewlap of cattle **d :** the wattle of a fowl **e :** a marked fullness and looseness of the flesh about the lower cheek and jaw usu. associated with aging — usu. used in pl. **2 :** the space and the soft tissues filling it between the branches of the lower jaw of a horse

3jowl \"\ *n* -s [ME *choll, cholle, jol, jolle*] **1** *obs* **:** HEAD 1 **2 :** a cut or dish of fish consisting of the head and usu. adjacent parts

4jowl \ˈjau̇(ə)l, ˈjōl\ *vb* -ED/-ING/-S [ME *chollen, jollen*, perh. fr. *choll, cholle, jol, jolle* head] *dial* **:** 1JOW

5jowl \"\ *n* -s *dial* **:** 2JOW

jowled \ˈjau̇(ə)ld *also* ˈjōld *sometimes* ˈjȯld\ *adj* [*2jowl* + *-ed*] **:** JOWLY ⟨his big, ~ countenance —W.A.White⟩

jowl·er \-lər\ *n* -s [*1jowl, 2jowl* + *-er*] *chiefly Scot* **:** a dog having extremely large jaws or jowls

jowly \ˈjau̇lē, -li *also* ˈjōl- *sometimes* ˈjȯl-\ *adj, often* -ER/-EST [*2jowl* + *-y*] **:** having marked jowls **:** full and usu. saggy of flesh about the lower cheeks and jaw area ⟨a silver-haired elderly man with a disillusioned ~ face, wrinkled as a leaky balloon —John Dos Passos⟩

jows·er \ˈjau̇zə(r)\ *sometimes* -au̇sə-\ *dial Eng var of* **1**DOWSER

jow·ter \ˈjau̇tə(r)\ *n* -s [origin unknown] *dial Eng* **:** a peddler or hawker esp. of fish

1joy \ˈjȯi\ *n* -s [ME *joye, joy*, fr. OF *joie, joye*, fr. L *gaudia*, pl. of *gaudium* joy, fr. *gaudēre* to rejoice; akin to Gk *gēthein* to rejoice, *gauros* proud, MIr *guāire* noble, Toch B *kāw-* to desire, Lith *džiaugiuos* I rejoice] **1 a :** the emotion excited by the acquisition or expectation of good **:** pleasurable feelings or emotions caused by well-being, success, or good fortune or by the prospect of possessing what one loves or desires **:** GLADNESS, DELIGHT **b :** an experience of such emotion **:** ENJOYMENT ⟨the ~ of books —Van Wyck Brooks⟩ **c :** the sign or exhibition of joy **:** GAIETY, JUBILATION, MERRIMENT ⟨after the victory there was great ~ in the town⟩ **d** — used interjectionally as an exclamation of delight esp. in the phrase *oh joy* **2 :** a state of happiness or felicity **:** BLISS **3 a :** a source or cause of joy ⟨motherhood is a ~ rather than a job —Kathleen H. Seib⟩ ⟨found many ~*s* in . . . rustic life —Ella E. Clark⟩ ⟨this book . . . is a ~ and an instruction —J.A.Michener⟩ ⟨a ~ to look at⟩ **b :** a small endearing or loved child **4** *of a planet* **:** astrological position in a house of agreeable quality or condition **:** an accidental dignity **syn** see PLEASURE

2joy \"\ *vb* -ED/-ING/-S [ME *joyen*, fr. OF *joir, jouir*, fr. L *gaudēre* to rejoice] *vi* **:** to experience or show pleasure or great delight **:** REJOICE, EXULT ⟨a happily married couple ~*ing* in a common ambition —Louise Mace⟩ ⟨could ~ in the purity of tone —W.M.Clark⟩ ~ *vt* **1** *obs* **:** to make joyful or happy **:** DELIGHT, GLADDEN **2** *archaic* **:** ENJOY **3** *obs* **a :** to greet with joy or welcome with honor **b :** CONGRATULATE **4** *obs* **:** to rejoice at

joy·ance \ˈjȯiən(t)s\ *also* **joy·an·cy** \-nsē\ *n, pl* **joyances** *also* **joyancies** [*joy* + *-ance, -ancy*] **1 :** the action of enjoying oneself **:** FESTIVITY, JUBILATION **2 a :** JOY, PLEASURE, DELIGHT **b** *archaic* **:** ENJOYMENT

1joyc·ean \ˈjȯisēən\ *adj, usu cap* [James Joyce †1941 Ir. writer + E *-an*] **:** of, relating to, or befitting the writer Joyce or his writings ⟨*Joycean* passages⟩ ⟨*Joycean* stream of consciousness⟩ ⟨*Joycean* bitterness —Ann F. Wolfe⟩

2joycean \"\ *n* -s *usu cap* **1 :** a specialist in the life and writings of James Joyce **2 a :** an imitator of the style or methods of writing of James Joyce **b :** one that is prone to defend Joyce against criticism or that favors Joyce's style or methods

joy·ful \ˈjȯifəl\ *adj, sometimes* **joyfuller**; *sometimes* **joyfullest** [ME, fr. *joye, joy* + *-ful*] **:** marked by joy: **a :** experiencing pleasure or delight **:** HAPPY, JUBILANT ⟨a mother who is ~ on the return of her lost son⟩ **b :** bringing or causing joy ⟨~ news⟩ **:** inspiring joy ⟨a ~ occasion⟩ **c :** showing joy ⟨a ~ countenance⟩ **syn** see GLAD

joy·ful·ly \-f(ə)lē, -li\ *adv* [ME *joyfully*, fr. *joyful* + *-ly*] **:** in a joyful manner ⟨~ singing Christmas carols⟩

joy·ful·ness \-fəlnəs\ *n* -ES [ME *joyfulnesse*, fr. *joyful* + *-nesse* -ness] **:** JOY

joy girl *n, slang* **:** PROSTITUTE

joyhouse \ˈ=,=\ *n, slang* **:** BROTHEL

joy–juice \ˈ=,=\ *n, slang* **:** an alcoholic liquor

joy·less \ˈjȯiləs\ *adj* [ME *joyles*, fr. *joy* + *-les* -less] **:** not experiencing joy ⟨a ~ man⟩ **:** not inspiring or causing joy ⟨a ~ occasion⟩ **:** UNENJOYABLE ⟨a ~ trip⟩ ⟨a ~ season⟩ — **joy·less·ly** *adv* — **joy·less·ness** *n* -ES

joy·ous \ˈjȯiəs\ *adj* [ME, fr. MF *joyeus*, fr. OF *joios*, fr. *joie, joye* joy + *-os* -ous — more at JOY] **:** JOYFUL **syn** see GLAD

joy·ous·ly *adv* **:** JOYFULLY, HAPPILY, MERRILY

joy·ous·ness *n* -ES **:** JOYFULNESS, MERRIMENT, JUBILATION

joy·pop \ˈjȯi,päp\ *vi, slang* **:** to use drugs only occasionally **:** use drugs as a joypopper

joy·pop·per \-äpə(r)\ *n, slang* **:** an occasional user of drugs **:** a drug user who is not yet totally addicted

1joyride \ˈ=,=\ *n* [*1joy* + *ride*] **1 :** a ride (as in car or plane) purely for pleasure **2 a :** a joyride taken esp. in a stolen car without regard for safety or consequences to oneself or others ⟨having stolen an automobile for a ~ —E.D.Radin⟩ **b :** any course of conduct or action marked by a seeking of pleasure with a reckless disregard of cost or consequences ⟨went on a ~, spending his inheritance heedlessly and improvidently⟩

2joyride \"\ *vi* **:** to go on a joyride ⟨after luncheon . . . I could ~ in a plane —C.L.Baldridge⟩ ⟨*joyriding* around in his car all evening⟩ — **joyrider** \ˈ=,==\ *n*

joys *pl of* JOY, *pres 3d sing of* JOY

joy·some \ˈjȯisəm\ *adj* **:** JOYFUL — **joy·some·ly** *adv*

joy stick *n* [perh. fr. E slang *joy stick* penis; fr. its position between the knees of the aviator] **:** CONTROL STICK

JP *abbr* **1** Japan paper **2** jet-propelled; jet propulsion

JP *abbr or n* -s *often not cap* justice of the peace

JPP *abbr* Japan paper proofs

jr *abbr* **1** journal **2** *often cap J* junior **3** juror

JS *abbr* joint support

j's *or* **js** *pl of* J

JSC *abbr* joint-stock company

JSD *abbr or n* -s **:** a doctor of juristic science

j–stick \ˈ=,=\ *n, cap J* **:** J-BAR LIFT

j–stroke \ˈ=,=\ *n, cap J* **:** a canoeing stroke in which the path of the paddle resembles the letter J used by a lone paddler to keep a straight course while paddling on one side of the canoe only

jt *abbr* joint

JTC *abbr* junior training corps

jtly *abbr* jointly

jua·ma·ve \(h)wəˈmävē\ *also* **juamave istle** *n* -s [perh. irreg. fr. *Jaumave*, town in eastern Mexico] **:** a high-grade istle derived from a Mexican agave (*Agave funkiana*) and characterized by long pale flexible fibers

jua·ne·ño \(h)wəˈnān(,)yō\ *n, pl* **juaneño** *or* **juaneños** *usu cap* [AmerSp, fr. *San Juan Capistrano*, Spanish mission in what is now southwestern California] **1 :** an extinct Shoshonean people of southwestern California speaking a dialect of Luiseño **2 :** a member of the Juaneño people

ju·ang \ˈjü,äŋ\ *n, pl* **juang** *or* **juangs** *usu cap* **1 a :** a Kol people of Orissa, India **b :** a member of such people **2 :** the Munda language of the Juang people

ju·ar \jəˈwär\ *var of* JOWAR

juárez *or* **juarez** *adj, usu cap* **:** CIUDAD JUÁREZ

ju·ba \ˈjübə\ *n* -s [origin unknown] **1 :** a Haitian dance of African origin having drum and stick accompaniment and performed as a work dance or as a dance for the dead **2 :** a dance of plantation Negroes in the South accompanied by complexly rhythmic hand clapping and slapping of the knees and thighs ⟨the sudden silence after the singing and ~ —R.P. Warren⟩

juba's–brush *or* **juba's–bush** \ˈjübəz,=\ *n, pl* **juba's–brushes** *or* **juba's–bushes** *usu cap J* [perh. fr. *Juba's*, genitive case of a name *Juba*] **:** an annual weed (*Iresine paniculata*) of the central U.S. and tropical America

ju·bate \ˈjü,bāt\ *adj* [NL *jubatus*, fr. L, having a mane, fr. *juba* mane + *-atus* -ate; akin to L *jubēre* to command — more at JUSSIVE] **:** fringed with long pendent hairs like a mane

jub·bah *or* **jub·ba** \ˈjübə, ˈjəbə\ *n* -s [Ar *jubbah*] **:** a long outer garment resembling an open coat, having long sleeves, and formerly worn in Muslim countries esp. by public officials and professional people ⟨arrayed in white cloth robes, a black ~, and a gold sash —John Buchan⟩

jub·bul·pore \ˈjəbəl,pō(ə)r\ *or* **ja·bal·pur** \ˈjəbəl,pu̇(ə)r\ *adj, usu cap* [fr. *Jubbulpore, Jabalpur*, city in Jubbulpore district, Madhya Pradesh, India] **:** of or from the city of Jubbulpore, India **:** of the kind or style prevalent in Jubbulpore

jubbulpore hemp *n, usu cap J* [fr. *Jubbulpore* district, Madhya Pradesh, India, where it is grown] **:** SUNN

ju·be \ˈyü(,)bā\ *n* -s [F *jubé*, fr. MF, fr. ML *Jube, Domine, benedicere* Deign, O Lord, to bless; prob. fr. the fact that in the medieval church the deacon stood at the rood screen or on the rood loft when pronouncing this benediction before the reading of the Gospel] **1 :** ROOD SCREEN **2 :** the gallery above a rood screen

ju·ber·ous \ˈjüb(ə)rəs, -bə(r)s\ *adj* [alter. of *dubious*] *South and Midland* **:** doubtful and hesitating **:** DUBIOUS

ju·bi·lance \ˈjübələn(t)s\ *n* -s [*jubilant* + *-ance*] **:** the quality or state of being jubilant **:** EXULTATION

ju·bi·lant \-nt\ *adj* [L *jubilant-, jubilans*, pres. part. of *jubilare* to jubilate] **1 :** making noises and demonstrations of joy or triumph ⟨shots fired by ~ cowboys in celebration of frontier legal victories —*Amer. Guide Series: Texas*⟩ **2 :** manifesting or expressing exultation or gladness ⟨~ strings and ceremonious percussion —Irving Kolodin⟩ ⟨the walls . . . were covered with ~ childish drawings —Oliver La Farge⟩ — **ju·bi·lant·ly** *adv*

ju·bi·lar·i·an \ˌ==ˈla(ə)rēən\ *n* -s [ML *jubilarius* jubilarian (fr. LL *jubilaeus* jubilee + L *-arius* -ary) + E *-an*, n. suffix] **:** one that celebrates a jubilee commemorating personal service in a state of life or profession; *esp* **:** a religious observing a jubilee

1ju·bi·late \ˈ==,lāt\ *vi* -ED/-ING/-S [L *jubilatus*, past part. of *jubilare*; akin to MHG *jū, jūch* (exclamation of joy), *jōlen* to yodel, Gk *iygē* shout, howling, Lith *yvas* owl] **:** to utter sounds or make demonstrations of joy and exultation ⟨the war was not officially ended but . . . a war-weary nation *jubilated* —Dixon Wecter⟩

2ju·bi·la·te \ˌyübəˈlä(,)tā, ˌjü-\ *n* -s [L, 2d pers. pl. imper. of *jubilare*; fr. the occurrence of this word at the beginning of Ps 99 in the Vulgate (Ps 100 AV and RSV)] **1 :** a song or outburst of joy and gladness ⟨Heaven's grand courts with ~*s* rang —*Tinsley's Mag.*⟩ **2** [L, 2d pers. pl. imper. of *jubilare*; fr. the occurrence of this word at the beginning of Ps 65 in the Vulgate (Ps 66 AV and RSV), used as the introit for the third Sunday after Easter] *usu cap* **:** the third Sunday after Easter

ju·bi·la·tio \ˌyübəˈlätsē,ō\ *n* -s [L, jubilation] **:** JUBILUS

ju·bi·la·tion \ˌjübəˈlāshən\ *n* -s [ME *jubilacioun*, fr. L *jubilation-, jubilatio*, fr. *jubilatus* (past part. of *jubilare* to jubilate) + *-ion-, -io* -ion] **1 a :** the action of jubilating ⟨we must not rejoice or give way to ~ —Sir Winston Churchill⟩ **b :** the state of being jubilant ⟨he expelled his pent-up ~ in a long whistle —F.G.Slaughter⟩ **2 :** an expression of joy or exultation ⟨the ~*s* of the garrison were short-lived —C.R.Low⟩

ju·bi·le·an \ˌjübəˈlēən\ *adj* [*1jubilee* + *-an*] **:** of or relating to a jubilee

1ju·bi·lee \ˈjübə,lē, ˌ==ˈ=\ *n* -s [ME, fr. MF & LL; MF *jubilé*, fr. LL *jubilaeus*, modif. (influenced by L *jubilare* to jubilate) of LGk *iōbēlaios*, fr. Heb *yōbhēl* ram's horn, trumpet, jubilee] **1** *also* **ju·bi·le** \"\ *often cap* **:** a year of emancipation and restoration provided by ancient Hebrew law for celebration every fifty years and held to be characterized by emancipation of Hebrew slaves, restoration of alienated lands to their former owners, and omission of all cultivation of the land — used esp. in the phrase *year of jubilee* ⟨the year of ~ . . . appears to have been calculated but not observed —T.W. Manson⟩ ⟨you shall hallow the fiftieth year . . . it shall be a ~ for you —Lev 25:10 (RSV)⟩ ⟨in this year of ~ ye shall return every man unto his possession —Lev 25:13 (AV)⟩ — compare SABBATICAL YEAR **2 a** (1) **:** a fiftieth anniversary or the completion of fifty years in an office, position, or condition ⟨the Australian florin commemorating the ~ of the constitution of the commonwealth —Lionel Thompson⟩ ⟨the ~ . . . of King George the Third in 1810 —E.J.Shears⟩ (2) **:** a special anniversary or the completion of a significant length of service involving a period other than fifty years — usu. used with qualifying adjective ⟨the seventieth ~ of the reign of the Emperor Francis Joseph —Hans Meyerhoff⟩ ⟨the approach of his thirty-year ~ may have supplied a . . . motive for retirement —W.F.Edgerton⟩ — compare DIAMOND JUBILEE, SILVER JUBILEE **b :** a celebration or commemoration of such an anniversary or of the completion of such a period of service ⟨the sesquicentennial vacation ~ scheduled for this year —*Stamps*⟩ **3 a :** a period of time (as a year) proclaimed by the Roman Catholic pope every 25 years or during a time of rejoicing (as an anniversary) as a time of special solemnity during which a special indulgence may be gained ⟨the first ~ was proclaimed in the year 1300 —Percy Winner⟩ **b** *or* **jubilee indulgence :** a special plenary indulgence granted during a year of jubilee to Roman Catholics who perform certain specified works of repentance and piety usu. including a pilgrimage to Rome ⟨the precise conditions for gaining each ~ are determined by the Roman pontiff —Herbert Thurston⟩ **4** [influenced in meaning by *jubilation*] **:** a state of joy or rejoicing **:** JUBILATION ⟨they . . . only thought of their triumph and abandoned themselves to ~ —W.H.Prescott⟩ **5** [influenced in meaning by *jubilation*] **:** the sound of jubilation **:** joyous shouting ⟨all along the crowded way was ~ and loud huzza —Sir Walter Scott⟩ **6 a** *obs* **:** a period of remission or restitution and sometimes license ⟨moved . . . a general ~ shall be for the debts —*House of Lords Debates*⟩ **b** [influenced in meaning by *jubilation*] **:** a season or occasion of celebration or rejoicing ⟨during the wild ~ of the Restoration —T.B.Macaulay⟩ ⟨we had a big ~ . . . to celebrate our victory —A.F.Harlow⟩ **7** *obs, often cap* **:** a period of fifty years ⟨I have lived among you almost a *Jubilee* —Ephraim Pagitt⟩ **8 :** a Negro folk song characterized by references to a future happy time or a time of deliverance from trials and tribulations ⟨the weary field hollers of the slaves were mingled with merrier elements of the ~*s* —*N. Y. Times Book Rev.*⟩ — compare HOLLER 3

2jubilee \"\ *adj* **:** FLAMBÉ 2 ⟨cherries ~⟩

ju·bi·lize \ˈ==,līz\ *vi* -ED/-ING/-S [prob. fr. *1jubilee* + *-ize*] **:** JUBILATE

ju·bi·lus \-ləs\ *n, pl* **jubi·li** \-,lī\ [ML, fr. LL, cry of joy, fr. L *jubilum*, fr. *jubilare* to jubilate] **:** the melisma on the last *a* of *alleluia* from which the sequence of the mass developed — called also *jubilatio*

ju·bus \ˈjübəs\ *var of* JUBEROUS

juca *var of* YUCA

juck \ˈjək\ *vi* -ED/-ING/-S [imit.] **:** to make the natural noise of a partridge settling down for the night

juco *abbr* junior college

jud *abbr* **1** judge; judgment **2** judicial; judiciary

judaean *var of* JUDEAN

judaeo- — see JUDEO-

1ju·dah·ite \ˈjüdə,īt\ *n* -s *usu cap* [*Judah*, 4th son of Jacob (Gen 29:35), the eponymous ancestor of the Judahites (Josh 15) + E *-ite*] **1 :** a member of the Hebrew tribe of Judah **2 :** a member of the Kingdom of Judah composed of the tribes of Judah and Benjamin

2judahite \"\ *adj, usu cap* **:** of or relating to the tribe or the Kingdom of Judah ⟨a place in *Judahite* territory —N.H. Snaith⟩ ⟨edited to suit a *Judahite* audience —L.A.Weigle⟩

ju·da·ic \(ˈ)jüˈdāik, -āēk\ *adj, usu cap* [L *judaicus*, fr. Gk *ioudaikos*, fr. *Ioudaios* Jew + *-ikos* -ic — more at JEW] **:** of, relating to, or characteristic of Jews or Judaism ⟨the . . . idea of particularism in Judaic thinking —F.S.Nichols⟩

ju·da·i·ca \jüˈdāəkə\ *n pl, usu cap* [L, neut. pl. of *judaicus* Judaic] **:** things Jewish; *esp* **:** literary or historical materials relating to Jews or Judaism ⟨a new publication devoted to *Judaica* —W.S. La Sor⟩ ⟨a large collection of *Judaica*

ju·da·i·cal \(ˈ)jüˈdāəkəl\ *adj, usu cap* [ME *judeicall*, fr. L *judaicus* + ME *-all*] **:** JUDAIC — **ju·da·i·cal·ly** \-k(ə)lē, -li\ *adv*

ju·da·ism \ˈjüdə,izəm, -dē,i- *sometimes* -(,)dā,i- *or* -,dīzəm\ *n* [LL *judaismus*, fr. Gk *ioudaismos*, fr. *Ioudaios* Jew + *-ismos* -ism] **1** *cap* **:** the religion of the Jews characterized by belief in one God and in the mission of Jews to teach the Fatherhood of God as revealed in the Hebrew Scriptures — see CONSERVATIVE JUDAISM, ORTHODOX JUDAISM, RECONSTRUCTIONISM, REFORM JUDAISM **2** *usu cap* **:** the quality or state of being a Jew **:** conformity to Jewish rites, ceremonies, and practices **:** adherence to the religion or culture of the Jews ⟨declared their *Judaism* openly —Cecil Roth⟩ **3** *usu cap* **:** the total complex of cultural, social, and religious beliefs and practices of the Jews **4** *usu cap* **:** the whole body of Jews **:** the Jewish community ⟨losses sustained by *Judaism* . . . by the oppression of Jews in Russia and Rumania —Herbert Loewe⟩

ju·da·ist \ˈjüdə·əst, -dēə-, -(,)dāə-\ *n* -s *usu cap* [*judaism* + *-ist*] **:** one that believes in or practices Judaism — **ju·da·is·tic** \ˌ=(,)=ˈistik, -tēk\ *adj* — **ju·da·is·ti·cal·ly** \-tək(ə)lē, -tēk-, -li\ *adv*

ju·da·iza·tion \ˌjüdə̇ə̇ˈzāshən, ˌjüdē|, ˌjü(,)dā|, ˌjü,dī|, |,īˈz-\ *n* -s *usu cap* **:** the act or process of judaizing or being judaized

ju·da·ize \ˈjüdə,īz, -dē,-, -(,)dā,-\ *vb* -ED/-ING/-S *often cap* [LL *judaizare*, fr. Gk *ioudaizein*, fr. *Ioudaios* Jew + *-izein* -ize] *vi* **:** to adopt the customs, beliefs, or character of a Jew **:** become Jewish ⟨they . . . prevailed on the Galatians to *Judaize* so far as to observe the rites of Moses in various instances —Joseph Milner⟩ ~ *vt* **1 :** to imbue with or deeply affect by the doctrines or practices of Judaism ⟨attempts to ~ the Christian Sunday into a sabbath⟩ **2 :** to make Jewish **:** convert to Judaism ⟨descendants of Slav tribes *Judaized* long after the Dispersal —Evelyn Waugh⟩

ju·da·iz·er \-,īzə(r)\ *n* -s *usu cap* **1 :** a Jewish Christian of the apostolic age who attempted to enforce conformity by all Christians to the precepts and practices of Judaism ⟨the *Judaizers* . . . thought that Gentiles, in order to be Christians, should be circumcised —J.W.Hunkin⟩ **2 :** a member of an heretical group arising in the Russian Orthodox Church in the 15th century and favoring an increased emphasis upon the doctrines and rituals of Judaism ⟨the *Judaizers* conducted a campaign of subversive activity within the Church —Serge Bolshakoff⟩

1ju·das \ˈjüdəs\ *n* -ES *often attrib* [after *Judas* Iscariot, apostle that betrayed Jesus] **1** *usu cap* **:** TRAITOR; *esp* **:** one that betrays under the pretense of friendship ⟨some *Judas* . . . gave the story to the one-party press —G.W. Johnson⟩ **2** *or* **judas window** *also* **judas–hole** *sometimes cap J* **:** a peephole usu. constituted by an aperture resembling a window with a sliding panel and used chiefly for inspection (as in the door of a house or a prison cell) ⟨the guard sprang to reconnoiter through a ~ —*N.Y.Sun*⟩ ⟨peering through the broken ~ in the door of the cell —John Hersey⟩ ⟨after a considerable time a ~ was opened —W.S.Maugham⟩ ⟨the *judas window* of the cell door slammed down —Dickey Chapelle⟩

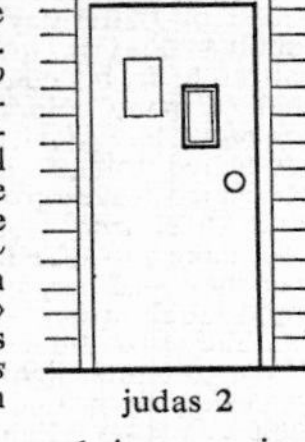
judas 2

2judas \"\ *adj, usu cap* **:** of, relating to, or being an animal used as a decoy or to lead other animals to slaughter ⟨a *Judas* duck⟩ ⟨as sheep are led by a *Judas* goat —James Reach⟩

judas–colored \ˈ==ˈ==\ *adj, usu cap J* [so called fr. a belief that Judas Iscariot had red hair] **:** RED, REDDISH — usu. used of hair ⟨there's treachery in that *Judas-colored* beard —John Dryden⟩

judas–ear \ˈ==,=\ *n, pl* **judas–ears** *usu cap J* [trans. of NL *auricula Judae* — more at JEW'S-EAR] **:** JEW'S-EAR

judas priest *interj, often cap J&P* [euphemism for *Jesus Christ*] — used as a mild oath

judas thorn *n, usu cap J* **:** a Judas tree (*Cercis siliquastrum*)

judas tree *n, usu cap J* [so called fr. a belief that Judas Iscariot hanged himself on a tree of this kind] **:** an often shrubby Eurasian tree (*Cercis siliquastrum*) that has glabrous shoots and rounded deeply cordate leaves and is widely cultivated in mild regions for its abundant purplish rose flowers which appear in early spring; *broadly* **:** a tree or shrub of the genus *Cercis*

jud·cock \ˈjəd,=\ *n* -s [perh. irreg. fr. *ged* + *cock*] **:** JACKSNIPE

1jud·der \ˈjədə(r)\ *vi* -ED/-ING/-S [prob. alter. (prob. influenced by *jar*) of *shudder*] **:** to vibrate with intensity **:** jar strongly ⟨the motors which clattered protestingly to life, backfiring and ~*ing* —J.L.Rhys⟩

2judder \"\ *n* -s **:** the action or sound of juddering ⟨they . . . found some comfort in the ~ of the engines —Audrey Barker⟩

1ju·de·an *also* **ju·dae·an** \(ˈ)jüˈdēən\ *adj, usu cap* [*Judea, Judaea*, southern division of Palestine under Persian, Greek, and Roman rule + E *-an*, adj. suffix] **:** of, relating to, or characteristic of ancient Judea ⟨*Judean* mountains⟩ ⟨the background of *Judaean* history —J.W.Jack⟩

²**judean** *also* **judaean** \"\ *n* -s *usu cap* [*Judea, Judaea* + E *-an*, n. suffix] **:** an inhabitant of ancient Judea ⟨the Israelites and *Judeans* . . . disclosed no interest in theoretical questions universal in scope —R.H.Pfeiffer⟩

judeo- *also* **judaeo-** *comb form, usu cap* [L *judaeus* Jewish, Jew — more at JEW] **1 :** of or relating to the Jews or Judaism ⟨*Judeo*phobia⟩ **2 :** Jewish and ⟨*Judeo*-Christian⟩ ⟨*Judeo*-Persian⟩

judeo-german \jü¦dā(,)ō, ¦jüdē(,)ō, jü¦dē(,)ō+\ *n, cap J&G* **:** YIDDISH

judeo-spanish \jü¦dā(,)ō, ¦jüdē(,)ō, jü¦dē(,)ō+\ *n, cap J&S* **:** the Romance language of Sephardic Jews in the Balkans, Greece, and Asia Minor

ju·dex \'jü,deks\ *n, pl* **ju·di·ces** \-də,sēz\ [L *judic-, judex*] **1 :** a private person appointed in Roman law to hear and determine a case and corresponding most nearly to a modern referee or arbitrator appointed by the court **2 :** JUDGE

judex or·di·na·ri·us \-,ȯ(r)dᵊn'a(a)rēəs\ *n, pl* **judices ordina·rii** \-rē,ī\ [ML, lit., regular judge] **:** a judicial magistrate having jurisdiction in his own right as a judge as distinguished from a judex appointed for a particular case

judex pe·da·ne·us \-pə'dānēəs\ *n, pl* **judices peda·nei** \-ē,ī\ [LL, lit., petty judex] **:** a judex appointed to hear petty causes

¹**judge** \'jəj, *dial* 'jej\ *vb* -ED/-ING/-S [ME *juggen*, fr. OF *jugier*, fr. L *judicare*, fr. *judic-, judex* judex, judge] *vt* **1 :** to form an authoritative opinion about **:** decide on the merits of ⟨a wall must be *judged* by the way it is built —Paul Potts⟩ ⟨humanity *judged* these authors . . . and found them worthy of enduring fame —Van Wyck Brooks⟩ **2 :** to hear and determine (as a litigated question) or decide in the case of (as a person) in or as if in a court of justice **:** sit in judgment upon **:** TRY ⟨the power of the court to ~ cases in interstate commerce⟩ ⟨*judged* and condemned to death for killing his mother —John Milton⟩ ⟨He shall come to ~ the quick and the dead —*Bk. of Com. Prayer*⟩ **3** *obs* **:** CONDEMN 3a ⟨some whose offenses are pilfering . . . they ~ to be whipped —Francis Bacon⟩ **4 :** to consider or pronounce to be usu. after inquiry and deliberation ⟨recommend . . . such measures as he shall ~ necessary and expedient —*U.S.Constitution*⟩ ⟨youngsters *judged* delinquent —Dorothy Barclay⟩ **5 :** to exercise paramount civil and military authority over **:** GOVERN, RULE — used of a Hebrew tribal leader in biblical times ⟨and he *judged* Israel in the days of the Philistines twenty years —Judg 15:20 (RSV)⟩ **6 :** to form an estimate or appraisal of ⟨he could ~ pace to a nicety —*Irish Digest*⟩ ⟨we ~ the distance from remembered comparisons —Weston La Barre⟩ **7 :** to hold as an opinion **:** THINK ⟨I ~ she was right —B.A.Williams⟩ ~ *vi* **1 :** to form an opinion: as **a :** to estimate esp. on the basis of a comparison of facts or ideas ⟨as near as I could ~, we were not twenty yards from the rocks —Frederick Marryat⟩ **b :** to form a conclusion from evidence ⟨when the mind assents to a proposition it ~s —J.S. Mill⟩ **c :** to form a critical evaluation — often used with *of* ⟨it is hard to ~ of the general style of the painting from such small portions —O. Elfrida Saunders⟩ **2 :** to hear and determine (as in causes on trial) **:** decide as a judge **:** pronounce judgment ⟨may the Lord ~ between you and me —Gen 16:5 (RSV)⟩ **syn** see INFER

²**judge** \"\ *n* -s [ME *juge*, fr. MF, fr. L *judic-, judex* judex, judge, fr. *ju-* (fr. *jus* right, law) + *-dic-, -dex* (fr. *dicere* to determine, say) — more at JUST, DICTION] **:** one that judges: **a** (1) **:** a public official invested with authority to hear and determine litigated questions; *esp* **:** the presiding magistrate in a court of justice usu. so named in his commission ⟨the ~ declares the law, the jury finds the facts —Edward Jenks⟩ ⟨European ~s are members of a hierarchically organized bureaucracy —C.J.Friedrich⟩ (2) **:** a person who performs one or more functions of such an official (as a justice of the peace or referee) or of any judicial officer — sometimes used as an honorific or courtesy title without much significance ⟨American law early . . . dignified every magistrate by calling him ~ —H.S.Commager⟩ **b** *cap* **:** GOD, CHRIST ⟨the coming of the Lord is at hand . . . behold, the *Judge* is standing at the doors —Jas 5:8-9 (RSV)⟩ **c** *often cap* **:** a tribal hero exercising paramount civil and military authority over the Hebrews in the biblical period of more than 400 years following the death of Joshua ⟨the Lord raised up ~s, who saved them out of the power of those who plundered them —Judg 2:16 (RSV)⟩ **d :** one appointed to decide in a contest or competition (as a trial of skill or speed between two or more parties) **:** UMPIRE ⟨the *Judge* . . . must occupy the judges' box at the time the horses pass the winning post —Dan Parker⟩ ⟨on election day the ~ helps decide disputes at the polls⟩ **e :** one that decides or determines any question, point at issue, or controversy **:** one that gives an authoritative opinion ⟨each house shall be the ~ of the . . . qualifications of its own members —*U.S.Constitution*⟩ ⟨the board shall be the ~ of what constitutes unprofessional conduct —G.B.Cummings⟩ ⟨the best ~ of what his book was about —Ellen Glasgow⟩ **f :** one that has sufficient knowledge or experience to decide on the merits of or to form an authoritative opinion about something (as a question or a work of art) **:** CONNOISSEUR, CRITIC ⟨was an extraordinary ~ of character —C.F.Smith⟩ ⟨a good ~ of poetry —John Dryden⟩

judge advocate *n, pl* **judge advocates :** a legal officer charged with the administration of military justice (as by acting as legal adviser or as prosecutor at a court-martial) and usu. serving on the staff of a military commander ⟨*judge advocates* shall perform their duties under the direction of the Judge Advocate General —*U.S.Code*⟩

judge advocate general *n, pl* **judge advocate generals** *or* **judge advocates general :** the senior legal officer and chief legal adviser in an entire military establishment (as the U.S. Department of Defense or the British army) ⟨the *Judge Advocate General* has ordered the case forwarded to the court for review —J.F.Spindler⟩

judge delegate *n, pl* **judges delegate :** a judge having delegated authority ⟨an extraordinary and rarely constituted court of *judges delegate* —*Nation*⟩ — compare JUDGE ORDINARY

judge lynch *n, usu cap J&L* **:** the lynch law personified ⟨*Judge Lynch* is not the sovereign spirit of America —*Nation*⟩

judge-made \'ꞏ¦ꞏ\ *adj* **:** created by judges or judicial decision — used esp. of law applied or established by the judicial interpretation of statutes so as to extend or restrict their scope

judge ordinary *n, pl* **judges ordinary** [trans. of ML *judex ordinarius*] **1 :** a judge having jurisdiction in his own right ⟨English prelates who were sitting . . . not as *judges ordinary* but as mere delegates of the pope —Frederick Pollock & F.W. Maitland⟩ — compare JUDGE DELEGATE **2 :** a judge having ecclesiastical or probate jurisdiction

judge·ship \'jəj,ship\ *n* **:** the jurisdiction or office of a judge ⟨the ~ for the western district of Pennsylvania provided for by the act —*U.S.Code*⟩ ⟨appointed him to a ~ in the circuit court of the United States —W.C.Ford⟩

judg·ess \'jəjəs\ *n* -ES **:** a female judge

judg·mat·i·cal \(')jəj¦mad·əkəl\ *also* **judg·mat·ic** \-d·ik\ *adj* [prob. irreg. (influenced by such words as *dogmatical, dogmatic*) fr. *judgment* + *-ical* or *-ic*] **:** JUDICIOUS ⟨his ~ introduction to this brief selection . . . of shorter poems —Leonard Bacon⟩ ⟨he . . . is nicely *judgmatic* for a man still in his twenties —E.A.Weeks⟩

judg·mat·i·cal·ly \-d·ək(ə)lē\ *adv* **:** in the manner of a judge **:** GRAVELY ⟨they need to be interpreted ~ —E.L.Bernays⟩

judg·ment *or* **judge·ment** \'jəjmənt\ *n* -s [ME *juggement*, fr. OF *jugement*, fr. *jugier* to judge + *-ment* — more at JUDGE] **1 a :** a formal utterance or pronouncing of an authoritative opinion after judging **b :** an opinion so pronounced; *esp* **:** an adverse opinion **:** CENSURE, CRITICISM **2 a** (1) **:** a formal decision or determination given in a cause by a court of law or other tribunal **:** COURT ORDER, SENTENCE — compare DECREE 3b(1), SUMMARY JUDGMENT (2) *Brit* **:** a record or statement of the reasons for a specific judicial decision — compare OPINION **b** (1) **:** an obligation (as a debt) created by decree of a court ⟨collection of . . . automobile ~s from uninsured motorists —*Harvard Law Rev.*⟩ — compare ESTOPPEL, QUASI CONTRACT (2) **:** an official certificate evidencing such a decision or decree **c** *archaic* **:** a definitive or authoritative decision usu. pronounced formally as if in a court of justice **3 a** *obs* **:** the action of trying a person or a cause in or as if in a court of justice **:** TRIAL **b** *usu cap* (1) **:** the final judging of mankind by God in which reward or punishment is meted out to each individual according to his deserts — usu. used with *the* ⟨the expected letting loose of . . . anger at the *Judgment* —C.A.Scott⟩ ⟨the dead . . . biding *Judgment*, in its fold have slept —Walter de la Mare⟩ (2) **:** JUDGMENT DAY 1a **4 a :** a divine sentence or decision; *specif* **:** a calamity held to be sent by God as a punishment for wrong committed or as a symbol of divine displeasure **b :** a divine decree **:** a law divinely given ⟨hear, O Israel, the statutes and ~s which I speak in your ears this day —Deut 5:1 (AV)⟩ **5** *obs* **:** JUSTICE, RIGHTEOUSNESS ⟨for I the Lord love ~, I hate robbery —Isa 61:8 (AV)⟩ **6 a :** the action of judging **:** the mental or intellectual process of forming an opinion or evaluation by discerning and comparing ⟨the author has sought to exercise some rigor of *judgement* —Ernest Barker⟩ **b :** an opinion or estimate so formed ⟨an economist should form an independent ~ on currency questions —Bertrand Russell⟩ **c** *obs* **:** a religious belief or opinion of a sectarian nature **:** PERSUASION ⟨those of the Presbyterian ~ —Oliver Cromwell⟩ **7 a :** the capacity for judging **:** the power or ability to decide on the basis of evidence ⟨~ is the highest of the human faculties —E.L.Godkin⟩ ⟨some of the sharpest men in argument are notoriously unsound in ~ —O.W.Holmes †1894⟩ ⟨a steadying and composing effect upon their ~ —Matthew Arnold⟩ **b** (1) **:** the exercise of the capacity to judge ⟨in cases where poor ~ was displayed —Harold Koontz & Cyril O'Donnell⟩ ⟨sound professional ~ —*Jour. of Accountancy*⟩ (2) **:** the wise or just exercise of this capacity **:** DISCERNMENT, DISCRETION — used without qualifier ⟨he was not a man of ~ and he allowed personal feeling to influence his action —Hilaire Belloc⟩ ⟨displays . . . tact, clarity, and ~ —*Saturday Rev.*⟩ **8** *obs* **:** one possessing good judgment **:** ²JUDGE f ⟨he's one o' th' soundest ~s in Troy . . . and a proper man —Shak.⟩ **9** *logic* **a :** the action of mentally establishing a relation between two or more terms; *esp* **:** the affirmation or denial of a predicate with respect to a subject — compare APPREHENSION **b :** a formal expression embodying such a logical conclusion; *esp* **:** a proposition viewed as a statement of something believed or asserted **10** *philos* **:** the capacity, power, or faculty of judging: as **a** *Scholasticism* **:** the capacity to arrive at a decision about the value of things **b** *Kantianism* (1) **:** the power of relating particular to general terms or concepts — see DETERMINATIVE JUDGMENT, REFLECTIVE JUDGMENT (2) **:** a capacity mediating between reason and the understanding; *broadly* **:** the critical faculty — **judgment not withstanding the verdict** *or* **judgment non ob·stan·te ve·re·dic·to** \-,nänəb'stantē,verə'dik(,)tō, -,nōn-\ **:** a legal judgment entered for one party because law and justice require it notwithstanding a verdict of the jury in favor of an opposing party **syn** see SENSE

judg·men·tal \(')jəj¦mentᵊl\ *adj* **:** of, relating to, or involving judgment ⟨emphasizing the ~ aspect of morality —Sing-nan Fen⟩ ⟨the right to correct ~ errors —H.F.Taggart⟩

judgment book *n* **1 :** a book in which the clerk of a court of record enters judgments **2** *usu cap J&B* **:** the record of all human acts to be opened at the Last Judgment ⟨the leaves of the *Judgment Book* unfold —Bayard Taylor⟩

judgment by default : a judgment entered as a result of the failure of a party to appear or to file a pleading or to perform some other act of an interlocutory nature required by law within the time allowed

judgment cap *n* **:** BLACK CAP

judgment creditor *n* **:** a creditor having a legal right to enforce execution of a judgment for a sum of money ⟨a suit in equity by two *judgment creditors* of an insolvent . . . corporation —*Corporation Jour.*⟩ — compare JUDGMENT DEBTOR

judgment day *n* **1 a** *usu cap J&D* **:** the day of the Last Judgment **:** DOOMSDAY 1 ⟨belief in . . . the *Judgment Day* at the end of the world —E.R.Pike⟩ **b :** a day of final judgment ⟨driven Congress . . . for the sake of a completed record before the *judgment day* of election —F.L.Paxon⟩ **2 :** the day fixed by statute, rule, or custom of a court on which judgments are pronounced or entered upon the court records

judgment debt *n* **:** a legal obligation to pay a debt or damages evidenced by a judgment entered in a court of record and enforceable by execution or other judicial process — compare QUASI CONTRACT

judgment debtor *n* **:** one whose obligation to pay a judgment debt remains unsatisfied ⟨order the appearance of a *judgment debtor* for supplementary examination as to financial ability —F.H.Myers⟩ — compare JUDGMENT CREDITOR

judgment lien *n* **:** a statutory lien usu. upon the real estate of a judgment debtor that becomes effective upon entry of a judgment by a court of record or upon filing notice of the judgment with the appropriate public official

judgment note *n* **:** a promissory note of a kind illegal in some states of the U.S. upon which the holder is enabled to enter judgment and take out execution ex parte in case of default in payment

judgment-proof \'ꞏꞏ¦ꞏ\ *adj* **:** of or being one (as a judgment debtor) from whom nothing can be recovered because he has no property or has fraudulently concealed or removed his property from the jurisdiction of the judgment ⟨an insolvent, *judgment-proof* tort-feasor —R.E.Keeton⟩

judgment rate *n* **:** an insurance rate based on the judgment of the rater instead of on a prescribed schedule

judgment roll *n* **1 :** a parchment roll or a book containing a record of the proceedings and judgment of a case in a court of law ⟨the cost of transcribing the *judgment roll* —*Ward v. Cruse*⟩ **2 :** a roll of papers constituted by a collection of the original records of a judicial proceeding

judgment seat *n, often cap J* **:** the seat of judgment where all are to be tried in the presence of God at the time of the Last Judgment ⟨we must all appear before the *judgment seat* of Christ —2 Cor 5:10 (RSV)⟩

judgment summons *n* **:** a summons issued in an English county court requiring a judgment debtor to appear and show cause why he should not be imprisoned

judgt *abbr* judgment

ju·di·ca·ble \'jüdəkəbəl\ *adj* [LL *judicabilis*, fr. L *judicare* to judge + *-abilis* -able — more at JUDGE] **:** capable of being or liable to be judged ⟨a ~ dispute⟩

ju·di·ca·tive \-,kād·iv\ *adj* [ML *judicativus*, fr. L *judicatus* (past part. of *judicare* to judge) + *-ivus* -ive] **:** having the power to judge **:** JUDICIAL ⟨all the ~ authority of the House of Lords —David Hume †1776⟩

ju·di·ca·tor \-ād·ə(r)\ *n* -s [LL, fr. L *judicatus* (past part. of *judicare*) + *-or*] **:** one that judges or acts as a judge ⟨the authority of its ~s called in question —William Robertson †1686⟩

ju·di·ca·to·ry \-kə,tōrē\ *n* -ES [ML *judicatorium* court of law, fr. L *judicatus* (past part. of *judicare*) + *-orium* -ory] **1 :** JUDICIARY 1a ⟨evidence in the Saxon *Judicatory* sometimes consisted in the . . . testimony of the fact itself —Nathaniel Bacon⟩ **2 :** JUDICATURE 2 ⟨the treaties of the U.S. had been . . . put in execution by state *judicatories* —Alexander Hamilton⟩ **3 :** one of the four governing bodies of the Presbyterian Church ⟨the General Assembly is the highest ~ of this Church —*Constitution of the United Presbyterian Church in the U.S.A.*⟩ — compare GENERAL ASSEMBLY, PRESBYTERY, SESSION, SYNOD

ju·di·ca·ture \-kə,chü(ə)r, -kəchər, -,kāchər\ *n* -s [MF, fr. ML *judicatura*, fr. L *judicatus* (past part. of *judicare*) + *-ura* -ure] **1 :** the action of judging **:** the administration of justice (as by courts of law) ⟨~ is nothing else but an interpretation of the laws —Thomas Hobbes⟩ ⟨the Supreme Court of *Judicature* in England⟩ **2 :** a court of justice **:** a legal tribunal ⟨the Court of the Lord Lyon in Scotland is one of the ~s of that country —F.J.Grant⟩ **3 :** JUDICIARY 1 ⟨the Lyon Court is a . . . part of the ~ of Scotland —L.G.Pine⟩

judices *pl of* JUDEX

ju·di·cial \(')jü¦dishəl\ *adj* [ME, fr. L *judicialis*, fr. *judicium* judgment (fr. *judic-, judex* judex, judge) + *-alis* -al — more at JUDGE] **1 :** of, relating to, or concerned with a judgment, the function of judging, the administration of justice, or the judiciary ⟨the ~ powers of Congress —W.S.Sayre⟩ ⟨the new ~ code⟩ ⟨a ~ circuit⟩ — compare ADMINISTRATIVE, EXECUTIVE, LEGISLATIVE **2 :** of or relating to judgment concerning the supposed influence of the heavenly bodies on things human ⟨prosecuted . . . for lecturing in ~ astrology —*Times Lit. Supp.*⟩ **3 :** ordered or enforced by a court or other legal tribunal ⟨it could not be the end of the law, whether moral or ~, to license a sin —John Milton⟩ ⟨a ~ sale⟩ — compare CONVENTIONAL **4** *obs* **:** JUDICIOUS ⟨showed himself so ~ and industrious as gave great satisfaction —John Smith †1631⟩ **5 :** of, characterized by, or expressing judgment **:** CRITICAL 1 c ⟨gave a cold, ~ look at his lapel —Claud Cockburn⟩ ⟨a biography . . . appreciative and yet ~ in purpose —Tyler Dennett⟩ **6 :** arising from a judgment of God **:** coming as a divine punishment ⟨a ~ pestilence⟩ **7 :** belonging or appropriate to a judge or the judiciary ⟨with stern ~ frame of mind —W.S.Gilbert⟩ ⟨weight of his ~ wig —Frank Yerby⟩

²**judicial** *n* -s [ME, fr. *judicial*, adj.] *obs* **:** a law or ordinance that is subject to enforcement by the courts — compare MORAL LAW

judicial act *n* **:** an act involving the exercise of judicial power; *esp* **:** one that determines controversies or questions of right or obligation

judicial administration *n* **1 :** the dispensing of justice according to law esp. through the functioning of a system of courts ⟨the people . . . see the processes of *judicial administration* at close range in thousands of local courts —E.F.Johnson⟩ **2 :** the management of the internal affairs of a system of courts ⟨effective *judicial administration* requires the establishment of businesslike methods —F.M.Vinson⟩

judicial astrology *n* **:** a branch of astrology that professes to foretell the fate and acts of nations and individuals — called also *mundane astrology*

judicial bond *n* **:** COURT BOND ⟨a *judicial bond* given where the law does not require any is not binding —*Hartford Accident & Indemnity Co. v. Abdalla*⟩

judicial combat *n* **:** TRIAL BY BATTLE

judicial committee of the privy council *usu cap J&P & both Cs* **:** a committee of the British Privy Council composed of leading jurists usu. from Great Britain and occasionally from Commonwealth countries that acts as the highest court of appeal from British colonies and from some of the nations of the Commonwealth ⟨appeal to the *Judicial Committee of the Privy Council* still lies from Ceylonese courts —Maurice Duverger⟩

judicial conference *n* **:** a conference composed of judges and sometimes other public officials and leaders of the bar and meeting to study problems and suggest reforms and improvements in the administration of the judicial system in a specific area ⟨each circuit has a *Judicial Conference* of the Circuit —F.M.Vinson⟩

judicial council *n* **:** a governmental agency usu. composed of judges and lawyers and established to study and make recommendations to the legislature on alterations in the laws and in the administration of the courts ⟨*judicial councils* . . . devise ways of simplifying judicial procedure —A.F.MacDonald⟩

judicial discretion *n* **:** the choice among possible decisions exercised by a judge according to the principles of justice and equity in the absence of a specific rule of law governing the case

judicial factor *n* **:** an administrator of an estate appointed under Scots law by the Court of Session — compare RECEIVER

ju·di·ci·al·i·ty \(,)jü,dishē'aləd·ē\ *n* -ES **:** the quality or state of being judicial ⟨characterized by Olympian ~⟩

judicial legislation *n* **:** laws held to be created by the pronouncements of a judge who departs from a strict interpretation of a law according to the manifest intention of the legislature — compare JUDGE-MADE

ju·di·cial·ly \(')jü¦dish(ə)lē, -li\ *adv* **:** in a judicial manner

judicial murder *n* **:** death caused by a court sentence held to be legal but unjust ⟨a revolution . . . with no massacres or *judicial murders* of people on the losing side —H.B.Parkes⟩

judicial notice *n* **:** the recognition by a court for the purposes of a case of the existence or truth of certain facts as being self-evident or common knowledge ⟨no evidence is necessary as to any matters of which the court takes *judicial notice* —H.J. Stephen⟩

judicial oath *n* **:** an oath required in the course of judicial proceedings esp. in a court — compare PERJURY

judicial process *n* **:** the series of steps in the course of the administration of justice through the established system of courts ⟨no valid basis within the *judicial process* for pursuing review of my rulings in the case —L.W.Youngdahl⟩

judicial review *n* **1 :** REVIEW 5 ⟨deportation orders shall not become final until the completion of *judicial review* —*Harvard Law Rev.*⟩ **2 :** a constitutional doctrine that gives to a court system and esp. to a supreme court the power to annul legislative or executive acts which the judges declare are contrary to the provisions of the constitution ⟨*judicial review* has . . . been termed America's distinctive contribution to the science of politics —F.A.Ogg & P.O.Ray⟩

judicial separation *n* **:** a separation of husband and wife sanctioned by an order of a court **:** a divorce a mensa et thoro — called also *legal separation*

judicial sequestration *n* **:** a mandate of a Louisiana court directing a sheriff to take possession of property in a dispute to await the order of the court as to who is entitled to possession

judicial township *n* **:** a political division of a county in some western states of the U.S. — compare CIVIL DISTRICT, ELECTION DISTRICT 2

judicial veto *n* **:** the power possessed by a court system and esp. a supreme court to annul legislative and executive acts by declaring them unconstitutional ⟨the explicit assumption . . . that the *judicial veto* is basically undemocratic —*Amer. Polit. Sci. Rev.*⟩

judicial writ *n* **:** a writ issued by a court under its own seal for judicial purposes — compare ORIGINAL WRIT

¹**ju·di·ci·ary** \jü'dishē,erē, -ri *also* -shər-\ *adj* [L *judiciarius*, fr. *judicium* judgment + *-arius* -ary — more at JUDICIAL] **:** of, concerned with, or relating to the judiciary **:** JUDICIAL ⟨the general principle of English ~ law —Edward Jenks⟩ ⟨the appointment of more women to higher ~ positions —*Current Biog.*⟩ ⟨the ~ committee⟩

²**judiciary** \"\ *n* -ES **1 a :** a system of courts of law in an area (as a nation or state) ⟨the judges are career members of the Italian ~ —Charles Fairman⟩ ⟨the federal ~ is responsible for the trial of cases involving federal laws —W.S.Sayre⟩ **b :** the persons (as the body of judges) constituting this system as an active agency ⟨in England . . . the ~ are recruited primarily from the ranks of practicing barristers —T.G.Lund⟩ **2 :** a branch of government in which judicial power is vested ⟨organization of the government into legislative, *judiciary* and executive —Thomas Jefferson⟩ ⟨the senate committee on the ~⟩ — compare EXECUTIVE 1, LEGISLATIVE

ju·di·cious \(')jü¦dishəs\ *adj* [MF *judicieux*, fr. L *judicium* judgment + MF *-eux* -ous] **1 :** having or exercising sound judgment ⟨a careful and ~ man —C.H.Lincoln⟩ ⟨this critic is admirably ~ —Milton Rugoff⟩ **2 :** directed or governed by sound usu. dispassionate judgment **:** characterized by discretion ⟨a ~ series of investments —Samuel Butler †1902⟩ ⟨the healthiest trees . . . have had the most ~ pruning —A.S. Igleheart⟩ ⟨compounded by a ~ mixture of ingredients —Malcolm Cowley⟩ **syn** see WISE

ju·di·cious·ly *adv* **:** in a judicious manner **:** with good judgment **:** WISELY ⟨the quality of hay can be . . . improved by ~ fertilizing the fields —*Farmer's Weekly (So. Africa)*⟩ ⟨an occasional word ~ designed to draw out reactions from others —A.T.Weaver⟩

ju·di·cious·ness *n* -ES **:** the quality or state of being judicious **:** sound judgment **:** SAGACITY ⟨~ is . . . apparent in the excellent job of selection —David Riesman⟩

ju·di·ci·um \yü'dikēəm\ *n, pl* **judi·cii** \-kē,ē\ [L] **:** JUDGMENT

ju·do \'jü(,)dō\ *n* -s [Jap *jūdō*, fr. *jū* weakness, gentleness (fr. Chin — Pek — *jou²* soft, gentle) + *dō* road, art, fr. Chin (Pek) *tao⁴* road, way] **:** a modern refined form of jujitsu utilizing special applications of principles of movement, balance, and leverage

ju·do·ka \'jüdō,kä, ꞏꞏ'ꞏ\ *n, pl* **judoka** [Jap *jūdōka*, fr. *jūdō*] **:** one who participates in judo

ju·do·pho·bia \,jüdə'fōbēə\ *n, usu cap* [prob. fr. *judo-* (alter. of *judeo-*) + *-phobia*] **:** ANTI-SEMITISM

ju·dy \'jüdē\ *n* -ES *usu cap* [fr. *Judy*, nickname for the name *Judith*] **:** GIRL ⟨as hep as the average *Judy* about such matters —John & Ward Hawkins⟩

juey \'hwā\ *n* -s [AmerSp] *Puerto Rico* **:** GREAT LAND CRAB

1jug \ˈjəg\ *n* -s [imit.] **:** a sound or note made by a bird (as the nightingale) ⟨the pretty birds do sing, cuckoo, *jug-jug* —Thomas Nash⟩

2jug \ˈ"\ *vi* **jugged; jugged; jugging; jugs :** to make the natural sound of a nightingale

3jug \ˈ"\ *n* -s [perh. fr. *Jug*, nickname for the name *Joan*] **1 a** *chiefly Brit* **:** a small pitcher usu. used as part of a table service ⟨holding the cream ~ poised above a cup —Frances Towers⟩ **b :** a large deep container usu. of earthenware or glass that has a narrow mouth, is fitted with a handle, and is used to hold liquids — compare BOTTLE **c :** the contents of a jug **2 :** JAIL, PRISON ⟨told them politely to discontinue their operations and get out of town or get thrown in the ~ —Frank Frederick⟩ **3** *slang* **:** BANK

jug 1b

4jug \ˈ"\ *vb* **jugged; jugged; jugging; jugs** *vt* **1 :** to stew in an earthenware vessel ⟨can ~ a rabbit well enough —Robert Browning⟩ **2 :** to commit to jail **:** IMPRISON ⟨is rudely pinched for stealing . . . and is *jugged* in an English jail —Edmund Gilligan⟩ ~ *vi* **:** to fish usu. for catfish by means of a hook and line attached to a floating jug

5jug \ˈ"\ *n* -s [fr. *Jug*, nickname for the name *Joan*] *obs* **:** WOMAN ⟨whoops, *Jug*, I love thee —Shak.⟩

6jug \ˈ"\ *vi* **jugged; jugged; jugging; jugs** [perh. fr. ²*jug*] *of quail or partridge* **:** to nestle or collect in a covey

juga *pl of* JUGUM

1ju·gal \ˈjügəl\ *adj* [L *jugalis*, lit., of a yoke, fr. *jugum* yoke + *-alis* -al — more at YOKE] **:** MALAR

2jugal \ˈ"\ *n* -s **:** a bone lying below the orbit in lower vertebrates and forming part of the cheekbone in some higher forms

jugal lobe *n* [*jugal* fr. *jugum* + *-al*] **:** the modified jugum of a primitive lepidopterous insect

jugal point *also* **ju·ga·le** \ˈjüˈga(ˌ)lē, -gä(-, -gā(-\ *n* -s [*jugal point* fr. ¹*jugal* + *point; jugale* fr. NL, fr. L, neut. of *jugalis* jugal] **:** the point at which lines following the margin of the frontal and temporal processes of the zygomatic bone are joined

ju·ga·tae \ˈjüˈgād.(ˌ)ē, -ˈgād·(ˌ)ē\ *n pl, cap* [NL, fr. fem. pl. of *jugatus* jugate] *in some classifications* **:** a division of Lepidoptera that is equivalent to Homoneura and consists of moths having the front wings provided with a jugum

ju·gate \ˈjüˌgāt, -gət\ *also* **ju·gat·ed** \-gād·əd\ *adj* [*jugate* prob. fr. (assumed) NL *jugatus*, fr. NL *jugum* + L *-atus* -ate; *jugated* fr. *jugate* + *-ed* — more at JUGUM] **1 a :** PAIRED **b :** having a jugum **2** [*jugate* fr. L *jugatus*, past part. of *jugare* to join, connect, fr. *jugum* yoke; *jugated* fr. L *jugatus* + E *-ed*] **:** CONJOINED, OVERLAPPING ⟨~ busts on a coin⟩

ju·ga·tion \jüˈgāshən\ *n* -s **:** the quality or state of being jugate

jug–eared \ˈ≡ˌ≡\ *adj* **:** having protuberant ears

juge d'in·struc·tion \zhüezhdaⁿstrüeksyōⁿ\ *n, pl* **juges d'instruction** \ˈ"\ [F, lit., judge of preliminary investigation] *French law* **:** a magistrate for criminal cases to whom complaints are made and who interrogates parties and witnesses, conducts investigations, and formulates charges

ju·gend·stil \ˈyügəntˌshtēl\ *n* -s *usu cap J* [G, lit., style of *Jugend*, fr. *Jugend*, illustrated periodical founded in Munich in 1896 + G *stil* style, fr. MHG, style, stylus, fr. L *stilus* — more at STYLE] **:** a late 19th century and early 20th century German decorative style parallel to art nouveau

ju·ger \ˈjüg|ə(r), ˈyüg|, ˈjüj\ *n, pl* **jugers** \|ə(r)z\ *or* **juge·ra** \ˈyügərə\ [L *jugerum*; akin to MHG *jiuch* morgen, Gk *zeugos* team, yoke (of oxen), L *jugum* yoke] **:** an ancient Roman unit of land area equal to 28,800 square Roman feet or 0.622 acre

jug·ful \ˈjəgˌfu̇l\ *n, pl* **jugfuls** *or* **jugs·ful** \-gˌfu̇lz, -gzˌfu̇l\ **1 :** the quantity held by a jug **2 :** GREAT DEAL — used in the phrase *not by a jugful* ⟨haven't seen anything yet — not by a ~⟩

jugged *past of* JUG

jug·ger *or* **jag·gar** \ˈjəgə(r)\ *n* -s [Hindi *jhagar*] **:** LUGGAR

1jug·ger·naut \ˈjəgə(r)ˌnȯt, -nät, *usu* |d.+V\ *n* -s [Hindi *Jagannāth* lord of the world (i.e. Vishnu, one of the principal Hindu gods), fr. Skt *Jagannātha*, fr. *jagat* world (fr. *jagat* adj., moving, living) + *nātha* lord; fr. a former belief that devotees of Vishnu sometimes allowed themselves to be crushed beneath the wheels of the car on which his image was being drawn in procession; akin to Skt *jigāti* he goes, *gamati* — more at COME] **:** a massive inexorable force or object that advances irresistibly and crushes whatever is in its path ⟨war has always been represented as a ~ —H.L.Matthews⟩ ⟨the tank . . . a formidable ~, is the modern scientific equivalent of the armored knight —G.R.Harrison⟩

2juggernaut \ˈ"\ *vt* -ED/-ING/-S **:** to crush under a juggernaut

jugging *pres part of* JUG

jug·gins \ˈjəgənz\ *n* -ES [prob. fr. the name *Juggins*] **:** one easily victimized **:** SIMPLETON ⟨was a clumsy ~ and let the ladder get out of control —Edith C. Rivett⟩

1jug·gle \ˈjəgəl\ *vb* **juggled; juggled; juggling** \-g(ə)liŋ\ **juggles** [ME *jogelen*, fr. MF *jogler* to joke, sing, fr. L *joculari* to joke, fr. *joculus* little joke, fr. *jocus* joke + *-ulus* — more at JOKE] *vi* **1 :** to perform the tricks of a juggler **:** engage in feats of manual dexterity ⟨the conjurer ~*s* with two oranges —R.L.Stevenson⟩ **2 :** to practice deceit **:** CHEAT, TRICK ⟨never ~*s* or plays tricks with her understanding —Charles Lamb⟩ **3 a :** to engage in manipulation esp. for the purpose of achieving a desired end ⟨the facts were unchangeable — it was useless to ~ with them —O.E.Rölvaag⟩ **b :** to make necessary adjustments **:** JIGGLE ⟨pilot bent to the instrument panel and ~*ed* quickly with his massed controls —Nevil Shute⟩ **4 :** to advance a ball by means of a juggle (as in girls' basketball) ~ *vt* **1 a** (1) **:** to practice deceit or trickery on **:** BEGUILE ⟨is't possible the spells of France should ~ men into such strange mysteries —Shak.⟩ (2) **:** to gain by deceit or trickery — usu. used with *out of* ⟨was simply ~*ing* money out of the pockets of the poor —S.E.Morison & H.S.Commager⟩ **b :** to engage in manipulation with esp. for the purpose of achieving a desired end ⟨~*ed* railroads as though they were letters in a Scrabble game —Bennett Cerf⟩ ⟨could ~ mathematical formulas in such a way as to make the ordinary man dizzy —A.W.Long⟩ **2 a :** to toss in or as if in the manner of a juggler ⟨~*s* nine balls at the same time⟩ ⟨a huge fire would already be ~*ing* its golden coronets in the fireplace —Osbert Sitwell⟩ **b :** to hold or balance insecurely or precariously ⟨tried to catch the ball but only *juggled* it⟩ **c :** to twist and turn **:** jiggle with ⟨~*s* the steering wheel to straighten the car⟩ **3 :** to advance (as a basketball) by means of a juggle

2juggle \ˈ"\ *n* -s **1 :** an act or instance of juggling: **a :** a trick of magic **b :** a show of manual dexterity **c :** an act of manipulation esp. for the purpose of achieving a desired end **:** DECEPTION, TRICKERY ⟨quieted by a ~ the apprehension about the size of the public debt —T.B.Macaulay⟩ ⟨a result of their royal father's unscrupulous ~ with the coinage —G.M.Trevelyan⟩ **2 :** the act of advancing a ball by tossing or tapping it into the air and catching it again usu. after taking several steps to gain ground (as in speedball or girls' basketball)

3juggle \ˈ"\ *n* -s [perh. alter. of ³*joggle*] **:** a block of timber cut to a specified length

4juggle \ˈ"\ *dial Eng var of* JOGGLE

jug·gler \ˈjəg(ə)lə(r)\ *n* -s [ME *jogelour*, *joglere*, fr. OE *geogelere*, fr. OF *joglere* joker (accus. *jogleour*), fr. L *joculator*, fr. *joculatus* (past part. of *joculari* to joke) + *-or*] **1 a :** one that performs tricks or acts of magic ⟨one of England's best generals with more tricks up his sleeve than a roving ~ —F.V.W.Mason⟩ **b :** one that is practiced in acts of manual dexterity; *esp* **:** one skilled in keeping several objects in motion in the air at the same time by alternately tossing and catching them **2 :** one that manipulates or deceives esp. for the purpose of achieving a desired end ⟨suave and unscrupulous ~ of words —H.J.Muller⟩

jug·glery \-glərē, -ri\ *n* -ES [ME *jogelrye*, fr. OF *joglerie*, fr. *jogler* to joke, sing + *-erie* -ery] **1 :** the art or practice of a juggler ⟨dances, acts of ~, prayers, and songs are climaxed by the weird fire dance —*Nat'l Geographic*⟩ **2 :** manipulation or trickery often designed to achieve a desired end ⟨the bill merely looks like a rather disingenuous piece of ~ —*Economist*⟩ ⟨the ~ with which . . . he proved whatever he had a mind to —W.S.Maugham⟩

jug–handled \ˈ≡ˌ≡\ *adj* [³*jug*] **:** not properly or fairly proportioned **:** ONE-SIDED ⟨trade between Canada and the U. S. is distinctly *jug-handled* —*Boston Herald*⟩

jughead \ˈ≡ˌ≡\ *n* **1** *chiefly West & Midland* **a :** MULE **b :** a wild or stubborn horse **2** *chiefly West & Midland* **:** a stupid person **:** LUNKHEAD

ju·glan·da·ce·ae \ˌjüˌglanˈdāsēˌē, -glən-\ *n pl, cap* [NL, fr. *Jugland-*, *Juglans*, type genus + *-aceae*] **:** a family of trees (order Juglandales) that include the walnuts and hickories and are characterized by odd-pinnate leaves, apetalous staminate flowers in catkins, pistillate flowers with a perianth and solitary or few in a cluster, and a drupe with a fibrous or woody epicarp and a nutlike seed — **ju·glan·da·ceous** \¦≡(ˌ)≡¦dāshəs\ *adj*

ju·glan·da·les \ˌ≡(ˌ)≡ˈdā(ˌ)lēz\ *n pl, cap* [NL, fr. *Jugland-*, *Juglans* + *-ales*] **:** an order or other group of Dicotyledoneae coextensive with the family Juglandaceae

ju·glans \ˈjüˌglanz\ *n, cap* [NL *Jugland-*, *Juglans*, fr. L *juglans*, *juglans* walnut, fr. *ju-* (fr. *Juppiter*, god of the sky) + *gland-*, *glans* acorn — more at DEITY, GLAND] **:** a genus (the type of the family Juglandaceae) of walnut trees characterized by the separation of the pith of the branchlets into thin plates and by the indehiscent husk and furrowed shell of the fruit — see BLACK WALNUT, BUTTERNUT, ENGLISH WALNUT

ju·glar \(ˈ)zhüˈglär\ *n* -s *usu cap* [after Joseph C. *Juglar* †1905 Fr. economist] **:** a business cycle of approximately nine years

ju·glone \ˈjüˌglōn\ *n* -s [ISV *jugl-* (fr. NL *Juglans*) + *-one*; orig. formed as G *juglon*] **:** a reddish yellow crystalline compound $C_{10}H_5O_2(OH)$ that is obtained esp. from green shucks of walnuts and is the chief active principle of the brown hair dye from walnuts; 5-hydroxy-1,4-naphthoquinone

jugoslavia *usu cap, var of* YUGOSLAVIA

jug plant *n* **:** a perennial evergreen herb (*Asarum arifolium*) having solitary basal flowers shaped like an urn

jugs *pl of* JUG, *pres 3d sing of* JUG

1jugu·lar \ˈjəgyələ(r) *sometimes* ˈjüg-, *chiefly in substand speech* ˈjəg(ə)l-\ *adj* [LL *jugularis*, fr. L *jugulum* collarbone, neck, throat; akin to L *jungere* to join — more at YOKE] **1 a :** of or relating to the throat or neck **b :** of or relating to the jugular vein ⟨~ pulsations⟩ **2 a** *of a fish* **:** having the ventral fins located on the throat anterior to the pectorals **b** *of a fin* **:** located on the throat **c :** of or relating to the fishes that have jugular fins

2jugular \ˈ"\ *n* -s **1 :** JUGULAR VEIN **2 :** a jugular fish

jugu·la·res \ˌjəgyəˈla(a)(ˌ)rēz, ˌjüg-\ *n pl, cap* [NL, fr. L, pl. of *jugularis* jugular] *in some esp former classifications* **:** an order or other group comprising teleost fishes with the ventral fins well forward on the throat that are now generally included in the order Percomorphi

jugular foramen *n* **:** a large irregular opening from the posterior cranial fossa that is bounded anteriorly by the petrous part of the temporal bone and posteriorly by the jugular notch of the occipital and that transmits the inferior petrosal sinus, the glossopharyngeal, vagus, and accessory nerves, and the internal jugular vein

jugular fossa *n* **:** a depression on the basilar surface of the petrous portion of the temporal bone

jugular ganglion *n* **:** SUPERIOR GANGLION

jugular process *n* **:** a lateral process of the occipital bone near each condyle articulating with the temporal bone

jugular vein *n* **:** any of several veins of each side of the neck: as **a :** a vein in man that collects the blood from the interior of the cranium, the superficial part of the face, and the neck, runs down the neck on the outside of the internal and common carotid arteries, and uniting with the subclavian forms the innominate vein — called also *internal jugular vein* **b :** a smaller and more superficial vein in man that collects most of the blood from the exterior of the cranium and deep parts of the face and opens into the subclavian vein — called also *external jugular vein* **c :** a vein in man that commences near the hyoid bone and joins the terminal part of the external jugular or the subclavian — called also *anterior jugular vein*

jugu·late \ˈjəgyəˌlāt, ˈjüg-\ *vt* -ED/-ING/-S [L *jugulatus*, past part. of *jugulare*, fr. *jugulum* collarbone, neck, throat] **:** to kill esp. by cutting the throat

jugu·lum \-ləm, ˈyügyəl-\ *n, pl* **jugu·la** \-lə\ [NL, fr. L, collarbone, neck, throat] **1 :** the lower throat or the part of the neck just above the breast of a bird **2 :** the jugum of an insect's wing

ju·gum \ˈjügəm, ˈyü-\ *n, pl* **ju·ga** \-gə\ *or* **jugums** [NL, fr. L, yoke — more at YOKE] **1 a :** one of the ridges commonly found on fruits of plants of the family Ammiaceae **b :** a pair of the opposite leaflets of a pinnate leaf **2 :** the most posterior and basal region of an insect's wing that is modified in the primitive Lepidoptera as a backwardly directed basal lobe on the inner margin of the fore wings and that serves to couple the fore and hind wings during flight **3 :** a more or less complicated crossbar linking the two arms of the brachidium of certain brachiopods

ju·gur·thine \jüˈgərthən, -ˌthīn\ *adj, usu cap* [L *jugurthinus*, fr. *Jugurtha* †104 B.C. king of Numidia defeated and captured by the Romans + L *-inus* -ine] **:** of or relating to Jugurtha or his reign ⟨the *Jugurthine* War⟩

1juice \ˈjüs\ *n* -s [ME *juis*, *jus*, fr. OF *jus* broth, gravy, juice, fr. L; akin to ON *ostr* cheese, Skt *yūṣa* soup, broth] **1 :** the extractable fluid contents of plant cells or plant structures ⟨tomato ~⟩ ⟨lime ~⟩ **2 a :** the extractable fluid contents of animal cells and flesh ⟨press all the ~ from the meat⟩ **b :** the natural fluids of an animal body (as blood, lymph, and secretions) **c :** the liquid or moisture contained in or coming from something ⟨mineral ~*s* in the earth —John Woodward †1728⟩ **3 a :** the inherent quality of a thing **:** inner warmth and vitality **:** ESSENCE ⟨merely as literary productions, they are bursting with authentic human ~*s* —G.W.Johnson⟩ **b :** robust life **:** strength and vigor **:** VITALITY ⟨in the old days there were the pioneers . . . full of ~ and jests —Sinclair Lewis⟩ ⟨dismiss any writing with the ~ of life in it as mere journalism —J.D.Adams⟩ **4 :** a fluid or medium (as electricity, gasoline, oil) that supplies power ⟨ship's scout-bombing groups had traveled just enough farther . . . to leave them short of ~ to get home —Fletcher Pratt⟩

2juice \ˈ"\ *vt* -ED/-ING/-S **1 a :** to extract the juice of ⟨*juiced* and canned the tomatoes⟩ **b** *dial* **:** MILK **2 :** to add juice to **:** supply with juice ⟨*juiced* the apple pies⟩

juiced rehearsal *n* **:** a dress rehearsal of a television program in which the mechanical equipment is used as if for the final production

juice·less \ˈjüsləs\ *adj* **1 :** lacking moisture **:** DRY **2 :** lacking interest or stimulation **:** LIFELESS ⟨dull and ~ as only book knowledge can be when it is unrelated to . . . life —John Mason Brown⟩

juice pear *also* **juicy pear** *n* **:** JUNEBERRY

juic·er \ˈjüsə(r)\ *n* -s **1 :** an electrician who arranges the lighting for a stage set (as for a theater or television) **2 :** an appliance with which juice is extracted from fruit or vegetables

juice up *vt* **:** to give life, energy, or spirit to **:** ANIMATE ⟨the show is *juiced up* by its stars —Wendell Brogen⟩ ⟨*juice up* an otherwise dull evening⟩

juic·i·ly \ˈjüsəlē, -li\ *adv* **:** in a juicy manner ⟨"how about a nice thick steak," she said ~ —Thomas Wolfe⟩

juic·i·ness \-sēnəs, -sin-\ *n* -ES **:** the quality or state of being juicy

juicy \ˈjüsē, -si\ *adj* -ER/-EST [ME *jousy*, fr. *jous*, *juis*, *jus* juice + *-y*] **1 :** abounding with juice **:** SUCCULENT ⟨ate red beef and ~ pork —F.V.W.Mason⟩ **2 :** having a high profit potential **:** financially rewarding **:** FAT 3a ⟨found the rewards of business *juicier* than the rewards of politics —Josephine Pinckney⟩ ⟨route over the old Spanish Main is a ~ strip for commercial flying —*Harper's*⟩ **3 a :** RAINY, MOIST, DAMP **b :** wet and sloppy underfoot ⟨sun was shining palely upon . . . roads ~ with black mud —Arnold Bennett⟩ **4 a :** rich in interest **:** COLORFUL, DISTINCTIVE ⟨~ human tradition that produced the masculine brown harmonies of the English pub —Lewis Mumford⟩ **b :** RACY, PIQUANT ⟨the story had all the elements of a ~ scandal —W.A.White⟩ **c :** lusty and full-blown **:** full of vitality ⟨as ripe and ~ a canteen manageress . . . as ever wore frilly crepe de chine —John Metcalf⟩ **d :** VIGOROUS ⟨had the distinct impression . . . that this particular kick had been a ~ one —E.F.Benson⟩

ju·jit·su *or* **ju·jut·su** *or* **jiu·jit·su** *or* **jiu·jut·su** \ˈjüˈjit(ˌ)sü *sometimes* -ˈjət- *or* -ˈjüt-\ *n* -s [Jap *jūjutsu*, fr. *jū* weakness, gentleness (fr. Chin—Pek—*jou²* soft, gentle) + *jutsu* art, fr. Chin (Pek) *shu⁴*] **:** the Japanese art of self-defense without weapons that depends for its efficiency largely upon the principle of making use of an opponent's strength and weight to disable or injure him — see JUDO

ju·ju \ˈjü(ˌ)jü\ *n* -s [of West African origin; akin to Hausa *djudju* fetish, evil spirit] **1 :** a fetish, charm, or amulet of West African tribes ⟨the ~ consisted of a bunch of chicken feathers well soaked in chicken blood and held together by strips of snakeskin —*Time*⟩ **2 :** the magic attributed to or associated with the use of a juju ⟨no one ever would have thought that the old man . . . was in any way connected with ~ —H.L.Ballowe⟩

ju·jube \ˈjüˌjüb\ *n* -s [ME, fr. ML *jujuba*, alter. of L *zizyphum*, fr. Gk *zizyphon*] **1 a :** an edible drupaceous fruit of a tree of the genus *Ziziphus* **:** CHINESE DATE **b** *also* **jujube tree :** a tree that produces jujubes; *broadly* **:** a tree of the genus *Ziziphus* **2 :** a fruit-flavored gumdrop or lozenge

juke \ˈjük, ˈju̇k\ *vi* -ED/-ING/-S [prob. alter. of ¹*jouk*] *chiefly South* **:** to mess around

juke·box \ˈjükˌbäks, *chiefly southern US* ˈju̇k,- *or* ˈjüt,-\ *or* **juke** *n, pl* **jukeboxes** *or* **jukes** [Gullah *juke*, *joog* disorderly, wicked] **:** a cabinet containing an automatic player and numerous phonograph records that are played by inserting a coin in a slot and usu. pushing a button to choose a record

juke joint *n* [Gullah *juke*, *joog* disorderly, wicked (in *juke house* brothel), of West African origin; akin to Wolof *dzug* to lead a disorderly life, Bambara *dzugu* wicked] **:** an establishment having a jukebox; *esp* **:** a small inexpensive establishment for eating, drinking, or dancing to the music of a jukebox

jukes \ˈjüks\ *n, pl* **jukes** \ˈ"\ *also* **jukeses** \-ksəz\ *usu cap* [*Jukes*, fictitious name of a family that was the subject of a study of hereditary tendencies to crime, immorality, disease, and poverty by Richard L. Dugdale †1883 Am. sociologist] **:** a stupid person ⟨before the Revolution, more than fifty thousand of England's *Jukes* . . . poured into the colonies —Charles Hamilton⟩ — compare KALLIKAK

ju·lep \ˈjüləp\ *n* -s [ME, fr. MF, fr. Ar *julāb*, fr. Per *gulāb* rose water, julep, fr. *gul* rose + *āb* water — more at ABKAR] **1 :** a drink consisting usu. of sweet syrup, flavoring, and water designed to soothe or stimulate ⟨a very soft well-flavored pleasant saccharine ~ —W.S.Coleman⟩ **2 a :** a tall drink made from gin, rum, or other alcoholic liquor and sometimes flavored with citrus juice ⟨gin ~⟩ ⟨orange ~⟩ **b :** a tall drink consisting of bourbon, sugar, and mint served in a frosted tumbler filled with finely crushed ice — called also *mint julep*

ju·lian \ˈjülyən\ *adj, usu cap* [L *julianus*, fr. Gaius *Julius* Caesar †44 B.C. Roman general and statesman + L *-anus* -an] **:** of, relating to, or characteristic of Julius Caesar

julian calendar *n, usu cap J* **:** a calendar introduced in Rome in 46 B.C. establishing the twelve-month year of 365 days with each fourth year having 366 days, the months each having 31 or 30 days except for February which has 28 or in leap years 29 days — compare GREGORIAN CALENDAR

julian day calendar *n, usu cap J* **:** a system used esp. by astronomers of numbering days consecutively from the arbitrarily selected point of the year 4713 B.C. instead of by cycles of days

julian day number *n, usu cap J* **:** the number of a day in the Julian day calendar (as 2,436,934 for Jan. 1, 1960)

ju·lian·ist \ˈjülyənəst\ *n* -s *usu cap* [*Julian*, 6th cent. bishop of Halicarnassus + E *-ist*] **:** a follower of Julian the Monophysite — compare APHTHARTODOCETAE

julian period *n, usu cap J* [*julian*, adj.] **:** a chronological period of 7980 Julian years that combines the solar and lunar cycles and the Roman indiction cycle and is reckoned from the year 4713 B.C. when the first years of these cycles coincided

julian year *n, usu cap J* **:** the year of exactly 365 days, 6 hours adopted in the Julian calendar

1ju·lid \ˈjüləd\ *adj* [NL *Julidae*] **:** of or relating to the Julidae

2julid \ˈ"\ *n* -s [NL *Julidae*] **:** a millipede of the family Julidae

ju·li·dae \ˈjüləˌdē\ *n pl, cap* [NL, fr. *Julus*, type genus + *-idae*] **:** a family of millipedes (class Diplopoda) having a cylindrical body composed of more than 30 rings and many eyes usu. crowded together in a cluster

ju·lien·ite \ˈjülyəˌnīt\ *n* -s [Flem *juliëniet*, fr. Henry *Julien* †1920 Belg. geologist + Flem *-iet* -ite] **:** a mineral $Na_2Co(SCN)_4.8H_2O$ consisting of a hydrous thiocyanate of sodium and cobalt that occurs in small blue needlelike crystals

1ju·lienne \ˌjülēˈen, (ˈ)jülˈyen, ˌzhü-, (ˈ)zhü-\ *n* -s [F, prob. fr. the name *Julienne*] **:** a clear soup containing julienne vegetables

2julienne \ˈ"\ *adj* **:** cut in long thin strips — used esp. of vegetables and fruit ⟨~ potatoes⟩ ⟨~ peaches⟩ ⟨garnished with ~ carrots⟩

ju·liet \ˈjülyət, ˈjülē|et *also* ˈjülēə *or* (ˈ)jülˈyet; *usu* |d.+V\ *n* -s [*Juliet*, heroine of Shakespeare's tragedy *Romeo and Juliet* (1594–95)] **:** a woman's slipper with a high front and back and low-cut sides — compare ROMEO

juliet cap *n, usu cap J* **:** a woman's skullcap that is often made of elaborately decorated mesh and used esp. for semiformal and bridal wear

ju·li·ett \ˈjülēˌet\ *usu cap* [prob. irreg. fr. *Juliet*] — a communications code word for the letter *j*

ju·lio *or* **giu·lio** \ˈjül(ˌ)yō\ *n* -s [It *giulio*, after Pope *Julius* II †1513 (It *Giulio* II)] **:** an Italian silver coin

ju·lius cae·sar cipher \ˈjülyə(s)ˈsēzə(r)-\ *n, usu cap J & 1st C* [after Gaius *Julius Caesar* †44 B.C. Roman general and statesman] **:** a substitution cipher replacing each plaintext letter by one that stands later in the alphabet

Juliet cap

jul·lun·dur \ˈjələndə(r)\ *adj, usu cap* [fr. *Jullundur*, city in northwestern India] **:** of or from the city of Jullundur, India **:** of the kind or style prevalent in Jullundur

ju·lus \ˈjüləs\ *n, cap* [NL, fr. Gk *ioulos* catkin, down, wood louse; perh. akin to L *volvere* to roll — more at VOLUBLE] **:** a widely distributed genus of millipedes that is the type of the family Julidae

ju·ly \(ˈ)jüˈlī, jəˈlī, ju̇ˈ-\ *n* -s *usu cap* [ME *julie*, fr. OE *julius*, fr. L, after Gaius *Julius* Caesar †44 B.C. Roman general and statesman who was born in this month] **:** the seventh month of the Gregorian year — see MONTH table

july hound *n, usu cap J* **:** a small chiefly white hound of U. S. origin

ju·ma·da \jəˈmädə\ *n* -s *usu cap* [Ar *jumādā*] **:** one of the two months Jumada I and Jumada II of the Muhammadan year — see MONTH table

ju·ma·no \ˌzhüməˈnō\ *n, pl* **jumano** *or* **jumanos** *usu cap* **1 :** a Uto-Aztecan people of northwestern Chihuahua, Mexico, and prob. a subdivision of the Suma **2 :** a member of the Jumano people

ju·mart \ˈjüˌmärt\ *n* -s [F, fr. Prov *gimerro*, *jamerro*, *chimarro*, fr. OProv *jumerra*, fr. L *chimaera* chimera] **:** a mythical offspring of a bull and a mare or she-ass or of a horse or ass and a cow

1jum·ble \ˈjəmbəl\ *vb* **jumbled; jumbled; jumbling** \-b(ə)liŋ\ **jumbles** [perh. of imit. origin] *vi* **1 :** to move in a confused or disordered mass **:** move in pell-mell fashion ⟨the soldiers *jumbled* through the door —Robert McLaughlin⟩ **2 a** *archaic* **:** to make discordant sounds **b :** to mingle in a confused or disordered manner **:** form a jumble ⟨entrances and exits tended to ~ —*Time*⟩ **3** *archaic* **:** to travel with jolts ~ *vt* **1 :** to mix in a confused mass **:** put or throw together without order — often used with *up* ⟨~*s* the stories up, giving no indication of when they were written —Edmund Wilson⟩ ⟨*jumbled* up the members of the chorus . . . to suit his pictorial effect —Edward Sackville-West⟩ **2** *archaic* **:** to stir, agitate, or jolt about **:** shake up ⟨a beast . . . whose trot would ~ me —William Cowper⟩

2jumble \ˈ"\ *n* -s **1 :** an assemblage of things mingled together without order, coherence, sequence, or plan **:** a confused, amorphous, or disordered mass **:** MEDLEY ⟨picturesque ~*s* of steep roofs, balconies, gables, dormers, and many chimneys —T.E.Tallmadge⟩ ⟨a ~ of fishing craft —Martin

Chisholm⟩ ⟨a thick ~ of technical terms and apparatus —Shirley A. Briggs⟩ ⟨our plans fell into a ~ —Carleton Beals⟩ ⟨an architectural ~⟩ **2** *archaic* **:** an instance of jolting or of being jolted **:** SHOCK, JOLT **3** *Brit* **:** articles for a rummage sale ⟨most of the stuff was very inferior ~ —Nigel Balchin⟩; *also* **:** RUMMAGE SALE ⟨they had a pair at the ~ —H.E.Bates⟩ **syn** see CONFUSION

[3]jumble *or* **jum·bal** \"\ *n* -S [*jumble* alter. (prob. influenced by [1]*jumble*) of earlier *jumbal*, prob. alter. of obs. *gimbal* finger ring — more at GIMBAL] **:** a small thin sugared cake usu. shaped like a ring

jumbled *adj* **:** lacking order, coherence, sequence, or plan **:** constituting a jumble ⟨a vast ~ waste —Henry Miller⟩ ⟨put his feet on the ~ desk —David Wagoner⟩ ⟨a ~ neighborhood of tenement houses, cheap stores —*New Yorker*⟩ ⟨my ~ memories fall harmoniously into patterns —David Daiches⟩

jum·ble·ment \-lmənt\ *n* -S **:** the act or an instance of jumbling **:** the fact of being jumbled

jumble sale *n, Brit* **:** RUMMAGE SALE

jum·bling·ly *adv* **:** in a jumbling manner

jum·bly \-blē\ *adj* **:** JUMBLED, CONFUSED

[1]jum·bo \ˈjəm(ˌ)bō\ *n* -S [fr. *Jumbo*, an elephant exhibited by P.T.Barnum] **1 :** a very large or huge specimen of its kind ⟨their size varies from the circumference of a small orange to ~*s* larger than a basketball —Charlotte D. Widrig⟩ **2 a :** a traveling carriage for mounting drills or saws or for transporting excavated material (as in tunnel driving) **b** (1) **:** a main-lead logging block (2) **:** a tongueless double sled used esp. for hauling logs short distances **c** (1) **:** a forestaysail esp. on an American schooner (2) **:** a triangular sail set point downward on the foreyard of a square-rigged ship or a topsail schooner in place of the regular foresail **d :** a record of car movements as posted on oversize sheets of paper maintained in a loose-leaf binder

[2]jumbo \"\ *adj* **:** being a very large specimen of its kind **:** HUGE ⟨a symphony does not need a ~ orchestra for its performance —Ross Parmenter⟩ ⟨flashed their ~ diamonds —Dawn Powell⟩

jum·bo·ism \-mbōˌizəm\ *n* -S **:** admiration for or worship of bigness ⟨too many Americans today are afflicted with ~ —*Springfield (Mass.) Union*⟩

jumbo roll *n* **1 :** the full-width roll of trimmed paper as it comes from the paper machine **2 :** a large roll of paper that is over 10 (or sometimes 12) inches in diameter and is to be used in converting operations

jum·buck \ˈjəmˌbək\ *n* [native name in Australia] *Austral* **:** SHEEP

jum·by *or* **jum·bie** \ˈjəmbē\ *n, pl* **jumbies** [modif. of Kongo *zumbi* fetish, spirit] *dial* **:** an evil spirit, ghost, or minor demon esp. in Negro belief and folklore

jumby bean *or* **jumby tree** *n* **1 a :** a West Indian necklace tree (*Ormosia monosperma*) **b** *West Indies* **:** the common lead tree (*Leucaena glauca*) **2** *or* **jumby bead :** the seed of a jumby bean

ju·melle \(ˈ)jüˈmel\ *adj* [F, fem. of *jumeau*, fr. MF, fr. OF *jumel*, fr. L *gemellus*, adj. & n., twin, dim. of *geminus* — more at GEMINATE] **:** TWIN, PAIRED — used of objects made or formed in pairs ⟨a ~ window opened upon the little balcony —John Bennett⟩

ju·ment \ˈjümənt\ *n* -S [ME, fr. L *jumentum;* akin to L *jungere* to join — more at YOKE] *archaic* **:** BEAST; *esp* **:** BEAST OF BURDEN

jum·ma \ˈjəmə\ *n* -S [Hindi *jama* collection, amount, fr. Ar *jamaʿ* total, aggregate] *India* **:** ASSESSMENT

jum·na·pa·ri \ˌjəmnəˈpärē\ *n, usu cap* [Hindi] **:** an Indian breed of milch goats

[1]jump \ˈjəmp\ *vb* -ED/-ING/-S [prob. akin to Sw *gumpa* to jump, LG *gumpen*] *vi* **1 a** (1) **:** to move or throw itself into or through the air ⟨a pretty stream ~*ing* and twisting down to sea⟩ **:** REAR ⟨the light ~*ed* up —Guy McCrone⟩ (2) **:** to rise and fall agitatedly or abruptly ⟨the formerly placid waters were . . . ~*ing* —Francis Birtles⟩ ⟨the snow ~*ed* in tiny cloud puffs —Victor Canning⟩ **b** (1) **:** to spring free from the ground or some other environing medium by the muscular action of the feet and legs or in some animals the tail **:** project oneself through the air **:** SPRING, LEAP, HOP ⟨a trout will ~ several feet —John Burroughs⟩ ⟨~*ed* on a moving bus⟩ ⟨~*ed* out of bed⟩ ⟨~*ed* down from the tree⟩; *also* **:** to rise to one's feet with a bound or other energetic movement ⟨~*ed* up and vigorously protested the chairman's action⟩ (2) **:** to make a sudden spasmodic movement as a result of surprise or other nervous shock **:** START ⟨~*ed* at his unexpected entry⟩ (3) *in board games* **:** to move over a position occupied by an opponent's man to a vacant one beyond and capture the man (as in checkers) or to so move merely to facilitate progress to one's goal (as in Chinese checkers) (4) **:** to pass over a regular or proper stopping point **:** SKIP ⟨this typewriter ~*s* and needs repairing⟩ (5) *of a published item* **:** to continue from one column or page to another (6) **:** to undergo a vertical or lateral displacement owing to improper alignment of the film on a projector mechanism ⟨images ~ on the screen⟩ (7) **:** to drop from an airborne airplane with a parachute (8) **:** to commence or launch upon a drive, march, expedition, or other enterprise **:** start out **:** BEGIN — used with *off* ⟨the campaign ~*ed* off to a good start⟩ ⟨~*ed* off for the distant mining country⟩; *specif* **:** to start forward in a military attack ⟨at 11:01 a.m. the assault companies ~*ed* off —P.W.Thompson⟩ ⟨the attack ~*ed* off in good weather —*Military Engineer*⟩ (9) **:** to move, obey, or act with energy or alacrity **:** HUSTLE ⟨when he spoke he expected people to ~ —T.O.Thoman⟩ ⟨said he wanted them to ~ to it —Earle Birney⟩ ⟨the first thing the new bureaucrat learns is this: when the phone rings — ~ —*Newsweek*⟩ **2 :** COINCIDE, AGREE, ACCORD — usu. used with *with* ⟨it ~*s* with my humor —Shak.⟩ ⟨that choice ~*s* with the spirit of the age —J.C.Powys⟩ **3 a** (1) **:** to pass or move haphazardly or aimlessly from one thing or state to another **:** shift abruptly ⟨the author ~*s* from region to region —*Geog. Jour.*⟩ ⟨~*ing* from job to job —Albert Deutsch⟩ (2) **:** to change or abandon employment esp. in violation of contract ⟨~*ed* to the Mexican League . . . and drew a five-year ban —*Springfield (Mass.) Daily News*⟩ ⟨~*ed* without notice —Fred Bradna & Hartzell Spence⟩ (3) **:** to rise or climb abruptly from one rank, status, or condition to another often with omission of intermediate stages ⟨~*ed* rapidly from captain through all the grades to colonel —H.H.Arnold & I.C. Eaker⟩ ⟨~*ed* from the Stone Age to the Iron Age without any intervening copper or bronze culture period —R.W.Murray⟩ (4) **:** to increase suddenly and sharply ⟨recruiting began to ~ that very evening —W.G.Shepherd⟩ ⟨population is ~*ing* —W.A.Bridges⟩ (5) **:** to make a jump bid in bridge **b** (1) **:** to make a judgment precipitately or without careful study of one's premises **:** make a mental leap ⟨inclined to ~ from some general observation to the first possible solution —W.J. Reilly⟩ ⟨before you ~ to that happy but unwarranted assumption —S.L.Payne⟩ ⟨no impressionist who ~*s* hastily to conclusions —C.I.Glicksberg⟩ (2) **:** to accept eagerly **:** take quick or immediate advantage — usu. used with *at* ⟨~*ed* at the job⟩ ⟨~*ed* at the chance⟩ (3) **:** to join, enter, or intervene with eagerness or alacrity — usu. used with *in* or *into* ⟨as unhealthy as if . . . the military ~*ed* in, in the recognition that a literate and educated population was important for the quality of future draftees —R.L.Meier & Eugene Rabinowitch⟩ ⟨~*ed* into this . . . business on twenty-four hour notice —F.D.Roosevelt⟩ and in such phrases as *jump aboard* ⟨finally ~*ed* aboard bolshevism —A.M.Rosenthal⟩ and *jump on the bandwagon* ⟨exhibiting a desire to ~ on the bandwagon —M. F.A.Montagu⟩ **4 a :** to attack suddenly or without warning **:** POUNCE — often used with *on* or *upon* ⟨~*ed* upon them without reason —*Pasadena (Calif.) Independent*⟩ **b :** to give a tongue-lashing **:** level severe criticism or censure ⟨~*ed* all over me for it⟩ — often used with *on* or *upon* ⟨people who ~ on modern poetry as obscure —*Time*⟩ or in the phrase *jump down one's throat* ⟨whenever I opened my mouth he ~*s* down my throat —W.S.Gilbert⟩ **5 a :** SWING ⟨the jazz they do blow is interesting and ~*s* —*Metronome Yearbook*⟩ ⟨whole thing ~*s* splendidly —*Jazz Jour.*⟩ **b :** to be very lively **:** bustle with gaiety or activity ⟨the joint was really ~*ing* with kids —Maritta Wolff⟩ ⟨the town was ~*ing* —*Springfield (Mass.) Daily News*⟩ ⟨the place is beginning to ~ already —Chandler Brossard⟩ ⟨Saturday night ~*ed* —Langston Hughes⟩ **~** *vt* **1 a** (1) **:** to pass over or across (a space or object) by or as if by a spring or leap **:** CLEAR ⟨~ a brook⟩ ⟨~ a hurdle⟩ ⟨took eight years before field trials ~*ed* the Atlantic —W.F.Brown b. 1903⟩ ⟨often ~ the border again the same day —*N.Y. Times*⟩ (2) *obs* **:** to expose to danger **:** RISK, HAZARD ⟨~ a body with dangerous physic —Shak.⟩ **b** *in board games* **:** to move over (a man) by jumping **c** (1) **:** to skip over or pass by **:** BYPASS ⟨the transmission of certain characteristics may ~ one or more . . . generations —Henry Wynmalen⟩ ⟨~ electrical connections⟩ (2) **:** to continue (as a newspaper story or article) from one column or page to another (3) **:** ANTICIPATE ⟨~ the green light⟩ ⟨~ the gun⟩ **d** (1) **:** to escape or run away from ⟨couldn't ~ his color —Thurston Scott⟩ (2) **:** to abandon or leave esp. hastily or furtively ⟨~ town without paying their bills —Hamilton Basso⟩ ⟨~*ed* their reservation and were on the warpath —P.A.Rollins⟩ (3) **:** to leave (employment) esp. in violation of contract or other obligation **:** breach (a labor contract) by leaving or taking other employment ⟨draft-age men ~*ing* essential war jobs —*Newsweek*⟩ ⟨wanted to ~ the show —Fred Bradna & Hartzell Spence⟩ ⟨~*ed* ship and settled in the United States —David Dodge⟩ ⟨~*ed* their indentures and bobbed up as journeymen in distant cities —*Newsweek*⟩ ⟨~ contract when tempted by more money —Harriot B. Barbour⟩ (4) **:** to turn off from (one's normal or appointed track or course) ⟨streams that ~*ed* their beds in the flood —*Springfield (Mass.) Union*⟩ ⟨a train ~*ed* the track⟩ (5) **:** to get aboard typically by jumping ⟨~*ed* a freight and rode it to town⟩ ⟨~ a crowded bus —W.J.Finn⟩ **2 a** (1) **:** to attack suddenly or unexpectedly **:** pounce upon ⟨thought he was snooping around and ~*ed* him —Lillian Hellman⟩ ⟨intended to ~ him, sitting or no —Shelby Foote⟩ ⟨suddenly ~*ed* by an enemy patrol party —Ed Cunningham⟩; *specif* **:** to attack (a target) suddenly with military aircraft (2) **:** to scold or criticize severely **:** assail verbally **:** bawl out ⟨that she would never do . . . unless she were ~*ed* into it —F. M.Ford⟩ — often used with *out* ⟨~*ed* the little foreman out —Ross Santee⟩ ⟨went down to ~ the inspector out —F.B. Gipson⟩ **b :** to seize or take possession of in violation of another's rights **:** occupy illegally ⟨~ another man's claim⟩ ⟨~*ing* an assignment for the first time in his life —Michael Foster⟩ **c :** to have coitus with — usu. considered vulgar **3 a** (1) **:** to cause to jump ⟨the wind can ~ those flames one mile or five —Stirling Silliphant⟩ ⟨it ~*s* me out of bed —J.W. Noble⟩ ⟨had to ~ her from the stiles —Jane Austen⟩ (2) **:** to cause (game) to break cover **:** START, FLUSH ⟨~*ed* a mule deer —D.C. Peattie⟩ (3) **:** to come upon suddenly ⟨~*ed* the trail and took cover —H.L.Davis⟩ **b** (1) **:** to elevate in rank esp. by skipping intermediate ranks ⟨one of many junior officers ~*ed* several ranks to fill the void —*Newsweek*⟩ ⟨~*ed* him from instructor to full professor in two years —*Time*⟩ (2) **:** to raise (a bridge partner's bid) by more than one rank (3) **:** to increase esp. swiftly or sharply ⟨~*ed* admission prices from fifty cents to a dollar —F.B.Gipson⟩ **4 :** to bore with a jumper (as in quarrying)

syn JUMP, LEAP, SPRING, BOUND, VAULT, and SALTATE mean, in common, to project oneself upward or through space by or as if by quick muscle action. JUMP, the most general, implies a muscular propelling, or any action resembling a muscular propelling, of the body upward or to a spot other than the one one is in, whether upward, on a level, or below one, or over some obstacle ⟨*jump* with fright⟩ ⟨*jump* three feet across a brook⟩ ⟨*jump* up onto a platform⟩ ⟨*jump* down from the truck⟩ ⟨*jump* over a wall⟩ LEAP, often interchangeable with JUMP, generally suggests a much greater muscular propulsion or a more spectacular result ⟨*leap* a high fence⟩ ⟨*leap* down from a platform⟩ ⟨go *leaping* across a field⟩ SPRING adds to JUMP or LEAP the idea of elasticity, lightness, or grace, stressing more the movement than the going to or over ⟨*spring* up into the air⟩ ⟨*spring* out of a cage⟩ ⟨a deer *springing* across the open field⟩ BOUND, like SPRING, emphasizes the movement but suggests vigor or strength and, often, a consequent forceful speed achieved by fast successive leaps forward ⟨a herd of antelope *bounding* gracefully across the plain⟩ ⟨the speaker, a large vigorous man, came *bounding* down the aisle and up onto the stage⟩ VAULT suggests a leap upward or over something with the aid of the hands laid on an object or with similar assistance ⟨rose to his feet . . . grabbed the sturdy milking stool by one leg, *vaulted* the fence, and plunged into the woods —C.G.D.Roberts⟩ ⟨an acrobat . . . was *vaulting* over chair backs —Margaret Deland⟩ SALTATE implies a jumping or leaping from place to place as in certain ballet movements

— jump bail : to abscond while at liberty under bail bonds **— jump over the broomstick** *or* **jump the broom** *dial* **:** to get married ⟨we ought to *jump the broom* —J.H.Stuart⟩ **— jump rope :** to jump over a rope held by its two ends by the jumper or by two other persons and swung around the jumper from head to foot, or back and forth under the feet **— jump the queue** *Brit* **1 :** to go ahead of a waiting line (as at a theater window) ⟨attempt to *jump the queue* is to court disaster —*London Calling*⟩ **2 :** to seek to obtain something in advance of one's turn **:** obtain preferential treatment ⟨*jumping the* allied *queue* and seeking a special arrangement —*Economist*⟩ **— jump the traces 1** *of a horse* **:** to jump over the traces **2 :** to cast off restraint **:** display a rebellious or nonconformist spirit ⟨might *jump the traces* and precipitate a new round of fighting —Lindesay Parrott⟩ ⟨*jumped the traces* more than once —Maurice Ries⟩

[2]jump *adv, obs* **:** EXACTLY, PAT

[3]jump \ˈjəmp\ *n* -S **1 a** (1) **:** an act of jumping **:** LEAP, SPRING, BOUND ⟨cleared the fence with a running ~⟩ (2) **:** any of several sports competitions featuring a leap, spring, or bound — see BROAD JUMP, HIGH JUMP (3) **:** a space cleared or traversed by a leap (4) **:** an obstacle to be jumped over (as on the course of a steeplechase) simulating natural obstructions met in fox hunting and of varied construction, dimensions, and number **b** (1) **:** a sudden spasmodic movement (as from surprise or other nervous shock) **:** START, TWITCH ⟨gave a ~ as she entered the room⟩ (2) **: jumps** *pl* **:** FIDGETS, WILLIES, NERVOUSNESS ⟨this place fairly gives me the ~*s* —G.K. Chesterton⟩ ⟨just got the ~*s*, I guess —Gore Vidal⟩ **c** *in board games* **:** a move made by jumping **d :** a descent by parachute from an airplane **e :** an act of coitus — usu considered vulgar **2** *obs* **a :** a critical point or crisis **b :** VENTURE, HAZARD **3 a** (1) **:** a movement made by the tube of a gun before a fired projectile leaves the muzzle (2) **:** a vertical deviation of the path of the trajectory from the line of elevation **b :** an abrupt interruption of level in a piece of brickwork or masonry **c** (1) **:** [4]BORE (2) **:** BREAKER 3a **d** (1) **:** a sharp or sudden increase ⟨the ~ in the size of the entering freshman class —J. K.Folger⟩ (2) **:** JUMP BID (3) **:** a sudden change **:** a qualitative or quantitative leap **:** an abrupt transition ⟨social progress proceeds by ~*s*⟩ ⟨the ~ from the liquid to the gaseous state⟩ (4) **:** the continuation of a published item (as a newspaper story or article) from one column or page to another; *also* **:** the portion of a published item comprising such a continuation — compare BREAKOVER **e** (1) **:** a quick or short journey esp. by air **:** HOP ⟨reluctant to start a new round of . . . plane ~*s* —*Newsweek*⟩ ⟨a convenient one-night ~ from either St. Louis or Memphis —*Amer. Guide Series: Ark.*⟩ (2) **:** one in a series of moves from one place to another ⟨usually going farther west at each ~ —Dixon Wecter⟩ ⟨kept one ~ ahead of the sheriff⟩ **4 :** an advantage esp. in time **:** START — usu. used in the phrase *get the jump* ⟨might get the ~ on the United States in the development of nuclear power —*N.Y. Times*⟩ ⟨desirous of getting the ~ on the competition —Elmer Davis⟩

syn JUMP, LEAP, SPRING, BOUND, and VAULT signify a single movement achieved by the corresponding action signified by the verb. SALTATION may indicate a sequence or group of such actions **syn** see in addition [1]JUMP

—on the jump *adv (or adj)* **:** on the go **:** very busy ⟨kept so much *on the jump* by the motel trade —W.L.Gresham⟩

[4]jump \"\ *adj* [prob. fr. [2]*jump*] **1** *obs* **:** EXACT, FITTING, PRECISE **2 :** constituting a jump bid in bridge ⟨~ response⟩ **3 :** SWING ⟨a ~ band⟩

[5]jump \ˈjümp, ˈjəmp\ *n* -S [prob. alter. of *jupe*] **1** *dial Brit* **:** a loose jacket for men **2** *dial Brit* **:** an underbodice worn usu. instead of stays by women — usu. used in pl.

jump·able \ˈjəmpəbəl\ *adj* **:** capable of being jumped

jump ball *n* **:** a method of putting a basketball into play by tossing it in the air between two opponents who jump up and tap it; *also* **:** a ball put into play in this manner

jump bid *n* **:** a bridge bid of more tricks than are necessary in the denomination specified to overcall the preceding bid — called also *jump*

jump boot *n* **:** a boot worn by paratroopers

jump dam *n* **:** a dam designed to prevent the migration of fishes into unsuitable spawning waters

jumped *past of* JUMP

jumped-up \ˈ=ˌ=\ *adj* **:** newly or recently sprung up or arisen ⟨this unconcern for pedigree leads people to suppose that the English lords are a *jumped-up* lot —Nancy Mitford⟩ ⟨the hatred of *jumped-up* genius —Hesketh Pearson⟩

[1]jump·er \ˈjəmpə(r)\ *n* -S [[1]*jump* + *-er*] **1 :** a person who jumps: as **a** *usu cap* **:** one of a revivalistic sect whose members jump, skip, hop up and down, clap their hands, shout, or otherwise demonstrate an intense spiritual excitation in their meetings — called also *Holy Jumper* **b :** a person who jumps another's claim **c :** a miner who drills with a jumper **d :** a person who quits his employment esp. in violation of contract or other obligation ⟨the special Army camp for drafted job ~*s* —*Newsweek*⟩ **e :** a delivery-route driver's helper **f :** an experienced employee who can help or substitute for one or more of the workers engaged in an industrial process — called also *handyman, utility man* **g :** a person who competes in a jumping event (as the broad jump or a ski jump) **2 a :** a drill or boring tool consisting of a bar which is jumped up and down in the borehole **b :** any of several sleds (as used by boys in coasting or for hauling merchandise over bare ground) **c :** JUMPER SLED **d :** a plowshare specially fitted for rough soil (as by having an upturned colter to cut roots); *also* **:** a plow having a moldboard so attached that it jumps out of the ground when it hits a stump **e :** SWAGE 2b **f :** stones used for leveling courses esp. in random-coursed ashlar **g** (1) **:** a short wire used to close a break or cut out part of a circuit (2) **:** the removable member of a train-line or truck-trailer coupling consisting usu. of two coupling plugs and a connecting cable **h :** HOSE BRIDGE **3 :** any of several jumping animals: as **a :** a saddle horse trained to jump obstacles **b :** SMALLMOUTH BLACK BASS

[2]jumper \"\ *n* -S *often attrib* [prob. fr. [5]*jump* + *-er*] **1 a :** a loose blouse, jacket, or smock worn esp. by workmen on the job **b :** a sleeveless dress or a skirt with a bib for women and girls worn usu. with a blouse or sweater **2 a :** a child's one-piece coverall for play or sleeping — usu. used in pl. **b :** a sailor's blouse having long sleeves and a broad square collar tapering to a V neck in front **c** *chiefly Brit* **:** a sweater for women or girls

jumper 1b

jumper sled *n* **:** a log sled having a high crosspiece on which one end of a log is supported while being dragged

jumper stay *n* **:** a stay or tackle set up esp. in heavy weather to prevent a yard or boom from jumping

jump fire *n* **:** a forest fire started some distance ahead of the main front of a larger fire by burning material carried ahead by wind

jump head *n* **:** a headline or heading identifying a jump (sense 3d[4])

jump-hop \ˈ=ˌ=\ *n* **:** a spring from both feet followed by a hop on one foot

jumpier *comparative of* JUMPY

jumpiest *superlative of* JUMPY

jump·i·ness \ˈjəmpēnə̇s, -pin-\ *n* -ES **:** the quality or state of being jumpy **:** NERVOUSNESS ⟨was better able to master his ~ —C.S.Forester⟩

jumping *adj* [fr. pres. part. of [1]*jump*] **1 a :** given to or characterized by making jumps ⟨a ~ animal⟩ **b :** used in making jumps ⟨a ~ pole⟩ **c :** featuring jumps ⟨a ~ race⟩ **2 :** SWING ⟨a ~ band⟩

jumping bean *or* **jumping seed** *n* **:** a seed of any of several Mexican shrubs of the genera *Sebastiania* and *Sapium* of the family Euphorbiaceae that tumbles about because of movements of the contained larva of a small moth (*Carpocapsa saltitans*)

jumping cactus *also* **jumping cholla** *n* **:** CHOLLA

jumping deer *n* **:** MULE DEER

jumping hare *n* [trans. of Afrik *springhaas*, fr. D *springen* to jump + *haas* hare] **:** a sciuromorph rodent (*Pedetes cafer*) of southern and eastern Africa that resembles a kangaroo in form, that is about two feet long, and that is tawny brown in color and of nocturnal and social habits — called also *springhaas*

jumping jack *n* **:** a toy figure of a man jointed and made to jump or dance by means of strings or a sliding stick

jump·ing·ly *adv* **:** in a jumping manner

jumping mouse *n* **:** any of several small hibernating No. American myomorph rodents (family Zapodidae) with long hind legs and tail and no cheek pouches

jumping mullet *n* **:** a very active Australian gray mullet (*Mugil argenteus*) reputed to leap into boats

jumping net *or* **jumping sheet** *n, chiefly Brit* **:** LIFE NET

jumping-off place \ˌ==ˈ=ˌ=\ *n* **1 a :** a place regarded as marking the farthest limit of civilization **:** a remote or isolated place **b :** the end or edge of the world ⟨seemed suddenly to be at the end of the world, the *jumping-off place* —*Nat'l Geographic*⟩ **2 :** a place from which some enterprise is launched **:** a point of departure ⟨a *jumping-off place* for the conquest of the rest of Europe —P.E.Mosely⟩ ⟨a *jumping-off place* for reflection — Maurice Valency⟩

jumping orchid *n* [so called fr. its habit of suddenly ejecting its pollen masses] **:** an orchid of the genus *Catasetum*

jumping pit *n* **:** the landing area for the high and broad jump and the pole vault events consisting of a pit filled with sawdust or soft loam to cushion the impact

jumping plant louse *n* [*jumping* + *plant louse*] **:** any of numerous jumping plant lice constituting the family Psyllidae

jumping rabbit *n* **:** FIVE-TOED JERBOA

jumping rat *n* **:** any of numerous jumping rodents (as the jerboa, jumping mouse, and kangaroo rat)

jumping shrew *n* **:** ELEPHANT SHREW

jumping spider *n* **:** a spider of the family Salticidae

jumping viper *n* **:** a small rough-skinned stout-bodied pit viper (*Bothrops nummifer*) of Central America and Mexico that slides its body forward when striking thereby considerably increasing its attacking range

jump joint *n* [[1]*jump*] **1 :** BUTT JOINT **2 :** a flush joint (as of plank or masonry)

jump line *n* **:** a directional line of print (as "continued on page 7, column 2") at the end of the first part of a divided story or article in a newspaper or periodical or a line (as "continued from page 1") at the continuation

jumpmaster \ˈ=ˌ==\ *n* **:** a person in charge of the jumping (as of parachute troops)

jump-off \ˈ=ˌ=\ *n* -S **1 :** an act of jumping off **:** a place from which to jump off **:** the start of a race or an attack ⟨the *jump-off* was at twelve —Dan Levin⟩ **2 :** an additional round of competition to determine the winner when two or more horses are tied after completion of the first round of jumping

jump page *n* **:** a page on which the continuation of a newspaper article appears

jump pass *n* **:** a pass executed by a player who jumps into the air and releases the ball before landing (as in football and basketball)

jump ring *n* **:** a circle of wire with ends meeting and not welded used as a connecting link in jewelry

jump rope *also* **jumping rope** *n* **:** a rope used in jumping rope — called also *skipping rope*

jumps *pres 3d sing of* JUMP, *pl of* JUMP

jump saw *n* **:** a crosscut circular saw in a sawmill that can be raised or lowered and is used for crosscutting timbers, boards, or slabs

jump scrape *n* **:** an implement resembling a plow that is used to complete ridges or levees for the check system of irrigation

jump seat *n* **1 :** a movable carriage seat **2 :** a folding seat between front and rear seats of a closed passenger automobile

jumpseed \'=,=\ *n* : VIRGINIA KNOTWEED
jump shot *n* **1** : a shot in billiards in which the cue ball is made to jump over an object ball **2** *also* **jump stroke** : a croquet shot made with a downward stroke of the mallet so that the ball jumps over an obstacle **3** : a shot made by a basketball player who jumps into the air and releases the ball with one or both hands at the peak of his jump
jump spark *n* : a spark produced by the jumping of electricity across a gap
jump suit *n* : a uniform worn by paratroopers for jumping
jump turn *n* **1** : a turn in the air executed by a skier who crouches, places the inner pole or both poles near the tip of the lower ski, pulls the knees up, jumps around the pole or poles, and lands in a crouch with the skis edged inward **2** : a turn in the air executed by a dancer who takes off with and lands on both feet
jump weld *n* : a butt weld in which one member is welded at right angles to a relatively larger part
jumpy \'jəmpē, -pi\ *adj* -ER -EST **1** : jumping or inducing to jump ⟨a ~ carriage⟩ : characterized by jumps or sudden variations ⟨the story . . . gets rather jerky and ~ —A.F.W. Plumptre⟩ **2** : NERVOUS, IRRITABLE, JITTERY ⟨if you didn't drink so much, you wouldn't be so ~ —Barnaby Conrad⟩ ⟨~ nerves⟩ : nervously apprehensive ⟨apprehension that bribes will be uncovered . . . makes senators as ~ as they are —R.H.Rovere⟩
jun *abbr* junior
junc *abbr* junction
jun·ca·ceae \,jəŋ'kāsē,ē\ *n pl, cap* [NL, fr. *Juncus*, type genus + *-aceae*] : a large widely distributed family of typically tufted herbs (order Liliales) resembling grasses and having a chaffy 6-parted perianth and a capsular fruit — **jun·ca·ceous** \;=;kāshəs\ *adj*
jun·cag·i·na·ce·ae \,jəŋ,kajə'nāsē,ē\ *n pl, cap* [NL, fr. *Juncagin-, Juncago*, type genus (fr. *Juncus*) + *-aceae*] : a family of marsh or bog herbs (order Naiadales) having leaves resembling rushes and small perfect flowers with 3 to 6 stamens and 3 to 6 carpels which separate at maturity
jun·co \'jəŋ(,)kō\ *n* [NL, fr. Sp, a bird, rush — more at JONQUIL] **1** *a cap* : a genus of small American finches found from the arctic circle to Costa Rica usu. having a pink bill, ashy gray head and back, conspicuous white lateral tail feathers and often reddish brown on the back and sides **b** *pl* **juncos** *or* **juncoes** : any bird of this genus — see CAROLINA JUNCO, SLATE-COLORED JUNCO **2** *pl* **juncos** *or* **juncoes** [AmerSp, fr. Sp, rush] : ALLTHORN
jun·coi·des \,jəŋ'kȯi(,)dēz\ [NL, fr. *Juncus*, genus of marsh plants + L *-oides* -oid] *syn of* LUZULA
¹junc·tion \'jəŋ(k)shən\ *n* -s [L *junction-, junctio*, fr. *junctus* (past part. of *jungere* to join) + *-ion-, -io* -ion — more at YOKE] **1** : the act or an instance of joining or meeting : the state of being joined ⟨a ~ of two armies⟩ ⟨operates a ~ between the French spirit and German ideas and . . . culture —MatthewArnold⟩ **2 a** : a place or point of union or meeting ⟨at the ~ of two . . . fences —Thomas Hardy⟩ **b** *or* **junction point** : a place or point at which carrier lines meet or interchange traffic **c** : an intersection of roads or highways esp. where one of the highways terminates **3** : something that joins: as **a** : JUNCTION BOX **b** : a logical connective **c** : a grammatical unit formed by qualified and qualifying terms (as "the red barn") — compare NEXUS, RANK
²junction \"\ *vb* -ED/-ING/-S : to join at a junction
junc·tion·al \-shənᵊl, -shnəl\ *adj* : relating to junction
junctional nevus *n* : a nevus that develops at the junction of the dermis and epidermis and is potentially cancerous
junction box *n* : a box (as of metal) for enclosing the junction of electric wires and cables
junc·tur·al \'jəŋ(k)chərəl, -)sh(ə)rəl\ *adj* : of or relating to grammatical juncture
junc·ture \'jəŋ(k)chə(r), -(k)shə(r)\ *n* -s [ME, fr. L *junctura*, fr. *junctus* (past part. of *jungere* to join) + *-ura* -ure — more at YOKE] **1** : an instance of joining : UNION, JUNCTION ⟨at the ~ of four fields —*Think*⟩ ⟨the ~ of the American Third and Seventh armies —E.K.Lindley & Edward Weintal⟩ ⟨emphasizes the ~ of poetry and music —Gilbert Highet⟩ **2 a** : JOINT, ARTICULATION, CONNECTION, SEAM **b** : the manner of transition between two consecutive speech sounds or between a speech sound and a pause **3** : a point of time; *esp* : one made critical or important by a concurrence of circumstances ⟨at certain ~s in the dancing, the skirts were raised high in the air —G.H.Fathauer⟩ ⟨at this ~ in history⟩
syn PASS, EXIGENCY, EMERGENCY, CONTINGENCY, PINCH, STRAIT (or STRAITS), CRISIS: these nouns all denote a critical or crucial time or state of affairs, as in the life of a person, an institution, or a country's history. JUNCTURE emphasizes the usu. significant concurrence or convergence of events ⟨we may now be at a vital *juncture* where the ideals of liberalism can best be achieved through separate institutions and not the omnicompetent state —P.W.Kurtz⟩ ⟨occasions when there may be genuine uncertainty as to who should become prime minister. At such a *juncture* it is highly desirable to have someone charged with the duty of inviting a suitable person to form a government —R.M.Dawson⟩ PASS is stronger than JUNCTURE in implying an evil or distressing concurrence or convergence of events or the condition induced by such a concurrence, or, sometimes, a dilemma brought about by it ⟨they did in a desperate *pass* the best they knew —J.J.Mallon⟩ ⟨the frightful *pass* to which destiny had brought her —Arnold Bennett⟩ EXIGENCY emphasizes the pressures brought to bear or the urgency of the demands created by a special situation, esp. a juncture or pass ⟨the *exigencies* of war⟩ ⟨such travel *exigencies* as having to scout around for a room when you're tired and want to hole up for the night —Richard Joseph⟩ ⟨social contacts for a presidential couple are pretty well restricted by official *exigencies* —S.H.Adams⟩ EMERGENCY, implying more of a crucial nature but less necessary difficulty than EXIGENCY, is a sudden, unforeseen juncture or pass calling for immediate action to avoid disaster ⟨a national *emergency*⟩ ⟨aid in helping to meet the *emergency* of a large number of unemployed youths —*Amer. Guide Series: Minn.*⟩ ⟨a great social *emergency*, teen-age delinquency —D.W.Maurer & V.H. Vogel⟩ CONTINGENCY is an event or concurrence of events that is fortuitous, only remotely possible, or uncertain of occurrence ⟨sense and ingenuity may be relied upon to cope with special *contingencies* —R.F.Heizer⟩ ⟨the bank had accumulated a surplus . . . which it held against future *contingencies* and risks —*Collier's Yr. Bk.*⟩ PINCH implies pressure or the need for action but without quite the same intensity as EMERGENCY or EXIGENCY ⟨could always in a *pinch* pawn my microscope for three pounds —W.S.Maugham⟩ ⟨ready in a *pinch* to ride roughshod over opposition —William Power⟩ STRAIT, now commonly STRAITS, applies to a troublesome situation from which escape is difficult because of hampering or binding circumstances ⟨a moment of financial *strait* —F.L. Paxson⟩ ⟨her father died and the family was left in dire financial *straits* —*Current Biog.*⟩ ⟨the army's truly desperate *straits* —F.V.W.Mason⟩ CRISIS applies to a juncture or pass whose outcome will make a decisive difference, esp. serving as a turning point as in a life, history, or the course of a disease ⟨her adolescence had passed without the trace of a religious *crisis* —Aldous Huxley⟩
jun·cus \'jəŋkəs\ *n* [NL, fr. L, rush — more at JONQUIL] **1** *cap* : a genus (the type of the family Juncaceae) of chiefly marsh plants of temperate regions that are perennial tufted glabrous herbs with mostly terete or channeled leaves **2** -ES : any plant of the genus *Juncus* — see RUSH
¹jun·dy *or* **jun·die** \'jəndi\ *n, pl* **jundies** [origin unknown] *Scot* : JOSTLE, JOG
²jundy *or* **jundie** \"\ *vb* **jundied; jundied; jundying; jundies** *Scot* : JOSTLE, JOG
¹june \'jün\ *n* -s *usu cap, often attrib* [ME *Junius, Juyn, June;* ME *Junius*, fr. OE & L; OE, fr. L, prob. fr. *Junius*, name of a Roman gens; ME *Juyn, June*, fr. MF & L; MF *juin*, fr. OF, fr. L *Junius;* prob. akin to L *Juno*, ancient Italian goddess] : the 6th month of the Gregorian calendar — see MONTH table
²june \"\ *vb* -ED/-ING/-S [origin unknown] *dial* : to drive briskly
ju·neau \'jü(,)nō\ *adj, usu cap* [fr. *Juneau*, Alaska] : of or from Juneau, the capital of Alaska : of the kind or style prevalent in Juneau
june beetle *or* **june bug** *n, often cap J* : any of numerous rather large leaf-eating scarabaeoid beetles that fly chiefly in late spring and have as larvae white grubs that live in soil and feed chiefly on the roots of grasses and other plants: as **a** : any of various large brown beetles (genus *Phyllophaga*) of eastern No. America **b** : GREEN JUNE BEETLE **c** : any of several European beetles (genus *Phyllopertha*) that are similar in appearance and habits to members of *Phyllophaga* **d** : any of several white-striped beetles (genus *Polyphylla*) of western No. America
june·berry \'jün — *see* BERRY\ *n, usu cap* **1** : any of various No. American trees and shrubs that constitute the genus *Amelanchier* and are sometimes cultivated for their showy white flowers or edible usu. purple or red fruits **2** : the fruit of a Juneberry
junebud \'=,=\ *n, usu cap* : REDBUD
june drop *n, usu cap J* : the falling of young fruit due to improper or incomplete fertilization, disease, or environmental factors at a maximum about June
junefish \'=,=\ *n* : SPOTTED JEWFISH
juneflower \'=,=\ *n, usu cap* : CANADA VIOLET
june grass *n, usu cap J* **1** : KENTUCKY BLUEGRASS **2** : a tufted grass (*Koeleria cristata*) abundant on prairies having narrow leaves and densely flowered terminal panicles like spikes — called also *crested hair grass, prairie June grass*
june pink *n, usu cap J* : SWAMP AZALEA
june·teenth \,jün-'tēn(t)th\ *n* -s *usu cap* [¹*june* + nine*teenth*] : June 19 observed as a general holiday by Negroes in Texas in celebration of the anniversary of the emancipation of slaves in the state
june week *n, usu cap J&W* : graduation week at West Point, Annapolis, and the U.S. Air Force Academy
june yellows *n pl but sing in constr, usu cap J* : a nonparasitic disease of strawberries due to a hereditary factor in some varieties and characterized esp. by yellow and green mottling and streaking of the leaves
jung \'jůŋ\ *n, pl* **jung** *or* **jungs** *usu cap* **1** : an ancient Tatar people of northwest China related to the Hsiung-nu, the Hu, and the Ti **2** : a member of the Jung people
jun·ger·man·nia \,jəŋgə(r)'manēə\ *n, cap* [NL, fr. Ludwig *Jungermann* †1653 Ger. botanist + NL *-ia*] : a formerly recognized genus of liverworts whose members are now included among various genera of the family Jungermanniaceae
jun·ger·man·ni·a·ce·ae \,=,=,manē'āsē,ē\ *n pl, cap* [NL, fr. *Jungermannia*, type genus + *-aceae*] : a family of liverworts comprising the acrogynous leafy members of the order Jungermanniales or in some esp. former classifications being coextensive with the order — see ACROGYNAE, ANACROGYNAE — **jun·ger·man·ni·a·ceous** \;=;=;=;āshəs\ *adj*
jun·ger·man·ni·a·les \,=,=,=ē'ā(,)lēz\ *n pl, cap* [NL, fr. *Jungermannia*, genus of liverworts + *-ales*] : a large and widely distributed order of predominantly tropical liverworts that grow from a definite apical cell, that are characterized by marked diversity of form but with simple primitive tissue organization, and that include the leafy liverworts together with certain lower forms with terrestrial habits and a simple branching thallus or a leafless thalloid shoot — compare ACROGYNAE, ANACROGYNAE; see JUNGERMANNIACEAE
¹jung·i·an \'yůŋēən\ *n* -s *usu cap* [Carl G. *Jung* †1961 Swiss psychologist and psychiatrist + E *-ian*] : an adherent of the psychological doctrines of C. G. Jung
²jungian \"\ *adj, usu cap* **1** : of or relating to C. G. Jung whose psychological doctrines stress the opposition of introversion and extroversion and the concept of mythology and cultural and racial inheritance in the psychology of individuals **2** : of, relating to, or having the characteristics of the psychological doctrines of Jung
¹jun·gle \'jəŋgəl\ *n* -s *often attrib* [Hindi *jaṅgal*, fr. Skt *jāṅgala*] **1** *India* **a** : uncultivated ground **b** : land overgrown (as with brushwood) **2 a** : an impenetrable thicket or tangled mass of tropical vegetation some parts of which can be lived in by native people or wild animals **b** : a tract overgrown with thickets or masses of vegetation **3** : a hobo camp ⟨stays here all the time and runs this ~ —Burl Ives⟩ **4 a** (1) : a confused or chaotic mass or assemblage of objects : TANGLE, JUMBLE ⟨a ~ of gigantic tanks and curiously shaped pipes —*Amer. Guide Series: Ark.*⟩ ⟨an old-fashioned used-car junkyard ~ —N.F.Busch⟩ (2) : something that baffles, perplexes, or frustrates by its tangled, complex, or deviously intricate character : MAZE ⟨a perfect ~ of minute regulations —John Buchan⟩ ⟨~s of official indifference and red tape —*Time*⟩ ⟨a bureaucratic ~ of double-talk and evasions —P.B.Williamson⟩ ⟨difficult . . . to find one's way through the medieval ~ —G.G.Coulton⟩ **b** : a place or scene of ruthless struggle for survival ⟨turned international economy into a ~ —W.L.Clayton⟩ ⟨the ~ philosophy of big-business capitalism —T.E.N.Driberg⟩ ⟨a tale of teen-age gang violence in the concrete ~ —Arthur Gelb⟩
²jungle \"\ *vi* -ED/-ING/-S **1** : to inhabit a jungle ⟨tiny beasts that have *jungled* in that pale forest —John Galsworthy⟩ **2** : to camp in a hobo jungle ⟨*jungled* up with four others beside a creek —Nelson Algren⟩
jungle ballot *n* : BLANKET BALLOT
jungle bear *n* : SLOTH BEAR
jungle cat *n* : a small grayish to tawny Asiatic wildcat (*Felis chaus*) with slightly crested back, somewhat tufted ears, and obscure blotching and striping
jungle cock *n* : a male jungle fowl
jun·gled \-ld\ *adj* [¹*jungle* + *-ed*] : overgrown with jungle
jungle fowl *n* **1** : any of several Asiatic wild birds of the genus *Gallus; esp* : a bird (*G. gallus*) of southeastern Asia from which domestic fowls are believed to have descended **2 a** : an Australian megapode (*Megapodius reinwardtii tumulus*) **b** : any Australian species of the genus *Megapodius*
jungle green *n* : a very dark green
jungle gym *n* [fr. *Junglegym*, a trademark] : a three-dimensional structure of vertical and horizontal bars upon which children can climb and play

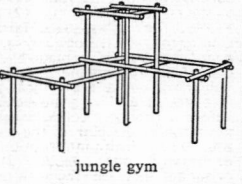

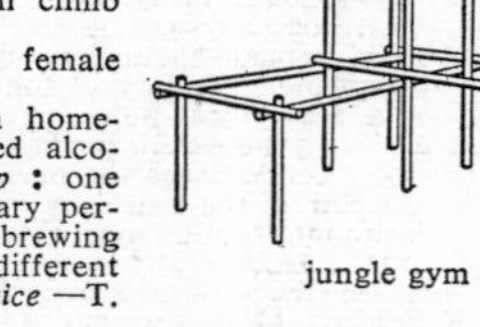
jungle gym

jungle hen *n* : a female jungle fowl
jungle juice *n* : a homemade or improvised alcoholic beverage; *esp* : one concocted by military personnel ⟨apt to be brewing on the ship fifteen different batches of *jungle juice* —T. O.Heggen⟩
jungle mouse *n* : any of several long-snouted often spiny-furred mice of southeastern Asia constituting the genus *Leggada*
jungle rice *n* : SHAMA MILLET
jungle yellow fever *n* : yellow fever endemic in or near forest or jungle areas in Africa and So. America and transmitted by mosquitoes other than members of the genus *Aedes* and esp. by those of the genus *Haemagogus*
¹jun·gli \'jəŋglē\ *n* -s [¹*jungle* + *-i* (as in *Hindi*)] : an inhabitant of an Indian jungle
²jungli *or* **jun·gly** \"\ *adj* **1** : inhabiting an Indian jungle : being or belonging to or characteristic of an inhabitant of such a jungle ⟨the ~ dialect was the only language we heard —S.T.Moyer⟩ **2** *India* : UNCOUTH, UNREFINED ⟨a rude, ~ individual —Alan Moorehead⟩
jun·gly \'jəŋg(ə)lē\ *adj* : of, relating to, or like a jungle ⟨an overgrown ~ garden⟩ ⟨a ~ world of high-pressure pluggers —*Time*⟩
juning *pres part of* JUNE
¹jun·ior \'jünyə(r)\ *n* -s [L, n. & adj.] **1 a** (1) : a person who is younger than another ⟨my ~s were already asleep —Jimmy O'Dea⟩ ⟨told his ~ that theological research was not compatible with longevity —H.J.Laski⟩ (2) *sometimes cap* [LL, fr. L] : a male child : SON ⟨in summer months ~ wears a coat of tan and nothing more —*N.Y. Herald Tribune*⟩ ⟨just as good for mother and the girls as for ~ —S.L.A.Marshall⟩ ⟨~ is improving in his understanding of numbers —Paul Woodring⟩ **b** (1) : a young person; *esp* : JUNIOR MISS ⟨coats and even skirts for teens and ~s —*Springfield (Mass.) Union*⟩ (2) : a clothing size for dresses, coats, and suits usu. for women and girls with slight figures that have youthful designs and little fullness in the bodice **c** : an immature or young animal — used esp. of small and pet stock **2** [ML, fr. L] **a** : a person holding a position of lesser standing in a hierarchy of ranks ⟨executives told their ~s that the day of the order taker was over —F.L.Allen⟩ ⟨the newest ~ on the staff —Albert Christen⟩ ⟨an officer one grade his ~ —Wirt Williams⟩ **b** (1) : a student in his next-to-the-last year before graduating from an educational institution (2) : a student in his third year or having third-year standing at a senior college (3) : a student in his first year at a junior college (4) : a student in his third year at a secondary school (5) : a pupil in a junior school (6) : a member of a church school or Sunday school age-level division that generally includes children of the ages 9 to 11 **3** : a barrister who has not taken silk **4** : a player (as the dealer in piquet) who receives cards later in the deal
²junior \"\ *adj* [L, compar. of *juvenis* young — more at YOUNG] **1 a** : less advanced in age than another : YOUNGER — used chiefly and often cap. to distinguish a son with the same given name as his father; opposed to *senior;* abbr. *Jr* or *jr* **b** (1) : of or relating to youth : YOUTHFUL, YOUNG ⟨some relatively ~ skins are as dry as bone —*Mademoiselle*⟩ (2) : designed for young people esp. of the adolescent age group ⟨a worthwhile ~ novel —Louise S. Bechtel⟩ **c** : of more recent date ⟨only six years ~ to Boston —H.L.Mencken⟩; *specif* : of more recent date and therefore inferior or subordinate as to right of preference ⟨a ~ lien⟩ **d** : ranking below another in point of time of service ⟨the ~ senator from Illinois⟩; *specif* : having less seniority than another ⟨resented having a ~ man get to be an engineer before him —*Time*⟩ **2 a** [ML, fr. L] : lower in standing or in rank esp. in a hierarchy of ranks ⟨a ~ partner⟩ ⟨made a ~ member —G.A.Wagner⟩ ⟨shifted himself, as ~ officer, to the general's left —J.G.Cozzens⟩ ⟨the task of teaching such courses is customarily assigned to ~ members of the staff —*Times Lit. Supp.*⟩ **b** : associated with another in a secondary or auxiliary role ⟨the ~ author of a methodological study⟩ **c** : duplicating or suggesting on a smaller or diminished scale something typically large or powerful ⟨the ~ hurricane that swept in —Mollie Panter-Downes⟩ ⟨the new store will be a . . . ~ department store —*Retailing Daily*⟩ **3 a** : composed of juniors ⟨the ~ class⟩ : of or relating to juniors, a junior class, or a junior school **b** : of or relating to a church school or Sunday school age-level division of juniors ⟨the ~ curriculum lessons⟩
jun·ior·ate *n* -s **1** : a course of high school or college study for the priesthood, brotherhood, or sisterhood; *specif* : one preparatory to the course in philosophy **2** : a seminary for juniorate training
junior captain *n* : a lieutenant in a fire department
junior church *n* : a program of worship, study, or project work for children carried on in churches during part or all of the adult worship service
junior college *n* **1** : an educational institution of post-high-school rank that offers two years of studies corresponding to the first two years of a senior college and prepares for transfer to such a college **2** : an institution complete in itself that serves the adults of its community by offering technical and vocational studies as well as courses in liberal education — compare COMMUNITY COLLEGE
junior common room *n* : a common room at a British college reserved for the use of undergraduates
junior high school *also* **junior high** *n* : a school organized to facilitate the transition from the elementary school to the high school usu. including the 7th and 8th grades of the elementary school and the 1st year of the high school — contrasted with *senior high school*
ju·nior·i·ty \jün'yȯrəd-ē, -yär-, -ətē, -i\ *n* -ES : the quality, state, or relation of being junior ⟨terms indicating relative rank of seniority or ~ —J.F.Embree & W.L.Thomas⟩
junior leaguer *n, often cap J&L* : a member of a league of young women organized for intelligent participation in civic affairs esp. through direct volunteer service to civic and social organizations and agencies for community betterment
junior levirate *n* : a form of the levirate in which a younger brother (as the next eldest one) marries the widow of the deceased husband
junior library *n, Brit* : a children's library
junior matriculation *n* : a certificate awarded to students who have successfully completed the ordinary course at a Canadian high school — compare SENIOR MATRICULATION
junior miss *n* **1** : an adolescent girl ⟨dresses in sizes for misses and *junior misses* —*N.Y. Times*⟩ **2** : JUNIOR 1b(2)
junior mortgage *n* : a second, third, or later mortgage
junior optime *n* : a man in the optime class at Cambridge University ranking one step below the senior optime and two steps below the wranglers
junior republic *n, usu cap J&R* : a self-governing industrial community for neglected or delinquent children
junior right *n* : the law of descent to the youngest son or in the absence of any issue to the youngest brother formerly existing by Anglo-Saxon custom in parts of England : BOROUGH-ENGLISH — compare PRIMOGENITURE, ULTIMOGENITURE
junior school *n* : a part of the British school system serving children from 7 to 11 years of age — compare INTERMEDIATE SCHOOL, SENIOR SCHOOL
junior seminary *n* : PREPARATORY SEMINARY
junior soldier *n* : a boy or girl between the ages of 7 and 13 who has met the requirements for enrollment as a junior member of the Salvation Army
junior varsity *n* : the members of a varsity squad lacking the experience or class qualification for the first team
junior yearling *n* : an animal of an age between 12 and 18 months on a date of the year specified by rules for livestock exhibits of the season
ju·ni·per \'jünəpə(r)\ *n* -s [ME *junipere, junipur*, fr. L *juniperus* — more at JONQUIL] **1 a** [NL *Juniperus*] : an evergreen shrub or tree of the genus *Juniperus; esp* : one having a prostrate or shrubby habit — see TREE illustration **b** : any of several coniferous trees resembling the juniper: as (1) : a white cedar (*Chamaecyparis thyoides*) (2) : LARCH **c** : RETEM **d** : BOX HUCKLEBERRY **2** : a dark grayish green that is bluer, lighter, and stronger than average ivy, lighter than Persian green, and yellower and lighter than hemlock green
juniper bay *n* [*juniper* + ⁹*bay*] : a swamp in which white cedar (*Chamaecyparis thyoides*) predominates and which often contains sweet bay
juniper berry *n* **1** : the fruit of a plant of the genus *Juniperus* (as the blue berrylike pungent-tasting cone of the common juniper) **2** : BOX HUCKLEBERRY
ju·ni·per·ic acid \'jünə¦perik-\ *n* [ISV *juniper-* (fr. NL *Juniperus*, genus that produces it) + *-ic*] : a crystalline hydroxy acid $HOCH_2(CH_2)_{14}COOH$ found in the waxy exudation from several conifers (as *Juniperus sabina*)
juniper oil *or* **juniper-berry oil** *n* : an acrid essential oil obtained from the dried ripe fruit of common juniper and used chiefly in gin flavors and liqueurs and esp. formerly in medicine as a diuretic and stimulant
juniper scale *n* : a tiny dull whitish round scale (*Diaspis carueli*) that feeds on junipers and related trees esp. in ornamental plantings
juniper-tar oil *or* **juniper tar** *n* : CADE OIL
juniper tree *n* **1** : a tree of the genus *Juniperus* **2** : TAMARACK 1a(1)
ju·nip·er·us \jü'nipərəs\ *n, cap* [NL, fr. L, juniper] : a large genus of evergreen shrubs or trees (family Cupressaceae) that have small appressed scale leaves or esp. on juvenile growth acerose leaves, minute solitary terminal flowers, and small cones resembling berries and that include some cultivated as ornamentals and some valued for their timber — see PENCIL CEDAR
juniper webworm *n* : the larva of either of two destructive European tortricid moths (*Phalonia rutilana* and *Dichomeris marginella*) introduced into No. America that devours the foliage of several junipers
¹junk \'jəŋk\ *n* -s *often attrib* [ME *jonke*] **1 a** *obs* : a piece of worn or poor rope or cable **b** : pieces of old cable or old cordage used for making such articles as gaskets, mats, swabs, or oakum **c** *chiefly Brit* : a thick piece or chunk of something : HUNK ⟨a ~ of cold salt mutton —E.O.Schlunke⟩ **d** : hard salted beef supplied to ships **e** : a part of the head of a sperm

whale between the case and the white horse containing oil and spermaceti **2 a** (1) : old iron, glass, paper, cordage, or other waste that may be treated so as to be used again in some form ⟨one third of the cars . . . are close to ~ in value —*Nation's Business*⟩ ⟨sold the old wreck for ~⟩ (2) : secondhand, worn, or discarded articles of any kind having little or no commercial value ⟨furnished the room with ~ obtained from relatives⟩ **b** : a product regarded as shoddy, cheap, or specious : something without intrinsic value : TRASH; *specif* : JUNK JEWELRY ⟨real jewelry, not ~ from Paris —Rose Thurburn⟩ ⟨newest ~ trinkets . . . made for her in Paris —Lois Long⟩ **c** : something devoid of meaning or significance : something that is intellectually worthless : BUNK, HOKUM, NONSENSE ⟨read no more ~ —Nathaniel Benchley⟩ ⟨will have nothing to do with protocol, formalities, and all that ~⟩ **3** : FISH 5e **4** *slang* : NARCOTICS; *esp* : HEROIN

²junk \"\ *vt* -ED/-ING/-S : to abandon or get rid of as no longer of value or use : SCRAP ⟨a dislike to ~ partially depreciated equipment —Harold Koontz & Cyril O'Donnell⟩ ⟨became the first big maker of electric appliances to ~ fair-trade pricing —*Newsweek*⟩ **syn** see DISCARD

³junk \"\ *n* -S [Pg *junco*, fr. Jav *joṅ*] : any of various characteristic boats of Chinese and neighboring waters having as common features bluff lines, very high poop and overhanging stem, little or no keel, usu. high pole masts carrying lug sails with battens running entirely across, and a rudder usu. dropping below the keel

junk

junk bottle *n* [¹*junk*] : a stout bottle of thick dark-colored glass

¹jun·ker \'yu̇ŋkə(r)\ *n* -S *usu cap, often attrib* [G, fr. OHG *junchērro*, fr. *junc* young + *hērro* lord, master — more at YOUNG, YOUNKER] **1** : a young German noble **2** : a member of the Prussian landed aristocracy characterized by extreme militarism, nationalism, and antidemocratic views ⟨the *Junkers*, the hard, ambitious governing class —*Auckland (New Zealand) Weekly News*⟩ ⟨*Junker* influence . . . in the German army —Hajo Holborn⟩

²junk·er \'jəŋkə(r)\ *n* -S [¹*junk* + -*er*] **1** *slang* : a narcotics addict **2** : an automobile of such age and condition as to be ready for scrapping ⟨wanted an old ~ —Gregor Felsen⟩

jun·ker·dom \'yu̇ŋkə(r)dəm\ *n* -S *usu cap* [¹*junker* + -*dom*] : the body of Junkers : Junker society ⟨lost in the anonymity of Prussian *Junkerdom* —V.L.Albjerg⟩

jun·ker·ism \-kə,rizəm\ *n* -S *usu cap* [¹*junker* + -*ism*] : the Junker system of government : Junker principles or policies ⟨*Junkerism* has greatly declined in influence —*N.Y. Times*⟩

¹jun·ket \'juŋkət, 'jəŋ-\ *n* -S [ME *jonket*, *junket*, fr. (assumed) ONF *jonquette* rush basket, dim. of OF *jonchee*, *jonchie*, fr. *jonc* rush, fr. L *juncus* — more at JONQUIL] *dial Brit* : BASKET; *esp* : one for carrying or catching fish

²jun·ket \'jəŋkət, *usu* -əd·+V\ *n* -S [ME *ioncate*, prob. fr. OIt *giuncata* cream cheese, fr. (assumed) VL *juncata*, fr. L *juncus* rush] **1 a** : a cream cheese or a dish of curds and cream **b** : a dessert of sweetened, flavored milk that is set in a smooth jelly by rennet **c** *obs* : a sweet dish, confection, or other delicacy **2 a** : a festive social affair : FEAST, BANQUET, PARTY ⟨the farm kitchen frequently was the setting for a country dance or ~ —Marilyn Fenno⟩ **b** (1) : a pleasure trip, cruise, or outing ⟨the ~*s* . . . attract hundreds of vacationers —Charles Rawlings⟩ ⟨a high-speed ~ to a tropical port —William McFee⟩ ⟨our first ~ by Italy's railroad system —Claudia Cassidy⟩ (2) : a pleasure trip or tour made by an official at public expense ostensibly for purposes of inspection, investigation, or other public business ⟨unnecessary ~*s* by state employees are taking big hunks out of the pockets of . . . taxpayers —*Springfield (Mass.) Union*⟩ ⟨this journey clearly is more than a ~ —W.H.Lawrence⟩ (3) : a tour or journey of any kind ⟨the best description of a lecturing ~ ever written —E.A.Weeks⟩ ⟨an agricultural ~ through nine European countries —*Newsweek*⟩ ⟨back from a business ~ through the eastern United States —E.T.Sager⟩

³junket \"\ *vb* -ED/-ING/-S *vi* **1** : to make an entertainment : FEAST, BANQUET **2** : to go on a junket : TOUR ⟨~*ed* like contemporary tourists —*N.Y. Herald Tribune*⟩ ~ *vt* : ENTERTAIN, FEAST ⟨these cowled academicians ~*ed* and entertained princes —Norman Douglas⟩

jun·ke·teer \,jəŋkə'ti(ə)r, -iə\ *also* **jun·ket·er** \'jəŋkəd·ə(r)\ *n* -S [³*junket* + -*eer* or -*er*] : a person who junkets; *esp* : an official who makes a pleasure trip at public expense ostensibly for purposes of inspection or other official business ⟨true ~*s* . . . are a small, potent minority who reflect on every study mission —H.A.Williams⟩

junketing *n* -S **1** : the act or an instance of junketing ⟨it will be political ~ —L.C.Wilson⟩ **2** *chiefly Brit* : FESTIVITY, FEASTING, CELEBRATION ⟨the feasting and ~ went on for days —Harold Albert⟩ ⟨there are to be big ~*s* —*Scots Mag.*⟩

junk·ie \'jəŋkē, -ki\ *n* -S [¹*junk* + -*ie*] **1** : JUNKMAN **2** *or* **junky** -ES \"\ *slang* : a narcotics peddler or addict

junk jewelry *n* [¹*junk*] : inexpensive costume jewelry

junk mail *n* [¹*junk*] : third-class mail (as circulars, leaflets, and other advertising matter) bearing no direct address or not bearing the recipient's name and typically addressed to "occupant", "householder", or "boxholder"

¹junk·man \'jəŋkmən\ *n, pl* **junkmen** [³*junk* + *man*] : a member of the crew of a junk

²junk·man \'jəŋk,man\ *n, pl* **junkmen** [¹*junk* + *man*] : a person who deals in resalable junk

junk ring *n* [¹*junk*; fr. its orig. use in confining the hemp packing round the piston of a steam engine] : a wide ring around the piston of an internal-combustion engine forming the base for piston rings

junks *pl of* JUNK, *pres 3d sing of* JUNK

junky \'jəŋkē, -ki\ *adj* -ER/-EST [¹*junk* + -*y* (adj. suffix)] : having the character of junk : constituting junk ⟨a ~ copy of a painting —John Howard⟩

junkyard \'=,=\ *n* [¹*junk* + *yard*] : a yard used to keep usu. resalable junk

ju·no·esque \,jünō'esk\ *adj, usu cap* [*Juno*, ancient Italian goddess, wife of Jupiter (fr. L) + E -*esque*] **1** : marked by stately or voluptuous beauty and generous proportions ⟨beautiful in a fine *Junoesque* fashion —Louis Bromfield⟩ ⟨her neck and head are *Junoesque* —P.B.Kyne⟩ **2** : PLUMP, BUXOM ⟨for the *Junoesque* figure —*Good Housekeeping*⟩ ⟨a *Junoesque* size 40 —*Women's Wear Daily*⟩

¹ju·no·nia \jü'nōnēə\ [NL, fr. LL *Junonia* (*ales*) peacock (lit., Juno's bird), fr. L *Junonia*, fem. of *Junonius* of Juno, fr. *Junon-*, *Juno*] *syn of* PRECIS

²junonia \"\ *n* -S [NL, fr. *junonia* (specific epithet of *Scaphella junonia*)] : a rare volute mollusk (*Scaphella junonia*) that is creamy white with brown or orange markings, that is much sought by shell collectors, and that is known to occur only in deeper water off the coasts of Florida

ju·no's bird \'jü(,)nōz-\ *n, cap J* [trans. of L *Junonis volucris* or LL *Junonia ales*] : PEACOCK

junr *abbr* junior

junt \'jənt\ *n* -S [prob. alter. (influenced by *chunk*) of *joint*] *chiefly Scot* : large amount : CHUNK

jun·ta \'hu̇ntə *also* 'hün- *or* 'jən- *sometimes* 'hün·(,)tä *or* 'hün(,)tä *or* 'həntə *or* 'jüntə\ *n* -S [Sp, fr. fem. of *junto* together, joined, fr. L *junctus*, past part. of *jungere* to join — more at YOKE] **1** : a council or committee for political or governmental purposes ⟨government by ~ is a characteristic feature —L.K. Caldwell⟩ ⟨abetted by the propaganda of exile ~*s* —G.W. Johnson⟩; *esp* : a closely knit group of persons composing or dominating a government esp. after a revolutionary seizure of power ⟨a military ~ with the trappings of a constitutional monarchy —E.K.Lindley⟩ ⟨called to account by a revolutionary ~ —Barbara Henderson⟩ ⟨some of the ruling ~*s* in the Arab countries —David Ben-Gurion⟩ **2** : a closely knit group of persons combined for some common purpose : JUNTO ⟨a literary ~⟩

jun·to \'jənt·(,)ō, -n·(,)tō\ *n* -S [prob. alter. of *junta*] : a closely knit group of persons combined for some common purpose and usu. meeting secretly or privately : CABAL, FACTION

ju·pa·ti *or* **ju·pa·ty** \'jüpəd·ē\ *or* **jupati palm** *n* -S [Pg *jupati*, fr. Tupi *jupati*, *jubati*] : a Brazilian palm (*Raphia taedigera*) attaining an overall height of 70 feet of which not more than 6 or 8 feet represents stem, the remainder consisting of extremely large leathery pinnatisect leaves that are arranged in a terminal crown and rise from long strong stems which are used locally for various structural purposes

jupe \'jüp\ *n* -S [ME *juype*, fr. OF *jupe*, fr. Ar *jubbah*] **1** *chiefly Scot* : a man's coat, jacket, or tunic **2** [F] *chiefly Scot* **a** : a man's shirt **b** : a woman's bodice **c** : STAYS — usu. used in pl. **3** : a woman's skirt

ju·pi·te·ri·an \,jüpə'tirēən\ *n* -S *usu cap* [(*Mount of*) *Jupiter* + E -*ian*] : a person that has a well-developed Mount of Jupiter and a long and large finger of Jupiter and that is usu. held by palmists to be characterized by ambition, leadership, and a religious nature ⟨with all his vanity the *Jupiterian* is warm-hearted —W.G.Benham †1944⟩

ju·pi·ter's-beard \'jüpəd·ə(r)z-\ *n, pl* **jupiter's-beards** *cap* [after *Jupiter*, ancient Roman god of the sky, fr. L *Juppiter*; trans. of L *barba Jovis* — more at DEITY] **1** : HOUSELEEK **2** : a silvery hairy European shrub (*Anthyllis barba-jovis*) with evergreen foliage and pale yellow flowers **3** : a fungus (*Hydnum barba-jovis*) **4** : RED VALERIAN

ju·pon \'jü'pän, '=,=\ *n* -S [ME *iopoun*, *iupone*, *iopon*, fr. MF *jupon*, fr. OF *jupe*] : a tight-fitting garment like a shirt often padded and quilted and worn under medieval armor; *also* : a late medieval jacket similar to the surcoat

jur \'jər\ *vb* -ED/-ING/-S [imit.] *dial chiefly Eng* : PUSH, JAR, BUTT

¹ju·ra \'yu̇rə\ *n pl* [L, pl. of *jur-*, *jus* law, right] : RIGHTS

²ju·ra \'ju̇rə\ *n, cap* [prob. fr. G, after *Jura*, mountain range between France and Switzerland, fr. L] : the Jurassic geological period or the rocks belonging to it

ju·ral \'ju̇rəl\ *adj* [L *jur-*, *jus* law, right + E -*al*] : of or relating to law : JURISTIC; *also* : of or relating to rights or obligations — **ju·ral·ly** \-əlē, -li\ *adv*

ju·ra·ment \'ju̇rəmənt\ *n* -S [L *juramentum*, fr. *jurare* to swear + -*mentum* -ment] *archaic* : OATH

ju·ra·men·ta·do \,hürəmən'tä(,)dō, ,jü-\ *n* -S [Sp, bound by oath] : a Muslim Moro who has taken an oath to die while engaged in killing Christians — compare AMOK

ju·ra·men·tum \,ju̇rə'mentəm, ,yü-\ *n, pl* **juramenta** \-tə\ [LL] *Roman, civil, & canon law* : OATH

ju·rane \'jü,rān\ *adj, usu cap* [ML *Juranus*, fr. *Jura* mountains + L -*anus* -ane] **1** : of or relating to the Jura mountains **2** : of or relating to the medieval duchy of Burgundy

ju·ra·ra \zhə'rärə, ¦zhürə¦rä\ *n* -S [Pg *jurará*, fr. Tupi *jurára*, *yurará*] : ARRAU

¹ju·ras·sic \jə'rasik, jü'-, -sēk\ *adj, usu cap* [F *jurassique*, fr. *Jura*, mountain range between France and Switzerland (fr. L) + -*ique* -ic] : constituting or relating to the period of the Mesozoic era preceding the Comanchean and succeeding the Triassic and the corresponding system of rocks — see GEOLOGIC TIME table

²jurassic \"\ *n* -S *usu cap* : the Jurassic period or system of rocks

ju·rat \'jü,rat\ *n* -S [ME *jurate*, fr. ML *juratus*, fr. L, past part. of *jurare* to swear — more at JURY] **1** : any of several public officials: as **a** : a municipal officer similar to an alderman in some English towns (as the Cinque Ports) **b** : a magistrate chosen for life in the Channel islands **2** : a person who has taken an oath; *specif* : one in late medieval England sworn to assist the administration of justice (as by giving information about crimes committed in his neighborhood) **3** [short for L *juratum* (*est*) it has been sworn] : a certificate added to an affidavit stating when, before whom, and in British practice where it was made

ju·ra·ta \jə'räd·ə\ *n* -S [ML] **1** *Old Eng law* : a jury of 12 men existing at common law and not by statute — compare ASSIZE **2** : JURAT 3

ju·ra·tion \jə'rāshən\ *n* -S [LL *juration-*, *juratio*, fr. L *juratus* (past part.) + -*ion-*, -*io* -ion] : a taking or an administration of an oath

ju·ra·to·ry \'ju̇rə,tōrē\ *adj* [LL *juratorius*, fr. L *juratus* (past part.) + -*orius* -ory] : relating to or comprising or expressed in an oath ⟨~ obligation⟩

juratory caution *n* [prob. trans. of F *caution juratoire*, trans. of LL *cautio juratoria*] **1** *Scots law* : a security consisting of a sworn inventory and pledge of the goods of the affiant **2** *admiralty law* : a suit in forma pauperis

jura-trias \'=='=\ *n* -ES *usu cap J&T* [²*jura* + *trias*] : the Jurassic and Triassic together

jura-triassic \¦==¦=='=\ *adj, usu cap J&T* : of or relating to the Jura-Trias

jure \'jü(ə)r\ *vt* -ED/-ING/-S [back-formation fr. *juror*] : to make a juror of

ju·rel \hü'rel\ *n* -S [Sp, fr. Sp. dial. *shurel* or Catal *sorell* fr. LL *saurus* horse mackerel, fr. Gk *sauros* horse mackerel, lizard — more at SAURIA] : any of several carangid food fishes of warm seas: as **a** : BLUE RUNNER **b** : a crevalle (*Caranx hippos*)

ju·re ux·o·ris \,jü(,)rē,ək'sōrəs\ *adv* [L] : in or by the right of a wife (as in a conveyance by a husband at common law of his wife's estate)

ju·rid·ic \jə'ridik, (')jü¦r-, -dēk\ *adj* [L *juridicus*, fr. *jur-*, *jus* right, law + -*dicus* (fr. *dicere* to say)] : JURIDICAL

ju·rid·i·cal \-dəkəl, -dēk-\ *adj* [L *juridicus* + E -*al*] **1** : of or relating to the administration of justice or the office of a judge : acting or used in the administration of justice **2** : of or relating to law in general or jurisprudence : LEGAL — **ju·rid·i·cal·ly** \-dək(ə)lē, -dēk-, -li\ *adv*

juridical days *n pl* [trans. of L *dies juridici*] : days on which courts are open

juridical person *n* : JURISTIC PERSON

juried *adj* : selected for exhibition by an art jury ⟨a ~ show of fine quality —*Craft Horizons*⟩

juries *pl of* JURY, *pres 3d sing of* JURY

ju·rin's law \'jürənz-\ *n, cap J* [after James Jurin †1750 Eng. physician] : a law of physics: the height of a capillary column of a liquid at a particular temperature is inversely proportional to the diameter of the tube

ju·ris·con·sult \,ju̇rə'skän,səlt ,ju̇rəskən's-\ *n* -S [L *jurisconsultus*, fr. *juris* (gen. of *jus* law, right) + *consultus*, past part. of *consulere* to consult] : a man learned in law, esp. international and public law

ju·ris·dic·tion \,ju̇rəs'dikshən, -əz', -ə'sti-\ *n* -S [ME *jurisdiccioun*, *jurediccioun*, fr. OF & L; OF *juridiction*, *jurediction*, fr. L *jurisdiction-*, *jurisdictio*, fr. *juris* (gen. of *jus* right, law) + *diction-*, *dictio* act of saying, delivery in public speaking — more at JUST, DICTION] **1** : the legal power, right, or authority to hear and determine a cause considered either in general or with reference to a particular matter : legal power to interpret and administer the law in the premises **2** : authority of a sovereign power to govern or legislate : power or right to exercise authority ⟨territory subject to the ~ of the U.S. —G.W. Johnson⟩ **3** : the limits or territory within which any particular power may be exercised : sphere of authority ⟨head of one of the world's smallest Masonic ~*s* —*Associated Press*⟩ : CONTROL ⟨an American theatrical trade union having ~ over dancers and singers —Anatole Chujoy⟩; *specif* : an assignment of organizing rights by a national labor federation to a constituent union **syn** see POWER

ju·ris·dic·tion·al \¦==¦dikshən°l, -¦sti-, -shnəl\ *adj* : of or relating to jurisdiction : involving a question of jurisdiction; *specif* : involving the right of one of two or more unions to organize and represent the employees of a plant, trade, or industry, the right to exclusive control over certain work, or the territorial limits of such jurisdiction ⟨a ~ dispute⟩ ⟨a ~ strike⟩ — **ju·ris·dic·tion·al·ly** \-°lē, -əlē, -i\ *adv*

ju·ris·dic·tive \-ktiv\ *adj* [*jurisdiction* + -*ive*] : of, relating to, or having jurisdiction

ju·ris·prude \'ju̇rə,sprüd\ *n* -S [back-formation (influenced by *prude*) fr. *jurisprudence*] : a person who makes ostentatious show of learning in jurisprudence and the philosophy of law or who regards legal doctrine with undue solemnity or veneration ⟨disclaims being a ~ —*New Republic*⟩

ju·ris·pru·dence \,ju̇rə'sprüd°n(t)s, ,jür- *also* '==,=='\ *n* -S [F & L; F, fr. MF, fr. LL *jurisprudentia*, fr. L *prudentia juris*] **1** *archaic* : knowledge of or skill in law **2 a** : a system or body of law : a department of law ⟨an exponent of sociological ~⟩ ⟨Roman ~⟩ — compare ANALYTICAL JURISPRUDENCE, FORENSIC MEDICINE **b** : the science or philosophy of law ⟨devoted himself to the study of ~⟩ **c** (1) : the course of court decisions as distinguished from legislation and doctrine ⟨a tendency that has become apparent in the ~ of the American courts —Bernard Schwartz⟩ (2) : the collected decisions of a court : REPORTS

ju·ris·pru·dent \¦==¦sprüd°nt\ *n* -S [LL *jurisprudent-*, *jurisprudens*, fr. L *juris* (gen. of *jus* right, law) + *prudent-*, *prudens* foreseeing, skilled, prudent — more at PRUDENT] : a person skilled in jurisprudence : JURIST

ju·ris·pru·den·tial \¦ju̇rə(,)sprü¦denchəl\ *adj* [LL *jurisprudentia* + E -*al*] : of or relating to jurisprudence — **ju·ris·pru·den·tial·ly** \-əlē\ *adv*

ju·rist \'ju̇rəst, 'jür-\ *n* -S [MF *juriste*, fr. ML *jurista*, fr. L *jur-*, *jus* law, right + -*ista* -ist — more at JUST] **1 a** : a person who practices law : LAWYER **b** : JUDGE ⟨replaced a ~ then under fire —R.G.Spivack⟩ **2** : a person skilled in the philosophy or science of the law : a scholar in the law ⟨19th century philosophical ~*s* —Roscoe Pound⟩

ju·ris·tic \jə'ristik, (')jü¦r-, -tēk\ *adj* : of or relating to a jurist or jurisprudence : relating to, created by, or recognized in law ⟨~ theory⟩ ⟨a ~ being⟩ — **ju·ris·ti·cal·ly** \-tək(ə)lē, -tēk-, -li\ *adv*

juristic act *n* : an act of a private individual directed to the origin, termination, or alteration of a right

juristic person *n* : a body of persons, a corporation, a partnership, or other legal entity that is recognized by law as the subject of rights and duties — called also *artificial person*, *conventional person*, *fictitious person*

ju·ror \'ju̇rə(r), 'jü- *also* -,rō(ə)r *or* -ō(ə)\ *n* -S [ME *juroure*, *jurrour*, fr. AF *jurour*, fr. OF *jurer* to swear + -*our* -or — more at JURY] **1 a** : one of a number of men sworn to deliver a verdict as a body : a member of a jury **b** : a person designated and summoned to serve on a jury **2** : a person who takes oath esp. of allegiance **3** : a member of a jury for awarding prizes or determining relative merit at a contest or exhibition

jurr *var of* JUR

juruk *usu cap, var of* YURUK

ju·ru·pa·ite \hə'rüpə,īt\ *n* -S [*Jurupa* mts., Riverside co., Calif. + E -*ite*] : a hydrous calcium magnesium silicate $(Ca,Mg)_2(Si_2O_5)(OH)_2$

¹ju·ry \'ju̇rē, 'jür-, -ri\ *n* -ES [ME *jure*, *jurie*, fr. AF *juree*, fr. OF *jurer* to swear, fr. L *jurare*, *jurari*, fr. *jur-*, *jus* law, right — more at JUST] **1** : a body of men sworn to give a verdict upon some matter submitted to them; *esp* : a body of men selected according to law, impaneled and sworn to inquire into and try any matter of fact, and to give their verdict according to the evidence legally produced — compare GRAND JURY, PETIT JURY, TRIAL JURY **2** : the body of dicasts of ancient Athens **3 a** : a committee for determining relative merit or awarding prizes at an exhibition or competition ⟨two *juries* for its third annual national exhibition —*Americana Annual*⟩ **b** : the director and four judges responsible for officiating at a fencing bout

²jury \"\ *vt* -ED/-ING/-ES : to select entries for (an art exhibit) ⟨inviting one man to ~ . . . its quadrennial exhibitions of contemporary American art —Aline B. Saarinen⟩ : judge the relative merits of (entries in an art exhibit) ⟨~*ing* the submissions at the invitation of the foundations —G.A.Wagner⟩

³jury \"\ *adj* [origin unknown] : improvised for temporary use esp. in an emergency : MAKESHIFT ⟨a ~ mast⟩ ⟨a ~ anchor⟩ ⟨a ~ rig⟩ ⟨~ repairs completed, they started again —Will Irwin⟩

jury box *n* : the place usu. enclosed by paneling where the jury sits at the trial of a court case

jury chancellor *n, Scots law* : the foreman of a jury

jury commission *n* : a body of public officers entrusted with the task of ascertaining the names and addresses of persons qualified by law to act as jurors and sometimes of actually selecting by lot a panel of such jurors

ju·ry·less \'==ləs\ *adj* : being without a jury

jury list *n* : a list of persons qualified to be drawn for jury service, summoned to court to serve as jurors, or sworn to act as jurors in a particular case

ju·ry·man \'==mən\ *n, pl* **jurymen** **1** : a person summoned to a sitting of a court to act as a juror if chosen **2** : JUROR

jury of the vicinage : a jury formerly drawn from the neighborhood and now drawn from the political subdivision in which the court is held

jury-packing \'=,==\ *n* : the practice or an instance of illegally or corruptly influencing a jury by making available for jury service persons known to be biased or partial in a particular case to be tried

jury-rigged \¦=¦=\ *adj* [³*jury*] : rigged for temporary service

jury room *n* [¹*jury*] : the place where a jury in arriving at a verdict deliberates in private

jury strut *n* [³*jury*] : an auxiliary strut used as a support for a primary strut

jury wheel *n* [¹*jury*] : a revolving device or circular box from which the names of persons to serve as jurymen may be drawn by chance

jurywoman \'==,=\ *n, pl* **jurywomen** : a female member of a jury

¹jus \'jəs\ *or* **ius** \'yüs\ *n, pl* **ju·ra** \'ju̇rə\ *or* **iu·ra** \'yu̇-\ [L — more at JUST] **1** : LAW **2** : a legal principle, right, or power

²jus \'zhüs, 'jüs, F 'zhüe\ *n, pl* **jus** [F — more at JUICE] : JUICE, GRAVY — compare AU JUS

jus *abbr* justice

jus ab·u·ten·di \-,abyə'tendē, -,dī\ *n* [L, right of abusing] *Roman & civil law* : a right to make full use of property even to wasting or destroying it : absolute and unlimited ownership with the power of free alienation — compare JUS UTENDI

jus ac·cre·scen·di \-,akrə'sendē, -,dī\ *n* [L, lit., right of increasing] *Roman & civil law* : a right of accrual (as the right of survivorship)

jus ad rem \-(')a'drem\ *n* [ML, right to a thing] *civil & canon law* : a right to acquire particular property arising out of another's legal duty : a jus in personam as distinguished from a jus in rem based on full ownership or possession of particular property : an inchoate as distinguished from a perfected right

jus ae·di·li·um \-ē'dilēəm\ *or* **jus ae·di·li·ci·um** \-,ēdə'lis(h)ēəm\ *n* [L, law of the aediles or law of an aedile] *Roman law* : the law of the curule aediles set forth in their edicts usu. relating to police and market regulations

jus al·ba·na·gii \-,albə'näjē,ī\ *n* [ML, right of alien confiscation] : DROIT D'AUBAINE

jus an·ga·ri·ae \-(,)aŋ'ga(a)rē,ē\ *n* [LL, lit., right of angaria] : ANGARY

jus ca·non·i·cum \-kə'nänəkəm\ *n* [ML] : CANON LAW

jus ci·vi·le \-sə'vī(,)lē\ *n* [L] : CIVIL LAW

jus com·mer·cii \-kə'mərshē,ī\ *n* [L, right of commerce] *Roman & civil law* : a right to make contracts, acquire, hold, and transfer property, and have business dealings

jus com·mu·ne \-kə'myü(,)nē\ *n* [L] **1** : the common law of England **2** : the common or public law or right as opposed to the jus singulare established for special cases

jus co·nu·bii *or* **jus con·nu·bii** \-kə'n(y)übē,ī\ *n* [L, lit., right of marriage, right of intermarriage] **1** : CONNUBIUM 2 **2** : the body of rules and conventions of a people or community governing intermarriage

jus de·li·be·ran·di \-də,libə'randē, -n,dī\ *n* [L, right of deliberating] *Roman & civil law* : a right granted to an heir to take a certain time to decide whether to accept the inheritance or not

jus dis·po·nen·di \-,dispə'nendē, -dī\ *n* [L, right of disposing] : a right of disposal as of property : power of alienation

jus ec·cle·si·as·ti·cum \-ə,klēzē'astəkəm, -e,k-\ *n* [LL] : ECCLESIASTICAL LAW

jus edi·cen·di \-,edə'sendē, -n,dī\ *n* [L, right of decreeing] *Roman law* : a right belonging to the curule aediles, praetors, and quaestors and presidents in the provinces of making edicts

jus fru·en·di \-frü'endē, -,dī\ *n* [L, right of enjoying] *Roman & civil law* : a right of enjoyment of another's property without destroying its substance

jus gen·ti·um \-'jenchēəm\ *n* [L, law of aliens, law of nations] **1** : a body of legal rules for the government of aliens subject to Rome and of the intercourse of Roman citizens with aliens **2** : INTERNATIONAL LAW

jus ho·no·ra·ri·um \-,änə'ra(a)rēəm\ *n* [L, magisterial law] *Roman law* : the law established by the edicts of the magis-

trates consisting chiefly of the praetorian law and the law of the curule aediles
ju·si *or* **hu·si** \'hüsē\ *n* -s [PhilSp, fr. Tag *husi*] : a fine sheer Philippine fabric for dresses or shirts that is made in plain weave from silk and vegetable fibers
jus in per·so·nam \'j'ə,sinpə(r)'sō,nam\ *n* [L, right against a person] : a right of legal action against or to enforce a legal duty of a particular person or group of persons — compare JUS IN REM
jus in re \-'rē\ *n* [ML, lit., right in a thing] : JUS IN REM
jus in rem \-'rem\ *n* [L, right against a thing] : a right enforceable against anyone in the world interfering with that right founded on some specific relationship, status, or particular property accorded legal protection from interference by anyone (as the right to be free from slander or to enjoy one's property)
jus in·ter gen·tes \-,intə(r)'jen-,tēz\ *n* [L, law among nations] : JUS GENTIUM
jus la·tii \-'lāshē,ī\ *n, cap L* [L, lit., right of Latium, ancient country of Italy] : the right of a person (as a Latin not a citizen of Rome) who has certain rights of or to Roman citizenship
jus na·tu·rae \-nə'tü(,)rē, -nə-'tyü-\ *n* [L, lit., law of nature] : NATURAL LAW
jus na·tu·ra·le \-,nachə'ra(,)lē, -rā(-, -rä(-\ *n* [L] : NATURAL LAW
jus per·so·na·rum \-,pərsə'na(a)rəm\ *n* [L, law of persons] : the law of persons occupying special relations to one another (as parent and child, husband and wife, guardian and ward) or of persons with limited rights (as aliens, minors, slaves, incompetent or insane persons)
jus post·li·mi·ni·i \-,pōstlə'minē,ī\ *n* [L, right of return to one's threshold] *Roman law* : POSTLIMINIUM
jus pri·mae noc·tis \-,prī(,)mē'näktəs\ *n* [L, right of first night] **1** : DROIT DU SEIGNEUR **2** : a right granted by the law or custom of a primitive people to some person other than the bridegroom of deflowering the bride
jus pro·pri·e·ta·tis \-p(r)ə,prīə'tād·əs\ *n* [ML, lit., right of ownership] : a right based on ownership of property irrespective of actual possession
jus pub·li·cum \-'pəbləkəm\ *n* [L] : public law including in Roman law the criminal and sacred law
jus re·lic·tae \-rə'lik(,)tē\ *n* [ML, right of a widow] *Scots law* : a widow's right to a share in the free movable estate of her deceased husband to the extent of one third if there are children and otherwise one half
jus re·lic·ti \-,tī\ *n* [ML, right of a widower] *Scots law* : a widower's right to share in the free movable estate of his deceased wife since 1881 to the extent of one third if there are children and otherwise one half
juss *abbr* jussive
jus san·gui·nis \-'saŋgwənəs\ *n* [L, right of blood] : a rule that the citizenship of the child is determined by the citizenship of its parents
jus·si·aea \,jəsē'ēə\ *n, cap* [NL, irreg. fr. Bernard de *Jussieu* †1777 Fr. botanist] : a genus of chiefly tropical aquatic or semiaquatic herbs (family Onagraceae) that are closely related to the evening primroses and have a many-seeded capsule and usu. entire alternate leaves — see PRIMROSE WILLOW
jus·si·ae·an \',=='ēən\ *or* **jus·si·eu·an** \-'yüən\ *also* **jus·si·e·an** \-'ēən\ *adj, usu cap* [fr. or irreg. fr. Bernard de *Jussieu* †1777 or Antoine Laurent de *Jussieu* †1836 Fr. botanists + E *-an*] : of or relating to the French botanists Bernard de Jussieu or Antoine Laurent de Jussieu ⟨*Jussiaean* classification⟩
jus sin·gu·la·re \-,siŋgyə'la(a)rē\ *n* [L, individual law, particular law] *Roman & civil law* : a law or right established for special cases as opposed to the jus commune
1jus·sive \'jəsiv, -sēv *also* səv\ *adj* [L *jussus* (past part. of *jubēre* to order) + E *-ive*; akin to W *udd* lord, Gk *hysminē* fight, battle, Skt *udyōdhati* it boils up, rages, *yudhyati* he fights] : expressing or having the effect of a command
2jussive \"\ *n* -s : a word, form, case, or mood expressing command
jus so·li \'jəs'sō,lī\ *n* [L, right of the soil] : a rule of the common law that determines the allegiance or citizenship of a child by the place of its birth — compare ALLEGIANCE
1just *var of* JOUST
2just \'jəst\ *adj often* -ER/-EST [ME *just, juste*, fr. MF & L; MF *juste*, fr. OF, fr. L *justus*, fr. *jus* right, law, justice, fr. OL *jous*; akin to OIr *huisse, uisse* right, just, Skt *yos* welfare, and perh. to L *jungere* to bind, join; basic meaning: tie, obligation — more at YOKE] **1 a** (1) : having a basis in fact : REASONABLE, WELL-FOUNDED, JUSTIFIED ⟨felt a ~ fear of the consequences of his actions⟩ (2) : conforming to fact or reason : not false : RIGHT, TRUE, ACCURATE ⟨had a very ~ notion of the boy's abilities⟩ ⟨one element in a ~ discrimination —John Dewey⟩ (3) *archaic* : agreeing closely or exactly with a pattern, model, or other original : FAITHFUL **b** *obs* : adapted to some end or purpose : APPROPRIATE, SUITABLE **c** (1) *obs* : regular or exact in operation : CONSTANT, UNIFORM (2) *obs* : being exactly the specified measure, dimension, quantity, or other result of calculation : not approximate but exact (3) : conforming to some standard of correctness : CORRECT, PROPER, FITTING ⟨tended to distort some of the concerto's ~ proportions —Winthrop Sargeant⟩ ⟨react in ~ measure against this naturalism —Irving Babbitt⟩ ⟨combines wit and sentiment in ~ proportions —Douglas Watt⟩ (4) *obs* : EQUAL, EVEN (5) : giving or sounding musical tones at the mathematically exact intervals of their vibration ratios ⟨~ intonation⟩ ⟨~ scale⟩ — compare TEMPERED **d** *archaic* : lacking nothing needed for completeness : COMPLETE, FULL **2 a** : righteous before God **b** (1) : acting or being in conformity with what is morally right or good : RIGHTEOUS, EQUITABLE ⟨a reward directed his way by a ~ providence —W.H.Whyte⟩ ⟨a ~ war⟩ ⟨that is justice, even if it is not ~ —Alan Paton⟩ ⟨his decisions quick and instinctively ~ —Norman Mailer⟩ (2) : MERITED, DESERVED ⟨won him that ~ affection and popularity —F.J.Mather⟩ ⟨received his ~ punishment⟩ **c** : conforming to or consonant with what is legal or lawful : legally right ⟨a ~ title⟩ ⟨~ compensation⟩ ⟨a ~ proceeding⟩ **syn** see FAIR, UPRIGHT
3just \(ˈ)jəs(t), (ˈ)jis(t), (ˈ)jes(t), *in rapid speech sometimes* (,)dis(t)\ *adv* [ME, fr. *just*, adj.] **1 a** : EXACTLY, PRECISELY ⟨some indication of ~ how nervous she was —C.B.Flood⟩ ⟨~ the words we often have to look up in a dictionary —G.A. Miller⟩ ⟨capturing . . . ~ the expression of terror which had baffled him —Laurence Binyon⟩ ⟨must always have his meals served ~ so⟩ ⟨has ~ the thing you need⟩ ⟨that's ~ the point in dispute⟩ ⟨you must take me ~ as I am⟩ ⟨an apartment project . . . that cost ~ $20 million —*Wall Street Jour.*⟩ **b** (1) : precisely at the time referred to or implied ⟨was ~ ten when he came in⟩ ⟨not here ~ now⟩ (2) : but a very short time ago : very recently ⟨has ~ been published⟩ ⟨was ~ here⟩ — often used in the phrase *just now* ⟨saw him ~ now⟩ **c** *Brit* : on the point of being — often used with *on* ⟨it was now ~ on eight o'clock —Paul Jennings⟩ **2** *obs* : in a precise or accurate manner : CORRECTLY, ACCURATELY **3 a** : by a very small margin : BARELY ⟨had only ~ time to get back —F.W.Crafts⟩ ⟨could ~ see the very high weathercock of the church —Arnold Bennett⟩ ⟨~ short of the record —*Current Biog.*⟩ ⟨it was ~ over fifty years ago —Alan Devoe⟩ ⟨should be adjusted to ~ clear the dial —W.E.Shinn⟩ ⟨has an entrance ~ within the . . . county line —*Amer. Guide Series: N.Y. City*⟩ **b** : in immediate proximity : IMMEDIATELY, DIRECTLY ⟨lies ~ west of here⟩ ⟨~ across from the campus⟩ ⟨~ down the hall —J.K.Blake⟩ **4 a** : ONLY, MERELY, SIMPLY ⟨~ a note to let you know⟩ ⟨turn it into ~ another automobile —R.C.Ruark⟩ ⟨to them it's ~ a business —*Irish Digest*⟩ ⟨asked for a copy and got it — ~ like that —M.S.Mayer⟩ ⟨there was ~ lots of scenery —J.F.Dobie⟩ ⟨seems incredibly large for ~ the aristocracy —H.P.Becker⟩ ⟨I'm ~ your interpreter —Ernest Hemingway⟩ ⟨I don't think about it; I ~ go —J.J.Godwin⟩ **b** (1) : QUITE, VERY, ABSOLUTELY, REALLY — used as an intensive ⟨that's ~ ducky⟩ ⟨~ had a wonderful time⟩ (2) *chiefly dial* : INDEED, TRULY ⟨I tried a master; but he confused me, ~ —Willa Cather⟩ ⟨couldn't he play the violin, ~ —*Wesjarmers News*⟩ — **just about** *adv* : ALMOST, APPROXIMATELY ⟨passes *just about* through the middle of the region —P.E.James⟩ ⟨is the work done? *just about*⟩ ⟨shown to *just about* every audience you can name —Cecile Starr⟩ — **just in case** *adv* : by way of precaution against a possible or anticipated eventuality ⟨surrounded the area *just in case* —*Springfield (Mass.) Union*⟩
just *abbr* justice
just·au·corps \ˌzhüstəˌkō(ə)r\ *or* **jus·ti·coat** \ˈjəstə̇ˌkōt\ *n, pl* **justaucorps** \-r(z)\ *or* **justicoats** \-ts\ [*justaucorps* fr. F, fr. *juste au corps* close to the body; *justicoat*, alter. (influenced by E *coat*) of *justaucorps*] : a fitted coat or jacket; *specif* : a man's knee-length coat with flaring and stiffened skirts worn in the late 17th and early 18th centuries

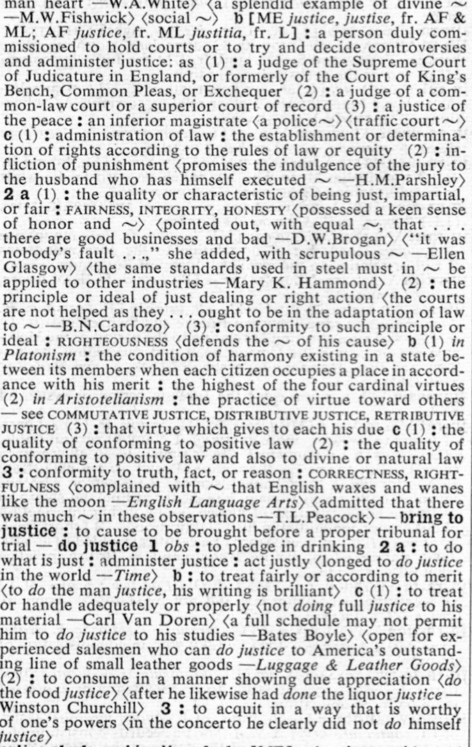
justaucorps

juste-mi·lieu \ˌzhüstmēlˈyə, -yər(·), -yə̄\ *n, pl* **juste-milieux** \-yə(z), -yər(·), -yərz, -yə̄(z)\ [F] : the just or golden mean; *esp* : a governmental policy characterized by moderation and compromise
jus·tice \ˈjəstəs\ *n* -s *often attrib* [ME *justice, justise*, fr. OE & OF; OE *justise*, fr. OF *justice, justise*, fr. L *justitia*, fr. *justus* just + *-itia* -ice] **1 a** : the maintenance or administration of what is just : impartial adjustment of conflicting claims : the assignment of merited rewards or punishments : just treatment ⟨meting out evenhanded ~⟩ ⟨the natural aspiration for ~ in the human heart —W.A.White⟩ ⟨a splendid example of divine ~ —M.W.Fishwick⟩ ⟨social ~⟩ **b** [ME *justice, justise*, fr. AF & ML; AF *justice*, fr. ML *justitia*, fr. L] : a person duly commissioned to hold courts or to try and decide controversies and administer justice: as (1) : a judge of the Supreme Court of Judicature in England, or formerly of the Court of King's Bench, Common Pleas, or Exchequer (2) : a judge of a common-law court or a superior court of record (3) : a justice of the peace : an inferior magistrate ⟨a police ~⟩ ⟨traffic court ~⟩ **c** (1) : administration of law : the establishment or determination of rights according to the rules of law or equity (2) : infliction of punishment ⟨promises the indulgence of the jury to the husband who has himself executed ~ —H.M.Parshley⟩ **2 a** (1) : the quality or characteristic of being just, impartial, or fair : FAIRNESS, INTEGRITY, HONESTY ⟨possessed a keen sense of honor and ~⟩ ⟨pointed out, with equal ~, that . . . there are good businesses and bad —D.W.Brogan⟩ ⟨"it was nobody's fault . . .," she added, with scrupulous ~ —Ellen Glasgow⟩ ⟨the same standards used in steel must in ~ be applied to other industries —Mary K. Hammond⟩ (2) : the principle or ideal of just dealing or right action ⟨the courts are not helped as they . . . ought to be in the adaptation of law to ~ —B.N.Cardozo⟩ (3) : conformity to such principle or ideal : RIGHTEOUSNESS ⟨defends the ~ of his cause⟩ **b** (1) *in Platonism* : the condition of harmony existing in a state between its members when each citizen occupies a place in accordance with his merit : the highest of the four cardinal virtues (2) *in Aristotelianism* : the practice of virtue toward others — see COMMUTATIVE JUSTICE, DISTRIBUTIVE JUSTICE, RETRIBUTIVE JUSTICE (3) : that virtue which gives to each his due **c** (1) : the quality of conforming to positive law (2) : the quality of conforming to positive law and also to divine or natural law **3** : conformity to truth, fact, or reason : CORRECTNESS, RIGHTFULNESS ⟨complained with ~ that English waxes and wanes like the moon —*English Language Arts*⟩ ⟨admitted that there was much ~ in these observations —T.L.Peacock⟩ — **bring to justice** : to cause to be brought before a proper tribunal for trial — **do justice 1** *obs* : to pledge in drinking **2 a** : to do what is just : administer justice : act justly ⟨longed to *do justice* in the world —*Time*⟩ **b** : to treat fairly or according to merit ⟨to *do* the man *justice*, his writing is brilliant⟩ **c** (1) : to treat or handle adequately or properly ⟨not *doing* full *justice* to his material —Carl Van Doren⟩ ⟨a full schedule may not permit him to *do justice* to his studies —Bates Boyle⟩ ⟨open for experienced salesmen who can *do justice* to America's outstanding line of small leather goods —*Luggage & Leather Goods*⟩ (2) : to consume in a manner showing due appreciation ⟨*do* the food *justice*⟩ ⟨after he likewise had *done* the liquor *justice* —Winston Churchill⟩ **3** : to acquit in a way that is worthy of one's powers ⟨in the concerto he clearly did not *do* himself *justice*⟩
justice clerk *n, pl* **justice clerks** [ME] : the vice-president of the High Court of Justiciary and the presiding officer of the Outer House of the Court of Session in Scotland — called also *lord justice clerk*
justice court *or* **justice's court** *n* : an inferior court not of record having limited criminal or civil jurisdiction, presided over by a justice of the peace, and existing in some states from which appeal usu. may be claimed
justice general *n, pl* **justices general** [ME] : the former presiding officer of the High Court of Justiciary in Scotland whose duties are now entrusted to the lord president of the Court of Session — called also *lord justice general*
justice in eyre *n* [ME, trans. of AF *justice en eire*] : an itinerant judge riding the circuit to hold court in the different counties
justice of the peace [ME] : a subordinate magistrate for the conservation of the peace in a specified district with sometimes other incidental administrative and financial powers specified in his commission and with the principal duties of administering summary justice in minor cases, of committing for trial in a superior court on cause shown, and in Great Britain of granting licenses and acting if a county justice as judge at quarter sessions
jus·tic·er \-sə(r)\ *n* -s [ME *justiser*, fr. MF *justicier*, fr. OF, fr. *justice*] *archaic* : one who maintains or administers justice : JUDGE
jus·tice·ship \-s,ship\ *n* : the office or dignity of a judge
justice's warrant *n* : a warrant issued by an inferior magistrate (such as a justice of the peace, alderman, or federal commissioner) as distinguished from a bench warrant issued by a court of record
justiceweed \'==,=\ *n* : a slender white-flowered herb (*Eupatorium leucolepis*) of the eastern U.S.
jus·ti·cia \ˌjəˈstishēə\ *n, cap* [NL, fr. James *Justice*, 18th cent. Scot. horticulturist + NL *-ia*] : a genus of perennial herbs or shrubs (family Acanthaceae) growing in water or wet places and having entire leaves and small flowers in long-peduncled axillary spikes or heads — see WATER WILLOW
jus·ti·cia·bil·i·ty \ˌjə,stish(ē)əˈbiləd·ē\ *n* -ES : the quality of being justiciable
jus·ti·cia·ble \ˌjəˈstish(ē)əbəl\ *adj* [F, fr. MF] : capable of being decided by legal principles or by a court of justice : liable to trial in a court of justice ⟨a ~ case⟩
jus·ti·ci·ar \ˌjəˈstishē(ə)r\ *n* -s [ME, fr. (influenced by ME *-ar*) ML *justiciarius, justitiarius*, fr. L *justitia* justice + *-arius* -ary — more at JUSTICE] **1** : a high royal judicial officer in medieval England; *esp* : a justice of one of the superior courts **2** [ML *justiciarius, justitiarius*] : the chief political and judicial officer of the Norman and later kings of England until the 13th century — called also *capital justiciar* **3** : either of two chief judges under early Scotch kings and with jurisdiction north and south respectively of Forth
jus·ti·ci·ar·ship \-(r),ship\ *n* : the office or dignity of a justiciar
jus·ti·ci·ary \ˌjəˈstishē,erē, -ri\ *n* -ES [ME *justiciarie*, fr. ML *justiciaria, justitiaria*, fr. L *justitia* justice + *-aria* -ary] **1** : the jurisdiction of a justiciar or of the High Court of Justiciary which consists of original and appellate jurisdiction in serious criminal cases and appellate jurisdiction from sheriff's decisions in civil matters in the small-debts court **2** [ML *justiciarius, justitiarius*] : JUSTICIAR
jus·ti·ci·es \ˌjəˈstishē,ēz\ *n, pl* **justicies** [ML, lit., you may bring to trial, 2d pers. sing. pres. subj. of *justiciare, justitiare* to bring to trial, fr. L *justitia* justice] *Eng law* : a writ addressed to a sheriff ordering him to do justice in a case (as trespass, vi et armis, or personal action involving not more than 40 shillings) he otherwise could not try
justicoat *var of* JUSTAUCORPS
jus·ti·fi·abil·i·ty \ˌjəstə,fīəˈbiləd·ē, -ətē, -i\ *n* -ES : the quality of being justifiable
jus·ti·fi·able \ˈjəstə,fīəbəl, ,==ˈ===\ *adj* [*justify* + *-able*] : capable of being justified : EXCUSABLE, DEFENSIBLE ⟨~ family pride —*Current Biog.*⟩

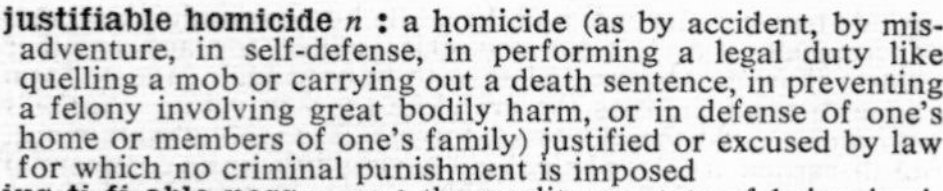

justifiable homicide *n* : a homicide (as by accident, by misadventure, in self-defense, in performing a legal duty like quelling a mob or carrying out a death sentence, in preventing a felony involving great bodily harm, or in defense of one's home or members of one's family) justified or excused by law for which no criminal punishment is imposed
jus·ti·fi·able·ness *n* -ES : the quality or state of being justifiable
jus·ti·fi·ably \-blē, -li\ *adv* : in a justifiable manner : DEFENSIBLY, EXCUSABLY ⟨~ classified as secret —D.W.Mitchell⟩ ⟨~ expects early action —H.S.Truman⟩
jus·ti·fi·can·dum \ˌjəstəfəˈkandəm\ *n, pl* **justifican·da** \-də\ [LL, neut. of *justificandus*, gerundive of *justificare* to justify — more at JUSTIFY] : something that is to be justified — compare JUSTIFICANS
jus·ti·fi·cans \ˌjəstəfəˈkanz\ *n, pl* **justifican·tia** \-nchēə\ [LL, pres. part. of *justificare*] : something (as a principle) that serves to justify
jus·ti·fi·ca·tion \ˌjəstəfəˈkāshən\ *n* -s [ME *justificacioun*, fr. LL *justification-, justificatio*, fr. *justificatus* (past part. of *justificare* to justify) + *-ion-, -io* -ion] **1 a** (1) : the act, process, or state of being justified by God **b** : the terms under which one is so justified **2 a** (1) : the act or an instance of justifying : VINDICATION, DEFENSE ⟨the ~ of barbarous means by holy ends —H.J.Muller⟩ (2) : the condition of being justified ⟨doubted the historical ~ of the Confiteor . . . in any Lutheran liturgy —S.G.Hefelbower⟩ (3) : something that justifies ⟨finds in it the ~ . . . of his own work —A.P.d'Entrèves⟩ ⟨its only logical ~ would have been swift military success —Hugh Gaitskell⟩ **b** (1) : the showing in court of a sufficient lawful reason why a party charged or accused did or failed to do that for which he is called to answer (2) : something that constitutes such a reason (3) : the justifying of sureties (as on a bail bond) **c** : the act or an instance of verifying or proving ⟨the purpose of ~ is to produce conviction in the hearer —John Ladd⟩ **3** : the process or result of justifying (as a line of type)
jus·ti·fi·ca·tive \ˈjəstəfə̇,kād·iv, jəˈstifə,kād·iv, ˈjəstəˈfikəd·iv\ *adj* [prob. fr. F *justificatif*, fr. MF, fr. LL *justificatus* (past part.) + MF *-if* -ive] : serving to justify : JUSTIFICATORY
jus·tif·i·ca·to·ry \ˌjəˈstifəkə,tōrē, ˈjəstəˈfikə,-, ˈjəstəfəkə-, -tȯr-, -ri, *esp Brit* ˈjəstifiˈkātəri *or* -ā·tri\ *adj* [LL *justificatus* (past part.) + E *-ory*] : tending or serving to justify : VINDICATORY
jus·ti·fi·er \ˈjəstə,fī(ə)r, -īə\ *n* -s : one that justifies: as **a** : a person who vindicates or absolves **b** : a graver for trimming the walls in enamel work
jus·ti·fy \ˈjəstə,fī\ *vb* -ED/-ING/-S [ME *justifien*, fr. MF or LL; MF *justifier*, fr. OF, fr. LL *justificare*, fr. L *justus* just + *-ficare* -fy — more at JUST] *vt* **1 a** (1) : to prove or show to be just, desirable, warranted, or useful : VINDICATE ⟨science *justifies* itself when it contributes to the desire to know —*Scientific American Reader*⟩ ⟨*justified* to herself his every fault —Ruth Park⟩ ⟨most cats must ~ themselves by catching mice —Charlton Laird⟩ ⟨~ the ways of God to man —John Milton⟩ ⟨undertaking to ~ a single scale of rates for the entire country —*Collier's Yr. Bk.*⟩ ⟨the welcome he received *justified* his visit —A.R.Forde⟩ (2) *obs* : to confirm, maintain, or acknowledge as true, lawful, or legitimate **b** : to prove or show to be valid, sound, or conforming to fact or reason : furnish grounds or evidence for : CONFIRM, SUPPORT, VERIFY ⟨their immediate jubilant reaction has been abundantly *justified* by the sales —Peter Forster⟩ ⟨attempts to ~ his definition of cartography —*Geographical Journal*⟩ ⟨insinuation of personal interest as a determining factor seems to me not *justified* by the facts shown —O.W.Holmes †1935⟩ ⟨*justified* my fondest hopes —D.G.Gerahty⟩ **c** (1) : to show to have had a sufficient legal reason (as that the libel charged is true or that the trespass charged was by license of the possessor) for (an act made the subject of a charge or accusation) (2) : to qualify (oneself) as a surety by taking oath to the ownership of sufficient property **2 a** *archaic* : to execute justice upon : administer justice to **b** *archaic* : to pronounce free from guilt or blame : ABSOLVE ⟨I think — or at least hope — you would have *justified* me —George Meredith⟩ **c** : to judge, regard, or treat as righteous, worthy of salvation, or as freed from the future penalty of sin ⟨God *justifies* with his forgiveness and grace the man who comes to him —Will Herberg⟩ **3 a** : to make level and square the body of (a typefounder's strike) **b** : to set to fit the measure or space closely (as a line of type, matrices, photocomposition, typewriting) or so that all full lines are of equal length and flush right and left (as typewritten matter) **c** : to cause to align evenly at the bottom (as letters of different size) **d** : to adjust to fit and lock up securely (set letterpress matter) ~ *vi* **1 a** : to show a sufficient lawful reason (as that the plaintiff consented to an act alleged to be a trespass) for an act done or not done **b** : to qualify as bail or surety by taking oath to the ownership of sufficient property ⟨the surety *justified* on the bail bond⟩ **2** : to accept and receive as just or righteous those who respond in wholehearted faith to God as revealed by Jesus Christ ⟨believing with all their being that God *justified* through faith —John Dillenberger & Claude Welch⟩ **3** *printing* **a** : to be capable of or susceptible of justification **b** : to become justified **syn** see EXPLAIN, MAINTAIN
justifying space *or* **justification space** *n* : a space that is set by striking the spacebar of a keyboard typesetting machine and that has no predetermined width
justing *var of* JOUSTING
jus·tin·i·an·ian *or* **jus·tin·i·a·ne·an** \ˌjəˌstinēˈānēən\ *adj, usu cap* [*Justinianian* fr. *Justinian* I †565 Byzantine emperor (fr. LL *Justinianus*) + E *-ian*; *Justinianean* fr. LL *Justinianeus* of Justinian (fr. *Justinianus* Justinian) + E *-an*] : of or relating to the Byzantine emperor Justinian under whom much of the Western Empire was reconquered and the laws codified in the Justinian Code ⟨the *Justinianean* ordinances on the subject of divorce were revived —B.J.Kidd⟩
justle *var of* JOSTLE
just·ly *adv* [ME, fr. *just* (adj.) + *-ly*] : in a just manner: as **a** *chiefly dial* : EXACTLY, PRECISELY, QUITE ⟨do not ~ know what your taste in reasons may be —Thomas Gray⟩ **b** : in conformity with law or justice : FAIRLY ⟨treated all his employees ~⟩ **c** : in conformity with fact or reason : CORRECTLY, PROPERLY ⟨~ ranked among the most wonderful efforts of the human hand —H.T.Buckle⟩ ⟨helps them to reason more ~ —M.R.Cohen⟩ **d** : in a manner appropriate to or required by the case : RIGHTLY, FITTINGLY, ACCURATELY ⟨essential that it be well developed and ~ proportioned to the other body measurements —H.G.Armstrong⟩ ⟨expresses quivering nervous strain more ~ than any player we have —*Current Biog.*⟩
just·ness \ˈjəs(t)nəs\ *n* -ES [ME *justnesse*, fr. *just* (adj.) + *-nesse* -ness] : the quality or state of being just: as **a** : RIGHTEOUSNESS, UPRIGHTNESS ⟨address as Jehovah a composite idea of authority, fatherhood, ~ —Joseph Macleod⟩ **b** : conformity with truth or reason : VALIDITY, FAIRNESS, SOUNDNESS ⟨the ~ and propriety of their sentiments —William Cowper⟩ **c** : conformity with some standard of aesthetic correctness or propriety : RIGHTNESS, ACCURACY, PRECISION, NICETY ⟨set forth with a ~ and care that proclaimed him a master orchestral artisan —Winthrop Sargeant⟩ ⟨estimating the ~ of the imitation —Irving Babbitt⟩ ⟨impressive in the absolute ~ of its design —R.M.Coates⟩ ⟨which he renders with a memorable ~ and beauty —Edward Sackville-West⟩
just-noticeable difference *n* : the minimum difference perceptible in any part of a series of sensory qualities ordinarily determined by reference to the corresponding stimulus conditions : the smallest perceptible change in a stimulus situation
just price *n* [trans. of ML *justum pretium*] **1** : a price conforming to the doctrine developed in antiquity and elaborated in the medieval period that price should in general correspond to the cost of production **2** : a price approved by common estimate, determined by a legal maximum, or conforming to some other standard of rightness or equity
justs *pl of* JUST
just the same *adv* : even so : NEVERTHELESS ⟨*just the same* I would trust him implicitly⟩
jus uten·di \ˌjəsyüˈtendē, -ˌdī\ *n* [L, right of using] : a personal right or servitude of one gratuitously for the needs of himself and his family and without profit to make use of another's property without consuming it or destroying its substance or capacity for future profit

[1]jut \'jət, *usu* -əd·+V\ *vb* **jutted; jutted; jutting; juts** [perh. back-formation fr. [1]*jutty*] *vi* **:** to shoot out or forward **:** PROTRUDE ⟨a cigar *jutting* from his teeth —J.A.Michener⟩ ⟨narrow bony shoulders *jutting* from his undershirt —James Jones⟩ ⟨cliffs *jutting* straight up —Peggy Durdin⟩ ⟨hurdles that ~ into the river —Murray Schumach⟩ **~** *vt* **:** to cause to jut ⟨*jutting* out his jaw humorously —Phelim Brady⟩ **syn** see BULGE

[2]jut \"\ *n* -s **:** something that projects or juts **:** PROJECTION ⟨passed behind a ~ of the shore —B.A.Williams⟩

[1]jute \'jüt, *usu* -üd·+V\ *n* -s *cap* [ME *Jute*, fr. ML *Jutae*, *Juti*, pl., Jutes, of Gmc origin; akin to OE *Eotas*, *Eotenas*, *Iotas* Jutes, ON *Jōtar*] **:** a member of one of the Low German peoples of Jutland of whom some settled in Kent in the 5th century — **jut·ish** \-üd·ish\ *adj*, *usu cap*

[2]jute \"\ *n* -s *often attrib* [Hindi & Bengali *jūṭ*, prob. fr. Skt *jūṭa* matted hair] **1 :** the glossy fiber of either of two East Indian plants (*Corchorus olitorius* and *C. capsularis*) used chiefly for sacking, burlap, and the cheaper varieties of twine **2 :** either of the two plants producing this fiber; *also* **:** any other plant of the genus *Corchorus*

jute board *n* **:** a strong plyboard containing no jute fiber but made typically from sulfate and wastepaper pulps and used esp. for shipping containers

jute butts *n pl* **:** fiber from the thick woody butt of the jute stalk used for bagging, twine, paper stock

jute paper *n* **:** a strong paper made largely from jute fiber — compare JUTE BOARD

jutia *var of* HUTIA

jut–jawed \'=¦=\ *adj* **:** having a jutting jaw ⟨his head was big, *jut-jawed* —Will Henry⟩

[1]jut·lan·dic \¦jət¦landik\ *adj*, *usu cap* [*Jutland*, Denmark + E *-ic*] **1 a :** of, relating to, or characteristic of Jutland **b :** of, relating to, or characteristic of the people of Jutland **2 :** of, relating to, or characteristic of the Jutlandic dialect

[2]jutlandic \"\ *n* -s *cap* **:** the Danish dialect of Jutland in western Denmark

jutting *adj* **:** PROJECTING, PROTRUDING ⟨the powerful ~ jaw —A.L.Kroeber⟩ — **jut·ting·ly** *adv*

[1]jut·ty \'jəd·ē\ *vb* -ED/-ING/-ES [ME *jutteyen*] *archaic* **:** to project beyond **:** JUT

[2]jutty \"\ *n* -ES [ME *jutte*, *jutty*, perh. alter. of *jette* jetty] **1** *archaic* **:** PIER, JETTY **2 :** a projecting part of a building ⟨an ugly assortment of *jutties*, ornaments, and blind windows —Joseph Wechsberg⟩

juv *abbr* **1** [L *juvenis*] young **2** juvenile

[1]ju·ve·nal \'jüvən°l\ *n* -s [L *juvenalis*, adj.] *archaic* **:** YOUTH ⟨forever . . . ~*s* in limb and spirit —*Observer*⟩

[2]juvenal \"\ *adj* [L *juvenalis*, fr. *juvenis* young person + *-alis* -al] **:** of, relating to, or being a juvenile ⟨~ bobwhite quail —*Wildlife Rev.*⟩

[3]juvenal \"\ *n* -s *usu cap* [after *Juvenal* † *ab* A.D. 140 Roman lawyer and satirist (fr. L D. Junius *Juvenalis*)] **:** a writer resembling or suggestive of the Roman poet Juvenal in his use of biting satire and pungent realism — **ju·ve·na·li·an** \¦jüvə¦nālēən\ *adj*, *usu cap*

juvenal plumage *n* [[2]*juvenal*] **:** the plumage of a bird immediately succeeding the natal down

ju·ve·nes·cence \ˌjüvə'nes°n(t)s\ *n* -s [[2]*juvenal* + *-escence*] **:** the state of being youthful or of growing young ⟨if she gave any evidence of ~, he had managed to overlook it —Josephine Pinckney⟩

[1]ju·ve·nile \'jüvəˌnīl, -ˌn°l *sometimes* -(ˌ)nil\ *adj* [F or L; F *juvénile*, fr. L *juvenilis*, fr. *juvenis* young person (fr. *juvenis* young) + *-ilis* -ile — more at YOUNG] **1 a :** of, relating to, or being a juvenile **:** physiologically immature or undeveloped **:** YOUNG ⟨the baby snake varies in color and markings from the ~ —*Farmer's Weekly* (*So. Africa*)⟩ ⟨his appearance was ~ —Elinor Wylie⟩ ⟨a ~ period that is essentially asexual —W.C.Allee⟩ ⟨gave her a most ~ and engaging look —Edna Ferber⟩ ⟨ten ~ years of my life —F.N.Souza⟩ **b :** being or remaining in a youthful stage of development; *specif* **:** being a plant in which the leaves are assumed to be similar to ancestral adult forms **c :** MAGMATIC ⟨~ waters⟩ **2 a :** of, relating to, characteristic of, or suitable for children or young people ⟨a ~ book⟩ ⟨a ~ phase of love not yet warmed into passion —C.W.Cunnington⟩ ⟨a ~ membership of 82,111 —C.W.Ferguson⟩ **b :** being or relating to an actor who plays a youthful part ⟨played the ~ lead in a new hit⟩ **3 :** reflecting psychological or intellectual immaturity **:** unworthy of an adult **:** CHILDISH ⟨the ~ customs of fraternities —Harold Taylor⟩ ⟨regarded their desperate rebellion as ~ melodrama —Paul Blanshard⟩ ⟨~ behavior⟩ **syn** see YOUTHFUL

[2]juvenile \"\ *n* -s **1 a :** a young person **:** CHILD, YOUTH ⟨observed some of the evil effects of factory labor upon ~*s* —Paul Woodring⟩ ⟨leader of a gang of ~*s* who stole a car recently —*Springfield* (*Mass.*) *Daily News*⟩ **b :** a book for children or young people ⟨a general trade book as well as a ~ —*Publishers' Weekly*⟩ **2 a :** a young individual fundamentally like an adult of its kind except in size and reproductive activity **b :** a bird in juvenal plumage **c :** a 2-year old racehorse **3 :** an actor who plays youthful parts; *sometimes* **:** an actress who plays such parts

juvenile court *n* **:** a court having special jurisdiction over delinquent and dependent children usu. up to the age of 18 and emphasizing in practice clinical and casework techniques with goals of delinquency prevention and rehabilitation of the child rather than punishment

juvenile delinquency *n* **1 :** a status in a juvenile characterized by antisocial behavior (as truancy, waywardness, incorrigibility) that is beyond parental control and therefore subject to legal action **2 :** a violation of the law of the U.S. that is committed by a juvenile and that is not punishable by death or life imprisonment

juvenile delinquent *n* **:** a person adjudged to be a delinquent under an age fixed by law (as 16 or 18 years or 21 years in a few states)

juvenile insurance *n* **:** insurance upon the life of a child usu. issued to a parent who signs the application and pays the early premiums

juvenile officer *n* **:** a police officer charged with the detection, prosecution, and care of juvenile delinquents — compare PROBATION OFFICER

ju·ve·ni·lia \ˌjüvə'nilēə\ *n pl but sometimes sing in constr* [L, neut. pl. of *juvenilis* juvenile] **1 :** artistic or literary compositions produced in the author's youth and typically marked by immaturity of style, treatment, or thought **:** youthful writing or other artistic work ⟨essentially ~ and are only interesting as such —*Times Lit. Supp.*⟩ ⟨a curious piece of ~ —Milton Crane⟩ ⟨is still ~ — magnificent ~ —Graham Greene⟩ **2 a :** artistic or literary compositions suited to or designed for the young ⟨the crown jewels of ~ —*Saturday Rev.*⟩ **b :** a book, film, or other composition of such character ⟨endow this ~ with what little verisimilitude it has —*Newsweek*⟩

ju·ve·nil·i·ty \ˌjüvə'niləd·ē, -ətē, -i\ *n* -ES [L *juvenilitat-*, *juvenilitas*, fr. *juvenilis* juvenile + *-itat-*, *-itas* -ity] **1 :** youthful condition or manner **2 a :** immaturity of thought or conduct **:** CHILDISHNESS ⟨reveals the fatal ~ . . . beneath the sophisticated surface —D.S.Savage⟩ ⟨the ~ of grown-up people —B.I.Bell⟩ **b :** an instance of such immaturity — usu. used in pl. ⟨pettiness, *juvenilities* —John Adams⟩

ju·via \'hüvēə, 'zhü-\ *n* -s [Sp & Pg, of Arawakan origin; akin to Baniva *iuíya*, *yuvíya* juvia, Baré *yuhíya*] **:** BRAZIL NUT

juxta- *comb form* [L *juxta*, adv. & prep., near, nearby — more at JOUST] **:** situated near ⟨*juxta*-articular⟩ ⟨*juxta*medullary⟩

jux·ta·pose \'jəkstəˌpōz *sometimes* ˌ==' =\ *vt* [prob. fr. E *juxtaposition*, after such pairs as *interposition: interpose*] **:** to place side by side **:** place in juxtaposition ⟨the huts were never closely *juxtaposed* —V.G.Childe⟩ ⟨words perpetually *juxtaposed* in new and sudden combinations —T.S.Eliot⟩ ⟨pain has been . . . *juxtaposed* to pleasure as a form of emotion —F.A.Geldard⟩

juxtaposed *adj* **:** placed side by side **:** being in juxtaposition **syn** see ADJACENT

jux·ta·pos·it \ˌ=='päzət\ *vt* -ED/-ING/-S [L *juxta* near + *positus*, past part. of *ponere* to place — more at POSITION] **:** JUXTAPOSE

jux·ta·po·si·tion \ˌjəkstəpə'zishən\ *n* -s [L *juxta* near + E *position*] **:** the act or an instance of placing two or more objects in a close spatial or ideal relationship ⟨the proper ~ of rocks, trees —D.C.Buchanan⟩ ⟨the ~ of abstract with concrete, of the homely with the far-fetched —C.D.Lewis⟩; *also* **:** the condition of being so placed ⟨forested mountains and the sea were in ~ —A.L.Kroeber⟩ ⟨the resulting ~ of popular epic and village song —G.F.Jones⟩ — **jux·ta·po·si·tion·al** \¦===¦zishən°l, -shnəl\ *adj*

JV *abbr* **1** Japanese vellum **2** junior varsity

JVP *abbr* Japanese vellum proofs

JW *abbr* junior warden

jwlr *abbr* jeweler

jyn·gine \'jinˌjīn, -njən\ *adj* [NL *Jyng-*, *Jynx* + E *-ine*] **:** of or relating to the genus *Jynx*

jynx \'jiŋ(k)s\ *n* [L *iynx*, fr. Gk] **1** -ES **:** WRYNECK **2** *cap* [NL, fr. L *iynx*] **:** a genus of woodpeckers consisting of the wrynecks

¹k \'kā\ *n, pl* **k's** *or* **ks** \'kāz\ *often cap, often attrib* **1 a :** the 11th letter of the English alphabet **b :** an instance of this letter printed, written, or otherwise represented **c :** a speech counterpart of orthographic *k* (as *k* in *kill, skill, like, joked,* or German *kühn*) **2 :** a printer's type, a stamp, or some other instrument for reproducing the letter *k* **3 :** someone or something arbitrarily or conveniently designated *k* esp. as the 10th or when j is used for the 10th the 11th in order or class **4 :** something having the shape of the letter K **5 :** a unit vector parallel to the z-axis

²k *abbr, often cap* **1** [L *kalendae*] calends **2** karat **3** [*kathode*] cathode **4** keel **5** keg **6** Kelvin **7** key **8** kilo- **9** kilogram **10** king **11** kip **12** kitchen **13** knight **14** knit **15** knot **16** kopeck **17** koruna **18** kran **19** krona **20** krone **21** kroon **22** kurus

³k *symbol* **1** *cap* [NL *kalium*] potassium **2** *often cap* constant **3** [G *konstant*] Boltzmann's constant **4** thermal conductivity **5 a** key — used as a cryptographic subscript ⟨B_p (D_k) = E_c means that D was used as the key letter when B was enciphered into E⟩; see VIGENÈRE CIPHER **b** *cap* a cryptographic numerical keying element or the numerical value of a key letter when the normal alphabet is numbered from 0 to 25 ⟨P + C = K is the Beaufort keying method⟩ **6** *cap* **:** dissociation constant **7** *cap* **:** ionization constant

¹ka *var of* KAY

²ka \'kō, 'kä\ *chiefly Scot var of* CALL

³ka \'kä\ *n* -s [Egypt] **:** the personality double believed in ancient Egypt to be born with an individual and after death to reside in the statue of the deceased in the tomb dependent upon the preservation and nourishment of the body

⁴ka *usu cap, var of* KHA

ka *abbr* [*kathode*] cathode

KA *abbr* king of arms

kaa·ba *or* **ka'·bah** *also* **ka'·bah** *or* **caa·ba** \'käbə, 'kabə\ *adj, usu cap* [Ar *ka'bah*, lit., square building, fr. *ka'b* cube] **:** of or relating to the Islamic shrine in Mecca that incorporates a sacred black stone and is the goal of Islamic pilgrimage and the point toward which all Muslims turn in praying — see QIBLA

kaa·ma \'kämə\ *n* -s [Hottentot (Nama dial.) *ǃxamap, Kamáb*] **:** HARTEBEEST

kaa·wi yam \'käwē\ *n* [origin unknown] **:** a yam (*Dioscorea aculeata*) of southern Asia and Polynesia with prickly stems and sweet tubers

kab *var of* CAB

ka·babish \kə'babish, -'bäb-\ *n, pl* **kababish** *or* **kababishes** *usu cap* **1 :** a nomadic Arab people in the Anglo-Egyptian Sudan **2 :** a member of the Kababish people

ka·ba·ka \kə'bäkə\ *n* -s [native name in Uganda] **:** the native king of Buganda in Uganda ⟨the Colonial Office a year ago exiled the *Kabaka* . . . of Buganda —*N.Y. Times*⟩

kabala *or* **kabbala** *or* **kabbalah** *often cap, var of* CABALA

kabalassou *var of* CABALASSOU

kabalist *var of* CABALIST

ka·ba·ra·go·ya \kə,bärə'gōyə\ *n* -s [origin unknown] **:** a large water monitor (*Varanus salvator*) of southeastern Asia, the Malay archipelago, and the Philippines that sometimes reaches a length of seven feet

ka·bar·din \¦kabər¦dēn, ¦käbər-, ¦kä,bär-\ *also* **ka·bard** \kə'bärd\ *n* -s *cap* **1 :** a member of a Circassian people of the Caucasus mountains who comprise over half the population of the Kabardino-Balkarian Autonomous Soviet Socialist Republic and whose religion is Islam **2** *or* **ka·bar·di·an** \kə'bärdēən\ **:** the Caucasic language of the Kabardins — **kab·ar·din·i·an** \¦kabər¦dinēən\ *adj, usu cap*

kabassou *var of* CABASSOU

kab·ba·lah \kə'bälə\ *n* -s [Heb *qabbālāh*, lit., received, fr. *qābēl* to receive] **:** a written certificate issued by a rabbi to a prospective shohet who has passed an examination testing his knowledge of and expertness in shehitah

kabbalist *var of* CABALIST

ka·bel·jou *also* **ka·bel·jau** *or* **ka·bel·jauw** \'käbəl,yaů, 'kab-\ *n* -s [Afrik *kabeljou*, fr. D *kabeljauw* cod] **:** a large South African sciaenid food fish (*Johnius hololepidotus*) having a liver extremely rich in vitamin A that is closely related to and sometimes held identical with the European maigre

kabinda *usu cap, var of* CABINDA

ka·bir·pan·thi \kə,bir'pən-,tē\ *n* -s *usu cap* [Hindi *kabīrpanthī* fr. *Kabīr* †1518 Hindu mystic poet + *panthī* follower] **:** a member of a reform sect of India originating in the 15th century with doctrines based on the teachings of Kabir

ka·bi·stan \¦käbə¦stän, ¦kabə¦stan\ *n* -s *usu cap* [*Kabistan, Kabristan*, locality in southeastern Dagestan, U.S.S.R.] **:** KUBA

ka·bob *also* **ka·bab** *or* **ke·bab** *or* **ke·bob** *or* **ca·bob** \'kä,bäb, kə'bäb; *when "shish" precedes*, kə,bäb\ *n* -s [Per, Hindi, Ar, & Turk; Per & Hindi *kabāb*, fr. Ar, fr. Turk *kebap*] **:** cubes of meat (as lamb) marinated and cooked with onions, tomatoes, or other vegetables esp. on a skewer — usu. used in pl.

kaboodle *var of* CABOODLE

ka·bui \kə'büē\ *n, pl* **kabui** *or* **kabuis** *cap* **1 :** a Naga people of the Naga hills on the Burma-Assam frontier west and northwest of Manipur valley **2 :** a member of the Kabui people

kab·u·kal·li \,kabə'kalē\ *n* -s [native name in British Guiana] **:** CUPIUBA

ka·bu·ki \kə¦büke, -'büke, *Jap approximately* 'käbü(,)kē\ *n, usu cap* [Jap, lit., art of singing and dancing] **:** traditional Japanese popular drama with singing and dancing performed in a highly stylized manner

ka·bul \'käbəl, -,bül, -,bůl; kə'bül, ka'-, -'bůl\ *adj, usu cap* [fr. *Kabul*, city in eastern Afghanistan, capital of Afghanistan] **:** of or from Kabul, the capital of Afghanistan **:** of the kind or style prevalent in Kabul

¹ka·bu·li \'käbə(,)lē; kə'bülē, -'bůlē\ *adj, usu cap* [Per *kābulī*, fr. *Kābul* Kabul] **:** of or belonging to Kabul, Afghanistan

²kabuli \"\ *n* -s *cap* **:** a native or resident of Kabul

ka·bu·ri \kə'bürē\ *n* -s [origin unknown] **:** a land crab (*Ucides cordatus*) common in mangrove swamps from the West Indies to southern Brazil

ka·byle *also* **ka·byl** \kə'bīl(ə)l, -bē(ə)l\ *n* -s *usu cap* [Ar *qabā'il*, pl. of *qabīlah* tribe] **1 :** a Berber belonging to a Muslim agricultural people of the mountainous coastal area east of Algiers including blond and brunet types and now speaking chiefly Arabic **2 :** the Berber language of the Kabyles

kacha *or* **kachcha** *var of* KUTCHA

ka·cha na·ga \¦kächə¦nägə\ *n, pl* **kacha nagas** *usu cap K&N* **1 :** a group of three allied Naga peoples including the Kabui, the Lyeng, and the Zemi and inhabiting the Naga hills near Manipur **2 :** a member of a Kacha Naga people

kachari *usu cap, var of* CACHARI

kache *usu cap, var of* KHA

kach·e·mak bay \¦kachə,mak¦bā\ *adj, usu cap K&B* [*Kachemak Bay*, locality south of Anchorage, south central Alaska, where remains of the culture were discovered] **:** of or relating to a Pacific Eskimo and Aleutian culture of about A.D.100–1700 characterized by sealing and by the development of southwest Alaskan types of artifacts and the introduction of foreign traits

¹ka·chin \kə'chin\ *n, pl* **kachin** *or* **kachins** *usu cap* **1 :** CHINGPAW **2 :** the Tibeto-Burman language of the Chingpaw people

²kach·in \'kachən\ *n* -s [perh. alter. of *catechin*] **:** pyrocatechol used as a photographic developer

ka·chi·na *or* **ka·tci·na** *also* **ka·tchi·na** *or* **ca·chi·na** \kə'chēnə\ *n* -s [Hopi *qačina* supernatural] **1 :** one of the deified ancestral spirits believed among the Hopi and other Pueblo Indians to visit the pueblos at intervals (as to bring rain) **2 :** one of the elaborately masked impersonators of the kachinas that dance at agricultural ceremonies **3** *or* **kachina doll :** a doll representing a kachina made from cottonwood root and given to Hopi children by the kachina dancers

k acid *n, cap K* **:** a crystalline sulfonic acid $NH_2C_{10}H_4(OH)(SO_3H)_2$ isomeric with H acid that is used as a dye intermediate; 8-amino-1-naphthol-3,5-disulfonic acid

kackle *var of* KECKLE

ka·da·ga \kə'dägə\ *n, pl* **kadaga** *or* **kadagas** *usu cap* **:** COORG

ka·dai \'kä,dī\ *n* -s *usu cap* **:** a language family of southern China and northern Vietnam held to be related to Thai

ka·dam·ba \kə'dambə\ *n* -s [Skt, of Dravidian origin; akin to Tamil-Malayalam *kaṭampu*] **1 :** an East Indian shade tree (*Anthocephalus cadamba*) of the family Rubiaceae having hard yellowish wood and globose clusters of flowers **2 :** the wood of the kadamba

kadarite *usu cap, var of* QADARITE

ka·da·ya gum \kə'dīə-\ *n* [*kadaya* modif. of Hindi *karāyal* resin] **:** STERCULIA GUM

kad·dish \'kädish\ *n, pl* **kad·di·shim** \kä'dishəm, -(,)-shēm\ *often cap* [Aram *qaddīsh* holy] **1 :** an ancient Jewish prayer in Aramaic recited in several forms by the cantor in the daily ritual of the synagogue and adopted for use on various occasions; *specif* **:** a mourner's prayer recited daily at public services during the first 11 months after the death of a parent or other close relative and on subsequent anniversaries of the death **2 :** the person (as traditionally a son) who recites the mourner's kaddish for the deceased

kadet *var of* ²CADET

kadi *also* **kadhi** *var of* QADI

kadiak bear *usu cap K, var of* KODIAK BEAR

ka·dir *also* **kha·dar** *or* **kha·dir** \'kädə(r)\ *n, pl* **kadir** *or* **kadirs** *usu cap* **:** a primitive jungle-dwelling people somewhat negroid in appearance who are remnants of the pre-Dravidian peoples of India and inhabit the Deccan plateau

ka·do·ha·da·cho \ka,dōhədə'chō\ *n, pl* **kadohadacho** *or* **kadohadachos** *usu cap* [Caddo *Kädohädächo*, lit., real chiefs] **1 :** a Caddoan confederacy of northeastern Texas and southwestern Arkansas including the Cahinnio, Kadohadacho proper, and Upper Natchitoches **2 :** a member of any one of the peoples of the Kadohadacho confederacy

kad·su·ra \'kädsərə, 'käts-\ *n* -s [modif. of Jap *katsura*] **:** KATSURA TREE

ka·du \'kä(,)dü\ *n, pl* **kadu** *or* **kadus** *usu cap* **1 a :** a people inhabiting chiefly the Katha district of Upper Burma east of Manipur, Assam **b :** a member of such people **2 :** the Tibeto-Burman language of the Kadu people

ka·dy *or* **ka·ty** *also* **ca·dy** \'kād¦ē, -ät¦, ¦i\ *or* **cad·dy** \'kad¦\ *n* -ES [perh. alter. of *caddie*; fr. its being worn by boys] **:** a man's hat (as a straw hat or derby)

kae \'kā\ *n* -s [ME (northern dial.) *ka*; akin to MD *ca* jackdaw, OHG *kāa, kā* — more at CHOUGH] *chiefly Scot* **:** JACKDAW

kae·ding petrel \'kādiŋ-\ *or* **kaeding's petrel** *n, usu cap K* [after Henry B. *Kaeding* †1913 Am. mining engineer] **:** a petrel (*Oceanodroma leucorhoa kaedingi*) of the coast and islands of Lower California that is closely related to the Leach's petrel but smaller and with a less forked tail

kaemp·fer·ol \'kempfə,rōl, -rōl\ *also* **kamp·fer·ol** \'kam-\ *n* -s [Engelbert *Kämpfer* †1716 Ger. physician + ISV *-ol*] **:** a yellow crystalline flavonol coloring matter $C_{15}H_{10}O_6$ found in the free form or in glycosidic combination in many plants

kaf *var of* KAPH

ka·fa *or* **kaf·fa** \'käfə, 'kafə\ *n, pl* **kafa** *or* **kaffa** *usu cap* **1 :** a native or inhabitant of the Kafa region in southwestern Ethiopia **2 :** the Cushitic language of the Kafa

kaf·er·i·ta \,kafə'rēdə\ *n* -s [blend of *kafir* and *feterita*] **:** a hybrid between kafir and feterita

kaf·fa \'käfə, 'kafə\ *n* -s *often cap* [*Kaffa, Kafa*, region and former province in southwestern Ethiopia] **:** a grayish reddish brown that is yellower and lighter than liver and redder and stronger than average taupe brown

kaf·fee·klatsch \'käfā,kläch, -fē,-, -lach\ *n* -ES *often cap* [G, fr. *Kaffee* coffee + *Klatsch* gossip] **:** COFFEE KLATCH

kaf·fir *or* **kaf·ir** \'kafə(r)\ *n* [Ar *kāfir* infidel] **1** *also* **caf·fer** *or* **caf·fre** \"\ *n, pl* **kaffir** *or* **kaffirs** *or* **kafir** *or* **kafirs a** *usu cap* **:** a member of a group of southern African Bantu-speaking peoples of Ngoni stock **b** *sometimes cap* **:** a South African of negroid ancestry — usu. used disparagingly **2** *also* **caffer** *or* **caffre** -s *sometimes cap* **:** one who is not a Muslim — usu. used disparagingly **3** -s *usu cap* **:** XHOSA — often used disparagingly **4** -s *usu cap* **:** a South African stock (as a land or mining share) traded on the London stock exchange — usu. used in pl. **5** *usu kafir or* **kafir corn** -s *sometimes cap K* **:** any of various grain sorghums that have stout short-jointed somewhat juicy stalks and erect heads

kaffir bean *n, usu cap K, Africa* **:** COWPEA

kaffir beer *n, usu cap K* **:** a beer prepared by the native population of southern Africa from grain

kaffir boom \-,bōm, -,büm\ *n, often cap K* [part trans. of Afrik *kafferboom*, fr. *Kaffer* Kaffir + *boom* tree, fr. D, fr. MD; akin to OE *bēam* tree — more at BEAM] *Africa* **:** CORAL TREE; *esp* **:** a coral tree (*Erythrina caffra*) with scarlet flowers and light soft wood sometimes used for fence posts or shingles

kaffir bread *n, usu cap K* **1 :** the farinaceous pith of the fruit of a plant of the genus *Encephalartos* (esp. *E. caffer*) used as food in southern Africa **2 :** a plant that bears Kaffir bread

kaffir cat *also* **caffer cat** *or* **caffre cat** *n, usu cap K or 1st C* **:** a widely distributed wildcat (*Felis ocreata*, syn. *F. caffra*) of Africa and Asia Minor that has a tawny striped coat and is regarded as one of the chief ancestors of domesticated cats

kaffir crane *n, usu cap K* **:** a slaty gray crane (*Balearica regulorum*) of southern Africa that has a crown of velvety black plumes

kaffir lily *n, usu cap K* **1 :** CRIMSON FLAG **2 :** a plant of the genus *Clivia*; *esp* **:** a plant (*C. miniata*) of southern Africa cultivated for its showy flowers

kaffir orange *n, usu cap K* **1 :** an East African tree (*Strychnos spinosa*) having rough bark, grayish green foliage, and dark green round aromatic fruit with hard rind and soft pulp **2 :** the fruit of the Kaffir orange

kaffir piano *n, usu cap K* **:** a marimba of southern Africa

kaffir plum *or* **kaffir date** *n, usu cap K* **1 :** an African tree (*Harpephyllum caffrum*) of the family Anacardiaceae **2 :** the edible fruit of Kaffir plum

kaf·fi·yeh *also* **kef·fi·yeh** \kə'fē(y)ə\ *n* -s [Ar *kūfīyah, kaffīyah* — more at CAFFA] **:** an Arab headdress consisting of a square of cloth folded to form a triangle and bound on the head with an agal

kaf·frar·i·an *also* **caf·frar·i·an** \ka'fra(a)rēən, kə'-\ *adj, usu cap* [*Kaffraria*, region of Cape Province, Union of South Africa + E *-an*] **:** of, relating to, or being the biogeographic province or subregion that includes the Union of South Africa and adjacent areas

kaf·ir \'kafə(r)\ *n, pl* **kafir** *or* **kafirs** *usu cap* [Ar *kāfir* infidel] **1 :** a people of the Hindu Kush in northeastern Afghanistan **2 :** a member of the Kafir people

kafi·ri \'kafərē, kə'firē\ *n* -s *usu cap* **:** the Dard language of the Kafir people

kaftan *var of* CAFTAN

ka·fu·an \kə'füən\ *adj, usu cap* [*Kafu* River, Uganda + E *-an*] **:** of, relating to, or being a Lower Pleistocene culture of Uganda typified by crudely chipped pebble tools

kagaba *usu cap, var of* CÁGABA

ka·go \'kä(,)gō\ *n* -s [Jap] **:** an open palanquin used in Japan

ka·go·shi·ma \¦kägə¦shēmə\ *adj, usu cap* [fr. *Kagoshima*, city on the south coast of Kyushu, Japan] **:** of or from the city of Kagoshima, Japan **:** of the kind or style prevalent in Kagoshima

ka·gu \'kä(,)gü\ *n* -s [native name in New Caledonia] **:** a crested flightless gruiform bird (*Rhynochetos jubatus*) confined to New Caledonia that is slaty gray with orange-red bill and feet and concealed bars of black, white, and rufous on the wings

ka·gu·ra \'kägə(,)rä\ *n* -s [Jap] **:** a stately dance of the Shinto religion that now forms a part of Japanese village festivals

ka·ha \'kä(,)hä, ='=\ *or* **kah·au** \-,haů, ='=\ *n* -s [native name in Borneo; fr. its cry] **:** PROBOSCIS MONKEY

ka·hal \'kä,häl\ *n* -s [Heb *qāhāl* community, gathering] **:** the local governing body of a former European Jewish community administering religious, legal, and communal affairs

ka·ha·la \kə'hälə\ *n* -s [Hawaiian] **:** an amberfish (*Seriola dumerili*) of Hawaiian waters

ka·har \kə'här\ *n* -s [Hindi *kahār*] **:** one of a Hindu caste whose caste occupation is that of a carrier

ka·ha·wai \'kähə,wī\ *n* -s [Maori] **:** AUSTRALIAN SALMON

ka·hi·ka·tea \'kīkə,tēə, 'kak-\ *n* -s [Maori] **:** a New Zealand evergreen tree (*Podocarpus dacrydioides*) valued for its light soft easily worked wood, its resin, and the sweet edible aril surrounding its seed — called also *white pine*

ka·hi·li \kə'hēlē\ *n* -s [Hawaiian] **:** a long pole decorated at one end with a cluster of feather plumes and used as a ceremonial emblem in Hawaii

kahili ginger *n, Hawaii* **:** a butterfly lily (*Hedychium gardnerianum*) that is native to northern India and is cultivated for its long spikes of lemon yellow flowers with bright red stamens

kahn test \'kän-\ *or* **kahn reaction** *or* **kahn** *n* -s *usu cap K* [after Reuben L. *Kahn* b1887 Am. bacteriologist] **:** a serum-precipitation reaction for the diagnosis of syphilis

ka·hu \'kä(,)hü\ *n* -s [Maori] **:** a common harrier (*Circus approximans*) represented by several distinct races in Australia and the East Indies

ka·hu·na \kə'hünə\ *n* -s [Hawaiian] **1** *Hawaii* **:** a native master of a craft or vocation **2** *Hawaii* **:** a native medicine man **:** a master of Hawaiian religious lore and ceremonial

kahuna ana·ana \ə'nä,nä\ *n, pl* **kahuna anaana** [Hawaiian, fr. *kahuna* + *'anā'anā* black magic] *Hawaii* **:** SORCERER; *esp* **:** one who prays his victims to death

kahuna la·pa·au \-lə'pä,aů\ *n, pl* **kahuna lapaau** [Hawaiian, fr. *kahuna* + *lapa'au* medicinal] *Hawaii* **:** a medical practitioner esp. skilled in herbal medicine

kai \'kī\ *n, pl* **kai** *or* **kais** *usu cap* **1 a :** a people on the Huon gulf, Territory of New Guinea **b :** a member of such people **2 :** the Melanesian language of the Kai people **3 :** KÄTE

kaibal *usu cap, var of* KOIBAL

kai·bar·tha *or* **kai·bart·ta** \kī'bərd·ə, -'bär-\ *n* -s *usu cap* [Beng *kaibartta*, fr. Skt *kaivarta* fisherman] **:** a member of a low caste of Mongoloid origin that is numerous in Assam and Bengal

kaid \'kīd, 'kä,ēd\ *n* -s [Ar *qā'id* leader, commander in chief, fr. *qād* to command] **:** a tribal chief or governor of a district or group of villages in northern Africa

kai·feng \'kī¦fəŋ\ *adj, usu cap* [fr. *Kaifeng*, city in east central China] **:** of or from the city of Kaifeng, China **:** of the kind or style prevalent in Kaifeng

¹kai-kai \'kī,kī\ *n, pl* **kai-kai** [Marquesan; akin to Hawaiian & Samoan *'ai* food, Maori & Tongan *kai*] **1** *or* **kai** *Austral* **:** FOOD **2** *Austral* **:** FEASTING

²kai-kai \"\ *or* **kai** *vt* -ED/-ING/-s *Austral* **:** EAT

kai·ka·ra \kī'kärə\ *n* -s [modif. of Ar *karākīy*, pl. of *kurkīy* demoiselle] **:** DEMOISELLE 2a

kai·ka·wa·ka \'kīkə,wäkə\ *n* -s [Maori] **:** either of two New Zealand evergreen trees of the genus *Libocedrus*: **a :** KAWAKA **b :** MOUNTAIN PINE 3b

kail *var of* KALE

kails \'kālz\ *n pl* [ME *kayles*; akin to MD *kegel* cone, ninepin, OHG *kegil* stake, peg, ON *kaggi* keg — more at KEG] **1** *dial Brit* **:** a set of bone or wooden pins used in playing ninepins **2** *usu sing in constr, dial Brit* **:** a game played with kails

¹kail·yard \'kā(ə)l,=\ *n* [Sc, fr. *kale, kail* + E *yard* — more at KALE] *Scot* **:** KITCHEN GARDEN

²kailyard \"\ *adj, often cap, of a school of writers* **:** characterized by sentimental description of Scottish life and considerable use of Scots dialect ⟨such various aspects of Scottish life as whiskey, deerstalking, salmon fishing, the *Kailyard* school of writers —Janet Adams Smith⟩

kail·yard·er \-də(r)\ *n* -s *often cap* **:** a writer of the kailyard school

kaim \'kām\ *chiefly Scot var of* COMB

kai·ma·kam *also* **qai·ma·qam** *or* **qaim·ma·qam** \¦kīmə¦käm\ *n* -s [Turk *kaymakam*, fr. Ar *qā'im maqām* deputy, fr. *qā'im* standing + *maqām* place] **:** a lieutenant or deputy in the service of the Ottoman Empire

kai·mi clover \'kīmē-\ *n* [origin unknown] **:** a West Indian tick trefoil (*Desmodium canum*) used as a pasture plant esp. in the humid tropics

¹kain *var of* ²CAIN

²kain \'kīn\ *n* -s [Malay] **:** SARONG

kai·nah \'kīnə\ *n, pl* **kainah** *or* **kainahs** *usu cap* [Blackfoot *ah-kai-nah*, lit., many chiefs] **:** BLOOD 9

kainga \'kīŋə\ *n* -s [Maori] **:** a Maori village usu. located on low ground — compare PA

kaingang *cap, var of* CAINGANG

¹ka·ing·in *also* **ca·ing·in** *or* **ca·iñg·in** \kä'ēŋən\ *n* -s [Tag *kaingin*] *Philippines* **:** SWIDDEN ⟨some lonely farmer hewing out a ~ in the jungle —Wallace Stegner⟩

²kaingin \"\ *adj, Philippines* **:** employing a technique of clearing land by slashing and burning underbrush and trees and plowing the ashes under for fertilizer ⟨well-known ~ system which has been enormously destructive of valuable timber —A.L.Kroeber⟩

kai·nite \'kī,nīt, 'kā,-\ *also* **kai·nit** \kī'nēt\ *n* -s [G *kainit*, fr. Gk *kainos* new, recent + G *-it* -ite — more at RECENT] **:** a natural salt $KMg(SO_4)Cl.3H_2O$ consisting of a hydrous sulfate and chloride of magnesium and potassium that occurs impure in irregular granular masses, whose color as determined by purity is white, gray, pink, violet, or black, and that is used as a fertilizer and as a source of potassium and magnesium compounds

kai·nos·ite \'kīnə,sīt, 'kän-\ *n* -s [Sw *kainosit*, fr. Gk *kainos* + Sw *-it* -ite] **:** a mineral $Ca_2(Ce,Y)_2(SiO_4)_3CO_3.H_2O$ consisting of hydrous silicate and carbonate of calcium, cerium, and yttrium

kainozoic *var of* CENOZOIC

kai·ros \(')kī¦räs\ *n, pl* **kai·roi** \-rōi\ [Gk, fitness, opportunity, time; perh. akin to Gk *keirein* to cut — more at SHEAR] **:** a time when conditions are right for the accomplishment of a crucial action **:** the opportune and decisive moment

kais *pl of* KAI

kai·ser \'kīzə(r)\ *n* -s [ME *keiser*, fr. ON *keisari*; akin to OE *cāsere* emperor, OHG *keisur*, Goth *kaisar*; all fr. a prehistoric Gmc word borrowed fr. L *Caesar*, cognomen of Gaius Julius *Caesar* †44 B.C. Roman general and statesman] **:** EMPEROR: as **a :** the head of an ancient or medieval empire (as the Roman Empire or the Holy Roman Empire) **b** [G, fr. OHG *keisur*] **:** the sovereign of Austria from 1804 to 1918 ⟨all the countries over which the Hapsburg ~s claimed personal lordship —*Century Mag.*⟩ **c** [G, fr. OHG *keisur*] **:** the ruler of Germany from 1871 to 1918 ⟨the appointment of the chancellor of the German Empire by the ~⟩

kaiser brown *n, often cap K* **:** GINGER 5

kai·ser·dom \-dəm\ *n* -s [prob. trans. of G *kaisertum*] **1 :** the office or authority of a kaiser ⟨opposition to ~ among many American groups⟩ **2 :** the territory ruled by a kaiser ⟨the most efficient economists of ~ —*N.Y.Times Mag.*⟩

kai·se·rin \'kīzərən\ *n* -s [G, fem. of *kaiser*] **:** the wife of a kaiser

kai·ser·ism \-,rizəm\ *n* -s *often cap* **:** a political system and practices existing under or symbolized by the rule of the German kaiser ⟨that *Kaiserism* must be repudiated in favor of some new and more liberal political system —F.A.Ogg & Harold Zink⟩ ⟨the . . . absolute political dogmas with which *Kaiserism* is associated —*New Republic*⟩

kai·ser·ship \-zə(r),ship\ *n* **:** the office of kaiser

kai·ta·ka \kī'täkə\ *n* -s [Maori] **:** a mat of fine flax worn as a cloak by the Maoris

kai·thi \'kīd·ē\ *n* -s *usu cap* [Hindi *kaithī, kāyathī* used by the Kayasths, fr. *kāyath* Kayasth, fr. Skt *kāyastha*] **:** an alphabet of Nagari type that is used in writing Bihari and eastern Hindi

kai·val·ya \kī'vəlyə\ *n* -s [Skt, fr. *kevala* exclusively one's own, alone, whole — more at CELIBATE] **:** the final state of Jain and Vedantic salvation characterized as absolute release of one's jiva from all entanglements with ajiva **:** self-directed liberation

kajak *var of* KAYAK

ka·jar \kə'jär, 'kä,j-\ *n, pl* **kajar** *or* **kajars** *usu cap* [Per *Qājār*, of Turk origin] **1 :** a people of northern Iran holding political supremacy through the dynasty ruling Persia from 1794 to 1925 **2 :** a member of the Kajar people

ka·ja·wah \kə'jäwə\ *also* **ke·dja·ve** \-ävə\ *n* -s [Hindi *kajāwa*, fr. Per] **:** a pannier used in pairs on camels and mules esp. in India

ka·ka \'käkə\ *n* -s [Maori] **:** an olive brown New Zealand parrot (*Nestor meridionalis*) that is marked with gray on the crown and red on the face, neck, abdomen, rump, and underwing coverts and that talks and mimics well in captivity

kaka beak *or* **kaka bill** *n* **:** an evergreen glory pea (*Clianthus puniceus*) that is a climbing shrub sometimes exceeding 12 feet in height, has brilliant red flowers growing in pendulous axillary racemes and distinguished by the very long pointed keel, and is native to New Zealand but now rare except in cultivation

ka·kap je·ram \¦kä,käpjə¦räm\ *n* [Malay *kakap jĕram*] **:** a fishing boat of the Malayan east coast

ka·ka·po \'käkə,pō\ *n* -s [Maori] **:** a New Zealand parrot (*Strigops habroptilus*) with soft green and brown barred plumage that has well-developed wings but little power of flight, lives in holes or burrows in the ground, and has nocturnal habits — called also *owl parrot*

ka·kar *or* **ka·kur** \'käkə(r)\ *n* -s [Hindi *kakar*] **:** MUNTJAC 1

kak·a·ral·li *also* **kak·a·rali** *or* **kak·e·ral·li** \,kakə'ralē\ *n* -s [native name in British Guiana] **1** *in British Guiana* **:** SAPUCAIA **2** *in British Guiana* **:** MANBARKLAK

ka·ka·ri·ki \'käkə,rēkē\ *or* **ka·ka·wa·ri·ki** \'käkəwə,-\ *n* -s [Maori] **1 :** either of two green parakeets of New Zealand: **a :** one (*Cyanorhamphus novae-zelandiae*) having a red crown **b :** one (*Cyanorhamphus auriceps*) having a yellow crown **2 :** a small green New Zealand lizard of the genus *Lygosoma*

kak·a·toe \,kakə'tō(,)ē\ *n, cap* [NL, perh. modif. of D *kaketoe* cockatoo — more at COCKATOO] **:** a genus of moderately large to very large parrots that are widely distributed in the Australasian area, are usu. predominantly white, and include numerous widely known cockatoos (as the pink cockatoo and the sulphur-crested cockatoo)

ka·ka·wa·hie \,käkəwə'hē,ā\ *n* -s [Hawaiian] **:** a bright scarlet flower-pecker (*Loxops maculata flammea*) of Molokai Island

ka·ke·mo·no \,käkə'mō(,)nō, ,kak-, -mōnə\ *n* -s [Jap] **:** a picture or writing on silk or paper that is suitable for hanging and that usu. has a roller at its lower edge — compare MAKIMONO

[1]**ka·ki** \'kä(,)kē\ *n* -s [Jap] **:** JAPANESE PERSIMMON

[2]**ka·ki** \kä'kē\ *n* -s [Maori] **:** a blackish stilt of New Zealand that is usu. considered a color phase of the white-headed stilt but is sometimes assigned to a separate species (*Himantopus novae-zelandiae*)

kak·i·dro·sis \,kakə'drōsəs\ *n, pl* **kakidro·ses** \-ō,sēz\ [NL, fr. *kak-*, *cac-* cac- + *-idrosis*] **:** secretion of sweat of a disagreeable odor

ka·ki·emon \,käkē'(y)ā,män\ *n* -s *usu cap* [after Sakaida *Kakiemon fl* 1650 Jap. potter] **1 :** a Japanese porcelain made in Arita and much copied in Europe **2 :** porcelain decoration in the manner of Kakiemon painted usu. in iron red, blue green, light blue, violet, or grayish yellow

kak·is·toc·ra·cy \,kakə'stäkrəsē\ *n* -ES [Gk *kakistos* (superl. of *kakos* bad) + E *-cracy* — more at CACK] **:** government by the worst men

kak·kak \'ka,kak\ *n* -s [Chamorro] **:** a small bittern (*Ixobrychus sinensis*) of Guam

kako- — see CAC-

kak·o·gen·ic \¦kakə¦jenik\ *adj* [*cac-* + *-genic*] **:** DYSGENIC

ka·kor·tok·ite \kə'kȯ(r)d·ə,kīt\ *n* -s [*Kakortok* (Greenland Eskimo name for Julianehaab), Greenland + E *-ite*] **:** a rock of variable composition occurring in Greenland in black, white, and red sheets — see AGPAITE

ka·ku \'kä(,)kü\ *n* -s [Hawaiian] *Hawaii* **:** GREAT BARRACUDA

kal *abbr* [L *kalendae*] calends

ka·la azar \,kälə·ə'zär\ *n* [Hindi *kālā-āzār* black disease, fr. Hindi *kālā* black + Per *āzār* disease] **:** a severe infectious disease chiefly of eastern and southern Asia that is marked by fever, progressive anemia, leukopenia, and enlargement of the spleen and liver and is caused by a flagellate (*Leishmania donovani*) which is transmitted by the bite of sand flies (genus *Phlebotomus*) and which proliferates in reticuloendothelial cells — called also *visceral leishmaniasis*

ka·lam \kə'läm\ *n* -s [Ar *kalām* word, speech] **:** Muslim scholastic theology — compare MUTAKALLIMUN, SHARI'A

Kal·a·mein \'kalə,mīn\ *trademark* — used for sheet metal used esp. on wooden doors to prevent the passage of fire

ka·la·mian \¦käləm¦yän\ *n, pl* **kalamian** *or* **kalamians** *usu cap* [native name in northern Sulu Sea] **1 :** a Christianized people inhabiting the Calamian islands of the Philippines **2 :** a member of the Kalamian people

kalan·choe \,kalən'kōē, kə'laŋkə(,)wē\ *n* [NL] **1** *cap* **:** a genus of chiefly African and Australian tropical herbs or shrubs (family Crassulaceae) having a four-parted calyx and including numerous forms cultivated as ornamentals **2** -s **:** any plant of the genus *Kalanchoe*

ka·lan·tas *or* **ca·lan·tas** \¦kalən·¦täs\ *n* -ES [Tag *kalantas*] **:** PHILIPPINE CEDAR

kal·a·poo·ia *or* **kal·a·pu·ya** *also* **cal·a·poo·ya** *or* **cal·a·pu·ya** \,kalə'püyə\ *n, pl* **kalapooia** *or* **kalapooias** *or* **kalapuya** *or* **kalapuyas** *usu cap* **1 a :** an Indian people of the Willamette basin, Oregon **b :** a member of such people **2 a :** a language family of Oregon including Kalapooia and Yoncalla **b :** a language of the Kalapooia family formerly spoken in the Willamette basin, Oregon

kal·a·poo·ian *or* **kal·a·pu·yan** \¦==¦=yən\ *adj, usu cap* **:** of or relating to the Kalapooia or their language

ka·la·sie \¦kälə¦sē\ *n* -s [Dayak (Ngadju dial.) *kalasi*] **:** a long-tailed monkey of Borneo (*Pygathrix rubicunda*) that has a tuft of long hair on the head

kale *or* **kail** \'kāl, *esp before pause or consonant* -āəl\ *n* -s [Sc, fr. ME (northern dial.) *cal*, *cale*, fr. OE *cāl* — more at COLE] **1 a :** COLE 1 **b :** a very hardy cabbage (*Brassica oleracea acephala*) that has curled often finely cut leaves which do not form a dense head and that is considered by some to be the original form of the cultivated cabbage **c** *Scot* **:** a plant of the family Cruciferae **2** *Scot* **:** BROTH, SOUP; *esp* **:** soup made with kale **3** *chiefly Scot* **a :** FOOD **b :** MEAL **4** *slang* **:** MONEY ⟨a ritzy neighborhood where everybody had the ~ —J.T.Farrell⟩

kaleege *or* **kaleej** *var of* KALIJ

[1]**ka·lei·do·scope** \kə'līdə,skōp *sometimes* -lēd-\ *n* [Gk *kalos* beautiful + *eidos* form + E *-scope* — more at CALLI-, IDOL] **1 :** an instrument that contains loose fragments of colored glass confined between two flat plates and two plane mirrors placed at an angle of 60° so that changes of position exhibit its contents in an endless variety of symmetrical varicolored forms **2 :** something resembling a kaleidoscope: as **a :** a variegated changing pattern or scene ⟨the lake a ~ of changing colors —Robert Gibbings⟩ **b :** a succession of changing phases or actions ⟨reduce all experience to a shifting ~ of meaningless incidents —John Dewey⟩ ⟨her day . . . became a ~ of things embarked upon and left for other things —Adrian Bell⟩

[2]**kaleidoscope** \"\ *vb* -ED/-ING/-S *vi* **:** to appear as if in a kaleidoscope ⟨pictures of the lights and the planes spinning and crashing . . . *kaleidoscoped* through his mind —Howard Hunt⟩ ~ *vt* **:** to view as if in a kaleidoscope ⟨poking . . . fun at our banalities and shortsightednesses as he ~*s* them with the long view of man's cultural achievement —Henry Hewes⟩

ka·lei·do·scop·ic \=¦==¦skäpik, -pēk\ *also* **ka·lei·do·scop·i·cal** \-pəkəl, -pēk-\ *adj* **1 :** of, relating to, or formed by a kaleidoscope ⟨gazed raptly at the ~ patterns within the instrument⟩ **2 :** having changing tints or variegated color ⟨~ color of the clouds at sunset⟩ **3 a :** constantly changing **:** rapidly shifting ⟨air was fretted with a ~ network of swifts . . . with swallows, martins, and if late enough, nighthawks —William Beebe⟩ ⟨a year of ~ change, of breathtaking developments crowding so rapidly one upon the other —Allan Taylor⟩ **b :** having infinite variety **:** possessing many facets ⟨such a being of ~ versatility . . . we call contemptuously a jack-of-all-trades —Havelock Ellis⟩ ⟨shocking inhumanity of the slave trade has been compressed within the pages of this ~ novel with romance and sea adventure —*N.Y. Herald Tribune*⟩ — **ka·lei·do·scop·i·cal·ly** \-pək(ə)lē, -pēk-, -li\ *adv*

ka·le·ma \kə'lāmə\ *n* -s [Pg] **:** a violent surf that occurs on the coast of the Guinea region, West Africa

kalendar *var of* CALENDAR — used esp. of ecclesiastical calendars ⟨the Episcopal ~⟩

kalends *var of* CALENDS

kale runt *or* **kale stock** *n* **:** the stem of kale

kaleyard \'=,=\ *chiefly Scot var of* KAILYARD

kal·gan \(')kal¦gan, (')käl¦gän\ *adj, usu cap* [fr. *Kalgan*, city in northern China] **:** of or from the city of Kalgan, China **:** of the kind or style prevalent in Kalgan

kalian *var of* CALEAN

kal·i·bo·rite \,kalə'bōr,īt\ *n* -s [G *kaliborit*, fr. *kali-* (fr. NL *kalium*) + *bor-* + *-it* -ite] **:** a mineral $KMg_2B_{11}O_{19}.9H_2O$ consisting of a hydrous borate of potassium and magnesium

ka·lic·i·nite \kə'lis^ən,īt\ *n* -s [G *kalicinit*, fr. F *kalicine* kalicinite (irreg. fr. NL *kalium* + F *-ine*) + G *-it* -ite] **:** a mineral $KHCO_3$ consisting of an acid carbonate or bicarbonate of potassium

ka·lig·e·nous \kə'lijənəs, (')ka¦l-\ *adj* [ISV *kali* alkali (fr. NL) + *-genous*] **:** forming alkalies — used of the alkali metals

kalij *or* **kaleege** *also* **kaleej** *or* **kal·lege** \'kalij, 'käl-,'kal-, -(,)lēj\ *n, pl* **kalij·es** *or* **kaleeg·es** *also* **kaleej·es** *or* **kalleg·es** [Nepali & Pahari *kālij*] **:** any of several related crested Indian pheasants (genus *Lophura* or *Gennaeus*) that are related to the Chinese silver pheasant

ka·li·na \kə'lēnə\ *n, pl* **kalina** *or* **kalinas** *usu cap* [Carib *calina* Caribs, strong men — more at CANNIBAL] **:** GALIBI

ka·lin·ga *also* **ka·ling·ga** \kə'liŋgə\ *n, pl* **kalinga** *or* **kalingas** *usu cap* [native name in northern Luzon] **1 a :** any of several peoples inhabiting northern Luzon, Philippines **b :** a member of such people **2 :** the Austronesian language of the Kalinga people

ka·li·nin \kə'lēnən, kəl'yēnyən\ *adj, usu cap* [fr. *Kalinin*, city in the west central part of European Russia, U.S.S.R.] **:** of or from the city of Kalinin, U.S.S.R. **:** of the kind or style prevalent in Kalinin

ka·li·nin·grad \-,grad\ *adj, usu cap* [fr. *Kaliningrad*, city in the western part of European Russia, U.S.S.R.] **:** of or from the city of Kaliningrad, U.S.S.R. **:** of the kind or style prevalent in Kaliningrad

kali·nite \'kalə,nīt, 'kāl-\ *n* -s [*kali-* (fr. NL *kalium*) + connective *-n-* + *-ite*] **:** a mineral $KAl(SO_4)_2.11H_2O$ consisting of a fibrous and birefringent hydrous sulfate of potassium and aluminum that is distinct from alum in crystallization and water content

kali·oph·i·lite \,kalē'äfə,līt, ,kāl-\ *n* -s [G *kaliophilit*, fr. *kalio-* (fr. NL *kalium*) + *-phil* -phile + *-it* -ite] **:** a colorless mineral $KAlSiO_4$ of volcanic origin consisting of potassium aluminum silicate that occurs in acicular crystals or fine threads (hardness 6, sp. gr. 2.5–2.6)

kal·i·spel \¦kalə¦spel\ *n, pl* **kalispel** *or* **kalispels** *usu cap* [Kalispel, lit., camas] **1 a :** a Salishan people of northern Idaho and northwestern Montana **b :** a member of such people **2 :** a language of the Kalispel and Spokan peoples — called also *Pend d'Oreille*

ka·li·um \'kālēəm\ *n* -s [NL, fr. *kali* alkali, potassium (fr. Ar *qily* saltwort) + *-ium*] **:** POTASSIUM — symbol *K*

ka·li yu·ga \,kəlē'yügə\ *n, usu cap K&Y* [Skt *kaliyuga*, fr. *kali* ace on a die + *yuga* yoke, age of the world; fr. the fact that the ace is the unluckiest throw in dice games — more at YOKE] **:** the depraved fourth and final age of a Hindu world cycle **:** dark age

kalka *usu cap, var of* KHALKHA

kal·kow·skite \kal'kȯf,skīt\ *n* -s [G *kalkowskyn* (irreg. fr. E. L. *Kalkowsky* †1938 Ger. mineralogist + G *-in* -ine) + E *-ite*] **:** a mineral $Fe_2Ti_3O_9$(?) consisting of an oxide of iron and titanium and usu. containing small amounts of rare-earth elements, niobium, and tantalum

kalk·vis \'kälk,fis\ *n* -ES [Afrik, fr. *kalk* lime (fr. D, fr. MD *calc*) + *vis* fish, fr. D, fr. MD *visch;* akin to OHG *kalk* lime and to OHG *fisc* fish — more at CHALK, FISH] **:** a cutlass fish (*Lepidopus caudatus*) of southern Africa

kal·li·kak \'kalə,kak\ *n* -s *usu cap* [*Kallikak*, fictitious name of a family having one branch consisting mainly of intelligent and successful persons and another branch containing a large proportion of mentally deficient and immoral persons that was studied by H. H. Goddard †1957 Am. psychologist, fr. Gk *kalli-* calli- + *kak-* cac-] **:** a stupid person ⟨rubber masks by means of which an ordinary citizen can transform himself into demon, witch . . . *Kallikak*, bumpkin —Bernard Wolfe⟩ — compare JUKES

kal·li·ma \'kaləmə\ *n, cap* [NL, prob. irreg. fr. Gk *kallimos* beautiful, fr. *kallos* beauty — more at CALLI-] **:** a genus of highly mimetic nymphalid butterflies of southern Asia and the Pacific islands that are often brilliantly colored above but when at rest with wings folded resemble dead leaves in color and markings

kal·li·type \'kalə,tīp\ *n* [ISV *kalli-* (fr. Gk *kalli-* calli-) + *type*] **:** a contact printing-out photographic process that uses paper sensitized with a ferric salt and silver nitrate and a developer containing borax and Rochelle salt

kal·mia \'kalmēə\ *n* [NL, fr. Peter *Kalm* †1779 Swed. botanist + NL *-ia*] **1** *cap* **:** a genus of No. American evergreen shrubs (family Ericaceae) with oblong to linear leaves and showy flowers that are borne in clusters in the axils of leaves or bracts and have a saucer-shaped basally 10-saccate corolla with an anther resting in each sac — see MOUNTAIN LAUREL, SHEEP LAUREL **2** -s **:** any plant of the genus *Kalmia*

kal·muck *or* **kal·muk** \'kal,mək, ='=\ *or* **kal·myk** \'kal(,)mik, ='=\ *also* **cal·muck** \'kal,mək, ='=\ *n* -s *usu cap* [Russ *Kalmyk*, fr. Kazan Tatar] **1 :** a member of a Buddhist Mongol people orig. of Dzungaria — called also *Eleut* **2 :** the Mongolian language of the Kalmucks

ka·lo \'kä(,)lō\ *n* -s [Hawaiian] **:** TARO

ka·lon \kə'län, (')ka¦l-\ *n* -s [Gk, fr. neut. of *kalos* good, beautiful — more at CALLI-] **:** the ideal of physical and moral beauty esp. as conceived by the philosophers of classical Greece

ka·long \'ka,lȯŋ, 'kä,l-, kə'l-, -läŋ\ *n* -s [Jav] **:** a large fruit bat of the Malay archipelago

ka·lop·a·nax \kə'läpə,naks\ *n* -ES [NL, fr. *kalo-* (fr. Gk *kalos* beautiful) + Gk *panax* panacea, fr. *panakēs* all-healing — more at PANACEA] **:** a showy Japanese tree (*Kalopanax ricinifolium*) of the family Araliaceae that has foliage like that of the castor-oil plant

kal·o·ter·mes \,kalə'tər(,)mēz\ *n, cap* [NL, fr. *kalo-* (fr. Gk *kalos*) + *Termes*] **:** the type genus of Kalotermitidae comprising many termites that are destructive pests of living trees or of dry timber — see CRYPTOTERMES

[1]**kal·o·ter·mi·tid** *also* **cal·o·ter·mi·tid** \¦==¦=_məd·əd\ *adj* [NL *Kalotermitidae*] **:** of or relating to the Kalotermitidae

[2]**kalotermitid** *also* **calotermitid** \"\ *n* -s [NL *Kalotermitidae*] **:** a termite of the family Kalotermitidae

kal·o·ter·mit·i·dae \,==(,)tər'mid·ə,dē\ *n pl, cap* [NL, fr. *Kalotermit-*, *Kalotermes*, type genus + *-idae*] **:** a family of primitive termites occurring in most warm regions and including many serious destroyers of wood and growing trees — compare CRYPTOTERMES; see DRY-WOOD TERMITE

ka·lox·y·lon \kə'läksə,län, -_lən\ *n, cap* [NL, fr. *kalo-* (fr. Gk *kalos*) + *-xylon*] **:** a form genus of fossil plants based only on roots

kal·pa \'kəlpə\ *n* -s [Skt] **:** a duration of time in Hinduism covering a complete cosmic cycle from the origination to the destruction of a world system — compare YUGA

kalpak *var of* CALPAC

kal·pis \'kalpəs\ *n* -ES [Gk; akin to OIr *cilornn* jar] **:** a hydria having a rounded shoulder and a small back handle

kal·si·lite \'kalsə,līt *also* -lts-\ *n* -s [prob. fr. *k*alium + *al*uminum + *sil*icon + *-ite*] **:** a rare mineral $KAlSiO_4$ consisting of aluminosilicate of potassium

kalsomine *var of* CALCIMINE

ka·lua \kə'lüə\ *adj* [Hawaiian *kālua*, fr. *kālua* to bake in a ground oven] *Hawaii* **:** baked in an earth oven ⟨~ pig⟩

ka·lum·pang \¦käləm¦päŋ\ *n* -s [Tag *kalumpáng*] *Philippines* **:** a large tropical Old World tree (*Sterculia foetida*) having foul-smelling blossoms that are followed by red pods enclosing oil-rich and protein-rich seeds sometimes used as food and yielding light soft wood that is sometimes used for carving

ka·lum·pit *also* **ca·lum·pit** \-¦pēt\ *n* -s [Tag *kalumpít*] **:** a common Philippine tree (*Terminalia edulis*) that yields a soft wood and dark red fleshy fruits used for preserves

ka·lun·ti \kə'lüntē\ *n* -s [Taw-Sug] **:** a lauan (*Shorea kalunti*) with yellow wood

kal·war \(,)kəl'wȯ(ə)r\ *n* -s *usu cap* [Hindi *kalvār*, lit., liquor seller, fr. Skt *kalyapāla*, fr. *kalya* liquor + *pāla* guard, keeper] **:** a member of a Hindu caste engaging in trade

kalymma *var of* CALYMMA

kam *dial var of* [2]CAM

ka·ma \'kämə\ *n* -s [Skt *kāma* love, wish, desire — more at CHARITY] **1 :** enjoyment of the world of the senses constituting one of the ends of man in Hinduism **:** PLEASURE **2** *in Buddhism & Theosophy* **:** the human principle of desire — compare KAMARUPA

ka·ma·ai·na \,kämə'īnə\ *n* -s [Hawaiian, fr. *kama* person + *'āina* land] **:** a long-time resident of Hawaii

ka·ma·chi·le \,kämə'chilē\ *or* **ka·man·chi·le** \,kämən'-\ *var of* CAMACHILE

kam·a·cite \'kamə,sīt\ *n* -s [obs. G *kamacit* (now *kamazit*), fr. Gk *kamak-*, *kamax* vine pole, shaft + G *-it* -ite; akin to MHG *hamel* pole, Skt *śamyā* stick, staff] **:** a mineral consisting of a nickel-iron alloy forming with taenite the mass of most meteoric iron

ka·ma·hi \kə'mähē\ *n* -s [Maori] **:** a New Zealand tree (*Weinmannia racemosa*) of the family Cunoniaceae that yields timber and firewood — called also *towai*

ka·ma·la *also* **ka·me·la** *or* **ka·mi·la** \'kəmələ\ *n* -s [Skt *kamala*, prob. of Dravidian origin; akin to Kanarese *kōmaḷe*, *kōvaḷ*] **1 :** an East Indian tree (*Mallotus philippinensis*) **2 :** a reddish cathartic powder from the capsules of the kamala tree that contains rottlerin and is used as an orange dye for silk and wool and as a vermifuge chiefly in veterinary practice

ka·ma·ni \kə'mänē\ *n* -s [Hawaiian] **1 :** MALABAR ALMOND **2 :** MASTWOOD

kamansi *var of* CAMANSI

ka·mao \kə'mä,ō, -maù\ *n* -s [Hawaiian *kama'o*] **:** a bird (*Phaeornis obscura myadestina*) of the family Turdidae found on Kauai Island, Hawaii

ka·mar \kə'mär\ *n, pl* **kamar** *or* **kamars** *usu cap* **1 :** a people of central India now engaged in the practice of plow agriculture **2 :** a member of the Kamar people

ka·ma·res *or* **ka·ma·rais** \kə'mä,res, -_rəs\ *n, pl* **kamares** *or* **kamarais** *usu cap* [fr. *Kamares*, cave on the south slope of Mount Ida, Crete, where it was discovered] **:** a gaily colored Minoan pottery reaching its peak of excellence about 2000 B.C.

ka·mar·e·zite \kə'marə,zīt\ *n* -s [G *kamarezit*, fr. *Kamareza*, *Kamariza*, near Laurium, Greece + G *-it* -ite] **:** a mineral $Cu_3(SO_4)(OH)_4.6H_2O$(?) consisting of a hydrous basic copper sulfate

ka·ma·rin·ska·ia \kə'märənzkəyə, -mar-, -nsk-\ *n* -s [Russ] **:** a Russian folk dance that is characterized by acrobatic knee bends, leaps, and leg extensions

ka·ma·ru·pa \,kämə'rüpə\ *n* -s [Skt *kāmarūpa*, fr. *kāma* desire + *rūpa* form] *Theosophy* **:** the form assumed by the kama after a person's death — compare ASTRAL BODY — **ka·ma·ru·pic** \¦==¦=pik\ *adj*

[1]**kamas** *or* **kamass** *var of* CAMAS

[2]**kamas** *pl of* KAMA

ka·ma·sin \¦kämə¦sēn, ¦kam-, -sin\ *also* **ka·mass** \'käməs, 'kam-\ *or* **ka·mas·sian** \kə'mashən, -asēən\ *or* **ka·mas·sin** *like* KAMASIN\ *n, pl* **kamasin** *or* **kamasins** *usu cap* [*Kamasin, Kamass, Kamassin* fr. Russ *Kamasintsy* (pl.), fr. Kamasin *Kangmāžə; Kamassian* prob. fr. *Kamass* + *-ian*] **1 a :** a Samoyed people on the upper Yenisei river, Siberia, who are ethnically largely extinct or absorbed into the Russian culture by intermarriage **b :** a member of such people **2 :** the Uralic language of the Kamasin people

ka·mas·si \kə'mäsē\ *n* -s [Afrik *kamassie*, prob. modif. of Xhosa *kamamasane*] **1 :** a tree (*Gonioma kamassi*) of the family Apocynaceae of southern Africa **2 :** the hard yellow wood of the kamassi

kam·ba \'kämbə\ *n, pl* **kamba** *or* **kambas** *usu cap* **1 a :** a Bantu people of central Kenya **b :** a member of such people **2 :** a Bantu language of the Kamba people

kam·bal \'kəmbəl\ *n* -s [Hindi, fr. Skt *kambala*] **:** a coarse woolen blanket or shawl worn in India

kam·ba·la \kəm'bälə\ *n* -s [Burmese] **1 a :** an East Indian tree (*Sonneratia apetala*) with strong reddish wood **b :** the wood of the kambala **2 :** IROKO

kam·ba·ra earth \kəm'bärə-\ *n, usu cap K* [fr. *Kambara*, town in Japan] **:** JAPANESE ACID CLAY

kam·boh \'kəm(,)bō, 'käm-\ *n* -s [Per] **:** a member of a low caste in the Punjab engaged chiefly in agriculture

kam·cha·dal *also* **kam·cha·dale** \¦kämchə¦däl\ *or* **kamchadele** \-del, -dē(ə)l\ *n, pl* **kamchadal** *or* **kamchadals** *usu cap* [Russ *Kamchadal* Kamchatkan] **1 a :** a Paleo-Asiatic people of southern Kamchatka who are chiefly hunters and fishers **b :** a member of such people **2 :** a Luorawetlan language of the Kamchadal people

[1]**kam·chat·kan** \(')kam¦chatkən\ *adj, usu cap* [*Kamchatka*, peninsula in the northeastern U.S.S.R. + E *-an*, adj. suffix] **:** of or relating to the Kamchatka peninsula

[2]**kamchatkan** \"\ *n* -s *usu cap* [*Kamchatka* + E *-an*, n. suffix] **:** KAMCHADAL

kamchatkan sea eagle *n, usu cap K* **:** an eagle (*Haliaeetus pelagicus*) that has white shoulders, rump, and tail when adult, feeds largely on fish, and is found on the coasts of the western north Pacific — called also *Steller's sea eagle*

[1]**kame** \'kām\ *now dial var of* COMB

[2]**kame** \"\ *n* -s [Sc, kame, comb, fr. ME (northern dial.) *camb* comb, fr. OE *camb* — more at COMB] **:** a short ridge, hill, or mound of stratified drift deposited by glacial meltwater — compare ESKER

ka·meel \kə'mē(ə)l, -mā(-\ *n* -s [Afrik, fr. D, camel, fr. MD *cameel*, fr. L *camelus* — more at CAMEL] *Africa* **:** GIRAFFE

ka·meel·doorn \-,dōrn\ *also* **ka·meel·do·ring bush** \-,dōriŋ-\ *or* **ka·meel·thorn** \-,thȯrn\ *n, pl* **kameeldoorns** *also* **kameelthorns** [*kameeldoorn* fr. obs. Afrik *kameeldoorn* (now *kameeldoring*), fr. Afrik *kameel* + obs. Afrik *doorn* thorn, fr. D, fr. MD *dorn; kameeldoring bush* fr. Afrik *kameeldoring* + E *bush; kameelthorn* part trans. of Afrik *kameeldoring;* akin to OE *thorn* — more at THORN] *Africa* **:** any of several acacia trees; *esp* **:** a tall tree (*Acacia giraffae*) on which the giraffe often browses

ka·me·ha·me·ha day \kə,māə'mā(,)hä-\ *n, cap K&D* [after *Kamehameha* I †1819 king of Hawaii] **:** June 11 observed as a holiday in Hawaii in celebration of the anniversary of the birth of Kamehameha I

kamela *or* **kamila** *var of* KAMALA

ka·me·lau·ki·on \,kämə'laùk,yȯn, -aùkē,ȯn\ *n* -s [MGk *kamēlaukion*, alter. (prob. influenced by Gk *kamēlos* camel) of LGk *kamelaukion*] **:** a tall brimless hat worn by priests and monks in some Oriental rites

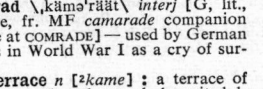

kamelaukions

ka·me·rad \,kämə'räät\ *interj* [G, lit., comrade, fr. MF *camarade* companion — more at COMRADE] — used by German soldiers in World War I as a cry of surrender

kame terrace *n* [[2]*kame*] **:** a terrace of stratified sand and gravel deposited by streams between a glacier and an adjacent valley wall

ka·mi \kä'mi\ *n, pl* **kami** [Jap, god] **:** a sacred power or force; *esp* **:** one of the Shinto deities including mythological beings, spirits of distinguished men, and forces of nature

ka·mia \'kämēə\ *n, pl* **kamia** *or* **kamias** *usu cap* [Kamia *Kamiyai, Kamiyahi*] **1 a :** an Indian people of southeastern California and northwestern Mexico **b :** a member of such people **2 :** a Yuman language of the Kamia people

ka·mias \kəm'yäs\ *n* -ES [Tag *kamyás*] *Philippines* **:** BILIMBI

ka·mik \'kämik\ *n* -s [Esk] **:** an Eskimo sealskin boat

[1]**ka·mi·ka·ze** \,kämə'käzē\ *n* -s [Jap, lit., divine wind, fr. *kami* god + *kaze* wind] **1** *often cap* **:** a member of a Japanese air attack corps assigned to make a suicidal crash on a target (as a ship) **2 :** an airplane containing explosives to be flown in a suicide crash on a target

[2]**kamikaze** \¦==¦==\ *adj, sometimes cap* **1 :** of, relating to, or resembling that of a kamikaze ⟨extending the ~ way of fighting to whole nations —Norbert Wiener⟩ **2 :** SUICIDAL ⟨the city's ~ taxi drivers⟩

kam·lei·ka \kam'līkə\ *also* **kam·e·lai·ka** \,kamə'l-\ *n* -s [Esk *kamleika*] **:** a waterproof pullover shirt made of dried animal intestines and worn in the Aleutians

kam·loops trout \ˈkam,lüps-\ *also* **kamloops** *n, usu cap K* [fr. *Kamloops,* city in Brit. Columbia] **:** a large black-spotted rainbow trout native chiefly to Lake Pend Oreille, Idaho, and widely introduced in western streams and lakes

käm·mer·er·ite \ˈkemərə,rīt\ *n* -s [Sw *kämmererit,* fr. A. A. *Kämmerer* 19th cent. scientist in St. Petersburg (Leningrad) + Sw *-it* -ite] **:** a reddish penninite

kampferol *var of* KAEMPFEROL

kam·pi·lan *or* **cam·pi·lan** \kämˈpē,län\ *n* -s [Tag *kampilan*] **:** a long straight-edged sheathed cutlass broadening toward the point that is used by the Moro peoples of Mindanao and Sulu

kam·pong *or* **cam·pong** \ˈkäm,pȯŋ, -päŋ, ⸗ˈ⸗\ *n* -s [Malay *kampong*] **:** a native hamlet or village in a Malay-speaking country

kamp·to·zoa \,kam(p)təˈzōə\ [NL, fr. *kampto-* (fr. Gk *kamptos* flexible) + NL *-zoa* — more at CAMPTO-] *syn of* ENTOPROCTA

ka·muk \kəˈmük\ *n, pl* **kamuk** *or* **kamuks** *usu cap* **:** a mountain people of northeast Thailand who practice primitive shifting agriculture and are related to the Kha of Vietnam

ka·mu·ning *or* **ca·mu·ning** \ˌkämüˌnēŋ\ *n* -s [Tag *kamuning*] **1 :** a tropical Asiatic tree (*Murraya exotica*) **2 :** the wood of the kamuning noted for its hardness

ka·na \ˈkänə\ *n, pl* **kana** *or* **kanas** *often attrib* [Jap] **1 a :** a Japanese system of syllabic writing dating from the 8th or 9th century A.D. and having characters that can be used exclusively for writing the language but are normally used only for foreign words, for grammatical inflections and function words not represented by kanji, or at the side of kanji to indicate pronunciation **b :** either of the two different but equivalent sets of characters that are used in the kana system and that each have 48 characters increased by the use of two diacritics to 73 — see HIRAGANA, KATAKANA **2 :** a single character belonging to the kana system of writing

kana-a \ˌkänəˌä\ *adj, usu cap* [origin unknown] **:** of or relating to a hard thin white to slate gray pottery of the Developmental Pueblo period that is either plain or decorated with black lines

kanaf *also* **kanaff** *var of* KENAF

ka·nai·ma \kəˈnīmə\ *n* -s [native name in British Guiana] **:** an evil spirit or a person possessed by an evil spirit believed by Indians of British Guiana and northwestern Brazil to be an avenger

ka·naka \kəˈnakə, -nakə; *in Hawaiian, sing & pl are both "kanaka" but sing is* ⸗ˈ⸗⸗ *& pl is* ˈ⸗⸗⸗\ *n* -s *often cap* [Hawaiian, person, human being] **:** POLYNESIAN, MICRONESIAN, MELANESIAN **:** SOUTH SEA ISLANDER

kana-majiri \ˌ⸗⸗ˈmäjərē\ *n* -s [Jap, fr. *kana* + *majiri* mixture] **:** the standard form of Japanese writing consisting of kanji supplemented by hiragana characters to indicate inflectional endings and function words and to show pronunciation esp. when that would otherwise be doubtful

ka·nam man \kəˈnam-\ *n, usu cap K* [fr. *Kanam,* locality on Lake Victoria, Kenya, where the type was discovered] **:** an extinct East African man known from a fragmentary fossil jaw and associated teeth found in early Pleistocene lake beds

kan·a·rese *also* **can·a·rese** \ˌkanəˌrēz, -ēs\ *n, pl* **kanarese** *also* **canarese** *usu cap* [*Kanara,* district in southwest India + E *-ese*] **1 a :** a Kannada-speaking people of Mysore, south India **b :** a member of such people **2 :** KANNADA **3 :** the script normally used to write Kannada

ka·na·ri *also* **ca·na·ri** \kəˈnärē\ *n* -s [Malay *kĕnari*] **:** JAVA ALMOND

ka·nau·ri \kəˈnau̇rē\ *or* **ka·na·wa·ri** \-näwərē\ *n* -s *usu cap* **:** a Tibeto-Burman language of Himachal Pradesh, India

ka·na·za·wa \kəˈnäzəwə\ *adj, usu cap* [fr. *Kanazawa,* city in western Honshu, Japan] **:** of or from the city of Kanazawa, Japan **:** of the kind or style prevalent in Kanazawa

kan·chil \ˈkänchəl\ *n* -s [Malay] **:** any of several small chevrotains of southeastern Asia formerly regarded as constituting several species but now usu. held to be varieties of one (*Tragulus kanchil*)

kan·de·lia \kanˈdēlēə, -lyə\ *n, cap* [NL, fr. Malayalam *kandel* tree of the genus *Kandelia* + NL *-ia*] **:** a genus of East Indian trees (family Rhizophoraceae) that are related to and resemble the common mangroves but have laciniate petals and 5-parted or 6-parted calyx

kandh *usu cap, var of* KHOND

¹kan·dy·an \ˈkandēən\ *adj, usu cap* [*Kandy,* town in central Ceylon, + E *-an,* adj. suffix] **1 :** of, relating to, or characteristic of Kandy, Ceylon **2 :** of, relating to, or characteristic of the people of Kandy

²kandyan \"\ *n* -s *usu cap* [*Kandy* + E *-an,* n. suffix] **:** a native or resident of Kandy, Ceylon

ka·neel·hart \kəˈnā(ə)l,härt\ *n* -s [prob. fr. D, fr. *kaneel* cinnamon (fr. MD *caneel, canele,* fr. MF *cannelle,* fr. ML *canella*) + D *hart* heart, fr. MD *herte, harte;* akin to OE *heorte* heart — more at CANELLA, HEART] **1 :** a tropical tree (*Licania cayennensis*) of Central and So. America **2 :** the very strong wood of kaneelhart

ka·nesh·ite \ˈkäni,shīt\ *n* -s *usu cap* [*Kanesh, Kanish,* ancient city of eastern Asia Minor + E *-ite*] **1 :** an inhabitant of ancient Kanesh in eastern Asia Minor **2** *or* **ka·nish·ite** \"\ **:** the principal dialect of Hittite — called also *Kanesian*

ka·ne·sian \kəˈnēzhən\ *or* **ka·ni·sian** \-nizh-\ *adj, usu cap* [irreg. fr. *Kanesh, Kanish* + E *-ian*] **:** of, relating to, or characteristic of the Kaneshites

kang *or* **k'ang** \ˈkäŋ\ *n* -s [Chin (Pek) *k'ang⁴*] **:** a brick platform built across one side or end of a room in a house in northern China or Manchuria, warmed by a fire beneath, and used for sleeping

kan·ga·ny *or* **kan·ga·ni** \kəŋˈgänē\ *n, pl* **kanganies** *or* **kanganis** [Tamil *kaṅkāṇi,* lit., one who sees with the eyes, fr. *kaṇ* eye + *kāṇ* to see] **:** an overseer of labor in Ceylon, India, and Malaya

¹kan·ga·roo \ˌkaŋgəˈrü, ˌkaiŋ-\ *n* -s [prob. native name in Queensland, Australia] **1 a :** any of various herbivorous leaping marsupial mammals (family Macropodidae) of Australia, New Guinea, and adjacent islands that have a small head, large ears, long powerful hind legs with the two larger hind toes armed with heavy nails, a long thick tail used as a support and in balancing, and rather small forelegs not used in progression — see MARSUPIALIA, WALLABY **b** (1) **:** the pelt or fur of the kangaroo (2) **:** leather made from the skin of the kangaroo resembling glazed kid in appearance **2** *Austral* **:** wild young cattle — usu. used in the pl. **3** *Brit* **:** AUSTRALIAN **4 :** KANGAROO CLOSURE ⟨the ~ saves parliamentary time —Derek Walker-Smith⟩

kangaroo

²kangaroo \"\ *adj* **:** of or relating to a kangaroo court ⟨these ~ qualities of justice that even of the courtroom . . . can make a jungle —Herbert Feinstein⟩

kangaroo acacia *or* **kangaroo thorn** *n* **:** a thorny Australian acacia (*Acacia armata*) often used for hedges

kangaroo apple *n* **1 :** an edible yellow egg-shaped fruit of Australia and New Zealand that has a mealy subacid pulp **2 :** a shrubby or herbaceous perennial plant (*Solanum aviculare*) that is sometimes cultivated in warm regions for its racemes of purple flowers and for the kangaroo apples that it bears

kangaroo bear *n* **:** KOALA

kangaroo beetle *n* **:** any of certain brilliantly colored Old World beetles with thick hind legs constituting the genus *Sagra* that is included in Chrysomelidae or made the type of a separate family

kangaroo closure *n* **:** the restriction of debate to those amendments judged by the presiding officer of a legislative body to be most appropriate ⟨the New Zealand House has not had to adopt . . . the *kangaroo closure* —Walter Nash⟩ — compare GUILLOTINE

kangaroo court *n* **1 :** a mock court in which the principles of law and justice are disregarded or perverted: **a :** one held by vagabonds or by prisoners in a jail or prison camp ⟨*kangaroo courts* . . . are vicious organizations controlled by the most perverted and brutal prisoners —J.V.B.Bennett⟩ ⟨non⸗Communist prisoners sentenced to death by Red *kangaroo courts* —*Army-Navy-Air Force Jour.*⟩ **b :** one involving comic procedures and ludicrous penalties designed for the amusement of the participants and spectators ⟨*kangaroo courts* — to which anyone not in Western garb can be hauled and fined —Helen Gould⟩ **2 :** a court or a similar body (as a legislative investigating committee) characterized by irresponsible, unauthorized, or irregular status or procedures ⟨in Czechoslovakia . . . *kangaroo courts* have been handing down stiff sentences for "labor sabotage" —C.L.Sulzberger⟩ ⟨two committee jobs which put him . . . in the position of conducting his own *kangaroo court* —*Atlantic*⟩

kangaroo dog *n* **:** an Australian breed of rough-haired dogs that resemble greyhounds and that are used for hunting kangaroos

kangaroo feathers *n pl, Austral* **:** NONSENSE

kangaroo grass *n* **:** any of several grasses of the genus *Themeda:* as **a :** a common perennial forage grass (*Themeda australis*) that is usu. held to occur from Australia across southern Asia and into eastern Africa and that is very closely related to and perhaps a variety of the African rooigras **b :** ULLA GRASS

kangaroo hare *n* **:** HARE WALLABY

kangaroo jerboa *n* **:** RAT KANGAROO

kangaroo mouse *n* **:** any of various small leaping rodents (as dwarf pocket rat, jumping mouse, or pocket mouse)

kangaroo paw *n* **:** an Australian sedgelike spring-flowering herb (*Anigozanthos manglesii*) of the family Amaryllidaceae having the clustered flowers covered with greenish wool except at their red bases — called also *kangaroo's-foot*

kangaroo rat *n* **1 :** RAT KANGAROO **2 :** any of numerous pouched nocturnal burrowing rodents (genus *Dipodomys*) of arid parts of the western U.S.

kangaroo's-foot \ˌ⸗⸗ˈ⸗,⸗\ *or* **kangaroo-foot plant** \ˌ⸗⸗ˈ⸗,⸗-\ *n, pl* **kangaroo's-foots :** KANGAROO PAW

kangaroo vine *or* **kangaroo grape** *n* **:** an Australian woody vine (*Cissus antarctica*) sometimes used as a houseplant

kan·ga·yam \ˌkaŋgəˌyäm\ *n* [*Kangayam,* cattle-breeding center in Madras state, southern India] **1** *usu cap* **:** an Indian breed of brown or gray cattle used chiefly for draft **2** -s *often cap* **:** an animal of the Kangayam breed

k'ang hsi \ˈkäŋˈshē\ *adj, usu cap K&H* [after *K'ang-hsi* †1722 Chin. emperor, second of the Ch'ing dynasty] **:** of, relating to, or having the characteristics of Chinese ceramic art or Chinese porcelain wares of the latter half of the 17th century or the first quarter of the 18th century

kang·li \ˈkäŋˈlē\ *also* **kang·la** \-lä\ *n* -s *usu cap* **:** one of the major divisions of the Great Horde

kan·gri \ˈkəŋ(,)grē\ *n* -s [Hindi *kāṅgṛī*] **:** a small portable earthenware-lined wicker basket used as a warming stove in Kashmir

kangs *pl of* KANG

k'angs *pl of* K'ANG

kan·ho·bal \ˌkänōˈbäl\ *n* -s *usu cap* **1 a :** an Indian people of western Guatemala **b :** a member of such people **2 :** a Mayan language of the Kanhobal people

ka·nin \ˈkänən\ *n* -s [Tag, fr. *kain* to eat] *Philippines* **:** boiled rice

kanishite *usu cap, var of* KANESHITE

kanisian *usu cap, var of* KANESIAN

kan·je·ra man \ˈkänjərə-\ *n, usu cap K* [fr. *Kanjera,* locality in Kenya where the type was discovered] **:** an extinct East African man known from parts of four thick-walled dolichocephalic skulls found in association with artifacts of Abbevillian type and regarded as a primitive form of *Homo sapiens* possibly belonging to the Middle Pleistocene

kan·ji \ˈkän(,)jē\ *n, pl* **kanji** *or* **kanjis** [Jap] **1 :** a Japanese system of writing based on the Chinese one and composed principally of characters borrowed or adapted from Chinese — see KANA, KANA-MAJIRI **2 :** a single character belonging to the kanji system of writing

kan·ka·nai \ˌkäŋkəˈnī\ *n, pl* **kankanai** *or* **kankanais** *usu cap* [native name in northern Luzon] **1 a :** a people inhabiting the southern part of Mountain Province of northern Luzon, Philippines — compare IGOROT **b :** a member of such people **2 :** an Austronesian language of the Kankanai people

kan·krej \ˈkän,krej\ *n* -ES [origin unknown] **:** GUZERAT

kan·na·da \ˈkänədə, ˈkan-\ *n* -s *usu cap* [Kanarese *kannaḍa*] **:** the major Dravidian language of Mysore, south India

ka·no \ˈkä(,)nō\ *adj, usu cap* [fr. *Kano,* city in northern Nigeria] **:** of or from the city of Kano, Nigeria **:** of the kind or style prevalent in Kano

kanon *var of* CANON

ka·no·ne \kəˈnōnə\ *n, pl* **ka·no·nen** \-ōnən\ [G, lit., cannon, fr. It *cannone* — more at CANNON] **:** an expert skier

ka·noon \kəˈnün\ *n* -s [Turk *kânun* — more at CANUN] **:** ZITHER

kanpur *usu cap, var of* CAWNPORE

kans \ˈkän(t)s\ *also* **kans grass** *n, pl* **kans** [Hindi *kās,* fr. Skt *kāśa*] **:** a common Indian grass (*Saccharum spontaneum*) found also in the West Indies that is used for thatching and for forage and in some areas is a troublesome weed — called also *glagah*

kan·sa \ˈkanzə, -n(t)sə\ *or* **kan·sas** *like* KANSAS\ *n, pl* **kansa** *or* **kansas** *usu cap* [native name in the Kansas river valley] **1 a :** a Siouan people of the Kansas river valley, Kansas **b :** a member of such people **2 :** a dialect of Dhegiha

¹kan·san \ˈkanzən, ˈkaan- *sometimes* -n(t)sən *or* ˈkain(t)s-\ *n* -s *cap* [*Kansas,* state in the central U.S. + E *-an,* n. suffix] **:** a native or resident of Kansas

²kansan \"\ *adj, usu cap* [*Kansas* + E *-an,* adj. suffix] **1 a :** of, relating to, or characteristic of the state of Kansas **b :** of, relating to, or characteristic of the people of Kansas **2 :** of or relating to the second glacial stage during the glacial epoch in No. America

kan·sas \-nzəs *also* -nzəz *sometimes* -n(t)səs *or* -zis *or* -ziz *or* -sis\ *adj, usu cap* [fr. *Kansas,* state in the central U.S., fr. *Kansa, Kansas* (Siouan people)] **:** of or from the state of Kansas ⟨*Kansas* wheatfields⟩ **:** of the kind or style prevalent in Kansas **:** KANSAN

kansas cit·i·an *also* **kansas city·an** \ˌ⸗zə(s)ˈsid·ēən, -itē- *also* -zəzˈsi- *sometimes* -sə(s)ˈsi-\ *n, cap K&C* **:** a native or resident of Kansas City

kansas city \ˌ⸗⸗ˈsid·|ē, -it|, |i, *in rapid speech* (ˈ)kanzˈsi- *or* (ˈ)kaan-\ *adj, usu cap K&C* **1** [fr. *Kansas City,* city in western Missouri] **:** of or from Kansas City, Mo. **:** of the kind or style prevalent in Kansas City **2** [fr. *Kansas City,* city in northeastern Kansas] **:** of or from Kansas City, Kans. **:** of the kind or style prevalent in Kansas City

kansas gay-feather *n, usu cap K* **:** a perennial herb (*Liatris pycnostachya*) having spikes of purplish flowers — called also *prairie button snakeroot*

kansas horse plague *n, usu cap K* **:** contagious equine encephalomyelitis

kansas thistle *n, usu cap K* **:** BUFFALO BUR

kan·tar *or* **can·tar** *or* **qan·tar** \kanˈtär, kən-\ *n* -s [Ar *qinṭār,* fr. LGk *kentēnarion* weight of 100 pounds, fr. LL *centenarium, centenarius* — more at CENTENARY] **:** any of various units of weight used in Mediterranean countries (as an Egyptian unit equal to about 99 pounds and a Turkish unit equal to about 124½ pounds)

kan·te·le *also* **kan·te·la** \ˈkäntələ, ˈkan-\ *n* -s [Finn *kantele*] **:** a traditional Finnish harp orig. having 5 strings but now having as many as 20 to 30 strings

kan·ten \ˈkan,ten\ *n* -s [Jap, lit., cold weather, fr. *kan* midwinter + *ten* sky] **:** AGAR 1a

kantharos *var of* CANTHARUS

¹kant·ian \ˈkantēən, ˈkän- *also* -nchən\ *adj, usu cap* [Immanuel *Kant* †1804 Ger. philosopher + E *-ian*] **1 :** of or relating to the German philosopher Immanuel Kant **2 :** of or relating to Kantianism

²kantian \"\ *n* -s *usu cap* **:** a follower of Kant or adherent to Kantianism

kant·ian·ism \-,nizəm\ *n* -s *usu cap* **:** the philosophy of Immanuel Kant that endeavors to synthesize the tradition of continental rationalism and British empiricism by holding that phenomenal knowledge is the joint product of percepts given to us through sensations organized under the forms of intuition of space and time and of concepts or categories of the understanding but that reason involves itself in fallacies if it tries to apply to the noumenal the principles of the understanding applicable only to the phenomenal so that the speculative ideas of God, the world, and the self although having heuristic import represent regulative knowledge as distinguished from the constitutive knowledge about the phenomenal at the same time that the ideas of God, freedom, and immortality represent necessary presuppositions for morality — compare CATEGORICAL IMPERATIVE, NOUMENON, PHENOMENON

kan·ti·ara \,kantēˈa(ə)rə\ *n* -s [origin unknown] **:** a spinose plant (*Carthamus oxycantha*) resembling the safflower that grows in troublesome clumps in Indian grasslands but can be made edible for livestock by beating off the spines

kantikoy *var of* CANTICO

kant·ism \ˈkant-,izəm, ˈkän-\ *n* -s *usu cap* **:** KANTIANISM

kant·ist \-ntəst\ *n* -s *usu cap* **:** KANTIAN

kantuta *var of* CANTUTA

ka·nuck *also* **ka·nuk** \kəˈnək\ *cap, var of* CANUCK

ka·nu·ka \ˈkänəkə\ *n* -s [Maori] **:** a shrubby New Zealand tree (*Leptospermum ericoides*) with strong resistant wood that is used for making fences — compare MANUKA

kanun *var of* CANUN

ka·nu·ri \kəˈnürē\ *n, pl* **kanuri** *or* **kanuris** *usu cap* **1 a :** a Negro people of the Muslim kingdom of Bornu west of Lake Chad whose history of dominance in that area goes back more than 500 years — compare TIBBU **b :** a member of such people **2 :** the language of the Kanuri people

kan·war \(ˈ)kanˈwär\ *n, pl* **kanwar** *or* **kanwars** *usu cap* **1 :** an indigenous people of central India esp. in the Bilaspur district many of whom are large landholders **2 :** a member of the Kanwar people

kan·ya butter \ˈkanyə-\ *n* [*kanya* perh. modif. of Hausa *ka³ˈda³nya¹* shea tree] **:** SHEA BUTTER

kanya tree *n* [*kanya* perh. modif. of Hausa *ka³ˈda³nya¹*] **:** SHEA TREE

kanyaw *var of* CANAO

kan·zu \ˈkan(,)zü\ *n* -s [Swahili] **:** a long white robe worn by African men (as the Swahili)

kao-chü-li \ˌkau̇chəˈlē\ *n, pl* **kao-chü-li** *usu cap* **:** a people of probable Tungusic affinities inhabiting the Yalu river region of Korea and Manchuria from the 1st to the 7th centuries A.D.

kaoh·siung \ˌkau̇ˈshēˈu̇ŋ, ˈgau̇-\ *adj, usu cap* [fr. *Kaohsiung,* city in Formosa, China] **:** of or from the city of Kaohsiung, Formosa, China **:** of the kind or style prevalent in Kaohsiung

kao·liang \ˌkau̇lēˈäŋ\ *also* **koa·liang** *or* **kow·liang** \ˌkōl-\ *or* \ˈkau̇l-, ˌkōl-\ *n* -s [Chin (Pek) *kao¹ liang²,* lit., tall grain, fr. *kao¹* high, tall + *liang²* grain] **1 :** any of various grain sorghums that have slender dry pithy stalks, open erect panicles, and small white or brown seeds and are grown chiefly in China and Manchuria for their grain which is used for food and stalks which are used for fodder, thatching, and fuel **2 :** a spirituous liquor made in China from the juice of kaoliang stalks

ka·olin *also* **ka·oline** \ˈkāələn, kāˈōl-\ *n* -s [F *kaolin,* fr. *Kao-ling,* hill in Kiangsi province, southeast China, where it was originally obtained] **:** a fine usu. white clay resulting from extreme weathering of aluminous minerals (as feldspar) that contains kaolinite as its principal constituent, that remains white on firing, and that is used chiefly in ceramics and refractories, as an adsorbent, as a filler or extender (as in paper or rubber or pigments), and in medicine — see CHINA CLAY; compare FIRECLAY

ka·olin·ic \ˌkāəˈlinik\ *adj* [ISV *kaolin* + *-ic*] **:** of, relating to, or resembling kaolin

ka·olin·ite \ˈkāələ,nīt, kāˈōl-\ *n* -s [*kaolin* + *-ite*] **:** a mineral $Al_2Si_2O_5(OH)_4$ consisting of a hydrous silicate of aluminum that is polymorphous with dickite and nacrite and constitutes the principal mineral in kaolin

ka·olin·it·ic \ˌkāələˈnid·ik, kāˌōl-\ *adj* **:** of, relating to, containing, or resembling kaolinite

ka·olin·iza·tion \,kāələnəˈzāshən, ˌkāə,lin-, kāˌōlən-, -,nīˈz-\ *n* -s [ISV *kaolinize* + *-ation*] **:** the development of kaolin by metasomatism

ka·olin·ize \ˈkāələ,nīz, kāˈōl-\ *vt* -ED/-ING/-s [ISV *kaolin* + *-ize*] **:** to convert (as feldspar) into kaolin

kaori *var of* KAURI

ka·pa \ˈkäpə\ *n* -s [Hawaiian] *Hawaii* **:** TAPA

ka·pai \käˈpī\ *adj* [Maori] *New Zeal* **:** GOOD

ka·pel·le *also* **ca·pel·le** \kəˈpelə\ *n, pl* **kapel·len** *also* **capel·len** \-lən\ *often cap* [G *kapelle,* fr. It *cappella* choir, chapel, fr. ML, chapel — more at CHAPEL] **1 :** the choir or orchestra of a royal or papal chapel **2 :** a musical organization; *esp* **:** ORCHESTRA

ka·pell·meis·ter *also* **ca·pell·meis·ter** \kəˈpel,mīstər\ *n, pl* **kapellmeister** *often cap* [G *kapellmeister,* fr. *kapelle* + *meister* master, fr. OHG *meistar,* fr. L *magister* — more at MASTER] **:** the musical director of a kapelle

kapellmeister music *n, often cap K* **:** music of uninspired correctness — usu. used disparagingly

kaph *also* **caph** *or* **kaf** \ˈkäf, ˈkȯf\ *n* -s [Heb *kaph,* lit., palm of the hand] **1 :** the 11th letter of the Hebrew alphabet — symbol כ or ך; see ALPHABET table **2 :** a letter of the Phoenician or another Semitic alphabet corresponding to Hebrew kaph

ka·pok *also* **ca·poc** \ˈkā,päk\ *n* -s [Malay *kapok*] **:** a mass of silky fibers that clothe the seeds of the ceiba tree and are used commercially as a filling for mattresses, cushions, life preservers, and sleeping bags and as insulation — called also *ceiba, Java cotton, silk cotton*

kapok oil *n* **:** a light-yellow semidrying oil obtained from the seeds of the kapok tree and used in foods and in soapmaking

kapok tree *n* **:** SILK-COTTON TREE

ka·po·te \kəˈpōd·ə\ *n* -s [Yiddish, fr. F *capote* — more at CAPOTE] **:** a man's long coat of medieval origin worn esp. by Jews of eastern Europe — compare CAPOTE

¹kap·pa \ˈkapə\ *n* -s [Gk, of Sem origin; akin to Heb *kaph*] **:** the 10th letter of the Greek alphabet — symbol Κ or κ; see ALPHABET table

²kappa \"\ *n* -s [NL, fr. Gk *kappa*] **:** a cytoplasmic factor in certain paramecia that mediates production of paramecin and thereby makes the medium in which such animals are grown toxic to members of strains not possessing the factor

kap·pa·rah \ˌkäpäˈrä, käˈpȯrə\ *n, pl* **kap·pa·roth** *or* **kap·pa·rot** \ˌkäpäˈrōt(h), käˈpȯrəs\ [Heb, lit., atonement] **1 :** a symbolic ceremony practiced by some Orthodox Jews on the eve of Yom Kippur in which typically a cock, hen, or coin is swung around the head and offered in atonement or as ransom for one's sins **2 :** SACRIFICE; *specif* **:** something used as a symbolic sacrifice in the kapparah ceremony

kap·pie \ˈkapē, ˈkäpē\ *n* -s [Afrik, fr. D *kapje* small cap, dim. of *kap* cap, fr. MD *cappe,* fr. LL *cappa* head covering — more at CAP] *Africa* **:** SUNBONNET ⟨her hair . . . covered by a big black linen ~ which came down over her shoulders —Stuart Cloete⟩

ka·pu \ˈkä(,)pü\ *n* -s [Hawaiian] *Hawaii* **:** TABOO

ka·pu·ka \ˈkäpəkə\ *n* -s [Maori] **:** a rather small New Zealand broadleaf evergreen tree (*Griselinia littoralis*) sometimes cultivated in warm regions as an ornamental

ka·pur \kəˈpu̇(ə)r\ *or* **ka·por** \-pō(ə)r\ *n* -s [Hindi *kapūr,* fr. Skt *karpūra* camphor — more at CAMPHOR] **:** a tree (*Dryobalanops aromatica*) that produces Borneo camphor

ka·put *also* **ka·putt** \käˈpu̇t, kə-, -ˈpüt\ *adj* [G, fr. F *capot* not having made a trick at piquet — more at CAPOT] **1 :** utterly defeated or destroyed **:** FINISHED, DONE FOR, RUINED ⟨after weeks of bombardment the city was ~⟩ **2 :** made useless or unable to function ⟨the TV production masterminds were caught with their cables and cameras ~ —R.L.Shayon⟩ **3 :** hopelessly outmoded or set aside ⟨the notion that reading is ~ each time a mammoth entertainment medium catches hold —Harvey Breit⟩ ⟨all those curls that used to take hours to do are ~ —Ethel Merman⟩

ka·ra·bagh \ˌkärəˈbäk\ *n* -s *usu cap* [fr. *Karabagh,* region in Azerbaidzhan, U.S.S.R.] **:** a small Caucasian rug showing considerable Persian influence in pattern and usu. having magenta, turquoise, and pale green as the prevailing colors

karabiner *var of* CARABINER

ka·ra·chai *also* **ka·ra·tchai** \ˌkärəˈchī\ *or* **ka·ra·cha·yevt**

\ˌ⸗⸗'chäyəft\ *n, pl* **karachai** *or* **karachais** *usu cap* [*karachai, karatchai* fr. *Karachai*, region on the northern slope of the western Caucasus mountains, U.S.S.R.; *karachayevt* fr. Russ *Karachayevtsi* (pl.) Karachai people, fr. *Karachai*] **1 :** a Turkic-speaking people of the Caucasus **2 :** a member of the Karachai people

ka·ra·chi \kə'rächē *also* -rachē\ *adj, usu cap* [fr. *Karachi*, Pakistan] **:** of or from the city of Karachi, Pakistan **:** of the kind or style prevalent in Karachi

ka·ra·dagh \ˌkärə'dä\ *n* -s *usu cap* [fr. *Karadagh*, mountain range in Azerbaidzhan province, northwestern Iran] **:** a Persian rug having a bold design and rich coloring

ka·ra·gan·da \ˌkarəgən'dä\ *adj, usu cap* [fr. *Karaganda*, city in the central U.S.S.R.] **:** of or from the city of Karaganda, U.S.S.R. **:** of the kind or style prevalent in Karaganda

kara·ism \'ka(a)rəˌizəm\ *or* **kara·it·ism** \-rəˌīd-ˌizəm\ *n* -s *usu cap* [*karaism* fr. *kara-* (fr. LHeb *qĕrāīm* Karaites, fr. Heb *qārā* to read) + *-ism*; *karaitism* fr. *karaite* + *-ism*] **:** a Jewish doctrine originating in Baghdad in the 8th century that rejects rabbinism and talmudism and bases its tenets on interpretation of the Scriptures

karait *var of* KRAIT

kara·ite \-rəˌīt\ *n* -s *usu cap* [*kara-* (fr. L Heb *qĕrāīm* Karaites) + *-ite*] **1 :** an adherent of Karaism **2 :** a Turkic dialect spoken by Karaite people from Crimea

karajá *or* **karaya** *usu cap, var of* CARAJÁ

ka·ra·ka \'kärəkə\ *n* -s [Maori] **:** a New Zealand tree (*Corynocarpus laevigata*) having orange-colored fruit with edible pulp and poisonous seeds that when cooked and dried are also edible and form an important article of native diet

kara·kal·pak *or* **qara·qal·paq** \ˌkärəkəl'pak, -rəkäl-\ *n, pl* **karakalpak** *or* **karakalpaks** *or* **qaraqalpaq** *or* **qaraqalpaqs** *usu cap* [Kirghiz, lit., black cap, fr. *kara* black + *kalpak* cap] **1 a :** a Turkic people living near Lake Aral, Central Asia **b :** a member of such people **2 :** the Turkic language of the Karakalpak people

kara kir·ghiz \ˌkarə(ˌ)kər'gēz, -arəˌkir'-\ *n, usu cap both Ks* [Kirghiz *Karakyrghyz*, lit., black Kirghiz, fr. *kara* black + *Kyrghyz* Kirghiz] **1 :** a Kirghiz people closely resembling the Mongols and dwelling chiefly in the Tien Shan highlands and the Great Pamir — called also *Black Kirghiz, Burut* **2 :** a member of the Kara Kirghiz people

kar·a·kul *also* **car·a·cul** \'karəkəl *also* 'ker-\ *n* [fr. *Karakul*, village in Uzbekistan, U.S.S.R., where the breed originated] **1 a** *usu cap* **:** a breed of hardy slender fat-tailed sheep from Bukhara with coarse wiry brown fur **b** -s *often cap* **:** a sheep of this breed **2** -s **:** the tightly curled glossy black coat of the newborn lamb of the Karakul breed valued as fur — compare ASTRAKHAN, BROADTAIL, PERSIAN LAMB

ka·ra·kurt \'karəˌkü(ə)rt\ *n* -s [Turki, fr. *kara* black + *kurt* wolf] **:** a venomous spider (*Latrodectus tredecimguttatus*) of eastern Europe and Siberia — called also *black wolf*

ka·ra·mo·jong \ˌkarə'mōˌjäŋ\ *or* **ka·ra·mo·jo** \-(ˌ)jō\ *n, pl* **karamojong** *or* **karamojongs** *or* **karamojo** *or* **karamojos** *usu cap* **1 a :** a pastoral people of northeast Uganda **b :** a member of such people **2 :** a Nilotic language of the Karamojong people

kar·a·mu \'karəˌmü\ *n* -s [Maori] **:** a New Zealand shrub or tree of the genus *Coprosma*

ka·ran·da \kə'randə, -ˌdä\ *var of* CARAUNDA

ka·ran·ka·wa \kə'raŋkəˌwō\ *n, pl* **karankawa** *or* **karankawas** *usu cap* **1 a :** an Indian people of the Gulf coast in Texas **b :** a member of such people **2 :** a language of the Karankawa people **3 :** a language family perhaps related to Coahuiltecan and Tonkawan that comprises the Karankawa language

kar·at *or* **car·at** \'karət *also* 'ker-\ *n* -s [prob. fr. MF *carat*, fr. ML *carratus* unit of weight for precious stones — more at CARAT] **:** a unit of fineness for gold equal to 1/24 part of pure gold in an alloy ⟨16-*karat* gold contains 16/24 pure gold⟩ ⟨24-*karat* gold is pure⟩ — abbr. *k* or *kt*

ka·ra·tas \'karəˌtas\ *n* [NL, fr. Tupi *carautá, caragoatá* karatas] **1** *cap* **:** a genus of tropical American plants (family Bromeliaceae) with the flowers in dense terminal heads **2** -ES **:** any plant of the genus *Karatas* (esp. *K. plumieri*) **3** -ES **:** SILK GRASS 3b

ka·ra·te \kə'rätē\ *n* -s [Jap, lit., empty hand] **:** a Japanese art of self-defense in which kicks and openhanded blows are delivered esp. to vulnerable parts of the body

karatto *var of* KERATTO

karaya *usu cap, var of* CARAJÁ

ka·ra·va gum *also* **karaya** \kə'rīə-\ *n* -s [*karaya* modif. of Hindi *karāyal* resin] **:** STERCULIA GUM; *esp* **:** a gum derived from an Indian tree (*Sterculia urens*)

¹kar·bi \'kärbē\ *n* -s [native name in Queensland, Australia] **:** a small stingless wild bee (*Trigona carbonaria*) of Australia that makes a spiral mass of honeycomb

²karbi \"\ *n, pl* **karbi** [Gujarati *kaḍbī*] *India* **:** dried stalks of Indian corn

ka·rel \kə'rel, 'karəl\ *n* -s *cap* [back-formation fr. *karelian*] **:** KARELIAN 2

ka·re·la \kə'rələ\ *n* -s [Hindi *karelā*, fr. Skt *kāravella, kāravellaka*] *India* **:** a large balsam apple (*Momordica charantia*) with an elongated warty yellowish to coppery fruit

¹ka·re·lian *also* **ca·re·lian** \kə'rēlēən, -lyən\ *adj, usu cap* [*Karelia*, region in northwestern U.S.S.R. + E *-an*, adj. suffix] **1 :** of, relating to, or characteristic of Karelia, a region of the northwestern U.S.S.R. and the adjoining borders of eastern Finland **2 :** of, relating to, or characteristic of the people of Karelia **3 :** of, relating to, or characteristic of the language of the Karelians

²karelian *also* **carelian** \"\ *n* -s *cap* [*Karelia* + E *-an*, n. suffix] **1 :** a native or inhabitant of Karelia **2 :** the Finno-Ugric language of the Karelian people that is closely related to Finnish and sometimes treated as a dialect of it

ka·ren \kə'ren\ *n, pl* **karen** *or* **karens** *usu cap* **1 a :** a group of peoples of eastern and southern Burma **b :** a member of any of such peoples **2 a :** a group of languages spoken by the Karen peoples that is held to be related to the Tibeto-Burman, Thai, or Mon-Khmer language groups **b :** a language of this group

ka·ren·ni \kə'renē\ *n, pl* **karenni** *or* **karennis** *usu cap* **1 :** one of several Karen peoples of eastern Burma the women of which elongate their necks by heavy coils of brass that thrust the head away from the body **2 :** a member of a Karenni people

ka·rez \kä'rez, '⸗ˌ⸗\ *n, pl* **karez** [Per *kārez*] **1 :** an underground irrigation tunnel bored horizontally into rock slopes in Baluchistan **2 :** a system of irrigation by underground tunnels

kari *var of* KARRI

kar·i·era \ˌkarē'erə\ *n, pl* **kariera** *or* **karieras** *usu cap* **1 :** a people of Western Australia **2 :** a member of the Kariera people

kar·in·gho·ta \ˌkarən'gōd·ə\ *n* -s [origin unknown] **:** NIEPA 1

kariri *usu cap, var of* CARIRI

kar·i·te *or* **kar·i·ti** \'karəd·ē\ *n* -s [F *karité*, of Niger-Congo origin; akin to Wolof *karité* karite] **:** SHEA TREE

karite butter *or* **karite oil** *n* **:** SHEA BUTTER

karl fisch·er reagent \'kärl'fishər-\ *n, usu cap K&F* [after *Karl Fischer*, 20th cent. Ger. chemist] **:** a colored solution of pyridine, sulfur dioxide, iodine, and anhydrous methanol that reacts quantitatively with water to form a colorless solution and is used to determine the amount of water in numerous substances

karls·bad salt \'kärlzˌbad-, -l(t)sˌbät-\ *n, usu cap K* [trans. of G *karlsbader salz*, fr. *Karlsbad* (*Karlovy Vary*), town in western Czechoslovakia renowned for its sulfur springs] **1 :** a mixture of mineral salts including esp. potassium sulfate and sodium sulfate that is obtained from the water of certain springs **2 :** an artificial mixture of potassium sulfate, sodium sulfate, sodium chloride, and sodium bicarbonate

karls·ru·he \'kärlzˌrüə, -l(t)sˌr-\ *adj, usu cap* [fr. *Karlsruhe*, city in southwest Germany] **:** of or from the city of Karlsruhe, Germany **:** of the kind or style prevalent in Karlsruhe

kar·ma \'kärmə, 'kər-\ *n* -s *often cap* [Skt *karman* (nom. *karma*) karma, work, office, fr. *karoti* he does, makes; akin to OIr *cruth* form, Lith *kurti* to build, Skt *kāra* doing, *kṛṇoti* he does, makes] **1 :** the force generated by a person's actions that is held in Hinduism and Buddhism to be the motive power for the round of rebirths and deaths endured by him until he has achieved spiritual liberation and freed himself from the effects of such force ⟨release from the ~ of recurrent existences —John Baillie⟩ — compare NIRVANA, SAMSARA **2 :** the sum total of the ethical consequences of a person's good or bad actions comprising thoughts, words, and deeds that is held in Hinduism and Buddhism to determine his specific destiny in his next existence ⟨as our desires shape themselves, so we act and build up our coming fate, our ~ —P.E.More⟩ **3 :** a subtle form of matter held in Jainism to develop in the soul and vitiate its purity, to lengthen the course of individual transmigration, and to postpone the possibility of final salvation ⟨the soul's chief problem . . . of managing to throw off or expel ~ matter from itself —J.B.Noss⟩ — **kar·mic** \-mik\ *adj, often cap*

kar·ma·dha·ra·ya \ˌkərmə'därəə, -ärəyə\ *n* -s [Skt *karmadhāraya*, fr. *karma-* (fr. *karman*) + *dhāraya* that holds, that maintains; perh. fr. the fact that such words maintain the same function throughout, inasmuch as the syntactic function of the entire compound is the same as the syntactic function of its final constituent would be if used alone; akin to Skt *dhārayati* he holds, carries, keeps — more at FIRM] **:** a class of compound words typically having a noun as second constituent and a descriptive adjective as first constituent (as *bluegrass, blackberry*), a noun as second constituent and an attributive noun as first constituent (as *houseboat*), or an adjective as second constituent and an adverb as first constituent (as *everlasting, widespread*) and having meanings that follow the formula "a *B* that is *A*" for nouns or "*B* in the manner expressed by *A*" for adjectives, where *A* stands for the first constituent and *B* for the second; *also* **:** a compound word belonging to this class

karma-marga \-'märgə\ *n* -s [Skt, fr. *karma-* (fr. *karman*) + *mārga* path, fr. *mṛga* deer, gazelle] **:** the strict observation of caste regulations and ritual duties regarded in Hinduism as one path to a happier life in an individual's next incarnation **:** salvation by works — compare BHAKTI-MARGA, JNANA-MARGA

karmatian *or* **karmathian** *usu cap, var of* QARMATIAN

karma-yoga \ˌ⸗⸗'⸗⸗\ *n* [Skt *karmayoga*, fr. *karma-* (fr. *karman*) + *yoga*] **:** yoga through disinterested service or the selfless performance of duties

kar·mouth *or* **kar·mout** \(')kär'müt\ *n* -s [Ar *qarmūṭ*] **:** any of several African siluroid fishes (genera *Clarias* and *Heterobranchus*) that have an accessory breathing organ enabling them to live for a time out of water

karn \'kärn\ *var of* CAIRN

ka·ro \'kä(ˌ)rō\ *n* -s [Maori] **:** either of two New Zealand plants of the genus *Pittosporum*: **a :** a shrub or small tree (*P. crassifolium*) with fastigiate branches **b :** an epiphyte (*P. cornifolium*) with whorled leaves

ka·rok \kə'räk\ *n, pl* **karok** *or* **karoks** *usu cap* [Karok *karuk* upstream] **1 a :** an Indian people of the Klamath river valley, California **b :** a member of such people **2 :** the Quoratean language of the Karok people **3 :** QUORATEAN

karolin *var of* CAROLIN

ka·ross \kə'räs\ *n* -ES [Afrik *karos*, perh. alter. of D *kuras* cuirass, fr. MF *curasse, cuirasse* — more at CUIRASS] **:** a simple garment or rug of animal skins usu. used by native tribesmen of southern Africa

kar·pas \'kärˌpäs\ *n* -ES [Heb *karpās*, fr. Aram *karpas*] **:** a piece of parsley, celery, or lettuce placed on the Passover seder plate as a symbol of spring or hope and dipped in salt water in remembrance of the hyssop and blood of the Passover in Egypt

kar·ree \kə'rē, -rā\ *also* **karree boom** \-ˌbüm, -ˌbōm\ *or* **kar·roo·boom** \-'rüˌb-\ *n* -s [*karree* fr. Afrik, prob. fr. Hottentot *karib*; *karree boom, karrooboom* fr. Afrik *karreeboom*, fr. *karree* + *boom* tree, fr. D, fr. MD; akin to OE *bēam* tree — more at BEAM] **:** a plant of the genus *Rhus* (esp. *R. viminalis*) of southern Africa

kar·ren \'karən\ *n* -s [G] **:** a ribbed and fluted rock surface resulting at least in part from differential solution

kar·ri *or* **kari** \'karē\ *n* -s [native name in Western Australia] **1 :** a large gum tree (*Eucalyptus diversicolor*) of Western Australia **2 :** the hard durable red wood of karri that constitutes one of the principal commercial timbers of Australia

karri-tree \'karē,\ *n* [origin unknown] **:** PRINCESS-TREE

kar·roo *or* **ka·roo** \kə'rü\ *n* -s [Afrik *karo*, perh. fr. Hottentot *garo* desert] **:** a dry tableland of southern Africa that often rises in terraces to a considerable elevation

karroo bush *also* **karroo shrub** *n* **1 :** a thorny acacia (*Acacia horrida*) that yields cape gum **2 :** a plant of the genus *Tetragonia* (esp. *T. arbuscula*)

karroo caterpillar *n* **:** the larva of a pyralidid moth (*Loxostege frustralis*) that seriously damages fodder in sheep-farming regions of southern Africa

kar·ru·sel \ˌkarə'sel, '⸗⸗ˌ⸗ *also* 'ker- *or* -zel\ *n* -s [prob. alter. of *carrousel*] **:** a revolving escapement that is designed to reduce position errors in a watch and is mounted in a carriage similar to that of a tourbillion but differs from it in slower speed of rotation and in having the fourth wheel contained inside the carriage

kar·shu·ni *also* **car·shu·ni** \kär'shünē\ *or* **gar·shu·ni** \gär-\ *n* -s *usu cap* [Ar *karshūnīy*, prob. fr. Syr *gershūn* alien, foreign + Ar *-īy* belonging to] **:** Arabic written in Syriac characters esp. as used in the Maronite ritual

karst \'kärst\ *n* -s [G] **:** a limestone region marked by sinks and interspersed with abrupt ridges, irregular protuberant rocks, caverns, and underground streams — **karst·ic** \-tik\ *adj*

kar·tik \'kärd·ik\ *n* -s *usu cap* [Hindi *kārtik*, fr. Skt *kārttika*, fr. *kṛttikā* Pleiades; perh. akin to Skt *kṛṇatti* he spins — more at HURDLE] **:** a month of the Hindu year — see MONTH table

kart·ve·lian \(')kärt'vēlēən, -lyən\ *also* **karth·li** \'kärtlē\ *or* **kart·vel** \'kärtˌvel\ *n* -s *usu cap* **1 :** a member of a group of related peoples of the Caucasus **2 :** the South Caucasic language family including Georgian, Mingrelian, Svanetian, and Laz

ka·ru·na \'kərüˌnä\ *n* -s [Skt *karuṇā* compassion; perh. akin to OE *hrēowan* to grieve, repent — more at RUE] **:** compassion that is a fundamental quality in the bodhisattva ideal of Mahayana Buddhism

kar·win·skia \kär'winzkēə, -n(t)sk-\ *n, cap* [NL, fr. Wilhelm *Karwinsky* von Karwin †1855 Ger. traveler + NL *-ia*] **:** a genus of shrubs or small trees (family Rhamnaceae) that are chiefly native to Mexico and the southwestern U.S. and have flowers with small hooded short-clawed petals and fleshy drupes

kary- *or* **karyo-** *also* **cary-** *or* **caryo-** *comb form* [NL, fr. Gk *kary-, karyo-* walnut, nut, kernel, fr. *karyon* — more at CAREEN] **1 :** nucleus of a cell ⟨*karyenchyma*⟩ ⟨*karyokinesis*⟩ — in cytological terms **2 :** nut **:** kernel ⟨*caryopsis*⟩

kary·en·chy·ma \ˌkarē'eŋkəmə, -enk-\ *n* -s [NL, fr. *kary-* + *-enchyma*] **:** KARYOLYMPH

kar·yo·chy·le·ma \ˌkarē(ˌ)ōˌkī'lēmə\ *n* -s [NL, fr. *kary-* + *-chylema* (as in *enchylema*)] **:** KARYOLYMPH

kar·yo·clasic \ˌkarēō'klāsik, -las-\ *or* **kar·yo·clas·tic** \-lastik\ *adj* [*karyoclasic* ISV *karyoclas-* (fr. NL *karyoclasis*) + *-ic*; *karyoclastic* fr. *kary-* + *-clastic*] **:** of or relating to karyoclasis

kar·y·oc·la·sis *or* **kar·y·ok·la·sis** \ˌkarē'äkləsəs\ *n, pl* **karyocla·ses** *or* **karyokla·ses** \-əˌsēz\ [NL *karyoclasis*, fr. *kary-* + *-clasis*] **1 :** disintegration of the cell nucleus **2 :** interruption of mitosis (as in colchicine poisoning)

kar·yo·gam·ic \ˌkarēō'gamik\ *adj* **:** of or relating to karyogamy

kar·y·og·a·my \ˌkarē'ägəmē\ *n* -ES [ISV *kary-* + *-gamy*] **:** the fusion of cell nuclei (as in fertilization) — compare PLASMOGAMY

kar·yo·kinesis \ˌkarē(ˌ)ō+\ *n* [NL, fr. *kary-* + *-kinesis*] **1 :** the nuclear phenomena characteristic of mitosis **2 :** the whole process of mitosis — compare CYTOKINESIS — **kar·yo·kinetic** \"+\ *adj*

karyokinetic figure *n* [*karyokinetic* ISV *kary-* + *kinetic*] *biol* **:** ACHROMATIC FIGURE

kar·y·o·log·ic \ˌkarēə'läjik\ *or* **kar·y·o·log·i·cal** \-jəkəl\ *adj* **:** of or relating to karyology — **kar·y·o·log·i·cal·ly** \-jək(ə)lē\ *adv*

kar·y·ol·o·gy \ˌkarē'äləjē\ *n* -ES [ISV *kary-* + *-logy*] **:** a branch of cytology that deals with the minute anatomy of cell nuclei and esp. the nature and structure of chromosomes

kar·yo·lymph \'karēō+,-\ *n* [ISV *kary-* + *lymph*; prob. orig. formed as G *karyolymphe*] **:** the clear homogeneous ground substance of a cell nucleus — called also *enchylema, nuclear sap*; opposed to *karyotin*

kar·y·ol·y·sis \ˌkarē'äləsəs\ *n* [NL, fr. *kary-* + *-lysis*] **:** dissolution of the cell nucleus with loss of its affinity for basic stains sometimes occurring normally but usu. in necrosis — **kar·yo·lyt·ic** \ˌkarēə'lid·ik\ *adj*

kar·y·ol·y·sus \-ləsəs\ *n, cap* [NL, fr. *kary-* + *-lysus* (fr. Gk *lyein* to loose, dissolve) — more at LOSE] **:** a genus of haemogregarines parasitic in reptiles

kar·yo·mere \'⸗⸗⸗ˌmi(ə)r\ *n* -s [ISV *kary* + *-mere*] **1 a :** CHROMOMERE **b :** a sperm head **2 :** a swollen vesicular chromosome (as in certain embryonic tissues) — called also *chromosomal vesicle*

kar·y·om·er·ite \ˌkarē'äməˌrīt\ *n* -s [ISV *kary-* + *-mere* + *-ite*; orig. formed as G *karyomerit*] **:** KARYOMERE 2

kar·yo·microsome \ˌkarē(ˌ)ō+\ *n* **:** a nuclear microsome

kar·yo·mi·to·ic \ˌkarēōˌmī'tōik\ *or* **kar·yo·mi·tot·ic** \ˌkarēō+\ *adj* [*karyomitoic* fr. *karyomitosis* + *-ic*; *karyomitotic* fr. *kary-* + *mitotic*] **:** of or relating to karyomitosis

kar·yo·mitome \ˌkarēō+\ *n* [ISV *kary-* + *mitome*] **:** the nuclear reticulum of a cell

kar·yo·mitosis \"+\ *n* [NL, fr. *kary-* + *mitosis*] **:** mitotic division of the nucleus of a cell

kar·y·on \'karēˌän\ *n* -s [NL, fr. Gk *karyon* nut — more at CAREEN] **:** the nucleus of a cell — **kar·y·on·tic** \ˌkarē'äntik\ *adj*

kar·yo·plasm \'karēō+ˌ-\ *also* **kar·yo·plas·ma** \ˌ⸗⸗⸗+\ *n* -s [ISV *kary-* + *-plasm, -plasma*; orig. formed as G *karyoplasma*] **:** NUCLEOPLASM 1 — **kar·y·o·plasmic** \ˌ⸗⸗(ˌ)⸗+\ *or* **kar·y·o·plasmatic** \"+\ *adj*

kar·yo·pyc·no·sis \ˌkarē(ˌ)ō+\ *n* [NL, fr. *kary-* + *pycnosis*] **:** KARYOCLASIS 1 — **kar·yo·pycnotic** \"+\ *adj*

kar·y·or·rhec·tic \ˌkarēə'rektik\ *adj* [*kary-* + Gk *rhēktikos* apt to burst, fr. *rhēktos* that can be broken (fr. *rhēgnynai* to break) + *-ikos* -ic] **:** of or relating to karyorrhexis

kar·y·or·rhex·is \ˌkarēə'reksəs\ *n, pl* **karyorrhex·es** \-kˌsēz\ [NL, fr. *kary-* + *-rrhexis*] **:** KARYOCLASIS 1

kar·y·os·chi·sis \ˌkarē'äskəsəs\ *n, pl* **karyoschi·ses** \-əˌsēz\ [NL, fr. *kary-* + *-schisis*] **:** KARYOCLASIS 1

kar·yo·some \'karēəˌsōm\ *n* -s [ISV *kary-* + *-some*; orig. formed as G *karyosom*] **1 :** CHROMOCENTER **2 :** ENDOSOME; *esp* **:** an endosome consisting of a nucleolar mass of heterochromatin as distinguished from one that is a plasmosome

kar·yo·systematic \ˌkarē(ˌ)ō+\ *adj* **:** of or relating to karyosystematics

kar·yo·systematics \"+\ *n pl but sing in constr* **:** a branch of systematics that seeks to determine natural relationships by the study of karyotypes

kar·yo·the·ca \ˌkarēō+\ *n* -s [NL, fr. *kary-* + *-theca*] **:** a nuclear membrane

kar·y·o·tin \'karēətən, -ˌtin\ *n* -s [ISV *kary-* + *-tin* (fr. *chromatin*); orig. formed as G *caryotin* (now *karyotin*)] **:** the reticular usu. stainable material of the cell nucleus — opposed to *karyolymph*

kar·yo·type \-ˌtīp\ *n* [ISV *kary-* + *type*; prob. orig. formed as F *caryotype*] **1 :** the sum of the specific characteristics of a cell nucleus including chromosome number, form, size, and points of spindle-fiber attachment **2 :** a diagrammatic representation of a physical karyotype — **kar·yo·typ·ic** \ˌkarēō'tipik\ *or* **kar·yo·typ·i·cal** \-pəkəl\ *adj*

¹kas *pl of* KA

²kas \'käs\ *n, pl* **kas** [D, fr. MD *casse, cas* chest, box, fr. ONF *casse* — more at CASE] **:** a Dutch cupboard or wardrobe common in the late 17th and the 18th centuries in the New Netherlands colony in America, often paneled, sometimes painted with floral designs, and equipped with two doors, heavy cornices, and usu. a drawer at the bottom

kasbah *or* **kasba** *usu cap, var of* CASBAH

kas·cam·i·ol \ka'skaməˌöl\ *n* -s [origin unknown] **:** a purple gallinule (*Porphyrula martinicas*) of the West Indies

ka·sha \'käshə\ *n* -s [Russ; akin to Pol *kasza* kasha, Lith *košti* to strain] **1 :** a mush made from coarse cracked buckwheat, barley, millet, or wheat **2 :** kasha grain before cooking

Kasha \'kashə\ *trademark* — used for a soft napped twilled fabric of fine wool and hair having a slight crosswise streaked effect

ka·shan \kə'shän\ *n* -s *usu cap* [fr. *Kashan*, city in central Iran] **1 :** a Persian rug of fine quality, soft color, and fluid floral designs **2 :** a heavy glazed pottery produced in eastern Mediterranean lands during the 16th, 17th, and 18th centuries

¹kasher *var of* KOSHER

²ka·sher \kä'she(ə)r, -eə\ *or* **ko·sher** \'kōshə(r)\ *vt* -ED/-ING/-s [*kasher* fr. Heb *kāshēr* to make kosher; *kosher* fr. Yiddish, n., kosher, fr. Heb *kāshēr* kosher, fit, proper] **:** to make (meat or utensils) kosher for use according to Jewish law

kash·gai *also* **khash·gai** \'kashˌgī\ *n* -s *usu cap* **1 :** a Turkic often nomadic people of southern Iran **2 :** a member of the Kashgai people

ka·shi \'käshē\ *n* -s [Ar *qāshīy* belonging to Kashan, fr. *Qāshān* Kashan, city in central Iran] **:** a Persian enameled tile made esp. in the 16th and 17th centuries

ka·shim \'kashəm\ *n* -s [Esk] **:** an Eskimo house of assembly

kash·mir \'kazhˌmi(ə)r, -aizh-, -iə; -ash-, -aa-,-ai-\ *var of* CASHMERE

kashmir goat *n, usu cap K* [fr. *Kashmir*, region in the northern part of the Indian subcontinent] **:** an Indian goat raised chiefly for its undercoat of fine soft wool that constitutes the cashmere wool of commerce

kash·miri *or* **cash·miri** \⸗'mirē\ *n, pl* **kashmiris** *or* **kashmiri** *usu cap* **1 :** a native or inhabitant of Kashmir **2 :** the Dard language of the Kashmir people

¹kash·mir·ian \(')⸗'mirēən\ *adj, usu cap* **1 :** of, relating to, or characteristic of Kashmir **2 :** of, relating to, or characteristic of the people of Kashmir

²kashmirian \"\ *n* -s *cap* **:** KASHMIRI

ka·shou·bish \kə'shübish\ *n* -ES *cap* **:** the Kashubian language

kash·ruth *or* **kash·rut** \käsh'rüt(h), '⸗ˌ⸗\ *also* **kash·rus** \'käshrəs, -rüs\ *n* -s [*kashruth, kashrut* fr. Heb *kashrūth, kashrūt*, lit., fitness, fr. *kāshēr* kosher, fit, proper; *kashrus* fr. Yiddish, fr. Heb *kashrūth*] **1 :** the state of being kosher according to Jewish religious law ⟨rabbinical approval of the ~ of the new scroll of the Torah⟩ **2 :** the Jewish dietary laws ⟨meals for Orthodox Jews who observe ~⟩ — compare HECHSHER

kashua *var of* CACHUA

ka·shube *or* **ka·shub** \kə'shüb\ *n* -s *cap* **1 :** a member of a Slavonic Pomeranian people who live just west of the mouth of the Vistula river **2 :** KASHUBIAN

ka·shu·bi·an \kə'shübēən\ *or* **kasubian** *or* **kas·su·bi·an** *also* **cas·su·bi·an** *or* **ca·su·bi·an** \kə'sü-\ *n* -s *cap* [*Kashube* + E *-ian*, n. suffix] **1 :** KASHUBE 1 **2 :** a West Slavic language closely related to Polish and spoken in the region of Danzig

kasida *var of* QASIDA

kas·ka \'kaskə\ *n, pl* **kaska** *or* **kaskas** *usu cap* **1 a :** an Athapaskan people of the Liard river valley of the Yukon and British Columbia **b :** a member of such people **2 :** the language of the Kaska people — called also *Nahane*; see MONTAGNARD

kaso·lite \'kasəˌlīt, kə'sōˌl-\ *n* -s [*Kasolo*, Katanga, Belgian Congo, its locality + E *-ite*] **:** a mineral $Pb(UO_2)SiO_4H_2O$ consisting of a hydrous uranium lead silicate that occurs in yellow-ocher monoclinic crystals

kas·sel *also* **cas·sel** \'kasəl, 'käs-\ *adj, usu cap* [fr. *Kassel*, city in central Germany] **:** of or from the city of Kassel, Germany **:** of the kind or style prevalent in Kassel

kas·site *or* **cas·site** \'kaˌsīt\ *n* -s *usu cap* **1 :** a member of a people inhabiting parts of the Iranian plateau south of the Caspian sea and ruling Babylon between 1600 and 1200 B.C. **2 :** the Elamite language of the Kassite people

kas·tu·ra \kə'stürə\ *n* -s [Hindi *kastūrī*, lit., musk, fr. Skt *kastūrikā*, fr. Gk *kastorion* castor, fr. neut. of *kastoreios, kastorios* of a beaver, fr. *kastor-*, *kastōr* beaver — more at CASTOR] **:** MUSK DEER

kaswa *var of* CACHUA

kat *or* **khat** *or* **qat** *or* **q'at** *or* **quat** *or* **cat** \'kät\ *n* -s [Ar *qāt*] **:** a shrub (*Catha edulis*) cultivated by the Arabs for its leaves that act as a stimulant narcotic when chewed or used as a tea — called also *African tea, Arabian tea*

ka·ta \ˈkä(,)tä\ *n* -s [Jap] **:** form practice in judo **:** a set of exercises in judo — compare RANDORI

kata- *or* **kat-** *prefix* [Gk — more at CATA-] **:** CATA-

katabanian *usu cap, var of* QATABANIAN

ka·tab·a·sis *or* **ca·tab·a·sis** \kəˈtabəsə̇s\ *n, pl* **kataba·ses** *or* **cataba·ses** \-bə,sēz\ [Gk *katabasis* descent, fr. *katabainein* to go down, fr. *kata-* cata- + *bainein* to go — more at COME] **1 :** a going or marching down or back **:** RETREAT; *esp* **:** a military retreat ⟨the Russian anabasis and ~ of Napoleon —Thomas DeQuincey⟩ ⟨the tragic and precipitate ~ of the UN troops —H.L.Ickes⟩ **2 :** a troparion sung after the two sides of the choir descend to the middle of the church at the end of each ode of the canon at matins in the Eastern Orthodox Church

kat·a·bat·ic \ˌkad·əˈbad·ik\ *adj* [LGk *katabatikos* of descent, fr. Gk *katabatos* descending (fr. *katabainein* to descend) + *-ikos* -ic] **:** of or relating to the downward motion of air (as in air drainage induced by surface cooling)

kat·a·bel·la \ˌkatəˈbelə\ *n* -s [origin unknown] *dial Brit* **:** HEN HARRIER

katabolism *var of* CATABOLISM

kata·chro·ma·sis *or* **cata·chro·ma·sis** \ˌkad·əˈkrōməsə̇s\ *n, pl* **katachroma·ses** *or* **catachroma·ses** \-mə,sēz\ [NL, fr. *kata-* or *cata-* + *chrom-* + connective *-a-* + *-sis*] **:** the mitotic nuclear transformations leading to formation of daughter nuclei from the chromosome groups separated in anaphase — compare ANACHROMASIS

katagenesis *var of* CATAGENESIS

ka·ta·ka·na \ˌkäd·əˈkänə\ *n* -s [Jap, fr. *kata* side + *kana*] **:** a set of symbols for writing Japanese kana having characters that are in general squarer and more angular than those of the hiragana

kata·mor·phism *or* **cata·mor·phism** \ˌkad·əˈmȯr,fizəm\ *n* -s [*kata-* or *cata-* + *-morphism*] **:** the breaking down of rock by chemical or mechanical processes — compare ANAMORPHISM, METAMORPHISM

kata·mor·pho·sis \ˌkad·əˈmȯrfəsə̇s *sometimes* -ˌmȯrˈfōs-\ *n* [NL, fr. *kata-* + *morphosis*] **:** evolutionary change based on or involving hypomorphosis

ka·ta·na \kəˈtänə\ *n* -s [Jap] **:** a single-edged sword that is the longer of a pair worn by the Japanese samurai

ka·tang \kəˈtäŋ\ *n, pl* **katang** *or* **katangs** *usu cap* **1 :** a Moi people of northern Vietnam **2 :** a member of the Katang people

katastate *var of* CATASTATE

kata·thermometer *or* **cata·thermometer** \ˈ|kad·ə+\ *n* [*kata-* or *cata-* + *thermometer*] **:** a large-bulbed alcohol thermometer used to measure the cooling effect of particular atmospheric conditions or to measure moderate air velocities by means of the cooling effect

katatonic *var of* CATATONIC

ka·ta·ya·ma \ˌkäd·əˈyämə\ *n, cap* [NL, prob. fr. *Katayama*, town in western Honshu, Japan] **:** a genus of Oriental freshwater snails (family Bulimidae) including important intermediate hosts of a human schistosome (*Schistosoma japonicum*) — see ONCOMELANIA

katcina *or* **katchina** *var of* KACHINA

[1]**kate** \ˈkāt, *usu* -ād·+V\ *n* -s [fr. *Kate*, nickname for the name *Catherine*] **1** *dial Eng* **:** HAWFINCH **2 :** PILEATED WOODPECKER

[2]**kâ·te** \ˈkätə\ *n, pl* **kâte** *or* **kâtes** *usu cap* **1 a :** a people of the Huon peninsula of the Territory of New Guinea **b :** a member of such people **2 :** the Papuan language of the Kâte people

kate green·a·way \ˈ|kāt'grēnə,wā\ *adj, usu cap K&G* [after *Kate* (Catherine) *Greenaway* †1901 Eng. painter and illustrator of children's books] *of clothing* **:** having a long full skirt, short waist and sleeves, round neck, and usu. a sash and ruffled edges ⟨in her green *Kate Greenaway* pelisse, with the long band of soft beaver running from neck to hem —Victoria Lincoln⟩

ka·tel \ˈkäd·ᵊl\ *n* -s [Afrik, fr. Pg *catel, catre* cot, fr. Tamil-Malayalam *kaṭṭil* bedstead, bier — more at COT] **:** a wooden hammock used in Africa as a bed in a wagon

ka·ter's pendulum \ˈkäd·ə(r)z-\ *n, usu cap K* [after Henry *Kater* †1835 Eng. scientist] **:** a compound pendulum with adjustable knife edges placed respectively at the center of suspension and near the center of oscillation and used to determine acceleration of gravity by means of the period of oscillation

ka·thak \kəˈtäk\ *n* -s [Beng, professional storyteller, fr. Skt *kathaka*, fr. *kathayati* he tells, narrates, fr. *kathā* talk, story, fr. *kathā* how; akin to Skt *ka* who? — more at WHO] **:** an intricate dance of northern India that includes passages of narrative pantomime — compare BHARATA NATYA, KATHAKALI, MANIPURI

ka·tha·ka·li \ˌkäd·əˈkälē\ *n* -s [Malayalam *kathakali* drama, fr. *katha* story (fr. Skt *kathā* talk, fr. *kathā* how) + *kaḷi* play; Skt *kathā* how akin to Skt *ka* who? — more at WHO] **:** a spectacular lyric dance drama of southern India based on Hindu literature and performed with acrobatic energy and highly stylized pantomime — compare BHARATA NATYA, KATHAK, MANIPURI

kat·hal \ˈkət,həl\ *n* -s [Hindi *kaṭ-hal*, fr. Skt *kaṇṭakaphala*, fr. *kaṇṭa* thorn + *phala* fruit] **:** JACKFRUIT 1

ka·tha·re·vu·sa *or* **ka·tha·re·vou·sa** \ˌkäthəˈrevə(,)sä\ *n* -s *cap* [NGk *kathareuousa*, fr. Gk, fem. of *kathareuōn*, pres. part. of *kathareuein* to be pure, fr. *katharos* pure] **:** modern Greek conforming to classic Greek usage and tending to reject non-Greek vocabulary — compare DEMOTIC 3

kath·a·robe \ˈkathə,rōb\ *n* -s [ISV *katharo-* (fr. Gk *katharos* pure) + *-be* (as in *microbe*)] **:** a katharobic organism

kath·a·robic \ˌ==ˈrōbik, -ˈräb-\ *adj* [*katharobe* + *-ic*] **:** living in or being a highly oxygenated medium free from organic matter — compare MESOSAPROBIC, SAPROBIC

kath·a·rom·e·ter \ˌ==ˈrämәd·ə(r)\ *n* [Gk *katharos* pure + E *-meter*] **:** an apparatus for determining the composition of a gas mixture by measuring thermal conductivity

katharsis *var of* CATHARSIS

kathen·o·theism \(ˈ)kat|henōthē,izəm, kaˈthe-; (ˌ)kat|henō|th-, ka|thenō|th-\ *n* [*katheno-* (fr. Gk *kath' hena* one at a time, fr. *kata* down, according to, by + *hena*, acc. sing. masc. of *heis* one) + *theism* — more at CATA-, SAME] **:** the worship of one god at a time as supreme without denying the existence of other gods and including the tendency to make different gods supreme one after the other — compare HENOTHEISM

kathen·o·the·ist \-ˌəst\ *n* [*kathenotheism* + *-ist*] **:** one whose worship exemplifies kathenotheism

ka·thi·a·wa·ri \ˌkäd·ēəˈwärē\ *n, usu cap* [prob. fr. Hindi or Gujarati *kāthiāwāḍī* of Kāthiāwād (Kathiawar), peninsula on the western coast of India] **1 :** a breed of small hardy horses of India of partially Arab ancestry **2** -s *often cap* **:** a horse of the Kathiawari breed

ka·this·ma *also* **ca·this·ma** \ˈkäthēzmə\ *n, pl* **kathisma·ta** \ˌkäˈthēzmətə\ [MGk *kathisma*, fr. Gk, sinking, settling down, fr. *kathizein* to seat, sit down, fr. *kata-* cata- + *hizein* to seat; akin to Gk *hezesthai* to sit — more at SIT] **:** one of the 20 sections into which the Psalter is divided for liturgical use in the Eastern Orthodox Church

kathodic *var of* CATHODIC

katholikos *var of* CATHOLICOS

[1]**kati** *var of* CATTY

[2]**ka·ti** \ˈkäd·ē\ *n, pl* **kati** *or* **katis** *usu cap* **1 :** a Kafir people of easternmost Kafiristan in the Hindu Kush mountains of Afghanistan **2 :** a member of the Kati people

ka·tik \ˈkäd·ik\ *n* -s *cap* [Hindi *kātik*, fr. Skt *kārttika* — more at KARTIK] **:** KARTIK

katin *usu cap, var of* KHATIN

kati·po \ˈkäd·ə,pō, ˈkad-\ *n* -s [Maori] **:** a small venomous spider (*Latrodectus hasselti* or *L. scelio*) of eastern Asia, Australia, and New Zealand related to the American black widow and commonly black with a red stripe on the abdomen — see REDBACK SPIDER

kat·man·du \ˌkat,manˈdü, -ˌmän- *also* ˌkät,män- *or* ˈkätmən-\ *adj, usu cap* [fr. *Katmandu*, Nepal] **:** of or from Katmandu, the capital of Nepal **:** of the kind or style prevalent in Katmandu

ka·to \ˈkäd·(,)ō\ *n, pl* **kato** *or* **katos** *usu cap* [Pomo, lake] **1 a :** an Athapaskan people of northwestern California **b :** a member of such people **2 :** a language of the Kato and Wailaki peoples

ka·tong lu·ang \ˈkä,tȯŋləˈwäŋ\ *or* **ka·ton luang** \-tȯnl-\ *n, pl* **katong luang** *or* **katon luang** *usu cap K&L* [Siamese, lit., savages of the yellow leaf] **1 :** a migratory pygmy people of mountainous regions of Thailand **2 :** a member of the Katong Luang people

ka·ton·kel \kəˈtäŋkəl\ *n* -s [Afrik] **1** *Africa* **:** BARRACUDA 2 **2** *Africa* **:** ATLANTIC BONITO

katoptrite *var of* CATOPTRITE

ka·to·wi·ce \ˌkäd·əˈvētsə\ *adj, usu cap* [fr. *Katowice*, city in southern Poland] **:** of or from the city of Katowice, Poland **:** of the kind or style prevalent in Katowice

kats *pl of* KAT

ka·tsu \ˈkät(,)sü\ *n* -s [Jap] **:** resuscitation of an unconscious judoka

katsup *var of* CATSUP

kat·su·ra tree \ˈkätsərə-\ *also* **katsura** *n* -s [Jap *katsura*] **:** a deciduous tree (*Cercidiphyllum japonicum*) of the order Ranales that has short spurs on its branches, broadly ovate leaves with crenate-serrate margins, and fruit which is a pod enclosing many winged seeds and that is sometimes cultivated as an ornamental esp. for its dark blue-green foliage which turns bright yellow or red in autumn

kat·su·won·i·dae \ˌkatsəˈwänə,dē\ *n pl, cap* [NL, fr. *Katsuwonus*, type genus (fr. Jap *katsuo* victorfish) + *-idae*] *in some classifications* **:** a family of scombroid fishes comprising the oceanic bonitos and closely related forms and including a type genus (*Katsuwonus*) that is commonly placed in the family Scombridae

ka·tu·ka \ˈkəd·əkə\ *n* -s [perh. fr. Skt *kaṭuka* sharp, bitter, fierce, fr. *kaṭu*, prob. of Dravidian origin; akin to Tamil *kaṭu* to be pungent, ache, Malayalam *kaṭu* pungent, extreme] **:** RUSSELL'S VIPER

ka·tun \ˈkä,tün\ *n* -s [Maya, fr. *ka* 20 + *tun* year of 360 days] **:** a period of 20 tuns in the Maya calendar — compare BAKTUN, PICTUN

katy *var of* KADY

ka·ty·did *also* **ca·ty·did** \ˈkād·|ē,did, -āt|, |i,- *sometimes* ,==ˈ=\ *n* -s [imit.] **1 :** LONG-HORNED GRASSHOPPER; *esp* **:** any of several large green American long-horned grasshoppers that have greatly elongated antennae, a long ovipositor, long hind legs, and stridulating organs on the fore wings of the males with which a loud shrill sound is produced **2 :** a pair of wheels usu. from 7 to 12 feet in diameter used with a heavy axle to transport logs in lumbering

katydid

katz·en·jam·mer \ˈkatsən,jamə(r)\ *n* -s [G, fr. *katzen* (pl. of *katze* cat, fr. OHG *kazza*) + *jammer* distress, misery, fr. OHG *jāmar*, fr. *jāmar*, adj., sad; akin to OE *geōmor* sad, OS *jāmar* — more at CAT] **1 :** the nausea, headache, and debility that often follow dissipation or drunkenness **:** HANGOVER ⟨asking you what you prescribe for a slight case of ~ —Malcolm Lowry⟩ **2 :** distress, depression, or confusion resembling that caused by a hangover ⟨forgetting the spiritual ~s from which men of culture periodically suffer in new . . . countries —*New Republic*⟩ **3 :** a discordant clamor ⟨during all this ~, divers . . . have been reconnoitering around the craft to learn the identity of its owner —S.J.Perelman⟩

kauch \ˈkäk\ *var of* KIAUGH

kau·mog·ra·pher \kȯˈmägrəfə(r)\ *n* -s [Gk *kauma* burning heat (fr. *kaiein* to burn) + E *-o-* + *-grapher* — more at CAUSTIC] **:** a worker who transfers designs, trademarks, or other printed material to cloth articles with a hot iron

kau·nas \ˈkaünəs\ *adj, usu cap* [fr. *Kaunas*, Lithuania] **:** of or from the city of Kaunas, Lithuania **:** of the kind or style prevalent in Kaunas

kau·ri *also* **kau·rie** *or* **kau·ry** *or* **kaw·rie** *or* **kaw·ry** *or* **cow·rie** *or* **kao·ri** \ˈkaürē\ *n, pl* **kauris** *also* **kauries** [Maori *kawri*] **1** *or* **kauri pine :** a tree of the genus *Agathis*; *esp* **:** a tall timber tree (*A. australis*) of New Zealand having fine white straight-grained wood **2 :** the wood of the kauri tree **3** *or* **kauri resin** *or* **kauri gum** *or* **kauri copal :** a light-colored to brown copal from the kauri tree found usu. as a fossil in the ground but also collected by tapping living trees and used chiefly in making varnishes and linoleum

kauri-butanol value *n* **:** a measure of the solvent power of a petroleum thinner for paints and varnishes that is determined as the number of milliliters of the thinner just causing turbidity in a standard solution of a hard kauri in normal butyl alcohol

ka·va *or* **ca·va** \ˈkävə\ *also* **ka·va·ka·va** \ˌ==ˈ==\ *n* -s [Tongan & Marquesan *kava*, lit., bitter] **1 a :** an Australasian shrubby pepper (*Piper methysticum*) from whose crushed root an intoxicating beverage is made **b :** the beverage made from kava **2 :** the dried rhizome and roots of the kava shrub formerly used as a diuretic and genitourinary antiseptic

ka·vass \kəˈväs\ *n* -ES [Turk *kavas*, fr. Ar *qawwās* bowman] **1 :** an armed constable or courier in Turkey **2 :** a consular guard in the countries of the eastern Mediterranean

kavil *var of* CAVEL

ka·vi·ka \kəˈvēkə\ *n* -s [origin unknown] **:** MALAY APPLE

ka·vi·ron·do \ˌkävəˈrän(,)dō\ *n, pl* **kavirondo** *or* **kavirondos** *usu cap* **:** BANTU KAVIRONDO

kav·va·nah *or* **kaw·wa·nah** \ˌkävəˈnä\ *n, pl* **kav·va·noth** *or* **kav·va·not** *or* **kaw·wa·noth** *or* **kaw·wa·not** \-ˈnōt(h), -ōs\ [Heb *kawanāh*, fr. *kawēn* to devote, intend] *Jewish relig* **:** intention to carry out a divine command or precept **:** devotion or fervor in prayer ⟨the women prayed with complete ~⟩

kav·ya \ˈkävyə\ *n* -s [Skt *kāvya*, fr. *kāvya*, adj., poetical] **:** poetic composition in Sanskrit and other Indic languages characterized by decorative elaboration

[1]**kaw** \ˈkȯ\ *n* -s *usu cap* **:** KANSA

[2]**kaw** \"\ *n, pl* **kaw** *or* **kaws** *usu cap* **:** AKHA

ka·wa \kəˈwä\ *n* -s *usu cap* **:** WA

ka·wa·gu·chi \kəˈwägə(,)chē\ *adj, usu cap* [fr. *Kawaguchi*, city in southeastern Honshu, Japan] **:** of or from the city of Kawaguchi, Japan **:** of the kind or style prevalent in Kawaguchi

ka·wai·isu \kəˈwīə(,)sü\ *n, pl* **kawaiisu** *or* **kawaiisus** *usu cap* **1 :** a Shoshonean people of the Tehachapi mountains of southern California **2 :** a member of the Kawaiisu people

ka·wa·ka \kəˈwäkə\ *n* -s [Maori] **:** a New Zealand timber tree (*Libocedrus plumosa*)

[1]**ka·wa·ka·wa** \ˈkäwə|käwə\ *or* **kawa** *n* -s [Maori] **:** KAVA 1

2 : a shrub or small tree (*Piper excelsum*) chiefly of New Zealand that has cordate to ovate aromatic leaves and is held to be sacred by the Maoris

[2]**kawakawa** \"\ *n, pl* **kawakawa** [Hawaiian] *Hawaii* **:** LITTLE TUNA

kaw·chot·ti·ne *also* **kaw·chod·in·ne** \kōˈchädənē\ *n, pl* **kawchottine** *or* **kawchottines** *usu cap* **:** HARE 3

ka·wi \ˈkäwē\ *or* **ka·vi** \-ävē\ *n* -s *usu cap* [Jav *kawi* poem, poetical, fr. Skt *kavi* wise, learned, poet or Skt *kāvya* poetical (fr. *kavi*); prob. akin to Gk *akouein* to hear — more at HEAR] **:** the ancient Austronesian language of Java

[1]**kay** \ˈkā\ *adj* [ME, left] *dial Eng* **:** LEFT, SINISTER

[2]**kay** *var of* KEY

[3]**kay** *also* **ka** \ˈkā\ *n* -s **1 :** the letter *k* **2 :** something having the shape of the letter K

kaya \ˈkīə, ˈkäyə\ *n* -s [Jap] **:** a Japanese tree (*Torreya nucifera*) with light red bark and yellow lustrous close-grained wood

[1]**kay·ak** *also* **ky·ak** *or* **cay·ak** *or* **ka·jak** \ˈkī,ak *also* -ī,yak\ *n* -s [Esk (Greenland dial.) *qajaq*] **1 :** a fully decked-in Eskimo skin canoe propelled by a double-bladed paddle — compare UMIAK **2 :** a canvas-covered portable canoe that resembles a kayak and is paddled or sailed widely in the U.S. — compare FALTBOAT

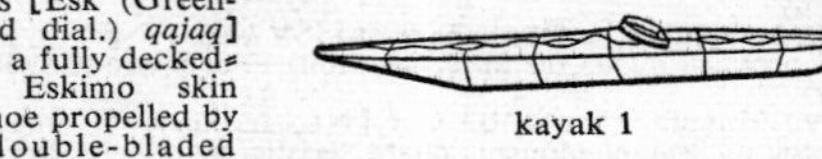

kayak 1

[2]**kayak** \"\ *vi* -ED/-ING/-S **:** to paddle or sail a kayak ⟨I was out ~ing for seal —D.B.Putnam⟩ — **kay·ak·er** \-akə(r)\ *n* -s

kay·an \ˈkīən\ *n, pl* **kayan** *or* **kayans** *usu cap* [native name in northern Borneo] **1 :** a Dayak people of north central Borneo sometimes regarded with the Kenya as a subdivision of the Bahau **2 :** a member of the Kayan people

kayapo *usu cap, var of* CAYAPO

ka·yasth \ˈkäyəst\ *or* **ka·yas·tha** \-stə\ *n* -s *usu cap* [Skt *kāyastha*, prob. fr. *kāya* body, group + *-stha* standing, being in; akin to Skt *cinoti* he gathers, heaps up and to Skt *tiṣṭhati* he stands — more at POET, STAND] **:** a member of a high Hindu caste esp. numerous in Bengal and Uttar Pradesh whose caste occupation is that of clerks, writers, and accountants

kay·en·ta \kīˈ(y)entə\ *adj, usu cap* [fr. *Kayenta*, village in northeastern Arizona, where remains of the culture were found] **:** of or belonging to the northern Arizona branch of the Anasazi culture that provides a record from the period of the earth-lodge villages to the Great Pueblo centers

kayles *var of* KAILS

[1]**kayo** \(ˈ)kā|ō\ *n* -s [pronunciation of *KO*, abbr. or n.] **:** KNOCKOUT

[2]**kayo** \"\ *vt* **kayoed; kayoed; kayoing; kayoes** *or* **kayos :** to knock out

kayuvava *or* **kayubaba** *usu cap, var of* CAYUVAVA

ka·zak \kəˈzak, -ˈzäk\ *n* -s *usu cap* [Kazak, lit., free person, adventurer, vagabond] **1** *or* **ka·zakh** \"\ **a :** a Turko-Tatar Muslim people of central Asia **b :** a member of the Kazak people **2** *or* **kazakh** *or* **qa·zaq** \"\ **:** TURKI **3 :** a bright-colored all-wool Caucasian rug woven by nomads often in sawtooth patterns or highly stylized plant or animal designs **4 :** OXBLOOD

ka·zan \kəˈzan, -ˈzän\ *adj, usu cap* [fr. *Kazan*, city in the eastern part of European Russia, U.S.S.R.] **:** of or from the city of Kazan, U.S.S.R. **:** of the kind or style prevalent in Kazan

kazan tatar *n, usu cap K&T* **1 :** a member of a group of Tatars living in the Tatar Republic, U.S.S.R. **2 :** the Turkic language of the Kazan people

kazarian *usu cap, var of* KHAZAR

kazi *var of* QADI

ka·zoo \kəˈzü\ *also* **ga·zoo** \gə-\ *n* -s [imit.] **:** a device into which a person sings or hums and which consists usu. of an open-ended tube with a membrane-covered side hole ⟨the ~ is that noisemaking toy that comes nowadays in Christmas stockings —Harlan Cleveland⟩ — called also *eunuch flute, mirliton, Tommy talker, zarah*

KB *abbr* **1** King's Bench **2** kitchen and bathroom **3** kite balloon **4** knight bachelor

KBP *abbr* kite balloon pilot

kc *abbr* **1** kilocycle **2** kilocycles per second

KC *abbr* **1** kennel club **2** king's counsel **3** knight commander

KČ *abbr* [Czech *koruna československý*] koruna

kcal *abbr* kilocalorie; kilogram calorie

k-capture \ˈ=,==\ *also* **k-electron capture** \ˈ|==ˈ=(,)=-\ *n, usu cap K* **:** the capture by an atomic nucleus of an electron from an inner energy level or orbit of the extranuclear electrons

kd *abbr* killed

KD *abbr* **1** kiln-dried **2** knocked down

KDCL *abbr* knocked down, in carloads

KDF *abbr* knocked down flat

KDLCL *abbr* knocked down, in less than carloads

kdm *abbr* kingdom

KE *abbr* kinetic energy

ke- — see KER-

kea \ˈkeə, ˈkēə\ *n* -s [Maori] **:** a large parrot (*Nestor notabilis*) of South Island, New Zealand, that is predominantly green with a very long heavy bill and that is normally insectivorous but sometimes attacks sheep, slashing the back to reach the kidney fat on which it feeds

kea·corn \ˈkā,kȯrn\ *n* -s [origin unknown] **1** *dial* **:** WINDPIPE **2** *dial* **:** GULLET

keat *var of* KEET

keats·ian \ˈkētsēən\ *adj, usu cap* [John *Keats* †1821 Eng. poet + E *-ian*] **:** of, relating to, or characteristic of the poet Keats or his poetry ⟨the manner of Keats is imitated to excess . . . and there is a similar profusion of *Keatsian* classical allusions —W.H.Gardner⟩

keawe *var of* KIAWE

kebab *or* **kebob** *var of* KABOB

keb·bie \ˈkebi\ *n* -s [prob. alter. of earlier *kibble*, fr. ME *kyble*] *chiefly Scot* **:** a rough hook-headed walking stick

keb·buck *also* **keb·bock** \ˈkebək\ *n* -s [ME (Sc dial.) *cabok*, fr. ScGael *ceapag* (also, piece of sod, barrow wheel)] *dial Brit* **:** a whole cheese

keb·yar \ˈkeb,yär\ *n* -s [Balinese] **:** a Balinese solo dance performed with the upper part of the body from a sitting position with crossed ankles

kechua *usu cap, var of* QUECHUA

kech·u·ma·ran \ˌkechəməˈrän\ *n* -s *usu cap* [*Kechua* + *Aymaran*] **:** a language stock comprising Aymara and Quechua

[1]**keck** \ˈkek\ *vi* -ED/-ING/-S [imit.] **:** to make the sounds of retching

[2]**keck** \"\ *n* -s [back-formation fr. [1]*kex*] *Brit* **:** WILD CHERVIL 1

[1]**keck·le** \ˈkekəl\ *dial var of* CACKLE

[2]**keckle** \"\ *also* **kack·le** \ˈkak-\ *vt* -ED/-ING/-S [origin unknown] **:** to wind with rope to prevent chafing

keck·ling \ˈkek(ə)liŋ\ *n* -s **:** old rope wound around a cable to prevent chafing

keck·sy \ˈkeksi\ *n* -ES [[1]*kex* + *-y*] *chiefly dial Eng* **:** KEX

ked \ˈked\ *n* -s [origin unknown] **:** SHEEP KED

ked·dah \ˈkedə, kəˈdä\ *n* -s [Hindi *khedā*] *in India* **:** an enclosure constructed to trap wild elephants

[1]**kedge** \ˈkej\ *adj* [ME *kygge*] *chiefly Scot* **:** BRISK, LIVELY

[2]**kedge** \"\ *vt* -ED/-ING/-S [ME *caggen*] **:** to move (a ship) from one position to another by means of a line attached to a kedge dropped at the distance and in the direction desired

[3]**kedge** \"\ *or* **kedge anchor** \"-\ *also* **kedg·er** \ˈkejə(r)\ *n* -s **:** a small anchor that is used in kedging or other light work

ked·ger·ee *or* **keg·er·ee** \ˈkejə,rē, ,==ˈ=\ *n* -s [Hindi *khicṛī*, fr. Skt *khiccā*] **1** *in India* **:** a mixture of rice, beans, lentils, and seasonings sometimes with smoked fish **2 :** cooked flaked fish, rice, hard-boiled eggs, and seasoning heated in cream

kedgy \ˈkejē, -ji\ *chiefly Scot var of* CADGY 1

kedjavé *var of* KAJAWAH

ked·lock \ˈked,läk, -ˌlək\ *n* -s [ME *ketelok*, fr. OE *cedelc*] **1 :** CHARLOCK **2 :** WHITE MUSTARD

ke·du·shah \kəˈdüshə\ *n, pl* **kedu·shoth** *or* **kedu·shot** \-ˌshōt(h), -ōs\ *usu cap* [Heb *qĕdhushshāh* holiness] **:** a recital of a prayer in the Jewish ritual introduced into the third benediction of the Amidah and sometimes including the responses

keech \ˈkēch\ *n* -ES [origin unknown] *dial Eng* **:** a fatty lump

[1]**keek** \ˈkēk\ *vi* -ED/-ING/-S [ME *kiken, keken*, prob. fr. MD *kiken* to look; akin to MLG *kīken* to look] *chiefly Scot* **:** PEEP, LOOK ⟨opened the low door and ~*ed* into the room —Alasdair Carmichael⟩

[2]**keek** \"\ *n* -s *chiefly Scot* **:** PEEP, LOOK ⟨take another ~ at the redcoats —R.L.Stevenson⟩

keekwilee-house \ˈkēkwə(,)lē-\ *n* [Chinook jargon *keekwilee* below, fr. Chinook *gigwalix*] **:** an earth lodge partially below the surface of the ground used by the Indians of the northwest coast of No. America — compare BARRABORA

[1]**keel** \ˈkēl, *esp before pause or consonant* -ēəl\ *vb* -ED/-ING/-S [ME *kelen*, fr. OE *cēlan*, fr. *cōl* cool — more at COOL] *vt* **1** *now dial* **:** COOL; *specif* **:** to keep esp. by stirring or skimming from boiling over ⟨while greasy Joan doth ~ the pot —Shak.⟩ **2** *obs* **:** to make less ardent or violent in feeling **~** *vi* **1** *now dial* **:** [4]COOL **2 :** to become less ardent or violent in feeling

[2]**keel** \"\ *n* -s [ME *kele*, fr. MD *kiel*; akin to OE *cēol* ship, OS & OHG *kiol*, ON *kjöll* ship, Gk *gaulos* milk pail, kind of ship, OE *cot* small house — more at COT] **1 a** (1) **:** a flat-bottomed ship; *esp* **:** a barge used on the Tyne to carry coal from Newcastle (2) **:** a barge load of coal **b :** a British unit of weight for coal based on the amount one keel can hold now equal to 21.2 long tons **2 :** a long ship of the early Norsemen

[3]**keel** \"\ *n* -s [ME *kele, keole*, fr. ON *kil-, kjölr*; akin to MD & MLG *kiel, keel* keel, OE *ceole* throat, beak of a ship — more at GLUTTON] **1 a** (1) **:** a longitudinal timber or series of timbers scarfed together extending from stem to stern along the center of the bottom of a boat, often projecting below the bottom, and constituting the boat's principal timber to which the ribs are attached on each side — compare CENTERBOARD, FALSE KEEL; see SHIP illustration (2) **:** a large keel plate or keel on a metal ship (3) **:** KEELSON (4) **:** BILGE KEEL **b** (1) **:** BOAT, SHIP (2) **:** a boat or ship having a keel as opposed to one having a centerboard or a flat bottom ⟨the shipyard laid down ten

new ~s in a year⟩ **c :** the assembly of members at the bottom of the hull of a semirigid or rigid airship that provides special strength to resist hogging and sagging and serves to distribute the effect of concentrated loads along the hull **2 :** a projection suggesting a keel **:** RIDGE: as **a :** a biological process forming a ridge **:** CARINA **b :** a keel molding or the ridge of one

[4]**keel** \"\ *vb* -ED/-ING/-S *vt* **1 :** to cause to turn or tip to the side away from a vertical plane or over esp. so that the bottom shows **:** OVERTURN, CAPSIZE — usu. used with *over* or *up* ⟨sailing vessels lying ~*ed* over at low tide in the harbors —Richard Joseph⟩ **2 :** to cause to collapse or faint — usu. used with *over* ⟨the continued heat ~*ed* over quite a few of the summer visitors⟩ **~** *vi* **1 :** to turn or tip away from a vertical plane or over esp. so that the bottom shows ⟨sailing craft ~ to the lee rail in a spanking breeze —*Amer. Guide Series: Conn.*⟩ **:** OVERTURN, CAPSIZE — usu. used with *over* or *up* ⟨the yacht swung across wind and ~*ed* over⟩ ⟨brakes squealing and slipping on the rails and engines ~*ing* over into drifts —Helen Rich⟩ **2 :** to fall in or as if in a faint **:** SWOON — usu. used with *over* ⟨so tired he ~*ed* over onto the bed⟩ ⟨just one drink, and ~*ed* right over —George Spanner⟩

[5]**keel** \"\ *or* **keel disease** *n* -S [[4]*keel*] **:** acute septicemic salmonellosis or paratyphoid of ducklings marked by sudden collapse and death of apparently healthy birds

[6]**keel** \"\ *n* -S [ME (Sc dial.) *keyle*, prob. fr. ScGael *cīl*] **1** *now chiefly dial* **:** a red ocher used for marking something (as lumber or sheep) **:** RUDDLE; *also* **:** a mark made with this material (as at the end of a warp of yarn to show whether the weaver has used the full length) **2 :** a colored marking chalk or crayon used by engineers and surveyors

[7]**keel** \"\ *vt* -ED/-ING/-S *Scot* **:** to mark with keel

keel·age \'kēlij\ *n* -S [[3]*keel* + *-age*] **:** a toll for a ship entering and anchoring or mooring in a port esp. in Great Britain

keelback \'=,=\ *also* **keelback snake** *n* [[3]*keel* + *back*] **:** a small aquatic Indian snake (*Natrix piscator*) with strongly keeled dorsal scales

keelbill *or* **keelbird** \'=,=\ *n* [[3]*keel* + *bill* or *bird*] **:** ANI

keelblock \'=,=\ *n* [[3]*keel* + *block*] **:** a block of hard wood used to support the keel of a ship when under construction or when docked

keelboat \'=,=\ *n* [[3]*keel* + *boat*] **1 :** a shallow covered riverboat with a keel that is usu. rowed, poled, or towed and used for freight **2 :** a yacht or other sailboat having a keel as distinguished from one having a centerboard

keel·boat·man \"mən\ *n*, *pl* **keelboatmen :** a member of the crew of a keelboat

keel–bully \'=,==\ *n* [[2]*keel* + *bully*] *Brit* **:** one of the crew of a keel

keeled \'kē(ə)ld\ *adj* [[3]*keel* + *-ed*] **:** having a carina ⟨~ breastbone⟩ ⟨~ flower⟩

keeled snake *n* **:** a snake with strongly keeled scales; *esp* **:** a venomous Australian elapid (*Tropidechis carinatus*)

[1]**keel·er** \'kēlə(r)\ *n* -S [ME *kelare*, a tub used for cooling liquids, fr. *kelen* to cool + *-are* -er — more at KEEL] *now chiefly dial* **:** a broad shallow tub (as for a liquid or washing something)

[2]**keeler** \"\ *n* -S [[2]*keel* + *-er*] *dial Eng* **:** KEELMAN

[3]**keeler** \"\ *n* -S [[3]*keel* + *-er*] **:** a boat having a keel; *esp* **:** KEELBOAT

kee·ler polygraph \"-\ *n*, *usu cap K* [after Leonarde *Keeler* †1949 Amer. criminologist, its inventor] **:** an instrument for making a graphic record of the changes in blood pressure and pulse and respiration rate of someone being questioned under or as if under suspicion of guilt — called also *lie detector*

keel·haul \'kē(ə)l,hȯl\ *also* **keel·hale** \-hāl, *esp before pause or consonant* -āəl\ *vt* [D *kielhalen*, fr. *kiel* keel (fr. MD) + *halen* to fetch, draw, pull, fr. MD — more at KEEL, HAUL] **1 :** to haul (a person) under the keel of a ship either athwartships or from bow to stern by ropes in punishment (as on a naval vessel) or torture (as by pirates) **2 :** to rebuke with great severity

kee·lie \'kēlē, -li\ *n* -S [imit.] **1 :** KESTREL **2** *dial Brit* **:** a street urchin **:** LOAFER

[1]**keeling** *pres part of* KEEL

[2]**kee·ling** \'kēliŋ\ *n* -S [ME *keling*, perh. of Scand origin; akin to Icel *keila* cusk, ON, arm of the sea; akin to OHG *kīl* wedge — more at CHINE] *chiefly Scot* **:** CODFISH; *esp* **:** a large codfish

kee·li·vine \'kēli,vīn\ *n* -S [origin unknown] *Scot* **:** PENCIL; *esp* **:** one of black lead

keel·less \'kē(ə)lləs\ *adj* [[3]*keel* + *-less*] **:** having no keel ⟨a ~ boat⟩

keel line *n* [[3]*keel* + *line*] **:** the bottom or lowest line of a boat esp. along the keel

keel·man \'kē(ə)lmən\ *n*, *pl* **keelmen** [[2]*keel* + *man*] **:** a member of the crew of a keel

keel molding *n* [[3]*keel*] **:** a brace molding with a central projecting fillet resembling a keel

keels *pres 3d sing of* KEEL, *pl of* KEEL

keel–shaped scraper \'=,=-\ *n* **:** a prehistoric flint scraper consisting of a small core chipped at both ends and sides and resembling the bottom of a boat in shape

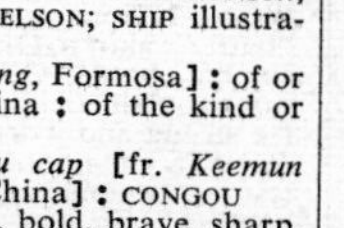

keel molding

keel·son *also* **kel·son** \'kelsən, 'kē(ə)l- *also* -lts-\ *n* -S [prob. of Scand origin; akin to Dan & Norw *kjølsvin*, Sw *kölsvin*, Norw dial. *kjølsvill*, prob. fr. *kjøl*, *köl* keel (fr. ON *kölr*) + *svin* pig, fr. ON *svīnn* — more at KEEL, SWINE] **:** a longitudinal structure in the framing of a ship to contribute stiffness, prevent local deformations, and distribute over a considerable length the effect of concentrated loads: **a :** a structure of timbers in a wooden ship parallel with and above the keel and fastened to it by long bolts passing through the floor timbers **b :** a deep continuous structure of plates and bars in a metal ship usu. in the form of a strong I beam secured at its ends to the stem and the sternpost and connected at its upper and lower edges to the reverse frames and keel plates respectively — called also *middle-line keelson*, *vertical keel;* see BILGE KEELSON, SIDE KEELSON; SHIP illustration

kee·lung \'kē¦lůŋ\ *adj*, *usu cap* [fr. *Keelung*, Formosa] **:** of or from the city of Keelung, Formosa, China **:** of the kind or style prevalent in Keelung

kee·mun \'kā¦mün, 'kē¦mən\ *n* -S *usu cap* [fr. *Keemun* (Ch'imen) district in Anhwei province, China] **:** CONGOU

[1]**keen** \'kēn\ *adj* -ER/-EST [ME *kene* wise, bold, brave, sharp, fr. OE *cēne* wise, bold, brave; akin to OHG *kuoni* bold, strong, MD *coene* bold, brave, ON *kœnn* wise, skillful, clever, OE *cnāwan* to know — more at KNOW] **1 a :** having a fine edge or point **:** SHARP ⟨a ~ blade⟩ ⟨a ~ sword⟩ **b :** affecting one as if by cutting **:** causing great distress to the mind or sensibilities ⟨~ sarcasm⟩ ⟨a ~ sense of guilt⟩ **c** (1) **:** affecting the senses or creating physical discomfort as if by cutting **:** PENETRATING, PIERCING ⟨a ~ wind⟩ ⟨~, cold winters —Edith Hamilton⟩ **:** STINGING ⟨a ~ slap⟩ **:** SHRILL ⟨a high ~ sound⟩ (2) **:** sharp or pungent to the sense ⟨a ~ scent⟩ **2 a :** characterized by intense interest, feeling, or desire **:** showing a quick and ardent responsiveness **:** EAGER, ENTHUSIASTIC ⟨a ~ swimmer⟩ ⟨fiery and dominant natures, eager to conquer, ~ to impress —A.C.Benson⟩ ⟨~ to go on a picnic⟩ ⟨both of them were ~ on skiing⟩ ⟨very ~ about the girl⟩; *also* **:** giving evidence of such qualities ⟨the features lean and ~ from restless intellectual energy —J.A.Froude⟩ **b** *of emotion or feeling* **:** INTENSE, GREAT ⟨a ~ desire to be in the forefront of activity⟩ ⟨the ~ delight in the chase —F.W.Maitland⟩ ⟨a ~ personal interest in the boy⟩ ⟨the ~ dread of the gods —M.R.Cohen⟩ **3 a :** acute or quick and penetrating (as in mental power) ⟨a ~ mind⟩ ⟨~ in their bargain —H.E.Scudder⟩ **:** intellectually sharp or incisive ⟨a ~ wit⟩ ⟨~ questions⟩ **:** ASTUTE ⟨~ businessmen —Gilbert Highet⟩; *also* **:** giving evidence of astuteness or the play of alert or carefully calculating minds ⟨~ competition⟩ ⟨debate was not as ~ as it might have been —Winston Churchill⟩ **b :** extremely sensitive in perception or in perceiving distinctions ⟨a ~ eyesight⟩ ⟨a ~ sense of smell⟩ **c :** marked by fine and extremely precise distinctions ⟨~ refinements of logic⟩ **4** *of ice in curling* **:** hard and clear **5** *Brit, of a price* **:** favorable to the purchaser **:** LOW ⟨outfits for all ranks and services at very ~ prices —*Nautical Mag.*⟩ **6** *slang* **:** WONDERFUL, DESIRABLE — a generalized expression of approval **syn** see EAGER, SHARP

[2]**keen** \"\ *adv* [ME *kene*, fr. *kene*, adj.] **:** KEENLY ⟨businessmen ~ set on practical affairs —J.W.Beach⟩

[3]**keen** \"\ *vt* -ED/-ING/-S [[1]*keen*] **:** to put a sharp edge on **:** SHARPEN ⟨the cutting edge of the knife is first ~*ed* up —J.V.A.Long⟩ ⟨~ the razor —Christopher Morley⟩

[4]**keen** \"\ *vb* -ED/-ING/-S [IrGael *caoinim* (I) lament, fr. OIr *coīnim*] *vi* **1 a :** to wail or bewail with a keen ⟨~*ed* like a squaw bereft —Minnie H. Moody⟩ **b :** to make a sound suggesting a keen ⟨the soft ~*ing* of the screech owls —A.W. Derleth⟩ ⟨the night was rent by ~*ing* sirens —*Time*⟩ ⟨the ~*ing* in the aerials rose to a witches' chorus —T.H.Raddall⟩ ⟨violins ~*ed* in the shadows —Albert Hubbell⟩ **2 :** to lament, mourn, or complain loudly **~** *vt* **:** to utter by keening ⟨~*ed* our sorrow —*Punch*⟩

[5]**keen** \"\ *n* -S [IrGael *caoine*] **1 a :** a lamentation or dirge for the dead uttered in a loud wailing voice **b :** a rhythmic recounting of the life and character of a dead person or an exhortation to vengeance for his death — compare CORONACH **2 :** a lamentation or cry of grief

keen·er \-nə(r)\ *n* -S [[4]*keen* + *-er*] **:** one that keens; *esp* **:** a professional usu. female mourner at a wake or funeral

keene's cement \'kēnz-\ *n*, *usu cap K* [after Richard W. *Keene*, 19th cent. Eng. inventor] **:** a hard-finish gypsum plaster to which alum has been added and which is used chiefly as a gauging plaster in lime mortar for walls (as of hospitals, stores, railroad stations) where an unusually tough and durable plaster is required

[1]**keening** *adj* [fr. pres. part. of [4]*keen*] **:** having the quality of or suggesting a keen ⟨the . . . cicada and his ~ cry —K.F. Weaver⟩ ⟨a long ~ scream like a rabbit caught in a gin trap —Hartley Howard⟩

[2]**keening** *n* -S [fr. gerund of [4]*keen*] **1 :** the act of keening ⟨mourning . . . is celebrated by self-laceration, the destruction of property, and daily ~ —William Lipkind⟩ ⟨~ was not confined to the period of death —Alfred Métraux⟩ ⟨the ~ of bagpipes —Lyn Harrington⟩ **2 :** [5]KEEN ⟨never had heard a ~ —Mary Deasy⟩

keen·ly *adv* [ME *kenely* boldly, bravely, sharply, fr. *kene* wise, bold, brave, sharp + *-ly* — more at KEEN] **:** in a keen manner ⟨stared at him ~ —Nevil Shute⟩ ⟨~ aware of the evils of the society —H.R.G.Greaves⟩ ⟨cleverly construed and ~ written —*Time*⟩

keen·ness \'kēnnəs\ *n* -ES [[1]*keen* + *-ness*] **:** the quality or state of being keen ⟨exhibited a ~ of judgment unusual in one his age⟩ ⟨the ~ of his desire to succeed⟩

keen–scented \'=¦==\ *adj* **:** having a keen sense of smell ⟨a *keen-scented* hound⟩

[1]**keep** \'kēp\ *vb* **kept** \'kept\ **kept**; **keeping**; **keeps** [ME *kepen* to observe, heed, seek, seize, keep, fr. OE *cēpan* to observe, heed, seek, seize; akin to OE *capian* to look, OS *kapōn*, OHG *chapfēn* to look, ON *kōpa* to stare, and perh. to Russ *zabota* care, worry] *vt* **1 a :** to observe or fulfill (something prescribed or obligatory) **:** adhere to or not swerve from or violate (as a faith) **:** practice or perform as a duty **:** not neglect **:** be faithful to (as a promise): as (1) **:** to notice with due, approved, or customary actions and feelings **:** act fittingly in relation to by refraining from anything inappropriate or unsuitable ⟨~*ing* a Sabbath day by ceasing from all work —H.G.Cowan⟩ (2) **:** to conform to in habits or conduct (as by regular attendance to or the performance of appropriate duties) or adjust one's schedule of activities to include ⟨~ chapel⟩ ⟨~ early hours⟩ (3) **:** to act (as in playing an instrument, singing, marching) in accord with (as a preestablished time, tempo, or rhythm) ⟨asked the musicians to ~ time with the metronome⟩ ⟨could not ~ the tricky rhythm of the Latin-American dance⟩ **b :** to reside at a British university long enough to complete the requirements of (a term); *esp* **:** to eat a sufficient number of dinners in hall at the Inns of Court to make (a term) count for the purpose of being called to the bar **2 :** PRESERVE, MAINTAIN: as **a :** to watch over and defend esp. from danger, harm, or loss ⟨prayed God to ~ and help his family⟩ ⟨anxious to ~ his son from illness and accident⟩ ⟨his sanguine nature *kept* him from worry⟩ **b** (1) **:** to have the care of **:** be responsible for **:** TEND ⟨the shepherd boy *kept* sheep on the moors at night⟩ ⟨*kept* a garden for his parents⟩ ⟨was paid to ~ the furnace⟩ (2) **:** to support by providing with a home, food, clothing, or other requisites of existence ⟨the foster parents *kept* the child for a year until his real parents could be found⟩ (3) **:** to maintain in a good, fitting, or orderly condition ⟨objected to ~*ing* the house⟩ ⟨a meticulously *kept* orchard⟩ (4) **:** to maintain habitually by undertaking the expense of ⟨what sort of table do they ~ —Jane Austen⟩ **c :** to continue to maintain **:** not cease from or intermit ⟨~ silence⟩ ⟨~ guard over the child⟩ **d** (1) **:** to cause to remain in a given place, situation, or condition **:** maintain unchanged **:** hold or preserve in a particular state ⟨~ valuables under lock and key⟩ ⟨*kept* all perishable food cold⟩ ⟨~ a person waiting⟩ — often used with a following prepositional phrase or adverb indicating place or direction ⟨*kept* the boys away from the house⟩ ⟨*kept* the top of the box down with weights⟩ ⟨*kept* the dog in the house⟩ ⟨*kept* the children in⟩ ⟨*kept* the cat out⟩ ⟨~ the birds off the antenna⟩ (2) **:** to preserve (food) in an unspoiled condition ⟨~ meat by packing it in ice⟩ ⟨~ potatoes in storage in a cool cellar⟩ **e** (1) **:** to have or retain in one's service or in an established position or relationship ⟨~ a maid and a butler⟩ ⟨~*s* two assistants⟩ — often used with *on* ⟨*kept* the cook on until she could find a new employer⟩ (2) **:** to possess (as a domestic animal) usu. for certain services or advantages ⟨~*s* a horse⟩ ⟨~*s* several head of cattle⟩ (3) **:** to maintain in exchange for sexual favors ⟨never married but *kept* a mistress for several years⟩ ⟨found the woman was ~*ing* a man several years her junior⟩ (4) **:** to control totally the policy, principles, and ideas of (as a newspaper) by one's money or economic power ⟨a *kept* press⟩ **f** (1) **:** to maintain a record in (as of daily occurrences or transactions) ⟨~ a journal⟩ ⟨~ books for a business firm⟩ (2) **:** to enter (as an account or record) in a book **g :** to have customarily in stock for sale ⟨bought the best sherry the store *kept*⟩ **3 a :** to restrain from departure or removal **:** not let go of **:** HOLD, DETAIN ⟨~ him as a prisoner for a week⟩ ⟨*kept* the children after school for disobedience⟩ ⟨nothing to ~ me in the hot city⟩ **b :** to hold back **:** RESTRAIN, PREVENT ⟨tried to ~ him from going out at night⟩ ⟨nothing *kept* him from going through with it⟩ **c :** SAVE, RESERVE, STORE ⟨asked the grocer to ~ a good cut of beef for her each week⟩ ⟨*kept* the hardest questions until the end of the examination⟩ **d :** to refrain from communicating, revealing, or betraying **:** not divulge ⟨~ a secret⟩ ⟨~ his counsel⟩ **4 a :** to retain or continue to have in one's possession or power esp. by conscious or purposive policy ⟨were able to conquer the island but were unable to ~ it⟩ ⟨found the money and figured he could ~ it⟩ ⟨the court decided the couple could ~ the child⟩ **b :** WITHHOLD ⟨*kept* most of his inheritance from him⟩ ⟨*kept* the sad news from the parents⟩ **c :** to have in control **:** not lose ⟨~ one's temper⟩ **5 :** to keep to ⟨ill and ~*s* her room —Jane Austen⟩ ⟨with a cold that has left her weak, so that she has *kept* the house for over a fortnight —O.W.Holmes †1935⟩ **6 a :** to continue in (as a course) **:** not deviate from ⟨~ the path rather than strike off through the woods⟩ ⟨~ the center of the road⟩ **b :** to stay or remain on or in usu. against opposition ⟨~ your seat⟩ ⟨~ the saddle despite the bucking of the horse⟩ ⟨~ the field under fire⟩ ⟨*kept* his ground even though attacked again and again⟩ **7 a :** CONDUCT, MANAGE ⟨~ a meeting⟩ **:** carry on ⟨~ a business⟩ ⟨the chairman was not there to ~ the yearly assembly⟩ ⟨*kept* a small tearoom⟩ **b** *archaic* **:** to keep up **c :** to make out or manage in respect to the welfare of (oneself) ⟨how have you been ~*ing* yourself⟩ **8 :** to associate with (company) ⟨concerned about the company she was ~*ing*⟩ **9** *dial Eng* **:** to frighten or scare away (birds) **~** *vi* **1** *now Brit* **:** LIVE, LODGE ⟨could not find where the man *kept* in town⟩ **2 a :** to maintain a course, direction, or progress **:** persevere in going ⟨~ along the main route for 10 miles⟩ ⟨*kept* to the south all day⟩ **b :** to continue usu. without interruption a particular action ⟨the fire *kept* burning all night⟩ ⟨~ smiling⟩ — often used with *on* ⟨*kept* on talking until he was told to stop⟩ **c :** to persist resolutely or stubbornly in a practice or a course of action often in spite of opposition or warning **:** continue firmly or obstinately ⟨~*s* asking us to go swimming⟩ — often used with *on* ⟨*kept* on drinking after the doctor told him to stop⟩ **3 a :** to stay or remain (as in a particular place or condition) ⟨~ in the house if it rains⟩ ⟨the wind *kept* to the east⟩ ⟨~ in a happy frame of mind⟩ ⟨~ out of the way⟩ ⟨~ in touch with friends⟩ ⟨*kept* warm with blankets and hot soup⟩ ⟨*kept* clean by washing daily⟩ **b :** to be in regard to health ⟨how are you ~*ing*⟩ **c :** to keep up ⟨was unable to ~ with the older boys on the hike⟩ ⟨it follows the herring schools and sometimes ~*s* with them for days —F.G.Kay⟩ **4 :** ABSTAIN, REFRAIN ⟨couldn't ~ from talking⟩ **5 a :** to remain in good condition **:** not go bad or deteriorate ⟨the food will ~ for a long time under refrigeration⟩ ⟨knowledge does not ~ any better than fish —A.N.Whitehead⟩ **b :** to remain undivulged ⟨knew the secret would ~ if he told nobody⟩ **c :** to call for no immediate action ⟨the matter will ~ until morning when we can see a lawyer⟩ **6 :** to be or remain in session ⟨school ~*s* five days a week⟩ **7 :** to keep wicket

syn KEEP, KEEP (*back*), KEEP (*out*), RETAIN, DETAIN, WITHHOLD, RESERVE, HOLD, and HOLD (*back*) can mean, in common, not to relinquish one's possession, custody, or control. KEEP is the most general term, carrying the common meaning ⟨*keep* one's car for another year⟩ ⟨*keep* one's balance⟩ ⟨*keep* one's right to vote⟩ KEEP (*back*) is interchangeable with any of the remaining terms ⟨*keep back* a part of an employee's pay⟩ ⟨*keep back* a person who wants to rush out into a storm⟩ ⟨*keep back* some tickets for a friend⟩ KEEP (*out*) applies to the keeping of some portion of a whole ⟨*keep out* a part of a week's pay for emergencies⟩ RETAIN implies continued keeping esp. against a threatened taking or loss ⟨*retain* one's possessions even in war⟩ ⟨*retain* one's sanity⟩ ⟨*retain* control of a company⟩ DETAIN implies a delay in letting go from one's control ⟨*detain* a man suspected of a crime⟩ ⟨*detain* a ship in quarantine⟩ WITHHOLD implies a delay in letting go or a refusal to give or let go ⟨*withhold* information⟩ ⟨*withhold* payments on a house⟩ ⟨*withhold* one's help⟩ RESERVE implies either a keeping in store or withholding from present use esp. for some future or special need or purpose ⟨*reserve* a certain percentage for emergencies⟩ ⟨*reserve* a space in a house for a playroom⟩ ⟨*reserve* seats at an opera⟩ HOLD and HOLD (*back*) are often used in place of WITHHOLD or KEEP (*back*) and sometimes in place of DETAIN or RESERVE when restraint in letting go is implied ⟨*hold* a portion of a week's pay as a fine⟩ ⟨*hold* a person suspected of a crime⟩ ⟨*hold back* some tickets that are on sale as a favor to a friend⟩ ⟨*hold* one's condemnation until a later date⟩ ⟨*hold back* one's judgment until all the evidence has been considered⟩

syn OBSERVE, CELEBRATE, SOLEMNIZE, COMMEMORATE: KEEP, along with others in this set, can mean the noticing or honoring of a day or occasion fittingly or duly. KEEP is rather mild in its implications and may suggest merely a customary or wonted notice without anything untoward or inappropriate; it implies opposition to *break* ⟨his build was all compact, for force, well-knit . . . he *kept* no Lent to make him meager —John Masefield⟩ OBSERVE may indicate a heightened solemnity, attention to correct details, and a proper attitude ⟨knowing that the usual ritual would have to be *observed* —T. B.Costain⟩ ⟨New Hampshire *observes* one holiday not possessed by any other state —*Amer. Guide Series: N.H.*⟩ In today's English and esp. in nonreligious contexts CELEBRATE is likely to suggest notice of an occasion by festivity or indulgence ⟨*celebrate* New Year's Eve⟩ ⟨*celebrating* a friend's good fortune⟩ ⟨many parties *celebrating* a football victory⟩ SOLEMNIZE is likely to carry a contrasting suggestion, that of grave dignity or splendid ceremony ⟨mysterious rites were *solemnized*, and . . . of those terrific idols some received such dismal service —William Wordsworth⟩ ⟨this blessed day ever . . . shall be kept festival: to *solemnize* this day the glorious sun stays in his course —Shak.⟩ COMMEMORATE stresses the idea of remembrance and suggests observance or ceremony, or a symbol or monument designed to ensure against forgetfulness and oblivion ⟨the first time it had ever been rung to *commemorate* the death of a monarch —*New Yorker*⟩ ⟨their six children all died in early youth, and the Bradleys determined to *commemorate* them by founding an educational institution —Marie A. Kasten⟩

— **keep an eye on :** to watch carefully although not continuously ⟨*keep an eye on* the pot so it doesn't boil over⟩ ⟨*keep an eye on* the children while I'm away⟩ — **keep at :** to persevere or persist in doing or concerning oneself with — **keep bach** *slang* **:** to live as a bachelor; *esp* **:** to keep house in the absence of one's wife — **keep cases 1 :** to be in charge of the casebox **2 :** to keep a watch on **:** keep tabs on — **keep company :** to go together as frequent companions or in courtship ⟨after marriage they could look back with pleasure on the time they were *keeping company*⟩ — **keep (one) company :** to stay or travel with (one) to provide companionship — **keep cut** *obs* **:** to keep one's distance **:** act warily — **keep face :** to retain one's poise or equanimity esp. under circumstances that would tend to destroy it — **keep faith :** to observe and live up to one's moral commitments (to something) **:** show steady loyalty — often used with *with* ⟨*keep faith* with one's religion⟩ ⟨*keep faith* with one's children⟩ — **keep hands off :** to refrain from interfering ⟨requested that the government *keep hands off* in the internal affairs of other countries⟩ — **keep house 1 :** to occupy or maintain a separate house or establishment as opposed to living with parents or relatives or boarding out ⟨is married and *keeping house*⟩ **2** *Brit* **:** to remain secluded at home to evade creditors — **keep mind** *Scot* **:** to keep in mind **:** REMEMBER — **keep one's end up** *or* **keep up one's end 1 :** to do one's fair share in an enterprise involving two and often more people or participants ⟨could *keep his end up* in a conversation on almost any subject⟩ **2 :** to preserve one's wicket by defensive play — used of a batsman in cricket — **keep one's feet :** to stay upright **:** keep one's balance — **keep one's hand in :** to keep in practice ⟨tried to *keep his hand in* at tennis by playing a little at least once a week⟩ — **keep pace :** to keep up ⟨had no trouble *keeping pace* with the faster runners⟩ ⟨did not wish to *keep pace* with the neighbors in social life⟩ — **keep standing :** to hold intact (as set type) — **keep step :** to keep in step ⟨*keep step* with the other marchers⟩ ⟨*keep step* with the times and turn it to your sales advantage —*Women's Wear Daily*⟩ — **keep the field :** to continue a campaign — **keep the peace :** to avoid or prevent a breach of the peace or any crime likely to result in such a breach — **keep to 1 a :** to confine oneself to **:** remain in **:** not leave ⟨*kept to* the house during his convalescence⟩ ⟨*kept to* the main roads in his travels⟩ **b :** to limit oneself to (as a particular kind of diet) **2 :** to abide by ⟨*keep to* the rules of the game⟩ **:** conform to ⟨*keep to* the hour decided on —Agnes M. Miall⟩ **:** not deviate from ⟨*keep to* the point⟩ — **keep to oneself 1 :** to keep secret ⟨knew what the facts were but *kept* them *to himself*⟩ ⟨*kept* their knowledge . . . *to themselves* and made no attempt to spread it —Sean MacCormac⟩ **2 :** to remain solitary or apart from other people **:** avoid social relations ⟨a shy girl who *kept* pretty much *to herself*⟩ — **keep wicket :** to play as wicketkeeper in cricket

[2]**keep** \"\ *n* -S [ME *kep*, *keep*, fr. *kepen* to keep — more at KEEP] **1** *archaic* **:** HEED, NOTICE — usu. used in the phrases *give keep*, *take keep* **2 :** the act of keeping or the state of being kept: as **a** *archaic* **:** CUSTODY, GUARD, CHARGE **b :** MAINTENANCE **3 :** one that keeps or protects: as **a :** STRONGHOLD, FORTRESS, CASTLE; *specif* **:** the strongest and securest part of a medieval castle often used as a place of residence esp. during a siege **b :** KEEPER ⟨has been made the ~ of an anticritical defensive system —F.R.Leavis⟩ **c :** PRISON, JAIL **d :** a cap or other mechanical device for retaining anything in place; *specif* **:** a light iron casting resting on the hanger at the bottom of a locomotive axle box to keep the lubricating pad in position **4 a :** the means or provisions by which one is kept ⟨the horse was hardly worth its ~⟩ **b** *Brit* **:** pasture for grazing or the grass in such pasture **c :** a conditioning tonic or regimen for game cocks **5 keeps** *pl but sing in constr* **:** a game of marbles played for keeps **6 :** a football play in which the quarterback fakes a pass but keeps the ball and runs with it **syn** see LIVING — **for keeps** *adv* **1 a :** with the provision that one keep what he has won ⟨the two men were playing the game *for keeps*⟩ **b :** with deadly seriousness **:** with the firm intention of winning or overcoming if at all possible ⟨found out that his rival was not fooling but competing with him *for keeps*⟩ **2 :** with the intention of remaining in a particular state or relationship for good **:** PERMANENTLY ⟨after his experience in foreign countries he came home *for keeps*⟩

3 : with finality **:** with the result of ending the matter ⟨stole their crown jewels . . . and *for keeps* —Ethel M. Thornbury⟩ ⟨plugged *for keeps* in a gun duel with a desperado —John McCarten⟩

keep·able \-pəbəl\ *adj* **:** capable of being kept for some time without deterioration ⟨some foods are ~ under refrigeration⟩

keep away *vi* **:** to sail less close to the wind ~ *vt* **:** to cause (a sailing ship) to keep away

keep back *vt* **1 :** RESTRAIN ⟨had a hard time *keeping* her *back*⟩ ⟨*kept* the man *back* from committing the crime⟩ **:** hold back **:** RETARD ⟨*kept* the completion of the plan *back* by a year⟩ **2 a :** to refrain from giving **:** WITHHOLD ⟨*kept* a portion of his pay *back*⟩ **b :** to refrain from divulging ⟨*kept* the information *back* until he was paid for it⟩ **c :** RESERVE, SAVE ⟨*kept* rare items *back* for customers who would pay the best prices⟩ ~ *vi* **:** to refrain from approaching or advancing near (as to something dangerous) ⟨asked the children to *keep back* while the fireworks were exploding⟩ **syn** see KEEP

keep down *vt* **1 a :** to hold in subjection **:** SUPPRESS ⟨had trouble *keeping* the insurgents *down*⟩ **b :** to keep in control ⟨*kept* the horse *down* with the curb⟩ **c :** LIMIT, RESTRICT ⟨tried to *keep* expenses *down*⟩ **d :** to prevent from growing, advancing, or succeeding ⟨can't *keep* a good man *down*⟩ **2 :** to prevent from regurgitating or vomiting ⟨felt sick but succeeded in *keeping* his dinner *down*⟩ **3 :** to set or leave set in lowercase in printing

¹keep·er \-pə(r)\ *n* -s [ME *keper*, fr. *kepen* to keep + *-er* — more at KEEP] **1 :** one that keeps something (as by watching over, guarding, maintaining, supporting, restraining) **:** as **a :** GUARDIAN, PROTECTOR ⟨am I my brother's ~ —Gen 4:9 (RSV)⟩ **b :** one that conforms to or abides by (as a custom, rite, or law) ⟨a ~ of the Lord's commandments⟩ **:** one that fulfills (as a promise or pledge) **c :** one that has charge of (as a prison, prisoners, inmates of an institution, the grounds or buildings of an estate, animals in a zoo); *specif* **:** GAMEKEEPER **d :** one that owns, maintains, or carries on (as a boarding house, castle, store) **e :** GUARD **f** *obs* **:** one that keeps a mistress **g :** one whose vocation or avocation is the care of (as bees) **h :** WICKETKEEPER **i :** CURATOR ⟨a ~ of manuscripts in a library⟩ **j :** one whose job is to keep something in good or satisfactory condition ⟨a boat ~⟩ ⟨a greenhouse ~⟩ **k :** an armature that preserves the intensity of magnetization of a permanent magnet **2 :** a device that keeps something in position **:** as **a :** LATCH **b :** the strike of a lock **c :** GUARD RING **d :** LOCKNUT **e :** a loop of string tied in the eye of a bowstring to keep it in place when the bow is unbraced **f :** the keep in a locomotive axle box **g :** a leather loop on a rifle sling for holding the sling tight on the arm when firing with the sling **3 :** a fruit or vegetable that keeps well **4 :** a fish large enough to be legally caught

²keeper \"\ *vt* -ED/-ING/-S *Brit* **:** to maintain (a game preserve) under the care of a keeper ⟨marsh . . . strictly ~*ed* and alive with fowl —*Country Life*⟩

keep·er·ing \-p(ə)riŋ\ *n* -s *Brit* **:** the occupation or work of a keeper (as a gamekeeper)

keeper of the broad seal *obs* **:** KEEPER OF THE GREAT SEAL

keeper of the great seal *or* **keeper of the seal :** a high officer of state in England and Scotland who has custody of the great seal **:** LORD CHANCELLOR

keeper of the privy purse : PRIVY PURSE 2

keeper of the privy seal [ME *keper of the prive seale*] **1 :** LORD PRIVY SEAL **2 :** an officer in Scotland and Cornwall analogous to the English lord privy seal

keep·er·ship \ˈkēpə(r),ship\ *n* **:** the office or position of keeper

keep in *vt* **1 a :** to keep from expressing **:** hold back ⟨*kept* his feelings *in* until he nearly burst⟩ ⟨was unable to *keep* the secret *in*⟩ **b :** to detain in the school after regular school hours as a punishment ⟨*kept* the children *in* for disobedience⟩ **2** *archaic* **:** to keep (a fire) burning ~ *vi* **1** *of a fire* **:** to keep burning **2 :** to stay on good or favorable terms ⟨anxious to *keep in* with the boss⟩

¹keeping *n* -s [ME *keping*, fr. gerund of *kepen* to keep — more at KEEP] **1 :** the act of one that keeps something **:** as **a :** CUSTODY, GUARD, MAINTENANCE ⟨left the small child in the woman's ~⟩ ⟨the ~ of the lighthouse⟩ **b :** the observance of a rule, obligation, or rite **c :** a reserving or preserving for future use **d** *obs* **:** the maintaining of a mistress **2 a :** the means by which something is kept **:** KEEP, SUPPORT, PROVISION, FEED ⟨provided good ~ for the cattle⟩ **b :** the state of being kept or the condition in which something is kept ⟨the house is in good ~⟩ **3 :** CONFORMITY, CONGRUITY, HARMONY, CONSISTENCY — usu. used in the phrases *in keeping* or *out of keeping* ⟨behavior in ~ with the solemnity of the occasion⟩ ⟨simplicity and restraint is in admirable ~ with the earnest purpose of the pioneers —*Amer. Guide Series: Minn.*⟩ ⟨a doctrine so out of ~ with the facts of Japanese life —Kazuo Kawai⟩

²keeping *adj* [ME *keping*, fr. pres. part. of *kepen* to keep] **:** of or relating to something that remains unspoiled over a period of time ⟨apples with good ~ quality⟩

keeping room *n, dial* **:** a family living room

keep off *vt* **1 :** to keep away **:** keep back ⟨had a hard time *keeping* the children *off* when he brought out the pony⟩ **2 :** to ward off **:** AVERT ⟨a charm to *keep off* disease and misfortune⟩ ~ *vi* **:** to keep back ⟨asked the spectators to *keep off* because the animal was unpredictable⟩

keep out *vt* **:** to keep back **:** WITHHOLD ⟨*kept* a portion of a man's paycheck *out*⟩; *also* **:** RESERVE, SAVE ⟨*keep* some of the best cuts of meat *out* for a good customer⟩ **syn** see KEEP

keeps *pres 3d sing of* KEEP, *pl of* KEEP

keep·sake \ˈkēp,sāk\ *n* [¹*keep* + *-sake* (as in *namesake*)] **1 :** something kept or given to be kept as a memento (as of a friend or a happy occasion) **2 :** GIFTBOOK 2 **3 :** a giftbook made up for a particular group or occasion and serving as a specimen of fine printing

keep under *vt* **:** to hold in subjection ⟨*kept* the conquered people *under* for 50 years⟩

keep up *vt* **1 :** to go on with **:** persevere in **:** continue usu. with persistence ⟨*kept* the talk *up* until midnight⟩ ⟨*kept* his criminal activity *up* until he was caught⟩ ⟨*kept up* their correspondence⟩ **:** MAINTAIN, SUSTAIN ⟨*kept up* a front for Mama, who was not to be worried —Andrea Parke⟩ ⟨*kept* their standards *up*⟩ **2 :** to prevent from diminishing or deteriorating **:** keep in good condition ⟨worked every day to *keep* the garden *up*⟩ ⟨*kept* his credit *up* by paying his bills regularly⟩ **3** *archaic* **:** to keep confined or penned up ~ *vi* **1 :** to stay even (as in acts of strength, endurance, or speed) ⟨although he was small he could *keep up* with the larger boys in sports⟩ **:** stay along (as in thoughts or studies) ⟨able to *keep up* with his class in school⟩ **2 :** to keep adequately informed — used with *on* or *with* ⟨*keep up* with the affairs of the office⟩ ⟨*keep up* on international relations⟩ **3 :** to continue without interruption **:** maintain a particular course, condition, or series of actions ⟨the rain *kept up* all night⟩ **4 :** to match one's neighbors or contemporaries in accomplishment or in the acquisition of material goods **:** be in fashion — usu. used with *with* ⟨*keeping up* with the professors —*Yale Rev.*⟩ ⟨farm folk seem to place less emphasis than city folk upon competitive consumption, or spending to *keep up* with the Joneses —Day Monroe⟩

keesh *var of* KISH

kees·hond \ˈkās,händ, -hȯn-, -nt\ *n* [D, prob. fr. *Kees* (nickname for *Cornelis* Cornelius) + *hond* dog, fr. MD; akin to OHG *hunt* dog — more at HOUND] **1** *usu cap* **:** a breed of small heavy-coated dogs like the pomeranians but larger, of uncertain origin, and long used in Holland on barges esp. as watchdogs and ratters **2** *pl* **kees·hon·den** \-ndən\ *often cap* **:** an animal of the Keeshond breed

keest \ˈkēst\ *n* -s [D, kernel, pit, marrow, fr. MD *keest, keeste*] *Scot* **:** inner vital substance **:** MARROW ⟨cold to the ~⟩

keester *var of* KEISTER

keet *or* **keat** \ˈkēt\ *n* -s [imit.] **:** GUINEA FOWL; *esp* **:** a young guinea fowl

keeve *or* **kieve** \ˈkēv\ *n* -s [ME *kive, keve*, fr. OE *cȳf*, prob. borrowed in prehistoric times fr. (assumed) VL *cupia*, fr. L *cupa* tub, vat — more at HIVE] **1 :** a tub or vat esp. for liquids (as a bleaching kier or dolly tub) **2** *Brit* **:** a rock basin hollowed out by water

kee·wa·tin \(ˈ)kēˈwātᵊn\ *adj, usu cap* [fr. *Keewatin* district, Northwest Territories, Canada] **:** of or relating to a division of the Archeozoic — see GEOLOGIC TIME table

kef \ˈkef, ˈkāf\ *or* **kif** \ˈkif\ *n* -s [colloq. Ar *kēf* (kayf) enjoyment, pleasure] **1 :** a state of dreamy tranquillity **:** LANGUOR **2 :** a smoking material (as Indian hemp) that produces kef ⟨basks there . . . smoking . . . his ~ —Hendrik de Leeuw⟩

kef·el \ˈkefəl\ *n* -s [W *ceffyl* horse, fr. L *caballus* horse, nag — more at CAVALCADE] *dial Brit* **:** a usu. old or worthless horse **:** NAG

keffiyeh *var of* KAFFIYEH

ke·fir *also* **ke·phir** \keˈfi(ə)r, kəˈf-, ˈkefər\ *n* -s [Russ *kefir*, fr. a native name in the Caucasus] **:** a slightly effervescent acidulous beverage of low alcoholic content made chiefly in southern Russia of cow's milk that is fermented by means of kefir grains

kefir grain *n* **:** a small mass resembling a tiny cauliflower, occurring in kefir, containing casein and other milk solids together with the yeasts and lactobacilli that cause the characteristic kefir fermentation, and serving as a starter to induce this fermentation when introduced into fresh milk

keg \ˈkeg, -ā-, ÷ -a-, ÷ -ai-\ *n* -s [alter. of earlier *cag*, fr. ME *kag*, of Scand origin; akin to ON *kaggi*, *-kaggr* keg, cask, Sw & Dan *kagge*; prob. akin to OHG *kegil* stake, peg, MD *kegge* wedge, Sw dial. *kage* tree stump, and perh. to Lith *žãgaras* dry twig; basic meaning: branch, stake] **1 :** a small cask or barrel having a capacity of 30 gallons or less **2 :** the contents of a keg

kegeree *var of* KEDGEREE

keg·ler *also* **kegel·er** *or* **kegel·ler** \ˈkeg(ə)lə(r), ˈkāg-\ *n* -s [G *kegler*, fr. *kegeln* to bowl (fr. *kegel* bowling pin, cone, fr. OHG *kegil* stake, peg) + *-er* — more at KEG] **:** ¹BOWLER

keg·ling *also* **kegel·ing** *or* **kegel·ling** \-g(ə)liŋ\ *n* -s [G *kegeln* to bowl + E *-ing*] **:** BOWLING

keg·meg \ˈkeg,meg\ *var of* CAGMAG

ke·gon \ˈkā,gän, -gȯn\ *adj, usu cap* [Jap, fr. *ke* lotus + *gon* glory] **:** of, relating to, or being a sect of Japanese Buddhism originating in the 8th century and teaching the unreality of phenomenal antitheses and the ultimate unity of all reality in and through the Buddha

ke·hil·lah *or* **ke·hil·la** \kəˈhilə\ *n, pl* **kehil·loth** *or* **kehil·lot** \-,lōt(h), -ōs\ [Heb *qĕhillāh* assembly, community] **:** the Jewish community of a city organized for the administration of charities and communal work

ke·hoe·ite \ˈkē(,)(h)ō,īt\ *n* -s [Henry *Kehoe*, 19th cent. Am. mineralogist + E *-ite*] **:** a mineral $Al_8(Zn,Ca)_3(PO_4)_6(OH)_{12}$·$21H_2O$(?) consisting of a massive basic hydrous calcium aluminum zinc phosphate (sp. gr. 2.3)

kei apple \ˈkā-, ˈkī-, ˈkəi-\ *n, usu cap K* [fr. Great *Kei* river, Cape Province, Union of South Africa] **1 :** the edible fruit of a southern African shrub (*Dovyalis caffra*) of the family Flacourtiaceae that is shaped like a small apple and is used for pickles and preserves **2 :** the shrub that bears the Kei apple

keik \ˈkēk\ *var of* KEEK

kei·ki \ˈkākē\ *n* -s [Hawaiian] **1** *Hawaii* **:** CHILD **2** *Hawaii* **:** an immature plant

keist \ˈkāst\ *Scot var of* CAST

keis·ter \ˈkēstə(r), ˈkīs-\ *or* **kees·ter** \ˈkēs-\ *n* -s [origin unknown] **1 :** SATCHEL, SUITCASE; *specif* **:** one carried by an itinerant peddler **2** *slang* **:** BUTTOCKS

keit·loa \ˈkītləwə, ˈkāt-, ˌ=ˈlōə\ *n* -s [Sechuana *kgetlwa, khetlwa*] **:** a black rhinoceros that has a posterior horn which equals or exceeds the anterior in length and that has been considered to constitute a distinct species

kek·chi *or* **quek·chi** \ˈkek(,)chē\ *n, pl* **kekchi** *or* **kekchis** *or* **quekchi** *or* **quekchis** *usu cap* **1 a :** an Indian people of north central Guatemala **b :** a member of such people **2 :** the Mayan language of the Kekchi people

ke·ku·lé formula \ˈkākə,lā-\ *n, usu cap K* [after Friedrich August *Kekule* von Stradonitz †1896 Ger. chemist] **:** a structural formula for an organic compound that depicts each valence bond as a short line; *esp* **:** the hexagonal ring formula for benzene — see BENZENE RING illustration

ke·ku·ne oil *or* **ke·ku·na oil** \kəˈkünə-\ *n* [prob. native name in Ceylon] **:** CANDLENUT OIL

ke·la·bit \kəˈläbət\ *n, pl* **kelabit** *or* **kelabits** *usu cap* [native name in Sarawak] **1 :** a Dayak people of northern Sarawak **2 :** a member of the Kelabit people

kelb–el–bahr \ˌkel,belˈbär\ *n* -s [Ar *kalb al-baḥr*, lit., the dog of the sea (river, Nile)] **:** any of several large formidable characin fishes of the Nile and rivers and lakes of tropical Africa that constitute the genus *Hydrocyon*, reach a length of about three feet, have strong teeth, and in form resemble a salmon

keld \ˈkeld\ *n* -s [prob. of Scand origin; akin to ON *kelda* spring, marshy place, prob. fr. *kaldr* cold — more at COLD] **1** *dial Eng* **:** SPRING, FOUNTAIN **2** *dial Eng* **:** the still part of a body of water

kel·e·be \ˈkelə(,)bē\ *n* -s [Gk *kelebē*, prob. of non-IE origin] **:** an ovoid krater having handles that drop almost vertically to the shoulder from horizontal extensions on the rim

kelebe

k electron *n, usu cap K* **:** an electron in the K-shell

k–electron capture *usu cap K, var of* K-CAPTURE

ke·lep \kəˈlep\ *n* -s [Kekchi *kelép*] **:** a Central American stinging ant (*Ectatomma tuberculatum*) that lives in small colonies in the ground esp. near clearings

kell \ˈkel\ *n* -s [ME (northern dial.) *kelle*, alter. of *calle* — more at CAUL] *dial Brit* **:** CAUL; *specif* **:** a net cap worn by women

kelleg *or* **kellock** *var of* KILLICK

kellin *var of* KHELLIN

kel·li·on \keˈlē,än, -ē,ȯn\ *n, pl* **kel·lia** \-ēə, -ē(,)ä\ [LGk, lit., little cell, fr. L *cella* cell + Gk *-ion* (dim. suffix) — more at CELL] **:** a small religious house of the Eastern Church occupied by not more than three monks and three lay brothers

kel·logg oak \ˈkel,ȯg-, -,läg-, -,ləg-\ *or* **kellogg's oak** *n, usu cap K* [after Albert *Kellogg* †1887 Am. botanist] **:** CALIFORNIA BLACK OAK

kel·lup·weed \ˈkeləp,=\ *n* [*kellup* (alter. of *kelp*) + *weed*] **:** OXEYE 1d

¹kel·ly \ˈkelē, -li\ *n* -ES [prob. by folk etymology (influence of the name *Kelly*) fr. *callow*] **:** the topsoil removed in order to secure clay for brickmaking

²kelly \"\ *vt* -ED/-ING/-ES **:** to cover (as a molding floor for bricks) with kelly

³kelly \"\ *or* **kel·lie** \"\ *var of* KILLIE

⁴kelly \"\ *n, pl* **kellies** *or* **kellys** [prob. fr. the name *Kelly*] **:** a man's stiff hat (as a derby or a flat-topped straw hat) ⟨only the dudes wore straw *kellies* —*New Yorker*⟩

⁵kelly \"\ *or* **kelly green** *n, often cap K* [fr. the common Irish name *Kelly*; fr. green's being a traditional Irish color] **:** a variable color averaging a strong yellowish green that is greener and duller than cyprus green and greener, stronger, and slightly lighter than emerald (sense 2b) ⟨comes in red, ~, white, or black —*Women's Wear Daily*⟩

⁶kelly \"\ *n* -s [prob. alter. of E dial. *kelp*, of unknown origin] *Austral* **:** CROW ⟨gave the ~s a rare blessing and left them to their feast —*Sydney (Australia) Bull.*⟩

⁷kelly \"\ *also* **kelly joint** *n* -s [prob. fr. the name *Kelly*] **:** GRIEF STEM

kelly pool *n, usu cap K* **:** a pool game in which each player draws a number and while playing on the object balls in numerical order aims to pocket the ball having his number on it and thereby win the game but if his ball is pocketed by another player he loses his chance of winning and continues to play with the aim of pocketing the balls of other players

kelm·scott \ˈke(l)mzkət, ˈkeūm-, -m(p)sk-; -mz,kät, -m(p)-,sk-\ *adj, usu cap* [fr. the *Kelmscott* Press, publishing firm in Hammersmith, England, fr. *Kelmscott*, England, home of William Morris †1896 Eng. poet and artist, its founder] **:** produced by the Kelmscott Press ⟨*Kelmscott* books⟩ ⟨the *Kelmscott* Chaucer⟩

ke·loid *also* **che·loid** \ˈkē,lȯid\ *n* -s [F *kiloïde, chéloïde*, fr. Gk *chēlē* claw + F *-oïde* -oid] **:** a thick scar resulting from excessive growth of fibrous tissue and occurring esp. after burns or radiation injury — **ke·loi·dal** \(ˈ)kēˈlȯidᵊl\ *adj*

kelp \ˈkelp, ˈkeūp\ *n* -s [ME *culp*] **1 a :** any of various large brown seaweeds of the orders Laminariales and Fucales — see GIANT KELP **b :** a mass or growth of large seaweeds; *esp* **:** a mass of those burned for the ashes **2** *also* **kelp ash :** the ashes of seaweed used formerly as a source of alkali and now as a source of iodine

kelp bass *n* **:** a dusky sea bass (*Paralabrax clathratus*) that is blotched with darker brown or gray above and silvery or yellowish below, is common in kelp beds along the California coast, and is an esteemed sport fish

kelp crab *n* **:** any of several spider crabs common among algae and eelgrass along the Pacific coast of No. America: as **a :** the common kelp crab (*Pugettia producta* syn. *Epialtus productus*) **b :** GRACEFUL KELP CRAB **c :** SHEEP CRAB

kelp·er \ˈ-pə(r)\ *n* -s **:** one that gathers or prepares kelp

kelpfish \ˈ=,=\ *n* **:** any of various fishes inhabiting kelp beds: as **a :** a large variably colored blenny (*Heterostichus rostratus*) found among kelp or eelgrass along the California coast or another member of the family Clinidae **b :** any of several brilliantly colored percoid fishes of the family Odacidae found along the coasts of Australia and New Zealand — called also *rock whiting*

kelp fly \ˈ=,=\ *n* **:** any of various rather large flattened two-winged flies that constitute the family Coelopidae and have larvae that feed on kelp

kelp goose *n* **:** a goose (*Chloephaga hybrida*) of littoral habits found in the Falkland islands and adjacent So. America

kelp greenling *n* **:** GREENLING 1a(2)

kelp gull *n* **:** a black-backed gull (*Larus dominicanus*) of the southern hemisphere

kelp hen *n* **:** a weka of South Island of New Zealand that feeds on marine animals and prob. represents a dark phase of a species (*Gallirallus australis*) though sometimes considered a separate species (*G. brachypterus*)

¹kel·pie *also* **kel·py** \ˈkelpē, ˈkeūp-\ *n, pl* **kelpies** [prob. of Celt origin; akin to ScGael *cailpeach, calpach, colpach* heifer, steer, colt, *colpa* cow, horse] **:** a water spirit usu. equine in form that is held esp. in Scottish folklore to delight in or bring about the drowning of travelers

²kelpie \"\ *n* -s [after *Kelpie*, an early specimen] **:** an Australian sheep dog of a breed developed in the 19th century in New South Wales by crossing the dingo with various British sheep dogs

kelp pigeon *n* **:** a sheathbill (*Chionis alba*) having a pinkish or yellowish black-tipped bill and occurring from the Falkland islands south to parts of Antarctica

kelp plover *n* **:** DOWITCHER

kelp raft *n* **:** a mass of floating kelp

kelpwort \ˈ=,=\ *n* **:** GLASSWORT 2

kelpy \ˈkelpē, ˈkeūp-\ *adj, sometimes* -ER/-EST [*kelp* + *-y*] **:** abounding in or characterized by kelp

kel·sey locust \ˈkelsē- *also* -ltsē-\ *n, usu cap K* [after Harlan P. *Kelsey* b1872 Am. horticulturist] **:** an American shrub (*Robinia kelseyi*) having rose or purple flowers, glabrous branches, and glandular hispid pods

kelson *var of* KEELSON

¹kelt \ˈkelt\ *n* -s [ME (northern dial.), prob. fr. ScGael *cealt*] **:** a salmon or sea trout that is weak and emaciated after spawning

²kelt \"\ *n* -s [ScGael *cealt*] *dial Brit* **:** homespun frieze cloth usu. of black wool with a mixture of white

³kelt \"\ *cap, var of* CELT

¹kelter *var of* KILTER

²kel·ter \ˈkeltər\ *vi* -ED/-ING/-S [origin unknown] *chiefly Scot* **:** to move restlessly **:** UNDULATE

³kel·ter \ˈkeltə(r)\ *n* -s [origin unknown] **1** *dial Eng* **:** property of any kind; *esp* **:** MONEY **2 :** RUBBISH, TRASH

keltic *usu cap, var of* CELTIC

kel·ty \ˈkeltī\ *n* -ES [origin unknown] *Scot* **:** an additional glass of liquor forced upon a reluctant drinker

kel·vin \ˈkelvən\ *adj, usu cap* [after William Thomson, Lord *Kelvin* †1907 Brit. physicist] **:** relating to, conforming to, or having a thermometric scale on which the unit of measurement equals the centigrade degree and according to which absolute zero is 0°, the equivalent of −273.16°C, and water freezes at 273.16° and boils at 373.16°

kelvin balance *n, usu cap K* [after Lord *Kelvin*] **:** a device for comparing the force produced by an electric current flowing through fixed and movable coils and the force of gravity

kelvin's law *n, usu cap K* [after Lord *Kelvin*] **:** a statement in electrical economics: the most economical cross-section area for an electric conductor is that for which the cost of energy lost in a given period equals the interest for the same period of the capital involved

ke·mal·ism \kəˈmä,lizəm\ *n* -s *usu cap* [*Kemal* Atatürk (Mustafa Kemal) †1938 Turkish general and statesman + E *-ism*] **:** the political, economic, and social principles advocated by Kemal Atatürk and designed to create a modern republican secular Turkish state out of a portion of the Ottoman empire

¹ke·mal·ist \-,ləst\ *n* -s *usu cap* [*Kemal* Atatürk + E *-ist*] **:** a follower of Kemal Atatürk **:** an adherent of Kemalism ⟨the economic policies of the *Kemalists*⟩

²kemalist \"\ *adj, usu cap* **:** of, relating to, or having the characteristics of Kemalism or Kemalists ⟨the modern *Kemalist* pattern of revolution —*Atlantic*⟩ ⟨the Ottoman empire collapsed and *Kemalist* Turkey was born — Necmeddin Sadak⟩

ke·man·cha \kəˈmänchə\ *n* -s [Ar *kamanjah*, fr. Per] **:** an Arabian violin that has usu. a single string and a gourd resonator and is held vertically when played

¹kemb \ˈkem\ *vt* **kembed** \-md\ *or* **kempt** \-m(p)t\ **kembed** *or* **kempt; kembing; kembs** [ME *kemben*, fr. OE *cemban*; akin to OS *kembian* to comb, OHG *kemben, chempen*, ON *kemba*; denominatives fr. the root of E ¹comb] *dial* **:** ¹COMB

²kemb \"\ *n* -s *dial* **:** COMB

ke·me·ro·vo \ˈkemə,rō(,)vō\ *adj, usu cap* [fr. *Kemerovo*, U.S.S.R.] **:** of or from the city of Kemerovo, U.S.S.R. **:** of the kind or style prevalent in Kemerovo

ke·mi·ri nut \kəˈmirē-\ *also* **kemiri** *n* -s [Jav *kĕmiri*] **:** CANDLENUT 1

¹kemp \ˈkemp\ *n* -s [ME *kempe*, fr. OE *cempa*; akin to OS *kempio* warrior, OHG *kempho*, ON *kappi*; all fr. a prehistoric WGmc-NGmc word derived fr. a word meaning "combat", "battle"; akin to OE *camp, comp* combat, battle, OHG *kamph* combat, battle, ON *kapp* contest, zeal; all borrowed fr. L *campus* plain, field, battlefield — more at CAMP] **1 a** *dial Brit* **:** a strong and worthy warrior or athlete **:** CHAMPION **b** *dial Eng* **:** an impetuous rogue **2** *dial Brit* **:** a competition or contest esp. among reapers in a harvest field

²kemp \"\ *vi* -ED/-ING/-S [ME *kempen*, prob. fr. *kempe*, n.] *chiefly Scot* **:** to contend or compete for championship esp. in a reaping contest

³kemp \"\ *n* -s [ME *kempe* coarse hair, of Scand origin; akin to ON *kampr* mustache; akin to OE *cenep* mustache, OFris *kenep* mustache, MD *canefbeen* cheekbone, and perh. to ON *knefill* pole, stake — more at KNAVE] **:** a coarse dead fiber esp. of wool or mohair that is usu. short, wavy, and white, has little affinity for dye, and is used in mixed woolls (as in carpets or for novelty effects)

kem·pas \ˈkempəs\ *n* -ES [Malay *kĕmpas*] **1 :** a leguminous Malayan tree (*Koompassia malaccensis*) with very hard heavy strong wood **2 :** the wood of the kempas

kemp·ite \ˈkem,pīt\ *n* -s [James F. *Kemp* †1926 Am. geologist + E *-ite*] **:** a mineral $Mn_2(OH)_3Cl$ consisting of a basic manganese oxychloride occurring in small emerald green orthorhombic crystals

kem·ple \ˈkempəl\ *n* -s [alter. of earlier *kimple*, of Scand origin; akin to ON *-kimbull* bundle, Icel *kimbill* small bundle, small haystack, Norw dial. *kimbel* bundle of grass] **:** a Scotch unit of measure for straw varying around 400 pounds

kemp's loggerhead *or* **kemp's turtle** \ˈkemps-\ *n, usu cap K* [fr. the name *Kemp*] **:** RIDLEY

kempt \ˈkem(p)t\ *adj* [ME, fr. past part. of *kemben* to comb — more at KEMB] **:** neatly kept **:** TRIM ⟨lips . . . unsmiling above the faintly grizzled and elegantly ~ imperial —Jean Stafford⟩

kempy \ˈkempē\ *adj, sometimes* -ER/-EST [³*kemp* + *-y*] **:** containing or resembling kemp ⟨a lean hairy animal . . . whose ~ wool brings only the lowest market prices —C.A.Amsden⟩

¹ken \ˈken\ *vb* **kenned** *also* **kend** \-nd\ *or* **kent** \-nt\ **kenned** *also* **kend** *or* **kent; kenning; kens** [ME *kennen*; partly fr. OE *cennan* to make known, declare, acknowledge; partly fr. ON *kenna* to perceive, know; both akin to OHG *kennen* to make known, Goth *kannjan*; causatives fr. the root of OE *cunnan* to know — more at CAN] *vt* **1** *archaic* **:** to have sight of : SEE ⟨as far as I could ~ thy chalky cliffs, . . . I stood upon the hatches in the storm —Shak.⟩ **2** *now dial* : to recognize by or as if by sight : DISCERN ⟨*kenned* in the beautiful lady the child of his friend —S.T.Coleridge⟩ **3** *now chiefly Scot* **a** : to have acquaintance with ⟨have *kend* every wench in the Halidome of St. Mary's —Sir Walter Scott⟩ **b** : to have knowledge of ⟨it was getting dark, and they didn't ~ the ground like us —John Buchan⟩ **c** : to have awareness or understanding of ⟨do ye ~ what ye're saying, man? —William Black⟩ **4** *Scots law* : to admit to ownership of heritable property ~ *vi* **1** *now chiefly Scot* : to have knowledge : KNOW ⟨it was his father then ye *kent* of —Sir Walter Scott⟩ **2** *obs* : to have the power of sight ⟨spaces distant from them as far as a man may ~ —Marchamont Needham⟩

²ken \"\ *n* -s **1** *obs* : the distance that bounds the range of ordinary vision esp. at sea ⟨are safely come within a ~ of Dover —John Lyly⟩ **2 a** : the range of vision ⟨then felt I like some watcher of the skies when a new planet swims into his ~ —John Keats⟩ **b** : the sight or view esp. of a place or person ⟨'tis double death to drown in ~ of shore —Shak.⟩ **c** : the power or exercise of vision ⟨searched with fixed ~ to know what place it was wherein I stood —H.F.Cary⟩ **3** : the range of recognition, comprehension, perception, understanding, or knowledge ⟨abstract words that are beyond the ~ of young children —Lois M. Rettie⟩ ⟨all knowledge and experience come within the historian's ~ —W.G.Carleton⟩ **syn** see RANGE

³ken \"\ *n* -s [prob. short for *kennel*] : HOUSE; *esp* : a rowdy resort for thieves and beggars ⟨has fishwives and boozing ~s enough to supply all of America —Kenneth Roberts⟩

⁴ken \"\ *n* -s [Jap, lit., fist] : a Japanese game of forfeits

ken- *or* **keno-** *comb form* [Gk, fr. *kenos;* akin to Arm *sin* empty, vain] : empty ⟨*keno*tron⟩

ke·naf *also* **ka·naf** *or* **ka·naff** \kə'naf\ *n* -s [Per] **1** : a valuable fiber plant (*Hibiscus cannabinus*) of the East Indies now widespread in cultivation **2** : the fiber of kenaf used for cordage and canvas manufacture — called also *ambari, bastard jute, Bombay hemp, deccan hemp, Java jute*

kench \'kench\ *n* -ES [origin unknown] : a bin or enclosure in which fish or skins are salted

ken·dal green \'kendᵊl-\ *also* **kendal** *n* -s *usu cap K* [ME, fr. *Kendal*, borough of Westmorland, England] : a green woolen cloth resembling homespun or tweed

kendal sneck bent *n, usu cap K* [prob. fr. *Kendal*, England] : a fishhook of wide squarish and curved pattern — see FISHHOOK illustration

ken·dle \'ken(d)ᵊl\ *dial var of* KINDLE

kend·na \'ken(d)nə\ [*kend* (past of ¹*ken*) + *na*] *chiefly Scot* : did not know

ken·do \'ken(,)dō\ *n* -s [Jap *kendō*] : a Japanese sport of fencing with staves

ken·dyr *or* **ken·dir** \(')ken¦di(ə)r\ *n* -s [Russ & Turk; Russ *kendyr'*, fr. Turk *kendir*] **1** : a strong bast fiber that resembles Indian hemp and is used in Asia as cordage and as a substitute for cotton and hemp **2** : an Old World dogbane (*Apocynum venetum*) cultivated chiefly in Asiatic Russia for the kendyr that it produces

ken·il·worth ivy \'kenᵊl,wərth-\ *n, usu cap K* [fr. *Kenilworth* Castle, Warwickshire, Eng.] : a delicate trailing Old World plant (*Cymbalaria muralis*) of the family Scrophulariaceae with palmately lobed and veined leaves and small pale violet flowers with a yellow palate

ke·nite \'kē,nīt\ *n* -s *usu cap* : a member of an ancient people of southern Palestine related to the Amalekites

ken·na \'ken(n)ə\ [¹*ken* + *na*] *chiefly Scot* : do not know

kenned \'kend\ *adj* [ME *kend*, fr. past part. of *kennen* to know — more at KEN] *chiefly Scot* : WELL-KNOWN, FAMILIAR ⟨wearying terribly for the sight of a ~ face —John Buchan⟩

ken·ne·dya \kə'nēdēə, 'kenə,dēə\ *n, cap* [NL, after Lewis *Kennedy* †1818, Eng. nurseryman] : a genus of Australian woody vines (family Leguminosae) bearing showy red or purplish flowers whose corolla has a long keel

¹ken·nel \'kenᵊl\ *n* -s [ME *kenel*, fr. (assumed) ONF *kenil*, fr. (assumed) VL *canile* (whence OF *chenil* kennel, F dial. *cani*), fr. L *canis* dog — more at HOUND] **1 a** (1) : a house for a dog or pack of hounds (2) : an establishment for the breeding or boarding of dogs — usu. used in pl. **b** : a house or other dwelling place regarded as unfit for human residence **2 a** : a pack of dogs or other animals **b** : a group of persons ⟨literary agent who has a ~ of eccentric clients —Martin Levin⟩ **3** : a bed or den of an animal (as a fox or otter) **4** : GABLE 2b

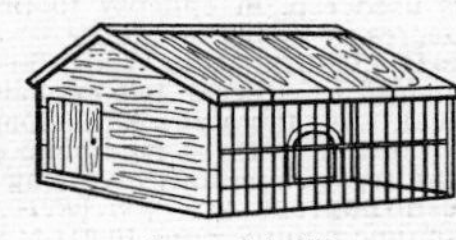

kennel 1a(1)

²kennel \"\ *vb* **kenneled** *or* **kennelled; kenneled** *or* **kennelled; kenneling** *or* **kennelling; kennels** *vi* **1** : to take shelter or lie in a kennel ⟨the fox ~s on the hillside⟩ **2** : to lodge in a dwelling place regarded as unfit for human residence ⟨the dull sodden faces of the man and woman who ~*ed* there —E.P.Roe⟩ ~ *vt* **1 a** : to put or keep in a kennel ⟨~ your hound for he has been well whipped —J.H.Wheelwright⟩ ⟨the apple trees under which the dogs were ~*ed* —Eve Langley⟩ **b** : to provide with a dwelling place regarded as unfit for human residence ⟨that quarter of the town where they are ~*ed* is . . . inhabited by strangers —Richard Steele⟩ **2** : to provide or seek lodging or shelter for esp. in a secluded place ⟨writers and painters . . . ~*ing* themselves in the depths of the country —*Times Lit. Supp.*⟩ **3** : to keep within bounds or under control : CONFINE, RESTRAIN ⟨indulge our enthusiasms while keeping our angers and envies ~*ed* —Brand Blanshard⟩ ⟨constantly striving to keep his quickly roused temper ~*ed*⟩

³kennel \"\ *n* -s [alter. of ²*cannel*] : a gutter in a street ⟨streets were ill-paved and . . . sloped down on both sides to the ~s —G.M.Trevelyan⟩

kennel club *n* : an association of dog fanciers concerned esp. with advancing the interests of one or more breeds of dogs usu. by establishing standards, providing competitions, or recording pedigrees

ken·nel·ly–heav·i·side layer \'kenᵊlē'hevē,sīd-\ *n, usu cap K&H* [after Arthur W. *Kennelly* †1939 Am. electrical engineer and Oliver *Heaviside* †1925 Eng. physicist, its discoverers] : IONOSPHERE

kennelmaid \'==,=\ *n* : a woman who takes care of kennels

ken·nel·man \'kenᵊlmən\ *n, pl* **kennelmen** : one who takes care of kennels

ken·ner·ly's salmon \'kenərl¦ēz-, -R -nəl| *or* -nᵊl|\ *n, usu cap K* [fr. the name *Kennerly*] : KOKANEE

ken·ni·cott's willow warbler \'kenəkəts-, -ə,käts-\ *n, usu cap K* [fr. the name *Kennicott*] : a warbler (*Acanthopneuste borealis kennicotti*) that breeds in Alaska

¹ken·ning \'keniŋ\ *n* -s [ME, fr. gerund of *kennen* to ken — more at KEN] **1** *obs* : range of sight : VIEW **2** *chiefly Scot* **a** : COGNITION, RECOGNITION **b** : a perceptible but small amount : LITTLE ⟨his father was . . . a ~ on the wrong side of the law —R.L.Stevenson⟩

²kenning \"\ *n* -s [ON, fr. *kenna* to perceive, know, name, name with a kenning + *-ing* — more at KEN] : a metaphorical compound word or phrase used esp. in Old English and Old Norse poetry ⟨Germanic verse . . . laid main stress upon the trope known as ~; the ocean is the "whale's bath," the "foaming fields", the "sea-street" —F.B.Gummere⟩

kenningwort \'==,=\ *n* [¹*kenning* + *wort*] : CELANDINE 1

ken·ny method *or* **ken·ny treatment** \'kenē-\ *n, usu cap K* [after Elizabeth *Kenny* †1952 Australian nurse, its developer] : a method of treating poliomyelitis consisting of application of hot fomentations to relax spasmodic contraction of affected muscles, reeducation through guided passive movement of the separate muscles with reestablishment of the patient's awareness of them, and guided active coordination

ke·no \'kē(,)nō\ *n* -s [modif. of F *quine* set of five winning numbers in a lottery, fr. OF *quines*, pl., throw at dice where each die shows 5, fr. L *quini* five each, fr. *quinque* five — more at FIVE] : a game resembling lotto in which numbers printed on pellets taken from a keno goose are announced to the players who cover the same numbers on cards and in which five numbers covered in the same horizontal row win for the player — see BINGO

keno- — see KEN-

keno goose *n* : a flexible sack with a narrow neck that releases one numbered pellet at a time for use in playing keno — called also *goose*

ke·no·sis \kə'nōsəs, kē'-\ *n* -ES [LGk *kenōsis*, fr. Gk, evacuation, action of emptying, fr. *kenoun* to purge, empty (fr. *kenos* empty) + *-sis* — more at KEN-] **1** : the act of Christ in emptying himself of the form of God, taking the form of a servant, and humbling himself to the extent of suffering death **2** : the act of voluntarily giving up personal rights and ambitions and accepting suffering as a follower of Christ

ke·not·ic \-nädˌik, -ät|, |ēk\ *adj* [Gk *kenōtikos* purgative, emptying, fr. (assumed) Gk *kenōtos* (verbal of Gk *kenoun*) + Gk *-ikos* -ic] : of, affirming, or marked by kenosis ⟨~ theories of the Incarnation that stem from Philippians 2:7⟩ ⟨a ~ Christology⟩ ⟨the ~ character of Russian Christianity⟩

ke·not·i·cism \|ə,sizəm\ *n* -s : the doctrine of or belief in the kenosis of Christ

ke·not·i·cist \-ˌsəst\ *n* -s : an advocate or adherent of kenoticism

ken·o·tron \'kenə·,trän\ *n* -s [*ken-* + *-tron*] : a high-vacuum diode used as a rectifier in appliances (as X-ray equipment and electrostatic precipitators) where high voltage and low current are required

kens *pres 3d sing of* KEN, *pl of* KEN

ken·sing·ton \'kenziŋtən, -n(t)siŋ-\ *n* -s [fr. the name *Kensington*] *dial* : a covered-dish supper

ken·speck·le \'kenz,pekəl, -n,sp-\ *or* **ken·speck** \-pek\ *adj* [prob. of Scand origin; akin to Norw *kjennspak* quick at recognizing, fr. *kjenne* to know, recognize (fr. ON *kenna*) + *spak* wise, gentle, tractable, fr. ON *spakr* — more at KEN] *chiefly Scot* : having a distinctive appearance : CONSPICUOUS

¹kent *past of* KEN

²kent \'kent\ *adj, usu cap* [fr. *Kent* county, England] : of or from the county of Kent, England : of the kind or style prevalent in Kent : KENTISH

³kent \"\ *n* -s [alter. of *quant*] *chiefly Scot* : STAFF, POLE: as **a** : a shepherd's staff **b** : a punting pole with a flange near the end

⁴kent \"\ *vb* -ED/-ING/-S *vi, chiefly Scot* : to push or propel a boat with a kent ~ *vt, chiefly Scot* : to push or propel with a kent

kent bugle *n, usu cap K* [prob. after Edward Augustus †1820 1st duke of *Kent*, Eng. soldier] : KEY BUGLE

ken·tia \'kentēə\ *n* [NL, fr. William *Kent* †ab 1828 Dutch gardener and traveler in the Orient + NL *-ia*] **1** *cap* : a genus of pinnate-leaved palms that are natives of Australia and the East Indies and have spadices with angled branchlets and flowers with six stamens **2** -s : any of several palms formerly assigned to the genus *Kentia:* as **a** : either of two feather palms (*Howea forsteriana* and *H. belmoriana*) from Lord Howe Island that are extensively cultivated for their ornamental foliage **b** : UMBRELLA PALM 1

kent·i·cism \'kentə,sizəm\ *n* -s *usu cap* [*Kent* county + *-icism* (as in *Anglicism*)] : a word or phrase peculiar to the Kentish dialect

kent·ish \'kentish\ *adj, usu cap* [ME, fr. OE *Centisc*, fr. *Cent* Kent + OE *-isc* -ish] **1** : of, relating to, or characteristic of the county of Kent, England **2** : of, relating to, or characteristic of the people of Kent

kentish glory *n, usu cap K* : an orange-brown moth (*Endromis versicolor*) with black-and-white markings that is common in parts of England and whose larva feeds on birch

kent·ish·man \-shmən\ *n, pl* **kentishmen** *cap* : a native or inhabitant of Kent

kentish nightingale *n, usu cap K, dial Eng* : BLACKCAP 2a

kentish plover *n, usu cap K* : a widely distributed ring plover (*Charadrius alexandrinus*) that sometimes breeds on the east coast of England

ken·tle \'kentᵊl\ *n* -s [by alter.] : QUINTAL

kent·ledge \'kent,lej\ *n* -s [origin unknown] : pig iron or scrap metal used as ballast

ken·tro·gon \'kentrə,gän\ *n* -s [Gk *kentron* sharp point, center of a circle + E *-gon* — more at CENTER] : a larva of a parasitic barnacle (order Rhizocephala)

ken·tro·lite \'kentrə,līt\ *n* -s [G *kentrolith*, fr. Gk *kentron* sharp point + G *-lith* -lite] : a dark reddish brown mineral $Pb_2Mn_2Si_2O_9$ consisting of a lead manganese silicate

¹ken·tuck \kən-'tək, (')ken¦t-, (')kän¦t-\ *adj, usu cap* [fr. *Kentucky*, the state] *dial* : KENTUCKIAN

²kentuck \"\ *n* -s *cap, dial* : KENTUCKIAN

¹ken·tuck·i·an \kən-'təkēən, -təkiən *sometimes* ken-·\ *adj, usu cap* [*Kentucky* + E *-an*] **1** : of, relating to, or characteristic of Kentucky **2** : of, relating to, or characteristic of the people of Kentucky

²kentuckian \"\ *n* -s *cap* : a native or resident of Kentucky

ken·tucky \-təkē, -ki\ *adj, usu cap* [*Kentucky*, state in the U. S., prob. of Iroquoian origin; akin to Iroquois *kenta* level, prairie] : of or from the state of Kentucky : of the kind or style prevalent in Kentucky : KENTUCKIAN

kentucky bass *or* **kentucky black bass** *n, usu cap K* : SPOTTED BLACK BASS

kentucky bluegrass *also* **kentucky blue** *n, usu cap K* : a valuable pasture and meadow grass (*Poa pratensis*) that has tall stalks and slender bright green leaves, is one of the chief constituents in mixtures of seed for lawns, and is found in both Europe and America where it reaches its finest development in the central U.S. — called also *bluegrass, June grass, meadow grass, smooth meadow grass*

kentucky cardinal *n, usu cap K* : ²CARDINAL 5

kentucky coffee tree *n, usu cap K* : a tall No. American tree (*Gymnocladus dioica*) of the family Leguminosae with bipinnate leaves and large woody brown pods whose seeds have been used as a substitute for coffee — called also *bonduc*

kentucky flat *n, usu cap K* : ARK 2b

kentucky green *n, often cap K* : a dark yellowish green that is yellower and less strong than holly green (sense 1), lighter and stronger than deep chrome green, yellower and darker than golf green, and yellower, lighter, and stronger than average hunter green

kentucky jean *n, usu cap K* **1** : a homemade jean woven with a cotton warp and a wool weft **2** : a garment of Kentucky jean

kentucky rifle *n, usu cap K* : a long-barreled flintlock of relatively small caliber developed in the early 18th century in Pennsylvania and extensively used on the American frontier

kentucky warbler *n, usu cap K* : a warbler (*Oporornis formosus*) of the eastern U.S. that is olive green above and yellow below and has the head marked with black

kentucky windage *n, usu cap K* [*Kentucky (rifle)*] : a windage correction made by aiming a firearm to the right or left of the target rather than by adjustment of the sights

¹ken·ya \'kenyə *also* 'kēn-\ *adj, usu cap* [fr. *Kenya*, country in eastern Africa] : of or from Kenya : of the kind or style prevalent in Kenya : KENYAN

²ken·ya *or* **ken·yah** \'kenyə\ *n, pl* **kenya** *or* **kenyas** *or* **kenyah** *or* **kenyahs** *usu cap* [native name in northern Borneo] **1** : a Dayak people of north central Borneo sometimes held with the Kayan to constitute a subdivision of the Bahau **2** : a member of the Kenya people

¹ken·yan \'kenyən *also* 'kēn-\ *adj, usu cap* [*Kenya* + E *-an*] **1** : of, relating to, or characteristic of Kenya **2** : of, relating to, or characteristic of the people of Kenya

²kenyan \"\ *n* -s *cap* : a native or inhabitant of Kenya

¹kep \'kep\ *vt* **kepped** \-pt\ **kep·pen** \-pən\ *or* **kip·pen** \'kipən\ **kepping; keps** [ME *keppen*, alter. of *kepen* to observe, heed, seek, seize, keep — more at KEEP] **1** *dial Brit* : to intercept and hinder ⟨~ him on his way home⟩ **2** *dial Brit* : to make a catch of : serve as a catch for

²kep \"\ *n* -s *dial Brit* : CATCH, HAUL

keph·a·lin \'kefələn\ *var of* CEPHALIN

kephir *var of* KEFIR

kepi \'kāpē, 'kepē\ *n* -s [F *képi*, fr. G dial. (Switzerland) *käppi*, dim. of *kappe* cap, fr. OHG *kappa* cloak, cape, fr. LL *cappa* head covering, cloak — more at CAP] : a military cap having a close-fitting band, a round flat top sloping toward the front, and a visor ⟨the forage cap was the American version of the French ~ —W.F.Harris⟩

kep·le·ri·an \(')ke¦plirēən\ *adj, usu cap* [Johannes *Kepler* †1630 Ger. astronomer + E *-ian*] **1** : of or relating to the astronomer Kepler **2** : being in accord with Kepler's laws

keplerian telescope *n, usu cap K* : a refracting telescope usu. used in astronomical observations including a positive objective lens and a positive eyepiece and giving an inverted image and a relatively wide field of view

kep·ler's law \'keplə(r)z-\ *n, usu cap K* [after Johannes *Kepler*] **1** : a statement in astronomy: the orbit of each planet is an ellipse that has the sun at one focus **2** : a statement in astronomy: the radius vector from the sun to each planet generates equal orbital areas in equal times **3** : a statement in astronomy: the ratio of the square of the revolution period to the cube of the orbital major axis is the same for all the planets

kept *past of* KEEP

ker- *also* **ke-** *prefix* [imit.] — used in onomatopoeic or echoic forms imitating the noise of a falling object ⟨*ker*plop⟩

ker·a·lan \'kerələn\ *n* -s *cap* [*Kerala* state, India + E *-an*] : a native or inhabitant of Kerala state, southern India

ke·ra·na *or* **ker·ra·na** \kə'ränə\ *n* -s [modif. of Per *karranāi*, fr. *nāi* reed, reed pipe] : a long Persian trumpet

ker·a·sin \'kerəsən\ *n* -s [ISV *keras-* (prob. fr. Gk *keras* horn) + *-in* — more at HORN] : a cerebroside $C_{48}H_{93}NO_8$ that occurs esp. in Gaucher's disease and that yields lignoceric acid on hydrolysis

kerat- *or* **kerato-** — see CERAT-

ker·a·ter·pe·ton \,kerə'tərpə,tän\ *n, cap* [NL, fr. *kerat-* + Gk *herpeton* creeping thing, snake] : a genus of broad-headed extinct amphibians similar to salamanders found in the Carboniferous of Ohio and Ireland

ker·a·tin \'kerəd·ən, -ətən\ *also* **ceratin** \'se-\ *n* -s [ISV *kerat-*, *cerat-* + *-in*] : any of various sulfur-containing fibrous proteins that form the chemical basis of epidermal tissues (as horn, hair, wool, nails, feathers), that are insoluble in most solvents and unlike collagen and other proteins are typically not digested by enzymes of the gastrointestinal tract, and that produce elastic properties of fibers — compare PSEUDOKERATIN

ker·a·tin·i·za·tion \,kerəd·ənə'zāshən\ *n* -s [ISV *keratinize* + *-ation*] : conversion into keratin or keratinous tissue

ker·a·tin·ize \'kerəd·ə,nīz\ *vb* -ED/-ING/-S [ISV *keratin* + *-ize*] *vt* : to make keratinous ⟨tissues *keratinized* by friction⟩ ~ *vi* : to become keratinous or converted into keratin ⟨a *keratinizing* scar⟩

ker·a·ti·no·phil·ic \kə¦ratᵊnō¦filik\ *adj* [*keratin* + *-o-* + *-philic*] : showing strong affinity for hair, skin, feathers, horns, and other keratinized material — used chiefly of fungi capable of growing on such materials

ke·rat·i·nous \kə'ratᵊnəs\ *adj* [Gk *keratinos*, fr. *kerat-*, *keras* horn — more at HORN] : HORNY

ker·a·ti·tis \,kerə'tīd·əs\ *n* -ES [NL, fr. *kerat-* + *-itis*] : inflammation of the cornea of the eye characterized by burning or smarting, blurring of vision, and sensitiveness to light and caused by infectious or noninfectious agents — compare KERATOCONJUNCTIVITIS

ker·a·to·conjunctivitis \¦kerəd·ō+\ *or* **cer·a·to·conjunctivitis** \¦serəd·ō+\ *n* [NL, fr. *kerat-*, or *cerat-* + *conjunctivitis*] : combined inflammation of the cornea and conjunctiva: **a** : a virus disease of man often epidemic and marked by pain, redness, and swelling with tenderness of adjacent lymph nodes and profuse watery discharge from the eyes — called also *pinkeye* **b** : a highly contagious rickettsial disease of cattle marked by inflammation of the conjunctiva and cornea and infective discharge from eyes and nose

ker·a·to·der·ma \,kerəd·ō'dərmə\ *n* [NL, fr. *kerat-* + *-derma*] : a horny condition of the skin

ker·a·to·gen·ic \¦===¦jenik\ *adj* [*kerat-* + *-genic*] : capable of inducing proliferation of epidermal tissues

ker·a·tog·e·nous \¦kerə¦täjənəs\ *adj* [*kerat-* + *-genous*] : producing horn or horny tissue

ker·a·toid \'kerə,tȯid\ *adj* [ISV *kerat-* + *-oid*] : HORNY

ker·a·toi·dea \,kerə'tȯidēə\ [NL, fr. *kerat-* + *-oidea*] *syn of* KERATOSA

Ker·a·tol \'kerə,tȯl, -tōl\ *trademark* — used for a pyroxylin-coated waterproof material used esp. in bookbinding

ker·a·tol·y·sis \,kerə'täləsəs\ *n* [NL, fr. ISV *keratin* + NL *-o-* + *-lysis*] **1** : the process of breaking down or dissolving keratin **2** [NL, fr. *kerat-* + *-lysis*] : a skin disease marked by peeling of the horny layer of the epidermis

¹ker·a·to·lyt·ic \¦kerəd·ō¦lid·ik\ *adj* [ISV *kerat-* + *-lytic*] : relating to or causing keratolysis

²keratolytic \"\ *n* -s : a keratolytic agent (as salicylic acid)

ker·a·to·ma·la·cia \,kerəd·ōmə'lās(h)ēə\ *n* -s [NL, fr. *kerat-* + *-malacia*] : a softening and ulceration of the cornea of the eye resulting from severe systemic deficiency of vitamin A — compare XEROPHTHALMIA

ker·a·to·phyre \'kerəd·ō,fī(ə)r\ *n* -s [ISV *kerat-* + *-phyre;* orig. formed as G *keratophyr*] **1** : any of various rocks resembling hornfels **2** : a compact porphyritic rock with anorthoclase as its prevailing feldspar and with or without quartz

ker·a·to·plas·ty \-,plastē\ *n* -ES [ISV *kerat-* + *-plasty*] : plastic surgery on the cornea; *esp* : corneal grafting

ker·a·tosa \,kerə'tōsə, -ōzə\ *n pl, cap* [NL, fr. *kerat-* + L *-osa* (neut. pl. of *-osus* -ous)] : an order of Demospongiae comprising the horny sponges with a spongin skeleton and without spicules and including the commercially important family Spongiidae

ker·a·tose \'kerə,tōs\ *or* **cer·a·tose** \'se-\ *adj* [NL *Keratosa*] : of or relating to the Keratosa

ker·a·to·sis \,kerə'tōsəs\ *n, pl* **kerato·ses** \-ō,sēz\ [NL, fr. *kerat-* + *-osis*] **1** : a disease of the skin marked by overgrowth of horny tissue **2** : an area of the skin affected by keratosis

ker·a·tot·ic \¦==¦täd·ik\ *adj* [fr. NL *keratosis*, after such pairs as NL *hypnosis:* E *hypnotic*] : of or relating to keratosis : affected by keratosis

ke·rat·to *also* **ka·rat·to** \kə'rad·(,)ō\ *n* -s [prob. native name in the West Indies] **1** : any of several West Indian agaves (esp. *Agave keratto*) **2** : the fiber from keratto

ke·rau·lo·phon \kə'rōlə,fän\ *also* **ke·rau·lo·phone** \-fōn\ *n* -s [*keraulophon* fr. G, fr. E *keraulophone; keraulophone* fr. Gk *keras* horn + *aulos* reed instrument like an oboe + E *-phone* — more at HORN, ALVEOLUS] : a labial pipe-organ stop of 8-foot pitch having metal pipes

kerauno- *comb form* [Gk — more at CERAUN-] : thunder

ke·rau·no·graph \kə'rȯnə,graf, -ràf\ *n* -s [ISV *kerauno-* + *-graph*] **1** : a figure impressed by lightning upon a body or material **2** : CERAUNOGRAPH — **ke·rau·no·graph·ic** \=¦==-¦grafik\ *adj* — **ker·au·nog·ra·phy** \,kerə'nägrəfē\ *n* -ES

kerb \'kərb\ *n* -s [by alter.] *Brit* : CURB 5 g, 6

ker·bau \'kər,baů\ *n* -s [Malay] *in Malaysia* : WATER BUFFALO; *esp* : a usu. black wide-horned variety of Siamese origin used chiefly in rice cultivation

¹kerch \'kərch\ *n* -ES [ME *kerche*, short for *kerchef*] : KERCHIEF 1a

²kerch \'kerch\ *adj, usu cap* [fr. *Kerch*, Crimea, U.S.S.R.] : of or from the city of Kerch, U.S.S.R. : of the kind or style prevalent in Kerch

ker·cher \'kəchə(r\ *n* -s [ME *kevercher, kercher*, modif. of MF *cuevrechief, cuerchief*] *dial Eng* : HANDKERCHIEF

¹ker·chief \'kərchə̇f, 'kəch-, 'kəich-, -,chē|\ *n, pl* **kerchiefs** *also* **ker·chieves** \|fs, |vz; *see pl at* HANDKERCHIEF\ [ME *courchef, kerchef, coverchief*, fr. OF *cuevrechief, couvrechef, cuerchief*, fr. *covrir* to cover + *chief, chef* head — more at COVER, CHIEF] **1 a** : a square of cloth worn usu. folded by women as a head covering **b** : a similar cloth worn about the neck or shoulders **2** : HANDKERCHIEF 1

kerchief 1a

²kerchief \"\ *vt* -ED/-ING/-S : to put a kerchief over ⟨~*ed* her hair before going out into the rain⟩

ker·chief·like \-f,līk\ *adj* : resembling a kerchief

¹ker·choo \kə'chü\ *n* -s [imit.] : the characteristic sound of a person sneezing

²kerchoo *vi* -ED/-ING/-S : to make a kerchoo

ke·re *or* **qe·re** \kə'rē\ *also* **qre** \'krē\ *n* -s [Heb *qĕrī* imper. of *qārā'* to read] : a reading that in the traditional

Jewish mode of reading the Hebrew Bible is substituted for one actually standing in the consonantal text with the consonants of the word or phrase to be read being usu. given in the margin and the vowel points if the text is vocalized being inserted in the text — called also *keri;* compare KETHIB

ke·rek \kə'rek\ *n, pl* **kerek** *or* **kereks** *usu cap* **1 a :** a people constituting a small branch of the Kamchadal-Koryak ethnic group **b :** a member of such people **2 :** the language of the Kerek containing elements of Eskimo

kere per·pe·tu·um \-pə(r)'pechəwəm\ *n* [NL, lit., perpetual kere] **:** a kere which is always substituted for a particular word in the Hebrew Bible and whose consonants are not written in the margin but are supplied by the reader from memory

ke·res \'kā,rās\ *n, pl* **keres** *usu cap* **1 a :** a Pueblo people of New Mexico including the Acoma, Cochiti, Laguna, San Felipe, Santa Ana, Santo Domingo, and Sia **b :** a member of the Keres people **2 :** the language of the Keres people constituting the Keresan family

ker·e·san \'kerəsən\ *n, pl* **keresan** *usu cap* **:** a language family consisting of Keres only and having no close relationship to any other language group

ke·re·wa \kə'rāwə\ *n, pl* **kerewa** *or* **kerewas** *usu cap* **1 a :** a Papuan people on the Gulf of Papua **b :** a member of such people **2 :** the language of the Kerewa people

[1]**kerf** \'kərf, 'kəf\ *n* -s [ME *kirf, kerf* (also, action of cutting), fr. OE *cyrf* action of cutting, something cut off; akin to MHG *kerbe, kerp* notch, OE *ceorfan* to carve — more at CARVE] **1 a :** a slit or notch made in cutting usu. by a saw or cutting torch **b :** the width of cut that a saw or cutting torch makes in wood or other material **2 :** GROOVE 2a(4) **3 :** a deep narrow cut in a face of coal (as to facilitate mining or to remove clay or dirt seams)

[2]**kerf** \"\ *vt* -ED/-ING/-S **:** to make a kerf in esp. by sawing; *specif* **:** to cut (as a beam) transversely along the underside in order to permit bending

kerf graft *n* **:** a graft similar to a cleft graft except that the cut in the stock is made with a saw

ker·flop \kə(r)'fläp\ *adv* [*ker-* + *flop*] **:** with or as if with a flop

ker·gue·len cabbage \'kərgələn-, ¦kərgə¦len-\ *n, usu cap K* [fr. *Kerguelen* island in the southern Indian ocean] **:** an herb (*Pringlea antiscorbutica*) of the family Cruciferae of the island of Kerguelen that is unique in its family in being wind-pollinated

ke·ri *or* **qe·ri** \kə'rē\ *also* **k'ri** *or* **kri** *or* **q'ri** *or* **qri** \'krē\ *n* -s [Heb *qĕrī* — more at KERE] **:** KERE

ke·ri·ah \kə'rēə\ *n, pl* **keri·oth** *or* **keri·ot** \-ē,ōt(h), -ōs\ [Heb *qĕrī'āh*] **:** the traditional act or ceremony among Jews of rending one's garment at the funeral of a near relative as a symbol of mourning

ke·ri·on \'kirē,än\ *n* -s [NL, fr. Gk *kērion* honeycomb — more at CERION] **:** inflammatory ringworm of the hair follicles of the beard and scalp usu. accompanied by secondary bacterial infection and marked by spongy swelling and the exudation of sticky pus from the hair follicles

keri perpetuum *n* [NL, lit., perpetual keri] **:** KERE PERPETUUM

ker·lock \'keələk\ *dial Eng var of* CHARLOCK

kerman *usu cap, var of* KIRMAN

ker·man·ji \kə(r)'mänjē\ *n* -s *cap* [Kurdish] **1 :** the western dialect of the Kurdish language spoken in the region of eastern Turkey **2 :** the Kurdish language

[1]**ker·man·shah** \¦kermən¦shä, kər'män,-\ *adj, usu cap* [fr. *Kermanshah*, Iran] **:** of or from the city of Kermanshah, Iran of the kind or style prevalent in Kermanshah

[2]**kermanshah** *usu cap, var of* KIRMANSHAH

[3]**kermanshah** \"\ *n* -s *often cap* **:** COCONUT 4

ker·mes \'kər(,)mēz, -,məs; kər'mes; *in sense 1b* 'kər(,)mēz\ *n* [F *kermès*, fr. Ar *qirmiz* — more at CRIMSON] **1 a** *pl* **kermes :** the dried bodies of the females of various scales (genus *Kermes*) that are found on the kermes oak of the Mediterranean region, are round and about the size of a pea, and constitute the oldest dyestuff known producing a red color resembling but much inferior to that of cochineal **b** *cap* [NL, fr. F *kermès* or E *kermes*] **:** a genus (the type of the family Kermesidae) of scales comprising those that form kermes and various related No. American and Australian scales **2** *pl* **kermes :** KERMES MINERAL **3** *or* **kermes scarlet** *pl* **kermes :** a somewhat variable color averaging scarlet

ker·mes·ite \'kərmē,zīt, -mə,sīt; kər'me,sīt\ *n* -s [F *kermésite*, fr. *kermès* + *-ite*] **:** a mineral Sb_2S_2O consisting of antimony oxysulfide occurring usu. as tufts of cherry-red capillary crystals and resulting from the alteration of stibnite

kermes mineral *also* **kermes** *n* **:** a soft brown-red powder consisting essentially of antimony trisulfide and antimony trioxide and used formerly as an alterative, diaphoretic, and emetic

kermes oak *also* **kermes** *n* **:** a dwarf often shrubby evergreen oak (*Quercus coccinea*) of the Mediterranean region that is the host of the kermes insect and has a bark rich in tannin

ker·mis \'kərməs, 'ke(ə)rm-\ *or* **ker·mess** \", kər'mes\ *or* **kir·mess** \kər'mes\ *n* -ES [D *kermis*, fr. MD *kercmisse, kermisse*, fr. *kerke, kerc* church + *misse* mass, church festival] **1 :** a local outdoor festival of the Low Countries orig. held annually on the feast day of the local patron saint **2 :** an entertainment and fair usu. given for the purpose of raising money

[1]**kern** \'kərn, 'kən\ *vb* -ED/-ING/-S [ME *curnen, kernen*, fr. (assumed) OE *cyrnen*, fr. OE *corn* — more at CORN] *vi, dial Eng* **:** to form kernels ⟨good weather for the grain to ~⟩ ~ *vt, dial Eng* **:** to form or set (as a crop of fruit) ⟨trees that had ~*ed* their best crop in years⟩

[2]**kern** \"\ *n* -s *dial Eng* **:** KERNEL, GRAIN ⟨~ of corn⟩ ⟨~*s* of sand⟩

[3]**kern** \"\ *also* **kerne** \", 'ke(ə)rn, 'keən\ *n* -s [ME *kerne*, fr. MIr *cethern* band of soldiers, fr. *cath* battle, fr. OIr; akin to Gaulish *catu-* battle, W *cad*, OE *heatho-*, OHG *hadu-*, ON *höth-* battle, Skt *śatru* enemy] **1 :** a foot soldier; *esp* **:** a light-armed soldier of medieval Ireland or Scotland ⟨those rough rugheaded ~*s* —Shak.⟩ — compare GALLOWGLASS **2 :** a rude or boorish countryman esp. from Scotland or Ireland

[4]**kern** \'kərn, 'kən\ *chiefly dial var of* KIRN

[5]**kern** \", 'kəin\ *n* -s [modif. of F *carne* corner, projecting angle, fr. F dial. (Picardy & Normandy), fr. L *cardin-, cardo* hinge — more at CARDINAL] **1 :** a part of the face of a typecast letter that projects beyond the body (as the upper or lower extremity of *f* or the tail of *Q*) **2 :** a corresponding part of a printed letter

[6]**kern** \"\ *vb* -ED/-ING/-S *vt* **1 :** to form with a kern (as a letter) **2 :** to smooth (type) about the kern ~ *vi* **:** to become kerned — used of a letter or some part of a letter

[7]**kern** \"\ *n* -s [G, core, kernel, nucleus, fr. OHG *kerno;* akin to ON *kjarni* kernel, core, OE *corn*] **:** NUCLEUS 2l

[1]**ker·nel** \'kərnᵊl, 'kən-, 'kəin-\ *n* -s [ME *curnel, kirnel, kernel*, fr. OE *cyrnel*, dim. of *corn* grain, seed — more at CORN] **1** *chiefly dial* **:** a fruit seed ⟨beaten . . . for picking a ~ out of a pomegranate —Shak.⟩ **2 :** the inner portion of a seed within the integuments — usu. used of edible seeds and of the contents of the endocarp in nuts, drupes, and similar fruits ⟨peach ~⟩ ⟨as brown in hue as hazelnuts, and sweeter than the ~*s* —Shak.⟩ **3 :** a whole grain or seed of a cereal ⟨~ of corn⟩ ⟨wheat and barley ~*s*⟩ **4** *chiefly dial* **a :** a hard swelling under the surface of the skin **b :** a small gland or body resembling a gland **5 :** a central or essential part: as **a :** the gist of a concept or idea ⟨a ~ of recognizable truth . . . which commands respect —*Wall Street Jour.*⟩ ⟨the ~ of this argument is made out to be a mere matter of logic —O.P.Wood⟩ ⟨recent tendency to regard myth, ritual, and magic as the ~ instead of the husk of religion —W.R.Inge⟩ **b :** the central structure or organization ⟨its position as a world power and the ~ of a great empire —Vera M. Dean⟩ **6 :** [1]CORE 1t

[2]**kernel** \"\ *vb* **kerneled** *or* **kernelled; kerneled** *or* **kernelled; kerneling** *or* **kernelling; kernels** [ME *kyrnellen*, fr. *curnel, kirnel, kernel*, n.] *vi* **:** to form or produce kernels **:** ripen into kernels ~ *vt* **:** to envelop or enclose as a kernel ⟨great artist ~*ed* in the . . . man of the world —Osbert Sitwell⟩

[3]**kernel** \"\ *vt* **kerneled** *or* **kernelled; kerneled** *or* **kernelled; kerneling** *or* **kernelling; kernels** [ME *kernelen*, fr. MF *querneler, kerneler*, var. of *creneler* — more at CRENEL] **:** CRENELLATE

ker·neled *or* **ker·nelled** \-ᵊld\ *adj* [[1]*kernel* + *-ed*] **:** having a kernel ⟨farms in this section produce a red ~ corn —*Amer. Guide Series: Pa.*⟩

ker·nel·late \'kərnᵊl,āt\ *vt* -ED/-ING/-S [ML *kernellatus*, past part. of *kernellare*, fr. ME *kernelen*] **:** CRENELLATE

ker·nel·ly \'kərnᵊlē\ *adj* [[1]*kernel* + *-y*] **1 :** having kernels or many kernels **2 :** resembling kernels

kernel smut *n* **:** COVERED SMUT

kernel spot *n* **:** a disease of the pecan kernel caused by a fungus (*Coniothyrium caryogenum*) and characterized by irregularly roundish dull brown spots

ker·nic·ter·us \kə(r)'niktərəs\ *n* -ES [NL, fr. G *kern* core, kernel, nucleus + NL *icterus* — more at KERN] **:** a condition marked by the deposit of bile pigments in the nuclei of the brain and spinal cord and by degeneration of nerve cells that occurs usu. in infants as a part of the syndrome of erythroblastosis fetalis

ker·nig sign \'kernig-\ *or* **kernig's sign** *n, usu cap K* [after Vladimir *Kernig* †1917 Russ. physician] **:** an indication usu. present in meningitis that consists of pain and resistance on attempting to extend the leg at the knee with the thigh flexed at the hip

kerning *pres part of* KERN

kern·ite \'kər,nīt\ *n* -s [fr. *Kern* co., Calif. + E *-ite*] **:** a mineral $Na_2B_4O_7.4H_2O$ that consists of a hydrous sodium borate occurring in colorless to white crystals and cleavage masses and that is an important source of borax — called also *rasorite*

ker·nos \'kər,näs\ *n, pl* **ker·noi** \-nȯi\ [Gk] **:** an ancient Greek vessel consisting of several small cups joined on a pottery ring or attached to the rim of a vase

kernos in cross section

kern river indian \'kərn-\ *n, usu cap K&R&I* [fr. the *Kern river*, in California] **:** an Indian of the Tübatulabal or a related people living on the Kern river in California

kern river trout *n, usu cap K&R* [fr. the *Kern river* in California] **:** a variety of rainbow trout occurring only in the Kern river in California

kerns *pres 3d sing of* KERN, *pl of* KERN

ker·o·gen \'kerəjən, -,jen\ *n* -s [Gk *kēros* wax + E *-gen* — more at CEREUS] **:** bituminous material occurring esp. in oil shale and yielding oil when heated — **ke·rog·e·nous** \kə'räjənəs\ *adj*

ker·o·sine *or* **ker·o·sene** \'kerə,sēn, 'kar-, ,==¦=\ *n* -s [*kerosine* alter. of *kerosene; kerosene* fr. Gk *kēros* wax + E *-ene* (as in *camphene*); fr. the use of paraffin in its manufacture — more at CEREUS] **:** a flammable hydrocarbon oil that is less volatile than gasoline, that is usu. obtained by distillation of petroleum, and that is used for burning in lamps and heaters or furnaces, as a fuel or fuel component for jet engines, and as a solvent or thinner (as in insecticide emulsions or paints) — see LAMP illustration

ker·plunk \kə(r)'pləŋk\ *adv* [imit.] **:** with a loud dull sound **:** with a thud ⟨a coconut which fell ~ at his feet⟩

kerrana *var of* KERANA

kerr cell \'kär-, 'kər-\ *n, usu cap K* [after John *Kerr* †1907 Scot. physicist] **:** a cell that contains electrodes immersed in nitrobenzene or other liquid, that exhibits double refraction in a high degree and with short time lag, and that is used in devices where the intensity of light is to be changed rapidly in accordance with the voltage applied to the electrodes (as in the recording of sound tracks for motion pictures) — compare KERR EFFECT 1

kerr effect *n, usu cap K* [after John *Kerr*] **1 :** the production of double refraction in various dielectrics when placed in a strong electric field **2 :** the rotation of the plane of polarization when plane-polarized light is reflected from the end of a magnet

[1]**ker·ria** \'kerēə\ *n* [NL, fr. William *Kerr* †1814 Eng. gardener + NL *-ia*] **1** *cap* **:** a genus of Chinese shrubs (family Rosaceae) with solitary yellow often double flowers **2** -s **:** any shrub of the genus *Kerria*

[2]**kerria** \"\ *n, cap* [NL, fr. Robert *Kerr* †1813 Eng. scientific writer + NL *-ia*] **:** a genus of aquatic New World oligochaete worms

ker·rie \'kerē\ *n* -s **:** KNOBKERRIE

ker·ril \'kerəl\ *n* -s [native name in India] **:** a sea snake (*Kerilia jerdoni*) of the Asiatic coast from the Persian gulf to Japan

[1]**kerry** \'kerē, -ri\ *adj, usu cap* [fr. County *Kerry*, Ireland] **:** of or from County Kerry, Ireland **:** of the kind or style prevalent in County Kerry

[2]**kerry** \"\ *n, usu cap* **1 :** an Irish breed of small hardy long-lived black cattle noted for their milk **2** -ES *often cap* **:** an animal of the Kerry breed

kerry blue terrier *n* **1** *usu cap K & B & T* **:** an Irish breed of medium-sized terriers of uncertain ancestry that has a long head, a deep chest, and a silky coat of blue of any shade, stands about 18 inches high, and weighs from 30 to 38 pounds **2** *usu cap K* **:** a dog of the Kerry blue terrier breed

kerry hill *n, usu cap K&H* [fr. *Kerry Hill* in Kerry, town in Wales] **:** a breed of hardy English mutton-type sheep

kers \'kərs, 'kärs\ *dial var of* CRESS

ker·sen·neh \kə(r)'senə\ *also* **ker·san·né** \-sanā\ *n* -s [Ar *kirsannah*] **:** ERS

[1]**ker·sey** \'kərzē, 'kəz-, -zi\ *n, pl* **kerseys** *also* **kersies** [ME, fr. *Kersey*, village in Suffolk, Eng.] **1 a :** a coarse ribbed woolen cloth for hose and work clothes woven first in medieval England **b :** a heavy wool or wool and cotton fabric made in plain or twill weave with a smooth surface and used esp. for uniforms and coats **2 :** a garment of kersey

[2]**kersey** \"\ *adj* **1 :** made of kersey **2** *obs* **:** HOMESPUN

ker·sey·mere \'==,mi(ə)r, -iə\ *n* -s [alter. (influenced by [1]*kersey*) of *cassimere*] **:** a fine woolen fabric with a close nap made in fancy twill weaves

ker·u·ing \'kerəwiŋ\ *n* -s [Malay *kĕruing*] **:** APITONG

ke·ryg·ma \kə'rigmə, kē-\ *also* **ke·rug·ma** \-rəg-\ *n, pl* **kerygma·ta** *also* **kerugma·ta** \-məd·ə\ [Gk *kērygma*, fr. *kēryssein* to proclaim, preach] **1 :** the preaching or proclamation of the Christian gospel esp. in the form found in the primitive Christian church **2 :** the original Christian gospel preached by the apostles

ker·yg·mat·ic \¦kerig¦mad·ik\ *adj* [Gk *kērygmat-, kērygma* + E *-ic*] **:** of, relating to, or based upon the kerygma

ker·yl \'kerəl\ *n* -s [*kerosine* + *-yl*] **:** a mixture of alkyl radicals that is derived from kerosine specially purified for making sulfonated anionic detergents and that consists chiefly of one or more radicals ranging in size from decyl to tetradecyl or hexadecyl ⟨condensation of ~ chloride with benzene yields keryl-benzene⟩

ke·rys·tic \kə'ristik, kē'-\ *adj* [fr. (assumed) Gk *kērystos* (verbal of Gk *kēryssein* to preach) + E *-ic*] **:** HOMILETIC

ke·sar \'kāzə(r)\ *archaic var of* KAISER

kest \'kest\ *dial Brit var of* CAST

kes·trel \'kestrəl\ *n* -s [ME *castrel*, fr. MF *cresserele, crecerelle, quercelle*, fr. *crecelle, cresselle* rattle, fr. (assumed) VL *crepicella*, alter. (influenced by L *crepare* to crack, rattle) of L *crepitacillum*, fr. *crepitare* to rattle, crackle — more at CREPITATE] **:** a common small European falcon (*Falco tinnunculus*) that is noted for its habit of hovering in the air against a wind, is about a foot long, and is bluish gray above in the male and reddish brown in the female; *broadly* **:** any of various related small Old World falcons — compare SPARROW HAWK

[1]**ket** \'ket\ *n, pl* **ket** [ME, flesh, meat, of Scand origin; akin to ON *kjöt* flesh, meat, OSw *köt, kiot, kiöt;* perh. akin to Skt *guda* bowel, rectum — more at COT] **1** *dial Brit* **a :** CARRION **b :** FILTH, RUBBISH **2** *dial Brit* **:** a good-for-nothing person

[2]**ket** \"\ *n, pl* **ket** [prob. alter. of [3]*cot*] *Scot* **:** a fleece of wool

[3]**ket** \"\ *n, pl* **ket** *or* **kets** *cap* **1 a :** a people of the middle Yenisei region of Siberia that constitutes the only western Paleo-Asiatic group **b :** a member of such people **2 :** the Yeniseian language of the Ket people

ket- *or* **keto-** *comb form* [ISV, fr. *ketone*] **1** *usu* **keto- a :** containing the ketone group ⟨*keto*hexose⟩ — in names of classes of compounds; compare ALD- 1 **b :** containing a ketone group regarded as formed by replacement of two hydrogen atoms in a methylene group by oxygen — in names of specific organic compounds ⟨*keto*propionic acid⟩; compare OX- **c** *usu ital* **:** containing an unmodified ketone group — in names of open-chain ketonic forms of specific sugars ⟨*keto*-D-fructose⟩; compare ALDEHYDO- 1 **2 :** related to a ketone ⟨*ket*oxime⟩ — compare ALD- 2

ke·ta \'kēd·ə\ *n* -s [Russ] **:** DOG SALMON 1

ke·tal \'kē,tal\ *n* -s [*ket-* + *-al*] **:** an acetal derived from a ketone

ket·a·pang \'ked·ə,paŋ\ *n* -s [Malay *kĕtapang*] **:** a low-grade variety of gutta

ke·ta·zine \'kēd·ə,zēn, -,zən\ *n* [ISV *ket-* + *azine*] **:** an azine $R_2C{=}NN{=}CR_2$ formed from a ketone

ketch \'kech\ *n* -ES [alter. of earlier *catch*, fr. ME *cache*, prob. fr. *cacchen* to chase, catch — more at CATCH] **:** a fore-and-aft-rigged boat similar to a yawl but having a larger mizzen and having the mizzenmast stepped farther forward typically of the rudderhead or of the after end of the waterline

ketch

ketchup *var of* CATSUP

ket·e·lee·ria \,ked·əˈlirēə\ *n, cap* [NL, fr. J.B.*Keteleer*, 19th cent. Belgian gardener + NL *-ia*] **:** a genus of Asiatic conifers (family Pinaceae) that resemble firs and have persistent cone scales and keeled upper leaf surfaces

ket·em·bil·la \,ked·əm'bilə\ *or* **kit·am·bil·la** \,kid-·\ *n* -s [Singhalese *kätämbilla*] **1 :** a hairy purple acid tropical fruit that is used esp. for preserves and is closely related to the kei apple **2 :** a small shrubby tree (*Dovyalis hebecarpa*) of the family Flacourtiaceae that is native to Ceylon and is cultivated in various tropical areas for the ketembillas it bears

ke·tene \'kē,tēn\ *n* -s [ISV *ket-* + *-ene;* orig. formed as G *keten*] **:** a colorless poisonous gaseous compound $CH_2{=}C{=}O$ of penetrating odor that is made by pyrolysis of acetic acid or acetone and used as an acetylating agent (as in making acetic anhydride from acetic acid or acetic esters from alcohols); *also* **:** any of various derivatives of this compound — see DIKETENE

ke·thib *or* **ke·thibh** *also* **ke·thiv** *or* **ke·tib** *or* **k'thib** *or* **kthib** *or* **k'thibh** *or* **kthibh** \kə't(h)ēv\ *n* -s [Heb *kĕthībh*, fr. Aram, written] **:** a reading in the consonantal text of the Hebrew Bible for which in traditional Jewish practice there is substituted a different reading whose consonants are usu. given in the margin — compare KERE

kethubah *var of* KETUBAH

ke·ti·mine \'kēd·ə,mēn, -mən\ *n* [ISV *ket-* + *imine*] **:** a Schiff base of the general formula $R_2C{=}NH$ or $R_2C{=}NR'$ formed by condensation of a ketone with ammonia or a primary amine

ke·to \'kēd·(,)ō, -ē(,)tō\ *adj* [*ket-*] **:** of or relating to a ketone **:** being or containing the ketone group — compare OXO

keto- — see KET-

keto acid *n* **:** a compound that is both a ketone and an acid ⟨acetoacetic acid is a beta *keto acid*⟩

ke·to·bem·i·done \,kēd·ō'bemə,dōn\ *n* -s [*ket-* + *carb*ethoxy + *methyl* + *-id* + *-one*] **:** a narcotic ketone $C_{15}H_{21}NO_2$ related chemically to meperidine

ke·to-enol tautomerism \'kēd·ō+ . . . -\ *n* [*ket-* + *enol*] **:** tautomerism in which the keto and enol forms of a compound (as ethyl acetoacetate) are in equilibrium

ke·to·gen·e·sis \,kēd·ō+\ *n* [NL, fr. *ket-* + L *genesis*] **:** the production of ketone bodies (as in diabetes and other conditions of impaired metabolism)

ke·to·genic \¦kēd·ə¦jenik\ *adj* [ISV *ket-* + *-genic*] **:** producing ketone bodies

ketogenic diet *n* **:** a diet that supplies a large amount of fat and minimal amounts of carbohydrate and protein and that is used esp. in epilepsy to produce a ketosis and alter the degree of bodily alkalinity

ke·to·glutaric acid \¦kēd·ō+(,)=¦== . . . -\ *n* [ISV *ket-* + *glutaric*] **:** either of two crystalline keto derivatives of glutaric acid; *esp* **:** the alpha keto isomer $HOOCCH_2CH_2COCOOH$ formed in various metabolic processes (as the Krebs cycle and transaminations involving glutamic acid)

ke·to·heptose \"+\ *n* [*ket-* + *heptose*] **:** a heptose of a ketonic nature — see HEPTULOSE

ke·to·hexose \"+\ *n* [ISV *ket-* + *hexose*] **:** a hexose (as fructose or sorbose) of a ketonic nature — see HEXULOSE

ke·tol \'kē,tōl, -tōl\ *n* -s [ISV *ket-* + *-ol*] **:** a compound (as an acyloin) that is both a ketone and an alcohol **:** HYDROXY KETONE

ke·tol·y·sis \kē'täləsəs\ *n* [NL, fr. *ket-* + *-lysis*] **:** the decomposition of ketones

ke·to·lyt·ic \¦kēd·ə¦lid·ik\ *adj* [ISV *ket-* + *-lytic*] **:** of, relating to, or characterized by ketolysis

ke·tone \'kē,tōn\ *n* -s [G *keton*, alter. of *azeton* acetone — more at ACETONE] **:** any of a class of organic compounds (as acetone) that are characterized by a carbonyl group attached to two carbon atoms usu. contained in hydrocarbon radicals (as in the general formula RCOR) or in a single bivalent radical and that are similar to aldehydes but are less reactive

ketone body *n* **:** any of the three compounds acetoacetic acid, acetone, and beta-hydroxybutyric acid recognized as products of fatty-acid catabolism and found in the blood and urine in abnormal amounts in diabetes mellitus and other conditions of impaired metabolism — called also *acetone body*

ketone group *n* **:** the characteristic group of ketones consisting of carbonyl attached to two carbon atoms

ke·to·ne·mia *or* **ke·to·nae·mia** \,kēd·ə'nēmēə\ *n* -s [NL, fr. ISV *ketone* + NL *-emia, -aemia*] **1 :** a condition marked by an abnormal increase of ketone bodies in the circulating blood **2 :** KETOSIS 2 — **ke·to·ne·mic** \¦==¦nēmik\ *adj*

ke·ton·ic \kē'tänik\ *adj* [ISV *ketone* + *-ic*] **:** relating to, containing, or derived from a ketone

ke·ton·imine \¦kē,tōn+\ *n* [ISV *ketone* + *imine*] **:** KETIMINE — used esp. of dyes

ke·to·nize \'kē,tō,nīz\ *vb* -ED/-ING/-S [*ketone* + *-ize*] *vt* **:** to convert into a ketone ~ *vi* **:** to become converted into a ketone

ke·to·nu·ria \,kēd·ə'n(y)urēə\ *n* -s [NL, fr. ISV *ketone* + NL *-uria*] **:** the presence in man and domestic animals of excess ketone bodies in the urine (as in diabetes mellitus, starvation acidosis, or other conditions involving reduced or disturbed carbohydrate metabolism)

ke·tose \'kē,tōs\ *n* -s [ISV *ket-* + *-ose*] **:** a sugar (as fructose or sorbose) containing one ketone group per molecule — contrasted with *aldose;* see MONOSACCHARIDE

ke·to·side \'kēd·ə,sīd\ *n* -s [*ket-* + *glycoside*] **:** a glycoside that on hydrolysis yields a ketose

ke·to·sis \kē'tōsəs\ *n, pl* **ke·to·ses** \-ō,sēz\ [NL, fr. *ket-* + *-osis*] **1 :** an abnormal increase of ketone bodies in the body in conditions of reduced or disturbed carbohydrate metabolism (as in uncontrolled diabetes mellitus) **2 :** a nutritional disease of cattle and sometimes sheep, goats, or swine that is marked by reduction of blood sugar and the presence of ketone bodies in the blood, tissues, milk, and urine, that is associated with digestive and nervous disturbances, that usu. results from long-continued feeding of coarse rations low in available sugar or from liver inefficiency associated with vitamin A deficiency, and that is esp. likely to occur in heavy milkers shortly after parturition — compare MILK FEVER 2a

ke·to·steroid \¦kēd·ō+\ *n* [ISV *ket-* + *steroid*] **:** a steroid (as androsterone, cortisone, or estrone) containing a ketone group ⟨excretion of 17-*ketosteroids* in the urine⟩

ke·tot·ic \kē'täd·ik\ *adj* [fr. NL *ketosis*, after such pairs as NL *hypnosis:* E *hypnotic*] **:** of or relating to ketosis **:** affected with ketosis

ke·tox·ime \kē'täk,sēm\ *n* [ISV *ket-* + *oxime*] **:** an oxime of a ketone

ket·tle \'ked|ᵊl, |tᵊl, ÷ 'kil; *some who have* ¦kil *in "teakettle" and/or "kettle of fish" have* ¦kel *in other contexts*\ *n* -s [ME *ketel*, fr. ON *ketill;* akin to OE *cietel* kettle, OHG *kezzil*, Goth *katilē* (gen. pl.); all fr. a prehistoric Gmc word borrowed fr. L *catillus* small bowl, dish, dim. of *catinus* bowl, pot; perh. akin to Gk *kotylē* cup, small vessel] **1 a** (1) **:** a metallic vessel in which liquids or semifluid masses are boiled; *esp* **:** TEAKETTLE (2) **:** a cooking utensil with a bail handle **b :** a quantity cooked in a kettle at one time ⟨could eat a whole ~ of stew⟩ **2 a** *obs* **:** KETTLEDRUM 1 ⟨let the ~ to the trumpet speak —*Shak.*⟩ **b :** the metallic bowl of a kettledrum across which the parchment head is stretched **3 a :** POTHOLE **b :** a steep-sided hollow without surface drainage esp. in a deposit of glacial drift and often containing a lake or swamp **4** *North* **:** a shallow metal pail ⟨dinner ~⟩

kettle base *adj* **:** ²BOMBÉ

kettle–bottomed \'==,==\ *adj, of a ship* **:** having a flat hull

kettledrum \'=,=\ *n* **1 :** a percussion instrument that consists of a hollow brass or copper hemisphere with a parchment head the tension of which can be changed by hand screws or foot pedal to vary the pitch, that is played with a pair of sticks with large padded heads, and that is used in pairs, threes, or fours of different sizes in both orchestra and concert band — see TIMPANI **2** *obs* **:** KETTLEDRUMMER **3 :** an informal party at which light refreshments are usu. served

kettledrum 1

ket·tle·drum·mer \"ə(r)\ *n* **:** one that plays the kettledrums

kettle front *adj* **:** ²BOMBÉ

ket·tle·man \'==mən\ *n, pl* **kettlemen :** an industrial worker who melts, cooks, or dyes substances in a heated container: as **a :** a brewery worker who makes the wort that is the basis for beer **b :** one who refines impure lead to secure a commercial grade **c :** one who cooks the ingredients of paints, varnishes, or oils **d :** BURNER MAN

kettle of fish *see* KETTLE\ **1 :** a bad state of affairs **:** MESS, PREDICAMENT ⟨here's a pretty how-de-do, here's a pretty *kettle of fish* —W.S.Gilbert⟩ **2 :** a thing to be considered or reckoned with **:** MATTER, AFFAIR ⟨books and discs . . . were two very different *kettles of fish* —Roland Gelatt⟩ ⟨a far different *kettle of fish* from the fictionalized life stories of Hollywood —Lee Rogow⟩

ket·tler \'ke|d·ᵊlə(r), |t(ᵊ)lə-, ÷'ki|\ *n* -s **:** a textile worker who prepares gums for use in mixing printing colors

ket·tle stitch \'ked·ᵊl-, -etᵊl-\ *n* [part trans. of G *kettelstich,* fr. *kettel* small chain (dim. of *kette* chain, fr. OHG *ketina,* fr. L *catena*) + *stich* stitch — more at CHAIN] *bookbinding* **:** a knot formed in the sewing thread at the ends of the sections to hold them together — called also *catch stitch*

ke·tu·bah *or* **ke·thu·bah** \,ke,t(h)ü'vä, kə'süvə\ *n, pl* **ketu·both** *or* **ketu·bot** \-,t(h)ü'vōt(h), -'sü,v-, -ōs\ *or* **ketubahs** *or* **kethuboth** *or* **kethubot** *or* **kethubahs** [Heb *kěthūbhāh* document] **:** a formal Jewish marriage contract that provides for a money settlement payable to the wife in the event of divorce or at the husband's death

ke·tu·pa \kə'tüpə\ *n* [NL, prob. fr. Malay *kětupok* fish owl] **1** *cap* **:** a genus of large chiefly tropical owls that is closely related to *Bubo* and contains various fish owls **2** -s **:** FISH OWL

ke·tyl \'kēd·ᵊl\ *n* -s [*ket-* + *-yl*] **:** any of a class of unstable compounds made by treating ketones with a metal (as sodium)

keuper \'kȯipə(r)\ *adj, usu cap* [G] **:** of or relating to the upper division of the German Trias — see GEOLOGIC TIME table

keur·boom \'kər,büm\ *also* **keur** \'kər\ *n* -s [Afrik *keurboom,* fr. *keur* choice + *boom* tree] **:** a pinnate-leaved shrub (*Virgilia capensis*) of southern Africa having purple flowers and being of the family Leguminosae

KEV *abbr, often not cap* kilo electron volt

ke·va·lin \'kävələn\ *n* -s [Skt, fr. *kevala* alone, pure, absolute — more at CELIBATE] *Jainism* **:** one who is set free from matter **:** a liberated soul

keva·zin·go \,kevə'ziŋ(,)gō, ,käv-\ *also* **ke·wa·sin·go** \,käwə'si-, -ə'zi-\ *or* **ke·wa·sin·ga** \-ŋgə\ *n* -s [native name in western Africa] **1 :** any of various African bubingas of the genus *Copaifera* **2 :** the wood of a kevazingo used esp. for decorative veneers

¹kev·el \'kevəl\ *or* **cav·el** \'kav-\ *n* -s [ME *kevile* pin, hasp, peg, fr. ONF *keville,* fr. L *clavicula* small key — more at CLAVICLE] **:** a strong timber, bollard, or cleat (as a cross timber in a bollard or a timber bolted across two stanchions)

²kev·el \'kevəl\ *n* -s [of Scand origin; akin to ON *kefli* stick of wood, *kafli* cut-off piece, Norw *kavle, kjevle* piece of wood, roller; akin to OFris *kavelia* to cast lots, MD *kavele* piece of wood for casting lots, Lith *žabas* branch, bunch of twigs] **:** CUDGEL, STAFF

³kevel \"\ *n* -s [ME *kevell*] **:** a hammer for roughly shaping or breaking stone

ke·wee·naw·an \¦kēwē¦nȯən\ *adj, usu cap* [*Keweenaw* Point, Mich. + E *-an*] **:** of or relating to a division of the Proterozoic see GEOLOGIC TIME table

kew·pie \'kyüpē, -pi\ *n* -s [alter. of *cupid*] **:** a fairy conceived of as a good-natured chubby winged baby with a topknot of hair

Kewpie \"\ *trademark* — used for a small chubby doll with a topknot of hair

kew weed \'kyü-\ *n* [prob. fr. *Kew* Gardens (Royal Botanic Gardens), London, Eng.] **:** FRENCHWEED 2

¹kex \'keks\ *n* -ES [ME] *dial chiefly Eng* **:** the dry stalk of various hollow-stemmed plants (as cow parsnip)

²kex \"\ *adj, dial Eng* **:** resembling kex **:** dry and hollow

³kex \"\ *n* -ES [Maya] **:** a Maya therapeutic rite in which an ailing person pledges an offering of food to the force or agency of his illness in return for his health

¹key \'kē\ *n* -s *often attrib* [ME *key, kay, keye,* fr. OE *cǣg, cǣga;* akin to OFris *kēi, kāi* key, MLG *keie, keige* spear, and perh. to OHG *kīl* wedge — more at CHINE] **1 a :** an instrument usu. of metal so designed that it may be inserted in a lock in order to operate the bolt or catch **b :** a tool with a shaft that fits into printers' quoins and is rotated to tighten or loosen them **c :** a small metal piece with a slot in one end used to roll up a strip of metal (as on a can of sardines) or to roll up the body of a collapsible metal tube (as a tube of toothpaste) **2 :** something that affords or prevents entrance, possession, or control **3 a :** something that serves to reveal or solve a problem, difficulty, or mystery ⟨the ~ to a riddle⟩ **b :** a simplified version that accompanies something as a clue to its explanation (as an outline map, a word-for-word translation, a book containing solutions to problems); *specif* **:** a list of words or phrases giving the value of symbols (as a pronunciation alphabet) **c :** an arrangement of the salient characters of a group of plants or animals or of species or genera for the purpose of determining the names and taxonomic relationships of unidentified members of a group **d :** the matter used to key an advertisement **e :** a map legend **4 keys** *pl* **:** spiritual authority in a Christian religion ⟨power of the ~*s*⟩; *specif* **:** the power or jurisdiction of the presidency in the Mormon Church **5 :** a tool or device used to transfer, wind, or otherwise move usu. in order to secure or tighten: as **a** (1) **:** COTTER PIN (2) **:** COTTER **b :** a keystone in an arch **c :** a wedge used to make a dovetail joint **d :** a wedge between two feathers to break a stone **e :** the last board laid in a floor **f :** a tapered block driven into a recess in a scarf joint between two timbers so as to draw them more firmly together **g :** a small wooden wedge that is forced into the dovetail joint at a corner of a stretcher frame of a painting in order to tighten the canvas **h :** a wedge used to split a tenon in a mortise or the upper end of a tool handle (as a hammer or ax) for the purpose of tightening **i :** any of the metal U-shaped devices used to secure the bands or cords in position in a bookbinder's sewing press **j :** a strip of wood inserted in a timber across the grain to prevent casting **k :** a small usu. metal parallel-sided piece that is flat or tapered on top and that is used for securing a part (as a pulley, crank, or hub) **6 a :** one of the levers (as a digital or pedal) of a keyboard musical instrument that actuates the mechanism and produces the tones **b :** a lever by which a vent is opened or closed in the side of a woodwind instrument (as a clarinet or bassoon) or a valve or piston is controlled in a brass instrument (as a French horn or trumpet) **c :** a depressible digital that serves as one unit of a keyboard and that works usu. by lever action to set in motion a character (as in a typewriter) or an escapement (as in some typesetting machines) **7 :** SAMARA **8 a :** a leading, prominent, or critical individual or principle ⟨a ~ actor⟩ ⟨the ~ features of a new car⟩ **b :** a component of a liquid mixture that is being separated by fractional distillation ⟨the least volatile of these components is the heavy ~ and the most volatile is the light ~ —E.G.Scheibel⟩ **9** [trans. of ML *clavis*] **a** *obs* **:** the lowest note or keynote of a scale **b** (1) **:** a system of seven tones based on their relationship to a keynote or tonic; *specif* **:** the tonality of a scale (2) **:** the total harmonic and melodic relations of such a system **10 a :** characteristic style, tone, or intensity of thought, feeling, or action **b :** the tone or pitch of a voice ⟨speaking in a plaintive ~⟩ **c :** the pervading tone and intensity of color (as in a painting) **d :** the predominant tone of a photograph with respect to its lightness or darkness — compare HIGH-KEY, LOW-KEY **11 :** a decoration or charm resembling a key **12 a** (1) **:** plastering forced between laths to hold the rest in place (2) **:** the hold that plaster has on a wall (3) **:** the roughness of a wall that causes plaster to adhere to it **b :** a hollow in a brick or tile to hold mortar **c :** the rough surface on the wrong side of a veneer to hold the glue **13 a :** a metallic lever for rapidly and easily opening and closing the circuit of telegraphic-station equipment **b :** a small switch for opening or closing an electric circuit **14 :** a projecting portion used to prevent movement at a construction joint (as of a floor, wall, pavement, footing, dam) into the adjacent section **15** *or* **keymove** \'=,=\ **:** the first move in the solution of a chess problem or combination **16 a :** the control of a cryptographic process (as a code book, grille, cipher alphabet, or set of alphabets) **b :** the enciphering or deciphering instructions for a cryptogram: as (1) **:** the settings of a ciphering machine (2) **:** the column sequence of a transposition (3) **:** KEYING SEQUENCE (4) **:** KEY WORD (5) **:** KEY LETTER (6) **:** an element in a keying sequence — see PERIODIC KEY, PERIOD KEY, RUNNING KEY, SPECIFIC KEY, VIGENÈRE CIPHER **17 :** KEYHOLE 4

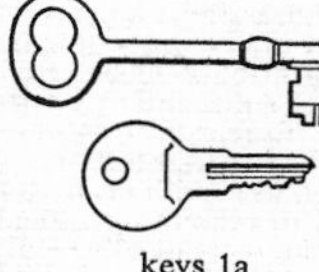

keys 1a

²key \"\ *vb* -ED/-ING/-s [ME *keyen,* fr. *key, kay, keye,* n.] *vt* **1 :** to lock with or as if with a key **:** FASTEN: as **a :** to secure by a key (as a hammerhead to a handle, a pulley on a shaft, plaster to lathing) **b :** to finish off (an arch) by inserting a keystone **c :** to expand and tighten (as a canvas stretcher on a painting) with keys **2 a :** to fix or determine the musical key of **b :** to regulate the musical pitch of ⟨~ the strings⟩ **c :** to control (a process) in cryptography ⟨in ~*ed* columnar transposition the column sequence is controlled by a key word⟩ — compare KEYING SEQUENCE **3 :** to apply color to (as a painting) in a particular key **4 :** HARMONIZE, ATTUNE ⟨remarks ~*ed* to a situation⟩ **5 :** to transmit by means of a telegraph key **6 :** to identify (a biological specimen) by means of a key **7 :** to insert in (an advertisement) some direction or other matter intended to identify answers **:** apply a symbol to (an advertisement) by means of which identification is effected **8 :** to produce or cause nervous tension in — used with *up* ⟨~*ed* up over an impending operation⟩ ~ *vi* **:** to use a key: as **a :** to permit of identification by means of a key — often used with *out* ⟨the specimen ~*s* out to a genus of common starfish⟩ **b :** to operate a telegraph key

³key \"\ *archaic var of* QUAY

⁴key \"\ *also* **kay** *like* ¹CAY\ *n* -s [modif. (influenced by ³*key*) of Sp *cayo,* fr. Lucayo *cayo*] **:** a low island or reef; *specif* **:** one of the coral islets off the southern coast of Florida

key·age \'kēij\ *archaic var of* QUAYAGE

keyaki *var of* KIAKI

ke·yau·wee \kə'yau̇(,)wē\ *n, pl* **keyauwee** *or* **keyauwees** *usu cap* **1 :** an extinct people of northern No. Carolina presumed to have been Siouan **2 :** a member of the Keyauwee people

keybank \'=,=\ *n* **:** a rectangular set of keys comprising one of the removable setting-key units of a monotype keyboard

key bargain *n* **:** the terms of a collective agreement that set a precedent for other companies or industries

key bed *n, geol* **:** a distinctive stratum or group of strata that serves to facilitate correlation in field mapping or subsurface studies **:** the horizon or bed on which elevations are taken or to which elevations are referred in making a structure contour map — called also *key horizon*

key bit *n* **:** the projection on a key for operating a tumbler lock

key block *n, chiefly Brit* **:** KEY PLATE

¹keyboard \'=,=\ *n, often attrib* [¹*key* + *board*] **1 a :** a bank of keys on which the performer on a musical instrument (as a piano) plays and which consists of a double row of seven white and five raised black keys to the octave **b :** one of several such banks constituting a set **:** MANUAL **c :** a set of manuals **2 :** an assemblage of systematically arranged keys by which a machine (as a typewriter) is operated **3 :** a board on which keys for locks (as of hotel rooms) are hung

part of the keyboard of a piano

²keyboard \"\ *vb* -ED/-ING/-s *vi* **:** to operate a keyboard typesetting machine ~ *vt* **:** to set by means of a keyboard typesetting machine — **keyboarder** *n*

keyboard paper *n* **:** a continuous roll of paper for use as a ribbon for a Monotype machine

key bolt *n* **:** a bolt secured at one end by a key or cotter

key brick *n* **:** a brick made so that each narrow side is inclined at the same angle toward the end of the brick

key bugle *n* **:** a bugle having six keys and a chromatic range of about two octaves

key button *n* **:** a lettered or numbered cover attachable to a key of a typewriter or typesetting machine

key chord *n, music* **:** a tonic triad

key–cold \'=¦=\ *adj, now dial Brit* **:** cold as a metal key **:** devoid of the warmth of life: as **a :** cold in death **b :** apathetic and indifferent

key deer *n, usu cap K* [⁴*key*] **:** a nearly extinct race of very small white-tailed deer native to the Florida keys

key desk *n* **:** CONSOLE 3a

key drawing \'=,=\ *n* **:** an outline drawing that indicates position of printed matter or that serves as a guide for color separation

keyed \'kēd\ *adj* [partly fr. ¹*key* + *-ed;* partly fr. past part. of ²*key*] **1 :** furnished with keys ⟨a ~ instrument⟩ **2 :** reinforced by a key or keystone ⟨a ~ arch⟩ **3 :** set to a key (as a tune) **4 :** ADJUSTED, ATTUNED, FITTED ⟨~ to the present situation⟩ ⟨every thought ~ to the reaction of the strangers —Agnes S. Turnbull⟩

keyed bugle *n* **:** KEY BUGLE

keyed horn *n* **:** BASS HORN

key·er \'kēə(r)\ *n* -s **:** a device (as a mechanical key or vacuum tube) that turns an electronic circuit on or off

key form *n* **:** the form that is run first of a set of forms used to print work in two or more colors

key fossil *n* **:** INDEX FOSSIL

key fruit *n* [so called fr. its growing in bunches suggesting a hanging bunch of keys] **:** SAMARA

key harp *n* **:** a keyboard musical instrument having tuning forks as vibrators

¹keyhole \'=,=\ *n* [¹*key* + *hole*] **1 :** a hole or aperture (as in a door or lock) for receiving a key **2 a :** a hole or groove in beams intended to be joined together to receive the key that fastens them **b :** a slot for a key or cotter **3 :** a hole made by a bullet that has keyholed **4 :** the free-throw area in basketball

²keyhole \"\ *vi* [¹*keyhole;* fr. the shape of the hole made by the bullet] *of a bullet* **:** to strike a target when (as from tumbling or ricocheting) the long axis of the bullet is not in the same line as the line of flight

³keyhole \"\ *adj* [¹*keyhole*] **1 :** revealingly intimate **:** INSIDE ⟨a ~ report⟩ ⟨a ~ view of private lives⟩ ⟨intimate, almost ~ narrative portrait —*New Yorker*⟩ **2 :** intent on revealing intimate details ⟨a ~ reporter⟩

keyhole limpet *n* [so called fr. the perforation at the apex of its shell] **:** a limpet of the genus *Fissurella*

keyhole neckline *n* **:** a neckline in the shape of a keyhole

keyhole saw *n* **:** a saw used for cutting short-radius curves that is similar to a compass saw but usu. has a narrower blade and finer teeth — see PISTOL GRIP illustration

keyhole urchin *n* **:** a flat sea urchin of the order Exocycloida with long narrow apertures occurring near the margin of the test

keyhole neckline

key horizon *n* **:** KEY BED

key industry *n* **:** an industry (as the production of machine tools or chemicals) whose output is essential to the successful operation of many other industries

¹key·ing \'kēiŋ, -ēēŋ\ *n* -s [¹*key* + *-ing* (n. suffix)] **:** the process of turning an electronic circuit off or on either manually or automatically ⟨such ~ represents the simplest possible form of modulation, and is applicable to all kinds of oscillators —W.A.Edson⟩

²keying \"\ *adj* **:** possessing the ability to turn an electronic circuit off or on ⟨a ~ device⟩

keying by *n* [fr. the gerund of *key by,* v.] **:** the action of clearing an automatic stop in an emergency and permitting a train to pass a signal set at danger

keying sequence *n* [fr. pres. part. of ²*key*] **:** a sequence of numbers or letters that enciphers or deciphers a polyalphabetic substitution cipher letter by letter

key job *n* **1 :** a critical or vital job **2 :** a job that can be evaluated accurately and then used as representative of other similar jobs

key·less \'kēləs\ *adj* [¹*key* + *-less*] **:** lacking or not requiring a key

keyless watch *n, Brit* **:** STEM-WINDER

key letter \'=,==\ *n* **:** a letter (as a letter of a repeated key word) functioning as an element in a cryptographic keying sequence

key light *n* **:** the main light illuminating a subject in photography

key line *n* **:** a line (as at the foot of a printed page) listing and explaining symbols used

keylock \'=,=\ *n* **1 :** a lock opened by a key **2 :** a wrestling hold in which a contestant uses both arms to lock an opponent's arm in a bent position

key·man \'kē,man, -maa(ə)n\ *n, pl* **keymen :** a person doing work of vital importance (as in a business organization) ⟨within ministry and cabinet alike, the prime minister is the ~ —F.A.Ogg & Harold Zink⟩

keyman insurance *n* **:** insurance upon the life of a valuable employee naming the employing firm as beneficiary — compare BUSINESS LIFE INSURANCE

key money *n* **1** *Brit* **:** a payment required of a tenant esp. of an apartment on taking possession of the key **2 :** a bribe paid by a prospective tenant in order to obtain housing ⟨the *key money* for an average studio in Paris is in the neighborhood of one thousand dollars —Paul Bowles⟩

keymove *var of* KEY

¹keynes·i·an \'kānzēən\ *adj, usu cap* [John M. *Keynes* †1946 Eng. economist + E *-ian*] **:** of or relating to Keynesianism

²keynesian \"\ *n* -s *usu cap* **:** an adherent or advocate of Keynesianism

keynes·i·an·ism \-ēə,nizəm\ *n* -s *usu cap* **:** the economic theories and programs ascribed to John Maynard Keynes and his followers; *specif* **:** the advocacy of monetary and fiscal programs by government to increase employment

¹keynote \'=,=, *in sense 1 sometimes* '=¦=\ *n* [¹*key* + *note*] **1 :** the first and harmonically fundamental tone of a scale **:** TONIC **2 :** the fundamental or leading fact or idea **:** the prevailing tone ⟨this simple statement may be taken as the . . . ~ of the whole system —C.H.Driver⟩ ⟨sadness is the ~ of this little collection —*Books Abroad*⟩

²keynote \'=,=\ *vt* **1 :** to set a keynote in ⟨the mood of compassion that ~*s* most of her writing —Ann F. Wolfe⟩ ⟨~ the overall color scheme . . . with a romantic mural —*N.Y. Herald Tribune*⟩ **2 a :** to deliver the keynote address at ⟨~ a Midwest farm political rally —*Wall Street Jour.*⟩ **b :** to declare in or as if in a keynote address ⟨"we want peace . . .," the secretary *keynoted* —*Newsweek*⟩

keynote address *or* **keynote speech** *n* **:** an address (as at a political convention) intended to present the issues of primary interest to the assembly but often concentrated upon arousing unity and enthusiasm ⟨the *keynote address* . . . is a highly emotional performance —D.D.McKean⟩ ⟨highlighting the convention's opening day is tonight's *keynote speech* —*TV Guide*⟩

key·not·er \'kē,nōd·ə(r), -ōtə-\ *n* **:** one that sets the keynote; *esp* **:** one that delivers a keynote speech ⟨to serve as temporary chairman and ~ of the Republican national convention —*Current Biog.*⟩

keynote speaker *n* **:** KEYNOTER

key of art **:** ALEMBROTH

key of life **:** ANKH

key pad *n* **:** a pad on a key of a wind instrument (as a flute or clarinet) making the hole leakproof

key pattern *n* **:** a Greek fret first found in the Geometric period and used throughout the classical era

key pipe *n* **:** a tubular opening in a lock for the shank of the key

key plate *n* **1 :** the part of a stove top in which the lids are placed **2 :** a protective usu. metal plate surrounding a keyhole **3 :** a plate that prints the central design on a bicolor postage stamp — compare DUTY PLATE **4 :** one of a set of color-printing plates that contains greater detail than the others and that is often the black plate

key plug *n* **:** the part of a lock into which the key is inserted

key punch *n* **:** a machine actuated by a keyboard and used to cut holes or notches in punched cards

keypunch \'=,=\ *vt* [*key punch*] **:** to cut holes or notches in (a punched card) with a key punch

keys *pl of* KEY, *pres 3d sing of* KEY

key seat *n* **:** a bed or groove in a mechanical part to receive a key

keyseat \'=,=\ *vt* [*key seat*] **:** to supply (as a mechanical part) with a key seat ⟨a ~*ed* shaft⟩

key·seat·er \'kē,sēd·ə(r)\ *n* **1 :** a machine for keyseating machine parts **2 :** one that operates a keyseating machine

key–sequence \'=,==\ *n* **:** KEYING SEQUENCE

key signature *n* **:** one or more sharps or flats placed immediately after the clef to designate the musical scale to be understood on the staff that in turn establishes the tonality

keyslot \'=,=\ *n* **:** a keyway esp. in a shaft

keysmith \'=,=\ *n* **1 :** a person who makes or repairs keys **2 :** an operator of a key-duplicating machine

key station *n* **:** a broadcasting station at which a network program originates

¹keystone \'=,=\ *n* [¹*key* + *stone*] **1 :** the wedge-shaped piece at the crown of an arch; *esp* **:** such a piece inserted last and locking the other pieces in place **2 :** something analogous to the keystone of an arch in position or function **:** a part or force on which associated things depend for support ⟨the ~ of his faith⟩ ⟨~ of a system of defense⟩: as **a :** crushed stone of small size used in bituminous bound roads to fill the voids of the large aggregate — compare COVER STONE **b :** a bondstone in masonry **c** *or* **keystone sack :** second base in baseball

keystone 1

²keystone \"\ *vt* **:** to support by means of a keystone

keystone effect *n* **:** a type of distortion in a television picture whereby a square pattern appears larger at the top than at the bottom

key·ston·er \'kē,stōnə(r)\ *n, usu cap* [*Keystone State,* nickname for Pennsylvania (fr. its central position among the original 13 states) + *-er*] **:** PENNSYLVANIAN 1 — used as a nickname

Key·tain·er \'kē,tānə(r)\ *trademark* — used for a small usu. leather case for carrying keys (as in the pocket)

key·trumpet *n* **:** a trumpet with side holes covered with keys that control its pitch

key turner *n, obs* : TURNKEY
key-type \ˈ=,=\ *n* : a single design used on the stamps of different colonies of a country
key valve *n* : a valve designed to be operated by a removable key to prevent unauthorized operation
keyway \ˈ=,=\ *n* **1** : a groove or channel for a key (as in a shaft or the hub of a pulley) : KEY SEAT **2** : the aperture for the key in a lock having a flat metal key **3** : a groove or channel for a key in a construction joint (as in a floor or wall) or underneath a retaining wall or dam
key word *n* : a word that is a key: **a** : a word exemplifying the meaning or value of a letter or symbol (as *then* in the statement "*th-* as in *then*") **b** : a word used as a cipher key: as (1) : a word that governs a transposition procedure (2) : a word from which a mixed alphabet is derived (3) : a word repeated to form a keying sequence
kg *abbr* **1** keg **2** kilogram **3** king
KGC *abbr* **1** knight grand commander **2** knight grand cross
kgm *abbr* **1** kilogram **2** kilogram-meter
KGPS *abbr, usu not cap* kilograms per second
k-gun \ˈ=,=\ *n, usu cap K* [ˈ*k*] : a naval depth-charge projector
kha *or* **ka** \ˈkä\ *also* **ka·che** \ˈkä(,)chā\ *n, pl* **kha** *or* **khas** *or* **ka** *or* **kas** *usu cap* **1 a** : a people of Nepal of mixed Mongoloid and Indo-Aryan blood **b** : a member of such people **2 a** : an agrarian aboriginal people of Laos **b** : a member of such people
kha·ba·rovsk \kəˈbärəfsk, -rəvzk\ *adj, usu cap* [fr. *Khabarovsk*, U.S.S.R.] : of or from the city of Khabarovsk, U.S.S.R. : of the kind or style prevalent in Khabarovsk
khadar *or* **khadir** *var of* KADIR
khad·dar \ˈkädə(r)\ *also* **kha·di** \ˈkädē\ *n* -s [Hindi *khādar*, *khādī*] : homespun cotton cloth worn by adherents of the movement for autonomy in India instead of the mill-made foreign product — compare SWADESHI, SWARAJ
kha·gan \kä'(g)än\ *also* **kha·kan** \-ˈ(k)än\ *n* -s [Turk *kağan*] : KHAN
khair \ˈkī(ə)r\ *n* -s [Hindi, fr. Skt *khadira*] : CATECHU 2
[1]**khaki** *also* **khakee** \ˈkak|ē, ˈkä|, ˈkȧ|, |ki, *Canadian often* ˈkär|\ *n* -s [Hindi *khākī* dusty, dust-colored, fr. *khāk* dust, fr. Per] **1 a** : a khaki-colored cloth; *esp* : a durable cotton or woolen cloth used for military uniforms **b** : a garment of khaki-colored cloth; *esp* : a military uniform — usu. used in pl. ⟨covered with mud to the eyes, in old ~*s* —F.M.Ford⟩ **2** : a light yellowish brown that is yellower and duller than walnut brown, yellower and less strong than cinnamon, and duller and slightly yellower than manila or fallow
[2]**khaki** *also* **khakee** \"\ *adj* : of the color khaki — used esp. of cloth
khaki bush *also* **khaki·bos** \-,bäs, -,bȯs\ *n* [*khakibos* fr. Afrik, fr. *khaki* + *bos* bush] *chiefly Africa* : AFRICAN MARIGOLD
khaki camp·bell \-ˈkam(b)əl, -aambəl\ *n* [after Mrs. Adale *Campbell*, 19th cent. Brit. duck breeder] **1** *usu cap K&C* : an English breed of small brownish upright ducks noted for their extensive production of large white eggs **2** -s *often cap K&C* : a bird of the Khaki Campbell breed
khaki election *n* : an election held during or shortly after a war in the expectation that the party in power will benefit from war enthusiasm
khaki weed *n, chiefly Austral* : CHAFF-FLOWER
khak·sar \(ˈ)käkˈsär\ *n* -s *usu cap* [Hindi *khāksār*, fr. Per *khāksār* humble, prob. fr. *khāk* dust + *-sār* like] : a member of a militant Muslim nationalist movement of India
kha·lal \kəˈläl\ *adj* [Ar *khalāl*] : of, relating to, or constituting the second of four recognized stages in the ripening of a date in which it reaches its full size and changes from green to red or yellow or a combination of the two colors — compare KIMRI, RUTAB, TAMAR
kha·lat *or* **khi·lat** \kəˈlat\ *n* -s [Hindi *khal'at*, *khil'at*, fr. Ar *khil'ah*] : a robe presented by a person of rank and worn as a mark of distinction in India
kha·lif \kəˈlēf\ *or* **kha·li·fa** \kəˈlēfə\ *var of* CALIPH
khal·kha *also* **khal·ka** *or* **kal·ka** \ˈkalkə\ *n* -s *usu cap* **1** : a member of a Mongol people inhabiting all but the western part of Outer Mongolia **2** : the language of the Khalkha people used as the official language of the Mongolian People's Republic
khal·sa \ˈkäl(t)sə\ *n* -s [Hindi *khāliṣa*, *khālsa* pure, genuine, fr. Per, fr. Ar *khāliṣah*] **1** : the exchequer of an Indian state **2** *usu cap* : a militant theocracy arising in the late 17th century and continuing today as one of the significant divisions of the Sikhs — compare NANAKPANTHI
kham·bu \ˈkäm(,)bü\ *also* **kham·ba** \-,bə\ *n, pl* **khambu** *or* **khambus** *also* **khamba** *or* **khambas** *usu cap* **1** : a Tibetan Mongoloid people of the southern slopes of the Himalayas **2** : a member of the Khambu people
kha·mir \kəˈmi(ə)r\ *n* -s *usu cap* : a dialect of the Cushitic language Agau
kham·sin *also* **kham·seen** *or* **cham·sin** \kamˈsēn\ *n* -s [Ar (*rīḥ al-*) *khamsīn* the wind of the fifty (days between Easter and Pentecost)] : a hot southerly Egyptian wind coming from the Sahara usu. in the spring and often carrying fine particles of sand ⟨the ~ . . . has been known to take paint off cars and force fine sand into camera shutters —G.E.Edgerton⟩ — compare SIROCCO
kham·ti \ˈkäm(p)tē\ *n, pl* **khamti** *or* **khamtis** *usu cap* **1 a** : a Tai people of northeastern Assam and Burma related to the Thais **b** : a member of such people **2** : a Thai language of the Khamti people
[1]**khan** \ˈkän, -a-, -aa(ə)-, -ȧ-\ *also* **cham** \ˈkam, -aa(ə)-\ *n* -s [ME *caan*, fr. MF, of Turkic origin; akin to Jagatai *khān*, Turk *han* prince, khan] **1** : a medieval sovereign of China and ruler over the Turkish, Tatar, and Mongol tribes ⟨at the critical moment . . . the great ~ died —Sir Winston Churchill⟩ **2** : a local chieftain or man of rank esp. in Afghanistan, Iran, and some areas of central Asia — used sometimes as a title of respect
[2]**khan** \"\ *n* -s [Ar *khān*, fr. Per] : a caravansary or rest house in some Asian countries ⟨huge ~*s* . . . still receive shipments of goods that wind into Aleppo by camel train —*N.Y.Times*⟩
khan·ate \-,nāt, -,nət, *usu* |d.+V\ *n* -s *sometimes cap* [ˈ*khan* + *-ate*] : the dominion or jurisdiction of a khan ⟨the capital of a semi-independent ~ —E.D.Laborde⟩
khan·jar \ˈkan,jär\ *or* **han·djar** \ˈha-\ *n* -s [Ar *khanjar*] : a short curved dagger of Muslim countries ⟨the broad silver-sheathed ~*s* — the mark of authority in the northern deserts —Ralph Hammond-Innes⟩
khan·kah \ˈkäŋkə\ *n* -s [Hindi *khānaqāh*, fr. Per *khāna* house + *gāh* place] : a dervish monastery
khan·sa·mah *or* **khan·sa·ma** \ˌkänsəˈmä, känˈsämə\ *n* -s [Hindi *khānsāmān*, fr. Per, fr. *khān* lord + *sāmān* stores] : a male servant in India: **a** : HOUSE STEWARD **b** : BUTLER **c** : COOK
khan·ty \ˈkäntē\ *n* -ES *usu cap* : OSTYAK
kha·num *or* **ha·num** \ˈhänəm, ˈkä-, =ˈnəm, =ˈnüm\ *n* -s [Per & Turk; Per *khānum*, fr. Turk *hanım*, fem. of *han* prince, sovereign, khan] : a woman of rank or position esp. in Turkey and Iran
kha·pra beetle \ˈkäˌprə, ˈka|\ *n* [Hindi *khaprā*, lit., destroyer, fr. Skt *kṣapayati* he destroys; akin to Skt *kṣiṇoti* he destroys — more at PHTHISIS] : a dermestid beetle (*Trogoderma granarium*) native to the Indian subcontinent and now a serious pest of stored grain in most parts of the world
kha·ria \ˈkärēə\ *n* -s *usu cap* **1** : a member of a people of western Bengal **2** : the Munda language of the Kharia people
kha·rif \kəˈrēf\ *adj* [Hindi *kharīf*, fr. Ar *kharīf* gathered, autumn, autumnal crop, fr. *kharafa* to gather] : of, relating to, or constituting India's autumn and lesser crop that consists chiefly of pearl millet, durra, and maize and that is sown in June just before the monsoon rains and is harvested from August on — compare RABI
kha·ri·jite \ˈkärə,jīt\ *n* -s *usu cap* [Ar *khārijī* one that departs, dissenter + E *-ite*] : a member of a Muslim secessionist sect establishing a radically democratic and puritanical reform community in the 7th century
khar·kov \ˈkär,kȯf, -rkə|, |v\ *adj, usu cap* [fr. *Kharkov*, U.S.S.R.] : of or from the city of Kharkov, U.S.S.R. : of the kind or style prevalent in Kharkov
[1]**kha·rosh·thi** \kəˈrōshtē\ *n* -s *usu cap* [Skt *kharoṣṭī*] : a cursive script of Aramaic origin used in northwestern India, Afghanistan, and Turkistan from about 300 B.C. to at least the middle of the 5th century A.D.
[2]**kharoshthi** \"\ *adj, usu cap* : of, relating to, or written in the script Kharoshthi
khar·toum \(ˈ)kärˈtüm\ *adj, usu cap* [fr. *Khartoum*, Sudan] : of or from Khartoum, capital of the Sudan : of the kind or style prevailing in Khartoum
khar·toum·er *also* **khar·tum·er** \=ˈ==ə(r)\ *n* -s *cap* [*Khartoum*, Sudan + E *-er*] : a native or inhabitant of Khartoum; *specif* : one of an organized Arab slaving company of the 19th century
khar·war \(,)kərˈwär\ *n, pl* **kharwar** *or* **kharwars** *usu cap* [Santali *kharwār*] **1** : a Bengal people speaking a Munda language **2** : a member of the Kharwar people
khashgai *usu cap, var of* KASHGAI
kha·si \ˈkäsē\ *or* **kha·sia** \-ēə\ *n* -s *usu cap* **1** : a member of any of several Mongoloid peoples of the Khasi and Jaintia hills of Assam **2** : the Mon-Khmer language of the Khasi people
khas-kura \ˈkäsˈkůrə\ *n* -s *usu cap* : an Indic dialect of Nepal
khat *var of* KAT
kha·tin *or* **ka·tin** \kəˈtin\ *n, pl* **khatin** *or* **khatins** *or* **katin** *or* **katins** *usu cap* : [4]TIN
kha·tri \ˈkə·trē\ *n* -s [Hindi *khatrī*, *khattrī*, fr. Skt *kṣatriya* — more at KSHATRIYA] : a member of a Hindu caste employed in trade who claim Kshatriya origin
khatti *usu cap, var of* HATTI
kha·tun \(ˈ)käˈtün\ *n* -s [Hindi *khātūn*, fr. Per *khānum*] : a woman of rank or position in Muslim countries
kha·wa·rij \kəˈwärij\ *n pl, usu cap* [Ar *khawārij*, pl. of *khārijī* one that departs, dissenter] : KHARIJITES
khaya \ˈkīə, ˈkäə\ *n* [NL, fr. Wolof *khaye* khaya tree] **1** *cap* : a genus of African timber trees (family Meliaceae) with wood closely resembling mahogany **2** -s : any tree of the genus *Khaya*
kha·zar *also* **kho·zar** *or* **cha·zar** \kəˈzär\ *or* **ka·za·ri·an** \-rēən\ *n, pl* **khazar** *or* **khazars** *usu cap* **1** : a Tatar people existing as a nation in the Caucasus and southeastern Russia from about the end of the 2d century A.D. to the end of the 11th century **2** : a member of the Khazar people
khe·dive \kəˈdēv, keˈ-\ *n* -s [F *khédive*, fr. Turk *hidiv*, fr. Per *khidīw* prince] : the ruler of Egypt from 1867 to 1914 governing as a semi-independent viceroy of the sultan of Turkey
khe·di·vi·al \-vēəl\ *also* **khe·div·al** \-vəl\ *adj, often cap* : of or relating to a khedive ⟨a bribe to some ~ minister —A.J. Liebling⟩ ⟨a *Khedival* decree —Salma Bishlawy⟩
khe·di·vi·ate \-vēət, -vē,āt\ *also* **khe·div·ate** \-vət, -,vāt\ *n* -s *often cap* : the government or dominion of a khedive
khel·la \ˈkelə\ *n* -s [Ar *akhillah*] : a bishop's-weed (*Ammi visnaga*)
khel·lin *also* **kel·lin** \ˈkelən\ *n* -s [*khella* + *-in*] : a crystalline compound $C_{14}H_{12}O_5$ obtained from the fruit of khella and used as an antispasmodic in asthma and a coronary vasodilator in angina pectoris
kher·wa·ri \ˈkə(r)ˈwärē\ *n* -s *usu cap* : any of a group of closely related Munda languages including Ho, Mundari, and Santali
khe·sa·ri \kəˈsärē\ *or* **khesari gram** *n* -s [Hindi *khesārī*, *khisārī*, *kisārī*] *India* : GRASS PEA
kheth *var of* HETH
khid·mat·gar *or* **khid·mut·gar** \ˈkidmət,gär\ *or* **khit·mat·gar** *or* **khit·mut·gar** \ˈkitm-\ *n* -s [Hindi *khidmatgār*, fr. Ar *khidmah* service + Per *-gār* (suffix denoting possession or agency)] *India* : a male waiter
khi·la·fat \ˌkiləˈfat, kəˈläfət\ *n* -s [Turk *hilâfet*, fr. Ar *khilāfah* caliphate] : the chief spiritual authority of Islam as exercised by the Turkish sultans
khilat *var of* KHALAT
khirghiz *usu cap, var of* KIRGHIZ
khi·tan *or* **ki·tan** \ˈkēˈtän\ *also* **chi·dan** *or* **chi·tan** \ˈchēˈdän\ *n, pl* **khitan** *or* **khitans** *or* **kitan** *or* **kitans** *usu cap* **1** : a conquering Tatar people maintaining hegemony of northern China in the Liao dynasty from the 10th to the 12th centuries **2** : a member of the Khitan people
khlyst \ˈklist\ *n, pl* **khlys·ty** \kliˈstē\ *or* **khlysts** *usu cap* [Russ, lit., whip, prob. of imit. origin] : a member of a secret Russian Christian sect that originated in the 17th century or earlier, taught that God becomes incarnate in many Christs through their suffering, and followed ascetic and ecstatic practices
khmer *or* **kmer** \kəˈme(ə)r\ *n, pl* **khmer** *or* **khmers** *or* **kmer** *or* **kmers** *usu cap* **1 a** : an aboriginal people of Cambodia noted for their architectural achievements ⟨the mighty *Khmer* empire . . . ruled most of Indo-China and bequeathed the matchless jungle temple of Angkor Wat to posterity —*Time*⟩ **b** : a member of such people **2** : a Mon-Khmer language of the Khmer people that is the official language of Cambodia — **khmeri·an** \-merēən, -mir-\ *adj, usu cap*
khmu \kəˈmü\ *n, pl* **khmu** *or* **khmus** *usu cap* **1** : the most numerous group of the Kha people of northern Laos **2** : a member of the Khmu people
khoa \kōˈwä\ *n* -s [Hindi *khoā*] : a semidehydrated whole-milk product of India
khoi·san \ˈkȯiˌsän\ *n* -s *usu cap* **1** : a group of African peoples speaking Khoisan languages **2** : a subfamily of African languages comprising Hottentot and the several languages known as Bushman and related to Sandawe and Hatsa with which it forms the Macro-Khoisan family
kho·ja *or* **kho·jah** \ˈkōjə\ *n* -s [Turk & Per; Turk *hoca*, fr. Per *khwāja*] **1** *also* **ho·dja** \ˈhō-\ **a** : a member of any of various classes (as wealthy merchants) in Muslim lands — used as a title of respect **b** : a Muhammadan teacher **2** *cap* [Hindi *khoja*, fr. Per *khwāja*] *India* : a member of an Ismaili sect surviving as a subsect of the ancient Assassins
kho·ka·ni \kōˈkänē\ *n, pl* **khokani** *or* **khokanis** *usu cap* **1** : a Durani people of Afghanistan **2** : a member of the Khokani people
khond *or* **kandh** \ˈkänd\ *n, pl* **khond** *or* **khonds** *or* **kandh** *or* **kandhs** *usu cap* **1** : any of several Dravidian peoples of Orissa, India **2** : a member of a Khond people
khon·di \-dē\ *n* -s *usu cap* : KUI
khor \ˈkō(ə)r\ *n* -s [Ar *khawr*] : WATERCOURSE, RAVINE
kho·ras·san *also* **khu·ra·san** \ˌkōrəˈsän\ *also* **khu·ra·san** \ˌkůr-\ *n, pl* **khorassan** *or* **khorassans** *usu cap* [fr. *Khorassan* or *Khurasan*, province of Iran] : a Persian rug or carpet often of Herat or animal pattern and vivid coloring
kho·shot \ˈkō,shät\ *n, pl* **khoshot** *or* **khoshots** *usu cap* **1** : a Kalmuck people converted to Lamaism in the early 17th century **2** : a member of the Khoshot people
kho·ta·na \kōˈtänə\ *n, pl* **khotana** *or* **khotanas** *usu cap* : KOYUKON
kho·ta·nese *n, pl* **kho·ta·nese** \ˌkōtᵊnˈēz, -ēs\ *usu cap* [*Khotan*, region in Turkistan, central Asia + E *-ese*] : an Iranian language of central Asia found in documents from the eighth century to the tenth century
kho·war \ˈkō,wär\ *n* -s *usu cap* : a Dard language of Chitral, northwest Pakistan
khozar *usu cap, var of* KHAZAR
khud \ˈkəd\ *n* -s [Hindi *khad*] *India* : RAVINE, PRECIPICE
khun·nong \kəˈnȯŋ, -näŋ\ *n, pl* **khunnong** *or* **khunnongs** *usu cap* **1** : a Tibeto-Burman people occupying the upper tributary region of the Irrawaddy river and dwelling in communal houses **2** : a member of the Khunnong people
khus·khus \ˈkəskəs\ *or* **khuskhus grass** *also* **khus** \ˈkəs\ *or* **kus·kus** *or* **cus·cus** \ˈkəskəs\ *n* -ES [Per & Hindi *khaskhas*] : an aromatic grass (*Andropogon zizamoides*) whose esp. fragrant roots yield an oil used in perfumery and are also made into mats in tropical India — called also *vetiver*
khut·bah *or* **khut·ba** \ˈkůtbə\ *n* -s [Ar *khuṭbah*] : a pulpit address of prescribed form that is read in mosques on Fridays at noon prayer and contains an acknowledgment of the sovereignty of the reigning prince
[1]**khwa·raz·mi·an** \kwəˈrazmēən, kwäˈ-\ *adj, usu cap* [*Khwarazm*, province of ancient Persia + E *-ian*] **1** : of or relating to Khwarazm **2** : of or relating to the Khwarazmian people
[2]**khwarazmian** \"\ *or* **khwa·rez·mi·an** \-rez-\ *or* **khwa·riz·mi·an** \-riz-\ *n* -s *usu cap* **1** : an Uzbek people **2** : a member of the Khwarazmian people
kHz *abbr* kilohertz
ki *var of* TI
ki *abbr* **1** kilocycle **2** king **3** kitchen
KIA *abbr* killed in action
ki·aat \kēˈät\ *n* -s [Afrik, prob. fr. native name in southern Africa] : a tree (*Pterocarpus angolensis*) of southern Africa having heavy strong durable wood that is used for furniture, joinery, and flooring
ki·a·boo·ca *or* **ki·a·boo·ka** *or* **ky·a·boo·ka** *also* **kya-bouka** \ˌkīəˈbükə\ *n* -s [origin unknown] : AMBOYNA 1
ki·aki *or* **ke·ya·ki** \kēˈ(y)äkē\ *n* -s [Jap *kiaki*] : a Japanese timber tree (*Zelkova serrata*) with fine hard wood
kia·mu·sze \jēˈämə,sə(r), -sē\ *adj, usu cap* [fr. *Kiamusze*, Manchuria] : of or from the city of Kiamusze, Manchuria : of the kind or style prevalent in Kiamusze
ki·ang *also* **ky·ang** *or* **ki·yang** \kēˈ(y)äŋ\ *n, pl* **kiangs** *also* **kiang** [Tibetan *kyaṅ* (written *rkyaṅ*)] : an Asiatic wild ass (*Equus hemionus*) typically having reddish back and sides, white underparts, muzzle, and legs, and a dusky stripe along the spine and occurring in many local races most of which have at various times been considered separate species
kia ora \ˌkēəˈōrə\ *interj* [Maori *kia ora*, lit., be well] — used as a salutation or toast in Australia and New Zealand
kiaugh \ˈkyäk\ *n* -s [prob. fr. ScGael *cabhag* hurry, trouble] *Scot* : TROUBLE, ANXIETY, STIR
ki·a·we *or* **ke·a·we** \kēˈäwä\ *n* -s [Hawaiian *kiawe*] : any of several mesquites introduced into and to some extent naturalized in Hawaii
kib·be *also* **kib·beh** \ˈkibə\ *n* -s [Ar *kubbah*] : ground lamb and wheat baked as a cake
[1]**kib·ble** \ˈkibəl\ *n* -s [G *kübel* tub, bucket, fr. OHG *-chubilī*, modif. of (assumed) VL *cupia* — more at KEEVE] *Brit* : a hoisting bucket used in mining
[2]**kibble** \"\ *vt* **kibbled; kibbled; kibbling** \-b(ə)liŋ\ **kibbles** [origin unknown] : to grind coarsely ⟨*kibbled* dog biscuit⟩ ⟨*kibbled* grain⟩
[3]**kibble** \"\ *n* -s : coarsely ground meal or grain
kib·butz \kiˈbůts, -üts\ *n, pl* **kib·but·zim** \(,)ki,bůtˈsēm, -büt-\ [NHeb *qibbūṣ*, fr. Heb, gathering] : a collective farm or settlement in Israel cooperatively owned and managed by the members and organized on a communal basis ⟨the ~ is one of four main types of agricultural settlement —John Hersey⟩ ⟨in each ~ the . . . living arrangements are centralized with a common dining hall and children's quarters —Joan Comay⟩
kib·butz·nik \kiˈbůtsnik, -büt-\ *n* -s [Yiddish *kibutsnik*, fr. *kibuts* kibbutz (fr. NHeb *qibbūṣ*) + *-nik* (n. suffix denoting a person engaged in or connected with — something specified —, fr. Pol & Russ)] : a member of a kibbutz
[1]**kibe** \ˈkīb\ *n* -s [ME *kybe*] : a chap or crack in the flesh caused by cold : an ulcerated chilblain esp. on the heel ⟨the clouted shoe of the peasant galls the ~ of the courtier —Sir Walter Scott⟩
[2]**kibe** \"\ *vt* -ED/-ING/-S : to affect with kibes ⟨make me as angry as a *kibed* heel —T.B.Costain⟩
ki·bei \(ˈ)kēˈbā\ *n, pl* **kibei** *also* **kibeis** *often cap* [Jap] : a son or daughter of issei parents who is born in America and esp. in the U.S. and educated largely in Japan — distinguished from *nisei*; compare SANSEI
ki·bit·ka \kəˈbitkə\ *n* -s [Russ, of Turkic origin; akin to Kazan Tatar *kibit* booth, stall, tent, Uighur *käbit*] **1** : a Kirghiz circular tent of latticework and felt **2** : a Russian covered vehicle on wheels or runners
kibitz \ˈkibəts *also* kəˈbits\ *vb* -ED/-ING/-ES [Yiddish *kibitsen*, fr. G *kiebitzen*, fr. *kiebitz* pewit, busybody, fr. MHG *gībitz* pewit, of imit. origin] *vi* : to act as a kibitzer ⟨observation which amounts, if not to democratic control, at least to democratic ~*ing* —Elmer Davis⟩ ⟨an awful thing to ~ on a man and his wife, and hear what they really talk about —J.M.Cain⟩ ~ *vt* : to observe as a kibitzer: **a** : to be a kibitzer at ⟨~*ing* a Pullman card game —Bob Broeg⟩ **b** : to watch the performance of as a kibitzer ⟨~*ed* him at poker —Theodore Sturgeon⟩
kibitz·er \-sə(r)\ *n* -s [Yiddish *kibitser*, fr. *kibitsen* + *-er*] : an outsider or nonparticipant who looks on and may offer unwanted advice or comment esp. at a card game ⟨contract bridge has achieved a following both of ~*s* and players probably never surpassed in the history of any nonathletic game —*N.Y. World-Telegram*⟩ ⟨nothing can be more of a trial at the scene of an illness or an accident than a ~ —Robert Rice⟩
kibla *or* **kiblah** *var of* QIBLA
[1]**ki·bosh** *also* **ky·bosh** \ˈkī,bäsh, kəˈbäsh\ *n* -ES [origin unknown] : something that serves as a check or stop — used chiefly in the phrase *to put the kibosh on* ⟨the directive puts the ~ on one of the few potentially valuable efforts that the United States has been making in the field of psychological warfare —R.H.Rovere⟩ ⟨might even be able to put the ~ on the plan before it was put into operation⟩
[2]**kibosh** \"\ *vt* -ED/-ING/-ES : BLOCK, FRUSTRATE ⟨a limited . . . budget ~*ed* the architects' first proposal —*Architectural Forum*⟩
ki·chai \ˈkē,chī\ *n, pl* **kichai** *or* **kichais** *usu cap* **1** : a Caddo people of north-central Texas **2** : a member of the Kichai people
kich·el \ˈkikəl\ *n, pl* **kich·lach** \-kləḵ\ *or* **kichel** [Yiddish *kikhel* small cake, dim. of *kukhen* cake, fr. OHG *kuocho* — more at CAKE] : a semisweet baked product made of eggs, flour, and sugar usu. rolled and cut in diamond shape and baked until puffed
kichua *usu cap, var of* QUECHUA
[1]**kick** \ˈkik\ *vb* -ED/-ING/-S [ME *kiken*] *vi* **1 a** (1) : to thrust out the foot or feet with force : strike out with the foot or feet (as in defense or bad temper or in effecting a swimming stroke); *esp* : to give impetus to something with a usu. fast blow with the foot (2) : THRUST, DRIVE ⟨the bomber's engines ~ with a 350,000-pound thrust⟩ **b** : to have a habit of kicking ⟨the horse ~*s* when men approach him with a saddle⟩ ⟨the boy ~*s* when he gets into fights⟩ **c** : to execute a kick in dancing **d** : to try to score or gain ground in a game of football by kicking the ball **e** : to engage in small annoying or harassing tactics ⟨~*ing* at neighboring countries to distract their own people from internal problems⟩ **2 a** : to show opposition : REBEL ⟨tends to ~ against authority⟩ **b** : to express discontent : COMPLAIN ⟨had studied very little and so had no reason to ~ about low grades⟩ **3** *slang* : DIE — compare KICK IN, KICK OFF **4** *of a firearm* : to recoil when fired — often used with *back* **5 a** *of a cricket pitch* : to cause a bowled ball to rebound erratically **b** *of a bowled ball in cricket* : to rebound erratically — often used with *up* **6** : to function with vitality and energy ⟨still alive and ~*ing* at 75 years⟩ ⟨continue to flourish and . . . wax fat and ~ —*Dock Leaves*⟩ **7 a** : to move or go erratically or jerkily as if being kicked ⟨an engine that ~*ed* a good deal when it was started in cold weather⟩ ⟨the jumping jack ~*ed* about on the floor until it ran down⟩ **b** : to move from one to another of or stay or rest in various successive places as circumstance or whim dictates ⟨an old chair that ~*ed* around the house for years⟩ ⟨during winters ~*ed* about Florida and other warm areas⟩ ~ *vt* **1 a** : to strike, thrust, or hit with the foot usu. with force **b** : to strike usu. suddenly with force as if kicking **c** : to impel or drive as if by kicking; *specif* : to cause (a railroad car) to be carried by momentum to a particular track position by uncoupling while still moving **d** : to cause (a racehorse or racing car) to show a sudden burst of speed ⟨~*ed* his car into the lead —*Newsweek*⟩ **2** : to score (a goal or point) by kicking the ball in a game of football **3** *chiefly dial* : to refuse (a person) after an invitation or an offer of marriage : JILT ⟨took to drink after being ~*ed* in favor of a rival⟩ **4** *slang* : to heap reproaches upon (oneself) ⟨~*ed* himself every time he thought of the lost opportunity⟩ **5** : RAISE 17a **6** *slang* : to free oneself of or break (a drug habit) **syn** see OBJECT — **kick against the pricks** : to feel or show usu. pointless opposition to or resentment of an often necessary authority one is subject to — **kick downstairs** : to kick out : EJECT — **kick one's heels** : to wait or pass the time aimlessly or futilely — **kick over the traces** : to cast off restraint : become insubordinate : throw off authority or control — **kick the beam** **1** : to be extremely lightly weighted **2** : to become or be of extremely small value ⟨the prices of building plots *kicked the beam* —Marguerite Steen⟩ — **kick the bucket** *slang* : DIE — **kick up one's heels** **1 a** : to show sudden extreme delight or energy inspired by such delight **b** : to have a lively time ⟨had no time to take a holiday and *kick up my heels* when I came back from the war —Rebecca West⟩ **2** *slang* : DIE
[2]**kick** \"\ *n* -s **1 a** : an act of kicking : a blow or sudden force-

ful thrust with the foot and esp. the toe ⟨felt the ~ so strongly that a pain shot up his leg⟩; *specif* : a sudden propelling (as of a ball) with a blow of the foot esp. in football — see DROP-KICK, FREE KICK, PLACE-KICK **b** : a forceful thrust or sudden drive ⟨the engine drove the car ahead in a series of ~s⟩ **c** : a vigorous elevation of a leg (as in dancing) ⟨a high ~ and then a pirouette⟩ **d** : the power to kick : degree of force in kicking **e** : a rhythmic often forceful motion of the legs used alone or in conjunction with arm movements to propel a swimmer through the water **f** : a burst of speed or the ability to exhibit a burst of speed in racing esp. as unleashed in the last part of a race **2** *slang Brit* : SIXPENCE **3** *archaic slang* : the latest fashion or style **4 a** : a sudden forceful jolt, jerk, jog, or thrust suggesting a kick ⟨felt the sudden ~ of the drill in his hand as the power was turned on⟩ ⟨a noticeable upward ~ in the barograph trace —G.H.T.Kimble⟩; *specif* : the recoil of a gun **b** : an electrical impulse or the deflection on a meter that records it **c** : a single automatic operation of a business machine **5** *slang* : DISMISSAL, DISCHARGE; *specif* : a dishonorable discharge from the armed forces ⟨the maximum penalty is . . . a year and a ~ —F.B.Wiener⟩ — compare ³BOOT 8b **6** *slang* : POCKET, POCKETBOOK ⟨without a dime in his ~ for a cup of coffee⟩ **7** *chiefly Brit* : KICKER 1b ⟨not a powerful ~, he is very accurate —Len Smith⟩ **8** : an indentation at the bottom of a molded glass bottle to lessen its holding capacity **9** *chiefly Brit* : a projection on a stock board or brick mold for forming a frog in the brick; *also* : the frog so formed **10 a** : a feeling of opposition or objection ⟨had a ~ against the new schedule⟩ **b** : an expression of opposition or objection ⟨heard all sorts of ~s against the administration⟩ **c** : the grounds for objection ⟨trying to find out what the ~ was⟩ **11 a** : a quick and forcible effect suggestive of a kick: as (1) : the effect or force of an explosive when exploded ⟨the high-test gasoline had quite a ~⟩ (2) : a marked physical effect (as of stimulation by alcohol) ⟨got a quick ~ out of drinking⟩; *also* : ability to produce such an effect ⟨a drink with no ~ in it⟩ **b** (1) : a feeling of pleasure or of marked enjoyment : THRILL ⟨get a ~ out of that music⟩ (2) : a source of such pleasure ⟨the play had a dramatic ~ that made it very successful⟩ **c kicks** *pl, slang* : PLEASURE, THRILLS, FUN ⟨playing for ~s, not money⟩ **d** *slang* : way of getting one's pleasure or livelihood : manner or style of behaving or performing ⟨the band is on a Dixieland ~⟩ ⟨went on a mystery-reading ~ —*Time*⟩ **12** : a sudden and striking surprise, revelation, or turn of events : TWIST ⟨the novel ended with an ironical ~⟩ **13** *slang* : RAISE ⟨a demand for a salary ~ —Pete Martin⟩ — **kick in the pants** : a humbling setback — **kick in the teeth** : a sudden usu. violent often contemptuous setback ⟨the pleased delegation . . . got a delayed *kick in the teeth* —*Time*⟩

kick·able \-kəbəl\ *adj* : capable of being kicked : fit or deserving to be kicked

kick·a·poo \'kikə,pü\ *n, pl* **kickapoo** *or* **kickapoos** *usu cap* [Kickapoo *kiwĕgapawa*, lit., he stands about] **1 a** : an Indian people orig. of Wisconsin but now living in Oklahoma and Chihuahua, Mexico **b** : a member of such people **2** : a dialect of Fox

kick around *vt* **1 a** : to treat in an inconsiderate or high-handed fashion ⟨business was so good he felt he could *kick* the customers *around* a little⟩ ⟨*kicks* his children *around* a good deal⟩ ⟨men and women who are so frequently *kicked around*, abused, misunderstood, and unappreciated —William Benton⟩ **b** *slang* : to treat in a casual, unsystematic, or experimental way ⟨*kicked* the music *around* for a while, trying it out⟩ **2** *slang* : to consider, examine, or discuss (as an idea) from all angles usu. by random suggestion or discussion ⟨*kicked* the notion *around* for an hour or so to see if it might be feasible⟩ ~ *vi* : to work in a hit-or-miss fashion or wherever work offers itself ⟨*kicked around* in stock companies —R.F.Shepard⟩

kick back *vi* **1** : to recoil upon one usu. in an unexpected way ⟨his accusations *kicked back* and he found himself in jail⟩ **2** : to pay a kickback ⟨forced to *kick back* out of every paycheck⟩ ~ *vt* **1** : to restore (something stolen) to the owner **2** : to give back (money) as a kickback ⟨asked to *kick* a dollar *back* each week⟩

kickback \'⸗,⸗\ *n* -s [*kick back*] **1** : the action or the effect of kicking back: as **a** (1) : the starting backward of an internal-combustion engine while being cranked (2) : the backward thrust of a piece of work being fed into a machine (as a circular saw) — called also *backkick* **b** : a strong esp. unfavorable reaction ⟨was unable to take the medicine because of a marked ~⟩ — called also *backkick* **2** : REFUND: as **a** : a percentage payment exacted as a condition for granting assistance by one in a position to open up or control a source of income or gain ⟨appointees paid a ~ to the ward boss out of each paycheck⟩ **b** : a usu. secret rebate of part of a purchase price by the seller to the buyer or to the one who directed or influenced the purchaser to buy from such seller **c** : a rebate given to a seller (as an automobile dealer) by a finance company that purchases the buyer's promissory note or installment paper **3** : high voltage produced (as in a radio transmitting set) by the sudden interruption of current in a low-voltage circuit — called also *backkick* **4** : KICKBOARD 1

kickball \'⸗,⸗\ *n* : a children's game that resembles baseball and is played with an inflated ball which is kicked instead of batted

kickboard \'⸗,⸗\ *n* **1** : one of two high boards on either side of the pit end of a bowling alley that separate adjacent alleys and keep flying pins in the right alley **2** : a buoyant rectangular board grasped with the hands by a swimmer while developing kicking techniques — called also *flutterboard*

kickdown \'⸗,⸗\ *n* -s [fr. *kick down*, v.] : a change to lower gear in an automotive vehicle; *also* : the manually operated or automatic device for making such a change

kicked *past of* KICK

kick·er \'kikə(r)\ *n* -s **1** : one that kicks: as **a** : an animal having the habit of kicking **b** : a member of a football team who makes or is designated to make dropkicks, place-kicks, or punts **c** : a person who protests, complains, or grumbles esp. habitually **d** : a sawmill device for throwing logs from the conveyor trough onto the log deck **e** : a mechanical part that gives a sharp push to some object (as for feeding or ejecting work from a machine) **f** : a device for opening a stove door or other object by pressure applied with the foot **g** : a ball (as in cricket and tennis) that rebounds erratically or high **h** : WILD-OAT KICKER **i** : a small internal-combustion engine in a boat; *also* : a boat driven by such an engine **j** : an aircrewman who releases or propels out of a cargo airplane bundles to be parachuted to a drop zone on the ground **2** : TEDDER **3** : a protective covering for the toes and instep of a goalkeeper in field hockey usu. made of canvas or soft leather with a padding of felt or sponge rubber **4** : an unmatched card retained with a pair or three of a kind when drawing cards in draw poker **5** : a machine for softening skins in tanning **6** : a line of newspaper type set above a headline usu. in a different typeface and intended to provoke interest in, editorialize about, or provide orientation for the matter in the copy it heads **7** : KICK 12

kickier *comparative of* KICKY

kickiest *superlative of* KICKY

kick in *vt, slang* : CONTRIBUTE ⟨asked to *kick* a dollar *in* for a present for the boss⟩ ~ *vi* **1** *slang* : DIE ⟨*kicked in* at the ripe old age of 90⟩ **2** *slang* : to make a contribution ⟨an unknown contributor *kicked in* with $1000⟩

kick-in \'⸗,⸗\ *n* -s [fr. *kick in*, v.] : a free kick in soccer used to put the ball in play after it has gone out of bounds over a sideline

kicking *pres part of* KICK

kicking-colt \'⸗⸗,⸗\ *n* : JEWELWEED a

kicking-horses \,⸗⸗'⸗⸗\ *n pl but usu sing in constr* : JEWELWEED a

kick·ish \'kikish\ *adj, now dial Eng* : IRRITABLE, CANTANKEROUS

kick off *vi* **1** : to start or restart the play in football by a place-kick from a point close to or at the center of the field **2** : to begin proceedings or undertake the initial move or action ⟨the entertainers *kicked off* with a fast song and dance⟩ **3** *slang* : DIE ⟨worth a cool million when he *kicked off*⟩ ~ *vt* : to start or signalize the beginning of (a concerted effort) ⟨*kick* the drive for funds *off* with a nationwide broadcast⟩

kickoff \'⸗,⸗\ *n* -s [*kick off*] **1** : the act of kicking off: as **a** : a kick that puts the ball into play in a football or soccer game **b** : COMMENCEMENT ⟨makes no bones about it being the ~ for his big bid for the Democratic Presidential nod —*Newsweek*⟩ ⟨is also hoping to round up some of its oldest living customers for this ~ party —Bennett Cerf⟩ **2** : a device (as a power-operated lever) for casting work off a machine table out of a cavity in a die

kick out *vi* **1** : to kick the ball deliberately over a touchline (as when stalling for time) in a soccer game **2** : to take a free kick after a touchback or safety in a game of football ~ *vt* : to turn out, dismiss, or eject usu. forcefully or summarily ⟨tried to keep the lad in his employ but finally had to *kick him out*⟩ ⟨when he entered the house he was *kicked out* immediately⟩ ⟨suggested *kicking* all enemy aliens *out*⟩

kickout \'⸗,⸗\ *n* -s [*kick out*] : the act of kicking out or of kicking something out

kick over *vi* : to begin to fire — used of an internal-combustion engine ⟨after a moment of cranking the motor *kicked over*⟩ ~ *vt* : to cause (an internal-combustion engine) to turn over and usu. begin to fire ⟨could not *kick* the motor *over*⟩

kickpipe \'⸗,⸗\ *n* : a short section of pipe to protect an electric cable from mechanical damage where it emerges from a floor or deck

kickplate \'⸗,⸗\ *n* : a protective plate (as of metal or plastic) applied to the bottom of a door or cabinet or to the riser of a step to prevent marring of the finish by shoe marks

kick pleat *n* : a short inverted pleat used to give breadth (as at the bottom of a skirt for ease in walking or at the bottom of a slipcover for ease in fitting the band around corners)

kicks *pres 3d sing of* KICK, *pl of* KICK

kick·shaw \'kik,shȯ\ *n* -s [by folk etymology fr. F *quelque chose* something, anything] **1** *or* **kickshaws** *pl but usu sing in constr* **a** : a fancy dish in cookery : TIDBIT, DELICACY **b** : something elegant but trifling : TRIFLE, TOY **2** *archaic* : a fantastic person

kick·sies \'kiksiz\ *n pl* [*kicks* trousers (fr. pl. of ²*kick*) + *-ie* + *-s*] *slang Brit* : TROUSERS, PANTS

kick-sled \'⸗,⸗\ *n* : a sled popular in Scandinavia that consists of a low seat on runners and that is propelled usu. by one holding the back of the seat, standing on a runner with one foot, and pushing with the other

kicksorter \'⸗,⸗⸗\ *n* : a device that sorts and records electrical pulses of given intensities (as pulses from an ionization chamber)

kickstand \'⸗,⸗\ *n* : a device for holding up a bicycle or motorcycle when not in use consisting of a metal bar or rod that is attached by a swivel device to the frame and may be kicked to a vertical position as a prop

kick starter *or* **kick start** *n* : a motor starter (as on a motorcycle) that is activated by a thrust of the foot usu. assisted by the body weight

kick through *vi* **1** *slang* : to kick in **2** *slang* : to make a confession ⟨*kick through* and tell me what it is —Erle Stanley Gardner⟩

kick turn *n* : a standing half turn in skiing made by raising one ski so that it is nearly vertical to the ground, turning the ski outward and downward so that it is finally brought down pointed backward, and bringing the other ski around parallel to it

kick up *vt* **1** : to cause to rise or be propelled upward forcefully ⟨the tires *kicked* little stones *up*⟩ ⟨clouds of dust *kicked up* by passing cars⟩ **2 a** : RAISE ⟨signal the auctioneer quietly and *kick* the bid *up* another thousand —Grant Cannon⟩ **b** : to stir up : PROVOKE ⟨*kicked* a row *up* over nothing⟩ ⟨*kick up* a fuss⟩ ~ *vi* **1** : to give evidence of disorder ⟨felt his stomach start to *kick up*⟩ **2** : to become insubordinate : act in a protesting or unexpectedly independent way ⟨when the New Woman began *kicking up* on the American scene in the middle of the 19th century —Lois Long⟩

kickup \'⸗,⸗\ *n* -s [*kick up*] **1** : a noisy quarrel : DISTURBANCE, ROW **2 a** : KICK 1c **b** : a method in speedball of converting a ground ball to an aerial ball by means of the foot **3** : KICK 8 **4** : an upward bend made in the frame of a motor vehicle to clear the rear axle

kick wheel *n* : a potter's wheel worked by a foot pedal or by kicking a heavy disk at the foot of the vertical shaft

kickx·ia \'kiksēə\ *n, cap* [NL, fr. Jean *Kickx* †1831 and his son Jean *Kickx* †1864 Belgian botanists + NL *-ia*] : a small genus of Old World creeping pubescent herbs (family Scrophulariaceae) having pinnately veined oval leaves and flowers with a prominent palate — see CANCERWORT

kicky \'kikē\ *adj* -ER/-EST **1** *chiefly dial* : SASSY, CONTRARY **2** : likely to kick

¹**kid** \'kid\ *n* -s [ME *kide*, of Scand origin; akin to ON *kith* kid, OSw *kidh*; akin to OHG *kizzī* kid; prob., like MIr *cit* sheep, Alb *qith* young male goat, fr. a cry to goats and sheep to return to the fold] **1 a** (1) : a young goat usu. under one year old (2) : a young individual of various related animals (as many antelopes and some deer) **b** : a young individual of various other animals ⟨a sea-otter ~⟩ **2 a** : the flesh, fur, or skin of a kid **b** : something made of kid: as (1) : KIDSKIN (2) : KID LEATHER (3) : KID GLOVE **3** : CHILD, YOUNGSTER ⟨took the ~s to the playground⟩ ⟨a ~ of eighteen —Dan Cushman⟩ ⟨grade-school ~s⟩ **4** *slang* : a young person marked by proficiency or expertness ⟨quite some ~ when it comes to staying in the public eye⟩

²**kid** \"\ *vi* **kidded; kidded; kidding; kids** [ME *kidden*, fr. *kide*, n.] : to bring forth young — used of a goat or an antelope

³**kid** \"\ *adj* [¹*kid*] **1** : of, relating to, or made of kid **2** : YOUNGER — used in the phrases *kid brother* and *kid sister*

⁴**kid** \"\ *vb* **kidded; kidded; kidding; kids** [prob. fr. ¹*kid*] *vt* **1** : DECEIVE, FOOL **2** : to make fun of usu. good-humoredly and often by innocent deception ⟨used to ~ him then about his intellectual face —G.W.Brace⟩ ⟨a medicine-show barker *kidding* the crowd⟩ ⟨any nation that could ~ its own foibles was . . . new and pleasant —*Time*⟩ ⟨*kidded* him into thinking the police were inquiring about him⟩ ~ *vi* **1** : to make fun of someone or something **2 a** : JOKE **b** : to indulge in good-humored fooling or horseplay — often used with *around* — **kid·der** \-də(r)\ *n* -s

⁵**kid** \"\ *n* -s [ME *kidde, kid*] *dial Eng* : a bundle of heath and twigs : FAGOT

⁶**kid** \"\ *vt* **kidded; kidded; kidding; kids** : to bind (fagots) in bundles

⁷**kid** \"\ *vi* **kidded; kidded; kidding; kids** [prob. alter. of earlier *cod*, fr. ¹*cod*] *dial Eng* : to form pods — used of a legume

⁸**kid** \"\ *n* -s [prob. alter. of ¹*cod*] *dial Eng* : the seed pod of a legume

⁹**kid** \"\ *n* -s [prob. alter. of ¹*kit*] : a small wooden tub; *esp* : a sailor's mess tub

kidcote \'⸗,⸗\ *n* [prob. fr. ¹*kid* (young goat) + *cote* (shed for animals); fr. the use of any available shed in small towns to house lawbreakers] *archaic* : JAIL

kid·der·min·ster \'kidə(r),minztə(r), -n(t)st-\ *or* **kidderminster carpet** *n* -s *usu cap* [fr. *Kidderminster*, borough in Worcester county, England] : ingrain carpet — called also *Scotch carpet*

kid·di·er \'kidēə(r)\ *also* **kid·der** \-də(r)\ *n* -s [origin unknown] *dial Eng* : a huckster esp. of agricultural produce

kid·ding·ly *adv* : in the manner of one that is kidding

kid·dish \'kidish, -dēsh\ *adj* : CHILDISH ⟨beginning to come along as well with her ~ admirers —W.C.Williams⟩ — **kid·dish·ly** *adv* — **kid·dish·ness** *n* -ES

¹**kid·dle** \'kid³l\ *n* -s [ME *kydle*, fr. ONF *quidel*, fr. MLG *kiedel*] : a barrier that extends across a river and that is designed to deflect the water and river fish through an opening across which a fishnet may be stretched

²**kiddle** \"\ *dial Eng var of* CUDDLE

kid·do \'ki(,)dō\ *n, pl* **kiddos** *or* **kiddoes** [¹*kid* + *-o*] — used as a familiar form of address ⟨don't worry about me, ~ —Max Arnold⟩ ⟨this means war, and ~, you're right in the middle —H.L.Spinner⟩

kid·dush \'ki(,)dush, -,dəsh; kə'düsh\ *n* -ES [Heb *qiddūsh* sanctification] : a Jewish ceremony that proclaims the holiness of the incoming Sabbath or festival and that consists of a benediction pronounced customarily before the evening meal over a cup of wine or two loaves of white Sabbath bread ⟨hurried home in time for ~ on Friday evening⟩

kiddush ha·shem \-hə'shām\ *n* [Heb *qiddūsh hashshēm* sanctification of the name (of God)] : a religious or moral act according to Jewish religion that causes others to reverence God : religious martyrdom — compare HILLUL HASHEM

kid·du·shin \kə'düshən, ⸗,⸗'shēn\ *n* -s [Aram *qiddūshīn*, pl. of Heb *qiddūsh*] : a betrothal ceremony preceding the Jewish marriage ceremony

kid·dy *or* **kid·die** \'kidē, -di\ *n, pl* **kiddies** [¹*kid* + *-y, -ie*] : a small child

kid finish *n* : a bookbinding finish of paper or boards resembling the surface of undressed kid leather

kid glove *n* : a dress glove made of kidskin or of some leather that resembles kidskin — **with kid gloves** *adv* : with special consideration : in a tactful manner ⟨never threatened to abuse or discriminate against him, instead treated him *with kid gloves* —*Time*⟩

kid-glove \'⸗'⸗\ *adj* [*kid glove*] **1** *or* **kid-gloved** \'⸗'⸗\ **a** : marked by a calculated fastidiousness and delicacy esp. in the avoidance of the rough or the uncouth in talk or action **b** : marked by extreme considerateness, care, and gentleness (as in handling) ⟨would no longer expect *kid-glove* treatment for their monarchist activities —*New Internat'l Yr. Bk.*⟩ ⟨I never thought I'd have a situation that called for such *kid-gloved* treatment —Francis Towle⟩ **2** *of a citrus fruit* : having an easily removable skin

kid-glove orange *n* : MANDARIN 4b(1)

kid leather *n* **1** : soft pliable leather made from either goatskin or kidskin and used for shoes, gloves, garments, and handbags **2** : a chrome tanned grain glove leather made from goatskin or lambskin

kid·let \'kidlət\ *n* -s [¹*kid* + *-let*] *slang* : KIDDY

¹**kid·nap** \'kid,nap\ *vt* **kidnaped** *or* **kidnapped; kidnaped** *or* **kidnapped; kidnaping** *or* **kidnapping; kidnaps** [prob. back-formation fr. *kidnapper*] **1** *obs* : to carry off to enforced labor esp. in the British colonies in America **2 a** : to carry (an unwilling person) away by unlawful force or fraud or to seize and detain for the purpose of so carrying away — compare ABDUCTION 2 **b** : to seize and carry or take away often wrongly ⟨*kidnapped* the children for the afternoon⟩ ⟨quite a business *kidnapping* pet dogs and watching the "Lost" columns for reward notices —T.W.Duncan⟩ ⟨*kidnapping* a sizable coastwise steamer —*Nat'l Geographic*⟩

²**kidnap** \"\ *adj* : of, relating to, or being a kidnapping ⟨a ~ plot⟩ ⟨the ~ car⟩

kid·nap·per *or* **kid·nap·er** \-pə(r)\ *n* -s [¹*kid* (child) + obs. *napper* thief, fr. *nap* (to seize) + *-er*] : one that kidnaps; *esp* : one that abducts a child for ransom

kidnapping *or* **kidnaping** *n* -s [fr. gerund of ¹*kidnap*] : the act or an instance of stealing, abducting, or carrying away a person by force or fraud often with a demand for ransom

kid·ney \'kidnē, -ni\ *n* -s *often attrib* [ME *kidenei, kidney*, fr. *kiden-, kidn-* (origin unknown) + *ei, ey* egg, fr. OE *ǣg* — more at EGG] **1 a** : one of a pair of vertebrate organs situated in the body cavity near the spinal column that serve to excrete urea, uric acid, and other waste products of metabolism, that in man are bean-shaped organs about 4½ inches long lying behind the peritoneum of the posterior part of the abdomen and embedded in a mass of fatty tissue, and that consist chiefly of nephrons by which urine is secreted, collected, and finally discharged into the pelvis of the kidney whence it is conveyed by the ureter to the bladder to be periodically discharged — compare MESONEPHROS, METANEPHROS, PRONEPHROS **b** : any of various more or less complex excretory organs of invertebrate animals — see GREEN GLAND; compare NEPHRIDIUM **2** : sort or kind esp. as regards persuasion, disposition, or temperament ⟨a nice helpful guy, of a different ~ entirely from the ubiquitous Secret Police functionaries —Paula Lecler⟩ **3** : a kidney-shaped aggregate of ore **syn** see TYPE

kidney bean *n* **1** : the seed of any cultivated bean derived from the common species (*Phaseolus vulgaris*); *esp* : any of certain rather large dark red kidney-shaped beans **2** : a plant producing kidney beans

kidney chop *n* : a loin chop (as of lamb or veal) containing a kidney whole or in part — see VEAL illustration

kidney corpuscle *n* : MALPIGHIAN CORPUSCLE

kidney cotton *n* [so called fr. the shape of the mass in which the seeds are found] **1** : a shrub or small tree (*Gossypium brasiliense*) yielding a long-staple cotton **2** : the fiber obtained from kidney cotton

kidney desk *n* : a desk that is kidney-shaped in top and horizontal section

kidney desk

kidney ore *n* [so called fr. its occurrence in kidney-shaped masses] : a mineral consisting of a variety of hematite

kidneyroot \'⸗⸗,⸗\ *n* [so called fr. the belief that such plants cure kidney diseases] **1** : JOE-PYE WEED **2** : COYOTE BRUSH

kidney-shaped \'⸗⸗,⸗\ *adj* : shaped like a kidney : RENIFORM

kidney stone *n* **1** : a kidney-shaped pebble **2** : RENAL CALCULUS

kidney table *n* : a usu. small side table with a kidney-shaped top

kidney vetch *n* : a perennial Eurasian herb (*Anthyllis vulneraria*) having heads of red or yellow flowers and formerly used as a remedy for renal disorders

kidney worm *n* : any of several nematode worms parasitic in the kidneys: as **a** : GIANT KIDNEY WORM **b** : a common and destructive black-and-white worm (*Stephanurus dentatus*) that is related to the gapeworm but attains a length of two inches and is parasitic in the kidneys, lungs, and other viscera of the hog in warm regions — called also *lardworm*

kidneywort \'⸗⸗,⸗\ *n* [so called fr. the use of such plants to cure kidney diseases] **1** : NAVELWORT 1 **2** : STAR SAXIFRAGE **3** : COYOTE BRUSH

kids *pl of* KID, *pres 3d sing of* KID

kidskin \'⸗,⸗\ *n* [¹*kid* + *skin*] **1** : the skin of a young goat **2** : KID LEATHER

kid stuff *n* **1** : something befitting or appropriate only to children ⟨realized that all that saluting and about-facing was *kid stuff* —T.W.Duncan⟩ **2** : something extremely simple or easy ⟨convinced him that running for the town council would be *kid stuff*⟩

kie·kie \'kēä,kēä, 'kē,kē, 'kī,kī\ *n* -s [Maori] : a New Zealand climbing shrub (*Freycinetia banksii*) with edible berries

kiel \'kēl, *esp before pause or consonant* -ēəl\ *adj, usu cap* [fr. *Kiel*, Germany] : of or from the city of Kiel, Germany : of the kind or style prevalent in Kiel

kiel·ba·sa \kil'bäsə, k(y)el-, kēl-\ *n, pl* **kielbasas** \-səz\ *also* **kielba·sy** \-sē\ [Pol *kiełbasa* sausage; akin to Russ *kolbasa* sausage, Czech & Slovenian *klobasa*] : uncooked smoked sausage

kier \'ki(ə)r\ *n* -s [prob. of Scand origin; akin to ON *ker* tub, vessel, Norw dial. *kjer*; akin to OHG *char* vessel, bowl, Goth *kas* vessel] : a large metal vat in which fibers, yarns, and fabrics are boiled off, bleached, or dyed

kier-boil \'⸗,⸗\ *vt* : to scour (as cotton) by boiling in a kier usu. with an alkaline solution

kier·ing \'kiriŋ\ *n* -s : the process of treating in a kier

¹**kier·ke·gaard·ian** \¦kirkə¦gärdēən, ¦kyerkə¦gȯrēən\ *adj, usu cap* [Sören Aabye *Kierkegaard* †1855 Danish philosopher + E *-ian*] : of or relating to the Danish philosopher Kierkegaard or his existentialist philosophy ⟨discourage the growth of a *Kierkegaardian* cult —James Collins⟩ — compare CHRISTIAN EXISTENTIALISM

²**kierkegaardian** \"\ *n* -s *usu cap* : a follower of Kierkegaard or an adherent of Kierkegaardian philosophy

kier·man \'kirmən\ *n, pl* **kiermen** : one who works at a kier

kie·sel·guhr *or* **kie·sel·gur** \'kēzəl,gü(ə)r, -üə\ *n* -s [G *kieselgur*, fr. *kiesel* pebble, flint + *guhr, gur* guhr] : loose or porous diatomite — compare TRIPOLI

kie·ser·ite \'kēzə,rīt\ *n* -s [G *kieserit*, fr. Dietrich G. *Kieser* †1862 Ger. physician + G *-it* -ite] : a mineral $MgSO_4{\cdot}H_2O$ that consists of hydrous magnesium sulfate and is white when pure

ki·ev \'kē,(y)e|f, -ēyə|, |v\ *adj, usu cap* [fr. *Kiev*, U.S.S.R.] : of or from the city of Kiev, U.S.S.R. : of the kind or style prevalent in Kiev

¹ki·ev·an \ˈkē,(y)efən, -evən\ *adj, usu cap* [*Kiev*, U.S.S.R. + E *-an*] **:** of or relating to Kiev, U.S.S.R.; *esp* **:** of the 11th and 12th centuries of Kiev's supremacy ⟨*Kievan* Russia⟩

²kievan \"\ *n* -s *cap* **:** a native or inhabitant of Kiev, U.S.S.R.

kieve *var of* KEEVE

kif *var of* KEF

Ki·ja·fa \kēˈ(y)afə, -)äfə\ *trademark* — used for a wine made from the juice and flavored with the pits of a small black Danish cherry

ki·kar \ˈkēkə(r), ˈkik-\ *n* -s [Hindi *kīkar*] **:** GUM ARABIC TREE

kike \ˈkīk\ *n* -s [prob. alter. of *kiki*, redupl. of *-ki*, common ending of names of Jews who lived in Slavic countries] **:** JEW — usu. taken to be offensive

ki·ke·pa \kēˈkāpə\ *n* -s [Hawaiian] **:** a tapa or sarong worn by Hawaiian women with the top under one arm and over the shoulder of the opposite arm

ki·kon·go \kēˈkäŋ(,)gō\ *n, usu cap* **:** KONGO

ki·ku \ˈkē(,)kü\ *n* -s [Jap] **:** CHRYSANTHEMUM 1

kiku·mon \ˈkikə,män, ˈkēk-\ *n* -s [Jap, fr. *kiku* + *mon* badge, crest] **:** CHRYSANTHEMUM 3

ki·ku·yu \kəˈkü(,)yü, kēˈ-\ *n, pl* **kikuyu** *or* **kikuyus** *usu cap* **1 a :** a Bantu-speaking agricultural negroid people of Kenya **b :** a member of such people **2 :** a Bantu language of the Kikuyu people

kikuyu grass *n, often cap K* **:** a southern African forage grass (*Pennisetum clandestinum*) introduced into Australia and So. America

kil *abbr* **1** kilderkin **2** kilogram **3** kilometer

kild *abbr* kilderkin

kil·dare \(ˈ)kil¦da(a)r\|(ə)r, -de\|, \|ə\ *adj, usu cap* [fr. County *Kildare*, Ireland] **:** of or from County Kildare, Ireland **:** of the kind or style prevalent in County Kildare

kildare green *n, often cap K* **:** a moderate yellow green that is greener, lighter, and stronger than average moss green, yellower and lighter than average pea green, and yellower and paler than apple green (sense 1)

kil·dee \ˈkildē\ *dial var of* KILLDEER

kildeer *var of* KILLDEER

kil·der·kin \ˈkildə(r)kən\ *n* -s [ME *kinderkin, kilderkin*, fr. MD *kindekijn, kinnekijn*, fr. ML *quintale* quintal + MD *-kijn* (dim. suffix) — more at QUINTAL, -KIN] **1 :** a cask about half the size of a common barrel and sometimes smaller **2 :** an English unit of capacity equal to ½ barrel or 18 imperial gallons

kiley *var of* KYLIE

kil·hig \ˈkil,hig\ *or* **kil·lig** \ˈkilig\ *n* -s [origin unknown] **:** a short thick pole used in logging to direct the fall of a tree

ki·lim \kēˈlēm\ *n* -s [Turk, fr. Per *kilīm*] **:** a pileless tapestry-woven carpet, mat, or spread made in Turkey, Kurdistan, the Caucasus, Iran, and western Turkestan

ki·li·wa \kəˈlēwə\ *or* **ki·li·wi** \-wē\ *n, pl* **kiliwa** *or* **kiliwas** *or* **kiliwi** *or* **kiliwis** *usu cap* **1 a :** an Indian people of northern Lower California, Mexico **b :** a member of such people **2 :** a Yuman language of the Kiliwa people

kil·ken·ny \(ˈ)kil¦kenē, -ni\ *adj, usu cap* [fr. County *Kilkenny*, Ireland] **:** of or from County Kilkenny, Ireland **:** of the kind or style prevalent in County Kilkenny

¹kill \ˈkil\ *vb* **killed** \-ld\ *or chiefly dial* **kilt** \-lt\ **killed** *or chiefly dial* **kilt**; **killing**; **kills** [ME *cullen, killen* to strike, beat, kill; perh. akin to OE *cwellan* to kill — more at QUELL] *vt* **1 a :** to deprive of life **:** put to death **:** cause the death of ⟨~*ed* by enemy fire⟩ ⟨this poison ~*s* rats⟩ ⟨the accident ~*ed* six people⟩; *also* **:** to terminate suddenly the life processes of (as in preparing tissue for fixing and microscopic examination) **b :** to destroy as if by killing ⟨~*s* whatever core of human decency he ever had in him —Aldous Huxley⟩ ⟨an industry ~*ed* by competition⟩ ⟨an unfavorable report would . . . ~ any chance of getting a license —*Wall Street Jour.*⟩ **c :** to slaughter (as a hog) for food **:** convert a food animal into (as pork) by slaughtering **d** (1) **:** to shatter (a clay target) by hitting in skeet shooting (2) *of a ship* **:** SINK ⟨~*ed* ships and . . . wounded ships staggering away from battle —Ira Wolfert⟩ **e :** to subvert completely the plans and hopes of **:** outwit with the result of putting in a hopeless position ⟨the calamitous failure of his plan ~*ed* him more than if he had lost all his money⟩ **2 a :** to put an end to esp. abruptly **:** cause to cease **:** stop esp. with finality ⟨knew he could not ~ the evil in the world⟩ ⟨~ the enterprise by denying it the money necessary to proceed⟩ ⟨the censors ~*ed* the play after its first week⟩ ⟨~*ed* the engine and got out of the car⟩ ⟨a snack to ~ her hunger⟩ ⟨the fire-*killing* power of the chemical⟩ **b :** to get rid of **:** ELIMINATE ⟨~ foam in pulp in paper mills⟩ **c :** DEFEAT, VETO ⟨the bill was ~*ed* on the first vote⟩ ⟨asked for a transfer but his petition was ~*ed*⟩ **d** (1) **:** to take out or omit or mark for omission (something published as in a newspaper or presented as on a stage) **:** mark for deletion (something designed for publication or presentation) ⟨~*ed* a good part of the article for political reasons⟩ ⟨~*ed* the story as it was written for the late edition⟩ ⟨~*ed* the second act and substituted a new one after the second week⟩; *also* **:** to order (as set type) to be destroyed or distributed (2) **:** to stop the use of (as a stage prop or broadcast microphone) or the functioning of (as a stage light) **3 a :** to destroy the vital or active or essential quality of ⟨~ a disease with antibiotics⟩ ⟨~*ed* the pain with drugs⟩ ⟨the heat ~*ed* the yeast⟩ ⟨believed that to explain a joke is to ~ it⟩ **b :** NEUTRALIZE ⟨threw an alkali in the solution to ~ the acid⟩ **c :** to deprive of the power to germinate ⟨~ the seed⟩ **d :** to do damage or injury to (as flour) by overheating **e :** SPOIL, RUIN ⟨the addition of the wrong color totally ~*ed* the portrait⟩ **f** (1) **:** to injure or hurt severely **:** cause extreme pain to ⟨my feet are ~*ing* me⟩ (2) *chiefly Irish* **:** to knock unconscious ⟨got ~*ed* in a fight and didn't come to until morning⟩ **g :** to tire or exhaust esp. almost to the point of collapse ⟨the heat and the heavy work ~*ed* him and he had to lie down for a while⟩ ⟨no use ~*ing* ourselves getting to the train —J.P. Marquand⟩ **h :** to lessen or impede markedly ⟨the frantic maneuver ~*ed* her speed —Joseph Millard⟩ **i :** to impress a cancellation mark upon (a stamp) ⟨the stamp was ~*ed* with a blue grid —E.R.Guilford⟩ **4 a :** to make a markedly favorable impression on **:** affect strongly ⟨on her first stage appearance she ~*ed* the audience⟩ **b** *slang* **:** to impress as hilariously funny or ridiculous ⟨his jokes ~*ed me*⟩ **5 :** to occupy oneself in some convenient way merely to pass (time or a unit of time) **:** fill in (time or a unit of time) ⟨ways in which to ~ an hour until train time⟩ ⟨~ an entire afternoon over a pot of tea —Lin Yutang⟩; *also* **:** to provide or serve as a convenient occupation or distraction to help pass (time or a unit of time) ⟨reading ~*ed* a good deal of time during the trip⟩ **6 a :** to treat in such a manner as to destroy undesirable properties and so make suitable for further treatment or for a specific purpose ⟨~ soap stock by boiling with alkali⟩ ⟨~ fur by means of chemicals in preparation for dyeing⟩ **b :** to cause (molten steel) to become quiet and free from bubbling by adding a strong deoxidizing agent (as aluminum) that combines with oxygen and minimizes reaction between oxygen and carbon during solidification **c :** KNOT 5 **d :** DE-ENERGIZE ⟨~ a live electrical circuit⟩ **e :** to reduce the strength of (plaster of paris) by mixing with an excess of water **7 :** to break or burn (an object in a mortuary rite of a nonliterate culture) for the purpose of separating from the material substance the spirit which may then accompany and serve the spirit of a recently deceased person **8 :** to play (a return shot) so hard in a racket game that one's opponent cannot make return — compare SMASH **9 a :** to consume (as an alcoholic beverage) totally ⟨~*ed* his drink and held out the glass —W.L.Gresham⟩ **b :** to consume the total contents of (as a bottle of liquor) ⟨~*ed* two bottles of wine over dinner⟩ ~ *vi* **1 a :** to perform the act of killing something **:** commit murder or slaughter **b :** to make an irresistible impression ⟨dressed to ~⟩ **c :** to produce exhaustion or fatigue ⟨a ~*ing* occupation⟩ **2 :** to undergo killing or slaughter — usu. used of a food animal

syn KILL, SLAY, MURDER, ASSASSINATE, DISPATCH, EXECUTE all mean, in common, to put to death. KILL merely states the fact ⟨*kill* a rabbit⟩ ⟨a man *killed* by a twenty-foot fall⟩ ⟨the drought *killed* most of the vegetation⟩ ⟨*kill* a proposal⟩ SLAY in being a more literary word implies a force and wantonness and a generally more dramatic action ⟨the law which forbade the sinful *slaying* of a cat —Agnes Repplier⟩ ⟨his heavy tales of how Dion O'Banion was *slain* in his flower shop —Herman Kogan⟩ ⟨in 1258 the terrible conqueror Hulagu swept over Baghdad and *slew* the Caliph with 80,000 of the faithful —*Times Lit. Supp.*⟩ MURDER implies motive and usu. premeditation in a criminal human act ⟨*murder* a wealthy man for his money⟩ ⟨the fear which drove Rome to *murder* Carthage and Corinth and her own character as well —Herbert Agar⟩ ⟨that theory is *murdered* by the brutal fact that there are many among the older generation who will not believe —G.W. Johnson⟩ ASSASSINATE implies the killing of a person by stealth or treachery, esp. of a person in governmental or political power ⟨*assassinate* a monarch⟩ DISPATCH in this connection stresses speed and directness in murdering or otherwise putting to death and is usu. used intentionally to avoid the violent or odious connotations of the other terms ⟨eight to twelve otters were *dispatched* before the main herd dispersed —*Nature Mag.*⟩ ⟨one of his first tasks was to *dispatch* a sick and dying horse with a sledgehammer —*Times Lit. Supp.*⟩ ⟨then reached up, caught Wright by the coat, drew him down on to him, and at one stab *dispatched* him —*Amer. Guide Series: La.*⟩ EXECUTE is the term used for putting to death one condemned to death by a legal or quasi-legal process ⟨*execute* a man convicted of murder⟩ ⟨the mob summarily *executed* the horse thief⟩

²kill \"\ *n* -s **1 a :** KILLING 1 ⟨an animal moving in for the ~⟩ ⟨indicted a man for a ~ in the downtown section of the city⟩ **b :** an act of hunting with the intent of killing for food ⟨an animal on a ~⟩ **c** (1) **:** the death or killing (as of weeds) by weed killers, insecticides, or other lethal preparations (2) **:** the ability to kill **:** a killing force (as of a weed killer) ⟨the residual ~ of DDT⟩ **2 :** something killed: as **a :** an animal or bird shot in a hunt; *collectively* **:** the animals or birds shot in a hunt, during a season, or in a particular period of time ⟨the annual ~ of cock pheasants is estimated at 750,000 —*Amer. Guide Series: Mich.*⟩ **b :** an enemy airplane shot down or otherwise destroyed by military action while in flight ⟨a group captain's determination to get maximum ~*s* at his fighter station —*Sydney (Australia) Bull.*⟩; *also* **:** an enemy submarine or ship destroyed **c :** something to be destroyed (as by gunfire) ⟨guide missiles to the ~ —J.J. Haggerty⟩ **d :** copy that has been omitted or marked for omission from a publication (as a newspaper) **e :** a return shot in a racket game that has been driven so hard that one's opponent cannot handle it **3 :** an order or instruction to kill (as set type matter or a news story) **4 :** KILLING 3 **5 :** an animal used as bait in big-game hunting — **on the kill 1** *of an animal* **:** having the intention of killing (as for food) **2 :** intending to stop at almost nothing to achieve one's end ⟨politicians *on the kill* in an election year⟩

³kill \"\ *n* -s *often cap* [D *kil*, fr. MD *kille*; akin to East Fris. *kille* watercourse, ON *kill* small bay, arm of the sea, and perh. to OHG *kil* wedge — more at CHINE] **:** CHANNEL, CREEK, RIVER, STREAM — used chiefly in place names in Delaware and the state of New York (as Catskill mountains)

kill·able \ˈkiləbəl\ *adj* **:** capable of being killed esp. legally ⟨fit to kill⟩

¹kil·lar·ney \kəˈlärnē, -lȧn-, -ni\ *adj, usu cap* [fr. *Killarney* mountains, Ontario, Canada] **:** of, relating to, or constituting mountain-making movements near the end of the Proterozoic era — see GEOLOGIC TIME table

²killarney \"\ *or* **killarney green** *n* -s *often cap K* [fr. *Killarney*, district in County Kerry, Ireland] **:** a moderate yellowish green to green that is stronger than Gretna green

kil·las \ˈkiləs\ *n* -ES [Corn *kyllas*] *Cornwall* **:** argillaceous slate

kill back *vt* **:** to kill (a tree or shrub) at the top ⟨low temperature *killed* the tree *back*⟩ ⟨the tops of all the garden shrubs were *killed back* by the storm⟩

kill-courtesy *n, obs* **:** BOOR

kill-cow \ˈ≈,≈\ *n* **1** *now dial* **:** a man of real or fancied importance **:** PERSONAGE **2** *now dial* **:** a serious or consequential matter

kill·crop \ˈkil,kräp\ *n* [LG *kīlkrop*] **:** a voracious infant **:** a fairy changeling

kill·dee \ˈkildē\ *dial var of* KILLDEER

kill·deer *or* **kil·deer** \ˈkil,di(ə)r, -iə\ *n, pl* **killdeers** *or* **killdeer** *or* **kildeers** *or* **kildeer** [imit.] **:** a plover (*Charadrius vociferus* syn. *Oxyechus vociferus*) found throughout temperate No. America and in southern areas in migration to So. America, being about 10 inches long, grayish brown above, ferruginous in the rump, and white below and with two black bands on the breast and neck, and having a much-repeated cry that is plaintive and penetrating

kill-devil \ˈ≈,≈≈\ *n* **1** *dial* **:** West Indian rum **2 :** liquor that is cheap or poor in quality

killed *past of* KILL

kil·le·fer *also* **kil·li·fer** \ˈkiləfə(r)\ *n* -s [fr. the name *Killefer*] **:** a tractor-drawn agricultural machine that is used for deep tillage and loosening of the subsoil and consists essentially of one or more wheel-mounted pointed horizontal knives or chisels

kill·er \ˈkilə(r)\ *n* -s *often attrib* [¹*kill* + *-er*] **1 :** one that kills: **a :** MURDERER; *esp* **:** a homicidal criminal or maniac **b :** SLAUGHTERER; *also* **:** one who buys animals for slaughter ⟨~*s* took a big share of the choice of low prime yearlings —*Chicago Daily Drovers Jour.*⟩ **c :** an effective bait in fishing **d :** something that has a forceful and usu. violent impact ⟨a backhand stroke that was a ~⟩ ⟨his punch was a ~⟩ **e** *slang* **:** one who gives an admirable or irresistible personal or sartorial impression ⟨she was no ~ on looks —Garson Kanin⟩ **2 :** an animal to be killed for food or other use **3** *or* **killer whale :** a fierce carnivorous gregarious whale (*Orcinus orca* syn. *Orca orca*) 20 to 30 feet long that is black with yellowish white areas on sides and underparts, has a high dorsal fin, powerful tail, and sharp strong teeth, and preys on large fishes, seals, and even in groups on the larger whales **4 :** a postal canceling stamp; *also* **:** a cancellation mark on a postage stamp

killer 4

killer bar *n* **:** a bar or line on a postmarking stamp or in the postmark it produces

killer boat *also* **killer ship** *n* **:** one of the small fast boats accompanying a factory ship in whaling and responsible for the pursuit and capture of a whale

killer-diller \ˌkilə(r)ˈdilə(r)\ *n* -s [redupl. of *killer*] *slang* **:** something highly and usu. factitiously sensational of its kind ⟨plot hocus-pocus and *killer-diller* battles between good and evil —Jean Garrigue⟩ ⟨*killer-diller* love scenes —C.J.Rolo⟩

killer plant *n* **:** an East African plant (*Adenia sinensis*) of the family Passifloraceae that contains a highly poisonous alkaloid — called also *modecca flower*

kil·lick \ˈkilik\ *also* **kel·leg** \ˈkeləg\ *or* **kel·lock** \ˈkelək\ *or* **kil·lock** \ˈkilək\ *n* -s [origin unknown] **1 :** ANCHOR; *esp* **:** a small anchor **2 :** a jury anchor formed by a stone usu. bound within sticks of wood

killickinnic *or* **killikinick** *or* **killickinnick** *var of* KINNIKINNICK

kil·lie *also* **kil·ly** \ˈkilē\ *or* **kel·ly** *or* **kel·lie** \ˈkelē\ *n, pl* **killies** *or* **kellies** [³*kill* + *-ie, -y*] **:** KILLIFISH

kil·li·fish \ˈkilē,fish, -li,-\ *n* [*killie* + *fish*] **1 :** any of numerous small oviparous fishes of the family Cyprinodontidae which are usu. striped or barred with black, which are much used as bait and in mosquito control, and some of which live equally well in fresh and brackish water or even in the sea — see GUDGEON, MAYFISH, MUMMICHOG **2 :** TOPMINNOW 1

killig *var of* KILHIG

¹kill·ing \ˈkiliŋ, -lēŋ\ *n* -s [ME, fr. gerund of *killen* to strike, kill — more at KILL] **1 :** the act of one that kills; *esp* **:** MURDER, HOMICIDE **2 :** KILL 2a **3 :** a sudden notable success esp. in stock speculation or business ⟨a ~ he made in railway securities —Robert Shaplen⟩

²killing \"\ *adj* [fr. pres. part. of ¹*kill*] **1 :** having the effect of killing: as **a :** producing death **:** FATAL, DEADLY ⟨a ~ disease⟩ ⟨a ~ drink⟩ **b :** having a marked deleterious or painful effect or impact extremely difficult to endure **:** ⟨the strain of concentration was ~, so he gave up⟩; *also* **:** calling for great strength, stamina, or endurance ⟨a ~ pace⟩ **c :** having an irresistible and notable effect ⟨a ~ humor⟩ ⟨a ~ dress⟩ **2 :** arousing the desire to kill ⟨as ~ a hatred between them as though they were two jungle beasts —Jean Stafford⟩

killing bottle *n* **:** a bottle containing a poisonous vapor (as cyanide) for killing insects to be preserved as specimens

killing frost *n* **:** a frost low enough in temperature to kill most exposed garden vegetation and fruit buds

kill·ing·ly *adv* **:** in a killing manner

kil·lin·ite \ˈkilə,nīt\ *n* -s [*Killiney*, bay and village, County Dublin, Ireland + E *-ite*] **:** a mineral consisting of a variety of pinite

killjoy \ˈ≈,≈\ *n* [¹*kill* + *joy*] **:** one that inspires gloom or counteracts joy or high spirits **:** one that tends to pessimism or a depressing solemnness esp. among people that are happy or optimistic **:** one that dispirits ⟨professional ~*s* whose chief fear it is that people . . . might get some fun out of life —T.P.Whitney⟩

kill-kid \ˈ≈,≈\ *n* [¹*kill* + *kid* (young goat); fr. the poisonous foliage] **:** SHEEP LAUREL

kill off *vt* **1 :** to destroy in large numbers or totally ⟨the flood of hunters *killed* the buffalo *off* rapidly until only a few were left⟩ ⟨the flowers were *killed off* by the first frost⟩ ⟨the lack of enthusiasm *killed* the project *off* quickly⟩ **2 :** to get rid of **:** ELIMINATE ⟨the low prices they asked *killed* their competition *off*⟩

kil·lo·gie \kəˈlōgi\ *n* -s [perh. irreg. fr. Sc *kill* kiln, fr. ME, alter. of *kilne* — more at KILN] *chiefly Scot* **:** the sheltered space before a kiln fire

kill out *vt* **:** to complete the curing of (tobacco) by exposing to high temperature to dry out the stem and stop further chemical change

kills *pres 3d sing of* KILL, *pl of* KILL

kill-time \ˈ≈,≈\ *n* **:** an occupation that serves to kill time

kill-wart \ˈ≈,≈\ *or* **killwort** \ˈ≈,≈\ *n* [*kill-wart* fr. ¹*kill* + *wart*; fr. its use to remove warts; *killwort* by folk etymology fr. *kill-wart*] **:** CELANDINE 1

killy fish *n* **:** KILLIFISH

kil·ly hawk \ˈkilē-\ *n* [*killy* of imit. origin] **:** SPARROW HAWK 2

kil·mar·nock willow \(ˈ)kil¦märnək-\ *n, usu cap K* [fr. *Kilmarnock*, burgh in Ayr county, Scotland] **:** a small Old World willow that is a variety (*Salix caprea pendula*) of the great sallow with crooked pendulous branches

¹kiln \ˈkil(n)\ *n* -s *often attrib* [ME *kilne*, fr. OE *cyln, cylen*, fr. L *culina* kitchen, fr. *coquere* to cook — more at COOK] **:** an oven, furnace, or heated enclosure used for processing a substance by burning, firing, or drying: as **a :** LIMEKILN **b :** BRICKKILN **c :** an oven with a heat-resistant lining used to fire ceramics **d :** a room or shed through which warm air is circulated for the removal of moisture (as from grain, lumber, or tobacco) — compare KILN EVAPORATOR

²kiln \"\ *vt* -ED/-ING/-S **:** to burn, fire, or dry in a kiln

kiln-dried \ˈ≈¦≈\ *adj* **:** dried or cured in a kiln ⟨*kiln-dried* lumber⟩

kiln-dry \ˈ≈,≈\ *vt* **:** to dry (wood) in a kiln **:** season artificially

kiln evaporator *n* **:** a room with a slatted floor through which heat is circulated for drying fruit

kilneye \ˈ≈,≈\ *or* **kilnhole** \ˈ≈,≈\ *n* **:** the mouth of a kiln; *specif* **:** an opening in a limekiln for removal of the lime

kiln·man \ˈ≈mən\ *n, pl* **kilnmen :** one who loads or fires a kiln or controls the drying or baking done therein

kiln-run \ˈ≈,≈\ *adj* **:** as taken from the kiln **:** not sorted as to quality ⟨*kiln-run* brick⟩

kiln scum *n* **:** WHITEWASH 3

¹ki·lo \ˈkē(,)lō, ˈki(-\ *n* -s **1 a** [by shortening] **:** KILOGRAM **b :** KILOWARE **2** [by shortening] **:** KILOMETER

²kilo \"\ *usu cap* — a communications code word for the letter *k*

kilo- *comb form* [F, modif. of Gk *chilioi* — more at MILE] **:** thousand — chiefly in names of units in the metric system ⟨*kilogauss*⟩ ⟨*kilojoule*⟩

kilo·calorie \ˈkilō+,-\ *n* [ISV *kilo-* + *calorie*] **:** CALORIE b(1)

kilo·cy·cle \ˈkilə,sīkəl\ *n* [ISV *kilo-* + *cycle*] **:** one thousand cycles; *esp* **:** one thousand cycles per second — used as a unit of radio frequency ⟨broadcasting on a frequency of 1250 ~*s*⟩; abbr. *kc*

kilo·gram *or* **kilo·gramme** \-,gram, -raa(ə)m\ *n* [F *kilogramme*, fr. *kilo-* + *gramme* gram — more at GRAM] **1 :** the basic metric unit of mass and weight equal to the mass of a platinum-iridium cylinder kept at the International Bureau of Weights and Measures near Paris and nearly equal to 1000 cubic centimeters of water at the temperature of its maximum density — see METRIC SYSTEM table; abbr. *kg* **2 :** a unit of force equal to the weight of a kilogram under standard gravity

kilogram calorie *n* **:** CALORIE b(1)

kilogram-meter \ˈ≈≈,≈¦≈≈\ *n* **:** the mks gravitational unit of work and energy equal to the work done by a kilogram force acting through a distance of one meter in the direction of the force **:** about 7.235 foot-pounds

kilo·hertz \ˈkilə +,-\ *n* [ISV *kilo-* + *hertz*] **:** a unit of frequency equal to one thousand hertz — abbr. *kHz*

kilo·liter \ˈkilə+,-\ *n* [F *kilolitre*, fr. *kilo-* + *litre* liter — more at LITER] **:** a metric unit of capacity equal to 1000 liters — see METRIC SYSTEM table; abbr. *kl*

kilome·ter \÷kəˈläməd·ə(r), \tə- *also* ˈkilə,mē\ *n* [F *kilomètre*, fr. *kilo-* + *mètre* meter — more at METER] **:** a metric unit of length equal to 1000 meters — see METRIC SYSTEM table; abbr. *km*

kilo·parsec \ˈkilə+\ *n* **:** one thousand parsecs

kilo·ton \ˈkilə,tən\ *n* [*kilo-* + *ton*] **1 :** one thousand tons **2 :** an explosive force equivalent to that of one thousand tons of TNT — used esp. in reference to an atom or hydrogen bomb — abbr. *kt*

kil·o·var \-,vär\ *n* -s [*kilovolt* + *ampere* + *reactive*] **:** the part of a kilovolt-ampere contributed by reactance

kilo·volt \ˈkilə,vōlt\ *n* [ISV *kilo-* + *volt*] **:** a unit of electromotive force equal to one thousand volts — abbr. *kv*

kilo·volt·age \-tij\ *n* **:** potential difference expressed in kilovolts

kilovolt-ampere \ˈ≈≈,≈¦≈,≈\ *n* **:** a unit of apparent power in an electric circuit equal to 1000 volt-amperes

kilo·ware \ˈkilə+,-\ *n* [*kilo* + *ware*] **1 :** packaged mixtures of unsorted postage stamps accumulated esp. by European post offices largely from parcel tags and sold by the kilogram **2 :** a package of unsorted stamps usu. sealed by the government to indicate that the mixture is as orig. assembled by the post office

kilo·watt \ˈkilə,wät, *usu* -äd.+V\ *n* [ISV *kilo-* + *watt*] **:** a unit of power equal to 1000 watts or about 1.34 horsepower — abbr. *kw*

kilowatt-hour \ˈ≈≈,≈¦≈\ *n* **:** a unit of work or energy equal to that expended in one hour at a steady rate of one kilowatt or to 3.6×10⁶ joules

kilp \ˈkilp\ *dial Eng var of* KELP

kil·roy \ˈkil,rȯi\ *n* -s *usu cap* [after *Kilroy*, mythical soldier of World War II whose name was inscribed in unlikely places all over the world by Amer. soldiers] **:** an inveterate traveler ⟨like the roamers *Kilroy* and Ulysses —Peter Viereck⟩; *esp* **:** a transient soldier ⟨of all the *Kilroys* of history who have passed through here . . . it was Napoleon who best summed up the strategic importance of Malta —J.P.O'Donnell⟩

¹kilt \ˈkilt\ *vb* -ED/-ING/-S [ME *kilten*, of Scand origin; akin to Dan *kilte* (*op*) to gather up (as a skirt), Sw dial. *kilta* (*sej*) to gather up one's skirts, ON *kjalta* fold made by a gathered skirt, OSw *kilta* lap, and perh. to Goth *kilthei* womb — more at CHILD] *vt* **1** *now chiefly dial* **:** to gather up or tuck in (as a skirt) for protection or freedom of action **2** *archaic* **:** to truss up **:** HANG ⟨brought the country to order by ~*ing* thieves and banditti with strings —Sir Walter Scott⟩ **3 :** to equip with a kilt ⟨insists that nominees prove Scottish relationship or extraction, or they don't get ~*ed* —*Sat. Eve. Post*⟩ ~ *vi* **:** to move nimbly

²kilt \"\ *n* -s **1 :** a pleated wraparound skirt usu. of tartan reaching from the waist to the knees worn by men and boys in Scotland and esp. by Scottish regiments in the British armies **2 :** something that resembles a Scottish kilt; *esp* **:** a short plaid skirt for women or girls

³kilt *chiefly dial past of* KILL

¹kilt·ed \ˈkiltəd\ *adj* [fr. past part. of ¹*kilt*] **1 :** gathered in or tucked up ⟨clam diggers with ~ skirts⟩ **2 :** gathered in vertical pleats **:** KNIFE-PLEATED ⟨yoke of ~ nylon⟩

²kilted \"\ *adj* [²*kilt* + *-ed*] **:** wearing a kilt ⟨a tall ~ Highlander⟩ ⟨~ regiment⟩

kil·ter \'kiltə(r)\ *also* **kel·ter** \'kel-\ *n* -s [origin unknown] **1 a :** good working condition : ORDER, ADJUSTMENT — usu. used in the phrase *out of kilter* ⟨the car wouldn't go because the engine was out of ~⟩ ⟨his nerves are out of ~ —James Hilton⟩ **b :** BALANCE, ALIGNMENT ⟨unexpected expenses threw the budget out of ~⟩ ⟨a truck rammed the house and pushed it out of ~⟩ **2 :** ⁴SKEET

kilt·ie \'kiltē, -ti\ *n* -s [²*kilt* + -*ie*] **1** *or* **kilty** \"\ -ES *often cap* : one who wears a kilt; *specif* : a member of a Highland regiment **2 a :** a shoe with a long slashed tongue that folds over the instep to cover the lacing **b :** SHAWL TONGUE

kiltie 2a

kim·ber·ley \'kimbə(r)lē\ *n* -s *often cap* [fr. *Kimberley*, town in northern Cape Province, Union of So. Africa] : a commercial grade of white diamond ranking below Wesselton

kimberley horse disease *n, usu cap K* [fr. *Kimberley*, district of Western Australia] : WALKABOUT DISEASE

kim·ber·lin \'kimbələn\ *n* -s [prob. alter. of ME *kymeling, comling* — more at COMELING] *dial Eng* : NEWCOMER, STRANGER

kim·ber·lite \'kimbə(r),līt\ *n* -s [*Kimberley*, Union of So. Africa + E -*ite*] : an agglomerate biotite-peridotite that occurs in pipes in southern Africa and less extensively in Kentucky and that is weathered yellow at the surface, is blue farther down, and often contains diamonds — called also *blue earth, blue ground, blue stuff*

kim·bun·du \kim'bün(,)dü\ *n, usu cap* : a Bantu language of northern Angola — called also *Mbundu*

kim·chi *also* **kim·ch'i** *or* **kim·chee** \'kimchē\ *n* -s [Korean] : a vegetable pickle seasoned with garlic, red pepper, and ginger that is the national dish of Korea

kim·mer \'kimər\ *var of* CUMMER

kim·me·ri·an \kə'mirēən, -mēr-\ *usu cap, var of* CIMMERIAN

kim·nel \'kimnᵊl\ *n* -s [ME *kymelyn, kymnelle*, prob. fr. OE *cumb*, a liquid measure — more at COOMB] *now dial Eng* : a large wooden tub for brewing, kneading, and salting meat

ki·mo·no \kə'mōnə *sometimes* -ō(,)nō\ *or* **ki·mo·na** \-ōnə\ *n* -s [Jap *kimono* clothes] **1 :** a loose wraparound robe with wide sleeves and a broad sash traditionally worn by Japanese men and women ⟨a neat waiting maid in striped ~ —*Outlook*⟩ **2 :** a loose dressing gown copied from the Japanese robe and worn chiefly by women and babies — **ki·mo·noed** \-nəd,-nōd\ *or* **ki·mo·naed** \-nəd\ *adj*

kimono sleeve *n* : a sleeve cut in one piece with the bodice

kim·ri \'kimrē\ *adj* [Ar] : of, relating to, or constituting the first of four recognized stages in the ripening of a date in which it makes its most rapid growth and remains green — compare KHALAL, RUTAB, TAMAR

kimono 2

kim·squit \'kimzkwət, -im(p)skw-\ *n, pl* **kimsquit** *or* **kimsquits** *usu cap* **1 :** a Bellacoola people of Dean Inlet on the Kimsquit river, British Columbia **2 :** a member of the Kimsquit people

¹**kin** \'kin\ *n, pl* **kin** *see sense 1a* [ME, fr. OE *cyn*; akin to OHG *kind* child, *chunni* family, race, ON *kyn*, Goth *kuni* family, race, L *genus* kind, race, *gignere* to beget, Gk *genea* birth, race, family, *genos* race, kin, kind, *gignesthai* to be born, Skt *janati* he begets, *jana* person] **1 a** *pl* **kins :** a group of persons of common ancestry : CLAN, STOCK ⟨chiefs of the ~s —P.A.Sorokin⟩ **b** *archaic* : LINEAGE, EXTRACTION, BIRTH ⟨some one perhaps of gentle ~ —Edmund Spenser⟩ **2 a :** one's immediate family : RELATIVES, KINDRED ⟨an outcast among . . . the ~ of his father —Ruth Benedict⟩ **b :** a blood relation : KINSMAN ⟨he wasn't any ~ to you —Jean Stafford⟩ — compare CONSANGUINITY **3** *obs* : the quality or state of being related : KINSHIP ⟨without a crime, except his ~ to me —John Dryden⟩ **4 a :** a related group : similar kind : ILK ⟨the positivists and their ~ —W.V.Quine⟩ **b :** one having community of interest or close affinity with another ⟨abstraction and generalization have always been recognized as close ~ —John Dewey⟩ — **of kin :** closely related : AKIN ⟨he was *of kin* to the . . . prizefighter —*Times Lit. Supp.*⟩

²**kin** \"\ *adj* : of the same nature or family : having affinity : KINDRED, RELATED ⟨Germany . . . is the ~ land of these people of Pennsylvania —G.P.Musselman⟩

³**kin** \'kēn\ *chiefly Scot var of* KIND

⁴**kin** \'kin\ *n* -s [ME *kyne, kynne*, alter. of *chin, chine* crack, fissure, chasm — more at CHINE] *dial Eng* : CRACK, CREVICE; *specif* : a chap in the skin

⁵**kin** \'kin\ *n, pl* **kin** [Jap] : CATTY

⁶**kin** \"\ *n* -s [Chin (Pek) *ch'in²*] : an ancient Chinese musical instrument resembling a zither and having from 5 to 25 silk strings — compare KOTO

⁷**kin** \'jin\ *n* -s *usu cap* [Chin (Pek) *Chin¹*] **1 :** a Tatar people founding an 11th century dynasty in China and being ancestral to the Manchus **2 :** a member of the Kin people

kin- *or* **kine-** *or* **kino-** *or* **cin-** *or* **cino-** *comb form* [Gk *kinēma* motion — more at CINEMATOGRAPH] : motion : action ⟨*kinesthesia*⟩ ⟨*kinoplasm*⟩ ⟨*kineplasty*⟩

-kin \kən\ *also* **-kins** \-nz\ *n suffix, pl* **-kins** [-*kin* fr. ME, fr. MD -*kin, -ken, -kijn*; akin to OS -*kîn*, dim. suffix, OHG -*chīn*; -*kins* fr. ME, suffix used to form surnames (as *Jenkins*), fr. -*kin* + -*s*, patronymic suffix (as in *Roberts*)] : little ⟨cat*kin*⟩ ⟨baby*kins*⟩

kinaesthesia *or* **kinaesthesis** *var of* KINESTHESIA

ki·nah *also* **qi·nah** \kē'nä\ *n, pl* **ki·noth** *or* **ki·not** *also* **qi·noth** *or* **qi·not** \-nōt(h)\ [Heb *qīnāh* dirge, lamentation] **1 :** a Hebrew elegy chanted traditionally on the Ninth of Ab **2 :** a dirge or lament esp. as sung by Jewish professional mourning women

kinah meter *n* : a Hebrew poetic meter typically having the line divided into two stichs with three stresses in the first stich and two stresses in the second

ki·nase \'kī,nās, 'ki,-\ *n* -s [ISV *kinetic* + -*ase*; orig. formed in G] **1 :** a substance (as enterokinase) that converts a zymogen into an enzyme — compare COENZYME **2 :** any of various enzymes (as hexokinases) that promote phosphorylation processes ⟨adenylic ~ or myosine catalyzes the transfer of phosphate groups among the adenosine phosphates⟩ — compare PHOSPHORYLASE

kin·car·dine·shire \kən'kärdᵊn,shi(ə)r, kiŋ'-, -,shər\ *or* **kincardine** *adj, usu cap* [fr. *Kincardineshire* or *Kincardine* county, Scotland] : of or from the county of Kincardine, Scotland : of the kind or style prevalent in Kincardine

kinch \'kinch\ *n* -ES [alter. of ³*kink*] *chiefly Scot* : a noose or loop in a rope

kin·chin \'kinchən\ *n* -s [G *kindchen*, dim. of *kind* child, fr. OHG — more at KIN] *slang* : CHILD ⟨~s . . . sent on errands by their mothers —Charles Dickens⟩

kin·cob *also* **kin·kob** *or* **kin·khab** \'kin,käb, -iŋ,-\ *n* -s [Hindi *kimkhāb, kamkhwāb*, fr. Per] : an Indian brocade usu. of gold or silver or both

¹**kind** \'kīnd\ *n* -s [ME *kind, kinde*, fr. OE *cynd, gecynd*; akin to OE *cyn* kin — more at KIN] **1 a** *archaic* : a universal order or inherent tendency in nature ⟨God holds us by laws of ~ —Nathaniel Fairfax⟩ ⟨lovers wanting sight shall follow ~ —Thomas Watson †1592⟩; *specif* : natural disposition **b :** a natural grouping without taxonomic connotations : SPECIES ⟨people . . . cut off by the desert or the frozen north from communication with their ~ —Ellen Glasgow⟩ ⟨the ways that mud turtles had found best for their ~ —J.W.Krutch⟩ ⟨search for the real essences of natural ~s —Stuart Hampshire⟩ **c** *archaic* : FAMILY, LINEAGE ⟨of a gentle ~ and noble stock —Shak.⟩ **d** *archaic* : a related grouping : SECT ⟨poets ever were a careless ~ —William Collins †1759⟩ **2 a** *archaic* : STYLE, ASPECT, MANNER, WISE ⟨mirthful . . . but in a stately ~ —Alfred Tennyson⟩ ⟨in no ~ desirous that his majesty should be under any obligation —Thomas Hale⟩ **b** *South & Midland* : WAY — used with superlative ⟨he's heartbroken the worst ~ over that little gal —*Amer. Guide Series: Tenn.*⟩ ⟨he's goin' to coax his father the hardest ~ —W.D.Howells⟩ **3 a** *obs* : SEX ⟨ask . . . what inquest made her dissemble her disguised ~ —Edmund Spenser⟩ **b** *archaic* : innate character : INSTINCT ⟨though fickle she prove, a woman has't by ~ —Robert Burns⟩ **c :** fundamental nature or quality : ESSENCE ⟨problems of social science differ from problems of individual behavior in degree . . . not in ~ —Edward Sapir⟩ **4 a :** a group united by common traits or interests : CATEGORY, CLASS ⟨examples of ~s of steel are: crucible, Bessemer, basic open-hearth —S.E.Rusinoff⟩ ⟨colonial houses . . . perfect of their ~ —R.W.Hatch⟩ ⟨there are ~s of madness which are really forms of inspiration —R.M.Weaver⟩ ⟨the ~ is satire —*Times Lit. Supp.*⟩ ⟨turned to Washington . . . to find companionship among his own ~ —Allen Johnson⟩ ⟨the people I have in mind are the ~ who assume most of the responsibility for unpaid . . . civic duties —J.W.Hoffman⟩ — sometimes used as a zero plural with a preceding *these* or *those* and a following *of* ⟨these ~ of sensational statements —Sir Winston Churchill⟩ **b** (1) **:** a specific variety : TYPE, BRAND ⟨one ~ of uniform for all . . . troops —L.H. Smith⟩ ⟨the ~ of analysis followed —W.D.Preston⟩ ⟨what ~ of car do you drive⟩ — often used in the phrase *kind of a* ⟨some ~ of a house is the first requirement of civilized man —L.F.Salzman⟩ ⟨what ~ of an organization —H.E.Gaston⟩ ⟨consider the ~ of a community in which they have faith —Eric Goldman⟩ ⟨that ~ of a girl —Hamilton Basso⟩ (2) **:** a recognized or desirable variety ⟨novel which won all ~s of praise —*Saturday Rev.*⟩ ⟨can be more ~s of a fool in a short time —W.C.Tuttle⟩ ⟨didn't figure that was any ~ of a life —H.S.Chippendale⟩ **c :** a doubtful or barely admissible member of a specified category — used with *of* and the indefinite article ⟨gave a ~ of snort —John Dos Passos⟩ ⟨the whole universe . . . turned a ~ of gray —H.A.Chippendale⟩ ⟨it's ~ of a vacation —W.H.Whyte⟩ ⟨~ of a blend of humor and pathos⟩ **d :** the same rank — used of playing cards ⟨four of a ~⟩ **5** *Christian relig* : either of the elements bread or wine used in the Eucharist ⟨Communion is given in one ~ only in Germany —C.B.Moss⟩ **6 a :** goods or commodities as distinguished from money ⟨economic measures providing aid in ~ rather than in cash —Frank Lorimer⟩ **b :** the equivalent of what has been offered or received ⟨reply in ~⟩ ⟨it hadn't seemed such a terrible thing to hurt him until she was paid back in ~ —William Heuman⟩ **7 :** AMOUNT — used in the phrase *that kind of money* ⟨he's got to be good to pull down that ~ of money —Richard Llewellyn⟩ **syn** see TYPE

²**kind** \"\ *adj* -ER/-EST [ME *kinde, kind*, fr. OE *gecynde*, fr. *cynd, gecynd*, n.] **1** *obs* : consistent with nature : NATURAL, FITTING ⟨is but ~ for a cock's head to breed a comb —Stephen Gosson⟩ **2** *now dial* : of a good variety or in thriving condition — used of crops ⟨graft . . . ~ fruits upon thorns —John Hales⟩ ⟨the cultivation having been perfect, the barley crop will be ~ —S.C.Scrivener⟩ **3** *now chiefly dial* **a :** of an affectionate nature : FOND, INTIMATE ⟨reserve your ~ looks and language for private hours —Jonathan Swift⟩ **b :** GRATEFUL ⟨should declare himself . . . ~ for all those benefits —*Homilies*⟩ **4 a :** of a sympathetic nature : FRIENDLY, OBLIGING ⟨was always ~ to the boy —A. Conan Doyle⟩ ⟨everyone is so friendly and ~ —A.J.McConnell⟩ **b :** of a forbearing nature : governed by consideration and compassion : GENTLE, LENIENT ⟨naturally you are ~ to pets —*Boy Scout Handbook*⟩ ⟨generally was ~ in his judgment of me —O.W.Holmes †1935⟩ **c :** arising from or characterized by sympathy or forbearance ⟨a ~ act⟩ **5** *now chiefly dial* **a :** of a pleasant nature : AGREEABLE ⟨the soft green . . . countryside is so ~ to your eyes —Richard Joseph⟩ **b :** soft and yielding to the touch ⟨the wool was . . . ~ to handle —*Westralian Farmers Co-op. Gazette*⟩

syn KIND, KINDLY, BENIGN, and BENIGNANT can mean, in common, having or manifesting a nature that is gentle, considerate, and inclined to benevolent or beneficent actions. KIND and KINDLY, often interchangeable, both suggest gentleness, humaneness, and a sympathetic interest in the welfare of others, KIND applying more often to the disposition to sympathy and helpfulness, KINDLY stressing more the expression of a sympathetic, helpful nature, mood, or impulse ⟨a *kind* person with a *kindly* interest in the problems of others⟩ ⟨a person *kind* to animals⟩ ⟨the *kindly* attentions of an elderly stranger⟩ ⟨the critics were by no means *kind* to the play —J.K.Newnham⟩ ⟨felt *kindly* and protective and superior —Christopher Isherwood⟩ BENIGN and BENIGNANT stress mildness and mercifulness and apply more often to the acts, utterances, or policies, gracious or patronizing, of a superior rather than an equal ⟨a *benign* master⟩ ⟨the *benign* rule of a benevolent despot⟩ ⟨the transformation of a *benign* personality into a belligerent one —Lewis Mumford⟩ ⟨looked up into his *benignant* face, as if she had come thither for his pardon and paternal affection —Nathaniel Hawthorne⟩ ⟨heaven was divinely merciful, infinitely *benignant*. It spared him, pardoned his weakness —Virginia Woolf⟩

³**kind** \"\ *adv, now dial* : KINDLY ⟨how ~ he puts it —Charles Dickens⟩

⁴**kind** *vt* -ED/-ING/-S [prob. fr. ¹*kind*] *obs* : BEGET

kind *abbr* kindergarten

kin·dal \'kindᵊl\ *n* -s [native name in India] **1 :** an Indian tree (*Terminalia paniculata*) with hard gray or grayish-brown wood that resembles black walnut **2 :** the wood of the kindal tree

kinder *comparative of* KIND

kin·der·be·weijs *also* **kin·der·be·wys** \,kində(r)bə'vīs\ *n* -ES [D *kinderbewijs*, fr. *kinder* (pl. of *kind* child) + *bewijs* proof] *Roman Dutch law* : a deed by a surviving spouse certifying and securing the amounts due to minor children out of the estate of a deceased

¹**kin·der·gar·ten** *R* 'kində(r),gär|tᵊn, |dᵊn, -*R* -də,gä|\ *n* -s [G, fr. *kinder* (pl. of *kind* child) + *garten* garden] **1 :** a school or division of a school below the first grade usu. serving pupils of the 4 to 6 age group and fostering their natural growth and social development through constructive play with blocks, clay, crayons and by group games, songs, and exercise **2 :** the room or building in which a kindergarten is housed

²**kindergarten** \"\ *adj* **1 :** of or relating to a kindergarten ⟨teaching at the ~ level⟩ **2 :** of or relating to an elementary level or initial phase ⟨a ~ lecture on the meaning of nationhood —Robert Trumbull⟩ ⟨have as yet only reached the ~ stage in learning how to manage our complex economic problems —A.H.Hansen⟩

kin·der·gart·ner *also* **kin·der·gar·ten·er** \|t(ᵊ)nə(r), |d(ᵊ)n-\ *n* -s [G *kindergärtner*, fr. *kindergarten* + -*er*] **1 :** a child attending kindergarten or of kindergarten age ⟨~s and first graders⟩ ⟨pajamas and robes for toddlers and ~s —*Parents Mag.*⟩ **2 :** a teacher at the kindergarten level ⟨~, experienced, summer camp —*N.Y.Times*⟩

kin·der·hook \'kində(r),hük\ *or* **kin·der·hook·ian** \¦≈≈-'hükēən\ *adj, usu cap* [fr. *Kinderhook*, Pike county, Ill.] : of or relating to the lowest formational division of the Mississippian series in the Mississippi valley or the epoch of its deposition — see GEOLOGIC TIME table

kindest *superlative of* KIND

kindhearted \'≈¦≈≈\ *adj* : having a sympathetic nature : HUMANE, COMPASSIONATE ⟨a ~ landlord — ever anxious to ameliorate the condition of the poor —Anthony Trollope⟩ — **kind·heart·ed·ly** *adv*

kind·heart·ed·ness *n* -ES : the quality or state of being kindhearted

¹**kin·dle** \'kindᵊl, *rapid* -nᵊl\ *vb* **kindled**; **kindled**; **kindling** \-(ᵊ)liŋ\ **kindles** [ME *kindlen*, fr. ON *kynda* to kindle + ME -*len* -le; akin to MHG *künten, künden* to kindle, OHG *cuntesal* fire] *vt* **1 :** to start (a fire) burning : LIGHT, IGNITE ⟨~ a fire with a match⟩ **2 a :** to awaken or intensify to awareness ⟨armies cannot be raised . . . unless the rage of the people is first *kindled* by lies and name-calling —Kenneth Roberts⟩ ⟨these two delightful . . . handbooks should ~ a child's imagination —Muna Lee⟩ **b :** to stir up : AROUSE, INSPIRE ⟨his enthusiasm ~s his comrades⟩ ⟨hopes that . . . *kindled* close to half of France —Janet Flanner⟩ **c :** to bring into being : INSTITUTE ⟨the Good Neighbor policy . . . which was *kindled* by Sumner Welles —A.C.Wilgus⟩ **3 :** to cause to glow : ILLUMINATE ⟨animation *kindling* his pale face —A.J.Cronin⟩ ⟨*kindling* with color the pale lichens —Thomas Vance⟩ ~ *vi* **1 a :** to start a fire ⟨some fire to ~ with —Stith Thompson⟩ **b :** to begin to burn : catch fire ⟨dry leaves ~ at the touch of flame⟩ **2 a :** to flare up : gather intensity ⟨their mutual resentment again *kindled* —Edward Gibbon⟩ **b :** to grow warm or animated : become stirred emotionally ⟨no boy will fail to ~ to the struggles of his California youth —Ethna Sheehan⟩ **3 :** to sparkle or become illuminated as if with fire : GLOW ⟨light *kindled* in the liquor —Frances G. Patton⟩ ⟨could see her eyes widen, ~ and flinch —John Fountain⟩

²**kindle** \"\ *n* -s [ME, prob. fr. *kinde, kind*, n., kind + -*le* — more at KIND] *now dial* : the young of an animal : LITTER ⟨a ~ of kittens⟩ — **in kindle :** PREGNANT — used chiefly of a rabbit

³**kindle** \"\ *vb* **kindled**; **kindled**; **kindling**; **kindles** [ME *kindlen*, prob. fr. *kindle*, n.] *vt* : to give birth to : BEAR ⟨one of our does *kindled* a single rabbit —*Amer. Small Stock Farmer*⟩ ~ *vi* : to bring forth young ⟨bred one of the Angora does to ~ about the time I would be making the move —*Standard Rabbit Jour.*⟩ — now used chiefly of a rabbit

kindle-coal *or* **kindle-fire** *n* [¹*kindle*] *obs* : one that stirs up strife ⟨Satan is the great *kindle-coal* —William Gurnall⟩

kin·dler \'kind(ᵊ)lə(r), *rapid* -n(ᵊ)l-\ *n* -s [ME, fr. *kindlen* + -*er*] **1 :** one that kindles **2 :** KINDLING 2

kind·less \'kīndləs, *rapid* -nl-\ *adj* [¹*kind* + -*less*] *obs* : INHUMAN ⟨remorseless, treacherous, lecherous, ~ villain —Shak.⟩ **2 :** DISAGREEABLE, UNSYMPATHETIC, UNCONGENIAL ⟨no thought less kindly — toward even thee that are ~ —A.C. Swinburne⟩ ⟨the unreturned of ~ land and sea —Walter de la Mare⟩ — **kind·less·ly** *adv*

kind·li·ness \'kīndlēnəs, -lin-, *rapid* -nl-\ *n* -ES [ME *kindlinesse*, fr. *kindly* + -*nesse* -ness] **1 :** the quality or state of being kindly : FRIENDLINESS, BENEVOLENCE **2 :** the quality or state of being agreeable or manageable : PLEASANTNESS, TRACTABILITY ⟨~ of climate⟩ ⟨~ of feel . . . makes esparto papers preeminent for their printing qualities —F.H.Norris⟩ ⟨steel of the future will be very different in ~ of working —William Metcalf⟩

¹**kin·dling** \'kindliŋ, -lēn, *rapid* -nl-\ *n* -s [ME, fr. gerund of *kindlen* to kindle (ignite) — more at ¹KINDLE] **1 a :** an act or instance of igniting ⟨the ~ of a bonfire⟩ **b :** an act or instance of exciting or causing to glow ⟨a ~ of enthusiasm⟩ ⟨looking at the sunset, watching the ~ of the clouds —Susan Ertz⟩ **2 :** easily combustible material of a convenient size for starting a fire ⟨crumpled paper makes good ~ for the stove⟩ ⟨a famous old covered bridge that was carried away and crushed to ~ . . . in the spring flood —*Amer. Guide Series: Conn.*⟩

²**kindling** \"\ *n* -s [ME, fr. gerund of *kindlen* (to give birth) — more at ³KINDLE] : an act of giving birth — used chiefly of a rabbit

kindling temperature *or* **kindling point** *n* : IGNITION TEMPERATURE

kindling wood *n* : wood of a size or kind to kindle readily — called also *fat pine, lightwood, pine, pitch pine, rich-pine*

¹**kind·ly** \'kīndlē, -li, *rapid* -nl-\ *adj* -ER/-EST [ME, fr. OE *cyndelic, gecyndelic*, fr. *cynd, gecynd* kind + -*līc* -ly — more at KIND] **1 a** *obs* : consistent with nature : NATURAL, APPROPRIATE ⟨the earth shall sooner leave her ~ skill to bring forth fruit —Edmund Spenser⟩ **b** *archaic* : related by birth or blood : HEREDITARY, LEGITIMATE ⟨their ~ possessions which . . . their predecessors and they had kept —John Spalding⟩ ⟨he must be a genuine or ~ son —W.E.Hearn⟩ **2 :** of an agreeable or beneficial nature : PLEASANT, FAVORABLE ⟨~ climate⟩ ⟨the soil is ~ to my feet —K.M.Dodson⟩ ⟨a ~ half century —Sinclair Lewis⟩ ⟨two of these periods . . . were most ~ toward his profession of architect —*Times Lit. Supp.*⟩ **3 :** KIND 2 **4 a :** of a sympathetic or generous nature : FRIENDLY, BENEVOLENT ⟨was greatly pleased and for that day . . . more ~ with her —Pearl Buck⟩ ⟨benefited greatly from their charity and ~ interest in him —Raymond Holden⟩ ⟨homespun, ~, shrewd men whose strength resided in their neighborliness —Norman Cousins⟩ **b :** expressive of a sympathetic nature ⟨~ look⟩ ⟨~ eye⟩ **5 :** SEA-KINDLY **syn** see KIND

²**kindly** \"\ *adv, sometimes* -ER/-EST [ME, fr. OE *cyndelīce, gecyndelīce*, fr. *cyndelic, gecyndelic*, adj.] **1 a :** in the normal way : NATURALLY ⟨old wounds which had healed ~ —*Amer. Mercury*⟩ **b :** in a natural way : READILY, SPONTANEOUSLY ⟨nearing the three furlongs he . . . was galloping ~ —*Sydney (Australia) Sunday Telegraph*⟩ — often used with *take to* ⟨a wild, fleet-footed people, who did not take ~ to restraint —R.A.Billington⟩ ⟨unadorned styles which some audiences take to more ~ than to . . . polished grace —Robert Bendiner⟩ **2 a :** in a kind manner : SYMPATHETICALLY, GENEROUSLY ⟨treats his horse ~ and never uses spurs⟩ ⟨the foundation is not looking ~ upon requests for grants⟩ **b :** in an appreciative manner : as a gesture of good will ⟨takes criticism ~⟩ ⟨would take it ~ if you would put in a good word for the boy⟩ **c :** in a gracious or considerate manner : COURTEOUSLY, OBLIGINGLY ⟨the party which I was ~ invited to join —Anthony Trollope⟩ ⟨the encipherer had ~ divided the words of his message off with commas —Fletcher Pratt⟩ ⟨~ fill out the attached questionnaire⟩ **3** *chiefly South* : in a way : RATHER ⟨going up the hollow was ~ like going up a big green tunnel —J.H.Stuart⟩

kindly tenant *n, Scots law, obs* : a tenant favored with a low or easy rent because his landlord wanted to favor him or believed him a descendant of an original possessor of the land

kind·ness \'kīnnəs *also* -ndnəs\ *n* -ES [ME *kindenesse*, fr. *kinde, kind* + -*nesse* -ness] **1 :** an act or instance of being kind : FAVOR ⟨a well-established lawyer did a great ~ in taking into his office this young man —Ruth P. Randall⟩ **2 a :** the quality or state of being kind : SYMPATHY, CLEMENCY ⟨man's supreme manifestation of the spirit is ~ —Albert Schweitzer⟩ ⟨cooler air . . . enwrapped him in its ~ —Joseph Whitehill⟩ **b** *archaic* : a feeling of fondness : AFFECTION, LOVE ⟨a lady for whom he had once entertained a sneaking ~ —Washington Irving⟩

kind of \'¦kīndə(v), -dē,-di,-dər\ *adv* : to a moderate degree or extent : RATHER, PARTLY ⟨I *kind of* like you all the same —Robert Westerby⟩ ⟨the wind *kind of* slowed up after while —Vance Randolph⟩

¹**kin·dred** \'kindrəd\ *n, pl* **kindred** *see sense 1a* [ME *kinrede, kindrede*, fr. ¹*kin* + -*rede* (fr. OE *rǣden* condition, rule, estimation, fr. *rǣdan* to advise, rule, guess, read) — more at READ] **1 a** *pl* **kindreds :** a natural grouping : PEOPLE, POPULATION ⟨every ~, every tribe on this terrestrial ball —Edward Perronet⟩ ⟨among the winter-scourged ~s —C.G.D.Roberts⟩ **b** (1) **:** a group of related individuals : FAMILY, CLAN ⟨the ~ has an organic quality; what happens to the individual member is felt by the whole group —A.D.Rees⟩ (2) **:** RELATIVES ⟨if his ~ still remain to him —Alexis de Tocqueville⟩ **c :** a genealogical group : LINEAGE ⟨study the incidence of cancer among members of a ~⟩ **2** *archaic* **a :** relationship by blood or marriage : KINSHIP ⟨a secret match . . . raised him to ~ with the throne —J.R.Green⟩ **b :** possession of similar qualities : AFFINITY ⟨thy ~ with the great of old — Alfred Tennyson⟩

²**kindred** \"\ *adj* **1 a :** of an allied nature : SIMILAR ⟨pamphlets of a ~ sort —G.C.Sellery⟩ ⟨an auditorium for concerts, lectures, and ~ events⟩ **b :** having common qualities or stemming from the same source : CONGENIAL, RELATED ⟨~ spirit⟩ ⟨~ arts of music, painting and letters —Elinor Wylie⟩ ⟨~ Germanic languages⟩ ⟨sound waves . . . penetrate to the listener's inner ear and there set up ~ vibrations —Charlton Laird⟩ **2** *archaic* **a :** of the same ancestry : COGNATE ⟨countries . . . already occupied by their ~ tribes —Edward Gibbon⟩ **b :** of, relating to, or done by a kinsman ⟨what ~ crime . . . am I decreed to expiate —Tobias Smollett⟩

kin·dred·less \-ədləs\ *adj* : not having kindred

kin·dred·ness *n* -ES : the quality or state of being related : KINSHIP

kin·dred·ship \-əd,ship\ *n* : KINSHIP

kinds *pl of* KIND, *pres 3d sing of* KIND

¹**kine** \'kīn\ *archaic pl of* COW

²**kine** \'kinē\ *var of* CINE

³**kine** \"\ *n* -s [by shortening] : KINESCOPE

kine- — see KIN-

ki·ne·ma \'kinəmə\ *var of* CINEMA

kinema red *n* : GOYA

¹**kin·e·mat·ic** \¦kinə¦mad·|ik, ¦kīn-, -at|, |ēk\ *also* **kin·e·mat·i·cal** \|ə̇kəl, |ēk-\ *adj* [back-formation fr. *kinematics*] **1 :** of or relating to kinematics or the motions of bodies **2 :** of or relating to mechanical elements having relative motion — compare PAIR 2a(8) — **kin·e·mat·i·cal·ly** \|ə̇k(ə)lē, |ēk-, -li\ *adv*

²**kinematic** \"\ *var of* CINEMATIC

kin·e·mat·ics \|iks, |ēks\ *also* **cin·e·mat·ics** \'sin-\ *n pl but sing in constr* [modif. (influenced by Gk *kinēmat-, kinēma* motion) of F *cinématique*, fr. Gk *kinēmat-, kinēma* + F -*ique* -ics — more at CINEMATOGRAPH] : a branch of dynamics that deals with aspects of motion (as acceleration and velocity) apart from considerations of mass and force

kinematic viscosity *n* : COEFFICIENT OF KINEMATIC VISCOSITY
kin·e·mat·o·graph \ˌkinə'mad·əˌgraf, ˌkīn-, -atə-, -ràf\ *var of* CINEMATOGRAPH
kin·e·ma·tog·ra·phy \ˌkinəmə'tägrəfē, ˌkīn-, -fi\ *var of* CINEMATOGRAPHY
kin·e·plas·ty \'kinəˌplastē, 'kīn-\ *var of* CINEPLASTY
kinepox \'=ˌ=\ *n* [[1]*kine* + *pox*] : COWPOX
kin·e·sal·gia \ˌkinə'salj(ē)ə, ˌkīn-\ *n* -s [NL, fr. *kinesis* + *-algia*] : pain occurring in conjunction with muscle action
[1]**kin·e·scope** \'kinəˌskōp\ *n* [fr. *Kinescope*, a trademark] **1** : a cathode-ray tube having at one end a screen of luminescent material on which are produced visible images (as television pictures or oscillograph curves) **2** : a motion picture made from a kinescope image
[2]**kinescope** \"\ *vt* **kinescoped**; **kinescoped**; **kinescoping**; **kinescopes** : to make a kinescope of (a television program)
kinesi- *or* **kinesio-** *comb form* [Gk *kinēsi-*, fr. *kinēsis* motion — more at KINESIS] : movement : motion ⟨*kinesi*meter⟩ ⟨*kinesi*ology⟩
-ki·ne·sia \kə'nēzh(ē)ə, ˌkī'-\ *or* **-ci·ne·sia** \sə'-, ˌsī'-\ *n comb form* -s [NL, fr. Gk *-kinēsia*, fr. *kinēsis*] : movement : motion ⟨hyper*kinesia*⟩ ⟨para*kinesia*⟩
ki·ne·si·at·rics \kəˌnēsē'a·triks, kīˌ-, -ēzē-\ *n pl but sing in constr* [ISV *kinesi-* + *-iatrics*] : KINESITHERAPY
ki·ne·sic \kə'nēs|ik (')kīˌn-, -ēz|\ *adj* [Gk *kinēsis* + E *-ic*] : of or relating to kinesics ⟨~ investigation⟩ — **ki·ne·si·cal·ly** \|ək(ə)lē\ *adv*
ki·ne·sics \kə'nēsiks, kī'-, -ēzi-\ *n pl but sing in constr* [Gk *kinēsis* + E *-ics*] : a systematic study of nonlinguistic body motion (as blushes, shrugs, waves) in its relation to communication ⟨man did not become truly human until he developed spoken language but one might guess that for millennia ~ was the . . . mode of communication —Stuart Chase⟩
kin·e·sim·e·ter \ˌkinə'simәd·ə(r), ˌkīn-\ *also* **ki·ne·si·om·e·ter** \kəˌnēsē'äm-, kīˌ-, -ēzē-\ *n* [*kinesi-* + *-meter*] : an instrument for measuring bodily movements
ki·ne·si·o·log·ic \kəˌnēsēəˌläjik, kīˌn-, -ēzē-\ *or* **ki·ne·si·o·log·i·cal** \-jəkəl\ *adj* : of, relating to, or involving the methods of kinesiology
ki·ne·si·ol·o·gy \=ˌnēsē'äləjē, -ēzē-\ *n* -ES [*kinesi-* + *-logy*] **1** : study of the principles of mechanics and anatomy in relation to human movement ⟨~ of corrective exercise⟩ ⟨~ of the ethnic dance⟩ **2** : KINESITHERAPY
ki·ne·sis \kə'nēsəs, kī'-\ *or* **ci·ne·sis** \sə'-, sī'-\ *n, pl* **kineses** *or* **cine·ses** \-ēˌsēz\ [NL, fr. Gk *kinēsis* motion, fr. *kinein* to move + *-sis;* akin to L *ciēre* to move — more at CITE] **1** : physical movement including quantitative, qualitative, and positional change **2** : movement that is induced by stimulation (as by light) and is not specifically orienting — compare TAXIS
-ki·ne·sis \kə'nēsəs, ˌkī'-\ *n comb form, pl* **-kineses** [NL, fr. Gk *kinēsis*] **1** : activation ⟨chemo*kinesis*⟩ ⟨photo*kinesis*⟩ **2** : division ⟨karyo*kinesis*⟩
ki·ne·si·therapy \kəˌnēsē, kīˌnēsē+\ *n* [ISV *kinesi-* + *therapy*] : the therapeutic and corrective application of passive and active movements (as by massage) and of exercise
kin·es·the·sia \ˌkinəs'thēzh(ē)ə *sometimes* ˌkīn-\ *or* **kin·es·the·sis** \-thēsəs\ *also* **kin·aes·the·sia** *or* **kin·aes·the·sis** \ˌkinəs'- *sometimes* ˌkīn-\ *n, pl* **kinesthesias** *or* **kinestheses** [NL, fr. *kin-* + *esthesia or esthesis*] **1** : a sense mediated by end organs that lie in the muscles, tendons, and joints and are stimulated by bodily movements and tensions : MUSCLE SENSE **2** : the sensory experience derived from the muscle sense
kin·es·thet·ic *also* **kin·aes·thet·ic** \ˌ==ˌthed·|ik, -et|, |ēk\ *adj* [fr. NL *kinesthesia*, after such pairs as NL *anesthesia*: E *anesthetic*] : of or relating to bodily reaction or motor memory ⟨get ~ pleasure from watching skaters waltz⟩ ⟨seldom had a ~ image of the first weight at the moment of lifting . . . the second —R.S.Woodworth⟩ — **kin·es·thet·i·cal·ly** *also* **kin·aes·thet·i·cal·ly** \|ək(ə)lē, |ēk-, -li\ *adv*
kinet- *or* **kineto-** *also* **cinet-** *or* **cineto-** *comb form* [Gk *kinētos* moving — more at KINETIC] : movement : motion ⟨*kineto*genic⟩
ki·net·ic \kə'ned·|ik, (')kīˌn-, -et|, |ēk\ *adj* [Gk *kinētikos* of motion, fr. *kinētos* moving (fr. *kinein* to move) + *-ikos* -ic — more at KINESIS] **1** : relating to kinetics or to the motion of material bodies and the forces and energy associated therewith **2 a** : of or relating to motion : ACTIVE, LIVELY ⟨modern dance has been called ~ pantomime⟩ ⟨a ~ world with mobility . . . as its keynote —F.D.Graham⟩ **b** : supplying motive force : ENERGIZING, DYNAMIC ⟨jumped to attention . . . upon the ~ arrival of the master —S.N.Behrman⟩ ⟨a ~ artist . . . inflames the passions of readers —*Saturday Rev.*⟩ ⟨a ~, creative force —*N.Y.Times*⟩ ⟨the complex civilization of which Rome was the ~ center —H.O.Taylor⟩ **3** : of or relating to kinesis ⟨~ occupational therapy⟩ ⟨response to light may be ~ —V.B. Wigglesworth⟩ **4** : KINESTHETIC ⟨in the concert hall . . . listening to actual musical sound enriched by the ~ force of human participation —Goddard Lieberson⟩
ki·net·i·cal·ly \|ək(ə)lē\ *adv* : in a kinetic manner
kinetic energy *n* : energy (sense 5) that is associated with motion
kinetic friction *n* : SLIDING FRICTION
kinetic potential *n* : the difference between the kinetic energy and the potential energy of a dynamic system expressed as a function of the position coordinates and their time derivatives — called also *Lagrangian function*
ki·netics \kə'ned·|iks, kī'-, -et|, |ēks\ *n pl but sing or pl in constr* **1** : a branch of dynamics that deals with the effects of forces upon the motions of material bodies **2 a** : a branch of physical science that deals with the rate of change in a physical or chemical system; *specif* : REACTION KINETICS **b** : the rate of change or reaction in such a system **c** : the mechanism by which a physical or chemical change is effected ⟨the ~ of the acid-catalyzed reaction between organic acids and alcohols —C.E.Leyes⟩
kinetic theory *n* : a theory in physics: the minute particles of a substance are in vigorous motion on the assumptions that (1) the particles of a gas move in straight lines with high average velocity, continually encounter one another and thus change their individual velocities and directions, and cause pressure by their impact against the walls of a container and that (2) the temperature of a substance increases with an increase in either the average kinetic energy of the particles or the average potential energy of separation (as in fusion) of the particles or in both when heat is added — called also respectively (1) *kinetic theory of gases*, (2) *kinetic theory of heat*
ki·ne·to·chore \kə'nē|d·|əˌkō(ə)r, kī'-, -ne|, |t|, |ōˌ-, -kȯ(ə)r\ *n* -S [*kinet-* + Gk *chōros* place — more at CHOR-] : CENTROMERE
ki·ne·to·gen·e·sis \=ˌ=='jenəsəs\ *n* [NL, fr. *kinet-* + L *genesis*] : evolution of animal structures presumed to be due to animal movements — **ki·ne·to·ge·net·ic** \=ˌ==jəˌned·ik\ *adj* — **ki·ne·to·ge·net·i·cal·ly** \-d·ək(ə)lē\ *adv*
ki·ne·to·graph \='==ˌgraf, -ràf\ *n* [*kinet-* + *-graph*] : an apparatus for taking a series of photographs of moving objects for examination with the kinetoscope — **ki·ne·to·graph·ic** \=ˌ==ˌgrafik\ *adj*
ki·ne·to·ne·ma \=ˌ=='nēmə\ *n, pl* **kinetonema·ta** \-məd·ə\ [NL, fr. *kinet-* + *-nema*] : a modified portion of chromonema associated with the centromere
ki·ne·to·nucleus \=ˌ==+\ *n* [NL, fr. *kinet-* + *nucleus*] : a kinetoplast formerly thought to be a secondary nucleus exclusively concerned with motor activities — compare TROPHONUCLEUS
ki·ne·to·phone \='==ˌfōn\ *n* [*kinet-* + *-phone*] : a machine combining a kinetoscope and a phonograph synchronized so as to produce the illusion of motion in a scene with accompanying sounds
ki·ne·to·phonograph \=ˌ==+\ *n* [*kinet-* + *phonograph*] : KINETOPHONE
ki·ne·to·plast \='==ˌplast\ *also* **ci·ne·to·plast** \sə'-, sī'-\ *n* -S [ISV *kinet-* + *-plast*] : a complex cell structure made up of basal granules, associated fibrils, and related bodies found in association with the base of certain flagella and undulating membranes and regarded as actively concerned with the motility of these structures
Ki·ne·to·scope \kə'==ˌskōp, kī'-\ *trademark* — used for a device for viewing through a magnifying lens a sequence of pictures of a changing scene on an endless band of film moved continuously over a light source and a rapidly rotating shutter that creates an illusion of motion
kin·e·to·sis \ˌkinə'tōsəs, ˌkīn-\ *n, pl* **kineto·ses** \-ōˌsēz\ [NL, fr. *kinet-* + *-osis*] : MOTION SICKNESS
kin·folk \'kinˌfōk\ *also* **kins·folk** \-nzˌ-\ *n pl* [*kinfolk* alter. of *kinsfolk; kinsfolk* fr. ME *kynsefolke*, fr. *kynse, kinnes* (gen. of [1]*kin*) + *folke, folk* folk] : RELATIVES
[1]**king** \'kiŋ\ *n* -S *except sense 13a, often attrib* [ME, fr. OE *kyning, cyning;* akin to OS & OHG *kuning, kunig* king, ON *konungr;* all fr. a prehistoric WGmc-NGmc compound whose first constituent is represented by E [1]*kin*, and whose second constituent is represented by E *-ing* (n. suffix)] **1 a** : a male monarch who reigns over a major territorial unit : the ruler of a kingdom ⟨~*s* were makers of the laws —James I⟩ ⟨distinguish between the ~ and the crown —C.H.McIlwain⟩ ⟨in . . . Britain the sovereign is not the *King* but the King-in-Parliament —W.H.Wickwar⟩ **b** : the paramount or an esp. important chief (as the head of an Indian or African tribe) ⟨occupied by Shingess, ~ of the Delawares —A.S.Withers⟩ **2** *cap* : GOD, CHRIST 1 ⟨to worship the *King*, the Lord of hosts —Zech 14:16 (RSV)⟩ ⟨that the *King* of glory may come in —Ps 24:7 (RSV)⟩ **3** : one that holds a supreme or preeminent position in a particular sphere or class; *esp* : a chief among competitors ⟨the cattle ~*s* rode up from the south —Alan Moorehead⟩ ⟨even if no longer ~, cotton remains the chief cash crop —Howell Walker⟩ ⟨this ~ of books —*Brit. Bk. Centre*⟩ ⟨their ~*s* of steel and oil and chemicals —*Nation*⟩ **4** *obs* : QUEEN BEE **5** : the principal piece in a set of chessmen that may move ordinarily one square in any direction and has the power of capture but is obliged never to enter or remain in exposure to capture **6** : a playing card marked with a stylized figure of a king and usu. the initial letter K **7** : one that occupies a position like that of or plays the part of a male monarch — often used in real or mock titles ⟨*King* of Arms of the Order of the Garter —A.L.Wagner⟩ ⟨a decorated float carrying the *King* of Misrule —*Springfield (Mass.) Daily News*⟩ ⟨in all the school games he was the ~ —Robert Graves⟩ ⟨~ of the club's annual hobby show —*Springfield (Mass.) Union*⟩ ⟨public opinion is ~ —L.W.Doob⟩ **8** : any of a class of fuller's teasels **9** : a checker that as a result of reaching an opponent's king row has been crowned and given the power of moving backward as well as forward **10** : the second officer in a Royal Arch chapter of Masons **11** : a sexually mature male termite **12** : KING SALMON ⟨fisherman who come . . . to catch the ~*s* —R.L.Haig-Brown⟩ **13 a** *usu cap* : an American breed of large vigorous utility pigeons developed to produce large numbers of squabs that weigh about one pound at four weeks of age **b** *often cap* : any pigeon of the King breed ⟨not bred so extensively as the white *King* —Rudolph Seiden⟩ **14** : a king-size cigarette
[2]**king** \"\ *vb* -ED/-ING/-S [ME *kingen*, fr. *king*, n.] *vi* : to act the king : RULE — usu. used with *it* ⟨in our . . . country science ~*s* it over the realm of intellectual discourse —Clifton Fadiman⟩ ~ *vt* **1** : to cause to be a king ⟨then am I ~*ed* again —Shak.⟩ **2** *archaic* : GOVERN ⟨England . . . is so idly ~*ed* —Shak.⟩
[3]**king** \"\ *usu cap* — a communications code word for the letter *k*
king al·fred's candle \-'alfrədz-\ *n, usu cap K&A* [after *Alfred* the Great †901 king of the West Saxons in England; fr. the belief that he developed such a device] : an early time-telling device consisting of a candle marked off in time bands to show the passage of time by the amount the candle burns down
king at arms *often cap K&A* : KING OF ARMS — not in official use
king auk *n* **1** : GREAT AUK **2** : DOVEKIE 2
king ball *n* : a red or black ball that is placed on a white spot in front of the holes on a bagatelle board and that must be struck by one of the other balls before a score can be made
kingbird \'=ˌ=\ *n, often cap* : any of various American tyrant flycatchers — see ARKANSAS KINGBIRD, CASSIN'S KINGBIRD, EASTERN KINGBIRD, GRAY KINGBIRD
king blossom *n* : the large central flower in a cluster of apple flowers on the fruiting spur
kingbolt \'=ˌ=\ *n* **1** : a vertical bolt by which the forward axle and wheels of a vehicle or the trucks of a railroad car are connected with the other parts **2** : an iron tie rod used in place of a king post in the construction of a roof
king carp *n* : MIRROR CARP
king charles's head \-'chärlz(əz)-\ *n, usu cap K&C* [after *Charles* I †1649 king of England, who was beheaded; fr. the habit of Mr. Dick, character in *David Copperfield*, novel by Charles Dickens †1870 Eng. novelist, of introducing the subject of King Charles's head into all discussions] : OBSESSION 3 ⟨that *King Charles's head* of modern America, the menace of Communism —*Times Lit. Supp.*⟩
king charles spaniel \-lz-\ *n, usu cap K&C* [after *Charles* II †1685 king of England, who was fond of such dogs] : a dog of a black and tan variety of the English toy spaniel
king closer *n* : a closer bigger than half a brick; *specif* : a brick with one corner cut away making the header at that end half the width of the brick — compare QUEEN CLOSER
king cobra *n* : a large and very venomous elapid snake (*Naja hannah*) found from India to southern China and the Philippines and attaining a length of 12 feet or more — called also *hamadryad*
king conch *n* : a large conch (*Strombus gigas*) with a pink outer shell often used in cameo cutting; *also* : any of certain other large conchs or helmet shells — compare QUEEN CONCH
king crab *n* **1** : any of several closely related large marine arthropods of eastern No. America and eastern Asia constituting the only surviving members of the order Xiphosura and class Merostomata and having a broad crescentic cephalothorax with a pair of large compound eyes and two simple eyes on the upper surface and six pairs of legs arising from the lower surface about the centrally placed mouth, a small abdomen articulated to the cephalothorax with its segments fused into a single piece, swimming appendages to which the flat leaflike gills are attached, and a long stiff movably articulated caudal spine; *esp* : an arthropod (*Limulus polyphemus* syn. *Xiphosurus polyphemus*) found on sandy and muddy bottoms on the coasts of No. America from Maine to Mexico and the West Indies that attains a length of nearly two feet — called also *horseshoe crab* **2 a** : a large European spider crab (*Maia squinado*) **b** : a large scarlet anomuran crab (*Lopholithodes mandtii*) of shallow water from California to Alaska **c** : the largest of the edible crabs (*Paralithodes camtschaticus*) often measuring five feet from claw tip to claw tip, weighing up to 15 pounds, and widely distributed in the No. Pacific
kingcraft \'=ˌ=\ *n* **1** : the art of governing as a king; *esp* : the use of clever tactics or cunning in exercising the functions of kingship ⟨a sort of correspondence course in ~ —Dorothy M. Stuart⟩ **2** : the craft or profession of a king ⟨to abolish ~, priestcraft, caste, monopoly —Walt Whitman⟩
king crow *n* : BLACK DRONGO
kingcup \'=ˌ=\ *also* **kingcob** \'=ˌ=\ *n* **1** : any of various common buttercups (as *Ranunculus bulbosus*, *R. acris*, or *R. repens*) **2** : a marsh marigold (*Caltha palustris*)
king devil *n* : any of various European hawkweeds (esp. *Hieracium praealtum*) that have been introduced into and are locally troublesome weeds in the northeastern U.S.
king·dom \'kiŋdəm\ *n* -S [ME, fr. OE *cyningdōm*, fr. *cyning* king + *-dōm* -dom — more at KING] **1** *obs* : KINGSHIP **2** : a major territorial unit subject to a monarchical form of government usu. headed by a king or queen : the realm of a king ⟨inclusion of additional provinces in the Italian ~⟩ ⟨when plantations were like small ~*s* —William Beebe⟩ ⟨travels through the ~*s* of Europe⟩ — compare EMPIRE 1a, PRINCIPALITY **3** : a politically organized community (as a nation or state) having a monarchical form of government usu. headed by a king ⟨the new Christian ~*s* found themselves at war with the Barbary —C.S.Forester⟩ ⟨decreed Spain a ~ (without a king) —S.G.Rich⟩ **4** *often cap* **a** : the eternal kingship or sovereignty of God ⟨Jesus, to whom the authority of the ~ is delegated, heals sickness —R.H.Strachan⟩ **b** : the spiritual realm over which God reigns as king : HEAVEN ⟨all I now have is what my Father is keeping . . . for us in His ~ —*Voice of Prophecy News*⟩ **c** : the fulfillment on earth of God's will esp. in complete perfection ⟨the time is fulfilled, and the ~ of God is at hand —Mk 1:14 (RSV)⟩ **d** : the invisible society of human beings in which God is held to be obeyed ⟨members of the ~ were to strive to be examples of the life which God deemed ideal for men —K.S.Latourette⟩ **5** : a realm or region in which something is dominant ⟨the rise of a ~ of wheat in the Old Northwest —W.O.Lynch⟩ ⟨in the untroubled ~ of reason —Bertrand Russell⟩ ⟨a cattle ~⟩ **6** : one of the three primary divisions into which natural objects are commonly classified — see ANIMAL KINGDOM, MINERAL KINGDOM, PLANT KINGDOM **7** : an area or sphere in which one exercises authority like a king ⟨his gambling ~ —Dean Jennings⟩ ⟨busy . . . increasing the size and ornamentations of our personal ~*s* —*Saturday Rev.*⟩ **8** : a hostel for men or for women that provides living quarters at low cost to members of a religious movement among Negroes in the U.S. known as Father Divine's Peace Mission Movement ⟨with Father Divine . . . at a meeting in one of his ~*s* —M.L.Bach⟩
kingdom come *n* [fr. the phrase *Thy kingdom come* in the *Lord's Prayer*] : the next world : HEAVEN ⟨the guns that would blow everyone to *kingdom come* —Meridel Le Sueur⟩
king·domed \'kiŋdəmd\ *adj* **1** : ROYAL ⟨~ Achilles in commotion rages —Shak.⟩ **2** : consisting of more than one kingdom — often used in combination ⟨a multi*kingdomed* confederation⟩
kingdom hall *n, usu cap K&H* : a local Jehovah's Witnesses meeting place where religious services are held
kingdomtide \'==ˌ=\ *n, often cap* : a season of the church year preceding Advent and observed by some Christians as a time for emphasizing the message of the kingdom of God
king eagle *n* : IMPERIAL EAGLE
kinged *past of* KING
king eider *or* **king duck** *n* : a circumpolar eider duck (*Somateria spectabilis*) having very large lateral gibbous processes at the base of the bill
king-emperor \'='=(=)=\ *n* : a king who is also ruler of an empire; *specif* : the British monarch in his onetime capacity as emperor of India ⟨the darling of the Saxon *king-emperors* —F.H.Cramer⟩ ⟨the . . . *king-emperor* of one fourth of the world —*Literary Digest*⟩
king fern *n* : ROYAL FERN
kingfish \'=ˌ=\ *n* **1 a** : any of several marine croakers of the family Sciaenidae: as (1) : a whiting (*Menticirrhus saxatilis*) of the No. American Atlantic coast (2) : a small silvery California food fish (*Genyonemus lineatus*) — called also *chenfish* (3) : MULLOWAY **b** : any of various scombroid fishes; *esp* : CERO **c** : any of various marine percoid fishes esp. of the family Carangidae (as an amberfish) **2** : an undisputed master in an area or group : COCK OF THE WALK ⟨the ~ in the gem trade in the whole Persian gulf —*Amarillo (Texas) Sunday News-Globe*⟩ ⟨the ~ of San Antonio's underworld —*Survey Graphic*⟩
king·fish·er \'kiŋˌfishə(r)\ *n* : any of numerous nonpasserine birds constituting the family Alcedinidae that are usu. crested and bright-colored with a rather short tail, long stout sharp bill, and weak syndactyl feet — see ALCEDO, BELTED KINGFISHER, DACELO, KOOKABURRA
kingfisher daisy *n* : a densely hairy annual herb (*Felicia bergeriana*) of the family Compositae found in southern Africa that is used as an ornamental and has bright blue ray flowers and a yellow disk
king hair *n* : GUARD HAIR
king har·ry \-'hari\ *n, usu cap K&H* [after one of the *King Henrys* of England; so called fr. its conspicuous crown] *dial Eng* : GOLDFINCH
kinghead \'=ˌ=\ *n* : GREAT RAGWEED
king·hood \'kiŋˌhu̇d\ *n* [ME, fr. *king* + *-hood*] : KINGSHIP
kinghunter \'=ˌ==\ *n* : KOOKABURRA
king-in-council \'=='==\ *n, pl* **kings-in-council** *often cap K&C* : the British monarch acting with the advice and consent of the privy council usu. as a formal means of giving legal effect to cabinet decisions ⟨executive decisions are reached by the *king-in-council*⟩
kinging *pres part of* KING
king-in-parliament \'=='===\ *n, pl* **kings-in-parliament** *often cap K&P* : the collective legal entity composed of the British monarch and the two houses of parliament acting together that constitutes the supreme legislative authority of the United Kingdom ⟨the lawmaking function is vested in the *king-in-Parliament* —F.A.Ogg & Harold Zink⟩
king-killer \'=ˌ==\ *n* : REGICIDE
king·klip \'kiŋˌklip\ *n* -S [short for *kingklipfish*, fr. *king* + *klipfish;* trans. of Afrik *koningklipvis*] : a mottled cusk eel of southern Africa (*Genypterus capensis*) that attains a length of five feet and is highly esteemed as food ⟨~ liver is of a delicacy and flavor unsurpassed by even chicken liver —J.L.B.Smith⟩
king·less \'kiŋləs\ *adj* [ME *kingles*, fr. *king* + *-les* -less] : lacking a king ⟨a ~ people —Lord Byron⟩
king·let \-ət\ *n* -S **1** : a weak or petty king; *esp* : one that rules over a small territory ⟨four eastern ~*s* receiving investiture at the hands of the emperor —*Century Mag.*⟩ **2** : any of several very small birds of the genus *Regulus* that resemble the warblers but have some of the habits of titmice — see GOLDCREST, GOLDEN-CRESTED KINGLET, GOLDEN-CROWNED KINGLET, RUBY-CROWNED KINGLET
king·li·ness \'kiŋlēnəs\ *n* -ES : the quality or state of being kingly
king·ling \-liŋ\ *n* -S [[1]*king* + *-ling*] : a little or petty king ⟨Germany has had more kings, ~*s*, and knights —*American*⟩
king lory *n* : KING PARROT
[1]**king·ly** \'kiŋlē, -li\ *adj* -ER/-EST [ME *kingly*, fr. *king* + *-ly*] **1** : having the status of king or royal rank ⟨before the murder of her ~ guest —William Stephenson⟩ **2** : of, suitable for, or usu. associated with a king ⟨symbolizing ~ power and justice —*N.Y.Herald Tribune*⟩ ⟨veneration of the ~ office —Charles Beadle⟩ ⟨venison was considered a ~ food —G.B.Saul⟩ ⟨a mere soldier, with few ~ qualities —J.R.Green⟩ **3** : having the character, qualities, or attributes of or usu. associated with a king ⟨a ~, i.e. self-ruling people —K.R.Popper⟩ **4** : characterized by having a king as ruler or as head of the state : MONARCHICAL ⟨the ~ form of government —Connop Thirlwall⟩
[2]**kingly** \"\ *adv, often* -ER/-EST : in a kingly manner ⟨and heard him ~ speak —Alfred Tennyson⟩
king mackerel *n* : a cero (*Scomberomorus cavalla*) esp. noted as a sport fish
kingmaker \'=ˌ==\ *n* : one that uses his power and influence to cause another to become a king; *esp* : one that exerts great influence over the selection of candidates for political office ⟨that great ~ Warwick —Samuel Daniel⟩ ⟨the chief financiers of some campaigns have been persons of great wealth, with no . . . ax to grind save the desire to be ~*s* —V.O.Key⟩
king monkey *n* : a guereza (*Colobus polykomus*) of Sierra Leone having a white forehead suggesting a crown
king mullet *n* : YELLOW GOATFISH
king nut *or* **king nut hickory** *n* : BIG SHELLBARK
king of arms *often cap K&A* [ME *king of armes*] : an officer of arms of the highest rank : a principal herald — called also *king at arms*
king of beasts [ME *king of bestes*] : LION
king of birds : EAGLE
king of heralds : a principal herald in medieval Europe
king of kings [ME *king of kinges*] : a monarch having other monarchs under him: as **a** : an earthly sovereign ⟨this forthright declaration by the *king of kings* . . . forms a fitting conclusion to the long story of Justinian's wars —P.N.Ure⟩ **b** *cap 1st K, often 2d K* : GOD, CHRIST 1 ⟨the blessed and only Sovereign, the *King of kings* and Lord of lords —1 Tim 6:15 (RSV)⟩ ⟨the deity is treated as the *King of Kings* —D.S. Sarma⟩
king of the anteaters : a So. American antbird (*Grallaria varia* syn. *G. rex*)
king-of-the-herrings \'==='==\ *n* : OARFISH
king of the mackerels : either of two large pelagic fishes of the family Molidae: **a** : a fish (*Ranzania truncata*) of the Atlantic ocean **b** : a fish (*Ranzania makua*) of the Pacific ocean
king of the mullets **1** : a European bass (*Labrax lupus*) **2** : CARDINAL FISH
king-of-the-salmon \'==='==\ *n* : a dealfish (*Trachypterus rex-salmonorum*) of the northern Pacific ocean

king of the vultures : KING VULTURE

king orange *n* **1 :** a citrus tree that produces a moderate sized fruit with a rich savory pulp enclosed in a thick deep orange-yellow to orange tuberculated rind and that may be a variety of the mandarin or a hybrid possibly between this and the sweet orange **2 :** the fruit of the king orange

king ortolan *n* **1 :** KING RAIL **2 :** FLORIDA GALLINULE

king parrot *n* **:** any of various Australian birds (genus *Alisterus*) of the family Psittacidae; *esp* **:** an Australian parrot (*A. scapulatus*) about 16 inches long that is chiefly bright scarlet on the head and underparts and green above

king penguin *n* **:** a large penguin (*Aptenodytes patagonica*) of the Falklands and Kerguelen

king penguin

kingpin \'⸗,⸗\ *n* **1 :** any of several bowling pins: as **a :** HEADPIN **b :** the number 5 pin **2 :** one that holds a chief or most prominent place in a group or undertaking ⟨~ of the great steel industry —F.L.Allen⟩ ⟨sought by the government . . . as the ~ of dope peddlers —*Associated Press*⟩ ⟨recognized ~ in the tailor-made car field —*Ethyl News*⟩ **3 a :** KINGBOLT 1 **b :** KNUCKLE PIN **4 :** one that holds together a complex system or arrangement ⟨the . . . chancellor is fully aware of the fact that he is the ~ of the constitutional setup —C.J.Friedrich & H.J. Spiro⟩

king plank *n* **:** the center plank of a wooden deck

king post *n* **1 :** a vertical member connecting the apex of a triangular truss (as of a roof) with the base — called also *crown post;* see ROOF illustration **2 :** a short strong tubular mast that supports the cargo boom of a shipboard derrick — called also *derrick post, samson post*

1 king post

king-post truss *n* **:** a truss having a vertical central strut

king quail *n, Austral* **:** PAINTED QUAIL b

king rail *n* **:** a rather large long-billed No. American rail (*Rallus elegans*) having plumage streaked above with black and tawny olive and a rufous or cinnamon-red breast when in full plumage

king rod *n* **:** KINGBOLT 2

king row *n* **1 :** a row of four playing squares on the edge of a checkerboard nearest each player **2 :** the men on a king row at the start of a game of checkers ⟨to keep a *king row* intact⟩

king rummy *n* **:** a card game of the contract rummy group

kings *pl of* KING, *pres 3d sing of* KING

king salmon *n* **:** a large usu. red-fleshed salmon (*Oncorhynchus tshawytscha*) of the northern Pacific ocean that attains an average weight of about 20 pounds but is reported to sometimes exceed 100 pounds and is of great commercial importance — called also *black salmon, Chinook salmon, quinnat salmon*

king's beadsman *n* **:** BEADSMAN 2b

king's bench *n, usu cap K&B* [ME *kyngesbenche*] **:** COURT OF KING'S BENCH

king's birthday *n, usu cap K&B* **:** the legal holiday on which the British monarch's birthday is publicly celebrated in the United Kingdom and many other parts of the Commonwealth and Empire

king's blue *n* **1 :** a light to moderate blue that is greener and less strong than bluet **2 :** SMALT 2 **3 :** COBALT BLUE 1a

king's books *n pl* **:** the crown taxation list of ecclesiastical benefices and preferments in England

king's champion *n, usu cap K&C* **:** one who formerly at the coronation of the sovereign of England declared his readiness to defend the sovereign's title to the crown against any challenger

king's color *n, often cap K&C* **1 :** a union jack carried on the right of the regimental color by most British regiments **2 :** a white ensign bearing the royal cipher used on ceremonial occasions by the Royal Navy

king's counsel *n, usu cap K&C* **1 :** a group of barristers of preeminence selected upon nomination of the lord chancellor to serve as counsel to the British crown and as such entitled to certain honorary privileges (as the wearing of a silk gown) **2 :** a member of this group of barristers ⟨the first woman attorney to win the high legal distinction of being a *King's Counsel* —P.J.Noel-Baker⟩

king's english *n, usu cap K&E* **1 :** standard, pure, or correct English speech or usage ⟨can think as speedily in classic Greek as . . . in the *King's English* —*Saturday Rev.*⟩ **2 :** English speech used by educated persons in southern England ⟨separating the *King's English* from the American language —M.A. Pei⟩

king's evidence *n, usu cap K* **:** one who gives evidence for the crown in British criminal proceedings ⟨willingness to turn *King's evidence*⟩ — compare STATE'S EVIDENCE

king's evil *n, often cap K&E* [ME *kinges evil;* fr. the belief that it could be healed by the touch of a king] **:** SCROFULA

king's-fern \'⸗,⸗\ *n, pl* **king's-ferns :** ROYAL FERN

king's friends *n pl, often cap K&F* **:** members of the British parliament supporting the attempts of George III to increase the personal power of the monarch ⟨the *King's Friends* . . . were in the main recruited from the ranks of the Tories —Sidney Low & F.S.Pulling⟩

king's-fruit \'⸗,⸗\ *n, pl* **king's-fruits :** MANGOSTEEN

king's grith *n* **:** KING'S PEACE 1

king·ship \'kiŋ,ship\ *n* **1 :** the office of king ⟨the traditional attributes of ~ —D.W.S.Lidderdale⟩ ⟨~ . . . has always been a symbol of national unity —Ernest Barker⟩ **2 :** the quality or state of being a king **:** MAJESTY ⟨the king is thus divested of his ~ and . . . becomes merely a corpse —J.G.Frazer⟩ **3 :** government by a king **:** a monarchical form of government headed by a king ⟨the medieval theory of ~ —G.H.Sabine⟩ ⟨whose contribution to the cause of ~ was less . . . enduring —Hector Bolitho⟩

king-size \'⸗,⸗\ *or* **king-sized** \'⸗;⸗\ *adj* **1 :** longer than the regular or standard size — used of a cigarette ⟨about the length of a *king-sized* cigarette —*Scientific Monthly*⟩ **2 :** much larger in size than is usual for a particular class of things **:** OVERSIZE ⟨regular or *king-size* portions —*N.Y.Times*⟩ ⟨a *king-size* cocktail⟩ ⟨*king-size* bed six by seven feet⟩ **3 :** exceeding others of the kind in some conspicuous quality **:** EXTRAORDINARY ⟨a *king-size* hobby —Barbara Lenox⟩ ⟨a *king-size* movie⟩ ⟨a *king-size* lightning storm⟩

king's man *n* **1 :** an adherent of the king; *esp* **:** a supporter of the British cause during the American Revolution ⟨neither *king's man* nor rebel —*Sat. Eve. Post*⟩ **2 :** a customhouse officer

king's mark *n, usu cap K* **:** an official mark consisting of a leopard's or lion's head crowned that is used as part of a hallmark

king snake *n* **:** any of numerous brightly marked colubrid snakes (genus *Lampropeltis*) of the southern and central U.S. that are voracious consumers of rodents — called also *milk snake*

king snapper *n* [so called fr. the markings on the young which suggest the mark the British Board of Ordance places upon government stores] **:** GOVERNMENT BREAM

king sora *n* **:** FLORIDA GALLINULE

king's paprika *n* [trans. of G *königspaprika*] **:** Hungarian paprika that is made from whole peppers including seeds and stalks

king's peace *n, sometimes cap K&P* [ME *kynges pees*] **1 :** the special protection secured by the monarch in Anglo-Saxon and medieval England to particular persons (as members of the royal household) or places (as the king's highway) and occas. to specific periods of time (as coronation days) ⟨the *king's peace* was to abide in his assembly and . . . extend to the members in coming to it and returning from it —T.E.May⟩ **2 :** the general peace for the protection of persons and property secured in medieval times to large areas and later to the entire royal domain by the law administered by authority of the British monarch ⟨the *king's peace* had . . . grown from an occasional privilege into a common right —Frederick Pollock⟩

king spoke *n* **:** the spoke of the steering wheel of a ship that is upright when the rudder is fore and aft and is usu. distinguished by a Turk's head

king's proctor *n, usu cap K&P* **:** an officer of the judiciary in England who may intervene in actions for divorce chiefly to prevent collusive proceedings

king's purple *n* **:** ROYAL PURPLE 2

king's ransom *n* **:** a very large sum of money ⟨a rare book sometimes sells for a *king's ransom* —R.D.Altick⟩

king's regulations *n pl, usu cap K&R* **:** regulations for the British armed forces issued by the crown

king's remembrancer *n, usu cap K&R* **:** an officer of the British judiciary who is responsible for the collection of debts due to the monarch

king's scholar *n, usu cap K&S* **:** a student in an English school or college who is supported by a foundation created by or under the auspices of a king ⟨a *King's Scholar* at Cambridge⟩

king's scout *n, usu cap K&S* **:** a boy scout who has achieved the highest rating in British scouting by earning ten proficiency badges including four from a required list

king's shilling *n* **:** a shilling whose acceptance by a recruit from a recruiting officer constituted until 1879 a binding enlistment in the British army ⟨he's taken the *king's shilling*⟩

king's silver *n, usu cap K* **:** POST-FINE

king's spear *n, Brit* **:** JACOB'S-ROD

kings·ton \'kiŋztən, -ŋ(k)st-\ *adj, usu cap* [fr. *Kingston,* Jamaica] **:** of or from Kingston, the capital of Jamaica **:** of the kind or style prevalent in Kingston

kingston valve *n, usu cap K* [prob. fr. the F. C. *Kingston* Co., Los Angeles, Calif.] **:** a conical valve opening outward from a ship and closed by the underwater pressure of the sea that is used esp. on a ballast tank of a submarine

king's x *interj, usu cap K&X* [prob. short for *king's excuse*] — used as a cry in children's games to claim exemption from being tagged or caught or to call for a time out ⟨how they make haste to cry with fingers crossed *King's X* — no fairs to use it any more —Robert Frost⟩

king's yellow *n* **1 :** arsenic trisulfide used as a pigment **2 :** ORPIMENT 2

king tody *n* **:** ROYAL FLYCATCHER

king truss *n* **:** a truss framed with a king post

king turtle *n* **:** a large No. American soft-shelled turtle (*Amyda spinifera*)

king vulture *n* **:** a large vulture (*Sarcoramphus papa*) ranging from Mexico to Paraguay that is creamy white in color with wings, rump, and tail black and the carunculate head and the neck colored scarlet, yellow, orange, and blue

king·wa·na \kiŋ'wänə\ *n, pl* **kingwana** *or* **kingwanas** *usu cap* **:** a dialect of Swahili widely used in the eastern Congo as a trade language

king whiting *n* **:** a whiting (*Menticirrhus americanus*) of the east coast of No. America from Maryland to Texas

king wil·liam pine \-'wilyəm-\ *n, usu cap K&W* [after *William* IV †1837 king of England] **:** a Tasmanian tree (*Athrotaxis selaginoides*) of the family Taxodiaceae with sharp-pointed leaves that curve inward and overlap loosely

kingwood \'⸗,⸗\ *n* **1 :** the wood of any of various trees esp. of the genus *Dalbergia; specif* **:** a handsome Brazilian wood from a tree (*D. cearensis*) of Ceará **2 :** a tree that yields kingwood **3 :** GONCALO ALVES 2

[1]**kink** \'kiŋk\ *vi* -ED/-ING/-S [ME *kinken* — more at CHINK] *dial* **:** to be seized with a kink **:** gasp convulsively (as in laughing or coughing)

[2]**kink** \"\ *n* -S *dial* **:** a fit or paroxysm of coughing or laughter ⟨the sister was in ~s of laughter —Donagh MacDonagh⟩

[3]**kink** \"\ *n* -S [D; akin to MLG *kinke* kink — more at CONGER] **1 a :** a short and often tight twist or curl caused by a doubling or winding of something (as a rope or hair) upon itself ⟨looped hose should be changed . . . to reverse folds and prevent ~s —G.E. Stecher⟩ **b :** a bend in something (as a line) otherwise straight **:** INDENTATION, PROJECTION ⟨a dozen curly streets with ~s in them —Thomas Wood †1950⟩ ⟨a ~ in a line on a graph⟩ **c :** a buckling of a railroad track due to longitudinal movement of the rails by creeping or expanding **2 a :** a twist or turn in a person's nature or disposition **:** a mental or physical peculiarity **:** ECCENTRICITY, QUIRK ⟨the ~ in his psychology which made him such a menace to society —P.G.Wodehouse⟩ ⟨a suspicious contempt for the intellectual life . . . is a ~ in the American character —J.J.Wright⟩ **b :** an odd notion **:** WHIM ⟨got a ~ in her head that diamonds she must have —Julian Hawthorne⟩ **3 :** a clever and often unusual idea or method of doing something ⟨every ~ . . . time-saver, or quality-improvement suggestion entered in the contest —*Textile Industries*⟩ ⟨cost-cutting shop ~s —*U.S. Daily*⟩ **4 :** a cramp or stiffness in some part of the body **:** CRICK ⟨taking the ~s out of his legs —Sinclair Lewis⟩ **5 a :** an imperfection (as in design or construction) that is likely to cause difficulties in the operation of something ⟨to spot the ~s . . . that get into an airplane as a result of faulty design —G.W.Gray b. 1886⟩ ⟨number of ~s . . . to be ironed out of the system —Cecile Starr⟩ **b :** a particular type of imperfection in a crystal that is important in the theoretical study of plastic deformation

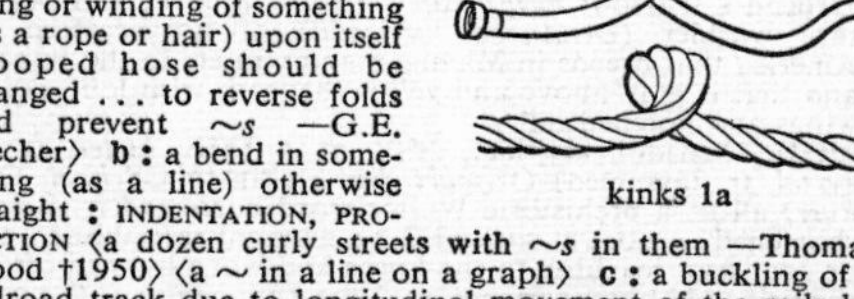

kinks 1a

[4]**kink** \"\ *vb* -ED/-ING/-S *vi* **:** to wind into or form a kink **:** become tightly twisted at one or more points ⟨vinyl hose . . . will not ~ —*Monsanto Mag.*⟩ ~ *vt* **:** to cause to form a kink **:** make a kink in ⟨the sinkers are projected forward to ~ the yarn around the needles —*Full-Fashioned Knitting Machine Primer*⟩

kin·kaid·er \kin'kādə(r)\ *n* -S *usu cap* [Moses P. *Kinkaid* †1922 Am. congressman + E *-er*] **:** a settler on free land in Nebraska under terms of the Kinkaid Act in 1904 which allowed each bona fide settler 640 acres upon payment of a filing fee of 14 dollars ⟨the place *Kinkaiders* make their home and prairie chickens freely roam —Carl Sandburg⟩

kin·ka·jou \'kiŋkə,jü\ *n* -S [F, of Algonquian origin; akin to Ojibwa *qwingwaage* wolverine — more at QUICKHATCH] **:** a nocturnal arboreal carnivorous mammal (*Potos caudivolvulus* syn. *Cercoleptes caudivolvulus*) of the family Procyonidae inhabiting Mexico and Central and So. America that is about three feet long with a slender body, long prehensile tail, large lustrous eyes, and soft woolly yellowish brown fur

kinkcough \'⸗,⸗\ *n* [[1]*kink* + *cough*] **:** WHOOPING COUGH

kink·er \'kiŋkə(r)\ *n* -S [prob. fr. [4]*kink* + *-er*] **:** an acrobat or other performer in a circus

kinkhab *var of* KINCOB

kink·host \'kiŋk,hōst\ *n* [ME (northern dial.), fr. *kinken* to gasp + *host* cough — more at CHINK, HOAST] *archaic Scot* **:** WHOOPING COUGH

kin·kle \'kiŋkəl\ *n* -S [[3]*kink* + *-le*] **:** a little kink ⟨to shake the ~s out o' back an' legs —J.R.Lowell⟩

kin·kled \-ld\ *adj* **:** having kinkles **:** KINKY ⟨~ hair⟩

kinkob *var of* KINCOB

kinks *pl of* KINK, *pres 3d sing of* KINK

kinky \'kiŋkē, -ki\ *adj* -ER/-EST **1 :** having or full of kinks **:** closely twisted or curled ⟨the Negro in Africa has short tight ~ hair —Weston La Barre⟩ **2 :** LIVELY, SPIRITED ⟨fresh and ~ horses —Will James⟩ **3 :** CROOKED 2 ⟨professional calligraphic swindler and ~ penman —*Graphic Arts Monthly*⟩

kin·less \'kinləs\ *adj* **:** having no relatives ⟨left for friendless and ~ souls —E.B.Tylor⟩

kin·nery \'kin(ə)rē\ *n* [[1]*kin* + *-ery*] *South & Midland* **:** KINFOLK, RELATIVES

kin·ni·kin·nick *also* **kin·ni·ki·nic** *or* **kin·ni·ki·nick** *or* **kin·ni·kin·nic** *or* **kin·ni·kin·nik** \¦kinəkə¦nik\ *or* **kil·lic·kin·nic** *or* **kil·li·ki·nick** *or* **kil·lic·kin·nick** \¦kiləkə-\ *n* -S [of Algonquian origin; akin to Natick *kinukkinuk* mixture, Ojibwa *kinikinige* he mixes by hand] **1 :** a mixture of the dried leaves and bark of certain plants (as sumac leaves and the inner bark of a dogwood, esp. the silky cornel) and sometimes tobacco smoked by the Indians and pioneers in the Ohio valley and the region of the Great Lakes **2 :** a plant used in kinnikinnick: as **a :** BEARBERRY **b :** SILKY CORNEL **c :** RED OSIER **d :** either of two sumacs (*Rhus virens* and *R. microphylla*) chiefly of the southwestern U.S. and Mexico

kin·nle \'kinᵊl\ *Scot var of* [2]KINDLE

kin·nor \kē'nȯ(ə)r\ *n* -S [Heb *kinnōr*] **:** an ancient Jewish lyre

[1]**ki·no** \'kē(,)nō\ *also* **kino gum** *n* -S [of African origin; akin to Mandingo *keno, kano* African kino] **1 :** any of several dark red to black tannin-containing dried juices or extracts obtained from various tropical trees: as **a :** the dried juice obtained usu. from the trunk of an East Indian tree (*Pterocarpus marsupium*) as brown or black fragments and used as an astringent in diarrhea — called also *East India kino, Malabar kino* **b :** BUTEA GUM **c :** EUCALYPTUS GUM **2 :** a tree that produces kino (esp. *Pterocarpus marsupium*)

[2]**kino** \"\ *n* -S [G, short for *kinematograph,* fr. F *cinématographe* — more at CINEMATOGRAPH] **:** a motion-picture theater in Europe ⟨fond of going to the ~ —Truman Capote⟩

kino- — see KIN-

kin·o·mere \'kinə,mi(ə)r, 'kīn-, -nō,-\ *n* -S [*kin-* + *-mere*] **:** CENTROMERE

kin·o·plasm \-,plazəm\ *also* **kin·o·plas·ma** \,⸗⸗'plazmə\ *n* [ISV *kin-* + *-plasm, -plasma;* orig. formed as G *kinoplasma*] **:** an active protoplasmic component held to form filaments and mobile structures (as cilia or spindle fibers) — opposed to *trophoplasm*

kin·o·rhynch \'⸗⸗,riŋk\ *n* -S [NL *Kinorhyncha*] **:** a worm of the class Kinorhyncha

kin·o·rhyn·cha \,⸗⸗'riŋkə\ *n pl, cap* [NL, fr. *kin-* + *-rhyncha* (fr. Gk *rhynchos* snout, proboscis)] **:** a class of Aschelminthes comprising minute marine worms of uncertain systematic position having certain resemblances to arthropods and annelids but prob. more closely related to the nematodes — see ECHINODERES

kin·o·ster·ni·dae \,⸗⸗'stə(r)nə,dē\ *n pl, cap* [NL, fr. *Kinosternon,* type genus + *-idae*] **:** a small family of No. American freshwater turtles comprising the mud turtles

kin·o·ster·non \-)nən\ *n, cap* [NL, fr. *kin-* + Gk *sternon* breast — more at STERNUM] **:** a genus (the type of the family Kinosternidae) of No. American freshwater turtles distinguished by fully hinged plastral lobes capable of completely closing the shell

kinot *or* **kinoth** *pl of* KINAH

kin·ross-shire \kin'rȯs(h),shi(ə)r, -,shər\ *or* **kin·ross** \kin'rȯs\ *adj, usu cap K* [fr. *Kinross-shire* or *Kinross* county, Scotland] **:** of or from the county of Kinross, Scotland **:** of the kind or style prevalent in Kinross

kins *pl of* KIN

-kins — see -KIN

kinsfolk *var of* KINFOLK

kin·sha·sa \kin'shäsə\ *adj, usu cap* [fr. *Kinshasa* (formerly *Léopoldville*), capital of Congo] **:** of or from Kinshasa **:** of the kind or style prevalent in Kinshasa

kin·ship \'kin,ship\ *n* [[1]*kin* + *-ship*] **:** the quality or state of being kin: as **a :** personal relationship by blood and sometimes by marriage ⟨her ~ with no less than twelve sovereigns —A.P. Stanley⟩ **b :** relationship by descent from a common ancestor or membership in a common group (as a clan) ⟨the Negroes . . . were already conscious of ~ with other men similarly marked throughout the world —Oscar Handlin⟩ ⟨the instinctive British feelings of ~ and common freedom —Barbara Ward⟩ ⟨a ~ of man with other animals —Weston La Barre⟩ **c :** the socially recognized relationship between people in a culture who are or are held to be biologically related or who are given the status of relatives by ritual **d :** a likeness in character or qualities **:** possession of common features ⟨its mineral waters . . . carry startling ~ to seawater —Helen A. Levin⟩ ⟨in . . . his character studies critics have found a ~ with the early Flemish masters —*Amer. Guide Series: Mich.*⟩ **e :** a community of interest; *esp* **:** a sense of oneness ⟨acquiescence when negation seems to question our ~ with the crowd —B.N.Cardozo⟩ ⟨a sense of professional ~ —Douglas Bush⟩ **f :** a close connection between things that resembles a blood relationship ⟨anthropology's ~ with the humanities⟩

kinship system *n* **:** the system of social relationships connecting people in a culture who are or are held to be related and defining and regulating their reciprocal obligations ⟨*kinship systems* vary in different forms of social organization —Thomas Gladwin⟩

kins·man \'kinzmən\ *n, pl* **kinsmen** [ME *kinnesman,* fr. *kinnes* (gen. of [1]*kin*) + *man*] **:** a man of the same race or family **:** one related by blood or sometimes by marriage **:** RELATION, RELATIVE ⟨Polynesians, distant *kinsmen* of the New Zealand Maori —Ernest Beaglehole⟩ ⟨a very great . . . American whom I am proud to call my ~ —A.E.Stevenson †1965⟩

kins·man·ship \-ən,ship\ *n* **:** KINSHIP

kins·people \'kinz+,-\ *n, pl* **kinspeople :** RELATIVES ⟨reach their sick ~ in Germany —B.J.Hendrick⟩

kins·woman \"+,-\ *n, pl* **kinswomen** [ME *kinneswoman,* fr. *kinnes* (gen. of [1]*kin*) + *woman*] **:** a female relative ⟨the murdered prince had married a ~ of the earl —E.A.Freeman⟩

kin·tra \'kintrə\ *Scot var of* COUNTRY

kin·try \-ri\ *Scot var of* COUNTRY

ki·nu·ra \kə'nürə\ *n* -S [prob. irreg. fr. Gk *kinyra,* a kind of lyre, fr. Heb *kinnōr*] **:** a small-scaled reed-organ pipe of thin nasal tone that is used in theater pipe organs for comic effects

ki·o·ea \,kēō'äə\ *n* -S [Hawaiian] **:** BRISTLE-THIGHED CURLEW

ki·o·ko \kē'ō(,)kō\ *n, pl* **kioko** *or* **kiokos** *usu cap* **:** CHOKWE 1

ki·o·re \kē'ōrē\ *n* -S [Maori] **:** the native rat (*Rattus exulan*) of New Zealand now wholly or nearly replaced by the introduced Norwegian and black rats

ki·osk *also* **ki·osque** \'kē,äsk *sometimes* ⸗'⸗ *or* 'kī,äsk\ *n* -S [Turk *kösk,* fr. Per *kūshk* portico, palace] **1 :** an open summerhouse or pavilion often having a roof supported by pillars and usu. built in gardens and parks ⟨~s on the heights above the Bosporus —*Manchester Guardian Weekly*⟩ **2** [F *kiosque,* fr. Turk *kösk*] **:** a structure resembling or felt to resemble a kiosk: as **a :** an outdoor newsstand ⟨the bountiful supply of newspapers displayed on every ~ —I.F.Fraser⟩ **b :** a structure housing the entrance to a subway **c** *chiefly Brit* **:** a stand or booth at which merchandise is sold or information is provided ⟨bought tea and buns at the station ~ —Lionel Shapiro⟩ ⟨the ticket ~ closed —T.W.Duncan⟩ ⟨a little information ~ —*Irish Digest*⟩ **d :** TELEPHONE BOOTH ⟨the red telephone ~s . . . at the side of the road —Richard Joseph⟩ **e :** a structure used as a receptacle or as housing for machinery ⟨transformer ~s for the distribution of electricity —*World*⟩

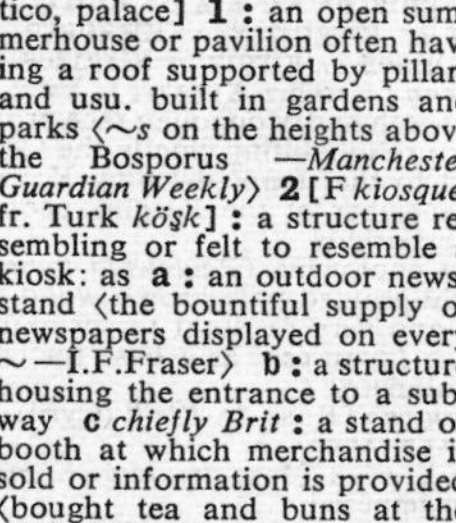

kiosk 1

ki·o·wa \'kīə,wä, -,wā, -əwə\ *n, pl* **kiowa** *or* **kiowas** *usu cap* [Kiowa *Gá-i-gwŭ, Ká-i-gwŭ,* lit., principal people] **1 a :** a Tanoan people in adjoining parts of Oklahoma, Kansas, Colorado, New Mexico, and Texas **b :** a member of such people **2 :** the language of the Kiowa people

kiowa apache *n, usu cap K&A* **1 a :** an Athapascan people associated with the Kiowa **b :** a member of such people **2 :** the language of the Kiowa Apache people

[1]**kip** \'kip\ *n* -S [obs. D, bundle of hides, bundle of flax, fr. MD; akin to MLG *kip* bundle of hides, bunch of fish, ON *kippi* bundle, sheaf] **1 :** a set or bundle of undressed hides of young or small animals (as calves, lambs, colts) **2 :** one of the undressed hides in a kip; *specif* **:** a skin coming from a bovine animal in size between a calf and a matured animal and weighing from 16 to 25 pounds in green salted condition

[2]**kip** \"\ *n* -S [origin unknown] *dial Eng* **:** the common tern

[3]**kip** \"\ *n* -S [perh. fr. Dan *kippe* cheap tavern] **1 :** BED ⟨ready for the ~ after this screwball day —K.M.Dodson⟩ ⟨was in ~ —Richard Llewellyn⟩ **2 :** SLEEP ⟨get some ~ —Paul Scott⟩

[4]**kip** \"\ *vi* **kipped; kipped; kipping; kips :** to lie in bed **:** SLEEP ⟨a ragged blanket to ~ in by nights —Richard Dehan⟩ — sometimes used with *down* ⟨you can ~ down . . . and get a bit of sleep —Edith Sitwell⟩

[5]**kip** \"\ *n* -S [G *kippe* edge, seesaw, arm of a balance, kip, fr. LG, point, edge, fr. L *cippus* stake, post — more at CEPE] **1 a :** a gymnastic feat that is executed when hanging by the hands from a piece of apparatus and consists of moving from

a position in which the legs are above the head to one with the head above the feet by flexing the hips and swinging the legs forward and upward above the head, then arching the back and thrusting with the chest and forcibly kicking the legs downward to raise the body — called also *upstart* **b :** a similar movement executed from a cross seat on the parallel bars by dropping backward with straight arms into position **2 :** a synchronized swimming stunt in which from a back layout position both knees are drawn to the chest and the trunk is submerged backward to a head down vertical position followed by extension of the legs and complete submersion of the body

6kip \"\ *vi* **kipped; kipped; kipping; kips :** to perform a kip in gymnastics or swimming

7kip \"\ *n* -s [*kilo* + *pound*] **:** a unit of weight equal to 1000 pounds used to express deadweight load

8kip \"\ *n* -s [origin unknown] **:** a small piece of wood from which the pennies are tossed in the Australian game of two-up

9kip \"\ *n* -s [Siamese] **:** the basic monetary unit of Laos from 1955 divided into 100 at — see MONEY table

kip·chak \kip'chäk\ *n* -s *usu cap* [Russ, fr. Jagatai] **1 a :** one of the ancient Turkic peoples of the Golden Horde related to the Uighurs and Kirghiz **b :** a member of the Kipchak people **2 :** the Turkic language of the Kipchak people

kipe \'kīp\ *n* -s [ME, fr. OE *cȳpa, cȳpe*; akin to MLG *kīpe* basket, Norw dial. *kaup* wooden vessel, OE *cot* (hut) — more at COT] *dial Eng* **:** a large basket used usu. for a measure

kip·fel \'kipfəl\ *n* -s [G, dim. of *kipf* wagon post, kipfel, fr. OHG *kipfa, chipf* wagon post, fr. L *cippus* post — more at CEPE] **:** a crescent-shaped cookie or roll

kip·ling·ese \ˌkipliŋ'ēz, -ēs\ *n* -s *usu cap* [Rudyard *Kipling* †1936 Eng. poet and novelist + E *-ese*] **:** the literary style of Rudyard Kipling ⟨write a chanty in *Kiplingese* —*Dial*⟩

kip·ling·esque \¦==¦esk\ *adj, usu cap* [Rudyard *Kipling* + E *-esque*] **1 :** of, resembling, or having the characteristics of the literary style of Rudyard Kipling ⟨the poems . . . were direct, *Kiplingesque* —Gertrude Stein⟩ **2 :** characterized by an attitude of superiority over and a responsibility for nonwhite peoples often associated with the writings of Rudyard Kipling ⟨a *Kiplingesque* condescension toward China —F.J.Brown & J.S.Roucek⟩

kip·page \'kipij\ *n* -s [modif. of F *équipage* (as in *être en piteux équipage* to be in a sorry plight) — more at EQUIPAGE] *Scot* **:** an excited or irritated state **:** COMMOTION, CONFUSION ⟨dinna pit yoursell into a ~ —Sir Walter Scott⟩

kip·peen \ki'pēn\ *n* -s [IrGael *cipín*] *chiefly Irish* **:** a short thin stick **:** SWITCH

kippen *past part of* KEP

1kip·per \'kipə(r)\ *n* -s [ME *kypre*, fr. OE *cypera*, prob. fr. *coper* copper; fr. the color — more at COPPER] **1 :** a male salmon or sea trout during or after the spawning season **2 :** a kippered herring or salmon

2kipper \"\ *vt* -ED/-ING/-s **:** to cure by splitting, cleaning, salting, and smoking

3kipper \"\ *adj* [origin unknown] *dial* **:** CHIPPER

4kipper \"\ *n* -s [native name in Australia] **:** a young Australian aborigine who has passed through the initiatory rite

kip·per·er \-pərə(r)\ *n* -s **:** one that kippers fish

kipp generator \'kip-\ *n, usu cap K* [after Petrus Jacobus *Kipp* †1864 Du. druggist and chemist] **:** a glass laboratory apparatus for generating a gas (as hydrogen sulfide by the action of an acid on ferrous sulfide)

kipping *pres part of* KIP

kips *pl of* KIP, *pres 3d sing of* KIP

kip·si·gis \'kip'sēgēs\ *or* **kip·si·kis** \-ēkəs\ *n, pl* **kipsigis** *or* **kipsikis** *usu cap* **1 a :** a predominantly pastoral people of west-central Kenya **b :** a member of such people **2 :** NANDI

kipskin \'=,=\ *n* [1kip + skin] **:** 1KIP 2

ki·pu·ka \kē'pükə\ *n* -s [Hawaiian] **:** an area of older land ranging in size from a few square feet to several square miles surrounded by later lava flows ⟨~s result from either topographic irregularities or the viscosity of the lava —H.T.Stearns & G.A.Macdonald⟩

kip-up *n* -s [fr. *kip up*, v.] **:** a kip executed from a supine position on the mat in tumbling

ki·ran·ti \kē'räntē\ *n* -s *usu cap* **:** a group of Tibeto-Burman dialects centering in eastern Nepal

kir·by \'kərbē\ *or* **kirby hook** *n* -s [fr. the name *Kirby*] **:** a fishhook of evenly curved pattern — see FISHHOOK illustration

Kipp generator

kirch·hoff's law \'kirk,hōfs-\ *n, usu cap K* [after Gustav R. *Kirchhoff* †1887 Ger. physicist] **1 :** a statement in physics: in an electric network the algebraic sum of the currents in all the branches that meet at any point is zero **2 :** a statement in physics: if any closed circuit is chosen from the branches of an electric network, the algebraic sum of the products formed by multiplying the resistance of each branch by the current in that branch is equal to the algebraic sum of the electromotive forces in the several branches forming the circuit **3 :** a statement in physics: the ratio of the emissive power to the absorptivity is the same for all bodies at the same temperature and equals the emissive power of a black body at that temperature

kir·ghiz *or* **kir·ghese** *or* **kir·ghis** *or* **kir·giz** *or* **khir·ghiz** \kir'gēz, kiə'-\ *n, pl* **kirghiz** *or* **kirghizes** *or* **kirghese** *or* **kirgheses** *or* **kirghis** *or* **kirghises** *or* **kirgiz** *or* **kirgizes** *or* **khirghiz** *or* **khirghizes** *usu cap* [Kirghiz *Kyrghyz*] **1 a :** a widespread people of Turkic speech and Mongolian race prob. with some Caucasian intermixture inhabiting chiefly the Central Asian steppes and related to the steppe-dwelling Kazak — see KARA-KIRGHIZ **b :** a member of the Kirghiz people **2 :** the Turkic language of the Kirghiz

ki·ri \'kērē\ *n* -s [Jap] **1 :** a paulownia (*Paulownia tomentosa*) **2 :** the light soft straight-grained pale brown wood of the kiri that is easily worked and very resistant to shrinking and swelling and that is used in Japan esp. as a base for lacquer work and in lining fine cabinetry

ki·ril·li·tsa \kə'riltsə\ *n* -s *usu cap* [Russ, fr. *Kirill* (Cyril) — more at CYRILLIC] **:** CYRILLIC ALPHABET

kiri·mon \'kirə,män, 'kērē,m-\ *n* -s [Jap, fr. *kiri* + *mon* badge, crest] **:** one of the two imperial badges of Japan consisting of three leaves of the paulownia surmounted by three budding stems — compare CHRYSANTHEMUM 3

ki·rin \'kē'rin\ *adj, usu cap* [fr. *Kirin*, Manchuria] **:** of or from the city of Kirin, Manchuria **:** of the kind or style prevalent in Kirin

ki·ri·ri \¦kērē¦rē\ *usu cap, var of* CARIRI

ki·ri·wi·na \ˌkērē'vēnə\ *n, pl* **kiriwina** *or* **kiriwinas** *usu cap* **:** an Austronesian language of the Trobriand islands

kirimon

1kirk *also* **kurk** \'ki(ə)rk, 'kərk, 'kiək, 'kə̄k\ *n* -s *often attrib* [ME (northern dial.) *kirke, kirk*, fr. ON *kirkja*, fr. OE *cirice* — more at CHURCH] **1** *chiefly Scot* **:** CHURCH ⟨bells in the city ~s —*Christian Century*⟩ ⟨coming to the ~ this morning —Guy McCrone⟩ **2** *usu cap* **:** the Church of Scotland as distinguished from the Church of England or the Episcopal Church in Scotland — usu. used with *the* ⟨the essential autonomy of the *Kirk* —J.Y.Evans⟩

2kirk \"\ *vt* **kirked** \-kt\ *or* **kirk·it** \-kət\ **kirked** *or* **kirkit; kirking; kirks** [ME (Sc dial.) *kirken*, fr. *kirke, kirk*, n.] **1** *chiefly Scot* **:** CHURCH **2** *Scot* **:** to take (a bride or couple) to church for the first time after the wedding ceremony ⟨I'm to be married the morn and *kirkit* on Sunday —Sir Walter Scott⟩

kirk·cud·bright·shire \kər'kübri,shi(ə)r, -ˌshər\ *or* **kirk·cud·bright** \¦=¦bri\ *adj, usu cap* [fr. *Kirkcudbrightshire* or *Kirkcudbright* county, Scotland] **:** of or from the county of Kirkcudbright, Scotland **:** of the kind or style prevalent in Kirkcudbright

kirk·er \'kərkər\ *n* -s *usu cap* [1kirk + -er] **:** a member or adherent of the Church of Scotland — see AULD KIRKER, FREE KIRKER

kirk·in·head \'kərkən,hed\ *n* [perh. irreg. fr. 1kirk + head] **:** JERKINHEAD

kirk keeper *n, Scot* **:** one that attends a kirk regularly

kirk·man \'kirkmən, 'kər-\ *n, pl* **kirkmen** [ME (northern dial.), fr. *kirk* + *man*] **1** *chiefly Scot* **:** CHURCHMAN **2 :** a member or adherent of the Church of Scotland

kirk·shot \'kərk,shät\ *n* [alter. of OE *ciricsceat* — more at CHURCHSCOT] **:** CHURCHSCOT

kirk·town \'kərk, taùn\ *also* **kirk·ton** \-ˌtən\ *n* [ME (Sc dial.) *kirktoun*, fr. *kirke, kirk* + *toun* town — more at TOWN] **1 :** the hamlet in the immediate neighborhood of the parish church in country parishes of Scotland **2 :** GLEBE 2a

kirk·yard \'kirk,yärd, 'kərk-\ *n* [ME (northern dial.) *kirkyard*, fr. *kirk* + *yard*] *chiefly Scot* **:** CHURCHYARD

kir·man \kir'män\ *or* **ker·man** \kər-, ker-\ *n* -s *usu cap* [fr. *Kirman* or *Kerman* province, Iran] **:** a Persian carpet or rug characterized by elaborate fluid designs and soft colors ⟨a *Kirman* is the only Persian carpet that looks feminine —Rumer Godden⟩

kir·man·shah \¦kirmən¦shä, kər'män,shä\ *or* **ker·man·shah** \¦kermən¦-, kər'män,-\ *n* -s *usu cap* **:** KIRMAN

kirmess *var of* KERMIS

1kirn \'kirn, 'kərn\ *n* -s [ME (northern dial.) *kirne*, fr. ON *kirna*; akin to ON *kjarni* churn — more at CHURN] *chiefly Scot* **:** CHURN

2kirn \"\ *vb* -ED/-ING/-s *chiefly Scot* **:** CHURN

3kirn \"\ *n* -s [perh. of Scand origin; akin to ON *korn* grain — more at CORN] **1** *chiefly Scot* **:** HARVEST HOME 2 ⟨the good old custom of the ~ —J.G.Lockhart⟩ **2** *chiefly Scot* **:** the last handful or sheaf reaped at the harvest — called also *mell*

kirn baby *or* **kirn doll** *or* **kirn maiden** *n* [3kirn] **:** HARVEST DOLL

ki·rom·bo \kə'räm(ˌ)bō\ *also* **ki·roum·ba** \-raùmbə\ *n* -s [Malagasy *kiròmbo*] **:** a crested conspicuously colored coraciiform bird (*Leptosomus discolor*) of Madagascar related to the rollers

ki·rov \'kērəf\ *adj, usu cap* [fr. *Kirov*, U.S.S.R.] **:** of or from the city of Kirov, U.S.S.R. **:** of the kind or style prevalent in Kirov

ki·rov·ite \'kērə,vīt\ *n* -s [Russ *kirovit*, fr. Sergei M. *Kirov* †1934 Russ. revolutionary leader + Russ *-it* -ite] **:** a mineral $Fe,MgSO_4 7H_2O$ consisting of a hydrous sulfate of iron and magnesium isomorphous with melanterite and pisanite

ki·ro·vo·grad \kə'rōvə,grad\ *adj, usu cap* [fr. *Kirovograd*, U.S.S.R.] **:** of or from the city of Kirovograd, U.S.S.R. **:** of the kind or style prevalent in Kirovograd

kir·pan \kir'pän, kər-\ *n* -s [Panjabi & Hindi *kirpān*, fr. Skt *kṛpāṇa* sword — more at HARVEST] **:** the sacred dagger of the Sikhs ⟨the right of every Sikh . . . to wear a ~ —J.C.Archer⟩

kirsch \'kirsh, -iəsh\ *also* **kirsch·was·ser** \-sh,väsə(r)\ *n, pl* **kirsches** *also* **kirschwassers** [*kirsch* fr. G, short for *kirschwasser*; *kirschwasser* fr. G, fr. *kirsche* cherry + *wasser* water] **:** a dry colorless brandy made in the Black Forest region of Germany, in Alsace, France, and in Switzerland that is distilled from the fermented juice of the black morello cherry and has a bitter almond flavor derived from the ground cherry pits placed in the juice prior to distillation

kirsch·ner value \'kirshnər-\ *n, usu cap K* [fr. the name *Kirschner*] **:** a value similar to a Reichert value that indicates the content in a fat of the water-soluble fatty acids (as butyric acid) having soluble silver salts

kir·se·baer \'kirsə,ba(ə)(ə)r\ *n* -s [Dan *kirsebær*, short for *kirsebærbrændevin*, fr. *kirsebær* cherry + *brændevin* brandy] **:** a Danish cherry liqueur

kir·sen \'kərsᵊn\ *now dial var of* 2CHRISTEN

kirt·land's owl \'kərtlən(d)z-\ *n, usu cap K* [after Jared P. *Kirtland* †1877 Am. naturalist] **:** SAW-WHET OWL

kirtland's warbler *n, usu cap K* [after Jared P. *Kirtland*] **:** a rare warbler (*Dendroica kirtlandii*) of northeastern No. America that breeds in Michigan and winters in the Bahamas and that is gray above and yellow beneath with long pointed wings and notched tail

1kir·tle \'kər|dᵊl, 'kə̄l, 'kəil, |tᵊl\ *n* -s [ME *kirtel*, fr. OE *cyrtel*, fr. (assumed) OE *curt* short; akin to OS *kurt*, OHG *kurz*; all fr. a prehistoric WGmc word borrowed fr. L *curtus* shortened — more at SHEAR] **1 :** a garment resembling a tunic or coat usu. reaching to the knees and worn by men often as the principal body garment until the 16th century **2 :** a long gown or dress worn during the middle ages by women usu. beneath a cloak and also in modern times as part of coronation robes ⟨wearing her . . . ~ of blue —H.W.Longfellow⟩

2kirtle \"\ *vt* -ED/-ING/-s **:** to cover or enwrap (as in a kirtle) ⟨the wild Albanian *kirtled* to his knee —Lord Byron⟩

kirve \'kərv\ *vi* -ED/-ING/-s [prob. alter. of *carve*] **:** to undercut coal in a mine

ki·saeng *also* **ki·sang** \'kē,saŋ\ *n, pl* **kisaengs** *or* **kisaeng** [Korean *kisaeng*] **:** a Korean professional singing and dancing girl

ki·san \kē'sän\ *n* -s [Hindi *kisān*, fr. Skt *kṛṣāṇa* one who plows, fr. *karṣati* he plows] **:** a small farmer or agricultural worker in India **:** PEASANT

1kish \'kish\ *n* -ES [IrGael *cis*, fr. MIr *cess*] **:** a large square wicker basket used in Ireland for carrying peat

2kish \"\ *also* **keesh** \'kēsh\ *n* -ES [prob. modif. of G *kies* gravel, pyrites, fr. MHG *kis*; akin to OHG *kisil* pebble — more at CHISEL] **:** graphite that separates on slow cooling of molten cast iron or pig iron rich in carbon

kish·en *or* **kish·on** \'kishən\ *n, pl* **kishen** *or* **kishon** [Manx *kishan*] **:** a Manx unit of capacity equal to 1.03 U.S. pecks or 1 British peck

kish·i·nev \'kishə,nef\ *adj, usu cap* [fr. *Kishinev*, U.S.S.R.] **:** of or from the city of Kishinev, U.S.S.R. **:** of the kind or style prevalent in Kishinev

kish·ke \'kishkə\ *n* -s [Yiddish, gut, sausage, of Slav origin; akin to Pol *kiszka* gut, sausage, Ukrainian *kyška*, Russ *kishka* gut; akin to Gk *kysthos* vulva — more at HOARD] **:** beef or fowl casing stuffed with a savory filling (as of matzoth flour, chicken fat, and onion) and roasted **:** stuffed derma

ki·si \'kēsē\ *n* -s [Hopi] **:** a bower of interwoven branches used for keeping snakes before a Hopi snake dance

kis·ka·dee \'kiskə(ˌ)dē\ *n* -s [imit.] **:** DERBY FLYCATCHER

kis kilim \'kēs-\ *n, often cap both Ks* [fr. *Kis Kilim*, a kind of carpet, fr. Turk *kızkilim*, fr. *kız* girl + *kilim*] **:** RUSSIAN CALF

kis·lev *or* **chis·lev** \'kisləf\ *n* -s *usu cap* [Heb *Kislēw*] **:** the 3d month of the civil year or the 9th month of the ecclesiastical year in the Jewish calendar — see MONTH table

kis·met \'kiz,met, -ˌmət\ *also* **kis·mat** \-ˌmət\ *n* -s *often cap* [Turk *kısmet*, fr. Ar *qismah* portion, lot] **:** FATE 1, 2a

1kiss \'kis\ *vb* **kissed** *also archaic* **kist** \'kist\ **kissed** *also archaic* **kist; kissing; kisses** [ME *kissen*, fr. OE *cyssan*; akin to OHG *kussen* to kiss, ON *kyssa*, Goth *kukjan*; denominatives fr. the root of OE *coss* kiss, OHG *kus, kuss*, ON *koss*; prob. akin (with phonological conservation due to the imit. nature of the word) to Gk *kynein* to kiss, Hitt *kuwassanzi* they kiss, Skt *cūṣati* he sucks] *vt* **1 a :** to touch or press with the lips (as in affection, greeting, reverence) **:** salute or caress with the lips ⟨~*ed* his wife on the mouth and the baby on the cheek⟩ ⟨~ the foot of the image⟩ **b :** to kiss with a smack ⟨~*ed* her loudly⟩ ⟨~ the children good-night⟩ **2 :** to put or effect by kissing ⟨~ away her tears⟩ **3 a :** to touch gently as if fondly or caressingly ⟨a soft wind that ~*es* the flowers⟩ **b :** to touch or hit lightly; *specif* **:** to contact (another billiard ball) lightly ~ *vi* **1 :** to make or give salutation with the lips **:** to salute or caress one another with the lips ⟨~ and be friends⟩ **2 :** to come in contact, touch, or collide gently **:** REBOUND ⟨the cue ball ~*es* from the red ball⟩ **3** *of duodenal ulcers* **:** to be directly opposite or lie against one another — **kiss good-bye 1 :** to take one's leave of **:** LEAVE ⟨*kissing* the old dump *good-bye* tonight —J.T.Farrell⟩ **2 :** to resign oneself to the loss of **:** part with ⟨whenever you have a ship ashore you can *kiss* a million bucks *good-bye* —J.W. Noble⟩ — **kiss hands :** to touch the hand of a sovereign or superior with the lips as a ceremonial sign of homage or submission (as on meeting or parting) ⟨was sent for by the king and *kissed hands* as prime minister⟩ — **kiss my foot** — used to express contempt (as in denying a request) — **kiss one's hand :** to kiss one's own hand with a motion toward another person in sign of affection — **kiss the book :** to touch with the lips the Bible, New Testament, or Gospels in taking an oath — **kiss the ground :** to prostrate oneself as a sign of homage — **kiss the rod :** to accept punishment or correction submissively

2kiss \"\ *n* -ES [ME, alter. (influenced by *kissen*, v.) of *cos*, fr. OE *coss* — more at 1KISS] **1 :** the act of kissing **:** a salute or caress with the lips **:** SMACK **2 a :** a gentle touch or contact **b :** the light contact or interference of one billiard ball with another — called also *kiss-off* **3 a :** a meringue sometimes with shredded coconut or other material added **b :** a bite-size piece of candy often wrapped in paper or foil ⟨chocolate ~⟩

kiss·abil·i·ty \ˌkisə'bilədē\ *n* **:** the quality or state of being kissable

kiss·able \'kisəbəl\ *adj* **:** so attractive as to invite kissing ⟨a ~ mouth⟩ — **kiss·able·ness** *n* -ES — **kiss·ably** \-blē\ *adv*

kis·sar \'kisə(r)\ *n* -s [colloq. Ar *qīsār* (Ar *qīthār*)] **:** a five-stringed lyre of northern Africa and Ethiopia

kiss-curl \'=,=\ *n* **:** a loose curl falling across the forehead or along the cheek

kiss·er \'kisə(r)\ *n* -s **1 :** one that kisses **2** *slang* **:** MOUTH ⟨a poke in the ~⟩ **3** *slang* **:** FACE ⟨threw the money in his ~⟩

kis·si \'kisē\ *n, pl* **kissi** *or* **kissis** *usu cap* **1 a :** an agricultural people of French Guinea, Liberia, and Sierra Leone **b :** a member of such people **2 :** a West-Atlantic language of the Kissi people

kiss impression *n* **:** impression (as of paper against an inked printing surface) that is extremely light

kissing bug *n* **:** CONENOSE

kissing cousin *or* **kissing kin** *n* **:** a cousin or other collateral relative whom one knows just well enough to kiss more or less formally upon occasional meeting ⟨distantly related but not *kissing cousins*⟩

kissing dance *n* **:** a social couple dance culminating in a kiss

kissing gate *n, dial Eng* **:** a gate swinging in a V-shaped enclosure that allows only one person to pass at a time

kiss·ing·ly *adv* **:** in a lightly touching manner

kiss-in-the-ring \'==='=\ *n* **:** drop the handkerchief in which the pursuing player may kiss the player he catches

kiss-me \'=,=\ *n* -s **:** any of various plants: as **a :** WILD PANSY **b :** LONDON PRIDE 1 **c :** HERB ROBERT

kiss-me-at-the-gate \'===='=\ *n* **:** a fragrant Chinese honeysuckle (*Lonicera fragrantissima*) grown in the southern U.S. for ornament

kiss-me-over-the-garden-gate \'==,==='=='=\ *n* **:** any of various plants: as **a :** PRINCE'S-FEATHER 2 **b :** ACHIMENES 2

kiss-me-quick \'==,=\ *n* -s **:** a small bonnet worn off the face esp. in the latter half of the 19th century

kiss of death [so called fr. the betraying kiss with which Judas pointed out Jesus in the garden of Gethsemane (Mark 14: 44–45)] **:** an act or association ultimately causing ruin ⟨track bucks baseball but this need not be the automatic *kiss of death* —Tommy O'Brien⟩ ⟨for an American to offer . . . friendship meant the *kiss of death* — for the Russian —Gouverneur Paulding⟩

kiss off *vt* **:** DISMISS ⟨*kisses* the other performers *off* as mere amateurs⟩

kiss-off \'=,=\ *n* -s [*kiss off*] **1 :** KISS 2b **2 a :** an event marking the end (as of a relationship) **b :** an act of dismissal

kiss of peace : a religious ceremonial kiss symbolizing fraternal unity and originating in the early church

kiss spot *n* **:** a spot appearing on vegetable-tanned leather caused by contact with another hide in tanning

1kist *archaic past of* KISS

2kist \'kist\ *n* -s [ME *kiste*, fr. ON *kista* — more at CHEST] *chiefly dial* **:** any of various chests: as **a :** a clothes or linen trunk **b :** COFFIN

3kist \"\ *n* -s **:** CIST

4kist \"\ *n* -s [Ar *qist*] *India* **:** an installment (as of land revenue) or the time for paying it

kist·vaen \'kist,vīn\ *n* -s [modif. of W *cistfaen*, fr. *cist* chest + *faen*, mutated form of *maen* stone] **:** 1CIST 1

kis·wa *or* **kis·wah** \'ki,swä\ *n* -s [Ar *kiswah*] **:** a black cloth covering the Kaaba

1kit \'kit, *usu* -id·+V\ *n* -s [ME *kitt, kyt*, prob. fr. MD *kitte, kit* jug, vessel] **1 a** *dial Brit* **:** a wooden tub or small barrel (as for butter, milk, water, fish) **b :** a round shipping container of wood or metal usu. having tapered sides, a solid bottom on the larger end, and a closure at or in the smaller end and holding about five gallons **2 a** (1) **:** a collection of equipment and often supplies typically carried in a box or bag **:** an outfit of necessary implements, effects, or materials ⟨a plumber's ~⟩ ⟨a first-aid ~⟩ (2) **:** a container (as a bag, box, or folder) for such a collection ⟨essential medical supplies in a clear plastic ~⟩ ⟨a big green ~ bulging with leaflets⟩ **b** *chiefly Brit* **:** an outfit of clothing and accouterments **:** UNIFORM, REGALIA ⟨troops in full battle ~ —Hal Lehrman⟩ ⟨the first game is won by players wearing their own ~ —Denzil Batchelor⟩ **:** DRESS, WEAR ⟨dressed in riding ~, a sleeveless brown silk shirt, breeches, and high boots —Eve Langley⟩ **c** *chiefly Brit* **:** EQUIPMENT, GEAR ⟨run over to my billet and get some overnight ~ —Lionel Shapiro⟩ **d :** a commercially packaged set of parts (as of a scale model, boat, or automobile accessory) usu. ready to assemble and often accompanied by finishing materials and tools **e :** a collection of printed material giving information or instruction on one subject and assembled (as in a folder) for distribution ⟨a free ~ which includes just about everything a prospective visitor should know about the state —*Springfield (Mass.) Republican*⟩ ⟨sent instruction ~s to every high school so youngsters can learn how to make out income-tax returns —*Newsweek*⟩ **3** *or* **kit and biling** *or* **kit and boodle** *or* **kit and caboodle :** a group of persons or things **:** LOT — used with *whole* ⟨sent the whole *kit and caboodle* of them home⟩ **4** *dial Eng* **:** BASKET; *esp* **:** one used for fish **5 :** a group of pigeons trained to fly together

2kit \"\ *vt* **kitted; kitted; kitting; kits** *chiefly Brit* **:** EQUIP, OUTFIT — often used with *up* ⟨enlisted in the Navy and went . . to be *kitted up* —A.P.Herbert⟩

3kit \"\ *n* -s [origin unknown] **:** a small violin formerly used by dancing masters

4kit *also* **kitt** \"\ *n* -s [short for *kitten*] **1 :** KITTEN 1 **2 a :** a young immature or much undersized individual of one of the smaller fur-bearing animals ⟨fox ~⟩ **b :** the skin or pelt of such an animal

5kit \"\ *vi* **kitted; kitted; kitting; kits :** to give birth to kits

ki·tab \kē'täb\ *n* -s [Ar *kitāb* book] *Islam* **:** a book esp. of sacred scripture and usu. of the scripture of the Jews, Christians, Zoroastrians, or Muslims

ki·ta·bi \-bē\ *n* -s [Ar *kitābī*, fr. *kitāb*] *Islam* **:** one who believes in a book of sacred scripture and with whom a Muslim may marry in what is deemed a lawful marriage

kit·a·mat *or* **kit·i·mat** \ˌkid·ə'mat\ *n, pl* **kitamat** *or* **kitamats** *or* **kitimat** *or* **kitimats** *usu cap* **1 :** a Wakashan people of Douglas Channel, British Columbia **2 :** a member of the Kitamat people

kitambilla *var of* KETEMBILLA

kitan *usu cap, var of* KHITAN

ki·ta·ne·muk \kə'tanə,mək\ *n, pl* **kitanemuk** *or* **kitanemuks** *usu cap* **1 :** a Shoshonean people living between the Tehachapi mountains and the Mojave desert, Calif. **2 :** a member of the Kitanemuk people

ki·tar *or* **kit·tar** \kə'tär\ *n* -s [Ar *qītār, qīthār* — more at GUITAR] **:** an Arabian guitar

kit bag *n* **1 :** KNAPSACK **2 :** a rectangular usu. leather traveling bag with sides that come together and fasten at the top or open to the full width of the bag and with two straps that wrap around the bag to secure it

kit boat *n* **:** precut parts of a boat that can be assembled by the purchaser into a complete boat

kit-cat *or* **kit-kat** \'kit,kat\ *n* [after *Kit* (*Christopher*) *Cat* or *Catling*, 18th cent. Eng. keeper of the tavern where the club originally met] **1** *usu cap K&C or both Ks* **:** a member of an early 18th century London club of Whig politicians and men of letters **2** [prob. so called fr. the portraits hung in a dining room

kit bag 2

of the Kit-cat club whose low ceiling made the smaller size necessary] **:** a portrait of less than half length but including the hands ⟨some thirty major portraits hanging on the walls, besides *kit-cats*, heads, sketches . . . and all the lesser oddities of a collection many years in the making —Clemence Dane⟩

¹kitch·en \'kichən\ *n* -s [ME *kichene, kichen*, fr. OE *cycene*; akin to OHG *chuhhina* kitchen, MLG *kökene*, MD *cokene, cökene*; all fr. a prehistoric WGmc word borrowed fr. LL *coquina*, fr. L, fem. of *coquinus* of cooking, fr. *coquere* to cook + *-inus* -ine — more at COOK] **1 a :** a room or some other space (as a wall area or separate building) with facilities for cooking **:** a place for preparing meals ⟨living room, dining room, and the ~⟩ ⟨a soup ~ where the starving villagers were fed⟩ ⟨a mobile ~ for soldiers in the field⟩ **b :** the personnel that prepares, cooks, and serves food ⟨send orders to the ~⟩ ⟨the ~ sent up a meal⟩ **c :** a combination of kitchen fixtures including cabinets and often stove, refrigerator, and sink marketed as a unit and installed as built-in equipment **2** *now chiefly Scot* **:** food from the kitchen; *specif* **:** food eaten as a side dish with other food **3 a :** any of a series of compartments in which sublimed arsenic fumes from a furnace for treating arsenical ore and baghouse dust are condensed **b :** the laboratory of a reverberatory furnace

²kitchen \"\ *adj* **1 :** of, relating to, or of a kind suitable for use in a kitchen ⟨mop the ~ floor⟩ ⟨~ clock⟩ ⟨a ~ stove⟩ **2 :** that works in a kitchen ⟨a ~ maid⟩ **3 :** used as a kitchen ⟨soldiers bringing supplies to the ~ tent⟩ **4 a :** constituting or having the characteristics of a pidgin language that is used largely for communication between servants and their employers when the two groups are not native speakers of the same language **b :** constituting or having the characteristics of a language as spoken by uneducated speakers ⟨want official acceptance of their language — a sort of ~ Dutch —Serge Fliegers⟩

³kitchen \"\ *vt* -ED/-ING/-S **1** *obs* **:** to furnish food to **:** entertain with kitchen fare **2** *chiefly Scot* **a :** to make palatable **:** SEASON **b :** to serve (food) as kitchen

Kitchen Bouquet *trademark* — used for bouquet garni

kitchen cabinet *n* **1 :** a cupboard with drawers and shelves designed to hold within easy reach utensils and materials used in preparing food **2 :** an unofficial and informal group of advisers to the head of a government who are held to have more influence with him than his official cabinet ⟨certain of our Presidents have turned to *kitchen Cabinets* to aid them —*Fortune*⟩

kitchen dresser *n, Brit* **:** KITCHEN CABINET 1

kitch·en·er \-ch(ə)nə(r)\ *n* -s [¹*kitchen* + *-er*] **1 :** the person in charge of a monastery kitchen **2** *Brit* **:** a cooking range

kitch·en·ette *also* **kitch·en·et** \,kichə'net, *usu* -ed·+V\ *n* -s [¹*kitchen* + *-ette*] **:** a very small compactly arranged room or an alcove containing cooking facilities

kitchen garden *n* **:** a household garden in which vegetables and often fruits and herbs are cultivated ⟨a flower garden on one side and a *kitchen garden* at the back⟩

kitchen kaffir *n, usu cap both Ks* [²*kitchen*] **:** a pidgin language based on Xhosa, Afrikaans, and English and sometimes used in communication between Europeans and Africans in So. Africa

kitchen match *n* **:** a wooden splint match that can be lighted by any friction surface

kitchen midden *n* [trans. of Dan *kökkenmödding*] **:** a refuse heap; *specif* **:** a mound (as a Neolithic shell heap) marking the site of a primitive human habitation ⟨army engineers, excavating for a mess hall . . . dig unexpectedly into the refuse heap of a prehistoric *kitchen midden* —Corey Ford⟩

kitchen police *n* **1 :** enlisted men detailed to assist the cooks in an army mess **2 :** the work of kitchen police — abbr. *K.P.*

kitchen rose *n* **:** CINNAMON ROSE

kitchen stuff *n* **1 :** food for cooking **:** kitchen requisites (as vegetables) **2 :** kitchen refuse or waste; *esp* **:** fat collected from pots and pans

kitchenware \'==,=\ *n* **:** hardware (as cutlery and cooking utensils) for kitchen use

kitch·ie \'kichi\ *Scot var of* KITCHEN

kitch·in \'kichən\ *n* -s *usu cap* [after Joseph A. *Kitchin* *b*1910 Amer. political scientist] **:** a business cycle formed by a recession of about three and a half years during a prosperity phase ⟨the *Kitchins* can be best observed, for all countries, on the chart of rates of changes —J.A.Schumpeter⟩

¹kite \'kīt, *usu* -īd·+V\ *n* -s [ME, fr. OE *cȳta*; akin to MHG *kūze* owl, ON *kȳta* to quarrel, Gk *goan* to lament, Lith *gausti* to sound, drone — more at COMELY] **1 :** any of various usu. rather small hawks of the family Accipitridae that have long narrow wings, a deeply forked tail, a weak bill, and feet adapted for taking such prey as insects and small reptiles, that feed also on offal, and that are noted for graceful sustained flight; *specif* **:** a common comparatively large European scavenger (*Milvus milvus*) with chiefly reddish brown plumage — compare BLACK KITE, BLACK-SHOULDERED KITE, SWALLOW-TAILED KITE, WHITE-TAILED KITE **2 :** a person that preys on others **3 :** a contrivance consisting of a surface of a light material stretched over a light often diamond-shaped framework, often provided with a balancing tail, and intended to be flown in the air at the end of a long string — see BOX KITE **4 a :** ACCOMMODATION BILL **b :** a check drawn against uncollected funds in a bank account **c :** a check that has been fraudulently raised before cashing **5 kites** *pl* **:** the lightest and usu. the loftiest sails (as skysails, spinnakers) ordinarily carried only in a light breeze — called also *flying kites* **6 :** something suggested or tried in order to see how people react **:** a tentative proposal or venture **:** TRIAL BALLOON, FEELER ⟨published what has all the appearance of being a ~ for his whole project —Peter Ure⟩ **7 a :** a drag to be towed under water at any depth up to about 40 fathoms that on striking bottom is upset and rises to the surface — called also *sentry* **b :** a device (as a heavy wooden platform) attached to a submerged line towed by a mine sweeper or between two vessels to make the line tow at a predetermined depth for clearing mined areas **8 a :** a heavier-than-air aircraft which is without propelling means other than the towline pull and whose support is derived from the force of the wind moving past its surfaces **b** *slang Brit* **:** AIRPLANE **9 :** a step cut for a gem having a diamond shape and eight quadrilateral facets **10 :** a letter smuggled past prison censorship

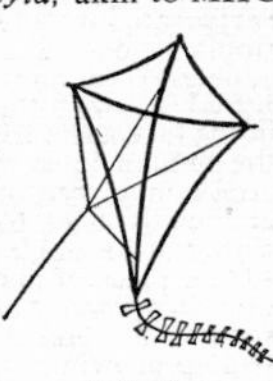
kite 3

²kite \"\ *vb* -ED/-ING/-S *vi* **1 :** to get money or credit by a kite; *specif* **:** to create a false bank balance by manipulating deposit accounts **2 :** to go in a rapid, carefree, or flighty manner: **a :** run or move very fast ⟨that dog went *kiting* down the street traveling all of 20 knots —Kenneth Roberts⟩ **b :** GALLIVANT ⟨would ~ off to the movies just about dishwashing time⟩ ⟨used to ~ around with the other kids in the evening⟩ **c :** rise rapidly **:** SOAR ⟨tin prices *kited* in world markets . . . to another record high —*Wall Street Jour.*⟩ **d :** leave suddenly **:** DECAMP ⟨walked out on me . . . took the boys and *kited* —Vance Bourjaily⟩ **3 :** to fly a hawk-shaped paper kite over the haunts of game birds (as grouse) to frighten them into lying close ~ *vt* **1 :** to cause to soar; *specif* **:** to inflate (as a price) in amount ⟨war-risk insurance has *kited* shipping costs skyward —*Time*⟩ **2 :** to use (a kite) to get money or credit ⟨had *kited* the worthless draft on innocent victims —M.M.Hunt⟩; *specif* **:** to raise the amount of (a check) by fraud before cashing it ⟨a $27.50 check could be *kited* to $327.50 —*Newsweek*⟩

kite balloon *n* **:** an elongated captive balloon with lobes that keep it headed into the wind for increased lift — abbr. *KB*

kite eagle *n* **:** a nearly black East Indian eagle (*Ictinaëtus malayensis*) having a short crest and a very large claw on the inner toe

kite falcon *n* **:** CUCKOO FALCON

kiteflying \'=,==\ *n* **:** the issuing of political news in such form that it may later be disavowed

kit·er \'kīd·ə(r)\ *n* -s **:** one that kites

kite-shaped \'=;=\ *adj, of a shield* **:** having a bowed top, long straight sides, and a pointed bottom

kite track *n* **:** a racetrack with only one turn and with the stretches converging to a point

kite track

kit fox *n* [⁴*kit*] **1 a :** a small fox (*Vulpes velox*) of the plains of western No. America **b :** a related species (*V. macrotis*) of the southwestern U.S. **2 :** the fur or pelt of the kit fox

kith \'kith\ *n* -s [ME *kiththe, kith*, fr. OE *cȳththu, cȳthth*, fr. *cūth* known — more at UNCOUTH] **1 :** familiar friends, neighbors, fellow countrymen, or acquaintances **2 :** KINDRED **3 :** a culturally homogeneous social group tending to be endogamous

kith and kin *n pl* [ME] **1 :** friends and kindred **2 :** KINDRED, RELATIONS

kith·a·ra \'kithərə, ki'thärə\ *var of* CITHARA

kithe *or* **kythe** \'kīth\ *vb* -ED/-ING/-S [ME *kithen, kythen*, fr. OE *cȳthan*, fr. *cūth* known — more at UNCOUTH] *vt, chiefly Scot* **:** to make known **:** MANIFEST, DECLARE ~ *vi, chiefly Scot* **:** to become known or manifest **:** APPEAR

kitimat *usu cap, var of* KITAMAT

kit-kat *var of* KIT-CAT

kit·ke·hah·ki \'kitkə,häkē\ *n, pl* **kitkehahki** *or* **kitkehahkis** *usu cap* **1 :** a people of the Pawnee confederacy **2 :** a member of the Kitkehahki people

kit·ksan \,kitkə'san\ *n, pl* **kitksan** *or* **kitksans** *usu cap* [Tsimshian, lit., people of the Skeena river] **1 a :** a division of the Tsimshian people in the upper Skeena river valley, British Columbia **b :** a member of such people **2 :** a dialect of Tsimshian

kit·ling \'kitlən\ *n* -s [ME, fr. ON *ketlingr*, fr. *katt-, kötte* cat + *-lingr* -ling — more at CAT] *dial Brit* **:** KITTEN

kit·man \'kitmən, -,man\ *n, pl* **kitmen** [¹*kit* + *man*] **:** an automobile-factory stock clerk who assembles matched hardware for each car

kitmutgar *var of* KHIDMATGAR

ki·tol \'kē,tōl, -tōl\ *n* -s [irreg. fr. Gk *kētos* sea monster, whale + E *-ol*] **:** a crystalline alcohol $C_{40}H_{58}(OH)_2$ obtainable esp. from whale-liver oil and capable of yielding vitamin A (as by heating)

kitool *var of* KITTUL

kits *pl of* KIT, *pres 3d sing of* KIT

kitsch \'kich\ *n* -ES [G, fr. *kitschen* to slap (a work of art) together, fr. G dial., to scrape up mud from the street] **:** artistic or literary material held to be of low quality, often produced to appeal to popular taste, and marked esp. by sentimentalism, sensationalism, and slickness ⟨the traditional gap . . . between ~ and literature —William Phillips b.1907⟩

kitt *var of* KIT

kittar *var of* KITAR

kitted *past of* KIT

kit·tel \'kid·ᵊl\ *n, pl* **kittel** [Yiddish *kitel*, fr. MHG *kitel, kietel* cotton or hempen outer garment, prob. fr. Ar *quṭn* cotton] **:** a white cotton or linen robe worn by Orthodox Jews on Rosh Hashana and Yom Kippur and at the Passover Seder and also used as a burial shroud

¹kit·ten \'kitᵊn\ *n* -s [ME *kitoun*, modif. (influenced by *kitling*) of (assumed) ONF *caton* (whence F dial. — Normandy — *caton*), dim. of ONF *cat*, fr. LL *cattus* — more at CAT] **1 a** (1) **:** a young cat (2) **:** a cat less than nine months old — used esp. in relation to competitive showing **b :** an immature individual of various other small mammals ⟨hamster ~⟩ ⟨rabbit ~⟩ **2 :** ⁴KIT 2b **3** *chiefly dial* **:** one of the rolls of dust that collect under furniture — usu. used in pl.

²kitten \"\ *vb* -ED/-ING/-S [ME *kytnen* fr. *kitoun*, n.] *vi* **:** to give birth to kittens **:** LITTER ~ *vt* **:** to give birth to ⟨that's what I've been called since I was ~*ed* —*Irish Statesman*⟩

kittenball \'==,=\ *n* **:** SOFTBALL

kitten-breeches \'==,==\ *n pl but sing or pl in constr* [so called fr. the shape of the blossoms] **:** DUTCHMAN'S-BREECHES

kit·ten·ish \'kit(ᵊ)nish, -nēsh\ *adj* **1 :** resembling or like that of a kitten **2 :** marked by coy or affected playfulness ⟨she was fat and over forty, but still ~ —*Farmer's Weekly (So. Africa)*⟩ — **kit·ten·ish·ly** *adv* — **kit·ten·ish·ness** *n* -ES

kit·ten·less \'kitᵊnləs\ *adj* **:** having no kitten ⟨a ~ cat⟩

kit·ter·een \,kid·ə'rēn\ *n* -s [origin unknown] **:** a two-wheeled one-horse carriage with a movable top

kitting *pres part of* KIT

kit·ti·wake \'kid·ē,wāk\ *n* -s [imit.] **:** any of various gulls of the genus *Rissa* having the hind toe short or rudimentary; *esp* **:** ATLANTIC KITTIWAKE

¹kit·tle \'kid·ᵊl, 'kitᵊl\ *vt* -ED/-ING/-S [ME (northern dial.) *kytyllen*, prob. fr. ON *kitla* — more at TICKLE] **1** *chiefly Scot* **:** TICKLE **2** *chiefly Scot* **:** ENLIVEN, TITILLATE **3** *chiefly Scot* **:** to flatter and please **4** *chiefly Scot* **:** to keep guessing **:** PERPLEX

²kittle \"\ *adj* -ER/-EST **1** *chiefly Scot* **a :** easily excited **:** TOUCHY, SKITTISH, FIDGETY **b :** QUICK, APT ⟨she's ~ of her hands —George Meriton⟩ **c :** VARIABLE, CAPRICIOUS ⟨Fortune will play ~ tricks —John Barr⟩ **d :** nicely balanced **:** DELICATE **2** *chiefly Scot* **:** hard or risky to deal with or do **:** TICKLISH ⟨to paint an angel's ~ work —Robert Burns⟩ ⟨it's a ~ thing to keep the likes o' him waitin' —S.R.Crockett⟩

³kittle \"\ *vi* -ED/-ING/-S [prob. of Scand origin; akin to Norw dial. *kjetla* to kitten, fr. *kjetling* kitten, fr. ON *ketlingr* — more at KITLING] **1** *chiefly Scot* **:** KITTEN **2** *chiefly Scot* **:** GENERATE, ARISE

kittle cattle *n, pl* **kittle cattle** *usu pl in constr* [²*kittle*] *chiefly dial* **:** a group of people that are difficult to manage and inclined to be capricious ⟨*kittle cattle* who do rather unpredictable things —*Country Life*⟩

kit·tling \'kitlən\ *var of* KITLING

kit·tlish \'kitlish\ *also* **kit·tly** \-li\ *adj* [¹*kittle* + *-ish* or *-y*] *chiefly Scot* **:** TICKLISH, KITTLE

kitt·litz's murrelet \'kitləts(əz)-\ *n, usu cap K* [after Baron Friedrich von *Kittlitz* †1874 Ger. officer, ornithologist, and traveler] **:** a murrelet (*Brachyramphus brevirostre*) having buff spots and ranging from Japan and Kamchatka to Alaska

kit·tly-benders \'kitlē+,-\ *n pl* [*kittly* (perh. fr. ¹*kittle* + *-y*) + *benders*, pl. of *bender*] **:** thin bending ice; *also* **:** the act of running over such ice

kit·tul *also* **kit·tool** *or* **ki·tul** \kə'tül\ *n* -s [Sinhalese *kitul, hitul*, fr. Skt *hintāla*] **1 a :** a brownish black fiber resembling horsehair yielded by the leafstalks of the Asiatic jaggery palm and used chiefly in making brushes for polishing linens and cottons and for brushing velvets — called also *black fiber* **b :** JAGGERY PALM **2 a :** a fiber derived from the gomuti palm resembling kittul **b :** GOMUTI PALM

¹kit·ty \'kid·ē, -it|, |i\ *n* -ES [fr. *Kitty*, nickname for *Catherine*] **1** *also* **kittie** \"\ *-s chiefly Scot* **:** a girl of easy virtue **:** WENCH **2 :** KITTY WREN

²kitty \"\ *n* -ES [⁴*kit* + *-y*] **:** CAT 1a; *esp* **:** KITTEN

³kitty \"\ *n* -ES [¹*kit* + *-y*] **1 :** a small bowl or other receptacle **2 a** (1) **:** a fund in a poker game accumulated by taking one or two chips from each large pot and used (as to pay expenses or buy refreshments) for the players (2) **:** a pool that belongs to all players in a game but that participates in the scoring or settlement of certain hands as though it were a player opposed to the bidder **b :** a sum of money or collection of goods usu. accumulated by occasional small contributions and often administered by or for the contributors **:** POOL, FUND ⟨enough in the ~ to make the trip —E.K.Gann⟩ ⟨a campaign ~ raised by oil and utility companies —*Time*⟩ ⟨the ground crew's ~ of cigarettes —Saul Levitt⟩ **c :** the widow in skat, pinochle, and other games — called also *blind* **3 :** JACK 2e(1)

⁴kitty \"\ *n* -ES [prob. alter. of *kidcote*] *dial chiefly Eng* **:** JAIL

⁵kitty \"\ *n* -ES [by shortening & alter.] **:** KITTIWAKE

kitty-corner *or* **kitty-cornered** *var of* CATERCORNER

kitty wren *n* [fr. the name *Kitty*] **:** a wren (*Troglodytes troglodytes*)

ki·tu·na·han \kə'tünəhən\ *n* -s *usu cap* **:** a language family of southwestern Canada and northwestern U.S. comprising Kutenai

ki·va \'kēvə\ *n* -s [Hopi] **:** a Pueblo Indian structure used as a ceremonial, council, work, and lounging room for men that is usu. round and is at least partly underground with entrance and lighting usu. from the roof and that includes a fireplace, altar space, and sipapu

¹kiv·er \'kivə(r)\ *n* -s [ME *kevere*, alter. of *keve, kive* keeve — more at KEEVE] *dial Eng* **:** a shallow vessel or wooden tub

²kiver \"\ *dial var of* COVER

ki·wai \kē'wäē\ *n, pl* **kiwai** *or* **kiwais** *usu cap* **1 a :** a Papuan people inhabiting islands at the mouth of the Fly River, Territory of Papua **b :** a member of such people **2 :** the language of the Kiwai people

ki·wa·ni·an \kə'wänēən\ *n* -s *usu cap* [*Kiwanis* (club) + E *-an*] **:** a member of one of the major service clubs

ki·wi \'kē(,)wē\ *n* -s [Maori, of imit. origin] **1** *also* **kiwi-kiwi** \'=(,)=;=(,)=\ **:** a flightless New Zealand bird of the genus *Apteryx* that is about the size of a domestic chicken, has very rudimentary wings, stout legs, a long straight or slightly curved bill with nostrils near the tip, and hairlike plumage of various shades of gray and brown, nests in burrows, and lays eggs as large as one fourth its weight which are incubated by the male **2** *usu cap* **:** NEW ZEALANDER — used as a nickname

kiwi

kiyang *var of* KIANG

¹ki-yi \(')kī'yī\ *interj* [origin unknown] — used to express exultation

²ki-yi \"\ *vi* **ki-yied; ki-yied; ki-yiing; ki-yis** [imit.] **:** YELP ⟨a . . . dog ran *ki-yiing* past us —Klondy Nelson & Corey Ford⟩

³ki-yi \"\ *n* -s **1 :** a bark or yelp (as of a dog) **2 :** DOG

⁴ki-yi \"\ *n* -s [origin unknown] *in the U.S. Navy* **:** a small brush for scrubbing clothing or canvas

ki·yi \'kē(,)yē\ *n* -s [origin unknown] **:** a small chub (*Leucichthys kiyi*) abundant in deep water in the Great Lakes

ki·zil \kə'zil\ *n, pl* **kizil** *or* **kizils** *usu cap* **1 :** a Russianized Mongolo-Tatar people around Achinsk, central Siberia **2 :** a member of the Kizil people

kiz·il·bash \,kizəl'bäsh\ *n, pl* **kizilbash** *or* **kizilbashes** *usu cap* [Turk *kızılbaş*, fr. *kızıl* red + *baş* head] **1 :** a Persianized Turk of a class devoted to business and professional pursuits in Afghanistan; *also* **:** a member of a community of Turkish or mixed-race colonists in Asia Minor **2 :** a community of Kurdish Turks in eastern Turkey who are Christians and whose women refuse to veil their faces **3 :** a nomadic people in the plains around Ankara, Karahisar, and Tokat professing the Muslim religion but practicing ancient pagan rites

kj *abbr* kilojoule

kjel·dahl \'kel,däl\ *adj, usu cap* [after Johan G. C. T. *Kjeldahl* †1900 Dan. chemist] **:** of, relating to, or being a method for determining the amount of nitrogen (as in an organic substance) by digesting a sample with boiling concentrated sulfuric acid and other reagents or by adding an excess of alkali, distilling, and collecting the ammonia expelled or by determining the ammonia by titration

kjeldahl flask *n, usu cap K* [after Johan G. C. T. *Kjeldahl*] **:** a round-bottomed usu. long-necked glass flask for use in digesting the sample in the Kjeldahl method

kjel·dahl·iza·tion \,kel,dälə'zāshən\ *n* -s *sometimes cap* **:** the process of kjeldahlizing

kjel·dahl·ize \'kel,dä,līz\ *vt* -ED/-ING/-S *sometimes cap* [*Kjeldahl (method)* + *-ize*] **:** to subject to the Kjeldahl method or a modification of this method

kl *abbr* kiloliter

klab \'kläb\ *n* -s [by shortening] **:** KLABERJASS

kla·ber·jass \'kläbə(r),yäs\ *n* [G] **:** a two-handed game played with 32 cards in which a player scores by holding a higher sequence than his opponent, by holding both the king and queen of trumps, by taking the last trick, and by taking scoring cards in tricks — called also *clabber, clob, clobber, jass, klab, klob*

Kjeldahl flask

klallam *usu cap, var of* CLALLAM

kla·man·tan *or* **kle·man·tan** \klə'män·,tän\ *n, pl* **klamantan** *or* **klamantans** *or* **klemantan** *or* **klemantans** *usu cap* [native name in Borneo; akin to Indonesian *Kalimantan* Borneo] **1 :** any of numerous Dayak peoples living in western, central, and northern Borneo **2 :** a member of any of the Klamantan peoples

klam·ath \'klaməth\ *n, pl* **klamath** *or* **klamaths** *usu cap* **1 a :** a Lutuamian people of southeastern Oregon and northern California **b :** a member of such people **2 :** a language of the Klamath people

klamath weed *n, usu cap K* [fr. *Klamath* river, Oregon and California] **:** a cosmopolitan yellow-flowered perennial St.-John's-wort (*Hypericum perforatum*) common in fields and waste places and useful for wildlife but a noxious weed when established in rangelands

klan \'klan, -aa(ə)n\ *n* -s *usu cap* [fr. (*Ku Klux*) *Klan*, a secret organization — more at KU KLUX] **1 :** an organization of Ku Kluxers **2 :** a subordinate unit of the Ku Kluxers' organization

klan·ism \'kla,nizəm, -laa,n-\ *n* -s *usu cap* **:** the beliefs or practices of Ku Kluxers

klans·man \'klanzmən, -laanz-\ *n, pl* **klansmen** *usu cap* **:** KU KLUXER

klap·match *or* **clap·match** \'klap,mach\ *n* [by folk etymology fr. D *klapmuts* cap with earflaps, hooded seal, fr. *klap, klep* brim, earflap + *muts* cap] **:** a female seal

klap·roth·ite \'klaprə,thīt\ *or* **klap·roth·o·lite** \kla'prōthə,līt\ *n* -s [*klaprothite* fr. G *klaprothit*, fr. Martin H. *Klaproth* †1817 German chemist + G *-it* -ite; *klaprotholite* alter. of *klaprothite*] **:** a steel-gray mineral $Cu_6Bi_4S_9$ consisting of a sulfide of copper and bismuth

klatch *or* **klatsch** \'klach, -ä-\ *n* -ES [G *klatsch* gossip, action of gossiping, fr. *klatschen* to gossip, of imit. origin] **:** a gathering characterized by informal conversation ⟨you meet him at a literary cocktail ~ —Victor Riesel⟩

klav·ern \'klavə(r)n\ *n* -s [blend of *klan* and *cavern*] **1 :** a meeting place of Ku Kluxers ⟨sallies forth to the ~ and there dons his resplendent robe —Stetson Kennedy⟩ **2 :** a local unit of the Ku Kluxers' organization

kla·vier \klə'vi(ə)r, klä'-, -iə\ *n* -s [G, fr. F *clavier* — more at CLAVIER] **:** CLAVIER 2

kla·vier·stück \-,shtik, *G* klä'vēr,shtuek\ *n* [G, fr. *klavier* piano + *stück* piece] **:** a piano piece

Klax·on \'klaksən\ *trademark* — used for an electrically operated horn or warning signal

klea·gle \'klēgəl\ *n* -s *often cap* [*klan* + *eagle*] **:** a high-ranking officer in the hierarchy of the Ku Kluxers' organization

kle·bels·berg·ite \'klābəlz,bər,gīt\ *n* -s [Hung *klebelsbergit*, fr. Kuno *Klebelsberg* †1932 Hung. statesman + Hung *-it -ite*] **:** a mineral consisting of a basic antimony sulfate found in the interstices between crystals in columnar aggregates of stibnite

kleb·si·el·la \,klebzē'elə, -epsē-\ *n* [NL, fr. Edwin *Klebs* †1913 Ger. pathologist + NL *-i-* + *-ella*] **1** *cap* **:** a genus of plump nonmotile gram-negative frequently encapsulated bacterial rods (family Enterobacteriaceae) commonly held to comprise a single variable species — see PNEUMOBACILLUS **2** -s **:** an organism of the genus *Klebsiella*

klebs-löff·ler bacillus \'kläps|'leflə(r)-, 'klebz|\ *n, usu cap K&L* [after Edwin *Klebs* and Friedrich A. J. *Löffler* †1915 Ger. bacteriologist] **:** a bacterium (*Corynebacterium diphtheriae*) that causes human diphtheria

kleene·boc \'klīn(ə),bäk, -lān-\ *n* -s [Afrik *kleinbok*, fr. *klein* small + *bok* male antelope] **:** ROYAL ANTELOPE

Klee·nex \'klē,neks\ *trademark* — used for a cleansing tissue

klein bottle \'klīn-\ *n, usu cap K* [after Felix *Klein* †1925 Ger. mathematician and inventor] **:** a surface that is closed in such a way that it is possible to pass from a point on one side to the corresponding point on the opposite side without passing through the surface and that is formed by passing the nar-

Klein bottle

row end of a tapered tube through the side of the tube and flaring this end out to join the other end

klein·ite \'klī,nīt\ *n* -s [G *kleinit*, fr. Karl *Klein* †1907 Ger. mineralogist + G *-it* -ite] **:** a mineral approximately $Hg_{12-}(NH_4)_6SO_4Cl_6(OH)_3O_3$ consisting of a basic oxide, sulfate, and chloride of mercury and ammonium

kleist·ian jar \'klīstēən-\ *n, usu cap K* [Ewald J. von *Kleist* †1748 Ger. scientist and dean of the cathedral of Kamin, Pomerania, one of its discoverers] **:** LEYDEN JAR

klemantan *usu cap, var of* KLAMANTAN

klen·du·sic \(')klen¦d(y)üsik\ *also* **klen·du·sive** \-siv\ *adj* [*klendusity* + *-ic* or *-ive*] **:** characterized by klendusity

klen·du·si·ty \=ˈ==sәd-ē\ *n* -ES [irreg. fr. Gk *kleidoun* to lock up (fr. *kleid-, kleis* key) + *endysis* entry, act of putting on + E *-ity* — more at CLOSE, ENDYSIS] **:** the tendency of a plant or variety to escape infection as a result of having some property (as a thick cuticle or hairy surface) that prevents or hinders inoculation **:** disease-escaping ability

klepht *or* **clepht** \'kleft\ *n* -s *often cap* [NGk *klephtēs*, lit., robber, fr. Gk *kleptēs* robber, fr. *kleptein* to steal] **:** a Greek belonging to one of several independent armed sometimes brigandish communities formed after the Turkish conquest of Greece — **kleph·tic** \-tik\ *adj, usu cap*

klept- *or* **klepto-** *comb form* [Gk, fr. *kleptein* to steal; akin to Goth *hlifan* to steal, L *clepere* to steal, OPruss *auklipts* concealed] **:** stealing **:** theft ⟨*kleptistic*⟩ ⟨*kleptomania*⟩

klep·to·ma·nia *or* **clep·to·ma·nia** \,kleptә'mānēә, -nyә\ *n* [NL, fr. *klept-* + LL *mania*] **:** a persistent neurotic impulse to steal esp. without economic motive in which the object stolen is usu. believed to have symbolic significance to the kleptomaniac

[1]**klep·to·ma·ni·ac** *or* **clep·to·ma·ni·ac** \-nē,ak\ *n* [*klept-* + *maniac*] **:** a person evidencing kleptomania

[2]**kleptomaniac** *or* **cleptomaniac** \;==;==,=\ *adj* **:** of, relating to, or having the characteristics of kleptomania or a kleptomaniac

k–level \'=,==\ *n, usu cap K* **:** the energy level of an electron in a K-shell

klez·mer \'klezmәr\ *n, pl* **klez·mo·rim** \klez'mȯrәm\ *or* **klezmer** [Yiddish, modif. of Heb *kᵉlēy zemer* musical instruments] **:** a Jewish instrumentalist; *specif* **:** a member of a band of folk musicians in eastern Europe hired to play at Jewish weddings and gatherings

klick·i·tat *also* **klik·i·tat** \'klikә,tat\ *n, pl* **klickitat** *or* **klickitats** *usu cap* [Chinook, lit., beyond (the Cascade mountains)] **1 a :** a Shahaptian people of southern Washington **b :** a member of such people **2 :** a language of the Klickitat people

klieg eyes *or* **kleig eyes** \'klēg-\ *n pl, sometimes cap K* [*klieg* (*light*) or *kleig* (*light*)] **:** a condition marked by conjunctivitis and watering of the eyes resulting from excessive exposure to intense light

klieg light *or* **kleig light** *n, sometimes cap K* [after John H. *Kliegl* †1959 & his brother Anton T. *Kliegl* †1927 Amer. lighting experts born in Germany] **:** a carbon arc lamp used in taking motion pictures

kline reaction *or* **kline test** \'klīn-\ *n, usu cap K* [after Benjamin S. *Kline* *b*1886 Amer. pathologist] **:** a rapid precipitation test for the diagnosis of syphilis

kling \'kliŋ\ *n* -s *usu cap* [Malay *këling*] **:** a Dravidian prob. of Tamil origin of the seaports of southeastern Asia and Malaysia

klink *var of* CLINK

kli·no·kinesis \;klī(,)nō+\ *n* [NL, fr. Gk *klinein* to lean, slope + NL *-o-* + *kinesis* — more at LEAN] **:** movement that is induced by stimulation and that involves essentially random alteration of direction

kli·no·kinetic \"+\ *adj* [Gk *klinein* + E *-o-* + *kinetic*] **:** of or relating to klinokinesis

klinostat *n* -s [G, fr. *klino-* clin- + *-stat*] **:** CLINOSTAT

kli·no·taxis \;klīnә+\ *n* [NL, fr. Gk *klinein* + NL *-o-* + *-taxis*] **:** directional orientation involving turning toward a stimulus

klip·bok \'klip,bäk\ *n* -s [Afrik, fr. *klip* cliff, rock + *bok* male antelope] **:** KLIPSPRINGER

klip·das·sie \'klip,däsē\ *or* **klip·das** \-äs\ *n, pl* **klipdassies** *or* **klipdases** [Afrik, fr. *klip* + *dassie* or *das*] **:** a hyrax (*Procavia capensis*) of southern Africa

klip·fish *or* **clip·fish** \'klip,fish\ *n* [in sense 1, part trans. of Dan *klipfisk*, Norw *klippfisk* & G *klippfisch*; Dan & Norw, prob. fr. G, fr. *klippe* rock near the sea, cliff + *fisch* fish; in sense 2, part trans. of Afrik *klipvis*, fr. *klip* rock, stone (fr. MD *klippe*) + *vis* fish; akin to OE *clif* cliff — more at CLIFF] **1 :** a fish (as cod) split open, salted, and dried **2 :** a fish of the family Clinidae **:** KELPFISH

klip·haas \'klip,häs\ *n* -ES [Afrik, fr. *klip* + *haas* hare] **:** ROCK HARE

[1]**klip·pe** \'klipә\ *n* -s [G, fr. Sw *klippa* to cut, shear, clip, fr. ON] **:** a coin with a square or lozenge-shaped flan (as in 17th century German necessity money)

[2]**klippe** \"\ *or* **klip** \'klip\ *n, pl* **klip·pen** \-pәn\ *or* **klips** [G *klippe* cliff, crag, rock near the sea, fr. MHG, fr. MLG; akin to OE *clif* cliff — more at CLIFF] **:** an outlying isolated remnant of an overthrust rock mass owing its isolation to erosion **:** OUTLIER

klip·salamander \'klip,==,=\ *n* [Afrik, fr. *klip* + *salamander*] **:** a spiny girdle-tailed lizard (*Cordylus cordylus*) that is widely distributed in rocky uplands of southern Africa and that exhibits black and yellowish or reddish color phases; *broadly* **:** GIRDLETAILED LIZARD

klip·spring·er \'klip,spriŋә(r)\ *n* [Afrik, fr. *klip* + *springer* springer, leaper] **:** a small antelope (*Oreotragus oreotragus*) that is somewhat like the chamois in habits and is found from Cape Colony to Somaliland — called also *klipbok*

klis·mos \'kliz,mäs, -,mos\ *n* -ES [Gk, fr. *klinein* to lean, recline — more at LEAN] **:** a chair of Greek design having a concavely curved back rail and curved legs

klis·ter \'klistә(r)\ *n* -s [Norw, lit., paste, fr. MLG *klīster*; akin to OE *clǣg* clay — more at CLAY] **:** a soft wax used on skis esp. for corn snow or crust

klm *abbr* kilometer

klob \'kläb\ *n* -s [by shortening and alter.] **:** KLABERJASS

klock·mann·ite \'kläkmә,nīt\ *n* -s [G *klockmannit*, fr. Friedrich *Klockmann* †1937 Ger. mineralogist + G *-it* -ite] **:** a mineral CuSe consisting of a selenide of copper found in tarnished blue-black granular aggregates

klomp \'klämp\ *n, pl* **klom·pen** \-pәn\ [D *klomp* lump, wooden shoe, fr. MD *clompe* clod, block; akin to LG *klump* lump, clump — more at CLUMP] **:** a wooden shoe worn in the Low countries

klomp

klompen dance *n* [part trans. of D *klompendans*, fr. *klomp* + *dans* dance] **:** a Dutch folk dance performed in wooden shoes

klon·dike \'klän,dīk\ *n* -s *usu cap* [fr. *Klondike*, region in Yukon territory, Canada, where a gold rush took place (1897-99)] **1 :** a source of valuable material or wealth ⟨every new road a *Klondike* to the country through which it passes —Cy Warman⟩ ⟨Yiddish represents a potential *Klondike* of barely tapped resources for Germanic and Slavic specialists —H.H. Paper⟩ **2 :** solitaire in which 28 cards are laid out in 7 piles consisting respectively of 1 to 7 cards with the top card of each pile face up and the remaining cards of the pack built in descending sequence of alternate colors as the player goes once through the rest of the pack one card at a time with the object of removing aces from the tableau as they become available and of building on them up to kings — called also *Canfield*

klon·dik·er \-kә(r)\ *n* -s *usu cap* [*Klondike* region + E *-er*] **:** an inhabitant of the Klondike region of northwestern Canada; *esp* **:** one who prospects for gold

klong \'klȯŋ, -äŋ\ *n* -s [native name in Thailand] **:** a canal in Thailand used for transportation and drainage ⟨the pond . . . narrowed into a ~ that rimmed the far width of the compound —Kathryn Grondahl⟩

kloof \'klüf, *Afrik* 'klüf\ *n* -s [Afrik, fr. MD *clove* cleft, crevice; akin to OHG *klobo* forked stick, fetter, OS *klobo* shackle for the foot, ON *klofi* cleft, OHG *klioban* to split — more at CLEAVE (split)] *Africa* **:** a deep glen **:** GORGE, RAVINE ⟨the narrow ~s of the echoing hills —Stuart Cloete⟩

klootch·man \'klüchmәn\ *also* **klooch** \-ch\ *n, pl* **klootchmen** *also* **klooches** [Chinook Jargon *klootshman*, fr. Nootka *łotssma* woman; wife] **:** an Indian woman of northwestern No. America

klop–klop *var of* CLOP-CLOP

klös·se *or* **kloes·se** \'klāsә, *among speakers of German descent in US often* 'klās *or* 'glās\ *n pl* [G *klösse*, pl. of *kloss* lump, clod, dumpling, fr. MHG *klōz* lump — more at CLOUT] **:** DUMPLINGS

kluck·er \'klәkә(r)\ *n* -s *usu cap* [by shortening & alter.] **:** KU KLUXER

klu·kia \'klükēә\ *n, cap* [NL] **:** a genus of early Mesozoic fossil ferns having large much divided fronds and sporangia arranged in spikes (as in ferns of the genus *Schizaea*)

klunk *var of* CLUNK

klux \'klәks\ *vt* -ED/-ING/-ES *often cap* [by shortening] **:** KU-KLUX

klux·er \'klәksә(r)\ *n* -s *usu cap* [by shortening] **:** KU KLUXER

klux·ery \-sәrē\ *n* -ES *usu cap* [short for *Ku-Kluxery*] **:** KLANISM

klux·ism \-,sizәm\ *n* -s *usu cap* [short for *Ku-Kluxism*] **:** KLANISM

Kly·don·o·graph \klī'dänә,graf, -räf\ *trademark* — used for an instrument that makes a photographic record of electric surges in power lines

klys·tron \'klīsträn\ *n* -s [fr. *Klystron*, a trademark] **:** an electron tube in which bunching of electrons is produced by subjecting them to acceleration and deceleration by high potential across a gap and which is used for the generation and amplification of ultrahigh-frequency current (as in radar)

km *abbr* **1** kilometer **2** kingdom

kmer *usu cap, var of* KHMER

KMPS *abbr, often not cap* kilometers per second

kmw *abbr* kilomegawatt

kmwh *abbr* kilomegawatt-hour

kn *abbr* knot

[1]**knack** \'nak\ *n* -s [ME *knak, knakke*] **1 a :** a task or chore requiring adroitness and dexterity **b :** a clever way of doing something **c :** TRICK, SCHEME, STRATAGEM **2 a :** a special ready capacity that is hard to analyze or teach for dexterous adroit performance esp. of the unusual, technical, or difficult ⟨the ~ of writing unforgettable, irresistible melodies —Roland Gelatt⟩ **b :** TRAIT, TENDENCY, INCLINATION; *esp* **:** one strictly individual and difficult to explain or analyze ⟨these rents in the interior of the earth had a ~ of enlarging themselves —Norman Douglas⟩ **3 a** *archaic* **:** an ingenious device **:** a cleverly made contrivance; *broadly* **:** TOY, TRINKET, KNICKKNACK **b** *obs* **:** a dainty article of food **:** DELICACY **c** *obs* **:** an ingenious literary device **:** CONCEIT **syn** see GIFT

[2]**knack** \"\ *n* -s [ME *knak*, of imit. origin like MHG *knacken* to make a cracking noise, OE *cnocian* to knock — more at KNOCK] **:** a sharp sound (as of the snapping of a finger)

[3]**knack** \"\ *vb* -ED/-ING/-S *vt, dial Brit* **:** to strike together so as to make a sharp snapping noise ~ *vi, now dial* **:** to make a sharp abrupt snapping noise **:** CRACK

knack·a·way \'nakә,wā, 'näk-\ *also* **knock·a·way** \'näk-\ *n* [by folk etymology fr. MexSp *anacua* — more at ANAQUA] **:** ANAQUA

knäck·e·bröd \(kә)'nekә,brә(r)d, -bәrd,-brēd,-bred\ *n* -s [Sw, fr. *knäcka* to break + *bröd* bread] **:** a very crisp and brittle unleavened rye bread made in large flat circular pieces often with a hole in the center

[1]**knack·er** \'nakә(r)\ *n* -s [[3]*knack* + *-er*] **:** something (as a castanet) used to make a sharp sound or noise; *esp* **:** one of two pieces of bone or wood held loosely between the fingers and struck together by moving the hand — usu. used in pl.

[2]**knacker** \"\ *n* -s [prob. fr. E dial. *knacker, nacker* harness-maker, saddle maker, prob. of Scand origin; akin to Icel *hnakkur* saddle; akin to ON *hnakki, hnakkr* back of the neck — more at NECK] **1** *also* **knacker·man** \-mәn\ *Brit* **:** one that buys worn-out domestic animals or their carcasses and disposes of the products for other purposes than use as human food (as for animal food or fertilizer) ⟨Jones will sell you to the ~, who will cut your throat and boil you down for the foxhounds —George Orwell⟩ **2** *Brit* **:** one that buys up old structures (as buildings or ships) for their constituent materials **3** *dial Eng* **:** an old worn-out domestic animal (as a horse)

knack·ery \'nakәri\ *n* -ES [[2]*knacker* + *-y*] *Brit* **:** the place of business of a knacker **:** RENDERING PLANT

knack·wurst *or* **knock·wurst** \'näk,=\ *n* -s [G *knackwurst*, fr. *knacken* to make a cracking noise (fr. MHG) + *wurst* sausage — more at KNACK, BRATWURST] **:** a sausage that is shorter and thicker than a frankfurter and more heavily seasoned

knacky \'nakē\ *adj* -ER/-EST [[1]*knack* + *-y*] *chiefly dial* **:** HANDY, INGENIOUS, CLEVER

knag \'nag\ *n* -s [ME *knagge, knagg*; akin to MLG *knagge* knot in wood, pin, peg, Sw *knagg* knot in wood, lump, Norw *knagg, knagge* pin, peg, handle, and perh. to OE *cnotta* knot — more at KNOT] **1 a** *obs* **:** short projection or spur esp. from a tree trunk or branch **b** *archaic* **:** a wooden peg for hanging things on **2** *obs* **:** a prong of an antler

knagged *adj* [ME, fr. *knagge, knagg* + *-ed*] *obs* **:** KNAGGY

knag·gy \'nagē\ *adj* -ER/-EST **:** full of or covered with gnarled knotty protuberances **:** CRAGGY, RUGGED, ROUGH ⟨the old dark — skull —Isak Dinesen⟩

knai·del \kә'nādәl, 'knā-\ *n, pl* **knai·dlach** \-dlәk\ [Yiddish *kneydel*, fr. MHG *knödel* — more at KNÖDEL] **:** DUMPLING 1a

[1]**knap** \'nap\ *n* -s [ME *knap*, fr. OE *cnæpp*; akin to OFris *knapp* button, MLG, hill, heel of a shoe, ON *knappr* button, OE *cnotta* knot — more at KNOT] *chiefly dial* **:** a top or crest of a hill **:** SUMMIT; *also* **:** a small hill or knoll

[2]**knap** *also* **nap** \"\ *n* -s [ME, of imit. origin] **:** a sharp or abrupt blow **:** RAP, KNOCK

[3]**knap** \"\ *vb* **knapped; knapped; knapping; knaps** [ME *knappen*, of imit. origin like MD *cnappen* to make a snapping noise, LG *knappen*] *vt* **1** *dial Brit* **:** to strike a sharp crisp blow to or with ⟨*knapped* his knuckles against the gatepost⟩ **:** RAP **2** *also* **nap :** to break with a quick jerk or blow; *esp* **:** to break up or dress (as flints) **3** *chiefly dial Brit* **:** to bite sharply or eagerly at **:** SNAP, CROP ⟨sheep *knapping* the new flush⟩ **4** *dial Brit* **:** to speak or utter brightly or affectedly **:** CHATTER ~ *vi* **1** *chiefly dial Brit* **:** to bite sharply or eagerly **2** *dial Brit* **:** to chatter smartly **:** BABBLE

knap·per *also* **nap·per** \-pә(r)\ *n* -s [[3]*knap* + *-er*] **:** one that knaps; *esp* **:** one that dresses flints or other stone by knapping

knap·ping hammer *also* **nap·ping hammer** \'napiŋ-\ *n* **:** a hammer having a medium-weight head with two slightly convex faces used for knapping stone

[1]**knap·sack** \'nap,sak\ *n* [LG *knappsack* or D *knapzak*, fr. LG & D *knappen* to make a snapping noise, bite into, eat + LG *sack* (fr. MLG *sak*) & D *zak* bag, sack, fr. MD *sac* — more at KNAP, SACK] **1 :** a bag or case often of canvas supported on the back by a strap over each shoulder and used esp. for carrying supplies while on a march **2** *or* **knapsack tank :** a container equipped with pressurizing and spraying devices, carried on the back, and used to transport materials (as insecticides or fire-extinguishing chemicals) to the point of application

knapsack 1

[2]**knapsack** \"\ *vb* -ED/-ING/-S *vt* **:** to equip with a knapsack ⟨~*ed* travelers⟩ ~ *vi* **:** to travel on foot dependent for supplies on the contents of a knapsack

knapsack sprayer *or* **knapsack pump** *n* **:** a spraying apparatus consisting of a knapsack tank together with pressurizing device, line, and sprayer nozzle, used chiefly in fire control and in spraying fungicides or insecticides

knapscull *also* **knapscap** *n* [ME *knapescall*] *obs Scot* **:** HELMET

knap·weed \'nap,=\ *n* [ME *knopwed*, fr. *knop* + *wed, weed* weed — more at KNOP, WEED] **:** any of various plants of the genus *Centaurea*; *esp* **:** a weedy perennial (*C. nigra*) that is native to Europe but widely naturalized and that has tough wiry stems and knobby heads of purple flowers

knarl *archaic var of* GNARL

knar·ry \'närē\ *adj* *also* **knarred** \-rd\ *adj* [*knarry* fr. ME, fr. *knarre* + *-y*; *knarred* fr. *knar* + *-ed*] **:** KNOTTY, GNARLED

knat *or* **knatte** *archaic var of* GNAT

knaur \'nȯ(ә)r\ *or* **knar** \'när\ *n* -s [ME *knarre* rough stone, knot in wood — more at KNUR] **:** a knot or burl on wood

knau·tia \'nau̇d·ēә\ [NL, fr. Christian *Knaut* †1716 Ger. physician + NL *-ia*] *syn of* SCABIOSA

[1]**knave** \'nāv\ *n* -s [ME (also, boy), fr. OE *cnafa* boy, male servant; akin to OHG *knabo* boy, OHG *knebil* piece of wood used in fastenings, ON *knefill* stick, pole, and prob. to OE *cnotta* knot — more at KNOT] **1** *archaic* **a :** a serving boy **b :** a male servant or menial **c :** a man of humble birth or position **2 :** a tricky deceitful fellow **:** an unscrupulous person **:** ROGUE, RASCAL **3 :** JACK 1 c (1) **syn** see VILLAIN

[2]**knave** \"\ *vb* -ED/-ING/-S *vt* **1** *obs* **:** to give the name of knave to **2** *obs* **:** to make a knave of (as oneself) ~ *vi, archaic* **:** to behave knavishly

knave bairn *n* [ME *knavebarn*, fr. *knave* + *barn* child — more at BAIRN] *chiefly Scot* **:** a male child

knav·ery \'nāv(ә)rē, -ri\ *n* -ES **1 a :** the practices of a knave **:** petty villainy **:** knavish action **:** FRAUD, TRICKERY, RASCALITY **b :** a roguish or mischievous trick **:** a rascally scheme — usu. used in pl. **2** *obs* **:** tricks of dress **:** quaint ornaments **:** TRINKETRY **3** *obs* **:** mischievous sportiveness **:** roguish mischief

knave·ship \'nāv,ship\ *n* **1 :** the condition of being a knave **:** the personality of a knave **2** *Scots law* **:** a small customary due formerly paid in meal to the miller's servant at a thirlage mill in return for grinding a quantity of grain

knav·ess \'nāvәs\ *n* -ES **:** a female knave

knav·ish \-vish,-vēsh\ *adj* [ME *knavyssh*, fr. *knave* + *-yssh, -ish* -ish] **:** having the characteristics of or appropriate to a knave: **a** *obs* **:** MISCHIEVOUS, ROGUISH ⟨a ~ lad, thus to make poor females mad —Shak.⟩ **b :** DISHONEST, FRAUDULENT ⟨~ booksellers put forth volumes of trash —T.B.Macaulay⟩

knav·ish·ly *adv* **:** in a knavish manner

knav·ish·ness *n* -ES **:** the quality or state of being knavish **:** KNAVERY

knaw \'nȯ, 'nå\ *dial Brit var of* KNOW

knaw·el \'nȯ(ә)l\ *n* -s [modif. of G *knäuel, knauel*, lit., ball of yarn, fr. MHG *kniuwel*, alter. of *kliuwel*, dim. of *kliuwe* ball of yarn, fr. OHG *kliuwa* — more at CLEW] **:** a low spreading Old World annual weed (*Scleranthus annuus*) with inconspicuous greenish flowers that is now widely distributed in No. America; *also* **:** any of several other weedy plants of this genus

knead \'nēd\ *vb* -ED/-ING/-S [ME *kneden*, fr. OE *cnedan*; akin to OS *knedan* to knead, OHG *knetan*, ON *knotha* to knead, OSlav *gnesti* to press, OPruss *gnode* trough for kneading bread, OE *cnotta* knot — more at KNOT] *vt* **1 a :** to work and press into a mass with or as if with the hands ⟨~*ing* clay to perfect smoothness⟩ **b :** to mix (as the materials of bread) into a well-blended whole by or as if by repeatedly drawing out and pressing together **c :** to make (as bread) by such a process **2 :** to manipulate or work on with or as if with a kneading motion ⟨~*ed* the shoulder muscles to relieve the stiffness⟩ **:** alter or affect with or as if with repeated small pressures ⟨gradually ~*ing* the idea into shape⟩ **3 :** to make kneading movements with ⟨~*ing* her fists into her waist —J.S. Redding⟩ ~ *vi* **:** to make kneading movements **:** perform the action of kneading with or as if with the hands ⟨a kitten ~*ing* on the bed⟩ ⟨~*ed* away at the cheeks —Constance Foley⟩

knead·able \-dәbәl\ *adj* **:** suitable for kneading; *esp* **:** having the proper texture for kneading with the hands ⟨flour that produces an excellent ~ dough⟩

kneaded eraser *also* **kneaded rubber** *n* **:** a soft pliable eraser of unvulcanized rubber used esp. to remove graphite or charcoal marks from drawing paper

knead·er \'nēdә(r)\ *n* -s **:** one that kneads

knead·ing·ly *adv* **:** in the manner of one that kneads **:** with a kneading movement ⟨pressed her fingers ~ against the cushion⟩

kneading table *n* **:** DOUGH TRAY

knead·man \'nēdmәn\ *n, pl* **kneadmen :** a worker that tends a machine which kneads flour paste for macaroni products

kne·bel·ite \'nābә,līt\ *n* -s [G *knebelit*, fr. Karl Ludwig von *Knebel* †1834 Ger. translator + G *-it* -ite] **:** a variously colored mineral $(Fe,Mn)_2SiO_4$ consisting of iron manganese silicate and occurring esp. in Sweden (sp. gr. 4.1)

[1]**knee** \'nē\ *n* -s *often attrib* [ME *kne, knee*, fr. OE *cnēow, cnēo*; akin to OHG *kneo* knee, ON *knē*, Goth *kniu*, L *genu*, Gk *gony*, Skt *jānu*] **1 a** (1) **:** a joint of the ginglymus type in the middle part of the human leg that is the articulation between the femur, tibia, and patella (2) **:** the part of the leg that includes this joint ⟨scrubbing the floor on hands and ~*s*⟩ **b :** the corresponding joint in the hind limb of a quadrupedal vertebrate formed by the femur above and the tibia or tibia and fibula below **2 a :** a bending of the knee (as in respect or courtesy) ⟨a man of parts well able to make a good ~⟩ **b :** a blow with the bent knee — usu. used with *the* ⟨got the ~ in the face as he tried to get up⟩ **3 :** something felt to resemble the human knee esp. in its angular bent form: as **a** (1) **:** a crook in a tree branch (2) **:** a piece of timber naturally or artificially bent for use in supporting structures coming together at an angle (as the framing and deck beams of a ship) (3) **:** a piece of metal of similar form and corresponding function **b** *archaic* **:** an angular joint in a grass **c :** a rounded or somewhat conical process arising from the roots of a few swamp-growing trees (as the bald cypress and tupelo gum) and projecting above the surrounding water — compare BUTTRESS ROOT **d :** the part of a cabriole furniture leg that curves outward immediately below the junction of leg and frame **e :** a vertical curve in a stair handrail that is convex on top — compare RAMP **f :** the part of the head block of a sawmill that is attached to the dogs holding a log **g :** the part of a composing stick which is attached and at right angles to the back rim and with which the measure is set **h :** an abrupt change in direction in a curve (as on a graph); *esp* **:** one approaching a right angle in shape **4 :** any of several bodily parts that are structurally or functionally comparable to the human knee: as **a :** the carpal joint of the forelimb of a quadrupedal vertebrate corresponding to the wrist in man — see HORSE illustration **b** (1) **:** the tarsal joint of a bird corresponding to the ankle of man (2) **:** the corresponding joint of a quadrupedal mammal — not used technically **c :** the joint between the femur and tibia of an insect **5 :** the part of a garment that covers the knee — **on one's knees :** in a state of serious or irremediable defeat or failure ⟨a great nation economically *on its knees*⟩ — **on the knees of the gods** [trans. of Gk *theōn en gounasi*] **:** beyond human control or knowledge — **over in the knees :** KNEE-SPRUNG — **to one's knees :** into a state of submission or defeat ⟨forced *to his knees* by competition⟩

[2]**knee** \"\ *vb* **kneed; kneed; kneeing; knees** [ME *knewen*, fr. OE *cnēowian*, fr. *cnēow, cnēo* knee] *vi* **1** *obs* **:** to bend the knee **:** bow low **:** KNEEL **2 :** to bend like a knee — often used with *over* ⟨heavy-headed grain may lodge or ~ over⟩ ~ *vt* **1** *archaic* **:** to bend the knee to in supplication or deference **2 :** to go over or traverse on the knees ⟨painfully ~*ing* his way up the stairs⟩ **3 a :** to strike or touch with the knee ⟨*kneed* his opponent repeatedly⟩ **b :** to move or cause to move with the knee ⟨*kneed* the door open⟩ **c :** to press the flanks of (a saddle horse) with the knees in alerting or encouraging **4 :** to repair or replace the knee of (as a garment) **5 :** to cut the knee of so as to disable ⟨~ a steer⟩ **6 :** to secure by a knee ⟨transoms must be *kneed* to the horn timber —Edwin Monk⟩

knee action *n* **:** a front-wheel suspension (as of an automobile) permitting independent vertical movement of each front wheel

knee baby *n, dial* **:** a baby barely able to walk ⟨a *knee baby* and a lap baby⟩

knee bend *n* **:** an exercise performed by dropping from an upright to a squatting position and resuming an upright position without using the hands

kneeboard \'=,=\ *n* **:** a low wall surrounding a riding ring

knee bone *n* **:** PATELLA

knee boot *n* **1 :** a cover for a knee or for the knees: **a :** a carriage boot for protecting the knees from rain or splatter **b :** a protective boot of padded leather used on the knees of a horse that tends to overreach or strike himself in the knee **2 :** a boot reaching to the knee ⟨wading in *knee boots*⟩

knee brace *n* **:** a bracing member of a structure that is placed diagonally from one to another of two adjoining principal members

knee breeches *n pl* **:** BREECHES

kneebrush \'=,=\ *n* **1 :** a tuft or brush of hair on the knees of some antelopes and other animals **2 :** POLLEN BRUSH

knee buckle *n* **:** a buckle used to fasten knee breeches at or just below the knee
kneecap \ˈ=,=\ *n* **1 :** PATELLA **2 :** a protective cover for the knee
knee colter *n* **:** a knee-shaped colter
knee-crooking \ˈ=,==\ *adj* **:** OBSEQUIOUS, FAWNING
kneed \ˈnēd\ *adj* [ˡ*knee* + *-ed*] **1 :** having a knee or knees ⟨a graceful ~ table⟩ — often used in combination ⟨a knobby-*kneed* boy⟩ **2 :** having a bend or angle like that of the bent human knee **:** GENICULATE ⟨steep ~ gables⟩
knee-deep \ˈ=ˈ=\ *adj* [ME *kne-depe*, fr. *kne, knee* knee + *depe, deep* deep — more at KNEE, DEEP] **1 :** rising to the knees **:** KNEE-HIGH ⟨*knee-deep* snow⟩ **2 a :** sunk to the knees ⟨men *knee-deep* in water⟩ **b :** deeply engaged or occupied **:** OVERWHELMED ⟨*knee-deep* in turmoil⟩ ⟨*knee-deep* in war⟩
knee drill *n* **:** a special Salvation Army service at which most of the time is spent on the knees in prayer
knee drop *n* **:** a fundamental trampoline stunt in which the performer drops to his knees on the bed and then rebounds to a standing position
knee-halter \ˈ=,==\ *vt* **:** to restrain (a horse) by passing a line from the halter or bridle to the knee of a foreleg so as to permit grazing but prevent free or fast movement
knee-high \ˈ=ˈ=\ *adj* **:** rising or reaching upward to the knees ⟨*knee-high* stockings⟩
knee-high blackberry *n* **:** SAND BLACKBERRY
kneehole \ˈ=,=\ *n* **:** an open space (as under a desk) for the knees
kneehole desk *n* **:** a flat-topped desk having a kneehole with flanking tiers of drawers
kneeing *pres part of* KNEE
knee jerk *n* **:** an involuntary forward jerk or kick induced by a light blow or sudden strain upon the patellar tendon of the knee that causes a reflex contraction of the quadriceps muscle

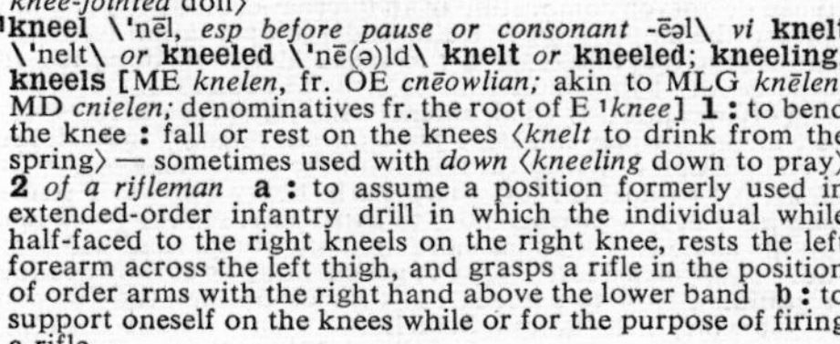
kneehole desk

knee joint *n* **1 :** KNEE 1a(1) **2 :** TOGGLE JOINT
knee-jointed \ˈ=ˈ=,=\ *adj* **1 :** GENICULATE, KNEED **2 :** having jointed knees ⟨a *knee-jointed* doll⟩
ˡ**kneel** \ˈnēl, *esp before pause or consonant* -ēəl\ *vi* **knelt** \ˈnelt\ *or* **kneeled** \ˈnē(ə)ld\ **knelt** *or* **kneeled; kneeling; kneels** [ME *knelen*, fr. OE *cnēowlian*; akin to MLG *knēlen*, MD *cnielen*; denominatives fr. the root of E ˡ*knee*] **1 :** to bend the knee **:** fall or rest on the knees ⟨*knelt* to drink from the spring⟩ — sometimes used with *down* ⟨*kneeling* down to pray⟩ **2** *of a rifleman* **a :** to assume a position formerly used in extended-order infantry drill in which the individual while half-faced to the right kneels on the right knee, rests the left forearm across the left thigh, and grasps a rifle in the position of order arms with the right hand above the lower band **b :** to support oneself on the knees while or for the purpose of firing a rifle
²**kneel** \"\ *n* -s **:** an act or instance of kneeling
kneel·er \ˈnēlə(r)\ *n* -s [ME *knelere*, fr. *knelen* to kneel + *-ere* -er] **1 :** one that kneels (as in worship) **2 :** something (as a cushion, stool, board) to kneel on **3 a :** a stone cut to provide a change of direction in masonry **b :** a stone so cut as to support and retain the coping of the slope of a gable
knee·let \ˈnēlət\ *n* -s [ˡ*knee* + *-let*] **:** a protective covering for the knee
ˡ**kneeling** *n* -s [ME *kneling*, fr. gerund of *knelen* to kneel — more at KNEEL] **1 :** the act of one that kneels **:** GENUFLECTION **2 :** a place or space for kneeling (as in a church)
²**kneeling** *adj* **:** suitable for use in kneeling ⟨a ~ cushion⟩ **:** designed to be used while kneeling ⟨~ desks⟩
kneel·ing·ly *adv* **:** in or from a kneeling position
knee mortar *n* **:** a light grenade discharger used by the Japanese during World War II
knee of head : an arrangement of timbers outside the stem and below the bowsprit that forms an overhanging bow in a wooden ship
kneepad \ˈ=,=\ *n* **:** a protective pad for the knee sometimes attached to a garment
kneepan \ˈ=,=\ *n* [ME *knepanne*, fr. *kne* knee + *panne* pan — more at KNEE, PAN] **1 :** PATELLA **2 :** a concavity at the distal end of the femur of an insect
knee plate *n* **1 :** a broad steel plate covering the thigh and projecting on each side and used chiefly in body armor for tilting **2 :** a plate for connecting a beam or girder to the frame of a ship
knee rafter *n* **:** a diagonal brace between a principal rafter and a tie beam
knee roll *n* **:** a padded margin sometimes introduced on the forepart of the skirt of an English saddle to keep a rider's leg from slipping forward
knee roof *n* **:** CURB ROOF
knees *pl of* KNEE, *pres 3d sing of* KNEE
knee·sie \ˈnēzē\ *n* -s [*knees* (pl. of ˡ*knee*) + *-ie*] *slang* **:** an action of flirting or becoming friendly or intimate ⟨played ~*s* under the table —Lane Foster⟩
knee-sprung \ˈ=,=\ *adj, of a horse* **:** having the knees bent when they should normally be straight; *esp* **:** having the knees protruding too far forward — compare BUCK KNEE
kneestone \ˈ=,=\ *n* **:** a kneeler for a gable slope
knee strap *n* **1 :** a strap to hold a shoe on a cobbler's knee **2 :** an iron strap or facing for a knee timber
knee-tied \ˈ=,=\ *adj, of a horse* **:** having a poor conformation in the front legs with the anteroposterior diameter of the leg just below the knee too narrow
knee timber *n* **1 :** timber with natural knees or angles in it **2 :** a piece of timber with a knee or angle in it
knee tool *n* **:** a knee-shaped tool holder; *usu* **:** a turret-lathe or screw-machine tool holder that supports tools for simultaneous turning and internal-cutting operations
knee wall *n* **:** a partition for supporting roof rafters when the span is great or for forming a side wall (as of a second-story room) under a pitched roof
kneif·fia \ˈnīfēə\ *n, cap* [NL, fr. F. G. *Kneiff* †1832 Ger. physician and botanist + NL *-ia*] *in some classifications* **:** a genus of No. American day-blooming herbs (family Onagraceae) having stamens of unequal length and a 4-angled ovary and often included in *Oenothera* — compare SUNDROPS
kneipp·ism \ˈnī,pizəm\ *also* **kneipp's cure** \ˈnīps-\ *or* **kneipp cure** *n, usu cap K* [*Kneippism* fr. Sebastian *Kneipp* †1897 Ger. priest who developed it + E *-ism*; *Kneipp's cure* or *Kneipp cure* after S. *Kneipp*, trans. of G *Kneippsche kur* or *Kneipp-kur*] **:** treatment of disease by forms of hydrotherapy (as walking barefoot in morning dew)
ˡ**knell** \ˈnel\ *vb* -ED/-ING/-S [ME *knillen, knellen*, fr. OE *cnyllan*; akin to MHG *erknellen* to resound, toll, MHG *knüllen* to strike, beat, ON *knylla*, and prob. to OE *cnotta* knot — more at KNOT] *vt* **1** *obs* **:** to ring (a bell) with slow solemnity **:** TOLL **2 :** to summon by or as if by a knell **3 :** to announce or proclaim by or as if by a knell ⟨the bell buoy ~*s* your hour —Marguerite J. Adams⟩ ~ *vi* **1 a** *of a bell* **:** RING; *esp* **:** to toll at a death, funeral, or disaster **b :** to sound a knell **2 a :** to give forth a sound like a knell ⟨the owl at its ~*ing* —Dylan Thomas⟩ **b :** to sound a warning or have a sound or import of evil omen
²**knell** \"\ *n* -s [ME *cnul, knel*, fr. OE *cnyll*, fr. *cnyllan*, v.] **1 :** a stroke or sound of a bell (as when tolled at a funeral or at the death of a person) **:** a death signal or passing bell **2 :** a warning of or a sound indicating the passing away of something ⟨this decision sounded the ~ of our hopes⟩
knelt *past of* KNEEL
kne·mi·do·kop·tes \,nēmədōˈkäp(,)tēz\ *n, cap* [NL, fr. Gk *knēmid-, knēmis* greave, legging + NL *-o-* + *-koptes* (fr. Gk *koptein* to smite, cut off); akin to Gk *knēmē* shinbone — more at CAPON, HAM] **:** a genus of itch mites attacking birds — see DEPLUMING MITE, SCALY-LEG MITE; compare SCALY LEG — **kne·mi·do·kop·tic** \ˌ===ˈ=,tik\ *adj*
knet *dial past of* KNIT
knettle *var of* NETTLE
knew *past or dial past part of* KNOW

knez \kəˈnez\ *n, pl* **knezes** *also* **knezi** [of Slav origin; akin to Serbo-Croatian *knez* prince, Russ *knyaz'*, OSlav *kŭnędzĭ*, of Gmc origin; akin to OHG *kuning* king — more at KING] **:** a Slavic prince or duke
knib \ˈnib\ *n* -s [by alter.] **:** NIB 6a, 6b
knicht *archaic var of* KNIGHT
knick \ˈnik\ *n* -s [*knick*point] **:** NICK 6
knick·er \-kə(r)\ *n* -s *often attrib* [short for *knickerbocker*] **1 knickers** *pl* **:** KNICKERBOCKERS **2 knickers** *pl* **:** pants for women or girls: as **a :** bloomers with fullness gathered on a band at the knee **b** *chiefly Brit* **:** UNDERPANTS **c :** sport or leisure pants similar in design to knickerbockers
knick·er·bock·er *R* ˈnikə(r),bäkər, *-R* ˈnikə,bäkə(r\ *n* -s *often attrib* [after Diedrich *Knickerbocker*, pretended author of *History of New York* (1809), by Washington Irving †1859 Am. author] **1** *usu cap* **:** a descendant of the old Dutch settlers of New York; *broadly* **:** NEW YORKER **2 a :** loose-fitting knee-length pants gathered at the knee on a band for sports and informal wear by men and boys — usu. used in pl. ⟨~*s* for golfing⟩ ⟨wearing a ~ suit⟩ **b :** KNICKER 2c **3 :** a wool and cotton clothing fabric resembling tweed and made from nubby yarns with flecks of color

knicker-bockers 2a

knick·er·bock·ered \-äkə(r)d\ *adj* **:** wearing knickerbockers
knick·ered \ˈnikə(r)d\ *adj* **:** wearing knickers
knick·knack \ˈnik,nak\ *n* [redupl. of *knack*] **1** *obs* **:** a petty trick or artifice **2** *or* **nick·nack** *or* **nic·nac :** a small or trivial article (as of furniture or dress) intended rather for ornament than for use; *esp* **:** a small functionless souvenir
knick·knack·ato·ry \-ə,tōrē\ *n* -ES [*knickknack* + *-atory* (as in *conservatory*)] *archaic* **:** a repository or collection of knickknacks
knick·knack·ery \-ak(ə)rē\ *n* -ES **:** a knickknack or knickknacks
knick·knacky \-akē\ *adj* **1 :** devoted to, characterized by, or concerned with knickknacks ⟨a cluttered ~ room⟩ ⟨such a ~ taste⟩ **2 :** FINICAL, TRIFLING, TRIVIAL
knickline \ˈ=,=\ *n* **:** a line formed by the point or angle of a nick in a slope (as of a hill)
knickpoint \ˈnik,=\ *n* [part transl. of G *knickpunkt*, fr. *knicken* to bend + *punkt* point] **:** a place in a stream bed where a nick occurs
ˡ**knife** \ˈnīf\ *n, pl* **knives** \-īvz\ [ME *knif*, fr. OE *cnīf*, prob. fr. ON *knīfr*; akin to MLG *knīf* knife, MD *cnijf*, OE *cnotta* knot — more at KNOT] **1 a :** a simple instrument used for cutting consisting of a sharp-edged usu. steel blade provided with a handle **b :** a weapon consisting of or resembling a knife **c :** a culinary utensil consisting of a knife usu. with blade of silver or steel and a handle of metal, ceramic, bone, or pearl ⟨dinner *knives*⟩ ⟨dainty fruit *knives*⟩ **d :** a sharp cutting blade or tool in a machine (as a band saw, a wood-planing machine, or a mowing machine) **e :** any of various instruments used in surgery primarily to sever tissues whether having the form of a conventional knife or scalpel or cutting by other means (as electric or radio-frequency currents); *also* **:** SURGERY — used with *the* ⟨finally decided to submit to the ~⟩ ⟨was under the ~ for several hours⟩ **2 :** MUMBLETY-PEG **3 :** the shape of an envelope flap as produced by the knife on the cutting machine ⟨the size, ~, and watermark of a stamped envelope⟩
²**knife** \"\ *vb* -ED/-ING/-S *vt* **1 :** to use a knife on: as **a :** to stab, slash, or wound with a knife **b :** to prune with a knife **2 a :** to cut or mark with a knife: as (1) **:** to shape or cut out (as shoe uppers) with a knife (2) **:** to trim (as shoe soles) with a knife **b :** to spread (as paint) with a knife **3 :** to try to defeat by underhand means (as a political candidate of one's own party) **:** to work secretly against (one justified in expecting support) **:** UNDERMINE ⟨aiding today those he knows will ~ him tomorrow⟩ **4 a :** to move like a knife in ⟨birds *knifing* the autumn sky⟩ **b :** to impart an action like that of a knife to ⟨*knifed* his hand against his opponent's neck⟩ ~ *vi* **:** to progress or cut a way with or as if with the blade of a knife ⟨the cruiser *knifed* through heavy seas⟩ ⟨a hot sun *knifing* down through the haze⟩ ⟨*knifed* rapidly along the bone⟩
knife and fork *n* **1** *Brit* **:** one that eats **:** TRENCHERMAN ⟨a good *knife and fork*⟩ **2 a knives and forks** *pl* (1) **:** paired and solitary cones of the common club moss (*Lycopodium clavatum*) (2) **:** a club moss that bears knives and forks **b :** a key fruit of the sycamore maple — usu. used in pl.
knife bar *n* **:** CUTTER BAR
knife bayonet *n* **:** a bayonet with considerable breadth of blade and a handle that enables it to be used as a knife, dagger, or entrenching tool
knifeboard \ˈ=,=\ *n* **1 :** a board on which knives are cleaned or polished **2** *Brit* **:** a seat on the roof of an old-fashioned omnibus
knife box *also* **knife case :** a receptacle for knives and other table cutlery: as **a :** an often ornate wooden container with sloping top used esp. during the 18th century in pairs for the storage of knives and spoons **b :** an open usu. handled tray or rack for the storage of table cutlery
knife-boy \ˈ=,=\ *n, Brit* **:** an underservant occupied primarily with the care of knives and general odd jobs about a large household
knife-edge \ˈ=,=\ *n* **:** a sharp narrow edge or margin like that of a knife: as **a :** a sharp wedge of steel or other hard material used as a fulcrum or axis of motion for a lever arm or beam in a machine or instrument of precision (as a scale, testing machine, pendulum) to minimize friction **b :** a narrow ridge (as of rock, ice, or sand) **c :** GIRDLE d
knife-edged \ˈ=,=\ *adj* **:** having an edge like a knife; *usu* **:** extremely sharp or precise ⟨*knife-edged* pleats⟩ ⟨a *knife-edged* wit⟩
knife file *n* **:** a tapered file with a triangular cross section suggesting that of a knife blade
knife fish *n* **:** any of several fishes sometimes kept in the tropical aquarium; *esp* **:** a small brownish green fish (*Gymnotus carapo*) from So. America related to the electric eel but lacking electric organs
knife·ful \ˈnīf,fu̇l\ *n, pl* **knives·ful** *or* **knife·fuls** \-īvz,fu̇l, -īf,fu̇lz\ **:** the quantity a knife will hold or convey
knife grinder *n* **1 :** one that grinds knives: as **a :** an itinerant tradesman who sharpens knives or other edged tools **b :** a device (as a grindstone or emery wheel) used for grinding or sharpening knives or other edged tools **2 :** a European nightjar (*Caprimulgus europaeus*)
knife-handle \ˈ=,==\ *n* **:** RAZOR CLAM
knife hook *n, obs* **:** SICKLE 1a
knife key *n* **:** a compass key having a knife at one end
knife lanyard *n* **:** LANYARD 3a
knife·less \ˈnīfləs\ *adj* **:** lacking a knife
knifelike \ˈ=,=\ *adj* **:** resembling or suggesting a knife: **a :** having a sharp edge or ridge ⟨a ~ ridge of land⟩ ⟨a narrow ~ profile⟩ **b :** keen and incisive ⟨icy ~ reasoning⟩ **c :** sharp and penetrating **:** PIERCING ⟨~ pains⟩ ⟨a ~ cold⟩
knife·man \ˈnīfmən\ *n, pl* **knifemen :** a man that uses or works on or works with knives (as a knife fighter or a knife grinder)
knife money *n* **:** ancient Chinese bronze money having the shape of knives
knife pleat *n* **:** one of a series of narrow sharply pressed pleats all turned in one direction
knif·er \ˈnīfə(r)\ *n* -s **:** one that knifes; *esp* **:** a person who stabs or slashes another with a knife
knife rest *n* **1 :** CHEVAL-DE-FRISE **2 :** a support on which a carving knife may be rested on the dining table when not in use
knif·er·man \ˈnīfə(r)mən\ *n, pl* **knifermen :** a slaughterhouse worker who severs hog heads and lets them hang by a thin strip of meat to expose neck glands for government inspection
knifes *pres 3d sing of* KNIFE
knifesmith \ˈ=,=\ *n* **:** a maker of knives **:** CUTLER
knife stone *n* **:** HONE 1; *esp* **:** a fine-grained whetstone for setting and finishing an edge

knife switch *n* **:** an electric switch in which contact is made by pushing one or more flat metal blades between the jaws of spring clips

knife switch

knife tool *n* **:** a tool suggestive of a knife: as **a :** a knife-shaped graver **b :** a small wheel used in seal engraving for cutting fine lines
knife urn *n* **:** an urn-shaped knife box popular in the late 18th and early 19th centuries
knifeway \ˈ=,=\ *n* **:** a long tapering usu. hardened straight bar (as a V bar)
knif·fin system \ˈnifən-\ *n, usu cap K* [after Wm. *Kniffin*, 19th cent. Am. horticulturist] **:** a system or method of training grapevines whereby a trunk is carried to the upper of two braced supporting wires along which the annually renewed fruiting canes are tied and from which the bearing branches are allowed to hang down
knifing *pres part of* KNIFE
ˡ**knight** \ˈnīt, *usu* -īd·+V\ *n* -s [ME, boy, youth, knight, fr. OE *cniht, cneoht* boy, youth, military follower; akin to OS & OHG *kneht* boy, youth, military follower, OE *cnotta* knot — more at KNOT] **1 a** (1) **:** a mounted man-at-arms of the European feudal period serving a king or other superior usu. in return for a tenure of land; *esp* **:** a man ceremonially inducted by a feudal superior into special military rank commonly immediately below that of baron usu. available only after completing regular periods of service as page and squire — compare DUB *vt* 1a (2) **:** a man upon whom a corresponding dignity has been conferred by a sovereign in recognition of personal merit (3) **:** a member of an order of knighthood or of chivalry ⟨a *Knight* of the Garter⟩ (4) **:** a member of a social or fraternal order ⟨*Knights* of Labor⟩; *also* **:** a member of such an order holding a particular degree or rank that is officially so designated ⟨members, acolytes, and ~*s* of the Inner Tabernacle⟩ **b** (1) **:** a person of ancient history or mythology of a rank equivalent to that of knight — often used to translate Latin *miles* (2) **:** EQUES **c :** KNIGHT OF THE SHIRE **d :** a man who devotes himself to a lady as her attendant or champion **e :** a man associated in his personal or professional character with something specified (as an implement, tool, place, material) — often used in trade or craft nicknames ⟨those petty rascals often called ~*s* of the bridewell⟩ ⟨a ~ of the quill earning a pittance by his writings⟩ **2 a :** a chess piece that may cross occupied squares and that has an L-shaped move of three squares of which two are in a horizontal or vertical row and one is perpendicular to the row **b :** a face card ranking between the queen and the jack in many European packs of playing cards **3 :** a small bitt with sheaves through which the running rigging of a ship is passed

knight 2a

²**knight** \"\ *vt* -ED/-ING/-S [ME *knighten*, fr. *knight*, n.] **:** to make a knight of **:** induct into the state or an order of knighthood **:** DUB
knight·age \-īd·ij\ *n* -s **1 :** knights or a body of knights ⟨the king and all his ~⟩ **2 :** a register and account of knights ⟨the several ~*s* and peerages that register men of nobility and note⟩ **3 :** KNIGHTHOOD ⟨hardy service may win a commoner ~⟩
knight bachelor *n, pl* **knights bachelors** *also* **knights bachelor :** a knight belonging to the most ancient but the lowest order of English knights and not a member of an order of chivalry — see KNIGHT BANNERET
knight banneret *n, pl* **knights bannerets** *also* **knights banneret** [ME] **:** a knight of an ancient English order of knighthood that was commonly conferred as a reward for valor on the field of battle and that entitled the holder to bear a banner rather than the pennon of a knight bachelor
knight baronet *n, pl* **knights baronets :** BARONET
knight commander *n, pl* **knights commanders :** a member of the second class in an honorary order (as the Order of the Bath) with more than one class of membership ranking below a knight grand cross and above a companion
knight-companion \ˈ==ˈ=\ *n, pl* **knights-companions** *also* **knight-companions :** a knight belonging to an order of knighthood having only one class (the Order of the Garter . . . consists of the sovereign and twenty-five *knights-companions* —Valentine Heywood)
knight-errant \ˈ=ˈ==\ *n, pl* **knights-errant** [ME *knight errant*] **:** a wandering knight; *esp* **:** one traveling at random in search of adventures in which to exhibit military skill, prowess, and generosity
knight-errantry \ˈ=ˈ===\ *n, pl* **knight-errantries 1 a :** the character or actions of a knight-errant **:** the practice of wandering in quest of adventures **b :** quixotic conduct **:** a quixotic or romantic adventure or scheme **2 :** KNIGHTS-ERRANT
knight·ess \ˈnīd·əs\ *n* -ES **1** *obs* **:** a woman filling the role of a knight either as a fighter or as a member of an order of chivalric import **:** female knight **2 :** the wife of a knight
knight·ful·ly \ˈnītfəlē\ *adv* **:** in the manner of a knight **:** BRAVELY, CHIVALROUSLY
knight grand commander *n, pl* **knights grand commanders :** a member of an honorary order (as the Star of India) that admits other than Christians to membership corresponding in rank to a knight grand cross
knight grand cross *n, pl* **knights grand cross :** a member of the highest class in an honorary order (as the Bath) with more than one class of membership — see KNIGHT COMMANDER
knighthead \ˈ=,=\ *n* [so called fr. its having been carved to represent knights] **1 :** one of two timbers rising in the bows of a wooden ship just within the stem with one on each side of the bowsprit — called also *bollard timber* **2 :** a triangular bulkhead just abaft the cutwater with a hole through which the bowsprit of a ship passes
knight·hood \ˈnīt,hu̇d\ *n* [ME *knighthod*, fr. *knight* + *-hod* -hood] **1 :** the rank, dignity, condition, profession, or vocation of a knight or of knights as a class ⟨won a ~ for his devotion to civic reform⟩ ⟨~ was at one time both a social obligation and a symbol of maturity⟩ **2 :** the character of a knight **:** qualities befitting a knight or knights as a class **:** KNIGHTLINESS, CHIVALRY **3 a :** knights as a class ⟨the early ~ held a place distinct from the great lords on the one hand and the working peasantry on the other⟩ **b :** a body of knights ⟨the legendary ~ of King Arthur⟩
knighthood-errant \ˈ=,=ˈ==\ *n* **:** KNIGHTS-ERRANT
knight hospitaler *n, pl* **knights hospitalers** *usu cap K&H* **:** HOSPITALER
knight·ia \ˈnīd·ēə\ *n, cap* [NL, fr. Thomas A. *Knight* †1838 Eng. plant physiologist + NL *-ia*] **:** a small genus of Australasian trees or shrubs (family Proteaceae) with alternate leathery leaves, showy racemose flowers, and follicular fruit — see REWA-REWA
knightless *adj, obs* **:** unbecoming a knight **:** UNCHIVALROUS
knight·li·hood \ˈnītlē,hu̇d\ *n* **:** KNIGHTLINESS
knightlike \ˈ=,=\ *adj* [ME *knightlik*, fr. *knight* + *-lik* -like] **:** KNIGHTLY 1
knight·li·ness \ˈnītlēnəs\ *n* -ES **:** the quality or state of being knightly; *broadly* **:** chivalrous courtesy or gracious kindness ⟨a natural ~ characterized all his relations with others⟩
knight·ling \ˈnītliŋ\ *n* -s **:** a knight of little worth or importance **:** petty knight
ˡ**knight·ly** \ˈnītlē, -li\ *adj* [ME, fr. *knight* + *-ly*] **1 a :** of or relating to a knight **b :** befitting a knight **:** CHIVALROUS **2 :** consisting or made up of knights
²**knightly** \"\ *adv* [ME, fr. *knightly*, adj.] **:** in a manner becoming a knight
knight marshal *n, pl* **knights marshals 1 :** a former military officer analogous to the modern quartermaster **2 :** a onetime officer of the British royal household who had judicial cognizance of transgressions committed in the royal household or verge and of contracts to which a member of the king's household was a party
knight of columbus *n, pl* **knights of columbus** *usu cap K&C* [after Christopher *Columbus* — more at COLUMBUS] **:** a member of a fraternal and benevolent society of Roman Catholic

men founded at New Haven, Conn., in 1882 to promote social and intellectual intercourse among its members, to aid its members and beneficiaries, to protect and promote Catholic interests, and to foster a spirit of fraternity among citizens of all races and creeds

knight of industry *n, pl* **knights of industry** [trans. of F *chevalier de l'industrie*] *obs* : SWINDLER

knight of labor *n, pl* **knights of labor** *usu cap K&L* : a member of a 19th century secret labor organization formed in 1869 to secure and maintain the rights of workingmen in respect to their relations to their employers

knight of malta *n, pl* **knights of malta** *usu cap K&M* [fr. *Malta*, island in the Mediterranean, the seat of the order from 1530–1798] : HOSPITALER

knight of pyth·i·as \-'pithēəs\ *n, pl* **knights of pythias** *usu cap K&P* [after *Pythias*, 4th cent. B.C. Pythagorean philosopher whose devotion to his friend Damon is legendary] : a member of a secret fraternal order founded at Washington, D.C., in 1864 for social and charitable purposes

knight of rhodes \-'rōdz\ *n, pl* **knights of rhodes** *usu cap K&R* [fr. *Rhodes*, city and island in the Aegean sea, former seat of the order] : HOSPITALER

knight of st. john of jerusalem *n, pl* **knights of st. john of jerusalem** *usu cap K&S & both Js* [after *St. John of Jerusalem* (John the Baptist), cousin of Jesus] : HOSPITALER

knight of the carpet *also* **knight of the chamber** *n, pl* **knights of the carpet 1** : a knight who is knighted in formal ceremony (as kneeling in a royal audience chamber) as distinguished from one knighted informally on the field of battle — compare CARPET KNIGHT **2** : a recipient of knighthood for service or distinction other than military

knight of the golden circle *n, pl* **knights of the golden circle** *usu cap K&G&C* : a member of a former American secret organization formed about 1855 to promote the interests of the South and the slavery cause

knight of the maccabees *n, pl* **knights of the maccabees** *usu cap K&M* [after *Maccabees*, 2d & 1st cent. B.C. Jewish family in Palestine] : a member of a secret beneficiary society formed in Ontario in 1878 and introduced into the U. S. in 1881 and having a ritual based on characteristics of the ancient Maccabean family

knight of the pestle *n, pl* **knights of the pestle** : APOTHECARY

knight of the post *n, pl* **knights of the post** : a professional false witness of 15th to 17th century England

knight of the road *n, pl* **knights of the road 1** *obs* : HIGHWAYMAN **2** : TRAVELING SALESMAN **3** : TRAMP

knight of the round table *n, pl* **knights of the round table** *usu cap K&R&T* : a knight belonging to the legendary order instituted by King Arthur

knight of the shire *n, pl* **knights of the shire** [ME] **1** : a knight selected by the freeholders to represent a shire in the House of Commons esp. in medieval times ⟨the *knight of the shire* was the connecting link between the baron and the shopkeeper —T.B.Macaulay⟩ **2** : a parliamentary representative from a shire or county as distinguished from a representative of a city or a borough ⟨the number of *knights of the shire* was increased to 159 —T.E.May⟩

knight of the sword *n, pl* **knights of the sword** *usu cap K&S* : a member of a German religious order of knights founded in 1202 by Bishop Albert of Riga in Livonia to convert the heathen Estonians and Livonians and appropriate their lands, confirmed by the pope in 1204, and merged into the Teutonic Order in 1237

knight of the temple *n, pl* **knights of the temple** *usu cap K&T* : TEMPLAR 1

knights *pl of* KNIGHT, *pres 3d sing of* KNIGHT

knight service *also* **knight's service** *n* [ME *knightes service*] **1** : the military service by rendering which a knight held his lands; *also* : the tenure of lands held on condition of performing military service **2** : service such as a knight can or should render; *broadly* : good or valuable service

knight's fee *n* [ME *knightes fee*] : the amount of land the holding of which imposed the obligation of knight service, being sometimes a hide or less and sometimes six or more hides

knight's-spur \'=,=\ *n, pl* **knight's-spurs** : LARKSPUR 1a

knight's-star \'=,=\ *or* **knight's-star lily** *n, pl* **knight's-stars** *or* **knight's-star lilies** : BARBADOS LILY

knight's tour *n* : a chess problem in which a knight makes a circuit of the board touching each square once

knight templar *n, pl* **knights templars** *or* **knights templar** *also* **knight templars** *usu cap K&T* **1** : TEMPLAR 1 **2** : a member of the Knights Templars, an order of Freemasonry conferring three degrees in the York rite — compare CHIVALRIC RITE

knip·ho·fia \nip'hōfēə, nī'fō-\ *n* [NL, fr. Johan H. *Kniphof* †1763 Ger. botanist + NL *-ia*] **1** *cap* : a genus of showy African herbs (family Liliaceae) having clumps of long radical leaves and tall scapes of red or yellow drooping flowers with reflexed perianths **2** -s : a plant of the genus *Kniphofia* — called also *tritoma*

knish \kə'nish\ *n* -ES [Yiddish, fr. Russ *knish, knysh*, a kind of cake; akin to Ukrainian *knyš*, Pol *knysz*] : a round or square of rich baking-powder dough folded over a savory meat or cheese filling and baked or fried

knis·te·neaux \kə,nistə'nō\ *n pl but sing in constr, usu cap* [modif. of F *Christenaux* — more at CREE] : CREE

¹knit \'nit, *usu* -id.+V\ *vb* **knit** *or* **knitted** *or dial* **knet** \'net, *usu* -ed.+V\ **knit** *or* **knitted** *or dial* **knet; knitting; knits** [ME *knitten*, fr. OE *cnyttan*; akin to MLG *knütten* to knit, knot together; denominatives fr. the root of E ¹*knot*] *vt* **1** *now chiefly dial* : to make fast or join with knots : tie together : form into a knot or into knots **2** : to cause to unite in a functional whole as if by knitting or knotting: as **a** : to link firmly or closely (as by interlocking, intertwining, or intertying) ⟨*knitted* her hands until the knuckles blanched⟩ : CONJOIN, CEMENT, CONSOLIDATE ⟨~ the timbers into a sturdy frame⟩ **b** : to cause to grow together ⟨time and rest will ~ the fractured bone⟩ **c** : to bind by immaterial (as social or legal) ties ⟨~ together by common interests⟩ **d** : to draw together : contract into wrinkles ⟨*knitting* his brow in thought⟩ **3 a** : to form (as a fabric or a garment) by the interlacing of a yarn or yarns in a series of connected loops by means of hand or machine needles ⟨*knitting* socks to match the sweater⟩ **b** : to form or bring into being (some immaterial tie) ⟨a new philosophy that *knitted* a new understanding between the classes⟩ ~ *vi* **1** : to make knitted fabrics or objects : do knitting ⟨some women ~, others sew⟩ **2** : to unite into a functional whole as if by being knitted or knotted: as **a** : to become compact : CONSOLIDATE **b** : to grow together ⟨fractures in old bones ~ slowly⟩ **c** : to become drawn together : contract into wrinkles **3** *now dial Brit* **a** (1) *of fruit* : SET (2) *of a plant* : to grow or set fruit **b** *of bees* : SWARM **4** *obs* : EFFERVESCE, FOAM

²knit \"\ *n* -s *often attrib* **1 a** : knitting or style of knitting **b** : knitted material **c** : KNIT STITCH **2** : a contraction or wrinkling up (as of the brow)

knitback \'=,=\ *n* [so called fr. its use to heal broken bones] : a coarse branching hairy comfrey (*Symphytum officinale*) sometimes cultivated for its white, yellowish, purple, or rose flowers

knitch \'nich, kə'n-\ *n* -ES [ME *knytche, knucche*, fr. OE *gecnycc* bond; akin to MLG *knocke* bundle, MHG *knock* back of the neck, *knoche* bone — more at KNUCKLE] *dial Eng* : BUNDLE, FAGOT

knit goods *n pl* **1** : knitted fabrics; *esp* : fabrics made on a knitting machine and used for underwear, hosiery, and other clothing **2** : articles made from such fabrics : knitted garments

knit stitch *n* : a basic knitting stitch usu. made with the yarn at the back of the work by inserting the right needle into the front part of a loop on the left needle, catching the yarn from the left side with the point of the right needle, and bringing it through the first loop to form a new loop — compare PURL STITCH

knit·ted \ˌnid·əd, -itəd\ *adj* : made or characterized by knitting ⟨~ garments⟩ — often used in combination ⟨hand-*knitted* woolens⟩

knit·ter \'nid·ə(r), -itə-\ *n* -s [ME, fr. *knitten* to knit + *-er* — more at KNIT] **1** : a person that knits by hand or operates a knitting machine **2** : a machine for making knit goods (as hose, jersey, sweaters)

knit·ting \'nid·iŋ, -it|, |ēŋ\ *n* -s [ME, fr. gerund of *knitten* to knit] **1** : the action or method of one that knits by hand or machine; *also* : the action of a machine that knits **2** : work in progress or products made by a person or machine that knits **3** : the occupation of operating a machine that knits **4** *obs* : FASTENING; *esp* : KNOT — **stick to one's knitting** *or* **tend to one's knitting** *also* **mind one's knitting** : to mind one's business : avoid interfering in or involving oneself with the affairs of others

knitting machine *n* : a machine for mechanically knitting fabrics (as jersey or tricot) and articles of wear (as sweaters or hosiery) — see CIRCULAR-KNIT, FLAT-KNIT

knitting needle *n* **1** : one of two or more slender rods with one or both ends pointed or a flexible rod with both ends pointed used for hand knitting and made usu. of metal, bone, or plastic — see NEEDLE illustration **2** : a spring needle or a latch needle used for machine knitting

knitting pin *n* : a single-pointed needle for hand knitting

knittle *var of* NETTLE

knit up *vt* **1 a** : to tie up : SECURE, UNITE **b** : to make or repair by knitting ⟨*knit up* several pairs of Christmas mittens⟩ ⟨*knit* a torn sleeve *up*⟩ **2** : to bring to an end : CONCLUDE ⟨to *knit* these remarks *up* briefly⟩

knitwear \'=,=\ *n* : knitted clothing including hosiery, underwear, and outerwear

knive \'nīv\ *vb* -ED/-ING/-S [fr. ¹*knife*, after such pairs as E *wife: wive*] : KNIFE

knives *pl of* KNIFE

knives and forks *pl of* KNIFE AND FORK

knivesful *pl of* KNIFEFUL

¹knob *also* **nob** \'näb\ *n* -s [ME *knobbe*; akin to MLG *knubbe, knobbe* knot on a tree, knob, Norw *knubb* block, ME *knoppe, knopp* bud, knob — more at KNOP] **1 a** (1) : a relatively small usu. rounded mass typically projecting from the surface or extremity of something : a usu. rounded projection or protuberance or protrusion ⟨a heavy club with ~s at one end⟩ ⟨his nose ends in a puggy ~ —N.M.Clark⟩ ⟨a skull having a couple of peculiar ~s⟩ (2) *archaic* : a small rather hard swelling (as a bump, pimple, pustule) on the surface of the skin (3) : a twisted knot or hard excrescence or protuberance esp. of wood : GNARL ⟨~s in the trunk of a tree⟩ (4) : a tiny ball, loop, or tuft (as of thread or hair) formed by twisting or coiling or otherwise tightly drawing together one or more strands; *specif* : KNOP c ⟨little ~s of wool or cotton in different colors —Mary Thomas⟩ (5) : ³BUN 2 ⟨dark hair drawn into a tight little ~ on the neck —Flora Thompson⟩ **b** (1) : a small rounded mass of often carved ornamental work (as a boss at the intersection of the ribs in a vaulting) topping or capping a larger piece of work or serving as a contrastive detail (2) : a small globular usu. ornamental body typically at the top or other extremity of something (as at the top or end of a finial or on the hilt of a sword or at the front and top of a saddlebow) : POMMEL (3) : FINIAL **c** (1) : a usu. rounded projection by which something can be grasped or otherwise manipulated or moved ⟨a metal bar with a ~ at one end⟩; *specif* : a usu. rounded handle (as of a drawer or door) ⟨a door with a heavy ~ of wrought metal⟩ (2) : a usu. rounded projection or a disk or dial typically having a guide mark or series of guide marks around the edge and capable of being turned or pulled or pushed so as to actuate or otherwise operate or control something (as a radio or television set) ⟨he reached to turn on the radio but she pushed his hand from the ~ almost angrily —E.K.Gann⟩ ⟨an expert at knocking ~s off safes —Paul McClung⟩ ⟨turns a control ~ on the instrument panel —T.W.Rodes⟩ **d** : a spool-shaped porcelain insulator for supporting electric wires — see INSULATOR illustration **2 a** (1) : a usu. rounded land prominence (as a knoll, hillock, hill, small mountain) with usu. steep sides; *esp* : an isolated prominent rounded hill (2) **knobs** *pl* : an area marked by a group of such prominences ⟨a rifleman from the east Kentucky ~s —I.S.Cobb⟩ **b** (1) : a usu. tapering upward projection from the summit of a hill or mountain : PEAK ⟨bare crags and ~s —W.M.Davis⟩ (2) : something (as a boulder or group of boulders or a stony area) projecting from the summit or sides of a hill or mountain ⟨erosion wore down the mountains, exposing ~s of harder granite —*Amer. Guide Series: Minn.*⟩ ⟨patches of ragged grass and ~s of boulders —Dixon Wecter⟩ **3** *chiefly Brit* : a small lump of something : a small piece ⟨a scraggly looking salad and a few ~s of cheese —Dawn Powell⟩ ⟨a ~ of coal⟩; *esp* : a small cube ⟨a ~ of sugar⟩ ⟨dropped a ~ of ice into the glass⟩ **4** *archaic* : HEAD ⟨a diminutive head like the ~ of a mannikin —George Santayana⟩ — **with knobs on** *adv* : in an esp. eminent manner : to an esp. notable degree ⟨anglophile though the first three pictures were, the new one is more so *with knobs on* —*Newsweek*⟩ ⟨whatever problem a town can have . . . we have it — *with knobs on* —Sam Pollock⟩

²knob *also* **nob** \"\ *vt* **knobbed; knobbed; knobbing; knobs 1** : to cause to have knobs : form knobs upon ⟨*knobbing* a sheet of metal⟩ **2** : to provide with a knob ⟨wrought-iron gates, *knobbed* on either side with stone balls —Edmund Wilson⟩

knob and tube wiring *n* : open electric-wiring work in which the wires are supported on knobs or cleats and encased in tubes where they pass through beams or partitions

knobbed \'näb(ə)d\ *adj* [ME, fr. *knobbe* knob + *-ed*] **1** : having a knob or knobs ⟨a ~ stick⟩; *specif* : ending in a knob ⟨a pole ~ at each extremity⟩ **2** : covered with knobs : KNOBBY ⟨a ~ tree trunk⟩

knobbed crab *n* : a spiny spider crab (*Mithrax caribbaeus*) of the West Indies and the northern coast of So. America

knobbed goose *n* : CHINESE GOOSE 2

knobbed wrack *n* : a common brown alga (*Ascophyllum nodosum*) of northern oceans

knob·ber \'näbə(r\ *n* -s [¹*knob* + *-er*] *Brit* : a two-year-old male deer

knob·bi·ly \'näbəlē\ *adv* : in such a way as to form protuberances ⟨her ~ corseted bulk —Marcia Davenport⟩

knob·bi·ness \-bēnəs\ *n* -ES : the quality or state of being knobby

knob·bish \-bish\ *adj* : rather knobby ⟨skinny as a rail, and kind of ~ at the joints —Helen Eustis⟩

knob·ble \'näbəl\ *n* -s [ME *knoble*, fr. *knob* + *-le* (dim. suffix)] : a little knob or lump

knob·bled \-ld\ *adj* : KNOBBLY

knob·bly *or* **nob·bly** \'näblē, -li\ *adj, often* -ER/-EST [¹*knob* + *-ly*] : KNOBBY; *esp* : having or covered with very small knobs ⟨a ~ pane of translucent glass⟩

¹knob·by \'näbē, -bi\ *adj, usu* **knobbier;** *usu* **knobbiest** [¹*knob* + *-y*] **1 a** : having knobs : having several or many knobs : covered with knobs: as (1) : having protuberances, projections, or protrusions ⟨~ bones⟩ ⟨~ knees⟩ ⟨~ knuckles⟩ : BUMPY ⟨grinned toothlessly and extended a ~ hand —Dorothy Sayers⟩ (2) : having usu. rounded land prominences : HILLY ⟨~ farmland⟩ **b** : shaped like or suggestive of a knob ⟨little ~ noses —Joseph Conrad⟩ **2 a** : involving difficulties : PERPLEXING, INTRICATE, KNOTTY ⟨some of the ~ problems of publishing —Harvey Breit⟩ **b** : resisting compromise or evasion or unequivocal solution : stubbornly unyielding : HARD, OBSTINATE ⟨prefer to turn away from the ~ facts of life —*Time*⟩

knob-ker-rie

²knobby \"\ *var of* NOBBY

knob celery *n* : CELERIAC

knob·cone pine \'=,=-\ *n* : a pine (*Pinus attenuata*) native to the Pacific coast of the U.S. with a prominent knob on each scale of the cone

knob grass *n* : HORSE BALM 1

knob·ker·rie *also* **knob·ker·ry** \'näb,kerē\ *n, pl* **knobkerries** [modif. (influenced by ¹*knob*) of Afrik *knopkierie*, fr. *knop* knob, bud (fr. MD *cnoppe*) + *kierie* stick, club, fr. Hottentot *kirri* — more at KNOP] : a rather short wooden club with a heavy round knob at one end that may be thrown as a missile or used in close attack and that is used esp. by aborigines of southern Africa

knob lock *n* : a door lock with a spring bolt operated by a knob and a dead bolt operated by a key

knobs *pl of* KNOB, *pres 3d sing of* KNOB

knobstick \'=,=\ *n* **1** : a stick, cane, or club with a rounded knob at its head; *specif* : KNOBKERRIE **2** *Brit* : STRIKEBREAKER, SCAB

knob·thorn *also* **knob·thorne** \'näb,thȯ(ə)rn\ *n* -s : an acacia (*Acacia nigrescens*) of southern Africa having a bark often dotted with thorn-tipped knobs

knobweed \'=,=\ *n* **1** : KNAPWEED **2** : HORSE BALM 1

knobwood \'=,=\ *n* **1** : a tree (*Zanthoxylum capense*) of southern Africa with compound leaves and greenish paniculate flowers **2** : the wood of the knobwood

¹knock \'näk\ *vb* -ED/-ING/-S [ME *knoken, knokken*, fr. OE *cnocian, cnucian*; akin to MHG *knochen* to press, ON *knoka* to hit, beat; all of imit. origin] *vi* **1** : to strike upon the surface of something (as a door) with a short sharp fairly heavy blow (as with the knuckles) esp. so as to indicate one's desire to gain admittance (as into a room) or otherwise to attract attention : RAP ⟨~*ed* on the green painted door and it was opened almost at once —Louis Bromfield⟩ ⟨stood there ~*ing* on the gate⟩ ⟨~*ed* on the table before beginning to speak⟩ **2** : to collide fairly heavily or jarringly with something : strike against or bump into something ⟨~*ed* into one person after another in the crowd⟩ ⟨his ~*ing* knees belied the bluster of his talk —W.F.Hambly⟩ **3 a** : to stir about or move along briskly, usu. noisily, and often clumsily or haphazardly : BUSTLE ⟨heard him ~*ing* round in the kitchen —Lucy M. Montgomery⟩ ⟨went ~*ing* rapidly down the road⟩ ⟨~*ing* along at a reasonable rate —Dillon Anderson⟩ **b** : to go or move about in an irregular, haphazard, or aimless way : travel about in a careless or indifferent manner and often with no particular objective : WANDER, ROAM, ROVE — usu. used with *about, around* ⟨~*ing* idly up and down the country⟩ ⟨decided to ~ around the world awhile⟩ ⟨~*ed* about the mountains for a couple of weeks⟩ ⟨spent a couple of hours ~*ing* around town⟩ **c** (1) : to lead an irregular life often in straitened difficult circumstances : live like a vagrant — used with *about, around* ⟨content to ~ about the world in a more or less disreputable way —R.W.Southern⟩ ⟨goes ~*ing* about the roads day and night —W.B.Yeats⟩ (2) : to exist in a condition of complete or nearly complete inaction, idleness, or neglect : pass the time inactively or idly : hang around : LOITER, DAWDLE — used with *about, around* ⟨used to ~ around that neighborhood⟩ ⟨would you have my pictures ~*ing* about some art dealer's place —Louis Bromfield⟩ **4 a** : to make a rattling, thumping, or pounding noise (as of loose connecting rods or loose bearings or other parts in a machine that strike against each other or another surface or as of improperly timed or uneven combustion in an internal-combustion engine) ⟨heard the motor ~*ing*⟩ **b** : to undergo detonation (sense 2) ⟨an engine fuel that ~*s*⟩ **5** : to speak ill of something esp. in a petty way : find fault with or criticize something adversely and often captiously ⟨malcontents who were perpetually ~*ing*⟩ **6** : to end the play in a card game (as gin rummy) and call for a comparison of hands ⟨at this point the player may ~⟩ ~ *vt* **1 a** (1) : to deal a short sharp fairly heavy blow to : strike sharply : deal a jarring blow to : HIT, RAP, BUFFET ⟨~*ed* him on the chin⟩ ⟨~*s* it about more than any rough road will ever do —Hardiman Scott⟩ (2) : to get rid of by or as if by dealing a stunning blow to : knock out : knock on the head ⟨he can ~ the worry if he takes a Scotch and soda —Ernest Hemingway⟩ ⟨an effective remedy for ~*ing* colds⟩ (3) : to affect in an indicated way by or as if by striking sharply, beating, battering, hammering, or pounding ⟨would ~ any road to pieces —Tom Wintringham⟩ ⟨~*ed* it apart⟩ (4) : to produce or make by so striking or battering ⟨~*ed* a hole in the wall⟩ ⟨a workroom composed of two or three servants' bedrooms ~*ed* into one —C.D.Lewis⟩ **b** (1) : to set forcibly into sudden movement ⟨kept ~*ing* the croquet ball along with her mallet⟩ or send flying ⟨swung hard with his bat and ~*ed* the baseball over the fence⟩ or drive in an indicated direction ⟨~*ed* the book away from his face⟩ or to, into, or onto an indicated thing, place, or position by a short sharp blow, thrust, or stroke or a series of such blows or thrusts ⟨~*ed* a nail up into the ceiling⟩ : give a sudden impetus to by driving with a short sharp blow : impel or propel suddenly and swiftly (2) : to drive out by so striking : force out or expel by or as if by a blow ⟨was ~*ing* the dust out of his clothes —Henry Baerlein⟩ ⟨threatened to ~ his brains out⟩ ⟨will ~ such notions out of your head —T.B.Costain⟩ ⟨can ~ all the interest out of it —H.L.Davis⟩ (3) : to drive forcibly off or down by or as if by so striking : cause to be so removed ⟨~*ed* the head off the statue⟩ ⟨~*ed* a considerable sum off the price⟩ (4) *of a dog* : to drive (game birds) from cover : FLUSH ⟨moved in and ~*ed* the birds —*Amer. Field*⟩ **c** : SHAKE, UPSET, BOTHER, DISTURB ⟨never gives up the idea that he can win, and nothing can ~ him —D.W.Maurer⟩ **d** *chiefly Brit* (1) : to knock out (sense 2a) ⟨struck him under the right eye with her clenched fist and ~*ed* him —Sigerson Clifford⟩ (2) : to make a strong impression on : produce a strong effect in; *esp* : to move to admiration or applause ⟨nothing ~*s* a country audience like a hornpipe —J.K.Jerome⟩ **2** : to cause to collide fairly heavily or jarringly with something : cause to strike against, run into, or bump into something ⟨~*ed* two oil drums against each other —Vicki Baum⟩ ⟨didn't look where they were going and ~*ed* their heads together⟩ **3** : to speak ill of esp. in a petty way : find fault with or criticize adversely and often captiously ⟨can satirize the manners and morals of our times and even ~ the government —Lee Rogow⟩ ⟨instructions were to keep smiling, ~ nobody —S.H.Adams⟩ **4** : to obtain by or as if by striking or beating ⟨a young man who can ~ some fun out of life —A.J.Cronin⟩ — **knock cold** : to knock out (sense 2a) ⟨ran his head into the wall and was *knocked cold*⟩ — **knock dead** : to move strongly esp. to admiration or applause : knock over ⟨a comedian who really *knocks* them *dead*⟩ — **knock for a goal** : to knock for a loop — **knock for a loop 1 a** : to overcome utterly : completely vanquish : ROUT ⟨*knocked* his opponent *for a loop*⟩ **b** : to make short work of : get rid of or demolish ⟨*knocked* his faith in human nature *for a loop*⟩ **2** : to make speechless : cause to be at a complete loss : OVERWHELM, BEWILDER, AMAZE, DUMBFOUND ⟨the news *knocked* them *for a loop*⟩ — **knock into a cocked hat 1 a** : to utterly demolish : RUIN ⟨*knocked* all our plans *into a cocked hat*⟩ ⟨threatened to *knock* the industry *into a cocked hat*⟩ **b** : to prove to be false : utterly disprove ⟨a theory that was finally *knocked into a cocked hat*⟩ **2** : to surpass eminently : excel by far ⟨something that'll *knock* all the other achievements of man *into a cocked hat* —John Galsworthy⟩ — **knock on the head** *or* **knock in the head 1** : to stun or kill by a blow on the head ⟨had been *knocked on the head* some dark night —R.L.Stevenson⟩ **2** : to check (as a plan, project, procedure) effectively or put an end to : SQUELCH, SQUASH ⟨has *knocked* this rumor *in the head* —*U.S. News & World Report*⟩ — **knock out of the box** : to cause (an opposing pitcher) to retire from a baseball game by hitting pitched balls with marked effectiveness — **knock spots off** *or* **knock the spots off** *also* **knock spots out of** : to surpass eminently : excel by far ⟨she *knocks spots off* anybody I've seen in London —J.B.Priestley⟩ — **knock together** : to make or assemble esp. hurriedly or in a makeshift way ⟨*knocked together* his own desk and bookcase⟩

²knock \"\ *n* -s [ME *knokke, knok*, fr. *knokken, knoken*, v.] **1 a** : a short sharp fairly heavy blow : RAP ⟨a loud ~ on the door⟩ **b** (1) : a blow of misfortune or hard treatment ⟨the school of hard ~*s* had given him a tenacious grasp on reality —Dixon Wecter⟩ ⟨some of the disappointments and hard ~*s* life has dealt —A.B.Herr⟩ ⟨takes the ~*s* of the world —M.N. Todd⟩ (2) : something that checks, interrupts, or reverses good conditions or progress : SETBACK, REVERSAL, UPSET ⟨appeared to receive a damaging ~ from the events —Mollie Panter-Downes⟩ **2 a** : a rattling, thumping, or pounding noise (as of loose connecting rods in a machine or as of uneven combustion in an internal-combustion engine) ⟨was worried by the ~ in his car⟩ **b** : DETONATION 2 ⟨a motor fuel that is not subject to ~⟩ **3** : a piece of often petty faultfinding or of adverse and often captious criticism ⟨likes praise but can't stand the ~*s*⟩ ⟨can take the ~*s*, not worrying what people say —Stella Molony⟩ **4** : an innings in cricket ⟨won the toss and decided to take first ~⟩

knock about *or* **knock around** *vt* **1** : to cause to move irregularly and abruptly from one point to another by or as if by repeated blows : JOLT, JAR ⟨the crowd pushed and shoved and the two boys got *knocked about*⟩ **2** : to treat roughly or subject to difficulties and hardship : mistreat physically or mentally ⟨has been pretty badly *knocked around* during his life⟩ ⟨come into life with large preconceived ideas and are *knocked about* in consequence —Lionel Trilling⟩

[1]knockabout \'=,=\ *adj* [*knock about*] **1** : designed or suitable for rough or casual informal use ⟨~ clothing⟩ ⟨a ~ travel valise⟩ **2 a** : noisy and rough : boisterously violent ⟨was especially fond of ~ games⟩ ⟨~ diversions⟩ **b** : marked by, given to, or skilled at boisterously funny antics and farce and often extravagant burlesque or slapstick ⟨a ~ film comedy⟩ ⟨a ~ vaudeville act⟩ ⟨~ comedians in baggy pants —*Time*⟩ **3** : marked by or given to irregular, haphazard, or aimless wandering about : traveling about carelessly or like a vagrant : ROAMING ⟨are afraid the place is full of ~ single men —O.E. Rölvaag⟩

[2]knockabout \"\ *n* -s [partly fr. [1]*knockabout;* partly fr. *knock about*] **1 a** (1) : a performer of knockabout comedy ⟨a couple of vaudeville ~*s*⟩ (2) : a performance or instance of knockabout comedy ⟨a grave ceremony that gradually turned into hilarious ~⟩ **b** : boisterous farcical humor of the kind found in knockabout comedy ⟨the rehearsal scene was good ~ —Leslie Rees⟩ **2 a** *Austral* : a handyman on a sheep station **b** : one that wanders about or travels in an irregular, haphazard, or aimless way : WANDERER, VAGRANT ⟨a man without family, a ~ —D.C.Peattie⟩ **3** : a sloop with a simplified rig marked by absence of bowsprit and topmast and by having a single headsail on the forestay **4** : something designed or suitable for rough or casual informal use: as **a** : an article of clothing (as a coat, hat) designed or suitable for such use **b** : an unpretentious vehicle esp. designed or suitable for short trips or other casual informal use ⟨a secondhand car that will serve as a ~⟩ ⟨was now in a one-cylinder ~ which in every way lived up to its name —William Beebe⟩

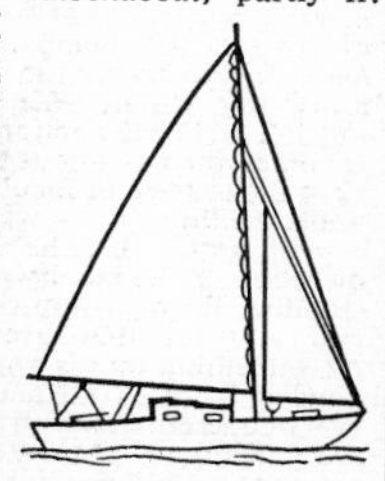
knockabout 3

knockaway *var of* KNACKAWAY

knock back *vt, chiefly Brit* : SWALLOW; *specif* : to toss down (an alcoholic beverage) ⟨smelt of the brandy they had just been *knocking back* —Bruce Marshall⟩

knock-back \'=,=\ *n* -s [fr. *knock back*, v.] *Austral* : REBUFF, REFUSAL ⟨he's had a *knock-back* from his old man —John Morrison⟩

knock down *vt* **1 a** (1) : to strike to the ground or lay low with or as if with a short sharp blow : FELL, PROSTRATE ⟨hit him on the chin and *knocked* him *down*⟩ (2) : to lower in degree : tone down : put down ⟨needs to have his self-esteem *knocked down*⟩ : HUMBLE, HUMILIATE ⟨try not to frustrate him or *knock down* his cap —*Education Digest*⟩ **b** : to hit with or as if with a projectile or other missile and cause to fall : shoot down ⟨thinking of ways to *knock* planes *down* from the skies —J.P. Baxter b.1893⟩ : bring down by a shot : POT ⟨*knocking down* game birds⟩ **c** (1) : to dispose of effectively : put out of the way : get rid of : ELIMINATE, QUASH ⟨each objection had been *knocked down* —*Times Lit. Supp.*⟩ (2) *Austral* : to spend (money) with abandon ⟨*knock down* their checks there — George Farwell⟩ **d** : to check or abate (flames or heat) at the edges of a blazing area **e** : to cause (a vessel) to heel over or list heavily or beyond recovery ⟨lets the wind blow on both sides of the sail . . . and the boat cannot be *knocked down* — Peter Heaton⟩ **2** : to dispose of to or as if to a bidder at an auction sale ⟨*knocked* the clock *down* for a trifling sum⟩ **3** : to take apart (something assembled) typically for convenience of moving, packing, storing, or shipping : DISASSEMBLE ⟨*knocked* the table *down* before boxing it⟩ **4 a** *slang* (1) : to appropriate dishonestly : STEAL ⟨*knocked down* plenty of the cash without getting caught⟩ (2) : ROB ⟨*knocked down* a bank⟩ **b** : to receive as income or salary : make by earning : EARN, DRAW, GET ⟨positions where they were able to *knock down* good money —*Infantry Jour.*⟩ ⟨were *knocking down* close to $150,000 a year —*Newsweek*⟩ **5** : to hammer out the round and joints of (a book to be rebound) after removal of the cover; *also* : to flatten out the frayed ends of (cords or bands) after lacing in **6** : to make a reduction in (an amount) : REDUCE, LOWER ⟨*knocked* the price *down* a dollar or two⟩ **7** : LOWERCASE ⟨*knocking down* an initial letter that had been printed as a capital⟩ ~ *vi* **1** : to be adaptable to being knocked down ⟨a portable device that easily *knocks down*⟩ **2** *of wind or a body of water* : to become tranquil : SUBSIDE ⟨the sea was *knocking down* steadily —R.F.Mirvish⟩

[1]knockdown \'=,=\ *n* -s [*knock down*] **1 a** (1) : the action of knocking down ⟨a general ~ of prices —*Newsweek*⟩ (2) : the condition of being knocked down; *specif* : the condition of a ship (as a sailboat) that is heeling over, listing heavily, or beyond recovery from the impact of wind or water **b** (1) : a temporary or permanent disordered state that is produced in an insect by an insecticide or other control agent and that is marked by cessation of the insect's normal activity and often followed by the insect's death (2) : the degree to which an insecticide or other control agent successfully incapacitates or kills insects (3) : the percentage of a test group of insects that is successfully incapacitated or killed by an insecticide or other control agent — compare KILL 1c **2 a** : a blow that knocks down ⟨watched for the first ~ in the fight⟩ **b** : an overwhelming or crushing blow (as of misfortune) : a severe setback ⟨it was a bad ~ for both of us —Lucien Price⟩ **3** : something (as a piece of furniture) that can easily be assembled or disassembled **4** *slang* : an introduction to a person ⟨give a guy a ~ to your girl friends —Jerome Weidman⟩

[2]knockdown \"\ *adj* [partly fr. *knock down;* partly fr. [1]*knockdown*] **1 a** : that knocks down or is capable of knocking down ⟨a ~ jab to the jaw⟩ : having such force or strength as to strike down : PROSTRATING, INCAPACITATING ⟨his schemes have met a ~ blow —Amy Lowell⟩ ⟨the ~ power of an insecticide⟩ **b** (1) : that cannot be successfully opposed : OVERWHELMING, OVERPOWERING ⟨a bewildering assortment of ~ arguments —J.W.Krutch⟩ ⟨would provide an almost ~ proof —A.G.N.Flew⟩ : CRUSHING ⟨a ~ defeat⟩ (2) : pushing hindrances or objections relentlessly aside by sheer force or drive : BULLDOZING ⟨his ~ style of polemics —W.E.Woodward⟩ : bluntly assured : CATEGORICAL ⟨he had his ~ answer for anyone who questioned his qualifications —Van Wyck Brooks⟩ **c** : KNOCK-DOWN-AND-DRAG-OUT ⟨can explode any moment into a ~ fight —*Newsweek*⟩ **2 a** : that can easily be put together or taken apart (as for convenience of storing or shipping) : made up of parts that are readily assembled or disassembled ⟨a ~ piece of furniture⟩ **b** : KNOCKED-DOWN **3 a** : lowest possible : MINIMUM ⟨the auctioneer set the ~ bid at $5.00⟩ **b** : extremely low ⟨can make the trip at ~ cost⟩ : REDUCED ⟨bought supplies at ~ prices⟩

[1]knock-down-and-drag-out \'=,='=,=\ *or* **knock-down, drag-out** \'=,=',=\ *adj* [*knock down* + *and* + *drag out*, v.] : marked by extreme violence or bitterness and by the giving of no quarter : carried to the last extremity ⟨a *knock-down-and-drag-out* fight⟩ ⟨*knock-down-and-drag-out* political debates⟩ ⟨one of the toughest *knock-down, drag-out* little battles ever fought —*Infantry Jour.*⟩

[2]knock-down-and-drag-out \"\ *n* -s : a knock-down-and-drag-out fight or controversy ⟨are both spoiling for a real *knock-down-and-drag-out* on this issue —*New Republic*⟩

knocked *past of* KNOCK

knocked-down \'='=\ *adj* [fr. past part. of *knock down*] : not assembled or only partly assembled : consisting of parts that can be assembled ⟨prefabricated *knocked-down* buildings⟩ — abbr. *K.D.*

knock·er \'näkə(r)\ *n* -s [ME *knokker*, fr. *knokken* to knock + *-er* — more at KNOCK] **1** : one that knocks: as **a** : a usu. ornamental fixture attached to the outer surface of a door and consisting typically of a metal plate to which a metal ring or bar or hammer is hinged that may be raised and lowered with sharp force against the surface of the plate or door so as to produce a rapping noise designed to indicate one's desire to gain admittance **b** *dial Eng* : a spirit or goblin believed to dwell in mines and to show by knocking where ore is **c** : a faultfinder or a person given to adverse often captious criticism ⟨when I see a ~ and a troublemaker I let him know what I think of him — L.B.Salomon⟩ **d** (1) : a slaughterhouse worker who stuns cattle with a sledgehammer before they are killed (2) : one that knocks ripe fruit (as prunes, olives, nuts) from trees typically with a rubber mallet and a pole (3) : CAKE PULLER **2** : BREAST — often considered vulgar **3** : TESTIS — often considered vulgar **4** *slang* : FELLOW ⟨that fish is a big ~⟩ : GUY ⟨hit the dirty ~ right in the jaw⟩ — **up to the knocker** *slang Brit* **1** : up to par ⟨didn't feel *up to the knocker*⟩ **2** : up to the fullest or best possible extent or degree ⟨was prepared *up to the knocker*⟩

knocker 1a

knocker-off \'=='=\ *n, pl* **knockers-off** *or* **knocker-offs** [*knock off* + *-er*] **1** : a worker who knocks temporary hoops from barrels by hand or by machine after heads and permanent hoops have been placed **2** : a worker who uses a chisel to break apart castings and remove sprues from molded and cast articles

knocking *pres part of* KNOCK

knocking over *n, pl* **knockings over** *or* **knocking overs** [fr. gerund of *knock over*] : the action of a knitting machine device that pushes the newly formed loops off the needles

knocking shop *n* [fr. gerund of *knock* "to copulate with", fr. [1]*knock*] *slang Brit* : BROTHEL

knock-knee \'=,=\ *n* : a condition in which the legs curve inward at the knees as a result of disease or unphysiologic stresses on the bones ⟨afflicted with *knock-knee*⟩

knock-kneed \'=;'=\ *adj* **1** : having knock-knee ⟨an emaciated *knock-kneed* child⟩ **2 a** : functioning or moving awkwardly or jerkily or laboriously ⟨a *knock-kneed* mind⟩ ⟨*knock-kneed* lines of verse⟩ : LIMPING, LAME, INEPT, WEAK ⟨a *knock-kneed* excuse⟩ **b** : devoid of smoothness and grace : CLUMSY, GAUCHE ⟨a *knock-kneed* collection of provincial practitioners —*Times Lit. Supp.*⟩ ⟨a *knock-kneed* vase in the foreground —H.L.Mencken⟩

knock-knees \'=,=\ *n pl* : knees that approach each other or knock together because of knock-knee ⟨developed *knock-knees* at an early age⟩

knock·less \'nākləs\ *adj* : having or producing no knock ⟨a ~ motor fuel⟩ : devoid of knocks ⟨the easy sheltered ~ unshocked life —*Forum*⟩

knock-me-down \'==,=\ *adj* : that overpowers or overwhelms : BULLDOZING ⟨*knock-me-down* Johnsonian pragmatism — George Saintsbury⟩ ⟨a *knock-me-down* doctrine —Joseph Conrad⟩

knockmeter \'=,==\ *n* : an instrument that measures the intensity of knock (sense 2)

knock off *vi* **1** : to discontinue doing something; *specif* : to cease from work or some other occupation ⟨*knocks off* for several days and lolls about in pajamas —E.P.Snow⟩ **2** *slang* : DIE ~ *vt* **1 a** : to do esp. in a hurried or routine way : take care of : get through with : attend to : DISPATCH ⟨*knocking off* routine duties with very little thought⟩ **b** : to produce esp. roughly or hastily : turn out hurriedly ⟨*knocks off* one book after another⟩ **2 a** (1) : to discontinue (work or some other occupation) : leave off ⟨arranged that they should *knock off* work at five —Nevil Shute⟩ : desist from : STOP, QUIT (2) : to cause to leave off from (work or some other indicated occupation) : DISMISS ⟨the foreman *knocked off* the workers for lunch⟩ ⟨told them he was tired of their talking and that he wished they would *knock it off*⟩ **b** : to dispense with : pass over : SKIP ⟨hoped that the usual inspection would be *knocked off*⟩ **3** : DEDUCT ⟨*knocked off* 20 cents to make the price more attractive⟩ **4 a** : to take into custody : SEIZE, ARREST, NAB ⟨had enough sense not to get *knocked off* by the police —Richard Llewellyn⟩ **b** : RAID ⟨*knocked off* a gambling joint⟩ **5 a** : KILL, MURDER ⟨*knocked off* two men, purely on mercenary grounds —Lewis Baker⟩ **b** : OVERCOME, DESTROY ⟨*knocked off* each center of rebellion⟩ **c** : to get rid of : ELIMINATE ⟨*knocked off* every objection⟩ ⟨usually has to *knock off* only one or two opponents —W.S.Carlson⟩ **d** : to dispose of to or as if to a bidder at an auction sale : knock down **6 a** *slang* (1) : STEAL ⟨*knocked off* a few trinkets in the store⟩ (2) : ROB ⟨*knocked off* a couple of banks⟩ **b** : RECEIVE, GET, OBTAIN ⟨*knocks off* a Nobel prize —Ethel Merman⟩ **7** : to swallow down : toss off : finish off ⟨ordered a schooner of beer and *knocked* it *off* with unaffected enthusiasm —A.J. Liebling⟩

knock-off \'=,=\ *n, pl* **knock-offs** [*knock off*] **1** : the action of knocking off; *esp* : the automatic coming to a halt of a machine or of a part of a machine through the action of a device actuated when the functioning of the machine becomes faulty **2** : a cam or other device designed to safeguard a machine or part of a machine from continuing to function when operation becomes faulty **3** : the time set for leaving off from work or from some other occupation ⟨finished the greater part of the job long before *knock-off*⟩

knock on *vt* : to knock onward : knock forward; *specif* : to knock (the ball in rugby) forward in the direction of the opponents' dead-ball line with the hand or arm

[1]knock-on \'=,=\ *n, pl* **knock-ons** [*knock on*] : the action of knocking on

[2]knock-on \"\ *adj* [*knock on*] : produced or projected as a result of the collision of an energetic particle (as a neutron or fission fragment) from outside an atom with an elementary particle inside ⟨a *knock-on* shower of particles⟩ ⟨a *knock-on* atom⟩ ⟨a *knock-on* electron⟩

knock out *vt* **1 a** : to produce esp. roughly or hastily : turn out hurriedly ⟨in that same month he *knocked out* eleven novelettes —*Time*⟩ **b** : to get through with : take care of esp. in a hurried or routine way : attend to : DISPATCH ⟨quickly *knocked out* the few things that had to be looked after⟩ **2 a** (1) : to fell (a boxing opponent) by hitting esp. on the chin and making unconscious or otherwise unable to rise or continue within a specified time ⟨*knocked* him *out* in the first round⟩ (2) : to make unconscious or to stupefy esp. by hitting on the head ⟨the flowerpot hit him on the head and *knocked* him *out*⟩ **b** (1) : to make the further use of impossible without replacement or repair : put out of commission : make inoperative ⟨telephone communications had been *knocked out*⟩ : DEMOLISH, DESTROY ⟨*knocking out* the bridges and an ammunition dump —Lee Rogow⟩ ⟨*knocked out* twelve transport aircraft —*Time*⟩ (2) : to put an effective end to : get rid of : ELIMINATE, CRUSH, SQUASH, SQUELCH ⟨*knocked out* commercial gambling —A.E.Stevenson †1965⟩ **3 a** : to make (as oneself) exhausted : tire out : wear out ⟨*knocked* themselves *out* with excessive work⟩ **b** : to exert (as oneself) to the breaking point or beyond endurance : exert to the utmost : drive to the point of exhaustion ⟨*knocking* myself *out* to get top grades —W.H.Whyte⟩ ⟨*knocked* ourselves *out* preparing for the grand opening —Polly Adler⟩ **4** : to strike (the inverted bowl of a pipe of tobacco) on something or with something so as to cause burning or burned tobacco to fall out ⟨*knocked* his pipe *out* before refilling it⟩ **5** : to knock out of the box ⟨the pitcher was *knocked out* in the fifth inning⟩

[1]knockout \'=,=\ *n* -s [*knock out*] **1** *Brit* : an auction or sale or similar transaction at which a combination (as of bidders) illegitimately forces out other potential competitors and arranges by prior agreement to have one member of the combination secure at a set price the thing being offered so as later to profitably dispose of the thing (as by reauctioning) **2 a** (1) : the act of knocking out or the condition of being knocked out (2) : a blow or attack that knocks out ⟨won the fight by a ~⟩ ⟨an attempted early ~ by the enemy —R.W. Stokley⟩ **b** (1) : termination of a bout in boxing that occurs when an opponent is knocked out (2) : TECHNICAL KNOCKOUT **3** : something sensationally striking or attractive : something altogether out of the ordinary or superlatively excellent ⟨she combines looks with poise and is a ~ at any party⟩ ⟨a hilarious book that is a real ~⟩ ⟨has produced a new film that is a ~⟩ **4 a** : something (as a set of pins in a die) that can be loosened or forced out typically to release or force out something else (as work in a punch or die) **b** (1) : a partially punched-out or cutout piece esp. in metal or plastic designed to be forced out when an opening is required; *esp* : such a partially punched piece in the side of a junction box (2) : the hole produced when such a piece is forced out

[2]knockout \"\ *adj* [partly fr. *knock out;* partly fr. [1]*knockout*] **1 a** : that knocks out: as (1) : that makes unconscious or stupefies ⟨delivered a ~ blow to the head⟩ ⟨mixed a ~ drink⟩ (2) : that incapacitates or puts out of commission or demolishes or destroys ⟨planned a ~ offensive against the enemy⟩ ⟨a ~ air attack⟩ (3) : that eliminates from competition ⟨only three teams were left in the running after the preliminary ~ matches⟩ **b** : that can be loosened or forced out ⟨removal of hot work from a press by means of ~ pins in the die⟩ or that is equipped with pieces that can be loosened or forced out ⟨metal file cases that are punched with ~ holes⟩ **2** : sensationally striking or attractive or unusual or excellent ⟨wore a ~ dress⟩ ⟨ideas for a ~ gift⟩

knockout drops *n pl* : drops of a solution of a drug (as chloral hydrate) put into a drink and designed to make the drinker unconscious or stupefied

knock over *vt* **1 a** (1) : FELL, PROSTRATE : knock down ⟨*knocked* him *over* with one blow⟩ (2) : to upset badly : greatly disturb : OVERWHELM ⟨was *knocked over* by the news⟩ **b** : to get rid of : dispose of : ELIMINATE ⟨*knocked over* every difficulty⟩ **c** : to get through with : finish up with : DISPATCH ⟨*knocked over* a book a day —R.L.Taylor⟩ **2 a** : STEAL; *esp* : HIJACK ⟨*knocks over* a truckload of merchandise —J.B. Martin⟩ **b** : ROB ⟨*knocking over* a jewelry store —John McCarten⟩ **3** : to receive as income or salary ⟨*knocks over* a good sum each year⟩ **4** : to move strongly esp. to admiration or applause ⟨which for really brilliant suddenness of perception *knocks* me *over* completely —H.J.Laski⟩

knockover \'=,==\ *n* -s [*knock over*] : the act of knocking over : the condition of being knocked over

knock poker *n* : a card game in which each player holds five cards and attempts to build a good poker hand but draws and discards as in rummy and may end the play by knocking

knock rummy *n* : rummy played by two to six players in which the winner is the player with the lowest count in unmatched cards and in which a player may end the play by knocking

knocks *pres 3d sing of* KNOCK, *pl of* KNOCK

knock under *vi, archaic* : to admit defeat : give in : give up : YIELD ⟨why should we *knock under* and go with the stream — H.D.Thoreau⟩

knock up *vt* **1 a** (1) : to arrange or devise esp. hurriedly or with little thought ⟨decided to *knock up* a tennis match⟩ : prepare quickly or without much care ⟨*knock up* a meal for us —Irwin Shaw⟩ (2) : to strike up casually ⟨*knocked up* an acquaintance with a few people⟩ **b** : to knock together ⟨two small wooden buildings, casually *knocked up* —Josephine Pinckney⟩ **c** : to practice informally with (as a tennis ball, shuttlecock) in warming up before a match (as in tennis, badminton, squash) **2** *Brit* : ROUSE, SUMMON; *specif* : to cause (as by knocking at the door) to awaken or rise from sleep or rest **3 a** : to make exhausted : knock out ⟨hurried too fast and it *knocked* me *up* —G.M.Hopkins⟩ **b** (1) : to put out of top condition : cause to deteriorate ⟨too much food and idleness had *knocked* them *up*⟩ (2) : to bring to an end : DESTROY ⟨unfair competition had *knocked up* the once flourishing business⟩ **c** : WOUND, HURT ⟨got pretty badly *knocked up*⟩ ⟨if I'm killed over there — that isn't likely, I'm more of the damned sort that gets *knocked up* —Ellen Glasgow⟩ **4 a** : to run up (as a score) : MAKE, ACHIEVE ⟨*knocking up* a good score⟩ **b** *Brit* : to receive as income or salary : EARN, GET **5** *slang* : to make pregnant ⟨no girls get married around here till they're *knocked up* —Ernest Hemingway⟩ **6** : to make uneasy : DISTURB, BOTHER ⟨felt rather *knocked up* by the news⟩ **7 a** *Brit* : to knock down (sense 5) **b** : JOG 4 ~ *vi* **1** : to become totally exhausted or otherwise unfit : break down ⟨a few of the beasts had *knocked up* and had to be abandoned —I.L. Idriess⟩ **2** : to chance upon or meet up with something indicated — used with *against* ⟨*knocked up* against formidable difficulties⟩ ⟨happened to *knock up* against an old friend⟩ **3** : to practice informally (as by volleying) in warming up before a match (as in tennis, badminton, squash)

knockup \'=,=\ *n* -s [*knock up*] : informal practice (as by volleying) in warming up before a match

knockwurst *var of* KNACKWURST

knod·den \'näd°n, kə'n-\ *adj* [fr. obs. past part. of *knead*] *dial Eng* : KNEADED

knö·del *or* **knoe·del** \kə'nœd°l\ *n, pl* **knödel** *or* **knödels** *or* **knoedel** *or* **knoedels** [G *knödel*, fr. MHG, dim. of *knode* knot, fr. OHG *knodo* — more at KNOT] : DUMPLING

knoe·ve·na·gel reaction \kə'nə(r)və,nāgəl-, kə'nāv-\ *or* **knoevenagel condensation** *n, usu cap K* [after Emil *Knoevenagel* †1921 Ger. chemist] : an aldol-type condensation catalyzed by amines that takes place between an aldehyde or ketone and a compound containing an active methylene group (as in esters of acetoacetic acid, malonic acid, or cyanoacetic acid)

[1]knoll \'nōl\ *n* -s [ME *knol*, fr. OE *cnoll;* akin to MHG *knolle* clod, lump, tuber, ON *knollr* mountaintop, OE *cnotta* knot — more at KNOT] **1 a** *now dial Eng* : the top of a hill **b** (1) : a usu. small rounded submerged elevation rising from the floor of a body of water; *esp* : the upper part or top of such an elevation (2) : a usu. rounded submerged projection of a shoal, reef, bank, or bar **2** : a usu. small rounded land eminence : MOUND, HILLOCK

[2]knoll \"\ *n* -s [ME, prob. alter. of *knel* — more at KNELL] *archaic* : KNELL

[3]knoll \"\ *vb* -ED/-ING/-S [ME *knollen*, prob. alter. of *knellen* — more at KNELL] *archaic* : KNELL

knolly \-lē\ *adj* : marked by knolls ⟨a ~ section of the country⟩

knoop hardness \'nüp-\ *n, usu cap K* [after F. *Knoop*, 20th cent. Am. chemist] : the relative hardness of a material (as a metal) that is determined by the depth to which the bluntly pointed diamond pyramid of a special instrument will penetrate it

knop \'näp\ *n* -s [ME *knoppe, knop*, fr. OE *-cnoppa;* akin to MLG *knuppe, knoppe* bud, MD *cnoppe* knob, bud, OHG *knopf* knot, bud, knob, ON *knӯfill* short horn, OIr *gnobh* knot in wood, OE *cnotta* knot — more at KNOT] : a usu. ornamental knob: as **a** : a small rounded or angular ornamental enlargement or protuberance that is usu. at the mid or upper part of the stem of a vessel (as a chalice, goblet) or at the same part of the shank or shaft of some other object (as a candlestick, andiron) and that usu. serves as an aid in grasping or holding **b** : KNOB 1b **c** : a tiny ball, loop, or tuft of a fiber (as wool, silk, cotton) that is formed in or on a yarn, thread, or cloth and that is often of a color varying from that of the yarn, thread, or cloth or from that of other balls, loops, or tufts formed in or on the yarn, thread, or cloth

knop·ite \'nä,pīt\ *n* -s [G *knopit*, fr. Adolf *Knop* †1893 Ger. mineralogist + G *-it* -ite] : perovskite containing cerium

knopped \'näpt\ *adj* [ME, fr. *knoppe* + *-ed*] : having one or more knops ⟨a glass bowl with a ~ stem⟩ ⟨~ yarn⟩

knop·per \'näpə(r)\ *n* -s [G; akin to OHG *knopf* knot, bud, knob] : a gall that is formed by a gall wasp on the leaves and immature acorns of various oaks and that is used in tanning and dyeing

knop·pie spider \'näpē-\ *n* [Afrik *knoppie*, dim. of *knop* knob, bud — more at KNOBKERRIE] : either of two venomous spiders (*Latrodectus geometricus* and *L. indistinctus*) of southern Africa that are closely related to the American black widow

knop's solution \'näps-, kə'nōps-\ *n, usu cap K* [after J. A. L. W. *Knop* †1891 Ger. chemist] : a nutrient solution used in growth experiments with higher plants and containing definite proportions of calcium nitrate, potassium nitrate, magnesium sulfate, monobasic potassium phosphate, and potassium chloride dissolved in water

knop yarn *n* : a ply yarn with knops that is often made by twisting one ply faster than another

knorhaan *also* **knoorhaan** *var of* KORHAAN

knor·ria \'nórēə, 'när-\ *n, cap* [NL, fr. Georg W. *Knorr* †1761 Ger. collector of petrified objects + NL *-ia*] : a form genus based on fossil stems of Carboniferous age that are intermediate in structure between those typical of the Lepidodendraceae and the Sigillariaceae

knosp \'näsp\ *n* -s [G *knospe*, lit., bud; akin to OHG *knopf* knot, bud, knob — more at KNOP] *archaic* : KNOP

knos·si·an *also* **cnos·si·an** \(kə)'näsēən, *chiefly Brit* -nōs-\ *adj, usu cap* [*Knossos* or *Cnossus*, city in ancient Crete (fr. Gk *Knōssos*) + E *-ian*] : of, relating to, or characteristic of the city of Knossos

1knot \'nät, *usu* -äd·+V\ *n* -s [ME *knotte, knot*, fr. OE *cnotta;* akin to OHG *knoto & knodo* knot, ON *knūtr* knot, *knūta* top of a bone, knuckle, Lith *gniùsti* to press, *gniùtulas* bale, paper, lump; basic meaning: to press together; something clumped together] **1 a** (1) **:** an intertwining, looping, bending, hitching, folding, gathering together, or tangling of one or more parts of a pliant relatively slender length of something in such a way as to produce a tying together, fastening, binding, or connecting of the length on, to, or with itself, another length, or some other thing ⟨a cord with ~*s* in it⟩ ⟨one rope was attached to another by a loose ~⟩ (2) **:** the interlacement or other disposition or arrangement or formation produced in a length by such manipulation ⟨wondered how to undo the ~⟩ (3) **:** a specific localized point or mass produced in a length by such manipulation; *esp* **:** a lump or knob or some other relatively tight mass produced in a length by such manipulation ⟨made heavy ~*s* in the rope every five feet⟩ (4) **:** a bow or rosette or cockade or epaulet or some other ornamental arrangement of a material (as ribbon) produced by such manipulation ⟨wore a faded red worsted ~, the emblem of his rank, on his left shoulder —F.V.W.Mason⟩ (5) **:** a length of hair rolled or coiled or twisted into a usu. tight mass on the head **:** BUN ⟨with iron-gray hair in a ~ on top of her head —Marcia Davenport⟩ **b :** something perplexingly intricate or involved or difficult **:** a problem or complication that cannot be easily solved ⟨a matter full of legal ~*s*⟩ **c :** something that ties or binds together **:** a bond of union ⟨the two nations renewed the ~ between them —R.W.Van Alstyne⟩; *esp* **:** the bond of marriage ⟨hoped to loose the ~ by divorce⟩ **d :** the central point or heart of something **:** the hard center **:** NUB, CORE, ESSENCE ⟨confront the ~ of meaning—*Western Rev.*⟩ ⟨the very ~ and center of my being —R.L.Stevenson⟩; *esp* **:** the heart of something complicated or problematical ⟨the very ~ of the difficulty —W.E.Gladstone⟩ **2 a** (1) **:** a usu. firm or hard lump or swelling or protuberance in or on a part of an animal body or bone or process ⟨a ~ in a gland⟩ ⟨a pendulous fold of flesh full of ~*s*⟩ ⟨a bone with two or three ~*s*⟩ ⟨a ~ at the end of the animal's horn⟩; *esp* **:** an often contorted lump or swelling or protuberance in a muscle ⟨strained at the oars until the muscles of their arms stood out in ~*s*⟩ (2) **:** a puckering or furrowing or wrinkling of the lower central area of the forehead typically occurring in deep concentration or as an indication of displeasure ⟨went over it slowly with the ~ between his brows —Vincent McHugh⟩ (3) **:** a tight constriction or the sensation of such a constriction ⟨music that dissolved the ~*s* in their minds —Van Wyck Brooks⟩ ⟨his throat caught in a dry ~, his head felt leaden —Marcia Davenport⟩ ⟨moving slowly, as in a dream, his stomach in a ~ —Gregor Felsen⟩ (4) **:** a constricted or contorted mass **:** a tight bundle ⟨I was tired and tense, my nerves were in ~*s* —Polly Adler⟩ **b :** a lump or swelling or protuberance in or on a part of a plant: as (1) **:** the node of a grass (2) **:** a protuberance or an excrescence on a stem or branch or root; *esp* **:** a hard irregular lump formed at the point where a branch grows out of the trunk of a tree ⟨the first American settlers employed . . . pine ~*s*, which were dipped in pitch and burned with a bright but smoky flame —A.L.Powell⟩ (3) *chiefly dial Brit* **:** BUD, BLOOM — used esp. in the phrase *in the knot* ⟨now the hawthorn is coming in the ~⟩ **c :** a relatively small concreted mass that may occur in rocks or in precious stones or in glass or in similar objects or substances and that is typically harder than the surrounding material or that otherwise differs (as in the direction of its grain) from the surrounding material **d :** a cross section of the hard lump on a tree trunk from which a branch grows out and which appears in a board as a rounded usu. cross-grained area that may fall out and leave an irregular hole **e :** a fungous disease of trees marked by the development of abnormal excrescences **3 a :** an ornamental usu. carved or hammered knob, boss, or stud **b :** an ornamental often functional mass (as a corbel or similar member or as the capital of a column) used in architecture and consisting typically of carved or sculptured foliage **4** *now dial Brit* **:** a hill or similar land eminence of moderate height; *esp* **:** a rocky hill of moderate height **5 a :** a small group of persons closely clustered together ⟨~*s* of people talking and arguing on street corners —S.V.Benét⟩ ⟨a chatty little ~ at the back of PTA meetings —Bice Clemow⟩ **b :** CLUMP ⟨a ~ of palm trees⟩ **:** BUNCH ⟨a ~ of drooping dandelions⟩ **6** *now chiefly dial* **:** KNOT GARDEN **7 :** a measured length of yarn, thread, or cord **8 a** (1) **:** one of the lengths marked off on a log line each of which is 47 feet 3 inches in extent and has the same relation to one nautical mile as 28 seconds has to one hour so that the number of such divisions running out from the log reel within a 28-second interval will indicate that the identical number of nautical miles will be covered within one hour by the ship if it maintains the same speed (2) **:** the point marking the dividing line between each such length **b :** one nautical mile per hour — used as a unit of measurement in expressing the rate of speed of seagoing ships and of airplanes and in expressing the relative strength of water currents and the degree of intensity of air currents ⟨a ship that logs 10 ~*s*⟩ ⟨a plane traveling 450 ~*s*⟩ ⟨a 30-*knot* wind⟩; abbr. *kn., kt., k.* **c :** one nautical mile ⟨the ship reached a speed of 12 ~*s* an hour⟩ — not used technically **9 :** an elevated land region formed by the juncture of several mountain regions **10 :** a space curve that is closed

2knot \"\ *vb* **knotted**; **knotted**; **knotting**; **knots** [ME *knott*] *vt* **1 a** (1) **:** to tie, fasten, bind, or connect with a knot **:** do up or secure with a knot ⟨*knotted* his clothes into a tight bundle⟩ (2) **:** to tie into a knot **:** form into a knot ⟨*knotted* the shoelace and couldn't untie it⟩ **b** (1) **:** to make a knot in or cause to be full of knots ⟨broad soft neckties, which he *knotted* in large loose bows —Laura Krey⟩ ⟨*knotted* the rope every five feet⟩ (2) **:** to make (lace, net, or other fancywork) by twisting and looping thread into knots to form designs **2 a** (1) **:** to unite closely or bind firmly together **:** cause to be closely joined or associated ⟨the ties of blood that were *knotted* into all the relationships of communal life —Oscar Handlin⟩ (2) **:** to group closely together ⟨their horses were *knotted* about an instructor —Hugh MacLennan⟩ (3) **:** to pull together ⟨official and private problems ~ the plot into an intriguing pattern —Fanny Butcher⟩ **b :** to cause to be joined in a confused or tangled way **:** ENTANGLE ⟨ligatures, i.e. combinations in which two or more letters are *knotted* together and lose their original shape —E.H.Minns⟩ ⟨creepers of many kinds . . . *knotting* the undergrowth into impenetrable thickets —C.D. Forde⟩ **3 :** to cause (the forehead or brows) to become knitted ⟨saw him ~ and unknot his eyebrows —Donn Byrne⟩ **4 :** to make (the score of an athletic contest or other competition) even **:** tie up **:** EQUALIZE ⟨slammed in a 30-footer to ~ it again at 3 all —John Drebinger⟩ **5 :** to cover the knots of (wood) with a conditioning preparation (as shellac) before painting ~ *vi* **1 a :** to form knots **:** become knotted ⟨wet cords tend to ~⟩ ⟨took a long drink, the raw alcohol *knotting* and burning in his chest —Irwin Shaw⟩ ⟨the men bent forward, grunting deep in their lungs, their belly muscles *knotting* with the pull of the oars —Frank Yerby⟩ — often used with *up* ⟨the tendons of his legs began to ~ up —Andrew Hamilton⟩ **b :** to form a constricted or contorted mass **:** form lumps ⟨planets . . . were formed by a process of shriveling and *knotting* —Waldemar Kaempffert⟩ **2 :** to become gathered together into a small group **:** cluster together ⟨commandomen, who roamed here and there, *knotting* into groups for the exchange of experiences —John Brophy⟩ **3 :** to make lace, net, or other fancywork by twisting and looping thread into knots to form designs

3knot \"\ *n* -s **:** any of several sandpipers (genus *Calidris*) that breed in the Arctic and winter in temperate or warm parts of the New and Old World: as **a :** a stocky gregarious Old World bird (*C. canutus*) whose plumage in the breeding season is chestnut and black above and that has a russet head and russet underparts **b :** a similar American bird that forms a subspecies (*C. canutus rufus*) and that is predominantly gray and spotted with black and ruddy brown above and that has a pale brown head and pale brown underparts **c :** a bird (*C. tenuirostris*) that is grayish brown to dark brown above with white underparts and white bars on the wings and tail and that breeds in northeastern Asia and winters southward to Australia — called also *great knot, Japanese knot*

knot bindweed *n* **:** BLACK BINDWEED 1

knot garden *n* **1 :** an elaborately designed garden esp. of flowers or herbs **2 :** a piece of ground marked by shrubbery or small trees arranged in an intricately formal pattern and typically trimmed into ornamental and often bizarre shapes **:** TOPIARY

knotgrass \'=,=\ *n* **1 :** a common cosmopolitan weed (*Polygonum aviculare*) with jointed stems, prominent sheathing stipules, and minute flowers **2 :** any of several grasses (as fiorin oat grass) with geniculate stems; *esp* **:** JOINT GRASS 1

knothead \'=,=\ *n* **:** a dull-witted blunderer **:** DUMBBELL, SIMPLETON

knothole \'=,=\ *n* **:** a hole in a board or tree trunk where a knot or branch has come out

knot·less \'nätləs\ *adj* **:** devoid of knots

knotroot \'=,=\ *n* **1 :** CHINESE ARTICHOKE **2 :** HORSE BALM 1

knotroot grass *n* **:** a No. American grass (*Muhlenbergia mexicana*) used as a soil binder and as hay

knots *pl of* KNOT, *pres 3d sing of* KNOT

knot sawyer *n* **:** one who saws defective parts from lumber

knot·ted \'näd·əd, -ätəd\ *adj* [ME, fr. *knotte, knot* knot + *-ed*] **:** KNOTTY; *esp* **:** twisted or contorted and marked by swollen joints ⟨had been wringing nothing but a scanty living from the soil with their gnarled and ~ hands —C.A. & Mary Beard⟩

knot·ter \-äd·ə(r), -ätə-\ *n* -s **1 :** one that makes knots: as **a :** a worker who makes nets by hand **b :** a device that knots threads **2 :** one that removes knots: as **a :** a device used in papermaking by which lumps are removed from paper pulp **b :** LIMBER

knotter bill *or* **knotter hook** *n* **:** KNOTTING BILL

knot·ti·ly \-äd·əlē\ *adv* **:** in a knotty manner ⟨a ~ involved problem⟩

knot·ti·ness \-äd·|ēnəs, -ät|, |in-\ *n* -ES **:** the quality or state of being knotty ⟨bewildered by the ~ of the legal points involved⟩

knotting *n* -s **1 :** fancywork produced by twisting and looping thread into knots to form designs **2 :** a conditioning preparation (as shellac) used to cover the knots of wood before painting

knotting bill *or* **knotting hook** *n* **:** a metal hook with a blunt point on which is formed the knot that secures a quantity of grain gathered up by a grain binder

knot·ty \'näd·|ē, -ät|, |i\ *adj, usu* -ER/-EST [ME *knotty*, fr. *knotte, knot* knot + *-y* — more at KNOT] **:** marked by or full of knots: as **a :** full of difficulties or complications **:** hard to solve or understand **:** INVOLVED, PUZZLING, INTRICATE ⟨the ~ problems of a complex society —V.L.Parrington⟩ ⟨~ points of international law —Lisle Bell⟩ **b :** tied in or with knots ⟨a ~ rope⟩ **c** (1) **:** twisted or contorted and marked by protuberances **:** GNARLED ⟨ancient ~ trees⟩ **:** BUMPY, KNOBBY ⟨her old ~ hands⟩ (2) **:** having many hard irregular lumps at the points where branches grow out ⟨cut down a ~ tree trunk⟩ (3) **:** showing cross sections of such lumps or having knotholes ⟨~ pieces of lumber⟩ **d :** marked by or indicative of robustness or ruggedness **:** WIRY, TOUGH ⟨a sinewy ~ strength —Jack London⟩ **syn** see COMPLEX

knotty brake *n* **:** MALE FERN

knotty gut *n* **:** NODULAR DISEASE

knotty guts *n pl* **1** *sing or pl in constr* **:** NODULAR DISEASE **2 :** intestines affected with nodular disease

knotty pine *n* **1 :** LODGEPOLE PINE **2 :** pine wood marked by an esp. decorative distribution of knots when finished for use unpainted esp. on walls or ceilings

knotty rhatany *n* **:** PERUVIAN RHATANY

knotweed \'=,=\ *n* **:** any of several plants of the genus *Polygonum; esp* **:** KNOTGRASS 1

knotweed spurge *n* **:** SEASIDE SPURGE

1knout \'nau̇t, 'nüt\ *n* -s [Russ *knut*, of Scand origin; akin to ON *knūtr* knot — more at KNOT] **:** a flogging whip with a lash of leather thongs twisted with wire used for punishing criminals

2knout \"\ *vt* -ED/-ING/-S **:** to flog with a knout

1know \'nō\ *vb* **knew** \'n(y)ü\ *or dial* **knowed** \'nōd\ **known** \'nōn *sometimes* -ōən\ *also dial* **knowed**; **knowing**; **knows** [ME *knowen, knawen*, fr. OE *cnāwan;* akin to OHG bi*chnāan* to recognize, ON *knā* I can, L *gnoscere, noscere* to become acquainted with, come to know, Gk gig*nōskein* to come to know, perceive, OSlav *znati* to know, Skt *jānāti* he knows] *vt* **1 a** (1) **:** to apprehend immediately with the mind or with the senses **:** perceive directly **:** have direct unambiguous cognition of ⟨taught that one could come to ~ objective truth⟩ (2) **:** to have perception, cognition, or understanding of esp. to an extensive or complete extent ⟨learning to ~ one's mind —Virgil Thomson⟩ ⟨insisted on the importance of ~*ing* oneself⟩ (3) **:** to recognize the quality of **:** see clearly the character of **:** DISCERN ⟨*knew* him for what he was⟩ ⟨~*s* him as honest and reliable⟩ (4) **:** to recognize in a specific capacity ⟨one glance and they ~ him as the one destined to lead them⟩ **b** (1) **:** to apprehend as being the same as something previously apprehended **:** recognize as being an object of perception identical with a previous object of perception **:** recognize as familiar ⟨*knew* her father as soon as she saw him⟩ ⟨said they would ~ that face anywhere⟩ (2) **:** to have acquaintance or familiarity with through experience or acquisition of information or hearsay ⟨*knew* no such restraints —Hugh Seton-Watson⟩ ⟨*knew* the law fairly well⟩ ⟨~*s* foreign languages⟩; *specif* **:** to have personal acquaintance with (a person) ⟨whom he had learned to ~ and love —Allen Johnson⟩ ⟨recognizes many people by sight but doesn't ~ them all⟩ (3) **:** to have experience of ⟨the region has *known* a steadily increasing . . . number of visitors —S.H.Holbrook⟩ ⟨*knew* great delight⟩ ⟨did not ~ happiness with the woman he married —Ruth P. Randall⟩ **c :** to apprehend as being distinct from something previously apprehended **:** recognize as being an object of perception distinct from a previous object of perception **:** recognize as distinct **:** DISTINGUISH ⟨barely able to ~ one thing from another⟩ **2 a :** to have cognizance, consciousness, or awareness of **:** have within the mind as something apprehended, learned, or understood ⟨*knew* they could never have what city folks had —M.W.Straight⟩ ⟨~*s* that this is quite true⟩ ⟨*knew* many would not believe him⟩ ⟨didn't ~ who she was or where she was going⟩ ⟨was *known* to be a friend of hers⟩ **b :** to have a practical understanding of or a distinct skill in through instruction, study, practice, or experience ⟨~*s* how to write vividly —William Clerk⟩ ⟨~*s* the fundamentals perfectly⟩ **3 :** to apprehend with certitude as true, factual, sure, or valid **:** perceive or have within the mind's grasp with clarity and the conviction of certainty **:** have certitude about and clear comprehension of ⟨~ what they want and intend to get it⟩ ⟨*knew* the solution to almost any problem⟩ **4** *archaic* **:** to have sexual intercourse with ~ *vi* **1 a :** to have perception or cognition or understanding of something esp. to an extensive or complete extent ⟨you ~ better⟩ ⟨people who ~ will not waste their time that way⟩ ⟨we want to ~, we will not be content with a fairy tale of love —L.O.Coxe⟩ **b :** to have cognizance, consciousness, or awareness of something **:** be aware of the existence or fact of something ⟨*knew* of her but had not yet met her⟩ ⟨*knew* about what had happened⟩ **2 :** to have information **:** have acquaintance with facts ⟨*knew* differently and therefore refused the offer⟩ **3 :** to have something within the mind's grasp with certitude and clarity ⟨do you ~, or is that only your opinion⟩ — **know one's onions :** to know one's stuff — **know one's stuff :** to be thoroughly proficient or highly skilled in a field of activity or an area of knowledge **:** know the ropes ⟨can rely on her completely because she really *knows her stuff*⟩ — **know the ropes :** to have experience and understanding of the details, methods, and procedures involved in accomplishing or furthering something esp. without unnecessary delay ⟨*knew the ropes* and soon had everything organized smoothly⟩ — **not know from nothing** *slang* **:** to know nothing about something **:** be completely ignorant ⟨do*n't know from nothing* —Erskine Caldwell⟩

2know \"\ *n* -s **:** the fact of knowing **:** KNOWLEDGE ⟨the inside ~ of a journalist —Douglass Cater⟩ — **in the know** *adv* (*or adj*) **:** in possession of confidential or otherwise relatively limited or exclusive knowledge, information, or awareness ⟨the sense of importance which comes from a feeling that one is *in the know* —Stanley Walker⟩ ⟨*in-the-know* intellectuals⟩

know·abil·i·ty \,nōə'biləd·ē\ *n* **:** capability of being known ⟨the question of the ~ of the external world —*Humanist*⟩

know·able \'nōəbəl\ *adj* **:** capable of being known ⟨the philosophical proposition that the external physical world around us and all its laws are fully ~ —*Atlantic*⟩ — **know·able·ness** *n* -ES

know-all *var of* KNOW-IT-ALL

knowe *or* **know** \'nō, 'nau̇\ *chiefly Scot var of* KNOLL

knowed *past of* KNOW

know·er \'nōə(r)\ *n* -s [ME, fr. *knowen* to know + *-er* — more at KNOW] **:** one that knows

know-how \'=,=\ *n* -s [fr. the phrase *know how*] **:** practical knowledge of how to do or accomplish something with smoothness and efficiency **:** ability to get something done with a minimum of wasted effort **:** accumulated practical skill or expertness ⟨business *know-how*⟩ ⟨needed the *know-how* of a good carpenter⟩ ⟨salesmanship *know-how*⟩ ⟨the *know-how* involved in producing a play⟩ ⟨developed his bowling *know=how*⟩; *esp* **:** technical knowledge, ability, skill, or expertness of this sort ⟨the company needed to use all its ingenuity and *know-how* to succeed in laying the oil lines⟩

1know·ing \'nōiŋ, -ōēŋ\ *n* -s [ME, fr. *knowen* to know + *-ing*] **1 a** (1) **:** the action or fact of knowing or understanding ⟨avoided their ~ about this⟩ ⟨her ~ was a source of comfort⟩ (2) **:** the process or faculty of getting to know or of arriving at understanding ⟨no ~ what may happen⟩ ⟨a power beyond his ~ —*Atlantic*⟩ **b :** the action of knowing by intuition or indirection or the faculty of getting to know or arrive at understanding through intuition or indirection ⟨the ~*s* of art are real . . . but they are not utterly reliable —H.J.Muller⟩ **c :** something that is apprehended or capable of being apprehended by such an action, process, or faculty ⟨underlying every concrete situation he sees the fusion of ~*s* and the known —J.R.Kantor⟩ **2 :** the condition or fact of possessing understanding or information or of being aware of something ⟨in private, in secret ~ —N.L.Rothman⟩

2knowing \"\ *adj, sometimes* -ER/-EST [ME, fr. pres. part. of *knowen* to know] **1 a :** having or reflecting knowledge, information, or insight **:** marked by understanding and intelligence **:** well-informed and marked by a ready capacity for further learning **:** KNOWLEDGEABLE ⟨a ~ student⟩ ⟨a ~ instructor⟩ **b** (1) **:** having or reflecting the keen awareness and insight and power of discernment typical of the specialist or expert **:** highly perceptive esp. in a specialized or exclusive field ⟨a ~ collector of rare books⟩ ⟨has done an excellent and ~ job in selecting the material for this book —J.C. Smith⟩ (2) **:** having or reflecting distinct skill ⟨~ brushwork on ceiling and doors —Claudia Cassidy⟩ **c** (1) **:** that indicates or is marked by awareness of and careful conformity to what is chic and currently in style **:** SMART ⟨a ~ selection of gloves and accessories⟩ (2) **:** marked by sophistication or snobbishness ⟨a distasteful air of pretentious smartness, of being altogether too ~ —Herbert Read⟩ **2 a** (1) **:** shrewd and keenly alert **:** QUICK-WITTED, ASTUTE ⟨a ~ handling of the business deal⟩ **:** WIDE-AWAKE ⟨any ~ person could have seen what was going on⟩ (2) **:** WORLDLY-WISE ⟨produces ~ chuckles —E.R.Bentley⟩ ⟨perhaps a bit too ~ and sensuous —Robert Lawrence⟩ **b :** that reflects or is designed to indicate possession of confidential, secret, or otherwise exclusive inside knowledge or information ⟨poised her fork and gave her guest a ~ look —Louis Bromfield⟩ ⟨a ~ wink⟩ ⟨maintain a discreet and ~ silence on the subject —Harry Gordon⟩ **:** that indicates an awareness or insight not generally shared ⟨the two young officers exchanged ~ glances —W.M.Thackeray⟩ **3 a :** that knows, is capable of knowing, or is the means of knowing **:** COGNITIVE ⟨in full possession of the ordinary ~ faculties⟩ **b** *archaic* **:** COGNIZANT ⟨~ to and familiar with the whole circumstances —George Catlin⟩ **4 :** that is done with awareness or deliberateness **:** that is intentional ⟨indiscriminate classification of innocent with ~ activity —*Civil Liberties*⟩ **syn** see INTELLIGENT

know·ing·ly *adv* [ME, fr. *knowing* + *-ly*] **:** in a knowing manner ⟨smiled ~⟩; *esp* **:** with awareness, deliberateness, or intention ⟨had never ~ hurt him —Max Peacock⟩

know·ing·ness *n* -ES **:** the quality or state of being knowing ⟨the brisk ~ of a competent journalist —C.J.Rolo⟩

1know-it-all \'==,=\ *also* **know-all** \'=,=\ *n, pl* **know-it-alls** *also* **know-alls :** one that rashly and annoyingly claims to know or acts as if knowing all about everything or nearly everything **:** one to whom nothing new can apparently be told or who views any advice or suggestion from others as of little or no value or as something that had already been considered and acted on or rejected ⟨loud cocky *know-it-alls*⟩ ⟨a humbling enigma for the *know-alls* —D.B.W.Lewis⟩

2know-it-all \"\ *also* **know-all** \"\ *adj* [1*know-it-all, know=all*] **:** of, relating to, or having the characteristics of a know-it=all ⟨a *know-it-all* attitude⟩ ⟨a *know-all* manner⟩ ⟨should not be so *know-it-all* about what the Almighty was up to —Gretchen Finletter⟩

knowledgable *var of* KNOWLEDGEABLE

1knowl·edge \'nälij, -lēj,-ləj, *Brit sometimes* 'nōl-\ *vt* -ED/-ING/-S [ME *knawlechen, knowlechen*, irreg. fr. *knowen, knawen* to know — more at KNOW] **1** *obs* **:** to recognize as being something indicated **:** admit the status, claims, or authority of **:** ACKNOWLEDGE **2** *obs* **:** to recognize, admit, or confess the fact or truth of

2knowledge \"\ *n* -s [ME *knawlage, knowlage, knawlege, knowlege*, fr. *knawlechen, knowlechen*, v.] **1** *obs* **a :** ACKNOWLEDGMENT **b :** COGNIZANCE **2 :** the fact or condition of knowing **a** (1) **:** the fact or condition of knowing something with a considerable degree of familiarity gained through experience of or contact or association with the individual or thing so known ⟨a thorough ~ of life and its problems⟩ ⟨has a fair ~ of the people of that country⟩ ⟨a remarkable ~ of human nature⟩ (2) **:** acquaintance with or theoretical or practical understanding of some branch of science, art, learning, or other area involving study, research, or practice and the acquisition of skills ⟨~ of advanced mathematics⟩ ⟨has little ~ of the techniques of drawing and painting⟩ ⟨a ~ of foreign languages⟩ **b** (1) **:** the fact or condition of being cognizant, conscious, or aware of something ⟨was elated by ~ of their success⟩ ⟨the ~ that it was really important⟩ ⟨his ~ of what she had had to endure⟩ (2) **:** the particular existent range of one's information or acquaintance with facts **:** the scope of one's awareness **:** extent of one's understanding ⟨said that to the best of his ~ the matter had not yet been attended to⟩ **c :** the fact or condition of apprehending truth, fact, or reality immediately with the mind or senses **:** PERCEPTION, COGNITION ⟨intellective ~⟩ ⟨the nature of ~⟩ **:** COMPREHENSION, UNDERSTANDING ⟨intuitive ~⟩ ⟨proceeding from the lower to the higher degrees of ~⟩ **d :** the fact or condition of possessing within mental grasp through instruction, study, research, or experience one or more truths, facts, principles, or other objects of perception **:** the fact or condition of having information or of being learned or erudite ⟨a man of great ~⟩ ⟨always seeking after more and more ~⟩ **3** *archaic* **:** CARNAL KNOWLEDGE **4 a :** the sum total of what is known **:** the whole body of truth, fact, information, principles, or other objects of cognition acquired by mankind ⟨adding to the vast store of ~⟩ ⟨all branches of ~⟩ **b** *archaic* **:** a branch of learning **:** ART, SCIENCE

syn KNOWLEDGE, SCIENCE, LEARNING, ERUDITION, SCHOLARSHIP, INFORMATION, and LORE agree in signifying what is or can be known. KNOWLEDGE applies to any body of known facts or to any body of ideas inferred from such facts or accepted as truths on good grounds ⟨a *knowledge* of languages⟩ ⟨a *knowledge* of the habits of snakes⟩ ⟨a *knowledge* of modern chemistry⟩ ⟨to benefit by the accumulated *knowledge* of centuries⟩ SCIENCE still sometimes interchanges with KNOWLEDGE but commonly applies to a body of systematized knowledge comprising facts carefully gathered and general truths carefully inferred from them, often underlying a practice, usu. connoting exactness, and often denoting knowledge of unquestionable certainty ⟨must bear in mind that geographic discovery also is *science*, and it was a scientific theory that impelled the venture of Columbus —I.M.Price⟩ ⟨the defense of nations had become a *science* and a calling —T.B.Macaulay⟩ ⟨the *science* of administration —A.S.Link⟩ ⟨the art of feeding preceded the *science* of nutrition by many centuries —F.B. Hadley⟩ ⟨the diagnosis of disease is no longer primarily guesswork but rather a *science*⟩ LEARNING applies to knowledge gained by study, often long and careful and sometimes connoting comprehensiveness and profundity ⟨to expose children to as much *learning* as possible⟩ ⟨a full, rich, human book, packed with information lightly dispensed and fortified with *learning* easily worn —Honor Tracy⟩ ⟨a man of great and profound *learning* but little common sense⟩ ERUDITION usu. stresses wide, profound, or recondite learning, sometimes suggesting pedantry ⟨often flabbergast their elders with their *erudition* — a scholarly but lively sense of words, a sound background in history and economics, the ability to translate or even to speak two or three foreign languages —Stanley Walker⟩ ⟨all the encyclopedic *erudition* of the middle ages —J.L.Lowes⟩ ⟨balancing an immense load of *erudition* upon a precarious foundation of fact —*Times Lit. Supp.*⟩ SCHOLARSHIP implies the learning, careful mastery of detail, esp. of a given field, and the critical acumen characteristic of a good scholar ⟨the immense and rapidly expanding *scholarship* not only in psychology but in history, sociology, and anthropology as well, which illuminates the study of the family —Lynn White⟩ ⟨unusually equipped in both scientific and classical *scholarship* in addition to his command of his own field, a brilliant and powerful lecturer —E.S.Bates⟩ ⟨his learning and general *scholarship* were universally recognized, and in his special sphere of law he had no peer in this country —T.D. Bacon⟩ INFORMATION generally applies to knowledge, commonly accepted as true, of a factual kind usu. gathered from others or from books ⟨this book, packed with *information* of the life and movements of big game —*Times Lit. Supp.*⟩ ⟨to seek *information* about a man from friends and credit records⟩ ⟨a book of *information* about early river boats⟩ LORE suggests special, often arcane, knowledge, usu. of a traditional, anecdotal character and of a particular subject ⟨fairy *lore*⟩ ⟨one of the most bizarre occurrences in railroad *lore* —Bennett Cerf⟩ ⟨bird *lore*⟩ ⟨taught the *lore* of medicinal herbs —*Amer. Guide Series: La.*⟩

knowl·edge·abil·i·ty *also* **knowl·edg·abil·i·ty** \,⸗⸗ə'biləd·ē, -lətē, -i\ *n* **:** the quality or state of being knowledgeable

knowl·edge·able *also* **knowl·edg·able** \'⸗⸗əbəl\ *adj* [²*knowledge* + *-able*] **1 a :** marked by or indicating intelligence or knowledge **:** mentally alert and well-informed **:** KNOWING ⟨~ about the technique of painting —Herbert Read⟩ ⟨the keenest and most ~ questions —Norman Cousins⟩ ⟨limousines with ~ chauffeur-guides —*advt*⟩ **b :** marked by a keen sense of discernment **:** marked by notable ability to evaluate and discriminate **:** highly perceptive **:** having awareness and insight ⟨a ~ critic⟩ ⟨sparse but ~ comments—*Newsweek*⟩ **2 a :** marked by an open receptive mind **:** not narrow-minded or otherwise intellectually cramped **:** not provincial in outlook **:** BROADMINDED, LIBERAL ⟨addressed himself to a ~ audience that he knew would not be shocked⟩ **b :** responsive and alive to intellectual or cultural stimulation ⟨an eager, ~ group of students⟩ **3 :** marked by deliberateness or awareness **:** INTENTIONAL, CONSCIOUS ⟨an intolerably ~ affectation —Eric Partridge⟩ ⟨not influenced by his ~ prejudices —A.C.Gimson⟩ — **knowl·edge·able·ness** *also* **knowl·edg·able·ness** *n* -ES — **knowl·edge·ably** *also* **knowl·edg·ably** \-blē, -bli\ *adv*

knowl·edged \-jd\ *adj* [²*knowledge* + *-ed*] **:** marked by or equipped with knowledge ⟨trained — at least in his own fashion — and ~ in our ways —S.E.White⟩

knowl·edge·less \-jləs\ *adj* **:** devoid of knowledge **:** IGNORANT ⟨naked and ~ —Carl Sandburg⟩

knowledges *pres 3d sing of* KNOWLEDGE, *pl of* KNOWLEDGE

knowledging *pres part of* KNOWLEDGE

¹**known** \'nōn *sometimes* -ōən\ *adj* [ME *knowen, knawen*, fr. past part. of *knowen, knawen* to know — more at KNOW] **:** that is apprehended or perceived by the mind or senses **:** that has become a part of knowledge ⟨a ~ truth that no one denies⟩ **:** familiar through knowledge or experience ⟨beyond the limits of the ~ world —A.C.Whitehead⟩; *esp* **:** generally recognized ⟨a ~ authority in this matter⟩

²**known** \"\ *n* -S **1 :** something known **:** something familiar or recognized; *specif* **:** a substance of known composition — used esp. in chemical analysis ⟨chemical determinations performed on ~s —A.A.Benedetti-Pichler⟩ **2 :** a letter (as in a^2+2ab) or some other symbol (as π) used in a mathematical equation to represent a known number or quantity

¹**know-noth·ing** \'nō,nəthiŋ, -thēŋ\ *adj* **1 :** extremely ignorant ⟨a *know-nothing* blunderer⟩ **2** *often cap K&N* **:** of, relating to, or characterized by know-nothingism ⟨the *Know-Nothing* party . . . proposed the political proscription of Roman Catholics —W.L.Sperry⟩ ⟨the *know-nothing* anti-intellectualism that parades . . . as anti-Communism —Stringfellow Barr⟩

²**know-nothing** \"\ *n, pl* **know-nothings 1 :** one that knows little or nothing **:** IGNORAMUS **2** *usu cap K&N* [so called fr. the fact that some members of the organization replied "I don't know" to any questions that were asked them about it] **:** a member of a 19th century short-lived secret American political organization prominent in the decade before the Civil War and hostile to the political influence of recent immigrants and Roman Catholics **3 :** AGNOSTIC **4 :** an exponent or adherent of 20th century political know-nothingism ⟨counting on the *know-nothings* . . . to exploit the present atmosphere of uncertainty and insecurity —Norman Cousins⟩ ⟨assaults upon intellectuals by political *know-nothings* —Richard Robbins⟩

know-noth·ing·ism \-ŋ,izəm\ *n* -S **1** *usu cap K&N* **:** the principles and policies of the 19th century Know-Nothings **2 :** the fact or condition of knowing nothing or of desiring to know nothing or the conviction that nothing can be known with certitude esp. in religion or morality ⟨an ethical *know-nothingism* in which there is no longer any certainty . . . as to what is and what is not evil —F.B.Millett⟩ **3** *sometimes cap K&N* **:** a political attitude or philosophy of the mid-twentieth century characterized chiefly by anti-intellectualism and exaggerated patriotism and by fear of foreign and subversive influences ⟨fighting the battle inside the government against the forces of hysteria and *know-nothingism* —Reed Harris⟩

knows *pres 3d sing of* KNOW, *pl of* KNOW

know-what \'⸗,⸗\ *n, pl* **know-whats** [fr. the phrase *know what*] **:** clear recognition of the objective of a selected course of action ⟨the know-why and the *know-what* which businessmen find necessary for all persons in administrative or executive positions —C.E.Henson⟩

know-why \'⸗,⸗\ *n, pl* **know-whys** [fr. the phrase *know why*] **:** understanding of the reasons underlying something (as a course of action) ⟨our frontier past and our industrialized present both incline us toward a preoccupation with technique, with know-how rather than *know-why* —Dwight Macdonald⟩

knox·ville \'näks,vil *esp S* -,vəl\ *adj, usu cap* [fr. *Knoxville*, Tenn.] **:** of or from the city of Knoxville, Tenn. ⟨a *Knoxville* industry⟩ **:** of the kind or style prevalent in Knoxville

knox·vil·lite \-vi,līt, -və,-\ *n* -S [*Knoxville*, town in Napa county, Calif. + E *-ite*] **:** MAGNESIOCOPIAPITE

knt *abbr* knight

knub \'nəb\ *n* -S [prob. fr. LG *knubbe*, fr. MLG *knubbe, knobbe*, knot on a tree, knob — more at KNOB] **1 a** *dial* **:** KNOB **b :** NUB 4 **2** *or* **knubs** *pl but sing or pl in constr* **:** FRISON

knubbly *var of* NUBBLY

knubby *var of* NUBBY

¹**knuck·le** \'nəkəl\ *n* -S [ME *knokel*; akin to MLG *knökel* knuckle, MHG *knöchel, knüchel*; diminutives fr. the root of MLG *knoke* bone, MLG *knoche*; akin to OE *cnycled* bent, ON *knykill* small knot, OE *cnotta* knot — more at KNOT] **1 a** (1) **:** the joint where the ends of two bones meet or articulate (2) **:** the tarsal or carpal joint and the parts including the flesh immediately above or below in a quadruped (as a pig) used for food; *specif* **:** the knee or hock joint and adjoining parts of a quadruped; *often* **:** the shank of a quadruped used as food (3) **:** the shoulder joint of a whale **b** (1) **:** a rounded prominence formed by bending a joint where two bones meet or articulate; *esp* **:** one of the prominences formed at each of the joints and bases of the fingers of the human hand when the hand is shut or when the fingers are clenched (2) **:** a projection at the carpal or tarsal joints of a quadruped **2 :** something that protrudes like a knuckle, that is shaped like a knuckle, or that is otherwise suggestive of a knuckle: as **a :** a sharply flexed loop of intestines incarcerated in a hernia **b** (1) **:** one of the joining parts of a hinge through which a pin or rivet passes (2) **:** KNUCKLE JOINT (3) **:** the rotating piece used for the coupling device in various forms of automatic car couplings (as the rotating hook of a railroad-car coupler designed to hook up with the coupler of another car) **c** (1) **:** the meeting of two surfaces at a sharp angle (as in a roof or as in the timbers of a ship) (2) **:** the outer part of a sharply angled jetty, a breakwater, or other construction at or along a shore **d :** a small, decorative, carved, or rolled terminal part esp. on a piece of furniture (as at the end of one of the arms of a chair) **e :** a chunk or knob of rock ⟨their bodies calloused by ~s of falling rock —Robert Payne⟩ **f :** a point or support on which something pivots or turns **:** pivotal point ⟨the ship used the end of the pier as a ~ for swinging around⟩ **3 knuckles** *pl but sing or pl in constr* **:** BRASS KNUCKLES — **near the knuckle 1 :** near the permitted, accepted, or tolerable limit of what can be said or done: as **a :** verging on the border line between decency and indecency ⟨jokes that were embarrassingly *near the knuckle*⟩ **b :** verging on what is offensive or injurious to one's sensibilities ⟨accusations too *near the knuckle* for them to ignore⟩ **2 :** near to what is of greatest importance, interest, or concern ⟨the real reasons for doing this are, perhaps, *nearer the knuckle* than they think —John Holloway⟩

²**knuckle** \"\ *vb* **knuckled; knuckled; knuckling** \-k(ə)liŋ\ **knuckles** *vi* **1 :** to knuckle under ⟨*knuckled* to no pressure groups —*Newsweek*⟩ **2 :** to project or protrude like a knuckle **3 :** to be affected with cocked ankles — usu. used of a horse or of an affected fetlock joint and often with *over* ⟨~s over badly on the off hind leg⟩ ⟨the fetlocks of colts may ~ for some time after birth without permanent harm⟩ ~ *vt* **1 :** to strike ⟨the seaman *knuckled* his forehead and wheeled around —Clark Russell⟩ or press or rub with the knuckles ⟨shook himself and rose, *knuckling* his eyes —Lawrence Durrell⟩ ⟨he *knuckled* his hair and he frowned —Thurston Scott⟩ **2 :** to shoot (a marble) from between the knuckle of the thumb and the bent forefinger **3 :** to form a bend or a knuckle joint in (as steel plates or wire fencing)

knuckle ball *n* **:** a baseball pitch made by gripping the ball with the knuckles or fingernails of the index and second and sometimes third fingers pressed against the top of the ball and thrown usu. with little speed or spin so as to give it a typically erratic course

knuck·le·ball·er \'nəkəl,bȯlə(r)\ *n* -S **:** a baseball pitcher that specializes in pitching knuckle balls

knucklebone \'⸗⸗,⸗\ *n* [ME *knokylle bone*, fr. *knokylle, knokel* knuckle + *bone, bon* bone] **1 a :** one of the bones forming a knuckle of a human finger **b :** a long bone with a knobbed end (as a femur or humerus); *also* **:** the knob of such a bone — now used only of animals **2 a :** the tetrahedral metacarpal or metatarsal bone of a sheep; *esp* **:** such a bone marked on its surfaces and used in ancient times in gaming and divination usu. through being tossed like one of a pair of dice **b knucklebones** *pl but sing in constr* **:** a game played with such marked bones or with small metal objects resembling such bones; *esp* **:** JACKS

knuck·led \'nəkəld\ *adj* **:** having knuckles

knuckle down *vi* **1 :** to place the knuckles on the ground preparatory to shooting a marble ⟨*knuckled down* and shot for the center hole⟩ **2 :** to apply oneself with seriousness or concentration **:** apply oneself earnestly ⟨let's have no more nonsense and *knuckle down* to business⟩ **3 :** to knuckle under

knuck·le-dust \'nəkəl,dəst\ *vt* [back-formation fr. *knuckle-duster*] **:** to strike with the fist; *specif* **:** to strike with brass knuckles

knuck·le-dust·er \-tə(r)\ *n* -S **1 :** BRASS KNUCKLES **2 :** one that specializes in or is given to attacking with the fists; *specif* **:** one that uses brass knuckles

knucklehead \'⸗⸗,⸗\ *n* **:** a stupid blunderer **:** DUMBBELL — **knuckleheaded** \¦⸗⸗¦⸗⸗\ *adj*

knuckle joint *n* **:** a hinge joint in which a projection with an eye on one piece enters a jaw between two corresponding projections with eyes on another piece and is retained by a pin or rivet

knuckle joint

knuckle-kneed \¦⸗⸗¦⸗\ *adj* **:** having projecting or bulging knees

knuckle line *n* **:** the line of meeting of two surfaces of a ship at an angle

knuckle man *or* **knuckle boy** *n* **:** a mine-car clipper who works at the top of a haulage slope attaching and detaching mine cars to and from cables and coupling trains of cars

knuckle pin *n* **:** a pin or rivet connecting the two parts of a knuckle joint

knuckle post *n* **:** the vertical post of an automobile steering knuckle on which the knuckle is pivoted

knuckle press *or* **knuckle-joint press** *n* **:** a punch press using a toggle joint **:** TOGGLE-JOINT PRESS

knuck·ler \'nək(ə)lə(r)\ *n* -S **1 a :** a marble that a player knuckles **b :** KNUCKLE BALL **2 :** a hydraulic-press operator who shapes steel parts for use in shipbuilding

knuckles *pl of* KNUCKLE, *pres 3d sing of* KNUCKLE

knuck·le·some \'nəkəlsəm\ *adj* **:** KNUCKLY

knuckle under *vi* **:** to admit defeat **:** give in **:** give up **:** YIELD, SUBMIT ⟨if it hadn't been for her pride, she'd have *knuckled under* and gone back home —Jane Woodfin⟩

knuckling *n* -S [fr. gerund of ²*knuckle*] **:** COCKED ANKLES

knuck·ly \'nək(ə)lē\ *adj, often* -ER/-EST **:** having bony protuberances; *specif* **:** having prominent knuckles ⟨~ fingers⟩

knucks \'nəks\ *n pl* [alter. of *knuckles*, pl. of ¹*knuckle*] **1** *sing in constr* **:** a game of marbles at the end of which the winner has the option of shooting a marble at the opponent's knuckles held on the ground **2** *sing or pl in constr* **:** BRASS KNUCKLES

knull·ing \'nəliŋ\ *n* -S [by alter.] **:** KNURLING

knur \'nər(·)\ *n* -S [ME *knorre*; akin to ME *knarre* rough stone, knot in wood; akin to MHG & MLG *knorre* burl, knot, OHG *chniurig* knotty, solid, Norw *knart, knort* knot, burl, OE *cnotta* knot — more at KNOT] **1 :** a hard excrescence (as on a tree trunk or stone) **:** GNARL **2** *dial Brit* **:** a usu. wooden ball (as used in the game of knur and spell)

knur and spell *n* **:** a game played in northern England that resembles trapball

¹**knurl** \'nərl, *esp before pause or consonant* 'nər·əl; 'nōl, 'nəil\ *n* -S [prob. blend of *knur* and *gnarl*] **1 a** (1) **:** a small protuberance, excrescence, or knob (2) **:** a small ridge or bead; *esp* **:** one of a series of small ridges or beads used on a usu. metal surface (as of a thumbscrew) as a means of ensuring a firm grip or as a decorative feature **b :** a contorted knot in wood **2 a** *chiefly Scot* **:** a short thickset person; *esp* **:** DWARF **b** *Scot* **:** a tangled mass (as of hair) **:** SNARL **3 :** a tool for knurling

²**knurl** \"\ *vt* -ED/-ING/-S **:** to provide (as a thumbscrew) with small ridges or beading (as for ensuring a firm grip) **:** make knurls on **:** MILL

knurled *adj* **1 :** GNARLED ⟨the ~ swollen knuckles of his other hand —Norman Mailer⟩ **2 :** provided with knurls ⟨a ~ thumbscrew⟩

knurling *n* -S **1 a :** the making of knurls **b :** the ridges on knurled work **:** knurled work **2 a :** a breaking up of a rounded molding as if for a bead and reel but usu. with more elaboration **b :** molding so treated

knurly \-ərlē, -əl-, -əil-, -li\ *adj, often* -ER/-EST [¹*knurl* + *-y*] **1 :** GNARLY **2 :** DWARFISH

knurry *adj* [*knur* + *-y*] *obs* **:** KNURLY

knut \(kə)'nət\ *n* -S [prob. alter. of ¹*nut*] **:** a fop of the late 19th or early 20th century

knys·na boxwood \(kə)'niznə-\ *or* **knysna** *n* -S [fr. *Knysna*, Union of So. Africa] **:** EAST LONDON BOXWOOD

ko \'kō, 'gō\ *n* -S *usu cap* [Chin (Pek) *ko*¹ elder brother] **:** a Chinese porcelain produced in the 12th century and distinguished by its dark clay and fine crackle

¹**KO** \(')kā¦ō\ *abbr or n, pl* **KO's** \-ōz\ *sometimes not cap* **:** KNOCKOUT

²**KO** \"\ *vt* **KO'd** \-ōd\ **KO'd; KO'ing; KO's** *sometimes not cap* **:** to knock out

KO *abbr* keep off

koa \'kōə\ *n* -S [Hawaiian] **1 :** a Hawaiian timber tree (*Acacia koa*) with light gray bark, crescent-shaped leaves, and white flowers in small round heads **2 :** the fine-grained red wood of the koa now used esp. for furniture

ko·ae \'kō'ä,ā\ *n* -S [Hawaiian] *Hawaii* **:** TROPIC BIRD

koa finch *n* **:** any of several Hawaiian birds of the genera *Pseudonestor* and *Psittirostra* (family Drepaniidae) that resemble the finches

koa ha·o·le \-hä'ō(,)lā\ *n* [Hawaiian] **:** LEAD TREE

ko·ala *also* **koala bear** *or* **co·ala** \kō'älə, kə'wä-\ *n* -S [*koala* native name in Australia] **1 :** a sluggish Australian arboreal marsupial (*Phascolarctos cinereus*) that is about two feet long and has large hairy ears, thick ashy gray fur, and sharp claws and that feeds on eucalyptus leaves — called also *kangaroo bear, native bear* **2 :** the pelt of the koala

ko·a·li \kō'ālē, kə'wä-\ *n* -S [Hawaiian] **:** any of several tropical morning glories of the genus *Ipomoea* (as *I. tuberculata* or *I. insularis*) used in Hawaii as cordage

koaliang *var of* KAOLIANG

ko·an \'kō,än\ *n, pl* **koans** *or* **koan** [Jap *kōan*, lit., public plan, fr. *kō* public + *an* proposal, plan] **:** a paradox used in Zen Buddhism as an instrument of meditation in training monks to despair of an ultimate dependence upon reason and to force them into sudden intuitive enlightenment

ko·asa·ti \,kōə'säd·ē\ *n, pl* **koasati** *or* **koasatis** *usu cap* **1 a :** a Muskogean people of northern Alabama **b :** a member of such people **2 :** the language of the Koasati people

¹**kob** \'käb, 'kōb\ *also* **ko·ba** \'kōbə\ *n, pl* **kob** *or* **kobs** [of Niger-Congo origin; akin to Wolof *koba* roan antelope, Fulani *kōba*] **:** any of various African antelopes (genus *Adenota*) related to the waterbucks

²**kob** \'käb\ *n* -S [by shortening & alter.] **:** KABELJOU

ko·ban \'kō,bän\ *also* **co·bang** *or* **ko·bang** \-bäŋ\ *n* -S [Jap *koban*, fr. *ko* small + *ban* size, format] **:** an oval Japanese gold coin of widely varying value issued from the 17th century to the 19th century

ko·be \'kōbē\ *adj, usu cap* [fr. *Kobe*, city in western Honshu, Japan] **:** of or from the city of Kobe, Japan **:** of the kind or style prevalent in Kobe

ko·bell·ite \'kōbə,līt\ *n* -S [Sw *kobellit*, fr. Franz von *Kobell* †1882 Ger. mineralogist and poet + Sw *-it* -ite] **:** a mineral $Pb_2(Bi,Sb)_2S_5$ consisting of a blackish gray sulfide of antimony, bismuth, and lead

ko·bird *also* **kow·bird** \'kō,⸗\ *n* [*ko-, kow-* (prob. imit.) + *bird*] **:** YELLOW-BILLED CUCKOO

ko·bold \'kō,bȯld, -bōld\ *n* -S [G — more at COBALT] **1 :** a gnome held esp. in German folklore to inhabit underground places ⟨looked like ~s from some magic mine —Rudyard Kipling⟩ **2 :** a domestic spirit often held in Germanic folklore to be mischievous

ko·bus \'kōbəs\ *n, cap* [NL, fr. E ¹*kob*] **:** a genus of antelopes containing the typical waterbucks

koch \'kōch\ *n, pl* **koches** *usu cap* **:** a member of a hinduized Mongoloid people of Assam

ko·chi \'kōchē\ *adj, usu cap* [fr. *Kochi*, city on south coast of Shikoku, Japan] **:** of or from the city of Kochi, Japan **:** of the kind or style prevalent in Kochi

ko·chia \'kōkēə\ *n* [NL, fr. W. D. J. *Koch* †1849 Ger. botanist + NL *-ia*] **1** *cap* **:** a genus of herbs (family Chenopodiaceae) having a turbinate perianth and broadly winged fruit — see SUMMER CYPRESS **2** -S **:** a plant of the genus *Kochia*

koch phenomenon \'kȯk-, 'kōk-,'kōk-,'käk-\ *n, usu cap K* [after Robert *Koch* †1910 Ger. bacteriologist] **:** the response of a tuberculous animal to reinfection with tubercle bacilli marked by necrotic lesions that develop rapidly and heal quickly and caused by hypersensitivity to products of the tubercle bacillus

koch's bacillus *or* **koch bacillus** *n, usu cap K* **:** a bacillus (*Mycobacterium tuberculosis*) that causes human tuberculosis

koch's postulates *also* **koch's laws** *n pl, usu cap K* **:** a statement of the steps required to establish a microorganism as the cause of a disease: (1) it must be found in all cases of the disease; (2) it must be isolated from the host and grown in pure culture; (3) it must reproduce the original disease when introduced into a susceptible host; (4) it must be found present in the experimental host so infected

koch-weeks bacillus \-'wēks-\ *n, usu cap K&W* [after Robert *Koch* †1910 and John E. *Weeks* †1949 Am. ophthalmologist, who discovered it independently] **:** a bacterium of the genus *Hemophilus* associated with human conjunctivitis

KO'd *past of* KO

ko·da·gu \'kōdə,gü\ *n, pl* **kodagu** *or* **kodagus** *usu cap* **1 a :** an aboriginal people of the mountainous region of Coorg in southern India **b :** a member of such people **2 :** the Dravidian language of the Kodagu people

ko·dak \'kō,dak\ *vb* -ED/-ING/-S [*Kodak*] *vi* **:** to take photographs with a Kodak camera ~ *vt* **:** to take a photograph of with a Kodak camera

Kodak \"\ *trademark* — used for a small hand camera

ko·da millet *also* **koda** \'kōdə\ *or* **ko·dra** \-drə\ *n* -S [*koda, kodra* fr. Panjabi *kodā, kodrā*, fr. Skt *kodrava*] **:** DITCH MILLET

ko·di·ak bear \'kōdē,ak\ *also* **ka·diak bear** \kəd'yak-, -yäk\ *or* **kodiak** *n* -S *usu cap K* [fr. *Kodiak* Island, southern Alaska, its habitat] **:** a brown bear (*Ursus middendorffi*) of Alaska that is larger and has shorter thicker claws than the grizzly and feeds largely on salmon

kod·kod \'kōd,kōd\ *n* -S [perh. native name in Chile or Argentina] **:** PAMPAS CAT

koe·ber·lin·ia \,kōbə(r)'linēə\ *n, cap* [NL, fr. C. L. *Köberlin*, 19th cent. Ger. clergyman and amateur botanist + NL *-ia*] **:** a monotypic genus of nearly leafless thorny shrubs of dry parts of the southwestern U.S. and adjacent Mexico that bear racemes of small white flowers and tend to form dense thickets and that are placed in the family Capparidaceae or sometimes isolated in a separate family

koech·lin·ite \'keklə,nīt\ *n* -S [Rudolf *Koechlin* †1939 Austrian mineralogist + E *-ite*] **:** a mineral Bi_2MoO_6 consisting of a bismuth molybdate

ko·el *or* **ko·il** \'kōəl, 'kȯi(ə)l\ *n* -S [Hindi *koel, koil*, fr. Skt *kokila* — more at CUCKOO] **:** any of several cuckoos (genus *Eudynamys*) of India, the East Indies, and Australia — called also *long-tailed cuckoo*

koel·lia \'kelēə\ [NL, fr. Johann L. C. *Kölle* †1797 Ger. physician and botanist + NL *-ia*] *syn of* PYCNANTHEMUM

koel·reu·te·ria \,kel,rȯi'tirēə, -rü'-\ *n* [NL, fr. Josef G. *Kölreuter* †1806 Ger. botanist + NL *-ia*] **1** *cap* **:** a small genus of Asiatic trees (family Sapindaceae) distinguished by large terminal panicles of flowers and inflated papery capsular fruit — see GOLDENRAIN TREE **2** -S **:** any tree of the genus *Koelreuteria*

koe·nen·ite \'kānə,nīt\ *n* -S [G *koenenit*, fr. Adolf von *Koenen* †1915 Ger. geologist + G *-it* -ite] **:** a mineral $Mg_5Al_2(OH)_{12}Cl_4$ consisting of a basic chloride of aluminum and magnesium

koenigsberg *usu cap, var of* KÖNIGSBERG

koe·pang·er \'kü,päŋə(r)\ *n* -S *usu cap* [*Koepang, Kupang*, city at the southwestern end of Timor + E *-er*] **:** a native or inhabitant of the city of Kupang on the Indonesian island of Timor

ko·e·ri *or* **ko·i·ri** \'kōərē\ *n, pl* **koeri** *or* **koeris** *or* **koiri** *or* **koiris** *usu cap* **1 :** an agricultural Aryo-Dravidian people of northeastern Hindustan **2 :** a member of the Koeri people

koet·tig·ite *or* **köt·tig·ite** \'ked·i,gīt\ *n* -S [Otto *Köttig*, 19th cent. Ger. chemist + E *-ite*] **:** a mineral $Zn_3(AsO_4)_2.8H_2O$ consisting of a hydrous arsenate of zinc

koettstorfer value *usu cap K, var of* KÖTTSTORFER VALUE

koft·ga·ri \'kōftgə(,)rē\ *n* -S [Hindi *koftgarī*, fr. Per *kōftgarī*, fr. *kōftgar* maker of koftgari, fr. *kōft* blow, beating + *-gar* doing; akin to Skt *kāra* doing — more at KARMA] **:** Indian damascene work in which steel is inlaid with gold

ko·fu \'kō(,)fü\ *adj, usu cap* [fr. *Kofu*, city in south central Honshu, Japan] **:** of or from the city of Kofu, Japan **:** of the kind or style prevalent in Kofu

ko·gas·in \kō'gasən, 'kō,g-\ *n* -S [G, fr. *ko-* (fr. *koks* coke, irreg. fr. E *coke*) + *gas* (fr. NL) + *-in* (fr. *benzin* benzine, gasoline)] **:** a liquid mixture of saturated and unsaturated aliphatic hydrocarbons made by reaction of carbon monoxide and hydrogen in the Fischer-Tropsch process

ko·gia \'kōjēə\ *n, cap* [NL] **:** a genus of whales consisting of the pygmy sperm whales

kogon *var of* COGON

ko·he·ko·he \¦kōē¦kōē\ *n* -S [Maori] **:** a New Zealand tree (*Dysoxylum spectabile*) of the family Neliaceae whose wood is used for furniture and interior finish

ko-hemp \'kō,⸗\ *n* [Chin *ko*² kudzu + E *hemp*] **1 :** KUDZU **2 :** a fiber of the kudzu vine

kohen *n, pl* **kohanim** *also* **kohens** *usu cap, var of* COHEN

koh-i-noor \'kōə,nu̇(ə)r\ *n, pl* **koh-i-noors** *often cap* [fr. *Koh-i-noor*, famous diamond that became part of the British crown jewels after the annexation of Punjab by Great Britain in 1849, fr. Per *Kōh-i-nūr*, lit., mountain of light] **:** something that is or is felt to be the best of its kind; *esp* **:** a usu. large and valuable diamond ⟨a young Spaniard with a *Koh-i-noor* of a diamond on his finger and pearls the size of camphor balls in his shirt front —W.J.Locke⟩

ko·hi·sta·ni \ˌkō(h)əˈstänē, -tanē\ *n* -s *usu cap* **1 a :** a Himalayan people of northern Pakistan **b :** a member of such people **2 :** a Dard language of the Kohistani people

¹kohl \ˈkōl\ *also* **co·hol** \ˈkōəl\ *or* **ko·hol** \ˈkōəl\ *n* -s [Ar *kuḥl*] **:** a preparation (as of antimony or soot mixed with other ingredients) used esp. in Arabia and Egypt to darken the edges of the eyelids

²kohl *usu cap, var of* KOL

koh·le·ria \kōˈlirēə\ *n, cap* [NL, fr. Michael *Kohler*, 19th cent. Swiss naturalist + NL *-ia*] **:** a genus of rhizomatous often shrubby tropical American herbs (family Gesneriaceae) that are widely cultivated for their soft velvety foliage and showy often scarlet flowers with four or five stamens and partly inferior ovary

kohl·ra·bi \kōlˈrabē, -räbē, ˈ=,==\ *n, pl* **kohlrabies** [G, modif. (influenced by G *kohl* cabbage) of It *cavoli rape*, pl. of *cavolo rapa* kohlrabi, fr. *cavolo* cabbage (fr. L *caulis*) + *rapa* turnip, fr. L — more at HOLE, RAPE] **1 a :** any of a race of cabbages having an edible stem that becomes greatly enlarged, fleshy, and turnip-shaped **b :** any plant of the kohlrabi type **2 :** BROMATIUM

kohlrabi

kohl·rausch flask \ˈkōl,raush-\ *n, usu cap K* [after Rudolf H. A. *Kohlrausch* †1858 Ger. physicist] **:** a volumetric flask that has an enlarged neck and usu. holds 100 or 200 milliliters

kohlrausch's law *n, usu cap K* [after Friedrich W. G. *Kohlrausch* †1910 Ger. physicist] **:** a statement in physical chemistry: the migration of an ion at infinite dilution is dependent on the nature of the solvent and on the potential gradient but not on the other ions present

kohs blocks *n pl, usu cap K* [after Samuel C. *Kohs* b1890 Am. psychologist] **:** a set of small variously colored blocks that are used to form test patterns in psychodiagnostic examination

ko·hua \kōˈhüə\ *n* -s [Maori] **:** a Maori earth oven

ko·hua·na \kōˈwänə\ *n, pl* **kohuana** *or* **kohuanas** *usu cap* **1 :** a Yuman people of the Colorado river valley in Arizona, California, and Mexico **2 :** a member of the Kohuana people

koi \ˈkȯi\ *n* -s [Jap] **:** CARP 1a

koi·a·ri \kȯiˈ(y)ärē\ *n, pl* **koiari** *or* **koiaris** *usu cap* **1 a :** a Papuan people inhabiting Papua **b :** a member of such people **2 :** the language of the Koiari people

koi·bal \(ˈ)kȯiˈbäl\ *also* **kai·bal** \(ˈ)kī-\ *n, pl* **koibal** *or* **koibals** *usu cap* **1 :** a tatarized Samoyed people of the East Siberian region **2 :** a member of the Koibal people

koil *var of* KOEL

koil·onych·ia \ˌkȯilōˈnikēə\ *n* -s [NL, fr. Gk *koilos* hollow + NL *-onychia* — more at CAVE] **:** abnormal thinness and concavity of fingernails occurring esp. in hypochromic anemias — called also *spoon nail*

koi·lo·rach·ic *or* **koi·lor·rhach·ic** \ˌkȯilōˈrakik, -lə-\ *adj* [*koilo-* (fr. Gk *koilos* hollow) + *rach-, rrhach-* (fr. Gk *rhachis* spine) + *-ic* — more at RACHI-] **:** having the lumbar region of the spinal column concave ventrally

koi·me·sis \ˈkēmēsəs\ *n* -ES [MGk *koimēsis*, fr. Gk, sleep, sleep of death, fr. *koiman* to put to sleep — more at CEMETERY] **:** a feast in the Eastern Orthodox Church commemorating the death and the corporeal assumption of the Virgin Mary now celebrated on August 15

koi·ne \(ˈ)kȯiˈnā *also* ˈkȯi,nē\ *n* -s [Gk *koinē*, fr. fem. of *koinos* common — more at CO-] **1** *usu cap* **:** the Greek language commonly spoken and written by the Greek-speaking population of eastern Mediterranean countries in the Hellenistic and Roman periods **2 :** a dialect or language of a region, country, or people that has become the common or standard language of a larger area and of other peoples — compare LINGUA FRANCA

KO'ing *pres part of* KO

koi·non \kȯiˈnän\ *n* -s [Gk, neut. of *koinos* common] **:** the common element in an apo koinou construction

koi·no·nia \ˌkȯinəˈnēə, ˌkēnə-\ *n* -s [Gk *koinōnia* communion, association, partnership, fr. *koinos* common] **1 :** the Christian fellowship or body of believers **2 :** intimate spiritual communion and participative sharing in a common religious commitment and spiritual community ⟨the ~ of the disciples with each other and with their Lord⟩

koiri *usu cap, var of* KOERI

koi·ro·pot·a·mus \ˌkȯirōˈpäd·əməs\ *n, cap* [NL, irreg. fr. Gk *choiros* pig + *potamos* river; akin to Gk *piptein* to fall — more at -CHOERUS, FEATHER] **:** a genus of wild hogs comprising the African river hogs

ko·ji \ˈkōjē\ *n* -s [Jap *kōji*] **1 :** a yeast or other starter prepared in Japan from rice inoculated with the spores of a mold (*Aspergillus oryzae*) and permitted to develop a mycelium **2 :** an enzyme preparation from koji that is similar to diastase from malt

ko·jic acid \ˈkōjik-\ *n* [*kojic* fr. *koji* + *-ic*] **:** a crystalline water-soluble phenolic-type toxic antibiotic $HOC_5H_2O_2CH_2OH$ derived from gamma-pyrone and made by fermentation (as of glucose with molds of the genus *Aspergillus*)

ko·ka·ko \kōˈkä(,)kō\ *n* -s [Maori] *New Zeal* **:** WATTLE CROW

ko·kam \kōˈkäm\ *n* -s [Malay *kukang, kongkang*] **:** LORIS 1b

ko·ka·ma \kōˈkämə\ *n* -s [Tswana *kukama*] **:** GEMSBOK

ko·kan \ˈkōkən\ *n* -s [Hindi] **:** an East Indian timber tree (*Duabanga sonneratioides*) of the family Sonneratiaceae

ko·kan·ee \kōˈkanē\ *also* **kokanee salmon** *n* -s [prob. fr. *Kokanee* creek, southeastern British Columbia] **:** a small landlocked sockeye salmon that rarely reaches a pound in weight but that is an important forage fish in certain inland waters

ko·ker·boom \ˈkōkə(r),büm, -bōm\ *n* [Afrik, fr. D *koker* quiver, sheath (fr. MD *coker*) + *boom* tree, fr. MD; akin to OE *cocer* quiver and to OE *bēam* tree — more at COCKER, BEAM] **:** QUIVER TREE

ko·kil \ˈkōkəl\ *or* **ko·ki·la** \-kələ\ *n* -s [Skt *kokila* — more at CUCKOO] **:** a koel (*Eudynamys scolopacea honorata*) of India

ko·klas *or* **ko·klass** \ˈkōkləs\ *n* -ES [native name in Nepal] **:** PUKRAS

¹ko·ko \ˈkō(,)kō\ *n* -s [prob. of Niger-Congo origin; akin to Twi *kɔ̀ˈkɔ̀* koko] **1 :** any of several araceous plants including the taro that are cultivated in tropical western Africa for their starchy edible roots **2** *also* **kok·ko** \ˈkä(,)kō\ [origin unknown] **:** LEBBEK

²koko \"\ *n* -s [Maori] **:** TUI

³koko \"\ *n, pl* **koko** *or* **kokos** *usu cap* **1 :** a group of numerous aboriginal peoples of northern Queensland **2 :** a member of any of the Koko peoples

ko·koon \kəˈkün\ *n* -s [Tswana *kgokoñ*] **:** BRINDLED GNU

ko·koo·na \kəˈkünə\ *n* [NL, fr. Singhalese *kokuṅ* kokoona] **1** *cap* **:** a genus of East Indian trees (family Celastraceae) having flowers with a 3-celled ovary and producing 3-angled fruit **2** -s **:** any tree of the genus *Kokoona*

ko·ko·pu \ˈkōkə,pü\ *n* -s [Maori] **:** any of various New Zealand fishes of the genus *Galaxias* that resemble the trout — compare GALAXIIDAE

ko·ko·wai \ˈkōkə,wī\ *n* -s [Maori] **1 :** red ocher used in New Zealand as a pigment esp. on woodwork **2 :** the earth from which kokowai is obtained

kokra \ˈkōkrə, ˈkäk-\ *also* **kokra wood** *n* -s [origin unknown] **1 :** COCOWOOD 1 **2 :** COCUSWOOD

kok-saghyz *or* **kok-sagyz** \ˌkōksəˈgēz, ˌkäk-, -giz\ *n* -ES [Russ *kok-sagyz*, fr. Turki *kok-sagiz*, fr. *kok* root + *sagiz* rubber, gum] **:** a perennial dandelion (*Taraxacum kok-saghyz*) native to the Kazakh republic of Russia that has fleshier leaves and more numerous flower heads than the common dandelion of No. America and Europe and is cultivated for its fleshy roots which have a high rubber content — called also *Russian dandelion*

kok·ta·ite \ˈkäktə,īt\ *n* -s [Czech *koktait*, fr. Jaroslav *Kokta*, 20th cent. Czechoslovak mineralogist + Czech *-it* -ite] **:** a mineral $(NH_4)_2Ca(SO_4)_2.H_2O$ consisting of a hydrous sulfate of calcium and ammonium

ko·ku \ˈkō(,)kü\ *n, pl* **koku** [Jap] **:** any of three Japanese units of capacity: **a :** a unit for dry measure equal to 5.12 bushels **b :** a unit for liquid measure equal to 47.65 gallons **c :** a unit for vessels equal to 10 cubic feet

ko·kum butter \ˈkōkəm-\ *also* **kokum** *or* **co·cum** \ˈkō-\ *n* -s [*kokum, cocum*, fr. Marathi *kokam, kokamb* mangosteen] **:** a semisolid fat or liquid oil obtained from the seeds of a small East Indian tree (*Garcinia indica*) and used in India for food — called also *Goa butter*

ko·ku·ra \ˈkōkərə, kōˈkúrə\ *adj, usu cap* [fr. *Kokura*, city in northern Kyushu, Japan] **:** of or from the city of Kokura, Japan **:** of the kind or style prevalent in Kokura

kol *or* **kohl** \ˈkōl\ *n, pl* **kol** *or* **kols** *or* **kohl** *or* **kohls** *usu cap* **1 :** a people of Bengal and Chota Nagpur, India **2 :** a member of such people

kola *var of* COLA

ko·lac·ky \kəˈläch(k)ē\ *or* **ko·lach** \ˈkō,läch\ *also* **ko·la·ce** \kəˈlächē\ *or* **ko·latch** \ˈkō,läch\ *n, pl* **kolacky** *or* **kolaches** [Czech *koláč*; akin to Russ *kolach* kolacky, Bulg *kolač* kolacky, OSlav *kolo* wheel — more at WHEEL] **:** a bun made of rich sweet yeast-leavened dough filled with jam or fruit pulp

ko·lam \kōˈläm\ *n, pl* **kolam** *or* **kolams** *usu cap* **1 :** a people of the Gond ethnic group in central India **2 :** a member of the Kolam people

ko·la·mi \kōˈlämē\ *n* -s **:** the Dravidian language of the Kolam people

ko·la nut *also* **kola** *or* **co·la nut** \ˈkōlə-\ *n* -s [²*cola* + *nut*] **:** the bitter caffeine-containing seed of a kola tree that is approximately the size of a chestnut and is chewed as a condiment and stimulant — see ²COLA 2a

ko·lar gold fields \ˈkō,lär-\ *adj, usu cap K&G&F* [fr. *Kolar Gold Fields*, city in southern India] **:** of or from the city of Kolar Gold Fields, India **:** of the kind or style prevalent in Kolar Gold Fields

ko·lar·i·an *also* **co·lar·i·an** \kōˈla(a)rēən\ *n* -s *usu cap* [prob. fr. *Kolar*, town in southern India + E *-ian*] **:** KOL

kola tree *or* **cola tree** *n* [²*cola* + *tree*] **:** a tree of the genus *Cola* (esp. *C. nitida*) native to tropical Africa but now cultivated in tropical America and Asia — see KOLA NUT

ko·lat·tam \kōˈläd·əm\ *n* -s [Tamil *kōl* stick + *āṭṭam* dance] **:** a folk dance of southern India accompanied by the striking together of sticks

kol·beck·ite \ˈkōl,be,kīt\ *n* -s [G *kolbeckit*, fr. Friedrich *Kolbeck* †1943 Ger. mineralogist + G *-it* -ite] **:** a mineral consisting of a hydrous silicate and phosphate of beryllium, aluminum, and calcium

kol·be reaction \ˈkōlbə-\ *or* **kolbe synthesis** *n, usu cap K* [after A. W. Hermann *Kolbe* †1884 Ger. organic chemist] **1 :** the synthesis of a hydrocarbon (as ethane) by the electrolysis of a salt (as sodium acetate) **2 :** the synthesis of salicylic acid by heating a mixture of sodium phenoxide and carbon dioxide under pressure at 180° to 200°C

kolbe-schmitt reaction *or* **kolbe-schmitt synthesis** \-ˈshmit-\ *n, usu cap K & 1st S* [after A. W. Hermann *Kolbe* †1884 and Rudolf *Schmitt* †1898 Ger. chemist] **:** a modified Kolbe reaction for synthesizing salicylic acid and other phenolic acids at temperatures of from 130° to 140°C

ko·lea \kōˈläə\ *n* -s [Hawaiian] *Hawaii* **:** a golden plover (*Pluvialis dominica fulva*) that commonly passes through Hawaii in its migratory flights

ko·lek \ˈkō,lek\ *n* -s [Malay] **:** a Malayan canoe often rigged with a rectangular sail

ko·lel \ˈkō,lāl\ *n, pl* **ko·le·lim** \kōˈlāləm, -ālem\ *also* **kolels** [NHeb *kōlēl*, fr. Heb *kālal* to comprise, include] **:** a community or congregation of Jewish settlers in Palestine receiving financial support from the halukkah fund

kole·ro·ga \ˌkōləˈrōgə, ˌkäl-\ *n* -s [Kannada *koleroga*, fr. *kole* rot + Skt *roga* disease] **:** a disease of an areca palm (*Areca catechu*) caused by a fungus (*Phytophthora arecae*)

kol·ha·pur \ˈkōlə,pù(ə)r\ *adj, usu cap* [fr. *Kolhapur*, city in western India] **:** of or from the city of Kolhapur, India **:** of the kind or style prevalent in Kolhapur

ko·li \ˈkōlē\ *n, pl* **koli** *or* **kolis** *usu cap* **1 :** a low-caste people of Bombay, Mysore, Andhra Pradesh, Madhya Pradesh, Rajasthan, and the Punjab, India **2 :** a member of the Koli people

ko·lin·sky \kəˈlinzkē, -n(t)skē\ *n* -ES [Russ *kolinskiĭ* of Kola, fr. *Kola*, town and peninsula in northwestern U.S.S.R.] **1** *or* **kolinski** \"\ **a :** any of several Asiatic minks (esp. *Mustela sibirica*) **b :** the fur or pelt of any of these minks — called also *red sable, Tatar sable* **2 :** LEAFMOLD

kol·khoz *also* **kol·koz** *or* **kol·khos** \(,)kəlˈkȯz, kōl-,käl-, -ȯs\ *n, pl* **kolkho·zy** \-ȯzē\ *or* **kolkhozes** [Russ *kolkhoz*, short for *kollektivnoe khozyaĭstvo* collective farm, fr. *kollektivnoe* (neut. of *kollektivnyĭ* collective) + *khozyaĭstvo* household, economy, farm] **1 :** a collective farm of the U.S.S.R. **2 :** a system of collectivized agriculture based on the kolkhoz and developed or enforced esp. among satellite countries

kol·khoz·nik \-ȯznik\ *n, pl* **kolkhozni·ki** \-nəkē\ *or* **kolkhozniks** [Russ, fr. *kolkhoz* + *-nik* (suffix indicating a person)] **:** a member of a kolkhoz

kolk·witz·ia \kōlˈkwitsēə, käl-\ *n* [NL, fr. Richard *Kolkwitz* b1873 Ger. biologist + NL *-ia*] **1** *cap* **:** a genus of Chinese shrubs of the family Caprifoliaceae having short-stipuled leaves and tubular flowers succeeded by ovoid bristly achenes **2** -s **:** any plant of the genus *Kolkwitzia*; *esp* **:** BEAUTY BUSH

kol·ler·gang \ˈkälə(r),gaŋ\ *n* [G, fr. *kollern* to roll + *gang* motion, course, route, fr. OHG, act of going — more at GANG] **:** EDGE RUNNER 2

kolm \ˈkō(l)m\ *n* -s [Sw] **:** a Swedish shale exceptionally high in uranium oxide U_2O_3

kol·mer \ˈkōlmə(r)\ *or* **kolmer reaction** *or* **kolmer test** *n* -s *usu cap K* [after John A. *Kolmer* b1886 Am. pathologist] **:** a complement fixation test for the diagnosis of syphilis

kol ni·dre \kōlˈni(,)drā, kōl-, -ˌdrē, -drə, ˌ=ˌniˈdrā\ *n, usu cap K&N* [Aram *kol nidhrē* all the vows; fr. the opening phrase of the prayer] **1 :** the recital of an Aramaic prayer in the synagogue on the eve of Yom Kippur asking for annulment of vows to God and forgiveness of transgressions **2 :** a traditional melody to which the words of Kol Nidre are sung or chanted

ko·lo \ˈkō(,)lō\ *n* -s [Serbo-Croatian, fr. OSlav, wheel — more at WHEEL] **:** a central European folk dance in which dancers form a circle and progress slowly to right and left while one or more solo dancers perform elaborate steps in the center

ko·loa ma·pu \kəˌlōəˈmä(,)pü\ *n* [Hawaiian, fr. *koloa* duck + *mapu* floating] *Hawaii* **:** PINTAIL 1a

koloa mo·ha \-ˈmō(,)hä\ *n* [Hawaiian, fr. *koloa* duck + *moha* shining] *Hawaii* **:** SHOVELER 2

kols *pl of* KOL

kol·skite \ˈkōlz,kīt, -l,sk-\ *n* -s [Russ *kolskit*, perh. fr. *Kolskiĭ Poluostrov* Kola Peninsula, northwestern U.S.S.R. + Russ *-it* -ite] **:** a mineral $Mg_3Si_4O_{13}.4H_2O(?)$ consisting of a serpentine

kol·son *or* **kol·sun** \ˈkōlsən\ *n* -s [native name in India] **:** DHOLE

ko·lusch·an \kōˈləshən, -lúsh-\ *n* -s *usu cap* [perh. irreg. fr. Aleut *kalukaq* wooden utensil, trough; fr. the trough-shaped labrets worn by Tlingit women] **:** TLINGIT 3

ko·mat·ik \kōˈmad·ik\ *n* -s [Esk (Labrador dial.)] **:** an Eskimo sledge with wooden runners and crossbars lashed with rawhide

komatik

kom·bu \ˈkäm(,)bü\ *n* -s [Jap, kombu, kelp, tangle] **:** a food prepared esp. in Japan from various broad-fronded kelps of the family Laminariaceae

ko·mi \ˈkōmē\ *n, pl* **komi** *or* **komis** *cap* [Zyrian] **1 a :** a people of north central U.S.S.R. — called also *Zyrian* **b :** a member of such people **2 :** ZYRIAN

kom·i·nu·ter \ˈkämə,n(y)üd·ə(r)\ *n* -s [G, fr. L *comminutus* (past part. of *comminuere* to crush, pulverize) + G *-er*, fr. OHG *-āri* — more at COMMINUTE, -ER] **:** a ball mill used in grinding raw materials or clinker in the manufacture of portland cement

ko·mi·tad·ji *or* **co·mi·tad·ji** *also* **ko·mi·ta·ji** \ˌkōməˈtäjē, ˌkäm-\ *n* -s [Turk *komitacı* rebel, member of a secret revolutionary society, fr. *komita* revolutionary committee, secret society] **:** a member of a guerrilla band in Macedonia or the Balkan countries

kom·man·da·tu·ra \kə,mandəˈtúrə\ *also* **kom·man·dan·tur** \ˌkämən,dan,tú(ə)r\ *or* **kom·man·dan·tu·ra** \ˌkämən,dan-ˈtúrə\ *n* -s *usu cap* [*kommandatura, kommandantura* prob. modif. of G *kommandantur* command post, fr. *kommandant* commandant (fr. F *commandant*) + *-ur* -ure; *kommandantur* fr. G, command post] **:** a military government headquarters; *esp* **:** a Russian or interallied headquarters in a European city subsequent to World War II

kommers *often cap, var of* COMMERS

kom·me·tje *or* **co·mi·tje** \ˈkäməchē\ *n* -s [obs. Afrik (now *kommetjie*), lit., mug, cup, fr. D, dim. of *kom* basin, bowl, fr. MD *com, comme*; akin to MHG *kumpf* bowl — more at COOMB] **:** a small depression common in parts of the African veld

kom·mos *or* **com·mos** \kəˈmäs, käˈ-; ˈkä,mäs, -məs\ *n* -ES [Gk *kommos* kommos, beating of the breast, fr. *koptein* to beat, smite — more at CAPON] **:** a lament in Greek tragedy sung in parts alternating between chief actor and chorus

ko·mo·do dragon \kəˈmō(,)dō-\ *or* **komodo lizard** *n, usu cap K* [fr. *Komodo* Island, Indonesia] **:** a dull brown or black monitor lizard (*Varanus komodoensis*) of Komodo and adjacent small islands lying east of Java that attains a length of 10 feet, weighs up to 300 pounds, and feeds largely on eggs but occas. on animals as large as wild pigs or small deer

ko·mon·dor \ˈkämən,dȯ(ə)r\ *n* [Hung] **1** *usu cap* **:** a Hungarian breed of large powerful shaggy-coated white dogs with black nose and dark brown eyes that are used as guard dogs and as herd dogs **2** *pl* **komondors** \-rz\ *also* **komondo·rock** *or* **komondo·rok** \-dərək\ *often cap* **:** a dog of the Komondor breed

kom·so·mol *or* **com·so·mol** \ˈkäm(p)səˈmȯl\ *also* **con·so·mol** \ˈkän(t)s-\ *n* -s *usu cap* [Russ *komsomol*, short for *Kommunisticheskiĭ Soyuz Molodezhi* Communist Union of Youth, fr. *kommunisticheskiĭ* communist + *soyuz* union + *molodezhi*, gen. of *molodezh'* youth] **:** a member of a Russian Communist youth organization with members between the ages of 16 and 23 years

ko·na \ˈkōnə\ *or* **kona storm** *n* -s [Hawaiian *kona*] **:** a storm of southerly or southwesterly winds and heavy rains in Hawaii

ko·nak \kōˈnäk\ *n* -s [Turk] **:** a large house in Turkey; *esp* **:** one used as an official residence ⟨we went to visit the big white ~ . . . which I loved so dearly —Selma Ekrem⟩

konakri *or* **konakry** *usu cap, var of* CONAKRY

ko·nar·i·ot \kəˈna(a)rēət, -ēät\ *or* **ko·nar·i·ote** \-ē,ōt, -ēət\ *n* -s *usu cap* [perh. irreg. fr. *Konya*, city and district in southwest central Turkey] **:** a Turk orig. from the Konya district of Asia Minor now settled in Macedonia

kond *or* **kondh** *usu cap, var of* KHOND

kon·de \ˈkän(,)dā\ *n, pl* **konde** *or* **kondes** *usu cap* **1 a :** a Bantu people of Nyasaland **b :** a member of such people **2 a :** a Bantu people of Tanganyika **b :** a member of such people **3 :** a Bantu language of either of the Konde peoples

kon·di·to·rei \ˌkōndētōˈrī\ *n* -s *often cap* [G, fr. *konditor* confectioner (blend of earlier *kanditor* confectioner — fr. *kandieren* to candy, fr. F *candir* or It *candire*, both fr. Ar *qandī* candied — and *kondieren* to preserve, fr. L *condire*) + *-ei* -y, fr. MHG *-īe*, fr. OF *-ie* — more at CANDY, CONDITE] **:** a shop selling confectionery or pastry

kon·dra·tieff \kənˈdräd·ē,ef\ *n* -s *usu cap* [after Nikolai D. *Kondratev* b1892 Russ. economist] **:** a business cycle with a periodicity of between 50 and 60 years

kon·fyt \kənˈfīt\ *n* -s [Afrik *konfyt*, fr. D *konfijt*, fr. MD *confijt*, fr. MF *confit* — more at COMFIT] *chiefly Africa* **:** PRESERVES

kon·go \ˈkän(,)gō\ *n, pl* **kongo** *or* **kongos** *usu cap* **1 a :** a Bantu people of the lower Congo river **b :** a member of such people **2 :** a Bantu language of the Kongo people used as a trade language in the western Congo and adjacent parts of western equatorial Africa and Angola — compare TSHILUBA

kon·go·ni *also* **con·go·ni** \käŋˈgōnē\ *n, pl* **kongoni** [Swahili] **:** a hartebeest (*Alcelaphus cokei*) of East Africa

kongs·berg·ite \ˈkäŋz(,)bərˌgīt\ *n* -s [F, fr. *Kongsberg*, town in southern Norway + F *-ite*] **:** a mineral consisting of a native silver mercury amalgam

ko·nia *or* **ko·ni·eh** \ˈkōnēə\ *n* -s *usu cap* [fr. *Konia, Konya*, district in southwest central Turkey] **:** a Turkish rug woven usu. in soft shades of red, blue, and yellow

kö·nigs·berg *or* **ko·nigs·berg** *or* **koe·nigs·berg** \ˈkānigz-ˌbərg, ˈkə(r)n-,ˈkən-, ˈkœniks,berk\ *adj, usu cap* [fr. *Königsberg* (now *Kaliningrad*), city in the former province of East Prussia, Germany] **:** of or from Königsberg **:** of the kind or style prevalent in Königsberg

ko·nim·e·ter \kōˈnimәd·ə(r)\ *also* **co·nim·e·ter** \ˌkōnē-ˈäməd·ə(r)\ *n* [*koni-* or *conio-* (fr. Gk *konia* dust) + *-meter* — more at INCINERATE] **:** a device for estimating the dust content of air (as in a mine or a cement mill)

ko·ninck·ite \ˈkōniŋ,kīt, -nən,k-\ *n* -s [F *koninckite*, fr. L. G. de *Koninck* †1887 Belg. geologist + F *-ite*] **:** a mineral $FePO_4.3H_2O$ consisting of hydrous ferric phosphate in yellow aggregates of radiated structure

ko·ni·ni \kəˈninē, -ˈnēnē\ *n* -s [Maori] **:** a tree fuchsia (*Fuchsia excorticata*) of New Zealand that often attains a height of 40 feet and that has pendulous showy flowers — called also *native fuchsia*

ko·nio·cortex \ˌkōnē(,)ō+\ *n* [*konio-* (fr. Gk *konia* dust) + *cortex*] **:** granular-appearing cerebral cortex esp. characteristic of sensory areas

ko·ni·ol·o·gy *also* **co·ni·ol·o·gy** \ˌkōnēˈäləjē\ *n* -ES [*konio-, conio-* (fr. Gk *konia* dust) + *-logy*] **:** a science that deals with atmospheric dust and its effects on plant and animal life

kon·jak \ˈkän,jak\ *n* -s [Jap *konjaku*] **:** a large aroid (*Amorphophallus rivieri*) grown in Japan for its large tuberous corms used for making flour

konk *var of* CONK

kon·ka·ni \ˈkäŋkə(,)nē, ˈkōŋ-\ *n* -s *usu cap* [Marathi *Koṅkaṇī*, fr. *Koṅkaṇ* Konkan, coast region of western India where it is spoken] **:** an Indic language of the west coast of India sometimes considered a dialect of Marathi

konk·er tree \ˈkäŋ[kə(r)-, ˈkōŋ]\ *n* [¹*conker* + *tree*] **:** HORSE CHESTNUT 1a

ko·no \ˈkō(,)nō\ *n, pl* **kono** *or* **konos** *usu cap* **1 a :** a peasant people of Sierra Leone **b :** a member of such people **2 :** a Mande language of the Kono people closely related to Vai

ko·no·hi·ki \ˌkōnəˈhēkē\ *n* -s [Hawaiian] **1 :** a headman of a Hawaiian land division who also controls fishing rights in adjacent waters **2 :** a Hawaiian land division with its accompanying fishing rights

kon·seal \ˈkän,sē(ə)l\ *n* [fr. *Konseals*, a trademark] **:** CACHET 3

-kont \ˌkänt\ *n comb form* -s [ISV, fr. Gk *kontos* pole, fr. *kentein* to prick — more at CENTER] **:** flagellum of a cell

kon·ta·kion *or* **con·ta·kion** \kənˈtäkyōn\ *n, pl* **konta·kia** *or* **conta·kia** \-yä\ [MGk *kontakion*, lit., scroll, prob. dim. of LGk *kontak-, kontax* pole, fr. Gk *kontos*] **:** a short hymn in the Eastern Orthodox Church in praise of a saint

kon·yak \ˈkän,yak\ *n, pl* **konyak** *or* **konyaks** *usu cap* **1 a :** a people of the Assam-Burma frontier area **b :** a member of such people **2 :** the Tibeto-Burman language of the Konyak people

kon·ze \ˈkänzə\ *n* -s [Konde *nkonzhe*] **:** an African hartebeest (*Alcelaphus lichtensteini*) of the Zambesi and Nyasa regions

koo·doo *or* **ku·du** *also* **kou·dou** \ˈkü(,)dü\ *n* -s [Afrik *koedoe*, prob. fr. Xhosa *iqudu, iquda*] **:** a large African antelope (*Strepsiceros strepsiceros* syn. *kudo*) that has large annulated spirally twisted horns and is grayish brown with vertical white stripes on the sides — compare LESSER KOODOO

koofah *var of* GUFA

kook·a·bur·ra \ˈkůkə,bərə\ *n* -s [native name in Australia] **:** a kingfisher (*Dacelo gigas*) of Australia that is about the size of a crow, has a call resembling loud laughter, and feeds in part on reptiles — called also *kinghunter, laughing jackass*

koo·le·tah \ˈkülə,tä\ *n* -s [Esk (Greenland dial.)] **:** an Eskimo coat made of caribou skin

koo·li·man \ˈkülə,man, -ˌmən\ *var of* COOLAMON

koo·lo·kam·ba \ˌkülōˈkambə, -käm-\ *n* -s [native name on the Gabon river, Gabon, equatorial Africa] **:** a dark-faced West African chimpanzee sometimes regarded as a separate species (*Pan koolokamba*)

koom·bar \'kümbə(r)\ *n* -s [Tamil *kumiṛ*] : an East Indian timber tree (*Gmelina arborea*) used esp. for building foundations and for boat decks
koom·kie \'kümkē\ *or* **koon·kie** \-üŋkē,-üŋkē\ *n* -s [Hindi *kumakī* helper, fr. Per] : a trained usu. female elephant used in India to decoy and train wild male elephants
koorajong *var of* KURRAJONG
koorhaan *var of* KORHAAN
koor·ka \'ku̇rkə\ *n* -s [origin unknown] : a coleus (*Coleus parviflorus*) native to Africa but cultivated widely in India for its edible tubers
kootch *var of* COOCH
koo·tcha \'küchə\ *or* **koo·tchar** \-chə(r)\ *n* -s [native name in Australia] : a small stingless wild Australian honeybee of the genus *Trigona*
kootenai *usu cap, var of* KUTENAI
kope \'kōp\ *chiefly Midland var of* ³COOP
ko·peck *or* **ko·pek** *or* **co·peck** \'kō,pek\ *n* -s [Russ *kopeĭka*, fr. *kop'e* lance; fr. the fact that the Czar was orig. depicted on the coin with a lance in his hand; akin to Russ *kopat'* to dig, hollow, Gk *koptein* to smite, cut off — more at CAPON] **1** : a Russian unit of monetary value equal to 1/100 of a ruble — see MONEY table **2** : a coin orig. of base silver representing one kopeck
koph *var of* QOPH
ko·pi \'kōpē\ *n* -s [Moriori] *New Zeal* : KARAKA
kop·je *or* **kop·pie** \'käpē\ *n* -s [Afrik *koppie* kopje, cup, fr. D *kopje* small head, cup, dim. of *kop* head, cup, fr. MD *cop, coppe* — more at CUP] : a small hill found esp. on the African veld sometimes reaching 100 feet above the surrounding country and often covered with scrub
kop·lik's spots \'käpliks-\ *also* **koplik spots** *n pl, usu cap K* [after Henry *Koplik* †1927 Am. pediatrician] : small bluish white dots surrounded by a reddish zone that appear on the mucous membrane of the cheeks and lips before the appearance of the skin eruption in a case of measles
kop·pa \'käpə\ *n* -s [Gk, of Sem origin; akin to Heb *qōph* qoph] : a letter of the early Greek alphabet replaced by kappa in the eastern Greek alphabet except for use as a numeral with the value 90 but retained in the western Greek alphabet and ultimately becoming the Latin letter *Q*
kop·pel·flö·te \'käpəl,flādə, -flōd-ə, *G* 'kɔpəl,flœtə\ *n* -s [G, fr. *koppel* tie, connection (fr. MHG *koppel, kuppel*, fr. OF *cople, couple* pair, bond) + *flöte* flute, fr. MHG *vloite*, fr. OF *flaute, fleute* — more at COUPLE, FLUTE] : an open flute stop in a pipe organ having a neutral tone and serving as a basis upon which to erect tonal pyramids of mutation ranks
kopp·ite \'kä,pīt\ *n* -s [G *koppit*, fr. Hermann F. M. *Kopp* †1892 Ger. chemist + G *-it* -ite] : a mineral consisting of a pyrochlore containing cerium, iron, and potassium
kopt *cap, var of* COPT
kor *also* **cor** *or* **core** \'kō(ə)r, 'kȯ(ə)r\ *n* -s [Heb *kōr*] : an ancient Hebrew and Phoenician unit of measure of capacity identical with the homer but used in later Old Testament times only in liquid measurement
ko·ra \'kōrə\ *n* -s [origin unknown] : WATER COCK
ko·rah·ite \'kōrə,īt\ *n* -s *usu cap* [*Korah*, great-grandson of Levi (Exod 6:21 (AV)) + E *-ite*] : a descendant of the biblical Levite Korah who founded a line of prominent temple musicians
ko·rai period \'kōr,ī-\ *n, usu cap K* [*Korai, Koryu*, dynasty ruling Korea from about A.D. 918 to 1392] : the historical and stylistic period from about A.D. 918 to 1392 in Korea
korait *var of* KRAIT
ko·ra·kan \'kōrə,kän\ *or* **ku·rak·kan** \'ku̇rə,kän\ *n* -s [Tamil *kurakkan*, fr. Sinhalese *kurakkan* raggee] : RAGGEE
ko·ran *or* **qur·'an** *or* **qu·ran** *or* **qo·ran** \kə'ran, (')kō¦r-, (')kȯ¦r-, (')ku̇¦r-, -rän, -raa(ə)n, -rän *sometimes* 'kōrən *or* 'kȯrən\ *n* -s *usu cap* [Ar *qur'ān*, fr. *qara'a* to read, recite] : the book composed of writings accepted by Muslims as revelations made to Muhammad by Allah and as the divinely authorized basis for the religious, social, civil, commercial, military, and legal regulations of the Islamic world
ko·ra·na \kə'ränə\ *n, pl* **korana** *or* **koranas** *usu cap* **1 a** : any of a group of racially mixed Hottentot peoples living along the Orange, Vaal, and Modder rivers in southern Africa **b** : a member of any of such peoples **2** : a dialect of Hottentot spoken by the Korana peoples
ko·ran·ic *or* **qur·'an·ic** \kə'ranik, kō'-, kȯ'-, ku̇'-, -rän-, -raan-, -rán-\ *adj, usu cap* : of, relating to, or prescribed by the Muslim sacred scriptures contained in the Koran ⟨they come to be able to sip alcoholic drinks without *Koranic* scandal —Hal Lehrman⟩
ko·ra·ri \'kōrə,rē\ *n* -s [Maori] : NEW ZEALAND FLAX
korban *var of* CORBAN
kor·dax *or* **cor·dax** \'kȯ(ə)r,daks\ *n* -ES [L *cordax*, fr. Gk *kordax*; akin to Gk *kradan* to shake, brandish — more at CARDINAL] **1** : a phallic dance by nude horned figures in the Dionysian orgies of ancient Greece **2** : a lewd coarse dance derived from the Dionysian kordax and incorporated into Greek and Latin comedy **3** : any of various lively Renaissance court dances
kor·do·fan gum \'kȯrdə,fan-\ *n, usu cap K* [fr. *Kordofan* province, Republic of the Sudan] : a superior gum arabic from the Kordofan district of the Republic of the Sudan
kor·do·fan·ian \,kȯrdə'fanēən\ *n, usu cap* [*Kordofan* province, Republic of the Sudan + E *-ian*] : a small group of languages spoken in the Kordofan district of the Republic of the Sudan constituting a language family
ko·rea \kə'rēə, *in rapid speech* 'krēə, *chiefly southern US* (')kō¦rēə\ *adj, usu cap* [fr. *Korea*, country in eastern Asia] : of or from Korea : of the kind or style prevalent in Korea : KOREAN
¹**ko·re·an** *also* **co·re·an** \-ēən\ *adj, usu cap* [*Korea* + E *-an*, adj. suffix] **1 a** : of, relating to, or characteristic of Korea **b** : of, relating to, or characteristic of the Koreans **2** : of, relating to, or characteristic of the Korean language
²**korean** *also* **corean** \"\ *n* -s *cap* [*Korea* + E *-an*, n. suffix] **1** : a native or inhabitant of Korea **2** : the language of the Korean people now usu. written in the Hankul alphabet
korean box *or* **korean boxwood** *n, usu cap K* : a compact slow-growing notably hardy box (*Buxus microphylla koreana*) with conspicuously winged branches and obovate leaves ¼ to ½ inch long
korean lawn grass *n, usu cap K* : an Asiatic grass (*Zoisia japonica*) used in China and Japan and more recently in America as a lawn grass — called also *Japanese lawn grass*
korean lespedeza *n, usu cap K* : a much-branched annual lespedeza (*Lespedeza stipulacea*) that is native to Korea but is widely cultivated for hay and forage esp. in regions of hot dry climate
korean pine *n, usu cap K* : a pine (*Pinus koraiensis*) of eastern Asia having reddish gray bark and differing from Swiss pine in having longer leaves with the margins toothed to the apex and cones four to six inches long
koreanspice viburnum \=¦==¦=-\ *n, usu cap K* : a much-branched spreading deciduous spring-flowering shrub (*Viburnum carlesii*) having both its young branchlets and its inflorescence tomentose and having clove-scented flowers with a cylindrical corolla tube
korean velvet grass *n, usu cap K* : MASCARENE GRASS
koreish *usu cap, var of* QURAISH
ko·resh·an \kō'reshən\ *adj, usu cap* [Heb *Kōresh* Cyrus (after *Cyrus* R. Teed †1908 Am. physician who founded Koreshanity) + E *-an*, adj. suffix] : of or relating to Koreshanity
ko·resh·an·i·ty \,kō,re'shanəd·ē\ *n* -ES *usu cap* [*koreshan* + *-ity*] : the doctrines and beliefs of a communal religious society founded in 1886 by Cyrus R. Teed to reestablish church and state upon a basis of divine fellowship
kor·haan \'kō(ə)r,hän\ *or* **knor·haan** *also* **knoor·haan** \'nō-\ *or* **koor·haan** \'kō-\ *n, pl* **korhaan** *or* **korhaans** *or* **knorhaan** *or* **knorhaans** [*korhaan, koorhaan* fr. Afrik *korhaan*, fr. D, black grouse, fr. *korren* to coo (fr. MD *curren*, prob. of imit. origin) + *haan* cock, rooster, fr. MD *hane*; *knorhaan, knoorhaan* fr. Afrik *knorhaan*, fr. D, black grouse, alter. (influenced by *knorren* to grumble, fr. MD *cnorren*, prob. of imit. origin) of *korhaan*; akin to OE *hana* rooster — more at CHANT] **1** : any of several African bustards **2** *usu* **knoorhaan** [so called fr. the sound they make when taken out of the water] **a** : any of several gurnards of southern Africa **b** : a large grunt (*Pomadasys operculare*) of the Indian ocean that is a food and game fish in southern Africa
koriak *usu cap, var of* KORYAK
ko·ri bustard \'kōrē-\ *n* [*kori* fr. a native name in southern Africa] : GOM-PAAUW
ko·ri·ma·ko \,kōrə'mä(,)kō\ *n* -s [Maori] : a New Zealand bellbird (*Anthornis melanura*)
ko·rin \'kōrən\ *n* -s [origin unknown] : a gazelle (*Gazella rufifrons*) of Senegambia, West Africa
Ko·ri·na \kə'rēnə\ *trademark* — used for limba wood
kor·ku \'kō(ə)r(,)kü\ *n, pl* **korku** *or* **korkus** *usu cap* **1 a** : a people inhabiting the forested hills of southern Madhya Pradesh, India **b** : a member of such people **2** : the Munda language of the Korku people
kor·nel·ite \'kȯ(r)nᵊl,īt\ *n* -s [Hung *kornelit*, fr. *Kornel* Hlavacsek, 19th cent. person otherwise unidentified + Hung *-it* -ite] : a mineral $Fe_2(SO_4)_3.7H_2O$ consisting of a ferric sulfate heptahydrate
kor·ne·rup·ine \,kȯ(r)nə'rü,pēn, -‚pən\ *n* -s [Dan *kornerupin*, fr. A. N. *Kornerup*, 19th cent. Dan. geologist + Dan *-in* -ine] : a mineral $(Mg,Fe,Al)_{20}(Si,B)_9O_{43}$ consisting of a magnesium aluminum iron borosilicate resembling sillimanite in appearance
ko·ro \'kōr(,)ō\ *n* -s [Jap *kōro*, fr. *kō* incense + *ro* hearth, furnace] : a squat broad-mouthed jar with bulging shoulder and usu. of porcelain or jade
ko·roa \kə'rōə\ *n, pl* **koroa** *or* **koroas** *usu cap* **1** : a Tunican people of the Yazoo and Mississippi river valleys, Mississippi **2** : a member of the Koroa people
kor·o·mi·ko \,kōrə'mē(,)kō\ *also* **kor·o·mi·ka** \-ēkə\ *n* -s [Maori] **1** : any of several shrubs of the genus *Veronica* (esp. *V. salicifolia* and *V. parviflora*) **2** : a drug obtained from a koromiko plant
ko·ro·na \'kōrə,nō\ *n, pl* **korona** *or* **koronas** [Hung, lit., crown, fr. L *corona* — more at CROWN] **1** : the basic monetary unit of Hungary 1892–1925 **2** : a silver coin representing one korona
Kor·o·seal \'kōrə,sē(ə)l\ *trademark* — used for a thermoplastic composition of polyvinyl chloride that is rubberlike and resistant to oil, sunlight, and flame and is used esp. in insulation, tank linings, gaskets, and coatings for textiles and paper
kor·ri·gan \'kȯrə,gän\ *n* -s [Bret, fem. of *korrig* gnome, dim. of *korr* dwarf] : a long-haired nocturnal often malevolent Breton fairy sorceress
kor·ri·gum \'kärəgəm\ *n* -s [modif. of Kanuri *kargum*] : a reddish fawn antelope (*Damaliscus korrigum*) of western Africa with black markings
kors *pl of* KOR
kor·sa·koff's psychosis *or* **korsakoff's syndrome** *also* **kor·sa·kow's psychosis** *or* **kor·sa·kow's syndrome** \'kȯ(r)sə,kȯfs-, -,kävz-\ *n, usu cap K* [after Sergei *Korsakov* †1900 Russ. psychiatrist] : an abnormal mental condition that is usu. a sequel of chronic alcoholism, is often associated with polyneuritis, and is characterized by an irregular memory loss for which the patient attempts to compensate through confabulation
ko·ru·na \'kȯrə,nä\ *n, pl* **ko·run** \-,rün\ *or* **ko·ru·ny** \-,rənē\ *also* **korunas** \-,rə,näz\ [Czech, lit., crown, fr. L *corona*] **1** : the basic monetary unit of Czechoslovakia — see MONEY table **2** : a coin representing one koruna
kor·wa \'kō(ə)rwə\ *n, pl* **korwa** *or* **korwas** *usu cap* **1 a** : a people of the western Chota Nagpur region of southwestern Bihar, India, apparently related to the Mundas **b** : a member of such people **2** : the Munda language of the Korwa people
kor·yak *or* **kor·iak** \'kȯrē,yak\ *n, pl* **koryak** *or* **koryaks** *or* **koriak** *or* **koriaks** *usu cap* **1 a** : an Americanoid people of northeastern Siberia **b** : a member of such people **2** : the Luorawetlan language of the Koryak people
KO's *pl of* KO, *pres 3d sing of* KO
ko·sam \'kō,sam\ *n* -s [origin unknown] : a small evergreen shrub (*Brucea amarissima*) of the family Simaroubaceae that is widely distributed in open country in much of southeastern Asia and in northern Australia, is noted for the bitterness of all its parts, and has various uses esp. in local medicine — see KOSAM SEED
kosam seed *n* : the very bitter fruit of the kosam sometimes used in the treatment of various diarrheas and dysenteries
ko·share \kō'sha(a)(ə)r\ *n, pl* **koshare** *or* **koshares** *often cap* [Keres] **1** : a Pueblo Indian clown society representing ancestral spirits in ceremonies invoking rain and fertility **2** : a member of the koshare
¹**ko·sher** \'kōshə(r)\ *or* **ka·sher** \kä'she(ə)r, -eə\ *adj* [Yiddish *kosher*, fr. Heb *kāshēr* fit, proper] **1** : sanctioned by Jewish law : ritually fit, clean, or prepared for use according to Jewish law ⟨~ meat⟩ ⟨a ~ scroll of the law⟩ **2** : selling, serving, or using food that is ritually fit according to Jewish law ⟨a ~ restaurant⟩ ⟨she keeps a ~ house⟩ **3** : GENUINE, LEGITIMATE, PROPER ⟨a strong minority feeling that Piltdown was not a very ~ specimen —*New Yorker*⟩ ⟨tried to stop me from withdrawing the money, sensing that something was not ~, but I wouldn't listen —Polly Adler⟩ ⟨the rifle report that followed shortly after seemed perfectly ~ at the time; after all, they do fire guns at army bases —Frederic Ramsey⟩
²**kosher** *var of* KASHER
kosher hide *n* : the hide of an animal slaughtered in accordance with rabbinical law by crosswise cutting of the throat — called also *cutthroat*
ko·sin \'kōsᵊn\ *n* -s [ISV *kos-* (fr. ¹*koso*) + *-in*] : a yellowish brown amorphous anthelmintic powder containing all of the constituents of brayera — called also *brayerin*
kosmos *var of* COSMOS
¹**ko·so** \'kō(,)sō\ *or* **kos·so** \'kä(-\ *or* **kous·so** \'kü(-\ *n* -s [prob. fr. Galla *kosso*] : BRAYERA
²**koso** \'kō(,)sō\ *n, pl* **koso** *or* **kosos** *usu cap* **1** : a Shoshonean people of southeastern California **2** : a member of the Koso people
kos·suth hat \(')käs¦süth-, (')kȯs¦süth-, 'kȯ,shu̇t-\ *n* [after Lajos *Kossuth* †1894 Hung. patriot and statesman] : a hat with a flat-topped crown and rolled brim

kossuth hat

kos·te·letz·kya \,kästə'letskēə\ *n, cap* [NL, fr. V. F. *Kosteletzky* †1887 Bohemian botanist] : a small genus of herbs of the family Malvaceae that are native chiefly to the southern U.S. and tropical America and that differ from the mallows in having a single ovule in each cell of the ovary
ko·stro·ma \,kästrə'mä\ *adj, usu cap* [fr. *Kostroma*, city in north central part of European Russia, U.S.S.R.] : of or from the city of Kostroma, U.S.S.R. : of the kind or style prevalent in Kostroma
kot \'kät, 'kōt\ *n, pl* **kot** *or* **kots** *usu cap* **1 a** : an extinct people once living along the Agul river tributary of the Yenisei river in Siberia **b** : a member of the Kot people **2** : the Yeniseian language of the Kot people
¹**ko·ta** \'kōd·ə\ *or* **ko·tar** \'kō,tär\ *n, pl* **kota** *or* **kotas** *or* **kotar** *or* **kotars** *usu cap* **1 a** : an artisan and buffalo-herding people of the Nilgiri hills of southwestern India **b** : a member of such people **2** : the Dravidian language of the Kota people
²**kota** \"\ *n, pl* **kota** *or* **kotas** *usu cap* **1** : a Bantu-speaking people of the interior of French Equatorial Africa noted in recent times for the quality of their carving esp. of wooden religious masks **2** : a member of the Kota people
ko·thor·nos \'käthər,näs, kō'thȯrnəs\ *n* -ES [Gk] : COTHURNUS 1
ko·to \'kōd·(,)ō\ *n* -s [Jap] : a long Japanese zither having 13 silk strings — compare ⁶KIN

koto

ko·to·ite \'kōd·ə,wīt\ *n* -s [G *kotoit*, fr. Bundjiro *Koto* †1935 Jap. geologist and petrographer + G *-it* -ite] : a mineral $Mg_3(BO_3)_2$ consisting of a borate of magnesium
ko·to·ko \kə'tō(,)kō\ *n, pl* **kotoko** *or* **kotokos** *usu cap* **1** : a people of the lower Shari-Logoni basin in the environs of Lake Chad **2** : a member of the Kotoko people
kotow *var of* KOWTOW
ko·tschu·be·ite \kə'chübē,īt\ *n* -s [F *kotchoubeïte*, fr. P. A. v. *Kochubey*, 19th cent. Russ. count + F *-ite*] : a rose-red mineral consisting of a chrome-bearing clinochlore
köttigite *var of* KOETTIGITE
kötts·torf·er value *or* **koetts·torf·er value** \'ket,stȯrfər-\ *n, usu cap K* [prob. fr. the name *Köttstorfer, Koettstorfer*] : SAPONIFICATION VALUE
ko·tu·ku \'kōd·ə,kü\ *n* -s [Maori] *NewZeal* : GREAT WHITE HERON 1
kot·wal *or* **cot·wal** \'kōt,wäl\ *n* -s [Hindi *kotwāl*, fr. Per] : a chief police officer or town magistrate in India
kot·wa·lee \'kōt,wälē\ *n* -s [Hindi *kotwālī*, fr. Per, fr. *kotwāl*] : a police station in India
kotyliform *var of* COTYLIFORM
kou \'kau̇\ *n* -s [Hawaiian] *Hawaii* : a tree (*Cordia subcordata*) of the Pacific islands whose wood is used for making household utensils
koudou *var of* KOODOO
koulan *var of* KULAN
kou·miss *or* **ku·miss** *or* **ku·mys** *or* **ku·myss** \kü'mis, 'küməs\ *n* -ES [Russ *kumys*, fr. Kazan Tatar & Kirghiz *kumyz*] : a fermented beverage made orig. by the nomadic peoples of central Asia from mare's milk and now also from cow's milk elsewhere — compare LEBEN
kou·prey \'kü(,)prā\ *also* **kou·proh** \-rō\ *n* -s [native name in Cambodia] : a blackish brown short-haired forest ox (*Bibos sauveli* or *Novibos sauveli*) of Cambodia that attains a large size, that has a long tail, large dewlap, and spreading recurved horns like those of the yak, and that may be an ancestor of the zebus
kourbash *var of* KURBASH
kou·ros \'kü,rȯs\ *n, pl* **kou·roi** \-rȯi\ [Gk *koros, kouros* boy — more at CRESCENT] : a sculptured figure of a Greek youth (as an athlete) of which many examples dating from classical antiquity are extant
¹**kouse** *also* **kous** \'kau̇(ə)s\ *n, pl* **kous·es** [by alter.] : COUS
²**kouse** *also* **kous** \'kau̇s\ *n, pl* **kous·es** [origin unknown] : PEARL MILLET
kouskous *var of* COUSCOUS
kousso *var of* KOSO
kousso flower *n* [*kousso* prob. fr. Galla *kosso* brayera] : BRAYERA
kov·no \'kȯv(,)nō, -‚nə\ *adj, usu cap* [fr. *Kovno* (*Kaunas*), Lithuania] : KAUNAS
kowbird *var of* KOBIRD
ko·whai \'kō,wī\ *n* -s [Maori] : a shrub or small tree (*Sophora tetraptera*) of Australasia and Chile that yields a hard strong wood
kowliang *var of* KAOLIANG
¹**kow·tow** *or* **ko·tow** \(')kau̇¦tau̇ *sometimes* kō'tau̇\ *n* -s [Chin (Pek) *k'o¹ t'ou²*, fr. *k'o¹* to strike, bump + *t'ou²* head] : an act of kowtowing
²**kowtow** *or* **kotow** \"\ *vi* -ED/-ING/-S **1** : to kneel and touch the forehead to the ground (as in old Chinese custom) in token of homage, worship, or deep respect ⟨everyone should ~ to the abbot, even the chief, but no one receives the abbot's kowtow —Ju-K'ang T'ien⟩ **2** : to show obsequious deference : FAWN ⟨you'll never find a Swiss ~*ing* or bootlicking —T.H. Fielding⟩ ⟨a brilliant scholar . . . ~*ed* to the regime and became an empty, self-hating shell of a man —*Time*⟩
ko·yem·shi \kō'yem(p)shē\ *n, pl* **koyemshi** *or* **koyemshis** *often cap* [Zuñi] **1** : a Zuñi Indian clown society whose members wear the mask of the mudhead and are credited with curing illness by their dancing and clowning **2** : a member of the koyemshi
ko·yu·kon \kō'yü,kän\ *n, pl* **koyukon** *or* **koyukons** *usu cap* **1 a** : an Athapaskan people of the Yukon river valley of west central Alaska **b** : a member of such people **2** : the language of the Koyukon people — called also *Khotana, Ten'a*
ko·zhi·kode \'kōzhə,kōd\ *adj, usu cap* [fr. *Kozhikode* (*Calicut*), India] : CALICUT
ko·zo \'kō(,)zō\ *n* -s [Jap *kōzo*] : PAPER MULBERRY
KP *abbr or n* -s kitchen police
KP *abbr* **1** king post **2** King's Proctor **3** knotty pine
kpel·le \kə'pelə\ *n, pl* **kpelle** *or* **kpelles** *usu cap* **1 a** : a people of central Liberia **b** : a member of the Kpelle people **2** : a Mande language of the Kpelle people
KPH *abbr* kilometers per hour
kr *abbr* **1** kiloroentgen **2** kran **3** kreuzer **4** krona **5** krone **6** kroon
Kr *symbol* krypton
kra \'krä\ *n* -s [Malay *kera*] : CRAB-EATING MACAQUE
¹**kraal** \'kräl, -ȧ-\ *n* -s [Afrik, fr. Pg *curral* pen for cattle, enclosure, fr. (assumed) VL *currale* enclosure for vehicles — more at CORRAL] **1 a** : a village of southern African natives (as Hottentots or Kaffirs) **b** : the organized social unit that the kraal represents : the native village community **2 a** : a single hut or group of huts in which natives in southern Africa live **b** : an enclosure for domestic animals in southern Africa **c** : an elephant corral in Ceylon, India, or Thailand **d** [D, fr. Pg *curral*] : an enclosure for keeping turtles, lobsters, or sponges alive in shallow water — called also *manyatta*
²**kraal** \"\ *vt* -ED/-ING/-S : to pen in a kraal
krae·pe·lin·i·an \,krepə'linēən *also* -rap-\ *adj, usu cap* [Emil *Kraepelin* †1926, Ger. psychiatrist + E *-ian*] : of or relating to Emil Kraepelin or to his system of psychiatric classification
kraft \'kraft, -aa(ə)-, -ai-, -ȧ-\ *n* -s *often attrib* [G, lit., strength, fr. OHG — more at CRAVE] : a strong paper (as most brown wrapping and bag papers) or board made from sulfate pulp ⟨~ paper⟩ ⟨~ process⟩ ⟨~ liner⟩
krait *or* **ko·rait** *also* **ka·rait** \'krīt, kə'r-\ *n* -s [Hindi *karait*] : any of several brightly banded unaggressive but extremely venomous nocturnal elapid snakes of the genus *Bungarus* that are native to eastern Asia and adjacent islands and frequent cultivated land and human habitations and feed esp. on other snakes
kra·ken \'kräkən\ *n* -s [Norw dial., the kraken, fr. Norw dial. *krake* kraken + Norw *-n* (suffixed definite article)] : a fabulous Scandinavian sea monster perhaps imagined on the basis of chance sightings of giant squids
krakow *usu cap, var of* CRACOW
kra·ko·wi·ak \krə'kōvē,ak\ *n* -s [Pol, fr. *Krakow, Cracow*, city and department in southern Poland] : a Polish usu. group folk dance that combines elements of the ancient round, the more recent square, and the modern polka ⟨read out bouncing ~ measures to the accompaniment of flute, fiddle, and accordion —H.M.Robinson⟩
¹**kra·ma** \'krämə\ *n* -s [Gk, mixture, mixed wine, fr. *kerannynai* to mix — more at CRATER] : the mingled and consecrated wine and water into which the consecrated bread is broken at the Eucharist in the Eastern Orthodox Church
²**krama** \"\ *or* **kro·mo** \'krō(,)mō\ *n* -s *usu cap* [Jav *krama*] : the form of Javanese used in speaking to or in the presence of social superiors
kra·me·ria \krə'mirēə\ *n* [NL, fr. J. G. H. and W. H. *Kramer*, 18th cent. Ger. botanists + NL *-ia*] **1** *cap* : a genus of shrubs that are usu. placed in the family Leguminosae but have sometimes been included among the Polygalaceae or isolated in a monotypic family, that have flowers with irregular petals and a one-celled ovary which are followed by indehiscent prickly fruits, and that in some cases have astringent roots which are sometimes used in pharmacy and tanning **2** -s : the dried roots of certain plants of the genus *Krameria* — see RHATANY — **kra·me·ri·a·ceous** \=¦==¦āshəs\ *adj*
kran \'krän\ *n* -s [Per *qrān*] **1** : the basic monetary unit of Persia from 1826 to 1932 **2** : a silver coin representing one kran
krang *var of* KRENG
krantz *also* **krans** \'kran(t)s, -ä-\ *n* -ES [Afrik *krans*, lit., wreath, fr. D, fr. MD *crans* — more at CRANCE] : a sheer cliff or precipice in southern Africa ⟨crawled forward and looked over the edge of the ~ —Stuart Cloete⟩

krantz·ite \'kran(t)‚sīt\ *n* -s [G *krantzit*, fr. A. *Krantz*, 19th cent. Ger. mineralogist + G *-it* -ite] **:** a fossil resin similar to amber

krap·fen \'kräpfən\ *n, pl* **krap·fen** [G *krapfen*, fr. OHG *krāpfo* hook, fritter — more at CRAVE] **:** BISMARCK

kra·pi·na man \'kräpənə-\ *n, usu cap K* [*Krapina*, locality in northern Croatia, Yugoslavia] **:** an early broad-headed Neanderthal man known from several fragmentary skeletons found associated with Mousterian artifacts in a rock shelter in northern Croatia

kra·sis \'kräsə̇s\ *n, pl* **kra·seis** \-ä(‚)sēs\ [Gk, mixing, combination, fr. *kerannynai* to mix — more at CRATER] **:** the act or practice of mingling water with wine in the Eastern Orthodox Eucharist **:** MIXED CHALICE — compare KRAMA

kras·no·dar \'kraznə‚där, ‚==ˈ=\ *adj, usu cap* [fr. *Krasnodar*, city in southern part of European Russia, U.S.S.R.] **:** of or from the city of Krasnodar, U.S.S.R. **:** of the kind or style prevalent in Krasnodar

kras·no·yarsk \'kraznə‚yärsk, ‚==ˈ=\ *adj, usu cap* [fr. *Krasnoyarsk*, city in west central Siberia, U.S.S.R.] **:** of or from the city of Krasnoyarsk, U.S.S.R. **:** of the kind or style prevalent in Krasnoyarsk

kra·ter *or* **cra·ter** \'krād·ər, krä'tā(ə)r\ *n* -s [Gk *kratēr* mixing bowl, krater — more at CRATER] **:** a vessel of Greek and Roman antiquity resembling an amphora but having a larger body and a wide mouth and used for mixing wine and water — compare KELEBE

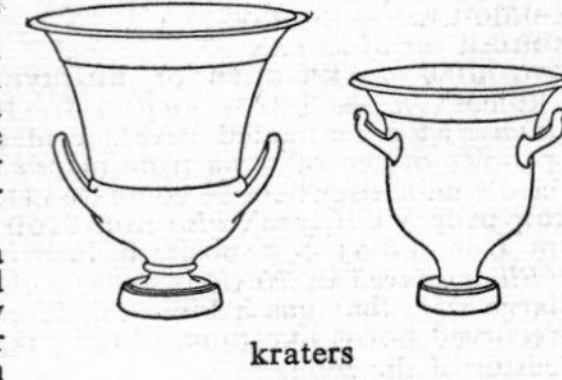
kraters

k ration *n, usu cap K* **:** a lightweight packaged ration of emergency foods developed for U.S. armed forces in World War II

kratoch·vil·ite \krə'tächvə‚līt, 'krad·ək‚vi‚l-\ *n* -s [ISV *kratochvil-* (prob. fr. Josef *Kratochvil* b1878 Czechoslovak petrographer) + *-ite*] **:** FLUORENE

krat·o·gen \'krad·əjən, -‚jen\ *n* -s [G, fr. *krato-* (fr. Gk *kratos* mastery, strength) + *-gen* — more at HARD] **:** a region that has remained undisturbed while an adjacent area has been affected by mountain-making movements — compare OROGEN — **krat·o·gen·ic** \;==ˈjenik\ *adj*

kra·ton \'krā‚tän, -ra‚t-\ *n* -s [ISV, perh. alter. of *kratogen*] **:** KRATOGEN

krau·rite \'krȯ‚rīt\ *n* -s [G *kraurit*, fr. Gk *krauros* brittle + G *-it* -ite] **:** DUFRENITE

krau·ro·sis \krȯ'rōsə̇s\ *n, pl* **krau·ro·ses** \-ō‚sēz\ [NL, fr. Gk *krauros* brittle + NL *-osis*] **:** atrophy and shriveling of the skin or mucous membrane esp. of the vulva where it is often a precancerous lesion — **krau·rot·ic** \(')=ˈräd·ik\ *adj*

[1]**krau·sen** \'krȯiz^ən\ *vt* -ED/-ING/-S [G *kräusen* to add herbs to brewing beer, fr. *krausen, kräusen* to curl back from the edge (said of foam), curl, fr. MHG *krūsen* to curl, fr. *krūs* curly — more at CURL] **:** to add strong newly fermenting wort to (beer) to produce natural carbonation — compare GYLE

[2]**krausen** \"\ *n* -s **:** fermenting wort

krau·se's corpuscle \'krau̇zəz-\ *n, usu cap K* [after Wilhelm *Krause* †1910 Ger. anatomist] **:** any of various rounded sensory end organs occurring in mucous membranes (as of the conjunctiva or genitals)

krause's end-bulb *n, usu cap K* **:** KRAUSE'S CORPUSCLE

krause's membrane *n, usu cap K* **:** one of the isotropic cross bands in a striated muscle fiber that consists of disks of sarcoplasm linking the individual fibrils

kraus·ite \'krau̇‚sīt\ *n* -s [Edward Henry *Kraus* b1875 Am. mineralogist + E *-ite*] **:** a mineral $KFe(SO_4)_2.H_2O$ consisting of a hydrous sulfate of potassium and iron

kraut \'krau̇t, *usu* -au̇d·+V\ *n* -s [G, sauerkraut, cabbage, plant, herb, fr. OHG *krūt* herb, cabbage — more at SAUERKRAUT] **1 a :** SAUERKRAUT **b :** turnips cured in the same way as cabbage kraut **2** *often cap* **:** a German soldier or civilian — usu. used disparagingly ⟨one of the . . . techniques of annoying the ~ today is to whistle at him —*Atlantic*⟩

kraut grass \'krau̇t,=\ *also* **kraut weed** \-au̇t‚=\ *n* [prob. alter. (influenced by *kraut*) of *crowd grass, crowdweed*] **:** CHARLOCK

krebs cycle \'krebz-\ *n, usu cap K* [after H. A. *Krebs* b1900 Eng. biochemist] **:** a cyclic sequence of reactions occurring in the living organism (as in muscle tissue) and forming a phase of the metabolic function in which acetic acid or acetyl equivalent is oxidized through a series of intermediate acids to carbon dioxide and water and thus provides energy for storage in the form of energy-rich phosphate bonds (as in adenosine triphosphate) that can make it available for use in other vital processes (as muscular work) — called also *citric acid cycle, tricarboxylic acid cycle*

kreef \'krāf\ *n* -s [Afrik, fr. D *kreeft* lobster, crayfish, fr. MD *creeft*; akin to OHG *krebiz* crab — more at CRAB] **:** CAPE CRAWFISH

kre·feld \'krā‚felt, -ld\ *adj, usu cap* [fr. *Krefeld*, Germany] **:** of or from the city of Krefeld, Germany **:** of the kind or style prevalent in Krefeld

kreis \'krīs\ *n, pl* **krei·se** \-īzə\ [G, lit., circle, fr. OHG *kreiz*; akin to MLG *kreit, krēt* circle, *krīt* enclosed combat area — more at KULTURKREIS] **:** a unit of local government in Germany corresponding to a county

kreit·to·nite \'krīt^ən‚īt, -rāt-\ *n* -s [G *kreittonit*, fr. Gk *kreittōn* stronger (compar. of *kratys* strong) + G *-it* -ite — more at HARD] **:** a black gahnite

kremers·ite \'kremər‚zīt, 'krām-\ *n* -s [G *kremersit*, after P. *Kremers*, 19th cent. Ger. chemist who described it + G *-it* -ite] **:** a volcanic mineral product $[(NH_4),K]_2FeCl_5.H_2O$ consisting of a hydrous chloride of potassium, ammonium, and iron that occurs in red octahedrons

[1]**krem·lin** \'kremlə̇n\ *n* -s [earlier *cremelena, cremelina*, prob. modif. of obs. G *kremelin*, modif. of Russ *kreml'*] **1 :** the citadel or fortress of a Russian city or town ⟨the ensembles of the fortified monasteries and ~s —Arthur Voyce⟩ **2** *usu cap* [fr. the *Kremlin*, citadel of Moscow now serving as the governing center of the U.S.S.R.] **a :** a governing center or executive stronghold usu. regarded as secretive and impenetrable ⟨there are many *Kremlins* outside Russia, whose secrets, too, are guarded —Irwin Edman⟩ ⟨some of the permanent secretaries and undersecretaries live in an invisible *Kremlin* —*Economist*⟩ **b :** the supreme governing oligarchy of Soviet Russia ⟨on both sides of the Iron Curtain the battle between *Kremlin* and Vatican continues —C.L.Sulzberger⟩

[2]**kremlin** \"\ *adj, usu cap* **:** of or relating to the Kremlin esp. as symbolizing the central government of the U.S.S.R. or its policies ⟨*Kremlin* leaders⟩

krem·lin·ism \-‚nizəm\ *n* -s *usu cap* **:** the policies and practices characteristic of the Soviet Russian government ⟨*Kremlinism* threatens the security and even the physical existence of mankind by keeping alive the global anarchy —H.D.Lasswell⟩

krem·nitz white *or* **crem·nitz white** \'kremnə̇ts-\ *n, usu cap K&C* [fr. *Kremnitz, Kremnica*, east central Czechoslovakia] **:** a white lead suitable esp. for use in inks and as an artist's color — called also *Krems white*

krems white *or* **crems white** \'kremz-, -m(p)s-\ *n, usu cap K&C* [perh. fr. *Krems*, city in Austria] **:** KREMNITZ WHITE

kreng \'kreŋ\ *or* **krang** *or* **crang** \'kraŋ\ *n* -s [D *kreng*, fr. MD *crenge* carrion, carcass; perh. akin to OE *cringan* to yield, fall in battle, die — more at CRINGE] **:** the carcass of a whale after removal of the blubber and baleen

kreng·ing hook \'kreŋiŋ-\ *or* **crang·ing hook** \'kraŋiŋ-\ *n* [*krenging, cranging* fr. *kreng, crang* + *-ing*] **:** a hook for holding the blubber of a whale while cutting it away

kren·ner·ite \'krenə‚rīt\ *n* -s [G *krennerit*, fr. J. S. *Krenner* †1920 Hung. mineralogist + G *-it* -ite] **:** a mineral $AuTe_2$ consisting of a gold telluride

kreo- — see CRE-

krep·lach *or* **krep·lech** *or* **crep·lich** \'krepləḵ\ *n, pl* **kreplach** *or* **kreplech** *or* **creplich** [Yiddish *kreplech*, pl. of *krepel*, fr. (assumed) MHG dial. *krepel* (whence G dial. *kräppel* fritter), dim. of MHG dial. *krape, krāpe* fritter; akin to OHG *krāpfo* hook, fritter — more at CRAVE] **:** triangular pockets of noodle dough filled with chopped meat or cheese, boiled, and eaten with soup or as a side dish

kreu·zer *also* **kreut·zer** *or* **creut·zer** \'krȯitsə(r)\ *n* -s [G *kreuzer*, fr. MHG *kriuzer* (trans. of ML *denarius cruciatus*, *cruciger*, fr. the cross marking them), fr. *kriuze* cross, fr. OHG *krūzi*, fr. L *cruc-, crux* — more at RIDGE] **:** a small coin of silver and later of copper used in Austria, Germany, and Hungary from the 13th to the mid-19th centuries

krex \'kreks, 'gr-\ *vi* -ED/-ING/-S [prob. fr. PaG *greckse* to grunt, ail, fr. G *krächzen* to croak, fr. *krachen* to crack, crash, roar, fr. OHG *krahhōn* to crack — more at CRACK] *dial* **:** GRUMBLE, COMPLAIN ⟨always something to ~ about⟩

k'ri *or* **kri** *var of* KERI

krib·er·gite \'kribər‚gīt\ *n* -s [Sw *kribergit*, prob. irreg. fr. *Kristineberg* mine, Västerbotten province, northern Sweden, its locality + Sw *-it* -ite] **:** a mineral approximately $Al_{16}(PO_4)_8$-$(SO_4)_3(OH)_{18}.10H_2O$ consisting of a hydrous basic sulfate and phosphate of aluminum

kri·der's hawk \'krīdə(r)z-\ *n, usu cap K* [fr. the name *Krider*] **:** a hawk of the central U.S. that is a variety (*Buteo jamaicensis kriderii*) of the red-tailed hawk and has the underparts almost pure white

krieg·spiel \'krēgz‚pē(ə)l, -ēg‚sp-, -ēk‚sp-\ *n* [G *kriegsspiel*, fr. *krieg* war + *spiel* game] **1 :** a game in which blocks, pins, and flags representing contending forces and guns are moved about according to rules based on war conditions **2 :** chess in which neither player sees the other's board but is given some information as to the opponent's moves by a referee who keeps track of all moves on a third board

krie·ker \'krēkə(r)\ *n* -s [perh. fr. D *krieken* to chirp, peep (of imit. origin) + E *-er*] **:** PECTORAL SANDPIPER

krig·ia \'krigēə\ *n* [NL, fr. David *Krig*, 18th cent. Am. plant collector + NL *-ia*] **1** *cap* **:** a genus of small branched yellow-flowered No. American herbs that are related to the chicories but resemble dandelions and have a pappus of both bristles and chaff and short achenes **2** -s **:** any plant of the genus *Krigia* — called also *dwarf dandelion*

krill \'kril\ *n* -s [Norw *kril* young fry of fish] **:** planktonic crustaceans and larvae that constitute the principal food of whalebone whales which feed by straining krill-containing water through their plates of baleen

krim·mer *also* **crim·mer** \'krimə(r)\ *n* -s [G *krimmer*, fr. *Krim* Crimea, peninsula in the southern part of European Russia, U.S.S.R.] **1 :** a gray fur resembling astrakhan or Persian lamb that is made from the pelts of young lambs of the Crimean peninsula region — compare BROADTAIL, KARAKUL **2 :** a pile fabric resembling krimmer fur

krim-saghyz *var of* KRYM-SAGHYZ

kris *or* **kriss** *also* **creese** \'krēs *sometimes* 'kris\ *n, pl* **krises** *or* **krisses** [Malay *kĕris*] **:** a Malay or Indonesian dagger often with two scalloped cutting edges and ridged serpentine blade ⟨the ~ of a noble or high-class family is a sacred possession —Virginia A. Oakes⟩

kris

kris dance *n* **:** a Balinese trance dance in which the dancer attacks himself with a kris

krish·na·ism \'krishnə‚izəm\ *n* -s *usu cap* [*Krishna*, eighth avatar of Vishnu, one of the principal Hindu gods + E *-ism*] **:** a widespread form of Hindu worship addressed to Krishna as eighth avatar of Vishnu

kri·ta yu·ga \‚krid·ə'yügə\ *n, usu cap K&Y* [Skt *kṛtayuga*, fr. *kṛta* best throw at dice (that of the four) + *yuga* yoke, age of the world — more at YOKE] **:** the first and best age of a Hindu world cycle

kri·voi rog \‚kri‚vȯi'rōg, kri‚vȯi'rōk\ *adj, usu cap K&R* [fr. *Krivoi Rog*, city in southeast central Ukraine, U.S.S.R.] **:** of or from the city of Krivoi Rog, U.S.S.R. **:** of the kind or style prevalent in Krivoi Rog

kroehn·kite *or* **kröhn·kite** \'kreŋ‚kīt\ *n* -s [modif. of Sp *krönnkite*, fr. B. *Kröhnke*, 19th cent. Ger. mineralogist + Sp *-ite*] **:** a mineral $Na_2Cu(SO_4)_2.2H_2O$ consisting of an azure-blue hydrous copper sodium sulfate that occurs massive

krom·draai ape-man \'kräm‚drī-\ *also* **kromdraai man** *n, usu cap K* [*Kromdraai*, town in Transvaal, So. Africa, site of the finds] **:** an australopithecine (*Paranthropus robustus* or *Australopithecus robustus*) known from skull and skeletal fragments from southern Africa and distinguished by an extraordinarily massive jaw — compare SWARTKRANZ APE-MAN

kro·mes·ki *or* **kro·mes·ky** *also* **cro·mes·ki** *or* **cro·mes·qui** \'krō'meskē\ *n, pl* **kromeskis** *or* **kromeskies** [modif. of Russ *kromochki*, pl. of *kromochka* slice of bread, dim. of *kroma* slice of bread] **:** a croquette wrapped in bacon, dipped in batter, and fried

krom·nek disease \'kräm‚nek-\ *n* [Afrik *kromnek*, fr. *krom* crooked (fr. D, fr. MD *crom, cromb*) + *nek* neck, fr. D, fr. MD *necke* nape of the neck; akin to OE *crumb* crooked and to OE *hnecca* neck — more at CRUMP, NECK] *in southern Africa* **:** TOMATO STREAK

kromo *usu cap, var of* KRAMA

kro·mo·gram \'krōmə‚gram\ *n* [alter. of *chromogram*] **:** the set of three photographic positives used in a chromoscope — called also *chromogram*

[1]**kro·na** \'krōnə\ *n, pl* **kro·nur** \-nə(r)\ [Icel *krōna*, lit., crown, fr. ON *krūna, krōna*, fr. MLG *krūne, krōne*, prob. fr. OF *corone, corune* — more at CROWN] **1 :** the basic monetary unit of Iceland — see MONEY table **2 :** a coin representing one krona

[2]**kro·na** \", 'krünə\ *n, pl* **kro·nor** \-‚nȯ(ə)r\ [Sw, lit., crown, fr. OSw *krūna, krōna*, fr. MLG *krūne, krōne*] **1 :** the basic monetary unit of Sweden — see MONEY table **2 :** a coin representing one krona

[1]**kro·ne** \'krōnə\ *n, pl* **kro·nen** \-nən\ [G, lit., crown, fr. OHG *corōna*, fr. L *corona* — more at CROWN] **1 :** the basic monetary unit of Austria from 1892 to 1925 **2 :** a coin representing one krone

[2]**krone** \"\ *n, pl* **kro·ner** \-nə(r)\ [Dan, lit., crown, fr. ODan *krūne, krōne*, fr. MLG] **1 a :** the basic monetary unit of Denmark — see MONEY table **b :** a coin representing one Danish krone **2 a :** the basic monetary unit of Norway — see MONEY table **b :** a coin representing one Norwegian krone

kroo \'krü\ *or* **kroo·boy** \-‚bȯi\ *n, pl* **kroo** *or* **krooboys** *usu cap* [*Kroo* alter. of *Kru*] **:** KRU 1b

kroon \'krün\ *n, pl* **kroo·ni** \-nē\ *or* **kroons** [Estonian *kron*, fr. G *krone*] **1 :** the basic monetary unit of Estonia from 1928 to 1940 **2 :** a coin or note representing one kroon

kru \'krü\ *n, pl* **kru** *or* **krus** *usu cap* **1 a :** an indigenous Negro people of Liberia skilled as boatmen **b :** a member of the Kru people — called also *Kruman* **2 :** a Kwa language of the Kru people **3 :** a language group containing Kru, Bassa, and Grebo

kru·bi \'krübē\ *n* -s [prob. native name in Sumatra] **:** a tropical East Indian aroid (*Amorphophallus titanum*) having a spathe that resembles the corolla of a morning glory and attains a diameter of several feet

kru·ken·berg tumor \'krükən‚bərg-\ *n, usu cap K* [after Friedrich E. *Krukenberg* b1871 Ger. pathologist] **:** a metastatic ovarian tumor of mucin-producing epithelial cells usu. derived from a primary gastrointestinal tumor

kru·man *or* **kroo·man** \'krümən\ *n, pl* **krumen** *or* **kroomen** *usu cap* **:** KRU 1b

krumm·holz \'kru̇m‚hōlts\ *n, pl* **krummholz** *usu cap* [G, fr. *krumm* crooked (fr. OHG *krumb, krump*) + *holz* wood, fr. OHG — more at CRUMP, HOLT] **:** stunted forest characteristic of most alpine regions — called also *elfinwood*

krumm·horn *also* **krum·horn** \'-‚hȯrn\ *n* [G *krummhorn* — more at CROMORNE] **1 :** an obsolete reed wind instrument with a curved tube — called also *cromorne* **2 :** CROMORNA

krummhorn with cap removed to show reed

krym-saghyz *or* **krim-saghyz** \'krimsə'gēz, -giz\ *n* -ES [Russ *krym-sagyz*, fr. *Krym* Crimea, peninsula in the southern part of European Russia, U.S.S.R. + Turki *sagiz* rubber, gum] **:** a small dandelion (*Taraxacum megalorrhizon*) of the Mediterranean region with yellow heads and a long rubber-containing taproot for which it is cultivated

kryo- — see CRY-

kry·o·gen yellow G \'krīōjən-, -‚jen-\ *n, usu cap K&Y* [*kryogen* perh. fr. *cry-* + *-gen*] **:** a sulfur dye — see DYE table I (under *Sulfur Yellow 3*)

kryokonite *var of* CRYOCONITE

kryolite *var of* CRYOLITE

krypt- *or* **krypto-** — see CRYPT-

kryp·ton \'krip‚tän, -‚tən\ *n* -s [Gk, neut. of *kryptos* hidden — more at CRYPT] **:** a colorless inert gaseous element that occurs in air to the extent of about one part per million by volume and in gases from thermal springs and other natural gases, that is obtained by separating from liquid air, and that is used in electric lamps (as small quartz lamps for extremely brilliant illumination) — symbol *Kr*; see ELEMENT table

k's *or* **ks** *pl of* K

KS *abbr* **1** keep standing **2** king's scholar

KSF *abbr, often not cap* kips per square foot

ksha·tri·ya *also* **kshat·tri·ya** *or* **ksat·ri·ya** \(kə)'sha·trē(y)ə, (kə)'shə-, 'ksh- *sometimes* 'ch-\ *n* -s *usu cap* [Skt *kṣatriya*, fr. *kṣatra* dominion, fr. *kṣayati* he possesses, rules — more at CHECK] **1 :** a twice-born Hindu of the second ancient varna assigned by classical law to a governing or military occupation **2 :** a twice-born Hindu belonging to one of a large group of modern upper castes traditionally derived from the ancient Kshatriya varna — compare SUDRA, VAISYA

k-shell \'=‚=\ *n, usu cap K* **:** the innermost shell of electrons surrounding an atomic nucleus and constituting the lowest available energy level for the electrons — compare L-SHELL, M-SHELL

k star *n, usu cap K* **:** a star of spectral type K — see SPECTRAL TYPE table

kt *abbr* **1** karat **2** kiloton **3** knight **4** knot

k'thib *or* **kthib** *or* **k'thibh** *or* **kthibh** *var of* KETHIB

KTL *abbr, often not cap* [Gk *kai ta loipa*] et cetera

k truss *n, usu cap K* **:** a building truss in which the vertical member and two oblique members in each panel form a K

kua·la lum·pur \'kwälə'lüm‚pu̇(ə)r, 'kwəl-, -'ləm-\ *adj, usu cap K&L* [fr. *Kuala Lumpur*, Federation of Malaya] **:** of or from Kuala Lumpur, capital of the Federation of Malaya **:** of the kind or style prevalent in Kuala Lumpur

kuan \'gwän, 'kw-\ *n* -s *usu cap* [Chin (Pek) *kuan*[1] official] **1 :** a type of Chinese pottery of the Sung period in the 12th century **2 :** imperial porcelain made at Ching-tê-chên

kuan hua \'gwän'(h)wä\ *n, usu cap K&H* [Chin (Pek) *kuan*[1] *hua*[4], fr. *kuan*[1] official + *hua*[4] speech, language] **:** MANDARIN

[1]**ku·ba** \'kü'bä\ *n* -s *usu cap* [fr. *Kuba*, town in northeast Azerbaidzhan, U.S.S.R.] **:** an eastern Caucasian carpet of coarse but firm weave resembling the Shirvan in design — called also *Kabistan*

[2]**ku·ba** \'kübə\ *n, pl* **kuba** *or* **kubas** *usu cap* **1 :** a Bantu-speaking people of the central Congo **2 :** a member of the Kuba people

ku·ba·chi \kü'bächē\ *n, pl* **kubachi** *or* **kubachis** *usu cap* **1 :** a Caucasian people of Dagestan **2 :** a member of the Kubachi people

ku·bong \'kü‚bȯŋ, -bäŋ\ *n, pl* **kubong** [Malay] **:** FLYING LEMUR

ku·bu \'kü(‚)bü\ *n, pl* **kubu** *or* **kubus** *usu cap* [native name in Sumatra] **1 :** an Indonesian Veddoid people of Sumatra **2 :** a member of the Kubu people

ku·che·an \(')kü'chēən\ *n* -s *cap* [*Kuche, Kucha*, town and oasis in west central Sinkiang, China + E *-an*] **:** TOCHARIAN B

ku·chen \'kükən, 'küḵ-\ *n, pl* **kuchen** [G, cake, fr. OHG *kuocho, chuohho* — more at CAKE] **:** any of several varieties of coffee cake typically made from sweet yeast dough and variously shaped, flavored, and frosted

ku·dize \'k(y)ü‚dīz\ *vt* -ED/-ING/-S [*kudos* + *-ize*] **:** grant honors to **:** PRAISE

ku·dos \-‚däs, -‚dōs\ *n, pl* **ku·dos** \-‚dōz\ [Gk *kydos*; akin to OSlav *čudo* wonder, Gk *akouein* to hear — more at HEAR] **1 :** fame and renown resulting from an act or achievement **:** PRESTIGE ⟨occupations linked to inferior castes in Africa and India bring no ~ to their practitioners, no matter how skilled the craftsman —E.A.Hoebel⟩ ⟨the curate's undaunted demeanor . . . was generally supposed to have terrified the burglars into flight and much ~ accrued to him thereby —Kenneth Grahame⟩ **2 :** praise given for achievement **:** ACCOLADE 3c ⟨a masterly study of primitive versus industrial society . . . with the ~ going to the pagan man —Betty Kirk⟩ ⟨they will compel new respect and admiration far beyond the ~ civilization finds itself obliged to pay —*Collier's*⟩

kudu *var of* KOODOO

kud·zu \'ku̇d(‚)zü\ *also* **kudzu vine** *n* -s [Jap *kuzu*] **:** a prostrate vine (*Pueraria thunbergiana*) of China and Japan that is used widely for hay and forage and for erosion control and soil improvement and that has tuberous edible roots and stems which yield a fiber — see KO-HEMP

kue *also* **ku** \'kyü\ *n* -s **:** the letter *q*

kufa *var of* GUFA

[1]**ku·fic** *also* **cu·fic** \'k(y)üfik\ *adj, usu cap* [*Al Kufa*, town in south central Iraq + E *-ic*] **1 :** of, relating to, or characteristic of Al Kufa, a city of Mesopotamia or of its inhabitants **2 :** constituting, belonging to, characteristic of, or written in the Arabic script Kufic

[2]**kufic** *also* **cufic** \"\ *n, usu cap* **1 :** a highly angular form of the Arabic alphabet orig. used at Al Kufa esp. for costly copies of the Koran **2 :** any angular variety of the Arabic alphabet — compare NESKHI

ku·gel \'kügəl\ *n* -s [Yiddish, lit., ball, fr. MHG *kugel, kugele* — more at CUDGEL] **:** a suet pudding made of noodles, potatoes, or bread, sometimes with raisins added

ku·gel·hof \-‚hōf\ *n* -s [modif. of G *gugelhupf, gugelhopf* — more at GUGELHUPF] **:** GUGELHUPF

ku·hio day \kü'hēo-, ‚==ˈ=-\ *n, usu cap K&D* [after Prince Jonah *Kuhio* Kalanianaole †1922 Hawaiian delegate to the U.S. Congress] **:** March 26 that is observed as a holiday in Hawaii to commemorate the birthday of Prince Jonah Kuhio Kalanianaole

kuh·lia \'külēə, -lyə\ *n, cap* [NL, fr. Heinrich *Kuhl* †1821 Ger. naturalist + NL *-ia*] **:** the type genus of Kuhliidae — see AHOLEHOLE

kuh·li·idae \kü'līə‚dē\ *n pl, cap* [NL, fr. *Kuhlia*, type genus + *-idae*] **:** a family of small Indo-Pacific marine and freshwater percoid fishes — see KUHLIA

kuh·nia \'k(y)ünēə\ *n, cap* [NL, fr. Adam *Kuhn* †1817 Am. physician and botanist + NL *-ia*] **:** a genus of No. American perennial herbs (family Compositae) with alternate resinous leaves and heads of cream-colored tubular flowers

kui \'küē\ *n, pl* **kui** *or* **kuis** *usu cap* **1 a :** a people of southeastern Thailand and adjacent Cambodia who are brachycephalic and of short stature **b :** a people of the Shan states **c :** a Dravidian people of central India **2 :** the Dravidian language of the Kui people of India

kui·by·shev \'kwēbə‚shef, 'küēb-, -ev\ *adj, usu cap* [fr. *Kuibyshev*, city in the eastern part of European Russia, U.S.S.R.] **:** of or from the city of Kuibyshev, U.S.S.R. **:** of the kind or style prevalent in Kuibyshev

ku·itsh \kü'ēch\ *n, pl* **kuitsh** *or* **kuitshes** *usu cap* **1 a :** an Indian people of the Pacific coast in Oregon **b :** a member of such people **2 :** a dialect of Siuslaw

ku·ja·wi·ak \kü'yävē‚ak\ *n* -s [Pol, fr. *Kujawy*, region in north central Poland] **:** a Polish couple dance resembling a waltz with lilting arm and body movements

kuke \'kyük\ *n* -s *usu cap* [by alter.] **:** KIKUYU

ku·ki \'kükē\ *n, pl* **kuki** *or* **kukis** *usu cap* **1 a :** any of numerous hill peoples in southern Assam, India **b :** a member of a Kuki people **2 :** a language of a Kuki people

kuki-chin \‚kükē'chin\ *n* -s *usu cap K&C* **:** a group of Tibeto-Burman languages spoken by the Kuki and Chin peoples

ku-klux \'k(y)ü‚kləks, *often* + 'klü- *by assimilation to the* kl *of* "*Klux*" *&* "*Klan*"\ *vt* -ED/-ING/-ES *often cap both Ks* [fr. *Ku-Klux, Ku-Klux Klan*, secret organization originating in the southern U.S. after the Civil War and advocating maintenance of white supremacy by violent methods] **:** to maltreat or terrorize in a way thought to be typical of Ku Kluxers ⟨*ku-kluxed* him by shooting him with bird shot —R.H.Collins⟩

ku klux·er \-əksə(r)\ *n, pl* **ku kluxers** *usu cap both Ks* **1** *also* **ku klux** *pl* **ku kluxes :** a member of a secret society advocating white supremacy and often using violent methods to intimidate Negroes in the South in the period following the Civil War **2 :** a member of a secret fraternal group achieving prominence in many parts of the U.S. in the second decade of the 20th century and believed to confine its membership to native Protestant whites ⟨wilder than the . . . stories about Catholics which are afloat among our own *Ku Kluxers* —*New Republic*⟩

ku klux·ism \-ək,sizəm\ *also* **ku klux·ery** \-əksərē\ *n, usu cap both Ks* **:** the principles and practices of Ku Kluxers ⟨the bitterness of the days of reconstruction and *Ku Kluxism* —*Amer. Missionary*⟩ ⟨the spirit of *Ku Kluxism* . . . among the older American elements —Samuel Lubell⟩

kuk·ri *also* **kuk·eri** \'ku̇k(ə)rē\ *n* -s [Hindi *kukrī*] **:** a curved short sword with a broad blade used principally by the Gurkhas of India

kukri

kuk·su \'ku̇k(,)sü\ *adj, usu cap* [origin unknown] **:** of or relating to an Indian religious cult or its rites practiced in the southern Sacramento valley of California

ku·ku \'kü(,)kü\ *n* -s [Maori] **:** a New Zealand fruit dove (*Hemiphaga novae-seelandiae*) that is locally important as a game bird — called also *kukupa*

ku·kui \kü'küē\ *n* -s [Hawaiian] **:** CANDLENUT 2

kukui oil *n* **:** CANDLENUT OIL

ku·ku·ku·ku \,kükə'kü(,)kü\ *n, pl* **kukukuku** *or* **kukukukus** *usu cap* **1 :** a people inhabiting parts of Morobe and Papua in eastern New Guinea **2 :** a member of the Kukukuku people

ku·ku·pa \'kükəpə\ *n* -s [Maori] **:** KUKU

ku·la \'külə\ *n, pl* **kula** [of Melanesian origin] **:** a Melanesian interisland system of exchange in which prestige items (as necklaces and arm shells) are ceremoniously exchanged with a concomitant trade in useful goods — compare EXCHANGE 1b

ku·lah \(')kü¦lä\ *n* -s *usu cap* [fr. *Kula*, town in western Turkey in Asia] **:** a Turkish rug that is often a prayer rug and that uses the Ghiordes knot

ku·lak \(')kü¦lak, -¦läk *also* (')kyü¦lak\ *n, pl* **kulaks** \-ks\ *also* **kula·ki** \⸗'lakē, ⸗'läkē\ [Russ, lit., fist, of Turkic origin; akin to Turk *kol* arm] **1 :** a prosperous or wealthy peasant farmer in 19th century Russia often associated with gaining profit from renting land, usury, or acting as a middleman in the sale of the products of other farmers **2 :** a farmer characterized by Communists as having excessive wealth usu. by possession of more than a minimal amount of property and ability to hire laborers or sometimes merely by unwillingness to join a collective farm and as a result denounced as an oppressor of less fortunate farmers and subjected to severe penalties (as heavy fines and confiscation of property) ⟨a large proportion of the ~s of the twenties were liquidated —L.K.Soth⟩

ku·la·man \'külə,män\ *n, pl* **kulaman** *or* **kulamans** *usu cap* [native name in southern Mindanao] **1 a :** a people inhabiting southern Mindanao, Philippines **b :** a member of such people **2 :** an Austronesian language of the Kulaman people

ku·lan *or* **kou·lan** \'kü,län\ *n* -s [Kirghiz *kulan*] **:** the wild ass of the Kirghiz steppe that is prob. a variety of the kiang

ku·la·na·pan \kü'länəpən\ *n* -s *usu cap* **:** a language family of the Hokan stock comprising several languages all known as Pomo

kula ring *n* **1 :** KULA **2 :** the circle of Melanesian islands participating in the kula exchange

kul·li \'kəlē\ *adj, usu cap* [fr. *Kulli*, locality in southern Baluchistan, Pakistan, site of the finds] **:** of or relating to a prehistoric culture of southern Baluchistan characterized by polychrome vases and small objects modeled in clay (as figurines of women and animals, bird whistles, carts)

kul·tur \ku̇l'tü(ə)r\ *n* -s *often cap* [G, fr. L *cultura* culture — more at CULTURE] **1 :** CULTURE 5b ⟨the dwindling survivors of New England *Kultur* —H.L.Mencken⟩ ⟨our ~ should have its own characteristics —*Irish Statesman*⟩ **2 :** culture chiefly of late 19th century Germans that is a state of civilization characterized by an emphasis on practical efficiency rather than on humanitarian refinements and subordination of the individual to a highly organized state **3 :** culture that is an ideal state of civilization unique to Germany chiefly to militant German expansionists during the Nazi and late Hohenzollern periods usu. to emphasize an alleged superiority of German material and political development over the cultures of other nations and peoples ⟨the ethnocentric doctrine of Germanic *Kultur* . . . utilized for political purposes to justify cultural and political absolutism —David Bidney⟩ ⟨German textbooks were fine-combed for the propaganda of *Kultur* —*Amer. Mercury*⟩

kul·tur·kampf \-,käm(p)f\ *n* -s *usu cap* [G, fr. *kultur* + *kampf* conflict, struggle, fr. OHG *kamph* combat — more at KEMP] **:** conflict between civil government and religious authorities esp. over control of education and church appointments ⟨the *Kulturkampf* . . . frets the life of practically every continental nation —*Christian Century*⟩ ⟨planning a protracted *Kulturkampf* against the Church —*Time*⟩

kul·tur·kreis \-,krīs\ *n, pl* **kulturkrei·se** \-īzə\ *usu cap* [G, fr. *kultur* + *kreis* area, circle, fr. OHG *kreiz* circular line, encirclement, district; akin to MLG *kreit*, *krēt* circle, enclosed dueling space, OHG *krizzōn* to scratch in (as letters), *krazzōn* to scratch — more at SCRATCH] **:** a culture complex developing in successive epochs from its center of origin and becoming diffused over large areas of the world ⟨the horse-raising peoples in the primary herding *Kulturkreise* —Lawrence Krader⟩ ⟨the concept of the *Kulturkreise* developed by the Vienna school of ethnology⟩

ku·ma·mo·to \¦küma¦mōd·(,)ō\ *adj, usu cap* [fr. *Kumamoto*, city in western Kyushu, Japan] **:** of or from the city of Kumamoto, Japan **:** of the kind or style prevalent in Kumamoto

kuman *usu cap, var of* CUMAN

ku·ma·ra \'kümərə\ *n* -s [Maori] *New Zealand* **:** SWEET POTATO

ku·ma·ra·hou \¦⸗⸗⸗¦hau̇\ *n* -s [Maori] *New Zealand* **:** any of several native woody plants: as **a :** a branching shrub (*Pomaderris elliptica*) with leaves lustrous above and whitish tomentose below and cymes of fragrant pale yellow flowers **b :** a small sometimes shrubby tree (*Quintinia serrata*) that is more or less covered with whitish scales and has shining leathery serrated leaves and cymes of pale lilac flowers

ku·ma·so \kü'mä(,)sō\ *n, pl* **kumaso** *or* **kumasos** *usu cap* **:** an indigenous Caucasoid people of Japan formerly inhabiting Kyushu — compare AINU

kumbh me·la \'kummə,lä\ *n, usu cap K&M* [Hindi *kumbh melā* festival in the sign of the zodiac Aquarius, fr. Skt *kumbha* pot, Aquarius + *melā* assembly — more at HUMP, MILITATE] **:** a Hindu festival occurring once every 12 years in one of four sacred sites where bathing for purification of sin is considered esp. efficacious

kum·bi \'ku̇mbē\ *n* -s [origin unknown] *India* **:** the silky fiber of the white silk cotton tree

kum·buk \'ku̇m,bu̇k\ *n* -s [origin unknown] **:** ARJUN

kum·har \(')ku̇m¦här\ *n* -s *usu cap* [Hindi *kumhār*, fr. Skt *kumbhakāra*, fr. *kumbha* pot + *kāra* maker; akin to Skt *kṛnoti* he does, makes — more at HUMP, KARMA] **:** a member of a potter caste of India

kumiss *or* **kumys** *or* **kumyss** *var of* KOUMISS

kum·kum \'ku̇m,ku̇m\ *n* -s [Hindi *kuṅkum*, fr. Skt *kuṅkuma* saffron, perh. of Sem origin; akin to Heb *karkōm* saffron, crocus — more at CROCUS] **1 :** red turmeric powder used for making the distinctive Hindu mark on the forehead **2 :** the mark on the forehead made with kumkum

küm·mel \'kiməl\ *n* -s [G, lit., caraway seed, fr. OHG *kumil*, *kumīn* cumin — more at CUMIN] **:** a colorless aromatic liqueur flavored principally with caraway seeds

kummi *usu cap, var of* KURMI

kum·quat *also* **cum·quat** \'kəm,kwät\ *n* -s [Chin (Cant) *kam kwat*, fr. *kam* gold + *kwat* orange] **1 a :** any of several small yellow to orange citrus fruits with sweet spongy rind and somewhat acid pulp that are used chiefly candied or in preserves **b :** a tree or shrub of the genus *Fortunella* that bears kumquats: as (1) **:** a Chinese tree (*F. margarita*) that is widely cultivated in warm regions and that bears ovoid orange-colored kumquats (2) **:** a tree (*F. japonica*) that is known only in cultivation and that bears spherical golden yellow kumquats **2** *Austral* **:** DESERT LEMON

ku·myk *also* **ku·mik** \(')kü¦mik\ *or* **ku·muk** \-¦mək\ *n* -s *usu cap* **1 a :** a Turkish people of the Caucasus **b :** a member of such people **2 :** the Turkic language of the Kumyk people

ku·nai \'kü,nī\ *n* -s [native name in eastern New Guinea] *New Guinea* **:** COGON

ku·na·ma \kü'nämə\ *n* -s *usu cap* **1 :** a language spoken in northern Ethiopia **2 :** a branch of the Chari-Nile language family containing only the Kunama language

kunbi *usu cap, var of* KURMI

kundt tube \'ku̇nt-\ *n, usu cap K* [after August *Kundt* †1894 Ger. physicist] **:** an acoustically resonating horizontal glass tube in which the standing-wave nodes are exhibited by the distribution of a fine powder and that is used to measure the velocity of sound in gases

kung *usu cap, var of* QUNG

kun·gu cake \'ku̇ŋ(,)gü\ *n* [*kungu* fr. Nyanja *nkungu* kungu fly] **:** a food made by the natives about Lake Nyasa consisting of compressed cakes of kungu flies

kungu fly *n* **:** any of certain small mayflies (genus *Caenis*) and midges (genus *Corethra*) that breed on Lake Nyasa — see KUNGU CAKE

kun·kur *or* **kun·kar** \'kəŋkə(r)\ *also* **con·ker** \'käŋ-\ *n* -s [Hindi *kaṅkar*, fr. Skt *karkara*] **:** a limestone used esp. in India for making lime and building roads

kunst·lied \'ku̇nzt,lēt, -n(t)st-\ *n* -s [G, fr. *kunst* art (fr. OHG, skill, knowledge) + *lied* song, fr. OHG *liod*; OHG *kunst* akin to OFris *kunst* knowledge, MD *const*, *cunst*, OS *kunst*, all fr. a prehistoric derivative of the verb represented by OHG *kunnan* to know, be able — more at CAN, LAUD] **:** ART SONG

kunz·ite \'ku̇nt,sīt\ *n* -s [George F. *Kunz* †1932 Am. gem expert + E *-ite*] **:** a variety of spodumene that occurs in beautiful pinkish lilac crystals and is used as a gem

kuo-yü \'gwō'yü\ *n* -s *usu cap* [Chin (Pek) *kuo²* *yü³*, lit., national language, fr. *kuo²* nation + *yü³* language] **:** a form of Mandarin taught in the schools and used in government

kupf·fer cell \'ku̇pfə(r)-\ *also* **kupf·fer's cell** *n, usu cap K* [after Karl Wilhelm von *Kupffer* †1903 Ger. anatomist] **:** a fixed histiocyte of the walls of the liver sinusoids that is stellate with large oval nucleus and the cytoplasm commonly packed with fragments resulting from phagocytic action

kupf·fer·ite \-fə,rīt\ *n* -s [ISV *kupffer-* (fr. Adolph T. *Kupffer* †1865 Russ. physicist) + *-ite*] **:** a green aluminous variety of amphibole

ku·phar \'küfə(r)\ *n* -s [Ar *quffah* basket] **:** GUFA

ku·ping tael \¦gü,piŋ-\ *n* [Chin (Pek) *k'u⁴* *p'ing²* treasury scale for silver (fr. *k'u⁴* treasury + *p'ing²* level, standard weight) + E *tael*] **:** the tael used for reckoning taxes and dues other than customs

kup·per \'kəpə(r)\ *n* -s [perh. fr. Sindhi *kapar*] **:** SAW-SCALED VIPER

ku·ra clover \kə'rä-, 'ku̇rə-\ *n, usu cap K* [perh. fr. *Kura*, river in Georgia and Azerbaidzhan, U.S.S.R.] **:** a perennial clover (*Trifolium ambiguum*) native to the Caucasus and Romania and introduced into America — called also *honey clover, pellett clover*

kurakkan *var of* KORAKAN

kur·bash *or* **kour·bash** *or* **cour·bash** *or* **cur·bash** \'ku̇(ə)r-,bash, ⸗'⸗\ *n* -ES [Turk *kırbaç*] **:** a lash or whip of hide used as an instrument of punishment

kur·chee bark *or* **kur·chi bark** \'ku̇rchē-\ *n* [*kurchee, kurchi* perh. of Indic origin; akin to Skt *kūrca* beard, brush, bundle of grass — more at QUILT] **:** a Tellicherry bark from a tree (*Holarrhena antidysenterica*) of the family Apocynaceae that contains conessine and other alkaloids

kurd \'ku̇(ə)rd, 'kərd\ *n* -s *usu cap* **1 :** one of a numerous pastoral and agricultural people inhabiting a large mountainous plateau region in adjoining parts of Turkey, Iran, Iraq, and Syria and in the Armenian and Azerbaidzhan sectors of the Soviet Caucasus **2 :** KURDISH

¹kurd·ish \-dish\ *adj, usu cap* **1 :** of, relating to, or characteristic of the region inhabited by the Kurds **2 :** of, relating to, or characteristic of the Kurds or their language

²kurdish \"\ *n* -ES *usu cap* **:** the Iranian language of the Kurds

kur·di·stan \¦ku̇rdə¦stan, ¦kər-; ¦ku̇rdə¦stän\ *n* -s *usu cap* [fr. *Kurdistan*, region inhabited by Kurds in Turkey in Asia, Iraq, and Iran] **:** one of the several varieties of rugs woven by the Kurds whose best examples are noted for fine colors and durability

ku·re \'k(y)u̇rē, 'kü(,)rā\ *adj, usu cap* [fr. *Kure*, city in southwest Honshu, Japan] **:** of or from the city of Kure, Japan **:** of the kind or style prevalent in Kure

kur·gan \(')ku̇(ə)r¦gän\ *n* -s [Russ, of Turkic origin; akin to Turk *kurgan* fortress, castle] **:** a burial mound of eastern Europe or Siberia

ku·rie plot \'kyu̇rē-\ *n, usu cap K* [after F. N. D. *Kurie* b1907 Am. physicist] **:** a graphic means of comparing theoretical and observed momentum distributions in continuous beta-ray spectra

¹ku·ril·ian \k(y)ü'rilēən, -rēl-\ *adj, usu cap* [*Kuril* islands, group of islands south of Kamchatka belonging to the U.S.S.R. + E *-ian*, adj. suffix] **1 :** of, relating to, or characteristic of the Kuril islands **2 :** of, relating to, or characteristic of the people of the Kuril islands

²kurilian \"\ *n* -s *cap* [*Kuril* islands + E *-ian*, n. suffix] **:** a native or inhabitant of the Kuril islands

kurios *usu cap, var of* KYRIOS

kurk *var of* KIRK

kur·ku \'ku̇(ə)r(,)kü\ *n, pl* **kurku** *or* **kurkus** *usu cap* **:** KORKU

kur·mi \'ku̇rmē\ *also* **kum·ni** \'ku̇mnē\ *or* **kun·bi** \'ku̇mbē, -ünbē\ *n* -s *usu cap* [Hindi *Kurmī*] **:** a member of an important agricultural caste distributed throughout India with the exception of the extreme south

kur·nai \'ku̇(ə)r,nī\ *n, pl* **kurnai** *or* **kurnais** *usu cap* **1 a :** a people of the southeastern coast of Australia living in permanent villages **b :** a member of such people **2 :** the language of the Kurnai people

kur·na·kov·ite \ku̇r'näkə,vīt\ *n* -s [Russ *kurnakovit*, fr. N. S. *Kurnakov* †1941 Russ. mineralogist + Russ *-it* -ite] **:** a mineral $Mg_2B_6O_{11}.13H_2O$ consisting of hydrous borate of magnesium

kur·ra·jong \'kərə,jȯŋ, -jäŋ\ *also* **koo·ra·jong** \'ku̇r-\ *or* **cur·ra·jong** \'kər-\ *n* -s [native name in Australia] **:** any of certain Australian shrubs or trees esp. of the family Sterculiaceae that have strong tough bast fibers used by the aborigines for making cordage, nets, and matting **:** BOTTLE TREE: as **a :** FLAME TREE a(1) **b :** a widely distributed eastern Australian tree (*Brachychiton populneum*) with soft light attractively grained wood sometimes used for interior finish, flowers whitish without and red and yellow within, and foliage that is an important emergency food for cattle — compare GREEN KURRAJONG

kurrajong leaf roller *n* **:** the destructive larva of an Australian pyralidid moth (*Sylepta clytalis*) feeding on kurrajong foliage

kur·rol's salt \'kərləlz-, 'ku̇r¦\ *n, usu cap K* [perh. fr. the name *Kurrol*] **:** an insoluble sodium metaphosphate or potassium metaphosphate; *esp* **:** a fibrous crystalline sodium metaphosphate $NaPO_3$ IV formed by seeding a melt at 550° C

kursk \'ku̇(ə)rsk\ *adj, usu cap* [fr. *Kursk*, city in central part of European Russia, U.S.S.R.] **:** of or from the city of Kursk, U.S.S.R. **:** of the kind or style prevalent in Kursk

kur·to·rach·ic \¦kərd·ə¦rakik\ *adj* [*kurto-* (irreg. fr. Gk *kyrtos* bulging, convex) + *rach-* (fr. Gk *rhachis* spine) + *-ic* — more at CYRT-] **:** having the lumbar region of the spinal column concave dorsally

kur·to·sis \,kər'tōsəs\ *n* -ES [Gk *kyrtōsis* convexity, fr. *kyrtos* convex + *-ōsis* -osis] **:** the state or quality of peakedness or flatness of the graphic representation of a statistical distribution

ku·ru·ba \kə'rübə\ *n, pl* **kuruba** *or* **kurubas** *usu cap* **:** a member of a pastoral people in Mysore and other parts of southern India

ku·rukh \'ku̇rək\ *n, pl* **kurukh** *or* **kurukhs** *usu cap* **1 a :** a primitive people of central India who antedate the Dravidians in India — called also *Oraon* **b :** a member of such people **2 :** the Dravidian language of the Kurukh people

ku·ru·ma \'ku̇rəmə\ *n* -s [Jap] **:** JINRIKISHA

ku·rum·ba \kə'rümbə\ *n, pl* **kurumba** *or* **kurumbas** *usu cap* **1 :** a member of a jungle people living on the slopes of the Nilgiri hills of southern India who are remnants of the oldest pre-Dravidian population of the Deccan **2 :** a member of a shepherd caste of southern India who are known for a variety of blanket that they weave

ku·ru·me azalea \'ku̇rə,mā-\ *n, often cap K* [fr. *Kurume*, city in northern Kyushu, Japan] **:** any of certain garden azaleas of variable hardiness with white, pink, rose, scarlet, or lavender flowers originating in Japan chiefly by selection from or hybridization of a native Japanese azalea (*Rhododendron obtusum*) with hairy shoots and evergreen or deciduous leaves

ku·rus \kə'rüsh\ *n, pl* **kurus** [Turk *kuruş*] **:** a Turkish piaster equal to 1/100 lira — see MONEY table

kur·vey \kə(r)'vā\ *vi* **kurveyed; kurveyed; kurveying; kurveys** [Afrik *karwei*, prob. fr. D *karweien* to do odd jobs, fr. *karwei* job, task, fr. MD *corweye* corvée, fr. MF *corvee* — more at CORVÉE] **:** to carry goods about in an ox wagon in southern Africa

kur·vey·or \-āə(r)\ *n* -s [modif. (influenced by E *-or*) of Afrik *karweier*, fr. *karwei* to kurvey + *-er* (fr. D, akin to OE *-ere* -er)] **:** a traveling trader in southern Africa who carries goods about in a large ox wagon

kus *pl of* KU

ku·sa *also* **ku·sha** \'ku̇(,)s(h)ä\ *n* -s [Hindi *kusā*, fr. Skt *kuśa*] **1 :** a grass (*Eragrostis cynosuroides*) of India used in Hindu ceremonies — called also *darbha* **2 :** KANS

ku·sai·an \(')kü¦sīən\ *n* -s *cap* [*Kusaie*, island in the eastern Caroline islands + E *-an*, n. suffix] **:** a Micronesian native or inhabitant of Kusaie in the eastern Caroline islands

ku·sam \'kü,sam\ *n* -s [origin unknown] **:** a tree (*Schleichera oleosa*) of the family Sapindaceae that grows in dry forests of southeastern Asia, has pinnate leaves, apetalous flowers, and dry fruits surrounded by pulpy arils and that yields a hard heavy reddish brown timber and from its seeds an oil that is used locally for cooking, illumination, and medicine — see MACASSAR OIL

ku·san \'küsᵊn\ *n, pl* **kusan** *or* **kusans** *usu cap* **1 a :** an Indian people of Oregon **b :** a member of such people **2 :** a language family in western Oregon including Coos

ku·shan \'kü,shän\ *n, pl* **kushan** *or* **kushans** *usu cap* **:** a Saka people invading India from central Asia, formerly having a ruling house with control extending over northwest India, much of present-day west Pakistan, and the Ganges valley to Benares, and eventually becoming absorbed as Kshatriyas or Sudras

ku·si·man·se \,küsə'man(t)sə\ *or* **ku·si·man·sel** \-səl\ *n* -s [prob. native name in Liberia] **:** a small dark brown burrowing carnivorous mammal that is a native of West Africa and related to the mongoose

¹kuskus *var of* KHUSKHUS

²kus·kus \'kü,skü̇s\ *var of* COUSCOUS

kuss·maul breathing \'ku̇,smau̇l-\ *or* **kussmaul respiration** *n, usu cap K* [after Adolf *Kussmaul* †1902 Ger. physician] **:** abnormally slow deep respiration characteristic of air hunger and occurring esp. in acidotic states

kus·ti \'kü(,)stē, ⸗'⸗\ *n* -s [Per *kustī, kushtī*, fr. *kusht* waist, side, fr. MPer *kust, kustak*] **:** the sacred cord or girdle worn by Parsis as a mark of their faith — compare SACRED SHIRT

ku·su \'kü(,)sü\ *n* -s [origin unknown] **:** any of several African striped mice

ku·sum \kə'süm\ *n* -s [Hindi, fr. Skt *kusumbha*] *India* **:** SAFFLOWER

kutch *var of* CUTCH

kutcha *or* **ka·cha** *or* **kach·cha** \'kəchə\ *adj* [Hindi *kaccā*] **:** being in a crude or raw state **:** MAKESHIFT, UNFINISHED ⟨where they cannot get a pukka railway, they take a ~ one —Lord Elgin⟩

ku·tchin \kü'chin\ *n, pl* **kutchin** *or* **kutchins** *usu cap* **1 a :** an Athapaskan people of the Yukon and Mackenzie river valleys, Alaska and northwestern Canada **b :** a member of such people **2 :** a language of the Kutchin people — called also *Loucheux*

ku·te·nai *or* **ku·te·nay** *also* **koo·te·nai** \'küt°n,ā, -t(,)nā, -tnē\ *n, pl* **kutenai** *or* **kutenais** *or* **kutenay** *or* **kutenays** *usu cap* **1 a :** a people of the Rocky mountains on both sides of the U.S.–Canada boundary **b :** a member of such people **2 :** the Kitunahan language of the Kutenai people

ku·ti·ra gum *also* **ku·tee·ra gum** \kə'tirə-\ *n* [Hindi *katīrā*] **:** any of several sterculia gums

kut·na·ho·rite \,kətnə'hȯr,īt, ,ku̇t-\ *n* -s [G *kutnahorit*, fr. *Kutná Hora*, western Czechoslovakia, its locality + G *-it* -ite] **:** a mineral $Ca(Mn,Mg,Fe)CO_3$ that consists of a carbonate of calcium, manganese, magnesium, and iron and that is isomorphous with either dolomite or calcite

kut·tar \kə'tär\ *n* -s [Hindi *katār*, fr. Skt (prob. Prakrit) *kaṭṭāra*, fr. Skt *kartati* he cuts — more at SHEAR] **:** a short dagger used in India with a handle consisting of two parallel bars joined by a crosspiece that is gripped with the hand

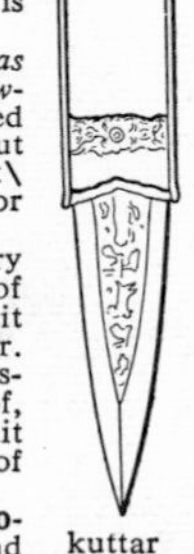
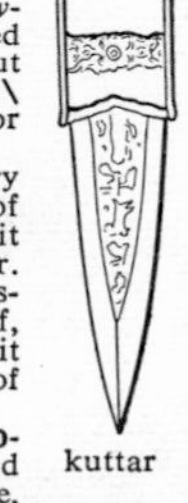
kuttar

ku·vasz \'ku̇,väs, 'kü,-\ *n* [Hung, fr. Turk *kavas* armed constable, guard, doorkeeper, fr. Ar *qawwās* bowman] **1** *usu cap* **:** a long-established Hungarian breed of tall and light-footed but sturdy white dogs **2** *pl* **ku·va·szok** \-vä,sȯk\ *often cap* **:** any dog of the Kuvasz breed used for centuries as guard and hunting dogs

ku·wait \kə'wāt\ *adj, usu cap* [fr. *Kuwait*, country on the Persian gulf] **:** of or from the country of Kuwait **:** of the kind or style prevalent in Kuwait

¹ku·wai·ti \-wād·ē\ *adj, usu cap* [Ar *kuwaytiy*, fr. *Kuwayt* Kuwait] **1 :** of, relating to, or characteristic of Kuwait, a country on the Persian gulf **2 :** of, relating to, or characteristic of the people of Kuwait

²kuwaiti \"\ *n* -s *cap* **:** a native or inhabitant of Kuwait

ku·yo·non \'küyō,nän\ *n, pl* **kuyonon** *or* **kuyonons** *usu cap* [Kuyonon, fr. *Kuyo* Cuyo, island in the central Philippines + Kuyonon *-non* people, language] **1 a :** a Christianized people inhabiting Cuyo and eastern Palawan islands and parts of other islands in the northern Sulu sea **b :** a member of such people **2 :** an Austronesian language of the Kuyonon people

kv *abbr* kilovolt

kva *abbr* kilovolt-ampere

kvah *abbr* kilovolt-ampere-hour

kvar *abbr* kilovar

kvarh *abbr* kilovar-hour

kvass *also* **kvas** \kə'väs, 'kfäs\ *or* **quass** *or* **quas** \", 'kwäs\ *n* -ES [Russ *kvas*; akin to OSlav *kvasŭ* sour drink — more at CHEESE] **:** a weak homemade beer of Eastern European countries (as Russia) made by pouring warm water over a mixture of cereals and allowing it to ferment

kvu·tzah *or* **kvu·tza** \kə,vüt'sä, ⸗'⸗(,)⸗\ *n, pl* **kvu·tzoth** *or* **kvu·tzot** \-sōt(h), -sōs\ *also* **kvutzahs** *or* **kvutzas** [NHeb *qĕbhūṣāh* (pl. *qĕbhūṣōth*), fr. Heb, group, gathering] **:** a Jewish communal and cooperative farm or settlement in Israel that is usu. smaller than a kibbutz and established on state-owned land

kw *abbr* kilowatt

kwa \'kwä\ *n, pl* **kwa** *usu cap* **:** a branch of the Niger-Congo language family that contains the Akan languages and Agni, Ga, Fon, Ewe, Yoruba, Ibo, Edo, and Nupe, and less certainly Kru, Bassa, and Grebo and that is spoken along the coast and a short distance inland from Liberia to Nigeria

kwa·ki·utl \¦kwäkē¦(y)üdᵊl, (')kwä¦k(y)ü-\ *n, pl* **kwakiutl** *or* **kwakiutls** *usu cap* **1 a :** a Wakashan people on both shores of Queen Charlotte Sound and on northern Vancouver Island **b :** a member of such people **2 :** the language of the Kwakiutl people

kwal·hi·o·qua \,kwäl(h)ē'ōkwə\ *n, pl* **kwalhioqua** *or* **kwalhioquas** *usu cap* **1 :** an Athapaskan people of southwestern Washington **2 :** a member of the Kwalhioqua people

kwang·ju \'gwäŋ¦jü, 'kw-\ *adj, usu cap* [fr. *Kwangju*, Korea] **:** of or from the city of Kwangju, Korea **:** of the kind or style prevalent in Kwangju

kwang·tung ware \'gwäŋ¦du̇ŋ-, 'kw-, -¦tu̇ŋ-\ *n, usu cap K* [fr. *Kwangtung*, province in southeast China] **:** a Chinese porcelanous stoneware that possibly originated in Sung times varying from almost white to dark brown or red and usu. having a variegated glaze

kwapa *usu cap, var of* QUAPAW

kwa·shi·or·kor \,kwäshē'ȯrkər, -ē,ȯr¦kō(ə)r\ *n* -s [native name in Ghana] **:** severe malnutrition in infants and children that is characterized by failure to grow and develop, changes in the pigmentation of the skin and hair, edema, fatty degeneration of the liver, anemia, and apathy and is caused by a diet excessively high in carbohydrate and extremely low in protein

kwa·tu·ma \kwä'tümə\ *n* -s [native name in southern Africa] : any of several moray eels (genus *Lycodontis*) of southern Africa

kwa·zo·ku \'kwäzō,kü, kwä'zō(,)kü\ *n, pl* **kwazoku** [Jap] : the class of nobility of both civil and feudal origin in the Japanese social scale — compare HEIMIN, SHIZOKU

kweek \'kwāk\ *n* -s [Afrik, fr. D, couch grass; akin to OE *cwice* couch grass — more at QUITCH] **1** *southern Africa* : a grass of the genus *Cynodon* **2** *also* **kweekgrass** \'=,=\ *southern Africa* : COUCH GRASS 1a

kwei·lin \'gwā¦lin, 'kw-\ *adj, usu cap* [fr. *Kweilin*, city in southeast China] : of or from the city of Kweilin, China : of the kind or style prevalent in Kweilin

kwei·yang \'gwā¦yäŋ, 'kw-\ *adj, usu cap* [fr. *Kweiyang*, city in southern China] : of or from the city of Kweiyang, China : of the kind or style prevalent in Kweiyang

kwe·ni \'kwānē\ *n, pl* **kweni** *or* **kwenis** *usu cap* : GURO

kwe·ri *also* **kwiri** \'kwirē\ *n* -s *usu cap* : a people of the southern British Cameroons

kwh *abbr* kilowatt-hour

kwo·ma \'kwōmə\ *n, pl* **kwoma** *or* **kwomas** *usu cap* **1 a** : a Papuan people of the Sepik district, Territory of New Guinea **b** : a member of such people **2** : the language of the Kwoma

kyabooka *also* **kya-bouka** *var of* KIABOOCA

ky·ack \'kī,ak *also* -ī,yak\ *n* -s [origin unknown] : a packsack to be swung on either side of a packsaddle

kyah \kē'(y)ä\ *n* -s [Beng] : an Indian partridge (*Francolinus gularis*) having a strong spur

kyak *var of* KAYAK

kyang *var of* KIANG

kyanite *var of* CYANITE

ky·a·nize \'kīə,nīz\ *vt* -ED/-ING/-S [fr. John H. *Kyan* †1850 Eng. inventor + E *-ize*] : to preserve (wood) by steeping in a solution of corrosive sublimate

kyat \kē'(y)ät\ *n* -s [Burmese] **1** : the basic monetary unit of Burma established in 1952 — see MONEY table **2** : a coin representing one kyat

kyathos *var of* CYATHUS

kybosh *var of* KIBOSH

kye \'kī\ *n pl* [ME *ky*, fr. OE *cȳ* — more at COW] *now dial* : KINE

kyle \'kī(ə)l\ *n* -s [ScGael *caol*, fr. *caol* narrow; akin to OIr *cōil, cōel* narrow, Latvian *kaîls* naked, bald] *Scot* : CHANNEL, SOUND, STRAIT ⟨at the widening mouth of the ~ —David Innes⟩

ky·lie *or* **ki·ley** \'kīlē\ *n, pl* **kylies** *or* **kileys** [native name in Australia] : an Australian boomerang having one side flat and the other convex

ky·lin \'kē'lin\ *n* -s [modif. of Chin (Pek) *ch'i*[2] *lin*[2], fr. *ch'i*[2] male kylin + *lin*[2] female kylin] : a unicorn of Chinese myth depicted with the tail of an ox and the legs and body of a deer — see FÊNG HUANG

ky·lix \'kīliks, 'kil-\ *or* **cy·lix** \'sīl-,'sil-\ *n, pl* **kyl·i·kes** \'kilə,kēz\ *or* **cyl·i·ces** \'sil-\ [Gk *kylix;* akin to Gk *kalyx* calyx — more at CHALICE] : a drinking cup that has two looped handles on a shallow bowl set upon a slender center foot

kylix

ky·loe \'kī(,)lō\ *n* -s *usu cap* [origin unknown] : WEST HIGHLAND

kym- *or* **kymo-** — see CYM-

ky·mat·i·on \kī'mad·ē,än, kə'-\ *var of* CYMATIUM

kym·ba·lon \'kimbə,län\ *n* -s [Gk — more at CYMBAL] : CYMBAL 1a

ky·mo·gram \'kīmə,gram\ *n* [ISV *cym-* + *-gram*] : a record made by a kymograph

ky·mo·graph \-raf,-råf\ *or* **cy·mo·graph** \'sī-\ *n* [ISV *cym-* + *-graph*] **1** : a recording device including an electric motor or clockwork that drives a usu. slowly revolving drum which carries a roll of plain or smoked paper and also having an arrangement for tracing on the paper by means of a stylus a graphic record of motion or pressure (as of the organs of speech, blood pressure, or respiration) often in relation to particular intervals of time **2** : a device for recording on a moving X-ray film the motion of an organ (as the heart) by means of a series of still images — **ky·mo·graph·ic** \¦==¦grafik\ *adj*

ky·mog·ra·phy \kī'mägrəfē\ *n* -ES [ISV *cym-* + *-graphy*] : the making of kymographic records

kymric *usu cap, var of* CYMRIC

kyn·uren·ic acid \¦ki\|nyə¦renik-, ¦kī\|\ *n* [*kynurenic* ISV *kyn-* (fr. Gk *kyn-, kyōn* dog) + *-uren-* (irreg. fr. Gk *ouron* urine) + *-ic* — more at HOUND, URINE] : a crystalline acid $C_9H_5N(OH)COOH$ occurring in the urine of dogs and other animals as one of the normal products of tryptophan metabolism

kyn·uren·ine \,=='re,nēn, -,nən\ *n* -s [ISV *kynuren-* (fr. *kynurenic*) + *-ine*] : an amino acid $NH_2C_6H_4COCH_2CH(NH_2)COOH$ occurring in the urine of various animals as one of the normal products of tryptophan metabolism and capable of forming kynurenic acid and other products; 3-anthranoyl-alanine

ky·oo·dle \(')kī¦(y)üdᵊl\ *vi* **kyoodled; kyoodled; kyoodling** \-d(ᵊ)liŋ\ **kyoodles** [imit.] : to make loud useless noises : HOLLER, YAP ⟨the dogs waved their tails happily and sought out a rabbit and went *kyoodling* after it —John Steinbeck⟩ ⟨quit listening to all this *kyoodling* from behind the fence —Sinclair Lewis⟩

kyo·to \kē'(y)ōd·(,)ō, -ō(,)tō *sometimes* 'kyō-\ *adj, usu cap* [fr. *Kyoto*, city in west central Honshu, Japan] : of or from the city of Kyoto, Japan : of the kind or style prevalent in Kyoto

ky·pho·scoliosis \¦kī(,)fō+\ *n, pl* **kyphoscolioses** [NL, fr. *kypho-* (fr. *kyphosis*) + *scoliosis*] : backward and lateral curvature of the spine

ky·pho·scoliotic \"+\ *adj* [fr. NL *kyphoscoliosis*, after such pairs as NL *hypnosis:* E *hypnotic*] : of, relating to, or marked by kyphoscoliosis

ky·phos·i·dae \kī'fäsə,dē\ *n pl, cap* [NL, fr. *Kyphosus*, type genus + *-idae*] : a family of chiefly tropical percoid shore fishes resembling bass and including a number of important herbivorous food fishes — see KYPHOSUS, RUDDERFISH

ky·pho·sis \kī'fōsəs\ *n, pl* **kypho·ses** \-ō,sēz\ [NL, fr. Gk *kyphōsis*, fr. *kyphos* humpbacked, bent + *-ōsis* -osis — more at CYPHELLA] **1** : abnormal backward curvature of the spine — opposed to *lordosis* **2** : the state of one who is affected with kyphosis — **ky·phot·ic** \(')=¦fäd·ik\ *adj*

ky·pho·sus \kī'fōsəs\ *n, cap* [NL, fr. Gk *kyphos* + L *-osus* -ose] : a genus that includes the Bermuda chub and is the type of the family Kyphosidae

kyr·i·a·le \,kirē'ä(,)lā\ *also* **kyr·i·al** \'kirēəl\ *n* -s *usu cap* [NL *kyriale*, fr. *kyrie* + ML *-ale* (as in *missale* missal)] : a liturgical book containing the text and plainsong notation of the parts of the ordinary of the mass (as the Kyrie, Sanctus, Agnus Dei) that are sung by the congregation

ky·rie elei·son \¦kirē,āə'lā(ə),sän, -lāsᵊn,-lāəsən, *in rapid speech* ,kirēə'l-\ *or* **kyrie** \'kirē,ā\ *n, pl* **kyrie eleisons** *or* **kyries** *often cap K&E* [*kyrie eleison* fr. LL, fr. Gk *Kyrie eleēson* Lord, have mercy; *kyrie* fr. NL, fr. LL *kyrie eleison*] **1** : a petitionary invocation (as in the ordinary of the mass and in the breviary) addressed to the Trinity and beginning with the words "kyrie eleison" **2** : either of two Anglican liturgical responses beginning with the words "Lord, have mercy upon us": **a** : one accompanying the decalogue **b** : one following the summary of the Law

kyr·i·elle \¦kirē¦el\ *n, pl* **kyrielle** [F, fr. OF *kyriele*, lit., kyrie eleison, fr. LL *kyrie eleison*] : a French verse form in short usu. octosyllabic rhyming couplets often paired in quatrains and characterized by a refrain which is sometimes a single word or sometimes the full second line of the couplet or fourth line of the quatrain

ky·ri·os \'kirē,äs\ *also* **ku·ri·os** \'kůr-\ *n, pl* **kyri·oi** \-ē,ȯi\ *or* **kyrios·es** \-ē,äsəz\ *also* **kuri·oi** *or* **kurios·es** *usu cap* [Gk *kyrios* lord, master, fr. *kyros* power, might — more at CURIOLOGIC] : LORD ⟨early Christians confessed Jesus Christ as their ~ instead of the emperor⟩

kyte \'kīt\ *n* -s [prob. fr. LG *küt* bowel; akin to MD *cuy* calf of the leg, *cuut* fish roe, MLG *kūt* calf of the leg, fish roe, G dial. (Bavarian) *kütz* part of the entrails, Skt *guda* bowel — more at COT] *chiefly Scot* : STOMACH, BELLY ⟨sit down and fill your ~ —R.L.Stevenson⟩

kythe *var of* KITHE

kyu·rin \kyə'rēn\ *n, pl* **kyurin** *or* **kyurins** *usu cap* : a member of a Lezghian people of the Caucasus mountains